The Encyclopedia of New York State

THE ENCYCLOPEDIA OF NEW YORK STATE

EDITOR IN CHIEF

Peter Eisenstadt

MANAGING EDITOR

Laura-Eve Moss

FOREWORD BY

Carole F. Huxley

Deputy Commissioner for Cultural Education
New York State Education Department

SYRACUSE UNIVERSITY PRESS

First Edition 2005
05 06 07 08 09 00 6 5 4 3 2 1

The paper used in this publication meets the minimum requirements of American National Standard for Information Sciences—Permanence of Paper for Printed Library Materials, ANSI Z39.48–1984.∞™

Designed by Christopher Kuntze
Proofreading by Nancy DeFranco Hayes
Index by Martin L. White

Printed and bound in New York State by
Maple-Vail Book Manufacturing Group,
Binghamton, New York.

LIBRARY OF CONGRESS CATALOGING-IN-PUBLICATION DATA
The encyclopedia of New York State / Peter Eisenstadt, editor in chief ; Laura-Eve Moss, managing editor ; with a foreword by Carole F. Huxley.— 1st ed.
p. cm.
Includes bibliographical references and index.
ISBN 0-8156-0808-X (alk. paper)
1. New York (State)—Encyclopedias. I. Eisenstadt, Peter R., 1954–
F119.E53 2005
974.7—dc22 2005001032

Manufactured in the United States of America

PROJECT STAFF

Editor in Chief
Peter Eisenstadt

Managing Editors
Edward H. Knoblauch (1999–2002)
Laura-Eve Moss (2001–4)

Deputy Managing Editor
Dan Streever

Assistant Managing Editors
Hadley Kruczek-Aaron
Tod M. Ottman

Chief Copy Editor
Kay Steinmetz

Community History Editor
Field Horne

New Netherland and Colonial Editor
Martha Dickinson Shattuck

Geography and Map Editor
James W. Darlington

Cartographer
Joseph Stoll

Assistant Editors
Jeanne Winston Adler
Andrew W. Arpey
Tricia A. Barbagallo
Pamela Cooper
Janet F. Daley
Sarah E. DeSanctis
John Farranto
Amybeth Gregory
Sean P. Guerin
Tanya M. Huelett
Michele A. Irwin
Mary Linnane
Jane Mackintosh
Mark A. Mastromarino
Sandra G. McClellan
Thomas Ross Miller
Roberta Newman
Douglas J. Pippin
Marianne Rahn-Erickson
Thomas Reimer
Cynthia K. Sauer
Eric Schillinger
Mary Beth Sullivan (illustrations)
Laura A. Ten Eyck
Jacqueline Villarrubia-Mendoza
Eric Waldemar
Bonita L. Weddle
Glenn Wright
Mary Ziegler

Copy Editors
Helen Glenn Court
Julie M. DuSablon
Kathryn Kraynik

Assistant Geography Editors
Mary Theresa Julien
Marc Korpus
Ethan D. Rogati

Editorial Assistants
David Call
Cynthia B. Childs
Marie E. DeFeo
Leigh Hall-Wilhelm
Alain Helfrich
Nekia T. Johnson
Heidi Knoblauch
Mollie T. Marchione
Brenden E. McNeil
Ichiro Okano
Ian Ostrander
Torey G. Ronan
Brittany Rostron
Rachel Rubin
Hannah M. Springer

Donors

This project would not be possible without the generous support of the following institutions, corporations, foundations, and individuals.

LEADERSHIP SUPPORT

Cultural Education Center in Albany

National Endowment for the Humanities

New York State Senate—Special Legislative Grants sponsored by Senator John A. DeFrancisco

Syracuse University

CORPORATE SPONSORS

Anoplate Corporation—Milton and Ann Stevenson

CSEA—New York's Leading Union

Empire Expo Center—Home of The New York State Fair
Peter Cappuccilli, Director

Frito-Lay Inc.

GE Foundation

The Maple-Vail Book Manufacturing Group

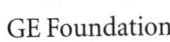

Marsh

Pepsi Bottling Group

Syracuse Banana Co., Inc.

Syracuse Federal Credit Union

Upstate Farms Cooperative, Inc.

CORPORATE PATRONS

Carrier Corporation

Crucible Materials Corporation

Lockheed Martin Ocean, Radar & Sensor Systems

Marsellus Casket Company

NBT Bank

Niagara Mohawk

Zogby International, Inc.

FOUNDATIONS

The Bernhill Fund

The Gladys Krieble Delmas Foundation

Furthermore: a program of the J. M. Kaplan Fund

The Lucius N. Littauer Foundation

The John Ben Snow Foundation

PATRONS

Ann L. Buttenwieser

Antje Lemke

FRIENDS

Dr. Patricia Bonomi

Eric Mower and Associates, Inc.

Jewels by Martha Conan and Absolute Weight Loss, Wellness and Sports Nutrition

Sensis Corporation

SUNYA Friends of the Libraries Board in memory of Dr. Mauritz Johnson, Jr.

Advisory and Editorial Boards

Contents

Foreword

IN THE WANING DAYS of the American Revolution, Gov George Clinton told the legislature in his annual message of the importance of "the promotion and encouragement of learning." Since forming in 1784 the New York State Board of Regents and the University of the State of New York, composed of all chartered educational institutions, have tried to honor Clinton's charge. They have had an expansive conception of educating New Yorkers, and this remains central to their mission today. The Office of Cultural Education, within the Education Department, has been delighted to be associated with *The Encyclopedia of New York State* since the project was in its formative stages. Surely, this exciting new publication responds to his vision in a way Gov Clinton would applaud.

Learning about New York State is a never-ending quest. Its history is unique and pivotal in the development of our country. Understandably, many volumes have been written on its importance in national and international affairs, the development of its communities, its many ethnic and racial groups, and its vast cultural achievements. The sources for New York State history are as diverse as its subject. The state's history can be found in books, newspapers, libraries, archives, and museums, at historic sites, on television and radio, and in the stories of New Yorkers. The *Encyclopedia* covers all of these topics and draws on all of these varied sources to provide a unique guide for those wishing to learn more about New York State.

We are proud of the final result. *The Encyclopedia of New York State* is one of the most ambitious works on the state's history to appear in many decades. It showcases the scholarship of over 1,200 authors on a vast range of subjects. For the student, for the casual browser, and for the expert alike, the *Encyclopedia* provides a new way of looking at and reading about New York State. We are also pleased that Syracuse University Press will distribute a free copy of the *Encyclopedia* to 780 public libraries in the state and will provide a discount to school libraries so that all of the state's citizens will be able to make use of this unparalleled resource.

Carole F. Huxley

DEPUTY COMMISSIONER FOR CULTURAL EDUCATION
NEW YORK STATE EDUCATION DEPARTMENT

Preface

TRYING TO COMPREHEND New York State as a whole was perhaps the greatest challenge that faced the editors and authors of this volume. Despite a momentous role in the history of North America and a rich legacy of first-rate scholarship and imaginative literature dating back to the 18th century, New York State resists tidy conceptualization. If grand personages, noteworthy events, and famous places come easily to mind, their connections often remain elusive. The focus of almost all of the best writing about New York State has concentrated on a particular locality or region.

Some think of New York State as little more than a historical accident, in which its disparate regions have little internal unity. There are legitimate grounds for this conception. In many ways New York is a state of peripheries. The state's strange shape, asymmetrical and elongated, makes it difficult to map. In one direction it thrusts north to Canada; in another it stretches west to the shores of Lake Erie. To the south and the east is an archipelago extending over 100 miles (160 km) into the Atlantic Ocean, where it shares a nautical border with Rhode Island. New York State is a regional crossroads. It is the only state on both the Atlantic Ocean and the Great Lakes and the only state bordering both Quebec and Ontario. In some instances New York State takes on the qualities of its adjacent areas: parts of eastern Long Island and the mid-Hudson Valley resemble New England; the Midwest is often said to begin either in Rochester or in Buffalo; parts of the Southern Tier form the northern end of Appalachia; and the French Canadian influence is strong in the North Country. And then there is New York City, in its own universe with over 40% of the state's population, self-contained and self-absorbed, with seemingly little in common with the rest of the state.

But if the state is an accident, it is an accident of long standing. New York State (and its Dutch predecessor, New Netherland) has had a coherent governmental structure for almost 400 years, almost twice as long as that of the United States itself. While New York, the Empire State, is not an empire, it has had to grapple with some classic imperial problems: maintaining order over a huge and incongruent dominion and respecting the unique qualities of each region while also creating coherent and distinctive political and cultural forms that provide a sense of unity. The difficulty is not merely that New York State is diverse; it is radically heterogeneous. No state except California has a more varied geology and topography. More than half of the state's population is crowded on three islands that constitute less than 5% of the state's area. The state has neighborhoods like Manhattan's Lower East Side, which at the turn of the 20th century was one of the most densely populated areas in the world, and regions like the central Adirondacks, in which Hamilton Co remains one of the least densely populated counties east of the Mississippi River (about 5,000 persons on over 2,100 mi^2/5,440 km^2). The need to develop institutions to govern the state and its disparate regions—urban, suburban, and rural—and their diverse populations gives New York State its distinctive character.

To deal with its untidy complexity, one is tempted to reduce the state to a series of dichotomies: upstate/downstate, rural/urban, cosmopolitan/provincial, and so on. They are all misleading. As for "upstate" and "downstate" there is no agreement on where those portions of New York State begin or end. Upstate is still often used as a synonym for rural, forgetting that few areas in the nation compare to the state north of New York City for their history of urbanization and industrialization. At the same time downstate has an ambiguous identity, including New York City as well as the adjacent suburbanized counties. In recent decades the suburban areas have increasingly formed their own identity separate from the New York City metropolis and now extend north to Orange and Dutchess Cos.

One problem with thinking of New York State in terms of regional dichotomies is that it obscures internal differences within a given region and the realities of class, race, and ethnicity that often account for the most salient internal divisions in particular areas. Regionalism also obscures what the state's areas share in their linked histories and what will be their common destiny. Many of the problems of the early 21st century (for example, deindustrialization, declining tax revenues, healthcare, urban poverty, and the quality of public education) extend statewide and call for statewide solutions.

The way to view New York State as a unified whole is by embracing its full complexity, not by trying to trim it to a single narrative. An encyclopedia has a unique ability to do this. *The Encyclopedia of New York State* contains entries that capture the special characteristics of every region, but it also includes entries on subjects ranging from environmentalism to higher education to railroads that show the connections that span those differences. New York City, for example, is treated both as the global city it is and as just one of the regions of the state. Through roughly 4,600 entries, including charts and tables, and over 100 maps and 500 illustrations, the *Encyclopedia* treats subjects in their specificity as well as through ties to the state as a whole.

We know the readers of *The Encyclopedia of New York State* will discover many connections between its entries and uses for the volume that we did not plan or fathom. If there is one thing we hope readers take away from the *Encyclopedia,* it is a renewed attention to "the idea of New York State," the various demographic, economic, political, cultural, and geographic skeins that have tied together the inhabitants of the state, as well as the various conflicts that have driven them apart. It is our fondest hope that this volume invigorates the study of New York State: by ordinary citizens, by persons in business, government, and science, by the newest immigrants, and by those who can trace their ancestry back to before European contact. Above all, we hope it is used by students of New York State at every level—grade school or graduate seminar—and that the next generation of scholars will be inspired to develop more sophisticated interpretations of the state's complex past. If we have succeeded, it will be clear to all that New York State is indeed greater than the sum of its splendid parts.

This is the first comprehensive, scholarly encyclopedia ever published about New York State, and it is a forum for the best in recent scholarly writing on its subject. We have tried to get leading experts to write each of the entries in the *Encyclopedia.* Their nuanced interpretations are found on each page. Every entry has been carefully fact checked. There is no greater burden that falls to the editors of reference works than avoiding the perpetuation of error, and we have treated this obligation with the greatest seriousness. We have also tried to make the *Encyclopedia* as comprehensive as possible, but this is a one-volume reference work, and there are many worthy entries and topics that do not appear in its pages.

Acknowledgments

THE IDEA FOR *The Encyclopedia of New York State* started with my discussions with members of Syracuse University Press in the winter of 1996–97. In the spring of 1998 initial funding for the project was secured from the New York State legislature through the efforts of Sen John A. DeFrancisco. His ongoing support, vision, and dedication were invaluable in ensuring the success of this project. After discussions with Carole F. Huxley, Deputy Commissioner for Cultural Education of the New York State Education Department, the *Encyclopedia* opened its office in the Cultural Education Center in Albany in October 1998. Advisory and Editorial Boards were soon put into place. A planning conference held at Syracuse University on 20–21 May 1999, with over 60 members of the Advisory and Editorial Boards in attendance, provided much direction on how we should proceed. With the help of the New York State Education Department, the New York State legislature, the National Endowment for the Humanities (NEH), private donors, and Syracuse University Press, we were able to finish the fact checking and initial editing by the end of April 2004.

A 2-million-word encyclopedia project is perhaps the scholarly equivalent of a Cecil B. DeMille motion picture: conceived on the largest possible scale, an extravaganza with a cast of thousands. I wish there were greater space in this section to thank everyone who had a hand in developing the *Encyclopedia.* There are many people who deserve special recognition.

The first debt is genealogical. Without *The Encyclopedia of New York City,* published by Yale University Press in 1995, this encyclopedia would not have been possible: first, because it is an exemplary and widely copied recent model for historical encyclopedias and, second, because I was a managing editor on that project and learned the reference editor's trade from Kenneth T. Jackson, Fred Kameny, and the late Edward Tripp. If it is not too immodest of me, I see the current volume as a companion to the older volume, an account of what has happened in New York State outside of the confines of the five boroughs. Our admiration and close study of *The Encyclopedia of New York City* will be obvious on every page of the current volume. One other reference editor who deserves a nod is John Homer French, editor of the *Gazetteer of the State of New York* (1860). A day has not gone by when we have not consulted French's *Gazetteer.*

When the *Encyclopedia* was first conceived in Rochester, Karl Kabelac, Ruth Rosenberg-Naparsteck, and Harold Wechsler were helpful in discussing the idea and providing encouragement. When the project was first brought to Syracuse University Press, former acquisitions editor Nicole Catgenova was instrumental in thinking broadly about an encyclopedia that would encompass the whole of New York State. No one played a more critical role in turning the early, vague plans into reality than Beth Rougeux, executive director of the Office of Government and Community Relations at Syracuse University, who worked with Sen DeFrancisco to arrange for legislative funding. There are many people at Syracuse University who supported this project with help on fund-raising, among them Lansing G. Baker, Deborah Freund, Mary Beth Hinton, Louis Marcoccia, Bill O'Brien, John Sellars, and Kenneth Shaw. The other major source of funding has been the NEH, which provided two major grants. Joe Herring, the *Encyclopedia*'s program officer at the NEH, directed us, like a shrewd Adirondack guide, through the wilds of the application process with friendly support, candor, and pointed stories around the campfire. We also received valuable advice and assistance from David Cronin and his staff at the New York Council for the Humanities. Several firms, foundations, and individuals assisted the project financially. I am grateful to each institution and individual listed on the donor list.

The *Encyclopedia* has been developed during the tenures of three directors at Syracuse University Press. Robert Mandel welcomed the *Encyclopedia* to the Press. Acting director John Fruehwirth has been a great friend to the project and helped it through some difficult times. Peter Webber, the current director of the Press, has been a strong supporter within Syracuse University, and the *Encyclopedia* has greatly benefited from his advice, counsel, and attention. The entire staff of Syracuse University Press has brought consistent and professional expertise to its work on *The Encyclopedia of New York State.* Kit Kuntze's talents as a designer are evident throughout the book.

It was the great fortune of the *Encyclopedia* to have been located at the Cultural Education Center in Albany. Close proximity to the magnificent resources of the New York State Library, the State Archives, and the State Museum was a continual boon. The staff members of the State Education Department were unfailingly gracious hosts, starting with Carole F. Huxley. Providing help with staffing, fund-raising, and many other matters were V. Chapman-Smith, former state archivist, and Christine Ward, current state archivist. Clifford Siegfried, director of the State Museum, provided much appreciated assistance. Among the many others who work at the Cultural Education Center who should be acknowledged are Warren Broderick, James Folts, Charles Gehring, Judy Hohmann, Dahlia Mazengia, Barbara Murray, Laurie Roberts, Kathleen Roe, Thomas Ruller, Bonita Walsh, Craig Williams, and the entire staffs of the State Archives, Library, and Museum.

The Editorial Board played a central role in establishing the entry list and in helping us assign and edit entries. Some members deserve special mention. Laurence Hauptman ensured that our treatment of American Indians was comprehensive and suggested knowledgeable authors for these entries. James Folts's awe-inspiring erudition on the history of the state government came to our rescue time and again, and he wrote or commented on many of the more difficult government-related entries. Natalie Naylor was extremely generous in sharing her remarkable knowledge of Long Island history. Her efforts were crucial in ensuring adequate coverage of one of the state's most populated regions. Other members of the Editorial Board whose advice and expertise helped the book immensely are Philip Bean, Gerald Benjamin, Dennis Connors, Deborah Gardner, Charly Gehring, William Graebner, F. Daniel Larkin, Robert Snyder, Judith Wellman, Harold Wechsler, Peter Wosh, and Gerald Zahavi. Members of the Advisory Board who provided assistance include historian Ann Buttenwieser and the Grand Old Man of New York State history, Wendell Tripp. Friends of the *Encyclopedia* who lent a helping hand include David Allen, Wesley Balla, Norman Carlson, Susan Conklin, Frances Dumas, James Eyre, Jaap Jacobs, Lisa Keller, Elaine Messere, Delia Robinson, and Mark Rothenberg.

Over the six years it took to develop the *Encyclopedia,* more than 60 persons joined the project. I regret that I cannot provide a personal acknowledgment to each of them for their unstinting efforts. Dan Streever, the deputy managing editor, and Laura-Eve Moss, the managing editor, are two of the finest persons it has ever been my pleasure to have as professional colleagues. Without their intelligence, their attention to detail, their incredible hard work and collegiality, this project never would have been completed. Their support for the goals of the *Encyclopedia,* in matters minor and not so minor, has been unwavering.

Edward and Heidi Knoblauch, Rachel Rubin, and Jacqueline Villarrubia-Mendoza helped prepare the over 200 tables in the book. Edward Knoblauch, the project's first managing editor, set up the database and first web site. Mary Beth Sullivan, with the assistance of Ian Ostrander, gathered and prepared illustrations. Bonita Weddle and John Farranto provided crucial assistance when the project was just getting started; Cindy Sauer and Eric Waldemar played an important role in the middle phase of the project; Janet Daley, Sarah DeSanctis, Amybeth Gregory, Michelle Irwin, Mary Linnane, Jane Mackintosh, Mark Mastromarino, Roberta Newman, Hannah Springer, and Mary Ziegler helped with the final push at the end. Tina Press was a valuable fund-raiser, strategist, and provider of encouragement and support during the first two years. Among the invaluable long-term personnel were Jeanne Winston Adler, Tricia Barbagallo, Pamela Cooper, Sandra McClellan, Douglas Pippin, Thomas Reimer, and Glenn Wright. Trish and Thomas were excellent assigners of entries and diligent editors; Jeanne, Pam, Sandy, Doug, and Glenn were expert fact checkers and editors on a wide variety of topical areas. Hadley Kruczek-Aaron and Tod Ottman worked as supervising editors and performed a number of critical editorial tasks. Hadley's editorial savvy and Tod's deep knowledge of 20th-century politics in New York State were much appreciated.

James Darlington provided the needed perspective of a geographer amidst a staff of historians. His work on the state's geography and cartography is of the highest order. He either wrote or closely edited each of the county physical descriptions. Jim worked with Joseph Stoll, cartographer at Syracuse University's Department of Geography, to create the *Encyclopedia*'s more than 100 maps. Their creativity and painstaking attention to detail is evident. Several others who helped with the geographic aspects are David Call, Mary Theresa Julien, Marc Korpus, Brenden McNeil, and Ethan Rogati.

Field Horne, a superb community historian, edited almost all of the 1,500 locality entries. The decision to include entries on all of the state's cities, towns, villages, and larger unincorporated localities was a high-risk gamble, and thanks to Field's diligence, tenacity, and aplomb we were able to pull it off.

Martha Shattuck, the terror of ill-informed writings on New York's Dutch period, pounced on inaccuracies and half-truths like a tiger on the prowl. Because of credulous histories, accounts of New Netherland are usually the weakest portion in state histories. In this encyclopedia, because of Martha, it is one of our strongest sections.

Kay Steinmetz has been the ideal copy editor for this project. Insistent and eagle-eyed, she has been properly impatient with errors of any kind. Kay's efforts were enhanced by the work of copy editors Helen Glenn Court, Julie DuSablon, Timothy Hayes, Kathyrn Kraynik, and D. J. Whyte. The final result is much clearer and more accurate and consistent than it otherwise would have been.

It has been my immense privilege to work with each and every one of the individuals associated with the *Encyclopedia* project. The most profound acknowledgments must be to the over 1,200 authors. They worked hard for little glory and meager compensation, submitted patiently to our intrusive fact checking and our demands for clarification and for more information, accepted constraints on entry length with grace, and fulfilled their authorial obligations in a timely fashion. One of the things that you discover when you work on an encyclopedia is that there are experts on just about everything, and we found them just about everywhere. Our authors range in age from 10 to over 90. They come from every region and every county in the state. And many of them come from most of the other 49 states and Canada. We also have authors from Germany, Sweden, Hong Kong, Israel, the Netherlands, New Zealand, the United Kingdom, and several other places that you cannot get to by the New York State Thruway. A few authors require special acknowledgment, including Scott Monje, who wrote 55 excellent entries on a great variety of topics, and the father-and-son team of William F. and William S. Helmer, who between them contributed 43 entries. (They are one of at least five parent-child tandems among our authors.) Kathleen LaFrank labored long on our state parks entry and its accompanying table. William McDermott, author of the Dutchess Co and Dutchess locality entries, was the gracious guinea pig while we tinkered with our procedures for editing locality entries. Other prolific authors include Marla Bennett, James Crawford, the husband-and-wife team of Bruce and Madelynn Fredrickson, Suzan Friedlander, and Jeffrey Kraus. I regret that space and time constraints and sometimes the reconceptionalization of portions of the *Encyclopedia* meant we were unable to edit and publish every entry that we commissioned. Each of the authors has a short biography in the back of this book, and reading through them will provide a sense of their remarkable accomplishments.

After this gargantuan catalog of acknowledgment, personal thanks seem a bit self-indulgent, but let me add just a few: to Amtrak and its conductors; to my good friends Dan Soyer and Rob Snyder; and to my brother Freddy, who drove me to Albany very early one morning when I badly needed a ride and provided other assistance. And the concluding acknowledgment is offered—conventionally, ardently, and uxoriously—to my wife, Jane, who made many sacrifices while I pursued the dream of this book.

Finally, much has happened in the six years that this book was gestating. Births are balanced with deaths. Two children were born to the families of project team members. Many people have passed away, including my father and my wife's father. Charles H. Canon, Loren Butler Feffer, Milton Goldin, Milton Klein, Herbert Kraft, Enayetur Rahim, Laura Lynne Scharer, Brother Denis Sennett, Annys Wilson, William Wilson, and Roger Wunderlich are among the authors and editors who did not live to see the *Encyclopedia* published. And the greatest loss New York State suffered during the preparation of the book was of course the almost 2,750 persons who perished in the destruction of the World Trade Center on 11 Sept 2001. To all the victims of that horrible day, and to all New Yorkers, past, present, and future, the *Encyclopedia* is dedicated.

Peter Eisenstadt
APRIL 2004

Using This Encyclopedia

SCOPE

The heart of any encyclopedia is its entry list. Determining what to include is a prolonged and difficult task, and worthy entries will inevitably be passed over, no matter how large the volume. The primary criteria of inclusion were connection and significance to New York State. The established guidelines were useful in developing comparable treatment of different themes and topics, but selection can never be an entirely objective process. In a few instances, the inability to find an appropriate author led to a reluctant decision to omit an entry. Entry lengths were determined by the scope and importance of the topic, also an inexact process. The availability of material and authors' different approaches influenced entry length as well.

Attempts were made to cover the entire scope of New York State, from its geologic history to events current in the early 21st century. The state's politics, economics, built environment, ethnicities, and faiths are among the topics covered in depth. There are biographical, geographical, institutional, and thematic entries, as well as more than 200 charts and tables and more than 100 maps. The *Encyclopedia* also contains a selection of sidebars that shed light on the related entries, either through a primary document or through an elaboration of a specific aspect of the entry. With a few exceptions, entries are structured in a chronological fashion.

Where possible, editors and writers have attempted to make information in the *Encyclopedia* current at least through 1 Mar 2004.

Biographical Entries

Biographical entries are limited to persons whose accomplishments in New York State the editors deemed to warrant an entry. Persons who were born or raised in the state but are primarily famous for what they did elsewhere (for example, Kirk Douglas or Leland Stanford, Charles Crocker, and Mark Hopkins [three of the Big Four who dominated California's railroads in the 19th century]) often do not have separate entries. In some topical areas, such as sports and classical and popular music, individual biographical entries are quite limited. Instead, biographical subjects are subsumed in a broader related entry; for example, Scott Joplin is discussed in the general entry about ragtime rather than in a separate entry. Biographical entries emphasize their subjects' careers in New York State, so, for example, the entry on Franklin D. Roosevelt is more concerned with his 4 years as state governor than his 12 years as president of the United States. The *Encyclopedia* includes entries on every state gov-ernor and popularly elected US senator. Entries about living and contemporary figures have been included, but the editors made some effort to avoid biographical entries about people who might prove to be of ephemeral significance.

Institutional and Thematic Entries

The *Encyclopedia* includes entries on every four-year college in the state and on every executive branch department of state government. Headings for institutional entries include New York or New York State if it would be confusing, misleading, or too informal to omit it (**New York Knickerbockers** and ***New York Times***), but for many entry titles, New York or New York State can be implied (**legislature**). For ease of use, schools that are part of the State University of New York are generally listed with short names under SUNY (**SUNY Plattsburgh**). Subjects are generally referred to with the name appropriate to the chronological point in the discussion.

Locality Entries

New York State has 62 counties and is divided between cities and towns. Incorporated villages fall only within the boundaries of towns, never within cities. Unincorporated communities can be within cities (and are generally called neighborhoods) or within towns (and are generally referred to as localities). The editors concluded that any attempt to separate "important" from "unimportant" communities would be arbitrary and invidious. Accordingly, there are entries on every county, city, town, incorporated village, and Indian reservation in the state. To provide comprehensive coverage of suburban areas, there are also entries on almost all localities that are Census Designated Places (CDPs) and that had a population in the 2000 census of greater than 4,500, as well as on some particularly notable localities that fall below the population threshold. With a handful of exceptions, the *Encyclopedia* covers neighborhoods (which are not CDPs and do no receive separate census counts) in the related city entries.

Locality entries have been combined in certain cases, such as when overlapping towns and villages have the same name. In some instances, especially for Long Island, adjacent localities that share a root name are combined in a single entry under the root name (for example, **Farmingdale** includes discussion of Farmingdale, East Farmingdale, and South Farmingdale). Indian reservations that bear the name of their nation are covered under the nation entry.

Entry headings for towns and villages indicate the political form, the population in the 2000 census, and the county. For villages and unincorporated localities the heading also identifies the surrounding town. Most locality entries have been edited to be as concise as possible. Because a focus for these entries is how people earned a living, economic and business histories and transportation access are major themes. Also highlighted are distinctive historical features, including landmarks, significant political developments or boundary changes, and persons of note. Information about the first settlers and the derivation of names, which is readily available in other sources, has often been excluded.

Pronunciation guides are provided for those localities whose names are likely to be mispronounced by speakers of standard English. These guides appear in small capital letters and use phonetic spellings; regular capital letters indicate the emphasized syllable (**Pulaski** [PUH-LASK-EYE]). All population figures in the headings of locality entries are from the 2000 US Census. There is additional information on the population for every town and city at 40-year intervals in tables in the relevant county entry. Most locality entries do not have bibliographic information because the best sources are often general county histories, and those works and many histories of individual localities can be found in the bibliographic essays at the end of country entries.

New York City

Determining how to handle New York City required much deliberation because there was no reason to duplicate the coverage in *The Encyclopedia of New York City* (Yale Univ Press, 1995). It would have been impossible, however, to make sense of New York State without providing a generous treatment of its largest city. The resulting compromise treats New York City at considerable length, but not with the depth given the rest of the state. The longest entry in the book is on New York City, but separate entries on places, persons, and things specific to the city have been limited. For example, only some of the most important neighborhoods have separate entries. Similarly, for biographical entries, the bar of significance needed for a separate entry was higher for persons with careers solely in New York City than for persons outside of the city. New York City and its significant residents are also treated in general thematic entries, and, as much as possible, developments related to New York City have been connected to the rest of the state. Entries for the five counties that make up New York City appear under their borough designations. Through 1898 New York City and New York Co were coterminous, and the city name is generally used. For references after 1898, the use of county and borough names is mixed.

USAGE

The *Encyclopedia* follows the *Chicago Manual of Style,* 14th ed., for Web addresses, 15th ed., and Webster's *New Collegiate Dictionary,* 10th ed., with some exceptions. For place-names we have generally relied on the New York State Department of Transportation's *New York State Atlas* (1998).

Alphabetization

The encyclopedia follows a letter-by-letter system, in which a heading of more than one word is treated as if it were spelled solid: spaces, hyphens, diacritical marks, and periods are disregarded, as are elements in brackets and parentheses. Headings beginning with "US" are alphabetized as if the abbreviation were spelled out. Corporate and institutional names that begin with a person's forename (such as R. H. Macy and the Solomon R. Guggenheim Museum) are alphabetized under the first letter of the forename, not the surname.

Abbreviations and Acronyms

This volume mirrors the practice of British reference works in eliminating the final periods of most abbreviations. Political and military offices are usually given in abbreviated form when directly preceding a proper name. Additionally, "County" is abbreviated when used with a county name (Madison Co, Monroe and Wayne Cos). Readers should refer to the separate list of abbreviations, which also includes acronyms that do not appear in expanded form on first references (NAACP, SUNY).

"New York," "Upstate," and "Downstate"

The *Encyclopedia* uses "New York State" as the name of the state, and "New York City" as the name of the city. New Netherland is used for the period 1609–64; New York Colony, Colony of New York, and Province of New York are used for the period 1664–1776. "New York" as a stand alone term is avoided unless the context is clear. The *Encyclopedia* also avoids the use of "upstate" and "downstate" in reference to particular areas because the terms lack geographic specificity. When the terms are used at all, they are generally in a political context with a reference involving New York City. Thus, upstate politicians can block a request from New York City, but a particular politician is from Syracuse, Onondaga Co, or Central New York rather than from upstate.

Geographic Regions

Regional designations are used in numerous entries as a way to quickly and concisely convey information. Other than for New York City and Long Island, though, there is no general agreement about regional borders, and the following allotment of regions makes no claim to be definitive. Unless otherwise indicated in entries, the *Encyclopedia* defines regions as follows:

Capital District: Albany, Rensselaer, Saratoga, Schenectady Cos
Central New York: Broome, Cayuga, Chemung, Chenango, Cortland, Madison, Oneida, Onondaga, Oswego, Schuyler, Seneca, Tioga, Tompkins Cos
Long Island: Nassau, Suffolk Cos
Lower Hudson: Putnam, Rockland, Westchester Cos
Mid-Hudson: Columbia, Delaware, Dutchess, Greene, Orange, Sullivan, Ulster Cos
Mohawk Valley: Fulton, Herkimer, Montgomery, Otsego, Schoharie Cos
New York City: Bronx, Brooklyn, Manhattan, Staten Island, Queens
Niagara Frontier: Erie, Niagara Cos
North County and Adirondacks: Clinton, Essex, Franklin, Hamilton, Jefferson, Lewis, St. Lawrence, Warren, Washington Cos
Southern Tier: Allegany, Cattaraugus, Chautauqua, Steuben Cos
Western New York: Genesee, Livingston, Monroe, Ontario, Orleans, Wayne, Wyoming, Yates Cos

The *Encyclopedia* deviates from using these regions when they are inappropriate to specific entries. For example, the table listing state parks is structured according to regions defined by the New York State Office of Parks, Recreation, and Historic Preservation rather than according to *Encyclopedia*-defined regions.

Geographic Place-Names and Anachronisms

On first mention in an entry, towns, cities, villages, and unincorporated places within New York State are followed in parentheses by the name of the county in which they are currently situated. Exceptions are well-known places, such as Albany or Buffalo; several localities that share the same name with their county, such as Schenectady or Oswego; series of five or more localities; and entries in which the county is clear from context, such as those about individual counties. Where several localities mentioned in a row are in the same county, the county identifier appears only after the last locality. Localities in the United States outside New York State are followed by their current state identifier, and localities in Canada are identified by their current provincial or territorial identifier. Localities elsewhere in the world are identified by their current country. Well-known cities and national capitals, such as Chicago or Tokyo, are not further identified. In some instances county identifiers appear after the names of institutions, but they are generally not used with parks, hydrographic features, and most physiographic features.

Places are referred to by the name and orthography that was in common use at the time of the discussion. However, the *Encyclopedia* does not indicate changes that solely involve punctuation or spacing; for example, Glen's Falls, the common spelling in the 18th and 19th centuries, is always rendered Glens Falls. The *Encyclopedia* uses a series of conventions in the text to indicate current place-names and locations for historical references:

[now . . .]
Indicates a change in the name of a locality, including cases where one name was directly changed to another and where one locality became part of another locality with different boundaries; a change in name of a broader jurisdiction such as county to county, state to state, or country to country; a change in name of both locality and broader jurisdiction.

For example: Skenesborough [now Whitehall, Washington Co]; Leningrad [now St. Petersburg, Russia]; Tryon Co [now Montgomery Co]

[now in . . .]
Indicates a change only in the name of a county or broader jurisdiction (no change in locality name); location of colonial manors and defunct Indian reservations

For example: Hempstead [now in Nassau Co]; Harpers Ferry [now in W Va]; Buffalo Creek Reservation [now in Erie Co]

[loc in . . .]
Indicates the locations of existing Indian reservations.

For example: Oil Spring Reservation [loc in Cattaraugus and Allegany Cos]

Measurements

The *Encyclopedia* uses English measurements and metric equivalents. Conversions are not provided for figures that are routinely measured in only one of these systems, for example, a football field goal of "47 yards" or a "15 km" race. Additionally, metric equivalents are not given for English measurements that required information not available for the conversion (board feet of lumber); for the non-numeric use of English measures ("the British forces, a few yards away"); or for some instances in which the unit of measure is used in a nonquantified manner ("she walked a mile"). Square or cubic measurements are indicated with superscripts (for example, ft^2 for square feet and m^3 for cubic meters). Temperatures are given in both Fahrenheit and Celsius.

Census Data and Racial Categories

Racial and ethnic information from the US Census appears throughout the *Encyclopedia* and is constrained by the census-defined categories and types of information collected. The 2000 census included the new categories of "two or more races" and "other race." This change, added to the four existing categories of White, Black, Asian, and American Indian/Pacific Islander, made the existing racial classifications less arbitrary and increased the possible ways in which individuals could define their racial identity. However, the additional categories, which permit 57 possible racial combinations tabulated by the census in 2000, can make the reporting of racial data more confusing. Most entries that use racial data from the 2000 census include the information from the single race categories of White, Black, Asian, and American Indian/Pacific Islander, but do not make use of the new mixed race and other race categories; thus the figures, when totaled, do not add up to 100%. Since 1970 Hispanic/Latino has been a separate category of ethnicity, not a category of race, making a total greater than 100% if one adds the Hispanic/Latino figures to those of census-defined racial groups.

The population tables appearing with each county entry provide racial data going back to 1790. To simplify the tables, the minority racial classifications have been combined into a single "nonwhite" category, consisting of everyone whose racial classification was not listed as White. Until 1970 this category would have been largely of African Americans. For 2000 the tables include mixed race and other race in the nonwhite category. Locality entries provide information about racial composition if there was a significant minority population in the community. Black and White are capitalized in the *Encyclopedia* when used as nouns.

Dates

Dates are given in day-month-year order, as in 18 July 1937. Life spans are provided for all biographical entries and in entry texts where relevant.

A conjectural date is one that is more likely than any alternative. For example, a conjectural date of "18 July" means the 18th of July is more likely than the 17th or the 19th. When an element is conjectural, this condition is indicated by a question mark before the uncertain element: "?18 July 1937" means that the day is conjectural, "18 ?July 1937" means that the month is conjectural, and "18 July ?1937" means that the year is conjectural. A day or month or both are omitted if less than conjectural, and a baptismal date *(bap)* is sometimes used if the date of birth is unknown.

When no one year is more likely than a particular alternative, but the year can be narrowed down to a span of years, it is indicated by *"ca"* (*ca* 1735). Years designated as such are generally given in multiples of five in the text; exceptions apply to photo captions. For dates of greater uncertainty, when birth and death years are unknown, *floruit*, *(fl)* is used. Unless otherwise indicated, all dates are given in new style and follow the Gregorian calendar. When significant to an entry to provide old-style dates, the corresponding new-style dates are also provided: "The Revolution broke out on 3 May *os*/10 May *ns* 1629." In reference to the destruction of the World Trade Center, the *Encyclopedia* sometimes uses the form September 11th or September 11th, 2001 because of its general prevalence.

Headings

Entry names are in boldface and have initial capital letters only when it would be appropriate in ordinary contexts. "The" is not included in some entry headings even though it may generally be used in referring to that item in everyday usage. Extant institutions are listed under their current names, while defunct institutions are listed under their best-known names. Honorific names are generally not used for headings, so readers will find an entry under **New York State Thruway** rather than under **Governor Thomas E. Dewey Thruway.** For in-stitutions commonly known by an acronym, the acronym may appear in the heading in paren-theses, as in **Boards of Cooperative Educational Services (BOCES).**

Biographical headings are styled to provide readers additional information about the subject of the entry and appear in the standard form:

Van Buren, Martin (*b* Kinderhook, Columbia Co, 5 Dec 1782; *d* Kinderhook, 24 July 1862).

Parentheses, with text in boldface, set off portions of a name that are not commonly used:

Anthony, Susan B(rownell)
Gehrig, (Henry) Lou(is)

Brackets, with text in lightface, indicate alternative names:

Balanchine, George [Balanchivadze, Georgi Melitonovich]
Red Jacket [Sagoyewatha]

The formula "née," in brackets and lightface, is used for women's birth family names:

Willard [née Hart], **Emma**

Individuals with patents of nobility are listed under their names and not their titles:

Alexander, William [Lord Stirling]
Hyde, Edward [Viscount Cornbury]

Titles of nobility are provided in lightface:

Andros, Sir **Edmund**

Common Names and Name Changes in Entries

When alternative or changed names of people or institutions appear in the body of an entry, they are given in parentheses: "the site of a famous concert by Bob Dylan (Robert Zimmerman)." When nicknames are the commonly used name, they do not appear in quotes (Babe Ruth), but when a given name and a nickname are both used, the nickname appears in quotes (Bill "Bojangles" Robinson). For institutional name changes, the construction "(now . . .)" means the institution is still operating, and the construction "(later . . .)" means the institution is defunct, such as King's College (now Columbia University) and Foster-Armstrong Piano Co (later American Piano Co).

Cross-References

Two kinds of cross-references are used to guide readers in the *Encyclopedia.*

1. Cross-references that appear as entry headings direct readers from an acronym or alternative name to another entry name (**fossils.** See ANCIENT LIFE).
2. Cross-references that appear at the end of an entry direct readers to other entries that contain a considerable amount of additional information about the topic of the original entry. For example, a cross-reference after the entry **colonial New York** might indicate See also RIOTS AND CIVIL DISTURBANCES. Such cross-references have been used sparingly. They do not include obvious related entries and only refer to entries with a substantial discussion of material not in the original entry where the cross-reference is found. Cross-references are just one tool for navigating between entries. They are not a substitute for the index and are not intended to preempt a reader's intuition.

Bibliographies

Most entries are followed by a list of suggested sources that provide more information about the topic. The bibliographies are arranged in alphabetic order. County entries are followed by a bibliographic essay.

Author Signatures

Entries with more than one author were created in a variety of ways and are indicated by the form of the author signature.

After entries for which two or more authors submitted a unified entry, the names appear in the order indicated by the authors, with "and" between them.

Entries in which the contributions of two or more authors are combined editorially into a single unified entry, without differentiation between the authors, the names appear in alphabetic order, with a comma between them.

For entries in which the contributions of two or more authors are combined editorially to form a single entry, with the contribution of each author kept separate, each individual section ends with italicized initials in the last line of text, with the full names in alphabetic order after the complete entry.

Abbreviations

AAS	Associate in Applied Sciences
AB	Artium Baccalaureus
AD	*anno Domini*
AFB	Air Force Base
AFL-CIO	American Federation of Labor–Congress of Industrial Organizations
AIDS	acquired immune deficiency syndrome
alt	altitude
Alta	Alberta
AM	Master of Arts
APNG	Advanced Practice Nurse in Genetics
AS	Associate in Science
Atty Gen	Attorney General
Ave(s)	Avenue(s)
b	born
BA	Bachelor of Arts
bap	baptized
BC	before Christ
BC	British Columbia
BD	Bachelor of Divinity
BFA	Bachelor of Fine Arts
bk	book
Blvd(s)	Boulevard(s)
BMus	Bachelor of Music
BOCES	Boards of Cooperative Educational Services
BP	before the present
Brig Gen	Brigadier General
Bros	Brothers
BS	Bachelor of Science
BSc	Bachelor of Science
bu	bushel
bur	buried
C	Celsius
ca	*circa*
CA	Certified Archivist
Capt	Captain
CAS	Certificate of Advanced Study
CBS	Columbia Broadcasting System
CD	compact disc
CDL	Center for Distance Learning
CEO	chief executive officer
CIA	Central Intelligence Agency
cm	centimeter
Co	County or Company
Col	Colonel
comp	compiler
Corp	Corporation
Cos	Counties
Cpl	Corporal
CUNY	City University of New York
cwt	US hundredweight
d	pence
d	died
DA	Doctor of Arts
DC	District of Columbia
DDS	Doctor of Dental Science or Surgery
DDT	dichlorodiphenyltrichloroethane
DH	Doctor of Humanities
diss	dissertation
DMA	Doctor of Musical Arts
DNA	deoxyribonucleic acid
DPh	Doctor of Philosophy
dr	dram
Dr	Doctor
DSc	Doctor of Science
DSI	Decision Sciences Institute
E	east
ed(s).	editor(s) or edition
EdD	Doctor of Education
Esq	Esquire
est	established
et al	*et alii* (and others)
f	following
F	Fahrenheit
FACD	Fellow of the American College of Dentists
FAIA	Fellow of the American Institute of Architects
FBA	Fellow of the British Academy
fd	founded
FICD	Fellow of International College of Dentists
fl	*floruit* (flourished)
Fr	Father
FRAeS	Fellow of the Royal Aeronautical Society
FRGS	Fellow of the Royal Geographical Society
FRS	Fellow of the Royal Society
FRSA	Fellow of the Royal Arts Society
frwd	foreword
ft	foot or feet
g	gram
gal	gallon
GED	General Equivalency Diploma
Gen	General
GI	"Government Issue" (World War II soldier)
GIS	geographic information system
Gov	Governor
Gov Gen	Governor General
h	hour
ha	hectare
HIV	human immunodeficiency virus
hl	hectoliter
HMO(s)	health maintenance organization(s)
HMS	Her (or His) Majesty's ship
hr	hour
Hz	hertz
in	inch
Inc	Incorporated
JD	Juris Doctor (Doctor of Laws)
Jr	Junior
K–8	kindergarten through grade 8
K–12	kindergarten through grade 12
kg	kilogram
km	kilometer
kph	kilometers per hour
kV	kilovolt
kW	kilowatt
kWh	kilowatt hour
l	liter
lat	latitude
lb	pound(s)
LLB	Bachelor of Laws
LLM	Master of Laws
loc	located
long	longitude
Lt	Lieutenant
Lt Col	Lieutenant Colonel
Lt Gen	Lieutenant General
Lt Gov	Lieutenant Governor
Ltd	Limited
m	meter
M/V	motor vessel
MA	Master of Arts
Maj	Major
Maj Gen	Major General
Man	Manitoba
MAT	Master of Arts in Teaching
MBA	Master of Business Administration
MCS	Master of Computer Science
MD	Doctor of Medicine
MEd	Master of Education
MFA	Master of Fine Arts
MGM	Metro-Goldwyn-Mayer
mi	mile
min	minute
ml	milliliter
Mlle	Mademoiselle
MLS	Master of Library Science
Mme	Madame
MPA	Master of Public Administration
mph	miles per hour
MPhil	Master of Philosophy
MS	manuscript
Msgr	Monsignor
MSSc	Master of Social Sciences
MT	metric ton
Mt(s)	Mount(s)
MUP	Master of Urban Planning
mW	megawatt
mya	million years ago
N	North
NASA	National Aeronautics and Space Administration
NB	New Brunswick
NBA	National Basketball Association
Newf	Newfoundland
NS	Nova Scotia
ns	new series or new style
NWT	Northwest Territories
NYC	New York City
NYS	New York State
NYSCA	New York State Council on the Arts
OBE	Officer of the Order of the British Empire
OD	Doctor of Optometry
Ont	Ontario
os	old series or old style
oz	ounce
p	pennies

PBS	Public Broadcasting Service
PCB(s)	polychlorinated biphenyl(s)
PE	Professional Engineer
PEI	Prince Edward Island
Pfc	Private First Class
PH	Professional Hydrologist
PharmD	Doctor of Pharmacy
PhD	Doctor of Philosophy
pk	peck
PLLC	professional limited liability company
PNP	Pediatric Nurse Practitioner
Pres	President
Priv	Private
pro	professional (sports contexts)
prt	part
psi	pounds per square inch
pt	pint
qt	quart
Que	Quebec
rd	rod
Rd(s)	Road(s)
Rear Adm	Rear Admiral
Rep	Representative
Rev	Reverend
RLA	Registered Landscape Architect
RN	Registered Nurse
rpm	revolutions per minute
Rte	Route
s	second or shillings
S	South
Sask	Saskatchewan
Sen	Senator
Sgt	Sergeant
SJ	Society of Jesus
Sr	Senior or Sister
St(s)	Street(s)
St.	Saint
STB	Bachelor of Sacred Theology/Bachelor of Theology
SUNY	State University of New York
Terr	Territory
ThD	Doctor of Theology
TNT	trinitrotoluene
trans	translator
Univ	University
USAF	United States Air Force
US	United States
USS	United States Ship
v	versus
V	volt
V-E Day	Victory in Europe Day
Vice Pres	Vice President
V-J Day	Victory in Japan Day
vol(s)	volume(s)
W	watt or west
yd	yard
YIVO	Yidisher Visnshaftlekher Institut (Yiddish Scientific Research Institute)
YMCA	Young Men's Christian Association
YM-YWHA	Young Men's and Young Women's Hebrew Association
Yukon	Yukon Territory
YWCA	Young Women's Christian Association

MAP ABBREVIATIONS

Cem	Cemetery
Cr	Creek
Expwy	Expressway
Ft	Fort
Hwy	Highway
Is	Island
L	Lake
Pkwy	Parkway
Pt	Point
R	River
Res	Reservation or Reservoir
Tnpk	Turnpike

New York State: An Introduction

Natural History

The oldest rock strata in New York State are at least 2.7 billion years old. The oldest record of life is found in fossil stromatolites, photosynthetic bacteria of 1.1–1.3 billion years of age. The state has a rich history of Paleozoic fishes and trilobites. The state fossil is the *Eurypterus remipes,* a relative of the crab and sea scorpion, that lived about 400 million years ago. The Adirondacks were formed about 1.2 billion years ago; the Catskills were formed about 400 million years ago. Although the state's rock strata are ancient and have a complex tectonic history, some of the most prominent geomorphical features, such as Niagara Falls and Long Island, are much younger (less than 20,000 years old). In the past 2 million years New York State has experienced several episodes of glaciation, most recently from 40,000 to 12,000 years ago, covering the entire state except for a bit of Cattaraugus Co.

The Hudson River, formed perhaps as much as 75 million years ago, is the one geological feature that determined the destiny of New York State beyond all others. One of the world's finest natural harbors is located where the Hudson River empties into the Atlantic Ocean, and the river remains broad, deep, and navigable 150 miles (240 km) inland, unlike any other major river on the East Coast. The Hudson and the Mohawk Rivers form the only break in the Appalachian barrier and together provide a water route to the Great Lakes, linking the western portions of the state to those in the east. This natural route was capitalized on and improved by the building of the Erie Canal, which became the principal thoroughfare between the Atlantic seaboard and the Midwest.

American Indians

Humans first entered New York State about 12,000 years ago, and the archaeological record of early peoples in the area has several distinct phases. Representatives of the Point Peninsula Culture moved into the state in the first millennium AD and were the ancestors of the Algonquian-speaking peoples of the Hudson Valley, New York City, and Long Island. Around AD 800, the ancestors of the Iroquois, bands of peoples from the Appalachian region, moved into the New York State area. Following AD 1300, after mastering the cultivation of beans, squash, and maize, the ancestors of the Iroquois, with their greater numbers, were able to dispossess or absorb the former inhabitants. The League of the Haudenosaunee (Iroquois Confederacy) was formed probably in the 15th or 16th century. On the eve of European contact it consisted of five nations—the Mohawk, Oneida, Onondaga, Cayuga, and Seneca—and stretched from the Hudson to the Genesee Rivers.

Europeans' demands on Indian land often led to disputes and sometimes open warfare, notably Kieft's War (1640–45). The relatively decentralized and small-scale settlements of the Algonquian-speaking Indians in the Hudson Valley were not well suited to make a sustained response to the various challenges that Europeans brought. By the end of the 17th century, most Indians had moved out of their original homelands, many to points beyond the control of Europeans. The Iroquois Confederacy, having stronger political and military organization and greater distance from the Europeans, was initially in a better position to resist.

New Netherland and Colonial New York

Dutch colonists established a small settlement at Fort Orange in 1624 and a settlement on Manhattan in 1626. The largest settlement of New Netherland was New Amsterdam, a small city on the tip of Manhattan Island. The fur trade was central to the economy, but the export of tobacco, wheat, and lumber was also important. After some difficult years in the early decades, the colony thrived under Petrus Stuyvesant, director general of New Netherland from his arrival in 1647 to 1664. The economy and standard of living in the colony grew after the mid-1650s with a diversification of the economy and rising immigration. By 1664 New Netherland had 16 towns with local governments, the city of New Amsterdam, and 1 patroonship, Rensselaerswijck. New Netherland's population in 1664 was approximately 7,000–8,000. Only a bare majority of the residents of New Netherland were ethnically Dutch. There were also substantial numbers of Germans, French, Scandinavians, Jews, Africans (the large majority of them enslaved), and representatives of many other nationalities. Stuyvesant's search for effective ways to control his far-flung and complex colony would have echoes in the state's later history.

With an overwhelming show of force and the offer of lenient terms of surrender, the English conquered New Netherland in 1664. Both the colony and its city were renamed after the new proprietor, James, Duke of York. The new colony continued the entrepreneurial bent set forth by the Dutch, and Dutch political, legal, religious, and cultural traditions remained vital throughout the colonial period. Anglicization of New York proceeded slowly and sporadically.

Many of the most powerful Dutch families, like the Van Rensselaers, Van Cortlandts, and Philipses, ingratiated themselves with the new English rulers and maintained and expanded their landholdings and political influence. Dutch enclaves persisted, and large segments of the Dutch mercantile community remained ambivalent to the English. The political interregnum provided by the Glorious Revolution in 1688 allowed Jacob Leisler to rise to power in New York, unleashing interethnic and interdenominational hostilities that had been building for many years. Although Leisler's tenure as governor ended with his beheading at the hands of his successor in 1691, disputes between Leislerians and anti-Leislerians remained a potent element in the colony's politics for many decades.

While the Dutch had encouraged patroonships, the only successful one in New Netherland was Rensselaerswijck, primarily in what are now Rensselaer and Albany Cos. It was confirmed as a manor by the English, and several other large-scale manors were established in the Hudson River valley, all renting land to tenants and, depending on the terms of the manor grant, retaining some form of legal jurisdiction over them. By 1700 four manors—Rensselaerswijck, Livingston, Cortlandt, and Philipsburg—covered over half the undeveloped land in the province. New York was a breadbasket and lumberyard for the British sugar colonies in the Caribbean and, in turn, a center of sugar refining, which remained a significant industry in the state for the next three centuries.

In the 18th century, of all colonies north of the Mason-Dixon Line, New York had the largest population and highest concentration of enslaved Africans, reaching its peak of approximately 16% of the colony's population around 1720. Many of the colony's enslaved Blacks worked in agriculture, often on relatively small farms with no more than two or three slaves, though they were also servants and worked in various trades. Slaves tried to escape bondage either by running away or through more coordinated revolts. A 1712 slave uprising in New York City led to the deaths of 9 Whites. After the rebellion was suppressed, participants were tortured, 21 slaves were executed, and a punitive slave code was enacted. Following the Negro Plot of 1741, 30 Blacks and 4 Whites (the alleged conspirators) were executed. Slavery had other faces as well. In 1760 Jupiter Hammon, a slave living on Long Island, became the first published African American author. After the Revolution, the number and pace of manumissions increased, and the state legislature was prodded into passing a gradual manumission act in 1799, though slavery was not ended in New York State until 1827.

With growing trade and artisanal activity in the Port of New York and flourishing agriculture in the Hudson Valley and Long Island, New York Colony thrived economically in the 18th century. Population increased rapidly. From the first fully reported colonial census (1698) to the last (1771), the colony's population increased from 18,067 to 168,007. The colony's northern four counties—Albany, Dutchess, Orange, and Ulster—experienced a population increase from 3,079 to 89,152. Although New York City's 1771 population of 21,863 made it the second-largest city in British North America, its share of the colony's population decreased from about 25% in 1700 to only 13% in 1771. Immigration from Europe, primarily English, Scots, Palatine Germans, and Irish, as well involuntary immigration from Africa, accounted for much of the increase. Migrants from hardscrabble areas of New England were also moving into the Hudson Valley, a foreshadowing of the much larger Yankee migration to come.

Politics in New York Colony was hard-fought and highly factional, with the merchant and landlord parties broadly representing distinct economic interests. Residents had the opportunity to be well informed about these struggles: 22 different newspapers were published between 1725 and 1776, and most were allied with specific factions. Perhaps the best-known was the *New-York Weekly Journal,* published by John Peter Zenger, whose 1735 trial and acquittal for seditious libel set a precedent in the evolution of the rights of the press. The franchise was fairly widely exercised. By the end of the colonial period about one-half of the adult men met the requirement for suffrage of £40 in property, and about one-half of those eligible actually voted. Nevertheless the colony's politics continued to revolve around prominent families, such as the Livingstons and the DeLanceys, and family connections, religious concerns, and long-standing feuds contributed to political developments.

Other conflicts of this period developed from the colony's geographic position in the struggle between the English and the French for North American supremacy. The Hudson River–Lake Champlain corridor became an invasion route between French Canada and New York and New England. The Mohawk corridor, which diverged from the Hudson near Albany, was a path of access to the Great Lakes and the interior of the continent. From 1609, when Samuel de Champlain fought a battle with the Mohawks near Ticonderoga, until the end of the French and Indian War, Iroquoia, the vast territory from the Mohawk River to the Niagara River, was at the center of imperial rivalries. A series of English and French forts across Iroquoia underlined its strategic significance; New York was one of the two colonies (South Carolina being the other) before 1755 with regular British troops, and it was the base of British operations during the French and Indian War.

The Dutch, French, and British all tried to exercise their sway in Iroquoia. At the same time, the Iroquois attempted to maintain their hegemony over the region, extending control over American Indian rivals while preserving their own often fragile internal unity. From the 1670s the English sought to bind the Iroquois through an array of treaties and agreements known as the Covenant Chain, and the French, after a series of punishing raids, exacted a pledge of neutrality in 1701. The complex three-sided battles and negotiations continued into the 1760s, when the French and Indian War removed the French counterbalance to the British; the subsequent steady encroachment of settlers meant the nations of the Iroquois Confederacy found their options increasingly limited.

The strength of the Iroquois Confederacy gave the New York frontier its distinctive character. The "middle ground" or frontier period west of the Hudson Valley began early with settlement, deep in the interior at Fort Orange, and endured as long as Indians controlled Iroquoia. The classic American frontier was in large measure defined in New York, characterized by relatively sparse patterns of European American settlement, presence of a borderland between contending sovereignties, existence of a large American Indian population, and a central role for trans-cultural intermediaries. The American frontier received its first lasting literary treatment by James Fenimore Cooper, who created from New York material many of the enduring frontier stereotypes.

Revolution and Independence

New York Colony's disenchantment with the British imperial machine began to emerge in 1765. The Stamp Act was bitterly resented by most New Yorkers. Although scheduled to go into effect on 1 Nov 1765, it never did. The plan was quashed after a crowd led by the Sons of Liberty forced the acting governor, Cadwallader Colden, to seek refuge aboard a British naval vessel in New York Harbor. The new social forces unleashed by the Stamp Act crisis did not go away after its repeal. The Sons of Liberty continued to agitate against the British. They represented a new "middling sort" of less wealth and education than those who had previously dominated New York's politics. The colony's great families continued to try to control succeeding events, but the "new men" retained their influence. Rioting flared on the Hudson River manors in 1766 as tenant farmers from Massachusetts challenged the legality of their leases. Continuing disputes about quartering British soldiers also roiled the colony. As the events in New York and other colonies came to a head, many prominent New York City merchants looked for a compromise between the patriots and the Crown. By April 1775, when the Battles of Lexington and Concord were fought, this middle ground ceased to exist.

New York's strategic significance ensured that it would be a primary battleground of the Revolution. By August 1776 the largest fleet assembled in the 18th century (over 30,000 British sailors and soldiers) had moored at Staten Island. In the fight for the New York City area over the next several months, Gen George Washington was lucky to escape with his army. New York City remained in British hands for the remainder of the war. Control of the Hudson-Champlain corridor was key for the domination of North America. If Gen John Burgoyne had been able to make contact with British forces moving north from New York City, the corridor would have been in British hands, New England would have been effectively sundered from the other colonies, and the American rebellion may well have been effectively repressed. But Burgoyne's armies were defeated at Saratoga in October 1777, which was immediately recognized as a potential turning point. The British had neither the military strength nor the political will needed to put down the rebellion.

The Revolution was not waged merely through great battles. Individuals grappled with their consciences to determine which side to support. Neighbors fought neighbors, and as much as in any colony, the struggle for American independence in New York was a civil war. These conflicts led the colony's inhabitants to wage conventional and guerrilla war upon one another. New York State emerged from the war transformed, with a new political order. Powerful families like the DeLanceys and the Philipses, who had supported the British, found themselves exiles, stripped of their estates. Some loyalist families fled to Britain. Others went to Nova Scotia and Canada, and the new province of Upper Canada [now Ont] had a large population of former New Yorkers.

With the end of the war, New York State's physical dimensions changed. The rebellious counties east of Lake Champlain broke away to form Vermont. Iroquoia, which had been ambiguously ruled by the British, became firmly under the control of New York State. The American Revolution had presented the nations of the Iroquois Confederacy with a series of impossible choices about whom to support. Many, out of a respect for traditional ties and fear of the American ambitions for their land, supported the British. The raids and counterraids across Iroquoia culminated in the 1779 Sullivan-Clinton campaign, which destroyed large numbers of Iroquois villages and settlements. Many Iroquois followed the British into exile at the conclusion of the war. Those who remained found that a return to their old ways of life was impossible. Demands for massive land sales and transfers could not be resisted. By 1797 Iroquois holdings in New York State were reduced to about a dozen small reservations, and by 1826 to 8, the number that remains today. The illegal treaties through which New Yorkers forced the Iroquois into alienating their land in the immediate post-Revolutionary decades are still being litigated.

The new political order began to take shape in April 1777 when a state constitution was promulgated. With a strong executive and sharp separation of powers, the constitution was an important precedent for the federal constitution of 1787. George Clinton was elected the state's first governor, and he remains the longest-serving governor in state history. Clinton was of modest family background and emblematic of the new classes that came to power after the Revolution, though many of the older families, such as the Schuylers, Van Rensselaers, and Livingstons, still retained considerable influence. The greatest champion of the former colonial aristocrats was Alexander Hamilton, an ambitious immigrant with no prominent family connections. He emerged as the leading advocate for mercantile interests and sought the creation of political, social, and legal structures to facilitate state and national commercial and financial advancement.

New Yorkers divided again over the ratification of the federal constitution in 1787. Antifederalists, primarily concentrated in the upper Hudson River valley and Albany, feared that a strong national government would circumscribe local autonomy; Federalists, centered in New York City, argued that strong national institutions would ensure the country's prosperity. Concern over ratification inspired passionate debate, none more famous than that found in the *Federalist Papers,* the 85 essays by Hamilton, James Madison, and John Jay published in New York City newspapers in 1787 and 1788. The Federalists' arguments did not sway many of the delegates, who only reluctantly ratified the Constitution at the state's 1788 convention in Poughkeepsie.

Hamilton became the leader of the Federalists in New York State. The other national political faction was variously known in its early history as the Democratic-Republicans, the Jeffersonians, and the Republicans, and was headed in the state by George Clinton. After several elections in which the Democratic-Republicans and the Federalists contested as equals, the Federalists became increasingly marginal electorally, and the faction disappeared as an organized unit soon after the War of 1812. New York State Republicans were the junior partners of the Virginia dynasty that produced four of the nation's first five presidents.

New York City became the national capital in 1785, when Congress under the Articles of Confederation started meeting. In 1790 George Washington was inaugurated there as the first president of the United States, but the federal capital moved to Philadelphia a few months later. In 1797 New York City lost the role of state capital to Albany. These shifts had little effect on the growth of New York City. The 1790 federal census showed it as the largest city in the United States. It was home to the nation's dominant port, largest commercial banks, and most liquid securities market. The city was a leader in mercantile pursuits and in industries as diverse as shipbuilding and garment making. New York City also soon became the center of the printing and publishing industries, and of literary, musical, and theatrical high and popular culture. The state as a whole was thriving, and by 1820 it was the most populated state in the country, a position it retained for almost a century and a half.

Erie Canal to Civil War

The opening of the Erie Canal in 1825 cemented the rise of New York City to economic supremacy and marked the emergence of Central and Western New York as important centers of commerce. Linking the Atlantic Ocean and the Great Lakes, the canal was an act of political will that joined the regions of the state, created a vast economic hinterland for New York City, and established a ready market for agricultural products from the state's interior. The year 1825 also marked the closing of the New York State frontier: all corners of the state that were to be settled had been settled, and county and municipal structures closely resembled their current organization.

The Erie Canal crossed the most dynamic region of the state. Between 1790 and 1830 the state's population increased from 340,120 to 1,918,608. Almost all of this increase can be attributed to the growth of Central and Western New York. By the 1790s, with the dispossession of the Iroquois, these regions and the Southern Tier rapidly opened up for settlement. Through the acquisitions of the Holland Land Co, the Phelps and Gorham Purchase, and other extensive land tracts, millions of acres were rapidly inventoried, systematically surveyed, divided into townships, and sold to prospective settlers and small-scale speculators. The fertile valleys of the Mohawk and Genesee Rivers and the Niagara Frontier were opened to land speculation and settlement. Rochester and Buffalo were two of the original "boomtowns," heavily promoted inland communities on favorable transportation routes that developed with remarkable rapidity. Rochester went from a village of 1,502 in 1820 to a city of 20,191 by 1840. By that year 6 of the 30 largest cities in the United States were in New York State: New York City (1st), Brooklyn (7th), Rochester (19th), Troy (21st), Buffalo (22nd) and Utica (29th).

New England culture dominated early Central and Western New York. A flood of Yankees left the rock-strewn soils of Vermont, Connecticut, and Massachusetts in search of more arable land in one of the first great internal migrations in the history of the United States. By 1850 over 15% of New York State's population had been born in New England, with a far higher percentage for those of New England descent. New Englanders brought with them their folkways, often reflected in the layout of village greens and house construction styles, and a commitment to entrepreneurialism and to education. For many decades, the New Englanders formed a distinctive culture, contrasting with that of the "Yorkers," those with longer roots in New

York State, often of Dutch, German, or Scots descent. Yankee and Yorker cultures were leavened by many people from Pennsylvania, New Jersey, and Maryland. With intermarriage and the passage of generations, however, the differences between Yankees and Yorkers ceased to be so sharply defined. At the same time, the habit of mobility persisted, and for many, New York State was not the final stop in their migration. In 1860 as many as a quarter of those born in New York State were living out of state.

Many of the newly settled regions of New York State, especially Central and Western New York State and the Southern Tier, were typical of emergent societies: rootless, lacking established institutions, and undergoing explosive commercial growth. Those seeking firmer moorings often turned to religion. The New England migrants drew on their inherited religious traditions, but by the early 19th century the harsher doctrines of Puritanism were in sharp decline. In contrast, the great religious revival in the early 19th century, led by the Methodists and Baptists, emphasized an individual's ability to choose salvation. Nowhere was this revival more fervent than in the recently settled areas of New York State. The area earned the name Burned-over District because of the many revivals that swept through western New York State. During the 1820s and 1830s, Charles Grandison Finney became the first great practitioner of the urban revival meeting. He established a model for successful revivalism that would be followed by evangelists into the 21st century.

What gave the area its special notoriety was its role as a laboratory for religious heterodoxy and communal experimentation, challenging conventional notions of religion and family arrangements. The Shakers, the largest communal religious sect in 19th-century America, got their start in the Albany area just after the Revolution. William Miller, raised in Washington Co, was a founder of the modern Adventist movement. The early history of Mormonism took place in Western New York and the Southern Tier: from 1820, when Joseph Smith Jr received his first vision from an angel, to the move of the church to Ohio in 1831. In the Book of Mormon, Smith presented a vast sacred history centered on New York State, which culminated in a great war of extinction between native civilizations in the Palmyra area. Modern spiritualism began in 1848 with the claims of the Fox sisters of Hydesville (Wayne Co) to be able to connect to the dead, and Lily Dale (Chautauqua Co) remains the national center of the spiritualist movement.

The Burned-over District was also a hotbed of utopianism and the belief that society could be remade and re-formed on a more equitable basis. John Humphrey Noyes's Oneida Community from the 1840s to the 1880s combined Perfectionist religious convictions with a rejection of conventional monogamy. Numerous short-lived Owenite and Fourierist socialist communities were formed in the antebellum decades. Modern Times was an anarchist community on eastern Long Island in the 1850s and 1860s.

The social and religious thought characteristic of the Burned-over District provided strong support to the movement against slavery. By continued attention to the problem of human bondage, abolitionists throughout New York State helped to make the issue of slavery the central political issue of the antebellum years. Lewis and Arthur Tappan, prominent New York City businessmen, formed the American Anti-Slavery Society in 1833. Another prominent businessman, Gerrit Smith of Peterboro (Madison Co), helped establish the Liberty Party, the first abolitionist party. Central New York was home to the Oneida Institute, the nation's first integrated institution of higher learning, and New York Central College, the nation's first college to have an integrated faculty. African Americans played a vital role in the state's abolitionist movement, sometimes working closely with white colleagues, sometimes working primarily with other Blacks. Sojourner Truth, born a slave in Ulster Co in the late 1790s, experienced the harshness of slavery in New York State before becoming a leading speaker for abolitionist causes. Frederick Douglass, an escaped slave from Maryland, moved to Rochester in 1847, where he became the best-known African American abolitionist in the country.

Attempts to effect the return of fugitive slaves were sometimes met by the forceful opposition of an outraged citizenry, as in the 1851 Jerry Rescue in Syracuse. The most famous of all conductors on the Underground Railroad, Harriet Tubman, a former Maryland slave, lived a half century in Auburn (Cayuga Co). Abolitionist John Brown was living in Timbucto, Gerrit Smith's colony for African Americans in the Adirondacks, when he embarked on his 1859 raid on the Harpers Ferry Arsenal in Virginia.

In addition to nurturing the crusade against slavery, western and central New York State witnessed the birth of the women's suffrage movement. Abolitionists Lucretia Mott and Elizabeth Cady Stanton organized the 1848 Seneca Falls Convention, which announced the agenda of the women's rights movement to a largely skeptical world. Stanton and her close friend and associate in Rochester, Susan B. Anthony, remained stalwarts of the movement for over half a century. New York State was at the center of the suffrage movement until the 19th Amendment was passed in 1920, and the influence of social-feminist reform became an important component of the state's politics. Early in the 20th century, Francis Perkins, the first female member of a presidential cabinet, and First Lady Eleanor Roosevelt, were two of its best-known representatives. The tradition was continued by another First Lady, Hillary Rodham Clinton, who in 2000 became the state's first female US Senator.

Reform movements flourished in New York State in the antebellum years, from peace reform to campaigns to change what people wore, what they ate, and how they spelled. An optimism about the possibilities of personal and societal transformation pervaded the thinking about social problems. Besides abolitionism and women's rights, temperance was an influential reform campaign. The first temperance society in the United States was founded in 1808 in Saratoga Co. The movement swelled and ebbed over the next century, but it was a persistent concern of Protestant reformers until the ratification of Prohibition by the legislature in 1919.

The opening of the Erie Canal also illuminated the increasing might of the state's manufacturing sector. Almost every 19th-century industry of consequence was represented in New York State, and on the eve of the Civil War, the state was a national leader in iron and steel, textiles, clothing manufacture, and grain processing. Notable innovations in transportation and communications had been emerging since the start of the century. The world's first successful steamboat debuted in 1807, when Robert Fulton established a route between New York City and Albany, and the nation's first passenger railroad line, extending between Albany and Schenectady, opened in 1831. Henry Wells and William Fargo started their express company in New York City 1852, and Western Union was founded in Rochester in 1856. Other transportation magnates from the state included Cornelius Vanderbilt, a one-time Staten Island ferry boat captain who by the 1860s controlled the New York Central, and his sometime collaborators and rivals, Daniel Drew and Jay Gould.

As powerful as commerce and industry became, they never eclipsed New York State's varied and prosperous agricultural sector. By 1830 New York State was the national leader in wheat and other field crops. Buffalo and Brooklyn were pioneers in the development of grain elevators, and the mills of Rochester earned it the nickname of Flour City. By the mid–19th century, the development of the Erie Canal, lateral canals, and the growing network of railroads pushed many farmers away from subsistence or semisubsistence agriculture into direct production for the market. New York State was also a center of agricultural periodicals and agricultural implement manufacture.

The state was a leader in the advance of education. The Common School Law of 1812 facilitated the establishment of local, largely publicly financed, schools. By 1843, 10,769 local school districts had been established. Academies were the main venues for secondary education. By 1855, 155 academies were recognized by the Board of Regents. The Emma Willard School (1821) in Troy was one of the first women's academies in the country that offered a rigorous academic curriculum. Joseph Henry, a leading scientist and scientific administrator in 19th-century America, started his professional career at the Albany Academy, where he performed his crucial experiments on electromagnetism before moving to the Smithsonian Institution in Washington, DC. Higher education in the state began with King's College (now Columbia University) in New York City in 1754. Union College, in Schenectady, was the second, founded in 1795. By the middle of the 19th century, a network of colleges, almost all with denominational affiliations, had been established across the state. Institutions that shaped the development of technological education include the US Military Academy (1802) at West Point and Rensselaer Polytechnic Institute (1824). New York State was a leader in the governmental sponsorship of research. The New York State Geological and Natural History Survey, which evolved into the New York State Museum, was founded in 1836 to survey the state's natural resources and is the oldest continuously operated geological survey in the United States.

Amid the general prosperity in New York State in the first half of the 19th century were two competing models of economic development. Starting with Alexander Hamilton, many political leaders in the state favored policies in which government aided and regulated business. Banking charters were doled out, with the approval for incorporation often requiring the exchange of political favors. Monopolies were sometimes granted by the legislature; for example, the legislature granted a monopoly in 1798 to Robert R. Livingston to operate steamboats on New York waters, which led to Livingston's and Robert Fulton's operation of steamboats between New York City and Albany. Hamilton's great successor in an expansive view of government in promoting business enterprise was De Witt Clinton. The Erie Canal was built with public expenditures and state borrowing and was the largest state-funded internal improvement of its era. When the US Supreme Court voided Livingston's monopoly in the landmark case *Gibbons v Ogden* (1824), it was an indication of a new way of thinking about the relation between government and business enterprise.

This new relationship between business and government is associated with Martin Van Buren. Clinton had played both sides of the aisle during his political career. In contrast, Van Buren was an advocate for party loyalty, the chief architect of the modern party system, a key founder of the modern Democratic Party, and a provider of crucial northern support for Andrew Jackson. Although Van Buren became the first New Yorker to become president of the United States in 1836, this was the least successful office of his career, and he dominated politics in New York State for several decades. Van Buren and his supporters, known as the Albany Regency, opposed many of Clinton's policies; they favored limiting the role of government in private business enterprise and banking and opposed the state taking on additional debt.

The 1821 New York State constitution represented the first important manifestation of this position. The constitution adopted principles that led to universal white male suffrage by 1826. The Democratic position on state government was enshrined in the 1846 Constitution, which embodied many Van Burenite principles. It rejected the quasi-feudal land tenure of the manors, an issue that had in the early 1840s led to the antirent agitation in the Hudson River valley. It also established strict and severe limits on state indebtedness and on the ability to finance improvements through bond sales. For the remainder of the century the state's politics, especially by the Democrats, reflected this laissez-faire approach to state government, trying to limit its expenditures and its role in the lives of average New Yorkers. The Clintonian approach, emphasizing more government support for business and internal improvements, was carried on by the Whig Party after De Witt Clinton's death in 1828. By 1840 Thurlow Weed and William H. Seward were leaders of the Whig Party at both state and national levels. They were also two of the founders of the new Republican Party in the 1850s. The Republican Party had immediate success in New York State, winning the gubernatorial election the first time out in 1854 with Fusion Republican candidate Myron H. Clark and winning the majority of the vote for US president in New York State in 1856 and 1860.

New York State was the birthplace of the first genuine third party, the Antimasonic Party, active in the late 1820s and early 1830s and later largely absorbed by the Whigs. An alternative for those who felt the two major parties were avoiding the issue of slavery was the abolitionist Liberty Party, active in the state in the 1830s and 1840s.

Contemporary developments in the state's arts and tourism industry served to connect regions of the state. The majestic Hudson River landscape inspired the nation's first authentic artistic movement, the mid-19th-century Hudson River school. New York City–based artists of this school symbolically affirmed the links between urban and rural New York by celebrating the forests, waterfalls, and mountains of the Hudson River area. Authors like Washington Irving and Joseph Rodman Drake wrote of the Hudson's "enchantments." Summer tourists sojourned to the Catskills, which were marked as a tourist destination with the 1823 opening of the Catskill Mountain House. Travelers often combined their trips to the Catskills with other tourist destinations, visiting such places as Saratoga Springs for its mineral waters or taking scenic tours along the Erie Canal with a stayover at Trenton Falls (Oneida Co) and terminating at Niagara Falls. By the 1850s and 1860s Saratoga Springs emerged as the most fashionable and prestigious summer resort in the United States.

The state was also a pioneer in other forms of leisure activities. The modern form of baseball was first played in the 1840s in the New York City area, which became home to some of the first great teams, including the Knickerbockers and Gothams of Manhattan and the Eckfords and Atlantics of Brooklyn. One of the central moments in 20th-century American sports occurred in 1947 when the Brooklyn Dodgers broke the color barrier in the major leagues with the signing of Jackie Robinson. The lack of credible evidence that baseball was invented in Cooperstown (Otsego Co) has not prevented that village from becoming the home of the National Baseball Hall of Fame. The Saratoga Race Course (1847) is the oldest major sports venue in the United States. Other sports with important New York State histories include football, basketball, ice hockey, boxing, and golf.

Civil War to the Early 20th Century

Hundreds of thousands of young men from New York State served in the Civil War. With the passage of the 15th Amendment to the US

Constitution in 1870, African Americans in New York State finally received the right to vote. The state's economy reached new heights. The National Banking Act of 1863 strengthened New York City's dominance of the nation's banking industry, and the financial markets of Wall St underwent a decade of growth in the 1860s. Eastman Kodak in Rochester, General Electric in Schenectady, and Endicott Johnson Shoes in Endicott (Broome Co) are only some of the best-known companies formed after the Civil War. By the 1890s hydroelectric power brought huge chemical and steel factories to the Buffalo and Niagara Falls area. Amsterdam and Yonkers were home to large carpet companies. The late 19th century was the state's agricultural heyday. The number of farms peaked at over 241,000 in 1880. Butter, cheese, and whole-milk farming replaced wheat as the state's leading agricultural product. Railroad and refrigeration technology expanded the "milkshed" for regular deliveries to the New York metropolitan area. From the middle to the end of the 19th century New York State led the nation in the number and value of farms and in improved acreage.

The religious culture of the Burned-over District underwent a slow cooling-off, and the frontiers of religious enthusiasm moved to the nation's South and West. Of the antebellum reform movements, only temperance remained an active and popular reform cause after the Civil War. The new temper of reform was symbolized by the Chautauqua Movement. Founded in western New York State in 1874, it became synonymous with morally earnest, Protestant-based adult education and lectures.

Although New York City had been the largest city in the state from the time of its founding, it was during the postwar period that it began to dwarf the state's other cities in population. In 1860, 20% of the state's population lived in New York City, with an additional 8% living across the East River in the City of Brooklyn. By 1900, the first census to include the consolidated five-borough New York City, 47% of the state's population lived in the city. By 1925 New York City had surpassed London and was the most populated city in the world.

The most significant reason for the increase in population was the heightened flow of immigration. Starting in the 1840s large numbers of immigrants came from Ireland and Germany. The potato famine of the 1840s pushed millions of Irish from their troubled homeland, with many settling in New York State. Catholic, Protestant, and Jewish Germans also arrived in large numbers. The new arrivals sought work in the state's rapidly growing industries and often occupied the lowest rungs on the economic ladder. A second wave of immigrants arrived from 1880 to 1920, with large numbers of Italians, Jews, ethnic Poles, and other immigrants from eastern and southern Europe. The immigration of the 19th century changed the religious character of the state. Roman Catholics challenged the use of Protestant texts in public schools, and Jews fought against persistent anti-Semitism. By the turn of the 20th century, New York City had more Jews than any other city in the world and a majority of the Jews in the United States. By the early 20th century 30–40% of the state's population was Roman Catholic, concentrated in New York City and the state's other big cities. In 1850, 46% of New York City's population was foreign-born; the figure was 37% in Erie Co (including Buffalo) and 30% in Monroe Co (including Rochester). The state's largest cities retained comparable levels of foreign-born into the mid–20th century.

By the Civil War years, a new pattern had been established in the state's politics that still remains largely in place. New York City was heavily Democratic, while much of the rest of the state was Republican. The dominant organization within the Democratic Party from the 1860s to the 1960s was Tammany Hall, the regular Democratic organization of New York City. Controlled by the Irish for most of its history, Tammany became a model for a successful urban machine. Although the Tweed Ring in the 1870s brought scandal and obloquy, Tammany quickly recovered and for nearly a century was one of the strongest political institutions in the state, holding the balance of power in many statewide elections. Too close an identification with Tammany was often a liability, however, and Democrats successful statewide during this period, such as Govs Samuel J. Tilden and Grover Cleveland, kept Tammany at arm's length and in the process developed national reputations.

The Republican Party also had its powerful statewide bosses, such as US senators Roscoe Conkling in the 1870s and early 1880s and Thomas C. Platt, "the Easy Boss," into the early 20th century. After 1894 the Republicans were able to redistrict the legislature in ways that, as Alfred E. Smith later lamented, made it "constitutionally Republican" by systematically underrepresenting New York City. The two parties nonetheless remained competitive. In the 37 presidential elections between 1856 and 2000, the Republicans have captured the state 19 times, the Democrats 18 times.

Although organized labor had been a force in the state dating back to the Working Men's Party of the 1820s, the labor movement became increasingly important after the Civil War. By 1882 the Knights of Labor local in New York City had 60,000 members, and locals had been organized in almost every county of the state. Though the Knights of Labor lost most of its influence by the turn of the 20th century, the Federation of Organized Trades and Labor Unions, founded in 1881 and renamed the American Federation of Labor in 1886, has remained the preeminent labor organization in the United States. With stronger organizations came increased political influence. As early as 1867 a state law was passed limiting some employees to eight-hour days. An 1895 state law limited bakery employees to 60-hour workweeks, but the law was voided by the US Supreme Court in 1905 in the landmark case *Lochner v New York*.

After the Civil War, the Adirondacks began to flourish as a tourist spot, and a number of wealthy families built "great camps" in the region. This helped spark an emerging concern about protecting pristine areas from commercial development, which became an increasingly important statewide political issue. The perceived tawdriness that had grown up around Niagara Falls led to state creation of one of the first state parks in the nation, the Niagara Reservation, in 1885. The Catskill and Adirondack preserves were created the same year. A more ambitious plan, one that curtailed development in a wide swath of the Adirondacks, culminated in the creation of the Adirondack Park in 1892, one of the founding acts in the modern environmental movement.

The literary traditions started by Washington Irving and James Fenimore Cooper evolved in the 19th century. Herman Melville, of Dutch ancestry and raised in New York City and Albany, wrote about New York City in several works and opened his great nautical novel, *Moby-Dick,* on the "insular city of the Manhattoes." A number of other figures drew on their experiences both in New York City and other areas of the state, including Stephen Crane, Edith Wharton, and Harold Frederic. The most acclaimed American writer of the late 19th century, Mark Twain (Samuel L. Clemens), married Olivia Louise Langdon from Elmira and spent many summers in the state. One of the centers of the late 19th-century arts and crafts movement, which rejected mass production in favor of personally fashioned items, was New York State. Syracuse was the center of the Stickley companies, producing classic Mission-style furniture. The Roycroft communities in East Aurora (Erie Co) made finely printed books, artworks, furniture, and a variety of other items.

Early 20th Century

In 1900 New York State was the wealthiest and most populated state in the United States and had the greatest industrial output. Impressive factories operated across the state, from the Lackawanna Iron and Steel Co plant (Erie Co) to the General Electric factories in Schenectady, textile factories in Little Falls (Herkimer Co) and Utica, and the giant Endicott Johnson boot and shoe factory in Endicott (Broome Co), the same village where a few years later the forerunner of IBM formed. In Rochester, Eastman Kodak had just introduced the Brownie camera. New hydroelectric power generation brought giant chemical and metallurgical factories to the Niagara and St. Lawrence Rivers.

The consolidation of New York City in 1898 as a five-borough city announced its arrival as an international center. Its symbol was the skyscraper. In 1913 the tallest building in the city, the Woolworth Building, was 792 feet (241 m). In the early 1930s the Chrysler and Empire State Buildings were over 1,000 feet (305 m). Other cities were also making bold claims about their prospects. In 1900 Buffalo was the ninth largest city in the United States and, to celebrate, held the Pan-American Exposition in 1901. The exhibit buildings, including the 375 ft (114 m) Electric Tower, were covered with electric lights, which provided fairgoers with the novelty of nighttime illumination. Rochester also experienced a renaissance in the early 20th century. The philanthropy of George Eastman, the founder of Eastman Kodak, helped spark a major expansion of the city's physical and cultural assets.

But New York State in the early 20th century had more than its share of serious social problems. Along with the promise of big city life came overcrowding in wretched tenements, backbreaking work in factories, child labor, poverty, corrupt urban political machines, and the full array of vice available in cities. The agricultural areas of the state had their own problems. Thoughtless extraction by the timber industry continued to strip the land of valuable natural resources. Although New York was still one of the leading agricultural states, by the early 20th century the number of farms and farmers was decreasing, and this pattern continued for the remainder of the century. Many rural towns and villages had declining population. Concerns about the weakening of agriculture spurred the birth of the Country Life Movement, started by Cornell University agronomist Liberty Hyde Bailey.

In many ways the division between the urban and rural areas of the state was stark. The rural areas were primarily Protestant and suspicious of the non-Protestant (Roman Catholic and Jewish) majorities in the cities. Nativism, immigration restriction, and, in the 1920s, the Ku Klux Klan would find a home in rural areas from Long Island to the Southern Tier. Prohibition was the great rural crusade of the era, and the state legislature voted for the 18th Amendment in 1919 over the strenuous objection of the urban areas. Although the cities had plenty of old-line Republicans, their populations and politics were dominated by immigrants and the children of immigrants, often with little knowledge of or interest in the rural areas.

These tensions were to a large extent overcome through a creative politics that emphasized the triad of strong government regulation, civic-minded business practices, and powerful labor unions. In no other state was this political synthesis, generally known as Progressivism, as important or long lasting. "The New York Idea," as the state's version of Progressivism was sometimes known, had a profound effect on the nation as a whole.

Republicans came to Progressivism through a legacy of high-minded reform dating to the era of abolitionism. Its main concerns included the righting of social ills, conservation, the discarding of ineffective and corrupt urban government, and control of trusts and other industrial combinations. Both in New York State and nationally, the movement's standard-bearer was Theodore Roosevelt. In 1912 he was the primary founder of the short-lived Progressive Party. Charles Evans Hughes, one of Roosevelt's Republican successors as governor, came to prominence investigating fraud in New York City's life insurance industry in 1905. Hughes believed in an expansive role for government, and among his innovations was the establishment of the forerunner of the Public Service Commission to control utility rates.

Democrats were active Progressives as well but were more concerned about factory labor and urban problems and had closer ties to immigrants and organized labor. New York City politicians such as Al Smith and Robert F. Wagner Sr were Tammany stalwarts, but the success of Republican Progressivism and catastrophic episodes like the Triangle Shirtwaist Factory fire in New York City in 1911 helped catalyze Democratic politicians into being proponents of reform, sponsoring factory investigation commissioners and pushing for workers' compensation, child labor laws, and other landmark legislation. The Democratic Party developed a new image—at once urban and reform minded, pro-immigrant, and welcoming to African Americans—that increasingly defined the northern Democratic Party.

Modern gubernatorial politics in New York State begins with Al Smith, elected for the first of his four terms in 1918. He greatly strengthened the power of the executive branch and gubernatorial control over state government, established a formal budgeting process, and increased support for housing, healthcare, labor, and public recreation and parks. Smith's record as an activist governor was expanded upon by his successor, Franklin D. Roosevelt. Faced with the unemployment of up to a quarter of the state's workers because of the depression, Roosevelt established the Temporary Emergency Relief Agency in 1931. New York State had the first comprehensive work relief program. Roosevelt was elected president in 1932 in part through his promises to expand the New York programs to the nation as a whole. Many of the leading figures of the New Deal, such as Frances Perkins, and Harry Hopkins, started their political careers with Roosevelt. Under Roosevelt's successor, Herbert H. Lehman, the first Jewish governor of the state, New York State developed a number of social programs in advance of similar New Deal legislation. The liberalism of Smith, Roosevelt, and Lehman was premised on extending equal rights and treatment to all of the state's citizens, primarily through an expansion of services. Their credo was enshrined in the 1938 New York State Constitution, which provided guaranteed rights for labor, required aid and support of the indigent, and established access to decent and affordable housing as a basic constitutional right.

The progressive commitment to public works on a grand scale had as its greatest exponent Robert Moses, a protégé of Al Smith and one of the most visible figures in state government from the 1920s to the 1960s. Moses left his mark from Long Island to the Niagara River to the St. Lawrence Seaway, building parks and the parkways to get to them and constructing bridges and highways to get people around and out of the large cities. He was an ardent believer in slum clearance and both displaced thousands of families from urban neighborhoods and built thousands of units of urban lower- and middle-class housing.

New York State at Midcentury

As early as 1840, Brooklyn Heights was perhaps the first real suburb in the United States. Westchester Co became, by the late 19th century, the first extensively suburbanized area in the nation. The automobile greatly sped up the process of suburbanization, which greatly expanded in the 1930s and 1940s. With the growth of the aviation industry during World War II, Nassau Co ex-perienced a remarkable population increase. Developments like Levittown, which opened in 1947, became national models for quickly constructed, inexpensive middle-class housing. In the course of the 1950s, Nassau Co's population increased from 672,765 to 1,300,171. Suffolk Co is now the most populated county in the state outside of New York City. More than half the population of the state outside of New York City now live in suburbs, and widespread suburbanization has changed the character of cities and put great pressure on the rural areas. In many urban counties, such as Erie and Monroe, from 1950 to 1990 the population underwent a reversal: from 75% of the population living in the central city to 75% living in the suburbs.

Along with suburbanization, the automobile led to the rise of new leisure patterns. Many classic 19th-century resorts such as the Catskill Mountain House and resorts in Saratoga Springs fell on hard times. New areas, such as the lower Catskill areas in Sullivan and Ulster Cos, opened to large-scale tourism, especially to Jews from New York City in the so-called borsht belt. New superhighways (eg, New York State Thruway and Adirondack Northway) made possible the building of new resorts in areas that had been largely inaccessible.

Twenty years of Democratic control of the statehouse ended in 1942, when Thomas E. Dewey was elected governor. He remained in that position until 1954. After one term with a Democrat (W. Averell Harriman), Nelson Rockefeller was elected governor and served through 1974. The heyday of postwar liberalism in New York State was dominated by Republicans. In many ways the governance of Dewey and Rockefeller continued the same broad themes of activist government established by their Democratic predecessors. Gov Dewey was the progenitor of the New York State Thruway. He was also the creator of the SUNY system (1948). As World War II ended, New York was the only state without a state university system. But persistent complaints about the underrepresentation of Jews, Blacks, and non-Protestants at the state's private colleges and the surge in college enrollment following the end of World War II led to the creation of SUNY. Rockefeller built on Dewey's legacy and established his own program of public works, including what is now the Governor Nelson A. Rockefeller Empire State Plaza in Albany. Rockefeller also greatly expanded SUNY, which within a few years had over 60 campuses, ranging from community colleges to medical schools and major research universities. Expansion of state services was closely connected to an expansion of citizens' rights. The Ives-Quinn Law in 1945 made New York the first state to prohibit racial discrimination in employment. This later extended to other areas of discrimination, such as public and private housing. In 1970 New York became the first state to legalize abortion, three years before *Roe v Wade.*

Recent History

One of the underlying assumptions of postwar liberalism was continued growth, mainly in urban areas. This, however, did not happen. The state's largest cities stopped growing after 1950. Only New York City has been able to reverse this trend and only since 1980, fueled by new immigrants. For some cities the loss of population has been little short of catastrophic. Between 1950 and 2000, Buffalo, the second largest city in the state, lost half of its population.

While suburbanization was one obvious cause of the depopulation of urban areas, another factor was the movement of many people out of New York State altogether. Between 1970 and 2000 the state's population increased less than 1%. During the 1970s New York State's population declined for the first time in census data going back to the 17th century. Sometime in the late 1960s, California passed New York State as the most populated state in the nation; Texas has also since surpassed New York State in population. New York State's declining industrial base is a critical reason for the population loss. Beginning in the 1940s factories relocated primarily though not exclusively to the south and the west because of lower taxes, lower wage rates, and the ability to hire a nonunion wage workforce. The largest carpet factory in Yonkers moved to Mississippi in the mid-1950s; textile factories in the Mohawk Valley closed at about the same time. In the late 1960s and 1970s the loss of factory jobs became a torrent. Near Buffalo, Bethlehem Steel's Lackawanna factory, which had employed 20,000 at its peak, closed; Long Island lost Grumman, Fairchild, Republic, and the other aviation companies; appliance manufacturers moved out of Syracuse and Utica; and New York City lost most of its garment factories. The trend of deindustrialization continued for the remainder of the century. By the early 21st century the remaining industrial giants that have not closed altogether, like General Electric, Eastman Kodak, and Xerox, retain a small fraction of their maximum employment.

The other main change in New York State in the second half of the 20th century was a transformation of the ethnic and racial mix of the population. At the start of the 20th century African Americans accounted for a little more than 1% of the state's residents. In the first wave of migration from the South (1915–30), Blacks fleeing the corrosive effects of racism and poverty moved to northern cities. There was also a large immigration of Blacks from the Caribbean. The numbers of African Americans in the state more than doubled between 1920 and 1940, when the census recorded 571,221 African Americans, about 4% of the state's population, and Harlem became known worldwide as a center of African American culture. The second migration from 1940 to 1960 had an even greater impact, nearly tripling the state's black population to almost 1.5 million. As many Whites moved to the suburbs, the residential segregation in cities rapidly increased, along with the attendant social problems from concentrated urban poverty. In 2000, 16% of the state's population was African American, much of it concentrated in the state's urban areas.

Puerto Ricans also came in large numbers, often moving to some of the same neighborhoods as African Americans. After federal immigration laws were changed in 1965, the pace of immigration from all over the world rapidly increased. Latinos from the Dominican Republic, Cuba, Mexico, and other nations in Central and South American came in large numbers. In 2000, 15% of the population of New York State was of Latino/Hispanic ethnicity. Chinese, Koreans, and Filipinos and people of various Asian ethnicities increased rapidly as well, making up 5.5% of the state's population in 2000. With large immigrant populations from the Middle East, Africa, and every other inhabited area of the world, in 2000, 3.9 million New Yorkers (20% of the state's population) were foreign-born.

By the 1960s and 1970s the combination of a slowing industrial base and a racially changing population provided the state's liberal traditions with a severe test. Poverty, unemployment, and welfare increased, as did levels of crime and residential segregation. Good-paying jobs seemed scarcer. Public schools, traditionally providing a path for upward mobility, were in crisis. The tenure of John Lindsay as mayor of New York City from 1966 to 1973, during which he went from liberal hero to a nearly universal scapegoat for the city's ills, is emblematic of the stormy path of liberalism during those years. Nelson Rockefeller's final years in office, marked by his mishandling of the 1970 Attica prison uprising, the slowing of the growth of SUNY, and the draconian Rockefeller Drug Laws, were notably more conservative than his earlier years.

During New York City's fiscal crisis of 1975, bankruptcy was narrowly avoided, but its resolution ushered in an era of financial austerity. Democrats regained the governorship in 1974 and held it for 20 years under Hugh Carey and Mario M. Cuomo. Although the Democrats remained firmly progressive, the political climate in both Albany and Washington had changed. Since the 1970s the main political challenge has been fiscal prudence rather than the expansion of services. Some of the state's most prominent Democrats in the last quarter of the 20th century, such as US senator Daniel Patrick Moynihan and New York City mayor Ed Koch, were distinctly more centrist than midcentury Democrats. The tradition of Republican liberalism largely died out after the 1970s. With US senator Alfonse M. D'Amato, Gov George E. Pataki, and New York City mayor Rudolph Guiliani, the state's Republican Party finally caught up with the more conservative trends in the party noticeable nationally since the 1960s. Still, in comparison with the rest of the country, New York State remains one of the most liberal states, and into the 21st century, politicians try to balance the need to attract new industry and keep taxes low with the mandate to provide adequate services for public schools, healthcare, welfare, housing, and other social needs.

New York State was transformed in the closing decades of the 20th century. Few areas in the nation navigated the transition to a postindustrial economy as successfully as New York City. In place of industrial employment came the variety of jobs in a modern service economy, especially the high-tech, communications, and financial services industries. Rather than large corporations employing thousands, smaller entrepreneurial companies flourished. The rising immigration to the city was a vote of confidence in its ability to incorporate and assimilate new immigrants and to meet the economic challenges at hand. The city's flourishing economy helped spark a cultural revival and attract the return of young professionals to urban areas in large numbers. The city remade itself into a center for all things chic and trendy, from fashion to fine dining. Disco, punk rock, and hip hop and rap all had strong roots in New York City. One change in the city's public culture was the new visibility of lesbians and gays. The modern gay rights movement began there after the Stonewall riots in Greenwich Village in 1969 and faced its greatest challenge with the AIDS crisis of the 1980s.

While New York City has prospered in a postindustrial economy, much of the rest of the state has not fared as well. The old factories were shuttered and for the most part were not replaced. Efforts to incubate smaller entrepreneurial firms, often in the computer and high-tech fields, have had mixed success. Urban centers continue to shrink and have become increasingly devitalized. Suburban areas continue to grow in physical size, even though the population of most of those areas does not exhibit positive growth. Statewide the number of farms continue to shrink, down to 30,000 by 1997. In some ways, at the beginning of the 21st century, the contrast between New York City and the rest of the state never seemed greater.

And then, in the course of one horrifying morning, differences between upstate and downstate and all of the petty differences that separate New Yorkers suddenly seemed irrelevant. The approximately 2,750 persons who died in the collapse of the World Trade Center on 11 Sept 2001 were a cross section of the population: rich and poor; native-born and immigrant; Jew, Christian, and Muslim; English speaking and Spanish speaking; gay and straight; urban and suburban.

New York in the early 21st century remains one of the largest and wealthiest states. The state has much to offer its citizens in terms of its economy, cities and suburban areas, and culture. Its problems, however, are equally substantial. Some complain that the political system is ossified. The peculiar situation (unlike any other state) in which Democrats and Republicans each remain in firm control in one house of the legislature has persisted since 1975, and with an incumbency rate approaching 100%, it is unlikely to change in the near future. This has, in the views of many observers, fostered government by "three men in a room" (the majority leaders of the two houses and the governor) in which outside input is not welcomed. The perennial lateness of the budget is another sign of a dysfunctional political system. The economy, particularly outside of New York City, is chronically underperforming, reflected in flat or negative population growth in many areas. Social services, particularly education and healthcare, are underfunded and characterized by sharp disparities between wealthier and poorer areas of the state. The new immigrants are a tremendous asset for the state's future, but their full incorporation into the social, economic, and political structures will not be easy. There is no doubt that New York State will rise to its current challenges. Over almost four centuries, New York State's greatest achievement has been the creation of political and social structures that unite its disparate regions and diverse citizens. The problems of the early 21st century may be unique to our times, but the solutions will draw on some of the enduring themes of the state's long history.

The Encyclopedia of New York State

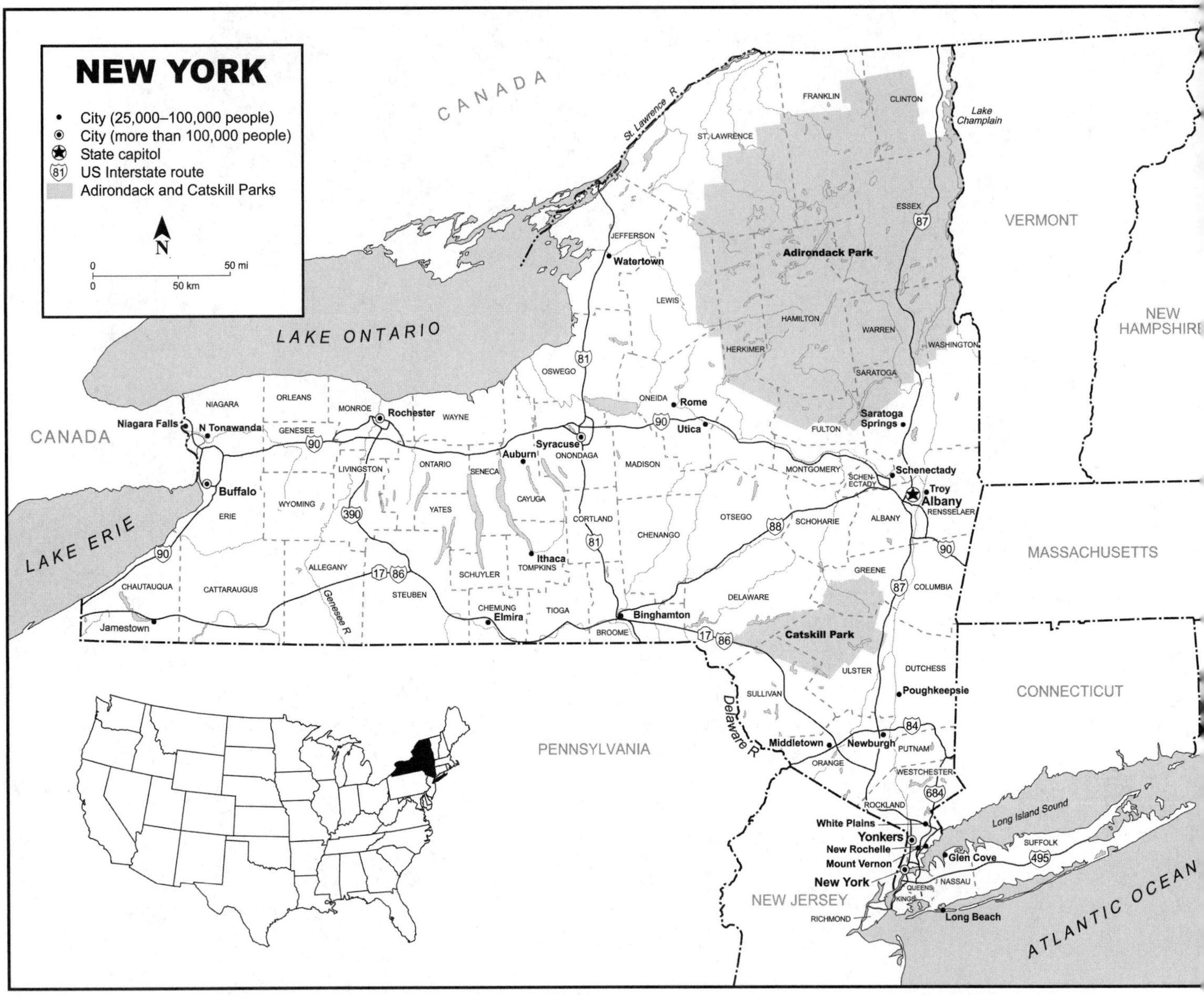
NEW YORK
City (25,000–100,000 people)
City (more than 100,000 people)
State capitol
US Interstate route
Adirondack and Catskill Parks
N
0
50 mi
0
50 km
CANADA
St. Lawrence R.
LAKE ONTARIO
CANADA
LAKE ERIE
Lake Champlain
VERMONT
NEW HAMPSHIRE
MASSACHUSETTS
CONNECTICUT
PENNSYLVANIA
NEW JERSEY
ATLANTIC OCEAN
Long Island Sound
Adirondack Park
Catskill Park
FRANKLIN
CLINTON
ST. LAWRENCE
ESSEX
JEFFERSON
Watertown
LEWIS
HAMILTON
WARREN
HERKIMER
WASHINGTON
SARATOGA
OSWEGO
ONEIDA
Rome
Utica
FULTON
Saratoga Springs
NIAGARA
ORLEANS
MONROE
Rochester
WAYNE
Niagara Falls
N Tonawanda
GENESEE
Syracuse
ONONDAGA
Auburn
MADISON
MONTGOMERY
SCHEN-ECTADY
Schenectady
Troy
Albany
RENSSELAER
LIVINGSTON
ONTARIO
SENECA
Buffalo
WYOMING
YATES
CAYUGA
CORTLAND
OTSEGO
SCHOHARIE
ALBANY
ERIE
CHENANGO
Ithaca
TOMPKINS
SCHUYLER
GREENE
COLUMBIA
ALLEGANY
Genesee R.
CHAUTAUQUA
CATTARAUGUS
STEUBEN
CHEMUNG
Elmira
TIOGA
Binghamton
BROOME
DELAWARE
Jamestown
ULSTER
DUTCHESS
SULLIVAN
Poughkeepsie
Delaware R.
Middletown
Newburgh
PUTNAM
ORANGE
WESTCHESTER
ROCKLAND
White Plains
Yonkers
New Rochelle
Mount Vernon
New York
Glen Cove
SUFFOLK
QUEENS
NASSAU
KINGS
RICHMOND
Long Beach
81
90
390
17
86
88
87
84
684
495

A

A&P [Great Atlantic and Pacific Tea Company]. In 1863 George Huntington Hartford and George Gilman established the Great American Tea Co and sold inexpensive teas from New York City through the mail. Renamed the Great Atlantic and Pacific Tea Co in 1869, the company became one of the first chain stores in the United States. By 1900 it had established nearly 200 stores in 28 states, with the majority in New York City. In addition to selling teas, A&P marketed its own brand of condensed milk, baking powder, spices, and Eight O'Clock blend coffee. After the death of Gilman in 1901, A&P incorporated under the laws of New Jersey and relocated its headquarters to Jersey City. In 1912 the company altered its traditional pattern of selling on credit and making home deliveries by opening a series of smaller cash-and-carry groceries. This strategy proved successful, and from 1917 until 1962 A&P remained the number one grocery chain in the United States. The company headquartered in New York City in 1925, operating out of the Graybar Building on Lexington Ave. From 1925 until 1950 A&P vertically integrated by purchasing fishing fleets and canneries in Alaska, a food manufacturing unit initially known as Ann Page foods, a produce buying unit, a commercial bakery, and the publication *Woman's Day.* After A&P was targeted by legislation in 1938 that focused specifically on eliminating chain stores and after a US Department of Justice probe into the monopolistic practices, the company divested many of its ancillary companies.

The period between 1950 and 1974 was one of decline as A&P continued its conversion, begun in 1937, from smaller groceries to larger supermarkets of 8,000 to 10,000 square feet (740–930 m^2) and closed thousands of its smaller, less-profitable operations. In 1974 the company moved to Montvale, NJ, and the Hartford heirs began to negotiate the sale of the business to the Germany-based Tengelmann Group, which gained majority control in 1979. Over the next two decades A&P purchased chains such as Food Emporium and Waldbaum's in the New York City metropolitan area, pared down the number of unprofitable stores, and built or upgraded to larger units. In 2001 A&P operated 752 stores under 11 names, and sales were $10.6 billion.

"Great A&P Tea Company," *Hoover's Handbook of American Business 2001* (Austin: Hoover's Business Press, 2000)

Walsh, William. *The Rise and Decline of the Great Atlantic and Pacific Tea Company* (Secaucus, NJ: Lyle Stuart, 1986)

Timothy W. Kneeland

Abbott, Berenice (*b* Springfield, Ohio, 17 July 1898; *d* Monson, Maine, 10 Dec 1991). Photographer. Abbott first arrived in New York City in 1918 and led a bohemian existence in Greenwich Village in Manhattan, experimenting with writing, acting, and sculpture. In 1921 she embarked for Paris, where she learned photography as a darkroom assistant in the studio of Man Ray. She was soon a successful portrait photographer in her own right, attracting sitters such as James Joyce and Peggy Guggenheim. Abbott met photographer Eugène Atget (1857–1927) in Paris, whose encyclopedic record of the city left a deep impression on her. Abbott was the principal custodian of Atget's legacy for many years. In 1929 she returned to New York City. Excited by the recent architectural changes, including the second great phase of skyscraper construction, she soon began to create a photographic record of the city. This cumulative portrait of New York City's built environment in the 1930s remains Abbott's best-known and most influential work. Funded by the Works Progress Administration's Federal Art Project from 1935 to 1939 and cosponsored by the Museum of the City of New York, the project culminated in the publication *Changing New York* (1939). Abbott initiated the photography program at the New School for Social Research, where she taught from 1934 to 1958. During the 1940s she photographed scientific subjects, work she continued in the 1950s while also turning her camera to the American landscape. Important solo exhibitions included those held at the Museum of the City of New York (1934, 1937), the Museum of Modern Art in New York City (1970), and the New York Public Library (1989).

For other illustrations see GUN CONTROL; HARLEM; NEW YORK CITY.

Van Haaften, Julia. *A Modern Vision: The Life of Berenice Abbott* (New York: Simon & Schuster, 2000)

Yochelson, Bonnie, and Berenice Abbott. *Berenice Abbott: Changing New York* (New York: New Press, 1997)

Amy Kurlander

Abercromby, James (*b* Glassaugh, Scotland, ?1706; *d* Glassaugh, 23 Apr 1781). British general. Enlisting in the British army and advancing to lieutenant colonel of the Royal Scots, Abercromby served during the French and Indian War as second in command under John Campbell, Earl of Loudoun. In 1756 he arrived in New York Colony and commanded operations at British military headquarters in Albany. Appointed commander in chief of the Royal American Regiment, he directed a full-scale campaign to gain control of Fort Ticonderoga [now in Essex Co] and on 4 July 1758 led 16,000 troops via Lake Champlain from Fort William Henry [now in Lake George, Warren Co] on Lake George to attack the fort. His army making ad-

Lower East Side chicken market, New York City. Photograph by Berenice Abbott, 1937.

vances 5–6 July, he ordered an attack on the fort breastworks on 8 July but calculated tactics poorly and lost 2,000 men. Because of this the campaign was considered a military disaster. Abercromby lost his commission that September and soon returned to Britain.

Bongard, David L., and Tom Magnusson, "Abercromby, James." In *The Harper Encyclopedia of Military Biography*, ed. Trevor N. Dupuy, Curt Johnson, and David L. Bongard (Edison, NJ: Castle Books, 1995)

Mark G. Spencer

abolitionism

Colonial Antislavery Efforts

During the first century and a half of the African presence in colonial New York, whether ruled by the Dutch or the British, few Whites publicly criticized the practice of chattel slavery. Africans sometimes ran away, and there were efforts to throw off the yoke of slavery, slave conspiracies, and rumors of conspiracies. The Colonial Assembly in 1705 passed "An Act to Prevent the Running Away of Negro Slaves out of the City and County of Albany to the French at Canada." The penalty for being recaptured beyond 40 miles (64 km) north of Sarachtoge [now Saratoga] was execution. In 1741, 31 Africans were executed in New York City, charged with being part of a revolutionary plot. Africans held in bondage had their own definition of abolitionism. If many white residents had become uneasy over the prospect of black slavery or black revolt, few were moved to denounce slavery in public.

The Quakers, or Society of Friends, were an exception. The first formal protest against slavery in colonial New York came at a 1767 meeting in Purchase (Westchester Co) when Quakers made a good faith effort to rid their communities of the sin of slavery. Several Quaker congregations even compensated individuals formerly held as slaves by their members. Elias Hicks, a Quaker from Long Island, traveled widely, speaking against slavery and participating in the free produce movement, wherein opponents of forced servitude refused to purchase or consume the products of slavery.

The Postrevolutionary Agenda

Egalitarian rhetoric fired by the struggle for American independence helped to stir interest in the plight of Africans held as slaves, who totaled 21,193 in New York State according to the 1790 federal census. In 1785 the Society for Promoting the Manumission of Slaves was established in New York City. Sponsors, including John Jay, Alexander Hamilton, and Philip Schuyler, advocated passage of a state emancipation bill. The New York Manumission Society also attempted to thwart the illegal importation and exportation of slaves for sale, assisted free Blacks illegally held in bondage, such as Austin Steward, who learned of his legal right to freedom in 1814 from members of the society, and promoted boycotts of merchants who profited from the slave trade. Supporters of the Manumission Society also sponsored New York City's African Free School (1787), one of a number of "free schools" set up across the state by antislavery proponents motivated by charitable as well as religious sympathies. In 1785 and again in 1788 New York State adopted laws that allowed owners to free a slave if that individual could become self-supporting. Prior to that time private manumissions were discouraged by a 1712 law requiring a bond of £200. Though the Manumission Society did not sharply criticize southern slavery, its work stimulated the growth of antislavery sentiment during the early national period.

Cazenovia Fugitive Slave Law Convention, 22 Aug 1850. Frederick Douglass is seated at the left end of the table; Gerrit Smith is standing behind him. To Smith's sides are the escaped slaves Mary *(left)* and Emily Edmonson. Dr Samuel J. May is standing behind the man seated at the right end of the table.

Africans held as slaves were caught up in the conflict between the colonists and England. Some obtained their freedom by seeking asylum with the British or by serving in loyalist militia organized by tories. Others fought with the Americans and received their freedom as a reward for siding with the patriot cause. The Revolutionary War underscored the paradox of slavery and freedom for Blacks and Whites. When the state's 1777 Constitutional Convention convened, slavery's critics held the majority.

After the War for Independence, New York State legislators intensified their efforts to weaken slavery's hold. A 1799 gradual emancipation law stipulated that females born after 1799 would be free at the age of 25 and males born after 1799 would be free at age 28. Legislators also sought to protect black residents with the 1808 Act to Prevent the Kidnaping of Free People of Colour. In 1817 New York State completed plans for emancipation in the state with a law that would manumit those born before 4 July 1799, effective 4 July 1827. African Americans celebrated the latter date as Emancipation Day, though events were often postponed until 5 July, to acknowledge the paradox of celebrating freedom in a country that permitted slavery. For this reason Frederick Douglass in 1852 delayed delivering his famous speech entitled "The Meaning of July Fourth for the Negro" to the Rochester Ladies' Anti-Slavery Society until 5 July.

The Evolving Antislavery Agenda

Many antislavery activists of the early 19th century were gradualists. This outlook was reflected in the movement for colonization and creation of the American Colonization Society (ACS) in Washington, DC, in 1816. Society members sought amelioration of the slavery question and a remedy to the perceived threat of the growing free black population in cities such as New York by proposing to send African Americans to Liberia in West Africa. Many white New Yorkers supported the ACS plan, believing that relocation was a reasonable alternative to total emancipation, especially with the prospect of bringing Christianity to Africa. But the colonization endeavor evoked strong black protest, including dissent from John B. Russwurm and Samuel E. Cornish, editors of New York City's *Freedom's Journal* (1827–29), the first black newspaper published in the United States. Russwurm, however, angered other free black leaders in 1829 when he went to Monrovia, Liberia, with support from the Maryland Colonization Society. Opposition also came from the "colored citizens" of New York City, Brooklyn, and Rochester, who denounced the ACS and drafted resolutions that the United States, not Africa, was their country.

African American leaders in New York State and elsewhere were instrumental in convincing Massachusetts-based William Lloyd Garrison that colonization was detrimental to their interests. On 1 Jan 1831 Garrison published a searing attack on the ACS in the first issue of the *Liberator*. Garrison's journal became the clarion call for immediate abolition. By 1833 immediatists had increased to the point where they felt the need for a national organization. A number of New Yorkers joined with the Garrisonians and immediatist-minded reformers from ten states to organize the American Anti-Slavery Society (AAS) at a December 1833 meeting in Philadelphia. The AAS embodied the Garrisonian philosophy of moral suasion, relying on the pen and the voice to persuade slaveholders to repent and free the enslaved. In the early years of the AAS, New Yorkers dominated the society, which was based in New York City and founded, in part, by brothers Arthur and Lewis Tappan, prominent merchants who were actively involved in religious and social reform.

New York State's first local abolitionist society dedicated to the principle of immediate abolition had been established in summer 1833 at Oneida Institute in Whitesboro (Oneida Co). The members of this student-sponsored society were young recruits from the revivals of Charles Grandison Finney, New York State's preeminent revivalist of the 1820s and 1830s. Though Finney did not directly attack the institution of slavery and shied away from the aggressive abolitionism of the AAS, his evangelical revivals helped inspire the formation of emancipationist voluntary societies in many communities. Particularly in Central and Western New York, the area that came to be known as the Burned-over District, his impact was crucial in the growth of the abolition movement.

Benevolent societies favorable to reform also emerged in New York City and its environs, where the Tappan brothers, John Rankin, and William Green Jr aided the emancipation cause by donating money, encouraging others to join organized abolition, and giving speeches. Both William Goodell's *Genius of Temperance* and Joshua Leavitt's *New York Evangelist* supported immediatism. The Rev Simeon S. Jocelyn, then a missionary to an African American congregation in New York City, and Theodore D. Weld, a former Oneida Institute student and general agent of the Society for Promoting Manual Labor in Literary Institutions, took up the cause.

Charles Stuart, white Jamaica native and retired captain of the British East Indies service, became the first traveling agent of the AAS. Assigned to New York State, Stuart was joined by Amos Phelps, William Goodell, Aaron Judson, and other lecturers who concentrated on regions west of Albany. They organized local and regional abolitionist societies and stirred support for immediatism. These lecturers were not always welcomed, and antiabolitionists brought in speakers to champion the ACS. Abolitionist activity often heightened antiblack sentiment and sometimes sparked violent reactions. A July 1834 antiabolition riot in New York City lasted a week, with crowds attacking the homes of such abolitionists as Lewis Tappan.

In some instances, abolitionist lecturers took refuge in African American churches. Though New York State's free black population numbered less than 45,000 according to the 1830 federal census, African Americans publicly supported immediatism, principally through their churches but also through voluntary associations such as literary societies and antislavery organizations. Blacks in 1835 created another immediatist organization, the New York Committee of Vigilance. Guided by David Ruggles and others, the committee evolved out of fights between Blacks and police officers who were protecting slave catchers in New York State. Abolitionists, business owners, and church members made up the committee, which aided Blacks newly escaped from the South and those most threatened with kidnapping.

Organizing State Abolitionists

When pro-colonization trustees took control of Western Reserve College in Ohio, Beriah Green and Elizur Wright Jr moved to New York State, where they became crucial figures in the immediate abolition crusade. Green became president of Oneida Institute in summer 1833 and continued the process of transforming the institution into an abolitionist school, training young men, black and white, for the ministry of reform. Alexander Crummell, Henry H. Garnet, Amos G. Beman, and William D. Forten, of the Forten family of Philadelphia, were among the African Americans who attended. Until its closing in 1844, Oneida Institute was New York State's most radical experiment in egalitarian education. Wright went on to New York City and became corresponding secretary of the AAS. New England Garrisonians still dominated the national body, however, and some abolitionists in Central New York, such as Utica lawyer Alvan Stewart, were eager to create a state-based society that had control of its own funds.

By 1835 abolitionist organizations, perhaps as many as 300, dotted the New York State landscape from Long Island to the Niagara Frontier. That October, Stewart and Green invited New York State abolitionists to gather in Utica to set up a state society. Approximately 600 immediatists attended the opening meeting held at Bleecker Street Presbyterian Church. Just as William Jay was reading the convention's declaration of sentiments, a mob of antiabolitionists, backed by "gentlemen of property and standing," stormed the church. In the midst of the chaos, Gerrit Smith, a wealthy landholder still affiliated with the ACS, spoke in defense of the abolitionists' right to free speech. He invited the delegates to reassemble in Peterboro (Madison Co), where the New York State Anti-Slavery Society (NYSASS) was chartered on 22 Oct 1835, with offices in Utica. The society's weekly newspaper, the *Friend of Man,* first appeared on 23 June 1836, with William Goodell as editor. The paper folded in 1842 and was replaced with the *Liberty Press* (1843–49) and the *Anti-Slavery Lecturer,* which began in 1839 as a monthly. In August 1838 the NYSASS declared its independence from the AAS and took control of its own financial affairs, pledging $10,000 to the national treasury.

Politicizing Abolition

The NYSASS served as a lodestar for abolitionists, particularly in Central and Western New York. Many in the organization were impatient with Garrison's rejection of running abolitionist candidates in elections. Though uneasy about entering into the morally ambiguous realm of electoral politics, upstate New York abolitionists were pragmatic enough to recognize that moral suasion alone would not end slavery. Some of them began to advocate a biblically based third party. Myron Holley of Rochester, Alvan Stewart, and William Goodell led the push for greater autonomy from the AAS. When delegates gathered for the seventh annual meeting of the national body in New York City in May 1840, the stage was set for a showdown between the Garrisonian loyalists, who favored moral suasion, boycotts, and publicity campaigns, and the politically minded abolitionists. It was "the woman question," however, that precipitated a division. After the New England–based Garrisonians gained control of the convention and elected Abby Kelly to the previously all-male Executive Committee, a rump faction withdrew and formed a rival national organization: the American and Foreign Anti-Slavery Society.

Lewis Tappan had a central role in organizing the new group. Unlike members of the AAS, who made women's rights one of their causes, members of the American and Foreign Anti-Slavery Society opposed diverting resources to women's rights and focused solely on ending slavery. Many New York State abolitionists favoring political action joined the new society. In Central and Western New York, those political abolitionists who maintained some confidence in Garrison increasingly turned to the NYSASS as the principal vehicle of their reform efforts.

The more radical political abolitionists set up a third party, the Liberty Party, in 1840. Members at an Albany convention that year nominated their own presidential candidate, James G. Birney, a former Kentucky slaveholder. Birney received only 7,059 votes nationally with 40% from New York State. In 1844 the Liberty Party faithful met in Buffalo and again nominated Birney for president. This time he garnered approximately 62,300 votes including about 15,000 from New Yorkers, but he lost to Democrat James K. Polk, an expansionist Jacksonian with proslavery leanings. Birney's strong showing in New York State actually took votes away from Whig Henry Clay, giving an important state and perhaps the election to Polk and the Democrats.

Much of the Liberty Party vote in New York State came from abolitionists who had organized "comeouter" churches, fellowships of Christians who either were forced out of conservative denominations or decided to set up their own evangelical communities in protest against the sin of slavery. In 1848 some Liberty Party supporters joined radical (antislavery) Democrats, called Barnburners in New York State, "Conscience" Whigs, and other fusion elements in organizing the Free-Soil Party at a convention in Buffalo. Members named Martin Van Buren their presidential candidate in 1848. With a platform that called for the prevention of slavery in the territories, Van Buren drew nearly 27% of the New York State vote, though winning just 10% nationwide. A Liberty Party remnant including stalwarts like Gerrit Smith and Beriah Green also remained, eventually setting up the Liberty League and, in the late 1850s, the Radical Abolition Society. But other abolitionists thought the Free-Soil movement had a better chance of gaining national political power. Those who threw their support to the Free-Soil Party included a cautious Frederick Douglass.

African American Abolitionists

African Americans had long been active in abolitionist circles in New York State. Like their white counterparts, they sometimes differed on tactics or means. Presbyterian clergyman Henry H. Garnet called for slave resistance in a stirring address given in 1843 in Buffalo, the site of the National Black Convention. Frederick Douglass was there and, true to the nonviolent moral suasion philosophy of the Garrisonians, opposed Garnet. Douglass moved to Rochester four years later and began to publish the *North Star,* which, like Samuel Ringgold Ward's *Impartial Citizen*, provided an important voice for black abolitionists. At the urging of Gerrit Smith and other Central New York abolitionists, Douglass broke with Garrison after concluding that the Constitution could be interpreted as an antislavery document that justified political abolition. Douglass operated out of Rochester for 25 years (1847–72). His home on South Ave, then in the country, was a stop on the Underground Railroad, and in 1848 he attended the Seneca Falls Convention for women's rights. Women's rights advocates Susan B. Anthony, also of Rochester, and Elizabeth Cady Stanton, whose husband Henry B. Stanton was an important New York State abolitionist, counted themselves among Douglass's friends and allies.

Douglass also worked with Harriet Tubman in her efforts to spirit slaves to freedom. After she herself escaped in 1849, Tubman operated out of Canada until settling in Auburn (Cayuga Co) in 1857. Former governor William H. Seward assisted her in buying a small acreage and house, to which she brought her elderly parents. Tubman's first biographer, Sarah Bradford, credited Tubman with bringing out approximately 300 slaves and making 19 trips south; recent research suggests that Tubman made about 9 to 11 trips, bringing north 60 to 80 individuals herself and inspiring others to escape from Maryland's Eastern Shore region. Other Underground Railroad agents also took active roles in the abolitionist movement. Jermain Loguen is said to have assisted as many as 1,500 runaways to move through Syracuse, and William Wells Brown assisted fugitives near Buffalo. Abel Brown, a leader in the Eastern New York Antislavery Society, helped runaways in the Albany area, and Eber Pettit was an important agent in Cattaraugus Co.

As the national debate over the runaway question escalated, vigilance societies continued to flourish. Gerrit Smith and Frederick Douglass were instrumental in calling together a convention of fugitives and their abolitionist allies in Cazenovia (Madison Co) in August 1850. On 1 Oct 1851 a biracial committee of abolitionists, including the Rev Samuel J. May, a staunch advocate of the Garrisonian principle of nonviolence, mobilized to rescue William "Jerry" Henry, a fugitive from Missouri who had been living and working in Syracuse. They spirited him to Canada in defiance of the 1850 US Fugitive Slave Act.

The passage of that law provoked black abolitionists to a higher degree of resistance. Some, such as Samuel Ringgold Ward, James McCune Smith, and James W. C. Pennington, urged political action, while others followed Martin R. Delany's lead in advocating emigration to Africa. Black nationalist sentiment increased. Delegates from 10 northern states gathered at Rochester's Corinthian Hall for the Colored National Convention on 6–8 July 1853. While rejecting emigrationism, they supported efforts to form black-directed national organizations for educational and economic advancement. The National Council of the Colored People, organized at the Rochester meeting, disbanded in 1855, in part because of ideological differences between separatists and integrationists.

Ending Slavery

Passage of the Fugitive Slave Act and agitation over the Kansas-Nebraska Act (1854) magnified sectional conflict and pushed more New Yorkers toward a Free-Soil position. During the subsequent Kansas conflict, Northerners opposing the extension of slavery coalesced in the new Republican Party, but their antisouthern sympathies did not necessarily translate into support for abolition or eradicate the existence of racial discrimination in the North. Many radical Free-Soilers joined the Republicans, following the lead of William H. Seward, and most New York State abolitionists, such as William J. Watkins, Joshua Leavitt, and Frederick Douglass, supported John C. Frémont, the Republican Party presidential candidate in 1856. This course upset abolitionists such as John A. Williams, pastor of the African Methodist Episcopal Zion Church in Troy (Rensselaer Co) and Beriah Green, who refused to endorse the Republicans. Williams spoke against pro-Republican resolutions at the suffrage convention of the Colored Citizens of New York in Troy on 14 Sept 1858.

The US Supreme Court's 1857 *Dred Scott v Sandford* decision, in which Chief Justice Roger B. Taney declared that African Americans were not and never had been American citizens, outraged abolitionists. Frederick Douglass deemed the ruling "judicial incarnation of wolfishness." The decision also greatly distressed many nonabolitionists, including the New York State legislature, which denounced the ruling. More radical antislavery efforts followed. In 1859 John Brown returned from Kansas Territory to his home in the Adirondacks and set in motion his daring assault upon slavery. Brown spoke about his planned raid to many in New York State, including Gerrit Smith and Frederick Douglass. Both were accused of conspiring with Brown after the assault on Harpers Ferry [now in W Va]. Douglass sought refuge in Canada, and Smith suffered an emotional breakdown and spent about seven and a half weeks in the New York State Lunatic Asylum. The actions of Brown, whose body lies in a grave at North Elba (Essex Co), stimulated new debate about how best to counteract southern demands for the perpetual continuation of slavery.

Once the Civil War began, most New York abolitionists threw their support behind the war aims of Pres Abraham Lincoln. Secretary of State Seward provided one of the strongest abolitionist voices in Lincoln's administration. Frederick Douglass also played an important role in bringing Blacks into the larger society, encouraging Lincoln to authorize the enrollment of African American troops. Like Jermain Loguen, Douglass helped recruit black troops once their services were sanctioned. Abolitionists condemned the draft riots that erupted in New York City in summer 1863 when white crowds, led by Irish Democrats, attacked African Americans.

Though emancipation was achieved in 1865, New York abolitionists continued to fight for the

New Yorkers in the Reconstruction Era. Rev Jermain Loguen of Syracuse toured Tennessee in 1865 and returned to New York State believing that "every strong man and woman, preacher and teacher, who can leave for a time their Northern laboring fields [should] go and spend all the time they can in the South." New Yorkers, black and white, responded to such calls to participate in the reconstruction of the South by aiding the newly freed people to read and write, plant and harvest, and exercise their political rights.

Edmonia Highgate belonged to the small army of schoolteachers who went South and were sponsored by the American Missionary Association (AMA). The daughter of free African American parents living in Syracuse, she informed AMA officials in 1864 of her interest in educational missionary work: ". . . I know just what self-denial, self-discipline and domestic qualifications are needed for the work and modestly trust that with God's help I could labor advantageously in the field for my newly freed brethren . . ." Highgate taught in rural Maryland and then in New Orleans as principal of the Frederick Douglass School, which was housed in a former slave pen. She resigned under protest rather than teach under a proposed segregated school system.

Rev Thomas James, a former slave long active in African Methodist Episcopal Zion circles in Central and Western New York, became an AMA agent in 1862. During the Civil War he established a Sunday school and day school for the homeless in Kentucky's contraband camps and sent some of these refugees from slavery north to find homes. He also supervised a federal hospital in Louisville, Ky. In 1878 James helped organize black churches in Ohio, despite opposition from white residents calling themselves Regulators. James went to Kansas in 1880 to assist the Exodusters, former slaves who had fled the South.

Raised in a Quaker household in Sherwood (Cayuga Co) and schooled in the tenets of Garrisonian abolitionism, reformer Emily Howland used education to assist Blacks in freeing themselves of the stigma of slavery and racism. She taught at Washington, DC's Miner School for Colored Girls and then during the Civil War in contraband camps surrounding the capital. After persuading her father, Slocum Howland, to purchase 400 acres (162 ha) of Virginia land, she established the Howland School for the children of Blacks and poor Whites. She returned to Cayuga Co in 1870 but continued to provide financial assistance to the Howland School until 1921, when it was incorporated into Virginia's public school system.

Sernett, Milton C. *North Star Country: Upstate New York and the Crusade for African American Freedom* (Syracuse: Syracuse Univ Press, 2002)

Milton C. Sernett

rights of African Americans during the Reconstruction Era (1865–76) and beyond. Many sons and daughters of the earlier generation of abolitionists were among the army of educators and missionaries who went south to help the newly freed people secure and protect their rights. Other abolitionists turned their energy and experience in new directions, battling for change in areas ranging from temperance to women's rights to civil service reform.

See also BURNED-OVER DISTRICT; SOCIETY OF FRIENDS (QUAKERS); TROY.

Barker, Anthony J. *Captain Charles Stuart, Anglo-American Abolitionist* (Baton Rouge: Louisiana State Univ Press, 1986)
Blackett, R. J. M. *Beating against the Barriers: Biographical Essays in 19th-Century Afro-American History* (Baton Rouge: Louisiana State Univ Press, 1986)
Burke, Ronald K. *Samuel Ringgold Ward: Christian Abolitionist* (New York: Garland, 1995)
Hodges, Graham Russell. *Root and Branch: African Americans in New York and East Jersey, 1613–1863* (Chapel Hill: Univ of North Carolina Press, 1999)
McFeely, William S. *Frederick Douglass* (New York: Norton, 1991)
McManus, Edgar J. *A History of Negro Slavery in New York* (Syracuse: Syracuse Univ Press, 1970)
Pease, Jane H. *They Who Would Be Free: Blacks' Search for Freedom, 1830–1861* (New York: Atheneum, 1974)
Ripley, C. Peter, ed. *The Black Abolitionist Papers,* 5 vols (Chapel Hill: Univ of North Carolina Press, 1985–92)
Sernett, Milton. *Abolition's Axe: Beriah Green, Oneida Institute, and the Black Freedom Struggle* (Syracuse: Syracuse Univ Press, 1986)
———. *North Star Country: Upstate New York and the Crusade for African American Freedom* (Syracuse: Syracuse Univ Press, 2002)
Sorin, Gerald. *The New York Abolitionists: A Case Study of Political Radicalism* (Westport, Conn: Greenwood, 1971)
Strong, Douglas M. *Perfectionist Politics: Abolitionism and the Religious Tensions of American Democracy* (Syracuse: Syracuse Univ Press, 1999)
Wellman, Judith. *Grassroots Reform in the Burned-over District of Upstate New York: Religion, Abolitionism, and Democracy* (New York: Garland, 2000)
White, Shane. *Somewhat More Independent: The End of Slavery in New York City, 1770–1810* (Athens: Univ of Georgia Press, 1991)

Milton C. Sernett

abortion. During the colonial period abortion was common and legal when performed before "quickening," the point at which the first motion of the fetus in the womb is felt by a pregnant woman (approximately the fourth month of pregnancy). In New York State this changed in 1828 when the legislature outlawed abortion, making it a misdemeanor when performed before quickening, and a felony when performed after. The main supporters of abortion law were male physicians who sought to establish control over reproductive medicine. Illegal abortions continued, however, even though women undergoing the procedure faced a high risk of illness or death. New York City was estimated to have about 200 abortion providers during the 1870s. The most famous was Madame Restell (Ann Trow Lohman), whose practice of abortion between 1831 and 1878 generated wealth for herself and hostility from her opponents, including Anthony Comstock.

Through the Gilded Age and Progressive Era, abortion opponents within the medical profession sought to enforce criminal abortion statutes and to drive out abortion providers. Although physicians had led the movement to outlaw abortion, they also led the movement to legalize it. In 1933 William J. Robinson and A. J. Rongy, members of the American Medical Association and New York State and county medical societies, published separate books urging the legalization of abortion. Despite the changing views of some physicians, governmental sanctions remained in place and were tightened. In 1942 the state legislature passed two laws intended to restrict illegal abortions even further. One required women who had undergone abortions to testify against the abortionist in criminal trials; the second made doctors who provided abortion referrals equally guilty with those who performed them. New York State had long allowed therapeutic abortions to preserve the life of the mother, with the vague definition of therapeutic abortion creating a legal loophole under which women obtained abortion legally. During the mid-1900s the number of therapeutic abortions fell dramatically after hospitals adopted a new system that required a woman seeking abortion to gain approval from a committee of physicians.

Toward Legalizing Abortion

Not until the 1960s did the movement to legalize abortion break into public view. Together with scholars and an emergent feminist movement, physicians assumed a position of leadership in the movement to legalize abortions, citing the health dangers associated with illegally obtained abortions. In New York State pressure to legalize abortion came from many quarters. In 1965, the *New York Times* endorsed reform of abortion laws. Clergy organized to coordinate abortion referrals; one such group was the Clergy Consultation Service on Abortion, established in New York City in 1967 by Rev Howard Moody, a Baptist pastor, and operated out of his Judson Memorial Church. Most significant was a revitalized feminist movement that campaigned for reproductive rights. In 1967 the National Organization of Women (NOW) became the first national group to advocate legalizing abortion. That year NOW–New York State adopted an abortion rights statement, and members, led by Betty Friedan, picketed a meeting of the New York State Constitutional Convention to call for abortion rights. Abortion reformers also took to the streets in 1969, when the radical feminist group Redstockings held a speak-out on abortion at Washington Square Methodist Church in New York City.

In 1970 the state legislature voted to legalize abortion performed by a licensed physician through the first 24 weeks of pregnancy, the most progressive abortion law in the country. The state senate approved the measure by a vote of 31 to 26, and the bill passed the state assembly by a single vote, that of Assemblyman George Michaels, a Democrat from Auburn (Cayuga Co). On 11 Apr 1970 Gov Nelson A. Rockefeller signed the bill into law. Immediately after the law went into effect on 1 July, the Women's Medical Center in New York City opened the state's first freestanding abortion clinic, and Planned Parenthood Center of Syracuse became the first affiliate to offer abortion services. In 1972 the legislature voted to repeal the law, but Gov Rockefeller vetoed the measure. When the US Supreme Court's decision in *Roe v Wade* (1973) held that abortion was a constitutional right and that states could not regulate abortion during the first trimester and could only regulate the procedure during the second three months for the protection of the women's health, New York was one of only four states (including Alaska, Hawaii, and Washington) in which abortions were legal and was the only state without a residency requirement. Legal abortions in the state peaked in 1973, when over 200,000 were performed.

Reactions to Legalization

Legalization brought immediate polarization and initiated a debate between the "pro-choice" advocates of abortion and their "pro-life" opponents. Although strong support for abortion rights exists, antiabortion forces also have a powerful presence. The genesis of the Right to Life Party (RTLP) was a group of women in Nassau Co who lobbied in 1969 against legalizing abortion. After abortion reform was enacted, the women continued their opposition. One of RTLP's founders was Ellen McCormack of Bellmore (Nassau Co), who would run unsuccessfully for US president in 1976 and 1980. Support for the antiabortion movement has been strongest within the Roman Catholic Church and among fundamentalist Protestants. During the 1980s New York State was a major center of direct-action protests organized by the right to life movement. The pioneer organization in these protests was Operation Rescue (1988), headquartered in Binghamton and led by Randall Terry, a Protestant minister from Rochester. In addition to engaging in direct action, blockading women's clinics and confronting those who sought entry, the group's members sought unsuccessfully to persuade government leaders to enact legislation that would define a fetus as a person and to endorse statutes stating that "life begins at conception." NOW–New York State won a permanent injunction in 1989 in the US District Court for the Southern District of New York against Operation Rescue for blockades in the New York City metropolitan area.

Tension increased between pro-life and pro-choice forces during the 1990s, often taking the form of harassing speech and actions, threats against providers, and physical violence. In one of the most violent actions, abortion doctor Barnett Slepian was slain in his Amherst (Erie Co) home on 23 Oct 1998; antiabortion activist James Kopp was charged with his murder in June 2002 and, after refusing a jury trial, was convicted of second-degree murder by a judge in March 2003 and sentenced to life in prison. In the 1990s officials began to enforce provisions of the federal Racketeer Influenced and Corrupt Organizations (RICO) statute and the federal Freedom of Access to Clinic Entrances (FACE) that limited protesters' proximity to clinics and to prosecute those using violence against women's clinics, holding antiabortion groups and their leaders financially responsible for the results of the violence they had sanctioned. The New York State Clinic Access and Anti-Stalking Act, which went into effect on 1 Dec 1999, included provisions that made it a crime to interfere with healthcare services. Pro-life activists have decreased access to abortion by driving practitioners from the field, thus making abortions more difficult to obtain. In 1996 New York State had 266 abortion providers, declining to 234 in 2000. A total of 164,630 women obtained abortions in the state in 2000, a rate of 39.1 abortions per 1,000 women of reproductive age. In 2002 New York State had no legislative restrictions on abortion; there was no requirement for a minor to obtain parental consent or notification; Medicaid funding was available for medically necessary abortions; and there was no waiting period. Sixteen counties in the state outside of New York City had abortion providers in 2002.

Solinger, Rickie, ed. *Abortion Wars: A Half Century of Struggle, 1950–2000* (Berkeley: Univ of California Press, 1998)

Penny Messinger

***Abrams v United States,* 250 US 616 (1919).** Free speech case. Jacob Abrams, Mollie Steimer, and three other Russian-born Jewish immigrants, all anarchists and socialists, were arrested in August 1918 for distributing leaflets in New York City. The leaflets, written in English and Yiddish, called Pres Woodrow Wilson a coward and urged a general strike by workers in ammunition factories to protest the sending of American troops to northern Russia following the 1917 Bolshevik Revolution. Convicted of violating the 1918 amendment to the Espionage Act of 1917, Steimer was sentenced to 15 years in prison, while the three men (the fourth died while in custody) each received a 20-year term. The Supreme Court voted 7–2 to reject the argument that the defendants had engaged in speech protected by the First Amendment. The *Abrams* case is notable for Justice Oliver Wendell Holmes's dissent (joined by Justice Louis Brandeis), which asserted that the pamphlets were not an immediate incitement to criminal activity. Holmes also articulated his famous "marketplace of ideas," arguing for the maximum amount of allowable speech, where the best ideas would eventually prevail. This was a departure from his position in previous incitement cases and marked the first of many dissents that would eventually lead to a more protective view of free speech. This revised view would come too late for the defendants in the *Abrams* case. In November 1921, having agreed to leave the United States in lieu of serving their prison terms, they were deported to the Soviet Union.

Polenberg, Richard. *Fighting Faiths: The Abrams Case, the Supreme Court, and Free Speech* (New York: Viking, 1987)

Timothy P. Gordinier

abstract expressionism. See ART, NEW YORK CITY AREA.

Abyssinian Baptist Church. Oldest African American Baptist congregation in New York State. Abyssinian, or Ethiopian, was a common term for African Americans in the early 19th century. The church was founded in 1808 as an outgrowth of First Baptist Church in Manhattan. Thomas Paul of the Boston Baptist community and a pioneering missionary to Haiti was called to be the first pastor of the church on Worth St. Under the leadership of William Spellman (1856–85) the congregation grew to a membership of 1,600 and built a large church on Waverly Place in Greenwich Village. In 1902 Charles Satchell Morris led the congregation to new facilities on West 40th St. During the pastorate of Adam Clayton Powell Sr (1907–37), the growing congregation moved to its current location at West 138th St. He was followed by his son, Adam Clayton Powell Jr (1937–72), who became a leader of the civil rights struggle in the US Congress and attracted national attention to the church. In the early 21st century, Abyssinian has become a national church of the black community. Its pastors include statesmen such as Samuel D. Proctor (1972–89) and Calvin O. Butts III (1989–). Its program has an emphasis on the fine arts and caring for human needs through housing and neighborhood action outreach, such as the Abyssinian Development Corp. Denominationally, it is affiliated with the American Baptist Churches in the USA.

Fitts, Leroy. *A History of Black Baptists* (Nashville: Broadman, 1985)

William H. Brackney

Abzug [née Savitzky], **Bella** (*b* New York City, 24 July 1920; *d* New York City, 31 Mar 1998). Congresswoman. The daughter of Russian Jewish immigrants, Abzug grew up as part of a politically aware household. She graduated from Hunter College (1942) and Columbia Law School (1947). As a left-leaning lawyer she defended communists and took civil rights cases. A feminist and peace activist, she helped found Women Strike for Peace. Also active in the reform Democratic movement, Abzug was elected to Congress in 1970 from Manhattan, served three terms, and was the first member of Congress to call for the impeachment of Richard M. Nixon. She narrowly lost the Democratic primary for US Senate in 1976, lost in the New York City mayoral primary in 1977, and tried unsuccessfully to return to the House of Representatives in 1978. She is remembered as a forceful, sometimes abrasive advocate for left-wing liberal and feminist ideas.

Abzug, Bella S. *Bella! Ms Abzug Goes to Washington.* Ed. Mel Ziegler (New York: Saturday Review Press, 1972)
Cook, Blanche Wiesen. "Abzug, Bella." In *Jewish Women in America: An Historical Encyclopedia,* ed. Paula E. Hyman and Deborah Dash Moore (New York: Routledge, 1997)

Susan Roth Breitzer

academies. From the 1770s to the 1880s, academies were the dominant form of postelementary schooling in New York State and throughout the United States. New York boasted the nation's largest and most highly organized system of state support for academies, administered by the Board of Regents. Hundreds of academies operated outside the Regents system as well. During the late 19th century, many academies converted to public high schools, private preparatory schools, state normal schools, or independent colleges.

DEFINITION

Academies possessed two chief features: breadth of curriculum and corporate legal status. Like private schools of the early republican era, which operated out of teachers' homes or rented public rooms, academies offered a range of studies in response to popular demand, backed by tuition dollars. Their curricula typically encompassed reading, writing, arithmetic, classical languages, and the "higher branches of English education," which included geometry, composition, history, rhetoric, chemistry, algebra, and the physical sciences. Most academies also offered applied subjects such as navigation, bookkeeping, surveying, music, painting, drawing, and needlework. The schools' market-oriented approach attracted a broader clientele than Latin grammar schools, which focused on classical languages. Academies were incorporated by the state and governed by boards of trustees instead of by individual schoolmasters. Thus in addition to tuitions, they drew funding from local communities, churches, or endowments, enjoying greater financial stability and longevity than private schools.

EARLY ACADEMIES

When the New York State legislature established the Board of Regents in 1784, a number of academies already existed. Schenectady Academy (1771), Washington Seminary (1776) in Claverack (Columbia Co), and Farmer's Hall (1784) in Goshen (Orange Co) first developed as Latin grammar schools and then broadened their curricula. Kingston Academy (1774) in Ulster Co and Washington Academy (1780) in Salem (Washington Co) were originally organized as academies. The first academies to receive Regents charters, both in 1787, were Clinton Academy of East Hampton (Suffolk Co) and Erasmus Hall of Flatbush (Kings Co).

Early academies arose in established areas such as the upper Hudson Valley, Long Island, and New York City. As New York State's commercial networks developed and new territories opened to settlement, academies followed. Canandaigua Academy was chartered in 1795, just a few years after the Town of Canandaigua (Ontario Co) became the headquarters for land sales in the Phelps and Gorham Purchase. In 1796 the nearly simultaneous founding of Cherry Valley and Otsego Academies resulted from competition between Cherry Valley and Cooperstown (Otsego Co) to attract prominent settlers.

In the early years most academies enrolled both male and female students. Only prestigious or well-endowed institutions, such as Albany Academy (1813), Canandaigua Academy, and New York City's Grammar School of Columbia College (1838), could afford to exclude half the potential clientele. Academies generally served a wide range of ages and grade levels, and their student bodies comprised children of farmers, crafters, and traders, as well as those of professionals and the elite. Though many academy principals personally favored the classical studies associated with college preparation, they depended on students of common school and advanced English subjects for most of their tuition. In 1804 thriving Erasmus Hall enrolled only 33 of its 107 students in classical studies.

Early academies were also ecumenical in affiliation as they sought to maximize funding and enrollment. While particular ministers might organize or teach at an academy, boards of trustees usually included members from multiple denominations, which was sometimes required by founding documents. Regents legislation of 1787 forbade religious tests for faculty and sectarian instruction at institutions with Regents charters.

EXPANSION

In New York State the heyday of canal building, railroad construction, and town building was also the heyday of academy building. By 1855, 155 Regents academies were open, more than triple the number in 1825. Even more dramatic was the increased number of students who qualified for Regents subsidies. In 1855 this group totaled 36,585 students, more than 10 times the number of subsidized students enrolled in 1825. In some small communities almost half of the youths attended a local academy at some time. The attendance rate was much lower statewide, 13–19%, but such figures compared favorably with the state's high school attendance rates as late as the 1890s.

Jacksonian politics spurred the growth of academies and enrollments as political leaders widely disseminated state benefits. Legislators opened up the incorporation process, making charters for academies available on easy terms. They also increased school funding and pressured the Regents to include "higher study" in the higher branches of English education as well as classical studies. This liberalization allowed additional academies, particularly female-only ones, to acquire Regents status and thus earn state funding. Once admitted to the Regents program, female academies proved the most popular and financially successful in the system. Celebrated institutions were Albany Female Academy (1821), Troy Female Seminary (1837) in Rensselaer Co, Utica Female Academy (1837), Rutgers Female Institute (1838) of New York City, Phipps Union Seminary (1840) of Albion (Orleans Co), and Brooklyn Female Academy (1845).

Religious revivalism and evangelical church organization also played a role in academy expansion. Academies were ideal locations for conversion, offering many youths an escape from both the religious identities and social destinies of their parents. Methodists worked to establish an affiliated academy in each of their conference territories, including Oneida Conference Seminary (1825) of Cazenovia (Madison Co), Genesee Wesleyan Seminary (1833) of Lima (Livingston Co), and Gouverneur Wesleyan Seminary (1828) in St. Lawrence Co. Other religiously affiliated academies included DeRuyter Institute of the Seventh Day Adventists (1836) in Madison Co and the Seventh Day Baptists' Alfred Academy (1843) in Allegany Co. The vast majority of academies remained coeducational and nondenominational, however, to meet the diverse demands of local populations. From elsewhere in their own counties or from neighboring counties they also drew older or advanced students, who boarded in local homes, rooming houses, or an institution's own facilities.

TRANSFORMATION

An 1853 state law enabled neighboring school districts to unite for the purpose of establishing a local "academical department," or public high school. In the decade after the law's passage, new union school districts organized 22 academic departments, half created from existing academies. Initially most of these institutions continued to charge tuition, but in 1864 and 1867, the legislature consolidated its authority over district schools and prohibited the collection of tuition. Some of the first school districts to take advantage of the new law inserted the word "free" into school names: Utica Academy (1814) became Utica Free Academy in 1853, Elmira Academy (1840) became Elmira Free Academy in 1859, and Franklin Academy (1824) of Prattsburg (Steuben Co) became Franklin Free Academy in 1870.

Independent academies continued to exist after 1870, with some new academies founded. But academies experienced increasing pressure either to become public high schools or to transform themselves into different institutions. A few, together with sponsoring towns, lobbied the state for money to become state normal schools, including Brockport Collegiate Institute (1842) in Monroe Co, which became Brockport Normal School in 1867; Cortlandville Academy (1843), which became Cortland Normal School in 1868; Fredonia Academy (1824) in Chautauqua Co, which became Fredonia Normal School in 1866; and St. Lawrence Academy (1816), which became Potsdam Normal School in 1868. Other academies became independent colleges or elite private preparatory schools. A number of female academies pursued such strategies. They had always enjoyed high social status relative to other academies and were unlikely candidates for conversion to public schools as few, if any, towns were willing to devote tax dollars to female-only schools. Thus Le Roy Female Seminary (1841) of Batavia (Genesee Co) became Ingham Collegiate Institute in 1852 and then Ingham University in 1857, Rutgers Female Institute became Rutgers Female College in 1867, and Wells Female Seminary (1868) of Aurora (Cayuga Co) became Wells College in 1870.

VARIATIONS

During the 19th century most New York State academies enrolled 75–90 students and employed 2–3 teachers. A few large institutions enrolled several hundred students and employed 10 or more teachers. Most were located in communities of fewer than 5,000 people, though a number of prestigious academies were located in Albany and New York City. Single-sex academies carried social distinction.

Some academies developed specialties. Albany Academy became a center of scientific learning in the 1810s–1820s as Joseph Henry, the future founder of the Smithsonian Institution, studied magnetism there. From 1809 a group of physicians formed a medical school attached to Fairfield Academy (1803) in Herkimer Co. Rensselaer Institute, founded in Troy (Rensselaer Co) as the Rensselaer School in 1824, held an academy charter for two decades beginning in 1841 and specialized in agricultural and mechanical sciences under Amos Eaton and others. Some academies originally founded as college preparatory schools—the Grammar School of Columbia College and the Grammar School of the University of the City of New York (1838)—operated in conjunction with colleges and universities. Geneva Academy (1813) in Ontario Co created Geneva College (1824), which became Hobart College; Genesee Wesleyan Seminary created Genesee College (1850), which became Syracuse University; and Alfred Academy created Alfred University (1857).

Into the 1880s chartered New York academies served white Anglo-Saxon Protestants almost exclusively. Though some Catholic and African American students entered Regents academies before the Civil War, few institutions recognized or welcomed them, and many standard texts expressed anti-Catholic and racist sentiments. One exception, with respect to African Americans, was the abolitionist, interracial Oneida Institute (1829) of Whitesboro (Oneida Co) that flourished into the 1840s. While institutions affiliated with Protestant denominations commonly received New York State funding under the Regents, the state's Protestant majority judged Catholic institutions "sectarian" and therefore ineligible for funding. The first Catholic academy to receive a state charter was Sacred Heart Academy of Rochester in 1849, followed by Sacred Heart Academy of New York City in 1851. But neither of these institutions acquired status as Regents institutions or received shares of the state's Literature Fund. Catholic academies did not begin receiving Regents charters until the late 1880s and the 1890s, when public high schools had become the dominant form of higher schooling.

See also LIBRARIES.

Beadie, Nancy. "Female Students and Denominational Affiliation: Sources of Success and Variation among 19-Century Academies," *American Journal of Education* 107 (Feb 1999): 75–115

Miller, George Frederick. *The Academy System of the State of New York* (Albany: J. B. Lyon, 1922)

O'Neil, Edward Herring. "Private Schools and Public Vision: A History of Academies in Upstate New York, 1800–1860" (PhD diss, Syracuse Univ, 1984)

Nancy Beadie

acid deposition. Environmental groups such as the Adirondack Council have recognized since the early 1970s that acid deposition, better known as acid rain, is a serious threat to New York State land, waters, and forests. The primary cause is the use of fossil fuels, and, due to its downwind location from large coal-fired utilities in the midwestern United States, New York State is particularly vulnerable. Combustion of fossil fuel produces sulfur dioxide (SO_2) and nitrogen oxide (NO_X), gases that react in sunlight with water, oxygen, and other chemicals to form sulfuric acid (H_2SO_4) and nitric acid (HNO_3). Ecosystems such as the Hudson Highlands and the Catskill and Adirondack Mountains are highly sensitive because of their high elevations and their low buffering capacity, which would provide resistance to changes in acidity. In urban environments, buildings and statues are susceptible to erosion. In rural environments, soil is depleted of calcium, magnesium, and potassium, and can also release aluminum, which washes into lakes, where it sometimes collects around fish gills and interferes with respiration. By the mid-1990s about one-sixth of the fish-inhabited lakes in the Adirondacks had lost one or more species of fish from the increased acidity of the water. The Rensselaer Plateau and sections of Long Island are also affected by acid rain. New York was the first state to pass legislation to control acid deposition; the New York State Acid Deposition Control Act of 1984 (SADCA) also created the New York State Acid Deposition Network to monitor changes in deposition. An Environmental Protection Agency study determined that there was a 38% drop from 1990 to 2000 in the number of acidic lakes in the Adirondack Park. A 2003 Syracuse University study determined that 50–60% of Adirondack lakes monitored since 1982 showed improvements in acidity.

Krochmal, Arnold. *Acid Deposition: The Controversy* (Kettering, Ohio: PPI Publishing, 1995)

Thomas Fletcher

acid rain. See ACID DEPOSITION.

Adams. Town (pop 4,782) and village (pop 1,624) in S central Jefferson Co. Settled in 1800, the town was formed from Mexico [now in Oswego Co] in 1802, and the village incorporated in 1851. The town specialized in growing peas and beans for seed (*ca* 1850–90) and in raising stock. Dairy farming and cheese making have been important since the mid–19th century and remain so in the early 21st century. In 2004 the Great Lakes Cheese Co operated a state-of-the-art cheese factory in town. The Rome, Watertown and Ogdensburg Railroad provided service beginning in 1851. Although Adams had only a small African American population, an August 1st celebration was held in 1855; hundreds attended from throughout New York and Ontario. Manufacturing included an oil-free paint producer (1898), the W. S. Rice Truss Factory (1886–1991), Hale's Household Ointment Co (1887–1960s), and Frazer Bros Small Engine Machine Shop (1905–40). I-81 was built through town in 1959. In the late 20th century canneries and an underwear factory were the main employers. Charles Grandison Finney (1792–1875) was working as a lawyer in Adams in 1821 when he underwent a religious conversion, the first step toward his becoming the most prominent revivalist of his era. Adams is known for the Jacquard coverlets made by Harry Tyler of Butterville between 1834 and 1858.

Laura Lynne Scharer

Adams, Samuel Hopkins (*b* Dunkirk, Chautauqua Co, 26 Jan 1871; *d* Beaufort, SC, 16 Nov 1958). Writer. Adams spent his boyhood in Rochester and graduated from Hamilton College in 1891. He was a reporter for the *New York Sun* newspaper (1891–1900) and then a medical writer for *McClure's* magazine (1900–1904). After 1904 he supported himself as a freelance writer. Adams wrote an exposé on "The Great American Fraud" in a series on patent medicines in *Collier's* in 1905. His muckraking articles helped gain passage of the federal Pure Food and Drug Act the following year. Adams moved to Auburn (Cayuga Co) in 1904 and established a summer residence on nearby Owasco Lake. Beginning in late 1936 he rented various accommodations in Beaufort, SC, each winter until his death.

His writing used New York State locales frequently and covered a broad spectrum from light novels to health nonfiction, from biography to detective stories, and from social to political commentary. His most debated novel, *Revelry* (1926), was based on the scandals of the Warren G. Harding administration. His Roaring Twenties novels, written under the pseudonym Warner Fabian, were epitomized by the title of the first, *Flaming Youth* (1923). Adams had a fascination with the Erie Canal, a focus for three of his historical novels, *Canal Town* (1944), *Banner by the Wayside* (1947), and *Sunrise to Sunset* (1950). He also published two popular juvenile books, the historical *Erie Canal* (1953) and the fictional *Chingo Smith of the Erie Canal* (1958). In addition he wrote reminiscences for *The New Yorker*, and these were collected in his *Grandfather Stories* (1955). New York City was the setting for some of his short stories, collected in *Our Square and the People in It* (1917), and the subject of his look at the Gilded Age in *Tenderloin* (1959), published posthumously. Adams authored 55 books and 450 articles and short stories, 20 of which were adapted into films, including the classic *It Happened One Night* (1934).

Kennedy, Samuel V., III. *Samuel Hopkins Adams and the Business of Writing* (Syracuse: Syracuse Univ Press, 1999)

Samuel V. Kennedy III

Addison. Town (pop 2,640) and village (pop 1,797) in SE Steuben Co. The first settlers arrived in 1791, attracted by the region's abundant timber and the Canisteo River, a tributary of the Chemung and Susquehanna Rivers. The town was formed as Middletown in 1796 and took its current name in 1808. The village was incorporated in 1854. The Erie Railroad was completed through town in 1851, and the Addison and Northern Pennsylvania (which continued to operate under various names until 1960) in 1882. Lumber-related businesses thrived throughout the 19th century, but after the timber stands were exhausted, dairy farming became important. Manufacturing in the village during the Gilded Age included furniture, boots and shoes, hoopskirts, sashes and blinds, and a foundry. The Mosaic Glass Co (1893) manufactured colored, embossed, and other decorative glass panels. Tobacco was grown on the bottomland of the Canisteo until the 1910s. Since the 1950s, after most local industries had left, many residents have worked in nearby Corning. A ski facility and a nine-hole golf course acquired by New York State opened in 1976 as Pinnacle State Park.

Virginia L. Wright and Jerry Wright

Adelphi University. Private university in Garden City (Nassau Co). Adelphi College opened in September 1896 in the same Brooklyn building as Adelphi Academy (1863), a preparatory school still operating in 2003. The college opened as a coeducational institution but, in its early years, enrolled only a few men and soon became known as a women's college, which it became formally in 1912. In 1929 it relocated to Garden City, where it has a 75-acre (30 ha) campus. In 1946 it became coeducational again to serve returning veterans. By 1950 the student body had grown to almost 2,500. In 1963 the college became a university. Offering professional certificates and graduate degrees in a number of fields, with schools of education, business, nursing, and social work, Adelphi is the home of a graduate center in clinical psychotherapy, the Gordon F. Derner Institute of Advanced Psychological Studies. Its intercollegiate athletic programs are particularly strong in men's and women's soccer and men's lacrosse. Enrollment in 2002 was above 6,000, with more than 500 full- and part-time faculty members.

Barrows, Chester Leonard. *Fifty Years of Adelphi College* (Garden City, NY: Adelphi College Press, 1946)

Lynda R. Day

Adirondack great camps. Throughout most of the 19th century large tracts of undeveloped Adirondack land were valued primarily for lumber. After the Civil War, when railroads provided better access, some sportsmen, as communal clubs or as individuals, acquired tracts for hunting preserves. William West Durant, son of national railroad promoter William Clark Durant, developed access by rail and water into the central Adirondacks and, beginning in 1877, built a model summer home for himself, Camp Pine Knot on Raquette Lake (Hamilton Co). Selling this property in 1895, Durant built other camps on nearby lakes, which he likewise sold to prominent businessmen from New York City. The model was the regional lumber camp, where local builders used native materials to construct a complex of detached log cabins. Picturesque rustic work employing twigs and saplings, combined with Alpine building forms as well as Japanese decorative work, contributed to a characteristic Adirondack style. In the 1890s Durant added the notion of self-sufficiency, placing farms on Adirondack estates.

The Adirondack great camps were often surrounded by estates exceeding 10,000 acres (4,000 ha), often in remote wilderness locations. Isolation fostered self-sufficiency, and some great camps, such as Camp Sagamore and Kamp Kill Kare in the Raquette Lake area, were veritable villages, where resident staff lived year-round, sometimes provided with a schoolhouse and even a church. Wealthy residents of New York City owned most of the great camps: Vanderbilts, Whitneys, Morgans, Huntingtons, Rockefellers, and others, who often traveled by means of private railroad cars. The huge establishments, requiring staffs of 40 or more people, were largely a phenomenon of the turn of the 20th century. The few large log villas that continued to be built until World War II were the last of the great camps. Preservation has been a difficult issue since the state has sought to acquire large tracts of land to incorporate into the Adirondack Forest Preserve while Article 14 of the New York State Constitution has been interpreted to preclude retention of buildings in the preserve. Saving Camp Sagamore (1897–98) twice became a crisis, but in 2000 it was designated a National Historic Landmark. Santanoni (1892) in Newcomb (Essex Co) likewise was a preservation problem for decades after acquisition by the state in 1971 but similarly was designated a National Historic Landmark in 2000. New York State's management plan provides for retention and restoration of its historic buildings. Some of the elaborate properties remain private residences, while others, including Sagamore and Santanoni, are open for public tours.

Gilborn, Craig A. *Adirondack Camps: Homes Away from Home, 1850–1950* (Syracuse: Syracuse Univ Press, 2000)

Paul Malo

Adirondack guideboat. This cross between a canoe and a rowboat, a design that originated in the central Adirondacks in the 1820s, holds a rower, one or two passengers, and their gear. The guide rowed from the bow, and passengers occupied the aft and middle seats. It measured 14–16 feet (4.3–4.9 m) long and 32–38 inches (81–97 cm) wide amidships with pointed bow and stern. Sportsmen and their guides needed a fast boat, light enough to carry overland but strong and spacious enough to haul supplies and game. "Church boats" were longer and were used to row passengers to and from church on Sundays. The earliest had skins of overlapping planking called lapstrake and closely spaced, naturally curved spruce root ribs. Some 3,000 brass screws joined planks to ribs, spruce joints were fastened by as many as 5,000 copper tacks, and several coats of varnish covered the boat. By the 1870s,

Guideboats at Saranac Lake, 1876.

quieter guideboats were built with smooth skins. Builders included Henry Dwight Grant, George W. Smith, Warren W. Cole, and Edmund and Caleb Judson Chase. Demand declined after the early 1900s when self-guided vacations and later motorboats became popular. A few crafters continued the tradition, however, and today there are several builders and annual races.

Bond, Hallie E. *Boats and Boating in the Adirondacks* (Blue Mountain Lake, NY: Adirondack Museum; Syracuse: Syracuse Univ Press, 1995)

Durant, Kenneth, and Helen Durant. *The Adirondack Guide-Boat* (Blue Mountain Lake, NY: Adirondack Museum, 1980)

Douglas McCombs

Adirondack guides. Hunters and experts in woodlore of New York State's northern mountain region who lead visitors on wilderness excursions. Settlers of European descent had moved to the Adirondacks after the Revolutionary War, soon displacing Native American hunters and gatherers. Like the original, probably seasonal, inhabitants of the region, the early settlers and their children depended largely on hunting and fishing for subsistence in the harsh, rocky environment. Adirondack residents thus gained remarkable skills in tracking, woodcraft, and lore. During the period 1838–65—sometimes described as the golden years of the Adirondacks—newly affluent and leisured tourists from northeastern industrial cities were drawn to this island of wilderness in the increasingly developed and civilized eastern United States. Because maps were poor and over two thousand lakes and streams functioned as the region's highways, a tourist could not venture far without a guide. Guides served clients of all types: those seeking scenic views, hunting and fishing adventures, or opportunities for scientific and economic exploration. William Wood and Matthew Beach, settlers in the Raquette Lake area in the 1840s and 1850s, guided the first tourists or "sports" to venture the area. In the mountainous region around Keene Valley, climbing guides worked, such as Orson "Old Mountain" Phelps, who cut one of the first trails up the state's highest peak, Essex Co's Mt Marcy, in 1861. Other noted guides of this period were Mitchell Sabattis, Alvah Dunning, and John Cheney. The guiding profession influenced development of an early workboat used by market hunters into the famed Adirondack guideboat, a boat stable enough to carry guides, sports, and game, but light enough to be carried between the many Adirondack lakes. Later in the 19th century, depletion of fish and game by an increasing number of tourists hunting and fishing lessened the demand for guides. They banded together to face this decline, forming the Adirondack Guides Association in 1891 and the Brown's Tract Guides' Association in 1898. The 1893 Forest Commission Report listed 626 Adirondack guides. The state began to license guides in 1919, making licenses mandatory in 1924, and from the 1980s has required that candidates pass a written test and have Red Cross certification. At the beginning of the 21st century, many guides were born outside the region and college educated; they have broadened Adirondack guiding to include such pursuits as white-water rafting and rock and ice climbing.

Brumley, Charles. *Guides of the Adirondacks: A History* (Utica: North Country Books, 1994)

Charles Brumley

***Adirondack League Club v Sierra Club*, 92 NY 2d 591 (1998).** Navigable waters, public right-of-use case. Litigation was triggered by a canoe and kayak journey down the South Branch of the Moose River 15 June 1991 sponsored by the Sierra Club, a nonprofit conservation organization. Participants paddled part way and portaged on some river sections. The Adirondack League Club, a private hunting and fishing club, had posted No Trespassing signs at the point where the river enters the club property, east of Old Forge (Herkimer Co), in anticipation of the challenge. In New York State, if a natural stream on private property may be used to convey persons or property from one point to another, then the watercourse is considered navigable and must be accessible to the navigating public. The New York Court of Appeals confirmed this principle in the case of *Adirondack League Club v Sierra Club.* It also held that evidence of a watercourse's suitability for recreational use may be enough to support a finding of navigability.

In its decision, the court acknowledged that its holding represented a departure from the common law of England but noted that the real break had been made in *Morgan v King* (1866), in which the suitability of a watercourse for commercial log driving had been enough to support a finding of "navigability." The court also held in the Adirondack Club case that a member of the navigating public commits no trespass if he or she resorts to the privately owned bed or banks to effect a passage around an obstacle. Curiously, however, he or she may commit a trespass simply by fishing from a floating watercraft. In *Douglaston Manor v Bahrakis* (1997), the court had held that the public right to navigate does not encompass the right to take fish and that exclusive fishing rights can be made a part of a riparian landowner's estate.

Helmer, William S. "Fanfare for the Common Law," *One on One* 21 (Spring 1999): 22

William S. Helmer

Adirondack lean-to. Used and popularized in the Adirondacks, this shelter is characterized by having three walls, an open front, and a roof that slants toward the back. Its origin remains unclear, but by the late 18th century hunters and trappers in northern New York State were constructing models from crotched poles covered with hemlock boughs. As the Adirondacks attracted more outdoors adventurers, the lean-to became a ubiquitous camp structure. Urban sportsmen and sportswomen relied on guides to build durable lean-tos that would last several days, if not weeks, while the party remained in the woods. Peeled bark from spruce, cedar, or other conifer trees usually covered roof and walls, while a thick layer of balsam boughs placed on the floor provided a comfortable and fragrant bed. Following the Civil War numerous

Two Guides, Winslow Homer, 1877. Copyright © Sterling and Francine Clark Art Institute, Williamstown, Massachusetts.

Adirondack lean-to, *ca* 1900.

hotels and other tourist accommodations opened throughout the Adirondacks, and wealthy families constructed elaborate camps for their own use. Lean-tos became regular features at these establishments. Frequently positioned on lakes, they were built more sturdily than their predecessors and served more as social gathering spots than basic shelters. Walls were frequently formed from logs, while roofs had sawed lumber and shingles. Lean-tos also appeared at both the Trudeau and Loomis Sanitoriums, where tuberculosis patients could convalesce in an open-air, rustic setting. The creation of the Adirondack Park in 1892 limited the building of lean-tos on state land. In 1913, to make the park more accessible to outdoor enthusiasts, the New York Forest Commission granted private individuals and groups permission to build lean-tos for public use from packed-in materials, that is, without on-site cutting down of trees. The commission did not build any itself until 1919. Published plans and building guides, such as the Adirondack Mountain Club's 1922 brochure *Open Camps,* tended to standardize the size of 8 ft x 12 ft (2 m x 4 m) and a construction of horizontal logs, shingled roof, and stone fireplace adjacent to the open front. Near the end of the century, around 260 lean-tos existed within the Adirondack Park and numerous others at private camps and scenic spots. Its form can be found in wilderness areas throughout the country and has become a symbol of outdoor life.

Brown, Eleanor. *The Forest Preserve of New York State: A Handbook for Conservationists* (Glens Falls, NY: Adirondack Mountain Club, 1985)

Gilborn, Craig. *Adirondack Camps: Homes Away from Home, 1850–1950* (Blue Mountain Lake, NY: Adirondack Museum, 2000)

Douglas McCombs

Adirondack Museum. This regional history and art museum in Blue Mountain Lake (Hamilton Co) interprets the Adirondack Park and North Country locales. Originally the idea of mining industry executive, philanthropist, preservationist, and local historian Harold K. Hochschild (1892–1981), the museum is located on the site of the Blue Mountain House resort hotel (1876–1950). It was chartered by the New York State Education Department in 1948 and opened to the public in 1957. The museum's mission is to explore and present the human, cultural, and environmental history of the Adirondacks and has consistently employed state-of-the-art exhibit and programmatic technique. The 205-acre (83 ha) campus is home to 42 buildings and 25 indoor and outdoor exhibition, education, and study/storage spaces. Object collections include tools for trades and industries, land and water vehicles, works of fine art and folk art, and artifacts representing domestic life, community, sport, and recreation. Other holdings are books, documents, historic photographs, films, and ephemera, as well as significant audio and oral history collections. The museum is noted for its 19th- and 20th-century art collection, including works by Thomas Cole, Winslow Homer, Arthur Fitzwilliam Tait, Frederic Remington, Harold Weston, and Rockwell Kent. Its large freshwater boat collection contains many examples of the region's signature artifact, the Adirondack guideboat. The Adirondack rustic furniture and decorative arts collection features objects unique to the region. The museum serves more than 115,000 people annually, including some 90,000 visitors during the five-month season when the museum is open to the public and approximately 25,000 year-round researchers.

Adirondack Museum, http://www.adirondackmuseum.org

Museum of the Adirondacks, rev ed. (Blue Mountain Lake, NY: Adirondack Museum, 1991)

Caroline M. Welsh

Adirondack Northway. See NORTHWAY.

Adirondack pack basket. Traditional woven wood basket. Used to carry the heavy loads needed for hunting, fishing, trapping, and other pursuits in the mountain wilderness, these baskets are among the oldest surviving traditions in the Adirondacks. While the origins are unverified, tradition attributes the basket style to the Abenaki Indians from Canada and New England in the 19th century. The pack basket (also known as a pack-basket, packbasket, or backpack basket) has historically been constructed of black ash, a wood that can be pounded apart into splints, and occasionally of white ash. Modern replicas are often made from imported reed. The lashed rim is a feature that distinguishes Adirondack pack baskets from those made in other regions, where rims may be nailed. Variations include plywood bottoms, wooden skids, carved wooden handles, and handles woven into the basket body. Harness straps, often made of leather or woven cotton, are attached for carrying. A small number of Adirondack craftspeople still make pack baskets for practical and decorative purposes and basketmaking workshops are offered in the region.

Camoin, Mike. *How to Make an Adirondack Packbasket* (Albany: Videos for Change, 2000), documentary film

Tracy N. Meehan

Adirondack Park. In 1872 a commission appointed by the New York State Assembly recommended creation of a state-owned park in the Adirondacks to protect the watershed and to preserve forests for recreation and a future timber supply. While the legislature failed to act on this recommendation, in 1885 it created the New York State Forest Preserve, comprising state-owned lands in both the Adirondacks and Catskills. But the forests thus protected were scattered and surrounded by vast tracts of private land over which the state had no control. In the Adirondacks, logging companies, wealthy families, and private clubs managed huge holdings, while smaller plots supported farms and villages. In 1892, finally convinced of the state's vital interest in protecting forests throughout the northern counties, the legislature created the Adirondack Park. The lawmakers indicated the area for expansion and consolidation of state holdings on a map, then believing the state would eventually own all land within the Blue Line, as the park boundary became known. The original park consisted of 2,807,760 acres (1,136,260 ha), of which several hundred thousand acres were state-owned forest preserve.

The legislature enlarged the park in 1912, 1931, 1956, and 1972 to encompass over twice the original acreage. It then contained 2,722,276 acres (1,101,666 ha) of state-owned forest preserve, protected as wild lands under Article 7 (later Article 14) of the New York State Constitution and managed by the New York State Department of Environmental Conservation (DEC), which succeeded two earlier managing bodies, the Forest Commission of 1885–1917 and the Conservation Commission (later New York State Department of Conservation) of 1911–70. The park also held 3,205,324 acres (1,297,149 ha) of private lands. It incorporated all of Essex and Hamilton Cos and parts of 10 other northern counties—Clinton, Franklin, Hamilton, Herkimer, Lewis, Oneida, St. Lawrence, Saratoga, Warren, and Washington—as well as New York State's highest mountains and the headwaters of the Hudson, Raquette,

Saranac, and Moose Rivers. In 1971 the legislature established the Adirondack Park Agency with authority over private lands as well as over the DEC's management of the forest preserve. Two years later the legislature approved the agency's controversial Private Land Use and Development Plan, which set zoning regulations for the park's private land. Environmentalists argued that the plan allowed too much development, while local politicians and business interests complained of the stifling effect on the Adirondack economy, where unemployment consistently ran higher than in the rest of New York State.

In 2000 the Adirondack Park was home to about 135,000 year-round residents, joined in summer by 70,000 seasonal residents and millions of tourists. Most full-time inhabitants of the Adirondacks lived in small communities dotting the park, which ranged from substantial villages like Saranac Lake (Franklin and Essex Cos) with a population of 5,280, to tiny hamlets like Raquette Lake (Hamilton Co) with a population of 130. New York State continues to make efforts to buy or preserve privately held lands within the park. A purchase agreement was made in 2003 to add approximately 6,000 acres (2,400 ha), including the land where Theodore Roosevelt was notified about the shooting of Pres William McKinley, to the state-owned forest preserve. In 2004 an agreement was made for the state to purchase development rights to more than 250,000 acres (101,200 ha) of private land across nine counties in the park. The arrangement would ensure state oversight of future development on those tracts.

Donaldson, Alfred L. *A History of the Adirondacks*, 2 vols (New York: Century, 1921)

Graham, Frank, Jr. *The Adirondack Park: A Political History* (New York: Knopf, 1978)

Terrie, Philip G. *Contested Terrain: A New History of Nature and People in the Adirondacks* (Blue Mountain Lake, NY: Adirondack Museum; Syracuse: Syracuse Univ Press, 1997)

Philip G. Terrie

Adirondack Park Agency. In 1968 the Temporary Study Commission on the Future of the Adirondacks, appointed by Gov Nelson A. Rockefeller, recommended creation of the Adirondack Park Agency (APA) to oversee management and protection of both New York State Forest Preserve lands—under immediate control of the state's Department of Environmental Conservation—and millions of acres of private land. The state legislature in 1971 established the agency in the executive branch, allowing the governor extensive control over its operations. Housed at Ray Brook (Essex Co), the agency has 11 members, 8 appointed by the governor, with no more than 5 from any one political party, as well as 3 ex officio members (commissioner of environmental conservation, commissioner of economic development, and secretary of state). In 2000 a professional staff of 60 also served the agency, whose yearly budget amounted to over $3.5 million and whose main function was the administration of the controversial Private Land Use and Development Plan. Since 1973 this plan has regulated development on the 3,205,324 acres (1,297,149 ha) of private land in the Adirondack Park. From the agency's creation both conservationists and business interests have often opposed its rulings, finding them either inadequate to protect the region's natural beauty or threatening to the local economy. The agency also runs the Adirondack Park Visitor Information Centers in Paul Smiths (Franklin Co) and Newcomb (Essex Co), which opened in 1989 and 1990, respectively.

Graham, Frank, Jr. *The Adirondack Park: A Political History* (New York: Knopf, 1978)

Liroff, Richard A., and G. Gordon Davis. *Protecting Open Space: Land Use Control in the Adirondack Park* (Cambridge, Mass: Ballinger Publishing, 1981)

Philip G. Terrie

Adirondack Railroad. Construction began in 1865 on this 60 mi (97 km) railroad, which ran from Saratoga Springs to a point just north of North Creek (Warren Co), incorporating land formerly belonging to the Adirondack Estate and Railroad Co. The line, owned by Dr Thomas C. Durant, began full operation in 1871, the year the North Creek station opened. Durant, who was also vice president of the Union Pacific Railroad Co, built the railroad to help develop his tourism and industrial holdings in the area. The railroad was purchased by the Delaware and Hudson Canal Co in 1889, becoming the Adirondack Branch of the D&H Railroad in 1902. After the decline of local tannery and titanium-mining operations, the line was abandoned in 1989. In the early 21st century the Upper Hudson River Railroad, a tourist line, offers excursions on an 8.5 mi (13.9 km) section of track running southeast from the refurbished North Creek station, and there are plans to extend service to Saratoga Springs. The line is not to be confused with the Adirondack Scenic Railroad, sections of which operate between Utica and Lake Placid (Essex Co).

Kudish, Michael. *Railroads of the Adirondacks: A History* (Fleischmanns, NY: Purple Mountain Press, 1996)

Michael I. Niman

Adirondack rivers. The rivers of the Adirondack Mountains drain laterally away from the billion-year-old metamorphic rock that makes up the central domed Adirondack region. This nonporous bedrock causes rapid runoff, and consequently there are no aquifers in the Adirondacks. The many swamps and bogs, particularly in the northwest flow, retard drainage, permitting excellent recreational paddling on its many placid rivers. The St. Lawrence River basin is the largest of the five major drainage systems in the Adirondack Park. Its major rivers are the Grass, Raquette, Oswegatchie, St. Regis, Salmon, and Chateaugay. They are considered young rivers geologically, their courses altered 10,000 years ago by the last Ice Age. The retreating glaciers left the region covered by glacial till (clay, sand, gravel, and boulders) and created the many waterfalls, gorges, lakes, ponds, eskers, and swamps. The rivers of the Lake Champlain basin, the Ausable, Boquet, Saranac, and Great Chazy, complete the so-called North Flow. Constituting the south and west flows are the rivers of the upper Hudson, Black, and Mohawk basins, including the Cedar, Indian, Boreas, Schroon, Sacandaga, Moose, and Black Rivers, and the Kunjamuk, East Canada, and West Canada Creeks. Altogether there are an estimated 30,000 miles (48,000 km) of navigable Adirondack rivers and streams.

Adirondack rivers were central to the colonization of this remote wilderness. With the arrival of European settlers between 1810 and 1820, rivers quickly became transportation highways, primarily for moving logs to mills. As loggers moved to higher elevations, broad rivers such as the Hudson, Raquette, and Grass, suitable for floating rafts of logs, quickly gave way to the new technique of "river drives," or floating individual logs down ever smaller tributaries, beginning with the first log drive in 1813 down the Schroon River. The pulp and tanning industries rapidly depleted the region's timber in the decades around 1900. Beginning in 1890 railroads gradually replaced rivers as transporters of logs and also enticed tourists and sports enthusiasts. The devastation caused by an unregulated timber industry along with the concern of New York City residents that watersheds would be destroyed gave rise to early conservation efforts. Deforestation, it was feared, would lead to desertification, as first suggested in 1864 by George Perkins Marsh in *Man and Nature*. In response the New York State legislature created the Forest Preserve in 1885 and the Adirondack Park in 1892. The "forever wild" clause of the state constitution was adopted in 1894.

Another early threat to the region's free-flowing rivers arose from efforts to build reservoirs to regulate flow and produce hydropower. A few were built, including the Sacandaga Reservoir [now Great Sacandaga Lake] in 1930. The reservoir was constructed by the Hudson River Regulating District following passage of an amendment by the state legislature in 1913 allowing up to 3% of Forest Preserve land to be used for reservoirs to regulate flow, maintain state canals, and provide municipal water supplies. Beginning in 1945 a drive by preservationists led by Paul Schaefer and Lithgow Osborne resulted in the Ostrander Amendment to the state constitution being ratified in 1953; it prohibited building any river-regulating reservoirs in the Forest Preserve. In the latter half of the 20th century, recreation superseded industry as the major use of rivers. As whitewater rafting and paddling grew in popularity, a long struggle ensued, led by guidebook author Paul Jamieson, to reopen Adirondack rivers and streams that had been closed for a century due to posting. By the late 20th century a series of favorable court decisions established the rights of recreationists to paddle on all navigable rivers and streams. The Adirondack Park Agency (APA) surveyed Adirondack rivers and devised protective regulations. In 1972 the APA established the Wild, Scenic and Recreational Rivers Act patterned after a similar federal program run by the US Forest Service. The APA oversees administration of the act, which provides that designated rivers "shall be preserved in free-flowing condition and that they and their immediate environs shall be protected for the benefit and enjoyment of present and future generations." In 2002 more than 1,300 miles (2,100 km) of Adirondack rivers were classified as wild, scenic, or recreational. All motor vehicles and new structures are prohibited on rivers classified as wild, and development on privately owned scenic and recreational river corridors is strictly controlled. This comprehensive legislation has become a model for the nation.

Graham, Frank, Jr. *The Adirondack Park: A Political History* (Syracuse: Syracuse Univ Press, 1984)

Christopher Angus

Adirondacks. A thinly populated region of mountains, rivers, lakes, and forests in northern New York State, roughly bounded by Lake

Champlain and the valleys of the St. Lawrence, Black, and Mohawk Rivers. The highest point in the state, 5,344 ft (1,629 m) Mt Marcy, is in the eastern Adirondacks. The Adirondack region includes the Adirondack Park, a mix of state-owned forest preserve protected by the state constitution and managed by the Department of Environmental Conservation, and private lands regulated by the Adirondack Park Agency (APA).

Early History

The Adirondack highlands are an extension of the Laurentian Plateau, which spreads across central Canada from Hudson Bay. The hard, igneous anorthosite of the high peaks is over a billion years old and was once the core of a series of rugged mountain ranges that arose and subsequently eroded. In recent millennia the Adirondack landscape was covered by a series of ice sheets, which rounded the peaks and valleys and left the many lakes and ponds that characterize the topography.

Archaeological remains suggest that parts of the Adirondacks served as hunting grounds and trade routes for various Native American cultures living in nearby river valleys, but there is little evidence that Indians lived permanently in the Adirondacks, except in fringe areas. Wildlife was more plentiful and agriculture more productive in the lowlands peripheral to the region.

The first European to see the Adirondacks was French explorer Jacques Cartier. On 3 Oct 1535 from a hill near a Huron village in what is now Montreal, he spotted mountains off to the southwest, though it was many years before a white man set foot in the region. On 30 July 1609 a band of French scouts and soldiers, led by Samuel de Champlain and accompanying an Algonquin war party, encountered and defeated a group of Iroquois near the future location of Fort Ticonderoga (Essex Co). Through the 17th and the first half of the 18th centuries, only the occasional military scout or trapper penetrated the heart of the Adirondack region, and detailed knowledge of most of the region was scant.

After the French and Indian War, speculators purchased much of the Adirondacks in several huge tracts: Totten and Crossfield Purchase of 1772, consisting of over 1 million acres (404,700 ha), with most of what would become Hamilton Co and parts of Herkimer and Essex Cos; Old Military Tract of 1781, of about 665,000 acres (269,100 ha) in what would become Clinton, Franklin, and Essex Cos and containing Keene Valley, Lake Placid, and the Chateaugay lakes; and Macomb's Purchase, sold by New York State to land speculator Alexander Macomb in a series of transactions between 1792 and 1798, of nearly 4 million acres (1,618,800 ha) in the northern Adirondacks and St. Lawrence Valley. The original owners never saw most of these lands; rather, the properties were sold to others or reverted to the state for unpaid taxes.

Slowly settlers began to arrive from other parts of New York State or from New England. Settlement in the Lake Champlain and Lake George valleys was established by 1790. From there and from the Mohawk Valley, slim fingers of settlement extended up Adirondack rivers with some settlers skipping ahead to the central lakes. These pioneers cleared land, built houses, and planted crops, reaching Keene Valley by 1797, Newcomb (Essex Co) by 1810, Saranac Lake (Franklin and Essex Cos) by 1819, and Long Lake (Hamilton Co) by 1830. Poor to begin with—as evidenced by their attempt to establish new lives in such a remote, harsh environment—they arrived with little but a willingness to work and endure hardship. They relied on hunting and fishing for much of their food, catching lake and brook trout, shooting bears, moose, and white-tailed deer, and slowly killing off the last of New York State's wolves and mountain lions. In laboriously cleared fields they planted hardy crops like rye, wheat, and potatoes, alongside vegetable gardens.

The Natural History Survey

Accurate knowledge of the Adirondacks reached the wider world largely through the explorations of the New York Natural History Survey. The survey began field research in 1836 following its establishment by the state legislature for the purpose of increasing knowledge of the state's natural resources. The geological research was divided among five prominent scientists, with Ebenezer Emmons, a professor at both Williams College and Albany Medical College, assigned most of the Adirondacks. On 5 Aug 1837 Emmons led the first recorded ascent of the mountain that he named after Gov William L. Marcy. The following year Emmons proposed the name "Adirondacks" for the surrounding mountains, believing it the name of an Indian tribe that had once used the region as a hunting ground, though more recent opinion holds that the term was an Iroquois epithet meaning "tree-eater," applied to Algonquin groups forced to live upon tree buds and bark during severe winters. Emmons's annual reports to the legislature, submitted from 1837 to 1841, along with his massive final report, *Geology of New-York, Part II: Comprising the Second Geological District,* contributed critical elements to the public perception of the Adirondacks. Emmons found the Adirondack region to be a land "unrivalled for its magic and enchantment." At the same time, Emmons was aware of the potential for economic development. In his view, this region of beautiful scenery offered both future sport for tourists and future wealth for entrepreneurs. Emmons predicted an extensive development of mining in the Adirondacks. The base camp for his 1837 ascent of Marcy was the McIntyre Iron Works on the upper Hudson River in Essex Co, and Emmons explored this area carefully, concluding that it held iron deposits of national significance. Yet like many Americans of his day, Emmons favored agriculture above all other types of land use, and he maintained high hopes of the Adirondacks someday supporting a population of prosperous farmers.

Lake Tear of the Clouds, source of the Hudson River, located near the summit of Mt Marcy.

Beginnings of Tourism and Recreation

After Emmons's descriptions of this hitherto largely unknown region, New Yorkers and other Americans began to view Adirondack peaks, lakes, and forests as ideal locales for wilderness recreation. One of the earliest Adirondack tourists was the Rev Joel T. Headley, who, assisted by local men hired as guides, climbed Mt Marcy and traveled by boat through the central lake region in the 1840s. His 1849 book, *The Adirondack; or, Life in the Woods,* helped to establish what became a major literary genre: books and articles about excursions into the Adirondack wilderness undertaken by urban, professional people. To serve such visitors, settlers scattered on rocky Adirondack farms and in isolated villages opened boardinghouses and primitive inns.

After the Civil War an 1869 bestseller, *Adventures in the Wilderness; or, Camp Life in the Adirondacks,* urged swarms of tourists to take their vacations in the Adirondacks. The author, William H. H. Murray, a Congregational minister from Boston, recounted marvelous tales of the redemptive powers of nature. Repeating a popular claim about the capacity of the mountain air to arrest tuberculosis, Murray depicted a miraculous landscape where all the physical, spiritual, and moral woes of modern life found their cure: "No portion of our country surpasses, if indeed any equals, in health-giving qualities, the Adirondack Wilderness." So many eager campers were lured to the Adirondacks by Murray's stories of idylls in the woods and arrived there so utterly unequipped for what they encountered that they became known as "Murray's Fools."

Large hotels soon sprang up in many locations to serve the flood of visitors. Among the better known were Paul Smith's, first built on Lower St. Regis Lake in 1861, and Prospect House, which opened on Blue Mountain Lake in 1882 and was the first hotel in the world to provide electric light in every guest room. Transportation to these and other hotels was often difficult. The first railroad into the central Adirondacks penetrated only as far as North Creek (Warren Co), work stopping there in 1871. The Delaware and Hudson then pushed a line up the Champlain Valley, by 1876 forging a direct rail link between Albany and Montreal, and in 1892, Dr William Seward Webb completed a line from Herkimer through the western Adirondacks to Malone (Franklin Co), which he sold to New York Central by 1905. From rail stations tourists boarded stagecoaches and endured long rides over often bumpy, muddy roads. Once travelers reached the central lakes, they might take a steamboat to their hotel. *Utowana* began carrying passengers across Blue Mountain Lake in 1878, while *Killoquah* operated on Raquette Lake the next year. By the end of the 19th century, the Adirondack region was known throughout the United States as a vacation mecca and a healthful retreat for tuberculosis patients. Leading the establishment of tuberculosis sanitariums was Dr Edward L. Trudeau, himself a sufferer from the 19th-century scourge, who came to Paul Smith's Hotel in 1873 and opened a retreat in Saranac Lake in 1884. Other specialized tourists were artists and intellectuals who flocked to Keene Valley. With tourism established as a fundamental part of the Adirondack economy, travelers could choose between staying at hotels or roughing it in the backcountry. Wealthy individuals, families, and clubs purchased huge estates, where they fished and hunted on lands closed to ordinary citizens. Typical of such "Great Camps" was Pine Knot on Raquette Lake, designed by William W. Durant in 1876 and sold to railroad magnate Collis P. Huntington in 1895. Among the private clubs were Adirondack League, founded near Old Forge (Herkimer Co) in 1891 and Tahawus, established in 1897 on lands originally owned by McIntyre Iron.

Steamer *Killoquah* on Raquette Lake, 1879.

Logging and the Origins of Conservation

Emmons's hopes for Adirondack mining and agriculture proved largely unrealized. The McIntyre development, disadvantaged by distance from markets and impurities in the ore, failed in 1857. Other iron mines—on Lyon Mountain and near the Chateaugay lakes and further south around Moriah, Au Sable Forks, and Schroon Lake (Essex Co)—lasted longer, but only Gore Mountain's garnet mine, opened by Henry H. Barton in 1878, continued in operation into the 21st century. The severity of Adirondack winters and relative thinness of the soil, underestimated by Emmons, ruled out development of commercial agriculture. While both mining and farming, especially in the eastern Adirondacks, formed important parts of the regional economy until early in the 20th century, timber emerged as the area's most important natural resource. Many were eager to benefit from this Adirondack treasure. The economic expansion in the US northeast during the Civil War and Reconstruction created a vast appetite for lumber. Adirondack logging began as a locally owned industry, which developed as new communities built sawmills to produce lumber. But by the 1860s loggers of the southern and eastern Adirondacks worked for large companies, capitalized by outside investors, that ran millions of logs down Adirondack rivers to bustling mill towns like Glens Falls (Warren Co).

Taking only virgin spruce and white pine, loggers left huge piles of brush and bark on the ground. In dry weather this debris turned into tinder waiting for a careless spark, and the threat of forest fires loomed during much of the year. Where a healthy, intact forest covered a slope, rain and snowmelt—held in a spongelike mass of topsoil, moss, and decaying leaves—gradually entered streams and rivers. But absent this forest cover, runoff occurred rapidly, leading to alternating flood and drought conditions. Since loggers worked primarily in the southern Adirondacks, the area that fed the Hudson River and Erie Canal, New York State transportation interests and others took alarm.

Verplanck Colvin, son of a prominent Albany attorney, was an early advocate of conservation in the Adirondacks. Colvin developed a passion for the Adirondacks as a teenager and later used his position as a state surveyor to advocate for protection of the area. In 1872 Colvin published an account of an 1870 ascent of a remote peak northeast of Long Lake, Mt Seward, which he and Raquette Lake guide and hunter Alvah Dunning were probably the first to climb. Colvin closed his description of this expedition with a ringing call for conservation. The chief argument for protecting the forests, in Colvin's view, was the need to preserve watershed. The steadily diminishing flow of water in principal canals and rivers, he maintained, threatened commerce. The source of the potential catastrophe was the "chopping and burning off of vast tracks of forest in the wilderness, which have hitherto sheltered from the sun's heat and evaporation the deep and lingering snows, the brooks and rivulets, and the thick, soaking, sphagnous moss which, at times knee-deep, half water and half plant, forms hanging lakes upon the mountain sides." Colvin proposed "the creation of an Adirondack Park or timber preserve." This is the earliest known appearance in print of the expression "Adirondack Park."

On 15 Mar 1872 the New York State Assembly began to consider a bill to appoint "Commissioners of Parks"; their chief mandate would be "to inquire into the expediency of providing for vesting in the State the title to the timbered regions lying within the counties of Lewis, Essex, Clinton, Franklin, St. Lawrence, Herkimer and Hamilton, and converting the same into a public park." Although the duly appointed commissioners enthusiastically recommended establishment of a state park in the Adirondacks, the legislature balked. Adirondack forests were open to exploitation by lumber barons until 1883, when the state withdrew its remaining Adirondack lands from public sale.

On 15 May 1885 the state legislature created the Adirondack Forest Preserve as part of the New York State Forest Preserve. The law defined the preserve as 681,000 acres (276,000 ha) of state land scattered within 11 (later 12) counties. But the legislation gave no clear indication of what the new preserve was designed to protect and no provision for expansion or consolidation of the public lands. With nothing done for the remaining millions of Adirondack acres, the region was scarcely protected. Moreover, logging was permitted in the forest preserve. Criticism of the law began almost immediately.

In his 1890 message to the legislature, Gov David B. Hill revived discussion of a state park for the Adirondacks. Hill hoped for a park of entirely public land, assembled over a period of time through exchange and purchase. He sidestepped the question of what would happen if the state was unable or unwilling to purchase all the privately owned land necessary. In 1892 the legislature passed, and Gov Roswell P. Flower signed a bill creating the Adirondack Park dedicated to public use, watershed protection, and a "future timber supply," thus confirming the state's interest in preserving the Adirondacks as a forested landscape.

The final act of this period of conservation activity was the inclusion of protections for the forest preserve in the new state constitution approved by voters in 1894. Mistrustful of both bureaucrats and loggers, the authors of the constitution sought protections stronger than those provided by legislative statute and won popular approval for Article 7, Section 7: "The lands of the state, now owned or hereafter acquired, constituting the forest preserve as now fixed by law, shall be forever kept as wild forest lands. They shall not be leased, sold or exchanged, or be taken by any corporation, public or private, nor shall the timber thereon be sold, removed or destroyed." The term "forever wild" caught the public imagination and remains strongly associated with the New York State Forest Preserve.

Public and Private Lands

During the 20th century the Adirondacks, within a day's journey of large, urban populations, became an evermore popular destination for Americans searching for glorious scenery and outdoor recreation far from the pressures of everyday routine. The chief agent in the growing popularity of the region was the automobile, which was widely affordable to middle-class Americans after World War I. The state paved roads originally designed for horse-drawn wagons and developed campsites and trails for auto-tourists. Meanwhile the private sector built motor courts and vastly expanded the number of moderately priced hotels.

The Conservation Commission, as the state conservation bureaucracy was called after 1911, moved swiftly to respond to public needs and to protect what it considered the public interest in the Adirondacks. Faced with clear-cutting high on privately owned slopes of Mt Marcy, for example, the state initiated condemnation proceedings in 1920 and added this critical parcel of land to the forest preserve. Even during the hard times of the Great Depression, public interest in and use of the Adirondacks remained strong, and when a new state constitution was created in 1938, efforts to dilute the protections of old Article 7, Section 7—renumbered that year as Article 14, Section 1—were unsuccessful.

During the 1920s and 1930s more people camped in the region than ever before, crowding state campgrounds. The Adirondacks, particularly the high peaks around Mt Marcy, drew enthusiastic hikers and climbers. Since the private lands through which these climbers drove to get to trailheads remained forested, the public paid little, if any, attention to the difference between the park and the forest preserve. The public image of the Adirondacks crystallized, almost exclusively, around the forest preserve. Throughout the first half of the 20th century, the status of private lands inside the park remained an unexamined but potentially explosive issue.

During the 1940s and 1950s, the issues of interrelationship of public and private lands and of the need for regionwide conservation surfaced indirectly in the controversy over plans of the Black River Regulating District to dam the South Branch of the Moose River, near

Panoramic illustration of the Adirondacks from Verplanck Colvin's *Annual Report on the Progress of the Topographical Survey of the Adirondack Region of New York (1883).*

McKeever (Herkimer Co). First proposed in 1919 the dam remained only an engineer's dream until after World War II, when the regulating district's aggressive effort to see it built resulted in an alliance between defenders of the forest preserve and private landowners. The battle over the dam, which required flooding several thousand acres of both public and private land inside the park, eventually involved the legislature, the governor, the courts, and three separate attempts to amend the New York State Constitution. The dam was never built.

In 1959 New York voters approved an amendment to the state constitution permitting the alienation of some 300 acres (120 ha) of the forest preserve for a super highway running north from Albany to the Canadian border. This stretch of I-87, completed in 1967 and known as the Northway, made accessing the region easier and quicker than ever before. At the same time the new environmentalism of the 1960s produced a dramatic jump in the number of campers and hikers, and many wanted to own an Adirondack summer cottage somewhere on the millions of acres of privately held Adirondack land with its hundreds of miles of undeveloped lake and river shore. Thus the combination of a new highway penetrating the region and an affluent population wishing to draw closer to nature created the potential for a widespread environmental catastrophe.

Tract subdivisions, theme parks, and a host of then permissible developments all endangered the forested nature of the park, and in 1967 a group of planners associated with conservationist Laurance S. Rockefeller proposed that the federal government create an Adirondack Mountains national park. This park was to contain 1,120,000 acres (453,000 ha) of forest preserve land and 600,000 acres (243,000 ha) acquired from private holdings. While not seriously considered as an answer to Adirondack problems, the park proposal stimulated investigation of other options. In 1968 Gov Nelson A. Rockefeller, Laurance's brother, appointed the Temporary Study Commission on the Future of the Adirondacks, charging it to examine the Adirondack Park and to make recommendations for its protection. The Temporary Study Commission found that "unguided development on the 3,500,000 acres [1,416,000 ha] of private land will destroy the character of the entire Park if immediate action is not taken" and recommended establishment of an Adirondack Park Agency with "planning and land use control powers over private land in the Park." After lengthy debate and significant diminution of the powers proposed for this agency, the legislature voted it into existence in 1971 and in 1973 approved—after further and often bitter debate—the agency's Private Land Use and Development Plan. This bold zoning plan restricted permissible development on most of the private land in the Adirondacks. Yet implementation of the private land plan failed to solve the problems of the Adirondacks. Many local residents saw the plan, controversial from the start, as a bureaucratic intrusion, while conservationists were disappointed with the compromises necessitated by legislative politics. Throughout the 1970s and 1980s, conservationists warned that the park's forested character was continuing to erode as developments, legal under the private land use plan, sprang up throughout the region.

The state responded to this call for better protections with a series of additions to the forest preserve. Between the establishment of the park agency in 1971 and 2000, the state enlarged the Adirondack Forest Preserve by over 300,000 acres (121,000 ha); at the end of the 20th century the Adirondack Forest Preserve held nearly 3 million acres. Much of this increase came from major purchases of spectacular tracts of lakes and forests. In 1998, for example, the state bought nearly 15,000 acres (6,000 ha) around Little Tupper Lake in northern Hamilton Co for $13.9 million. In another response to concerns over failure of the existing land-use plan, Gov Mario M. Cuomo in 1989 appointed a new special commission to study the park. During this same year the United Nations Educational, Scientific, and Cultural Organization (UNESCO) designated the Adirondack region a world biosphere reserve, along with neighboring parts of Vermont, citing it as a model working landscape combining permanent human residence and strict environmental protections. Though such reserves remain under the sovereign jurisdiction of the countries in which they are located, property rights advocates in the Adirondacks insisted that this designation was part of a plot to further deprive them of control of their land. Against this background and following hearings throughout the state, in spring 1990 Gov Cuomo's Commission on the Adirondacks in the 21st Century concluded that serious modification of the private land-use plan was necessary to prevent permanent loss of the Adirondack Park's forested open space.

Local government and business interests condemned the report, charging undue influence by environmentalists. They also asserted that no crisis existed and that the commission's recommendations, if implemented, assured destruction of an already precarious local economy. On 11 May 1990 the report's opponents drove vehicles in a "freedom drive" that created a traffic gridlock on the Northway between Exits 20 and 28. Two weeks later a second motorcade of over 1,000 cars and trucks traveled from Exit 34 near Elizabethtown (Essex Co) to Clifton Park (Saratoga Co), where it turned and headed north to a rally at Frontiertown in North Hudson (Essex Co). Faced with this level of hostility, Gov Cuomo retreated from the report's recommendations. During the 1990s, in addition to groups antagonistic to the park agency, grassroots support of conservation emerged in the Residents Committee to Protect the Adirondacks. And environmental organizations drawing members from all of New York State and beyond—Adirondack Council, Adirondack Mountain Club, and Association for the Protection of the Adirondacks—pushed for more effective conservation.

The Adirondacks in the 21st Century

In 2000 the Adirondacks remained a complicated mix of state-owned forest preserve and privately owned lands. As in nearly all of early 21st-century rural America, unemployment rates were high, especially in winter. The major sources of employment for year-round residents were state and local government, tourism, and logging. Though hostility to the recommendations of the 21st Century Commission continued to be widespread, local sentiment for protecting the rural way of life adjoining the forest preserve was also strong.

In addition to inappropriate development, airborne acid pollution posed a further menace to the Adirondack environment at the beginning of the 21st century. This pollution destroyed fish populations in some Adirondack lakes and ponds and threatened the health of forests on the higher slopes of Adirondack mountains. But even amid such losses, the environment was also capable of recovery. A century after an era of ruthless logging and devastating fires, a largely intact forest covered millions of acres, and moose, wiped out by the time of the Civil War, had returned—without human aid—by the 1980s.

See also Climate and weather; Environmental conservation, department of; Environmentalism; Geology and plate tectonics; Logging and lumbering; Mining and mineral industry; Tourism.

Bond, Hallie. *Boats and Boating in the Adirondacks* (Blue Mountain Lake, NY: Adirondack Museum; Syracuse: Syracuse Univ Press, 1995)

Donaldson, Alfred L. *A History of the Adirondacks,* 2 vols (New York: Century, 1921)

Gilborn, Craig. *Adirondack Camps: Homes Away from Home, 1850–1950* (Blue Mountain Lake, NY: Adirondack Museum; Syracuse: Syracuse Univ Press, 2000)

Graham, Frank, Jr. *The Adirondack Park: A Political History* (New York: Knopf, 1978)

Headley, Joel T. *The Adirondack; or Life in the Woods* (New York: Baker & Scribner, 1849)

Kaiser, Harvey. *Great Camps of the Adirondacks* (Boston: David R. Godine, 1982)

McMartin, Barbara. *The Great Forest of the Adirondacks* (Utica: North Country Books, 1994)

———. *Perspectives on the Adirondacks: A Thirty-Year Struggle by People Protecting Their Treasure* (Syracuse: Syracuse Univ Press, 2002)

Murray, William H. H. *Adventures in the Wilderness; or, Camp-Life in the Adirondacks* (Boston: Fields, Osgood, 1869)

Terrie, Philip G. *Wildlife and Wilderness: A History of Adirondack Mammals* (Fleischmanns, NY: Purple Mountain Press, 1993)

———. *Forever Wild: A Cultural History of Wilderness in the Adirondacks* (Syracuse: Syracuse Univ Press, 1994)

———. *Contested Terrain: A New History of Nature and People in the Adirondacks* (Blue Mountain Lake, NY: Adirondack Museum; Syracuse: Syracuse Univ Press, 1997)

Welsh, Peter C. *Jacks, Jobbers and Kings: Logging in the Adirondacks, 1850–1950* (Utica: North Country Books, 1995)

White, William Chapman. *Adirondack Country* (New York: Knopf, 1954)

Philip G. Terrie

Adirondack Scenic Railroad. William Seward Webb's Adirondack and St. Lawrence Railroad opened in 1892. By linking existing lines at Remsen (Oneida Co) and Malone (Franklin Co), it became the first railroad to completely traverse the Adirondacks and provided service between Herkimer and Montreal. In 1893 the railroad became New York Central's Adirondack Division, soon hauling the most passengers and freight, mainly forest products, in the region. After decades of mill closings and highway competition, service declined and was abandoned in stages between 1960 and 1972. In 1980 Adirondack Railway Corp, assisted by state funding, revived the line by running Utica–Lake Placid trains that brought rail service to Lake Placid (Essex Co) for the 1980 Winter Olympics and the ensuing tourist season. In 1992 Adirondack

Railroad Preservation Society, also with state assistance, reopened the line as Adirondack Centennial Railroad between Thendara and Minnehaha (Herkimer Co). Renamed Adirondack Scenic Railroad in 1994, service extended to the Carter rail junction, 6 miles (9.6 km) north of Thendara, in 1995, to Utica in 1998, and added shuttle service between Lake Placid and Saranac Lake (Franklin and Essex Cos) in 2000. The 148 mi (238 km) line is expected to be fully operational between Utica and Lake Placid.

Harter, Henry A. *Fairy Tale Railroad: The Mohawk and Malone through the Adirondacks to the Saint Lawrence—the Golden Chariot Route* (Sylvan Beach, NY: North Country Books, 1979)

Michael Kudish

adjutant general. Head of the Division of Military and Naval Affairs. The primary responsibilities are to direct state military forces in carrying out their missions, recruitment, and training; to establish a joint unified command of the New York Army National Guard, New York Air National Guard, New York Naval Militia, and New York Guard; to act as the state director of civil defense; and to command, as required when the governor does not act as commander in chief, the state military forces.

After 1786 and before a 1792 federal statute mandated the office in each state, the adjutant general in New York State was appointed by the governor to supervise the militia and military establishments. The state constitutions of 1821 and 1846 confirmed this responsibility of the governor, and that of 1894 gave the governor the authority to appoint a military secretary, who, along with the adjutant general, supervised the state's defense forces until 1926. The adjutant general took on the duties of all staff officers beginning in 1909. In 1945 the adjutant general was named chair of the Veterans Affairs Commission, an advisory body to the newly created Division of Veterans Affairs to assist World War II veterans returning from service. Four years later the chief of staff to the governor (a new position) replaced the adjutant general as head of the Division of Military and Naval Affairs. In 1988 the chief of staff to the governor was redesignated by military law to again be the adjutant general.

Michael J. Stenzel

adoption. Legal adoption began in the United States in the mid–19th century, and the first New York State adoption law, passed 25 June 1873, defined adoption as the legal act whereby an adult person takes a minor into the relation of child. The law specified that both biological parents of the child had to consent to the adoption, unless they were legally separated, and that children over age 12 had to agree to be adopted. Consent of the biological parents was not required if they had previously been deprived of civil rights due to conviction for a serious crime, adjudged guilty of adultery or cruelty, insane, or if they were known to be habitually drunk.

Adoptions grew in popularity at the same time that concerns were raised about foster and institutionalized care for children. As early as 1908, periodicals popularized adoption and recruited prospective parents. Specialized agencies or adoption services within agencies, such as the State Charities Aid Association, New York Foundling Hospital, and the predecessor agency to Louise Wise Services, placed infants, a few toddlers, and young children. A few services were not actual agencies but were run by volunteers who, before placing children for adoption, first prepared them to adapt into reputable families. By the early 1920s agency social workers, following then current eugenic theories, were reluctant to place children who were thought to have an inherited predisposition to social degeneracy, including many from ethnic and racial groups deemed inferior. Those with physical disabilities were also deemed not adoptable.

Prospective parents were thoroughly screened. All agencies, public and private, had age, income, and religious requirements. Infertility was required. Prospective adopters rejected by the agencies could attempt to adopt privately, finding children through biological mothers, physicians, and others. Without an agency, they could petition the court to approve the adoption. Judges had to be satisfied that the "moral and temporal interests" of the children would be furthered by the adoptions. Of about 2,300 children adopted in New York State in 1940, roughly 70% were adopted privately.

Adoption agencies failed to outlaw nonagency adoption but successfully mandated court investigations of prospective adoptive parents. Beginning in the 1950s, a few agencies attempted adoption for minority or slightly disabled toddlers but often failed because they continued to use screening standards ill-suited to new circumstances. Agencies without special training or awareness did not realize that prospective parents for difficult-to-place children might need to be recruited and might include older, less affluent, single individuals, or families with their own biological children. Adoptees' birth certificates were originally available in New York State, but in 1924 legislation permitted judges to have them sealed. In 1935 all adoption records were required to be sealed, a provision still in effect in the state. Beginning in 1969 financial subsidies were available for foster parents so that they could adopt children already placed in their homes. Adoption subsidies were subsequently expanded to include all adoptive parents. This and the development of adoption advocacy organizations such as the New York Council on Adoptable Children and New York State's Citizen's Coalition for Children led to an increase in the number of adoptions of older children, minority children, and children with special medical or psychiatric needs. In 1978 more than 1,000 of the 1,840 adoptions were subsidized. In 2001, 95.5% of New York State Office of Children and Family Services adoptions were subsidized.

There are 56 public (county or city), 107 voluntary, and 16 out-of-state agencies authorized to arrange adoptions in New York State. Private agencies generally charge fees to adoptive parents, while public agencies do not. New York State requires that an adoption be in the best interest of the child, but because values differ not all agencies or judges agree about what makes a suitable parent. Although current law does not prohibit single people, including gays and lesbians, from adopting, married couples are generally preferred. Prospective parents must have a legal means of support and must be able to meet the needs of the child they are adopting. In agency adoptions, visits are made to adoptive families following placement and until the adoption becomes legal, usually about a year. The New York State Adoption Service maintains a list of authorized agencies and a photolisting of children legally eligible for adoption.

Gilman, Lois. *The Adoption Resource Book* (New York: Harper Resource, 1998)
Karp, Wayne E. *Family Matters* (Cambridge, Mass: Harvard Univ Press, 2000)
New York State Department of Health Adoption Registry, http://www.health.state.ny.us/nysdoh/vr/forms/registry.htm

Eve P. Smith

Adventists. Christian sects that focus on the fulfillment of prophecies about the Second Coming (or Advent) of Christ, the apocalypse, and the millennium. Adventist churches and sects developed in New York State during widespread revivalism from 1820 to 1840 that earned the regions of Central and Western New York the label of Burned-over District. William Miller (1782–1849) of Hampton (Washington Co) was the principal founder. Experiencing a religious conversion while serving in the military during the War of 1812, Miller moved from deism to evangelical Christianity. Bible study revealed to him that prophecies in the Books of Daniel and Revelation about the apocalypse and Second Coming of Christ would be fulfilled "some time in 1843." In 1831 he began publicizing his views, lecturing, and publishing a pamphlet and book of lectures, and Millerism quickly spread throughout the Champlain, Hudson, and Mohawk Valleys. A revival that resulted from Miller's lectures in Lansingburgh (Rensselaer Co) gained publicity for his views and a team of three powerful preachers to help spread them—Emerson Andrews, Charles Cole, and E. B. Crandall. Several other Baptist, Christian Connexion, and Methodist preachers volunteered their labors on his behalf—Truman Hendryx, an itinerant Baptist preacher; Isaac Fuller of Poultney, Vt; and Joseph Marsh of New York Mills (Oneida Co).

After a group of professional Boston and New York City reformers took over the management of the movement in 1840 it spread west rapidly. The leaders undertook an intensive crusade throughout Western New York in 1842–43 called the Great Enterprise, using as a promotional device a huge tent that could seat thousands of listeners. Again local leaders arose in large numbers to proclaim the imminent end of the world. These included Elon Galusha, an influential Baptist pastor in Lockport (Niagara Co), Joseph Marsh, who published a Millerite newspaper called the *Voice of Truth* in Rochester, and Hugh Hancock, who worked in Syracuse. Women often found a public voice for the first time by preaching in the movement—Lydia Richmond in Chautauqua Co, Elvira Fassett of Seneca Falls (Seneca Co); and Olive Maria Rice who itinerated throughout Western New York.

The Millerite message attracted considerable scorn and ridicule. Thousands of Adventists left their congregations or were expelled because of their beliefs, including William Miller and his family. The small Baptist chapel he had built near his farmhouse in Hampton became an Adventist meetinghouse. Millerites in Syracuse, Rochester, and Ithaca built their own "tabernacles," separate from the churches, which they loudly condemned as allied with the Antichrist. When 1843 passed uneventfully, various Adventist leaders established more precise deadlines, the last one being 22 Oct 1844, a date that Miller himself endorsed just a few days before the deadline, but this, too, led to disappointment.

Nevertheless Miller's views had gained thousands of believers, probably up to 5,000 in New York State alone. A small group of believers, undeterred by the Great Disappointment, provided the core of new Adventist denominations after 1845. The first, the Advent Christian Church, was founded in 1860 at a general conference of Adventists in Providence, RI. One of its first additions was the Adventist chapel on the Miller farm. Much larger is the Seventh-day Adventist Church, founded by former Millerites principally from Maine. Combining belief in the imminent end of the world, vegetarianism, and Saturday worship, it was organized by representatives of 100 congregations who met in Battle Creek, Mich, in 1863. Later successors to the Millerites include the Church of the Nazarene and a number of much smaller groups. Altogether the Adventist denominations have small memberships in New York, concentrated in the lower Hudson Valley and in the Rochester, Utica/Rome, and Buffalo regions, which had all hosted strong Millerite communities in the 1840s.

Doan, Ruth Alden. *The Miller Heresy, Millennialism, and American Culture* (Philadelphia: Temple Univ Press, 1987)

Knight, George R. *Millennial Fever and the End of the World: A Study of Millerite Adventism* (Boise, Idaho: Pacific Press Publishing, 1993)

David L. Rowe

advertising industry. The industry comprises companies and individuals who consult with and work for advertisers, often on a range of marketing needs and opportunities, including analysis of sales methods and of competitors, advertisement text and design, purchase of media time and space, and consumer research. It includes market and public opinion researchers, direct-mail companies, media that sell and carry advertisements, and other related firms.

New York City has played a leading role in almost every development in advertising. During the 1730s *New-York Weekly Journal* (1733–51) edited by John Peter Zenger—defendant in a 1735 libel trial that raised freedom of the press issues—devoted four to five times as much space to advertising as any other American newspaper of the period. Publisher James Parker's *New-York Weekly Post-Boy* (1743–47) in New York City soon topped the *Weekly Journal*'s ad volume, with the *Post-Boy* employing three of its four pages for ads. They published both display ads—ads that have either a headline, graphic, or noticeable white space—and line notices in large typeface. Francis Childs's *New-York Commercial Advertiser* (1831–89) adopted a similar advertising-heavy format.

Newspapers, not magazines, pioneered most advertising tactics. Another New York City newspaper, Benjamin Day's *Sun* (1833–1950), which claimed a circulation of 20,000 by 1834, vigorously pursued display ads, marriage and death notices, and "wants," or classifieds. In addition, the *Sun* charged low prices—contracts at 1¢ per line per day—with Day writing most advertising text (copy) himself. Resulting ad volume forced him to use larger paper sheets and made the *Sun* highly profitable for his successors. James Gordon Bennett Sr founded *New York Morning Herald* in May 1835 (from August 1835 to 1924, *New York Herald*) and adopted similar practices through the late 1840s when it banned display ads because other advertisers complained they were unable to afford the larger displays. The paper still carried the most advertising of any US paper for about 50 years. From its founding, Robert Bonner's *New York Ledger* (1855–98) published advertising directed to women, advertised for readership in other newspapers, and broke the custom of not accepting display ads. After the Civil War two major New York City department stores, Lord and Taylor and Macy's, took advantage of new publisher flexibility and purchased two-column display ads, often featuring large logos or typefaces.

New York City–based magazines also became advertising pioneers, although the publishers of some, such as *Harper's Magazine* (1857–1916), believed advertising cheapened their publications' images. In 1880 New York City–based Cyrus H. K. Curtis began to publish magazines primar-ily as advertising, rather than as literary vehicles. That year New York City's Business Address Co became the first modern direct-mail advertising firm, although individual companies had advertised by mail for decades. Over time, most publications ran increased and larger advertisements that contained more illustrations, and by the 1890s magazine advertisements commonly used color inks. Also during this time the extensive wiring of New York City for electricity led to the creation of illuminated, often large, signs, with Broadway known as the Great White Way by 1893.

Volney B. Palmer (with offices in New York City, Boston, Philadelphia, and Baltimore by 1846) and John L. Hooper introduced use of multiple publications for advertising campaigns, agency-written and designed ads, and integration of advertising into overall marketing. In 1865 George P. Rowell opened a Manhattan agency that bought space from newspapers and resold smaller blocks to advertisers. Four years later he launched his annual *American Newspaper Directory* and still later founded a precursor of the American Association of Advertising Agencies (1917). Rowell sold his agency in 1892 to focus on his advertising trade magazine *Printer's Ink* (1888–1967).

By 1900 New York City dominated the advertising agency industry, housing 25 agencies, including one of the nation's three largest, J. Walter Thompson. The other two were Philadelphia's N. W. Ayer and Son and Chicago's Lord and Thomas. Stanley Resor, from 1912 vice president and general manager of J. Walter Thompson, bought the agency in 1916, integrating new social science and psychology research methods into the agency's work. Resor, who would head the agency for 39 years, specialized in the "hard sell." The city's agencies boomed from 1918 to 1929, before and after radio's introduction. Young and Rubicam, started in Philadelphia in 1923, moved to New York in 1926, and pollster George Gallup oversaw its research from 1932 through the late 1940s.

The advertising community in New York City launched organizations for its professionals. One was the Advertising Club (1915), which taught skills, set ethical standards, held advertising expositions, and formed the Advertising Hall of Fame in 1949. The Newspaper Advertising Bureau, or NAB (1913–92), promoted standard advertising contracts, provided materials and ideas to newspapers and promoted them as an advertising medium, and conducted research on the newspaper and advertising industries. The American Marketing Association's New York City chapter has held the EFFIE Awards since 1968 to recognize the year's most successful advertising campaigns. New York City–based trade publications such as the newspapers *Advertising Age* (1930), *Adweek* (1959), and *Editor and Publisher* (1901), and the magazine *Folio* (1972) also appeared at this time.

Following the Great Depression and World War II the industry boomed again, spurred especially by the widespread introduction of television in 1948 and the subsequent move of radio networks into the new medium. The advertising industry influenced television programming, and in 1958–59, it was charged that Madison Ave advertising executives seeking higher ratings corrupted participants in *The $64,000 Question* quiz show. New York City's agencies tended to pass through common creative phases as well as common phases in corporate structure. The 1960s creative revolution led by Brooklyn native William Bernbach of Doyle Dane Bernbach, developed messages of simple language aimed at average consumers, such as his Think Small campaign for Volkswagen. Many small or specialized agencies originated during this decade. During the 1970s agencies largely reverted to hard-sell tactics, with most—including J. Walter Thompson, Doyle Dane Bernbach, Ogilvy and Mather, Foote, Cone and Belding, and Grey Advertising—becoming publicly traded companies. Young and Rubicam bought the public relations firm and Manhattan-headquartered Burson-Marsteller, and other agencies became full-service marketing firms by creating in-house public relations capability. Some New York City firms merged, and eventually the three Manhattan giants, BBDO International, Doyle Dane Bernbach, and Needham Harper Worldwide, would merge to form Omnicom Group (1986). In 1986 Saatchi and Saatchi, a British agency founded in 1970, bought New York City agencies Ted Bates Worldwide, Backer and Spielvogel, and Dancer Fitzgerald Sample. Young and Rubicam, publicly traded in 1998–2000, merged with London-based WPP Group, which had acquired J. Walter Thompson and Ogilvy and Mather in 1986.

At the beginning of the 21st century, advertising agencies, major media corporations, and advertising trade publications and organizations, such as American Association of Advertising Agencies, Association of National Advertisers, and Direct Marketing Association, continue to maintain New York City's position as the world's advertising headquarters. At the same time, more than a dozen agencies, which came into existence primarily in the latter decades of the 20th century, serve clients from headquarters in Syracuse, Albany, Rochester, and Buffalo. Syracuse-based Eric Mower and Associates is the largest of these, ranking in the top 75 advertising firms worldwide, with 2003 billings of over $130 million and with branch offices in Albany, Rochester, and Buffalo as well as in Portsmouth, NH, and Atlanta, Ga. In 2003 Mower clients included Carrier Corp, Corning Inc, Bristol-Myers Squibb, Niagara Mohawk, and Syracuse and Clarkson Universities. Other Central, Northern, and Western New York firms are Syracuse's MRA Group (billings of $36 million) and Ryan Communications ($2.5 million); Albany's Media Logic ($45 million); Rochester's Jay Advertising ($100 million), Sigma Marketing Group ($98 million), and Roberts Communications ($52 million).

Fox, Stephen R. *The Mirror Makers: A History of American Advertising and Its Creators* (New York: William Morrow, 1984)

Goodrum, Charles, and Heley Dalrymple. *Advertising in America: The First 200 Years* (New York: Harry N. Abrams, 1990)

Marchand, Roland. *Advertising the American Dream: Making Way for Modernity, 1920–1940* (Berkeley: Univ of California Press, 1985)

Dane S. Claussen

Afghanis. See CENTRAL ASIANS.

AFL-CIO. See LABOR.

African Americans

New Netherland

The history of Africans in New York State begins with their appearance in about 1626 as Dutch West India Co slaves in New Amsterdam. Without a specific date recorded of their arrival, 1626 is generally accepted and is based on the manumission by Director Willem Kieft and council of 11 slaves and their wives in 1644 "who have served the Company for 18 or 19 years." The freeing of the slaves both for their long service to the West India Co and the need to support their growing families was the start of a small free black community. They were given land and expected to earn their living by agriculture. It was called a "half freedom" because the Africans were to pay the West India Co each year "30 schepels [approximately 22 bu/775 l] of maize or wheat, pease, or beans, and one fat hog worth 20 guilders." They were also to serve the company when called upon, for which they would receive "fair wages." However, their children, "born or yet to be born," were to remain slaves in service to the company. Included in the *Remonstrance of New Netherland,* which cited numerous complaints from New Netherland to the States General in 1650, was the concern that keeping children of manumitted slaves enslaved was "contrary to all public law." In response, the colonial secretary, Cornelis van Tienhoven, said that the children of the former slaves were "treated the same as Christians" and that "no more than three" were then in service.

It is not known if the company changed its policy regarding children of half-freed slaves, but there is evidence that their children could be manumitted for a cash payment. Moreover, 26 Africans, slave and free, were married in the Dutch Reformed Church in New Amsterdam between 1641 and 1664. Baptized in the church were 50–60 African children; their parents hoped that by doing so their chances for freedom would be increased. After 1655 only one baptism is recorded; the ministers had adopted a more restrictive definition of religious understanding for membership, affecting the number of black children to be baptized. They refused baptism, wrote one minister, "partly" because the parents' "lack of knowledge and faith" and "partly" because of the "wrong-aim" of parents "who sought nothing else by it than the freeing of their children from material slavery, without pursuing piety and Christian virtues."

Slave or free, Africans had legal rights in the court and could testify and sue and be sued. Following Dutch custom, they also petitioned for various rights, as did four women slaves who asked for and received manumission. In 1664 eight half-free Africans petitioned to be manumitted and "made entirely free," which was granted. Free Blacks could own and will their property. They also apprenticed their children or signed them to contracts to secure a better future for them.

Colonial New York

By the time of the English takeover of the colony in 1664, it is estimated that of the probable 375 Blacks in New Amsterdam, about 75 were free. Under the more restrictive English law, however, between 1664 and 1698 the number of Blacks manumitted declined in New Amsterdam. In the earliest extant colonial census (1698), there were 2,170 Africans, with 700 in New York City. Almost all of them were slaves. New York Colony had the highest percentage of slaves of any northern colony, peaking at about 16% of the population around 1720. At this time New York City had the largest slave population of any city on the North American mainland. Although the numbers of African Americans would increase throughout the colonial period, both through natural increase and new slave importations (reaching 19,883 in 1771), their percentage, because of white migration and immigration, would decrease to 11.8%. The slave trade to New York remained active throughout the colonial period. At least through the middle of the century, a majority of the slaves brought to New York Colony were from the Caribbean. There was a thriving internal trade in slaves in New York Colony, and few slaves stayed with one master throughout their lifetime; many were sold several times.

African slaves worked in many positions within the economy. In urban areas they often worked as assistants to artisans or as domestics, although most domestics had a number of duties besides domestic service. In the Hudson Valley and Long Island, they generally worked on small farms, usually in communities of no more than five slaves. There were some larger plantations, such as Philipsburg Manor (Westchester Co), on which there were up to 60 slaves. In some rural areas slaves were the primary source of farm labor.

Some denominations, such as the Dutch Reformed and Huguenot congregations, actively discouraged slave conversions for fear that the newly Christianized slaves would have to be freed (a fear legally unwarranted). However, the Society for the Propagation of the Gospel in Foreign Parts (SPG), the missionary arm of the Church of England, attempted to convert slaves in the colony. From 1706 to 1722 Elias Neau had a school at which he attempted to catechize slaves, but only a relatively small percentage (no more than 1 in 10) attended, and the vast majority of slaves maintained their own religious practices outside of the churches of their owners. Neau's experiment met with considerable resistance from his fellow Anglicans, who barred Africans from burial in the churchyard of Trinity Church. Africans developed their own burial ground near Collect Pond north of the developed part of the city. Between 10,000 and 20,000 persons were buried there between about 1715 and 1795.

Africans expressed their resistance to slavery in numerous ways. Some slaves sued their masters for their freedom. Many escaped bondage, and colonial newspapers were filled with advertisements for freedom seekers. (Slave advertisements, often noting that slaves could speak English, Dutch, French, Welsh, Spanish, or various African languages, evidenced the diverse background of the enslaved.) Free black communities grew slowly in colonial New York; by

Detail of African Americans parading in celebration of the adoption of the 15th Amendment, New York City, from *Frank Leslie's Illustrated Newspaper,* 30 Apr 1870.

midcentury there was a growing population in New York City and small settlements in the Hudson Valley and Long Island.

There were two slave rebellions in colonial New York City. In 1712 slaves started a fire and killed nine Whites who came to put out the blaze. In the aftermath 22 slaves were executed, and a strict slave code was adopted, further restricting the possibility of manumission. In the 1741 "Negro Plot," an arrest of several slaves for arson led to the arrest of numerous slaves and some of their supposed white supporters. Thirty Blacks and four Whites, the alleged conspirators, were executed. Thirteen of the Blacks were burned at the stake. Seventy other slaves were banished to the West Indies.

A different aspect of slavery was seen in the case of rural slave Jupiter Hammon, who handled accounts for his master in Queens Village [now Lloyd Neck, Suffolk Co] and who in 1760 became the first published African American author. Hammon's position on slavery was ambiguous, and his published writings are dominated by exhortations to accept Christianity. Although the extremely pious Hammon was far from a militant critic of slavery, his final work, *An Address to the Negroes in the State of New York* (1787), recounted a lifetime of accumulated humiliations. "If we should ever get to Heaven," he wrote, "we shall find nobody to reproach us for being black, or for being slaves."

The Revolutionary War and Its Aftermath

The political and social instability surrounding the American Revolution presented an opportunity for New York's slaves. Some Blacks had fought for the American side after responding to early calls for volunteers, although New York patriots prohibited recruitment of slaves for militia service with the Militia Act of 1775, a policy reaffirmed by the Continental Congress when it formed the Continental army that same year. Some African Americans served in the militia in spite of the policy. Other enslaved New Yorkers escaped bondage to fight for the British, who promised freedom in exchange for military service; Virginia's royal governor, John Murray, Earl of Dunmore, issued a proclamation to this effect in November 1775. Many were informally organized into black loyalist companies, such as the Black Pioneers and the Black Brigade, that raided patriot positions on Long Island and along the Hudson River.

Americans responded with strict punishments for fugitive slaves caught behind British lines and for black loyalists recruiting others to join them, such as those jailed in Albany in 1779. But, initially, patriot leaders refrained from making similar promises of freedom for military service. Military necessity compelled a change in this policy, and in 1781 New York's legislature freed slaves who provided three years of service or who were regularly discharged. A visitor to Washington's army at White Plains (Westchester Co) in 1781 observed that a quarter of the troops were Blacks. In addition to fighting, Blacks performed fatigue duty and other service jobs for the American military forces. Henry Bakeman, who enlisted at Stone Arabia (Montgomery Co) in 1781, served as a courier in the Mohawk Valley until frostbite crippled him during the Continental army's unsuccessful raid on Fort Ontario in Oswego in February 1783. At war's end in November 1783, around 3,000 black loyalists gathered in New York City, where they evacuated with the British amid fears that their masters were coming to reclaim them. Many left for Nova Scotia and eventually went on to Sierra Leone in 1792. A sizable free black population, which in 1790 numbered over 1,000, remained in New York City. At the end of the war the percentage of free Blacks among New York State's African American population was larger than ever. Still, 82% of the 25,875 black New Yorkers enumerated in the 1790 census were enslaved.

The rhetoric of the American Revolution, with its doctrines of life, liberty, and the pursuit of happiness as articulated in the Declaration of Independence, resonated with some patriot leaders and provided a basis for challenging the institution of slavery. In 1785 the Society for Promoting the Manumission of Slaves (later New York Manumission Society) was organized in New York City, and its members, who were white and mostly Quaker, named John Jay president and Alexander Hamilton secretary. The group unsuccessfully lobbied for passage of a gradual emancipation bill in 1785, although other antislavery efforts were successful. The legislature limited the slave trade, eliminated a bond required of masters freeing slaves since 1712, and provided slaves some legal rights in measures passed in the 1780s. In 1787 the society founded the first African Free School, which offered instruction in reading, writing, the domestic arts, and navigation; its official building did not open until 1796.

Several subsequent attempts to end slavery in the state also failed, and the number of slaves actually increased in some communities during this period. From 1790 to 1800 New York City's slave population grew to approximately 2,500 (a 25% increase), and Albany's slave population peaked in 1790 at 572. Antislavery sentiment, however, had strengthened enough to prompt passage of a gradual emancipation law in 1799. The law, which enabled New York State slaveholders to keep the next generation of slaves in bondage through their most productive years, held that female slaves born after 4 July 1799 were freed at age 25, while male slaves born after that date were freed at age 28. An 1817 law gave freedom to all enslaved New Yorkers on 4 July 1827. Black New Yorkers celebrated Emancipation Day in communities across the state with parades and speeches on 5 July 1827. Churches, such as New York City's African Zion Church, Albany's African Baptist Church, and Cooperstown's (Otsego Co) Presbyterian Church, provided the venue for many of these celebrations.

Toward Freedom

In the wake of manumission's slow progress, enslaved New Yorkers physically resisted slavery through theft or violence, while others made attempts to free themselves before 1827. Some purchased their freedom with their own money, others petitioned their masters or negotiated to be freed in a master's will, and some infant children of slaves were freed by masters through the state's abandonment policy (1799–1817). Many ran away; Peter Wheeler of Ludlowville [now in Tompkins Co], for example, escaped slavery in 1806, and Thomas James of Canajoharie (Montgomery Co) found freedom in Canada in 1821 before returning to Rochester and opening a school for African American children in 1828. For all of these reasons, there was a significant rise in the state's free black population prior to 1827, when all New Yorkers became free. From 1790 to 1810 the number of free Blacks in the state increased from 4,682 to 25,333, from 22% to 62% of the state's African American population. The rate of manumission varied greatly from county to county, with urban areas having a much higher percentage of free Blacks. In 1820 only 5% of the approximately 11,000 African Americans in New York City were enslaved, while across New York Bay, on Staten Island, 85% of the Blacks were still in bondage. By 1830, the year of the first postslavery census, the African American population in New York State numbered 44,870, more than 60% of whom lived in seven counties in southern New York State: New York (13,959), Queens (3,108), Dutchess (2,486), Orange (2,223), Westchester (2,115), Suffolk (2,013), and Kings (2,007). Other sizable communities (larger than 1,000) clustered in Albany, Columbia, Rensselaer, and Ulster Cos, with much smaller groups living in the emerging cities of central and western New York State in 1830.

In many of these communities, free Blacks lived in close proximity to each other, and churches and schools were key institutions. In New York City the African Zion Church was founded after Peter Williams left the John Street Methodist Church in 1796 to form a black congregation within the Methodist Episcopal Church; this eventually became the African Methodist Episcopal Zion (AMEZ) Church, the "mother" church of the AMEZ denomination. The Abyssinian Baptist (1808), St. Philips (Protestant Episcopal) (1818), African Methodist Episcopal (AME) (1820), and First Colored Presbyterian (1821) Churches also served the city's large black population. New York City's first African Free School proved so successful that a second was opened in May 1815. Brooklyn's first school for Blacks opened the same year. The success of these early schools demonstrated the capability and enthusiasm of African Americans at a time when supporters of slavery were using racist arguments to defend the institution.

In early 19th-century Albany, most Blacks were communicants of St. Peter's Episcopal Church, but many later joined the Methodist Episcopal Church (1813) or black churches, such as the Israel AME Church (1828). Albany's African American children attended the Albany School for People of Color, an institution established by Albany Blacks who successfully petitioned the legislature for its creation in 1816. Located on Malcolm St (now Broad St), it received financial support mostly from Blacks but also from a few Whites and the city's Lancaster School; 60 students attended in 1823. The Wilberforce School, named for British abolitionist William Wilberforce, was established by the city in 1844 and was its first public school for black children; black and white teachers educated 148 students in 1862.

In Rochester the local AME Society established a church in 1823, and 10 years later an African Methodist Church (which became an AMEZ Church in 1835) opened on Favor St. Thomas James, the fugitive from Canajoharie, attended a Sabbath school in Rochester organized by businessman Austin Steward and schoolmaster Zenas Freeman before ministering and teaching at Rochester's AMEZ Church in the 1830s. These religious schools, which aimed

Kept In, depiction of a one-room schoolhouse near the art colony in Cragsmoor (Ulster Co), by Edward Lamson Henry, 1889. In the 1880s there were still at least 20 segregated schools in rural school districts in New York State.

to teach youngsters not only about Christianity but also the rudiments of learning, served the community's African American youth until 1841, when the local board of education established a school on the city's west side. Churches took an early role in African American education elsewhere, including Buffalo, where its black churches also conducted Sunday school classes. By the eve of the Civil War, Buffalo's fledgling community supported three churches, the Vine Street AME, Michigan Avenue Baptist, and St. Philips Episcopal Churches. Lyceums, such as those founded by Buffalo's Debating Society and the Ladies Literary Society before 1837, offered a creative alternative for Blacks to improve their reading and writing skills. They also encouraged literary expression by providing its members with literary critics and sources for publication.

In Syracuse James also helped establish the city's AMEZ Church, which was formally organized in 1842. Members of the black community worshiped as well at the Second Congregation Church in the 1850s. In Ithaca nine African American residents founded the St. James AMEZ Church in 1833, and a school was serving black children there by 1841. In Geneva (Ontario and Seneca Cos) a black congregation met at the High Street Sabbath School, the Second Baptist Church, and the First Wesleyan Methodist Church in the 1830s and 1840s.

Antebellum Agitation

Out of New York State's black churches, schools, and communities emerged some of the nation's most vocal abolitionists, who, after celebrating the end of slavery in the state in 1827, accelerated their fight to end slavery elsewhere and to improve the social, economic, and political position of free Blacks. The best-known African American activists in New York State were three former slaves: Sojourner Truth, Frederick Douglass, and Harriet Tubman. Born into slavery in Ulster Co in 1797, Sojourner Truth escaped to New York City in 1826. Spurred on by her religious convictions, she earned acclaim as a preacher and lecturer for African American and women's rights throughout the 1840s–1860s; her memoirs were published in 1850. Douglass, who escaped slavery in Maryland and fled to New York City in 1838, eventually settled in Massachusetts, where he befriended William Lloyd Garrison and became an agent for the American Anti-Slavery Society. In 1847 he moved to Rochester and established the *North Star* (later *Frederick Douglass' Paper*). A Rochester resident until 1872, he shifted his allegiances from the Garrisonians to the political abolitionists of central and western New York State by the early 1850s. Harriet Tubman, also born a slave in Maryland, moved to Auburn (Cayuga Co) after William H. Seward gave her a home there in 1857. She led dozens of freedom seekers to safety, served as a scout and a nurse in the Union army during the Civil War, and established a home for the aged in Auburn after 1896.

Numerous others, although less well known, emerged as leaders in communities across the state. Black women founded charitable societies, such as the Albany Female Lundy Society (1833) and the African Female Benevolent Society of Troy (1833). Susan Douge, a prominent black activist in Albany, was the first president of the Lundy Society, which not only assisted poor families but promoted education for black children. In Buffalo William Wells Brown, an abolitionist and writer, became active in the Western New York Anti-Slavery Society after escaping slavery in Kentucky in 1836. In New York City Samuel E. Cornish, a Presbyterian minister and agent for the African Free School, agitated for African American rights via *Freedom's Journal* (the country's first African American newspaper) and later the *Colored American* beginning in 1827. David Ruggles helped found the New York Committee of Vigilance, which offered support to freedom seekers and others accused of being runaways beginning in 1837; the committee, which was created after the federal Fugitive Slave Act of 1793 mandated that local law enforcement officers return freedom seekers to their owners, sent fugitives on to Boston, Albany, and Troy. James McCune Smith, an African Free School graduate, was an abolitionist, writer, and the first African American to earn a medical degree (1837). He then maintained a practice and pharmacy in New York City. Other students of African Free Schools included abolitionist Henry Highland Garnet, who pastored at the Liberty Street Presbyterian Church in Troy in the 1840s before helping organize a black congregation and school in Geneva, and Samuel Ringgold Ward, also an abolitionist and pastor, who ministered in South Butler (Wayne Co) and Cortland in the 1840s. Ward, Garnet, and other abolitionists including Jermain Loguen, a fugitive slave and AMEZ minister in Syracuse, attended the interracial Oneida Institute in Whitesboro (Oneida Co).

Many of these leaders became active in the black convention movement, which originated in Philadelphia in 1830. National conventions were held in five New York State communities: New York City (1834), Buffalo (1843), Troy (1847), Rochester (1853), and Syracuse (1864). Notable debates among convention attendees took place in Buffalo, where Garnet delivered an impassioned speech calling for slave uprisings if owners refused to free them. In Troy leaders debated the merits of Gerrit Smith's gift of 40-acre (16 ha) parcels of Adirondack land to free Blacks; about 200 took Smith up on his offer and moved to the settlement called Timbucto in Franklin and Essex Cos. Rochester's meeting featured a speech by Frederick Douglass, who argued against Martin Delany's call for emigration. At other meetings, attendees discussed which candidates and political parties to endorse. Garnet, Ward, Loguen, Douglass, and others became strong supporters of political abolitionism, and they often used their pulpits and their newspapers to agitate for Liberty Party candidates. Of special interest to all of these leaders at the state level was black suffrage, which was limited at the Constitutional Convention of 1821 to black males holding $250 worth of property; in 1826, of an approximate black population of 12,000 in New York Co, only 16 met this qualification to vote. Activists lobbied to remove the qualification via a referendum in 1846, but it failed; subsequent referendums also failed in 1860 and 1869.

In the 1850s black protest surged after the Fugitive Slave Act (1850) passed. The law, which made freedom seekers and those who assisted them subject to arrest or reenslavement, led many African Americans in New York State to be uncertain of their legal and civic status in the United States, and many considered emigration. Those who remained in the state organized protest meetings, such as the one held in a Cazenovia (Madison Co) apple orchard on 22 Aug 1850, formed additional vigilance committees, and openly violated federal law by continuing to assist freedom seekers. In Syracuse in October 1851, a few months after Massachusetts senator Daniel Webster visited and pledged that the law would be enforced, Loguen, Ward, and others helped free William "Jerry" Henry from federal custody by storming the jail in which Henry was being held and ferrying him off to Canada via Oswego. Both Loguen and Ward, escaped slaves themselves, went to Canada for safety after the rescue.

A similar rescue happened in April 1860 in Troy, where community members (led in part by Harriet Tubman, who was visiting Troy) broke Charles Nalle out of custody. They helped him escape to Niskayuna (Schenectady Co) and eventually purchased his freedom. The use of violence as a means to end slavery was increasingly debated in black activist circles, and in the years leading up to the Civil War more leaders came to believe that slavery would inevitably "go out in blood." After the Kansas-Nebraska Act passed in 1854, Frederick Douglass and James McCune Smith supported John Brown in his battles against proslavery settlers in Kansas Territory. Smith, Loguen, and Tubman provided Brown counsel and support during planning stages for his invasion of the South. Although Douglass chose not to condone the plan, he was identified as a co-conspirator after Brown was captured following his raid on Harper's Ferry [now in W Va] in October 1859; Douglass traveled to England for a speaking tour and avoided arrest. Executed two months later, Brown was celebrated as a martyr by many African Americans, who considered his North Elba (Essex Co) farm a pilgrimage site.

Civil War and Draft Riots of 1863

If most Americans viewed the political crisis of 1860 with fear for the future, African Americans in New York State and elsewhere welcomed the coming of conflict. They knew, perhaps better than leading politicians, that a war between the North and South would not leave the institution of slavery unchanged. As Douglass wrote in March 1861, "The contest must now be decided, and decided forever, which of the two, Freedom or Slavery, shall give law to this Republic. Let the conflict come." Although Pres Abraham Lincoln called for volunteers for the Union cause in April 1861, it was not until the summer of 1862 that black troops were officially allowed to enlist. This delay caused much bitterness among New York State's African Americans, who in numerous public meeting and petitions demanded the right to serve.

African Americans served with distinction. Beginning in 1864 more than 4,000 black troops trained at Rikers and Hart Islands [now in Bronx Co] and served in the 20th, 26th, and 31st of the United States Colored Troops (USCT). In addition to native New York State Blacks, black Canadians and foreign Blacks also served in the state's regiments. Several black New Yorkers became commissioned officers. Commitment to the war effort was not limited to men of service age. Harriet Tubman returned South, this time to work as a nurse with the troops. Starting in 1862 and continuing through Reconstruction, many African American men and women went to areas liberated by Union forces to proselytize or teach, such as Edmonia Highgate, from a black family in Syracuse, who starting in 1864 taught in Maryland and New Orleans.

The home front remained troubled, with frequent reminders to Blacks of their second-class status. On the eve of the Civil War, in 1860, New York State voters rejected an amendment to the state's constitution, by a vote of 345,791 to 197,889, that would have eliminated the property requirement for black male suffrage. But the most chilling indication of racism took place during the draft riots of 1863. Under the Enrollment Act of that year, most white men were subject to military duty but could avoid service through the payment of a $300 commutation fee, well beyond the means of working-class families. There were protests against the draft in many New York State cities, especially in New York City, where beginning 11 July 1863 mobs of over 50,000 Whites, largely working-class Irish, rioted for three days. They burned the Colored Orphan Asylum on 5th Ave between 43d and 44th Sts and terrorized those they thought supported the draft and the African Americans who came in their path. Estimates of the death toll in New York City range from 100 to over 1,000, making it one of the most extreme episodes of violence against Blacks in the nation's history. Racism was also expressed in less violent ways. In 1869, just before the ratification of the 15th Amendment made it moot, New York State voters once again kept the property qualification for black suffrage (282,403–249,802).

Although civil rights triumphs in succeeding decades would be few, in 1873 the state legislature passed a civil rights law prohibiting discrimination in access to public schools and public transportation. William H. Johnson, an Albany barber who was a former president of the Colored State Convention and an active Republican, aggressively lobbied for its passage. The law provided African Americans in New York State an impetus to struggle for school integration.

This struggle had begun in the 1840s, with the first efforts by African Americans to gain admittance to predominantly white schools in Buffalo and Rochester. In 1856, after a campaign of sev-

Negro Laborers at Work under the "Storm King," Hudson River, drawn by John Alexander, from *Harper's Weekly,* 20 Aug 1881.

eral years spearheaded by Frederick Douglass, Rochester became the first city in the state to close its separate school for black pupils. African Americans were sometimes ambivalent about the closing of all-black schools, because the only African American teachers in the school system were in the black schools. In 1883 and 1884 the Cities of Brooklyn and New York opened all of their white schools to black pupils, but the black schools were not closed, primarily to keep the jobs of black teachers. It was only in 1896 that the first African American was licensed to teach in one of New York City's traditionally white public schools.

Niagara Movement, NAACP, and Organizational Life

In addition to churches and religious groups, African Americans formed fraternal and benevolent organizations dating to the late 18th century. In the late 19th century, at a time when the civil rights of African Americans were eroding, organizations became an increasingly important focus for African Americans. Many of these organizations espoused an ethos of self-help, advancement, and racial pride. Although they were influenced by the accommodationist policies of Booker T. Washington, the most powerful African American leader at the turn of the 20th century, organizations in New York State played a critical role in pushing the African American agenda toward a more overt civil rights stance.

Many black organizations were separated by gender. The Prince Hall Masons, for example, was formed as an all-male group, with the Eastern Stars as its female counterpart. The first intercollegiate Greek organization for male African American undergraduates (Alpha Phi Alpha) was founded at Cornell University in December 1906. The oldest African American sorority (Alpha Kappa Alpha) had chapters in New York State soon after its founding in 1908. The National Association of Colored Women's Clubs was founded in 1896, and the state's women were prominent in the movement. Alice Wiley Seay founded an affiliate, the Empire State Federation of Women's Clubs (1908), in Brooklyn in 1908. The club had two main goals: "to uplift work amongst young girls and women" and to care for the quite elderly Harriet Tubman in her home in Auburn. Another affiliate, the Buffalo Phyllis Wheatley Club, protested the stereotypical representations of Blacks at the Pan-American Exposition in 1901 and successfully advocated the inclusion of a "Negro exhibit." It also invited the National Association for the Advancement of Colored People (NAACP) to organize in Buffalo in 1910. In 1919 women in Arbor Hill, in the northern part of the City of Albany, founded the Maria C. Lawton Club, a branch of the Empire State Federation of Women's Clubs, and Victoria Earle Matthews organized the White Rose Mission in 1897 in Brooklyn. In 1900 the mission, which sought to protect young migrant women from exploitative employers and the vicissitudes of urban life, moved to 217 East 86th St in Manhattan and established a settlement house.

At opposite ends of the state, the Niagara Movement, the NAACP, and the National Urban League—three of the most significant national civil rights organizations of the early 20th century—were founded. W. E. B. DuBois, who had become the leader of black opposition to Booker T. Washington, was a leader in the organization of the Niagara Movement in 1905. Those present at the early meetings at the Buffalo home of Mary Burnett Talbert and wealthy realtor husband William H. Talbert included Ida B. Wells, the antilynching crusader. Unable to find a meeting place that would rent to African Americans on the New York side of the falls, the 29 male founders eventually met in Niagara Falls, Ont. The Niagara Movement was outspoken in its rejection of Washington's accommodationist policies and demanded full civil liberties and enforcement of the 14th and 15th Amendments. Despite its great early promise, by 1910 the Niagara Movement, hobbled by a weak organization and financial problems, had disbanded. It was superseded by the NAACP, which proved longer lasting. Unlike the Niagara Movement, the NAACP was organized as an interracial movement. It was founded in 1909 in Manhattan following an interracial civil rights meeting in the apartment of William English Walling that called for civil and political rights for African Americans. A series of race riots that took place in various communities, including Springfield, Ill, where a white mob killed two African Americans and destroyed black businesses and homes in 1908, prompted the meeting. DuBois, the only African American among the four or five most prominent persons in the organization's earliest years, was editor of the NAACP's magazine, the *Crisis*, from 1910 to 1934. Another important organization set up at this time was the National Urban League, which formed in 1911 from the merger of three groups founded in New York City: the Committee on Urban Conditions among Negroes (1910), the Committee for the Improvement of Industrial Conditions among Negroes in New York (1906), and the National League for the Protection of Colored Women (1905). The National Urban League was first called the National League on Urban Conditions among Negroes and adopted its present name in 1920. It was created to help ease the economic and social problems exacerbated by the increased influx of southern Blacks to northern states.

Marcus Garvey's Universal Negro Improvement Association (UNIA) rejected collaboration with sympathetic Whites and the emphasis on integration. A Jamaican immigrant who first came to Harlem in 1916 to study Booker T. Washington's education program, Garvey developed a huge following over the next decade for his advocacy of economic development and black self-determination. The movement declined greatly in influence after Garvey's conviction for mail fraud and eventual deportation to Jamaica in 1927.

World War I and the Great Migration

To many African Americans World War I was an ongoing reminder of discrimination and segregationist policies within the United States. Nevertheless, many hoped that their military contributions and sacrifice would aid in the struggle to end these policies. One division, the 369th Regiment (formerly the 15th New York Regiment), also known as the Harlem Hellfighters, did engage, and with distinction, in direct combat. The 369th included Sgt Henry L. Johnson, a former Albany Union Station worker and the first American to be awarded France's highest award of gallantry for his single-handed battle with a German raiding party. Almost one-third of the Harlem Hellfighters were killed or wounded. New York State was the training ground for another black regiment, the 367th, also known as the Buffaloes. The 367th trained at Camp Upton in Suffolk Co and departed for France in 1918, ultimately serving on the frontline. Although the 369th was honored with a parade down 5th Ave after the war, Blacks were not awarded any medals by the US government, and their contributions were often downplayed. A large number of black nurses qualified to provide services overseas, but their applications were rejected by the American Red Cross because the military did not accept the service of black women.

The Great Migration of southern Blacks to the North during the early 20th century created large urban concentrations of African Americans in the state's largest cities, especially in New York City. Oppressive conditions in the post–Reconstruction South and greater job opportunities in the North provided the impetus. The greatest influx of Blacks occurred during the war because of the industrial labor boom that it created. By 1920 Harlem, which started to be developed as a black community around 1904, had a wide variety of religious, social, and literary institutions. Artists, writers, and musicians—Alain Locke, Claude McKay, Zora Neale Hurston, Langston Hughes, James Weldon Johnson, W. E. B. DuBois, Aaron Douglas, Duke Ellington, Paul Robeson, among others—created what became known as the Harlem Renaissance.

The increased African American population of Harlem in the 1920s was not solely the result of southern migration. As much as one-quarter of Harlem's population was of Caribbean birth and ancestry. Marcus Garvey was a Jamaican immigrant, and many of Harlem's leading political and intellectual figures were of Caribbean background. Many black nationalists and socialists, including Cyril Briggs, W. A. Domingo, Frank Crosswaith, Richard B. Moore, and Hubert H. Harrison, were from the Caribbean, as was poet and novelist Claude McKay. Another leading figure of the Harlem Renaissance of Caribbean ancestry was the Puerto Rican–born black scholar and bibliophile Arthur A. Schomburg, whose extensive collection documented the experiences of people of African descent throughout the world. His collection formed the core of the Schomburg Center for Research in Black Culture, Harlem's world-renowned research library. The black population of Harlem reached 115,000 during the 1920s.

Cities elsewhere in New York State also experienced an increase in their black populations. By the start of the 20th century Buffalo's black population had reached about 1,000, making up less than .5% of the city's population. It had climbed to 9,000 by 1925. Even though the population was small, Buffalo Blacks had developed a legacy of struggle. Blacks from the southeastern states gradually began to trickle into the city. With the outbreak of World War I the population expanded as Blacks sought to take advantage of opportunities to work in the wartime industries, which first came in 1916 when they were hired to replace striking maritime workers. For the first time black workers retained their jobs after the strike was settled. Subsequently, other industries such as the railroads and steel mills began to em-

Fenimore Hotel employees on Otsego Lake, Cooperstown, 1912. Summer resorts such as Cooperstown and Saratoga Springs were major sources of employment for African Americans.

ploy African Americans. Although black women experienced deplorable working conditions and limited access to jobs, two-thirds of them found it necessary to work. Over half worked in domestic service, mainly as chambermaids and domestics in private homes and hospitals; a few found employment as porters, waitresses, or day workers.

In 1920 the African American population of Rochester was only 1,500, but it soon grew as southern Blacks, initially from Sanford, Fla, joined the Great Migration to the North. By 1965 this population had reached 33,000. Most came because of the chain migration from Sanford; others traveled from Louisiana, Virginia, and the Carolinas. The black community's infrastructure of churches and community organizations grew. The African Methodist Episcopal Zion Society (1823) and the Mount Olivet Baptist Church (1908) established institutions to educate and provide aid to the black community. African American–owned businesses included the Douglas Grocery Co in 1920, and Rochester's first licensed black physician, Dr Charles T. Lunsford, began his practice in 1921. Noted architect Thomas W. Boyde Jr came to Rochester in 1930 to help design the Monroe County Home and Infirmary, Star Market supermarkets, and the Community Child Center. Musician R. Nathaniel Dett, one of the first significant African American classical composers, taught at the Eastman School, from which the great baritone William Warfield, who grew up in Rochester, graduated in 1942.

Post–Great Depression and World War II

Although the depression that started in 1929 was difficult for all Americans, African Americans were hit especially hard. The migration of Blacks from the South was severely curtailed. The African American population of the state, which had more than doubled in the 1920s (and would almost do so again in the 1940s), increased only 28% from 1930 to 1940. Still this represented a significant increase in the state's black population, which for the most part remained confined to increasingly crowded segregated neighborhoods. In Albany southern Blacks settled in the city's South End after Rev Louis Parson, who moved to Albany in 1927 and established a branch of the First Church of God in Christ, encouraged families from his hometown of Shubuta, Miss, to move north. Although city officials told Parson to discourage the migration, by the late 1940s over 500 persons from Shubuta lived in the South End. There were also black neighborhoods along Orange St and in the vicinity of Livingston Ave. By 1943 a black suburb was being developed in the still unsettled Rapp Rd area in western Albany, and local residents built their own houses; the community was designated a National Historic District in 2003. In 1935 an Albany chapter of the NAACP was organized.

In the wake of harsh economic conditions and racial prejudice during the 1930s, Buffalo's African Americans worked to develop their own institutions and businesses. Community events were highlighted in the local black newspaper, the *Buffalo American.* Black business owners in 1935 organized the Buffalo Cooperative Economic Society, under the leadership of Dr Ezekial Nelson. The Michigan Avenue YMCA, founded by Blacks in 1922, provided community-based education programs and recreational programs. Blacks began to make inroads into the political process during the 1930s. They were selected to serve on various boards and commissions, and a few were appointed as police officers.

The lack of employment opportunities for African Americans in the 1930s spurred "don't buy where you can't work" campaigns in various communities, including one in Harlem that achieved some success. In the wake of the Harlem riot of 1935, in which three persons were killed, a commission appointed by Mayor Fiorello LaGuardia recommended the vigorous anti-discrimination efforts in housing and municipal employment. Little was done to implement these recommendations, and a more serious riot took place in Harlem in 1943, in which six persons were killed and 185 were injured. Despite these problems, Harlem continued to be a cultural and political center for black America during the 1930s and 1940s. The Apollo Theater opened its doors in 1934. The novelists Ralph Ellison and Richard Wright wrote about Harlem in the Federal Writers' Project (FWP). African American politics remained vibrant as well. The Communist Party, with its forthright stance on civil rights, was a powerful force in Harlem politics, attracting many visible supporters, among them Paul Robeson and Langston Hughes, and elected a member of the party to the New York City Council, Benjamin Davis, from 1943 to 1947. The two major parties attracted much support as well. The Republicans were the traditional party for black New Yorkers, and under Mayor LaGuardia, black Republicans achieved considerable recognition. In 1939 La Guardia appointed Jane M. Bolin to the Domestic Relations Court, and she became the first black female judge in the United States. But it was the Democrats that achieved the greatest success, and African Americans, supporting New Deal programs, started to vote Democratic in large numbers. The greatest beneficiary of this switch in African American voting was the Rev Adam Clayton Powell Jr, pastor of the Abyssinian Baptist Church, the largest congregation in Harlem. He was first elected to the House of Representatives in 1944. The first African American representative from New York State, he would dominate black politics in New York City and State for a generation.

The coming of World War II was a watershed event for black America, as support for the mobilization for war against Axis powers was tempered by the reality that African Americans still faced systematic discrimination in both employment and in segregated military units. A. Philip Randolph organized the March on Washington Movement in 1940, threatening to lead tens of thousands of Blacks to a march on Washington, DC, in protest in the summer of 1941. The prospect motivated Pres Franklin D. Roosevelt into issuing Executive Order 8802, which barred discrimination in defense industries and federal bureaus, and created the Fair Employment Practices Committee (FEPC). Yet Blacks still remained in segregated units throughout the war. For many black Americans, the war represented a "double-V": victory over the Axis Powers, and victory over Jim Crow at home. Due in large part to the efforts and protests of the National Association of Graduate Colored Nurses (founded in 1908 in New York City) led by Mabel Staupers and the NAACP, by the end of the war over 500 nurses had been commissioned and gained full integration in professional nursing organizations. The commitment to full racial equality received a boost during the war years that would help start the modern Civil Rights Movement.

Postwar History

The 1940s–1960s have often been called the "Second Great Migration." Although perhaps less celebrated than the first, its demographic consequences were considerably more significant. This was the period of greatest migration of southern Blacks to New York State. Between 1910 and 1940 there was a total African American internal migration (movement from other states to New York) of 371,800. For the period 1940–70, the same figure was 917,000, and the

African American population increased from 6% to 21% of the state's population.

The war years culminated with the 1945 passage of the landmark Ives-Quinn Law by the New York State legislature, the first bill passed by a state legislature banning employment discrimination. The African American population of the state, leading organizations such as the NAACP, organized labor (particularly the Congress of Industrial Organizations [CIO]), and large segments of both major political parties seemed united in their commitment to civil rights. In 1947 Jackie Robinson joined the Brooklyn Dodgers, becoming the first African American Major League baseball player in the 20th century. The next year, with much less publicity, the Buffalo Bills of the All-America Football Conference signed its first black player, Edward Conwell. In 1949 Leeland Jones Jr, who was the first African American to play for the University of Buffalo football team, became Buffalo's first black elected official.

Progress on civil rights, however, proved more difficult than many anticipated. The Cold War in the late 1940s and 1950s often frayed the previously close relationships between progressives and black activists. Although the scope of Ives-Quinn had expanded to cover public accommodations (1952), public housing (1955), and private housing (1961), enforcement proved difficult and sporadic. Outside of urban areas, black families seeking to purchase houses often faced numerous hurdles and the prospect of hostile neighbors. In cities the problem was often one of keeping white families in a neighborhood after the black presence passed the "tipping point." In any event, the combination of suburbanization and continued migration from the South rapidly remade the state's largest cities and in ways that often increased the existing residential and educational segregation. The criticism of the Civil Rights Movement by Malcolm X, the charismatic leader of the Harlem Mosque of the Nation of Islam from the mid-1950s to 1964, spoke to the growing frustration of many African Americans in the cities of New York State who, despite the move to the North, remained mired in poverty, inadequate housing, police harassment, and unequal educational opportunities.

The 1960s were a time of great turmoil for African Americans in the urban North. Although there was passage of significant civil rights legislation by the US Congress, such as the Civil Rights Act of 1964, there were also outbreaks of violence in urban areas. In July 1964 there were protests against police brutality in Harlem and the Bedford-Stuyvesant section of Brooklyn. Although begun as a peaceful protest sponsored by the Congress of Racial Equality (CORE), it erupted into full-fledged riots that ended two days later with one fatality and hundreds injured and arrested.

In Rochester, a three-day riot began in July 1964 following a dance. Although Gov Nelson A. Rockefeller called in the National Guard, which arrived on 27 July, property damage exceeded $1 million, and 4 people died and hundreds were injured. Response by the black community was swift. The Inner-City Ministry of the Rochester Council of Churches invited noted organizer Saul Alinsky to organize the city's response, and the following year a black organization, FIGHT (Freedom, Integration, God, Honor and Today) formed. FIGHT immediately set forth a series of demands, including more black representation in neighborhood and city organizations, better schools, and increased and better employment opportunities. Local companies like Kodak, Xerox, and Bausch and Lomb were targeted and responded by increasing the number of African Americans employed and promoted.

In the summer of 1967 there were a number of serious riots in major cities, including Chicago, Detroit, Newark, and Buffalo. The Buffalo riot, which lasted 6 days (26 June–1 July), nearly shut down the city and ended with over 40 injured, many with gunshot wounds, and over 200 arrested.

The civil unrest that pervaded the nation in the 1960s culminated in the organization of black militant groups seeking to end black oppression, unemployment, police brutality, and racism. Eighty students from Cornell University belonging to the Afro-American Society (AAS) seized Willard Straight Hall in 1969 armed with guns demanding a black studies program and an end to racism on campus. The incident achieved considerable national notoriety. The Black Panther Party (BPP), formed by Bobby Seale and Huey Newton in 1966, became a national symbol of this militancy and the turn to "black power." In 1968 David Brothers opened a branch in Brooklyn, and a few months later Lumumba Shakur opened one in Harlem. Although they offered practical help to their neighborhoods, such as free breakfast programs to inner-city children, free health clinics, and clothing drives to promote self-reliance in the black community, they also carried weapons and had frequent run-ins with the police and other legal authorities. By the 1980s the Panthers and similar organizations had largely unraveled because of a combination of internecine fights and the efforts of the FBI and other police organizations to weaken their influence. Following a police raid in 1969, 21 panthers were charged with conspiracy to blow up the New York Botanical Gardens and other public buildings. In 1971, after the longest trial in New York City history (known as the Panther 21 trial) and 45 minutes of jury deliberations, they were acquitted of all charges.

During the early 1970s violence erupted in New York State's prison system, in which most inmates were black and most guards were white. In addition to smaller disturbances at the Manhattan House of Detention and the Auburn Correctional Facility in 1970, an uprising involving over 1,000 inmates, many of whom were black militants, at Attica Correctional Facility (Wyoming Co) ended with 32 inmates and 11 prison employees dead in September 1971. Rioters demanded an end to racism and brutality in the prison system, improved wages and living conditions, parole reform, and increased political and religious freedom. After negotiations stalled Gov Nelson A. Rockefeller authorized forces from the National Guard and State Police to retake the prison; coroner reports indicated that all deaths resulting from this effort were caused by state shotgun fire. Rioting inmates were indicted (though charges were eventually dropped), and a special commission formed in 1972 to make recommendations for prison reform.

At the same that black militancy was on the rise, African Americans made steady progress in more conventional politics. In 1966 Robert C. Weaver, former New York State rent commissioner (1955–59), became the first African American to serve in a presidential cabinet when he was Pres Lyndon Johnson's secretary of Housing and Development; he later served as president of Baruch College in Manhattan (1969–70). In 1970 Charles B. Rangel defeated Adam Clayton Powell Jr in a primary for his Harlem seat. In 2004 Rangel was serving his 17th term as representative. Shirley Chisholm became the first African American woman elected to Congress in 1968 when she was voted into the House of Representatives from a district in Brooklyn. In 1972 she made a bid for the US presidency, becoming the first black woman to take on this challenge. In 1978 Clifton R. Wharton Jr became the chancellor of the SUNY system, serving until 1987. In 1993 he served as Pres Bill Clinton's deputy secretary of state.

By the 1970s a number of African American politicians in New York State were seeking office as mayor in some of the state's largest cities. Arthur O. Eve, first elected to the state assembly in 1966, became the first black Democratic mayoral candidate in New York State in 1977. Although he lost the mayor's race, he was named deputy speaker of the state assembly in 1979, a position he held until retiring in 2002. In 1989 David Dinkins, the former borough president of Manhattan, became the first African American mayor of New York City. In 1994 William A. Johnson Jr, who had arrived in Rochester in 1973 as president of the local National Urban League chapter, became the first African American mayor of Rochester, and he was reelected in 1997 and 2001.

The two most prominent black politicians in New York State at the turn of the 21st century were the Rev Alfred C. "Al" Sharpton and H. Carl McCall. Sharpton, a Brooklyn native who became a controversial figure following his advocacy for Tawana Brawley (the teenager who many believe falsely accused police of sexual molestation), helped publicize instances of brutality based on race. An advocate of racial, economic, and environmental justice, he has run unsuccessfully for various offices, including the US Senate and presidency. In 1993 McCall was elected state comptroller, becoming the first African American elected to a statewide office. In 2002 he was the losing Democratic candidate for governor.

Although there has been much change in the status of African Americans in recent decades and much progress in advancement in politics and business, many social problems continue. In 2000 the largest cities had a substantial black presence: Albany (28%), Buffalo (38%), New York City (27%), Rochester (37%), and Syracuse (25%). In many of these cities, the percentage of African American children under the poverty line is 50% or greater.

Although the African American population in New York State remains predominantly urban, increased suburbanization has taken place in recent decades. By 2000 the residential and educational segregational problems encountered in the rapidly growing African American populations in Westchester (14%), Rockland (11%), and Nassau (10%) Cos, for example, are found in the suburbs. The long struggle of African Americans for full and equal justice in New York State continues.

See also BASEBALL; EDUCATION DEPARTMENT AND UNIVERSITY OF THE STATE OF NEW YORK; ETHNIC PRESS; FOOTBALL; JAZZ; LABOR; PHYSICIANS;

PUBLIC EDUCATION; SUFFRAGE; TENNIS; UNITED STATES MILITARY ACADEMY (WEST POINT).

Berlin, Ira. *Many Thousands Gone: The First Two Centuries of Slavery in North America* (Cambridge, Mass: Harvard Univ Press, 1998)
Biondi, Martha. *To Stand and Fight; The Struggle for Civil Rights in Post-War New York City* (Cambridge, Mass: Harvard Univ Press, 2003)
Gellman, David N., and David Quigley. *Jim Crow New York: A Documentary History of Race and Citizenship, 1777–1877* (New York: New York Univ Press, 2003)
Goodfriend, Joyce D. *Before the Melting Pot: Society and Culture in Colonial New York City, 1664–1730* (Princeton, NJ: Princeton Univ Press, 1992)
Greenberg, Cheryl Lynn. *"Or Does It Explode?" Black Harlem in the Great Depression* (New York: Oxford Univ Press, 1991)
Grover, Kathryn. *Make a Way Somehow: African-American Life in a Northern Community, 1790–1965* (Syracuse: Syracuse Univ Press, 1994)
Harris, Leslie M. *In the Shadow of Slavery: African Americans in New York City, 1626–1863* (Chicago: Univ of Chicago Press, 2003)
Mabee, Carleton. *Black Education in New York State: From Colonial to Modern Times* (Syracuse: Syracuse Univ Press, 1979)
Osofsky, Gilbert. *Harlem: The Making of a Ghetto* (New York: Harper & Row, 1963)
Trotter, Joe William. *The Great Migration in Historical Perspective* (Bloomington: Indiana Univ Press, 1991)
Williams, Lillian Serece. *Strangers in the Land of Paradise: The Creation of an African American Community, Buffalo, New York, 1900–1940* (Bloomington: Indiana Univ Press, 1999)
Williams-Myers, A. J. *Long Hammering: Essays on the Forging of an African American Presence in the Hudson Valley to the Early 20th Century* (Trenton, NJ: Africa World Press, 1994)
Young Armstead, Myra B. *Mighty Change, Tall Within: Black Identity in the Hudson Valley* (Albany: SUNY Press, 2003)

Lillian S. Williams, Amybeth Gregory, Hadley Kruczek-Aaron

African Burial Ground. Containing the remains of between 10,000 and 20,000 people within 5 to 6 acres (2 to 2.4 ha) in Lower Manhattan, it is the oldest known African cemetery in urban America. Once called the Negro (or Negros) Burial Ground, it was used from as early as 1712 to about 1795. Barred from the cemeteries of many New York City churches, including Trinity Church in 1697, free and enslaved Africans buried their dead on the outskirts of the developed city beyond Wall St near Collect Pond, where 18th-century free Blacks also owned land. By 1812 builders had deposited up to 25 feet (7.6 m) of fill over the burials, which remained largely forgotten until 1991, when archaeologists unearthed them. Knowing of the possible existence of the burial ground, the federal General Services Administration (GSA) contracted archaeologists to document and remove remains during construction of a $275 million federal office building at 290 Broadway, on one section of the cemetery. Concerned citizens, including many African Americans, organized protests and pressured politicians to halt the excavation when they learned construction crews had destroyed burials, improper storage had damaged remains, and the archaeological project lacked a proper research design and African American involvement. A 1992 federal law stopped excavation of the burials and allocated $3 million for on-site reburial and a memorial. The GSA contracted new scholars to study the remains; artifacts stayed in New York City, but the skeletal remains were transferred to Howard University. Though the identities of those buried remain unknown, analysis revealed that most excavated individuals had been placed in wooden coffins and buried facing east. Most were wrapped in white shrouds fastened with copper pins, and some were buried with objects, including coins, shells, glass, buttons, beads, clay pipes, coral, and quartz crystal. Approximately 45% of the burials were of children under age 12. Many individuals were malnourished, and some suffered from severe arthritis, muscle tears, and bone fractures caused by intense physical labor. In 1993 the site earned National Historic Landmark status, the GSA established an Office of Public Education and Interpretation for the African Burial Ground, and New York City's Landmark Preservation Commission created the African Burial Ground and Commons Historic District, a designation requiring review of any construction or excavation projects proposed for the area. The office building was completed in 1994. The excavated remains will be reburied upon completion of research, and an interpretive center and memorial are planned to honor those buried in the African Burial Ground.

Cantwell, Anne-Marie E., and Diana diZerega Wall. *Unearthing Gotham: The Archaeology of New York City* (New Haven, Conn: Yale Univ Press, 2001)
Frohne, Andrea E. "The African Burial Ground in New York City: Manifesting and Representing Spirituality of Space" (PhD diss, SUNY Binghamton, 2002)
LaRoche, Cheryl, and Michael L. Blakey. "Seizing Intellectual Power: The Dialogue at the New York African Burial Ground," *Historical Archaeology* 31 (1997): 84–106

Andrea E. Frohne

African Female Benevolent Society of Troy. In February 1833 a dozen members of the black community in Troy (Rensselaer Co) formed the African Female Benevolent Society (AFBS). Troy's African American population at the time numbered roughly 400 in a city of approximately 12,000 persons. Predicated on spiritual uplift, education, and community service, the AFBS grew to over 60 members by 1834 and collected over $100, providing financial assistance to sick members. Although it had at least one white member, the society remained predominately black, its members comprising a black elite of Troy, both in terms of their status and their focus on distributing aid and promoting education. Many adherents came from Troy's black churches, but the AFBS transcended links to any single religious denomination. Equally important, it published some of its proceedings in pamphlet form. In 1834 secretary Elizabeth Wicks printed an address outlining the society's educational mission and religious underpinnings; attached was a "Eulogy" delivered by member Eliza Dungy on the death of a white patron. These documents reveal the expanding reform efforts of African American women throughout New York State during the 1830s and the growth of black communities in emerging market towns such as Syracuse, Rochester, and Buffalo. Although not much is known about its dissolution, the society functioned for at least 15 years, because Henry Highland Garnet delivered an address to its members in 1848.

Newman, Richard, Patrick Rael, and Philip Lapsansky, eds. *Pamphlets of Protest* (New York: Routledge, 2000)

Richard Newman

ON SLAVERY

Slavery! oh, thou cruel stain,
Thou dost fill my heart with pain:
See my brother, there he stands
Chain'd by slavery's cruel band.

Could we not feel a brother's woes,
Relieve the wants he undergoes;
Snatch him from slavery's cruel smart,
And to him freedom's joy impart?

—George R. Allen, student at African Free School, aged 12 years, Oct. 21, 1828

Andrews, Charles C. *The History of the New-York African Free Schools* (New York: Mahlon Day, 1830)

African Free Schools. The chief schools for Blacks in New York City from 1787 to the mid–19th century. On 1 Nov 1787 Trinity Church reopened their Episcopal catechism school in a private home on Cliff St in Lower Manhattan, renaming it the African Free School. The New York Manumission Society employed white teachers and administrators and paid expenses until 1834. A female teacher was hired in 1791 to instruct girls in needlepoint. Enrollment had increased to 110 students by 1800, making it the largest public school in the city. It became a meeting place for Blacks, and in 1807 the end of the legal slave trade was celebrated there. In 1809 administrators adopted the Lancasterian method, a leading teaching style where older advanced students taught younger pupils. The Free School burned in a neighborhood fire in 1814 and reopened on Doyer St. With private donations and city support, a new schoolhouse for 200 students opened January 1815 at 245 William St. That spring an annex, a sewing school for girls, was added. Another school was built in 1820 on Mulberry St to accommodate 500 male students, and the William St school was designated for female students.

By 1824 the schools had received state aid from the Common School Fund and the curriculum expanded. Students in both facilities took basic lessons and geography and diction. There were regular lessons on the evils of human bondage, and students declaimed antislavery poetry and prose in class and for visitors. Girls made eight types of clothing, including shirts, as well as pillowcases, seat covers, and pocketbooks. Boys built carts, wagons, and furniture, and were instructed in navigation and astronomy. Four more schools opened by 1827. In 1832 the Manumission Society acceded to the demands of parents and hired black administrators and teachers. In 1834 most of the black teachers were dismissed when the New York Public School Society took over administration of seven Free Schools and the 1,441 enrolled students. Renamed Colored Free Schools in 1838 the schools gradually declined. In 1853 they were absorbed by the city's Board of Education. The African Free Schools cultured a generation of the state's black leaders, including Ministers Samuel E. Cornish, Alexander Crummell, and Henry Highland Garnet. Sarah J. Smith Thompson, Garnet's wife, taught in the African Free School in 1845 and became the first African American woman principal in New York City.

Andrews, Charles C. *The History of the New York African Free Schools* (1830; repr New York: Negro Univ Press, 1969)
Mabee, Carleton. *Black Education in New York State* (Syracuse: Syracuse Univ Press, 1979)

April Harris

African Methodist Episcopal (AME) Church. Formed as an independent denomination for African Americans in Philadelphia in 1816, it was first organized in New York State in 1818. Richard Allen, the first bishop of the AME Church, commissioned William Lambert to establish the AME Church in New York City, and in July 1820 it was consecrated on Mott St. The first New York State conference was held on 8 June 1822. At that time there were preachers stationed in Brooklyn, Manhattan, White Plains (Westchester Co), and New Bedford (Westchester Co). By 1856 there were 10 circuits throughout the state, serving congregations in locations such as New York City, Albany, and Flushing (Queens Co). The church experienced rapid growth after the Civil War, and by 1916 there were 548,355 members nationwide. Reverdy C. Ransom, pastor of Bethel AME in Manhattan, was a nationally known church leader and editor of the *AME Review* from 1912 to 1918. Floyd Flake served as a Democratic congressman from 1986 to 1997, at which time he returned to the Allen AME Church in Queens to pastor full-time while overseeing eight nonprofit corporations. There were 61 AME churches in New York State in 2002.

See also METHODISM.

Lincoln, C. Eric, and Lawrence H. Mamiya. *The Black Church in the African American Experience* (Durham, NC: Duke Univ Press, 1990)
Payne, Daniel Alexander. "History of the African Methodist Episcopal Church." In *The American Negro: His History and Literature,* ed. William Loren Katz (New York: Arno Press, 1969)

Amanda Blohm

African Methodist Episcopal Zion (AMEZ) Church. The African Chapel, the nucleus of the later denomination, was founded in New York City in October 1796 by slaves and free black members of the John Street Methodist Episcopal Church, led by Peter Williams and William Miller, who left the older congregation because of segregated seating and other discriminatory practices. In 1801 their congregation was incorporated as the African Chapel, or African Methodist Episcopal Church of the City of New York. On 21 June 1821 African Methodists from New York, Pennsylvania, and Connecticut met in New York City and decided to leave the Methodist Episcopal Church. They also rejected affiliation with Richard Allen's African Methodist Episcopal Church, though confusingly they used the same name until 1848, when they added Zion to the denomination's name. In 1822 James Varick, pastor at the AME Zion Church (formerly the African Chapel), was elected the first superintendent (known as bishop after 1868) of the AMEZ Church. In the antebellum period, the AMEZ Church in New York State was known for its commitment to abolitionism and included among its members Harriet Tubman, Frederick Douglass, and Sojourner Truth. By 1886 there were 14 churches with full-time pastors and 12 without permanent clergy in the state. Other prominent New York figures in the AMEZ Church were Bishop Alexander Walters, a spokesman for the Democratic Party in the 1912 election, and T. Thomas Fortune, a noted journalist and political essayist in the late 19th and early 20th centuries. The AMEZ churches in New York State experienced rapid growth during the time of African American migration to the North after World Wars I and II. As of 1990 there were 123 congregations with 174,000 members in the state.

See also METHODISM.

Lincoln, C. Eric, and Lawrence Mamiya. *The Black Church in the African American Experience* (Durham, NC: Duke Univ Press, 1990)
Walls, William J. *The African Methodist Episcopal Zion Church: Reality of the Black Church* (Charlotte, NC: AME Zion Publishing House, 1974)

Amanda Blohm

Africans. There was minimal voluntary immigration by sub-Saharan Africans to the United States and New York State until the middle of the 20th century. Most who came in the 1930s and 1940s were students in New York City, plus a few professionals, traders, and workers. After the 1965 immigration reforms, however, the African population increased. The majority were at first Liberians and Nigerians. Driven by devastating droughts and continued political instability, another wave of immigrants arrived in the 1980s and 1990s, a sizable proportion of whom were undocumented. In 1986 thousands were amnestied and so able to bring over their families, while others were recognized as political refugees. In 1990 the US census counted 44,000 people born in sub-Saharan Africa living in New York State, all of them in New York City. In 2000 the figure was 72,347. There still is a large undocumented immigration, and community activists estimate the number, including children, at up to 450,000. Although since 1990 a larger number of immigrants have come from former French colonies like Senegal and Mali, most are still from former British colonies, such as Ghana and Nigeria, where English is the official language. The 2000 census counted 10,334 immigrants born in East Africa, 2,310 in central Africa, 4,477 in southern Africa (including a substantial population of European descent), and 55,226 in western Africa. Among the latter, 17,000 came from Ghana and 19,000 from Nigeria. The African immigrant population is fairly spread over the city, although concentrations exist in the Bronx and Harlem, Clifton on Staten Island, and in Brooklyn. As a group, immigrants since the 1980s earn less than the earlier group, many working as laborers, often as taxi drivers or street vendors, and hoping to return home with savings. Some have shops and restaurants. Most are Christian or Muslim; a smaller number are animists.

They come from over 40 states in sub-Saharan Africa, and many states are further divided by ethnicity. A large number of organizations cater to African immigrants by country or ethnic group. Ghanese organizations include the First Ghana Seventh-day Adventist Church in Manhattan, the Ghanaian Presbyterian Reformed Church in Brooklyn, and the National Council of Ghanaian Associations; also the Ga-Adangme Kpee supports those of Ga and Dangme ethnicity from southeastern Ghana. For Nigerians, there is the Nigerian Catholic Community and the Nigerian Community Help Center. Many of the smaller groups have their own organizations. Associations catering to African immigrants at large include the African Services Committee in Manhattan, the Africa Business Community, and the United African Congress (UAC). There is also a small African press in New York City, published in English, which includes the weekly *African Sun Times* (1989), now published in East Orange, NJ, the biweekly *West African News* in Brooklyn (1993), and the monthly *Nigerian* in the Bronx (1995).

Africans tend to remain apart from African American organizations. But the fatal shooting of Guinean immigrant Amadou Diallo on 4 Feb 1999 by New York City police galvanized the community and brought it closer to African American organizations, as did the shooting of Ousmane Zongo, from Burkina Faso, in May 2003. Shared concerns about immigration law and civil rights issues have promoted cooperation with other African American and immigrant advocacy groups. Some Africans have achieved prominence in New York City as musicians, such as the Nigerian drummer Babatunde Michael Olatunji, who helped popularize African drumming styles at the Center for African Culture in Harlem that opened in 1958, and Godfrey Lukongwa Binaisa, a former Mount Vernon (Westchester Co) resident who had served as president of Uganda (1979–80) and returned to a position with the New York City government after his overthrow.

African Services Committee, http://64.177.81.13/AboutAfricanCommunity.php
Arthur, John A. *Invisible Sojourners: African Immigrant Diaspora in the United States* (Westport, Conn: Praeger, 2000)
Ogbaa, Kalu. *The Nigerian Americans* (Westport, Conn: Greenwood, 2003)

Thomas Reimer

Afton. Town (pop 2,977) and village (pop 836) in SE Chenango Co. Settled in 1786, the town was formed from Bainbridge in 1857 and is divided by the Susquehanna River. The Albany and Susquehanna Railroad (1867) opened up a market for dairy produce. The village incorporated in 1892. About that time fluid milk became dominant, and a Borden milk station was built in 1905. Later strawberry farms were established along the river, and two such farms remained in 2002. From 1914 to 1922 Ansco manufactured nitrocellulose for film manufacturing. I-88 was completed in 1975 and transformed Afton into a bedroom community for Binghamton and Oneonta (Otsego Co). In the 1990s IVCI (electronics) became the largest Afton employer. Joseph Smith Jr, the founder of Mormonism, lived on an Afton farm in the late 1820s. While living there in 1827 he married his first wife, Emma Hale.

Michele A. McFee

Aging, Office for the. State agency responsible for programs and services for New Yorkers aged 60 years or over. This agency, one of America's first state agencies dedicated to the needs of the elderly, was preceded by several committees. The Joint Legislative Committee to Study the Problems of the Aging was the first created in 1947 by the state legislature and reconstituted each year by legislative action until 1969. In 1955 Gov W. Averell Harriman established the Interdepartmental Committee on Problems of the Aging, composed of the heads of 12 state agencies, to advise the governor on issues affecting older New Yorkers.

In 1960 a state committee was created to study problems associated with aging, and in 1961 a White House conference convened on the same topic. Gov Nelson A. Rockefeller then created by executive order the Office for the Aging in 1961 within the Department of Social Welfare. Its first mission was to administer the programs of the Interdepartmental Committee. After the Interdepartmental Committee was abolished in 1974, the Office for the Aging took on an increasingly expanded role. In 1965 the Office for the Aging was transferred to the Executive Department, where it remained in 2003. In the 21st century the office requires each county within the state to submit an annual plan detailing community services available to the elderly, which the office approves and helps fund. The office also reviews state legislation affecting older New Yorkers and administers federal programs for the elderly, including Title III-C, which in part provides nutritional programs for seniors at more than 1,000 sites throughout the state; Title V, which offers low-income persons 55 years and older part-time employment; and Title VII, which investigates and resolves complaints about services provided at nursing care and other health-related facilities. The office also publishes a resource guide for seniors, the newsletter *Aging News*, hosts *Aging and You*, a cable television program, and provides a toll-free senior citizens hotline. In 2003 the Office for the Aging served the 3.2 million New Yorkers who are 60 years and older.

Office for the Aging, http://www.aging.state.ny.us

Christine Karpiak

agricultural cooperatives. Businesses collectively owned by and operated for the mutual benefit of farmers and rural residents to market products, purchase supplies, and obtain services. Some of the first in the United States were begun in New York State. In 1844 dairy farmers formed the Orange County Milk Association to represent members in bargaining for prices received for their milk from cheese processors. The association was short-lived, however. The New York City milkshed soon expanded beyond the local counties into surrounding states not represented by the association. In 1863 a fertilizer purchasing cooperative was formed in Riverhead (Suffolk Co) to help farmers buy boatloads of guano. In the 1880s associations of New York State apple and cherry growers were formed in the Hudson Valley and Western New York to market members' fruit.

The Order of the Patrons of Husbandry, also known as the Grange, played a key role in organizing purchasing cooperatives toward the end of the 19th century. In April 1868 the first permanent local Grange was organized in Fredonia (Chautauqua Co) five months after the formation of the National Grange. In 1874 the Grange studied the Rochdale Pioneers Cooperative in England to improve management of Grange-sponsored cooperatives in the United States. This led to the successful growth of several New York State purchasing cooperatives, including the Union Grange Trade Association in Monroe Co, which in 1882 had a total farm supply purchasing volume of over $1 million from farmers in 21 counties.

The Dairymen's League, formed in 1907 by a group of Orange Co dairy farmers, comprised producers in both New York State and New Jersey. The league (now Dairylea) became a leading organization in the US dairy industry and in 2001 was the largest raw-milk marketer in the Northeast. In 1911 the first county Farm Bureau was formed in Broome Co. The Farm Bureau county agents were the predecessors of the US Department of Agriculture Extension Service and a source of information for farmers on cooperatives. The New York State Federation of County Farm Bureaus was established in 1917. On 22 June 1920 the Grange, Dairymen's League, and the New York State Federation of County Farm Bureaus formed one of the most influential supply cooperatives of its day, the Cooperative Grange League Federation Exchange (now Agway).

The State College of Agriculture and Life Sciences at Cornell University has played a key role, beginning in 1908, in conducting research on cooperatives as well as in providing educational programs to cooperative organizers and leaders. A number of faculty, including Liberty Hyde Bailey, Howard E. Babcock, William I. Myers, Elmer S. Savage, George Warren, and Glen Hedlund, were instrumental in developing agricultural cooperatives in New York State as advisors, researchers, and, in some cases, managers. The New York State Council of Farmer Cooperatives was created in 1949 as an educational organization with links to Cornell University to enhance the performance of cooperatives and, in 1990, expanded into New England to become the Northeast Cooperative Council, with headquarters in Ithaca.

The number of cooperatives in New York State peaked in 1951, with 1,303 marketing and supply cooperatives, 145 cooperatives for services such as artificial breeding, dairy herd and seed improvement, and 169 mutual associations for farm services such as credit, electrification, and insurance. In the mid-1950s the number of cooperatives declined as associations merged, consolidated, or went out of business because of decreasing profit margins and increasing economies of scale. In 2001 New York State had 79 marketing, 8 supply, and 5 service cooperatives with a net business volume of $2.8 billion.

Knapp, Joseph G. *The Rise of American Cooperative Enterprise: 1620–1920* (Danville, Ill: Interstate Printers and Publishers, 1969)

Brian M. Henehan

agricultural implement manufacture

The 19th Century

Through the 19th century the invention of agricultural devices followed the actual work of agriculture, as farmers sought physical and mechanical assistance according to their own ingenuity and desire to experiment. Village blacksmiths and iron molders were the means by which farmers modified their tools or realized equipment of their own design. An example of this partnering is the creation of the cast-iron plow designed and patented in 1814 by Jethro Wood of Poplar Ridge (Cayuga Co), the first practical version of a plow with interchangeable parts. Blacksmith Elias Rogers of nearby Moravia worked eight months with different iron ores to cast the device, which some farmers viewed skeptically because they thought iron somehow tainted the soil, and Rogers was reluctant to invest in production. Steady manufacture was accomplished in 1821 after years of proving the plow's value and of overcoming production difficulties, but Wood could not keep up with patent protection or market competition, and versions of his plow were manufactured widely. The Wiard family first had success with a 1798 wrought-iron plow design patented by Thomas Wiard Sr, and the family operated a plow business in Avon (Livingston Co) for several decades. The business was moved in 1876 to Batavia (Genesee Co), where it operated as Wiard Plow Co until 1954. Grandson Harry Wiard was an organizer in 1879 of Syracuse Chilled Plow, which manufactured a chilled-iron plow less brittle and prone to breakage than cast iron. Deer River (Lewis Co) and H. H. Lovejoy (Washington Co) also had some success with plow design later in the century.

The manufacture of other agricultural equipment across New York State either led or kept pace with national developments. At the Albany Agricultural Fair of 1835, six threshers were shown—some with newly patented horse powers (whereby horses generate power either walking on a treadmill or in a circle)—including the new design of Hiram and John Pitts, who are credited with inventing the American threshing machine, which also winnowed grain. John Pitts set up manufacturing in Rochester and then Buffalo; Hiram moved to Illinois. John's company became known as Buffalo Pitts about 1847.

The success of one man's design did not discourage others from creating similar equipment based on personal theory, experience, or landscape. Cyrus McCormick of Virginia, who began developing his famous reaper in 1831, came to New York State and licensed William Seymour and Dayton Morgan of Brockport (Monroe Co) to manufacture and improve the device from 1844 to about 1848. Seymour and Morgan were already established manufacturers whose reaper was exhibited with those of McCormick and four others at the 1851 Agricultural Fair in Rochester. George Westinghouse Sr began building threshing machines about 1835 at Central Bridge (Schoharie Co), moving to Schenectady in 1856. Walter A. Wood of Hoosick Falls (Rensselaer Co) began building farm equipment in 1852 and established his namesake Mowing and Reaping Machine Co in the 1860s. Cyrenus Wheeler received the first of 17 patents in 1854 for harvesters that he manufactured at Poplar Ridge, then Auburn (Cayuga Co), where he moved to in 1860. In 1866 he became president of Auburn's Cayuga Chief Manufacturing Co, maker of the successful self-raking reaper, and in 1874 merged with D. M. Osborne, maker of the Kirby mower and Osborne binding reaper. Adriance Platt of Poughkeepsie started making harvesting equipment in 1855 and eventually built binders, rakes, and harrows.

Lyman Bickford and Henry Huffman began making seed drills at Macedon (Wayne Co) in 1842 and founded a company that excelled with mechanical planters for 60 years. P. K. Dederick of Albany patented a hay press, the earliest machine baler, in 1843 and manufactured without competition for many years. Manure spreaders were new to American farmers when introduced by Kemp and Burpee of Syracuse in 1880. C. J. Cummings of Tully (Onondaga Co) claimed in 1895 to have built over 75 different kinds of potato diggers in the previous 12 years; Warsaw-Wilkinson in Wyoming Co made ensilage cutters; and Grant-Ferris of Troy made seeders and commercial fanning mills.

Dairy Manufacture

In the mid–19th century all dairy work was by hand. Cream was separated from milk by skimming or by a gravity-based system. Wood-cased gravity separators were manufactured by at least one company in the state, John S. Carter in Syracuse, before centrifugal separation became standard. Swede Gustav de Laval patented a continuous discharge centrifugal cream separator in 1877 and established his company DeLaval Separator in New York City in 1885. Under license to Phillip Sharples, DeLaval separators were manufactured at a new factory in Poughkeepsie in 1890. America's DeLaval became a dairy industry leader and developed a successful automatic milking machine between 1894 and 1918 after trying 19 different designs. It also made power devices for milking machinery and lighting systems for barns. Another aid to the dairy farmer was the laminated wood Unadilla silo, which replaced open storage of feed and silage. Begun by Frank Van Cott in 1906, the company operated at Unadilla (Otsego Co), Sidney (Delaware Co), and briefly in Iowa and Texas. During the 1950s the company changed its focus from silos to laminated wood rafters and other large structural elements for barns and similarly sized buildings.

The 20th Century

Few New York State agricultural manufacturers survived on their own in the 20th century. Bickford and Huffman merged with five other firms (one from New York, four from the Midwest) to form the American Seeding Machine Co of Springfield, Ohio, in 1903. Syracuse Chilled Plow became part of John Deere Co in 1912. Johnston Harvester of Brockport (1847) and Batavia (1882) diversified to produce binders, harrows, and spreaders and was purchased by Massey-Harris in 1917. Westinghouse made threshers from the 1850s to the 1920s and then licensed smaller Pioneer Thresher of Shortsville (Ontario Co) to continue manufacture, which they did into the 1950s.

More recently, DeLaval became Alfa Laval and continued in Poughkeepsie until 1990; it was essentially the state's only agricultural equipment manufacturer of the late 20th century. In 2003 three companies produced agriculture-related equipment: Fluid Metering of Syosset (Nassau Co), which made pumps, Superflex of Brooklyn, which made hose, and Hannay Reels of Westerlo (Albany Co), which made hose reels.

Danhof, Clarence H. *Change in Agriculture: The Northern United States, 1820–1870* (Cambridge, Mass: Harvard Univ Press, 1969)

Gates, Paul Wallace. *The Farmer's Age: Agriculture, 1815–1860* (New York: Holt, Rinehart & Winston, 1960)

Hedrick, U. P. *A History of Agriculture in the State of New York* (New York: Hill & Wang, 1966)

Mills, Robert K., ed. *Implement and Tractor: Reflections on 100 Years of Farm Equipment* (Overland Park, Kans: Intertec Press, 1986)

Partridge, Michael. *Farm Tools through the Ages* (New York: Promontory Press, 1973)

Wendel, C. H. *Encyclopedia of American Farm Implements and Antiques* (Iola, Wisc: Krause Publications, 1997)

Jane Mackintosh

agricultural publishing. Farming periodicals of the 19th and 20th centuries helped to establish a distinctly American agricultural science by encouraging experimentation, promoting agricultural education and new technology, and discussing issues relevant to American soils and climates. For the isolated farmer, the periodicals were an important source of new and shared information. The earliest printed contributions to agriculture in New York State include the annual *Transactions of the Society for the Promotion of Agriculture, Arts, and Manufactures* (Albany), consisting mainly of the addresses given at annual society meetings and published from 1792 to 1799. The earliest New York State agricultural almanac may be the *Farmer's Calendar* (Albany), published in 1798 by Fry and Southwick. Similar almanacs, not explicitly directed at farmers but often containing agricultural information, were published in New York City as early as 1695. Early almanacs included brief weather predictions and miscellaneous notes, but their most important feature was the standard calendar noting sunrise and sunset, and the phases of the moon. By the 1830s farmers' almanacs were published across the state. They contained standard calendars and general and agricultural information. Agricultural periodicals in other states began to appear in the 1820s and were well established by 1850. Published monthly or weekly, most of the journals were available by subscription for a modest price. By 1860 there were between 50 and 60 active periodicals; circulation approached 250,000.

The *Plough Boy* (Albany), one of the earliest agricultural newspapers in the United States, was the first of its kind to be printed in New York State. Established by Albany printer and postmaster Solomon Southwick in 1819, this weekly paper ran until 1823 and was the instrument of the State Board of Agriculture. Luther Tucker, an experienced printer, founded the *Genesee Farmer* (Rochester) in 1831. This weekly paper advocated a scientific approach to agriculture and encouraged agricultural education. Leading agriculturalists contributed articles, making it one of the first agricultural periodicals to be written from practical experience. It was published through 1839, when Tucker purchased the *Cultivator.* This Albany weekly had been started in 1834 by Jesse Buel and was one of the most popular and influential newspapers of the period. It was read nationally and internationally, and its circulation frequently reached 20,000 or more. It was sponsored by the New York State Agricultural Society until its second year, when Buel was made controlling editor. The *Cultivator* advocated scientific farming methods and also emphasized agricultural education. Tucker continued to publish the *Cultivator* until 1865 when it was absorbed by the *Country Gentleman* (Albany, New York City, and Philadelphia), which he had established in 1853. This broad publication addressed matters of rural taste, society, and education, as well as general and agricultural news. A well-illustrated newspaper, the *Country Gentleman* appealed to a broader audience, was published weekly, and continued until 1955. Brothers A. B. and R. L. Allen edited the *American Agriculturist* (New York City), established in 1842. Their monthly magazine campaigned for better breeding methods, but it also discussed general news and foreign agriculture, and had a popular children's column, making it appealing to the entire family. Still published in 2002, it had a nationwide circulation of nearly 2 million. Dutchess Co agriculturalist Henry Morgenthau Jr, who later served as secretary of the treasury under Pres Franklin D. Roosevelt, was the publisher from 1922 to 1933. In 1964 it incorporated the *Rural New Yorker,* founded in 1850.

Reliable and affordable watches, advertising calendars, and daily newspapers led to the decline of almanacs from 1850 to 1875, but nostalgic trade variations were published throughout the 20th and into the 21st centuries. In 2003 agricultural periodicals and society publications are highly specialized and remain an important source of information in New York State.

Demaree, Albert Lowther. *The American Agricultural Press, 1819–1860* (New York: Columbia Univ Press, 1941)

Suzan D. Friedlander

agriculture. At the end of the 20th century, 7,254,470 acres (2,935,780 ha), or one-quarter of the state's land, were in some form of agricultural production. In 1997 there were 31,757 farms in operation. In 1998 the state ranked 2d in the nation in apple production, 3d in dairy production and corn silage, 4th in tart cherries, 7th in strawberries, and 10th in potatoes. The nursery industry continues to flourish and remains concentrated on Long Island, although the Rochester area retains its importance. Livestock and related products brought in over $1.8 billion to New York State in 2000, and muckland remains productive for vegetables. Forest cover was far greater in 2000 than it was a century earlier, reflecting a decline in the number of farms. At the same time, though, the average farm size for those that remain has grown over the past half century to the largest it has ever been. But the present agricultural scene no more than hints at the agricultural activities and accomplishments of a past that predates European settlement.

Geography of Farming

New York State's physical environment is pivotal for agriculture. The lay of the land, the character and quality of the soil, the growing season, and the timing and amount of rainfall can all be limiting factors. Some, like soil quality or growing season, can be partially counterbalanced by using appropriate fertilizer or planting climate-compatible crops. Others, like an early frost, a dry May, or a very wet harvest season, are beyond control, although sometimes a last minute adjustment is possible. A late spring or a failed early crop, for instance, may cause a farmer to plant buckwheat, a fast-maturing but less-

Downtown farmers' market in Syracuse, 1980.

profitable alternative to a slower-maturing, more-profitable crop that would not reach maturity in a shortened growing season. The tremendous diversity of the state's physical base contributes to differences in the regional and local character of agriculture. The growing season in Franklin Co ranges from 97 to 135 days, while in Suffolk Co it is from 200 to 210 days. Average temperature may vary on a single farm by a degree or two depending on elevation, and soil quality can vary tremendously within a short distance, making appropriate crop selection and land utilization decisions challenging.

The Adirondack and Catskill regions are least hospitable to farming because of shallow, often acidic, infertile soils, excessive slopes, and short growing seasons. The Tug Hill Plateau, much of the Delaware Hills, and the more rugged sections of the Cattaraugus Hills are only marginally better. Other upland areas offer more favorable farming terrain. The Finger Lakes region of the Appalachian Plateau has deep, fertile soils and broad, sweeping valleys. Elsewhere on the plateau the wider, alluvial-floored valleys provide excellent farming conditions, often in sharp contrast to the shallow, sour soils and more difficult terrain of the surrounding hilltops. The intermediate land (between the bottomlands and excessive slopes and hilltops) lacks the heavy soil and forest of the bottomlands yet is decidedly more fertile than the hilltops. The Genesee Valley arguably contains the finest farmland in the state. Other areas of prime farmland include extensive sections of the counties bordering the south shore of Lake Ontario; much of Madison, southern Oneida and Herkimer, and western Montgomery Cos in the state's central region; the Black River valley in the north; and the flatter parts of Orange and Ulster Cos in the southeast. Long Island's soils are primarily sandy loams suitable for crops if adequately fertilized and for pasturage, especially on the eastern end of the South Fork. There are many other localized areas of high-quality farmland scattered throughout the state.

Other key factors besides the physical environment have affected agricultural patterns across the state, such as cultural traditions regarding food preferences and farming practices, and the understanding and knowledge of soil husbandry and other environmentally friendly practices. Market forces have grown in importance. Technology, not just in relation to farm tools and machinery but also to drainage systems and transportation, agricultural research, and government policy have all helped shape and transform the agricultural scene.

Colonial Era Agriculture

The American Indians in what became New York State had a well-developed agricultural tradition. Their slash-and-burn farming methods centered upon the "three sisters"—beans, corn, and squash—grown by the Iroquois beginning in the 1300s. From nutritional and ecological perspectives, the combination was complete. Intercropped, the beans fixed nitrogen in the soil, the corn served as a pole for the beans, and the broad leaves of the ground-hugging squash kept the weeds at a minimum. Further it was far more complex than the name suggests, because multiple varieties of each crop were grown, many of which were completely unknown to Europeans. A village's agricultural complex later also included apple and peach orchards sometimes of 1,000 or more trees. Evidence also indicates that the Iroquois deliberately altered the composition of the surrounding forest by planting black walnut and other species they found particularly useful. Overall, the Dutch and English settlers learned much from the Indians. For example, farmers on Long Island were shown that the tiny fish menhenden made an excellent if strong-smelling fertilizer.

Europeans brought their farmways to the New World, including such crops as wheat, rye, oats, and barley. For the Dutch, wheat was the most important, followed by rye and oats. Fruits transplanted from Europe included cherries, peaches, apricots, plums, persimmons, figs, currants, gooseberries, thorn apples, and foreign stocks of grapes. Most houses had a kitchen garden with a wide variety of vegetables: cabbages, parsnips, carrots, beets, endive, succory, sorrel, radishes, leeks, and onions. Livestock consisted chiefly of horses, cattle, hogs, sheep, and barnyard fowl. The Dutch West India Co sent 103 horses and cattle to Manhattan Island in 1625 alone. Honey bees arrived early as well. Later the Dutch attempted to breed horses. Sir William Johnson was recognized as a breeder of horses and other improved livestock in the mid-1700s. By the late colonial period there is evidence that the Oneida and conceivably other Iroquois groups were raising domesticated cattle and swine.

Archaeological findings indicate that the early European farmers selected Indian old fields, which did not require clearing, for their farm sites. In the Hudson Valley during English rule, many of these plots were leased from manor lords rather than owned outright by the farmers, and historians have long debated whether the prevalence of leaseholds held up agricultural development in the colony. Although records indicate the Dutch had sold and traded farm surpluses, including wheat from Esopus [now in Ulster Co] in New Amsterdam [now New York City] and Rensselaerwijck [now in Albany, Columbia, and Rensselaer Co] and tobacco from Long Island in the Netherlands, the primary concern of farmers was to provide food and produce for the family. The other exception to this semisubsistence agriculture was on the Hudson Valley manors, where wheat was produced in surplus quantities for sale to the southern colonies and the Caribbean. As early as 1678 New York Colony was reported to have exported 60,000 bushels (2.1 million l). A century later wheat production had spread west along the Mohawk River and into adjoining country, so much so that the Schoharie Valley earned the title Breadbasket of the Revolution. During the 18th century New York colonists also built up a profitable trade shipping salted meat to the West Indies.

The Agricultural Frontier

The Sullivan-Clinton campaign of 1779 devastated Iroquois agriculture in Central and Western New York, although the crops that were destroyed showed participating troops the agricultural potential of the region. At war's end an estimated 5,000 Whites lived west of Schenectady. Slow at first, the movement of settlers gained momentum once the Iroquois were stripped of nearly all their lands in the 1790s. By 1820 the population west of Schenectady exceeded 700,000, and all parts of the state that would eventually be farmed could boast of at least some agricultural settlement.

In a typical pattern, a prospective pioneer farmer traveled west in the fall after his crops were harvested to select and purchase (or lease) a piece of land. The parcel was normally chosen on the basis of forest cover, water availability, and preference for either fecund, densely vegetated bottomland or more thinly vegetated, more easily cleared and worked intermediate land. Early settlers usually avoided hilltops, where soils tended to be shallow and sour. (These highlands were generally settled only much later by families unable to afford to

FARMS AND FARMLAND BY COUNTY

	1850		1900		1950		1997		
	Farms	Acres Hectares	Farms	Acres Hectares	Farms	Acres Hectares	Farms	Acres Hectares	County Land in Farms (%)
Albany	2,903	297,382 120,346	3,281	298,656 120,862	1,453	160,858 65,097	396	56,782 22,979	16.9
Allegany	3,173	378,289 153,088	5,082	593,888 240,338	2,604	416,425 168,521	724	157,744 63,837	23.9
Bronx	—	— —	—	— —	19	235 95	—	— —	—
Broome	2,497	289,462 117,141	4,410	417,022 168,763	2,345	294,942 119,359	511	85,804 34,724	19.0
Cattaraugus	3,655	408,709 165,399	5,976	672,561 272,176	3,508	513,321 207,734	946	192,015 77,706	22.9
Cayuga	4,228	398,496 161,266	5,039	413,924 167,509	2,934	353,569 143,084	846	251,820 101,908	56.8
Chautauqua	5,163	592,314 239,701	7,404	614,303 248,600	5,336	499,746 202,240	1,557	244,921 99,116	36.0
Chemung	2,170	233,272 94,402	2,438	233,976 94,687	1,280	155,628 62,980	313	59,272 23,987	22.7
Chenango	4,406	501,991 203,149	4,473	543,884 220,102	2,689	416,052 168,370	801	183,312 74,184	32.0
Clinton	2,095	236,082 95,539	3,764	435,825 176,372	2,275	400,390 162,032	488	148,677 60,168	22.4
Columbia	2,511	359,549 145,504	2,944	375,904 152,123	1,692	259,998 105,218	464	114,883 46,492	28.2
Cortland	2,465	260,759 105,526	2,754	303,254 122,723	1,414	238,985 96,714	452	120,838 48,901	37.8
Delaware	4,747	644,904 260,984	5,232	795,997 322,129	3,234	630,038 254,968	717	183,667 74,327	19.8
Dutchess	3,208	475,127 192,277	3,537	466,453 188,767	1,729	303,763 122,929	539	106,749 43,200	20.8
Erie	4,880	462,706 187,251	7,929	571,084 231,110	4,611	376,353 152,305	973	143,234 57,965	21.4
Essex	1,872	303,561 122,847	2,412	401,912 162,648	1,156	196,741 79,618	197	48,196 19,504	4.2
Franklin	1,647	167,349 67,724	3,721	429,452 173,793	2,074	305,427 123,602	476	163,017 65,971	15.6
Fulton	1,361	164,535 66,585	2,234	208,687 84,453	830	92,261 37,337	176	34,291 13,877	10.8
Genesee	2,574	273,579 110,714	3,286	294,316 119,106	2,112	257,379 104,158	516	170,878 69,152	54.0
Greene	2,672	314,418 127,241	2,746	337,909 136,747	1,300	171,835 69,539	244	48,770 19,737	11.8
Hamilton	261	37,532 15,189	510	63,832 25,832	75	7,306 2,957	13	788 319	0.1
Herkimer	2,723	340,182 137,667	3,227	383,180 155,068	1,869	282,277 114,234	583	141,847 57,403	15.7
Jefferson	5,490	598,339 242,139	6,052	745,093 301,529	3,440	585,983 237,139	916	291,103 117,805	35.7
Kings	363	20,862 8,443	360	6,480 2,622	65	219 89	8	8 3	trace
Lewis	2,374	233,051 94,312	3,838	494,165 199,982	1,701	320,626 129,753	623	179,696 72,720	22.0
Livingston	2,503	316,700 128,164	3,267	373,660 151,215	1,835	326,831 132,264	625	197,408 79,888	48.8
Madison	3,845	456,595 184,778	4,144	388,866 157,369	2,360	317,578 128,519	692	185,924 75,241	44.3
Monroe	4,113	386,496 156,410	5,889	381,941 154,566	3,147	285,005 115,338	480	103,097 41,722	24.4
Montgomery	1,883	239,128 96,772	2,407	236,934 95,884	1,473	204,612 82,804	542	134,940 54,608	52.1
Nassau	—	— —	1,658	88,452 35,795	618	27,334 11,062	55	1,390 563	0.8

FARMS AND FARMLAND BY COUNTY (continued)

	1850		1900		1950		1997		
	Farms	Acres Hectares	Farms	Acres Hectares	Farms	Acres Hectares	Farms	Acres Hectares	County Land in Farms (%)
New York	168	2,673 1,082	184	3,461 1,401	—	— —	2	—[a] —	trace
Niagara	3,143	280,792 113,633	4,356	305,456 123,614	3,362	247,904 100,323	687	127,355 51,539	38.1
Oneida	6,292	666,241 269,618	7,232	657,748 266,181	3,909	485,052 196,294	928	216,094 87,450	27.8
Onondaga	4,595	430,571 174,246	6,305	453,934 183,701	3,405	334,822 135,498	602	147,109 59,533	29.5
Ontario	3,058	365,377 147,863	4,328	405,003 163,899	2,507	303,255 122,723	692	185,924 75,241	45.1
Orange	3,426	423,698 171,465	3,966	402,519 162,894	2,958	273,820 110,811	624	94,771 38,352	18.1
Orleans	2,271	217,454 88,001	2,964	237,600 96,153	1,878	201,125 81,392	456	143,397 58,031	57.2
Oswego	4,497	363,280 147,014	6,914	492,935 199,484	3,339	335,462 135,757	605	102,537 41,495	16.8
Otsego	4,764	548,162 221,833	5,634	612,224 247,758	3,261	478,771 193,752	865	206,985 83,764	32.2
Putnam	989	120,845 48,904	1,141	133,899 54,187	319	42,935 17,375	48	3,433 1,389	2.3
Queens	2,303	169,646 68,653	1,188	25,649 10,380	111	542 219	2	—[a] —	trace
Rensselaer	2,930	349,746 141,537	3,668	365,007 147,713	1,822	227,697 92,146	459	98,965 40,050	23.6
Richmond	212	15,174 6,141	290	11,724 4,745	113	2,036 824	7	29 12	0.1
Rockland	682	77,403 31,324	939	62,050 25,111	408	17,376 7,032	21	561 227	0.5
St. Lawrence	6,124	639,713 258,883	8,353	1,068,798 432,528	5,091	886,855 358,898	1,363	396,406 160,420	23.1
Saratoga	3,465	412,989 167,131	3,805	406,079 164,334	1,795	200,349 81,078	472	72,928 29,513	14.0
Schenectady	1,040	105,831 42,828	1,194	119,577 48,391	600	60,501 24,484	151	18,168 7,352	13.8
Schoharie	2,439	311,189 125,934	3,437	367,023 148,529	1,940	289,090 116,991	518	110,773 44,828	27.8
Schuyler	—	— —	2,103	196,718 79,609	1,118	143,301 57,992	318	65,281 26,418	31.0
Seneca	1,555	167,478 67,776	2,303	194,591 78,748	1,275	153,602 62,161	413	117,426 47,521	56.5
Steuben	5,797	675,396 273,323	8,179	825,334 334,001	3,833	632,295 255,881	1,295	348,971 141,224	39.2
Suffolk	2,323	353,904 143,220	3,277	276,860 112,041	2,187	123,346 49,916	606	35,858 14,511	6.1
Sullivan	1,889	236,255 95,609	3,887	478,783 193,757	1,881	191,978 77,691	311	58,067 23,499	9.4
Tioga	2,026	221,351 89,578	3,134	305,061 123,454	1,870	246,035 99,567	497	109,356 44,255	32.9
Tompkins	3,193	327,497 132,533	3,270	285,721 115,627	1,662	201,822 81,675	447	95,451 38,628	31.3
Ulster	3,539	440,997 178,465	5,184	522,113 211,292	2,552	227,497 92,065	409	68,989 27,919	9.6
Warren	1,505	221,840 89,776	2,121	286,945 116,123	547	73,712 29,830	58	9,187 3,718	1.7
Washington	3,037	402,044 162,702	3,715	454,502 183,931	2,349	384,889 155,759	738	194,962 78,898	36.5
Wayne	3,957	331,460 134,137	5,286	363,211 146,986	3,643	317,957 128,673	840	167,190 67,659	43.2
Westchester	2,587	251,929 101,952	2,326	184,512 74,669	664	48,545 19,645	91	7,528 3,046	2.7

continued on page 32

FARMS AND FARMLAND BY COUNTY (continued)

	1850		1900		1950		1997		
	Farms	Acres Hectares	Farms	Acres Hectares	Farms	Acres Hectares	Farms	Acres Hectares	County Land in Farms (%)
Wyoming	3,360	350,280 141,753	3,519	367,894 148,882	2,217	325,661 131,790	702	194,902 78,874	51.4
Yates	1,673	186,500 75,474	2,504	203,568 82,381	1,183	156,772 63,443	657	104,790 42,407	48.4
Total	170,621	19,059,084 7,712,944	226,720	22,648,109 9,165,373	124,977	16,016,721 6,481,743	31,757	7,254,470 2,935,782	24.0

Sources: US Census; *1997 Census of Agriculture.*

[a]In the *1997 Census of Agriculture,* total acreage was withheld for New York and Queens Cos to avoid disclosing data for individual farms.

migrate to superior lands in the Midwest.) The prospective settler then erected a crude shelter, cut away the underbrush and girdled the trees on a patch of ground; broke up the soil as much as possible, working around the trees and root systems; and sowed some winter wheat. He then returned to his home and family. Late the following winter, while the ground remained frozen and covered with snow (making traveling easier), family members packed their belongings and headed off to the new farm, arriving in time to take advantage of the upcoming growing season. The years immediately following involved erecting a more substantial log dwelling, a livestock shelter, crop storage facilities, and fences; clearing and breaking land; and planting and harvesting crops. Besides patches of various crops, forest openings were, according to Elkanah Watson, the site of "stumps, half burnt logs, girdled tress, and confusion."

Early agriculture was highly diversified and directed toward self-sufficiency. A typical farm contained a combination of grain, vegetables, fruit, grass, and livestock. Grains included corn, oats, barley, rye, buckwheat, and, often, flax in the era of homespun clothing. Although wheat eventually became the favored cash crop, corn was the initial subsistence crop on nearly every farm. It was hardier than wheat, less susceptible to insects and disease, yielded more per acre, and required little land preparation or tending other than some early-season weeding. It grew on marginally drained land, did not demand immediate harvest, and could be used without being milled. Fruit included apples, pears, plums, and, where the climate permitted, peaches, along with grapes, berries, and currants. Besides vegetables for family consumption, hops, peppermint, and various herbs were grown. Horses, a few head of beef cattle, a milk (milch) cow, a yoke of oxen, some hogs and sheep, and assorted chickens, turkeys, and geese made up the livestock. During the early years of a farm settlement, the animals were let to wander and fend for themselves. Pigs were particularly adept at surviving on mast (acorns, beechnuts, and chestnuts). On Long Island they fattened on shellfish. Sheep were the most vulnerable to predators. Only in the dead of winter were the animals fed on whatever hay the farmer had found time to harvest and store.

During the settlement period agriculture involved forest exploitation as much as plant and animal husbandry, with the forest providing wood for buildings and fences, and fuel for cooking and warmth. It was most often the only source of much needed cash, chiefly from the sale of potash (potassium carbonate), which was extracted from the ashes of deciduous trees burned during the process of clearing land. An essential ingredient in gunpowder, soap, and fertilizer, and critical in paper and textile manufacture, potash brought an immediate cash return and helped finance farm building. Over $250,000 worth of potash was produced annually in the state in the decades following the Revolution, when the central and western regions were being opened for settlement. Some farmers produced charcoal for cash or exchange with local blacksmiths. Where there was a convenient and ready market, like the saltworks at Salina [now in Onondaga Co] or a growing urban center, cordwood and sawn timber were sold. Some farmers exploited the local stands of oak and manufactured barrels or butter firkins during the winter months. Some cut stands of hemlock and sold the bark to tanneries. Maple syrup was the standard household sweetener, with surpluses traded or sold. Ginseng, wild honey, and beeswax were other cash crops gathered from the forest. While supplies lasted, mink and beaver were trapped and the pelts sold. Finally, the forest contributed to a family's larder with game, berries, and grapes.

Early 19th Century

Farm creation required at least as much labor as capital, plus a good measure of endurance and some luck. Labor involved all able-bodied members of the family and, when larger tasks or those requiring special skills were involved, neighbors. Within a few years of establishment, pioneer farms were largely self-sustaining in terms of clothing and food; a family of six was said to be able to feed itself on 12 acres (4.9 ha) of crops. Nevertheless, limited amounts of cash were needed for items that could not be locally grown or made and for payment of debts, the largest of which were outstanding land payments and the accompanying compound interest. Earning cash required a ready market and an efficient means of transporting products to it. For wheat the ultimate market was Europe, and the challenge was getting wheat or flour to a seaport. For Hudson and Mohawk Valley farmers, access to the Port of New York was comparatively straightforward via bateaux and sloops on the respective rivers.

In contrast, it took time before central, western, and northern New York State farmers could prepare enough land for surplus crops, and then the cost of getting a load of wheat or flour to Mohawk or Hudson markets tended to exceed the revenue received. Instead, those farmers shipped northeast to Montreal via Lake Ontario schooners or south to the Chesapeake and Baltimore via river arks on the Susquehanna. A standard 70 x 16 ft (21 x 5 m) ark carrying 1,200 bushels (42,300 l) of wheat could be, in times of high water, sent out from the Cohocton River settlement of Avoca (Steuben Co) and make the 350 mi (563 km) trip to the Chesapeake in five to seven days. But it was not until after the War of 1812 that farmers in the western parts of the state began shipping significant amounts of wheat and flour out of the region. In 1818, 26,000 barrels of flour were shipped from the mouth of the Genesee River to Montreal; two years later 67,000 barrels were sent along the same route. Before the Erie Canal, farmers in the Susquehanna watershed tended to be as successful as their counterparts on the Ontario Lake Plain in the north. More cost effective than ship-

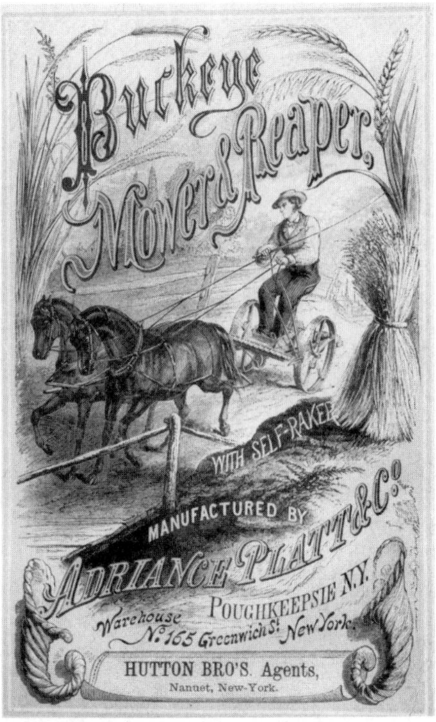

19th-century agricultural implements catalog cover.

ping surplus crops was hauling the more highly valued forest products to markets closer to home, such as potash to Ithaca, where the price in 1821 was $90 per ton. Alternatively the ash could be sold to a local merchant at $2.50–$3.00 per 100 pounds (45 kg). Another option was to drive cattle, swine, turkeys, and geese to stockyards and slaughterhouses in Albany, Catskill (Greene Co), and other Hudson River towns.

The process of creating a farm was long and slow. It was estimated that 10–15 acres (4–6 ha) could be cleared in a year (not including stump removal), depending on the nature of the forest. Land clearing normally continued for decades. Despite the cries of Jesse Buel and other advocates of scientific farming, most farmers during this period saw land as a disposable commodity and gave little thought to long-term consequences. Thus animal manure was considered a necessary nuisance to be dealt with in the most expeditious manner, such as dumping it into streams instead of recycling it as fertilizer. A field was often planted with the same crop year after year until yields dropped to a fraction of what they had been. Fertility decline spread from east to west. In 1813 Horatio Gates Spafford proclaimed Hudson Valley soils to be exhausted. Repetitive cropping also encouraged the spread of plant diseases and insect infestation, most especially smut and the Hessian fly.

1820–50

The transition from semisubsistence farming to surplus production or market economy agriculture did not come quickly or uniformly across the state for many reasons. As crop yields in the east waned and as land farther west was cleared and broken, the center of wheat production shifted. Unable to compete effectively, farmers in the Hudson and Mohawk Valleys turned to livestock and barley production. In 1820 two-thirds of the nation's barley crop were grown in New York State, largely in the Mohawk Valley. By then Hudson Valley farmers had turned their attention to livestock, primarily beef cattle in the low country and sheep and beef cattle in the high. As farmers reduced grain acreage and cleared more land, they prepared the fields for hay and pasture, sowing them with a mix of European grasses, usually some combination of white clover, red clover, timothy, and redtop. Although most farmers had sheep, the number during the colonial and pioneer periods was low and the quality poor. The largest flocks were on Long Island, where conditions were best, and in Dutchess Co. Sheep raising first spiked between 1810 and 1815 in conjunction with hostilities with Britain, the establishment of domestic woolen mills, and the consequent demand for quality fleece. The crash that followed cost many Long Island and Hudson Valley farmers dearly as their investments in Spanish merino stock proved shortsighted. Beginning in the 1820s the wool market started a recovery that once again prompted Long Island and hill country farmers bordering the Hudson Valley to turn to wool and tallow as surplus crops. Sheep raising soon spread rapidly west across the Appalachian Upland.

The opening of the Erie Canal, beginning in 1819, solidified and encouraged the expansion of these trends for a time. Farther west, the canal's presence stimulated the wheat trade and shifted its direction to the east, away from outlets to the north and south. By 1820 wheat had become the surplus crop of central New York State farmers, and with a cheaper, more convenient means to market, Genesee Country farmers increased their land-clearing efforts and focused on wheat production, repeatedly sowing the same fields in white flint, the variety they made famous. At that time the crop was produced entirely by hand, and it took 250–300 hours to produce 100 bushels (3,524 l) of wheat on 5 acres (2 ha) of land. Among western farmers the labor seemed justified because "Genesee flour" commanded premier prices in Europe and North America. In 1831 Rochester milled 240,000 barrels of flour, virtually all of the grain supplied by farmers in the region. Some was shipped west to tide over pioneer families in the Old Northwest, but the bulk moved east via canal barge. Throughout the 1830s Genesee Country thrived as the nation's center of wheat production. In 1839 the Genesee Valley wheat crop was estimated at $3,740,000, but by then strong competition from the burgeoning Midwest was at hand. A year later 1 million bushels (35 million l) of wheat were transshipped from Buffalo eastward on the canal. The Erie, which had given western New York State farmers a market edge 15 years earlier, now gave that advantage to their western competitors. Market farmers in the Southern Tier had turned toward cattle and sheep raising and away from surplus grain production.

The agricultural press began advising specialization in the 1830s: "The farmer should apply his labor to such objects as will ensure him the best profit." And a growing number were doing just that. An 1836 survey in the Utica area reported that only about one-fifth of the wheat consumed by that region's inhabitants was locally grown, whereas only a few years earlier wheat had been the region's principal crop. Competition from the Genesee Country and insect infestation pushed central and western New York State farmers to turn to raising cattle and sheep and to growing potatoes, a relatively new commercial crop. Farmers throughout the state were enduring painful transitions as they lost the competitive advantage on one product and were forced to find another. Beginning in the 1830s barley production shifted from the Mohawk Valley to Onondaga Co and the eastern Finger Lakes region. A number of farmers in southern Oneida Co, adjacent Madison Co, and nearby Otsego Co successfully entered the volatile hop market. Some Montgomery, Schenectady, and Schoharie Co farmers turned to broomcorn as a cash crop. Faced with mounting western competition, some Rochester and Geneva (Ontario and Seneca Cos) agriculturists developed a highly successful commercial niche cultivating fruit, ornamental tree, and shrub species as well as other nursery stock. The first commercial orchards in the state were established in the Hudson Valley around 1820. Farmers near the south shore of Lake Ontario followed in the 1840s, taking advantage of the lake's temperature-moderating influence, and began cultivating extensive apple and peach orchards. In addition Orleans Co became the nation's center for navy bean production, a crop that remained locally important throughout the century. Farmers on eastern Long Island and in parts of the Hudson Valley marketed cordwood harvested from their woodlots to New York City and Brooklyn.

The most significant change during this period was the rise of dairy farming. From the time of early settlement, the offerings of the family milch cow (milk, butter, and, to a lesser extent, cheese) had been important components of a farm family's diet. Unlike other farm products, early dairy production was largely managed by women. Settlers from Cheshire Co, Conn, initiated surplus cheese production in Herkimer Co before 1810, and a few farms in that county contained herds of 30 or more milk cows in 1815. But large-scale commercial cheese production did not begin until the mid-1820s in southwest Herkimer and adjacent Oneida Cos. In 1832 farm families in a six-town area produced over 1,000 tons (900 MT), which were purchased by agents who shipped to eastern markets. Facilitated by the expanding canal system, cheese making soon spread to nearby areas and down the Black River valley to Jefferson and St. Lawrence Cos. Dairy herds grew accordingly. Cortland Co farmers claimed nearly 34,000 cows in 1841, and two years later 24 million pounds (10.9 million kg) of cheese passed through Albany, most of it cheddar and destined for Britain. In 1845 families in the Town of Fairfield (Herkimer Co) produced 1,356,000 pounds (615,000 kg) of cheese. In Dutchess and Orange Cos, farm women began producing surplus butter for sale in the New York City market. Orange Co butter, especially that produced in the area around Goshen, soon gained the reputation of being of particularly high quality, and Goshen butter became the national standard by which all butter was judged.

The marketing of whole milk did not begin until a fast and reliable means of transportation became available. Before then city dwellers were offered highly adulterated milk produced by malnourished cows fed little but distillery mash and brewery swill. In 1842 Orange Co farmer Philo Gregory made the first rail shipment of fluid milk to New York City via the Erie Railroad. Two years later the Erie was carrying 17,000 quarts (18,700 l) of milk to the city daily, and by 1847 it operated a scheduled milk train. Soon the Harlem Railroad was doing likewise. Profits from dairy farming enticed thousands of sheep farmers, confronted with low wool prices and a disappearing tallow market, to sell their flocks and turn their pastures over to dairy cattle.

In the 1840s farmers across the state began to perceive the value of their land not in its resale value but in its productive capacity, and with that changing perception came a growing concern for nurturing the land. By decade's end, for example, manuring fields was a common practice. At midcentury, despite the competition from the Midwest and the seemingly constant need to make painful adjustments in crop production, New York State farmers had reason to be proud. Although certainly not the largest state in area, New York contained the greatest acreage of improved farmland, and its farmers owned farm equipment and machinery valued at nearly twice that of Pennsylvania, its nearest rival. In crop production New York ranked first in oats, barley, and buckwheat and had only recently been overtaken in wheat and rye. The state was the nation's leading producer of butter and cheese, orchard and garden produce, potatoes, poultry, maple sugar, and fuelwood. It also led the nation in number of cattle, total value of livestock, and animals slaughtered, and had just fallen behind Ohio in sheep and wool production. Yet, only about half of the state's 170,000 farms were in the market economy.

1850–1900

Stimulated by numerous affordable manufactured goods and a doubling of agricultural prices relative to consumer goods, farm families adopted the strategies of producing beyond the rural household's food, seed, and stock needs and of selling the surplus. Demands presented by new markets and by the Civil War further accelerated the abandonment of traditional semisubsistence farming strategies. By 1865 two out of three New York State farmers produced a marketable surplus. That proportion rose to almost 100% in the decades following, as farm commodity prices rose and transportation facilities improved.

Adjustment remained necessary for the 321,930 farmers listed in the 1855 state census. Despite a record harvest of over 13 million bushels (458.1 million l) in 1850, New York dropped to third in wheat production among states. The legacy of repeated cropping, a serious infestation of the wheat midge, black stem rust, the Hessian fly, and even stronger competition from the West resulted in an absolute and relative decline in production in the years following. New York ranked only sixth in wheat production, and Genesee Country farmers were turning to barley, horse breeding, and sheep raising by the end of the 1850s. Potato production grew significantly during this time, especially in Jefferson, Franklin, Saratoga, Rensselaer, and Washington Cos. Acres dedicated to specialty crops like hops also increased. Flocks of 1,000 or more sheep were not uncommon during the mid-1860s, when over 4 million grazed on the upland pastures of eastern New York State.

Dairy farming exhibited the most important growth in whole milk, butter, and cheese as increasing numbers of farm families chose the twice-a-day regimen of milking over commercial crop production. For hillside farmers it was an especially prudent decision. Butter producers often capitalized on their by-products and raised hogs on a diet of whey, sour and skim milk, and buttermilk. Also, a major adjustment in cheese making began in 1851 when Rome (Oneida Co) area farmer Jesse Williams established the first cheese factory. By 1864 an estimated 205 cheese factories produced 33% of the state's cheese, rising to 900 factories and over 90% of the cheese by 1875. The change in venue from family farmsteads to crossroads cheese factories took the work away from the farmwife, effectively altering her role from a critical co-worker in farm production to domestic manager of the family. The oversight of farm production became "masculinized" and more scientific and businesslike.

Rather than deal with crop adjustment, a substantial but unknown number of New Yorkers sold their farms and migrated west, where they purchased land and joined the competition. According to the 1860 federal census, nearly one-quarter of native-born New Yorkers had moved out of state, chiefly to the upper Midwest, where land was cheap and exceptionally fertile and the crops bountiful. In their place came other farmers: some were from nearby farm families, and others were from further afield, such as the foreign-born southern Germans and Irish who settled parts of the Tug Hill. By the early 20th century other foreign groups were taking over old farms and altering the local culture, including Jewish poultry farmers in Ulster and Sullivan Cos, Polish and Italian laborers working the mucklands of southern Orange and northern Madison Cos, and Finns in northwest Tioga Co.

In the decade and a half following the Civil War the national and the state rail networks expanded dramatically. National network growth encouraged western cereal crop and livestock production, thus further undermining the competitive position of New York farmers. Conversely the expansion of the local rail net permitted larger numbers of local farmers to enter into higher-value, labor-intensive production of goods for which freshness and thus proximity to rapidly expanding urban markets was a decided advantage. This was especially important in dairy farming. Railroads instituted scheduled milk train service over expanding distances; milk destined for the New York City market was being hauled from as far away as Rome on the Ontario and Western Railway in 1889. By 1891 Rochester's milkshed extended over 100 miles (160 km), and Buffalo was receiving about half a million 40 qt (44 l) cans of fresh milk daily via seven different railroads.

In 1880 the number of farms in the state exceeded 241,000, the most ever enumerated. New York State farmers faced the problem of overproduction for the first time, and farm prices and incomes faltered. In response farmers organized. Government involvement in agriculture, interest in agricultural education, systematic scientific research in livestock and crop production, and implementation of the research all expanded. Market gardening and fruit and potato production increased, while cereal crop acreage and some specialty crop production declined. The state's dairy herd continued to expand but not as rapidly as milk production because of improved breeding. Whole milk more often became the end product as the years passed. Farming methods continued to evolve, and new crop varieties enhanced production. Animal feed was improved, and the introduction of the silo allowed green fodder crops, principally field corn, to be stored in a succulent rather than a dry condition. An ensilage diet had at least two advantages: it lengthened a cow's lactation period, thereby increasing productivity, and it allowed farmers to maintain larger herds on the same amount of land because its nutritional value was greater than that of the traditional hay and grain diet.

Mechanization continued to increase production efficiency, encouraging farmers to expand their operations. In 1890 it took a farmer 40–50 hours to produce 100 bushels of wheat. In 1850 a bushel (35 l) of corn required four and one-half hours of labor, and in 1894 just 41 minutes. During most of this half century, New York surpassed other states in the manufacture of farm implements and machinery. D. M. Osborne and the Kirby reaper, R. L. Howard and the Ketchum mower, and Walter A. Wood were household names in agricultural areas well beyond New York State. In 1870 factories in the state produced one-half of America's mowers and one-third of its reapers and grain cradles. This new, horse-drawn field machinery was largely suited for level or rolling land, thereby placing farmers with crops on steeper slopes and hilltops at a further disadvantage, leaving them with few options but to quit farming. Other less conspicuous changes were the introduction of improved crop strains and more productive milk cows. Field tiling, first tried in Seneca Co, helped improve productivity across the state. The advent of the tin can in 1885 gave rise to a new dimension in fruit and vegetable preservation, and counties directly south of Lake Ontario (notably Wayne) quickly began producing large quantities of sweet corn, green and lima beans, peas, and other vegetables for a much wider market.

Despite the many improvements in production, by the turn of the 20th century New York had fallen from first place in nearly every category listed in the federal census. Nevertheless, there were over 225,000 farms covering more than 22 million acres (8.9 million ha), two-thirds of it improved. More than 196,000 of those farms reported dairy production. St. Lawrence Co led in whole milk sales (over 39 million gal/148 million l), followed by Orange, Chenango, Jefferson, and Oneida. Chautauqua led cheese production (more than 287,000 lb/130,000 kg sold), followed by Herkimer, Erie, Allegany, and Oneida. Delaware Co was the largest butter producer (over 5 million lb/ 2.3 million kg sold), then Schoharie, Otsego, Steuben, and Greene. Steuben Co stood out in bushels of potatoes harvested, followed by Monroe, Erie, Suffolk, and Washington. The county ranking for total orchard products was Niagara, Orleans, Wayne, Ontario, and Dutchess. The top five counties in total value of farm goods produced were St. Lawrence, Monroe, Chautauqua, Erie, and Steuben.

Agricultural Organization and Education

One reason for New York State's agricultural prominence was the leadership role it took in the agricultural-improvement movement of the 19th century. Agricultural associations, books and periodicals, county and state fairs, schools, colleges, and experiment stations disseminated the new principles of scientific agriculture and improved animal husbandry, increasingly with state support. The elite founders of the state's first agricultural association, the New York Society for the Promotion of Agriculture, Arts and Manufactures (New York City, 1791), pursued an enlightenment program of patriotism, publications, and patronage. Its *Transactions* publicized agricultural observations of local gentlemen along with experiments in Europe and America. Reorganized in 1804, the society in 1824 became part of the Albany Institute (now the Albany Institute of History and Art). The New York State Agricultural Society was founded in 1832. Two years later the *Cultivator* became the group's official mouthpiece and was a publication more readily accepted by farmers skeptical of "book farming" and resentful of the patronizing tone of earlier publications. The editors of such periodicals as the *Plough Boy* (Albany, 1819), *Genesee Farmer* (Rochester, 1831), and *American Agriculturalist* (New York, 1842) enjoyed circulations in the 10,000s by reporting on agricultural improvements, providing practical advice for farm families, reviewing market conditions, and, overall, raising farming's image to the level of a noble profession.

The speeches, premium lists, prizewinning essays, and other printed materials associated with agricultural fairs stressed exposition, entertainment, emulation, and friendly competition, and provided the agricultural press with much useful material. Inspired by Elkanah Watson's Berkshire County Agricultural Society in Massachusetts and with his assistance after his return to Albany, local elites organized countywide societies to hold annual fairs and exhibitions across the state during the 1810s. County fairs encouraged farm families to familiarize themselves with the latest agricultural improvements while coming together to socialize. After 1867 picnics sponsored by the more politically minded Grange met many of the same needs.

Agricultural organizations received modest state assistance before midcentury. Under Watson's lobbying, the legislature in 1819 created the Board of Agriculture and annually appropriated money to be distributed as premiums at fairs (less than $43,000 was granted over the next six years). In 1841 the legislature gave the New York State Agricultural Society the first of five annual $8,000 grants. All but $700 each year was earmarked for the county societies; the remainder supported a state fair held at various locations until 1890, when the society acquired a permanent fairground site near Syracuse. To assist the financially strapped fairgrounds, the state purchased it in 1899, establishing a State Fair Commission in 1900. It came under the jurisdiction of the Department of Agriculture, which was created out of the Dairy Commission in 1893 to take over distribution of the fair grants. In 1917 the Department of Farms and Markets was created from the Department of Agriculture, the Department of Foods and Markets (1914), and the Office of the State Superintendent of Weights and Measures (1851). It became the Department of Agriculture and Markets in 1926.

The state also supported formal agricultural education. From 1792 to 1796 the legislature funded a professorship in natural history, chemistry, and agriculture at Columbia College. In 1824 Stephen Van Rensselaer founded the Rensselaer School (now Rensselaer Polytechnic Institute) at Troy, which originally had a strong agricultural education component. In 1833, 1842, 1843, 1845, 1849, 1851, and 1852, the legislature failed to pass bills establishing public agricultural schools or colleges. It incorporated a state agricultural college in 1853, but the institution failed with the sudden death of John Delafield, its chief proponent and president. Amos Brown, principal of the Ovid Academy (Seneca Co), successfully lobbied for state matching grants and maneuvered to have an agricultural college established there, but mismanagement and the outbreak of the Civil War ended the venture. The legislature incorporated the People's College in Havana [now Montour Falls, Schuyler Co] in 1853 to promote literature, science, arts, and agriculture. It was located at the farm of chief benefactor Charles Cook. After Congress passed the Morrill Land Grant Act in 1862, which granted New York State 990,000 acres (400,639 ha) of public land to support at least one college to teach subjects related to agriculture and the mechanical arts, the legislature in 1863 voted to give the People's College the federal land grant money. The school, however, failed to meet the property, faculty, and building conditions attached to the state appropriation act. In 1865 the legislature gave the entire land grant fund to Cornell University, which had an Agriculture Department and later a College of Agriculture with its own farm, herd, and faculty; the state assumed fiscal responsibility for the expanded college in 1904. An experiment station was organized at Ithaca in 1879 to be governed by a board of the college's faculty, representatives of the New York State Agricultural Society, the Grange, and six other farm organizations. In 1880 a second experiment station was established by the state, this time at Geneva. It was placed under the College of Agriculture in 1923. The college sponsored the state's first Farmers' Institute in 1886. A cooperative extension service, supported by the US Department of Agriculture (1862) in conjunction with Cornell, served all but two counties of the state by the late 1910s.

The 20th Century and Beyond

At the turn of the 20th century, crops and markets in New York State were established in patterns that essentially hold true a century later. Farming in the state in the 20th century entailed mechanization, changes in market forces, and a progressive reduction of its physical extent, but not large and sudden shifts in cash crops, which had characterized much of the 19th century. It was also marked by ever increasing yields but shrinking profit margins. The mechanization of farming parallels mechanization in the larger society, but given the ages-old methods of farming, it is perhaps more striking in the former. By 1900 farming districts were experiencing some of the impacts of electricity, telephones, automobiles, and improved roads, even though most users were urbanites. The first steam-powered tractor was patented in 1850 and used primarily in stationary applications such as powering threshing machines; they were in common but not universal use by the end of the 19th century. The gasoline-powered tractor was invented in 1892, but its impact began only in the World War I era. Internal combustion tractors and farm trucks came into common use during the 1920s, and although the economic woes of the 1930s and gas rationing from 1942 to 1945 tended to retard their spread, World War II's heavy drain on human resources worked to encourage their use. After 1945 the tractor became universal on well-capitalized New York State farms, and combines, mowers, and balers were widely used.

Electrification transformed rural life. About the time of World War I, some farmers began installing their own generating systems. The cheapest was a water turbine that converted a small stream of flowing water into mechanical energy, which could drive a one-half-horsepower motor for tasks like pumping water or lighting bulbs. Electrical machinery included 100 gal (379 l) butter churns, vacuum milkers, cattle cleaners, washing machines, vegetable peelers, pea hullers, corn crackers and huskers, ensilage cutters, wood splitters, feed grinders, and pumps. General Electric (GE) and Westinghouse both took an early interest in rural electrification, and one-fifth of GE's magazine advertising in 1925 was directed to the rural market. Some benefits of electrification were unexpected, such as in chicken farming. Two 40 W lightbulbs in the henhouse turned on a few hours before dawn raised egg production by as much as 50% during the winter months. The Rural Electrification Act of 1936 helped finance the extension of the power grid to farmers and other rural dwellers. On the eve of systematic rural electrification, somewhere between 30% and 45% of New York State farms were electrified.

New York State was equally affected by strides in dairy technology. The Babcock butterfat tester, the DeLaval cream separator, and competing models revolutionized the handling of milk by the turn of the 20th century, but milking remained a manual task, and whole milk was still shipped in 40 qt cans. The DeLaval Separator Co was the first in the United States to develop a practical milking machine in 1918, and with improvements, it was gradually adopted. Bulk tanks appeared after 1938, and Ancram and Copake (Columbia Co) farmers were among the first New York users in 1948. Their adoption changed the rhythms of dairy farming. In a little more than a decade, most dairy farmers had adopted the new systems, and transporters and processors began to phase out the old methods. When bulk tanks became required, some poorly capitalized, generally older farmers chose to go out of business rather than to make the substantial investment.

Although the number of dairy farms and the number of cows have continued to decline, the state's milk production increased to record levels. This was because of efficiencies of scale (the state average is 69 cows per farm, but an increasing number have 250 or more), advances in breeding and feeding, and the impact of bovine growth hormone (bGH), which since the late 1980s has stimulated milk production. In 2002 New York ranked third in the nation in total milk production.

The state and federal governments played an ever increasing role in agricultural policy in the 20th century. As the state government grew under Govs Alfred E. Smith and Franklin D. Roosevelt and their successors, it took over more town and county responsibilities, alleviating some of the tax burden on rural counties. Diversification of the tax structure away from an overreliance on property tax also helped cash-strapped farmers. Also helping farmers was the Reforestation Law of 1929 (and its Hewitt amendment of 1931), which authorized the Conservation Department to acquire land (by purchase of gift) for reforestation outside the boundaries of the Catskill and Adirondack Parks. Over 500,000 acres (202,000 ha) of some of the poorest farmland in the state was acquired and converted into multiple-use areas. A similar effort led to the acquisition of more than 200,000 acres (81,000 ha) of former farmland as wildlife management areas. These programs offered undercapitalized farmers on targeted, marginal land a buyout to help them start over in town or on better land. There was also concern over the loss of fertile farmland. The Purchase of Development Rights (PDR) strategy was developed in the early 1970s to keep land in production and was first implemented in New York State in Suffolk Co in 1973. New York State established a statewide PDR program in 1996.

A more direct form of assistance for farmers—price supports—emerged during the New Deal with the passage of the Agricultural Adjustment Acts of 1933 and 1938. The impact of price supports peaked in the 1970s, and such supports remain in effect for a variety of farm crops in the state, from apples to dairy products. Government purchase of agricultural surpluses also helps maintain agricultural production.

Perhaps the most unexpected changes of the last quarter of the 20th century were the fresh-foods movement and other environmentally driven changes in farming practices. Concern about pesticides grew following the publication of Rachel Carson's *Silent Spring* (1962) and after the environmental movement coalesced around Earth Day in 1970. By the late 1970s organic farming was sufficiently well established to form NOFA-NY (Northeast Organic Farming Association of New York, Inc), which incorporated in 1985. A NOFA-NY subsidiary company, accredited by the US Department of Agriculture, is one of the organizations in the state that certifies qualifying farms as organic. The number of organic producers has climbed since the 1980s, although most farmers continue to use agrochemicals. The system called Integrated Pest Management (IPM), another result of environmental consciousness, was endorsed by a 1985 amendment to the state Agriculture and Markets Law, authorizing Cornell involvement in its development and application.

Parallel to the recognition of organic farming and contributing significantly to its success has been the return to fresh-foods marketing. Through most of the 20th century supermarkets had been increasingly ubiquitous, and direct marketing of produce and other foods such as meats had declined in consequence. Few of the market houses that once anchored urban downtowns remained in operation. Driven partly by demand for healthful food and partly by small farmers' need to increase income in an economy that favored large-scale production, farmers' markets emerged and were well established by the 1980s. Present not only in the state's largest cities (as in New York, where the Union Square market draws farmers from beyond a 100 mi/161 km radius) but also in modest-sized county seats and small villages, these markets have helped spur other commercial activity in communities.

The average farm in New York State became larger during the 20th century, increasing from 99.8 acres (40.4 ha) in 1900, to 128.1 acres (51.8 ha) in 1950, to 228.4 acres (92.4 ha) in 1997. Mechanization and electrification of farming practices especially contributed to the growth in farm size, making economies of scale increasingly profitable as the costs of remaining competitive producers steadily increased. Some observers lamented for the decline of the family farm, and while that institution in New York State is beleaguered, it remains viable. Private and public land conservancies often try to arrange deed covenant agreements with individual farmers and help them resist the blandishments of suburban developers. Nevertheless, 3 of the state's major agricultural regions—Hudson Valley, Finger Lakes, and Long Island—are listed by the American Farmland Trust as among the top 20 endangered agricultural areas in the United States. Dairying retains its agricultural preeminence and is responsible for exactly half of farm receipts, but it is undergoing consolidation, and the trend to large farms will no doubt continue. Other important sectors are nurseries and greenhouses (11% of receipts), hay, apples, and cattle and calves (each 3–4% of receipts).

Old farm families and newcomers continue to face abundant challenges. As younger generations have opted out of farming, finding adequate agricultural laborers has proven increasingly difficult and has brought with it many social problems linked to the low wages and poor living conditions provided for some of the migrant workers. By the last decades of the 20th century, Mexican immigrants were the primary migrant farmworkers, assuming the roles of post–World War II southern and Caribbean blacks. In 1986 one-third of New York's farmers were hired workers, and by the early 21st century the number was over one-half.

The numbers involved in farming have dramatically decreased over the course of the 20th century, especially after 1950 with massive postwar suburbanization and farm consolidation. In 1950 the state had 124,977 farms on 16,016,721 acres (6,481,743 ha). By 1997 those figures had dropped to 31,757 farms on 7,254,470 acres (2,935,782 ha), and the 2000 census counted only 54,372 New York State residents (a mere .6% of the labor force) as holding jobs in agriculture, forestry, and mining. Although these figures reflect profound changes in the nature of agriculture, New York State remains among the top national producers for a variety of crops, and it is likely that agriculture will continue to be a key element of the state's economy into the 21st century and beyond.

See also FARMSTEADS; MIGRANT FARMWORKERS.

Atack, Jeremy, and Fred Bateman. *To Their Own Soil: Agriculture in the Antebellum North* (Ames: Iowa State Univ Press, 1987)

Bidwell, Percy Wells, and John I. Falconer. *History of Agriculture in the Northern United States, 1620–1860* (New York: Peter Smith, 1941)

Bruegel, Martin. *Farm, Shop, Landing: The Rise of a Market Society in the Hudson Valley, 1780–1860* (Durham: Duke Univ Press, 2002)

Butcher, Donald G. *New York Agriculture 2000* (Albany: NYS Department of Agriculture and Markets, [2000])

Cohen, David Steven. *The Dutch-American Farm* (New York: New York Univ Press, 1992)

Conklin, Howard E., and Robert E. Linton. *The Nature and Distribution of Farming in New York State* (Albany: NYS Office of Planning Coordination, 1969)

DuPont, Patricia, Carl H. Feuer, and Jean Kost. "Black Migrant Farmworkers in New York State: Exploitable Labor," *Afro-Americans in New York Life and History* (Jan 1988): 7–26

Gates, Paul W. "Agricultural Change in New York State, 1850–1890," *New York History* 50 (Apr 1969): 114–41

Gold, David M. "Jewish Agriculture in the Catskills, 1900–1920," *Agricultural History* 55 (Jan 1981): 31–49

Hart, John P. "Rethinking the Three Sisters," *Journal of Middle Atlantic Archaeology* 19 (2003): 73–82

Hedrick, U. P. *A History of Agriculture in the State of New York* (New York: Hill & Wang, 1966)

Linder, Marc, and Lawrence S. Zacharias. *Of Cabbages and Kings County: Agriculture and the Formation of Modern Brooklyn* (Iowa City: Univ of Iowa Press, 1999)

McMurry, Sally. *Transforming Rural Life: Dairying Families and Agricultural Change, 1820–1885* (Baltimore: Johns Hopkins Univ Press, 1995)

McNall, Neil Adams. *An Agricultural History of the Genesee Valley, 1790–1860* (Philadelphia: Univ of Pennsylvania Press, 1952)

Parkerson, Donald H. *The Agricultural Transition in New York State: Markets and Migration in Mid-19th-Century America* (Ames: Iowa State Univ Press, 1995)

James W. Darlington

Agriculture and Markets, Department of. State agency responsible for regulating, promoting, and conducting research on New York State agriculture. The department has responsibility for more than 37,500 farms throughout New York State covering nearly 7.6 million acres (3.1 million ha), about one-quarter of the state's land area. In 2002 these farms collectively produced and sold approximately $3.4 billion in products. The department began in 1884 as the New York State Dairy Commission to inspect dairy production and sales facilities; milk-borne diseases such as scarlet and typhoid fevers, diphtheria, and septic throat were common during the Gilded Age. In 1893 the commission was abolished, and its functions merged into the Department of Agriculture. The new department inspected farms, set agricultural quality standards, and operated agricultural experimental stations, including the Geneva Experiment Station (Ontario Co), which opened in 1880 and became part of Cornell University in 1923. A separate Department of Foods and Markets was created in 1914 to establish standards for grading and selling food, supervise markets, and publish bulletins on daily prices and marketing methods. In 1917 these two agencies, along with the Office of the State Superintendent of Weights and Measures, created in 1851, were consolidated into a new Department of Farms and Markets headed by the newly created Council of Farms and Markets. This new department was also assigned some duties from the State Department of Health, including ensuring sufficient milk supplies within cities, regulating exchanges and boards of trade, and mediating controversies between producers and distributors.

The current Department of Agriculture and Markets was established as part of the general reorganization of state government in 1926 under Gov Alfred E. Smith and assumed all functions and powers of Farms and Markets and of the State Fair Commission, created in 1900. The last organizational change came in 1935 when the legislature abolished the Council of Farms and Markets, granting the governor power to appoint the commissioner. In the early 21st century the department's work includes investigating animal and plant diseases, regulating food safety and labeling, promoting the state's agricultural sector, and administering the annual New York State Fair.

Department of Agriculture and Markets. Records. New York State Archives, Albany

Christine Karpiak

Agway. Agricultural cooperative headquartered in Syracuse and formed in 1964 through the merger of the Cooperative Grange League Federation Exchange (GLF), Eastern States Farmers Exchange, and the following year the Pennsylvania Farm Bureau Cooperative. The Ithaca-based GLF, established in 1920, purchased livestock feeds, fertilizers, and seeds in bulk, and passed along the savings to farmer-members. The GLF later marketed farm products and, following mechanization, sold gasoline, tires, and agricultural equipment. In the first year after the 1964 merger, Agway reported $338 million in sales and served 85,000 members. The cooperative has developed four main business segments: the animal feed and nutrition division, which sells feed and technical services to producers, primarily dairy farmers, through a network of feed mills and centers in the northeastern United States; Agway Energy Products, which markets heating oil, propane, retail gasoline, and air-conditioning and heating equipment; the fresh produce division (Country Best Products), which purchases and sells produce to large chain stores and major grocers in the eastern United States; and the agricultural technologies division, which promotes new technologies in such areas as food preservation. Agway also meets the needs of urban gardeners, fruit and vegetable growers, and pet owners. Regional Agway centers serve the public, but only active farmers may be members. A 15-member board of directors, elected by Agway members, determines policies.

In 2001 Agway had 69,000 members, with net sales and revenues of $1.1 billion. Consolidated net sales and revenues were $899,934,000 in 2002. After declaring bankruptcy in October 2002, Agway streamlined, selling four business operations by the end of that year: Telmark, which offered farmers lease financing for equipment, buildings, and vehicles; Agway Insurance Co; Agronomy, which sold fertilizer, farm seed, and crop protectants; and Seedway. Agway planned to continue its agriculture, country products group, and energy segments.

Knapp, Joseph G. *Seeds That Grew: A History of the Cooperative Grange League Federation Exchange* (Hinsdale, NY: Anderson House, 1960)

Suzan D. Friedlander

AIDS [acquired immune deficiency syndrome]. On 3 July 1981 the US Centers for Disease Control (CDC) reported 26 cases of an unusual cancer, Kaposi's sarcoma, among homosexual men in New York City and California. One month earlier the CDC had published an account of the appearance of the deadly *pneumocystis carinii* pneumonia (PCP) in Los Angeles. These reports marked the official start of the AIDS epidemic. AIDS is the advanced form of infection by the human immunodeficiency virus (HIV), which compromises the immune system and often manifests as an opportunistic illness after a long latency period. HIV is spread by exchange of body fluids through sexual contact, among drug users who share injection equipment, during pregnancy, and through blood transfusions. At the onset of the AIDS epidemic, New York City had a large intravenous drug-using population and a thriving gay community. In the years leading up to 1984, 57% of new AIDS cases were among gay men, and 35% among drug users.

The first decade of the epidemic was marked by conflict between AIDS activists and proponents of measures that might be viewed as intrusions on individual rights. In 1985 and 1986 public health officials moved to close the bathhouses where some gay men congregated for sexual contact. Later controversies swirled around the question of whether the New York State Department of Health should collect the names of individuals infected with HIV for a confidential registry, as it was already doing with people with AIDS, and whether newborns should be screened for the presence of HIV infection without maternal consent. In both cases civil libertarians ultimately lost out to measures that would restrict privacy in the name of public health. When the antiviral azidothymidine (AZT) was shown to slow the progression of AIDS in some cases, the AIDS Coalition to Unleash Power (ACT UP) demonstrated on Wall St to bring down the price of the drug. Pressed by AIDS activists to provide sterile injection equipment to drug users as a way of interrupting the spread of HIV, health officials had to overcome opposition from those who saw this approach as support for behavior that was illegal and had destructive consequences. With great reluctance New York State made funds available to community groups providing needle exchange. By 1990 gay men constituted 35% of the new cases, and intravenous drug users made up 52%.

HIV-AIDS CASES AND DEATHS IN NEW YORK STATE

	New Cases	Deaths
Before 1980	15	13
1980	36	31
1981	153	141
1982	544	510
1983	1,189	1,112
1984	2,053	1,887
1985	3,224	2,948
1986	4,695	4,317
1987	5,982	5,377
1988	7,418	6,522
1989	8,066	7,038
1990	9,067	7,675
1991	10,756	8,751
1992	13,102	9,640
1993[a]	15,147	9,775
1994	14,570	7,784
1995	13,902	5,455
1996	11,272	2,856
1997	8,537	1,563
1998	6,103	849
1999	4,689	448
Total	140,520	84,692

Source: NYS Department of Health, *AIDS in New York State,* 2001–2 ed.

Note: Death information is from the New York State Department of Health Bureau of Production Systems, the National Death Index, and voluntary reporting of deaths of known New York State residents by other states.

[a]On 1 Jan 1993 the AIDS Surveillance Case Definition for adults with HIV infection was expanded to include pulmonary tuberculosis, recurrent pneumonia, invasive cervical cancer, and severe immunodeficiency. Data for 1998 and 1999 are incomplete because of the lag in case reporting and time required for case confirmation.

A 1994 research study determined that providing AZT to pregnant women infected with HIV could reduce the rate of transmission to their unborn children by two-thirds. While 172 cases of HIV were diagnosed among infants and children in New York City in 1994, only 8 cases were reported in 1999. In 1995–96 combinations of therapeutic agents were used to treat individuals with HIV infection. New cases of fully developed AIDS dropped dramatically, as did deaths from AIDS-related complications. New York ranked first among states in annual cases per 100,000 at the end of the 1990s, largely due to the prevalence of AIDS in New York City, exceeded only by Washington, DC. Of all cases, 31% were gay men, and 46% were intravenous drug users. Outside New York City there were 23,000 cases and 13,000 deaths in New York State between 1981 and 2000. The occurrence of AIDS throughout the state mirrored the situation in New York City, where the most affected neighborhoods had a rate of HIV infection 14 times higher than that of the least affected neighborhoods.

See also PUBLIC HEALTH.

Arno, Peter S., and Karyn L. Feiden. *Against the Odds: The Story of AIDS Drug Development, Politics, and Profits* (New York: Harper Collins, 1992)

Bayer, Ronald. *Private Acts, Social Consequences: AIDS and the Politics of Public Health* (New York: Free Press, 1989)

Joseph, Stephen C. *Dragon within the Gates: The Once and Future AIDS Epidemic* (New York: Carroll & Graf Publishers, 1992)

Ronald Bayer

airlines. See AVIATION; COMMUTER AIRLINES; and individual airlines.

Airmont. Village (pop 7,799) in Ramapo (Rockland Co). The Erie Railroad (1841) established a stop at Tallman, and a post office by the same name followed in 1860. In the early 20th century, cut flowers and strawberries were among the products of its farms before suburbanization accelerated. Residents of the hamlets of Airmont, South Monsey, and Tallman incorporated as Airmont in 1991 to better control zoning. The NASA-designed Challenger Space Science Center (1999) provides services to school systems.

airports

EARLY FACILITIES

Once aircraft began flying with regularity in the 1910s, there was a need for increasingly improved ground facilities. Early airports consisted of a small terminal or office along with either wooden or cinder-block hangars that housed perhaps 10 aircraft. When Charles Lindbergh took off on his record-breaking flight from New York City to Paris in 1927, most runways were little more than small fields of dirt and weeds displaying a yellow or orange wind sock to detect wind direction. Runways in smaller communities often had surfaces of only hard-packed sod or cinders, or were surrounded by dangerous high-tension wires. In 1929, when Colonial Airways began airmail service between Albany and Buffalo, these cities' airports added boundary lights and floodlights, with revolving beacon lights every 10 miles (16 km) along the routes to guide pilots flying at night. The next year American Airways purchased Colonial, which also flew between Newark, NJ, and Boston, and expanded airmail service. American flew from Buffalo, Rochester, Syracuse, Utica, Schenectady, Albany, and Newark, adjacent to New York City. By the 1930s there were three main airways in the state, one running between Buffalo and Newark, another between Buffalo and Albany, and another between Albany and Newark. Despite the era's economic depression, most airports began installing radio ranges that assisted pilots flying on instruments, with all the major facilities in the state acquiring the ranges by 1940.

The federal government's Works Progress Administration (WPA) began modernizing many airports during the depression, and millions of WPA dollars paid for longer, concrete or macadam runways, more advanced lighting,

Inside the control tower at Syracuse Hancock International Airport, 1970s.

new hangars, and drainage systems; these investments led to overall airport expansion. In 1935 Rochester Airport installed one of the first control towers, which utilized a portable light-gun system using red and green lenses for safer and more efficient movement of aircraft. By 1938 all the state's airports had experienced steady increases in commercial flights, with American Airlines serving as a main carrier in northern and central New York State. In New York City, North Beach Airport in Queens, originally established in 1929 as Glenn H. Curtiss Airport, was remodeled and reopened as New York Municipal Airport–La Guardia Field in 1939. Floyd Bennett Field in Brooklyn opened in 1930 as New York City's first municipal airport, but its distance from Manhattan made it an inconvenient location for commercial flights, and it was sold to the US Navy in 1942. Airport construction was frozen during World War II except for military airfields: Griffiss Air Force Base in Oneida Co, Stewart Airfield (later Stewart Air Force Base) in Orange Co, and Suffolk County Airport (now Francis S. Gabreski Airport).

Postwar Changes

In 1947 the Port of New York Authority took over operations at New York Municipal Airport–La Guardia Field, renaming it La Guardia Airport, and launched work on Idlewild International Airport in Queens. Idlewild, opened in 1948, served 222,620 passengers as La Guardia served 4,284,244 in 1949. Both Idlewild and La Guardia generated a tremendous amount of activity during the postwar years. Idlewild grew rapidly during the 1950s, adding nine new passenger terminals to accommodate increased ridership brought by commercial jet aircraft beginning in 1958. By December 1963, when Idlewild became John F. Kennedy International Airport (JFK), more than 9 million passengers had passed through the facility. Buffalo Municipal Airport expanded its passenger terminal in 1955 and became Greater Buffalo International Airport in 1959. New York State operated the Buffalo facility through the Frontier Port Authority from 1956 until 1967 and then through the Niagara Frontier Transportation Authority. The airport at Rochester acquired a new control tower in 1949 and built new runways in 1950, extending these a decade later. Traffic at Albany Airport, cited in 1939 for inadequate runways and an obsolete control tower, increased fivefold between 1938 and 1955 as improvements were made. Albany Co took over the facility from the city in 1959 and built a new terminal in 1962.

Developing technologies contributed to the growth of flying. From the 1960s many airports began employing a new navigational tool, the instrument landing system (ILS), which used two superimposed radio beams to guide aircraft down to a safe altitude in stormy or foggy weather. With improvements the system permitted larger jet aircraft to land on certain runways in near zero-zero weather conditions.

The state's airports also underwent significant transformation as many military bases either disappeared or converted to civilian uses in a trend extending into the 1990s. In Garden City (Nassau Co) Roosevelt Field was turned into a shopping center in 1951, and Mitchel Field, closed in 1961, was occupied by Hofstra College and Nassau Community College. In 1970 Hancock Field in Syracuse became Syracuse Hancock International Airport, and Stewart Air Force Base turned into Stewart International Airport. The military relinquished all use of Suffolk County Airport after 1970. Renamed the Francis S. Gabreski Airport in 1991, it boasted a 9,000 ft (2,743 m) runway, one of the state's longest. The military ceded Floyd Bennett Field to the Department of the Interior in 1971, and Gateway National Recreation Area, the US Coast Guard, and the New York City police heliport took over use of the site. In 1995 the USAF Strategic Air Command base at Plattsburgh, opened in the mid-1950s, became Clinton County Airport, and Griffiss Air Force Base was reborn as Griffiss Airpark. At the same time smaller civilian airports faced some instability, largely caused by the development of homes, shopping centers, and office parks. Between 1967 and 1995 the number of New York State airports decreased by 55.

Recent Developments

In the 1990s Buffalo, Rochester, and Albany expanded and modernized their terminals and sought to attract new airlines; at New York City airports, record numbers of passengers and volatile weather brought delays. A new regional system, terminal radar approach control facilities (TRACONs) mitigated these delays and provided an orderly air traffic flow for JFK, Newark, and La Guardia Airports extending 100 miles (161 km) around New York City. The Port Au-

COMMERCIAL SERVICE AIRPORTS

	Locality (County)	Number of Airlines (May 2003)
Adirondack Regional Airport	Harrietstown (Franklin)	1
Albany International Airport	Colonie (Albany)	12
Buffalo Niagara International Airport	Cheektowaga (Erie)	16
Chautauqua County/Jamestown Municipal Airport	Ellicott (Chautauqua)	1
Clinton County Airport	Plattsburgh (Clinton)	1
Elmira-Corning Regional Airport	Horseheads (Chemung)	2
Greater Binghamton Airport–Edwin A. Link Field	Maine (Broome)	5
Greater Rochester International Airport	Rochester (Monroe)	15
John F. Kennedy International Airport	Queens Co	71[a]
La Guardia Airport	Queens Co	20[b]
L. I. MacArthur Airport	Ronkonkoma (Suffolk)	10
Massena International Airport/Richards Field	Massena (St. Lawrence)	1
Ogdensburg International Airport	Ogdensburg (St. Lawrence)	1
Stewart International Airport	Newburgh (Orange)	6
Syracuse Hancock International Airport	Syracuse (Onondaga)	13
Ithaca/Tompkins Regional Airport	Ithaca (Tompkins)	1
Watertown International Airport	Watertown (Jefferson)	1
Westchester County Airport	White Plains (Westchester)	13

Source: NYS Department of Transportation, *Directory of New York State Commercial Service Airports.*

[a]14 domestic, 57 foreign.

[b]19 domestic, 1 foreign.

thority of New York and New Jersey's aviation facilities, including Port Authority-Downtown-Manhattan/Wall St Heliport together with Teterboro Airport in New Jersey, constituted one of the biggest and busiest regional aviation complexes in the world by the end of the 20th century. La Guardia generated more than $6 billion in 2003 and employed 9,000 people. JFK, which in 2003 generated over $23 billion and employed 35,000 people, had 10,000 ft (3,050 m) runways and a 321 ft (98 m) control tower, one of the tallest in North America. The facility accommodated the largest aircraft, including the Boeing 747 and the British Concorde, and became a hub for foreign airlines. Although the state's 20 largest commercial airports flourished at century's end, a 1999 report of the Aircraft Owners and Pilots Association (AOPA) discussed threats to the approximately 450 smaller facilities, where many new pilots trained, citing shortages of flight crews, unsympathetic local governments, and ongoing pressure from land developers.

The terrorist raid of 11 Sept 2001 closed all New York State and US airports for three days, and in its wake airports tightened security procedures and placed national guard patrols at all airports. The number of passengers using the state's airports dropped after the attack, from 34,244,334 enplanements in 2000 to 31,361,310 in 2001. Passenger traffic slowly recovered, with the State Department of Transportation reporting 34,686,913 enplanements in 2003. That year New York State had 160 airports (including heliports and seaplane bases) for public use and 382 airports for private use; a total of 6,622 aircraft—including jets, gliders, and helicopters—used those facilities. Activities related to New York State's airports, including passenger travel and air cargo, generated more than $35 billion in 2002–3.

See also WORKS PROGRESS ADMINISTRATION (WPA).

New York State. Department of Transportation. *New York State Inventory of Aviation Facilities* (Albany: Author, 1999)

Petzinger, Thomas J. *Hard Landing* (New York: Random House, 1995)

Paul Roxin

air shows and airplane racing. After the Wright brothers' first airplane flight in 1903, aviators were spurred by prizes, air shows, and races. Many of these early aerial exhibitions occurred in New York State skies. On 4 July 1908 New Yorker Glenn Curtiss flew a fabric-winged biplane over Hammondsport (Steuben Co) and claimed the trophy offered by *Scientific American* for the first public airplane flight of a kilometer. The next year thousands attended an air show in New York City; among other events, Wilbur Wright flew routes between Governors Island and Grant's Tomb. Meanwhile, the *New York World* offered $10,000 for the first one-day flight between Albany and New York City. On 29 May 1910 Curtiss took off from Albany and, stopping twice, landed at Governors Island after 156 minutes in the air. Later that year French and British aviators met their American counterparts for races at Belmont Park in Elmont (Nassau Co). And in 1911, spurred by William Randolph Hearst's $50,000 offer, Calbraith Rodgers undertook the first flight across the United States. Leaving Brooklyn on 17 September, Rodgers suffered accidents, crashes, and broken bones during the flight. With crutches strapped to the Wright biplane's struts, Rodgers finally landed in Pasadena, Calif, on 5 November. Pioneer feats were soon eclipsed by advances stemming from World War I. After the war New York State was no longer a major racing venue, but it was the starting point for many record-setting trips. The first transatlantic flight took place in 1919 from the Naval Air Station Rockaway in Queens. Charles Lindbergh's 1927 nonstop solo flight to Paris and Wiley Post's 1931 round-the-world flight both originated from the Roosevelt Field airstrip. After World War II individual flying displays were superseded by larger air shows, many of which featured vintage airplanes. Renowned shows include the Orleans Flying Machine and Hot Air Balloon Family Fest in Albion (Orleans Co), the Thunder over Niagara show at Niagara Falls, the Wings of Eagles Air Show at the Elmira-Corning Regional Airport in Horseheads (Chemung Co), and the pioneer plane exhibitions at the Old Rhinebeck Aerodrome in Rhinebeck (Dutchess Co).

Casey, Louis S. *Curtiss: The Hammondsport Era, 1907–1915* (New York: Crown Publishers, 1981)

Villard, Henry S. *Contact! The Story of the Early Birds* (New York: Crowell, 1968)

James Maas

Akron. Village (pop 3,085) in Newstead (Erie Co). A post office was established at Akron in 1833. Limestone and gypsum were discovered in 1839, making its economy based on manufacturing, especially of cement and plaster. Akron was served by a railroad beginning in 1840 that later became part of the New York Central system. The village was incorporated in 1849. By 1860 there was a tannery, a foundry, and seven mills of various kinds. In the early 21st century, manufacturing remained economically important, especially Ford Gum (*ca* 1915) and Perry's Ice Cream (1918). The Rich-Twinn octagonal house (1849) is a landmark.

Andrew C. Maines

Akwesasne (St. Regis Indian Reservation). An Iroquois, primarily Mohawk, reservation of about 26,000 acres (10,500 ha) on both the Canadian and the New York State sides of the St. Lawrence River. Akwesasne ("Where the Partridge Drums") is the name for the community on both sides of the border, but the territory within New York State, located in Franklin Co, is also known as the St. Regis Indian Reservation. This boundary has created a historically complex relationship between Akwesasne Mohawks and the local and national governments on both sides of the border.

A Jesuit mission was established at Akwesasne in the 1750s, from which the New York side of the territory takes its name, but according to Mohawk oral tradition the area had been inhabited for generations. In 1802 the Akwesasne Mohawk in New York, unlike other Iroquois reserves of the time, adopted a system of elected officials rather than the traditional system of league chiefs. Conflict on both sides of the border continues between elected council officials and Mohawks who follow the traditional Longhouse religion. There are three major governmental organizations at Akwesasne in the early 21st century. The traditional Mohawk Nation Council of Chiefs is recognized by the Iroquois Confederacy as the official government of the Mohawk people. The St. Regis Mohawk Tribal Council is recognized by New York State and the federal government. The Mohawk Council of Akwesasne is recognized by Canadian governments.

The reservation's land base on both sides of the border was substantially reduced from 1816 to 1845 through a series of controversial leases and sales. During this time residents successfully farmed the rich shore lands and established numerous dairies, and also worked as lumbermen, river pilots, and guides. Since the latter part of the 19th century, Akwesasne Mohawks have been nationally renowned as expert basketmakers, makers of lacrosse sticks, and ironworkers.

Akwesasne has been a source of visible American Indian political consciousness and activism since the 1940s. In 1968 the bridge connecting Cornwall, Ont, and Massena (St. Lawrence Co), passing through the reservation, was blockaded by Akwesasne residents protesting the collection of tolls and customs duties at the border. These restrictions were interpreted as a violation of the 1794 Jay Treaty that guaranteed Indians unimpeded movement across the US-Canadian border. The following year *Akwesasne Notes* began publication and became a leading national and international journal of Indian news. The Ronathahonni Cultural Center (formerly Native North American Indian Traveling College) on Cornwall Island, Ont, and the Akwesasne Cultural Center in Hogansburg (Franklin Co) both educate visitors about Iroquois culture and history. The Akwesasne Freedom School was founded in 1980 to teach, preserve, and protect Mohawk language and culture. Created in 1987, the Akwesasne Task Force on the Environment turned scientific attention to the toxic pollutants of large industries on the St. Lawrence River.

The introduction of gambling at Akwesasne has been controversial for decades, but pro-gambling officials succeeded in establishing a casino in Hogansburg, which opened in April 1999. As of the 2000 census, 2,699 people were enrolled in New York State; the 2002 Canadian census listed 9,771 individuals, although Akwesasne residents can be enrolled on both sides.

Fenton, William N., and Elizabeth Tooker. "Mohawk." In *Northeast,* ed. Bruce G. Trigger, vol 15 of *The Handbook of North American Indians* (Washington, DC: Smithsonian Institution, 1978)

Joel S. Cadbury

Alabama. Town (pop 1,881) in NW Genesee Co. Part of the town is in the Tonawanda Indian Reservation. A Seneca village on this land preceded the 1806 white settlement. In 1816 the Oak Orchard Acid Springs were discovered, inspiring a health resort for a time. The town was formed from Shelby (Orleans Co) and Pembroke in 1826 as Gerrysville; the name was changed to Alabama in 1828. The town's primary income base is dairy farming, but the primary income source is employment in neighboring cities. The Iroquois National Wildlife Refuge and Tonawanda State Wildlife Management Area are in the northwest part of town and encompass a large part of the Tonawanda Swamp, which is the largest swamp remaining in New York State.

Susan L. Conklin

A. L. A. Schechter Poultry Corp v United States, 295 US 495 (1935). In the 1930s New York City had the largest live poultry market in the United States. The 1934 Live Poultry Code, promulgated under the 1933 National Industrial Recovery Act (NIRA), attempted to regulate the market. A wholesale kosher poultry dealer in Brooklyn, the A. L. A. Schechter Poultry Corp, charged with selling "unfit chickens" and with other relatively minor violations, legally challenged the code's regulatory reach. On 27 May 1935, by a vote of 9 to 0, the Supreme Court ruled the Live Poultry Code and a portion of NIRA unconstitutional, holding that Congress could not transfer its core legislative functions to the president in what Justice Benjamin Cardozo labeled in his concurrence "delegation running riot." This effective overturning of the NIRA, a key act in the first phase of the New Deal, greatly increased Pres Franklin D. Roosevelt's ire at what he felt was a conservative and obstructionist court.

Bressman, Lisa Schultz. "*Schechter Poultry* at the Millennium: A Delegation Doctrine for the Administrative State," *Yale Law Journal* 109 (April 2000): 1399–442

Timothy P. Gordinier

Albanians. A people from southeastern Europe, tracing their origins to the ancient Illyrians, who have settled in large numbers in New York City, with smaller communities in Jamestown (Chautauqua Co), Buffalo, Rochester, and Albany. At the beginning of the 21st century, there were, by some estimates, 250,000–300,000 Albanian Americans in New York State who came from Albania and from Albanian populations in neighboring Montenegro, Kosova (the Albanian name for Kosovo), and Macedonia. Their homelands in the western Balkans were long the crossroads of empires: Roman, Byzantine, and later Ottoman. Reflecting this history there are Roman Catholic, Orthodox Christian, and Muslim Albanians, but a strong ethnic and linguistic identity as Albanians overrides religious differences. Since World War II New York has become the US state with the largest Albanian population and serves as a political, cultural, and publishing center for all Albanian Americans.

Settlement

Albanians first came to New York State at the end of the 19th century and during the first two decades of the 20th century. The earliest arrivals were Orthodox Christians from the region of Korça in southern Albania. In the 1910s they were joined by Muslims, also from southern Albania. Both groups sought economic opportunity and political stability; the breakup of the Ottoman Empire had brought warfare and economic decline to Albania. At first only young Albanian men came, finding work across New York State on the railroads, in factories, and in restaurants. After World War I they began to bring their wives and children. A second wave of Albanian immigrants arrived after World War II. These were largely refugees from the Communist regime of Enver Hoxha; they came from all regions of Albania and settled in New York City. A third and much larger wave, initiated by the oppression of Albanians in Yugoslavia as well as by the easing of US immigration laws, began to flow into New York State in the late 1960s and continued into the 21st century. These Albanians came first from Montenegro and Macedonia, and later from Kosova (all regions of Yugoslavia until 1992), and in the 1990s from Albania as well.

Community Development and Cultural Life

An early Albanian community formed in Jamestown. Orthodox Christian Albanians were drawn to work in the furniture factories of the region, whose natural beauty resembles that of Albania. In 1905 they founded the first Albanian nationalist organization in America, Malli i Memedheut (Longing for the Motherland). In 1911 members of the same community founded St. Elia Albanian Orthodox Church, the first such church in the state. Astronaut William Gregory (1957–), an Albanian American from Lockport (Niagara Co), was baptized at St. Elia.

In New York City Fan Noli, the first priest of the Autocephalous [Independent] Albanian Orthodox Church, was ordained in 1908 by the Russian Orthodox archbishop, though the seat of the Albanian Orthodox Church was in Boston. It was not until 1942 that St. Nicholas Albanian Orthodox Church was founded on West 48th St in Manhattan. Fr Arthur Liolin, who became chancellor of the Albanian Orthodox Archdiocese and dean of St. George, was raised in New York City's St. Nicholas community. St. Nicholas Albanian Orthodox Church moved to Jamaica (Queens Co) in 1970.

The Bronx, Brooklyn, and Staten Island also became the sites of dynamic, densely populated Albanian communities. Beginning in the 1970s Albanians from Macedonia, Montenegro, and Kosova found work in construction and as superintendents of apartment buildings, where they worked as whole families and learned additional skills. Gradually, working multiple jobs and with loans from fellow Albanians, many of the new immigrants bought apartment buildings and renovated them. With economic betterment came growth of community institutions. New York State's first Albanian American Islamic Center, led by Imam Isa Hoxha, was founded in Brooklyn in 1972. Other such centers formed and expanded in Staten Island, the Bronx, and Queens. In the mid-1970s Monsignor Zef Oroshi founded the state's first Albanian Catholic Church in the Bronx. His Albanian Catholic congregation, later led by Fr Rrok Mirdita and Fr Pjetër Popaj, built a new church, Our Lady of Shkodra, in Hartsdale (Westchester Co), which opened in 1998.

Since the 1970s Albanian musicians and singers and a folklore troop (Rozafati) have performed regularly in the New York metropolitan area, and since 1990 Albanian festivals have been held every fall in the Bronx. In the mid-1990s the Albanian American Soccer League established its headquarters in Staten Island.

Political Activism

From the mid–20th century, political organizations flourished in New York City. Free Albania Committee (1949–91), Balli Kombëtar (National Front), the royalist Legaliteti, and Independent Block were largely anticommunist organizations, while Albanian American Civic League, founded in 1989, and an important branch of LDK (Democratic League of Kosova), founded in 1990, supported Albanians in Kosova. Vatra, the oldest ongoing Albanian organization, founded in Boston in 1912 to work for the survival of Albania as a nation, moved its headquarters to New York City in 1991. Most of these organizations had their own publications. In 1991 the widely read, bilingual newspaper *Illyria* began publication in the Bronx, moving to Manhattan in 2002. At the beginning of the 21st century, the Bronx was home to the Albanian newspapers *Dielli* and *Bota Sot.*

New Yorkers played a central role in founding the National Albanian American Council (NAAC) in Washington, DC, in 1996. During the Kosova crisis of 1998–99, NAAC educated US leaders on the Balkans and advocated for Albanians in Kosova, as Albanian communities in New York City raised funds to help support 800,000 refugees from Kosova. A group of Albanian Americans, mainly New Yorkers and known as the Atlantic Brigade, traveled from New York City to Kosova to fight in the 1998–99 conflict. From the 1990s Rep Eliot Engel from New York's 17th Congressional District, led the Albanian Issues Caucus in Congress.

Conclusion

In the last decades of the 20th century, Albanians revitalized the northern Bronx. Statewide they have worked in real estate, food service, commercial cleaning, and construction. Notable Albanian American professionals have also contributed to the state: advertising executive Stan Dragoti originated the "I Love New York" campaign; photographer Gjon Mili supplied images for the collections of Manhattan's Museum of Modern Art; historian Stavro Skendi taught at Columbia University; David Avdul served as dean of education at Pace University; mathematician Nikolla Cako taught at Queens College; and investment banker Richard Lukaj has helped direct Manhattan-based Bear, Stearns and Co.

Federal Writers' Project of the Works Progress Administration of Massachusetts. *The Albanian Struggle in the Old World and New* (1939; repr New York: AMS Press, 1975)

Hall, Derek. *Albania and Albanians* (New York: St. Martin's Press, 1994)

Trix, Frances. *Albanians in Michigan: A Proud People from Southeast Europe* (East Lansing: Michigan State Univ Press, 2001)

Frances Trix

Albany. City (pop 95,658) and state capital. First settled by the Dutch in 1624 and organized as Beverwijck in 1652, it was renamed Albany in 1664 and chartered as a city in 1686.

Native Inhabitants and White Settlement

When *Half Moon (Halve Maen),* captained by Henry Hudson, arrived on 19 Sept 1609 at the area that would become Albany, it was greeted by the Mohican (Mahican) Indians, an eastern Algonquian-speaking group that had numerous villages in the area. To their west were the Mohawk Indians, the easternmost nation of the Iroquois League. The report of the furs that the Mohicans offered Hudson's crew eventually reached his employer, the Dutch East India Co. As early as 1611 the first traders sailed up the river to trade with the native peoples. By 1614 a trading fort, Fort Nassau, was built on Castle Island [now in Port of Albany]. Continually flooded, the fort was abandoned in 1617, but trade with the Indians continued until 1621, when the Dutch West India Co (WIC) was founded, ending open trade to New Netherland.

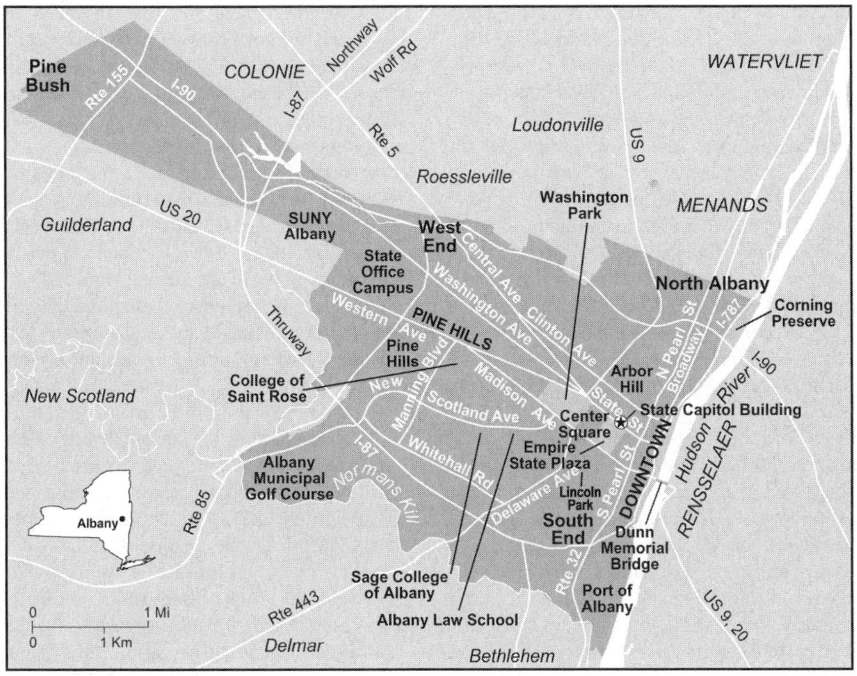

In 1624, 30 families, mostly Walloons, arrived in New Netherland. Sent as support personnel for trading posts on the Connecticut, Delaware, and Hudson Rivers, 18 of the families went to Fort Orange, which was erected in 1624. (The site of the fort is in the vicinity of Broadway, Pruyn St, and I-787.)

Trade was carried on at the fort with the Mohawk and the Mohican. Despite instructions to Director Willem Verhulst (1625–26) that the Dutch were not to interfere in Indian affairs, the fort's commissary, Daniel van Crieckenbeeck, took the Mohican side in a war with the Mohawk. The Mohicans, van Crieckenbeeck, and six of his soldiers were ambushed by the Mohawks in the spring of 1626, not far from the fort; van Crieckenbeeck and three soldiers were killed. The Mohicans fled to their lands east of the river. Director Peter Minuit (1626–32), concerned about possible Indian retaliation, recalled the people from Fort Orange and trading posts on the Delaware and Connecticut Rivers and settled them on Manhattan Island, leaving only military personnel at the forts. It would be four years before the Fort Orange area was settled permanently.

In 1629 the WIC, hoping to increase the new colony's population, enacted the Freedoms and Exemptions, which allowed company members to purchase land from the Indians 12 miles (19 km) along one side of a river or 6 miles (10 km) on each side and inland "as far as the situation allowed." In 1630 Kiliaen van Rensselaer, a WIC director, received a charter for Rensselaerswijck. Land was purchased for him on both sides of the Hudson River near Fort Orange. Van Rensselaer intended that the nucleus of his agricultural colony be on the east side of the Hudson, but in 1631 some settlers reoccupied the vicinity of the fort. In 1648 the director of Rensselaerswijck, Brant van Slichtenhorst, granted building lots to nonagricultural settlers on the west side of the river near the protection of the fort, giving them access to the fur trade. The director general of New Netherland, Petrus Stuyvesant (1647–64), objected and ordered all building stopped within 3,000 feet (915 m) of the fort. The dispute between the two men lasted until 1652, when the company's jurisdiction around the fort was proclaimed by ordinance. In April 1652 an Inferior Court of Justice was established at Fort Orange and the adjacent village of Beverwijck, the fur trading entrepôt of the colony and core of the city of Albany. Beverwijck residents were a diverse group occupationally, including farmers, sawyers, brewers, millers, shoemakers, blacksmiths, carpenters, gunstock makers, bakers, tailors, and coopers. Equally diverse were their countries of origin. Most were from the Netherlands, and Germans were the largest minority group, with significant populations from Norway, Sweden, England, France, Ireland, Scotland, the Spanish Netherlands, and Africa. This was a commercial town, geared to fur trading and other enterprises such as brick and tile making and lumbering. The river trade increased as boats hauled commodities from Beverwijck and grain from Esopus [now Kingston, Ulster Co] for sale in Manhattan to be shipped abroad and returned with goods from the Netherlands and Manhattan for sale in Beverwijck. This carrying trade continued and expanded under the English. The village flourished and grew fairly rapidly. In 1652 Beverwijck had 100 houses and close to 370 people; by 1657 the minister counted "a potential" of 600 people for the church and 120 houses with others "springing up daily." A reasonable estimate of the 1660 population is 1,000.

When the English took possession of the colony in 1664, Beverwijck was renamed Albany after the colony's proprietor, James, Duke of York and Albany. Initially there was little ethnic or governmental change in the community. In 1673 the Dutch took back the colony for 14 months and renamed the community Willemstadt, and the fort, Fort Nassau. With the arrival of Gov Edmund Andros in 1674 the name Albany was restored, and the English legal and governmental system was imposed more extensively. In 1676 the English built a fort on the high ground above the settlement and garrisoned it with soldiers recruited in Europe and paid by the province. Some English and Irish newcomers married Dutch women, and soldiers became Albany's first English-speaking population.

The Landscape

Beverwijck developed approximately 200 feet (60 m) west of the Hudson River floodplain and east of a hill, a major defining feature of the area. The village had two main thoroughfares. Joncker St [now State St] ran east-west and bisected the community. It ended at Court and Market Sts [now Broadway], which paralleled the river. The site was crossed by three watercourses, the Beverkil, Ruttenkil, and Vossenkil (Fox Kill), which cut the hillside and flowed into the Hudson. In the 17th and 18th centuries the most substantial structures were built between these streams on high ground, along the present-day State St and generally between Madison and Clinton Aves. By 1800 the riverfront was filled in, creating several blocks for commercial use. The three streams created wetlands and inhibited development, but beginning in the 1790s drainage became more effective and streams were channeled through culverts into the Hudson. The few lakes within city limits resulted from damming streams. As the terrain was modified for housing, development commenced along Broadway, Pearl St, and new cross streets running west, ultimately merging into what are now Washington, Western, and Central Aves.

Albany's soils are chiefly dense clay, but an area known in the 18th century as the Pine Barrens has sandy soils, which were deposited by postglacial rivers during the last period of the Ice Age; it originally extended from the State Capitol west to Rte 155. In 1988 the legislature created the Albany Pine Bush Preserve Commission to protect what was left of this rare ecosystem. It includes 2,750 acres (1,113 ha) and has mostly pitch pines, scrub oaks, and specialized communities of grasses, shrubs, and herbs.

Colonial and Revolutionary Albany

Gov Thomas Dongan granted Albany a municipal charter on 22 July 1686, establishing the city as the colony's second incorporated entity. The Dongan Charter defined boundaries and set up a municipal political structure that included a Common Council, giving Albany control over internal affairs. It endowed the city with substantial privileges, including the sole right to negotiate with local Native Americans (chiefly through the fur trade) and rights to channel exports from the upper Hudson Valley region, and gave it investment lands at Fort Hunter [now in Montgomery Co] and Schaghticoke [now in Rensselaer Co]. City officials were appointed by the governor, and prominent fur trader Pieter Schuyler was named first mayor. After the Revolutionary War the Council of Appointment named city officers. The city was divided into three wards, each served by locally elected aldermen, assistants, firemasters, and constables. The charter also fixed the city's boundaries: the east boundary was, of course, the river; the north boundary was just beyond the Foxenkill; the southern boundary was approximately a half mile south of the former location of Fort Orange; and the western boundary was 16 miles (26 km) from the river. The Dutch Reformed Church was constructed in the middle of Albany's main intersection of Joncker, Court, and Market Sts. The 1679 census counted 143 households, and the 1697 census enumerated 714 persons, although the census data may not have included transients living in Albany. The city's population grew slowly, with 1,128 recorded in 1714 and an estimated 1,500 by 1750. The city was the site of the 1754 Albany Congress and was designated British military headquarters during the French and Indian War. In 1756 a British inventory counted more than 330 structures in the community. The war brought large numbers of soldiers, opportunists, and émigrés to Albany.

Two decades later, frustrated by British restrictions on trade and development, most of the community's leaders supported the Revolutionary cause and took the lead in persuading rank-and-file citizenry to do the same. They rooted out tories and would-be neutrals throughout Albany Co. During the Revolutionary War, merchants were major suppliers to the army, and with a significant military hospital Albany became a center for medicine. Members of almost every city household participated in the war effort or the home-front infrastructure. Native sons Gen Philip Schuyler and Gen Abraham Ten Broeck were the most prominent of the dozens of Albany men who served as officers with the patriot forces. After the war Albany's population increased, the growth fueled by an influx of newcomers from New England along with others from states to the south and from Europe. At the same time many members of the community's founding families moved to western New York State and the Old Northwest. The city's population reached 3,498 in 1790, when the slave population peaked at 572.

Economic Development

From its earliest days, Albany's main enterprises have been commerce, service, government, and education. The city had a viable production economy, particularly repair and refurbishing of boats. After the Revolution, home-based businesses and trades gave way as enterprises began to employ wage laborers in workshops, warehouses, and yards. By 1800 small factories and processing complexes were established along streams north and south of the city. By 1823 an island pier was constructed in the Hudson, and the 8-acre (3.2 ha) space was lined with storehouses. The water between the shore and the pier was called the Albany Basin. Over the next century the industrial revolution created a production economy, and larger factories and plants were opened north and south of the city core. They included coach, sleigh, and iron factories, and distilleries. State St and Broadway were reserved for banking, legal services, and government-related enterprises. The Bank of Albany (incorporated 1792) opened on Broadway in 1795. Printing, publishing, and brewing became leading enterprises in the early 1800s, while heavy industry gravitated more to the other cities of the Capital District. Irish and German immigrants established piano and iron factories, and North Albany was home to a major cut stone business. Important enterprises in the South End in the early 20th century included cigar, baseball, and shirt factories, which used immigrant labor.

Albany was the northernmost port on the Hudson River and the only place where cargoes could be loaded from vessels onto wagons for shipment into the interior, and furs, grains, and lumber were collected at Albany and shipped to New York City and beyond. Albany sloops dominated the river trade while cross-river transit was provided by ferries and small boats. After 1763 roads radiating from Albany were improved as Watervliet, Bethlehem, New Scotland, and Guilderland (Albany Co) became more populated. Before the 1780s even the main thoroughfare, the King's Highway to Schenectady, was little more than a trail worn through dense undergrowth. Around 1800 the first turnpikes enabled newcomers to travel westward, while city streets were improved and extended to serve growing residential and business needs. Robert Fulton's first steamboat trip to Albany in 1807 ushered in a new era of transportation, and steam power quickly eclipsed sail on the Hudson for both freight and passengers. Completion of the Champlain (1823) and Erie (1825) Canals intensified Albany's role as a transportation interchange and created a major service industry of its own. Over the next century hundreds of steamboats, steam tugs, and sail-driven vessels carried passengers and cargoes from the ocean to Albany. Freight was stored on the waterfront and then reloaded for overland, canal, or rail transit.

The Mohawk and Hudson Railroad's *De Witt Clinton,* which embarked from Madison Ave for Schenectady on 24 Sept 1831, launched a new transportation era that made Albany a railroad hub, interchange, and train-building center. The New York Central Railroad established its headquarters in Albany in 1853 and was the most important railroad for over a century. Its West Albany repair shops and stockyards occupied 350 acres (142 ha) and provided jobs for hundreds of residents during that period. The shops included 10 buildings for engine fabrication and repair. By 1850 the stockyard was said to be the largest depot for cows, sheep, and pigs in the nation. One thousand carloads of cattle arrived weekly by 1866, leading to the establishment of meatpacking businesses nearby, which were major industries until the 1880s. Because railroad tracks were constructed along the waterfront, the river was inaccessible by the end of the Civil War. Trains replaced water and road transportation for most long-distance travel by the 1870s. Albany began to turn away from the river, and new construction was aligned to the railroads rather than the water.

Public transportation began in 1862 when private companies formed to equip the city with horse-drawn streetcars. They were supplanted by electric streetcars beginning in 1888. In 1915 bus service was initiated, and the last electric trolleys ceased running in 1949. Bus companies folded into the Capital District Transportation Authority (CDTA) in 1970, which provides public transportation in Albany, Schenectady, Rensselaer, and Saratoga Cos. In 2003 CDTA served 350,000 customers daily with a fleet of 250 vehicles. The city is served by the Albany International Airport in Colonie (1928; originally Albany Municipal Airport).

Politics

Since the late 1700s Albany has been a political center, and municipal and state governments have been important sources of employment. The legislature first met in Albany in January 1780, but sessions were also held in New York City, Kingston, and Poughkeepsie. Beginning in 1797 state government met solely in Albany, although it was not officially designated as the state capital until 1971. State leaders met first in Albany's City Hall and then in the first State Capitol (1809) at Public Square, on Eagle St. The capitol housed the municipal government until a new city hall was built in 1829. The growth of state government in the 1840s and 1850s made the existing statehouse inadequate. Work began on a new building in 1867. It opened in part in 1879, although it was not finished until 1897.

Municipal government was established by the 1686 charter, and during the 17th and early 18th centuries the mayor, recorder (assistant mayor), and three Common Council members managed city affairs. The Common Council had authority to enact laws while the mayor oversaw operations. The governor appointed Albany's mayor until 1821, when that privilege was given to the city's aldermen. The first public mayoral election was in 1840. By 1821 the Common Council had 10 elected members, one for each city ward. The Albany Regency, a group of Democrats, dominated Albany politics in the 1830s, but by the 1840s, with the influence of powerful newspaper editor Thurlow Weed, Albany was considered predominantly a Whig city. After the collapse of the Whigs in the 1850s, the Democrats, bolstered by a large Irish population, dominated city politics for the remainder of the century. Only four Republicans held seats in municipal government between 1856 and 1898. In 1899 the Republican Party, running as reformers, took power in the city, led by Thurlow Weed's grandson, William J. Barnes Jr, publisher of the *Albany Evening Journal.* He permitted many Democratic officeholders to change parties and retain their positions. Barnes's operation soon became indistinguishable from other urban machines. In 1921 Barnes was ousted by a Democratic coalition led by the O'Connell and Corning families. Behind-the-scenes leader Daniel P. O'Connell orchestrated countywide patronage-based operations until his death in 1977, while Erastus Corning 2d served as mayor of Albany for 42 years until his 1983 death, the longest mayoral term in the country.

The 1686 charter was revised in 1998 and the revision adopted by referendum. In the early 21st century, municipal government and services are well established. Numerous departments as well as professional police and firefighting forces serve the city's 15 wards and provide essential services, constituting an important element of the city's workforce. In 2004 city government consisted of 4 elected officials, the mayor, treasurer, comptroller, and treasurer; 15 elected Common Council members, 1 from each ward; and an elected council president. The Common Council has legislative authority and passes municipal laws and ordinances, and the mayor oversees all departments, which in 2004 numbered nine, along with a housing and parking authority and the Albany Port District Commission. The newest municipal divisions include Economic Development and Neighborhood Revitalization.

Religion and Culture

The Dutch Reformed Church (now First Church) is the oldest congregation, formed in 1642. For much of the church's first 150 years, most Albany families received spiritual comfort there, and it was the community's premier social institution. The Episcopal Church dates to the formation of

St. Peter's Anglican parish, established in 1708 to serve garrison soldiers and other residents of English background. Lutheran services were held in German beginning in the mid-1650s, although a minister did not permanently reside in Albany until after the Revolution. Scottish traders built a Presbyterian meeting house in the 1760s. St. Mary's was founded in 1797, the second Roman Catholic Church in the state. By 1813 Albany had 10 Christian churches. The first synagogue was incorporated as Congregation Beth El in 1838. In 1846 Rabbi Isaac Mayer Wise, later a founder of American Reform Judaism, came to the Beth El pulpit. The first Albany Masonic Lodge has operated continuously since 1768.

The Albany Institute of History and Art had its origins in 1791. The Albany Public Library, formed in 1790, provides a range of services at five locations throughout the city. The New York State Museum (1836), the New York State Library (1818), and the New York State Archives (1971) have been housed in the Cultural Education Center since 1978. Scottish brothers Alexander and James Robertson were Albany's first printers; they published the *Albany Gazette* in 1771. After the Revolution, the *Gazette* (1784–1817) was reborn and other papers followed. The *Albany Argus* (1813–25, 1828–56), the *Albany Evening Journal* (1830–1925), and the *Knickerbocker News* (1937–88) were nationally known. Albany's only remaining daily newspaper is the *Times-Union* (1891).

Education

Albany has long educated lawyers and physicians. The city's military army hospital (built by 1757) became a center for medical education during the French and Indian and Revolutionary Wars because Albany was a hub for military operations. Professional training was formalized with the establishment of Albany Medical College (1839) and Albany Law School (1851), which became part of Union University in 1873. The State Normal School (1844) was created to educate teachers and, in 1948, became part of the SUNY system, which is headquartered in the former Delaware and Hudson Building on Broadway. Other institutions of higher learning within the city are the Albany College of Pharmacy (1881), the College of Saint Rose (1920), Sage Colleges (1957), and Maria College (1958). Medical care and research facilities are major employers and include Albany Medical Center (1849), St. Peter's Hospital (1869), and the Stratton VA Medical Center (1951). The Albany City Free Dispensary (1868), a homeopathic hospital, is now Albany Memorial Hospital.

For children, a schoolmaster was present in Beverwijck in 1657, and Gov Richard Nicolls licensed an English schoolmaster for Albany in 1665 and a Dutch schoolmaster in 1670. Albany's first important private school, Albany Academy, opened in 1780 and was granted a charter in 1813; it counts many distinguished men among its graduates, including novelist Herman Melville and scientist Joseph Henry. Education remained private for many years with 19 male and female teachers listed in the first city directory published in 1813. Public education began with the establishment of a Lancasterian School (1812–36). In 1822 a total of 50 schools, both public and private and including an African Free School, were operating in the city. A common school system was at last established in 1830. The Free Academy opened in 1868, becoming Albany High School in 1873. Today Albany is served by a dozen public elementary schools, two middle schools, a high school, two charter schools, and private schools.

With Albany's large Catholic population, parish schools and parochial high schools were opened beginning in 1829. Once numbering as many as 20, they educated thousands of city children until low enrollment and financial difficulties forced many to close during the 1970s. Christian Brothers Academy operated in the city from 1859 to 1998 when it moved to Colonie. In the early 21st century only the Academy of Holy Names, Bishop Maginn High School, and seven Catholic grade schools remain. The interfaith Doane Stuart School, founded in 1852 as Kenwood Academy, and nonsectarian Albany Girls Academy round out the city's educational network.

Neighborhoods

Following the French and Indian War, settlement spread north along the river into a part of Rensselaerswijck known as Watervliet, which held almost twice as many people as the city in 1790. That area was an important part of Albany's economy and was annexed by the city in 1815. It later became a close-knit Irish American neighborhood known as North Albany. After 1790 Albany lost some of its peripheral lands, including tracts at Schaghticoke and Fort Hunter, that had been in the original city charter. Along the river, factories, warehouses, and lumberyards were established around the Van Rensselaer Manor House. The south part of Albany was developed after the Dutch Reformed Church began selling its pastures in 1791, and following the death of Gen Philip Schuyler in 1804, his heirs sold property surrounding his mansion. By the early 1800s the area was residential, and houses filled in the newly platted streets. For more than a century, the South End became a first home for thousands of Albany newcomers and included the city's first free Black enclave, established by 1810 along South Pearl St.

The city population was 5,289 in 1800 and increased to 33,721 by 1840, when Albany was the ninth largest city in the country. This increase came chiefly from immigrants who settled the South End from Ireland and Germany, the latter group including Albany's first substantial Jewish population. As immigrants settled, they influenced long-standing residents to relocate to the western portion of the city, a process that continued into the late 1920s. In 1870 Albany acquired two large tracts, north and south of the city, and both were developed as working-class neighborhoods. The area north of Central Ave was developed for employees of the New York Central Railroad shops, and another part along the river was developed for people who worked in the lumberyards. The south part of the city was called Groesbeckville in the 1860s and extended to Second Ave; it was developed for those who worked in South End factories. An intricate network of horse-drawn trolleys connected all neighborhoods by 1880.

Because of immigration Albany's population had reached nearly 100,000 by end of the 19th century. Settlement followed the Great Western Turnpike (US 20) and the Schenectady Rd (Rte 5) as immigrants settled along what was called the Bowery (along Central Ave) or far away from the river. By 1900 multifamily houses were built on most Albany streets to the west near Allen St. On the north side Arbor Hill (named for the grape arbors at Gen Ten Broeck's 1798 mansion) and the West End provided city homes and a sense of community for immigrant workers in the West Albany shops and in the lumber district. Businesses and institutions along Northern Blvd and Watervliet Ave served ethnic neighborhoods. By the early 20th century, the Albany Basin was becoming obsolete. Electric trolley lines connected uptown residences with the factories, shops, and downtown shopping district. By 1910 there were distinct ethnic neighborhoods. In Arbor Hill, Polish and eastern European immigrants found homes between the railroad and lumberyards. Downtown had individual ethnic neighborhoods, including Little Italy, west of South Pearl along Grand St. Jews lived east of South Pearl near Ferry, and Germans lived in what was called Kraut Town, north of Central in the vicinity of Lexington Ave. Uptown or western settlement began in 1900 and included areas in Pine Hills, along Madison Ave, Washington and New Scotland Aves (Helderberg Heights), southwest along Whitehall Rd, and south along Delaware Ave. Urban architectural styles were modified to accommodate one or two families on lots that sometimes included substantial yards. These were occupied by South Enders and Northsiders who moved uptown and by newcomers (particularly Italians) who sought to work and farm close to family members.

Immigration prompted the city to annex tracts north and west of Washington Park in 1910 and 1916, and two southern areas in 1916. All were developed for housing. Along the river 200 acres (81 ha) were annexed in 1926 to develop the Albany Port District, which opened June 1932. Substantial immigration from southern and eastern Europe took place during the first two decades of the 20th century. The ethnic composition of the city has changed in recent decades as well, with the arrival of many immigrants from India, Pakistan, and elsewhere in Asia, and the growth of the Latino population. In 2000 Albany's population was 63% white, 28% African American, and 3% Asian. Six percent of the population was of Latino heritage.

Decline and Revival

In 1950, during Erastus Corning 2d's tenure, Albany reached its peak population of 134,995. Suburbanization had begun in the 1920s, when the popularity of the automobile and the construction of roads opened the countryside to personal travel. The Dunn Memorial Bridge (1932, rebuilt 1969) improved automobile access to Rensselaer Co. After World War II buses replaced trolleys, and automobiles became increasingly widespread. Rail service continued at Albany's Union Station until 1968, when the station was moved to Rensselaer. In 1967 work began on the network of arterial highways and beltways that now facilitate access to the city from all directions. The Town of Bethlehem deeded parcels to Albany for I-787 (north-south) and I-90 (east-west) in 1967 and 1977. These interstate road and the Arterial (Rtes 85 and 85A) south to Delmar made it easier to get in and out of the city and increased suburban growth.

Albany Co grew in population because many residents moved to the suburbs, but the city's population declined to 94,301 by 1990. Retail businesses relocated, away from the once vibrant

Flooding on Broadway, Albany, 1913.

Pearl St shopping district, first to Westgate and Stuyvesant Plazas and then to larger shopping malls such as Colonie Center and Crossgates Mall. Highways made numerous strip malls in the surrounding suburbs easily accessible. The children of immigrants were able to escape downtown urban decline for western Albany, Colonie, and other suburban towns. During the 1950s and 1960s another burst of residential construction filled in marginal lots that had been bypassed earlier with suburban-style housing, while urban renewal replaced deteriorated buildings with high-rise public housing in the South End and in Arbor Hill. Since then, more appealing low-income apartments and townhouses have replaced many of the old "projects." By the end of the century, with the number of viable building lots fast decreasing, residential development had extended to the city's outermost borders along Washington Ave Extension, where new housing is located alongside new office buildings and a small African American community in the Rapp Road National Historic District (2003).

In the second half of the 20th century, Albany lost much of its industrial base. The state government solidified its position as the city's largest employer. In 1930 state operations were centralized in the Alfred E. Smith State Office Building, a 34-story skyscraper. As the scope of state government expanded during the mid–20th century, the 12-building W. Averell Harriman State Office Campus (1954) was built on a 350-acre (142 ha) tract in the western part of the city. The massive Empire State Plaza, later renamed for its chief sponsor, Gov Nelson A. Rockefeller, opened in 1977. Its construction required the leveling of some 40 city blocks in a residential and commercial neighborhood adjacent to downtown. Although the project had (and has) many critics, it redefined the surrounding neighborhood and, as the plaza filled, satellite agency buildings were constructed in the western part of the city. As a result, the number of state workers in Albany increased, totaling over 20,000 in 2001.

The historic preservation movement in the 1970s helped restore the downtown Pastures, Mansion Hill, and Center Square districts. A number of 19th-century buildings on Broadway and along Clinton and Madison Aves were also restored and adapted to modern use. The Empire State Convention Center and the Albany County Civic Center (opened 1989; now Pepsi Arena) provide venues for large popular events. Around the turn of the 21st century, urban revitalization has focused on the downtown area and has led to the opening of new attractions, making Albany an increasingly appealing destination for conventions, meetings, and cultural tourism. New garages have reduced a chronic parking problem. The proliferation of neighborhood associations and the politicization of quality-of-life issues in every part of the city have worked to stem Albany's half century of population loss.

The new millennium brought a significant change for Albany when, in 2002, Gov George E. Pataki announced that International Sematech, a consortium of nanotechnology firms, would build a microchip plant on the SUNY Albany campus. The first workers arrived in 2003. It was anticipated that, in addition to conducting research that would position the city as a center of technology, the plant would attract other computer-based industries. Within months Tokyo Electron announced its plans for a research and development facility near Sematech.

See also AFRICAN AMERICANS; SUBURBANIZATION; TURNPIKES; WATER SUPPLY AND USE (NON–NEW YORK CITY WATERSHED).

Barbagallo, Tricia, Cynthia Sauer, and John Warren. *Albany, New York: Historic Crossroads, State Capital, City of Neighborhoods* (Albany: National Council on Public History, 1997)

Colonial Albany Social History Project, http://www.nysm.nysed.gov/albany

Grondahl, Paul. *Mayor Erastus Corning: Albany Icon, Albany Enigma* (Albany: Washington Park Press, 1997)

Howell, George Rogers, and Jonathan Tenney. *The Bicentennial History of the County of Albany, NY, from 1609 to 1886* (New York: W. W. Munsell, 1886)

Hughes, Mirian I. *Refusing Ignorance: The Struggle to Educate Black Children in Albany, New York, 1816–1873* (Albany: Mount Ida Press, 1998)

Kennedy, William. *O Albany!* (New York: Viking Press, 1983)

McEneny, John J. *Albany: Capital City on the Hudson* (1981; repr Sun Valley, Calif: American Historical Press, 1998)

Munsell, Joel, comp. *Annals of Albany* (Albany: Author, 1850–59)

———. *Collections on the History of Albany* (Albany: Author, 1865–71)

Rittner, Don. *Images of America: Albany* (Charleston, SC: Arcadia, 2000)

Shattuck, Martha Dickinson. *A Civil Society: Court and Community in Beverwijck, New Netherland* (Lincoln: Univ of Nebraska Press, forthcoming)

Tantillo, L. F. *Visions of New York State: The Historical Paintings of Len Tantillo* (Wappingers Falls, NY: Shawangunk Press, 1996)

Venema, Janny. *Beverwijck: A Dutch Village on the American Frontier, 1652–1664* (Albany: SUNY Press, 2003)

Weise, Arthur, J. *The History of the City of Albany* (Albany: E. H. Bender, 1884)

Stefan Bielinski

Albany College of Pharmacy. Private, coeducational institution founded in 1881 as the Department of Pharmacy of Union University, a federation of autonomous institutions established in 1873 and associated with Union College in Schenectady. It is the state's oldest continuously operating pharmaceutical college. The college's program has reflected state and national changes in pharmacy practice and education. In 1904 New York was the first state to require that all candidates for licensure be graduates of a college of pharmacy. Originally located on Eagle St in Albany, the first major expansion occurred in 1927 with the construction of a new building on nearby New Scotland Ave. Over the years the college expanded its initial two-year curriculum, becoming a six-year PharmD program in 1998. By the late 1990s the college also was a partner in the University Heights Association, a consortium of four colleges developing a 31-acre (13 ha) shared campus. The college is unusual among colleges of pharmacy in that it is private, has a wide range of science and liberal arts courses in addition to professional courses, and maintains a strong sports program. The college offers a BS in pharmaceutical science, the doctor of pharmacy, PharmD, and the nontraditional doctor of pharmacy program for licensed pharmacists. In 2002 the college enrolled 670 students with 64.5% women and 35.5% men. A restoration of the Throop Drugstore (1800) of Schoharie (Schoharie Co) is located in the college's main building.

Albany College of Pharmacy, http://www.acp.edu

Kenneth J. Blume

Albany Congress. In June and July 1754, delegates from the British colonies of New York, Massachusetts, New Hampshire, Connecticut, Rhode Island, Pennsylvania, and Maryland met in Albany to negotiate a treaty with the Iroquois Confederacy and to form a plan for greater intercolonial cooperation. The catalyst for the congress was a speech Mohawk chief Hendrick had made a year earlier, when he declared the Covenant Chain alliance between the Iroquois Confederacy and the British broken because the New Yorkers had been neglecting their diplomatic obligations to his people.

After hearing of Hendrick's speech, the British Crown called for a general treaty with the Iroquois, bringing an unprecedented number of colonial representatives to Albany in 1754. In the ensuing negotiations, the visiting colonial delegations teamed up with William Johnson to form an alliance against Lt Gov James DeLancey's management of Indian affairs. Three years earlier Johnson had resigned as New York's Indian agent to challenge the authority that the New York Colony governor and Albany merchants traditionally held over the Covenant Chain. Working with Hendrick and the Mohawks, the delegates negotiated a restoration of the alliance that rested on a generous donation of goods and the understanding that Johnson would be reinstated as their agent. The following year Johnson was appointed superintendent of Indian Affairs, after which the locus of Anglo-Iroquois diplomacy shifted from Albany to Fort Johnson [now in Montgomery Co].

While in Albany the delegates also drafted a plan for colonial union, intended to improve financial and military coordination between the colonies. The Albany Plan of Union called for an intercolonial grand council, to be presided over by a president general appointed by the Crown. Among its constitutional innovations, the plan provided for the intercolonial administration of western lands, frontier defenses, Indian affairs, and even taxation imposed by the council. Pennsylvania delegate Benjamin Franklin was the plan's chief author and advocate, but it was soundly rejected by the colonial assemblies and British ministry in 1755. Some scholars have claimed that the Albany Plan of Union was modeled after the Iroquois Confederacy, but there is no evidence in any contemporary source that Franklin or his fellow delegates received advice from or consulted with the Indians present at the Albany Congress as they drafted and debated the plan.

Jennings, Francis. *Empire of Fortune: Crowns, Colonies, and Tribes in the Seven Years War in America* (New York: Norton, 1988)

Shannon, Timothy J. *Indians and Colonists at the Crossroads of Empire: The Albany Congress of 1754* (Ithaca: Cornell Univ Press; Cooperstown, NY: NYS Historical Association, 2000)

Timothy J. Shannon

Albany County (523 mi²/1,355 km²; pop 294,565). The county was created on 1 Nov 1683, confirmed 1 Oct 1691 as one of the original 12 counties, and named for King James II's earlier title, Duke of York and Albany. It originally encompassed the entirety of the state north of Ulster and Dutchess Cos and the entire state of Vermont. Two counties now in Vermont, Cumberland and Gloucester, were formed in 1766 and 1770, respectively, from parts of Albany Co. In 1772 Tryon and Charlotte Cos [now Montgomery and Washington Cos] were taken off. Further removals and subdivisions created Columbia Co in 1786, Rensselaer and Saratoga Cos in 1791, and Schenectady Co in 1809. Other portions were taken in the creation of Schoharie Co in 1795 and of Greene Co in 1800. Albany Co is subdivided into 3 cities and 10 towns that contain 6 incorporated villages. Albany, the state capital, serves as county seat.

Elevation ranges from less than 70 feet (21 m) above sea level along the Hudson River to over 2,160 feet (658 m) on an unnamed summit just south of Triangle Lake in the Town of Rensselaerville. Albany Co lies within two physiographic provinces. The northeastern half is in the Hudson Valley subregion of the Hudson-Mohawk Lowland; more specifically, the area is part of the Glacial Lake Albany sand plain. Elevations increase from the Hudson to roughly 400 feet (120 m) at the base of the steep Helderberg Escarpment except in the far west, where it rises to over 800 feet (240 m). The sand plain's average elevation is 300 feet (90 m), and relief is modest; but there are a number of well-preserved shoreline features, such as deltas and beach strands. Sand deposits are typically less than 50 ft (15 m) deep and cover Ordovician-age bedrock of sandstones (graywackes) and shales. The Helderberg Hills subregion of the Appalachian Upland extends behind the imposing escarpment, which rises 1,300 feet (400 m) above sea level. Sometimes referred to as mountains, the Helderbergs consist of a series of cuestas facing north-northeast with very gentle, southwest slopes. The cuestas are dissected by several narrow, steep-walled through valleys. The escarpment is composed of Devonian age limestone, and the bedrock beyond is Devonian sandstone and shale. The Wisconsinan glaciation was the most recent of at least four such periods that covered the region with a thick mantle of ice. Besides the sand plain, other glacial-related features include an exceptionally thick layer of till and a series of drumlins in the Helderberg region. With one partial exception, Albany Co lies entirely within the Hudson River watershed. That exception is an area drained by Fox Creek and its tributaries that empty into Schoharie Creek and then the Mohawk River, which enters the Hudson at Cohoes. Three major streams flow southeast directly into the Hudson: Normans Kill, Hannacrois Creek, and Catskill Creek. With limited exception the county's soil is not especially well suited to support modern commercial agriculture.

Albany Co's climate is humid-continental. Mean January temperatures range from 21°F (-6°C) at the Alcove Reservoir in the south to 23°F (-5°C) near Cohoes. Winter lows can be expected to fall below 0°F (-18°C) a few times every year. Mean July temperatures range from less than 70°F (21°C) in the southwest to 73°F (23°C) in the far northeast. Daytime highs reach 90°F (32°C) at least a few times each year. Average annual precipitation amounts range from 38 inches (97 cm) in the northeast to 41 inches (104 cm) at the Alcove Reservoir in the south. Higher amounts are estimated to fall in the southwest. Seasonal snowfall totals vary from 41 inches (104 cm) near Cohoes to over 80 inches (203 cm) in the Helderbergs. Primeval forest cover consisted of three communities. Central hardwoods dominated by beech, sugar maple, and basswood occupied the eastern third of the county; dwarf oak and pitch pine covered much of the sand plain between the present cities of Albany and Schenectady; the rest of the county was covered by Alleghenian hardwoods where beech, sugar maple, hemlock, white pine, and basswood were the dominant species.

Settlement

During the first years of European contact, the present Albany Co was occupied by the Mohican (Mahican), an Algonquian-speaking people. To the west were the Mohawk, the easternmost nation of the Iroquois Confederacy. There were at least two clashes between these peoples, in 1626 and 1628, the second resulting in the Mohican abandoning the west side of the river and many, if not most, relocating to what became Stockbridge, Mass. Land titles derive principally from purchases made from the Mohican.

Henry Hudson, an Englishman employed by the Dutch East India Co, anchored just north of present-day Albany for four days in September 1609. His positive reports on the availability of

ALBANY CO POPULATION CENSUS FIGURES

	White	Nonwhite	Total Population	Foreign-Born
1790	71,642	4,094	75,736	—
1800	31,882	2,161	34,043	—
1810	33,023	1,638	34,661	—
1820	36,845	1,271	38,116	321
1830	51,925	1,595	53,520	3,552
1840	67,279	1,314	68,593	—
1850	92,085	1,194	93,279	27,444
1860	112,979	938	113,917	34,288
1870	131,957	1,095	133,052	39,314
1880	153,510	1,380	154,890	37,977
1890	163,122	1,433	164,555	37,267
1900	164,013	1,558	165,571	31,531
1910	172,392	1,274	173,666	32,764
1920	184,497	1,609	186,106	29,395
1930	209,093	2,860	211,953	29,760
1940	217,806	3,509	221,315	25,050
1950	233,100	6,286	239,386	20,924
1960	261,414	11,512	272,926	18,256
1970	269,945	16,797	286,742	15,902
1980	262,779	23,130	285,909	15,849
1990	260,692	31,902	292,594	16,127
2000	245,060	49,505	294,565	19,228

Notes: "Nonwhite" includes African Americans, Asians, American Indians, and Pacific Islanders and, for 2000, also the mixed race and other race categories. Through the 1960 census these figures primarily reflect the African American population. Foreign-born figures for 1820 and 1830 include only those not naturalized, and for 1930 and 1950, the foreign-born totals include Whites only. Other years include all foreign-born in the population.

furs encouraged Dutch fur traders to visit the area regularly beginning in 1611 and to establish the trading posts of Fort Nassau [now Port of Albany] (1614) and Fort Orange [now Albany] (1624). Permanent settlement began in 1630 with the founding of the colony of Rensselaerswijck [now in Albany, Columbia, and Rensselaer Cos], which surrounded Fort Orange. Following the 1664 English takeover, some English settled in the area and, as time passed, grew in numbers. Palatine Germans arrived from 1710 until the Revolutionary War, settling particularly in Guilderland and New Scotland. Population growth in Albany Co was relatively slow at first. The 1698 census counted 1,476 residents, increasing to 2,273 by 1703 and to 5,693 by 1723. Rural areas remained somewhat isolated. Dutch and German were usually spoken in homes, shops, and churches.

Albany was the staging area for colonial expeditions against Canada during the four wars between France and Britain, bringing soldiers and merchants from other colonies and from Great Britain into both the city and its surrounding areas. There was a rapid population increase in the county in the middle decades of the 18th century: from 14,805 in 1756 to 38,829 in 1771. Many soldiers and merchants settled in the 1760s following the last colonial war. The first federal census in 1790 listed 75,736 residents and, in 1800, in a much smaller territory close to the current boundaries, 34,043.

Revolutionary and Early National Period

During the Revolutionary War period the territory between Albany and military headquarters at Cohoes was (as it had been during the French and Indian War) an assembly point for armies and their suppliers and civilian support, this time preparing for war against British and loyalist forces from Canada. This activity, together with investigation of persons of uncertain loyalty by the Albany County Committee of Safety, kept loyalist sentiment to a minimum. Several prominent individuals, notably Albany mayor Abraham C. Cuyler, were arrested in 1776 by the Committee of Safety and sent to the prison for loyalists in Hartford, Conn. Thereafter, such loyalist sentiment tended to be in the farther reaches of Rensselaerswijck and just beyond its borders.

Following the war, many people who had come to Albany in connection with war efforts elected to stay. To this number was added the many land-starved New Englanders who took up leaseholds in Rensselaerswijck, which grew from 500 farms in 1750 to 3,400 by 1800. The territory of Rensselaerswyck Manor was made a district in 1772; after the Revolution the portion west of the Hudson River became the West Manor, which in 1788 became the Town of Watervliet [now Colonie].

Transportation

Albany, with its natural port on the Hudson River, has been an international port for four centuries. In colonial times, waterways separated by short portages allowed trade with Montreal, while the Mohawk River brought trade from the interior, and the Hudson carried goods to and from New York and beyond. Because of sandbars in the river, traffic was generally restricted to shallow-draft craft. In 1795 there were about 90 commercial sloops operating between New York and Albany, and by 1848 there were 331 sloops and 284 schooners engaged in trade.

Albany was the principal gateway to the west, but in the colonial period the few roads that existed were poor. Several turnpikes starting in Albany were in operation in 1805, with stagecoach service by 1811. The Champlain Canal (1823) extended direct water travel into northern New York and Canada and diverted trade away from Lower Canada [now Que]. Two years later the Erie Canal extended water traffic west to the Great Lakes, opening up trade with the Midwest.

The Mohawk and Hudson Railroad began regular service in 1831 between Albany and Schenectady, allowing travelers and, later, shippers to circumvent the Erie Canal's first 18 time-consuming locks. Railroads were soon crisscrossing Albany Co, and communities developed around the stations as they had on the turnpikes wherever there was sufficient distance between destinations to require a way station: two railroads were built in 1863 through Altamont, already a popular stopping place on the Schoharie Rd. With the county's first railroad bridge across the Hudson in 1866 opening the route east to Boston and south to New York City and with track southwest to Binghamton completed in 1869, railroads, turnpikes, and waterways ran in every direction from Albany. In 1883 the West Shore Railroad linked Albany to Weehawken, NJ, with connections to New York City. Ports developed along the river at several places where there were products to ship and a reasonably good harbor. Winne's dock in Bethlehem shipped locally grown oats to feed New York City's horses, but most of the river traffic originated between Albany and Cohoes.

Economic Development

A number of Yankee merchants settled in the City of Albany in the late 18th and early 19th centuries. More fast paced than established business owners, they became community leaders and, by 1820, largely controlled Albany commerce and manufacturing. The principal manufacturing area was along the Hudson River from Albany north to Cohoes and included Menands, West Troy [now Watervliet], and Green Island. Albany's development in the post-Revolutionary period was based on its preeminent position in trade with the western part of the state via the Mohawk River and, later, the Erie Canal. Its importance increased as turnpikes and railroads radiated from Albany to the interior of the state and to New York, Boston, and Montreal.

As Albany grew it absorbed neighboring manufacturing communities in North Albany, West Albany, and northern Bethlehem (including Groesbeckville and two ironworks on Van Rensselaer Island). The lumber district in the North Albany area extended more than a mile along the river. West Albany had railroad repair shops and stockyards. Cohoes was an agricultural community until the completion of the Champlain and Erie Canals in 1823–25. By harnessing the waterpower produced by a series of power canals and the Cohoes Falls in the Mohawk River, Cohoes became a major industrial city supplying world markets but declined sharply after 1930. The present city of Watervliet similarly became a manufacturing community because of the canals. Watervliet Arsenal (1813) has produced ordnance for the US armed forces. Green Island was the site of extensive railroad shops beginning in 1840.

Towns elsewhere in the county also developed

POPULATIONS OF TOWNS AND CITIES, ALBANY CO

Town or City, Year Founded	1800	1840	1880	1920	1960	2000
Albany (city), 1686	5,289	33,721	90,758	113,344	129,726	95,658
Berne, 1795	3,486	3,740	2,616	1,371	1,542	2,846
Bethlehem, 1793	3,733	3,238	3,752	4,430	18,936	31,304
Coeymans, 1791	3,095	3,107	2,912	4,147	5,622	8,151
Cohoes (city), 1869	—	—	19,416	22,987	20,129	15,521
Colonie, 1788[a]	4,992	10,141	22,220	10,196	52,760	79,258
Green Island, 1896	—	—	—	4,411	3,533	2,278
Guilderland, 1803	—	2,790	3,459	3,117	16,710	32,688
Knox, 1822	—	2,143	1,694	975	1,320	2,647
New Scotland, 1832	—	2,912	3,251	2,470	5,818	8,626
Rensselaerville, 1790	4,560	3,705	2,488	1,345	1,232	1,915
Watervliet (city), 1896	—	—	—	16,073	13,917	10,207
Westerlo, 1815	—	3,096	2,324	1,240	1,681	3,466

Note: In 1800 Albany Co included the City of Schenectady and the Towns of Duanesburg and Princetown [now in Schenectady Co].

[a]Informally considered a district by 1767; made district of West Manor of Rensselaerswijck, 1779; recognized as town, 1788; named Watervliet 1788–1895.

industries, especially mills along their streams. Ice cutting on the Hudson was important for Coeymans and Bethlehem; icehouses in Coeymans were converted to mushroom-growing facilities after natural ice was eclipsed in the 20th century. From shortly after the Revolution until 1815, Guilderland had a glass factory, which was among the first in America. A Berne factory produced axes beginning about 1821. Knox and New Scotland had tanneries. Westerlo quarried flagstone. Rensselaerville with its many mills was the business and manufacturing hub for an agricultural region from the end of the Revolution until after 1910.

In the colonial period the great cash crop was wheat. The opening of the Erie Canal brought increased competition from western grain. After the 1830s the emphasis in farm products shifted to spring grains, dairying, stock raising, and gardening for the Troy and Albany markets. Present Colonie supplied milk to Albany. Farmers in Bethlehem shipped hay, straw, apples, and other farm products from Winne's dock, which was also a steamboat landing. As industrialization proceeded, farming declined. In 1880 Albany Co had 3,325 farms and in 1920, 3,000; but only 1,927 existed 10 years later, and 1,450 in 1950. In 1997 there were 181 full-time farms.

Immigration and Ethnicity

The settlers in the Dutch period represented many European nationalities, but the English in the 17th century sent primarily British and French subjects. In the 18th century, immigration into the county consisted largely of Germans, Scots, Scots-Irish, and English and, immediately after the Revolution, of New Englanders in both urban and rural areas. Sizable numbers of Irish arrived early in the 19th century, and many eventually settled in the City of Albany. Around midcentury its Irish, German, and Jewish populations grew dramatically. Beginning in the 1890s, there was a considerable immigration of Italian and Slavic people. Francophone Canadian immigration early in the 20th century was directed toward the mill towns of Cohoes, Watervliet, and Green Island.

One African is mentioned in the Rensselaerswijck records in 1646, possibly a Dutch West India Co employee or slave. By 1820 there were 1,271 African Americans in Albany Co, including 109 slaves in the city and 308 in the rest of the county. The county's black population in 1830, when all were free, was 1,595. Following emancipation, a rural black community developed near Beckers Corners in Bethlehem, where descendants still reside. In 1848 the Schuyler Steamboat Tow Line was started by Samuel Schuyler, an African American who became a wealthy and highly regarded member of the Albany business community.

The county's greatest growth came between 1820, when it had 38,116 residents, and 1880, when it had 154,890. The City of Albany was always the county's center of population. As the corridor from Albany to Cohoes became heavily industrialized in the late 19th century, the population became even more concentrated in the former. The wealthy of Albany had country homes as early as the 18th century, and as transportation improved, New York City and Albany city business owners created country estates in Guilderland and on the Helderberg Escarpment beginning about 1844. By the 1880s Altamont was a popular summer retreat, and Guilderland in general was a resort town. Suburbanization began in the last quarter of the 19th century with the advent of regularly scheduled streetcar service. Loudonville and Menands became suburban early in the 20th century; although the Village of Colonie was agricultural, it had close ties to the urban industrial areas and quickly became suburbanized.

Religion, Education, and Culture

Under the Dutch, public worship was restricted to the Reformed Church, with Lutherans and Roman Catholics meeting clandestinely. The earliest churches were all in the City of Albany, and there seems to have been no organized congregation with a permanent minister elsewhere in the present county prior to the Revolutionary War. Methodists began meeting informally by 1765, but the first Methodist society was organized only in 1789. In 1796 St. Mary's Church, the second Roman Catholic church in the state, was incorporated. In 1776 the Shakers, led by Mother Ann Lee, settled in present Colonie on a 3,500-acre (1,420 ha) farm, from which their form of Christianity spread to other parts of the state and nation. The first Jewish synagogue was organized and incorporated in Albany in 1838 as Beth El.

Beverwijck [now Albany] had a schoolmaster by 1657. Before 1670 there were two teachers for Dutch children and later an English teacher. The development of schools outside the city came slowly, and they were poorly funded and irregular. By 1820 Bethlehem had 25 schools, Coeymans 15, Westerlo 16, Rensselaerville 18, Berne 30, Guilderland 11, and Watervliet 12. Private academies offered the only dependable education well into the 19th century. Albany Academy was founded in 1813 and Albany Academy for Girls in 1814. By midcentury there were private academies in Berne, Rensselaerville, Knox, and Coeymans. Even early in the 20th century, there were districts that offered only a grammar school education. In 2003 the county had 10 central school districts and 3 city school districts. In addition, Heatly School in Green Island offers kindergarten through senior high school, and Maplewood School in Watervliet and Menands School offer elementary programs. Albany also has two elementary-level charter schools. The Roman Catholic Diocese of Albany lists eight elementary and three secondary schools in Albany, elementary schools in Cohoes, Delmar, Latham, Loudonville, and Watervliet, and a high school in Loudonville. There are also schools sponsored by Baptist, Lutheran, Jewish, Seventh-day Adventist, and other faiths. Because there were strong private and parochial school programs in the City of Albany, the public schools were underfunded by city government through much of the 20th century. Siena College in Loudonville is the only college in the county outside of the City of Albany.

The principal newspapers have always been published in the City of Albany. The *Albany Gazette* (1771) was the first. In 2003 the *Albany Times-Union* is the regional daily, while weeklies are published for Altamont, Colonie, Delmar, Guilderland, Loudonville, and Ravena. The Albany River Rats (1993), a minor league hockey team, is the only professional sports franchise in the county, although minor league baseball teams were located in Albany and its suburbs through much of the 20th century. The Altamont Fairgrounds offers a variety of events in addition to the annual fair for Albany, Schenectady, and Greene Cos; its annual Scottish Games are among the largest in the nation. The Rensselaerville Institute, founded in 1963 as the Institute of Man and Science, develops self-help programs for failing small communities and focuses on improving skills in government and private agencies that advance the human condition.

Politics

The party that controls the City of Albany has generally controlled the county as well. In the 1840s and 1850s, the Whigs won 10 of 14 city elections, but, after the party collapsed, the Democratic machine won 17 of 21 elections from 1858 to 1898. The Republicans controlled the City of Albany's politics from 1899 to 1921 under the leadership of William Barnes Jr. In 1921 a revitalized Democratic organization led by the brothers Edward and Daniel P. O'Connell, who organized immigrants, working-class, and ethnic wards in the city, and by Edwin and Parker Corning, who brought along affluent defectors from the Republican patrician class, gained control of city and then county offices. Following the death of Edwin Corning in 1934 and of Edward O'Connell in 1939, Daniel P. O'Connell and Erastus Corning 2d controlled local politics for the rest of their long lives (until, respectively, 1977 and 1983). Although the Democratic Party continues to control the city, county politics have been more volatile. Beginning in the 1960s, with Joseph Frangella of Ravena as chairman, Republicans have been able to win a number of county offices outside the city. In part they have been able to take advantage of political infighting in the Democratic Party, chiefly among families of Irish American heritage. Between 1960 and the mid-1990s, Republicans have been elected county executive, district attorney, and treasurer, as well as to Congress and to state legislative offices. Democrats still maintain a two-to-one enrollment in the county and an overwhelming edge in the city. The Republican Party, however, has been able to maintain control in several of the towns for a century and more.

Recent History

After midcentury, general trends away from industrialization and toward suburban living were exacerbated by machine politics. Manufacturers and other businesses did not find the city administration receptive to their needs, and much of the City of Albany's economic base fled to the suburbs. Towns adjacent to the city, particularly Republican Colonie, were more amenable to business development and were the principal beneficiaries. This left the city dependent primarily on state government, colleges, and hospitals for its economic base. In 1958 only 168 factories, employing 4,900 workers, remained in the city, and in 1963 only 24% of the workforce was in manufacturing, well below the national average. Increasing taxes and quality-of-life issues sent the population fleeing as well. From a high of 134,000 in 1950, the population declined to 94,000 by the century's end, equaling roughly that of 1890. The demolition of over 1,000 buildings in the 1960s for the building of Empire State Plaza, displacing many thousands of residents, exacerbated this process. At the same time, the city's black population grew between 1950 and 2000 from 1.5% to 28% of the population. The relocation of the general population to the suburbs, however, has extended the metropolitan area. In the same time period that the City of Albany's population declined by 40,000, that of the rest of the county grew from 109,000 to 200,000, with neighboring Colonie increasing from about 30,000 in 1950 to almost 80,000 in 2000. There has been considerable revitalization of the City of Albany since the 1970s, with renewed attention to its theaters, arenas, and public parks, and to the expansion of the SUNY Albany and the Albany Medical Center.

See also SUBURBANIZATION.

The only countywide historical monographs are George Rogers Howell and Jonathan Tenney, *Bicentennial History of Albany County* (1886); Amasa J. Parker, *Landmarks of Albany County* (1897); and C. R. Roseberry, *Albany: Three Centuries a County* (1983). Every town and village has published some sort of book or pamphlet. John J. McEneny, *Albany Capital City on the Hudson: An Illustrated History* (1981), covers the population center. Others include Floyd I. Brewer, *Bethelehem Revisited: A Bicentennial Story, 1793–1993* (1993); [Arthur H. Masten], *The History of Cohoes* (1877, repr 1969); *The Town of Colonie: A Pictorial History* (1980); Mary Fisher Torrance, *Old Rensselaerville* (1939); *People Made It Happen Here: History of the Town of Rensselaerville* (1977); Dennis Sullivan, *Voorheesville, NY: A Sketch of the Beginnings of a 19th Century Railroad Town* (1988); and Gary L. Dohhardt's *Indian Ladder: A History of Life in the Helderbergs* (2001).

Peter R. Christoph

Albany Institute of History and Art. Museum and library. Founded in New York City in 1791 as the Society for the Promotion of Agriculture, Arts and Manufactures, the organization moved to Albany in 1797. It was renamed the Society for the Promotion of Useful Arts in 1804. The society merged with the Albany Lyceum of Natural History in 1824 to create the Albany Institute. In 1829 the institute began collecting art, historical, and bibliographic materials. In 1900 it merged with the Albany Historical and Art Society located at 176 State St and formed the Albany Institute and Historical and Art Society, which opened a larger museum on Washington Ave in 1908. The name was changed to the Albany Institute of History and Art in 1926, and the museum focused on collecting and interpreting the art, history, and culture of the upper Hudson Valley. During the 1960s the museum acquired the Rice House and annex, doubling the size of the structure. In 2001 a storage facility and atrium were added, and the main building was restored. Major art collections include limner portraits, Hudson River school art, Erastus Dow Palmer sculptures, and Walter Launt Palmer paintings. The institute also has major decorative arts collections, including New York State furniture, glass, and silver, Albany and Troy cast-iron stoves, ceramics, and clothing and textiles. The library has books, manuscripts, photographs, and ephemera. More than 100,000 people visit annually; 36 members serve on the institute's board of trustees.

Groft, Tammis K., and Mary Alice Mackay, eds. *Albany Institute of History & Art: 200 Years of Collecting* (New York: Hudson Hills Press, 1998)

Mary Alice Mackay

Albany Law School. Private law school. Founded in 1851 as part of the new University of Albany, the institution is among the oldest independent law schools in the United States. In 1873 it became part of Union University, together with Union College in Schenectady and the Albany Medical College. After renting rooms in several buildings in downtown Albany, the school moved in 1854 to the campus of Albany Medical College at Lancaster and Eagle Sts. In 1879 it bought and relocated to the former German Evangelical Church building on State St, which was sold to New York State in 1926 to make room for the Alfred E. Smith Building. After three years in a former factory on Lancaster St, the school moved to its present campus at 80 New Scotland Ave. In addition to the JD degree, it offers an MS in legal studies and an LLM in several legal specializations. Its most famous alumnus is Pres William McKinley, class of 1867. In 2001 the institution enrolled 646 full-time and 41 part-time students.

Allen, Elizabeth K., and Diana S. Waite. *Albany Law School, 1851–2000: A Tradition of Change* (Albany: Albany Law School in association with Mount Ida Press, 2000)

Yayin Chu-Reimer

Albany Medical Center. Albany Medical College opened its doors at the former Lancaster School at Eagle and Lancaster Sts in 1839, conferring its first degrees the same year. Albany Hospital, the state's first private hospital outside of New York City, was incorporated in 1849 and became a teaching hospital for the college. From Lydius St [now Madison Ave] and Dove St (1849–51), the hospital moved to a former jail at Hudson and Eagle St (1851–98) near the med-

Aerial view of the Port of Albany, 1951. *Left:* Albany, *right:* Rensselaer.

Aerial view of Albany Hospital, 1951.

ical college. The hospital moved out of downtown Albany in 1898, opening a new building at New Scotland and Holland Aves. The college moved to an adjacent location in 1928. In the mid-1950s the Albany Hospital became the Albany Medical Center Hospital. In October 1982, renamed the Albany Medical Center, the hospital and medical college were united within a single institution. The medical center had approximately 630 beds, with seven off-campus facilities, and enrolled about 600 students in 2002.

Rue Moore

Albany Pine Bush. A gently rolling sandy plain between Schenectady and Albany southwest of the confluence of the Mohawk and Hudson Rivers. During the last glaciation the Mohawk River deposited a delta of large quantities of sand from the melting ice sheet at its mouth on Glacial Lake Albany. The lake drained about 12,000 years ago, and wind and stream action formed the dunes and ravines that make up the landscape. The area is dominated by a globally imperiled pitch pine scrub oak barrens community characterized by a sparse canopy of pitch pine trees, a shrub layer of scrub oak and dwarf chestnut oak, a low shrub layer of black huckleberry, blueberries, and sweet fern, and a ground layer of grasses, legumes, and other plants tolerant of the dry, acidic, nutrient-poor, fire-swept conditions. Under natural conditions this community type is maintained by wildfires every 6 to 15 years. Rare pine barrens vernal ponds and a small, rich, sloping fen community occur in the Pine Bush along with several rare plants, amphibians, reptiles, and insects, including the endangered Karner blue butterfly. Dozens of fungus, plant, and insect species were first discovered there.

Indians and European settlers used the Albany Pine Bush as a hunting ground and transportation corridor from the Hudson Valley to the western frontier along the Mohawk Valley. Settlers logged it heavily for firewood and lumber but found the area unproductive for farming. Between the 1860s and 1920s, vast amounts of sand were removed for use in foundry molding operations, and sand mining for the construction industry continued until the mid-1970s. During the last half of the 19th century and the first half of the 20th century, the Pine Bush also served as an important railroad corridor, an informal recreational area, and a prominent naturalists' collecting ground. In the early 1950s transportation, housing, and commercial development intensified. With natural wildfires no longer allowed to burn, fire-dependent communities began to deteriorate. By the last quarter of the 20th century, only a small fraction of the Pine Bush remained undeveloped and was the target of a major conservation effort involving private, state, and municipal cooperation. The state legislature established the Albany Pine Bush Preserve Commission in 1988 to coordinate preservation efforts, including land acquisition and prescribed burns, and to oversee development of recreational activities, such as nature study and hiking. Approximately 2,600 acres (1,100 ha) of the 25,000 acres (10,100 ha) that originally made up the Pine Bush have been preserved.

Rittner, Don, comp and ed. *Pine Bush: Albany's Last Frontier* (Albany: Pine Bush Historic Preservation Project, 1976)

Jeffrey K. Barnes

Albany Railroad Bridge. Also known as the Livingston Avenue Bridge, it crosses the Hudson River between Albany and Rensselaer. Albany citizens first petitioned for a bridge over the Hudson in 1814. Debate continued in the courts and legislature over the next half century, as rival cities Troy (Rensselaer Co) and Albany pursued public support for their own commercial interests. Troy residents opposed the bridge, arguing that it would seriously obstruct coastal trade, while Albany residents supported it, hoping to forge a seamless rail network between Buffalo and Boston. The desperate wrangling over the issue led several railroad companies to consider tunneling under the river as late as 1851. Albany gained the upper hand in 1856 when the state legislature chartered the Hudson River Bridge Co. But an 1857 court injunction, brought by Troy shipping interests, suspended work until 1864. Construction was finally completed two years later. The swing bridge featured a wooden Howe truss for the main structure and incorporated a novel iron turntable to meet the charter's requirement for an especially large draw, allowing sizable ships to pass. The compromise nature of the bridge design indicated that the shipping interests still retained significant power. Costing over $1 million, the bridge spanned 2,020 feet (616 m), and the turntable opened to reveal twin 131.75 ft (40.2 m) spans. Including approaches it extended nearly 1 mile (1.6 km). The bridge was rebuilt in the early 20th century, and the swing feature is still used. Both passenger and freight trains cross the bridge, which CSX Corp acquired in 1997.

Salsbury, Stephen. *The State, the Investor, and the Railroad: The Boston & Albany, 1825–1867* (Cambridge, Mass: Harvard Univ Press, 1967)
Testimony Taken before the Senate Committee in the Matter of Bridging the Hudson River at Albany: Transmitted to the Legislature, February 29, 1856 (Albany: C. Van Benthuysen, 1856)

Michael R. Fein

Albany Regency. The name given the coterie of politicians centered on Martin Van Buren and based largely in Albany. Within New York State they sought to bring disciplined coherence to the Bucktail Republicans opposed to De Witt Clinton and, on the national level, to coordinate the exercise of power in Washington, DC, and in Albany. Condemning Clinton for ambition, they emphasized party devotion and support for policies formulated among the group and confirmed by caucus, arguing that these principles fostered true democracy and national unity. Their number initially included Van Buren's law partner, Benjamin F. Butler, Judge Roger Skinner of the Federal Court of the Northern District of New York, Comptroller William L. Marcy and his manufacturer father-in-law, Benjamin Knower, Edwin Croswell of the *Albany Argus*, Azariah C. Flagg of the *Plattsburgh Republican*, St. Lawrence Co surrogate Silas Wright, Atty Gen Samuel A. Talcott, New York City merchant Churchill C. Cambreleng, and Albany banker Thomas W. Olcott. They built on a hunger for patronage sharpened by the Panic of 1819 and took shape during the Bucktail ascendancy that led to constitutional revision in 1821. In 1824 they backed Van Buren's unsuccessful presidential candidate, William H. Crawford of Georgia, struggled with Bucktails supporting Henry Clay for president, blocked the popular election of presidential electors, and threw De Witt Clinton off New York State's Canal Commission. When Gov Joseph C. Yates, denied renomination by the Van Burenites, called a special session of the legislature to approve the electoral reform, Regency discipline held, denying change.

After this session the name Albany Regency became firmly attached to the group. First used artfully in early 1823 by Union College president Eliphalet Nott in thwarting a Bucktail-led probe into his school's finances, the name reappeared in September 1823 in the *New-York American*, a newspaper edited by Van Buren's erstwhile Federalist allies. New York State newspapers had followed the recent parliamentary adultery trial of Queen Caroline, consort of England's profligate George IV; New Yorkers knew of the abuse of power during his regency. "Regency" therefore connoted oppression by a secretive cabal of corrupt leaders. The Van Burenite leadership survived despite defeat in the presidential contest, failure to elect a majority of assemblymen in 1825, and loss of the governor's office to Clinton. Maneuvering carefully, they fostered an uneasy détente with Clinton, after which Van Buren established the Regency as a prime backer of Andrew Jackson, Clinton's 1824 presidential candidate. Into the 1840s the Regency-led *Argus* guided a network of state newspapers, and loyal Regency members and supporters were frequently appointed to positions from which they fostered Regency policy. After Clinton's death in 1828, Van Buren won the governorship before becoming US secretary of state in 1829. Marcy was elected governor in 1832, 1834, and 1836 before losing in 1838; Wright, after service in Congress, won that office in 1844 but lost it in 1846. The Regency served as one prototype for later capital-centered state machines, but local squabbling and factional splinters at the state level limited its control over New York State's Republican and later its Democratic Party, which emerged to support Jackson. Regency leaders pragmatically cultivated as many regions and groups in New York State as possible, but Democrats in areas such as New York City, Western New York, and the Southern Tier proved restive. Differences within the Regency over New York State's economic development were exacerbated by Pres Van Buren's monetary and banking policies and fatally undermined its unity. Some members wanted rapid growth by credit freely provided through state banks, protection of manufactures, and government spending for improvements. Others, favoring coin over bank-issued scrip, demanded adequate taxation and economy in government. Following the lead of Flagg, this group engineered passage of the Stop and Tax Law of 1842 and built fiscal restrictions on spending into the 1846 Constitution. These changes marked the death throes of the Regency.

Hanyan, Craig. "King George, Queen Caroline and the Albany Regency: The Origins of a Political Term," *New York History* 76 (Oct 1995): 349–78

Remini, Robert V. "The Albany Regency," *New York History* 39 (Oct 1958): 341–55

Craig and Mary L. Hanyan

Albany Times-Union. Primary daily newspaper of New York State's capital city. It descended from the *Morning Times* (1856). The *Times-Union* (the name was hyphenated until recent years) was created in 1891 when the *Morning Times* and *Albany Evening Union* merged. The *Times-Union* thrived in a crowded newspaper field under the leadership of Martin H. Glynn, a native of Kinderhook (Columbia Co) and rising star in Democratic politics at the turn of the century. Glynn abandoned the paper's neutral stance in politics by attacking Republican boss William "Billy" Barnes, publisher of the *Albany Evening Journal.* Glynn was elected to several political offices, including lieutenant governor in 1912, and served briefly as governor (1913–14) after the impeachment of Gov William Sulzer. The *Times-Union* battled in a circulation war with the *Knickerbocker Press* and its sister publication the *Evening News,* which was purchased in 1928 by Frank E. Gannett. Glynn sold a controlling interest in the *Times-Union* just before his death in 1924 to William Randolph Hearst, setting the stage for a showdown between two newspaper titans. Gannett merged his two papers into the *Knickerbocker News* in 1937, and Hearst immediately countered by shifting the *Times-Union* from an afternoon to a morning publication, which was a prescient move amid changing readership patterns.

By 1950 *Times-Union* circulation climbed to 60,000 daily and 120,000 on Sundays. Hearst Corp bought out rival Gannett's *Knickerbocker News* in 1960 and moved operations into a modern downtown office, creating Capital Newspapers with Gene Robb as publisher. The papers' critical coverage of the Albany Democratic machine led to a land dispute, which caused Hearst to move the paper out of the city and into a new office in suburban Colonie (Albany Co) in 1970. Harry M. Rosenfeld, an editor of Watergate coverage at the *Washington Post,* became editor in 1978, and circulation peaked in the mid-1980s for the morning *Times-Union.* Steady declines of the afternoon *Knickerbocker News* led Hearst to halt publication in 1988. The *Times-Union* added color photography in 1987 and launched an on-line edition in 1996. Rex Smith was named editor in 2002, replacing Jeff Cohen, and was faced with a challenge: to boost sagging circulation (100,000 daily and 150,000 on Sundays) while covering a wider regional base.

Kennedy, William. *O Albany!* (New York: Viking Press; [Albany]: Washington Park Press, 1983)

McEneny, John J. *Albany: Capital City on the Hudson* (Albany: Windsor Publications, 1981)

Paul Grondahl

Albertson. Locality (pop 5,200) in North Hempstead (Nassau Co). In 1874 a new stop on the Long Island Rail Road was named in honor of local landowner Richard Albertson. The area remained primarily agricultural until development began in the 1920s. The Long Island Motor Parkway, constructed in 1908 by William K. Vanderbilt Jr, passed through the southern border of this community. A post office opened in 1928. In 1946 William J. Levitt began intensive development of housing in the area. Albertson is the site of the Searing-Roslyn United Methodist Church (1788), the oldest Methodist church building on Long Island, as well as the 12-acre (5 ha) Clark Botanic Garden and the National Center for Disability Services. Its 2000 population was 14.5% Asian.

Richard A. Winsche

Albion. Town (pop 9,409) and village (pop 5,992) in central Orleans Co. Settled in 1811, the village was known as Newport until the Erie Canal was completed in 1824 and a post office named Canal opened. It was renamed Albion in 1826 and incorporated in 1828. It serves as the county seat and was the site of an important lumber trade and of commission houses, both dependent on the canal. In 1852 the village became a station on the Niagara Falls Branch of the New York Central Railroad. In 1860 it had gristmills, furnaces, a woolen factory, a tannery, a cabinet shop and a planing mill. It was also a center of Medina sandstone quarrying. The town was formed from Barre in 1875. In 1896 the village, which lies in the Towns of Albion and Gaines, became the site of the first dial telephone placed in use in the world. In the mid–20th century General Foods operated a plant in the village. In the early 21st century some residents commute to Rochester or Batavia; a number of small industries, including a mortgage call center, and Albion Correctional Facility (1894; founded as the Western House of Refuge) and Orleans Correctional Facility (1984) provide employment. Landmarks include Mount Albion Cemetery (1842) and the Pullman Memorial Universalist Church, with its Tiffany windows, a gift of George M. Pullman (1831–97), who lived in Albion as a carpenter from 1848 to 1855.

See also ARCHITECTS AND ARCHITECTURE, ROCHESTER AND WESTERN NEW YORK.

Cheryl Staines

Albion. Town (pop 2,083) in central Oswego Co. Settled in 1812 the town was formed in 1825 from Richland. Its economy was based on forest products; in 1860 the town had 38 sawmills and 3 tanneries, and logs were also floated down the Salmon River from the northern part of the town to mills in Richland. By the end of the 19th century dairy farming was important. In the early 21st century, farming has declined and most residents commute for employment. The Happy Valley State Wildlife Management Area lies in the southeastern corner of town.

Barbara J. Dix

Albion Correctional Facility. Medium security state correctional facility for females aged 16 and older. Established in 1893 as the Western House of Refuge for Women at Albion (Orleans Co), it was the second women's reformatory in New York State, opening six years after the House of Refuge at Hudson (Columbia Co). Both were established through the efforts of noted social reformer Josephine Shaw Lowell. Albion received women aged 16 to 30 convicted of misdemeanors from courts in Central and Western New York. During its early years it maintained a family-like environment with academic, household, and religious training based on the popular cottage plan. The name was changed to Albion State Training School in 1923. In 1931 its reformatory function was eliminated, and it became the Institution for Mentally Defective Delinquent Women, replacing Bedford (Westchester Co) as the place of confinement for New York State's female inmates judged defective delinquents. In 1932 the name reverted to Albion State Training School, but the function remained the same. The inmate population peaked in 1939 at nearly 400.

By the mid-1950s theories of defective delinquency were losing favor, and Albion's defective population was gradually phased out. In 1957 the Western Reformatory for Women was established as a separate unit. Another unit, for addicted inmates, operated by the Drug Addiction Control Commission, opened in 1967. In 1971, with the state in fiscal crisis, the entire facility was closed, and inmates were sent to other institutions. The facility reopened a year later as a medium security, all-male facility and was renamed the Albion Correctional Facility. In 1977 women returned to the institution at a medium security unit separate from the men. By 1986 Albion was again an all-female facility. In 2003 inmates numbered approximately 1,200 and staff 590.

"Albion Correctional Facility," *DOCS Today* (Sept 1998): 14–17
Albion State Training School, Albion, N.Y.: Its History, Purpose, Makeup, and Program (Albany: NYS Department of Correction, 1949)

Richard Andress

Albright-Knox Art Gallery. Located at 1285 Elmwood Ave, across from Buffalo State College, the museum is governed by the Buffalo Fine Arts Academy, one of the nation's oldest public arts organizations. Though it did not open until 1905, the original Albright Art Gallery, designed by local architect Edward B. Green and funded by entrepreneur John J. Albright, was initially planned as the Fine Arts Pavilion of the 1901 Pan-American Exposition held in Buffalo. With contributions from the family of Seymour H. Knox Jr and others, a new wing, designed by Gordon Bunshaft, was opened in 1962, and the building became the Albright-Knox Art Gallery. Its special strengths are in the artistic legacy of the 20th century. Works by such figures as Pablo Picasso, Henri Matisse, and Joan Miró document cubism, surrealism, and other early 20th-century movements, while abstract expressionism, pop art, and art from the 1970s and beyond are represented through works by Louise Nevelson, Arshile Gorky, Jackson Pollock, Andy Warhol, Jasper Johns, Anselm Kiefer, and Chuck Close. An extensive program of lectures, concerts, films, and art classes relating to special exhibitions and the permanent collection is offered throughout the year. The museum attracts over 125,000 visitors annually.

For illustration see ART, BUFFALO AND THE NIAGARA FRONTIER.

Spaulding, Karen Lee, ed. *Masterworks at the Albright-Knox Art Gallery* (New York: Hudson Hills Press in association with the Albright-Knox Art Gallery, 1999)

Cheryl Orlick

ALCO. See AMERICAN LOCOMOTIVE CO (ALCO).

Alcoholic Beverage Control, Division of. The agency is mainly responsible for issuing licenses and permits for the manufacture, distribution, and sale of alcoholic beverages; investigating violations of the Alcoholic Beverage Control (ABC) Law and invoking penalties such as fines, license suspensions, and revocations; and regulating trade and credit practices regarding sale and distribution of alcoholic beverages. The division was established after the end of Prohibition by the 1933 ABC Law. The following year the State Liquor Authority (SLA) was created as its governing board, with five members, reduced to three in 1995. SLA commissioners are appointed by the governor and serve three-year terms, one is appointed as chair, and no more than two can be from the same political party.

The SLA maintains offices in Albany, Buffalo, Syracuse, and New York City and handles licensing applications. The SLA Enforcement Bureau operates out of the offices in New York City, Albany, and Buffalo and investigates possible ABC Law violations, referring any to SLA's governing board or police, because the SLA lacks authority to make criminal arrests. Some conflict arises between the SLA and the businesses it regulates as tavern owners face heavy penalties for not detecting the use of high-quality forged identification cards, which, with advancements in computer technology and visual reproduction, are extremely difficult to distinguish from genuine IDs. For the 2002–03 fiscal year, the agency's budget was $13.7 million, and there were 172 full-time equivalent positions.

Division of Alcoholic Beverage Control, State Liquor Authority, http://abc.state.ny.us

Jon Lines

alcoholism. See DRUG ADDICTION AND TREATMENT.

Alden. Town (pop 10,470) and village (pop 2,666) in E Erie Co. Settled in 1810, the town was formed from Clarence in 1823. Many Germans settled in town in the 1830s and 1840s. The Attica and Buffalo Railroad (1842; later New York Central) was the first of four lines crossing the town east to west. Although Erie Co's first antislavery society was organized in Alden in 1823, sentiments on the slavery question were divided. In 1861 the hamlet of Town Line attempted to secede from the Union by a two to one vote in 1861. The Village of Alden incorporated in 1869. Black mineral water, discovered in 1891, was used in the Alden Black Water Bath House (1904–63). Other 20th-century industries included the New York Glass Works (1901–*ca* 1915) and a dashboard factory (1906), which became Bennett Manufacturing Co. Wende Correctional Facility (1983) is a maximum security prison. Dairy and grain farming are the predominant land uses in the early 21st century.

Andrew C. Maines

Aldridge, George W(ashington) (*b* Michigan City, Ind, 28 Dec 1856; *d* Rye, Westchester Co, 13 June 1922). Political leader. Aldridge's family moved to Rochester soon after his birth. He was educated in city schools and then at De Graff Military Institute of Rochester and Cary Collegiate Seminary at Oakfield (Genesee Co). His father, a Rochester contractor and politician, died in 1877, and Aldridge took over his business. He was elected as a Republican to the Rochester Executive Board, which controlled city expenditures and patronage, for four terms beginning in 1883, and he became chairman in 1891. Elected mayor in 1894, he resigned the following year when Gov Levi P. Morton appointed him New York State Superintendent of Public Works, a post he held until 1899. Pres Warren G. Harding appointed Aldridge collector of the Port of New York in 1921. By personality and pragmatic decision making, Aldridge controlled Rochester/Monroe Co politics for nearly 40 years.

McKelvey, Blake. "Some Former Rochesterians of National Distinction," *Rochester History* 21 (July 1959): 3–4

Karl S. Kabelac

Alexander. Town (pop 2,451) and village (pop 481) in S Genesee Co. Alexander Rhea, for whom the town and village are named, recorded the first deed in 1802. Alexander had the first public library in the county (1811). The town was formed from Batavia in 1812; the village incorporated in 1834. The Buffalo and Rochester Railroad (after 1853, New York Central) came through in 1843; two other lines followed. The Alexander Classical School (1837–86) was housed in a three-story cobblestone building, and it is listed on the National Register of Historic Places and is the town hall and museum. Dairy, crop, and vegetable farms, and small businesses provide livelihoods. The Western New York Gas and Steam Engine Association's annual rally is held in the fall.

Susan L. Conklin

Alexander, De Alva Stanwood (*b* Richmond, Maine, 17 July 1845; *d* Buffalo, 25 Jan 1930). Congressman and historian. An Ohio Volunteer Infantry veteran of the Civil War, Alexander graduated from Bowdoin College in Brunswick, Maine, in 1870 and had a varied career as teacher, Republican newspaper editor, and lawyer in the Midwest before being appointed US Treasury Department auditor in 1881. In 1885 he moved to Buffalo and served as US district attorney for the Northern District of New York from 1889 to 1894. Elected to Congress in 1896, he served seven terms and chaired the Rivers and Harbors Committee. Alexander, a supporter of the Port of Buffalo, was instrumental in acquiring $8.5 million in federal funding for its development. In 1910 he lost his House seat by a single vote, a defeat attributed to the factional struggles that divided the Republican Party; Alexander had sided with the party's regular, pro-Taft, wing.

While in Congress Alexander began work on the historical series for which he is best known, *A Political History of the State of New York,* with the first two volumes published in 1906 and a third in 1909. *Four Famous New Yorkers: The Political Careers of Cleveland, Platt, Hill, and Roosevelt,* published in 1923, is considered the fourth volume of his political history. Alexander discussed the history of a state or nation as that of its leaders. His books were praised by contemporary reviewers for the anecdotal color and vigor of his political portraits. They were criticized, however, for their failure to explore in any depth the themes of increasing academic interest: social and economic change, urban growth and its relation to the rise of Tammany Hall, third party movements, or other developments not directly reflected in the party and personal battles at the state capital. Alexander's *The History and Procedure of the House of Representatives,* published in 1916, was less controversial and better received.

American National Biography, sv "Alexander, De Alva Stanwood"

Robert P. Kerker

Alexander, Lee (*b* Jersey City, NJ, 18 May 1927; *d* Syracuse, 25 Dec 1996). Mayor. The son of Greek immigrant parents, Alexander received undergraduate (1950) and law degrees (1955) from Syracuse University. He was first elected to public office as a Democrat on the Syracuse Common Council in 1966. As mayor of Syracuse from 1970 to 1985, the longest mayoral tenure in the city's history, Alexander oversaw the construction and rehabilitation of nearly 12,000 housing units for the poor and elderly, as well as new schools, firehouses, and other public buildings. He served as president of the US Conference of Mayors in 1977–78 and the National Conference of Democratic Mayors in 1980, achieving a national reputation as a crusader for state and federal aid for cities. In 1987 he was indicted by a federal grand jury for operating an extortion racket and collecting kickbacks during his years in office. The following year he pleaded guilty to counts of racketeering, conspiracy, and tax evasion, and served five and a half years in prison. After his release, he worked for a time as the maître d'hôtel of a Syracuse restaurant next door to City Hall.

Fish, Mike. "Larger Than Life," *Syracuse Herald-Journal*, 26 Dec 1996

Dick Case

Alexander, William [Lord Stirling] (*b* New York City, 25 Dec 1726; *d* Albany, 15 Jan 1783). Revolutionary War general. Born to one of the wealthiest families in colonial America and proprietor of an extensive estate in New Jersey, Alexander served as a staff officer to Massachusetts governor William Shirley during the French and Indian War (1754–63). When Shirley was recalled to England in 1757, Alexander accompanied him, attempting while there to claim title to the Scottish earldom of Stirling. Unsuccessful, he adopted the title regardless and was referred to as such when he returned to America in 1761. Commissioned a brigadier general early in the Revolutionary War, Alexander commanded the Continental army's right flank in the Battle of Long Island on 27 Aug 1776. He saved the army from annihilation by leading his outnumbered Maryland troops in a series of charges that covered the American retreat. Captured during the battle, he rejoined the army after a prisoner exchange. He fought at the Battle of Trenton on 26 Dec 1776 and was promoted to major general two months later. In 1781 he was sent to Albany to command the Northern Department of the Continental army, a position he held until his death from gout.

Nelson, Paul D. *William Alexander, Lord Stirling* (University: Univ of Alabama Press, 1987)

John G. Staudt

Alexandria. Town (pop 4,097) in N Jefferson Co. Settled in ?1816, the town was formed in 1821 from Brownville and Le Ray. Lumbering and timber rafting were important early activities, and cylinder glass was manufactured at Redwood beginning in 1833. Since the mid–19th century, tourism has been Alexandria's most important industry, centered on the St. Lawrence River and the Thousand Islands. Much of Wellesley Island is part of the town, including Westminster Park (1875), a cottage colony. The Thousand Islands Bridge (1938) connects the town to Ontario; I-81 was completed from the south in 1965 and extended to the bridge in 1971. Boldt Castle (1904) is a major attraction. Alexandria continues to be one of the main agricultural areas of Jefferson Co, with a small number of large dairy farms. It is the site of Kring Point and Keewaydin State Parks. The locality of Plessis, according to a well-attested local legend, was named after the pet dog of land proprietor James Le Ray de Chaumont.

Laura Lynne Scharer

Alexandria Bay. Village (pop 1,088) in Alexandria (Jefferson Co). It was platted in 1818 by the proprietor, James Le Ray de Chaumont, who built a tavern and store to serve loggers. Since a hotel was built in 1848, the main industry has been tourism. In 1872 the Thousand Island House and Crossmon House, resort hotels, were built, and a visit by Pres Ulysses S. Grant in that year drew national attention and resulted in rapid growth. The village was incorporated in 1878. Known locally as "the Bay," it is rebuilding its waterfront and rehabilitating its downtown in hopes of attracting more families and extending the short summer season.

Laura Lynne Scharer

Alfred. Town (pop 5,140) and village (3,954) in E Allegany Co. Settled in 1807, the town was formed in 1808 from Angelica. The Erie Railroad (1851) helped develop the town's dairy industry. A concentrated community of Seventh Day Baptists founded Alfred Select School (1836), which grew into Alfred University (1857). As late as the mid–20th century, village businesses were closed Saturday and open Sunday. The Celadon Terra-Cotta Co Ltd (1889–1909) produced roofing tile and architectural terra-cotta. Its showpiece Terra Cotta Building (1892) is on the National Register of Historic Places. Celadon is partly responsible for the birth of the state-supported College of Ceramics (1900) at Alfred University. The Alfred Clay Co (1892–?1911) manufactured brick at Alfred Station. The State University College of Technology at Alfred (1908) originated as an agricultural school. The Alfred Village Historic District includes much of the downtown. Attractions on the university campus include the Davis Memorial Carillon (1937), composed of 16th- and 17th-century Flemish bells, the Schein Joseph International Museum of Ceramics (1991), and the Steinheim (1876), a replica of a medieval German castle.

Alfred State. See SUNY ALFRED.

Alfred University. Private university. Founded in 1836 by Seventh Day Baptists, Alfred Select School became Alfred University in 1857 and is New York State's oldest coeducational college. Women were enrolled on the same terms as men in the early 1850s, and in 1860 a full 40% of the student body were women. The university added the New York State School of Clayworking and Ceramics (now SUNY College of Ceramics) in 1900 and was home to the New York State School of Agriculture (now Alfred State College) from 1908 to 1948. Business programs were added to its core offerings of liberal arts and sciences in 1939. The curriculum has expanded dramatically since World War II, with notable graduate offerings in ceramics, materials science, and psychology. Engineering programs were added in 1985. In the early 21st century, Alfred serves about 2,000 undergraduate and 400 graduate students on its 232-acre (94 ha) campus.

Horowitz, Gary S., and Alan Littell, eds. *A Sesquicentennial History of Alfred University: Essays in Change* (Alfred, NY: Alfred Univ Press, 1986)

Thomas H. Rasmussen

Algonquin Round Table. Informal group of writers, actors, and other celebrities of the 1920s, who met daily in the dining room of Manhattan's Algonquin Hotel. Most of the members of the Algonquin Round Table were associated with the magazine *Vanity Fair,* particularly Robert Benchley and Dorothy Parker, or with the Broadway theater, either as writers (George S. Kaufman, Robert Sherwood) or as performers (Harpo Marx, Helen Hayes). Other important members were newspaper columnists Franklin P. Adams, the group's main publicist, and Alexander Woollcott. Many other contemporary celebrities, such as James Thurber, Edna Ferber, Noël Coward, and Irving Berlin occasionally joined the group.

The Round Table began in the early 1920s with an afternoon roast of Woollcott (then the *New York Times* drama critic). The group enjoyed the event so much that they met the next day, and many days to come, encouraged by Algonquin manager Frank Case. Ostensibly meeting for lunch their real business was the trading of wisecracks, put-downs, and other clever remarks. The contemporary press fell enthusiastically on these witticisms and created the group's contemporary celebrity. While their literary reputations have largely faded, the members of the Algonquin Round Table are a lasting symbol of the sophisticated and sardonic literary culture of New York City during the interwar years. A vestige of their style of wit remains in the fast-paced, wisecracking comedies of Kaufman and Moss Hart, particularly in *The Man Who Came to Dinner* (1939), whose overbearing leading character, Sheridan Whiteside, is transparently based on Woollcott.

Gaines, James R. *Wit's End: Days and Nights of the Algonquin Round Table* (New York: Harcourt Brace Jovanovich, 1977)

David Raymond

Alien and Sedition Acts. Confronted with increasing political partisanship and the Quasi-War with France, Congress adopted the Alien and Sedition Acts in 1798 to restrain foreign radicals and to muzzle domestic critics. These acts were especially controversial in New York City, a haven for immigrants fleeing political prosecution in Britain and home to several opposition presses. The government used both common-law libel actions and the Sedition Act to prosecute newspaper editors. The most outspoken paper was New York City's *Time Piece* (1798), edited by John Daly Burk, a radical Irish immigrant who supported Democratic-Republicans and was associated with Aaron Burr. As Congress debated the alien and sedition statutes, Judge John Sloss Hobart on 6 July 1798 charged Burk under the federal common law with libeling Pres John Adams. He was indicted on 4 Sept 1799. Fearing deportation under the Alien Act, Burk promised to leave the country, and the paper folded. He found sanctuary in Virginia. A second federal libel prosecution followed when William Durell, publisher of the insignificant *Mount Pleasant (Westchester Co) Register,* was charged on 19 July 1798 with republishing an article critical of the president but was not indicted until September 1799. He was left dangling, which served to muzzle him, and he abandoned publishing even though he was not tried and found guilty until April 1800. He was the only editor pardoned by Pres Adams. Mrs Ann Greenleaf, editor of the influential New York City *Argus* (1795–1800), was indicted under the Sedition Act in 1799, but the case never came to trial.

The Sedition Act also was used to prosecute Assemblyman Jedidiah Peck, a nominal Federalist who circulated petitions in Otsego Co calling for its repeal. The Democratic-Republicans believed citizens enjoyed the unrestricted right to petition government, whereas Federalists, such as Rep William Cooper (who initiated proceedings against Peck), warned constituents that signing these petitions violated the act.

Various congressmen, including Republican Edward Livingston, who had vehemently opposed the Alien Act, presented petitions to Congress to repeal it early in 1799. Although a congressional committee upheld the constitutionality of the Alien and Sedition Acts, the protracted public debate strengthened the political opposition that they were designed to curb. The acts were never repealed but lapsed because of their sunset clauses: the Alien Friends Act automatically expired two years from its adoption, and the Sedition Act on 3 Mar 1801, at the inauguration of the victor of the 1800 presidential election.

Durey, Michael. "Tom Paine's Apostles: Radical Emigrés and the Triumph of Jeffersonian Republicanism," *William and Mary Quarterly,* 3d ser, 44 (Oct 1987): 661–88

Smith, James Morton. *Freedom's Fetters: The Alien and Sedition Laws and American Civil Liberties* (Ithaca: Cornell Univ Press, 1956)

Taylor, Alan. *William Cooper's Town: Power and Persuasion on the Frontier of the Early American Republic* (New York: Knopf, 1995)

Whitman H. Ridgway

Allan, Indian [Ebenezer] (*b* ?Morristown, NJ, 17 Sept 1752; *d* Delaware [now in Ont], 13 Apr 1813). Pioneer. Allan fought for the British in the American Revolution with Col John Butler's Corps of Rangers (1777–81) and in the Indian Department under Sir John Johnson (1781–83). Sent to the Genesee Valley as a spy in 1782, he established himself as a settler and trader near present-day Mount Morris [now in Livingston Co], where he lived with a Seneca woman. In 1783 the British notified Allan of his discharge. Angered at this and anxious to protect his property, he acted as an intermediary in the peace process between the US government and the Six Nations; this led to a 10-month imprisonment by the British. In 1788 land speculators Oliver Phelps and Nathaniel Gorham gave Allan 100 acres (40 ha) to build and operate grist- and sawmills near the falls of the Genesee, now the site of the Blue Cross Arena in downtown Rochester. These mills failed, but soon new mills nearby formed the core of the settlement that became Rochester. Allan married a white woman in 1788 and in 1792 returned to his original Genesee Valley farm, where he encountered difficulties with authorities over land titles. He moved with his family in 1794 to Delaware Township in Canada, where he was granted 2,000 acres (809 ha) for his past military service. He promoted the US cause during the War of 1812 and was imprisoned by the British in 1813.

Turpin, Morley Beebe. "Ebenezer Allan in the Genesee Country." In *Centennial History of Rochester, New York,* vol 2, ed. E. R. Foreman (Rochester, 1931–34)

Joann Minor

Allegany. Town (pop 8,230) and village (pop 1,883) in SE Cattaraugus Co. Settled by 1820, the town was formed from Great Valley in 1831 as Burton; the name was changed in 1851. The original settlers worked at lumbering, rafting the logs down the Allegheny River; as late as 1860 the town was 90% forested. The first tannery opened in 1854 and the first cheese factory in 1867. The Erie Railroad (1851) brought Irish laborers; Nicholas Devereux of Utica, a large landowner, offered them land and was also responsible for the creation of Franciscan-run St. Bonaventure University (1858). A successful oil well was drilled in 1877, and by the end of 1878 Allegany had 100 producing wells. Working wells were still found in town at the beginning of the 21st century. The Village of Allegany was surveyed in 1837, but its growth awaited the railroad; it was incorporated in 1905. Rte 17 (I-86) was built across town in 1984. Aside from farming, residents work at St. Bonaventure or in Olean. The Allegany Indian Reservation has sovereignty over a part of the town's extent. Rock City Park, a tract of gigantic exposed quartz conglomerate rocks taking the form of large buildings divided by streets and alleys, is an attraction. The oil boom of the 1870s led to a population peak of 4,044 in 1880, followed by a subsequent decline. With the suburbanization of Olean, Allegany's population doubled between 1940 and 2000 (from 3,919 to 8,230).

Bruce D. Fredrickson and Madelynn P. Fredrickson

Allegany County (1,030 mi^2/2,668 km^2; pop 49,927). It was created in 1806 from Genesee Co and named for the Allegewi, early inhabitants driven from the area by the Iroquois. A portion of Steuben Co was annexed in 1808, and a section was lost to Genesee Co in 1811. In addition, substantial areas were lost to Wyoming Co in 1846 and to Livingston Co in 1846 and 1857. Allegany Co is divided into 29 towns containing 10 incorporated villages. The Seneca Nation's Oil Spring Indian Reservation straddles the county's western border. Belmont is the county seat. Elevations vary from 2,548 ft (776.6 m) high Alma Hill, the highest point in western New York State to a low of 1,137 feet (346.6 m) above sea level on the banks of the Genesee River where it exits the county in the north. The entire county lies within the Cattaraugus Hills subregion of the Appalachian Plateau physiographic province. The land rises to the south. With limited exception hilltops range between 2,200 and 2,400 feet (670–730 m) in the more rugged south, and 1,900 to 2,100 feet (580–640 m) in the more rolling north. Larger valley bottoms lie 500–700 feet (150–210 m) below surrounding hilltops. The county is glaciated throughout, as evidenced by the rounded hilltops and an omnipresent mantle of glacial till that varies in thickness from less than 1 foot (.3 m) on some hilltops to over 100 feet (30 m) in some valley bottoms. Bedrock consists almost entirely of near horizontal beds of Devonian sandstone and shale. Oil deposits lie within Upper Devonian sandstones and Upper Silurian and Middle Devonian carbonate rocks in the county's southern half. The Cuba oil spring, reported by a Franciscan missionary in 1627, is one of a number of oil seeps in the region. Drilling began in 1860, and oil production peaked during the 1880s and again in the 1940s with secondary recovery techniques. A modest 34,516 barrels was pumped in 2000, which was the second highest production among New York State counties.

The north-flowing Genesee River drains over three-quarters of Allegany Co; the Susquehanna drains the northeast; the Allegany River watershed extends into the southwest corner; and the streams in the northeast are tributaries to the

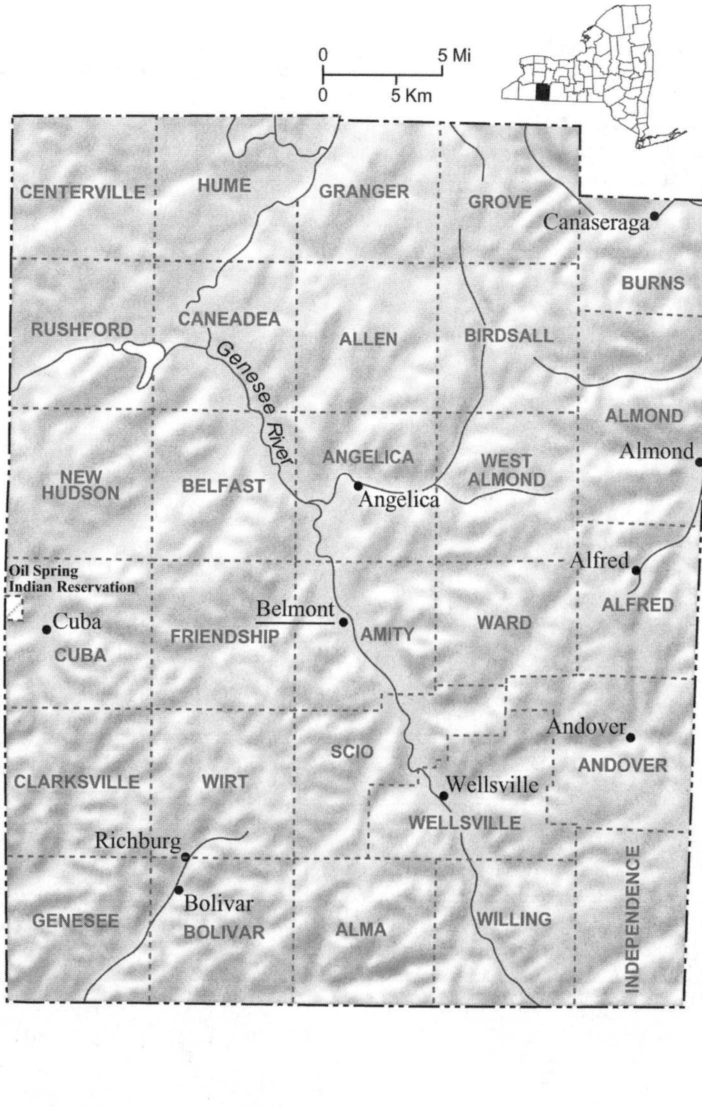

Canisteo River and to the Susquehanna River system. A small area in the far northwest drains to Lake Erie. Almost all of the soils are glacial in origin. The most arable are associated with outwash material along the Genesee River north of Wellsville and portions of Black Creek. Areas of good agricultural land are scattered, notably in the southeast and northwest corners, but over one-half of the county's lands hold little or no agricultural value.

The climate is humid-continental. Mean temperatures in the deeper valleys range from about 21°F (-6°C) in January to 66°F (19°C) in July. Hilltops tend to be a few degrees cooler. Below 0°F (-18°C) temperatures are part of every winter as are 90°F (32°C) or higher temperatures each summer. The annual precipitation varies from 35 in (89 cm) in the Genesee Valley to 43 inches (109 cm) at Friendship. Seasonal snowfall ranges from about 56 in (142 cm) in the Genesee Valley near Wellsville to over 100 inches (250 cm) at the highest elevations in the southwest. Primeval forest cover consisted of Alleghenian hardwoods dominated by beech, sugar maple, hemlock, white pine, and basswood, except in the Genesee River valley, where oak-chestnut forest predominated. More than 65% of the county is presently covered with later growth forest.

Settlement

Under growing pressure from white intruders, Native American inhabitants surrendered title to their lands in western New York State at the Treaty of Big Tree (1797). Several land speculators, notably Oliver Phelps, Nathaniel Gorham, Joseph Elliott, and Philip Church, bought huge tracts of land for pennies an acre. Their land agents based in Bath (Steuben Co), Batavia (Genesee Co), and Angelica typically sold "first quality" land to settlers in 50–100-acre (20–40 ha) parcels for about $2 an acre. Agents complained that their tenants were not in a hurry to repay the debt on their land, preferring to buy goods to improve farm and home. However, once settlers invested sweat equity in improving their land, they had every incentive to repay their loans rather than to risk losing their farms. In Allegany Co, a survey of 583 mortgages found that only 13 (2%) ended in foreclosure. It was not uncommon for early settlers to improve their land, sell at a higher price, and move to the Middle West, where land was available at an average price of $1.25 per acre in 1830. Improved land in Allegany Co sold for about $3.75 in 1836, $4.25 in 1845, and $9.00 in 1855.

The first order of business for the Allegany Co settler was to fell enough trees to build a small log cabin and to clear enough land to plant crops. Log cabins were soon replaced with framed houses sided with sawed lumber, allowing second stories and more windows. The original log cabins were dismantled or used to store goods or shelter animals. In 1895, 100 years after initial settlement, there were only six occupied log cabins according to historians.

Population grew from 1,200 to 40,000 between 1810 and 1850. Early 19th-century settlers tended to select their farms close to earlier migrants. Neighbors provided companionship and protection, and together they could support school and church, general store and sawmill. Villages were located astride the roads that ran along the valley floors. The mean distance between 32 neighboring 19th-century Allegany Co hamlets was 4 miles (6.4 km). Most farmers could travel to town and return home in less than a day.

Nathaniel Dyke, the first permanent settler in the county in 1795, built along Dyke Creek, a tributary of the Genesee River. Many first-generation migrants settled in the Susquehanna River basin. They carved roads from Pennsylvania following the Susquehanna and Canisteo Rivers along present-day US 15. Others moved westward from overpopulated holdings in New England. An important settler and land speculator, Philip Church, moved westward through Karr Valley to reach his 100,000-acre (40,500 ha) tract of land at Angelica in the Genesee River basin in 1801. He followed the relatively flat valley sculpted by Ice Age glaciers and early postglacial rivers along the route of the present-day Rte 17 (I-86).

ALLEGANY CO POPULATION CENSUS FIGURES

	White	Nonwhite	Total Population	Foreign-Born
1810	1,921	21	1,942	—
1820	9,301	29	9,330	30
1830	26,197	79	26,276	16
1840	40,833	142	40,975	—
1850	37,680	128	37,808	2,332
1860	41,617	264	41,881	3,216
1870	40,465	349	40,814	3,546
1880	41,433	377	41,810	3,187
1890	42,900	340	43,240	3,208
1900	41,146	355	41,501	2,374
1910	41,086	326	41,412	2,200
1920	36,622	220	36,842	1,469
1930	37,848	177	38,025	1,204
1940	39,517	164	39,681	867
1950	43,627	157	43,784	901
1960	43,817	161	43,978	712
1970	46,207	251	46,458	559
1980	51,210	532	51,742	786
1990	49,695	775	50,470	787
2000	48,444	1,483	49,927	920

Notes: "Nonwhite" includes African Americans, Asians, American Indians, and Pacific Islanders and, for 2000, also the mixed race and other race categories. Through the 1960 census these figures primarily reflect the African American population. Foreign-born figures for 1820 and 1830 include only those not naturalized, and for 1930 and 1950, the foreign-born totals include Whites only. Other years include all foreign-born in the population.

Economic Development

Settlers floated lumber and potash down creeks and rivers to Chesapeake Bay during the spring of the year. Two workers were able to construct a flat-bottomed ark drawing 2 feet (.6 m) of water in two weeks. The 350 mi (563 km) trip down the Canisteo River to the Susquehanna to Baltimore took six days and a crew of four. After dismantling the ark and selling the lumber, the crew made its way back to New York. Other settlers developed farms along Turnpike Rd, constructed in 1802 to connect the county's eastern gateway at Almond with Church's large landholding at Angelica. By 1830 many migrants used Turnpike Rd to reach the Allegheny River at Olean (Cattaraugus Co), where they headed downstream to settle new lands in Ohio.

Completion of the Erie Canal in 1825 shifted Allegany Co's orientation from the Susquehanna Valley to the booming economic centers of Rochester and Buffalo. The Genesee River flows northward through the center of the county, emptying into Lake Ontario. The Erie Canal lowered the cost of transporting goods to frontier villages and farmers' exports of potash and lumber to markets back east by a factor of 10. All Genesee Valley towns grew rapidly in response to the Erie Canal. By 1840 four of the most populous towns in the county—Hume, Cuba, Caneadea, and Belfast—were located in that valley. Belfast was the center of Genesee River lumber shipment. During the fall and winter, logs were floated downriver to large sawmills at Portageville (Wyoming Co) and Mount Morris (Livingston Co).

For the first 50 years, lumber was the principal source of cash for Allegany Co residents. Low-value, unprocessed logs could not be profitably shipped by team over rough roads, so settlers processed the timber to reduce the weight and bulk and to add value. The 1845 census reported 257 sawmills on Allegany Co's rivers and creeks. Frederick Douglass, who gave a series of anti-slavery lectures in the county in October 1851, observed that "sawmills are dotted all over Allegany's valleys. So profitable is the lumber business that many of the men engaged in it think it more for their interest to buy their produce than to cultivate their land, of which they have abundance. Timber is to Allegany what gold is to California and these must be exhausted before there will be much cultivation of the soil in either." Technological advances, especially the circular saw, and a major flood in 1855 wiped out most small sawmills.

The Erie Railroad, its Buffalo Division, and the Genesee Valley Canal were completed in the 1850s, increasing the importance of lumbering.

POPULATIONS OF TOWNS, ALLEGANY CO

Town, Year Founded	1840	1880	1920	1960	2000
Alfred, 1808	1,630	1,526	1,269	3,730	5,140
Allen, 1823	867	818	524	306	462
Alma, 1854	—	865	643	871	847
Almond, 1821	1,434	1,567	1,121	1,373	1,604
Amity, 1830	1,354	1,972	1,843	2,006	2,245
Andover, 1824	848	1,988	1,809	1,801	1,945
Angelica, 1805	1,257	1,620	1,502	1,335	1,411
Belfast, 1824[a]	1,646	1,470	1,279	1,265	1,714
Birdsall, 1829	328	890	464	160	268
Bolivar, 1825	408	1,029	1,979	2,441	2,223
Burns, 1826	867	1,671	1,214	1,238	1,248
Caneadea, 1808	1,633	1,764	1,183	1,911	2,694
Centerville, 1819	1,513	956	668	491	762
Clarksville, 1835	326	852	770	840	1,146
Cuba, 1822	1,768	2,203	2,395	3,116	3,392
Friendship, 1815	1,244	2,127	1,788	2,020	1,927
Genesee, 1830	578	974	911	1,193	1,803
Granger, 1838[b]	1,064	1,086	590	429	577
Grove, 1827[c]	623	1,125	602	469	533
Hume, 1822	2,303	1,905	1,701	1,729	1,987
Independence, 1821	1,440	1,186	1,028	1,004	1,074
New Hudson, 1825[d]	1,502	1,034	663	612	736
Rushford, 1816	1,512	1,453	1,118	995	1,259
Scio, 1823	1,156	1,555	1,062	1,513	1,914
Ward, 1856	—	620	400	234	390
Wellsville, 1855	—	4,259	6,171	8,278	7,678
West Almond, 1833	808	803	416	293	353
Willing, 1851	—	1,267	755	1,208	1,371
Wirt, 1838	1,207	1,225	974	1,117	1,215

Note: In 1840 Allegany Co included the Towns of Ossian, Nunda, and Portage [now in Livingston Co] and the Towns of Eagle and Pike [now in Wyoming Co].

[a]Orrinsburgh until 1825.

[b]West Grove until 1839.

[c]Church Tract until 1828.

[d]Haight until 1837.

The cost of transporting lumber to ready markets along the Erie Canal and in Atlantic seaboard cities fell dramatically, and the cost of importing manufactured goods declined. The population of towns along canals and railroads increased. In the Towns of New Hudson and Alma, for example, a new generation of lumberjacks joined a few hundred isolated farmers. In the spring of 1853, 14 million board feet of lumber lined the banks of the canal in Belfast and Caneadea awaiting shipment northward to Rochester.

After lumbermen stripped the hills of trees, farmers converted them into pastures for dairy cattle. Milk was made into cheese for shipment to urban markets on the Erie Railroad. In the early 1900s the worldwide price for cheddar cheese was set in weekly meetings in the Village of Cuba, the third-largest cheese market in the state. After 1915, when Wisconsin surpassed New York as the leading dairy state, the dairy industry began a long decline. The key to dairy profitability was cheap feed, and feed was expensive in Western New York. Indeed, farmers found it cheaper to import feed from western states than to grow their own.

The expansion of industrial and commercial activity following the Civil War provided new economic opportunities. Many residents moved from farms to villages and took jobs in dozens of small factories. After 1900 commercial blocks were built in brick in about a dozen villages and hamlets to supply prosperous citizens with goods and services. The Village of Wellsville grew rapidly as a railroad center, provider of services to the oil industry, and home to many businesses serving the population within a 10–15 mi (16–24 km) radius. Discovery of oil near Petrolia in 1879 and Allentown and Richburg in 1881 also contributed to prosperity. Allegany Co quickly became New York State's largest oil producer. Refineries were built in Bolivar, at the center of the oil field, and in Wellsville, its transportation hub and legal and financial service center. By 1895, 3,500 wells were producing \$2.3 million in oil revenues per year. Production slowed in the 1950s in the face of competition from new fields in Texas and Saudi Arabia. In the early 21st century, most oil wells in Allegany Co are capped, awaiting higher petroleum prices or development of advanced recovery techniques.

Religion, Education, and Culture

Settlers built churches in all of the 32 villages and hamlets of Allegany Co, and they were centers of community life in the 19th century. One large contingent of Seventh Day Baptists came from Rhode Island, settling in the southern part of the county. Some churches have closed, and some struggle to survive with small congregations. New churches have been formed whose congregations are committed to a literal reading of the Bible and the quest for personal salvation.

K–12 schools are centers of community activity and sources of local pride. Most of the one-room schools within walking distance of farms have been abandoned, and large consolidated schools offer a specialized curriculum and varied student services. Four major institutions of higher education also serve the area: Alfred University (1857), offering varied programs in the fine arts; Houghton College (1923), specializing in musical performance; New York State College of Ceramics at Alfred University (1900); and Alfred State College (1908), providing a program in culinary arts. Several libraries and museums offer information services, including the Wellsville Public Library, the Jean B. Lang Western New York Historical Collection at Alfred State College, the Herrick Library's Special Collections at Alfred University, the Allegany County History Museum at Belmont, and the Pioneer Oil Museum at Bolivar.

Most early Allegany Co settlers were of English ancestry, immigrating from New England and Pennsylvania. At midcentury many Irish immigrants came to build the railroads and the Genesee Valley Canal. After construction was completed, some bought land and remained. Most of the small black, Latino, and Asian populations are associated with the colleges in Alfred as staff and students. In recent years numerous Amish households have moved to western Allegany Co, where they engage in labor-intensive dairy production, woodworking, or other crafts.

Politics

In the early 19th century, school districts and town governments were responsible for providing essential public services such as operating schools and maintaining roads. The first county seat was Angelica. In 1859 it was moved to Belmont, located on the new Erie Railroad and the geographic and economic center of the county. Whigs and Democrats competed for Allegany Co votes prior to the Civil War. Whigs supported state financing of a canal network and railroads, and their supporters successfully championed construction of the Genesee Valley Canal in 1853. Democrats supported the party of Andrew Jackson, who championed the cause of poor western farmers against eastern seaboard commercial interests. Mostly, political factions gravitated toward one party or another on the basis of local political considerations rather than of broader questions of state policy or political philosophy. The Republican Party was formed in 1854 over the issue of the extension of slavery and quickly became the dominant party in Allegany Co. Whigs joined the Republican Party, and Democrats lost favor because of their strong association with Irish Catholicism, New York City machine politics, and southern white resistance to Reconstruction. The Republican identification of the Democratic Party with "rum, Romanism, and rebellion" rang true among post–Civil War voters. As New York City continued to grow during the industrial revolution, the upstate/downstate split came to define Republican and Democratic political competition. Allegany Co has remained a pillar of Republican strength.

Local officials and attentive citizens are often skeptical of decisions made in Albany. Unfunded state mandates in social services and public works are seen to impose burdens on local taxpayers. In 1989 a siting commission's search for sites to store low-level radioactive waste evoked intense county opposition. The commission rather clumsily decreed that Allegany Co, meeting basic geological and demographic characteristics, was likely to be selected. Residents waged an effective nonviolent protest campaign. Over a 15-month period in 1989 and 1990, many protest meetings were held, the credibility of Siting Commission studies was attacked, and nonviolent protesters were arrested for interfering with commission activities. Ultimately Gov Mario M. Cuomo announced that New York State would no longer consider sites in Allegany Co.

Centralization of public services is a continuing issue. The county has taken over some solid waste management and road and bridge maintenance responsibilities from town governments. In education, larger central schools are replacing smaller schools. Advantages are a greater range of courses and services, less duplication of staff, and lower per pupil cost; disadvantages are long bus rides for students, less personal school settings, and loss of community identification in the cases where schools have closed. County government has professionalized its operations. The number of legislators has been consolidated from 29 to 15, a committee system permits legislators to specialize, and higher salaries encourage them to devote more time to county business. A professional county administrator oversees daily operations.

RECENT HISTORY

Allegany Co has fallen upon hard economic times since World War II and ranks near the bottom of New York State counties in per capita income. It has a relatively large percentage of young and old residents and is short of workers in the 25–64 age range. For many residents, the nearest large village for shopping and employment is in a neighboring county. The demise of the railroad hurt the economy, as did construction of the Interstate Highway System, which bypassed Allegany Co. Many small, aging industries that filled local and regional market niches during the early 20th century closed or moved during the 1950s and 1960s. Manufacturing continues to employ about one-quarter of the workforce, the largest manufacturing employers being Alstom Power Air Preheater Corp, Current Controls, Dresser Rand, Acme Electric Co, Empire Cheese, and Friendship Dairies.

Dairy production has not declined, but the number of farms has dropped, and agriculture now employs only 6% of the labor force. The county's economic base provides services for the 50,000 residents who prefer to buy groceries, obtain professional services, repair cars, or dine out close to home. Allegany Co has valuable resources to strengthen its economic base. Rte 17, rebuilt as a four-lane highway in 1973–74, was designated I-86 in 1999, and several industrial parks are under development. The higher education institutions enroll over 5,000 students, employ about 20% of the county labor force, and create high-technology jobs. The Ceramic Corridor Innovation Center in Alfred hosts several promising start-up companies. Recreation and tourism also strengthen the economy. In 2000 hunters tagged 18,600 deer, up from 7,600 in 1983. Much underutilized pastureland is owned by people living out of Allegany Co who have built cabins for summer vacation getaways and hunting trips in the fall. Projects that build on recreation and tourism are favored, such as making more intensive use of 51,000 acres (20,600 ha) of state forest and of the Genesee River. Swain ski area is a downhill facility.

The county's population has remained relatively constant since 1840, while New York State's population increased from 2.4 million to 18 million. Therefore, Allegany and the other Southern Tier counties have less influence in New York State politics today. The east-west-oriented 31st Congressional District, which represented five rural Southern Tier counties, followed the Erie Railroad and Rte 17 (I-86). Today, economic links are oriented northward, and the 31st was divided between Rochester and Buffalo congressional districts following the 2001 redistricting.

See also PETROLEUM AND NATURAL GAS INDUSTRY.

Allegany Co's earliest years are covered by Orsamus Turner, *Pioneer History of the Holland Patent* (1849). The standard reference, *History of Allegany County* (1879), is one of the least useful of centennial era histories, but John S. Minard, *Allegany County and Its People* (1896) is above the average of its period. Early town histories include John S. Minard, *Hume Pioneer Sketches* (1888), Helen Gilbert, *Rushford and Rushford People* (1910), and Cortez R. Clawson, *History of the Town of Alfred* (1926). One of the better examples among the more recent town histories of varying quality is *The History of Friendship* (1964). Thomas V. Peterson, *Linked Arms: A Rural Community Resists Nuclear Waste* (2002), describes the successful Allegany Co protest movement of the late 1980s and early 1990s. Thomas Rasmussen is currently preparing a book on the county's social and economic history.

Thomas H. Rasmussen

Allegany Indian Reservation. Created at the Treaty of Big Tree in 1797, this tract [loc in Cattaraugus Co] is one of the Seneca Nation of Indians' three federally recognized reservations. Originally surveyed to comprise some 30,469 acres (12,330 ha) along both banks of the Allegheny River, it encompassed several important and long-standing Seneca communities.

Because of the rich timber resources and the railroad, an increasing number of white settlers began to encroach on the reservation by the mid-1800s. Some had leased illegally from individual Senecas. Congress legitimized these transactions, which included the Village (now City) of Salamanca, for five years in 1875. In addition to Salamanca, there were five other so-called congressional villages (Carrolton, Great Valley, Red House, Vandalia, West Salamanca) occupying some 12,000 acres (4,900 ha) of reservation lands whose leases were renewed in 1880 and then extended for 99 years in 1892. The approaching expiration of the 99-year lease resulted in considerable agitation among the non-Indian leaseholders in the congressional villages and antagonism against the Seneca. In 1990 a newly revised lease more favorable to Seneca interests was negotiated and remained in place in 2003. The Allegany Reservation was affected by the Kinzua Dam reservoir, completed in 1965, which flooded approximately 10,000 acres (4,050 ha) of the reservation and forced Seneca communities to relocate. In 1981, after years of negotiation and a land swap involving 795 acres (322 ha), I-86 was built through the reservation. The Seneca received in return an equal amount of land, much of it from Allegany State Park, but tensions with state and federal authorities over land use remain.

Abler, Thomas S., and Elisabeth Tooker. "Seneca." In *Northeast,* ed. Bruce G. Trigger, vol 15 of *Handbook of North American Indians,* ed. William C. Sturtevant (Washington, DC: Smithsonian Institution, 1978)

Abrams, George H. J. *The Seneca People* (Phoenix, Ariz: Indian Tribal Series, 1976)

George H. J. Abrams

Allegany State Park (65,000 acres/26,000 ha). Located in Cattaraugus Co and part of the Appalachian mountain range, it is the third-largest state park in New York after the Adirondack and Catskill Parks. There are approximately 700 acres (280 ha) of old growth hemlocks and northern hardwoods within the park. The region has been home to the Seneca Indians since the mid–17th century, and the park is bordered on the west and north by the Allegany Indian Reservation of the Seneca Nation. The area was the site of commercial logging beginning in 1828 and peaking between 1890 and 1895; the last sawmill closed around 1910. The park opened on 30 July 1921. The grounds have a variety of flora and fauna and contain several interesting geological formations, such as Thunder Rocks and the Bear Caves. There is also an observational stone tower with an elevation of 2,200 feet (670 m) built by the federal Civilian Conservation Corps, which worked at the park from 1933 to 1937. Summer activities include boating, cycling, fishing, hiking, horseback riding, and swimming. Winter visitors can enjoy ice fishing, skiing, sledding, snowshoeing, and snowmobiling. An estimated 1.5 million people visit the park annually.

Congdon, Charles E. *Allegany Oxbow: A History of Allegany State Park and the Allegany Reserve of the Seneca Nation* (Little Valley, NY: Straight Publishing, 1967)

Mary E. Gabriel

Allegheny Airlines. The company was founded on 5 Mar 1937 as All American Aviation to introduce a unique form of airmail service in which a mail container was suspended on a wire strung between two poles and picked up by a trailing line from a low-flying aircraft. After an experimental period the airline launched its service with routes radiating from Pittsburgh on 12 Aug 1940 to dozens of points in the Allegheny Mountains region of Pennsylvania, but one tentacle of the web served Jamestown (Chautauqua Co) in western New York State. With a change of status to serve as a local service airline, All American began passenger service on 7 Mar 1949, and the Jamestown route was extended to Buffalo via Dunkirk/Fredonia (Chautauqua Co). The pickup mail service ended on 30 June 1949. At that time Mohawk Airlines served all of New York State, connecting with All American at Buffalo. On 1 Jan 1953 All American changed its name to Allegheny Airlines and advertised Buffalo as a co-terminal with Niagara Falls. During the 1960s it introduced twin-engined pressurized airliners and became known customarily as a regional airline. The company removed Dunkirk from service in 1967 because of the expanding network of interstate highways and made a second entry into New York State from Philadelphia to Albany in 1970. Operating in a well-populated commercial and industrial region and under the energetic leadership of Leslie Barnes, the airline began to promote itself as the Allegheny Air System.

On 12 Apr 1972 Allegheny merged with Mohawk Airlines, whose service area included cities along the Mohawk Valley, with branchlines to smaller communities such as Watertown (Jefferson Co), Ogdensburg, and Massena (St. Lawrence Co). By this time Allegheny had set up the Allegheny Commuter System, and this included Air North, which took over some low-density routes in 1970 at points in the northern part of New York State that had been acquired with the Mohawk merger. Under the terms of the Airline Deregulation Act of 1978, in which airlines were ranked by the size of annual revenues, USAir was classed as a major airline. During that year the airline carried almost 13 million passengers and had an operating revenue of $566,754,000. The final stage of expansion came on 28 Oct 1979 when Allegheny Airlines changed its name to USAir, reflecting the scope of its routes. Having acquired Piedmont Airlines and Air California, USAirways is a nationwide airline and, as of 2002, ranked fifth in the United States in passenger numbers and operated across the Atlantic as well as New York State at many cities, such as Albany, Syracuse, Buffalo, and Rochester.

Davies, R. E. G. *Airlines of the United States since 1914* (1972; repr McLean, Va: Paladwr Press, 1998)

Lewis, W. David, and William F. Trimble. *The Airway to Everywhere* (Pittsburgh: Univ of Pittsburgh Press, 1988)

R. E. G. Davies

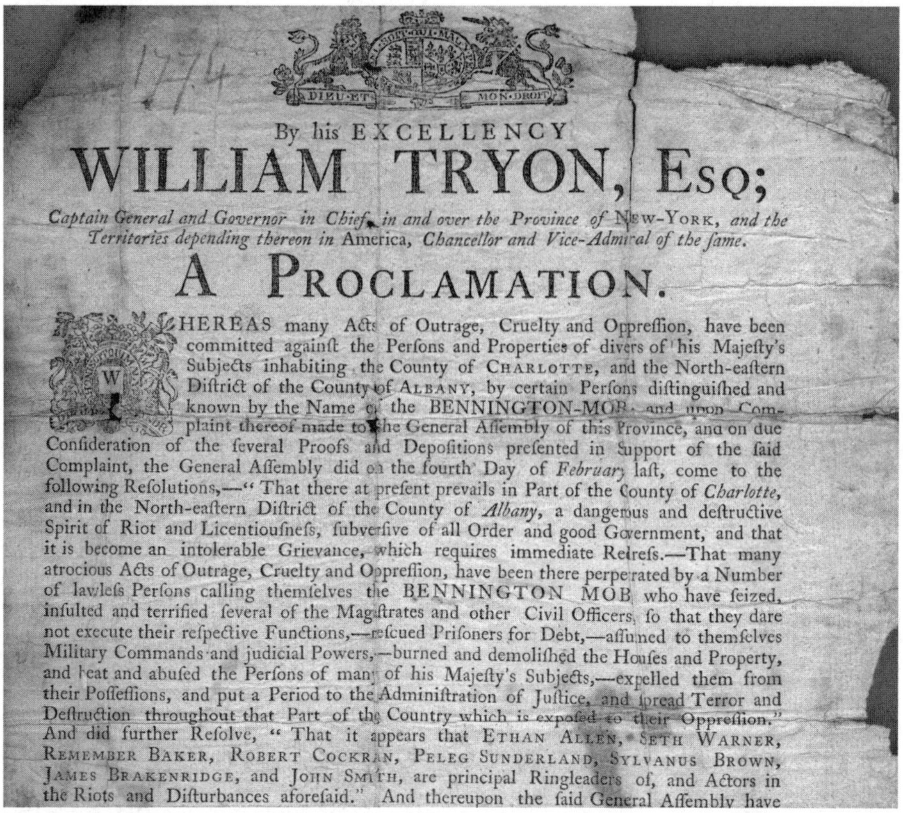

By his EXCELLENCY
WILLIAM TRYON, Esq;
Captain General and Governor in Chief, in and over the Province of NEW-YORK, *and the Territories depending thereon in* America, *Chancellor and Vice-Admiral of the ſame.*

A PROCLAMATION.

WHEREAS many Acts of Outrage, Cruelty and Oppreſſion, have been committed againſt the Perſons and Properties of divers of his Majeſty's Subjects inhabiting the County of CHARLOTTE, and the North-eaſtern Diſtrict of the County of ALBANY, by certain Perſons diſtinguiſhed and known by the Name of the BENNINGTON-MOB; and upon Complaint thereof made to the General Aſſembly of this Province, and on due Conſideration of the ſeveral Proofs and Depoſitions preſented in Support of the ſaid Complaint, the General Aſſembly did on the fourth Day of *February* laſt, come to the following Reſolutions,—" That there at preſent prevails in Part of the County of *Charlotte*, and in the North-eaſtern Diſtrict of the County of *Albany*, a dangerous and deſtructive Spirit of Riot and Licentiouſneſs, ſubverſive of all Order and good Government, and that it is become an intolerable Grievance, which requires immediate Redreſs.—That many atrocious Acts of Outrage, Cruelty and Oppreſſion, have been there perpetrated by a Number of lawleſs Perſons calling themſelves the BENNINGTON MOB who have ſeized, inſulted and terrified ſeveral of the Magiſtrates and other Civil Officers, ſo that they dare not execute their reſpective Functions,—reſcued Priſoners for Debt,—aſſumed to themſelves Military Commands and judicial Powers,—burned and demoliſhed the Houſes and Property, and beat and abuſed the Perſons of many of his Majeſty's Subjects,—expelled them from their Poſſeſſions, and put a Period to the Adminiſtration of Juſtice, and ſpread Terror and Deſtruction throughout that Part of the Country which is expoſed to their Oppreſſion." And did further Reſolve, " That it appears that ETHAN ALLEN, SETH WARNER, REMEMBER BAKER, ROBERT COCKRAN, PELEG SUNDERLAND, SYLVANUS BROWN, JAMES BRAKENRIDGE, and JOHN SMITH, are principal Ringleaders of, and Actors in the Riots and Diſturbances aforeſaid." And thereupon the ſaid General Aſſembly have

Detail of a proclamation declaring Ethan Allen and the "Bennington Mob" to be ringleaders of "atrocious Acts of Cruelty, Outrage and Oppression," 1774.

Allegheny River (325 mi/523 km). Rising in headwaters in Potter Co, Pa, the Allegheny River flows north into New York State at Genesee (Allegany Co) before arching west and south back into Pennsylvania at South Valley (Cattaraugus Co) and joining the Monongahela at Pittsburgh to form the Ohio River. In New York State, the river serves as a northern boundary for Allegany State Park, and some 40 miles (64 km) of it run within the Allegany Indian Reservation of the Seneca Nation. In earlier centuries, the Allegheny was an important transportation route for American Indians and, later, for white settlers who envisioned it as the main avenue to the west because it linked with the Ohio and Mississippi Rivers. However, the river's fluctuating water levels within New York State made year-round navigation difficult, and the Erie Canal (1825) proved a more reliable and appealing route to western lands. Industries located along the Allegheny River, especially in the Town of Olean (Cattaraugus Co), which was linked to other cities by rail during the 1850s. Many of the region's industries centered around the transportation and processing of oil. The upper and lower sections of the river were divided in 1965 when the US Army Corps of Engineers completed the Kinzua Dam in northern Pennsylvania. In 2002 issues about the Allegheny River revolved around environmental contamination from runoff from old industrial sites in Olean and vicinity and from agricultural fertilizers.

Schafer, Jim, and Mike Sajna. *The Allegheny River: Watershed of the Nation* (University Park: Pennsylvania State Univ Press, 1992)

Penny Messinger

Allen. Town (pop 462) in N central Allegany Co. Settled in 1806, the town was formed in 1823 from Angelica. Sheep raising was eclipsed by dairying after the Civil War. A German community developed in the 1850s and formed St. Paul's Lutheran Church (1868). In 2003 several farms continue to ship milk, and other residents commute. The town has many hunting camps, two campgrounds catering to outdoor recreation, and a famous restaurant, the Maple Tree Inn, which operates during sugaring season. Part of the 2,421-acre (979.7 ha) Allen Lake State Forest is in the town. In 1989–90 Allen was one of five Allegany Co towns selected for possible nuclear waste dumps, which it successfully resisted.

Allen, Ethan (*b* Litchfield, Conn, 10 Jan 1738; *d* Burlington Intervale [now Burlington, Vt], 12 Feb 1789). Militia leader in Revolutionary War and in struggle for an independent Vermont. In 1757 Allen served briefly in the French and Indian War as part of the Connecticut militia. He married Mary Brownson in 1762, and between 1763 and 1779 they had five children. In 1762 he also started operating an iron forge in Salisbury, Conn, but moved in 1770 to the Green Mountains (now in Vermont but was at the time claimed by New York Colony) and invested in land titles granted by New Hampshire. In the summer of 1770 he organized the Green Mountain Boys and led the mostly nonviolent resistance to New York Colony's jurisdiction over land in the New Hampshire Grants, as the area was also known. In 1772 New York governor William Tryon offered a £100 reward for Allen but otherwise did little to crush what proved, within four years, to be a successful rebellion in New York's northern territory, with Allen insisting as early as 1773 on the people's right to create their own state outside "the kingdom."

After the fighting at Lexington and Concord, Allen led the Green Mountain Boys in a surprise attack on Fort Ticonderoga [now in Essex Co] on 10 May 1775. Along with some Massachusetts militia and aided by Benedict Arnold, Allen's poorly armed forces captured control of Lake Champlain without a single casualty. Every British soldier in the area was taken captive, and essential military stores were seized. Allen became a national hero on the basis of this first offensive victory of the Revolutionary War. After the capture of Ticonderoga, Allen's cousin Seth Warner was given command of the Green Mountain Boys upon its appointment as a unit of the Continental army. Later in 1775, Ethan Allen recruited Indians and Canadians to support Gen Richard Montgomery's invasion of Canada. Taken prisoner in a premature and ill-conceived attack on Montreal in September, Allen spent two years in England and New York City as a prisoner of war. Exchanged in May 1778 for Lt Col Archibald Campbell, Allen soon after wrote a very successful captivity narrative that went through eight editions in two years.

In 1777 Vermont settlers declared their independence from both New York State and Great Britain, but the Continental Congress, pressured by New York, did not accept their claim of statehood. The Vermont republic faced unrelenting but ineffective opposition from New York for most of its existence from 1777 to 1791. Allen became a key figure in the independent state upon his return from captivity, holding a variety of offices, including commander in chief of Vermont's military forces. In 1781 he began negotiations with Gov Frederick Haldimand, British commander in Canada, indicating a willingness to have Vermont join the British Empire. For three years Allen negotiated between the Continental Congress and Great Britain while keeping Vermont on an entirely independent course. Partly in response to Vermont's neutrality in Shays's Rebellion, the New York State legislature, despite the opposition of Gov George Clinton, gave up its effort to reclaim Vermont in 1786.

Although he lacked a formal education, Allen aspired to win acceptance as a writer. Between 1781 and 1785 he wrote *Reason the Only Oracle of Man,* the first deistic work written by an American. Allen devoted one-third of this long theological study to showing Christianity's failings and the other two-thirds to putting forth a deistic religion of nature. The book found few readers. He dedicated the last years of his life to his family's farm in what is now Burlington, Vt. He died in 1789, two years before Vermont became the 14th state.

Allen, Ethan, and Ira Allen. *Ethan and Ira Allen: Collected Works,* 3 vols, ed. J Kevin Graffagnino (Benson, Vt: Chalidze Publications, 1992)

Bellesiles, Michael A. *Revolutionary Outlaws: Ethan Allen and the Struggle for Independence on the Early American Frontier* (Charlottesville: Univ of Virginia Press, 1993)

Michael A. Bellesiles

Allen, Horatio (*b* Schenectady, 10 May 1802; *d* East Orange, NJ, 31 Dec 1889). Civil engineer. An 1823 graduate of Columbia College, he began work in 1824 as a resident engineer for Chesapeake and Delaware Canal Co at St. George's, Del. In 1826 he became assistant engineer of Delaware and Hudson (D&H) Canal Co, which also planned to build a railroad. D&H chief engineer, John B. Jervis, sent Allen to England to study railroad construction and to order locomotives and iron rail. In 1829 Allen made a successful run with the British locomotive Stourbridge Lion on the D&H line—likely the first run of a commercial locomotive in North America. Later that year he became chief engineer of South Carolina Canal and Rail Road Co. In 1837 Jervis hired Allen as his principal assistant for the Croton Aqueduct project. Allen served as president of the New York and Erie Railroad from 1843 to 1844, and as consulting engineer (1849) and chief engineer (1851) of the company. In 1844 he partnered in Novelty Iron Works (later Stillman, Allen and Co), which manufactured engines, hydraulic presses, and other machinery in New York City. Officer and president of the firm between 1844 and 1870, Allen also invented new steam-valve gear (1853–57) and consulted on the Brooklyn Bridge project. He was president of the American Society of Civil Engineers (1871–73).

Forney, Matthias N. *Memoir of Horatio Allen* (New York: Burr, 1890)

Stover, John F. *American Railroads,* 2d ed. (Chicago: Univ of Chicago Press, 1997)

Albert S. Eggerton Jr

Allen, Woody [Konigsberg, Allan (Stewart)] (*b* Brooklyn, 1 Dec 1935). Filmmaker, writer, and actor. Allen grew up in Brooklyn's Midwood section of Flatbush. While attending Midwood High School he began writing jokes for Broadway columnists. After graduating in 1952, he adopted his current name and attended New York University, leaving in 1953. Allen began his career as a stand-up comedian, often appearing in Greenwich Village nightclubs, and achieved considerable renown. He has also been a writer of comic vignettes for the *New Yorker* since 1966 but is best known for his work in film. He directed, co-wrote, and starred in his breakthrough film, *Annie Hall* (1977), the story of an ill-fated Manhattan love affair. His films are often set among the wealthy and intellectual populations of Manhattan's Upper East Side and West Side. The ethnic Jewish culture of his youth forms a major component of his humor, and his comic persona is the neurotic New Yorker who is forever in therapy, lost whenever separated from his beloved Manhattan, and endlessly looking for love but not knowing what to do when he finds it. Many of his movies, from *Annie Hall* and *Manhattan* (1979) to *Manhattan Murder Mystery* (1993) and *Everyone Says I Love You* (1996), are valentines to Manhattan's urban beauty. Others with New York City settings include *Broadway Danny Rose* (1984), *Hannah and Her Sisters* (1986), *Radio Days* (1987), *Crimes and Misdemeanors* (1989), and *Bullets over Broadway* (1994). Allen received much public attention in 1993 after he split with his long-time companion, actress Mia Farrow, following his romance with her 21-year-old adopted daughter, Soon-Yi Previn, whom he married in 1997.

Allen, Woody. *Woody Allen on Woody Allen: In Conversation With Stig Bjorkman* (New York: Grove Press, 1995)

Allied-Signal. Formed as the Solvay Process Co and named after Belgian chemists Ernest and Alfred Solvay, it engaged in the large-scale production of sodium carbonate (Na_2CO_3), or soda ash, an alkali essential in producing a wide variety of common products such as glass, soap, and other industrial chemicals. The brainchild of Oswego native William Cogswell, the company was incorporated in 1881 with the financial backing of Ernest Solvay and Rhode Island industrialist Rowland Hazard. A plant was built in the Town of Geddes (Onondaga Co), close by two of the three primary raw materials required: calcium carbonate ($CaCO_3$) in the form of limestone, quarried at Split Rock and later Jamesville (Onondaga Co), and sodium chloride (NaCl), common salt, collected as brine at Tully (Onondaga Co). Production began 10 Jan 1884, quickly reaching 20 tons (18 MT) a day, and the company became the first successful large-scale manufacturer of an alkali in the nation. A year later production exceeded 50 tons (45 MT) daily, and other products soon followed; bicarbonate of soda ($2NaHCO_3$), baking soda, was the best known (marketed as Arm and Hammer and Cow Brand).

By 1900 the company employed over 3,000 workers, providing them with employee benefits that included hospital care, sick pay, educational and recreational programs, and facilities for workers and their families. Semet-Solvay Co, an offshoot company, established a picric acid and trinitrotoluene production facility at the former Split Rock quarry site in 1903. Solvay Process expanded to meet munitions needs during World War I. Although a major explosion on the night of 2 July 1918 resulted in the death of 50 workers, the company prospered and continued to grow and in 1920 consolidated with four other chemical companies to form Allied Chemical and Dye Corp, later named Allied Chemical Corp (1958) and then Allied Corp (1981). The other companies were Semet-Solvay Co (coke and coke by-products), Barrett Co (coal-tar products), General Chemical Co (acids), and National Aniline and Chemical Co (dyestuffs).

Success did not come without an environmental price. The Solvay plant generated large quantities of waste materials and pollutants. Gases such as ammonia and hydrogen sulfide were periodically discharged into the atmosphere, as were countless tons of particulate matter. Large volumes of effluent, at times containing various heavy metals and other toxic substances, were emptied into local waters, primarily nearby Onondaga Lake. In addition hundreds of acres of tailings ponds were constructed north and west of the plant to hold solid wastes. Declining product demand and outdated facilities prompted permanent closure of the facilities in 1986, thereby placing over 1,500 employees out of work. In 1999 AlliedSignal (as it was known since 1985) announced its intention to clean up and rectify the environmental problems the chemical plant caused during its century of operation. Later that year AlliedSignal merged with Honeywell.

Allied Chemical. *1700 Milton Avenue: The Solvay Story, 1881–1981* ([Solvay, NY: Author], 1981)

Haber, Ludwig F. *The Chemical Industry, 1900–1930: International Growth and Technical Change* (Oxford, England: Clarendon Press, 1971)

James W. Darlington

Alline, Anna Lowell (*b* East Machias, Maine, 1864; *d* Iowa, 16 Dec 1934). Nurse educator. Alline graduated in 1893 from the Brooklyn Homeopathic Hospital Training School for Nurses, after which she was hired as assistant to the school's superintendent, Linda Richards. In 1900 Alline was one of two students to enroll in the hospital economics course at Teachers College, Columbia University. After completing the program she became its director (1900–1906) and worked at supervising students and expanding the program. Alline was New York State's first inspector of nurse training schools (1906–9), and she worked to standardize nursing education methods and practices. In 1910 she became superintendent of the Buffalo Homeopathic Hospital (1910–12). Alline worked for the Red Cross during World War I and served as director of the laboratory and outpatient department at Albany Homeopathic Hospital (1918–23). In 1923 Alline married E. Wilton Brown and retired from nursing.

Julie M. Pavri

Alling, Joseph T(ilden) (*b* Rochester, 19 Jan 1855; *d* Rochester, 20 Sept 1937). Businessman and civic leader. Alling grew up in Rochester and graduated from the Rochester Free Academy (1872) and the University of Rochester (1876), where he received his AB degree. Upon graduation he went to work at Alling and Cory, the paper company his father was associated with in Rochester. He worked at the firm until his death, serving as president from 1908 to 1935. Interested in education, Alling served as a trustee at the University of Rochester from 1892 to 1937 and as trustee chairman from 1932 to 1937. His 45-year tenure as a University of Rochester trustee was during the university's period of greatest growth, when it evolved from a small men's college to a university and grew from one campus to four. He led Rochester's Good Government League from 1895 to 1912. During his tenure the league accomplished the election of a reform mayor and the removal of the local school board of education from political control. He also was active in the YMCA, the Central Presbyterian Church, and the Community Chest. He was president of the Rochester YMCA from 1891 1897. During World War I he was involved in YMCA work at Camp Dix.

McKelvey, Blake. "Civic Medals Awarded Posthumously," *Rochester History* 22 (Apr 1960): 18–19

Karl S. Kabelac

Alma. Town (pop 847) in S Allegany Co. Settled in 1833, the town was formed in 1854 from Willing. Early industries were lumbering and tanning. Irish immigrants arrived in the early 1840s and Germans late in the same decade. Oil was prospected beginning in 1877, creating a boom. Allentown was platted in 1881 by an oilman. Oil was pumped until the late 1980s. Between the world wars potatoes were grown commercially. The town includes Alma Hill, the highest point in the Southern Tier at 2,548 feet (776.6 m).

Almond [AL-MOND]. Town (pop 1,604) and village (pop 461) in NE Allegany Co. Almond was settled in 1796, primarily from the Wyoming Valley of Pennsylvania. Legendary frontiersman and surveyor Moses Van Campen (1796–1849) was among the first comers. The town was formed in 1821 from Alfred and was crossed by the Lake Erie Turnpike from Bath to Olean (1810–11), and as a result many immigrants came prior to the Erie Canal. Industries included tanning and shoe manufacturing, the Phoenix Woolen Mill (1848–early 1870s), and hay-rake manufacturing. The Erie Railroad crossed the town in 1851. The village, of which a small part is in Hornellsville (Steuben Co), was incorporated in 1921. The World Horse Traders' Convention took place in Almond from the mid-1920s until it was moved to the county fairgrounds in 1953. Rte 17 (I-86) was completed through Almond in 1974. Reforestation in the 1930s resulted in Turnpike (4,744 acres/1,920 ha), Bully Hill (3,513 acres/1,422 ha), and Klipnocky (2,612 acres/1,057 ha) State Forests.

almshouses and poorhouses. The Dutch Reformed Church established the first poorhouses in New Netherland, initiating a poor relief program based on Calvinist principles they practiced in the Dutch Republic. In Beverwijck [now Albany] church officials established a poorhouse by 1652, said to be the first in North America, and deacons in New Amsterdam [now New York City] managed another in 1653. When the British took over the colony in 1664, the Dutch Church system, similar to England's poor laws (1601) requiring local parishes to assist the indigent, remained intact. In 1683 a provincial poor law was enacted stipulating that churches assist all community paupers, not only parishioners, which led denominations throughout New York Colony to develop a relief system.

By the early 1700s both church and community leaders in New York City and Albany and Westchester and Suffolk Cos provided housing for the poor. Some paupers lived in church poorhouses, but most stayed in private residences—hence the term "boarding out"—with church or city leaders paying the homeowners rent. Churches and municipalities also housed paupers in homes they owned, thus creating small neighborhood poorhouses. Many poor received outdoor relief, such as cash, food, and clothes, from local churches. In 1700 New York City officials bought a vacated residence and established the city's first municipal poorhouse. It built a larger structure in 1736 in the pasture area referred to as the Commons, near the site of the current City Hall, which, although designed to serve the poor, was also a hospital and house of correction. Residents were called inmates, lived structured lives, and were forced to eat, sleep, work, and pray at designated times, making it more of a reformatory for social deviants. In 1766 New York City improved the poorhouse and in 1775 built the Bridewell next door, an almshouse correctional facility. During the Revolutionary War, New York City paupers were deported to Westchester Co, forcing many towns to establish poorhouses. State legislation in 1784 required each city, town, and district to establish a relief program. Poorhouses were not mandated, however, and boarding out and outdoor relief were the main forms of assistance.

By 1820 poorhouses, always small, existed in many communities, but larger structures, built specifically to house paupers and known as almshouses, also existed. These institutional-style buildings were set away from residences and businesses and offered workshops, schools, and farms in an effort to rehabilitate the poor. New York City paupers lived at Bellevue, north of the city core on the East River, in an almshouse built by 1816. The state's 1824 Yates Report, the first inclusive survey of poor housing and relief programs in the country, counted 2 county almshouses, 2 under construction, and 22 poorhouses in towns, villages, and cities in 24 of the state's 54 existing counties. Yates exposed that paupers were mistreated and neglected and that multiple forms of relief were not cost effective. This prompted the legislature to pass the County Poorhouse Act (1824), which required all counties (except Oneida and Ulster Cos) to build and manage almshouses. The report ushered in an ideology that institutional housing, combined with work and education programs, would rehabilitate and benefit paupers, a system that continued into the early 20th century. New York Co had the state's largest almshouse, on Blackwell's Island [now Roosevelt Island], which opened in 1848.

An 1858 state survey, conducted after the panic of 1857, counted 13,422 poorhouse residents, of whom 6,503 were immigrants and 2,313 physically or mentally impaired. Of all New York State residents, 10.5% lived in poorhouses or received public aid, and in New York Co 17.5% received temporary relief. There were 57 county almshouses with teachers, superintendents, keepers, physicians and farms tended by inmates. In most, men and women lived in separate, dormlike quarters. Many institutions lacked bathing facilities, and in some paupers were confined to cells and shackled. Poverty increased with immigration during the 1840s and 1850s, prompting charity and religious organizations to establish poorhouses. Facilities were privately run, usually in mansionlike homes, and were targeted to assist specific social groups, such as women, women and children, orphans, veterans, the elderly or infirm, and immigrants. In 1867 the State Board of Commissioners of Public Charities formed to oversee county almshouses. It became the Board of Charities in 1873 and managed state- and county-operated almshouses and independently owned poorhouses and old-age homes. The mentally ill and children under 16 were then moved out of almshouses and into separate facilities. Erie Co built an almshouse and farm in Buffalo in 1889, and mentally disabled people lived there even though it was prohibited by state law.

In 1890 the legislature enacted the New York State Care Act, creating separate poorhouse and treatment centers for the mentally ill, a first in the nation. In the 1890s, as child labor and child welfare were becoming public issues, poor children lived in the stricter environment of the orphan asylum. By the 1910s almshouse residents were adults and were either European immigrants, without family, suffering from alcohol addiction, or considered social deviants. The institutional system began to decline in the 1920s as social work became a profession and both national and state laws, such as the workers' compensation acts, state pension law, and unemployment and health insurance laws, were passed. Policies targeted causes of poverty and provided state or national aid giving more poor people the option to live at home on lower income. Almshouses were crowded during the depression, but by the late 1930s were less so, mainly because of New Deal legislation that essentially reestablished the 18th-century relief program, outdoor relief, where the majority of poor lived in their own homes and received public assistance. By the early 1940s many almshouses were converted into old-age homes. Although never politically abolished, poorhouses were nonexistent by the 1950s. The 21st-century almshouse takes shape as the city mission or the homeless or women's shelter, in which most occupants have no surviving relatives, are veterans, or suffer from personal problems or mental or physical diseases.

See also CHILD WELFARE; HOMELESSNESS; MENTAL HEALTH CARE; POVERTY.

Cray, Robert E., Jr. *Paupers and Poor Relief in New York City and Its Rural Environs, 1700 to 1830* (Philadelphia: Temple Univ Press, 1988)
Mohl, Raymond. *Poverty in New York, 1783 to 1825* (New York: Oxford Univ Press, 1971)
Schneider, David M., and A. Deutsch. *The History of Public Welfare in New York State, 1867–1940* (Chicago: Univ of Chicago Press, 1941)
Trattner, Walter. *From Poor Law to Welfare State: A History of Social Welfare in America* (New York: Free Press, 1998)

Altamont. Town (pop 6,137) in SW Franklin Co. Settled *ca* 1840, its lumber industry developed *ca* 1850. The first resort hotel was the Mount Morris House (1868). The town was formed from Waverly in 1890. Faust, also called Tupper Lake Junction, is the former junction point of the New York and Ottawa (1890) and the Mohawk and Malone (1892) Railroads, as well as the privately owned Brooklyn Cooperage Railroad. Principal industries are tourism, pulp, lumber, and wood products. Beginning in 1960 the main attraction was Big Tupper Ski Area; it closed in the 1990s. The town's population remained relatively stable during the 1990s despite difficult economic conditions; in 2000, 64% of the residents lived in the Village of Tupper Lake.

Thomas W. Perrin

Altamont. Village (pop 1,737) in Guilderland (Albany Co). The locality acquired a post office named West Guilderland in 1829, which was renamed Knowersville in 1840 for the recently deceased proprietor of its hat factory. Business grew with the Schoharie and Albany Plank Road (1849) and with the Albany and Susquehanna Railroad (1863). It became a summer resort, noted for the Hotel Kushaqua (1885) and for private cottages. After changing its name to Altamont in 1887, the village incorporated in 1890 and has held the Altamont Fair since 1892. The hotel, located outside the village limits, became the LaSalette Seminary in 1924; a new building was completed in 1953. In the early 21st century Altamont is a suburban village; much of its Main Street is a National Register historic district.

alternative medicine. Several alternatives to standard medical practices were fostered in New York State by the early 19th century. Common treatments such as bloodletting and use of poisonous purgatives, emetics, and mineral drugs often debilitated and harmed patients. Dissatisfaction with these therapies led to popular health crusades and the growth of competing medical systems. While some health reform movements addressed only laypersons and home health practices, others founded hospitals, medical schools, and professional organizations like those of the existing medical establishment, competing successfully for patients and stimulating reforms in therapies. Medical reform paralleled and often intersected other 19th-century reform movements, including temperance, women's rights, abolitionism, and religious reform. Part of a national democratic impulse to make social, religious, and political institutions more inclusive, movements such as Thomsonism, hydrotherapy, eclecticism, homeopathy, and Christian Science lauded gentle, natural remedies, the mind/body relationship in healing, and the restorative powers of the body's nonmaterial "vital force" or energy.

BOTANICAL MOVEMENTS

In the 1820s New Hampshire native Samuel Thomson developed a numbered system for administering botanical drugs based on "cleansing and strengthening" theories popular in folk medicine. Beginning as a self-help movement of laypersons, Thomsonian healers established "friendly societies" promoting self-treatment. In the 1840s practitioners led a successful battle to repeal New York State's law prohibiting the unlicensed practice of medicine, though by this time, Thomsonism had developed into a movement of professional practitioners, thereby losing much of its popular appeal.

In the 1830s another botanical healer and physician, Wooster Beach, formulated a "reformed system of medical practice," which he termed "eclectic." Lacking a specific therapeutic philosophy, the eclectic school utilized salutary therapies from various schools of medicine while rejecting their "defects." Beach later employed and marketed concentrated botanical medicines. Unlike Thomsonism the eclectic movement established a parallel medical profession, including local and state medical societies and colleges with curricula similar, in most respects, to those of mainstream medical schools. Seven eclectic medical colleges were established in New York State: New York Reformed Medical College (1836–38); Metropolitan Medical College (1852–62); Eclectic Medical College of the City of New York (1866–1913); and US Medical College (1878–82), all located in New York City, plus Central Medical College of New York, located in Syracuse (1848–55), Syracuse Medical College (1850–57), and Rochester Eclectic Medical College (1848–52). Despite these schools the number of eclectic physicians remained small, estimated at only 4% of the nation's physicians between 1850 and 1900. In 1886, 1,883 regular physicians, 224 homeopaths, and 53 eclectics practiced medicine in New York City. Eclectic schools were noted for their early admission of women; Clemence Sophia Lozier, founder of New York State's first women's medical college, graduated from Syracuse Medical School in 1853. Eclectic medicine provided an important avenue to medical degrees for women, as did homeopathy.

HOMEOPATHY

Developed by German physician Samuel Hahnemann in the late 1700s, homeopathy was introduced into the United States in 1825 by Hans Burch Gram, a German immigrant physician and New York City resident. Hahnemann's Law of Similars held that a drug causing particular symptoms when tested or "proved" on a healthy person was able, in fractional doses, to cure an ill individual with similar symptoms. Thus homeopaths prescribed only minute doses of drugs. The first US homeopathic dispensary was established in 1845 in New York City. By 1860 between 3 and 4% of the 55,000 physicians in the United States were homeopaths, with New York State claiming the largest number (699).

During the 1860s Manhattan's New York Homeopathic Dispensary became an important center for homeopathic education and practice. Along with the New York Ophthalmic Hospital and School, which operated as a homeopathic institution from 1867, New York City claimed two other early and long-lived homeopathic medical colleges: New York Homeopathic Medical College (1860–1936) and New York Medical College and Hospital for Women (1863–1918). The latter school was New York State's first women's medical college and the nation's third, graduating about 370 women before merging in 1918 with formerly all-male New York Homeopathic Medical College. The last third of the 19th century was the heyday of homeopathy; its physicians then formed 8% of all doctors, and 21 medical colleges and hundreds of hospitals, dispensaries, and medical societies were in operation throughout the United States. Homeopathy attracted a wealthy, educated, primarily urban clientele who viewed this "new school" of medicine as part of a progressive agenda of social reform. Providing early opportunities for women, homeopathy was linked with women's rights. By 1936, after gradually eliminating homeopathic subjects from its curriculum, New York Homeopathic College, once one of the nation's largest and most important homeopathic schools, became New York Medical College.

HYDROPATHY

Thomsonism, eclecticism, and homeopathy, which claimed large numbers of converts by the mid–19th century, all advocated the administration of botanical or mineral drugs or remedies. In contrast, hydropathy or "water cure," which enjoyed nationwide popularity by the 1840s, largely abandoned drug therapy, deeming it incompatible with the human system. Founded by Silesian peasant Vincent Priessnitz in the 1820s, water cure used internal and external applications of cold water along with dietary and hygenic principles of "right living." In 1843 physician Joel Shew and his wife Marie Louise treated patients in their New York City home, establishing the first water cure in the United States. A year later physician Russell Thatcher Trall opened a second, more extensive facility nearby, and in 1851, health reformer and prominent practitioner and teacher of hydropathic therapeutics Mary Gove Nichols founded American Hydropathic Institute, the nation's first water-cure college in New York City. Trall's New York Hydropathic and Physiological School, later the New York Hygeio-Therapeutic College, replaced Nichols's school within two years, and on the founding of the Water Cure College in Dansville (Livingston Co) in 1861, New York State became the US water-cure center. Between 1840 and 1900 there were over 200 hydropathic establishments in the country. Two of the longest-lived were located in New York State: Elmira Water Cure (1852–1959) in Chemung Co and Dansville Water Cure (1854–1914).

RISE OF SCIENTIFIC MEDICINE

By the beginning of the 20th century, mainstream medicine developed a new identity rooted in laboratory experimentation rather than in medical theory and tradition. Reforms in medical therapies and training, the reinstitutionalization of licensing, and the rise of scientific medicine resulted in professional consensus and consolidation. Prominent voices in the medical community warned patients against the "quackery" of homeopathy and other nonmainstream traditions. By 1920 most eclectic and homeopathic medical schools had closed or discarded their sectarian identities. Although many alternative practitioners assimilated into the medical mainstream, alternative medicine continued to exist, either practiced by sharply reduced numbers, as in the case of homeopathy, or by adapting 19th-century teachings to the modern world, as with Christian Science healing. New alternative practices also emerged and gained adherents. During the 20th century, Missouri native Andrew Taylor Still's system of osteopathy, inspired by the tenets of magnetic healing and maintaining that illness resulted from a misaligned skeleton, acquired a strong following. From 1898 his American School of Osteopathy in Kirksville, Mo, trained students to treat chronic ailments with spinal manipulation, and by 1990 the New York College of Osteopathic Medicine was among the nation's 14 osteopathic medical schools. Osteopathy developed educational and training standards similar to those of mainstream medicine. Another form of alternative healing, Canadian Daniel David Palmer's chiropractic system, founded in 1895 and resembling osteopathy in its focus on alignment of the vertebrae, created a new professional model. Most mainstream physicians and osteopaths refused to recognize chiropractic therapy for many years. But in 1981 civil lawsuits, including one brought by New York State, resulted in cooperation agreements between chiropractors and other doctors.

RENAISSANCE OF ALTERNATIVE MEDICINE

In the 1970s alternative medicine resurfaced as one of many movements seeking to reform American society. As in the 19th century, this rise of alternative medical practices sprang from a critique of established medicine and also signaled a broad shift in social values. For many, modern technological medicine embodied impersonal, fragmented, market-oriented, and harmful aspects of postmodern life. Increasing numbers of people turned to healing practices relying on less technological and more human and individual approaches to healthcare. These approaches ranged from the old self-care therapies of folk remedies and personal prayer to newer ones such as the use of vitamins and practitioner-based therapies like homeopathy, naturopathy, chiropractic, massage, and acupuncture. In the last decade of the 20th century, alternative or "complementary" medicine moved closer to the mainstream. In 1991 the US Congress created the Office of Alternative Medicine, overseen by the National Institutes of Health, to fund studies in alternative medicine. New York State medical schools incorporated alternative therapies into their curricula. By 1997 both Columbia University's College of Physicians and Surgeons and SUNY Stony Brook established major centers for the study and practice of alternative or complementary medicine.

On 14 Dec 1993 two New York State Assembly committees held hearings on consumer demand for alternative healthcare and on issues of patients' rights and medical freedom. As a result the state amended Education Law 6527(4) on 26 July 1994 to legalize physicians' use of nonconventional therapies in the treatment of disease. At the turn of the 21st century, New York was one of nine states with laws protecting patients' rights to use complementary and alternative medicine with the help of licensed physicians.

See also HEALTHCARE AND HOSPITALS; PHYSICIANS.

Donegan, Jane B. *Hydropathic Highway to Health: Women and Water-Cure in Antebellum America* (Westport, Conn: Greenwood Press, 1986)

Fuller, Robert C. *Alternative Medicine and American Religious Life* (New York: Oxford Univ Press, 1989)

Gevitz, Norman, ed. *Other Healers: Unorthodox Medicine in America* (Baltimore: Johns Hopkins Univ Press, 1988)

Kirschmann, Anne Taylor. "A Vital Force: Women Physicians and Patients in American Homeopathy, 1850–1930" (PhD diss, Univ of Rochester, 1999)

Rothstein, William G. *American Physicians in the 19th Century: From Sects to Science* (Baltimore: Johns Hopkins Univ Press, 1985)

Anne Taylor Kirschmann

Altmar. Village (pop 351) in Albion (Oswego Co). Originally called Sand Bank, its first house was erected in 1813. Waterpower was available from the Salmon River; the community's growth was advanced by the Rome branch of the Rome, Watertown and Ogdensburg Railroad (1851), and many residents worked on the railroad. The village incorporated in 1876. Altmar has become a center of sportfishing. The Salmon River Fish Hatchery (1981) is located in the village, and on a self-guided tour visitors can watch hatchery operations and view different exhibits including mounted and live fish.

Barbara J. Dix

Altona. Town (pop 3,160) in N Clinton Co. Settled in 1800 from New England and Canada, Altona was formed from Chazy in 1857. Though its land is not very fertile, it has good waterpower, and Altona prospered in the 19th century with iron forges and forest products; mixed farming was succeeded by dairying. Milk was shipped on the Northern Railroad (1848; later Rutland Railroad). The Mohawk Nation established its Ganienkeh community on 5,700 acres (2,310 ha) of former state parkland at Miner Lake in 1977, operating businesses and pasturing cattle on the tract. In 1983 the former Altona Central High School was converted into the medium security Altona Correctional Facility. Lumbering and farming remain important to the economy.

Thomas A. Rumney

aluminum industry. In 1888 in Pennsylvania, Charles Martin Hall opened the Pittsburgh Reduction Co (PRC; after 1907, Alcoa), which used a commercially successful method of smelting aluminum through electrolysis. This new process made the production of aluminum feasible for applications in industry and in consumer goods. A PRC rival, the Cowles Electric Smelting and Aluminum Co in Lockport (Niagara Co), was producing aluminum electrothermally by 1891, using a somewhat different process; after a series of patent infringement lawsuits Cowles withdrew from aluminum smelting. In 1895 PRC took advantage of cheaper hydroelectric power by becoming the first customer of the new Niagara Falls Power Co in Niagara Falls. It opened a smelting facility there that August, approximately 1.25 miles (2.01 km) upriver from the falls. The following year PRC opened another smelter below the falls. The company opened additional capacity in Massena (St. Lawrence Co) in 1904; sited on 3,500 acres (1,416 ha), this massive facility boasted a smelter and fabrication and wire-making plants. Massena became a leading source of aluminum wire and cable for the nation and during World War I became the principal fabricator for US naval airships. In the 1920s Alcoa enhanced Massena's capacity to make aluminum bodies for automobiles and trains. Workers at the site consisted of large numbers of foreign-born; Alcoa recruited heavily in New York City's immigrant communities in the 1910s and 1920s.

During the Great Depression concerns about job security and wage standardization led to union organization within the industry, initially by the American Federation of Labor (AFL). Nationally numerous Alcoa plants went on strike in 1934, including the Massena and the Niagara Falls facilities, but resulted in little gain for labor. Anger from many workers over the AFL's failures eventually led the Niagara Falls plants to organize with the United Steelworkers of America (USWA) in the Congress of Industrial Organizations (CIO). World War II vastly increased aluminum demand. A critical material for airplane bodies, production of the metal swelled 600% during the war. Alcoa's inability to meet this demand forced the US government, through the federal Defense Plant Corp, to construct new aluminum plants to be leased and operated by Alcoa, two of which were in New York State. A smelter in Queens opened in 1942 and employed some 1,375 workers. The other plant, St. Lawrence, opened in 1941 and was adjacent to Alcoa's Massena works, reaching full capacity in 1943 with almost 10,000 employees. In 1945 the Queens plant was shuttered, and the St. Lawrence was acquired by Reynolds Metals as a part of the settlement of a long-standing antitrust suit brought by the US government against Alcoa for its monopolistic control of the aluminum industry. Other changes were underway in the 1940s: Alcoa's Niagara Falls plants were closed in 1949, their advanced age making them obsolete. But Massena expanded with smelter capacity upgraded in 1959 after the state Power Authority opened its nearby hydroelectric facility. Electricity from this project, sold at production cost production to Alcoa, greatly increased cost efficiencies at the site. In 2002 Alcoa's Massena facility was the world's oldest operating aluminum plant, producing tube, wire, rod, and bar products. Moreover, as a consequence of the merger of Reynolds with Alcoa in 2000, Alcoa once again operated the St. Lawrence smelter in Massena. In the 1990s PCBs were found in sections of the Grass and St. Lawrence Rivers adjacent to the two plants. Small sections of the St. Lawrence were dredged in 2001; remediation efforts are ongoing. In 2002 Alcoa's North Country operations had 1,500 employees; these workers were represented by the USWA.

Smith, George David. *From Monopoly to Competition: The Transformation of Alcoa, 1888–1986* (New York: Cambridge Univ Press, 1988)

Douglas McCombs

Alvord, Thomas G(old) (*b* Onondaga, Onondaga Co, 20 Dec 1810; *d* Syracuse, 26 Oct 1897). Lieutenant governor, state legislator, and salt manufacturer. Alvord's father, Elisha, was an early salt manufacturer in the works near Onondaga Lake, but the family resettled in Lansingburgh (Rensselaer Co). Alvord graduated from Yale College in 1828, apprenticed at law, and began practicing in Salina (Onondaga Co) in 1833. Alvord became a partner in various Syracuse area salt-production companies in the 1840s, an interest he maintained until death. He served as a village and town clerk before election to the state assembly as a Democrat in 1843 representing Onondaga Co. He continued to serve in the assembly over the next four decades (1858, 1862, 1864, 1870–72, 1874–75, 1877–82). Members chose Alvord to be Speaker of the assembly in 1858 and again in 1864 and 1879 after he had become a Republican. He was elected as lieutenant governor for a two-year term in 1864 and as a delegate to the New York State Constitutional Conventions of 1867 and 1894. Alvord promoted the state's canals and railroads, opposed the corrupt Tammany Hall ring, and labored especially to sustain New York State's salt manufacturing interests, centered in his home district. This latter activity earned him the political nickname Old Salt.

Bruce, Dwight H, ed. "Thomas G. Alvord." In *Onondaga's Centennial: Gleanings of a Century,* vol 2 (Boston: Boston History, 1896)

Dennis J. Connors

Amagansett U-boat Landing. World War II incident. On 13 June 1942 a German submarine, the *U-202,* surfaced off Amagansett Beach (Suffolk Co) and dispatched a team of four saboteurs on a mission to disrupt the American war effort. Shortly after landing on the beach the Germans were challenged by a coastguardsman. Speaking fluent English, the saboteurs claimed they were fishermen from Southampton (Suffolk Co) whose vessel had run aground. They declined the guardsman's offer to take them to the Coast Guard station where they could remain until dawn and instead offered him a bribe. Pretending to agree, the guardsman took the money and returned to the small Coast Guard station house where he sounded an alarm. In the meantime the Germans disappeared into the night and caught the 7:10 AM train from Amagansett into New York City. The invaders left parts of German uniforms, cigarettes, and small incendiary bombs on the beach, exposing their true identity and purpose and setting off an intensive 15-day manhunt. The search came to an end when one of the saboteurs turned the others in and provided information about a second team of saboteurs that had landed in Florida. They were also apprehended. Convicted in a military tribunal, six of the Germans were hanged while the two who had cooperated with the government received prison sentences.

Epstein, Jason, and Elizabeth Barlow. *East Hampton: A History and Guide* (Wainscott and Sag Harbor, NY: Medway Press, 1978)

Richard F. Welch

Amalgamated Clothing Workers of America. First industrial union to emphasize immigrant clothing workers. Disillusioned with the conservatism of the United Garment Workers (UGW), Sidney Hillman led a majority of workers to bolt the 1914 UGW convention in Nashville, Tenn, and to form the Amalgamated Clothing Workers of America (ACW). The founding convention in New York City on 26 Dec 1914 laid the groundwork for major innovations in collective bargaining with a system featuring impartial arbitration. The ACW also introduced an ambitious plan of social reform, espousing welfare programs in housing, unemployment insurance, and banking. Strengthened by Hillman's contacts with Progressive Era leaders and the government's need for military clothing during World War I, the fledgling ACW easily overtook the UGW, growing from under 30,000 members at its founding to nearly 175,000 in 1920. The ACW pioneered a number of social services to its members and the broader community: opening the Amalgamated Bank of New York in 1923, offering free checking to working people, and in 1926 breaking ground on their first cooperative apartments in the north Bronx. Labor's reversals in the 1920s and the Great Depression led the ACW to join briefly with the American Federation of Labor (AFL) in 1933, but dissatisfaction with the AFL's narrow craft unionism led the ACW to withdraw in 1935 and to join the Committee of Industrial Organization (after 1938 the Congress of Industrial Organizations), which Hillman helped establish that year. Hillman was an important advisor for the New Deal, and ACW philosophy substantially influenced Franklin D. Roosevelt's labor policy. The ACW merged with the Textile Workers Union of America in 1976 to become the Amalgamated Clothing and Textile Workers Union (ACTWU). In 1995 the ACTWU merged with the International Ladies' Garment Workers' Union (ILGWU) to create UNITE, the Union of Needletrades, Industrial and Textile Employees, which is headquartered in New York City.

Amalgamated Clothing Workers of America. Archives. Martin P. Catherwood Library, Cornell Univ, Ithaca
Fraser, Steve. *Labor Will Rule* (New York: Free Press, 1991)

Christopher Martin

Amboy. Town (pop 1,312) in E Oswego Co. Settled in 1805 it received a large influx of settlers in 1822–23; the town was formed from Williamstown in 1830. Lumbering, including shingle making, and farming, especially cheese making, provided employment. The 150-acre (60 ha) Amboy 4-H Environmental Center, operated by Oswego County Cooperative Extension, provides programs and trails, including a trail accessible to people with disabilities.

Barbara J. Dix

Amenia. Town (pop 4,048) in E central Dutchess Co. Part of Great Nine Partners Patent (1697), it was settled in the 1730s by New Englanders and others. It was formed as a town in 1788. When the Harlem Railroad (1850) opened up New York City's fluid-milk market, it became a strong dairying region. In 1861 Gail Borden established his condensed milk plant at Wassaic. In 1916 and 1933 the Amenia Conferences on civil rights were held in town. During most of the 20th century the Wassaic State School, a New York State institution for the developmentally disabled, was the principal employer; the town's population (7,546 in 1960) dropped sharply when it closed. It has become a bedroom and weekend-home community.

William P. McDermott

Amenia Conferences. Two meetings held in 1916 and 1933 to forge a strategy for advancing civil rights for black Americans. Both meetings took place at Troutbeck, the estate of Joel E. Spingarn, in Amenia (Dutchess Co). Spingarn, a dedicated white member of the NAACP, first suggested the 1916 conference, of which the guiding spirit was W. E. B. DuBois. After the death of Booker T. Washington in November 1915, Spingarn and DuBois saw an opportunity to close ranks within the movement by developing a strategy on which both Washington's accommodationist supporters and DuBois's activist NAACP could agree. Spingarn sent personal invitations to approximately 200 black and white leaders, carefully avoiding the appearance that the NAACP was sponsoring the event. Together concluding that the conference would be better served by their absence, the white invitees sent their regrets, although some white visitors were present.

On 24 Aug 1916, 50 women and men assembled at Troutbeck. Under DuBois's guiding hand, those gathered created a Unity Platform with seven resolutions later summarized by DuBois as "a plea for education, a warning against factionalism, a need for interracial understanding, and a forward movement." The resolutions, presented at the close of the conference on 26 August, acknowledged that methods in the South would necessarily diverge from those appropriate in the North. No specific program for implementation was adopted. Nevertheless, the conference was widely perceived as a success. The entry of the United States into World War I and the general upheaval that followed, however, limited its effects.

By the early 1930s the NAACP had been weakened by the Great Depression and internal tensions. In 1932 Spingarn, then NAACP president, and DuBois proposed a new conference, in part to rejuvenate the black civil rights movement and also to redefine the mission of the NAACP. The reluctant leadership eventually called the conference but only under the threat of Spingarn's resignation. Spingarn again discouraged institutional NAACP participation and this time also opposed direct white participation. The conference began on 18 Aug 1933 with 33 black professionals attending, one-third of whom were women. Apart from four elder activists, including DuBois, the average age of the participants was about 30, demonstrating the organizers' conviction that the struggle for civil rights had to pass to a new generation. Active behind the scenes, DuBois refrained from taking a visible role in the proceedings.

While affirming cultural nationalism, the conference rejected black separatism. Perhaps its central determination was that black economic (and hence social and political) advancement was of necessity linked to the white labor movement, and conferees resolved to promote integrated industrial unions in a new labor alliance. The conference concluded on 21 Aug 1933. By the time the conference's committee drew up recommendations in 1935 for carrying out its resolutions, DuBois had resigned from the NAACP, and the organization as an institution did little to pursue the conference's goals. Individual members did, however, take active roles in labor organizing in the later 1930s.

DuBois, William Edward Burghardt. "The Amenia Conference: An Historic Negro Gathering." In *W. E. B. DuBois: A Reader,* ed. David Levering Lewis (New York: Henry Holt, 1995)
Ross, Barbara Joyce. *J. E. Spingarn and the Rise of the NAACP: 1911–1939* (New York: Atheneum, 1972)

Veronica F. Towers

American Ballet Theatre. See BALLET; DEMILLE, AGNES.

American Federation of Labor (AFL). See LABOR.

American Indian architecture. Native American houses in the Hudson-Champlain corridor and Long Island prior to the 18th century were typically wigwam-style dwellings. Flexible saplings were set in the ground in a circular pattern about 10–17 feet (3–5 m) in diameter. The upper ends of the saplings were bent over the middle and lashed to form a hemispherical framework. This in turn was sheathed with bark or mats. A small doorway was left for access, a sleeping bench typically built around the interior wall, and a hearth placed in the middle of the floor for heat and cooking. A smoke hole above the hearth allowed smoke to exit but enough remained to irritate the eyes of those inside. The wigwam was a snug and warm home for a typical family of five even in cold weather.

Extended families sometimes built larger elongated wigwams, rounded at the ends and no higher than the smaller single-family wigwams. An adult could stand only near the center. These and the smaller domed wigwams were temporary dwellings. Families typically cycled through a small number of regularly used locations during the course of a year. If mats were used as coverings, they would often be taken along to the next location where the skeleton of a previous year's wigwam stood ready for repair and reoccupation. The Munsee of the southern Hudson Valley and western Long Island apparently used a somewhat larger elongated house form having compartments for nuclear families occupying the center and a side, with an aisle along the other side.

The most formidable of regional house styles was the Iroquois longhouse, the standard form across the area between what are now Albany and Buffalo. The floor plan of the typical longhouse was 19.8 feet (6 m) wide and accommodated a central aisle 6.6 feet (2 m) wide and living areas on both sides. Outer bark-sheathed walls were 11.5–13 feet (3.5–4m) high, and wall posts were ideally made of rigid rot-resistant cedar. The vertical posts were rarely more than about 4 inches (10 cm) in diameter. Arched flexible saplings were used in the roof arbor, and the houses were about as high as wide. The whole framework was sheathed with large sheets of elm bark peeled from trees in the springtime when the sap was running and the bark loose. Moss was used to chink the spaces where the bark sheets overlapped. The harvesting of bark sheets accompanied the girdling of trees and forest clearing for farming. Villages were relocated every 10 or 20 years as fields wore out, and bark longhouses were designed to last about the same amount of time.

Longhouses were partitioned at roughly 20 ft (6 m) intervals. A hearth located somewhere between doorways in the partitions was shared by the two nuclear families occupying the living spaces in the compartment. Rather than building a bench for sitting and sleeping along the entire outer wall of its compartment space the family built and used a berth 7–10 feet (2–3 m) long and about 7 feet deep for that purpose. The sides of the berth were enclosed and topped by a ceiling about 7 feet high. The lower bench was about 1.5 feet (.5 m) high, convenient for seating. Spaces above and below were used to store pots and other household belongings.

The Iroquois longhouse was typically long enough to house a large extended matrilineal family. While six pairs of compartments might have been common, archaeological examples approaching or even exceeding 330 feet (100 m) in length are known. The ends of the longhouses, where access doors were located, were typically left flat to accommodate additional compartments as the matrilineage grew. Unless village space was at a premium, temporary storage rooms were often built at one or both ends for bins of maize and to buffer the interior from winter winds.

Native houses of all forms were surrounded by protective palisades in times of warfare or when there were nearby political frontiers. Palisades sometimes had multiple walls of upright posts and easily protected access corridors. Both palisades and longhouses vanished in the 18th century. By that time firearms had made palisades ineffective against attack, and people came to depend instead on retreat to nearby forts. Many native groups adopted European-style log or frame dwellings, which tended to be dispersed to accommodate the demands of an emerging agriculture that incorporated European crops and animal domesticates along with native crops.

See also ARCHITECTS AND ARCHITECTURE, MOHAWK VALLEY; FORTIFICATIONS.

Snow, Dean R. *The Archaeology of New England* (New York: Academic Press, 1980)

———. "The Architecture of Iroquois Longhouses," *Northeast Anthropology* 53 (1997): 61–84

Sturtevant, William C. "Two 1761 Wigwams at Niantic, Connecticut," *American Antiquity* 40 (1975): 437–44

Dean R. Snow

American Indian missions. The earliest mention of American Indian missions in New York State is in 1627 when Joseph d'Aillon, a French Recollet, visited the region around Niagara Falls. Jesuit father Isaac Jogues and two French coadjutors, René Goupil and Guillaume Couture, were captured by Mohawks in 1642 and taken deep into Mohawk territory. There they met different fates: Goupil quickly succumbed to mistreatment while Couture was adopted by the Mohawks. Jogues survived torture, and the following year he achieved freedom while visiting Fort Orange [now Albany] and returned to France. Jogues was allowed to return to Mohawk country in 1646 and pursue missionary work, but in October of that year he and John LaLande were executed at Ossernenon [now Auriesville, Montgomery Co]. In 1930 Goupil, Jogues, and Lalande were canonized as members of "The Eight North American Martyrs." After Jogues's death and recurrent uneasy relations between the Iroquois Confederacy and French envoys, Jesuits pursued little work south of Lake Ontario and the St. Lawrence River, with sporadic ventures among the Onondaga and Cayuga in the 1650s being the only subsequent efforts worthy of note. While French Catholics explored the St. Lawrence Valley, Dutch colonists farther east conducted a missionary enterprise of greater effectiveness and duration. In 1642 Johannes Megapolensis had been brought to New Netherland by the patroon, Kiliaen van Rensselaer, and settled at Rensselaerswijck. His central charge was to provide pastoral care for white settlers, but he soon became acquainted with Mohawks who lived northeast of the Dutch outpost. Initial interest led to fascination, and Megapolensis made Indian missionary work an important, though always secondary, feature of his seven-year tenure. He gradually learned the local language and produced a rudimentary grammar. Always respectful of native values and customs, he cooperated with trading agent Arent van Curler to cement good relations with the Mohawk.

Megapolensis left Rensselaerswijck in 1649, and missionary work languished until 1683, when a new dominie, Godfreidus Dellius, arrived to renew pastoral activities on all fronts. Possessed of a patient temperament and great linguistic ability, Dellius continued the tradition of preaching in native idioms and respecting precontact customs. To the body of literature he contributed a Mohawk translation of the Decalogue, Psalms, and a catechism in Calvinistic doctrine. He labored for 16 years (1683–99) and in that time helped establish an independent Mohawk church near Albany that eventually grew to over 200 members. The first Dutch Reformed clergyman to be ordained in this country was Peter Tesschenmaeker in 1679; he settled in Schenectady and assisted Dellius in extending missionary outreach to the Mohawk. His work with them was cut short by Comte de Frontenac's raid in 1690, which destroyed the settlement and killed half the population. From 1690 to 1699 Tesschenmaeker was a schoolteacher and minister to white congregations. After a 10-year hiatus, Bernardus Freeman resumed missionary work (1700–1705) with fluent sermons in Mohawk, contributing also a translation of parts of both biblical testaments, the Athanasian Creed, and, indicating a shift in political influence, the Anglican liturgy. English patterns increasingly predominated, but a final Dutch missionary worth noting was Peter Henry van Driessen (1712–38). This last in a long line of dominies who made Indian missions an additional facet of their parish work continued to respect native culture. His discussion of Christianity did not impose any changes regarding speech, dress, habitation, property rights, or work habits. As a result Driessen reaped the benefit of what his predecessors had initiated. He witnessed professions of faith in every palisaded settlement along the Mohawk Valley and, in each, conducted morning and evening prayer, taught catechism classes, and continued to preach in the rich native tongue.

When England succeeded Holland as the dominant power in the area, the groundwork for cordial relations with Iroquoian peoples had already been laid. In 1704 Thoroughgood Moore spent a year in Albany as representative of the Society for the Propagation of the Gospel in Foreign Parts (SPG). William Andrews (1712–19) followed with work at Upper and Lower Mohawk Castles in Canajoharie [now in Montgomery Co] and Ticonderoga [now in Essex Co], respectively. John Miln (1727–31) reopened missions while residing in Albany, and Henry Barclay (1735–46) continued the work at Fort Hunter [now in Montgomery Co]. SPG agents tried to teach native youths English speech, habits, and worship. They sought to influence native power blocs so they could be used against competing interests, enlisting Iroquois support first against the French and then against colonial republicans. Throughout the 18th century they tried simultaneously to serve the British crown and promote the Church of England. After the American Revolution the field for Indian missions diminished considerably. In 1798 Quakers established a school for Senecas at Genesinguht near the Allegany Reservation [loc in Cattaraugus Co]; in 1803 they added one nearby at Tunessassa; another appeared in 1821 on the Tonawanda Reservation [loc in Genesee, Erie, and Niagara Cos]. They embodied the basic approach of most missions, namely to equate Christianity with American civilization and to urge natives to accept both in order to flourish in the new nation. By the 1820s and 1830s additional groups appeared at various sites, preaching a common acculturating gospel with few variations. Baptists made efforts on Seneca reservations at Cattaraugus [loc in Cattaraugus and Erie Cos] and Buffalo Creek [now in Erie Co]. Later efforts at Cattaraugus included representatives of the New York Missionary Society, the American Board of Commissioners for Foreign Missions, and finally, in the 1870s, Presbyterians. All of these white missionaries pursued evangelical efforts in the hope of turning back what they perceived as the twin threats of pagan belief and barbaric practices. Most missionary work ended by the turn of the 20th century.

See also MOHICANS (MAHICANS); NEW FRANCE; TUSCARORA NATION.

Bowden, Henry Warner. *American Indians and Christian Missions: Studies in Cultural Conflict* (Chicago: Univ of Chicago Press, 1981)
Calam, John. *Parsons and Pedagogues: The S.P.G. Adventure in American Education* (New York: Columbia Univ Press, 1971)
Jameson, John Franklin, ed. *Narratives of New Netherland* (New York: Charles Scribner's Sons, 1909)
Kittler, Glenn D. *Saint in the Wilderness: The Story of St. Isaac Jogues and the Jesuit Adventure in the New World* (Garden City, NY: Doubleday, 1964)
Talbot, Francis. *Saint among the Hurons: The Life of Jean de Brebeuf* (New York: Harper, 1949)

Henry Warner Bowden

American Indians: Before contact. The territory of the modern State of New York has been occupied by human beings for at least 12,000 years. Glacial ice covered the region around 15,300 years ago, still covering most of the state 2,000 years later. As warmer conditions evolved and the ice stagnated, there emerged a bleak landscape of moraines, till, and vast glacial lakes. It was centuries before vegetation and animal populations were reestablished.

Paleo-Indians

While archaeological sites document earlier human occupations on unglaciated territory south of New York, the earliest occupants here were Paleo-Indians carrying portable tool assemblages that included classic Clovis fluted points. Clovis culture was widespread but short-lived in North America (lasting about 500 years), flourishing mainly between 11,400 and 10,900 BC.

These people were highly mobile hunters and foragers who depended upon large game animals, such as mammoths, bison, caribou, and elk. Their principal weapon was a small spear (or dart) propelled by a spear thrower (or atlatl), a short, hooked shaft that articulated with the end of the spear and effectively lengthened the thrower's arm. The device increased the velocity and distance of the thrown spear without compromising accuracy. Fluted and barbless chert points on the spears allowed them to penetrate deeply but fall out easily. Hunters could reuse the same spears several times in a single hunt.

While smaller game, fish, and plant resources must have been harvested also, the landscape was still changing too rapidly for more specialized food-gathering and preparation techniques to emerge. Isolated Clovis point finds are scattered across the state. A few Paleo-Indian campsites have been investigated more thoroughly. The best known is the site atop West Athens Hill (Greene Co) in the Hudson Valley. From there hunters could observe the movements of herd animals migrating along the largely treeless, postglacial landscape of the valley. While Paleo-Indians are known to have hunted mammoths and other now extinct game animals elsewhere in North America, there is no direct evidence for it in New York.

Paleo-Indian bands were small and scattered, and, like similar bands that survived into the 19th century, they probably depended upon mutual assistance when food was scarce or supplies were erratic. Interaction with neighboring bands over long distances was also necessary if young band members were to find marriage mates. Evidence for these kinds of connections is found in the widespread distribution of fluted points made from high-quality cherts from distant quarries. For example, finished points of red chert (jasper) from eastern Pennsylvania were found at West Athens Hill, while equally fine points of Onondaga chert from Central New York were discovered in central Pennsylvania. The last few centuries of the Paleo-Indian period in New York are not well known. Small mobile bands probably continued to roam the landscape, carrying spears tipped by unfluted projectile points of the Plano tradition.

Archaic Period

Archaeologists refer to the long time span between the disappearance of Paleo-Indians and the rise of horticulture and ceramic production as the Archaic period, which has been subdivided into shorter periods. The hallmarks of these periods are reasonably distinctive projectile point types, many featuring barbs, which unlike earlier Paleo-Indian points would have stayed in a wounded animal. Early Archaic assemblages are dominated by barbed points with split bases, called bifurcate based points. The change in points was probably related to the extinction of mammoths, mastodons, and other very large game animals and to the movement northward of caribou and other smaller surviving species. The Archaic period features growing human dependence upon the game animal species that still survive. Thus the shift to deer and moose began as early as the beginning of the early Archaic period, around 10,000 years ago or 8000 BC.

The middle Archaic period began around 6000 BC and lasted for two millennia. Evidence for occupations in this and the earlier Archaic period is scanty, partly because of the youth and instability of the early postglacial environment. Much evidence is probably buried under deep alluvial deposits in the state's major river valleys. Despite the paucity of evidence, archaeologists generally accept that these were periods in which human populations settled into subsistence adaptations that made increasingly sophisticated and specialized use of local food resources. Tool inventories expanded to include less portable items, such as grinding stones. While populations might have remained highly mobile, they now moved in regular ways between fixed campsites, where seasonally abundant resources were harvested, preserved, and stored for later use. For example, spring fish runs might find a group at a particularly good weir on a major river, while the nesting of passenger pigeons later found them camped near a traditionally productive stand of beech trees.

The regularization of the seasonal round and the preservation and storage of seasonally abundant resources changed the relationships between human communities. Earlier long-distance trade and exchange ceased as the number and sizes of bands increased. Indian people were no longer dependent upon distant neighbors for marriage mates and insurance against starvation. The advent of storage technologies not only tied them to traditional camps but gave them something that had to be protected from theft or the pleading of improvident neighboring groups. The result was that the Archaic was a time during which social and consequently linguistic boundaries were established across the American landscape. Communities came to choose carefully with which other communities they would trade, share, and intermarry. Social boundaries tended to coincide with the highlands separating river drainages or other natural boundaries. Where there had once been widespread uniformity in the styles of key archaeological artifacts, there emerged a mosaic of first dozens then hundreds of local styles across the continent.

By the beginning of the late Archaic, around 4000 BC, the territory of modern New York State is best thought of in terms of a half dozen archaeological regions. Sites of this period are numerous, partly because the population was larger, partly because their tool types were distinctive, and partly because environmental stabilization made them easier for modern archaeologists to discover. Regional adaptations varied from fishing and moose hunting in the

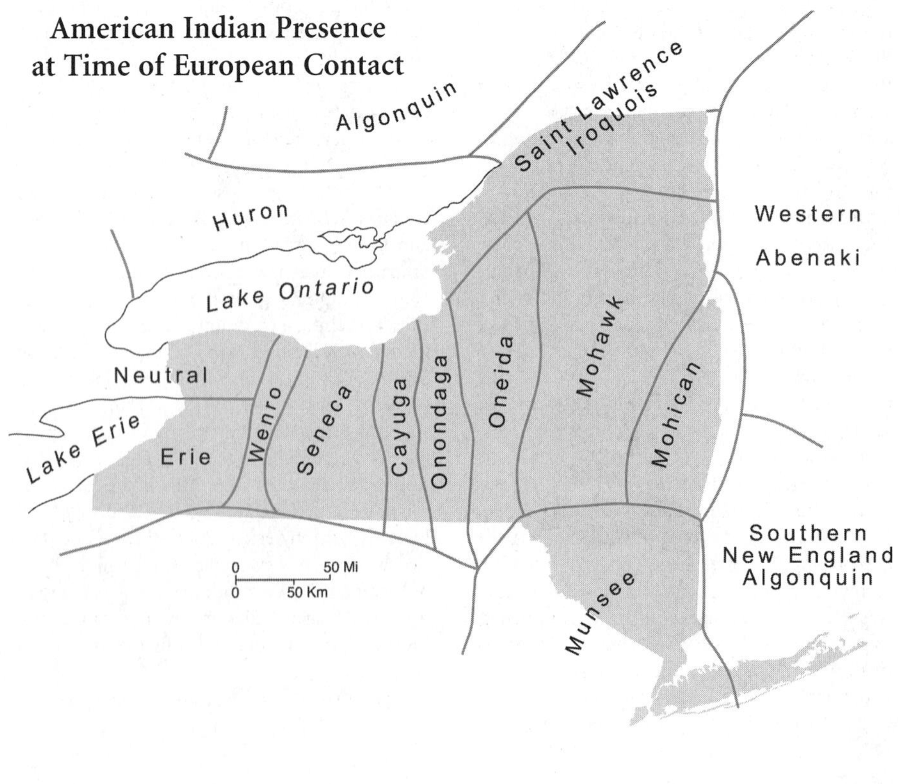

boreal forests flanking the Great Lakes and St. Lawrence River, to the smaller but more abundant game in the mast forests farther south. The migratory fish that entered by way of the St. Lawrence were different in kind and number from those that migrated northward up the Hudson, Delaware, and Susquehanna Rivers. The mast forest produced acorns, butternuts, and other nuts that were scarce or unavailable in the boreal forest of the northern part of the region. Not surprisingly, the kinds of artifacts and their styles found for this period reflect these differences in adaptation. The Laurentian tradition, whose hallmarks are broad-notched points, bannerstones, adzes, plummets, and ground slate tools, dominated in northern New York. Meanwhile the more southerly mast forest Archaic featured small stemmed points and grinding stones for the preparation of meal from acorns and other nuts. Evidence is growing that people in this period were exploiting local plants so intensely that their practices amounted to cultivation. Various *Chenopodium* species (goosefoot or pigweed) were heavily used, with the result that charred seeds, found in archaeological sites, show the early signs of domestication. Other plants, like wild onion, were artificially transported beyond their natural ranges and still survive in patches around archaeological sites dating to the late Archaic.

The late Archaic period gave way to the Terminal Archaic, which lasted from about the middle of the second millennium to the middle of the first millennium BC. By this time, and probably earlier, the establishment of numerous regional cultural boundaries had prompted the development of social mechanisms to facilitate new trade and exchange across them. The clan system of eastern North American Indian nations probably dates to this time, if not earlier. Although this system was later used for other social and political purposes, it likely emerged as a means to allow travel and trade across barriers of language and culture. A man belonging to the Bear Clan in one community was the fictive kinsman of a Bear Clan member in another community, no matter how far removed they were from each other in space. The protocols that grew up around this fictive kinship allowed for the development of long-distance trade and exchange, often facilitated by long journeys, unlike the down-the-line movement of objects that prevailed in the more mobile Paleo-Indian period. In the Terminal Archaic period, the manufacture and trade of vessels made of soapstone (steatite) also developed. These vessels, or more often fragments of them, are found on sites across New York. There are only a few quarries that produce suitable soapstone, and the nearest are located in Connecticut. Others are known in the Mid-Atlantic region. Soapstone vessels tend to be found in sites near large rivers, suggesting that they spread largely in association with canoe travel.

Woodland Period

Pottery vessels quickly replaced soapstone ones in New York in the first millennium BC. Crude pots appeared along the Gulf Coast as early as 2500 BC. Their appearance in New York marks the beginning of the period referred to as the early Woodland by archaeologists. Meadowood culture dominated the period in central and western New York. The hallmarks of Meadowood are fine chert blades, often deposited in caches, as well as gorgets, and birdstones. Meadowood was contemporaneous with Adena culture, which was centered in southern Ohio. Adena traders roamed the eastern woodlands to acquire exotic raw materials, and their finished artifacts often ended up in earthen burial mounds. Thus burial mounds first proliferated across the Eastern Woodlands. Those few that were constructed in New York State were once assigned to a separate "Middlesex" phase, but it is now clear that the Adena burial ritual and its associated mounds and artifacts were grafted on to indigenous Meadowood culture.

Adena culture held on later in a few places, but it was replaced by Hopewell culture around 200 BC in southern Ohio. Many archaeologists use its advent to mark the beginning of the middle Woodland period. Like Adena communities, Hopewell villages were sustained by domesticates native to the Eastern Woodlands. Hopewell architects built vast complexes of geometric earthworks, and their traders traveled far beyond the limits of their Adena predecessors. Obsidian was imported from the Rockies, shell from the Gulf Coast, copper from the upper Great Lakes, and quartz crystals from the Mohawk Valley. As was the case with Adena, Hopewell ritual was adopted by some New York communities, but burial mounds are modest and scarce in the state. Sometimes referred to as a separate "Squawkie Hill" phase, the Hopewellian mounds of western New York State are more likely the products of Point Peninsula culture.

Point Peninsula spread into New York in the first millennium AD. The dominance of Point Peninsula people in the region probably relates to the bow and arrow, with which they were apparently equipped. The new weapon was superior to the old spear thrower in the dense woods of the region and more suited to hunting deer, by then the principal game animal. Point Peninsula culture was also distributed through New England and southern Quebec and Ontario, and it is likely that this widespread culture was carried by people speaking one or more Algonquian languages. Their adoption of pottery facilitated the spread of this craft beyond the limits of native plant cultivation, once thought to be a limiting condition to the spread of ceramic vessels.

Hopewell culture and its vast trading network that was centered in Ohio waned by AD 400. Point Peninsula culture persisted longer at the northeastern margin, but profound changes were overtaking Indian cultures farther south. A new tropical species of squash replaced the native species in the Eastern Woodlands, and maize spread with it northward out of Mexico. Farmers in the Eastern Woodlands experimented with the new crops and discovered that they formed a nearly complete diet when supplemented by native plants and traditional game foods. They also found that intensive maize and squash cultivation facilitated the year-round occupation of densely packed villages. The new mode of settlement made them dominant over smaller, less permanent, communities of hunters and foragers.

Formation of Longhouse Communities

One set of communities in the Appalachians used their new dominance to expand their range beginning around AD 800. They adopted a matrilineal system and lived in multifamily houses organized internally by related women. The matrilocal system made it possible for tribal communities of up to several hundred people to maintain peace among competing groups of men without the need for more complex political institutions. One set of communities moved to the Carolina Piedmont, where their post-Contact successors were known as the Tuscarora and related tribes. Others moved north to what are now New York State and Ontario, displacing or absorbing the thinner Point Peninsula population.

The expanding longhouse communities were the founders of the various northern Iroquoian nations. They were well established in New York, where their culture has been referred to as Owasco, by AD 950. Their permanent compact villages tended to be on broad hilltops and surrounded by fertile upland soils. Maize and squash combined with deer, fish, and native plants to fill out their subsistence. Most of the basic elements of post-Contact Iroquois culture were already in place. Tropical beans spread to Owasco farmers in New York by around AD 1350, completing the famous "three sisters" set of staple crops. Iroquoian potters abandoned cord decorating and took up incised decorating at about the same time. With these shifts emerged classic Iroquois culture across most of New York. A period of internecine warfare engulfed many of these communities in late pre-Contact times. This led to the creation of the League of the Iroquois sometime in the 16th century. This political innovation, linking the Mohawk, Oneida, Onondaga, Cayuga, and Seneca, was built upon the old clan structure and funeral ritual. It brought internal peace to the Iroquois nations, deflecting violence outward against neighboring nations in the region.

Descendants of Algonquian-speaking Point Peninsula communities persisted in eastern New York and Long Island. They too eventually adopted maize horticulture, but they did not adopt the strongly matrilineal social and political system of the Iroquois. The native people of the northeastern Adirondacks, the Hudson Valley, and Long Island retained their principal cultural connections with their linguistic relatives in New England.

See also Cartography and mapping; Munsee; Prehistoric archaeology.

Ritchie, William A. *The Archaeology of New York State* (Harrison, NY: Harbor Hill Books, 1980)

Ritchie, William A., and Robert E. Funk. *Aboriginal Settlement Patterns in the Northeast* (Albany: University of the State of New York, State Education Department, 1973)

Snow, Dean R. *The Iroquois* (Cambridge, Mass: Blackwell, 1994)

Dean R. Snow

American Indians: Colonial period

New Netherland

The year 1609 marked the beginning of the interactions of the Iroquois and Algonquian-speaking Indians with the colonial powers in what would become New York State. In that year Henry Hudson encountered Munsee Indians along the lower Hudson River valley as he sailed north from Sandy Hook on the shore of what is now New Jersey. When he reached the area of Beverwijck [now Albany], he was met by Mohicans (Mahicans) bearing furs and welcome. That same year, Samuel de Champlain, with Algonquin and Montagnais allies, while exploring the lake that would later bear his name, fought a battle with the Mohawk near Ticonderoga [now in Essex Co] in which several Mohawks were killed.

The Algonquian-speaking Indians in the lower Hudson Valley, New Amsterdam, and Long Island soon found the Dutch encroaching on their land. The fur trade enabled them to exchange for European goods but changed the traditional ways of providing for themselves and made them increasingly dependent on the Dutch. The grazing of Dutch livestock on Indian agricultural plots and the ill-advised plan of New Netherland director Willem Kieft to collect taxes from local Indians helped release pent-up Indian resentment. During Kieft's War (1640–45), the Raritan, Wekquaesgeck, Hackensack, and other Alquonquian-speaking groups fought with colonists and Dutch West India Co soldiers. Skirmishes were fought in a number of places in the lower Hudson Valley, including Long Island and Staten Island. Not until the spring of 1644, when a combined force of Dutch settlers and English mercenaries killed nearly 500 Indians at what is now Pound Ridge [Westchester Co] in a fiery massacre, did the tide of the war begin to turn. Some Indians remained at war, and it was not until the next year that peace was achieved.

There would be other conflicts in the lower Hudson Valley. The Peach War of 1655 was a three-day rampage by 600 Indians starting in Manhattan and destroying settlements on Staten Island and Pavonia [now Hoboken and Jersey City, NJ]. In 1659 some 500 Esopus Indians, after years of growing tension, laid siege to Wiltwijck [now Kingston, Ulster Co]. After reinforcements came the Dutch forced the Esopus to sign a treaty in which they surrendered most of their lands in the vicinity of the settlement. Another outbreak in 1663 required Director General Petrus Stuyvesant's presence at Wiltwijck in May 1664, several months before he surrendered the colony to the English. The Dutch maintained good relations with both the Mohawks and the Mohicans at Beverwijck, as the desire to trade preserved peace. Out of mutual necessity, Fort Orange [now Albany] became a pragmatic middle ground, where the interdependence spawned by the fur trade forced Indians and traders to tolerate each other.

Under the English, the Algonquian-speaking Indians found themselves further pushed to the margins of society. They were largely bypassed in the fur trade, and most bands would in time alienate all of their remaining land. By 1700 the Canarsee were no longer living in Brooklyn, nor were the Kichtawank and Wekquaesgeck living in Westchester Co. By 1750 the Esopus Indians and the Mohican had largely left the Hudson Valley. Some merged into the local population, often marrying with poor Whites and free Blacks. (The Ramapo Mountain People, who currently live near the New York State–New Jersey border in Rockland Co—and whose origins remain extremely controversial—may be the descendants of such a community.) Some moved east to Christian mission towns such as Schaghticoke, Conn, or Stockbridge, Mass. Others moved west to multi-Indian towns in the Susquehanna River valley, such as Oquaga [now Windsor, Broome Co] and Otsiningo [now Binghamton], until the Revolution brought further dislocation and movement west. The Indians on Long Island fared marginally better than those in the Hudson Valley. Two reservations, the Poospatuck Indian Reservation and the Shinnecock Indian Reservation [both loc in Suffolk Co], remain, as do the reservation-less Montaukett (Montauk) Indians on the tip of Long Island.

The Iroquois and the Covenant Chain

After his arrival in 1674, Gov Edmund Andros began to forge closer ties to the Five Nations of the Iroquois, whom he believed could facilitate his imperial charge to contain the French on the north side of Lake Ontario, secure the loyalty of the colony's Dutch population, and bring order to Indian-European relations. The resulting Covenant Chain made a powerful Anglo-Iroquoian alliance. It enabled the Five Nations to absorb many of the defeated southern New England Algonquian-speaking peoples to their east, ravaged by the interracial violence of King Philip's War in New England. Andros's promotion of Iroquois interests came at a price. He and his successors, who saw in the Covenant Chain the best interests of the colony and the empire, wanted Iroquois assistance in England's imperial warfare with the French. The French and their Indian allies had attacked the Seneca at Ganondagan [now Victor, Ontario Co] in July 1687, Mohawk villages now in Montgomery Co in February 1693, and the main villages of the Onondaga and Oneida now in Onondaga and Oneida Cos in August 1696. Continued warfare against the French was costly, and after the English-French détente at the Treaty of Ryswick of 1697, the neutralist Iroquois negotiated the "Grand Settlement" with the French at Montreal in 1701 and a similar agreement with the English that same year. To halt the bloodshed and to bring peace to the huge expanse of territory occupied by the Five Nations, the Iroquois through these agreements opted for a policy of playing one power against the other.

Nevertheless, both the English and the French continued to pressure the Five Nations. Iroquois leaders learned that they could trust neither European power. The French and the English fortified sites in Iroquoia to control access to the lands they claimed in the west. Indians in New York, increasingly unable to live without the Europeans because of the dependence that had developed for arms, ammunition, and trade, struggled to avoid the devastating consequences of war. During the three imperial wars that followed the Iroquois declaration of neutrality (Queen Anne's War, 1702–13, King George's War, 1744–48, and the French and Indian War, 1754–63), the Iroquois managed to maintain a fragile neutrality, although individual nations often formed temporary alliances with one power or the other. Only after the final defeat of the French in 1763 and the collapse of Pontiac's War in 1763 did the Iroquois finally attach themselves to the English and the Crown's superintendent for Indian Affairs for the Northern Department, Sir William Johnson.

The relative stability of Iroquoia in the 18th century made it a haven for other Indians seeking refuge from wars and dispossession elsewhere in British North America, especially for groups with Iroquoian connections. The Tuscarora moved from North Carolina to Oneida territory and in 1722 became the sixth nation of the Iroquois Confederacy. The Tutelo and Saponi were adopted by the Cayuga in 1753. Oneida settlements in the Susquehanna Valley, such as Oquaga, became a home for Munsees, Mohicans, Delawares, and many other Indian groups. Urged by British officials, the Midwestern Fox Indians (also known as Mesquakie, Muskwaki, or Outagamie Indians) moved to Seneca territory on the Genesee River in different migrations from 1712 to 1730.

Revolution in Iroquois Country

The relationship between the Iroquois and English imperial officials faced new challenges as tensions deepened between the Crown and its American subjects. The New England minister Samuel Kirkland established successful missions among the Oneida and Tuscarora. Initially Sir William Johnson welcomed efforts to Christianize and to civilize the Indians, but by 1771 he had begun actively to disrupt Kirkland's efforts, fearing that the missionary's teachings would pull the Oneida and Tuscarora into an alliance with the growing resistance movement and weaken their attachment to the king. Also, colonists began to encroach on Iroquois lands, especially on those of the Mohawk and Oneida. Settlement moved rapidly westward along the Mohawk River. Johnson, the king, and Parliament all wanted to protect England's Indian allies after the war. The Proclamation of 1763 prohibited English settlement west of the Appalachians and required that colonists settled in violation of its provisions abandon their farms. In New York the 1768 Treaty of Fort Stanwix drew a similar line, from Wood Creek east of Oneida Lake, south along the Unadilla River over to the bend in the Delaware, and west and then south along the Susquehanna. This helped the western Iroquois, but the Mohawk found their lands entirely to the east of the Stanwix treaty line. They, especially, looked to the Crown and Sir William Johnson to protect their lands from the aggressions of frontier settlers.

The Iroquois could not stay out of the growing conflict between the colonists and Britain, as both sides pressed the Iroquois for their support. In 1775 the Indian Committee of the Second Continental Congress undertook diplomatic efforts to secure Iroquois neutrality in any conflict with the British. Guy Johnson, Sir William's nephew and successor as the Crown's superintendent of Indian Affairs, encouraged the Six Nations to continue to hold to the Covenant Chain and to remember that it was the king, not the provincials, who protected them and their lands.

Most of the Iroquois Confederacy favored neutrality. When fighting between the Americans and the British began in the spring of 1775, the Oneida told Connecticut's governor, John Trumbull, that the quarrel between the colonists and the Crown "seems to be unnatural. . . . We are unwilling to join in either side in such a contest." Thus, in the same year that the colonists went to war with the British, the Iroquois tried to secure their independence from both. But the Revolutionary War, like the imperial wars that preceded it, would not tolerate Iroquois neutrality. The forces faced by the Six Nations were too powerful. The ties to Kirkland, along with other factors, were sufficiently strong to pull the Oneida and Tuscarora into alliance with the rebels. For the rest of the Six Nations, the inability of the Continental Congress to support Iroquois neutrality with gifts and supplies, the atrocities committed by frontier settlers, and continuing encroachment on Indian lands by American farmers all made neutrality untenable. The Confederacy was shattered, and the council fire at Onondaga was extinguished.

In the following years, the Revolutionary War would be fought back and forth in raids and counterraids. The most prominent supporter of the British was the Mohawk Joseph Brant, who, with loyalist troops, attacked the American settlement at Cherry Valley [now in Otsego Co] in November 1778, leaving dozens dead and spreading terror. In response, an American army of approximately 4,000 men under the command of Gens John Sullivan and James Clinton in 1779 systematically destroyed Iroquois settlements in central and western New York State, making few distinctions between Indian friends, foes, and neutrals. Thousands of dispossessed Iroquois moved to the vicinity of Fort Niagara [now in Porter, Niagara Co], and many of them followed Brant into Canada at the conclusion of hostilities to the Grand River Reservation. Those who stayed in New York State and tried to resume their lives soon found that the pressure from Americans to sell their land would be impossible to resist. Although the individual Iroquois nations would battle tenaciously and heroically over the next two centuries to retain a portion of their historic homeland, Iroquoia was lost forever.

Dennis, Matthew. *Cultivating a Landscape of Peace: Iroquois-European Encounters in 17th Century America* (Ithaca: Cornell Univ Press, 1993)

Graymont, Barbara, *The Iroquois and the American Revolution* (Syracuse: Syracuse Univ Press, 1972)

Richter, Daniel K. *The Ordeal of the Longhouse: The Peoples of the Iroquois League in the Era of European Colonization* (Chapel Hill: Univ of North Carolina Press, 1992)

Tooker, Elisabeth. "The League of the Iroquois: Its History, Politics and Ritual." In *Northeast,* ed. Bruce G. Trigger, vol 15 of *Handbook of North American Indians* (Washington, DC: Smithsonian Institution, 1978)

Trelease, Allen W. *Indian Affairs in Colonial New York: The 17th Century* (Ithaca: Cornell Univ Press, 1960)

Michael Leroy Oberg

American Indians: Policies since 1776. New York State has government-to-government relations with nine American Indian nations: the Cayuga, Mohawk, Oneida, Onondaga, Seneca Nation of Indians, Tonawanda Band of Seneca, and Tuscarora (the Iroquois) and the Shinnecock and Poospatuck, or Unquachog-Quiripis (the Long Island Algonquian). All but the Long Island Algonquians are federally recognized Indian nations. The state ranks 10th in size of native populations in the country. There are over 80,000 American Indians residing in New York State, spread across 10 reservations, a specially leased parcel of land at Altona (Clinton Co) called Ganienkeh, a recently established Mohawk community in Fonda (Montgomery Co) called Kanatsiohareke, and five major urban Indian communities in Buffalo, New York City, Niagara Falls, Rochester, and Syracuse. There are also Indian populations recognized by neither New York State nor the federal government: the Ramapo Mountain People, or Ramapo Mountain Indians, of Orange and Rockland Cos, the Matinecock Indians of Queens and Nassau Cos, and the Montaukett Indians of Suffolk Co. As many as half of the American Indians in New York State are from other states or from Canada, having relocated here in search of better opportunities.

Original American Indian Reservations

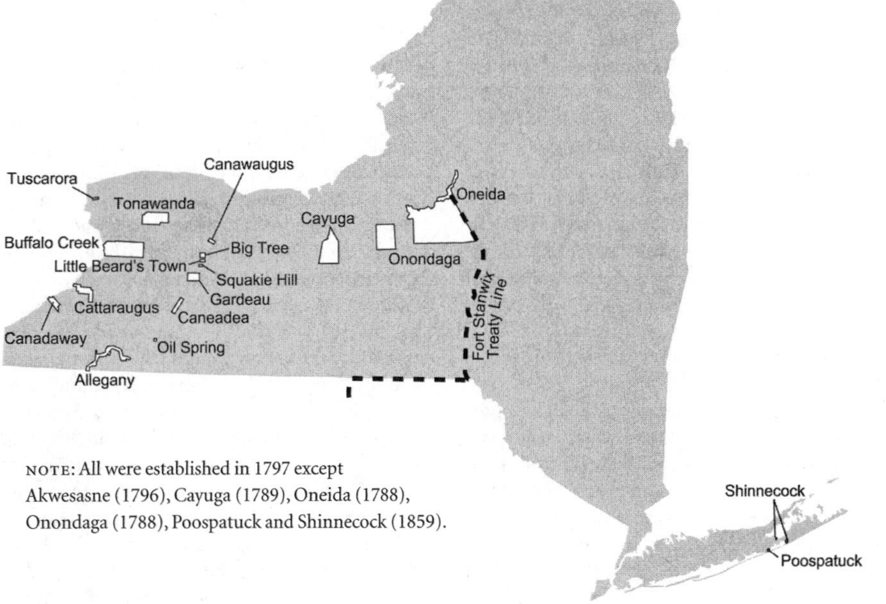

NOTE: All were established in 1797 except Akwesasne (1796), Cayuga (1789), Oneida (1788), Onondaga (1788), Poospatuck and Shinnecock (1859).

Reservations in 2003

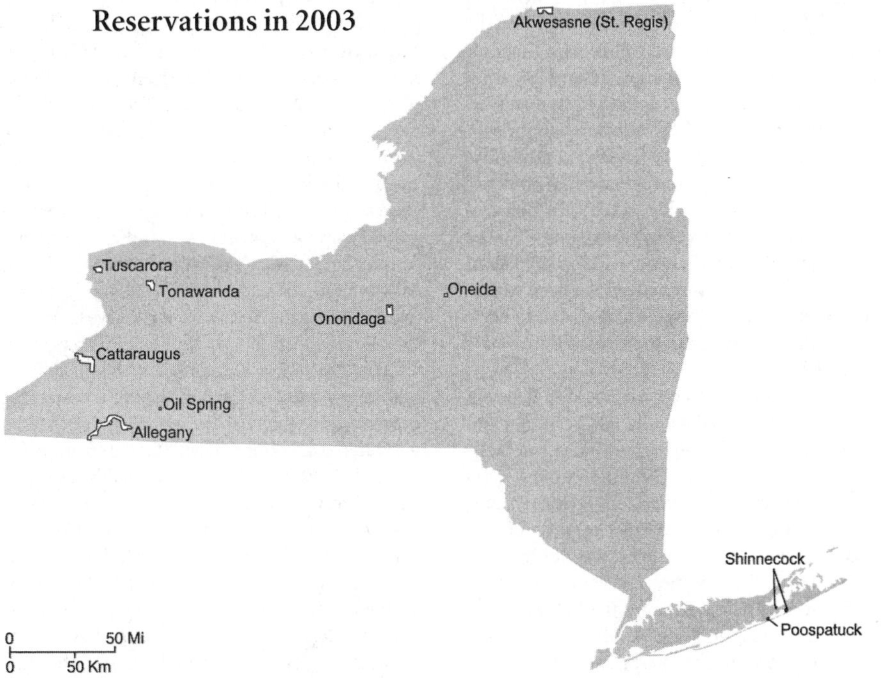

TREATY MAKING AND EXPANDING CONTROL

New York State officials initiated treaty making with the Iroquois at Fort Herkimer in 1785. The resulting Oneida cession was the first in a series of post-Revolutionary negotiations into the 1840s that state officials made with separate Iroquois nations, especially with the Cayuga and Onondaga. Only two of the nearly three dozen state treaties made with the Iroquois had a US commissioner present, as required by federal law. Only two, in 1798 and 1802, were ratified by the US Senate and proclaimed by the US president. Land purchased by state treaty for 50¢ an acre was sold for 7–10 times its original purchase price. Meanwhile, the state was building its transportation network and encouraging the settlement of the central and western portions of the state. With the development of the Erie Canal, Indians in the affected areas soon found themselves surrounded by Whites who coveted their lands. By the 1830s and 1840s, railroads further added to the land rush. The dispossession of the Indians' land between 1785 and 1846 has led to major land claims suits by the Cayuga, Mohawk, Oneida, Seneca, and Stockbridge-Munsee and to Shinnecock efforts seeking federal recognition.

Albany policy makers also sought increasing control over Indian affairs during and after the American Revolution. The reduction of Indian sovereignty was manifest in state statutory law.

The legislature first became involved in Indian statutory law in 1813, with regulations banning the cutting of timber on tribal lands. In 1821 it transferred the enforcement of the 1813 law to county district attorneys. By 1835, without federal approval, the legislature began permitting and ratifying leases made by non-Indians on the Allegany Indian Reservation. By 1840 and 1841 New York State attempted to tax Indians for the first time, efforts that continue to be a source of tensions and conflicts into the early 21st century. Moreover, the state built canals, roads, and turnpikes through Indian lands, beginning in the 1790s and continuing to the construction of the New York State Thruway in the 1950s and of Rte 17 (I-86) in the 1970s and 1980s.

Education and Welfare

In 1846 the state legislature enacted a law providing for school buildings and annual appropriations for the education of American Indians on four reservations: Allegany, Cattaraugus, Onondaga, and Akwesasne (St. Regis). Later, state-administered schools were specifically established at Shinnecock in 1848, Tonawanda and Tuscarora in 1855, Oneida in 1857, and Poospatuck in 1875. The schools at Oneida were closed in 1889. The rest, except for schools at Onondaga, Akwesasne, and Tuscarora, were also closed, starting with Tonawanda in 1931 and ending with the Allegany Reservation School in 1965. These closings were results partly of the general movement to centralize rural schools and partly of efforts to integrate the races rather than to maintain separate Indian educational institutions. Historically the educational philosophy of these schools was largely to assimilate American Indians into American life; however, in a major reversal of policy in 1975, the Board of Regents announced a position paper, "Native American Education"; number 22 in the Board of Regents series, it emphasized the need to recognize the worth of Indian cultures and to work with Native American communities to improve educational services.

In a move promoted by the Board of Regents, the legislature passed a bill in 1977 creating and appropriating $175,000 for an Indian public library system, the first of its kind in the United States. The act also provided for specific means of acquiring and accepting surplus library books, a specific formula of apportionment of state aid to Indian libraries, and a mechanism for distributing state aid to either the Indian library board of trustees or directly to the tribal government for a contract for library services.

In 1867 the legislature created the Board of Commissioners of Public Charities (renamed New York State Board of Charities in 1873), whose tasks included administering poorhouses; institutions for people with mental and physical disabilities, including lunatic and idiot asylums; and reformatories and orphanages for dependent children. In 1875 the board took over administration of a formerly private Indian orphanage, the Thomas Asylum (1856; later Thomas Indian School), which continued in operation until 1957. From the 1930s successor agencies have also provided social services to the Indians at the Tonawanda Indian Community House at Akron (Erie Co). For much of the 20th century, the Department of Social Welfare and then the Department of Social Services were the lead agencies in handling day-to-day services to American Indians across the state. Since 1998 the Office of Children and Family Services has fulfilled many of those responsibilities.

Evolving Status

Throughout the late 19th and early 20th centuries, the New York State legislature conducted a series of investigations into what its members considered "the Indian problem." American Indians were faced with the prevailing white societal attitude that native peoples should be absorbed into mainstream US society through forced assimilation. One of the most significant investigations occurred in 1888 and was chaired by Assemblyman J. S. Whipple of Salamanca (Cattaraugus Co). This special committee and its report of 1889 held Indian family life, customs, land claims, lifestyle, and religious practices and traditions in contempt. The Whipple Report concluded that the Indian problem could be solved only by ending the Indians' separate status, giving them full citizenship, and absorbing them into the broader American populace. It also maintained that reservation lands, especially Onondaga, Allegany, and Cattaraugus, be allotted in severalty among tribal members, with suitable restrictions as to alienation of lands to Whites and protection from judgments and debts.

In sharp contrast, a special committee appointed by the state legislature in 1920 and chaired by Assemblyman Edward Everett, reported in 1922 that New York State had illegally seized over 6 million acres (2.4 million ha) of land from the Iroquois after the American Revolution. This report, although never accepted by the legislature or governor's office, became proof positive to Indians that they were entitled to justice and further ignited their legal efforts to seek redress and their lost lands back. State efforts to extend control over American Indians, nonetheless, continued with legislative hearings and draft bills in 1900, 1915, and 1930. On 8 Mar 1943, the legislature created the Joint Legislative Committee on Indian Affairs, which issued its report on 15 Mar 1945. It included two draft bills recommending congressional approval of transferring criminal and civil jurisdiction to New York State and offered to cooperate with Congress in securing these laws. The Congress passed the criminal jurisdictional transfer bill, which was signed into law on 1 July 1948. Within 26 months, Congress transferred civil jurisdiction over Indians to New York State. Despite extensive criticism by Indians of these moves, both of the bills passed overwhelmingly. In more recent times, despite tensions caused by jurisdictional transfer, the state and three Indian nations (Oneida Nation, Mohawk Nation, Seneca Nation of Indians) have signed gaming compacts under the federal Gaming Act of 1988, allowing the creation and operation of three Indian-owned casinos in the state.

Continuing Struggles

In the three-decade period after World War II, the Iroquois lost substantial acreage to power projects and road development that was supported by New York State (and Pennsylvania) officials. The Tuscarora Reservoir sought by the New York State Power Authority flooded 550 acres (223 ha) of the Tuscarora Indian Reservation; the St. Lawrence Seaway, pushed by the St. Lawrence Development Corp, condemned 130 acres (53 ha) of Akwesasne lands; and the Kinzua Dam, largely advocated by Pennsylvania politicians but supported by local non-Indian officials in southwestern New York who feared an alternative plan, flooded over 9,000 acres (3,600 ha)—the entire Cornplanter Grant of the Seneca Nation—and led to the forced removal and resettlement of over 500 Senecas to new homesteads at Steamburg and Salamanca (Cattaraugus Co).

In the early 21st century, Indian remembrances of past land loss and opposition to New York State's attempts to tax Indians and Indian-owned reservation-based enterprises have led to continued tensions between the Indian nations and Albany. Despite federal court decisions favorable to Indian land claims in 1974, 1985, 1990, and 2001, Albany officials have not lessened these tensions because they have failed to settle any and all outstanding Indian land claims, unlike their counterparts in Connecticut, Maine, Massachusetts, Rhode Island, and South Carolina.

Graymont, Barbara. "New York State Indian Policy after the American Revolution," *New York History* 58 (Oct 1976): 438–74

Hauptman, Laurence M. *Formulating American Indian Policy in New York State, 1970–1986: A Public Policy Study* (Albany: SUNY Press, 1988)

———. *Conspiracy of Interests: Iroquois Dispossession and the Rise of New York State* (Syracuse: Syracuse Univ Press, 1999)

New York State. Legislature. *Report of the Special Committee to Investigate the Indian Problem of the State of New York, Appointed by the Assembly of 1888,* 2 vols. Assembly Document No. 51 (1889; repr Rochester: Monroe Abstract & Title, 1989)

Upton, Helen M. *The Everett Report in Historical Perspective: The Indians of New York* (Albany: NYS Bicentennial Commission, 1980)

Vecsey, Christopher, and William Starna, eds. *Iroquois Land Claims* (Syracuse: Syracuse Univ Press, 1988)

Venables, Robert, ed. *The Six Nations of New York: The 1892 United States Extra Census Bulletin* (repr Ithaca: Cornell Univ Press, 1995)

Laurence M. Hauptman

American Indians in literature: Indigenous authors. The work of indigenous writers within New York State covers an array of topics, including the complicated issues surrounding American Indian identity, geography, and intellectual property. While writers outside of the Haudenosaunee (Iroquois) cultures are represented in contemporary literature in the state, most Indian writers fall within Haudenosaunee communities and fit loosely into three categories: those concerned with documentation of the heritage, with its creative reclamation, and with its transformation.

Documentation

In a period of coerced assimilation into the larger identity of the United States, several individuals attempted to document the traditional cultures and stories of their communities in formal ethnographic style. David Cusick (*ca* 1780–*ca* 1840), a Tuscarora, is the author of *Sketches of Ancient History of the Six Nations . . .* (1827), the first recorded document of Haudenosaunee culture written by one of its members. This volume, which includes interpretive illustrations by Cusick, predates the conventions of modern anthropology and appears to be the product of the author's personal concern for posterity. Tuscarora anthropologist J. N. B. Hewitt (1857–1937) published studies of Iroquois cosmology and Seneca mythology in the early 20th century. His work is more formally anthropological than Cusick's but reveals similar characteristics, in particular the ways in which Western thought and ideology are embedded in even the most basic cultural elements. For instance, the Haudenosaunee creation story, in both Cusick and Hewitt, reflects the Western motif of good conquering evil, while other versions of the story, such as those in Arthur C. Parker's *Seneca Myths and Folk Tales* (1923) and Jesse J. Cornplanter's *Legends of the Longhouse* (1938), have good and evil operating in balance. Parker and Cornplanter, both Seneca, also document other traditional stories from Haudenosaunee cultures with an eye toward coherence, accessibility, and historical value.

RECLAMATION

The second stage of Haudenosaunee literature is manifested in writing that, while not otherwise homogeneous, represents 20th-century Indian life in its richness and complexity, without the romanticized notions and clichés non-Indian writers often employed when writing about Indians. An influential early work, addressing 20th-century reservation life in earnest terms, is the novel *The Reservation* (1976), by the Tuscarora writer Ted C. Williams. The narrative is not linear but cyclical, documenting the narrator's growth not only as a contributing member of his community but as an arbiter of cultural history and identity. The impact of Williams's unorthodox use of language, time, and narrative structure can be seen in subsequent American Indian literature. American Book Award winners Maurice Kenny, in *Carving Hawk* (2002), *Tekonwatonti: Molly Brant* (1992) and *The Mama Poems* (1984), and Peter Blue Cloud (Aroniawenrate), in *Elderberry Flute Song* (1982), infuse their work with the aesthetic of contemporary Mohawks, encompassing worldviews not limited by Western cultural influence. Seneca author Duwayne Bowen, in *One More Story* (1991) and *A Few More Stories* (2001), employs a matter-of-fact, conversational tone that captures an essence of contemporary oral style.

TRANSFORMATION

A third major Haudenosaunee aesthetic development is represented by the work of multidisciplinary artists, consciously referring to earlier departures from formal verbal narrative by Indian authors, who understand that some concepts cannot be expressed exclusively with words. Mohawk poet James Thomas Stevens, in *Combing the Snakes from His Hair* (2002), makes his own images integral elements of the work rather than mere adornment and in fact engages in an explicit dialogue with David Cusick's pictorial imagery. Mohawk Alex Jacobs (Karoniaktatie) balances word and image in his major series, *Pow-Wow Highway (Crossroads)*, as well as engages this form in his installation work. Onondaga author Eric Gansworth is the author of three novels that integrate visual images with written narrative and of as a collection of poems and paintings, *Nickel Eclipse: Iroquois Moon* (2000). These writers, along with Beth Brant, notably in her *Mohawk Trail* (1985), bring a postmodern, self-reflective sensibility to their work. They and their contemporaries are keenly aware of the traditional stories preserved during the first literary wave and the value of the contemporary Indian world embraced in the second, but they synthesize those approaches in new ways, exemplifying the adaptability that has allowed indigenous groups to maintain their cultural identities through periods of great duress.

Two anthologies of contemporary Haudenosaunee literature, *New Voices from the Longhouse* (1989) and *Iroquois Voices, Iroquois Visions* (1996), reveal the diversity and steady growth of American Indian literary voices in recent years. While many writers represented in these collections have not gone on to develop full-length works, their inclusion speaks to the many ways in which Haudenosaunee literary culture has survived and thrived. Among those included are poets David Back, Salli Benedict, Francis Boots (Ateronhiatakon), William T. Laughing (Atonwa), Amber Coverdale Sumrall, Tahnahga, and Daniel Thompson (Rokwaho) (Mohawk); Pam Colorado, Melanie M. Ellis, and Bruce King (Oneida); Audrey Shenandoah, Diane Shenandoah, and Gail Tremblay (Onondaga); Lisa Fuller and Carol Snow (Seneca); Tom Huff (Seneca/Cayuga); and Shirlee Winder (Seneca/Oneida).

While the American Indian literature of New York State is dominated by writers from Haudenosaunee communities, the state's complex history is also manifested in works by writers of other indigenous affiliations. Joseph Bruchac, most explicitly in *Translator's Son* (1994) and *Bowman's Store* (1997), explores contemporary Indian life from the perspective of an Abenaki who has discovered this heritage later in life. Muriel Miguel, Gloria Miguel, and Lisa Mayo, three sisters of Kuna and Rappahannock background and the core members of the New York City–based Spiderwoman Theater, have published plays that address feminist issues: "Winnetous's Snake-Oil Show from Wigwam City," in *Playwrights of Color* (1999); "Power Pipes," in *Seventh Generation: An Anthology of Native American Plays* (1999); and "Sun, Moon, and Feather," in *Stories of Our Way: An Anthology of American Indian Plays* (1999).

Brydon, Sherry. "Ingenuity in Art: The Early 19th-Century Works of David and Dennis Cusick," *American Indian Artist Magazine* (Spring 1995)
Hill, Rick. *Creativity Is Our Tradition* (Santa Fe, N Mex: IAIA Museum, 1992)
Judkins, Russell A., ed. *Iroquois Studies: A Guide to Documentary and Ethnographic Resources from Western New York and the Genesee Valley* (Geneseo, NY: SUNY; The Geneseo Foundation, 1987)

Eric Gansworth

American Indians in literature: Nonindigenous authors. The fictional responses to American Indians in New York State by non-Indians in works intended for teenagers and adults is extensive and has played an important role in shaping general attitudes to Indians.

NATIVE AMERICAN STEREOTYPES

From the beginning, representations of New York State's Indians in American literature and popular culture in general have tended to follow two prevailing stereotypes: the majority of Native Americans have been depicted as brutish, bloodthirsty, ignoble savages, while some are shown to be honorable, sagacious "noble savages." American history supposedly demonstrated that the native population was capable of unspeakable barbarism. Well-publicized incidents of cruelty, such as the killing of Jane McCrea by Huron Indians near Fort Edward (Washington Co) in 1777, however isolated from a larger historical perspective, justified the ignoble portrayal. The earliest works, including Ann Eliza Bleecker's *The History of Maria Kittle* (1779) and the anonymous story "Oneyo and Marano" (1795), depict Indians primarily as barbarians. The noble savage was also present in American literature from the colonial era and was popularized rather than invented by James Fenimore Cooper in novels like *The Last of the Mohicans* (1826). A convenient foil to the ever-present ignoble savage in literary themes and plots, the noble savage was distinguished by wisdom, even temperament, generosity, and other virtues, while being thoughtful enough to recognize that this way of life was doomed to extinction from expanding white settlement. Noteworthy examples of the noble savage type appear in John Gardiner Calkins Brainerd's *Letters Found in the Ruins of Fort Braddock* (1824) and Ambrose Walker's *The Highlands* (1826). Most Native American literary characters seem unreal to the modern reader. Indeed, the "wooden Indians" of literature for many years provided American readers no factual information on the lives of any Indians, as few white authors possessed firsthand knowledge of the tribes they depicted. Thus ignorance as well as racial bias perpetuated the stereotypes.

The Indians of New York State have received somewhat different literary treatment from their counterparts across the country. First of all, the majority in the former are Iroquois, and authors sometimes found it difficult to classify them according to the twin stereotypes of the noble and ignoble savage. Some Iroquois committed atrocities against settlers during the American Revolution, but at the same time the Six Nations were renowned for their famous confederacy and considered by many as a model of republican government. Likewise, the lives and exploits of certain Iroquois leaders, such as the Mohawk Joseph Brant and Red Jacket of the Seneca, were well known, which made it difficult to oversimplify them using stereotypes. The literary portrayals of the Christian Mohawk Kateri Tekakwitha, the French/Seneca leader Madame Montour and her granddaughter Queen Catharine, and the adoptive Seneca Mary Jemison are exceptional in granting these women distinct, if not wholly realistic, personas. Of the Iroquois, the Oneida are often shown to be ennobled because of their alliance with the American cause during the Revolutionary War. The Huron and other native peoples aligned with the French during the colonial period are generally depicted as barbaric. The Lenape, Manhattan, Mohican (Mahican), Munsee, Wappinger, and other Algonquian-speaking groups are mostly shown as peace loving and more highly civilized.

Most literary works dealing with New York State's Indians are pieces of prose fiction. Examples of poetry and drama are almost nonexistent; they generally use the same Native American stereotypes but tend to be more sentimental and melodramatic than the fictional works. Shorter sentimental poems about Indians are often so unspecific that no geographic setting or historical time frame is recognizable. A number of early poems feature dying Indian chiefs, noble savages who have come to recognize their individual doom and that of their race. Henry Wadsworth Longfellow's *Song of Hiawatha* (1855) is a largely imaginary interpretation of the legend of the Iroquois Confederacy's founding, unconnected to authentic Iroquois traditions and mistakenly set in the western Great Lakes.

White Stock Characters

Three stereotypical white genre characters populate many works dealing with the Indians of New York State. Foremost is the frontiersman, also referred to as a scout or ranger in a number of works. Natty Bumppo of Cooper's Leatherstocking Tales (1822–41) was by far the best-known representative of the type. The frontiersman may have been rude in his dress or behavior but possessed a knowledge of the frontier, of woodcraft, and of Indians that few others could match. His intentions and actions are universally noble. The "Indian hater" and "renegade" are characters unique to American frontier literature. The renegade is a white man who not only spurned civilization but turned against other Europeans, a man more depraved than the ignoble savages whose company he often kept. An important prototype for the renegade character was the Revolutionary era defector Simon Girty, who on behalf of the British instigated Indian attacks on white Americans in Pennsylvania and Ohio. The Indian hater is another type of "white savage," but unlike the renegade his antisocial and barbaric behavior is justified by authors. Usually members of the Indian hater's family were killed by Indians when he was young, and he became consumed by a thirst for revenge. The Indian hater appeared in the earliest works and is often associated with the historical Tom Quick, a Delaware Valley pioneer who devoted his life to killing Indians. The justification of the Indian hater's murderous conduct in books like James E. Quinlan's *Tom Quick, the Indian Slayer* (1851) reveals the racial bias of authors toward American Indians.

History and Folklore

Despite the prevalence of stereotypes, the increasing remoteness of colonial and Revolutionary era conflicts and the rise of ethnographic interest in American Indians in the first half of the 19th century led some New York State authors to present detailed (if not always accurate) historical background material, including information on American Indian history, culture, and folklore. Charles Fenno Hoffman, a prominent New York State author, published four lively tales based on Native American history and lore in *Wild Scenes in the Forest and Prairie* (1839), while Nathaniel Sylvester, well-known folklorist and author of county histories, published four stories in his *Indian Legends of Saratoga and of the Upper Hudson Valley* (1884). Harrison Chamberlain's *Legend of Silver-Thread Falls* (1909) preserves a traditional Seneca tale. John L. E. W. Shecut authored two popular books in the Cooper era praising the political and religious heritage of the Iroquois: *Ish-noo-ju-lut-sche* (1841) and *The Scout* (1844). Some significant short stories from this period drawing on legendary or historical sources are the anonymous "Ben Pie, or The Indian Murderer" (1825), Francis Herbert's "The Cascade of Melsingah" (1828), William Cullen Bryant's "The Indian Spring" (1830), and Mary Chase's "Kaunameek" (1847). With ethnologists like Lewis Henry Morgan and Henry Rowe Schoolcraft stressing the need to collect and preserve Indian legends and folklore, poets too exhibited a far greater interest in this material, especially in the years following the Civil War. The best examples are John McNaughton's *Onnalinda* (1884), Clinton Scollard's *Skenandoa* (1896), Benjamin Hathaway's *League of the Iroquois* (1882), John Sanborn's *Day-yu-da-gont* (1904), and John Minard's *Story of the Old Indian Council-House* (1912).

Dime Novel Era

Many works dealing with New York State's indigenous peoples are highly melodramatic, verbose, and sometimes confusing, filled with bombastic rhetoric and stilted dialogue. The speech of Indians, and of frontiersmen and African American characters, is contrived and reflects the biases of the times. These qualities are most evident in fiction of the "dime novel" era, between 1860 and *ca* 1915. Dime novels were inexpensive, action-packed adventure stories with a romantic subplot, about 100 pages in length, and targeted to a mostly adolescent readership. About 60 such tales, including a number by W. J. Hamilton (Charles Clark), present Indians in New York State settings, mainly during the French and Indian War or the American Revolution. Novels published in the traditional format during these years, while longer and with more complicated plots, mostly contained similar Indian characters. Works by prolific novelist Edward Ellis were published in both dime novel and traditional fiction format, the most significant being *Iron Heart* (1899) and *Red Jacket* (1900). James Mark Allerton's *Hawk's Nest* (1892) is notable for its in-depth portrayal of the Delaware Valley Cahoonshee.

The 20th Century

While earlier stereotypical treatments of American Indians as brutal savages continued, often defended on grounds of historical accuracy, authors in the early 20th century began to feel the need to present more realistic portrayals of Indian characters. Two well-researched novels of the period, *The White Seneca* (1911) and *At Seneca Castle* (1912), were written by William Canfield, a western New York State historian. Kenneth Roberts depicted Indians as individuals with distinct personalities in his novels set in the colonial and Revolutionary eras, *Rabble in Arms* (1933) and *Northwest Passage* (1937). Other significant novels of the first half of the century include the acclaimed *Drums Along the Mohawk* (1936) and *In the Hands of the Senecas* (1947) by Walter D. Edmonds. A number of Indian-themed novels for young adult audiences were also published around midcentury. Meanwhile, poetry of the era continued to draw on American Indian folklore. Carleton Burke published two short poetic works on Iroquois folklore associated with the Genesee Valley, *The Indian and His River* (1933) and *Symphony Iroquoian* (1937), while Arnold Bellows' *The Legend of Utsayantha* (1945) contains a number of poems dealing with Mohican folklore of the northern Catskills.

A number of novels published since 1970 have presented American Indian characters in depth and with considerable sensitivity to their lives and culture. Many of these works valorize traditional Indian religious practices, as filtered through "new age" spiritual sensibilities. Robert Moss's trilogy of novels set in the pre-Revolutionary heyday of Sir William Johnson emphasizes Indian dreams and shamanism: *Fire along the Sky* (1990), *The Firekeeper* (1995), and *The Interpreter* (1997). Early settlers and their Native American neighbors in the upper Sacandaga Valley provide the backdrop for Sara Donati's trilogy, comprising *Into the Wilderness* (1998), *Dawn on a Distant Shore* (2000), and *Lake in the Clouds* (2002). Kate Cameron's *Orenda* (1991) features wise and powerful Iroquois matron figures, while Harold Thomas Beck's *Cornplanter Chronicles* (2001) details the life of the Allegany Seneca leader, Ganiodieu. Four noteworthy novels present Native Americans in contemporary settings in Indian Nation territory or in New York City: Jack Ishmole's *Walk in the Sky* (1972), Robert Lipsyte's *The Brave* (1991), Jesse Browner's *Turnaway* (1996), and Marlene Carvell's *Who Will Tell My Brother?* (2002), the latter dealing with the controversial issue of Indian school mascots and athletic team names. Elizabeth Speare's *The Prospering* (1967) and Alan Firstone's *Son of the Silvery Waters* (2001) are remarkable for their treatments of the Mohican and Cayuga Indians, respectively. Two young adult novels with historical settings are Katherine Kirkpatrick's *Trouble's Daughter* (1998), based on an event that occurred in 1643 in what is now the Bronx, and Betsy Urban's *Waiting for Deliverance* (2000), about the post–Revolutionary War Finger Lakes frontier. American Indians also figure prominently in a few mystery novels, including Thomas Perry's widely read Jane Whitefield series published between 1995 and 1999, Margaret Clark's *Mystery Horse* (1972), and Harriet Feder's *Death on Sacred Ground* (2001).

See also LITERATURE, BEYOND NEW YORK CITY.

Barnett, Louise. *The Ignoble Savage: American Literary Racism, 1790–1890* (Westport, Conn: Greenwood, 1975)

Beam, Joan, and Barbara Branstad. *The Native American in Long Fiction: An Annotated Bibliography* (Lanham, Md: Scarecrow Press, 1996)

Beidler, John, and Marion F. Egge. *The American Indian in Short Fiction: An Annotated Bibliography* (Metuchen, NJ: Scarecrow Press, 1979)

Haas, Marilyn. *The Seneca and Tuscarora Indians: An Annotated Bibliography* (Metuchen, NJ: Scarecrow Press, 1994)

Keiser, Albert. *The Indian in American Literature* (New York: Oxford Univ Press, 1933)

Pearce, Roy Harvey. *Savagism and Civilization: A Study of the Indian and the American Mind,* rev ed. (Baltimore: Johns Hopkins Univ Press, 1967)

Warren F. Broderick

American Jewish Committee (AJC). Jewish voluntary organization. The committee was founded in New York City in 1906, in the wake of the persecution of Jews in Russia, to defend Jewish civil and religious rights worldwide through lobbying and education. Initially consisting of upper-class German Jews, it disavowed political Zionism. Under Syracuse-born Louis Marshall, its president from 1908 to 1929, the AJC fought anti-Semitism, immigration restriction, and lynching. By the end of World War II it had become a mass-membership organization, supporting the creation of a Jewish state and increasing work toward ending prejudice toward minorities. It founded the journal of opinion *Commentary* in 1945 and had 26,000 members by the late 1950s. In the late 20th and early 21st centuries it has continued to be a staunch defender of Israel and of Jewish interests generally.

Cohen, Naomi W. *Not Free to Desist: The American Jewish Committee, 1906–1966* (Philadelphia: Jewish Publication Society, 1972)

Susan Roth Breitzer

American Jewish Congress (AJCongress). Jewish voluntary organization. The AJCongress was founded in New York City in 1918 as a temporary delegation to the Paris Peace Conference to lobby for the inclusion of treaty guarantees of Jewish minority rights in the defeated countries. The growing demand for a more democratic and representative alternative to the largely self-selected American Jewish Committee, however, resulted in the reestablishment of the AJCongress as a permanent body in 1922, two years after disbanding. It was distinguished by both its Zionism and its aggressive approach to issues of discrimination. In the 1930s the AJCongress, led by Rabbi Stephen S. Wise, organized a boycott of German goods and staged anti-Nazi rallies at Madison Square Garden, most notably in 1933. Following World War II the AJCongress was active in the Civil Rights Movement in the 1960s, supported feminist causes in the 1990s, and continued, in 2002, to support strong ties between American Jews and the State of Israel, with about 50,000 members nationwide.

Svonkin, Stuart. "American Jewish Congress." In *Jewish Women in America: An Historical Encyclopedia*, vol 1, ed. Paula E. Hyman, Deborah Dash Moore, and Phyllis Weisbard (New York: Routledge, 1997)

Susan Roth Breitzer

American Labor Party. Founded in 1936 by David Dubinsky, Sidney Hillman, and Alex Rose, the American Labor Party (ALP) consisted of labor union leaders, socialists, and other members of the Left. The initial goal of the party was to give socialist and communist voters an alternative line to choose Democratic candidate Franklin D. Roosevelt in the 1936 presidential election. The ALP's membership was centered in New York City and consisted primarily of voters from working-class ethnic neighborhoods. The ALP primarily cross-endorsed Democratic and Republican candidates it considered progressive. In elections where no candidate fit the ALP platform, it ran its own. In the 1936 national elections, the ALP endorsed Roosevelt for president and Herbert H. Lehman for governor of New York State, providing more than 274,924 votes for Roosevelt and 262,192 for Lehman. Fiorello La Guardia received 482,790 ALP votes (21% of his total votes) in his election as mayor of New York City in 1937, and the following year the ALP obtained nearly 45% of the votes for East Harlem congressman Vito Marcantonio's reelection.

In its first few years, the ALP grew into a major political force, especially in New York City politics, providing the winning margin in a number of elections. Michael J. Quill, president of the Transport Workers Union, was elected to the New York City Council in 1937, 1943, and 1945 on the ALP ballot. The ALP fielded African American and Hispanic candidates to push for minority representation, and its endorsement of Adam Clayton Powell Jr was key to his congressional victory in Harlem in 1944 by providing more than 14,000 votes. However, there were divisions by 1940 between the Far Left and liberal members of the ALP concerning policy toward the Soviet Union. In 1944 Dubinsky and Rose led an anticommunist faction that left the ALP and formed the Liberal Party. In 1948 the ALP polled over 500,000 votes for presidential candidate Henry A. Wallace in New York State, but many members withdrew in opposition to his candidacy. The ALP lost its place on the New York ballot in 1954 by failing to receive at least 50,000 votes for its gubernatorial candidate, and the party officially dissolved in 1956.

Meyer, Gerald. *Vito Marcantonio: Radical Politician, 1902–1954* (Albany: SUNY Press, 1989)
Waltzer, Kenneth. "The Party and the Polling Place: American Communism and the American Labor Party in the 1930s," *Radical History Review* 23 (Autumn 1980): 104–29

Brian Keough

American Locomotive Company (ALCO). The Schenectady Locomotive Engine Manufactory Co was established in 1848 by John Ellis and Platt Potter, who invited the locomotive-building Norris brothers of Philadelphia to help set up the enterprise. Land was purchased from Union College near the Erie Canal, and $50,000 was raised by subscription. About a year later their first locomotive, Lightning, was built for the Utica and Schenectady Railroad, but it was too heavy for the rails and had poor steaming capacity. With no more orders forthcoming, the Norrises withdrew, and the company was sold for taxes in 1851. The same group, without the Norris brothers, created the Schenectady Locomotive Works in May 1851. During the next six years they built over 200 locomotives and supplied 84 to the US Military Railroad during the Civil War. In 1868 the 4–4–0 type locomotive Jupiter was built for the Central Pacific Railroad, one of two that met at Promontory Point, Utah, to celebrate the completion of the transcontinental railroad. The Ellis family retained control through the end of the century with their chief engineer, Walter McQueen, developing and producing a variety of well-respected locomotives, including the New York Central and Hudson River Railroad's 4–4–0 speedster, Locomotive 999. By 1901 the Schenectady Locomotive Works had built 6,300 locomotives.

On 24 June 1901 Schenectady's Big Shop, as the works were known, merged with seven other locomotive builders in the Northeast, including Brooks Locomotive Works of Dunkirk (Chautauqua Co), to form the American Locomotive Co. Two other companies were acquired by 1905, including Montreal Locomotive Works (MLW) in 1904. After this consolidation most of the fabrication was moved to Schenectady. During the early years of the 20th century ALCO contributed significantly to development of the steam locomotive, including building the nation's first Hudson type 4–6–4 for the New York Central in 1927. The company also built a number of electric locomotives in conjunction with the General Electric Co (GE) of Schenectady and developed diesel-electric locomotives with GE and the McIntosh and Seymour Engine Co in Auburn (Cayuga Co), which ALCO purchased in 1929. The first diesel-electric passenger locomotive was built for the New York Central in 1928.

During World War II the War Production Board restrained ALCO from building diesel road locomotives, allowing only switcher locomotives, to maximize plant utilization, which allowed General Motors to gain production expertise and a market foothold that would adversely affect ALCO in the postwar years. In 1946 ALCO's production was 75% diesel, with the last steam locomotives built in 1948. Although ALCO enjoyed 30% of the locomotive business in 1948, other competitors, including GE, were capturing the market. Despite expanding into nuclear and heavy industrial manufacturing and a new line of superpower locomotives, the company faltered. Renamed ALCO Products Inc in 1955, Worthington Corp (later Studebaker-Worthington) purchased the company in 1964. By the end of 1969 the Schenectady plant was closed and leased to GE for steam turbine production, with the locomotive design rights transferred to MLW. ALCO design engines and parts are still available, but the corporate identity has disappeared.

Kirkland, John F. *American Locomotive Company and Montreal Locomotive Works*, vol 2 of *The Diesel Builders* (Pasadena, Calif: Pentrex Media Group, 1989)
Steinbrenner, Richard T. *The American Locomotive Company: A Centennial Remembrance* (Kutztown, Pa: Kutztown Publishing, 2002)

Jim Shaughnessy

American Missionary Association. Founded in Albany on 3 Sept 1846 by New School Congregationalists with abolitionist principles, the American Missionary Association (AMA) was headquartered in New York City and served as an organization of reform, humanitarianism, and religious and secular education. Important early leaders include New York City abolitionist and businessman Lewis Tappan, and the African American ministers Samuel Ringgold Ward and Samuel E. Cornish. Providing for the educational needs of African Americans was a significant mission for the AMA, and after 1865 the group established a variety of schools for former slaves in the South, employing more than 525 teachers by 1867. The organization also played a critical role in establishing institutions of higher learning for African Americans, including Fisk, Howard, Hampton, and Atlanta Universities. By 1938 the AMA was absorbed into the Home Missions Department of the Congregational Church.

Brownlee, Frederick L. *New Day Ascending* (Boston: Pilgrim Press, 1946)
Richardson, Joe. *Christian Reconstruction: The American Missionary Association and Southern Blacks, 1861–1890* (Athens: Univ of Georgia Press, 1986)

David B. Malone

American Museum of Natural History. Albert Smith Bickmore, a former student of the naturalist Louis Agassiz, started planning a natural history museum in the late 1860s with the aid of patrons such as Joseph H. Choate and J. P. Morgan. Calvert Vaux and Jacob Wrey Mould designed a Gothic-style building for the new American Museum of Natural History (AMNH), which opened 22 Dec 1877 on Manhattan Square, an area across from Central Park between West 77th and 81st Sts. The AMNH emphasized educational programs for public schools as well as the work of scholars, such as anthropologist Franz Boas and zoologist Joel A. Allen. After becoming AMNH president in 1908, conservationist Henry Fairfield Osborn sponsored Roy Chapman Andrews on the Central Asiatic Expeditions from 1921 to 1930, which yielded the discovery of numerous early mammal and dinosaur fossils, including the frilled dinosaur *Protoceratops andrewsi.* Before he retired in 1933, Osborn initiated the construction of the Hayden Planetarium, which opened in 1935. Margaret Mead developed AMNH projects in social and cultural anthropology during the mid–20th century. Paleontology and astronomy continue to be popular attractions at the AMNH; the five-story-high *Barosaurus* display was installed in 1991, and the Rose Center for Earth and Space opened 19 Feb 2000. At the beginning of the 21st century the museum comprised 23 buildings and 42 exhibit halls, listed an endowment at $472.4 million, and received over 5 million visitors annually.

American Museum of Natural History, http://www.amnh.org

Preston, Douglas J. *Dinosaurs in the Attic: An Excursion into the American Museum of Natural History* (New York: St. Martin's Press, 1986)

Rosenzweig, Roy, and Elizabeth Blackmar. *The Park and the People: A History of Central Park* (Ithaca: Cornell Univ Press, 1992)

Dorothy M. Browne

American Revolution: Military history. When war erupted in April 1775 between the British government and most of its American colonies, which were united by a decade of resistance to British laws and policies, New York's geographical location and topography made it a battleground for the next eight years. The New York City seaport, the navigable Hudson River linked by the Champlain corridor to Canada, and the Mohawk Valley leading westward gave New York its strategic importance. From no other place on the Atlantic coast south of Canada was it possible to penetrate by water so deeply into the American interior. With rebellious New England to the northeast and the rich colonies of Pennsylvania, Virginia, and South Carolina to the south, New York became the strategic keystone of the war.

Campaigns of 1775–76

Soon after the outbreak of war in Massachusetts, New Englanders led by Ethan Allen and Benedict Arnold seized Fort Ticonderoga [now in Essex Co] on the New York shore of the south end of Lake Champlain. A Yankee blow as much against New York's northeastern boundary claims as against British authority, New England's capture of Ticonderoga led to an American invasion of Canada via Lake Champlain and the Richelieu River. The invasion's commander was a prominent New Yorker, Philip Schuyler, but most of his troops were New Englanders. Schuyler delegated field command to Richard Montgomery, a former British officer who had married into the New York elite family of the Livingstons, and concentrated on supplying Montgomery's army and on persuading the Iroquois Confederacy west of Albany not to join the British. Montgomery, a capable leader, captured Montreal in November and soon linked up with a force from Boston for a winter attack on the British stronghold at Quebec. The attack failed, Montgomery was killed, and by May 1776, when the ice broke up in the St. Lawrence River and British reinforcements arrived, the American retreat from Canada had become a rout. In October 1776 near Valcour Island in Lake Champlain, a small American navy under Arnold lost a battle but stopped further British advance until the next year.

Frustrated at Boston in its military campaign of 1775 to smash armed American resistance, the British high command shifted its headquarters to New York in 1776. Unlike the solidly united New Englanders, New Yorkers were more divided and hesitant about plunging into war with the mother country. Royal governor William Tryon was not unpopular, and New York's extralegal revolutionary military companies needed help from Connecticut militia when they tried to disarm New Yorkers who opposed the decision of the Continental Congress in Philadelphia to declare American independence in July 1776.

To the south more than 30,000 British and hired German troops had massed on Staten Island by mid-August 1776, and a large British fleet controlled the waters around the New York islands. George Washington, appointed by Congress in June 1775 to command the revolutionary Continental army, had about 20,000 ill-trained men, many of them digging in at Brooklyn Heights (Kings Co) but the rest on Manhattan and Governors Island and in Westchester Co. On 22 August the British landed at Gravesend Bay (Kings Co), quickly expanded their beachhead, and on the 27th sent 10,000 men and 28 guns around the American left flank at Jamaica (Queens Co). In what are now the neighborhoods of Park Slope and Brooklyn Heights, the British overwhelmed and routed Washington's force in the Battle of Long Island.

On the night of 29–30 August, Washington evacuated more than 10,000 of his defeated army by having them rowed across the East River and on to Manhattan. Two weeks later a large British force landed at the foot of what is now East 34th St and moved north against American defenses on Harlem Heights. Washington had his troops dig in on the high ground north of present-day 130th St, and as the British advanced roughly along what is now Broadway, driving in the American outposts, Washington ordered a counterattack. A small battle took place 16 September on the line of present-day West 120th St. Again the Americans lost but fought much better than on Long Island, and the British advance stopped.

In British-captured New York City, which in 1776 had only the lower tip of Manhattan developed, on the night of 20 September fire broke out, destroying hundreds of buildings, about one-quarter of the city. Who set the fire remains a mystery. Both sides accused the other of setting the fire. Washington was delighted at the news, because the British had planned to quarter their forces in the city, but Congress had forbidden him to burn it. In 1778 another fire destroyed almost 100 houses, adding to the miseries of an occupied city.

In mid-October 1776, British forces landed on the Westchester Co shore, at Throgs Point and Pell's Point [now Rodman's Neck in Bronx Co], forcing Washington to withdraw from Harlem, across King's Bridge, to a new defensive position at White Plains (Westchester Co). Moving cautiously, the British attacked the White Plains position on 28 October. After spirited resistance the Americans withdrew when their right flank was crushed. Washington had left behind almost 3,000 men in Upper Manhattan to hold Fort Washington [now Fort Tryon Park]. This fort and another on the New Jersey shore, Fort Lee, were supposed to stop British warships moving up the Hudson. In mid-November, a British-German force stormed Fort Washington from three sides.

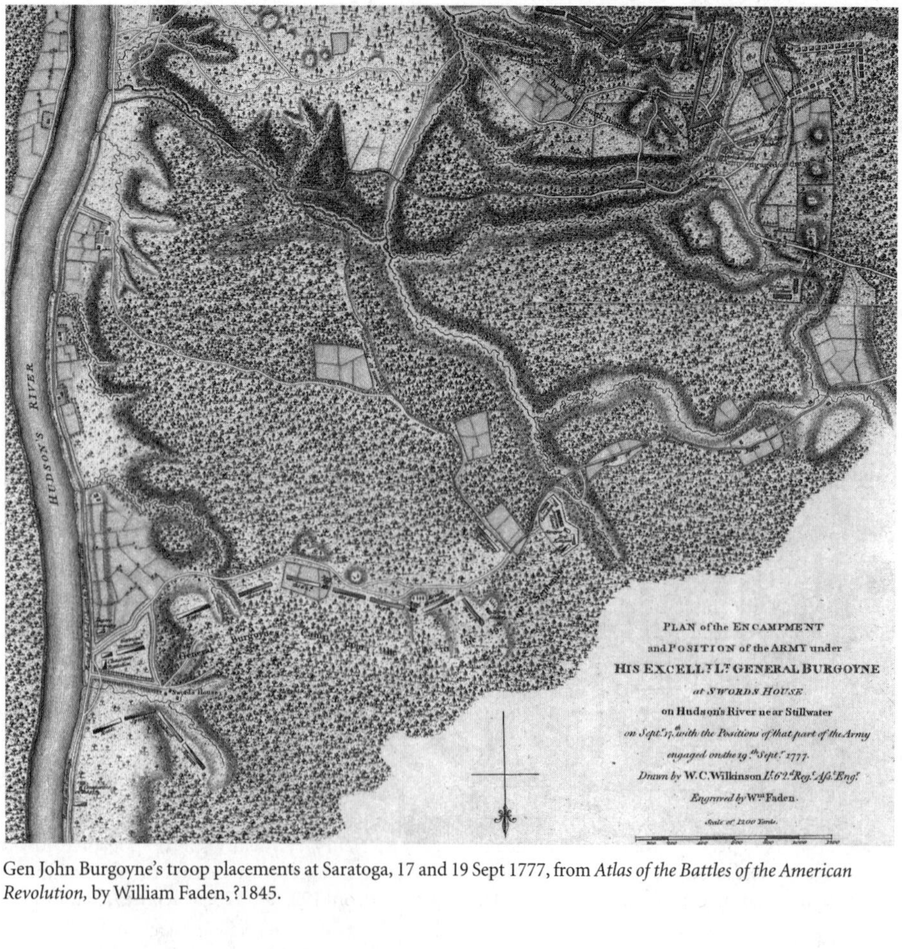

Gen John Burgoyne's troop placements at Saratoga, 17 and 19 Sept 1777, from *Atlas of the Battles of the American Revolution,* by William Faden, ?1845.

After fierce fighting and heavy casualties on both sides, Fort Washington surrendered. Fort Lee fell a few days later. After his defeat at White Plains and the loss of the Hudson River forts, Washington took what was left of his army to New Jersey, leaving New York State to look after itself. The British army and navy established themselves firmly on Manhattan and western Long Island, with strong outposts in lower Westchester Co and New Jersey. From his New York base the British commander Gen William Howe sent raids into Connecticut and a major expedition in December 1776 to occupy Newport, RI. On the northern frontier, beyond Albany, Schuyler tried to keep the Iroquois Confederacy friendly and prepared to meet a renewed British advance in 1777.

Campaign of 1777

British strategy for 1777 centered on New York State. A large force from Montreal under Gen John Burgoyne drove southward to the upper Hudson Valley, and a smaller force moved from Lake Ontario into the Mohawk Valley. The British army and navy based in Manhattan were expected to assist with this northern invasion that was intended to break the links between New England, which had provided much of the labor and supplies for the rebellion, and the Americans living west and south of the Hudson. But Gen Howe and his brother, Adm Richard Howe, calculated that they had ample time to force Washington to fight a decisive battle in defense of the American capital, Philadelphia. Washington remained a threat to the British, regrouping his bedraggled army in late 1776 to overwhelm British outposts (Trenton and Princeton) in New Jersey. The Howes' decision to go south against Washington in 1777 was to deal with an active and dangerous enemy.

Schuyler faced more than British invasion in the north. Embroiled in the historic conflict between New York State and New England, he was disliked and mistrusted by the Yankees under his command. When the key to his defenses, the position at Ticonderoga, fell easily to Burgoyne's army in June, Schuyler's critics in Congress sent Horatio Gates, a former British officer but popular in New England, to take command. Even before Gates's arrival, Burgoyne's advance had become bogged down. Schuyler's men blocked the route south of Skenesborough [now Whitehall, Washington Co] leading to the Hudson, while a mixed force of British and Germans, Indians, and American loyalists, sent eastward by Burgoyne to replenish his dwindling supplies, was wiped out in August by a much larger force of New Englanders at Walloomsac [now in Rensselaer Co] in what is called the Battle of Bennington. Also in August the smaller British invasion down the Mohawk Valley routed the local militia sent against it at Oriskany [now in Oneida Co] and besieged the garrison of Fort Stanwix [now Rome, Oneida Co] on the route from Lake Ontario. Discouraged by their heavy losses at Oriskany, the Indian allies of the British began to leave, and Schuyler, a week before he gave up command to Gates, sent Arnold with a small force to relieve Fort Stanwix. Arnold chased the weakened invaders out of the valley and quickly moved his troops back down the Mohawk to support the American forces against Burgoyne. Gates, the new American commander, faced Burgoyne on the hilly ground of Bemis Heights near Saratoga, in what is now Stillwater (Saratoga Co).

Gates, as the commander, got credit for the decisive American victory in October 1777 at Saratoga, when Burgoyne's army, unable to fight its way forward or backward, was forced to capitulate, but Schuyler deserves a share. Gen Henry Clinton, left by Howe to hold the New York City base, tried to rescue the trapped British army, sending seaborne forces up the Hudson as far north as Kingston (Ulster Co), which they burned. But it was too little, too late. The British defeat at Saratoga brought France, with its navy, army, and immense wealth, into the war on the American side. After Saratoga major military operations moved out of New York State. But even when the main British army, with Gen Clinton its new commander, marched out of Philadelphia and back to New York in the summer of 1778, the war of big battles did not return. The British hunkered down around New York City, while Washington took up strong positions on the Hudson at West Point (Orange Co) and near Peekskill (Westchester Co), as well as at Morristown, NJ, and the war became one of forays and skirmishes fought over the terrain separating the two armies.

War in the Lower Hudson Valley

Westchester Co, like parts of eastern New Jersey, became a bloody, dangerous ground of armed patrols, guerrillas, bandits, spies, and fearful residents. Prominent New Yorkers like James DeLancey and Beverly Robinson, loyal to the Crown, raised whole regiments of fellow New York loyalists in British pay, so that this shadow war north and west of New York City was to some extent a civil war. New York State's government at Poughkeepsie struggled to mobilize resources, with most of its people under British occupation and the rest highly insecure and hard pressed by wartime conditions.

Memories and legends arising from this protracted civil war in lower Westchester are an enduring part of New York history, as much from the stories told by Washington Irving and James Fenimore Cooper as from the historical record. This area between two field armies—the British on Manhattan and the American based in the Hudson Highlands—was contested from mid-1776 onward because each side feared that the

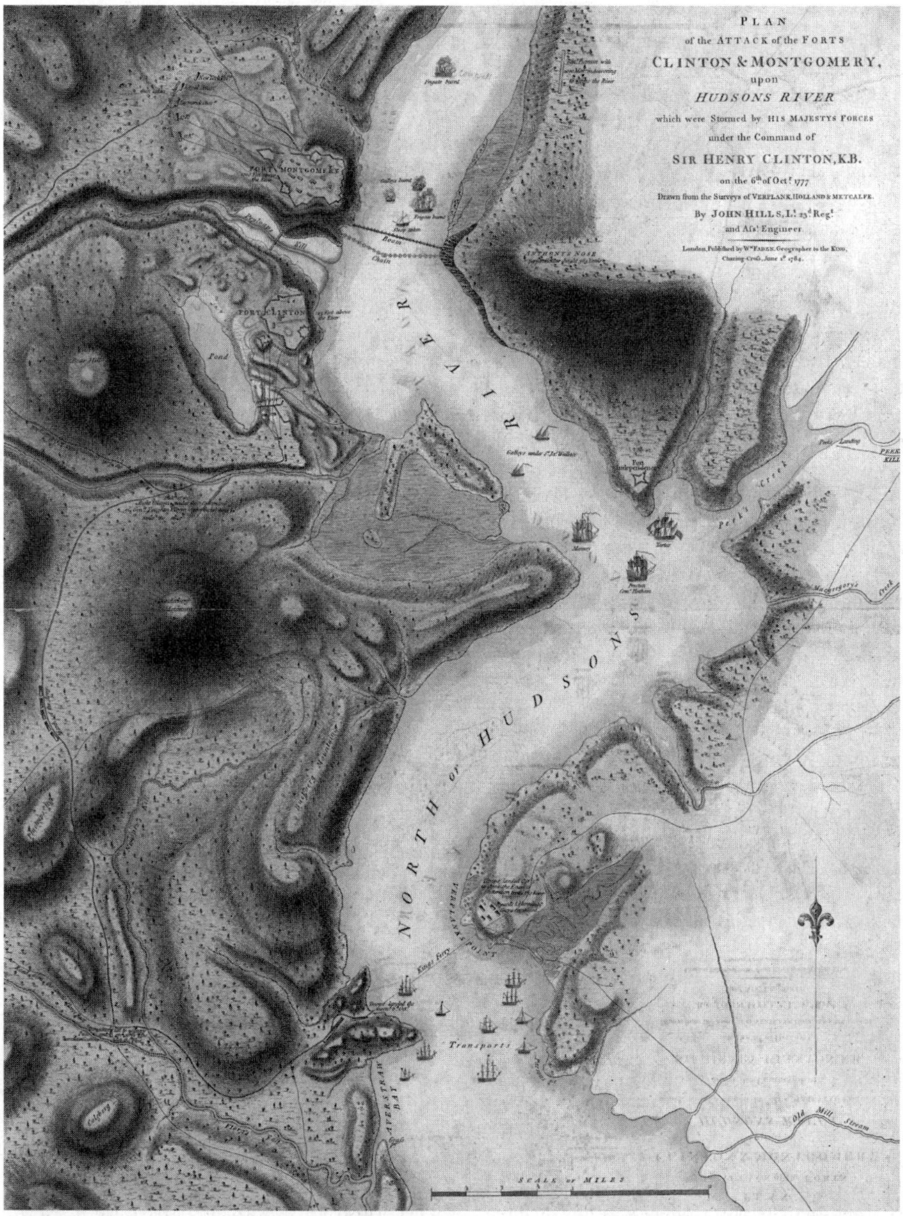

Plan of Attack of Forts Clinton and Montgomery, 6 October 1777, drawn by William Faden, *ca* 1845, depicting British positions just prior to the attack on American fortifications.

other would launch a surprise attack through the area. The consequence for the civilian population was a breakdown of anything resembling law and order, every family prey to whatever armed band appeared at its door. With soldiers from both sides roaming and ambushing one another for more than five years, banditry flourished, and even American privateers coasting the east side of the Hudson contributed to the social chaos. Refugees from Westchester under British protection, enlisted and led by DeLancey and known to the other side as "Cowboys," were blamed for many atrocities, especially the killing of about 20 rebel soldiers trying to surrender in May 1781. But American "Skinners," as they were called by their enemies, were equally blamed. One problem exacerbating the conflict was that many of the American loyalists fighting on the British side served without pay and were expected to compensate themselves with "rebel" property. But the political identity of any particular farmstead was often unclear. In the warfare on the lower Hudson, the Americans scored a spectacular victory in July 1779, surprising and destroying a regiment of British regulars at Stony Point, in what is now Rockland Co, a British outpost on the west shore. Aside from raising American morale, the Stony Point action changed nothing in this shadow war. Large seaborne expeditions were dispatched by the British from New York City to the West Indies, Georgia, and South Carolina, but neither side—Washington in the Hudson Highlands or Clinton on Manhattan—was strong enough to defeat the other.

The Sullivan-Clinton Campaign

Living on the Mohawk frontier was even more dangerous than living in Westchester. A large force of armed loyalists operating from Fort Niagara [now in Porter, Niagara Co], joined by a sizable Iroquois contingent, in November 1778 surprised the fortified American settlement at Cherry Valley [now in Otsego Co], killing dozens and spreading terror throughout the region. Under pressure after the "massacre" at Cherry Valley and an earlier raid on Wyoming, Pa, Washington reluctantly agreed in 1779 to send a large detachment from his army to punish the New York State Indians and, if possible, to capture Fort Niagara. An American army of about 4,000, under the command of Maj Gen John Sullivan and Brig Gen James Clinton (brother of Gov George Clinton) and including four New York regiments, assembled in mid-August at Tioga [now in Tioga Co] and began moving slowly up the Chemung River. On 29 August, the loyalist Iroquois and their New Yorker allies made a stand near Newtown [now Elmira] but could not resist superior American numbers and artillery in the only pitched battle of the campaign. The expedition cut a terrible swath through Cayuga and Seneca settlements along the east side of Seneca Lake and as far west as the Genesee River, burning villages and crops and killing anyone it could catch. The expedition made no distinction between those who had joined the British and others, such as most of the Oneida Nation, who supported the Americans or those who had tried to stay neutral. The 1779 expedition effectively destroyed the homelands of the western Iroquois nations and embittered its Indian survivors, who wreaked vengeance along the New York State and Pennsylvania frontier in 1780 and 1781.

The War Strikes Home

Major battles and campaigns inevitably get most of the attention in a military history of New York State's part in the war, but for many New Yorkers minor incidents often had the greatest impact. Two examples illustrate this point. Nathan and William Pearce governed Pawling (Dutchess Co) during the war. Nathan collected taxes for the Poughkeepsie government and fines from the many Quakers settled east of Pawling who refused military service; William was captain of the local militia whose main task was to keep local loyalists in check. One night, late in the war, a gang ambushed Nathan in his own home and beat him to death in front of his wife and children. Capt William Pearce relentlessly tracked his brother's killers, caught and wounded the leader, and bayoneted him to death as he begged for mercy. Much further north, northeast of Albany, many German members of the Gilead Lutheran Church in Hoosick [now in Rensselaer Co] armed themselves and followed Francis Pfister, a former lieutenant in the British army, to Bennington, Vt, in 1777. These German Lutheran loyalists supported royal authority, hated the rebellion, and welcomed Burgoyne's invasion as liberation from democratic tyranny. But in the first few minutes of the Battle of Bennington, August 1777, "Colonel" Pfister was mortally wounded, and most of his Lutheran soldiers were killed, wounded, or captured. Dozens of incidents like these constitute an unknown history of the Revolutionary War in New York.

Treason and Victory

Treason in 1780 came close to breaking the stalemate between the armies of Washington and Clinton. Many Americans were discouraged and weary of endless warfare. Congress was bankrupt, with Continental paper money officially revalued at less than 3% of face value. Joint operations with the French had proved unsuccessful. News from the South was uniformly bad. Off Manhattan and Kings Co, thousands of American prisoners of war were sick and dying, packed into unhealthy buildings and onto prison ships. Regiments in Washington's army were growing mutinous over lack of food, clothing, and pay. In this year of despair, a wounded American hero, Benedict Arnold—secretly in touch with Gen Clinton since 1779 and in 1780 made commandant of West Point, the key to Washington's position—concocted a plan to deliver West Point to a sudden British attack. The plan ripened in mid-1780 and by September was on the verge of being carried out when Arnold's British contact, Maj John André, was captured by American militiamen at Tarrytown (Westchester Co), which blew the plot. Warned, Arnold and his wife fled to a British warship in the Hudson, while André was tried and hanged for espionage.

Arnold's treason sent shock waves through the American army and the young American republic. Major mutinies erupted in January 1781 among troops near Morristown. New England soldiers marching from West Point put down the mutiny in the New Jersey regiments, but the Pennsylvania mutineers shot a few of their officers and marched on Congress in Philadelphia before finally agreeing to return to duty. The commander of the small French expeditionary force based in Rhode Island received a secret plan of action in case the Americans collapsed, as many predicted they would in 1781, but that tear proved instead to be the year of American victory.

Knowing that something decisive had to be done soon, Washington planned a joint Franco-American attack on the well-fortified British base on Manhattan. The key to his plan was cooperation with the French navy, one of whose fleets would be bringing reinforcements from the West Indies. The French commanders were polite but not enthusiastic about the plan. The American war was going very badly in the South, and Washington agreed that he would give up his plan and march with the French to Virginia if the as-yet-unknown destination of the West Indies fleet was Chesapeake Bay and not a northern port. In mid-August 1781 the news arrived that the West Indies fleet was indeed headed for Chesapeake Bay. Furious, Washington kept his bargain, joined forces with the French from Rhode Island, and marched rapidly through New Jersey and Philadelphia in time to trap the southern British army under Gen Charles Cornwallis at Yorktown, Va. The united French navy won a crucial battle to block the resupply or evacuation of Cornwallis, who surrendered his army, like Burgoyne at Saratoga, in October 1781. Washington's plan to attack Manhattan had not failed: rumors and leaks to Clinton's headquarters of an imminent attack froze the British garrison in New York State in place while the French and Americans marched past it on the road to Virginia.

The War Plays Out

News of Yorktown brought down the British ministry, and a new government started serious peace negotiations. But peace did not officially come for another two years, during which time lower New York State remained under British occupation, and Indian raids kept the Mohawk frontier on full alert. Guy Carleton, a more capable and aggressive commander, replaced Clinton at British headquarters on Manhattan, while Washington resumed his wary and watchful position around West Point but with an ever shrinking army. American patrols continued to scour Westchester, mainly to gather information and chase notorious bandits, while the peace negotiations dragged on in Paris. The last event of the bloody frontier war was farcical. The British had ceased active operations in mid-1782, but an American attack on the Lake Ontario post of Oswego in February 1783 failed when its Oneida guide apparently got lost in the woods, leading the American force in circles until dawn broke and surprise was lost. Even after hostilities were declared to be at an end, months rolled by before Gen Carleton in November 1783 presided over the evacuation of the British army from New York City. Unpaid American soldiers furloughed from Washington's army were drifting down the river, getting in fights with local loyalists and signing on as sailors in the transports that would carry British soldiers home. Although the British still held forts at Niagara, Oswego, Point au Fer [now Champlain, Clinton Co], and Oswegatchie [now Ogdensburg, St. Lawrence Co] and would not evacuate them until 1796, the war was over. The British forces formally took leave of New York City on 25 Nov 1783, or Evacuation Day, celebrated as a major public holiday for over a century. The last act came on 4 Dec 1783 when Washington took a tearful and graceful leave of his officers at Fraunces Tavern on Pearl St on Manhattan, while out in the harbor the British fleet finally set sail.

See also AFRICAN AMERICANS; CARTOGRAPHY AND MAPPING; WAR MEMORIALS.

Barck, Oscar T. *New York City during the War for Independence* (New York: Columbia Univ Press, 1931)

Bliven, Bruce, Jr. *Battle for Manhattan* (New York: Henry Holt, 1956)

East, Robert A., and Jacob Judd, eds. *The Loyalist Americans: A Focus on Greater New York* (Tarrytown, NY: Sleepy Hollow Restorations, 1975)

Fischer, Joseph R. *A Well-Executed Failure: The Sullivan Campaign against the Iroquois, July–September 1779* (Columbia: Univ of South Carolina Press, 1997)

Gerlach, Don R. *Proud Patriot: Philip Schuyler and the War of Independence, 1775–1783* (Syracuse: Syracuse Univ Press, 1987)

Graymont, Barbara. *The Iroquois in the American Revolution* (Syracuse: Syracuse Univ Press, 1972)

Jones, Thomas. *History of New York during the Revolutionary War,* 2 vols (New York: New-York Historical Society, 1879)

Klein, Milton M. *New York in the American Revolution: A Bibliography* (Albany: NYS American Revolution Bicentennial Commission, 1974)

Ranlet, Philip. *The New York Loyalists* (Knoxville: Univ of Tennessee Press, 1986)

Van Doren, Carl. *Secret History of the American Revolution* (New York: Viking Press, 1941)

Ward, Christopher. *The War of the Revolution,* 2 vols (New York: Macmillan, 1952)

Willcox, William B. *Portrait of a General: Sir Henry Clinton in the War of Independence* (New York: Knopf, 1964)

John Shy

American Revolution: Social and political history

Background to Rebellion

During the mid-1760s New York was a crucible of resistance to Britain. Its revolutionary movement emerged from three factors. The first was the British victory over France in the French and Indian War (1754–1763), much of which was either fought or staged in New York Colony. There were large numbers of British troops in New York City and Albany. Merchants and farmers profited from supplying them and the fleet. The war's end led to a major depression that severely affected the market sector. The second factor was uncertainty about what New York comprised. Contemporary maps did not show the state's modern outline. The most complete, drawn by Claude-Joseph Sauthier, emphasized New York's claim to the Green Mountains in Vermont and suggested that New York reached into both Massachusetts and Connecticut. The map showed the territory of the Six Nations of Indians exactly as it depicted neighboring colonies: white space beyond New York's boundaries. The third factor was uncertainty and upheaval within the colonial community. New York politics was bitterly factious, with endless disputes among such great families as the Livingstons, DeLanceys, Morrises, Van Rensselaers, and Schuylers. Although they liked to cast themselves as innocents in the corrupt world of imperial politics, these families understood how to work the system for their own benefit. Dealings between the elite and ordinary white colonists easily became tumultuous, whether in the two major centers, Albany and New York City, over elections and issues of consumption, or in the countryside over landownership.

From Stamp Act Crisis to Revolution

The British government brought all of these matters into relief when it set out to reorganize finance and administration. In August 1765 New York City hosted the Stamp Act Congress, with delegates from nine provinces to consider Britain's new policy of taxing them directly. The congress gave a strong lead, but its resolutions were not enough to frustrate London's plans. New York City's people played a major role in turning words into action. By the day of the Stamp Act's enforcement, 1 Nov 1765, they rendered it a dead letter with street demonstrations, which forced the resignation of the stamp distributor. They also forced the resignation of Maryland's distributor when he was discovered in the city.

From then until the autumn of 1776, crowds sacked theaters, brawled with soldiers from the resident garrison, harassed importers of British goods, and dumped tea. Few incidents were accidental. Sons of Liberty emerged during the Stamp Act crisis, negotiating a mutual-aid pact with its Connecticut counterparts. A popular leadership, comprising artisans like instrument maker John Lamb and candle maker Isaac Stoutenburgh, as well as small merchants like Isaac Sears and, after 1769, Alexander McDougall, was emerging. These men previously might have voted, if they had enough property, and observed the doings of the great, but nothing more.

Although they worried about Britain's claim to absolute power over the colonies, they were concerned with other issues as well. New York newspapers ran pieces about conspicuous consumption in a time of deprivation. McDougall's public career began with his 1769 diatribe "To the Betrayed Inhabitants of the City and Colony of New York," directed against the assembly for complying with Parliament's Quartering Act, which required colonial assemblies to supply British troops in the colonies. The problem of the soldiers illustrates all the issues involved as New York City moved toward revolution.

New York had had a garrison since the English seized it from the Dutch. During the French and Indian War, the garrison swelled with British soldiers, who remained when peace returned. On duty they were constantly visible; off duty they competed for scarce jobs. To ideologues they portended ever grasping power because their job was to do their officers' bidding. The provincial assembly's earlier refusal to supply them was an astute political move, but it led to Parliament's act of 1767 forbidding the New York Assembly to do anything until the soldiers' needs were met.

The New York Suspending Act of 1767 became one of the grievances of John Dickinson in his widely read *Letters from a Farmer in Pennsylvania.* McDougall's broadside "To the Betrayed Inhabitants" proved equally important, both as a cry of outrage and as a marker of the emergence of lesser men than the wealthy, highly educated Dickinson. McDougall directed his anger toward the assembly's leaders (the DeLancey faction) for complying with the act. Outraged in their turn, the assembly leaders had McDougall arrested and jailed, but that served only to make him a martyr. McDougall went on to a major generalship in the Continental army, the state senate, and the presidency of the Bank of New York. The DeLanceys ended the Revolution in exile with their great colonial era fortune confiscated.

Resistance to Britain was mainly urban, but there was also upheaval in the country, particularly in Dutchess, Westchester, and Albany Cos and in the Green Mountains. The issue—land—was provoked both by border uncertainty and differing visions of how and by whom the land ought to be owned, occupied, and used.

New York's boundary with Massachusetts was still being negotiated. The Province of New York's original claim reached to the Connecticut River, and Sauthier's map showed dense settlements and grants from there to the Hudson, as if to include them within New York. But Yankee migrants believed the border was much nearer to the Hudson than it is now. They set up towns under Massachusetts authority on land also claimed within New York's manors and patents. There had been ferment along the disputed boundary for decades, and in 1766 the east bank of the Hudson erupted in a tenant uprising. British troops armed with artillery squelched it. The leaders were tried by a court that included politicians from the Stamp Act resistance. One British officer observed that the British believed nobody was entitled to riot "except themselves."

Other Yankees were settling in the Green Mountains with titles from New Hampshire, although the Privy Council had awarded the region to New York in 1764. They had no objection to land speculation; their leader Ethan Allen's Onion River Land Co acquired some 13,000 acres (5,300 ha). But they wanted nothing to do with great holdings on the New York model or with New York's county governments. By roughly 1770 they were in open resistance to New York authority, which they nullified by 1773. The colonial government responded in 1774 with the "Bloody Act," which condemned Allen and other leaders to death. The settlers briefly reconciled with New York when war broke out in 1775, and Allen accepted a militia commission, but Vermont declared its own independence early in 1777. In New York's view its citizens were "revolted subjects," and Vermont remained a "pretended state" until 1790.

There were hardly any tremors felt in the Mohawk Valley before 1775, but stress was rising along the fault lines that would split both the Six Nations and settler society. Sir William Johnson's great estate was a combination of quasi-feudalism, with Johnson dominating loyal Scottish immigrant tenants, and middle ground, where Indian and white cultures mingled. By negotiating with Johnson in 1768, the Six Nations had breached the British proclamation of 1763 that restrained white settlement east of the Appalachian crest. The land they sold was in what is now Ohio, and other Indians believed the Six Nations had no right to sell it. Pressure from settlers and traders was also building up east of Johnson Hall in what is now Johnstown (Fulton Co).

The crisis that led to war and independence began in 1773, when Parliament set out to rescue the British East India Co by letting it sell tea with British taxes directly to the colonies (circumventing the typical intermediaries). A committee met the vessel bearing New York City's consignment outside the harbor limits, offered its crew food and fresh water, and persuaded it to turn around. But early in 1774 the city had its own tea party, when word leaked that there was tea on board the recently arrived *London*. Before "Mohawks" could finish dressing, a crowd boarded the vessel and dumped the tea.

About the same time, committees of correspondence began to form. Some, like New York City's Committee of Fifty-One, operated openly. Others, like the committee in Tryon Co on the western frontier, remained secret. In the autumn of 1774, under goading from the First Continental Congress, some of these became committees of observation, empowered not only to share information but to enforce the boycott of British commerce in response to Britain's punishments for the destruction of the tea at Boston. Committee formation brought many men with humble backgrounds into the revolutionary process.

New York at War

When war broke out in April 1775, new elections created larger committees of safety, which began to claim local governing power. The first of five provincial congresses assembled in New York City. A crowd led by "King" Isaac Sears broke into the city's arsenal, seized the weapons, and paraded. Unlike Massachusetts, where colonial era institutions collapsed in 1774, the old power structures remained, at least for a time. Courts stayed open through 1775. The mayors of New York City and Albany continued to do their jobs. When newly appointed Gen George Washington and royal Governor William Tryon arrived in New York City on the same day in June 1775, crowds welcomed them, though they avoided each other. By the end of 1775 Tryon had moved to a British ship in the harbor, but he still called an assembly election to revive his collapsing government. The provincial congress called an election, too, lest Tryon's assembly should interfere with "political subjects." In fact, the new assembly never met.

New York's delegates to the First and Second Continental Congresses were not street leaders or artisans. They were the likes of Robert R. Livingston and John Jay. They committed themselves to resistance, but they balked at independence until the last moment. Nevertheless, they retained their preeminence. The British helped them by invading and conquering New York City and the surrounding Southern District of Long Island, Manhattan, Staten Island, and Westchester just after independence was declared, thus giving revolutionaries every reason to make common cause.

Jay dominated the drafting of a state constitution. It provided a strong governorship, a state senate designed to represent property, and property qualifications for voting. Philip Schuyler, a candidate for governor in 1777 who supported these principles, observed that the voters might "chuse who they will, I will command." Schuyler did command an army as a Continental major general, but he never led New York State. Its first governor was George Clinton of Ulster Co, and he served until 1795. Clinton was also a general and had been an assemblyman, but to Schuyler his "family and connections" did "not entitle him to so distinguished a predominance." Clinton was one of many "new men" who entered or rose in public life. They became a coherent force, initially over treatment of loyalists, price controls against inflation, and taxation. By 1785 they were voting together on many issues, predicting their alignment against the Constitution in 1788. Early in the 1780s the Jays, Schuylers, and Livingstons began leaving state politics, some for private life, some for Continental affairs.

The war touched everybody. The British invaders of July 1776 formed the largest maritime expedition since ancient Rome, too big and too skilled for Washington's Continental troops and militia to resist. The British nearly trapped the Americans in Brooklyn. Washington retreated to Manhattan and then to Westchester Co and New Jersey, while New York City burned. He lost significant numbers of troops both on Long Island and at Fort Washington on Upper Manhattan. In the Mohawk Valley the Johnson tenants stayed loyal, while motley freehold farmers and small traders chose the Revolution. Under pressure from both sides, the Seneca, Cayuga, Onondaga, and Mohawk went with the British, and the Oneida and Tuscarora chose the Americans.

Others also were making difficult decisions. They included elite figures like the brothers (patriot) Nicholas and (loyalist) Isaac Low and tenant farmers who gathered in secrecy to decide which side was "right." New York City patriots went into exile, but the mostly loyalist farmers of Staten Island, Long Island, and lower Westchester accepted the British conquest. The great estate counties east of the Hudson saw popular loyalism, with resistance to militia service and taxes, safe houses for spies, and one outright uprising, but in the small-farmer counties across the river there was relatively little of it.

In late summer and autumn 1777 Gen John Burgoyne tried to break New York State's revolution, leading British troops, hired German Hessians, and white and native loyalists south from Montreal. A smaller force under Lt Col Barry St. Leger started eastward from Oswego. The initial response was panic, and an ambush devastated patriot militia at Oriskany [now in Oneida Co]. But a ruse by Benedict Arnold, who led a rescue force westward, scattered St. Leger's force, while Burgoyne's army floundered in the Champlain–upper Hudson corridor. New Englanders defeated a foraging expedition at Bennington, Vt, and militiamen rallied around Continental soldiers commanded successively by Philip Schuyler and Horatio Gates. The armies collided at Saratoga, where Burgoyne ran out of supplies and energy. As his defeat neared, a smaller force under Henry Clinton pillaged up the Hudson but with no possibility of saving Burgoyne.

Thereafter fighting shifted westward, despite Arnold's treason at West Point (Orange Co) and Anthony Wayne's conquest of a British post at Stony Point [now in Rockland Co]. Pro-British Indians and loyalists based at Niagara waged an offensive across the Mohawk, Delaware, and Susquehanna Valleys in 1778, but an expedition under John Sullivan and James Clinton sacked the Iroquois country in 1779. The destruction hindered but did not end the Indians' ability to fight or their determination to protect what was theirs. Frontier conflict continued even after the British gave up the large struggle in 1781, but by 1783 the war was over.

Postwar Settlement

New York State regained the Southern District and also started gaining control over the whole territory that it now contains. A plan to evict the pro-British Indians and to shift the Oneida and Tuscarora to the Niagara region failed. But the four pro-British nations had been defeated, the Johnsons and what they stood for were gone, and the way was open for settlement. By an agreement worked out in Hartford, Conn, Massachusetts gained title to all the land west of Seneca Lake and some land on the Southern Tier as a private holder under New York jurisdiction. There, and where New York claimed ownership as well as jurisdiction, the initial task was to "extinguish" Indian title. That proved complicated, involving the Six Nations, both states, and ultimately the federal government, and raising problems that are not yet resolved. Nevertheless, settlers began pouring west, and speculators began acquiring large tracts.

In New York City, there was struggle over the treatment of the loyalists, leading to continuing punitive legislation, despite the terms of the peace treaty with Britain. Alexander Hamilton, rising lawyer and former aide to Washington, took it upon himself to rally men of property around the causes of moderation toward loyalists, regularity in taxation and legislation, and strength for the central Continental authorities, his blueprint for the Federalist constitutional project.

The only issue that did not fit into the split between his forces and those surrounding Gov Clinton was an attempt in 1785 to abolish slavery gradually, sponsored by the Manumission Society established the previous year. The issue went through many votes in the legislature. The Council of Revision (the governor and the highest judges) rejected the bill because it would render Blacks permanently inferior to Whites. Not until 1799 did the state begin abolition, but destroying slavery had become a public issue. Slaves themselves, who constituted perhaps one-fifth of the whole population, had a big hand in raising that issue, joining both sides during the war for the sake of their own freedom. Thousands departed with the British forces in 1783, despite efforts by many masters to reclaim them. Women in other states were beginning to raise their voices, but during the Revolution few spoke out for themselves in New York State. Elizabeth Cady Stanton and the women of Seneca Falls were years in the future.

In 1784 and 1786 the state rejected proposals to grant taxing power to the Continental Congress. Most New Yorkers who cared about politics agreed that the state was in fine shape, but in New York City plebeians and gentry alike were starting to think otherwise, not the least because they were coming to understand that their future was best served in a large economy. Hamilton saw that most clearly. The sheer force of his personality won him a place on New York's delegation to the Constitutional Convention in 1787, but the other two delegates were there specifically to counteract him. To the convention Hamilton contributed little, but he joined John Jay and Virginia's James Madison to produce *The Federalist*, the most trenchant and influential essays in support of adopting the Constitution. The essays were addressed to "The Considerate Citizens of New York." New York State Antifederalists, particularly Melancton Smith and Albany's Abraham Yates, also made strong arguments.

Clinton, who was strongly Antifederalist, presided over the state's ratifying convention in Poughkeepsie in the summer of 1788. Despite 46 Antifederalist delegates and only 19 Federalists, the Constitution was ratified. *The Federalist* may have contributed, and threats that New York City would separate and ratify on its own certainly did. But by the time the vote was called 10 other states had decided to accept the Constitution, which meant that New York could not defeat it. Antifederalism collapsed, with the "full confidence" that amendments to the Constitution would follow.

More than a little ironically, New York City became the new Republic's first capital, and New York State gained more greatly than any other from the Republic's existence. On its own, New York State might have become a minor republic. Within the union its burgeoning capitalism was the perfect context for the financial dominance, advanced transportation, industrial development, and productive agriculture that transformed a second-tier colony into the Empire State.

See also AFRICAN AMERICANS; RIOTS AND CIVIL DISTURBANCES.

Becker, Carl Lotus. *The History of Political Parties in the Province of New York, 1760–1776* (Madison: Univ of Wisconsin Press, 1909)

Countryman, Edward. *A People in Revolution: The American Revolution and Political Society in New York, 1760–1790* (Baltimore: Johns Hopkins Univ Press, 1981)

De Pauw, Linda Grant. *The 11th Pillar: New York State and the Federal Constitution* (Ithaca: Cornell Univ Press, 1966)

Graymont, Barbara. *The Iroquois in the American Revolution* (Syracuse: Syracuse Univ Press, 1972)

Kaminski, John. *George Clinton: Yeoman Politician of the New Republic* (Madison, Wisc: Madison House, 1993)

Mintz, Max M. *The Generals of Saratoga: John Burgoyne and Horatio Gates* (New Haven: Yale Univ Press, 1990)

Tiedeman, Joseph S. *Reluctant Revolutionaries: New York City and the Road to Independence, 1763–1776* (Ithaca: Cornell Univ Press, 1997)

White, Shane. *Somewhat More Independent: The End of Slavery in New York City, 1770–1810* (Athens: Univ of Georgia Press, 1991)

Young, Alfred F. *The Democratic-Republicans of New York: The Origins, 1763–1797* (Chapel Hill: Univ of North Carolina Press, 1967)

Edward Countryman

American Tract Society. Protestant missionary organization. During the first two decades of the 19th century, devout Christians established several local and regional transdenominational tract societies that coalesced into the American Tract Society (ATS), which was founded in New York City in 1825. This new national organization specialized in publishing and distributing inexpensive, popular religious literature and soon emerged as one of the largest and most innovative publishing houses in antebellum America. The society pioneered in employing modern printing technology, sophisticated managerial techniques, and novel distribution methods to support its mission. Its popular product line included moral reform pamphlets, anti-Catholic literature, children's stories, and such Christian classics as John Bunyan's *Pilgrim's Progress.* Traveling colporteurs, who combined Christian witness with aggressive fund-raising and sharp sales techniques, constituted the cornerstones of the ATS's mass distribution efforts throughout the 19th century. Christian unity proved an elusive goal. Denominational controversies, sectional schisms, and abolitionist dissatisfaction plagued the society's antebellum existence. Still the ATS survived the Civil War relatively intact and actually experienced a brief postbellum resurgence by establishing southern regional agencies and working closely with the Freedmen's Bureau to produce educational literature for emancipated slaves. Beginning in the 1870s, however, the society entered a protracted period of stagnation. A disastrous decision to construct a massive 20-story skyscraper in New York City at Nassau and Spruce Sts in 1894 plunged the organization into significant debt. Economic depressions, competition from denominational publishing houses, leadership turnover, and a decision to concentrate primarily on foreign language publications also took their financial toll. The ATS only began reviving its fortunes in the late 1940s by exercising careful stewardship, marketing more aggressively, pursuing new outreach ventures, and forging closer ties with the burgeoning evangelical and fundamentalist movements. The organization left New York City in 1962, relocating first to Oradell, NJ, and eventually to Garland, Tex.

Nord, David Paul. "The Evangelical Origins of Mass Media in America, 1815–1835," *Journalism Monographs* 88 (May 1984)

Slocum, Stephen Elmer. "The American Tract Society, 1825–1975: An Evangelical Effort to Influence the Religious and Moral Life of the United States" (PhD diss, New York Univ, 1975)

Valois, Karl Eric. "To Revolutionize the World: The American Tract Society and the Regeneration of the Republic, 1825–1877." (PhD diss, Univ of Connecticut, 1994)

Peter J. Wosh

American Tragedy, An. Theodore Dreiser based his 1925 novel on the highly publicized 1906 case of Chester Gillette, a Cortland factory functionary who was accused of drowning Grace Brown, his pregnant girlfriend, in Big Moose Lake in Herkimer Co. Gillette's trial, held in Herkimer, captured attention statewide. Newspapers covered the trial in great detail. With no eyewitnesses and no confession, the circumstances of the event were unclear: according to the prosecution, Gillette took Brown to a secluded section of the lake and brutally stunned her with a tennis racket before dumping her overboard; Gillette claimed that a distraught Brown committed suicide by jumping into the water rather than tell her parents about her pregnancy. Gillette was found guilty of murder and executed in Auburn (Cayuga Co) in 1908.

This episode is easily identifiable in Dreiser's fictional narrative, where Clyde Griffiths, a factory supervisor, secretly dates Roberta Alden, another worker. Roberta's pregnancy complicates Clyde's intention to abandon her in favor of Sondra Finchley, an attractive socialite, and unable to arrange an abortion, he makes plans to kill Roberta. Alone with her on a remote North Woods lake, he loses his courage, but she drowns when their boat overturns accidentally. At a trial dominated by the political ambitions of the rival lawyers, the evidence of Clyde's plotting and concealment overwhelms the defense that he is a "mental and moral coward" and had decided at the last moment to marry Roberta. He is executed in the electric chair.

Dreiser figures Clyde's story as an American tragedy by emphasizing economic success and social status as the objects of weak but relentless human desire. His novel revived interest in the Gillette trial, and yet, with the introduction of such fictional elements as the Sondra Finchley character, it also led to inaccurate versions of the historical events. In 1931 a film adaptation of Dreiser's novel appeared, and showings in Herkimer, Old Forge (Herkimer Co), and Norwich (Chenango Co) prompted displays of Gillette-related artifacts. In addition to two stage versions of the novel, another film version, *A Place in the Sun* (1951), retold Dreiser's story but moved the setting to California. The "American Tragedy," which has come to refer to both Dreiser's novel and the events on which he based it, has been a subject of Adirondack lore through folksongs, rumors of the mysterious disappearance of Gillette's boat, and stories of ghost sightings at Big Moose Lake.

Brandon, Craig. *Murder in the Adirondacks: "An American Tragedy" Revisited,* 2d ed. (Utica: North Country Books, 1986)

Brownell, Joseph W., and Patricia A. Wawrzaszek. *Adirondack Tragedy: the Gillette Murder Case of 1906* (Interlaken, NY: Heart of the Lakes Publishing, 1986)

David J. Nordloh

Ames. Village (pop 173) in Canajoharie (Montgomery Co). Settled mostly by New Englanders, Ames had developed as a hamlet by the 1790s. It provided services to the farmers in the surrounding countryside with a gristmill, sawmill, wheelwright shop, and, briefly, pottery and nail factory in the early 19th century. First known as Bowman's Creek, it acquired in 1819 a post office, which was renamed Ames in 1832. Incorporated in 1924, the village remains a small service and residential village surrounded by farmland.

James Crawford

Ames, Ezra (*b* Framingham, Mass, 5 May 1768; *d* Albany, 23 Feb 1836). Artist. A self-taught painter who produced at least 700 works, Ames is best known for his portraits and miniatures. Son of Jesse Emes and Betty Bent, his widower father remarried and moved the family to Staatsburgh (Dutchess Co). In his early 20s Ezra changed his name to Ames. He settled in Albany in 1793 and painted miniatures, signs, and carriages. A year later Ames married Zipporah Wood, with whom he had three children. In the 1800s Ames painted portraits for elite clients, including the Livingstons, Van Rensselaers, and Lansings. By the 1810s Ames received commissions from the legislature and state politicians. He gained national prominence for his portraits of Vice Pres *George Clinton* (1812), *De Witt Clinton* (1811 and 1818), and the series *Portraits of Seven Governors of New York* (1813–29), which earned him election to the American Academy of Fine Arts in 1824. Ames was celebrated for his versatile use of oils and watercolors in his portraits, miniatures on ivory, and landscapes. Throughout his life Ames produced ornamental work, specialized in Masonic regalia, and was active in the civic affairs of Albany.

Bolton, Theodore, and Irwin F. Cortelyou. *Ezra Ames of Albany: Portrait Painter, Craftsman, Royal Arch*

The Fondey Family, by Ezra Ames, 1803. The Fondeys were a prominent merchant family in Albany.

Mason, Banker, 1768–1836, and a Catalogue of His Works (New York: New-York Historical Society, 1955)

Mary Alice Mackay

Amherst. Town (pop 116,510) in N Erie Co. Settled in 1798, the town was formed in 1818 from Buffalo. The Erie Canal (1825) brought settlers to the northern portion of town, but it remained agricultural, producing grain and cattle. German, Alsatian, and French immigrants followed the first settlers; German Mennonites settled in the southern part of Amherst, where they quarried limestone. The Canandaigua and Niagara Falls Railroad (later New York Central and called the Peanut Line) crossed the town in 1853, and the Lehigh Valley Railroad followed in 1896. When an electric railroad (1893–1930) was completed from Williamsville to Buffalo, city residents began moving outward, at first the wealthy on large estates and then others into suburban developments such as Amherst Estates (1910) and the 1,300-home Cleveland Park Terrace (1926) in Eggertsville. Suburbanites patronized University Plaza (1941), the first shopping center in Western New York. Growth resumed after World War II; superhighways such as the New York State Thruway (1954) and I-290 (1965) promoted it. The population nearly tripled between 1950 and 1970 because of large housing developments in the northern part of town. In the early 21st century Amherst is primarily a bedroom community, with commercial and office complexes such as Centerpointe. Ingram Micro (1992), worldwide wholesalers of computers and related products, employed 1,500 workers in 2003. The Mennonite Meeting House (1834) and St. Mary of the Angels Motherhouse (1926) are listed on the National Register of Historic Places. Amherst is the site of Daemen College (1947), Erie Community College (1959), and the vast University of Buffalo North Campus (constructed beginning in 1970).

Nancy B. Mingus

Amherst, Jeffery (*b* Riverhead, England, 29 Jan 1717; *d* Sevenoaks, England, 3 Aug 1797). British army commander. After a celebrated military career in Europe, Amherst served the army in North America, achieving fame after capturing two key Canadian forts and Fort Duquesne [now Pittsburgh]. On 18 Sept 1758 he replaced James Abercromby as commander in chief of the Royal American Regiment. Amherst led two major expeditions during the French and Indian War. In 1759 he directed a campaign to take control of French defenses on Lake Champlain, marching 11,000 troops from Albany to Lake George [now in Washington Co] and taking possession of Fort Ticonderoga and then Crown Point [now in Essex Co], which the French had abandoned. In 1760 he orchestrated a concentric march on Montreal. Leading 10,000 soldiers via the Mohawk River, through German Flatts [now in Herkimer Co], down the Oswego River for Lake Ontario, Amherst continued down the St. Lawrence River and captured Montreal, a major achievement for the British. His victories secured his military and political career and he was appointed governor of North America in 1760. His distrust for Native Americans led to restrictive political policies that precipitated Pontiac's Rebellion in 1763, however, and that year he returned to Britain. He died at his residence, Montreal Park.

Amherst, Jeffery. *The Journal of Jeffery Amherst, Recording the Military Career of General Amherst in America from 1758 to 1763.* Ed. J. C. Webster (Chicago: Univ of Chicago Press, 1931)

Long, John C. *Lord Jeffery Amherst: A Soldier of the King* (New York: Macmillan, 1933)

Mark G. Spencer

Amish. See ANABAPTISTS.

Amity. Town (pop 2,245) in central Allegany Co. Settled in 1803, the town was formed in 1830 from Angelica and Scio. Lumbering was the chief industry in the early 19th century and was succeeded by dairying. The Erie Railroad crossed town in 1851. Christ Episcopal Church (1860) at Belvidere is listed on the National Register of Historic Places. Amity has several dairy farms and considerable recreational land use. The majority of 1,666-acre (674.2 ha) Plumbottom State Forest is in Amity. Belmont, the county seat, is the business center of the town.

Amityville {Amityville, village (pop 9,441) in Babylon, Suffolk Co; North Amityville, locality (pop 16,572) in Babylon}. The area was called Huntington West Neck South until the Amityville post office was established in 1850. The South Side Rail Road (1867) made resort development possible, including large hotels and summer cottages and, later, homes for commuters. Large sanatoriums and hospitals were established during the 1880s. The village was incorporated in 1894. In 1918 Lawrence Sperry launched the first guided missile from an Amityville site. Automobile access was improved by Sunrise Highway (1929). Boatyards on the Great South Bay were a 20th-century industry of some importance; in the early 21st century, Amityville produces pharmaceuticals, aircraft parts, and electronic equipment. North Amityville, settled as early as the 1780s, is one of the oldest African American communities on Long Island. In the 19th century Blacks continued to arrive, largely from the south, to work on farms and in Amityville hotels. Ronek Park was a 1950s development catering to World War II veterans and the black middle class. It is the site of Bethel African Methodist Episcopal Church (1844), former home of an African American congregation founded in 1815 and the oldest African American church structure on Long Island. In 2000 the population of North Amityville was 69% black, and that of Amityville was 85% white.

Eileen Effrat

Amityville Horror, The. This book and film had origins in a gruesome set of murders on 13 Nov 1974, when 23-year-old Ronald DeFeo Jr shot to death his parents and four younger siblings (ranging in age from 9 to 18) in their home in Amityville (Suffolk Co). Convicted on multiple counts of murder in 1975, DeFeo was sentenced to six concurrent life sentences in state prison. George and Kathy Lutz purchased the DeFeo house in December 1975 but abandoned the property after less than a month, driven out by what they claimed were demons in the home. Self-identified ghost hunters descended on the property, and in 1977 Jay Anson published a book, *The Amityville Horror,* in which he detailed the Lutzes' battle with these evil spirits, a story that Anson claimed was true. A lurid film of the same title was released in 1979, and the number of people harassing the new owners of the home increased. In an effort to discourage the curious, the house was painted a different color, the street number was changed, and many local children have deliberately given wrong directions when asked for the location.

Kaplan, Stephen. *The Amityville Horror Conspiracy* (Laceyville, Pa: Belfry Books, 1995)

Ammann, Othmar H(ermann) (*b* Schaffhausen, Switzerland, 26 Mar 1879; *d* Rye, Westchester Co, 22 Sept 1965). Civil engineer and bridge builder. Ammann graduated from the Swiss Federal Polytechnical Institute in 1902 and worked in Switzerland before moving to the United States in 1904, where he gained respect and recognition among engineers for his report investigating the 1907 collapse of the cantilever bridge in Quebec. Hired in 1912 by bridge designer Gustav Lindenthal, Ammann served in 1917 as Lindenthal's deputy chief engineer during construction of the Hell Gate Bridge over the East River in New York City. In 1923 Ammann left Lindenthal's company and opened his own consulting firm. In 1925 the federal government and the states of New York and New Jersey approved plans for construction of the George Washington Bridge linking Manhattan and New Jersey over the Hudson River. The Port of New York Authority chose Ammann as chief engineer for the project. Construction began in 1927, and the bridge opened in 1931. Ammann was chief engineer of the authority from 1930 to 1937 and served as the director of engineering from 1937 to 1939. In his tenure with the Port of New York Authority, Ammann oversaw construction of the Bayonne Bridge (1932) between Staten Island and New Jersey, the Triborough Bridge (1936) and the Bronx-Whitestone Bridge (1939), both in New York City, and the Lincoln Tunnel (1937), between Manhattan and New Jersey. He retired from the Port Authority in 1939 and returned to private practice. In 1954 the Port Authority hired his firm, Ammann and Whitney, to oversee construction of the Verrazano-Narrows Bridge connecting Staten Island and Brooklyn. The bridge, Amman's last major project, was the world's longest suspension span when it opened to traffic in November 1964. Many of the bridges Ammann designed and constructed are considered architectural and aesthetic masterpieces because of his innovative use of steel and the simplicity of the design.

Rastorfer, Darl. *Six Bridges: The Legacy of Othmar H. Ammann* (New Haven, Conn: Yale Univ Press, 2000)

Frank E. Griggs Jr

amphibians and reptiles. There are 32 species of amphibians and 36 species of reptiles native to New York State. Amphibians include salamanders, frogs, and toads. Reptiles include turtles, snakes, and lizards. Collectively known as herpetofauna, or "herps," amphibians and reptiles are cold-blooded vertebrates. Because their activity is determined by the temperature of their surroundings, they must retreat to subterranean or aquatic habitats in winter to survive the subfreezing climate found in New York State. Only the sea turtles *(Chelonia, Caretta, Lepidochelys, Dermochelys),* which frequent the coastal areas of Long Island and New York City, are capable of migrating to warmer climates in the winter.

The typical life cycle of an amphibian begins with eggs, laid in water, that hatch into aquatic larvae, commonly known as tadpoles or pollywogs. In most cases, the gill-breathing aquatic stage is followed by an air-breathing, terrestrial stage. The larval period can take just two weeks for the spadefoot toad *(Scaphiopus holbrookii)* or as long as six years for the mud puppy *(Necturus maculosus),* a salamander. Whereas all of the state's frogs and toads begin with the aquatic stage, some of its salamanders, such as the red-backed salamander *(Plethodon cinereus),* forgo the aquatic stage and develop directly from an egg deposited on land into a terrestrial juvenile. At the other end of the spectrum, the mud puppy remains aquatic throughout its life, and, while it loses its larval coloration by six years of age, it retains external gills as an adult. Some amphibians have a life span of only a couple of years, whereas a salamander like the hellbender *(Cryptobranchus alleganiensis)* may live as long as 70 years.

The typical life cycle of turtles, lizards, and some snakes also begins with the egg deposited in a "nest" on land and left unattended. Eggs hatch in late summer, producing juveniles that look very similar to adults. Some snakes, such as the garter snake *(Thamnophis sirtalis)* and the timber rattlesnake *(Crotalus horridus),* give birth to live young. A box turtle holds the longevity record for New York State reptiles; it was over 100 years old when found on Long Island in 2002.

Amphibians and reptiles are found in most habitats throughout the state; some even reach the tops of the highest Adirondack peaks. Most species are rarely seen, although there are notable exceptions, such as the widespread and abundant garter snake, the painted turtle *(Chrysemys picta),* and the snapping turtle *(Chelydra serpentina).* Frogs are commonly seen but often only as a sudden movement and splash as they jump to safety, giving little time to recognize species. But frog calls are unique for each species, allowing identification by ear rather than by eye. Surpris-

AMPHIBIANS AND REPTILES NATIVE TO NEW YORK STATE

Order	Scientific Name	Common Name
Caudata: Salamanders	*Desmognathus ochrophaeus*	Allegheny Mountain dusky salamander
	Ambystoma laterale	blue-spotted salamander
	Necturus maculosus maculosus	common mud puppy
	Cryptobranchus alleganiensis alleganiensis	eastern hellbender
	Plethodon cinereus	eastern red-backed salamander
	Ambystoma tigrinum tigrinum (E)	eastern tiger salamander
	Hemidactylium scutatum	four-toed salamander
	Ambystoma jeffersonianum	Jefferson salamander
	Eurycea longicauda longicauda	long-tailed salamander
	Ambystoma opacum	marbled salamander
	Desmognathus fuscus	northern dusky salamander
	Pseudotriton ruber ruber	northern red salamander
	Plethodon glutinosus	northern slimy salamander
	Gyrinophilus porphyriticus porphyriticus	northern spring salamander
	Eurycea bislineata	northern two-lined salamander
	Notophthalmus viridescens viridescens	red-spotted newt
	Ambystoma maculatum	spotted salamander
	Plethodon wehrlei	Wehrle's salamander
Anura: Frogs and Toads	*Rana catesbeiana*	American bullfrog
	Bufo americanus americanus	eastern American toad
	Acris crepitans crepitans (E)	eastern cricket frog
	Scaphiopus holbrookii	eastern spadefoot
	Bufo fowleri	Fowler's toad
	Hyla versicolor	gray treefrog
	Rana septentrionalis	mink frog
	Rana clamitans melanota	northern green frog
	Rana pipiens	northern leopard frog
	Pseudacris crucifer crucifer	northern spring peeper
	Rana palustris	pickerel frog
	Rana sphenocephala utricularia	southern leopard frog
	Pseudacris triseriata	western chorus frog
	Rana sylvatica	wood frog
Testudines: Turtles	*Emydoidea blandingii* (T)	Blanding's turtle
	Glyptemys muhlenbergii (E)	bog turtle
	Terrapene carolina carolina	eastern box turtle
	Kinosternon subrubrum subrubrum (E)	eastern mud turtle
	Chelydra serpentina serpentina	eastern snapping turtle
	Apalone spinifera spinifera	eastern spiny softshell
	Chelonia mydas (T)	green sea turtle
	Lepidochelys kempii (E)	Kemp's ridley sea turtle
	Dermochelys coriacea (E)	leatherback sea turtle
	Caretta caretta(T)	loggerhead sea turtle
	Malaclemys terrapin terrapin	northern diamond-backed terrapin
	Graptemys geographica	northern map turtle
	Chrysemys picta	painted turtle
	Clemmys guttata	spotted turtle
	Sternotherus odoratus	stinkpot
	Glyptemys insculpta	wood turtle

continued on page 80

AMPHIBIANS AND REPTILES NATIVE TO NEW YORK STATE (continued)

Order	Scientific Name	Common Name
Squamata: Lizards (suborder Lacertilia)	*Eumeces fasciatus*	common five-lined skink
	Sceloporus undulatus (T)	eastern fence lizard
	Eumeces anthracinus anthracinus	northern coal skink
Squamata: Snakes (suborder Serpentes)	*Thamnophis sirtalis*	common garter snake
	Nerodia sipedon sipedon	common water snake
	Heterodon platirhinos	eastern hognose snake
	Sistrurus catenatus catenatus (E)	eastern massasauga
	Lampropeltis triangulum triangulum	eastern milk snake
	Elaphe alleghaniensis	eastern rat snake
	Thamnophis sauritus	eastern ribbon snake
	Carphophis amoenus amoenus	eastern worm snake
	Coluber constrictor constrictor	northern black racer
	Storeria dekayi dekayi	northern brown snake
	Agkistrodon contortrix mokasen	northern copperhead
	Storeria occiptomaculata occiptomaculata	northern red-bellied snake
	Diadophis punctatus edwardsii	northern ring-necked snake
	Regina septemvittata (E)	queen snake
	Thamnophis brachystoma	short-headed garter snake
	Opheodrys vernalis	smooth green snake
	Crotalus horridus (T)	timber rattlesnake

Source: New York State Amphibian and Reptile Atlas Project.
Note: (E) = endangered; (T) = threatened.
Compiled by Alvin R. Breisch

LENGTHS OF NEW YORK STATE AMPHIBIANS AND REPTILES

Salamanders
Smallest: four-toed salamander, 4 in (10.2 cm)
Largest: Eastern hellbender, 29 in (73.7 cm)

Frogs
Smallest: Eastern cricket frog, .9 in (2.3 cm)
Largest: American bullfrog, 8 in (20.3 cm)

Turtles
Smallest: bog turtle, 4.5 in (11.4 cm)
Largest: leatherback sea turtle, 74 in (188.0 cm)

Snakes
Smallest: Eastern wormsnake, 13 in (33.0 cm)
Largest: Eastern ratsnake, 101 in (256.5 cm)

Compiled by Alvin R. Breisch

ingly, the 5 in (12.7 cm) red-backed salamander is the most abundant vertebrate in northeastern hardwood forests, exceeding all species of birds and mammals, not just in numbers of individuals but also in total weight of the organisms.

In 1829 James Macauley published the earliest book describing the animals of New York State, listing 25 species of herps, but his imprecise descriptions make modern identification of many of the listed species impossible. Contributing to the confusion, Macauley referred to salamanders as "lizards" and considered turtles to be amphibians rather than reptiles. Physician James E. DeKay made the first scientific effort to describe the state's amphibians in his *Zoology of New York* (1842). DeKay, long associated with New York City's Lyceum of Natural History, established in 1817 (after 1877, New York Academy of Sciences), listed 63 species of amphibians and reptiles. He included some appearing in adjacent states, expecting, correctly in most cases, that they would eventually be found in New York. While DeKay, unlike Macauley, described exact species in a recognizable way, he made some errors, such as describing the red eft and the red-spotted newt as separate species, when they are actually two stages of the same organism *(Notophthalmus viridescens).* Subsequent checklists by Spencer Baird (1854) and Edwin Eckel and Frederick Paulmier (1902) corrected earlier mistakes in nomenclature but added little to scientists' knowledge of these organisms. From the 1940s, two nationally prominent herpetologists, Sherman C. Bishop and Albert Hazen Wright, greatly advanced knowledge of New York State's herpetofauna. Working as a zoologist at the New York State Museum in Albany, Bishop produced *Salamanders of New York* (1941), at the time the most comprehensive treatment of salamanders published by any state. Wright, a professor of zoology at Cornell University, collaborated with his wife, Anna W. Wright, on numerous studies. Together they produced the *Handbook of Frogs and Toads* (1949) and *Handbook of Snakes* (1957), both still considered primary references at the beginning of the 21st century.

While loss of habitat poses the greatest threat to amphibians and reptiles, unregulated collection of the animals for food, bait, or pets has contributed to the decline of several species. Protection of streams and wetlands is important as a conservation tool, but fragmentation of habitat by roads can eliminate populations that migrate from an overwintering habitat to breeding ponds or wetlands. To help alleviate this problem, the first amphibian tunnel in the state was constructed in the Town of Guilderland under Albany Co's Meadowdale Rd in 1999. This project has significantly decreased the number of frogs and salamanders killed on this road.

Although the decline of amphibians is recognized as a global problem, possibly caused by global warming or increases in ultraviolet (UV) radiation, the situation in New York State is unclear. More than 300 years of land-use changes in the Northeast partly mask changes in the state's amphibian populations. Since the early 1900s, much forest that was cut for timber or converted to agriculture has reverted back to forest, benefiting animals that rely on forested ecosystems. With relatively little historic data compared to those available for birds, mammals, and fish, it is difficult to quantify changes in most herp populations. In 1990, as part of an effort to establish a baseline from which to measure future changes, the New York State Department of Environmental Conservation (DEC) began a 10-year atlas project to document the distribution of all amphibians and reptiles occurring in the wild.

Breisch, Alvin. "The Status and Management of Turtles in New York." In *Status and Conservation of Turtles of the Northeastern United States,* ed. T. F. Tyning (Lanesboro, Minn: Serpent's Tale Natural History Books, 1997)

New York State Amphibian and Reptile Atlas Project, http://www.dec.state.ny.us/website/dfwmr/wildlife/herp/

Wright, Albert H., and Anna A. Wright. *Handbook of Snakes of the United States and Canada,* 2 vols (Ithaca: Cornell Univ Press, 1994)

Wright, Albert H., Roy McDiarmid, and Anna A. Wright. *Handbook of Frogs and Toads of the United States and Canada* (Ithaca: Cornell Univ Press, 1994)

Alvin R. Breisch

Amsterdam. Town (pop 5,820) and city (pop 18,355) in NE Montgomery Co. Settled by Palatine Germans *ca* 1720, Amsterdam formed as a town from the extinct town of Caughnawaga in 1793. The nucleus of the modern city was called Veedersburg until the Amsterdam post office opened in 1803 and streets and lots were platted in 1807; it incorporated as a village in 1831. Several streams provided good waterpower for manufacturing, including a gristmill, sawmills, a scythe factory, an oil mill, and a tannery. The present city was crossed by the Erie Canal (1822), the Utica and Schenectady Railroad (1836; later New York Central), and the West Shore Railroad (1883). In 1842 John Sanford and partners established a large carpet mill; by 1878 Sanford Mills employed 700 people and produced over 15,000 feet (4,600 m) of carpet daily. Shuttleworth Bros (1878) and McCleary, Wallin, and Crouse (1886) were two other major carpet manufacturers. Knitting mills, introduced in 1857, became Amsterdam's second-largest industrial sector; other products included needles, shoes, linseed oil, soap, paper, brooms and brushes, buttons, and coffins. The city was incorporated in 1885. Port Jackson, south of the Mohawk River, was annexed from the Town of Florida in 1888. Factory work attracted many immigrants, especially Germans,

Carpet manufacture at McCleary, Wallin, and Crouse Mill in Amsterdam.

Poles, Italians, and Jews. In 1920 Shuttleworth Bros and McCleary, Wallin, and Crouse merged to form Mohawk Carpet Mills, and in 1929 Sanford and Sons merged with Bigelow-Hartford Carpet Co to form Bigelow-Sanford Carpet Co. At their peak in the 1920s, the two large carpet factories in the "Carpet City" employed about 9,300 workers. In 1955 Bigelow-Sanford pulled out, and Mohawk Carpet's successor, Mohasco, ended production in 1968.

Concentrated efforts by the city initiated in 1954 attracted new industry, but the population began a dramatic decrease. From a peak of 34,817 in 1930, it had declined to 18,355 by 2000. The city's plight was not helped by one of the state's most destructive urban renewal programs (1965–79), which gutted the business district and surrounded it with four-lane arterials. In the early 21st century plans are underway to rehabilitate the waterfront and some mill buildings. Major employers in 2003 were Cranesville Block Co (1950; 425 workers), Ward Products (antennas; 340 workers), and Noteworthy Corp (1954; specialty advertising; 300 workers). Actor Kirk Douglas (1916–) is a native. Amsterdam is the site of Guy Park State Historic Site (1773), the Walter Elwood Museum, and the Noteworthy Indian Museum, all in the city, and Old Fort Johnson (1749) in the town. In 2000, 16% of the city's population was of Latino ethnicity.

James Crawford

Amtrak. Registered trademark of the National Railroad Passenger Corp. An act of US Congress formed this body, effective 1 May 1971, to create a national rail passenger network and to relieve private, freight rail carriers of unprofitable passenger services. The advent of paved roads, automobiles, and motortrucks had seriously eroded all rail services by 1950. The 1956 opening of the New York State Thruway from New York City to Buffalo, which paralleled New York Central Railroad's (NYC's) famed Water Level Route, was a fatal blow to the state's major rail passenger carrier. Amtrak inherited a mélange of outdated, undermaintained equipment that operated over a hodgepodge of routes, serving decrepit and often inconvenient stations. The key to Amtrak's survival was a simultaneous crisis in freight railroading; the tax-funded Interstate Highway System had proved equally ruinous to many rail freight carriers. On 1 Apr 1976 Penn Central, the short-lived company resulting from the 1968 merger of NYC and Pennsylvania Railroad, and six other bankrupt northeastern carriers combined as Consolidated Railroad Corp, or Conrail. Their government-directed merger allowed Amtrak to purchase the Northeast Corridor, the valuable rail route extending from Boston to Washington, DC; outside this corridor Amtrak contracted with various private freight rail companies to gain track routes for other intercity passenger services. Although still operating subject to the winds of congressional politics and dependent on other carriers, Amtrak became a real railroad with tracks, stations, and related facilities and real estate. It soon launched the Northeast Corridor Improvement Project with an overhaul of tracks and signals to permit 125 mph (201 kph) operation and acquisition of new passenger cars and locomotives. In 1983 Amtrak began to hire its own engineers, conductors, and other employees rather than contracting with the various freight carriers; this provided both operational and financial savings.

During the 1980s and 1990s Amtrak in New York State, assisted by both state and federal funds, augmented basic corridor services and opened new routes. Amtrak's Adirondack (1974) ran between New York City and Montreal along a scenic route paralleling the Hudson River and Lake Champlain, while an agreement between Via Rail Canada and Amtrak supported daily service aboard Maple Leaf (1978) between Toronto and New York City. Both Vermont and New York State funds supported Ethan Allen Express (1996) service from New York City to Rutland, Vt, and Amtrak's Lake Shore Limited (1975) connected Chicago with New York City and Boston. But at the beginning of the 21st century, the heart of Amtrak service in New York State is the Empire Corridor, stretching from New York City's Penn Station to Buffalo and Niagara Falls via Albany. The busiest section, New York City to Albany, boasts near hourly service; it ranks second only to the Northeast Corridor in traffic volume, making Albany-Rensselaer station the third busiest in the nation. New York State has been actively involved in the development of the corridor, lobbying first Conrail and then CSX, which was the owner of most of the former Conrail track structure west of Albany and as far south as Poughkeepsie since 1 July 1999, to upgrade track and signals to permit 110–125 mph (177–201 kph) operation. Although Amtrak owns 7.8 miles (12.55 km) of direct line west of Schenectady and an additional 12 miles (19.3 km) connecting Albany-Rensselaer station with New England routes, it is still dependent on contracts with freight carriers for rail route access north and west of Albany. Beginning in 1998 New York State funds supported the remanufacture of seven turbo-liner train sets, semipermanently coupled trains with both power cars and passenger cars, able to provide 125 mph (201 kph) service; the first set was completed in 2002. Amtrak completed full electrification from Boston to New Haven, Conn, on the Northeast Corridor in 1999 and commenced 150 mph (241 kph) Acela service from Boston to Washington, DC. In 2002 new or rehabilitated stations serve, or are under construction, at Rhinecliff, Hudson, Albany-Rensselaer, Utica, Rome, and Syracuse, with plans under consideration for others at Buffalo, Niagara Falls, Lyons, and Dunkirk.

In 2002 the New York State legislature passed rail real estate property tax relief, designed to encourage the state's major rail carriers to invest in rail improvements primarily of benefit to rail passenger service. It is hoped these will lead to the replacement of the second main track between Albany and Schenectady, a long-standing bottleneck to improved service and proposed commuter rail operations in the Capital Region. The debate over Amtrak's future includes proposals to break up the passenger carrier, privatizing some elements and routes; various plans have been suggested to fund and structure desired services. Amtrak, the unwanted stepchild of the freight carriers, may yet emerge as a true national asset, offering a viable, widely accessible alternative to highway and air travel.

Schafer, Mike. *All Aboard Amtrak* (Piscataway, NJ: Railpace Co, 1991)

David R. Gould

amusement parks. In the mid–19th century, New York City became the site of America's first large-scale amusement resort when Jones's

Wood opened in Manhattan between Third Ave and the East River between 66th and 75th Sts. Inspired by European pleasure gardens, Jones's Wood featured attractions such as billiards, bowling, a shooting gallery, donkey rides, dancing, concerts, and a beer garden. Although successful, the park was quickly consumed by the growth of the city, closing in the 1860s. During the same era Coney Island, located on a peninsula in Kings Co, became a popular seaside getaway. Development began in 1829 with the opening of the first hotel, followed by bathhouses, restaurants, and dance halls. The first major amusement device, a 300 ft (91.4 m) observation tower, opened at Coney Island in 1877. In 1879 Rochester and Lake Ontario Railroad opened Sea Breeze in Rochester; this park featured athletic fields and facilities for picnicking, dancing, and bathing, plus other common diversions of the era. Similar parks soon followed: the Bowery (1886) in Queens Co; South Beach (1886) on Staten Island; Ontario Beach (1887) in Charlotte (Monroe Co); Island Park (1889) in Auburn (Cayuga Co); Lakeside Park (1891) in Syracuse; and Celoron Park (Chautauqua Co) near Jamestown.

In 1884 former textile factory owner LaMarcus Thompson built the world's first roller coaster, the Switchback Railway, at Coney Island. The simple device boasted two parallel 600 ft (182.9 m) long tracks; from a 50 ft (15.2 m) peak, a six-person car traveled to the end of one track and then was manually pushed to the top of a second peak for a return trip on the other track. In 1895 Chicago entrepreneur Paul Boyton created Coney Island's first amusement park, Sea Lion Park, featuring a range of rides, and two years later Steeplechase Park, named for its simulated horse-race ride, also opened at Coney Island. This park boasted the 5-acre (2 ha) Pavilion of Fun with indoor amusements. In 1903 Luna Park rose on the old site of Sea Lion Park; its elaborate architecture outlined with 250,000 electric lights revolutionized amusement park design. Its success inspired nearby Dreamland (1904), which featured a 375 ft (114.3 m) tower and 1 million electric lights adorning opulent buildings. Amusement parks opened at a rapid pace throughout the state, their numbers increasing from 28 to 62 between 1899 and 1905. Among those opening during this period were Rockaway Playland (1901) in Queens, Carnival Court (1904) in Buffalo, Dreamland (1905) in Albany, Kaydeross Park (1905) in Saratoga Springs, Happyland (1906) on Staten Island, and White City (1906) in Syracuse.

A fire destroyed Dreamland in 1911, signaling the beginning of Coney Island's decline, in part caused by growth of amusement parks in suburban areas surrounding New York City. One of the most influential of these opened in 1928 in Rye (Westchester Co). The Westchester County Park Commission razed two seedy, private parks—Rye Beach and Paradise Park—and constructed the first totally planned amusement park, Playland. Landscape architect Gilbert D. Clarke laid out the grounds, which included 7,900 feet (2,408 m) of beach and boardwalk, a lake for boating, a swimming pool, picnic area, miniature golf course, and ice-skating rink. Architects Stewart Walker and Leon Gillette developed the overall plan of the park, and Fred Church designed the Dragon roller coaster. A wide mall connected by covered colonnades led to the different attractions, with kiddie rides placed in a separate area. Playland with its consistent landscape and architectural design foreshadowed the theme parks of the later 20th century.

The depression of the 1930s badly hurt New York State's amusement parks, with about half closing by 1939. Luna Park burnt in 1944. After World War II, two major developments, kiddielands and theme parks, dominated the industry. Kiddielands developed in response to the postwar Baby Boom and grew with the suburbs in the 1950s. One of the earliest, Nunley's in Baldwin (Nassau Co), opened in 1939 and operated until 1995, and Fairyland (1952) in Brooklyn remained in business until 2003. Harris Hill Park (1947) in Elmira and Hoffman's Playland (1952) in Latham (Albany Co) continue to operate in the early 21st century.

A number of pioneering theme parks opened. Santa's Workshop opened in North Pole (Essex Co) in 1949, and in 1954 entrepreneur Charles Wood launched Storytown, originally a small, roadside attraction featuring recreations of famous nursery rhymes, in Lake George (Warren Co). Now a major theme park known as Great Escape, it offers over 30 rides, a water park, and since 1984 the Comet roller coaster, relocated from 1989-shuttered Crystal Beach near Buffalo. Another early theme park, Freedomland, opened in the Bronx in 1960. Designed as a miniature United States, the park's rides, attractions, and displays celebrated the nation's history; it survived until 1964.

In 1962 Astroland, showcasing many modern rides of European manufacture, opened on Coney Island; Steeplechase closed in 1964. At the beginning of the 21st century, Coney Island's amusement area is only a fraction of its original size, but it is home to two National Historic Landmarks, the Cyclone roller coaster (1927) and the Wonder Wheel (1920). The state's newest theme park, Six Flags Darien Lake, originated as a campground in Darien Center (Genesee Co) in 1965. By 1981 it had grown into a major park, and in 1999 joined the Six Flags chain. It is home to Superman, the state's largest roller coaster. At the beginning of the 21st century, New York claims some two dozen amusement parks, including Midway Park (1898) in Maple Springs (Chautauqua Co), Enchanted Forest (1956) in Old Forge (Herkimer Co), Martin's Fantasy Island (1960) on Grand Island (Erie Co), Adventureland (1962) in East Farmingdale (Suffolk Co), and Nellie Bly Amusement Park (1965) in Brooklyn.

Adams, Judith A. *The American Amusement Park Industry: A History of Technology and Thrills* (Boston: Twayne Publishers, 1991)

Cartmell, Robert. *The Incredible Scream Machine: A History of the Roller Coaster* (Bowling Green, Ohio: Bowling Green State Univ Popular Press, 1987)

Kyrazi, Gary. *The Great American Amusement Parks* (Secaucus, NJ: Citadel Press, 1976)

James Futrell

Anabaptists. Religious bodies descended from a radical wing of the English Reformation. The main Anabaptist groups in New York State include the Amish, Bruderhof Communities (Society of Brothers), Church of the Brethren, and Mennonites. The historical experiences of these groups differ, but they share basic Protestant beliefs. Each also attempts to re-create their ideal of a primitive Christian community, which gives rise to a number of nonconformist practices, including adult baptism, nonresistant pacifism, plain dress and appearance, communalism, and resistance to certain technologies. Church structures encourage small, local, loosely linked, and sometimes schismatic communities.

Various 17th-century documents identify several individuals in New Netherland and then New York Colony as Anabaptist or Mennonite. In 1663 Pieter Cornelisz Plockhoy established a New Netherland community of Mennonites near what is today Lewes, Del, but the settlement was destroyed in Anglo-Dutch warfare the following year. Not until the early 19th century did persistent groups appear, when Mennonites from southeastern Pennsylvania settled in the Niagara Frontier. From the 1830s to the 1870s, Lewis Co attracted one of the largest Anabaptist settlements, Amish who emigrated from the Alsace-Lorraine and Swiss regions of Europe. In the early 21st century, Lewis and Jefferson Cos continued to host one concentration of Mennonites in the state, with congregations that evolved from Amish to Amish Mennonite to a variety of Mennonite conferences. There were other mid–19th-century Mennonite settlements in Fayette (Seneca Co), Amherst and Clarence (Erie Co), and Livonia (Livingston Co).

In recent decades the Central New York and Southern Tier regions have had a growing concentration of Mennonites, the majority of them Old Order groups. A third and smaller concentration was in the New York City metropolitan area, a legacy of mission activity that began in 1949. In 1998 the Church of the Brethren presence was limited to New York City congregations, again the result of mission work, which began in 1896. The Amish, whose multiplying communities continue to proscribe automobiles and electricity, established their oldest extant New York State settlement in Cattaraugus Co in 1949. Other Amish settlements, the majority in the Southern Tier, started after 1974, in Steuben and Chautauqua Cos, with other settlements in Montgomery and St. Lawrence Cos. The Bruderhof Communities, founded in Germany in the 1920s, established a communal settlement called Woodcrest in Rifton (Ulster Co) in 1954 under the leadership of Heini (Johann Heinrich) Arnold (1913–82), son of the movement's founder. Their communal beliefs led to an intermittent, uneasy affiliation with the Hutterian Brethren of the western United States and Canada. By 2000 no longer connected with the Hutterian Brethren, Bruderhof Communities had nine settlements, including five in New York State, Bellvale (Chester and Walden, Orange Co), Fox Hill (Walden), Catskill (Elka Park, Greene Co), Maple Ridge (Ulster Park, Ulster Co), and Woodcrest.

Historically, many Anabaptist groups have relied on and been shaped by a rural social base and agricultural or other small-scale economies. The spread of Amish and Mennonite communities has typically been driven by a search for farmland. The Bruderhof Communities have succeeded by producing educational toys (Community Playthings) and aids for people with physical disabilities (Rifton Equipment), both in Orange Co. At the same time, urban evangelism also had an impact, and by the 1980s the New York City Council of Mennonite Churches included numerous African American and Spanish-speaking congregations. Although the diversity of these groups makes generalizations difficult, their legacies include an ongoing emphasis on community life and peacemaking. If the communal Bruderhofs and the extensive mutual aid of the technologically resistant Amish are the most distinctive expressions of Anabaptism, the Mennonites and Church of the Brethren have institutionalized their modern peace stances in service organizations such as Mennonite Central Committee (1920) and Brethren Volunteer Service (1948).

Oved, Iaacov. *The Witness of the Brothers: A History of the Bruderhof* (New Brunswick, NJ: Transaction Publishers, 1996)

Schlabach, Theron F., ed. *The Mennonite Experience in America,* 4 vols (Scottsdale, Pa: Herald Press, 1985–96)

M. J. Heisey

anarchists. They believe that all forms of government are both unnecessary and undesirable, and advocate a society based on voluntary cooperation and free association of individuals and groups. Modern Times, in Islip (Suffolk Co), founded in 1851 by Josiah Warren and Stephen Pearl Andrews exemplified the anarchist principles within antebellum abolitionism and radical reform. It had no governing rules and a barter system to exchange services for necessary goods, but disputes over "free love" led to its end in 1864. Refugees from Europe brought continental antistatist views to New York City. In 1849 Wilhelm Weitling, a one-time colleague of Karl Marx (who had denounced Weitling in one of his polemics), immigrated to New York City and published *Die Republik der Arbeiter (Worker's Republic),* 1849–55.

New York City became the US center for the anarchist movement after the 1886 Haymarket riot in Chicago and the subsequent hanging of five anarchist proponents. One of the most notorious of the era was Johann Most (1846–1906), who immigrated to New York City in 1882. His journal, *Freiheit* (1882–1910), urged workers to rise up against capitalists to free themselves, and Most saw dynamite and homemade bombs as weapons that could help in equalizing the odds against the proletariat in the class struggle. Although the violent "anarchism of the deed" was not unknown among proponents in the movement, it was generally more theoretical than actual. Most supporters in the late 19th century were German, Russian Jewish, Italian, and Spanish immigrants who put forth their radical political ideas in foreign language journals, including the Yiddish *Fraye Arbeter Shtime* (1890–1977) and the Italian *L'Anarchico.*

After the 1901 assassination of Pres William McKinley in Buffalo by Leon F. Czolgosz, who claimed that anarchist literature inspired his action, anarchism was denounced, and political restrictions were placed on immigrants seeking asylum. Anarchists in New York City, however, continued to meet, publish, and articulate the problems that faced a nation in the throes of change. Emma Goldman, a Russian immigrant who moved to Rochester as a teenager in 1885 before moving to New York City in 1890, helped anarchism reach a larger audience by beginning the English language journal *Mother Earth* (1906–19). Between 1912 and 1916 speakers such as Goldman and Alexander Berkman held political meetings at Cooper Union. The anarcho-syndicalist Industrial Workers of the World led strikes among hotel workers in New York City (1911–12) and a major strike among textile workers at Little Falls (Herkimer Co) in 1912, and was the subject of a famous pageant held at Madison Square Garden in 1913, supporting a strike among silk workers in Patterson, NJ.

When registering for the draft became compulsory in 1917, anarchists formed the No Conscription League, and neither threats of deportation nor arrests stopped their efforts. The period of intense repression of dissidents, known as the Red Scare, occurred after the passage of the 1918 Sedition Act. In 1919 Goldman and Berkman were arrested on conspiracy to interfere with the draft, imprisoned, and deported in 1919 along with 245 other dissidents, including Molly Steimer, a defendant in the *Abrams v United States* Supreme Court case. Carlo Tresca, an Italian immigrant who edited many newspapers, including *L'Avvenire* and *Il Martello,* supported Nicola Sacco and Bartolomeo Vanzetti, two Massachusetts anarchists on trial for murder and robbery. The case had been widely publicized beginning with their arrest in 1920 until their executions in 1927. Tresca, a labor organizer and outspoken leader of the Anti-Fascist League, criticized American supporters of Benito Mussolini and was assassinated in New York City in 1943, probably as a mob hit.

The combination of state repression and the popularity of communism among the left led to a gradual decline in anarchism by the 1930s, but the movement remained strong in New York City. Prominent intellectual, writer, and critic Dwight Macdonald challenged the militarization and lethargy of Western society, ideas reflected in his periodical *Politics* (1944–49), and kept anarchist principles in the public eye. The Ferrer movement, named after Spanish anarchist Francisco Ferrer y Guardia, was a radical effort at unstructured education for children. The Modern School movement it engendered established progressive schools in Manhattan in 1914 and inspired several short-lived utopian communities, including one founded by Harry Kelly in 1925 at Lake Mohegan (Westchester Co). Ralph Borsodi was a New York City writer who advocated decentralized living and self-sufficiency without state support and established several colonies in Rockland Co in the 1930s.

Libertarianism, a conservative variant of antistatist philosophy, has had several prominent advocates in New York City. Albert Jay Nock was the editor of the *Freeman* (1920–24) and the author of *Our Enemy, The State* (1935). Ayn Rand, who migrated to the United States from Russia in 1926 and spent several decades living in New York City, developed objectivism, a type of radical individualism. She is best known for her novels *The Fountainhead* (1943) and *Atlas Shrugged* (1957). Murray Bookchin, born in New York City in 1921 and the author of many works (among them, *Post-Scarcity Anarchism,* 1971) has been influential among both anarchists and libertarians.

Avrich, Paul. *Anarchist Voices: An Oral History of Anarchism in America* (Princeton, NJ: Princeton Univ Press, 1995)

DeLeon, David. *The American as Anarchist: Reflections on Indigenous Radicalism* (Baltimore: John Hopkins Univ Press, 1978)

Linnea Goodwin Burwood

Fossil of trilobite.

ancient life. Paleontology includes the study of animals (including humans), plants, bacterias, and bacteria-like forms through Earth history. Though few of these organisms were ever preserved as fossils (the remains or indications of ancient organisms), fossils provide important clues about the nature of ancient life. The upper age limit for their remains to be considered "ancient" or a fossil is vague. However, the appearance of preliterate humans in North America more than 12,000 years ago and just before the end of the Ice Age (an informal name for this long glacial period) overlapped with ancient life.

Paleontology became an important science in the late 1700s in western Europe with the understanding that fossils were the remains of ancient life. Scientists came to use fossils in locating coal and other economic deposits and in relative age dating of rocks. This use of fossils followed from a new philosophical approach based on the fossil record. This can be broadly stated as "God's creation somehow was not perfect" because rocks record extinct organisms. Extinction allowed late 18th- and early 19th-century scientists to use fossils to calibrate rocks in a sequence from oldest to youngest and to make relative time correlations between the rocks of widely separated regions. This use of paleontology in relative time determination is called biostratigraphy. Geochronology, the dating of rocks and some biological materials (such as wood) in terms of years ago based on the decay of radioactive elements, was perfected later in the 20th century.

Early Study of Fossils

New York State's ancient life was documented quite early and became a standard for worldwide comparison because fossiliferous rocks cover much of the state. In addition, the Geological Survey established by Gov William L. Marcy in 1836 to evaluate the bedrock for economic potential employed a number of energetic scientists who described many fossils for the first time. Even before the survey, there were some notable discoveries in the state. The skeleton of an elephant-like mastodon was found in 1705 in Claverack (Columbia Co). This oldest report of a mastodon in the Americas was discussed in 1712 by Massachusetts minister Cotton Mather as evidence of an antediluvian "giant man." Subsequent mastodon finds were primarily in southeast New York State, in 1807–18 at Chester (Orange Co) and in 1845 near Newburgh (Orange Co). A possible mastodon (the specimen was not collected) was found in 1835 at Coeymans (Albany Co), and other reports extended across the state to Goat Island in the Niagara

EON	ERA	GEOLOGIC PERIOD AND AGE IN MILLIONS OF YEARS		MAJOR EVENTS IN LIFE HISTORY IN NEW YORK STATE AND ELSEWHERE
PHANEROZOIC (time of abundant fossils)	Cenozoic	Quaternary		Mastodons, mammoths, condors, marine mammals, early humans in New York State
			2	"Ice Age" begins, oldest humans appear
		Tertiary		No Tertiary rocks or fossils in New York
				Diverse mammals evolve, first primates
			65	Dinosaur extinction
	Mesozoic	Cretaceous		Fossil plants on Long and Staten Islands, including early flowering plants
			138	
		Jurassic		Earliest birds
			195	
		Triassic		Dinosaur tracks in Rockland Co
				Oldest dinosaurs and mammals
			225	
	Paleozoic	Permian		Mammal-like reptiles appear
				No Permian rocks or fossils in New York
			280	
		Carboniferous		Oldest reptiles appear
				Marine shells and land-plant fossils, Allegany State Park region
			345	
		Devonian		Earth's oldest forests, Gilboa
				Marine fossils of Finger Lakes region
				Diverse marine fossils, Helderberg Mountains
			418	
		Silurian		Eurypterids common in central New York
				Abundant fossils, Rochester and Niagara Falls
			440	
		Ordovician		Early land-plant spores in Niagara Frontier rocks
				Graptolites and trilobites in Mohawk and Black River valleys
				Earth's oldest coral reefs (Chazy area)
				Tropical seas cover New York, many mollusk fossils
			489	
		Cambrian		Stromatolites near Saratoga Springs
				Oldest fish on earth
				First animal fossils in New York (Claverack)
				Oldest trilobites (Siberia)
				Origin of modern marine animal groups
			543	
PRECAMBRIAN			575	First large multicellular animals
			1,000	Adirondack and Hudson Highlands rock forms, most fossils destroyed by metamorphism
			1,300	New York's oldest fossils (Balmat stromatolites)
			3,200	Oldest bacteria fossils on earth
			3,800	Oldest geochemical evidence for life
			4,600	Origin of solar system and earth

River, where a mastodon tooth was found in 1841.

An 1832 report by Jacob Green described new North American trilobites, extinct marine animals that resembled sow bugs, including species from Trenton Falls (Oneida Co). Amos Eaton, founder of what became Rensselaer Polytechnic Institute in Troy, published a textbook in 1830 that noted trilobites and other fossils from the Helderberg Escarpment near Albany to the Lake Erie bluffs near Hamburg-on-the-Lake (Erie Co). Eaton's knowledge of these fossils likely stemmed from his 1823–24 geological survey of the Erie Canal. The Geological Survey's map, completed in 1838, showed that almost all of the state's rocks predated the early abundance of land plants in the period called the Coal Age, or Carboniferous period, 362–286 million years ago (mya).

Geologist and State Paleontologist James Hall maintained the Geological Survey as a research unit. His 13-volume *Palaeontology of New York* began to appear in 1847 and provided the first descriptions of fossils later found across North America. His work with Edwin B. Hall (no relation) led to the description and publication of the latter's late Devonian, *ca* 375 mya, fossil sponge collection from Allegany and Chautauqua Cos. Unfortunately, the great fossil collection that James Hall assembled in the State Museum based on research across North America was sold during a budget crisis. This material was the basis for the American Museum of Natural History's (AMNH's) collection in New York City, with other specimens going to the Field Museum in Chicago and elsewhere.

Hall's greatest achievement was using fossils to show that the earth had changed greatly through time and that its mountains were not formed during a biblical creation. Hall's conclusion was based on an understanding of New York State's slate belt and its fossils. The slate belt enters northernmost Washington Co from Vermont and extends to Beacon (Dutchess Co), near Poughkeepsie. In 1849 Ebenezer Emmons compared trilobites from Washington Co with the oldest trilobites of Wales to demonstrate the great age of some slate belt rocks. Silas W. Ford, a telegraph operator from Troy, published articles showing that the area of Troy to Castleton-on-Hudson in Rensselaer Co had particularly old fossils. The problem was that these rocks, from the Cambrian period (543–489 mya), overlie late Ordovician rocks (*ca* 470 mya) east of the Hudson River in Rensselaer and Columbia Cos. The older Cambrian should lie beneath the Ordovician. Hall noted faults (breaks in the rocks that show disruption and movement) at the base of the slate belt and realized that the Cambrian slate belt rocks had been pushed from the east onto the late Ordovician rocks. Hall used fossils to demonstrate mountain-building processes, and his model for mountain building was used to interpret the Alps in Europe.

New York City artist Charles R. Knight used the latest paleontological research to depict the way ancient plants and animals would have looked in life. Knight was the dominant figure in prehistoric re-creations of his era. He worked with Henry Fairfield Osborn of the AMNH to create paintings, murals, and sculptures of ancient life, most notably dinosaurs that were displayed in museums across America. His renditions of dinosaurs and their habitats still appear in popular culture as well as institutions, and continue to influence our conceptions of these extinct creatures.

Fossil Distribution

Fossiliferous rocks are not uniformly distributed across New York State. Nonfossiliferous rocks dominate the Adirondacks, the high Taconic Range, and the Westchester Co–Manhattan area. Adirondack Mountain rocks are so old that they predate complex life-forms and so metamorphosed (changed by heat and pressure into new rocks) that few fossils have been found. Much younger rocks of the high Taconics and much of the New York City area had their fossils destroyed by recrystallization and shear during metamorphism and mountain building. Rocks of other areas represent environments that supported or preserved few organisms. These conditions are recorded, for example, at Ausable Chasm and the Shawangunk Mountain ridges in northeastern and southeastern New York State, respectively. Ausable Chasm, a canyon in Upper Cambrian Potsdam Formation sandstones (*ca* 494 mya), and the rocks of the Shawangunks (Upper Silurian, *ca* 420 mya) reflect high-energy conditions in which few marine animals lived. In addition, these rocks have low calcium carbonate ("lime") content, and most limy fossil fragments dissolved away during diagenesis (processes by which sediment becomes rock).

The fossiliferous rocks that cover much of the state reflect high sea levels and extensive seas in the early and early middle Paleozoic (543–*ca* 380 mya). With the filling of these seas with sediment eroded from mountains in the Appalachian belt, fossiliferous Upper Paleozoic marine rocks were restricted to the Southern Tier. Remnants of these youngest marine rocks (*ca* 362–282 mya) cap the hills in Allegany State Park. The subsequent fossil record is scanty and comes from Mesozoic rocks in Rockland Co, Staten Island, and Long Island. Fossils from the last stage of New York State's geologic evolution at the end of the Ice Age are widespread. The stream, river, lake, and swamp deposits of this time have fossils that range from mastodons to plant pollen.

Precambrian Eon

The Precambrian is the long interval from the origin of Earth (*ca* 4.5 billion years ago) to the beginning of the Cambrian (543 mya). The oldest rocks and fossils in New York State record geologic events from the latter part of the Proterozoic eon, the later half of the Precambrian. The Balmat stromatolites in St. Lawrence Co are the oldest fossils in the eastern United States. Their age is more than 1.1 billion years—the age of metamorphism of Adirondack rocks. Their upper age limit is 1.3 billion years—the age of the now metamorphosed volcanic rocks that form part of the Adirondacks. The Balmat stromatolites were found in the early 1980s by geologist William De Lorraine, who noted domelike structures with a layered appearance up to 12 inches (30 cm) high and 18 inches (46 cm) wide. Modern stromatolites (layered rocks) are constructed by cyanobacteria, photosynthetic bacteria with blue-green chlorophyll. Cyanobacteria also produce the feltlike mats on the bottom of old rain puddles. In aquatic environments, cyanobacteria grow upward to trap sediment grains that fall on the mats. The stirring up of bottom sediment by waves or currents led to internal lamination, the wavy layers in stromatolites.

Simple stromatolites like those at Balmat are found as fossils in much older rocks (3.2 billion years ago) and persist until the present. The Balmat stromatolites indicate shallow-water formation in the zone of photosynthesis. Their form, with the domes pointing downward, shows the rocks are overturned. Evidence shows that shallow tropical seas covered parts of the state 1.3–1.1 billion years ago. Giant stromatolite reefs occur in the Proterozoic elsewhere in North America and probably occurred in New York State. Although Proterozoic rocks also form the Hudson Highlands and parts of the Westchester Co–Manhattan region, Proterozoic fossils are known only from the northwest Adirondacks.

Cambrian Period

The seas of the Cambrian period (543–489 mya) featured the early evolution of almost all major marine animal groups. Fragments of the trilobite *Olenellus* and tiny, cap-shaped phosphatic remains of *Discinella* from Beacon Hills and Stissing Mountain in Dutchess Co indicate marine incursion about 515 mya, when Cambrian seas inundated the area. Trilobites are often the most frequently found fossils of the Cambrian period, but the shallow-water rocks of New York State have mollusks (snails and relatives) as the commonest fossils. Trilobites are arthropods, with external skeletons of a starchlike material called chitin strengthened by calcium carbonate. The three "lobes" of a trilobite are defined by two depressions that parallel the axis of the animal. Sparse trilobite-dominated animal life with snails and hyoliths, extinct mollusk-like forms with a conical shell and trap door-like operculum to close the shell, show that shallow seas reached Fort Ann (Washington Co) around 505 mya. Shortly afterward the shoreline moved across New York State, as recorded by middle late Cambrian fossils in the rocks at Ausable Chasm in Clinton Co, Chateaugay Chasm in Franklin Co, Greenfield Center (Saratoga Co), and the Noses water gap on the Mohawk River in Montgomery Co. The first deposits were typically sandstones; at Mooers (Clinton Co), they have tracks up to 8 inches (20 cm) wide called *Climachtichnites* that appear to have been made by giant snaillike animals. Limestone and dolostone in Washington Co and in the Poughkeepsie–Wappingers Falls area of Dutchess Co have latest Cambrian stromatolites, trilobites, and mollusks, including chitons (mollusks with eight valves), and North America's oldest cephalopods. These cephalopods lived in the outer chamber of an elongated, internally partitioned shell and pumped nitrogen gas in and out of the other chambers to control buoyancy. Modern cephalopods include the spiral-shelled *Nautilus,* octopuses, and squids. Spectacular stromatolites formed in shallow water occur at Petrified Gardens and Lester Park near Saratoga Springs.

The oldest shelled animal fossils in eastern North America appear in the deep-water Cambrian rocks of the Taconic slate belt. Among these remains, recently documented at Claverack, are tiny mollusks, including *Fordilla troyensis,* Earth's oldest clam (first discovered in Troy), and brachiopods, marine animals with two shells somewhat similar to clams. They were swept from the shallow tropical sea in eastern New York State into the deep water. Other forms include trilobites and archaeocyathans, extinct calcareous sponges that had porous skeletons used to filter water. Archaeocyathans produced the oldest animal-constructed reefs and were first reported in North America at Beaman Park in Troy. The latest Cambrian saw the appearance of conodonts, extinct marine vertebrates with tiny phosphatic teeth that had the ecologic role of small predatory fish. These fossils allow finely resolved correlations between the slate belt and the shallow tropical sea rocks in eastern New York State.

Ordovician Period

The Ordovician period (489–438 mya) began with a sea-level rise that brought tropical seas across the United States. Earliest Ordovician limestones of the Tribes Hill Formation (named for that area in Montgomery Co) are exposed from Washington Co to Herkimer Co and reappear in the Halcyon Lake area of Dutchess Co. Near-shore facies (the general depositional environment and type of sedimentary rock) of the Tribes Hill Formation are primarily mollusk dominated with some snails and cephalopods. Deeper facies have trilobites and abundant fragments of echinoderms—starfish, crinoids (sea lilies), and their relatives—at Canajoharie and Amsterdam (Montgomery Co) and other Mohawk Valley communities. Late early Ordovician dolostones near Ogdensburg (St. Lawrence Co) have a few trilobites in a mollusk-dominated fossil assemblage. With exception of the trilobite-rich Fort Cassin Formation at the top of the Lower Ordovician in Washington Co and near Beekmantown (Clinton Co), the higher Lower Ordovician rocks have a poorly preserved near-shore variety of fossils, mostly snails and cephalopods with a few trilobites. The early Ordovician ended with a fall in sea level. The earliest Middle Ordovician rocks hold small bivalved crustaceans called ostracodes, best seen on southern Isle La Motte in Lake Champlain.

Earth's oldest coral reefs, which appeared during a sea-level rise in the Middle Ordovician, were first recorded in New York State. Composed of coral and stromatoporoids, an extinct group of calcareous sponges, these reefs appear in limestone quarries in Plattsburgh and further south along Lake Champlain to Crown Point in Essex Co. The coral reefs were wave-resistant structures and as such provided new habitats for a wide variety of marine animals that appear in the Upper Ordovician. Continuing sea-level rise in the Ordovician brought shallow marine life and limestones across the Adirondacks. These mollusk-rich limestones are seen along the Black River from Watertown to Lowville (Lewis Co). The last deposition of Ordovician limestone in New York occurred about 450 mya. These limestones are thinly bedded and rich in trilobites, horn corals, and bryozoans, colonial "moss-animals" that produced calcareous structures. They are exposed in New York State Thruway road cuts from Amsterdam to Utica.

Advanced graptolites, colonial marine organisms with organic skeletons that often look like pencil marks on dark mud rocks, appeared in the earliest Ordovician in the deep-water Taconic slate belt. During the late 1800s Dr Rudolf Ruedemann, originally a high school teacher from Utica who later published extensively in paleontology and received international acclaim for his work, documented graptolites from Rensselaer Co. The graptolites include very early Ordovician forms at Schaghticoke Gorge and forms ranging into the early Middle Ordovician on the Deep Kill. Ruedemann's work in New York State led to a worldwide correlation standard for North America that was published in 1947, two years after his death. Younger Middle Ordovician graptolites at Normans Kill gorge on the south side of Albany, and Mt Merino in Glenmont (Albany Co), complement this succession and allow correlation of Taconic rocks with those in Australia, China, and western Europe.

The Ordovician ended with the thrust of the slate belt into eastern New York State and depression of this area under its enormous weight. A deep marine trough, the ancient Utica Sea, was formed and received mud and sands eroded from the Taconic highlands. The first deposit was the graptolite-rich Utica Shale, seen in many black shale road cuts on the Thruway in the Mohawk Valley. Rare bottom-dwelling animals in the Utica Sea include the trilobite *Triarthrus,* a form adapted to low-oxygen conditions. Specimens of *Triarthrus,* described by Charles E. Beecher in 1893–94 north of Rome (Oneida Co), are replaced by the mineral pyrite (fool's gold) and provided the first evidence of the legs and antennae of trilobites. These fossils helped resolve their evolutionary relationships to other arthropods. Increased sand input into the Utica Sea is recorded by the deep-water, sandstone-rich Schenectady Formation, a unit with sparse graptolites that is exposed in cliffs along the Mohawk River and in long road cuts on I-88 north of Schoharie Creek. Filling of the Utica Sea led to the accumulation of Upper Ordovician shallow-water sandstones with mollusk-dominated faunas, characteristic of the Tug Hill Plateau east of Lake Ontario. Exposed along the Lake Ontario shore from Rochester to the Niagara Gorge, the red sandstones and shales of the Queenston Formation contain few fossils. The Queenston is important because microscopic spore tetrads recovered from it provide the earliest record of the existence of primitive land plants (mosses) at the end of the Ordovician.

Silurian Period

Fossiliferous rocks from the Silurian period (438–418 mya) are largely limited to western New York State and the Niagara Falls area, as the state east of Syracuse was not covered by seas until later in the period. Earliest Silurian rocks, best seen low in the Niagara Gorge, contain the same types of bivalve, snail, and ostracod fossils that appear in near-shore Ordovician deposits. The trace fossil *Arthrophycus* long segmented-appearing horizontal burrows up to 1 inch (2.5 cm) wide, characterizes the middle Medina Group and ranges from New York to Alabama. Open-marine conditions in the western Lake Ontario lowlands are indicated by the over 200 species of trilobites, corals, bryozoans, cephalopods, crinoids, and others in the Rochester Shale of the Genesee River Gorge at Rochester and west into Ontario.

Late Silurian rocks often lack any fossils, although the corals and stromatoporoids at the base of the Helderberg Escarpment are exceptions. Times of more normal marine salinity are recorded in slightly older late Silurian rocks in central and western New York by thin intervals with brachiopods, ostracods, large algae, and eurypterids, extinct arthropods similar to horseshoe crabs. A thin interval of late Silurian rock that extends west from southern Herkimer Co to Ontario Province yields the most prolific eurypterids in North America, with some species reaching 12 feet (3.7 m). The commonest eurypterid, *Eurypterus remipes,* was designated the New York State Fossil in 1984. Accompanying these fossil fauna are small, washed-in Y-shaped fossils of *Cooksonia,* Earth's oldest vascular land plant. *Cooksonia* had tissues that acted as vessels to transport water and gave the plant rigidity, but it lacked differentiated roots, stem, and leaves.

Devonian Period

Continuous marine deposition from the Silurian into the Devonian period (418–362 mya) is recorded in the lower part of the Helderberg Escarpment in eastern New York State. With little change in most fossils, certain conodont species are used to define the base of the Devonian. Down-warping of the eastern edge of ancestral North America and gentle elevation of central New York State mean that early Devonian rocks occur only east of Syracuse. The lowest Devonian (Helderberg Group) records progressive deepening followed by a shallowing. The deepest marine unit (New Scotland Formation) in the middle Helderberg Group extends from Albany Co south to Port Jervis (Orange Co) and has fossils that resemble those of the Rochester Shale in variety and type.

The distribution of Devonian organisms and rock types after deposition of the Helderberg Group was controlled by alternations of mountain building and quiescence in the interior of the Appalachians. Gentle uplift after Helderberg Group deposition was followed by submergence and deposition of the thin Oriskany Sandstone. Along its outcrop belt from Syracuse to Port Jervis, the Oriskany Sandstone has large, thick-shelled brachiopods that preferred high-energy, wave-dominated environments. Brachiopods, corals, bryozoans, trilobites, and fish fragments are common through much of the lower middle Devonian Onondaga Limestone, which extends west from the Port Jervis–Helderberg escarpment belt to Buffalo. Small coral reefs are seen in outcrops, such as Roberts reef in southern Albany Co, while reefs up to several hundred feet high and a half mile wide are encountered in oil wells in central and western New York State.

The oldest in situ fossil forests known in the world are the *ca* 380 mya stumps of giant lycopods (club mosses) and ferns in the subaerial and fluvial deposits along Schoharie Creek near Gilboa (Schoharie Co). The fossil forests also yield fossil mites, spiders, and other insects that inhabited early terrestrial ecosystems. Associated ancient stream deposits record Earth's oldest freshwater clams, *Arcanodon,* in the Grand Gorge area of Delaware Co. The Catskills have produced fragments of early freshwater fish, such as jawless ostracoderms, armored placoderms (possible shark cousins with armored head shields and jaws), and air-breathing bony fish as well as apparent burrows made by lungfish of this period. Further offshore, muddy, and somewhat limey marine deposits of the Hamilton Group extend from the Finger Lakes to the Lake Erie bluffs. These deposits record diverse middle Devonian fossils that include the trilobite *Phacops rana* and crinoids, which were often buried by storms and are complete.

In the early 1960s, Dr John Wells, who taught in the Geology Department of Cornell University, examined fine growth lines on Hamilton Group brachiopods and corals and recognized monthly and annual bands. He concluded the middle Devonian year had 395 days, a figure earlier suggested by physicists who reasoned that tidal friction between the earth and the moon slows their rotation and leads to fewer days in a year over geologic time. The later part of the late Devonian featured relatively shallow-water clam and brachiopod faunas that can be seen in stream and quarry cuts in the Southern Tier along Rte 17 (I-86) from Friendship (Allegany Co) to Mayville (Chautauqua Co). By the late Devonian some marine animals had developed the ability to breathe on land and amphibians evolved.

Carboniferous Period

The Carboniferous period, or Coal Age (362–286 mya) is noted for the formation of coal from great forests in Europe and North America, both of which then had equatorial climates. Amphibians were the dominant fauna, but reptiles appeared early in the Carboniferous and had the advantage of the amniote (closed) egg, which did not require a freshwater environment for reproduction. Carboniferous period rocks in New York State are limited to a few hilltops in southern Allegany, Cattaraugus, and Chautauqua Cos. Near-shore marine sandstones with clam-dominated faunas and transported plant debris are interbedded with conglomerates (rocks made of pebbles and coarser fragments) and represent only the lowest and part of the middle Carboniferous. Mammal-like reptiles appeared during the Permian period (286–225 mya), but no Permian rocks or fossils have been found in the state. In the late Permian there were mass extinctions among animals in the ocean as well as among amphibians and reptiles.

Mesozoic Era

The Mesozoic Era, or "Age of Dinosaurs" (225–65 mya) comprises the Triassic period (225–195 mya); the Jurassic period (195–138 mya); and the Cretaceous period (138–65 mya). Mesozoic rocks are limited to southeast New York State, where the only known dinosaur tracks in the state were discovered in Blauvelt (Rockland Co) by Dr Paul Olsen of Columbia University in 1972. The three-toed tracks, made in red mud, probably belonged to a *Coelophyses*-like dinosaur, a small meat-eating animal that walked on two legs. This site also has dinosaur teeth and in situ tree stumps. As at other latest Triassic to earliest Jurassic sites along the Connecticut River in Massachusetts and Connecticut *ca* 220–190 mya, the Blauvelt site records very early dinosaurs that inhabited intermountain valleys. Flowering plants, the angiosperms, developed in the late Mesozoic and increased the variety of food supply available to herbivores. Middle Cretaceous (*ca* 100 mya) sandstones and shales underlying southeast Staten Island and Long Island yielded leaves and branches of a diverse flora of early flowering trees, such as magnolias and figlike forms, and conifers. About 100 million years separate the Cretaceous floras from Pleistocene plant and animal fossils found across New York State. The Cretaceous ended with a mass extinction of many land and marine animals, including the dinosaurs.

Pleistocene Epoch

The Cenozoic era began 65 mya and comprises two periods, the Tertiary (65–2 mya) and the Quaternary (2 mya–present). No Tertiary rocks or fossils have yet been discovered in New York State. The Quaternary period is divided into the Pleistocene epoch, or Ice Age (2 mya–10,000 years ago) and the Holocene (or Recent) epoch (10,000 years ago–present). With melting and retreat of the continental ice sheets beginning *ca* 14,000 years ago, plants and animals (likely also humans about 12,000 years ago) returned to New York State. Depression of the earth's surface by more than 550 feet (168 m) under the continental ice sheet, followed by its melting, led to incursion of seawater into Lake Champlain and the upper St. Lawrence about 12,000 years ago. Marine Pleistocene fossils are found in northern New York State. In 1987 bones of a white whale, or beluga, were found in a gravel pit 6 miles (10 km) southeast of Massena (St. Lawrence Co). Associated clams, ostracods, and single-celled foraminiferans indicate a cold, brackish habitat for this 10,800 year-old animal. Similar finds are possible along the Lake Champlain valley, where oyster shell banks record brackish water in the northern part of the basin.

Pleistocene land animals include mastodons, wooly mammoths, several species of peccaries, caribou, elk, rare giant beavers, and the woodland bison. Other Pleistocene animals still resident in New York State include deer, moose, and foxes. Remains may occur in any late and post-glacial stream and bog deposit. A farmer in Byron (Genesee Co) discovered bones and bird feathers in a bog in the mid-1980s; the remains proved to be mastodon, caribou, and the first condor from the eastern United States. Abundant conifer twigs at the site are crushed and chopped into short lengths and may represent a winter "starvation" diet of the mastodons. A mastodon now displayed in the Museum of the Earth in Ithaca was found in 1999 in a pond near Hyde Park (Dutchess Co).

Goldring, Winifred. *Guide to the Geology of John Boyd Thacher Park* (1933; repr, ed. Ed Landing and John B. Skiba, Albany: NYS Museum, 1997)

Isachsen, Yngvar W., et al, eds. *Geology of New York: A Simplified Account,* 2d ed. (Albany: NYS Museum, 2000)

VanAller Hernick, Linda. *The Gilboa Fossils* (Albany: NYS Museum, 1996)

Whitley, Thomas E., Gerald J. Kloc, and Carlton E. Brett. *Trilobites of New York* (Ithaca: Cornell Univ Press, 2002)

Ed Landing

Ancient Order of Hibernians. Irish Catholic social and benevolent society. The Ancient Order of Hibernians (AOH) draws its inspiration from a 16th-century secret society in Ireland known as the Defenders, a group that sought to protect Irish society from English colonial powers. In the United States the AOH was originally conceived to preserve the culture of Irish individuals living there. It was founded in New York State in 1836, and the first meeting took place at St. James Church in Manhattan. The order provided an important outlet for Irish immigrants to socialize and adjust to life in the new world. It also promoted business ties, provided charity in the era before welfare, and ensured burials for the dead. The AOH provided a social foundation that strengthened Irish political organization at a time of nativism and anti-Catholic sentiment. The organization became a national movement in 1871. The order's motto—Friendship, Unity, and Christian Charity—reflects its stated goals to promote education, Catholic faith, Irish nationalism, and ethnic pride. The New York State AOH is organized into eight districts statewide, each subdivided into local divisions; members join their local division. The division that a prospective member joins is usually dictated by the county where the family originated in Ireland. *Empire State Hibernian* is the state order's published journal. The New York State AOH is best known for sponsoring St. Patrick's Day parades, most notably in New York City, where AOH has run the parade for more than 150 years. In 1990 the AOH refused to allow the Irish Lesbian and Gay Organization to march under its own banner in the parade, spurring an ongoing controversy.

Bayor, Ronald H., and Timothy J. Meagher, eds. *The New York Irish* (Baltimore: Johns Hopkins Univ Press, 1996)

Ridge, John T. *Erin's Sons in America: The Ancient Order of Hibernians* (New York: Ancient Order of Hibernians, 1986)

Jennifer Steenshorne

Ancram. Town (pop 1,513) in SE Columbia Co. Settled by Scots in 1741 and later by Dutch and German farmers, the town was the site of New York State's first iron furnace (1743), which used ore from Salisbury, Conn to produce bar iron and cast-iron goods. Three different iron mines and a lead mine operated at various periods between 1775 and 1900. The town formed from Livingston in 1803 as Gallatin, and the name was changed in 1814. In the mid–19th century Ancram was the county's largest sheep-farming town, and with Harlem Railroad (1852) service, farmers began to ship fluid milk to New York City from Ancramdale (1872). The Poughkeepsie and Eastern (1872) and Rhinebeck and Connecticut (1874) Railroads provided east-west service. In 1854 a paper mill was built on the site of the ironworks and produced straw, manila, tissue, and ultimately specialty papers. In 2003 it was operated by Schweitzer-Mauduit Corp. In 1948 Ancram and neighboring Copake were among the first US users of bulk tanks for milk. In the early 21st century much of the land remains in agriculture, and most residents commute. Second homes, however, have resulted in growth. In 1853 a famous prizefight was held at Boston Corner, then part of Massachusetts, between John Morrissey and Yankee Sullivan, because Massachusetts law enforcement could not cross the intervening mountain range; the locality was ceded to New York State the same year. Since 1976 Ancram has been the site of the Grey Fox Bluegrass Festival.

Anderson, Warren M(attice) (*b* Bainbridge, Chenango Co, 16 Oct 1915). New York State Senate majority leader. He graduated from Colgate University in 1937 and from Albany Law School in 1940, before serving as assistant Broome Co attorney (1940–42) and in the army during World War II (1943–46). In 1952 Anderson won a seat in the New York State Senate as a Broome Co Republican, was elected chairman of the Finance Committee in 1966, and was elected majority leader of the senate in 1972. His ability to work with Democrats enabled him to meet the greatest challenge of his political career, the bailout of New York City during the fiscal crisis of 1975. Other accomplishments credited to Anderson while he was majority leader include the creation of the Tuition Assistance Program (1974); the $13 million three-theater Anderson Center at SUNY Binghamton (1985) named for his father, Floyd; the establishment of Oquaga Creek State Park (1979) and of I-88; and the expansion of Broome Community College. Although he never formally announced his candidacy, he contemplated running for governor in 1978. Anderson retired from the New York State Senate in 1988 having served as majority leader for 16 consecutive years.

"A Master of the Politics of Understatement," *New York Times*, 2 June 1988

"Anderson Makes History," *New York Times*, 1 Jan 1984

"Andy: A Profile of New York's Top Republican," *Binghamton Sunday Press*, 17 June 1981

Joann Lindstrom

Andes. Town (pop 1,356) in SE Delaware Co. Settled *ca* 1770 but abandoned during the American Revolution, it was resettled beginning in 1781, and the town was formed from Middletown in 1820. Located on the East Branch of the Delaware River, Andes, named for its rugged terrain, includes Mt Pisgah, which at 3,440 feet (1,049 m) is the highest peak in the county. Lumbering and butter making featured prominently in the 1800s. Late in the 19th century, a wood acid factory fostered the growth of the hamlet of Shavertown. The town includes a National Historic District and the restored Hunting Tavern, site of several incidents in the antirent conflict in the 1840s. Pepacton Reservoir (1955) inundated the hamlets of Shavertown and Union Grove. In the 20th century the decrease in small farms was followed by an influx of second-home owners and a focus on tourism. Murphy Hill State Forest offers hiking and hunting opportunities. The Village of Andes, which was incorporated in 1861 and had a population of 289 in 2000, was dissolved on 31 Dec 2003.

Dorothy Kubik

Andover. Town (pop 1,945) and village (pop 1,073) in SE Allegany Co. Settled in 1796, the town was formed in 1824 from Independence. Pine timber made up a high proportion of its virgin forest, and the lumber industry was important until the Civil War era. The Erie Railroad came through in 1851. Late 19th-century manufacturers included a tannery, a foundry, and a woolen mill, and dairying was important. Two silk mills (1903–73), two condenseries (1908–69), a tinware and enamelware stamping company, and a cutlery firm (1917–20) provided employment, as did Niagara Electron Laboratories (electronics, 1946–91). Certified Traffic Controllers (1983) employed 100 workers in 2003, manufacturing signs and other traffic control devices.

Andros, Sir Edmund (*b* London, 6 Dec 1637; *d* London, 19 Feb 1714). Royal governor of New York and New Jersey (1674–80). Staunch royalists, the Andros family during Edmund's childhood followed Charles II into exile after his 1651 defeat at the Battle of Worcester. In the Netherlands Edmund served as a page to Elizabeth, queen of Bohemia. He began his military career in 1656 as an ensign, serving under the command of Prince Henry of Nassau, whose Dutch army fought with the Danes against Sweden. After the 1660 Restoration of Charles II, Andros continued his military career in Barbados at the rank of major during the Second Anglo-Dutch War (1665–67). Andros served in England during the Third Anglo-Dutch War (1672–74), rising to the rank of lieutenant colonel. During this war the Dutch seized New Netherland, renamed New York by the English, but at the war's conclusion the province was returned to the English. Its proprietor, James, Duke of York, named Edmund Andros as governor.

Andros quickly overcame the antipathy of the many Dutch residents, unhappy at the prospect of being returned to English rule, by assuring them that they would be free to practice their own religion. Andros also overcame the resistance of Puritan settlers on Long Island, who particularly objected to the nonrepresentative government Andros reinstituted at the duke's order. Andros also attempted to seize control of East New Jersey's government from the Carteret family. Despite his attempts to intimidate the jury that tried Gov Philip Carteret for illegally governing East New Jersey, Carteret was found not guilty.

One of Andros's most significant achievements in New York was to keep the Five Nations of the Iroquois Confederacy from joining King Philip in the war Philip and his allies waged on New England. Instead, Andros urged the Mohawk, the easternmost Iroquois tribe, to attack Philip, hastening the end of the war. He then, in 1677, negotiated the Covenant Chain agreement with the Iroquois, which included New York, New England, and the Chesapeake colonies. Favored by the king and his brother, the duke of York, Andros was rewarded with knighthood in 1678. Two years later he was recalled to face charges of favoritism and misappropriation of funds brought by some discontented New Yorkers. Andros was exonerated of all charges and appointed a gentleman in ordinary of the king's privy chamber, serving Charles II until the king's death in 1685. James II appointed Andros to his next post as governor of the newly created Dominion of New England, which eventually included New York. After the 1688 Glorious Revolution in England, the Dominion government was overturned in 1689, causing Andros and his closest advisors to be incarcerated for almost a year in Boston. Released and returned to England at the order of the new king, William III, Andros was exonerated of all charges. He held his last American colonial post in Virginia from 1692 until his resignation in 1698 because of ill health. Appointed lieutenant governor of Guernsey by Queen Anne, he served from 1703 to 1707, spending his last years in London. Andros implemented a fair system of taxation in the colonies he governed and organized a united government in New England, New York, and New Jersey. An effective agent of centralization, Andros helped to establish England's presence firmly in North America.

See also COLONIAL NEW YORK.

Christoph, Peter R., and Florence A. Christoph, eds. *The Andros Papers,* 3 vols (Syracuse: Syracuse Univ Press, 1989–91)

Lustig, Mary Lou. *The Imperial Executive in America: Sir Edmund Andros, 1637–1714* (Madison, NJ: Fairleigh Dickinson Univ Press, 2002)

Matson, Cathy. *Merchants and Empire: Trading in Colonial New York* (Baltimore: Johns Hopkins Univ Press, 1998)

Mary Lou Lustig

Angelica. Town (pop 1,411) and village (pop 903) in central Allegany Co. Settled in 1801 under the proprietorship of Judge Philip Church (1778–1861), the town was formed in 1805 from Leicester (Livingston Co). In that year Judge Church welcomed some French royalist refugees, but they did not remain long. The village, on Angelica Creek, a tributary of the Genesee, was laid out in 1805 and incorporated in 1835. It served as the Allegany Co seat from 1806 to 1859 and as its half-shire until 1892. It lost its status of county seat because there was no railroad, but it was later served by the Pittsburg, Shawmut and Northern (1903–46). A paper mill provided employment after the Civil War. Rte 17 (I-86) was completed through town in 1974. Angelica Park Circle Historic District, including the 1819 courthouse, is on the National Register of Historic Places. The American Hotel (1808) is the village's oldest business. In the southwest corner of town, Belvidere (1804), Judge Church's house, is also on the National Register. The Allegany County Fair (1843) takes place in July and the Heritage Days festival in August. Angelica's Park Circle has one of the few clay roque courts in the United States, used for a version of croquet played in the village since the 1880s.

Anglo-Dutch Wars. See DUTCH RESTORATION; NEW NETHERLANDS.

Angola. Village (pop 2,266) in Evans (Erie Co). Created by a station on the Buffalo and State Line Railroad (1852), it was incorporated in 1873. By 1882 it was crossed by three parallel sets of track. Industries included Lythe Tile (1888–mid-1920s), Candee Lock Factory (1896), Angola Macaroni Manufacturing Co (1903), Emblem Bicycle Co (1904–1930s), Pickering Co (1919; grape juice), Bison Canning Co (1928), and Enzinger Union Works (1933; brewing equipment). It was crossed by the Thruway in 1957 but didn't have an interchange until 1972. In the early 21st century Angola is a summer resort, and water treatment and filtration systems are manufactured. On 18 Dec 1867 it was the site of the Angola Horror, when two railroad cars fell into Big Sister Creek and burned, killing 50.

Andrew C. Maines

animal feeds industry. Animal feeds are scientific formulations of as many as 30 ingredients for dairy cattle, poultry, and other farm animals and pets. Major end products for the industry in New York State are milk, meat, eggs, turkey, and chicken. The industry began in the 19th century with many small mills mainly processing oats for feed to draft animals. The first formula feed, for calves, was produced in 1875. In the first half of the 20th century larger mills evolved. By 1930 there were high-volume terminal mills in Buffalo, some reaching capacities of 100 train carloads a day, nearly 1 million tons (.9 million MT) a year. Smaller milling centers were at Albany, Binghamton, Olean (Cattaraugus Co), and Oneonta (Otsego Co). As with other grain-milling industries, Buffalo's commanding position has eroded since the mid-1950s, partly because of freight-shipping patterns but also because management realized that concentration of operations facilitated organized labor activity and made the industry vulnerable to work stoppages. None of the 11 animal feed mills operating in Buffalo in 1945 remain in use. Smaller local mills again predominate but in an industry declining overall. The statewide workforce of over 5,000 in 1947 stood at 1,677 in 1997.

Major producers have included the farmers' cooperative Agway, which began business in 1920 as the Cooperative Grange League Federation Exchange, with a mill in Buffalo. Headquartered in Syracuse, Agway has important feed mills in Batavia, Binghamton, Canton, Salem, Sangerfield, and elsewhere in the Northeast. In the 1980s Blue Seal Feeds, a New England company established in 1868, expanded into New York State with plants in Chatham (Columbia Co), Bainbridge (Chenango Co), Arcade (Wyoming Co), and Watertown. Independents such as Reisdorf Bros of North Java (Wyoming Co) serve regional markets within the state. In 2002 Canadian miller Shur-Gain purchased a large mill in Strykersville (Wyoming Co), primarily for production of dairy feed. Some mills are owned by and serve a single producer, such as turkey processor Plainville Farms in Onondaga Co.

While formulas vary greatly across animal species, common ingredients include corn, oats, other grains, millfeed (a by-product of flour milling), molasses, fish oil, vitamins, and minerals. To prevent the introduction of bovine spongiform encephalopathy (mad cow disease), the US Food and Drug Administration in 1997 banned the use of protein from mammals in livestock feeds. Feeds are often pelletized so that the animals cannot pick and choose among ingredients. Nutritional science has done much to improve animal health, growth rates, and feeding efficiency, producing more usable pounds of animal per pound of feed consumed and thus helping to hold down the price of animal products. In 1997 there were 52 manufacturers of animal feeds in the state, with combined shipments valued at $997,115,000. Production by weight exceeded 2,770,000 tons (2,513,000 MT) in 2000.

Lockwood, Joseph Flawith, and Anthony Simon. *Provender Milling: Manufacture of Feeding Stuffs for Live Stock,* 3d ed. (Liverpool, England: Northern Publishing, 1949)

Milliman, Thomas E., and Frances E. Sage. *The GLF Story, 1920–1964: A History of the Cooperative Grange League Federation Exchange* (Ithaca: Wilcox Press, 1964)

Pfost, Harry B., ed. *Feed Manufacturing Technology* (Arlington, Va: American Feed Manufacturers Association, 1976)

United States. Bureau of the Census. *Economic Census (Manufacturing), 1909–*

Henry H. Baxter

Annsville. Town (pop 2,956) in NW Oneida Co. Settled in 1793, the town was formed from Lee, Florence, Camden, and Vienna in 1823. At Taberg, a hamlet on East Branch Fish Creek named for a Swedish iron-mining town, the Oneida Iron and Glass Manufacturing Co (1809) began operating a blast furnace in 1811. The town attracted a large number of Irish immigrants, and the cutting of timber was an important local industry. After the Civil War factories produced cheese, especially Limburger. In the 1930s New York State purchased large blocks of the town's marginal land for reforestation. Farming is the chief occupation for some residents in 2002. Glenmore Reservoir supplies water to the City of Oneida, and Fish Creek Reservoir supplies water to the City of Rome. Nonfarm residents commute to Camden or Rome or work at Harden Furniture (1902), a McConnellsville business that employed 600 workers in 2002.

Ansco. See GAF CORPORATION.

Anthony, Susan B(rownell) (*b* Adams, Mass, 15 Feb 1820; *d* Rochester, 13 Mar 1906). Woman suffrage advocate. Susan B. Anthony was the second daughter of seven children born to Quaker farmer and entrepreneur Daniel Anthony and Lucy Read Anthony. Her education was encouraged by her father's belief in self-sufficiency but varied with his fortunes. After her father moved from farming into textile manufacture, first in Massachusetts and subsequently in Battenville (Washington Co), she attended a private school founded by her father for his children and workers. While in school she also helped her mother with the domestic burdens imposed by a dozen boarders and in summers served as a governess for nearby families. When old enough she and her sister were sent to a Quaker boarding school outside Philadelphia. After one year there her family's bankruptcy forced Anthony to leave school to supplement the family income. She taught first in New Rochelle (Westchester Co) then at home in Washington Co before moving with her family to a farm near Rochester in 1845. The next year she took a teaching position at Canajoharie Academy in Montgomery Co and gained a new sense of independence, which prompted her to abandon the plain speech and

Susan B. Anthony, 1887.

dress of her Quaker heritage, though she pursued the values of her Quaker family by joining the Daughters of Temperance. By the 1850s Anthony found the local Quakers insufficiently committed to the antislavery cause, and she affiliated with the First Unitarian Church of Rochester.

ANTEBELLUM REFORM

By 1849, dissatisfied with teaching, Anthony returned to Rochester, devoted more time to temperance activities, and participated in a radical antislavery circle that met at the Anthony farm. Both Frederick Douglass and William Lloyd Garrison joined this group on occasion, and some members attended the 1848 Rochester women's rights meeting organized by Elizabeth Cady Stanton. In 1851 Anthony visited temperance activist Amelia Bloomer in Seneca Falls (Seneca Co) and met Stanton, who became Anthony's political collaborator for the next 50 years. In 1852 Stanton helped Anthony organize the Women's New York State Temperance Society, which paid Anthony to lecture across the state during the next year. The rejection of women's autonomous activities by conservatives in the temperance movement plus Anthony's frustration in trying to organize women who lacked economic independence shifted her focus to women's rights. In 1853 she began a petition drive for married women's property rights and woman suffrage, and in 1854–55 she continued to work—lecturing and gathering petitions—for these causes as an agent of the New York State Woman's Rights Committee. In 1856 the American Anti-Slavery Society hired her to organize in New York State. Using her considerable political skills and statewide contacts, Anthony spent the next few years speaking against slavery, facing down hostile crowds, including one Syracuse mob that dragged her effigy through the streets in 1861. Anthony interspersed this abolitionist work with ongoing efforts on behalf of women's rights, speaking out also for coeducation.

WOMAN SUFFRAGE ABOVE ALL

As the Civil War began, Anthony temporarily suspended her women's rights work. In 1863 she and Stanton founded the Women's Loyal National League, which ultimately delivered 400,000 antislavery petition signatures to Congress. After the war Anthony orchestrated the first national petition drive for woman suffrage and helped form the American Equal Rights Association (AERA), which sought universal suffrage regardless of race or gender. In 1867, on behalf of AERA, Anthony and Stanton petitioned the New York State Constitutional Convention in support of woman suffrage and also spoke in Kansas where a woman suffrage referendum appeared on that state's November ballot. Feeling betrayed by Republican leaders who opposed woman suffrage in both Kansas and New York, Stanton and Anthony accepted in fall 1867 the aid of racist millionaire Democrat George Francis Train, who lectured alongside them in Kansas and helped fund their suffrage newspaper, the *Revolution,* first published in 1868 from New York City.

Anthony's experience as publisher of the *Revolution* nurtured her long-term interest in laboring women, and in 1868 she urged women in the printing and sewing trades of New York City to form workingwomen's associations; she sought to persuade these workers that suffrage was a vital tool for wage justice. By 1869 Anthony's commitment to woman suffrage, above all else, fueled her opposition to the 15th Amendment, which enfranchised black men but did not enfranchise women. Conflict over the amendment dissolved the AERA. Anthony and Stanton then formed the National Woman Suffrage Association to continue the campaign for a constitutional amendment. Lucy Stone and others who favored the 15th Amendment founded the American Woman Suffrage Association to work for the vote on a state-by-state basis.

STRATEGIST, POLITICIAN, LEADER

In 1870 Anthony was forced to sell the *Revolution* and to assume responsibility for its $10,000 debt. She spent most of the next decade lecturing to earn this sum. Between lecture tours, in November 1872, Anthony registered and voted in Rochester's Eighth Ward to test women's de facto rights under the 14th and 15th Amendments. She was arrested for violating federal election law, convicted, and fined in a US district court in June 1873. For the remainder of the 1870s Anthony pursued woman suffrage nationwide independent of Stanton, but in the 1880s they collaborated to write their three-volume *History of Woman Suffrage* and to unite women's rights movements across the globe in the International Council of Women. Anthony and Lucy Stone also reconciled, merging the two US suffrage organizations in 1890. Although the new National American Woman Suffrage Association (NAWSA) elected Stanton president at Anthony's insistence, Anthony—organizing, fundraising, and strategizing—remained its leader. While her strategy focused on Congress, numerous state battles, like the 1894 New York State Constitutional Convention, enabled her to build a following among younger suffragists, who elected "Aunt Susan" president of NAWSA in 1892. Anthony retired from leadership in 1900 but remained active, publishing a fourth volume of the *History of Woman Suffrage* in 1903 and traveling to Europe in 1904. Anthony had long been active in Rochester civic affairs and local women's groups, and she played a central role persuading the University of Rochester to admit women, in part by raising $50,000 for that purpose. She attended a suffrage convention one month before her death. Susan B. Anthony lived at 19 Madison St in downtown Rochester from 1866 to 1906. It is now the Susan B. Anthony House, a museum and research center dedicated to maintaining her legacy. In 1979 the US Mint issued a new dollar coin with Anthony's likeness, making her the first American woman and the second New Yorker to appear on American coinage.

Anthony, Susan B., and Elizabeth Cady Stanton. *The Papers of Elizabeth Cady Stanton and Susan B. Anthony.* Ed. Patricia G. Holland and Ann D. Gordon (Wilmington, Del: Scholarly Resources Microfilms, 1991)

Barry, Kathleen. *Susan B. Anthony: A Biography of a Singular Feminist* (New York: New York Univ Press, 1988)

DuBois, Ellen Carol. *Feminism and Suffrage: The Emergence of an Independent Women's Movement in America, 1848–1869* (Ithaca: Cornell Univ Press, 1978)

Harper, Ida Husted. *The Life and Work of Susan B. Anthony,* 3 vols (1898; repr New York: Arno and New York Times, 1969)

Laura E. Free

Antifederalists. Political faction that opposed ratifying the US Constitution. When New York's convention convened at Poughkeepsie in June 1788, 46 of the 65 delegates were there to reject the proposed constitution for the new republic. These included Gov George Clinton, who presided, and one of Antifederalism's best thinkers, merchant Melancton Smith, who represented Dutchess Co. Like most of the newly independent states, New York's institutions offered possibilities for political participation that the colonial order had denied. The senate and assembly were much larger than the old council and assembly, and both were elected. Farmers, small traders, and artisans moved into both houses, usually after intense experience in the committees and provincial congresses of the independence crisis. They were not in politics to struggle with other Americans, but most did bring an attitude of suspicion toward "high-flyers," as Albany's Abraham Yates described people like his neighbor and rival Philip Schuyler or Schuyler's son-in-law Alexander Hamilton. To the Antifederalists, such men stood for continued dominance by the elite rather than for democracy.

Antifederalists did not begin as a self-conscious political party but instead coalesced during the legislative session of 1779 around the issues of taxation, punishment of loyalists, and wage and price controls to combat wartime inflation. Initially Clinton was not with the Antifederalists on any of those counts. Clinton worked well with the likes of Schuyler and John Jay, and he may not have known that the high-flyers thought him unfit for his office, because as late as 1783, for example, Hamilton was expressing respect for Clinton's conduct as governor.

By war's end, however, Clinton came to believe that state needs outranked federal, and he learned to cooperate with the rural, plain-people politicians he would lead in Poughkeepsie. By 1785 the Clintonian legislators were voting as a bloc (though the word Clintonian never was used). In 1784 and in 1786 they rejected proposals to give an independent taxing power to Congress, believing New York's absolute control over taxation within its borders was too important to yield. Abraham Yates called taxing power "that precious jewel, sovereignty." It was precisely to overcome such men and their attitudes, not just in New York but in other states as well, that people like Hamilton, George Washington, and James Madison coalesced into Federalism.

The attitude and the organization that acquired the semipejorative label Antifederalist during the ratification struggle existed well before 1787. They represented three major themes of the American Revolution: the expansion of political participation, the primacy of the separate states, and a degree of class awareness and class hostility. Nowhere was Antifederalism more fully developed or, for a time, more successful than in New York State.

See also US CONSTITUTION RATIFICATION.

Cornell, Saul. *The Other Founders: Anti-Federalism and the Dissenting Tradition in America, 1788–1828* (Chapel Hill: Univ of North Carolina Press, 1999)

Countryman, Edward. *A People in Revolution: The American Revolution and Political Society in New York, 1760–1790* (Baltimore: Johns Hopkins Univ Press, 1981)

De Pauw, Linda Grant. *The Eleventh Pillar: New York State and the Federal Constitution* (Ithaca: Cornell Univ Press, 1966)
Young, Alfred F. *The Democratic-Republicans of New York: The Origins, 1763–1797* (Chapel Hill: Univ of North Carolina Press, 1967)

Edward Countryman

Antimasonry. A 19th-century religious and political movement that emerged in New York State. Antimasons were antagonistic to Freemasonry and, in a larger sense, to secret societies and social elitism. Freemasonry had been well established in New England in the 1790s when emigrants from that region settled in Western and Central New York and brought their lodge organizations with them. At times it was difficult to move from one local lodge to another, owing to elites in a given community. When William Morgan, a stonemason, attempted to transfer from the Le Roy Lodge (Genesee Co) to a newly established lodge in nearby Batavia in 1825–26, he was denied membership, reputedly because of his questionable community standing—by some accounts he was unemployed and drank heavily. Their action led Morgan, with the help of publisher David C. Miller of Batavia, to write an exposé of Masonic secrets, *Illustrations of Masonry,* which was published in August 1826. Morgan was jailed in Canandaigua (Ontario Co) on trumped-up charges of petty theft, then abducted, presumably by Masons, and taken to Fort Niagara in Porter (Niagara Co), where he was seen alive for the last time. Stories circulated widely, ranging from his drowning in Lake Ontario to his escaping to Canada. In 1827 newspapers sensationalized the story as an act of conspiracy. When a body washed up on the shore of Lake Ontario, Thurlow Weed of Rochester declared it "Good enough Morgan," his goal being to build political capital rather than to resolve Morgan's fate. Gov De Witt Clinton spearheaded an investigation, but its inconclusive results were widely interpreted as a cover-up.

Hostility to Freemasonry, fomented by the Morgan incident, first coalesced into a primarily religious Antimasonic movement. Evangelical Christian leaders organized a religious crusade focused on Masonry as a false religion and an antidemocratic association. The crusade had a wide impact on Baptists, Methodists, and Presbyterians, although several Baptist regional associations were divided between Masonic and Antimasonic ministers and congregations. Out of religious Antimasonry emerged a slate of political candidates for the election of 1827 whose rhetoric was evangelical in tone and content. A series of local conventions or gatherings of sympathizers was held, culminating with the "Declaration of Independence" Convention at Le Roy on 4–5 July 1828, at which former Masons publicly renounced their previous affiliation. The Antimasonic Party's 1828 gubernatorial ticket ran Solomon Southwick, who finished third with 12% of the vote. The majority of votes for the Antimasons were in what Martin Van Buren called the "Infected district," a bloc of 16 counties west of the Finger Lakes. The election of 1828 was to be the high watermark of the religious crusaders, bringing statewide attention to the perceived evils of Masonry and a host of locally elected officials. Thereafter the religiously oriented Antimasons took up the cause against all secret societies and wrote polemics to be circulated across all religious denominations.

Political Antimasonry, led by Thurlow Weed, outmaneuvered the religious purists and outlasted them at the polls. This movement, essentially different from religious Antimasonry, was effectively created at meetings in Utica in August 1828, when Weed and Frederick Whittlesey proposed a statewide political strategy. Seeking a full investigation of the Morgan incident and prosecution of all potential criminals involved, their larger purpose was to unite a coalition against the Albany Regency, Andrew Jackson, and the Democrats, and they had distinct success. In 1828, 4 state senators and 17 assemblymen were elected as Antimasons, including Weed and Millard Fillmore. By 1830 the Antimasonic Party was the leading opposition to the Democrats in the state. The gubernatorial candidate it supported, Francis Granger, received 47.9% of the vote, and it added 3 more senators and 33 additional assemblymen to its roster. In 1832 the party held the nation's first presidential convention.

That year a coalition of Antimasons and National Republicans lost to the Democrats in the state and national elections, and the Antimasons then declined rapidly, keeping only nine seats in the 1833 assembly. Most of the party's leaders, like Weed and William H. Seward, transferred their alliance to what became, by 1834, the Whig Party. But before ending its brief political life, the Antimasonic Party rose from its Western New York roots and became a national party, the first genuine third party in American history. Its veterans, who had learned how to effectively fuse evangelical Christian fervor with populist politics, would shape the fortunes of the Whig and later the Republican Party in New York State for decades to come.

Brackney, William H. "Religious Antimasonry: The Genesis of a Political Party" (PhD diss, Temple Univ, 1976)
Ratner, Lorman. *Antimasonry: The Crusade and the Party* (Englewood Cliffs, NJ: Prentice-Hall, 1969)
Vaughn, William Preston. *The Antimasonic Party in the United States, 1826–1843* (Lexington: Univ Press of Kentucky, 1983)

William H. Brackney

antirent movement. Tenant farmers' movement from 1839 to 1852 that decisively influenced New York State politics in the 1840s and helped destroy the system of tenanted estates, replacing them with owner-operated farms. With 25,000–60,000 supporters, it was the most extensive farmers' movement in the United States before the Civil War and one of the most influential popular movements of the antebellum era.

LEASEHOLD ESTATES

New York State's leasehold estates originated in land grants made by the Dutch and English colonial governments in the 17th and 18th centuries. Grants ranged in size from a few thousand to hundreds of thousands of acres, totaling tens of millions of acres in all. Several recipients created leasehold estates or tracts on which tenant families held their land through long-term leases, paying an annual rent. Beginning in the 1730s the population of these estates grew dramatically

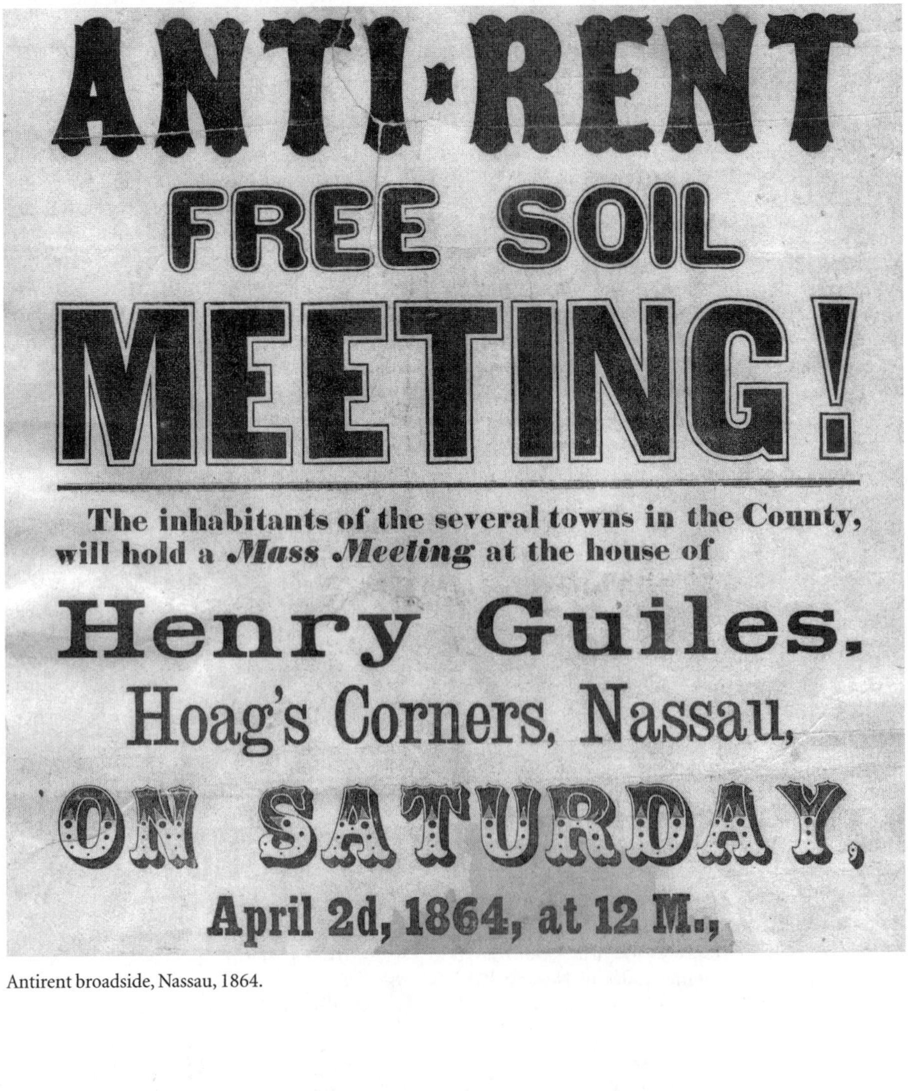
ANTI-RENT
FREE SOIL
MEETING!
The inhabitants of the several towns in the County, will hold a *Mass Meeting* at the house of
Henry Guiles,
Hoag's Corners, Nassau,
ON SATURDAY,
April 2d, 1864, at 12 M.,

Antirent broadside, Nassau, 1864.

as migrants from New England, southern and eastern New York State, Scotland and the German states took leases, but with an embargo placed on European goods in 1807 and an ensuing depression, migration to frontier areas was temporarily halted. By the 1810s some two dozen tenanted estates, totaling about 2 million acres (809,000 ha), spread across 16 counties in the mid-Hudson Valley and the surrounding mountains, the foothills of the Catskills, and the Mohawk and Susquehanna Valleys. By the 1840s leasehold tenants numbered about 260,000 people, about one-tenth of the state's population.

Legally, the relationship between landlords and estate farmers was modern and nonfeudal, founded on civic equality and the cash nexus. Tenants were legally free and could sell out and leave at any time. They owed landlords a specified yearly rent and were obliged to abide by certain restrictions on their use of the land. Typically, landlords reserved all mineral and manufacturing rights on the land as well as part of the sale price whenever a tenant sold his farm, but this contractual connection was embedded in a broader patron-client relationship. Landlords maintained tenant loyalty by tolerating irregular payments, occasionally forgiving a portion of the rent, assisting poor tenants, and subsidizing community institutions. In return, tenants deferred to their superiors, publicly affirming their loyalty and affection and voting as directed. But they also made the most of landlords' lenience, minimizing their rent payments (a strategy that led to large accumulations of unpaid rents) and ignoring landlords' prohibitions against cutting timber on unleased estate lands. Landlords' and tenants' embrace of benevolence and deference may not have been sincere, and not all tenants were deferential as antilandlord rebellions erupted in the 1750s, 1760s, 1790s, and 1810s. But these practices defined the normal relationship between them, ensuring widespread social peace on the estates for 50 years.

Origins of the Movement

Peace between landlords and tenants broke down between 1819 and 1840. After the American Revolution, landlords began dividing their estates among several heirs and ended their former practice of marrying to consolidate different families' fortunes, which diminished the size of estates and incomes enjoyed by heirs. To make up for lost income proprietors after 1819 intensified pressure on tenants to pay rents, and most began suing them. They also ended their tolerance of standing-timber theft, bringing unauthorized lumbermen to court. In several counties, including Ulster, Schoharie, and Montgomery, large numbers of landlords replaced their long-term leases with those of between one and five years, ending tenants' status as economically secure, semi-independent proprietors. Tenants responded by dragging out court proceedings, organizing rent boycotts, and legally challenging their landlords' titles to their estates. These efforts were sporadic and local, and a unified, well-organized movement did not emerge before 1839.

The conflict between landlords and tenants became a crisis on 26 Jan 1839 with the death of Stephen Van Rensselaer III, the proprietor of the 750,000-acre (304,000 ha) estate of Rensselaerswyck [now in Albany and Rensselaer Cos]. His personal debts totaled $400,000, about the amount owed him by his tenants. Van Rensselaer had instructed his executors to pay his debts by collecting the rent owed him; if they failed, his heirs would assume the debt. Stephen Van Rensselaer IV, heir of the half of Rensselaerswyck that lay in Albany Co, began prosecuting selected tenants in the courts. After a failed attempt at negotiating, tenants in the towns of the Helderberg Mountains in Albany Co initiated a rent boycott. During the summer and fall of 1839, Albany Co lawmen marched into the hill towns to serve legal process on boycotting tenants. Farmers threatened, assaulted, and robbed them of their legal papers. The sheriff sent out increasingly larger posses, which were met by ever larger groups of farmers. By early December 1,500 tenants turned back 500 men sent by the sheriff, and Gov William H. Seward sent in the state militia, while publicly urging tenants to seek legislative redress and promising his office's help in doing so. The insurgents embraced the governor's offer. The crowds in the hill towns went home, and the antirenters (as they began to call themselves) began a petition campaign.

Antirent at Flood Tide

Between 1839 and 1845, the antirent movement gained momentum from the western half of Rensselaerswyck to a score of estates in 11 counties (Albany, Rensselaer, Schoharie, Columbia, Delaware, Greene, Ulster, Sullivan, Otsego, Montgomery, and Washington), with the most powerful antirent presence in the first 5. People signing antirent petitions in 1845 numbered 25,000, and a movement newspaper claimed that 50,000–60,000 tenants actively supported the cause.

The antirent campaign was never a monolithic movement but had three wings, each pursuing a distinct strategy. Antirenters created town and county associations that oversaw rent boycotts, collected funds, coordinated legal campaigns against the landlords, lobbied the legislature, and mobilized tenants through meetings, picnics, dances, and rallies. Starting in 1844, they also entered electoral politics, fielding their own candidates for town and county offices and the state legislature. Finally, they formed the "Indians," heavily armed and grotesquely disguised bands of boys and young men dressed in calico gowns and masks of sheepskin or painted muslin, who protected tenant boycotters by driving landlords' agents and lawmen off the estates. The Indians also intimidated and assaulted tenants who supported the landlords or paid rent, ensuring unanimous support for the antirent cause.

For all their diversity, the antirenters shared a common vision and set of demands. Their core aims were to end landlords' control over estate lands and to distribute those lands among the tenants who farmed them. They justified these objectives on the grounds that the landlords' titles were fraudulently obtained, a legitimate claim in most cases. And, drawing on a long tradition of antimonopoly and republican thought in the United States, they declared that large accumulations of land stripped laborers of the freedom promised by the American Revolution. Freedom, they argued, could only be realized when every head of household owned the land he farmed. In petitioning the legislature, antirenters demanded a legal prohibition on landlords' right of distress. In petitioning the legislature, antirenters voiced three demands: a legal prohibition on landlords' right of distress—the power to seize and sell tenants' personal property to recover unpaid rent; taxation of landlords' rent income; and a law enabling tenants sued for back rents to challenge the validity of their landlords' titles as a defense.

Antirenters in Politics

The antirenters gained significant influence in the political arena. In 1845 they sent seven antirent candidates to the state assembly and one to the state senate, elected a US congressman, and convinced the leaders of both major parties that they would provide the swing votes to determine the next gubernatorial election. Whig and Democratic Party activists both made alliances with the antirenters, serving the tenants as speakers, newspaper editors, lobbyists, and candidates for elective offices, as did members of the National Reform Association, a land reform organization based in New York City. In 1846 the legislature abolished landlords' right of distress and taxed landlords' rent income. The leaders of both parties also endorsed a law that would allow tenants to buy their farms at the death of the current landlords. That law failed to pass because the leaders of each party were unwilling to allow their partisan rivals to take credit for its passage.

The heyday of the antirenters' political power was also a moment of political frustration. The demands that the legislature granted were minor. Most legislators opposed the insurgents' main demand—a law allowing tenants to "plead title" when sued for unpaid rents—as violating the federal constitution and the rights of property. Moreover, the antirenters' electoral gains came just as the Indians were being crushed. When the Indians killed Deputy Sheriff Osman Steele at a distress sale in Andes (Delaware Co) in August 1845, Gov Silas Wright declared Delaware, Columbia, and Schoharie Cos in insurrection and called out the militia. Posses and the militia swept through Delaware and Columbia Cos, making mass arrests, intimidating antirenters, destroying property, and serving legal papers on tenants who boycotted rents. In the face of this repression, the Indians disbanded, leaving thousands of tenants vulnerable to eviction.

The movement also suffered from bitter internal divisions. From early 1845 on, antirenters fought over whether to disband the Indians. Beginning in May 1845, Whig and Democratic allies of the antirenters engaged in a fierce factional dispute with Thomas Ainge Devyr, a National Reformer and editor of the antirent *Albany Freeholder.* Devyr and his supporters campaigned to win the antirenters over to the National Reform Association's program for national land reform and to forge an electoral alliance between the two movements. His Whig and Democratic rivals sought to make similar alliances between the antirenters and the reform wings of their parties. This conflict reached a climax during the 1846 gubernatorial election. While Devyr and the National Reformers worked to create an independent land-reform party, Whig activists won control of the state antirent convention, pushing through the nomination of the Whig gubernatorial nominee, John Young. The National Reformers and several Democrats bolted the convention and formed a separate Free Soil ticket, but Young triumphed in November, when the vast majority of antirent votes gave him the margin of victory over his Democratic rival.

Decline of the Movement

The 1846 election marked the high point of antirent electoral strength. In addition to providing the swing votes that won Young the governorship, tenant militants sent 11 antirent representatives to the state assembly. But Young's nomination by the antirent state convention had alienated militants who had hoped for an independent antirent political organization and had convinced Democratic antirenters that their Whig rivals had won control of the movement. From 1847 on, the campaign was beset by partisan squabbles, as Democratic and Whig antirenters sought to win control of county and state nominating conventions. Amidst these conflicts, antirent voting strength collapsed, and militants lost their former influence in the legislature. Between 1848 and 1860, not a single antirent measure passed the legislature.

At the same time, the suppression of the Indians left landlords free to prosecute or evict rent boycotters, and proprietors flooded their estates with eviction notices. In this context of political stalemate and legal prosecution, tenants began to buy out their landlords' interest in their farms. All but a handful of tenants did so or left the estates, and the antirent movement collapsed. The *Albany Freeholder,* the last surviving antirent newspaper, closed its doors in 1851, and the antirent state central committee declined to call a state convention in 1852. Rump movements survived in Albany, Rensselaer, Montgomery, and Otsego Cos, but these were sporadic, weak remnants. By the late 1880s, these insurgencies had also ended.

Legacies

The antirent movement left a lasting impact on New York State's society and politics. Throughout their campaign, the antirenters had refused landlords' offers to sell their land, so tenants' buyout of their landlords' property after 1846 marked the defeat of the insurgency, not its victory. Nevertheless, that buyout destroyed the leasehold system in New York State and the United States, ending a system of property and class relations that had shaped the lives of over a quarter of a million people. The antirenters' political influence was just as decisive. The movement created bitter divisions between conservatives and reformers in both the Whig and Democratic Parties, contributing to the collapse of the Whig Party after 1852. Just as important, the antirenters influenced the policies and ideologies of the major political parties. By 1845 a new, bipartisan consensus emerged that the leasehold system was hostile to American liberties. More generally, political leaders came to oppose any set of class relations that smacked of deference, seemed to create permanent inequalities, or retarded the free exchange of land. Many endorsed a radically new state power, that of weakening or destroying systems of property and class relations that undermined freedom. Finally, the antirenters injected the land issue into New York State politics. Antirent leaders were the first major party politicians in the state, and among the first in the nation, to call for a homestead act. In the mid-1850s, these innovations found their way into the ideology and platform of the Republican Party.

Christman, Henry. *Tin Horns and Calico: A Decisive Episode in the Emergence of Democracy* (New York: Henry Holt, 1945)

Huston, Reeve. *Land and Freedom: Rural Society, Popular Protest, and Party Politics in Antebellum New York* (New York: Oxford Univ Press, 2000)

McCurdy, Charles W. *The Antirent Era in New York Law and Politics, 1839–1861* (Chapel Hill: Univ of North Carolina Press, 2001)

Reeve Huston

anti-Semitism. Discrimination and violence against Jews. Gov Petrus Stuyvesant tried to exclude Jews from New Netherland and implemented discriminatory laws against them when the Dutch West India Company (WIC) ordered him to admit 23 Jewish refugees in 1654. Some regulations were overturned after Jewish appeals. The English, concerned about the loyalty of their new subjects, guaranteed existing rights and extended some new ones, allowing Jews to own land, participate in retail trade, and worship in public, although they were denied citizenship. New York Colony was the only British colony that allowed Jews the franchise, but this was not untroubled. After a disputed election in 1737, the Colonial Assembly unanimously passed a resolution asserting that Jews could not vote in provincial elections, but they nonetheless remained on the election rolls. In 1743 a mob attacked a Jewish funeral procession in New York City, and there were reports of vandalism at the Jewish cemetery off Chatham Square at 55 St. James Place in 1746 and 1751. However, by the New York State Constitution of 1777, the state became the first political jurisdiction within the Christian world to guarantee the free exercise of religion without discrimination or preference and political equality regardless of religion. These rights did not mean that anti-Semitism was a thing of the past. The rise of Naphtali Phillips to the vice presidency of the Democratic-Republican Society in New York City in 1795, for example, drew "tribe of Shylock" jibes from his opponents. Prominent newspaper publisher James Gordon Bennett used anti-Jewish slurs to vilify the Jewish politician Mordecai M. Noah (1785–1851) in the *New York Herald.* The *Herald*'s revival of the Damascus blood libel incident contributed to a mob attack on a Brooklyn synagogue in 1850.

Discrimination against Jews in employment, business, residence, and accommodation persisted well into the 20th century. When the practice of credit reporting developed in the 1840s, negative stereotypes pervaded reports on Jewish businesses. In 1866 seven major fire insurance companies secretly agreed not to insure Jewish businesses, causing widespread Jewish protests when they were exposed. Anti-Semitism increased in the late 19th century as the numbers of Jews increased. In 1877 Henry Hilton set off a wave of discrimination in public accommodations that would last nearly a century when he had his Grand Union Hotel in Saratoga refuse to honor the reservation of a prominent Jewish banker, a practice that led to the establishment of alternative Jewish accommodations and resorts. Two years later Hilton sponsored a meeting of an American Society for the Suppression of the Jews, held at his Saratoga hotel. The Lake Placid Club, founded by Melvil Dewey in 1895, was another grand hotel that excluded Jews, although when knowledge of this became widely known, Jewish complaints forced Dewey in 1905 to resign from his long-time position as state librarian.

Early 20th Century

In 1902 the funeral procession of Rabbi Jacob Joseph was attacked by factory workers in Manhattan. Police arrived and clubbed the Jewish mourners. An official investigation condemned the police, but those involved went unpunished and police harassment continued. In 1916 the first Jewish intern at Kings County Hospital was physically attacked, and the hospital stayed entirely non-Jewish for another decade. In 1914 a dean at Columbia University expressed concern over rising Jewish enrollments, and quotas against Jewish students were applied extensively after 1922, dramatically dropping their percentage from roughly 40% to 20%. Elsewhere in the state the discrimination in private colleges, especially outside of New York City, was even more pronounced, as was pervasive discrimination in many professional schools. Widespread employment discrimination extended from elite law firms to large segments of education, utilities, insurance, and banking industries. In small towns like Amsterdam (Montgomery Co), Jewish boys could not even deliver newspapers. In New York City, where Jews were the best-educated quarter of the population, they held only 10% of white-collar jobs. Jews who earned adequate incomes found themselves barred from much of the state's better housing, particularly in suburbs and some upscale New York City neighborhoods, through court-enforced clauses in real estate contracts that restricted sales to Christians.

Discrimination worsened under the pressure of the Great Depression and the influence of anti-Semitic propaganda stemming from Rome and Berlin. Nazi Germany's agents infiltrated German American organizations statewide, and the German-American Bund developed a strong following among recent immigrants from Germany. They allied with the mostly Irish American followers of the radio priest Charles Coughlin in the Christian Front, which issued a call to "liquidate the Jews" in 1938. Christian Front gangs initiated least 40 violent assaults on Jews around New York City in the late 1930s, attacks often ignored by a police force that had more than 400 Christian Front members in its ranks. Christian Fronters helped pack the Bund's 1939 rally in Madison Square Garden in Manhattan with 19,000 enthusiasts chanting "Heil Hitler." Violent attacks against Jews continued during the war years, and polling data suggest that anti-Semitism increased through 1946.

After World War II

The steady rise in anti-Semitism, combined with revulsion over revelations about the Holocaust, created a backlash after the war. The mass media campaigned against prejudice, and in 1945 the state outlawed religious bias in hiring. In 1948 restrictive covenants in real estate transactions were declared unconstitutional by the US Supreme Court. The same year New York State created the SUNY system, in part in response to Jewish and African American complaints about discrimination at the state's private colleges, and passed legislation outlawing college discrimination. By the end of 1949, 64% of commercial employment agencies admitted accepting discriminatory orders, down from 88% in 1946. Although discrimination in college admissions was outlawed, the practice continued at some level. For example, in Ithaca, Cornell University's Medical School continued to accept white Protestant applicants at five times the rate of Jewish applicants into the 1950s.

Several dozen incidents of anti-Semitic vandalism marred the New York metropolitan area in 1959–60. By the 1960s open discrimination against Jews was declining rapidly in New York State, but anecdotal evidence suggests that prejudice remained strong in many small towns and rural areas. Anti-Jewish prejudices also remained strong among African Americans, becoming a public issue in the mid-1960s during desegregation struggles in Mount Vernon (Westchester Co) and in the 1968 conflict over school decentralization in New York City. By 1985 the Nation of Islam was the leading force in promoting African American anti-Semitism, and a rally at Madison Square Garden attracted more than 20,000. Black-Jewish relations have remained strained, especially when rioters in Brooklyn killed a Hasidic Jew after a rabbi's driver ran down a black child in 1991. New York State's 352 reported anti-Semitic incidents in 1999 greatly outnumbered those of any other state, but these were most likely attributable to its large number of Jews rather than to any particular prevalence of anti-Semitism.

Dinnerstein, Leonard. *Antisemitism in America* (New York: Oxford Univ Press, 1994)
Gerber, David A., ed. *Anti-Semitism in American History* (Urbana: Univ of Illinois Press, 1986)
Sarna, Jonathan D. *Jacksonian Jew: The Two Worlds of Mordecai Noah* (New York: Holmes & Meier, 1981)

Stan Nadel

antiwar movements. See PEACE AND ANTIWAR MOVEMENTS.

Antwerp. Town (pop 1,793) and village (pop 716) in NE Jefferson Co. Settled in 1803, the town was formed from Le Ray in 1810. At the village, a dam was built across the Indian River in 1805; the Village of Antwerp was incorporated in 1853, acquiring railroad service from the Rome, Watertown and Ogdensburg in 1855. Iron mining, particularly at the Sterling and Parish mines, brought great prosperity from 1836 through the 1880s. Dairy farming, however, was the town's most important industry through World War II. It supported several cheese factories, including the large Baumert plant (1889). In 1931 the US government annexed one-third of the town for Pine Camp (now Fort Drum), devastating the dairy industry. The Baumert factory, bought by Borden in 1928, closed in 1947. The town benefited little from Fort Drum's 1984–89 expansion, and it is primarily a bedroom community for other parts of the county.

Laura Lynne Scharer

Apalachin meeting. On 14 Nov 1957 federal alcohol tax unit agents accompanied by state and local authorities arrived at the Apalachin (Tioga Co) home of Joseph Barbara, a bottling-plant owner, to investigate possible organized crime activity. State police had learned that Barbara's son was booking rooms at a nearby motel and spotted out-of-state license plates at the Barbara home. They suspected the meeting had been called to discuss control of the garbage-hauling racket or the recent death of mob boss Albert Anastasia, although the actual explanation for the meeting was never identified. After a foot chase through wooded terrain bordering the property and a police roadblock, 65 men were apprehended, including some prominent names associated with underworld activity such as Vito Genovese, Carlo Gambino, and Paul Castellano. In all, 153 arrests were made. The incident caused FBI director J. Edgar Hoover to focus more heavily on mob activity. The publicity generated by the raid sparked a new fascination with organized crime in popular culture.

"65 Hoodlums Seized in a Raid and Run Out of Upstate Village," *New York Times,* 15 Nov 1957

Joann Lindstrom

Appalachia. A geographical region in the eastern United States marked by hills, mountains, and plateaus. Also a term linked with a pattern of economic development based on extractive industries and the exploitation of natural resources that often results in poverty. The word describes a folk culture, claimed by some as a precious heritage but repudiated by others as the source of derogatory stereotypes. Washington Irving's Catskill Mountains character Rip Van Winkle, which first appeared in 1820, was in many ways a prototype of the fictional "hillbilly" stereotype.

The Appalachian Upland region encompasses half of New York State. Although lands north and east of the Hudson and Mohawk Valleys are part of the Appalachian range, the territory is generally not considered part of Appalachia because of social and cultural differences. Starting from the Hudson and Mohawk Valleys, seven subsections of New York's Appalachia are commonly identified: the Catskill Mountains, the Delaware Hills, the Helderberg Hills, the Susquehanna Hills, the Finger Lakes Hills, the Cattaraugus Hills area, and the Allegheny Hills. Throughout the 17th and 18th centuries, the Iroquois controlled the natural corridors of access to the continental interior. Despite periods of peaceful coexistence between American Indians and white settlers in areas such as the upper Susquehanna River basin, English competition with the French over control of the inland region of New York Colony at first limited white settlement in the upland.

The western portion of the upland was not settled until after 1810. Germans and Scots-Irish were strongly represented among the immigrants who entered the region in the late 18th and early 19th centuries and had an influence in the southern Appalachians as well. Later arrivals would change this ethnic mixture, creating patterns similar to those in other parts of the Appalachian region. Particularly important in the Southern Tier were Irish workers who arrived with the canals and railroads of the mid–19th century and southern and eastern European immigrants who came to the region's industries later in the century.

Although contemporary scholars delineate the area of Appalachia differently, the most recognized boundaries are those of the Appalachian Regional Commission (ARC), a federal agency established in 1965 to address the economic problems of Appalachia. The original ARC boundary in the legislation did not include New York State, but by August the counties of Chautauqua, Cattaraugus, Allegany, Steuben, Schuyler, Chemung, Tompkins, Tioga, Cortland, Broome, Chenango, Otsego, and Delaware were admitted to ARC membership. In 1967 Schoharie was included. Many political leaders and activists in the Appalachian South viewed the effort to expand the scope of the ARC as a boondoggle, an attempt to deflect federal antipoverty initiatives from economically devastated areas such as the coalfields of eastern Kentucky and West Virginia that had long been considered as part of the Appalachian region. New York governor Nelson A. Rockefeller and US senator Robert F. Kennedy urged that the New York counties be included so that the state could use ARC funds for highway construction and economic development.

Despite the lack of a historic Appalachian identity, the counties of New York's Southern Tier are tied to the rest of the Appalachian region by geography, settlement history, and economics. Geographically the region is part of the Appalachian Plateau. It is predominantly rural, sprinkled with small cities and towns and one major metropolitan area (Binghamton). Major industries include agriculture, recreation (especially in the Catskills), and extractive industries based on timber, stone, clay, glass, and oil (in the western area). Reliance on extractive industries and exploitation of natural resources has limited economic development. As with other parts of Appalachia, patterns of economic decline and stagnation and a high rate of out-migration have marked the region since 1950. The area is also marked by declining agriculture on marginal farmland. All of the Appalachian counties were below the New York State median household income for 1999 of $43,393. From 1990 to 2000 populations declined in 10 of 14 ARC counties in New York State.

See also CLIMATE AND WEATHER.

Raitz, Karl B., and Richard Ulack, with Thomas R. Leinbach. *Appalachia, A Regional Geography: Land, People, and Development* (Boulder, Colo: Westview Press, 1984)

Penny Messinger

Appalachian Trail. Continuously marked walking path from Maine to Georgia. Eighty-eight miles (142 km) of the Appalachian National Scenic Trail meander through southeastern New York State on the footpath's 2,167 mi (3,487 km) journey from Mt Katahdin, Maine, to Springer Mountain, Ga. Regional planner Benton MacKaye of Massachusetts first proposed the trail in a 1921 journal article. He envisioned it as a nature retreat where eastern urbanites could recreate and recuperate from city living. MacKaye's vision prompted construction by volunteers from the newly formed New York–New Jersey Trail Conference, and the first section of trail built solely as part of the Appalachian Trail opened in 1923 in Bear Mountain State Park. In 1937 the trail was completed with the construction of the last section in Maine. The National Trails Systems Act of 1968 designated the Appalachian Trail the first National Scenic Trail and made provisions for acquiring the trail's right-of-way, both inside and outside federal lands. The Appalachian Trail Conference, under the auspices of the National Park Service, administers the trail, which is largely maintained by volunteers through local hiking clubs and trail conferences.

In New York State the Appalachian Trail passes just 28 miles (45 km) outside New York City. On the Connecticut side, the footpath enters New York State in the Town of Dover (Dutchess Co) and exits to New Jersey west of Greenwood Lake. On a ridge overlooking this lake is Prospect Rock, the trail's highest point in New York State at 1,433 feet (437 m). North of Pawling (Dutchess Co), the Metro-North Railroad from New York City has an Appalachian Trail stop for hikers. The trail still serves MacKaye's intended purpose. In 2000 the trail had 564 through hikers (those who walked the entire trail) and thousands of day hikers.

Appalachian Trail Conference, http://www.appalachiantrail.org

Chazin, Daniel D., ed. *Appalachian Trail Guide to New York–New Jersey*, 14th ed. (Harpers Ferry, W Va: Appalachian Trail Conference, 1998)

MacKaye, Benton. "An Appalachian Trail: A Project in Regional Planning," *Journal of the American Institute of Architects* 9 (Oct 1921): 325–30

Julie Polhemus

Apple Boy. In September 1940 a handsome, curly-haired, 15-year-old boy, thousands of miles away from his home in Wales Hollow (Erie Co), was caught in the act of stealing an apple from a refrigerator. When his parents heard from him in December, he had been tried, convicted, and sentenced to a three-year term in Louisiana's state penitentiary, having elected prison over the indeterminate, reform-school punishment he would have received had the court known he was a juvenile. The Apple Boy, as the press labeled John Robert Swanson, became a national cause célèbre, a symbol of wronged innocence and of judicial malfeasance. Amid public cries of injustice, Swanson's charges were reduced to juvenile delinquency, and he was released to the custody of his mother, who brought him back to Western New York, where it was widely expected that Swanson would temper his rebellious conduct and rejoin the community. "Never again," he said as he stepped off the bus in Buffalo. "No 'open road' for me."

But the Apple Boy's troubles were far from over. In March 1942 he took a car, stole guns and ammunition in Fredonia (Chautauqua Co), robbed a diner near Silver Creek (Chautauqua Co) at gunpoint, and was caught by police after a high-speed chase along the Lake Erie shoreline. Pleading guilty to a reduced charge, Swanson received an indefinite sentence in the state industrial school at West Coxsackie (Greene Co). Three years later he was dead on a battlefield in Luxembourg, a rebel in an age of conformity.

Graebner, William. "The Apple Boy: Individual and Community in the Era of the Second World War," *New York Folklore* 10 (Summer–Fall 1984): 77–88

William Graebner

apples. Apples were introduced to the United States by European colonists in the 17th century, and by the early 18th century orchards were established in the Hudson and Mohawk River valleys. By the 1730s the first commercial apple tree nursery was operating in Oyster Bay [now in Nassau Co], and by the 1750s, somewhat farther west on Long Island in Newtown [now Elmhurst, Queens Co], the Newtown Pippin became the first widely known American apple variety. By the turn of the 19th century other New York State apple varieties became popular, including the Esopus Spitzenburg in the Kingston (Ulster Co) area, the Wagener in Penn Yan (Yates Co), and the Northern Spy in East Bloomfield (Ontario Co). Settlers in Central and Western New York brought apple seedlings with them, and apple trees were soon ubiquitous. Around 1800 the peripatetic nurseryman John Chapman (1774–1845), better known as Johnny Appleseed, spent a year in Olean (Cattaraugus Co) before moving to points farther west.

Apple cultivars proliferated during the 19th century with the development of the state as a national center of horticulture and fruit production. The 1855 census reported 13,668,830.75 bushels (481,676,000 l) of apples produced in New York State. Except for New York Co, apples were grown in every county of the state, with three in Central New York—Oneida, Onondaga, and Otsego, in that order—leading the state in production. Commercial fruit growing expanded following the Civil War, and cultivars that did well in shipping and in cold storage, such as Baldwin, gained importance.

Most new cultivars came from chance seedlings discovered to have desirable qualities. For example, Jonathan, an Esopus Spitzenburg seedling on the farm of Philip Rick in Woodstock (Ulster Co), and Northern Spy, from seeds planted in the orchard of Heman Chapin in East Bloomfield (Ontario Co), were recognized as useful commercial varieties in the mid–19th century. They were disseminated widely in apple-growing areas of the state. With the opening of the New York State Agricultural Experiment Station in Geneva (Ontario Co) in 1882, controlled breeding programs replaced reliance on haphazard discovery. Nurserymen such as George Ellwanger and Patrick Barry in Rochester and William and Thomas Smith in Geneva, among others, contributed scions to be grafted on 695 existing apple trees on the 125-acre (51 ha) farm purchased for the fledgling station. Apple breeding at the station began in 1888 with the planting of open-pollinated seedlings. In 1899 New York State was the nation's largest producer of apples with 24,111,257 bushels (849,656,500 l).

There were at least 345 different cultivars of apple growing in the state in 1900, and examples of each were presented in the New York horticultural exhibit at the Pan-American Exposition in Buffalo in 1901. These apples for exhibition were placed in the Buffalo Cold Storage Co at 34°F (1.1°C). Samuel D. Willard, the Geneva nurseryman and fruit grower who superintended the exhibition, used this opportunity to test their keeping qualities. At that time the ammonia-compression technology was new, and the variables involved in storing fruit for market were not yet well understood. Still, by the early 20th century, cold storage, which extended the season for apple sales, was transforming the way apples were marketed. In late 1902, for example, there were a million barrels of apples in cold storage in the state, two-thirds of them in warehouses west of Syracuse.

In 1905 *The Apples of New York* by S. A. Beach, N. O. Booth, and O. M. Taylor described nearly 700 named cultivars of apple, 123 originating in the state. At that time Baldwin and Rhode Island Greening accounted for two-thirds of the apples produced for market. The Geneva Experiment Station continued to introduce new varieties of apples throughout the 20th century, includ-

NEW YORK STATE APPLE CULTIVARS, 1904 AND 1999–2001

1904	1999–2001
Baldwin	McIntosh[a]
Rhode Island Greening	Empire
Northern Spy	Rome
Tompkins King	Red Delicious
Roxbury	Ida Red
Golden Russet	Cortland
Hubbardston	Golden Delicious
Esopus Spitzenburg	Crispin (Mutsu)
Black Gilliflower	Rhode Island Greening
Ben Davis	Jonamac
Tolman Sweet	Jonagold
Twenty Ounce	Paula Red
Pumpkin Sweet	Spartan
Swaar	Twenty Ounce
Westfield Seek-No-Further	Macoun
Fameuse	Northern Spy
Fall Pippin	Gala
Yellow Bellflower	Gingergold

Sources: S. A. Beach, N. O. Booth, and O. M. Taylor, *The Apples of New York*, 2 vols (1905); New York Agricultural Statistics Service, 2001 Annual Summary, http://www.nass.usda.gov/ny/01jan/frt0102.htm.

Note: Listed in order of commercial significance by bushels.

[a]In 1904 the McIntosh was the 26th most widely produced cultivar.

Compiled by Paul Grebinger

ing the Cortland (1915), Macoun (1924), Lodi (1924), Empire (1966), Jonagold (1968), and Jonamac (1972). During the 1930s and 1940s Cornell University scientists pioneered the development of "controlled atmosphere" storage, which significantly slows the ripening process and extends the time apples may be stored. The marketing of apples developed over the course of the century, and new apple products were introduced. The Duffy-Mott Co, the combination of the Mott Co founded in Bouckville (Madison Co) in 1842 and the Rochester-based W. B. Duffy Cider Co and known primarily for its cider and vinegar, introduced its first applesauce in 1930. Trade organizations were formed, such as the Western New York Apple Growers Association in 1950.

The list of apple cultivars grown in New York State in the early 21st century reflects significant change from the list of 100 years earlier. This transformation in apple cultivars can be ascribed to changes in consumer taste. Apples for cider were replaced by apples for the table, and consumers have demanded apples that are more flavorful and sweeter, have firmer texture, and are more attractive and colorful. In 2001 McIntosh and Empire accounted for almost 30% of the apples produced for market (based on total bushels produced for 1999–2001). State apple production of 23,810,000 bushels (839,040,400 l) that year was second only to Washington State. At that time there were 695 farms in New York State growing apples on a total of 44,563 acres (18,034 ha), and the top apple-producing counties and acreage were Wayne, 17,156 acres (6,943 ha); Ulster, 5,669 acres (2,294 ha); and Orleans, 4,805 acres (1,945 ha).

Beach, S. A., N. O. Booth, and O. M. Taylor. *The Apples of New York,* 2 vols. Report of the New York Agricultural Experiment Station for the Year 1903 (Albany: J. B. Lyon, 1905)

Chapman, P. J., and E. H. Glass. *The First 100 Years of the New York State Agricultural Experiment Station at Geneva, NY.* Ed. R. E. Krauss (Geneva, NY: NYS Agricultural Experiment Station, 1999)

Grebinger, Paul, and Ellen M. Grebinger. *To Dress and Keep the Earth: The Nurseries and Nurserymen of Geneva, New York* (Geneva, NY: Geneva Historical Society, 1993)

Way, Roger D. "Apple Cultivars Introduced by the New York State Agricultural Experiment Station, 1914–1968," *Search* (Mar 1971): 1–84

Paul Grebinger

apportionment and districting. Apportionment is the distribution of specific numbers of seats in a legislative body among geographic areas. Districting is the drawing of electoral boundary lines within geographic areas. Apportionment and districting are generally the most overtly political, partisan, and personal subjects with which legislators deal. They have a direct impact on the fortunes of the parties and the careers of individual politicians, and because the processes are critical in determining the composition of a legislative body, they affect the disposition of every issue. The legislature generally redistricts following each decennial federal census, subject to gubernatorial veto. From 1825 to 1925, however, state censuses allowed more frequent actions; court rulings have at times necessitated intermediate revisions; and political circumstances once caused a 26-year interval.

Independence to 1894

The first state constitution (1777) established a 24-member senate and 70-member assembly. The state was divided into four senate districts, each apportioned a number of senators to be chosen at large by the district's electors, constitutionally defined as "freeholders . . . possessed . . . of the value of £100 over and above all debts and incumbrances." Assembly seats were apportioned to whole counties, some of which were combined. In counties with more than one member, all were elected at large. A year after the 1790 census, both houses of the legislature were reapportioned, with additional future seats authorized based on each area's growth. The 1801 convention enlarged the assembly to 100 members. The 1821 Constitutional Convention changed the apportionment base to "inhabitants excluding aliens, paupers and persons of colour not taxed," amended in 1874 to "inhabitants excluding aliens," a formulation that remained in effect until replaced in 1969 by total population.

The 1821 Constitution divided the state into eight senate districts with four seats each, prohibited the division of counties to form senate districts, and required every county except Hamilton (since its founding by far the least populated county in the state) to have at least one assembly seat. This ensured representation for all eligible residents but made it impossible to achieve population equality among districts. The 1846 convention mandated single-member districts in both houses. It authorized the legislature to draw senate district boundaries everywhere except in New York Co, where the Board of Supervisors was thus empowered. Counties apportioned two or more assembly seats were to be districted by their governing bodies.

Until the late 19th century, these procedures caused relatively little controversy. There were occasional clashes over differing interpretations and alleged violations of the rules, but these were generally not of an "upstate versus downstate" nature. However, as the urban centers, and especially New York City, began to grow rapidly due to the post–Civil War increase in immigration, the disputes took on more overtly sectional, partisan, and ethnic tones. It became clear that trying to equalize populations among districts, even within the limits imposed by various restrictive rules, would inevitably lead to significant decreases in the rural counties' representation. Thus, when the 1875 state census indicated that 12 upstate counties would lose assembly seats if past procedures were followed, the legislature waited for four years and then arbitrarily awarded several smaller counties more seats than others with larger populations.

To ensure passage of a controversial 1892 reapportionment, several rural counties were awarded additional assembly seats that under the traditional procedures would have gone to the most populated counties. The act was thus highly unpopular in urban areas, but it was attacked in rural regions too, because use of an alternative apportionment method could have enabled several upstate counties to retain seats they had lost. The reapportionment was legally challenged but upheld on grounds that the legislature had discretion to interpret constitutional provisions as it saw fit. Nevertheless, wide dissatisfaction was a major factor leading to a constitutional convention in 1894.

The 1894 Formulas

The 1894 convention devised complex new rules designed to protect rural counties from the political consequences of urban growth. That objective was so successfully accomplished that each reapportionment that took place between 1907 and 1953 resulted in the urban (and, after World War II, suburban) counties becoming ever more underrepresented as their populations grew relative to the rest of the state. To apportion senate seats after 1894, the state's citizen population was divided by 50, the number of seats in 1894. The resulting number was called the "first ratio." Counties with populations between three and four times this figure received three seats, those between four and five times the ratio got four, and so on. The total number of seats held by each county with three or more times the ratio would then be compared to the number it had in 1894. Because they had constituted single counties in 1894, New York and Bronx Cos were calculated together, as were Queens and Nassau Cos. If any of these larger counties were entitled to more seats than they had in 1894, total senate membership was increased by that number. This guaranteed that new urban seats would not be taken from those previously held by the more sparsely populated counties. A "second ratio" was then calculated by dividing the combined citizen populations of the counties with less than three times the first

APPORTIONMENT OF POPULOUS COUNTIES UNDER 1894 ASSEMBLY FORMULA

	Average Citizen Population of Assembly Districts	
Year Ratio[b]	Counties with More than 1.5 Times Ratio[a]	Counties with Less than 1.5 Time
1894	40,733	36,010
1907	50,657	41,602
1917	60,998	41,424
1943	97,366	52,187
1953	112,477	57,648

Source: D. Wells, *Legislative Representation in New York State,* rev ed. (1964).

[a]Greater than or equal to 1% of state citizen population.

[b]Less than 1% of state citizen population.

APPORTIONMENT OF POPULOUS COUNTIES UNDER 1894 SENATE FORMULA

	Average Citizen Population of Senate Districts	
Year	Counties with More than 3 Times Ratio[a]	Counties with Less than 3 Times Ratio[b]
1894	120,682	112,835
1907	148,594	130,189
1917	170,288	147,994
1943	267,909	178,299
1953	301,178	195,859

Source: D. Wells, *Legislative Representation in New York State,* rev ed. (1964).

[a]Greater than or equal to 6% of state citizen population.

[b]Less than 6% of state citizen population.

ratio (ie, less than 6% of the state's citizen population) by the remaining number of seats, which were distributed on the basis of the second ratio among those smaller counties. This system survived court challenges in 1907 and 1943. Additional rules designed to further limit the representation of the New York City region were also adopted by the 1894 Convention.

The assembly apportionment system was less complex but equally effective in suppressing the more populated counties' representation. First, every county but Hamilton, which was combined with an adjacent county for apportionment purposes, received a seat. Next, each county with at least 1.5 times the assembly ratio (the state's citizen population divided by the constitutionally prescribed total of 150 assembly seats) was given another seat. Finally, the leftover seats were distributed among counties with at least twice the ratio. The inherent problem was that so many seats—61 of 150—were distributed in the first step that too few were left to provide an equitable share for the more populated counties.

These rules created major disadvantages for the urban areas, where the political strength of the Democratic Party was concentrated, thus giving Republicans a marked edge in achieving legislative control. Republicans were often able to win substantial majorities of the seats despite Democratic majorities at the polls. While the system was in effect, Republicans held control of both houses for 62 years, Democrats for 6. With each successive reapportionment under the 1894 formulas, urban and suburban underrepresentation grew more severe. Barring a constitutional convention, however, only the legislature itself had the power to change the formulas, so the system was self-perpetuating, until the 1960s.

The 1960s Rulings

New York was not the only state where a clearly inequitable apportionment system prevailed, and almost everywhere the growing urban and suburban areas were disadvantaged. This began to change with the landmark 1962 US Supreme Court decision in *Baker v Carr,* which held for the first time that federal courts could consider whether representation in a state legislature was sufficiently inequitable to constitute a violation of the 14th Amendment's guarantee of equal protection. In combination with similar lawsuits from other states, *WMCA v Lomenzo,* a suit challenging New York's apportionment system, came before the US Supreme Court. On 15 June 1964 the Court ruled that legislatures must be apportioned substantially on an equal population ("one person, one vote") basis. Because it made wide population disparities unavoidable, New York's complex formula was ruled constitutionally invalid. The following year, in *In re Orans,* the New York State Court of Appeals sought to clarify whether any of the state constitution's rules survived. It determined that the federal constitutional violations related exclusively to the formulas for apportioning seats among the counties. The senate's two-ratio feature was therefore invalid, as was the assembly's guarantee of at least one seat to each county except Hamilton. It would no longer be possible, the court said, to confine all districts within county lines or to permit county-governing bodies to delineate districts. Other rules not in direct conflict with "one person, one vote," such as the formula for determining the total number of senators, were allowed to stand, as were certain rules governing the placement of boundaries. These rulings revolutionized the politics of the state. Henceforth, no area would be over- or underrepresented, and no party could assume permanent control of the legislature.

Largely to revise the truncated state constitutional apportionment provisions, the legislature summoned a constitutional convention for 1967. That Democratic-controlled convention completely rewrote the rules, transferring power over the process from the legislature to a bipartisan commission, making the drawing of congressional lines subject to constitutional rules for the first time, and explicitly prohibiting gerrymandering (the drawing of district lines in ways calculated to give one party a chance to win more seats than it would likely get if partisan considerations played no role). But because the electorate turned down the entire proposed 1967 constitution due to struggles over other issues, the parts of the old constitution that had not been invalidated, plus the relevant court rulings, remained the only guidelines.

Congressional Districting

While apportionment of seats in the US House of Representatives is done by Congress, delineation of congressional districts is left to the states. The federal constitution does not require that states be divided into separate districts. Indeed, until 1842, many states (including New York) elected members from multimember districts. In that year, however, Congress passed legislation mandating single-member districts. In New York State the power to draw congressional district lines is exercised by the legislature, with the governor's approval. Because the state's congressional delegation has always been among the nation's largest, the way congressional lines are laid out in New York State has been of considerable national political significance.

In contrast to state legislative districting, which is based on rules set forth in the state constitution, the legislature, until the 1960s, had unrestricted power to carve out congressional districts in any way it chose. The party in control has never hesitated to use that power to secure partisan advantage. Extensive partisan manipulation of New York State's congressional districts can be traced back to districts drawn by the then dominant Federalists well before the word "gerrymander" was coined in the early 19th century. Since the 1960s, with numerical inequality having been eliminated, skillful gerrymandering has become common at both levels.

There are numerous ways to gerrymander. In areas where the party in control is usually in the minority, it can connect small, scattered concentrations of its own political strength to form winnable districts while "dumping" large numbers of opposition party voters into adjacent districts where they will merely add to opposition majorities without costing additional seats. This often produces bizarrely shaped districts. In regions where the controlling party is strong, it can "chop up" concentrations of opposition strength and dilute them by attaching areas of its own strength to the separate pieces. While frequently ignored state constitutional provisions call for compact and contiguous senate and assembly districts, no such restrictions exist regarding congressional lines. Until the 1960s another widely used method of gerrymandering was to give districts created to favor the controlling party smaller populations than those likely to be won by the opposition, thus enabling the dominant party to win more seats with fewer votes. But the Supreme Court effectively ended this practice nationally in *Wesberry v Sanders* (1964) and in New York in *Wells v Rockefeller* (1969). All congressional districts within a state must now have equal populations.

Since the 1960s

Every redistricting since the 1960s rulings has been subjected to legal challenges in federal or state courts, or both. Invalidation of the old constitutional system made redistricting necessary, but when a politically divided legislature in 1966 was unable to agree on a plan, a special commission appointed by the Court of Appeals drew new lines. In 1971–72 the legislature, under complete Republican control, enacted a redistricting plan, but the strong post-Watergate tide of 1974 enabled the Democrats to gain assembly control. From 1975 through the end of the century and beyond, the legislature remained politically divided. In both 1982 and 1992, following extended partisan deadlock, complex litigation, and intervention by the US Department of Justice, the legislature adopted plans that solidified each party's position in the house it already controlled. Because neither party has been in full control of redistricting since the early 1970s, there have been no single-party gerrymanders at the congressional level. Nevertheless, because the drawing of congressional districts remains essentially unregulated, a bipartisan form of gerrymandering has evolved in which the parties, after preliminary skirmishing, reach agreement to protect selected representatives in each party.

While the rulings in the 1960s outlawed certain practices, they did not end controversy surrounding districting and apportionment. Several major issues remain. Among the most contentious is whether the state should either require or permit race and ethnicity to play a role in the delineation of districts, or, conversely, whether such factors should be prohibited from consideration. Arguments persist over the advisability of various proposals to control partisan gerrymandering, including the adoption of a more enforceable set of districting rules, the transfer of districting power to a bipartisan commission, the clarification of existing constitutional provisions mandating geographically compact and contiguous districts, a prohibition on the unnecessary crossing of county lines in districting, and the extension to cities of constitutional protections for county and town boundaries. Although much has changed, the process of drawing district lines remains as politically volatile as ever.

Grofman, Bernard, et al, eds. *Representation and Redistricting Issues* (Lexington, Mass: Lexington Books, D. C. Heath, 1982)
Lincoln, Charles Z. *The Constitutional History of New York,* 5 vols (1906; repr Buffalo: William S. Hein, 1994)
Silva, Ruth. "Apportionment in New York," *Fordham Law Review* 30 (1961–62): 581–650
———. "Apportionment of the New York Assembly," *Fordham Law Review* 31 (1962–63): 1–72
Wells, David I. *Legislative Representation in New York State,* rev ed. (New York: International Ladies' Garment Workers' Union, 1964)
———. "Redistricting in New York State: It Is a Question of Slicing the Salami," *Empire State Report* 4 (Oct–Nov 1978): 9–13
———. "The Reapportionment Game," *Empire State Report* 5 (Feb 1979): 8–14
———. *Legislative Districting and the New York State Constitution* (Albany: Nelson A. Rockefeller Institute of Government, 1995)

David I. Wells

Arabs. The first groups of Arabs to immigrate to New York State were Christians from the Ottoman province of Greater Syria [now Syria, Lebanon, Israel, Palestine, and Jordan]. Emigration from the Ottoman Empire was illegal then but tolerated for Christians. Beginning in the late 1870s these "Syrian," also called Syro-Lebanese, immigrants primarily settled in New York City, though in Utica and other cities as well. By 1900 the area around Rector St in Lower Manhattan was known as Little Syria. Atlantic Ave in Brooklyn was another popular settlement area. Although accurate estimates are impossible because official reports did not distinguish between Arabs and other migrants from the Ottoman Empire, one rough estimate suggests that between 150,000 and 250,000 Arabs migrated to the United States during the first wave. The Immigration Act of 1924 cut the immigration of Arabs.

These first Arab immigrants were overwhelmingly single men who came to the United States to accumulate savings and then return to their hometowns. They worked in industrial plants in New York City and other industrial towns, while others became peddlers, often specializing in Christian devotional items. Some opened stores, bakeries, or restaurants, or joined the professions by becoming doctors, dentists, and lawyers. The money remitted by these emigrants to their families helped fuel economic development in greater Syria. This early Arab American community in New York City had a great impact on subsequent Arab settlements in the United States and also influenced Arab society through the newspaper *Al-Hoda* (1898–1992).

In the 1950s Palestinian refugees, expelled from their homeland, and Arab Jews, especially from Syria, came to the United States as well-educated professionals and business owners. In 1965 the quota system of immigration ended, and Arab immigration increased. Since 1970 Yemenis have made up the largest group of Arab immigrants to New York City. Unlike pre–World War II immigrants, postwar Arab immigrants often came with their families, which reflects the political realities of the Middle East and the unlikelihood of returning. In 2000 the US Census reported 121,925 people of Arab birth or ancestry in New York State, although some community activists place the number close to 280,000. The majority lived in the New York City area, with large centers around Albany, Binghamton, Buffalo, Rochester, Syracuse, and Utica. Arabs in New York State are diverse in their origins, representing the 22 Arab nations and Muslims, Christians, and Jews. In New York City most Arabs are still of Syro-Lebanese origin, followed by those of Palestinian, Yemeni, and Jordanian descent.

With the second wave of immigration, there has been a geographic shift of communities within New York City. Most Arab American communities are still found in Brooklyn, such as in Brooklyn Heights, Park Slope, and Bay Ridge, and more recently in Cobble Hill and Sunset Park, but new neighborhoods are growing outside Brooklyn, notably in Astoria (Queens Co), and they have more Muslims than the older Christian Arab areas. The community supports a large number of societies and religious institutions, such as the Arab American Family Support Center in Cobble Hill in Brooklyn and the Arab American Council in Yonkers. A strong concern of the community is media stereotyping of Arabs and Muslims and resulting incidents of discrimination, harassment, and violence, especially during periods of tension, such as the Arab-Israeli wars of 1967 and 1973, the oil embargo of 1973, the Gulf War of 1991, the World Trade Center bombing of 1993, and the destruction of the World Trade Center on 11 Sept 2001. To correct stereotyped images Arab American leaders founded in 1980 the Arab-American Anti-Discrimination Committee (ADC). Famous Arab Americans from New York State include the writer Khalil Gibran, former US Secretary of Health Donna Shalala, actor F. Murray Abraham, and Edward Said of Columbia University. Utican James Zogby founded the Arab American Institute (1985), an advocacy organization, and his brother John founded Zogby International (1984), a polling organization.

Kayal, Philip, and Kathleen Benson, eds. *A Community of Many Worlds: Arab Americans in New York City* (Syracuse: Syracuse Univ Press, 2002)
Naff, Alixa. *Becoming American: The Early Arab Immigrant Experience* (Carbondale: Southern Illinois Univ Press, 1985)

John VanderLippe

Ararat. Proposed Jewish homeland. Mordecai M. Noah (1785–1851), a prominent member of New York City's Jewish community, sought to establish a refuge for the world's Jewish Diaspora, to be situated on Grand Island in the Niagara River between Tonawanda (Erie Co) and Fort Erie, Ont. Noah, an attorney, former US consul to Tunis, newspaper editor, and sheriff of New York Co, hoped to transform the entire 27 mi^2 ($70\ km^2$) island into a utopian Jewish colony named for the mountain on which the biblical Noah's ark came to rest. In 1820 Noah presented his plan to the New York State legislature and began private negotiations to buy sections of Grand Island, envisioning the colony as a temporary home for Jews who would one day safely move on to the ancient Jewish homeland in Palestine. In the meantime, they would live as a "Jewish Nation under the auspices and protection of the constitution and laws of the United States of America." In September 1825 Noah, who by then owned a modest tract of land on Grand Island, proclaimed the founding of the City of Ararat by unveiling a sandstone tablet reading, "Ararat, a City of Refuge for the Jews," and later leading a parade through nearby Buffalo. At the ceremony, which included a visit to the island by Seneca chief Red Jacket, Noah proclaimed himself "Judge of Israel," a title he created for the leader of Ararat. Despite this celebratory start, Ararat failed to win colonists, with many Jewish leaders deriding Noah as a real estate swindler or would-be messiah. Noah gave

Ararat foundation stone, 1825. Hebrew inscription is the Sh'ma, the central prayer of Judaism: Hear O Israel! The Lord our God, the Lord is One.

up on Ararat by 1833, when he sold the property to a timber company. Returning to New York City, he resumed his career as an influential editor and politician. The original Ararat tablet is now permanently housed in the Buffalo and Erie County Historical Society Museum in Buffalo.

Adler, Selig, and Thomas E. Connolly. *From Ararat to Suburbia: The History of the Jewish Community of Buffalo* (Philadelphia: Jewish Publication Society, 1960)

Michael I. Niman

arboretums. See BOTANICAL GARDENS.

Arbus [née Nemerov], Diane (*b* New York City, 14 Mar 1923; *d* New York City, ?26 July 1971). Photographer. Born to a successful commercial family, Arbus began her photographic career in the 1940s, working as a fashion photographer with her husband, Allan Arbus. During this period her work followed traditional photographic conventions. In the mid- or late 1950s she studied formally with Lisette Model and shared Model's fascination with eccentric subjects. Arbus's first photo-essay, published by *Esquire* in 1960, anticipated the urban, edgy character of her mature work. She soon began to make what would become her most famous photographs: portrayals of individuals and groups on the margins of contemporary society, or with physical abnormalities, such as midgets, giants, transvestites, and middle-aged nudists, in New York City and its environs. Her subjects address the camera head-on, challenging the viewer's notions of normalcy and difference. In 1962 Arbus switched from a 35 mm camera to a square format, resulting in images that have the directness of enlarged snapshots. Financial support came from magazine assignments, grants, and teaching, including appointments at the Parsons School of Design (1965–66) and Cooper Union (1968–69) in New York City. In 1967 the Museum of Modern Art in New York City featured Arbus's work in the *New Documents* exhibition, which explored the changing social landscape of America. Arbus's bouts of depression and eventual suicide prompted many accounts of her photography as the manifestation of an artist's psychological torment. Recent observers, however, point out that some of Arbus's most "freakish" subjects were shot on assignment for magazines and that her eccentric approach reflected larger trends in American culture in the 1960s.

Arbus, Doon, and Marvin Israel, eds. *Diane Arbus: Magazine Work* (Millerton, NY: Aperture, 1984)
Bosworth, Patricia. *Diane Arbus: A Biography* (New York: Knopf, 1984)

Amy Kurlander

Arcade. Town (pop 4,184) and village (pop 2,206) in SW Wyoming Co. Settled in 1807, the town was formed from Sheldon in 1818 as China; the name was changed to Arcade in 1866. Manufacturing began with the Arcade Woolen Mills (1819–1926). Sandstone was quarried *ca* 1900. Arcade's first rail connection was the Buffalo, New York and Philadelphia Railroad (1871; later the Pennsylvania). Rail shipment helped Arcade become New York State's largest cheese market west of Utica. Products have included yarn, knit goods, shoe last blocks, bowling pins, powdered milk, hydraulic jacks, and precision instruments. Lee J. Drennan Enterprises produced automobile radio tuners and was sold in 1955 to Motorola, which left town *ca* 1990. In the early 21st century, Arcade's manufacturers produce automobile alternators, electronic components, and welding positioners. Pioneer Credit Recovery (1980), a subsidiary of Sallie Mae, is a large employer. Farming in the town is centered on dairying, potatoes, and hay. Arcade was the summer residence of Francis Striker, creator of radio shows *The Lone Ranger* and *The Green Hornet.* Incorporated in 1917 the Arcade and Attica Railroad has attracted travelers for steam excursions since 1962 and was added to the National Register of Historic Places in 1980.

Arcadia. Town (pop 14,889) in S central Wayne Co. Settled in 1791, Arcadia was formed from Lyons in 1825. It was crossed by the Erie Canal (1822) and the New York Central Railroad (1853). Modern spiritualism was born in Hydesville in 1848, when the Fox sisters reported hearing "rappings" from a murdered man. Farmers in Arcadia raise bison and produce milk, fruit, vegetables, and corn. Light industry is concentrated in Newark. In the north is Zurich Bog, a 414-acre (168 ha) National Natural Landmark that is a glacial-age formation hosting a dozen native species of orchids and other rare flora and fauna.

Scott C. Monje

archaeology. See HISTORICAL ARCHAEOLOGY; PREHISTORIC ARCHAEOLOGY; UNDERWATER ARCHAEOLOGY.

architects and architecture. Buildings are objects in a living museum, in which every structure qualifies as a cultural artifact from which much can be learned. Many buildings are handsome works of design and contribute to the environment as a source of constant pleasure. A number can be deeply moving works of art and appear in art history courses taught around the world, such as Louis Sullivan's rich and delicate Guaranty Building (1896) in Buffalo or Frank Lloyd Wright's strange and "organic" Guggenheim Museum (1959) in New York City. However, any number of buildings throughout the state could qualify equally as works of art, such as the simple and beautiful Greek Revival houses, certain dynamic Victorian designs, or the modest but perfect bungalows in the Craftsman style.

New York State played a major role in the development and dissemination of the architecture of the United States. Its waterways (eg, the Hudson and Mohawk Rivers and the Erie Canal) and the railroads that later followed their shorelines opened up a lush landscape to the west, devoid of mountain barriers, reaching deeply into the heartland of the new nation. This pathway generated a powerful current pulling westward a population of pioneers, drawn by the open land carrying with them the building practices and architectural styles of east coast America and of New York State.

The one-story, graystone Dutch farmhouse is still a distinctive feature of the Hudson Valley landscape. In the 18th century, manor houses in the Georgian Colonial style, such as the Schuyler Mansion (1763) in Albany, marked the transformation of New Netherland into a British colony. After the War of Independence, the Federal style flourished with the prosperity that accompanied the western movement passing through Albany and Schenectady. A variation on the Late Georgian style of Robert Adam in England, with its distinctive fanlight entranceways, the Federal style (like the Federalist Party in power) symbolized the new Republic's reluctance to finalize its divorce from England.

In the 1830s the Federal style evolved into the Greek Revival, which, in its domestic form, had no counterpart elsewhere in the world. The first style to spread the length of the state, the Greek Revival was a vivid architectural symbol of the democratic ideal. Resembling the new government buildings of Washington, DC, with its white-columned porches, the Greek Revival house was a declaration of the average American's confidence of being as much a part of the government of the country as was the president of the United States.

It was in the Victorian styles that followed the Greek Revival, beginning in the 1840s, that New York made a major contribution to the development of American architecture. Away from the major cities, the Victorian styles still dominate New York's built environment. Designated in their day as the "picturesque styles," they were a manifestation of the Romantic movement's passion for nature. All the Victorian styles shared in common nature's rich colors, asymmetrical arrangements, and broken patterns. Alexander Jackson Davis's Gothic Revival Lyndhurst (1838) in Tarrytown (Westchester Co) was the first great house in America in a picturesque style. Andrew Jackson Downing of Newburgh (Orange Co) and Calvert Vaux of Kingston (Ulster Co) disseminated both picturesque theory and picturesque form in their popular architectural books. The Victorian styles spread rapidly across New York State. They appeared in a sequence of stylistic fashions: first the Gothic Revival, then the Italianate styles before the American Civil War, followed by the Second Empire style (called French Renaissance in its day) with its mansard roofs, and then the High Victorian Gothic, known in the 1870s and 1880s as Modern Gothic, and, finally, in the 1880s and 1890s, the Romanesque Revival and its domestic version, the Queen Anne style. A variation of the Queen Anne style, the great camps of the Adirondacks, was one of New York State's most important contributions to the history of American architecture.

During this same time, the industrial revolution manifested itself in major factory architecture throughout the state, such as the surviving examples in Cohoes (Albany Co), the machines turned by the power of the Mohawk. New York City's technical contributions to architecture were its mass-produced but beautifully designed iron-framed buildings of the 1850s and 1860s, and Elisha Graves Otis's first safety elevator, invented in his Yonkers factory in 1852. Both made possible the development of the skyscrapers of a later generation.

Although the 20th century in New York State began with a return to the past in the Beaux Arts classical style of the state's libraries, museums, and public buildings, there also appeared in New York City some of the important examples of skyscraper architecture, from the beautiful "Gothic" Woolworth and Art Deco Chrysler Buildings (Cass Gilbert, 1913, and William Van Alen, 1930) to the first glass-slab skyscraper, Lever House on Park Ave (Skidmore, Owings and

Merrill, 1952). The Lever House design is a pure and perfect example of the 20th-century International Modern style. Its ordered, clear, functional design touched base at every point with the machine aesthetic of modernism. An expression of the industrial revolution that drove the modern age, a factory form lies behind typical examples of the style, but a factory purified and dematerialized by delicate details and shimmering glass.

In the 1960s and 1970s a Late Modern style reflected a reaction against minimalist modernism, with a broken pattern of massive shapes arranged like free-formed sculpture. Exposed, unadorned concrete was the preferred material. The great masterpiece in this Late Modern manner is Louis I. Kahn's First Unitarian Church (1967) in Rochester. In the final years of the 20th century, antimodern postmodernism invaded every aspect of US culture, never more conspicuously than in the art of architecture. Every principle of modernism was overturned. No greater example of this deconstruction of modernism exists than in the brilliant but outrageous Westin New York (Arquitectonica, 2002) at Times Square in New York City. Eccentrically shaped, gaudily colored in a number of hues, the lower stories covered with signs and symbols, the design violates functional logic and every principle of symmetry and decorum. From Dutch farmhouses to postmodernist efforts in deconstruction, New York State has produced a rich architectural legacy.

James K. Kettlewell

architects and architecture, Adirondacks and North Country. During the 18th- and 19th-century conflicts between the French and British and later between the British and American colonists, the St. Lawrence River, Lake Champlain, and Lake George were strategically important water routes. Having control of them was vital to the outcome of the French and Indian War, Revolutionary War, and War of 1812. To strengthen their positions in this corridor, the antagonists built several fortifications, some based on the star-shaped designs of the French military engineer Sébastien le Prestre de Vauban. From this period are the restored Fort Carillon [now Fort Ticonderoga] at Ticonderoga (Essex Co), the ruins of two forts at Crown Point (Essex Co), the reconstructed Fort William Henry at Lake George (Warren Co), and a host of archaeological sites on these waterways.

Northern New York State buildings of the settlement period often retained forms brought from New England, Quebec, and elsewhere in the state. Yankees who largely populated the Lake Champlain and St. Lawrence Valleys east and north of the Adirondacks erected buildings much like those of Vermont. The Penfield Homestead (1828) and the Congregational Church (1843) in Ironville (Essex Co) are but two examples of this tradition. Settlers of the southern Adirondacks and the Lake Ontario shore more frequently came from Massachusetts, Connecticut, and other parts of New York State, but their building traditions were the same. For this reason, much of the 19th-century vernacular architecture of the region is similar to that of lower New York State regions likewise settled by New Englanders.

More distinctive was the French influence, coming southward from Quebec and brought directly from France by émigrés who colonized Jefferson Co, among others, along the northern tier. The steep roof of the *maison québécoise* is common in early vernacular houses of the North Country. An elite class of French émigrés built distinctive country houses, such as the Neoclassical villa of James Le Ray Chaumont, extant at Fort Drum (Jefferson Co), as is the fine stone house of his son at Cape Vincent and another Le Ray house at Chaumont (Jefferson Co). Later waves of Francophone Canadian immigrants, coming to work in the busy mills and deep woods of the region, also occasionally left their mark, as in the towering Romanesque Revival church, St. Jean le Baptiste (1903) in the town of Ausable (Clinton Co).

Although trees and lumber were plentiful, many early builders favored native stone, where it was close to the surface. Limestone, found extensively in the St. Lawrence River valley and in parts of the Champlain Valley, was used for substantial stone churches, houses, mills, and warehouses. The hamlet of Essex (Essex Co), with some 150 buildings listed on the National Register of Historic Places, boasts more than a dozen limestone buildings, as does Waddington (St. Lawrence Co). Sandstone is found in a broad band across the region between the Ausable River in the east and the Potsdam/Canton area in the west and was used for utilitarian structures (mills and bridges) and to build churches, public buildings, and houses in the early 19th century. The largest clusters of these are in the Town of Potsdam (St. Lawrence Co), where there are 41 National Register–listed sandstone buildings, and the Village of Keeseville (Clinton and Essex Cos). The Laurentian Shield provided granite for the monumental summer homes of the Thousand Islands of the St. Lawrence River.

Early settlers also built log structures, such as the Samuel Adsit Cabin (*ca* 1794) on Willsboro Point (Essex Co), now open to the public. Several builders in the area around Big Moose Lake used a half-log palisades construction technique to build camps and hotels during the period before sawed lumber was common. They used a pit saw to cut their logs lengthwise, then placed the half-logs upright to create the building's walls. The rounded bark side became the exterior surface and the flat surface became the interior wall, which was finished with batten strips. In the last quarter of the 19th century and during the beginning of the 20th century, the log cabins of early settlers and the ephemeral lumber camps became the model for large rustic camps, built for the region's summer elite. At the same time, new railroads made the Thousand Islands and the interior of the Adirondacks more accessible to summer visitors.

Styles familiar elsewhere in New York State characterize buildings in North Country cities and towns, and a variety of architects designed public and private buildings throughout the region. An important architectural work is the Roswell P. Flower Memorial Library (1904) in Watertown, a splendid marble structure designed in the Beaux Arts style by Watertown architect Addison F. Lansing. Sumptuous interiors were designed by the nationally prominent New York City architect Charles R. Lamb. The nearby brick Paddock Building contains the Paddock Arcade, a remarkable survival of the mall precedent. Built in 1850, it is one of the oldest, continuously operated shopping arcades in America. Watertown's public square is one of New York State's most notable civic spaces, distinguished for its large size, the distinctiveness of the buildings that surround it, and the well-preserved state of most of them. John Russell Pope, best known for designing monumental Neoclassical structures like the Jefferson Memorial in Washington, DC, the Plattsburgh City Hall (1912), and that city's 135 ft (41.2 m) high Macdonough Monument (1926). These projects, along with associated urban renewal work of the City Beautiful Movement era (1893–*ca* 1909), transformed the city's Saranac River waterfront. Pope also designed much of

Sagamore, Vanderbilt family great camp in Raquette Lake.

Kamp Kill Kare, a rustic Adirondack camp in the Raquette Lake area in Hamilton Co.

Isaac Perry, who grew up in Keeseville and was the son of a local builder, became an architect based in Binghamton. He was eventually hired to complete the New York State Capitol and, as the first state architect, designed many hospitals and armories across the state and in the region, including the St. Lawrence State Hospital [now St. Lawrence Psychiatric Center] in Ogdensburg (St. Lawrence Co) and armories in Malone (Franklin Co), Glens Falls (Warren Co), and Ogdensburg. Architect William Coulter came to Saranac Lake (Franklin and Essex Cos) to be treated at Edward Livingston Trudeau's tuberculosis sanatorium. He established a practice in the village and, between 1896 and 1907, produced hundreds of projects, including large rustic camps, sanatorium buildings, churches, houses, commercial and civic buildings in a variety of turn-of-the-century architectural styles. Coulter was the first resident, professional architect of the Adirondack Park region.

Everest, Allan S. *Our North Country Heritage: Architecture Worth Saving in Clinton and Essex Counties* (Plattsburgh: Tundra Books, 1972)

Gallos, Philip L. *Cure Cottages of Saranac Lake: Architecture and History of a Pioneer Health Resort* (Saranac Lake, NY: Historic Saranac Lake, 1985)

Gilborn, Craig. *Adirondack Camps: Homes Away from Home, 1850–1950* (Blue Mountain Lake, NY: Adirondack Museum; Syracuse: Syracuse Univ Press, 2000)

McGowan, Robert Harold. *Architecture from the Adirondack Foothills* (Malone, NY: Franklin County Historical and Museum Society, 1977)

Steven Engelhart and Paul Malo

architects and architecture, Albany and Capital District. Rich with facades of red brick, brownstone, granite, and marble, Albany and Troy (Rensselaer Co) rank among the most architecturally distinguished and well-preserved cities in America. Although the cities are linked by the Hudson River and common construction traditions, their architectural manifestations are remarkably different: through its monumental buildings Albany establishes its place as the capital of the Empire State, while the architecture of Troy reflects its history as an important center of industry, trade, and education.

ALBANY

The first known buildings in what is now the City of Albany were constructed at Fort Nassau in 1614. At Fort Orange traders associated with the Dutch West India Co, like other early American immigrants, followed building traditions of their homeland. By 1664, when the English took New Netherland and Beverwijck was renamed Albany, more than 100 houses had been constructed, typically having brick facades and gables facing the street, much like contemporary urban houses in the Netherlands. Today, only drawings, a few photographs, and archaeological traces of these 17th-century structures survive; the most visible legacy of early Albany is the irregular street pattern in the area east of Pearl St between Hudson Ave and Orange St.

The early 18th century was more peaceful, and there was significant construction within the Albany stockade. The Dutch Reformed congregation enlarged a stone church at the foot of State St in 1714–15 (not extant). A three-story stone courthouse, erected on Broadway in 1740, later welcomed the Albany Congress of 1754 and served as the first state capitol (1797–1807, not extant). Two dwellings, constructed in the Dutch tradition, survive from the mid-18th century: the Quackenbush House (*ca* 1736), now a restaurant, and the Johannes Radliff House (*ca* 1759). Once the British conquered Canada and attacks by the French and Indians ceased, outlying farms were resettled and elegant country seats appeared. Schuyler Mansion (1761–64) was embellished with wallpaper and hardware sent from London and is now a state hstoric site. The great Van Rensselaer Manor House (1765) was demolished in 1893, but a room is displayed at the Metropolitan Museum of Art. A generation later Philip Van Rensselaer built the two-story, gambrel-roofed residence (1787) still known as Cherry Hill, now a museum.

New York's first state capitol built for that purpose was completed in 1809 to the designs of Albany architect Philip Hooker. With its Ionic portico overlooking a public square, the new capitol firmly established State St hill as the center of state government. Hooker's capitol and the nearby city hall (1829–32) were destroyed in the early 1880s, but two other important downtown buildings that he designed survive: the twin-towered Dutch Reformed Church (1797–99; now First Church) and the former Albany Academy (1814–17; now Albany City School District administrative offices), its red sandstone facades enriched with fluted pilasters.

It took three decades and four architects—Thomas Fuller (1867–76), Leopold Eidlitz and H. H. Richardson (1876–83), and Isaac Perry (1883–99)—to complete the present state capitol, built of granite with red-tiled roofs, two magnificent legislative chambers, and elaborately carved staircases. While in Albany, Richardson designed a new city hall (1880–83) just across Eagle St from the capitol, with granite faces, brownstone archways, and a 200 ft (61 m) high tower. Next door, in the New York State Court of Appeals, is Richardson's splendid carved-oak courtroom, moved from the capitol in 1916.

West Capitol Park, created in the 1920s, is framed by the capitol and other monumental state buildings. On the north is the block-long terra-cotta colonnade of the New York State Education Building (1908–12), designed by Palmer and Hornbostel; inside is the original, soaring Guastavino-vaulted space used as the reading room of the New York State Library until 1978, and outside are two electroliers with bronze figures of industrious children sculpted by Charles Keck. The west side of the park is enclosed by the 32-story, Art Deco–inspired Alfred E. Smith Building (1926–30), erected to accommodate burgeoning state agencies.

Many other architects and builders—some nationally known, others locally based or just starting their careers—were hired by Albany residents or government officials intent on erecting distinctive buildings: Henry Rector, New York State Court of Appeals (1832–42); Richard Upjohn, St. Peter's Church (1859–60), tower by his son Richard M. Upjohn (1876); Daniel Badger's Architectural Iron Works of New York City (1861) at 51–53 North Pearl St; Fuller and Wheeler, YMCA (1886–87); Robert W. Gibson, Cathedral of All Saints (1884–88); Isaac Perry, New York State Armory (1889–91); and Shepley, Rutan and Coolidge, Union Station (1899–1900). Washington Park was developed beginning in the 1870s by engineer William S. Egerton.

Long a center of interstate commerce, downtown Albany is filled with bank buildings, many designed by nonresident architects and firms

Stevenson and Wendell Houses, State Street, Albany, ca 1810, by James Eights, 1849.

often incorporating notable interiors: Russell Sturgis, 41 State St (1874–75); York and Sawyer, 60 State St (1901–3); Henry Ives Cobb, 69 State St (1927); and Denison and Hirons, 11 North Pearl St (1927). Competing successfully with well-known outsiders was an Albany architect educated at Columbia University, Marcus T. Reynolds, who often imbued his creations with carefully studied historical references. He designed a Venetian palazzo with a vermiculated facade of creamy yellow terra-cotta (1896–97) at 385–389 State St and integrated Flemish Gothic tracery made of cast stone into the facades of the Delaware and Hudson Building (1913–18) on Broadway at the foot of State St, which was part of a complex planned with Arnold W. Brunner and is now SUNY Plaza.

More recent buildings include Edward Durell Stone's uptown campus of SUNY Albany (1962–71) and Cannon Corp's Center for Environmental Sciences and Technology Management (1997), also part of SUNY Albany. The most ambitious and controversial architectural project in Albany in the 20th century was the Gov Nelson A. Rockefeller Empire State Plaza (1962–78), adjacent to the capitol. It is a 98-acre (40 ha) complex of marble-clad office towers designed by architect Wallace K. Harrison in concert with Gov Rockefeller.

TROY

Lansingburgh, now part of Troy, was originally laid out in 1771 with a village green and a grid of streets that were soon lined with houses built by families from New England. In 1793 the four-year-old settlement of Troy wrested from Lansingburgh the designation of county seat. With an economy based on commerce and industry, Troy soon boasted sophisticated residences: the Vail House (1818; now home of the president of Russell Sage College), the Hart-Cluett Mansion (1827; now home of Rensselaer County Historical Society), the Gothic Revival St. Paul's Episcopal Church (1828), and two significant Greek Revival monuments: First Presbyterian Church (1834–36), designed by James H. Dakin, and the block-long ensemble known as Washington Place (1840), overlooking private Washington Park. The Warren family, prosperous from trade and intellectually curious, commissioned architects from New York City to erect a crenellated residence called Mount Ida (1838–39), designed by Alexander Jackson Davis, the Church of the Holy Cross (Davis, 1843; Upjohn, 1848; Henry Dudley, 1859), and a family vault and chapel (1860) in Troy's Oakwood Cemetery designed by Dudley. Laid out by John C. Sidney in 1848 with miles of picturesque carriageways, Oakwood was soon studded with obelisks, mausoleums, and ironwork designed in the latest idioms: Greek, Roman, Gothic, Egyptian, Romanesque, and Neoclassical. The interior of Gardner Earl Memorial Chapel and Crematorium (1884), by Fuller and Wheeler, is embellished with oak, marble, and mosaics.

An 1862 fire that consumed acres of downtown buildings prompted a young architect from Utica, Marcus F. Cummings, to settle in Troy. Over the next six decades, he and his Rensselaer Polytechnic Institute (RPI)-trained son, Frederick M. Cummings, designed many of Troy's landmarks: First United Presbyterian Church (1864–65), classrooms and dormitories at Russell Sage College (1890s), the Rensselaer County Courthouse (1894–98), Whitman Court (1906), and Emma Willard School (1910).

New York City architects also came to Troy. George B. Post bested the Cummings firm in an architectural competition for the Troy Savings Bank building (1875) and produced an acoustically renowned music hall upstairs. W. and L. E. Gurley, world-famous manufacturer of surveying instruments, hired Diaper and Dudley to design a handsome factory (1862), now Gurley Precision Instruments. Iron magnate Henry Burden commissioned Robert H. Robertson for his office building (1881–82), now headquarters of Hudson-Mohawk Industrial Gateway and the Burden Iron Works Museum. The polychrome Hall-Rice Building (1871) is attributed to Calvert Vaux. The firm Barney and Chapman was called in to create the elegant Hart Memorial Library (1895–97; now Troy Public Library), which has tooled-marble facades and glass-floored stacks. Mortimer L. Smith and Son, of Detroit, friends of the owner, designed the extravagant department store known as Frear's Cash Bazaar (1897–1900), which now used for offices. Several churches and the library have stained-glass windows produced by the Tiffany Studios. Efficient yet handsome, scores of brick and cast-iron stores, warehouses, and factories were erected along River St, from Congress St as far as North St. More recent buildings include Levatich and Miller's Chapel and Cultural Center (1967–68), affiliated with RPI.

RESIDENTIAL HOUSING

Sometimes architect designed, sometimes contractor initiated, the 19th-century brick and brownstone row houses built for the upper, middle, and working classes in Albany and Troy rival contemporary housing in Manhattan and Brooklyn. Many of their railings were created by the architectural ironworks established by James McKinney in Albany or by Michael Mahony in Troy. As both cities grew, new neighborhoods with frame and masonry houses, both large and small, spread over the hills, away from downtown commercial and industrial areas. The cosmopolitan Caldwell apartment building (1907) in Troy had its own dining room and roof garden.

See also SKYSCRAPERS; URBAN HOTELS.

Historic Albany Foundation. *Albany Architects: The Present Looks at the Past* (Albany: The Foundation, 1978)

Waite, Diana S. *Ornamental Ironwork: Two Centuries of Craftsmanship in Albany and Troy, New York* (Albany: Mount Ida Press, 1990)

———, ed. *Albany Architecture: A Guide to the City* (Albany: Mount Ida Press, 1993)

Diana S. Waite

architects and architecture, Buffalo and the Niagara Frontier. The Niagara River flowing northward from Lake Erie to Lake Ontario borders the New York State counties of Erie and Niagara, jointly called the Niagara Frontier. Old Fort Niagara [now in Porter, Niagara Co], at the mouth of the river, is the site of the oldest masonry building between Central New York and Santa Fe, N Mex. The fortified stone chateau built by the French in 1726 was designed by the military engineer of New France, Joseph-Gaspard Chaussegros de Léry. It was restored in 1926 with the help of Buffalo architect James A. Johnson of the firm Esenwein and Johnson. Two stone blockhouses, also in Fort Niagara, designed by British military architect John Montresor and built in 1770 and 1771, are components of the most complete collection of 18th-century military architecture in the United States.

THE 19TH CENTURY

At the head of the Niagara River, the City of Buffalo is justly considered a treasure of landmark American architecture, including major works by H. H. Richardson, Louis Sullivan, and Frank Lloyd Wright. The Village of Buffalo was surveyed and laid out by Joseph Ellicott in 1804 on a radial plan taking advantage of the waterfront location. A prominent structure on Buffalo's waterfront is the 1833 lighthouse. The sophisticated design is in the form of a precisely tapered octagon. As a witness to the growth of the city and its harbor, the lighthouse has become a symbol.

Buffalo has two very different examples of early Gothic Revival churches inspired by English architect A. W. N. Pugin, who helped popularize the movement. Architect Richard Upjohn, known for his 1846 Gothic Revival design of Trinity Church in New York City, designed Buffalo's St. Paul's Episcopal Cathedral (1851). Upjohn turned the restrictions of a difficult, sloping triangular site to advantage with his design of a picturesque, asymmetrically massed, dark red sandstone building of such variety that it has no primary facade. Upjohn considered St. Paul's his best work. The 270 ft (82.3 m) stone spire was the highest point in the city at the time. In 1870 Buffalo photographer C. L. Pond used the tower to take a series of panoramic stereoscopic views of the surrounding urban landscape.

In downtown Buffalo, the Gothic Revival St. Joseph's Roman Catholic Cathedral (1851) was built to the design of the prolific, Irish-born architect Patrick Keeley, who worked under Pugin in Ireland. St. Joseph's symmetrical cruciform massing and Celtic interconnection of gray and yellow stone contribute to making it one of Keeley's best Gothic Revival churches. The rural cemetery movement in the United States was related to the aesthetic of the picturesque, an informal and asymmetrical arrangement based on the appearance of natural landscape or of landscape painting. Forest Lawn, Buffalo's major cemetery, is a prime example of a rural cemetery. It opened in 1850 on the northern outskirts of urban development. Charles Clarke laid out the grounds to conform to the hilly natural landscape bordering the meandering Scajaquada Creek. It is a cemetery that is also a park, arboretum, and museum of history, art, architecture, and landscape design.

Landscape architect Frederick Law Olmsted and his partner Calvert Vaux designed the Buffalo park system and interconnecting parkways beginning in 1868. In spite of some serious intrusions it is still considered the most complete Olmsted system. Delaware Park, the major park, adjoined and expanded upon the green space of Forest Lawn. In 1887 Olmsted and Vaux designed roadways and paths for the Niagara Reservation, New York's first state park (1885) at Niagara Falls. Olmsted also designed the grounds of H. H. Richardson's monumental Romanesque Revival New York State Insane Asylum (1869–95). It was in the course of designing this massive complex of buildings that the architect developed the heavy masonry style later referred to as the Richardsonian Romanesque. The state-owned buildings, now known as the H. H. Richardson complex, are on the grounds of the Buffalo Psychiatric Center and have been largely vacant over the past 25 years. In November 2002 State Supreme Court justice John A. Michalek ruled that New York State must repair and preserve the buildings. Rochester architect Andrew Jackson Warner, who was Richardson's assistant on the asylum project, designed Buffalo's Old County Hall. The gray granite Romanesque landmark was dedicated on the American centennial 4 July 1876.

Modernism and the 20th Century

The Guaranty Building (1896) in Buffalo is a masterwork of architect Louis Sullivan. One of the state's first significant skyscrapers outside New York City, the 13-story Guaranty is a mature expression of Sullivan's revolutionary design ideals and ornament. The building was extensively restored in 1985. Although Sullivan opposed the use of Classical Revival–styled buildings, they had caught the public imagination through architect Daniel Burnham's famous 1893 World's Columbian Exposition at Chicago. In 1896 Burnham's firm completed Buffalo's Ellicott Square Building in a Classical Revival style. At the turn of the century two Buffalo-based firms gained prominence employing Classical Revival styles. Edward B. Green of the firm Green and Wicks produced the Market Arcade (1892) and the Dun Building (1893) with early Italian Renaissance Revival elements and details. His 1900 Buffalo Savings Bank (now M & T Bank), now recognizable for its golden dome, was a High Renaissance composition. The firm of Esenwein and Johnson designed the prominent white-glazed terra-cotta General Electric Tower (now Niagara Mohawk Building), completed in 1912. Within Delaware Park are the Buffalo and Erie County Historical Society (1901), originally the New York State Building at the Pan-American Exposition, and the Albright-Knox Art Gallery, opened in 1905 as the Albright Art Gallery. Nationally, Stanford White of the firm McKim, Mead and White was the most prominent practitioner of Academic Classicism. Three of Buffalo's Delaware Ave mansions were designed by White. He began work in the office of H. H. Richardson, producing Romanesque Revival- and Shingle-style buildings. His first building in Buffalo of that early period, the James F. Metcalfe House (1882), was demolished in 1980. Two rooms from that house have been installed in the American Wing of the Metropolitan Museum of Art.

Buffalo has a large stock of architecturally distinctive housing that has been the focus of preservation efforts in the 20th century. The Allentown Historic District protects a variety of brick and wood buildings from the third quarter of the 19th century. The residential Linwood Avenue District has outstanding examples of the Shingle style, including the greatest concentration anywhere of Joseph Lyman Silsbee houses. Buffalo also has the largest concentration of Frank Lloyd Wright residential architecture east of Chicago, all related to Wright's famous icon of modern architecture, the Larkin Administration Building (1906). Although the building was demolished in 1949–50, five "Prairie House" residential works survive in the city. The Darwin D. Martin House (1904), one of Wright's greatest Prairie Houses, is undergoing a $25 million restoration that began in the 1990s. Spatial continuities, structural cantilevers, natural materials, and abstractions of natural forms characterize what Wright called "organic" architecture. His last work in the area is Graycliff (1927), the Martin family summer home on Lake Erie in Derby (Erie Co). It is Wright's realization of his ideal, the indigenous natural house, conceptionally and physically integrated into a spectacular landscape, foreshadowing his most famous house, Fallingwater (1937, Merion, Pa).

One of the most important centers of the American arts and crafts movement was the Roycroft Campus in East Aurora (Erie Co), founded by Elbert Hubbard in 1895. The colony supported itself on handcrafted pottery, furniture, metalwork, and printing. Most of the major buildings of the Roycroft Campus survive, including the restored Roycroft Inn (1903). In Buffalo the Arts and Crafts and Mission styles are reflected in the buildings of the Parkside neighborhood. On a series of concentric curvilinear streets planned by Olmsted to border his major park, there is a rich variety of bungalows, Craftsman cottages, and vernacular housing with Arts and Crafts elements.

Buffalo has two significant examples of Art Deco civic architecture. The City Hall, designed by John Wade with the assistance of New York State Architect Sullivan Jones, was dedicated in 1932 to commemorate the centennial of the city. The power, fully massed, energetically ornamental monument to civic pride dominates the main public square of the Joseph Ellicott plan. A soaring 375 ft (114.3 m) tower, enhanced by stepped angular setback massing, evokes *The Metropolis of Tomorrow* (1929) visions of New York City architectural illustrator Hugh Ferriss. Buffalo's New York Central Terminal (1929) is one of two major Art Deco railroad stations built in the United States, both designed by Fellheimer and Wagner architectural firm. Their Cincinnati station has become the Museum Center, but the more elaborate Buffalo complex has remained vacant for over 20 years. The Art Deco tower of the terminal, rising from one corner of the barrel-vaulted concourse, remains a highly visible landmark on the city's east side.

In the first decades of the 20th century the wooden grain elevators of the Buffalo waterfront at the eastern terminus of Great Lakes shipping were rapidly being replaced by monumental concrete structures. The Buffalo River has one of the greatest collection of these starkly geometric, functional structures in the world. They had a direct influence on and were an inspiration to a generation of major European modern architects, including Eric Mendelsohn, Walter Gropius, and Le Corbusier. More recently, they were the inspiration of architectural critic Reyner Banham's *A Concrete Atlantis* (1986). South of Buffalo in Lackawanna (Erie Co), better known for its steel mills, is Our Lady of Victory Basilica and National Shrine (1925). Designed by architect Emile Ulrich, it calls to mind the great baroque churches of 17th-century Rome. The lavishly ornamental interior space successfully serves the baroque intention of creating awe in the spectator. Four spiral columns supporting a gilded baldachin over the main altar are a direct invocation of Gian Bernini's great baldachin in St. Peter's in Rome. Kleinhans Music Hall (1938–40), the home of the Buffalo Philharmonic Orchestra, is a National Historic Landmark designed by the father and son team of Eliel and Eero Saarinen. World-renowned for its acoustic excellence and streamlined functionalism, it continues to inspire architects and musicians. Buffalo-born architect Gordon Bunshaft of Skidmore, Owings and Merrill was one of the first to introduce the architecture of Ludwig Mies van der Rohe to postwar Manhattan with his Lever House (1952). In 1960 Bunshaft designed the Miesian wing of Buffalo's Albright Art Gallery. The building represents an epitome of the harmonious joining of modern and traditional architecture, respecting and reflecting the proportions and precision of the original classical building such that each enhances the other. The new terminal of the Buffalo Niagara International Airport in Cheektowaga (Erie Co), designed by Kohn Pedersen Fox Associates, gained immediate recognition as an architectural landmark when it opened in 1997. The building is a dramatically sculptural and gracefully confident combination of aesthetics and functionality.

See also Shopping centers and malls.

Banham, Peter Reyner, ed. *Buffalo Architecture: A Guide* (Cambridge, Mass: MIT Press, 1981)

Conlin, John H. *Buffalo City Hall: Americanesque Masterpiece* (Buffalo: Landmark Society of the Niagara Frontier, 1993)

Fox, Austin M. *Erie County's Architectural Legacy* (Buffalo: Erie County Preservation Board, 1983)

———. *Designated Landmarks of the Niagara Frontier* (Buffalo: Meyer Enterprises, 1986)

John H. Conlin

architects and architecture, Long Island (Nassau and Suffolk Counties)

Colonial Period and the 19th Century

From its early settlement period in the 17th century through the first quarter of the 18th century, close to 100 First Period (pre-1730) buildings survive on Long Island, a number probably second only to Essex Co, Mass. The restored Old House (1649) in Southold (Suffolk Co) is likely the oldest and exhibits the narrow clapboards, massive central chimney, and leaded-pane casement windows that are so associated with the medieval appearance of these buildings. The Thompson House (*ca* 1700) in Setauket, whose "saltbox" appearance is derived from an integral lean-to, the Mulford House (1680) in East Hampton, and the Halsey House (*ca* 1648) in Southampton (Suffolk Co) are among the best examples of the region's earliest domiciles and are today historic house museums. While many of these buildings exhibit that hallmark of English construction, the summer beam (supporting floor joists arranged at right angles), the Schenck House at the Old Bethpage Village Restoration (Nassau Co) does not. The Dutch features of this 18th-century house, which was originally situated in Manhasset (Nassau Co), are a reminder that Long Island was first settled from its ends and that Dutch buildings could be found from Brooklyn into what is now Nassau Co.

Long Island also retains a legacy of 18th-century architecture. The Joseph Lloyd Manor House (1767) on Lloyd Neck in Huntington and Sylvester Manor (1733) at Shelter Island (Suffolk Co) and Rock Hall (1768), a high-style Georgian country house in Lawrence (Nassau Co) are noteworthy examples. As a breadbasket for New York City in the 18th century, the region was renowned for the quantity of its grain and still possesses the largest concentrations of windmills and tide mills on the eastern seaboard. In Lloyd Harbor (Suffolk Co) the Van Wyck–Lefferts Tide Mill (1793–97) retains most of its wooden machinery. The Old First Church (1784) in Huntington, the Caroline Church (*ca* 1724) in Setauket, the brick-ended Clinton Academy (1785) in East Hampton, and the Montauk (1797) and Eatons Neck (1799) lighthouses, designed by New York City architect John J. McComb, are also significant examples of the region's architectural heritage from the period. Sag Harbor (Suffolk Co), a thriving whaling port during the 19th century, is the site of two masterpieces by the New York City architect Minard Lafever: the Egyptian Revival First Presbyterian "Old Whalers" Church (1844) and the Benjamin Huntting House (1845; now Sag Harbor Whaling Museum), along with a sampler of mid-19th-century Revival styles. Garden City (Nassau Co) was another community that stood apart. Developed by Manhattan department store and hotel magnate A. T. Stewart for his workers, the planned community, with its own rail line, was designed (1869–71) by New York City architect and Long Island native John Kellum. Henry G. Harrison's perpendicular Gothic Cathedral of the Incarnation (1876–83) and Edward Harris's Ruskinian Gothic St. Paul's School (1879) were later built here as memorials to Stewart.

The 20th Century

In the decades leading up to World War I, Long Island became one of the most desirable residential areas of the country and a cradle of suburban innovation as a litany of transportation improvements, including the Long Island Motor Parkway and the East River railroad tunnel, helped spur development. "Country homes with their mile-long driveways are continuous for a hundred miles," reported the *New York Herald* in 1902. The area on the North Shore from Great Neck (Nassau Co) to Huntington (Suffolk Co), studded with millionaires' mansions, became known as the Gold Coast. The phenomenon brought some of the country's most noted architectural firms and architects, including McKim, Mead and White, Carrère and Hastings, Delano and Aldrich, and John Russell Pope. Among the nationally important country houses was the enlarged farmhouse (alterations 1886, 1892, and 1902) in St. James (Suffolk Co) that was architect Stanford White's country retreat and architectural laboratory. Box Hill's eclectic interior illustrates the architect's synthesis of many different styles and has been called a landmark of interior design. Harbor Hill (1899–1905, not extant) in Roslyn (Nassau Co), his chateau for Clarence Mackay, was a seminal design ushering in the taste for masonry houses and European precedent.

Other significant country dwellings included Laurelton Hall (1902–5, not extant) in Laurel Hollow (Nassau Co), Louis C. Tiffany's "supreme creation," an Art Nouveau treasure house where his favorite artwork was installed; Pope's Caumsett (1927) in Lloyd Neck (Suffolk Co), the vast estate designed in the manor style of an English country seat for Marshall Field III; Delano and Aldrich's Gertrude Vanderbilt Studio (1913) in Old Westbury (Nassau Co); and Richard Morris Hunt's work for William K. Vanderbilt, Idle Hour (1878–79, not extant) in Oakdale (Suffolk Co). White was not alone in residing on Long Island amidst his clients. Among the other architects who designed and built their own country houses were William A. Delano (Muttontown Corners, 1914–15, in Muttontown, Nassau Co); Philip Goodwin (Goodwin Place, 1917, not extant, in Woodbury, Nassau Co); Thomas Hastings (Bagatelle, 1910, in Old Westbury); and Harrie T. Lindeberg's home (*ca* 1926, in Matinecock, Nassau Co).

As the country house era drew to a close, a new mode of architecture evidenced itself in the 1920s and 1930s, often amidst the country houses. A. Conger Goodyear's Modernist hilltop retreat (1938) in Old Westbury, designed by Edward Durell Stone and based on Ludwig Mies van der Rohe's Barcelona Pavilion (1927), helped introduce European Modernism to America. Frank Lloyd Wright's Rebhuhn House (1936–37) at Great Neck Estates (Nassau Co) is an early example of his Usonian design. Another architect of the Modern movement, Wallace K. Harrison, built his avant-garde home and studio (1931) in Huntington. It was here that Harrison worked on designs for the New York World's Fair of 1939–40, including its symbols, the Trylon and Perisphere. Showcasing the suburban innovations of master builder Robert Moses, the fair was reached by the nation's most developed parkway system and linked to amenities that could only be accessed by the automobile, such as Jones Beach State Park (1929) off Long Island's South Shore. The World of Tomorrow was the fair's theme, and its design requirements attracted dozens of talented Modernists to the region. No part of the country was to be more transformed in succeeding decades by the experiment in automotive suburbia. America's first great postwar community, Levittown (1947–51) in Nassau Co, with 17,447 houses, was a car-dependent development, as was Roosevelt Field Shopping Center (1956), one of the first (open-air) megamalls, which opened with 11,000 parking spaces.

Marcel Breuer's Geller House (1945) in Lawrence is considered to have been one of the most influential American houses of the 1940s. Its distinctive "butterfly" roof is also seen in the Hanson House (1951) in Lloyd Harbor. After World War II, Long Island's wealth of domestic architecture was enriched by Philip Johnson's Robert Leonhardt House (1956, not extant) in Lloyd Neck and Peter Blake's Pin Wheel House (1954) in Water Mill (Suffolk Co). Two of the most celebrated Modernist houses of the 1960s are the Gwathmey House and Studio (1965) in Amagansett (Suffolk Co), designed by architect Charles Gwathmey, and Richard Meier's Saltzman House (1967–69) in East Hampton. As the century drew to a close, there were also award winning commissions by Paul Rudolph, Julian and Barbara Neski, Andrew Geller, Robert A. M. Stern, Michael Harris Spector, Mojo-Stumer, Bentel and Bentel, among other architects and firms. Of particular note were Meier's North American headquarters building for Swissair (1995) in Melville and his Federal Building and US Courthouse (2000) in Islip (Suffolk Co), winner of the American Institute of Architects National Honor Award.

See also COURTHOUSES.

American Institute of Architects, Long Island Chapter, and Society for the Preservation of Long Island Antiquities. *AIA Architectural Guide to Nassau and Suffolk Counties, Long Island* (New York: Dover, 1992)

Baker, Anthony, Robert B. MacKay, and Carol A. Traynor. *Long Island Country Houses and Their Architects, 1860–1940* (New York: Norton, 1997)

Gordon, Alastair. *Weekend Utopia: Modern Living in the Hamptons* (New York: Princeton Architectural Press, 2001)

Robert B. MacKay

St. Paul's School in Garden City, designed by Edward Harris, 1879.

architects and architecture, Mid-Hudson. Between Albany and New York City the Hudson River extends about 140 miles (225 km) through a valley noted for its beautiful and varied landscape, natural resources, and valuable agricultural lands, and punctuated by a European-based architectural history approaching 400 years old.

Colonial Period

The region's earliest buildings, known only from written descriptions and some archaeological evidence, consisted of dug-out, wood-lined cellars or posthole structures. By the third quarter of the 17th century, the Dutch medieval house became the standard form for domestic and agricultural architecture for the next 100 years. Its wooden framing system was made of massive H bents consisting of two vertical timbers mortised with a brace about three-quarters of its height with a horizontal timber that served as both ceiling beam and rafter for the garret floor. The bents supported heavy plate beams that in turn held the rafters, which were joined at the peak with a peg, forming a steeply pitched roof. The exterior was clad in brick or wide boards. In the majority of surviving stone houses from this time, the same kind of steep roof and horizontal beams were usually supported by shelves built in at the top of masonry walls. The famous Dutch half-doors were split horizontally in the middle so that the upper half could be open while the lower half was closed. Dwellings built by French Huguenots and German Palatines shared many features of the Dutch house and possibly added characteristics of their own native regions, such as multileveled dwellings in New Paltz (Ulster Co), where houses on Huguenot St give a strong impression of an 18th-century village built environment. On Main St in Hurley and at Stone Ridge (Ulster Co), built largely by the Dutch, are other examples of village environments. The gambrel roof was introduced to the mid-Hudson Valley in the 1760s by migrating New Englanders. Along with the roof form came the center hall and center entryway. Although the English had governed the colony since 1664, the Dutch and other European populations were slow to copy prevailing English Georgian styles, especially in the rural areas of the colony. Robert Livingston's (1688–1775) mansion (1730; burned by the British 1777; renovated 1779–82) built at Clermont (Columbia Co) is the only known example of Georgian architecture in the Hudson Valley until the 1760s.

Lyndhurst, Alexander Jackson Davis, 1865.

Federal Period and the 19th Century

The Federal period spans 1790–1825, and in Kingston (Ulster Co), Hudson (Columbia Co), and Poughkeepsie, some early examples of Federal style appeared. The Fred J. Johnston House in Kingston and the Robert Jenkins House (Daughters of the American Revolution, Hendrick Hudson Chapter house) in Hudson are examples open to the public. It was not until the 1810s that the style was widely adopted in rural areas, where it was used until after the 1850s. In upland areas on the east and west sides of the Hudson River, less elaborate versions built entirely in frame often show strong New England influences. The style is characterized by a central entry flanked by sidelights and often topped with an elliptical, arched transom window. The pink brick then being made from native clays gives the form a distinctive regional expression, as does the frequent use of leaded glass in the sidelights and transoms. New river cities such as Poughkeepsie and Hudson developed with surveyed streets, blocks, and house lots that echoed a modern order. A graceful vernacular version of the style is found in the Shaker community (1787–1947) at Mount Lebanon (Columbia Co).

Among the French émigrés who began to arrive in New York State in the 1780s and 1790s were some trained artisans and engineers who left their design marks on the layout of small towns, notably Tivoli (Dutchess Co) and Athens (Greene Co), and on some of the residential architecture. These designs reflected strong Classical influences and sometimes offered a hybridized version of republican Roman style—most influential in the Federal era—and democratic Greek forms. It was in this period, too, that a group of houses now called the Hudson River Estates began to be built at riverside. Grand country houses would also come to be located on many prominent heights along the river. While some were exotic at the time they were built, such as the Livingston houses—the Clermont mansion (1792; burned 1909; ruins extant) of Chancellor Robert R. Livingston (1746–1813) in Clermont, John R. Livingston's Massena (1793; not extant) in Barrytown (Dutchess Co), Janet Livingston Montgomery's Montgomery Place (1804–5) at Annandale-on-Hudson (Dutchess Co)—and Frederic Edwin Church's Olana (1870–74; with renovations by Church through 1899), most started as less complex residences that would be embellished and elaborated later in the 19th century. Nevertheless, presaging the American landscape movement, siting a house on the river became as much an aesthetic choice as a practical one for access to river transportation. This 32 mi^2 (83 km^2) district from Staatsburg (Dutchess Co) through Clermont is a National Historic Landmark District.

Largely because of pattern books such as Minard Lafever's *Modern Builder's Guide* (1833), Greek Revival design swept the country between 1832 and 1855. An early New York State practitioner was Alexander Jackson Davis. His remarkable design for the Dutch Reformed Church (1835) at Newburgh (Orange Co) copied the proportions and details of a Greek temple at Illissos. The style was widely popular in vernacular architecture. Andrew Jackson Downing, a Newburgh native and designer with a picturesque aesthetic, carried American architecture and design to new heights. In addition to Davis, English architects Calvert Vaux and Frederick C. Withers came to his Newburgh office. Downing's inspiration remained influential in American architecture and landscape design well into the 21st century. The Gothic Revival style is most ambitiously expressed in Tarrytown's (Westchester Co) Lyndhurst (1838), a house designed by Davis for William Paulding and enlarged by Davis (1864–67). Its turrets, towers, large tracery windows, and asymmetry evoke a castle, and it marked a startling change in American architecture. The design became a popular vernacular form for houses of all sizes. Ornamental details were shaped from wood, and when millwork technology emerged after the Civil War, a wide range of fanciful ornament emerged.

Italianate Revival designs, characterized by a low-pitched roof over a tall building, with an asymmetrical outline and ornamental bracketing at roof overhangs, were extremely popular and many survive. Martin Van Buren hired architect Richard Upjohn to design Italianate renovations and additions for Lindenwald (1797; renovations 1848), his late Georgian mansion at Kinderhook (Columbia Co). Like the Greek Revival style of a decade or so before, Italianate detail was successfully applied to many older buildings during the second half of the 19th century, such as the porches and bracket ornamentation designed by Davis for the Plumb-Bronson house (*ca* 1811; Davis renovations 1839, 1849) on the outskirts of Hudson. Kingston's Dutch Reformed Church (1852), designed by Minard Lafever, manifests the detailed ornament of Renaissance Revival, while Withers employed the High Victorian Gothic style in designing the Hudson River State Hospital (1871; now Hudson River Psychiatric Center) in Poughkeepsie. Landscape architects Frederick Law Olmsted and Calvert Vaux designed the grounds of this innovative mental health facility, which featured New York State's first Kirkbride building, a 19th-century, state-of-the-art, functionally designed structure for the care of the mentally ill.

The high purpose of academy buildings of the first half of the 19th century, typically vernacular adaptations of the Federal style such as Clermont (1834) and Kinderhook (1836) Academies, was expressed in their relatively large scale. By the midcentury, colleges like Bard, begun as St. Stephen's College (1860) in Annandale-on-Hudson, and Vassar (chartered in 1861) in Poughkeepsie, employed imposing architectural styles evocative of historic English buildings.

Bard continues to build architecturally innovative buildings, such as the Richard B. Fisher Center for the Performing Arts (2003), designed by Frank Gehry.

Mills and an early ironworks (1743; 19th- and 20th-century refittings) in Ancram (Columbia Co) flourished in the colonial era. The industrial revolution added a significant dimension with quite larger buildings: textile mills large enough to employ a workforce of 100 or more people were at the forefront of this trend. Early mills, such as the Ancram and Stuyvesant Falls mill (*ca* 1824, with alterations), were sometimes refitted and enlarged over the 19th century as manufacturing expanded and technology changed. Remains of enormous brick kilns at Copake (Columbia Co) reveal the scale of later 19th-century ironworks. Other manufactories and warehouses were built at river landings and, after 1854, at other locations where the railroads opened the commercial frontier. Bannerman's Castle (1901–18), built as a safe island warehouse for munitions storage, is in the 21st century best known as an exotic ruin on Pollepel Island in the Hudson River and is owned by the New York State Office of Parks, Recreation, and Historic Preservation.

After 1854, when rails first linked New York City and Albany, transportation had a significant impact on Hudson Valley design. In the last quarter of the 19th century a vacation in the Catskill Mountains was available not only to the wealthy and to exploratory artists but to a large number of people from urban areas; they came to places like the Hotel Kaaterskill (1881; not extant) in Haines Falls (Greene Co), the greatly enlarged Catskill Mountain House (1824; not extant) in Catskill (Greene Co), and the Mohonk Mountain House (1869) in New Paltz. Individual rustic dwellings at private enclaves, such as Onteora and Twilight Parks (Greene Co), expressed a rural ideal.

The 20th Century

In the late 19th and early 20th centuries, railroads affected where and how people lived. Railroad depots, designed with new functional spaces serving travelers and freight, were built in many small communities, such as Chappaqua (1901) in Westchester Co. In the Hudson Valley, suburban landscape design followed a strong landscape aesthetic. Tuxedo Park (Orange Co), developed in 1886, exemplifies exclusive subdivision with architect-designed houses, but most suburban developments were small and had a wider appeal. Frank Lloyd Wright's Usonian houses (1947–53) at Pleasantville (Westchester Co), displaying an open-plan design derived from his early Prairie House style, was an influence on post–World War II domestic architecture in the Hudson Valley but probably not nearly as much as the communities and subdivisions that evolved on the model of affordable small houses established at Levittown (Nassau Co). The growth and home building that concentrated in Westchester, Rockland, and Orange Cos attracted business from the city to the suburban valley. Distinguished corporate architecture sometimes offered an imposing presence, such as IBM's corporate headquarters (1963) at North Castle (Westchester Co), designed by Skidmore, Owings and Merrill, with a glass atrium by I. M. Pei. Such design influenced regional hospitals. More often, however, architecture of the later 20th century is represented by commercial shopping malls and single-story ranch houses in Cape Cod- or Prairie-derived style. A quite recent innovation is the return to older Revival styles, often interpreted in imposing scale.

See also AMUSEMENT PARKS.

Downing, Andrew Jackson. *Landscape Gardening and Rural Architecture* (1865; repr New York: Dover, 1991)

Dwyer, Michael Middleton. *Great Houses of the Hudson River* (Boston: Bulfinch Press, 2001)

Eberlein, Harold Donaldson, and Cortlandt Van Dyke Hubbard. *Historic Houses of the Hudson Valley* (1942; repr New York: Bonanza Books)

McAlester, Virginia, and A. Lee McAlester. *A Field Guide to American Houses* (1984; repr New York: Knopf, 2000)

Reynolds, Helen Wilkinson. *Dutch Houses in the Hudson Valley before 1776* (1928; repr New York: Dover, 1965)

Ruth Piwonka

architects and architecture, Mohawk Valley.

The Mohawk were the primary inhabitants of the area in the centuries immediately before European contact. They had considerable architectural sophistication and prowess. At a 16th-century Mohawk site near Garoga (Fulton Co), recent excavations have revealed a complex palisaded village of at least 13 longhouses.

Colonial Period

European presence in the Mohawk Valley began in the mid–17th century. In 1661 Arent van Curler purchased the land that would become Schenectady. The settlement was burned to the ground, and most of its inhabitants were killed or captured in the French and Indian raid of 1690. Despite this crippling blow, Schenectady started to rebuild shortly thereafter. More than 80 historic buildings, dating from 1690 to 1930 and in Dutch, Federal, Greek Revival, Gothic, and Victorian architectural styles, survive in the Stockade Historic District in downtown Schenectady. It is one of the largest areas of colonial and early national structures in the United States, with over 40 buildings over two centuries in age. The Glen Sanders Mansion (1658, expanded in 1713) in Scotia, built by Scottish immigrant Alexander Glen, is now a restaurant.

Beginning in the 1720s, the Palatine Germans settled in the Mohawk Valley, building landmarks such the Herkimer House (*ca* 1750), the grand Georgian house of Revolutionary War general Nicholas Herkimer in Danube (Herkimer Co) that is now a state historic site, and the Georgian-style Palatine Church (1770) in St. Johnsville (Montgomery Co). A number of important buildings are associated with Sir William Johnson, a land magnate and superintendent of Indian Affairs for the Crown. His Georgian homes, Fort Johnson (1749) in the village of that name in Montgomery Co and Johnson Hall (1763) in Johnstown [now in Fulton Co], are both museums. Johnson joined with the Iroquois in 1769 to build the Indian Castle Church, an Anglican mission church in the Town of Danube. The church is now owned by the Indian Castle Church Restoration and Preservation Society. Johnson also was responsible for the Tryon County Courthouse and Jail (both 1772) at Johnstown, which are still in government use.

Much vernacular architecture survives from the colonial period. European medieval architecture is a clear influence on many early farm structures, such as the Mabee House (*ca* 1706–10) at Rotterdam Junction (Schenectady Co), which has a steeply pitched roof, stone construction, and many Dutch details. The Schenectady County Historical Society acquired the farm in 1993 for educational uses. Another medieval survivor is the Palatine House (1743), a frame dwelling in Schoharie (Schoharie Co), restored as a museum in 1971 by the Schoharie Colonial Heritage Association. An important building type in the region is the New World Dutch barn, derived from Dutch and Palatine German prototypes, but making use of the area's plentiful large timber. These barns have a distinctive shape: nearly square in plan, with a broad, steeply gabled roof, double wagon doors centered in the gable end, and, often, low side walls. They have a unique H-shaped structural frame, which provides a rigid core supporting the roof and walls. The wagon door may be divided into upper and lower halves in the Dutch fashion. The barns were built by Dutch and German settlers, and by others as well, from the mid-1600s to the early 1800s. Examples abound, although most of the earliest structures were destroyed during the American Revolution. Those open to the public include the Nilsen Barn (*ca* 1760) at the Mabee Farm, the Schaeffer Barn (*ca* 1780) now at the Old Stone Fort Museum in Schoharie, and the Klock Barn (perhaps early 18th century) at Fort Klock in St. Johnsville.

The 19th and 20th Centuries

After the Revolution, turnpike roads were constructed to handle the influx of settlers to the Mohawk Valley. Important buildings began to appear along these turnpikes, where settlers from Connecticut, Massachusetts, and eastern New York brought the Federal style. The recessed arches and refined classical details of the Delos White House (*ca* 1812) in the Village of Cherry Valley (Otsego Co) illustrate this trend. At about the same time Union College in Schenectady was designed by French architect and landscape planner Joseph Jacques Ramée in 1814 as the first planned campus in America; the 16-sided, High Victorian Gothic Nott Memorial (1875) by Edward Tuckerman Potter is a later, important addition.

With the opening of the Erie Canal in 1825, the Mohawk Valley welcomed large numbers of foreign immigrants from Ireland, Germany, England, and Scotland. Significant structures proliferated along the Mohawk River and beyond. A major Greek Revival building—one of the largest in the United States—is the former New York State Lunatic Asylum (1837–43) at Utica, a 550 ft (167.6 m) long limestone structure with a monumental Doric portico, designed by William Clarke. The building, on the grounds of the Mohawk Valley Psychiatric Center, was vacated in the 1970s and 1980s, and the first floor is being renovated by the Office of Mental Health to house medical archives and an exhibition space devoted to the history of mental health care in New York State. In 19th-century residential architecture, the Greek Revival style predominates in the region. One of the most strikingly situated Greek Revival residences is Hyde Hall (1817–35), overlooking Otsego Lake in Springfield (Otsego Co). Designed by Albany architect Philip Hooker, the limestone mansion in the Doric order was built for George Clarke as a country home. In 1963 New York State acquired the property, and it is now part of Glimmerglass State Park. A later style, the Italian Villa, is represented by another historic house in museum use, Fountain Elms (1850–52) in Utica.

Along US 20 are towns that in the 19th century were resorts known for their mineral water treatments. Much of the resort grandeur of Richfield Springs (Otsego Co) in the 1880s and 1890s was lost after World War I, but still extant are numerous Victorian houses along Main St, Spring House Park, and a bandstand in the center of town. Sharon Springs (Schoharie Co) is undergoing revitalization with the recent restoration of the American Hotel (1847–51), a Greek Revival frame structure built near the mineral springs, and the Roseboro Hotel (1830s–1915), a Renaissance Revival resort. In Cobleskill (Schoharie Co), the Hotel Augustan, built soon after the railroad arrived in 1865, catered to travelers; it is Italianate in style, with a striking two-story bracketed veranda.

Schenectady, which grew rapidly beginning in the 1890s, is the site of the General Electric Realty Plot, an important example of a planned residential development; 100 structures built between 1900 and 1927 are mostly Georgian Revival or Colonial Revival, but there are some Queen Anne, Shingle, and Mission houses. Schenectady also had the most important industrial architecture in the region; the immense GE complex has been substantially reduced by demolition but still contains many utilitarian but graceful brick laboratories and offices with ornamentation related to the architecture current at the time of construction.

Although rich in 18th- and 19th-century architecture, the Mohawk Valley also contains notable examples of 20th-century architecture. One of the most conspicuous structures is the Holy Trinity Russian Orthodox Monastery (1946–50) in Jordanville (Herkimer Co). With its Byzantine style and ogee domes, the complex is a striking contrast to the surrounding farmland. Philip Johnson's art museum building (1960) at the Munson-Williams-Proctor Institute in Utica is a windowless masterpiece of modernism. Two recent additions to the landscape celebrate the region's agricultural heritage. Hugh Hardy's postmodern/contextual design for the Alice Busch Opera Theater (1987) on Otsego Lake near Cooperstown evokes the vernacular tradition of area dairy farms and provides a spectacular setting for the Glimmerglass Opera's summer performances. Kurt Ofer and Teresa Drerup of Cooperstown's Altonview Architects recall the local hops industry, albeit with Belgian references, at Brewery Ommegang (2000) in Milford (Otsego Co), built on the foundation of an old hops barn.

Kelly, Virginia B. *Wood and Stone: Landmarks of the Upper Mohawk Region* (Utica: Central New York Community Arts Council, 1972)

Maston, Bruce. *An Enclave of Elegance* (Schenectady: GERPA Publications, 1983)

Schull, Diantha Dow. *Landmarks of Otsego County* (Syracuse: Syracuse Univ Press, 1980)

Kerry Dean Carso and Ned Pratt

architects and architecture, New York City. The Manhattan skyline is the quintessential representation of New York City's architecture. For almost four centuries, a vast array of building types and styles have been characteristic of the metropolis, both influencing and being influenced by architecture elsewhere in the state. The city's Gothic-style churches influenced those in Utica and Hudson Valley towns; row houses of the late 19th century were similar to their counterparts in Albany; Brooklyn's waterfront grain elevators resembled those built in Buffalo. The density of development and the height of residential and commercial buildings, however, have been unique to the city.

Colonial Era to the Mid–19th Century

The Dutch and English settlers of the 17th and 18th centuries brought with them building types that closely resembled those of their home countries. No Dutch era buildings survive in Manhattan, although archaeologists have found cisterns and the footings of several buildings. The original street pattern has been preserved and landmarked along Stone St and adjacent blocks in the warren of streets below Wall St. The only remnants of Dutch-style architecture in New York City are about two dozen farmhouses located in Queens, Brooklyn, and Staten Island. The two oldest are the Pieter Claesen Wyckoff House (*ca* 1652) in Flatlands, Brooklyn, and the John Bowne House (1661) in Flushing, Queens. Most of the other Dutch farmhouses date from the late 17th to the early 18th centuries and with their swooping rooflines are similar in appearance to those in the Hudson River valley. The city's oldest house of worship is the Friends Meeting House (1694) in Flushing. Richmondtown Restoration, operated by the Staten Island Historical Society, has collected a number of buildings dating from the late 17th to the 19th centuries, including a 1695 schoolhouse, the oldest in the state.

With the arrival of the English in 1664 until their departure in November 1783, the appearance of New York City was influenced by buildings from London and England's seaport towns. The design of churches, such as St. Paul's Chapel (1766) at Broadway and Fulton St, and Georgian-style mansions and public buildings were drawn from imported architectural pattern books. The proliferation of building types, reflecting a more complex economy and housing an ever expanding and diverse population, began in the early 19th century. Along the streets fronting the East River, and later the Hudson River, landfill composed of sunken ships, ballast, and other materials had expanded the property available for development. Countinghouses like those preserved in the Fraunces Tavern block on Pearl St or at the South Street Seaport rose to four or five stories, the limit for the building technologies and work conditions of the day. There were numerous warehouses similar to the Empire Stores (1869), just north of the Brooklyn Bridge on Water St. Also reflective of New York City's role as the chief American port were two Wall St buildings constructed after an 1835 fire destroyed much of the downtown area: the Greek Revival US Custom House (1842), since 1955 known as Federal Hall National Memorial, and the colonnaded Merchants' Exchange (1841), used later as a customhouse, a bank, and a hotel.

During the first decades of the 19th century, people of various classes were housed within fairly close proximity to one another because of the need of all to be close to work. People with the lowest incomes lived in small wooden houses, middle-class tradesmen and their families lived in the modest brick row houses of the Federal era like those on Grand St, and the wealthy lived in grand urban mansions and seasonally decamped to country houses in Upper Manhattan, Queens, or Staten Island, of which only a few survive. They include Gracie Mansion (1801), the official residence of the city's mayor since 1942, and the Grange (now Hamilton Grange National Memorial), the home of Alexander Hamilton (1802), both in Manhattan. As surface transportation improved, wage earners could live farther away from their work. New neighborhoods appeared at the edge of Manhattan's settled areas, first in Greenwich Village and then in Chelsea. Increasingly strict fire laws began to push wooden structures to the outskirts of Manhattan, and their construction continued only in the other four boroughs. Occasionally factory owners built housing for their workers adjacent to their manufacturing plants. This happened in Queens, where William Steinway built a new piano factory and workers' housing (1879) nearby. On Staten Island the owner of the Kreischer Brick Works built a church and houses (*ca* 1890) for his employees. The mix of industrial and residential activities continued in all the growing areas of the city, except portions of Manhattan, until the early 20th century, when the first major zoning law (1916)

Hyde Hall on Otsego Lake, designed by Philip Hooker, built 1817–19, now in Glimmerglass State Park.

began to regulate land use and the height and bulk of buildings.

One of the most important influences on New York's architecture was the imposition of the street grid plan in 1811. Created to bring order to the development of Manhattan above 14th St, the grid provided for wide north-south avenues and a regular pattern of east-west streets with a number of extra broad crosstown streets. The basic unit of land division was the 25 x 100 ft (7.6 x 30.5 m) lot, which encouraged the building of row houses, and their serried ranks moved north along the side streets of Manhattan from the 1820s to the 1910s—from Chelsea to Morningside Heights on the West Side and from Murray Hill to Harlem on the East Side—and filled the streets of Brooklyn after the 1830s. The urban row house was infinitely adaptable to family size and income as well as to the resources of the speculators and developers who built a few houses or filled an entire block. Over the course of a century, the urban row house evolved from the modest vernacular buildings of two or three stories to the four or five stories of the 1840s and after, with their basement kitchens and attic rooms for servants. Later, brownstone and limestone facades were common for larger and more ornate row houses. These were more likely to be designed by trained architects than the earlier rows, which had been erected mainly by local builders. Many hundreds of row houses were converted to rooming houses or apartments during the 1920s and 1930s and then returned to single-family use with the regentrification of brownstone neighborhoods beginning in the late 1960s.

The Late 19th Century to the Mid–20th Century

If the row house was the defining residential type until the 1880s, the apartment house soon supplemented it and then supplanted it. Multiple dwellings for all classes emerged after the Civil War. The tenement house became the prime dwelling for the poor and for the vast numbers of immigrants who came to New York seeking a new life. Dark, dank, and mostly without indoor plumbing, these five- and six-story walk-ups housed a million people by 1900 in neighborhoods that dominated the East Side of Manhattan, starting at the Lower East Side and continuing north to edges of Harlem. On the West Side they were built north of 14th St to where Lincoln Center for the Performing Arts now stands, including Hell's Kitchen (now known as Clinton). Tenements were also built in Brooklyn in Williamsburg and Brownsville, but most surviving examples are in Manhattan in Chinatown and in what was known as Little Italy. The Lower East Side Tenement House Museum on Orchard St is located in a tenement built in 1863. The Tenement House Law of 1901 outlawed the worst features of these structures, and many "New Law" buildings, as they were known, were built in Manhattan, the Bronx, and Brooklyn.

The first true apartment houses, or "French flats" (a building type that originated in Paris), had amenities that made them attractive to middle- and upper-class families, such as elevators, full plumbing, servants' quarters, and services like doormen, laundries, and restaurants. The largest and best known, of which the picturesque Dakota (1884, Henry J. Hardenbergh) on Central Park West and 72d St is perhaps the most famous, were built from the 1880s to the 1910s, occupied large lots, sometimes half or even full blocks, and preserved a large inner courtyard for a carriageway or garden. With the high cost of real estate, the apartment houses created the distinctive 20th-century residential landscape of the city. Apartment houses of 12 and 14 stories lined Park and Madison Aves in Manhattan, and the taller towers of Tudor City (1928), with over 3,000 apartments and a hotel, were a striking feature in the east 40s. As new sections of the city opened up, five- to eight-story buildings in the traditional styles of the 1920s and Art Deco of the 1930s lined the Grand Concourse in the Bronx and Ocean and Eastern Parkways in Brooklyn. Vast swatches of Queens were developed from the 1920s to the 1950s with garden apartments, which ranged from two- to three-story complexes to the five- to six-story co-ops built around interior garden courts in Jackson Heights. Medium and then towering apartment houses were a feature of the second half of the 20th century in every borough except Staten Island. Single-family homes remained features of parts of Brooklyn, Queens, Staten Island, and even the Bronx, particularly in Riverdale and Fieldston, but apartment living became synonymous with New York City.

The city hosted several interesting experiments in urban housing. These included "model tenements" for the working class, funded by philanthropically minded investors who agreed to low returns on their investments to keep rents down and to provide quality apartments. In Brooklyn, A. T. White built the Tower and Home Buildings (1877, 1879) in Cobble Hill and the Riverside Apartments (1890) in Brooklyn Heights. In Manhattan the City and Suburban Homes Co built several groups, the largest at 79th St and York Ave (1900–1913). In Queens, the Phipps Gardens (1931) were built in Sunnyside. While these projects did not influence the economics of the private housing market, aspects of their designs, such as large central garden courts, did have a positive influence on middle-class housing. Two other experiments with single-family and attached homes were found at Forest Hills Gardens, a garden suburb sponsored by the Russell Sage Foundation (1913) and with row houses at Sunnyside Gardens (1928) in Queens.

Commercial and Public Architecture through World War II

As Manhattan land grew more expensive and businesses sought to remain close to other services and government entities, office buildings grew taller because of new technologies, including the passenger elevator, fireproof iron and steel framing, steam-powered construction equipment, electric light, and air-conditioning. The use of cast iron in particular was trendsetting. The structural use of iron columns to carry heavier loads resulted in larger open spaces because less footage was required than that needed for masonry walls. Builders of factory loft buildings took advantage of cast-iron framing and facades, which permitted larger window openings; eventually this would lead to a completely self-supporting steel frame system, known as the curtain wall, to which the exterior windows and wall material would be attached. Beginning in the 1870s, the race was on to build taller and taller structures using first iron and then steel. By 1914 the famous skyline image of the cluster of tall buildings at the Battery signified New York City. One building succeeded the next, holding the record for months, a few years, or perhaps decades. First to exceed Trinity Church's 284 ft (86.6 m) steeple was the New York World Building (1889, demolished) at 309 feet (94.2 m), followed by the Park Row Building (1899) at 391 feet (119.2 m), the Singer Tower (1908) at 47 stories, the Metropolitan Life Insurance Tower (1909) at 700 feet (213.4 m), and the terra-cotta Gothic-style Woolworth Building (1913) at 792 feet (241.4 m), which held the record for 17 years. It was outdistanced, in rapid succession, by the Manhattan Co (1930) at 927 feet (282.6 m), the Chrysler Building (1930) at 1,046 feet (318.8 m), and the Empire State Building (1931), topping out at 1,250 feet (381 m). Its record would last until 1970, when the 110-story, 1,350 ft (411.5 m) World Trade Center North Tower was completed.

By the late 19th century, office towers, as well as many other kinds of significant public and private buildings, were designed increasingly by architects who had studied in the new American schools of architecture, including Cooper Union, Pratt Institute, Columbia University, Cornell University, and Massachusetts Institute of Technology, and abroad, particularly in Paris at the Ecole des Beaux-Arts. By 1900 architects were part of a profession with its own organizations, including the American Institute of Architects, founded in New York City (1867) and the Architectural League of New York (1881), later housed in the French-style American Fine Arts Society building (1892) on 57th St with the Art Students League.

It was during this era when the monumental inspired style of the classically based Beaux Arts came to prominence, and New York City architects trained in Paris were adept at applying its aesthetic and planning principles to a wide variety of building types, including those of financial organizations, such the Classical-style New York Stock Exchange (1903) and the Dime Savings Bank (1908) on DeKalb Ave in Brooklyn, and Manhattan's Pennsylvania Station (1910) and Grand Central Terminal (1913), which became the models for transportation centers around the country. The evolution of Columbia University and New York University (NYU) from local colleges to major centers for graduate training and research was expressed in the new campuses designed for them in the 1890s by McKim, Mead and White, the leading architecture firm in the country. The Roman grandeur of the New York Public Library (1911, Carrère and Hastings) at 42d St and 5th Ave sheltered a research repository that drew people from around the world. Among the best known of the private libraries were the J. Pierpont Morgan Library (1907) on 36th St in Murray Hill and the Henry Clay and Adelaide Frick House and Library (1914) at 70th St and 5th Ave. Among the dozens of extraordinary mansions were the Gertrude Rhinelander Waldo House (1898) on Madison Ave (now a showcase store) and the 64-room Andrew and Louise Carnegie House (1903) (now Cooper-Hewitt National Design Museum, Smithsonian Institution) at 91st St and 5th Ave.

The immense wealth flowing through the city underwrote the construction of hospitals, zoos, botanic gardens, theaters, performance spaces like Carnegie Hall (1891) and Brooklyn Academy of Music (1908), and numerous private clubs like the Century Association (1891), New York Yacht Club (1900), and University Club (1900), all in Midtown Manhattan. Great private fortunes also paid for the construction of many extraordinary religious buildings from before the Civil War era to the 1920s. St. Peter's (1840) on Barclay St and St. Joseph's (1834) at 365 6th Ave were Greek Revival Roman Catholic churches. Quakers favored simple buildings in accord with their spiritual austerity. The Gothic Revival design of Trinity Church (1846) by Richard Upjohn at the head of Wall St started a trend for Episcopal and other Protestant denominations. The elegant new Roman Catholic St. Patrick's Cathedral (1858) on 5th Ave and 50th St in the French Gothic style had twin 330 ft (100.6 m) towers. Episcopalians melded Gothic and Romanesque in their huge Cathedral of St. John the Divine (1892) in Morningside Heights, unfinished into the 21st century. The Baptists, with the help of Rockefeller money, built the modern Gothic-style Riverside Church (1930) at Riverside Drive and 120th St with a 392 ft (119.5 m) tower and 72-bell carillon. Synagogues were built in various historic styles, but the Moorish and Romanesque were favored by a number of congregations, including Central Synagogue (1872) at Lexington Ave and 55th St and Eldridge Street Synagogue (1887). Russian Orthodox congregations built their churches in the eastern style with onion-domed cupolas, as at the Russian Orthodox Cathedral of the Transfiguration of Our Lord (1921) in Greenpoint, Brooklyn. As the Buddhist, Hindu, and Islamic populations grew in the second half of the 20th century, they built their own distinctive halls of worship. The first purpose-built mosque opened in 1991 as the Mosque of New York and Islamic Cultural Center at 3d Ave and 96th St in Manhattan, combining traditional and modern features.

The early 20th century was a time when municipal and other public buildings, such as firehouses, police stations, public baths, subways, and the 60 branches of the New York Public Library funded by a gift from Andrew Carnegie, were considered worthy of the design services of talented architects. The College of the City of New York (now City College of the City University of New York) at Convent Ave and West 138–140 Sts (1897) was housed in a Collegiate Gothic campus designed by George B. Post. Many of the city's public schools were designed by C. B. J. Snyder, a Board of Education architect. His English Gothic building for Hunter College (1913) remains at 68th St and Lexington Ave, and numerous elementary and high schools designed by him survive in several boroughs. The city greatly expanded the century-old Bellevue Hospital (1908) and built Sea View Hospital (1911) on Staten Island to care for tuberculosis patients. The majestic new US Custom House (1907) at Bowling Green provided an appropriate and even elegant setting for government business. The city's new Municipal Building (1914) at Chambers St towered above the City Hall built in 1811. Many future citizens of the consolidated city would soon come through the great halls of the US Immigrant Station on Ellis Island (1900) in the harbor, having sailed past one of New York's icons, the Statue of Liberty (1886). World War I slowed new construction in New York City. One of the most unusual projects was built to meet the needs of the military when America entered the war in 1917. The austere, reinforced concrete Brooklyn Army Terminal complex (2d Ave at 58–65 Sts) was completed in a matter of months in early 1918, and from its piers the majority of American soldiers and goods were shipped to Europe.

In the 1930s, with the advent of the depression, publicly financed construction surged while private investment declined, with a few exceptions. The 50-story Art Deco tower of 1 Wall St and the Empire State Building (both 1931) were the last major office towers built until the early 1950s. John D. Rockefeller Jr was one of the few developers who could afford to take advantage of low wages and cheap materials. He had the Rockefeller Center complex (1932, Associated Architects) constructed, with its stylish, organized grouping of limestone-clad office buildings, low-rise retail structures, the glamorous 6,200-seat Radio City Music Hall, central promenade, pioneering underground shopping concourse, and art-bedecked interiors and grounds. The entire complex became a model for urban redevelopment when cities resumed building after World War II.

Tenements were torn down in the 1930s, and the first public housing projects in the country, including First Houses (1936) on the Lower East Side and the Harlem River Houses (1937), were built in New York for working-class families, often with public health clinics and recreational facilities. The larger-scale projects such as the Williamsburg Houses (1937) were developed on superblocks, after the famous "tower in the park" model developed by Swiss architect Charles E. J. Le Corbusier that would exert a powerful influence on postwar apartment housing, both public and private, in New York and elsewhere. In 1939 and 1940 New York City hosted the World's Fair in Flushing Meadow Park, Queens, providing the thousands who visited with a glimpse of the future.

Architecture after World War II

A new generation of skyscrapers was built in the 1950s and 1960s. Those in the 1960s were influenced by zoning changes in 1961 that prescribed a tower straight up from the sidewalk with adequate open space at its base, which contrasted with the base and tower or base and setbacks configurations that had resulted from the 1916 zoning regulation. These new towers, often characterized by unembellished facades reflective of the building structure and by large panes of glass set in a steel framework, were the epitome of curtain-wall construction and would dominate skyscraper design for the rest of the 20th century. The first of these new structures was Lever House (1952), a slim tower set above low horizontal pavilions designed by Gordon Bunshaft of Skidmore, Owings and Merrill (SOM), which became one of the largest and most influential architecture firms of the second half of the century. Also on Park Ave was the Seagram Building (1958), a slender bronze tower designed by Ludwig Mies van der Rohe with Philip Johnson. Together these two buildings set the aesthetic tone of an International style that would persist for 40 years, until postmodern design added some Classical embellishments, and architects experimented more radically with form. The UN Secretariat Building (1950), designed by an international committee of architects, was also a pathbreaker in this idiom.

Redevelopment in Lower Manhattan was spurred by two important projects. The Chase Manhattan Bank Tower (1960, SOM), one of the first new office buildings constructed in Lower Manhattan since the depression, had a large plaza area ornamented with a sunken garden by Isamu Noguchi and plaza sculpture by Jean Dubuffet. The second major development was the clearing of a vast multiblock site of small retail and wholesale businesses for the construction of the World Trade Center (WTC), an ambitious project of the Port Authority of New York and New Jersey to reclaim for New York City the distinction of hosting the world's tallest building and to improve transportation access from New Jersey for the Port Authority Trans-Hudson (PATH) lines. Two identical towers, both 110 stories and 1,350 feet (411.5 m) high, were designed by Minoru Yamasaki, and their square tops were immediately distinctive among the spires of older skyscrapers. Adjacent mixed-use developments, connected by bridges, were built on the 92 acres (37.2 ha) of landfill created by the excavation for the WTC. Battery Park City (1979) was built following the guidelines of a master plan that included residential buildings; at the southern end the Museum of Jewish Heritage (1996) and the Ritz Carlton Hotel (2003) with the Skyscraper Museum (2004) were built; and at its northern end Stuyvesant High School (1992) was constructed. North of Battery Park City, private developers built the World Financial Center (1985), with its vaulted glass and steel Winter Garden (1988, rebuilt 2003, Cesar Pelli), four office towers, and stores. An esplanade and series of parks filled with art, performance spaces, and a variety of recreational areas start at the Battery and extending north to Chambers St and link the two developments.

Midtown Manhattan was also the site of much new skyscraper construction, including an extension of Rockefeller Center on 6th Ave, new sloped towers such as those of the W. R. Grace Building (1974, SOM) at 6th Ave and 43d St, and the significant redevelopment of the East Side along 1st, 2d, and 3d Aves with large office buildings displacing tenement housing. The first tall office building outside Manhattan since the 512 ft (156 m) Williamsburg Savings Bank Tower (1929) on Atlantic Ave in Brooklyn was constructed in 1989 at Hunters Point in Queens by Citicorp (SOM). Its 663 ft (202.1 m) height was a visual anomaly in a neighborhood of two- and three-story buildings until the Queens West development a decade later.

Postwar housing also changed in scale. Targe-scale development on superblocks that started in the 1930s would be an influential model for apartment housing, both public and private. Urban renewal projects carried out by private developers with public clearance assistance created thousands of units of moderate-income housing. The Metropolitan Life Insurance Co developed Parkchester (1942) in the Bronx to house 40,000 people and later sponsored Peter Cooper Village (1947) and Stuyvesant Town (1947), located between 14th and 23d Sts on Manhattan's East Side. They were upscale versions of the large public housing projects that were built later in Manhattan, Brooklyn, Queens, and the Bronx in the 1950s and 1960s, with more spacious grounds and better internal finishes, but remarkably similar in their plain brick facades. The union-sponsored Co-op City (1970) in the Bronx housed 55,000 people in large towers and provided them with parking, schools, and shopping. A unique residential development was planned and built by the New York State Urban Development Corp on historic Roosevelt Island (1975) in the East River; cars were banned, and access was by aerial tramcar or subway.

Urban renewal was also used as a tool for nonresidential projects. Blocks of tenements were leveled for what became the Lincoln Center for the Performing Arts (1962), a long-desired consolidation of performing arts groups in one location. It had the secondary effect of sparking a great deal of private redevelopment in the surrounding blocks. Other venues for the visual arts were built in this period: the Solomon R. Guggenheim Museum (1959) at 5th Ave and 89th St (the only major work by Frank Lloyd Wright in New York City, except for a modest prefabricated house on Staten Island built in 1959) and the Whitney Museum of American Art (1966, Marcel Breuer) at 77th St and Madison Ave.

With the exception of the WTC, there was little innovation in commercial architecture in New York City in the 1970s, 1980s, and early 1990s, although large projects were undertaken once the city recovered from the financial crisis of the 1970s. Metrotech Center (1986) was built in downtown Brooklyn, with bulky office towers and a hotel looming over small open spaces but with a positive effect on the downtown area. Many CUNY campuses were modernized, including the construction of two glass and concrete towers at Hunter College (1983, Ulrich Franzen) at 68th St and Lexington Ave and the Baruch College Academic Complex (2002, Kohn Pedersen Fox) at Lexington Ave and 24th St, a vertical campus curving up to the sky with a 10-story atrium that dominates the surrounding streets. In the 1990s a large-scale planned residential development, Queens West (1998), was constructed. Across from Midtown Manhattan along the East River, it comprised a group of apartment buildings, a waterfront recreation area, and Gantry Plaza State Park, which commemorated the former industrial use of the site. The theater district became the focus of redevelopment efforts, and new office towers and entertainment complexes replaced tawdry peepshows in older buildings. Design guidelines for the Times Square district called for special lighting and signage to continue the tradition of the brilliantly lit "Great White Way" that had drawn crowds since the early 1900s. Several historic Manhattan theaters were renovated, including the New Victory (1899, 1995) and New Amsterdam (1903, 1997), both on 42d St, with preservation plans by Hardy Holzman Pfeiffer.

The historic preservation movement traces its roots to the 1920s, when architect and historian I. N. Phelps Stokes and others tried to save parts of or entire historic buildings. The movement expanded with the destruction of Pennsylvania Station in 1963. Within two years, New York City had the Landmarks Preservation Commission (LPC), which designated historic districts, starting with Brooklyn Heights (1965). Structures 30 years or older were eligible for landmark status if they were architecturally, historically, or culturally significant. In 1978 the US Supreme Court upheld the LPC law in a decision that had wide ramifications for landmark preservation laws elsewhere in the United States as well as for other areas of property law. By 2003 the LPC had designated 79 historic districts, 1,200 individual and interior landmarks, and 9 scenic landmarks, with a total of some 22,000 buildings. By the late 1990s, the LPC was designating buildings from the 1960s, including the Seagram Building, the flight-invoking form of the Trans World Airlines Terminal (1962) at JFK International Airport, and the Ford Foundation (1967) headquarters on 42d St, with its pathbreaking interior atrium garden.

Whether buildings were official landmarks, many were converted to new uses when they became redundant. Between 1970 and 2000, the cast-iron manufacturing spaces of SoHo (South of Houston St) became housing and gallery spaces for artists and then commercial galleries and retail space. Factories and schools in Brooklyn, Staten Island, and the Bronx were converted to apartments, as were office buildings in Lower Manhattan as a glut of space left many vacant. The neighborhood of DUMBO (Down Under the Brooklyn Bridge) was gradually transformed as apartments filled vacant manufacturing buildings. The Greek Revival complex of Sailors' Snug Harbor (1833) on Richmond Terrace in Staten Island went from sheltering retired sailors to hosting cultural programs and a botanic garden as the Snug Harbor Cultural Center. The Italian Renaissance–style B. Altman department store (1906) on 5th Ave and 34th St became home in the 1990s to a university press, a branch of the New York Public Library, and the CUNY Graduate School. In a wonderful turnabout, the grand colonnaded US General Post Office (1913, McKim, Mead and White), which is now the Farley Post Office and occupies a full block at 31st St and 8th Ave, will be transformed into a new Pennsylvania Station.

Some of the most interesting architectural work in the city in the 1990s and after was commissioned by museums and corporations. The American Folk Art Museum (2002) built a new home on West 53d St, with its irregularly angled front and compact interior making full use of a narrow site. Its design, by Tod Williams Billie Tsien and Associates, signified the arrival of a new generation of architects. Down the block, the Museum of Modern Art (1939) went through a major expansion and rebuilding (2004) designed by Yoshio Taniguchi. His work was a sign of the increasing presence of European architects in the city. Christian de Portzamparc of Paris designed the LVMH (Moët Hennessy, Louis Vuitton) offices (1999) at 57th St with its singular "folded" glass facade. Sir Norman Foster of London designed a faceted glass design for a new tower to arise out of the Hearst Magazine Building (1928) at 8th Ave and 56th St. The Classical-style Brooklyn Museum built a contemporary new entrance pavilion of glass and reconfigured parts of its interior (2004, Polshek Partnership). The museum's choice of glass was part of a trend emerging in the 1980s, with imaginative new uses of the material beginning with the Jacob K. Javits Convention Center (1986, James Ingo Freed of I. M. Pei and Partners) at 34th St and 12th Ave. Glass was also selected for the Frederick Phineas and Sandra Priest Rose Center for Earth and Sciences (2000, Polshek Partnership), a glowing box enclosing a great globe, at the American Museum of Natural History. Glass was also the distinguishing characteristic of the Time Warner and AOL Center (2004, David Childs for SOM) at Columbus Circle, which combines a hotel, shops and restaurants, performing arts spaces, and residential units in one immense structure whose facade curved to conform with the great traffic circle on which it was located.

The most challenging project of the 21st century is the redesign and rebuilding of the WTC site. The destruction by terrorists of the two great towers and their auxiliary buildings on 11 Sept 2001 altered a skyline that had been familiar for over three decades. The gaping hole in the landscape symbolized the loss and grief felt by all who love the city. A limited competition was held to select a master plan for the site, and the proposal of Studio Daniel Libeskind was selected for development. The final appearance of the area will evolve over the course of a decade and will reflect the conversations and debates among the public, the architects, the sponsoring agency (the Port Authority), the leaseholder, government officials, the families of the victims, and numerous others, including landscaper designers, engineers, transportation planners, and federal officials.

See also AMUSEMENT PARKS; BOTANICAL GARDENS; BRIDGES AND TUNNELS; NATIONAL PARK SERVICE AREAS; OLMSTED, FREDERICK LAW; URBAN HOTELS; WORLD TRADE CENTER; WORLD'S FAIRS.

Dolkart, Andrew S., and Matthew A. Postal. *Guide to New York City Landmarks* (New York: Wiley, 2004)
Jackson, Kenneth T., ed. *Encyclopedia of New York City* (New Haven, Conn: Yale Univ Press, 1995)
Stern, Robert A. M., Gregory Gilmartin, and John Massengale. *New York 1900: Metropolitan Architecture and Urbanism, 1890–1915* (New York: Rizzoli, 1983)
Stern, Robert A. M., Gregory Gilmartin, and Thomas Mellins. *New York 1930: Architecture and Urbanism between the Two World Wars* (New York: Rizzoli, 1987)
Stern, Robert A. M., Thomas Mellins, and David Fishman. *New York 1960: Architecture and Urbanism between the Second World War and the Bicentennial* (New York: Monacelli Press, 1995)
———. *New York 1880: Architecture and Urbanism in the Gilded Age* (New York: Monacelli Press, 1999)
White, Norval, and Elliot Willensky. *AIA Guide to New York City*, 4th ed (New York: Three Rivers Press, 2000)

Deborah S. Gardner

architects and architecture, Rochester and Western New York. The Rochester area contains buildings that reflect its history as a prosperous milling, horticultural, and manufacturing center.

ROCHESTER

Rochester's central business district comprises buildings that illustrate the wide range of styles and scale of business construction over the course of 150 years. The earliest commercial buildings include the United States Hotel (*ca* 1830), now divided into commercial spaces, and two rows of brick commercial buildings from the late Greek Revival period. The Powers Building (1869–91) is a large-scale office block built in the French Second Empire style. Beginning with a masonry corner block at West Main and State Sts, the building was soon expanded with cast-iron wings, two additional mansard floors, and a tower, making it for a time the tallest building in Rochester at 175 feet (53.3 m). Diagonally across Main St is the 170 ft (51.8 m) Wilder Building (1888), an early example of the skyscraper. The Romanesque style, steel-frame building is clad with brick, with principal elevations composed in the "column" arrangement of base, shaft, and capital typical of early tall buildings. Another early skyscraper, the similarly composed Granite Building (1893), draws on classical ornament. The central business district retains two major department stores of the early 20th century. The former Duffy-Powers Department Store (1906), now known as City Place, is a well-preserved example of the use of decorative, Neoclassical white terra cotta exterior cladding. The former Sibley, Lindsay and Curr Department Store (1904), now known as the Sibley Building, is a more modern design, frankly expressing its structure with restrained ornament on a brick facade, large plate-glass display windows, and broad Chicago-style windows on the upper floors.

The downtown skyline is dominated by office towers of the mid- to late 20th century. Perhaps the most distinctive of these silhouettes is that of the Genesee Valley Trust Building/Times Square Building (1930). This Art Deco–style tower features an exterior of gray sandstone that terminates in four upraised wings. Other signature elements of the skyline include the Lincoln First tower (1973; now Chase tower), whose facade is composed of white marble ribs that flare out at the lower stories; the massive charcoal gray Xerox tower (1968) that rises from an elevated plaza; and the Bausch and Lomb tower (1995), surmounted by a multifaceted pyramid.

Architecturally notable churches in the downtown area include St. Luke's/St. Simon Cyrene's Episcopal Church (1824), which combines Federal period form and massing with simple Gothic decoration; St. Joseph's Roman Catholic Church (1846), gutted by fire in the mid-1970s but whose burned-out Neoclassical shell has been creatively preserved as the enclosure for an urban park; the Romanesque Revival Brick Presbyterian Church (now Downtown United Presbyterian Church) complex (1860, 1903, 1909, 1941) with later Tuscan-style towers; and the First Universalist Church (1908), an unusual square brick building by local architect Claude Bragdon that combines Tuscan sources using the Arts and Crafts aesthetic.

Most major civic buildings are clustered on the west side of downtown and include the Italian Renaissance Revival Monroe County Courthouse (1894), built from designs by J. Foster Warner, the austere Modern 1960s Civic Center complex, and New City Hall (1874–75). The latter is the former city hall, a very restrained work by Andrew Jackson Warner, father of J. Foster Warner, and constructed of rough-finished Lockport graystone with cut stone trim and punctuated by vertical bands of high narrow windows, all surmounted by high-pitched roofs. The City Hall since 1978 has been the renovated former Federal Building (1885–89), a large Romanesque structure with corner tower; the interior features a large multistory, sky-lit and arcaded atrium. On the east side of the river, the Rundel Memorial Building (1933–36), an important example of Art Deco/Art Moderne design, houses the Rochester Public Library.

The surrounding residential areas include buildings that illustrate the entire period of European settlement. Notable surviving first-generation buildings are the Stone-Tolan House (?1792), operated as a house museum by the Landmark Society of Western New York and the more elaborate and sophisticated Oliver Culver house (1816), originally located on the same road as the Stone-Tolan House. Rochester's first surge of prosperity followed the completion of the Erie Canal in 1825, coinciding with the peak in popularity of the Greek Revival style. A large stock of Greek Revival–style domestic buildings survives in the region, ranging from modest one- and one-and-a-half-story workers' cottages and farmhouses to large and elaborate mansions. The Third Ward near downtown Rochester contains a large collection of these houses. Less flamboyant versions of the style are more common, incorporating Greek ornament without the expensive porticos associated with the style. The late 1840s marked the fading in popularity of the Greek Revival style and the emergence of more picturesque styles associated with Romanticism. Italianate-style houses are common, including the familiar cube form, with or without cupola, and the more rambling form with towers. Following the American Civil War, Rochesterians embraced the various national styles that emerged for residential construction. Rochester and the surrounding area contain numerous high-style examples of French Second Empire-, Queen Anne-, and Shingle-style houses as well as large numbers of middle- and working-class examples of these styles.

In the late 19th and early 20th centuries, there were major expansions of Rochester's residential areas, and it represented a time when western New York State was a major center of the Arts and Crafts movement in architecture and related design fields. Lands that had been devoted to the local horticultural industry and to other more agrarian uses were subdivided for new residential developments. Among the major local designers working in this vein were the regionally important architects Claude Bragdon and Ward Wellington Ward and the Rochester firms of Gordon and Madden (1902–18) and Gordon and Kaelber (1919–32). Ward's domestic designs freely combine Tudor- and Colonial Revival–style planning and decorative elements and employ simple handworked details in leaded and stained glass, handmade decorative tile, and richly textured exteriors of various wood and masonry materials. Gordon and Kaelber worked in a similar vein, producing a large number of stock designs that recur with slight variations in many of the Rochester area's subdivisions of the 1910s and 1920s, located in the outer areas of the city and in the adjacent Towns of Irondequoit and Brighton (Monroe Co). A particularly important residence from this period is a house on East Blvd designed by Frank Lloyd Wright, a small example of his Prairie houses. The influence of these design trends can also be seen in large tracts of more modest middle-class housing of the period. Residential construction during the Great Depression and World War II was limited, but the development of suburban residential subdivisions resumed following World War II and continues into the early 21st century. These newer subdivisions contain examples of nationally popular forms of the period, including one-story ranch houses, split-levels and modified "colonials."

Rochester has several architecturally notable campuses. The University of Rochester's River Campus, dedicated in 1930, is situated on a broad bend of the Genesee River and is dominated by formally arranged red brick and sandstone buildings of Neoclassical and Colonial Revival styles. In contrast, the Wilson Commons student union building, completed in 1974 from designs by I. M. Pei, is a large red brick cube with a bold diagonal skylight and corner windows over a central atrium, oriented to provide a dramatic view of the dome of the main library building. The Colgate Rochester Divinity School campus, constructed beginning in 1928 of similar materials in the Collegiate Gothic mode, dominates a hilltop to the east of the university and the intervening Mount Hope Cemetery (1838) and Highland Park (1890), the latter designed by Frederick Law Olmsted. The Rochester Institute of Technology campus in Henrietta (Monroe Co), dating from the 1960s, is a starkly modern assemblage of sleek cubic forms faced with dark brick.

Surrounding Communities

Outside of the immediate Rochester area are several communities that prospered as ports and manufacturing centers on the Erie Canal during the 19th century and that retain significant concentrations of Victorian and earlier period commercial buildings. In particular, Brockport (Monroe Co) and Medina and Albion (Orleans Co) boast business districts of several blocks of two- and three-story commercial buildings of brick or stone or both. Many of the buildings in Medina and Albion were either entirely constructed of the local red Medina sandstone or trimmed with the material. In these communities, the surrounding residential areas reflect the evolving national tastes in domestic architecture, from the Greek Revival style of the first period of prosperity when the canal opened in 1825 through the years following World War II.

In Albion the sophisticated Greek Revival–style Tousley-Church House (1844) features elaborate interior and exterior Greek moldings and an unusual staircase supported by a cluster of four columns under the landing. The Orleans County Courthouse (1858–59), also in the Greek Revival style and from designs by W. B. M. Barlow, is surmounted by a large dome and dominates the middle of the village. The Pullman Memorial Universalist Church (1894), a gift of former Albion resident George M. Pullman, is a sophisticated building that combines the heavy masonry of the Richardsonian Romanesque with pointed openings. Built from designs by Solon S. Beman, a Chicago architect and former student of Richard Upjohn, the building is constructed of the local red Medina sandstone and features windows by the Tiffany Glass and Decorating Co.

The canal villages immediately to the east of Rochester are generally smaller than those to the west and consequently have smaller commercial cores, although several boast notable examples of 19th-century architecture. The most striking building in the Village of Pittsford (Monroe Co) is the three-story brick, Federal-period Phoenix Building. The village also has a compact commercial area of mid- to late 19th-century commercial buildings and a rich collection of middle-class domestic architecture spanning the final three-quarters of the 19th century and all of the 20th century. Palmyra (Wayne Co) is notable for the recently restored Federal-period store where the first Book of Mormon was printed in 1830, its collection of 19th-century commercial buildings stretching along the main street (Rte 31), and the four 19th-century churches at the intersection of Rte 31 with Rte 21. The churches are the High Victorian Gothic Revival–style Zion Episcopal Church (1877), the Greek Revival–style Western Presbyterian Church (1832), and the Romanesque Revival–style First Methodist

(1866) and First Baptist (1871) Churches. In Lyons (Wayne Co) is the Greek Revival–style County Courthouse, completed in 1854 from designs by Rochester architect Henry Searles.

Although much of Batavia's (Genesee Co) 19th-century core has been lost, several notable buildings remain along the main street. The Holland Land Office (1815) is a National Historic Landmark. It is a modest-sized but refined example of Federal-period stone commercial architecture, featuring delicate Adamesque detailing inside and out, and remarkable for its sophistication, given its construction on what was then the frontier. The imposing gray Greek Revival–style Genesee County Courthouse (1841), a few blocks to the east, dominates a commanding west-facing view at the junction of several major roads. Batavia's main street also boasts major examples of ecclesiastical architecture, including the Gothic Revival–style First Presbyterian Church, (1856, 1892, 1919), the Richardsonian Romanesque–style First Baptist Church (1891), designed by the prominent regional firm of Pierce and Dockstader of Elmira, and the Neo-Gothic–style Saint James' Episcopal Church (1908), designed by Robert North.

Of particular note in Canandaigua (Ontario Co) are the Greek Revival courthouse surmounted by a dome (?1858, major renovations *ca* 1910), the Federal-period City Hall (?1824), and the Federal-period First Congregational Church (?1812, ?1872). Perhaps the most unusual building in the city is the Granger Homestead (1815), constructed by Gideon Granger following his service as postmaster general under Presidents Thomas Jefferson and James Madison. While typical of high-style American Federal domestic architecture in its decoration, the building's unusual form is reminiscent of period estate architecture in Europe, featuring a full two-story oblong mass with a smaller third story, all topped by low-pitched roofs with balustrades. Geneva (Ontario Co) is notable for its collection of row houses, a rare form west of the Hudson Valley, located along South Main St on a bluff overlooking Seneca Lake and dating from the first third of the 19th century. Proceeding south, these houses give way to a collection of large-scale freestanding residences spanning the period from the 1830s through the early 20th century.

See also URBAN HOTELS.

Hamlin, Talbot. *Greek Revival Architecture in America* (New York: Dover, 1944)

Landmark Society of Genesee County. *The Architectural Heritage of Genesee County, New York* (Batavia, NY: Landmark Society of Genesee County, 1989)

Malo, Paul. *Landmarks of Rochester and Monroe County: A Guide to Neighborhoods and Villages* (Syracuse: Syracuse Univ Press, 1974)

Reisem, Richard O. *200 years of Rochester Architecture and Gardens* (Rochester: Landmark Society of Western New York, 1994)

Robert Englert

architects and architecture, Saratoga County. Saratoga Co begins, at its southern extreme, where the navigable Hudson ends, at the Village of Waterford. From here the Great Rd followed the Hudson north to the Schuyler property in Saratoga, renamed Schuylerville in 1831. Saratoga Co was separated from Albany Co in 1791. The only obviously Colonial building to survive before this date is the Philip Schuyler House in Schuylerville. It was rebuilt in 1777 after it was destroyed during the second Battle of Saratoga. Few structures of any importance, beside fortifications, were built north of Albany until after the War of Independence because of the threat of incursions during the French and Indian War. After the war, from the 1790s to the 1830s, Federal-style houses appeared everywhere. The Fitch House (1798) on Fitch Rd in the Town of Saratoga, with the delicate colonnaded temple front, is characteristic of the finest examples of this style.

George Washington's visit on 27 July 1783 to the High Rock Spring, at the site of what later became Saratoga Springs, attracted national attention to the area. Almost immediately visitors arrived, drawn by the health-giving waters, and by the 1830s it had become a famous international resort. While fine buildings occur throughout Saratoga Co, the most important were in Saratoga Springs, continuing into the 21st century with Antoine Predock's extraordinary postmodern Tang Teaching Museum and Art Gallery (2000) at Skidmore College. Gideon Putnam, the founder of Saratoga Springs, built in 1802 his Boarding House, the first large-scale accommodation for guests. Putnam's Boarding House later expanded into Union Hall (later Grand Union). In 1811 Putnam constructed a much more impressive building, Congress Hall, fronted with the first colonnaded porch in Saratoga Springs running the length of a long facade. The design was intended to be a reference to the colonnaded porch of Washington's Mount Vernon. Monumental porches became the principal architectural symbol of the great hotels of Saratoga and of resort hotels across the country. A third large hotel, the United States, was added in 1824. The three great hotels were continually added to and rebuilt. In the 1870s the final rebuilding of them was achieved in a massive Second Empire style. With powerful mansarded roofs and towers dominating the skyline, the sheer scale of these hotels made Saratoga Springs famous throughout the western world. With their destruction in the 20th century (Congress Hall in 1913, United States in 1946, and Grand Union in 1953), the city's world-famous architectural environment came to an end. Only the architecture of the Saratoga Race Course (renovation, 1902) retains the grandeur of the great hotels, while the perfectly restored Adelphi Hotel (1877), on a smaller scale, survives as a fine example of the style of the period.

The most important architectural symbol of Saratoga's gambling past, John Morrissey's Italian style Club House (1871–72; now called the Casino) can still be visited in Congress Park. More important for architectural history was the design of the park itself, created by the team who created Central Park in New York City, landscape architect Frederick Law Olmsted and architect Calvert Vaux. In 1876 Olmsted designed Congress Park, while Vaux provided an exquisite High Victorian structure that included a restaurant with pavilions for the Congress and

The rebuilt United States Hotel in Saratoga Springs, opened for guests in 1874.

Columbian Springs. Sections were taken down beginning in 1915. The last structure to survive, the Columbian Spring pavilion, was razed in 1931. Also important for architectural history was Richard Upjohn's Bethesda Episcopal Church (1842). It is one of the earliest true Gothic Revival churches, and, up to this date, the most perfect expression of Upjohn's high church ideals.

Impressive houses in all of the Victorian styles were erected on the major streets of Saratoga Springs in the late 19th century. The most extraordinary for its aggressive originality was the High Victorian George Sherman Batcheller Mansion (1873). The most significant architectural complex erected in Saratoga Springs encompasses the buildings of the Saratoga Spa State Park, a project that began in 1915 and climaxed with the completion of the Hall of Springs in 1934. In 1911 civic leaders of Saratoga Springs developed an ambitious plan to create a bathing spa to rival the spas of Europe. The first building completed was the beautiful Washington Baths (1918; now National Museum of Dance). Designed by State Architect Lewis Pilcher, the style is a large-scale version of Gustav Stickley's domestic Craftsman style. The Lincoln Baths, a converted factory, burned in 1927. It was replaced in 1929 with a monumental Beaux Arts design by State Architect William Haugaard. Like so many American architects in this period, Haugaard had been trained at the Ecole des Beaux-Arts in France. When the final building phase of the spa began in 1930, an Ecole des Beaux-Arts graduate, Joseph Freedlander, was hired as architect in charge. He created one of the most impressive and original examples of Beaux Arts design in America (1934), a grand architectural composition, partly Italian Renaissance, partly Williamsburg Colonial in style. Colonnaded temple fronts and long arcades, including the Hall of Springs, the Administration Building, and the two Roosevelt Baths (1934) surround a central mall with reflecting pool. Crossing malls extend to the temple-fronted Victoria Pool (1934) at one end and to the Late Modern Saratoga Performing Arts Center at the other. This last was begun in 1964, when Gov Nelson A. Rockefeller took on the Saratoga Spa State Park as a favorite project, and completed in 1966.

Kettlewell, James K. *Saratoga Springs: An Architectural History, 1790–1990* (Saratoga Springs, NY: Lyrical Ballad Bookstore, 1991)

Swanner, Grace Maguire. *Saratoga, Queen of Spas* (Utica: North Country Books, 1988)

Sweeney, Beatrice, and Marion Taub. *Bibliography of Research Materials on Saratoga Springs, New York* (Saratoga Springs, NY: Saratoga Springs Public Library, 1977)

James K. Kettlewell

architects and architecture, Southern Tier (eastern)

Binghamton and Surrounding Regions

Until the middle of the 19th century, most of the small cities and towns of the eastern Southern Tier of New York State did not have a population large enough for a resident architect. A few superior designs were built when the client had the means and sophisticated taste. In Binghamton, Whitney Place, an 1824 flush-boarded, bowfronted Adamesque manse patterned after a Manhattan example, was exceptional by any measure. While the Federal structures are generally modest, the Greek Revival designs of the region reflected its increased wealth and soon began to rival the best known in the country. John A. Collier's Ingleside (1837–38), whose principal Classical portico overlooked the Chenango Canal, is but one of several examples that remain much more obvious in communities such as Owego (Tioga Co), where there was less subsequent development. Projects in Binghamton by architects from outside Binghamton include Christ Church (1853–55), designed by New York City–based Richard Upjohn and built by contractor J. Stuart Wells, and the First Presbyterian Church, erected during the Civil War and designed by J. J. Lyons of New York City. The First National Bank is often cited as the first architect-designed building in Binghamton.

By the mid–19th century, Binghamton's architects catered to the local market. In the early 1860s, at the request of Dr J. Edward Turner, Isaac Perry, one of the state's best-known designers (then based in Manhattan), secured the commission of the New York State Inebriate Asylum, the first single-purpose hospital in the country to treat alcoholism as a disease. This castellated Gothic structure on a hill east of Binghamton was also enlarged under his direction. By 1863 Perry's work was demanding enough that he left New York City and established an office to serve the Southern Tier and northern Pennsylvania. In Binghamton his Gothic vocabulary is also evident in Centenary Methodist Episcopal Church (1866–68), St. Patrick's Church (1867), and First Baptist Church (1870–72). The first major business block he designed was for Cyrus Strong, in 1864, and several others followed. The 1876 cast-iron Perry Block, a building he designed for himself, was testimony to his ability to experiment freely with new materials. After spending a number of years working on the State Capitol in Albany, Perry returned to Binghamton in 1899 to supervise the construction of the Carnegie Library, one of his last projects before retiring.

The many members of the Lacey architectural family provided hundreds of designs in the tri-city area of Binghamton, Johnson City, and Endicott (Broome Co) from 1872 through 1930. T. I. Lacey's contribution included the 10-story Security Mutual Building (1904), which ranks as Binghamton's first true "skyscraper." Arthur T. Lacey's steel frame Beaux-Arts Press Building (1904) provides some insight about his abilities, while his firm continued to produce a wide range of industrial and hospital buildings in the model manufacturing village of Johnson City. Sanford Lacey's Binghamton schemes included the Bijou Theatre (1893), Boston Department Store (1899), and the Exchange Street Public Library (1904).

Setting up office in 1903, Walter H. Whitlock was also one of Binghamton's better-known architects. Among his works are the Doctor's Memorial Building and the Nurses' Home at City Hospital in Binghamton; the Harry L. Johnson and Lincoln Schools in Johnson City; and St. Thomas Aquinas, Port Dickinson Baptist, and Calvary Baptist Churches, all in Binghamton. Nearer the end of his career, he was responsible for the US Post Office in Endicott (1937), with an interior mural by Douglass Crockwell, and for the Broome County Office Building, an Art Deco masterpiece, largely completed in 1939.

Charles H. Conrad, a Beaux-Arts Institute of Design in Manhattan graduate, was the first president of the Binghamton Society of Architects, which formed in 1916. Conrad was also a cofounder, with Cornell graduate George Bain Cummings, of a firm that would last well into the second half of the 20th century. The first major commission of the Cummings-Conrad partnership was the Benjamin Franklin School (1926) in Binghamton, which led to the firm's specialization in providing modern centralized schools. Their most well-known post–World War II project was the Civic Center complex in Binghamton, with City Hall and state and county office buildings on a common plaza.

Ithaca and Environs

Elsewhere around the eastern Southern Tier, the same transition from itinerant builder-architects and outside designers to a locally established professional cadre occurred. For example, the largest Greek Revival house in Tompkins Co and probably in the region is the Hermon Camp House, in Trumansburg, designed and constructed in 1845 by carpenter-architect Thomas Judd. Similarly pretentious was the triple-gabled Gothic Revival Thomas Jefferson Williams House, Sunny Gables, constructed in 1851–52 just south of Ithaca, one of three such houses in the region. The architect and contractor was Sam Graham, another talented builder who quickly moved from the region. Like Binghamton's master builder Wells, Ithaca's Ira Tillotson had to broaden his services to include building, surveying, and holding various public offices. Tillotson, likely the designer of the impressive Greek Revival Clinton House hotel that opened in 1832, provided midcentury designs for the Presbyterian, Dutch Reformed, and First Methodist congregations.

Alfred B. Dale, an English-born carpenter and builder, became Ithaca's first resident architect after serving a year in the office of Isaac Perry in Binghamton. Dale's career rose following a disastrous Ithaca fire in August 1871, when he designed several business blocks and fashionable residences nearby, including the Griffin Block (1872), the second Ithaca Hotel (1871), and the Blood Building (1870). A better-known early designer is William H. Miller. Having become involved in local construction, Miller was noticed by the first president of Cornell University, Andrew Dickson White, and enlisted to supervise the construction of his house, in 1871, drawn from a Calvert Vaux design as revised by Miller's partner George Hathorne. Miller's achievements, however, lie in the studio he sponsored for a number of young designers. His work remains obvious locally in a number of large houses for prominent Cornell benefactors, notably those for the Sage family and Jennie McGraw-Fiske from 1875 to 1881, several fraternities, and the execution of the Romanesque Uris Library at the university, dedicated in 1891.

Cornell University provided a stimulating setting and new ideas. Its initial period of construction depended upon the mansard schemes of out-of-town firms and architects such as Wilcox and Porter, and Archimedes Russell to frame the dimensions of the quadrangle during the 1860s. Pres White's search for Cornell's first professor of architecture, the Rev Charles Babcock, shifted the approach with Ruskin-inspired Gothic schemes for Sage Chapel and Sage College for Women, as well as Franklin and Lincoln Halls, which led to a markedly stylish collection. The Department of Architecture at Cornell University was established in 1871, becoming one of the earliest architecture schools in the nation; some of its graduates, such as Alvah Bugbee Wood, practice nearby for decades. The university, especially under Bryant Fleming's chairmanship of the newly established Department of Landscape Art, was also important for fostering landscape architecture. A large percentage of modest work in the Ithaca area was done in the office of Arthur N. Gibb and Clinton L. Vivian, who had worked together in William Miller's office. Their taste, tending toward the classical in houses and commercial blocks through World War I, is evident in examples such as the Robert B. Williams house (1904–5) and the Jared T. Newman residence (1903, 1909).

Cortland

By comparison to Ithaca, Cortland's 19th-century commercial and residential development benefited from the designs of few local architects, chiefly M. F. Howes and H. W. Beardsley. Many of the large commissions went to out-of-town designers. For example, when the prominent industrialist Chester F. Wickwire decided to build his limestone castle in 1888, two New York City–based professionals, architect Samuel Burrage Reed and decorator Joseph Burr Tiffany, were called upon to execute the scheme. Reed also provided the design for the local Presbyterian Church (1889–90). The firm of Henry C. Allewelt and Sons, of Syracuse, completed the interior, and the work was found to be so attractive that that firm was subsequently responsible for the interiors of the Baptist Church, the Grace Episcopal Church, and the residence of Lawrence J. Fitzgerald. In 1890, when T. H. Wickwire attempted to outdo his brother with the construction of his sandstone "palace," he chose Charles S. Sedgwick, of Minneapolis. Even as late at 1923, the Wickwires pushed for the expansion of the Presbyterian Church with the famed New York City firm of George Kramer and Son. The same year, the Cortland County Courthouse was completed under the direction of architect James Reily Gordon, of New York City, apparently modeled on St. Paul's Cathedral in London, with a landscaped park by Professor Laurie Cox of Syracuse University. Perhaps the most important Cortland architect was Carl W. Clark, best known for his commercial work and school facilities. Clark opened his office in Cortland in 1914. His firm designed over 55 school buildings in central New York State.

Elmira and Environs

Elmira gained importance as a shipping center in the region because transportation up the Chemung River beyond this point was unreliable. A pride of place is obvious in the striking Chemung County Courthouse Complex, with the Romanesque courthouse (1861–62) by Syracuse architect Horatio Nelson White, alongside the classically inspired County Clerk's Office (1875; annex, 1895) and the Greek Revival District Attorney and Treasurer's Office.

Elmira's best-known architects were J. Q. Ingham and the firm of Pierce and Bickford, both in practice throughout the region. Joseph H. Pierce and Hiram H. Bickford maintained a successful 27-year partnership from 1890 to 1917. Pierce first learned under the tutelage of Elmira architect Eugene B. Gregory but by 1881 was working alongside William H. Hayes, the first graduate of the architecture program at Cornell. He later practiced alone and with engineer Otis Dockstader, from 1883 to 1890, specializing in residential and church architecture, such as the First Baptist Church in Elmira (1889). Bickford joined Pierce in 1890, and larger commissions followed, including the Mansfield Normal School (1891); Elmira Free Academy (1890); St. Patrick's Parochial School (1892); Clifton Springs Sanitarium (1891); and Steele Memorial Library (1921–23). Perhaps their most distinctive single building is the richly decorated stone and terra-cotta-clad Elmira City Hall (1895). Their 1922 stucco YMCA building is a Renaissance palazzo that would be at home in Florence.

Bath and Corning

The Steuben Co communities of Bath and Corning blossomed only with the advent of the railroad. In Bath the 120 ft (37 m) tall stone spire of St. Thomas's Episcopal Church (1869–71) follows the approved ecclesiological principles of the period. New York City architect Henry Dudley was the architect. Yet another spire by another Manhattan-based designer would top it. First Presbyterian Church (1874–77), initiated at the request of wealthy land speculator John Davenport, was the vision of designer Jacob Wrey Mould. While the polychromatic Gothic exterior is striking, the interior sports an exposed arch system with stubby colonnettes and Tiffany glass, added later.

The railroad coal car adopted by Corning in 1847 in its village seal captured the local idea of progress, and two years later the Erie Railroad finally made its debut. Corning Flint Glass Works (now Corning Inc), established in 1868, made the City of Corning world famous. The expansion of the glass company's manufacturing continued to stimulate the local housing market, so that entire subdivisions were built for its workers. The first carpenter-architect of note was Henry G. Tuthill, whose earliest commissions date to 1877. Other architects and firms, such as Otis Dockstader and Pierce and Bickford contributed prominent houses and business blocks. One of the several striking religious structures is the stone Christ Episcopal Church (1893–94) by architect R. W. Gibson, which features stained glass by the Tiffany and Lamb companies. The most important event of the 20th century was the flood that devastated Corning in June 1972, in the wake of Hurricane Agnes, when water covered much of the valley. Corning Glass renewed its commitment to the area, and many of the business blocks that were remodeled with glass in the 1930s were restored with the guidance of the Market Street Restoration Agency.

Alfred and Cuba

Allegany Co's communities are relatively small and remain in an agrarian context. The office and display center of the Celadon Terra-Cotta Co, built in 1892 in Alfred, is important in representing the effort of a group of investors who made use of local clays and finished their brick and ware with a greenish glaze, said to resemble Chinese ceramics. The roofing and decorative products were featured in offices in New York and Chicago. Although the tile works burned in 1906, the company was in part responsible for the establishment of what became the SUNY College of Ceramics at Alfred University. That institution's role in the community is obvious in local monuments such as the Chapel (1852), which became Alumni Hall, and the stone manse built by university president Jonathan Allen, now known as the Steinheim Museum (1879). The most pretentious designs in Cuba often were provided by out-of-town architects and executed by local builders. The mail order firm of George F. Barber, in Knoxville, Tenn, provided the frame Romanesque scheme for J. H. Setchel (1888) east of town and others along Robie St. The McKinney Stables (1907–9), built for trotter breeder William Simpson, at the southern perimeter of Cuba, is one of the most impressive agricultural buildings in the state for its 347 ft (106 m) length. Reportedly costing $200,000, the cast stone and poured concrete structure featured Celadon terra cotta, made in Alfred. It was designed by architect John Coxhead of Buffalo.

Bothwell, Lawrence. *Broome County Heritage: An Illustrated History* (Woodland Hills, Calif: Windsor Publications, 1983)

Foote, Keith G. "Binghamton Architects: 1863–1916." MS, 1981

Rash, David A. "The Works of Clinton L. Vivian, Architect of Ithaca." MS, 1987

Reed, Roger G. *Architects of Standing: Pierce and Bickford, Elmira, NY, 1890–1932* (Elmira: Chemung County Historical Society, 1983)

Snodderly, Daniel R. *Ithaca and Its Past* (Ithaca: DeWitt Historical Society of Tompkins County, 1982)

Michael A. Tomlan

architects and architecture, Southern Tier (western)

Early Builders and Styles

The western part of New York State's Southern Tier—Chautauqua and Cattaraugus Cos—has a remarkably wide representation of the complete record of architecture and the built environment, including vernacular and high style, commercial and industrial, with every major mode of design represented. Documented builders of simple, early vernacular housing, such as Aaron Putnam of Fredonia (Chautauqua Co), were craftsmen and farmers as well as carpenters. The earliest vernacular dwellings, few of which had survived except in photographic and early history records, were of log construction, soon supplanted by timber framing with vertical board sheathing (which was an economical replacement for more traditional studding), and then traditional timber framing with 4 x 4 in (10.2 x 10.2 cm) studs. Balloon framing is found by the 1850s.

A few Federal-style houses in Chautauqua Co survive, including the Cyrus D. Angell House (early 19th century) in Forestville, the James McClurg House (1818) in Westfield, and the Zattu Cushing House (?1818) in Fredonia, and the rare Federal-style public building exists, such as the Town Hall (1829) in Ellicottville (Cattaraugus Co). The largest body of sophisticated 19th-century building, however, is from the Greek Revival. By the 1840s there was a boom in Greek Revival dwellings and public buildings, based largely on a selection of standard New England types; hundreds, from the simple to the grand, still stand. Many used pattern book doorways and other details from the standard contemporary books (specifically those of architects Asher Benjamin and Minard Lafever). John Jones and Aaron Hall are two of Chautauqua Co's better-known Greek Revival builder-architects.

Local architects who prospered in the 19th to early 20th centuries often began their careers as carpenters and then, with the aid of book study, became architects. This was the case for Enoch A. Curtis, who centered in Fredonia after the Civil War. He had a thriving regional business in domestic and public buildings throughout western New York State and northwestern Pennsylvania, all in the most current styles; some models traced to the popular *American Architect and Building News* periodical as well as to pattern books of the day. Oliver P. Smith, active in the southern part of Chautauqua Co, published his own pattern book, *The Domestic Architect* (1854), in Buffalo. Another documented 19th-century builder-architect was Elias S. Barger of Westfield, whose elegant Austin Smith House (whose cornerstone is dated 1830) predates the famous Lafever pattern book of that type.

Professional Designers and Catalog Fashion

While carpenter-builders made notable contributions to the built environment, the architectural sophistication of the whole region, which includes notable dwellings in Gothic Revival, Italianate, Octagon mode, Second Empire, Queen Anne, Richardsonian Romanesque, Colonial Revival, and most of the 20th-century Revival styles, was also influenced by professional architects whose designs arrived via the printed page or mail order plans. Dwellings by, or adapted from, Andrew Jackson Downing (Newburgh), Samuel Sloan (Philadelphia), E. C. Hussey (New York City), George F. Barber (Knoxville, Tenn), and G. W. Ashby and W. F. Schroeder (Chicago) are all found in the region, often multiple times. Sears, Aladdin, and other catalog dwellings from the first part of the 20th century can be seen throughout both counties.

Lewis Miller, a founder of the Chautauqua Institution, designed one of the most interesting houses of the area. His Cottage (1875) at that center for education is an excellent Stick-style dwelling. It was precut in Akron, Ohio, and shipped to the site for assembly. Especially in this region, prefabricated architectural elements (eg, cast-iron lintels and storefront piers, or interior millwork and fireplaces for houses) were ordered from Buffalo, New York City, or elsewhere and are found in numerous communities.

In the early 20th century sophisticated local architectural firms, such as Beck and Tinkham of Jamestown (Chautauqua Co), built throughout the region, but designers from outside the region were also employed. For example, E. E. Jarolemon (Niagara Falls) designed both the beautiful Beaux Arts Classical library (1905) and a Tudor Revival parsonage (1906) in Westfield, and G. Wesley Stickle (Erie, Pa), erected a fine Neo-Colonial home (1932) in Fredonia, although the initial blueprints were based on a design published in 1930 by Standard Homes Co in Washington, DC.

In the 20th century a number of Modernist-inclined architects worked in the region as well, most notably the firm of I. M. Pei and Partners (Henry N. Cobb, partner in charge), who designed and built from 1967 to 1971 a dozen new structures for the expanded SUNY Fredonia campus. Combining the severity of Bauhaus design with the robust forms of Le Corbusier, the main structures in poured concrete have surfaces animated by subtle form-board imprints. More recent construction at the campus includes a library addition (1989–91) by Pasanella and Klein from New York City.

Planned Communities

In the early 19th century, many communities, whether they grew organically or were laid out in a grid plan, had a public common at their center (eg, Fredonia, Westfield, Silver Creek, Mayville, and Ellicottville), around which the civic and religious buildings were clustered on one or two sides, with commercial structures completing the composition. The Barker Common in Fredonia retains two cast-iron J. W. Fiske fountains from 1901.

Chautauqua Lake in the 19th century was surrounded by resort hotels, both elaborate and modest, and communities. The Chautauqua Institution (founded 1874) grew organically along the lakeshore, with a focus on early assembly areas such as Miller Park, planned quadrangles such as Bestor Plaza, and key buildings such as the Athenaeum Hotel, the Amphitheater, the Hall of Christ, with the rich array of dwellings from the 1870s to the present often oriented to take advantage of lake views. Across the lake is Point Chautauqua, a community laid out by Frederick Law Olmsted in 1875; much of the original plan still exists. On nearby Cassadaga Lakes is Lily Dale, a spiritualist community established in 1880.

The SUNY Fredonia campus by I. M. Pei and Partners in the late 1960s and early 1970s was an especially challenging planning problem, for the firm had to integrate new buildings with 10 existing structures (erected mainly 1940–60) and to try to animate a flat site. By weaving the new construction among the old with an L axis and creating new quadrangles, the two were handsomely and meaningfully integrated. This mix of styles is typical of many of the communities in the region, notably Silver Creek, Dunkirk, Fredonia, Westfield, and Jamestown (Chautauqua Co), and Cattaraugus, Ellicottville, Franklinville, Olean, and Salamanca (Cattaraugus Co).

Conkling, Edgar C. *Frederick Law Olmsted's Point Chautauqua: The Story of an Historic Lakeside Community* (Buffalo: Canisius College Press, 2001)

Fancher, Pauline. *Chautauqua: Its Architecture and Its People* (Miami, Fla: Banyan Books, 1978)

Lindquist, Marlene, and Therold Lindquist. *Architecture in Westfield: An Historical Survey* (Fredonia, NY: Lakeshore Association for the Arts, 1975)

Reiff, Daniel D. *Architecture in Fredonia, New York, 1811–1997: From Log Cabin to I. M. Pei* (Fredonia, NY: White Pine Press, 1997)

———. *Houses from Books: Treatises, Pattern Books, and Catalogs in American Architecture, 1738–1950: A History and Guide* (University Park: Pennsylvania State Univ Press, 2000)

Thompson, Dolores. *Jamestown and Chautauqua County: An Illustrated History* (Woodland Hills, Calif: Windsor Publications, 1984)

Daniel D. Reiff

architects and architecture, Syracuse and Central New York

Early 19th-Century Architecture

It was not until after the Revolutionary War that people of European descent undertook extensive building in the area, much of it, like the settlers, representing vernacular traditions from New England. From the Connecticut River valley came the massive Yankee houses with their central chimneys, an example of which is the Needham Maynard House (1787) in New Hartford (Oneida Co). Transmitted from the Hudson Valley by way of the canal system, the one-and-a-half-story house known as the upright and wing—composed of two intersecting gabled pavilions—became common in the region beginning in the 1820s and maintained its popularity for most of the 19th century.

Examples of all of the 19th century's predominant architectural styles are common throughout the region. Among the best extant examples of the Federal and Neoclassical styles are the Deacon William McCullins House (*ca* 1805) in Eaton (Madison Co); Whitestown Town Hall (1807) in Whitesboro (Oneida Co) and Lorenzo (1807–9), John Lincklaen's house in Cazenovia (Madison Co), both by John Hooker; Hulbert House Hotel (1812) in Boonville (Oneida Co); Delphi Baptist Church (1815–18) in Pompey (Onondaga Co); Hamilton College Chapel (1827) in Clinton (Oneida Co) by Philip Hooker; the Clinton House (1828–29, Ira Tillotson; 1872, William H. Miller) in Ithaca; and Whig Hill (1833) in Lysander (Onondaga Co). Numerous examples of modest dwellings in Neoclassical style are located in the region, including 80 New Hartford St (*ca* 1825) in New York Mills (Oneida Co).

Many of the earliest builders in the region had their roots in Albany. Philip Hooker and his brother John and father Samuel were influential during the first two decades of the 19th century. With the continued expansion of permanent settlements and the establishment of an urban culture, builder-architects settled in the area. One of the earliest in this group was Edward Crane, who was active in Utica during the 1820s. Professional architectural offices were established during the middle decades of the 19th century. S. E. Hewes, in Syracuse, became nationally known through publications on schoolhouse design.

Architectural Revivals of the 19th Century

Central New York is well known for its Greek Revival architecture, some of the best examples of which include the Richard Berry House (*ca* 1835) in Poolville (Madison Co); Cayuga County Courthouse (1835–36, John I. Hagaman) in Auburn (Cayuga Co); Blinn Harris House (1838) in Norwich (Chenango Co); Rose Hill (1837–39) in Geneva (Seneca Co); Utica State Hospital (1837–43), William Clarke) and Mechanics Hall (1838, Benjamin Bourne), both in Utica. Additional examples include the Lisle Post Office (*ca* 1840) in Broome Co; Presbyterian, Baptist, and Unitarian Churches (1843–44) in Holland Patent (Oneida Co); and Hatheway Homestead (1844) in Solon (Cortland Co). The Oswego County Courthouse (1860, Horatio Nelson White) in Oswego and the Schuyler County Courthouse (1867) in Watkins Glen (Schuyler Co) are prominent later examples of

Greek Revival. In the latter building, elements of the Italianate are integrated in a design that is Greek Revival in its massing and major details. Many dwellings continued to be constructed in the Greek Revival style, which became in essence the regional vernacular, through to the third quarter of the 19th century. Cobblestone construction was a regional favorite during the period 1825–60; most extant examples are in the Greek Revival style.

The Gothic Revival in church architecture was promoted by the ecclesiastical movement in England and was adopted by the Episcopal Church in New York State at an early date. Among the best of the region's extant Gothic Revival churches is St. Thomas' Episcopal Church (1846–47, Richard Upjohn) in Hamilton (Madison Co). Churches constructed in the Gothic style before the 1840s were influenced by English Romanticism, as in St. Luke's (1828) in Harpursville (Broome Co). The style was later adapted to domestic and public applications, including the Reuel E. Smith House (1849–52, Alexander Jackson Davis) in Skaneateles (Onondaga Co), Fowler House (*ca* 1850) in Owego (Tioga Co); Eccleson House (?1853) in Oxford (Chenango Co); Second Tompkins County Courthouse (1854, John F. Maurice) in Ithaca; the Oswego City Library (1855–56, Hewes and Rose); and Grace Episcopal Church (1856–60, Richard Upjohn) in Utica.

Experimental and High Styles

Increased access to the visual cultures of the past, promoted by a dramatic expansion of publishing, stimulated experimentation with various architectural styles. This is evidenced in the Tuscan style of the John Munn House (1854, A. J. Davis) in Utica, Italianate Jonathan Wells House (*ca* 1850) in Norwich, Anglo-Norman Chemung County Courthouse (1862, H. N. White) in Elmira, and Oswego City Hall (1870, H. N. White), as well as in the Byzantine-modeled St. John's Church (1869) in Utica and in the Second Empire–styled Tioga County Courthouse (1871–73, Miles F. Howe) in Owego. The Italianate predominated and is represented further by the Weeks-Burns House (*ca* 1870) in Harpursville and the Sherman D. Phelps House (*ca* 1870, Isaac Perry) in Binghamton. From the 1850s to the 1870s a squarish two-story house type, surmounted by a cupola and using a combination of Italianate detailing and Neoclassical massing, became popular, particularly in Oneida Co. The dramatic increase in availability of engraved views of European buildings promoted an eclectic approach toward the application of historical motifs on American buildings beginning in the middle of the 19th century.

Among the most prominent architects to base their practices in this region during the later 19th century were Archimedes Russell (1840–1915), Horatio Nelson White (1814–92), and Joseph Lyman Silsbee (1848–1913), all based in Syracuse, and Isaac Perry (1822–1904), active in Binghamton. These architects designed structures throughout Central New York in the sophisticated hybrid styles popular during their era. Chief among their works include the White Memorial Building (1876, Silsbee), the Syracuse Savings Bank (1876, Silsbee), and the Hall of Languages at Syracuse University (1873, White), all in Syracuse. Perry was responsible for the design of many of the state's armories.

Late 19th-century high-style architecture is well represented in the region. Richardsonian Romanesque became a popular style for homes of the wealthy and for public buildings beginning in the late 1880s through to the first decade of the 20th century. The First Baptist Church (1888–89, Melvin Hubbard) in Oneida (Madison Co); Scrooby (1889, R. S. Stephenson Jr), the Benjamin Brewster House in Cazenovia; the Jim Stevens House (1890) and St. Peter's Church (1897) in Rome; the Kanatenah Apartments (1897) and the Olbiston Apartments (1898) in Utica; and the Methodist Church (1909) in Canastota (Madison Co) are all fine examples of the style.

Sophisticated examples of the Queen Anne style include the DiIorio House (1879) at 1024 Park Ave in Utica, and Hillcrest, the Robert Benson Davis House (1905) in Cazenovia. Other eclectic styles are represented by the Albright House (*ca* 1895) in Utica and the Rome City Hall (1894). The Beaux Arts aesthetic was promoted as American Empire style at the World's Columbian Exposition in Chicago in 1893. Examples include the Binghamton City Hall (1897, Raymond F. Almirall) and the Savings Bank of Utica (1900). It became popular for the design of academic buildings and can be seen in examples by William H. Miller, of Ithaca, and Green and Wicks on the Cornell University campus. The post office (1934–35) in Watkins Glen was designed in the Colonial Revival style, a related aesthetic frequently used for smaller buildings. Both styles used Classical language in their detailing and were popular until the advent of World War II.

The 20th Century

Gustav Stickley is perhaps the most well known architect working in the region during the first quarter of the 20th century. Stickley's *Craftsman Homes* had widespread influence in the United States and in Europe and offered an astylar alternative to the overwrought Neoclassical work then popular. Ward Wellington Ward was another Syracuse-based architect who excelled at Arts and Crafts design and who enjoys a widespread reputation. Other architects and firms promulgating this aesthetic included Sackett and Park, whose Cortland Fire Headquarters (1914) also mined Flemish Renaissance architecture for its details.

The State Tower Building (1927, Thompson and Churchill of New York City) and the Niagara Mohawk Building (1932, Melvin L. King, Syracuse, and Bley and Lyman, Buffalo), both in Syracuse, are important examples of the Art Deco style. Their bold lines articulate a love of material and form over florid detail.

After World War II an increasing proportion of large regional commissions went to architectural firms based in New York or other large cities. Following national trends, corporate architects including I. M. Pei and Skidmore, Owings and Merrill were asked to design high-profile campus architecture. Pei's work is particularly well represented: the Everson Museum and the S. I. Newhouse School of Public Communications (both 1961–64) in Syracuse and the Herbert F. Johnson

Yates Castle in Syracuse, designed by James Renwick Jr, built 1852–54, demolished in 1954.

Museum of Art (1968–73) in Ithaca are good examples of his work. Philip Johnson designed the new pavilion for the Munson-Williams-Proctor Arts Institute (1957–60) in Utica. This trend continued to the end of the century, with Boston architects Koetter, Kim and Associates responsible in part for the design of two buildings on the Syracuse University campus: Science and Technology Center (1989) and the Dorothea Ilgen Shaffer Art Building (1990). Despite these trends, local talent continued to generate quality work. Among the best known of the later 20th-century architects of the region are Gordon A. Wright and Carl W. Clark. Architect Arthur McDonald's own house in Syracuse (1981) is a good example of late 20th-century residential work. Syracuse-based architectural firm Sargent Webster Crenshaw and Folley, founded in 1946, was perhaps the largest architectural firm in the region during the 1970s and 1980s. It designed the James M. Hanley Federal Building complex (1977) in Syracuse and specialized in academic and institutional work in Syracuse and throughout the state. Subsequent to the development of the historic preservation movement in the 1960s, firms such as Schopfer Architects of Syracuse began to specialize in renovation of older structures.

See also ARCHITECTS AND ARCHITECTURE, SOUTHERN TIER (EASTERN); SHOPPING CENTERS AND MALLS; URBAN HOTELS. For illustration see SYRACUSE UNIVERSITY.

Hardin, Evamaria. *Syracuse Landmarks: An AIA Guide to Downtown and Historic Neighborhoods* (Syracuse: Onondaga Historical Association; Syracuse Univ Press, 1993)

Jeschke, Carol T., ed. *Onondaga Landmarks: A Survey of Historic and Architectural Sites in Syracuse and Onondaga County,* rev ed. (Syracuse: Estabrook Publishing, 1981)

Montillon, Eugene D. *Historic Architecture in Broome County, New York, and Vicinity* (Binghamton: Broome County Planning Department; Broome County Historical Society, 1972)

Przybycien, Frank E. *Utica, a City Worth Saving* (Utica: Dodge-Graphic Press, 1976)

Wellman, Judith, ed. *Landmarks of Oswego County* (Syracuse: Syracuse Univ Press, 1988)

Williams, Emily. *Canal Country: Utica to Binghamton* (Rome: Canterbury Press, 1982)

Walter Richard Wheeler

archives. Individuals, governments, businesses, and nonprofit entities create and use records every day in the conduct of their normal activities. Those records that are deemed to have long-term significance are retained as archives. Archival records serve multiple purposes, of which historical research is certainly one. Public records, for example, are maintained in part to guarantee the rights of citizens and to help hold government accountable for its actions.

Archival Development

Archival repositories can be classed into two broad categories. The first includes those that care for the records of the institution of which they are a part. This group includes repositories for public records, such as the New York State Archives and the Westchester County Archives, and institutional archives, such as the Ford Foundation Archives and the Syracuse University Archives. Other archival repositories focus on collecting records produced by individuals, businesses, and organizations outside of the repository. Most historical societies and manuscript and special collections departments of college and university libraries fall into this group. Many archives combine both internal and external collecting programs.

Archivists who work in institutional archives are typically interested in the management of both the current and the historical records of the institution. This records management function is important in helping ensure that archives expend resources only on maintaining essential records. Typically, only about 3–5% of the records created by government or business are important enough to be retained as archival records. The New York State Archives, for example, creates schedules that identify which records created by state agencies and local governments are to be retained permanently and how long other records must be kept before they can be discarded.

In New York State the development of repositories to collect and maintain archival records generally followed a pattern found in the United States as a whole. During the 19th century, efforts to maintain such records were carried out primarily by historical societies and individual collectors. These collections consisted mostly of personal papers of individuals or families of national, state, or local prominence. In the 20th century colleges and universities began to develop collecting programs as well as programs to maintain their own institutional records. At the same time greater attention was paid to the proper care of the vast amount of government records created by New York State government and by the more than 4,000 local government entities across the state.

In the 19th century numerous historical societies were established across the state and formed libraries that usually included manuscript materials important for local and state history. The New-York Historical Society, established in 1804, took the whole of the United States as the scope of its collections, but most such societies had a more localized focus. In addition to collecting local manuscript materials, the larger historical societies often published the texts of documents in their collections, which became the chief means of disseminating their holdings. The New York State Historical Association in Cooperstown (Otsego Co), founded in 1899 in Lake George (Warren Co), combines a large museum program with a library of books and historical records focusing on American, New York State, and local history. This combination of functions is replicated on a smaller scale at county and local historical societies across the state.

Professionalization and Specialization

Formal attention to caring for public records was slow to develop in the United States. (The first state archives program was not established until 1901, in Alabama, and the National Archives was established only in 1934.) The New York State legislature first gave attention to the state's public records in 1847, when it directed the secretary of state to turn over historic documents to the New York State Library (1818). However, most of the state's early records held by the library were tragically lost in the 1911 fire in the State Capitol. The library became the custodian of state records, although a formal archives and records program was launched much later with the creation of the New York State Archives, established in 1971 and opened in 1978. Although its primary focus has been on the records of state government, with roughly 130 million documents from the 17th century on, the State Archives has also done significant work to improve record-keeping practices across the state. Through its Documentary Heritage Program, established in 1988, the State Archives has provided grants and technical assistance to many small repositories and historical societies. In addition, the Local Government Records Management Improvement Fund, established in 1989, allows the archives to assist local governments in providing better care for their archival and nonarchival records. The New York State Historical Records Advisory Board helps promote overall planning and coordination for the care of historical records across the state.

In the 20th century important programs for the collection of archival records were developed by manuscript programs in college and university libraries. Led by major universities, such as Columbia, Cornell, Syracuse, and New York University, the state's institutions of higher education have amassed large collections of important records in a variety of areas, including literature, publishing, and labor relations, among many others. At the same time some colleges and universities have developed strong internal archival programs that document their own histories and serve as important resources for the schools' own administrations.

The late 20th century was also a time of growth of many specialized archives caring for the records of religious groups, businesses, and nonprofit agencies. Examples of such repositories in the state include the Maryknoll Mission Archives, which collects items related to its United States–based Catholic mission, and the Rockefeller Archive Center, with items such as the papers of Rockefeller family members and affiliated institutions. Another characteristic of recent archival work in New York State, as well as throughout the rest of the country, has been the attempt to expand the scope of collections to ensure that all elements of society are represented in archives and that important contemporary records are collected as avidly as historical records.

Using Archives

A major factor stimulating the use of archives in recent years has been the increased interest in genealogical research, which has brought many new researchers into archival repositories and promoted greater interest in local records. Guides to researching county records published by Cornell University *ca* 1990 and the development of county halls of records have facilitated increased public access to these records. Archivists are also working actively with school teachers to incorporate the use of historical records into social studies curriculum.

According to ArchivesUSA, a national directory, there were more than 600 archival repositories in New York State in the early 21st century. Despite the growth in the number of archival programs, however, many programs remain small and poorly funded. Even better established programs have difficulty sustaining themselves and dealing with the ever increasing amount of records produced today. The popularity of the Internet, however, has had an incredible impact on archival records. While the transition from paper to electronic records poses tremendous challenges to archivists as they seek to preserve adequate and permanent documentation of contemporary society, the Internet has made information on records more widely available, increasing the use of records at repositories of all sizes.

Dearstyne, Bruce W. "Archival Politics in New York State, 1892–1915," *New York History* 66 (Apr 1985): 165–84
Hackman, Larry J. "State Government and Statewide Archival Affairs: New York as a Case Study," *American Archivist* 55 (Fall 1992): 578–99
New York State Archives, http://www.archives.nysed.gov
Whitehill, Walter Muir. *Independent Historical Societies: An Enquiry into Their Research and Publication Functions and Their Financial Future* (Boston: Boston Athenæum, 1962)

Philip B. Eppard

Ardsley. Village (pop 4,269) in Greenburgh (Westchester Co). Called Ashford before it became Ardsley in 1883, the village incorporated in 1898. Early business included three pickle factories. The railroad that eventually became the Putnam Division of the New York Central (1880–1958) stimulated residential development, and growth spurts followed both world wars. The Saw Mill River Parkway (1930) and the New York State Thruway (1955) further improved access, although portions of the village were razed in the building of each. Ardsley is a suburban residential community with some manufacturing. Purdue Pharma and other corporations maintain research and development facilities at Ardsley Park Science and Technology Center.

Scott C. Monje

arena football. Introduced as a test game in Rockford, Ill, in 1986, arena football is a scaled-down version of traditional American football: games are played on indoor fields that are roughly half the size of most outdoor fields, with eight players on the field for each team. The professional Arena Football League (AFL) season runs from February to June. The AFL made its New York State debut in 1988. The New York Knights, based at Madison Square Garden, posted a 2-10 record and then folded, due in part to low attendance. The AFL returned to New York State in 1990 when co-owners Glenn Mazula and Joe O'Hara established the Albany Firebirds. Playing at the Knickerbocker Arena (now Pepsi Arena), the Firebirds tied for fourth place among six teams in their inaugural season. They were third in league attendance, averaging 10,153 fans. Led by offensive specialist Touchdown Eddie Brown, the Firebirds hosted ArenaBowl XIII in 1999, defeating the Orlando Predators, 59-48. It was the first ArenaBowl appearance for any New York–based team. Though the Firebirds averaged 10,049 fans per game and qualified for the playoffs in 2000, the owners decided Albany could no longer support a team in the growing league and moved the team to Indianapolis. The AFL's New York CityHawks played at Madison Square Garden in 1997 and 1998. The team had a 4-24 record and drew well under the average league attendance before being relocated to Hartford, Conn. Buffalo was awarded an AFL franchise in 1997, and the Buffalo Destroyers began play at the Marine Midland Arena (now HSBC Arena) in 1999. The Iowa Barnstormers moved to the Nassau Coliseum in Uniondale (Nassau Co) and became the New York Dragons before the start of the 2001 season. Additionally, arenafootball2 (af2), a minor league version of the AFL, was introduced in 2000. The Rochester Brigade joined the af2 in 2001, and Albany fielded a team in 2002.

Arena Football League Official Record and Fact Book, 2001 (Kingston, NY: Total Sports, 2001)
Arena Football League, http://www.arenafootball.com
Foley, Jeff. *War on the Floor: An Average Guy Plays in the Arena Football League and Lives to Write about It* (Lincoln, Nebr: Writer's Club Press, 2001)

Jeff Foley

Argentineans. The first wave of Argentinean migration to New York State took place during the 1960s when some professionals left the country in search of better employment opportunities. However, there were Argentineans living in New York State as early as the beginning of the 20th century. During the period of military authoritarian rule in Argentina, 1976–83, professionals (mainly physicians, engineers, and scientists) and some entrepreneurs, students, and others immigrated to New York State. In the late 1980s and throughout the 1990s there was a significant rise of immigration. Like most Latino groups, they were predominantly Catholic, but there are also Jews, Muslims, and Protestants, which reflects Argentina as a magnet of immigration for diverse nationalities during the first half of the 20th century.

Argentineans have developed numerous cultural, professional, religious, and entrepreneurial organizations. The Asociación Nuestra Señora Luján was founded in the state in 1977, when the image of the most venerated virgin of Argentina was officially brought to New York City. They also celebrate patriotic holidays, such as Independence Day (9 July), and promote the celebration of the International Tango Day (11 December). In addition, Argentineans have humanitarian organizations and groups working in New York State whose targeted groups are in Argentina; for example, the Atagualpa Yupanqui and Ayuda Ya send aid to different groups of disadvantaged Argentineans in Argentina. According to the 2000 US census, there were 17,906 foreign-born Argentineans living in New York State, the majority (11,268) living in New York City. Almost half of these (5,608) live in Queens. Outside of New York City, Argentineans are concentrated in Nassau and Suffolk Cos (3,324); the remainder (3,314) are scattered throughout the state.

Logan, John. "The New Latinos: Who They Are, Where They Are," http://mumford1.dyndns.org/cen2000/HispanicPop/HspReport/page6.html

Ana Margarita Cervantes-Rodríguez

Argyle. Town (pop 3,688) and village (pop 289) in central Washington Co. Argyle Patent was granted with township powers in 1764 and settled in the following year chiefly by families that had immigrated in 1738–40 from the islands of Islay and Jura in Scotland. Town meetings began in 1771, and it was confirmed as a town in 1786. The county poorhouse (1827) became the county-run Pleasant Valley Infirmary in 1963. The village incorporated in 1838. Irish immigrants arrived in 1850–70. Potatoes and dairy were the chief crops in the Civil War era. Catheter manufacturing in Argyle began in 1955, and by 1979 three such firms were in operation. In 2002 agriculture remained the predominant land use. The town includes Summit and Cossayuna Lakes, on which there are many summer cottages. Argyle has been a dry town since 1846.

R. Paul McCarty

Arietta. Town (pop 293) in central Hamilton Co. The first white settlers were a group of Shakers who lived along the West Branch of the Sacandaga for a few years in the 1810s. Permanent settlement began in 1827, and the town was formed from Lake Pleasant in 1836. Andrew K. Morehouse platted Piseco hamlet that year, and in 1843 he invited a group of workers from New York City to form a Fourierist community. Despite his offer of free land, however, the Morehouse Union, as it was known, lasted less than a year, and by 1860 Piseco was nearly deserted. After the Civil War lumbering, tanning, and spruce-gum gathering sustained residents until the beginning of the 20th century. The Piseco Lake Trout Club (1830–51) was an early sportsmen's group. The tourist economy began with private camps in the 1890s and improved roads in 1912 and was fully formed by 1915. Snowmobiling created a strong winter season beginning in the late 1960s. Piseco Lake and 640 ft (195 m) T-Lake Falls are the town's primary natural features.

Arkport. Village (pop 832) in Hornellsville (Steuben Co). Beginning in 1800 Arkport was the construction and embarkation point for river craft known as "arks." Farmers from the surrounding country brought potash, wheat, flour, corn, cured pork, butter, and cheese to the village to be transported down the Canisteo River to Chesapeake Bay markets, trade that flourished until the Erie Canal was completed in 1825. The village, incorporated in 1912, was located on the Buffalo Division of the Erie Railroad (1852). Produce farming grew more and more important, with potatoes a leading crop. By 2003 the village had become the headquarters of Silk Road Transport, a long-distance trucking firm.

Virginia L. Wright and Jerry Wright

Arkwright. Town (pop 1,130) in NE Chautauqua Co. Settled in 1807, the town was formed in 1829 from Pomfret and Villenova. A hilly town, it is best suited to grazing. Its first cheese factory was built around 1861. Dairy farming, cattle raising, horse farming, and, more recently, deer and elk farming are means of livelihood, along with maple sugaring. Privately owned Arkwright Falls on Canadaway Creek is a natural attraction, and the Canadaway Creek State Wildlife Management Area encompasses 2,200 acres (890 ha).

Beatrice Houck Curtin

Arlen, Harold [Arluck, Hyman] (*b* Buffalo, 15 Feb 1905; *d* New York City, 23 Apr 1986). Composer, songwriter, and singer. Arlen's father was the cantor at Buffalo's Temple Beth-El, and Arlen sang in the synagogue choir at age 7. At 15 he became a jazz pianist in local groups, one of which, the Buffalodians, was successful locally and in New York City in the mid-1920s. Arlen wrote arrangements for the Fletcher Henderson Orchestra, sang with the Arnold Johnson Orchestra in *George White's Scandals of 1928* on Broadway, and contributed songs to the *Scandals* series and many other New York revues. With lyricist Ted Koehler he created his first hit song, "Get Happy" (1930), as well as several revues between 1930 and 1934 for the famous Cotton Club in Harlem, where he introduced "Between the Devil and the Deep Blue Sea" (1931) and "Stormy Weather" (1933). The versatile Arlen also recorded as a vocalist, including a 1931 session with Joe Venuti's Rhythm Boys. From the mid-1930s he alternated between Broadway and Hollywood, where in 1939 Arlen and lyricist E. Y. "Yip" Harburg wrote the score for the film *The Wizard of Oz.* He worked with such notable lyricists as Ira Gershwin, Leo Robin, and especially Johnny Mercer, with whom he wrote "Blues in the Night" (1941) and "That Old Black Magic" (1942). For Broadway, Arlen and Harburg scored the hits *Bloomer Girl* (1944) and *Jamaica* (1957). Less commercially successful, but more highly regarded, were Arlen's scores for *St. Louis Woman* (1946, with Mercer) and *House of Flowers* (1954, with Truman Capote). His last Broadway musical was the unsuccessful *Saratoga* (1959). Arlen's music combined melodic and harmonic elements of blues and jazz with more traditional theater music style. He also wrote several jazz-influenced instrumental works and in the late 1950s a blues opera, *Free and Easy.*

Jablonski, Edward. *Harold Arlen: Rhythm, Rainbows, and Blues* (Boston: Northeastern Univ Press, 1996)

David Raymond

Arlington. Locality (pop 12,481) in Poughkeepsie (Dutchess Co). Earlier known as Leetown and later as Bull's Head, it was the site of a tollhouse on the Dutchess Turnpike (1807) until 1888. There was also a racetrack that became part of the campus of Vassar College, which opened in 1865. The development of the college and real estate expansion eastward from Poughkeepsie resulted in a horsecar connection in 1872, and it was designated East Poughkeepsie. Renamed Arlington in 1882, it developed a small commercial center serving Vassar, capturing a few businesses leaving Poughkeepsie in the 1960s. The Arlington Central School District (organized in 1951) extends far into other towns.

William P. McDermott

Armenians. A few Armenian students and travelers had settled in New York State before 1880, largely in New York City, but the first substantial wave of immigration came thereafter, as the Ottoman Empire increased its persecution of Armenians. Seeking jobs and stability, about 64,000 Armenians had arrived in the United States by 1915. In New York State outside of New York City, many settled in factory towns. As a rule Armenian women did not work outside the home, but it was acceptable for them to be employed in fields considered appropriate for women, and many worked in the garment trade, especially in Troy (Rensselaer Co). Other settlements were established near factories in Schenectady, Massena, Utica, Herkimer, Syracuse, Rochester, Binghamton, Endicott, Elmira, and Niagara Falls, with Armenian churches established in many of these communities.

Few of the early immigrants who took factory jobs made their employment a lifetime career. In comparison with other southern and eastern European groups, a high proportion of Armenians had been skilled traders, merchants, or professionals in their home country. Soon the Armenians opened small shops or businesses, often groceries, tailor shops, and stores for rug cleaning, repair, and sales. Young men from rural environments sought work as farmhands, and some managed to buy their own farms. An "Armenian Road" in Sherman (Chautauqua Co) was once home to 8–10 Armenian-owned farms. In New York City Armenians were best known for their involvement in the photoengraving industry and import business, including oriental rugs. The *Armenian Encyclopedic Almanac* of 1925 lists Armenian businesses in 25 cities and towns throughout New York State.

A second wave of Armenian emigration to the United States took place following the Armenian genocide of 1915, which left about 30,000 survivors. Abruptly curtailed to 100 or less per month by the quotas of the Johnson-Reed Immigration Act of 1924, immigration slowed until the 1960s, after which began a third wave of over 200,000 newcomers from overseas, primarily from the Middle East, Eastern Europe, and Soviet and post-Soviet Armenia. Los Angeles had replaced New York City and Boston as the cultural hub of US Armenians by the 21st century. The older neighborhoods from the 1920s in Manhattan's East Side and Washington Heights dwindled, to be replaced by the newcomer neighborhoods with Armenian storefronts in Queens, especially in Jackson Heights, Flushing, Rego Park, Douglaston, and Elmhurst. Communities outside of New York City have slowly declined. In the early 21st century, the estimated number of Armenians in the Troy region, at 3,000, was still the largest in the state outside of the metropolitan New York City area, although reduced from its peak of 3,500 during the 1960s and 1970s. An estimated 500 Armenians reside in the Niagara Falls area, 250 in Syracuse, and 130 in Binghamton.

Armenian Churches

About 80% of Armenians are members of the Armenian Apostolic Church, whose head, the Catholicos, resides in Etchmiadzin, Armenia. A second Catholicos is based in Lebanon. Roughly 10% are Protestants, primarily Evangelical, Congregationalist, and Presbyterian. A Protestant prayer group formed in Manhattan in 1881 and became an Evangelical congregation with its own church in 1921. Some 3% are members of the Armenian Rite of the Roman Catholic Church. Apostolic church groups began forming in New York State's Armenian communities in the 1890s, and in 1898 Rev Khat Markarian became pastor to the Armenians of New York City. St. Peter's Armenian Apostolic Church in Troy was founded in 1899, followed by St. Gregory the Illuminator in Manhattan in 1903. The United Armenian Calvary Congregational Church was established in Troy in 1906. Apostolic parishes were formed in Syracuse (1911) and Binghamton (1923), and parish boards were established in Niagara Falls and Massena (St. Lawrence Co) soon after. In 1898 Armenian Apostolic churches in the United States were placed under the jurisdiction of the Armenian Catholicos. The diocesan seat for the United States was moved from Boston to New York City in 1927. After the Armenian Republic was taken over by Soviet Union in 1920, there was a schism within the Apostolic Church, culminating in 1933 with the assassination of the primate, Archbishop Ghevont Tourian, during Christmas Eve services in Holy Cross Armenian Church in New York City. From this time forward the divided communities proceeded separately, with both groups headquartered in Manhattan. The group that had supported Primate Tourian is based at St. Vartan Cathedral. The Diocese of the Armenian Church of America governs Armenian Apostolic churches throughout the eastern United States and has 10 churches in New York State, from Holy Martyrs Armenian Church in Queens, with about 1,500 members, to St. Paul in Syracuse, with about 35. There is also a mission parish in Rochester. St. Nersess Armenian Seminary, founded in 1962 in Evanston, Ill, relocated to New Rochelle (Westchester Co) in 1967 and is the only Armenian seminary outside of Armenia and the Middle East. The other faction, the Prelacy of the Armenian Apostolic Church of America, is based at St. Illuminator Armenian Apostolic Church. The Prelacy operated independently until it was placed under the jurisdiction of the Catholicos in Lebanon. The Prelacy has 5 churches in the state. There are 18 Armenian churches in New York State.

The Armenian Community

Compared with other new arrivals, Armenians in New York State suffered little bigotry. "Hyes" (as Armenians call themselves) were multilingual, white Christians with entrepreneurial values coming in small, tight-knit families and entering in such modest numbers that they remained unnoticed. Typically arriving with a trade or profession, Armenians and their families thrived, many achieving prosperity, education, even wealth within their first generation on American soil. Rapid growth of the communities was reflected in the emergence of political parties, transplanted from the homeland to the New World, charitable societies, social educational groups, and athletic societies. Enjoying the advantage of numbers, the Armenian community in greater New York City has a vibrant network of over 50 ethnic organizations of all sorts—athletic, cultural, dance, educational, music, political, religious, service, and youth. The world's largest English-language Armenian weekly newspaper, the *Armenian Reporter,* was founded in Flushing in 1967. Prominent Armenians in New York State have included Khachadur Osganian, who immigrated in 1834, becoming a writer for the *New York Herald Tribune* and president of the New York Press Club; director Rouben Mamoulian; Metropolitan Opera stars Lili Chookasian and Ara Berberian; writer Eric Bogosian; educator Vartan Gregorian; poet Peter Balakian; artist Arshile Gorky, and Democratic politician and lawyer Edward Costikyan.

Mesrobian, Arpena S. *"Like One Family": The Armenians of Syracuse* (Princeton, NJ: Gomidas Institute, 2000)

Mirak, Robert. *Torn between Two Lands: Armenians in America, 1890 to World War II* (Cambridge, Mass: Department of Near Eastern Languages & Civilizations, Harvard Univ, 1983)

Takooshian, Harold. "Armenian-Americans." In *Gale Encyclopedia of Multicultural America,* vol 1, eds. R. Vecoli, J. Galens, A. Sheets, R. V. Young (Detroit, Mich: Gale Research, 1995)

Vassilian, Hamo, ed. *Armenian American Almanac,* 8th ed. (Glendale, Calif: Armenian Reference Books, 2001)

Zakian, Christopher Hagop, ed. *The Torch Was Passed: The Centennial History of the Armenian Church of America* (New York: St. Vartan Press, 1998)

Arpena S. Mesrobian and Harold Takooshian

Armstrong, John, Jr (*b* Carlisle, Pa, 25 Nov 1758; *d* Red Hook, Dutchess Co, 1 Apr 1843). Military officer, writer, and politician. In 1776 Armstrong abandoned his studies at the College of New Jersey (now Princeton University) to join the Continental army and, with the rank of major, served in the Battle of Saratoga (1777). While stationed at Newburgh (Orange Co) in 1783, Armstrong anonymously wrote the Newburgh Addresses. His essays criticized Gen George Washington for not advocating for soldiers' and officers' rights. Armstrong suggested a mutiny if Congress would not resolve issues such as the lack of pay. Although many praised Armstrong's writing style, his criticism negatively affected his reputation, and he returned to Pennsylvania to pursue politics. After marrying Alida Livingston, sister of Chancellor Robert R. Livingston, in 1789, he settled on a 25,000-acre (10,117 ha) estate in Red Hook and held numerous political positions. A Republican, he was elected to the US Senate (1801–2, 1803–4); he was US minister to France (1804–10) and army brigadier general (1812–13); and under Pres James Madison he served as secretary of war (1813–14). Considered a notable writer, Armstrong authored political pamphlets and books, such as the two-volume *Notices of the War of 1812* (1836, 1840).

Skeen, Carl Edward. *John Armstrong, Jr., 1758–1843: A Biography* (Syracuse: Syracuse Univ Press, 1981)

Mark G. Spencer

Armstrong, Louis. See JAZZ.

Armstrong investigations. An inquiry conducted in 1905 by the New York State legislature into financial manipulation and corruption in the life insurance industry. Public demand for the investigations was sparked by extensive press coverage of the struggle for control of the Equitable Life Assurance Society, which led to exposure of abuses by major New York City–based life insurance companies Equitable, Mutual, and New York Life. Acting upon the recommendation of Gov Frank W. Higgins, the legislature created a joint committee to investigate and make recommendations for reform. William W. Armstrong, a Republican senator from Rochester, was named chairman. Charles Evans Hughes, who led the legislative investigation of utility rates in New York City earlier in 1905, was appointed counsel.

Through rigorous questioning of insurance company executives during four months of public hearings, Hughes amassed substantial evidence of abusive practices. These included payment of exorbitant salaries and commissions, investment of policyholders' money in risky enterprises, improper deferral of dividend payments, self-dealing by directors and officers, and concealment of large cash balances used to support trust companies in which industry officials held interest. Testimony of industry executives and pillars of the New York political establishment, such as US senators Thomas C. Platt and Chauncey M. Depew, also revealed that insurance companies had made campaign contributions (including to Pres Theodore Roosevelt's 1904 election bid) to purchase, in effect, protection against hostile legislation and had maintained a centralized office to influence legislation throughout the United States, dividing the country into four districts for lobbying purposes.

When the hearings concluded, Hughes oversaw preparation of the committee's report and the drafting of bills to carry out its recommendations. The ensuing legislation became the model for insurance industry regulation nationwide. Among the most significant and enduring reforms were those that limited the annual amount of insurance a company could write, placed greater strictures upon self-dealing, and increased the review powers of the New York State Insurance Department. Standardized policy forms, limits to salaries, campaign contributions, and annual dividend payments, and registration of lobbyists also were legislated.

Hughes, Charles E. "The Gas and Insurance Investigations 1905–1906." In *The Autobiographical Notes of Charles Evans Hughes,* ed. David J. Danelski and Joseph S. Tulchin (Cambridge, Mass: Harvard Univ Press, 1973)

Robert A. Klump

Army football. In 1890 Naval Academy midshipmen challenged Army cadet Dennis M. Michie to a football contest. Michie organized the United States Military Academy's first football team, and the two military schools played at West Point (Orange Co) on 29 November. Navy beat Army, 24-0, to initiate one of college football's most intense rivalries. For much of the next century, though, Army was the dominant major college team in New York State and a national power. Cadets had 32 consecutive winning seasons (1907–38), during which future generals Dwight D. Eisenhower, Omar N. Bradley, and James A. Van Fleet lettered as Army football players. Michie Stadium, Army's current home field, opened 15 Nov 1924. Named for the cadet who started Army football and was killed in action during the Spanish-American War (1898), the stadium is one of the most spectacular scenic locations for sports events in the country.

Army's zenith spanned 1944 through 1950 when it had a 57-3-4 record under Coach Earl H. "Red" Blaik (1941–58). Undefeated through five of those seven seasons, including 32 consecutive games (1944–47), Blaik's teams were the 1944 and 1945 national champions. Army's outstanding players in this period included backs Felix A. "Doc" Blanchard ("Mr Inside") and Glenn W. Davis ("Mr Outside"), who won the Heisman Memorial Trophy as the nation's best college player in 1945 and 1946, respectively. Quarterbacks Arnold Y. Tucker and Arnold A. Galiffa, end Henry C. "Hank" Foldberg, and guard Joseph B. Steffy were Army All-Americans. In perhaps the most exciting college game in history, Army's 25-game winning streak ended before 74,121 fans at Yankee Stadium on 9 Nov 1946 when the cadets battled Notre Dame to a scoreless tie.

Misfortune struck in 1951 when 90 cadets, including 37 football players, were dismissed from the Military Academy for violating the corps' honor code. Army football finished with two victories and seven losses that year, but the team recovered quickly and went undefeated in 1958. Halfback Peter M. Dawkins led that last of Blaik's Army teams and became the third Army player to win the Heisman Trophy. Army regained touches of the old glory during three successful years under Coach Thomas B. Cahill (1966–68) and won its first two bowl victories under Coach James C. Young (1984, 1985). Army and Navy met for the 100th time in 1999; the Army cadets ended the 20th century by leading that series with 48 victories to 45 for Navy, with 7 ties.

Army Football '99 Media Guide (West Point, NY: US Military Academy Sports Information Department, 1999)
Blaik, Earl H. *The Red Blaik Story* (New Rochelle, NY: Arlington House, 1974)
White, Gordon S., Jr, and Mervin D. Hyman. *Coach Tom Cahill: A Man for the Corps* (New York: Macmillan, 1969)

Gordon S. White Jr

Arnold, Benedict (*b* Norwich, Conn, 14 Jan 1741; *d* London, 14 June 1801). General. At 13 Arnold was apprenticed to a Norwich, Conn, apothecary. In 1762 he went to New Haven, Conn, and became a prosperous merchant and sea captain, trading with Canada and the Caribbean. In April 1775 Capt Arnold marched his militia company to Boston, where he convinced Massachusetts authorities of the importance of seizing cannon at Britain's Lake Champlain forts of Ticonderoga and Crown Point [now in Essex Co]. Commissioned colonel, Arnold left alone and met two forces en route; one was the Green Mountain Boys led by Ethan Allen, and the other was from Connecticut. Arnold shared command with Allen, and the forts were taken in May. When Arnold's troops arrived they captured a British war sloop and took the northern lake post of St. John [now in Quebec], preventing the retaking of Ticonderoga. Arnold began building a navy to prepare for the invasion of Canada, but Massachusetts would not support him, preferring a Connecticut force to lead the campaign. Arnold resigned his commission.

Later in 1775 Arnold, a newly commissioned Continental army colonel, led troops on a march through Maine's wilderness to help Brig Gen Richard Montgomery, advancing from Montreal, take Quebec City. Though the Americans lost, the Continental Congress, impressed by Arnold's march, promoted him brigadier general in January 1776. In May Arnold retreated from Canada to New York, where under Maj Gen Philip Schuyler's command, he built a navy at Skenesborough [now Whitehall, Washington Co] on Lake Champlain to prevent the British from retaking Ticonderoga. In October the British defeated Arnold's navy at Valcour Island, but their advance was halted temporarily. Nevertheless Arnold's critics called him incompetent. In February 1777 Congress passed Arnold over for promotion to major general. In May he was made major general, but his seniority was not restored and Arnold resigned his commission in July. Encouraged by commander in chief George Washington, who admired Arnold's military prowess and fighting spirit, he withdrew his resignation to help Schuyler against Gen John Burgoyne's army, which had retaken Ticonderoga. In August Arnold marched with 1,200 men to the relief of besieged Fort Stanwix [now at Rome, Oneida Co], preventing British control of the Mohawk Valley and blocking a British force from joining Burgoyne. By now

Gen Horatio Gates commanded in Schuyler's place. In September at the first Battle of Saratoga at Freeman's Farm, Arnold and Gates disagreed over the plan of battle, and after the armies clashed Arnold returned to headquarters prompting Gates to relieve him. When Burgoyne attacked at Bemis Heights [now in Saratoga Co] in October, Arnold returned to the front and led successful charges. Burgoyne soon surrendered. In June 1778 Washington appointed Arnold, whose seniority had been restored, military governor of Philadelphia. Arnold's poor political skills, speculative ventures, lavish living, and marriage to tory sympathizer Peggy Shippen put him on a collision course with Pennsylvania authorities, who charged him with corruption and misuse of power. In January 1780 the court acquitted Arnold of fraud but convicted him of abuse of power. It sentenced him to be reprimanded by Washington, who did so mildly.

Following his April 1779 marriage, Arnold began plotting treason, using his wife's connections to contact the enemy. The British wanted the fortifications at West Point (Orange Co), so Arnold had to convince Washington to give him that appointment. Washington preferred that Arnold command the army's left wing but in August 1780 granted Arnold's request. British commander Henry Clinton agreed to give Arnold £10,000 for defecting and £20,000 for West Point's surrender (with 3,000 troops). In September Arnold met secretly with British Maj John André about the surrender, but after the meeting André was captured and Arnold's treason was discovered. Arnold escaped and became a British brigadier general but received only some of the promised money. After the war the Arnolds lived in England and Canada, shunned even by loyalist exiles, his name ever after a byword for treason.

Martin, James Kirby. *Benedict Arnold, Revolutionary Hero: An American Warrior Reconsidered* (New York: New York Univ Press, 1997)

Wallace, Willard M. *Traitorous Hero: The Life and Fortunes of Benedict Arnold* (New York: Harper & Bros, 1954)

Gaspare J. Saladino

art, Adirondacks and North Country. For 200 years, pictorial views of the Adirondacks have been changing from evocations of the sublime, to realistic transcriptions, to contemporary and abstract constructs of nature, humanity, and politics.

First Views

Among the earliest pictorial images of the Adirondack landscape were 18th-century maps of the Lake George and Champlain waterway, wood engravings of Fort William Henry and Fort Ticonderoga, and scenes of Lake George and the Hudson River above Albany. Flora and other natural details were drawn by Swedish botanist Peter Kalm (1716–79), who visited Lake Champlain in 1749. Jacques Gerard Milbert (1766–1840), a French naturalist and artist, collected natural history specimens between 1815 and 1818, and made many drawings of the southern Adirondack region and other places in New York State. His wash drawings of the Hudson River were lithographed in Paris and published as *Itineraire pittoresque du fleuve Hudson* (1828–29). Twenty watercolor sketches of the region north and west of Lake George by English artist William Guy Wall (1792–1864) were published as aquatints in a landmark publication, *The Hudson River Portfolio* (1821–25). Charles Cromwell Ingham (1796–1863) ascended the state's highest peak, Mt Marcy, in 1836 and produced one of the earliest oil landscape paintings, entitled *The Great Adirondack Pass, Painted on the Spot* (1837).

Thomas Cole (1801–48) and Asher B. Durand (1796–1886) are credited with founding an American school of landscape painting popularly known as the Hudson River school. Their work embodied a nationalistic fervor and optimism about the promise of the United States as portrayed in images of the grandeur of the American landscape. During the 1830s and 1840s, these two artists traveled into the Adirondacks, capturing its wild beauty in their paintings. Works such as Cole's *Schroon Mountain* and *Adirondacks* (1838) inspired other artists to venture to the northern wilderness. Artists were attracted to Lake George because of its scenery and the popular demand for images. Printmakers William Henry Bartlett (1809–54) and Harry Fenn (1845–1911) produced an enormous number of engravings, while others produced lithographs after paintings or documented the lake and its visitors for the popular press. Photographs were also made works of art for commercial purposes. Landscape artist John Frederick Kensett (1816–72) made at least a dozen formal compositions of the lake beginning in 1850, the most important being *Lake George* (1869). Alfred Thompson Bricher (1837–1908) created appealing Lake George views from two sketchbooks made in 1867. David Johnson's (1827–1908) highly detailed views of lake scenery and boating are among his finest works.

Artists' Mecca

After 1850 improved transportation to the Adirondacks and increased knowledge of the area, communicated in part through paintings and prints, attracted more artists. Inspired by dramatic vistas, they produced paintings, drawings, and watercolors. Many works were reproduced as engravings or chromolithographs as publishers recognized the magnetism of the region for the public, especially city dwellers. Arthur Fitzwilliam Tait (1819–1905) was one of the best-known and most productive 19th-century painters of American animals and sporting life. Lithographs by Currier and Ives after his paintings of Adirondack animals, hunting, and fishing scenes, such as *Autumn Morning, Raquette Lake* (1872) and *A Good Time Coming* (1862), helped popularize the region as a sports enthusiast's paradise.

The first artists' colony in the Adirondacks was in Keene Valley (Essex Co) during the 1850s. After the Civil War artists came to the region for longer stays, built studios, and stimulated an economic boom in tourism and wilderness recreation. Landscape artists like Durand, American pre-Raphaelite William Trost Richards (1833–1905), and Alexander Lawrie (1828–1917) came to the valley and nearby Elizabethtown (Essex Co). They were followed by Roswell Morse Shurtleff (1838–1915), who lived and painted there for more than four decades, and artists of the 1870s, including John Lee Fitch (1836–95), Samuel Colman (1832–1920), George Smillie (1840–1921), James David Smillie (1833–1909), and Winslow Homer (1836–1911). Homer's Adirondack watercolors of the 1880s and 1890s are acclaimed by critics as masterpieces of the medium. Levi Wells Prentice (1851–1935) produced some 70 landscapes during the 1870s. His hard-edged, realistic style depicted nature's botanical details and lakeside vistas like *Smith's Lake, Adirondacks, N.Y.* (1883) as well as campsites. During the 1880s George Inness (1825–94), Alexander Wyant (1836–92), Julian Alden Weir (1852–1919), and others arrived.

20th-Century Views

Popular taste for landscape painting declined during the 20th century. During the second decade of the century an artists' colony led by illustrator Charles Sarka (1879–1960) and wildlife artist Paul Bransom (1885–1979) emerged at Canada Lake (Fulton Co). Photographer Alfred Stieglitz (1864–1946) and sculptor David Smith (1906–65) were nationally prominent artists inspired by the region during the first half of the century. Stieglitz was a frequent visitor to Lake George beginning in the 1880s, and the first generation of American modernists followed him there in the 1920s. They included John Marin (1870–1953), Georgia O'Keeffe (1887–1986), Edward Steichen (1879–1973), Marsden Hartley (1877–1943), Arthur Dove (1880–1946), Alfred Maurer (1868–1932), and Max Weber (1881–1961), representing the Adirondacks in semiabstract compositions. Smith created his first welded steel artwork in 1933 in a garage in Bolton Landing (Warren Co). Abstract expressionist artists Helen Frankenthaler (1928–), Robert Motherwell (1915–91), and Kenneth Noland (1924–) came to work and visit. Eccentric modernist Florine Stettheimer (1871–1944), also a friend of Stieglitz and O'Keeffe, frequented Lake Placid and added one work, *Lake Placid*, to the Adirondack canon in 1919. In the 1930s nationally renowned portrait artist Wayman Adams (1883–1959) founded a summer art school in Elizabethtown, attracting major artists like Stanley Turnbull (1888–1966) and students from across the country. During the 1940s German expressionist painter George Grosz (1893–1959), Japanese American Bumpei Usui (1898–1994), Jacob Asanger (1887–1941), and other artists visited the area and painted images of its scenery.

Other post–World War I painters of the Adirondacks were full-time residents. The Adirondack landscape was the greatest influence on the paintings and murals of rugged expressionist Harold Weston (1894–1972). Amy Jones (1899–1992), painter, printmaker, and sculptor, won national recognition in the 1930s as a Works Progress Administration muralist while living in Saranac Lake (Essex and Franklin Cos). Rockwell Kent (1882–1971), printmaker, painter, graphic artist, and designer of international reputation, lived half his life near Au Sable Forks (Clinton and Essex Cos). Norwegian American Jonas Lie (1880–1940) came to the Adirondacks during the 1920s and 1930s and made the woods and villages his subject.

Since the 1970s artists such as Stephen Story (1915–88), Mark Potter (1929–95), Allen Blagden (1938–), and Don Wynn (1942–), like many earlier Adirondack painters, are realists who draw their subjects from the natural grandeur they see. One exception to post-

1970 realism is the work of nonobjective color-field painter Ludwig Sander (1906–75), who created 15 geometric abstract works of the Adirondack landscapes in 1972. Locally, nationally, and internationally recognized artists continue to work, live, and teach in the region.

Major museums in the Adirondacks and North Country include the Adirondack Museum (1957) at Blue Mountain Lake (Hamilton Co), with a strong collection of 19th- and 20th-century Adirondack paintings and decorative arts. The Hyde Collection Art Museum (1963) at Glens Falls (Warren Co) has an excellent collection of European paintings, including works by Sandro Botticelli, Raphael, Rembrandt, Georges Seurat, and Adirondack artists such as Winslow Homer. Other museums include the Akwesasne Museum in Hogansburg (Franklin Co) with a collection of Mohawk arts, the Plattsburgh State Art Museum, and the Frederic Remington Art Museum at Ogdensburg (St. Lawrence Co).

See also CERAMICS AND POTTERY.

Barnhill, Georgia G. *Wild Impressions: The Adirondacks on Paper* (Blue Mountain Lake, NY: Adirondack Museum, 1995)
Cadbury, Warder H., and Marsh, Henry P. *Arthur Fitzwilliam Tait: Artist in the Adirondacks* (Newark, Del: Univ of Delaware Press, 1986)
Mandel, Patricia C. F. *Fair Wilderness: American Paintings in the Collection of the Adirondack Museum* (Blue Mountain Lake, NY: Adirondack Museum, 1990)
Tatham, David. *Winslow Homer in the Adirondacks* (Syracuse: Syracuse Univ Press, 1996)
Welsh, Caroline Mastin, ed. *The Adirondack Prints and Printmakers: The Call of the Wild* (Syracuse: Syracuse Univ Press, 1998)

Caroline M. Welsh

art, Albany and the Capital District, Upper Hudson, and Mohawk Valley. The arts have flourished in Albany and the upper Hudson and Mohawk Valleys since the early 1700s. Dutch settlers who came to the area in the 17th century brought with them cultural traditions characterized by a communal unity, skills in agriculture and commerce, and an appreciation of fine and decorative arts. By the early 18th century, prosperous merchants and landowners began to commission itinerant artists referred to as limners (term used to denote a painter) to paint family portraits and Scripture paintings for their homes. After the heyday of limners and at the time of the French and Indian War, a group of English-born artists came to the region. Thomas McIlworth, John Durand, and John Wollaston were successful itinerant artists who painted portraits of people living in the region.

After the Revolutionary War the region's increasing commercial prosperity drew many new immigrants, and a strong portrait tradition continued. One of the most significant artists was Ezra Ames, who painted portraits of prominent area residents and New York State governors. More landscapes were produced during this period for topographical purposes and recorded natural wonders, such as John Vanderlyn's series of paintings of Niagara Falls (1801–3). History and genre paintings also were popular, and the best-known area artists included Vanderlyn, John T. Peele, and A. D. O. Browere. These types of painting required of the artists (and the audience) a grounding in literature, history, and the classics.

Hudson River School and Landscape Painting

From about 1825 until the 1870s the picturesque setting of the Hudson River valley attracted and supported a number of Hudson River school landscape painters, such as Thomas Cole, Asher B. Durand, Frederic Edwin Church, William Hart, James M. Hart, John Frederick Kensett, Sanford Robinson Gifford, and Homer Dodge Martin. Most of these artists established their careers by painting wilderness and pastoral views of the region, such as Church's *Niagara* (1857) and Durand's *Hudson River Scene* (1846), and they were referred to as the Hudson River school. During the 1850s and 1860s the studio of Albany sculptor Erastus Dow Palmer, whose Neoclassical sculpture is now internationally known, also served as a center for artistic activities. Self-taught, Palmer is best known for *White Captive* (1861), now in the Metropolitan Museum of Art, and *The Angel at the Sepulchre* (1868), a monument in Albany Rural Cemetery. Other notable, late 19th-century artists working in the region include Palmer's son, Walter Launt Palmer, a landscape impressionist whose works include *Library at Arbor Hill* (1878) and *Silent Dawn* (1919), and muralists Will H. Low and David C. Lithgow. The leading African American sculptor of the 19th century, Edmonia Lewis, was born in Greenbush [now Rensselaer] in 1845.

At the Turn of the Century

The art activity in the region prior to World War I can best be described as adhering to the American Renaissance ideology of cosmopolitanism, patriotism, and idealism. In 1907 the Albany Institute of History and Art (founded 1791) erected a new building to house its regional collections of American art and an important collection of European art donated by John Townsend Lansing. Together these collections became the foundation of the region's first cosmopolitan art museum. The New York State Museum was founded in 1836 after the establishment of the State Geological and Natural History Survey and in 1975 moved to the Cultural Education Center, where it regularly stages artistic exhibitions. In the spirit of patriotism, Albany commissioned in 1909 a major war memorial, *Memorial to the Soldiers and Sailors of the Civil War.* The commission was awarded to noted American sculptor Hermon Atkins MacNeil and dedicated in 1912 in Washington Park. Leading sculptors John Quincy Adams Ward and Daniel Chester French collaborated on an equestrian statue of Gen Philip Sheridan (1916), guarding the eastern approach to the State Capitol.

Other notable art activity during this period included the Troy School of Arts and Crafts founded by Henry Albright in 1908 and the Albany Art League founded in 1903 by J. Rapp, David C. Lithgow, and Samantha Huntley. The Albany Art Colony (1923) presented a notable exhibition of regional artists in the Municipal Gas Company Auditorium. Other artists who were born, lived in, or worked in this region include children's book illustrators Dorothy Lathrop and Louis Slobokin, surrealist painter Kay Sage, sculptor Edward McCarten, and painter Edouard Buyck. The Print Club of Albany, founded in 1934 by a group of collectors associated with the Albany Institute of History and Art, has provided the region with exhibitions by master printmakers and an annual presentation print.

20th-Century Art

Founded in 1936 at the Albany Institute, the annual juried Exhibition by Artists of the Mohawk-Hudson Region pays tribute to artists working within a 100 mi (161 km) radius of Albany.

A Sculptor's Studio, depiction of Albany sculptor Erastus Dow Palmer's studio, by Tompkins Harrison Matteson, 1857.

Artists such as David Smith, Dorothy Dehner, John Carlson, and George Ault, among many others from the Woodstock art colony south of Albany in Ulster Co, were frequent exhibitors. One of the largest publicly owned collections of art in the country was purchased by the state during the 1960s to complement a new government center. The Governor Nelson A. Rockefeller Empire State Plaza Art Collection includes over 90 works by modern and contemporary artists such as Alexander Calder, Robert Motherwell, Mark Rothko, and Louise Nevelson. More recently the vitality of art departments in area colleges and universities has enhanced the diversity of art activity in the region with museum exhibitions, regional art centers, and a host of commercial galleries, and the Albany Institute remains a major repository. Many artists of international and national prominence, as well as those with rising reputations, are presently living, working, and exhibiting art in the area, which has created a stimulating atmosphere for producing and enjoying the arts.

Mohawk Valley and Upper Hudson Valley Art

Institutions in the Mohawk and Hudson Valleys also have major collections of fine arts, the result of affluent New Yorkers who acquired private collections. Collections in the Mohawk Valley comprise works at the New York State Historical Association's Fenimore Art Museum in Cooperstown (Otsego Co), collected by Stephen C. Clark Sr, which includes Gilbert Stuart's portrait of the Mohawk leader, *Joseph Brant* (1786). In 1995 the museum added the American Indian Wing to exhibit the Eugene and Clare Thaw Collection of Indian Art, which includes more than 700 objects. Dia:Beacon, in Beacon (Dutchess Co), is a museum of contemporary art that opened in 2003 and features large and oversized works of art. There is also a wealth of art found at Olana, the home of Hudson River school artist Frederic Edwin Church at Greenport (Columbia Co), and at museums at SUNY New Paltz and Vassar College in Poughkeepsie. Numerous galleries can also be found in Hudson (Columbia Co) and Woodstock.

Beech-Nut president Bartlett Arkell founded an art gallery in the Canajoharie Library (Montgomery Co) in 1926, which features works by European and American artists, namely Winslow Homer. Arkell also collected rural landscapes of the Hudson and Mohawk River valleys and decorative arts, sculpture, and furniture from the Stickley company in Syracuse. Art was central to the lives of Louis Hyde and his wife Charlotte Pruyn Hyde. Beginning in 1913 the two traveled throughout Europe and purchased works by European masters, building a significant collection for their Glens Falls (Warren Co) mansion. They obtained 2,800 objects including fine and decorative arts, furniture, and sculpture, and their collection became the Hyde Collection art museum in 1962. Works such as Sandro Botticelli's *Annunciation* (?1492) and the *ca* 1620 painting *Head of a Negro,* by Peter Paul Reubens are exhibited. In Saratoga Co, Yaddo was formed as an artists' retreat in 1926 at the estate of Katrina and Spencer Trask. Writers, composers, visual artists, performance artists, and choreographers have lived at Yaddo since it opened.

See also Arts and crafts movement; Ceramics and pottery; Hudson river school; Prints and printmaking; Sculpture, public.

Groft, Tammis K., and Mary Alice Mackay, eds. *Albany Institute of History and Art: 200 Years of Collecting* (New York: Hudson Hills Press, 1997)

Johnson, Ken. *20th Century Art of the Albany Region* (Albany: Albany Institute of History & Art, 1989)

Tammis Groft

art, Buffalo and the Niagara Frontier. When the Erie Canal opened in 1825, it connected Albany and the Hudson River with Buffalo, creating one of the country's most significant trade routes for transporting grain and goods from the Northeast to the Midwest and beyond. Movement and change also permeated the arts in this region. Niagara Falls inspired a pilgrimage by hundreds of artists, including the internationally renowned Albert Bierstadt (1830–1902), Frederic Edwin Church (1826–1900), and John Vanderlyn (1775–1852).

Painting and Sculpture

The first artists to settle in the region were itinerant portraitists. Ammi M. Farnham (1846–1922), born in Silver Creek (Chautauqua Co), and Burr H. Nicholls (1848–1915), born in Lockport (Niagara Co), were among the few native figurative and landscape painters. Swedish-born Lars Sellstedt (1819–1911), who settled permanently in Buffalo in 1842, was one of the founders of the Buffalo Fine Arts Academy in 1862, which became the governing body of the Albright-Knox Art Gallery, established in 1905 as the Albright Art Gallery. A portrait, genre, and landscape painter, Sellstedt also was active in teaching and promoting the arts, and wrote a comprehensive history, *Art in Buffalo* (1910). Among his colleagues were William Holbrook Beard (1824–1900), known for portraits and allegorical animal vignettes; Thomas LeClear (1818–82), a genre painter; and William Wilgus (1819–1953), a portrait and landscape painter.

Founded in 1891, the Buffalo Society of Artists is the oldest artists' organization in Western New York, and its members are elected. James Francis Brown (1862–1935) served as its first president. Alexis Jean Fournier (1865–1948), called "the Barbizon painter of East Aurora, New York," painted idyllic landscapes that concentrate on atmosphere and light. He was also a member of the Roycroft arts and crafts movement community founded in East Aurora (Erie Co) in 1895 by Elbert Hubbard (1856–1915). Claire Shuttleworth (1868–1930) produced an important series of more than 100 paintings of Niagara Falls and the Niagara Gorge, which included industrial horizon lines contrasting the waterways. Preeminent watercolorist Charles Burchfield (1893–1967) moved to Buffalo in 1921 and settled a few years later in Gardenville (Erie Co). While the tragic beauty of city and harbor subjects interested him during the 1930s, his masterworks are metaphoric landscape paintings of seasonal changes and the visualization of music and natural sounds. In 1966 a museum now known as the Burchfield-Penney Art Center was established at Buffalo State College to honor his work. Robert N. Blair (1912–2003), who lived in Holland (Erie Co), took a more traditional approach to watercolor in his firsthand documentation of World War II in Europe and later gestural landscapes of New York, New England, and the Southwest.

The Patteran Society was founded in 1933 by a

Albright Art Gallery (now Albright-Knox Art Gallery) in Buffalo, *ca* 1905.

group of 38 artists who wanted to separate from the Buffalo Society of Artists, which they considered to be too conservative. Founders included Ruth Erb Hoffman (1902–), Harold L. Olmsted (1886–1972), Louisa Robins (1898–1962), and Martha Hamlin Visser't Hooft (1906–94). The society disbanded in 1983. The Art Institute of Buffalo was launched in 1931 as part of the Buffalo Education Service under the Works Progress Administration. Faculty included Edwin Dickinson (1891–1978), who painted large, dreamlike hallucinations with bizarre spatial shifts, social realist Isaac Soyer (1902–81), and Charles Burchfield. It closed in 1956.

Between 1933 and 1934, the federally funded Public Works of Art Project made possible the production of murals by Pascal Scime, Angelo Scibetta, William B. Rowe (1910–55), Raphael Beck (1858–1947), and Eugene M. Dyczkowski (1899–1987). More contemporary Western New York muralists include William Y. Cooper (1934–), a painter, printmaker, and teacher in the Buffalo Public Schools system whose jewel-colored abstractions pay homage to African subjects and the achievements of African Americans. In 1941 Philip C. Elliott (1903–85) and Virginia Cuthbert (1908–2001), his wife, moved from Pittsburgh to Buffalo to head and teach at the Albright Art School. This leading arts institution merged in 1954 with the University of Buffalo. Elliott was most accomplished as a formalist photographer. Cuthbert's paintings changed stylistically from Ashcan school to magic realism. Other influential faculty included abstract painters Harriet Greif (1924–88) and Seymour Drumlevitch (1923–89), her husband. Masters of realism include painters Donald R. Haug (1925–99) of Evans (Erie Co), Catherine Catanzaro Koenig (1921–) of Kenmore (Erie Co), Walter R. Garver (1927–) of East Amherst (Erie Co), Bruce Kurland (1938–) of Buffalo, and Thomas Aquinas Daly (1937–) of Arcade (Wyoming Co).

Contemporary arts in Buffalo were transformed when founding artists Charles Clough (1951–), Nancy Dwyer (1954–), Robert Longo (1953–), and Cindy Sherman (1954–) created the exhibition space Hallwalls in 1974. In addition to mentors Joseph Piccillo (1941–) and Paul Sharits (1943–93), others soon to join them were Michael Zwack (1949–), Diane Bertolo (1953–), and Andrew Topolski (1952–). The artist-run gallery has had a profound effect on the artistic community that continues to cultivate challenging art. Roberley Bell's (1955–) sculpture and installations traverse issues of power as it affects women, health, and the environment. *Transhistory* (2002), a public art-in-transit project, was done in collaboration with Alison Slein and Courtney Grim for the Genesee Valley Transit Authority in Batavia (Genesee Co). Sharon McConnell (1960–) of Belmont (Allegany Co) uses unorthodox materials, such as animal gut, fabric, and embroidery thread, to make sculptures and installations that comment metaphorically on female identity and the tenuousness of life. Peter D. Stephens (1958–) of Buffalo reinterprets idyllic 19th-century landscapes in paintings and bromoil photographs that look antique yet contemporary. Born in Cuba, Alberto Rey (1960–) of Fredonia (Chautauqua Co) works in a variety of materials to express symbolically his cultural heritage and personal experiences. Sculptors who teach at the SUNY College of Ceramics at Alfred University (Allegany Co) include Wayne Higby (1943–), a raku master who reveres Western and Eastern landscape forms, and Anne Currier (1950–), who defies the malleable quality of clay with nonobjective, hard-edged forms. The sculpture and installations of Patrick Robideau (1965–) of Niagara Falls evoke black, sooty pollution and eerie dull light in vignettes that convey the monumental environmental disasters left behind by steel companies in the rust belt region and the horrors of Love Canal. He collaborated with artist Kurt von Voetsch (1963–) in 2002 for a psychologically compelling performance in a three-story diorama-like set.

Photography

At the beginning of the 20th century, Buffalo played an important role in helping establish photography as an art form, primarily through the efforts of the Photo-Pictorialists, originally a group of eight men who in 1906 had broken from the more traditional Buffalo Camera Club (1888–1938). Their soft-focus carbon- and platinum-print portraits, landscapes, and still-life subjects mimicked painting in images that had impressionist and romantic qualities. The strongest member of this group was landscape photographer Wilbur H. Porterfield (1873–1958). Notable later members include Augustus J. Thibaudeau (1866–1939), who often blurred his images more radically than his colleagues dared, and Howard D. Beach (1867–1954), who invented blended bifocal lenses and the mutotone. Alfred Stieglitz (1864–1946) exhibited the first International Exhibition of Pictorial Photography at the Albright Art Gallery in 1910. Pictorialist Clara E. Sipprell (1885–1975), who left Buffalo in 1915, produced portraits using only natural light. The Photo-Pictorialists of Buffalo last exhibited together in 1914, when clear-focus photography and social documentation began to take precedence over manipulated images.

Social documentary photographer Milton Rogovin (1909–) of Buffalo focused on humanitarian portraits of working men and women around the globe. Beginning in 1958 with African American subjects in storefront churches of Buffalo, Rogovin's Western New York photographs include diptychs of steelworkers at work and at home, and triptychs or quartets of the city's Lower West Side residents taken over a 33-year span. Landscape photographer John Pfahl (1930–) of Buffalo pursues the picturesque and the sublime, in which Nature's wild, brutal power humbles human perspective. His exquisite images sometimes address issues of environmental pollution. Bonnie Gordon (1941–) utilizes photography and self-discovered techniques to produce two- and three-dimensional works that merge images with words and dictionary definitions in undulating, interwoven patterns. Photographer and educator Robert N. Muffoletto (1947–) founded the Center for Exploratory and Perceptual Arts (CEPA) in 1974 and served as its first director. CEPA now occupies multiple spaces in Buffalo's Market Arcade. Exhibitions, workshops, programs, and publications of photography and other media serve the public. During the 1970s and 1980s, Les Krims (1943–), professor of fine arts at SUNY Buffalo State, used female nudes as props, often covered and surrounded by countless objects from popular culture, in scenes that mimic staged vignettes from the 19th century. Buffalo-born Ap. Gorny (1950–), formerly known as Anthony-petr Gorny, teaches at Buffalo State. His prints, photographs, and mixed-media works address gender issues. Photographer and former CEPA director Robert J. Hirsch (1949–) is also the author of significant publications on photography, including *Exploring Color Photography* (1996) and *Seizing the Light: A History of Photography* (1999).

See also ARTS AND CRAFTS MOVEMENT; CERAMICS AND POTTERY; PRINTS AND PRINTMAKING.

Bannon, Anthony. *The Photo-Pictorialists of Buffalo* (Buffalo: Media Study, 1981)

Ehmke, Ronald, ed., with Elizabeth Licata. *Consider the Alternatives: 20 Years of Contemporary Art at Hallwalls* (Buffalo: Hallwalls Contemporary Arts Center, 1996)

Gerdts, William H. *Art across America: Two Centuries of Regional Painting, 1710–1920* (New York: Abbeville Press, 1990)

Heacock, Lee F. *The Buffalo Artists' Register*, vol 1 (Buffalo: Heacock Publishing, 1926)

Krane, Susan, with contributions by William H. Gerdts and Helen Raye. *The Wayward Muse: A Historical Survey of Painting in Buffalo* (Buffalo: Albright-Knox Art Gallery, 1987)

Sellstedt, Lars Gustaf. *Art in Buffalo* (Buffalo: Matthews-Northrup Works, 1910)

Nancy Weekly

art, New York City area

European Styles in Colonial America

While Boston stood at the center of artistic activity in the colonial period, New York City also had an active artistic community. European traditions dominated via art brought to the colonies and engravings of famous works. Most artists, such as John Wollaston and the Duyckinck family, made their livings painting portraits of prominent citizens. The names of most 17th- and 18th-century artists have been lost, including the painter of *Governor Peter Stuyvesant* (*ca* 1660). Limners, or itinerant artists with little formal training, produced the majority of art in the colonial period. The first public sculptures in the city, by Joseph Wilton—*George III* (1770) and *William Pitt the Elder* (1770)—were destroyed after the reading of the Declaration of Independence in July 1776. Landscape painting flourished; William Winstanley, with patronage from George Washington, created images of the Hudson River and Genesee Falls, and city views including harbor scenes by William Burgis were engraved and sold in England.

Antebellum 19th-Century Painting and Sculpture

At the beginning of the 19th century, the styles and subjects prevalent in the 18th century still dominated. Francis Guy produced street scenes, including *Winter Scene in Brooklyn* (*ca* 1817), while William Guy Wall published landscapes in the collection *Hudson River Portfolio*. The most prominent portraitists were John Wesley Jarvis, his student Henry Inman, and Samuel F. B. Morse. Commissioned by the city, Morse painted the full-length portrait *Marquis de Lafayette* (1825–26). New York City had become the economic capital of the country after the Revolutionary War, and leading citizens soon established it as the cultural capital. Painter John Trumbull presided over the American Academy of Fine Arts, which promoted history painting and the fine arts through exhibitions of Old Masters and plaster casts. To acknowledge contemporary American artists, Morse and others formed the National Academy of Design (1825), which offered local artists educational and exhibition opportunities. Painter William Dunlap wrote the first published history of American art, *History of the Rise and Progress of the Arts of Design in the United States* (1834). Businessman Luman Reed's collection was opened to the public as the New York Gallery of Fine Arts in 1844 and was acquired by the New-York Historical Society in 1858. By collecting works of American artists, Philip Hone and Jonathan Sturges encouraged the arts. Brooklyn hosted a vibrant artistic community as well. The Brooklyn Institute (now Brooklyn Museum of Art), founded as the Brooklyn Apprentices Library (1823), held annual exhibitions of local and nationally known artists, while the Graham Art School and Brooklyn Academy of Design provided art instruction.

With the growth of nationalism in the early 19th century, artists sought to define America visually, and landscape painting emerged as the vehicle. In richly detailed landscapes of the Hudson River valley, Thomas Cole strove to reveal the presence of God in nature and the cycles of history. Others, including Asher B. Durand and Frederic Edwin Church, also used realistic depictions of nature to express broad ideas. Together with Albert Bierstadt, Jasper Francis Cropsey, John Frederick Kensett, Worthington Whittredge, and others, these artists were integral to what became known as the Hudson River school. Many of them worked at the Tenth Street Studio Building, the first building designed specifically for artists; it remained a hub of artistic activity for much of the century. Genre painting, or scenes of everyday life, became popular at midcentury. William Sidney Mount explored contemporary social and political issues in his genre paintings of life on Long Island, including *Farmer's Nooning* (1836), commissioned by Sturges. John Quidor produced paintings based on the stories of James Fenimore Cooper and Washington Irving. Other popular genre painters in the mid- and late 19th centuries included Winslow Homer, Eastman Johnson, and Lily Martin Spencer. Before the Civil War, sculpture in the city was dominated by portraits of war heroes and civic leaders, including Henry Kirke Brown's *George Washington* (1856) in Union Square and Robert Ball Hughes's *Alexander Hamilton* (1835, destroyed). Exhibited in 1853 at London's Crystal Palace, Hiram Powers's nude statue *Greek Slave* attracted much attention and admiration.

City residents' main familiarity with art was through prints and exhibitions. Currier and Ives, which commissioned genre paintings from well-known artists, produced over 7,500 different prints between 1834 and 1907. James Herring founded the Apollo Association (1839), which became the American Art Union (AAU, 1848–60). The AAU and the Cosmopolitan Art Association (1854–?61) introduced art to the public through annual exhibitions, distribution of prints to subscribers, and a lottery for artworks. The small statuettes of everyday life by John Rogers reached a wide audience through mass production and mail order.

Post–Civil War: The Academic Style and Its Rivals

In earlier decades artists such as Bierstadt, Johnson, Whittredge, and Emmanuel Leutze had studied at Germany's Düsseldorf Academy, but later American students studied at academies in Munich and Paris. Frank Duveneck, an American artist living in Munich, influenced a generation of artists including Edward Lamson Henry, William Merritt Chase, and Julian Alden Weir. In Paris, students including Childe Hassam and Augustus Saint-Gaudens flocked to the Académie Julian and the Ecole des Beaux-Arts. When these students returned to New York City advocating new trends in art, they were not welcomed by the National Academy of Design. Therefore, in 1877, several artists founded the progressive Society of American Artists to encourage new forms of art. One new trend was impressionism. In 1886, 300 French impressionist works were exhibited by the American Art Association and French art dealer Paul Durand-Ruel, who opened a gallery in the city in 1888. American collectors including Henry O. and Louisine Havemeyer purchased modern French works. Chase and Hassam applied the lighter palette and more fluid brushstroke of impressionism to local scenes, Chase painting Prospect Park and Washington Square, and Hassam 5th Ave. Both were members of the Ten, a group of American impressionists from Boston and New York City who exhibited jointly beginning in 1898. At this time Long Island, especially eastern Suffolk Co, became a popular destination for artists because of the open air and light. Several artists, including Hassam and Thomas Moran, established studios in East Hampton in the 1870s and 1880s. Chase set up a studio in 1892 and later a school in nearby Shinnecock Hills, and the Parrish Art Museum (1897) opened in Southampton.

Public commissions for monuments and statues honoring military heroes flourished after the Civil War. Saint-Gaudens designed the memorial *Admiral David Farragut* (1878–81) that stands in Madison Square Park, and John Quincy Adams Ward created the heroic statues *Henry Ward Beecher* (1891) in Brooklyn's Columbus Park (now Cadman Plaza) and *Horace Greeley* (1890) in City Hall Park. Civic pride was also manifest in the openings of the Metropolitan Museum of Art in 1870 and of the Brooklyn Museum's (now Brooklyn Museum of Art's) new home in 1893 on Eastern Parkway.

1900–1950s: Realism, Abstraction, Modernism

In direct contrast to the refined European sensibilities of the Ten, several artists produced gritty depictions of urban life, for which they were nicknamed the Ashcan school. A heterogeneous group, including John Sloan and Stuart Davis and many of whom had started as newspaper illustrators, their styles ranged from realism to symbolism. One member, Robert Henri, helped organize a 1908 exhibition at the Macbeth Gallery of a group that came to be called the Eight. In a challenge to the traditionalism of the National Academy of Design, such artists as Rockwell Kent and George Bellows joined the Eight to organize the *Exhibition of Independent Artists* in 1910. At the same time, photographer and art dealer Alfred Stieglitz established the 291 Gallery devoted to the works of the Photo-secessionists, including Gertrude Kasēbier and Edward Steichen, who emphasized the artistic properties of photography over its documentary capabilities. This gallery became a center of artistic photography and a showcase for European artists, as well as for artists working in New York City including Arthur Dove, Marsden Hartley, Georgia O'Keeffe, Joseph Stella, and Max Weber. Countering the American scene painting of the Eight, they were influenced by European abstraction (although often still working in a representational mode) and inspired by the energy and architecture of the city.

The controversial 1913 International Exhibition of Modern Art (better known as New York Armory Show) was an epoch-making event in the introduction of modern art to the United States. Organized by the Association of American Painters and Sculptors, it featured over 1,000 works by modernists, including fauves and cubists, at the 69th Regiment Armory. While the critical response to the show was mainly derisive, its effect on American art in the coming years was enormous. Dada, the anarchic movement that rejected traditional artistic expression, began in World War I era Zurich, Paris, and Berlin; it was practiced in New York by Marcel Duchamp, Man Ray, and the eccentric Baroness Elsa Von Freytag-Loringhoven. Abstraction continued to influence artists in the 1920s and 1930s. Artists such as Charles Demuth and Charles Sheeler utilized hard lines and geometric shapes, a style known as precisionism, to depict the industrial landscape, while Dove and O'Keeffe reduced natural forms to abstract shapes. Meanwhile Thomas Hart Benton, Isobel Bishop, Edward Hopper, Reginald Marsh, and others still focused on stylized figurative paintings of the American scene. Later in the century, more literal figurative representation found proponents, such as Russian Jewish émigrés Moses and Raphael Soyer, who were influenced by socialist realism, innovative modernist realist Philip Pearlstein, and portraitist Alice Neel. The Art Students League (1875), founded to provide life drawing classes to a wide range of students, continued to function as the most important educational center in New York City, with influential teachers including Benton, Henri, Davis, Sloan, and Walter Shirlaw.

Numerous private collections, notably those of Henry Clay Frick and J. P. Morgan, opened as public museums. Avant-garde artists were supported by collectors such as Louise and Walter Arensberg, Mabel Dodge Luhan, Katherine Dreier, the artist Florine Stettheimer and her sisters Ettie and Carrie, and Gertrude Vanderbilt Whitney. Lillie P. Bliss, Abby Aldrich Rockefeller, and Mary Quinn Sullivan formed the Museum of Modern Art (MoMA, 1929). Whitney, a sculptor whose *War Memorial* (1923) stood at Broadway between 167th and 168th Sts, founded the Whitney Museum of American Art (1930). The collection of Solomon R. Guggenheim became the Solomon R. Guggenheim Museum of Non-Objective Painting (1939, now known as the Guggenheim Museum); its landmark curvilinear building, designed by Frank Lloyd Wright, was completed in 1959.

While there was a major upheaval in painting in the first decades of the 20th century, most new public sculpture continued to be monuments and memorials in the style of the Ecole des Beaux-Arts. Saint-Gaudens's *William Tecumseh Sherman* (1902) and Frederick MacMonnies's bronzes *Army* and *Navy* (1901) in Brooklyn's Grand Army Plaza, and Daniel Chester French's *Four Continents* (1907) at the US Custom House (now Museum of the American Indian, Smithsonian Institution) were among the many major monuments dedicated in the city during this period. Although designed by the artists, most were carved by the six Piccirilli brothers, who had a studio in the Bronx; brothers Attilio and Furio achieved individual fame. The 1930s Federal Art Project of the Works Progress Administration hired painters and muralists to create artworks for schools, housing projects, post offices, and other public buildings. Berenice Abbott's dramatic photographs of the city were published as *Changing New York* (1937) by the New York City Federal Art Project. Lewis Hine and Margaret Bourke-White received commissions to photograph the new skyscrapers, including the Chrysler and Empire State Buildings.

A key figure in the Harlem Renaissance of the late 1920s and the 1930s was Aaron Douglas, who created a large mural entitled *Aspects of Negro Life* (1934) for what is now the Schomburg Center for Research in Black Culture. Sculptor Augusta Savage, who had studied at Cooper Union and the Pratt Institute, opened the Savage Studio of Arts and Crafts (1932) to encourage young artists; its students included Romare Bearden and Jacob Lawrence.

Abstract Expressionism: The New York School

During the World War II years, exiled European artists, among them Salvador Dalí, Max Ernst, and Roberto Matta, involved in surrealism and other modern art movements arrived in the city, influencing a generation of American artists. Among the latter was the reclusive Joseph Cornell, who from the basement of his family home on Utopia Parkway in Queens, produced boxed assemblages of surrealist images, text, and objects evoking mysterious visions of the past. Also influenced by the émigrés were a number of young painters who focused on abstraction and the process of making art itself. Jackson Pollock, working in his eastern Long Island studio, developed a masterful technique of splattering large canvases with paint. His unique method and closely allied styles became known as action painting, a term coined by critic Harold Rosenberg. Led by Pollock, the New York school of abstract expressionism included diverse nonrepresentational artists such as gestural abstractionists Willem de Kooning, Lee Krasner, and Arshile Gorky, color-field painters Mark Rothko, Barnett Newman, and Clyfford Still, and such kindred spirits as Philip Guston, Franz Kline, and David Smith. Gathering frequently at Cedar Tavern in Greenwich Village, several of them exhibited at Betty Parsons's gallery and Peggy Guggenheim's Art of This Century Gallery between 1943 and 1946. With the success of the New York school, New York City displaced Paris after World War II as the perceived center of the international art world. In the 1950s the enthusiastic support of critics Rosenberg, Clement Greenberg, and Meyer Schapiro coalesced into a hegemonic stylistic orthodoxy. By the late 1950s, the turn away from pure abstraction was being led by Jasper Johns and Robert Rauschenberg, whose mixed-media canvases incorporated curatorial icons, newspaper images, and found objects.

The 1960s

In contrast to abstract expressionism's focus on the materials and processes of painting, the Pop artists of the late 1950s and the 1960s including Red Grooms, Roy Lichtenstein, Claes Oldenburg, and Andy Warhol took as their inspiration popular images from advertising, movies, comic strips, and shop windows. Warhol's Factory was a center of 1960s alternative culture. Fluxus, a playful and conceptual antiart movement begun in Europe by George Maciunas, spread to New York in 1961 at Maciunas's A/G gallery. New York art world figures associated with the international Fluxus movement include Henry Flynt, Al Hansen, Geoffrey Hendricks, Dick Higgins, Alison Knowles, Larry Miller, Yoko Ono, and Nam June Paik. Carolee Schneeman's feminist performance art kinetically explored the erotics of the female body. Happenings, organized by Allan Kaprow, Jim Dine, and others in the early to mid-1960s, were interactive theater and art events mixing performance and visual installations in an exploration of the boundary zone between life and art.

David Smith's monolithic sculptures, particularly his monumental 1961–65 Cubi series, influenced the minimalists of the 1960s to mid-1970s, including Carl Andre and Donald Judd. Although its exploration of new geometric forms was mainly sculptural, minimalism also involved nonrepresentational painters Ellsworth Kelly, Brice Marden, Agnes Martin, Ad Reinhardt, Robert Ryman, and Frank Stella. The Storm King Art Center in Mountainville (Orange Co), an outdoor museum of modern sculpture set in a scenic landscape, was founded in the 1960s by Ralph E. Ogden and H. Peter Stern. Public sculpture in New York City was encouraged by the so-called plaza law of 1961 requiring new buildings to have street-level open courts. Lincoln Center (1962), the performing arts complex on Manhattan's West Side, installed works by

Entryway to the Guggenheim Museum in New York City, designed by Frank Lloyd Wright, opened in 1959.

Alexander Calder and Henry Moore, and a 1967 Parks Department initiative temporarily placed 29 sculptures throughout Manhattan.

SINCE 1970

The young artists of the 1960s and 1970s did not embrace a single style. One dominant theme was conceptual art, which defined a work of art as an idea rather than as a physical object and rejected the materiality of an object that could be bought and sold on the market. Earthworks, performance, video, body, process, and installation art were just a few of the forms of 1970s art spawned by conceptualism. Site-specific installation art challenged preconceptions by questioning received notions of art. Richard Serra's *Tilted Arc,* a 120-ton (109 MT) curving wall of steel commissioned by the US General Services Administration for Federal Plaza, was installed in 1981. Public response to the sculpture was extreme, resulting in a national controversy and its removal by federal officials at night in 1989. While object and representational painting returned in the 1980s, postmodernism and performance art also rose to prominence. In the work of Jean-Michel Basquiat, Keith Haring, and Kenny Scharf, underground subway graffiti and cartooning met the high-art establishment. Jenny Holzer displayed her text-based "truisms" in light-emitting diode (LED) displays in the Guggenheim Museum and Times Square. Other 1980s artists who in different ways exemplified the eclecticism of postmodernism included Eric Fischl, Vitaly Komar and Alex Melamid, Jeff Koons, Mark Kostabi, Barbara Kruger, Sherrie Levine, David Salle, Julian Schnabel, Cindy Sherman, and David Wojnarowicz.

Art critics and art historians began to acknowledge the contributions of previously marginalized groups, and a new breed of museums, including the Studio Museum of Harlem (1968), El Museo del Barrio (1969), P.S.1 Contemporary Art Center (1971), and the New Museum (1977), provided venues for art and artists shut out of the increasingly conservative MoMA and other museums. The Guerrilla Girls, a band of anonymous feminists wearing gorilla masks, crashed numerous art events in the 1980s to draw attention to the misogyny of the art world and the underrepresentation of female artists in major museums. Attracted by large warehouse spaces ideal for studios and the arrival of galleries such as Paula Cooper, artists moved to SoHo and later to Tribeca. Galleries such as Mary Boone, Leo Castelli, Sonnabend, and Pace/Wildenstein flourished. In Chelsea, the Dia Art Foundation (1974) opened Dia Center for the Arts (1981; now Dia:Chelsea). The rise in prices and speculation in the art market contributed to the celebrity status of art dealers and artists. For a brief period in the mid-1980s, the East Village replaced SoHo as the center of the downtown art scene. SoHo regained its prominence after the 1987 stock market crash but faded in the 1990s because of high rents.

In the 1990s galleries such as Matthew Marks and Luhring-Augustine became the focus of activity. With decreases in arts funding, there was a reaction against the commercialism of the 1980s. Video, process, sound art, and political art achieved wider recognition, as exemplified in several controversial Whitney Biennial exhibitions during this period. In 1999 New York City Mayor Rudolph Guiliani attempted unsuccessfully to revoke the lease of the Brooklyn Museum of Art in response to the exhibition of Chris Ofili's *The Holy Virgin Mary* (1996), a depiction of a black Madonna decorated with dried elephant dung (considered a sacred substance in some African Christian traditions). The terrorist attacks of 11 Sept 2001 destroyed the World Trade Center (WTC) studios of World Views, an art residency program administered by the Lower Manhattan Cultural Council. Artist in residence Michael Richards was killed in the attacks, and several sculptures at the WTC plaza were partially or totally destroyed. In the economic downturn after 11 September, museums cut staff, reduced programming, and modified renovations in response to decreased tourism.

A considerable expansion of the region's art museums in the late 20th century had usually coincided with flush economic times. Some major projects continued in the new century despite the economic slide. In 2003 Dia Art Foundation opened Dia:Beacon, a permanent home for its collection of post-1960 art, on the Hudson River shore in Beacon (Dutchess Co). MoMA temporarily relocated to a converted staple factory in Queens while its Manhattan building underwent a renovation and expansion by architect Yoshio Taniguchi, slated to reopen in 2004. The Guggenheim's satellite branch in SoHo drew large crowds when it opened in 1992 but closed at the end of 2001. The economic downturn of the early 21st century provided further impetus for galleries and museums to leave SoHo. Many relocated to Chelsea, which had become a center for art galleries in the 1990s; others reopened in Williamsburg and DUMBO (Down Under the Brooklyn Bridge), the Brooklyn waterfront neighborhoods where as many as 10,000 artists have moved in recent years.

See also ART MUSEUMS, COLLECTING, AND PATRONAGE; ARTS AND CRAFTS MOVEMENT; CERAMICS AND POTTERY; GLASS; HUDSON RIVER SCHOOL; MURALS; PHOTOGRAPHY; PRINTS AND PRINTMAKING; SCULPTURE, PUBLIC; WORLD'S FAIRS.

Ashton, Dore. *The New York School: A Cultural Reckoning* (New York: Viking, 1972)

Belknap, Waldron Phoenix. *American Colonial Painting: Materials for a History* (Cambridge, Mass: Belknap Press of Harvard Univ Press, 1959)

Brown, Milton W. *American Painting from the Armory Show to the Depression* (Princeton, NJ: Princeton Univ Press, 1955)

Craven, Wayne. *Sculpture in America* (Newark: Univ of Delaware Press, 1984)

Gerdts, William H. *American Impressionism* (Seattle: Henry Art Gallery, 1980)

Kirby, Michael, ed. *Happenings* (New York: E. P. Dutton, 1965)

McCarthy, Kathleen D. *Women's Culture: American Philanthropy and Art, 1830–1930* (Chicago: Univ of Chicago Press, 1991)

Nygren, Edward J. *Views and Visions: American Landscape Painting before 1830* (Washington, DC: Corcoran Gallery of Art, 1986)

Rosenblum, Naomi. *A World History of Photography,* 3d ed. (New York: Abbeville Press, 1997)

Jamie W. Johnson

art, Rochester area and the Southern Tier. Rochester developed as a center for artists early in its history. John Lee Douglas Mathies (1780–1834) was active in Canandaigua (Ontario Co) as early as 1815 before moving to Rochester in 1823. His most noted work is an 1820 portrait of the Seneca chief Red Jacket. Helen Searle Pattison (1830–84) was a specialist in still life. Eugene Sintzenich (1792–1852) relocated to Rochester after visiting Western New York in 1831. He, along with Henry Van Ingen (1833–99), produced works that reflected their academic training and European influences. Other artists in Rochester in the 1840s, portraitists and itinerant genre scene painters, included Jean-Baptiste Roy Audry (1798–?1848), Alvah Bradish (1806–1901), and Cornelius Krieghoff (1815–1871).

The Rochester Academy of Art was founded in 1874 to sponsor exhibitions of national and local artists. It was soon supplanted by the Powers Art Gallery (1875–97), an elegant gallery created by a prominent Rochester banker. The Rochester Art Club (1877) provided the first professional art school in the city. Among its instructors was landscape painter Horatio Walker (1858–1938), who worked in a manner reminiscent of the French Barbizon school. In Le Roy (Genesee Co), Lemuel Wiles (1826–1905) became a noted painter and instructor. Charles Gruppe (1860–1940) spent much of his career in Holland but maintained his connection with Rochester through exhibitions and patronage; his son, Emile Gruppe (1896–1978), also attained a substantial reputation as one of America's finest landscape painters. Emma Lampert Cooper (1860–1920), originally from Nunda (Livingston Co), who painted largely European subjects, achieved international success. By 1891 the Rochester Athenaeum and the Mechanics Institute (now Rochester Institute of Technology) would supplant the Art Club as the leading source of instruction for Rochester students. In 1908 a show of impressionist paintings in Rochester provoked a minor sensation. In 1913 the Memorial Art Gallery opened on the campus of the University of Rochester. It would become the city's major art museum and acquired the collection of George Eastman.

Rochester and Western New York regional artists in the early 20th century were distinguished in many genres. They were important exponents of the arts and crafts movement. Harvey Ellis (1852–1904), at first a painter and art instructor, is best known today for his designs for the Stickley Furniture Co. Ellis's knowledge and integration of international movements, such as Secessionist, Art Nouveau, Pre-Raphaelite, and Japonism, extended to the painters Ada Howe Kent (1858–1942) of Rochester and M. Louise Stowell (1861–1930) of Hornell (Steuben Co). Charles Livingston Bull (1874–1932), a student of both Ellis and Stowell, Clifford Ulp (1885–1957), a student of Charles Gruppe, and impressionist John J. Inglis (1867–1946) provided strong influences for generations of students who fell under their tutelage at the Mechanics Institute. Two Rochester-born artists who won acclaim after moving to New York City were Louise Upton Brumback (1872–1929), who specialized in vibrantly colored landscapes and seascapes, and George Renouard (1885–1954), a painter and printmaker whose work is aligned with the New York City Ashcan School. Carl W. Peters (1897–1980) of Fairport (Monroe Co) was one of the region's most noted artists, with many impressionistic landscapes focused on the Genesee. His murals adorn the Genesee Valley

Trust Headquarters, Rochester Academy of Medicine, and Fairport Public Library. Ralph Avery (1906–76) and Roy Mason (1886–1972) were noted watercolorists. James D. Havens (1900–1960) and John C. Menihan (1908–1992) were masters of the color wood-engraving print. William Ehrich (1897–1960) was an imaginative and socially conscious sculptor.

In the 1930s the Works Progress Administration's Federal Art Project in Rochester stimulated much local art, such as the innovative Seneca Arts Project at the Rochester Municipal Museum (now Rochester Museum and Science Center), including depictions of Iroquois creation myths by Seneca painter Ernest Smith (1907–75). In addition to the Memorial Art Gallery, other important museums in the area are the Rockwell Museum and the Corning Museum of Glass (Steuben Co). Rochester Contemporary is an institution dedicated to the exhibition and promotion of contemporary artists from Rochester and Western New York. The Chautauqua Institution has sponsored art programs and exhibitions since the late 19th century.

See also CERAMICS AND POTTERY; PHOTOGRAPHY; PRINTS AND PRINTMAKING.

Gerdts, William H. *Art across America: Two Centuries of Regional Painting* (New York: Abbeville Press, 1990)

McKelvey, Blake. "The First Century of Art in Rochester—to 1925," *Rochester History* 17 (Apr 1955): 1–24

———. "The Visual Arts in Metropolitan Rochester," *Rochester History* 32 (Jan 1970): 1–24

David F. Martin and Michael L. James

art, Syracuse, Ithaca, Utica, and Central New York

EARLY ARTISTS

Portrait painting by itinerant artists was common in early 19th-century rural America. Abraham Tuthill (1776–1843) and Sheldon Peck (1797–1868) were two such Central New York artists. Tuthill's range extended even farther to Buffalo and Vermont. Peck lived in Jordan (Onondaga Co), where he painted portraits on wood panels. Sanford Thayer (1820–80) maintained a studio in Syracuse. In 1845 he completed an important portrait of the Onondaga Indian chief Ossahinta. Francis B. Carpenter (1830–1900) of Homer (Cortland Co) studied briefly with Thayer. In 1851 Carpenter moved to New York City, where he had many distinguished sitters, among them Presidents John Tyler, Millard Fillmore, Franklin Pierce, and Abraham Lincoln. His large painting representing Pres Lincoln signing the Emancipation Proclamation hangs in the Capitol building in Washington, DC. Henry Inman (1801–46) and Charles Loring Elliott (1812–68) were two other Central New York artists who moved on to New York City and made their reputations there. Inman, a Utica native, became the leading portrait painter of his time and was the first vice president of the National Academy of Design. Elliott, born in Scipio (Cayuga Co), studied in New York City with John Trumbull and John Quidor. He then spent the next 10 years as an itinerant portrait artist in Central and Western New York and was particularly active in the Skaneateles (Onondaga Co) area.

Susan Waters (1823–1900) of Binghamton is a rare example of a female itinerant artist. Self-taught, she worked in southern New York State and in Pennsylvania as a photographer and painter. From 1843 through 1846, she painted portraits in many small towns in the Southern Tier. Andrew J. Russell (1839–79), who grew up in Nunda (Livingston Co) painted the Finger Lakes area extensively; *View of Bath from the West* (1859) is a notable example of his work. In 1868 he was commissioned to make a photographic record of the construction of the Union Pacific portion of the transcontinental railroad. Russell's photo of the historic moment, *The Meeting of the Rails at Promontory Point,* has been widely reproduced.

PAINTERS IN THE 20TH CENTURY

Henry Ward Ranger (1858–1916), who was raised in Geneseo (Livingston Co) and Syracuse, enrolled in Syracuse University's College of Fine Arts but did not graduate. As a student in France, he became involved with the Barbizon school of painting but later became a committed tonalist. Utica native Arthur B. Davies (1862–1928) organized the landmark Armory Show of 1913 at the 69th Infantry Regiment Armory in New York City, a defining event in American modernism. After Davies's death, the Museum of Modern Art's first president credited him with that institute's conception. Another important artist from the region was Arthur Dove (1880–1946), who was born in Canandaigua (Ontario Co). A student at Hobart College and Cornell University, Dove is thought to be the first innovative abstract painter in America. Ithaca native Louis Agassiz Fuertes (1874–1927) is considered the most notable ornithological artist since John James Audubon. Cornell University has a large collection of Fuertes's bird illustrations and personal papers, including the journal he kept during the 1899 E. H. Harriman Expedition.

Syracuse native Beatrice Wose Smith (1908–71) studied painting at Syracuse University. Following graduation, she went to New York City, where she studied with artist George Luks, a member of the Ashcan school, and her later paintings bore the distinctive mark of that style. By 1932 she had returned to Syracuse, where she spent the remainder of her career. Her work is in the permanent collection of the Everson Museum of Art in Syracuse. Merrill Bailey (1909–81) of Cazenovia (Madison Co) graduated from Pratt Institute and Syracuse University and later taught art in Cazenovia schools. A member of the National Watercolor Society, his work received national notice, and a collection of his watercolors are displayed at the historic Lincklaen House Inn in Cazenovia. Portrait artist Robert Hofmann (1889–1987) in 1939 fled his birthplace in Austria and in 1956 moved

The Connoisseurs, by Sanford Thayer, 1845.

to Syracuse, where he resided for the rest of his life.

SCULPTORS AND CERAMISTS

Ceramist Adelaide Alsop Robineau (1865–1929) worked from her studio in Syracuse and was widely recognized as the preeminent pottery artist in America. Her famed 1911 scarab vase, *The Apotheosis of the Toiler,* is in the Everson Museum Ceramics Collection, along with a large portion of her work. Harry G. Aitken distinguished himself as the head of design at Onondaga Pottery/Syracuse China for which he had been hired in 1904. He painted many of the china decorations himself, and these items are now highly sought by collectors. He was a member of the Associated Artists of Syracuse and exhibited his oil paintings in various regional shows during his career. Sculptor Rodger Mack (1938–2003) taught at Syracuse University. Notable artists such as Anthony Caro (1924–), Kenneth Noland (1924–), and Helen Frankenthaler (1928–) worked with him on a variety of projects. With Caro, Mack established the Triangle Artists Workshop, held in Pine Plains (Dutchess Co) as well as in London and Barcelona, Spain. A native New Englander transplanted to Syracuse, George F. Welch (1926–2003) worked as a painter but is known primarily for his unique copper enameling. He also created the artwork for the paper covers and dust jackets of 10 books published by Syracuse University Press.

MUSEUMS AND ART CLUBS

The Everson Museum of Art was founded in 1896 by Dr George Fisk Comfort as the Syracuse Museum of Fine Arts. He established the first regular museum education program in America. Comfort was succeeded in 1910 by Fernando Carter, who initiated the museum's extensive ceramic collection with the purchase of 31 pieces by Robineau. Anna Wetherill Olmsted succeeded Carter in 1931 and was instrumental in founding the Ceramic National Exhibition in memory of Robineau. The Munson-Williams-Proctor Art Institute in Utica, chartered in 1919, has an extensive art school and has formed an alliance with Pratt Institute, known as Pratt at MWP. Students spend the first two years of their bachelor of fine arts program in Utica and complete their degree at Pratt's main campus in Brooklyn.

High-quality, professional art museums are also found in some of the region's smaller cities. These include Auburn's (Cayuga Co) Schweinfurth Memorial Art Center, constructed in 1979–80, and the Roberson Museum and Science Center in Binghamton, founded in 1954. The Rome Art and Community Center (Oneida Co), founded in 1967, also bears witness to the vitality of the regional art scene. Many colleges and universities in the area also maintain their own first-rate museums and galleries, such as the Lowe Art Gallery at Syracuse University and the Johnson Museum at Cornell. The Lowe Gallery is associated with Syracuse University's School of Visual and Performing Arts, which encompasses five schools and departments. Syracuse has the nation's first degree-granting College of Fine Arts, originally housed in the Romanesque Crouse College building, designed by architect Archimedes Russell and built in 1889.

The first art club or guild in Central New York was the Associated Artists of Syracuse (AAS), which was founded in 1926 by a group of art professors from Syracuse University. In 1929 the group began a close affiliation with the Syracuse Museum of Fine Arts (now Everson Museum), where annual juried exhibits were held. These shows were open to all; artists whose work was accepted were invited to join AAS. Grandma Moses received her first award at one of these exhibitions. These AAS-sponsored exhibits continued until 1952, when the museum began to offer its own juried regional show. AAS opened a cooperative gallery in 1966 and maintained an exhibit facility for 17 years until a shortage of available volunteers forced its closing. AAS, which is still active in the region, served as prototype for Central New York's myriad art guilds and associations. Some of the more notable examples include the Onondaga Art Guild, North Syracuse Art Guild, Syracuse Ceramics Guild, and the Camillus Art Guild.

See also ARTS AND CRAFTS MOVEMENT; CERAMICS AND POTTERY; GLASS.

Finger Lakes Artists List, http://www.westlakeconservators.com/artists3.htm
Reed, Cleota, and Stan Skoczen. *Syracuse China* (Syracuse: Syracuse Univ Press, 1997)
Resource Library Magazine: America's Magazine for Representational Art, http://www.tfaoi.com/resourc.htm

Sallie Naatz Bailey

Arthur, Chester A(lan) (*b* Fairfield, Vt, 5 Oct 1829; *d* New York City, 18 Nov 1886). US president. He graduated from Union College in Schenectady in 1848 and began practicing law in New York City in 1854. An early member of the Republican Party, Arthur supported abolitionist causes and was an attorney in New York State's victory in the *Lemmon v the People* (1860) slave freedom case. In 1861 Gov Edwin D. Morgan appointed him assistant quartermaster general and then quartermaster general (1862–63), bureaucratic positions that entailed provisioning Union soldiers passing through New York City. In the late 1860s Arthur befriended Sen Roscoe Conkling and clung to his coattails as Conkling gained national prominence. In 1871 Arthur was appointed collector of the Port of New York, the most lucrative federal patronage post. At the Customs House, Arthur performed his duties no better but no worse than his predecessors, earning the sobriquet "Gentleman Boss" for his sophistication, education, appearance, and good manners. In 1878 Pres Rutherford B. Hayes, bent on civil service reform, defied Conkling and the New York Republican machine and displaced Arthur. At the 1880 Republican National Convention, the Conkling "Stalwarts" could not prevent James A. Garfield's nomination. To balance the ticket the Republicans nominated Arthur for vice president, a pairing that helped Garfield win New York State and the presidency.

On 2 July 1881 a deranged office seeker, Charles Guiteau, shot Pres Garfield and told the arresting policeman, "I am a Stalwart and Arthur will be president." Garfield's death on 19 Sept 1881 made Arthur president under most difficult circumstances. Yet, despite his reputation for machine politics and doubts about his ability and integrity, his administration proved relatively honest and dignified. Arthur effectively supported the Civil Service Reform Act of 1883, vetoed one Chinese exclusion bill (although he supported another), vetoed a pork-filled "River and Harbor" bill, and vigorously if fruitlessly prosecuted the people involved in the post office scandals known as the Star Route trials. In foreign affairs he supported the creation of a steelship navy and sought an American interest in an interoceanic canal. In the New York State gubernatorial election of 1882, the president supported Charles Folger; but Folger's defeat by an obscure Democratic mayor of Buffalo, Grover Cleveland, and Arthur's deteriorating health, led Arthur to decide not to seek actively renomination in 1884. Nomination went to his longtime rival, James G. Blaine. Arthur's refusal to support Blaine contributed to Blaine's loss in New York State to Cleveland by a mere 2,000 votes. Arthur died of a cerebral hemorrhage two years later and was buried in his family plot in the Albany Rural Cemetery.

Doenecke, Justus. *The Presidencies of James A. Garfield and Chester A. Arthur* (Lawrence: Regents Press of Kansas, 1981)
Howe, George. *Chester A. Arthur: A Quarter-Century of Machine Politics* (1935; repr New York: F. Ungar, 1957)
Reeves, Thomas. *Gentleman Boss: The Life of Chester Alan Arthur* (New York: Knopf, 1975)

Jon Sterngass

art museums, collecting, and patronage

EARLY NEW YORK CITY COLLECTIONS

Museums were established in the state during the 19th century by merchants, attorneys, and other prominent citizens. The New York Academy of the Fine Arts (later American Academy of Fine Arts), organized in 1802 through the efforts of Edward and Robert R. Livingston, acquired reproductions of famous sculptures and heroic paintings but failed by 1842. The New-York Historical Society (NYHS), established in 1804, drew prominent New York families to give time, funding, and artifacts from their own attics to create exhibits on New York State and American history and art. Many of New York City's wealthy collected art, but grocery merchant Luman Reed was one of the very few who permitted wide access to his paintings. The gallery on the third floor of Reed's Greenwich St house, completed in 1832, was open to the public one day a week. Consisting primarily of Hudson River school works by Thomas Cole and Asher B. Durand and paintings by William Sidney Mount and George Whiting Flagg, Reed's collection went to the NYHS in 1858. The Van Cortlandt, Livingston, and Van Rensselaer families were among those contributing decorative art and furniture for exhibits in the first part of the 19th century. After the Civil War, significant donations were more likely to come from Vanderbilts, Carnegies, and Rockefellers.

The Metropolitan Museum of Art (the Met) was founded in 1870 by members of the Union League Club, including George Putnam Palmer, Joseph H. Choate, John Frederick Kensett, and William T. Blodgett, who were primarily interested in the Old Masters and antiquities from abroad. J. P. Morgan was one of the wealthy patrons who helped build museum collections after the Civil War. Whenever a prized item became available, his buyer was dispatched and usually outbid other collectors. Between 1890 and 1913 Morgan used up approximately half of his fortune on $60 million worth of art, according to his estate appraisers, and much of it went to the Met. Upon attaining the presidency of that institution, Morgan invited Henry Clay Frick and other wealthy individuals to join the board of trustees. Trustees gave generously and encouraged their friends, relatives, and colleagues to do likewise. Their wealth and power gave other donors confidence that the Met would be a stable and flourishing institution in which to invest. Both Morgan's and Frick's Manhattan mansions became museums that held the remainder of their remarkable collections.

Federal legislation also encouraged American donors to support museums. The Payne-Aldrich tariff of 1909, sponsored in the House of Representatives by Sereno E. Payne of Auburn (Cayuga Co), added original artworks over 20 years old to the duty-free list of items that could be imported, making it easier for private collectors and museum curators to acquire valuable art from abroad. The Payne-Aldrich tariff also established the charitable deduction for estate taxes. A few years earlier, J. P. Morgan had confided to Sen Nelson Aldrich and the Monetary Commission that he wished to donate his paintings to the Met but that it would cost him over $1 million in taxes to do so. Payne-Aldrich passed, and Morgan's collection went to the Met upon his death. The charitable deduction for income and gift taxes established under Payne-Aldrich encouraged Americans to donate both money and art after federal income tax was instituted in 1913.

Museum Collections beyond New York City

Significant collections were also being developed in other parts of the state. Matthias Hollenback Arnot, president of the Chemung Canal Bank, began collecting contemporary American and European art in 1869, moved to acquiring Old Masters during the 1880s, and built a gallery in his family home in Elmira to display the paintings. Arnot bequested his collection in 1910, and the 1833 Neoclassical mansion that housed it became the Arnot Art Museum, which opened in Elmira in 1913. George Fisk Comfort, an art educator and member of the Union League Club, founded the Syracuse Museum of Fine Arts, opened in 1900. The museum, which became the Everson Museum of Art in 1968, began in 1911 to specialize in American paintings, sculpture, graphics, and ceramics. In 1916 the museum acquired 32 porcelains by Adelaide Alsop Robineau and in 1932 established the Ceramic National exhibitions in his honor.

Buffalo philanthropist John J. Albright provided the Albright Art Gallery (1905). Significant donations from entrepreneur Seymour H. Knox Jr enhanced the collection, which adopted the name Albright-Knox Art Gallery in 1962. The same year, it moved into a new Gordon Bunshaft–designed building, displaying its strong collection in 20th-century art. The Memorial Art Gallery in Rochester was founded in 1913 by Emily Sibley Watson, prospering through substantial patronage from George Eastman and presenting an international survey of art. Utica's Munson-Williams-Proctor Arts Institute was founded in 1919 around American and European paintings and decorative arts donated by the Williams and Proctor families. Bartlett Arkell, the first president of the Beech-Nut Packing Co, helped found the Canajoharie Library and Art Gallery (Montgomery Co) in 1924 and donated paintings that celebrated rural New York State, especially the Mohawk and Hudson Rivers. The Hudson River Museum in Yonkers, the oldest museum in Westchester Co, was founded in 1915 by sculptor Isidore Konti and other local citizens as the Yonkers Art Association. It opened in 1924 in the Glenview mansion and now boasts both an art museum and a science museum. The art museum displays works by Hudson River school artists, such as Jasper Francis Cropsey and Samuel Colman Jr, as well as later American artists, such as Andy Warhol.

Seneca effigy ladle, *ca* 1760, in the Thaw Collection at the Fenimore Art Museum, Cooperstown.

Female Art Patrons

Women used a different style of patronage, one that required less cash and more of their own time. As women seldom had access to huge sums, they often favored buying less expensive types of art, such as decorative arts, or buying the work of living artists. Their personal involvement began with locating and purchasing art themselves, including buying directly from artists, and sometimes extended to cataloging and curating exhibits. When powerful male donors became involved, women often deferred to them, voluntarily or involuntarily. Catharine Lorillard Wolfe was the only woman among the 106 founders of the Met. The collection of paintings she bequeathed to the Met in 1887 started its European Painting Collection. Amy, Sarah, and Eleanor Hewitt founded the Cooper Union Museum of Art and Decoration (now Cooper-Hewitt, National Design Museum) in 1897 to house their collection of textiles and decorative arts. The sisters purchased the objects on trips abroad; the prices they paid were moderate, as textiles and decorative arts were not as valued as paintings and sculptures by famous artists. Once patrons such as George A. Hearn and J. P. Morgan became trustees, the sisters ceded control. The Museum of the City of New York (officially a historical museum but with an early emphasis on furniture and decorative arts) was the brainchild of May Van Rensselaer, who opened the exhibits of decorative arts with artifacts she and her friends had taken from their family homes. After the exhibits were in place, the charter was given by the state to publisher Henry Collins Brown in 1923, and the women were relegated to advisory committees and social functions. Louisine Havemeyer left many Impressionist and Postimpressionist works to the Met at her death in 1929.

Gertrude Vanderbilt Whitney used her personal fortune to found the Whitney Museum of American Art in 1930 because her husband Harry Whitney, though wealthy, was unsupportive of her project. Whitney and director Juliana Reiser Force often bought work from artists for display or simply because they knew that the artist needed the money. The modern art that Whitney and Force purchased in the beginning did not command high prices, as American art was relatively unheralded and inexpensive; for example, Force paid Stuart Davis $900 for three abstract paintings from his Eggbeater series. The Whitney has continued the tradition of supporting living artists through its Biennial Exhibitions of contemporary American art. The competitions began in 1932, without juries or awards, and artists could choose their own works for display. Although curators have taken over that role, the Biennials continue to showcase the talents of undiscovered artists.

Lillie P. Bliss, Mary Quinn Sullivan, and Abby Aldrich Rockefeller also promoted modern art, founding the Museum of Modern Art (MoMA) in 1929. They remained active in the museum and influenced the elements of the early collection, but A. Conger Goodyear, the first president, and Albert Barr, the first director, began to emphasize European modernism and what they called the International style: art and architecture characterized primarily by abstraction. Although Abby Rockefeller was uninspired by surrealist and abstract art, she yielded to Barr's advice that the museum collect it.

Corporate and Government Support

The climate of social responsibility that convinced Morgan, Whitney, and Rockefeller to bring fine art to the masses also influenced big business and government. During the 20th century the arts benefited from the largesse of corporations and corporate foundations. The Carnegie Foundation made significant donations to New York State museums and organizations to give the public better access to art through educational projects. Many corporations underwrote exhibits that specifically highlighted their industries. The first Museum of the City of New York building and endowment drive received funds from the New York Stock Exchange for an exhibit on its history and from AT&T for an exhibit on communications. By the late 20th century, major exhibitions often featured banners and promotional materials emblazoned with the names of corporate sponsors.

Government also became a patron of the arts. The City of New York provided municipal funds to pay maintenance bills for the Met and other museums, often donating city property as well. The federal government provided aid through the Federal Art Project (FAP) of the Works Progress Administration (WPA), initiated in 1935. This support paid for the clerical, maintenance, and security staff that allowed museums to remain open and maintain public programs during the depression. The FAP promoted the work of living artists to highlight New York culture in new ways. The FAP sponsored *Changing New York*, an exhibit at the Museum of the City of New York of Berenice Abbott's photographs of skyscrapers and modernist construction contrasted with crumbling tenements and old stables. Congress created the National Endowment for the Arts in 1965 to encourage presentations of works that might not have wide followings. The New York Foundation for the Arts, established in

1971, is a national leader in funding artists and arts organizations. The New York State Council on the Arts (NYSCA) subsidizes artistic programs through the Decentralization (DEC) Program, developed in 1977. Highly controversial exhibitions have brought notoriety, as the Brooklyn Museum found during its *Sensation* exhibit in 2000, when Mayor Rudolph Giuliani attempted to force the museum to change the exhibit or have its funding revoked because of a controversial painting. Yet, with the increasing cost of upkeep of acquisitions and permanent collections, museums have found that government contributions help to create more inclusive exhibits and provide better access to the public by subsidizing longer hours and free days of admission.

Many museums attracted visitors through innovative approaches to collecting and display. In 1960 business partners Ralph E. Ogden and H. Peter Stern founded the Storm King Art Center in Mountainville (Orange Co) to show paintings of the Hudson Valley. Ogden's outdoor arrangement of 13 sculptures by Bolton Landing (Warren Co) artist David Smith against the landscape of Schunnemunk and Storm King Mountains formed the nucleus of the permanent collection of post-1945 sculptures set among 500 acres (202 ha) of "green galleries." In May 2003 the Dia Foundation opened a museum in Beacon (Dutchess Co) that concentrated on post-1945 artworks and artists who began their careers in the 1960s and 1970s.

See also ART, ADIRONDACKS AND NORTH COUNTRY; ART, ALBANY AND THE CAPITAL DISTRICT, UPPER HUDSON, AND MOHAWK VALLEY.

Cabanne, Pierre. *The Great Collectors* (New York: Farrar, Straus, 1961)

Levine, Lawrence. *Highbrow, Lowbrow: The Emergence of Cultural Hierarchy in America* (Cambridge, Mass: Harvard Univ Press, 1988)

McCarthy, Kathleen D. *Women's Culture: American Philanthropy and Art, 1830–1930* (Chicago: Univ of Chicago Press, 1991)

Meyer, Karl. *The Art Museum: Power, Money, Ethics* (New York: William Morrow, 1979)

Scott, William B., and Peter M. Rutkoff. *New York Modern: The Arts and the City* (Baltimore: Johns Hopkins Univ Press, 1999)

Dorothy M. Browne

arts and crafts movement. The movement developed in the latter decades of the 19th century out of a reaction against the machine production of goods and was dedicated to the fashioning of handcrafted household items. At the turn of the 20th century, the height of the arts and crafts movement nationwide, New York State was home to many flourishing craft workshops and hosted several important arts colonies and publications.

Arts and Crafts Communities

Four artistic communities established in the state were loosely based on the socialist ideals of British arts and crafts movement leaders William Morris and John Ruskin. Roycroft (1895–1938) in East Aurora (Erie Co), founded by Elbert Hubbard (1856–1915), was the only one that was commercially successful, beginning as a book-publishing venture but soon expanding into fine bookbinding, leather, metalwork, and furniture.

The Byrdcliffe Colony in Woodstock (Ulster Co) was founded by Ralph Whitehead (1854–1929) in 1902. In the early years there were nearly 30 buildings on the campus, including residences, studios, a dairy, and a theater, and summer courses in various arts and crafts were offered. Furniture production, initially the main commercial venture, ended in 1905, and by the 1910s ceramics were the only remaining commercial product. When Whitehead died in 1929 the colony closed its doors. His son Peter bequeathed the property to the Woodstock Guild of Craftsmen in 1975, and in 2003 the guild operates it as a performance venue and summer arts colony.

Briar Cliff (or Briarcliff) (?1904–?11) manufactured furniture in Ossining (Westchester Co) in conjunction with an enterprise known simultaneously as the Craftsman's Shop, the Craftmanshop, and the Craft Settlement Workshop. Furniture was mostly fashioned from oak, with chair seats made of leather, tapestry, and rushes collected along the Hudson River. *Elverhöj* (1913), in Milton-on-Hudson (Ulster Co) was a short-lived summer school offering coursework in a variety of fine and decorative arts. Few works produced at Elverhöj exist today.

Ceramics, Metal, and Glass

New York State produced some of the finest ceramics in the arts and crafts style. Adelaide Alsop Robineau was an innovative potter who experimented with different clays and glazes at her Robineau Pottery in Syracuse and published an important magazine, *Keramic Studio* (1899–1924). Frederick Walrath (1871–1921) of Walrath Pottery produced work distinguished by delicate floral designs and subtle glazes, and was an instructor at the Mechanics Institute in Rochester. Volkmar Pottery was established by Charles Volkmar in 1879 in Greenpoint (Kings Co). He and his son Leon in 1903 established Volkmar Kilns in Metuchen, NJ. Other notable potteries included Jervis Pottery, founded by William Percival Jervis in Oyster Bay (Nassau Co) in 1908, and the Durant Kilns in Bedford (Westchester Co), established by Jean Rice in 1911.

The best-known metalwork was manufactured at Roycroft, but workshops like the Benedict Art Studios in Syracuse and the Art Crafts Shop in Buffalo (later Heintz Art Metal) also produced quality pieces. In the area of glass, Louis C. Tiffany, based in New York City, was at the forefront, though two others stand out. The Quezal Art Glass and Decorating Co in Brooklyn was established in 1901 by two of Tiffany's former employees, and in 1903 Frederick Carder came to Corning (Steuben Co) from England to found the Steuben Glass Works.

Furniture and Architecture

There were several leaders in arts and crafts furniture design. In Eastwood (Onondaga Co) in 1899 Gustav Stickley (1858–1942) established the Gustav Stickley Co, forerunner to the Craftsman Workshops. *The Craftsman* (1901–16) became the most important periodical of the movement in America. In 1906 Stickley moved his showrooms and headquarters to New York City but by 1915 was forced to declare bankruptcy. He firmly believed in a democratic art form, and over the years the Craftsman Workshops produced numerous decorative arts including furniture, metalwork, textiles, and house designs. Beginning in 1902 Leopold and J. G. Stickley manufactured their own arts and crafts–style furniture in Fayetteville (Onondaga Co). Although producing items similar to their brother's, they did not replicate his work, and the business continued into the 1920s.

Charles Rohlfs began his furniture making as a hobby, but by 1890 this had developed into a full-fledged business. Establishing his shop in Buffalo, he believed in keeping quality high and avoiding mass production. His work garnered international recognition. Joseph P. McHugh and Co was probably the first to establish what is synonymous with arts and crafts–style furniture in the early 21st century—the mission style, characterized by uncomplicated beauty in harmony with its surroundings. As early as 1898 McHugh marketed his products at the Popular Shop in New York City, but it was the 1901 Pan-American Exposition in Buffalo that established him as a leader in this field. The exposition was an important moment in the promotion of the arts and crafts style in the United States. For the arts and crafts display, Tiffany designed the exhibition court, and the furniture was contributed by Stickley and McHugh. In 1903 Stickley arranged and promoted the massive Arts and Crafts Exhibition, which included over 1,000 objects from the United States and Europe. It opened in Syracuse at Stickley's Craftsman Building followed by a showing in Rochester at the Mechanics Institute.

Architecture in New York State also reflected the arts and crafts style. In Buffalo and Rochester Frank Lloyd Wright constructed several homes in his prairie style, and Harvey Ellis and Claude Bragdon designed arts and crafts buildings in Rochester. Frederick R. Lear and Ward Wellington Ward both designed arts and crafts–style homes in Syracuse, and the firm of Ogden and Van Guysling was active in the Albany area.

There were numerous organizations around the state in the early decades of the 20th century that fostered enthusiasm for the arts and crafts style, including the Guild of Applied Art and the Guild of Allied Arts in Buffalo; the Rochester Arts and Crafts Society; and in New York City, the National Arts Club, the National Society of Craftsmen, the New York Society of Keramic Art (absorbed into the National Society of Craftsmen around 1912), and the New York Society of Decorative Arts (1877), founded by Candace Wheeler.

Evans, Paul. *Art Pottery of the United States* (New York: Feingold & Lewis, 1987)

Ludwig, Coy L. *The Arts and Crafts Movement in New York State, 1890s–1920s* (Hamilton, NY: Gallery Association of NYS, 1983)

Nancy E. Green

Art Students League of New York. Art school founded 2 June 1875 by disaffected students of the National Academy of Design who sought a rigorous course of academic figure study. In reaction to the academy's preoccupation with organizing exhibitions for professional artists, they created an institution devoted entirely to the instruction of art students. The league began as a group of studios, each autonomous and directed by a different artist. This framework, based upon the 19th-century French atelier system, enabled an instructor to evaluate students through periodic critiques of classroom work, without assigning grades. In addition to classes in drawing, painting, sculpture, and printmaking, the league has, at various times, provided instruction in commercial art fields: editorial and fashion illustration, advertising layout and design, textile design, and lettering. The school is governed by a 12-member board of artists, six of whom, elected annually by the membership, appoint six others for one-year terms. It has been housed since 1892 in the American Fine Arts Society Building at 215 West 57th St in New York City. The French Renaissance structure, equipped by architect Henry J. Hardenbergh with north-lit studios, expanded the school's exhibition space and afforded it visibility in a Midtown area dotted with galleries and studio buildings. Prominent instructors have included Munich- and Paris-trained artists (William Merritt Chase, Augustus Saint-Gaudens), members of the Eight (Robert Henri, John Sloan), the Fourteenth Street School (Kenneth Hayes Miller, Reginald Marsh), social realists (George Grosz, Raphael Soyer), and modernists (Jan Matulka, Hans Hofmann). For many years (1906–22, 1947–79) the Art Students League operated a summer school in Woodstock (Ulster Co) that further cultivated the American landscape tradition. In 1996 it opened the Vytlacil School of Painting and Sculpture in Sparkill (Rockland Co). After World War II, when the growing credibility of degrees from university art departments led many independent art schools in New York City to close, merge with universities, or apply for accreditation, the Art Students League adhered to its original aim: the cultivation of artists' manual skills without prescribed curricula or time limits. In the early 21st century, the league continues to offer its student body of 2,500 open enrollment, low tuition, monthly registration, and a roster of nearly 80 instructors. Its gallery is open to the public year-round and features a student concours (exhibition series), holiday sale, and special exhibitions.

Landgren, Marchal E. *Years of Art: The Story of the Art Students League of New York* (New York: R. M. McBride, 1940)

Stephanie Cassidy

Asharoken. Village (pop 625) in Huntington (Suffolk Co). Asharoken is located on Eatons Neck, which was purchased from the Matinecock Indians in 1646 by Theophilus Eaton, governor of New Haven colony. Eatons Neck Lighthouse (1798), second oldest on Long Island, was built by the federal government to warn ships of a dangerous reef, the site of more than 200 shipwrecks. Sand and gravel were mined from 1854 to 1964. Asharoken Beach was developed *ca* 1900 as a summer destination for New York City residents arriving by steamboat or rail. By 1915 it had become a summer resort for well-to-do families. The village was incorporated in 1925. In the early 21st century Asharoken is an affluent residential community and the site of a US Coast Guard station. Antoine de Saint-Exupéry wrote *The Little Prince* (1942) while renting a house in Asharoken.

Eileen Effrat

Ashford. Town (pop 2,223) in N Cattaraugus Co. Settled in ?1816, the town was formed from Ellicottville in 1824. Many Germans settled by the mid–19th century. Farming in Ashford shifted to dairy, with maple sugar and fruit as side crops. Ink was manufactured close to East Ashford, near present Riceville, in the late 1870s. The Buffalo, Rochester and Pittsburgh Railway (1878) served the town. In 1966 a nuclear fuel reprocessing center opened, but in 2000 it was restructured to be a remote handled waste facility. In the early 21st century Ashford was developing an office park. Griffis Sculpture Park (1966) at Ashford Hollow is a 425-acre (172 ha) outdoor art gallery, featuring more than 200 sculptures that visitors are encouraged to touch and climb. Gooseneck Hill Waterfowl Farm (1983) features 300 kinds of ducks, geese, and swans along with the two largest covered aviaries in the world.

Bruce D. Fredrickson and Madelynn P. Fredrickson

Ashland. Town (pop 1,951) in S Chemung Co. Settled in ?1785, the town was formed in 1867 from Chemung, Southport, and Elmira. Newtown Battlefield Reservation, site of the 29 Aug 1779 Battle of Newtown during the Sullivan-Clinton campaign, is located in Ashland. The town was served by the Erie Railroad (1849). It was a commercial tobacco-growing town from 1858 to the 1930s but emphasized dairying; a tannery (1859) and creamery (1879) were located at Wellsburg. Rte 17 (I-86) was completed through Ashland in the 1970s. In the early 21st century, its economy was supported by tourism, agriculture, and Wellsburg industry; most residents work in Elmira.

Heather A. Wade

Ashland. Town (pop 752) in NW Greene Co. In the Batavia Kill valley, between parallel spurs of the Catskill Mountains along its north and south borders, the town was settled by New Englanders shortly after the Revolution. Irish Catholics, drawn by tannery work, arrived in the 1830s. The town was set off from Windham and Prattsville (Greene Co) in 1848 and named for the home of Henry Clay. For a brief period around 1860 it was a center of hat manufacturing. Early in the 21st century its residents find jobs in nearby towns and more distant cities.

Field Horne

Association Island. In Henderson (Jefferson Co), this island is situated just off the coast in Lake Ontario, near the outlet of the St Lawrence River. From 1907 until the mid-1950s the island's approximate 100 acres (40 ha) served as a summer recreation retreat and conference center for managers and engineers from the National Electric Lamp Co and later the General Electric Co (GE), National's corporate parent. The island brought together GE engineers, scientists, managers, and, later, line-level supervisors from the firm's widely scattered factories, research centers, and service and marketing departments, and helped forge a collective identity while promoting departmental teamwork. Island invitees met, mingled, and shared ideas, and listened to the firm's leaders spell out yearly goals and elaborate on new business initiatives. The island also reinforced GE corporate culture through ritual and play, activities that novelist Kurt Vonnegut satirized in fiction in *Player Piano* (1952). By the mid-1950s, however, the "Spirit of the Island," which emphasized building corporate fraternalism through play, ritual, and social interaction, grated against the efficiency-striving, no-nonsense, bottom-line ideals of new GE bureaucrats. In September 1959 GE donated Association Island to the New York State branch of the YMCA. In 2002 part of the island serves as a campground and a recreational vehicle park.

Nye, David E. *Image Worlds: Corporate Identities at General Electric, 1890–1930* (Cambridge: MIT Press, 1985)

Gerald Zahavi

Association of the Bar of the City of New York. The leading professional association for attorneys in the New York City area. It was established in 1870 by lawyers seeking to combat the legal and judicial corruption prevalent in Mayor William M. "Boss" Tweed's administration. It created codes of conduct for lawyers and judges, and inspired the founding of a Brooklyn bar association (1872), an Albany-headquartered New York State group (1876), and a national group (1878). In 1884 the New York State Supreme Court recognized the New York City association's power to oversee the conduct of all members of the city's legal profession. The relatively small, elite group—it had fewer than 1,400 members in 1896—enjoyed great prestige and influence extending from city matters to state, national, and international legal questions. It proposed standards for international arbitration to the Hague Conference of 1899, spurred the investigations that forced Mayor Jimmy Walker from office in 1932, and condemned federal loyalty oaths in 1954–55. Membership was enlarged in the 1960s, and during this decade the association defended the Civil Rights Acts (1964–65) and protested intervention in Cambodia (1970). In 1980 the state assumed disciplinary oversight of lawyers. At the beginning of the 21st century, the group claims about 21,000 members and continues to work for political, legal, and social reform in local, national, and international arenas. At the city level, the association evaluates candidates for judgeships and reports on governance and business. It is located in an 1895 limestone building designated as a landmark at 37 West 43d St in Manhattan.

Leonard Benardo

Astor, John Jacob (*b* Waldorf, Germany, 17 July 1763; *d* New York City, 29 Mar 1848). Businessman. The son of a butcher, Astor spent several years in London before arriving in New York City in 1784. By 1786 he was established as a dealer in both musical instruments and furs. Over the next two decades he extended his fur-trading networks to the Great Lakes region and Canada. In 1808 the New York State legislature chartered his American Fur Co, which would eventually monopolize the trade in the western states and territories. The company established the outpost of Fort Astor [now Astoria, Oreg] at the mouth of the Columbia River in 1811 but was forced to sell it to the British Northwest Co two years later, at a fraction of its worth, under threat of seizure. By this time, however, Astor was worth over $2 million and owned a large private fleet that maintained a lucrative trade in furs and other items with Europe, China, and other regions.

In the 1810s Astor invested heavily in government bonds, banking, and New York City real estate. He lived primarily in Europe from 1819 to 1834. On his return to the United States he sold his fur business but kept the real estate holdings that made him "the landlord of New York." The Astor House, a huge Manhattan luxury hotel, opened in 1836. Around this time the Town of Astor [now Green Bay, Wisc] was founded on the western shore of Lake Michigan, where the American Fur Co had long traded. At his death Astor was the richest man in America, with a fortune valued at $20 million. His $400,000 bequest created the Astor Library, which opened in New York City in 1849. Its collections are now held by the New York Public Library.

Madsen, Axel. *John Jacob Astor: America's First Multimillionaire* (New York: John Wiley, 2001)

Porter, Kenneth Wiggins. *John Jacob Astor: Business Man,* 2 vols (1931; repr New York: Russell & Russell, 1966)

Martin Stahl

Athens. Town (pop 3,991) and village (pop 1,695) in NE Greene Co. Part of a 1665 purchase later patented and named Loonenburg, it was settled shortly thereafter. The Village of Athens was incorporated in 1805, combining colonial Loonenburg with Esperanza, a riverfront community surveyed in 1794. The town was formed from Catskill and Coxsackie in 1815. In the 19th century Athens residents quarried limestone and manufactured lime and bricks. Athens was especially noted for stoneware (1805–1900) and shipbuilding, which expanded after the Civil War when nearby towns' shipyards declined. The last boat made in Athens was built in 1938. Aerobilt made truck bodies from about 1950 until 1981. The company that surveyed 1,651 lots in 1971 for the huge resort development Sleepy Hollow Lake (on the northern border with Coxsackie) went bankrupt three years later. Under new management, sales continue into the early 21st century, as well as a scattering of manufacturing enterprises. An important landmark is the Hudson-Athens Lighthouse (1874).

Field Horne

Atlantic Beach. Village (pop 1,986) in Hempstead (Nassau Co). Located on the western end of the Long Beach barrier beach, this area remained part of the Town of Hempstead common lands until after the Civil War. In 1889 development was begun by the Atlantic Beach Co, and, while a failure, it gave the community its name. Atlantic Beach was little more than a sandbar until Freeport developer Stephen Petit began its successful development in 1925 as a beach resort, which required dredging the bay for vast amounts of fill. The post office was established three years later. The village incorporated in 1962 to control access to the beaches and its 1 mile (1.6 km) of oceanfront. Development was largely complete by 1970.

Richard A. Winsche

Attica. Town (pop 7,806) and village (pop 2,597) in N Wyoming and S Genesee Cos. About 4,000 of the town's residents are prisoners. Settled in 1802 and located in the Tonawanda Valley, the town was formed in 1811 from Sheldon. The village, which is partly in Alexander (Genesee Co) was incorporated in 1837. In addition to the large Attica Mills, a foundry (1828–73) produced threshing machines. Dairying expanded with cheese factories starting in 1866. Westinghouse Castings (1904–86) was a gray-iron foundry. The maximum security Attica Correctional Facility (1929) and medium security Wyoming Correctional Facility (1985) are the town's largest employers. In 1971 a riot in Attica Correctional Facility made international headlines. Aside from prison work, the town remains largely dairy country. The Attica Rodeo has been held annually since 1958.

Attica Correctional Facility. Maximum security penitentiary. Established in 1931 as Attica State Prison (Wyoming Co), the facility is under the control of the New York State Department of Correctional Services. Severe overcrowding in state prisons in the mid-1920s prompted plans for a new high-security penitentiary. In May 1928, under the leadership of Gov Alfred E. Smith, a state legislature commission recommended locating the facility in Attica. An appropriation of $3.5 million was used to buy 697 acres (282 ha) in the middle of the village. Ground was broken in October 1929. Gov Franklin D. Roosevelt allowed the project to proceed despite the social and economic hardships of the Great Depression. The plans called for four main cell blocks forming the sides of a square, with connecting walkways dividing the exercise yard into quadrants. When the penitentiary opened in 1931 with William Hunt as its first warden, newspapers touted it as a "convict's paradise." The inmates were to receive beds with springs and mattresses, sunlit cells, quality cafeteria food, recreation rooms, and a radio in every cell. In reality, however, the finished prison resembled other state penitentiaries in most ways, with the exception of its distinct and imposing Gothic architecture. By the time the last cell block opened in 1938 expenses had risen $2 million over projected costs to approximately $9 million, making it at that time the most expensive prison ever built. The institution took its current name in July 1970.

Originally intended to house primarily upstate prisoners, Attica became in the 1960s an overflow facility for New York City–area offenders, leading to racial and social tensions between the predominantly urban, minority inmate population and the mostly local white guards. On 9 Sept 1971 the prison made national news when inmates rioted and took control of two cell blocks. They were protesting, among other issues, an unfair state parole system; religious, racial, and political persecution; lack of adherence to state labor laws; and inadequate recreational and educational opportunities. Four days later Commissioner of Correctional Services for the State of New York Russell Oswald, under directions from Gov Nelson A. Rockefeller, ordered New York State Police and National Guard troops to retake the prison. In all, 32 inmates and 11 prison employees died. Following the uprising, minority officers were recruited to diversify the workforce, and across the state new training requirements for correction officers were put in place. In June 2002 the facility had 803 employees and housed 2,204 inmates, of whom 1,173 were black, 418 white, and 575 of Latino ethnicity.

Murphy, Helen Kollwitz. *The Development of Attica, N.Y.* (Attica: Author, 1977)

New York State Special Commission on Attica. *Attica: The Official Report of the New York State Special Commission on Attica* (New York: Praeger, 1972)

Rebecca Partise

Attica uprising. The events of September 1971 in the Attica Correctional Facility (Wyoming Co) that claimed the lives of 32 inmates and 11 prison employees had its roots in an overcrowded and inadequately supervised prison system, as well as in the racial tensions of the early 1970s. Originally meant to house inmates mainly from upstate New York, in the 1960s Attica became an overflow facility for predominantly minority offenders from the New York City area. At the time of the uprising the prison population was 54% black, 37% white, and 9% of Latino ethnicity. Relations with the overwhelmingly white corps of guards drawn from the local population were frequently characterized by hostility and mutual incomprehension. If the prisoners often saw the guards as the representatives of what they considered a ruthless and dehumanizing system, the correction officers, each responsible for 85–90 men, with little or no formal training in psychology or criminology, often felt outnumbered and uncomfortable in their duties.

Beginning of the Crisis

The Attica uprising was played out on a background of increasing racial tension within the New York State prison system. In 1970 there had been three significant prison disturbances, one

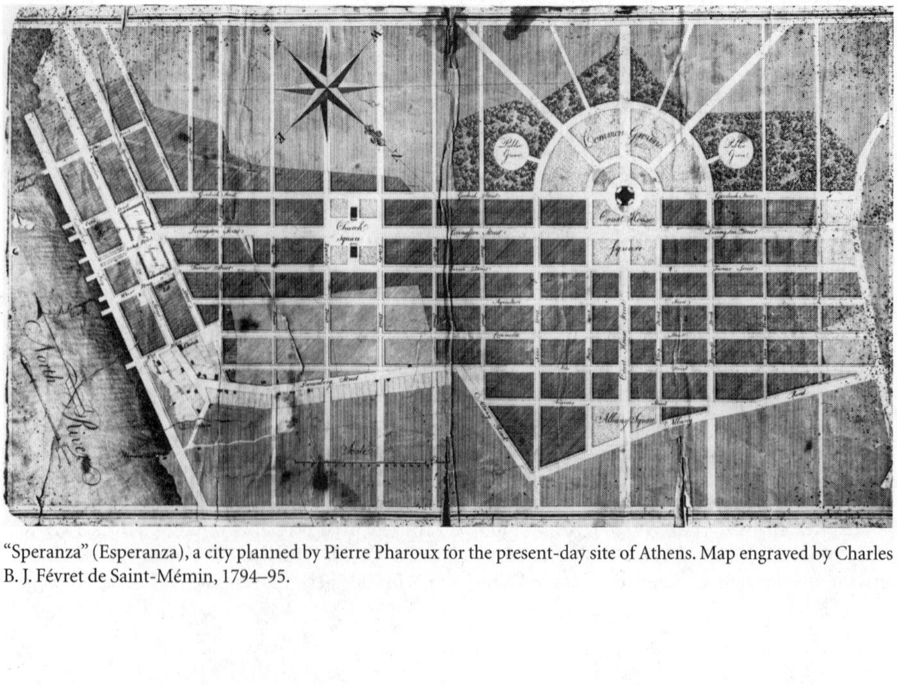

"Speranza" (Esperanza), a city planned by Pierre Pharoux for the present-day site of Athens. Map engraved by Charles B. J. Févret de Saint-Mémin, 1794–95.

at the Manhattan House of Detention, known as the Tombs, in reaction to severe overcrowding, and a work stoppage in the Attica metal shop on 19 July protesting the paltry wages for inmate workers. The most serious, at the Auburn Correctional Facility (Cayuga Co) on 4 November, began as a sit-down to demand a black solidarity day and evolved into a riot, including the taking of hostages. Several of the leaders of these rebellions ended up in Attica, creating the largest congregation of radicalized prisoners in the state, including substantial contingents of the Nation of Islam, the Black Panther Party, and the Weather Underground.

Two events in the summer of 1971 contributed to a volatile prison environment. In July a group of prisoners calling themselves the Attica Liberation Faction presented Commissioner of Correctional Services Russell Oswald with a list of demands, including reform of the state parole system, application of wage and labor laws, improved living conditions, the right to profess their religious and political beliefs openly, and an end to what they saw as the continuing racism and brutality of the state prison authorities. On 21 Aug 1971 George Jackson, a prisoner at San Quentin Correctional Facility in California, was fatally shot by prison guards during an attempted escape. The next day, Attica prisoners called a hunger strike in Jackson's honor. This proved popular with many of the disparate racial and political factions within Attica.

The Attica facility's four cell blocks (A, B, C, and D) formed the sides of a square. Tunnels leading from each of the blocks intersected at a control point known as Times Square and divided the exercise yard into four sections. The administration buildings, workshops, kitchen, mess halls, school, and chapel were on the perimeter of the cell block square, and the whole complex was surrounded by 30 ft (9.1 m) walls dotted with guard towers. On the afternoon of 8 September a scuffle between two inmates in the A Yard ended with a belligerent exchange between inmates and correction officers. When the A Block was locked down for the evening, one man was forcibly taken to solitary confinement, and another prisoner reportedly struck an officer on the head with a can of soup. The following morning a rebellion broke out in the A Tunnel as inmates were returning from breakfast. Some of the badly outnumbered guards were overpowered and others retreated to Times Square, while prisoners took control of A Yard and A Block. Now armed with pipes, sticks, and rakes, they broke into Times Square and gained access to the other tunnels. They forced their way through the gates at the ends of the tunnels, overran the remaining cell blocks, and advanced into the outbuildings. Forty-two prison officials and civilian employees were taken hostage, and many of the guards were stripped naked or beaten. Close to 1,300 inmates participated in the riot; over 800 did not, and spent the remainder of the rebellion in A and C Blocks, which reverted to state control when the rioters decided to concentrate in D Yard. Four of the most severely injured hostages were released immediately. The rest were kept in the center of D Yard under the watch of Muslim guards.

Negotiations and Decision to Intervene

The inmates negotiated with Oswald on the same fundamental issues they had listed in July, with the additional demands of complete amnesty and transportation to a "non-imperialistic" country for all rebels. The prisoners also requested the formation of an impartial committee of civilian observers to aid in the negotiations. Their ranks included radical attorney William M. Kunstler; Assemblyman Arthur O. Eve from Buffalo; representatives from the Prisoners' Solidarity League and the Young Lords; Clarence Jones, publisher of New York City's *Amsterdam News;* James Ingraham of the *Michigan Chronicle* in Detroit; Dave Anderson of the Urban League of Rochester; Tom Wicker of the *New York Times;* and Richard Roth of the *Buffalo Courier-Express.* Oswald added, among others, Congressman Herman Badillo and Assemblyman John Dunne of Nassau Co. Over the course of the rebellion, close to 35 outside observers would participate in the negotiations. The inmate negotiating committee included some of the most prominent political inmates in Attica at the time, such as Roger "Champ" Champen, Jerry Rosenberg, Richard X Clark, and Herb Blyden.

The confrontation went on for four days amid intense media scrutiny. The rebellion's leaders permitted some journalists onto the prison grounds to hear statements from the inmates and get updates on the condition of the hostages. Negotiating sessions took place in D Yard, first involving Oswald directly and later making use of the citizens' observer committee. On the afternoon of 11 September, news arrived that Officer William Quinn had died of massive head injuries received from inmates in the early moments of the riot. The media carried unsubstantiated reports that Quinn's death was the result of being thrown from a window or down a flight of stairs, though the official examiner listed the cause of trauma as unknown. These reports heightened tensions outside and inside the prison and stalled negotiations. Oswald proposed 28 points of reform that addressed many of the inmates' concerns, but Quinn's death dramatically raised the stakes in the amnesty issue and caused both the state and the prisoners to dig in their heels. When negotiations ended late on the night of the 11th, the inmates, state officials, and observer committee members had reached a stalemate.

The following day members of the observer committee made public appeals for Gov Nelson A. Rockefeller to come to Attica, as did several hostages in televised interviews urging compliance with the inmates' demands. Rockefeller, however, declined to go to Attica, leaving matters in the hands of the state representatives already there. While the observers and the families of hostages continued to press for a negotiated resolution, Oswald had lost faith in the talks, and Rockefeller apparently feared that, given the worldwide media coverage, extended negotiations or concessions would encourage armed revolutionary movements around the world. On the morning of 13 September, Oswald, with Rockefeller's approval, authorized New York State Police and National Guard troops to retake the institution by force. Helicopters dropped tear gas on D Yard, and a hostage rescue detail armed with shotguns and handguns was sent into the yard under cover of rifle fire from atop D Yard walls. When the smoke cleared 26 inmates and 9 hostages lay dead, 33 hostages and 85 inmates were wounded, and several would later die of their injuries. The inmates were stripped naked and made to crawl through mud, and many were subjected to beatings. The bodies of three more inmates, killed by rebelling prisoners prior to the assault, were also found. In all, the death toll rose to 43.

Aftermath

The events of 13 September remain highly controversial. It continues to be extremely difficult to document the precise sequence of events. On the afternoon of the action, Deputy Commissioner Walter Dunbar reported to the press and the general public that several of the hostages had had their throats slit and that a surviving hostage had been castrated. The Monroe Co coroner was asked to verify these claims, but his report, released the following morning, indicated instead that state shotgun fire had killed all inmates and hostages. It was subsequently determined that none of the prisoners had firearms. Numerous commissions have investigated the events at Attica. In December 1972 the official investigation handed down 62 indictments, totaling over 1,200 felony counts, against inmates involved in the riot. No guards or other prison officials were ever indicted, and charges of reckless endangerment against a single trooper were dropped before coming to trial. The 1972 New York State Special Commission on Attica, composed of nongovernmental officials and chaired by New York University Law School dean Robert McKay, was concerned largely with prison and correctional reform. The hearings of the McKay Commission, as it was popularly known, were televised and its findings were published. Several of its recommendations were adopted within Attica and across the state: a major overhaul of the parole system; more and better opportunities for recreation, vocational training, and education; wage increases for prison labor; the establishment of an inmate grievance procedure; improved counseling and religious services; less restricted interactions between prisoners and the outside world; and a schedule rearrangement that would allow inmates more time out of their cells. Prison administration was transformed through mandated riot plans, a statewide effort to hire minority guards, increased training requirements, and even uniform changes.

In 1974 the Attica Brothers Legal Defense, an advocacy group for inmates injured in the retaking of the prison, filed civil suit against the state. The following year Malcolm Bell, chief assistant to the special Attica prosecution, went public with charges that the state was covering up official wrongdoing on the part of police, guards, and administration, and that relevant records had either been destroyed or hidden. Gov Hugh Carey declared a general amnesty for both inmates and authorities in 1976, citing a lack of usable evidence. All outstanding inmate indictments were dropped, seven inmates who had pled guilty were pardoned, and the sentence of John Hill, one of two men convicted of killing Quinn, was commuted. In August 2000 a US district judge awarded the Attica Brothers Legal Defense and the families of slain inmates a $12 million settlement. The Forgotten Victims of Attica, a group representing surviving hostages, their families, and the families of prison employees killed during the uprising, emerged at this time. In late 2001 Gov George E. Pataki formed a task force to hear testimony from the group, which is seeking an annual memorial service, counseling, access to all sealed riot records, a formal apology for wrongdoing, and monetary damages beyond the workers' compensation that most Attica widows accepted shortly after the crisis and that technically barred them from suing the state for additional awards.

The Attica uprising remains an unhealed wound. It is not forgotten and, by observers and living participants on all sides, largely not forgiven. Russell Oswald resigned in 1973. Gov Rockefeller's reputation never overcame the widespread sense that his reluctance to get publicly involved made a very difficult situation worse. Amid a series of race-related riots and incidents in the late 1960s and early 1970s, Attica stands out as the most violent in terms of loss of life and use of police power. The events of September 1971 at the Attica Correctional Facility shook New York State and the nation to the core. The interpretation of the Attica uprising is likely to remain bitterly controversial, though few would disagree that by the time over 40 men lay dead in the prison yard something had gone terribly wrong.

Badillo, Herman, and Milton Haynes. *A Bill of No Rights: Attica and the American Prison System* (New York: Outerbridge & Lazard, 1972)

Bell, Malcolm. *The Turkey Shoot: Tracking the Attica Cover-Up* (New York: Grove Press, 1985)

Clark, Richard X. *The Brothers of Attica.* Ed. Leonard Levitt (New York: Links, 1973)

New York State Special Commission on Attica. *Attica: The Official Report of the New York State Special Commission on Attica* (New York: Praeger, 1972)

Useem, Bert, and Peter Kimball. *States of Siege: U.S. Prison Riots, 1971–1986* (New York: Oxford Univ Press, 1991)

Wicker, Tom. *A Time to Die: The Attica Prison Revolt* (Lincoln: Univ of Nebraska Press, 1975)

Rebecca Partise

attorney general. The functions of the official serving as attorney general are established primarily by common law. In New York Colony, the first Crown officer to bear the title was Thomas Rudyard, appointed by Gov Thomas Dongan in 1684. Suggesting the early diversity of the colony, both Dongan, a Catholic, and Rudyard, a Quaker, were dissenters from the English religious establishment. Atty Gen Richard Bradley earned a special place in history by prosecuting, but not convicting, John Peter Zenger for seditious libel in 1735 and by prosecuting and securing the executions of more than three dozen slaves and poor Whites for their participation in the supposed "popish" conspiracy of 1741, when Roman Catholics were believed to be plotting a slave rebellion to seize control of the colony. The last incumbent prior to the Revolutionary War was John Kempe, and all colonial offices became defunct with the ending of the British military occupation in November 1783. In the meantime, the New York convention in Kingston (Ulster Co) had created, on 8 May 1777, an independent Office of the Attorney General and had appointed Egbert Benson, a friend of the young Alexander Hamilton, as the first incumbent. Under the Constitution of 1777, selection of the attorney general was a function of the Council of Appointment of the state legislature, and some men of talent and ambition served in the office in the early years of the Republic, among them Aaron Burr (1789–91) and Martin Van Buren (1815–19).

From 1821 to 1846 the state legislature appointed the attorney general directly, and the considerable prosecutorial powers that the attorney general enjoyed at common law were redistributed to locally elected district attorneys. At the same time, the state's rapidly expanding economy prompted the legislature to add steadily to the attorney general's civil functions and responsibilities. The continued importance of the office was recognized by the Constitution of 1846, which provided for the popular election of the attorney general. This new independence sometimes led to friction with the equally independent governor, and in 1900 Gov Theodore Roosevelt prevailed on the legislature to establish an Office of Counsel to the governor within the Executive Chamber.

There was a renewed emphasis on the prosecutorial function in the 20th century, at least in the area of white-collar crime. In the wake of World War I, the public clamored for a return to normalcy, and the attorney generals at both the federal and state levels found themselves assuming new roles in response to the public's unease. While US attorney general A. Mitchell Palmer was arresting and deporting hundreds of suspected radicals in the great Red Scare, New York attorney general Charles D. Newton was presented by the legislature with sweeping new powers under the Martin Act of 1921, one of the most encompassing blue sky laws enacted by any state legislature for the protection of security investors. Under it, the state attorney general wields uniquely powerful investigative and prosecutorial weapons aimed at speculators who promise to produce wealth from nothing more substantial than a "blue sky."

The Constitution of 1938 provided for 20 departments of state government, including the Department of Law headed by the attorney general. With the enactment of the Environmental Conservation Law in 1972, the responsibilities of the attorney general in the area of criminal law enforcement began to grow rapidly. Atty Gen Robert Abrams (1979–93) took full advantage of this trend, establishing an Environmental Crimes Unit in 1984. Further new criminal responsibilities in the areas of Medicaid fraud and organized crime were added in the 1980s. In recognition of the expansion of the attorney general's criminal portfolio, Atty Gen Dennis Vacco (1995–98) created a separate Criminal Division of the Office of Attorney General in 1995. Vacco's successor, Eliot Spitzer, made extensive use of the Martin Act in his campaign to reform the business practices of Wall St brokers and bankers.

The two other major divisions within the Department of Law are the Division of State Counsel and the Division for Public Advocacy. The first manages the bulk of the general responsibilities of the attorney general, defending the state in the Court of Claims, appearing in federal and state courts on behalf of state agencies, rendering legal opinions to state and municipal officials on questions of state law, and pursuing the state's claims for compensation and damages. The second handles matters relating to the environment, consumer fraud, antitrust, investor protection, civil rights, charities, and similar areas. Typically, state agencies look to the Office of the Attorney General for in-court representation, although a number of agencies, such as the Department of Public Service, represent themselves in some or all legal proceedings. State authorities usually represent themselves through staff attorneys or outside counsel, but some large authorities, such as the Thruway Authority, are represented by the attorney general.

Office of New York State Attorney General Eliot Spitzer, http://www.oag.state.ny.us

Swanson, Karl T. W. "The Background and Development of the Office of Attorney General in New York State" (PhD diss, Syracuse University, 1954)

William S. Helmer

Auburn. City (pop 28,574) in central Cayuga Co. Located at the foot of Owasco Lake, the city grew up at the site of a number of Indian settlements where the ancient Genesee Trail crosses the Owasco Lake Outlet. Fort Hill Cemetery, with its stone monument to the famous Cayuga orator, Logan, occupies the site of a substantial defensive fort built during the Archaic period. The Cayuga Nation, which displaced Algonquian-speaking people during the 13th century, maintained a permanent village called Wasco ("River Crossing Place") along the Owasco Outlet near the present site of Auburn Correctional Facility. Most Cayuga left the area after the scorched-earth Sullivan-Clinton campaign of 1779. The Cayuga ceded title to most of their lands, including Auburn, in 1789–90. A few Cayugas remained at Wasco until 1797, when they abandoned their longhouses and migrated to western New York State. Earthworks at Fort Hill Cemetery are all that remain of the presence of Native Americans in Auburn.

SETTLEMENT

Between 1789 and 1791, New York State awarded more than 1.6 million acres (650,000 ha) of the New Military Tract to Revolutionary War soldiers or their assignees in bounties of 600 acres (243 ha). Auburn is located on six of the best of those 600-acre lots near the center of the tract. Indeed, the locale's perceived promise is reflected in the purchase by John L. Hardenburgh, a Revolutionary War veteran and one of the tract's surveyors, of one of the lots in 1792 for the purpose of founding a manufacturing city. Hardenburgh moved to his land and became Auburn's first white settler. He was one of several pioneers who brought slaves, who, following manumission, formed the core of Auburn's small African American community.

Rapid growth followed settlement. Hardenburgh built the first gristmill; another settler built a saw- and gristmill in 1798, and William Bostwick erected a hotel in 1803. In 1797 the state routed the Genesee Road through Hardenburgh's Auburn property, partly because of the political influence of Hardenburgh's brother, Abraham. The road was improved as

Harriet Tubman Home in Auburn.

the Seneca Turnpike in 1802–3, and a substantial bridge was built across Owasco Outlet. Until the statewide completion of the Erie Canal in 1825, most westward migration through central New York State passed through the community. Auburn became the seat of Cayuga Co in 1805, an incorporated village in 1815, and a city in 1848. For much of the first half of the 19th century, it was the largest city in central New York. German, Irish, and English immigrants, along with New Englanders, New Yorkers, and other Americans, fueled Auburn's early growth. Although situated in the heart of a farming region settled heavily by New Englanders, Auburn's early merchants and lawyers were drawn to its commercial potential from varied locations, including Albany, New York City, western Massachusetts, southern Connecticut, New Jersey, Virginia, Scotland, and England.

Economic Development

Auburn's economy was initially dominated by retailing and services for the immediate region: grist-, saw-, and fulling mills, distilleries, breweries, and tanneries. Auburn's first bank was established in 1817, in part to support the creation of the Auburn Prison, which began accepting inmates in 1818. Many of the city's most important 19th-century industries emerged from prison workshops and from the market provided by westward migration. From the prison came garment, shoemaking, carpet-weaving, woodworking, and tool-making industries, producing goods for distant markets. To serve the prison workshops, Auburn's workforce became highly skilled. During the first half of the 19th century the city became an important manufacturing center for tools, hardware, shoes, textiles, carpets, grain, alcoholic beverages, books, and confectioneries. Metalworking skills fostered Auburn's most important 19th-century business, the nationally known D. M. Osborne and Co, which manufactured farm machinery such as mowers and reapers. Founded in 1858, it became a division of International Harvester in 1903. Other products of 19th-century manufacture included carriage hardware, buttons, locomotive engines, and musical instruments.

Auburn's many wealthy investors provided capital for railroads and banks. By 1837 Auburn capitalists had acquired enough capital to provide most of the funds needed to build the Auburn and Syracuse Railroad (1838). The city was also connected to Rochester by rail in 1841. In 1848 six Auburn investors capitalized the highly profitable Oswego Starch Factory, which produced approximately one-third of the world market's cornstarch during the second half of the 19th century and brought considerable wealth to its investors, who were mostly Auburnites.

After the Civil War, immigrants from eastern Europe and southern Italy came to take jobs in Auburn's growing factories. By 1900 the population had stabilized at around 30,000. It remained a highly diverse community with a wide range of religious and other institutions and little ethnic conflict. Labor movements emerged in the factories in the early 20th century, when Auburn's industrial sector specialized in shoes, agricultural machinery, locomotive engines, iron and steel, pumps, and rope. After 1950 most of these factories closed.

Cityscape

The stagnation in 20th-century industrial growth is evident in the city's townscape. A number of individuals made significant fortunes in Auburn in the 19th century, and many of their residences remain on Genesee, West Genesee, North, and South Sts. Because the city had an abundance of capital, workers were also able to acquire homes of their own. Present neighborhoods reflect earlier patterns of homeownership at all social levels. There are few apartment buildings in the city. Its industrial buildings have nearly all been razed, and many of its oldest retail and commercial buildings were removed for the Rte 5 arterial in 1976. The Auburn Correctional Facility is still a dominant feature along the Owasco Outlet.

Culture and Politics

The Auburn Theological Seminary was established in 1819 and for more than a century trained scholars for missions throughout the expanding West and around the globe. It was incorporated into the Union Theological Seminary of New York City in 1939; all that remains in Auburn is the Willard Chapel, preserved because of its Tiffany interior. Cayuga Community College was originally founded as Auburn Community College in 1953. Auburn's first permanent library was organized in 1876. The Cayuga Museum of History and Art (1936) and the Schweinfurth Art Center (1981) interpret history and art.

Auburn's 19th-century capitalists created an aggressive and entrepreneurial culture that combined an innovative spirit with political and legal astuteness. One of the state's governors, Enos T. Throop, was an Auburn lawyer. William H. Seward practiced law for many years in Auburn before serving as governor, senator, and US secretary of state. Theodore M. Pomeroy, another Auburn lawyer, became Speaker of the House. Several Civil War generals, including Ulysses and Abner Doubleday, were raised in Auburn, as were John Foster Dulles, US secretary of state, and his brother, Allen Welsh Dulles, director of the CIA.

Auburn's notable innovators include David Munson Osborne, founder of the D. M. Osborne and Co; William Kirby, inventor of the Kirby reaper; Cyrenus Wheeler, inventor of the Cayuga Chief reaper; William G. Fargo, partner with Henry Wells in the Wells, Fargo and Co; William Burroughs, inventor of the first mechanical calculator; William Bundy, inventor of an industrial punch clock that led to the creation of IBM; and Theodore Willard Case, an inventor of sound movies. After the Civil War, Harriet Tubman moved to Auburn, where she died in 1913.

Auburn has had a strong tradition of baseball. There has been minor league baseball since 1877; the 1899 team played as the Auburn Prisoners. For 34 years, beginning in 1901, the National Association of Professional Baseball Leagues, the association of the minor leagues, was headquartered in the city. Auburn's first minor league club organized in 1938 and played in the Canadian-American Class D League. Auburn had a Class A Border League club from 1946 to 1951 and a Class A New York–Pennsylvania League club since 1958. The Auburn Doubledays, named for resident Abner Doubleday and part of the Toronto Blue Jays organization, have been the local team since 1996.

The 20th Century

Auburn's most important industries included Dunn and McCarthy (shoe manufacturing), McIntosh and Seymour Engine Co (steam engines and power plants), International Harvester, and the Columbia Rope Factory. In the early 21st century the city's most important industries include Bombardier Transportation (locomotive engine manufacturing), Auburn Steel Co, TRW Electronics Division, and Goulds Pumps. Auburn's population decreased 8.6% in the 1990s but is otherwise quite stable, with little immigration or demographic change. In 2000, 8% of the population was African American, and those of Latino ethnicity constituted 3%.

Scott W. Anderson

Auburn Correctional Facility. A maximum security prison for males, located on 6 acres (2.4 ha) along the Owasco Lake Outlet in Cayuga Co. The oldest currently operational state prison in New York was established in 1816 as Auburn Prison. The facility gave its name to one of the 19th century's most widely imitated prison innovations, the Auburn system. Under the system prisoners worked together in silence during the day but, unlike at other institutions, occupied single cells at night. They wore striped suits and closely cropped hair, marched in lockstep, followed rigid rules, and endured swift and severe punishments, including floggings. Both Charles Dickens and Alexis de Tocqueville traveled to the United States in part to observe the Auburn system. Tocqueville recommended it to the French government in 1833 in preference to the continual isolation of Philadelphia's penitentiary system, and it became commonplace in Europe and in much of the United States. Between 1828 and 1890 inmates were employed in prison shops as contract labor for outside industries. In 1890 the world's first execution by electric chair took place at Auburn Prison, and the state's first facility for female felons operated there from 1893 to 1933. The Auburn system came to an end in part because of the efforts of Thomas Mott Osborne, who chaired a state commission on prison reform in 1913. Osborne's reforms aimed at the rehabilitation rather than punishment of offenders and included initiatives such as the Mutual Welfare League, a self-help organization that prepared prisoners to return to free society. The league was discontinued following riots on 28 July and 11 Dec 1929, during which hostages were taken and much of the prison was burned. This led to the modernization of what had become an overcrowded and outmoded facility. The prison took its current name in 1970. In the early 21st century the institution employs approximately 500 civilians and has a population of approximately 1,700 inmates. Many prisoners work in its large industrial facilities, producing state-use items such as license plates.

Miskell, John M. "Why Auburn? The Relationship between Auburn and the Prison," http://www.correctionhistory.org/auburn&osborne/miskell/miskell_index.html

Scott W. Anderson

Auburn Theological Seminary. Established in Auburn (Cayuga Co) on 16 Aug 1818 by action of the Presbyterian Synod of Geneva (Ontario and Seneca Cos). After dropping the plan for a college-level "academical" department, the synod obtained a charter from the New York State legislature on 14 Apr 1820 for a postbaccalaureate theological seminary. The seminary matriculated its first class in October 1821 and grew quickly. The charter provided that the seminary's board be elected by Presbyterian bodies in New York State, but it also stipulated that "no student of any Christian denomination shall be excluded," and the Roman Catholic bishop of Boston contributed books to the seminary's original library. Following the 1837 division of the Presbyterian Church along Old School and New School lines, the seminary became a center of the New School church, which was less rigid in Calvinist doctrine and more flexible in matters of church government. When the northern Old and New School churches reunited in 1870, Auburn joined in a compact with other Presbyterian seminaries but, unlike most of them, declined to amend its charter to transfer control from New York State Presbyterian bodies to the national General Assembly.

Under Pres George Black Stewart in the early 20th century, the seminary began to grant degrees and took on other characteristics of a modern graduate school. The seminary built on its progressive educational heritage by developing programs for laypersons and opening the seminary to women; in 1917 Ida Thorne Parker, a minister in the Society of Friends, became the first woman to graduate from the seminary. Auburn's theologically liberal graduates, along with those of Union Theological Seminary in New York City, dominated the Presbyterian churches of New York State. Auburn also educated students from Southeast Asia and established strong ties with churches there. The seminary's freedom from national church control permitted its faculty to take major roles on the liberal side of Presbyterian Church conflicts over fundamentalism. The liberal manifesto that contributed to the defeat of the fundamentalists was drafted by Robert Hastings Nichols, a professor at the seminary, and the final version, published in Auburn in 1924, became generally known as the Auburn Affirmation.

The seminary was severely weakened in the Great Depression. In 1939 it closed its Auburn campus and moved to the New York City campus of Union Theological Seminary, where it works in close cooperation with Union; no merger occurred, and Auburn's relationship to the presbyteries of New York State continued. Since the move Auburn has conducted programs for Union's Presbyterian students and nondegree theological education programs for ordained and lay religious leaders of many faith traditions. One of these, the 1971 Susquehanna Valley Project, created courses in preaching and ministry for Presbyterian pastors in the area between Binghamton and Oneonta (Otsego Co). In 1991 the seminary established the Auburn Center for the Study of Theological Education, an educational research center. The seminary does not currently enroll students for degrees or make regular faculty appointments, but several thousand persons each year participate in its educational programs.

Adams, John Quincy. *A History of Auburn Theological Seminary, 1818–1918* (Auburn, NY: Auburn Seminary Press, 1918)

Nichols, Robert Hastings. *Presbyterianism in New York State: A History of the Synod and Its Predecessors* (Philadelphia: Westminster Press, 1963)

Barbara G. Wheeler and Mark N. Wilhelm

Audit and Control, Department of. See COMPTROLLER.

Augusta. Town (pop 1,966) in SW Oneida Co. Part of the town was occupied by Stockbridge Indians beginning in 1784. European American settlers came in 1793, and the town was formed from Whitestown in 1798. The Augusta Academy (1834–78) was located in a unique semicircular building. Located mostly on two limestone ridges, Augusta's land provided good grazing and, beginning in 1861, supported cheese factories. Hops were grown extensively after the Civil War and, in the years up to the 1930s, peas and beans were important crops. In the late 20th century Mennonite farmers bought farms in town. Farm products include milk, grain, hay, corn, and beans. In 2002 Benchmark quarried limestone.

Aurelius. Town (pop 2,936) in central Cayuga Co. Settled in 1788, the town was formed in 1789. A sulfur spring near Aurelius Station was the site of a bathhouse around 1840. The Auburn and Rochester Railroad (later New York Central) crossed the town in 1841; the Cayuga Lake Railroad (1873–1971; later Lehigh Valley) followed. Its land supports dairy farming and corn tillage; Cowles Dissolver Co manufactures tools for industry.

Auriesville Shrine. See NORTH AMERICAN MARTYRS.

Aurora. Town (pop 13,996) in central Erie Co. Formed in 1804 as Willink, the name was changed in 1818. The area of the present town was settled in 1804. The Buffalo, New York and Philadelphia Railroad (1867; later Pennsylvania Railroad) crossed Aurora, meeting the shipping needs of grain and dairy farmers. Beginning in the 1870s the town was known for breeding and training trotters; it had a covered mile track with glass windows on both sides (1885–1918). In the early 21st century, polo is still played in town. The Rte 400 four-lane highway (1966–68) made commuting to Buffalo more practical. Employment is available in several industries in the Village of East Aurora, and other residents commute to suburban towns nearby.

Andrew C. Maines

Aurora. Village (pop 720) in Ledyard (Cayuga Co). The first settlement (1789) of the New Military Tract, it served as the county seat of Onondaga Co (1794–99) and of Cayuga Co (1799–1807). Incorporated as a village in 1837, it was the site of Cayuga Academy and successor institutions (1800–1916) and continues as the site of Wells College (1868), established by Henry Wells (1805–78), organizer of the American Express and Wells Fargo companies. It was served by steamboats (1820–1907) and by the Cayuga Lake Railroad (1873–1971). Long-lived enterprises are the Aurora Inn (1833) and Shakelton Hardware (1905), still occupying their original buildings. In 2002 residents worked at the college, in nearby cities, or at MacKenzie-Childs, manufacturer of tableware and furnishings. The entire village is listed on the National Register of Historic Places. Significant restoration, funded by a wealthy Wells alumna, was begun in 2001.

Sheila Edmunds

AuSable. Town (pop 3,015) in SE Clinton Co. Bordered on the east by Lake Champlain and on the south by the Ausable River, it was settled about 1794 and was formed from Peru in 1839. Iron ore was discovered in 1806, and an iron rolling mill at Keeseville became the nucleus of an industrial village in 1815. Iron mining and fabrication, lumbering, and woodworking were the town's economic base until the mid–20th century. Today many residents commute to Plattsburgh. The 2 mi (3.2 km) Ausable Chasm, carved deep into rock by the Ausable River, has been a privately owned tourist attraction since 1870.

Thomas A. Rumney

Austerlitz. Town (pop 1,453) in E Columbia Co. Settled *ca* 1750 by squatters from Connecticut and Massachusetts, the town was formed from Canaan, Chatham, and Hillsdale in 1818. At Spencertown, 19th-century industries included a foundry, machine shop, and hat factory, and it began to attract summer boarders in the 1870s. Poet Edna St. Vincent Millay (1892–1950) lived at Steepletop (now Millay Colony for the Arts; 1973). The Taconic State Parkway (1963) made Austerlitz more accessible for second homes. Historic sites include Spencertown Academy (1847), now a performing arts center. Austerlitz is home to both Beebe Hill (1965) and Harvey Mountain (1998) State Forests. At 2,065 feet (629.4 m), Harvey Mountain is the highest point in the county.

automobile industry. See MOTOR VEHICLE INDUSTRY.

automobile landscapes. The development of automobile transportation in the early 20th century brought notable changes to roadways and surrounding communities. Wagon and coach roads were organic in that they were rarely constructed or engineered but simply followed tracks across the countryside, often angling sharply to follow property boundaries instead of cutting through property to achieve a relatively straight-line distance between two points. Turnpikes built during the 19th century began providing more direct routes, and roads engineered for the automobile were less a product of local conditions and more in concert with state and national priorities of reliability, speed of travel, and safety. Early automobile roads carried names such as Liberty Rd, which ran through Wellsville (Allegany Co) in the Southern Tier; the Great Western Turnpike, through Finger Lakes country; and the Cherry Valley Turnpike, which ran east from the Finger Lakes to Cherry Valley (Otsego Co).

To help cross-country travelers navigate through open country, highway booster organizations adopted painted symbols, often strips painted on telephone poles or fence posts, to guide people along a route. The nation's first state-supported limited-access highway, the Bronx River Parkway, was opened in 1925 and included landscaped right-of-way and cut stone bridge abutments. In 1926 a federal law standardized the national highway numbering system, and the Great Western and Cherry Valley Turnpikes became part of US 20, which crossed the breadth of the state from New Lebanon (Columbia Co) on the Massachusetts border to the Pennsylvania state line at the community of State Line (Chautauqua Co).

Prior to the early 1920s automobile travelers

had little choice in roadside accommodations other than those available in established and usually centrally located city or town hotels. From the 1920s onward, automobile services began to appear at roadsides on the edge of many communities, where land was cheaper than it was on main streets. Local rural landowners might subdivide their road frontage property into small piano-key lots with narrow frontages. Entrepreneurs built gas stations, car sale establishments, repair garages, and restaurants catering to local and traveling clientele. Roadside landowners and many municipalities set up campgrounds for motorists. Some camp operators added cabins for rent by the night; the roadside motel evolved from linking cabins with a single common roof. Old cabin camps are rare but can often be found along major highways, such as those near Carlisle (Schoharie Co) on US 20.

During the 1950s locally owned independent motels found new competition from major motel franchise chains, which offered standardized rooms and furnishings complete with amenities such as on-site swimming pools and restaurants, all conveniently advertised to the motorist by large signs right on the roadside. Other roadside business experiments included dance halls, skating rinks, retail stores, and drive-in theaters, such as the Transit Drive-in near Lockport (Niagara Co), and curio shops based upon local features, such as the Petrified Creatures Museum of Natural History in Richfield Springs (Otsego Co). Another addition to the automotive landscape was the farmers' market, which appeared when local people began to realize the marketing potential of a convenient location passed by thousands of motorists each day. Roadside business competitors found that success was related as much to their visibility and physical presentation to the motoring public as to the quality of their products or services. They installed large signs and painted their buildings in bright colors to attract customers. One notable example is Big Duck, an icon created by farmers Martin and Jueule Maurer, who built a 20-ft (6.1 m) tall concrete and frame duck near Flanders (Suffolk Co) to advertise their ducks and eggs merchandise.

After World War II national automobile ownership exceeded 50 million, and roadside businesses were increasingly franchised and standardized although locally owned motels and restaurants, such as Tom Wahl's in Avon (Livingston Co) and Doug's Fish Fry in Skaneateles (Onondaga Co), continued to thrive. Large-scale auto-oriented suburbs, pioneered by William Levitt with his 1947 development at Levittown (Nassau Co), were copied and reproduced by real estate developers across the state and nation. The Interstate Highway System bypassed many old highways, isolating businesses from automobile traffic. New business clusters, primarily gas stations, motels, and fast food restaurants, developed at major interstate interchanges and were advertised to the highway traveler by stilt signs visible for a mile or more. Some old roadside businesses continue to operate, but many were closed or converted. Some former motels now serve as retirement facilities or provide housing for low-income families.

In 1985, 9.6 million motor vehicles were registered in New York State. By 2000 gasoline station franchises at large interstate interchanges near urban areas were reconfigured with multiple pumps and large overhead canopy roofs that served as shelter from the weather and as a safety light reflector at night. These stations are also adopting "co-branding," or sharing their retail space with fast food restaurants, such as Subway and Dairy Queen, to increase sales potential.

Balasco, Warren J. *Americans on the Road: From Autocamp to Motel, 1910–1945* (Baltimore: Johns Hopkins Press, 1979)

Hugill, Peter J. "Good Roads and the Automobile in the United States, 1880–1929," *Geographical Review* 72 (July 1982): 327–49

Raitz, Karl. "American Roads, Roadside America," *Geographical Review* 88 (July 1998): 363–87

Karl Raitz

automobile racing. The first formal motor sports contest in New York State was a "reliability trial" called the Cosmopolitan Race on Memorial Day, 1896, from Kings bridge [now in Bronx Co] to Irvington-on-Hudson (Westchester Co), a distance of 30 miles (48.3 km). Frank Duryea won the race, and his brother Charles came in second. In 1900 a 50 mi (80.5 km) race was staged on Long Island. Such city-to-city races were derived from the European tradition of road racing and, in turn, were inspired by bicycle *épreuves,* or tests. The American taste for oval races, however, was shortly established, and tracks at county fairs became the principal venue for the dangerous and exciting events. The famous 1 mi (1.6 km) track at the State Fairgrounds in Syracuse staged its first race in 1901.

Road Racing

The most prestigious event, however, remained a road race: the Vanderbilt Cup, held from 1904 to 1906 and from 1908 to 1910 along open roads on Long Island. Appallingly dangerous, the race drew huge crowds of eager spectators. In 1908 a New York City–to–Paris race was held, attracting a quarter of a million spectators in Manhattan for the start. A board track was constructed in Brooklyn at Sheepshead Bay, which attracted the best and most daring drivers of the day and great crowds of enthusiastic spectators. The Sheepshead Bay Speedway operated from 1915 to 1919. The signal event of the era, however, was a tragedy: on 11 Sept 1911, before a crowd of 50,000 at the Syracuse fairgrounds, Lee Oldfield crashed through the infield fence and 11 spectators were killed. The race was not stopped, however, and the famous Ralph DePalma took the victory. This tragedy and World War I curtailed racing at Syracuse for several years, and few events continued to be held around the state. After the war, automobile racing in New York State continued to be hugely popular at Middletown (Orange Co), Sheepshead Bay, Syracuse, and countless county fairgrounds. Throughout the 1920s purses for the racers were enormous, but the danger and carnage remained. Despite the Great Depression, racing proved immensely popular, particularly in the form of the even-more-dangerous midget racers. These small cars raced at tracks all over the state at stadiums and fairgrounds. At the other end of the spectrum were the glamorous Vanderbilt Cup races, which were revived in 1936 and 1937 at Roosevelt Raceway near Westbury (Nassau Co), attracting Europe's finest champions. Road racing's renaissance continued at Alexandria Bay (Jefferson Co) on the St. Lawrence River, where the Automobile Racing Club of America (ARCA) staged races from 1936 to 1939 on the streets of the small village in "The Race Round the Houses." ARCA also sponsored a special race in 1940 at the New York World's Fair at Flushing Meadow in Queens. The start of World War II terminated racing in the state.

Stock-Car Racing

The enthusiasm of both racers and fans sprang back after the war. The American Race Drivers Club sanctioned popular midget races, and Middletown, Goshen (Orange Co), Buffalo, and Syracuse staged highly successful events. A major shift after the war was to stock-car racing. More accessible to the average fan, a secondhand family car could be turned into a racer and compete at the local quarter mile dirt track. For the fans the stock cars offered marquee familiarity, and the racing was relatively safer. In 1948 sports-car road racing was revived at Watkins Glen (Schuyler Co), sanctioned by the village and the Sports Car Club of America. Races through the streets of the village and into the hills in the area on a twisting 6.6 mi (10.6 km)

The US Grand Prix was held at the Watkins Glen International raceway from 1961 to 1980.

course attracted huge crowds until a crash in 1952 caused the death of a young spectator. Races thereafter were held on a temporary course in the Town of Dix (Schuyler Co) until a permanent road course was built and first used in 1957, and the US Grand Prix was held in 1961. Subsequently, sports-car and Grand Prix racing at Watkins Glen attracted huge crowds. In 1957 a road course for sports cars was built at Bridgehampton (Suffolk Co) that was used until 1998.

Stock-car racing constituted the main portion of racing in New York State, on both paved and dirt tracks, for professional and amateur racers. Brewerton Speedway (Onondaga Co) was built in 1948, and many other tracks were constructed for stock cars. In 1950 the Oswego Speedway was founded, where supermodifieds achieved terrific speed. The Driver's Independent Race Tracks (DIRT) of Central New York, a sanctioning body formed in 1976, has been the most successful regional organization, and the National Association for Stock Car Auto Racing (NASCAR) has sanctioned races at several New York State tracks. The State Fairgrounds at Syracuse has had races almost continuously over the 20th century. In 2002 there are nearly 60 tracks operating in New York State (dirt, paved, road, and drag), and in the course of the 20th century there have been over 200 tracks. These short tracks have produced some legendary drivers, including Dutch Hoag, Richie Evans, Jim Shampine, Shirley Muldowney, and Geoffrey Bodine.

GRAND PRIX RACING

In the course of hosting the Grand Prix from 1961 to 1980, Watkins Glen International has attracted the preeminent Formula 1 drivers in the world. British World Champion Graham Hill became a particular local favorite when, after an accident, he spent an extended stay in an Elmira hospital. Following the last Grand Prix in Watkins Glen in 1980, the track had a few lean years until it was purchased by Corning Enterprises in 1983. NASCAR came to Watkins Glen in 1986, and since then the August Winston Cup race at the track is one of the largest sporting events in the state, attracting as many as 180,000 spectators. Small-track racing in New York State is often a family enterprise and one that absorbs a large proportion of a family's financial means. A few modified drivers and teams have major sponsorship, which allows them to compete professionally, but the majority of drivers build their own cars in their spare time and race to infrequent success on the weekends. Track owners struggle, for the most part, and few tracks other than Watkins Glen International are financial successes.

Spaid, Gary and Henry Schramm. *"Car Coming": An Auto Racing History of New York State* (Oswego: Speedway Press, 1990)

Phil McCray

Ava. Town (pop 725) in N Oneida Co. Settled in 1798 the town was formed from Boonville in 1846. The first post office (1828) was named Crontbaf, an anagram of Postmaster John Bancroft's name, but in 1830 it was changed to Ava after the capital of Burma at that time. Lumbering was the town's most important industry, declining in the late 19th century. Many Germans settled in the northern part of town before 1850. Some Poles settled in town after World War I. Ava was the home of Hiram Cronk (1800–1905), the last survivor of the War of 1812. Thanks to reforestation in the 1930s, Ava's lumbering has revived and provides employment, including an industrial-scale sawmill. Dairy farming also continues. The Ava Test Annex (1957–97) supported research and development for Griffiss Air Force Base. Camp Kingsley (1920) is a 430-acre (174 ha) Boy Scout facility in town.

avant-garde film. See FILM, AVANT-GARDE.

Avery, Milton (*b* Sand Bank [now Altmar, Oswego Co], 7 Mar 1885; *d* New York City, 3 Jan 1965). Painter. From age 13 Avery lived in Wilson Station and later East Hartford, Conn, where as an adult he worked in various jobs as a machinist, assembler, clerk, and construction worker to support his mother and other family members for nearly two decades. A late bloomer, Avery received limited recognition as an artist and during this time painted part-time. He exhibited in group shows and in 1919 attained top honors in painting and life drawing at the School of the Art Society of Hartford. A turning point came in 1926 with his marriage to Sally Michel, a Brooklyn-born illustrator who was almost 20 years his junior. The couple took up permanent residence in Manhattan, and supported by Sally's work as a freelance illustrator, Avery was able to paint full-time. He encountered European modernism, which rapidly transformed his style. Whereas his earlier work was mostly plein air (outdoor) painting, he henceforth painted in the studio from sketches, and his work became more simplified and abstract, showing the influence of Henri Matisse.

Avery's career evolved steadily in New York City. He exhibited his work with the Valentine Gallery (1935–43); with two French-run galleries, Durand-Ruel and Paul Rosenberg (1945–50); and with the Grace Borgenicht Gallery beginning in 1951. He had his first museum show in the Phillips Memorial Gallery in Washington, DC (1944), and the Baltimore Museum of Art (1952) and the Whitney Museum of American Art (1960) held survey exhibitions of his work. Avery's canvases were thinly painted, usually with austere compositions, which have been interpreted as embodying the Yankee values of thrift, practicality, and understatement. While he courted abstraction, simplifying and distorting his preferred subjects of human figures, animals, and the landscape, Avery's art never completely broke with realism.

Haskell, Barbara. *Milton Avery* (New York: Whitney Museum of American Art in association with Harper & Row, 1982)
Hobbs, Robert. *Milton Avery* (New York: Hudson Hills Press, 1990)

Chris Gilbert

aviation. Lighter-than-air aviation feats in New York State include balloon ascensions by 1830 and Carl Myers's experiments with pedal-operated dirigibles at Frankfort (Herkimer Co) after 1889. Around 1900 Charles P. Steinmetz flew gliders at Hoffmans (Schenectady Co), as did Charles R. Wittemann on Staten Island. Matthias C. Arnot, Charles Teasdale, and possibly Augustus Herring also may have experimented near Elmira. In 1906 Thomas S. Baldwin brought his powered dirigible business to Hammondsport (Steuben Co). The state's heavier-than-air aviation history truly began in 1908 with Alexander Graham Bell, Glenn H. Curtiss, and their Aerial Experiment Association in Hammondsport. This group flew perhaps the first airplanes in the hemisphere outside the Wright camp, and Curtiss began manufacturing his own aircraft in 1909. He quickly became the nation's most prominent maker of aircraft, developing business and service infrastructure along with machines. Other manufacturers such as Kirkham and Thomas sprang up nearby.

The Curtiss and Wright companies both incorporated in New York State at a time when most aviation opportunities lay in experiments, exhibitions, and speculative military applications. New York City and environs—with connections to capital, transport, communications, science, and industry throughout the world—spawned manufacturing and exhibition firms such as those of John and Albert Moisant, Baldwin, and Wittemann. The metropolitan region, including Long Island with its flat fields and sparse population, provided fine flying grounds. The area hosted many early air events: the 1909 Hudson-Fulton Celebration that featured a flight by Wilbur Wright; Curtiss's 1910 Albany–New York City flight, and the 1911 Nassau Blvd air meet in which participants carried the first official airmail.

WORLD WAR I AND THE INTERWAR YEARS

World War I sparked an aviation boom. Curtiss set up a factory in Buffalo and a research corporation in Garden City (Nassau Co), each bigger than the original Hammondsport plant, which continued operations alongside Curtiss licensees such as Willys-Morrow in Elmira. Thomas moved from Bath (Steuben Co) to Ithaca, where by 1918 the company ranked as the fourth largest aircraft firm in the United States. The falloff in aircraft demand after the war eliminated many firms and reduced others, but some small operators, such as Mercury Aircraft in Hammondsport and Taylor Bros in Rochester, launched ambitious design and production programs during the 1920s.

Scheduled airline service also appeared in the 1920s, with seaplane carriers based in New York City using Curtiss flying boats for some of the first routes. American Airways, founded in 1926 as Colonial Western, became an important New York State carrier. Eastern Air Lines, founded in 1927 as Pitcairn Aviation, and All American Aviation came into being during the interwar period as well. Mail contracts supplemented meager passenger and cargo business, with the earliest mail routes all serving New York City. By the mid-1920s airmail routes extended to Western New York, and improved technology slowly made airlines more practical. Recreational and private flying formed significant parts of the state's aviation business. The new industry created such ancillary businesses as Buffalo's parachute maker Irving Air Chute Co, while long-established Corning Glass Works (Steuben Co) began to produce lenses for beacons and runway lights as night flying grew in importance.

By 1924 Consolidated Aircraft Corp joined Curtiss in Buffalo. Across the state, manufacturers Grumman Aircraft Corp and Loening thrived on the aeronautic activity of Long Island. This

Buffalo Airport, *ca* 1955.

region's airfields served as bases for some of the earliest and greatest feats in aviation. On 20 May 1927 Charles Lindbergh took off from Roosevelt Field in Garden City and landed 33 h 30 min 30 s later to a crowd of 150,000 in Paris, accomplishing the first nonstop transatlantic flight. And on 30–31 Jan 1929 the 17-year-old Elinor Patricia Smith of Freeport (Nassau Co) broke the women's solo record for a nonrefueled endurance flight over Garden City. During the 1920s Chance Vought Corp of Long Island City (Queens Co) and the firms of Sikorsky Aero Engineering Corp and Fairchild Aviation Corp, opening offices in Manhattan, also established themselves in the state. Communities sought airfields as eagerly as they had once desired canals or railways. Many of these fields never materialized or they gained limited significance, but the predecessors of such giants as La Guardia—world's busiest airport in 1940—and Buffalo Municipal Airport were established during this decade.

The Great Depression hit aviation hard, throttling the brief boom created by Lindbergh's flight and thwarting efforts by newly merged Curtiss-Wright Corp to establish vertical consolidation of the industry. New York State boasted 56 airfields in 1929 and 82 at the end of 1930. The number rose to 98, with 25 of them lighted, at the beginning of 1935 but five years later only reached 99, with 27 lighted fields. The state had 1,047 aircraft in 1930, about 14% of the national total; of these, over half were open-cockpit biplanes. The state's aircraft numbers fell to 814 planes in the depression year of 1935, rising again to 937 at the beginning of 1940. The number of pilots rose from 1,004 in 1929 to 1,444 in 1935, and to 2,636, plus 30 glider pilots, in 1940. —*KWH*

World War II and the Postwar Era

World War II led to a massive expansion of New York State's aviation industry. At the height of war production in 1944–45, more than 100,000 New Yorkers were employed by the Long Island aircraft makers of Grumman and Republic Aviation, and 50,000 worked for Bell Aircraft Corp and Curtiss-Wright of the Buffalo area. Aviation was the most critical of New York State's industries to the American war effort. By June 1945 the state would rank second nationally, trailing California, in the number of military aviation contracts let by the US government. Of all US government defense contracts awarded in New York State, these aircraft contract made up 35% and totaled $7.5 billion. Aircraft produced in New York State included Curtiss-Wright's P-40 Tomahawk fighter and Bell Aircraft's P-39 fighter, both built for the US Army Air Force. Grumman Aircraft turned out for the US Navy the F4F Wildcat and the F6F Hellcat. Extraordinarily agile, the Hellcat after 1942 was the US Navy's principal fighter. Republic Aviation Co in Farmingdale (Nassau Co) produced during the war over 9,000 P-47 Thunderbolts. One of the most rugged aircraft of World War II, the Thunderbolt served as America's mainstay aircraft in Europe as a fighter, and after the Allied landings in Normandy on 6 June 1944, it had a significant ground-attack role.

The aviation sector's tremendous expansion during the war brought significant social changes to New York State, changes that would persist after 1945. As increasing numbers of men were drafted into the military, larger and larger numbers of the state's aviation workers were women. By 1945, 40% of all aviation workers in the state were female. Labor shortages, along with civil rights agitation, led to the racial integration of the state's aeronautical plants. In March 1941 the state government formed its own committee to place minorities at aircraft firms. This pathbreaking program, spawned by aeronautical labor needs, led to the May 1945 creation of the State Committee against Discrimination, America's first permanent fair employment agency.

Following 1945 state manufacturers developed new civilian aircraft; one of the first was Republic Aviation's amphibious Seabee, modestly priced to reach a broader civilian market. Schweizer Aircraft manufactured the crop-dusting AG-Cat biplane, which was a Grumman product and design. Starting in 1946, Bell Aircraft manufactured its renowned helicopter, the Model 47, improved many times since and used currently in a variety of capacities, including rescue work and monitoring of traffic conditions. Military orders, however, still remained central to the industry's financial health, a reliance that deepened through the years of the Cold War. Bell Aircraft produced the X-1A, a rocket-powered plane that Capt Chuck Yeager piloted to break the sound barrier on 14 Oct 1947. That same year Fairchild Republic (formerly Republic Aviation) began production of the F-84 Thunderjet, the US Air Force's main fighter during the Korean War; production lasted until 1953 with 4,450 planes built. Two years later Fairchild Republic began production of the F-105, the US Air Force's next generation of fighter. The F-105 was the lead aircraft of America's ill-fated Rolling Thunder campaign in Vietnam.

In response to the growing demand for passenger air travel, American Airlines, serving New York City and some cities in northern and central New York State, began converting military four-engine C-54s into the popular DC-4s. By 1946 Trans World Airlines (TWA), flying out of New York City, introduced the 60-passenger Lockheed Constellation and in 1948 replaced DC-3s with CV-240 Convairs, which were faster and doubled passenger capacity. Other airlines underwent various mergers. Mohawk Airlines, originally Robinson Aviation, began operation in 1945 with service to Utica, Elmira, Binghamton and other cities. United and Capital Airlines soon joined it in serving northern and central New York State. In 1972 Allegheny Airlines acquired Mohawk, becoming USAir in 1979. In 1986 Piedmont Airlines, flying routes across New York State, New England, and the Mid-Atlantic states, acquired Empire Airlines, which linked Buffalo and Albany with Boston and Newark, NJ. USAir then acquired Piedmont in 1987.

The End of the Cold War

Grumman and Fairchild Republic continued to turn out military aircraft through the 1980s. For the US Navy, Grumman built E2C Hawkeyes (1960–73), A-6 Intruders (1960–87), and F-14 Tomcats through 1987. Fairchild's A-10 Thunderbolt II, the current ground-attack aircraft for the US Air Force, remained in production through 1979. Yet New York State's aviation industry, which was so heavily dependent upon the defense sector, slowly contracted. From 1953, when postwar US defense spending crested at 14% of gross domestic product (GDP), military spending fell to 9% of GDP by 1968, 6% by 1986, and 3% by 2001. Although there were reverses in this downward trend during the Kennedy and Reagan years, in the long run New York State's aircraft industry began to either exit the business or to consolidate. Bell Aircraft was acquired in 1966 by Lockheed-Martin Corp of Maryland, with most of Bell's Buffalo-area plants closing in the ensuing decades (as of 2001 only 30 employees were left in the state). In 1987 Fairchild Republic shuttered its Long Island factories and exited the aircraft sector completely. In 2002 Fairchild Republic was a communications equipment maker in Virginia. After a series of layoffs in the early 1990s, Grumman merged with Northrop of California in 1994. In 2002 Northrop-Grumman employed only 2,000 workers at its Long Island facilities.

In 1980 the US government deregulated the airline passenger industry. The purpose of deregulation was to increase competition among airlines, thereby lowering costs and greatly increasing the public's air travel opportunities. Hence new, smaller airlines emerged, such as People Express, that offered low-fare routes in New York State. However, deregulation made it difficult for upstate cities to retain carriers and competitive service. By 1998 the average airline fare in this region was 30% higher than the national average. Since 1999 the state and federal governments have worked aggressively to bring cheaper and more frequent air service to the state, viewing it as integral to the revitalization of the state economy. In 2000 JetBlue Airways, a budget line, started to provide regular service to Buffalo and Rochester, and in 2001 to Syracuse. To facilitate this new coverage, starting in 2000 Gov George E. Pataki undertook a state-funded, multiyear $650 million capital program to rebuild airports around the state. In 2002 AirTran Airways joined JetBlue to offer low-cost service connecting Rochester to major airline hubs. —*PR*

See also WORLD WAR II.

Dade, George C., and Frank Strnad. *Picture History of Aviation on Long Island, 1908–1938* (New York: Dover, 1989)

Petzinger, Thomas, Jr. *Hard Landing* (New York: Random House, 1995)

Schweizer, William. *Soaring with the Schweizers* (New York: Rivolo Books, 1991)

Kirk W. House, Paul Roxin

Avoca. Town (pop 2,314) and village (pop 1,008) in NW Steuben Co. Settled in 1794 by Scots-Irish who were joined by Dutch and German migrants from the Mohawk Valley by 1820, the town was formed in 1843 from the towns of Bath, Cohocton, Howard, and Wheeler. Farm and forest products were first transported to market at Baltimore by raft along the Cohocton River, but the railroads (Erie in 1852 and Delaware, Lackawanna and Western in 1882) brought prosperity. In the late 19th century, Avoca products included lumber, beehives, sash and blinds, chairs, cheese, brooms, wheels, and bricks. Beginning in 1938 farmers from Maine's Aroostook Valley revitalized the potato culture. By 1940 village factories made spools and reels, hockey sticks, potato graders, and trunks. The Haines Manufacturing Co, established in 1946, produces equipment for vegetable harvesting and grading. Southern migrant workers were employed to harvest the crops of chipping potatoes until the 1970s. Avoca lies at the junction of Rte 17 (I-86), completed in 1969–70, and I-390, completed in 1976.

Virginia L. Wright and Jerry Wright

Avon [AV-ON]. Town (pop 6,443) and village (pop 2,977) in NW Livingston Co. The Canawaugus settlement of Seneca Indians was located at Avon Springs. The first settlers, primarily from the New England states, arrived about 1789, and the town was formed in 1797 as Hartford. The name was changed to Avon in 1808. Its sulfur springs were developed for health and tourism beginning in 1821. Avon Springs Downs (1836) was a harness racetrack in the 19th and 20th centuries. The Genesee Valley Canal, two miles (3.2 km) west of the Genesee River in Caledonia, carried freight for Avon farmers from 1840 to 1878. Two railroads built in the early 1850s (both later incorporated into the Erie) made Avon more accessible. The village incorporated in 1853. East Avon was home to the Wiard Plow Works (*ca* 1830–77) until its move to Batavia. The town's rich land was used for wheat and later dairy. From 1935 to 1965 the Jockey Club operated the Lookover Stallion Station in Avon; it was later run by the Genesee Valley Breeders' Association. I-390 opened through town in 1982. General Foods operated a Birds Eye frozen foods plant in Avon for many years until 1988, when the facility became the world's only producer of Kraft's Cool Whip. In the early 21st century the town was widely regarded as good horse country.

Joyce Rapp

Ayer, William Ward (*b* Shediac, NB, 7 Nov 1892; *d* St. Petersburg, Fla, 18 Nov 1985). Fundamentalist minister. The youngest of 10 children, Ayer left home secretly on a train for Brooklyn, where he lived with a brother and peddled newspapers on the streets. Other siblings in Lynn, Mass, then took William in and helped him to complete an eighth-grade education. In 1916 while living in Boston, a Billy Sunday revival meeting inspired him to preach the Christian message. After graduating from Chicago's Moody Bible Institute in 1919 and serving pastorates in the Midwest, in 1936 he accepted a call as pastor of the Calvary Baptist Church, founded in 1847, in New York City. Ayer's evangelical radio broadcasts attracted a monthly audience of 2 million listeners on New York City station WMGM, and worshippers crowded into the services of the congregation's "sky-scraper church" at 57th St between 6th and 7th Aves. In 1944 Ayer became founding president of the National Religious Broadcasters. A rival radio station, WOR, conducted a poll in 1947 to determine "New York's Number One Citizen," and listeners gave Ayer the third highest vote, preceded only by Francis Cardinal Spellman and Eleanor Roosevelt. Ayer retired from Calvary Baptist in 1949 and went on to write several books and numerous articles.

Beale, David O. *In Pursuit of Purity: American Fundamentalism since 1850* (Greenville, SC: Bob Jones Univ Press, 1986)

De Plata, William R. *Tell It from Calvary* (New York: Calvary Baptist Church, 1997)

Larson, Mel. *God's Man in Manhattan: The Biography of Dr. William Ward Ayer* (Grand Rapids, Mich: Zondervan, 1950)

David Beale

B

Babcock, Stephen Moulton (*b* Bridgewater, Oneida Co, 22 Oct 1843; *d* Madison, Wisc, 1 July 1931). Agricultural research chemist. Babcock's parents were farmers, and as a youth he worked on the family farm in Bridgewater. After attending Tufts College in Medford, Mass, and receiving his BA in 1866, Babcock did farmwork and was employed part-time at a chemistry laboratory at Cornell University from 1868 to 1872. He enrolled in the University of Göttingen in Germany in 1877, receiving his PhD in chemistry in 1879. A chemistry instructor at Cornell from 1881 to 1882, Babcock was the first chemist at the New York State Agricultural Experiment Station at Geneva (Ontario Co), a position he held from 1882 to 1888.

Professor of agricultural chemistry at the University of Wisconsin at Madison, Babcock was the chief chemist at the Wisconsin Agricultural Experiment Station (1887–1913). There he developed the Babcock butterfat test (1890), which he did not patent but released to the public. This practical test determined the fat content of milk samples accurately, inexpensively, and rapidly, helping revolutionize the dairy industry. It was the first successful method of testing butterfat content outside of a laboratory and the prime factor in transforming dairying from an art acquired through practice into a reliable science. Creameries and cheese factories could adjust milk prices based on quality rather than quantity, which discouraged milk adulteration and thinning. By testing individual milk samples, farmers could provide appropriate care and determine the quality of individual cows, encouraging improved livestock care and the development of better dairy strains. Babcock retired as emeritus professor at the University of Wisconsin in 1913 and spent his next two decades in basic research on the nature of matter and its relation to energy.

Russell, Harry L. *Stephen Moulton Babcock* (Madison: Wisconsin Alumni Research Foundation, 1943)

Suzan D. Friedlander

Babylon {Babylon, town (pop 211,792) in Suffolk Co; Babylon, village (pop 12,615) in Babylon; North Babylon, locality (pop 17,877) in Babylon; West Babylon, locality (pop 43,452) in Babylon}. The first purchase of land in Babylon was in 1657; it was part of the Town of Huntington and was called Huntington South when a post office was established in 1802, but it was named Babylon in 1803 by Nathaniel Conklin. The post office name was changed in 1830. Salt hay was harvested from its marshes by Huntington farmers, and bluefishing and eeling in the bay became significant in the 19th century. Industries included a woolen mill (*ca* 1810) and a straw paper mill (*ca* 1849). While the Surf Hotel (1856) on Fire Island and some other resort activity preceded it, Babylon was made a resort by the South Side Rail Road (1867; now Long Island Rail Road), but it also resulted in the loss of its pine forests due to sparks from steam locomotives. Because of Huntington town expenditures on New York Ave (1871) in the hamlet of Huntington, the residents of the south side decided to form their own town in 1872. The village was incorporated in 1893. Guglielmo Marconi (1874–1937) operated the first commercial wireless station in 1901 in the village. North Babylon was the site of the Nursery, August Belmont II's horse farm and private track created in 1865; his widow sold the land in 1925. Before World War II North Babylon was the site of summer homes, and the 459-acre (186 ha) Belmont Lake State Park was created from part of the Nursery in the 1930s.

The Southern State Parkway (1929) and the Sunrise Highway (1929) made Babylon more accessible by automobile. West Babylon developed during the 1950s as part of the postwar housing boom, during which the town's population exploded from 24,297 in 1940 to 142,309 in 1960. Babylon is the site of the 2,000-acre (809 ha) Pinelawn Cemetery (1902), including Long Island National Cemetery, and of Republic Airport (1928). Famous residents have included civil servant Robert Moses (1888–1981) and Bob "Captain Kangaroo" Keeshan (1927–2004). Babylon's Cuban Giants baseball team was the first all-Black professional team when it played its home games at the Argyle Hotel in 1885. In 2000 Babylon's racial composition was 76% white and 16% black. Those of Latino ethnicity made up 10% of the population, but the largest ethnic group was Italian American, with 30% of the total. Babylon is governed by a town board, composed of a supervisor and four elected council members.

Bacheller, Irving (*b* Paradise Valley, St. Lawrence Co, 26 Sept 1859; *d* White Plains, Westchester Co, 24 Feb 1950). Novelist and journalist. Bacheller's parents, along with many other farmers, migrated from Vermont to northern New York. He attended Canton Academy and graduated from St. Lawrence University in 1882, remaining a devoted alumnus, a member of the board of trustees, and a recipient of an honorary degree. Bacheller left for New York City that year to become a journalist. In 1884 he started the New York Press Syndicate, known as the Bacheller Syndicate, selling literary works, including Stephen Crane's *Red Badge of Courage,* to newspapers in serial form. By 1890 it was a thriving business, with over 56 newspapers as customers. Bacheller also wrote fiction, and in July 1900 his hugely successful novel *Eben Holden* was published. It was full of local color and characters based on farm people known from his boyhood. A prolific writer, Bacheller published 29 novels, the last in 1949, on subjects as diverse as religion, American political heroes, and Adirondack guides. Unfortunately his characters were stereotypes—a manly hero, an unblemished heroine, an unconvincing villain—and his plots were repetitive. Bacheller also became a successful lecturer, creating a simple, optimistic philosopher, Socrates Potter, who became his beloved public persona. Though Bacheller proclaimed nostalgia for his rural roots and his novels reflected his North Country heritage, he loved his country clubs, his winter home in Winter Park, Fla, and his summer home, Robinhood, a 1,000 acre (400 ha) estate near Tupper Lake in the Adirondacks.

Bergmann, Frank, ed. *Upstate Literature: Essays in Memory of Thomas O'Donnell* (Syracuse: Syracuse Univ Press, 1985)
Samuels, Charles E. "Irving Bacheller: A Critical Biography" (PhD diss, Syracuse Univ, 1952)

Shirley S. Samuels

"Backside Albany." First African American dialect song by a white American, written *ca* 1815. The title refers to the location of Lake Champlain and Plattsburgh. The lyrics, written by musician and humorist Micah Hawkins (1777–1825), celebrate the American victory over the English in the Battle of Plattsburgh on 11 Sept 1814, as told in a comical style by a fictional black sailor. The melody is the traditional Irish fiddle tune "The Boyne Water," originally a ballad lamenting a famous English victory in 1690 in Ireland. African American volunteers among the American seamen served with distinction when Commodore Thomas Macdonough, commanding the *Eagle* and the *Saratoga,* defeated the British flagship, killing its commander and forcing the British to retreat. An exuberant celebration of African American patriotism, the song was premiered in February 1815 in a play about the battle, probably performed by Hopkins Robinson, an early specialist in blackface performance. The text appeared in the *Columbian Harmonist,* an anthology printed in Albany, the same year. In 1837 an arrangement of the music by William Clifton was published in New York City, and the song remained popular for about three decades.

Mahar, William J. " 'Backside Albany' and Early Blackface Minstrelsy: A Contextual Study of America's First Blackface Song," *American Music* 6 (Spring 1988): 1–27

Elliott S. Hurwitt

bagels. The bagel originally came to New York State with the large influx of eastern European Jewish immigrants in the late 1800s. Bagels, made of flour and boiled before they are baked, resemble doughnuts and are noted for a hard outer crust and a soft interior. Because of New York City's large Jewish population, the city became closely identified with bagels. Vendors selling bagels on the streets of Manhattan's Lower East Side were ubiquitous, and by 1907 New York City was home to newly founded Bagel Bakers Local 338 of the International Bakers Union, representing more than 300 of the city's bagel makers by 1910. Bagel bakers regarded bagel making as an art, with techniques that were closely guarded secrets. In the mid-1960s automation overtook hand manufacture, and in 2003 most bagels in the United States were mass produced by companies outside of New York State (New York City still retained many traditional bagel establishments). The image of the superior New York bagel persists. In the late 1980s, when Americans began seeking a low-fat alternative to doughnuts, chains such as Noah's New York Bagels (*ca* 1973) and Manhattan Bagels (1987) spread throughout the United States, although neither company is based in New York. Bruegger's Bagels, founded in Troy (Rensselaer Co) in 1983 and now based in Burlington, Vt, is the largest bagel retailer in New York State. Another well-known company, H&H Bagels (1972), began producing bagels at a store at Broadway and 80th St in New York City but now has a plant that produces millions of bagels annually for the wholesale market. Today bagels come in numerous varieties, from the traditional plain, poppy, and onion, to the more unusual blueberry or chocolate chip, and while they are especially popular in New York State, they are no longer considered just an East Coast ethnic food.

Gabaccia, Donna R. *We Are What We Eat* (Cambridge, Mass: Harvard Univ Press, 1998)

Donna L. Halper

Bahá'í. The Bahá'í faith entered New York State within a half century of the religion's beginnings in Iran in 1844. In December 1892 Ibrahim George Kheiralla, born in what is now Lebanon, arrived in New York City, claiming that the faith's founder, Bahá'u'lláh (1817–92), sent him to America. He headed west, settling in Chicago, where the Americans first became Bahá'ís in 1894. Several Bahá'í families moved to the New York City area in late 1897 and invited Kheiralla to give a series of Bahá'í classes in the winter and spring of 1898. Bahá'í teachings include the unity of humankind, equality of the sexes, establishment of world peace, universal education, and selection of a universal auxiliary language. Religious practices include daily obligatory prayer, an annual fasting period in March, and commemoration of Bahá'í holy days. In New York City the 150–200 converts often were middle- and upper-middle-class white Protestants, with such exceptions as Olive Jackson, a dressmaker and the first African American Bahá'í woman.

'Abdu'l-Bahá, son of Bahá'u'lláh and head of the faith, arrived in New York City on 11 Apr 1912, making it his headquarters for the next nine months and greatly strengthening the Bahá'í community. In May 1912 he visited the Mohonk Mountain House in Rochester to attend a peace conference. He stopped in Buffalo and Niagara Falls while en route from Toronto to Chicago. The period from 1913 to 1950 saw steady growth of the Bahá'í faith, and the New York Bahá'ís, who included some successful business people and a few intellectuals, contributed significantly. In 1925 the US Bahá'í Publishing Committee moved to New York City. In 1932 the Spiritual Assembly of the Bahá'ís of New York City, the nine-member elected governing body of the local Bahá'í community, was legally incorporated, and its bylaws became the model for local Bahá'í communities worldwide. Horace Holley, a resident of New York City, was elected to the National Spiritual Assembly in 1923 and was elected secretary in 1924. This brought the national Bahá'í organization to New York City, where it remained until 1939, when construction of a national Bahá'í house of worship in Wilmette, Ill, prompted Holley to move there, followed by the Bahá'í Publishing Committee in 1940.

Expansion of the Bahá'í faith across the state has been steady. By 1912 small groups of Bahá'ís with fewer than nine members existed in Jamestown (Chautauqua Co), Ithaca, Utica, and Buffalo. By 1926 Bahá'í communities with nine-member local spiritual assemblies existed in Buffalo, Geneva (Ontario Co), and Yonkers. Localities throughout New York State to elect spiritual assemblies were Ithaca (1928), Binghamton (1932), Rochester (1936), Jamestown (1940), Syracuse (1944), Waterloo (1946), and Hamburg (Erie Co) and Mount Vernon (Westchester Co) in 1950. The Geneva Bahá'í community was distinguished in the late 1930s by its integration of African Americans and European Americans. Prominent African American Bahá'ís include Alain Locke, who made a central contribution to the Harlem Renaissance, and Dizzy Gillespie, a leading jazz musician. By 1963 New York State had spiritual assemblies in 18 localities. In 2000 the state had 4,300 Bahá'ís and 34 spiritual assemblies. While white Protestants remain the principal source of converts, New York Bahá'ís include a significant number of former Catholics and Jews, American Indians, and immigrants from Iran, Southeast Asia, and Spanish-speaking countries.

Stockman, Robert H. *Origins, 1892–1900*, vol 1 of *The Bahá'í Faith in America* (Wilmette, Ill: Bahá'í Publishing Trust, 1985)
Ward, Allan L. *239 Days: 'Abdu'l-Bahá's Journey in America* (Wilmette, Ill: Bahá'í Publishing Trust, 1979)

Robert H. Stockman

Bailey, Liberty Hyde (*b* South Haven, Mich, 15 Mar 1858; *d* Ithaca, 25 Dec 1954). Horticulturist, educator, and author. Bailey grew up on his family's fruit farm in Michigan and took an early interest in nature. He studied botany at Michigan's State Agricultural College (now Michigan State University in East Lansing) and received his BS degree in 1882. He worked as an assistant to botanist Asa Gray at Harvard University from 1883 to 1884, returned to his alma mater to teach horticulture, received his MS degree there in 1886, but left in 1888 to become professor of horticulture at Cornell University. Best known for his wide-ranging writings and long and productive career at Cornell, Bailey also served as dean of the Agricultural College and director of its agricultural experiment station (1903–13). Under his direction and influence, the New York State College of Agriculture at Cornell became a center for plant studies, and horticulture became a recognized academic field. His publications became the standard for study on such topics as pomology and horticulture. Bailey was also much interested in agricultural education in rural schools and promoted a widely adopted system of nature studies that aimed to foster a child's native curiosity about the natural world. He became involved in the Country Life Movement and was appointed by Pres Theodore Roosevelt to report on rural life in 1908, although Bailey was skeptical of the romantic notions of farming that many in the movement harbored. He retired from Cornell at the age of 55 to write and travel the world collecting plant specimens, presenting his collection to Cornell in 1935. His remarkably active career ended shortly before his death at the age of 96.

Dorf, Philip. *Liberty Hyde Bailey: An Informal Biography* (1956; repr Ithaca: Wilcox Press, 1979)

Suzanne Etherington

Bailey, Theodorus (*b* Fishkill, Dutchess Co, 12 Oct 1758; *d* New York City, 6 Sept 1828). US senator, congressman, and militia officer. He attended rural schools, studied law, and was admitted to the bar in 1778, entering practice in Poughkeepsie. A militia officer during the American Revolution, he ended his service as brigadier general of the New York State militia in 1805. Vigorously Antifederalist he lost his first two congressional campaigns, winning election after a bitter campaign against his brother-in-law, James Kent, and serving in Congress from 1793 to 1797 and from 1799 to 1803. In 1802 he was a Dutchess Co representative to the state assembly. Named to the US Senate in 1803, he served one year, resigning to become postmaster of the City of New York, a position he held until his death.

Biographical Directory of the American Congress, 1774–1971 (Washington, DC: Government Printing Office, 1971)

William P. McDermott

Bainbridge. Town (pop 3,401) and village (pop 1,365) in SE Chenango Co. The first European settlers were displaced by settlers from Vermont, known as the Vermont Sufferers, in 1786. The town was formed in 1791 as Jericho, which was part of Tioga Co until 1798, and changed to Bainbridge in 1814. The village incorporated in 1829. Manufacturing developed late in the 19th century: Gilbert Manufacturing Co (1883–98) made children's sleds, the Crump firm (1891–94) canned condensed coconut milk, and cigars were manufactured (1882–1932). Most plants, however, grew out of the dairy industry, starting with the Bainbridge Creamery (1889). The National Milk Sugar Co (1898) and the Casein Manufacturing Co (1904) used milk by-products, the latter using casein for early plastics manufacture. The American Separator Co (1895–*ca* 1960) manufactured cream separators for farm use. Borden purchased the milk by-products plants in 1929 and it remained, as Elmer's Products, the largest employer in 2003. When I-88 was completed through Bainbridge in 1975, residents began traveling to Binghamton and Oneonta (Otsego Co) for work and shopping. Jedediah Strong Smith (1799–1831), explorer and mountain man, was born in town.

Michele A. McFee

Baker, Nelson Henry (*b* Buffalo, 16 Feb 1841; *d* Lackawanna, Erie Co, 29 July 1936). Roman Catholic priest. Following a late calling to the ministry after a life in the grain and feed business, Baker was educated at Our Lady of Angels Seminary at Niagara Falls and ordained in the Diocese of Buffalo in 1876. Assigned to St. Patrick's Church at Limestone Hill, West Seneca (Erie Co), in 1882 he became pastor and the superintendent of the St. John's Protectory/Boys Home and St. Joseph's Orphan Asylum in nearby Lackawanna. The remainder of his life was dedicated to building a comprehensive charitable enterprise in Lackawanna devoted to homeless and destitute children, including trade schools and an infant and maternity hospital. A pioneer in national fund-raising techniques, he established the Associates of Our Lady of Victory for the spiritual and financial support of "Father Baker and His Boys from Buffalo," winning a national reputation as an American "apostle of charity." In 1926 he fulfilled a lifelong dream when the National Shrine and Basilica of Our Lady of Victory was consecrated, a permanent monument in Lackawanna to his piety and charity. The Roman Catholic Church he served named him a Servant of God in 1987, the first step toward canonization as a saint.

Anderson, Floyd. *Father Baker* (Milwaukee: Bruce Publishing, 1960)

Kathleen L. Riley

baker's dozen. In 1836 Hudson Valley writer and statesman James Kirke Paulding (1778–1860) published "The Origin of the Baker's Dozen" in the *Book of Saint Nicholas.* Paulding's story described a visit by St. Nicholas in the disguise of an old woman to a 17th-century Albany baker named Volckert Jan Pietersen. To make a point about charity, the woman insisted that a dozen consisted of 13 cookies and blighted the baker's work until he agreed. Although purportedly translated from a local Dutch folktale, thus far no version of that folktale has been found antedating Paulding's story. Best remembered as Washington Irving's coauthor of the *Salmagundi* pamphlets (1807–8), Paulding is known to have fabricated other folktales. The baker's dozen custom persists in New York State at the turn of the 21st century as many bakeries and bagel shops automatically include 13 or more items in a dozen.

Brewer, Ebenezer Cobham, and Adrian Room. *Brewer's Dictionary of Phrase and Fable,* 16th ed. (New York: Harper Resource, 1999)

Nancy Groce

baking industry. Baking in New Netherland was overwhelmingly a domestic industry. The first commercial bakery on record opened in New Amsterdam [now New York City] in 1645, and for the next two centuries such businesses would remain primarily urban. Both Dutch and English colonial governments closely regulated the price and weight of bread. As in Europe, bakers sold their products from storefronts because street vending was usually prohibited, but most baked goods were made to order. An exception, establishing a basic division within the industry that would last well into the 20th century, was nonperishable hard bread, sold wholesale to shipping companies as sailor's tack.

There were 12 bakeries in New York City when independence was declared in 1776. British forces quickly recaptured the city, and in 1777 the military administration reestablished price controls on bread to ensure that this staple remained within reach of the general population. Although evading the controls could result in seizure and imprisonment, prices continued to rise. New York State bakeries in the late 18th century were typically established and run by immigrants, particularly Irish, Scottish, and German. In the first half of the 19th century the baking industry expanded with New York City's population, much of it housed in units without ovens suitable for home baking. There was explosive growth in the 1840s, from 38 retail bakeries to 476 over the course of the decade. At the same time the baking trade became more German, with several decades of heavy German immigration starting in the 1810s leading to complete domination of the industry in New York State by midcentury.

Industrialization, Expansion, and Consolidation

The history of the baking industry from *ca* 1850 is one of increasing automation, with larger companies absorbing many of the small local bakeries, and factory-style manufacturers establishing regional and eventually national distribution networks. This was first evident in cracker and biscuit manufacturing, where recent inventions like kneading and rolling machines could be more easily applied. Moreover, the long shelf life of these foodstuffs meant that they could be distributed outside the local market, encouraging mass production. In 1889 numerous bakeries in New York State and the Northeast consolidated to form the New York Biscuit Co, with wholesale distribution throughout the region. Within just nine years New York Biscuit Co and other regional wholesalers merged to form the National Biscuit Co, comprising over 114 bakeries, 19 in New York State. Later known as Nabisco, the company was acquired by Kraft Foods in December 2000.

By contrast, the making of fresh breads and pastries remained throughout the 19th century an industry of small retail shops, most with only a handful of employees and little or no automation. Most New York City bakeries were located in the cellars of tenement buildings, where space was cheap but conditions often unsanitary and ventilation poor. Home delivery was a standard service for these neighborhood shops. Although at the turn of the 20th century 75% of America's bread was still baked at home, the figure represented a 15% decline over 50 years. A larger retail market, the growth of urban centers outside the New York City area, the use of mechanical mixers and molding machines, and the expansion of rail networks allowed wholesale bread-baking companies to emerge in the early 20th century. The Ward baking family established a presence in New York State in 1849, when Hugh Ward opened a one-oven shop on Broome St in Manhattan. Robert B. Ward organized the Ward Bread Co in 1900, with locations in Manhattan, Brooklyn, and Newark, NJ. Eleven years later a merger with other Ward enterprises created the Ward Baking Co. William B. Ward combined Buffalo's seven Ward and Ward plants, Rochester's three Ward Bros plants, and the nine plants of a Kansas City company to form United Bakeries Corp in 1922, but further consolidation led to intervention by the Justice Department and the divestiture of part of the Ward empire four years later. Among the brands manufactured by Ward-owned companies were Tip-Top Bread, Wonder Bread, and Hostess snack cakes. Ward Baking Co's New York City headquarters was eliminated during a reorganization in 1974, and the enterprise left the baking business entirely in 1981. From 1924 until his death in 1953 Ralph Ward was president of East Coast snack cake manufacturer Drake's Bakeries, with facilities in the Bronx, Manhattan, and Brooklyn. Drake's is now owned by Interstate Bakeries Corp.

By the 1920s wholesalers were in command of the industry, with distribution in grocery stores overshadowing bakeshop retailers. Nevertheless, continuity with the era of home delivery was maintained by companies like Entenmann's Baking Co and Charles A. Freihofer Baking Co, which sent their products house-to-house by horse-drawn cart and later by truck. German immigrant William Entenmann started his business in 1898 with a bakery in the Flatbush neighborhood of Brooklyn, relocating in the early 1900s to Bay Shore (Suffolk Co). Brothers of the Freihofer baking family opened a bakery in Troy (Rensselaer Co) in 1913, and within five years were baking in Schenectady, Albany, and New Paltz (Ulster Co). Other early baking companies incorporated in New York State include Tri-State Baking Co (1919), later absorbed by Purity Baking Co, and Cushman Sons (1914), which combined 40 stores in the New York City area. A significant event in New York State's baking history was Adolph Levitt's invention of an automated doughnut machine in 1920. Levitt used the machines in his own chain of doughnut shops and made them commercially available through Levitt's Donut Machine Corp (later DCA Industries), thereby enabling an enormous increase in doughnut production nationwide. Some New York City bakeries, such as Silvercup Bread (1929) of Long Island City (Queens Co) and Stella D'oro Biscuit Co (1930) in the Bronx, were able to make the transition from local retailing to high-volume wholesaling. Others survived by catering to niche markets in the city's ethnic neighborhoods. In 1931 there were over 600 Jewish retail bakeries in New York, selling bagels, hamantaschen, Passover cake, and other specialties. Bagels, once closely identified with Jewish bakeries in New York City, have become standard fare across the country.

Labor

Bakers in colonial New York observed an apprenticeship system inherited from their European precursors but lacked the strong guild structure that safeguarded the industry's interests in the Old World. While the cost of bread was regulated, that of most ingredients was allowed to fluctuate, leading to periodic conflicts with civic authorities. In April 1741 New York City bakers launched a strike, or "combination," in an effort to force an increase in bread prices. They were prosecuted for conspiracy, but no convictions were made. Although retail baking retained a craft character well into the industrial era, the Germans who dominated the trade from the early 19th century brought with them a robust tradition of labor solidarity. Workers set up employment services to "advise and protect" new immigrants entering the trade and to ensure that their often desperate circumstances did not negatively affect labor standards.

Still, in 1880 the average baker worked an estimated 108 hours per week. Journeymen bakers in New York City were normally required to lodge with the bakery owners, and many would sleep in the cellar bakeries themselves, on beds made of rags. Rheumatism, baker's asthma, tuberculosis, and other ailments were rampant. To improve working conditions, approximately 3,200 bakers in the metropolitan area, most of them German, formed the Journeymen Bakers Union (1880). On 2 May 1881 the union began a largely unsuccessful strike aimed at reducing bakers' hours to 12 hours a day during the week and 14 on Saturday. The union collapsed, but the appearance of a German language, bakery workers' journal in 1885 stimulated organization, and approximately 700 German bakers in New York City and Brooklyn unionized that year. On 13 Jan 1886 the Journeymen Bakers National Union of the United States was formally established, with New York City as the seat of its National Executive Committee. In 1895 the New York State legislature unanimously passed a bakeshop act, setting hygiene standards and limiting work to 8 hours a day or 60 a week. Utica bakery owner Joseph Lochner challenged the act in 1902; it was upheld by New York State courts but overturned on appeal by the US Supreme Court in 1905, dealing a blow to the labor movement nationally. Since 1999 the industry's labor force has been represented by the Bakery, Confectionery, Tobacco Workers and Grain Millers International Union, which in 2004 had five locals in New York State. However, the acquisition of unionized companies by nonunion ones has caused the state's union membership to decline.

RECENT TRENDS

Since the 1980s there has been an explosive growth in the popularity of handmade, "artisan"-style breads, with total sales in the category rising from $918 million nationwide in 1994 to $1.775 billion in 2002. The Bread Bakers Guild of America, formed in 1993 to support the artisan industry, has more members in New York than in any other state. Notable artisan breadmakers include Daniel Leader, author of *Bread Alone* (1993), with Bread Alone bakeries in Rhinebeck (Dutchess Co), Kingston, Woodstock, and Boiceville (Ulster Co), and Amy Scherber, who started Amy's Bread in New York City in 1992. Additionally, independent corner bakeries have reestablished a strong market niche in New York City neighborhoods and around the state. Responding to the appeal of these high-quality shops, many supermarkets have increased the size and sophistication of their bakeries and now offer a wide range of European-style and ethnic breads and pastries.

Ongoing consolidation continues to erode the wholesale baking industry in New York State. Between 1992 and 1997 the number of wholesale bakeries dropped from 423 to 374, total sales from $1.768 billion to $1.448 billion, and employment from 13,800 to just over 11,000. Nevertheless, some independent wholesalers remain competitive, mostly serving regional markets. At the same time the number of retail bakeries has increased, led by the resurgent market in the New York metropolitan area. By the end of 2000 there were 1,365 wholesale and retail baking companies in New York City, with 12,414 employees.

See also LOCHNER V NEW YORK.

Alsberg, Carl L. *Combination in the American Bread-Baking Industry* (1926; repr New York: Arno Press, 1973)

Bakery, Confectionery, Tobacco Workers and Grain Millers International Union, http://www.bctgm.org

Bakery Production and Marketing (Chicago: Gorman Publishing, 1966–)

Kaufman, Stuart Bruce. *A Vision of Unity: The History of the Bakery and Confectionery Workers International Union* (Kensington, Md: Bakery, Confectionery, & Tobacco Workers International Union, 1986)

New York Industrial Retention Network. "Baked in New York: Special Report to the Consortium for Worker Education and the Artisan Baking Center." Feb 2002

Tammy Popejoy

Balanchine, George [Balanchivadze, Georgi Melitonovich] (*b* St. Petersburg, Russia, 22 Jan 1904; *d* New York City, 30 Apr 1983). Choreographer, dancer, and cofounder of the New York City Ballet. Balanchine was trained in classical dance at the Imperial Ballet School in St. Petersburg [later Petrograd, then Leningrad], from 1914 until 1921, when he joined the corps of the Maryinsky Ballet, by then renamed the State Theater of Opera and Ballet. In 1924 he began a tour of western Europe and while performing in London was hired by impresario Sergei Diaghilev and within a year became the chief choreographer for the Ballets Russes.

In 1933 Balanchine moved to New York City, accepting Lincoln Kirstein's offer to collaborate first on the School of American Ballet (1934) and then on a company that became the New York City Ballet in 1948. Balanchine also choreographed for the Metropolitan Opera and for Broadway productions of *On Your Toes* (1936) and *The Boys from Syracuse* (1938) as well as Hollywood movies including *The Goldwyn Follies* (1938).

His neoclassical style combined Russian classical technique with the energy, athleticism, and freshness of American dancers that created a truly American classical dance. Balanchine's most significant ballets include *Serenade* (1934), *Concerto Barocco* (1941), and *Jewels* (1967). A lifelong collaboration with Igor Stravinsky produced a number of significant works, including *Danses Concertantes* (1944), *Orpheus* (1948), and *Agon* (1957). Several works, such as *Western Symphony* (1954), *Square Dance* (1957), and *Stars and Stripes* (1958), had specifically American themes. Balanchine's new vision of choreography and performance and the institutions he founded changed the course of classical dance. The George Balanchine Foundation was founded in 1983 to preserve his legacy and interpretations of classical ballet and continue the development of dance throughout the world.

Taper, Bernard. *Balanchine*, 2d ed. (New York: Times Books, 1984)

Anya Peterson Royce

Baking bread at On the Rise Bakery, Syracuse, 1989.

Baldwin. {Baldwin, locality (pop 23,455) in Hempstead, Nassau Co; Baldwin Harbor, locality (pop 8,147) in Hempstead}. Located on the south side of Long Island, the area was known as Hicks Neck by 1660; in 1686 a mill was built, and the locality took the name Milburn. It served as a fishing and oystering port and, by 1830, as a sportsmen's resort. In the 19th century it was named variously Baldwins and Baldwinsville after a prominent local family. The South Side Rail Road (now the Long Island Rail Road) made it a station stop in 1867; the new post office (1871) shortened the name to Baldwin. In the 1920s it grew rapidly as a commuting community, which it remains today. Baldwin Harbor, located south of Atlantic Ave, was first developed in the same era with large homes, many with private docks. The town-operated Baldwin Harbor Park (147 acres/59 ha) has sport and recreational facilities. Actor George "Gabby" Hayes (1885–1969) was a native of Baldwin.

Lynda R. Day

Baldwin. Town (pop 853) in E Chemung Co. Settled in 1813, the town was formed from Chemung in 1856. Lumbering was the first industry, followed by dairy farming in the mid–19th century. The population declined in the 20th century, reaching 457 in 1940, and then began gradual growth. Residents commute to work in Chemung, Elmira, and Horseheads.

Heather A. Wade

Baldwin, Thomas S(cott) [Sackett] (*b* ?Decatur, Ill, ?30 June 1854; *d* Buffalo, 17 May 1923). Pioneer aeronaut. While a circus performer Baldwin made the first parachute jump from a balloon in 1888, also creating the first all-fabric parachute. In 1904 he built and flew the first successful US dirigible, powered by a Curtiss motorcycle engine. In 1906, after the San Francisco earthquake destroyed his shop, "Captain Baldwin" worked on balloons and dirigibles at the Curtiss plant in Hammondsport (Steuben Co). Baldwin aided the 1908 Aerial Experiment Association, a group that included Glenn Curtiss and Alexander Graham Bell, in developing aircraft. Also that year he and Curtiss created the dirigible SC-1, the army's first powered aircraft. In 1909–10 Baldwin designed and produced two prototype airplanes at Curtiss, contracting with Wittemann Bros of Staten Island to manufacture the craft. From bases in Mineola (Nassau Co) and later Staten Island, Baldwin toured America and the Far East, demonstrating the planes with his Red Devil exhibition team (1911–14). Advancing age and Wright brothers' litigation led him to give up the business. During World War I Baldwin served as a major in the US Army balloon section. Following the war he worked for Goodyear Tire and Rubber Co.

Eklund, Don Dean. "Captain Thomas S. Baldwin: Pioneer American Aeronaut" (PhD diss, Univ of Colorado, 1970)

Roseberry, C. R. *Glenn Curtiss: Pioneer of Flight* (Garden City, NY: Doubleday, 1972)

Kirk W. House

Baldwinsville. Village (pop 7,053) in Lysander and Van Buren (Onondaga Co). Settled in 1797, Baldwinsville is divided by the Seneca River and was the site of its first bridge (1806). Its post office, first called McHarrie's Rifts and then Columbia, opened in 1815. An important flour-milling locality, it benefited from the Baldwinsville Canal (1807–1919), which bypassed rapids in the Seneca River. Other products included axes, woolen cloth, tissue paper, pumps, and farm tools. The village, which incorporated in 1848, over time became a residential suburb of Syracuse. In the early 21st century, the Female Charitable Society (1817) still meets regularly.

Barbara S. Rivette

Baldwinsville Canal and Seneca River Towing Path. Built by Dr Jonas C. Baldwin in 1807 and 1808, this short (.6 mi/1 km), one-lock canal permitted boats to bypass the rapids in the Seneca River known as McHarrie's Rifts at Baldwinsville (Onondaga Co). In 1809 Baldwin received authorization from the state legislature to collect tolls. The river being naturally navigable below the site, a 7.5 foot (2.3 m) dam built in conjunction with the canal allowed slack water navigation for 11.75 miles (18.91 km) upstream to Jack's Reef. The canal was enlarged in 1831. Acquired by the state in 1853, it was subsequently further enlarged and improved. In 1919 Erie Barge Canal Lock 24 was built directly across the river from the old canal, which thereafter only provided waterpower to adjacent mills. The Baldwinsville Canal was completely filled in by 1965.

Whitford, Nobel Earl. *History of the Canal System of New York State,* 2 vols (Albany: Brandow Printing, 1906)

David W. Beebe

Ball, Lucille (Désirée) (*b* Jamestown, Chautauqua Co, 6 Aug 1911; *d* Los Angeles, 26 Apr 1989). Actress, comedian, and television producer. Lucille Ball created one of television's most enduring comic characters, Lucy, and starred in several series on CBS from 1951 to 1974. Her first television series, *I Love Lucy,* remains one of the touchstones of American popular culture and has probably been seen by more people more often than any other program in history. Ball's father died when she was 4. Her mother remarried and left the Jamestown area four years later, but Ball remained, living with relatives. As an adolescent she was active in school and community theater projects. At age 15 Ball went to New York City to study acting and supported herself by modeling. She briefly appeared in Broadway chorus lines, but her first noticeable role was as a showgirl in the 1933 movie musical *Roman Scandals,* starring Eddie Cantor. Encouraged by the initial success, Ball moved to Hollywood and appeared in numerous movies for RKO Pictures and MGM. For almost 20 years she was a respected actress, comfortable in musicals, comedies, and dramas.

From 1947 to 1951 her comic talents were on display in the CBS radio series *My Favorite Husband.* CBS wanted to transfer the show to television as a live situation comedy from New York City. Ball resisted, preferring to costar with her husband, Cuban bandleader Desi Arnaz, and stay close to her West Coast home. Arnaz and executive producer Jess Oppenheimer devised a technique to film a weekly comedy before a live Hollywood audience. *I Love Lucy* debuted on 15 Oct 1951, with Ball as redheaded screwball wife Lucy Ricardo. The premise—a couple with different backgrounds living in Manhattan's East 60s, both seduced by the allure of show business—gave the series a New York City flavor. *I Love Lucy* was the country's most popular program for most of its six seasons and established the situation comedy as the dominant television genre. The cast reprised their roles in a series of specials (1957–60). Ball divorced Arnaz in 1960, and two years later assumed sole ownership of their production company, Desilu, becoming the first woman to head a television studio. She returned to Broadway for the musical *Wildcat* (1960) and produced new programs featuring her staple character: *The Lucy Show* (1962–68) and *Here's Lucy* (1968–74). In 1985 she startled her fans by playing a homeless woman in the television movie *Stone Pillow.* The Lucy Desi Museum in Jamestown, opened in 1996, sponsors a festival each spring.

Andrews, Bart. *Lucy and Ricky and Fred and Ethel: The Story of "I Love Lucy"* (New York: Dutton, 1976)

Brady, Kathleen. *Lucille: The Life of Lucille Ball* (New York: Hyperion, 1994)

Ron Simon

ballet. The company of Alexandre Placide, the first major ballet company appearing in New York City, performed at the John Street Theater from January to May 1792. The troupe included John Durang, the first internationally known American dancer. Durang also performed in the city with Lewis Hallam's Old American Co and partnered Gardie, a popular ballerina of the day. Notable dancers who performed in New York City over the next several decades included Charles and Mme Ronzi Vestris, Marius and Jean-Antoine Petipa, French dancer Mlle Augusta, Paul Taglioni and his wife Anna Galster, and American Mary Ann Lee, who made her New York City debut in 1839. Austrian Fanny

Lucille Ball at the helm of *City of Jamestown* on Chautauqua Lake, 1946.

Elssler began her triumphant US tour at New York City's Park Theatre on 14 May 1840. After 15 performances, eight dancers from the theater joined her company for the tour.

A new era in American dance started with *The Black Crook*, first seen at Niblo's Garden Theatre in New York City on 12 Sept 1866, a four-act extravaganza with the Great Parisienne Ballet Troupe with Marie Bonfanti and Rita Sangalli. It played for 16 months before going on tour and employed hundreds of dancers, giving a push to ballet in America. Niblo's Garden followed this success with *The White Fawn* (1868), and among the attractions in these productions were the bared legs of some of the female dancers. Musical and dance productions continued in a similar vein for the remainder of the century, such as the lavish spectacles of the Hungarian Imre Kiralfy in the 1870s and 1880s. The Metropolitan Opera, founded in 1883, also regularly employed ballet dancers and in 1909 founded the first American ballet school for its corps de ballet.

Early Russian Visitors

By the turn of the century the center of the ballet world had shifted to Russia. Anna Pavlova first visited New York in 1910 and until her last tour in 1929 traveled the country extensively. She inspired generations of girls to dance and opened schools in New York and other cities, convincing people that ballet was an art worthy of patronage and development. Pavlova's partner in 1910 was Mikhail Mordkin, and they were engaged by the Metropolitan Opera House and its franchise, the New Theatre. Pavlova brought primarily short solo pieces or pas de deux but began to stage larger works as she gathered a small troupe. The most ambitious was her *Sleeping Beauty*, opening at New York City's Hippodrome on 31 Aug 1916. For six weeks, 5,000 people came to each of 12 shows a week. On 17 Jan 1916 Serge Diaghilev's *Ballets Russes* opened at the Century Theater in New York City and then set off on a tour that took them to Albany and other centers. Their second New York season opened 3 Apr 1916 at the Metropolitan Opera House, and the last of the Diaghilev-inspired companies came to New York City in December 1933.

Resident Companies in New York City

Prominent Russian choreographer and dancer Michael Fokine came to the United States in 1919, debuting at the Metropolitan Opera House. He settled in New York City in 1921, opened a ballet school, performed at various ballet and musical theater venues, and choreographed works for several prominent companies. His *Les Elfes* premiered at the Metropolitan Opera in 1924, and an all-Fokine performance at Lewisohn Stadium in Upper Manhattan drew 17,000, with thousands turned away. New York City's first two major ballet schools opened in 1934: the Ballet Russe de Monte Carlo under Serge Denham and the School of American Ballet under Lincoln Kirstein and George Balanchine. The American Ballet gave its first performance in June 1934 in White Plains (Westchester Co), premiering Balanchine's *Serenade*. A similar pupil-based company, the Mordkin Ballet, was created in 1937 by Mikhail Mordkin and became professional in 1938. Lucia Chase was its principal dancer, and in 1940 Chase, Richard Pleasant, and a small group of the Mordkin company formed the American Ballet Theatre.

Ballet Society, founded by Kirstein and Balanchine, encouraged dance by producing new works and gave Balanchine the opportunity to create a truly innovative company. The first performance on 20 Nov 1946 at Manhattan's Central High School of the Needle Trades presented *The Four Temperaments*, a work Balanchine choreographed to a score composed for the piece by Paul Hindemith, which like many of his later creations displayed the speed and clarity of American dancers in neoclassical style. Ballet Society became the New York City Ballet in 1948 and the resident company of the New York City Center for Music and Drama. In 1964 the company moved to the New York State Theater at Lincoln Center, which was built to Balanchine's specifications. The company's 1972 Stravinsky Festival celebrated the long collaboration between the composer and Balanchine. On Balanchine's death in 1983, Peter Martins and Jerome Robbins took over direction of the company. Robbins left in 1990, but Martins has continued, maintaining the Balanchine repertory as the foundation but adding other choreographers, such as renowned English dancer Christopher Wheeldon. The school continues to train strong, classical dancers.

American Ballet Theatre (ABT), founded as Ballet Theatre in 1940, took a different direction, establishing itself as a repertory company with choreographers such as Michael Fokine, Antony Tudor, and Agnes de Mille, later adding Birgit Cullberg, Jerome Robbins, and Kenneth Macmillan. The company was given an official home at the Metropolitan Opera House in 1977. Mikhail Baryshnikov was its artistic director from 1980 to 1989, both strengthening the classical base and adding new works by modern choreographers such as Paul Taylor, Merce Cunningham, Mark Morris, and Twyla Tharp. Its stars over the decades have included Nora Kaye, Cynthia Gregory, Fernando Bujones, Leslie Browne, Paloma Herrera, Julio Bocca, and Ethan Steifel. Under the direction of Kevin McKenzie since 1992, ABT has its own performing company, the Ballet Repertory Co.

New York City has supported other ballet companies. Among the best known is the Dance Theater of Harlem, founded in 1969 by Arthur Mitchell, a principal dancer with New York City Ballet and the first African American male dancer to become a permanent member of a major ballet company. Its first performance was at the Guggenheim Museum and featured three chamber ballets by Mitchell. The repertory includes 20th-century classics by de Mille, Balanchine, Robbins, and Vaslav Nijinsky, but also works that draw upon the company's African American heritage. The Joffrey Ballet School–American Ballet Center was founded by Robert Joffrey and Gerald Arpino in 1960. Its company, the Robert Joffrey Ballet Concert, gave its first performance in 1954 at the 92d Street Y. Joffrey and Arpino choreographed for the company but also invited choreographers such as Twyla Tharp, Jiri Kylián, and Mark Morris to create works. In 1966 the company was invited to become the resident company of New York City Center. After Joffrey's death in 1988, Arpino took on sole responsibility, eventually moving the company to Chicago in 1995.

By the 1960s New York City was one of the major ballet centers in the world and an obligatory stop for any touring company. The Bolshoi Ballet performed there in 1959, as did the Kirov in 1961. Within a short time, three of the Kirov's greatest dancers had defected to the West: Rudolf Nureyev in 1961, Natalia Makarova in 1970, and Mikhail Baryshnikov in 1974. Both Makarova and Baryshnikov made their home in New York City and were instrumental in shaping the repertory of ABT. A number of influential dance critics were based in New York City, among them John Martin, a major critic for the *New York Times* from 1927 to 1962, and Edwin Denby, a dance critic for *Modern Music* and the *New York Herald-Tribune* and a contributor to such magazines as *Ballet, Dance Magazine, Mademoiselle*, and *Evergreen Review*.

Ballet Outside of New York City

New York City's status as a ballet center has led to a network of schools and companies throughout the state, including the Rochester City Ballet, Ithaca Ballet (1961), Ballet Regent School (1979) in Saratoga Springs, and the Greater Buffalo Youth Ballet (1997). The Saugerties Ballet Co (Ulster Co) is the official school of the Ulster Ballet Co (1977) and showcases the talent found in the Hudson Valley. The New York City Ballet gives a summer season at Saratoga Performing Arts Center in Saratoga Springs, where the National Museum of Dance is located. The summer of 2004 marked the 35th year of the schools that make up the New York State Summer School of the Arts (NYSSA), held at Skidmore College in Saratoga. Their School of Ballet accepts 60 students, using guest teachers from the New York City Ballet in July, and has been under the direction of Damian Woetzel, its internationally acclaimed principal dancer, since 1994. The Eglevsky Ballet was founded by renowned Russian dancer André Eglevsky in New Hyde Park (Nassau Co) and is the only professional company on Long Island. The New York State Council of the Arts has been one source of support for companies both in New York City and statewide.

Anawalt, Sasha. *The Joffrey Ballet: Robert Joffrey and the Making of an American Dance Company* (Chicago: Univ of Chicago, 1997)

Garafola, Lynn, ed. *Dance for a City: 50 Years of the New York City Ballet* (New York: Columbia Univ Press, 1999)

Jacob, Ellen, and Christopher Jonas. *Dance in New York* (New York: Quick Fox, 1980)

Kaye, Elizabeth. *American Ballet Theatre: A 25-Year Retrospective* (Kansas City: Andrews McMeel Publishing, 1999)

Anya Peterson Royce

ballooning and balloon festivals. Using hot air or lighter-than-air gases to leave the ground and relying on the whim of the wind to travel, balloons have graced the skies of New York State since the late 1780s when spectators in New York City paid to watch the launch of crewless balloons. New York City was just one stop for touring European balloonists who by the late 18th century were ascending with their crafts. Charles Durant was among the first Americans to take to the air, making the first of several flights from Manhattan's Castle Garden on 9 Sept 1830. Exhibition flights at fairs and other venues attracted crowds across the state and country for the rest of the century. Perhaps the best known was Carlotta, the aerial name of Mary Hawley Myers, whose debut ascent was witnessed by an audience of 15,000 on 4 July 1880 at Little Falls (Herkimer Co). Her husband, Carl Myers, used balloons to conduct scientific experiments and sought to improve balloon construction. Their home in Frankfort (Herkimer Co) became known as the Balloon Farm in part because of the many half-inflated balloons on the grounds. Balloons also became the means in the late 19th century for high-altitude acrobatic performances. In the early 1900s twins Edward and Edgar Allen of Dansville (Livingston Co) gained fame by ascending in "smoke balloons" filled with hot air from fires on the ground, then parachuting back to earth. Edward, known as Captain Eddie, made over 3,000 ascensions and parachute jumps at carnivals and air shows throughout the country. His children, raised in Batavia (Genesee Co), continued "The Flying Allens" performances into the 1950s. As the interests of the aeronauts, who had worked throughout the 19th century to improve ballooning technology and the distances that could be covered, turned to aviation in the early 20th century, wealthy amateurs took up the sport. The international distance contest for the James Gordon Bennett Cup, named after the publisher of the *New York Herald,* is still regarded as the premier balloon event. After a hiatus in sports ballooning in the 1940s and 1950s, the development of propane burners in the 1960s ignited interest in the sport once again. Although gas balloons continue to be used for distance contests, popular at balloon festivals and also used in commercial operations are the colorful, seven-story crafts made of synthetic nylon fabrics and filled with hot air. Balloons are governed by the Federal Aviation Administration (FAA), and balloonists must have an FAA license to fly. Two of the largest festivals in the state are the Adirondack Balloon Festival, held every September at the Warren County Airport in Glens Falls with about 100 balloonists, and the New York State Festival of Balloons, held every Labor Day in Dansville with over 75 balloons. Some of the other annual balloon festivals in the state are held in Binghamton, Jamesville, Wellsville, Poughkeepsie, and Jamestown.

Crouch, Tom D. *The Eagle Aloft: Two Centuries of the Balloon in America* (Washington, DC: Smithsonian Institution Press, 1983)

Greg Livadas

Ballston. Town (pop 8,729) in SW Saratoga Co. Settled by Irish-born Michael and Nicholas McDonald in 1763, it was named for Rev Eliphalet Ball, who arrived in 1771 with a church colony from Bedford (Westchester Co). Formed as a district under Albany Co in 1772, it was recognized as a town in 1788. It was chiefly agricultural, and there were not enough good mill sites to encourage industry. Ballston Lake is 4 miles (6 km) long, attracting a trolley line (1902) and amusement park (1904) that stimulated modest Schenectady-oriented suburban development. Rte 50 (*ca* 1935) reinforced the town's Schenectady orientation and aided suburbanization after World War II.

Field Horne

Ballston Spa. Village (pop 5,556) in Ballston and Milton (Saratoga Co). Settlement began in 1771 when the Iron Spring was discovered. Benajah Douglas built the first lodgings in 1787 and five years later a hotel now operated as a museum by the Saratoga County Historical Society. Ballston Spa was incorporated as a village in 1807 and named the county seat in 1816. Nicholas Low, proprietor of most of the village's land, built the Sans Souci Hotel (1804–87), a three-story building 150 feet (46 m) long, with gaming rooms and lodging for 250 people. Visitors declared Ballston Spa the most splendid watering place in America. In the 1820s Ballston and Saratoga Springs were equal in size and reputation. As a result, the second railroad built in New York State connected Ballston Spa to Schenectady in 1832. Ballston declined for a number of reasons: the limited number of freely flowing springs, Saratoga Spring's vigorous promotion and infrastructure development, and Low's absentee-landlord status. By the 1830s visitors had drifted to Saratoga Springs, and Ballston Spa's fame faded. The village re-created itself by midcentury as an industrial village; the Gordon and Kayaderosseras Creeks provided waterpower for factories employing more than 1,100 workers, producing paper, textiles, clothing, ironwork, and lumber. George West's large paper bag factory (1868) was the most prominent. In the 20th century industrial employment was anchored by Howes Leather Co (1882–1960), Bischoff Chocolate Co (1919–47), and Tufflite Plastics (1949–96), but the Kesselring Site of Knolls Atomic Power Laboratory in adjacent Milton and Galway became the chief employer in the 1950s. In the second and third quarters of the century most of the factories closed, and Ballston Spa reinvented itself as a Capital District suburb. It is the site of the National Bottle Museum and was the birthplace of Civil War hero Gen Abner Doubleday.

band music. The American brass band developed from "field music" played by brass and drums, primarily in military contexts, in the decades before the Civil War, largely displacing earlier, softer wind ensembles dominated by woodwinds. Music instruction at West Point (Orange Co) began in 1817 when Richard Willis, a keyed bugle virtuoso from Ireland, became bandmaster. Rochester had its own town band by around 1819, and Buffalo gained a military band within about a decade.

New York City and Brooklyn have long been the dominant centers for band music in New York State. In the mid–19th century the dominant force in the city's brass music was the Dodworth family, publishing influential instruction manuals such as Allen Dodworth's *Brass Band School* (1853). Another leading bandmaster, Claudio S. Grafulla (1810–80) from the Spanish island of Minorca, was connected with New York State's Seventh Regiment. Town bandmasters entered military service with their bands during the Civil War, resulting in a great increase in production of brass instruments and a need for disciplined, precise players. Saxhorns, a family of brass instruments introduced *ca* 1838 and dominant during the war, included large "over-the-shoulder blasters" easily played on horseback, but they became obsolete in the 1870s. They were replaced by the standard family of trumpet, trombone, and tuba. Irish-born Patrick Gilmore (1829–92) took over direction of New York State's 22d Regiment Band in 1873 and soon turned it into the nation's leading band. By 1878 it boasted 66 pieces, including 35 woodwinds, and was a training ground for many future leaders in band music, including cornetists Herman Bellstedt and Jules Levy. In 1888 Gilmore began the tradition of New Year's Eve celebrations in Manhattan's Long Acre Square (now Times Square).

The golden age of American band music from 1865 to 1930 was a time when almost every town and village in the state had a brass band, and most of the great bandleaders were headquartered in New York City or, like John Philip Sousa (1854–1932), visited frequently. Sousa's famous march *Manhattan Beach* (1893) commemorates his engagement at a Brooklyn resort. Among New York City bandleaders, Edwin Franko Goldman (1878–1956) was the most important, composing and commissioning new repertoire and leading an excellent band. *On the Mall* (1923), celebrating Central Park, is probably his best-known march. In 1922 Ithaca College's Conway Military Band School was founded by Patrick Conway (1867–1929) from Troy (Rensselaer Co). He was an important bandleader in Ithaca since the 1890s when his band vied with other ambitious ensembles at the annual conventions of the Central New York Volunteer Firemen's Association.

Ernest S. Williams (1881–1947) began teaching privately in 1922 and founded a band academy, the Ernest S. Williams School of Music, that thrived in the Bedford section of Brooklyn from 1931 to 1943. Among the finest American bands of the mid–20th century was the Eastman Wind Ensemble, founded in Rochester by Frederick Fennell in 1952 and led by Donald Hunsberger (1965–2002) and Mark Scatterday (2002–). Under Fennell and Hunsberger, the Eastman Wind Ensemble recorded much of the standard repertoire for symphonic band. The West Genesee Wildcat Marching Band of Camillus (Onondaga Co), winner of several national high school championships, has won the New York State Field Band Conference competition, as of 2003, 28 times since the annual event began in 1972. Many towns still have marching bands, pep bands, and small volunteer bands, and there are several prominent concert bands in the state. The Macy's Thanksgiving Day Parade in Manhattan showcases about a dozen of the nation's finest marching bands.

Camus, Raoul. "Bands." In *New Grove Dictionary of American Music,* vol 1, ed. H. Wiley Hitchcock (New York: Macmillan, 1988)

Newsom, Jon. "The American Brass Band Movement," *Quarterly Journal of the Library of Congress* 36 (1979): 114–39

Elliott S. Hurwitt

Bangladeshis. In the 2000 census there were 45,277 New York State residents who identified themselves as born in Bangladesh, 48% of the US total. Nearly 95% lived in the New York City metropolitan area, 59% in Queens (primarily in Woodside, Elmhurst, Ravenswood, Jamaica, and Hillcrest), and 22% in Brooklyn (primarily in Kensington and Windsor Terrace). There are small communities in Albany, Columbia, Monroe, and Rockland Cos. Modest but steadily increasing numbers emigrated from the former Indian state of East Bengal [later East Pakistan and now Bangladesh] to the United States in the first half of the 20th century; far more came after the Immigration Act of 1965. In the 1990s Bangladeshis were among the fastest-growing immigrant groups in New York City. Factors in Bangladesh propelling emigration include professional underemployment, inadequate opportunities for graduate education, and periodic disenfranchisement of minorities. Many men immigrating to New York City stay initially with relatives and bring their wives and children only after establishing themselves.

Bangladeshis have had a diverse work experience in New York State. Immigrants before 1965 were predominantly professionals. In the 1980s and 1990s, male immigrants pioneered or developed several distinctive niches including Indian restaurants, brownstone renovation, and subway newsstand operations. By 2001 there were 7,500 Bangladeshi taxi drivers in New York City (up from a handful in 1990), two-thirds of whom owned their taxicabs. During the 1990s more than 200 Bangladeshis were drawn to Hudson (Columbia Co) to work in the Emsig button factory, which closed in 2002. Some professionals take entry-level jobs while trying to resume work in such fields as medicine, computer science, and university teaching.

Typically, first-generation immigrants remain active in Bangladesh politics. Smaller numbers of US Bangladeshis have sought elective office at the state level, are active in local New York City politics, and have created lobbying groups such as the Bangladesh Caucus to bring their issues to the US Congress. The Bengali language, Bangla, is at the heart of social life. There are at least six weekly newspapers published in New York City, including the *Thikana, Bangla Patrika,* and *Bangalee.* At annual conventions and celebrations of major national days, performances of traditional and modern songs and dances attract wide participation. More specialized groups are organized around particular professions or the regions of Bangladesh.

The Bangladeshi community is predominantly young adult and male. The 2000 census gives the median age as 29 years and the ratio of men to women as 148:100. Bangladeshis are predominantly Muslims, attending about 50 mosques throughout New York City. Between 15 and 20 mosques serve solely Bangladeshi congregations; most of these are located in Astoria, Jamaica, and Brooklyn. Some religious groups provide support to newcomers and classes in Bangla language and culture for children. Bangladeshis have been affected in many ways by the World Trade Center attacks of September 2001. They were among those killed outright, others lost nearby businesses, and as of June 2003 Bangladeshis were still among the post–September 11th detainees. (None have been charged in connection with terrorism, but some have been charged with immigration violations.)

Angell, Dorothy, and Enayetur Rahim. "Bangladeshis in the United States: Community Dynamics and Cultural Continuity." In *Contributions to Bengal Studies: An Interdisciplinary and International Approach,* ed. Enayetur Rahim and Henry Schwarz (Dhaka, Bangladesh: Pustaka, 1998)

Lobo, Arun Peter, Joseph J. Salvo, and Vicky Virgin. *The Newest New Yorkers, 1990–1994* (New York: New York City Department of City Planning, 1996)

Rutherford, Dorothy Angell. "Bengalis in America: Relationship, Affect, Person, and Self among 'Those Away from Home' " (PhD diss, American Univ, 1984)

Dorothy Angell and Enayetur Rahim

Bangor. Town (pop 2,147) in NW Franklin Co. Settled ?1806 from Vermont, the town was formed from Dickinson in 1812. Potatoes were manufactured into starch, and the first such factory was built in 1846; there were eight factories at various times but all closed before World War I. The Northern Railroad (later Rutland Railroad) was built through the town in 1850. Hops were grown in the late 19th century. Bangor became a dairying town with a creamery (1870) and a condensery (1904–47). Refrigerated railroad cars shifted the town's primary product from butter to milk in 1908. The last cheese factory closed in the late 1950s. In the early 21st century Bangor remains a dairying town.

Thomas W. Perrin

Banking Department. The oldest such agency in the nation, the Banking Department regulates and supervises state-chartered or licensed banking entities, including bank holding companies, commercial banks, savings banks, savings and loan associations, safe deposit companies, credit unions, and branches of international banks. It oversees mortgage bankers and brokers, check cashers, licensed lenders, budget planners, and money transmitters. Assets of the 3,400 regulated institutions totaled nearly $2 trillion at the end of 2002.

The emerging banking system of the early 19th century was unstable because of insufficient capitalization, inadequate controls, and political interference. The legislature granted bank charters individually; the recipients were generally selected through party politics and occasionally bribes. Statutes of 1804 and 1818 barred private associations and individuals from banking activities, thus giving chartered banks a lucrative monopoly. Banks issued their own circulating notes, and in many cases the total value of this currency far exceeded a bank's assets. Some fiscal controls were included in bank charters starting in 1816. The legislature in 1825 authorized court appointment of receivers to protect and distribute the assets of insolvent banks. The Revised Statutes of 1828 standardized the powers of newly chartered banks, while the landmark Safety Fund Act of 1829 placed caps on the value of a bank's circulating notes and bills and of its loans and discounts. Banks were required to contribute 3% of their capital to a bank insurance fund, the first in the nation; if a bank failed, the fund would help redeem its banknotes and reimburse its depositors. Banks were to be supervised and regularly examined by bank commissioners appointed by the governor.

After the financial panic of 1837, every bank in the state suspended payments, several large banks failed, and the bank fund was empty. In response, the Free Banking Act of 1838 authorized the granting of a bank charter to anyone who met the requirements of the law, opening the door again to private banks. Newly chartered banks did not contribute to the safety fund but were required to secure their banknotes by depositing a specified proportion of their value, mostly in government bonds, with the state comptroller. The state bank commissioners were abolished in 1843 and regular bank examinations eliminated. The result of free banking was a rapid increase in the number of banks and in the number of bank failures. In 1851 the legislature established a Banking Department headed by a superintendent, who was appointed by the governor with senate approval. The superintendent assumed the responsibility for registering all banknotes and maintaining the engraving plates. As "safety fund" bank charters expired, the banks reincorporated as "free banks." New York State's bank currency had become the strongest in the country, but in 1866, the federal government imposed a tax of up to 10% on state banknotes to support the new national currency (greenbacks). Because note issuance had been one of their main functions, most state banks now failed, closed, or converted to national banks.

State-chartered banks revived after the Civil War because of the steady growth in commercial loans and in regular and checking deposits. The department's jurisdiction and authority were expanded, often in response to financial panics and bank failures. Besides banks, other entities—savings banks (1857), trust companies (1874), and savings and loan associations (1875)—were required to report to the superintendent, who was empowered to examine them periodically. Regular examinations of all banks were authorized in 1884 and of savings and loan associations in 1887. Starting in 1895 the Banking Department incorporated personal loan companies, later called licensed lenders, as an alternative to unscrupulous loan sharks. The financial panic of 1907 prompted legislation limiting the excesses of some trust companies and banks and requiring careful scrutiny of stockholders of new banking organizations. The superintendent also received authority to liquidate insolvent banks, under court supervision. A major recodification of the banking law in 1913 enabled state banks to join the new Federal Reserve System. Superintendent Eugene Lamb Richards recommended and the legislature established in 1914 the Land Bank of the State of New York, a consortium of savings and loan associations that sold bonds and channeled the proceeds into mortgage loans to farmers and homeowners. It became a model for similar federal agencies.

In early 1929 a Moreland Act commission, headed by Robert Moses, recommended still stricter supervision of banking, especially protection for thrift accounts in commercial banks. In 1930 the legislature gave the department more comprehensive examination powers and full jurisdiction over private (unincorporated) banks. In 1932 a Banking Board was established to charter banking organizations, issue organization certificates and licenses, promulgate and enforce regulations for institutions under its control, and advise the superintendent. It is chaired by the superintendent and today has 16 other members appointed by the governor and confirmed by the senate for three-year terms. Eight of the members represent the banking community, and the rest represent the public. While the New York State legislature disregarded Gov Franklin D. Roosevelt's pleas for a law to protect thrift deposits, as president he signed legislation to create the Federal Deposit Insurance Corp (FDIC).

The first branch bank in New York State opened in 1898. The state was divided into nine banking districts in 1934, and banks were limited to opening branches only within their own district. A 1961 law permitted New York City banks to establish suburban branches, and a 1971 law authorized statewide banking branches by 1976. The resulting wave of bank mergers greatly altered the banking landscape. Consumer protection has become a priority. The agency enforces laws banning geographic discrimination in loans, or redlining (1978), and in deposit accounts (1994). In 1997 New York became the first state to designate Banking Development Districts to promote banking services to underserved communities. The Holocaust Claims Processing Office assists survivors and heirs seeking financial restitution from foreign banks. After terrorist attacks in 2001, the Banking Department and federal authorities froze suspect accounts in state-regulated banks.

In 2004 the department had about 570 employees, about 75% of them bank examiners. State-regulated institutions pay fees, which fund the department's budget, about $73 million. The main office is near Wall St in New York City; Albany and Syracuse host branch offices. The Banking Department supervises most foreign banking activity in the United States. Alone among state bank regulators, it maintains overseas offices in London and Tokyo.

See also SAVINGS BANKS.

Dillistin, William H. *Historical Directory of the Banks of the State of New York* (New York: NYS Bankers Association, 1946)

Hubbard, J. T. W. *For Each, the Strength of All: A History of Banking in the State of New York* (New York: New York Univ Press, 1995)

Christine Karpiak

banks. See COMMERCIAL BANKS; SAVINGS BANKS; SECURITIES INDUSTRY.

Baptists. Protestant denomination. Baptists, a nonconformist group related to the Puritans but opposed to infant baptism, emerged in 17th-century England. They came to be distinguished by literal interpretation of Scripture, congregational government, and the ordinance of believers' baptism by immersion. As various Puritan groups migrated to the American colonies in the mid-1600s, Baptists settled in New England and the Middle Colonies from 1638.

Arrival and Expansion

The first Baptists in what is now New York State apparently came from Rhode Island and Connecticut. The first recorded Baptist presence occurred in New York City before 1669 when William Wickenden of Providence, RI, was imprisoned for four months for his beliefs. About 1700 William Rhodes began to preach at Oyster Bay [now in Nassau Co], and in 1712 Nicholas Eyres founded the First Baptist Church in New York City. A third significant Baptist beginning was the creation of a congregation at Middlebush, near Fishkill Baptist Church (Dutchess Co) in 1782.

As tolerance grew for dissenters in the 18th century, more congregations formed, which in turn joined the Philadelphia Baptist Association for broader fellowship. The first association in the state was the New York Association (1791), centered in New York City and the lower Hudson Valley. With the settlement of Central and Western New York, the association in 1796 took on a missionary interest, and Baptists arriving from New England started congregations and formed missionary and evangelical organizations, the first of which were the Lake Baptist Missionary Society (1807) and the Baptist Missionary Society of Western New York (1814). The latter group published one of the earliest missionary journals in the United States, the *Western New York Baptist Magazine* (1814–25). The Baptist churches in the New York City region cooperated in an ecumenical mission directed by Elkanah Holmes to the Seneca and Tuscarora along the Niagara frontier, later forming the New York Baptist Missionary Society. By 1816 there were Baptist congregations in most of the villages along the Mohawk River, with others scattered in Western New York. Domestic Baptist missionaries started churches in the Hudson River valley and along the lakes and rivers of the Adirondack region, although these congregations were historically weak and isolated. Individual Baptist families were attracted to the area, and a colony of Baptists settled at Rush (Monroe Co).

In Central New York, Hamilton (Madison Co) became an epicenter for Baptist activity, which continued for much of the 19th century. The Lake Baptist Missionary Society, formed in 1807 and renamed the Hamilton Baptist Missionary Society in 1808, became in 1825 the Baptist Missionary Convention of the State of New York, representing all of the state's congregations. The convention commissioned John Peck in 1825 as a traveling missionary, the state's first full-time executive Baptist ministerial appointment. In 1819 the Hamilton Literary and Theological Institute (now Colgate University) was founded. The school enjoyed wide support, preparing students for domestic pastoral and mission work as well as overseas assignments. Nathaniel Kendrick, Ebenezer Dodge, William Newton Clarke, Nathaniel Schmidt, and T. J. Conant all taught at Colgate. A number of important overseas missionaries were trained at Colgate or lived there, including William Dean, Jonathan Goble, and Emily C. Judson.

Baptists published scores of tracts and books, many of them printed in Utica by Cephas Bennett, then by the firm of Bennett and Bright in the 1830s and 1840s. Baptist newspapers were published in the 19th century in Albany, Morrisville, Warsaw, Utica, and New York City, such as the *New York Baptist Repository* (1829–30) and the *Examiner* (1865–95). The *Signs of the Times* was started in Middletown (Orange Co) in 1833 and continues today.

Prominent churches were located in Utica (1801), Albany (1811), Rochester (1818), Syracuse (1821), Buffalo (1822), and the New York City area. New York City Baptist ministers, such as John Gano, Spencer H. Cone, Archibald Maclay, Henry L. Morehouse, and, in the 20th century, Harry Emerson Fosdick and Stephen Olford led the denomination nationally. Rochester Baptists in particular grew in numbers and congregations and started a rival to Hamilton in the University of Rochester and Rochester Theological Seminary, both commenced in 1850. Prominent among the Baptist educators in Rochester were Augustus H. Strong, Walter Rauschenbusch, and Helen B. Montgomery. Among the so-called regular, or convention, Baptists, there were approximately 937 congregations with 149,000 members and 10 educational institutions across the state by 1900. This represented the high-water mark of mainstream Baptist unity in New York. From 1900 to the present, the majority of white Baptist congregations have been affiliated with the Northern Baptist Convention, which changed its name to the American Baptist Convention in 1950 and since 1973 has been called the American Baptist Churches of New York State, counting 48,184 members and 329 churches in 2003. Nationally, their affiliation is with the American Baptist Churches in the USA.

Theological and Ethnic Divisions

Issues surrounding local church protectionism, ethnic identity, urban/rural conflicts, polity, the social gospel, and other theological concerns brought great diversity to Baptists in New York. As early as the 1820s, Freewill Baptists migrated from New England and planted churches in Western New York. Close in affinity to the Freewill group were the Free Communion Baptists, formed in the state in the 1830s. The Freewill Baptists and the Free Communion Baptists merged in 1841 to form the Free Baptists and started a biblical school at Whitestown (Oneida Co), which was later moved to New Hampshire. The eminent Arminian theologian, John J. Butler, taught at Whitestown. Some Baptist churches, particularly in the south-central upstate counties, were opposed to missionary and educational activities and loosely identified themselves as Old School, Hard-Shell, or later Primitive Baptists, joining similar coalitions in Maryland and the Ohio Valley in the 1830s. A unique brand of Baptists, the Seventh Day Baptists, originated in England and grew in Rhode Island and New Jersey; they were firmly situated in Allegany Co in the 1830s, and a sabbatarian community, a university, and a theological school were established at Alfred. The Antimasonic movement divided Baptists in western New York State from the 1820s to 1860. More denominational variation occurred along ethnic and racial, as well as theological, lines. The German Baptist churches in the Rochester and Buffalo areas formed associations in cooperation with the 1850 national German Baptist Conference (later North American Baptist Conference). Many of those who were opposed to the theology of the Social Gospel movement and Rochester Seminary in particular in the 1920s and after joined either the General Association of Regular Baptists, the Conservative Baptist Association, or one of several fundamentalist groups, like the Baptist Bible Fellowship, in the mid–20th century. In Binghamton and later in Johnson City (Broome Co), the Practical Bible Training Institute provided theological education for many of these churches, as did Houghton College in Allegany Co and Gordon College in Massachusetts. Beginning in the 1950s Southern Baptists, operating from a support base in Maryland, began mission work in New York City and spread across the state, forming the Baptist Convention in New York, with about 250 churches and 22,000 members in 2000.

Black Baptists formed separate congregations in New York City at Abyssinian (1808) and in Brooklyn Concord (1847), which provided national leaders like Adam Clayton Powell (Sr and Jr) and Samuel D. Proctor and from which came historically black churches in New York, Washington, and Philadelphia. Many of the black churches are affiliated with the National Baptist Convention in the USA, the National Baptist Convention of America, the Progressive National Baptist Convention, the American Baptist Churches in the USA, or with several of these. While pastor at Concord Baptist

Church in Brooklyn, Gardner C. Taylor was a founder with Martin Luther King Jr of the Progressive National Baptist Convention in the USA. Elsewhere in the state, prominent black Baptist congregations are Mount Olivet (1910) and Aenon Missionary (1923) in Rochester, Monumental (1880) in Elmira, Bethany (1887) in Syracuse, and Antioch (1889) in Bedford Hills.

NEW YORK CITY

New York City has been an important venue for Baptist events and organizations. In 1832 the General Missionary Convention of the Baptist Denomination in the United States for Foreign Missions met for its triennial national convention at Oliver Street Baptist Church. At an adjourned session of that meeting, the American Baptist Home Mission Society was founded at Mulberry Street Baptist Church. The American Bible Union, largely under the auspices and patronage of Baptists, was headquartered in New York (1850–*ca* 1880), as were the national offices of the American Baptist Foreign Mission Society (1814–1962). The Ministers and Missionaries Benefit Board, one of the largest religious trusts in the United States, is located at the Interchurch Center, an ecumenical building in Morningside Heights in Upper Manhattan. The Baptist Congress, an international Baptist scholarly forum, met frequently in New York during the late 19th century, and the local city associations of Baptist churches conducted missions to seamen and ethnic populations in New York neighborhoods that became models for other cities and religious groups.

Educational institutions in New York begun or maintained by Baptists include Colgate University (1819), Brockport Collegiate Institute (1841), DeRuyter Institute (1836), Whitestown Seminary (1844), New York Central College (1849), University of Rochester (1850), Marion Collegiate Institute (1855), Alfred University (1857), Pike Seminary (1859), Cook Academy at Montour Falls (1873), Keuka College (1888), Rochester Theological Seminary (1850), the German Baptist Seminary in Rochester (1928), and the Empire State Baptist Seminary at Jamesville (1975). Vassar College was started by a Baptist layman, Matthew Vassar, but it was never officially related to the denomination. Deacon William Colgate (1784–1857) of New York City and his two sons, Samuel and James, underwrote the expenses of many benevolent projects for the denomination statewide. The Samuel Colgate Baptist Historical Collection of the American Baptist Historical Society is located at the Colgate Rochester Divinity School. As of 2000, various types of Baptists in New York State number more than 200,000 and are affiliated with approximately 1,000 churches.

Brackney, William H. *The Baptists* (New York: Greenwood, 1988)

Brooks, C. W. *A Century of Missions in the Empire State* (Philadelphia: American Baptist Publication Society, 1900)

Kane, H. Victor. *The River That Flowed Upstream: The Story of American Baptists in New York State* (Syracuse: American Baptist Churches of NYS, 1982)

William H. Brackney

bar associations. See ASSOCIATION OF THE BAR OF THE CITY OF NEW YORK; NEW YORK STATE BAR ASSOCIATION.

Barber, Samuel (*b* West Chester, Pa, 9 Mar 1910; *d* New York City, 23 Jan 1981). Composer. Barber began composing at age 7 and attended Philadelphia's Curtis Institute of Music (1924). His *Overture to "The School for Scandal"* (1931) and *Music for a Scene from Shelley* (1933) were quickly taken up by famous conductors. In 1938 Arturo Toscanini and the NBC Symphony premiered Barber's *First Essay for Orchestra* and *Adagio for Strings*, which became one of the best loved of all American concert works. From 1943 to 1974 Barber lived in Mount Kisco (Westchester Co) with composer Gian Carlo Menotti. Barber's music, largely tonal and romantic in style, also includes two symphonies; concertos for violin, cello, and piano; a piano sonata (1949); *Knoxville: Summer of 1915* for soprano and orchestra (1947); and the ballet *Medea (The Cave of the Heart)* (1946) written for Martha Graham. Barber had two operas premiered by the Metropolitan Opera, *Vanessa* (1958), with a libretto by Menotti, and *Antony and Cleopatra* (1966), which inaugurated the new opera house at Lincoln Center for the Performing Arts.

Heyman, Barbara. *Samuel Barber: The Composer and His Music* (New York: Oxford Univ Press, 1992)

David Raymond

Bard College. Private college. Founded in Annandale-on-Hudson (Dutchess Co) in 1860 as St. Stephen's College, the school provided a classical education for young men planning to enter Episcopal seminaries. The natural and social sciences were added to the curriculum following Bernard Iddings Bell's appointment as warden in 1919. In 1928 St. Stephen's became an undergraduate college of Columbia University, leading to further innovations: the arts were recognized as integral to undergraduate education, and the classics, though still offered, were no longer required. In 1934 the institution took the name Bard College, honoring John Bard, one of its founders. With enrollment shrinking because of World War II, Bard began admitting female students in 1944, thus ending its relationship with Columbia, which permitted only Barnard College to grant degrees to women. Leon Botstein became president of Bard in 1975. Beginning in the 1980s the school added graduate programs in fine arts, environmental policy, curatorial studies, and decorative arts, and has hosted an annual classical music festival since 1990. It operates two schools that offer college-level programs to students of high school age: Simon's Rock College of Bard in Great Barrington, Mass (acquired in 1979), and Bard High School Early College in New York City (2001). At the start of the 21st century, enrollment stood at 1,200.

Kline, Reamer. *Education for the Common Good: A History of Bard College—The First 100 Years, 1860–1960* (Annandale-on-Hudson, NY: Bard College, 1982)

Annys Wilson

Barge Canal. See ERIE CANAL.

Barker. Town (pop 2,738) in central Broome Co. Barker is on the Tioughnioga River, an important waterway for Native Americans. Settled around 1787, the town was formed from Lisle in 1831. Early industries included lumbering, salt mining, and rope making. The Syracuse, Binghamton and New York Railroad came through in 1854. I-81 was completed through town in 1968. Farming continues, although agriculture has declined in importance.

Charles J. Browne

Barker. Village (pop 577) in Somerset (Niagara Co). Settled in 1815 by David Barker, who, with his family, was active on the Underground Railroad, the locality became a station on the Rome, Watertown and Ogdensburg Railroad (1876). In 1881 building lots were surveyed, and Barker attracted farm-related businesses serving the surrounding fruit-growing region: evaporators, a maker of farm sprays, produce storage, and canneries. The village was incorporated in 1908. The Springville Canning Co (1888) became part of Southland Frozen Foods in 1953, which closed *ca* 2000. The David Barker House (1834) is a landmark.

Nancy B. Mingus

barley. An annual cereal crop of the grass family (Gramineae). Barley, an ancient grain grown in a wide variety of climates and soil conditions, has traditionally been used both for malting in beer production and for animal feed. It is now a minor crop, but New York State was once the leading producer in the nation.

The earliest Dutch settlers introduced the grain to New Netherland. Once settlement in the Mohawk Valley began, New York rose to dominate American barley production. In 1849 nearly 70% of the national crop was produced in the state, with the highest concentration in Onondaga, Cayuga, and Madison Cos. In the 1850s, the state's dominance declined as production increased in California and elsewhere. By 1859 California surpassed New York as the leading producer.

Between 1859 and 1889 barley production in the United States increased from 15 million to 80 million bushels (529 million to 2.8 billion l). Although New York State continued to increase production, the national importance of its crop declined. Barley production was shifting within the state as well, declining in the eastern counties and concentrating in the corridor between Rochester and Syracuse. In 1889 Cayuga, Onondaga, and Ontario Cos produced 25% of the state's barley crop; Cayuga Co alone produced nearly 1 million bushels (35 million l).

By the 1890s the demand for malt from New York State plants exceeded the state's supply of barley, and maltsters were forced to import from Canada. An 1890 tariff raised the price of imported Canadian barley so high that the cost of producing malt in the Midwest and shipping it east was cheaper than producing it in New York from Canadian barley. Having thus lost a significant market, New York State barley farmers cut production from 8.2 million bushels (290 million l) in 1889 to 1.9 million bushels (67 million l) in 1909.

Decline in production brought another geographic shift. In 1910 Cayuga Co continued to lead the state but at less than one-third of its 1890 production level. Farmers in Schoharie, Saratoga, Schenectady, and Rensselaer Cos increased their production tenfold but only temporarily. In the early 1970s, when three malting facilities operated in the state, there was an attempt to revive a market for malting barley. Cornell University plant scientists developed a new malting variety, and a crop was delivered to the plant in Buffalo. Problems with quality and crop failure in a subsequent crop put an end to the experiment. In 1999, 969,000 bushels (34 million l) of New York State barley were harvested, largely for animal feed, and by 2003 there were no commercial malting facilities in the state.

Bidwell, Percy Wells. *The History of Agriculture in the Northern United States: 1620–1860* (New York: P. Smith, 1941)

Weaver, John C. "Barley in the United States: A Historical Sketch," *Geographical Review* 33 (1943): 56–73

Anne M. Derousie

Barnard [née Jenkins], **Hannah** (*b* ?Dutchess Co, ?1754; *d* Hudson, Columbia Co, 27 Nov 1825). Quaker minister. Though possibly born in Nantucket, Mass, she was raised in Dutchess Co. She became a member of Oblong Monthly Meeting in 1772. In 1779 she married Peter Barnard and in 1784 moved with her husband and stepchildren to Hudson. An active member of Hudson Monthly Meeting and an acknowledged minister, she traveled several times to Quaker meetings in New York State and New England between 1793 and 1796. From 1798 to 1801 she traveled as a minister in England and Ireland. While in Britain she publicly expressed disbelief in certain passages of the Old Testament justifying war, the miraculous conception of Jesus, and miracles. London Yearly Meeting, charging her with rejecting the authority of the Bible, silenced her as a minister and asked her to return to America. She returned to Hudson in 1801. Hudson Monthly Meeting silenced her as a minister in 1802 and then, noting her "contentious disposition" and refusal to accept the authority of the meeting, disowned her. Though never rejoining the Society of Friends, she occasionally attended meetings. In 1820 she published *Dialogues on Domestic and Rural Economy* and about the same time helped organize a peace society in Hudson. Though the Barnard controversy of 1801–2 seems to have had only a minor impact on New York Quakers at the time, Barnard was later seen as a precursor of the Hicksite-Orthodox controversy, which divided Quakers in New York State and elsewhere in the 1820s.

Maxey, David W. "New Light on Hannah Barnard, a Quaker Heretic," *Quaker History* 78 (Fall 1989): 61–86

Christopher Densmore

Barnard College. Private women's liberal arts college. Founded in 1889 in New York City and affiliated with Columbia University, Barnard was one of the first schools in the nation to make higher education available to women. The school was named after Frederick A. P. Barnard, president of Columbia College (1864–88), who had labored, but failed, in an effort to make Columbia coeducational. Barnard College's first group of 14 students attended class in a rented brownstone on Madison Ave. Barnard and Columbia moved to their present locations in Morningside Heights in Manhattan in 1897 and established their formal affiliation in 1900. Barnard now occupies a 4-acre (1.6 ha) campus across the street from Columbia University, and Barnard students have open access to the university's facilities and classes. Barnard maintains its own independent administration, faculty, and board of trustees, and has its own endowment. Barnard graduates receive their BA degrees from Columbia University, signed by presidents of both schools. Notable alumnae include Zora Neale Hurston, Jeanne Kirkpatrick, Margaret Mead, and Jacqueline Barton. Undergraduate enrollment in 2003 was 2,297.

White, Marian Churchill. *A History of Barnard College* (New York: Columbia Univ Press, 1954)

Marianne Rahn-Erickson

Barnburners. Democratic Party faction formed in the late 1830s when conflict developed within the party over the state's economic policies. Originally called the Radical wing of the party, the faction was led by former president Martin Van Buren, his son John, Azariah C. Flagg, and Silas Wright. Use of the term Barnburners suggested its members' alleged willingness to burn down the barn (the party) to rid it of its rats (its enemies). Unlike their party opponents, the Hunkers, the Barnburners favored balanced budgets and hard money, and opposed state funding for canal and road construction, a national bank, and the liberal speculative activities of state banks. After the Panic of 1837, they fiercely resisted Whig governor William H. Seward's successful plans, supported by the Hunkers, to use state funds for spending policies, including canal building, aimed at promoting development. Democratic divisions intensified after Martin Van Buren's failed renomination bid in 1844 and new Democratic president James K. Polk's mishandling of the state's factional differences. Polk failed to recognize the Barnburners' election efforts on his behalf, including Wright's successful run for governor, which helped Polk win New York State, and he favored the Hunkers through patronage. In the late 1840s the Barnburners antagonized their Democratic opponents by supporting the Wilmot Proviso, which challenged Polk's attempt to add new slave territory in the West. The state Democratic Party formally split in 1847; thereafter two Democratic organizations fought each other as well as the Whigs. In 1848 the Barnburners joined with antislavery Whigs to form the national Free Soil Party, with Martin Van Buren as its presidential candidate; they opposed the Democrats and Whigs, each of which, Barnburners argued, favored the expansion of slavery. Placing second in New York State, they denied the state to Democratic candidate Lewis Cass, an opponent loathed for contributing to Van Buren's 1844 renomination defeat. In the election aftermath, with Polk gone and the territorial issue being compromised in Congress, the Barnburners and Hunkers began a painful process of reuniting to keep the Whigs at bay. Many Barnburners, however, would join the antislavery Republican Party later in the 1850s.

Cole, Donald B. *Martin Van Buren and the American Political System* (Princeton, NJ: Princeton Univ Press, 1984)

Donovan, Herbert D. A. *The Barnburners* (1925; repr Philadelphia: Porcupine Press, 1974)

Joel H. Silbey

Barnes, William, Jr (*b* Albany, 17 Nov 1866; *d* Mount Kisco, Westchester Co, 25 June 1930). Politician and newspaper publisher. An 1888 Harvard College graduate, Barnes in 1889 acquired control of the *Albany Evening Journal,* a Republican newspaper founded by his grandfather Thurlow Weed. The "boy leader" won control of the Republican Party in Albany in 1891 and subsequently challenged the long-dominant Democratic organization of D. Cady Herrick. Barnes's success in electing a Republican mayor in 1899 led to his increasingly active role in state and national politics, where he aligned himself with Thomas C. Platt, the boss of the state Republican Party. Often at odds both philosophically and personally with such progressive Republicans as Theodore Roosevelt and Charles Evans Hughes, Barnes served as floor manager of the Taft forces at the 1912 national convention and was credited with turning back Roosevelt's challenge. Indeed, Roosevelt attributed his loss of the Republican presidential nomination to "Boss Barnes of Albany, a corrupt boss." Barnes sued Roosevelt for libel. The protracted trial in Syracuse in 1915 attracted national attention, and Barnes was thereafter widely known as Boss Barnes.

Avoiding elective public office, Barnes served as a member of the Republican State Committee (1892–1915) and National Committee (1912–16), and as state chairman (1911–14). His organization controlled the city and county of Albany from 1900 to 1921, although it was the target of legislative investigations following the Democratic resurgence in the state in 1910, and its later years were marked by charges of corruption and Barnes's open hostility to Prohibition, woman suffrage, the direct primary, and organized labor. These issues, coupled with local Republican factionalism, which was exacerbated by Barnes's increasingly long absences from Albany, ultimately led to the election of a Democratic mayor in 1921 and the triumph of the organization headed by Edwin Corning and Daniel P. O'Connell.

Robinson, Frank S. *Machine Politics: A Study of Albany's O'Connells* (New Brunswick, NJ: Transaction Books, 1977)

Robert P. Kerker

Barneveld. Village (pop 332) in Trenton (Oneida Co). Settled in 1793 under the Holland Land Co, it was named Olden Barneveldt and incorporated under that name in 1819; the name was changed to Trenton in 1833. Early industries included a woolen mill, tannery, and foundry. The Black River and Utica Railroad came through in 1855. In 1901 a large commercial carnation greenhouse business was established. The post office and railroad station changed to Barneveld in 1902, and in 1975 the village's name was also changed. In 2003 Sampo (fishing equipment) and Square Stamping (metal sheet for aircraft and automobiles) were employers. Francis Adrian Van der Kemp (1752–1829), a Barneveld resident, was the first to translate New York State's Dutch colonial documents (1817–22).

Barnum, P(hineas) T(aylor) (*b* Bethel, Conn, 5 July 1810; *d* Bridgeport, Conn, 7 Apr 1891). Museum and circus proprietor. Following his tradesman father's death, Barnum moved to Brooklyn at age 16 to become a grocery store clerk. In 1829 Barnum married Charity Hallet and in 1835 launched his career in public amusements by acquiring the services of African-born Joice Heth, who was reportedly 161 years old and George Washington's former nurse. Barnum, though aware these claims about Heth were false, exhibited her throughout New York State and New England as the "Greatest Natural and National Curiosity in the World."

In 1841 Barnum purchased John Scudder's American Museum, located on Broadway and Ann St in New York City, adding to its collection of natural and fabricated curiosities and broadening the enterprise to include a theater, aquarium, science laboratory, freak show, menagerie, and circus. The Feejee Mermaid was one infamous exhibit in the museum's collection: Barnum promoted a fish body sewn to the head of a baboon as the exotic curiosity from the Fiji Islands. The museum's theatrical attractions included a flea circus, ventriloquists, puppet shows—perhaps the first Punch and Judy show in the United States appeared in Barnum's museum—and musical performances by singers such as Jenny Lind. Freak shows featured Charles Stratton, the midget better known as Gen Tom Thumb. By 1847 Barnum's highly successful venture was drawing up to 400,000 visitors a year. But the museum burned in 1865, and Barnum then attempted other amusement businesses with lesser degrees of success until he established his traveling circus.

In 1870 P. T. Barnum's Grand Traveling Museum, Menagerie, Caravan and Circus, featuring freak shows, wild animal acts, and performances by jugglers, fire-eaters, clowns, acrobats, and contortionists, began to journey across the United States and England. In 1873 only weeks after the death of his first wife, Barnum married an English woman 40 years his junior, Nancy Fish, and opened his circus at the New York Hippodrome (later the first Madison Square Garden) on 27th St and Madison Ave in New York City. In 1882 Barnum shipped one of his more notable attractions from England to be exhibited in his US circus. This was Jumbo, an 11 ft 6 in (3.5 m) high and 6.5-ton (5.9 MT) elephant. Jumbo toured North America until he met an untimely death in 1885 when struck by a train. In 1889 the elephant's skeleton was donated to New York City's American Museum of Natural History. Barnum partnered with James Bailey in 1887 to form Barnum and Bailey Circus, which became known as "The Greatest Show on Earth." Barnum died at his home in Bridgeport, Conn. *Barnum,* Cy Coleman's musical comedy based on the showman's life, enjoyed a long run on Broadway in the 1980s, and at the beginning of the 21st century a descendant of Barnum's circus continues to entertain the public.

Barnum, P. T. *Barnum's Own Story* (New York: Dover, 1961)

Kunhardt, P. B., Jr, P. B. Kunhardt III, and P. W. Kunhardt. *P. T. Barnum: America's Greatest Showman* (New York: Knopf, 1995)

Laura Dickstein Thompson

Barre [BAR-RY]. Town (pop 2,124) in S Orleans Co. Settled in 1815, the town was formed from Gaines in 1818. Wheat was its first crop, succeeded by beans; apple orchards were planted after the mid–19th century. Other early industries were potash making, lime burning, and, briefly, threshing machine manufacturing (1830–34). The draining of Barre's muckland began with state appropriations in 1865 and 1867 and was completed between 1900 and 1910 on 3,500 acres (1,420 ha) by Western New York Farms Co, which operated until 1917. In the early 21st century, the muck, now in private ownership, produces lettuce, onions, and potatoes. Pine Hill (742 ft/226 m) is the highest point in the county.

Helen Mathes

barrel jumping. Speed skaters circle an ice rink a few times, gaining enough speed to jump 5–6 feet (1.5–1.8 m) in the air over a row of about a dozen or more barrels. The sport provided entertainment during ice shows or in between speed-skating competitions in the early 20th century. The first barrel-jumping record may have been set in 1925 at Saranac Lake when Edmund Lamy jumped 27 feet 8 inches (8.4 m). Irving Jaffee developed rules and held the first world championship barrel-jumping competition in 1951 at Grossinger's Resort in Liberty (Sullivan Co) in the Catskill Mountains. Jaffee, a New York City native and 1932 Olympic speedskating gold medalist, promoted the sport throughout the country as president of the Amateur Speedskating Union. Barrel jumping gained popularity through the middle and late 20th century, receiving coverage on network television sports broadcasts.

Vehe, Bob. "World Barrel Jumping Championships," *Racing Blade,* Feb 1997

George W. Garner

barrier beaches and islands. Created by water and wind, the barrier beaches of Long Island's South Shore stretch approximately 116 miles (187 km) from the Rockaway Peninsula in Queens and Nassau Cos to Montauk Point in Suffolk Co. The barrier islands are one beach system, consisting of four major islands (Long Beach and Jones Beach in Nassau Co and Fire Island and Westhampton Beach in Suffolk Co), two large sand spits (the Rockaways in Queens and Nassau Cos and Southampton in Suffolk Co), headlands (Southampton to Montauk), and hundreds of small islands. This barrier system constantly shifts, changing over short and long terms. Littoral, or long shore, drift moves sand generally from east to west, while storm waves carry away sand, decreasing the berm, the crest of the beach and natural wall that protects the coast. Gentler waves then deposit sand. Severe storms, such as hurricanes and nor'easters, can breach the dunes, allowing sand to invade bayside marshes, eventually causing barriers to migrate shoreward.

The beauty of the barrier islands has proved irresistible to people who come as visitors to national, state, and county parks or as seasonal and permanent residents. Jones Beach State Park (1929) offers amenities from water sports to summer music concerts and attracts more than 7 million visitors each year. Fire Island National Seashore (1964), which encompasses 80% of Fire Island, contains the 1,300-acre (526 ha) Otis Pike Wilderness Area, the only such federally protected preserve in New York State. The islands and beaches west of Jones Inlet in Nassau Co and east of Moriches Inlet in Suffolk Co are primarily residential areas, excluding Montauk Point, a state park (1924) protected from development.

Development on the barrier beaches has created controversy through the beginning of the 21st century. Houses built on dunes alter the physical environment, and subsequent attempts to stabilize beaches with groins, bulkheads, and revetments cause down-drift erosion. In addition, the tangle of federal, state, and local laws, and homeowners and environmental groups with opposing agendas make it difficult to manage the barrier system consistently. These issues reflect competing approaches to nature—one accepting the force of nature and the other depending on technology to preserve property—that must be balanced to protect the barrier beaches.

Leatherman, Stephen P., Sandra E. Shumway, and Douglas W. Christel. *The Hampton's South Shore: A History of Beach Changes and Storm Impacts* (Southampton, NY: Eastern Long Island Coastal Conservation Alliance; Southampton College of Long Island Univ, 1999)

McCormick, Larry R., et al. *Living with Long Island's South Shore* (Durham, NC: Duke Univ Press, 1984)

Marsha Hamilton

Barrington. Town (pop 1,396) in S central Yates Co. Permanent settlement began in 1799, and the town was formed from Wayne (Steuben Co) in 1822. Crystal Spring was discovered in 1865 when attempts were made to drill for oil. A hotel was built, and building lots were surveyed. After the Civil War grapes were grown near Keuka Lake, along with peaches, apples, and berries. In 1894 the town had 85 vineyards. Much of Barrington's recent population growth (85% increase between 1960 and 2000) is due to an influx of Groffdale Conference Mennonites from Pennsylvania beginning around 1980. About 50% of Barrington is in forest with many steep slopes. The rest is composed of family farms and lakefront cottages, with several wineries. Barrington is the site of the Windmill Farm and Craft Market, which draws up to 10,000 visitors each Saturday in season.

Gwen Chamberlain

Barry, Patrick (*b* near Belfast, Ireland, 24 May 1816; *d* Rochester, 23 June 1890). Horticulturist and nurseryman. At the age of 18 Barry became a teacher in one of the Irish national public schools. Immigrating to New York City in 1836, he found work in Flushing (Queens Co) as a clerk in William Prince's Linnaean Botanic Garden, a leading nursery firm in antebellum America. In 1840 he joined George Ellwanger as co-partner in the Mount Hope Botanical and Pomological Gardens in Rochester. Together Ellwanger and Barry created the 19th century's premier wholesale nursery business in North America.

As editor of the *Genesee Farmer* (1845–55) and the *Horticulturalist: A Journal of Rural Art and Rural Taste* (1852–55), Barry established his reputation as a leading advocate for improvements in horticulture and pomology, in particular. In 1851 he published *The Fruit Garden,* a practical guide for the home gardener that continued in print until 1915. For the American Pomological Society in 1862, Barry prepared *A Catalogue of Fruits, for Cultivation in the United States and Canadas,* the authoritative source on the classification of fruit varieties for the remainder of the century. From 1864 until his death Barry served as president of the Western New York Horticultural Society. To improve the competitive advantage of New York State fruit growers, he advocated scientific improvement of fruit varieties. He served on the original Board of Control (1882) of the New York State Agricultural Experiment Station in Geneva (Ontario Co).

Grebinger, Paul, and Ellen M. Grebinger. "George Ellwanger, Patrick Barry, and the Ellwanger and Barry Mount Hope Nurseries." In *Pioneers of American Landscape Design,* ed. Charles A. Birnbaum and Robin Karson (New York: McGraw-Hill, 2000)

Paul Grebinger

Barton. Town (pop 9,066) in SW Tioga Co. Settled in 1791, the town was formed from Tioga in 1824. The early economy was based on the timber and tanning industries. Most farming was concentrated in the valleys. The Erie Railroad came through in 1849, and the Southern Central Railroad in 1872. Feed for farm livestock and birds was produced by the Tioga Mill and Elevator Co (later Tioga Mills) from 1908 to 1973. For a number of years starting in 1938, the J. E. Ranch served as winter quarters for rodeos that toured nationally. Most residents commute to Sayre, Pa, Elmira, or the Triple Cities metropolitan region (Binghamton, Endicott, and Johnson City in Broome Co).

Joann Lindstrom

Baruch College. Public college. The College of the City of New York introduced business courses in 1907; an expanded business curriculum led to the establishment of the college's School of Business and Civic Administration at 17 Lexington Ave and East 23d St in 1919. It was renamed for financier Bernard Baruch, an 1889 City College graduate, in 1953. The Baruch School of Business and Civic Administration of City College was elevated to a separate four-year college within the City University of New York (CUNY) system in 1968. The institution administers the CUNY doctoral program in business and also offers degree programs through its schools of arts and sciences and public affairs. The institution has offered extensive continuing education programs, including a Division of Vocational Subjects and Civic Administration that offered courses to prepare candidates for Civil Service examinations. As of 2001 Baruch College's Zicklin School of Business had the largest undergraduate enrollment of any collegiate school of business in the nation (10,995). Baruch's vertical campus (2001), which covers the block from 24th St to 25th St between Lexington and Third Aves near Gramercy Park, received the 2003 Honor Award from the American Institute of Architects. In fall 2002 Baruch enrolled 12,653 undergraduate and 2,708 graduate students.

Berrol, Selma. *Getting Down to Business: Baruch College in the City of New York, 1847–1987* (New York: Greenwood, 1987)

Barbara J. Dunlap

Baryshnikov, Mikhail (*b* Riga, Latvia, 27 Jan 1948). Dancer and choreographer. Baryshnikov studied at the Riga Dance School starting in 1959 and then with Alexander Pushkin at Leningrad's Vaganova School (1964–67), developing an impeccably pure classical technique. He joined the Kirov company in 1967. Defecting during a Toronto stay in 1974, his first appearance in New York City was with former Kirov dancer Natalia Makarova in the American Ballet Theatre production of *Giselle.* From 1974 to 1976 he danced worldwide in some 26 roles, including *Push Comes to Shove* (1976) and *Once More, Frank* (1976), his first collaborations with choreographer Twyla Tharp, and also with Makarova in Jerome Robbins's *Other Dances* (1976). His primary affiliation was with the American Ballet Theatre, where his partnership with Gelsey Kirkland gave new life to the classics. He choreographed the troupe in a full-length *Nutcracker* for television in 1976 and in a new production of *Don Quixote* (1978).

Seeking new challenges and movement idioms, Baryshnikov worked with Martha Graham, Paul Taylor, and Alvin Ailey, and in 1978, to learn the Balanchine repertoire, danced one season with the New York City Ballet. His film credits include Herbert Ross's ballet film *The Turning Point* (1977) with Shirley MacLaine and Ann Bancroft, for which he received an Oscar nomination, and *White Nights* (1985) with Gregory Hines (1946–2003). In 1980 he returned to American Ballet Theatre as its artistic director and principal dancer. He expanded the repertoire with the work of choreographers such as Merce Cunningham, Eliot Feld, Martha Graham, Jiri Kylian, and Paul Taylor, and restored works by August Bournonville and Sir Frederick Ashton. In 1989 he left American Ballet Theatre and in 1990 founded the White Oak Dance Project with choreographer Mark Morris to bring modern dance to new audiences.

Aria, Barbara. *Misha: The Mikhail Baryshnikov Story* (New York: St. Martin's Press, 1989)

Anya Peterson Royce

baseball. Although historians have debunked the myth that West Point cadet Abner Doubleday invented baseball in 1839 on a dirt field near Cooperstown (Otsego Co), they continue to debate whether New York State is the true birthplace of modern baseball. Beyond dispute is the state's significant role in the evolution of the sport from the European games of rounders and cricket. Newspaper accounts from as far back as 25 Apr 1823 indicate that an organized version of baseball was being played in Manhattan, and there are reports of a game similar in style emerging in Rochester, Syracuse, Buffalo, and other areas of the state, both urban and rural, during the same period. As the 19th century progressed, New Yorkers found themselves with more leisure time, and they wanted a pastime they could call their own, rather than a holdover game from the days of British rule. Initially, baseball was an elite game played by businessmen and politicians. In time, though, the sport's popularity spread to the masses, with games being played in urban parks and streets throughout the state.

The Early Amateur Game

Alexander J. Cartwright, a New York City bank employee, is regarded by many as the father of the modern game. Cartwright organized the Knickerbocker Base Ball Club in 1845 and is credited with codifying rules such as the diamond-shaped infield with pitcher in the center and the standard distance of 90 feet between bases. The first game using these rules took place on 19 June 1846 at Elysian Fields in Hoboken, NJ, and involved two New York City teams. Word spread throughout the baseball world, and Cartwright's rules became standard in the sport. During the next 15 years more than 60 baseball clubs sprang up in the New York City area. There was parallel growth in cities like Rochester, where teams were organized according to neighborhood, vocation, and race. In 1866 Rochester fielded an all-black team probably featuring the son of the former slave and abolitionist leader Frederick Douglass. In the early years of baseball, many towns and cities had no official playing fields, so players, to the annoyance of many, would turn public squares and quiet neighborhoods into ball diamonds. In 1845 baseball had become so popular in Syracuse that city officials banned the sport from Clinton and Hanover Squares because it caused too much congestion.

Baseball of Abner Graves on display at the National Baseball Hall of Fame and Museum in Cooperstown. Graves, of nearby Fly Creek, was a major proponent of the theory that Abner Doubleday invented baseball.

New York State newspapers contributed to the sport's growth. In the late 1850s Henry "Father" Chadwick, an Englishman and former cricket standout, became the first reporter to give baseball serious coverage, disseminating reports to various New York City newspapers. He is credited with coining the term "national pastime" and with inventing the box score, a statistical summary of games. Chadwick later wrote the first hardcover book about the sport, *The Game of Base Ball* (1868), and was instrumental in significant rule changes and the development of several individual statistical categories that are still in use. In 1938 Chadwick would become the only writer voted into the regular wing of the National Baseball Hall of Fame in Cooperstown.

Organization and Professionalization

The National Association of Base Ball Players, the game's first governing body, was formed in 1858. Cartwright's rules were tweaked slightly. It was decided that games would end after nine innings rather than when a team reached 21 aces (runs), and balls caught on the first bounce would no longer be considered outs. The dramatic growth in the game's popularity came at a cost. On 20 July 1858 the first admission fee (50¢) was charged to watch a contest between the New York All-Stars and Brooklyn All-Stars at the Fashion Race Course in what is now Corona (Queens Co). Two years later the Brooklyn Excelsiors embarked on what is believed to be baseball's first extensive road trip, a 10-day tour involving contests in Albany, Troy, Buffalo,

PROFESSIONAL BASEBALL TEAMS IN NEW YORK STATE, FROM 1871

Yrs in League	Team	League
Albany (Albany-Colonie)		
1877	Nolans	LA
1879	—	NA
1881	Capital City	EL
1885	Senators	NYSL
1886	—	HRL
1888	Governors	IL
1890	Senators	NYSL
1891–93	Senators	EL
1895	Senators	NYSL
1896	Senators	EL
1899–1916	Senators	NYSL
1920–32	Senators	EL
1932–36	Senators	IL
1937	Senators	NYPL
1938–59	Senators	EL
1983–84	A's	EL
1985–94	Yankees	EL
1995–98	Diamond Dogs	NEL
1999–2002	Diamond Dogs	NOL
Amsterdam (Montgomery Co)		
1894	—	NYSL
1895	Red Stockings	NYSL
1938–42	Rugmakers	CAL
1946–51	Rugmakers	CAL
Amsterdam-Johnstown-Gloversville		
1902	Jags	NYSL
1903–4	Hyphens	NYSL
1905–8	Jags	NYSL
Auburn (Cayuga Co)		
1877	—	LA
1879	—	NA
1888–89	Maroons	NYSL
1897–98	Maroons	NYSL
1899	Prisoners	NYSL
1905–7	—	ESL
1938	Bouleys	CAL
1940	Colts	CAL
1946–50	Cayugas	BL
1951	Falcons	BL
1958–61	Yankees	NYPL
1962–66	Mets	NYPL
1966–	Doubledays	NYPL
1967–71	Twins	NYPL
1972–77	Phillies	NYPL
1978	Sunsets	NYPL
1979	Red Stars	NYPL
1980	Americans	NYPL
1982–95	Astros	NYPL
Babylon (Suffolk Co)		
1885	Argyle Hotel Athletics	AAI
Batavia (Genesee Co)		
1897	Reds	NYSL
1939–53	Clippers	PONYL
1957–59	Indians	NYPL
1961–65	Pirates	NYPL
1966–87	Trojans	NYPL
1988–97	Clippers	NYPL
1998–	Muckdogs	NYPL
Bath (Steuben Co)		
1890	—	WNYL
Binghamton		
1877	—	LA
1885	Bingoes	NYSL
1886–87	Crickets	IL
1888	Crickets	CL
1892–94	Bingoes	EL
1895	Crickets	NYSL
1899	Bingoes	NYSL
1900	Crickets	NYSL
1901–17	Bingoes	NYSL
1918–19	Bingoes	IL
1923–37	Triplets	NYPL
1938–63	Triplets	EL
1964–66	Triplets	NYPL
1967–68	Triplets	EL
1992–	Mets	EL
Brooklyn		
1872	**Eckfords**	NA
1872–75	**Atlantics**	NA
1877	Chelseas	LA
1881–82	Trolley-Dodgers	EA
1883	Grays	INA
1884	Greys	EA
1884	**Atlantics**	AA
1885–87	**Grays**	AA
1888–89	**Bridegrooms**	AA
1890	**Bridegrooms**	NL
1890	**Ward's Wonders**	PL
1890	**Gladiators**	AA
1891–95	**Grooms**	NL
1896–98	**Bridegrooms**	NL
1899–1910	**Superbas**	NL
1905–22	Royal Giants	AAI
1911–12	**Dodgers**	NL
1913	**Superbas**	NL
1914–31	**Robins**	NL
1914–15	**Tip-tops**	FL
1923–27	Royal Giants	ECL
1932–57	**Dodgers**	NL
1933	Royal Giants	NNL
1934–41	Royal Giants	AAI
2001–	Cyclones	NYPL
Buffalo		
1877	—	LA
1878	Bisons	IA
1879–85	**Bisons**	NL
1886–90	Bisons	IL
1891–98	Bisons	EL
1899	Bisons	WL
1900	Bisons	AL
1901–11	Bisons	EL
1912–70	Bisons	IL
1914	**Buffeds**	FL
1915	**Blues**	FL
1979–84	Bisons	EL
1985–97	Bisons	AA
1998–	Bisons	IL
Canandaigua (Ontario Co)		
1888–89	—	NYSL
1897–98	Rustlers	NYSL
Canastota (Madison Co)		
1888	—	CNYL
Canisteo (Steuben Co)		
1890	—	WNYL
Catskill (Greene Co)		
1903	—	HRL
Celeron (Chautauqua Co)		
1894	—	NYSL
1898	Acme Colored Giants	IOL
Cobleskill (Schoharie Co)		
1890	Giants	NYSL
Constableville (Lewis Co)		
1888	—	CNYL
Corning (Steuben Co)		
1951–52	A's	PONYL
1953	Independents	PONYL
1954–56	Red Sox	PONYL
1957–58	Red Sox	NYPL
1959	Cor-Sox	NYPL
1960	Red Sox	NYPL
1968–69	Royals	NYPL
Cortland		
1888	—	CNYL
1897–1901	Wagonmakers	NYSL
1905	—	ESL
1910	—	CNYL
Dunkirk (Chautauqua Co)		
1890	Dandies	NYPL
1898	—	IOL
Elmira		
1885	Colonels	NYSL
1888	Babies	CNYL
1889	—	NYSL
1891	Gladiators	NYPL
1892	Gladiators	EL
1895	Maple Cities	NYSL
1900	—	ATL
1900	Pioneers	NYSL
1908–17	Colonels	NYSL
1923	Red Jackets	NYPL
1924–31	Colonels	NYPL
1932–34	Red Wings	NYPL
1935–36	Pioneers	NYPL
1937	Colonels	NYPL
1938–55	Pioneers	EL
1957–61	Pioneers	NYPL
1962–70	Pioneers	EL
1971	Royals	EL
1972	Pioneers	EL
1973–95	Pioneers	NYPL
1996–98	Pioneers	NEL
1999–	Pioneers	NOL
Fishkill (Dutchess Co)		
1994–	Hudson Valley Renegades	NYPL
Fulton (Oswego Co)		
1905–7	—	ESL
Geneva (Ontario Co)		
1897	—	NYSL
1905–7	—	ESL
1910	—	CNYL
1947	Red Birds	BL
1948–51	Robins	BL
1958–62	Redlegs	NYPL
1963–68	Senators	NYPL
1969	Pirates	NYPL
1970–72	Senators	NYPL

PROFESSIONAL BASEBALL TEAMS IN NEW YORK STATE, FROM 1871 (continued)

Yrs in League	Team	League
1973	Twins	NYPL
1977–93	Cubs	NYPL
Glens Falls (Warren Co)		
1980–85	White Sox	EL
1986–88	Tigers	EL
1993	Red Birds	NYPL
1995–98	Adirondack Lumberjacks	NEL
1999–	Adirondack Lumberjacks	NOL
Glens Falls–Saratoga Springs		
1906	—	HRL
Gloversville (Fulton Co)		
1895	Mitten Makers	NYSL
1937	Glovers	CAL
Gloversville-Johnstown		
1890	Jays	NYSL
1908	Jags	NYSL
1938–42	Glovers	CAL
1946–51	Glovers	CAL
Haverstraw (Rockland Co)		
1888	—	HRL
Hornell (Steuben Co)		
1878	Hornells	IA
1890	—	WNYL
1906	Pigmies	INL
1914	Green Sox	INL
1915	Maple Leafs	INL
1942–47	Maples	PONYL
1948–49	Maple Leafs	PONYL
1950–56	Dodgers	PONYL
1957	Redlegs	NYPL
Hudson (Columbia Co)		
1886	—	HRL
1903–7	Marines	HRL
Ilion (Herkimer Co)		
1901–4	Typewriters	NYSL
1905	—	ESL
Islip (Suffolk Co)		
2000–	Long Island Ducks	ATL
Jamestown (Chautauqua Co)		
1890–91	—	NYPL
1905	Hill Climbers	NYPL
1906	Oseejays	NYPL
1914	Giants	NYPL
1915	Rabbits	NYPL
1939	Jaguars	NYPL
1940–56	Falcons	NYPL
1957	Falcons	NYPL
1961–65	Tigers	NYPL
1966	Dodgers	NYPL
1967	Braves	NYPL
1968–72	Falcons	NYPL
1973	Expos	NYPL
1977–93	Expos	NYPL
1994–	Jammers	NYPL
Kingston (Ulster Co)		
1886	—	HRL
1888	—	HRL
1903–6	Colonials	HRL
1907	Colonial Colts	HRL
1913	Colonials	NYNJL
1947	Dodgers	NATL
1948	Hubs	COL
1949–50	Colonials	COL
1951	Colonials	CAL
Little Falls (Herkimer Co)		
1977–88	Mets	NYPL
1995	Mohawk Valley Landsharks	NEL
Lockport (Niagara Co)		
1942	White Sox	PONYL
1943–44	Cubs	PONYL
1945	White Sox	PONYL
1946	Cubs	PONYL
1947–50	Reds	PONYL
1951	Locks	MAL
Lowville (Lewis Co)		
1888	—	CNYL
Lyons (Wayne Co)		
1897–98	—	NYSL
1905	—	ESL
1907	—	ESL
Malone (Franklin Co)		
1887	—	NENL
Maspeth (Queens Co)		
1886	Long Island A's	EL
Massena (St. Lawrence Co)		
1936	Grays	CAL
Middletown (Orange Co)		
1913	Middies	NYNJL
1914	Middies	ATL
Mountaindale (Sullivan Co)		
1995	Sullivan Mountain Lions	NEL
1996	Catskill Cougars	NATL
1997–98	Catskill Cougars	NEL
2000	Catskill Cougars	NOL
Newark (Wayne Co)		
1968–79	Co-Pilots	NYPL
1983–87	Orioles	NYPL
1995–96	Barge Bandits	NATL
Newburgh (Orange Co)		
1886	Cobblestone Throwers	HRL
1903–5	Taylor-mades	HRL
1906	Hill Climbers	HRL
1907	Hillies	HRL
1913	Dutchmen	NYNJL
1914	Hillclimbers	ATL
1946	Hummingbirds	NATL
1995–96	Nighthawks	NEL
1998	Black Diamonds	ATL
New York		
1871–75	**Mutuals**	NA
1876	**Mutuals**	NL
1881	Metropolitans	EA
1883–84	**Gothams**	NL
1883–87	**Metropolitans**	AA
1885–1957	**Giants**	NL
1887	Gorhams	NCL
1888–91	Gorhams	AAI
1890	**Giants**	PL
1896	Metropolitans	ATL
1903–12	**Highlanders**	AL
1911–22	Lincoln Giants	AAI
1912	Knickerbockers	USL
1913–	**Yankees**	AL
1914–16	Lincoln Stars	AAI
1916–22	Cuban Stars East	AAI
1917–19	Pennsylvania Red Caps	AAI
1923–26	Lincoln Giants	ECL
1923–28	Cuban Stars East	ECL
1927	Lincoln Giants	AAI
1928	Lincoln Giants	ECL
1929	Cuban Stars East	ANL
1929	Lincoln Giants	ANL
1930	Lincoln Giants	AAI
1932–35	Black Yankees	AAI
1935–36	Cubans	NNL
1936–48	Black Yankees	NNL
1939–48	Cubans	NNL
1949–50	Black Yankees	AAI
1949–50	Cubans	NAL
1962–	**Mets**	NL
Niagara Falls		
1908	—	IL
1939–40	Rainbows	PONYL
1946–47	Frontiers	MAL
1950–51	Citizens	MAL
1970–79	Pirates	NYPL
1982–85	Sox	NYPL
1989–93	Rapids	NYPL
1995	Mallards	NATL
Norwich (Chenango Co)		
1888	—	CNYL
Nyack (Rockland Co)		
1946–48	Rocklands	NATL
Ogdensburg (St. Lawrence Co)		
1936–39	Colts	CAL
1940	Senators	CAL
1946–51	Maples	BL
Olean (Cattaraugus Co)		
1891	—	NYPL
1898	—	IOL
1905–7	Refiners	INL
1908	Candidates	INL
1914	Refiners	INL
1915–16	White Sox	INL
1939–51	Oilers	PONYL
1952–53	Yankees	PONYL
1954	Giants	PONYL
1955–56	Oilers	PONYL
1957–58	Oilers	NYPL
1959	A's	NYPL
1961–62	Red Sox	NYPL
Oneida (Madison Co)		
1888	—	CNYL
1889	—	NYSL
1905	—	ESL
1910	—	CNYL

continued on page 156

PROFESSIONAL BASEBALL TEAMS IN NEW YORK STATE, FROM 1871 (continued)

Yrs in League	Team	League
Oneonta (Otsego Co)		
1890	Indians	NYSL
1924	Indians	NYPL
1940–42	Indians	CAL
1946–51	Red Sox	CAL
1966	Red Sox	NYPL
1967–98	Yankees	NYPL
1999–	Tigers	NYPL
Ossining (Westchester Co)		
1903	—	HRL
Oswego		
1885	Sweegs	NYSL
1886–87	Starchboxes	IL
1888	—	EIL
1898	Starchmakers	NYSL
1899	Oswegos	NYSL
1900	Grays	NYSL
1905–7	Starchmakers	ESL
1910	—	CNYL
1936–40	Netherlands	CAL
Palmyra (Wayne Co)		
1897–1898	Mormons	NYSL
1905	—	ESL
Peekskill (Westchester Co)		
1888	—	HRL
1903	—	HRL
1905	—	HRL
1946–49	Highlanders	NATL
Penn Yan (Yates Co)		
1888	—	NYSL
1906	—	ESL
Plattsburgh		
1907	Brewers	NHSL
Port Chester (Westchester Co)		
1947–48	Clippers	COL
Poughkeepsie		
1886	—	HRL
1894	—	NYSL
1903–7	Colts	HRL
1913	Honey Bugs	NYNJL
1914	Honey Bugs	ATL
1947	Giants	COL
1948–50	Chiefs	COL
Queens		
2000	Kings	NYPL
Rochester		
1855	Flour Cities	NYSL
1877–78	Red Wings	IA
1879	Red Wings	NA
1886–87	Maroons	IL
1888–89	Jingoes	IL
1890	**Hop Bitters**	AA
1891–92	Hop Bitters	EL
1895–96	Browns	EL
1897	Blackbirds	EL
1898	Patriots	EL
1899–1911	Bronchos	EL
1912–20	Hustlers	IL
1921	Colts	IL
1922–27	Tribe	IL
1928–	Red Wings	IL
Rome (Oneida Co)		
1898	Noble Romans	NYSL
1899–1901	Romans	NYSL
1905	—	ESL
1910	—	CNYL
1937–42	Colonels	CAL
1946–51	Colonels	CAL
Rouses Point (Clinton Co)		
1895	—	EIL
Saratoga Springs		
1886	—	HRL
Saugerties (Ulster Co)		
1903–5	—	HRL
Schenectady		
1895	Electrics	NYSL
1899–1902	Electricians	NYSL
1903	Frog Alleys	NYSL
1904	Electricians	NYSL
1913–15	Mohawk Giants	AAI
1946–50	Blue Jays	CAL
1951–57	Blue Jays	EL
Seneca Falls (Seneca Co)		
1888–89	Maroons	NYSL
1905–7	—	ESL
Staten Island		
1999–	Yankees	NYPL
Syracuse		
1877	Stars	LA
1878	Stars	IA
1879	**Stars**	NL
1885	Stars	NYSL
1886–89	Stars	IL
1890	**Stars**	AA
1891–92	Stars	EL
1894–1901	Stars	EL
1902–17	Stars	NYSL
1918	Stars	IL
1920–27	Stars	IL
1928–29	Stars	NYPL
1934–55	Chiefs	IL
1956–57	Chiefs	EL
1961–96	Chiefs	IL
1997–	SkyChiefs	IL
Troy (Rensselaer Co)		
1871–72	**Haymakers**	NA
1877	—	LA
1879–82	**Trojans**	NL
1886	Trojans	HRL
1888	Trojans	IL
1890	Trojans	NYSL
1891–93	Trojans	EL
1894	Washer Women	EL
1895	Collars	NYSL
1899–1900	Washerwomen	NYSL
1901–16	Trojans	NYSL
2002	Tri-City Valley Cats	NYPL
Utica		
1878	Utes	IA
1879	—	NA
1885	Pentups[a]	NYSL
1886	Pentups	IL
1887	Pent Ups	IL
1889	Pentups	NYSL
1898–1900	Pentups	NYSL
1901–9	Pent-Ups	NYSL
1910–17	Utes	NYSL
1924	Utes	NYPL
1939–42	Braves	CAL
1943	Braves	EL
1944–50	Blue Sox	EL
1977–80	Blue Jays	NYPL
1981–2001	Blue Sox	NYPL
Walden (Orange Co)		
1946	Hummingbirds	NATL
Waterloo (Seneca Co)		
1888	—	NYSL
Watertown		
1888	—	CNYL
1936	Bucks	CAL
1946–51	Athletics	BL
1983–88	Pirates	NYPL
1989–98	Indians	NYPL
Waverly (Chemung/Tioga Cos)		
1901	Wagonmakers	NYSL
Wellsville (Allegany Co)		
1914–16	Rainmakers	INL
1942–46	Yankees	PONYL
1947–49	Nitros	PONYL
1950	Senators	PONYL
1951–52	Rockets	PONYL
1953–56	Braves	PONYL
1957–61	Braves	NYPL
1963–65	Red Sox	NYPL
Yonkers		
1888	—	HRL
1905	—	HRL
1907	—	HRL
1995	Hoot Owls	NEL

Minor League Abbreviations

AA	American Association (1902–62, 1969–97)
AL	American League (1900)
ATL	Atlantic League
BL	Border League
CAL	Canadian-American League
CL	Central League
CNYL	Central New York League
COL	Colonial League
EA	Eastern Association
EIL	Eastern International League
EL	Eastern League
ESL	Empire State League
HRL	Hudson River League
IA	International Association
IL	International League
INA	Interstate Association
INL	Interstate League
IOL	Iron and Oil League
LA	League Alliance
MAL	Middle Atlantic League
NA	National Association (1879–80)
NATL	North Atlantic League
NEL	Northeast League
NENL	Northeastern League
NHSL	New Hampshire State League

PROFESSIONAL BASEBALL TEAMS IN NEW YORK STATE, FROM 1871 (continued)

Minor League Abbreviations (cont.)

NOL	Northern League
NYNJL	New York–New Jersey League
NYPL	New York–Pennsylvania League
NYSL	New York State League
PONYL	PONY League
USL	United States League
WL	Western League
WNYL	Western New York League

Major League Abbreviations

AA	American Association (1882–91)
AL	American League (1901–)
FL	Federal League
NA	National Association (1871–75)
NL	National League
PL	Players League

Negro League Abbreviations

AAI	African American Independent
ANL	American Negro League
ECL	Eastern Colored League
NAL	Negro American League
NCL	National Colored League
NNL	Negro National League

Sources: Baseball-Reference.com, http://www.baseball-reference.com; P. Filichia, *Professional Baseball Franchises* (1992); L. Johnson and M. Wolff, *The Encyclopedia of Minor League Baseball,* 2d ed. (1997); Mike McCann's Minor League Baseball Page, http://www.geocities.com/big_bunko/total.htm; Negro League Baseball Players Association, http://www.nlbpa.com; J. A. Riley, *Biographical Encyclopedia of the Negro Baseball Leagues* (1994).

Notes: List is sorted alphabetically by city designation, then chronologically by league and use of team name. Major League team names are in bold. Table includes independent, nonleague African American (AAI) teams of major-league caliber, as listed by Riley.

[a]Utica used several variations for this team's name.

Compiled by Dan Streever

Rochester, and Newburgh. "The Star Spangled Banner" was played before a game at the Union Base Ball Grounds in Brooklyn on 15 May 1862, the first time the future national anthem was performed at a sporting event. During this time fenced parks became the rule among leading teams, and although clubs were supposed to be made up solely of amateurs, highly skilled players began receiving money under the table. Gambling became a growing problem among fans, and there were instances of umpires, players, and managers receiving bribes. The National Association, whose membership had ballooned to 300 clubs by 1867, could stop neither the gambling nor the game's inexorable movement toward professionalism. In 1869 the New York Mutuals became the first baseball team to pay all of its starters, but by the end of the year the Cincinnati Red Stockings were paying every player on the roster. Stocked with top talent and nearly unbeatable, the Red Stockings went on a barnstorming tour that included stops in New York State. They were finally defeated by the Atlantics, 8-7, in front of a large crowd in Brooklyn on 14 June 1870.

During the latter part of the 19th century, the presence of women at ballparks was tolerated and occasionally encouraged. On 16 June 1883 the first "ladies' day" in baseball history was hosted by the New York Gothams at the original Polo Grounds north of Central Park. Women were admitted free. Owners hoped more female fans would result in heftier gate receipts and have a calming effect on crowds that occasionally became unruly. Many of the first female players were college students. In 1866 students at Vassar College, an all-women's school in Poughkeepsie, formed two teams. By 1879 the campus league comprised seven clubs. But ballplaying was viewed as an inappropriate activity for Victorian era females, and social mores put an end to their league before the arrival of the 20th century. "Bloomer Girls" teams formed in the 1890s and despite the name generally fielded both male and female players. The New York Bloomer Girls (1910–33) traveled from town to town, challenging men's amateur and semiprofessional teams. These exhibition teams were the forerunners of the Colorado Silver Bullets, an all-female touring professional team that played several games against men's amateur teams in cities throughout New York State in the 1990s.

Birth of the Major Leagues

On 17 Mar 1871 a meeting at Collier's Café in Lower Manhattan led to the formation of the National Association of Professional Base Ball Players, hastening the demise of the sport's amateur governing body founded 13 years earlier. The professional association is considered the first major league, and it included three teams from the New York City area—the New York Mutuals (1871–75), Brooklyn Atlantics (1872–75), and Brooklyn Eckfords (1872)—as well as the Troy Haymakers (1871–72). In 1876 a group of owners formed the National League of Professional Baseball Clubs, better known today simply as the National League. Three upstate franchises played in the league: the Buffalo Bisons (1879–85), Syracuse Stars (1879), and Troy Trojans (1879–82). A New York City team called the Gothams joined in 1883 and, renamed the Giants in 1885, won titles in 1888 and 1889. In 1883 another major league, called the American Association, was established. The New York Metropolitans had the league's best record in 1884 but lost the first World Series to the National League champions. The Brooklyn franchise won the league title (as the Bridegrooms) in 1889 before jumping to the National League. There the Bridegrooms claimed another title in their first season, thus becoming the only team in major league history to win consecutive titles in different leagues. In 1890 three upstate cities briefly fielded major league teams: the Buffalo Bisons in the Players League, formed by National League players upset with salary constraints imposed by the owners, and the Syracuse Stars and Rochester Hop Bitters in the American Association. (There were eight major league teams playing in New York State in 1890, with three in Brooklyn and two in New York City.) The Players League disbanded after one season, and the American Association ceased play the following year. Buffalo was the last upstate city to host a major league franchise, competing in the short-lived Federal League in 1914–15.

Race and the Negro Leagues

The impact of African Americans on baseball was felt in the years following the Civil War. On 18 May 1878—68 summers before Jackie Robinson famously broke baseball's color barrier—Bud Fowler, who was born in Fort Plain (Montgomery Co) and raised in Cooperstown, joined the Lynn (Mass) Live Oaks and became the first African American to play in the white professional leagues. Also among the handful of Blacks competing alongside Whites during this era were Moses Fleetwood Walker and Robert Higgins with the Syracuse Stars and Frank Grant with the Buffalo Bisons. Black players were routinely subjected to epithets and physical harm. Cap Anson, the most influential player of his time and an avowed racist, urged baseball at all levels to refrain from offering any more contracts to "colored players." Blacks vanished from the white pro leagues entirely in the late 1880s and would not reappear for nearly six decades.

In the interim, determined African Americans created their own opportunities to play ball for a living. Frank P. Thompson helped found the first professional all-black team at an 1885 meeting at the Argyle Hotel in Babylon (Suffolk Co), where most of the early members of the team worked. The club, known as the Athletics, wound up going 6-2-1 against local competition in its inaugural season and soon changed its name to the Cuban Giants. In 1920 Rube Foster formed the Negro National League, the first all-black professional sports league, and other black leagues soon followed. New York City teams in the Eastern Colored League, which formed in 1923, included the New York Lincoln Giants and the Brooklyn Royal Giants. Led by exceptional players such as pitcher Smokey Joe Williams and shortstop John Henry Lloyd of the Lincoln Giants, the Negro Leagues drew large, appreciative crowds. But both the Negro National League and the Eastern Colored League disbanded at the onset of the depression because of financial difficulties. In 1933 a second Negro National League was formed, and it lasted through 1948. New York State was represented there by the Brooklyn Eagles, New York Black Yankees, and New York Cubans. The Cubans also played in the Negro American League in 1949 and 1950. Barnstorming teams featuring Negro League stars such as catcher Josh Gibson and pitcher Satchel Paige played numerous games against semipro teams while touring cities across New York State. The signing of Robinson to a minor league contract by the Brooklyn Dodgers in 1945 finally reopened the door for talented African American players to compete in the major leagues. The integration of the game would be the death knell of the Negro Leagues.

The 20th Century: Major Leagues

The birth of a number of baseball traditions can be traced to early 20th-century New York City. Hot dogs were sold at a ballpark perhaps for the first time *ca* 1900 at the new Polo Grounds in Coogan's Hollow between 157th and 159th Sts, and "Take Me Out to the Ballgame," written by New Yorkers Al Von Tilzer and Jack Norworth, was sung at games for the first time in 1908. The American League was formed in New York City in 1901 and two years later was recognized as a major league. The addition of the Junior Circuit, as the league would come to be known, led to a revival of the World Series against the National League champion. From 1903 to 1924 the National League's New York Giants were the most powerful and profitable team in baseball. Under the guidance of Truxton (Cortland Co) native John McGraw, a future Hall of Fame manager, they won 10 league titles and 3 World Series (1905, 1921, 1922), outdistancing the success of their league rivals from Brooklyn (then formally known as the Robins), who won two pennants during that span (1916, 1920).

A third New York team, the Highlanders of the American League (1903), whose first stadium was in the Washington Heights area of Upper Manhattan, became tenants of the Giants at the Polo Grounds in 1913. The Highlanders would later become known as the Yankees after newspapers began referring to them by that name in headlines. The Yankees were long overshadowed by McGraw's Giants, but that all changed with the acquisition of Babe Ruth from the Boston Red Sox in 1920 and the construction in 1923 of the massive 70,000-seat Yankee Stadium at East 161st St and River Ave in the Bronx, which would become the sport's most hallowed ground. Ruth, a prodigious slugger whose flamboyance on and off the diamond epitomized America during the 1920s, took the sport to new heights of popularity. He would be followed in Yankee pinstripes by Lou Gehrig, Joe DiMaggio, and Mickey Mantle, and the team known as the Bronx Bombers would accumulate 29 league pennants and 20 World Series from 1921 to 1964. The Yankees and Giants met in six World Series (which became known as Subway Series) during that span, with the Giants prevailing twice: in 1921, the first World Series to be broadcast on radio, and 1922. The Yankees won the matchups in 1923, 1936, 1937, and 1951. During the 1940s and 1950s the Dodgers became a formidable team in the National League. Propelled by the successes of players such as Jackie Robinson, Duke Snider, and Pee Wee Reese, the club fondly referred to as "Dem Bums" went to seven World Series, winning one (1955) and losing six (1941, 1947, 1949, 1952, 1953, and 1956), all to their Bronx rivals.

Media coverage, especially with the emergence of television, expanded baseball's appeal to an even larger audience during this era. Famous broadcaster Red Barber announced the first televised baseball game from Brooklyn's Ebbets Field in 1939. Nearly 25 New York City newspapers chronicled the drama of Bobby Thomson's "shot heard 'round the world," a home run that propelled the New York Giants to the 1951 National League pennant over the Brooklyn Dodgers; as many papers reported of the only perfect game in World Series history, tossed by the Don Larsen of the Yankees in 1956. Sportswriters began referring to New York City as the capital of baseball. The designation disappeared, however, after the 1957 season when the owners of its National League teams announced plans to move to California—the Giants, with popular center fielder Willie Mays, to San Francisco and the Dodgers to Los Angeles.

Not until 1962, when the New York Mets began play as a National League expansion team, would the wounds begin to heal. The Mets, under former Yankees manager Casey Stengel, became lovable losers, winning just 40 of 160 games in their inaugural season. But just seven seasons later, they became known as the Amazin' Mets after upsetting the heavily favored Baltimore Orioles in the World Series. They became more popular in New York City than the Yankees were, who fell upon lean times once their seemingly endless talent pipeline went dry in the 1960s. With controversial owner George Steinbrenner's purchase of the team from CBS in 1973, however, the Bronx Bombers experienced a revival. The Yankees won back-to-back World Series in 1977 and 1978, but Steinbrenner's impatience and his meddlesome management style led to a drought that did not end until the Yankees, under the unflappable leadership of manager Joe Torre, won four World Series titles in a five-year span (1996, 1998–2000). Although they failed to repeat their championship in 2001, losing a dramatic seven-game World Series to the Arizona Diamondbacks, the Yankees postseason run gave the city something to rally around after the shocking destruction of 11 September.

The 20th century: Minor Leagues

With the exception of Buffalo's Federal League franchise, baseball north of New York City in the 20th century has centered on the minor leagues and the cultivation of future big league players. The New York State League—precursor to the modern International League, now the oldest functioning minor league in baseball—was formed in 1885. Albany, Binghamton, Oswego, Rochester, Syracuse, and Utica fielded teams, with Buffalo coming aboard a year later. The league dissolved in 1890, but the following year Charles D. White of Utica revived it as the Eastern League (or Eastern Association). Building successful franchises was complicated because minor league clubs often lost their best players to major league teams without receiving any compensation. The idea of working agreements between major and minor league teams came about only in the early 1920s. Having talent climb through the rungs of a "farm system" was the brainchild of St. Louis Cardinals general manager Branch Rickey, who would later sign Jackie Robinson to a Dodgers contract. Rickey made the Syracuse Stars a farm club for his Cardinals in 1921 and seven years later established what would be a long and productive relationship with the Rochester Red Wings. St. Louis paid for the building of a $400,000 stadium in Rochester and loaded the Wings with talented players who would go on to win four consecutive pennants (1928–31). The 1930 team, led by Rip Collins, who drove in an International League–record 180 runs, is regarded as one of the finest minor league clubs of all time. Rochester became the model minor league affiliate, spending 33 years with the Cardinals and 42 years with the Baltimore Orioles before joining forces with the Minnesota Twins in fall 2002.

Watching the development of superstar players such as Cal Ripken Jr in Rochester, Johnny Bench in Buffalo, and Robin Yount in Newark (Wayne Co) was part of the appeal of the minor leagues. Equally attractive was the opportunity to watch journeyman players like Luke Easter, a mountainous slugger who wowed fans in both Buffalo and Rochester with his tower-clearing homers and friendly demeanor. Easter, who played past age 50, became a folk hero in each city, and wound up having his jersey number retired by both the Bisons and the Red Wings. Of the thousands of minor league games involving New York State teams, none could top the 18 Apr 1981 contest between the Red Wings and Pawtucket (RI) Red Sox for drama and duration. After 32 innings, play was suspended in the wee morning hours of 19 April, and the game was not completed until the next visit of the Wings to Pawtucket that June. The Red Sox won 3-2, and several artifacts from the game remain on display at the National Baseball Hall of Fame.

With franchises in both major leagues and three minor circuits in 2003, New York boasts more professional baseball teams than any state but California. At one time or another in the 20th century, every major town and village in the Empire State fielded either a professional or semiprofessional team. While the International League is the last rung on the ladder before the big leagues, the New York–Pennsylvania League, which formed in Buffalo on 8 Mar 1939 (and known as the PONY League through 1956), has been the first stop in the careers of many future major league stars, including Pete Rose, Robin Yount, Don Mattingly, Nolan Ryan, Tony Perez, and Mel Stottlemyre. The league made history on 24 June 1972, when Bernice Gera, after protracted legal struggles, became the first female umpire to work a professional game. However, Gera resigned after just one game, citing hostility from several fronts, including other umpires.

During the 1980s and 1990s several new ballparks were built in cities around the state. Before the start of the 1988 season, the Bisons moved from the dilapidated War Memorial Stadium ("the Rockpile" but best known as the setting for Robert Redford's classic baseball film, *The Natural* [1984]) to Pilot Field (now Dunn Tire Park), a $42 million, 19,500-seat stadium in downtown Buffalo. The Bisons established a minor league attendance record when they sold 1,240,951 tickets in 1991. Rochester and Syracuse followed with new parks in the mid-1990s. Brooklyn fielded a New York–Penn League team in 2001, marking the return of professional baseball to the borough for the first time since the Dodgers departed 44 years earlier.

Conclusion

New York State's impact on the game continues to be felt in a number of ways that transcend the playing field. Dolgeville (Herkimer Co), longtime home of the Adirondack Bat Co, remains the second largest manufacturer of major league bats, trailing only the Louisville Slugger Co. Much of the northern white ash used to make the bats comes from New York State forests. While Cooperstown's status as the birthplace of baseball has been challenged, it retains a unique place in baseball history as the site of the sport's

Vassar College Resolutes, *ca* 1876.

shrine, the National Baseball Hall of Fame and Museum (1939). Home to many of the game's most precious artifacts, the Hall of Fame attracts more than 300,000 visitors annually.

Dixon, Phil, with Patrick Hannigan. *The Negro Baseball Leagues, 1867–1955: A Photographic History* (Mattituck, NY: Amereon House, 1992)
Levine, Peter. *A. G. Spalding and the Rise of Baseball: The Promise of an American Sport* (New York: Oxford Univ Press, 1985)
Mandelaro, Jim, and Scott Pitoniak. *Silver Seasons: The Story of the Rochester Red Wings* (Syracuse: Syracuse Univ Press, 1996)
The New Bill James Historical Baseball Abstract (New York: Free Press, 2003)
O'Neal, Bill. *The International League: A Baseball History, 1884–1991* (Austin: Eakin Press, 1992)
Robinson, Ray, and Christopher Jennison. *Yankee Stadium: 75 Years of Drama, Glamor, and Glory* (New York: Penguin Studio, 1998)
Seymour, Harold. *Baseball*, 3 vols (New York: Oxford Univ Press, 1960–90)
Thorn, John, and Pete Palmer, eds. *Total Baseball: The Official Encyclopedia of Major League Baseball*, 7th ed. (Kingston, NY: Total Sports, 2001)

Scott Pitoniak

Baseball Hall of Fame. See NATIONAL BASEBALL HALL OF FAME AND MUSEUM.

basketball. While other popular American sports, including baseball and football, developed haphazardly from European roots, basketball was invented in the United States by Dr James Naismith (1861–1939), a Canadian-born instructor at the YMCA Training School (now Springfield College) in Springfield, Mass. In 1891, asked to introduce an indoor team sport to the local YMCA's winter schedule, he compiled a list of 13 rules for a game to be played on the gymnasium floor. The object was to score points by tossing a ball into peach baskets erected on balconies at both ends of the court. Players were forbidden to run with the ball and were required to either pass or shoot upon possession (dribbling was a later innovation). The game caught on quickly, attracting both male and female players. By the late 1930s rules had been published in at least 30 languages, and there were estimated to be some 20 million players worldwide.

High School and College Men's Basketball

In New York State Buffalo and New York City were among the first cities in the nation to organize play on the high school level. In 1903 Luther Gulick, a colleague of Naismith's at the Springfield YMCA, founded the Public Schools Athletic League in New York City, personally helping to supervise construction of basketball courts in school gymnasiums throughout the five boroughs. Partly because of its relatively low budgetary demands and spatial requirements, basketball developed into the most commonly played interscholastic sport in New York State by the 1920s. Dominant high school basketball programs have included Power Memorial High School (Manhattan), which featured Lew Alcindor (Kareem Abdul-Jabaar), Elgin Nathan, and Eddie Moss; St. Nicholas of Tolentine (Bronx), whose stars included Malik Sealy (who led them to a High School National Championship in 1988), Gary Voce, and Adrian "Red" Autry; Buffalo Traditional High School, which has the distinction of being the only team to win three straight New York State championships (Class C) in 1999, 2000, and 2001; Boys High School (Brooklyn), which produced Connie Hawkins, Dwayne "Pearl" Washington, Richard Gordon, Lennie Willkins, and Mel "Killer" Davis; and Christ the King High School (Queens), which in the 1990s featured future college and professional stars Lamar Odom, Craig "Speedy" Claxton, Eric Barkley, and Omar Cook.

The state was the site of much early intercollegiate play, with Columbia and Cornell Universities instrumental in launching competition in the Eastern Intercollegiate Basketball League (now Ivy League) in 1900. By 1910 top-level college teams were fielded by New York University, Syracuse University, University of Buffalo (now SUNY Buffalo), University of Rochester, St. Lawrence University, Colgate University, and Union College. The college game transformed from a somewhat genteel sport to a big-time, big-money media attraction in the 1930s after promoter Ned Irish arranged popular college basketball doubleheaders at Madison Square Garden in 1934. The events brought the best teams from around the country to play the major New York City area powers, especially New York University, Long Island University, and St. John's University. He later helped to arrange the first postseason college championship, the National Invitation Tournament (NIT), which began at Madison Square Garden in 1938. In 1950 New York City college basketball reached the zenith of its influence when the City College of New York (CCNY) won both the NIT and the NCAA (National Collegiate Athletic Association) postseason tournaments, the only team ever to accomplish this feat. Less than a year later, however, the New York City college basketball scene was devastated after members of the CCNY team were arrested in a point-shaving scandal that soon spread to other area schools. By the beginning of the 21st century, only two New York State schools continued to play top-caliber schedules: St. John's University and Syracuse University, both of which are members of the Big East Conference. In 2003 Syracuse, led by freshman Carmelo Anthony, defeated Kansas to become the second team (after CCNY) from New York State to win the NCAA Division I men's championship.

In Western New York, Niagara University, Canisius College, and St. Bonaventure University developed what came to be known as the "Little Three Rivalry." Niagara and Canisius are members of the Metro-Atlantic Athletic Conference, as are Siena College, Iona College, and Manhattan College. The University of Rochester, a member of the University Athletic Association, won the NCAA Division III National Championship in 1990.

Semiprofessional and Professional Men's Basketball

Organized professional basketball started in 1898 with the establishment of the National Basketball League (NBL), whose five members included teams representing New York City and Brooklyn. Before World War II, however, the professional game was dominated not by league play but by barnstorming teams who crisscrossed the country playing any competition that could meet their price and supply a venue. These were often factory teams that otherwise played in industrial leagues. New York State was home to some of the greatest barnstorming teams, including the Buffalo Germans, Original Celtics (Brooklyn), Harlem Renaissance Five (the Rens), New York Wanderers, the Rochester Centrals, and Troy Trojans.

The Celtics (an all-white team) and the Rens (an all–African American team) were perhaps the two most powerful barnstorming dynasties of the 1920s and 1930s. Formed as the New York Celtics in 1917 and re-formed as the Original Celtics in 1918, the Celtics played their early games at armories and gymnasiums in Brooklyn and Manhattan and were among the first sports teams to tour by automobile. The Celtics joined the professional American Basketball League for the 1927–28 season, but after compiling a record of 109-11, they were expelled for being too good. Some of the most famous Celtics players went on to become great coaches, including Nat Holman at CCNY, Joe Lapchick at St. John's University, and Red Auerbach with the National Basketball Association's (NBA's) Boston Celtics. Formed in 1922, the Rens, who were named for the Harlem Renaissance Casino where they played their home games, dominated the black barnstorming circuit with equal ferocity, compiling an astounding record of 473-49, including an 88-game winning streak. Stars included Clarence "Fat" Jenkins, Bill Yancey, John "Casey" Holt, and Wee Willie Smith. Their stop-and-go speed, tough defense, and sudden reverses were characteristic of the less conservative "city game" played in the schoolyards of Harlem, Bedford-Stuyvesant, and other African American urban neighborhoods. The Harlem Globetrotters, a black barnstorming team founded in Chicago in 1926, continue to tour in the 21st century. Although the Rens disbanded in 1948, marking the end of the barnstorming period, their style of play eventually influenced the game as a whole after Brooklyn-born Red Auerbach broke the color line in the NBA by signing Chuck Cooper, the league's first African American player, to the Boston Celtics in 1950. Later that year the New York Knickerbockers signed Nathaniel "Sweetwater" Clifton, who left the Harlem Globetrotters to join them.

The NBA was born in 1949 by the merger of two existing leagues, the NBL and the Basketball Association of America. Three New York State teams were among the 17 original NBA franchises: the New York Knickerbockers, Rochester Royals, and Syracuse Nationals. Each brought the NBA championship to the state: Rochester in 1951, Syracuse in 1955, and New York in 1970 and 1973. As the NBA grew into a major national enterprise, the league's smaller venues, including Rochester and Syracuse, lost their franchises to larger cities; the Royals went to Cincinnati after the 1956–57 season, and the Nationals moved to Philadelphia after the 1962–63 season. The Buffalo Braves entered the NBA as an expansion team in 1970, but they too departed for a bigger fan base after the 1977–78 season. In 1976 the New York Nets, champions of the collapsing American Basketball Association in 1974 and 1976, were admitted to the NBA. A season later they became the New Jersey Nets after moving from Nassau Coliseum in Uniondale to the Meadowlands Sports Complex in East Rutherford, NJ.

Women's Basketball

Women's basketball achieved extraordinary popularity soon after the invention of the game, even though controversy sometimes surrounded it. Progressives tended to advocate basketball as a health-promoting and liberating activity, while some conservatives, including clergy, denounced the public exhibition of the female body and deplored what they saw as the glorification of aggressive traits in women. The first recorded women's intercollegiate game in New York State was played in 1898, with Syracuse University defeating Cortland Normal School (now SUNY Cortland) by a score of 6-2. After a dormant period during the mid–20th century, women's college basketball had a period of tremendous growth after 1972, when Title IX was enacted into federal law, forcing schools with male-oriented athletic programs to allocate resources reflecting the percentage of female students at the institution. Syracuse and St. John's have had the strongest women's college programs in the state, each having been invited to the NCAA Division I championship tournament three times as of 2003. Other schools that have fielded competitive teams include Division I contenders Hofstra, Columbia, and Cornell Universities; Division II's Queens College, which participated in the first women's basketball game played in Madison Square Garden in 1975; and New York University, which won the NCAA Division III championship in 1997.

On the professional level, the New York Stars played in the short-lived Women's Basketball League (1978–81), and the New York Liberty was one of eight founding franchises in the Women's National Basketball Association (WNBA), which was formed in 1997. In 1999 Madison Square Garden, the Liberty's home court, sold out for the WNBA's first all-star game, and in 2001 the Liberty led the WNBA in attendance. They appeared in four of the league's first six championship series.

Cohen, Stanley. *The Game They Played* (New York: Carroll & Graf Publishers, 2001)

National Basketball Association, http://www.nba.com

National Collegiate Athletics Association Sports, http://www.ncaasports.com

Taragano, Martin. *Basketball Biographies: 434 US Players, Coaches, and Contributors to the Game, 1891–1990* (Jefferson, NC: McFarland, 1991)

Women's National Basketball Association, http://www.wnba.com

David Marc

Basques. Thought to be the oldest surviving ethnic group in Europe, the Basque people live in a small geographic region that constitutes parts of north central Spain and southwestern France. Like much of Europe, the Basque country suffered from agricultural and political upheaval in the mid–19th century, thereby fostering widespread migration to the United States. Although the great majority of Basque immigrants settled in the American West, a substantial Basque colony developed in New York City, the main point of arrival on the Atlantic coast. Consisting of as many as several thousand people in 1910, New York's Basque community centered around Cherry and Water Sts in Lower Manhattan, a multiethnic neighborhood also populated by Italians and other southern European immigrants. In 1913 New York's Basques founded Centro Vasco Americano (now Basque House of New York), a mutual aid society offering illness and death insurance benefits and providing a social center for Basques; it is one of the oldest Basque organizations in the United States. By the beginning of the 21st century, Basque New Yorkers have successfully assimilated into American society, but Basque House of New York continues to flourish along with some Basque feast day and food traditions. One of the most important Basque holidays is the Feast of St. Ignatius of Loyola (31 July), the Basque founder of the Jesuit order and Basque patron saint. The US census of 2000 reported 43,839 persons in New York State who claimed Basque ancestry, with most living in New York City and its immediate suburbs.

Douglass, William A., and John Bilboa. *Amerikanuak: Basques in the New World* (Reno: Univ of Nevada Press, 1975)

Zubiri, Nancy. *A Travel Guide to Basque America: Families, Feasts, and Festivals* (Reno: Univ of Nevada Press, 1998)

Nicholas P. Ciotola

Batavia. Town (pop 5,915) and city (pop 16,256) in central Genesee Co. The Seneca called the area Deo-on-go-wa, "The Great Meeting Place," because it was at the junction of two major Indian trails, one from Lake Erie to the Hudson River and the other from Lake Ontario to the Susquehanna River. In 1801 Benjamin Ellicott, working for his brother Joseph and the Holland Land Co, built a dam and sawmill at the bend in Tonawanda Creek, and within a year at least 30 families lived there. The site was selected because of its location at the trail junction. The town, formed in 1802, initially included the entire Holland Purchase. In the same year, Batavia was selected as the site of the Holland Land Co office and then as seat of the new Genesee Co. After the burning of Buffalo during the War of 1812, Batavia became a haven for refugees fleeing the Niagara frontier. In 1823 Batavia incorporated as a village. Three years later William Morgan, local author of *Freemasonry Exposed: Illustrations of*

Masonry, was arrested on the streets of Batavia, and his subsequent disappearance at the hands of the Masons created Antimasonic sentiment throughout the Northeast and led to the formation of the Antimasonic Party.

In 1837 the first railroad pulled into Batavia. It became a major stop along the New York Central line because its second president, Dean Richmond, lived there. With the railroad came the first Irish residents. By 1870 there was enough of a German population to support two German churches. Italian migration began in the 1880s with the building of additional railroads, and in 1908 a new parish, St. Anthony of Padua, was formed to serve them. The Polish came from Buffalo for farm employment in the late 19th century and formed their own church, Sacred Heart of Jesus, in 1904.

By the time Batavia became a city in 1915 there were more than 12 industrial plants. The largest was Johnston Harvester Co (later Massey-Harris, 1882–1958). Other companies that called Batavia home included Wiard Plow Co (1876–1954), Baker Gun Co (1889–1919), E. N. Rowell Co (paper boxes, 1888–1981), and F. E. Mason and Sons (embossed labels, 1907–77). In 1958 the Batavia Industrial Center, an early example of a business incubator, began renting small parcels for industry. Today the large firms are gone, but Batavia has many smaller plants: Graham Corp (heat exchangers and surface condensers), R. E. Chapin (insect sprayers), and P. W. Minor and Son together employ more than 1,000. Funding for an urban renewal project was approved in 1962; the project proceeded to demolish the heart of the city's downtown. The first tenants in the newly built downtown occupied stores in 1976. Much of the retail business in the early 21st century is in shopping plazas in the town. Batavia is home to the Holland Land Office Museum and the minor league baseball team Batavia Muckdogs.

See also ARCHITECTS AND ARCHITECTURE, ROCHESTER AND WESTERN NEW YORK.

Patrick Weissend

bateau. Flat-bottomed vessel. Well suited to the natural inland waterways of North America in the 18th century, where frequent shallows and numerous portages restricted transport, the bateau in New York State was used often in the rivers and streams linking the Great Lakes to the Hudson River–Lake Champlain corridor. It was a generic flat-bottomed boat, double ended, and driven by poles in the shallows, oars in deeper water, and occasionally a small sail that could be set up and taken down quickly. Built in a range of sizes averaging 30 feet (9 m) in length, it was suited to various military, commercial, and private tasks. Normally two polemen stood in the bow, and a steersman controlled the craft with a long oar lashed to the stern post. Bateaux could be carried around obstacles, and at the major portages specially fitted wagons were usually kept to assist in the overland passage. They were generally replaced by larger Durham boats around 1800.

Gardner, John. *The Dory Book* (Camden, Maine: International Marine, 1987)

Philip L. Lord Jr

Bath. Town (pop 12,097) and village (pop 5,641) in central Steuben Co. In 1793 Col Charles Williamson, agent for Sir William Pulteney of Bath, England, identified this wide valley at the head of navigation on the Cohocton River as a good village site. The town and county were formed in 1796. Bath became the county seat and was incorporated as a village in 1816 and again in 1836. During the early 19th century it was a launching point for lumber rafts and cargo boats called arks. After the mid–19th century, agriculture, especially dairy farming, became important to the town's economy. Rail service was provided first by the Erie Railroad Rochester Division (1852) and later by the Delaware, Lackawanna and Western Railroad (1882). Two humanitarian agencies have been important: the Davenport Home for Female Orphans (1864–58) and the New York State Soldiers' and Sailors' Home (1878), since 1929 operating as the federal Bath VA Medical Center. In 2003 the Medical Center had a capacity of about 900 beds. Bath National Cemetery is located on its grounds. Significant employers in 2003 included county government and manufacturers Babcock Ladder Co, Lane Pipe Co (road culverts), Netherlands-based Royal Philips Electronics (high-intensity light bulbs), and Mercury Aircraft (industrial components). Bath has highway access via Rte 17 (I-86), constructed through the town in 1970–73, and is the site of the annual Steuben County Fair, which dates to 1819. The Bath Presbyterian Church has a Louis C. Tiffany interior.

See also ARCHITECTS AND ARCHITECTURE, SOUTHERN TIER (EASTERN).

Virginia L. Wright and Jerry Wright

Battle of Boonville. Milk strikes by independent milk producers against the prices paid by New York City milk dealers date back to the 1880s. At times these confrontations edged into violence against those transporting the milk of nonstriking farmers, as in the Orange Co milk war of 1883. The most noted and most violent milk strike occurred in 1933 against the backdrop of a declining demand and predatory competition among New York City dealers, which put severe downward pressure on wholesale milk prices. Faced with the loss of their farms, small commercial farmers again turned to milk strikes as a way of disrupting the market and extracting concessions. In 1933 violent clashes erupted across Central and Western New York. On 1 August in Boonville (Oneida Co), 50 state troopers equipped with steel helmets and submachine guns teargassed a crowd of 300–400 farmers peacefully picketing a local milk plant and beat farmers and bystanders alike as they chased them through the streets of town. The *Boonville Herald*, with a long history of opposing milk strikes, called the action by the troopers "an outrageous example of blood-thirsty savagery." Two weeks later near the Revolutionary War battlefield in Oriskany (Oneida Co), 150 farmers took their revenge as they hurled stones, swung clubs, and swarmed over state troopers escorting milk trucks to local plants. Stunned by the spectacle of such violence, a *New York Times* reporter declared, perhaps with justifiable exaggeration, that the 1933 milk strikes "brought New York State closer to martial law than any time since the Revolutionary War."

Kriger, Thomas J. "Syndicalism and Spilled Milk: The Origins of Dairy Farmer Activism in New York State, 1936–41," *Labor History* 38 (Spring–Summer 1997): 266–86

Wilson, Edmund. "The Second Battle of Oriskany." In *The American Earthquake* (Garden City, NY: Doubleday, 1958)

Thomas J. Kriger

Battle of Golden Hill. Urban riot. In early 1770 tensions between British soldiers and New York City residents had been growing for months. Coming into office as acting governor in September 1769 Cadwallader Colden, working in concert with the DeLancey faction of the Colonial Assembly, enacted legislation in December that gave Colden his salary, granted the British army £2,000 for supplies, and authorized the emission of £120,000 in paper money. The bill aggravated several contentious issues: the presence of a standing army, the competition between soldiers and laborers for jobs, and Parliament's claim in the Quartering Acts (1765, 1767) that it could order the assembly to appropriate money or suspend it for refusing to do so. The Sons of Liberty commenced a propaganda campaign and held protest meetings at the Liberty Pole, which stood in the Fields (now City Hall Park) near the army barracks. Soldiers countered by twice attempting to destroy the pole. Three thousand residents consequently agreed on 17 January that employers should not hire soldiers and that the city should demolish the barracks. When soldiers distributed their own broadside on 19 January, Liberty Boys dragged several redcoats before the mayor. After other soldiers came to their rescue, the group retreated to Golden Hill (at the top of John St) where they were joined by more reinforcements. The troops then charged the civilians who were following them. Before officers could restore order, several people on both sides were injured. Calm was restored only after the military and the city's Common Council agreed on 22 January that an officer must accompany soldiers outside the barracks. The Battle of Golden Hill (and the subsequent Boston Massacre of 5 Mar 1770) demonstrated how the military's presence endangered rather than strengthened Britain's grip on the colonies.

Boyer, Lee R. "Lobster Backs, Liberty Boys, and Laborers in the Streets: New York's Golden Hill and Nassau Street Riots," *New-York Historical Society Quarterly* 57 (October 1973): 280–308

Shy, John. *Toward Lexington: The Role of the British Army in the Coming of the American Revolution* (Princeton, NJ: Princeton Univ Press, 1965)

Tiedemann, Joseph S. *Reluctant Revolutionaries: New York City and the Road to Independence, 1763–1776* (Ithaca: Cornell Univ Press, 1997)

Joseph S. Tiedemann

Battle of Newburgh. Conflict over welfare policy. With the closing of major industries and a rapid increase in the number of people needing financial help, the City of Newburgh (Orange Co) was spending 31% of its budget to cover welfare costs by 1961. To reduce these costs, that year Newburgh began requiring assistance recipients to pick up their checks at police headquarters. The city also sought to force those on assistance to work. City Manager Joseph Mitchell blamed much of the community's ills on a recent influx of black residents—Newburgh's black population had more than doubled between 1950 and 1960—and the relief efforts quickly took on racial overtones. While

Blacks constituted only 17% of the Newburgh citizenry in 1960, they were 39% of the people receiving assistance.

The State Department of Social Welfare struck down Newburgh's new work requirement, and in response the city announced in 1961 its intention to decline all state welfare funds in the following year. This allowed city leaders to shape completely their own program, which was slated to include work requirements, vouchers for food instead of cash, benefit caps, and the denial of additional benefits to women who bore children out of wedlock while on assistance. Radical at the time, the intended program drew strong public reaction as conservatives like Sen Barry Goldwater from Arizona applauded Newburgh's efforts while the liberal *New York Times* rejected them as cruel. Capturing national attention, the controversy was quickly dubbed the Battle of Newburgh by the media. Angered by Newburgh's intended plan, Gov Nelson A. Rockefeller directed Atty Gen Louis J. Lefkowitz to seek an injunction to block it. This succeeded in December 1961, and the Newburgh plan was dead, though it would find echoes in subsequent debates on welfare policy. Following this defeat Newburgh abandoned further attempts at cutting its rolls, and the city quickly receded from the spotlight. As a sign of how much the political culture has turned against poverty programs since 1961, many proposals similar to those of Newburgh were enacted by the US government in 1996, when legislation abolished the Aid to Families with Dependent Children program and instituted work requirements to receive assistance.

Ritz, Joseph P. *The Despised Poor: Newburgh's War on Welfare* (Boston: Beacon Press, 1966)

Tod M. Ottman

Baum, L(yman) Frank (*b* Chittenango, Madison Co, 15 May 1856; *d* Hollywood, Calif, 6 May 1919). Children's author. Baum's wealthy family moved to Syracuse in 1862 and six years later settled at an estate in Centreville [now Mattydale, Onondaga Co] called Rose Lawn. Due to a weak heart, Baum received tutoring at home. He briefly stayed at the Peekskill Military Academy (Westchester Co) in 1868 and attended the Syracuse Classical School in 1873. Once home Baum published a juvenile newspaper called the *Rose Lawn Home Journal.* Baum was fond of making up nursery rhymes, and he assembled his stories for a play, *Mother Goose in Prose,* performed in Syracuse on 3 Dec 1879 and published as a book in 1897 with illustrations by Maxfield Parrish. In 1882 Baum wed Maud Gage in Fayetteville (Onondaga Co); they had four children. Matilda Joslyn Gage, Maud's mother, was one of the leaders of the suffrage movement. Baum also toured with his original play, *Maid of Arran,* in 1882. Baum and his family moved in 1888 to Aberdeen, S Dak, where he opened a store, Baum's Bazaar, and later worked for a newspaper. In 1891 they moved to Chicago, where Baum eventually started his own magazine to help store owners develop window displays.

In 1900 Baum published *The Wonderful Wizard of Oz,* a children's book of adventure on a yellow brick road that led to the magical Land of Oz. Full of fanciful characters, such as the Tin Woodman, Scarecrow, Munchkins, and Winged Monkeys, the best-selling book became a classic American fairy tale. Baum's text has often been examined for symbolism and connections to the author's own experiences. Several events that occurred in Central New York during Baum's adolescence seem to appear in his famous work. Rose Lawn was situated by one of the first plank roads built in the United States, the Syracuse and Central Square Plank Road. The road was made of hemlock, a golden-colored wood, and its appearance as well as its importance to the local economy may have been the inspiration for Baum's yellow brick road. And a possible model for the Wizard of Oz was Prof C. C. Coe of Rome (Oneida Co), who in 1871 landed his hot air balloon in downtown Syracuse's Clinton Square.

Ferrara, Susan E. *The Family of the Wizard: The Baums of Syracuse* (Philadelphia: Xlibris, 2000)

Susan E. Ferrara

Bausch and Lomb. An optics and ophthalmology company based in Rochester. John Jacob Bausch, an immigrant, founded the company in 1853 as a small optics shop. Initially importing small numbers of eyeglasses from his brother in Germany, Bausch then began grinding lenses from imported optical glass and making frames. In need of funds, he borrowed $60 from his friend Henry Lomb, a cabinetmaker, promising to make Lomb a partner if the business succeeded. A breakthrough came when Bausch developed vulcanite (hard rubber) frames in the late 1850s. In addition to its own innovations, the company negotiated the US manufacturing rights from German optical firm Karl Zeiss. By the end of the century the Rochester company manufactured binoculars, microscopes, and telescopes and made camera lenses for Eastman Kodak. Bausch and Lomb and companies founded by former employees made Rochester a center of the optics industry in the United States. In 1903, its 50th anniversary, it employed 1,200 people.

The approach of World War I pushed the company in new directions. In cooperation with the federal government, Bausch and Lomb became the first US firm to produce optical glass to reduce US dependence on European imports. It produced 70% of the optical glass used by the government during the war. In 1929 the Army Air Corps contracted Bausch and Lomb to produce lenses that would reduce sun glare for pilots; the result was available to the public in 1936 as Ray-Ban sunglasses. The firm also produced range finders, gun sights, periscopes, and aerial cameras. In the 1960s it developed lenses for satellite and missile systems.

Bausch and Lomb Place, the company's headquarters building in Rochester, was built in 1995.

Labor relations at Bausch and Lomb suffered in August 1919, a time of heightened labor tensions generally, when the locally organized Amalgamated Optical Workers initiated a strike. Company officials denounced the strike as "IWW, anarchist, and bolshevist" and refused to negotiate. The strike began crumbling later that month. The firm announced a wage increase but also reduced its labor force and screened returning workers. Later it attempted to keep unions out by mimicking Eastman Kodak's "high-wage policy." The company also participated in the Rochester Plan (1931–38), one of the nation's first industry-organized unemployment insurance programs.

Bausch and Lomb acquired optical and scientific equipment firms in the 1960s. In 1971 it introduced the soft contact lens and began to specialize in contact lens manufacture. In the 1980s the firm sold off some noncore divisions and moved into medical products and research. It was hit by investigations (including those by the Securities and Exchange Commission) and class-action lawsuits in the mid-1990s, when pressure for major financial growth had given rise to questionable accounting and marketing tactics. It sold more noncore divisions during this time but also acquired companies manufacturing surgical equipment. At the beginning of the 21st century, defining itself as an "eye health company," Bausch and Lomb manufactured contact lenses, lens care products, ophthalmologic pharmaceuticals, and products for cataract, vitreoretinal, and refractive surgery. By the time of its 150th anniversary in 2003, Bausch and Lomb employed 11,500 people worldwide with annual revenues of $1.8 billion.

Eisenhart, M. Herbert, *J. J. Bausch (1830–1926): American Pioneer* (New York: Newcomen Society, 1948)

Scott C. Monje

Baxter Estates. Village (pop 1,006) in North Hempstead (Nassau Co). Settled about 1643 the land was owned by the Baxter family beginning in 1741. Around the time of the Civil War, sand mining was conducted on a large scale. Percy Baxter and Charles Hyde began development of the family property in 1910. The village, encompassing just .2 mi^2 (.52 km^2), was incorporated in 1931. It includes substantial single-family homes and a small commercial district. Landmarks include the Port Washington Public Library and the historic Baxter House (*ca* 1705).

Joan Gay Kent

baymen. See LONG ISLAND BAYMEN.

Bayport. Locality (pop 8,662) in Islip (Suffolk Co). Its territory was part of a 1697 patent to William Nicoll, but the first settlement seems to have been only in 1786. During its first century, the area was known as Middle Road, and its residents were farmers, baymen, or shipyard workers. The South Side Rail Road (1869) encouraged industries including fish oil factories, commercial nurseries (late 1890s), and the Bayport Barrel Co (1904–1930s), as well as cottages for summer residents. A Bayport post office was established in 1871. The nearby Brookhaven National Laboratory (1947) employed 200 Bayport residents in the late 1960s and encouraged residential development that replaced most of the nurseries, although Bayport Flower Houses (1932) was still in business in 2003. The Bayport Aerodrome, an unpaved historic airstrip, is home to several dozen vintage aircraft. A 20 ft (6.1 m) model of the Egyptian sphinx, built in Blue Point in the 1890s, is a Bayport landmark.

Daria E. Merwin

Bay Shore {Bay Shore, locality (pop 23,852) in Islip, Suffolk Co; North Bay Shore, locality (pop 14,992) in Islip; West Bay Shore, locality (pop 4,775) in Islip}. Purchased from the Secatague Indians in 1701, the area's primary occupations were fishing, clamming, and oystering in the 18th and 19th centuries. It acquired a post office in 1849 named Penataquit. When the South Side Rail Road came through in 1868, the name was changed to Bay Shore, and it became a fashionable summer resort for wealthy New Yorkers. Vitagraph Studios made movies there in 1915–16. The Southern State Parkway (1929) and Sunrise Highway helped open it up for residential development, which rapidly expanded after World War II. Bay Shore is the site of Touro College's School of Health Sciences (1970) and of the century old Entenmann's Bakery, a major employer. North Bay Shore is a predominantly Latino (50.7%) community, originally Puerto Rican but growing in diversity with new arrivals from South and Central America; the Puerto Rican/Hispanic Day Parade is an annual event. North Bay Shore is the site of the South Shore Mall, a large regional shipping center. West Bay Shore is the site of Sagtikos Manor (1697), now a museum, and of the 231-acre (93 ha) Gardiner County Park on Great South Bay.

Eileen Effrat

Bayville. Village (pop 7,135) in Oyster Bay (Nassau Co). Located on land originally called Oak Neck and Pine Island, it was purchased from several native Matinecocks in 1658 and used as pasture. It was named Bayville in 1869. Shellfishing has always been important locally, and Bayville remains the home of Frank M. Flower and Sons (1887), an oyster and clam dredging company. The widespread cultivation of asparagus in the 19th century was ended by Bayville's growth as a summer community, when a number of hotels and cottages were built, along with Bayville Casino (1913). The village incorporated in 1919 and by 1940 had a population of 1,516; most growth took place in the 1950s and 1960s. A 1965 proposal to build a bridge to Rye (Westchester Co) would have altered the village irreparably and was opposed by village residents and others; it was ultimately defeated.

Tom Kuehhas

Baywood. Locality (pop 7,571) in Islip (Suffolk Co). Located on land patented to Thomas and Richard Willetts (1695) and Stephanus van Cortlandt (1697), it was little used except for farming and cordwood cutting. The Long Island Rail Road came through in 1842. After the Sagtikos State Parkway was completed in 1952, residential development created suburban housing.

Daria E. Merwin

beaches. See BARRIER BEACHES AND ISLANDS.

Beacon. City (pop 13,808) in SW Dutchess Co. Formed in 1913 from the merger of two adjoining villages, Fishkill Landing and Matteawan, and named after signal fires lit on the 1,500 ft (457 m) Mt Beacon during the Revolution. Fishkill Landing was an important 18th-century river port, and good waterpower resulted in the growth of industries there and across Fishkill Creek at Matteawan, especially machine shops but also manufacturers of bricks, cotton goods, tools, hats and felt goods, clothing, carpets, and steam engines. During its peak there were 6,000 factory jobs in the villages. With some old factories housing small industrial enterprises, by 2000 Beacon had become racially and ethnically diverse; 20% of the population was African American, and 17% was of Latino ethnicity. Historic preservation downtown, along with antique shops, the Howland Cultural Center, and the Dia:Beacon art museum attracts tourists. Beacon was the birthplace and home of James V. Forrestal (1892–1949), US secretary of the navy (1944–47) and secretary of defense (1947–49), and of Pete Seeger, folksinger and activist.

William P. McDermott

bear, black *[Ursus americanus].* New York's only bear species and the state's largest mammal until the return of the moose in the 1980s. Adult bears stand 2.5–3 feet (.76–.91 m) high at the shoulder and weigh an average of 200 pounds (91 kg). Some may reach 6 feet (1.8 m) tall, balanced on their hind legs, and weigh 600 pounds (272 kg); the state record is 750 pounds (340 kg). Shy and secretive, the black bear prefers mature forest habitat interspersed with areas of open meadow; these conditions foster bear populations in the Adirondacks and Catskills as well as in the Alleghenies of the state's Southern Tier.

This species is almost always black in New York State but shows some color variation elsewhere in North America. An omnivorous feeder most active at dawn and dusk, the bear normally eats a variety of fruit, nuts, acorns, insects, succulent greens, and animal flesh. It consumes plant and animal products almost continually during its active season, building fat reserves for yearly hibernation. Depending on weather conditions, black bears usually enter hibernation by the end of November and reemerge around April. Bears wander large areas, with home ranges for yearlings of 1–2 miles (1.6–3.2 km) in diameter, for adult females 2–6 miles (3.2–9.7 km), and for adult males 8–15 miles (12.9–24.1 km). Paths often connect several feeding areas. Tree-climbing abilities, high intelligence, average eyesight, and superior sense of smell and hearing help bears search for food and avoid enemies.

At maturity, 3–7 years old, the sex ratio settles at one male per two to five females. Mating occurs from late May through early July, with females producing one to four cubs during January and early February. Young remain with the sow about one and a half years, and sows produce a new cub or litter every two to four years. Bears can live as long as 21 to 33 years but average 3 to 5 in hunted populations. Since the colonial period, habitat alteration has transformed the distribution of black bears in New York State. After near extinction during the early 1900s, the population has resurged. In 2003, though still absent from their colonial era range on Long Island, a few bears were sighted on the Great Lakes Plain, the Adirondacks harbored approximately 5,000, the Catskills near 700, and the Alleghenies perhaps 200.

New York State permits the hunting of black bears in the Adirondack, Allegheny, and Catskill regions. Hunting outside these areas is permitted only in special circumstances, such as livestock depredation and nuisance bears. Licensed bear-

Black bears in New York State live in the Adirondack, Allegheny, and Catskill Mountains.

tracking dogs may be used. From 1993 through 2000, 4,987 bears were taken by hunters in the Adirondack region, 1,882 in the Catskill region, and 473 in the Allegheny region. The New York State Department of Environmental Conservation (DEC) has made efforts to control bear-human interactions resulting from an increase in bear ranges accompanied by greater human impingement into bear habitat. The DEC advises general good housekeeping to decrease bear attractants, as well as keeping garbage indoors, removing or masking food odors after outdoor cooking, and minimizing summer bird feeding.

Fair, Jeff, and Lynn Rogers. *Great American Bear* (Minocqua, Wisc: North Word Press, 1990)

Richard Wojtowicz

Bear Mountain and Harriman State Parks. Two adjacent parks in Orange and Rockland Cos established in 1910. The combined 53,463-acre (21,636 ha) preserve is one of New York State's earliest and largest state park areas. Bear Mountain and Harriman were developed by the Palisades Interstate Park Commission (PIPC), an interstate agency (New York and New Jersey) formed in 1900 to preserve the Hudson River Palisades. Until 1910 the PIPC focused on protecting the endangered cliffs along the southwest bank of the river. The acquisition of a large inland tract was precipitated by the New York State Prison Commission's 1908 plan to relocate Sing Sing Prison to a scenic 5,000-acre (2,000 ha) parcel above the Hudson River. The scheme drew considerable opposition, including that from E. H. and Mary Williamson Averell Harriman, who owned more than 30,000 acres (12,100 ha) adjacent to the site. After her husband's death in 1909, Mary Harriman donated 10,000 acres (4,000 ha) for a park in his memory, provided that the state relocate the prison, develop its site as a park, and pledge funds for additional park acquisition and development. The state dropped its prison relocation plan in 1910 and that same year began to develop the site. These two tracts were the nucleus of Bear Mountain and Harriman State Parks.

The parks occupy rugged, sparsely settled mountainous land in the Hudson Highlands and Ramapo Mountains. The naturalistic designed landscape incorporates artificial lakes, scenic roads, trails, and hundreds of rustic buildings and features constructed of native stone and chestnut. Two important linear recreation systems traverse the parks: the Appalachian Trail (1923) and the Palisades Interstate Parkway (1947–61). The most prominent feature in Bear Mountain State Park is the Bear Mountain Inn (1915), a monumental rustic-style lodge, while the park's tallest peak is Bear Mountain at 1,306 feet (398 m).

The preserve's proximity to metropolitan New York City inspired the development of innovative programs to link urban populations to public parkland. The organized group camping program, established in 1913, continues to provide camping and nature education programs for hundreds of urban children each summer. Bear Mountain and Harriman provide opportunities for picnicking, camping, hiking, swimming, fishing, boating, sledding, skating, cross-country skiing, and organized sports, serving 3.2 million patrons in 2002.

Palisades Interstate Park Commission. *60 Years of Park Cooperation: NY-NJ Palisades Interstate Park Commission, a History, 1900–1960* (Bear Mountain, NY: Palisades Interstate Park Commission, 1960)

Kathleen LaFrank

beaver *[Castor canadensis].* The largest rodent in North America, the beaver is a herbivore with a large flat tail, glossy dark brown fur, and chisel-like incisors used for cutting trees. Beavers mate for life and produce a litter of one to four kits each spring. Adept at building dams, beavers can remain submerged for up to 20 minutes. Beavers occupied almost every aquatic habitat in North America, prior to European colonization. The unregulated fur trade of the 17th and 18th centuries, the later draining of lands for agriculture, and forest harvesting drove the beaver nearly to extinction by 1900, reducing the population across the continent from an estimated 60–400 million to just a few thousand. In New York State, wildlife biologists estimate that the number of beavers in 1894 was five—just one colony of related beavers in the Adirondacks.

Since beavers are a keystone species, their demise affected numerous other species. Beavers back up streams by building dams, thus controlling the water level and obscuring the underwater entrances to their homes, which protects them from predators. The consequent ponds and wetlands that these dams create support waterfowl, aquatic invertebrates, fish, reptiles and their predators, moose, and many wetland plant species. The activities of beavers also heighten and control the local water table, modify the structure and composition of the riparian zone, and decrease stream velocity, which increases sediment deposition and decreases erosion. Watersheds lost their wetlands when beavers were trapped out of an area and their dams collapsed, and combined with the draining of land for agricultural use and development, an estimated 75,000–100,000 mi^2 (195,000–260,000 km^2) of wetlands became dry land across North America between 1834 and 1970.

Beavers have returned to North America and New York State due to reintroduction efforts. Between 1901 and 1907 the New York State Conservation Commission, predecessor to the New York State Division of Fish, Wildlife and Marine Resources, released 34 beavers from Wyoming into New York State. By 1915 there were an estimated 15,000 beavers in the state. Throughout the state beaver trapping seasons were opened by 1955. The state's current estimated population of 70,000 beavers is controlled by trapping seasons that vary in length annually to account for population fluctuations. The pelts of 15,000 beavers trapped every year in the state go to North American, Asian, and European fur markets. The return of the beaver has not been without problems; their dams can cause flooding, resulting in damage to property, highways, crops, and roads. The beaver has been the official state animal since 1975, on the New York City flag since 1915, and a component of the city's seal since the Dutch period. Though Albany is no longer known as Beverwijck ("district of the beavers"), there are over 130 place names in New York State with a beaver connection, including the Beaver Kill, a major tributary of the Delaware River; 11 Beaver Creeks, 19 Beaver Ponds, and 20 Beaver Brooks.

Naiman, Robert J., Carol A. Johnston, and James C. Kelley. "Alteration of North American Streams by Beaver," *BioScience* 38 (Dec 1988): 753–62
Outwater, Alice. *Water: A Natural History* (New York: Basic Books, 1996)

Julie Polhemus

Beck, T(heodoric) Romeyn (*b* Schenectady, 11 Aug 1791; *d* Albany, 19 Nov 1855); **Beck, John B(rodhead)** (*b* Schenectady, 18 Sept 1794; *d* ?New York City, 9 Apr 1851); and **Beck, Lewis C(aleb)** (*b* Schenectady, 4 Oct 1798; *d* ?Albany, 20 Apr 1853). Physicians and scientists. Two of the brothers, T. Romeyn (1807) and Lewis (1817), graduated from Union College, while John was educated in Rhinebeck (Dutchess Co). T. Romeyn earned a medical degree in 1811 from the College of Physicians and Surgeons, now part of Columbia University. From 1815 to 1840 he taught at a branch of the College of Physicians and Surgeons, Fairfield Medical College (Herkimer Co). In 1829 he served as president of the state's Medical Society. He attended inmates at Albany's jail and almshouse but resigned, complaining that maniacs were treated as criminals rather than as medical cases. Beck's theory on treating the mentally ill precipitated the establishment of the state's Lunatic Asylum (now Mohawk Valley Psychiatric Center) in Utica

Beaver.

(1842), where he served on the board until 1854. His *Elements of Medical Jurisprudence* (1823) addressed insanity, poisoning, and sexual issues such as rape, infanticide, and illegitimacy. He taught at Albany Medical College (1841) and was principal of the Albany Academy (1817–53).

John Beck received a theology degree from Columbia College (1813) and a medical degree from the College of Physicians and Surgeons in 1817. In 1822 he was a founder of the *New-York Medical and Physical Journal.* Beck was a pioneer in the study of pregnancy, spontaneous and induced abortion, and neonatal physiology. The Becks opposed physicians who performed abortions. As the state's criminal code was being revised in 1828, they were instrumental in inserting a clause that would penalize doctors who performed abortions. Considered a model law, it was copied by other states. Lewis was a natural scientist and taught mineralogy and botany at the Rensselaer School (now Rensselaer Polytechnic Institute) and chemistry at Albany Medical College. He conducted a chemical study of the salt springs in Salina (Onondaga Co) and wrote *A Manual for Chemistry* (1844). In 1829 he was appointed state mineralogist and surveyed mineral resources. His *Report of the Mineralogy of New York State* (1842) became the foundation for mineral study in the state. A noted botanist, he collected herbaria (vascular plants), mosses, and liverworts, principal components of New York State Museum's collections. The Becks were committed to modernizing scientific and medical research and education. Their commitment did not end at death: all three donated their bodies to science.

Donhauser, Joseph, et al. *The Life and Career of Dr. T. Romeyn Beck* (Schenectady: Union College, 1950)
Gilman, C. R. *Sketch of the Life and Character of John B. Beck* (New York, 1851)
Sebring, Lewis Beck. *Life of Lewis C. Beck, M.D.* (1934)

Tricia A. Barbagallo

Becker, Carl L(otus) (*b* Black Hawk Co, Iowa, 7 Sept 1873; *d* Ithaca, 10 Apr 1945). Historian. His parents were from Carthage (Jefferson Co). Becker earned a bachelor's degree from the University of Wisconsin in 1896 while studying with, among others, historian Frederick Jackson Turner; after graduation, he attended the university's graduate school. Between 1898 and 1902 he was a fellow at Columbia University and an instructor at two other schools. In 1902 Becker began teaching at the University of Kansas while pursuing a doctorate from Wisconsin. He finished his dissertation under Turner in 1907; two years later it appeared as *The History of Political Parties in the Province of New York, 1760–1776,* the first of his 16 books. In this landmark of progressive historiography, Becker argued that the American Revolution represented two movements, the first for "home-rule or independence," the second for "who should rule at home." The latter movement, epitomized by a class conflict to democratize politics, was fundamental.

Becker served on the *American Historical Review*'s editorial board from 1914 to 1922 and in 1931 was elected president of the American Historical Association. In his presidential address, published in 1932, Becker dismissed complete objectivity as an ideal goal of historians; historical writing, he argued, was "an imaginative creation" upon which historians impressed their own experiences, needs, and tastes. Becker remained at Kansas until 1916 when he left for the University of Minnesota. In 1917 he moved to Cornell University in Ithaca, where he taught only European history, though he continued to publish scholarship on American history. His important books at Cornell included *The Eve of the Revolution* (1918), in which he employed the novelist's methods to explicate and depict the American Revolution, and *The Declaration of Independence: A Study in the History of Political Ideas* (1922), in which he fused psychology, political theory, and popular philosophy. These interpretative works demonstrated his preoccupation with the operation of people's minds and the reasons for their behavior. In 1927 Becker published "The Spirit of '76," originally a lecture of his fictional synopsis of *Political Parties* in which he explained why an imaginary New York merchant became a revolutionary while his merchant father-in-law remained loyal. Retiring in 1941 Becker became Cornell University's historian and two years later published his Messenger lectures on Cornell's founders and founding. An enlightened humanist and a consummate stylist, Becker's books, essays, articles, lectures, and book reviews, studded with psychological insights, philosophical thoughts, and literary allusions, have encouraged historians to ruminate about the nature of history and its social uses.

Becker, Carl L. *The Spirit of '76.* Ed. Louis L. Tucker (Albany: NYS American Revolution Bicentennial Commission, 1971)
Klein, Milton M. "Detachment and the Writing of American History: The Dilemma of Carl Becker." In *Perspectives on Early American History: Essays in Honor of Richard B. Morris,* ed. Alden T. Vaughan and George Athan Billias (New York: Columbia Univ Press, 1973)
Smith, Charlotte Watkins. *Carl Becker: On History and the Climate of Opinion* (Ithaca: Cornell Univ Press, 1956)

Gaspare J. Saladino

Bedford. Town (pop 18,133) in NE Westchester Co. Purchased from Indians in 1680 by 22 proprietors, it was settled in 1681 as a farming community in Connecticut until a boundary dispute placed it in New York Colony in 1700. It was confirmed as a town by the state in 1788. The hamlet of Bedford Village was burned by the British in 1779; it served as the county's half-shire town (1784–1868), and the Bedford Courthouse (1787) remains a landmark. Bedford Hills developed around the Harlem Railroad (1847) and housed workers. Another railroad hamlet, Katonah, was moved in 1897 to make room for the enlargement of the Croton Reservoir. After the Civil War Bedford became an estate community. The Bedford Hills (1901) and Taconic (1973) Correctional Facilities are located in the town. Chief Justice John Jay's Katonah farm is now the John Jay Homestead State Historic Site.

Lynne Ryan

Bedford Falls. The fictional setting of Frank Capra's 1946 film *It's a Wonderful Life.* Based on the 1943 short story "The Greatest Gift" by Philip Van Doren Stern, the film focuses on George Bailey (James Stewart), the owner of a family building and loan business in Bedford Falls. Bailey dreams of a life of travel and adventure, but instead remains within the confines of his hometown because of his social responsibilities to its people; he alone stands in the way of the domination of a wealthy banker, Mr. Potter. Through the intervention of his guardian angel on Christmas Eve, the suicidal Bailey experiences a grittier version of Bedford Falls called Pottersville in a fantasy sequence. Capra exposes the seedy undercurrent of the American dream, allowing George to see his own value within the community. Despite its bleak premise and its poor performance at the box office upon its release, the film ascended to perennial holiday classic status beginning in the 1970s, and Bedford Falls came to symbolize the ideals and values of small town America, its existence continually threatened by greed and corruption. There are references throughout the film to Western New York locations like Elmira and Rochester, and residents of the former factory town of Seneca Falls (Seneca Co) have claimed their community was the inspiration for Bedford Falls, and much ingenuity has been expended in elaborating this argument. Another account suggests that Stewart's hometown of Indiana, Pa, inspired Capra. Neither of these scenarios has been verified, and it is likely that Capra created Bedford Falls as a composite to better suit the universal appeal that he intended.

Carney, Ray. *American Vision: The Films of Frank Capra* (1986; repr Hanover, NH: Wesleyan Univ Press, 1996; distributed by Univ Press of New England)

Matt Kirsch

Bedford Hills Correctional Facility. The New York Reformatory for Women opened in 1901 in Bedford (Westchester Co) with reformer Katherine B. Davis as the first superintendent. The institution held approximately 250 women, aged 16 and older, convicted of misdemeanors from courts in eastern New York State. For the first decade Davis managed the institution as a school, stressing education and fresh air activities based on the popular cottage plan. A growing number of incorrigible inmates, however, forced changes in the reformatory concept. A laboratory of social hygiene, privately financed by John D. Rockefeller Jr, opened in 1911 and used new psychological and intelligence testing to identify large numbers of "psychopaths" and "feebleminded" women who needed special custody. In 1916 and 1920 respectively, a psychopathic hospital and a division for "mentally defective delinquent women" were established to house these inmates.

Renamed Westfield State Farm in 1931, the facility closed its defective division and sent those inmates to Albion Correctional Facility (Orleans Co). A prison division, separate from the reformatory, opened in its place and received inmates from the women's prison at Auburn (Cayuga Co), which had closed. In 1970 Westfield was again reorganized and renamed the Bedford Hills Correctional Facility. The reformatory was closed, and the new institution had separate sections for men and women. Men remained at Bedford Hills until 1973, when their section was separated and renamed Taconic Correctional Facility. In 2003 Bedford Hills was the state's only maximum security prison for women, housing approximately 840 inmates with a staff of 627. The facility also serves as the orientation and classification center for all women's prisons in the state's correctional system. A national model for family-centered prison programs, its

Children's Center contains the oldest prison nursery in the country, opening in 1901.

"Bedford Hills Correctional Facility," *DOCS Today* 8 (May 1999): 12–15
Rafter, Nicole H. *Partial Justice: Women in State Prisons, 1800–1935* (Boston: Northeastern Univ Press, 1985)

Richard Andress

Beecher family. The children of clergyman Lyman Beecher (1775–1863) and his first two wives included prominent New York State pastors Henry Ward Beecher (1813–87) and Thomas Kinnicut Beecher (1824–1900), five other sons in the Protestant ministry, writer Harriet Beecher Stowe (1811–96), author of the hugely popular abolitionist novel *Uncle Tom's Cabin* (1852), education reformer Catharine Esther Beecher (1800–78), and women's rights champion Isabella Beecher Hooker (1822–1907).

Lyman Beecher, after college at Yale, served the East Hampton Presbyterian Church on Long Island from 1798 to 1810, marrying Roxana Foote in 1799. At the Congregational Church in Litchfield, Conn, he established a national reputation for evangelistic preaching and leadership of social reform and missionary societies from 1810 to 1826. Soon after his wife's death, he married Harriet Porter in 1817. As pastor of Hanover Street Church in Boston (1826–32), in 1827 he called Presbyterian and Congregationalist leaders to the New Lebanon Conference in Columbia Co to address concerns about the revival methods of Mohawk Valley Presbyterians led by Charles Grandison Finney. In 1832 Beecher assumed the presidency of Lane Seminary and the pastorate of Second Presbyterian Church in Cincinnati. Harriet died in 1835, and he married Lydia B. Jackson the next year. In 1856 he retired to Brooklyn.

Henry Ward Beecher, a graduate of Amherst College and Lane Seminary, served in Presbyterian churches in Indiana before his 1847 call to the newly formed Plymouth Church in Brooklyn Heights. He preached to huge crowds there for 40 years, perhaps becoming America's best-known clergyman. He vocally opposed slavery and supported women's rights, and his progressive theological liberalism stressed human goodness and God's love in ways that reflected Victorian culture. He edited the *Independent* (1861–63) and the *Christian Union* (1870–81), both based in New York City, and he published many books of sermons, prayers, and lectures. His affectionate relationship with parishioner Elizabeth Tilton led to adultery charges and a sensational trial in 1875. Commonly presumed guilty at that time and since, the jury nonetheless split nine to three in favor of the popular preacher. He resigned his membership in the New York Congregational Ministerial Organization in 1882 because of his outspoken belief in evolution but retained his large following.

Thomas Beecher was educated at Illinois College and ordained in 1851 as pastor of New England Congregational Church in Williamsburg [now in Brooklyn]. In 1854 he moved to the Independent Congregational Church of Elmira, where his unconventional style focused on the earthly needs of parishioners, especially children and the poor. In 1871 the congregation changed its name to Park Church and constructed a vast, elaborate new building, one of the first "institutional churches" in the United States, designed as a social, educational, and cultural center as well as for worship.

George Beecher (1809–43) pastored in Batavia (Genesee Co) and Rochester in the 1830s, and William (1802–89) followed him in Batavia. James (1828–86) served in Oswego and Poughkeepsie from 1867 to 1876, when he became the "hermit preacher" of Ulster Co. Edward (1803–95), abolitionist president of Illinois College and pastor in Illinois and Boston, retired to Brooklyn in 1871 to write and assist Henry in editing the *Christian Union.*

Caskey, Marie. *Chariot of Fire: Religion and the Beecher Family* (New Haven, Conn: Yale Univ Press, 1978)
Snyder, Stephen H. *Lyman Beecher and His Children* (Brooklyn: Carlson Publishing, 1991)

Charles E. Hambrick-Stowe

Beech-Nut. Food manufacturer. In 1891, five Canajoharie (Montgomery Co) businessmen formed the Imperial Packing Co, a business that produced bacon, ham, and sliced beef, sold mostly in bulk through commercial and government contracts. Headquartered in Canajoharie, it was the first company to pack meat products in glass jars for the retail market (1893) and the first to use vacuum-sealed jars for jam, peanut butter, catsup, and mustard (1897). In 1898 it formally incorporated as Beech-Nut Packing Co, taking the name of the brand that had become its main product line. After introducing further food products shortly before World War I, the company opened additional plants in San Jose, Calif (1911), Canajoharie (1917), and Rochester (1919), and from 1913 space was rented at the Bush Terminal Building in Brooklyn.

Bartlett Arkell, the company's president (1891–1943), had experience as an advertising executive. At Beech-Nut, he used commercial art and celebrity endorsements as promotional tools. These included paintings by Edward Gay, Norman Rockwell, and Cushman Parker, and endorsements from Gene Tunney and Amelia Earhart. In 1931 Beech-Nut introduced baby food, its best-known and longest manufactured product. Approximately 3,000 workers were employed at the three New York State plants in 1940. The company was sold to Life Savers in 1956, and its name changed to Beech-Nut Life Savers. Port Jefferson (Suffolk Co) became the new headquarters, serving as such through 1967, when continued financial troubles led to a second sale of the company, this time to Squibb Pharmaceuticals. Squibb was headquartered in New York City until it moved to Princeton, NJ, in 1971. With various Squibb divestitures between 1971 and 1985, several companies acquired the rights to manufacture one or more Beech-Nut products. In 2003 Beech-Nut Nutrition Corp is a subsidiary of the Milnot Holding Corp of St. Louis, which purchased the company in 1999 from Ralston-Purina. Beech-Nut baby food is still manufactured at a plant in Canajoharie and a plant in Fort Plain (Montgomery Co), which employ approximately 350 workers.

"Beech-Nut Packing," *Fortune* (Nov 1936): 85–93

James Crawford

beef on weck. A sandwich of thinly sliced, rare roast beef dipped in its own juices and piled high on a crusty, hard kümmelweck. The roll, also known as a kaiser or Vienna roll, is covered with caraway or cumin seeds and coarse salt. A frequent garnish is horseradish. The sandwich, also known as beef on wick, has been a staple of bars and taverns in Buffalo and Erie Co for years. It is believed to have been created in Buffalo's German American community about the turn of the 20th century. Two sources are commonly claimed: Schwabl's Restaurant in West Seneca (Erie Co), which remains a favored destination for lovers of the sandwich, and Carl Meyer, who served beef on weck as early as 1901 in his family's first restaurant at Jefferson and Broadway in Buffalo.

Brady, Karen. "Scrumptious Kümmelweck: Buffalo's Treat to Itself," *Buffalo Evening News,* 12 Jan 1966
Jayes, Paul. "What Says Buffalo Like Roast Beef on Weck?" *Buffalo Courier Express,* 23 Mar 1975

Vicki Weiss

Beekman. Town (pop 11,542) in SE Dutchess Co. Part of the Beekman Patent (1697), it was first settled by Palatine Germans in the 1720s. It was formed as a town in 1788. Its only industry was some small iron mines and furnaces. Starting in the 1970s it became a home for workers from Westchester Co and New York City seeking affordable housing; population soared 345% from 1960 to 2000. Irish immigrant Daniel D. Delaney (1802–80) discovered and operated an iron mine at Sylvan Lake.

William P. McDermott

Beekman Patent. Land patent granted 22 Apr 1697 to Henry Beekman Sr (1652–1716) of Kingston (Ulster Co), a member of the colonial legislature. At approximately 100,000 acres (40,500 ha) it comprised the towns now known as Beekman and Union Vale and parts of LaGrange, Dover, and Pawling in Dutchess Co. The original patent did not adequately describe its boundaries, so Beekman applied for and received a new grant in 1703. It was divided among Beekman's heirs and leased to tenants beginning in the 1720s, with formal leases executed *ca* 1740. William Prendergast, seeking secure leases at reasonable rates, led a tenant revolt in 1766. He was accused of treason and sentenced to death but pardoned due to intervention by his wife, Mehitabel Wing. Most leases were converted to freehold status in the 19th century.

Doherty, Frank J. *Settlers of the Beekman Patent, Dutchess County, New York* (Pleasant Valley, NY: Author, 1990)

William P. McDermott

Beekmantown. Town (pop 5,326) in E Clinton Co. Bounded on the east by Lake Champlain, the territory was incorporated in a large grant to speculator William Beekman in 1769 and settled in 1783. Its residents harried the British en route to the Battle of Plattsburgh in 1814. The town was formed in 1820 from Plattsburgh. Since the 1880s apples and dairying have been primary agricultural pursuits. Proximity to Plattsburgh and the presence of the Northway (1965) resulted in the doubling of Beekmantown's population between 1960 and 1990. It is the site of Point Au Roche State Park.

White, Philip L. *Beekmantown, N.Y.: Forest Frontier to Farm Community* (Austin: Univ of Texas Press, 1979)

Thomas A. Rumney

Beekmantown Patent. Land patent in Clinton Co. On 27 Mar 1769 Gov Henry Moore awarded a patent on 30,000 acres (12,000 ha) of land on New York's northern frontier to William Beekman of New York City, a merchant and speculator, and a number of associates. Although the French had granted the same tract several times prior to 1763, a British government decision of 1768 treated their grants south of Quebec as invalid, thus opening the territory for disposition. The patent authorized the township of Beekmantown with the right of town government, but proprietors' early efforts to settle or dispose of the tract were unsuccessful. A 1773 plan to settle Highland Scots in Beekmantown was a failure, as were three attempts to sell it outright. The proprietors charged a surveyor with laying out farm-sized lots in 1785, and sales began in 1787. Initially they offered 21-year leases at £7 annually per 100 acres (40 ha) after 2 years gratis, or sales at 14s to 20s per acre. Soon after settlement began, North Hero, an island in Lake Champlain included in the patent, was awarded to the new state of Vermont, and the proprietors exchanged a southern portion of the grant, adjoining lands of Zephaniah Platt, for a piece of Platt's land north of Beekmantown. These adjustments resulted in a net area of 28,647 acres (11,593 ha). The proprietors and their agents never experienced major conflicts with tenants, and in 1849, when the land had been nearly all settled and most of it sold, agent William Swetland wrote that "a satisfied, contented and kind feeling prevails throughout the whole tenancy."

White, Philip L. *Beekmantown, N.Y.: Forest Frontier to Farm Community* (Austin: Univ of Texas Press, 1979)

Thomas A. Rumney

beer and brewing. Brewing and beer drinking was a significant part of the culture of New Netherland and New York Colony. The climate and terrain of New Netherland were well suited to brewing beer and to growing beer's essential ingredients: barley and wheat (to make malt) and hops. During the 18th century, New York City emerged as a brewing center, where, between 1695 and 1786, 25 brewers and maltsters were active. Most beer brewed in the United States until the middle of the 19th century was top-fermenting ale or porter, styles most commonly found in England and Ireland. Consumer demand for beer during these years reflected not only the colonists' taste for well-made ales but also their awareness that much of the water supply was unsafe to drink. New York brewers continued to use locally grown ingredients, but at times hops had to be imported from other colonies.

In the decades after the American War of Independence, America's drinkers moved away from beer toward distilled drinks such as rum and whiskey. Nevertheless, many brewers started their own businesses during the early 19th century. In 1810 there were 129 breweries in the United States, 42 of which were located in New York State (mainly in the New York City area). New York breweries that year produced nearly 67,000 barrels of beer valued at $340,000. In 1855 the state census listed 128 breweries. The counties with the largest number of breweries were New York (19), Erie (18), Monroe (16), Kings (12), Albany (9), Oneida (8), and Rensselaer (8).

Along with the many new breweries beginning operations during this period was an older firm that James Vassar had founded in Poughkeepsie in 1797. In 1810 Vassar's two sons, Matthew and John, had assumed control of the brewery. Despite a devastating fire in 1811 and the death of John Vassar, Matthew persevered. By the early 1840s the Vassar brewery was producing nearly 15,000 barrels of ale and porter each year, a tremendous figure for the period. By 1860 its 50 employees were turning out 30,000 barrels a year, making it among the nation's largest breweries. In 1860 Matthew Vassar used his earnings from the brewery to endow Vassar College.

Late 19th-Century to Prohibition

According to the 1860 census, New York State accounted for 220 of the nation's 1,269 breweries. The state's emergence as the nation's dominant brewing center—a position it would retain until after World War II—paralleled an important transformation in the type of beer that was brewed. After the 1840s bottom-fermenting lager beers characteristic of central European brewing regions such as Bavaria and Bohemia began to take hold in the United States. German immigrants in New York State began many lager breweries, although some regions with significant Anglo-Irish communities, such as Albany, resisted this trend and continued brewing large amounts of ale in addition to the new lager. New York State's production rose from 5 million barrels in 1880 to 13.1 million barrels in 1915. During these decades, immigrants (particularly German) started many breweries in New York cities and towns. Manhattan and especially Brooklyn were the largest brewing centers. In 1877, 5 of the 10 largest breweries in the United States were located in New York City and Brooklyn. Because these breweries enjoyed direct access to the nation's largest beer drinking community, they, unlike the major Midwestern breweries, did not need to look for customers in distant cities and never developed an extensive regional distribution system. Despite intense competition from large Midwestern firms over the next several decades, New York City breweries continued to thrive. In 1895, 5 of the industry's top 13 breweries were still based in the city, along with countless small breweries with an annual production of less than 1,000 barrels. Many of these firms invested in artificial refrigeration, which permitted year-round brewing. Yet, because New York's breweries generally focused on local markets, they distributed most of their beer in wooden kegs and invested much less into bottling than large breweries in other parts of the country.

The rise of Brooklyn, especially its Bushwick section, as a brewing center occurred after 1859, when clean, soft lake water, ideal for brewing, began to be pumped into the area from eastern Long Island. In 1866 George Ehret started the Hell Gate Brewery in Yorkville. By 1877 it was the largest brewery in the nation, producing 138,000 barrels of beer per year. In the 1890s, at an annual production rate of 500,000–600,000 barrels, it remained one of the nation's top four breweries. Like many locally oriented breweries, Hellgate sold much of its beer in nearby saloons that it either owned or controlled. Critics in the growing temperance movement, however, disapproved of this close relationship between breweries and saloons. Other Bushwick breweries included Piels Bros (1883), John F. Trommer's Evergreen Brewery (1897), and Rheingold, which was founded in 1854 by Samuel Liebmann, a German Jewish immigrant, and which merged in 1924 with the family-owned Liebmann Breweries. F. and M. Schaefer was founded in 1842 by Frederick and Max Schaefer from Germany. Originally located in Manhattan, the brewery moved in 1916 to Bushwick.

Around 1900 the City of Albany supported about 20 breweries, including Hinckel's, Hedrick's, and Quinn and Nolan's. In Rochester there was Bartholomay Brewing, one of the largest breweries in the country by the turn of the century, and the Genesee Brewing Co. In Syracuse notable breweries included Haberle (1855) and Greenway (1850). The major breweries in Buffalo were Lang's Park Brewery, founded as Born and Lang (1840), Lake View Brewing Co (1885), and Iroquois Brewing Co (1892).

Prohibition and Repeal

These enterprises, however, were rendered practically worthless by the passage in 1920 of the 18th Amendment to the US Constitution, which

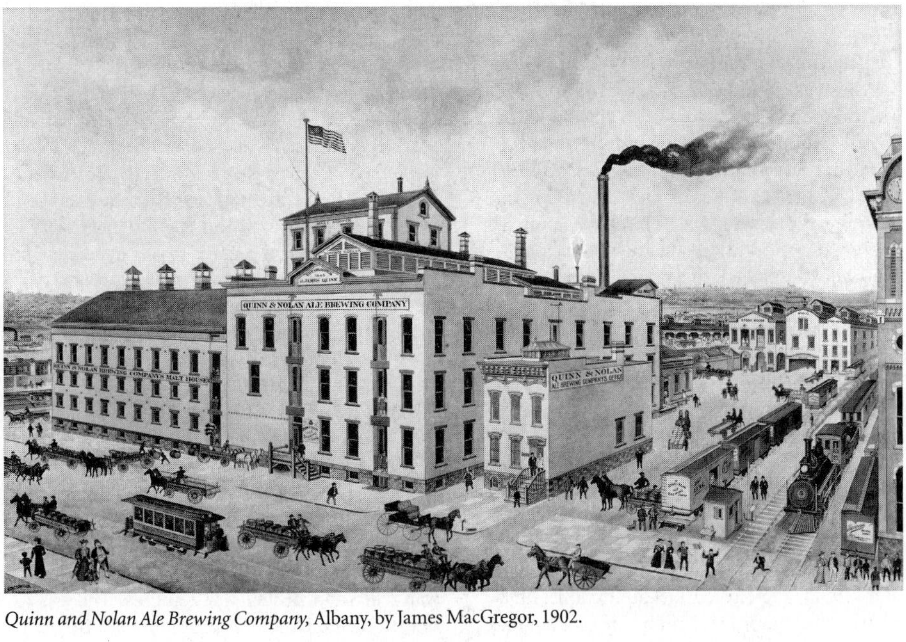

Quinn and Nolan Ale Brewing Company, Albany, by James MacGregor, 1902.

prohibited the production, distribution, and sale of alcoholic beverages throughout the United States. National Prohibition remained in effect until December 1933, although breweries were allowed to begin brewing 3.2% beer in April 1933. This 13-year gap in legal production drove hundreds of breweries out of business. Some continued to produce related products—malt syrup, malt tonic, soft drinks—in an effort to continue plant operations, but many more sold their plants and equipment at a loss. As a result, the post-Prohibition brewing industry consisted of far fewer firms. Also, smaller breweries were harmed by new legislation forbidding them from owning saloons and requiring them to sell their beer to wholesalers, who in turn distributed the beer to retailers. Many local and regional New York breweries that entered the market in the first decade after the repeal of Prohibition closed, despite a new demand for bottled beer and, after 1935, for canned beer, both of which became available at that time in grocery stores.

Only four breweries reopened in Albany after repeal. Of the eight firms that started operations in Rochester, only three survived beyond 1940. In Syracuse only Haberle and Greenway survived more than a few years after the end of Prohibition, finally closing their doors in 1952 and 1962, respectively. Although New York managed to regain its position as the leading brewing state in the 1930s, its share of total production continued to decline. In 1939 it produced 8.7 million of the nation's 52.9 million barrels, or 16%. During the 1940s New York City's largest breweries began to see their production levels fall increasingly behind those of the nation's top breweries. Trommer's, badly hurt by a strike in 1949, closed in 1951. By the early 1970s only one New York City brewery, F. and M. Schaefer, still ranked among the industry's top firms, but its 5 million barrels in 1973 put it far behind the nation's largest brewery, Anheuser-Busch of St. Louis, which sold nearly 30 million barrels. Schaefer closed its Brooklyn plant in 1976, four years after opening a large brewery near Allentown, Pa. In Buffalo the Beck-Mangus Brewery closed in 1955, the Lang's Park Brewery, in 1949, and the Iroquois Brewing Co, in 1971. Even though F. X. Matt in Utica and the High Falls Brewing Co in Rochester survived, New York's rich brewing tradition seemed to be nearing an end. However, since 1980 scores of brewpubs and microbreweries have begun small-scale production of high-quality craft beers. In 1997 Brewery Ommegang, specializing in Belgian-style beers, was opened in Cooperstown (Otsego Co). Also, in 1999 Samuel Liebmann, a descendant of the original founder of Rheingold, opened a new Rheingold brewery in White Plains (Westchester Co).

See also PROHIBITION.

Downward, William. *Dictionary of the History of the American Brewing and Distilling Industries* (Westport, Conn: Greenwood, 1980)

Van Wieren, Dale. *American Breweries II* (West Point, Pa: Eastern Coast Brewiana Association, 1995)

Martin Stack

Belarusians [Byelorussians]. The Republic of Belarus, between 1919 and 1991 the Byelorussian Soviet Socialist Republic (BSSR), lies between Poland to the west, Russia to the east, Ukraine to the south, and Lithuania and Latvia to the north. The majority of Belarusians, about 80%, belong to the Eastern Orthodox religion, and about 18% are Roman Catholic. During the 18th and 19th centuries, Belarusian lands fell under Russian domination, with Eastern Orthodoxy proclaimed the state religion, and by 1859 the Belarusian language was outlawed.

Mass emigration from Belarus to the United States began in the late 19th century and lasted until World War I. This movement included a large number of Jews who generally did not identify themselves as Belarusians. Small numbers from Belarus entered the United States between the two world wars. A much larger wave arrived after World War II. Perhaps a total of 600,000 to 650,000 persons from Belarus settled permanently in the United States. New York City was the main port of entry, with Castle Garden, in what is now Battery Park, and later Ellis Island the principal processing points. While the industries of New York City, Yonkers, Binghamton, Beacon, Albany, Buffalo, Syracuse, and Rochester drew Belarusians to New York State, many also settled in the state's rural areas, close to Polish farmers with whom they had good relations. Belarusians became garment workers, laborers, and farmers in large numbers.

During the 1920s efforts were made to organize a Roman Catholic–affiliated "Landsmen Circle" in Buffalo, and in 1923 delegations of Belarusians from New York State took part in the All Belarusian–American Congress in Chicago. In 1926 the All-American Committee for Assistance to the Peoples of West Belarus was established in New York City with branches in Yonkers and Syracuse. Two years later left-oriented Belarusian Progressive People's Societies formed in Buffalo and Brooklyn. Most of these organizations, the products of socialist aspirations, faded away with the arrival of post–World War II anticommunist immigrants committed to restoration of a democratic state, the Belarusian Democratic Republic, which was proclaimed in 1918 but whose government had quickly been driven into exile. During 1949 and 1950 a US jurisdiction of the Belarusian Autocephalous Orthodox Church was established, with St. Cyril's of Turau Cathedral at 401 Atlantic Ave in Brooklyn dedicated in 1957. Between 1969 and 1972 a new church of St. Cyril of Turau was organized in Richmond Hill (Queens Co)and administered by the Ecumenical Patriarchate. The postwar immigrants also organized the Belarusian-American Association, which was chartered in Albany on 26 July 1950, had several hundred members within its first year, and had several branches in New York City, Beacon (Dutchess Co), Krumville (Ulster Co), and Hempstead (Nassau Co). The association has published a monthly newspaper, *Belarus*, since 1950 and has aided the affiliated Belarusian-American Youth Organization (1951), Union of Belarusian Veterans (1951), and Belarusian-American Women's Association (1953). Through the latter half of the 20th century and into the 21st century, these groups have expressed views on Eastern European problems, such as the Chernobyl catastrophe of 1986 and the dictatorial post-Soviet regime in Belarus. Other active New York State societies include Belarusian Institute of Arts and Sciences (1951), Belarusian-American Relief Organization (1957), the Kreceuski Foundation (1958), Belarusian-American Union of New York (1965), and Fund for Chernobyl Victims in Belarus (1989).

The Belair Miensk resort in Glen Spey (Sullivan Co) is a popular summer vacation spot for Belarusians. The Chapel of the Smalensk Adyhitrija in Glen Spey, founded in 1970, provides services from May to October, and the chapel's annual altar feast on 10 August draws attendees from throughout the eastern United States. Notable Belarusian New Yorkers include poets Natalla Arsiennieva and Masiej Siadnieu, editor and critic Anton Adamovich, biblical scholar Vitaut Tumash, literary scholar Uladzimir Siadura, painter Piotra Miranovich, and civic leader Anton Shukieloyts.

Kipel, Vitaut. *Belarusians in the United States* (Lanham, Md: Univ Press of America, 1999)

Zaprudnik, Jan. *Historical Dictionary of Belarus* (Lanham, Md: Univ Press of America, 1998)

Vitaut Kipel

Belfast. Town (pop 1,714) in central Allegany Co. Settled in 1803, the town was formed from Caneadea as Orrinsburgh in 1824. The name was changed in 1825. The Genesee Valley Canal (1853–78) stimulated the growth of Belfast hamlet, which was later served by three railroads. Sandstone for grindstones was quarried in the late 1870s a mile above the mouth of White Creek and at Rockville. John L. Sullivan trained in Belfast for the last heavyweight championship boxing match under native William Muldoon; the match, against Jake Kilrain, took place 8 July 1889. The 141 ft (43 m) high, 3,119 ft (950.7 m) long Genesee Viaduct (1910–84) carried the Erie Railroad across the Genesee Gorge. In the 1980s an Amish community settled in town and made their living with farming, sawmilling, furniture making, and working in a machine shop. Other residents mostly commute to work in nearby cities. The Rail and Titsworth Warehouse, which served the canal, is a landmark.

Belgians. The Kingdom of Belgium was created in 1830 and is inhabited by Dutch-speaking Flemish, French-speaking Walloons, and a small number of German speakers. A large number of immigrants came from that area to the New Netherlands in the 17th century but were quickly assimilated into Protestant Dutch culture. After 1830 small numbers of individuals settled in New York State. In the 1840s Flemish farmers settled in Sheldon (Wyoming Co), though most Belgian immigrants in the state worked in industries and crafts. Prominent New Yorkers of Belgian descent include Brooklyn-born George Washington Goethals, the engineer of the Panama Canal, and chemist Leo Baekeland, inventor of the early plastic Bakelite. In 1865 the Belgian manufacturer Ernest and Alfred Solvay created a chemical plant in the village of Solvay (Onondaga Co), but few employees came from Belgium. In 1900, 1,787 Belgian-born persons lived in New York State, with about 1,200 in New York City. The Flemish tended to join Dutch Catholic or German parishes before World War I, and the Walloons joined French and Francophone Canadian societies. Because of their small numbers and ethnic divisions, there have been few Belgian associations, save during the two world wars when Belgians collected for war relief and hosted war refugees. There is a branch of the Union Francophone des Belges à

L'Etranger (French Speaking Union of Belgians Abroad), of Vlamingen in de Wereld (Flemish in the World), and the Manhattan Chapter of the Orden van den Prince with Dutch and Flemish membership. Notable post–World War II Belgian Americans in New York State include cell biologist Albert Claude (Nobel Prize in medicine 1974), artist Jan Yoors, and writer Luc Santé. Since 1997 Brewery Ommegang in Cooperstown (Otsego Co) manufactures high-quality Belgian-style beer and holds festivals highlighting Belgian culture. In 2000 the US Census noted about 7,000 people of Belgian ancestry in New York State, most in the New York City area and about 2,000 in Monroe Co.

Sabbe, Philemon D., and Leon Buyse. *Belgians in America* (Tielt, Belgium: Lannoo, 1960)

Thomas Reimer

Belizeans. Emigrants from this northeastern Central American country first came to the United States in the 1940s, when the government recruited men to work in agriculture in the South. Since then there has been a small but continued flow of immigrants. One contributing factor during the 1960s was hurricane Hattie of 1961, which devastated Belize. More recent immigration has been attributed to a lack of economic opportunities, high unemployment rates, and poor standards of living in Belize. The majority of Belizeans coming to the United States are either Garifuna or Creole, the country's two black ethnic groups. Many of the Garifuna in New York State live in Brooklyn. Belizeans are English speakers, and a large percentage of immigrants have high levels of education. A large part of the workforce, both male and female, come to the United States as part of a strategy to diversify the family income at home. Belizean women usually find work in the service sector. Approximately 6,840 people in New York State claim Belizean descent. They tend to gather to celebrate traditional Belizean holidays, including their Independence Day of 21 September.

Woods, Louis A., et al. "International Migration and Ruralization of Belize, 1970–1991." In *Belize: Selected Proceedings from the Second Interdisciplinary Conference*, ed. Michael D. Phillips (Lanham, Md: University Press of America, 1996)

Ana Margarita Cervantes-Rodríguez and Michael C. English

Bell Aircraft Corporation. Company founded in 1935 in Buffalo by Lawrence Bell (1894–1956). Raised in Santa Monica, Calif, Bell worked for aircraft maker Glenn L. Martin from 1913 to 1917. In late 1917 he became manager of newly formed Glenn L. Martin Aircraft Co in Cleveland, directing construction of new bombers ordered by the US Army following Billy Mitchell's post–World War I bombing demonstration. In 1928 Bell joined Consolidated Aircraft Co in Buffalo as vice president and general manager. When Consolidated moved to San Diego in 1935, Bell remained in Buffalo to launch Bell Aircraft Corp in the vacated Consolidated plant, serving as president and aided by Ray Whitman as vice president and Robert Woods as chief designer. In 1936 the US Army Air Corps contracted with Bell to develop XFM-1 Airacuda, an innovative five-place bomber-destroyer featuring wing nacelles holding 37mm cannon, and the gunner's seat forward of the pusher-mounted Allison V-12 engine. Bell also built wing panels for Consolidated's PBY-1 Catalinas.

In 1938 Pres Roosevelt sent Larry Bell to Europe to survey military aviation there. On his return Bell applied German innovations in factory design to plans for a new Bell plant in Wheatfield (Niagara Co), built in 1940. Also in 1938 Bell delivered a prototype of the P-39 single-seat fighter Airacobra. Novel features of the craft included a turbo-supercharged Allison V-12 engine mounted amidships, tricycle landing gear, and a 37mm cannon that fired through a hollow propeller shaft. Nearly 10,000 Airacobras were delivered from early 1941 to mid-1944. In 1943 Bell began delivery of over 3,300 of the more capable P-63 King Cobra fighters, with nearly 7,000 Airacobras and King Cobras sent to US allies during World War II.

In late 1941 Bell had launched a top-secret program in Buffalo to develop P-59A Airacomet, the first American jet aircraft, and in October 1942 shipped XP-59A, disguised with a fake propeller, to California's Muroc Air Base (now Edwards Air Force Base) for testing. At this time Bell diversified operations with the successful test of its Model 30 helicopter by Arthur M. Young in 1942 and acquisition of a Burlington, Vt, producer of gun mounts in 1943. During the war Bell also managed a large plant in Marietta, Ga, which built Boeing-designed B-29 Superfortresses.

From a peak of 28,000 in mid-1944, employment at Bell's Buffalo and Wheatfield plants dropped to 5,300 in June 1945, with the company shifting focus to helicopters, rockets, missiles, spacecraft, and the technology of supersonic flight. On 8 Mar 1946 Bell's Model 47 helicopter received the world's first commercial helicopter license. The Wheatfield facility built helicopters for the US military and export markets until 1952, when production moved to Texas. In 1947 Maj Chuck Yeager piloted Bell XS-1 on the first flight to break the sound barrier. In the same year Bell's X-1E reached a speed of 1,450 mph (2,334 kph), or Mach 2.21, more than twice the speed of sound. In 1951 the company's X-5 tested the aerodynamics of variable-sweep design, and five years later, its swept-wing X-2 reached Mach 3.196. In the early 1950s Bell also created the automatic aircraft carrier landing system (ACLS) for the navy, and after Larry Bell's resignation in 1956 the company continued to innovate. The military tested Bell's X-22A vertical/short takeoff and landing (VTOL/STOL) aircraft in 1965, while during the same decade, Bell divisions pioneered air cushion vehicles (ACV) and built rocket engines for Lockheed satellites and subsystems for the Apollo space program. In April 1966 Lockheed-Martin Corp, headquartered in Bethesda, Md, acquired most Bell facilities in Western New York. During the 1980s these facilities produced inertial subsystems for ballistic missiles. At the beginning of the 21st century, about 30 employees produced gravitational instruments for Western New York's Lockheed-Martin.

Norton, Donald J. *Larry: A Biography of Lawrence D. Bell* (Chicago: Nelson-Hall, 1981)
Pelletier, Alain J. *Bell Aircraft since 1935* (Annapolis, Md: Naval Institute Press, 1992)

Richard Byron

Bellerose. Village (pop 1,173) in Hempstead (Nassau Co). In the 1880s florists and seed growers began using land here that had previously been used for general farming. In 1893 the Citizens Realty Co of Brooklyn planned a development named Bellerose but failed. In 1910 Helen Marsh of Lynn, Mass, began developing the area. Having formed the United Holding Co (1906) to acquire 77 acres (31 ha) of flower farms, she proceeded to build homes on speculation. Bellerose is also the name of an abutting neighborhood in Queens. The portion in Nassau Co incorporated as a village in 1924. Bellerose Terrace, adjacent to the village on the west, added 600 houses in the 1920s. The new development was divided by the construction of the Cross Island Parkway (1939) but surpassed the village in population; in 2000 it was 20% Latino. In the early 21st century Bellerose remains comfortably middle to upper middle class.

Richard A. Winsche

Belle Terre. Village (pop 832) in Brookhaven (Suffolk Co). Situated on the east side of Port Jefferson Harbor, the site was purchased in 1902 by developer Dean Alvord, who created Belle Terre as a 1,300-acre (530 ha) waterfront playground for the rich and famous. His dream was unrealized due to inadequate sales, and the land went into receivership in 1913. In the 1920s sand and gravel mining threatened to turn the end of the neck into an island. To control the mining, residents incorporated as a village in 1931, and there were 89 residents in 1940. The village's "anti-grouper" ordinance (prohibiting unrelated individuals from renting houses) was upheld by the US Supreme Court in 1974.

Victoria R. Aspinwall

Bellevue Hospital Center. Municipal hospital in New York City and the oldest continuously operating public hospital in the United States. Bellevue's institutional ancestor, the city almshouse, opened in 1736 on the present site of City Hall. It relocated to Chambers St around 1794 and moved to a new complex in 1816 on what had been Belle Vue Farm, at 27th St and 1st Ave. In the 1830s and 1840s many of the groups served by the almshouse, such as orphans and pauper children, the able-bodied poor, the insane, and prisoners, were moved to other institutions, leaving the sick and injured to be cared for in what from 1825 was called Bellevue Hospital. The hospital was administered by the city public charities department (under various names) until 1902, by a separate city department called Bellevue and Allied Hospitals from 1902 to 1928, by the city's Department of Hospitals from 1928 to 1970, and by the New York City Health and Hospitals Corp from 1970 on. Bellevue was the first hospital to use hypodermic syringes (1856) and to provide an ambulance service (1869).

Bellevue is a highly acclaimed teaching hospital. In 1873 it became home to America's first professional nursing school. Starting in the late 19th century, three medical schools trained their students in its wards: New York University (NYU) School of Medicine, Columbia University College of Physicians and Surgeons, and Cornell University Medical College. After World War II, NYU gradually expanded its presence and in 1968 assumed full responsibility for the hospital's clinical services. In the early 21st century Bellevue is particularly well known for its psychiatric services and its Emergency Department, which is New York City's designated emergency treatment location for the US president. In 2001 the hospital maintained about 1,000 beds, admitted approximately 25,000 inpatients, provided ambulatory care to almost 490,000 patients, and treated nearly 90,000 people in its Emergency Department.

See also PHYSICIANS.

Opdycke, Sandra. *No One Was Turned Away: The Role of Public Hospitals in New York City since 1900* (New York: Oxford Univ Press, 1999)

Sandra Opdycke

Bellmont. Town (pop 1,423) in NE Franklin Co. Settled in 1816, the town was formed from Chateaugay in 1833. The Banner House (1816), a hotel on Lower Chateaugay Lake, was still in operation in 2003. State legislation to improve the Salmon River resulted in the state dam at Mountain View (1855–57). Locally mined iron ore and ore brought from Lyon Mountain in Clinton Co were processed in the Catalan forge of the Bellmont Iron Works (1874–93). Much local timber was used for charcoal. The town was reached by the Chateaugay Railroad (1886; later Delaware and Hudson Railroad) and the New York Central (1892). In the early 21st century it remains a lumbering town, with resort development on the lakes near Mountain View.

Thomas W. Perrin

Bellmore {Bellmore, locality (pop 16,441) in Hempstead, Nassau Co; North Bellmore, locality (pop 20,079) in Hempstead}. Bellmore is bounded in the south by East Bay, part of Great South Bay. Both localities were settled by Anglo American farmers: North Bellmore in 1655, Bellmore in 1676. North Bellmore was called Little Britain in the Revolutionary War era; it was later called Smithville and acquired a post office named Smithville South in 1867, renamed North Bellmore in 1920. Bellmore was first known as Little Neck, then New Bridge (crossing what is now Newbridge Creek) from 1818 until the South Side Rail Road (now Long Island Rail Road) established a Bellmore stop in 1869; a post office opened in 1883. In North Bellmore grain and vegetable culture dominated until the cut-flower industry became more important (*ca* 1880–1950). The Brush area of Smithville, south of Jerusalem Ave, was home to free Blacks and Native Americans from the 1790s to the 1930s. Modest development of Bellmore began in the 1920s, and the Southern State Parkway improved automobile access when opened in 1930. A central high school district was created in 1935. North Bellmore, which had a population of 3,519 in 1940, underwent considerable growth in the 1950s, and Bellmore, with a population of 6,793 in 1940, grew significantly in the 1950s and 1960s. Bellmore's waterfront offers access to East Bay for pleasure boaters via 14 canals with bulkheads and three natural creeks. Bellmore's family festival takes place in September; North Bellmore holds a strawberry festival in June. Landmarks are the Southard House (*ca* 1655) and the Bedell House (?1689).

Kenneth M. Foreman

Bellport {Bellport, village (pop 2,363) in Brookhaven, Suffolk Co; North Bellport, locality (pop 9,007) in Brookhaven}. The area was settled in 1655. Bellport residents in the 18th and early 19th centuries were whalers and cordwood cutters. In 1829 the Bell brothers opened a shipyard and platted streets, and the Bellport post office opened in 1834. A great storm closed the harbor in 1837, and fires decimated the forests, ending those industries. The Long Island Rail Road opened a station in Bellport in 1852. From the 1840s through the 1930s, Bellport was a noted resort. Jacqueline Bouvier spent her childhood summers there. It was also where the patented ball bearing (1866) and the scooter, a type of iceboat, were invented. Incorporated in 1908, the village was the home of Suffolk Novelty Fireworks Co (Grucci's, 1929–83). Since 1950 it has been the site of the Gateway Playhouse (now Suffolk County Center for the Performing Arts). Many of its residents are employed at Brookhaven National Laboratory (1947). North Bellport, originally farmland, was first developed as an 1890s real estate venture, with many of its lots sold to Italian Americans; Pace Developers built 300 small houses in the mid-1950s. Bellport declined in the 1960s because of losses in nearby defense employment, but in the late 1990s community housing alliances and an Economic Development Zone designation improved its fortunes.

Bronwyn Hannon

Belmont. Village (pop 952) in Amity (Allegany Co). Located at the Philipsburgh Mill Reserve, an important waterpower site, sawmills and gristmills were built at an early date. The village was incorporated in 1853 as Philipsville and changed to Belmont in 1859, the year it became the county seat due to its Erie Railroad (1851) service. The Belmont Manufacturing Co (1866) produced mowing machines and circular-saw mills. By 1889 it was in the business of manufacturing equipment for electricity plants. Clark Bros operated a plant in Belmont during the first decade of the 20th century, moving to Olean after a fire and becoming Dresser Rand. In the 20th and 21st centuries, Belmont's chief business has been county government. Other employers include Genesee Valley Central School, William Laidlaw and Co (machining), and Accord Corp (community service agency). The Italianate Whitney-Halsey Mansion (Americana Manse, 1870) is a museum.

Belmont Park. This American thoroughbred racetrack is located just outside Queens in Elmont (Nassau Co). A group headed by William C. Whitney and August Belmont II opened Belmont Park in 1905 and named it after Belmont's father, a leader of horse racing after the Civil War. The park not only boasted a $^1/_2$ mi track (still the longest in the United States) but until 1920 ran its races clockwise in the English style. The park experienced several problems in its early years. It shut down in 1911 and 1912 because of state antigambling legislation, and a series of huge fires destroyed the grandstand in 1917, though horse races continued to be run. Within three years the track was restored, and Belmont Park hosted some of the most exciting races in the country, including the 1923 defeat of Epsom (or English) Derby champion Papyrus by Kentucky Derby champion Zev and the 1947 victory of Armed, owned by Calumet Farm of Kentucky, over Assault, fielded by the King Ranch of Texas.

The New York Racing Association (NYRA) bought the track from the Belmont group in 1955. Structural problems caused the park to close in 1963, but an entirely rebuilt $31 million Belmont Park opened in 1968. Three years later, however, it was challenged by OTB, a public benefit corporation operating off-track betting parlors that threatened attendance and income at the tracks. Highly publicized races still drew both fans, such as the 82,694 who witnessed Pass Catcher's defeat of Canonero II in the 1971 Belmont Stakes, and money, such as the $10.5 million that was bet at the Breeders' Cup races at Belmont in 1990. But in recent years neither Belmont Park nor NYRA's Aqueduct racetrack in Queens have been able to outmaneuver OTB and bring in the crowds on a daily basis. Belmont Park has a capacity of 85,000 to 90,000, including seating for 32,941. It has two race meetings: early May to mid-July and early September to late October. It also operates year-round as a thoroughbred training center.

Hotaling, Edward. *They're Off! Horse Racing at Saratoga* (Syracuse: Syracuse Univ Press, 1995)

Edward Hotaling

Belmont Stakes. A celebrated horse race for three-year-olds at Belmont Park in Elmont (Nassau Co). It is the third leg in the Triple Crown of American thoroughbred horse racing, the first two segments being the Kentucky Derby and the Preakness Stakes. The race is held in June, three weeks after the Preakness. Named after banker August Belmont, this contest was first run 19 June 1867 at Jerome Park in Fordham [now in Bronx Co]. It was initially run at a distance of $1^5/_8$ miles, and the first winner was a filly named Ruthless in a time of 3 min 5 s.

Several venues have hosted the race: Jerome Park (1867–89), Morris Park [now in Bronx Co] (1890–1904), Aqueduct in Queens (1963–67), and Belmont Park (1905–62 excluding 1911–12, and 1968–). Since 1925 the race has been $1^1/_2$ miles, making it the longest leg of the Triple Crown. The 2001 purse was $1 million. The largest crowds for the Belmont Stakes have seen the victories of Lemon Drop Kid in 1999 (85,818) and Conquistador Cielo in 1982 (82,894). Among the most memorable Belmont Stakes finishes were Man o' War's 1920 win by 20 lengths in a world record 2 min 14.2 s for $1^3/_8$ miles, and Secretariat's 1973 victory by 31 lengths in a world record 2 min 24 s for $1^1/_2$ miles. The latter still stands as a dirt-track world record. In addition to Secretariat, the classic's Triple Crown laureates include Sir Barton (1919), Gallant Fox (1930), Omaha (1935), War Admiral (1937), Whirlaway (1941), Count Fleet (1943), Assault (1946), Citation (1948), Seattle Slew (1977), and Affirmed (1978).

Hotaling, Edward. *They're Off! Horse Racing at Saratoga* (Syracuse: Syracuse Univ Press, 1995)

Edward Hotaling

Bemis, James D(raper) (*b* Spencer, Mass, 1 July 1783; *d* Canandaigua, Ontario Co, 2 Nov 1857). Printer and publisher. Known as the Father of Western New York Press, Bemis started as a book clerk for the Backus and Whiting booksellers in Albany, where he apprenticed for seven years. In 1803, en route to open a branch store in Little York [now Toronto, Ont], bad road conditions forced him to stop in Canandaigua. He decided to open the store there instead but sold it within a year to buy half interest in a local printshop. His partner was John K. Gould, publisher of the *Western Repository.* After Gould died in 1808, Bemis became sole owner and remained involved in publishing the paper, under the name *Ontario Repository,* through 1828. Bemis expanded the business by buying several bookbinding and printing companies and establishing the first printing presses and bookstores in Erie, Wayne, Livingston, and Onondaga Cos. He also printed the region's first almanac in 1814, *The Farmer's Diary; or, Western Almanack.* Bemis and his wife, Ruth Williams, had three daughters.

Stern, Madeleine B. *Imprints on History: Book Publishers and American Frontiers* (Bloomington: Indiana Univ Press, 1956)

Matt Leingang

Bemus Point. Village (pop 340) in Ellery (Chautauqua Co). Located at the narrows on Chautauqua Lake, evidence of Paleo-Indian, Archaic, and Late Woodland occupation was found here. A few Seneca families occupied the point from 1782 to *ca* 1800. It was settled by William Bemus in 1806. A ferry across the lake began in 1811 and has been operated by Chautauqua Lake Historic Vessels since 1982. Hotels (starting in 1871), boardinghouses, and summer cottages were built to accommodate summer vacationers, still the village's chief business. Vacationers originally came by steamboat. The Chautauqua Lake Railroad was completed along the lakeshore in 1887. The village incorporated in 1911.

Mary Jane Stahley

Bennington. Town (pop 3,349) in NW Wyoming Co. Settled in 1802 along the Indian path from the Genesee River to the Buffalo Creek Reservation [now in Erie Co], the town was formed from Sheldon in 1818. The Cowlesville Furnace (1844) produced iron. Germans settled in the town *ca* 1840. Franklin Mineral Springs were discovered in 1865 while drilling for oil. Bennington is a dairy farming town, with nonfarm workers commuting to Buffalo, Rochester, and elsewhere.

Bennington, Battle of. In August 1777 a British campaign under Lt Gen John Burgoyne pushed southward along the Champlain-Hudson corridor trying to capture Albany before winter. In an attempt to resupply his main army for the final push to Albany, Burgoyne dispatched an expedition eastward from Fort Miller [now in Saratoga Co]. The goal was to capture stores at a Continental military depot at Bennington in the Hampshire Grants [now in Vt], just over what is now the New York State border. Commanded by German lieutenant colonel Frederick Baum, the expedition consisted of approximately 200 Brunswick dragoons, two crews of Hesse-Hanau artillerymen, each of the latter with a 3-pounder cannon, a small number of British marksmen, 150 loyalists from Peter's Provincial Corps, about 50 Canadian and provincial volunteers, and over 100 Caughnawaga Mohawks. Believing he was in a strongly loyalist district, Baum expected to see large numbers of volunteers joining his ranks.

While Baum departed the main British army, Gen John Stark of the New Hampshire Militia was raising men and supplies in western New England to defend the region. As Baum's expedition halted on 13 August a few miles west of the mill at Sancoick [now Hoosick, Rensselaer Co], Stark sent out a reconnaissance force of over 200 men west along the main road. Early on 14 August Baum's troops confronted Stark's advance force at the mill and drove them off after a brief skirmish. Now aware of the location and size of the approaching forces, Stark sent his entire army west to oppose them. Because records are sparse, the number of his troops cannot be reliably estimated. Baum sent immediately back to Burgoyne's headquarters for reinforcements.

By midday on 14 August, the British expedition and New England forces stood facing each other across a broad area of low farmland on the Walloomsac River, east of the hamlet of Walloomsac [now in Rensselaer Co]. Both armies occupied advantageous high ground, and neither wanted to venture forward across the floodplain to engage the other. Baum quickly built earth and log redoubts on several points west of the river, and Stark established a camp just over the New York State border but sent out parties to observe and harass the expedition. At dawn on 15 August the relief force under Col Heinrich Breymann, about 500 German troops supported by two 6-pounder cannons, was dispatched from the main army. It rained most of the day, preventing any general engagement along the Walloomsac River and delaying the arrival of Breymann's column. Unable to engage Stark's forces because of inclement weather and apparently unwilling to do so without reinforcements, the British improved their fortified positions while the Americans harassed the margins of their defenses.

The weather delay allowed the New England forces to grow to approximately three times the numbers of the British, since units of the Vermont and Massachusetts Militia arrived late in the night of 15 August. The weather gradually improved on the morning of 16 August, and over 1,000 men from the New England units were positioned to execute Stark's plan for an encircling movement around the expedition and a simultaneous attack on all fronts. By afternoon a general assault on the British entrenchments began. Early in the battle the Mohawks fled through a ravine and escaped westward to the main army. The loyalist force posted at a smaller redoubt was easily overwhelmed. Dragoons in the large redoubt eventually ran out of ammunition and were driven out, withdrawing to the main army. The British position at the river was also overrun, and Baum was mortally wounded.

Breymann's relief column arrived and engaged the New England troops, who were chasing down scattered British units attempting to escape. Supported by the two cannons, Breymann's column pushed back the New Englanders to the western edge of the hills they had just captured from Baum. At this critical point, newly arrived Continental army troops under Col Seth Warner came up to reinforce the American front. As Breymann's casualties mounted and his ammunition ran out, he was forced to withdraw in the approaching darkness, leaving the Americans in control of the battlefield.

In frustrating the excursion into Bennington and denying the British an opportunity to resupply, the Americans helped to starve the main British Army. American morale was also boosted by this first victory against British artillery. In many ways, Bennington was the mortal wound that eventually led to the British surrender at Saratoga [now Schuylerville, Saratoga Co].

Lord, Philip, Jr. *War over Walloomscoick: Land Use and Settlement Pattern on the Bennington Battlefield—1777* (Albany: NYS Museum, 1989)

Philip L. Lord Jr

Benson. Town (pop 201) in SE Hamilton Co. Settled prior to 1810, the town was formed from Mayfield [now in Fulton Co] and Hope in 1860. Until the 1890s lumbering and small farms sustained the economy, and some women sewed for Northville glove shops. The population peaked in 1880 at 399 and in 1960 was only 87. In the early 21st century lumbering and seasonal recreation are its main land uses.

Benton. Town (pop 2,640) in NE Yates Co. Gen John Sullivan's expedition destroyed a Seneca village in the northeastern part of town on 8 Sept 1779. Two French traders established a European American presence in the 1780s, and permanent settlement followed in 1789. The town was formed from Jerusalem in 1803 as Vernon, and its name was changed to Snell in 1808 and to Benton in 1810. The Northern Central Railway crossed the town in 1851. Yates Co's first vineyard was planted in the town's southwestern corner in 1855, but Benton's level land is chiefly valued for dairy, with the northeastern quarter in crop farming. Beginning in the 1890s its farming was dominated by Danes. Mennonite families began moving to town around 1980.

Gwen Chamberlain

Bergen [BER-JEN]. Town (pop 3,182) and village (pop 1,240) in NE Genesee Co. Settled in 1801 the town was formed from Murray in 1813. Buffalo Rd (Rte 33) was built in 1810, and the Tonawanda Railroad reached Bergen in 1837. The village incorporation, authorized in 1877, was completed in 1886. By 1890 Bergen's rich, level farmland grew wheat and barley. A canning factory (now Agrilink) opened in 1907 and uses seasonal migrant labor. Liberty Pumps (1965) manufactures pumps for nationwide sale. The Bergen Swamp, which is 2,000 acres (809 ha) of wet forest, was designated (1965) as a National Natural Landmark, and the west side of the village is on the National Register of Historic Places. As a result of I-490 (1966), which has an exit in town, Bergen came within commuting range of Rochester, Brockport (Monroe Co), and Le Roy. Between 1990 and 2000 the population grew nearly 14%.

Susan L. Conklin

Bergholz. Locality in Wheatfield (Niagara Co). A group of German Lutherans, migrating because they opposed the Prussian Church Union, acquired 2,120 acres (858 ha) in 1843 and surveyed a compact agricultural village; each male community member received one of 121 parcels. New Bergholz, as it was first known, was the largest of four communities they established. They brought with them a distinct culture and, for many years, welcomed only German Lutherans as new residents, retaining that identity until the World War II era. Thirty-seven migrated to Michigan in 1854, and more in following decades. In 2003 the community is suburban to Niagara Falls and Buffalo, and the site of Das Haus, one of the original 1843 log dwellings operated as a museum by the Historical Society of North German Settlements in Western New York. The Bergholz Band of Western New York (1971) continues the locality's German brass band tradition.

Joseph Golombek Jr

Berkshire. Town (pop 1,366) in NE Tioga Co. Settled in 1791 from Stockbridge, Mass, the town was formed from Tioga in 1808. A brickyard operated from 1827 to 1835, and a tannery opened in 1849, becoming part of United States Leather Co in 1893. The Southern Central Railroad (later Lehigh Valley Railroad) came through in 1871, and small industries followed, including fashioners of rakes, novelties, butter tubs, and wagon wheels. Beginning in 1906 the Howland Bros Co timbered and shipped hardwood and remained one of the town's chief employers in 2003. Howland Apiaries (1930s) produces honey. Agriculture and lumbering contribute to the town's economy, while many residents commute to Owego, Ithaca, or beyond. Part of Jenksville State Forest is located in Berkshire.

Joann Lindstrom

Berlin [BER-LIN]. Town (pop 1,901) in E Rensselaer Co. Settled around 1765, the town was formed in 1806 from Petersburgh, Schodack, and Stephentown. Most of its population lives in the narrow valley of the Little Hoosic, between high ridges to the east and west. At West Berlin a number of Bavarian immigrant families settled in 1834 and manufactured charcoal. The Harlem Railroad Extension (later Rutland Railroad) served the town from 1869 to 1953. Dyken Pond was created in 1902 by damming the Poesten Kill, and Cherry Plain State Park was developed from a Civilian Conservation Corps site. Longtime employers in Berlin include W. J. Cowee Co (1900), manufacturer of turned wood products, and Henry J. Seagroatt Co (1927; now Seagroatt Riccardi), a large grower of roses. Some residents commute to the Capital District and to Pittsfield, Mass.

Kathryn T. Sheehan

Berlin, Irving [Beilin, Israel] (*b* Tyumen, Russia, 11 May 1888; *d* New York City, 22 Sept 1989). Songwriter. Berlin emigrated in 1893 with his family and settled on the Lower East Side of Manhattan. Leaving school at 14 to work as a singer and song plugger in Bowery saloons, he wrote the lyrics to "Marie from Sunny Italy," his first published song (1907), followed by his great hit "Alexander's Ragtime Band" (1911), for which he wrote the words and music. In 1912 he married Dorothy Goetz, who died of typhoid five months later. He became a citizen in 1918, joined the army, and at Camp Upton in Yaphank (Suffolk Co) wrote *Yip! Yip! Yaphank,* featuring "Oh! How I Hate to Get Up in the Morning," performed by Berlin himself. He wrote "A Pretty Girl Is Like a Melody" for the *Ziegfeld Follies of 1919.* In 1921, with producer Sam Harris, he built and opened the Music Box Theatre on 45th St and went on to write four editions of the *Music Box Revue.* In 1926 he married Ellin Mackay, daughter of telegraph magnate Clarence Mackay, who promptly disinherited her. From this period came the songs "Blue Skies" (1926) and "Puttin' on the Ritz" (1927). *Face the Music* (1932), with songs by Berlin, book by Moss Hart, and direction by George S. Kaufman, opened on Broadway at the New Amsterdam Theatre in February and ran for 165 performances. Hart and Berlin collaborated on *As Thousands Cheer* (1933), one of the biggest hits of the decade. Built on the idea of a living newspaper, the musical included "Heat Wave" and "Easter Parade."

Berlin had contributed to film scores since the earliest talkies, although his greatest successes in the genre were three films starring Fred Astaire and Ginger Rogers: *Top Hat* (1935), which included "Cheek to Cheek" and "Top Hat, White Tie and Tails"; *Follow the Fleet* (1936), including such tunes as "Let's Face the Music and Dance" and "Let Yourself Go"; and *Carefree* (1938). Berlin scored the films *On the Avenue* (1937) and *Alexander's Ragtime Band* (1938), which loosely followed his own life story and included 30 of his tunes.

In 1938 Kate Smith introduced Berlin's "God Bless America" on her radio program. Originally written for *Yip! Yip! Yaphank,* with only minor word changes, the song became an unofficial national anthem. *Louisiana Purchase* premiered on Broadway in 1940, and in 1941 Berlin worked on the movie score that became *Holiday Inn* (1942), starring Fred Astaire and Bing Crosby, which included "White Christmas." Another all-soldier Broadway revue, *This Is the Army* (1942), earned more than $2 million for the Army Emergency Relief Fund. Berlin's most successful musical and the first to feature a strong book was *Annie Get Your Gun* (1946), including such hit songs as "Anything You Can Do," "I Got the Sun in the Morning," "There's No Business Like Show Business," and "They Say It's Wonderful." While Berlin would write other stage musicals, notably *Call Me Madam* (1950), and would see his songs featured in additional movies, he had by this time accomplished his most intense creative work. Successful in forms of entertainment from vaudeville to revue to musicals to film scores, he helped form the American character by defining its dreams clearly and simply, with intuitive understanding, in song.

Bergreen, Laurence. *As Thousands Cheer: The Life of Irving Berlin* (New York: Viking, 1990)
Jablonski, Edward. *Irving Berlin: American Troubador* (New York: Henry Holt, 1999)

Joan Morris

Berne. Town (pop 2,846) in W Albany Co. Settled *ca* 1750 by Germans, the area was the site of a massacre (the only one in Albany Co during the Revolution) of eight members of the Deitz family by tories and Indians in 1780. After the war, Berne's population increased with influxes of New Englanders and Scots-Irish. The town was formed from Rensselaerville in 1795. Berne was the site of agitation during the antirent war between 1839 and 1846, and as late as 1860 due to the persistence of leases in town. The first antirent convention took place at the Berne Lutheran Church in 1845. Berne was the initial home of the Simmons axe factory (1825–33), woolen cloth was produced in the 1860s, and Helderberg bluestone remains an important product. Warner and Thompsons Lakes became resorts after the Civil War; the second featured the Lake View House (*ca* 1876). In the early 21st century the agricultural town is primarily a bedroom community for the Capital District.

Bernstein, Leonard (*b* Lawrence, Mass, 25 Aug 1918; *d* New York City, 14 Oct 1990). Composer and conductor. After attending Harvard University and Philadelphia's Curtis Institute of Music, he moved to New York City, which became his personal and professional base. When he was in his early 20s he performed in a revue with Betty Comden and Adolph Green at the Village Vanguard. In 1943, at age 25, he was named assistant conductor of the New York Philharmonic and made an electrifying impression as a last-moment substitute for the ailing Bruno Walter on a broadcast concert that November. From 1945 to 1948 he conducted the short-lived New York Symphony (succeeding Leopold Stokowski), concentrating on 20th-century repertoire. In 1957 he became co-director (with Dimitri Mitropoulos) of the New York Philharmonic, then, in 1958, the Philharmonic's first American music director. In this capacity he influentially championed the music of Charles Ives and Gustav Mahler. Building on an ingenious series of television specials beginning in 1954, he invigorated the Philharmonic's Young People's Concerts as a nationally televised medium for music education. Breaking with traditional music appreciation, he refused to sanctify famous music; rather, he dismantled it to see how it worked or juxtaposed it with Beatles and Elvis Presley tunes.

As a composer, Bernstein merged the worlds of George Gershwin and Aaron Copland. His eclectic concert idiom draws upon jazz and popular song. His symphonic works include the much-performed *Serenade for Violin, Strings, and Harp* (1954), but none of his three symphonies has entered the mainstream repertoire. For Broadway, he aspired to synthesize American musical theater with opera. His crowning creative achievement, *West Side Story* (1957), retells the Romeo and Juliet story in a racially severed Manhattan slum. His Broadway musicals *On the Town* (1944) and *Wonderful Town* (1953) are also set in New York, as is the ballet *Fancy Free* (1944). *Candide* (1956), after Voltaire, is more remarkable for its score than for its theatrical possibilities; its overture is Bernstein's most-performed single composition.

After leaving the New York Philharmonic in 1969 and becoming the orchestra's conductor laureate, Bernstein increasingly based his career in Europe. As a composer, his most ambitious later work is the little-remembered opera *A Quiet Place* (1984), a mirror of personal disillusionment and compositional discomfort. More admired is his *Songfest* (1977) for vocal soloists and orchestra (1977), an American tapestry setting poets as diverse as Edgar Allan Poe, Walt Whitman, Frank O'Hara, and Lawrence Ferlinghetti. His Norton Lectures (1973), published as *The Unanswered Question,* document his estrangement from contemporary popular culture (which he found vulgar) and high modernism (which he found unduly esoteric). He will be remembered for the ebullience and versatility of his talents. No previous American achieved comparable international eminence as a classical musician.

Bernstein, Leonard. *The Joy of Music* (New York: Simon & Schuster, 1959)
Burton, Humphrey. *Leonard Bernstein* (New York: Doubleday, 1994)

Joseph Horowitz

Bernstein, Philip S(ydney) [Feivel Shimmel] (*b* Rochester, 29 June 1901; *d* Rochester, 3 Dec 1985). Rabbi. The son of Lithuanian immigrants, Bernstein attended Rochester's East High School and graduated from Syracuse University (1921) and the Jewish Institute of Religion in New York City (1926). He was ordained in 1926. After post-graduate study he returned to Rochester and became rabbi of Temple B'rith Kodesh in 1927. Of humble Orthodox roots, Bernstein restored to the Reform congregation some Jewish traditions, including the return of the Sabbath celebration from Sunday to Friday evening. Beyond his congregation, he stirred Rochester by such activities as inviting birth control pioneer Margaret Sanger to speak at his temple in 1932 and beginning a campaign for public housing as early as 1928. A leading Jewish pacifist for much of the 1930s, he warned about the rise of Hitler in sermons and articles from as early as 1931 but later forsook his antiwar position to become a leading supporter of war preparedness. From 1942 to 1946 Bernstein held a position with the Jewish Welfare Board supervising all Jewish chaplains of the US armed forces. In 1946–47 he served as adviser on Jewish affairs to Gen Joseph T. McNarney, commanding general of Allied forces in Europe. In this capacity, Bernstein began the process of helping displaced Jews establish new lives in Europe, Palestine, the United States, and elsewhere. After the massacre of 41 Jews in the Kielce (Poland) pogrom on 4 July 1946, he convinced military authorities to keep the Polish borders open and helped more than 110,000 Holocaust survivors leave that country.

Bernstein was active in establishing the state of Israel and was an ardent Zionist. An important ambassador for his faith, his book *What the Jews Believe* (1950) was a best-seller. He retired from Temple B'rith Kodesh in 1973. As his last public appearance, he gave the commencement address at Nazareth College in Rochester in 1978.

Eisenstadt, Peter. *Affirming the Covenant: A History of Temple B'rith Kodesh, Rochester, New York, 1848–1998* (Rochester: Temple B'rith Kodesh, 1999; distributed by Syracuse Univ Press)

Joann Minor

Berra, Yogi [Lawrence Peter] (*b* St. Louis, 12 May 1925). Baseball player. Raised in St. Louis he signed with the New York Yankee organization in 1942. A superlative catcher Berra was a central figure on a Yankee team that appeared in 14 World Series during his 18 seasons with the club (1946–63). His records for the most games and hits in World Series play still stand. He managed the Yankees to the World Series in 1964 only to be fired after the season. Berra joined the New York Mets as a coach in 1965, the year he made his final appearances as a player, and later managed the club (1972–75), taking them to the 1973 World Series. His second stint as Yankee manager (1984–85) ended with an unceremonious firing by Yankee owner George Steinbrenner. Berra's feud with Steinbrenner lasted until 1999. Berra's reputation for coining naive though cunning catchphrases, "Yogi-isms" (many of them apocryphal) such as "It ain't over 'til it's over," enhanced his public standing, but his reputation rests on his baseball prowess. Inducted into the Baseball Hall of Fame in 1972, he was one of two catchers voted onto Major League Baseball's All-Century Team in 1999.

Bannon, Joseph J., Bill Madden, and Joanna L. Wright. *Yogi Berra: An American Original* (Champaign, Ill: Sports Publishing, 1998)

Berra, Yogi. *The Yogi Book: "I Really Didn't Say Everything I Said!"* (New York: Workman Publishing, 1998)

Berra, Yogi, and Tom Horton. *Yogi: It Ain't Over* (New York: McGraw-Hill, 1989)

Scott Pitoniak

Berrigan, Daniel J(oseph) (*b* Virginia, Minn, 9 May 1921) and **Berrigan, Philip F(rancis)** (*b* Two Harbors, Minn, 5 Oct 1923; *d* Baltimore, 6 Dec 2002). Roman Catholic priests and political activists. In the 1930s the Berrigans' father, a trade unionist, moved the family to Syracuse where the brothers grew up and graduated from high school. After serving in the US Army during World War II (1943–46), Philip enrolled in the College of the Holy Cross, graduating in 1950 with a BA in English. Daniel joined the Society of Jesus and was ordained a priest in 1952, while Philip was ordained a Josephite priest in 1955. Daniel taught at Brooklyn Preparatory School and later at LeMoyne College in Syracuse (1957–62). Philip was assigned to New Orleans, where he became active in the Civil Rights Movement, leading to a transfer in the mid-1960s to a Josephite seminary in Newburgh (Orange Co). His preaching against the Vietnam War caused him to be reassigned to Baltimore. In 1964 the brothers helped to found the Catholic Peace Fellowship in New York City. Daniel became a chaplain at Cornell University in 1967, and both brothers became increasingly active in protesting the Vietnam War. The Berrigans gained widespread notoriety in 1968 when, along with seven others, the Catonsville Nine burned hundreds of draft files with homemade napalm in a Baltimore suburb. Sent to federal prison in 1970, the Berrigans were paroled in 1973, and Philip was excommunicated following his marriage to Elizabeth McAlister, a nun. During the next several decades the brothers continued their pacifist activities, often through the Plowshares movement, a peace group against nuclear weapons, and were repeatedly arrested and imprisoned. Philip was released from an Ohio prison for a Plowshares action just a year before his death. Daniel remained a Jesuit priest, committed to social justice, and for many decades has lived in New York City.

Polner, Murray, and Jim O'Grady. *Disarmed and Dangerous: The Radical Life and Times of Daniel and Philip Berrigan* (New York: Basic Books, 1997)

J. Justin Gustainis

Bethany. Town (pop 1,760) in SE Genesee Co. Settled in 1803 the town formed in 1812 from Batavia. The Genesee County Home and Infirmary was built in 1827 and relocated to Batavia in 1974. In the mid–19th century Bethany attracted a number of Irish and German immigrant farm families. The Genesee County Forest and Park (444 acres/179.7 ha) began with the purchase of a wood lot in 1882 and was designated a county forest in 1935, the first in New York State. Farms have become larger through consolidation, and many residents commute to Batavia or larger cities.

Susan L. Conklin

Bethel. Town (pop 4,362) in central Sullivan Co. Settled ?1798, it was rendered more accessible to settlers by the Newburgh and Cochecton Turnpike (1801). Bethel lies on the high ridges that form the watershed between the Delaware and Mongaup Rivers. The town was formed from Lumberland in 1809. Lumbering and tanning were its early industries, and when lumber and tanbark grew scarce, dairying took over. White Lake was a fashionable summer resort by the time of the Civil War, but its small hotels faded during the county's transition to the borscht belt; the Mansion House (1848) was among the first resort hotels in the county and is the oldest hotel standing. Beginning in 1928 Smallwood was developed as a Gentiles-only resort community; in the 1950s its development resumed, and had a mixture of primary and second homes as well as of Gentiles and Jews. The Woodstock Art and Music Fair took place in Bethel in 1969. It is home to Lake Superior State Park and the Sullivan County International Airport.

John Conway

Bethlehem. Town (pop 31,304) in E Albany Co. Settled under Rensselaerswijck [now in Albany, Columbia, and Rensselaer Cos] in 1634, the town was formed from the old town of Watervliet in 1793. Its fertile soil made it excellent for farming, and wheat, dairy, vegetables, and fruit remained major products until past the mid–20th century. Molding sand was quarried at Glenmont from the 1830s to the 1950s. Callanan Road Improvement Co (1883) at South Bethlehem remains a large gravel producer. The Albany and Susquehanna (1863) and West Shore (1883) Railroads made possible summer residences and, especially after World War I, suburban homes for wealthy Albanians. Bethlehem's population more than quadrupled between 1920 and 1960. In 1924 the New York Central Railroad moved its vast freight classification yards to Selkirk. With excellent highway access from the New York State Thruway (1954), this suburban town was also the site of large industrial facilities in 2003, including Niagara Mohawk's steam-generating plant (1952) at Glenmont, GE Plastics (1966), and Owens-Corning (1976). National Register landmarks include the Nicoll-Sill House (1735) and a Whipple bowstring truss bridge (1867; reconstructed at its present site *ca* 1900). Price Greenleaf (1961), a nursery, is the successor to the Albany Seed Store (1831), making it one of New York State's oldest businesses.

George Wise

Bethlehem Steel Company. The Lackawanna Iron and Steel Co, a Pennsylvania-based corporation with origins back to 1857, began construction of a massive steel mill in 1902 in Lackawanna (Erie Co), a location chosen for proximity to Great Lakes shipping and nearby low-cost electrical power. The plant started production three years later, though the facility was not fully completed until 1907. The Lackawanna plant cost $60 million, with the site encompassing 1 mile (1.6 km) of Lake Erie shoreline and occupying approximately 1,600 acres (650 ha). The mill transformed Lackawanna into an industrial center soon known as the Steel City of the Great Lakes and attracted an ethnically and racially diverse workforce that included many Croats, Serbs, Poles, and Blacks. The plant, one of the world's largest steel factories, had a complete fabricating works to make steel, as well as its own ship canal, and giant storage areas for limestone and coal. After the site's original owners encountered financial difficulties, Bethlehem Steel Co, another Pennsylvania-based corporation, purchased Lackawanna in 1922, initiating a modernization program in 1929. The onset of the depression halted improvements until a return to profitability in 1934–40. Bethlehem Steel was notably antiunion, but in 1941 the plant was unionized by the Steel Workers Organizing Committee, renamed United Steel Workers of America in 1942. During World War II sales increased markedly, exceeding $1 billion for the first time in 1943. At its peak of production in 1966, the plant employed 21,500 workers and produced 6.6 million tons (6 million MT) of steel. Steel production was reduced in the 1970s as foreign steel firms competed aggressively with domestic producers. Bethlehem stopped most of the plant's operations in 1983. The facility's reduction destroyed much of Lackawanna's employment base, and its population declined steeply in the latter 20th century. In 2002 only 420 people were employed at the facility, with most of the site slated for redevelopment. In addition to the Lackawanna mill, Bethlehem Steel briefly operated an iron ore mine at Mineville (Essex Co). Owning a significant interest in this mine from 1909 to 1918, and again from 1922 to 1938, Bethlehem used ore from the facility to supply its steel-making operations. The Adirondack mine was sold by Bethlehem in 1938.

See also DEINDUSTRIALIZATION.

Leary, T. E., and E. C. Sholes. *From Fire to Rust* (Buffalo: Buffalo and Erie County Historical Society, 1987)

Jack Westbrook

Bethpage. Locality (pop 16,543) in Oyster Bay (Nassau Co). Quakers settled this part of the 1695 Bethpage Purchase, establishing Bethpage Preparative Meeting (1698) and a school (1741). Growth followed the Long Island Rail Road (1841), which established Jerusalem Station between 1850 and 1857; a post office was instituted in 1857, and its name was changed to Central Park in 1867. Confusion with Manhattan's Central Park led to calls for a name change. After Bethpage State Park opened nearby in 1931, the post office was renamed Bethpage in 1936. In the following year Grumman Aircraft Engineering Corp began operations here and grew into Long Island's largest employer. Large-scale suburbanization occurred during the 1950s and 1960s. Grumman merged with Northrop Aviation in 1994, which divested much of the local property. The elite Beau Sejour Hotel was a landmark from 1908 to 1974.

William J. Johnston

Bethune [née Graham], **Joanna** (*b* Fort Niagara [now in Porter, Niagara Co], 1 Feb 1770; *d* New York City, 28 July 1860). Religious and charitable society founder. The daughter of Isabella Marshall Graham and Dr John Graham, a British army surgeon, Joanna Graham was raised in Scotland. She moved to New York City with her widowed mother and two sisters in 1789. Her happy marriage to Divie Bethune in 1795 followed a wrenching evangelical conversion experience. Joanna, her mother, and her husband formed a "happy trio" in the work of religious benevolence. Her career in religious benevolence began in 1797 when she and her mother founded the Society for the Relief of Poor Widows with Small Children, one of the earliest women's charitable societies in the United States. She was involved with a Sunday School in 1803; she had a lifelong passion for the Orphan Asylum Society, for which she worked from 1806 until her retirement in 1858 and which later became Graham-Windham Services; and in 1814 she helped provide work to women impoverished by the War of 1812 through her duties in a house of industry. In these and other endeavors, Bethune drew upon the financial contributions, political connections, and support of friends and associates from New York City's leading mercantile, commercial, and professional families. After her husband's death in 1824, Bethune's concerns focused increasingly on children. Having taken the lead in founding the New York Female Union Society for the Promotion of Sabbath Schools in 1816, she sponsored the New York Infant School Society in 1827 and subsequently opened nine schools for infants in New York City. As late as 1840 she was still teaching a Sunday School class of "infant scholars." During those years she also gave time to the female branch of the New York Religious Tract Society and a Liberian colonization society. Bethune made an impact on New York City by channeling the religious energies of Protestant women into organizational forms and turning women's organizations into sources of social discipline and social service provision in the burgeoning city.

Benson, Mary Sumner. "Joanna Graham Bethune." In *Notable American Women* (Cambridge, Mass: Harvard Univ Press, 1971)
Bethune, George Washington. *Memoirs of Mrs. Joanna Bethune* (New York: Harper & Bros, 1863)
Bethune, Joanna Graham. Autobiography (1814) and Diaries (1824–53). Clements Library, Univ of Michigan

Anne M. Boylan

Bethune [Jennie], **Louise Blanchard** (*b* Waterloo, Seneca Co, 21 July 1856; *d* Buffalo, 18 Dec 1913). Architect. Jennie Louise was the daughter of teachers Dalson Blanchard and Emma Williams. Educated at home, she moved to Buffalo in 1866 with her family and graduated from Buffalo High School in 1874. Exhibiting interest in architecture, from 1876 to 1881 she worked as a drafter in the Buffalo firm of Richard A. Waite. She opened her own firm in October 1881 and was the first professional woman architect in the United States. Two months later she married colleague Robert Armour Bethune, who became her business partner. In 1883 Bethune had her only child. The firm of Bethune, Bethune, and Fuchs designed industrial, educational, and commercial structures throughout Western New York, including police stations, an armory, the Woman's Prison of the Erie County Penitentiary in Alden, and Buffalo's Lafayette Hotel (1902–4) and annex (1908) at 391 Washington St. Her firm designed 18 public schools between 1881 and 1904, including the Lockport Union High School. In 1888 Bethune became the first woman voted into the American Institute of Architects. She retired in 1908.

Barbasch, Adriana. "Louise Blanchard Bethune: The AIA Accepts Its First Woman Member." In *Architecture: A Place for Women,* ed. Ellen Perry Berkeley (Washington, DC: Smithsonian Institution Press, 1989)
Fox, Austin. "Louise Blanchard Bethune: Buffalo Feminist and America's First Woman Architect," http://ah.bfn.org/a/archs/beth/bethfox.html

Nancy Knechtel

Beverwijck. See ALBANY.

Biasone, Danny [Daniel] (*b* Miglianico of Chieti, Italy, 22 Feb 1909; *d* Syracuse, 25 May 1992). Basketball executive. Biasone moved to Syracuse with his family at age 10. Later the owner of a liquor store, he purchased a franchise from the National Basketball League, a forerunner of the National Basketball Association (NBA), in 1946. Three years later the Syracuse Nationals, as he named the team, joined the NBA. But NBA attendance dwindled because of slow play and limited scoring. In 1954 Biasone convinced team owners to adopt a 24-second shot clock, a concept he devised with the aid of Nationals general manager Leo Ferris. Team owners met in Syracuse in August 1954 to view the first-ever demonstration of the shot clock at Biasone's alma mater, Blodgett Vocational High School. The invention, adopted for NBA use for the 1954–55 season, quickly increased scoring in games, leading to increased attendance. NBA commissioner Maurice Podoloff later called the 24-second clock the greatest invention in the history of basketball. After Biasone sold the Nationals in 1963, he oversaw his bowling alley/restaurant, the Eastwood Sport Center, on James St in Syracuse. In 2000 Biasone was elected to the Basketball Hall of Fame.

Ramsey, David. *The Nats: A Team, a City, an Era* (Utica: North Country Books, 1995)

David Luke Ramsey

bible camps. See CAMP MEETINGS AND BIBLE CAMPS.

Bible conferences. During the late 19th century, Protestants from several Calvinist traditions began gathering in fellowship for summer excursions at resort locales where they explored biblical themes, preached their common doctrines, and systematically studied prophecy. The movement initially took shape at an informal conference convened by several prominent millenarian leaders in New York City in 1868. Within evangelical and fundamentalist circles, some of the prominent initiators of the early Bible conferences included James H. Brookes, Adoniram J. Gordon, and William J. Erdman. Annual meetings began in 1875 and were occasionally held at such New York State venues as Watkins Glen (Schuyler Co), Clifton Springs (Ontario Co), and Point Chautauqua (Chautauqua Co). Between 1883 and 1897 the group settled at Niagara-on-the-Lake, Ont. The annual meetings there, which became known as the Niagara Conference, served as influential gathering places for a loosely defined yet rapidly coalescing corps of Christian conservatives who advocated the dispensational and millennial doctrines most closely associated with early 20th-century fundamentalism. The 14-point Niagara Creed, formulated in 1878 and adopted in 1890, articulated most of the group's core beliefs, including the verbal inerrancy of the Bible, a strong emphasis on human depravity, and an affirmation of the premillennial Second Coming of Christ. Despite the importance of the conferences in providing both a physical space and recognizable leadership for the movement, schisms occasionally occurred. Arno C. Gaebelein, for example, broke with his colleagues over a biblical dispute involving the church's relationship to the time of tribulation and initiated his own influential series of Bible conferences at Sea Cliff (Nassau Co) in 1901. Bible conferences expanded and remained important in fundamentalist and evangelical movements throughout the 20th century, offering wholesome recreational environments for devout Christian families and featuring special programs for young adults. Bible study, inspirational preaching by a nationally recognizable network of fundamentalist celebrities, and old-fashioned revivalism held sway at these gatherings. Beginning in the early 20th century, the movement shifted geographically away from New York State and toward other locales, including Winona Lake, Ind, Rumney, NH, Montrose, Pa, and Mount Hermon, Calif.

Carpenter, Joel A. *Revive Us Again: The Reawakening of American Fundamentalism* (New York: Oxford Univ Press, 1997)
Sandeen, Ernest R. *The Roots of Fundamentalism: British and American Millenarianism, 1800–1930* (Chicago: Univ of Chicago Press, 1970)
Weber, Timothy P. *Living in the Shadow of the Second Coming: American Premillennialism, 1875–1925* (New York: Oxford Univ Press, 1979)

Peter J. Wosh

Bible schools. Emerging in the early 20th century as an alternative to more conventional forms of theological education, these secondary and sometimes college-level schools had a theologically and culturally conservative position that usually included a central focus on the Bible as the word of God, evangelism, premillennialism, and missions. Students usually fulfilled a fieldwork component by evangelizing and teaching. Because they judged prospective students on the basis of their consecration rather than on their educational attainments, the schools were often more inclusive than other institutions and admitted large numbers of women.

The most important early Bible schools in New York State were the Missionary Training Institute sponsored by the Christian and Missionary Alliance, located in Manhattan from 1882 to 1897 and then in Nyack (Rockland Co), now Nyack College; the Bible Teachers Training School (1900), a hybrid that resisted participation in the fundamentalist-modernist controversy and eventually became New York Theological Seminary; the National Bible Institute (1907) in Manhattan, later Shelton College in New Jersey; Union Missionary Training Institute (1885) in Brooklyn and Niagara Falls, which merged with the National Bible Institute in 1916.

The Bible schools fell outside the pale of new accrediting agencies, since most of these institutions were neither high schools nor colleges. Later some of the more prominent schools, such as Nyack College, became liberal arts colleges. For those schools that retained the essential marks of a Bible school, the Accrediting Association of Bible Colleges was created in the early 1940s in connection with the establishment of the National Association of Evangelicals.

Brereton, Virginia L. *Training God's Army: The American Bible School, 1880–1940* (Bloomington: Indiana Univ Press, 1990)

Virginia Lieson Brereton

Bible societies. Christian organizations dedicated to Scripture distribution, publication, and translation. Bible societies began appearing throughout the United States during the first decade of the 19th century. New Yorkers played a disproportionately prominent role in the early movement, establishing 27% of all Bible societies by 1815. Societies typically were organized by religious leaders in cities (Albany, 1810) and counties (Otsego, 1812), as well as by women (Geneva, Ontario Co, 1813), youths (Kingston, Ulster Co, 1809), students (Union College, 1815), and denominations (New York City's Episcopalians, 1809). In 1816, 56 delegates from these local organizations across the United States, including 33 New York State representatives, gathered in New York City to federate and establish the American Bible Society (ABS). This new national organization defined its core mission as circulating the Scriptures without doctrinal note or commentary. Throughout the 19th century the ABS relied heavily on local auxiliaries for financial support and volunteer distributors; New Yorkers proved particularly generous. By the 1830s every New York State county except Niagara contained an ABS auxiliary, Scripture distribution in New York State exceeded 58,000 Bibles and testaments annually, and state residents made up 60% of the ABS's major donors. Especially active ABS affiliates existed in New York City, Albany, and Long Island, as well as in the following counties: Dutchess, Fulton, Hamilton, Monroe, Oneida, Orange, Rensselaer, and Westchester.

By 1855 the ABS constituted one of the largest and most technologically innovative publishers in the United States, producing unprecedented quantities of inexpensive Scriptures at its Bible House printing plant and supporting an extensive translation program that included Mohawk portions for use near the border between New York State and Canada. Denominational disagreements, however, fragmented the Bible movement. Baptists charged that the ABS erred in its translations policies, thus violating core doctrines, and most withdrew in 1837 to establish the American and Foreign Bible Society (AFBS). A subsequent translation controversy within the AFBS resulted in the formation of the American Bible Union in 1850. Territorial tensions also surfaced within the ABS. Most auxiliaries disintegrated as the parent body became more centralized in the late 19th century. Relations between the ABS and the New York Bible Society (NYBS) proved particularly acrimonious. This New York City auxiliary, which reorganized several times between 1807 and 1913, actively distributed Scriptures at humane and criminal institutions, naval and military stations, hotels, and Ellis Island. Conflicts emerged with the ABS over fund-raising practices, distribution boundaries, and the auxiliary's increasingly evangelical focus. The local organization initially declared its independence from the ABS in 1913, and continuing tension resulted in a final rupture in 1971. The NYBS supported the translation of the very successful New International Version (1978), directed primarily at an evangelical readership. Eventually the NYBS reincorporated as the International Bible Society (1983) and relocated to Colorado Springs (1989). Remaining in New York City, the ABS strengthened its international commitments through participation in the United Bible Societies (1946) and broadened its denominational partnerships to include Roman Catholics in the 1960s. Thematic Scripture selections, such ABS-produced common language versions as the Good News Bible (1976), and multimedia translations dominated its diversified late 20th-century product line.

Gutjahr, Paul C. *An American Bible: A History of the Good Book in the United States, 1777–1880* (Stanford, Calif: Stanford Univ Press, 1999)
Lacy, Creighton. *The Word-Carrying Giant: The Growth of the American Bible Society (1816–1966)* (South Pasadena, Calif: William Carey Library, 1977)
Wosh, Peter J. *Spreading the Word: The Bible Business in 19th-Century America* (Ithaca: Cornell Univ Press, 1994)

Peter J. Wosh

bicycling (manufacture). The hobbyhorse, a European-designed, two-wheel device propelled by the rider's feet pushing on the road, appeared in New York City in 1819. Local coach maker Richard P. Lawrence took orders in late May, and the first US velocipede patent was granted to William K. Clarkson of New York City in June. But cyclists soon tired of riding circles on indoor tracks or negotiating rough roads. Interest in cycling revived when a similar vehicle, but with a pedal mechanism attached to the front hub, appeared in late 1868. Utilizing a patent granted to Pierre Lallement, New York City carriage maker Calvin Witty manufactured the new velocipede and licensed others to build it. Known also as boneshakers, most velocipedes utilized carriage technology of wrought iron and wood. Despite the introduction of tubular frames and precision machining by Pickering and Davis in New York City, the uncomfortable velocipedes enjoyed only brief popularity.

Interest in crank-driven bicycles remained, however, and the display of English high-wheel bicycles at the Philadelphia Centennial Exposition in 1876 prompted their importation and manufacture in New England. Ball bearings, wire suspension wheels, and rubber tires combined with tubular frames to create a vehicle lighter and more responsive than the boneshaker. By 1880 wealthy young men in urban areas had taken up recreational cycling on the mechanically sophisticated and exhilarating but unstable machines, and the League of American Wheelmen was formed to advocate for bicyclists' interests. The safety bicycle, with chain drive and the rider mounted between two equal-sized wheels, arrived from England around 1890. Now women in skirts and others previously excluded from cycling took to the stable and easy-riding vehicles. Still, participants in the recreational cycling boom that swept the country at mid-decade faced societal disapproval of Sunday riding, the occasional wrath of horse-drawn vehicle drivers reluctant to share the road, and unimproved rural roads. Side paths were alternative venues for riding; licenses issued by the operating authorities allowed use of the smooth, usually paved paths often adjacent to public roads.

Previously only marginally involved in bicycle fabrication, the state's industry was quick to respond to the market demand of the 1890s. Manufacturing centers arose in New York City, Buffalo, and Syracuse, where in 1896 it is estimated one-eighth of the population was sustained by five major companies employing 3,000 people. Factories were also located in such places as Rochester, Jamestown (Chautauqua Co), Little Falls (Herkimer Co), and Elmira. By 1896 New York State's bicycle manufacturers were experiencing overproduction, a depressed economy, and bankruptcy, and the formation in 1899 of the short-lived American Bicycle Co bicycle trust by 44 US firms resulted in the elimination of more of the state's bicycle producers. Manufacture continued for a time at such locations as Pierce Cycle Co in Buffalo and Emblem Manufacturing Co in Angola (Erie Co), while bicycle manufacture at the H. P. Snyder Manufacturing Co in Little Falls and the Chain Bike Corp in Brooklyn lasted through the mid-1970s. Except for small-scale specialty makers, bicycle production has disappeared from New York State.

Dodge, Pryor. *The Bicycle* (Paris: Flammarion, 1996)
Stein, Geoffrey N. "Buffalo Diamond, Elmira Clipper, and New York Flyer: A History of Bicycle Manufacturing in New York State," MS prepared for the NYS Museum, Albany, 1985

Geoffrey N. Stein

bicycling (sport). Bicycle racing became a popular sport with the invention of the safety bicycle during the 1890s. One of the initial functions of Manhattan's Madison Square Garden was as an indoor velodrome, and its famous six-day bicycle races were first held there in 1891. The race was a solo competition until 1899, after which two-person teams competed. Marshall Walter "Major" Taylor, one of the first African American athletes to achieve national renown and an international cycling champion, raced at Madison Square Garden, sometimes under the auspices of the South Brooklyn Wheelmen. Velodromes in other urban centers, including five in the Buffalo area, also hosted track racing. In a different sort of competition, on 30 June 1899 Charles "Mile-A-Minute" Murphy was the first bicyclist to reach 60 mph (96.6 kph) when he rode on wood planks directly behind a Long Island Rail Road (LIRR) train. After World War I bicycling as a sport gradually declined in popularity in the United States and New York State, though interest in it as a form of recreation and a means of transportation continued. Madison Square Garden's six-day bicycle races were last held in 1939. Renewed interest in bicycling, as a form of good exercise, developed during the 1950s, while mountain biking (in which cyclists traverse off-road trails) and BMX racing (bicycle motocross, in which cyclists race on jump-filled dirt tracks) emerged during the mid-1970s.

In Manhattan, bike messenger services rose in number in the 1970s as a way to maneuver crowded streets, and one veteran of this occupation, cycling courier Nelson Vails, won the silver medal in the sprint at the 1984 Summer Olympics. Other elite racers with connections to New York State include US Postal Service pro rider George Hincapie, 1992 world pursuit champion Mike McCarthy, and 1999 US national cyclocross champion Marc Gullickson. New York City's Central Park offers miles of road riding, and since 1977 the annual Five Borough Bike Tour takes 30,000 participants through Manhattan, the Bronx, Queens, Brooklyn, and Staten Island in a day. Additionally, stages of the now defunct Tour de Trump passed through New York City in 1989 and 1990.

Elsewhere in the state, the Blue Mountain Reservation in Peekskill (Westchester Co) offers secluded trail time to mountain bikers, and the Lake Placid (Essex Co) area has annual road and mountain bike races that include some of the longest climbs on the East Coast. In Western New York the Genesee Valley Greenway follows abandoned railbeds and canals along the Genesee River, while major portions of the 230 mi (370.2 km) Canalway Trail System follow former Erie Canal towpaths. The Pedaling History Bicycle Museum in Orchard Park (Erie Co), perhaps the world's largest bicycle museum, features hundreds of historical bikes and artifacts.

See also ROADS.

Burgwardt, Carl F. *Buffalo's Bicycles* (Orchard Park, NY: Pedaling History Bicycle Museum, 2001)
Meinert, Charles Willis. *A History of Bicycling in the Hudson-Mohawk Region of New York State, 1880–1900* (Delmar, NY: Author, 1996)
Perry, David B. *Bike Cult: The Ultimate Guide to Human-Powered Vehicles* (New York: Four Walls Eight Windows, 1995)

Sean Coffey

Big Apple. Nickname for New York City. Its origins are unknown but might be related to New York State's reputation as an apple-growing region. The phrase first appeared in print in *The Wayfarer in New York* (1909) where editor Edward S. Martin used it in an extended metaphor about New York City's relationship to the Midwest. In the 1920s black stable hands at New Orleans racetracks used the term, and John J. FitzGerald, sports reporter for the *Morning Telegraph*, heard it and appropriated it for his racing column, "Around the Big Apple." In 1937 bandleader Tommy Dorsey had a modest hit with a dance called "The Big Apple," by lyricist Buddy Bernier and composer Bob Emmerich. The term and its variants were widely used by black jazz musicians during the 1930s and 1940s, as in Charlie Parker's 1947 recording "Scrapple from the Apple." By the 1950s the term had become passé, and it dropped out of popular usage until 1971. That year Charles Gillett, president of the New York Convention and Visitors Bureau, revived it as part of a successful advertising campaign. Since the 1970s the Big Apple has been the most recognized nickname for New York City.

Groce, Nancy. *New York: Songs of the City* (New York: Billboard Books, 1999)

Nancy Groce

Big Duck. Landmark of roadside architecture in Flanders (Suffolk Co). Inspired by a California coffee shop in the shape of a coffeepot, Riverhead (Suffolk Co) duck farmers Martin and Jueule Maurer built the Big Duck in 1931 to sell ducks and eggs. The cement-covered frame of wood and wire mesh stood 20 feet (6.1 m) high, 15 feet (4.6 m) wide, and 30 feet (9.1 m) long. Moved by the Maurers to Flanders in 1936, it was in the way of land development in 1987, and its then owners donated it to Suffolk Co, which moved it to Sears Bellows County Park nearby. Listed on the National Register of Historic Places, the duck houses a gift shop selling "duck-a-bilia." The Big Duck was the prototype for duck architecture popularized by Robert Venturi and Denise Scott Brown in *Learning from Las Vegas* (1972).

Davies, Carolyn L'Hommedieu. "Creating a Landmark: Hatching the Big Duck," *Long Island Forum* 55 (Winter 1993): 30–35
Wick, Steve. "It's a Tall Tail but True," *Long Island: Our Story* (Melville, NY: Newsday, 1998), 224
Yeager, Edna Howell. "The Big Duck," *Long Island Forum* 51 (1988): 66–70

Natalie A. Naylor

Big Flats. Town (pop 7,224) in W Chemung Co. Settled in 1787, the town was formed from Elmira in 1822. In the early years of the Chemung Feeder Canal (1832), lumbering sustained the economy. The town derives its name from the rich alluvial flats along the Chemung River, where tobacco was grown from 1850 to 1953, peaking in the decade prior to World War I when 1,000 acres (405 ha) were under cultivation. The Erie (1851) and the Delaware, Lackawanna and Western (1882) Railroads served Big Flats. In the late 19th and early 20th centuries, cigar manufacturing was a source of employment. Suburbanization began with Golden Glow Heights (1924). Big Flats gained its enduring reputation as the Soaring Capital of the World during the 1930s when it hosted national glider competitions and the Schweizer Aircraft Corp (1938) opened a factory. The federal Big Flats Plant Materials Center (1940) was established as a nursery and Civilian Conservation Corps camp; during World War II it became a conscientious objector camp; in the early 21st century it is a site for research on erosion, water quality, and sustainable agriculture. After World War II agriculture declined as suburbanization increased. The population of Big Flats increased 86.5% during the 1960s. A Corning Glass Works plant opened in 1958. Rte 17 (I-86) was completed as a four-lane highway in 1985. By 2000 Big Flats had three distinct commercial centers: Arnot Mall (1967), Consumer Square (1992), and Airport Corporate Park (1995). Big Flats is also the site of Elmira-Corning Regional Airport (1944), the National Soaring Museum (1969), and the National Warplane Museum (1983). Community Days (1954) is an annual June event.

Heather A. Wade

bigfoot. A creature also known as sasquatch, one of New York State's most enduring rural legends. In the early 19th century the Tuscarora Indian David Cusick wrote of the Iroquoian legend of the Otneyarhed (stonish giants), gruesome monsters that once overran the countryside like locusts, eating everything and everyone they found. Early pioneers reported occasional brushes with the creature. In New York State one of the earliest recorded sightings in modern times took place in Ellisburg (Jefferson Co) in August 1818, when a witness of "unquestionable veracity" purportedly spotted "the Wild Man of the Woods," as reported in the *Exeter Watchman* from New Hampshire. Although most often associated with the Pacific Northwest, bigfoot sightings have been reported in 28 counties in New York State by the Bigfoot Field Researchers Organization (BFRO), one of numerous web sites that collect information on the creature. Eyewitnesses describe a cross between a human and an ape, standing 6–10 feet (2–3 m), weighing 300–900 pounds (136–408 kg), with feet 14–18 in (36–46 cm) long. In 2002 BFRO received reports of sightings near Smyrna (Chenango Co), Mineville (Essex Co), and Bath (Steuben Co). Favorite haunts in New York State include the forests of the Southern Tier and the Adirondack Mountains. Skeptics note that neither body parts nor fossils of bigfoot have ever been found, and the creature has rarely been taken seriously by the scientific community.

Krantz, Grover S. *Big Footprints: A Scientific Inquiry into the Reality of Sasquatch* (Boulder, Colo: Johnson Books, 1992)
Bigfoot Field Researchers Organization, www.bfro.net

John Pitcher

Big Tree, John [Karontowanen] (*b* unknown; *d* Philadelphia, ?1794). Seneca chief. During the Revolutionary War Big Tree negotiated with Gen George Washington through the Oneida to convince a faction of the Seneca to side against the British and in 1778 was a part of the Iroquois delegation to Philadelphia. Despite these diplomatic efforts, he took part in the British and Indian raid that destroyed Cherry Valley [now in Otsego Co] and killed almost 50 Continental solders and civilians in November 1778. In 1779 he lost credibility with the Seneca after the American campaign under Gen John Sullivan burned villages and displaced the Seneca and Cayuga from their homeland in the western part of the state. His village of Adjuste [now Conesus, Livingston Co] was among those destroyed. After the war, in the hope of gaining a privately owned parcel of land, Big Tree urged the Seneca to accept American terms. In 1790 he returned to Philadelphia and, with several other Seneca chiefs, delivered an important oration to Washington about attempts to remove the Seneca from their homeland in New York State and the Seneca's ability to retaliate. He committed suicide in Philadelphia during the winter of 1793–94 after being publicly dishonored for his pro-American stance.

Parker, Arthur C. *The History of the Seneca Indians* (Port Washington, NY: I. J. Friedman, 1967)

Christina B. Rieth

Big Tree Reservation. An 18th-century Seneca Indian village. Ga-on-do-wa-nuh, or Big Tree, was upon a bluff opposite Geneseo [now in Livingston Co], just north of present-day Cuylerville. It was the home of the Seneca orator Big Tree, who had served the British and their Tory Rangers commanded by Walter Butler during the American Revolution. The village bordered Little Beard's Town of the Seneca on the south and a Tuscarora village on the north. In 1797, at the federal treaty with the Seneca at Big Tree, the US government recognized the Big Tree Reservation, a 2 mi^2 (5.2 km^2) parcel of land on the west side of the Genesee River, as Seneca territory. Besides Chief Big Tree, the prominent Seneca leader, Half Town (Achiout or Ga-ji-ot) also resided in the territory. The Seneca lost the Big Tree Reservation in the Treaty of Buffalo Creek of 1826, a fraudulent federal treaty that was never ratified by the US Senate.

Hauptman, Laurence M. *Conspiracy of Interests: Iroquois Dispossession and the Rise of New York State* (Syracuse: Syracuse Univ Press, 1999)

Laurence M. Hauptman

bilingual education. Instructional programs designed to provide equal educational opportunity to students with limited English proficiency (LEP). The federal Bilingual Education Act of 1968 provided funding for bilingual programs within schools, and in 1969 the Office of Bilingual Education was formed. Part of the New York State Education Department, it was created to assist schools in establishing and maintaining bilingual educational programs. The 1974 US Supreme Court decision *Lau v Nichols* further strengthened bilingual education by ruling that English-only instruction denied LEP students equal access to education and that school districts had an obligation to provide them with alternative programs. Implementation of bilingual education began on a widespread basis in New York State in 1975 with the Aspira Consent Decree, the result of a successful federal lawsuit against the New York City Board of Education by the advocacy organization Aspira. The decree required that bilingual programs be available to Spanish-speaking students scoring in the bottom 20% on English proficiency tests in schools with sufficient numbers of LEP students.

There are two basic types of bilingual education programs: transitional and two-way. Most bilingual programs in New York State are transitional, with students receiving content instruction in their native language for approximately two to three years, over which time instruction in English is gradually introduced and increased. The goal is for students to transition from native language instruction to English-only instruction as quickly as possible. Students receive additional instruction in English as a Second Language (ESL) classes for three to nine hours per week depending on language proficiency and grade. In the two-way bilingual education programs, English-speaking and LEP students study together, the goal being that each group becomes fluent in the other's language. There are eight school districts within New York City that provide two-way bilingual education programs and six other school districts throughout the rest of the state. While the vast majority of two-way programs are Spanish-English, there is also a Haitian/Creole-English program and a Chinese-English program, both in New York City. According to a New York State Department of Education report, 165,245 students were enrolled in bilingual education programs in 2001–2. The majority of LEP students were Spanish-speaking, 102,833 (62%); followed by Chinese, 8,670 (5%); Russian, 5,009 (3%); and a number of other languages making up less than 3% each.

Bilingual education remains a hotly debated topic in the state. Mayor Rudolph Giuliani appointed a New York City Task Force on Bilingual Education that maintained in December 2000 that the methods used in city schools to teach English to LEP students were in need of reform. According to a mayoral study conducted in 2000, over half of the students enrolled in bilingual education classes did not transfer to regular classes within the three years the state requires. Additionally, in 2002 the Lexington Institute found over 83% of ninth graders entering the LEP program could not test out after four years. Some proposals to modify bilingual education programs include giving parents of LEP students the choice between programs, setting time limits for achieving English proficiency, and improving teacher quality. Beginning in spring 2003, the New York State English as a Second Language Achievement Test (NYSESLAT) was administered to LEP students grades K–12 to test their achievement in English proficiency and their continued eligibility for LEP programs. This will help determine the success of LEP programs throughout the state. Additionally, a lack of qualified LEP teachers led to the funding of 13 Bilingual Education Technical Assistance Centers throughout the state that address the needs of teachers and the districts.

Crawford, James. *Bilingual Education: History, Politics, Theory and Practice,* 4th ed. (Los Angeles: Bilingual Educational Services, 1999)

John K. Fitzer

bill of rights. See CONSTITUTIONS AND CONSTITUTIONAL CONVENTIONS.

Binghamton. Town (pop 4,969) and city (pop 47,380) in Broome Co. Located at the confluence of the Chenango and Susquehanna Rivers, near the Pennsylvania state line, the city is the county seat. Most of the present city is situated on a wide outwash plain of the Ice Age Susquehanna River. Underlying shale, siltstone, and sandstone of the late Devonian Sonyea Group yield many fossils. The hills of the city's south side and of the town beyond are made up of more recent shales of the West Falls Group. Etienne Brûlé may have been the first European to reach the site, in 1618. The area was presumably used by the Susquehannock before their dispersal by the Iroquois in 1675 and thereafter by the Onondaga, Tuscarora, and Cayuga, as well as groups of Nanticokes, Mohicans (Mahicans), and Delawares. The Indian presence in the area was largely destroyed during the Sullivan-Clinton campaign in August 1779, although a small reserve provided under the Boston Purchase treaty survived near the mouth of Castle Creek until ?1794.

European Settlement

European settlement began in ?1785, from the Hudson Valley, New England, and the Wyoming Valley. The earliest area of settlement was north of the present city on lands of the Boston Purchase. The territory around the river confluence was included in a 1786 patent of Philadelphia merchant William Bingham. His liberal policies and the promotional talents of his agent, Joshua Whitney, encouraged many of the pioneers to buy land in Bingham's Patent, forming a settlement called Chenango Point in ?1799. Broome Co was formed in 1806, with the new post office hamlet of Chenango Point as the county seat. Chenango Point had been renamed Binghamton by 1813, although the post office retained the old name until 1830; the village was incorporated in 1834. The Town of Binghamton was created from the Town of Chenango in 1855, and the village remained part of the town until chartered as a city in 1867.

Economic Development

Chenango Point began with a subsistence economy based on hunting and fishing. Shad were particularly bountiful. Oak, white pine, and hemlock provided the raw material for the lumber and tanning industries that came to dominate the economy. Log rafts were constructed each spring to carry the lumber down the Susquehanna River to Baltimore. Hardwood trees also produced wood ash (leached to make lye and potash) and pearl ash. Timber industries remained more significant than agriculture for half a century.

Farming began in valley clearings left by the Indians. Grain was raised until the soil was exhausted. Later, cultivation moved up the hills, adapting between 1845 and 1875 to sustained commercial agriculture, with apple orchards and cattle grazing predominant and dairying assuming primary importance by the period's end. Both the Chenango and Susquehanna Rivers were dammed by 1828, generating waterpower for mills. The Chenango Canal (1837–78) allowed shipment of Pennsylvania coal north to the Erie Canal after 1852 and greatly increased Binghamton's trade with outside markets. Further expansion was fueled by service of the Erie

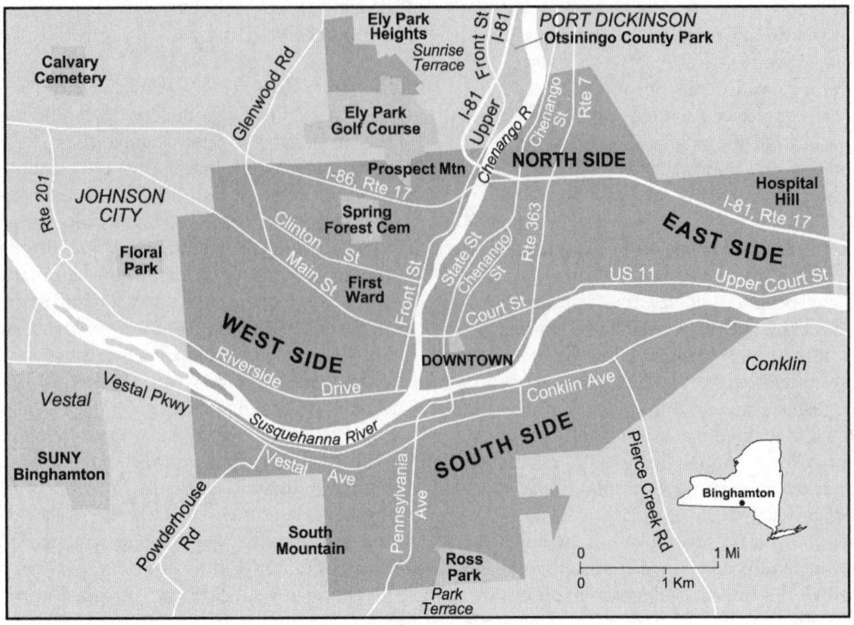

Railroad (1848), the Delaware, Lackawanna and Western (1869), and lines to Syracuse (1854) and Albany (1869).

Before the Civil War, Binghamton grew rapidly as a commercial and industrial village, manufacturing soap, candles, crockery, carriages, and agricultural implements. Several iron foundries were in operation, including Binghamton Iron Works (1854). After the war economic growth accelerated. In the 1870s a building boom took place as banks, office buildings, and government buildings were erected. In the late 19th century Binghamton produced a great variety of goods, including steam engines, glass, combs, buttons, tools, carriage hardware, scales, and beer. Swamproot patent medicine, one of the community's most famous products, was first produced in 1881 by Dr. Kilmer & Co. Willis Kilmer inherited the company and founded the *Binghamton Press* (1904), the city's major newspaper. Gustav Stickley, a major figure in the arts and crafts movement, the Stickley brothers, and Stickley-Brandt all manufactured furniture in Binghamton between 1883 and 1914. Kroehler Manufacturing was another important furniture maker through 1984. Carriages, wagons, sleighs, and toy sleds were made by companies such as Sturtevant-Larrabee Co. Trucks were later made by Larrabee-Deyo.

Binghamton achieved increasing renown as a manufacturing center. By 1872 the city had four tanneries and six shoe factories, the most important of which was Lester Bros (1854), which moved in 1891 to Johnson City, where it developed into the Endicott Johnson Co. Cigar making, first undertaken locally in 1857, grew *ca* 1870 into a large enterprise, employing about 5,000 (about one-third of the community's industrial workers) in 1890. About 40% of the cigar making workforce was female, increasing to 85% by 1927. By 1900 Binghamton had approximately 70 cigar manufacturers and was one of the largest cigar-making cities in the nation. The business in Binghamton collapsed after it was automated in the 1930s. Another industry with a heavily female workforce was clothing manufacture, with many small factories specializing in outerwear. The fire at the Binghamton Clothing Co on 23 July 1913 killed 32 people and demonstrated that the statewide factory safety measures put in place after the 1911 Triangle Shirtwaist Factory fire in New York City were still inadequate.

Famous products originating in Binghamton include those made by Eureka Tent, originally Binghamton Tent and Awning Co, and in 2003 it still operated in Conklin (Broome Co). The Whirlpool brand was created by the 1900 Washer Co (1898). Valvoline engine oil was patented in 1873 by the Continuous Oil Refining Co (1866) of Binghamton. The Bundy Manufacturing Co was incorporated in 1889 and became International Time Recording Co (1901), moving to Endicott in 1907 and later becoming a part of IBM. Anthony and Scovill (1902; incorporated in 1907 as Ansco and later as German-owned Agfa-Ansco), manufacturer of cameras, film, and photographic supplies, became Binghamton's largest employer by the 1920s. In 1942 the company, by then the GAF Corp, was seized by the US government. Link Aviation (1935), maker of flight simulators and other products, grew out of Edwin Link's trainer for pilots, which was patented in 1929; it moved to Kirkwood (Broome Co) in the late 1960s. Stow Manufacturing (1875–1997; flexible shafts), Fairbanks Valve (?1908–85), and Vail-Ballou Press (1910–90) were large late 20th-century industries important to Binghamton.

Organized labor has had a continuing presence. An 1890 strike by unorganized cigar workers lasted for about 10 weeks and was one of the longest in the city's history. The Binghamton Central Trades and Labor Assembly was organized in 1888 and replaced by the Binghamton Central Labor Union in 1897. Strikes in 1937 and 1941 by the Amalgamated Street Railway and Motor Coach Employees against the Triple Cities Traction Corp were settled with concessions, but the firm went into bankruptcy in 1942.

Population

Binghamton settlers were nearly all European, but a small African American community was present from the beginning. Binghamton was a major station on a minor route of the Underground Railroad. An African American, Tom Crocker, was elected mayor in 1872 over a Republican candidate, but the election was overturned by ballots being thrown out for "irregularity." The canal and the railroads brought Irish immigrant workers. The first Roman Catholic church organized in 1838. A German land association promoted a neighborhood whose streets were named for German composers. German Jewish immigrants arrived concurrently and were followed by larger Jewish groups from eastern Europe. Population growth was particularly dramatic between 1880 and 1905. Slovaks, Italians, Lithuanians, ethnic Russians, and Poles arrived in large numbers through 1920, along with smaller numbers of Armenians, Greeks, and Syro-Lebanese.

Politics

Federalists such as the wealthy land speculator Joshua Whitney dominated Binghamton's politics in the early period, although Whigs and

Cigar rollers in Binghamton, *ca* 1885.

Democrats vied for power in pre–Civil War years; the foremost figure was Daniel S. Dickinson, a conservative Hardshell Democrat who served as village president, lieutenant governor, and US senator. Republicans have dominated Binghamton politics since the Civil War. When the city was incorporated in 1867, it formed a common council composed of aldermen and a mayor, all elected to one-year terms, which became two-year terms in 1889. The Ku Klux Klan began recruiting in Binghamton in 1923 and bought a building for its state headquarters in 1924. Common Council president Hubert D. Ballard presided at a Klan rally and was later Binghamton's kleagle. The Klan attempted to dominate local Republican politics, but its influence sharply declined after 1925. A city council system was instituted in 1932. Since 1928 its mayors have served four-year terms. Local politics in the 20th century were dominated by a succession of Republican leaders, including Harvey Hinman, active from about 1904 to 1920, William Henry Hill (1877–1972), who dominated local politics for almost four decades starting in 1920, and State Sen Warren M. Anderson (1915–), a powerful majority leader of the New York State Senate. Nevertheless, the Republican dominance has not been complete. The Democrats have maintained a few seats on the City Council and occasionally (as with Juanita Crabb [1981–93]) put a Democrat in the mayor's office.

Cityscape and Culture

Binghamton in 2002 is a small city in a setting surrounded by hills and divided by rivers. The downtown core of offices, banks, restaurants, and shops is close to the rivers' confluence. Security Mutual Life Insurance Co of Binghamton (1886) occupies one of the taller office buildings, a 10-story structure built in 1904. The Press building (1904; 12 stories) and the State Office Building (1972; 18 stories) dominate the skyline. Binghamton has often pictured itself as a progressive community in the area of social welfare. The New York State Inebriate Asylum (1854) was the first hospital in the nation to treat alcoholism as a disease (1858); taken over by the state in 1867, it became an insane asylum in 1879 and was ultimately renamed Binghamton Psychiatric Center. The Susquehanna Valley Home (1869–1980) took in children from surrounding counties after a state law prohibited housing children in county poorhouses.

Binghamton continues as a major center of government services and federal, state, and county offices. It is also a center of culture, home of the Roberson Museum and Science Center (1953), Broome County Veterans Memorial Arena (1972), Binghamton Philharmonic (1955), Tri-Cities Opera (1949), Ross Park Zoo (1875), Discovery Center (1983), and The Forum (Broome Center for the Performing Arts; 1975). NYSEG Stadium, offering both sports and musical events, opened in 1992. Among Binghamton's educational institutions, Ridley-Lowell Business and Technical Institute (1859) is one of the nation's oldest business schools, and Broome Community College (1946) has been located nearby in Dickinson since 1956. SUNY Binghamton (1946), though located in Vestal, is a source of recognition and pride for the city. Rod Serling (1924–75), writer and creator of *The Twilight Zone* television series, was raised in Binghamton and began his career in the city.

Recent History

Just before World War II, Binghamton was the anchor of a powerful manufacturing region. The Triple Cities (Binghamton, Endicott, and Johnson City) had 107 manufactories employing 34,500 people in 1940. From 1880 through 1930 Binghamton's population increased as rural communities dwindled, increasing 102% in the 1880s alone. After 1930 Binghamton grew more slowly than surrounding communities, and, since its 1950 peak of 80,674, its population has decreased significantly. The region's economic health was adversely impacted when factories started closing after 1960, and its defense-related industries lost business at the end of the Cold War. Retail businesses struggle to survive, and many storefronts are vacant. A disproportionate percentage of elderly and poor citizens reside in the urban core, further straining resources. Attempts to reverse this course included urban renewal programs (1960–87), which successfully cleared slums but also destroyed adequate and affordable houses, replacing them with access roads, a government complex, office buildings, parking facilities, housing for the elderly, and a few garden apartment complexes. Highways, particularly Rte 17 (I-86) (1971), were constructed through neighborhoods, destroying community cohesion while giving commuters easier access to Binghamton workplaces. Asian, Latin American, and Ukrainian immigrants predominate among recent arrivals, as do refugees from Bosnia, Cuba, Somalia, and elsewhere. By 2000 Binghamton's nonwhite population, which had been under 1% in 1950, was 10% black or black biracial and nearly 4% Asian. In addition almost 4% were of Latino ethnicity. Although the minority populations remain small, the increased diversity in the area during the 1980s and especially the 1990s is notable.

Suburban housing and shopping malls, as well as two county-built industrial parks, have pulled retail commerce and tax revenue from Binghamton. Binghamton Plaza (1961) was the first automobile-based shopping center. The Oakdale Mall (1975) in Johnson City diverted retail business from Binghamton's downtown, and development along Vestal Parkway, including the Town Square Mall (1992), continued the process. Rte 17 (I-86) and I-81 (completed through the city in 1966) brought commerce to the city but have also encouraged industrial construction outside city limits.

Industry remaining within city limits in 2003 included E. H. Titchener (1881; wire), Titchener Iron Works (1920), Mechanical Specialties (1955; machinist), Lander Co (1920; soap), Crowley Foods (1915), Elliott Manufacturing Co (1916; flexible shafts), and Buckingham Manufacturing Co (?1896; pole-climbing equipment). Binghamton remains a center for simulation technology, with Doron Precision Systems (1973), Binghamton Simulator Co (1990), and the successor firms to Link (in Kirkwood). Binghamton is still known as the Parlor City and one of the Triple Cities, and it plays the leading role in regional government, finance, and commerce.

See also Architects and architecture, southern tier (eastern).

Lawyer, William S., ed. *Binghamton: Its Settlement, Growth and Development and the Factors in Its History, 1800–1900* (Binghamton: Century Memorial Publishing, 1900)

Smith, Gerald R. *The Valley of Opportunity: A Pictorial History of the Greater Binghamton Area* (Norfolk, Va: Donning, 1988)

Smith, H. P., ed. *History of Broome County* (Syracuse: D. Mason, 1885)

Wilkinson, J. B. *The Annals of Binghamton, and of the Country Connected with It, from the Earliest Settlement* (Binghamton: Cooke & Davis, 1840)

Charles J. Browne

Binghamton University. See Suny binghamton.

bird decoy art. Originally functional tools for hunting and now highly prized as folk art, bird decoys have existed in New York State since pre-Columbian times. Intended to lure different kinds of waterfowl into the range of hunters, decoys often present a highly realistic appearance. While decoys were carved in nearly every region of the state, several areas stand out for the quality and quantity of decoys produced. Carvers near the St. Lawrence River and Lake Ontario focused on the redhead and scaup ducks that frequented the area. Alexandria Bay (Jefferson Co) produced a trio of great craftsmen in the early 1900s: Samuel Denny (1874–1953), Chauncey Wheeler (1862–1937), and Frank Coombs (1882–1958). The Stevens Factory, a family-run operation in Weedsport (Cayuga Co), produced notable decoys from approximately 1865 to 1902. Stevens's specialties, advertised in sporting journals, included canvasbacks, mallards, and redheads.

The art may have reached its pinnacle on Long Island, where hunters were attracted by the abundance and variety of waterfowl. Market gunning—the mass hunting of birds to supply New York City hotels, restaurants, and hat factories—had its heyday between 1860 and 1920. As hunters sought plovers, curlews, and other kinds of shorebirds, as well as ducks, decoy carvers (who were often hunters themselves) responded to the demand. William Bowman (1824–1906) of Lawrence (Nassau Co) made exceedingly lifelike shorebirds. An extremely rare Bowman Hudsonian curlew was sold at auction in 2000 for $464,500. Obediah Verity (1813–1901), known for his whimsically plump decoys, was the foremost carver of Seaford (Nassau Co). Carved eyes and S-shaped wing patterns were hallmarks of Seaford crafters, who used chewed twigs as paintbrushes, dipping them into dark paint and swirling the color onto a lighter background to replicate feathering.

The US Migratory Bird Treaty Act of 1918 and other federal and state legislation ended unlimited hunting across New York State, slowing the

Greenback plover shorebird decoy, attributed to John Dilley of Quogue, late 19th century.

need for decoys. As decoy carving continued, the emphasis gradually shifted from function to beauty of form. Decoys were exhibited in museums for the first time during the 1920s, and the 1934 publication of Joel Barber's *Wild Fowl Decoys* increased interest in collecting. The Long Island Museum of American Art, History, and Carriages in Stony Brook (Suffolk Co) features an exhibition of its permanent collection of decoys, *The Baymen's Art: Wildfowl Decoys of Long Island.*

Engers, Joe, ed. *The Great Book of Wildfowl Decoys* (San Diego: Thunder Bay Press, 1990)
Townsend, E. Jane. *Gunner's Paradise: Wildfowling and Decoys on Long Island* (Stony Brook, NY: Museums at Stony Brook, 1979)

Joshua Ruff

birds. Inhabitants of Earth for more than 100 million years, predating mammals and following reptiles in the fossil record, birds form the most diverse and conspicuous group of vertebrates in New York State. They are unique among all living organisms in having a body covering of feathers, which provide protection from weather and injury and make another distinctive ability, powered flight, possible. Flight allows almost complete freedom of movement and enables birds to make annual migrations over great distances. The bobolink *(Dolichonyx oryzivorus),* a small songbird that nests in hayfields and pastures across New York State, for example, spans two hemispheres in traveling to Argentina in winter and back to New York in spring. Of the nearly 250 different kinds of birds that nest in the state, approximately 72% are migratory, leaving each fall to spend the winter in warmer climates and returning to nest in spring.

New York State boasts a rich store of information on its birds. The ease with which they may be observed and a 150-year tradition of contributions by volunteer and professional observers have made birds one of the best-documented groups of animals in the state. Significant publications, beginning with James E. DeKay's pioneering *Zoology of New York State* (1844) and continuing through works of the early 21st century, chronicle the natural history of New York State's birds. Volumes by Elon H. Eaton (1910, 1914), John Bull (1974), Robert Andrle and Janet Carroll (1988), and Emanuel Levine (1998) are part of this continuum, and, in addition, contain extensive bibliographies. The quarterly journal of the New York State Ornithological Association (known from 1947 through 2003 as the Federation of New York State Bird Clubs), the *Kingbird* (1950–), periodically updates the bibliography of New York State ornithology and publishes in each issue details of recent and seasonal observations of birds throughout the state. Since 1989 the association has maintained and occasionally published separately the official checklist of the birds of New York State.

The variety of birds observable in the state reflects the return to the region, over the past 10,000–12,000 years, of species forced southward during the last glaciation. None of the birds in New York State are endemic (limited only) to the state. The New York State Department of Environmental Conservation (DEC) maintains a list of the species of fish and wildlife that are extirpated (no longer occurring or exhibiting traditional patterns of use in the state), endangered (in imminent danger of extirpation or extinction), threatened (likely to be endangered in the near future), or of special concern (documented risk of endangerment). Species formerly occurring in New York State but now extinct include the Labrador duck *(Camptorhynchus labradorius),* by 1875, and the passenger pigeon *(Ectopistes migratorius),* by 1899. The latter became extinct most likely because of unregulated hunting and loss of forested habitat. John Bull's 1974 review of historical reports of the Carolina parakeet *(Conuropsis carolinensis)* concluded that the species likely never occurred in New York State. A distinct eastern subspecies of greater prairie chicken *(Tympanuchus cupido),* the heath hen *(Tympanuchus cupido cupido),* disappeared from New York State *ca* 1835, however, with conversion of the native prairies of Long Island's Hempstead Plains to villages and farmland. The Eskimo curlew *(Numenius borealis)* was last reported as a migrant species in the state in the early 1890s. Although still seen during migration, the golden eagle *(Aquila chrysaetos)* and loggerhead shrike *(Lanius ludovicianus)* are extirpated from the state as breeding species, with the last known successful eagle nesting reported in 1970 and the last known shrike nesting reported in 1988.

Blue jay nesting, Arcade.

As of 1999, 455 species of resident and migratory birds, representing 19 orders and 62 families, had been documented within the state. By the same date, 6 of the 455 were either extirpated or extinct. As of 2002, among the 449 extant species, 39 (9%) receive special consideration through identification as endangered, threatened, or of special concern by the DEC. In addition, 244 of the 449 extant species were known as breeding birds, and 118 (26%) were of such rarity that the Avian Records Committee of the Federation of New York State Bird Clubs requested written documentation of sightings. Although much sought after by bird watchers, these rare or "accidental" species contribute modestly to the functional avian diversity.

In addition to recognized species, at least three hybrid forms are listed among the breeding birds of the state: those resulting from the interbreeding of mallard *(Anas platyrhynchos)* with American black duck *(A rubripes),* and the morphologically distinctive hybrids of blue-winged warblers *(Vermivora pinus)* and golden-winged warblers *(V chrysoptera),* identified for more than 100 years as Brewster's and Lawrence's warblers.

At the beginning of the 21st century, perhaps the greatest threat is habitat conversion and degradation. Of those New York breeding birds showing significant declining population trends, 45% are affected by losses of open land and shrub-land habitats through human activities and natural ecological "succession" of those habitats to forested lands. Of forest and woodland species, most of which are long-distance migrants to Central and South America, 32% are in decline. Unlike exploitation via unregulated hunting and trapping for food at the beginning of the 20th century, habitat conversion and degradation are diffuse threats, affecting species on both breeding and wintering ranges. Trends in habitat change caused by ecological succession are challenging and expensive to reverse or stabilize across a land area the size of New York State. Monitoring of bird populations and the habitats necessary for bird survival and reproduction remains critical to conservation of New York State's rich and varied bird resources.

Andrle, Robert F., and Janet R. Carroll, eds. *The Atlas of Breeding Birds in New York State* (Ithaca: Cornell Univ Press, 1988)
Bull, John. *Birds of New York State* (Garden City, NY: Doubleday Natural History Press, 1974)
DeKay, James E. "Birds." In *Zoology of New York; or, The New York Fauna,* vol 2 of *Natural History of New York* (New York: D. Appleton; Wiley & Putnam, 1844)
Levine, Emanuel, ed. *Bull's Birds of New York State* (Ithaca: Cornell Univ Press, 1998)

Charles R. Smith

Birdsall. Town (pop 268) in NE Allegany Co. Settled in 1816, the town was formed in 1829 from Allen and Almond. In the mid–19th century it received an influx of Irish immigrants. The Allegany Chemical Works (1875) at Hiltonville produced alcohol, acetate of lime, and charcoal. Dairy products, hay, and potatoes were late 19th-

BIRDS OF NEW YORK STATE

Order	Family	Common Names of Species (No. of Species)
Gaviiformes	Gaviidae	loons (4)
Podicipediformes	Podicipedidae	grebes (5)
Procellariiformes	Diomedeidae	albatrosses (1)
	Procellariidae	shearwaters and petrels (9)
	Hydrobatidae	storm-petrels (3)
Pelecaniformes	Phaethontidae	tropicbirds (2)
	Sulidae	boobies and gannets (2)
	Pelecanidae	pelicans (2)
	Phalacrocoracidae	cormorants (2)
	Anhingidae	darters (1)
	Fregatidae	frigatebirds (1)
Ciconiiformes	Ardeidae	bitterns, egrets, and herons (12)
	Threskiomithidae	ibises and spoonbills (4)
	Ciconiidae	storks (1)
	Cathartidae	American vultures (2)
Anseriformes	Anatidae	swans, geese, and ducks (42)
Falconiformes	Accipitridae	kites, eagles, and hawks (15)
	Falconidae	falcons (4)
Galliformes	Phasianidae	partridges, grouse, and turkey (6)
	Odontophoridae	New World quail (1)
Gruiformes	Rallidae	rails, gallinules, and coots (11)
	Gruidae	cranes (1)
Charadriiformes	Charadriidae	plovers and lapwings (7)
	Haematopodidae	oystercatchers (1)
	Recurvirostridae	stilts and avocets (2)
	Scolopacidae	sandpipers and phalaropes (41)
	Laridae	jaegers, gulls, and terns (39)
	Alcidae	auks, murres, and puffins (8)
Psittaciformes	Psittacidae	parrots (1)
Cuculiformes	Cuculidae	cuckoos (2)
Strigiformes	Tytonidae	barn owls (1)
	Strigidae	typical owls (9)
Caprimulgiformes	Caprimulgidae	goatsuckers (3)
Columbiformes	Columbidae	pigeons and doves (4)
Apodiformes	Apodidae	swifts (1)
	Trochilidae	hummingbirds (3)
Coraciiformes	Alcedinidae	kingfishers (1)
Piciformes	Picidae	woodpeckers (10)
Passeriformes	Tyrannidae	tyrant flycatchers (17)
	Laniidae	shrikes (2)
	Vireonidae	vireos
	Corvidae	jays, magpies, and crows (6)
	Alaudidae	larks (2)
	Hirundinidae	swallows (7)
	Paridae	chickadees and titmice (3)
	Sittidae	nuthatches (3)
	Certhiidae	creepers (1)
	Troglodytidae	wrens (7)
	Regulidae	kinglets (2)
	Sylviidae	gnatcatchers (1)
	Turdidae	thrushes (14)
	Mimidae	mockingbirds and thrashers (4)
	Sturnidae	starlings (1)
	Motacillidae	pipits (1)
	Bombycillidae	waxwings (2)
	Parulidae	wood warblers (40)
	Thraupidae	tanagers (3)
	Emberizidae	towhees and sparrows (32)
	Cardinalidae	grosbeaks and buntings (8)
	Icteridae	blackbirds (13)
	Fringillidae	finches (12)
	Passeridae	Old World sparrows (1)

Sources: American Ornithologists Union, *Check-list of North American Birds* (1998); Federation of New York State Bird Clubs, *Checklist of the Birds of New York State* (1999).

Compiled by Charles R. Smith

century crops. The Pittsburg, Shawmut and Northern Railroad (1903–46) provided service. A large part of Birdsall was reforested in the 1930s, encompassing 2,408-acre (974.5 ha) Keaney Swamp, 2,332-acre (943.7 ha) Gillie Hill, and 2,263-acre (915.8 ha) Gas Springs State Forests, as well as the 707-acre (286.1 ha) Keaney Swamp State Wildlife Management Area.

bird watching. Recreational activity involving identification and observation of birds, often by enticing them to viewing areas with feeders containing seeds or other foods. Bird watching as a leisure-time activity grew significantly in the United States throughout the 20th century. Theodore Roosevelt, New York State governor (1899–1900) and US president (1901–9), watched, studied, and wrote about birds from his boyhood onward. In 1900 Frank M. Chapman, curator of birds at New York City's American Museum of Natural History (1908–42), originated the annual Christmas Bird Count (CBC) as an alternative to the practice known as the Christmas Side Hunt, when hunters would choose an area to hunt and shoot as many different kinds of animals (including birds) as possible from the area on Christmas Day. The CBC became a bird-watching activity still popular at the beginning of the 21st century. Chapman also wrote an early guide to help bird watchers in 1927: *Handbook of Birds of Eastern North America,* illustrated by Louis Agassiz Fuertes, an artist and bird watcher who also illustrated Elon H. Eaton's *Birds of New York* (1910, 1914). The growth in popularity of bird watching was facilitated by the publication of *A Field Guide to the Birds* (1934) by Jamestown (Chautauqua Co) native Roger Tory Peterson. Following art training in New York City, teacher and bird lover Peterson prepared this mass-audience guide, one of the first nonscholarly works on birds, which grouped illustrations by easy-to-recognize features. In its fifth edition at the beginning of the 21st century, the guide popularized the modern bird-watching movement.

Bird watchers have contributed significantly to knowledge of New York State birds. From 1980 through 1985, more than 4,000 volunteers supplied observations to the state's first breeding bird atlas (1988), which documented geographic distributions for breeding birds. In 1965 the US Fish and Wildlife Service launched the Breeding Bird Survey, with nearly 100 volunteer bird watchers participating in its New York State surveys each year. In 2000 work began on a second New York State breeding bird atlas, making New York the first North American state or province to launch a second such largely volunteer-dependent birding project. The largest bird-watching organization in the state, the New York State Ornithological Association (known from 1947 through 2003 as the Federation of New York State Bird Clubs), represents more than 10,000 members and more than 50 bird clubs.

Andrle, Robert F., and Janet R. Carroll, eds. *The Atlas of Breeding Birds in New York State* (Ithaca: Cornell Univ Press, 1988)

New York State Ornithological Association, http://www.nybirds.org/

Peterson, Roger T., and Virginia M. Peterson. *A Field Guide to the Birds of Eastern and Central North America,* 5th ed (Boston: Houghton Mifflin, 2002)

Charles R. Smith

EXTINCT, ENDANGERED, THREATENED, AND SPECIAL CONCERN BIRDS OF NEW YORK STATE, 2003

Species Name	Common Name
Extinct (after 1800)	
Tympanuchus cupido cupido	heath hen
Camptorhynchus labradorius	Labrador duck
Ectopistes migratorius	passenger pigeon
Endangered	
Laterallus jamaicensis	black rail
Chlidonias niger	black tern
Numenius borealis	Eskimo curlew
Aquila chrysaetos	golden eagle
Lanius ludovicianus	loggerhead shrike
Falco peregrinus	peregrine falcon
Charadrius melodus	piping plover
Sterna dougallii	roseate tern
Asio flammeus	short-eared owl
Falcipennis canadensis	spruce grouse
Threatened	
Haliaeetus leucocephalus	bald eagle
Sterna hirundo	common tern
Ammodramus henslowii	Henslow's sparrow
Rallus elegans	king rail
Ixobrychus exilis	least bittern
Sterna antillarum	least tern
Circus cyaneus	northern harrier
Podilymbus podiceps	pied-billed grebe
Cistothorus platensis	sedge wren
Bartramia longicauda	upland sandpiper
Special Concern	
Botaurus lentiginosus	American bittern
Catharus bicknelli	Bicknell's thrush
Rynchops niger	black skimmer
Dendroica cerulea	cerulean warbler
Gavia immer	common loon
Chordeiles minor	common nighthawk
Accipiter cooperii	Cooper's hawk
Vermivora chrysoptera	golden-winged warbler
Ammodramus savannarum	grasshopper sparrow
Eremophila alpestris	horned lark
Accipiter gentilis	northern goshawk
Pandion haliaetus	osprey
Melanerpes erythrocephalus	red-headed woodpecker
Buteo lineatus	red-shouldered hawk
Ammodramus maritimus	seaside sparrow
Accipiter striatus	sharp-shinned hawk
Pooecetes gramineus	vesper sparrow
Caprimulgus vociferous	whip-poor-will
Icteria virens	yellow-breasted chat

Source: Endangered, Threatened, and Special Concern Fish and Wildlife Species of New York State, http://www.dec. state.ny.us/ website/dfwmr/wildlife/endspec/etsclist.html.

Compiled by Charles R. Smith

birth control

The 19th Century and the Comstock Era

Although the term "birth control" came into use during the 20th century, women have always sought to limit and control fertility. During the colonial and early national periods of New York State's history, common techniques included douching, coitus interruptus, and abortion. There was a decrease in birth rates in the 19th century, and white, native-born women of the middle and upper classes experienced the greatest declines. The total fertility rate for Whites (the average number of children born to the women of this group who survived to menopause) fell from 7.04 children per woman in 1800 to 3.87 in 1890 and continued to fall until after World War II, rising with the Baby Boom, and declining again in the mid-1960s. The sharpest declines in fertility during the 19th century were not primarily due to new birth control techniques, contraception, or abortion (illegal in the state after 1828), but to continence or abstinence, both of which were associated with the movement for "voluntary motherhood" that took hold midcentury and grew in influence through the Gilded Age. Voluntary motherhood was popular both with suffragists, such as Elizabeth Cady Stanton, and with free love advocates, including New York City residents Victoria Woodhull and her sister, Tennessee Claflin. Nativists raised the fear of "race suicide" and pressed for restricting access to birth control to increase birth rates among native-born Whites.

In 1868, through the efforts of the Young Men's Christian Association (YMCA), the New York legislature passed a law entitled An Act for the Suppression of the Trade in and Circulation of Obscene Literature, Illustrations, Advertisements, and Articles of Indecent or Immoral Use, and Obscene Advertisements of Patent Medicines. From his New York City base, Anthony Comstock, with backing from his affiliation with the YMCA, led the effort against public circulation of information about reproduction as part of his crusade against "obscene" materials. In 1873 the US Congress approved legislation, known as the Comstock Law, which prohibited the mailing of obscene materials, including information on contraception, and New York State adopted its own Comstock Law that same year. As a special agent of New York State and the US Post Office, Comstock held authority to enforce the laws and arrest violators. He exercised this power for more than four decades, until his death in 1915. All forms of contraception were illegal in the state from 1869 to 1881, when physicians gained authority to prescribe contraception to prevent the spread of disease, although in practice some physicians interpreted the law broadly to authorize birth control for those who sought it out and who had the means to pay for it.

Margaret Sanger and Planned Parenthood

The Comstock Law greatly limited public discussion of birth control, but activists in Manhattan's Greenwich Village, including Emma Goldman, Elizabeth Gurley Flynn, and Crystal Eastman, began to defy the restrictions during the 1910s. Goldman argued that controlling reproduction was a woman's right and advocated birth control to advance working-class interests. Goldman's ideas strongly influenced Margaret Sanger, who would become the leader of the American birth control movement. Sanger, who maintained that advocacy of birth control grew directly from her work as a public health nurse on the Lower East Side, publicized birth control through standard grassroots approaches such as pamphleteering and street corner oration. She called for birth control, female emancipation, and world revolution in her journal, the *Woman Rebel*, launched in March of 1914. Sanger was indicted for violating state obscenity laws, but the charges were dropped in 1916. On 16 Oct 1916, Sanger, her sister Ethel Byrne, and Fania Mindell opened the nation's first birth control clinic in an immigrant, working-class neighborhood in the Brownsville section of Brooklyn. Days later, she and the clinic's staff were arrested and charged with violating state obscenity statutes and with maintaining a public nuisance. Although Sanger spent 30 days in the Queens County Penitentiary, the resolution of the case was a victory for birth control advocates. The state's Court of Appeals, ruling in *People v Sanger* (1918), upheld Sanger's conviction but interpreted the law to permit contraception under a physician's direction.

The way was prepared for a system of birth control clinics operating under medical direction. Most of these clinics were affiliated with Sanger's American Birth Control League (ABCL), which she founded in 1921 in New York City. On 2 Jan 1923 Sanger opened the first legal birth control clinic in the country, the Clinical Research Bureau, at 17 West 16th St, which served 1,208 patients in its first year of operation. Renamed the Birth Control Clinical Research Bureau in 1928, the facility had 15,200 patients by 1929. By the 1930s it served over 10,000 women per year and was the largest birth control clinic in the country. In 1930 Sanger opened an affiliate in Harlem. In 1933 Esther Sawyer and May Carter established the Family Relations Institute in Buffalo, one of the first birth control clinics to open outside of New York City. The following year the ABCL opened a clinic in Rochester. Sanger's Research Bureau and the ABCL joined in 1939 to form the Birth Control Federation of America, which in 1942 became Planned Parenthood Federation of America (PPFA), with headquarters in New York City.

The state's large Roman Catholic population has been influential in opposing the birth control movement, whose growth during the 1920s led the Catholic Church to organize and become politically active. The National Catholic Welfare Conference (NCWC) condemned birth control and the endorsement of birth control by the New York State Federation of Women's Clubs during the 1930s, and NCWC representatives campaigned through circulars, magazines, and lobbyists against contraception as a "national menace." A tense debate over contraception and abortion has marked national politics since the 1960s. The introduction of Enovid-10, the first oral contraceptive ("the pill"), in 1960 was revolutionary; it was simple to use, more effective than other techniques, and allowed women control over contraception. Because of these characteristics, the pill quickly became the most popular form of birth control, and it remains the most popular nonsurgical method of birth control. After the constitutional right to contraception for married couples was established by the Supreme Court in *Griswold v Connecticut* (1965) and extended to the unmarried in *Eisenstadt v Baird* (1972), attention shifted to the debate over abortion. New York State legalized abortion three years before the US Supreme Court issued its decision in *Roe v Wade* (1973), which made abortion legal throughout the nation. In 1971 the US Congress repealed the Comstock Law's anticontraception provisions.

Margaret Sanger, 1920s.

Recent History

Since the 1970s, exercising reproductive rights has become largely a matter of gaining access to existing reproductive services. While feminists defend women's right to control fertility, their opponents seek to restrict access to contraception and abortion. Well-organized opposition targeting abortion providers has increased the financial expense of providing reproductive services and the physical risks associated with working at clinics that provide a full range of reproductive services. Since contraception has been established as a legal right, costs of birth control methods and devices have decreased, and new, more reliable products have been introduced. Also, New York State underwrites the cost of some forms of contraception. Much of the opposition to birth control is religiously based, including fundamentalist Christians as well as Catholics. Much of the remaining debate over birth control concerns social behaviors, for instance, does birth control education increase sexual intercourse among teenagers? In addition to the pill, condoms, barriers, and the intrauterine device (IUD), there are several recent innovations in contraception, including surgical implants, injections, the contraceptive patch, and the vaginal ring. In September 2000 the federal Food and Drug Administration approved RU-486 (mifepristone), which operates by blocking the receptors of progesterone and thus preventing pregnancy, for use in the United States to terminate early pregnancy (up to 49 days). Although the teen pregnancy rate in New York State fell between 1985 and 1996 (from 117 to 108 pregnancies per 1,000 women aged 15–19), the state had the third highest rate of teen pregnancy in 1996. PPFA is the largest organization in New York State providing birth control services with 14 affiliates located throughout the state in 2002.

Chesler, Ellen. *Woman of Valor: Margaret Sanger and the Birth Control Movement in America* (New York: Simon & Schuster, 1992)

Solinger, Rickie, ed. *Abortion Wars: A Half Century of Struggle, 1950–2000* (Berkeley: Univ of California Press, 1998)

Tone, Andrea, ed. *Controlling Reproduction: An American History* (Wilmington, Del: Scholarly Resources, 1997)

Penny Messinger

bisexuals. See Lesbians, gays, bisexuals, and transgendered people.

Black, Frank S(wett) (*b* Limington, Maine, 8 Mar 1853; *d* Troy, Rensselaer Co, 22 Mar 1913). Governor. After graduating from Dartmouth in 1875, Black became editor of the *Johnstown Journal* (Fulton Co) but moved to Troy within a year, where he was admitted to the bar in 1879 and soon entered private practice. In 1893 he became chair of the Rensselaer Co Republican Committee, which he unified and solidified, and he also handled the receiverships of Troy Steel and Iron Co and Gilbert Car Co. In 1894 he was elected to Congress; after serving one term he was nominated for governor in 1896 and won by a large majority. As governor, he advocated a sensible civil service code and backed a bill giving appointing officers greater prerogatives. He also approved (1897) New York City charter legislation. His party chose Theodore Roosevelt for the 1898 gubernatorial nomination, and Black returned to private life, practicing law in New York City.

Kathryn T. Sheehan

Black Brook. Town (pop 1,660) in SW Clinton Co. Bounded on the south by the Ausable River, it was settled before 1825 by Yankees, and the town was formed from Peru in 1839. By midcentury there was a significant Francophone Canadian population. Lumber, iron, and charcoal were its early industrial products, thanks to its excellent waterpower. Between 1870 and 1966 many residents worked in the J. and J. Rogers Co ironworks and, later, in its pulp and paper mill at Au Sable Forks (Essex and Clinton Cos). Nearly all Black Brook residents work out of town in the early 21st century.

Thomas A. Rumney

black convention movement. Prompted by an 1829 race riot in Cincinnati, free black leaders inaugurated the first national convention of African Americans in Philadelphia (1830). Numerous subsequent conventions met at the state level and, from 1830 to 1864, 12 at the national level to plan tactics, protest political disfranchisement, and debate issues relevant to the black struggle for justice. New York City, Buffalo, Troy, Rochester, and Syracuse each hosted a national convention.

As before, attendees at the fourth annual convention meeting in New York City (1834) focused on the threat of colonization. American Colonization Society members in the North and South encouraged slaveholders to manumit the enslaved, secure in the knowledge that Blacks would be colonized elsewhere. William Hamilton, president of the fourth convention, countered their position, arguing in a public address that Blacks must remain in America and organize as a potent but respectable public force. After a hiatus, prompted in part by the deaths of early leaders such as Richard Allen and Hamilton, the black convention movement was revived in Buffalo (1843). This new locale heralded the leadership of activists from beyond the major Northeastern black communities of Boston, Philadelphia, and New York City. Over the next 20 years, conventioneers would come from Western New York, Ohio, Michigan, and even from the South. Frederick Douglass and Henry Highland Garnet (both had escaped bondage in Maryland) emerged as national leaders at the Buffalo convention. They battled over Garnet's famous "Address to the Slaves," in which he advocated the direct, even physical, confrontation of masters by the enslaved. After much debate, Douglass's motion not to print the address prevailed; he feared that it would be tactically unwise and would lead to much bloodshed.

The next convention met in Troy (Rensselaer Co) in 1847, and it too considered a significant proposal: white abolitionist Gerrit Smith's offer to donate 120,000 acres (48,600 ha) of Adirondack land to Blacks. Smith hoped to encourage Blacks to settle in rural rather than urban areas and to become independent landowners and thereby eligible voters in New York State. Convention leaders expressed appreciation for Smith's donation, noting that black "freedom, independence, and steadiness" would flow from it. Smith's plan resonated with delegates hoping to inculcate moral uplift values, such as industry, sobriety, and piety, in black communities. Some antebellum black activists, such as Martin Delany, criticized such efforts for not confronting the realities of black subjection. Blacks should focus less on improving black behavior and image, Delany argued, and more on removing themselves from oppressive white power structures, such as by forming their own nation beyond America. In the 1853 national convention in Rochester, Douglass offered one of the powerful speeches against emigrating from America. "We address you as American citizens asserting their rights of their own native soil," he proclaimed. During the Civil War, Blacks organized another national convention, chaired by Douglass, at Syracuse in 1864. Attendees called for the end of slavery, suffrage for black men, and equal rights regardless of race. Viewed as a way both to coordinate black protest activities and to present black reformers as a thoughtful, intelligent group deliberating on weighty matters, the conventions influenced later generations of reformers.

Newman, Richard, Patrick Rael, and Phillip Lapsansky. *Pamphlets of Protest: An Anthology of Early African-American Protest Literature, 1790–1860* (New York: Routledge, 2001)

Rael, Patrick. *Black Identity and Black Protest in the Antebellum North* (Chapel Hill: Univ of North Carolina Press, 2002)

Richard Newman

Black Diamond. Express passenger train of the Lehigh Valley Railroad. The name Black Diamond was chosen in a contest and honored the anthracite coal carried as the railroad's main cargo. First called Black Diamond Express, the train began service on 18 May 1896 as part of the railroad's 50th anniversary celebrations. It ran a 450 mi (724 km) route between Buffalo and Jersey City, NJ, near New York City. From 1918 onward Black Diamond and other Lehigh Valley passenger trains served Manhattan directly at Penn Station, using Pennsylvania Railroad tracks. Touted as "Handsomest Train in the World" by Lehigh Valley, Black Diamond was first pulled by a Camelback steam locomotive, with the engineer's cab straddling the boiler. In April 1940 designer Otto Kuhler restyled the train. Kuhler used Pacific-type steam locomotives (those with four leading wheels, six driving wheels, and two trailing wheels) with bullet-nosed shrouding for a modern look. Black Diamond was painted the bright crimson of Cornell University, which the train passed. Accents of black and white added to the train's vivid appearance. Competition from air and highway travel forced Black Diamond to cease operations on 11 May 1959.

Archer, Robert F. *Lehigh Valley Railroad: The Route of the Black Diamond* (Berkeley, Calif: Howell-North Books, 1977)

Karl Zimmermann

black nationalism. Calls for "Black Power" and kindred expressions of black identity have a long tradition in New York State. This sentiment has generated a history of community organizing and a wider sense of racial pride and, sometimes, separatism. One of the first exponents was Alexander Crummell (1819–98). He grew up in New York City, attended the African Free School, where he met Henry Highland Garnet (1815–82), another black nationalist. Crummell and Garnet eventually became enamored with the idea of "colonization," that is, trying to establish a homeland for African Americans in Liberia. From here American blacks would help "civilize" the continent. Although the results of the Liberian experiment were at best equivocal, the efforts to inculcate Western values made it clear that black nationalism had conservative tendencies. These tendencies lived past the Civil War and into the age of Booker T. Washington, when nationalists sometimes accommodated the realities of segregation, both North and South.

By the early 20th century black nationalism became associated with Harlem, where the great migration of African Americans north and the segregated real estate practices created a city within a city. Here W. E. B. DuBois (1868–1963) stationed offices of the NAACP (1909), but his leadership and broadly integrationist vision were challenged by the nationalist Marcus Garvey and his Universal Negro Improvement Association. Garvey stoked up race pride among Harlem residents along with Hubert H. Harrison (1883–1927). Harrison had abandoned Marxism by the 1920s for black nationalism and was an intellectual who could speak to great crowds. Garvey's race pride and Harrison's calls for community control eventually inspired the Buy Black movement that inspired Harlem's citizens in the 1930s and thereafter. By the depression Du Bois, Garvey's fiercest opponent, expressed a renewed interest for black nationalism, and some communists and left-wing activists, typically integrationists, also saw validity in the idea of a black nation.

After the depression the Nation of Islam (NOI) started a movement to organize black power. Originating in Detroit in the 1930s, this religion offered a theological justification for black nationalism. NOI faithfuls felt that Blacks were the original race, while a mad scientist Yacub had created the white race to avenge Allah. Equating Whites with devils, the NOI made separatism its core theology. Leader Elijah Muhammad spread the faith and recruited Malcolm X as a minister. A reformed drug dealer and burglar, Malcolm X was familiar with the social culture of Harlem and turned himself into an influential public speaker. He broke from the NOI in 1964 and turned his Harlem ministry over to Louis Farrakhan, but remained connected to black nationalism and Harlem. He formed the Organization of Afro-American Unity, which translated the black nationalist message into a more overtly leftist, and less overtly antiwhite, message. He criticized the Civil Rights Movement and called on African Americans to identify with Third World struggles. While bringing cases against the United States at the United Nations, he was still searching for a coherent set of policies when assassinated in February 1965.

Malcolm X left behind a somewhat vague legacy for younger black nationalists. Organizers within the Student Nonviolent Coordinating Committee (SNCC) grew enamored with his militancy and expelled Whites from the organization in 1966. Its new leader, Stokely Carmichael, had come of age in Harlem and had become a young radical at the Bronx High School of Science. Carmichael developed the idea of black power, arguing for community control within segregated areas, and this nationalist ferment had an impact on the movement for the community control of schools, which culminated in the bitter struggle between the Ocean Hill–Brownsville Community School Board (Brooklyn) and the United Federation of Teachers in 1968.

Formed in 1966, the Black Panther Party (BPP) merged black nationalism and Marxism, distancing itself from a more conservative stance of black nationalism. Although known for its policy of armed self-defense against police, the BPP also performed community organizing (most famously its Breakfast Program). In New York City, however, some members of the BPP broke with Huey Newton's call to focus on community organizing and electoral politics, and forged an alliance with the radical faction of Students for a Democratic Society (SDS), the Weather Underground Organization (Weathermen), and started calling for armed insurrection. They eventually formed the Black Liberation Army (BLA). The best-known member of this group was Assata Shakur, who was jailed after a shootout with police on the New Jersey Turnpike. In 1979 she escaped from the Clinton Correctional Institution for Women in New Jersey, eventually making her way to Cuba, showing through her escape that the BLA, though small, was still active beyond the tumultuous 1960s. So too was the connection between black power and armed vanguardism. The Panthers left behind a sense of black nationalism, as did the Black Arts Repertory Theater/School (BARTS), a performing arts center started by the poet LeRoi Jones (Amiri Baraka) in Harlem. With support from numerous jazz artists, this short-lived experiment attempted to create a separatist black aesthetic. Outside of New York City, organizations like FIGHT (Freedom, Integration/Independence, God, Honor, Today) in Rochester in the mid-1960s had strong nationalist elements.

Black nationalism continues to veer between militancy and traditional community organizing. During the 1980s and 1990s Rev Al Sharpton reacted to white racist behavior by organizing grassroots protests and legal actions (questionably, it should be pointed out, in the Tawana Brawley case). He has built power in Harlem and black neighborhoods of Brooklyn. In 2003 the NOI was still strong, and Louis Farrakhan continued to accuse the US government of conspiring to spread drugs through the black community, while demanding financial reparations for the legacy of slavery. Some rap musicians (many based in New York City) appropriate the styles of militant confrontation left behind by the BPP and Malcolm X. All of this suggests that black nationalism and black power continue to exert a great deal of influence in New York State.

Cruse, Harold. *The Crisis of the Negro Intellectual* (New York: William Morrow, 1967)
Moses, Wilson Jeremiah. *The Golden Age of Black Nationalism, 1850–1925* (Hamden, Conn: Archon Books, 1978)
Umoja, Akinyele Omowale. "Repression Breeds Resistance: The Black Liberation Army and the Radical Legacy of the Black Panther Party." In *Liberation, Imagination, and the Black Panther Party,* ed. Kathleen Cleaver and George Katsiaficas (New York: Routledge, 2001)

Kevin Mattson

blackouts. Brief localized power outages have occurred frequently since the 1880s, when electric power was first used in New York City. In 1888 a blizzard knocked over lines and shut down power transmission for several hours. In 1936 a fire in a generating station caused electricity to be shut off in Manhattan north of 59th St and the Bronx. On 17 Aug 1959 and 13 June 1961 limited local blackouts occurred in parts of New York City.

At approximately 5:15 PM on 9 Nov 1965, an incorrectly adjusted relay in Queenston, Ont, caused a transmission line near Niagara Falls to fail. Power surges backed up, causing massive overloads and rapidly triggering systemwide shutdowns. Within minutes almost all of New York State and most of the northeastern United States were without any electrical power, and some 30 million people were plunged into darkness. Rochester lost power at 5:18 PM, and New York City went dark at 5:28 PM. Rush-hour commuters were stranded, including some 800,000 in New York City subways and many others in elevators. Rescue workers, engineers, and citizens managed to free almost all of them by 10 PM. Some emergency generators failed, but most hospitals and radio stations were able to operate on auxiliary power supplies. Full service was not restored to New York City for 13.5 hours, with Manhattan coming back on-line by 4:44 AM on 10 November. The overall response of the public was cheerful fellowship and camaraderie, and only 96 people, considered an extraordinarily low number, were arrested. The experience of what became known as the Great Northeast Blackout entered popular folklore. "Where were you when the lights went out?" was a favorite topic of conversation, and a false urban legend circulated of a spike in the birthrate nine months later. Changes put in place afterward included the creation of the New York Power Pool (1966), the Northeast Power Coordinating Council (1966), and the National Electric Reliability Council (now North American Electric Reliability Council, 1968). The new safeguards passed their first test in 1971, when the system recovered quickly from line failures affecting Baldwinsville (Onondaga Co), Oswego, and parts of Long Island.

Lightning struck twice on the hot summer evening of 13 July 1977, when successive thunderbolts at 8:37 and 8:55 PM crippled two double-circuit 345 kV power lines running between Millwood (Westchester Co) and Pleasant Valley (Dutchess Co). The lightning severed feeder lines and knocked out the Indian Point generating station in Rockland Co; mechanical failure and human error in systemwide load shedding

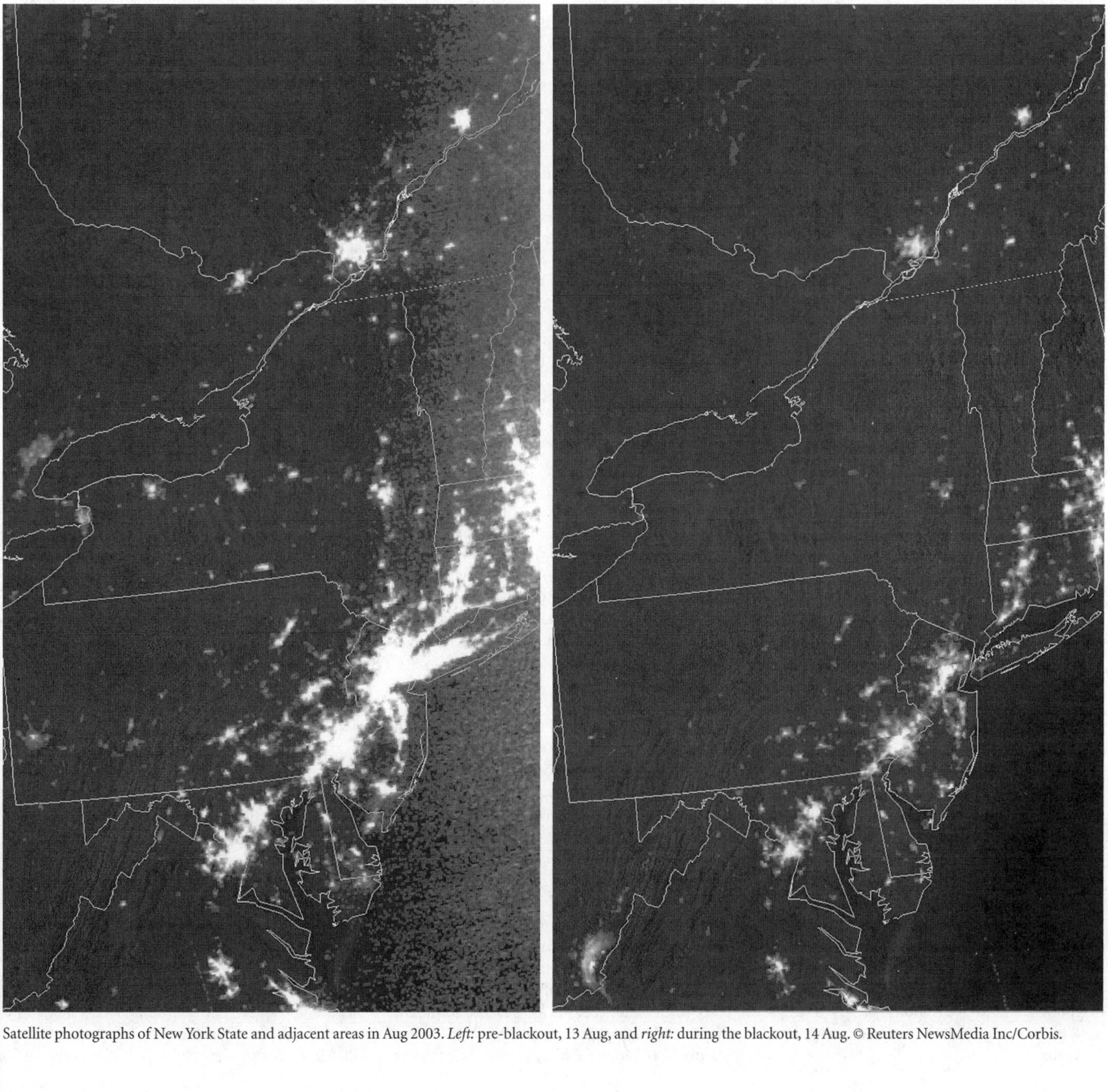

Satellite photographs of New York State and adjacent areas in Aug 2003. *Left:* pre-blackout, 13 Aug, and *right:* during the blackout, 14 Aug. © Reuters NewsMedia Inc/Corbis.

resulted in a massive shutdown of the electrical grid. By 9:36 PM, more than 8 million people in the New York City metropolitan area were without electricity for up to 25 hours. Although most people reacted calmly, within half an hour spontaneous looting erupted in all five boroughs. Widespread disorder broke out simultaneously in neighborhoods across the city. More than 1,600 stores were damaged, firefighters sought to control 1,037 fires, and 31 neighborhoods suffered extensive damage. Hardest hit were Bushwick, Crown Heights, Bedford-Stuyvesant, and Flatbush in Brooklyn, the central and south Bronx, the Upper West Side, and East Harlem. In Brooklyn, hundreds of stores were looted. On Jerome Ave in the Bronx, a crowd broke into a Pontiac dealership and drove 50 cars out through a single door. Merchants' estimated losses exceeded $350 million. It was the largest and most costly collective theft in the city's history and, with an estimated 3,776 looters caught by police, the largest mass arrest. The police were badly outnumbered, and most reinforcements did not arrive until after midnight. Seriously injured were 18 officers; 400 others suffered minor injuries. Police behavior was deliberately a model of restraint. Although two rioters were killed by shopkeepers, no one was shot, killed, or severely wounded by either police or crowds. In the aftermath, prosecutors and judges were tougher on looters than on ordinary criminals.

The hardest hit neighborhoods were overwhelmingly poor, African American, and Hispanic. In Bushwick, the site of the heaviest looting, there was significant destruction and arson. The disturbances during the 1977 blackout were confirmation for many that New York City had entered a period of rapid decline and fraying social institutions. The federal government refused to declare the city a disaster area, the real estate market in blighted urban neighborhoods subsequently collapsed, many business owners fled, and buildings were abandoned. Decades later, Bushwick had still not fully recovered.

Several smaller blackouts occurred between 1977 and 2003. An ice storm on 8 Jan 1998 knocked out power to much of northern New York State, in some areas for weeks; Potsdam (St. Lawrence Co) was without electricity for 23 days. Many Con Edison customers, including those in much of northern Manhattan, went without electricity during a heat wave on 6 July 1999; the same day storm blackout affected another 75,000 people in northern New York State. On 14 Aug 2003 the lights went out around 4:30 PM in the most massive blackout in US history, including much of the Northeast and all of New York State. Evidently triggered by an overload surge originating with the malfunction of damaged equipment in Ohio, the cascading power failure lasted between 28 and 44 hours in different areas, prompting politicians to call for nationwide modernization of the power grid. That the power outage occurred several hours before sundown gave officials and citizens time to prepare for the night of darkness. While there were a few sporadic burglary incidents and 850 arrests in New York City (100 fewer than on a typical summer night), crime slowed during the blackout. Contrasts to the riotous behavior during the 1977 blackout were widely noted. The calm, neighborly, and festive response of New Yorkers was taken as a sign that the city had changed for the better.

The Blackout History Project, http://blackout.gmu.edu/
Curvin, Robert, and Bruce Porter. *Blackout Looting!* (New York: Gardner Press, 1979)
Doheny-Farina, Stephen. *The Grid and the Village: Losing Electricity, Finding Community, Surviving Disaster* (New Haven, Conn: Yale Univ Press, 2001)
Goodman, James. *Blackout* (New York: North Point Press, 2003)
Lurkis, Alexander. *The Power Brink: Con Edison, a Centennial of Electricity* (New York: Icare Press, 1982)

Thomas Ross Miller

Black River (112 mi/180 km). Arising from the woods of the central and western Adirondacks and the core forest of Tug Hill, the Black River passes through wilderness, farmland, and city before ending its northwest flow to Lake Ontario at Dexter (Jefferson Co). The river provided much of the water and electricity that built the North Country, including paper mills and manufacturing plants. A feeder canal at Forestport and Boonville (Oneida Co) can divert water from the river through the historic Black River Canal (1848–1924) south to Rome (Oneida Co) and the Erie Canal. In 1919 the Black River Regulating District was formed to control the river's flow and to reduce flooding. Several small dams span the river as it flows west out of North and South Lakes in the Black River Wild Forest of the Adirondack Park to Forestport and then north to Lyons Falls (Lewis Co). The flat water stretch of the river from Lyons Falls north to Carthage (Jefferson Co) is noted for fishing—walleye, smallmouth bass, northern pike, bullhead, pickerel, and rock bass—and recreational boating. The Adirondack tributaries of the Moose, Otter, and Independence Rivers, the hydropower-developed Beaver River, and several Tug Hill tributaries, including the Deer River, also join the Black River in this area. From Carthage to Lake Ontario, the river again tumbles downhill, providing additional hydropower and whitewater recreation. In 2003 the river is the cleanest it has been in well over a century and supplies drinking water for Watertown.

Thomas, Howard. *Black River in the North Country* (Prospect, NY: Prospect Books, 1978)

Robert R. Quinn

Black River. Village (pop 1,285) in Rutland and Le Ray (Jefferson Co). Settled in 1806 (in Rutland) and 1829 (in Le Ray), the village was incorporated in 1891. A prosperous manufacturing community, its first major industry was furniture making; the H. C. Dexter Chair Co (1839–1912) and the Black River Bending Co (1860–89) were the best known. Paper mills, notably Jefferson Paper Co (1888–1928) and H. Remington and Sons Pulp and Paper Co (?1890–1928) replaced the furniture factories. Some factories remained after the paper mills closed, but Black River's manufacturing era was over. In the early 21st century the village is primarily a bedroom community to Watertown and Fort Drum.

Laura Lynne Scharer

Black River Canal. In 1825 residents of Herkimer, Oneida, Lewis, and Jefferson Cos petitioned the state legislature for a canal to link the Black River with the Erie Canal, citing the Black River Valley region's fertile land, abundant timber, and high-grade iron ore. By 1828 the legislature hired James Geddes, a principal engineer on the Erie Canal, to survey possible routes. The lawmakers chose a line running from Rome (Oneida Co) on the Erie, through Boonville (Oneida Co) to High Falls [now Lyons Falls, Lewis Co] on Black River and requiring 1,122 feet (342 m) of lockage. The private Black River Canal Co was organized that year and capitalized at $400,000 but failed after three years, having accomplished little. In 1832 a second Black River Co incorporated with double the capital but failed by 1835. State intervention came with a canal bill passed the following year, and work began in 1838 under chief engineer Porteus Root. Root oversaw the excavation—35 miles (56.3 km) long, 42 feet (12.8 m) wide, and 4 feet (1.2 m) deep, and containing 109 lift locks, or an average of 15 locks every 5 miles (8 km). The Erie Canal enlargement, also under construction, averaged only 1 lock per 5 miles. Black River was dredged to allow for navigation from High Falls to Lake Ontario. Construction halted on state canals in 1842 because of the Stop and Tax Law passed to reduce state debt. Work resumed on the Black River Canal in 1848 and was completed in November 1855 at a cost of $3,157,296, $1 million above estimate. Canal commerce peaked in 1889 at 143,561 tons (130,236 MT) and fell rapidly thereafter; railroad competition and depletion of the area's natural resources caused the decline. Black River Canal was not merged into the Barge Canal system. It closed 24 July 1924 when the last boat was "locked down" to Rome. The canal contributed little to the growth of the Black River Valley region but survived longer than most of New York's state-operated canals.

Larkin, F. Daniel. *New York State Canals: A Short History* (Fleischmanns, NY: Purple Mountain Press, 1998)

F. Daniel Larkin

Black Rock. Extinct town in Erie Co, now a neighborhood of the City of Buffalo. The state put land along the Niagara River up for sale in 1802, and the young Black Rock community competed for trade with Buffalo. From 1811 the collector of customs was housed at Black Rock save during the winter, when he was at Buffalo. Both Black Rock and Buffalo were burned by the British and their Indian allies during the War of 1812. Through the influence of Gen Peter B. Porter, Black Rock was chosen as the western terminus of the Erie Canal, but Buffalo interests questioned the safety of its harbor and eventually secured a bill early in 1825 authorizing a canal along the river to Buffalo, which was completed in 1842. Black Rock incorporated as a village in 1837, formed as a town in 1839, and was annexed by Buffalo in 1853. Germans arrived beginning in the 1840s, Poles in the 1880s and after World War II, and Ukrainians and Hungarians in the early 20th century, making Black Rock a strong working-class neighborhood. Employment included milling, iron founding, steam engine fitting, and glass manufacture, but Black Rock was hard hit by the factory closings of the 1970s.

Joseph Golombek Jr

Blacksnake [Tenh-Wen-Nyos] (*b* Kendaia [now in Seneca Co], ?1753; *d* Allegany Indian Reservation [loc in Cattaraugus Co], 1859). Seneca leader and orator. Born in a Seneca village on Seneca Lake, he lived his early life at Canawaugus [now Avon, Livingston Co]. He served the

British during the American Revolution, like many other Senecas. After the war he attended nearly all of the federal-Iroquois councils accompanying his uncle, Cornplanter. In 1788 Blacksnake, then known as Gov Blacksnake, moved to the Cornplanter Grant in northern Pennsylvania, close to the Allegany Indian Reservation. At the Cornplanter Grant on 15 June 1799 he witnessed the catatonic-like trance of his uncle Handsome Lake, the Seneca prophet who was having his first vision, leading to the founding of the Gaiwiio, or Good Word. As one of the prophet's major disciples of the Longhouse religion, Blacksnake preached this Code of Handsome Lake, which condemned whiskey, witchcraft, love potions, and abortion. Besides proselytizing the new religion, Blacksnake served as the prophet's major advisor.

With the pressures of land companies, transportation interests, and Albany politicians intent on ridding the state of its Indian population, Blacksnake became one of the great defenders of the Senecas after the death of the prophet in 1815. Until his own death Blacksnake led his Seneca peoples, helped institutionalize the religion espoused by Handsome Lake, and resisted efforts at removing Indians westward. He was especially important in the case *Seneca Nation of Indians v Philonus Pattison* (1855–61), an ejectment case against white squatters on the Oil Spring Reservation [loc in Allegany and Cattaraugus Cos]. As a result of his testimony on 27 and 28 Aug 1858, the court ruled in favor of Seneca ownership of this mile-square parcel, leading to the ejectment of the squatters. "Nephew" is a major family name among the Seneca as a tribute to Blacksnake, the nephew of Handsome Lake.

Abler, Thomas S., ed. *Chainbreaker: The Revolutionary War Memoirs of Governor Blacksnake as Told to Benjamin Williams* (Lincoln: Univ of Nebraska Press, 1989)

Hauptman, Laurence M. *Conspiracy of Interests: Iroquois Dispossession and the Rise of New York State* (Syracuse: Syracuse Univ Press, 1999)

———. "Governor Blacksnake and the Seneca Indian Struggle to Save the Oil Spring Reservation," *Mid-America* 81 (Winter 1999): 51–73

Wallace, Anthony F. C. *The Death and Rebirth of the Seneca* (New York: Knopf, 1969)

Laurence M. Hauptman

black suffrage referendums. Statewide canvasses in 1846, 1860, and 1869 considered the fate of a constitutional provision discriminating against black voters. The 1821 state constitution introduced race into suffrage requirements by dropping property qualifications for white men while requiring a $250 freehold for black men. Debate centered on the ability of black men to vote independently because of their alleged economic dependence on white economic elites. Free Blacks formed associations to protest this and other forms of discrimination. White abolitionists also joined the fight, and by 1846 the issue, now linked to slavery in national politics, surfaced prominently at the state constitutional convention. Delegates voted primarily along party lines (Democrats for; Whigs against) to retain the property qualification for Blacks. Submitted for separate voter consideration, equal suffrage was defeated 224,336 to 85,406 (2.6 to 1). Support for equal suffrage came principally from western and northern counties settled by New Englanders and where Whigs, hoping to attract Liberty Party voters, supported the measure. Opposition centered in the southeastern, formerly slaveholding, counties.

Partisan realignment brought most supporters of equal suffrage into the new Republican Party in the 1850s. Republican legislators prepared a constitutional amendment removing the property qualification for submission to voters in 1860. Fear that the race issue might damage Abraham Lincoln's chances in the presidential election, however, caused many Republicans to ignore the referendum. The result was massive Republican abstentions and the defeat of the equal suffrage provision once again, this time 345,791 to 197,889 (1.7 to 1). As Republicans nationally required southern states to accept black suffrage during Reconstruction, party radicals in New York State used a new constitutional convention to bring their state into conformity with the South. In a final referendum in 1869, 53.1% of the electorate, dividing largely on party lines, again voted to keep the property qualification by a vote of 282,403 to 249,802 (1.1 to 1). The ratification of the 15th Amendment to the US Constitution in 1870 finally ended the discriminatory qualification.

Field, Phyllis F. *The Politics of Race in New York: The Struggle for Black Suffrage in the Civil War Era* (Ithaca: Cornell Univ Press, 1982)

Phyllis F. Field

Blackwell, Antoinette Louisa Brown (*b* Henrietta, Monroe Co, 20 May 1825; *d* Elizabeth, NJ, 5 Nov 1921). Minister, author, and social activist. She was educated at Monroe County Academy and Oberlin College. While a student at Oberlin and thereafter, Antoinette Brown lectured on women's rights, temperance, and antislavery. A delegate to the 1853 World's Temperance Convention in New York City, she received national attention after being heckled off the platform by those who believed that women should not speak in public to a mixed-gender gathering. Brown was the first woman in the United States formally appointed to a post within a recognized denomination; she was ordained by the First Congregational Church of South Butler (Wayne Co) in 1853. That same year, in Rochester, she was the first woman to perform a marriage ceremony. She resigned her pulpit in 1854 and became a Unitarian. In 1855 she volunteered in the slums and prisons of New York City and wrote about her experiences for the *New York Tribune*. In 1856 Brown married Samuel Blackwell, and they had seven children. She produced works on evolution and social science, a novel, and a volume of verse. Blackwell served as vice president of the Association for the Advancement of Women, founded the Unitarian Church in Elizabeth, NJ (1908), encouraged women to enter ministerial and scientific careers, and lived long enough to cast her ballot in a national election.

Cazden, Elizabeth. *Antoinette Brown Blackwell: A Biography* (Old Westbury, NY: Feminist Press, 1983)

David E. Bumbaugh

Blackwell, Elizabeth (*b* Counterslip, England, 3 Feb 1821; *d* Hastings, England, 31 May 1910). Physician and medical educator. After emigrating in 1832, her family settled in New York City and later moved to Jersey City, NJ, and Cincinnati, Ohio. She studied medicine privately in North Carolina, South Carolina, and Pennsylvania before matriculating at Geneva Medical College (Ontario Co) in 1847. Blackwell was admitted when the faculty, reluctant to admit a woman but nervous about rejecting such a qualified candidate, submitted the choice to the students, who believed her application was a hoax. On 23 Jan 1849 at the top of her class, she became the first woman to earn a medical degree in the United States. Following postgraduate study in Paris and London, she returned in 1851 to New York City, where she maintained a practice (1851–57) and cofounded the New York Infirmary for Women and Children (1857) with her sister Emily and Marie Zakrzewska. Additionally Blackwell trained nurses and organized relief efforts during the Civil War. In 1869 she permanently settled in England, where she established a prosperous private practice and taught gynecology at the London School of Medicine for Women (1875–1907). She was a prolific author of books and pamphlets promoting hygiene, preventive medicine, sex education, social welfare, and reform of women's roles.

Wilson, Dorothy Clarke. *Lone Woman: The Story of Elizabeth Blackwell, the First Woman Doctor* (Boston: Little, Brown, 1970)

Eric v. d. Luft

Blasdell. Village (pop 2,718) in Hamburg (Erie Co). Blasdell owes its start to the Erie and Nickel Plate Railroads. A post office opened in 1885, and the village was incorporated in 1898. Heavy manufacturing sustained the village through much of the 20th century, including Seneca Iron and Steel Co (1907; later Bethlehem Steel Co) and the Ford Motor Co stamping plant. Steel production declined in the 1970s, leaving light manufacturing as the driving economic force.

Andrew C. Maines

blasphemy. A crime under English common law and by statute in some jurisdictions but not in New York State. Blasphemy has been variously defined as denying the truth of Christian religious doctrine or as speaking disrespectfully of God, the Bible, religious figures, or religion in general. The most famous blasphemy case in New York State, and the first reported in the state, occurred in December 1810 when a freethinker named Timothy Ruggles was indicted in Salem (Washington Co) for the common-law crime of having said "Jesus Christ was a bastard, and his mother must be a whore." In June 1811 Ruggles was found guilty in a Court of Oyer and Terminer in Salem, sentenced to jail for three months, and fined $500. His lawyer appealed, arguing there was no state law against blasphemy. Chief justice of the Supreme Court of New York James Kent upheld the constitutionality of the prosecution in *People v Ruggles* (1811). Kent held that blasphemous utterances were a threat to public welfare and morality and constituted a common-law "offence against the public peace and safety." *Ruggles* has never been explicitly overruled, but it is incompatible with state and federal constitutional prohibitions of religious establishment and guarantees of free exercise.

Levy, Leonard W. *Blasphemy: Verbal Offense against the Sacred, from Moses to Salman Rushdie* (New York: Knopf, 1993)

Perry, Kenneth A. *The Fitch Gazetteer: An Annotated Index to the Manuscript History of Washington County, New York*, vol 1 (Bowie, Md: Heritage Books, 1999)

William M. Wiecek

PROSUFFRAGE VOTING BY COUNTIES

	1846 (%)	1860 (%)	1869 (%)
Albany	25.6	34.5	44.9
Allegany	35.1	61.5	65.3
Broome	21.1	44.3	56.2
Cattaraugus	53.7	56.5	57.9
Cayuga	23.6	57.3	59.6
Chautauqua	40.1	57.9	65.2
Chemung	24.5	33.7	42.4
Chenango	25.5	46.9	52.4
Clinton	72.8	47.1	44.5
Columbia	11.2	25.0	43.8
Cortland	52.5	60.6	62.0
Delaware	33.3	44.7	50.7
Dutchess	11.6	21.9	50.4
Erie	28.2	31.3	63.4
Essex	70.8	57.8	58.0
Franklin	58.8	52.3	54.9
Fulton and Hamilton	15.1	24.7	47.1
Genesee	43.6	59.7	59.1
Greene	5.3	10.8	33.9
Herkimer	31.4	48.0	49.5
Jefferson	38.1	48.4	54.0
Kings	20.3	19.1	41.8
Lewis	42.5	42.7	51.5
Livingston	27.2	49.0	56.3
Madison	53.1	62.2	59.9
Monroe	47.0	42.2	51.6
Montgomery	13.4	10.6	43.7
New York	14.6	13.9	29.6
Niagara	27.8	37.8	47.8
Oneida	39.4	46.6	51.7
Onondaga	39.3	52.8	55.4
Ontario	36.5	51.4	56.9
Orange	6.9	10.2	47.8
Orleans	37.1	53.8	58.8
Oswego	57.8	57.3	61.6
Otsego	22.4	44.0	48.1
Putnam	2.3	7.0	32.9
Queens	2.1	7.7	38.5
Rensselaer	38.6	40.0	47.4
Richmond	4.5	5.4	38.9
Rockland	3.6	2.4	35.5
St. Lawrence	34.7	66.8	75.4
Saratoga	14.6	27.5	43.8
Schenectady	16.0	19.9	36.0
Schoharie	7.2	18.0	38.7
Schuyler	24.1	48.3	53.0
Seneca	21.5	35.4	44.1
Steuben	19.1	47.8	52.6
Suffolk	7.9	19.0	45.9
Sullivan	8.4	10.7	38.6
Tioga	26.7	43.6	55.4
Tompkins	26.2	48.7	58.9
Ulster	4.4	13.1	39.4
Warren	56.3	48.0	47.1
Washington	60.0	56.2	56.9
Wayne	30.9	50.2	50.2
Westchester	4.1	11.3	42.7
Wyoming	57.7	58.2	61.8
Yates	35.4	60.7	58.4
Entire State	27.6	36.4	46.9

Source: Adapted from P. F. Field, *The Politics of Race in New York: The Struggle for Black Suffrage in the Civil War Era* (1982), App B.

Blatch, Harriot (Eaton) Stanton (*b* Seneca Falls, Seneca Co, 20 Jan 1856; *d* Greenwich, Conn, 20 Nov 1940). Woman suffrage leader. Daughter of reformer and suffrage pioneer Elizabeth Cady Stanton, who wanted to raise her free of traditional gender stereotypes, and Henry Brewster Stanton, from whom she acquired a love of politics, Harriot graduated from Vassar College in 1878 and helped her mother write the *History of Woman Suffrage.* She traveled to Europe in 1880, married Englishman Harry Blatch in 1882, and lived in England until 1902. Returning to New York City that year, and finding the suffrage movement largely moribund, Harriot initiated measures that modernized and revitalized the campaign in New York State, and made it a mass movement. These changes were brought in part through the Equality League of Self-Supporting Women, which Blatch established in 1907. This organization, renamed the Women's Political Union in 1910, led the referendum campaigns for woman suffrage in the state from 1913 to 1915.

Blatch tried to create alliances across economic classes by emphasizing two issues that she believed drew women together in modern society: the need to achieve financial independence and the struggle to balance the demands of work and family. Blatch's organization aimed at altering the stereotype of "strong-minded" suffragists, cultivating a public image of diversity and playfulness. They produced romantic suffrage movies, sponsored suffrage shops where people could buy memorabilia of the cause, and between 1908 and 1912 organized suffrage parades in New York City, the first in the nation. After 1915 Carrie Chapman Catt and Alice Paul overshadowed Blatch, although their emphasis on lobbying and militant tactics owed a great deal to Blatch's work. Following the successful passage of the 19th Amendment in 1920, Blatch continued to rejected narrow single-issue approaches to women's rights. She connected the liberation of women with other social justice causes, such as labor relations and world peace. Refusing to support protective legislation for women, she withdrew from organizations like the Women's Trade Union League and the Socialist Party. Blatch's many activities helped shape the 20th-century women's rights movement.

Blatch, Harriot Stanton. *Challenging Years: The Memoirs of Harriot Stanton Blatch* (1940; repr Westport, Conn: Hyperion, 1976)

DuBois, Ellen Carol. *Harriot Stanton Blatch and the Winning of Women Suffrage* (New Haven: Yale Univ Press, 1997)

Jon Sterngass

Blatchford, Samuel (*b* New York City, 9 Mar 1820; *d* Newport, RI, 7 July 1893). US Supreme Court justice. Educated in private schools in Pittsfield, Mass, and New York City, Blatchford graduated from Columbia College at 17. His father's friend William H. Seward helped Blatchford's professional rise. Blatchford completed his legal training as Gov Seward's private secretary. He was admitted to the bar in 1842 and practiced with his father's New York City firm. In 1844 Blatchford joined Seward and Christopher Morgan in an Auburn (Cayuga Co) partnership. After the breakup of that firm, in 1854 he set up the New York City firm of Blatchford, Seward, and Griswold, which was, like his Auburn firm, a predecessor of Cravath, Swaine, and Moore. His work as a court reporter, covering admiralty and Civil War prize cases as well as US Second Circuit opinions, began in 1852 and enhanced Blatchford's reputation for expertise. After declining a seat on the state supreme court in 1855, Blatchford was appointed in 1867 to the District Court for the Southern District of New York, was promoted to the Second Circuit in 1872, and was appointed to the "New York seat" on the US

Supreme Court in 1882. Transferring his court reporter habits of industry and thoroughness to his work on the bench, Blatchford did more than his share of work on the Court, particularly in patent and admiralty cases. Meanwhile his reputation for following precedent gave weight to the Court's modification of the *Munn* (1877) doctrine that states could "regulate business in the public interest"; in *Chicago, Milwaukee and St. Paul Railway Co v Minnesota* (1890), he ruled that statutes had to allow courts to rule on the "reasonableness" of such regulations. Blatchford's service on the Court ended with his death.

Paul, Arnold. "Samuel Blatchford." In *The Justices of the United States Supreme Court, 1789–1969: Their Lives and Major Opinions,* ed. Leon Friedman and Fred L. Israel, 5 vols (New York: Chelsea House in association with Bowker, 1969–78)

Swaine, Robert T. *The Cravath Firm and Its Predecessors, 1819–1947* (New York: Ad Press, 1946)

Donald M. Roper

Blauvelt. Locality (pop 5,207) in Orangetown (Rockland Co). Part of the Tappan Patent (1686–87), the locality was settled by the Dutch and was known as Greenbush. In 1828 a post office was established, called Blauveltville until 1886, when the name was shortened. The Erie Railroad came through in 1841; a second station was established on the West Shore Railroad in 1883. German Catholic farmers arrived in the mid–19th century, forming the Church of St. Catherine of Alexandria (1868). The St. Dominic Convent (1878) continues to care for children in the early 21st century. Extensive suburban development followed the end of World War II. Blauvelt is the site of Dominican College (1952). The state's only known dinosaur tracks were discovered at Blauvelt in 1972.

Mary R. Cardenas

Bleecker. Town (pop 573) in N central Fulton Co. Most of the town's waterways flow northward and drain into the Great Sacandaga Lake. Settled around 1800, the town was formed in 1831 from Johnstown. A substantial German immigrant community developed in the mid–19th century. Lumbering and tanning provided work for residents through most of the 19th century; thin mountain soils supported little agriculture. The town is entirely within in the Adirondack Park, hindering further development. In 2003 Bleecker has camps and summer cottages, and some year-round residents drive southward to jobs.

James Crawford

Bleecker [née Schuyler], Ann Eliza (*b* New York City, Oct 1752; *d* Schaghticoke, Rensselaer Co, 23 Nov 1783). Author. Ann Eliza Schuyler was raised in a prosperous merchant family and exhibited a talent for poetry at an early age. She moved from Poughkeepsie to Schaghticoke in the early 1770s along with her husband John J. Bleecker. They lived near the junction of Tomhannock Creek and Hoosic River, a few miles west of the modern settlement of Tomhannock in Pittstown [now in Rensselaer Co]. In the summer of 1777 her family was forced to flee to Lansingburgh [now in Rensselaer Co] for safety, for fear of attack by Indians in league with British Gen John Burgoyne. The terror Bleecker experienced on that occasion led her in 1779 to compose a short novel based on an Indian attack and captivity incident in Schaghticoke in 1711. Although it was not published until 1790–91, *The History of Maria Kittle* is regarded by most literary scholars as America's first novel by a woman. This novel, also included in Bleecker's *Posthumous Works* (1793), introduced to American fiction the "ignoble savage" and "noble savage" stereotypes of the Native American as well as the literary character known as the "Indian hater." Also included in *Posthumous Works* were 36 poems, most with patriotic, sentimental, or highly personal themes. In 1781 Bleecker's neighbor James Yates horribly murdered his family with an ax. Bleecker penned an account of these murders, which appeared in *New-York Magazine* and *Philadelphia Minerva* in 1796. Her article furnished America's preeminent novelist, Charles Brockden Brown, with the plot of his landmark Gothic novel *Wieland* (1798). Despite her premature death Bleecker has earned an important place in US literature for both her early treatment of Native Americans and her role as one of America's first female poets and novelists.

Broderick, Warren F. "Fiction Based on 'Well Authenticated Facts': Documenting the Birth of the American Novel," *Hudson Valley Regional Review* 4 (Sept 1987): 1–37

Giffen, Allison. "Ann Eliza Bleecker." In *American Women Prose Writers to 1820,* ed. Carla Mulford, Angela Vietto, and Amy Winans, vol 200 of *Dictionary of Literary Biography* (Detroit: Gale Research, 1999)

Warren F. Broderick

Blenheim. Town (pop 330) in S central Schoharie Co. Settled by Dutch and Palatine Germans before 1761 and by New Englanders after the Revolution, the town was established in 1797. Difficult terrain and shallow soils limited farming to a few crops, which included hops and broom corn. On 13 Mar 1990 a Texas Eastern Transmission Corp petroleum pipeline (1963) exploded in North Blenheim, killing two people and destroying eight houses. In the early 21st century, the principal occupations are dairying and logging. The northwest quarter of the town is mostly state forest land. The 210 ft (64 m) Blenheim covered bridge, Mine Kill State Park, and Lansing Manor (?1818) are located in town, as is the Blenheim-Gilboa Pumped Storage Power Project of the New York Power Authority.

Peter Johnson and Dawn Johnson

blindness

Education

Dating back to the colonial era, the indigent blind were housed in almshouses. Large numbers of children confined to them suffered from eye diseases. There was no systematic attempt at educating the blind until 1831, when John Dennison Russ, Samuel Wood, and Samuel Akerly incorporated the New York Institution for the Blind in New York City. They recruited the first class of three boys from the city almshouse on 15 Mar 1832. The school was held at various locations around the city before moving into its own building at 34th St and 9th Ave, and in May 1834 provision was made to admit pupils to the school at state expense. In 1912 the school was renamed the New York Institute for the Education of the Blind to stress its focus on education. The institute did away with its manufacturing department in 1916, emphasizing the intellectual rather than manual education of its pupils. In 1922 construction began on a new facility in the Bronx located on Pelham Parkway, the school's present location. The institute changed its name in 1986 to the New York Institute for Special Education (NYISE) to reflect the expansion of its services to children with an assortment of disabilities.

The New York State School for the Blind was founded at Batavia (Genesee Co) in 1866 to serve blind children in the western and central parts of the state. The school opened in 1868 with 74 pupils and initially gave enrollment preference to veterans blinded in the Civil War. In 1919 the school came under the control of the State Education Department.

Because most schools for the blind were residential, the majority of students were required to be away from family for long periods of time, causing some families to keep the children at home rather than to send them away for school. When New York State made education compulsory for blind children in 1911, several parents began to lobby for day schools. New York City imitated Chicago, dividing the city into grids and providing a special room for blind students in one school per sector. The students spent most of the day in regular classes, accompanied by special teachers. Demand for special education classes in regular public schools exploded as a result of epidemics of retinopathy of prematurity (ROP) and rubella in the 1950s and 1960s, creating a rapid increase in the number of blind children and a shortage of both programs and teachers. Starting in the 1960s, federal funding allocated for the training of special education teachers shifted the focus to preparing teachers for instructing students with multiple disabilities in a variety of settings.

US Congress in 1967 created the Helen Keller National Center for Deaf-Blind Youths and Adults (HKNC), located in Sands Point (Nassau Co), as a training and research center and residential school. The facility provides diagnostic assessments, short-term vocational rehabilitation, assistance with jobs and residential placement for deaf-blind Americans. Services and training are offered across the nation through HKNC's 10 regional offices and 40 affiliated agencies.

Reading and Writing

In the mid–19th century there was no standard reading code for the blind. Louis Braille devised a raised dot system in France in 1829, and his system was modified in Britain and in the United States. In 1866 William Bell Wait, principal of the New York Institution for the Blind, began studying raised dot reading codes and in 1868 published a new system, called New York Point. Wait's system was endorsed and recommended for use by the American Association of Instructors of the Blind in 1871. Wait also created the Kleidograph, a machine like a typewriter with 12 keys, designed for use by only one hand (allowing the other hand to read) to emboss New York Point in 1894. Debates over the proper code to use waged for years. In 1918 the American Printing House for the Blind (APH), the major publisher of textbooks for blind students, agreed to print only revised Braille type. Standard Braille was adopted by the APH in 1932. Braille remains the international writing and reading code. The Computer Center for Visually Impaired People was established in 1978 at Baruch College in Manhattan to use computers equipped with speech synthesizers, print enlargement, and Braille printers to help visually impaired people increase their access to education.

The New York State Talking Book and Braille Library (TBBL), located in Albany, loans Braille and recorded reading materials along with audio equipment to residents of New York State who are not capable of reading typical printed materials because of visual or physical disabilities. Founded in 1896 as the New York State Library for the Blind, the library originally provided embossed books for blind adults. In 1974 the library was renamed the New York State Library for the Blind and Visually Handicapped, and became the TBBL in 1995. The Andrew Heiskell Library for the Blind and Physically Handicapped, located in Manhattan, was named in honor of a former chairman of the New York Public Library's Board of Trustees and opened in 1991. The barrier-free library includes circulating collections of special-format materials along with audio playback equipment for listening to recorded books and magazines.

INCREASING AUTONOMY

Numerous organizations provide information on blindness and operate as clearinghouses for reading materials in Braille. Lighthouse International was founded in 1905 in New York City as the New York Association for the Blind. Lighthouse provides numerous services to blind children and adults, including a workshop and summer camps. The National Braille Association was founded in Rochester in 1945, creating the Braille Book Bank in 1963. Organizations like the New York State Commission for the Blind and Visually Handicapped, located in Syracuse, and the Jewish Guild for the Blind, founded in 1914 in New York City, provide vocational rehabilitation services, medical and vocational evaluation, educational sponsorship, and job training for legally blind consumers seeking employment. The American Foundation for the Blind (AFB), founded in 1921 in New York City, provides information on blindness to Congress, conducts surveys, and records talking books. The AFB's M. C. Migel Memorial Library holds the Helen Keller Archives.

Several developments during the 20th century have increased the independence of the blind. The Lion's Clubs International has been attributed with introduction of the white cane to the United States in 1930. Although the blind had used canes before this date, the emphasis on painting the cane white increased its visibility to approaching motorists. The cane was widely used to help blind veterans of World War II gain some mobility at home. State law dictates that every driver approaching an intersection or crosswalk yield the right-of-way to a pedestrian accompanied by a guide dog or using a white or metallic cane. Many organizations were established to train guide dogs after World War II, including the Guide Dog Foundation for the Blind (1946) in Smithtown (Suffolk Co), Guiding Eyes for the Blind (1954) in Yorktown Heights (Westchester Co), Canine Companions for Independence (1975) in Medford (Suffolk Co), and the Upstate Guide Dog Association (1992) in West Bloomfield (Ontario Co). These organizations rely on volunteer puppy raisers to train a puppy for about a year. The dog is then sent for intensive training at the facility and later matched with a future owner. The new owner and guide dog train together at the organization for two to three weeks before returning to the owner's home. A 1986 New York State law mandates that guide dogs can accompany their owners in public places and on public transportation at no extra fee.

Holbrook, M. Cay, and Alan J. Koenig, eds. *Foundations of Education,* 2d ed. (New York: American Foundation for the Blind Press, 2000)
New York Institute for Special Education, http://www.nyise.org
New York State Commission for the Blind and Visually Handicapped, http://www.ocfs.state.ny.us/main/cbvh/

Sarah E. DeSanctis

blizzard of 1888. Beginning in New York State around midnight on 12 Mar 1888 and continuing for over 24 hours, a classic nor'easter—a cyclone spinning counterclockwise—hit along the Atlantic coast from Maryland to Maine. Winds up to 50 miles per hour (80 kph) created snowdrifts as high as 30 feet (9 m). Caught unaware, New York City residents were unprepared when heavy rains changed to freezing rain and ice and when snowfall and winds drastically increased. Several elevated trains were immobilized, with passengers trapped inside, for 36 hours. Scores of horses died carrying much needed provisions, coal supplies were quickly exhausted, stores ran out of foodstuffs, and heavy ice and snow pulled down the city's overhead wires. Some shop owners dug tunnels through the snow for patrons, and others used torches to melt a path, only to be confronted with flooded basements. Although New York City reestablished outside contact in a few days, it was several weeks before all the snow melted. The "white hurricane" moved up the Hudson River valley, pummeling Troy (Rensselaer Co) and Albany with about 50 inches (127 cm) of snow, approximately twice the amount that fell on New York City. Areas to the west of the Hudson received snow, but the blizzard did not greatly affect daily life. The storm caused the deaths of 400 people on the East Coast and $25 million in damages. In addition to sparking public interest in subways, the storm led to Mayor Hugh J. Grant's directive to move New York City's overhead wires underground to mitigate the effects of future storms.

Cable, Mary. *The Blizzard of '88* (New York: Atheneum, 1988)

Gregory Dehler

Clearing the sidewalk outside the Leland Opera House after the blizzard of 1888, Albany.

Block, Adriaen (Courtsz) (*b* Amsterdam, *ca* 1567; *bur* Amsterdam, 7 Apr 1627). Early skipper, explorer, and trader. Working for a cartel of Lutheran merchants, Block searched for the river explored by Henry Hudson in 1609. Instead of approaching the mouth of the river from the south, he struck land around Cape Cod. By following the Connecticut coast he entered all major waterways along the way. During his four voyages to this area from 1611 to 1614, he developed a lucrative trade in sewan (wampum) produced by the Pequot in Connecticut for furs offered by the Mohawk on the upper Hudson. Block was so active in this trade that the island that served as his base of operations still carries his name. Block recorded his knowledge of the region on the 1614 map attributed to him and Cornelis Doetsz. It not only indicates "Adrian Blox eyland" but also describes the architectural features of the trading post called Fort Nassau [now Port of Albany]. While wintering over on Manhattan Island in 1614 Block's ship, the *Tijger,* caught fire and burned to the waterline. His crew built a yacht called the *Onrust* as a replacement vessel. Block and his crew have the distinction of being the first Europeans to winter over and the first to build a ship on Manhattan. Block traded with the *Onrust* along the coast of Connecticut as far as Cape Cod, where he boarded a Dutch ship bound for the Netherlands. He never returned to the New World.

Hart, Simon. *The Prehistory of the New Netherland Company, Amsterdam Notarial Records of the First Dutch Voyages to the Hudson* ([Amsterdam]: City of Amsterdam Press, 1959)

Charles T. Gehring

blood libel. The erroneous belief that Jews murdered Christian children has been a staple of anti-Jewish persecution since at least the 12th century. Though there have been few accusations of this activity in the United States, the two best-known instances took place in New York State. On the basis of a sensationalist *New York Herald* story of the ritual murder of a child, 500 men led by local police in New York City, ransacked a synagogue in September 1850, the eve of Yom Kippur. Perhaps the most notorious blood libel incident in American history took place in Massena (St. Lawrence Co) on 22 Sept 1928, when 4-year-old Barbara Griffith disappeared in the nearby woods. While a search was conducted, Greek immigrant Albert Comnas, a local restaurateur, sparked the rumor that she had been murdered so that her blood could be used for Yom Kippur. The rumor spread and was embellished, and the local Jewish community was harassed. Mayor W. Gilbert Hawes called the state police, and a trooper harshly questioned the local rabbi. The next day Barbara Griffith was found unharmed, but the incident provoked a national outcry and demands for investigation. Hawes asserted that Jews had released the child only when their plot was discovered and organized a boycott of Jewish businesses. Rabbi Stephen S. Wise, chairman of Manhattan's American Jewish Congress, persuaded Gov Alfred E. Smith, then a presidential candidate, to speak in defense of Massena's Jews. Hawes publicly apologized, apparently under pressure from the national Republican Party, and the state trooper who had investigated the rabbi was reprimanded and reassigned. Nevertheless the incident soured interreligious relations in the Massena community for some time.

Dinnerstein, Leonard. *Anti-Semitism in America* (New York: Oxford Univ Press, 1994)
Friedman, Saul S. *The Incident at Massena: The Blood Libel in America* (New York: Stein & Day, 1978)

Susan Roth Breitzer

Bloomer [née Jenks], Amelia (*b* Homer, Cortland Co, 27 May 1818; *d* Council Bluffs, Iowa, 30 Dec 1894). Dress reformer and feminist. The daughter of clothier Ananias Jenks and his wife, Lucy Webb, Amelia attended Homer schools and by age 17 began work as a teacher in Clyde (Wayne Co). After serving as a governess in Waterloo (Seneca Co), in 1840 Amelia married Seneca Falls (Seneca Co) newspaper editor Dexter C. Bloomer. With her husband's encouragement she began to write anonymous reform-minded articles, contributing many to the *Water Bucket* newspaper of the Seneca Falls Temperance Society that she helped found. Bloomer believed that women had a duty to speak on their own behalf as well as on worthy causes, and she participated in the 1848 Seneca Falls Convention for women's rights. In 1849, frustrated by the reluctance of male temperance advocates to include women fully in the movement, Bloomer founded the *Lily,* the first newspaper published by a woman; it became a forum for women writing on abolition, women's rights, and other progressive matters. In 1851 Bloomer adopted a light and comfortable style of dress originated that year by Elizabeth Smith Miller, daughter of Peterboro (Madison Co) abolitionist Gerrit Smith. The style featured a skirt that reached just below the knee, worn over moderately full trousers that gathered above the footwear. Traditional women's attire of the era included a voluminous trailing skirt that picked up dust and filth, a minimum of six full petticoats, and a tightly laced whalebone corset that occasionally damaged internal organs; such an outfit weighed 12 to 15 pounds (5.4 to 6.8 kg), made normal daily activity a challenge, and often left the wearer gasping for breath. Bloomer published patterns in the *Lily* for the new "Turkish costume" and daguerreotypes of herself and Elizabeth Cady Stanton wearing it. Other papers noted the design and attributed it to Bloomer. The style lasted about three years and enjoyed only a limited popularity among women in the Northeast and West. Women wearing "bloomers" were frequently harassed in public. The costume gained publicity for the feminist movement—it increased the *Lily*'s circulation eightfold—but by 1854, in Bloomer's view, it was drawing attention away from greater issues such as a woman's right to the ballot, a good education, and better pay and employment opportunities.

Bloomer was elected corresponding secretary of the New York Woman's Temperance Society in 1853, and she joined Susan B. Anthony on speaking tours at a time when it was unconventional for women to speak in public, much less to lecture before an audience. She advocated strict prohibition of alcohol and became a famed lecturer for women's rights. In 1853 Bloomer and the *Lily* moved to Mount Vernon, Ohio, where her husband had purchased a newspaper. In 1855 she sold the *Lily* and moved with her husband to Council Bluffs, Iowa, where they adopted two children. Bloomer remained active in temperance and women's causes until her death.

Gattey, Charles N. *The Bloomer Girls* (New York: Coward McCann, 1968)
Kleinberg, Susan J. Frwd. *Life and Writings of Amelia Bloomer,* by Dexter C. Bloomer (New York: Schocken Books, 1975)

Caryn E. Neumann

Bloomfield. Village (pop 1,267) in East Bloomfield (Ontario Co). The hamlet of East Bloomfield originated on the state road from Utica to Avon (authorized 1794). Another hamlet, Bloomfield Station, later called Holcomb, developed less than a mile away around a depot on the Canandaigua and Niagara Falls Railroad (1853). The two villages incorporated a few weeks apart in 1917, merging to become the Village of Bloomfield in 1990. The original state road, macadamized in 1911, is now Rte 5 and US 20. The Antique Wireless Association Museum is located on the village green in the original East Bloomfield Academy building (1838). Residents commute to Canandaigua and Rochester. Holcomb is the site of Gannongarae, a Seneca village destroyed by Marquis de Denonville in July 1687.

Marla A. Bennett

Bloomingburg. Village (pop 353) in Mamakating (Sullivan Co). It acquired a post office in 1811 and was incorporated in 1833. Before it was bypassed by the Delaware and Hudson Canal (1828), Bloomingburg was a minor commercial center, headquarters of lumber merchants. It was the site of Sullivan Co's first school (1784), printing office (*ca* 1810), and newspaper (1821). In one of his sketches, Washington Irving called it "the beautiful village of Bloomingburgh." Ontario and Western Railroad service (1871–1953) built its resorts, which were located on the ridge outside village limits. Cut off from the rest of the county by the Shawangunk Mountains and bypassed by Rte 17 (I-86) in 1958, Bloomingburg's hotel business was largely gone by 1960.

John Conway

Blooming Grove. Town (pop 17,351) in central Orange Co. Settled in 1706, many of the town's early residents came from Suffolk Co. J. Hector St. John de Crèvecoeur purchased a Blooming Grove farm in 1769, and his *Letters from an American Farmer* (1782) reflected his experiences there. A forge and powder mill operated during the Revolution at Craigville, which had a paper mill and a cotton factory *ca* 1790; another paper mill was located at Salisbury Mills a decade later. The town was formed in 1799 from Cornwall. Rail service began with the Erie at Oxford Depot in 1841. The Brotherhood Winery (1839) at Washingtonville is believed to be America's oldest continuously operating winery; it produced sacramental wines during Prohibition. Iron was mined on Pedlar Hill beginning in 1861. In the late 19th century, Alexander Hornby produced "steam-cooked cereals" at Craigville, creating HO Oats. Mountain Lodge was developed as a summer resort in the early 1920s; in the late 20th century many of its cottages were converted to year-round use. Rte 17 (I-86) provided a limited-access highway through town beginning in 1954, and Blooming Grove began attracting blue-collar New York City workers beginning in the early 1960s, joined later by white-collar commuters. The town's population quadrupled between 1960 and 2000. Museum Village (1950) is a large collection of restored and rebuilt 19th-century buildings. The Grape Harvest Festival has been held in October since 1997.

Jeanne Versweyveld

Blue Point. Locality (pop 4,407) in Brookhaven (Suffolk Co). Its 19th-century residents made their living as farmers and baymen, and Blue Point oysters found in the muddy bay bottom became world famous; they were seeded beginning in 1815. A post office opened in 1856, and in 1868 it acquired a station on the South Side Rail Road (now Long Island Rail Road). Large hotels were built and a resort developed. Greenhouses were significant before World War I. The oyster industry was profitable until 1931, when storms created a new inlet and increased salinity in the Great South Bay. Blue Point's population nearly tripled in the second half of the 20th century as the locality became a bedroom community. In 2003 it was the site of the Blue Point Brewing Co, a microbrewery, and of a large marina.

Joan Ryan, CSJ

B'nai B'rith. The oldest Jewish fraternal order in the United States. The name literally means "sons of the convenant" in Hebrew but idiomatically means members of the Jewish people. The order, founded in a saloon on Manhattan's Essex St in 1843 by 12 immigrants from Germany, combined mutual aid, social service, and recreational and cultural activities. Though modeled on Freemasonry, B'nai B'rith featured specifically Jewish elements in its rituals. By 1861 it had established lodges in all major Jewish communities in New York State and throughout the United States. The first chapter outside the country was formed in Berlin in 1882. In 1913 the order created the B'nai B'rith Anti-Defamation League (ADL) to combat a wave of antisemitism, sparked by large-scale immigration of eastern European Jews. In 1925 B'nai B'rith adopted Hillel Foundation, founded two years earlier by Rabbi Benjamin Frankel at the University of Illinois, to meet the religious and social needs of Jewish college students. During the 1930s the order offered vocational programs in New York City. By the 1940s the ADL was the largest of its agencies, and in 1946 it was separately incorporated with headquarters in Manhattan. B'nai B'rith expanded after World War II, providing a range of adult education services. Its headquarters moved from Manhattan to Washington, DC, in 1957. At the beginning of the 21st century, B'nai B'rith is the largest international Jewish fraternal organization, and together with subsidiary groups, works to preserve Judaism through education and communal activity.

Moore, Deborah Dash. *B'nai B'rith and the Challenge of Ethnic Leadership* (Albany: SUNY Press, 1981)

Rachel Rojanski

Board of Commissioners of the Land Office. The state legislature designated commissioners of the land office in 1784 to dispose of the "waste and unappropriated lands" belonging to the state. During the 19th century the Board of Commissioners included the secretary of state (chair), lieutenant governor, speaker of the assembly, comptroller, treasurer, attorney general, and surveyor general (after 1846, state engineer and surveyor). "Unappropriated lands" refer to all state-owned lands not used for public purposes. They have included lands belonging to the Crown in 1776, lands ceded by various Indian nations starting in 1784, lands acquired or designated in the early 19th century as investments for the common school fund and the canal fund, lands reverting to the state through mortgage foreclosure or lack of heirs (escheat), abandoned canal lands, and other lands no longer needed by the state. The state also derived from the Crown title to lands under navigable rivers and lakes and some near-shore lands under water in the vicinity of New York City.

After survey, appraisal, and sale of a parcel of unappropriated land, land under water, or abandoned canal land, the state grants letters patent for that parcel. Most of the several million acres of unappropriated lands were granted by 1860. The board was abolished in 1960. Since then the Office of General Services has been responsible for the disposition of unneeded state-owned lands.

James D. Folts

Board of Regents. See EDUCATION DEPARTMENT AND UNIVERSITY OF THE STATE OF NEW YORK.

Boards of Cooperative Educational Services (BOCES). Regional organizations that enable school districts to share resources. BOCES were created in 1948 as part of a broader effort by the New York State Education Department (SED) to reduce costs, improve educational quality and equity, and enable more effective central control of the state's 5,112 school districts, which were then grouped into 181 supervisory districts. The quality of education and the available resources varied widely among school districts, the number of which had already been reduced by almost half since the SED was created in 1904. Though the 1947 *Master Plan for School District Reorganization in New York State* called for reducing the number of school districts to 560, further consolidation was resisted because of concerns about loss of local control, transportation, expense, and the diminishment of community.

A 1948 law created intermediate districts (IDs) as formal arrangements by which school districts could share educational and administrative services and costs. IDs were expected to take over the functions of the supervisory districts, reducing their number to 65, each including at least 5,000 students, and to promote consolidation of schools and districts. This legislation also created BOCES as a temporary transition to get wary districts accustomed to working together before forming an ID. BOCES were intended as vehicles for the sharing of specialized staff, such as nurses, and unlike IDs they could not own or lease buildings, did not replace district superintendencies, and had no authority to tax or to expand their functions or domain.

As federal and state legislation during the 1960s and 1970s mandated an increasing number of specialized services, particularly vocational programs and services to pupils with disabilities, BOCES became the vehicle for providing them. BOCES also began to offer clerical and administrative services, research, professional development for teachers, administrators, and school boards, distance learning, adult education, foreign languages, and gifted and talented programs. In 1967 BOCES were authorized to purchase and operate facilities. The law that created IDs was repealed in 1972, BOCES having become a de facto replacement for them. Since 1988 all BOCES programs and services must be approved by the commissioner of education, and since 1997 BOCES have been required to provide annual reports on pupil performance, programs, and expenditures per pupil.

BOCES are created by the commissioner of education at the request of component school boards and are governed by a board of 5 to 15 members elected for three-year terms by those school boards. The BOCES board appoints the district superintendent, subject to the commissioner's approval, to serve as its chief executive officer. Funding for BOCES primarily comes from contracts with member districts for specific services, with the state or federal government, or with other specified agencies. BOCES have gradually become coterminous with supervisory districts, which have been reduced to 38, equal to the number of BOCES, and they have aided in reducing the number of school districts, as of 2000, to 705. BOCES have played an important role in the development and consolidation of a comprehensive, statewide system of elementary and high school education, providing needed services to rural areas and helping to mediate between state and local governments. The SED has advanced its goal of creating a unified, comprehensive, and equitable school system, though it has not yet achieved its desired degree of consolidation and administrative control, in part because of the effectiveness of BOCES in offering services to rural areas and mediating between local and state control.

Kachris, Peter Thomas. "A History of the District Superintendency and BOCES, 1910–1982" (PhD diss, Syracuse Univ, 1987)

Pugh, Thomas J. "Rural School Consolidation in New York State, 1795–1993" (PhD diss, Syracuse Univ, 1994)

Thomas J. Mauhs-Pugh

bobsledding. Competitive Olympic winter sport. Stephen Whitney of Albany, vacationing in Davos, Swtizerland, during the winter of 1888–89, helped develop the competitive bobsled, which was derived from the American clipper sled. Modern competitive bobsledding consists of two- and four-person events for men and women. Team members push the sleds to accelerate, jump in, and speed downhill, taking the best line in the iced, 1,500 m (4,921 ft) track with 15–20 curves and a vertical drop of up to 423 feet (129 m). Bobsledding first came to the United States at Lake Placid in the winter of 1930–31 as the community prepared to host the Winter Olympics in February 1932. Several sleds were built, and a temporary seven-curve run was laid out on a hillside next to the Intervales ski jump, enabling the Americans to train while construction began on the 1.5 mi (2.4 km) Olympic bobsled run on Mt Van Hoevenberg. This was the only bobsled run in the United States until Salt Lake City's opened in 1978. As driver of a four-person sled, William Fiske Jr won his first Olympic gold medal in 1928 at St. Moritz, Switzerland, and his second in 1932 at Lake Placid. Stanley DeLong Benham of Lake Placid was a member of the two- and four-person teams that won the silver at the 1952 Oslo Games. Benham's personal popularity built the sport in the United States during bobsledding's early years. Until the late 1960s most bobsled competitors were from the Adirondack region.

Women drove bobsleds in competition during the early years in Lake Placid; in 1940 Kathryn Dewey of Lake Placid, daughter of library classification developer Melvil Dewey, won the four-person national title. After her victory, all major competitions were restricted to men. After the 1980 Winter Olympics were held at Lake Placid, women began qualifying as drivers of two-person sleds. Among the first was Julie Walzak of Lake Placid. During the 1997–98 winter season, women began international competition in two-person World Cup events.

In the 1990s NASCAR driver Geoffrey Bodine, a native of Chemung (Chemung Co), and his auto-racing team designed American sleds to meet international standards. The Bodine sleds won three medals at the 2002 Winter Olympics at Salt Lake City. The women took the gold, and the men earned silver and bronze medals in the four-person events. Lake Placid is the home of the United States Bobsled and Skeleton Federation (USBSF). In 2000 a new combination track for bobsled, luge, and skeleton was built on Mt Van Hoevenberg, next to the 1932 track, which is still used for training. The first world championship on the new track was held in 2003.

Ortloff, George Christian, and Stephen C. Ortloff. *Lake Placid: The Olympic Years, 1932–1980* (Lake Placid, NY: Macromedia, 1976)

Laura Viscome

BOCES. See BOARDS OF COOPERATIVE EDUCATIONAL SERVICES.

Bodine, Geoffrey (*b* Chemung, Chemung Co, 18 Apr 1949). Race car driver. Bodine's family in Chemung had long been involved in auto racing. His grandfather, Eli H. Bodine Sr, was a passionate devotee of stock-car racing in the 1940s. His father, Eli Jr, owned and managed the Chemung Speedrome, a $^1/_4$ mi dirt oval track that opened in 1951, for many years. Geoffrey and his two brothers, Brett and Todd, have since the 1970s achieved success in short track racing and in the National Association for Stock Car Auto Racing's (NASCAR) Winston Cup events. Following a successful career in modified pavement racing across New York State and the East Coast, Geoffrey had his first full Winston Cup season in 1982 and won in 1986 NASCAR's Daytona 500 in Florida, as well as 17 other Winston Cup races through 2002, including the 1996 race at Watkins Glen (Schuyler Co). Geoffrey was a safety innovator, being the first to introduce power steering and the use of a full-face helmet. Brett won the 1990 Winston Cup North Wilkesboro race in North Carolina, and Todd has won several Busch Division races, the immediate support series of Winston Cup. Together they have made over 1,000 starts in NASCAR-sanctioned events. Geoffrey's son Barry has begun a career in stock-car and truck racing, and a cousin Eric has raced in NASCAR's Busch North series. Geoffrey, Brett, and Todd Bodine live in North Carolina.

Geoffrey Bodine Fan Club Online, http://www.geoffbodinefanclub.com

Phil McCray

Bogardus, James (*b* Catskill, Greene Co, 14 Mar 1800; *d* New York City, 13 Apr 1874). Inventor and builder. At 14 Bogardus apprenticed with a local watchmaker, invented a prize-winning clock, then moved to New York City in 1828. After seeing iron used architecturally in London he conceived of constructing self-supporting cast-iron building facades using prefabricated, mass-produced components molded to simulate ornately carved stone. In Lower Manhattan he erected the first total cast-iron fronts: the Milhau Pharmacy (1848) and the Laing Stores (1849), and an all-iron factory for himself (1849). Bogardus acquired 1 British and 13 US patents. Despite his patent for iron construction (1850), his principles entered the public domain and iron fronts proliferated. Bogardus built at least 40 iron structures, half of them in New York City. These included the Harper Building (1855), a storefront at 75 Murray St (1857), a commercial building at 254 Canal St (1856–57), and two iron towers for making lead shot (1855–56), which were precursors of skyscraper construction. He erected Albany's first cast-iron structure, the Ransom Building (1857), and the Ironclad Building (1862) in Cooperstown (Otsego Co). Bogardus's pamphlet (1856, revised 1858) championed cast-iron design. He ceased construction after 1862 but occasionally exhibited his inventions.

Gayle, Margot, and Carol Gayle. *Cast-Iron Architecture in America: The Significance of James Bogardus* (New York: Norton, 1998)

Carol Gayle and Margot Gayle

Bohemia. Locality (pop 9,871) in Islip (Suffolk Co). Founded in 1855 by Czech Protestants who had fled religious persecution, it became known as New Tabor by 1859. By 1873 it was known as Bohemia, and a post office by that name opened in 1885. The residents, numbering 300 by the 1870s, were farmers and laborers; cigar making was significant from 1876 to about 1930, and a pearl button factory opened in 1922–23. Access was improved by the Sunrise Highway (1929). The population increased after World War II from under 1,000 to 8,926 in 1970, and industrial parks were created. In 2003 the largest employers were ILC Industries (software), NBTY (vitamins), and Dayton T. Brown (engineering and test facility). Landmarks include a statue of Jan Hus (1893) in Union Cemetery and the Bartunek House (1915).

Daria E. Merwin

Bolivar [BAHL-I-VIR]. Town (pop 2,223) and village (pop 1,173) in SW Allegany Co. Settled in 1819, the town was formed in 1825 from Friendship. A tannery (*ca* 1835) and shoe factory provided employment, but the town was chiefly a farming town until the boom caused by the 1881 oil strike at Richburg. Businesses developed to support oil extraction, such as hardware, drilling tools, engines, and a nitroglycerine plant (1895). There was also a cigar factory (1893). Town and village were served by the Pittsburg, Shawmut and Northern Railroad (1903–46). The oil business declined after World War II. It remains the site of the Pioneer Oil Museum. Frank E. Gannett (1876–1957) graduated from Bolivar High School in 1893 and went on to build a newspaper syndicate.

Bolivians. See SOUTH AMERICANS.

Bolton. Town (pop 2,117) in E Warren Co. Lying on the shore of Lake George, this mountainous town is distinguished by the rugged Tongue Mountain Range, which extends into the lake as a peninsula. Settled after the Revolutionary War, the town was formed from Thurman in 1799. A hamlet called The Huddle was the site of a gristmill, sawmill, and tannery built by John Vandenburgh, but extensive lumbering stripped the forests by 1820. Bolton's economy has depended on tourism since the Civil War era. The best-known hotel remains the Sagamore, first built in 1883, at Bolton Landing. Motels, hotels, and campsites host visitors throughout the summer. Bolton is the site of the Marcella Sembrich Opera Museum (1937) and of the Darrin Fresh Water Institute.

Marilyn J. Van Dyke

Bombay. Town (pop 1,192) in NW Franklin Co. Settled in 1803, the town was formed from Fort Covington in 1833 and named by Michael Hogan (1765–1833) for his wife's former home in India. Irish immigrants from Montreal arrived *ca* 1825, and the Roman Catholic congregation dates from 1827. Akwesasne (St. Regis Indian Reservation), Mohawk Nation territory, adjoins the town on the north. In Hogansburg a significant Mohawk presence has included the Indian Girls' Industrial School (1880), run by the Sisters of Mercy, and the Shields Bros factory (1918), which produced moccasins, playsuits, and sports uniforms. Hogansburg was the home of Rev Eleazer Williams, the controversial Indian agent in the early 19th century who claimed to be the lost French dauphin. Bombay remains a dairy town in the early 21st century; Gildan Activewear manufacturers tee shirts in town.

Thomas W. Perrin

Bonackers. In its narrowest definition, Bonacker refers to a handful of East Hampton (Suffolk Co) fishing families who trace their ancestry back to 17th-century settlers at Accabonac Creek and Three Mile Harbor in Springs, a few miles north of Amagansett (Suffolk Co). These Bonackers are recognized by a distinctive mode of speech traced to the south coast of England, especially Dorset and Kent, and an independent way of life. They lived mostly by harvesting clams, eels, lobsters, and scallops from bays and harbors around Springs. For cod fishing and near-shore whaling, they went the few miles south to the ocean; deep-sea whaling dominated the eastern Long Island economy during the first half of the 19th century. The Long Island Railroad (1895) and trucks over the next quarter century allowed for expedient transport of the catch to New York City.

The Bonacker tradition was both threatened and romanticized as East Hampton and its locality of Springs grew famous as home to wealth, celebrity, and tourism. Starting in the 1870s a three-decade influx of landscape and genre painters came to Springs. Some returned seasonally, and others stayed year-round. In the 1940s a second wave brought Jackson Pollock and Lee Krasner, part of a colony of artists whose members bought property in Springs and East Hampton. In the 1980s, as the Bonackers faced increasing economic pressures from declining stocks and state-mandated catch restrictions, Peter Matthiessen's *Men's Lives* sympathetically documented their lives and characteristic speech, focusing especially on the haul seiners, who launched dories into the surf with nets that they then drew back to shore. Well-organized groups of sports fishers urged New York politicians to impose restrictions on this method, and in 1983 the Department of Environmental Conservation asked the state assembly to pass the first of several initiatives to control the number and size of striped bass caught and kept, a law that fell most heavily on the Bonackers. With the various restrictions and the growth of a brown algae bloom beginning in 1985, fishers began to abandon bays and harbors in greater numbers. In the early 21st century, what remain are a small number of traditional Bonackers and a term rich in history. Meanwhile, to the dismay or amusement of some of the old Springs families, local fire companies, high school sports teams, and recent residents of East Hampton have appropriated the name Bonacker for themselves.

Matthiessen, Peter. *Men's Lives: The Surfmen and Baymen of the South Fork* (New York: Random House, 1986)

Rattray, Everett T. *The South Fork: The Land and the People of Eastern Long Island* (1979; Wainscott, NY: Pushcart Press, 1989)

Catherine A. McKeen

bonded indebtedness. Money borrowed by New York State or other public entities and secured by a bond or some other certificate of debt, specifying amounts and timing of redemption, the rate of interest, and any assets pledged as security by the borrower. Few issues have been more important in the political, economic, or monetary history of New York State government than the financing of public works. Moreover, this subject has had a significant impact on the state's constitutional development. Along the way four main issues have been debated: what constraints should be placed on the legislature's ability to borrow money, the purposes for which the state may borrow money, the extent of state liability for debts incurred by entities created by but not part of the state government, and the extent to which restrictions placed upon the New York State government might be applicable to counties, cities, towns, villages, or other incorporated subdivisions within the state.

EARLY HISTORY

New York State's first constitution, which went into effect in 1777, placed few constraints on the state's ability to borrow money, and beginning in 1797 it began to borrow on a regular basis. These borrowings occasionally covered operating deficits, but they also enabled the state to purchase the debt instruments of fledgling banks or to make loans to farmers, merchants, or county governments. Nevertheless, New York State, like other states, began the 19th century with a comparatively clear balance sheet. In 1790 the US government approved legislation that assumed the debts of the states as one of the critical building blocks establishing the strong federal presence recommended by Secretary of the Treasury Alexander Hamilton.

The Erie Canal project and the innovative financing involved in its construction had an enormous impact on the constitutional development of New York State. Because of the huge capital outlay, canals generally received either direct or indirect financing by state governments. With the state's appeal for federal funding rejected and thrown back on its own resources, one of the New York's major contributions to the canal era was to demonstrate that it was possible to finance large public works through the sale of state bonds. In addition, the state constitution adopted in 1821 provided that the tolls plus the revenue from two reliable sources of state income, salt and auction duties, were to be deposited in a sinking fund, known as the canal fund, for the ordinary servicing of the debt. The success of the Erie Canal led to numerous proposals for lateral, or branch, canals. Beginning in 1825 the state financed their construction by selling bonds, or, as they were then called, transferable certificates of stock.

Although the Erie Canal continued to attract a growing volume of traffic, a cluster of problems emerged that were to affect debt and debt policy in New York State. First, revenue from many of the branch canals, particularly those extending south of the Erie, fell short of expectations. Second, the Erie required widening and deepening to accommodate larger and more numerous boats. Third, a spreading railway network began to compete for canal traffic and for both public and private capital. And, fourth, a nationwide banking crisis lasting from 1837 to 1841 made it difficult to market public debt; it also reduced state revenue and led to defaults on state obligations throughout the country. Appeals by the states for federal assistance, citing the assumption of state debt in 1790 as a precedent, were rejected.

Although New York State did not default, it was still skirting close to bankruptcy. By 1843, however, with the crisis easing, its bonds were again selling at par, and it was reported to be the only state with a large existing debt that increased its borrowing in the early 1840s. Extensive enlargements of the Erie Canal accounted for much of the growth, but aid to private companies for the construction of railroads was an increasingly vigorous competitor for public aid and credit. Such aid, which had begun in 1827, took various forms. The state sold its own bonds using the proceeds to buy stocks or bonds from the private companies; it exchanged its obligations directly for such stocks or bonds; and it guaranteed the bonds of private companies, enabling them to sell bonds that were otherwise unmarketable or only disposable at high rates of interest.

As in the case of the lateral canals, the enthusiasm for railroads often exceeded their economic viability. Many companies failed, leaving their debt a burden on the state's general fund or their bonds a valueless asset in the state's treasury. The state's largest investment in railroads began in 1836 when it approved the issuance of $3 million in debt to the New York and Erie and authorized the railroad company to sell the certificates at public auction. The state extended this aid to meet the needs of the Southern Tier, which was remote from the Erie Canal and lacked access to either the Great Lakes or New York City.

Debt Becomes a Constitutional Issue

The era of major canal expansion was coming to an end, but maintenance and improvement of the existing structure continued to send the state to the credit markets, and there was growing unease about lending state credit to railroad companies. Although structural changes inspired by Jacksonian Democracy were reflected in the 1846 Constitution, the first achievement of the 1846 Constitutional Convention was reformation of the laws governing state debt. As adopted, the constitution, most significantly in terms of the state's financial policy, prohibited borrowing without a referendum and required each project to have a separate vote. Attempts to bypass this restriction on the creation of state debt began as early as 1851. They rested on the implicit assumption that the state would have a "moral obligation" to honor obligations incurred by an agency or other entity created by the state, even if the debt had not been authorized by a vote of the people in a referendum. This became a central issue in the debate over state debt policy with the emergence of the public authority in the 1920s and with the financing of comprehensive public construction programs since 1960.

The convention of 1846 also dealt with a related issue, the gift or loan of state money or credit to private corporations or associations. Such gifts or loans had contributed significantly to the expansion of state debt in the two decades before the convention, and the constitution approved by the voters in 1846 prohibited the state from continuing the practice. At the same time, however, cities and towns were substantially increasing their own gifts to railroads. Moreover, beginning in 1851 the legislature encouraged cities to aid railroad construction, authorizing them to borrow money to invest in railroad stock and bonds or to lend their credit as the state had done prior to 1846. Overbuilding, shaky finances, competition, and periodic banking crises forced many of the companies into default or bankruptcy in the years following the Civil War, and an amendment severely restricting the ability of localities to incur debt was sponsored by a constitutional commission and adopted in 1874. An additional amendment prohibiting counties, cities, towns, and villages from giving or loaning "their property or credit" to private corporations or associations was overwhelmingly adopted.

Although the canal debt was paid off in 1893 and for a brief period the state was free of debt, the continuing revolution in transportation gave rise to new demands. New York was among the first states to finance highway construction by borrowing, and in 1905 the voters approved a constitutional amendment authorizing the state to issue $50 million in bonds for highways. When this money ran out in 1912, with only 50% of the planned work completed, the voters approved another $50 million. Meanwhile, despite a steady decline in tonnage after 1880, the canals began to place new burdens on the state's debt structure. A referendum in 1895 authorized $9 million in bonds to finance canal repairs, but this sum permitted completion of only half the work; in 1903 the electorate authorized the state to issue $101 million in 18-year bonds. Two years later voters approved extending the period to 50 years. By 1916 New York State accounted for almost one-third of the total state debt in the country, even though the consensus appeared to be that the state should limit its public improvements to those that could be accommodated within current income. In the following decade the aggressive building program of Gov Alfred E. Smith won the support of the electorate for further use of bonded debt: $50 million for hospitals and charitable institutions in a 1923 referendum, $15 million for parks and parkways in 1924, $300 million for the elimination of railroad-highway grade crossings, and $100 million for additional public improvements in 1925. Challenging the supposed bias in favor of pay-as-you-go, Smith campaigned vigorously for the bond issues on the grounds of efficiency and rapid state development. The Great Depression of the early 1930s demonstrated that bonded debt could serve purposes other than construction. With the collapse of the state's revenue base, both Gov Franklin D. Roosevelt and his successor, Herbert H. Lehman, reluctantly but successfully supported bond issues to help finance relief payments between 1932 and 1936, while still upholding the pay-as-you-go principle for anything other than permanent improvements.

Emergence of the Public Authority

The establishment of the public authority, or public benefit corporation, turned a new page in the history of bonded indebtedness in New York State. The Port of New York Authority (now Port Authority of New York and New Jersey) formed in 1921 and, modeled on an Elizabethan entity created to manage the London docks, was designed to overcome the jurisdictional problems inherent in a harbor lying between two states and requiring the participation of a variety of municipalities. However, the authority's ability to issue debt without the restrictions imposed on the states was of almost equal importance and increasingly useful in the construction of highways, bridges, tunnels, parks, hydroelectric power sources, ports, and other major projects. By the time of the 1938 Constitutional Convention, there were 33 such entities in New York State, and the proliferation of the authority and its implications became a critical item on the convention's agenda. Supporters of the authorities, such as former governor Al Smith and Robert Moses, stressed their ability to achieve results and argued against a new article to regulate them. Contemporary critics stressed the risks inherent in the authority's ability to sidestep constitutional safeguards. Particularly ominous in the light of later developments had been a decision of the Court of Appeals in 1926 that bonds issued by a state authority, even if they were not legally enforceable obligations, nonetheless represented a "moral obligation" and could be paid if the legislature so authorized. Another decision in 1935 had explicitly confirmed that public authorities could issue "non-guaranteed" bonds without regard to constitutional debt restrictions.

More than any other individual, Robert Moses grasped the possibilities inherent in the public authority. It could not only operate with the independence of a private company but exercise many of the regulatory powers normally possessed by sovereign states. In specific cases it could be granted the power of eminent domain. With the threat posed by the convention of 1938 behind him, Moses proceeded in the late 1930s and next two decades to build an extensive interlocking network of public authorities in and around New York City. The legislative charters of these authorities, influenced and at times drafted by Moses, generally insulated them from the control of either state or city officials, enabled them to continue to function long after their initial purposes had been achieved, and seemed to acquire the attributes of a fourth branch of government.

During World War II, New York State and other states were able to build large surpluses through tax increases, full employment, and deferral of civil construction because of the war effort, promising for a time a return to a policy of pay-as-you-go. For a brief period following the war the state was indeed able to finance its capital projects from the postwar reconstruction (later capital construction) fund. The establishment of the fund was considered by Gov Thomas E. Dewey a hallmark of his administration.

Even the New York State Thruway, begun in 1946 under the direction of the Department of Public Works, was constructed on a pay-as-you-go basis in its initial stages. Progress was slow, however, as the state soon faced the erosion of its resources because of cost increases and competing construction in the private and other parts of the public sectors. The Division of the Budget predicted that at the rate funds could be made available the project would not be completed until 1965. After extensive debate it was decided in 1950 to create a new state authority, with the power to finance, construct, and operate the Thruway. The authority was able to issue bonds and to fix fees and other charges for the use of the highway, which, it was anticipated, would be self-liquidating. Presenting arguments similar to those of Al Smith in the 1920s, an interagency committee appointed by Gov Dewey insisted that without the ability to issue bonds construction would proceed so slowly that there would be little hope of making the project self-liquidating.

Innovation and Crisis

Nelson A. Rockefeller's election as governor in 1958 was to have a dramatic impact on the debate over the nature, legitimacy, and economic consequences of bonded indebtedness in the next three decades. The Rockefeller administration initially sought support for new projects at the polls. In 1961 the voters approved constitutional amendments explicitly making the state liable for the obligations of both the Port of New York Authority, resulting from the acquisition of locomotives and passenger equipment used in commuter service within the port district, and the new Job Development Authority. At the same election, however, the voters also rejected a proposal authorizing funds for the expansion of the state university system and another amendment authorizing the state to contract debt for two or more "specific" (but unnamed) purposes "in the event of a recession."

The defeat of the university referendum in 1961 significantly affected debt policy and came on the eve of a comprehensive reorientation and reorganization of state government inaugurated by Gov Rockefeller. At its heart was an enormous effort to overhaul the state's system of public higher education, care of the mentally ill and disabled, public transportation, water supply and purity, criminal justice, middle-income housing, and the aging cores of the state's major cities. This effort went far beyond reorganization, although there were critical changes in the structure and scope of New York State government. It also involved vast building programs, which were managed by new construction agencies independent of existing state departments and largely free from the personnel, procedural, and budgetary restrictions that governed established agencies; new public authorities that could bridge agency and intergovernmental boundaries; and a new financing entity, the Housing Finance Agency (HFA). Initially a public authority created to finance middle-income housing projects, the HFA became the vehicle for financing construction of the university system, mental hygiene institutions, and other programs of the 1960s.

The new tools enabled the state to proceed with its construction projects at a rapid pace, bypassing the controls and jurisdictional disputes that had frustrated such "builders" as Smith and Moses. The use of public authorities also enabled the state to avoid referendums on a project-by-project basis and to keep the debt technically off the state's books. In effect, it reopened the doors that the Convention of 1846 had attempted to close and raised again the issue of moral obligation. In a report to the state legislature in June 1971, Comptroller Arthur Levitt called attention to the growth and changing character of state debt within the preceding decade while simultaneously acknowledging the value and importance of the projects for which it had been incurred. He also discussed the attendant problems in the complicated debt structure, which were compounded by the multiplicity and diversity of the agencies created for the completion of capital works.

Although there is some variation in the classification of state debt, the major distinction lies between borrowing that is "guaranteed" and borrowing that is "nonguaranteed." The former includes debt authorized by the voters for a specific purpose. The state constitution requires the comptroller to pay principal and interest on such borrowing as it becomes due, even if the legislature has failed to provide the necessary funds in a state appropriation. It is thus said to be backed by "the full faith and credit of the state." Nonguaranteed debt is not backed explicitly by the state's full faith and credit, although it may be supported by some form of lease-purchase or other contractual arrangement or by a moral obligation. In lease-purchase arrangements an authority created by the state would sell bonds and construct a facility. The state government would lease space in the facility, paying rent at a level that would enable the authority to service the debt as well as operate the facility. The debate over moral obligation debt reemerged with renewed force. In the 1960s the obligation was enhanced by the addition of a so-called "make-up clause," which required an agency that had sold bonds to notify the governor and the state budget director of potential problems in servicing its debt and of the amount required to restore its debt reserve.

The debt of New York State's authorities took center stage in the mid-1970s, when one of the state's most prominent and innovative authorities, the Urban Development Corp, was unable to meet a payment due on its bond anticipation notes. Concurrently there was concern in the money market about the increasing burden of New York City's short-term debt. The ensuing fiscal crisis, which dominated the political and economic life of New York State and its major cities for a decade, ranks as one of the major events in state history. The state's authorities and its major city were denied access to the market, and the entire financial structure of New York State government was perilously close to collapse. Indeed, throughout the United States municipalities found their ability to borrow money seriously impaired. The reasons for the fiscal crisis were complex, but the role of debt as its trigger brought the nature of borrowing and of the obligations it entailed once again into the limelight. Although the basic issue framed by Gov Smith in the 1920s regarding the best way to satisfy perceived public needs expeditiously was still critical, there was general agreement about the need for better control over the purpose, volume, and timing of the creation of debt. In 1976 the state established the Public Authorities Control Board, an agency appointed by the governor but with two of its three members recommended by the leaders of the two legislative houses. At the same time, legislation repealed most of the make-up clauses that implied the state's moral obligation from the laws that had governed the incurrence of debt by public authorities since the 1960s.

Administrative and statutory changes alone did not still the debate over debt policy, however, and for the next two decades the issues were argued at length, if inconclusively, in the courts. In a 1994 case, which reached the state's highest court, Chief Justice Judith Kaye commented on the longevity and intensity of the debate concerning state financing of public works. She concluded, however, that the reform of state borrowing practices was an issue more appropriately placed in the public arena, where state borrowing practices and policies merited and, in her view, were receiving serious consideration.

The state did indeed address the issue directly in the comprehensive Debt Reform Act of 2000. This law resolved the thorny question of debt incurred by its public authorities by defining "state-supported debt" as "any bonds or notes . . . issued by the state or a state public corporation" for which the state is "constitutionally" or "contractually" obligated to pay debt service "subject to an appropriation." The act also provided that no debt could be contracted unless the total outstanding principal of state-supported debt was less than a designated percentage of the total personal income of the state. It limited such debt to the financing of "capital works or purposes" and required the governor to submit quarterly financial plans to the heads of the legislative finance committees that would demonstrate that the limitations on the issuance of state-supported debt set forth in the law were being observed. Although capital construction costs continued to rise in response to the state's perceived needs, the statutory restrictions appeared to have had some effect. The proportion of such construction financed by debt fell from 47% in fiscal year 1988–89 to 41% in 2002–3.

The emergency borrowing during the depression of the 1930s aside, the state has essentially limited its borrowing to the financing of capital construction since the constitutional changes of 1846. In recent years, however, there have been two exceptions. In 1990, in an effort to eliminate the annual short-term borrowing that enabled the state to advance funds to local governments and, especially, school districts, the state established a local government assistance corporation. It converted the short-term debt to long-term obligations and made it possible to put future local assistance on a pay-as-you-go basis. In addition, in anticipation of the penalties assessed in lawsuits against tobacco companies, the state sold $4.6 billion in bonds in 2003. The debt, defined as a contingent contractual obligation, is being liquidated with monies received from the settlements.

Axelrod, Donald. *Shadow Government: The Hidden Hand of Public Authorities—and How They Control over $1 Trillion of Your Money* (New York: John Wiley & Sons, 1992)

Griffith, Janice C. "Moral Obligation Bonds: Illusion or Security?" *Urban Lawyer* 8 (Winter 1976): 54–93

New York State. Division of the Budget. *The Executive Budget in New York State: A Half-Century Perspective.* Ed. Robert P. Kerker (Albany: Author, 1981)

Quirk, William J., and Wein, Leon E. "A Short Constitutional History of the Entities Known as Authorities," *Cornell Law Review* 56 (Apr 1971): 521–97

Ratchford, B. U. *American State Debts* (Durham, NC: Duke Univ Press, 1941)

Utevsky, Michael D. "The Future of Non-guaranteed Bond Financing in New York," *Fordham Law Review* 45 (Mar 1977): 860–84

Robert P. Kerker

Book of Mormon. Published in 1830 in Palmyra (Wayne Co) by Joseph Smith Jr (1805–44), the Book of Mormon has become the foundational scripture of the Utah-based Church of Latter-day Saints (Mormon); the Community of Christ, formerly the Reorganized Church of Jesus Christ of Latter Day Saints (Independence, Mo); and other minor groups. The book purports to be a religious history of two ancient American nations: the Jaredites, who crossed the ocean following the corruption of language at the tower of Babel (Gen 11), and the Lehites, who escaped the Babylonian captivity of Jerusalem in the 6th century BC. The majority of the Book of Mormon covers the thousand-year rivalry between Lehi's sons and their descendants (the Nephites, who struggle to maintain their Jewish religion and belief in the coming of the Messiah) and the Lamanites, who believe in false traditions. God curses the latter group with dark skins, thus explaining the origin of Native Americans. The centerpiece is the appearance of the resurrected Jesus and the establishment of a theocratic government. After about 200 years, the Nephites and Lamanites return to their old ways. Finally, in AD 385, the Lamanites succeed in exterminating the Nephites, the last great battle taking place in Western New York. Anticipating the destruction of his people, Mormon engraved the history of the Nephites on gold plates and hid them in the Hill Cumorah, now located in Manchester (Ontario Co).

Smith, who by age 17 was a practicing scryer (one who locates buried treasure or lost objects by means of a special stone used much like a crystal ball), claimed that on the night of 21 Sept 1823 a spirit, whom he later identified as Moroni, Mormon's son, appeared to him three times and revealed the location of the plates. The next morning, Smith said he went to the nearby hill and discovered the plates, which had been carefully hidden in a stone box under a large rock. Smith was not permitted to remove the plates at this time but was instructed to meet with Moroni annually. When Smith finally obtained the plates in 1827, he was prohibited from showing them to anyone; however, he allowed his family and friends to feel them through a cloth covering. Later, Smith obtained an affidavit signed by three men claiming that an angel had shown them the plates, and an additional statement by eight others affirming that they had seen and handled the plates. Persecution drove Smith from Manchester to Harmony, Penn, where most of the Book of Mormon was subsequently "translated" from "reformed Egyptian." Smith's method of translating was similar to his scrying for treasures. After placing his seer stone in the crown of his hat and putting his face into the same, he claimed he saw the translation in shining letters on the stone, which he dictated to a scribe. This process was followed from April to June 1829, when Smith relocated to Fayette (Seneca Co) and boarded with the family of Peter Whitmer Sr. Here Smith completed the Book of Mormon by early July. Even before it was finished, Smith began negotiating with Palmyra publisher Egbert B. Grandin, who initially declined to print the book. Grandin finally consented to print 5,000 copies of the book for $3,000 provided Martin Harris, a believer in Smith's revelations, would mortgage his farm as collateral. Printing began in August 1829 and the first copies were available for sale in March 1830. Initially sold at $1.25, collectors might well pay more than $50,000 for this rare edition.

Quinn, D. Michael. *Early Mormonism and the Magic World View* (Salt Lake City: Signature Books, 1987)

Vogel, Dan. *Indian Origins and the Book of Mormon: Religious Solutions from Columbus to Joseph Smith* (Salt Lake City: Signature Books, 1986)

Dan Vogel

Boonville. Town (pop 4,572) and village (pop 2,138) in N Oneida Co. Settled in 1795 under the Holland Land Co, the town was the site of an unsuccessful experiment in commercial maple sugar production in its first years. It was formed in 1805 from Leyden (Lewis Co); the village incorporated in 1855. Located on a natural transportation route, Boonville has been served by a turnpike (1817), plank road (1848), canal (1850–1924), railroad (1855), and state highway (1912). Manufacturing has included cooperage, tanning, iron, chairs, canal boats, textiles, and Limburger cheese. During a milk strike in August 1933, state troopers attacked a crowd of protesters and bystanders in the so-called Battle of Boonville. State reforestation planted 3,604 acres (1,458.5 ha) in town in the 1930s. Important employers in 2002 were furniture maker Ethan Allen with 340 employees, wood chair maker N. M. Sargent and Sons (1851), Boonville Manufacturing Corp, Boonville Enterprises, Nirvana Spring Water, and Baillie Lumber Co. The Boonville Fair (1888) is held in July, and the New York State Woodsmen's Field Days are in August. Boonville was the home of Walter D. Edmonds (1903–98), author of *Drums along the Mohawk,* and is the site of Pixley Falls State Park (1932). The Boonville Historic District was created in 1979.

boot and shoe manufacturing. New York State's boot and shoe industry dates back to the colonial era, when production was heavily concentrated in New York City and individual shoemakers and small workshops provided order or custom work to their customers. It became a significant industry only in the late 19th century. Improved transportation and communications networks, expanding markets, abundant raw materials, and new labor markets shaped the development of the industry in the state. By the 1890s New York State ranked second (behind Massachusetts) in the nation in the production of boots and shoes. Manufacturers tended to specialize in women's, misses', and children's footwear; in 1900 these constituted 65% of all footwear manufactured in New York State, compared to 38% in Massachusetts.

For most of the late 19th through mid–20th centuries, boot and shoe manufacturing in the state concentrated in Broome, Monroe, Kings, and New York Cos. By the early 20th century, these companies were responsible for just under 80% of the state's footwear production. New York City, with its vast labor pool, equally large market, and advantageous coastal location, had the largest number of manufacturers throughout the 19th and 20th centuries. By the 1920s, for example, Brooklyn had around 150 shops manufacturing men's and women's boots and shoes, as well as another 50 firms producing shoe manufacturing supplies and components. Manhattan, too, had large numbers of manufacturers (around 90 in 1927).

The City of Binghamton and the Villages of Endicott and Johnson City (all in Broome Co), where Dunn and McCarthy, Gotham Shoe Manufacturing, Collingwood Shoe Co, and the vast Endicott Johnson Co works were located, became a major center for American shoe production in the late 19th century. Footwear manufacturing had emerged in the region with the completion of rail and canal links with New York City, Scranton, Pa, Syracuse, and the Great Lakes in the 1850s and 1860s. The industry grew exponentially in the first half of the 20th century, mainly due to the expansion of Endicott Johnson. Other manufacturing centers in the state included Rochester, where boot and shoe production emerged earlier than in most other areas. With its advantageous location along the Erie Canal, Rochester was one of the first cities to benefit from the westward spread of shoe manufacturing out of New England. Dozens of small- and medium-sized manufacturers sprang up in the early 19th century, employing hundreds of operatives. By 1900 over 50 firms were operating in the city. In the late 1920s, with around 30 firms still in business, Rochester remained a significant center of boot and shoe manufacturing. But its glory days had passed, with many of the firms moving to the Midwest. Smaller concentrations of boot and shoe manufacturing also took hold in Long Island City (Queens Co), a center of women's and children's shoe manufacturing; Auburn (Cayuga Co), the home base of Dunn and McCarthy, manufacturers of women's shoes; Buffalo, with 24 factories and over 800 workers in the industry in 1900; and Syracuse, home of the world-famous A. E. Nettleton Co, manufacturers of fancy men's shoes.

Along with the rise of boot and shoe factory production in the 19th and 20th centuries came unions. The Knights of St. Crispin, one of the first boot and shoe unions, emerged in the 1860s as machinery, unskilled labor, and increased factory production began to encroach on the status, position, and autonomy of skilled shoe workers. The Knights of St. Crispin spread through New England and into New York State. The union led strikes in New York City, Albany, Rochester, Binghamton, and many of the state's smaller communities. Rochester was a major center of St. Crispin activity in the state in the 1860s and 1870s, and strikes were frequent. In the 1860s, 600 members of the local Crispin lodge successfully struck and did away with the contracting system in that city. But the Knights of St. Crispin hardly slowed the growth of factory production or exploitative shop management, and the union was short-lived. The International Order of the Knights of St. Crispin declined just as rapidly as it had grown, disappearing almost entirely by 1873, a year that marked the beginning of a major national depression. In its place came the Knights of Labor, which took on abuses by subcontractors in the trade and was active in the 1870s and 1880s in many New York State communities. It challenged egregiously exploitative practices, such as the use of foremen-contractors who took a percentage of employees' earnings. The Knights of Labor too was short-lived, all but disappearing by the late 1880s and replaced by the American Federation of Labor's (AFL's) Boot and Shoe Workers Union, and finally by the Congress of Industrial Organization's (CIO's) United Shoe Workers of America. In 2002 these unions were absent in New York State.

In 1900 there were 223 boot and shoe factories operating in New York State, and around 16,000 workers were employed in the industry. In the 1950s one firm alone, the Endicott Johnson Co, employed around 20,000 workers. In fact, the 1950s marked the heyday of the industry in New York State. From midcentury on, production declined, factories closed, and manufacturing moved overseas, mainly to Asia. In 2002 there were about two dozen firms still in business in the state, employing fewer than 1,000 workers. China was responsible for more than 70% of all shoe imports to the United States in 2002, and shoe imports have essentially replaced domestic production.

Zahavi, Gerald. *Workers, Managers, and Welfare Capitalism: The Shoeworkers and Tanners of Endicott Johnson, 1890–1950* (Urbana: Univ of Illinois Press, 1988)

Gerald Zahavi

Borden. One of the first national dairy chains, organized as a company in 1858 to produce condensed milk. Gail Borden Jr (1801–74) of Norwich (Chenango Co) learned the difficulty of preserving food on the frontier. Returning east he patented a process for condensing milk in a vacuum over low heat in 1856. Borden built condenseries in Connecticut, set cleanliness standards for suppliers, and, financed by Jeremiah Milbank, founded the New York Condensed Milk Co in 1858 in Burrville, Conn, to capture the New York City milk trade. The public accepted canned condensed milk only hesitantly. During the Civil War, the federal government bought the entire production of the company's expanded facilities in Wassaic (Dutchess Co), Brewster (Putnam Co), and Elgin, Ill, to supply Union soldiers. The lasting taste they developed ensured postwar sales for the company, which was reorganized in 1899 as the Borden Condensed Milk Co. The creation of a single large milk purchaser changed farmers' lives near Borden facilities, and the company's market domination spurred the formation of cooperatives to improve farmers' bargaining power. By the 1930s fresh milk and store distribution were displacing canned milk and home delivery.

The fresh milk trade had been based on local markets until 1923, when the National Dairy Products Corp (now Kraft Foods) was formed and began buying up facilities. The growing Borden Co, as it was renamed in 1919, reacted by buying 207 dairy enterprises in 18 states between 1928 and 1932. Its control of markets was modest nationally (6.8% in 1934) but substantial in individual cities. In 1937 the New York State attorney general found that Borden and other large distributors colluded to dictate milk prices, and in 1938 a joint federal-state price control program was initiated for the New York City milkshed. Borden's subsidiary in New York City, Dairy Sealed, earned praise in 1945 for its low-cost distribution methods, which generated savings that could be passed on to consumers.

Because increasing government price regulations eroded profit margins on milk, Borden diversified in the 20th century, manufacturing ice cream and powdered milk (1928), cheese (1929), glue (1929), chemicals (1940s), snack foods (1960s), and pasta (1980s). During World War II it provided the US Army with instant coffee. Overextended, Borden's market value plummeted in the early 1990s. An investment firm took control of the company in 1994, selling the cheese division (Borden Dairy) to a Missouri-based cooperative in 1997 and the Eagle brand of condensed milk in 1998 (both new companies use Elsie the Cow, a Borden trademark since 1939), before buying the kitchenware division of Corning Inc. Divisions of Borden Inc (so named since 1968) surviving into the 21st century are Borden Foods, Elmer's Products, Borden Chemical, and World Kitchen. None are headquartered in New York State, but one of World Kitchen's acquisitions, Corningware, is in Corning (Steuben Co).

Frantz, Joe B. *Gail Borden: Dairyman to a Nation* (Norman: Univ of Oklahoma Press, 1951)

Scott C. Monje

borscht belt. Common term given to the Jewish resort area of the Catskills, comprising eastern Sullivan Co, western and northern Ulster Co, a small part of southern Greene Co, and a tiny sliver of southeastern Delaware Co. Beginning in the 1890s, Jews, mainly from New York City, farmed, vacationed, and worked in the area, creating a major cultural presence in hotels, bungalow colonies, boardinghouses, adult camps, Zionist camps, both secular and religious children's camps, and local municipalities. The resort area enabled Jews to have a proper vacation like other Americans but in a very Jewish milieu. Additionally, working in the resorts provided major financial support to people, mostly of the first generation, to attend college and professional school.

The Term Borscht Belt

The term borscht belt, largely used by journalists, writers, and the general public since the 1930s but not by the people involved in the area, is based on the popularity of the eastern European beet soup that was widely served in the resorts. Very infrequently the term extends to the entertainment circuit of singers and comics who play in other Jewish resort areas, especially the Poconos in Pennsylvania and parts of New Jersey and the Adirondacks. "Borscht belt comic" remains an appellation for a stand-up comedian. Some people find the phrase borscht belt derisive or sarcastic. It was rarely employed by the people in the area; they referred to "the Catskills" or simply "the mountains." Because of its reference to a mainstream of Jewish cuisine, the term highlights the significance of the Catskills resort area for American Jewish life and also for the general culture.

Origins of the Resort Area

In the late 1890s the Jewish resort experience began with a few boardinghomes and grand hotels, though most of the hotels started small and expanded gradually. These places were started because antisemitic restrictions kept Jews out of existing resorts and also because many Jews at the time wanted kosher food and a Jewish environment. The Jewish Agricultural Society supported the development of farming, and by 1908 it recorded 500 Jewish farms in Sullivan and Ulster Cos, a noteworthy presence because many farms turned into boardinghouses and then into hotels. Well-known hotels, such as Tamarack, Grossinger's, Nemerson, Brickman, Windsor, Raleigh, Nevele, Fallsview, and Kutsher's, began as farms in localities including Greenfield Park, Ellenville, Monticello, South Fallsburg, Liberty, Woodbourne, Loch Sheldrake, and White Lake. The farmers, along with local business operators, formed a year-round source of support for synagogues and Jewish organizations.

The Resorts

Boardinghouses were the simplest form of resort, lodging up to 30 people. A variant of the boardinghouse was the *kuchalayn* (Yiddish for "cook yourself"), where renters had privileges to part of a stove and a refrigerator, as well as their own table at which to eat. By the post–World War II period, few of these types of facilities remained. Bungalow colonies were groups of small cottages, usually in a semicircle or oval. People rented these for the entire season, July 4th weekend to Labor Day weekend. Individual bungalows might have had as little as one bedroom and a living room/kitchen combination; others might have been more substantial. Colonies with a dozen or more bungalows typically had a social hall (usually called a "casino"), but only larger colonies provided outside entertainment. Handball courts, basketball courts, softball diamonds, and, later, pools provided recreation. Commonly there was an owner-operated store where people bought food and household items. Peddlers came on a daily basis to sell clothing, linens, household supplies, and food that that store did not carry, such as fresh meat and chicken. Starting in the 1950s, children's day camps became prevalent.

Hotels ranged from small ones, holding 50 guests, to the largest, Grossinger's and the Concord, which held between 1,000 and 2,000 guests. Although guests could stay a day or a weekend, one- and two-week stays were common, and some guests stayed for the whole season. In both bungalow colonies and hotels, it was common for husbands to work in New York City and come up only for the weekend. Hotels, especially the larger ones, had a wide range of facilities, including indoor pools, riding stables, ski slopes, toboggan runs, and tennis courts. The hotels were noted for their all-inclusive "American Plan," providing three meals a day. These large meals were a major part of the legend of

Catskills resort culture. Catskills hotels pioneered the idea of a separate children's dining room, so that the day camp and the children's dining room freed parents from their children virtually all day. Camp counselors on night patrol allowed guests to enjoy the entertainment after putting their children to sleep.

Entertainment was a central component of the resorts. Before World War II, many hotels had resident entertainment staffs that put on original and takeoff productions of Broadway shows. Danny Kaye and Moss Hart were among the famous show people who worked in those settings. In the post–World War II period, outside entertainers were more common, sometimes performing at three or four hotels and bungalow colonies a night. Sid Caesar, Red Buttons, Alan King, Jerry Lewis, Henny Youngman, Leslie Uggams, Billy Eckstine, Totie Fields, Jackie Mason, Buddy Hackett, Billy Crystal, Milton Berle, Eddie Fisher, Phil Foster, Myron Cohen, Jack Carter, Jan Murray, Robert Merrill, Neil Sedaka, Joey Bishop, Don Rickles, and many other comics and singers got their start in the Catskills. It is widely accepted that modern American stand-up comedy has its roots in the Catskills's comedians. Some very small hotels (50–100 guests) might not have provided large shows (usually a singer and a comedian) on a regular basis. Large hotels (500 guests or more) would have singers and comics up to four nights a week, while small- (up to 250 guests) and medium-sized (250–500 guests) hotels would only have such shows on Friday and Saturday nights. Other activities would include a movie, a champagne night (dance exhibition and contests), amateur night (guests and staff), and bingo (and sometime other gambling) night. Daytime activities included tennis, basketball, softball, Simon Says, swimming at the pool, boating on the lake, arts and crafts lessons, nature hikes, calisthenics, mah-jongg, and cardplaying.

The resorts had a strong sense of community. Bungalow colony residents lived among each other for a whole summer, often returning each year. Hotel guests frequently came from neighborhood networks and knew each other all year. As a result, these resorts developed miniature societies where people knew much about each other and created intricate relationships in a neighborhood and family mentality that would not be found at an ordinary resort. The "golden era" of the Catskills resort area was the 1950s–1960s. In 1952 an industry census counted 509 hotels and boardinghouses in Sullivan Co; an equal number of bungalow colonies dotted the area. This figure is widely quoted, but more recent research finds that nearly 1,000 hotels and boardinghouses existed in Sullivan and Ulster Cos at various times in the 20th century. It is estimated that 1 million guests vacationed each summer in the 1950s and 1960s.

The Present

Beginning in the late 1960s, the resort industry began a steady decline. Changes in family structure, such as higher divorce rates and more mixed marriages, made it less comfortable to stay in Jewish-identified and family-oriented hotels. More women in the workplace and women's rejection of the centrality of domestic roles made it less palatable to take care of the children while the husbands were away, especially in the bungalow colonies where women did all the cooking and cleaning. Family and religious ties weakened, including the historic reliance on kosher food, making the Catskills resorts less in demand. Jews exhibited increased geographic mobility, leaving them too far away to vacation in the Catskills. The aging of the older population of Catskills guests meant there were fewer veterans to return. People wanted to have a wider variety of vacation experiences, instead of the ones they had been tied to for two or three generations. The decline in anti-Semitism allowed Jews to vacation more freely. On top of those changes, the resorts themselves were old, built over the decades in a quirky and incremental fashion and hence too old-fashioned to please customers and too expensive to maintain. The particularities of family partnership, ownership, and management made it hard to operate the resorts productively and profitably. As well, the economic downturn beginning in 1973 was troublesome. By the 1980s the majority of hotels had ceased to operate, and by 2000 only a half dozen or so remained. The flagship Concord and Grossinger's were closed in the 1990s, although they are currently being redeveloped. A large number of bungalow colonies remained, largely populated by Orthodox and Hasidic Jews. Because of the cultural impact of the borscht belt experience, reunions and other gatherings of ex-Catskills workers and guests are common. Many ashrams, yeshivas, Orthodox Jewish camps, self-help centers, and mental health facilities have taken over the former hotels. There are two separate annual gatherings of Sullivan Co veterans in southern Florida, as well as the Catskills Institute's History of the Catskills Conference held in Sullivan Co. Many guests and workers from various hotels and bungalow colonies also hold reunions.

Brown, Phil. *Catskill Culture: A Mountain Rat's Memories of the Great Jewish Resort Area* (Philadelphia: Temple Univ Press, 1998)

———, ed. *In the Catskills: A Century of the Jewish Experience in "The Mountains"* (New York: Columbia Univ Press, 2002)

Catskills Institute, http://Catskills.brown.edu

Richman, Irwin, *Borscht Belt Bungalows: Memories of Catskill Summers* (Philadelphia: Temple Univ Press, 1998)

Phil Brown

Boston. Town (pop 7,897) in S central Erie Co. Settled in ?1805, the town was formed from Eden in 1817. In the second half of the 19th century Boston was home to the largest cowbell manufacturing company in the United States. Boston was on a short-lived (1906–16) railroad route from Buffalo to Wellsville (Allegany Co). The town's population more than doubled between 1950 and 1960. US 219 was completed as a four-lane highway as far as North Boston in 1972 and to the south end of town in 1978–79, making possible an easy commute to greater Buffalo.

Andrew C. Maines

Boston and Maine Railroad. Chiefly operating in New England, it extended into New York State to Troy (Rensselaer Co), Rotterdam Junction (Schenectady Co), and Saratoga Springs. The Troy and Boston (T&B) opened from Troy to North Adams, Mass, 48 miles (77 km) long in 1852 with a 5 mi (8 km) branch from North Hoosick (Rensselaer Co) to the Town of White Creek (Washington Co). With completion of the Hoosac Tunnel in 1875, through service to Boston was established via the Troy and Greenfield Railroad in Massachusetts. In 1879 the Boston, Hoosac Tunnel and Western Railroad (BHT&W) was completed to a point on the Erie Canal at Rotterdam Junction. This line paralleled the T&B for 20 miles (32 km) west from North Adams, then continued west to Mechanicville (Saratoga Co) and Rotterdam Junction. A branch route was built to Saratoga Springs and Schuylerville (Saratoga Co) from Mechanicville and opened for service in 1882. The Fitchburg Railroad acquired the T&B and the BHT&W in 1887, and the Boston and Maine (B&M) took over the Fitchburg Railroad in 1900. Guilford Transportation Industries (GTI) bought the B&M in 1983. The Saratoga branch was sold to outside interests in the 1940s and the Troy branch, 16.3 miles (26.2 km) from Johnsonville (Rensselaer Co), was abandoned in 1972. In 2002 the line ran from Rotterdam Junction east to the Massachusetts border and was owned by GTI.

Baker, George P. *The Formation of the New England Railroad Systems: A Study of Railroad Combination in the 19th Century* (1937; repr New York: Greenwood, 1968)

Harlow, Alvin F. *Steelways of New England* (New York: Creative Age Press, 1946)

Jim Shaughnessy

Boston Post Road. The first official mail route between New York City and Boston. The Post Road, most likely a redeveloped American Indian travel route, was initiated in 1672 by King Charles II and earned the nicknames Great Road and King's Highway. Gov Francis Lovelace and Connecticut governor John Winthrop dispatched the first official post rider on 22 Jan 1673. In New York Colony the route was 30 miles (48 km), extending from the Battery in New York City to Port Chester [now in Westchester Co] near the Connecticut border. At New Haven, Conn, the Post Road branched into three sections, Lower, Middle, and Upper, all of which terminated at Boston. By 1776, at the insistence of Postmaster General Benjamin Franklin, milestone markers were installed. In the late 18th century, the road was used as a main stage route. Sections of the former road can still be found in the Bowery in Manhattan and on Boston Road in the Bronx. US 1 outside of New York City largely follows the contours of the original.

Holbrook, Stewart Hall. *The Old Post Road: The Story of the Boston Post Road* (New York: McGraw-Hill, 1962)

Mark G. Spencer

Boston Ten Towns. First known as the Chenango Purchase, the Boston Ten Towns (also called the Boston Purchase) was a 230,400-acre (93,240 ha) tract between the Tioughnioga and Chenango Rivers and Owego Creek, north of the Susquehanna River. The former Cayuga land, alienated by them in 1785, was ceded to Massachusetts in 1786 by New York State to settle a long-standing border dispute. In 1787 a company of 11, later increased to 60, and virtually all from Stockbridge and Lenox in Berkshire Co, Mass, bought the tract for 3,333 Spanish milled dollars. Three townships along the Susquehanna's north bank (Owego, Chenango, and Nanticoke) were surveyed first; James McMaster was already living on the present site of the Village of Owego but settled his claim in exchange for the western half of

Owego township. Immediately north of those three towns, the Grand Division of 600 lots was surveyed in 1789–90. Rather than selling these lots, the proprietors attracted as settlers many of the generation born just before the Revolution in Stockbridge and Lenox. As finally surveyed, the Boston Ten Towns became the Towns of Owego, Richford, Berkshire, and Newark Valley (Tioga Co); of Lisle, Nanticoke, Maine, Union, Barker, and Chenango (Broome Co); and small parts of the Towns of Caroline (Tompkins Co) and of Harford, Lapeer, and Marathon (Cortland Co). The tract sustained a strong New England cultural identity for many years. Richford, Newark Valley, and Berkshire hamlets all have village greens. The first church (1803) was affiliated with the Stockbridge, Mass, church, and some men returned to Stockbridge to marry. Many of the next generation went west and established Brownhelm, Ohio.

Darlington, James W. "Peopling the Post-Revolutionary New York Frontier," *New York History* 74 (Oct 1993): 341–81

Gay, W. B. *Historical Gazetteer of Tioga County, New York, 1785–1888* (Syracuse: 1887)

Mancall, Peter C. *Valley of Opportunity: Economic Culture along the Upper Susquehanna, 1700–1800* (Ithaca and London: Cornell Univ Press, 1991)

Jessie Ravage

botanical gardens. Although there were some efforts to create botanical gardens in colonial New York, permanent scientific gardens, in which research was a top priority along with public display, were not built until the early 19th century. One of the most prominent horticulturists of the early national period was David Hosack, a physician and professor of medicine at Columbia College in New York City. During this era botany was an integral part of medical education. In the late 1790s Hosack petitioned Columbia and the state legislature for money to develop an educational botanical garden, but these efforts failed. Thus in 1801 Hosack purchased with his own funds a 20-acre (8 ha) parcel in an isolated section of Manhattan (now the site of Rockefeller Center). He arranged specimens of rare plants, both native and exotic, in discrete beds, each representing different botanical families. He erected a conservatory for the culture of tropical plants and kept a herbarium of dried plant specimens. By 1806 Hosack's Elgin Garden contained over 2,000 species. Hosack ran into financial trouble, however, and after attempts to secure public support for his garden failed, he was forced in 1810 to sell the property to New York State, which turned it over to Columbia four years later. Columbia, to raise funds, rented the land to local farmers.

In 1818, as the Elgin Garden withered, a group of professional horticulturists from the New York City area founded the New-York Horticultural Society at an inn on Broadway in Manhattan. The nation's first organization devoted exclusively to horticulture, the society was a socially fashionable organization and, under the guidance of David Hosack, prospered, sponsoring lavish exhibitions and social functions. It sought a permanent site to build a botanic garden. To secure a land grant the society approached both Columbia College and New York City, but neither was interested. In 1835 Hosack died and within a few years the society, lacking effective leadership, disbanded.

In New York City

In the 1880s the New-York Horticultural Society revived as both a prominent social organization for the elite as well as an informal trade association. Nathaniel Lord Britton, a botanist at Columbia, now courted society members and other affluent individuals in an effort to build a botanic garden. Legislation adopted in 1891, the same year the garden was incorporated, provided the mechanism for acquiring the necessary land. In 1895 Britton secured 250 acres (101 ha) of land bordering Bronx Park from New York City. In the next few years he solicited donations from wealthy New Yorkers, including $25,000 apiece from J. P. Morgan and Andrew Carnegie, to fund construction, and by the second half of the 1890s ground was broken for many of the major buildings that would constitute the New York Botanical Garden. In 1896 Britton became director of the new garden, where he headed a staff of botanists who, over time, compiled one of the most comprehensive collections of plant life in the Western Hemisphere. A museum and an outdoor park designed for education, recreation, and civic prestige was built. Renowned conservatory builder Lord and Burnham Co (then based in Irvington, Westchester Co) erected a stately series of glasshouses where the garden staff cultivated thousands of tropical plants. In 1910 C. S. Gager, a former employee of Britton, helped found the Brooklyn Botanic Garden, a 39-acre (16 ha) parcel adjacent to Prospect Park. Like its Bronx neighbor, the Brooklyn garden boasted a conservatory and plantings arranged in systematic displays. Its research facilities were housed in a building designed by McKim, Mead and White. Other botanical gardens in New York City include the Queens Botanic Garden, located in Flushing on a 39-acre site, formerly a part of the grounds of the World's Fair of 1939–40; the Staten Island Botanic Garden, home to the Chinese Scholar's Garden; and Wave Hill in Riverdale (Bronx Co), located along the banks of the Hudson River and containing a center for landscape history research.

In May 2002 the New York Botanical Garden dedicated its newly renovated library headquarters. After just over a century, the library was actually returning to its original home atop the museum building erected at the turn of the 20th century. The area under the building's dome, long inaccessible to the public, was once again an integral part of the library space. The library itself had been modernized, with Internet terminals, an on-line catalog, and permanently reserved, climate-controlled exhibition space in which the garden's first-rate collection of rare botanical volumes, maps, and prints could be displayed in rotation to the public. The herbarium, numbering over 6.5 million specimens, had moved into new headquarters in the state-of-the-art International Plant Science Center.

Elsewhere in the State

The Buffalo and Erie County Botanical Garden, located in Lackawanna, is a part of Erie Co's South Park, designed by Frederick Law Olmsted in 1893. Dominated by a Lord and Burnham conservatory, this greenhouse was one of the world's largest when it was completed in 1899. The garden itself was opened in stages starting in the mid-1890s. John Cowell, who became the first director in 1894, was a collaborator of Britton. The two botanists made several trips to the Caribbean to collect plants during the first two decades of the 20th century. The garden helped in part to showcase Buffalo during the Pan-American Exposition held in the city in 1901. The Fall Chrysanthemum Show, an event started by Cowell in November 1906, remains the garden's most popular annual exhibit; the Spring Bulbs and the Winter Poinsettia Shows are also popular yearly attractions in the 21st century.

Cornell University in Ithaca maintains a large botanical garden as part of its massive Plantations facility. Founded by Cornell horticulturist

Brooklyn Botanic Garden.

Liberty Hyde Bailey in 1944, the Cornell Plantations rests on 1,000 acres (405 ha) of university land. Comprising orchards, gardens, woodlands, and farm fields, the Plantations was, in Bailey's view, designed to be a complete enterprise in which every part of the agricultural and horticultural process was observable. Bailey's efforts at Cornell were part of his long-standing desire to preserve natural habitats near colleges and universities as outdoor classrooms for students. All aspects of the landscape, Bailey asserted, needed to be preserved using a master plan designed to bring together various ecological resources into an overall educational effort. Once established, the Plantations staff began publishing an influential quarterly, the *Cornell Plantations,* which was read eagerly by administrators at other state agricultural universities. In 2003 the botanical garden consists of 14 separate gardens; some are devoted to decorative floral displays, and some to vegetables and herbs. Cornell's herbaria are among the most important in the United States.

Highland Botanical Park, located in Rochester, the so-called Flower City, is famous for its 1,200-specimen collection of lilac shrubs. The park, founded in 1888 after the renowned nursery firm of Ellwanger and Barry donated 20 acres to the city, was designed by Olmsted and includes the Lamberton Conservatory, built in 1911. The lilacs were first planted in 1892, and the festival started six years later; the festival continues in the 21st century and draws approximately .5 million visitors each May. The Sonnenberg Gardens in Canandaigua (Ontario Co) consist of the former home and gardens of Frederick Ferris and Mary Clark Thompson. The centerpiece is a Lord and Burnham conservatory completed in 1915. The gardens were designed by John Handrahan between 1902 and 1919 and include large decorative floral displays of species from Europe and Asia and a butterfly garden.

Baatz, Simon. *Knowledge, Culture, and Science in the Metropolis: The New York Academy of Sciences, 1817–1970* (New York: New York Academy of Sciences, 1990)

Robbins, Christine Chapman. *David Hosack: Citizen of New York* (Philadelphia: American Philosophical Society, 1964)

Sloan, D. "Science in New York City, 1867–1907," *Isis* 71 (1980): 35–76

Peter Mickulas

botanists and naturalists. Botanists and naturalists have played key roles in developing the natural and life sciences in New York State. A number of botanists and naturalists led the state to scientific prominence, with their legacy enduring into the 21st century in internationally acclaimed universities, botanical gardens, and museums, as well as in a tradition of amateur naturalist studies.

Creating Order

New York Colony's first botanists and naturalists, like those elsewhere in British North America, faced the daunting challenge of describing a natural world almost entirely new to them. They focused on exploring the region's rivers and mountains, recording its climatic patterns, and above all, on gathering, describing, and classifying plants, animals, and minerals. They collected specimens from early settlements along the Hudson River, sending many to Europe for identification and naming according to European taxonomic systems. In an age with few scientific journals, they exchanged information and specimens with one another and with European scientists in the course of much lively correspondence. They also published the colonial era's most reliable accounts of the region's botany and natural history. Leaders of this early group were Cadwallader Colden (1688–1776), who wrote his *Plantae Coldenhamiae* (1744) before serving as lieutenant governor of New York Colony between 1760 and 1776; the first native-born American botanist, John Bartram (1699–1777), author of *Observations on the Inhabitants, Climate, Soil, Rivers, Productions, Animals . . . from Pennsylvania to . . . Lake Ontario* (1751); Swedish naturalist Peter Kalm (1716–79), author of *Travels in North America* (1753); and Colden's daughter Jane Colden (1724–60), who is considered the first American woman botanist. The works of Cadwallader Colden, Bartram, and Kalm all contain initial lists of New York's plant and animal species, as well as descriptions of its landforms, soils, and climate.

Between the American Revolution and the mid–19th century, New York State was home to many prominent botanists and naturalists who advanced the taxonomic work of their colonial predecessors and who began to establish an institutional structure to support their studies. They founded the state's earliest scientific societies, botanical gardens, natural history museums, and scientific journals. They also filled its first college professorships in materia medica (as pharmacology was then known), botany, and natural history, and produced numerous publications, rivaling the output of botanists and naturalists working in Philadelphia, another center of such studies.

In 1791 landed statesman and diplomat Robert Livingston Jr (1746–1813) cofounded New York State's first scientific society, the practically oriented Society for the Promotion of Agriculture, Arts, and Manufactures. The society provided a venue for discussions of research, particularly regarding agriculture, and awarded financial support to scientists and farmers; it met in Manhattan until relocating to Albany in 1793. In 1792 botanist and naturalist Samuel Latham Mitchill (1764–1831) was appointed first professor of natural history and botany at Manhattan's Columbia College (now Columbia University), and five years later cofounded the era's leading scientific journal, *Medical Repository,* based in Manhattan; in 1817 he served as a cofounder of the Lyceum of Natural History of New York (now New York Academy of Sciences) located in Manhattan's Old Almshouse. In 1801 physician and botanist David Hosack (1769–1835) established the state's first botanical garden, the Elgin Botanic Garden in Manhattan (on land now occupied by Rockefeller Center); in 1804 he cofounded the New-York Historical Society, headquartered in Manhattan. In 1807 he became the first professor of materia medica at the newly founded College of Physicians and Surgeons (now part of Columbia University). In 1817 geologist and botanist Amos Eaton (1776–1842) published the first edition of his popular *Manual of Botany* and a year later cofounded the Troy Lyceum of Natural History. In 1824 wealthy landowner and scientific patron Stephen Van Rensselaer (1764–1839) established scientifically oriented Rensselaer Institute (now Rensselaer Polytechnic Institute) in Troy.

From 1836 to 1843 John Torrey (1796–1873) served as botanist for the New York Natural History Survey, which published illustrated volumes on the state's zoology, botany, mineralogy, horticulture, and paleontology. From 1838 to 1843 Torrey and Asa Gray (1810–88), the two most prominent American botanists of the mid–19th century, published their *Flora of North America,* the first comprehensive attempt to describe all of the plants growing north of Mexico according to the "natural system" of classification. This system considered all plant parts and challenged the older, narrower Linnaean method.

Ascent of the Sciences

In the later 19th and 20th centuries, the world of botanists and naturalists in New York State changed in a number of fundamental ways. Botany, geology, and the other natural and life sciences broke from the matrix of natural history and became increasingly specialized, reflecting a shift from the more taxonomic research of Torrey and earlier generations of botanists and naturalists to a consideration of the inner workings of organisms. Following the work of the great theorists like naturalist Charles Darwin and botanist Gregor Mendel, botany splintered into plant anatomy, morphology, physiology, genetics, pathology, and a host of applied specialties, such as agriculture and forestry. At the same time, support for research and institutions devoted to the work of botanists and naturalists increased dramatically, underwritten by business interests, philanthropic foundations, and local, state, and federal governments. Among the most important federal contributions was the 1862 Morrill Land Grant Act, which supported the founding of Cornell University in 1865. Other institutional advances included Torrey Botanical Society in New York City (?1866), American Museum of Natural History in Manhattan (1869), Brooklyn Botanic Garden (1910), and numerous colleges, universities, and local herbaria. Business, philanthropic, and government money often combined to support the endeavors of scholars like Columbia University's botanist Nathaniel Lord Britton, who founded in 1891 the New York Botanical Garden in what is now the Bronx. The increase in support led to the mounting importance of academic departments and to burgeoning numbers of scientists and academic journals.

The state's distinguished 20th-century botanists include internationally famed Henry Gleason (1882–1975) and Arthur Cronquist (1919–92). Having received a PhD in botany from Columbia University, Gleason spent 30 years at the New York Botanical Garden, principally developing its South American collection. Pioneering in the fields of taxonomy and ecology, his work influenced ecological and geographical studies of vegetation. After Cronquist joined the New York Botanical Garden in 1943, he and Gleason collaborated on publications such as their *Manual of Vascular Plants of Northeastern United States and Adjacent Canada* (1963), known to botany students as the Green Bible. Cronquist also contributed to the field of plant classification, authored textbooks on introductory botany, and served as adjunct professor at Columbia University and CUNY.

From the early 20th century, the term "naturalist" has increasingly described the more popular or philosophical work of generalists, covering a wide spectrum of researchers, writers, and speakers, ranging from the scientifically trained to untrained members of local garden and bird clubs. Long Beach (Nassau Co) native Stephen J. Gould (1941–2002) represents the scientific edge of this spectrum. Receiving a Columbia University PhD in paleontology and evolutionary biology, he became a professor of geology and zoology at Harvard University. Gould published nearly 20 books and hundreds of essays and articles. He is best known for writings on the theory of evolution as well as for a monthly column (1974–2002) in *Natural History*, the magazine of the American Museum of Natural History.

Greene, John C. *American Science in the Age of Jefferson* (Ames: Iowa State Univ Press, 1984)
Pauly, Philip J. *Biologists and the Promise of American Life: From Meriwether Lewis to Alfred Kinsey* (Princeton, NJ: Princeton Univ Press, 2000)
Rodgers, Andrew Denny. *John Torrey: A Story of North American Botany* (Princeton, NJ: Princeton Univ Press, 1942)

George Vrtis

Bouck, William C. (*b* Fultonham, Schoharie Co, 7 Jan 1786; *d* Schoharie Co, 19 Apr 1859). Governor. With little formal education, Bouck entered public life at an early age. After serving as county sheriff (1812), he became a state assemblyman (1814–16, 1818), state senator (1820–21), and canal commissioner (1821–40). Though Bouck was defeated in the 1840 governor's race, the debate over canal expansion and state debt relief motivated the Democrats to nominate him again in 1842. Without incumbent governor William H. Seward in the race, Bouck, who favored canal expansion and had the support of both the conservative and radical factions of the Democratic Party, won convincingly. His governorship was marked by calling out the militia in response to the developing antirent movement. Perceived as a weak candidate for reelection during a presidential election year, he was not renominated and instead served on the Board of Regents (1846–49) and as a constitutional convention delegate (1846). After serving as assistant US treasurer in New York City (1846–49), he retired to his farm in Fulton (Schoharie Co).

Alexander, DeAlva Stanwood. *A Political History of the State of New York*, 4 vols (1906; repr Port Washington, NY: I. J. Friedman, 1969)

John Marino

Boughton, Smith (Azer) (*b* Stephentown, Rensselaer Co, 1 Sept 1810; *d* Alps, Rensselaer Co, 14 Nov 1888). Physician, reformer, and agrarian leader. The son of a farmer on the 750,000-acre (304,000 ha) tenant estate of Rensselaerswijck, Boughton attended school in Washington Co and studied medicine at Middlebury College in Vermont. After receiving his MD in 1831, he participated in the unsuccessful Patriots' War of 1837 in Canada and practiced medicine briefly in several towns before marrying Mary Bailey, daughter of a leading citizen of Alps, and settling there. In 1843 Boughton joined the antirent movement, becoming its agent to the state legislature. He led the effort to organize the tenants of Columbia Co in 1844, earning the alias of Big Thunder as an orator and antirent vigilante "Indian" (dressed in Indian garb for protests). Authorities arrested Boughton in December 1844, charging him with several crimes—such as manslaughter, theft of legal papers, assault, riot, and conspiracy—committed by various Columbia Co "Indians." They held him without bail until his trial the following March, when lack of evidence saved him from the more serious charges, but at his second trial in September he was sentenced to life imprisonment. Pardoned in 1847 by Gov John Young, who also restored his rights of citizenship, Boughton resumed his medical practice and position in the antirent movement's leadership. After the cause's collapse in 1852, he remained active in the antislavery and land reform movements until his retirement in 1880.

Boughton, James. *Bouton-Boughton Family* (Albany: Joel Munsell's Sons, 1890)

Reeve Huston

Bovina. Town (pop 664) in E central Delaware Co. Settled in 1792 by New Englanders who were joined by Scots *ca* 1800, the town was formed in 1820 from Delhi, Stamford, and Middletown. Bovina farmers were noted for fine cattle and for butter production. Lake Delaware (26 mi²/67 km²) is part of the 3,000-acre (1,214 ha) Gerry estate, inherited by Louisa Livingston Gerry (1835–1920) and owned by her descendants in 2003; St. James Church Lake Delaware (1922) was designed by Ralph Adams Cram as a Gerry memorial. The population of the town steadily declined after an 1845 peak but increased more than 20% in the 1990s. Farming has almost disappeared. Most residents travel to work in surrounding areas, but second-home owners and bed-and-breakfast establishments contribute to the local economy.

Dorothy Kubik

bowling. Nine-pin bowling, in which the pins are placed in a diamond pattern, was a popular recreation in New Netherland and colonial New York, though lawn bowling was probably the more popular pastime. Dutch authorities prohibited nine-pin rolling on Sundays in 1656. The association of the Dutch with nine-pin bowling endured, most famously in Washington Irving's 1820 story in which Rip Van Winkle encountered nine-pin playing elves dressed in "antique Dutch fashion." Under the English the sport was associated with taverns, which often had adjacent alleys for bowling. Wooden balls gradually replaced rounded stones, and dirt- or wood-smoothed playing surfaces replaced bumpier terrain and enabled year-round play indoors.

Though ten-pin bowling, in which pins are arranged in a triangle, was played in New York State as early as 1803 in Suffolk Co, nine-pin bowling remained dominant for most of the 19th century. Advertisements in Buffalo in 1843 promised an invigorated nervous system from visits to canal-district bowling saloons. German immigrants brought their love of bowling, or kegeling, with them, and helped spark the opening around 1840 of establishments like Manhattan's Knickerbocker Alleys, which featured the sport's first indoor clay-baked surface. New York City boasted approximately 400 bowling alleys by 1850. The taint of gambling and other vices somewhat sullied bowling's reputation after midcentury, though by 1890 there were bowling leagues in Buffalo, New York City, Brooklyn, and Rochester.

Ten-pin bowling supplanted nine-pin bowling as the game of choice during this period, yet standardization remained a problem. The first national attempt to standardize occurred in 1875, when representatives from 11 Brooklyn and New York City bowling clubs formed the National Bowling Association and agreed to common pin dimensions, a 60 ft (18.3 m) long alley, and prohibitions on lofted balls. More extensive regulations came in 1895 when the American Bowling Congress (ABC) formed at New York City's Beethoven Hall. Under the stewardship of Louis Stein and Sam Karpf, representatives agreed to 12 in (30.5 cm) spacing between pins, a maximum of two shots per frame, and a 300-pin total count per game. Women created a separate governing body, the Women's National Bowling Association (now Women's International Bowling Congress [WIBC]), in 1916. The Professional Bowlers Association, formed in 1958, held its first tournament, the 1959 Empire State Open, at Schade's Bowling Academy in Albany.

Though most leagues initially formed from voluntary associations such as singing societies, physicians' meetings, and groupings of saloon owners, leagues attracted a broader audience in the first half of the 20th century. Bowling became a national game that appealed to New Yorkers seeking a year-round sport. High ratings for bowling television shows, such as Buffalo's *Beat the Champ*, during the post–World War II era reflected the sport's appeal and nurtured its popularity in the state. Twenty-five ABC and WIBC annual tournaments were hosted at Syracuse, Niagara Falls, Rochester, Buffalo, and New York City venues during the 20th century. Though individual and informal group bowling rose in the late 20th century, league bowling in the state and nationwide has declined since the 1980s. With fewer leagues, many lanes have closed, bringing greater consolidation within the industry. In 1997, 417 bowling establishments operated in New York State, collecting over $188 million in receipts.

The Bowling Hall of Fame includes West Nyack's (Rockland Co) John Koster, who was the first to win four ABC tournaments, Buffalo's Frank Caruana, who in 1924 was the first to roll consecutive 300 games, and Lockport's (Niagara Co) Allie Brandt, who held the highest score in a three-game series (886) from 1939 to 1988. Brooklyn's Jimmy Smith and Andy Varipapa were well-known exhibition bowlers, and Rochester's Mildred Ignizio was the first to win three WIBC tournaments. Buffalo's Doris Coburn and her daughter Cindy Coburn-Carroll also captured WIBC individual championships; they both performed in the Women's Professional Bowlers Association, which formed in 1959.

Adelman, Melvin L. *A Sporting Time: New York City and the Rise of Modern Athletics, 1820–1870* (Urbana: Univ of Illinois Press, 1986)
Reiss, Steven A. *City Games: The Evolution of American Urban Society and the Rise of Sports* (Urbana: Univ of Illinois Press, 1989)

Kevin J. Grzymala

boxing. Modern boxing is a combat sport in which two opponents attempt to inflict maximum physical damage upon one another within official parameters. The first important American fighter was Bill Richmond, a free Black, born a slave on Staten Island in 1763 but made his career in England. The 1816 New York City fight between Jacob Hyer and Tom Beasley became the first widely publicized American match. The *New York Evening Post* was the first newspaper to cover boxing with its report of a 8 July 1823 bout at Gardner's wharf near Cherry St. The *Post* article documented the presence of referees and a demarcated ring as well as a $200 purse. In 1838 new rules prohibited the more brutal tactics of bare-knuckle fighting but did not prevent the death of Thomas McCoy in his 13 Sept 1842 bout with Christopher Lilly at Hastings-on-Hudson (Westchester Co). The tragedy suppressed boxing in New York State, and New York's Tom Hyer (son of Jacob) won the first national championship by defeating Yankee Sullivan in Maryland on 7 Feb 1849. A 1853 match for the heavyweight championship between Sullivan and John Morrissey, born in Ireland but raised in Troy (Rensselaer Co), was held at Boston Corners [now in Columbia Co] on the border of New York, Connecticut, and Massachusetts to avoid state interference.

In summer 1857 Buffalo became a center for boxing when Izzy Lazarus brought three major bouts to his saloon. When Morrissey fought John C. Heenan on 20 Oct 1858, the bout was held at Long Point [now in Ont]. Morrissey defeated the much younger Heenan, who was also born in Ireland and raised in Troy, where his father was a foreman at the Watervliet Arsenal. The wild celebrations that followed in Buffalo and New York City confirmed the views of those who regarded boxing as a progenitor of depravity. Contenders often came from the lower economic strata and were sometimes employed by politicians to intimidate rivals. These factors, along with the accompanying gambling activities, contributed to widespread disapproval of boxing.

Queensberry Rules

From its 1866 beginning the New York Athletic Club (NYAC) presented amateur bare-knuckle fighting as a respectable sport governed by rules and suitable for its middle-class members. The 1867 publication of the Queensberry Rules, which stipulated timed rounds, one-minute rests between rounds, and the use of padded gloves, increased the acceptance of boxing. While professional boxing in New York State declined during the 1870s and 1880s, amateur boxing drew increasing support as a healthful pursuit for sedentary white-collar workers and upper-status youth, such as Theodore Roosevelt. In 1878 the NYAC held the first national championships in amateur boxing.

The application of the Queensberry Rules to prize-money bouts helped revitalize professional boxing, as did the state's Horton Act of 1896, which permitted matches within the proprietary holdings of athletic clubs. Boxing by now was filmed and replayed for profit; a Coney Island fight between Jim Jeffries and Tom Sharkey on 3 Nov 1899 may have been the first match filmed under artificial lights. The 11 May 1900 heavyweight championship bout, held in Coney Island, in which James J. Corbett defeated Jeffries, brought in a gate of $60,000. The Horton Act was repealed in 1900, but professional matches continued in private New York City clubs. Realistic depictions of boxers in art, such as George Bellows's 1909 oil painting *Stag at Sharkey's*, showing a bout at a small New York City club, confirmed their place in American culture. The Frawley Act (1911–17), permitted a restricted sport with contests limited to 10 rounds with no allowance for referee decision.

Dempsey to Ali

In 1920 New York State passed the Walker Law, which legalized prizefighting. It allowed judges to decide matches after 12 rounds and created an unpaid supervisory commission; still, boxing became connected to organized crime, with gangsters managing athletes and promoting fights. As professional boxing was reestablished, New York City journalist Nat Fleischer founded the magazine the *Ring* in 1922. Madison Square Garden became the center of New York boxing, although a number of famous bouts were conducted elsewhere, such as Jack Dempsey's defeat of Luis Angel Firpo on 14 Sept 1923 at the Polo Grounds. Dempsey (1895–1983; heavyweight champion 1919–26) became the most glamorous boxer of his era, owning a Manhattan restaurant for many decades after his retirement from the ring. His successor, Gene Tunney (1898–1978; heavyweight champion 1926–28), a native of New York City, had won the American Expeditionary Forces light heavyweight title in Europe in 1919. As a heavyweight Tunney's most famous bouts were wins over Dempsey on 23 Sept 1926, which gave Tunney the title, and on 22 Sept 1927, in a bout that came to be known as the "long count" bout. After retiring undefeated in 1928, Tunney had a career in business as a corporate executive; during World War II, he served as director of physical fitness for the US Navy.

In addition to serving as a venue for many important bouts, New York City dominated American boxing through the number of great boxers who were born or grew up there, such as Tunney, Benny Leonard (Benjamin Leiner, 1896–1947; lightweight champion 1917–25), "Slapsie" Maxie Rosenbloom (1904–76; light-heavyweight champion 1930–34), James J. Braddock (1905–74; heavyweight champion 1935–37), Barney Ross (Barnet Rosofsky, 1909–67; welterweight champion 1934, 1935–38). Boxers from elsewhere in the state include the "Herkimer Hurricane" Lou Ambers (Luigi Giuseppe D'Ambrosio, 1913–95; lightweight champion 1936–38, 1939–40) of Herkimer and Jack Sharkey (Juozas Zukauskas, 1902–94; heavyweight champion 1932–33), born of Lithuanian parentage in Binghamton. Joe Louis (Joe Louis Barrow, 1914–83; heavyweight champion 1937–50) fought many memorable fights in New York City, including a one-round knockout of Max Schmeling at Yankee Stadium on 22 June 1938, avenging his only professional defeat (and by defeating a representative of Nazi Germany became a national hero), and a 13-round knockout of Billy Conn at the Polo Grounds on 18 June 1941.

Three New York City middleweights dominated the weight category in the 1940s and 1950s. Rocky Graziano (Thomas Rocco Barbella) and Jake (Giacobe) LaMotta were born and grew up in New York City, overcoming poverty and delinquency to achieve success in the ring. Both served time in what is now Coxsackie Correctional Facility (Greene Co) in their adolescent years, and LaMotta learned to box there. Graziano, born 1 Jan 1921, became a professional boxer in 1942 and held the world middleweight title from July 1947 to June 1948. After retiring from boxing in 1952 he appeared in television shows and wrote his biography, *Somebody Up There Likes Me* (1955), which became a 1956 motion picture. He died on 22 May 1990. LaMotta, born 10 July 1921, became a professional boxer in 1941 and held the world middleweight title from June 1949 to February 1951. Graziano introduced LaMotta to acting, and the latter appeared in 19 motion pictures. LaMotta's biography, *Raging Bull* (1970), became a motion picture in 1980. LaMotta's nemesis, Sugar Ray Robinson (Walker Smith Jr, 1921–89), who moved to New York City at age 12, was a five-time middleweight champion and is generally acknowledged to be the best boxer ever in his weight category. Another champion boxer in the middleweight categories was Carmen Basilio, born on 2 Apr 1927 in Canastota (Madison Co); he was welterweight champion in 1955 and 1956 and middleweight champion from September 1957 to March 1958.

New York City has also been a center for training. Bobby Gleason (Peter Robert Gagliardi) opened Gleason's Gym in the Bronx in 1937. Angelo Dundee came to New York City in the late 1940s to pursue a career as a boxing trainer; his first titleholder was Carmen Basilio. Dundee later trained Muhammad Ali and Mike Tyson. Cus D'Amato founded the Empire Sporting Club around 1930 to develop boxers at the Gramercy Gym. Floyd Patterson trained under D'Amato to win a gold medal in boxing at the 1952 Olympics and the heavyweight title in 1956. José Luis Torres, silver medallist in the 1956 Olympics, also turned professional under D'Amato's guidance. D'Amato would not match his boxers with those of the corrupt International Boxing Club, attempting to undercut the its influence. After retirement both Patterson and Torres served on the New York State Athletic Commission. Robert Arum grew up in Crown Heights (Kings Co) and graduated from New York University in 1953 and from Harvard Law School in 1956. In 1962 he investigated boxing scandals at the request of Attorney General Robert F. Kennedy. Arum began promoting fights in 1966 and became one of the country's top boxing promoters starting in the 1970s.

On 8 Mar 1971 Madison Square Garden was the site of the "Fight of the Century" between Muhammad Ali, the former heavyweight champion who had been stripped of his title because of his 1967 refusal to serve in the army, and Joe Frazier, the unbeaten heavyweight champion. Frazier won by decision after 15 rounds. The bout drew a closed-circuit television audience of over 300 million and gate revenue of $1.3 million.

Boxing in Recent Decades

The most successful New York State boxer in recent decades has been Mike Tyson. Tyson was the protégé of Cus D'Amato, who opened a gym in Catskill (Greene Co), where he met the teenage Michael Tyson, then a resident at a reformatory. D'Amato became Tyson's mentor but died in 1985 before Tyson, born in Brooklyn on 30 June 1966, became the youngest heavyweight champion of the world, winning the World Boxing Council title on 22 Nov 1986. Tyson went on to win the World Boxing Association title in March 1987 and the International Boxing Federation title in August 1987, although he probably is destined to be remembered more for his extremely wayward career than for his remarkable boxing prowess. Riddick Bowe, born in Brooklyn on 10

Aug 1967, held the world heavyweight title from 13 Nov 1992 until 6 Nov 1993.

In the late 20th century bouts at Madison Square Garden were increasingly rare, and major fights often were held in resorts. On 8 Oct 1999 Laila Ali (daughter of Muhammad Ali) defeated April Fowler at Turning Stone Casino and Resort in Verona (Oneida Co). Gleason's Gym moved to Manhattan in 1974 and then to Brooklyn in 1984. As boxing became a popular form of exercise among young professionals, Gleason's began its monthly White Collar show in 1988. In 1998 Gerry Cooney founded the Fighters' Initiative for Support and Training (FIST) to help retired boxers in the New York metropolitan area with vocational, financial, and health issues. Cooney grew up in Huntington (Suffolk Co), won a New York Golden Gloves title in 1972, and turned professional in 1977; he fought Larry Holmes for a shot at the heavyweight title in 1982. On 11 Feb 2003 FIST became affiliated with the AFL-CIO as the Boxer's Guild in Local 153, Office of Professional Employees International Union.

Carpenter, Harry. *Masters of Boxing* (South Brunswick, NJ: A. S. Barnes, 1964)
Fleischer, Nat, and Sam Andre. *An Illustrated History of Boxing* (Secaucus, NJ: Citadel Press, 1997)
Gorn, Elliott J. *The Manly Art: Bare-Knuckle Prize Fighting in America* (Ithaca: Cornell Univ Press, 1986)
Mead, Chris. *Champion: Joe Louis, Black Hero in White America* (New York: Charles Scribner's Sons, 1985)
Seltzer, Robert. *Inside Boxing* (New York: MetroBooks, 2000)

Pamela Cooper

Boyle, T(homas) Coraghessan (*b* Peekskill, Westchester Co, 2 Dec 1948). Writer. The son of working-class parents, Boyle spent his childhood in Peekskill. At 17 he changed his middle name, John, to Coraghessan, from his mother's side of the family. A 1964 graduate of Lakeland High School in Shrub Oak (Westchester Co), Boyle received his BA in English and history at SUNY Potsdam (1968), where a creative writing class sparked his interest in fiction. He taught English for four years at Lakeland High School and also wrote short stories. In 1972 Boyle was accepted into the University of Iowa's Writer's Workshop, where he earned an MFA (1974) and a PhD in literature (1977). The following year he was hired to teach in the University of Southern California's English department, where he has remained. Boyle's first novel, *Water Music,* was published in 1981 and demonstrated the irreverent and satiric humor that would become his trademark. He received widespread attention with his 1987 book, *World's End,* a historical account of three families in the Hudson River valley, which earned him the PEN/Faulkner Award for best novel of the year. *The Road to Wellville* (1993), a satire on health-food fanatics during the 1800s, was made into a film the following year starring Matthew Broderick and Anthony Hopkins. His most recent novel is *Drop City* (2003). Boyle lives in Montecito, Calif.

Appell, David. "Earthquakes, Critics and the 600 Nitro: An Interview with T. Coraghessan Boyle," *Hayden's Ferry Review* 18 (Spring–Summer 1996): 9–27

J. Justin Gustainis

Boylston. Town (pop 505) in NE Oswego Co. Settled in 1812 the town was formed from Orwell in 1828. Prior to 1850 only the west half of town was settled; lumbering and grazing were its economic bases. Work in the lumbering trades attracted French and English Canadians. Fishing and hunting have become major draws for visitors. Maple sugar is an important product, and lumbering continues on extensive tracts of both state and private land. Most residents commute to work outside of town. Its highest points, 700–800 feet (210–40 m) above sea level, provide a wonderful panoramic view of Lake Ontario.

Barbara J. Dix

Bradford. Town (pop 763) in E central Steuben Co. Settled in 1793, its early population was drawn from New Jersey, Pennsylvania, and Maryland; the town was formed in 1836 from the old town of Jersey [now Orange (Schuyler Co) and Bradford]. The early economy revolved around timber; approximately 100,000 feet (30,500 m) of lumber was sent via the Susquehanna to Baltimore in 1798. Later 19th-century products included flour, maple sugar, and livestock. In the 1920s, after an influx of ethnic Polish farmers, Bradford became known as Little Poland; for almost 60 years (1926–85) an annual Polish picnic attracted thousands.

Virginia L. Wright and Jerry Wright

Bradford, William (*b* Barnwell, England, 20 May 1663; *d* New York City, 23 May 1752). Royal printer. After an apprenticeship with a Quaker printer, in 1685 Bradford immigrated to Pennsylvania and became a printer for Pennsylvania Colony and the Society of Friends. In 1692 he was imprisoned for sedition after printing anti-Quaker literature, spent several months in jail awaiting trial, but was never convicted. He then left Philadelphia and in 1693 became New York Colony's first government printer. Setting up a press in New York City, Bradford abandoned the Quakers and joined the Church of England. In 1694 he printed the first version of the colony's laws, often called Bradford's Laws, titled *The Laws of Her Majesties Province of New-York.* He printed almanacs, dramas, and history books and the first newspaper in the colony, the *New-York Gazette,* which debuted 8 Nov 1725. The paper supported government policies, unlike the *New-York Weekly Journal* edited by John Peter Zenger, a former apprentice to Bradford. The editors engaged in a war of words that led Zenger to be tried for seditious libel in 1735.

Thomas, Isaiah. *History of Printing in America.* Ed. Marcus A. McCorison (New York: Weathervane Books, 1970)

Mark G. Spencer

Bradstreet, John (*b* Annapolis Royal, NS, 21 Dec 1714; *d* New York City, 25 Sept 1774). British army officer. Bradstreet received his initial ensigncy with the 40th Regiment of Foot at Canso, NS, on 23 Aug 1735. He rose to prominence in 1745 during King George's War (1744–48) in the campaign against French-held Louisbourg on Isle Royale [now Cape Breton Island, NS]. His conduct there was rewarded with the lieutenant governorship of St. John's, Newf, and command of a regular company in the 51st Regiment of Foot. During the French and Indian War (1754–63) his endeavors with a corps of armed boatmen to maintain communication between Albany and Oswego won him a captain's commission in the newly formed 60th (Royal American) Regiment of Foot. On 27 Aug 1758, shortly after promotion to colonel, he led the attack that severed the French supply line between Montreal and interior garrisons through the capture of Fort Frontenac [now Kingston, Ont], at the head of the St. Lawrence River. In partnership with Philip Schuyler, Bradstreet speculated heavily in Indian land following the war and left his heirs an estate valued at £15,000.

Godfrey, William G. *Pursuit of Profit and Preferment in Colonial North America: John Bradstreet's Quest* (Waterloo, Ont: Wilfrid Laurier Univ, 1982)

Alexander V. Campbell

Brainerd, David (*b* Haddam, Conn, 20 Apr 1718; *d* Northampton, Mass, 9 Oct 1747). Presbyterian missionary. According to his diary young Brainerd frequently experienced morbid fears of physical and spiritual death. This inner tumult continued until he underwent a conversion experience on 12 July 1739. That same year he entered Yale College and continued to support revival meetings, an activity frowned upon by college authorities. When he made disparaging remarks about that policy in 1742 he was required to make a public apology and, upon refusal to do so, was expelled without receiving a degree. Despite this setback Brainerd was determined to become a preacher and on 20 July 1742 was licensed to preach by the Congregationalist Association of Ministers. He soon traveled to New York City and received a commission from the Society in Scotland for the Propagation of Christian Knowledge to serve as a missionary to American Indians. His first charge was to work among the Housatonics, an Algonquian-speaking group located principally at Kaunaumeek, a settlement midway between Stockbridge, Mass, and Albany. Brainerd's missionary activities at Kaunaumeek (1 Apr 1743–3 Nov 1744) were not a marked success. His frail health and mental depressions impeded serious work, and eventually the Housatonics moved closer to Stockbridge while Brainerd left to try further ventures among the Delawares. He died three years later. Many readers of his posthumously published diary (1749) were inspired by his pious dedication and are said to have volunteered for missions in emulation, but contemporary opinions of Brainerd have been shaped by his negative views toward native peoples and his responsibility for infecting American Indians with tuberculosis.

Day, Richard E. *Flagellant on Horseback: The Life Story of David Brainerd* (Philadelphia: Judson Press, 1950)
Edwards, Jonathan, ed. *An Account of the Life of the Late Reverend Mr. David Brainerd* (Boston: D. Henchman, 1749)
Wynbeek, David. *David Brainerd: Beloved Yankee* (Grand Rapids, Mich: Wm. B. Eerdmans, 1961)

Henry Warner Bowden

Brandon. Town (pop 542) in NW Franklin Co. Settled in 1820, the town was formed from Bangor in 1828. Santa Clara was taken off in 1888, reducing Brandon to about 20% of its previous land area and taking a large part of Brandon's nonresident taxpayers. The northern part of town is agricultural; the rest is in forestry. The population increased by 39% between 1990 and 2000.

Thomas W. Perrin

Brant. Town (pop 1,906) in SW Erie Co. Settled in 1816 primarily by farmers from Pennsylvania and New England, the town was formed from Evans and Collins in 1839. Brant was crossed by the first of three railroads in 1852. German immigrants came to town in the mid–19th century, followed by French and Italian immigrants. A region of fruit and vegetable farming, Brant had a number of canneries and packing companies. The Sprague Corn Sheller Manufacturing Co burned in 1896. The New York State Thruway opened through town in 1957. From 1956 to 1971 Brant held an annual strawberry festival, but it was discontinued when the crop declined. In 2003 the town was an important farming area. It is the site of Evangola State Park and adjoins the Cattaraugus Indian Reservation.

Andrew C. Maines

Brant, Joseph [Thayendanegea] (*b* Cuyahoga Valley [now in Ohio], ?1742; *d* Burlington Bay [now Burlington, Ont], 24 Nov 1807). Mohawk warrior and diplomat. Born to Mohawk parents of the Wolf Clan in the Ohio Country, Brant was raised in Canajoharie [now in Montgomery Co], where his stepfather, Brant Canagaraduncka, was a leading Turtle Clan sachem with close ties to Sir William Johnson. As a young man Brant participated, with the British, in a few campaigns of the French and Indian War. From 1761 to 1763 he attended Eleazar Wheelock's Indian school in Connecticut, learning something of English language and culture. Sir William Johnson, superintendent of Indian Affairs, employed Brant as an interpreter in the Indian Department. Brant's and Johnson's connection was close also because Brant's sister Molly, an influential pro-British Mohawk, was Johnson's common-law wife. After Sir William's death in 1774, Brant became secretary to Guy Johnson, the new superintendent. During the Revolutionary War, Brant emerged as a Pine Tree chief who vigorously promoted Iroquois loyalty to Britain. He became a transatlantic dignitary after his trip to London in 1775–76 with Guy Johnson and other loyalists, representing Mohawk grievances over land to the British government.

After returning to America, Brant participated in the British and Iroquois expeditions in the New York and Pennsylvania frontiers that tied down large numbers of American troops, forced thousands of settlers to abandon the frontier, and denied supplies to the American armies. He fought at the Battles of Oriskany in 1777 and Newtown during Maj Gen John Sullivan's 1779 invasion. From 1778 to 1780 he frequently coordinated offensives with the Seneca warrior Sayenqueraghta against settlements in the Susquehanna, Mohawk, and Schoharie Valleys. The Americans vilified him as "Monster Brant" for his attacks on frontier settlements and because they believed he was involved in the July 1778 Wyoming Valley massacre in Pennsylvania, although he was not. Some Iroquois resented his pretentiousness and British officers' favoritism of him. Brant gained in stature however, after his third marriage in 1779 to Catharine Croghan (Adonwentishon), a Mohawk Clan matron and a relation of the sachem Henry Tekarihogen. After 1780 Brant's attention turned to the Ohio Valley, where he hoped to promote unity between the Six Nations and the western Indian nations.

When Brant learned of the 1783 Treaty of Paris, he excoriated the British for betraying faithful allies and failing to mention Iroquois interests. He became a forceful advocate of Indian unity in the face of American expansion and a leader of the Mohawks' resettlement in Canada along the Grand River on the Niagara peninsula. Brant remained a transatlantic figure through correspondence with British elites and a visit to London in 1785–86 to secure compensation for the Mohawk. He also acted as the principal spokesman for the Grand River Indians and advocated assimilation with the British. Some Iroquois vehemently opposed his policies. Living in an opulent style, Brant invited white farmers to settle on Grand River, believing that they would improve the Mohawks' economic security. A long-time patron of the Anglican Church, he assisted in translating numerous prayer books and biblical texts into Mohawk. Throughout his life he ably negotiated between two cultures to strengthen the Anglo-Iroquois alliance and the Mohawks' welfare.

Joseph Brant, by Gilbert Stuart, 1786, painted when both men were in London.

Graymont, Barbara. *The Iroquois in the American Revolution* (Syracuse: Syracuse Univ Press, 1972)

Kelsay, Isabel Thompson. *Joseph Brant, 1743–1807: Man of Two Worlds* (Syracuse: Syracuse Univ Press, 1984)

David L. Preston

Brant, Molly [Mary] [Konwatsi tsiaienni] (*b* ?1736; *d* Kingston [now in Ont], 16 Apr 1796). Mohawk matron and diplomat. Molly Brant, much like her brother Joseph Brant, emerged as a prominent leader of the Iroquois in the late 18th century. While her exact birthplace is unknown, she was most likely born at the Mohawk town of Canajoharie [now in Montgomery Co] and acquired the name Brant after her mother's second marriage to Brant Canagaraduncka, an important Mohawk sachem. Through him she came into contact with Sir William Johnson, superintendent of Indian Affairs for the Northern Colonies and a frequent visitor to the Brant household. By 1759 Johnson's first wife had died, and Brant, who had already moved into Johnson's frontier estate as housekeeper, gave birth to the first of their eight children. Living at Fort Johnson [now in Montgomery Co] and later Johnson Hall [now Johnstown, Fulton Co] along the Mohawk River, Molly Brant was at the center of Indian affairs in colonial New York. Both estates functioned as important meeting grounds for Indian and colonial diplomats. Brant and Johnson never married, but she gained a reputation as a gracious hostess and proved indispensable to him as a cultural mediator. Using the authority and status Iroquois culture assigned to women, Brant assisted Johnson in his diplomatic affairs with Indians.

Following Johnson's death in 1774, Brant returned to Canajoharie with her children and a substantial inheritance to establish a trading store. After the outbreak of the American Revolution, Brant found new opportunities as a leader in the Mohawk Valley. A staunch ally of the British, Brant aided loyalists with shelter, ammunition, and military intelligence. Her most famous act was to warn British military officials, engaged in the siege of Fort Stanwix [now Rome, Oneida Co], of advancing American troops in August 1777. This enabled the British to organize a successful ambush, resulting in the Battle of Oriskany on 6 Aug 1777. Her role as informant compelled her to seek protection for her children and herself among the western nations of the Iroquois Confederacy, whom she chastised in public council for their wavering support of the British. By late 1777 Brant relocated to Fort Niagara [now in Porter, Niagara Co], a major military base and refuge for displaced Indians. Throughout her stay, she kept the commanding officer informed on the disposition of the Iroquois. By summer 1779 crowded and uncomfortable conditions prompted Brant to move first to Montreal and several months later to Carleton Island [now in Jefferson Co] at the head of the St. Lawrence River, where she spent the remainder of the war. At this post she continued her valuable work as a cultural broker, counseling the Iroquois to remain loyal and defusing tensions between the British military and loyalists in Canada. At the war's end, Brant moved to Cataraqui [now Kingston, Ont]. In a show of gratitude for her wartime assistance, the British government built her a house and granted her an annual pension of £100. She and her family successfully assimilated into Canadian society. Five of her daughters married Canadian men of military and professional standing, and one remained unmarried. Her older son Peter died fighting for the British in Philadelphia at the Battle of Mud Island in 1777. Brant maintained an active involvement in the Anglican Church. She was buried at St. George's Church (now St. Paul's Church) in Kingston.

Earle, Thomas. *The Three Faces of Molly Brant: A Biography* (Kingston, Ont: Quarry Press, 1996)

Huey, Lois M., and Bonnie Pulis. *Molly Brant: A Legacy of Her Own* (Youngstown, NY: Old Fort Niagara Association, 1997)

Gail D. MacLeitch

Brasher [BRAY-ZHER]. Town (pop 2,337) in NE St. Lawrence Co. Settled in 1817, the town was formed from Massena in 1825. Settlers from New England were joined by Irish immigrants entering via Montreal; "Brasher Irish" names such as McGreavy and Dawson are still common. Brasher Iron Works included a furnace (1825) and bog-ore extraction (1836). Brasher Falls, on the St. Regis River, developed into an industrial center from 1845 on, producing woolen cloth, agricultural implements, leather, pumps, and potato starch. Lumbering and dairy farming were the most common occupations. Some farming continues, but many residents work in Massena. The 22,195-acre (8,982 ha) Brasher State Forest was created by reforestation of small farms that failed during and after the Great Depression. The octagonal Italianate Buck-Stevens House (1855–57) is listed on the National Register of Historic Places.

Richard E. Mooers

Brasher doubloon. During the Articles of Confederation period, several of the newly independent American states had their own coinage. Though New York State never officially authorized production of coins, several issues of coins were privately minted. In 1787 Ephraim Brasher, a New York City silver- and goldsmith, produced a set of inexpensive coins, the *Nova Eborac* (New York) coppers, as well as gold coins, the so-called Brasher doubloons. The doubloons, with the legend *Nova Eboraca* and an image of the state seal on one side and of the US eagle on the other, are among the most highly valued of all American coins. Only seven specimens are known to exist; one sold in 1979 for $725,000. The coin was at the center of a successful 1947 film, *The Brasher Doubloon,* based on a novel by mystery writer Raymond Chandler.

Louis, Jordan. "Brasher's Doubloons 1786–1787: Introduction," http://www.coins.nd.edu/ColCoin/ColCoinIntros/Brasher.intro.html

Peter Eisenstadt

Brasher doubloon, 1787.

Brazilians. Although the 23 Jewish refugees from Dutch Brazil who arrived in New Amsterdam in 1654—marking the beginning of Jewish settlement in North America—were likely the first immigrants from Brazil to come to what would become New York State, there was little sustained Brazilian presence until the 20th century. Beginning in the 1920s scattered populations of Brazilians were present in the United States, and by the middle to late 1960s small Brazilian enclaves formed in New York City and the Catskill Mountain region. Some of the first Brazilian immigrants of the 1960s came from Governador Valadares, a city of 230,000 in the state of Minas Gerais in south-central Brazil. Immigrants from Minas Gerais dominated New York State's Brazilian communities until the 1980s. During the 1970s and early 1980s the rate of emigration from Brazil began to increase, then soared in the mid-1980s. Brazilians fled economic problems in their homeland: low wages, underemployment, a high cost of living, and until 1994 runaway inflation. During the first major wave of immigration in the mid-1980s, men accounted for 70% of the immigrant population. Most were young and single between the ages of 20 and 40 with few over 50. Children were only a small segment of this population, and most of the immigrants were at least nominally Roman Catholic.

The immigration profile changed in the 1990s with Brazilians from Rio de Janeiro, São Paulo, and other cities in the southern part of the country also moving to New York State, though natives of Governador Valadares still made up a major segment of the Brazilian community in the Catskills. During the 1990s men only slightly outnumbered women, and the greater presence of children reflected the growing number of older, married immigrants. Also, increasing numbers belonged to various Protestant denominations, especially evangelical churches such as Assembly of God. These later immigrants, like earlier ones, largely found employment in the low-wage service sector of the economy. In New York City they worked in restaurants and as household servants, street vendors, and shoeshiners. In the suburbs they performed landscaping and unskilled construction work, and in the Catskills they filled jobs as waiters and chambermaids in the region's resorts. But some, resident in the state for several years, moved on to white-collar and professional positions.

The large number of undocumented immigrants makes it difficult to estimate population size. The 2000 US Census counted only 22,265 Brazilians in New York State, but that year Brazil's Ministry of Foreign Relations estimated that 300,000 Brazilians were living in its New York consular district, which covers New York, New Jersey, Connecticut, Pennsylvania, and Delaware. This second figure suggests that the largest concentration of Brazilians in the United States, close to 40% of the total, lived in the greater New York City metropolitan area. By 2000 the state's Brazilian population was concentrated in New York City, particularly in the Astoria and Long Island City sections of Queens and in several surrounding suburbs, including White Plains, New Rochelle, Mount Vernon, Port Chester, and Mineola. A few thousand Brazilians resided in the Catskill Mountain resort villages of Ellenville (Ulster Co) and Monticello (Sullivan Co).

At the beginning of the 21st century, Brazilians represented a recent migration stream into New York State. Since some were undocumented and few had become citizens, with many planning on returning to Brazil, they did not yet wield political or economic power in the state. Sometimes called an invisible minority, New York's Portuguese-speaking Brazilians are often confused with Spanish-speaking Hispanics. Brazilian immigrants did not create distinctive neighborhoods. Even the Manhattan block of West 46th St between 5th Ave and Avenue of the Americas, containing several Brazilian-owned businesses and dubbed "Little Brazil" by Mayor Rudolph Giuliani in 1996, was little known as such.

Margolis, Maxine L. *An Invisible Minority: Brazilian Immigrants in New York City.* New Immigrants Series, ser ed. Nancy Foner (Boston, Mass: Allyn & Bacon, 1998)

———. *Little Brazil: An Ethnography of Brazilian Immigrants in New York City* (Princeton, NJ: Princeton Univ Press, 1994)

Maxine L. Margolis

Breitel, Charles D(avid) (*b* New York City, 12 Dec 1908; *d* New York City, 1 Dec 1991). Jurist. Breitel received his BA from the University of Michigan (1929) and his law degree from Columbia (1932). A Republican, he had a long association with Thomas E. Dewey, serving under him as an attorney from 1935 to 1937, aiding Special Prosecutor Dewey's rackets investigation. After Dewey was elected as governor of New York State, Breitel was appointed as counsel to the governor (1943–50). In this position he was influential in persuading Dewey to enact legislation in 1948 to ban religious and racial discrimination in the state's private colleges and to create the SUNY system. Two years later Breitel was appointed to the New York State Supreme Court. He was elected a justice on the Court of Appeals, the state's highest court, in 1967, serving as chief judge from 1974 to 1978. There he was most noted for his 1972 decision that upheld the state's liberal abortion law and five years later for his opinion that sustained landmark status for Grand Central Terminal in Manhattan. From 1978 to 1985 he was a partner at Proskauer, Rose, Goetz, and Mendelsohn, a New York City law firm.

Smith, Richard Norton. *Thomas E. Dewey and His Times* (New York: Simon & Schuster, 1982)

Mitchell C. Newton-Matza

Brentwood. Locality (pop 53,917) in Islip (Suffolk Co). Located in the pine barrens in the center of Long Island, it was founded in 1851 as Modern Times, a utopian settlement. Never larger than 150 people, Modern Times began to fail during the 1857 financial panic and ended in 1864, when the area was renamed Brentwood. It acquired a railroad station in 1869 and a post office in 1870. A pine forest created by a private owner became the site of the Austral Hotel in 1888; in the same year building lots were platted. The hotel became the motherhouse, novitiate, and academy of the Sisters of St. Joseph of Brentwood in 1896. Pilgrim State Hospital (1930) grew into the world's largest mental facility, housing 13,875 patients in 1954. Skillcraft Corp began building Cape Cod houses in 1949, and with extensive development Brentwood's 1950 population of 2,803 underwent a 20-fold increase by 2000. It is the site of a campus of Suffolk County Community College. In 2000 Brentwood's population was 18.1% black, and 54.3% of residents claimed Latino ethnicity.

Joan Ryan, CSJ

brewing. See BEER AND BREWING.

Brewster. Village (pop 2,162) in SE Putnam Co. In 1848 Walter and James Brewster began development in anticipation of a station on the Harlem Railroad (1849) that became the depot for local factories producing hats, shoes, and paper. Brewster was home to a Borden Condensed Milk Co plant from 1864 to 1918. Iron was mined from 1806 to *ca* 1900. Brewster was the home base of Howes' Circus (1828–70). The village incorporated in 1894. After I-84 and

I-684 were completed in 1967, bypassing the village, shopping centers sprouted on state highways nearby, and Brewster's historic downtown lost much of its retail trade. In the early 21st century Brewster struggled to revitalize, becoming home to Latino day laborers and small business owners; its population increased 38% in the 1990s.

Sallie S. Sypher

Briarcliff Manor. Village (pop 7,696) in Ossining and Mount Pleasant (Westchester Co). In the late 19th century Scarborough hamlet attracted prominent New Yorkers who built mansions overlooking the Hudson River. Beginning in 1890 retired carpet manufacturer Walter W. Law built Briarcliff Farms near Whitson's Corners as a model dairy farm and school of practical agriculture and horticulture. After settling employees on the farm, Law arranged to incorporate it as the Village of Briarcliff Manor in 1902 and built a grand hotel, Briarcliff Lodge. The village annexed Scarborough in 1906. Development, stimulated by the Hudson River Railroad (1849, at Scarborough) and the Taconic State Parkway (1932), accelerated after World War II. Briarcliff Lodge became the evangelical The King's College (1955–94), and Briarcliff College educated upper-class women from 1904 to 1977, when it became a facility of Pace University. Briarcliff Manor is an affluent residential community. Philips Electronics operates a research laboratory in the village.

Scott C. Monje

brick industry. Bricks were made at least as early as 1630 near Beverwijck [now Albany] for local use, and Manhattan had a brickyard in operation between 1647 and 1664. In the first half of the 19th century, where the essential ingredients of clay and sand were available, rural homesteads were sometimes built with bricks made on site, while larger brickyards operated in scattered urban areas across New York State. From approximately 1820 to 1960 brickmaking as an industry for wider markets was concentrated in several small cities and villages along a 120 mi (193 km) stretch of the Hudson River between Haverstraw (Rockland Co) and Albany. This industry produced the world's largest yearly output of bricks in the first decade of the 20th century, with 131 sites producing 1.3 billion bricks annually in the peak years 1905 and 1906. Hudson Valley yards specialized in molded "common" bricks used for inner walls, as opposed to "face" bricks used for exteriors. Brickyards of Rockland and Westchester Cos clustered around Haverstraw and dominated production until the late 19th century. Brickyards further north clustered around Kingston (Ulster Co), Newburgh (Orange Co), and Beacon (Dutchess Co), and took the lead in production in the early 20th century. Brickmaking was concentrated in these areas because of abundant clay and sand, a large immigrant labor force, and the Hudson River itself, which offered transport to the largest market for bricks, New York City. Smaller markets included the Midwest and New England, also accessed by water. New York City's demand for bricks began with a need for fireproof building material after the Great Fire of 1835, a demand that grew as population and services expanded between 1880 and 1920. Bricks were used for residential and business structures, and for subway, sewer, and water tunnels, and sidewalks, too.

Brickmaking was labor intensive, done mostly by hand up through its early 20th-century heyday. Clay was dug by hand, machines mixed the ingredients and molded the bricks, and the blocks were dried. Handwork resumed with stacking to make a kiln, firing the kiln, unstacking to load wheelbarrows, and filling boats one load at a time. Because clay excavation was precluded by ground freezing, production was limited to late spring, summer, and early autumn. The Hudson River yards, on average, employed 66 people in the early 20th century, although in 1913 the Washburn Brickyard in Glasco (Ulster Co) employed 232 and the Rose Brickyard in Roseton (Orange Co) 226. Wages were comparable to other industrial work and improved when the entire Hudson Valley brick industry unionized in 1938 (some yards had unionized earlier). The workforce was mainly European immigrants—Irish, German, Italian, Polish, and Hungarian—and southern Blacks. Most yards provided year-round company housing for workers and extended credit at the company store. The community of Roseton was created by brickyard owner John Rose at the turn of the 20th century specifically for his brickworkers and included a schoolhouse and commons building with club rooms, a reading room, and billiards. Children carried breakfast and lunch pails to workers for small pay.

The Hudson Valley brick industry declined soon after its zenith years. The number of yards dropped 60% to 53 in 1925 and to 12 in 1945. Major causes were the rise in preference for concrete during the 1920s and in the 1940s competition from southern brickyards that had higher-quality clay and more months each year for production. The longest-running New York State brickyard (115 years), Hutton in Kingston, closed in 1980. That left just one in the state still operating, Powell and Minnock at Coeymans (Albany Co), which stopped making bricks in 2001 but continued to crush and sell existing flawed bricks for landscaping.

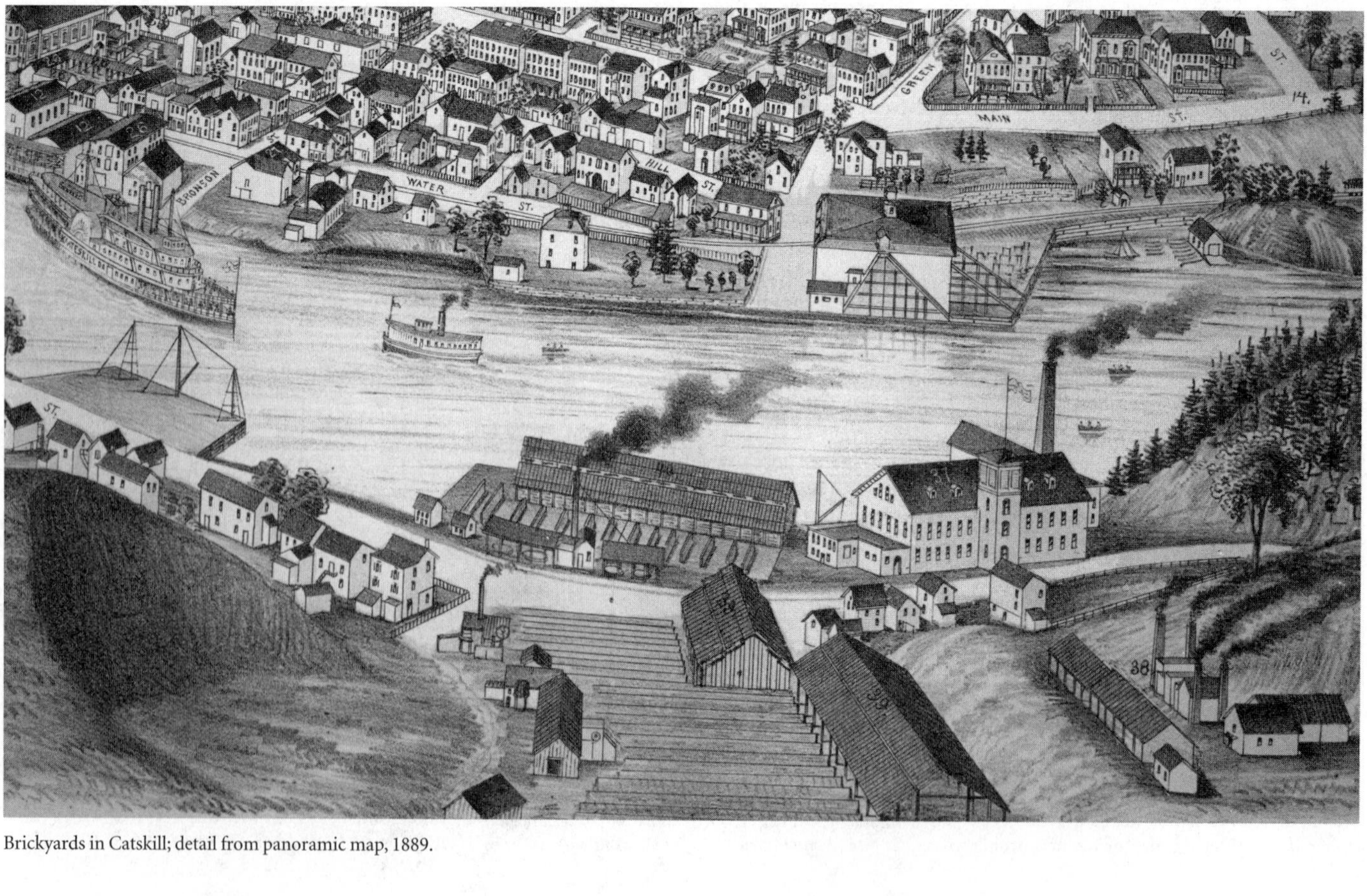

Brickyards in Catskill; detail from panoramic map, 1889.

deNoyelles, Daniel. *Within These Gates* (Haverstraw, NY: Author, 1982)
Hall, Charles E. "The Story of Brick," *Building Trades Employers Association Bulletin* (July 1905)
Hutton, George V. *The Great Hudson River Brick Industry* (Fleischmanns, NY: Purple Mountain Press, 2003)
O'Connor, Richard P. "The History of Brickmaking in the Hudson Valley" (PhD diss, Univ of Pennsylvania, 1987)
Serravallo, Vincent. "Why Working Class Parents Inspire: Class Culture and Socialization for Mobility Over Three Generations" (PhD diss, City Univ of New York, 1994)

Vincent Serravallo

Bridge Authority, New York State. Public benefit corporation that operates five toll bridges in the mid-Hudson Valley region. New York State Bridge Authority (NYSBA) was created in 1932, making it the third oldest public authority in the state, when Gov Franklin D. Roosevelt signed legislation creating an authority to finance and build Rip Van Winkle Bridge over the Hudson River between Hudson (Columbia Co) and Catskill (Greene Co). Initial financing for the $2.4 million project came from toll revenue bonds purchased by the federal Reconstruction Finance Corp; the cantilevered bridge with suspended deck trusses opened in July 1935. Prior to the opening of the Rip Van Winkle Bridge, NYSBA had also assumed ownership of the Mid-Hudson Bridge (Franklin D. Roosevelt Bridge) (1930), a $5.9 million wire cable suspension bridge constructed by the State Department of Public Works to connect Poughkeepsie and Highland (Ulster Co).

In September 1940 NYSBA purchased Bear Mountain Bridge (1924) from Bear Mountain–Hudson River Bridge Co; this suspension bridge of parallel wire cables connected Peekskill (Westchester Co) and the Rockland-Orange Cos border. Built at a cost of $2.9 million, it was the first Hudson River crossing south of Albany and north of New York City and, briefly, the longest suspension bridge in the world. In May 1946, at the behest of the state legislature, NYSBA took over the Kingston-Rhinecliff Ferry, a privately owned ferry service in operation for 190 years until December 1942. In July 1954 construction began on the Kingston-Rhinecliff Bridge (since 1999, George Clinton Kingston–Rhinecliff Bridge); this continuous under-deck truss bridge, built at a cost of $17.5 million, opened in February 1957.

In 1956 NYSBA took over the Newburgh-Beacon ferry service. Newburgh-Beacon Bridge opened in 1963, replacing a 220-year-old ferry route. During the 1970s, in response to growing congestion on Newburgh-Beacon, construction began on a second bridge just south of the original $19.5 million articulated-deck truss structure. The Federal Interstate Highway Trust Fund paid 90% of the $94 million construction cost of the second bridge, also called Newburgh-Beacon, which opened in November 1980; the original Newburgh-Beacon then closed for three and a half years so that it could be widened; it now carries I-84 across the Hudson River.

Governance of NYSBA is vested in its five-member Board of Commissioners. Members, who must reside in the counties served by the authority, are appointed by the governor and serve without compensation for five-year terms. The board appoints an executive director to manage day-to-day operations. The Civil Service Employees Association, Local 50 represents NYSBA's employees. In 1999 the NYSBA board approved the Bridges for the 21st Century Program, a five-year, $121 million capital improvement program. In 2001 NYSBA's five bridges carried 55,849,012 vehicles. Toll revenue from the bridges in 2001 was $37,358,311. NYSBA headquarters is in Highlands (Orange Co).

Moffett, Glendon L. *To Poughkeepsie and Back: The Story of the Poughkeepsie-Highland Ferry* (Fleischmanns, NY: Purple Mountain Press, 1994)

Jeffrey Kraus

bridge companies. Beginning the late 1700s, bridges were needed in New York State as company after company built turnpikes and private toll bridges. After the Civil War, with an increased availability of iron, bridge building entered a new era. A number of small companies were established in New York State, all relying on the railroads to transport iron produced in western Pennsylvania to job sites. Chief among them was the Groton Iron Bridge Co (Tompkins Co), incorporated in 1877 and one of the largest bridge builders in the state during the 1880s. Bought by J. P. Morgan's American Bridge Co in 1899, it continued operating under the Groton name until at least 1920. In 1901 400 people worked in its Groton plants.

Other notable companies included the Leighton Bridge and Iron Works and Alden and Lassig Bridge Works, both in Rochester. John Alden, chief engineer for Leighton, formed a partnership with Moritz Lassig of Chicago in 1881. The partnership crumbled four years later, with Alden retaining control of the company's Rochester division and changing its name to Rochester Bridge and Iron Works in 1886. In 1889 that enterprise engaged in its most notable project, construction of the Seneca Park Bridge spanning the Genesee River Gorge in Rochester, but by the end of the 19th century the firm had sold out to American Bridge Co. In New York City Nathaniel Rider organized the Iron Bridge Co in 1848, but in 1850, after Rider's death, its name changed to the New York Iron Bridge Co. The company competed for the contract to build the Brooklyn Bridge but lost to the New York Bridge Co founded by J. W. Shipman. Bridge companies in Albany included the Hilton Bridge Co and later the Albany Iron and Machine Works, which functioned under three separate owners between 1866 and 1882. Competition between companies was fierce, and failures, mergers, and buyouts were frequent in the late 19th century. By the turn of the 20th century, the American Bridge Co had purchased many smaller regional companies, and the age of the small, independent bridge-building firm drew to a close.

Darnell, Victor. *A Directory of American Bridge-Building Companies, 1840–1900* (Washington, DC: Society for Industrial Archeology, 1984)

Frank E. Griggs Jr

bridges and tunnels. New York State's excellent transportation system unified the state and provided access to the Great Lakes and midwestern markets. Numerous streams and varied terrain were obstacles that engineers who built the turnpikes, canals, railroads, highways, and subways had to overcome. Thousands of such structures, built by some of the world's greatest engineers, were thrust across the state's major rivers—Hudson, East, Harlem, Delaware, Genesee, Susquehanna, St. Lawrence, and Niagara—and their tributaries. Many of the engineers trained in the state's own civil engineering schools.

STONE, WOOD, IRON, AND STEEL

The oldest surviving bridges are stone bridges on old turnpikes. For example, a late 18th-century, four-span bridge of stone arches carried the Susquehanna Turnpike over Catskill Creek at Leeds (Greene Co) and still carries Greene Co Rte 23B. Some 24 wooden covered bridges survive in the state. The longest—with a span of 210 feet (64 m)—is the bridge across Schoharie Creek (1855) at North Blenheim (Schoharie Co). Closed to traffic since 1931, it was named both a national and civil engineering historic landmark in 1983. In addition to the bridges carrying roads and railroads over canals, canals required water-bearing bridges or aqueducts to cross other waterways. At the beginning of the 21st century, the remains of the Erie Canal's 624 ft (190.2 m) Schoharie Aqueduct (1841) of 14 stone arches are on view at the Schoharie Crossing State Historic Site at Fort Hunter (Montgomery Co). Rochester's aqueduct (1842) was later used by trolley cars of the Rochester subway and still carries Broad St across the Genesee River. The Delaware Aqueduct (John Roebling, engineer, 1849), built to carry the Delaware and Hudson Canal across the Delaware River at Minisink Ford (Sullivan Co), is a four-span, 535 ft (163.1 m) suspension bridge and was restored for automobile use by the National Park Service in 1983. It is the oldest surviving wire suspension bridge as well as the oldest surviving Roebling bridge in the United States.

In 1841 Squire Whipple patented the first scientifically designed iron-truss bridge and six years later wrote the first authoritative American treatise on bridge design. Many bridges of Whipple design were built over the Erie Canal; a restored Whipple bowstring truss carries a footpath over a stream on the Union College campus in Schenectady. Numerous ornamental bridges adorn the state's parks and parkways. Of the three dozen stone and iron bridges in New York City's Central Park, the beautiful Bow Bridge (Vaux and Mould, 1862) ranks as one of the oldest cast-iron bridges in the nation. Three very different bridges cross the Ausable River at Keeseville (Clinton and Essex Cos): a 110 ft (33.5 m) stone arch (1843), a two-span, 214 ft (65.2 m) wrought-iron truss (1878), and a 240 ft (73.2 m) pedestrian suspension bridge (1888). All three were designated Civil Engineering Landmarks in 1987.

INTERNATIONAL BRIDGES

The challenge of spanning the international boundary at the Niagara River gorge attracted the world's foremost engineers, beginning with Roebling, who built the 821 ft (250.2 m) Niagara Railway Suspension Bridge in 1855. Four bridges span the gorge early in the 21st century. From south to north, they are Waddell and Hardesty's 950 ft (289.6 m) steel-arch Rainbow Bridge of 1941; William Perry Taylor's and H. Ibsen's 640 ft (195.1 m) steel Michigan Central Arch Bridge of 1925, a railway bridge; Leffert L. Buck's 550 ft (169.6 m) steel-arch Whirlpool Rapids Bridge, which replaced Roebling's bridge in 1897; and

Hardesty and Hanover's 1,000 ft (304.8 m) steel-arch Lewiston-Queenston Bridge of 1962. In 1992 the American Society of Civil Engineers collectively designated these bridges as an International Civil Engineering Landmark. Two additional bridges cross Niagara River at Buffalo: the 3,651 ft (1,112.8 m) multiple-span truss International Railroad Bridge (1873) and the Peace Bridge (1927), a 5,800 ft (1,767.8 m) vehicular bridge of one truss and five steel-arch spans. At the beginning of the 21st century, a proposed replacement for Peace Bridge is embroiled in controversy.

Three St. Lawrence River bridges link New York State and Canada. Thousand Islands International Bridge (Robinson and Steinman, 1938) near Alexandria Bay (Jefferson Co) is an 8.5 mi (13.68 km) island-hopping, multiple-span crossing that includes two suspension spans—an 800 ft (243.8 m) American span and a 750 ft (228.6 m) Canadian span—and extends I-81 into Ontario. The 1,150 ft (350.5 m) suspension span of the Ogdensburg-Prescott International Bridge (1961) connects Ogdensburg (St. Lawrence Co) and Prescott, Ont. The Three Nations Bridge Crossing (1960), known as Seaway International Bridge prior to 1 Jan 2000, is a suspension bridge and three-span continuous truss that connects Rooseveltown (St. Lawrence Co) and Cornwall, Ont.

Hudson River Bridges

Until 1867 ferries provided the only transportation across the Hudson River. That year a railroad bridge at Albany completed a continuous railroad route between New York City and Albany, supplanting the Erie Canal as the state's principal transportation artery. At the outset of the 21st century, ten bridges and five tunnels penetrate the Hudson barrier south of Albany, facilitating movement of people and goods. Of these crossings, the first built was the 6,767 ft (2,062.6 m) Poughkeepsie Railroad Bridge (1888), a multiple-span, cantilever-truss bridge and the largest railroad bridge in the United States at the time of its construction, connecting New England railroads with the South and West. Though closed since a 1974 fire, an environmental group hopes to reopen the bridge as a recreational walkway.

The Hudson's first highway crossing to the south of Albany (US 6) was Bear Mountain Bridge (Howard C. Baird, engineer, 1924), a 1,632 ft (497.9 m) suspension span that ranked as the world's longest for two years. The 1 mi (1.6 km) multiple-span truss Alfred H. Smith Memorial Railroad Bridge (1924) at Castleton (Rensselaer Co), named for a New York Central Railroad president, eased freight train congestion around Albany. It has a 600 ft (182.9 m) main span and is the only 21st-century rail freight crossing south of the state capital, necessitating a 200 mi (321.9 km) detour for freight trains traveling between New Jersey and New York City. Mid-Hudson or Franklin D. Roosevelt Bridge (Modjeski and Moran, engineers, 1930) at Poughkeepsie is a 1,500 ft (457.2 m) suspension span. The George Washington Bridge (Othmar H. Ammann, engineer, 1931), connecting Manhattan with Fort Lee, NJ, doubled the suspension span record to 3,500 feet (1,066.8 m). Rip Van Winkle Bridge (Frederick S. Greene, engineer, 1935) between Hudson (Columbia Co) and Catskill (Greene Co) is a 5,041 ft (1,536.5 m) long 13-span cantilever, with a main span of 800 feet (243.8 m). The 3 mi (4.8 km) Gov Malcolm Wilson Tappan Zee Bridge (Madigan-Hyland, engineers, 1955), with a 1,212 ft (369.4 m) cantilever main span, crosses the Hudson at its widest point. Kingston-Rhinecliff Bridge (David B. Steinman, engineer, 1957) is a continuous truss with an 800 ft (243.8 m) main span. The 5,330 ft (1,624.6 m) Castleton-on-Hudson multiple-span cantilever bridge (Madigan-Hyland, engineers, 1959) adjacent to the Castleton railroad bridge carries NYS Thruway's Berkshire Spur connecting the Thruway and the Massachusetts Turnpike. The 7,800 ft (2,377.4 m) parallel trusses, with a 1,000 ft (304.8 m) main span, of Beacon-Newburgh Bridge (Modjeski and Masters, engineers, 1963 and 1980) carry I-84 connecting New England and Pennsylvania. From Albany north, numerous smaller bridges crossing the Hudson are community assets. For example, Troy (Rensselaer Co) is improving six bridge approaches, largely through landscaping, to enhance its waterfront.

New York City Bridges and Tunnels

The numerous waterways that divide New York City once inhibited travel and the flow of commerce. Until replaced by bridges and tunnels, dozens of ferries plied these waterways. The promise of better transportation through bridges and subways led to the consolidation of the five boroughs as one greater city in 1898. At the beginning of the 21st century, there are over 2,000 bridges in the city, 76 over water. From 1693 to 1917 King's Bridge connected Manhattan and lower Westchester Co [now Bronx Co], giving the Kingsbridge section of the Bronx its name. The city's oldest bridge is the landmark multiple-span, stone High Bridge (John B. Jervis, engineer, 1848) of Roman arches, built to carry Croton Aqueduct across the Harlem River to Manhattan. During the great era of waterway bridge construction in the city, 1883–1910, 23 significant bridges were built. John and Washington Roebling's Brooklyn Bridge (1883) across the East River, boasting a 1,596 ft (486.5 m) suspension span, was the wonder of its day. Williamsburg Bridge (Buck, engineer, 1903), connecting Delancey St in Manhattan and Brooklyn, was the first major bridge to employ steel towers; it exceeded Roeblings' span by 4.5 feet (1.37 m) and remained the world's longest bridge for 21 years until surpassed by Bear Mountain Bridge. The 1,470 ft (448.1 m) suspension span of Manhattan Bridge (O. H. Nichols and Leon Moisseiff, engineers, 1909) at Canal St carries four subway tracks. The cantilever Queensboro, or 59th St, Bridge (Gustav Lindenthal, engineer, 1909), with a 1,182 ft (360.3 m) main span, opened the cornfields of Queens to development. Lindenthal also built Hell Gate Bridge (1917), which at 977 feet (297.8 m) between hinges was the longest steel arch until 1931 and is now a vital link in Amtrak's high-speed Northeast corridor.

The region was further unified by six Othmar H. Ammann bridges: George Washington (1931), at 3,500 feet (1,066.8 m) the world's longest suspension span for 6 years; Bayonne (1931), at 1,675 feet (510.5 m) the world's longest steel arch for 46 years; 3.5 mi (5.63 km) long Triborough (1936), which boasts a 1,380 ft (420.6 m) suspension span and a 310 ft (94.5 m) lift span; Bronx-Whitestone (1939), a 2,300 ft (701 m) suspension span; Throgs Neck (1961), a 1,800 ft (548.6 m) suspension span; and Verrazano-Narrows (1964), the world's longest suspension span at 4,260 ft (1,298.5 m) for 17 years. Harlem River has 15 bridges, 7 of which are movable swing bridges, probably the largest collection of swing bridges in the world. Four bridges link Staten Island with New Jersey: Goethals (Waddell and Hardesty, engineers, 1928), a cantilever truss with a 672 ft (204.8 m) main span; Outerbridge Crossing (Waddell and Hardesty, 1928), a cantilever truss with a 750 ft (228.6 m) main span; Bayonne; and Arthur Kill Railroad Bridge (Parsons Brinckerhoff, engineers, 1959) with the world's longest vertical lift span at 558 ft (170.1 m). Outerbridge Crossing, named after Eugenius H. Outerbridge, first chairman of the Port Authority of New York and New Jersey, is in fact the city's outermost bridge.

New York City projects advanced the art of tunnel building, with 22 subaqueous vehicular and rail tunnels unifying the city. Construction of the nation's first underwater tunnel, under the North, or Hudson, River, began in 1874, but because of construction and financial difficulties, the tunnel (now the uptown PATH tunnel) was not completed until 1908. A companion tunnel to Lower Manhattan was added in 1909. Pennsylvania Railroad built two tubes under North River and four under East River to access Penn Station (1910). New York City's subway system, built largely between 1900 and 1940, contains 14 underwater tunnels. While most were built by the shield method, the Lexington Ave subway tunnel (1918) under the Harlem River was one of the first constructed by the immersed-tube method, as was the 63d St subway tunnel (1989). Some of the world's greatest tunnel engineers, Clifford M. Holland and Ole Singstad, among others, developed their skills building the city's subway tunnels. Holland, with his assistant Singstad, developed the mechanical ventilation system still used in road tunnels. After Holland's premature death, Holland Tunnel (1927) was named in his honor. Singstad went on to build Queens-Midtown Tunnel (1940) and Brooklyn-Battery Tunnel (1950). At 9,117 feet (2,778.9 m) Brooklyn-Battery is the longest underwater highway tunnel in the nation. The Port Authority of New York and New Jersey under Ammann and Ralph Smillie built three-tube Lincoln Tunnel (1937, 1945, 1957), the world's busiest vehicular tunnel.

The Future

At the beginning of the 21st century, there are nearly 20,000 bridges in the state. Environmental and traffic concerns make construction of large new bridges unlikely. Instead there is emphasis on bringing older bridges into good repair, replacing obsolete spans, preserving historic bridges, and introducing new technology. Studies are under way to evaluate possible replacement of bridges such as Tappan Zee, Batchellerville (Saratoga Co) over Great Sacandaga Lake, and the Peace Bridge, with plans for a Long Island Sound bridge dormant. The rehabilitation of Williamsburg Bridge may be the most expensive such repair in the history of any state or nation. In 1998 the state built two innovative "channel bridges," composed of precast concrete segments, in Dutchess and Orange Cos, and in 2000 a cable-stayed pedestrian bridge was completed over East 63d St in New York City.

Pedestrians crossing the Brooklyn Bridge, *ca* 1891.

Prospects for new tunnels are more promising, with several large projects under consideration for the New York metropolitan area, including a new Hudson River rail tunnel.

Petroski, Henry. *Engineers of Dreams: Great Bridge Builders and the Spanning of America* (New York: Knopf, 1995)
Plowden, David. *Bridges: The Spans of North America* (New York: Norton, 1974)
Rastorfer, Darl. *Six Bridges: The Legacy of Othmar H. Ammann* (New Haven, Conn: Yale Univ Press, 2000)
Reier, Sharon. *The Bridges of New York* (1977; repr Mineola, NY: Dover, 2000)

Robert A. Olmsted

bridges of the Niagara Gorge. Between the falls of Niagara and Lake Ontario, four international bridges span the gorge of the Niagara River, which separates the Province of Ontario, Canada, and Niagara Co. From south to north these bridges are the Rainbow Bridge (1941), the Michigan Central Arch Bridge (1925), the Whirlpool Rapids or Lower Steel Arch Bridge (1897), and the Lewiston-Queenston Bridge (1962).

The steel arch Rainbow Bridge is approximately 550 feet (168 m) downstream of the 1898 Falls View or Upper Steel Arch Bridge (also known as the Honeymoon Bridge) that was destroyed by an ice jam on the river in 1938. The 1898 bridge had replaced the Niagara Falls and Clifton, or Upper Suspension Bridge, of 1869. The Rainbow Bridge has a span of 950 feet (289.6 m), carrying highway traffic 200 feet (61 m) above the level of the river approximately 1,500 feet (457 m) downstream of the American Falls. Construction began 4 May 1940, and the bridge opened for traffic 1 Nov 1941. The bridge was designed by the Edward P. Lupfer Corp of Buffalo.

The Michigan Central Arch Bridge replaced the Canada Southern or Michigan Central Cantilever Bridge of 1883, located approximately 50–100 feet (15–30 m) upstream. This steel arch railroad bridge has a span of 640 feet (195.1 m) and is located about 1.75 miles (2.8 km) below the American Falls. Work on the bridge started in 1924, and it was opened to rail traffic 21 Feb 1925. William Perry Taylor designed the bridge, H. Ibsen enhanced the design, and J. L. Delming, chief engineer of the Michigan Central Railroad supervised construction. Rail operations on this bridge ceased in 2002. Proposals have been made to convert it into a highway bridge exclusively for trucks to alleviate traffic at the other highway crossings.

Just north of the Michigan Central Arch Bridge, the Whirlpool Rapids Bridge, designed by Leffert L. Buck of Canton (St. Lawrence Co), was the first arch bridge to span the Niagara Gorge. This bridge was built directly beneath John Roebling's 1855 Niagara Railway Suspension Bridge. Roebling's bridge was the permanent replacement for Charles Ellet Jr's temporary 1848 Niagara Suspension Bridge, also at this location. Work commenced 9 Apr 1896 and when completed, 27 Aug 1897, the portions of Roebling's Niagara Bridge not used in construction of the new bridge were removed. The bridge was officially opened in September 1897. The double-deck structure is 550 feet (167.6 m) in length and carries rail traffic above and highway traffic below.

Connecting the Villages of Lewiston (Niagara Co) and Queenston, Ont, the Lewiston-Queenston steel arch highway bridge is about .7 mile (1.1 km) upstream from the bridge it replaced, the 1899 Lewiston and Queenston Suspension Bridge. The 1899 bridge was built to carry trolley cars across the gorge at the site of the Lewiston and Queenston Suspension Bridge of 1851, which had been destroyed in a gale in 1864. The third Lewiston-Queenston Bridge was designed by engineers from Hardesty and Hanover, the successor firm to Waddell and Hardesty, consultants on the Rainbow Bridge. Construction began 2 Nov 1960, and the bridge opened 1 Nov 1962. The $16 million bridge has a deck length of 1,600 feet (487.7 m) and is 370 feet (112.8 m) above the river. The bridge's 1,000 ft (304.8 m) span made it, at the time of its construction, the world's longest fixed-end steel arch bridge. Most truck traffic crossing the Niagara Gorge uses this bridge.

The Rainbow, Lewiston-Queenston, and Whirlpool Rapids Bridges are owned and maintained by the Niagara Falls Bridge Commission, an agency formed in 1938 and composed of commissioners from the United States and Canada. The only purely railroad bridge, the Michigan Central Arch Bridge, is owned and maintained by the Canadian Pacific Railway.

Greenhill, Ralph. *Spanning Niagara: The International Bridges, 1848–1962* (Lewiston, NY: Niagara Univ, 1984; distributed by Univ of Washington Press)
Seibel, George A. *Bridges over the Niagara Gorge; Rainbow Bridge, 50 Years, 1941–1991* (Niagara Falls, Ont: Niagara Falls Bridge Commission, 1991)

Paul J. Bartczak

Bridgewater. Town (pop 1,671) and village (pop 579) in SE Oneida Co. Settled in 1789 the town was formed from Sangerfield in 1797. The land consists of a rugged plateau in the west, hills in the east, and a fertile valley, Bridgewater Flats, between them. The Cherry Valley Turnpike (1810) gave a start to the village, which incorporated in 1825. Hops were grown extensively, and an unusual round cobblestone hop kiln still stands on Rte 8. The Utica, Chenango and Susquehanna Valley Railroad (1869) served the town; the Unadilla Valley Railroad (1895–1959) from Sidney (Delaware Co) terminated in the village. Hop culture was succeeded by dairying and the cultivation of grains, beans, and potatoes. In 2002 Bridgewater remains a farming town, due largely to the vast Curtin Bros dairy farm, which milks 2,000 cows and plants 2,000 acres (809 ha) in corn. Most residents commute to Utica for work. Everett Holmes, elected village mayor in 1973, is believed to have been the first black mayor in the state. Bridgewater was the childhood home of Stephen Moulton Babcock (1843–1931), whose invention of the Babcock butterfat test (1890) revolutionized the dairy industry by discouraging adulteration and encouraging pricing based on content.

Brigham, Amariah (*b* New Marlborough, Mass, 26 Dec 1798; *d* Utica, 8 Sept 1849). Physician. Orphaned at age 11, he was adopted by Origin Brigham, his physician uncle who lived in Schoharie (Schoharie Co). Between 1812 and 1821 he apprenticed with his uncle and two other physicians, Edmund C. Peet in New Marlborough, Mass, and Ovid Plumb in Canaan, Conn. During this time he also visited hospitals and attended medical classes in Europe. He practiced medicine first in Enfield and Greenfield, Mass, then in Hartford, Conn (1831–40). Brigham lectured at the New York College of Physicians and Surgeons (1837–38) and was superintendent of the Hartford Retreat (1840–42). He served as the first superintendent of the New York State Lunatic Asylum (1842–48) at Utica, which opened on 16 Jan 1843. His goal was to create a model institution of humane, patient-centered care. Brigham argued that insane asylums should be therapeutic, not custodial. To promote his views he founded the *American Journal of Insanity* (now the *American Journal of Psychiatry*) in 1844.

Bell, Leland V. "Brigham, Amariah." In *Dictionary of American Medical Biography,* 93 (Westport, Conn: Greenwood, 1984)

Eric v. d. Luft

Brighton. Town (pop 1,682) in SE Franklin Co. Settled by 1815, the town was formed from Duane in 1858. Paul (Apollos A.) Smith (1825–1912) arrived in 1859 and built a hotel; situated in a 30,000-acre (12,000 ha) private park, it expanded to accommodate 500 guests and employ 250 workers. His son transformed it into Paul Smith's College (1937). The adjacent Lower St. Regis Lake is surrounded by private camps belonging to wealthy urbanites. The town was the site of Gabriels Sanitorium (1897–1963) and Rainbow Sanitorium (1910–34), both caring for tuberculosis patients. The hamlet of Gabriels grew with railroad access in 1892 and today is the center of a significant seed-potato growing district; Camp Gabriels (1982), a minimum security prison, occupies the former Gabriels Sanitorium property.

Thomas W. Perrin

Brighton. Town (pop 35,588) in central Monroe Co. Franciscan missionaries built a chapel in the present town in 1679. Resettled in 1790, it was the site of a promising landing on Irondequoit Creek called Tryon from 1797 to 1818. The town, formed in 1814 from the old town of Smallwood, included the Village of Rochester and extended to Lake Ontario. Brighton was a canal port beginning in 1822 and a stop on the Auburn and Rochester Railroad beginning in 1840. In the 19th century it manufactured brick and tile, glue, threshers, baskets and boxes, fertilizer, gunpowder, and barrel hoops and heading. From an early date its residents engaged in truck farming, nurseries, and dairies for the Rochester market. Suburbanization began around 1900 and took off rapidly after 1930. Its 1920 population of 3,027 increased ninefold by 1960 and has since leveled off. Brighton has a large Jewish population and Monroe Co's largest Asian American population (8%). The town is part of Rochester's inner ring of suburbs, and government leaders are trying to revitalize aging retail areas while maintaining residential character. Town Supervisor Sandra Frankel (1991–) was the Democratic candidate for lieutenant governor in 1998. Since 1968 Brighton has been the site of Monroe Community College. The Stone-Tolan House (1792) is a landmark.

Carolyn Vacca

Brightwaters. Village (pop 3,248) in Islip (Suffolk Co). In 1907 Brooklyn developer Thomas Benton Ackerson (1856–1924) began buying land between the Great South Bay and the Montauk Highway, creating a planned community on 1,173 acres (475 ha), which included a 4,000 ft (1,200 m) boat canal and 100 homes, ranging from $3,500 bungalows to $20,000 mansions. A post office opened in 1912, and the village incorporated in 1916.

Joan Ryan, CSJ

Bristol. Town (pop 2,421) in SW Ontario Co. Settled in 1788, the town was formed in 1796. The hamlet of Bristol Center is noted for the "burning spring," a sulfur spring set aflame by explorer René-Robert Cavalier de la Salle in 1669. Muttonville (later Vincent) was named *ca* 1845 because of the presence of a large tallow chandlery. Later it was a center of merino sheep breeding and hop culture. The tributaries of Mud Creek contain many beautiful waterfalls. The suburbanization of Canandaigua led to a 250% increase in Bristol's population between 1960 and 2000.

Marla A. Bennett

Bristol-Myers Squibb. See PHARMACEUTICAL INDUSTRY.

Broadalbin. Town (pop 5,066) and village (pop 1,411) in E central Fulton Co. In 1761 Sir William Johnson built a retreat called Castle Cumberland on Summer House Point, now under the Great Sacandaga Lake. The town was settled *ca* 1770. It was formed from the old town of Caughnawaga in 1793 and named for Breadalbane, Scotland. Paper mills utilized the waterpower of Frenchman's Creek at Union Mills (1828–77), and a straw paper mill was located at Stevers Mills. Broadalbin Knitting Co (1884–1950), several glove factories, and a tire factory in the World War I era employed Broadalbin residents. The Fonda, Johnstown and Gloversville Railroad branchline came in 1895. The village incorporated in 1924. The creation of Great Sacandaga Lake (1930) inundated much of the town's best farmland. After World War II Ukrainian refugees settled near Union Mills and built St. Basil's Church, which is now closed. A late 20th-century employer was Korkay (chemicals, 1968), though it ceased operating around 1990. Its location was a Superfund site in 2003. Fiber Conversion Co (1906) continued to recycle textile materials in the early 21st century. Robert W. Chambers (1865–1933), author of historical romances, was a resident. The Hotel Broadalbin (1854) is a local landmark.

broadcasting (radio and television)

Origins

Public demonstrations of Samuel F. B. Morse's electromagnetic telegraph around 1838 marked a turning point in the era of instantaneous long-distance communication. Morse's wire-borne system, however, did nothing to solve the pressing problems of ship-to-shore and ship-to-ship communication. A race ensued among scientists to achieve an airborne system of telegraphy, culminating in a breakthrough by Italian physicist Guglielmo Marconi, who patented a wireless telegraph in 1896. Also known as the radiotelegraph, or radio, it could cast its signal radially, or simultaneously in all directions. There is little evidence that Marconi or any of the other scientists whose work contributed to wireless telegraphy had conceived of it as anything but a two-way communication system for military and commercial shipping.

It was not long, however, before the radio learned to talk. The Audion, invented in 1906 by Dr Lee De Forest, an Iowa-born resident of the Bronx, went beyond the dots and dashes of the Morse and Marconi telegraphs by allowing for the transmission of a range of natural sounds audible to the human ear. In 1908 De Forest's 4th Ave Radio Telephone Co began a series of experimental transmissions of voice and music. In one of history's first electronic media events, De Forest broadcast the voice of Enrico Caruso from the stage of the Metropolitan Opera House in 1910. Although De Forest would successfully defend most of his patents on legal technicalities, the authenticity of his invention was challenged because he was unable to explain how the technology worked. Many historians prefer to give credit for the invention of analog sound broadcasting to the Canadian inventor Reginald Fessenden, whose laboratory De Forest had visited in 1905.

The pivotal contribution of another New Yorker to the development of radio broadcasting is beyond dispute. In 1912 Edwin Armstrong, who was born in New York City, patented the regenerative circuit while still an undergraduate at Columbia University. His circuit allowed for a degree of signal stability that for the first time eliminated the need for headphones, a crucial step in making radio listening a user-friendly activity that could attract general audiences. In the 1930s, as a Columbia University physics professor, Armstrong developed frequency modulation (FM) broadcasting, the standard system used today for superior radio sound quality and for television audio.

A Mass Medium

Radio's life as an entertainment and information medium began among backyard inventors and amateur performers. Between 1913 and 1917 the US Bureau of Navigation, which then regulated radio, issued approximately 8,500 licenses to individual amateur operators for purposes other than maritime commerce. These hobbyists entertained each other with jokes, poems, political commentary, sermons, weather reports, music, and whatever else they could think of, earning them the old theatrical sobriquet of "hams," from which came the term ham radio.

David Sarnoff, a Russian Jewish emigrant who had grown up in the tenements of Manhattan's Lower East Side, was among the first to foresee a commercial mass market application for the improved radio sound made possible by the Armstrong circuit. In 1916 he proposed to his superiors at the Marconi Wireless Telegraph Co of America (American Marconi) in New York City that the company broadcast music at its own expense to create an incentive for the public to buy a new line of cheap receiver-only radios, which American Marconi would manufacture specifically for this purpose. These "Music Boxes" were to be "affordable home appliances . . . in the same sense as the piano or phonograph . . . to be placed on a table in the parlor or living room. . . ." The plan, however, was rejected by management. In 1920 the Westinghouse Co, a rival manufacturer, pursued the same plan by launching KDKA, a station in its hometown of Pittsburgh. The quick sale of thousands of radios at a local department store chain proved the commercial viability of selling receiver-only sets to the public, and the age of radio broadcasting began. Before the end of 1921, New York State had three radio stations. General Electric Co (GE) of Schenectady was first with WGY-Schenectady, which continues to serve the Capital District as the state's oldest broadcasting entity. The Radio Corporation of America (RCA), a corporate descendant of America Marconi, established WJY-New York. WEAF, also located in New York City, was a venture of the American Telephone and Telegraph Co (AT&T).

While GE and RCA, like Westinghouse, could recoup their broadcasting expenses and make profits from the sale of home radio sets, AT&T was a regulated utility and thus forbidden from retail manufacturing. Instead, the telephone company pursued a business it called "toll broadcasting" in which it sold time to customers on its radio station, much as it did on its long-distance telephone lines. The very first broadcast commercial, which aired on 28 Aug 1922, was a 12-minute sales pitch for a cooperative apartment development in Jackson Heights (Queens Co), for which AT&T billed the Queensboro Corp $100. As the market for home radios became saturated in the mid-1920s, all for-profit radio broadcasters in the United States accepted the sale of time to advertisers.

The Commercial Radio Broadcasting Industry

Several factors led to New York City's emergence as the national center of the new commercial radio broadcasting industry during the 1920s. As an advertising-based industry, American radio quickly became dependent on the Madison Ave agencies, which took responsibility for program content and for negotiation of program placement and billing rates. Many of the agencies built radio studios in their own office suites, where they produced both commercials and shows. Young and Rubicam and Batten, Barton, Durstine, and Osborn (BBD&O) became leading national powers in the new field of radio advertising.

In 1926 RCA announced the formation of a new subsidiary, the National Broadcasting Co (NBC), with David Sarnoff at its helm. NBC operated two radio networks, both emanating to affiliates around the country from flagship stations in New York City. Other radio networks, including the Columbia Phonograph Broadcasting System (now Columbia Broadcasting System, or CBS), in 1927 made their corporate and production homes in New York City as well. The Mutual Broadcasting System, a program-sharing cooperative of independent stations, was dominated by two stations, WOR-New York and WGN-Chicago. The majority of network radio programs from 1927 until the television era were fed live to the nation from New York City. Local radio stations ranging from 50,000 W clear-channel broadcasters to 500 W daytime-only operations sprouted up across New York State during the 1920s. In 1925 the Western New York Network was formed, linking stations WGY-Schenectady, WHAM-Rochester, WFBL-Syracuse, and WMAK-Lockport/Buffalo, for broadcasts of regional interest. Since 1948 the Rural Radio Network, headquartered in Ithaca, brought farm market news and other programs to agricultural communities, from Central New York dairy farmers to Adirondack loggers, otherwise divided geographically.

The US Department of Commerce's 1922 listings of licensed "Stations Broadcasting Market or Weather Reports, Concerts and Lectures" included nine stations assigned to New York State. By 1926 the list had grown to 39. In addition to the various electronics manufacturers that had entered the field to sell their radios, the growing list of broadcasters reflected a widening interest in the new medium. Licensees included Madison Square Garden (WMSG-New York), the People's Pulpit Association (WBBR-Rossville, Richmond Co), the Onondaga Hotel (WFBL-Syracuse), and Cornell University (WEAI-Ithaca). Wanamaker's (WWZ) and Gimbel's (WGBS) informed their customers of new products and discount sales. The Third Avenue Railway Co announced delays and service changes over its station, WEBL. In 1922 Staten Island's *Times-Dispatch* became the state's first newspaper to operate a radio station (WBAZ), and the practice soon became widespread. WBEN was founded by the *Buffalo Evening News* in 1934; in 2002 it was the oldest of such stations in the state. The *New York Times* entered the broadcasting business in 1944 when it purchased WQXR, which became the flagship of a statewide classical music and news network; in 2003 it was one of the nation's few commercially successfully classical music stations.

By the mid-1930s all of New York State's largest cities had several radio stations, including both network affiliates and independents, while most localities with populations greater than 10,000 had at least one station. Listeners in the North Country and along the shores of Lake Ontario had the added advantages of clear reception of French and English language stations from Montreal, Toronto, and other Canadian cities. In New York City some of the nation's first non-English language radio stations were started. WCDA, licensed to the Italian Education Foundation in 1925, offered a full schedule in Italian, even carrying several programs in Sicilian dialect. WEVD was licensed to the New York State Socialist Party; its call letters honored the party's five-time presidential candidate, Eugene Debs. At first the station offered mostly Yiddish language broadcasts for Jewish immigrants, but over the years it added blocks of programming in Spanish, Mandarin Chinese, and other immigrant languages. At the start of the 21st century three all-Spanish language commercial stations, including WADO, WLXE, and WSKQ, competed for the large audience of Spanish speakers living in the New York City metropolitan area.

Noncommercial Radio Broadcasting

The history of noncommercial broadcasting in New York State originates in 1924, when the Federal Communications Commission (FCC) granted licenses to the City of New York (WNYC) and the Seneca Vocational School (WSVS-Buffalo). Before 1970 almost all public broadcasting was restricted to educational institutions, with the exception of municipally owned WNYC, which was sold to the WNYC Foundation in 1995. New York State's college radio stations have been sponsored by both private institutions (eg, WAER-Syracuse University, WKCR-Columbia University) and SUNY schools (eg, WRVO-SUNY Oswego, WSUB-SUNY Buffalo). Until the late 1960s these stations provided the only alternative to commercial broadcasting in most regions of the state.

After passage of the Public Broadcasting Act of 1967, federal funds and state matching grants became available to nonprofit community foundations wishing to establish public radio and television stations. Some of the leading public radio stations that blanket the state are WAMC-Albany, WSKG-Binghamton, and WNED-Buffalo. They serve minority musical tastes with programs featuring classical, jazz, and folk music, and produce local public affairs and talk shows. Most are affiliated with National Public Radio (NPR) and carry the network's news and cultural programming. While public radio stations solicit direct financial contributions from their listeners, they also request contributions from corporate sponsors. WBAI-New York, a fully noncommercial listener-supported station founded in 1960, is an exception. The station is licensed to the Pacifica Foundation, a free speech organization.

Radio in the Age of Television

With the advent of television in the late 1940s and early 1950s, radio lost its position as New York State's (and America's) primary mass medium. The mass culture genres developed for radio during its golden age, including the soap opera, situation comedy, police and detective dramas, migrated to television as radio reshaped itself to serve niche audiences. With most New Yorkers spending an increasing amount of time in their cars, drive time became the center of commercial concern.

During the 1950s and early 1960s, some of the state's maximum-wattage amplitude modulation (AM) radio stations, such as WABC-New York and WKBW-Buffalo, enjoyed great success with top-40 music formats directed at the youth market. In the late 1960s, however, the long suppression of FM broadcasting ended. Most musical programming migrated to the FM band, where it could be broadcast static free and in two-channel stereo, while talk radio came to dominate the AM dial. Talk formats include all-news (eg, WINS-New York, WCBS-New York), call-up (WABC-New York, WROW-Albany), and all-sports (WFAN-New York, WHEN-Syracuse). Religious formats on both AM and FM were first broadcast in the state in the 1920s, but they have become an increasingly important factor in the state's radio mix since the 1980s. Some stations are operated directly by churches, such as WZXV-Rochester, a service of the Calvary Chapel of the Finger Lakes. Others, like WGKR-Grand Gorge (Delaware Co), are commercial stations offering religious-oriented entertainment formats, such as contemporary Christian music. At the start of the 21st century the great majority of the state's FM stations were commercial operations dedicated almost exclusively to the airing of demographically targeted recorded music. Reflecting national trends in all areas of American commercial media culture, the stations largely targeted homogeneous audiences segregated for advertisers by factors such as age, race, and taste.

In 2002 FCC-licensed commercial and noncommercial radio stations operating in New York State in 2002 included 169 on AM and 291 on FM, with 122 additional translator stations carrying the signals of these stations to communities beyond transmission range. Some stations have made their signals available worldwide via the Internet, a practice known as bitcasting. In addition, a new kind of audio service makes itself available only via the Internet, although a debate continues on whether this activity can be defined as radio broadcasting.

The Coming of Television

Demonstrations of television actually predate the existence of radio. In 1884 the German inventor Paul Nipkow successfully transmitted images via a spinning disk, a mechanical system that occupied the interest of researchers for decades. Advances on the Nipkow system were made by Charles Francis Jenkins, who transmitted a 10-minute film for US government officials across a distance of 5 miles (8 km) to Washington, DC, in 1925, and John Logie Baird, who offered a successful demonstration of television transmission to the Royal Academy of Science in London in 1926. AT&T invested heavily in the development of a mechanical television, as this method did not make use of any of the radio patents held by rival companies. In 1928 Herbert E. Ives of AT&T's Bell Telephone Laboratories conducted a spectacular demonstration of a system based on the Nipkow model, transmitting color images of a bouquet of roses and an American flag on a closed circuit carried by AT&T long-distance telephone lines between New York City and Washington, DC. As late as the 1940s, CBS advocated the Nipkow model specifically for its superior color transmission system.

The radio patent-holders group, composed of RCA, GE, and Westinghouse, pushed for an all-electronic system of television that would force all manufacturers to pay for patent rates, just as they did for radio. GE was one of the first companies in the world to begin television research. Its scientists successfully transmitted images as early as 1902, and by the 1920s the company had set up two of the first experimental television stations in the world. Some of the notable achievements in the development of the medium took place in Schenectady under the direction of GE engineers E. F. W. Alexanderson and Ray D. Kell. These included the first telecast of a dramatic production, *The Queen's Messenger* by J. Manners Hartley, in 1928, and the first successful public presentation of television by means of closed-circuit, big-screen projection, an event held at Proctor's Theatre in Schenectady in 1930.

RCA, headquartered in New York City, fostered the system that eventually came to dominate American and world television broadcasting, although the company did not make the original breakthrough. Philo T. Farnsworth, an independent inventor from Idaho held the patent for the iconoscope, the first tube-based, all-electronic television transmission system. Forced to pay Farnsworth for patent rights, RCA mounted research and development to elaborate on his work. Vladimir Zworykin, a Russian physicist who had immigrated to New York after the Bolshevik Revolution, headed the company's effort. In 1929 RCA demonstrated its image dissector system of electronic television to reporters and investors at the company's Manhattan headquarters. Through its NBC division, RCA established an experimental television station at Van Cortlandt Park in the Bronx in 1929, erecting a transmitter atop the Empire State Building the following year. Other New York State companies that played pioneering roles in the invention of television include Norton Laboratories of Lockport (Niagara Co), which transmitted the first television signal in Western New York in Kenmore (Erie Co), near Buffalo, in 1928; the Pilot Electric Manufacturing Co of Brooklyn, which made breakthroughs in electronic tubes, and the United Research Corp of Long Island City (Queens Co), which developed transmitting equipment.

While the nation suffered through the Great Depression of the 1930s, television research and development accelerated, fueled by the profits of radio advertising. It culminated in an unofficial presentation of the medium to the public at the 1939 New York World's Fair in Flushing Meadow Park (Queens Co). Franklin D. Roosevelt became the first US president to appear on television during the live telecast of the fair's opening ceremonies, an event that was viewed on monitors placed throughout the fairgrounds as well as on the approximately 1,000 sets in the New York City area, which were owned mostly by employees of electronic companies. Visitors to the RCA Pavilion, which was shaped like a giant electronic tube, could pass in front of a television camera and view themselves on a video monitor, a feature so popular that it was later reinstalled as a permanent tourist attraction at the company's Rockefeller Center headquarters.

In 1941 the FCC formally recognized that the experimental stage of television development had come to an end, approving uniform technical standards and issuing the first 10 commercial station licenses. Four of these went to New York State companies: RCA (WNBT), CBS (WCBS-TV), and DuMont Electronics (WABD) were assigned to New York City and GE (WRGB) to Schenectady. The nation's entry into World War II halted the general diffusion of commercial television that was ready to take place, although research in radar and other military technologies provided new advances that helped improve and refine the medium. Momentum was quickly recovered after the war. By the late 1940s the nation's three coast-to-coast radio networks, NBC, CBS, and ABC (American Broadcasting Co), all had established embryonic commercial television networks that were to be built on the model of their national radio networks. A fourth network, operated by DuMont, also took to the air. A technology company with no experience in radio broadcasting or show business, it left the air in 1955.

Post–World War II Growth

When television was introduced, there was little of the entrepreneurial experimentation that took place with radio in the 1920s. Commercial radio broadcasting had since revealed itself as a multibillion dollar industry and large corporations saw the promise of even greater profits from television, even while it was still a laboratory curiosity. RCA, as the nation's dominant communication company during the 1950s, led a fight to minimize competition in television. For example, the company favored the 12-channel VHF (very high frequency) spectrum and opposed the 69-channel UHF (ultrahigh frequency) spectrum, refusing to even build sets that could receive UHF stations until forced by Congress to do so with passage of the All-Channel Receiver Act in 1961.

As of 1948, 108 television station licenses had been granted by the FCC, with about half of the licensees operative and others in various stages of building and testing. Almost all stations were concentrated in the Northeast, the Great Lakes cities, and coastal California, with the rest of the country anxiously waiting for stations. That year, reacting to complaints of technical problems (including cross-station signal interference), the FCC imposed a freeze on new licenses until solutions could be worked out and new standards imposed. It lasted until 1952. During this four-year period, New York State led the nation with 13 commercial television stations, all operating by the end of 1950, in seven cities. They included Binghamton (WNBF, 1949), Buffalo (WBEN, 1948), New York City (WNBT, 1941; WABD 1941; WCBS, 1941; WJZ, 1948; WPIX, 1948; WOR, 1949), Rochester (WHAM, 1949), Schenectady (WRGB, 1941), Syracuse (WHEN, 1948; WSYR, 1950), and Utica (WKTV, 1949).

New York City, as the home of the radio companies and advertising agencies that ruled the new medium, became the center of early television production, most of which was presented live. The three national networks headquartered their news and sports divisions in New York City as well, and two programming genres, both reflecting the city's theatrical culture, dominated the early years of prime-time television: teleplays (stage dramas performed in front of the camera) and variety programs (video approximations of vaudeville). In 1947 the teleplay premiered in New York City with *Kraft Television Theatre,* the first televised dramatic anthology series. A number of other teleplays, including *Marty* (*Goodyear Playhouse,* 1953) by Paddy Chayevsky (born in the Bronx), *Twelve Angry Men* (*Studio One,* 1954) by Reginald Rose, and *Patterns* (*Kraft Television Theatre,* 1955) by Rod Serling (born in Binghamton), won great critical acclaim. In variety entertainment, Milton Berle, who was born and raised in Uptown Manhattan, became television's first great star in the 1940s and 1950s. Sid Caesar of Yonkers and Jackie Gleason of Brooklyn were among the relatively unknown comedians who achieved sudden stardom in their own weekly series, presented "live from New York" during the early 1950s. Lucille Ball, the first star of the situation comedy genre, hailed from Jamestown (Chautauqua Co), although her series, *I Love Lucy,* was one of the few produced on film in Los Angeles when it premiered in 1951. *New York Daily News* gossip columnist Ed Sullivan, who was born in New York City in 1902, became a national figure by presenting television audiences with an eclectic array of show business acts each week. The *Ed Sullivan Show,* originally titled *Toast of the Town* after his column, aired on CBS every Sunday night from 1948 to 1971.

Following the end of the FCC's freeze on licensing in 1952, scores of new stations sprouted up across the country. One effect of the expansion of the television audience was the decline of New York City as a center of television production. Believing that the city's highbrow theater traditions, as well as the ethnic and racial diversity of its comedy and music cultures, were liabilities in cultivating large national audiences, network executives opted for new programs that were filmed and edited at California's movie studios. While network management and news operations remained in New York City, the bulk of production was shifted to southern California by 1960.

By 2002 there were some 55 fully licensed television stations licensed in New York State, including 9 noncommercial stations that were affiliated with the Public Broadcasting System (PBS). The neighboring five states and two Canadian provinces supply the region with dozens of additional broadcast stations. WXNY, a low-power UHF station in New York City, is the only station in the state that broadcasts exclusively in Spanish, although many New York City area residents can access two other Spanish language stations from northern New Jersey. North Country viewers are within range of French language stations in Quebec.

No true calculation can be made of the choices offered to contemporary television viewers because of the opportunities for signal importation offered by cable systems and direct satellite reception. A household subscribing to a digital cable service may receive hundreds of channels from all over the world, while a next-door neighbor opting for a tabletop antenna might receive just two or three, depending upon the day's weather conditions.

See also PUBLIC BROADCASTING (RADIO AND TELEVISION); TELEVISION, CABLE.

Banning, William Peck. *Commercial Broadcasting Pioneer; The WEAF Experiment, 1922–1926* (Cambridge, Mass: Harvard Univ Press, 1946)
Barnouw, Erik. *A History of Broadcasting in the United States,* 3 vols (New York: Oxford Univ Press, 1966–70)
———. *Tube of Plenty: The Evolution of American Television,* 3d ed. (New York: Oxford Univ Press, 1990)
Buffalo Broadcast Pioneers, http://www.buffalobroadcasting.com
Jaker, Bill, Frank Sulek, and Peter Kanze. *The Airwaves of New York: Illustrated Histories of 156 AM Stations in the Metropolitan Area, 1921–1996* (Jefferson, NC: McFarland, 1998)
Lewis, Tom. *Empire of the Air: The Men Who Made Radio* (New York: E. Burlingame Books, 1991)
Ritchie, Michael. *Please Stand By: A Prehistory of Television* (Woodstock, NY: Overlook Press, 1994)
Sterling, Christopher H., and John M. Kittross. *Stay Tuned: A Concise History of American Broadcasting,* 2d ed. (Belmont, Calif: Wadsworth Publishing, 1990)
Sturcken, Frank. *Live Television: The Golden Age of 1946–1958 in New York* (Jefferson, NC: McFarland, 1990)

David Marc

Brockport. Village (pop 8,103) in Sweden and Clarkson (Monroe Co). When, in 1822, it became known that the locality would be the temporary western terminus of the Erie Canal, it was platted into lots and settled, taking advantage of the farm trade from three directions. The village was incorporated in 1829. Cyrus McCormick manufactured the first reapers at Globe Iron Works in 1846, and two village plants produced them through 1892. Other 19th-century manufactures included carriages, rotary pumps, mowers, foundry products, vinegar, and cooling boards for undertakers. Shoes were produced from 1881 to 1927, and Quaker Maid Canning operated from 1929 to 1964. Brockport author Mary Jane Holmes (1828–1906) sold over 2 million copies of her novels, over 50 titles in all. Brockport Collegiate Institute, founded in 1841 and incorporated a year later, evolved into a normal school and teachers college, and became SUNY Brockport in 1948. Village negotiations with companies such as 3M and General Electric for testing, remediation, and cleanup of pollution they left behind began in the late 1990s. Main St is a historic district including 45 commercial buildings ending at the lift bridge, 1 of 16 still in operation on the Barge Canal.

Carolyn Vacca

Brockway, Zebulon Reed (*b* Lyme, Conn, 28 Apr 1827; *d* Elmira, 21 Oct 1920). Penologist. Brockway popularized indeterminate sentencing, parole, and other practices that became standard in the field of criminal justice. Beginning his career as a clerk in Wethersfield Prison in Connecticut, Brockway served in a succession of leadership positions, including assistant superintendent of New York State's Albany Co Penitentiary (1851) and superintendent of Monroe Co Penitentiary (1854) and later of Michigan's Detroit House of Correction (1861–72). In 1870 he helped write the Declaration of Principles at the influential National Congress on Penitentiary and Reformatory Discipline. Brockway gained national attention during his tenure as superintendent of Elmira Reformatory (1876–1900), where he experimented with the adult reformatory concept based on the medical model of crime, which stated that the roots of crime could be found in biological and environmental causes and that criminals could be reformed through training. Brockway emphasized that the ultimate goal of corrections was to protect society from crime by socializing antisocial convicts and reforming them into good citizens. His inmates were released only after completing a rigorous program of physical, industrial, and military training, as well as religious and academic education. He increasingly devoted attention to reforming mentally impaired inmates, who Brockway considered a major source of crime. He served as president of the National Prison Association from 1897 to 1898. Investigations by the State Board of Charities during 1893 and 1894 disclosed that excessive inmate punishment and administrative mismanagement were the reality at Elmira, contrary to Brockway's persistent claims of success. He was forced to resign from his post at Elmira in 1900 but remained active in the corrections field, becoming honorary president of the 1910 International Prison Congress. In 1912 Brockway published his autobiography, *Fifty Years of Prison Service.*

Pisciotta, Alexander W. *Benevolent Repression: Social Control and the American Reformatory-Prison Movement* (New York: New York Univ Press, 1994)

Richard Andress

Brocton. Village (pop 1,547) in Portland (Chautauqua Co). Resident Elijah Fay is credited with planting the first vines in Chautauqua Co in 1818. The first winery opened in 1859, and table grapes were first shipped from Brocton in 1877. The village incorporated in 1894. Brocton is one of the few communities that has preserved its lighted double arch over US 20 (Main St). It has been the home of George M. Pullman (1831–97), inventor of the Pullman sleeping car; Brad Anderson, creator of the syndicated cartoon character Marmaduke; and Donald C. Reinhoudt, titled the World's Strongest Man from 1973 to 1980.

Michelle Henry

Brodhead, John Romeyn (*b* Philadelphia, 2 Jan 1814; *d* New York City, 6 May 1873). Editor and historian. Retiring from practicing law in 1837 to care for his ill father in Saugerties (Ulster Co), Brodhead joined the staff of his relative Harmanus Bleecker, the chargé d'affaires at The Hague, in 1839. In 1841, on Bleecker's recommendation, the New York State legislature appointed him agent in charge of collecting documents relating to the state's colonial history from European repositories. Despite resistance from the British and the destruction of the Dutch West India Co documents, Brodhead succeeded in preserving a significant number of records. The multivolume works were published as *The Documentary History of The State of New-York* (1853–87), edited by Edmund Bailey O'Callaghan. Among Brodhead's publications were the two-volume *History of the State of New York* (1853, 1871). He served as secretary to the American legation in London under George Bancroft (1846–49) and was an active member of the New-York Historical Society, contributing documents and papers on New Netherland history to the society's publications.

Barnouw, Adriaan J. "John Romeyn Brodhead," *de Halve Maen* 39 (Oct 1964): 3, 11–12
Howard, Ronald. "John Romeyn Brodhead," *de Halve Maen* 59 (Jan 1959): 7–10, 27

Jennifer Steenshorne

Bronx [Bronx County] (42 mi²/109 km²; pop 1,332,650). On 1 Jan 1898, the Annexed District of New York City (the area of the city north of the Harlem River) became the Borough of the Bronx. The new borough remained a part of New York Co until 1 Jan 1914, when Bronx Co became the 62d and last county in the state to be organized.

AMERICAN INDIANS AND COLONIAL SETTLEMENT

Paleo-Indians arrived in the area about 12,000 years ago. At the time of European contact, there were several settlements of Algonquian-speaking bands in the area of what became the Bronx, with the Siwanoy, the Wiechquaeskeck, and the Rechgawawank being the most common names in 17th-century records. Tensions between the Dutch and English settlers exploded in Kieft's War from 1640 to 1645 with substantial casualties on both sides. In the war's aftermath, the Indian population was greatly diminished in the area, and by the end of the century most of the Indians had moved to regions further away from Europeans. (However, some Indians have returned in recent decades. In the 2000 census Bronx Co has the highest number of persons who listed their race as American Indian of any county in the state. Many of these were Central and South American natives of indigenous descent.)

In 1639 Jonas Bronck, a sea captain born in Sweden and residing in the Netherlands, was the first European settler, along with his Dutch, German, and Danish servants. His property was near the Harlem River and extended only to modern 150th St. New England settlers came into the area and asked the Dutch permission to stay. In 1642 English families from Rhode Island led by John Throckmorton established a settlement on the peninsula in Long Island Sound later called Throgs Neck. Anne Hutchinson, fleeing from religious persecution in Massachusetts, came from Rhode Island to what was later named the Hutchinson River. During Kieft's War the Throckmorton colony was expelled in 1643, the same year Hutchinson and most of her family were massacred. Bronck died of natural causes in 1643, and the people in his settlement dispersed, but his name remained and eventually was associated with the Bronx River.

In 1646 Englishman Thomas Cornell and his family came from Rhode Island and established a farm on Long Island Sound at what is now Clason Point. In 1653 Dutch lawyer Adriaen van der Donck acquired his patroonship, Colendonck, along the Hudson River straddling the current Bronx-Westchester Co line. Eventually his prop-

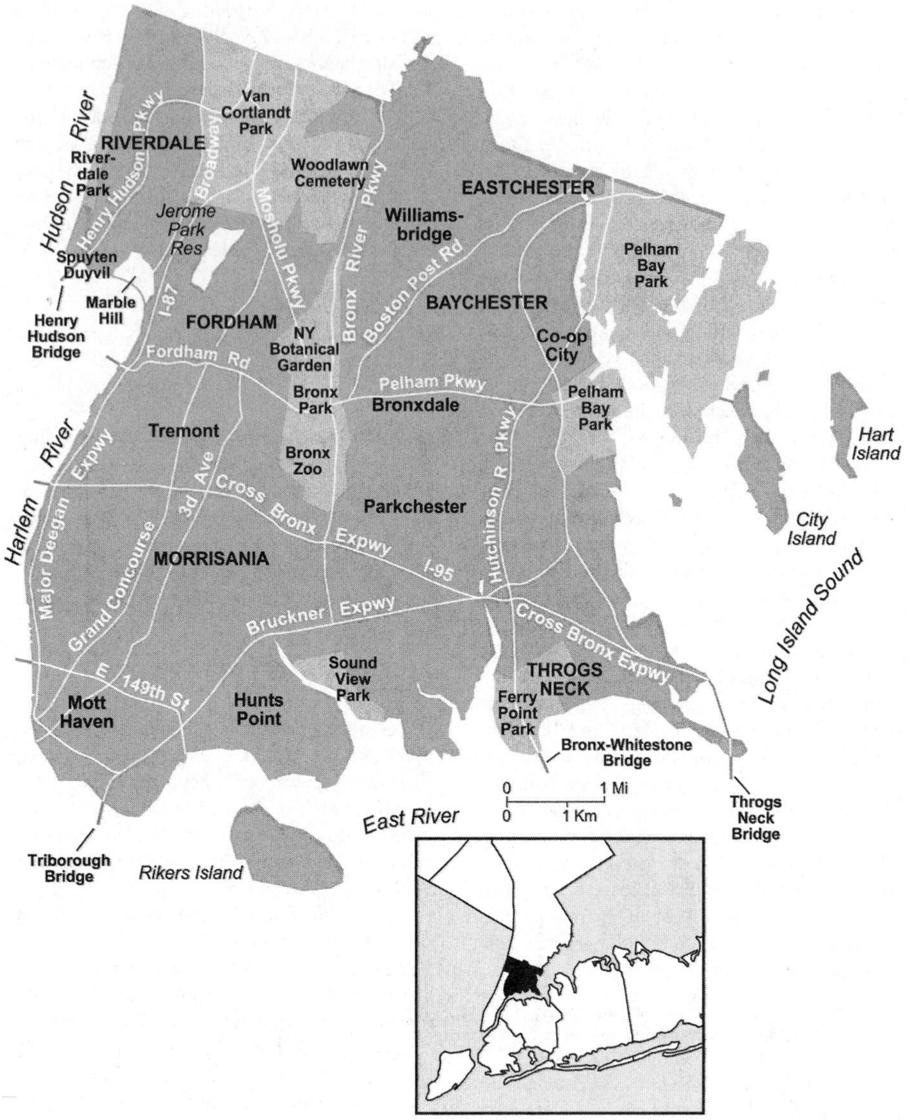

erty was called Yonkers. In 1654 Thomas Pell of Connecticut purchased the eastern half of today's Bronx and a portion of what is now Westchester Co from local Indians and settled 15 families from Connecticut in a new village called Vreedlant by the Dutch and Westchester by the English. This is the oldest continuously settled community in the county. A sporadic struggle ensued between New Netherland and Connecticut for control. This was resolved in 1664 when English forces captured New Netherland, and it became the Colony of New York. Pell was granted a manor, later called Pelham, by Gov Richard Nicolls in 1666, and he established the Village of Eastchester in 1667, straddling the current Bronx-Westchester Co border. John Archer purchased much of the land between the Bronx and Harlem Rivers, which was made into the Manor of Fordham in 1671. Richard and Lewis Morris, brothers from Monmouthshire in Wales, came via Barbados in 1670 to purchase Bronck's old farm and its neighboring lands, which in 1697 became the Manor of Morrisania. They brought black slaves to work the farm. Frederick Philipse I obtained the Yonkers land that became part of his Manor of Philipsburg in 1693. He also erected the King's Bridge over Spuyten Duyvil Creek [now Harlem River], becoming the first land link to Manhattan.

In 1683, with the creation of the county system, all of what is now Bronx Co became part of Westchester Co. Westchester was the county seat until the courthouse burned down in 1758. In 1696 the town was given a charter making it a borough. It had the right to have a mayor's court and a mayor elected by its inhabitants not just by its freeholders, the right to elect its own assembly members, and the right to hold two fairs each year.

In the colonial period, economic activity was almost exclusively agricultural. Cattle, sheep, horses, and pigs were raised. Wheat, made into flour, was the cash crop, but vegetables were grown for family use. Orchards produced mostly apples, some of which were made into cider. There was a thriving cloth industry. Sheep were raised for wool that was carded and spun by women. Grist- and sawmills were built on Westchester Creek, the Bronx River, and at the lake in modern Van Cortlandt Park. Commercial ships went from New York City to Westchester twice a week and to Eastchester once a week. Society was highly stratified. About 10–15% of the population was black, almost all of whom were slaves.

Revolutionary and Early National Period

In the American Revolution, a large portion of the population either supported the British or remained neutral. The Anglican rector of Westchester, Samuel Seabury (1729–96) wrote the Tory pamphlet *Letters from a Westchester Farmer* (1775). The leading patriot, Lewis Morris of Morrisania (1726–98), signed the Declaration of Independence. The patriot victory at the Battle of Pell's Point (in what is now Pelham Bay Park) on 18 Oct 1776 enabled George Washington to regroup and fight the Battle of White Plains. Most of what is now Bronx Co remained behind British lines, but residents were subject to periodic raids by irregular American troops. In 1787 Gouverneur Morris of Morrisania (1752–1816) took a leading part in drafting the US Constitution. In 1788 New York State established Morrisania, Westchester, Eastchester, Pelham, and Yonkers as towns. When the first federal census indicated that Morrisania had too few inhabitants to elect a town government, the legislature dissolved it in 1791 and annexed it to the Town of Westchester. The area remained rural, but the War of 1812 stimulated paint, glass, and pottery manufacturing on the Bronx River at West Farms. This disappeared once cheap English goods became available after the war. With the completion of the Erie Canal, the influx of wheat from the growing states of the Midwest caused farmers to shift production to dairy and meat products for the New York City market.

1874–1945

Lower Westchester Co was increasingly tied to commerce in Manhattan. In 1841 the New York and Harlem Railroad started service to the area. The Hudson River Railroad, on a New York City-to-Albany route, opened in 1849. The High Bridge, part of the Croton Aqueduct system, opened in 1848. In 1841 Jordan L. Mott (1798–1866), inventor of the coal-burning stove, moved his iron foundry to Mott Haven. Population growth pushed the state legislature in 1846 to divide the Town of Westchester, creating the Town of West Farms west of the Bronx River. In 1855 further immigration led the legislature to divide West Farms in half, the southern part becoming a new Town of Morrisania. By mid-19th century a failed revolution and economic hardship caused large numbers of Germans to come to Morrisania. They established small businesses, beer gardens, and breweries. In the 1890s and early 20th century, Italians came to the Belmont area in search of a better livelihood, and there was a substantial influx of eastern European Jews to the southern areas of the borough.

Since the approval of the Commissioners' Plan of 1811, the urbanized area of Manhattan seemed on an inevitable path of northward expansion. In 1873 the state divided the Town of Yonkers, and its southern part became the new Town of Kingsbridge. In 1874 the legislature approved the annexation of Kingsbridge, West Farms, and Morrisania (ie, those parts of the future Borough of the Bronx west of the Bronx River) to New York City. The area became known as the Annexed District, or the North Side. In 1888 a state-sanctioned committee purchased Van Cortlandt, Bronx, Pelham Bay, Crotona, Claremont, and St. Mary's Parks and Pelham, Mosholu, and Crotona Parkways for the city, thus starting Bronx Co's park system, which currently occupies 24% of the land. In 1895 the legislature approved New York City's annexation of land east of the Bronx River: the Town of Westchester, the southern portions of the Towns of Pelham and Eastchester and Wakefield (incorporated as a village in 1888). The two annexed areas had never had a common name or political identity. Three years later, in 1898, the Annexed District became a separate borough in consolidated New York City, named after the area's most distinctive feature, the Bronx River, becoming the Borough of the Bronx.

By the 1890s a continuous urban area had developed along the Harlem Railroad axis from Mott Haven northward through Melrose and Morrisania to the Tremont and Belmont areas south of Fordham Rd. The remainder of the Annexed District was a mixture of scattered urban development, suburban villages and farms, but undeveloped areas were rapidly filled with new urban development. On 26 Nov 1904 the first subway line opened in the Bronx, less than a month after the opening of the first subway in Manhattan, providing perhaps the single greatest spur to development. By 1940 there was no undeveloped land left in the borough. The recorded census population of the areas that became the Borough of the Bronx in 1898 rose explosively from 88,908 in 1890 to 1,265,258 in 1930. In the early 20th century, the Bronx was the fastest-growing borough of New York City, and its rapid growth was accompanied by massive expansions in infrastructure, transit systems, and residential development.

The early leaders, most notably Louis F. Haffen, an engineer of German American and Irish descent who served as commissioner of street improvements (1893–97) and then as borough president (1898–1909), envisioned a high-density development of Manhattan-style apartments that would cover most of the borough for an anticipated population of 8 million. Early development from the 1890s to the 1920s followed this pattern and filled most of the southwestern portion of the borough (south of Fordham Rd and west of the Bronx River) with 3–10 story apartment buildings. The flagship urban development project was the construction of a 4.5 mi (7.2 km) north-south avenue on a ridge on the west side of the borough known as the Grand Concourse, initiated in 1902 and inaugurated in 1909. Large numbers of apartment buildings were constructed along the concourse axis in the first four decades of the 20th century, and during the same period an extensive network of subway and elevated routes was developed to connect most of the borough with Manhattan. The Bronx offered superior apartments at a lower price, with more parks and greenery and with excellent transit connections to Manhattan, and it attracted many upwardly mobile households from overcrowded areas like the Lower East Side. Instead of replicating the high densities of the west Bronx, most of the east and north Bronx was filled with lower-density, newer development, including large areas of single- and two-family dwellings, in part because of the lack of subway service. Housing developments included the Amalgamated Cooperative Apartments in the 1920s, the first significant housing cooperative in New York City. Parkchester was an extensive rental housing development of over 12,000 units built by the Metropolitan Life Insurance Co (1938–42).

The Bronx in the first half of the 20th century was dominated by European immigrants and their children. In 1930, of the approximately 1.26 million residents, over 475,000 (38%) had not been born in the United States. The single largest ethnic group were the Jews, accounting for at least one-third of the borough's population and by some estimates almost one-half. (The Bronx had the highest percentage of Jewish population of any of the boroughs.) Much of the area south of Tremont Ave was over 80% Jewish. For many Jews, life in the Bronx was a step up from the overcrowded tenements of the Lower East Side. The Belmont neighborhood around Arthur Ave emerged as the borough's "Little Italy." The Irish were a significant presence in Kingsbridge, Norwood, Highbridge, and Mott Haven. Germans moved from Morrisania to Throgs Neck and to the northern section of the Bronx. Numerous other European nationalities were present, most notably immigrants from Russia, Poland, Austria, Hungary, and Romania. There was also a small but growing presence of Puerto Ricans, immigrants from the Caribbean and Latin America, and African Americans. The Harlem riot of 1943 provided an impetus for many in Harlem and East Harlem to seek better housing in adjacent areas across the Harlem River. Among the immigrants were the Jamaican-born parents of the future secretary of state, Colin Powell, who settled in the Longwood neighborhood.

Bronx Borough Hall, illuminated for the Hudson-Fulton Celebration, 1909.

Education and Culture

The romantic poet Rodman Drake in his posthumously published 1835 poem "Bronx" offered a tribute to the area's natural beauties, and many Manhattan residents went to lower Westchester Co for excursions and occasionally to settle. Edgar Allan Poe lived in Fordham from 1846 to 1849. His cottage is still extant. Bronx Park is home to two of the city's preeminent cultural institutions, the Wildlife Conservation Park (1899), commonly known as the Bronx Zoo, and the New York Botanical Garden (1891). Yankee Stadium, a cultural institution of a different sort, opened in 1923 as the home of baseball's New York Yankees, often known as the Bronx Bombers. The Bronx is home to 14 institutions of higher learning, including Fordham University (1840), Lehman College (1931), Bronx Community College (1957), and Hostos Community College (1968.) New York University operated a campus in the Bronx from 1894 to 1973. Bronx natives who have written extensively about their home borough include the novelists Herman Wouk and E. L. Doctorow and essayists Irving Howe and Kate Simon. Composer Béla Bartók and conductor Arturo Toscanini resided in the Bronx.

The Bronx has a vibrant musical tradition and a history as an incubator of popular musical styles. In the dance halls in Hunts Point and along Southern Blvd in the 1940s and 1950s, "Mambo Kings" such as Tito Puente, Machito, and Tito Rodríguez held forth, later joined by a later generation of Bronx-raised innovators in the 1960s and 1970s, among them Eddie Palmieri, Willie Colón, Johnny Pacheco, and Ray Barretto, who helped craft the distinctive amalgam of Latino and American music known as salsa. In 1954 the Chords, a group of Bronx African American teenagers, had a huge hit on both the rhythm and blues and pop charts with "Sh-Boom," helping to usher in the genre of doo-wop. Dion (DiMucci) was one of the most successful doo-wop performers of the late 1950s and early 1960s, often accompanied by the Belmonts, named after the Bronx's Belmont Ave. The most influential genre of popular music over the past quarter century, rap and hip hop, was born in the Bronx, in jams in the 1970s in the Bronx River Houses and elsewhere. Among the borough's rap pioneers were Afrika Bambaataa, DJ Kool Herc, Grandmaster Flash, and the Sugar Hill Gang. Later hip hop musicians from the Bronx include the Puerto Rican rap artist Big Pun.

Politics

Throughout the 20th century the Borough of the Bronx was predominated by Democratic voters and administrators. The Bronx Democratic organization emerged from under the shadow of Tammany Hall under the leadership of Edward J. Flynn (1891–1953), who was its leader after

BRONX (BRONX CO) POPULATION CENSUS FIGURES

	White	Nonwhite	Total Population	Foreign-Born
1900[a]	136,665	2,584	139,249	61,258
1910[a]	277,715	4,330	282,045	148,935
1920	726,990	5,026	732,016	267,194
1930	1,251,747	13,511	1,265,258	477,342
1940	1,370,319	24,392	1,394,711	463,453
1950	1,351,662	99,615	1,451,277	373,894
1960	1,256,284	168,531	1,424,815	306,592
1970	1,080,859	390,842	1,471,701	229,210
1980	554,046	614,926	1,168,972	215,313
1990	431,318	772,471	1,203,789	274,793
2000	398,003	934,647	1,332,650	385,827

Notes: "Nonwhite" includes African Americans, Asians, American Indians, and Pacific Islanders and, for 2000, also the mixed race and other race categories. Through the 1960 census these figures primarily reflect the African American population. For 1910, 1930, and 1950, the foreign-born totals include Whites only. Other years include all foreign-born in the population.

[a]Bronx County not formed until 1914; figures for Bronx Borough.

1922. His liberal politics, avoidance of scandal, and close relationship with Franklin D. Roosevelt gave him access to federal patronage at a time when Roosevelt and Tammany were at loggerheads. When he was chairman of the Democratic National Committee (1940–44), he was one of the most powerful Democrats in the county. With Flynn's support, James J. Lyons served as Bronx borough president from 1933 to 1961. Flynn's successor, Charles A. Buckley, lost influence after opposing New York City mayor Robert F. Wagner Jr's reelection bid in 1961. Herman Badillo, borough president 1966–69, was the first powerful Puerto Rican politician in the city, and Bronx politics has been dominated by Latinos since the late 1980s, including Fernando Ferrer, borough president from 1987 to 2001.

Recent History

With the move of Puerto Ricans and African Americans to the Bronx in substantial numbers in the 1940s, a growing socioeconomic contrast was emerging in the borough between the densely populated southwest quadrant, which came to be known as the South Bronx, and the less densely populated northern and eastern portions of the borough. (The term South Bronx is an amorphous one, defined as much by race and class as geography, and a term that over time came to cover an increasing swath of the Bronx.) Although it included some elegant middle-class apartments, notably along the Grand Concourse, the South Bronx had most of the older urban development, including many tenements and most of the industrial, warehousing, and port areas, and it had higher levels of congestion and pollution. Parts of the South Bronx were scheduled for slum clearance and urban renewal, and several major public housing projects were constructed. Highways were built to accommodate automobile traffic to new suburbs. The controversial Cross Bronx Expressway, built by Robert Moses, ripped through a number of neighborhoods in the southern and central Bronx from 1953 to 1961, displacing thousands of families. Co-op City, the largest cooperative housing project in the world with over 15,000 apartments, was constructed in the northeast Bronx in the late 1960s, promoted by the United Housing Federation led by Abraham Kazan.

The population of the South Bronx swiftly changed from a majority of European immigrants with a strong Jewish and Catholic presence to a majority of Puerto Ricans and African Americans. As the older Bronxites moved northward and eastward, the South Bronx became stigmatized as a poor and transitional area. During the 1970s there was a rapid growth in drug dealing and crime as well as the abandonment and arson of a substantial part of the housing stock. The borough's population peaked at around 1.5 million in the late 1960s; in the 1970s the Bronx lost over 300,000 persons, more than 20% of its population. The Charlotte St area in the Morrisania and Crotona Park East neighborhoods attracted great national attention when on 5 Oct 1977 Pres Jimmy Carter stood in the ruins and compared the devastation to the bombing of German cities during World War II. Eventually the area was cleared, and in the mid-1980s the South Bronx Development Organization and MBD Community Housing Corp redeveloped the area with suburban-style ranch houses, part of a broader strategy to promote new construction for affordable homeownership.

The South Bronx remains the poorest quadrant of the borough, but it is no longer a minority enclave in a predominantly European American population. The borough is home to large numbers of recent immigrants from eastern Europe, the Middle East (both Arabs and Israelis), Asia, Africa, the Caribbean, and Central and South America. In 2000, 29% of the its residents were foreign-born, and the racial composition of the Bronx was 37% African American and 3% Asian. Those of Latino ethnicity made up 48% of the population. (In 2000 the Bronx had the lowest percentage of Whites and by far the highest percentage of Latinos of any of the city's boroughs.) The contemporary Bronx is ethnically and culturally diverse, with a strong Latino and Caribbean presence. The Riverdale and Fieldston neighborhoods to the northwest have many prosperous residents, and some other northern and eastern neighborhoods, such as Woodlawn, Pelham Parkway, Pelham Gardens, City Island, and County Club, have a stronger middle-class homeowner presence. Most of the borough's population, however, is low to middle income and rents far more than owns homes. As a result of recent immigration, many Bronx neighborhoods are by and large no longer sharply defined by single ethnic groups. Many groups live side by side, and many of the old neighborhood names and boundaries are being superseded. Residents often identify their section of the borough with their street name alone. Still, some ethnicities remain concentrated in one or two neighborhoods, for example, the English-speaking Caribbean population in the Williamsbridge and Wakefield neighborhoods or the Jewish population in Riverdale and Pelham Parkway. The Hunts Point Market is the largest wholesale distributive food market in the world. Major shopping areas include Fordham Rd, the Hub at 149th Street, and Bay Plaza near Co-op City.

Lloyd Ultan has written several histories of the Bronx, among them *The Beautiful Bronx: 1920–1950* (1979); with Gary Hermalyn, *The Bronx in the Innocent Years,*

POPULATIONS OF FORMER TOWNS, BRONX (BRONX CO)

Town	Years in Existence	1790	1800	1810	1820	1830	1840	1850	1860	1870	1880	1890
Morrisania[a]	1788–91; 1855–74	133	258	—	—	—	—	—	9,245	19,609	—	—
Westchester	1655–1895[b]	1,203[c]	992	1,969	2,162	2,362	4,154	2,492	4,250	6,015	6,789	10,029
West Farms	1846–74	—	—	—	—	—	—	4,436	7,098	9,372	—	—

Note: Only towns wholly within the current territory of the Bronx are included.

[a]Created as a town in 1788, then dissolved in 1791. Regardless, the US Census counted population in 1800. The town was re-created in 1855.

[b]Earliest town meeting record is 1655.

[c]As printed in 1790 census; total of columns is actually 1,141.

1890–1925 (1985); *The Bronx: It Was Only Yesterday, 1935–1965* (1992); and *The Birth of the Bronx: 1609–1900* (2000). Another history is by Barbara Unger, *Bronx Accent: A Literary and Pictorial History of the Borough* (2000). Borough president Louis F. Haffen's proud volume, *Borough of the Bronx: A Record of Unparalleled Progress and Development* (1909) remains useful. John McNamara has compiled a street gazetteer, *History in Asphalt: The Origin of Bronx Street and Place Names* (1989). Jill Jonnes, *South Bronx Rising: The Rise, Fall, and Resurrection of an American City* (2002) is a valuable account of the borough's recent history. There have been many memoirs of life in the Bronx. Two of the best are Edward J Flynn, *You're the Boss: My Story of a Life in Practical Politics* (1947) and Kate Simon, *Bronx Primitive: Portraits in a Childhood* (1982). City Lore has produced an excellent annotated map of the borough's musical history: *From Mambo to Hip Hop: Latin Music and Hip Hop Trail in Harlem and the Bronx* (2002).

Ray Bromley and Lloyd Ultan

Bronx River Parkway. Roadway from Bronx Park (Bronx Co) to Valhalla (Westchester Co), considered the first limited-access automobile parkway in the United States. In 1907 the Bronx Parkway Commission, funded by New York City and Westchester Co, was authorized to acquire property in the Bronx River valley, install sewage control systems for the polluted Bronx River, and develop the adjacent land as a scenic preserve. Although the primary goal was conservation, the introduction of parks, trails, and a scenic drive also allowed recreational use of the reclaimed land. The design of the serpentine 15.5 mi (24.9 km) parkway (1917–24) included features that helped to transform driving into recreation, such as a uniform roadway with controlled access, limited cross traffic, smooth driving surfaces, gentle grading, and a landscape designed to be experienced from the automobile. The parkway's designers included engineer Jay Downer, one of the architects of the New York State park system, and Gilmore D. Clark, one of the preeminent landscape architects of the 20th century. Even before the parkway officially opened, 17,000 vehicles were counted in a 13-hour period in 1924. By 1927, 35,000 cars were counted on weekends and holidays, and by 1931, 30,000 on weekdays. The enormous popularity of the preserve proved a catalyst for economic development and local planning, and the design of the parkway set the precedent for scenic roads built across America. The parkway increased property values along its route, and the improved transportation made commuting easier, greatly increasing everyday traffic on the scenic road. The most significant parkway improvement projects, such as widening and straightening, took place in the 1950s and 1960s. In the early 21st century, the parkway carried approximately 100,000 vehicles per day in the southern Bronx, 75,000 in the northern Bronx, and 60,000 through Westchester Co.

Downer, Jay, and James Owen. *Public Parks in Westchester County* (New York: Lewis Historical Publishing, 1925)

Kathleen LaFrank

Bronxville. Village (pop 6,543) in Eastchester (Westchester Co). A Harlem Railroad station was established at Underhill's Crossing in 1844; the Bronxville post office followed in 1852. William Van Duzer Lawrence bought a hilltop farm in 1890 and set about developing a colony of writers, artists, and talented professionals. The Gramatan Inn, a fine hotel, and the short commute to Grand Central Terminal were among its selling points. The village incorporated in 1898. Houses, many of them substantial, were built before the depression. After World War II development resumed until the village was "built out." The new residents tended to be corporate executives, and zoning initiated in 1958 has created a rather formal village.

Field Horne

Bronx Zoo. Located on 264 acres (106.8 ha) at the southern end of Bronx Park, the Bronx Zoo is among the largest urban zoos in the United States. It is operated by the Wildlife Conservation Society (prior to 1998, officially the New York Zoological Society) on land owned by New York City. The zoo plays a leading role in the preservation of endangered species and in wildlife conservation research. The possibility of establishing a metropolitan zoo emerged in 1888, when a state-mandated committee bought parkland north of Manhattan for New York City. With the backing of lawyer Madison Grant, Theodore Roosevelt, and others concerned about the extinction of big game in the United States, a bill incorporating the New York Zoological Society passed the state legislature in 1895. William Temple Hornaday, the society's first director, chose the southern portion of Bronx Park for the zoo's site because its combination of ridge, hollow, glade, meadow, rock, river, lake, and virgin forest was suitable for every species of animal. The stated purposes of the zoo were to exhibit animals for the public, encourage interest and education in animal life, and preserve animals from destruction. With the help of a $30,000 appropriation from New York City, the zoo was opened on 8 Nov 1899 by former governor Levi P. Morton, the president of the society. Although named the New York Zoological Park, it was known to the public as the Bronx Zoo.

In the first of many successful efforts by the institution to propagate vanishing wildlife, the American Bison Society was established at the zoo in 1905 to save the American buffalo. Beginning with the African Plains exhibit in 1941, the zoo strove to provide more naturalistic habitats, although this meant a decline in the total number and variety of animals that could be supported. The zoo was officially renamed the Bronx Zoo/Wildlife Conservation Park in 1993. Zoo personnel conduct research and establish national parks throughout the world. In 2001 the zoo's total revenues of almost $110 million included $25 million from New York City, over $2 million from the state, and over $4 million from federal agencies. Exhibits of more than 4,000 animals and well over 500 species draw about 2 million visitors yearly.

Bridges, William. *Gathering of Animals: An Unconventional History of the New York Zoological Society* (New York: Harper & Row, 1974)

Lloyd Ultan

Brookfield. Town (pop 2,403) in SE Madison Co. Settled in 1791, the town was formed from Paris (Oneida Co) in 1795. The Brookfield Agricultural Society's annual fair (1849) became the official county fair late in the 19th century. A number of local firms manufactured agricultural implements, including Leonardsville Manufacturing (1852–57) and Brookfield Manufacturing (1853–1860s); the Craine triple-wall silo was invented in Brookfield and manufactured by Craine until its 1966 sale to Agway. The town was served by the Utica, Chenango and Susquehanna Valley Railroad (1870; now New York, Susquehanna and Western) and the Unadilla Valley Railroad. Reforestation in the 1930s created the 13,000-acre (5,261 ha) Brookfield State Forest, containing over 100 miles (160 km) of bridle trails. In the early 21st century some dairy farming continues, but most residents commute. The Wheeler House Complex (1874) in Leonardsville is listed on the National Register. Brookfield native Myrtilla Miner (1815–64) ran a school for Blacks in Washington, DC, from 1851 to 1860.

William F. Helmer

Children with bird at the Bronx Zoo, *ca* 1990.

Brookhaven. Town (pop 448,248) in central Suffolk Co. The largest town in the county in size and population, it covers 323.5 mi^2 (837.9 km^2) between the Atlantic Ocean and Long Island Sound. Glacial deposits created its two terminal moraines, Harbor Hills and Ronkonkoma. The north shore is rocky and hilly, and the south a wide, sandy plain. Fire Island, a barrier beach, is part of the town. Occupied by two Algonquian-speaking groups, the Setalcott in the north and the Unquachog in the south, the area was first settled by Whites at Setauket in 1655, where a town government began functioning by 1659, the date of the earliest surviving minutes. Residents farmed, fished, gathered oysters, conducted offshore whaling expeditions, and cut cordwood. During the Revolutionary War, the British occupied much of the town. On 22 Aug 1777 a battle was fought at Setauket Green and, in November 1780, Maj Benjamin Tallmadge led a successful raid on Fort St. George and burned British hay stored at Coram. After the Revolution, shipbuilding blossomed in every harbor on both north and south shores. Three rail lines ran through Brookhaven: the main line of the Long Island Rail Road (1844), the South Side Rail Road (1868), and the Port Jefferson line (1873), which extended to Shoreham (1895). Electrical pioneer Nikola Tesla worked in a laboratory in Shoreham in the early 20th century. Camp Upton near Yaphank was built as a training camp during World War I and became, after serving as a CCC camp and then a military installation during World War II, Brookhaven National Laboratory (1947). Suburban development, begun around 1900, intensified after World War II, and Brookhaven became more accessible by the Long Island Expressway, completed across town in 1970. Brookhaven is the site of SUNY Stony Brook (1957), Briarcliffe and St. Joseph's Colleges, and a campus of Suffolk County Community College at Selden. After a fourfold population increase in the four decades beginning 1960, Brookhaven's racial composition in 2000 was 4% Black, and 3% Asian. People of Latino ethnicity made up 8%. Council districts were established in 2003 after more than 250 years of townwide representation.

See also CAROUSELS.

Suzanne Johnson

Brookhaven National Laboratory. Opened in 1947 as a facility for basic scientific research at former US Army Camp Upton (Suffolk Co), Brookhaven National Laboratory (BNL) was founded by a consortium of northeastern universities and funded by the federal Atomic Energy Commission. In 1950 scientists at BNL built the first nuclear reactor in the United States specifically for peacetime research. What was then the world's most powerful particle accelerator, the Cosmotron, was completed in 1952. The lab's second generation of large instruments included the Alternating Gradient Synchrotron (1960) and the High Flux Beam Reactor (1965). The third generation of facilities includes the National Synchrotron Light Source (1981) and the world's largest accelerator for nuclear physics, the Relativistic Heavy Ion Collider (2000).

Discoveries at Brookhaven have led to four Nobel Prizes in physics (1957, 1976, 1980, and 1988). In addition to pioneering research into nuclear technology and high energy physics, the lab also has been involved in biomedical and environmental sciences. BNL scientists in 1961 began to pioneer research with a medical imaging technique known as positron emission tomography (PET) to explore in particular the link between dopamine and addiction. Medical breakthroughs also include establishment of the connection between salt and hypertension, resulting in the recommendation to restrict salt intake (1960s); synthesis of the first human insulin to replace animal insulin for use by diabetics (1960s); use of L-dopa for relief of Parkinson's symptoms (1970s); development of FDG (fluorodeoxyglucose), a key radiotracer now used worldwide to diagnose cancer, brain disease, psychiatric illnesses, and heart disease (1970s); and research into Lyme disease (1990s). Brookhaven scientists developed the first video game as a toy for visitors (1958) and a version of lawn tennis, and were awarded a patent for magnetically levitated trains (1968). BNL also has focused on researching air pollution, brown tide, and global warming; a new direction is nanoscience research with a focus on designer materials.

Brookhaven was named a federal Superfund site in 1989 because of past use and disposal practices, common until that time, that had resulted in the contamination of a small portion of the lab's 5,300 acres (2,145 ha). Problems beset the lab in 1997 when the spent fuel pool of the High Flux Beam Reactor leaked water containing low concentrations of radioactive tritium into the soil, though the leak (a total of 5 curies) did not pose a health hazard. The US Department of Energy fired the lab's contractor, Associated Universities, and replaced it with Brookhaven Science Associates, which was established by the Research Foundation of SUNY Stony Brook (Suffolk Co) and Battelle Memorial Research Institute, headquartered in Columbus, Ohio. Brookhaven drew about $425 million in federal money to New York State in 2002 and had 3,000 employees. It attracts annually over 4,000 visiting scientists to its facilities.

Crease, Robert P. *Making Physics: A Biography of Brookhaven National Laboratory, 1946–1972* (Chicago: Univ of Chicago Press, 1999)

Robert P. Crease

Brooklyn [Kings County] (81 mi^2/210 km^2; pop 2,465,326). Kings Co was created in 1683. Since 1896, when it became coterminous with the City of Brooklyn, it has had no internal political subdivisions. In 1898 Brooklyn became a borough of New York City. Located on the western end of Long Island, it is bounded by the Borough of Queens, the East River, New York Bay, the Atlantic Ocean, Rockaway Inlet, and Jamaica Bay. Its natural shoreline covers 65 miles (105 km) including 7 miles (11 km) of beaches with 595 acres (241 ha) of adjacent parkland and, in Jamaica Bay, about one-quarter of the Gateway National Recreation Area, or 7,000 acres (2,833 ha). Geographically, Brooklyn is in the northern section of the Atlantic coastal plain, a terminal moraine and the broad outwash plain created by a retreating glacier about 13,000 years ago. The highest natural land elevation is 220 feet (67.1 m) in Green-Wood Cemetery; the lowest is sea level. The soil is a sandy loam. Newtown Creek and Gowanus River are inlets off the East River. Much of the southern portion of Brooklyn was lowland and consisted of discrete islands until filled through development. The lowland had a marshy character, which is retained in Jamaica Bay.

American Indians and Colonial Settlement

The Canarsee, a Delaware Indian nation, lived in various sites in the area, including Marechkawick, a village in what is now downtown Brooklyn, Nayack, near present-day Fort Hamilton, and Kesh-eachquereren, near what is now Canarsie. The Canarsee were among the local Indians who fought the Dutch during Kieft's War (1640–45). Canarsee leaders signed 22 land conveyances between 1636 and 1684, and most Canarsee had left Kings Co by the end of the 17th century. Brooklyn was part of New Netherland from its founding to 1664. Dutch settlement in the area began around 1636 with land purchases by Director Wouter van Twiller in what is now Flatbush. When these fledgling communities had sufficient numbers to establish their own Inferior Court of Justice, villages were established. Established were Breuckelen [now Brooklyn], centered at Fulton Ferry, in 1646; Amersfoot [now Flatlands] and Midwout [now Flatbush] in 1654; and Boswijck [now Bushwick] and Nieuw Utrecht [now New Utrecht] in 1661. Their charters were reconfirmed after the beginning of English rule in 1664, when they were commonly known as the Five Dutch Towns. The sole English settlement in what became Kings Co prior to 1664 was Gravesande [now Gravesend], the village granted to English religious dissenter Lady Deborah Moody in 1645.

Throughout the colonial period Kings Co retained a largely Dutch character. However, there were also people from other ethnicities, such as Hans Hansen Bergen, a Norwegian who settled in 1647 in the area now known as Bergen Beach, and Joris de Rapelje, a Flemish immigrant who acquired land on Wallabout Bay in the vicinity of what became the Brooklyn Navy Yard. Population growth was slow; Breuckelen recorded no more than 131 inhabitants by 1661. In the first colonial census of 1698, Kings Co had 2,017 people; by the final colonial census of 1771, it had only 3,623. Kings Co's percentage of the population of New York Colony declined from 11% to 2% in this period. The most important demographic shift in colonial Kings Co was the steady growth of the African population, almost all of whom were enslaved. Already a substantial 15% in 1698, it rose to 33% by the time of the first federal census in 1790, by far the highest proportion of slaves of any county in the state. In that year a mere 3% of the African Americans in Kings Co were free, far less than in neighboring New York City. Slaves had a variety of roles, especially on the large farms in rural Kings Co. In 1830, after the abolition of slavery in New York State in 1827, the federal census recorded 2,007 African Americans, many of them in the communities of Weeksville and Carrville in central Brooklyn.

Although the white residents of Kings Co were generally neutral on the question of independence, the county was the site of one of the war's major battles, variously known as the Battle of Brooklyn or Battle of Long Island, in August 1776, when Gen William Howe, with a force of 32,000 troops, attempted to seize Kings Co and trap the patriot forces. Howe succeeded in the first goal but not in the second, as most of Gen

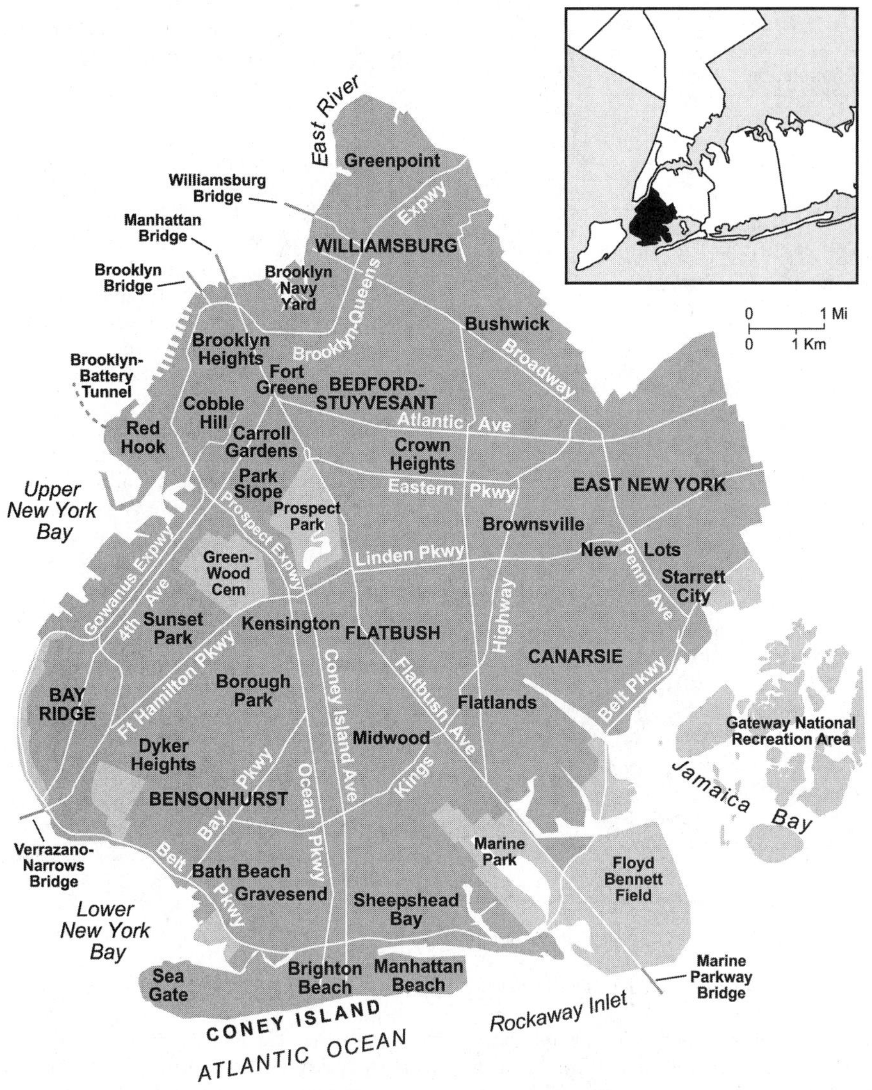

George Washington's forces were able to escape to Manhattan. Wallabout Bay housed numerous prison ships from 1776 to 1783, and in these fetid conditions, an estimated 11,000 patriot soldiers died during their captivity. The Prison Ship Martyrs' Monument, erected in Fort Greene Park in 1844 and rebuilt by McKim, Mead and White in 1908, is a tribute to Americans who died on the ships.

Urbanization

Although most of Kings Co remained rural in the decades after 1790, the area around the landing for the ferry to Manhattan, adjacent to Brooklyn Heights, was the site of increasing business activity. The *Brooklyne Hall Super-Extra Gazette* began publishing in 1782 and was followed by the *Courier, and Long Island Advertiser* in 1799. In another area along the East River, Secretary of the Navy Benjamin Stoddart established the Brooklyn Navy Yard in Wallabout Bay in 1800. Between 1790 and 1810 Brooklyn's population tripled with housing, stables, and taverns rising around the ferry landing. Brooklyn became a village in 1816 and inaugurated John Garrison as its first president. He passed sanitary rules, constructed brick walks, and appointed a master chimney sweep and an official in charge of catching loose pigs. In 1834 Brooklyn was incorporated as a city. Brooklyn Heights was emerging as one of the first suburbs in the nation, as many of its well-to-do residents daily took the ferry to Manhattan. Kings County Hospital was founded in 1831 and Kings County Penitentiary in 1854. Green-Wood Cemetery opened in 1838, serving as not just a burial ground but also a park.

Within a few decades, the population of the City of Brooklyn began to dwarf that of the rest of the county. By the 1840 census it had supplanted Albany as the second largest city in the state, and by 1860 it was the third largest city in the nation. Brooklyn's growth occurred in part because of annexation of adjacent areas. Williamsburgh [now Williamsburg], near Wallabout Bay, and Bushwick were annexed by Brooklyn in 1854. (Williamsburg had been incorporated as a village in Bushwick in 1827, as a separate town in 1840, and as a city in 1852.) By 1860 96% of the 279,122 persons living in Kings Co were residents of the City of Brooklyn. The remainder of the county was rural and often retained a distinctly Dutch character. It was annexed to Brooklyn in stages, although not without much grumbling and resentment in some quarters. The Town of New Lots (formed from Flatbush in 1852) was annexed in 1886, the Towns of Flatbush and New Utrecht in 1894, and the Town of Flatlands in 1896.

Economic Development

For the remainder of the 19th century, Brooklyn retained a strong agricultural base, and 360 farms existed in 1900. In the late 19th century, before urbanization swallowed up much of the remaining farmland, it was one of the leading market gardening areas in the county, selling its fruits and vegetables to Manhattan consumers. However, as Manhattan expanded northward, businesses and industry crossed the East River because of Brooklyn's excellent port facilities. Shipbuilding became a natural industry of the waterfront of Greenpoint and Fort Greene where the Navy Yard developed in 1800. Soon other trades and industries dotted the area. Peter Cooper started a glue factory in Bushwick in the 1840s. By the middle of the century, the main industries of Greenpoint and Williamsburg became known as the "five black arts": printing, ceramics, petroleum, glassmaking, and iron founding. Other industries along the East River included sugar and fine chemical production. Some of the leading firms included Havemeyer's Sugar (1856; now Domino and Amstar), Union Porcelain Works (1861), Continental Iron Works (1859). Also established were publishers D. Appleton (1868) and A. S. Barnes (1880) and pharmaceutical manufacturers Pfizer (1842) and E. R. Squibb (1858). Standard Oil set up operations on the East River in 1874. The Brooklyn Flint Glass Works (1823) moved to Corning (Steuben Co) in 1868. By the 1880s Brewers Row in Bushwick had 45 breweries, including Liebmann (makers of Rheingold), and F. and M. Schaefer. Other companies included Eberhard Faber (1851), pencil manufacturers, and Dugan Brothers Bakery (1878). The huge Bush Terminal complex in Sunset Park, a series of piers, warehouses, and factory lofts, started opening in 1890. At its greatest extent it encompassed about 200 acres (80 ha).

Transportation

The phenomenal increase in Brooklyn's population and industry in the 19th century was based in part on improvements in transportation, which permitted a far wider dispersion of people. Transportation across the East River started with rowboats in the 1640s. By 1704 ferries sailed between New York City and Brooklyn, and the first stagecoach began runs between Brooklyn and Sag Harbor (Suffolk Co). Early roadways rambled through the county, originating from cow paths and Indian trails, and Kings Highway and Flatbush Ave still bisect the borough on strange angles, wreaking havoc with grid patterns. After settlement increased, some of these trails became turnpikes and toll roads, such as Flatbush and Jamaica Aves, and the bridges to Coney Island.

By 1814 Robert Fulton began steam ferry service between streets bearing his name in Manhattan and Brooklyn to ease the commute for city workers who lived in Brooklyn. At the service's peak, there was a ferry crossing the East River every seven minutes. The Brooklyn and Jamaica Railroad Co was founded in 1832, connecting East New York with Brooklyn and Jamaica. In 1834 it became the Long Island Rail Road Co, chartering a route between Brooklyn and Greenport (Suffolk Co). In 1883 the Brooklyn Bridge opened; it was the first permanent link across the East River and perhaps the most beloved of all of New York City's public structures. The bridge greatly facilitated ties between the two cities, hastening their subsequent consolidation.

Local public transportation began with the stagecoach, which transported riders east and

BROOKLYN (KINGS CO) POPULATION CENSUS FIGURES

	White	Nonwhite	Total Population	Foreign-Born
1790	3,017	1,478	4,495	—
1800	3,929	1,811	5,740	—
1810	6,450	1,853	8,303	—
1820	9,426	1,761	11,187	308
1830	18,528	2,007	20,535	1,073
1840	44,767	2,846	47,613	—
1850	134,817	4,065	138,882	56,201
1860	274,123	4,999	279,122	109,077
1870	414,254	5,667	419,921	153,811
1880	590,201	9,294	599,495	188,312
1890	826,555	11,992	838,547	272,895
1900	1,146,909	19,673	1,166,582	355,697
1910	1,610,487	23,864	1,634,351	572,512
1920	1,984,953	33,403	2,018,356	660,778
1930	2,488,448	71,953	2,560,401	868,770
1940	2,587,951	110,334	2,698,285	778,054
1950	2,525,118	213,057	2,738,175	630,526
1960	2,245,859	381,460	2,627,319	516,349
1970	1,905,788	696,224	2,602,012	456,636
1980	1,249,486	981,450	2,230,936	530,973
1990	1,079,762	1,220,902	2,300,664	672,569
2000	1,015,728	1,449,598	2,465,326	931,769

Notes: "Nonwhite" includes African Americans, Asians, American Indians, and Pacific Islanders and, for 2000, also the mixed race and other race categories. Through the 1960 census these figures primarily reflect the African American population. Foreign-born figures for 1820 and 1830 include only those not naturalized, and for 1930 and 1950, the foreign-born totals include Whites only. Other years include all foreign-born in the population.

west in the northern part of the county or from the north to Cropsey's Inn at Coney Island. Those who objected to the bumpy unpaved roadways could opt for an excursion boat to Norton Point at Sea Gate after 1847. The Brooklyn City Railroad introduced the horse-drawn omnibus by 1853. Steam excursion trains started after the Civil War, and the 1870s became a period of great expansion for rail transportation. Most lines ran from north to south with Coney Island or its ancillary amusements as their destination; among the major lines constructed were the Brooklyn and Rockaway Beach Railroad (1865), Brooklyn, Bath and Coney Island Railroad (1867), Prospect Park and Coney Island Railroad (1875), New York and Sea Beach Railroad (1877), and the Brooklyn, Flatbush, and Coney Island Railroad (1878). For two years a primitive monorail even ran from Bensonhurst to Brighton Beach. By 1896 these privately owned lines had been absorbed by the Brooklyn Rapid Transit Co.

In 1908, with the opening of the Brooklyn Interborough Rapid Transit (IRT) line from Borough Hall to Atlantic Ave, the first subway opened in Brooklyn. Over the next 20 years, numerous subway lines would be built. In 1918, during a labor strike, tragedy struck with the Malbone St tunnel wreck; 94 passengers were killed. In its aftermath the Brooklyn Rapid Transit declared bankruptcy and was replaced by the Brooklyn-Manhattan Transit Co in 1923. In 1936 the Independent Subway System opened service in Brooklyn, and by 1940 the borough's subways were owned by the city.

Politics in the Late 19th and Early 20th Centuries

Politics in 19th-century Kings Co and Brooklyn was dominated by wards and ward bosses. The Irish, as in New York City, dominated politics after midcentury. Among the Brooklyn Democratic bosses was Hugh McLaughlin, who started as a dockworker in the Navy Yard and dominated the city's politics for a half century after 1862. Henry Murphy served as state senator, member of congress, ambassador to the Netherlands, and publisher of the *Brooklyn Daily Eagle.* A less honored politician was John McKane, a contractor and the notorious boss of the Town of Gravesend (which included the area of Coney Island) who rose through the police ranks to become a boss holding 17 positions in the town before his downfall in 1893 and subsequent imprisonment for election fraud.

As in New York City, reformers, running as Republican or anti-machine Democrats, sometimes crafted successful Fusion campaigns. Seth Low was mayor of Brooklyn (1881–85) and introduced the merit system into its government. He then served as president of Columbia University (1890–1901) and as mayor of New York City (1901–3), the only person to be mayor of the state's two largest cities. William J. Gaynor, elected justice of the state supreme court from Brooklyn, served a term as a reform-minded mayor of New York City (1909–13).

Brooklyn's leaders and residents had abundant civic pride in the late 19th century. Frederick Law Olmsted and Calvert Vaux's masterpiece, Prospect Park, opened in 1867. Their plans for broad Parisian-like boulevards to radiate from the park were largely abortive, but two broad thoroughfares were built, Eastern Parkway (1868) and Ocean Parkway (1880), signaling the intention of city leaders to rival New York City, if not Paris itself. New neighborhoods with stately mansions were built, such as Park Slope, midway between Manhattan and Coney Island and bordering on Prospect Park. The Academy of Music (1861) and the Long Island Historical Society (1863; now Brooklyn Historical Society) provided culture downtown. Brooklyn was preparing to build a new central library building and a gargantuan museum to match any in the world.

POPULATIONS OF FORMER TOWNS AND CITIES, BROOKLYN (KINGS CO)

Town	Years in Existence	1790	1800	1810	1820	1830	1840	1850	1860	1870	1880	1890
Brooklyn	1646 (town) 1834–98 (city)	1,603	2,378	4,402	7,175[a]	15,394[a]	36,233	96,838	266,661	396,099	566,663	806,343
Bushwick	1661–1854 (town)	540	656	798	930	1,620[b]	1,295	3,739	—	—	—	—
Flatbush	1652–1894 (town)	941	946	1,159	1,027	1,143	2,099	3,177	3,471	6,309	7,634	12,338
Flatlands	1647–1896 (town)	423	493	517	512	596	810	1,155	1,652	2,286	3,127	4,075
Gravesend	1645–1894 (town)	426	489	520	534	565	799	1,064	1,286	2,131	3,674	6,937
New Lots	1852–86 (town)	—	—	—	—	—	—	—	3,271	9,800	13,655	—
New Utrecht	1657–1894 (town)	562	778	907	1,009	1,217	1,283	2,129	2,781	3,296	4,742	8,854
Williamsburgh	1840 (town) 1852–54 (city)	—	—	—	—	—	5,094	30,780	—	—	—	—

[a]Includes Village of Brooklyn, chartered 1816.

[b]Includes Village of Williamsburgh, chartered 1827.

Some Brooklynites talked of overtaking New York City's commercial preeminence because of Brooklyn's natural harbor.

But there were other powerful actors in Brooklyn, Manhattan, and the rest of the state who thought that a combined city offered the best chance for economic and civic preeminence. Among them were Brooklynite James Stranahan, promoter of the Brooklyn Bridge and Prospect Park, and Manhattan resident Andrew Haswell Green, director of the Central Park Commission and for many decades a tireless proponent of a greater New York City. US senator Thomas C. Platt, from Owego (Tioga Co), the boss of the state's Republican Party, supported the idea, in part because he thought it would weaken the power of Tammany Hall. Most Democratic politicians in both cities were opposed to greater New York, seeing a possible diminution of their power. St. Clair McKelway, editor of the *Brooklyn Daily Eagle,* wrote vitriolic editorials opposing the annexation on the grounds that it would hurt Brooklyn's commercial prospects and tax base. Some of the wealthy in Brooklyn feared that consolidation would encourage poor immigrants from Manhattan to seek refuge across the East River. Economic concessions helped smooth the path to consolidation. Brooklyn's city coffers were depleted in the depression of 1893, and many people in the burgeoning areas of southern Brooklyn complained of tainted well water and poor streets. Brooklyn was promised a new water supply, benefits of the newly proposed subway system, new bridges, and a 10-year tax break if it agreed to consolidation. The state legislature approved a consolidation bill, and on 1 Jan 1898 Brooklyn went from being the fourth largest city in the United States to being the second most populated borough of New York City. It is still debated whether this was in the best long-term interests of Brooklyn and its residents.

The change of political status did little to stop the growth of the borough. Between 1900 and 1930, Brooklyn's population more than doubled and soared to 2,560,401. It supplanted New York Co as the most populated county in the state, a status it has retained ever since. Much of the growth of Brooklyn from the middle of the 19th century through the 1920s was fueled by immigration. In 1910, 35% of Brooklyn's residents were foreign-born. The Irish worked in the shipyards and lived in Vinegar Hill or Irishtown. Italians, many of whom also worked as laborers, gravitated to East New York and areas along the rail right-of-way such as Bensonhurst and Canarsie. Jews moved from the Lower East Side across the Williamsburg Bridge into Williamsburg and to Brownsville and other areas. Poles moved to Greenpoint; Norwegians, Danes, and Swedes settled in areas that overlooked the Narrows, such as Bay Ridge; and Finns stayed farther north in Sunset Park.

Opening of the Brooklyn Elevated Railway, drawing by W. P. Snyder, from *Harper's Weekly,* 13 May 1885.

Religion, Education, and Culture

The Reformed Dutch Church was founded in Flatbush (1654) as the official church. The current church structure on the site was built in 1793. Bridge Street African Wesleyan Methodist Episcopal Church, Brooklyn's oldest black church, was founded in 1818. The cornerstone for St. James Church, the first Roman Catholic church on Long Island, was laid in 1822 to serve the growing Irish population. The same year the Brooklyn auxiliary of the American Society for Meliorating the Condition of the Jews was established. Brooklyn's Protestants convinced the state legislature to award the city an Anniversary Day in 1860 to honor the founding of the Brooklyn Sunday School Union in 1812, currently celebrated as Brooklyn-Queens Day, an official school holiday.

In the middle of the 19th century Brooklyn developed a full range of cultural institutions. Besides the Brooklyn Academy of Music and the Long Island Historical Society, the Brooklyn Academy of Art (founded 1823) began as the Apprentices Library and evolved into a museum of art, natural history, and science collections; in 1890 it was incorporated into the Brooklyn Institute of Arts and Sciences, which included several other Brooklyn cultural institutions. The current home of what is now the Brooklyn Museum of Art opened in 1897. Only one-sixth of architect Stanford White's grandiose plan was completed. A new entrance and public space opened in 2004. In 1900 five daily newspapers were published in Brooklyn. The best known was the *Brooklyn Daily Eagle* (founded 1841). Walt Whitman was its editor from 1846 to 1848.

In the late 19th century, the pleasure grounds in the southern portions of Brooklyn were vastly expanded. As early as 1824, Coney Island Causeway opened along with the Terhune brother's Coney Island House, the shore's first public house. The growth of Coney Island began in earnest with the building of grand hotels—the Manhattan Beach (1877), Brighton Beach (1878), and the Oriental (1880)—and of several thoroughbred racing tracks—Brighton Beach (1879), Sheepshead Bay (1886), and Gravesend (1886). When the tracks were forced by the state to close in 1910, they did not reopen, but from 1912 to 1916 there was automobile racing at Sheepshead Bay. And, finally, Coney Island became famous for its amusement parks, especially Steeplechase (1897–1965), Luna Park (1903–44), and Dreamland (1904–11); there were also amusement parks in nearby Canarsie (Golden City Amusement Park, 1907) and Bergen Beach (Percy Williams Amusement Park, 1905). Brooklyn was a center of the new sport of baseball from the 1850s on and had a major league franchise as early as 1873. The team that would be best known as the Brooklyn Dodgers first played in 1883. Their famous stadium, Ebbets Field, opened in 1913.

Erasmus Hall Academy was founded in 1787 at Flatbush and Church Aves and was the first secondary school chartered by the New York State Regents. It would be another half century before Brooklyn had its own board of education, created in 1843. The Brooklyn Female Academy began in 1845, but a fire destroyed the institution in 1853. Harriet Putnam Packer (1820–92) donated money to reestablish the school as the Packer Collegiate Institute, which opened in 1854 on Joralemon St in Brooklyn Heights. Brooklyn is home to many private and public colleges: Polytechnic University (1854), St. Francis College (1859), Pratt Institute (1887), Brooklyn Law School (1901), St. Joseph's College (1916), Long Island University (1926), Brooklyn College (1930) , New York City Technical College (1946), Kingsborough Community College (1964), and Medgar Evers College (1968).

Recent History

Brooklyn reached its peak population in 1950 at 2,738,175. During World War II its economy had seemed to be the picture of health. Brooklyn Navy Yard operated in full production, employing 75,000 workers around the clock, while docking facilities, such as the Brooklyn Army Terminal, boomed with war workers. Fort Hamilton teemed with servicemen, the New York Maritime Training Center at Sheepshead Bay prepared merchant marines for ocean duty, and Floyd Bennett Field was converted to a naval air station. Following the war, however, fortunes began to change for Brooklyn as industries downsized because of cheaper labor elsewhere and an aging industrial infrastructure. One by one, Brooklyn's 50 breweries disappeared; Brooklyn's trolley cars were replaced; the *Brooklyn Daily Eagle* closed in 1955; the Brooklyn Paramount and Fox theaters closed in the early 1960s; and, finally, the Brooklyn Navy Yard closed in 1966. Arguably the most wrenching and best-remembered loss of the era was the decision of the Brooklyn Dodgers to relocate to Los Angeles after the 1957 season, shortly after winning their only World Series championship in 1955.

By 1980 the borough's population was half a million less than that of 1950. As many white Brooklynites were relocating to the suburbs of Long Island, African American, Latinos, and Asians were moving into the borough in large numbers. The changes wrought by these movements cannot be underestimated. On the eve of World War II, in 1940, 4% of the population of Brooklyn was not white. By 1980 that percentage was up to 44% and by 2000, 59%. Fewer Whites lived in Brooklyn in 1990 than in 1900. Blacks began to assume positions of importance in the borough's politics. In 1968 Shirley Chisholm became the first African American member of Congress from Brooklyn and the first black woman elected to the House of Representatives. The same year a bitterly divisive school strike over the decentralization plans of the Ocean Hill–Brownsville Community School Board, in

Winter Scene in Brooklyn (1820), by Louisa A. Coleman, 1853.

which allegations of racism and anti-Semitism were exchanged, revealed some of the tensions in the new racial realities in Brooklyn. There would be other ugly incidents in Brooklyn: for example, widespread looting during the 1977 blackout and a riot between Hasidic Jews and Africans in Crown Heights after an unfortunate traffic accident in 1991.

The development of public housing and roadways caused urban upheaval. With the creation of the New York City Housing Authority (1934), the city would become the landlord for hundreds of thousands. The first projects dealt with the need for housing during the depression: Williamsburg Houses (1938), Red Hook Houses (1939), and, for veterans, Fort Greene Houses (1944). The postwar projects became synonymous with low-cost housing for minorities, such as the Farragut Houses in Fort Greene (1952) and the Van Dyke Houses in Brownsville (1955). Major arterial roadways had a disruptive effect on many Brooklyn neighborhoods. Robert Moses planned to circle the city with a "circumferential highway." The Belt Parkway (1941) began on the southern border and continued along the western shore and north along the East River, slicing through Canarsie, Sheepshead Bay, Gravesend, and Bay Ridge. The Gowanus Expressway (1939–64) effectively cut off Red Hook from the rest of the borough. The Brooklyn-Queens Expressway (1937–64), built on the pillars of the old Third Avenue Elevated Train, cut through Gowanus, Brooklyn Heights, and Williamsburg. The last massive construction project of the 20th century, the Verrazano-Narrows Bridge (1964) and its approach roads, disrupted life in Bay Ridge.

Amid the changes and upheavals of recent decades, there is much evidence of a new urban revival. Brooklyn Heights became the state's first landmarked historic district in 1966, and in the early 21st century, there are 16 historic districts in Brooklyn. King's Plaza (1970), Brooklyn's largest indoor mall, thrives in the Mill Basin area. The former Floyd Bennett Field became part of Gateway National Recreation Area in 1972. Starrett City (1974; now Spring Creek Towers) is a complex of 46 apartment buildings in East New York that spurred the development of Gateway Plaza and the adjacent Gateway Houses. Major corporations, such as Chase, Morgan Stanley, and Goldman Sachs, developed Metrotech Center (1987), a 10-block complex in downtown Brooklyn. Nearby, the New York Marriot at the Brooklyn Bridge opened in 1998, the first new hotel in the borough in 40 years. The Brooklyn Academy of Music (BAM) began hosting the Next Wave Festival in 1983, a regular opera series began in 1989, and the Rose Cinemas opened in 1998, featuring independent art films. The Botanic Garden–Steinhardt Conservatory (1988) opened at Brooklyn Botanic Garden.

Revitalization and gentrification of neighborhoods attracted a younger generation to Brooklyn in Park Slope, Greenpoint, Kensington, and other neighborhoods. Some neighborhoods were redefined when historic districts were created during the 1970s; for example, Gowanus became Cobble Hill and Carroll Garden. Chinese immigrants congregated in Sunset Park, Middle Eastern shopkeepers on Atlantic Ave, Mexicans near Borough Park, and Russians in Brighton and Manhattan Beaches.

Between 1980 and 2000, Brooklyn gained over 200,000 residents, many of whom reflected the new ethnic mix of the borough, with substantial numbers of African and Caribbean immigrants, Latinos, Chinese, and Hasidic and Russian Jews. The annual West Indian-American Day and Parade, held on Eastern Parkway since 1967, is one of the city's most colorful ethnic festivals. In the early 21st century, Brooklyn's residents represent racial, ethnic, and religious groups from over 150 countries. In the 2000 census, the racial composition of Brooklyn was 41% White, 36% African American, 8% Asian, and 14% mixed or other race. Those of Latino ethnicity made up 20%.

See also BEER AND BREWING; CAROUSELS; FINNS; OLMSTED, FREDERICK LAW; STREET RAILWAYS; WATERFRONTS.

Standard older histories are Henry R. Stiles, *The Civil, Political, Professional, and Ecclesiastical History of the City of Brooklyn* (1884); Ralph Foster Weld, *Brooklyn Village, 1816–1834* (1938); and Harold C. Syrett, *City of Brooklyn, 1865–1898* (1944). More recent histories include David Ment, *The Shaping of a City: A Brief History of Brooklyn* (1979); Elliot Willensky, *When Brooklyn Was the World: 1920–1957* (1986); Ellen M. Snyder-Grenier, *Brooklyn! An Illustrated History* (1996); and John B. Manbeck, with Zella Jones, *The Brooklyn Century* (2001). Accounts of the borough's neighborhoods can be found in John B. Manbeck, ed., *The Neighborhoods of Brooklyn*, rev ed. (2004), and significant studies of individual neighborhoods include Jonathan Rieder, *Canarsie: The Jews and Italians of Brooklyn against Liberalism* (1985) and Wendell Pritchett, *Brownsville, Brooklyn: Blacks, Jews, and the Changing Face of the Ghetto* (2002). Charles Denson's *Coney Island: Lost and Found* (2003) is representative of an enormous literature. Jerald E. Podair's *The Strike That Changed New York* (2002) is the best study of the 1968 Ocean Hill–Brownsville controversy. Studies on specific topics include Marc Linder and Lawrence S. Zacharias, *Of Cabbages and Kings County: Agriculture and the Formation of Modern Brooklyn* (1999) on 19th-century agriculture; Brian J. Cudahy, *How We Got to Coney Island: The Development of Mass Transportation in Brooklyn and Kings County* (2002); David G. McCullough, *The Great Bridge* (1972) on the Brooklyn Bridge; and Jeffrey I. Richman, *Brooklyn's Green-Wood Cemetery: New York's Buried Treasure* (1998). Craig Wilder's *Covenant with Color: Race and Social Power in Brooklyn* (2000) is a comprehensive history of African Americans, and two distinctive Brooklyn-based Jewish populations are profiled in Annelise Orleck, *The Soviet-Jewish Americans* (1999) and Jerome R. Mintz, *Hasidic People: A Place in the New World* (1992). The Jackie Robinson era of the Brooklyn Dodgers and its denouement are discussed in Roger Kahn, *The Boys of Summer* (1971) and Michael Shapiro, *The Last Good Season* (2003).

John B. Manbeck

Brooklyn, Battle of. See LONG ISLAND, BATTLE OF.

Brooklyn Academy of Music (BAM). Performing arts center. Founded in 1861 in Brooklyn Heights, BAM moved in 1908 to its current location in the Fort Greene neighborhood at 30 Lafayette Ave, a building designed by Henry Beaumont Herts and Hugh Tallant. Isadora Duncan, Arturo Toscanini, and Sarah Bernhardt performed at BAM. Enrico Caruso appeared there many times, most tragically on 11 Dec 1920, when a performance of Donizetti's *L'Elisir d'Amore* was stopped when he suffered a throat hemorrhage, a sign of the cancer that would take his life within a year.

With the appointment of Harvey Lichtenstein as executive director in 1967, BAM began to reassert itself as a major cultural force. The Next Wave Festival, founded in 1983, showcased avant-garde music, dance, and theater, often featuring the work of minimalist composers like Philip Glass and John Adams. A regular opera series, started in 1989, brought in notable European companies. In 1991 the Brooklyn Philharmonic became BAM's resident orchestra. The Rose Cinemas opened in 1998, featuring independent and foreign films on four screens. In the early 21st century, live performances were given in a 2,100-seat opera house and a 900-seat theater. BAM's new-found vitality and trendiness has paralleled the revival of its surrounding neighborhoods, Fort Greene and downtown Brooklyn.

McGowan, Martha. *Growing Up in Brooklyn: The Brooklyn Academy of Music, Mirror of a Changing Borough* (Brooklyn: Brooklyn Academy of Music, 1983)

Andrea Olmstead

Brooklyn Bridge. Pioneering suspension bridge. With a span of 1,596 feet (486.5 m), it was built between 1868 and 1883 over the East River between Brooklyn and Manhattan, then two separate cities. It was proposed and designed by wire-rope pioneer John A. Roebling. When he died in 1869 from injuries sustained on the site, his son, Washington A. Roebling, went on to complete the bridge after years of difficulties with corrupt contractors and politicians. The most challenging part of the project was sinking the foundations by using compressed air in caissons, which were dug to greater depths than ever before. The high air pressures led to debilitating illness for many workers from caisson disease, or the bends, the cure for which was then unknown. Working alongside the men, Washington Roebling's health was destroyed by the bends in 1872. From then until 1883 he supervised construction from a house in Brooklyn Heights within sight of the bridge. His wife Emily Warren Roebling conveyed his instructions and took over on-site supervision.

The structure was built to carry rapid transit trains in its center lanes, carriages on outer lanes, and pedestrians on a wide promenade over the center lanes. Its massive masonry towers with Gothic arches over the roadways, the soaring steel truss roadway, and steel suspension cables webbed by diagonal stays from the towers all combined to give the Brooklyn Bridge a unique aesthetic power. Technically the project pioneered the use of steel in bridge construction as well as the use of compressed air in caisson work and also spurred new design of wire rope. Celebrated in poetry, painting, and photography perhaps more than any other American engineering work, the bridge reinforced the natural linkages between Brooklyn and Manhattan and aided the political consolidation of the two cities in 1898. At the beginning of the 21st century, the Brooklyn Bridge retains its unique promenade offering spectacular views of the city, while all lower lanes accommodate automobile traffic.

McCullough, David. *The Great Bridge* (New York: Simon & Schuster, 1972)
Trachtenberg, Alan. *Brooklyn Bridge: Fact and Symbol* (New York: Oxford Univ Press, 1965)

Thomas R. Flagg

Brooklyn College. Public college. Between 1917 and 1924 the College of the City of New York and Hunter College established centers in Brooklyn that, in 1926, were organized as the Brooklyn Collegiate Center, offering the first two years of college work in response to the increased need for access to public higher education in that borough. The Board of Higher Education authorized Brooklyn College in 1930 as the third New York City municipal liberal arts college and the first to be coeducational. Its lovely neo-Georgian campus in the Midwood section of Brooklyn (1936) is architecturally distinguished. Harry Gideonse, a well-known political scientist and intellectual, was president of the college from 1939 to 1966. Brooklyn College maintains a strong focus on the liberal arts, and in 1980 the faculty instituted a widely praised core curriculum. Outstanding alumni include US Congresswoman Shirley Chisholm (1946), New York State Assembly Speaker Stanley Fink (1956), and US Senator Barbara Boxer (1962). In 2002 the college offered more than 60 undergraduate majors and programs and 39 master's programs, and enrolled 10,767 undergraduate and 4,868 graduate students.

Horowitz, Murray M. *Brooklyn College, the First Half-Century* (New York: Brooklyn College Press, 1981)

Barbara J. Dunlap

Brooklyn Dodgers. The Brooklyn Baseball Club played its first season with the minor league Interstate League in 1883 and in 1884 transferred to the major league American Association. The team was referred to as the Brooklyns, or the Grays, from the color of the uniforms. When they won their first pennant in 1889 they were called the Bridegrooms or Grooms because a number of players had married in the off-season. Other early nicknames included the Gladiators (1890), the Superbas (1899–1910), and the Robins (1914–31). The many trolley tracks near the team's home at Washington Park in the Park Slope or Gowanus section of Brooklyn led to the nickname Trolley Dodgers, which was shortened to Dodgers, but not until 1932 did this became the official name. The team joined the National League in 1890. Charles C. Ebbets became president in 1898, bringing in star players such as Wee Willie Keeler, Hughie Jennings, Joe Kelley, and Joe McGinnity, who led Brooklyn to first-place finishes in 1899 and 1900.

Ebbets Field in Flatbush opened on 5 Apr 1913, and Wilbert Robinson became manager in 1914. An infusion of new talent including Jake Daubert and Zack Wheat helped the Dodgers take home the pennant in 1916 and 1920, although they lost the World Series both times. After 1920 the Dodgers finished as high as third place only twice in the next 18 years. The team wore the name Dodgers on their jerseys for the first time in 1933. By then their chronic ineptness had earned them another nickname, Dem Bums, an image immortalized in a famous 1937 cartoon by Willard Mullin.

New general manager Leland Stanford "Larry" MacPhail Sr hired Walter "Red" Barber to broadcast Dodger games over the radio in 1937, introduced night baseball to Brooklyn, and added players Dolph Camilli, Pee Wee Reese, Pete Reiser, Dixie Walker, and Joe Medwick. The Dodgers brought the National League championship back to Brooklyn in 1941, but a dropped third-strike pitch by Dodgers catcher Mickey Owen in game four of the 1941 World Series allowed the New York Yankees to win the game and the World Series. The following year, MacPhail was succeeded by Branch Rickey. In 1947 Rickey introduced the major leagues' first African American player in the 20th century, Jackie Robinson. Led by Robinson, Reese, Gil Hodges, Roy Campanella, Duke Snider, and Carl Furillo, the Dodgers played in the World Series six times between 1947 and 1956, all "subway series" against the crosstown New York Yankees. The Yankees won all of the contests except for the one in 1955, when the Dodgers won their only World Series victory.

Soon after becoming the president of the Dodgers in 1950, Walter O'Malley began negotiations with New York City for land on which to build a domed, 52,000-seat stadium. Thwarted in his attempts to acquire a parcel at Flatbush and Atlantic Aves, O'Malley accepted an offer of land and financial incentives to move the team to Los Angeles. To the great anger and sadness of their many fans, the Dodgers played their last game as a Brooklyn team on 29 Sept 1957.

Kahn, Roger. *The Boys of Summer* (New York: Harper & Row, 1971)
McNeil, William F. *The Dodgers Encyclopedia* (Champaign, Ill: Sports Publishing, 1997)
Shapiro, Michael. *The Last Good Season: Brooklyn, the Dodgers, and Their Final Pennant Race Together* (New York: Doubleday, 2003)

Larry McGill

Brooklyn Navy Yard. The facility—known officially as US Naval Shipyard, New York—lies on the Brooklyn shore of the East River at Wallabout Bay, anchorage of British prison ships during the American Revolution. Secretary of the Navy Benjamin Stoddart established the yard in 1800, and during the Civil War its workers built 16 warships for the Union navy and also fitted out numerous vessels, including the pioneering, armor-plated USS *Monitor* for blockading service. With the coming of the "new steel navy" in the 1890s, the yard produced turreted battleships, including ill-fated USS *Maine,* destroyed under mysterious circumstances in Havana Harbor in 1898, and USS *Arizona,* sunk at Pearl Harbor in 1941.

During World War II the yard ranked as the largest and busiest shipyard in the world and the largest industrial plant in New York State, employing 75,000 men and women and generating monthly payrolls of $15 million. After wartime expansion the yard included 6 dry docks, 2 building ways, 8 piers, 270 buildings, 30 miles (48 km) of railroad track, and a huge hammerhead crane for lifting battleship turrets into position. From 1941 to 1945 the facility built 18 navy warships, including the USS *Missouri,* 2 other battleships, and 5 aircraft carriers. The Brooklyn yard handled countless damaged vessels as well, repairing or modifying 345 ships in 1942, 869 in 1943, and 1,539 in 1944. The yard performed routine repairs on 6 cruisers, 262 destroyers, 825 destroyer escorts, and 103 auxiliary ships in 1944. It also converted 11,138 transports and assembled 3,581 prefabricated landing craft. A day-and-night, 7-days-a-week wartime production schedule clocked 2,479,830 worker hours in 1942, rising to 6,591,203 worker hours in 1944. With the coming of the Cold War, the navy shifted production from New York City, viewed as a prime nuclear target, to shipyards in Bath, Maine, Newport News, Va, and Pascagoula, Miss. The Brooklyn yard closed in 1966. At the beginning of the 21st century, the site holds an industrial park.

Berner, Thomas F. *The Brooklyn Navy Yard* (Charleston, SC: Arcadia, 1999)

Joseph F. Meany Jr

Brooks, Louise (*b* Cherryvale, Kans, 14 Nov 1906; *d* Rochester, 8 Aug 1985). Actress, dancer, and writer. The daughter of a prosperous lawyer and an amateur pianist, Brooks studied dance from an early age, debuting in a local charity event at age 4. In the summer of 1921 she moved to New York City to attend Ted Shawn's summer dance school. Impressed by her considerable talent, Shawn and his colleague Martha Graham invited her to join his Denishawn dance company. Dismissed after two seasons, most likely due to her extracurricular interests in men and alcohol, she found work in the chorus of *George White's Scandals* and in 1925 appeared in Florenz Ziegfeld's *Louie the 14th,* which led to a five-year contract with Paramount Pictures, then filming at Famous Players–Lasky studios in Astoria (Queens Co). Between 1925 and 1929 she appeared in 14 films, including Howard Hawks's *A Girl in Every Port* (1928). Her striking beauty and sensual screen presence caused a sensation. When Paramount reneged on a contracted raise, Brooks traveled to Berlin to star in two films directed by Georg Wilhelm Pabst, *Pandora's Box* (1929) and *Diary of a Lost Girl* (1929). After her refusal in 1929 to cooperate with Paramount and dub her part in a silent film the studio hoped to release as a talkie, the studio instigated the false rumor that her voice was unsuitable for sound films. When Brooks moved to Hollywood, Calif, in 1930 without a contract and burdened by her reputation as a difficult employee, she was reduced to occasional supporting roles. After completing her last film, *Overland Stage Raiders* (1938) starring John Wayne, Brooks returned to Wichita and in 1940 opened a dance school. When it failed she decamped to New York City, arriving by January 1943. She endured years of obscurity and poverty until a new generation of French fans led by Henri Langlois of the Cinémathèque Française rediscovered her in the 1950s and film archivist James Card encouraged both her move to Rochester in 1956 and her interest in writing. From 1956 to 1977 she published a series of essays recounting her experiences in Hollywood and abroad in various film journals; these were collected in the volume *Lulu in Hollywood* in 1982.

Paris, Barry. *Louise Brooks* (New York: Knopf, 1989)

Ellen Prokop

Brooks Locomotive Works. Manufacturer of steam locomotives in Dunkirk (Chautauqua Co). The company was shaped by Horatio G. Brooks, who was born 30 Oct 1828 in Portsmouth, NH. Brooks apprenticed in his cousins' machine shop and developed an interest in locomotives. He worked at the Boston and Maine Railroad shops in Andover, Mass, becoming a road fireman and then a locomotive engineer by age 21. New York and Erie Railroad hired Brooks to drive an engine from Boston to Dunkirk, where he moved to work as an engineer on the Erie line. He drove the first train along the newly opened Erie route on 13 May 1851 but left after helping to lead a strike by engineers. New management brought him back to the Erie in 1859. He worked as master mechanic and Western Division superintendent, and in 1865 became the line's superintendent of motive power and machinery. In 1868 the railroad moved its main facility to Buffalo. With four other men, Brooks leased the empty Dunkirk shops and organized Brooks Locomotive Co in November 1869. He became president and superintendent with Marshall L. Hinman as secretary-treasurer. The new company produced 32 engines in 1870, all purchased by the Erie. The panic of 1873 hurt the company, but Brooks persevered. With better business conditions, the company built 100 locomotives in 1880 and 200 in 1882. During these same years Horatio Brooks served as village president and later as city mayor after Dunkirk's incorporation in 1880. Brooks bought the Erie shops in 1883, erected new buildings, and acquired more acreage. The Brooks locomotives also won top awards at the Chicago Industrial Exposition that year. On 22 Feb 1884 the company completed its 1,000th locomotive. After Horatio Brooks's death in 1887, the company faced hard times, mostly caused by national depression in the 1890s. But, headed by son-in-law Edward H. Nichols and later by Hinman, the Brooks Works continued to turn out engines ranging from tiny tank locomotives for the New York Elevated to some of the largest railroad engines in the nation. Prosperity returned in 1901 when Brooks merged with Schenectady Locomotive and other engine builders to form American Locomotive Co (ALCO), headquartered in Schenectady. From 1915 to 1917 the company produced raw materials. After World War I the Dunkirk division developed three-cylinder locomotives and emerged as ALCO's number two locomotive shop. By 1921 the plant boasted 4,500 employees. Brooks Locomotive Works and Dunkirk ALCO produced more than 13,000 locomotives between 1869 and 1928, when ALCO consolidated all locomotive work at Schenectady.

Hungerford, Edward M. *Men of Erie* (New York: Random House, 1946)
White, John H. *American Locomotive Builders* (Washington, DC: Bass, 1982)

Albert S. Eggerton Jr

Brookville {Brookville, village (pop 2,126) in Oyster Bay, Nassau Co; Old Brookville, village (pop 2,167) in Oyster Bay; Upper Brookville, village (pop 1,801) in Oyster Bay}. The area was settled in the 17th century by Dutch farmers, and Indian fighter Capt John Underhill was given a tract of land there in 1663. Brookville was known as Wolverhampton and Wolver Hollow until 1848, when the inhabitants decided to change the name to Brookville. Old Brookville was one of the areas that supplied corn to the Duryea Corn Starch Factory at Glen Cove in the 19th century. In the 1910s and 1920s, estates were created throughout the area. Old Brookville incorporated in 1929, Brookville in 1931, and Upper Brookville in 1932. Arthur H. Dean, Upper Brookville's mayor from 1952 to 1958, was simultaneously US ambassador to South Korea. In 1958 the federal government built a Nike missile installation in Brookville. The C. W. Post Campus of Long Island University (1954) is located in Brookville; Banfi Vintners, Nassau County's only vineyard (55 acres/22.3 ha), and the 409-acre (165.5 ha) Planting Fields Arboretum State Historic Park (1949) are in Upper Brookville.

Tom Kuehhas

Brookwood Labor College. See WORKERS' EDUCATION.

broomcorn. A variety of sorghum, *Sorghum vulgare,* first grown as a commercial farm crop in New York State late in the 18th century. While broomcorn is a grain, it has for the most part been cultivated for its bristles. Only the panicle, the seed-bearing stalk at the top of the plant, is of value in broom making, the rest is waste. The broom industry in New York State may have begun at the Shaker community established in the late 1770s at Niskayuna [now Watervliet, Albany Co]. The Shakers are credited with manufacturing the first commercially produced flat brooms. The earliest cultivation of broomcorn in New York State may have been in the Mohawk Valley between Albany and Amsterdam, but it had become a significant farm crop elsewhere in the state by the mid–19th century. Farmers in Schoharie Co produced and sold thousands of tons. Some of these farmers also made brooms as a cottage industry, as did others in the state. The state's 1855 agricultural census reported that four factories in the Village of Schoharie (Schoharie Co) produced a total of 77,800 brooms and purchased 40 tons (36 MT) of broomcorn, at a cost of $180 per ton. The *History of the County of Schenectady, NY* (1866) noted there were so many broom factories in Schenectady during the 19th century that it was called "the City That Sweeps the World." Production reached its peak there between 1840 and 1860 with about a million brooms and brushes manufactured in Schenectady annually. Some broomcorn was still being grown in the Mohawk Valley in 1950, but by that time New York State broom factories were purchasing broomcorn from western states and Mexico.

Doris Lange

Broome. Town (pop 947) in SE Schoharie Co. Tory and Indian raids during the Revolution drove out the original Dutch and Palatine settlers, but emigrants from older Schoharie Co settlements and New England resettled Broome after the war. Formed from Schoharie in 1797 as Bristol, the town was renamed Broome in 1808. Among early residents was Daniel Shays (1747–1825), leader of the 1786–87 Shays's Rebellion in Massachusetts; when he left, his farm near Livingstonville was taken up by David Williams (1754–1831), one of the captors of Maj John André. Hilly uplands and deep ravines border the valley of the Catskill Creek, which rises near Franklinton. Dairying and logging were the chief economic activities by the early 21st century.

Peter Johnson and Dawn Johnson

Broome County (607 mi²/1,572 km²; pop 200,586). It was created from Tioga Co in 1806, but the Towns of Berkshire and Tioga were ceded back to Tioga Co in 1822. Named after Lt Gov John Broome, the county is currently divided into the City of Binghamton (the county seat) and 16 towns that contain 7 incorporated villages. Broome Co is located entirely within the Appalachian Upland physiographic province. The bulk lies within the Susquehanna Hills subregion. The remainder, known as the Delaware Hills, lies immediately east of the Susquehanna River. It contains the highest elevations (over 2,000 ft/610 m) and the strongest relief (up to 700 ft/210 m) between valley floor and hilltop in the county. The lowest elevation of 810 feet (247 m) occurs where the Susquehanna River exits the county at its western border. Bedrock is of Upper Devonian age throughout and consists primarily of shale and siltstone. All of Broome Co was glaciated, as evidenced by the many well-rounded, rolling hills. The large valleys served as major meltwater channels and, as a result, contain substantial amounts of unconsolidated sediments. Other glacial features include eskers, kames, kame terraces, and kettle lakes. Approximately 90% of the soils were formed from unsorted glacial till. The better-quality soils are primarily found scattered in the larger valleys, where the most economically viable farms are also found.

Broome Co's climate is humid-continental. Average January and July temperatures are 22°F (-6°C) and 69°F (21°C), respectively, in the larger valleys (1°–3° colder in higher elevations). In a typical year daytime summer temperatures occasionally rise above 90°F (32°C); nighttime winter lows sometimes drop below 0°F (-18°C). Seasonal snowfall ranges from over 80 inches (203 cm) in the higher elevations to less than 40 inches (102 cm) in some of the major river valleys. Average annual precipitation ranges from 35 inches (89 cm) at Whitney Point in the northern part of the county to over 43 inches (109 cm) at Deposit in the extreme southeast corner. Major rivers include the Susquehanna, Chenango, Tioughnioga, and Delaware. The Susquehanna flows south into Pennsylvania, reenters the county, and flows west before exiting a second time. Broome Co lies almost entirely within the greater watershed of the Susquehanna. The exception is a small area in the extreme southeast corner that drains into the Delaware, which serves as a county boundary south of Deposit. Primeval forest cover consisted of three different communities, and three principal valleys contained central hardwood communities dominated by beech, sugar maple, basswood, oak, and chestnut. The Delaware Hills supported a spruce-fir forest, while the rest of the uplands were blanketed by an Alleghenian hardwood community consisting primarily of beech, sugar maple, hemlock, white pine, and basswood.

Native Inhabitants

Fluted point discoveries in the Towns of Kirkwood and Dickinson indicate Paleo-Indian presence from 10,000 to 8000 BC. By 2000 BC an Archaic culture developed in the advancing forest area but was replaced by a much later Native American culture by AD 1000. Owasco settlements existed in western and central Broome Co. From the mid-1720s until the late 1770s, the area along the Chenango River from its juncture with the Tioughnioga to its confluence with the Susquehanna was one of the most tribally mixed areas in Iroquoia. The largest village was Oquaga (Onoquaga), near what is now Windsor; although under Oneida control, it was populated by a mixture of Indian groups, Iroquois and non-Iroquois, as was Otsiningo, an Onondaga-controlled village near present-day Binghamton.

The first known European visitor was Etienne Brûlé in 1618. Conrad Weiser, who came in 1737, wrote a description of the region. Moravian missionaries from Pennsylvania arrived by 1748, but the 1768 Treaty of Fort Stanwix excluded further white settlement. During the early years of the American Revolution, Mohawk chief Joseph Brant used Oquaga as a base of operations from which to raid New York Colony frontier settlements. In response, Oquaga was destroyed in 1778 by Col William Butler's colonial forces. A year later Gens John Sullivan and James Clinton led Revolutionary troops through the area to destroy remaining Iroquois opposition. Clinton's forces reached Otsiningo only to find it had been destroyed by its inhabitants. They then joined with Sullivan's troops in what is now the Town of Union before marching west to Newtown [now Elmira]. Most of the Native American population fled the area, with many joining Brant in Canada. Evidence suggests that about 200 Native Americans lived near the present hamlet of Castle Creek [now in Chemung Co] until about 1794.

Settlement

The resolution of the boundary and jurisdictional dispute between Massachusetts and New York following the Revolution resulted in the former being awarded ownership of the 230,400-acre (93,240 ha) tract known as the Boston Ten Towns, which included northern and much of western Broome Co. Massachusetts then sold the entire tract to a 60-member company at 12.5¢ per acre (.4 ha). New York Colony patented and sold the rest of the present county's land to speculators including Robert Harpur, John Jay, William Smith, and Marinus Willett. William Bingham bested competing bidders and acquired 10,000 acres (4,000 ha) of land at the confluence of the Susquehanna and Chenango Rivers in 1787. European American settlement began *ca* 1785 and consisted primarily of transplanted New England Yankees from Massachusetts, Connecticut, Vermont, and northern New England, some of them by way of the Hudson Valley. Many purchased lands from proprietors of large tracts, while some squatted and only later purchased the land. African Americans made up about 1.5% of the county's population during its first century, the earliest arriving as slaves with their New England owners. A few upper-class residents purchased slaves as late as the early 1820s. Working primarily as domestics, many Blacks settled in Binghamton, but a few families located in rural towns like Vestal and Triangle. After 1840 Pennsylvanians joined the earlier arrivals, coming from Susquehanna and Lackawanna Cos and from the Wyoming Valley.

Economic Development

The initial economy centered on agriculture and small-scale milling operations. Clusters of pioneer settlement began at the future Village of Union [now Endicott] in 1785 and at Chenango Point [now Binghamton] in the late 1780s. Other central places, including Lisle, Harpursville, and Castle Creek, were established by the late 1790s. The convergence of the Chenango, Tioughnioga, and Susquehanna Valleys made the area a natural hub of traffic and trade. Commercial river traffic was dominated by rafts of lumber floated south to Pennsylvania and Chesapeake markets. A limited quantity of agricultural produce was shipped as well. Early development was handicapped by a small population base and an inefficient transport network. The Chenango Canal opened in 1837, linking Binghamton and Broome Co to the Erie Canal at Utica. The canal facilitated shipment of foodstuffs, furniture, and other consumer goods

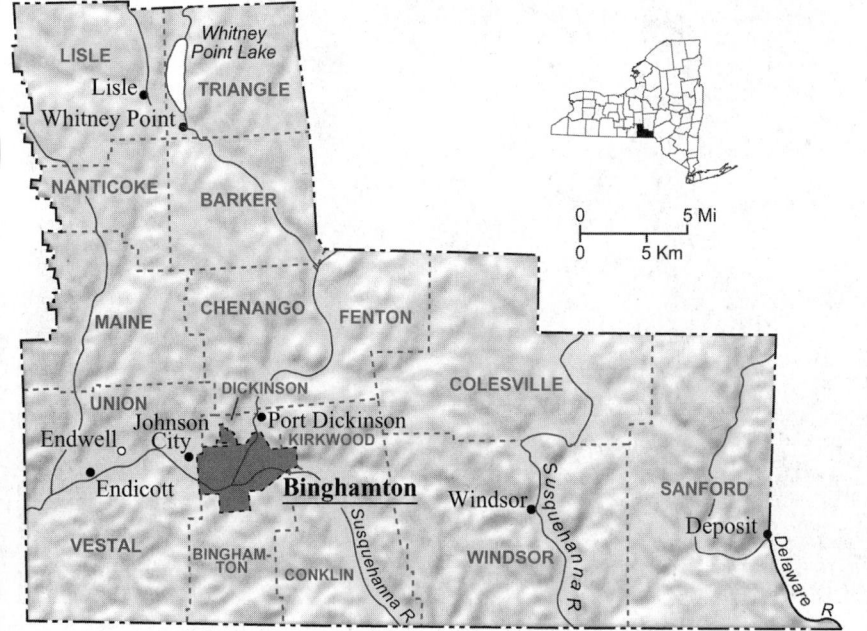

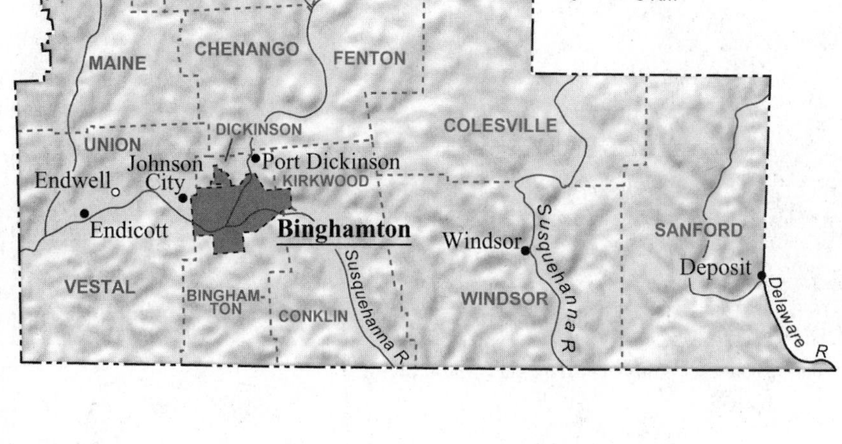

from the county and enhanced the range and quantity of dry goods for sale locally. Places grew up to handle canal traffic, such as Port Dickinson and Port Crane. Eleven years later the New York and Erie Railroad provided the first rail service. Initially constructed from the Hudson River to Lake Erie, the Erie became an important east-west trunk line and contributed substantially to the economic rise of Binghamton and the surrounding area over the next 100 years. North-south rail service was first available in 1854, and Binghamton became a significant rail center. Railroad competition resulted in closure of the Chenango Canal in 1878.

Grain was the most profitable cash crop in early years, and cattle raising and apple growing were also important. Farming turned increasingly to milk from the mid–19th century onward, but some crops such as oats and corn were produced for market. Dairy producer Crowley moved its operations to Binghamton from Poughkeepsie in 1915. The first Farm Bureau in the country began in Broome Co in 1911 to educate farmers about new agricultural methods.

Post–Civil War assembly line factories brought new industries, and cigars became a major product. Starting with one firm *ca* 1870, over 70 factories employed 5,000 workers and produced 100 million cigars annually by the turn of the century. Most of the factories were in Binghamton, and production ranked second in the nation after New York City. The influx of immigrants in the late 1800s, an expanded rail system, and undeveloped land in the urban core all encouraged industrial expansion. In addition to cigars, patent medicine, furniture, time recorders, shoes, and nearly 200 other products were made in the late 19th century. Labor unrest was common, especially in the cigar industry, and labor organizations took hold.

Immigration and Ethnicity

The county began with largely English, Scots, and Scots-Irish roots. By the 1850s an influx of Irish and Germans changed that profile. The Irish were split between the farming communities and the urban area. Some worked in factories, while others worked in canal operations. The Germans were largely from the mercantile class. The mid–19th century also marked the arrival of the first Jewish immigrants, many of whom operated dry goods and similar stores. Transportation improvements brought large numbers of immigrants in the late 1800s and early 1900s. Population increases were dramatic: from 44,103 in 1870, to 78,809 in 1900, to 113,610 in 1920. Thousands of eastern Europeans, Russians, and Italians immigrated, settling around Binghamton's factories and following the expansion of what became Endicott Johnson Co to the company towns of Johnson City and Endicott beginning in 1888. Women played an important role in the development of industry. Some worked in factories prior to the Civil War, and thousands were employed in the manufacture of cigars, shoes, patent medicines, and other products.

Religion, Education, and Culture

The earliest known congregation was a short-lived Baptist church (1789) on the west bank of the Chenango River. By 1825 Broome Co included most of the major Protestant denominations: Episcopalian, Methodist, Presbyterian, Congregational, and Baptist. In 1838 the first Catholic church and two African American churches organized, and in 1899 the first synagogue opened in Binghamton. In the first half of the 20th century, a number of Orthodox churches were established; their gilt, onion-shaped domes now number over 20.

The first public schools were established in the 1790s, and the first private academy in 1799. The number of schools grew after limited state funding was enacted in 1812, and the system grew more sophisticated after adoption of the Union Free School Act (1853). School consolidation began in 1931 in the Windsor district and continued until Johnson City completed the process in 1964. There are 11 central school districts and one city district. Private schools such as the Lady Jane Grey School, a finishing school, parochial schools, and business schools such as the Ridley-Lowell Business and Technical Institute (1859) increased educational opportunities. As a response to the needs of returning veterans, Harpur College (now SUNY Binghamton) was founded in 1946. Broome Community College also opened in 1946.

The first newspaper, the *American Constellation,* began publication in 1800, and the current daily newspaper, the *Press and Sun-Bulletin,* has origins in the mid–19th century. The Ross Park Zoo, the fifth oldest zoo in the nation, opened in 1875. Both the Binghamton Philharmonic (1955) and the Tri-Cities Opera (1949) perform regularly at the Broome County Center for the Performing Arts (1975), known as The Forum. The Roberson Museum and Science Center (1953) and the Discovery Center (1983) are widely respected museums. Radio arrived with WNBF in 1929, and the first television station, also WNBF, went on the air in 1949. Among famous natives and residents are Rod Serling, Richard Deacon, Hugh Herbert, William Prince, and Slam Stewart.

Politics

Broome Co has traditionally been a conservative area, with a largely Republican majority in most governmental bodies. However, the area's most prominent 19th-century politician, Daniel S. Dickinson (1800–1866), was a Democrat and served as Binghamton's mayor, US district attorney, state lieutenant governor, and US senator. The most prominent 20th-century politician was Warren M. Anderson (1915–), majority leader of the state senate from 1972 to 1988. Broome Co government consisted of a four-member board of supervisors that began in 1806, but the structure was changed in 1969 to a legislative system to better reflect one person–one vote representation. Daily operations are overseen by an elected county executive.

The 20th Century

Broome Co experienced enormous economic growth between 1900 and 1920. Much of it was dependent on the influx of immigrant labor, the expanding cigar industry, and growing assembly line systems using the railroads to ship goods. Endicott Johnson became the area's largest employer, surpassing 20,000 workers in the 1947–52 period. The renaming of Endicott's Computing, Tabulating and Recording Co (C-T-R) as International Business Machines (IBM) in 1924 helped position that company in the international market. Link Aviation began in 1929 and cornered the market on the flight simulator. In 1940 the Triple Cities (Binghamton, Endicott, and Johnson City) had 107 manufacturing concerns employing 34,500 workers. World War II resulted in many local industries changing product lines to meet war demands, such as boots and guidance systems.

The end of World War II did not end industrialization, and many industries became closely tied to the Cold War. IBM moved its product line into the computer world. Link Aviation merged with other firms to produce items for defense use and space exploration. The development of better highways, especially I-81 (1961–68), Rte 17 (I-86) (four-lane, 1950–68), and I-88 (1976), allowed for the growth of suburbs. Urban population declined, and the population of many outlying towns increased in the second half of the 20th century. School population similarly increased outside the cities, while the number of

Crowley Foods employees inspecting milk at Binghamton plant, *ca* 1940.

BROOME CO POPULATION CENSUS FIGURES

	White	Nonwhite	Total Population	Foreign-Born
1810	8,077	53	8,130	—
1820	14,255	88	14,343	51
1830	17,483	96	17,579	112
1840	22,115	223	22,338	—
1850	30,229	431	30,660	1,580
1860	35,442	464	35,906	2,770
1870	43,622	481	44,103	4,045
1880	48,890	593	49,483	3,956
1890	62,332	641	62,973	5,869
1900	68,512	637	69,149	5,154
1910	78,071	738	78,809	8,776
1920	112,863	747	113,610	14,042
1930	146,170	852	147,022	17,624
1940	164,942	807	165,749	16,719
1950	183,799	899	184,698	15,172
1960	211,174	1,487	212,661	13,203
1970	218,699	3,116	221,815	10,129
1980	207,791	5,857	213,648	9,971
1990	203,387	8,773	212,160	9,105
2000	183,153	17,383	200,536	10,536

Notes: "Nonwhite" includes African Americans, Asians, American Indians, and Pacific Islanders and, for 2000, also the mixed race and other race categories. Through the 1960 census these figures primarily reflect the African American population. Foreign-born figures for 1820 and 1830 include only those not naturalized, and for 1930 and 1950, the foreign-born totals include Whites only. Other years include all foreign-born in the population.

POPULATIONS OF TOWNS AND CITIES, BROOME CO

Town or City, Year Founded	1800	1840	1880	1920	1960	2000
Barker, 1831	—	1,259	1,333	1,003	1,683	2,738
Binghamton, 1855	—	—	2,555	672	3,475	4,969
Binghamton (city), 1867	—	—	17,317	66,800	75,941	47,380
Chenango, 1791	1,149	5,465	1,590	1,183	9,858	11,454
Colesville, 1821	—	2,528	3,208	2,311	3,773	5,441
Conklin, 1824	—	1,475	1,420	796	4,347	5,940
Dickinson, 1890	—	—	—	1,975	6,591	5,335
Fenton, 1855[a]	—	—	1,555	1,111	5,920	6,909
Kirkwood, 1859	—	—	1,344	899	4,651	5,651
Lisle, 1801	660	1,560	2,399	1,219	1,587	2,707
Maine, 1848	—	—	2,129	1,360	3,931	5,459
Nanticoke, 1831	—	400	999	444	794	1,790
Sanford, 1821	—	1,173	3,495	2,681	2,489	2,477
Triangle, 1831	—	1,692	2,073	1,458	2,019	3,032
Union, 1791	921	3,165	2,596	25,651	64,423	56,298
Vestal, 1823	—	1,253	2,184	1,910	16,806	26,535
Windsor, 1807	—	2,368	3,286	2,137	4,373	6,421

Note: In 1800 the Towns of Chenango, Lisle, and Union were part of Tioga Co.

[a]Port Crane until 1867.

high schools decreased in Binghamton to one in 1985, and several elementary schools closed to adjust for the declining school-age census. Urban blight resulted in the adoption of urban renewal programs (1960–87) for Binghamton that, unfortunately, did not hold up to their promise of revitalization.

The population of the county reached its zenith in the 1970s and began a slow slide downward. It has continued to decline as many older industries, such as Endicott Johnson and those tied to defense contracts, closed or were forced to downsize or reconfigure product lines. Locally owned department stores closed, and malls and plazas have shifted the retail focus away from Binghamton into the Town of Vestal and the Oakdale area of Johnson City. The destruction wrought by urban renewal reawakened the need to preserve historic structures, and historic districts were created in several municipalities.

Broome Co has one of the earliest county histories. J. B. Wilkinson, *The Annals of Binghamton and of the Country Connected with It, from the Earliest Settlement* (1840), is filled with anecdotes of the pioneer era. Unfortunately, the standard history, H. P. Smith, *History of Broome County* (1885), adds little to it, but a 20th-century work, William F. Seward, *Binghamton and Broome Co: A History,* 3 vols (1924), is useful. Adding to knowledge of the settlement period is a recent work based on the personal and business papers of major land developers: Marjory B. Hinman, *Bingham's Land, Whitney's Town* (1996). In the second half of the 20th century, almost every town's history was chronicled in local publications of varying quality. Two recent countywide books are Lawrence Bothwell, *Broome County Heritage: An Illustrated History* (1981) and Gerald R. Smith, *Valley of Opportunity: A Pictorial History of the Greater Binghamton Area* (1986). Ross McGuire and Nancy Grey Osterud's *Working Lives: Broome County, NY, 1800–1930* (1980) is a superlative study that grew out of a museum exhibition and that explores both agricultural and industrial development. There are two important academic studies of labor: Scott Nash, "Parlor City Cigar Makers in the Gilded Age: Binghamton, NY, 1877–1894" (BS thesis, Cornell Univ, 1988), and Gerald Zahavi, *Workers, Managers, and Welfare Capitalism: The Shoeworkers and Tanners of Endicott-Johnson, 1890–1950* (1988).

Gerald R. Smith

Brotherhood of Sleeping Car Porters. See INTERNATIONAL BROTHERHOOD OF SLEEPING CAR PORTERS (BSCP).

Brotherton. By the 1770s white settlement in New England and Long Island had reduced Native American populations to scant numbers. Samson Occom, a Mohegan Indian and ordained Presbyterian minister, felt that removal to western lands was the key to their survival, and he explored the possibility of gaining sanctuary among the Oneida Nation of the Iroquois Confederacy. After delays caused by the American Revolution, in 1785 Occom led groups of Montauks, Narragansetts, Mohicans (Mahicans), Nanticokes, Pequots, and his own nation to a tract of land in the Oriskany Valley centered in what is now Marshall (Oneida Co). This area measured 6 mi^2 (16 km^2), and the newly arrived remnants of New England tribes called it Eeayam Quittoowauconnuck, in Algonquian, or Brothertown or Brotherton. A year later the Indians of today's Stockbridge-Munsee band of Mohicans were allowed an allocation nearby at New Stockbridge [now Stockbridge, Madison Co], and Occom served as spiritual leader of both groups. As he itinerated throughout Central New York, preaching at white churches, he also raised money to aid native settlements. Several hundred Christian Indian refugees settled in the new territory and resumed farming as their customary livelihood. Although the Indian nations in this new, forced proximity abandoned their local dialects and adopted English as the lingua franca, accepting "the Brotherton" as a collective label, they never succeeded in sufficiently suppressing cultural differences to attain a cohesive new community, despite some attempts to do so. When Occom died in 1792, no successor could prevent factions from arising. From the time of settlement there was severe pressure on the Brotherton to sell their land to white settlers, and by the early 19th century they had lost over two-thirds of their initial holdings. The Oneida faced similar pressure to sell their land and in the 1820s purchased land from the Menominee Nation in Wisconsin. The Brotherton followed their lead, began to move to Wisconsin in 1831, and continued to arrive for another decade. Dispossessed of their Wisconsin lands starting in 1839, the Brotherton Indian Nation has no reservation in the early 21st century and is currently seeking tribal recognition from the federal government. There are about 2,200 members, most of whom live in the area of Fond du Lac, Wisc.

Trigger, Bruce G., ed. *Northeast,* vol 15 of *Handbook of North American Indians* (Washington, DC: Smithsonian Institution, 1978)

Henry Warner Bowden

Brown, Charles Brockden (*b* Philadelphia, 17 Jan 1771; *d* Philadelphia, 22 Feb 1810). Novelist and editor. Born a Quaker, Brown was educated in Philadelphia from 1781 to 1786 at the Friends' Latin School, where he displayed an early enthusiasm for writing. In Philadelphia he studied law and met Elihu Hubbard Smith, a medical student, whose friendship eventually drew Brown to New York City for several extended stays. There Brown participated with Smith in the Friendly Club, an intellectual circle energized by the radical British novelist and political theorist William Godwin. For several years Brown moved between states, dabbled in periodical writing, and by early 1798 completed *Alcuin,* a dialogue on women's rights influenced by Mary Wollstonecraft, and two novels, *Sky-Walk,* which is now lost, and *Wieland.* Brown remained in New York City for his longest stay from 1798 until 1801, during which time he undertook his most well known writing. Brown survived the 1798 yellow fever outbreak, the worst in the city's history, which left his friend Smith among the 2,000 dead. The experience fueled his next novels, *Ormond* (1799) and the two-volume *Arthur Mervyn* (1799, 1800). Also in 1799 he founded *The Monthly Magazine* with the Friendly Club's support and published *Edgar Huntly.* The four major novels share preoccupations with human agency, sensory experience, social disorder, and the scientifically aberrant. Unlike these works, which were influenced by European Gothicists but set firmly on American soil, his final two novels, *Clara Howard* and *Jane Talbot* (both 1801), turned from horror and suspense toward domesticity. His novels were never a great commercial success, and he spent the remainder of his life editing journals. Brown influenced other writers like the British author Mary Shelley and Americans Edgar Allan Poe, Nathaniel Hawthorne, Margaret Fuller, and Herman Melville. In his later years Brown grew more conservative. Returning to Philadelphia in 1801, he married Elizabeth Linn (the daughter of prominent New York City minister William Linn) in 1804. At his death Brown was engaged in his family business, magazine ventures, and political pamphleteering. Contemporary scholars view Brown as the first American novelist with a substantial body of work.

Watts, Steven. *The Romance of Real Life: Charles Brockden Brown and the Origins of American Culture* (Baltimore: Johns Hopkins Univ Press, 1994)

Bryan Waterman

Brown, Jim [James Nathaniel] (*b* St. Simons Island, Ga, 17 Feb 1936). Football player and actor. Raised in Manhasset (Nassau Co), Brown was a star athlete in five sports at Manhasset High School. Though he entered Syracuse University at age 16 without an athletic scholarship, Brown is regarded as the school's greatest football player and all-around athlete. An All-American in football and lacrosse, Brown was also a double-figure scorer in basketball and ran track, finishing fifth in the national decathlon championship in his sophomore year. As a senior halfback in 1956, he scored 43 points (6 touchdowns and 7 kicked points-after) in a game against Colgate and led the team to the Cotton Bowl. Brown ran for 986 yards in just 8 games that season but finished fifth in balloting for the Heisman Trophy. The low placement likely reflected the reluctance of many sportswriters to vote for a black player. Brown ended his Syracuse career with 2,091 running yards, averaging 5.8 yards per carry. The Cleveland Browns made him their top pick in the 1957 National Football League (NFL) draft, and he was named the league's best rookie that year. Brown never missed a game in nine seasons, played in nine Pro Bowls, ran for 12,312 yards, led the NFL in rushing eight times (1957–61, 1963–65), and was twice named the NFL Most Valuable Player (1958, 1965). Though he retired at age 30 to pursue an acting career, Brown is regarded by many as the greatest professional football player of all time. He was inducted into the Pro Football Hall of Fame (1971), Lacrosse Hall of Fame (1984), and College Football Hall of Fame (1995), the only person honored by all three halls. Brown became active in political and social reform and in 1988 he created Amer-I-Can, a nationwide program to improve life-management skills of inner-city youth.

Brown, Jim, and Steve Delsohn. *Out of Bounds* (New York: Kensington Pub, 1989)

Bob Snyder

Jim Brown playing lacrosse at Syracuse University *ca* 1955.

Brown, John (*b* Torrington, Conn, 9 May 1800; *d* Charlestown [now Charles Town, W Va], 2 Dec 1859). Abolitionist. Raised in Hudson, Ohio, Brown received ministerial training before working as a tanner in Pennsylvania and Ohio. He went bankrupt during the panic of 1837, mostly because of his poor business skills and failed land speculations, and spent the rest of his life in or near poverty. A fervent opponent of slavery, by the late 1840s he had committed himself to fighting bondage and helping Blacks. In 1848, after a failed attempt at wool brokering in Springfield, Mass, he contacted Peterboro (Madison Co) philanthropist Gerrit Smith, who had pledged 120,000 acres (48,600 ha) of Adirondack land to free Blacks willing to settle and farm there. Brown asked Smith for a land donation so that he could live among the settlers and help "these poor despised Africans to try and encourage them." Smith did not agree to this, but in 1849 he sold Brown 244 acres (99 ha) in North Elba (Essex Co) at a dollar an acre. At the settlement called Timbucto, Brown lived and worked with African Americans, treating them as social equals and with a respect that was unusual for the period.

North Elba remained Brown's home for the last decade of his life, but Brown was often away, at antislavery conventions, attending to lawsuits over his failed wool business, and organizing Blacks to resist fugitive slave laws. In 1855 he went to the Kansas Terr to join in the fight over slavery's status. There he directed the massacre of five proslavery activists and settlers at Pottawatomie and fought slavery's supporters in numerous armed battles. He later entered Missouri, where he helped 11 enslaved African Americans escape to Canada. From 1857 to 1859 Brown planned an invasion of the South by abolitionists who would start a guerilla war against slavery. One of Brown's main financial backers was Gerrit Smith, who offered his support after meeting to discuss the plan in Peterboro in February 1858. Other New York State abolitionists, including Jermain Loguen and Harriet Tubman, supported him; Frederick Douglass urged caution, although Brown had drafted a provisional constitution for a postinvasion interim government at Douglass's Rochester home in 1859.

In October 1859 Brown led 18 men in a raid on the national armory at Harpers Ferry [now in W Va]; among them were two of Brown's sons, as well as William and Dauphin Thompson of North Elba and Shields Green of Rochester. The raid was a fiasco, and almost all of Brown's men were captured or killed. Brown was wounded but immediately put on trial, convicted, and sentenced to death. After his sentencing, Brown wrote hundreds of letters to supporters and sympathizers, and in the process made himself a martyr for the antislavery cause. He was hanged on 2 Dec 1859 and his body shipped back to North Elba. He was buried as a hero to the cause of liberty in the eyes of most Blacks and many white northern opponents of slavery and as an arch-villain to many northern conservatives and southern whites. Brown's North Elba farm is a National Historic Landmark and state historic site.

Finkelman, Paul, ed. *His Soul Goes Marching On: Responses to John Brown and the Harpers Ferry Raid* (Charlottesville: Univ Press of Virginia, 1995)

Paul Finkelman

Brownell, Herbert (*b* Peru, Nebr, 20 Feb 1904; *d* New York City, 1 May 1996). US attorney general. Brownell was raised in Lincoln, where his father was a science education professor at the University of Nebraska. He graduated from the University of Nebraska in 1924. After receiving his law degree from Yale University in 1927, Brownell took a position at Root, Clark, Buckner and Ballantine, a New York City law firm. He moved to Lord, Day and Lord, a crosstown rival in 1929, and became a partner in 1932. From 1933 to 1937, as a Republican, he served in the state assembly from Manhattan. At Albany he supported unemployment insurance and other measures to help families affected by the Great Depression. He declined to run for reelection to devote more time to his law practice. In 1942 Brownell directed Thomas E. Dewey's successful campaign for governor of New York State. Brownell centralized and unified the New York Republican Party's organization to back Dewey. The campaign emphasized the entire Republican ticket and encouraged the loyalty of county leaders by providing them with funds collected statewide. He also managed Dewey's failed presidential campaigns in 1944 and 1948. In 1944 Dewey secured Brownell's election as chairman of the Republican National Committee. Brownell worked to unify the internationalist and isolationist wings of the national party. He established links with ethnic groups that had previously supported the Democratic Party, beginning the slow breakdown of the New Deal coalition created by Pres Franklin D. Roosevelt. He stepped down as chairman in 1946, the year the Republican Party regained control of Congress. At the 1952 Republican National Convention, Brownell worked with Dewey to advance the successful presidential candidacy of Dwight D. Eisenhower. Newly elected Pres Eisenhower named Brownell attorney general of the United States in January 1953. As attorney general he was noted for his hard stand against communism, though his position on civil rights was more progressive than that of other members of the Eisenhower administration. He resigned after guiding the Civil Rights Act of 1957 through Congress and returned to his law practice, where he worked until stepping down as senior partner in 1977. In 1964 he briefly returned to New York State politics to manage the reelection campaign of Sen Kenneth B. Keating, who lost to Robert F. Kennedy. A cautious attorney, in 1971 he urged the *New York Times* not to publish the Pentagon Papers. He retired from law and public service in 1989.

Brownell, Herbert, with John P. Burke. *Advising Ike: The Memoirs of Attorney General Herbert Brownell* (Lawrence: Univ Press of Kansas, 1993)

John David Rausch Jr

brownstone architecture. A 19th-century style of building facade for which New York State, particularly New York City, is renowned. Brownstone, also known as Jersey freestone, is formed of iron-stained sandstone. Its original reddish-brown color, deriving from a high concentration of iron, weathers to a rich chocolate color. The vast majority of the brownstone utilized by New York State builders came from quarries in neighboring Connecticut and New Jersey, in particular from Connecticut's Central Valley. Prior to the 1830s most row-house construction in New York State involved brick or wood facades. There were alternatives, such as marble and granite, but the difficulty of transporting these heavy stones and cutting them by hand made their cost prohibitive for most residential construction. By the 1840s an emerging urban middle class sought a building material more durable than wood and more elegant than standard brick. Steam-powered machines could saw the relatively light, soft brownstone into 4 or 6 in (10 or 15 cm) thick sheets, which could then be fastened to a brick structure. Soon a brownstone dwelling came to be defined as a one-family row house faced with the soft stone and standing three to four stories high. Such narrow-fronted but deep houses typically featured raised basement kitchens and stone steps leading up to a high stoop before the first-floor entrance. Brownstone also became a favored material for places of worship, university buildings, and other institutions. Significant examples of brownstone construction include the Cathedral of the Immaculate Conception (1852) in Albany, Cooper Union (1859) in Manhattan, Annunciation Church (1901) in Buffalo, and many stately homes in Troy (Rensselaer Co) as well as more modest single-family homes throughout Brooklyn. Architectural historian Lewis Mumford has dubbed the late 19th century "the Brown Decades," largely because of the popularity of this stone. By the 20th century brownstone had begun to lose its appeal as other materials, particularly limestone, came into fashion. For homeowners, brownstone often became both an aesthetic and a structural liability. Consisting of layers of compressed sediment, water easily seeped in, causing cracks and flaking. Following the late 20th-century boom in restoration and preservation, a market for brownstone has reemerged.

Lockwood, Charles. *Bricks and Brownstone: The New York Row House, 1783–1929: An Architectural and Social History* (New York: McGraw-Hill, 1972)
Mumford, Lewis. *The Brown Decades: A Study of the Arts in America, 1865–1895* (New York: Dover, 1931)

Leonard Benardo

Brownville. Town (pop 5,843) and village (pop 1,022) in W central Jefferson Co. Settled by Brig Gen Jacob Brown in 1799, the town was formed from Leyden [now in Lewis Co] in 1802. The village was incorporated in 1828. During the Embargo of 1807 the village was a terminus of the county's main smuggling route, and during the War of 1812, it was a gathering place for the militia, since Brown served as commander of the northern frontier. The town became dairy country, but its villages and hamlets were manufacturing centers; the Village of Brownville's industries included textile mills, a stove factory, and a lithic paint company. The Rome, Watertown and Ogdensburg Railroad came through in 1851. In the last quarter of the 19th century, pulp and paper mills predominated, including Brownville Paper Co (1892–1973) and Brownville Board Co (1901–54). In 2003 there were few farms and little manufacturing in town; many residents commuted to Watertown.

Laura Lynne Scharer

Bruce, Louis R(ook), Jr (*b* Onondaga Indian Reservation [loc in Onondaga Co], 30 Dec 1906; *d* Arlington, Va, 20 May 1989). US commissioner of Indian Affairs. A Mohawk-Oglala Sioux Indian, Bruce was born on the Onondaga Indian Reservation, where his father, Louis R. Bruce Sr, was the resident Methodist minister. Louis R. Bruce Jr was educated at nearby Syracuse University, where he excelled as a student. Eleanor Roosevelt saw to Bruce's appointment as head of the National Youth Administration's Indian programs in New York State in the mid-1930s; in that capacity he helped design programs of Iroquoian cultural retention. After World War II Bruce operated a dairy farm in Richfield Springs (Otsego Co), worked in the advertising industry in New York City, and in the late 1940s and 1950s was on the board of the National Congress of American Indians. On 8 Aug 1969 Bruce became the third Native American to become US commissioner of Indian Affairs. Much to his credit his time in office was a major turning point in the history of the administration of Indian affairs: Pres Richard M. Nixon ended the termination policies of the 1950s and 1960s; Blue Lake, considered a sacred site, was returned to the Taos Pueblo; more money was allocated for Indian health, education, and social services; and more Indians were appointed to management positions in the Bureau of Indian Affairs. Yet Bruce was blamed for listening too much to activists. He was dismissed by Nixon in December 1972, unfairly blamed for "allowing" Red Power activists to take over the Bureau of Indian Affairs building. For the remainder of his life, Bruce headed a consulting and lobbying firm for Native American nations.

Cash, Joseph H. "Louis Rook Bruce, 1969–73." In *The Commissioners of Indian Affairs, 1824–1977,* ed. Robert M. Kvasnicka and Herman J. Viola (Lincoln: Univ of Nebraska Press, 1979)
Hauptman, Laurence M. *The Iroquois and the New Deal* (Syracuse: Syracuse Univ Press, 1981)
———. *The Iroquois Struggle for Survival: From World War II to Red Power* (Syracuse: Syracuse Univ Press, 1986)
———. "Eleanor Roosevelt and the American Indian: The Iroquois as a Case Study," *Hudson Valley Regional Review* 16 (Mar 1999): 1–15

Laurence M. Hauptman

Bruno, Joseph L(ouis) (*b* Glens Falls, Warren Co, 8 Apr 1929). State senator. Bruno grew up poor, working from an early age to help support his family. After serving as an infantry sergeant in the Korean War, he earned a business degree at Skidmore College in Saratoga Springs with the help of the GI Bill and went on to build a successful telecommunications business. Becoming involved in Republican politics and working on Gov Nelson A. Rockefeller's 1966 reelection campaign and joining the legislative staff in 1968, Bruno was first elected to the state senate in 1976 from Rensselaer Co, where he had served as Republican county chairman. He became majority leader and temporary president in 1995, with backing from incoming Republican governor George E. Pataki, positions to which he was reelected in 1997, 1999, 2001, and 2003. Gaining a reputation as a plainspoken and pragmatic politician who eschewed ideology in favor of practical politics and legislative results, Bruno worked with Democratic speaker of the assembly Sheldon Silver in 2003 to pass a budget that was at odds with Gov Pataki's budget proposal and drew 119 gubernatorial vetoes. He advocated tax cuts for business development but also expanded spending on public schools and used his position to steer major public projects to his home base of Rensselaer Co. In 2002 the Joseph L. Bruno Stadium opened at Hudson Valley Community College in Troy and hosts the Tri-City Valley Cats, a Class A baseball team affiliated with the Houston Astros.

Rosen, Hy, and Peter Slocum. *From Rocky to Pataki: Character and Caricatures in New York Politics* (Syracuse: Syracuse Univ Press, 1998)

Peter Slocum

Brunswick. Town (pop 11,664) in central Rensselaer Co. Settled by Palatines prior to 1742, the town was formed from Troy in 1807. Small manufacturing developed along Poesten and Quacken Kills. About 1840 Brunswick and Vanderheyden Lakes were enlarged to provide drinking water for Troy. In the mid–19th century, "brush blocks" and handles were made for Lansingburgh's brush-making industry. The town's proximity to a ready market in Troy resulted in extensive truck farming in the late 19th century. Suburbanization began after World War I with the Country Club of Troy (1927) and Brunswick Hills, a residential development. A small shopping center opened in 1969 at Clums Corners. Although quite suburban, in 2002 Brunswick continued to support a number of successful farms, and a stone quarry (1951) and asphalt plant (1957) provided industrial jobs. It is the hometown of Joseph L. Bruno, majority leader of the state senate (1995–).

Kathryn T. Sheehan

Brushton. Village (pop 479) in Moira (Franklin Co). Brushton was first settled by Robert Watts, who sold his real estate improvements to Henry Neilson Brush; the village incorporated in 1925. The Northern Railroad (later Rutland Railroad) came through in 1850. A minor mineral spring at Brushton was the site of a sanatorium (*ca* 1865) operated by Dr H. G. Parker, an African American. From 1872 to 1878 the village's agricultural society operated a fairground and racetrack south of the railroad station. In the early 21st century Brushton remains a dairy-farming community.

Thomas W. Perrin

Brutus. Town (pop 4,777) in central Cayuga Co. Settled in 1795, the town was formed from Aurelius in 1802. After the Erie Canal was completed from Utica in 1819, Weedsport became the canal port for Auburn shippers until the railroad reached Auburn in 1838. Later Brutus was crossed by the New York Central (1853) and the Southern Central (1869–1957, after 1888 the Lehigh Valley) Railroads. Brothers Harvey and George Stevens produced high-quality wooden duck decoys from the late 1860s to 1894. The Thruway was built through town in 1954 with a Weedsport exit. In the early 21st century general crop farming is the predominant land use.

Jeanne L. Baker

Bryant, William Cullen (*b* Cummington, Mass, 3 Nov 1794; *d* New York City, 12 June 1878). Poet and editor. Bryant attended Williams College in Williamstown, Mass, later studied law, and was admitted to the Massachusetts Bar. He married Frances Fairchild in 1821, and they had two daughters. Leaving the practice of law, Bryant moved to New York City in 1825 and edited the *New York Review* before being hired by the *New York Evening Post* in 1827. Two years later he became editor in chief and part owner, positions he held for nearly 50 years. The "American Wordsworth" gave the *Post* a literary style with a free trade, antislavery bent. Bryant's journalism was socially committed but avoided the sensationalism of his penny press competitors. His more than two dozen books of poetry and prose include his perhaps most famous poem "Thanatopsis" (1817), *Poems* (1821), and translations of *The Iliad* (1870) and *The Odyssey* (1871). Bryant's myriad civic activities comprised advocacy for the establishment of Central Park and the Metropolitan Museum of Art. Bryant Park, adjacent to the New York Public Library, bears his name. The restored Cedarmere, the Roslyn Harbor estate Bryant bought in 1843 and site of his many botanical experiments, is a museum administered by Nassau Co.

Brown, Charles Henry. *William Cullen Bryant* (New York: Scribner, 1971)

Eric Newton

Brydges, Earl W(illiam) (*b* Niagara Falls, 25 May 1905; *d* Niagara Falls, 30 Mar 1975). Republican legislative leader. Attending Niagara University and graduating from the University of Buffalo Law School in 1926, Brydges practiced law until he was elected to the state senate in 1948. There he became a specialist in school finance and a strong advocate for aid to parochial schools. As majority leader (1965–72), he presided during a time when the legislature was largely subservient to the governor. Although he himself was more conservative, Brydges supported the expansionist policies of Republican governor Nelson A. Rockefeller. These led to a vast growth in state government, including the nation's most generous health insurance program for the poor and near poor. A devout Roman Catholic, Brydges opposed liberalization of divorce laws and legalization of abortion, but he did not use his significant parliamentary powers to block those proposals from coming to a vote. He wept openly when the senate voted to make New York the first state to legalize abortion in April 1970. Brydges retired from the senate two years later. A state park containing a performing arts center, the Earl W. Brydges Artpark, opened in Lewiston (Niagara Co) in 1974.

Peter Slocum

Buchanan. Village (pop 2,189) in Cortlandt (Westchester Co). Buchanan formed around a station of the Hudson River Railroad (1849) serving Verplanck and was known as Centreville. The station relocated a little to the south about 1862. The locality had a post office named Lyell (1860–63) and East Haverstraw (1863–66). Growth began with the founding of Standard Oilcloth Co (1874–1974, later Standard Coated Products, then part of American Cyanamid). The village incorporated in 1928. The Hudson River Day Line created Indian Point Park (1923–56) as a destination for its cruises. The 320-acre (130 ha) site was sold to Consolidated Edison in 1954 and developed for the three Indian Point nuclear plants (1962, 1973, 1976). In 2003 concern about evacuation plans led to calls for closure of the plants, then being operated by Entergy Corp. Buchanan is otherwise a quiet suburban village. The Gallon Measure Service Station (?1927), with its office in the shape of an oil can, is a landmark.

Francis B. Stein

Buck, Leffert L(efferts) (*b* Canton, St. Lawrence Co, 5 Feb 1837; *d* Hastings-on-Hudson, Westchester Co, 17 July 1909). Civil engineer and bridge builder. Growing up in Canton, Buck apprenticed in a machine shop before attending St. Lawrence University, but his education was cut short when he entered the army in 1861. He served until 1865, rising to the rank of captain, and fought at Antietam, Chancellorsville, and Gettysburg. Following the war, he was awarded a retroactive BS degree and earned a master's degree at St. Lawrence University. He then received a civil engineering degree at Rensselaer Polytechnic Institute in Troy in 1868. His first major engineering project was the construction of the Verrugas Viaduct in Peru, the highest bridge in the world when completed in 1873. Buck oversaw the restoration of the Roebling Railroad Suspension Bridge across the Niagara River between 1877 and 1884. He drew the plans for the replacement arch for that bridge and designed the Clifton Bridge just below Niagara Falls, by far the longest arch bridge in the world when it opened in 1897. Buck also built two bridges in Rochester over the Genesee River Gorge during the 1890s. One still exists; the other was taken down in 1996. His largest project was the Williamsburg Bridge over the East River in New York City, which, when it opened in 1903, was the world's longest suspension span, at 1,600 feet (487.7 m), surpassing the previous champion, the Brooklyn Bridge. Buck's development of steel-arch bridge structures remains his legacy to the field of civil engineering.

Griggs, Francis E. "Leffert Lefferts Buck: Bridge Maker," *Journal of Bridge Engineering (ASCE)* 5 (Nov 2000): 276–83

Petroski, Henry. *Engineers of Dreams: Great Bridge Builders and the Spanning of America* (New York: Knopf, 1995)

Frank E. Griggs Jr

Buckley, James L(ane) (*b* New York City, 9 Mar 1923). Senator and federal judge. Buckley was raised in Dutchess Co. After serving in the navy and graduating from Yale Law School, he became vice president and director (1953–70) of the New York City–based family business Catawba Corp, an oil and mineral exploration services company. In 1965 he managed the unsuccessful New York City mayoral campaign of his younger brother, William F. Buckley Jr. James was the candidate in 1968, with an unsuccessful run for the US Senate on the Conservative ticket. Two years later he won the seat, and as senator he aligned with the Republican Party in advocating fiscal conservatism and limited government, though his environmentalism set him apart from most of his conservative colleagues. Buckley's challenge of the federal campaign finance law resulted in the Supreme Court decision *Buckley v Valeo* (1976), which struck down limits on campaign spending. He lost his bid for reelection in 1976 and was defeated again in 1980 when he ran for senator from Connecticut. Pres Ronald Reagan appointed Buckley to a series of federal positions and in 1985 to the District of Columbia Circuit of the US Court of Appeals, where he served until his retirement in 2000.

Buckley, James L. "Bucks and Buckley: The Plaintiff Makes His Case," *National Review,* 27 Sept 1999

———. *If Men Were Angels: A View from the Senate* (New York: Putnam's, 1975)

Timothy Sullivan

Buckley, William F(rank), Jr (*b* New York City, 24 Nov 1925). Author and editor. After graduating from Yale University and working briefly for the Central Intelligence Agency in Mexico City, Buckley captured national attention in 1951 with his first book, *God and Man at Yale*, which denounced liberal education's neglect of religion. In 1955 Buckley founded *National Review*, a conservative journal. Based in the Murray Hill section of Manhattan, it became the premier forum for conservative intellectuals, journalists, and politicians. Buckley's 1959 *Up from Liberalism* summarized his conservative philosophy, and during the 1960s his influence and prominence increased dramatically. He helped found the Young Americans for Freedom and the Conservative Party of New York State, and in 1962 began his nationally syndicated weekly newspaper column "On The Right." In 1965 Buckley attracted national attention by running for New York City mayor on the Conservative Party ticket, ultimately losing the election to Republican John Lindsay. The following year Buckley began a New York City–based weekly television show, *Firing Line*. On the show he waged an often fierce rhetorical battle with a succession of liberal politicians, writers, and academics. Buckley's erudite manner and caustic wit made him an easily recognizable, even parodied, personality. He wrote a series of spy novels and remained a prominent conservative spokesman, even after stepping down as *National Review* editor and ending *Firing Line* in the 1990s.

Buckley, William F., Jr. *Up from Liberalism* (New York: Obolensky, 1959)
Judis, John B. *William F. Buckley, Jr: Patron Saint of the Conservatives* (New York: Simon & Schuster, 1988)

Timothy Sullivan

Bucktails. A political term designating a portion of the Republican Party that flourished from 1818 to 1828 and that opposed De Witt Clinton and his supporters. The group earned its name from the buck's tail originally worn on the hats of members of the Tammany Society of New York City. Consistent with Native American themes raised by early Tammany members, the tail suggested the ideal of a free man, roaming to hunt the animals of the forest. Transformed from a fraternal order into a political organization, by 1808 Tammany was led by the "Martling Men" (named after Abraham Martling's tavern, where Mayor Clinton's foes had held a critical meeting), who opposed Clinton and supported the Madison administration. After Clinton's election as governor in 1817, the Tammany emblem became the name of the statewide opposition to his administration. The Clintonian Republicans sought to define their opponents throughout New York State as a cabal of discontented political hacks who blindly followed Tammany's lead in party regularity: calling them "buck-tails" seemed to drive the point home. Condemning Clinton as a man of "unchastened ambition," anti-Clintonians embraced the name, with its connotations of personal independence. Bucktails resented Clinton's emphasis on the primacy of executive authority over legislative leadership and his appointment of unreconstructed Federalists to office, and they expressed concern about the expansion of state debt that would come with the building of the Erie and Champlain Canals.

The Bucktails were successful in eroding Clinton's legislative following by 1820. Their leaders embodied many of their political objectives—for example, shortening the governor's term from three to two years and vesting much of the power to appoint in the state legislature—in the new constitution formulated by the 1821 convention and temporarily forced Clinton from office, when he declined to run for governor in 1822. Their successes came despite internal divisions between Tammany Hall members, sensitive to the power vested in the government at Albany, and upstate Bucktails, whose leaders were often obliged to defend their New York City colleagues accused of stirring urban disorder. Lacking a foe to unite them after Clinton's departure, Bucktail unity frayed especially during the 1824 presidential election when many failed to support William H. Crawford of Georgia, the presidential candidate favored by Bucktail leader Martin Van Buren. Clinton's restoration to the governorship by the People's Party in the 1824 election gave new life to the Bucktails. Though the Albany Regency, which sought to guide and maintain Bucktail unity, ran William B. Rochester against Clinton in 1826, Van Buren sought accommodation with the governor, in part to ease the Bucktails into the camp of Andrew Jackson, Van Buren's and Clinton's choice for president. Drawing from a variety of social and political elements, including ex-Federalists, and deferring to the leadership of Van Buren and the Albany Regency, the Bucktails constituted an effective faction that laid claim to the Jeffersonian Republican heritage. They brought about constitutional revision in New York State in 1821 and formed much of the substance of the emerging Democratic Party.

Fox, Dixon Ryan. *The Decline of Aristocracy in the Politics of New York, 1801–1840* (1919; repr New York: AMS Press, 1976)
Kass, Alvin. *Politics in New York State, 1800–1830* (Syracuse: Syracuse Univ Press, 1965)

Craig and Mary L. Hanyan

buckwheat. Technically not a grain but the seed of a fruit-bearing plant native to Manchuria, buckwheat has been grown in the Old World for millennia. After hulling, the triangular, gluten-free seeds are known as groats and may be roasted, boiled, and eaten whole like rice in the dish called kasha in Jewish and eastern European cuisines. They may also be ground into a black-flecked, gray flour. Dutch and German settlers introduced this food into New York State in the 1600s, calling it *bockweit* (beech wheat) because its seeds resemble beechnuts in shape. Reliable, hardy, nearly impervious to disease, and with a short growing season, buckwheat was a diet staple throughout rural New York State in the early 1900s and was used primarily in griddle cakes raised with sour milk. Nearly every farm grew 1–2 acres (.4–.8 ha) for domestic use. Samuel Deane, a New England agricultural writer of the late 1700s, also recommended buckwheat for fattening hogs and poultry. Buckwheat could be planted at midsummer where winter wheat had been harvested, and cut in early fall. It could also be planted where a spring-sown crop had failed. At the beginning of the 21st century, buckwheat is often used as a cover crop to hold soil in place after another crop has been harvested. Central and Western New York and the Pacific Coast produce most of the nation's crop. Most New York State production is processed into groats. Birkett Mills, in operation in Penn Yan (Yates Co) since 1797, packages and sells roasted groats as Wolff's Kasha in grocery stores nationwide. Ground buckwheat flour is also available in a range of specialty shops, and buckwheat hulls are often used for pillow stuffing.

Schlebecker, John T. *Whereby We Thrive: A History of American Farming, 1607–1972* (Ames: Iowa State Univ Press, 1975)

Jessie Ravage

Buddhism. Immigrants have practiced Buddhism in New York since the 19th century. European American interest in Buddhism also has a long history, dating from at least 1875 when Helena Petrovna Blavatsky, a Russian immigrant, and Henry Steel Olcott, a journalist, founded the Theosophical Society in Manhattan. The two later moved to South Asia, converted to Buddhism, and built theosophy into an important Buddhist-inspired spirituality that is a source for much of the current New Age movement. Japanese Zen, the first form of traditional Asian Buddhism practiced among European American converts, took root in 1931 when Sokei-An Sasaki, a missionary teacher, founded the First Zen Institute in New York City. After his death in 1945 his wife, Ruth Fuller, remained a prominent American Buddhist. Zen greatly benefited from the work of Daisetz Teitaro Suzuki, a scholar and translator who taught at Columbia University in the 1950s. His lectures attracted psychoanalysts and writers, among them the Beat poets. Together they inaugurated the "Zen boom," a major expression of popular interest in Buddhism that set the stage for the more extensive interest expressed in the 1960s. In 1966 Phillip Kapleau founded the Rochester Zen Center, America's first monastic-style Zen training center. Zen Studies Center was established in New York City to support Suzuki and was directed by Eido Tai Shimano beginning in 1965. The Zen Community of New York, headquartered in Yonkers, was founded by Bernard Glassman in 1979, and Zen Mountain Monastery was established by John Loori in 1980 in Mount Tremper (Ulster Co). Several other Japanese traditions have roots in ethnic communities. The New York Buddhist Church practices Jodoshinshu Pure Land Buddhism. The Myosetsuji Temple in Queens practices the Japanese Nichiren Shoshu tradition. Soka Gakkai International, which has centers in Manhattan and Buffalo, was expelled from Nichiren Shoshu in conflicts over its proselytizing and fund-raising practices.

In the Tibetan tradition, which has also flourished among European Americans, noteworthy institutions include Tibet House in New York City, founded in 1987 at the request of the Dalai Lama by Columbia University professor Robert Thurman; Namgyal Monastery Institute of Buddhist Studies (1992) in Ithaca, the US branch of the Dalai Lama's home monastery in India; and Karma Triyana Dharmachakra in Woodstock (Ulster Co), founded in 1979 as the North American seat of the Karma Kagyus, an important religious order of Tibet. The Kadampa order's first temple in the United States was under construction in 2004 at the Kadampa Meditation Center, established in Glen Spey (Sullivan Co) in 2000, and there are Kadampa centers in Long Island, White Plains (Westchester Co), and Manhattan.

A leading Buddhist publisher is Snow Lion Press (1980) in Ithaca, and *Tricycle* (1991) is a nonsectarian Buddhist magazine based in New York City.

Since the 1965 liberalization of immigration laws, there are numerous temples in various traditions found throughout the state that are an integral part in Asian ethnic communities. The Mandarin Chinese, one of the largest of the Buddhist immigrant populations in New York State, sponsors the Buddhist Association of the United States, which was founded in New York City in 1964 by immigrant Chia Theng Shen. Headquartered in the Bronx, the association also maintains Chuang Yen monastery near Carmel (Putnam Co). The Ch'an Meditation Center in Elmhurst (Queens Co), established in the late 1970s, practices the Chinese tradition that is the precursor to Japanese Zen. In 2002 other ethnic Buddhist organizations in New York State include Wat Lao Samakhitham, a Laotian temple in Castle Creek (Broome Co); the America Burma Buddhist Association, founded in New York City in 1981; the Jotanaram Temple in the Bronx, which serves the Cambodian immigrant community; and the Staten Island Buddhist Vihara, which follows the Sri Lankan Theravada tradition. The Manhattan Won Buddhist Center and Modern Buddhism of America in Queens serve Korean Buddhists, and the Thai tradition has centers in New York City, Buffalo, and Long Island.

Fields, Rick. *How the Swans Came to the Lake: A Narrative History of Buddhism in America,* 3d ed. (Boston: Shambhala International, 1992)

Seager, Richard Hughes. *Buddhism in America* (New York: Columbia Univ Press, 1999)

Richard Hughes Seager

Budget, Division of the. Agency in the Executive Department under the direct supervision of the governor. The director of the budget assists in carrying out responsibilities assigned to the chief executive by Article 7 of the state constitution. These include preparing and presenting to the legislature an annual budget containing a complete plan of expenditures and estimated revenues. The division prepares and publishes the executive budget and all appropriation bills and related financial legislation, helps the governor negotiate differences with the legislature over priorities or estimates, and administers the financial plan throughout the fiscal year. In fulfilling these tasks, division staff undertakes management studies, conducts hearings on funding requests, monitors the flow of expenditures and revenues, and initiates corrective action as necessary to fulfill the financial plan.

The division was created in 1927 as an integral part of a comprehensive overhaul of New York State government initiated by Gov Alfred E. Smith and carried out in the mid-1920s with the aid of such allies as Charles Evans Hughes, Henry L. Stimson, and Robert Moses. The reforms included establishing an "executive budget," a central component of the Progressive Era agenda that centered responsibility for the financial management of government in the hands of the chief executives at the national, state, and local levels.

New York was a relative latecomer to the ranks of the states adopting the executive budget, largely because Smith insisted on giving the budget a constitutional rather than simply a legislative base. New York State's political leaders and scholars nonetheless played a critical role in developing the theoretical underpinnings of the "strong executive" system, of which the executive budget was a critical element. The New York Bureau of Municipal Research, a private group founded in 1906, for example, worked with the President's Commission on Economy and Efficiency (appointed in 1910 by Pres William H. Taft), which recommended an executive budget at the national level. The bureau also contributed significantly to the work of the New York State Constitutional Convention of 1915, which focused on the role of the chief executive in state government. Although the constitution proposed by the 1915 convention was rejected by voters, it had included establishing an executive budget among its major reforms. It would have made the governor, the chief executive, responsible for presenting a comprehensive financial plan and budget to the legislature, replacing the prevailing practice under which each agency offered its requests independently and directly to the legislative finance committees. Under this system, the governor could exercise some political influence, and certainly use the item veto, but there was no overall plan, and revenue requirements were determined by adding up the total amounts of the appropriations.

During the decade that followed the rejection of the proposed constitution the state experimented with a variety of approaches to budgetary reform. Although the Sage-Maier Act of 1916 established a legislative budget process, there was general agreement on the need for a more defined role for the governor. To this end, legislation in 1921 established a joint executive legislative body, the Board of Estimate and Control, to manage the system. The board consisted of the chairs of the Senate Finance and Assembly Ways and Means Committees, the governor, and the state comptroller. Smith, who had lost office in 1920, returned as governor in 1922. Thereafter, the staff, theoretically responsible to a multimember board, gradually became part of the executive for all practical purposes.

At the same time, Smith continued to make the case for sweeping changes in state government. Reelected in 1924, following a campaign based largely on the need to reorganize the executive branch, the governor successfully promoted the adoption of a constitutional amendment establishing an executive budget. Legislation in 1927 transferred the personnel of the Board of Estimate and Control to a new agency, the Division of the Budget, whose head was responsible to the governor alone. The staff of the division numbered around 20 at the time of its foundation in 1927. The first budget prepared under the new constitutional provisions was presented to the legislature by Gov Franklin D. Roosevelt in 1929, although Gov Smith and the legislative leaders arranged to use the new procedures as a test case in presenting the budget in 1928. Thereafter, all state agencies were obliged to supply the division with estimates of their financial needs and defend their requests at hearings conducted by the budget director and appropriate staff of the division. Separate staff units, varying from time to time in response to the perceived need of the division for particular specialized services, began to appear in the 1930s.

The influence of the Division of the Budget has ebbed and flowed over the years, reflecting the relative importance of fiscal issues and the personal priorities and relationships of the director, the governor, and other leading figures within the administration. The division's work, once seasonal, has become more intense throughout the year, as legislative sessions have lengthened and debates over fiscal policy and budgetary priorities have become more acute. In addition, the complexity of intergovernmental funding flows has increased dramatically, requiring division staff to track financial and programmatic changes pending in Congress or in federal agencies and to evaluate their impact on the state financial plan. Nevertheless, the essential budgetary responsibilities of the governor, as defined in the constitution, and of the Division of the Budget as the principal agent of the governor in carrying out these responsibilities, have remained essentially unchanged. Its internal organizational structure has increasingly focused on broad program categories (eg, education, health, social services, transportation, environment) rather than on the methods by which the state funds and provides these services (eg, capital construction, institutional care, state operations, local assistance). In 2003 the division had a staff of about 340 and a budget of $65 million.

See also EXECUTIVE BRANCH.

Dahlberg, Jane S. *The New York Bureau of Municipal Research: Pioneer in Government Administration* (New York: New York Univ Press, 1966)

Kerker, Robert P. "The State of the Executive Budget." In *Governing New York State,* 3d ed, eds. Jeffrey M. Stonecash, John Kenneth White, and Peter W. Colby (Albany: SUNY Press, 1994)

New York State. Division of the Budget. *The Executive Budget in New York State: A Half-Century Perspective.* Ed. Robert P. Kerker (Albany: Author, 1981)

Robert P. Kerker

Buel, Jesse (*b* Coventry, Conn, 4 Jan 1778; *d* Danbury, Conn, 6 Oct 1839). Publisher and agriculturalist. The son of farmers, Buel was apprenticed to a printer in 1792. Five years later he started his first newspaper, the *Northern Budget,* in Lansingburgh (Rensselaer Co). After living in Poughkeepsie and Kingston (Ulster Co), where he established weekly newspapers, he moved to Albany in 1813 to launch the *Argus,* an influential newspaper that would become a Democratic Party mainstay. In 1821 Buel, long interested in agriculture, purchased property in what was known as the Sandy Barrens west of Albany and began to practice "scientific farming." He was named recording secretary of the State Board of Agriculture in 1822 and was elected the following year to the New York State Assembly, serving in the state legislature on and off for the next 13 years. He was recording secretary and then served several terms as president of the New York State Agricultural Society (1832). Sponsored by the society, Buel in 1834 established the weekly *Cultivator* (Albany), soon the most popular farm journal in the country and an important advocate for agricultural education and scientific farming. It helped to break down the opposition to scientific approaches by presenting the results of the editor's own experiments and improvements, and by printing articles written by a variety of acknowledged experts. Buel published the *Cultivator* until his death, when it was purchased by Luther Tucker. Buel ran unsuccessfully as Whig candidate for governor in 1836 and was a regent of the University of the State of New York at his death.

Carman, Harry J. "Jesse Buel, Albany County Agriculturalist," *New York State Historical Association Proceedings* 31 (1933): 241–49

Suzan D. Friedlander

Buffalo. City (pop 292,648) in W Erie Co, the second most populated city in New York State. Buffalo is located along the US border with Canada on a plain at the point where Lake Erie joins the Niagara River. The site gradually rises 127 feet (38.7 m) from the lakeshore to the northeastern city line. Its altitude above sea level is between 572 and 699 feet (174.4–213.1 m). The city has a land area of 42.7 mi^2 (110.6 km^2). Little Buffalo Creek in southeast Buffalo supplied water in the 1820s for the Hydraulics, a milling and light manufacturing area in South Buffalo. Buffalo and Cazenovia Creeks join in the southeast corner of modern Buffalo to form the Buffalo River, which meanders west through the city before turning north and entering Lake Erie. The Erie Canal, coming into the city along the Niagara River from the north, terminated in the city. Paralleling the north-south section of the river is the City Ship Canal. Just east of the river, land rises 25 feet (7.6 m) from a marshy area to the Terrace. The harbor and its wharves, materials handling and support facilities, and, eventually, steel mills grew along the river and to the area south and west. Boatyards were established, as well as a community of squatters along the spit formed by Lake Erie and the Ship Canal. The downtown commercial district developed above the Terrace, and the major rail lines entered just north of the river, where stockyards, lumberyards, and other industries also clustered. On the East Side the Iron Island neighborhood took its name from being completely surrounded by rail lines and yards. Immigrant neighborhoods developed near the industrial sections: Germans, Poles, and Russians settled on the East Side; Irish congregated in the Old First Ward on the south side near the waterfront; and later Italians occupied the West Side.

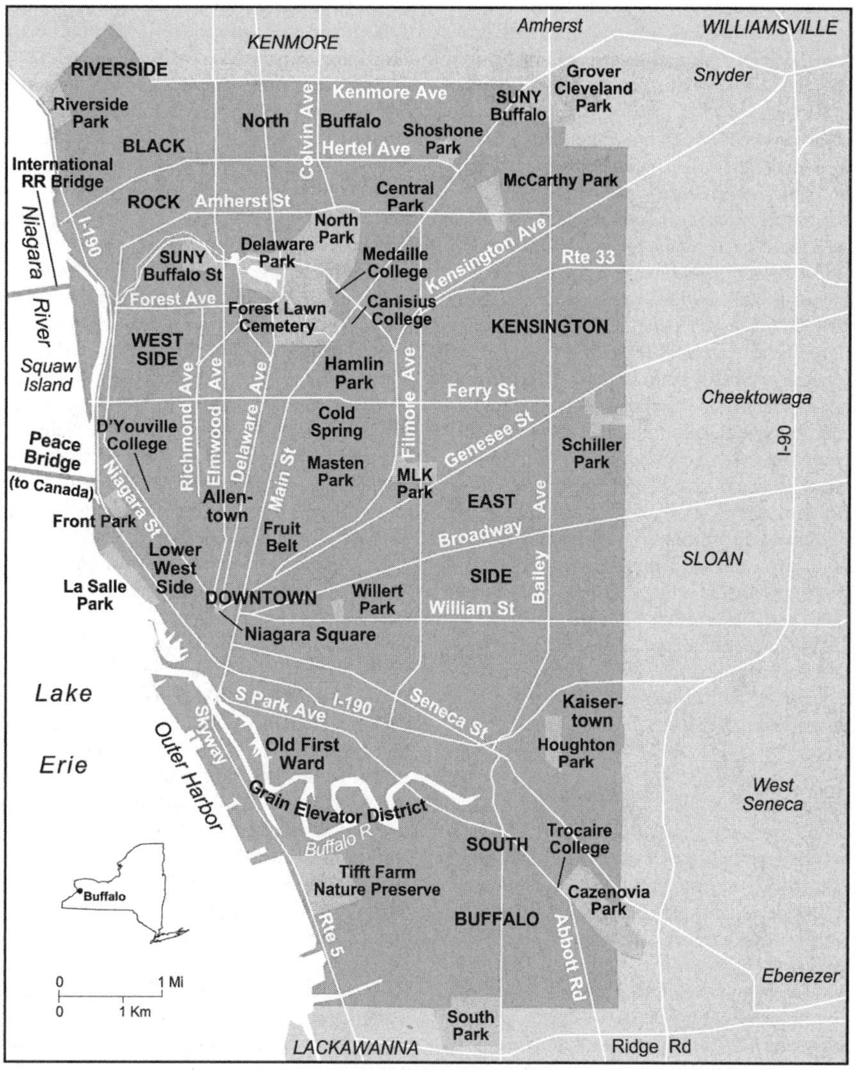

Daniel-Marie Chabert de Joncaire trading post and farm established a European presence at the site of Buffalo in 1758. Soldiers' reports of rich land encouraged settlement of the Western New York region after the Revolution. By the Treaty of Big Tree, the Seneca had been relegated to reservations, including one at Buffalo Creek (1798). The Ogden Land Co took part of the reservation in the 1826 Treaty of Buffalo Creek, forcing some of the Senecas and other nations to Kansas. The 1838 Treaty of Buffalo Creek ceded the remainder of the reservation land to the city in 1839.

Black Rock was once a separate town and village along the Niagara River north of downtown. Farther north, Scajaquada Creek flows from east to west through the entire city. Middle-class neighborhoods grew between downtown and the Scajaquada in the 19th century and expanded north of the creek into the 20th. The Belt Line Railroad circled the entire city from 1883, allowing industry to expand to the northwest and along its route to the east. Immigrant workers followed, settling in such areas as Riverside and Assumption Parish.

Buffalo's lakeside location moderates the climate. Lake Erie cools summer temperatures and stores heat, which extends the fall growing season. The average temperatures are 25°F (-4°C) in January and 71°F (22°C) in July. Annual snowfall averages 92 inches (233.7 cm) and rainfall, 9 inches (22.9 cm). From June through August, 67% of the days are on average sunny.

Settlement

Human beings have occupied Western New York for over 12,000 years. Sites in Buffalo were occupied from about 1540 AD. The Kahkwa, Erie, Wenro, and Neutral peoples controlled the area before the Seneca came from the east and displaced them in the mid–17th century. Seneca commerce and warfare incorporated members of many native nations. Jesuit missionaries in the 1650s found people from 11 Indian nations living in one Seneca village.

Removal of the British garrison at Fort Niagara [now in Porter, Niagara Co] in 1796 and resolution of conflicting land claims opened the region for settlement. In 1791 Robert Morris purchased the preemption right to the site of Buffalo, later selling it to the Holland Land Co. The first non-Indian settlers included Englishman William Johnson, Dutch trader Cornelius Winney, German cooper Martin Middaugh, and African American storekeeper Joseph Hodge. In 1804 the Holland Land Co's agents, Joseph Ellicott and Augustus Porter, surveyed streets and lots on a radial plan mimicking that of Washington, DC. New Englanders displaced the early settlers and changed the town's name from New Amsterdam to Buffalo Creek and later to Buffalo. In 1810 Buffalo was formed as a town from Clarence, and in 1813 the town's lakefront core was incorporated as a village.

Economic Development

In 1804 Peter B. Porter established a rival community named Black Rock just north of Buffalo. Its sheltered natural harbor facilitated movement of goods around Niagara Falls. Porter's influence as congressman secured placement of the Customs House at Black Rock during the shipping season and in Buffalo during the winter. British soldiers attacked Black Rock's navy yard in the summer of 1813, and Buffalo served as a staging area for invading Canada and capturing Fort George the same year. In retaliation for the destruction of Newark [now Niagara-on-the-Lake, Ont], British troops crossed the Niagara River on 30 Dec 1813 and torched both Black Rock and Buffalo. Americans reclaimed the sites in 1814 and launched a successful expedition to capture Fort Erie on the Canadian side. The situation remained largely unchanged until war ended in 1815.

Buffalo and Black Rock competed for designation as the western terminus of the Erie Canal. Buffalo won in 1823 after Samuel Wilkeson created a harbor by building a breakwater at the mouth of Buffalo Creek. When the canal opened in 1825, Buffalo's population was 2,412, and Black Rock's was 1,039, but Buffalo grew rapidly (to 8,653 in 1830 and to 19,215 in 1835), was chartered as a city in 1832, and finally annexed Black Rock in 1853. The canal lowered freight rates between Buffalo and New York City from $100 to $10 per ton. In 1827 civic leaders launched efforts to develop manufacturing, and soon Buffalo was producing lumber, flour, hats, beer, ironwork, and woolens. In 1842 Joseph Dart and Robert Dunbar introduced the world's first steam-powered grain elevator for unloading and storing grain, which mechanized grain transfers from lake vessels to canalboats. Dart and Dunbar's elevator had a capacity of 55,000 bu (1.9 million l). By 1857, 10 elevators with a total capacity of 1.5 million bu (52.9 million l) surrounded Buffalo harbor. Before the Civil War, Buffalo had become the largest grain port in the world.

Commerce quickly became Buffalo's principal industry. The Marine Bank (1850) was an essential component, but manufacturing grew as well. By the 1850s, 1,600 residents worked in iron industries, 500 in tanning leather, 200 in agriculture implement manufacture, and 200 in shipbuilding. Transportation played a major role in the rapid growth, starting with the canal. Railroads, beginning with the 3 mi (5 km) horse-drawn Buffalo and Black Rock Railroad (1834) and the Attica and Buffalo Railroad (1842; later New York Central), enhanced Buffalo's position as a commercial and transshipment center in the 19th century; by 1860, 14 trunk lines served the city.

Ethnicity, Race, and Religion

Buffalo's numerous ironworks, breweries, lumberyards, mills, and grain elevators created jobs for thousands of immigrants. For hundreds of escaping slaves, Michigan Street Baptist Church, the American Hotel, and other sites were final stops for them before finding safe haven in Canada. Proximity to Canada also made Buffalo an immigration point of entry well into the 20th century. Buffalo residents actively smuggled Chinese immigrants across the border during the period of the Chinese Exclusion Act (1882–1943). The city continues to be a point of entry for illegal immigrants. In the 1866 Fenian raid, Irish nationalists crossed the river at Buffalo in an abortive attempt to capture a stronghold in Canada and to disrupt Canadian shipping as a bargaining chip for Irish independence.

Immigrants from the German states between the 1830s and 1850s brought skills and some capital. They clustered on Buffalo's East Side, and Buffalo elected a German-born mayor in 1876. In contrast, Irish immigrants arrived with little wealth, and many worked at unskilled waterfront jobs. Poles, Italians, Hungarians, Jews, and others arriving in the late 19th and early 20th centuries located on the periphery of older ethnic neighborhoods near the waterfront, railroads, or heavy industries. In 1900 almost 30% of the population was foreign-born. Of the foreign-born in 1920, approximately one-quarter were Polish, and their community centered on St. Stanislaus Church (1874). As Poles and Jews left the Broadway-Fillmore neighborhood, African Americans moved into the area. In recent decades Latinos have established themselves in the old West Side Italian neighborhood, and Native Americans have have taken up residence in the Polish section of Black Rock.

Nativist movements and the Ku Klux Klan sought to exclude or "Americanize" new arrivals. Newcomers felt tension between conflicting desires: maintenance of familiar identities versus assimilation. All created institutions that changed both the immigrants and the society around them. Religious institutions both preserved traditions and languages and served integrative roles, providing for social as well as spiritual needs. John Timon, the first Roman Catholic bishop of Buffalo (1847), invited religious orders to the area to organize schools and other institutions. In 1855 there were 12 Roman Catholic parishes in the city. The 43 Protestant churches in 1855 represented many denominations and included 3 African American congregations; Temple Beth Zion was founded in 1850. By 1880 there were 21 Catholic, 73 Protestant, and 3 Jewish congregations.

In response to economic and labor problems, Protestant Church leaders formed the Charity Organization Society (COS) in 1877, which initiated a system of "friendly visits" to separate the "deserving" from the "undeserving" poor. Its casework marked the beginning of professional social work, and it encouraged a network of benevolent societies to provide support. The Fitch Crèche (1880), for example, provided childcare for working mothers, operated a kindergarten, and trained nursery maids. Following the panic of 1893 the COS established a district plan, assigning responsibility for poor relief to neighborhood churches. Westminster Presbyterian Church opened Westminster Settlement House in 1894, and the Unitarian Church of Our Father opened Neighborhood House. Each provided penny banks, libraries, public nursing, and instruction in various job skills to immigrants within its service area. The organizations merged in 1981 to form the Buffalo Federation of Neighborhood Centers, which continues to help people escape poverty.

Emerging immigrant middle classes advocated secular management of education and social services. The Turnverein and the German Young Men's Society sought to preserve German culture but also defended the rights of naturalized citizens. Italian Louis Onetto organized the city's first mutual benefit society in 1874. German Jews organized the Jewish Welfare Society in the 1880s to assist eastern European Jews. In the early 20th century Poles and Italians championed better public schools with vocational training. Dr Charles Borzilleri founded Columbus Hospital in 1908 to care for Italians. Polish mutual aid societies flourished on the East Side and in North Buffalo. Dom Polski, with its Polish library, afforded immigrants an opportunity to learn about American society. The Michigan Avenue YMCA provided recreation, social support, and cultural enrichment to the growing East Side African American community.

Politics

Whig politicians Millard Fillmore and his law partners Nathan Hall and Solomon Haven

Buffalo Harbor from the Village, by George Catlin, 1825.

wielded political power in Buffalo for over 30 years. Fillmore and Hall served in the New York State Assembly; all three served in Congress. Haven was elected mayor in 1846, and Fillmore won national office in 1848 as Zachary Taylor's vice president and succeeded to the presidency in 1850. During and after the Civil War, Fillmore turned his efforts to building many of the cultural and educational institutions that remain central to Buffalo's civic life today.

By 1870 two relatively equally divided party organizations dominated Buffalo politics. Ethnic ward politicians organized political machines controlled by bosses, exemplified by Democrat William F. "Blue-Eyed Billy" Sheehan (1880–95). Party newspapers fueled genuine fears of political corruption and self-service. A product of the system, Democrat Grover Cleveland won office as Erie Co sheriff in 1870. He was elected mayor in 1881 on a reform platform. His success made his tenure short-lived, as he was elected governor in 1883 and president in 1884. The presidential election, over the local opposition of the Sheehan machine, was an aberration. Patronage gave the machines control of local politics, although city charters in 1891 and 1916 sought to curb some of the bosses' power. The 1891 Charter attempted to separate technical from political issues by distributing administrative power among three commissioners. Legislative power was lodged in a two-house city council. The 1916 Charter placed policy and administrative power in the hands of five elected commissioners (safety, work, finance, parks and buildings, and welfare), but in 1928 another charter created a strong mayor and a 15-member common council. Republicans controlled both city and county governments in the early 20th century. While Democrats made significant advances uniting behind Franklin D. Roosevelt, city Republicans retained the advantage in registered voters until the 1950s.

With the strong-mayor form, the power of party chairmen began to reemerge. In the 20th century most notable was Edwin F. Jaeckle, Republican boss from 1935 to 1948. An advocate of consolidated city/county services, he achieved national prominence as a campaign manager for Thomas E. Dewey's 1948 bid for the presidency. Democratic gains beginning in the 1940s were spearheaded by Peter J. Crotty (chair, 1947–64). His protégé and successor, Joseph R. Crangle (chair, 1965–88), engineered Democratic majorities in the state assembly beginning in 1974. His service to national political figures including Robert F. Kennedy and Hubert H. Humphrey caused Humphrey to name him the "Best County Chairman in the Country." Crangle achieved nationwide recognition for his advocacy of minority and women's participation in the party at the 1968 Democratic National Convention.

Through the early years of the century German Americans exercised considerable influence, occupying the mayor's office from 1910 through 1937. Subsequently the office was occupied by people of Irish, Polish, and Italian descent as they gained political strength. Since 1951, when Leeland Jones Jr became the first African American elected to the Common Council, African Americans have increased their political influence, briefly holding a majority on the council in the late 1990s, while Arthur O. Eve became one of the highest ranking state officials in 1979 when he was elected deputy speaker of the state assembly.

Cityscape

Based on Frederick Law Olmsted's plans for Buffalo's park and parkway system, the first coordinated park design plan in the United States, the Centennial Exposition proclaimed Buffalo the "best planned city . . . in the United States." Civic leaders had invited Olmsted to Buffalo in 1868 to create a physical presence matching the city's boundless aspirations. He maximized green space by connecting the grounds of Buffalo State Hospital (now Buffalo Psychiatric Center) and Forest Lawn Cemetery with Delaware Park. Broad parkways linked Delaware Park to the Parade and the Front and provided settings for much of Buffalo's great architecture. He also redesigned downtown public spaces in the 1870s and added South (1894) and Cazenovia (1894), and Riverside (1898) Parks. Many of the nation's leading architects designed for Buffalo, among them H. H. Richardson, Dankmar Adler, Louis Sullivan, Daniel Burnham, and Frank Lloyd Wright. As the children of earlier immigrants sought more stylish homes reflecting their middle-class status, public transportation in the 1890s allowed them to build in comfortable settings within the city. Parkside featured a street layout by Olmsted. North Park and Central Park, South Buffalo, the Kensington-Bailey neighborhood, and North Buffalo's Nye Park all prospered at the turn of the 20th century.

Between 1880 and 1890 Buffalo grew from 155,000 people to 256,000. In 1900, at 352,387, it was the eighth largest city in the United States. To commemorate its surging civic growth, Buffalo hosted the Pan-American Exposition in 1901. Planners intended to promote the development potential of electricity, which was successfully transmitted to Buffalo from Niagara Falls in 1896. Built on 350 acres (142 ha) north of Delaware Park, the exposition featured a 410 ft (125 m) high Electric Tower. Over 8 million people visited the exposition with its spectacular lighting display outlining the buildings with 200,000 ten W lightbulbs. Today it is best remembered for Pres William McKinley's assassination.

Culture

Buffalo's first theaters opened in the early 1820s. They hosted itinerant actors, opera companies, and bands. Buffalo's first resident band, organized in 1824, played at public events including the Marquis de Lafayette's visit in 1824 and the opening of the Erie Canal in 1825. The Academy of Music with a performance hall was established in 1852. Three of the premier cultural institutions are products of Civil War prosperity. The Buffalo Academy of Fine Arts (which runs the Albright-Knox Art Gallery), the Buffalo and Erie County Historical Society, and the Buffalo Society of Natural Sciences have each amassed internationally significant collections. Other museums and heritage organizations have followed, including the Buffalo Lighthouse Association, Theodore Roosevelt Inaugural Site Foundation, the Landmark Society of the Niagara Frontier, the Preservation Coalition of Erie Co, and the Michigan Street Preservation Corp. Galleries in addition to the Albright-Knox include the Burchfield-Penney Art Center, Hallwalls Contemporary Arts Center, CEPA Gallery, and the Buffalo Arts Studio.

The Young Men's Association Library (1836) and the Grosvenor Library (1871), a separate reference library, were the genesis of the public library system. The Young Men's Association Library became the Buffalo Public Library in 1897, and various town libraries merged to form the Erie County Public Library in 1948. The three entities merged to form the Buffalo and Erie County Public Library in 1954. A modern central library was completed downtown in 1963. The Buffalo Philharmonic Orchestra was orga-

Buffalo City Hall, designed by John Wade, with the assistance of Sullivan Jones, built between 1929 and 1931.

nized in 1932 and moved into its new home, Eero and Eliel Saarinen's Kleinhans Music Hall, in 1940. From the beginning, outstanding conductors built a nationally respected orchestra. Buffalo was a stop for traveling theater and vaudeville companies in the 19th and early 20th centuries. Buffalo's vaudeville impresario, Michael Shea, developed movie theaters in the 1920s, including the luxurious Buffalo Theatre (1926), now Shea's Performing Arts Center and anchor of Buffalo's Theatre District. Studio Arena Theatre (1927), a regional company supporting new works, is a major component of the district. Smaller companies include Shakespeare in Delaware Park, Irish Classical Theatre Co, and Alleyway Theatre.

Successive waves of immigrants from the 19th century onward have enriched Buffalo's cultural life. The Germania Society, Liedertafel, Saengerbund, Irish Emerald Brass Band, and Seneca Indian National Band performed in the 1840s and 1850s. The Polish Adam Mickiewicz Library and Dramatic Circle, Polish Singing Circle, Chopin Singing Society, Kalina Singing Society, and Polish Arts Club followed between the 1860s and 1940s. The Dante Alighieri Society organized in 1935 to preserve an interest in Italian literature and poetry. African American women formed a variety of organizations to support the arts, among them the Phyllis Wheatley Club. A lively jazz scene originated after World War I. Clubs like the Little Harlem hosted America's best-known African American performers in the 1930s and 1940s. Other organizations founded since the late 1950s, including the African American Cultural Center, the Langston Hughes Institute, and the Juneteenth Festival, present African American culture.

The city's colleges include the University of Buffalo, founded as a medical school by Millard Fillmore in 1846. Part of the SUNY system since 1962, it is now the largest public university in the state. German Jesuits founded Canisius College in 1870. Buffalo State College, created as a normal school in 1871, became part of the SUNY system in 1948. The Grey Nuns of the Sacred Cross founded D'Youville College in 1908 as the first degree-granting college for women in Western New York. Medaille College (1875) and two-year institutions— Trocaire (1958), Villa Maria (1960), and Erie Community (1971) Colleges— broaden educational opportunities. Among their cultural facilities are SUNY Buffalo's Center for Creative and Performing Arts, Canisius's Montante Culture Center, Buffalo State's Rockwell Hall Performing Arts Center, and D'Youville's Kavinoky Theatre.

Blue-Collar City

At the turn of the 20th century, Buffalo was well furnished with railroad, canal, and lake transportation and with hydroelectric power from Niagara Falls. Access to iron ore discovered in Minnesota in 1892, to Pennsylvania coal, and to Midwestern markets encouraged Lackawanna Iron and Steel Co to move to Buffalo. Local investors bought $2.5 million in stock in one day in 1899 and eventually owned one-sixth of the $30 million issue. In 1903 the plant, in West Seneca just south of the city line, rolled its first steel in the country's first fully integrated iron- and steelmaking plant.

Steel attracted automobile manufacturers, such as the luxury Pierce Arrow (1908–37) and General Motors (GM; 1923). Inexpensive hydroelectric power made production of tough, lightweight ferroalloys for components feasible. By 1910, 10,000 men worked in iron and steel plants in and around Buffalo. Another 3,600 worked in automobile manufacturing, 3,400 made and repaired railroad cars, and 1,800 worked in copper manufacturing. The presence of a skilled labor force and the location near the Canadian border induced Glenn H. Curtiss to move his aircraft plant to Buffalo in 1914 after receiving a British Admiralty contract for flying boats and trainers; it remained until 1946. Chemical and refractory industries benefited from the cheap electricity. Plants located along the Niagara River and the Lake Erie shore between Niagara Falls and Hamburg sustained the economy for much of the 20th century.

By 1918, 500,000 people, almost one in four foreign-born, lived in Buffalo, the nation's eighth-largest manufacturing center and one of its greatest grain ports and leader in marketing sheep. The Lackawanna Steel plant produced nearly 2 million tons (1.8 MT) of ingots in 1920. Buffalo produced manufactured goods worth $634 million in 1919. Five hundred freight trains a day moved raw materials and finished products to and from Buffalo. Innovations like the windshield wiper (Trico Products Corp, 1916) and moisture-proof cellophane (DuPont, 1927) helped create jobs and wealth between the wars.

The labor movement in Buffalo originated in the Working Men's Party (late 1820s) and the Mechanics' Association (1836), but its real momentum began late in the century with the first efforts at federation (1884). During the 19th century, craft unions successfully addressed some of the problems associated with industrial expansion; for example, brewers and builders established an eight-hour day for public contract work by 1894. Even unskilled workers had some success organizing. A grain-scoopers strike in 1899 won improved working conditions and hiring practices and better wages for some waterfront workers. But many were bitterly hostile to unions. A force of specially deputized sheriffs put down the 1877 railroad strike within a week. In 1892, 8,000 National Guardsmen ended a railroad switchmen's strike. While semiskilled workers won a modest wage increase and improved working hours after the 1913 streetcar strike, violence and bombings during the 1922 streetcar strike undermined public sympathy. Antiunion sentiment after World War I generally occasioned the use of police, state troopers, and the National Guard to break strikes, undermining any hope of success during the steel strike of 1919.

Buffalo's industry began to shift to outside ownership in the 1920s, and the loss of local control would ultimately be disastrous. In the meantime, industrial organization brought further gains for organized labor in the 1930s. In 1936 the Steel Workers Organizing Committee (SWOC) began organizing Republic Steel and Bethlehem Steel workers, building a racially integrated union. The United Automobile Workers' (UAW's) successful 1937 sit-down strike against GM gained the UAW a foothold in Buffalo. Recognition of SWOC as bargaining agent at Bethlehem Steel (which had purchased the Lackawanna works in 1922) followed a 1941 strike and the intervention of Labor secretary Frances Perkins. Republic Steel and Ford granted union recognition that summer. Buffalo ranked sixth in the value of prime World War II contracts, and Bethlehem was a major steel producer. Bell Aircraft and Curtiss-Wright supplied fighter planes and transports. Chemical plants delivered everything from high explosives and dyes to insect repellent, and held numerous Manhattan Project contracts. Automobile makers supplied tanks, trucks, and other vehicles, while boatyards turned out landing craft.

Recent History

In the 1950s Buffalo was still dependent on its steel and automotive industries, but plants were outdated and owners were reluctant to reinvest in them. Population peaked at 580,132 in 1950, although Buffalo's thriving postwar economy lasted until the early 1970s. This apparent success masked serious problems. The signs of a downward trend were apparent by the 1950s. The St. Lawrence Seaway, completed in 1959, diverted traffic from Buffalo, reducing Buffalo's grain trade by 50% in its first year. Businesses that had sustained the economy for most of the 20th century closed or moved. Curtiss-Wright relocated to Columbus, Ohio, in 1946. Spencer Kellogg and Sons (linseed oil) left in 1952. Allied Chemical acquired National Aniline and moved it to Virginia the same year, and DuPont and Hooker built new plants for new products outside the area. American Ship Building closed in 1962, and National Gypsum, Carborundum, Houdaille, and Western Electric left in 1977. In the meantime, the flour-milling industry was bought by out-of-town owners who closed five Buffalo mills in 1966 alone. Even the brewing industry suffered. The last major brewery, Iroquois Brewing, closed in 1972. The trend culminated in the closing of Lackawanna's Bethlehem Steel plant in 1983; employment had already dwindled at the site to 7,300 from 21,500 workers in 1965.

With industrial decline came an equally dramatic decline in population. In 1950 a population density of 23,000 per square mile made Buffalo more crowded than any American city but Milwaukee. The Niagara Section of the New York State Thruway (1951), Scajaquada Expressway (1957), Youngman Expressway (*ca* 1962), and Kensington Expressway (1967) afforded the middle class easy escape to the suburbs. SUNY Buffalo's new suburban campus (1974) drew still more people from the city. The tax base shrank as welfare costs grew. Suburban shopping centers eroded the main commercial district. The 2000 population was 292,648, about 50% of the 1950 peak.

The changing relationship between the city and the county and issues of ethnicity and race shaped 20th-century politics. At the beginning of the century, 81% of Erie Co's population lived in Buffalo, and city residents balked at the cost of extending utilities to surrounding towns. By 1990 outmigration to the suburbs left it with only 33% of the county's population, a shrinking tax base, and a disproportionate share of social welfare costs. How to share tax revenues equitably to alleviate city financial problems remains a contentious issue in the early 21st century.

The first proposal for metropolitan government in 1929 foundered with the onset of the depression. Although other such proposals surfaced several times between the 1940s and 1970s, none proceeded to a vote. A proposal for a countywide police force was defeated in 1968. Other consolidations, however, have succeeded. City and county welfare departments merged in the 1930s, and the county assumed control of the city's Meyer Memorial Hospital (now Erie County Medical Center). Erie Co also subsequently assumed responsibility for public health, libraries, the airport, public transportation, central police services, and cultural organization funding. More recently it has taken over operation of the convention center and some city parks.

An incident on the excursion boat *Canadiana* in 1956 and urban rioting in 1967 exposed serious racial divisions. The riots revealed the strength of the African American neighborhood organization, BUILD (Build Unity Integrity Liberty Dignity), which secured improved playground facilities in the inner city and a pledge of jobs for African American youth. In 1972 a number of African Americans sued the Buffalo Board of Education for systematically segregating the public schools. Federal judge John Curtin decided in their favor in 1976. Under court supervision, which ended in 1997, the city created inner-city magnet schools to encourage voluntary desegregation by attracting white students. This avoided the violence that accompanied desegregation elsewhere. However, the community remains divided over the racial implications of releasing the first African American school superintendent in 1999 and of downsizing both the Buffalo Common Council and the Erie Co legislature in 2002.

As of 2003 the largest numbers of workers employed in Buffalo's manufacturing industries made automobiles, automotive engines, axles, brass, china, frozen foods, cereals, and cheese. Among more unusual product manufacturers, QRS Musical Technologies (1900) continued to make piano rolls and digital player piano systems.

Strategies to rebuild Buffalo include creating a medical research corridor anchored by the Roswell Park Cancer Institute and the Hauptman-Woodward Medical Research Institute. In 2002 SUNY Buffalo created the Center for Excellence in Bioinformatics to capitalize on advances made in the medical field and to encourage ongoing research. Similarly, the university's Institute for Earthquake Engineering Research (1986) stimulates job creation in civil engineering.

Business and government view sports as an economic development tool and have invested heavily to retain the Buffalo Bills football franchise (which plays home games in Orchard Park) and the Buffalo Sabres hockey franchise. A new baseball stadium for the Buffalo Bisons Triple A baseball team (1988) and a downtown hockey arena (1996) are part of the investment plan. A new airport opened in 1997, and low-cost airlines have since helped reduce the cost of doing business. Other efforts to capitalize on Buffalo's crossroads location have stalled. Plans to build a new international bridge to facilitate truck traffic have been on hold as questions of design and location are addressed. Under Joel Giambra, a city resident elected Erie Co executive in 1999, discussion of regionalization and consolidation has become intense, with the suggestion that the city disappear as a separate political entity. A financial crisis resulted in the state's June 2003 creation of the Buffalo Fiscal Stabilization Authority, charged with creating a long-term strategy to strengthen city finances by restructuring debt, financing short-term cash flow, and issuing bonds. It also has power to approve city labor contracts and city, school board, or municipal authority contracts above $50,000.

See also African Americans; Communists; Great Lakes shipping lines and watercraft; Iron and steel industry; Labor; Motor vehicle industry; Policing; Street railways; Suburbanization; Waterfronts; Water supply and use (non–New York City watershed).

Adler, Selig, and Thomas Connolly. *From Ararat to Suburb: The History of the Jewish Community of Buffalo* (Philadelphia: Jewish Publication Society, 1960)
Dunn, Walter S., Jr, ed. *History of Erie County, 1870–1970* (Buffalo: Buffalo & Erie County Historical Society, 1972)
Eberle, Scott, and Joseph A. Grande. *Second Looks: A Pictorial History of Buffalo and Erie County* (Norfolk, Va: Donning, 1987)
Gerber, David. *The Making of an American Pluralism, Buffalo, 1825–1860* (Urbana: Univ of Illinois Press, 1989)
Goldman, Mark. *High Hopes: The Rise and Decline of Buffalo, NY* (Albany: SUNY Press, 1983)
———. *City on the Lake: The Challenge of Change in Buffalo, NY* (Buffalo: Prometheus Books, 1990)
Graebner, William. *Coming of Age in Buffalo: Youth and Authority in the Postwar Era* (Philadelphia: Temple Univ Press, 1990)
Leary, Thomas E., and Elizabeth C. Sholes. *From Fire to Rust: Business, Technology, and Work at the Lackawanna Steel Plant, 1899–1983* (Buffalo: Buffalo & Erie County Historical Society, 1987)
Williams, Lillian Serece. *Strangers in the Land of Paradise: The Creation of an African-American Community; Buffalo, New York, 1900–1940* (Bloomington: Indiana Univ Press, 1999)

William H. Siener

Buffalo and Erie County Historical Society. Millard Fillmore and 17 associates founded the Buffalo Historical Society in 1862 to collect materials from the recent past that would inform and inspire future generations. It quickly assembled papers and artifacts documenting the early years of European settlement and individuals associated with that period; for example, Red Jacket's Washington Peace Medal, the figurehead from the *Caroline,* and the first edition of Louis Hennepin's *Nouvelle Decouverte.* Toward the end of the 19th century the collection grew more diverse, reflecting the city's cosmopolitan aspirations. Buffalo travelers brought back such items as Egyptian mummies and a bronze reproduction of Michelangelo's *David.* Three locations in downtown Buffalo housed collections before the society moved to its present location, the Pan-American Exposition's New York State Pavilion, in 1902.

By the 1950s the society returned to collecting regional materials from the recent past. In 2003 it owns approximately 100,000 three-dimensional artifacts, 2,000 manuscript collections, 200,000 photographs, and 20,000 books. Holdings include outstanding collections of art, Holland Land Co records, Fillmore's incoming correspondence, Pan-American Exposition artifacts (including the pistol of Leon F. Czolgosz), papers and artifacts documenting local industry (including one of the earliest snowblowers), and Lackawanna Steel Workers Organizing Committee records. To reflect its countywide service area and increased Erie Co funding, the society was renamed the Buffalo and Erie County Historical Society in 1960.

The main building, a National Historic Landmark in Frederick Law Olmsted's Delaware Park, is an integral part of the city's Museum District. Some 75,000 visitors use the research library and museum each year. The society reaches over 50,000 additional people per year through outreach programs to schools and community organizations. In the 1990s it acquired the Julia Boyer Reinstein Center and the former International Railway Corp's streetcar barn to accommodate expanded programs and collections. Exhibition space in the streetcar barn opened in 2001.

Brown, Richard C., and Bob Watson. *Buffalo: Lake City in Niagara Land* ([Woodland Hills, Calif]: Windsor Publications, 1981)
Donovan, Timothy J. "The Growth of the Museum," *Niagara Frontier* 9 (Summer/Autumn 1962): 45–48
Park, Julian. "Highlights of 100 Years," *Niagara Frontier* 9 (Summer/Autumn 1962): 37–44

William H. Siener

Buffalo and Susquehanna Railroad. Freight and passenger railway that linked western New York State with lumber and coal regions in Pennsylvania. In the 1880s Frank H. Goodyear of Buffalo constructed railroad lines to carry lumber from his land near Galeton to Keating Summit, Pa. In 1893 these lines merged into the Buffalo and Susquehanna Railroad (B&S). Over the next five years, B&S created important connecting routes with other major railroads. It opened a 37 mi (60 km) route from Galeton to Erie Railroad–served Wellsville (Allegany Co), acquired Addison and Pennsylvania Railroad, which ran between Erie-served Addison (Steuben Co) and Gaines, Pa, and also built a spur from Gaines to New York Central Railroad–served Ansonia, Pa. As the lumber lands were played out, B&S expanded south to Sinnemahoning, Pa, and to soft coalfields owned by Goodyear near Dubois and Sykes, Pa. Between 1902 and 1906 B&S laid 85 miles (137 km) of track from Wellsville to Buffalo. For a few years the company operated passenger trains from Buffalo to Ansonia, Pa, and from Addison to Sagamore, Pa, as well as day excursions along its Grand Scenic Route. An engineering flaw handicapped B&S: switchbacks over a mountain west of Galeton, rather than a tunnel through it, ruled out heavy loads. Three years after Goodyear's death in 1907, B&S entered receivership. Reorganized in 1914 the new company sold the Wellsville-Buffalo line, which was scrapped in 1916. In 1932 Baltimore and Ohio Railroad (B&O) bought the Dubois-Sinnemahoning section as part of a scheme, never realized, for a low-grade Chicago–New York freight line. In 1942 a flood washed out the line north of Galeton. The last portion of ex-B&S to go was B&O's line from Dubois to Weedville, Pa, which disappeared in the 1970s.

Dunn, Edward T. *A History of Railroads in Western New York* (Buffalo: Canisius College Press, 2000)

Edward T. Dunn

Buffalo Bills. Professional football team. In 1959 Detroit entrepreneur Ralph C. Wilson Jr established a franchise in the new American Football League (AFL) in Buffalo after failing to get a stadium lease in Miami, Fla. The Bills played poorly in their first two seasons (1960–61), winning 11 games with 16 losses and 1 tie. New head coach Lou Saban (1962–65, 1972–76) shaped a winning team. The acquisition of Jack Kemp (1962–69) provided the Bills with a quality quarterback. With Kemp, running back Cookie Gilchrist (1962–64), twice a touchdown-scoring champion, and superb defenders such as defensive tackle Tom Sestak (1962–68), the Bills won AFL titles in 1964 and 1965. Saban garnered AFL Coach of the Year honors both seasons but resigned over a personnel dispute with Wilson before the 1966 season.

Several difficult years followed with the Bills posting losing records from 1967 to 1972. In 1968 the Bills finished last in their division with 1 win, 12 losses, and 1 tie. A year later the AFL merged with the National Football League (NFL), and Buffalo drafted Heisman Trophy winner O. J. Simpson. The Bills play improved with the addition of Simpson, who led the American Football Conference (AFC) in rushing four times (1972–73, 1975–76), and the return of Saban as coach. In 1973 the Bills moved from the antiquated War Memorial Stadium (known to fans as the Rockpile) into the new 80,000-seat Rich Stadium in the Buffalo suburb of Orchard Park (Erie Co). The Bills reached the playoffs again in 1974 but lost a first-round game to the Pittsburgh Steelers. From 1976 to 1978 the Bills won just 10 of 44 games, finishing last in their division three times.

The hiring of head coach Chuck Knox (1978–82) and a revamped roster including quarterback Joe Ferguson (1973–84), running back Joe Cribbs (1980–83, 1985), and nose tackle Fred Smerlas (1979–89) helped Buffalo reach the playoffs in 1980 and 1981. Disrupted by the NFL Players Association strike in 1982, the team finished last in their division in 1984 and 1985 with only two victories each season. Attendance dwindled so badly that Wilson considered moving the Bills to another city, but shrewd maneuvering by new general manager Bill Polian (1984–92) set the foundation for the franchise's turnaround. Polian drafted standout players for the core of his team, including defensive end Bruce Smith (1985–98), wide receiver Andre Reed (1985–98), and running back Thurman Thomas (1988–98). He also signed quarterback Jim Kelly (1986–95) and hired head coach Marv Levy (1986–96), who would become the most successful coach in team history with 123 wins and 78 losses.

Levy guided the Bills to an unprecedented four consecutive Super Bowls (1990–93), though the team lost all four contests. The most painful Super Bowl loss was to the New York Giants in 1991, when a last-second 47 yd field goal attempt by Scott Norwood sailed wide right. Kelly retired as the team's all-time passing leader after the 1996 season, and Levy retired a year later. Head coach Wade Phillips (1998–2000) and quarterback Doug Flutie (1998–2000) led Buffalo to consecutive playoff appearances in 1998 and 1999. Ralph Wilson Jr has been the only owner of the Bills. His initial 1959 investment of $25,000 to acquire a franchise had appreciated to $250 million by 2000. Despite playing in the NFL's third smallest market, the Bills have led the league in attendance nine times, including six consecutive seasons (1988–93).

Maiorana, Sal. *Relentless: The Hard-Hitting History of Buffalo Bills Football* (Lenexa, Kans: Quality Sports Publications, 1995)

Pitoniak, Scott. *The Buffalo Bills Official Trivia Book* (New York: St. Martin's Press, 1989)

———. *The Buffalo Bills All-New Official Trivia Book II* (New York: St. Martin's Press, 1992)

Scott Pitoniak

Buffalo Bisons. Baseball team. Professional baseball in Buffalo dates to 1879, when the Buffalo Bisons began play in the National League. The next year pitcher Jim Galvin won 20 games and, on 20 August, threw a no-hitter. Hugh Ignatius Daily, the first of only two one-armed players in the majors, pitched for the Bisons in 1882 and won 15 games. After the 1885 season the team moved to the newly formed International League. In 1886 it signed its first African American player, second baseman Frank Grant, who hit .366 and led the league in home runs in 1887. Buffalo won its first Eastern League Championship in 1891. It played the 1900 season in the American League, the franchise's last year in a major league before being dumped in favor of a franchise in Boston before the start of the 1901 season.

The Bisons rejoined the Eastern League for the first decade of the 20th century, won the championship in both 1904 and 1906, and remained when it became the International League in 1912. Buffalo won the International League pennant under manager Patsy Donovan in 1915 and 1916 but would not win another championship until 1927, when first baseman Del Bissonette hit .365, with 31 home runs and a league-leading 167 runs batted in. Outfielder Frank McGowan, the league's Most Valuable Player, led Buffalo to another championship in 1936 when they finished at 94-60. Buffalo suffered through most of the 1940s and 1950s, winning championships only twice (1949, 1959), despite stars like Luke Easter. A combination of poor play through the 1960s, fiscal struggles, a deteriorating stadium, and dwindling attendance caused the forfeiting of franchise in 1970 to the parent club Montreal Expos. After playing only 38 games of the season, the Expos relocated the team to Winnipeg, Man.

Professional baseball returned to the area in 1979, when Buffalo native and Eastern League umpire Pete Calieri suggested to the league president that a team in Buffalo enter the league to replace a recently folded franchise in New Jersey. A conference with Buffalo mayor Jimmy Griffin followed, setting in motion the plan for a Double-A farm franchise named, once again, the Buffalo Bisons. Initial start-up cost, estimated at $90,000, was covered by a group of 90 independent Buffalo citizens, who each pledged $1,000. An agreement with the Pittsburgh Pirates linked the club to that Major League team's farm system. The Bisons set record marks for attendance in their first season and led the Eastern League again in their second season. Ticket sales topped 130,000 both years, when no other team in the Eastern League sold over 100,000. After six years of play in the Double-A Eastern League, the team moved to the Triple-A American Association and began a two-year relationship with the Chicago White Sox in 1985. In 1986 the Bisons set a record attendance mark at over 425,000. They spent the 1987 season as a Cleveland farm team but reunited with the Pittsburgh Pirates in 1988. That season the team moved into the $40 million Pilot Field (since 1999, Dunn Tire Park) in downtown Buffalo, one of more than a dozen parks that Bisons teams have called home since 1879.

Buffalo ended a 32-year title drought in 1991 when it won the American Association Eastern Division title, which it also won in 1992. In 1995 Buffalo reestablished an affiliation with Cleveland. The following year the Bisons won the Eastern Division but did not win the overall American Association championship until 1997. The team moved to the Triple-A International League before the start of the 1998 season. League champions that year, they won in dramatic fashion as they came from behind to move into first place on the final day of the season. Baseball in Buffalo continues to be an important part of the city's image, and hopes remain that one day the Bisons franchise will return to the major leagues.

Overfield, Joseph M. *The 100 Seasons of Buffalo Baseball* (Kenmore, NY: Partners' Press, 1985)

Leslie Heaphy

Buffalo Braves. Professional basketball team. The history of major league professional basketball in Buffalo begins in 1946 with the Buffalo Bisons, a founding franchise of the National Basketball League, a forerunner of the National Basketball Association (NBA). After just one season, the team left the city, eventually becoming the Atlanta Hawks. As part of league expansion, the Buffalo Braves, an NBA franchise owned by Philip J. Ryan and Peter J. Crotty, was awarded to the city in 1970; Ryan and Crotty sold the team to Paul L. Snyder before its first game was played. Coached by Dolph Schayes, a central and western New York State fan favorite who had starred for the Syracuse Nationals, the Braves debuted on 14 Oct 1970, defeating Cleveland before a crowd of 7,129 at Buffalo Memorial Auditorium. Under the leadership of Coach Jack Ramsay (1972–76), Buffalo reached three consecutive Eastern Division playoffs (1974–76) and produced a succession of young stars. Three Braves took NBA Rookie-of-the-Year honors during the team's eight-year history: Bob McAdoo (1973); Ernie DiGregorio (1974); and Adrian Dantley (1977). Although the National Hockey League Buffalo Sabres thrived, professional basketball in Buffalo never caught on at the box office. John Y. Brown, who bought a majority share in the team in 1977, declared a need for 8,000 season ticket holders per game to break even on his investment. During the 1977–78 season the Braves sold only 2,200 season tickets, making their departure a certainty. In an extraordinary deal, Brown swapped franchises with Boston Celtics owner Irv Levin. Upon taking title, Levin moved the Braves to California, where they became the San Diego Clippers (now Los Angeles Clippers).

Original Buffalo Braves Site, http://www.geocities.com/collinskev121

David Marc

Buffalo Creek Reservation. The Seneca established their claim to the Niagara Frontier by the conquest, dispersal, and amalgamation of the Neutral, Wenro, and Erie Indians between 1638 and 1680. Other Senecas entered this region in 1687 after the French invasion known as the Denonville expedition. They moved to the area in large numbers especially after the Sullivan-Clinton campaign in 1779. By 1783 about 2,000 Indians lived from Buffalo to Fort Niagara. The Seneca named their lands along Buffalo Creek Dosyoua-oo-sah Tiyoos-yo-wa, meaning "at the place that abounds with basswood," a wood used to carve "false face" masks. The Iroquois Confederacy's council fire was maintained here from 1784 to 1847.

Significant settlement at the Buffalo Creek Reservation commenced in 1780, in the area that is now West Seneca (Erie Co), with the arrival of the Seneca chief Old Smoke. Many other Seneca population clusters followed. In 1797, at the federal treaty with the Seneca at Big Tree [now in Livingston Co], the US government recognized the Buffalo Creek Reservation, a rectangular plot of 83,557 acres (33,814 ha), as Seneca territory. (This land is now most of the City of Buffalo and its eastern suburbs.) Before the War of 1812 a log council house was constructed in Seneca Village, about 300 feet (90 m) north of present-day Little and Archer Sts in South Buffalo. By the 1820s the village had two mission houses, a school, and a church. Within Seneca Village were two neighborhoods: the so-called Pagan Village, also known as Red Jacket's Village, and the Christian Village, headed by Capt Pollard and later Seneca chiefs Young King and Seneca White.

Other Indians sought protection in Seneca territory. By the 1780s there were two Onondaga settlements at Buffalo Creek along Cazenovia Creek, while the Cayuga formed their community on the northern edge of the reservation along William St and Cayuga Rd in today's City of Buffalo. Many Iroquoian and non-Iroquoian peoples lived at Buffalo Creek, primarily Senecas, Onondagas, Cayugas, Oneidas, Munsees, and Mohicans (Mahicans), but also Saponis, Tutelos, and other Indian groups. But the Buffalo Creek Reservation proved short-lived. Its land, located on what was a prime transportation route, was coveted by many non-Indians. The Seneca were dispossessed in the Buffalo Creek Treaty of 1838 and the Compromise Treaty, also known as the Supplemental Treaty of Buffalo Creek, in 1842.

Hauptman, Laurence M. *Conspiracy of Interests: Iroquois Dispossession and the Rise of New York State* (Syracuse: Syracuse Univ Press, 1999)

Houghton, Frederick. *The History of the Buffalo Creek Reservation.* Buffalo Historical Society Publications 24 (Buffalo: Buffalo Historical Society, 1920)

Karas, Faith E. "Material Culture on the Buffalo Creek Reservation, 1780–1842" (MA thesis, SUNY Buffalo, 1963)

Laurence M. Hauptman

"Buffalo Gals." A song from the 1840s. Briefly popular in minstrelsy, the tune and base lyrics stayed in circulation for generations under a wide variety of names. "Bowery Gals" was among the best-known variants in the mid–19th century, but others included "New York Gals," "Charleston Gals," and "Mobile Gals." The song, which may have had folk origins, was first published as a minstrel song in 1848, deriving in part from the earlier "Lubly Fan" (1844), but by the 1850s its run in minstrelsy was practically over. By this time there was a new move toward gentility among the minstrel troupes. The Buffalo Gal, as depicted in various versions of the lyrics, is a lower-class woman encountered in the street. She is alone, meaning, in the social code of the time, either unprotected or intentionally available. Sometimes she is a "yellow gal," meaning either a light-skinned black woman or a woman of easy virtue. She is, in any event, not dainty, and in some versions her feet take up the entire sidewalk. Often she is the gal "with a hole in her stocking." The singer invites her to "come out tonight" and "dance by the light of the moon." "Buffalo Gals" was particularly associated with the very popular Christy's Original Virginia Minstrels, who originated in Buffalo and began their career touring New York State from 1843 to 1845. It remains a favorite, and through a 1982 hip hop version by Malcolm McLaren and the Bronx-based World Famous Supreme Team, variants have been sampled and recorded by numerous rap artists, including Eminem.

Mahar, William J. *Behind the Burnt Cork Mask: Early Blackface Minstrelsy and Antebellum American Culture* (Urbana: Univ of Illinois Press, 1999)

Elliott S. Hurwitt

Buffalo General Hospital. Buffalo's second public hospital opened one wing in 1858, ten years after the opening of Sisters of Charity Hospital. Local Protestant business leaders established the hospital as an alternative to the Roman Catholic hospital. Antebellum hospitals such as Buffalo General provided care for the poor, and physicians provided their services without charge. However, provisions were also made to accept paying patients. During its first decade the hospital served predominately male patients because the institution lacked a separate women's ward. In 1869 the Ladies Hospital Association formed and assumed responsibility for rooms and wards for female patients. The institution, plagued early by financial problems when local fund-raising proved inadequate, had opened with only one-third of its physical plant in place. Financial woes persisted throughout the 19th century, and hospital construction was not finished until 1899. From its inception the hospital served as the teaching hospital for the University of Buffalo Medical College. In 1877 it opened the city's first training school for nurses and in 1883 began Buffalo's first ambulance service. A children's ward was added in 1884 and a maternity ward in 1885. Buffalo General operated an accident ward within Fitch Institute from 1886 to 1901. After Buffalo Medical College hired prominent Chicago physician Roswell Park (1883), he was appointed as attending surgeon at Buffalo General Hospital. At the beginning of the 21st century Buffalo General was a 742-bed acute medical care center and teaching hospital. Doctors at the hospital were the first in the Buffalo area to use X-ray machines (1902) and insulin (1922), and in 1954 they developed a new type of blood dialyzer.

Richardson, Jean. "Catholic Religious Women as Institutional Innovators: The Sisters of Charity and the Rise of the Modern Urban Hospital in Buffalo, NY, 1848–1900" (PhD diss, SUNY at Buffalo, 1996)

Jean Richardson

Buffalo Historical Marionettes. Work relief theater program. Established in Buffalo in 1933 by Esther Wilhelm and initially part of the Erie County Emergency Relief Program (then the federally funded Civil Works Administration), the Buffalo Historical Marionettes (BHM) moved onto the rolls of the Works Progress Administration's Federal Theatre Project in December 1935 and employed more than 200 Buffalonians. Wilhelm contended that her project focused on "visual education," and BHM plays such as *Rip Van Winkle* and *The Niagara Frontier* addressed regional and national history, while others dealt with race relations, automobile safety, and public health. The BHM performed at numerous New York State venues, primarily in Western New York, including public and parochial schools, playgrounds, Civilian Conservation Corps camps, nursing homes, orphanages, asylums, Kiwanis and Rotary clubs, and even Attica State Prison. Within the BHM a troupe of eight African Americans, called the Jubilee Singers, manipulated marionettes representing Blacks and Whites and sang quartet style. Although most of the troupe had pursued working-class service jobs such as porters, chauffeurs, and domestics, they were deeply rooted in Buffalo's African American middle class. Supported by the BHM's playwrights and costume, puppet, and scenery makers, the Jubilee Singers performed separately (though to the same range of audiences and venues), sometimes accompanied by a "Colored orchestra." Their repertoire included *Eli Whitney and the Invention of the Cotton Gin, The Life of Stephen Foster,* and *Uncle Tom's Cabin,* and the performance of spirituals and gospel songs. Their plays challenged the dominant representations of race then current in American popular culture: their black puppets were realistically designed, avoiding the minstrel images that were typical on other stages; their black characters were not sources of buffoonery; and many of their primary white characters were economic failures and the victims of exploitation. By 1939, when national funding for the Federal Theatre Project ceased and their work ended, the Buffalo Historical Marionettes and the Jubilee Singers had entertained approximately 2.5 million people.

Federal Theatre Project. Photos and scripts. Library of Congress, Washington, DC

Works Progress Administration, Federal Theatre Project. Records. National Archives and Records Administration, Washington, DC

Peter Rachleff and Beth Cleary

Buffalo Museum of Science. Founded in 1861 the museum had been relocated in 1929 from a west side building to Humboldt Parkway on Buffalo's east side. Governed by the Buffalo Society of Natural Sciences since its founding, it maintains a collection of almost 700,000 specimens. The museum supports teaching and research locally and internationally in anthropology, zoology, botany, entomology, mycology, and paleontology with over 70 people on staff. In 1990 the museum and Buffalo in a joint effort added the Dr Charles R. Drew Science Magnet Elementary School building onto the museum building, facilitating a unique specialized science education program. The museum operates the 264-acre (107 ha) Tifft Nature Preserve, located near Lake Erie, as well as a 42,000-volume library, an astronomical observatory, and a 400-seat auditorium. Almost 100,600 people visited the facility in 2000.

Buffalo Museum of Science, http://www.sciencebuff.org

The Official Museum Directory, 31st ed., vol 1 (Washington, DC: National Register Publishing, 2001)

David W. Sawicki

Buffalo News. Publication first appearing as the afternoon *Buffalo Evening News* on 11 Oct 1880. Its publisher, Edward H. Butler, who had launched the *Buffalo Sunday News* in 1873, entered a competitive market of two morning and two afternoon newspapers with this penny paper. Butler's son, Edward Jr, became publisher upon his father's death in 1914 and was succeeded by his son-in-law, James H. Righter, in 1956 and by Edward Jr's widow, Kate, in 1971. Alfred H. Kirchhofer was managing editor from 1927 to 1966. By 1982, with the closing of the *Courier* and *Express,* it became Buffalo's only daily newspaper, changing its name to the *Buffalo News,* and began publishing morning editions.

Under the Butlers, the *Buffalo Evening News* was a pioneer in local broadcasting when it opened radio station WBEN in 1930 and began the area's first FM radio station (WBEN-FM) and the first television station (WBEN-TV) in the late 1940s. The paper was purchased in 1977 by investor Warren Buffett. With a daily circulation at 224,500 and Sunday's at 307,500 in 2001, it had the highest penetration rate of any newspaper in the nation's top 50 markets. *Buffalo News* staff has won three Pulitzer Prizes: Edgar S. May (1961) for local reporting on welfare abuse and Bruce M. Shanks (1958) and Tom Toles (1990) for editorial cartoons.

Dillon, Michael J. "'A Smart, Live Journal': E. H. Butler's *Buffalo News* and the Rise and Decline of an Open Public Forum, 1873–1914" (PhD diss, Pennsylvania State Univ, 1995)
Goldberg, Jerry. "Edward H. Butler and the Founding of the *Buffalo Evening News:* The Life and Times of One of the Last Publisher Editors" (MA thesis, SUNY Buffalo, 1995)
Headlines and History: Celebrating 120 Years of the "Buffalo News" (Buffalo: Buffalo News Publishing, 1999)

W. Richard Whitaker

Buffalo Peace Bridge. International highway bridge across the Niagara River connecting Buffalo and Fort Erie, Ont. Construction began 17 Aug 1925, and the $4.5 million bridge opened 7 Aug 1927. Named in commemoration of a century of peace between the United States and Canada, the bridge's designer was Edward P. Lupfer. Consulting engineers were William Russell Davis and John F. Stevens. Composed of five steel arch spans varying in length from 346.5 feet (105.6 m) to 432.5 feet (131.8 m) and a through truss span of 360 feet (109.7 m), the bridge carries the roadway 100 feet (30.5 m) above the Black Rock ship canal. This vertical clearance requirement, imposed by the US Army Corps of Engineers, resulted in an asymmetrical design. By the late 1990s, with the bridge at capacity (6,000 trucks per day), proposals were made to twin the bridge or to replace it entirely. The construction of the current bridge resulted in the destruction of Fort Porter and a major incursion into Frederick Law Olmsted's Front Park in Buffalo. Further loss of parkland has been one of the key issues in the debate over the form and end points of a replacement span. The Buffalo and Fort Erie Public Bridge Authority, a 10-member board with equal representation from New York State and Canada, oversees the bridge.

Greenhill, Ralph. *Spanning Niagara: The International Bridges, 1848–1962* (Lewiston, NY: Niagara Univ, 1984; distributed by Univ of Washington Press)
Peace Bridge Authority, http://www.peacebridge.com/history.html

Paul J. Bartczak

Buffalo Plan. A voluntary program of student dress developed for the Buffalo public schools. The dress code, known as Dress Right, was created in 1955 under the aegis of Dr Joseph Manch, associate superintendent for Pupil Personnel Services. Concerned about juvenile delinquency, convinced that dress had a significant impact on behavior, and committed to involving students in the problem-solving process to harness the authority of the peer group, Manch approached the Inter-High School Student Council with his idea for a dress code. Separate recommendations were presented for boys and girls, as well as for academic and vocational high schools. The code emphasized modesty for girls and discouraged boys from wearing T-shirts, sweatshirts, and especially motorcycle boots, which were identified with delinquent youth and gangs. The somewhat more informal dress deemed appropriate for vocational students was in part an acknowledgment of class differences. Dress Right was enforced through voluntary measures, including editorials in student newspapers, assembly programs, and in one school a mirror inscribed with the words, "Look! This is you. Are *You* satisfied?" Compliance was general, although hardly complete. After the first year, school principals agreed that the program had improved student dress, and several of them believed that students were better behaved as a result of the code. A small minority of parents objected, some for financial reasons, others because they believed that Dress Right was illegal. In response the New York State Education Department emphasized the voluntary nature of the program. Packaged as the Buffalo Plan, Dress Right found a receptive national audience. By fall 1957 many schools across the nation, including 31 in New York City, had adopted the program.

Graebner, William. "The 'Containment' of Juvenile Delinquency," *American Studies* 27 (Spring 1986): 81–97
———. *Coming of Age in Buffalo: Youth and Authority in the Postwar Era* (Philadelphia: Temple Univ Press, 1990)

William Graebner

Buffalo River (8 mi/13 km). Extending from the confluence of the Buffalo and Cayuga Creeks to the eastern end of Lake Erie and the northbound Niagara River, the Buffalo River divides the southern third of Buffalo from the rest of the city. Known as Buffalo Creek through the 19th century, from 1797 until its illegal expropriation in 1838, most of the river flowed through the Seneca's Buffalo Creek Reservation. There were few white settlers until the Holland Land Co surveyed the future city of Buffalo in the early 1800s. In 1819–20 Samuel Wilkeson led a successful effort to deepen and widen the river's mouth and to create a harbor to convince the New York State legislature to name Buffalo as the western terminus of the Erie Canal rather than neighboring Black Rock. Starting in 1826 the US Army Corps of Engineers began to improve the harbor and in 1901 assumed the responsibility for deepening the channel and stabilizing the banks.

Major industries situated on the Buffalo River in the 19th century included tanning, maritime services, iron working, and meat processing. Iron and steel, chemicals, and oil refining played an increasing role along the river's banks in the 20th century, including National Aniline, which produced more than half of the coal-tar dye used in the United States by 1917. Republic Steel and Bethlehem Steel processed Great Lakes iron ore at Lake Erie's easternmost point, resulting in dyes coloring the river's water, oily slicks, occasional fires on the water's surface, and thick sediments laden with heavy metals and complex chemical compounds. The sediments remained in 2002, and the Environmental Protection Agency has designated the Buffalo River Harbor one of 43 toxic hot spots in the Great Lakes basin. However, industrial emissions and waste from combined sewer overflows channeled into the river have been dramatically reduced since 1975. Increased greenery and wildlife support and substantiate calls from citizen groups and local governments for more recreation on the river. In 2002 the river still hosted the largest collection of grain elevators in the country. About half of the river tonnage in 2002 was grain being barged into three remaining corporate elevators.

Rossi, Mary C. "An Historical Evaluation of Industrial Growth and Its Environmental Impacts on the Buffalo River, New York" (MS thesis, SUNY College at Buffalo, 1998)

Kenneth S. Mernitz

Buffalo, Rochester and Pittsburgh Railway. Coal-hauling and passenger railway that connected Buffalo and Rochester with western Pennsylvania. Buffalo, Rochester and Pittsburgh (BR&P) inherited routes from two older companies; Rochester and State Line Railroad was completed from Rochester to Salamanca (Cattaraugus Co) in 1878, and Rochester and Pittsburgh (R&P) Railroad was completed from Salamanca to Punxsutawney, Pa, in 1883. Through subsidiaries, R&P also ran a 48 mi (77 km) line from Ashford Junction (Cattaraugus Co) to Buffalo and a 9 mi (14 km) spur from Lincoln Park in Rochester to Lake Ontario. New York City financier Adrian Iselin purchased R&P in 1885 and created BR&P two years later. Rochester coal merchant Arthur G. Yates became president in 1890 and extended branches to his mines near Dubois, Pa. A 59 mi (95 km) subsidiary was built in 1898 from near Punxsutawney to Butler, Pa, which enjoyed trackage rights over the Baltimore and Ohio Railroad (B&O) to Pittsburgh. The company flourished through World War I under Pres William T. Noonan but faltered when nonunion mines in West Virginia began competing with Pennsylvania mines. In 1932 B&O bought BR&P to acquire Butler-Dubois trackage for a projected New York City–Chicago route, which was never built. In 1986 Genesee and Wyoming Inc bought the former BR&P lines from the Chessie System, which had acquired B&O, and formed Rochester Southern Railroad and Buffalo and Pittsburgh Railroad. Some ex-BR&P routes have since been abandoned.

Drury, George H., ed. *The Historical Guide to North American Railroads* (Waukesha, Wisc: Kalmbach Publishing, 1985)
Pietrak, Paul. *The Buffalo, Rochester and Pittsburgh Railway,* 2d ed. (Rochester: S. R. Ames Enterprises, 1992)

Edward T. Dunn

Buffalo Sabres. This National Hockey League (NHL) franchise built on local enthusiasm for the minor league Bisons, which played in Buffalo (1928–36, 1940–70) and won five Calder Cups (1943, 1944, 1946, 1963, 1970). Rejected in the NHL's first expansion in 1967, the Sabres ownership group, led by brothers Seymour and Northrup Knox, was granted a team in 1969, and the Sabres supplanted the Bisons at Memorial Auditorium. Led by Coach and General Manager George "Punch" Imlach, the team selected center Gilbert Perreault with the first pick in the 1970 expansion draft. During his 16 years with the Sabres, Perreault scored 512 goals and led the team to 11 consecutive playoffs (1975–85) and the 1975 Stanley Cup finals. Philadelphia won the cup in six games; game three, which took place on the fog-covered ice of Memorial Auditorium, became known as the Fog Game. During the 1970s Perreault teamed with wingers Rene Robert and Rick Martin to form the French Connection line. In the mid-1980s the team missed the playoffs twice as Perreault retired and the roster changed. Winger Alexander Mogilny (1989) and center Pat LaFontaine (1991) joined the team, but the Sabres struggled in the playoffs during the early 1990s. In 1996 the Sabres moved to Marine Midland Arena (now HSBC Arena). In the late 1990s Buffalo found success with goaltender Dominik Hasek, who was named the NHL's best goaltender six times (1994, 1995, 1997–99, 2001) and the league's Most Valuable Player twice (1997, 1998). The team played in the Eastern Conference finals (1998) and lost to the Dallas Stars in the Stanley Cup finals (1999) before trading Hasek and center Michael Peca in 2001. After the 2001–2 season, the team's regular season record was 1158-921-381. Hall of Famers with Sabres links include players Perreault, Tim Horton, and Dale Hawerchuk, coaches Imlach, Scotty Bowman, and Marcel Pronovost, and owner Seymour H. Knox III. In 2003 a group headed by Rochester-area resident B. Thomas Golisano purchased the team.

Bailey, Budd. *Celebrate the Tradition, 1970–1990: A History of the Buffalo Sabres* (Orchard Park, NY: Boncraft, 1989)

Sal Maiorana

Buffalo State College. See SUNY BUFFALO STATE.

Buffalo subway and light rail line. In the early 1980s city government envisioned a downtown pedestrian mall as a means of revitalizing Buffalo's central business district. Early construction (1978) connected the SUNY Buffalo North Campus to the downtown business district via an underground light rail line. By 1984 the entire line opened, with a free fare zone (primarily located above ground) to encourage shopping on downtown's Main St.

Operated by the Niagara Frontier Transit Authority (NFTA), the line is 6.6 miles (10.6 km) long, with 1.2 miles (1.9 km) at-grade through a pedestrian mall in the central area and 5.4 miles (8.7 km) in tunnel, of which 1.6 miles (2.5 km) were built using the cut-and-cover technique and 3.9 miles (6.2 km) were excavated by boring machines. The system runs modern broad-gauge light rail cars with both high-level doors for platforms in the subway and low-level doors for street operation. Power comes from overhead catenary. The underground section is completely accessible to people with disabilities, but the pedestrian mall segment offers small ramps located around entrances; elsewhere passengers climb steps. Transfers to local buses are provided. Approximately 26,000 riders per day use the system. An extension between the North and South Campuses of SUNY Buffalo, located 3.3 miles (5.3 km) apart, has been in the planning stage for years, but because of the lack of success of the light rail system in revitalizing and bringing new development and activity to downtown, it will most likely not be built.

Middleton, William D. *Metropolitan Railways: Rapid Transit in America* (Bloomington: Indiana Univ Press, 2003)

David Babson

Buffalo wings. Chicken wings covered, traditionally, with a mixture of butter and hot sauce and served with blue cheese dressing and celery. This snack was created at Teressa and Frank Bellissimo's Anchor Bar at 1047 Main St, Buffalo. There are several accounts of the origin of Buffalo wings. The most popular version is that the Bellissimos cooked up a batch as a late night snack for their son Dominic and his friends in 1964. Because the wings were thought of as scrap and usually thrown out, Teressa decided to serve them as a cheap snack that night. In another account, the restaurant received a shipment of wings by accident and, rather then waste them, found a use for them. News of the dish spread quickly through the community, and soon wings were on the restaurant's regular menu. By 1975 they had spread to south Florida, a destination of Buffalo retirees and "snow birds." In 1977 the city named 29 July as Chicken Wings Day. Calvin Trillin further spread the news with a 1980 *New Yorker* article, in which he documented what was known of their origin. With more publicity, the popularity of Buffalo wings rapidly increased. By the mid-1990s, fast food chains like Domino's and Pizza Hut were distributing wings nationally. The annual National Buffalo Wing Festival, "Wing Stock," in which area restaurants compete for the title of "Best Wings in the City," was inaugurated in 1996. In 2002 more than 20 tons of chicken wings were used. Wings are Buffalo's currency of choice when making bets with rival cities. They are generally served at four degrees of spiciness: mild, medium, hot, and "suicidal."

Trillin, Calvin, "An Attempt to Compile a Short History of the Buffalo Chicken Wing," *New Yorker* 25 Aug 1980, 82–27

Andrew C. Maines

Burchfield, Charles (Ephraim) (*b* Ashtabula Harbor, Ohio, 9 Apr 1893; *d* West Seneca, Erie Co, 10 Jan 1967). Painter. Burchfield was raised in Salem, Ohio. Memories of his childhood, particularly the hours spent in nature, exerted a powerful influence on his art. Burchfield attended the Cleveland School of Art (now Cleveland Institute of Art) from 1912 to 1916. Upon graduation he received a scholarship to the National Academy of Design in New York City. Although Burchfield remained in the city only a few months, he made crucial contacts in the art world. After a brief return to Salem and a six-month stint in the army, Burchfield became a wallpaper designer for M. H. Birge and Sons Co in Buffalo in 1921, working there until he began to paint full-time in 1929. He married Bertha Kenreich in 1922, and the couple had five children. In 1925 they moved to the Buffalo suburb of Gardenville (Erie Co), where he lived and worked until his death.

In the early 1920s Burchfield, along with Edward Hopper, was heralded by art world critics as a pioneer of the American scene. In 1930 Burchfield became one of the first American artists to have a solo exhibition at the Museum of Modern Art in New York City. This exhibition focused attention on his pre-1920 works, which were highly expressionistic responses to his childhood experiences. In 1943 Burchfield began creating the large-scale expressionistic depictions of nature that dominated the remainder of his career. One of the preeminent 20th-century watercolorists, Burchfield is acclaimed for his introduction of large-scale compositions and innovative use of opaque color. Representative masterworks include *Church Bells Ringing, Rainy Winter Night* (1917), *Ice Glare* (1931–33), and *The Moth and the Thunderclap* (1961). His late years were filled with honors, including retrospectives at the Albright Art Gallery (1944) in Buffalo and the Whitney Museum of American Art (1956) in New York City. The Charles Burchfield Art Center (now Burchfield-Penney Art Center) at SUNY Buffalo was established in 1966. The Charles E. Burchfield Nature and Art Center was built in 1999 in West Seneca, near the artist's home, and celebrates Burchfield's love of nature and the inspiration it provided him as an artist.

Maciejunes, Nannette V., and Michael D. Hall, et al. *The Paintings of Charles Burchfield: North by Midwest* (New York: Abrams, 1997)

Nannette V. Maciejunes

Burdett. Village (pop 357) in Hector (Schuyler Co). Settled in 1799 and known as Hamburg, it was renamed Burdett in 1819 soon after it acquired a post office. In 1860 a foundry, a tannery, a woolen mill, and an agricultural implement factory provided employment. It was served by the Lehigh Valley Railroad (1892–1976). Burdett incorporated as a village in 1898. In 1921 many village residents were retired farmers, but Burns Produce operated a processing plant. In the early 21st century Burdett's residents work in Elmira, Corning (Steuben Co), Ithaca, or elsewhere in Schuyler Co.

Glenda Gephart

Burgoyne, John (*b* London, ?24 Feb 1723; *d* London, 4 Aug 1792). British general. After a successful military career in Europe he was promoted to major general and in 1775 was sent to North America to advise Massachusetts Colony's Gov and Gen Thomas Gage and Maj Gen Guy Carleton on military tactics, although he returned to England. He was sent to Canada in 1777 to direct major military campaigns. He is credited with being the chief architect of the Campaign of 1777, where three British movements planned to attack military strongholds and then simultaneously meet in Albany. In May 1777 Burgoyne pushed south from Canada with nearly 9,000 men; Col Barry St. Leger advanced east from the Mohawk Valley, and Gen William Howe marched north from New York City. Burgoyne took Fort Ticonderoga [now in Essex Co] 2–5 July 1777, securing the lake country. On 15 September he was at Schuylerville [now in Saratoga Co] and on 19 September was defeated at Freeman's Farm (first Battle of Saratoga). Burgoyne led a second battle there 7 October but was beaten again at Bemis Heights (second Battle of Saratoga). Ten days later he surrendered. He returned to England in 1778 and was stripped of his military titles. He spent the final years of his life writing stage plays.

Mintz, Max M. *The Generals of Saratoga: John Burgoyne and Horatio Gates* (New Haven: Yale Univ Press, 1990)

Mark G. Spencer

Burke. Town (pop 1,359) and village (pop 213) in N Franklin Co. Settled ?1797 primarily from Vermont, the town was formed from Chateaugay in 1844. In 1850 the Northern Railroad (later Rutland Railroad) came through town. A refrigerated car began operating the following year, and Burke farmers began shipping their butter; within two years the farms along the line doubled in value. The first creamery opened in 1874. A variety of small industries provided employment, including asheries, tanneries, sandstone quarries, starch factories, brick-making establishments, and an iron foundry. Burke's Democratic Party sympathies were expressed on 4 July 1861 by a mob that raised a Confederate flag over the hamlet. Almanzo Wilder of *Farmer Boy* and other books by Laura Ingalls Wilder lived in Burke from 1857 to ?1875; his childhood home is a museum. The village of Burke incorporated in 1922. In the early 21st century the town remains a dairying district, with maple syrup also being produced.

Thomas W. Perrin

Burleigh, Harry (Henry) T(hacker) (*b* Erie, Pa, 2 Dec 1866; *d* Stamford, Conn, 12 Sept 1949). Spirituals arranger, composer, and baritone. A leading figure in the development of the spiritual and a key figure in African American music, Burleigh came to New York City in 1892. He was befriended by the Czech composer Antonín Dvořák, who taught at Jeannette Thurber's National Conservatory of Music from 1893 to 1895. Burleigh helped spark Dvořák's fascination with American music and with spirituals, in particular. Famed for his fine baritone voice, Burleigh long held two prestigious sacred music singing positions, one at St. George's Episcopal Church on Stuyvesant Square from 1894 to 1946 and the other at Temple Emanu-El on 5th Ave and 43d St from 1900 to 1925. His Palm Sunday singing became so popular that hundreds were turned away at the door annually. He was involved in the founding of ASCAP (American Society of Composers, Authors and Publishers) in 1914 and was its first African American officer. It was in his famous arrangements that many of the greatest spirituals, including "Deep River," entered the national consciousness. His outstanding art songs include the song cycle *Five Songs of Laurence Hope.*

Simpson, Anne K. *Hard Trials: The Life and Music of Harry T. Burleigh* (Metuchen, NJ: Scarecrow Press, 1990)

Elliott S. Hurwitt

burlesque. Form of theater featuring variety acts, musical numbers, comics, and scantily clad showgirls. Popular from the late 19th century through the 1930s, burlesque developed in New York City. Although it owed much to the circus sideshow cootch dancers and dance hall honkytonk music, the concept was sparked by an 1866 New York City musical and comic revue, *The Black Crook,* which had in its cast a troupe of female ballet dancers wearing tights. The vogue for such "naked" spectacles gained momentum in 1869 with Lydia Thompson and her British Blondes, a troupe that toured New York State in a musical "burlesque" (parody of Greek drama). The British Blondes first introduced Americans to the showgirl, and by the 1880s, showgirls May Howard and Rose Sydell were well-known performers, with several New York City theaters, including the Eighth Avenue Theatre (1881), regularly offering burlesque entertainment.

By 1900 the form of the burlesque show was well established, although producers such as the Minsky brothers (Abe, Billy, Herbert, and Morton) would continue to borrow ideas from Broadway's *Ziegfeld Follies* and legitimate theater for their less expensive, popular entertainments. Early burlesque (1870s–1920s) emphasized music, dance, and performances by comedians like Bert Lahr and Fanny Brice over female nudity. Funnymen Ed Wynn and Jackie Gleason also got their start in burlesque comedy. But the showgirls and comic material of the early period were still racy enough to inspire New York theatrical producer and director Tony Pastor to create an alternative, family-oriented entertainment known as vaudeville in 1881. Vaudeville became a second successful genre, emphasizing comedy and musical and variety acts, but eliminating sketches and songs with sexual content. At the same time, over the second decade of the 20th century, burlesque routines became more overtly sexual, featuring such comic bits as "Desire under the El," "The Sway of All Flesh," and "Panties Inferno."

From 1905 touring agencies, called wheels—Columbia, Empire, Eastern, and Mutual among them—booked burlesque shows into theaters along the Eastern seaboard for runs of several weeks. The wheels helped establish burlesque houses throughout the state before their eventual demise in the 1930s. By the first decade of the 20th century, most large cities in New York State had one or two "class" houses in addition to shoestring operations. In the years before World War I Buffalo became both a vaudeville and a burlesque hub. Its Court Street Palace and Gaiety, Teck, and Star Theaters all booked burlesque and vaudeville entertainments. Burlesque houses in Albany, Troy, Utica, Syracuse, Rochester, and Buffalo sometimes shared managements and rotated shows. The Gaiety Theaters in Albany and Troy operated in this way; these houses were torn down in the 1930s and 1940s. Burlesque also developed borscht belt touring, so-called because it served Catskill Mountain summer resorts catering to New York City Jews of Russian and central European origins, through the 1930s. Borscht belt shows also emphasized comedy over nudity and became training vehicles for such famed comedians as Phil Silvers, (Bud) Abbott and (Lou) Costello, and Red Skelton.

Burlesque's popularity peaked just prior to World War I, with the striptease not incorporated until the late 1920s. The strippers Mary Dawson ("Mlle Fifi"), Georgia Southern, Margie Hart, and Rose Louise Hovick ("Gypsy Rose Lee") revived business at New York City's National Winter Garden, Park, Apollo, and Little Apollo, but moved burlesque closer to the edge of legality. Despite harassment of burlesque producers by the New York Society for the Suppression of Vice (1873) throughout the 1920s, Mayor Jimmy Walker discouraged any official censorship. The resurgence of burlesque during the Great Depression, when cheap tickets and bawdier entertainment once again packed houses, brought new attention from moral arbiters and local government, which precipitated its demise. Despite the 1933 formation of the Burlesque Artists Association, which improved working conditions, increased salaries, and helped to correct booking inequities, pressure from church organizations, the *New York Daily Mirror* and other newspapers, and various reform groups resulted in Mayor Fiorello La Guardia's and License Commissioner Paul Moss's targeting of burlesque shows for closure. One by one the shows were found to be lewd, obscene, and contributory to immoral conduct, and one by one, the burlesque houses were turned into movie houses or sold. Even though talkies and radio were drawing audiences from live entertainment anyway, La Guardia and Moss succeeded in putting burlesque out of business abruptly by 1937. Stripper Ann Corio would briefly revive interest in the form with her Broadway show *This Was Burlesque* (1964).

Allen, Robert Clyde. *Horrible Prettiness: Burlesque and American Culture* (Chapel Hill: Univ of North Carolina Press, 1991)
Zeidman, Irving. *The American Burlesque Show* (New York: Hawthorn Books, 1967)

Nan Mullenneaux

Burlington. Town (pop 1,085) in W central Otsego Co. Part of the Croghan Patent (1770), it was acquired by William Cooper in 1786. Settled in 1790 by New Englanders, the town was formed from Otsego in 1792. Population peaked in 1810 at 3,196. In the 19th century a variety of products were made in small shops at Burlington Green, including combs, hats, leather, ironwork, wool cards, and furniture; ladles and wool cloth were made at West Burlington. A hilly upland, the town continues some farming but it is increasingly a bedroom community for neighboring urban areas. The village green at Burlington Flats and the Carpenter Gothic Christ Church at West Burlington are landmarks.

Hugh C. MacDougall

Burned-over District. Roughly defined as the area of Central and Western New York, extending north to St. Lawrence Co and south into areas of the Southern Tier during the period 1800–1860, when the area was characterized by successive waves of religious excitement. It received its name from Ministers Lyman Beecher and Charles Grandison Finney, two of the leading disseminators of evangelical religion in the area, who wrote, not approvingly, of the "wild excitement passing through that region." The term was popularized for recent generations of scholars by Whitney Cross in his seminal book *The Burned-over District* (1950). Although many of Cross's original conceptions have been challenged and revised, his volume initiated much of the subsequent scholarly interest in the antebellum religious history of Central and Western New York.

The Second Great Awakening

The Burned-over District was part of a larger, national religious movement, the Second Great Awakening. It began in New England congregations in the 1790s, manifesting itself in a concern for religion, responsiveness to preaching, increased church attendance, and greater attention to public morality. Early 19th-century settlers of Central and Western New York came chiefly from New England and brought this influence with them. Fervent revivalism was a part of many transplanted Yankees' lives from birth. The settlers can be divided into two general groups: mainstream Protestants who formed the great majority, carrying forward the evangelism that had prevailed among their Puritan ancestors for centuries, and a small but significant minority who deviated from orthodoxy and were given to unusual metaphysical notions, often joining movements and designing crusades for the perfection of humanity and the attainment of millennial bliss. The term "religious ultraism" was used to describe the extremes of the Burned-over District as early as 1835, when Presbyterian William B. Sprague published a sermon in Albany.

Although the turmoil of the Burned-over District came to full fruition after the completion of the Erie Canal in 1825, the symptoms are to be detected from the first settlements. The canal opened up an enormous part of New York's middle west to economic development, and the demand for laborers and practitioners of every enterprise brought tens of thousands of migrants into the region. Soon there was a new wealthy class of bankers, jobbers, merchants, and owners of mills and factories. For the residents of the Burned-over District, all of this meant upheaval, rapid socioeconomic change, and, often, a search for religion and religious experiences that could make sense of their new circumstances.

Isolated Protestant revivals had continued in New England towns after the Great Awakening of the 1740s had run its course. Particularly in Connecticut, from 1770 to 1800, there were scattered awakenings. Shortly thereafter, the Second Great Awakening would become powerful throughout much of the new nation and would continue for four decades. It was the frontier—Kentucky, Tennessee, western Pennsylvania, and western New York State—where the revival reached its peak intensity. The well-known Cane Ridge, Ky, camp meeting of 1801 drew as many as 20,000. With over 1,000 camp meetings and crowds sometimes numbering in the tens of thousands, Methodists, Baptists, Presbyterians, and other denominations hastened to consolidate revivalists' gains into established churches throughout the frontier. Although there could be emotionalism in Burned-over District revivals, they were, on the whole, far more sedate than they were in the South. Revival styles varied, perhaps, because of the difference in religious styles between the Scots-Irish Presbyterianism of western Pennsylvania and the upper South, and the more decorous Congregationalism of New England colleges, where the eastern awakening began in earnest. Numerous graduates of these colleges entered the ministry, most were in favor of revivalism, and many moved to New York State in the 1790s and 1810s. In New York State the years 1799 and 1800 were known as the Great Revival. The war years temporarily distracted attention from religion, but the number of new adherents after the War of 1812 surpassed all previous gains.

The Congregationalists and Presbyterians recorded impressive gains in the early 19th century, largely because of local revivals. Two pro-revival denominations, the Congregational and the Presbyterian, sent numbers of pastors into the Burned-over District to further the awakening and to found churches, which stressed an educated clergy and orderly worship. Growing cooperation between the two led to the adoption of the Plan of Union in 1801, proposed by Jonathan Edwards Jr, president of Union College in Schenectady. This plan allowed Presbyterians and Congregationalists in any community to form one congregation and to elect a pastor from either denomination, because their theology was substantially the same. This "presbygational" arrangement first operated in New York State and eventually spread into Ohio, Indiana, Illinois, Kentucky, Tennessee, and Missouri.

Charles Grandison Finney, mid–19th century.

After the War of 1812 the new nationalistic spirit called for a program of home missions on a national level, again fostering interdenominational cooperation. The most important of these new national agencies was the American Home Missionary Society (AHMS). By the 1820s there were numerous local missionary groups throughout New York State. In addition, there were numerous Bible, tract, and Sunday school societies. In 1826 local branches banded together with societies of other states to form the AHMS, supported by the Congregational, Presbyterian, Dutch Reformed, and Associate Reformed denominations. One year later the AHMS was fielding 169 evangelists, 120 of whom were laboring in New York State. Other denominations were equally active, and many of the migrants from New England coming into the state were young and indifferent to which denomination was available in their area.

The Methodists were particularly aggressive in attracting new members. Its circuit riders traveled hundreds of miles each month, over rugged terrain, to widespread communities. Their efficient circuit-rider system gained many converts. Lorenzo Dow (1778?–1847), a powerful and well-known evangelist, visited Western (Oneida Co) often after 1808 and made it the base of the most important Methodist circuit of central New York State. Baptists were no less determined to promote revival meetings and gain converts. In Monroe and Ontario Cos especially they held intense campaigns and their numbers increased rapidly. Freewill Baptist revivals were held in Erie Co on the shore of Lake Ontario and in the Susquehanna Valley from 1811 through 1820.

Old School and New School Protestants

The fervor of the awakening had progressed for two decades, and many people had been added to the churches, but there was a decline in intensity around 1820. But after just a short fallow period, a new theological trend would bring the Burned-over District to its highest pitch. With the orthodox clergy, in both New York State and throughout New England, particularly among the Presbyterians and the Congregationalists, two groups had been forming that traced their positions back to the 1740s. Both agreed that humans needed salvation and that faith brought justification before a holy God. Beyond this agreement they split. Old School pastors accepted revivals but were cautious, often needing proof that it was a work of God, and holding to the old Puritan ideas of original sin inherited from Adam, predestination, and the need for sinners' prolonged period of conviction before the Holy Spirit might grant faith. The New School thinking revolved around strong approval of revivals and the view that the sinners' decision for salvation must be immediate, not prolonged, and that they did indeed have free will to choose.

While these ideas had been developing for decades, it was the driving insistence of the influential professor of theology Nathaniel William Taylor (1786–1858), who taught at Yale from the 1820s to the 1850s, that brought the matter to a boil. Taylor taught his many students that people become sinful only by their own breaches of God's law and that "sin is in the sinning," not because of Adam and Eve's sin. The doctrine of original sin and the traditional waiting to be moved by the Holy Spirit were seen as impediments to conversion and revivals. Taylor taught instead that Christians had free will in the choice of conversion and could make an immediate decision for salvation. This provided a new impetus and urgency to evangelism and revivals. This so-called New Haven Theology penetrated deeply into the Plan of Union churches and would lead to a complete schism in the Presbyterian Church in 1837.

Charles Grandison Finney (1792–1875), a proponent of Taylor, was the leading figure in the second phase of the awakening. Finney grew up in Oneida Co and became an apprentice lawyer in Adams (Jefferson Co). He underwent conversion in 1821, and almost immediately he was determined to enter the ministry; he received Presbyterian ordination in 1824. Finney became a missionary in the rural Lake Ontario region, preaching to congregations in Jefferson and St. Lawrence Cos. From October 1825 through 1827 his extended preaching stints and revivals, first in the Oneida Co locales of Western, Rome, and Utica and in Auburn (Cayuga Co) and Troy (Rensselaer Co), attracted national attention. In Utica, Finney acquired his most famous convert, Theodore Dwight Weld (1803–95), who later became an abolitionist leader. Finney pioneered the concept of citywide campaigns supported by numerous committees for publicity and prayer. He was an early proponent of the importance of giving women significant and public roles in the revivals. After conducting revivals in Philadelphia, New York City, Boston, and elsewhere, he led his most powerful revival in Rochester for six months in 1830–31, ushering in the national awakening of 1830–32.

Finney eschewed emotionalism in his sermons and in Rochester ministered primarily to the professional classes, which responded in great numbers to his dignified meetings. The churches of the region cooperated, and for a period simultaneous meetings conducted by other speakers were held throughout Monroe and surrounding counties, in Ovid (Seneca Co) and as far away as Ithaca. Finney's methodology was broad and nondenominational and could be accepted by almost all Christian groups. Lyman Beecher claimed that 100,000 were converted across the nation within a year, an event "unparalleled in the history of the church." Beginning in 1832 Finney gave up full-time evangelism and began as a pastor at New York City's Chatham Street Chapel, always devoting a part of each year to revivals elsewhere. His career as an evangelist firmly established the connection between Central and Western New York and religious fervor, and he created a model for evangelical revivals that would be emulated by his successors, from D. L. Moody to Billy Graham.

Ultraism and Communalism

In addition to these orthodox expressions of religious awakenings in New York State in the beginning of the 19th century, there were a number of movements that deviated, sometimes wildly, from Christian orthodoxy. Jemima Wilkinson (1752–1819), the "Public Universal Friend," in 1794 set up a short-lived community called Jerusalem on the west side of Seneca Lake. More successful was Ann Lee, or Mother Ann Lee (1736–84), founder of the Shakers in Manchester, England. Her trances and visions convinced others and then herself that Christ's Second Coming would be in the form of a woman and that she was that woman. After experiencing rejection in England, she moved to the United States with eight followers in 1774 and settled at Watervliet (Albany Co), organizing a celibate community in which everything was owned in common. By 1794 there were 12 communities, 2 in New York State and the remainder in New England. The community at New Lebanon (Columbia Co) remained the center of authority.

The full blossoming of ultraism in New York State came in the 1820s. William Miller (1782–1849) of Hampton (Washington Co) maintained a fascination with calculating the date of Christ's return to earth. In 1828 he began to preach that Jesus would return "about 1843." He was ordained a Baptist minister in 1833, and between 1840 and 1843 meetings were held all across the nation, with Miller himself lecturing over 300 times during one six-month period. Condemnation came from many quarters. He then calculated that Jesus would return between 21 Mar 1843 and 21 Mar 1844. When this did not happen, Miller reset the date at 22 Oct 1844, and again many who trusted felt betrayed. Millerism after the "Great Disappointment" soon dwindled, although followers formed the core of later Adventist sects nationwide.

Mormonism also began in the Burned-over District. In 1830 Joseph Smith Jr (1805–44) was disturbed by the competition among the area's religious groups and sought to re-create the primitive church. He published the Book of Mormon in Palmyra (Wayne Co), translated, he claimed, from golden plates inscribed in "reformed Egyptian," and in Fayette (Seneca Co) founded the Church of Jesus Christ of Latter-Day Saints. Smith and most of his early followers, such as Brigham Young from Mendon (Monroe Co), were New Yorkers of New England background, looking for spiritual assurance amid an abundance of religious choices. Smith's doctrinal heterodoxies put the new sect at odds with existing Christian denominations, and in 1831 he and his followers left New York State for an uncertain future. In time, however, they would emerge as one of the most distinctive American religious groups.

Perfectionism, the belief in human beings' capacity for perfect holiness, took several forms. Whereas the Shakers sought perfection in celibacy, John Humphrey Noyes (1811–86), who believed that conversion brought complete release from sin, rejected monogamous marriage. After proselytizing throughout New York State and New England from 1834 to 1837, he founded the Putney Community in Vermont. Driven out of Vermont, he took his community to Oneida (Madison Co) in 1848, where it lasted until 1880, when it was reorganized and "complex marriage" was repudiated.

Communalism of a less explicitly religious nature also flourished in the Burned-over District. The Oneida Community was only the best known of the numerous utopian communities founded in the area, and in the 1830s and 1840s, numerous short-lived Owenite and Fourierist socialists organized utopian communities. Many believed that they were on the cusp of movements that would usher in radical new forms of human relationships.

In 1848 Spiritualism shook the Burned-over District and much of the nation. It was rooted in the writings of the Swedish mystic Emmanuel Swedenborg (1688–1772) and in mesmerism, which used hypnotic trances, claiming to unlock the mysteries of life after death. At Hydesville (Wayne Co) in 1848 and then in Rochester, sisters Margaret, Leah, and Kate Fox imitated spirit "rappings" that responded to specific questions. Crowds gathered, and the sisters and their rappings became famous everywhere. Spiritualism made important converts, such as Horace Greeley, editor of the *New York Tribune*, and claimed at its height, in the mid-1850s, 67 periodicals and thousands of adherents. Although an investigating committee later discovered that the Fox sisters produced the rapping sounds with their toe joints, this did not diminish the faith of the general public. Spiritualism also provided an impetus for communalism; for example, in the short-lived Kiatone Community in the 1850s in Randolph (Cattaraugus Co) and in Thomas Lake Harris's Brotherhood of the Good Life in Dutchess and Chautauqua Cos in the 1850s and 1860s. A remnant of the Spiritualist interest in communal organizations survives at Lily Dale (Chautauqua Co).

Political and Social Impact

The district's concern for spiritual matters often led to political involvements, and one of its legacies to the nation was an intense commitment to social reform, both within and without the standard political organizations. A new form of reform politics was shaped. One of the first manifestations was New York State's Antimasonic movement, which began after Freemason William Morgan of Batavia (Genesee Co) published an exposé of the secret society in 1826. Jailed on trumped-up charges, he was abducted from prison and last seen alive in Youngstown (Niagara Co). This caused an enormous furor, which led to the emergence of the Antimasonic Party in the election of 1828. Mostly absorbed by the Whig Party by 1836, the movement substantially shaped that party's fusion of evangelical fervor with populist politics. Other reform causes—ranging from temperance, women's rights, and pacifism, to vegetarianism and spelling reform—took root in the Burned-over District.

Although temperance was undoubtedly the most popular of the reforms, the movement with the greatest political impact was abolitionism. Along with the Boston-based group led by William Lloyd Garrison, the Burned-over District established itself as one of the cores of the antislavery movement. While Finney confined himself to evangelism, many of his followers, such as Weld, became leaders of the abolitionist movement. Also strongly aligned with Finney were the Tappan brothers, Arthur (1786–1865) and Lewis (1788–1873), wealthy New York City merchants and founders of the American and Foreign Anti-Slavery Society, who throughout their lifetimes generously supported a host of reforms and causes, inspiring other business owners to similar stewardship. Leaders in the area comprised Frederick Douglass in Rochester, Ministers Samuel J. May and Jermain Loguen in Syracuse, and Gerrit Smith in Peterboro (Madison Co). Abolitionist education institutions including the Oneida Institute in Whitesboro (Oneida Co) and New York Central College in McGrawville [now McGraw, Cortland Co]. The Burned-over District became the home of numerous African American leaders of the struggle against slavery, which in addition to Douglass and Loguen included Henry Highland Garnet, William Wells Brown, and Harriet Tubman. The Liberty Party, the most important abolitionist political party, had its core of support in the area in the 1840s, and area abolitionists generally sought political influence as well as "moral suasion." Thus it was no accident that William H. Seward—governor, US Senator from New York State, Pres Abraham Lincoln's secretary of state, and one of the most successful political abolitionists—came from the area (Auburn). It also made sense that the Burned-Over District was the site of the revolutionary meeting in Seneca Falls in 1848 that initiated the modern women's rights movement, which had close ties to abolitionism. That movement's two best-known early leaders, Elizabeth Cady Stanton and Susan B. Anthony, had deep roots in the area, reflecting the commitment to spiritual freedom, personal equality, and societal transformation so characteristic of religious-inspired reform in the Burned-over District.

The coming of the Civil War marked an end to the heyday of the Burned-over District. The intense Protestantism of the region (increasingly leavened by a large Roman Catholic population) remained, but for the most part the revivalistic and evangelical fervor and the evangelically based connection to social reform did not.

Religious associations such as the Holiness movement, which were largely shaped in the environment of antebellum New York State, went on to greater postbellum successes elsewhere in the United States, notably in the South and West. Temperance became the most important religious-based reform in the decades after the Civil War in New York State. Perhaps the Chautauqua Movement, founded in the state in 1874, was the most significant expression of American Protestant social thought to develop in the area in the decades after the Civil War. Its relative gentility and its disinclination to advocate either radical social and religious positions were signs that the Burned-over District had cooled.

Barkun, Michael. *Crucible of the Millennium: The Burned-over District of New York in the 1840s* (Syracuse: Syracuse Univ Press, 1986)

Cross, Whitney R. *The Burned-over District: The Social and Intellectual History of Enthusiastic Religion in Western New York, 1800–1850* (Ithaca: Cornell Univ Press,1950)

Hambrick-Stowe, Charles E. *Charles G. Finney and the Spirit of American Evangelicalism* (Grand Rapids, Mich: William B. Eerdmans, 1996)

Hardman, Keith J. *Charles Grandison Finney, 1792–1875: Revivalist and Reformer* (Syracuse: Syracuse Univ Press, 1987)

Hatch, Nathan O. *The Democratization of American Christianity* (New Haven, Conn: Yale Univ Press, 1989)

Perciacante, Marianne. *Calling Down Fire: Charles Grandison Finney and Revivalism in Jefferson County, New York, 1800–1840* (Albany: SUNY Press, 2003)

Strong, Douglas M. *Perfectionist Politics: Abolitionism and the Religious Tension of American Democracy* (Syracuse: Syracuse Univ Press, 1999)

Keith J. Hardman

Burnet, William (*b* The Hague, Netherlands, March 1688; *d* Boston, 7 Sept 1729). Royal governor of New York and New Jersey (1720–28). Burnet, who trained as an attorney at the Inns of Court, was controller of customs in London from 1714 to 1720, when he exchanged posts with Robert Hunter, governor of New York and New Jersey. On his arrival in New York, Burnet favored Hunter's allies, who were predominantly landowners, and kept the agreeable assembly elected during Hunter's tenure. Merchants complained to English authorities when Burnet banned the lucrative Albany-Montreal trade, which was benefiting the French enemy. In New Jersey Burnet overcame initial resistance from the proprietary party by calling for assembly elections. Burnet, in 1727, was transferred to the government of Massachusetts and New Hampshire. Arriving in Boston in 1728, he died before monetary issues with the assembly could be resolved. A competent governor, Burnet was generally respected by colonists but was less successful than his predecessor, Robert Hunter, primarily because his inflexible nature alienated potential allies.

See also COLONIAL NEW YORK.

Nelson, William, ed. *Original Documents Relating to the Life and Administrations of William Burnet, Governor of New York and New Jersey, 1720–1728* (Paterson, NJ: Press Printing & Publishing, 1897)

Mary Lou Lustig

Burns. Town (pop 1,248) in NE Allegany Co. Settled in 1805, the town was formed in 1826 from Ossian [now in Livingston Co]. The Buffalo Division of the Erie Railroad came through in 1852, making possible such local industry as a mill at Garwoods that manufactured lumber and shipped stove wood. Later the Pittsburg, Shawmut and Northern Railroad (1903–46) also served town. Reforestation in the 1930s created 1,132-acre (458.1 ha) Slader Creek State Forest. In the early 21st century some dairy farms continue to ship milk.

Burr, Aaron (*b* Newark, NJ, 6 Feb 1756; *d* Port Richmond, Richmond Co, 14 Sept 1836). Vice president and US senator. Burr was born into a prominent ecclesiastical family. He graduated from the College of New Jersey (now Princeton University) in 1772 and joined the Continental army in 1775. Burr participated in the Canadian expedition and the Battles of Long Island and Monmouth. He served at Valley Forge but did not receive Gen George Washington's favor and, in poor health, resigned as a lieutenant colonel in 1779. He studied law and was admitted to the New York State Bar in January 1782, and the following year he moved to New York City. In 1784–85 he served in the state assembly but was not active or particularly partisan. He did not take a public position on the newly proposed Constitution of 1787, although he was assumed to be an Antifederalist.

As part of Gov George Clinton's new coalition of steadfast Antifederalists, Burr was appointed state attorney general in 1789 and party leaders identified Burr as the person the legislature should (and did) vote for to replace Philip Schuyler as US senator in 1791. Burr aligned himself with Thomas Jefferson's Democratic-Republicans. He received 30 electoral votes for president in the 1796 election, but, with Federalists in control of the state legislature, Burr was not reelected as US senator in early 1797. He was elected to the state assembly in 1798 and orchestrated the 1800 assembly race in New York City that provided a Republican majority, which virtually assured Jefferson's party a majority of the electoral votes in the 1800 presidential election. A grateful Jefferson accepted Burr as his vice presidential candidate. When both men received 73 electoral votes, Burr sought the presidency in the lame duck, Federalist-controlled US House of Representatives. Alexander Hamilton warned various Federalists that Burr was a dangerous man, and after 36 ballots Jefferson was elected. Although ostracized by Jefferson, Burr served well as president of the Senate. With his national political prospects ruined, he ran for governor of New York State in 1804. Again Hamilton spoke against Burr. Burr challenged Hamilton to a duel and mortally wounded him in July 1804, further jeopardizing Burr's political career.

For the next two and a half years Burr conspired to capture Mexico and the western United States and to establish an independent nation there. He was arrested for treason in January 1807 but was acquitted in a celebrated trial in Richmond, Va, for which Chief Justice John Marshall presided as circuit judge. From 1808 to 1812 Burr traveled through Europe seeking support for his clandestine operations. He returned to the United States in May 1812. He continued to practice law in New York City until his death.

Lomask, Milton. *Aaron Burr,* 2 vols (New York: Farrar, Straus & Giroux, 1979, 1982)

Melton, Buckner F. *Aaron Burr* (New York: John Wiley, 2002)

John P. Kaminski

Burroughs, John (*b* Roxbury, Delaware Co, 3 Apr 1837; *d* eastern Ohio, 29 Mar 1921). Writer and naturalist. Raised on a farm in the Catskills, Burroughs learned to tap maple trees, shear sheep, and thresh oats, and also found time to fish, watch birds, and read. At Cooperstown Academy (Otsego Co) he encountered the works of Samuel Johnson and Ralph Waldo Emerson, and decided to become a writer. Beginning in 1854 he taught in rural schools in New York State, New Jersey, and Illinois, and in 1857 married Ursula North of Olive (Ulster Co). By 1863 he worked for the US Treasury in Washington, DC. While there he wrote essays on his native state and, inspired by reading John James Audubon, made frequent bird-watching trips to the Catskills and Adirondacks. In Washington, DC, he befriended Walt Whitman, and chat-filled walks along woodland trails with the poet inspired Burroughs's first book, *Notes on Walt Whitman as Poet and Person* (1867). Burroughs then published his Catskill essays as *Wake-Robin* (1871), achieving marked literary success. Another Washington, DC, friend, Myron Benton, introduced Burroughs to the writings of Henry David Thoreau, and in 1872 Burroughs returned to the Catskills, living at Riverby, the house he built in West Park (Ulster Co), to work as a writer and fruit farmer. Between 1875 and 1886 he published a half dozen volumes dealing with nature, including *Winter Sunshine, Locusts and Wild Honey,* and *Signs and Seasons.* In 1899 he joined the E. H. Harriman Expedition to Alaska along with John Muir and George Bird Grinnell. Burroughs's 1903 essay "Real and Sham Natural History," which condemned writers who sentimentalized animals, won praise from Pres Theodore Roosevelt, and the two men later camped and traveled together. Between 1908 and 1921 Burroughs summered near Roxbury, where he wrote *Summit of Years, Time and Change,* and other works. These late volumes deal directly with philosophy and theology. Burroughs, who helped establish the nature essay as a literary genre, died during a train trip from Chicago to New York City. His writings on camping, mountain climbing, bird watching, and the protection of endangered flora and fauna helped launch the first conservation movements in New York State.

Renehan, Edward. *John Burroughs: An American Naturalist* (Post Hills, Vt: Chelsea Green, 1992)

Richard F. Fleck

buses. See INTERCITY BUS LINES.

business and industry. For entries in business and industry topics in the colonial period see FUR TRADE; MERCHANTS (17TH CENTURY); MERCHANTS (18TH CENTURY). General entries on business topics include DEINDUSTRIALIZATION; LABOR; MINORITY-OWNED BUSINESSES; NEW YORK CITY AS METROPOLIS; WOMEN-OWNED BUSINESSES. See also entries on particular businesses, eg, IBM and XEROX CORPORATION, and industries, eg, GARMENT INDUSTRY; IRON AND STEEL INDUSTRY; POWER AND LIGHTING.

Busti [BUST-EYE]. Town (pop 7,760) in SE Chautauqua Co. Settled in 1810 it was formed in 1823 from Ellicott and Harmony and named for Paul

Busti of the Holland Land Co. In the early 19th century the Frank family developed a combined tannery, shoe shop, and last factory. Small shops made many goods, including baskets and bowls. The Atlantic and Great Western Railroad came through in 1860–61 but without a stop until 1874. Swedes came, fleeing the crop failures of 1867–69 and forming two churches (1878, 1906). The short-lived Art Metal office furniture factory (1968–71) employed 1,500, and Cummins Engine took over the building in 1974. Busti's population increased almost fourfold between 1920 and 1960 as Jamestown's population spread outward. Since then its population has remained largely unchanged. It had a number of dairy farms in the early 21st century. Town native Kate Stoneman was the first woman to be admitted to the New York Bar (1886), and her brother George was a Civil War general and governor of California (1883–86). The town is known for the annual Busti Apple Festival (1975).

Michelle Henry

Butler. Town (pop 2,277) in E Wayne Co. Settled about 1803, Butler was formed from Wolcott in 1826. In the 19th century, tobacco was grown and lime was produced. South Butler developed from the 1820s as a crossroads trading and milling center. Samuel Ringgold Ward, an African American abolitionist, was the pastor of an all-white congregation (1841–43), and Antoinette Brown Blackwell became the first ordained woman minister in the United States in 1853, both at the South Butler Congregational Church. In 1989 the state opened the minimum security Butler Correctional Facility and the medium security Butler Alcohol and Substance Abuse Correctional Treatment Center in northern Butler, boosting the town's population. The town's economy is largely agricultural, producing a variety of fruits, vegetables, and grains. Part of the village of Wolcott lies in the town.

Scott C. Monje

Butler, Benjamin F(ranklin) (*b* Kinderhook Landing [now Stuyvesant, Columbia Co], 14 Dec 1795; *d* Paris, 8 Nov 1858). Lawyer and political leader. Son of a politically active tavern keeper and merchant, Butler studied law under Martin Van Buren while serving as a bank lobbyist. In 1818 he married Harriet Allen, who shared his Presbyterianism. He presided for a year over the Washington and Warren Bank of Sandy Hill [now Hudson Falls, Washington Co] and then returned to the law in 1820. A member of the Albany Regency, he helped shape its strategy and served as Albany Co district attorney (1821–25). Butler led the 1824 effort to reformulate and order New York State's laws, making them more suited to a commercial society. He defended that code as a state assemblyman (1828) and worked on the 1833 commission to settle the New York–New Jersey boundary dispute. Butler served under Andrew Jackson and Martin Van Buren as US attorney general (1833–37) and as ad interim secretary of war (1836–37). He also cultivated a lucrative law practice in New York City. In 1838 Butler became southern New York State's federal district attorney and the principal professor of law at the University of the City of New York (now New York University). Dismissed as federal district attorney in 1845 by Pres James K. Polk, Butler supported the Free-Soilers in 1848, condemned the Kansas-Nebraska Act, and joined the Republican Party. Butler died of Bright's disease. Butler is not to be confused with Benjamin F. Butler (1818–93), the Massachusetts politician and Civil War general.

Driscoll, William D. *Benjamin F. Butler: Lawyer and Regency Politician* (New York: Garland Publishing, 1987)
Ekirch, Arthur A., Jr. "Benjamin F. Butler of New York: A Personal Portrait," *New York History* 58 (Jan 1977): 47–68

Craig and Mary L. Hanyan

Butler, John (*b* New London, Conn, ?1728; *d* Newark [now Niagara-on-the-Lake, Ont], 13 May 1796). Loyalist military commander and Indian agent. Butler's home was in the Mohawk Valley at Butlersbury [now Mohawk, Montgomery Co]. An Indian agent and interpreter for Sir William Johnson, Butler served during several campaigns of the French and Indian War, including the 1759 siege of Fort Niagara [now in Porter, Niagara Co]. He fled the valley in 1775 at the start of the American Revolution and from Fort Niagara began recruiting loyalists for military duty. As deputy superintendent of Indian Affairs, he worked to keep the Iroquois as British allies and in the summer of 1777 led loyalist and Indian forces at the siege of Fort Stanwix [now Rome, Oneida Co] and on 6 Aug 1777 at the Battle of Oriskany. In September 1777 Butler received a commission to raise a corps of rangers. Acting under his orders, Butler's Rangers and allied Indians attacked frontier settlements in New York and Pennsylvania, including Cherry Valley [now in Otsego Co] on 11 Nov 1778. Butler personally commanded the raid on Pennsylvania's Wyoming Valley on 3–4 July 1778 and at the Battle of Newtown, in what is now the Town of Elmira on 29 Aug 1779. Following the war he continued to serve as deputy superintendent and attended Indian treaties and councils. He engaged in trade and speculated in real estate, both in New York and Canada, but met with little commercial success.

Cruikshank, Ernest. *The Story of Butler's Rangers and the Settlement of Niagara* (1893; repr Owen Sound, Ont: Richardson, Bond & Wright, 1975)
Swiggett, Howard. *War Out of Niagara: Walter Butler and the Tory Rangers* (New York: Columbia Univ Press, 1933)

Christine Sternberg Patrick

butter. See DAIRY INDUSTRY.

Butterfield, Daniel (*b* Utica, 31 Oct 1831; *d* Cold Spring, Putnam Co, 17 July 1901). Businessman and Civil War general. After he graduated from Union College (1849), Butterfield studied law, worked for the American Express Co in New York City, and was active in the New York State Militia. Following the outbreak of the Civil War, he was rapidly promoted to colonel of the 12th Regiment of the militia (later known as the 12th New York State National Guard). His gallantry in the 1862 Peninsular Campaign at Gaines' Mill, Va, earned him a congressional Medal of Honor (1892). While serving with the Third Brigade in the Army of the Potomac in 1862, he modified an earlier military tune into the bugle call known as "Taps." He was wounded at Gettysburg, Pa, while working as chief of staff for Gen George Gordon Meade. After the war Butterfield supervised the army's recruiting efforts and commanded forces at New York Harbor. He worked briefly as assistant US treasurer at the New York Subtreasury, beginning in 1870, and then resumed work with American Express. He later served as president of the Albany and Troy Steamboat Co, and he helped direct several New York City banks, while being active in Republican Party politics. Although Butterfield never attended the US Military Academy, he is buried in one of the West Point Cemetery's most ornate tombs.

Stephen B. Grove

Butterfield, John (*b* Berne, Albany Co, 18 Nov 1801; *d* Utica, 14 Nov 1869). Express company entrepreneur. Raised in Berne, he intermittently attended the local public schools. Moving to Utica in 1822, Butterfield became a stagecoach driver and eventually the owner of most stage lines in Central New York. He invested in several local projects, including barges on the Erie Canal, a steamboat operation on Lake Ontario and the St. Lawrence River, and a street railway company in Utica. In the mid-1840s Butterfield established the New York, Albany and Buffalo Telegraph Co in conjunction with Samuel F. B. Morse, Ezra Cornell, Amos Kendall, Henry Wells, and Theodore Faxton. His firm of Butterfield, Wasson and Co, formed in 1849 to provide express service between New York City and Albany, joined with two competing firms owned by Henry Wells and William G. Fargo to create the American Express Co in 1850. The company, initially located in Buffalo, moved its headquarters to New York City within the decade. Butterfield established the Butterfield Overland Mail Co in 1857 upon winning a federal government contract and subsidy to carry mail between Missouri and San Francisco. He served as mayor of Utica in 1865.

Grossman, Peter Z. *American Express: The Unofficial History of the People Who Built the Great Financial Empire* (New York: Crown Publishers, 1987)

Sharon Ann Murphy

Butternuts. Town (pop 1,792) in SW Otsego Co. Settled in 1786 by farmers from England and New England, the town was formed from Unadilla in 1796. Its name derives from three butternut trees growing from a single stump that marked one corner of the town. The town was an important cheese and butter producer for a century. In the early 21st century nearly all residents commute to jobs outside town, 46% of them outside the county. Landmarks include architect William Ralph Emerson's Romanesque-style Tianderah (1885).

Hugh C. MacDougall

butter sculpture. Since 1969 the New York State Fair has exhibited a sculpture each year made entirely of butter. These life-size creations, sponsored by the American Dairy Association and Dairy Council, are made from 600–1,000 lb (270–450 kg) of unsalted butter and displayed in a large, refrigerated case. A different subject is portrayed each year. Scenes of domestic and farm life are common subjects, such as a home milk delivery, *Milk Memories* (1998), and a mother relaxing in a milk bath, *Milk Maid: Queen for a Day* (2001). Renowned artists Ray Macintosh of Canada, Sharon BuMann of Central Square (Oswego Co), and Jim Victor, a nationally known Pennsylvanian sculptor, are among the New York State Fair butter sculptors. Butter sculptures are also displayed at other agricultural fairs in the state, such as *The Blues Brothers* (2000) and *Out of this World* (1997) sculptures at the Erie County Fair in Hamburg.

Hannah M. Springer

button industry. New York City and Rochester emerged as centers of the ready-to-wear clothing industry following the Civil War, and New York State became a leader in the production and distribution of button accessories. New York City was a center for the manufacture of covered, crochet, rubber, and Galalith (casein) buttons and for the distribution of buttons through jobbers who sold to clothing manufacturers. Rochester was a leading producer of finished freshwater and ocean pearl buttons and by 1910 emerged as the national center for the manufacture of vegetable ivory buttons made from the seed of the tagua palm. Auburn (Cayuga Co) was the home of the leading producer of composition buttons. Dominating production were the M. B. Shantz Co, Rochester Button Co, and German-American Button Co, which changed its name to Art In Buttons during World War I. In 1919 there were 243 firms manufacturing buttons in the state, employing 42.2% (6,568) of all wage earners in the industry and producing 44.7% of the total value of button products in the country.

By the mid-1920s excess production capacity, passage of federal quota laws that drastically reduced immigration, and style changes in women's wear precipitated a crisis in the industry that was exacerbated by the onset of the Great Depression. M. B. Shantz and Rochester Button consolidated with Superior Ivory Button Co of Newark, NJ, under the Rochester name. Art In Buttons ceased operations by the late 1940s. In the late 1950s the US industry was threatened by competition from Italian and Japanese producers, and Rochester Button moved manufacturing to rural Virginia, where labor was cheaper and not unionized. In June 1961, 200 workers represented by the Amalgamated Clothing Workers of America went on strike when the company announced plans to close the Rochester operations. In response costs were cut, some jobs consolidated, and the plant at 300 State St remained open. Rochester Button continued as a leading national manufacturer, with the largest market share through the 1980s. Leveraged buyouts by companies with no experience in button making weakened the firm, and US Plastics and Chemical Corp, a smaller button manufacturer in Connecticut, bought and then closed Rochester Button in the spring of 1990.

Grebinger, Paul. "Button Man: How One Rochester Executive Guided His Firm through the Great Depression," *Rochester Museum and Science Center Focus,* Winter 1985

McKelvey, Blake. "The Men's Clothing Industry in Rochester's History," *Rochester History* 22 (July 1960): 1–31

Paul Grebinger

Byelorussians. See BELARUSIANS.

Byron. Town (pop 2,493) in NE Genesee Co. Settlement occurred in 1807–8, and the town was formed from Bergen in 1820. Byron was located on the main line of the New York Central Railroad (1852). In the late 19th century the town was home to McElver and Sons Agricultural Works and Genesee Mills (1880), a large grain milling operation. One of the richest Ice Age paleontological sites in North America was discovered in 1959, and since 1983 teams of specialists from the Buffalo Museum of Science have excavated this prime mastodon site annually. The Byron Heritage Festival is celebrated each July.

Susan L. Conklin

C

Cabrini, Francesca Xavier [Mother Cabrini] (*b* Sant'Angelo, Lombardy, Italy, 15 July 1850; *d* Chicago, 22 Dec 1917). Missionary and saint. Educated as a teacher, Cabrini was rejected by convents because of frail health. She eventually took vows in 1877 and established her own order, the Missionary Sisters of the Sacred Heart of Jesus, in 1880. Pope Leo XIII sent members of the order to New York City to assist Italian immigrants in 1889. Mother Cabrini worked in Little Italy, opened an orphanage for Italian girls, and assisted the homeless, uneducated, and indigent. In 1890 she founded the Sacred Heart Orphan Asylum in West Park (Ulster Co) on a 450-acre (182 ha) tract along the Hudson River. (The institution is now the St. Cabrini Home, and the West Park site also includes Cabrini-on-Hudson, a facility for senior citizens.) Mother Cabrini opened the charity Columbus Hospital (now Cabrini Medical Center) in New York City in 1892, and she established an additional 67 institutions in the United States, including an orphanage at Dobbs Ferry (Westchester Co) in 1914. She was naturalized in 1909. Buried in Chicago upon her death, her body was reinterred at West Park in 1918, and then moved in 1933 to Mother Cabrini High School at 701 Fort Washington Ave in the Bronx. Her remains are exhibited in a glass casket in the school's chapel, and her head was returned to Italy. Mother Cabrini was beatified in 1938 and canonized 7 July 1946, the first American citizen to be so recognized. She was proclaimed the patron of immigrants in 1950.

Sullivan, Sr Mary Louise. *Mother Cabrini: Italian Immigrant of the Century* (New York: Center for Migration Studies, 1992)

Tricia A. Barbagallo

Caffè Lena. Coffeehouse in Saratoga Springs. Caffè Lena was opened in 1960 by Lena Spencer (Pasqualina Rosa [Nargi] Spencer) to supplement her husband's earnings as an artist. Folksingers regularly performed Friday, Saturday, and Sunday evenings. An art gallery adjacent to the performance area provided a venue for Bill Spencer's work and was open sporadically after his departure in 1962 and the couple's subsequent divorce. Experimental theater began in May 1961 and remained a frequent feature of the operation until Lena Spencer's death. In the 1960s and early 1970s, hootenannies and later open mic nights added an informal stage for local musicians and were revived in the mid-1980s.

Lena Spencer continued her business alone for 27 years, providing a venue for many acoustic musicians early in their careers; among them were Bob Dylan, Arlo Guthrie, Tom Paxton, Don McLean, Bernice Johnson Reagon, Maria Muldaur, David Bromberg, Dave Van Ronk, Loudon Wainwright III, Tom Chapin, Christine Lavin, Papa John Phillips, and hundreds of others. Although the community was at first skeptical of the beatnik and hippie ambience of the establishment, by the late 1970s Spencer was a respected local figure. The size of the café's audience diminished along with the popularity of folk music, and Lena Spencer's death placed the future of the business in jeopardy. A nonprofit corporation purchased it from her estate and kept the name. It is one of the oldest continuously operated coffeehouses in the United States.

Banner, Mae G., " 'She Had a Place That Will Live Forever': Caffè Lena Founder Dies at 66," *The Saratogian*, 24 Oct 1989, 1A
" 'Grand Lady of the Folk Circuit,' Lena Spencer, 66, Dies after Fall," *Schenectady Gazette*, 24 Oct 1989

Field Horne

Cahan, Abraham (*b* Podberezy [now Pabrade, Lithuania], 7 July 1860; *d* New York City, 31 Aug 1951). Editor. The son of a teacher in Vilna, Cahan was forced to flee Russia due to his involvement in the Narodnaya Volya, an anti-czarist group. Arriving in New York City on 6 June 1882, he settled in the Jewish community on Manhattan's Lower East Side and became a labor activist, organizing in 1884 the state's first Jewish tailors' union. He wrote for both Yiddish newspapers and English language papers, including the *New York Sun* and the *New York World*. In 1897 he helped launch the Yiddish language *Forverts (Jewish Daily Forward)*, and as its chief editor from 1903 to 1946, he transformed the paper into America's most influential Jewish daily. His short stories and novels address immigrant acculturation in the United States. Cahan's first novel in English, *Yekl: A Story of the New York Ghetto* (1896), provides insight into this conflict between Old World values and the process of Americanization. This theme is also developed in Cahan's novel *The Rise of David Levinsky* (1917), which is set in New York City and the Catskill Mountains. Cahan and *Forverts* were committed to the union movement and a pragmatic, non-Marxist socialism. Cahan wielded considerable political influence within liberal circles in New York City and in 1936, along with labor leaders Sidney Hillman and David Dubinsky, helped establish the American Labor Party, which helped bolster Jewish support for Democratic president Franklin D. Roosevelt. During World War II and the early postwar, Cahan continued to remain active as a journalist and political commentator, espousing anti-Stalinist and antifascist views.

Marovitz, Sanford. *Abraham Cahan* (New York: Twayne Publishers, 1996)

Mark Noon

Cairo [KAY-RO]. Town (pop 6,355) in central Greene Co. The town was first settled by its patentee, the Englishman James Barker, in 1765 and benefited from the Susquehanna Turnpike, constructed westward from Salisbury, Conn, through Catskill in 1801. The town was formed as Canton in 1803 from Catskill, Coxsackie, and Freehold [now Durham, Greene Co]; the name became Cairo in 1808. The crest of the eastern Catskills forms its western boundary, and Catskill Creek flows southeast through the town. The first resort, Winter Clove at Round Top, opened in 1838. In the 1920s–1930s many resorts acquired distinct German or Italian character. It remains a summer resort, though the traditional ethnic hotels have declined in popularity.

Field Horne

Calder, William M(usgrave) (*b* Brooklyn, 3 Mar 1869; *d* Brooklyn, 3 Mar 1945). US representative and senator. Calder attended Brooklyn public schools, became a carpenter's apprentice at age 13, and later studied during the evening at the Cooper Institute (now Cooper Union) in New York City. He entered the construction industry in 1893 and worked briefly as the Brooklyn Borough buildings commissioner in 1902–3. He served five terms in the US House of Representatives (1905–15) as a Republican from New York State's Sixth District. Elected to the US Senate in 1916, Calder chaired the Senate Committee to Audit and Control the Contingent Expense (1919–23). He was a supporter of woman suffrage but opposed American involvement in the League of Nations. He was a delegate to eight Republican National Conventions between 1908 and 1940. After being defeated for reelection in 1922, Calder returned to New York City and was known as a major real estate developer in Brooklyn.

"Calder, William Musgrave." In *Biographical Directory of the United States Congress* (Washington, DC: Government Printing Office, 1989)

Jeffrey Kraus

Caledonia. Town (pop 4,567) and village (pop 2,327) in NW Livingston Co. Settled in 1795, the town was formed from the old town of Northampton in 1802 as Southampton; its name was changed in 1806. Scots from Perthshire, recruited by Pulteney land agent Charles Williamson, settled in 1798; others arrived in 1804 from Inverness. The town was the site of the Canawaugus Reservation from 1797 to 1826. In early years Caledonia grew wheat on its valley land and had a woolen factory (1822) and gypsum quarries; five railroad lines, beginning in 1838, made it more accessible. The Genesee Valley Canal (1840–78) passed through town, transporting produce and freight. In 1864 Seth Green opened the first fish hatchery in the United States, which was taken over by the state in 1875 and remains an important state hatchery in the early 21st century. The town produced agricultural implements, including grain cradles, plows, and sowers *ca* 1880. The village was incorporated in 1891. Among employers in town in the early 21st century are Allen-Bailey Tag and Label Co (1911), Jones Chemical (1939), and CEN Electronics (1949; industrial battery chargers and specialty magnetics). The Big Springs Museum, in part, commemorates a late 19th-century African American community that relocated from Culpeper, Va. At 3.5%, Caledonia's 2000 black population was the highest in Livingston Co, and many of those are descendants of former slaves who arrived in Caledonia after the Civil War.

Joyce Rapp

Callicoon. Town (pop 3,052) in W Sullivan Co. A road was cut through the present town in 1807, but the first settlers did not come until 1814 and growth was slow until the 1830s. The town, formed from Liberty in 1842, is generally thought to have gotten its name from the Dutch word *kalkoen* (wild turkey). Its early industries were lumbering and tanning. Irish laborers at five large tanneries used local tanbark in the mid–19th century, but the tanneries closed after the Civil War. Beginning around 1840, Callicoon was home to a large German and Swiss population, thanks to German language circulars promoting settlement; in 1860 one-third of the population was German. They preserved their language and culture for a time, and there were picnic grounds and dance pavilions scattered around town. In the early 21st century Callicoon remains largely agricultural, despite an influx of new residents from the metropolitan area.

John Conway

Calverton. Locality (pop 5,704) in Riverhead (Suffolk Co). A post office was established in 1868 and named for Postmaster Bernard J. Calvert. Calverton was a center of cranberry production from the late 19th century until 1976. In 1953 the US Navy purchased 4,000 acres (1,619 ha) in Calverton, leasing it to Grumman Aircraft Corp for use as a testing facility. In 1995, following Grumman's closure, the navy returned it to the Town of Riverhead; its future use remains under discussion. Calverton is also the site of the 1,052-acre (426 ha) Calverton National Cemetery. Since the 1970s suburban housing has been making deep inroads into this former farming community.

Richard F. Welch

Cambodians. See SOUTHEAST ASIANS.

Cambria. Town (pop 5,393) in W central Niagara Co. Settled in 1801, the town was formed from Willink [now Aurora, Erie Co] in 1808 and was coextensive with Niagara Co until 1812. The primary industry is fruit growing; historically, apples were the staple product, along with pears, peaches, and quinces. There were stone quarries on the Mountain Ridge. A railroad, which became the Lockport and Niagara Falls, crossed town in 1836. Lockport Air Force Station (1965–79) was located in town. Cambria was the home of the Seven Sutherland Sisters, whose floor-length hair made them a popular Barnum and Bailey Circus attraction starting in 1884. It remains a largely agricultural area, although proximity to Buffalo and Niagara Falls significantly increased suburbanization in the late 20th century.

Nancy B. Mingus

Cambridge. Town (pop 2,152) and village (pop 1,925) in SE Washington Co. Patented in 1761, Cambridge was probably settled in the same year and became a district in 1772. In 1781 residents chose to be part of the Vermont republic and sent a representative, but quickly changed their minds. The town was formed in 1788 and annexed to Washington Co in 1791. The seed-packing business began in 1816 at Coila; what became Jerome B. Rice Seed Co got underway in 1832. Cambridge was served by the Northern Turnpike (1799) and by the railroad (1852; later Delaware and Hudson), a part of which provided freight service and excursions in 2003 as the Batten Kill Railroad (1994). The village, partly in the town of White Creek, incorporated in 1866; a large part of it had become a historic district by the 21st century. The seed company was sold to Asgrow in 1939 and closed in 1976. Bentley Seeds continued the seed business in 2003 and farming remains the predominant land use in town. The Hotel Cambridge (1885), where pie à la mode is said to have originated, was restored in 1998. The cultural life of a large part of Washington Co and adjacent Vermont centers on Hubbard Hall, the village's 1878 opera house, restored by community effort beginning in 1976.

R. Paul McCarty

Camden. Town (pop 5,208) and village (pop 2,330) in NW Oneida Co. Settled around 1797, the town was formed from Mexico (Oswego Co) in 1799. Located on the road from Rome to the Salmon River, the village, incorporated in 1834, was made more accessible in 1850 by a railroad later known as the Rome, Watertown and Ogdensburg Railroad. Nineteenth-century industries included a foundry producing turbines, a woolen factory, knitting mill, tannery, and furniture factory. Stone was quarried in town. Several packing companies canned local corn starting *ca* 1855. Modern industries have included Rochester Shoe Tree Co, J. M. Young and Sons Furniture (1890–1970s), Camden Wire Co (1929), and Laribee Wire Co (1947); the latter two were part of International Wire Co in 2003. In the same year, the Mystic Stamp Co was a large mail-order philatelists' firm employing hundreds of workers. Since the Civil War the Camden Continental Fife and Drum Corps has been a source of local pride.

Cameron. Town (pop 1,034) in central Steuben Co. Settled in 1800, the town was formed from Addison in 1822. Settlers were attracted by stands of prime timber, especially pine, which were used for ships' spars. After the coming of the Erie Railroad in 1850 made it possible to ship livestock to markets, Cameron established a stockyard rail depot. Farming and population declined in the late 19th and early 20th centuries. Beginning in the 1930s, New York State acquired almost 2,000 acres (800 ha) of abandoned farmland in the town, from which it created state forestland, including the 165-acre (66.8 ha) West Cameron State Wildlife Management Area. After reaching its 20th-century low of 587 (1960), Cameron's population rebounded, nearly doubling by 2000. Cameron resident Gen William Woods Averill (1832–1900) secured patents on asphalt paving.

Virginia L. Wright and Jerry Wright

Camillus [KA-MIL-US]. Town (pop 23,152) and village (pop 1,249) in W central Onondaga Co. Settled *ca* 1790, the town was formed in 1799 from Marcellus. The first discovery of gypsum in the United States was made in town by William Lindsay in 1792; it was quarried beginning in 1809. Camillus's location on the North Branch of the Seneca Turnpike (1807–8) promoted settlement. The Erie Canal (1819) and the Syracuse and Auburn (1838) and Rochester and Syracuse (1851) Railroads placed it on important east-west routes. The village was incorporated in 1852, the same year that more than 300 Camillus citizens formed the New Party, whose candidates won office espousing the principles on which the Republican Party was founded four years later. Nineteenth-century products included woolens, brick, clay smoking pipes, pottery by Syracuse Pottery (1875–1993), knit goods, drain and sewer tiles, and Portland cement. Onondaga Co's first commercial airport (1919–49) was at Amboy. Twentieth-century employers included a maker of player pipe organs (1928–34) and Sylvania Electronic Products (1956–95; data processing). Major early 21st-century employers were Southern Container Corp (corrugated cardboard) and Camillus Cutlery Co (1894). After World War II both residential and retail development occurred, and the town's 1950 population of 6,735 nearly tripled in the following decade. Fairmount Fair and Camillus Plaza made the town a shopping destination for the vicinity by the early 1960s. The Erie Canal bed is now a park with a canal store museum and summer boat rides. In 2003 eggs were the town's chief farm product.

Barbara S. Rivette

campaign finance. Concerns about the role of campaign contributions have led to periodic enactments of comprehensive election law to regulate the process. New York State's first such legislation was enacted in 1906 and significantly revised in 1949 and 1976. These laws specify how much can be given and how contributions must be reported. Individuals can give much higher amounts in state and local elections than in federal. As of 2003 an individual can give as much as $33,900 to a statewide candidate and $8,500 to a state senate candidate. The maximum an individual can contribute to all campaigns within a calendar year is $150,000. A family can give as much as $100,000 to a single statewide or legislative candidate.

There is concern that the high success rate of incumbents—90% for state legislature incum-

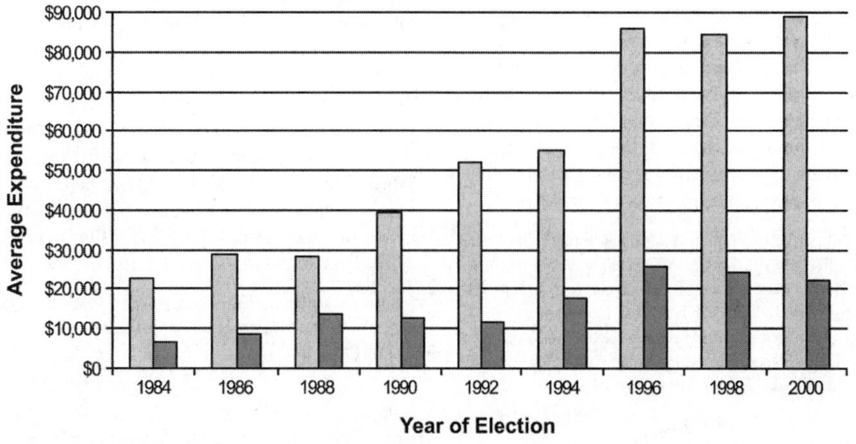

Fig 1. Incumbent and challenger average campaign expenditures, 1984–2000, New York State Assembly. ▒ incumbent; ■ challenger.

bents for the entire 20th century—is based on their greater access to campaign funds. For elections in the 1990s in the state assembly incumbents spent almost four times as much as challengers, and for 2002 in the state senate almost three times as much (Fig 1).

Even though there is concern, it is not clear that money is as significant in elections as some critics allege. With regard to reelection rates in New York State, the political parties represent very different constituencies. Democrats are much more likely to come from less affluent, urban, and liberal districts, many with a high percentage of racial minorities. Republicans are more likely to come from more affluent, suburban-rural, and more conservative districts, many with a high percentage of Whites. Most party members run and win by large margins in districts that are already heavily Democratic or Republican. They are typical of their districts, and their primary concern is to represent their constituents. The reason they win by large margins may have more to do with the lopsided partisan inclinations in many districts than with the expenditure of money.

Further, the ability of money to determine a state legislative election is limited by the ability of each party to match the other when a race is close. If a district is a swing district, that is, diverse and not dominated by one party, each party can funnel large sums of money to their candidates, resulting in relatively equal expenditures by both candidates. In such cases, message and strategy can play a more important role than money. Finally, the ability of interest groups to sway legislators hostile to their views may also be limited. Interest groups generally give to their friends and not to their enemies. If contributions have an effect, it is to incline legislators to be careful to listen to a group's argument. Contributions buy access but not necessarily success, and it is difficult to determine whether the money or persuasion have any effect in pushing legislators away from their initial positions.

The public appearance of elected officials taking large sums of money does undermine society's confidence in government. In response to concerns, New York State has chosen to require regular disclosure of receipts and expenditures during campaigns. Following passage of the 1976 election law, candidates must file a report with the local or the State Board of Elections that indicates all sources of funds and specific expenditures. These reports are open to the public, and the reports for state officials are available on the State Board of Elections web site. This practice allows each side to scrutinize reports and to draw attention to contributions deemed inappropriate. The logic of requiring disclosure is that it will inhibit New York State's politicians from accepting some contributions, and, if money is accepted, the public record of acceptance will constrain legislators from looking as if a contribution swayed their views.

Stonecash, Jeffrey M., and Amy Widestrom. "Political Parties and Elections." In *Governing New York State*, 5th ed., eds. Robert F. Pecorella and Jeffrey M. Stonecash (Albany: SUNY Press, forthcoming)

Stonecash, Jeffrey M., and Sara E. Keith. "Maintaining a Political Party: Providing and Withdrawing Campaign Funds," *Party Politics* 2 (July 1996): 313–28

Jeffrey M. Stonecash

Campbell [CAMP-BELL]. Town (pop 3,691) in SE Steuben Co. Settled *ca* 1800, the town was formed from Hornby in 1831. Large stands of hemlock supported prosperous shoe leather tanneries in Campbell and Curtis hamlets. The town acquired railroad service from the Rochester Division of the Erie in 1852 and from the Delaware, Lackawanna and Western in 1882. The independent not-for-profit Watson Homestead Retreat and Conference Center, previously operated by the United Methodist Church, is located on the former East Campbell farm where IBM founder Thomas J. Watson (1874–1956) was raised. Campbell's major industry is a Pollio cheese factory (1936). The town is largely a bedroom community for nearby Corning.

Virginia L. Wright and Jerry Wright

camp meetings and Bible camps. Revivalistic and evangelistic tool of many different denominations. The camp meeting was often held in wooded areas where participants camped for days at a time. Francis Asbury, founding bishop of the Methodist Church in America, called camp meetings a battle-ax and a weapon of war against wickedness after experiencing gatherings like the four-day camp meeting held 20 miles (32 km) northeast of New York City, possibly Philipse Manor in Westchester Co, that had attracted roughly 3,000 people in 1806.

By the 1840s the enthusiastic style and potential for disorder caused a decline in camp meetings among Baptists and Presbyterians, but they remained the staple of Methodists and related Holiness groups. Methodism laid the groundwork for reaching common folk and individuals in rural areas. Many farmers and pioneers enjoyed this large communal form of religious gathering with its forceful preaching and singing. Camp meetings, such as those held in Berne (Albany Co), Sing Sing [now Ossining, Westchester Co], Watertown, and throughout Western New York, became regular events. Campgrounds were established near Round Lake (Saratoga Co) in 1868 and Shelter Island (Suffolk Co) in the 1870s and developed to meet the recurring needs of religious life. The summer Methodist camp meetings at Round Lake continued for 60 years, permanent cottages were built in the area, and in 1969 Round Lake was incorporated as a village.

By the late 1870s and 1880s camp meetings began to change as protracted revivals held in churches became the norm and as campgrounds began to be used for other purposes. Chautauqua Institution on Chautauqua Lake had begun on the Fair Point camp meeting site and symbolized the changes in American religious culture, moving from emotional revivalism to more reserved educational courses. As older camps transformed their missions, new religious movements and groups established their own camps. Examples of the new breed of camps with long histories are Word of Life Bible Camp in Schroon Lake (Warren Co), begun in 1946, and Camp-of-the-Woods in Speculator (Hamilton Co), established in 1900.

See also CHAUTAUQUA INSTITUTION.

Johnson, Charles A. *The Frontier Camp Meeting: Religion's Harvest Time* (Dallas: Southern Methodist Univ Press, 1955)

David B. Malone

camps. See CAMP MEETINGS AND BIBLE CAMPS; HIKING AND CAMPING; LEFT-WING SUMMER CAMPS; MUSIC CAMPS; SUMMER CAMPS.

Camp Upton. The mobilization and training camp named for Civil War general Emory Upton was mandated northeast of Yaphank (Suffolk Co) on 16 May 1917. Crews cleared scrub oak and pines and built accommodations, services, and administration buildings on 2 feet (.6 m) of loam over sand, with the camp eventually including barracks for about 40,000 troops and covering 18 mi^2 (47 km^2). The first group of 2,000 draftees arrived at Camp Upton in mid-September 1917. The major unit that mobilized was the 77th Infantry, the "Liberty Division," consisting mostly of New York City and Long Island troops. Songwriter Irving Berlin was among those billeted at Upton. His musical *Yip! Yip! Yaphank* was produced in New York City in the summer of 1918, and the song "Oh, How I Hate to Get Up in the Morning" was probably inspired by his training at Upton. After the camp closed in 1921, the buildings were auctioned and removed, but the camp reopened in 1941 as a reception center for World War II troops. As of January 1947 the Brookhaven National Laboratory has occupied the site.

Dwyer, Norval, "The Camp Upton Story, 1917–1921," *Long Island Forum*, Jan–Mar 1970

Michael J. Stenzel

Camp Wikoff. Federal demobilization and quarantine camp. It was named for Col Charles Wikoff, 22d Infantry, killed in the July 1898 assault on San Juan Heights in Cuba, and was established in August 1898 on about 5,000 acres (2,000 ha) in the vicinity of Fort Pond Bay, Montauk Point (Suffolk Co). The prevalence of communicable diseases such as yellow fever and malaria among troops returning from fighting in Cuba and Puerto Rico during the Spanish-American War necessitated a quarantine section separate from the recovery camp; each had its own hospital. The first troops arrived on 14 August, before the facilities were completed, and the population eventually reached a peak of 21,000. Camp personnel included 300 female nurses to help staff the hospitals. The units processed through Camp Wikoff included the 1st US Volunteer Infantry (Rough Riders), the 9th US Infantry (based at Madison Barracks in Jefferson Co), and the 71st New York Volunteer Infantry. Camp Wikoff closed in October 1898, but the National Guard used the site for training into the 1920s.

Heatley, Jeff, ed. *Bully! Colonel Theodore Roosevelt, the Rough Riders and Camp Wikoff, Montauk, New York, 1898* (Montauk, NY: Montauk Historical Society, 1998)

Michael J. Stenzel

Canaan. Town (pop 1,820) in NE Columbia Co. Settled *ca* 1750 by New Englanders, it was formed as Kings District in 1772, renamed Canaan District in 1778, and recognized as a town in 1788. Along Stony Kill mills produced gunpowder, linseed oil, leather, paper, cotton wadding, woolen cloth, grain cradles, and scythe rifles. Canaan was home to two Shaker "families" from 1813 to 1897. The town was crossed by the Hudson and Berkshire (1838) and Albany and West Stockbridge (1842) Railroads. A dairying town, it began to attract a summer population by the 1880s. Berkshire Farm (1886) for at-risk youth now operates as Berkshire Farm Union Free School. The Berkshire Extension of the New

York State Thruway (1957) cut across many of its farms. Canaan was depicted in Susan Warner's best-selling books, *The Wide, Wide World* (1850) and *Queechy* (1852). Red Rock, a hamlet, was named in 1825 when a boulder was painted and topped with a wooden shaft, replaced in 1860 by a marble column.

Canada. Canada has always framed its evolution through its changing political, economic, and cultural relationships with the United States. New York State, the only state to border on both Quebec and Ontario, is part of a Great Lakes borderland region that is increasingly within an interconnected North American industrial heartland and an integrated global economy.

Early New York–Canada Relations

North-south intermingling occurred well before Europeans settled and long before the border was demarcated, as the Iroquois developed a trade system that transcended the region. There were several waves of loyalist migrations to Canada during the course of the Revolutionary War, but the greatest came at the end of the hostilities and the demarcation of the border in the Treaty of Paris in 1783. While Nova Scotia received the wealthier and more educated loyalists from eastern seaboard communities, 80% of the loyalists settling in the part of Quebec that became Upper Canada [now Ontario] were frontier farmers from the Hudson and Mohawk Valleys. In 1784 British officials reported that there were 3,463 loyalists settled in the townships along the St. Lawrence River and the eastern end of Lake Ontario. Although their origins are not specified, there is little doubt that the greatest number of Upper Canada–bound loyalists came from nearby New York State. The same can be said for those who settled along the Niagara River. Another group of loyalists were members of the Iroquois Confederacy under Joseph Brant, who came to the Grand River area in 1784. Lower Canada [now Quebec], particularly Montreal and the eastern townships, were attractive to American millers, merchants, and lumbermen.

The natural water routes connecting Ontario and Quebec with New York State facilitated the cross-border migration of people. Early in the 19th century, this movement was predominantly northward as loyalists were followed by the "late loyalists," a restless group of land seekers from New York and other states attracted by cheap Crown land. After the Genesee Rd was extended to Niagara, increasing numbers of land seekers crossed the river and traveled by military roads to newly opened areas in southwestern Upper Canada. However, after the War of 1812, Upper Canada, in an environment of growing attachment to the Crown and distrust of the United States, passed legislation making it difficult for Americans to purchase Crown land, effectively reducing their in-migration. Yet even while unfavorable legislation reduced the flow of people northward, the Rush-Bagot Treaty (1817) eased tensions along the border as both the United States and Great Britain agreed to limit their naval forces to three small ships each on the Great Lakes and one each on Lake Champlain. And even though cross-border migration slowed considerably during the first half of the century, trade continued. Much of the timber, potash, and flour exported from Montreal and Quebec City in the early 19th century originated in New York and Vermont, and Montreal merchants, many American-born, began to import consumer goods by way of New York City and Albany-Troy.

Never again would tensions be as great within the region as they had been during the War of 1812, but the United States and Britain were brought to the brink of war during the *Caroline* Affair. In 1837 William Lyon Mackenzie, the Reform Party leader and advocate of self-rule, led a party of several hundred disgruntled farmers frustrated with the unresponsiveness of British rule in a march on Toronto to seize arms. The revolt failed and Mackenzie escaped to Buffalo, where he and a sympathetic audience of Americans formed the "patriot army," occupying Canada's Navy Island [now in Ont] in the Niagara River on 13 Dec 1837. Canadian loyalist Col Sir Allan McNab ordered a party of militia to cross the river on 29 December to seize and burn the American steamer *Caroline*, which was used to supply the rebels. This attack on US soil sparked a rapid response by the American government, which dispatched Gen Winfield Scott to assume command of US regulars and state militia on the border. Two weeks later the patriots abandoned the island and the crisis was over.

Canals and Railways

The natural water corridor connecting Canada and New York State was later extended and reinforced with the development of a railway network that crossed the border at several points. The construction of the Erie Canal, completed in 1825, was partly a reaction to complaints made by Americans forced to pay shipping duties at British-controlled Great Lakes and St. Lawrence ports. In response, the British built the Welland Canal connecting Lake Ontario and Lake Erie, and the Rideau Canal, stretching from Kingston [now in Ont] on Lake Ontario to the Ottawa River, not only as preventative measures against the threat of invasion but as a means to secure Canadian transportation routes to and between the Great Lakes. Competition in this borderland region for the Great Lakes hinterland spurred the development of extensive canal systems on both sides of the border, in turn stimulating the cross-border flow of entrepreneurs and investment. When trade liberalized in the 1840s, Canadian wholesale merchants in Toronto and Hamilton [now in Ont] feared that their Buffalo and Rochester counterparts would capture the retail trade with small cities and towns along Lake Ontario. The Canadian merchants responded by importing American goods directly from New York City, and in this way they controlled both import routes from the largest American and Canadian cities, such as Montreal.

The railways first augmented and then replaced the canal system and served to strengthen intranational and international links. The same serve-and-volley pattern of response to transportation expansion continued. After the Americans built the Erie Railroad in the early 1850s, the British constructed the Grand Trunk Railway (GTR), likewise going from the Champlain Valley to the Niagara Frontier. The GTR and the Great Western Railway (GWR) also served as direct channels into America's most expansive market, much of it based in New York State, and served to further connect Canada West and Canada East, which became Ontario and Quebec in 1867, to their neighbors. As unprocessed raw materials left Canada, finished consumer goods from cities in New York entered the country along the same international rail system including the GTR, GWR, and New York Central Railroad. Trade links developed over time, even after the end of Reciprocity, a limited free trade policy (1854–66), and the introduction of National Policy tariffs in 1879 by the John A. Macdonald government. New York State capital flowed north into Canada, particularly Ontario, as Americans purchased land and invested in branch-plant manufacturing as well as power and mineral development. No Canadian national market existed until the Canadian Pacific Railway was completed in 1885, so Ontario and Quebec looked for viable borderland region markets, transporting their products into adjacent states, the most important being Michigan and New York. Likewise, American border cities such as Detroit and Buffalo found ready markets in Canada.

Economic Changes

While New York provided Upper Canada and, to a lesser extent, Lower Canada with people early in the century, it would later lure their descendants away in significant numbers. Economic stagnation in the midst of a series of global recessions during the period 1873–96 hit Canada particularly hard. In Ontario the decline of the wheat staple brought about by land shortages, soil depletion, western competition, and the ending of imperial preferences meant that farmers had to find markets for new exports; meanwhile lower prices and smaller profits triggered an exodus from the countryside. During this same period, New York State's industrial growth burgeoned, due to the abundance of native and immigrant labor to work in its factories, a network of financiers and entrepreneurs, and proximity to raw materials. Eventually the Canadian economy improved and emigration decreased, though American direct investment in Canada and particularly in Ontario increased after 1900. Before the National Policy tariff, many Canadian firms relied heavily upon New York supplies to make their products. For example, during the 1860s and 1870s, A. Harris and Sons of Brantford, Ont, manufacturers of harvesting machinery, depended on Rochester and Buffalo for pig iron and Auburn (Cayuga Co) for harvester parts. This company and others drew heavily upon New York for designs, materials, parts, machinery, technical skills, and advice. But by the 1880s the foundries, shops, and associated services, often replicas of those found in New York, were established in Ontario, and their necessary inputs were provided from Ontario and Quebec sources. Yet the market for Ontario broadened throughout the Great Lakes region as its products and raw materials were sold in adjacent states. One consequence of the National Policy system of tariffs was to encourage American capital to relocate to the Canadian side of the Great Lakes. Proximity to America's manufacturing belt encouraged industries to locate branch plants in Ontario, and both these and Canadian firms benefited from their ready access to the huge market of the Northeast and the Midwest.

Expansion of Trade and Investment

North-south trade across the lakes has existed for two centuries, but it was only after the completion of the St. Lawrence Seaway system in 1959 that the full potential of this great inland waterway was realized. The seaway in effect forms a fourth coastline for both countries and plays a major role in overseas and US-Canadian trade, permitting oceangoing vessels to navigate between the Great Lakes and the Atlantic Ocean and making many lake cities important seaports. During the construction of the seaway, both Ontario and New York cooperated in the building of the St. Lawrence–Franklin D. Roosevelt Power Project at the International Rapids section of the river. The generating capacity produced by the project is shared equally by the United States and Canada. The relationship between Canada and New York has entered a new era as the reduction in tariffs under the North American Free Trade Agreement (NAFTA) in 1993 and resulting trade liberalization has served to weaken traditional east-west economic bonds within Canada. Most of the investment still flows northward, but increasingly Canadian firms are investing south of the border. In 1989 Toronto alone received 41.5% of American direct investment in Canada, with other Ontario locations accounting for an additional 27% of the total. In contrast Montreal received only 4.3% of US direct investment. In that same year New York was the location of 16.6% of the American headquarters investing in Canada, followed by California (12.1%) and Illinois (7.2%). In 1998 Ontario traded over 90% of its exports to the United States, with Michigan (33%) and New York (13.4%) as the major destinations for its products. The Toronto area economy attracts most of its investment from the core of American financial capital, and New York City lies at the center of that core. Ontario now has a reduced role in domestic trade as it has restructured itself under free trade to serve the larger North American market. In this sense it has become even more dependent on the American economy and has aligned itself more with the industrial heartland of the United States. Increasingly economists are viewing Canada as a series of north-south economies, with Ontario and New York constituting perhaps the most important of these cross-border regional structures.

BORDERLAND

The international boundary between Canada and New York bisects what has been termed the Great Lakes borderland region. Despite the differing policies and occasional disputes that have at times impaired migration and trade, the border has been largely open, and the result has been the development of an international region where the boundary itself, especially in this era of free trade, is viewed by many as an obstacle to ties of geography and economy. Indeed, until the Canadian dollar plummeted in the early 1990s, Canadian shoppers flooded across the border to contiguous New York communities, specifically to large outlets built partly in response to this particular market. The flow reversed as New Yorkers took advantage of a favorable exchange rate, although visitors from New York State are smaller in number and travel on a more infrequent basis to the larger but more distant cities of Toronto and Montreal. Yet while the border has become increasingly permeable and, in the eyes of some, irrelevant, it is still viewed by many Canadians as a reference for Canadian culture. This is most pronounced where communities face each other across the boundary, and yet the milieus among these twin centers differ. Along the St. Lawrence at Prescott, Ont, and Ogdensburg (St. Lawrence Co), the association with a British colonial and loyalist past serves to differentiate the former from the latter. Cultural conversion is evidenced at the two Niagara Falls, important linkage points in the Ontario–New York corridor. Yet it is in these two similar places that the different meanings assigned to the border are most evident. Patrick McGreevy has identified Niagara Falls as the "end of America" and "the beginning of Canada," the place where Anglophone Canadian nationalism was born and where American Manifest Destiny ended. The forces of globalization have challenged the traditional Canadian view of the border as a territorial symbol of sovereignty and separation. Over time Ontario and Quebec, particularly the former, have increasingly become extensions of the American manufacturing belt. But this is not a one-sided relationship, as the Niagara Falls region suggests, in which the Niagara River separates the Canadian city, a tawdry and thriving resort, from its poor and depressed American cousin. The prolonged economic doldrums in Western New York is also heightening a sense of connection to Canada in the early 21st century, as cities like Rochester vie to establish a fast ferry service to Toronto, in part to take advantage of the latter city's growing reputation as the cultural center of the entire Lake Ontario region. Finally, the presumption that globalization was making the American-Canadian boundary irrelevant was called into question by the heightened border security after the terrorist attack of 11 Sept 2001.

See also NEW FRANCE; PLANNING AND REGIONAL PLANNING ASSOCIATIONS; PROHIBITION; ST. LAWRENCE SEAWAY.

McGreevy, Patrick. "The End of America: The Beginning of Canada," *Canadian Geographer* 32 (1988): 307–18

McNaughton, Rod. "U.S. Foreign Direct Investment in Canada, 1985–89," *Canadian Geographer* 36 (1992): 181–89

Widdis, Randy W. *With Scarcely a Ripple: Anglo-Canadian Migration into the United States and Western Canada, 1880–1920* (Montreal and Kingston: McGill-Queen's Univ Press, 1998)

Winder, Gordon. "The North American Manufacturing Belt in 1880: A Cluster or Regional Industrial System or One Large Industrial District?" *Economic Geography* 75 (2001): 71–92

Randy William Widdis

Buffalo Peace Bridge across the Niagara River connecting Canada with the United States.

Canada and Nova Scotia Refugee Tract. At the beginning of the Revolution, American forces invaded Canada in an attempt to join that colony with the newly separated colonies to the south. A number of Canadian residents, including Quebecois French and transplanted New Englanders, supported the Americans. When the American forces withdrew from Canada in 1776, these Canadian "patriots," organized into two regiments, fled Canada with their families. In Nova Scotia a similar though smaller uprising also produced a number of refugees who fled to the United States, many of whom joined the American army, serving with the Canadian regiments. These regiments merged in 1781 and served until the end of the war, attached administratively to the New York Continental Line. Along with other New York regiments, the Canadians and Nova Scotians were granted lands for their service. Under the leadership of officers including Moses Hazen, James Livingston, Edward Antill, and Benjamin Mooers, the former soldiers were granted 131,500 acres (53,216 ha) in what is now Clinton Co by New York State in 1786. The grant, on the Canadian border just east of the Old Military Tract, was settled by 227 former military personnel, making a largely Quebecois cultural area close to family and friends still in Canada. The tract is now in the Towns of Champlain, Mooers, and Altona, with portions in Dannemora and Saranac.

Everest, Allan. *Moses Hazen and the Canadian Refugees in the American Revolution* (Syracuse: Syracuse Univ Press, 1976)

Thomas A. Rumney

Canadaway Reservation. Under the provisions of the Treaty of Big Tree, a federal Indian treaty signed on 16 Sept 1797 that confirmed an agreement between the Holland Land Co and the Seneca Nation, Canadaway was reserved as Seneca land. This parcel, in what is now Chautauqua Co, lay between Cattaraugus Creek and Canadaway Creek east of Lake Erie. On 30 June 1802, in another federal treaty that confirmed an agreement with the Holland Land Co, the Seneca

Nation ceded this parcel as well as much of their land along Lake Erie near what is now Cattaraugus Indian Reservation.

Abrams, George H. J. *The Seneca People* (Phoenix, Ariz: Indian Tribal Series, 1976)

Laurence M. Hauptman

Canadiana incident. An episode of racial violence, which involved Buffalo teenagers and occurred Memorial Day, 30 May 1956. The incident took place in stages. The first was at Crystal Beach, an amusement park in Ontario, Canada, on Lake Erie's northern shore. Violence between Blacks and Whites broke out during the afternoon at the beach. Eyewitnesses reported the use of knives and other weapons, and four people were hospitalized. The Canadian provincial police made nine arrests—five Blacks and four Whites—all Buffalo residents. The second altercation occurred aboard the SS *Canadiana*, a recreational boat, during the ship's 9:15 PM run from Crystal Beach to Buffalo. Most of the 1,000 passengers were teenagers, about 80% of whom were black. Problems started as the passengers were boarding and continued as the ship reached open water. Eyewitnesses claimed gangs of black girls roamed the ship and harassed and attacked white girls. Firecrackers exploded frequently. Anxious and fearful, Whites took refuge in the ship's dining room. One white teenage boy was hit in the face with a beer bottle. The overmatched crew of the ship radioed Buffalo police for assistance, and three people were arrested after the ship reached port.

Youth played a role in sparking the violence; none of those arrested was older than 22. Buffalo civic leaders highlighted the immaturity of the offenders to deemphasize tones of racial violence. Alcohol consumption was another factor, suggested by the use of beer bottles as weapons. Youth gangs, often representing conflicts over turf in Buffalo, were another factor; many girls involved in the violence aboard the *Canadiana* wore jackets bearing the names of different gangs and clubs. The *Canadiana* incident can be seen as indicative of racial tensions in the northern United States and perhaps, too, as a precursor of the racial violence that swept through US cities in the mid-1960s.

Graebner, William. *Coming of Age in Buffalo: Youth and Authority in the Postwar Era* (Philadelphia: Temple Univ Press, 1990)
"Terror Marks Boatride," *Buffalo Courier Express*, 31 May 1956

Doing History class, SUNY Fredonia, Spring 2001

Canadians, Anglophone. Canadians, traditionally those of British descent, whose primary language is English.

Settlement

A certain amount of emigration from Canada took place during the early 19th century, starting with disenchanted loyalists returning to their former homes. But by the 1850s economic change, high rates of natural increase, and progressively unfavorable population-to-land ratios conspired to increase the flow out of the country. From 1861 to 1931 the net migration of Canadians to the United States has been estimated at over 2 million, with the out-migration peaking during the 1880s. Emigration during the latter part of the 19th century was framed by the decomposition of rural society, a sluggish pace of industrial development in the midst of a global recession, and the expansion of urban-industrial opportunities in nearby border states.

New York State was a major destination for Ontarians and Anglo-Quebeckers. The 1900 census records 90,336 "English" Canadian born and 27,199 "French" Canadian born in the state. The preference for certain jobs and short-distance travel explains the settlement of Anglophone Canadians in both the United States in general and New York State in particular. Because the distances were so short, associations defined by kinship and kith also significantly influenced the emigration of Canadians into New York State. Through a process of chain migration, communities on the Canadian side were directly attached to communities across the line. Migrants from eastern Ontario and southwestern Quebec settled in the northeastern and north-central parts of the state, while those from south-central and southwestern Ontario located primarily in Western New York. Small border cities such as Ogdensburg (St. Lawrence Co) and Oswego retained small, sharply focused migration fields, attracting rural craft workers from townships along the St. Lawrence and the Bay of Quinte, respectively. The migration fields for larger and more prosperous centers such as Buffalo, Syracuse, and particularly New York City were greater and more dispersed. The latter attracted migrants from all over Canada, drawing people of a more diverse and generally higher-skilled range of occupations. A number of migrants from the St. Lawrence townships chose to cross the river in winter by foot, sleigh, or stagecoach, and most crossed into Western New York by rail.

Employment

Though almost exclusively of British origin, Anglophone Canadians did not constitute a unified element. Socioeconomic distinctions and regional separation reinforced ethnic and religious divisions. The 1900 census reveals that Anglophone Canadians were distributed widely among different occupations in the larger cities of New York but were concentrated primarily in blue-collar occupations in the smaller centers. Rural unskilled and semiskilled male workers and their families were more attracted to smaller cities such as Watertown (Jefferson Co), while New York City was a magnet for urban white-collar workers, professionals, and young, single females who worked as secretaries, nurses, and domestics. After the turn of the 20th century, movement from Canada was somewhat diminished because of increased industrial opportunities in Ontario and Quebec and the expansion of the wheat economy in the West. Canadians, however, continued to immigrate to New York State. The 1950 census records 99,730 Canadians of "other" origin, most presumably of Anglo-Celtic ethnicity, and 18,254 "French" Canadian-born. Yet since the end of World War II, changing economic demands and immigration policy have considerably modified the nature of Canadian emigration. The United States has selectively attracted increasing proportions of well-trained professional workers, and New York is just one of many states attracting Canadians possessing high-technology skills and professionals. As a result, Anglophone Canadians do not generally have as significant a role in New York communities as they once did, at least in terms of numbers. The Census Bureau indicates that approximately 39,000 Canadians, both Anglophone and Francophone, lived in the state in 1997, constituting 7% of the total number of this group in the United States. Anglophone Canadians in New York State now encompass a wide variety of ethnicities, including a substantial Jewish and Caribbean population.

Social Life

During the zenith of emigration at the end of the 19th century, Anglophone Canadians played a major role in the social and economic development of many New York communities. In 1880, Canadians, primarily from Ontario, formed 14% of the foreign-born population in Rochester and 12% in both Buffalo and Syracuse. They were even more important in smaller centers such as Watertown, where in 1900 they were 52% of the foreign-born population. Their presence was, however, rarely noted. Unlike their Francophone Canadian counterparts, Anglophone Canadians seldom established formal ethnic institutions. Most Anglophone Canadians joined established American religious congregations, so the church played virtually no role in preserving cultural heritage. Social institutions were also rare; the one or two that existed, such as the Canadian Club of New York City, served the elite business fraternity. Even in Watertown, arguably the most Anglophone Canadian of all cities in New York, this group was seldom mentioned in newspaper discussions relating to the "immigrant" dimension of the community. The generally receptive attitude on the part of the host society toward this group made the transition to American life relatively easy.

Communities

Anglophone Canadians were not a homogeneous group and were not completely willing assimilators. As Canadians they had experienced different conceptions of government, social welfare, and economic organization from their neighboring Americans. The structural conditions of the receiving communities and the composition of particular migration streams created a variable Anglophone Canadian experience at the turn of the 20th century. In Watertown a rigid class division ensured that this group would be congregated in a separate social and economic space. Such barriers, along with the lack of industrial and entrepreneurial skills held by this predominantly rural group, meant that most would work in unskilled and semiskilled occupations. In that city Anglophone Canadians relied on kin and boarders of the same nationality to supplement the family economy. Many lived in multiple-dwelling units and exhibited a significant rate of endogamy. They also were, in comparison to other Anglophone Canadian groups, the least likely to give up their former citizenship and the most likely to return to Canada. Anglophone Canadians in Syracuse, in contrast, showed a greater diversity of occupations, with proportionately more engaged in clerical, professional, and business positions, and a higher occupational status with length of residence, indicating that there were more opportunities for upward mobility than there were in Watertown. New York City, which was much larger, offered a wide variety of opportunities and, consequently, more avenues of mobility.

The city attracted Anglophone Canadians of various backgrounds but was especially inviting to those possessing certain professional skills, such as doctors and nurses, business people who could take advantage of the huge local market, and clerical workers, both male and female, who found plenty of job opportunities in the city's expanding service sector.

As a group, contemporary Canadian immigrants in New York State are smaller in number, more metropolitan oriented, and higher skilled than their predecessors. The few Canadian organizations that do exist, such as the Canadian Society of New York, the Canadian Club of New York, the Canadian Women's Club of New York City, and various Canadian university alumnae and alumni groups, attract the attention of only a small number of expatriates.

Canadian Consulate General in New York, http://canada-ny.org/English/organiz.htm

Widdis, Randy W. *With Scarcely a Ripple: Anglo-Canadian Migration into the United States and Western Canada, 1880–1920* (Montreal and Kingston: McGill-Queen's Univ Press, 1998)

Randy William Widdis

Canadians, Francophone. The Francophone Canadian population of New York State can be traced to two French colonies founded at the beginning of the 17th century: Acadia and New France, most settlers having come from what is today the province of Quebec. In 1755 the British deported thousands of Acadians for their refusal to swear allegiance to the Crown. Some 300 came to New York Colony, although few settled permanently. In 1782 New York State voted to naturalize and give land to Francophone Canadians who had fought for the American cause. The veterans were settled in the Canada and Nova Scotia Refugee Tract on the western shores of Lake Champlain and founded the Towns of Champlain and Chazy and the Village of Rouses Point (Clinton Co).

Many partisans of the failed Papineau rebellion of 1837–38 fled to northern New York State. Their leader, Louis Joseph Papineau, remained in Albany for two years before moving to France and later returning to Canada. His followers helped establish the first French Canadian parish in New York State, Saint Joseph de Corbeau, in Clinton Co in 1842. After 1840 economic pressures replaced political ones as the principal reason for Francophone Canadian migration. In Nova Scotia, farming, fishing, and lumbering provided little more than subsistence. In Canada East (after 1867, Quebec), land was growing less productive and the population was rapidly increasing. Most emigrants went to New England, but some settled in New York State, mainly the North Country and Adirondacks, such as in Watertown and Ogdensburg (Clinton Co), the Capital District, especially in Cohoes (Albany Co) and Troy (Rensselaer Co), and New York City. By 1900 there were 19,000 Francophone Canadian immigrants with 36,800 US-born children in New York State. The Great Depression ended the era of mass migration.

Community Life

Francophone Canadians typically immigrated as families and tended to settle near others from their village or region of origin. In rural areas they worked in agriculture and lumber. In cities many found jobs as day laborers in construction or as employees in small businesses, but the majority held modest-paying factory jobs. Generally, all members of the family needed to work to ensure its economic survival, especially in the textile industry. Many lived in factory-owned tenements, such as those built by Harmony Mills in Cohoes.

The close-knit communities were further bound by the ideology of *la survivance*, which supported the tenacious preservation of the "ancestral heritage" of the Catholic faith and the French language. Each community founded a French Catholic parish as soon as possible. By 1891 there were 34 parishes in the Diocese of Ogdensburg and 17 in the Dioceses of Albany and Syracuse, whose membership (approximately 86,940) was entirely or mostly Francophone Canadian. Many had parish schools in which French was the primary language, taught by members of Francophone Canadian teaching orders, such as the Sisters of Saint Anne, which began work in Oswego in 1866.

Francophone Canadians also founded fraternal benefit associations. There was a Société Saint-Jean-Baptiste in Malone (Franklin Co) as early as 1848; in 1850 Gabriel Fanchère founded the Société de Saint-Jean-Baptiste des Etats-Unis in New York City, which became the most influential association among Francophone Canadians. Also very important for the cohesion of the community were the national conventions for the discussion of common social and political concerns. Between 1865 and 1901, 19 were held in the United States, 7 of which took place in New York State: New York City (1865, 1866, 1874), Troy (1867), Glens Falls (1875), Cohoes (1882), and Albany (1884).

The third pillar of *la survivance* was the French language press. Francophone Canadian newspapers read in New York State often were published in New England. They were characteristically highly political and generally short lived. In New York State there were, among others, the *Ruche Canadienne,* published in Troy in the 1851, the *Phare des Lacs,* published in 1858 in Watertown, and *La Patrie Nouvelle,* published in Cohoes from 1876 to about 1890 by Joseph M. Authier and his family. The *Journal des Dames* (1875–76), published in Cohoes by Virginie Authier, was the first Francophone American publication intended specifically for a female audience.

Survival and Assimilation

Prior to 1930 the steady arrival of new immigrants and the infrastructures of *la survivance* were effective tools against two constant threats to French cultural maintenance: American nativism and the Irish dominance of the American Roman Catholic Church. However, when immigration ended and the depression and World War II triggered widespread social changes on both sides of the border, support for the traditional culture declined rapidly. By the mid-1960s, most Francophone Canadians were no longer transmitting French to their children, and the language had largely disappeared from the community infrastructure.

In 2000, 151,080 New Yorkers reported their ancestry as "French Canadian." But Francophone Canadians often identify themselves simply as "French," and many of the 477,730 New Yorkers who classified themselves as such probably are more specifically Francophone Canadian than French. In the late 1970s, when they began defining themselves as part of a larger Franco-American group, they rediscovered their history and culture in New York State. The nonprofit Fédération Franco-Américaine du New York, founded in Cohoes in 1982, has been an active sponsor of activities designed to create awareness of the North American French heritage and to foster its expression among Franco-Americans.

Brière, Eloise, ed. *J'aime le New York: A Bilingual Guide to the French Heritage of New York State.* Franco-American Quebec Heritage Series (Albany: SUNY, 1986)

Van Lent, Peter C. *The Hidden Heritage/héritage caché: The French Folk Culture of Northern New York* (Malone, NY: Malone Arts Council, 1988)

Cynthia A. Fox

Canadice. Town (pop 1,846) in SW Ontario Co. A family from New Jersey settled in the area in 1795, without others settling until 1804. The town was formed in 1829 from Richmond. Canadice lies between Hemlock and Honeoye Lakes, and Canadice Lake lies in the center of town. Canadice and Hemlock Lakes have supplied drinking water to Rochester since 1876. Hemlock Lake was a well-known resort in the late 19th century, and its attractions included the Port House, ingeniously situated at the end of a long pier to avoid the liquor restrictions in Canadice, a "dry" town. The lakeside dwellings were torn down by the early 20th century for sanitary reasons. Canadice's population more than tripled between 1960 and 1990. In 2003 the town is primarily farmland with dairy and beef herds, sheep, grapes, and berries. Cottages surround Honeoye Lake.

Marla A. Bennett

Canajoharie. Town (pop 3,797) and village (pop 2,257) in S central Montgomery Co. The name, a Mohawk word meaning "the pot that washes itself," refers to Canajoharie Creek, where there is a famed 20 ft (6.1 m) diameter pothole. Settled probably in the 1740s, Canajoharie was formed as a district in 1772 and as a town in 1788. During the Revolutionary War forces under Gen James Clinton camped there prior to marching south to meet Gen John Sullivan's troops in the 1779 campaign against the Iroquois. The seven Kane brothers operated an important forwarding and shipping firm there approximately from 1790 to 1805. The Central Asylum for the Instruction of the Deaf and Dumb (1823–36) was located at Buel, in the southern part of Canajoharie; a newspaper, the *Canajoharie Radii,* had a deaf editor and developed a national reputation among the deaf. Canajoharie became an Erie Canal port in 1825 but did not have a railroad on its side of the Mohawk until the West Shore came through in 1883. The village was incorporated in 1829. Three large industries supported the community in the late 19th and early 20th centuries: Arkell and Smith (1859–1952; makers of and pioneers in paper bags for flour, sugar, and cement), limestone quarrying, and the Imperial Packing Co (1891), which became Beech-Nut Packing Co, makers of baby food (from 1931) and Life Savers candy (from 1956). The New York State Thruway came through the village and town in 1954. Beech-Nut has remained the main employer, although it sold Lifesavers in 1967, and local manufacture of that candy ceased in 1988. Its plant is now operated by Joyco USA, another candymaker. The town's land remains mostly in agriculture. The Canajoharie Library and Art Gallery (1924), founded by Bartlett Arkell, president of Beech-Nut, contains an excellent collection of American representational art.

James Crawford

Canal Board. Administered the operation, expansion, and reconstruction of the Erie Canal system. Created by statute in 1826, the board was composed of the canal commissioners (three, four, or five in number, until that office was abolished in 1878) or their successor, the superintendent of public works; the surveyor general (after 1846, the state engineer and surveyor); and the lieutenant governor, comptroller, treasurer, secretary of state, and attorney general. The latter six officials also served as commissioners of the canal fund, established in 1817 to manage canal investments and debts. The Canal Board established canal tolls and exercised great patronage powers. It appointed toll collectors until tolls were abolished in 1882, superintendents of repairs until 1894, and division and resident engineers from 1850 until 1876. Another duty was hearing appeals of decisions of the Board of Canal Appraisers (after 1883, the Board of Claims), which assessed money damages for lands appropriated for or affected by canal construction or repairs.

The Canal Board granted or denied numerous petitions from landowners seeking use of canal lands or surplus waters or requesting bridges, docks, slips, culverts, and other structures. Between 1835 and 1878 the board issued general canal regulations, formerly issued by the canal commissioners and the canal fund commissioners and subsequently by the superintendent of public works. The Canal Board also authorized all major repairs or improvements to the canals. However, contractors and superintendents of repairs were only loosely supervised, and major legislative investigations in 1846 and 1852 found flagrant abuses and cost overruns. The legislature established an office of auditor of the Canal Department in the Comptroller's Office (1848–83) and a canal contracting board (1854–70) to exercise appropriate fiscal controls. After further contracting scandals, the Canal Board was again given full control over canal contracts and repairs in 1870 and major investigative powers in 1876. During the early 20th century the board's principal business was to oversee construction of the Barge Canal System. The board was abolished in 1926, and its responsibilities were transferred to the Department of Public Works.

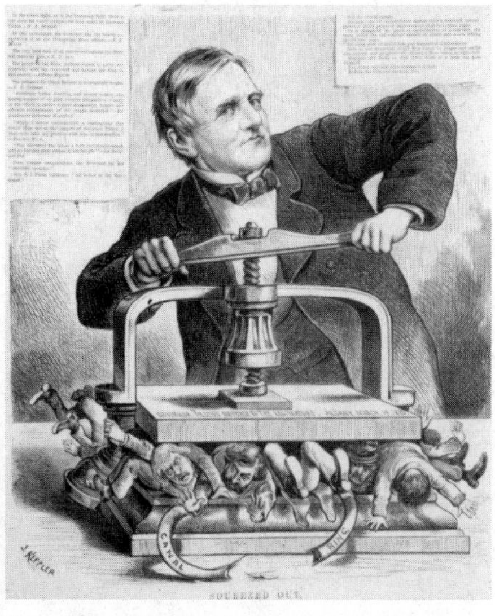

Gov Samuel J. Tilden putting the squeeze on Canal Board corruption, political cartoon from *Frank Leslie's Illustrated Newspaper*, 1875.

Sheriff, Carol. *The Artificial River: The Erie Canal and the Paradox of Progress, 1817–1862* (New York: Hill & Wang, 1996)

Whitford, Noble E. *History of the Canal System of the State of New York*, 2 vols (Albany: NYS Library, 1906)

James D. Folts

canalboats. The boats used on New York State's first canal, the Western Canal or canalized Mohawk River (1795), built by the Western Inland Lock Navigation Co, were flat bottomed with sharp ends, low sides, and open decks, and were propelled by square sails, oars, and poles. Known as bateaux or Durhams, these boats were replaced by a class of vessels known as canalboats after the 1825 opening of the Erie Canal. Canalboats were larger and stronger, and had a more boxlike shape than the Mohawk River bateaux and Durham boats. A variety of vessels including scows, packets, line boats, lakers, and bullheads made up the vessel class of canalboats. Their design continually changed as a result of innovations in ship construction and alterations that occurred in the canal prisms, lock sizes, overhead obstructions, types of cargoes carried, and methods of towing and operating the canalboats. Most 19th-century canalboats were propelled through the canals by horses or mules. The flat-bottomed scow was the most popular all-purpose canalboat, built with square sloped ends and an optional deck and crude cabin. Packets, which carried only passengers, had sharp ends and a cabin that ran nearly the entire length of the vessel. With the Erie's opening about 200 canalboats were operating in New York State, but the number grew to 1,853 vessels by 1833 as the state's canals exceeded 660 miles (1,062 km). Until the 1850s freight companies operated line boats (of similar construction to packets) that hauled both passengers and cargo. Lake boats were stronger, higher-sided freighters designed for the open water of the rivers and lakes that connected to the canals. With a flat bottom, lakers had a round bow and watertight decks and hatches. Some were equipped with one or two masts for sails, which were removed before entering the canal. Bullheads, or heavily built freighters, had a cabin similar to packets to keep their cargo dry, and both lakers and bullheads usually had an onboard stable for tow animals.

Initially any reasonably skilled carpenter could build a canalboat. As boats became more specialized, however, shipbuilding centers developed at important canal communities, such as Rondout (Ulster Co), terminus of the Delaware and Hudson Canal, Tonawanda (Erie Co), and Skenesborough [now Whitehall, Washington Co] on the Champlain Canal. The boats constructed at these yards met the differing environmental and work needs of each region. A boat's dimensions could not exceed the size of the smallest lock that it was to pass through. Most boats were owned by a few men, one of which might serve as the vessel's captain. Often entire families were living aboard part of the year or all year round. Well-constructed and maintained boats often lasted 15 years before having to be rebuilt. The numbers of canalboats in New York State increased to 3,867 by 1859, when the canal system exceeded 1,000 miles (1,610 km). However, by that time railroads had already begun to challenge canals. To counter this threat the first practical steam-driven canal tugs were introduced on the Erie Canal in 1871. During the state's navigable canal season, which generally ran from May through December, most boats operated 24 hours a day, seven days a week. Boats were limited to a speed of 4 mph (6 kph) by a New York State law issued by the Canal Board. Although, with the typical delays they probably traveled about 2 mph (3 kph) on average, thereby covering about 48 miles (77 km) per day. In 1878, about the time when many New York State canals were being abandoned, there were 8,558 canalboats operating. The total number of boats probably never exceeded 10,000 as they began to decline quickly in the 1880s when the railroad finally achieved near complete dominance of the freight trade. Only a few thousand boats were operating when the Barge Canal system opened in 1918. Crewless steel barges, which were pushed or pulled by tugboats, replaced the remaining wooden canalboats by 1950. These steel barges continued to transport freight through the state's canals until the 1990s, when commercial use of the canals essentially stopped.

Canal Museum. *A Canalboat Primer on the Canals of New York State* (Syracuse: Canal Museum, 1981)

Scott A. McLaughlin

Canal Ring. A loose alliance of Democratic and Republican state legislators who illegally pocketed a share of the money appropriated for repairing and extending the Erie Canal and its feeder canals during the 1860s and 1870s. The state-owned Erie Canal required constant maintenance. The contractors, ostensibly competing with each other, instead auctioned among themselves the right to submit the winning bid. The losers divided the auction price, and the winner guaranteed himself a sizable profit by submitting an "unbalanced bid"—that is, offering to do the major parts of the project at a low rate but charging exorbitant prices for minor ones. Canal Ring politicians then received kickbacks from favored contractors. The Canal Ring was not a tightly knit conspiracy but had considerable influence on both political parties along the routes of New York State's major canals: in Buffalo, Lockport, Oswego, Rochester, and Syracuse. Two state Democrats, Sen Jarvis Lord from Rochester and Assemblyman Willard Johnson from Oswego, led the Ring's forces in the legislature, and the Syracuse firm of Belden and Denison seems to have been its major beneficiary.

At the Constitutional Convention of 1867, former legislator Erastus Brooks charged that canal repair contracts were being awarded to the highest rather than lowest bidder. The resulting investigative committee reported the next year that "gross and monstrous frauds" existed, but only one canal commissioner was impeached. Appropriations for Extraordinary Repairs, the program that disguised the worst frauds, reached a high of $4.1 million in 1872. Democrat

Canalboats moored on the Hudson River, *ca* 1850.

Samuel J. Tilden, fresh from his triumph against William M. "Boss" Tweed in New York City, won the governorship in 1874, singling out corruption in Albany as the key issue. Tilden acted cautiously, however. In March 1875 he unveiled a detailed account of the machinations of the Canal Ring, noting that in the previous five years, tolls had exceeded ordinary expenses by $5.8 million, but the $10.9 million spent on extraordinary repairs had obliterated this profit.

Despite considerable opposition, the legislature authorized a commission of investigation under the chairmanship of the Republican secretary of state, John Bigelow of Malden (Ulster Co). In February 1876 the Bigelow Commission issued a 3,000-page report substantiating Tilden's charges. These findings led to the indictment for fraud, bribery, and conspiracy of 10 men, including 8 Democrats, an astonishing development in an era of extreme partisanship. Most of the guilty avoided jail, however, and former assemblyman George Lord's conviction for bribery was reversed, as was a $387,000 judgment against Belden and Denison. Tilden's success in smashing the Canal Ring made him a national political figure, and in 1876 he won the Democratic nomination for president.

Archdeacon, Thomas. "The Erie Canal Ring, Samuel J. Tilden, and the Democratic Party," *New York History* 59 (Oct 1978): 408–29

Jon Sterngass

canals. No state has been shaped by canals to a greater extent than New York. Located on the sole water-level route through the Appalachian barrier, New York State seized the opportunity to create canals and improve rivers to channel freight through its ports. This process began early. When, in 1727, a trading house was built at Oswego, its factors began to travel the Mohawk-Oneida corridor with greater frequency in the customary bark and dugout canoes, but also in larger bateaux. In 1730 a small cut was made in a narrow neck near the present city of Utica to bypass an oxbow of the Mohawk. This cut remained New York's only canal-related engineering project until the 1790s.

Westward population expansion made improvements to the route desirable. In 1792 the Western Inland Lock Navigation Co was chartered to improve the waterway to Lake Ontario. Beginning the following year, it cleared the Wood Creek channel, shortened it 7 miles (11 km) by cuts through its sharpest bends, built a canal with locks at Little Falls (Herkimer Co), built a short canal at Rome, and after 1800 constructed four locks on Wood Creek. These improvements allowed the use of Durham boats that had eight times the freighting capacity of bateaux. Overall the company's achievements were limited. The Northern Inland Lock Navigation Co, also chartered in 1792 with the mandate to improve navigation from the upper Hudson River to Lake Champlain, accomplished nothing.

A proposal to create what became the Erie Canal was made in 1808; a survey followed, and in 1811 the first enabling legislation was enacted. The War of 1812 made the development of the canal more pressing so in 1817 the legislature passed acts to authorize both the Erie and Champlain Canals. Though canal transportation was never swift, it was cheap, and the canals (completed 1825 and 1823 respectively) drove down shipping costs, produced substantial revenue for the state, and solidified New York City's position as the nation's leading port. The two largest Finger Lakes were linked to the completed Erie Canal by the Cayuga and Seneca Canal (1826–28), and the Oswego Canal (1825–28) connected the Erie to Lake Ontario.

Demand for the advantages of a canal, both practical and economic, was so great that a number of laterals were constructed to the Erie: the Chemung Canal (1830–33) between Seneca Lake and the Susquehanna River, the Crooked Lake Canal (1831–33) between Keuka and Seneca Lakes, the Chenango Canal (1834–36) from Utica to Binghamton, the Genesee Valley Canal (built 1837–61), and the Black River Canal (built 1838–55). None of the laterals was profitable, and the Crooked Lake, Chenango, Genesee Valley and Chemung closed in 1877–78. A few canals were constructed independent of the state system. The Delaware and Hudson Canal (built 1825–29) and the Junction Canal (built 1853–58) were created by private corporations to ship coal northward from Pennsylvania. The Shinnecock and Peconic Canal (built 1884–92) crossed Long Island's South Fork.

The heyday of canals in New York State was relatively brief. Competition was not long in coming, with the first railroad operating between Albany and Schenectady in 1831; although initially it was not allowed to carry freight, it was permitted to do so in 1844. Despite the railroads, the tonnage on the Erie Canal increased through 1880. Passenger traffic, which enjoyed a brief heyday on packet boats traveling the Erie Canal, turned immediately to rail when track was complete from Albany to Buffalo in 1842.

The modernization of four canals—Erie, extending 340 miles (547 km) with 36 locks; Champlain, 63 miles (101 km) with 11 locks; Cayuga and Seneca, 27 miles (43 km) with 4 locks; and Oswego, 24 miles (39 km) with 7 locks—between 1903 and 1918 created the New York State Barge Canal. But the construction of

19th-Century Canal System

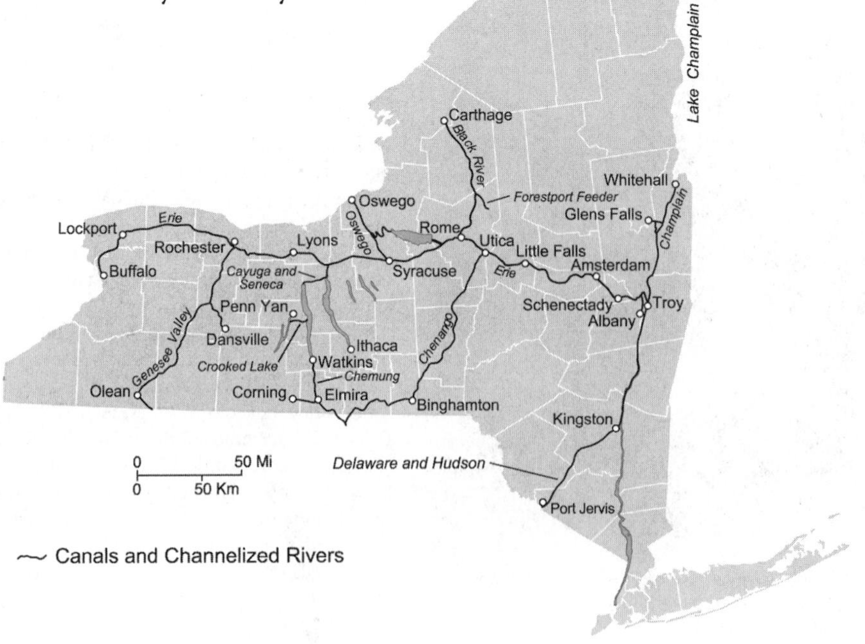

19TH-CENTURY NEW YORK STATE CANALS

Canal	Construction	Length in Miles (km)	No. Locks	Total Vertical Lockage in Feet (m)	Original Cost	Navigation Ended
Baldwinsville Canal	1808	.6 (1.0)	1	10 (3.1)	—[a]	—[b]
Erie Canal[c]	1817–25	363 (584.2)	83	675.5 (205.9)	$7,143,789[d]	—[e]
Champlain Canal and Glens Falls Feeder	1817–23	66 + 12 (106.2 + 19.3)	32	311 (94.8)	1,013,000	—[e]
Delaware and Hudson Canal[f]	1825–29	108 (173.8)	110	950 (289.6)	1,424,000	1898
Oswego Canal	1825–28	38 (61.2)	18	154.9 (47.2)	565,000	—[e]
Cayuga and Seneca Canal[g]	1826–28	23 (37.0)	11	83.5 (25.5)	214,000	—[e]
Chemung Canal and Feeder	1830–33	39 (62.8)	52	516 (157.3)	314,395	1878
Crooked Lake Canal	1831–33	8 (12.9)	22	277.8 (84.7)	157,000	1877
Old Oneida Lake Canal[h]	1832–35	6.5 (10.5)	7	57.7 (17.6)	79,000	1862
Chenango Canal and Feeders	1834–36	97 + 13 (156.1 + 20.9)	114	1,015 (309.4)	2,316,186	1878
Genesee Valley Canal and Dansville Branch[i]	1837–61	125 (201.2)	112	1,128 (33.8)	5,663,183	1878
Seneca River Towing Path	1838–39	5.8 (9.4)	0	0	14,864	—[b]
Black River Canal and Feeder	1838–55	35.5 + 10 (57.1 + 16.1)	109	1,082 (329.8)	3,157,296	1924
Oneida River Improvement	1839–50	19 (30.6)	2	6.3 (1.9)	79,346	—[j]
Junction Canal[f]	1852–58	18 (29.0)	11	72 (22.0)	530,637	1871
Black River Improvement	1854–61	42.5 (68.4)	2	9.3 (2.8)	—[k]	1918
Chenango Extension Canal[l]	1865–72	40 (64.4)	10	8.3 (2.5)	1,600,889	1878
New Oneida Lake Canal	1867–77	5.3 (8.5)	6	62 (18.9)	444,000	1887
Shinnecock and Peconic Canal	1884	.8 (1.2)	0	0	98,000	—[j]

Source: N. E. Whitford, *History of the Canal System of the State of New York,* 2 vols (1906).

[a]Information not available.

[b]Completely filled in by 1965.

[c]The Enlarged Erie Canal, with construction between 1842 and 1862, extended 350 miles (563.3 km).

[d]Cost through 1862.

[e]Route incorporated into the New York State Barge Canal system.

[f]Built and operated privately.

[g]Began as a private undertaking in 1813, but the state purchased it in 1826, improved it, and made it a lateral of the Erie.

[h]Constructed privately and purchased by the state in 1841.

[i]Completed from Rochester to Mount Morris in 1840; to Dansville, 1841; to Olean, 1857; to Mill Grove, 1861.

[j]Still in operation.

[k]Included in the cost of the Black River Canal and Feeder.

[l]Work never completed.

the St. Lawrence Seaway (1954–59), in which the United States and Canada cooperated, created a more direct route from the Great Lakes to the Atlantic that siphoned off most of the canal's business. The shipping of freight on the Barge Canal ended in 1994.

In 1992 legislation transferred responsibility for the system from the Department of Transportation to the Thruway Authority and its subsidiary, the New York State Canal Corp. That same year the Barge Canal was renamed the New York State Canal System, and the four component canals reverted to their original names. Additionally, a Canal Recreationway Commission was established to supervise development and promotion. In the early 21st century, leisure use of the canal is increasing.

See also BONDED INDEBTEDNESS.

Larkin, F. Daniel. *New York State Canals: A Short History* (Fleischmanns, NY: Purple Mountain Press, 1998)

Shaw, Ronald E. *Canals for a New Nation: The Canal Era in the United States, 1790–1860* (Lexington: Univ of Kentucky Press, 1990)

Whitford, Noble E. *History of the Canal System of the State of New York,* 2 vols (Albany: Brandow Printing, 1906)

Field Horne

Canandaigua [CAN-AN-DAY-GWA]. Town (pop 7,649) and city (pop 11,264) in central Ontario Co. Canandaigua was built near the site of a Seneca village, Ganundagwa, that was destroyed by the Sullivan-Clinton expedition in 1779. Oliver Phelps and Nathaniel Gorham, the purchasers of the land (1787), ordered a village surveyed at the site. It was settled in 1789 and became the county seat with the formation of Ontario Co the same year. The town was formed in 1790. A road from Utica provided a route for migrants by 1791, and Canandaigua soon became the leading settlement in Western New York, surrounded by a rich farming district. In 1794 the Treaty of Canandaigua (also known as Pickering Treaty) was signed, establishing peace and friendship between the Six Nations of the Iroquois and the United States. The village incorporated in 1815. The Ontario Female Seminary (1825–75), a pioneer institution in the education of women, incorporated in 1824. *Lady of the Lake,* Canandaigua's first steamboat, was launched in 1827. When the village was bypassed by the Erie Canal, it entered a period of relative dormancy until the mid-1850s. Early settlers of Yankee origin were joined by Irish immigrants at midcentury and by Germans and by Italians early in the 20th century. Canandaigua acquired rail service in 1840 upon the opening of the Auburn and Rochester Railroad. Rail connections to Syracuse (1851) and Batavia (1853) further improved accessibility. Among 19th-century industrial enterprises were J. and A. McKechnie Brewing Co (1843–1919), gristmills, a planing mill, and a brick and tile works. Canandaigua's best-known industry was the Lisk Manufacturing Co (1892–1966), producer first of tinware, then of galvanized ware, enamelware, and solenoids after 1948. The village became a city in 1913.

A Veterans Administration hospital opened in 1930. Finger Lakes Community College began accepting students in 1967. Other major employers in 2002 were Canandaigua Wine, Labelon office products, Wegmans Food Markets, Tenneco Packaging, and Thompson HealthCare. A beautiful and well-preserved small city, it attracts considerable tourism due to its architecture and lakefront setting. Attractions include the Finger Lakes Performing Arts Center (1983), the Granger Homestead (1816), and Sonnenberg Gardens (1902). Its attractiveness has led to a combined population growth in city and town of 25% between 1960 and 2000, in part because of the growth of the greater Rochester area. Henry Johnson (1822–) was an African American barber in the village who read law, became a lawyer, and ultimately was attorney general (1870–71) of the Republic of Liberia. Myron H. Clark (1806–1892) was New York State governor from 1855 to 1857. Gideon Granger (1767–1822) was a politician and former US postmaster general (1801–14) who settled in the village in 1816 and established a political power base, which was used by his son, Francis Granger (1792–1868), a congressman in the 1830s and 1840s. The 1873 trial of Susan B. Anthony for voting illegally was conducted at the Ontario County Courthouse.

See also ARCHITECTS AND ARCHITECTURE, ROCHESTER AND WESTERN NEW YORK; BOTANICAL GARDENS.

Marla A. Bennett

Canandaigua Lake (16.5 mi²/42.7 km²). The fourth largest of the Finger Lakes is located in Ontario and Yates Cos. It is 15.5 miles (24.9 km) long with 35.9 miles (57.8 km) of shoreline, and at its deepest, it is 276 feet (84.1 m). Canandaigua Lake was formed by glacial action. During the settlement period, the lake was the primary means of movement within the region. Lake trout were the only salmonid in the lake until 1925, when the Conservation Commission introduced whitefish and burbot smelt. Rainbow trout, alewife, and brown trout were introduced in 1936, 1953, and the early 1970s, respectively. The lake serves as a public water supply for Canandaigua, Newark, Palmyra, Rushville, and Gorham. During the steamboat era (1827–1935) the transportation system created an economic boom throughout the watershed. The *Canandaigua Lady* operates in summer. Roseland Amusement Park (1925–85) was on the lake's north shore. In 2002 Roseland Waterpark is a popular family attraction. At the turn of the 20th century there were 160 cottages scattered along the shores, 1,163 in 1945, and 1,450 residences in 1992. Cottage City in Gorham (Ontario Co) began as a steamboat landing with cottages (1878). In 1929 the large Crystal Beach resort development was surveyed but never developed. In 2002 less than 3% of the shoreline is publicly accessible for recreation. In 1996 the City of Canandaigua invested $4.5 million in a lakefront redevelopment project to refurbish its 7-acre (2.8 ha) waterfront park and roadways, and add 1,000 feet (305 m) of shoreline to the public park. Canandaigua Lake is a natural resource that is crucial to the region's economic health.

Burnes, Pauline. "The Inventory of Significant Geological, Geographical, Historical, Cultural, and Scenic Resources" (MA thesis, SUNY College of Environmental Science and Forestry, 1992)

Maus, Henry, et al. *Glimpses of Canandaigua and the Lake* (Canandaigua, NY: Ontario County Historical Society, 1982)

Simpson, Robert. "Studies in Populational Geography, Canandaigua Lake Region, New York" (PhD diss, Clark Univ, 1931)

Marla A. Bennett

Canarsee Indians. A general term often used to identify Indians living in and around Kings Co during the first centuries of European colonization. Although documented place and personal names indicate that the Canarsee spoke Delaware, it is unclear whether it was the Munsee or the Unami dialect. Translations of meaning of the word in Delaware range from "fenced place" to "long grassy ground." It is preserved on modern maps as the Canarsie section in southern Brooklyn. Dutch and English records show that the Canarsee location, also known as Kesheachquereren in early Dutch records, was only one of several Delaware villages within present-day borough boundaries occupied at various times during the colonial era. Others include a town overlooking the Narrows in the Fort Hamilton section identified as Wichquawanck in 1639 and as Nayack (the Delaware word for point or neck of land) in later documents, a village called Techkonis near what is now Prospect Park, another known as Marechkawick in downtown Brooklyn, and Maspeth at Newtown Creek in what is now Queens. Colonial records also show that Penhawitz, Tackapousha, Matteno, and other Canarsee leaders put their marks to 22 deeds conveying title to lands in and around Kings Co between 1636 and 1684.

Venerable local traditions, such as the story identifying Canarsees as the Indians who sold Manhattan to the Dutch in 1626 and another claiming that Mohawk raiders destroyed them following their refusal to make customary wampum tribute payments, are not corroborated in documentary sources. Extant records show that the Canarsee were among the west Long Island Indians fighting against the Dutch during Kieft's War (1640–45). Other records show that these same communities sent 70 warriors to assist the Dutch in their wars with the Munsee-speaking Esopus Indians and their allies in the mid-Hudson Valley between 1659 and 1664. Increasingly unable to resist colonial expansion onto their lands, most Indians left Brooklyn by 1700. Many moved among friends and relatives farther from the center of European settlement in northern New Jersey, southern New York State, and central Long Island. The majority were gradually forced into exile in Ontario, Wisconsin, and Oklahoma by the end of the 19th century. Others tracing descent to Canarsee Indian ancestors continue to make their homes in and around the New York City metropolitan area.

Grumet, Robert S. *Native American Places Names in New York City* (New York: Museum of the City of New York, 1981)

Robert S. Grumet

Canasatego (*b* unknown; *d* Onondaga territory, 6 Sept 1750). Onondaga leader. Canasatego played a prominent role in Anglo-Iroquois diplomacy in the mid–18th century, participating in treaty conferences at Easton (1742) and Lancaster, Pa (1744), Albany (1745), and Philadelphia (1749), speaking on behalf of a pro-British faction among the Onondaga and acting as an intermediary between colonial governments and other Indian nations. At the Easton conference he asserted Iroquois Confederacy power over the Delaware and sped their dispossession by ordering them off of land in eastern Pennsylvania. He also made a famous speech at the 1744 Lancaster Treaty, in which he urged the colonists to maintain union and peace with each other. He died a few days before a planned meeting with Pennsylvania Indian agent Conrad Weiser. Weiser and his companion Daniel Claus thought Canasatego may have been murdered by French emissaries who were encouraging the Onondaga to move to the Jesuit mission community of Oswegatchie [now Ogdensburg, St. Lawrence Co].

Jennings, Francis. *The Ambiguous Iroquois Empire: The Covenant Chain Confederation of Indian Tribes with English Colonies* (New York: Norton, 1984)

Timothy J. Shannon

Canaseraga [CAN-A-SIR-AY-GA]. Village (pop 594) in Burns (Allegany Co). Located on the Buffalo Division of the Erie Railroad (1852), Canaseraga benefited from the lumber industry. The village incorporated in 1892. The Four Corners Historic District (2002) encompasses 16 brick buildings constructed after an 1895 fire. Located five miles from Swain ski area, the village's tourist business is growing in the early 21st century and features the Canaseraga Fall Harvest Festival in September. Canaseraga Central School District is the largest employer. Other residents are self-employed or commute, some as far as Rochester.

Canastota. Village (pop 4,425) in Lenox (Madison Co). Canastota grew because of its location on the Erie Canal (1819) and the Syracuse and Utica Railroad (1839; later New York Central). The village incorporated in 1835. Nineteenth-century manufacturing included Spencer Telescope Co (1846–76), Canastota Knife Co (1874–95), Canastota Glass Co (1881–1920s), Patten and Stafford (1882; wheel rakes), and Smith and Ellis (1888; furniture). The firm of Marvin and Casler played a major role in the invention of the Mutoscope and Biograph motion picture machines (1898). The village's population became heavily Italian in the 20th century due to the concentration of vegetable farms in Lenox owned by Italian families. Their produce was marketed through the Canastota Growers Co-operative Association (1932–68). Canastota was crossed by the New York State Thruway in 1954. Late 20th-century industry included Henney Motors (1956; truck bodies) and General Electric (1957, closed-circuit televisions), but by 2003 only Diemolding Corp (1920; plastics) and Owl Wire and Cable (1966) remained. Canastota is the birthplace of welterweight and middleweight champion Carmen Basilio (1927–) and the site of the International Boxing Hall of Fame (1989) and of the Canal Town Museum.

William F. Helmer

Canawaugus Reservation. In 18th-century Canawaugus (Ga-no-wau-ges), meaning "fetid waters," was a Seneca village located at Avon Springs [now Avon, Livingston Co] on the east bank of the Genesee River. The village was the home of Gayasuta, who led the western (Chenussio) Seneca during Pontiac's War of 1763, and was the birthplace of the great Seneca prophet Handsome Lake, Gayasuta's nephew, and of his half-brother, the war chief Cornplanter. The village was destroyed in 1779 during the Sullivan-Clinton campaign. In 1797, at the federal treaty with the Seneca at Big Tree [now Geneseo], the US government recognized Canawaugus, a 2 mi² (5.2 km²) reservation on the west bank of the Genesee River. The Seneca lost the reservation in the 1826 Treaty of Buffalo Creek. The fraudulent treaty was never ratified by the US Senate.

Doty, Lockwood L. *History of Livingston County, New York*, 2d ed., 2 vols (Jackson, Mich: W. J. Van Deusen, 1905)

Hauptman, Laurence M. *Conspiracy of Interests: Iroquois Dispossession and the Rise of New York State* (Syracuse: Syracuse Univ Press, 1999)

Turner, Orsamus. *History of the Pioneer Settlement of Phelps and Gorham's Purchase* (Rochester: William Alling, 1851)

Laurence M. Hauptman

Candor. Town (pop 5,317) and village (pop 855) in N central Tioga Co. Settled in 1794, it was formed from Spencer in 1811. A woolen mill operated from 1824 to 1842. The Ithaca and Owego Railroad (later the Cayuga division of the Delaware, Lackawanna and Western Railroad) came through in 1834, fostering small manufacturing that included ironworks, tanneries, and a chair factory, but especially the Ironclad blanket factory, which produced 50,000 annually before closing *ca* 1920, and the Wands Glove Co (1895–1957). The Utica, Ithaca and Elmira Railroad (built 1872–75) provided a second line. The village was incorporated in 1900. The town is crossed by a Mobil Pipeline Co oil pipeline (1941). Candor was the subject of the 1958 book *Small Town in Mass Society: Class, Power and Religion in a Rural Community* by Arthur Vidich and Joseph Bensman. Agritourism has become significant to the local economy, with attractions including a pumpkin farm, deer and goat farms, a fish hatchery, and a lumber mill. Many residents are employed in Ithaca. The town is the site of Fairfield State Forest, of part of Shindagin Hollow State Forest, and of Buckridge, a naturist resort.

Joann Lindstrom

Caneadea. Town (pop 2,694) in NW Allegany Co. The site of an important Seneca village, part of the present town was in the Caneadea Reservation (1797–1826), along with the towns of Hume and Granger. European settlement began in 1800, and the town was formed in 1808 from Angelica. Houghton and Oramel were business localities on the Genesee Valley Canal (1851–78). Oramel, a village created by the canal, incorporated in 1856. Germans from Rochester and from Europe settled near the Allen border starting about 1851. Although later served by the Erie and Pennsylvania Railroads, the canal's closing ended the town's commercial boom. The Caneadea Dam (1927) of Rochester Gas and Electric created an artificial lake, mostly in the Town of Rushford. Caneadea's major employer is Houghton College (1923), an outgrowth of Wesleyan Seminary (1884). During the 1990 nonviolent protest against siting a nuclear waste dump in town, Belgian horses were used effectively to block a road, keeping out the commissioners sent to inspect a potential site.

Caneadea Reservation. In 1797, at the federal treaty with the Seneca at Big Tree, north of present-day Cuylerville (Livingston Co), the US government recognized Caneadea Reservation, a 16 mi^2 (41 km^2) parcel on the west bank of the Genesee River opposite the present-day Hume (Allegany Co), as Seneca territory. It had existed as a Seneca village from at least 1765, and its name is derived from a Seneca word for "where the heavens rest upon the earth." The village was the home of John Hudson (Do-ne-ho-ga-weh) and Capt Shongo (Gah-nee-son-go). The most southward and mountainous of the Seneca Nation's Genesee River valley villages, Caneadea was not sacked by the American army in the Sullivan-Clinton campaign of 1779. In 1826 the Seneca were dispossessed of the Caneadea Reservation by the Ogden Land Co in a fraudulent federal treaty, one that was never ratified by the US Senate. In the early 1870s the Seneca Council House at Caneadea was moved and reassembled at Letchworth State Park, where it remains.

Hewitt, J. N. B. "Caneadea." In *Handbook of American Indians North of Mexico,* vol 1, ed. Frederick Webb Hodge (Washington, DC: Government Printing Office, 1907)
Minard, John S. *History of Allegany County, New York* (Alfred, NY: W. A. Ferguson, 1896)
Morgan, Lewis Henry. *League of the Ho-De-No-Sau-Nee, or Iroquois* (Rochester: Sage & Bros, 1851)

Laurence M. Hauptman

Canisius College. Private coeducational college. Founded in 1870 as a Jesuit institution, the school started with a single structure. By 2002 it had 45 buildings on 36 acres (15 ha) in a residential neighborhood in the north-central section of Buffalo. It is made up of the College of Arts and Sciences, the Wehle School of Business, and the School of Education and Human Services. For the past several years Canisius has been working with the adjacent neighborhood to assist homeowners in beautifying the community they share. The school offers associate, bachelor's, and master's degree programs. In the fall of 2003, enrollment was 2,983 full-time undergraduate and 1,492 graduate students, with about 45% men and 55% women.

Brady, Charles A. *The First 100 Years: Canisius College* (Buffalo: Canisius College, 1969)
Canisius College, http://www.canisius.edu

Joseph Golombek Jr

Canisteo [CAN-IS-TEE-OH]. Town (pop 3,583) and village (pop 2,336) in SW Steuben Co. Before permanent European settlement in 1789, the area contained the Seneca town of Canisteo, which was destroyed by a force of Mohawks sent by Sir William Johnson in 1764. The town was formed in 1796. Settlers turned to lumbering, and the wood was rafted down the Canisteo River to be sold in Chesapeake Bay markets. After the Erie Railroad (1850) came through, industry developed, particularly wooden goods such as sash and blinds, chairs, and tables. Significant firms included Flohr Brothers Tannery (1875–1919) and a silk mill (1905–80) that employed over 200 in the 1920s. The village was incorporated in 1873. Still maintained is a living sign spelling the name Canisteo; made up of 260 Scotch pine trees, it was planted on a hillside plot in 1933. In 2003 the village is chiefly a bedroom community for those who work in Hornell. The Steuben Gas Storage Co (1991) operates a natural gas storage field and compressor station in Canisteo.

Virginia L. Wright and Jerry Wright

canning. Industry devoted to the preservation of food in cans or jars. The practice of preserving food in containers originated in France and was patented by the Englishman Peter Durand in 1810. The English immigrant Thomas W. Kensett established the first American canning company in New York City in 1818. His firm, Kensett and Daggett, received the first US patent for "vessels of tin" in 1825.

Development of the Industry

At first the new market of canned foods attracted the wealthy, who bought canned luxury items, and sailors, who found canned goods useful for long voyages. Kensett and Daggett specialized in salmon, oysters, and lobsters. Other firms canned meats, fruits, soups, and vegetables. The gold rush of 1849 gave the industry a boost, since prospectors in the little developed California countryside had trouble finding provisions locally and were uninterested in growing their own food. Widespread acceptance of canned goods came with the Civil War, when the US government ordered provisions both for troops and for the starving populations in occupied areas of the South. Hundreds of thousands of people thereby became accustomed to canned foods for the first time.

The canning industry remained largely concentrated in port cities, but in New York State fruit and vegetable canning dispersed itself into rural areas where the crops were produced. The migration began with Ezra A. Edgett, who established the country's first inland cannery at Camden (Oneida Co) in 1851, canning corn and then beef and poultry for the army during the Civil War. In 1863 the firm moved to Newark (Wayne Co), where the Erie Canal approached the Lake Ontario fruit belt, canning fruits and vegetables there until 1964. In 1879, 40% of the canneries in the state were located in either Monroe or Wayne Co. Erie Co, with a smaller number of canneries, had the highest output.

In the 50 years after the war, the canning industry in the United States expanded both in volume of output and in technological innovation.

FRUIT AND VEGETABLE CANNERIES, BY COUNTY, 1879

	No. of Canneries	Value of Products ($)
Erie	7	561,743
Genesee	3	82,900
Livingston	1	25,000
Madison	1	92,175
Monroe	20	427,760
Niagara	8	156,365
Oneida	9	82,300
Onondaga	2	60,000
Queens	3	193,500
Suffolk	1	20,000
Wayne	15	160,601

Source: E. F. Keuchel Jr, "The Development of the Canning Industry in New York State to 1960" (PhD diss, Cornell Univ, 1970).

Among New York State innovators was Harvey Hemingway, who in Syracuse developed the gun cooker, a steam-heated tube that cooked corn as it passed to the can. On the whole, however, New York State canners lagged technologically behind the canning industry throughout the rest of the country. Because rural workers had only modest expenses, few alternative employment opportunities, and no organization, they accepted far lower wages than their urban counterparts. In 1880 a can capper in Baltimore could make $2.50 a day; in Buffalo, $1.25; but in Newark, only $0.60. Rural canners in the state were therefore under less financial pressure to invest in labor-saving devices.

By the end of the 19th century, a unified national market for canned goods had developed, and canned fruits and vegetables from New York State were being sold across the country. As a consequence, firms faced increased competition from canners in other regions and a rising tide of confusing and often contradictory state regulations regarding food. Although canners had a history of opposing government regulation, a national meeting of canners in 1905 publicly endorsed regulation at the federal level to establish a uniform set of standards. Congress passed the Pure Food and Drug Act in 1906.

Growth and Consolidation

Around 1900 the first modern can was perfected by the Sanitary Can Co of Fairport (Monroe Co). Prior to this, most canners in the state had continued to manufacture their own cans by hand during the off season. Cans everywhere had been filled through a hole in the end and then capped with solder and acid. Leakage, swelling, bursting, and solder contamination had been persistent problems. The new "sanitary cans" were machine produced, open on the end for easy filling, and closed by a machine that crimped a lid onto the sides. Although large corporations were already consolidating the canning industry in California, Alaska, and Hawaii, the commercial availability of the new mass-produced cans spurred the further proliferation of small rural canneries in New York State. Their number peaked at 515 in 1919. In the early decades of the 20th century, the government and trade associations experimented with ways to improve standardization and quality grading. Freezing became a new option for food processors, and some canners switched wholly or partly to that method.

Spurred by increasing competition and technological changes following World War I, the process of consolidation finally penetrated the New York State canning industry, beginning with the combination of local firms. This included the merger of six canneries in Albion (Orleans Co) to form New York Canners (later Snider Packing) in 1919 and the merger in the Lake Ontario–Finger Lakes region of seven canneries and a brokerage to form Comstock Canning in 1937. Later these and other firms were purchased by large corporations that came to dominate the industry in New York State after World War II. Some, such as Glidden Paints, were already established in other fields and desired to diversify into the food industry through the acquisition of successful enterprises. More recently, the trend has favored food-oriented corporations.

Most large firms operate in several states and engage in other forms of food processing in addition to canning. Some of the largest firms have their roots in New York. For example, Seneca Foods, with operations in five states, began in 1949 as a grape juice producer in Dundee (Yates Co). Headquartered since 2001 in Marion (Wayne Co), Seneca runs plants in Marion, Geneva (Ontario Co), and Leicester (Livingston Co) and also has a warehouse in East Williamson (Wayne Co). It sells 9% of its output under its own labels (including Libby's, Aunt Nellie's, Farm Kitchen, and Seneca), but most of its output is sold to other companies, the largest share appearing under the Green Giant label. With its acquisition of Chiquita Processed Foods in 2003, Seneca became the nation's largest producer of canned vegetables.

The company known since 2003 as Birds Eye Foods also has a long history in New York State. Initially called Curtice-Burns, it was formed in 1961 through the merger of Curtice Bros (1868) of Rochester and Burns-Alton (1900) of Wayne Co. About the same time some 700 western New York State farmers formed the Pro-Fac Cooperative, and the company and the cooperative formed a joint venture. In 1973 Curtice-Burns sold company stock to the public. Between 1994 and 2002, the corporation was a wholly owned subsidiary of the Pro-Fac Cooperative, but in 2002 Pro-Fac sold 51% of its stock to an investment firm. Acquisitions in the 1990s included the Birds Eye label. The company changed its name to Agrilink Foods in 1997 and then to Birds Eye Foods in 2003. The firm, based in Penfield (Monroe Co), operates facilities from Georgia to California; New York State facilities include those in Barker, Bergen, Brockport, Fulton, and Oakfield.

Reflecting a larger trend in the food-processing industry, Birds Eye is shifting away from canning to concentrate on frozen vegetables, of which it is the nation's largest producer. Its last New York State plant without a freezing facility, located in Red Creek (Wayne Co), closed in 2002. Nevertheless, according to the 1997 economic census, New York State at that time had 57 cannery establishments employing over 3,800 people and had the third largest value of output in the nation (after California and Florida), with $1.3 billion.

The Almanac of the Canning, Freezing, Preserving Industries (Westminster, Md: Edward E. Judge & Sons, 1915–)

Keuchel, Edward F., Jr. "The Development of the Canning Industry in New York State to 1960" (PhD diss, Cornell Univ, 1970)

Scott C. Monje

Can of Worms. The highway interchange in Rochester and Brighton (Monroe Co) characterized by a complex "weave" pattern in the lanes, exits, and entrances. Patterned after a similar interchange near San Francisco, it was designed in 1956 and completed between 1962 and 1964. The Can of Worms (named by Mitchell Kaidy, a Rochester-area reporter), then a state-of-the-art highway design, connected what are now I-490, I-590, East Ave, and University Ave and allowed the New York Central Railroad to travel through the interchange. The locations of I-490 and I-590 were influenced by the location of the former Rochester subway system, which provided some rights-of-way, defining the interchange's location. The interchange of Northern State and Meadowbrook Parkways in North Hempstead (Nassau Co) has a similar design. Reconstruction of the Can of Worms from 1988 to 1991 involved 11 new bridges. The interchange cost $4 million to construct and $129.2 million to replace.

Eric L. Kline

Canton [CANT-N]. Town (pop 10,334) and village (pop 5,882) in central St. Lawrence Co. Settled in 1800, the town was formed in 1805 from Lisbon. The village, county seat since 1828, was incorporated in 1845. It was served by the Rome, Watertown and Ogdensburg Railroad (1854). Canton had a bloom forge before 1812 and a pocket furnace in 1827 that made stoves and Jethro Wood plows. Iron pyrite was mined at High Falls on the Grass River from around 1832 to 1836; 60–80 hands processed it to make copperas and alum. Other 19th-century products included leather, furniture, carriages, edge tools, tailors' pressing machines, and the noted canoes (made 1873–1916) of J. Henry Rushton. Outside the village, dairy farming became important after the Civil War and remains so in the early 21st century. The Dairy Farmers Union was formed in Canton in 1938 and led a far-reaching milk strike in 1939. The village is the site of St. Lawrence University (1856) and SUNY Canton (1906). The Upper and Lower Lakes State Wildlife Management Area is located on the Indian Creek carry, a natural, seasonal canal (6 mi/9.7 km) between the Grass and Oswegatchie Rivers. Canton was the birthplace of artist Frederic Remington (1861–1909) and the home of Gov Silas Wright (1795–1847). The village contains several historic districts; landmarks include the Harison Grist Mill (1840), being restored, and Trinity Episcopal Church (1870–1), both at Morley. Employers include county government, a Kraft Foods cheese plant, and Corning.

Richard E. Mooers

Cape Vincent. Town (pop 3,345) and village (pop 760) in NW Jefferson Co. Bordered by the St. Lawrence River and Lake Ontario, the town includes Carlton and Grenadier Islands. Settled in 1801 and augmented starting in 1815 by French and German immigrant families, it was a point of lumber shipment on the St. Lawrence. In 1818 a small contingent of aristocratic French émigrés arrived, many of them associates of Napoleon, for whom they built the strangely designed Cup and Saucer House as a refuge. While numerically insignificant (in 1855, 244 French-born, 7% of the population) this group has always colored the town's identity. The village, first settled in 1809, did not develop until the Rome, Watertown and Ogdensburg Railroad arrived in 1852; it incorporated in 1853. Industries included commercial fishing, shipbuilding (1819–*ca* 1877), and ice harvesting (through World War II). Agricultural pursuits included hay, market gardening, and seed growing, notably for the A. B. Cleveland Seed Co (1885–*ca* 1920). Since the 1950s tourism, particularly boating and sportfishing, has been the major industry. The town is the site of the Cape Vincent Correctional Facility (1988) and the state-run Cape Vincent Fisheries Research Station (1965), which has an aquarium and visitors' center. The keeper's house at the Tibbetts Point Lighthouse is a youth hostel; the light was automated in 1976.

Laura Lynne Scharer

capital punishment. Except for a 30-year period from 1965 to 1995, capital punishment has always been part of New York State law. Because of its age and large population, New York has conducted more known executions than any state except Virginia.

Colonial Period

New York's 17th-century criminal codes imposed death for a list of crimes that seems surprisingly long today, including offenses like sodomy and adultery, though it was much shorter than England's. The colony added more capital crimes in the 18th century, an era when criminal codes were growing harsher throughout the British Empire. The death penalty was instituted for counterfeiting in 1709, for instance, and for certain forms of perjury in 1772. The most significant expansion of capital punishment took place after the slave revolt of 1712, when New York appears to have become the first colony in British North America to enact extra capital statutes applicable only to slaves. The idea behind the 1712 statute subjecting slaves to execution for attempted rape and attempted murder would be widely copied over the next 150 years in other colonies and states, especially in the South.

Death was inflicted by hanging, the traditional English method of execution. Hangings took place in public and often attracted crowds numbering in the thousands. The hanging itself was just the last act in a ceremony that could take several hours to complete, a ritual that encompassed a procession from jail to the gallows, a sermon from a minister, and a speech by the condemned, who typically warned spectators not to follow the same path. The more publicity accompanying an execution, it was thought, the greater capital punishment's deterrent effect would be. Attending an execution was understood to be a wholesome, educational experience, and for that reason parents often brought their children. At most hangings spectators seem to have been somber and respectful. Today's popular image of the carnivalesque execution crowd is largely an invention of 19th-century reformers. In the 18th century just over half of the criminals sentenced to death in New York were pardoned. As in the other colonies, New York's capital laws were much harsher on paper than in practice, because executive clemency played a much larger role in sentencing than it does today. In an era before prisons, clemency allowed officials some flexibility in tailoring the punishment to the offender, and in an era before convictions were normally reviewed on appeal, clemency allowed mistakes to be corrected.

1790–1860

In 1796, after the issue had been debated in the press for a decade, New York became one of the first states to abolish capital punishment for crimes other than murder and treason. (New Jersey and Virginia did so in the same year, and Pennsylvania had done so two years earlier.) Many of the criminals who would have been sentenced to death were now sent to the first state prison, Newgate, in Manhattan's Greenwich Village. Prison provided an alternative that caused many to perceive the death penalty as less necessary than it had once been. With the exception of arson, which became a capital crime in 1808, murder would be the state's only capital crime in the 19th and 20th centuries. In this respect New York was typical of other northern states. Horace Conklin, hanged in 1851 for setting a series of fires in Utica, appears to have been the last person executed by any northern state for a nonmilitary crime other than murder.

New York was one of the first states to abolish public execution when it moved hangings into the jail yard in 1835. (Connecticut had been the first, in 1830.) Public execution would be abolished throughout the North and much of the South by 1860, though it would linger on in parts of the South until the early 20th century. The arguments against public hanging were the same in New York as elsewhere: it was said to increase the rate of crime by acclimating spectators to violence, to cause spectators to sympathize unduly with the criminal, and to be widely viewed as entertainment rather than as instruction. Jail yard hangings still attracted crowds of several hundred people, despite a statute limiting the number of spectators to 12. Local sheriffs accommodated demand simply by issuing temporary appointments as deputies. Thousands of people sometimes gathered outside the jail's walls, often hoping for a view from a neighboring tree or rooftop.

Abolishing capital punishment completely became a major political issue throughout the North in the 1840s and 1850s. Michigan, Rhode Island, and Wisconsin abolished the death penalty between 1846 and 1853, and several other states, including New York, came close. The leader of the movement to abolish capital punishment in New York State was the lawyer and publisher John O'Sullivan, a member of the state assembly in the early 1840s. Assembly committees recommended abolition in 1841, 1845, 1846, 1847, 1851, 1859, and 1860, but none of the bills passed. In 1860 the legislature did divide murder into degrees, as several states had already done, with capital punishment available only for murder in the first degree.

1860–1965

The state became the focus of international attention in 1888, when it became the first jurisdiction in the world to adopt electrocution as its method of execution. Dissatisfaction with hanging had been growing since the middle of the century, because hanging was often very painful for the condemned. Electricity was first brought into the home in the 1880s, and after hundreds of fatal accidents caused by the new networks of wires, the ability of electricity to produce instant death was well known. With the responsibility of building the first electric chair, prison officials found themselves in the middle of one of the major commercial battles in US history, between Thomas Edison's firm, which sold electrical systems using direct current, and George Westinghouse's firm, which sold systems using alternating current. Edison persuaded prison officials to use alternating current for the electric chair, hoping that the public would associate Westinghouse's electricity with death. After

EXECUTIONS, 1700–1963

	Executions	Male	Female	White	Nonwhite and Latino
1700–1709	12	9	3	6	6
1710–19	35[a]	28	5	7	26
1720–29	11	11	0	8	3
1730–39	8	7	1	6	2
1740–49	46	43	3	9	37
1750–59	24	24	0	22	2
1760–69	20	18	2	15	5
1770–79	72	67	5	65	7
1780–89	62	61	1	57	5
1790–99	21	17	4	12	9
1800–1809	14	13	1	9	5
1810–19	67	64	3	62	5
1820–29	22	20	2	17	5
1830–39	25	25	0	22	3
1840–49	35	33	2	30	5
1850–59	45	44	1	40	5
1860–69	28	28	0	27	1
1870–79	40	40	0	32	8
1880–99	53	52	1	48	5
1890–99	51	50	1	37	14
1900–1909	66	65	1	59	7
1910–19	121	121	0	102	19
1920–29	125	124	1	100	25
1930–39	153	150	3	124	29
1940–49	114	113	1	70	44
1950–59	55	53	2	39	16
1960–63	10	10	0	2	8

Source: D. A. Hearn, *Legal Executions in New York State: A Comprehensive Reference, 1639–1963* (1997).

[a]In 1719, 2 people were executed for whom gender and race are unknown.

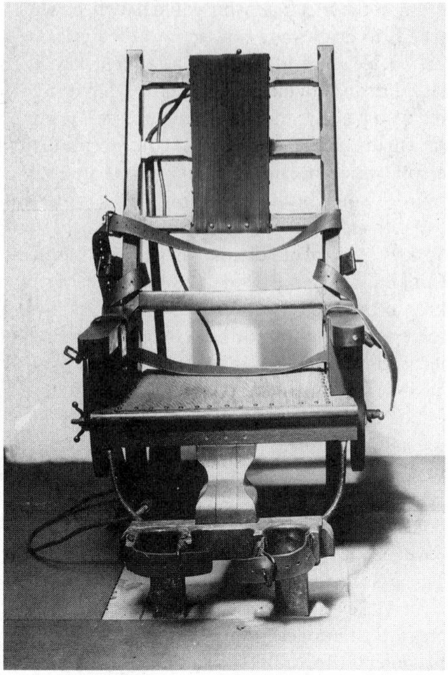

Electric chair at Sing Sing Prison.

many tests conducted in Edison's own laboratory, the state did use alternating current, but the cost advantages of alternating current were enough for it to prevail despite the unfavorable publicity.

In 1890 at Auburn Prison (Cayuga Co), William Kemmler of Buffalo became the first person executed by electricity. The execution was a disaster. Kemmler received a 17-second jolt, but as the warden was removing the electrode from his head, Kemmler's chest began heaving. Terrified that Kemmler was not yet dead, the warden ordered the electricity reapplied for more than a minute. The capillaries on Kemmler's face ruptured, and beads of blood appeared like sweat on his face. The smell of burned flesh filled the room. Spectators were nauseated, and the execution was sharply criticized in the press. Later electrocutions went more smoothly, and within a few years the electric chair had proven to be, on average, less painful and less gruesome than hanging. Most states eventually followed New York in abandoning hanging in favor of the electric chair.

In the middle of the 19th century, many began to complain that juries were acquitting defendants who were guilty of first-degree murder because they were unwilling to send defendants to their deaths. This widening discomfort with the death penalty caused state after state to abandon mandatory capital sentencing and to give juries discretion to choose between death or prison in cases of first-degree murder. The trend was a gradual one, encompassing no more than eight states and no fewer than two in any decade between the 1860s and the 1930s. New York held on to the mandatory death penalty until 1963, longer than any other state.

Between 1907 and 1917 nine more states abolished capital punishment, and although New York was not one of them, the issue was prominent in the state legislature and at the state's 1915 Constitutional Convention. Some of the leading proponents for abolition in the first half of the century were New Yorkers, including Thomas Mott Osborne and Lewis E. Lawes, both wardens at Sing Sing Prison in Ossining (Westchester Co). The frequency of executions in the state began to decline in the mid-1930s, as it did throughout the rest of the North, as dissatisfaction with capital punishment continued to grow. New York conducted an average of 15.3 executions per year in the 1930s, 11.4 per year in the 1940s, and only 5 per year from 1950 to 1963, the year Eddie Lee Mays became the last person executed in New York State as of 2003.

1965–2003

Finally, in 1965, in the midst of a flurry of anti-death penalty legislative activity in several states, New York abolished capital punishment except for the murder of a police officer or a murder committed by a prisoner serving a life sentence. Even these remnants of the death penalty were in effect abolished soon after by the US Supreme Court, which in 1972 declared every state's capital sentencing scheme unconstitutional. Most states immediately reestablished capital punishment according to new procedures approved by the Supreme Court in 1976, but New York was not one of them. Bills that would have reintroduced the death penalty were passed by the legislature every year between 1977 and 1994, but all were vetoed by the governor. In the latter year George E. Pataki defeated Mario M. Cuomo in the gubernatorial election, after a campaign in which Pataki declared his support for capital punishment. In 1995, in the very first statute of the Pataki administration, capital punishment returned. Execution is to be by lethal injection, in Clinton Correctional Facility in Dannemora (Clinton Co). As of April 2003, five men had been sentenced to death, though none had yet been executed.

Banner, Stuart. *The Death Penalty: An American History* (Cambridge, Mass: Harvard Univ Press, 2002)
Hearn, Daniel Allen. *Legal Executions in New York State: A Comprehensive Reference, 1639–1963* (Jefferson, NC: McFarland, 1997)
Mackey, Philip English. *Hanging in the Balance: The Anti-Capital Punishment Movement in New York State, 1776–1861* (New York: Garland Publishing, 1982)

Stuart A. Banner

Carborundum Company. Western New York State manufacturer of silicon carbide, or carborundum. Edward G. Acheson founded the company in 1891 in Monongahela City, Pa. In an 1890 experiment, Acheson had discovered silicon carbide, a crystalline substance that was extremely hard, sharp, and refractory. An ideal abrasive, silicon carbide was initially used in whetstones and grinding wheels but later in other capacities such as heating elements. With large amounts of electricity required to make silicon carbide, in 1895 Acheson sited his first plant on a 4-acre (1.6 ha) plot in Niagara Falls, approximately .5 mi (.8 km) from Niagara Falls Power Co. The company eventually had five plants in Erie, Chautauqua, and Niagara Cos, and its Niagara plant employed more than 3,000 workers and produced more than 5,000 tons (4,500 MT) of silicon carbide annually. Independent until 1977, Carborundum Co was acquired by a succession of companies before its purchased by St. Gobain Industrial Ceramics, headquartered in France, in 1996.

Dubpernell, George, and J. H. Westbrook, eds. *Symposium on Selected Topics in the History of Electrochemistry, 1977, Philadelphia, Pa* (Princeton, NJ: Electrochemical Society, 1978)

Jack Westbrook

Cardiff Giant. A well-orchestrated scheme that evolved into a huge archaeological hoax. After an argument with an Iowa minister in 1866 over the literal interpretation of biblical passages in the Book of Genesis referring to giants, George Hull, a cigar maker from Binghamton, devised a plan to fool the public and make money. While on a trip to Fort Dodge, Iowa, in 1868, Hull purchased a 5-ton (4.5 MT) block of gypsum and

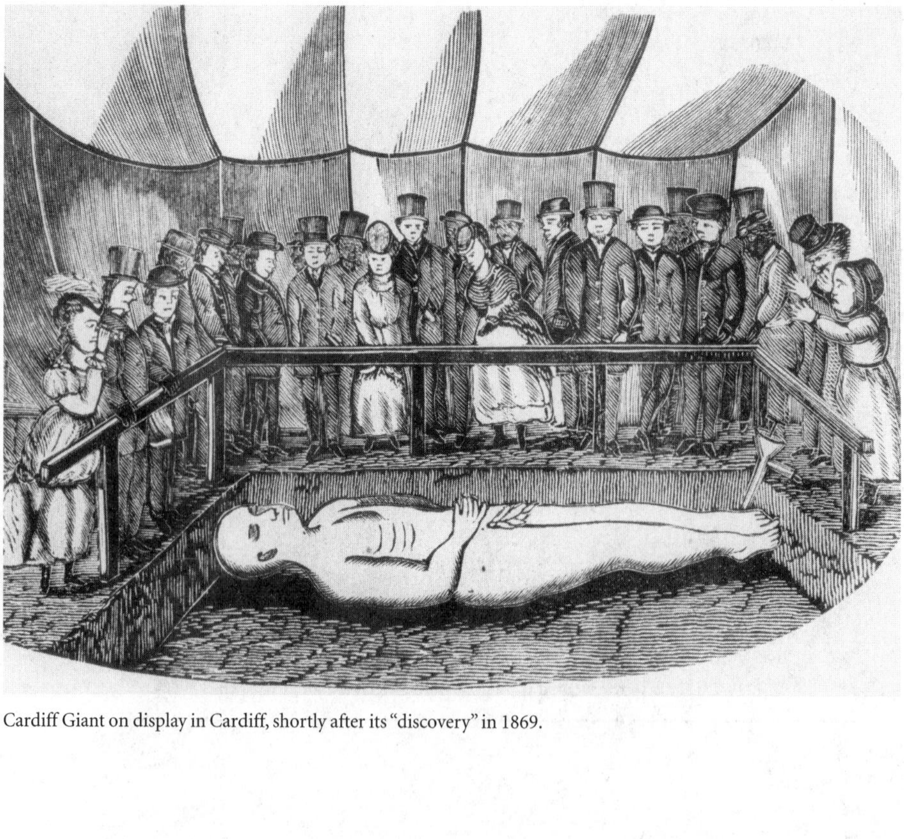

Cardiff Giant on display in Cardiff, shortly after its "discovery" in 1869.

sent it to a Chicago stonecutter, Edward Burghardt, who used Hull as a model to carve a figure 10 feet (3 m) tall and weighing over 3,000 pounds (1,400 kg). The giant was buried in Cardiff (Onondaga Co) on the farm of Abe "Stub" Newell, Hull's brother-in-law, and remained there until 16 Oct 1869 when it was unearthed during the digging of a well. A tent was erected over the site, and hundreds of people each paid 50¢ to see the giant. On 5 Nov the giant was moved to Syracuse, where the New York Central Railroad set up a stop to accommodate the large crowds. Controversy about the origin of the giant was immediate, with theories ranging from a petrified aboriginal being, to a statue carved by Jesuit priests, to a fraud. Exposure of the hoax began in November when reporters questioned the activities of Hull and Newell, and in December Hull admitted the ruse. Interest in the giant gradually dwindled. In 1901 it was exhibited at the Pan-American Exposition in Buffalo and from 1913 through the 1930s was displayed at fairs in New York State and Iowa. The New York State Historical Association purchased the Cardiff Giant in 1947. It remains on display at the Farmers' Museum in Cooperstown (Otsego Co).

Ross, Irwin. "The Cardiff Giant Hoax," *American History Illustrated* 3 (Aug 1968): 38–41

Mary E. Gabriel

Cardozo, Benjamin N(athan) (*b* New York City, 24 May 1870; *d* Port Chester, Westchester Co, 9 July 1938). New York State Court of Appeals judge and US Supreme Court justice. In 1871 the Association of the Bar of the City of New York charged his father, Albert Cardozo, a justice of the New York State Supreme Court and a Tammany Hall stalwart implicated in the Tweed Ring scandal, with corruption. In 1872 Albert, a Sephardic Jew, resigned his judgeship to avoid impeachment. Benjamin was tutored at home, and one of his instructors was Horatio Alger Jr, author of the popular rags-to-riches stories for boys. After Albert Cardozo's death in 1885, Benjamin lived with his older sister Ellen until her death in 1929.

He attended Columbia University (1885–89) and Columbia University Law School (1889–91), was admitted to the bar in 1891, and joined his brother's law firm, where he practiced commercial law until 1913. He successfully ran as an anti-Tammany Democrat for a seat on the New York State Supreme Court in 1913. Less than a month after Cardozo took office, Gov Martin H. Glynn appointed him to a three-year term on the New York State Court of Appeals, the first Jew to sit on that court. Cardozo soon distinguished himself with important decisions such as *MacPherson v Buick Motor Co* (1916), a ruling that made car manufacturers responsible for the safety of their vehicles. In 1917 he won election to an additional 14-year term, during which he would write more than 500 opinions.

In 1927 he was elected chief judge of the New York State Court of Appeals, where he issued further landmark decisions, among them *Palsgraf v Long Island Railroad* (1928). In this case, Cardozo reformulated negligence law, ruling that companies could not be held liable for accidents resulting from unforeseeable hazards. He was a member of the Committee on the Establishment of a Permanent Organization for the Improvement of the Law in 1922–23 and helped to found the American Law Institute (ALI) in 1923.

In 1932 Pres Herbert Hoover appointed him to the US Supreme Court, where he voted, at first in the minority, to uphold much New Deal legislation and served until his death. Cardozo was a trustee of Columbia University (1928–38) and a board member of both the American Jewish Committee (1929–32) and the Zionist Organization of America (1918–32). His views on the relation of law to social change (often termed sociological jurisprudence), expressed not only in his opinions but in books such as *The Nature of the Judicial Process* (1921) and *The Growth of the Law* (1927), made him one of the most influential US judges in the first half of the 20th century.

Kaufman, Andrew L. *Cardozo* (Cambridge, Mass: Harvard Univ Press, 1998)

Polenberg, Richard. *The World of Benjamin Cardozo: Personal Values and the Judicial Process* (Cambridge, Mass: Harvard Univ Press, 1999)

Jeffrey Kraus

Carey, Hugh (Leo) (*b* Brooklyn, 11 Apr 1919). Governor. Enlisting in the National Guard, Carey saw active service in World War II and reached the rank of colonel. He received his law degree from St. John's University Law School, passed the bar in 1951, and entered private practice. Elected to Congress as a Democrat in 1960, Carey took the seat of a four-term incumbent in a district that had been designed as Brooklyn's Republican stronghold. Carey, with liberal leanings and an Irish working-class support base, was reelected six times by increasingly comfortable margins.

Assigned to the House Education and Labor Committee, he was considered the architect of the Elementary and Secondary Education Act of 1965. Carey also demonstrated a strong interest in legislation to benefit people with mental illnesses or disabilities, which was to continue throughout his public career. Shifting to the Ways and Means Committee in 1971, he became a strong advocate of federal revenue sharing and, unsuccessfully, of more tax breaks for the parents of children attending parochial schools.

Originally a proponent of American involvement in Vietnam, Carey became increasingly critical of the US military presence there in the mid-1960s. He ran for president of the New York City Council in 1969, finishing a close second in a multicandidate Democratic primary. In 1974 he was overwhelmingly elected governor with the third largest plurality in state history to that point; he was reelected in 1978. The first of his many crises was a judgment in the case of the Willowbrook Developmental Center on Staten Island, which forced the state to undertake a complete and rapid reorientation of the nature, scope, and funding of its care of people with developmental disabilities or mental illnesses. The second was the fiscal crisis in New York City in spring 1975. Carey took the lead in marshaling the business community, organized labor, the state and city administrations, the state legislature, and even the federal government behind the comprehensive, but often fragile, rescue and rehabilitation program. His personal ability to bring together widely disparate coalitions for drastic and often controversial measures and to win bipartisan support for the structural and fiscal reforms was significant in bringing about economic recovery. Gov Carey played a key role in resolving the Love Canal chemical landfill crisis, which surfaced in western New York State in 1978. He inaugurated the I Love New York program, instituted the Empire State Games, and established the Conference of Northeast Governors (CONEG). Carey married Helen Owen Twohy on 27 Feb 1947; they had 14 children. Helen Carey died in March 1974 on the eve of his first campaign for governor. In 1983 Hugh Carey returned to the practice of law.

See also DEINDUSTRIALIZATION; EXECUTIVE BRANCH.

Kramer, Daniel C. *The Days of Wine and Roses Are Over: Governor Hugh Carey and New York State* (New York: Univ Press of America, 1997)

Robert P. Kerker

Carle Place. Locality (pop 5,247) in North Hempstead (Nassau Co). Named after a 19th-century estate, it was renamed Mineola Park after a real estate development begun in 1895, but the post office (1916) and railroad station (1923) resumed the original name. Most of the area was in small farms where Irish, German, and Polish farmers raised potatoes. William J. Levitt began a housing development in 1946, and its population increased from 991 in 1940 to 5,625 in 1960. It is a comfortable middle-class locality with extensive commercial development along Old Country and Glen Cove Rds in the last decades of the 20th century.

Richard A. Winsche

Carleton, Guy [Baron Dorchester] (*b* Strabane, Ireland, 3 Sept 1724; *d* Berkshire Co, England, 10 Nov 1808). Governor of Quebec and British army officer. Carleton arrived in North America during the French and Indian War with Maj Gen James Wolfe for the 1759 expedition against Quebec. He was appointed lieutenant governor of the new British possession on 7 Apr 1766 and governor on 12 Apr 1768. One of his first duties was to meet with New York Colony governor Sir Henry Moore and establish an equitable boundary line between the two provinces. He was able to prevent the fall of Quebec City during the American invasion of Canada in 1775–76 but failed to crush the attacking army during its retreat. After leading a counterinvasion into New York in the fall of 1776, Carleton withdrew into winter quarters shortly after the Battle of Valcour Island on Lake Champlain on 11 Oct 1776. He was passed over for command of the invasion the following year, in favor of Lt Gen John Burgoyne. Carleton resigned his office of governor on 27 June 1777. He later replaced Sir Henry Clinton as commander in chief of British land forces in North America on 2 Mar 1782 and oversaw the evacuation of British supporters from New York City following the armistice. In April 1786 Carleton received simultaneous commissions as governor of Quebec, Nova Scotia, and New Brunswick. He returned to England with his family from 1791 to 1793 but retained his position as governor. Returning briefly, he retired and left Canada permanently in July 1796.

Dictionary of Canadian Biography, sv "Carleton, Guy, 1st Baron Dorchester"

Alexander V. Campbell

Carlisle. Town (pop 1,758) in N Schoharie Co. Settled by Palatine Germans in 1760 and then by

New Englanders, the town was formed from Cobleskill and Sharon in 1807. It lies on a high ridge, a massive limestone karst formation, separating the Mohawk and Cobleskill Valleys. Through much of the 19th century Carlisle Foundry (1846) produced plows. Grove Seminary (1853–*ca* 1865) was a boarding school for 300 students. Agriculture is the major economic activity in the early 21st century, but where hops were once cultivated, dairies, livestock, organic vegetables, and maple syrup dominate.

Peter Johnson and Dawn Johnson

Carlisle, Floyd Leslie (*b* Watertown, Jefferson Co, 5 Mar 1881; *d* Glen Cove, Nassau Co, 9 Nov 1942). Paper and utility executive. Attending Watertown public schools, Carlisle went on to Cornell University, where he graduated with a BA in 1903, then read law at a Watertown law firm, and in 1905 was admitted to the New York State Bar. In 1916 he and other businessmen bought the locally based St. Regis Paper Co, where he served as president from 1916 to 1934 and as board chairman from 1934 to 1942. At St. Regis he was instrumental in ending acrimonious relations between labor and management and in initiating a large forest-replanting program, making the company a conservation leader within the industry. In 1926 he transformed it into a utility named Northeastern Power Corp, providing electricity to most of the North Country. In 1929 Carlisle was the leading architect in merging Northeastern with other state utilities to form Niagara Hudson Power Corp, for which Carlisle served as board chairman from 1929 to 1942. By now Carlisle was one of America's most influential utility executives. In 1930 he was appointed director of New York Edison Co. Carlisle's penchant for deal making led to his biggest merger ever, when in three separate moves between 1936 and 1937 he merged New York Edison with five separate New York metropolitan region utilities, forming Consolidated Edison (Con Edison), a public utility monopoly providing gas and electrical service to New York City and Westchester Co at significantly reduced rates. Carlisle served as chief executive of Con Edison.

Throughout his career Carlisle was a strong proponent of the holding company setup that dominated the structure of public utilities. The notorious practices of many of these firms, with misleading financial statements and creative bookkeeping, however, led to calls during the New Deal for their abolition. To avert government action, Carlisle formed the Edison Electric Institute, a trade group that championed straightforward business practices. He and other utility industry figures can be widely credited with helping thwart significant federal intervention into the utility sector. Although the federal government enacted the Public Utility Holding Co Act in 1935, actions by Carlisle and others led to substantially weaker legislation than originally outlined. The act did not ban all holding firms, for example, but banned only certain types, leaving the rest to operate under greater regulatory oversight. By 1942, in Carlisle's capacities as Niagara Hudson's board chairman and Con Edison's chief executive, he oversaw the production and distribution of 75% of all the electricity in New York State. The two firms were the world's largest electrical utilities at the time.

"Floyd Carlisle Dies," *Around The System: Published Monthly for Employees of Consolidated Edison System Companies*, December 1942

William S. Pretzer

Carlson, Chester F(loyd) (*b* Seattle, Wash, 8 Feb 1906; *d* New York City, 19 Sept 1968). Inventor. After graduating from the California Institute of Technology in 1930, he joined Bell Laboratories in New York City. He began as a research engineer but soon transferred to the patent department. Laid off in 1933, he worked with patent attorneys processing applications and earned a law degree from New York Law School in 1939. His experience in preparing patents led him to search for a mechanical method of making quick, dry copies of documents. He conducted experiments in his apartment in Jackson Heights (Queens Co). With Otto Kornei, a physicist who had fled the Nazi regime in Germany, he set up a laboratory behind his mother-in-law's beauty shop in Astoria (Queens Co). On 22 Oct 1938 they produced the first electrostatic image. In 1942 Carlson received a US patent for the process he called electrophotography. He had considerable difficulties convincing potential investors of the commercial viability of his invention and finally entered into a royalty sharing agreement with Battelle Memorial Institute of Columbus, Ohio, in 1944. Battelle later licensed its rights to the Haloid Co of Rochester. In 1948 Carlson moved to Rochester to oversee development of Haloid's photocopier, demonstrated publicly on 22 October of that year under the trade name Xerox. Eventually he realized $150 million in royalties from his original patent and others related to the process. His generous philanthropy is reflected in the University of Rochester's Carlson Science and Engineering Library and the Rochester Institute of Technology's Chester F. Carlson Center for Imaging Science, both named posthumously. Carlson had an interest in Eastern spirituality and supported the establishment of the New York Zendo in New York City and of the Dai Bosatsu Zendo in Livingston Manor (Sullivan Co).

Dinsdale, Alfred. "Chester Carlson, Inventor of Xerography: A Biography," *Photographic Science and Engineering* 7 (1963): 1–4

Hall, Dennis G., and Rita M. Hall. "Chester F. Carlson: A Man to Remember," *Optics and Photonics News*, Sept 2000

Laura Zelasnic

Carlton. Town (pop 2,960) in N Orleans Co. The first settlement in the county was made at Manilla on the east side of Oak Orchard Creek's mouth in 1803. The town was formed from Gaines and Ridgeway in 1822 as Oak Orchard; the name was changed in 1825. As early as 1804 residents manufactured ladles, bowls, and rolling pins to market in Canada. The town was served by the Rome, Watertown and Ogdensburg Railroad (1876; called the Hojack). By 1883 Oak Orchard-on-the-Lake was the site of cottages and hotels. Carlton became a fruit-growing town with both dry houses and cold storage and in the early 20th century had what was thought to be the world's largest quince orchard. Lakeside Beach State Park (1968) was one of the motivations for the Lake Ontario State Parkway (1970) and draws Rochesterians for summer recreation. By 1980 the town had become known for salmon and trout fishing. A number of cobblestone houses are landmarks. George Coles Stebbins (1846–1945), composer of the hymn "There Is a Green Hill Far Away" was a native.

Lysbeth Hoffman

Carmel. Town (pop 33,006) in central Putnam Co. The town was formed in 1795 from part of the old town of Frederickstown. It was selected as the seat of the new county in 1812; the first courthouse (1814) remains in active use. Financier Daniel Drew (1797–1879), a Carmel native, funded Drew Seminary (1850–1952) for girls; its site is now the headquarters of *Guideposts* magazine. In 1881 the New York and Northern Railroad (later Putnam Division of New York Central Railroad) reached the hamlet. New York City incorporated the hamlet's Lake Gleneida into its reservoir system in 1893, requiring the relocation of all lakeshore structures. From 1950 to 2000, subdivisions increased Carmel's population fivefold and transformed it into a bedroom suburb. Carmel was the home of Enoch Crosby (1750–1835), said to be the inspiration for Harvey Birch in James Fenimore Cooper's *The Spy*. Anna Hyatt Huntington's equestrian bronze of Sybil Ludington (1961) stands on the lakeshore.

Sallie S. Sypher

Carmer, Carl (Lamson) (*b* Cortland, 16 Oct 1893; *d* Bronxville, Westchester Co, 11 Sept 1976). Folklorist and writer. Schooled in Albion (Orleans Co), where he grew up, Carmer graduated from Hamilton College in 1914. After earning an MA in English literature from Harvard University the following year, he began a teaching career that involved stints at Syracuse University, the University of Rochester, Hamilton, and the University of Alabama. He also served as an artillery officer during World War I. Carmer left education for journalism in 1927, moving to New York City a year later as an assistant editor at *Vanity Fair* magazine. He became associate editor of *Theatre Arts Monthly* in 1929 and began publishing poetry. A poetic sensibility would continue to be reflected in his prose work, to which he dedicated himself full-time beginning in 1933. The initial result was *Stars Fell on Alabama* (1934), based on folklore he had collected while in the southern United States. The book became a best-seller, encouraging him to focus on the folkways of his "real home country," central and western New York, which he liked to call "York State." His many works on state themes include three notable collections of stories and lore, *Listen for a Lonesome Drum* (1936), *Dark Trees to the Wind* (1949), and *My Kind of Country* (1966); a historical novel, *Genesee Fever* (1941); and an account of the New York State years of Joseph Smith Jr, *The Farm Boy and the Angel* (1970). He served as one of the principal editors for the acclaimed 65-volume Rivers of America anthology series, writing *The Hudson* (1939) and *The Susquehanna* (1955), and editing *Songs of the Rivers of America* (1942). In the mid-1940s Carmer moved into the architecturally significant Octagon House in Irvington-on-Hudson (Westchester Co). He also edited an anthology of upstate literature *The Tavern Lamps Are Burning* (1964) and wrote many books for young readers with his wife, Elizabeth, including a book on the antirent wars, *Rebellion at Quaker Hill* (1954). A committed environmentalist and adoptive member of the Seneca Nation, Carmer is best remembered as a master storyteller whose engaging, conversational prose style belied the depth of research underlying his work.

"Carmer, Carl Lamson." In *World Authors, 1900–1950*, ed. Martin Seymour-Smith and Andrew C. Kimmens, vol 1 (New York: H. W. Wilson, 1996)

Frank K. Lorenz

Carnegie Hall. Music hall on the southeast corner of 57th St and 7th Ave in New York City. Its doors opened on 5 May 1891 with composer Peter Tchaikovsky conducting a five-day music festival of his own works. The structure was designed by architect William B. Tuthill with the consulting firm Adler and Sullivan, and was built by Isaac A. Hopper and Co. Conductor Walter Damrosch convinced industrialist Andrew Carnegie to underwrite its $1 million cost, and in 1894 it was officially renamed Carnegie Hall. With warm acoustics and favorable sight lines it became New York City's premier concert venue and was home of the New York Philharmonic and its predecessor organizations from its opening until 1962. Among the best-known compositions receiving a world premier there were Antonín Dvořák's symphony *From the New World* (1893) and George Gershwin's *An American in Paris* (1928). To play in Carnegie Hall—especially after the spectacular American debuts of violinist Jascha Heifetz (1917) and pianist Vladimir Horowitz (1927)—became an ambition of most performing artists. A nondiscriminatory seating and performing policy helped it become an important venue for jazz and other forms of popular music. Notable concerts featured James Reese Europe (1912), Benny Goodman (1938), and the New York premier of Duke Ellington's *Black, Brown, and Beige* (1943). Its favorable acoustics made the hall a platform for thousands of nonmusical events as well as appearances by important politicians, civic and religious leaders, scientists, comedians, authors, and dancers. To generate additional income for the building, two towers, designed by Henry J. Hardenbergh, were constructed in 1894 and 1896–97 and contained 150 studio offices and residences. After Carnegie's death the ownership of Carnegie Hall passed from him to his wife, Louise, who sold it to real estate developer Robert E. Simon in 1924. The announcement in 1955 of plans for the Lincoln Center for the Performing Arts put Carnegie Hall dangerously close to demolition; the property was sold and a skyscraper was designed to be built on its site. Carnegie Hall was saved by a coalition of musicians, politicians, and civic figures, led by violinist Isaac Stern, and the City of New York purchased it in 1960. It became a registered National Landmark in 1964.

The building contains four public performance spaces: the Main Hall, known since 1997 as the Isaac Stern Auditorium, seating 2,804; the Chamber Music Hall, renamed the Carnegie Recital Hall in 1898 and the Joan and Sanford I. Weill Recital Hall in 1986, seating 268; the Chapter Hall, used for lectures, meetings, and religious services, renamed the Alice and Jacob Kaplan Space in 1985; and the Recital Hall, which became the Carnegie Lyceum in 1898, the Carnegie Playhouse in 1960, the Carnegie Hall Cinema in 1970, and the Judy and Arthur Zankel Hall in 2003. In 1986 the hall established its first archives.

Schickel, Richard. *The World of Carnegie Hall* (1960; repr Westport, Conn: Greenwood, 1973)
Walsh, Michael, and Richard Schickel. *Carnegie Hall: The First 100 Years* (New York: Abrams, 1987)

Gino Francesconi

Carnegie libraries. A dedicated philanthropist, the Scottish-born steel magnate Andrew Carnegie spent over $56 million on the construction of over 2,500 public libraries throughout the English-speaking world between 1886 and 1919. Of these approximately 1,680 stood in the United States, 107 of which were built in New York State; only Indiana (164) and California (142) exceeded that total. Academic libraries received funds from Carnegie as well, resulting in the construction of 108 US college libraries, including those at Alfred (Allegany Co) and Syracuse Universities, and Wells College in Aurora (Cayuga Co).

An advocate for the concept of the stewardship of wealth, Carnegie was convinced that he had a responsibility to use his riches for the public good but also was anxious about the pauperizing effect of indiscriminate charity. Thus he settled on libraries as the best way "to help those who will help themselves," as he stated in an essay entitled "Wealth" in *North American Review* (June 1889). Initially Carnegie followed a paternalistic pattern of giving, financing elaborate multipurpose cultural institutions in Pennsylvania communities where he had personal or business connections. In 1901, however, Carnegie's library philanthropy entered a new phase, when he offered an unprecedented $5.2 million to New York City to finance the construction of 65 local branch libraries (67 branches were eventually built). At the same time Carnegie began to accept applications from any community that would provide a site and an annual library maintenance fund equal to 10% of the initial construction grant. In New York State many communities took advantage of Carnegie's offer. Particular areas of concentration were along the Hudson River; around Buffalo, where Lackawanna (Erie Co) was the last New York State town to secure a Carnegie grant of $30,000 in May 1917; around Syracuse, which received $200,000 in 1901, the largest Carnegie grant for a single building in New York State; and in the Southern Tier, where Franklinville (Cattaraugus Co) received only $2,200, one of the four smallest Carnegie library grants in the United States. In 1911 Carnegie established the Carnegie Corp of New York (CCNY) to oversee the program. Although the CCNY still exists, it has not made new grants for public library buildings since 1919.

The Carnegie program helped revolutionize American public library architecture, particularly in giving readers free access to the bookshelves and in devoting substantial space to children's use. In Manhattan three firms oversaw in that borough the design of 41 Carnegie-financed branches: McKim, Mead and White; Carrère and Hastings; and Babb, Cook, and Willard. Aiming at a uniformity that would identify these buildings as libraries, the architects modeled each on the Italian Renaissance palazzo. Each branch was three or four bays wide with an end bay devoted to the stairs leading to the building's upper stories. Although readers had direct access to the books, their movements were controlled by large circulation desks that created narrow passages and required them to exit the library single file, past a librarian's watchful eye.

In other parts of New York State, Carnegie libraries stood on open lots and followed the single-story arrangement preferred by professional librarians, taking on an architectural form that became closely associated with the Carnegie name throughout the country. In these open-plan buildings, a single librarian supervised the entire library from a centrally located delivery desk, while readers fetched their own books from shelves lining perimeter walls. Architects who marketed themselves as specialists in Carnegie library design rendered most of these libraries in a restrained Classicism. Among the New York City–based architects who designed Carnegie libraries in the state were Edward L. Tilton at Olean (Cattaraugus Co), Mount Vernon, and Ossining (Westchester Co), and Albert Randolph Ross at Gloversville (Fulton Co), New Rochelle (Westchester Co), Penn Yan (Yates Co), and Port Jervis (Orange Co). With the donor's encouragement, many Carnegie libraries included basement lecture rooms, which allowed these buildings to serve as multipurpose community centers. In the late 20th century, approximately 60% of New York State's Carnegie-financed buildings were still in use as community-oriented public libraries.

Van Slyck, Abigail A. *Free to All: Carnegie Libraries and American Culture, 1890–1917* (Chicago: Univ of Chicago Press, 1995)

Abigail A. Van Slyck

carnivores. At the time of European contact in the early 17th century, the area that is now New York State was home to a large number of carnivores. The largest of these was the black bear *(Ursus americanus)*, which continues to thrive into the early 21st century with about 5,000 in the Adirondacks, 700 in the Catskills, and 200 in wooded sections of western New York State. At least three species of the family Canidae—the gray wolf *(Canis lupus)*, red fox *(Vulpes fulva)*, and gray fox *(Urocyon cinereoargentus)*—once inhabited the state as well. The first of these was exterminated in the 1890s. In 1999 plans were made to reintroduce the gray wolf. Both species of foxes survive, and their ranges extend throughout the state.

It has been suggested that coyotes *(Canis latrans)*, which are spreading rapidly in the 21st century, were also native to the state, but most authorities view them as recent arrivals. They are abundant in the north but are also found everywhere in the state except New York City and Long Island. Into the 19th century the Felidae, or cats, were represented by the mountain lion *(Felis concolor)*, lynx *(Lynx canadensis)*, and bob-

Nighttime photograph of a coyote in the Adirondacks.

cat *(Lynx rufus)*. Only the last of these species survived into the 20th century in New York State. In the early 1990s efforts to reintroduce the lynx resulted in the release of over 100 in the Adirondacks, but a viable population failed to establish itself. The raccoon *(Procyon lotor)* has thrived in contact with humans in rural, urban, and suburban environments, though occasionally representing a serious rabies hazard: a 1993 study indicated that 53% of tested raccoons carried the disease, and in 2000, 32% of tested raccoons showed positive for rabies. The Mustelidae, or weasel family, remains well represented by the fisher *(Martes pennanti)*, striped skunk *(Mephitis mephitis)*, mink *(Mustela vison)*, ermine *(Mustela erminea)*, long-tailed weasel *(Mustela frenata)*, and river otter *(Lutra canadensis)*. The last, which survives in the Adirondacks and the Catskills, was largely extirpated elsewhere in the state, where it is the subject of reintroduction efforts.

Davis, Mary Bird, ed. *Eastern Old Growth Forests: Prospects for Rediscovery and Recovery* (Washington, DC: Island Press, 1996)
New York Conservationist (1946–)

Brad Coon

Caroga. Town (pop 1,407) in N central Fulton Co. Settled ?1783, the town was formed in 1842 from Johnstown, Stratford, and Bleecker. The land is not suitable for farming, and settlers worked at lumbering or tanning. Nick Stoner (?1762–1853), a legendary Adirondack frontiersman, lived in Caroga beginning around 1802. The Wheeler-Claflin Co bought 20,000 acres (8,094 ha) in 1865, about two-thirds of the town, and built a large tannery at Wheelerville and a number of sawmills. The tannery closed in 1888, but the firm continued harvesting timber for some years. The first large resort hotel was the Canada Lake House (1868). In the 1880s the lakes began to attract summer residents, including urban industrialists and, by the 1900s, a number of New York City artists, illustrators, and celebrities, including illustrator Paul Bransom and watercolorist Charles Sarka. Sherman's Arcade (1921) is an amusement park on West Caroga Lake, and the town's population swells to over 7,000 in August. Royal Mountain Ski Area (1955) draws winter sports enthusiasts.

James Crawford

Caroline. Town (pop 2,910) in SE Tompkins Co. Settled in 1795, the town was formed from Spencer (Tioga Co) in 1811 and was taken from Tioga Co in 1823. Four families from Virginia and Maryland settled in 1805, bringing with them 32 enslaved African Americans. The Ithaca and Owego Railroad (1834) skirted the west edge of town, but the Utica, Ithaca and Elmira Railroad (1872–75, after 1905 the Lehigh Valley Railroad) provided more accessible service. Mineral water was discovered at Slaterville Springs in 1871, and two hotels were constructed. Industries in Brooktondale hamlet included a gun shop, a furniture factory, and two woolen mills. Dairying developed after the Civil War, but over 7,000 acres (2,800 ha) of marginal farmland were reforested by Civilian Conservation Corps campers (1933–41). Rte 79, once part of the Catskill Turnpike (1804), is the link between Ithaca and major highways to large East Coast cities and serves many of the town's commuting residents.

Jane Dieckmann

***Caroline* Affair and the Canadian Rebellion of 1837.** In 1837 William Lyon Mackenzie led a rebel force seeking the independence of Upper Canada [now Ont] from British colonial rule. After British authorities crushed the rebellion in December, Mackenzie fled to the United States, where he found a receptive audience in Buffalo. With the help of Rensselaer Van Rensselaer and a small group of American volunteers, he seized Navy Island, on the British side of the Niagara River, as a base of operations in mid-December. Sympathizers leased the steamboat *Caroline* from Buffalo to ship arms, ammunition, and supplies from the Town of Niagara to the men on Navy Island.

British authorities organized the Canadian militia, under the command of Andrew Drew, to attack the invasion force at Navy Island. Scrapping plans to seize the *Caroline* in Canadian waters, Drew decided to follow the vessel to the American side on 29 Dec 1837. In the ensuing melee one American was killed, and several on both sides were wounded. The Canadians seized the *Caroline* and set it on fire on the Niagara River, where it sank. The American and Canadian rebels, beset by internal divisions and having lost their supply vessel, withdrew from Navy Island on 14 Jan 1838. Pres Martin Van Buren sent Maj Gen Winfield Scott to enforce American neutrality laws, and Scott arranged for the departure of the rebels from Canadian soil. Simultaneously, Van Buren requested that neutrality legislation be revised and that the British pay reparations, and he formally protested the invasion of American territory. The British argued that they had practiced legitimate self-defense in curbing treason and that the *Caroline*'s supplying arms to rebels amounted to piracy, allowing the British to attack the vessel under international law. Both governments, however, wanted to downplay the diplomatic incident and restore friendly relations.

New York State supporters of the Canadian Rebellion made their own foreign policy when they organized the Canadian Refugee Relief Association at Lockport (Niagara Co) on 19 Mar 1838. This spawned secret societies of "Patriot Hunters," who invaded Canada between 1838 and 1842. Van Buren instructed New York's governor William L. Marcy and Maj Gen Alexander Macomb, commander of the US Army, to stop the raids. Then, on 12 Nov 1840, Canadian Alexander McLeod was arrested in Lewiston (Niagara Co) for participation in the burning of the *Caroline*. Van Buren left the matter to local courts, and the British threatened retaliation if McLeod were found guilty. Crisis was averted when a Utica jury found him not guilty on 21 Oct 1841 and released him. The British government, as part of the Webster-Ashburton Treaty of 1842, made an indirect apology for the *Caroline* attack, and the United States agreed that the British had acted in self-defense, abandoning the American claim for reparations.

Corey, Albert. *The Crisis of 1830–1842 in Canadian-American Relations* (New Haven, Conn: Yale Univ Press, 1941)
Ireland, John. "Andrew Drew: The Man Who Burned the *Caroline*," *Ontario History* 59 (Sept 1967): 137–56

Harvey Strum

carousels. The merry-go-round, or carousel, originated in 17th-century France, where knights training for lavish tournaments called "carrousels" rode carved wooden horses that revolved around a center pole. They practiced for spearing contests by lancing rings as they rode, and these devices also became known as "carrousels." In the mid–19th century, French and German artisans created magnificent carved wooden carousels as amusement park rides for children. Some of the artisans immigrated to the United States and began making carousels in New York City and Philadelphia.

After 1870 the application of steam power allowed bigger and better devices, including deco-

Merry-go-round in Children's World at the 1939 World's Fair, New York City. Photograph by Carl Van Vechten, 4 July 1939.

rative panels and band organ musical accompaniment. A number of early carousels appeared at Coney Island in Brooklyn. Notable designers included Charles I. D. Looff, who arrived from Europe in 1870 and whose factory operated in Greenpoint in Brooklyn from 1880 to 1905. Trained as a furniture maker, he built his first carousel from spare parts around 1876 for Balmer's Bathing Pavilion; it was the first carousel at Coney Island. Looff's Coney Island–style carousels featured carved horses elaborately adorned with painted jewels and gold leaf. The oldest surviving American carousel, the Flying Horses, was made by Charles W. F. Dare of Brooklyn in 1876. It was used for two years at Coney Island before being moved to Oak Bluffs at Martha's Vineyard, Mass, where it is now restored and operated as a National Historic Landmark. Marcus Charles Illions, born in Russia, came to the United States around 1888 and carved horses at Coney Island for William F. Mangels, who later entered partnership with carver Charles Carmel. In 1909 Illions opened his own factory nearby.

Allan Herschell, a native of Scotland, built a steam-powered carousel in 1882 for his firm, the Armitage-Herschell Co in North Tonawanda (Niagara Co). This was the first American carousel manufacturer to make its own barrel organs instead of importing them from Europe. By 1891 Herschell was turning out 100 carousels a year and had traveled to India looking for export trade. Domestic demand continued, but heavy land investments and a depressed real estate market caused the company to collapse in 1899. Herschell and his brother-in-law, Ed Spillman, formed a new company, Herschell-Spillman, which soon became the world's largest manufacturer of outdoor amusements and survived under various names until 1945. Spillman made park carousels that were 50 feet (15.2 m) in diameter with carved horses three and four abreast. His company also produced portable carousels, with horses two and three abreast, that could be put up and taken down in one day and moved to the next town. The brothers-in-law split up, and the Allan Herschell Co, founded in 1915, produced over 3,000 hand-carved wooden merry-go-rounds, more than any other manufacturer. The North Tonawanda factory site, now the Herschell Carrousel Factory Museum, boasts the restored 1916 No. 1 Special, featuring a chariot with seated lady and a lovers' tub.

In 2000 there were at least 28 carousels existing in New York State, including a dozen built by Herschell and his partners, several by Mangels, Carmel, and Illions, and a 1905 Gustave Dentzel carousel at Ontario Beach Park in Rochester. The oldest known working carousel in the state is an Armitage-Herschell portable model, which was probably made in the 1890s and has been located since the 1920s at the Church of the Assumption in Redford (Clinton Co). It uses sleighs for chariots and has musical accompaniment provided by a truck-mounted calliope.

The first carousel in New York City's Central Park opened in 1872, turned by a mule and a blind horse. The present large carousel, built in 1908 by Solomon Stein and Harry Goldstein and first used at Coney Island, has been operating on the site since 1951 and still uses its original Ruth Sohn band organ playing 150 Wurlitzer music rolls. George F. Johnson, president of Endicott Johnson Shoes, donated six carousels to Broome Co parks on the condition that rides would always remain free. The merry-go-round at Syracuse's Carousel Center mall, refurbished during the 1920s, was restored in 1990 to its original 1909 style. Seabreeze Amusement Park in Rochester operates a 1914 carousel rebuilt in 1996 after a fire, featuring realistic detailed paintwork. A 1918 Herschell portable model at Rochester's Strong Museum was restored to service in 1995. A 1907 carousel featuring a famous pair of lovers' chariots is at the Palisades Center mall in West Nyack (Rockland Co). The Heckscher Carousel, made around 1920 by Illions and restored in the 1980s, has operated at Hempstead Lake Park in West Hempstead (Nassau Co) since 1931. Rye Playland Park in Rye (Westchester Co) has two carousels, including one of only two surviving 1920s Racing Derby machines in the United States. The New York State Museum carousel at Albany was restored to operation in 2001 together with an original Wurlitzer band organ. Built at the Herschell-Spillman factory *ca* 1915 and featuring horses carved by Dare in the 1890s, it may be one of the largest traveling carousels ever made, with 40 horses, chariots, and a lovers' tub. The Stadel brothers of Wellsville (Allegany Co) moved it by train throughout the Southern Tier and Pennsylvania until 1929 and then to Olcott Beach (Niagara Co). It was the main attraction at Olivecrest Park on Cuba Lake (Allegany Co) from 1933 to 1972, when it was acquired by the museum.

The Empire State Carousel, opened in 2003 in Brookhaven (Suffolk Co), was conceived of as a New York State history museum in motion. Construction was begun in Islip (Suffolk Co) in 1984 by Gerry Holzman, who was later joined by carver Jim Beatty and more than 1,000 New York State folk artists. Every riding figure represents an animal native to the state (including a beaver, duck, loon, brook trout, and moose), and bench rides include a miniature Erie Canal barge boat. Center panels feature murals of important events in the history of New York State and historical or folkloric characters such as Susan B. Anthony, Jackie Robinson, Irving Berlin, Walt Whitman, Capt Kidd, and Adirondack hermit Noah John Rondeau. Every year one figure will be replaced by a new one, representing the changing nature of the state and providing an outlet for future woodcarvers.

The Carousel News and Trader, (1985–)
Fried, Frederick. *Pictorial History of the Carousel* (New York: Bonanza Books, 1964)
Weedon, Geoff, and Richard Ward. *Fairground Art* (New York: Abbeville Press, 1985)

John L. Scherer

Carpatho-Rusyns. Slavic people from central Europe, also known as Carpatho-Russians, Carpatho-Ukrainians, Lemkos (a subdivision of the Carpatho-Rusyns), Ruthenians, and Rusnaks. Before World War I their homeland was part of the Austro-Hungarian empire. Then it was divided between Czechoslovakia and Poland, after World War II mostly annexed by the Soviet Union, and in 2003 is split between Slovakia, Poland, and Ukraine. Because of this complicated political history, Carpatho-Rusyn immigrants and their descendants have identified themselves under all these ethnicities and states, making it impossible to determine their actual numbers in New York State.

Most Carpatho-Rusyn immigrants to New York State came between the 1880s and 1914, mainly to New York City, Yonkers, Binghamton, Endicott, and Johnson City. They were generally single males who left for economic reasons and subsequently sent for their families. After World War II a few thousand political refugees fleeing Communist rule came as well. Most immigrants worked in light industrial enterprises and service industries. The vast majority belonged to the Byzantine Ruthenian Catholic Church (formerly called Greek Catholic), the Orthodox Church in America, and the American Carpatho-Russian Orthodox Church. Community life has traditionally been centered on the group's Eastern-rite Christian parishes.

The main Carpatho-Rusyn community organizations are based in western Pennsylvania, with branches in New York State. Others are based in New York State, including several church choirs still active in 2003. In New York City there was an immigrant home (1920) on East 4th St in Manhattan, a Democratic Party political club (1930s–1940s), a radio program (1940s), and cultural organizations asserting that Carpatho-Rusyns are either a branch of the Ukrainians (Carpathian Research Center, 1958) or a distinct people (Carpatho-Rusyn Research Center, 1978). New York City was also home to several groups supporting different political solutions for the Carpathian homeland in Europe. The League for the Liberation of Carpatho-Russia (1917) called for joining a democratic, non-Communist Russia or for establishing an independent state. The Carpatho-Russian National Committee (1939) favored joining the Soviet Union, the Organization for the Defense of the Lemko Land (1940) supported joining an independent non-Communist Ukraine, while the Council of Free Carpatho-Ruthenia in Exile (1951) supported returning to Czechoslovak rule. In Yonkers the Carpatho-Russian American Center (Lemko Hall, 1939–99) hosted social and cultural events and housed the Lemko Association, which has published since 1939 the weekly newspaper *Karpatska Rus'/Carpatho-Rus.* The Lemko Association supported the summer resort Lemko Park (1958–97) in Monroe (Orange Co).

In 1990, 1,315 persons in New York State identified their ancestral heritage as Carpatho-Rusyn or Ruthenian, and only 548 people in 2000 indicated their ancestry as Carpatho-Rusyn. It is likely, though, that about 85,000 persons of Carpatho-Rusyn heritage actually live in the state. As a group, Carpatho-Rusyns have been too small and divided along religious and national lines to have much impact on state politics and culture. Their onion-domed, Eastern-rite churches do, however, stand out in the communities where they are located. A few individuals of Carpatho-Rusyn background have been prominent in New York State, such as pop artist and experimental filmmaker Andy Warhol, former New York State assistant attorney general Orestes Mihaly, and chief of the New York Public Library's Slavic Division, Edward Kasinec.

Magocsi, Paul Robert. *Our People: Carpatho-Rusyns and Their Descendants in North America,* 3d rev ed. (Toronto: Multicultural History Society of Ontario, 1984)

Paul Robert Magocsi

carpet industry. New York State, along with New England and Philadelphia, was an early center of

"I . . . crossed the track, went up the wooden steps and through some big green doors into a deafening, roaring, clanging clack in which one had to shout to make oneself heard. We were on the lower weaving-floor, where I suppose more than a hundred power-looms were in full work. All the floor on each side of the gangway was filled with looms, nearly all in action. The shuttles were stabbing and clacking, the belts were humming, the swords were coming back with a bang, and the appalling ceiling of advancing spools shook and jerked overhead. The noise was like nothing that I had ever heard. The air was already filled with wool-dust, and sweepers were moving along the gangway with their great brooms to sweep away the coloured dust."

—John Masefield, Poet Laureate of Britain, describing his first impressions of the Alexander Smith mill in Yonkers, where he worked in the early 1890s.

Masefield, John. *In the Mill* (New York: Macmillan, 1941), 6–7. (Courtesy of the Society of Authors as the Literary Representative of the Estate of John Masefield.)

carpet production in the United States. Before the American Revolution there was no real domestic carpet industry in the colonies. The wealthiest colonists imported carpets from England, and the less affluent made their own rugs for household use. Home producers used a variety of techniques, such as sewing strips of fabric together, sewing or embroidering on a cloth foundation, knitting homespun wool yarn, braiding strips of cloth, and weaving on very simple hand looms.

Although small carpet-weaving workshops sprang up in the Philadelphia area during the early national period, it was not until the 1820s and 1830s that carpet factories began to develop. By 1830 there were three carpet mills in Columbia Co, one of which also made woolen cloth. Mills were also operating in Catskill (Greene Co), Rochester, and, by the mid-1830s, Poughkeepsie. Factories also opened in and around New York City. Some New England mills were organized or financed by New York City merchants. By 1845 there were 56 carpet mills in the country, concentrated in Massachusetts, Connecticut, Philadelphia, and Columbia Co, in populated areas close to waterpower and transportation.

Major Manufacturers

One of the most prominent carpet makers in New York State history was Alexander Smith, who began operations in West Farms [now in Bronx Co] in 1845. In 1864 after his factory was destroyed in fires that he attributed to weavers angry about the introduction of power machinery, Smith relocated to Yonkers, where the company operated for 90 years. As Yonkers's top employer, Smith quickly achieved a position of prominence. In November 1878 he was elected to Congress on the Republican ticket, but he died on the night of the vote. By the late 1880s Alexander Smith and Sons Carpet Co, with more than 3,000 employees, was the largest carpet maker in the country and the second largest in the world. By 1929 the company had 7,000 employees. Yonkers was also briefly home to several smaller carpet companies, whose labor forces ranged in size from several dozen to 300. These firms failed in the 1890s after the panic of 1893.

Another leading carpet manufacturer, John Sanford, began operating in Amsterdam (Montgomery Co) around 1842. In 1853 his son Stephen took over the business; he became a civic leader and served in Congress in the early 1870s. In 1929 Sanford and Sons merged with Bigelow-Hartford Carpet Co, which itself had evolved from earlier mergers of old-line New England carpet manufacturers and E. S. Higgins Carpet Co, a Manhattan-based firm that began making carpets in 1847 and employed more than 2,000 workers by 1880. The new firm, Bigelow-Sanford Carpet Co, maintained plants in Amsterdam and in Thompsonville, Conn. Amsterdam was the site of several other major carpet companies, including Shuttleworth Bros (founded in 1878) and McCleary, Wallin, and Crouse (1886). In 1920 these two firms merged to form Mohawk Carpet Mills. By 1929 Amsterdam's two carpet mills, Bigelow-Sanford and Mohawk, employed about 9,300 workers in a city whose population was just 35,000. Amsterdam became known as Carpet City, the carpet capital of the world. New York State was home to some smaller carpet companies as well. Firth Carpet Co operated a plant at Firthcliffe (Orange Co) from the mid-1880s, adding mills in Auburn (Cayuga Co) in 1922 and Newburgh (Orange Co) in 1932. Another Auburn firm, Nye and Wait Carpet Co, was organized around 1871.

New York State's Leadership

New Yorkers were responsible for some of the industry's most significant technological advances. Throughout the mid- and late 19th century, carpet makers sought to develop power-driven machinery, which increased productivity while reducing dependence on skilled labor and allowing manufacturers to exert greater control over employees. A major breakthrough came in 1856 when Halcyon Skinner, an engineer who worked with Alexander Smith, invented a power loom that could weave Axminster carpet, a luxurious variety that was expensive and time consuming to make by hand. The new machinery, perfected and patented by the late 1870s, allowed carpet makers to increase production 10-fold while slashing labor costs.

By the late 19th century, New York firms dominated the trade. Philadelphia carpet mills were more numerous but tended to produce a cheaper grade of carpet. As higher-quality goods became more popular, New York State's leadership was secured. In 1880 Smith, Sanford, and Higgins employed nearly one-third of the nation's carpet workers and produced nearly one-fourth of mill output. In 1929 there were 67 domestic carpet establishments. Although 32 of these were in Philadelphia, fully half of the industry's nearly 33,000 wage earners were located in New York State. By 1941 four New York–based firms—Smith, Bigelow-Sanford, Mohawk, and Firth—accounted for nearly 55% of all domestic carpet sales. New York City was the center for marketing and sales. Historically, carpeting was a luxury item, and because the nation's upper classes tended to cluster in the Northeast, especially the New York City area, carpet consumption was concentrated there as well. In 1939, 15% of retail sales of all domestically produced floor coverings, including carpets, took place in New York State; New York City residents alone accounted for 10.5% of sales. In addition, many carpet firms maintained offices and showrooms in Manhattan, where they displayed their wares in seasonal openings each year. The carpet industry's trade association, founded in 1927 by the major firms, moved from Washington, DC, to New York City in 1930 and remained there for many years. Some of the industry's leading trade journals were also based in New York City from the late 19th century.

Union Organizing

Carpet executives were not alone in uniting to protect their interests. In 1846 skilled hand-weavers from 31 carpet factories in Yonkers, Amsterdam, Philadelphia, Haverstraw (Rockland Co), and elsewhere gathered at Tammany Hall in New York City to form a national association. Hoping to block an attempt by the manufacturers to reduce wages, the unionists elected officers and established shop committees. In response to the organizing, employers stepped up efforts to introduce power machinery that would eliminate the need for skilled weavers. To tend the new machines, mill owners began hiring young women and new immigrants, who they believed would be easier to control.

These new hiring practices, however, did not prevent labor unrest. In the early 1880s carpet workers began swelling the ranks of the Knights of Labor. Nearly all Smith, Sanford, and Higgins employees signed on, and in November 1884, in response to wage cuts, Sanford employees staged a walkout that sparked an industry-wide strike. The most dramatic action occurred in Yonkers, where thousands of workers, mostly young Irish women, swept out of the Smith mills on 20 Feb 1885. The strikers, incensed by pay cuts and despotic work rules, were buoyed by the support of other unions and local merchants. The workers declared victory in mid-July when Smith executives agreed to restore and even hike wages, promised to establish a grievance process, and vowed that no worker would be fired for union membership. In the wake of the settlement, Sanford and Higgins granted their employees a 10% raise.

The Knights declined dramatically in the late 1880s and 1890s, but the upsurge in labor activism in the 1930s brought New York State's carpet workers back into the union fold. In the early 1930s, amid the economic hardships of the depression, carpet workers began to join the United Textile Workers of America, affiliated with the American Federation of Labor. In early 1937 national union leaders launched the Textile Workers Organizing Committee, and in 1939 they founded the Textile Workers Union of America (TWUA), affiliated with the Congress of Industrial Organizations. The workers at Bigelow-Sanford's Amsterdam plant received the first charter issued by the TWUA. Smith workers followed their example by voting to unionize in June 1937.

Carpet executives bitterly resisted the union campaign. When organizers charged Smith with violating the National Labor Relations Act by forming a "company union" and firing union activists, company officials declared the law unconstitutional. (Smith only agreed to comply after the US Supreme Court upheld the act in April 1937.) In May 1938 Bigelow-Sanford slashed workers' wages by 10%, despite the existence of a collective bargaining agreement. Mohawk officials managed to keep the union out until 1942. Firth workers tried to organize in the late 1930s but faced so much opposition that they were never able to sustain a union presence. During World War II, however, the labor movement gained in strength, and by the war's end most carpet workers carried union cards.

In addition to their involvement in local unions, New Yorkers were instrumental in building carpet unionism as a whole. From the early 1940s to 1952, Jack Rubenstein, the TWUA's director of organizing for New York State, also headed the union's carpet division. In 1955 William DuChessi of Amsterdam, a former Bigelow-Sanford employee who joined the union's staff in 1937, became the carpet division director, a post he held for many years.

Carpet Mills Move South

During the 1950s New York State's importance as a site of carpet production began to wane. After World War II companies invested heavily to increase productive capacity, but their product remained too costly to capture a mass market, and they were left with excess capacity within a few years. Also, the old-line northeastern firms faced competition from a group of upstart carpet makers, largely based in northwest Georgia. These new entrants used a technology called tufting, which turned out goods much more quickly and at far lower cost than traditional weaving. Finally, the proportion of overseas imports was on the rise.

Northern carpet manufacturers responded to these developments by adopting cheaper raw materials, lobbying for high import duties, and in a very few cases, installing tufting machinery in their northern plants. Their principal strategy, however, was to head south themselves. In the early 1950s, Bigelow-Sanford and Mohawk invested in southern tufting operations. Around the same time, Alexander Smith opened an Axminster weaving mill in Mississippi and soon afterward closed the Yonkers plant. In 1955 Smith merged with Mohawk, and the new company, Mohasco, moved part of Mohawk's Amsterdam operation to Smith's Mississippi site. Similarly, in the late 1950s Bigelow-Sanford began shifting production from Amsterdam to other locales. Mohasco took over Firth in early 1962 and quickly phased out Firth's plants. By the late 1960s, Mohasco had ceased all Amsterdam operations, and in 1988 its headquarters moved south. In December 1969 the trade association for the woven carpet industry, then known as the American Carpet Institute, merged with the Tufted Textile Manufacturers Association. The new organization, renamed the Carpet and Rug Institute, was based in Dalton, Ga, which replaced Amsterdam as the carpet capital.

By the early 1970s carpet manufacturing had all but disappeared from New York State. The impact of the loss varied by location. By the late 1950s Amsterdam's unemployment rate was nearly 25%, and the federal government classified the city as an economically distressed area eligible for special forms of aid. By the early 1970s Amsterdam's population had dropped to 25,500. In 1998 the carpet mill site was included in a state-designated Economic Development Zone (EDZ). Yonkers, as a whole, fared better because of its larger size and more diversified economy. However, within 10 years after the Smith plant closing, the area surrounding the mill complex had become the most economically depressed section of Yonkers, and it became part of an EDZ in 1988. In these communities and elsewhere, the old carpet mill buildings—often neglected, gutted by fire, or occupied by marginal enterprises and storage firms—still stand as crumbling monuments to a thriving industrial past.

Cole, Arthur H., and Harold F. Williamson. *The American Carpet Manufacture: A History and an Analysis.* Harvard Economic Studies, no. 70 (Cambridge, Mass: Harvard Univ Press, 1941)

Friedman, Tami J. "Communities in Competition: Capital Migration and Plant Relocation in the US Carpet Industry, 1929–1975" (PhD diss, Columbia Univ, 2001)

Levine, Susan. *Labor's True Woman: Carpet Weavers, Industrialization, and Labor Reform in the Gilded Age* (Philadelphia: Temple Univ Press, 1984)

Tami J. Friedman

Carrier Corporation. Climate control manufacturing company founded by Willis Haviland Carrier, a mechanical engineer from Angola (Erie Co). In 1901, upon graduating from Cornell University, Carrier began working for the Buffalo Forge Co. The following year he designed an air-conditioning unit, the first in the world to control temperature and humidity, for the Sackett-Wilhelms Lithographing and Publishing Co in Brooklyn. A patent followed in 1906 for "An Apparatus For Treating Air," along with improvements in design. In 1915 Carrier and six associates raised $32,600 and founded the Carrier Engineering Co with headquarters in Buffalo. After moving the headquarters to Newark, NJ, four years later, Carrier designed the "centrifugal refrigeration machine" in 1922, the first practical method of cooling large spaces. In 1925 Carrier air-conditioned the Rivoli Theater in New York City, and his success there, in addition to several theaters in Texas, won national publicity. Business boomed, and in 1928 Carrier air-conditioned the chambers of the US Congress. In 1937 the company moved its headquarters to Syracuse. Demand for nonindustrial air-conditioning decreased during the Great Depression and World War II, but in 1950 Carrier introduced the first window unit. Business flourished, and employment in Syracuse approached 6,000. United Technologies Corp purchased Carrier in 1979. That same year Carrier moved its world headquarters to Farmington, Conn, dividing its North American operations into two divisions: residential and light commercial systems, and commercial systems and services. The latter business was based in Syracuse and employed 3,500 in 2001. In addition to manufacturing, the Syracuse operations include research and development and marketing. Carrier contributed $2.75 million in 1979 to Syracuse University for construction of the Carrier Dome, an enclosed stadium. Carrier is the world's largest manufacturer of air-conditioning, heating, and refrigeration equipment. Its total employment force in 2001 was 42,600 with revenue of $8.9 billion. In 2003, however, the company announced it would close its manufacturing plants in DeWitt (Onondaga Co), leading to the layoff of more than a thousand workers; office, warehouse, and research jobs remain in the Syracuse area.

Ford, Barbara. *Keeping Things Cool: The Story of Refrigeration and Air Conditioning* (New York: Walker, 1986)

J. Brooks Flippen

Carrier Dome. Syracuse University sports arena. Built between April 1979 and September 1980 on the site of old Archbold Stadium, the Carrier Dome is the main arena for Syracuse University athletics and the largest on-campus domed stadium in the nation. Construction costs totaled $28 million, with $2.75 million coming from the Carrier Corp to purchase the naming rights. The Dome's teflon-coated fiberglass fabric roof is inflated by fans 65 feet (19.8 m) in diameter. During the winter, warm air is forced between the roof's fabric layers to melt snow. In 1999 new

The Carrier Dome.

fabric panels replaced the original ones. A capacity crowd of 50,564 turned out on 20 Sept 1980 for Syracuse University's first football game in the new building. A 2003 basketball game between Syracuse and Rutgers University drew 33,071 spectators and set an NCAA on-campus attendance record for the sport. The Carrier Dome has also hosted nonuniversity events, including the Empire State Games, the Moscow Circus, and concerts by Frank Sinatra, Bruce Springsteen, Elton John, and the Rolling Stones. The building stimulates important economic activity in Central New York, and its bubble roof has become one of Syracuse's most prominent and oft-photographed features.

Syracuse University Athletics, Carrier Dome, http://www.suathletics.com/sports/gen/2001/carrierdome.asp

Syracuse University Football Media Guide (Syracuse: Syracuse Univ Sports Information Department, 1999)

Scott Pitoniak

Carroll. Town (pop 3,635) in SE Chautauqua Co. Settled in 1809 the town was formed from Ellicott in 1825. The town's early economy was based on the lumber industry and included the production of barrel staves; farming later replaced lumbering in importance. The hamlet of Frewsburg grew around furniture factories, a cannery, and dairy processing. Ethan Allen, a furniture company, operated a Frewsburg plant until 2001. Swedish Americans make up a significant portion of the population.

Michelle Henry

Carrollton. Town (pop 1,410) in S central Cattaraugus Co. Settled in 1814, the town was formed from Great Valley in 1842. Carrollton is divided by the Allegany Indian Reservation. Lumbering was the important early industry with logs floated down the Allegheny River; sawmills, a planing mill (1871), and a handle factory were established. The Erie Railroad (1851), its Bradford Branch (1866), and the Buffalo, Rochester and Pittsburgh (1878) provided transport. Irish immigrants who had fled the potato famine in County Clare settled New Ireland in the 1850s. The Limestone Tannery (*ca* 1858) employed 70 in 1878; the Vandalia Chemical Works (1874) extracted tannin. In 1864 oil was discovered along Tuna Creek (shortened form of Tunungwant Creek), the pace accelerating in 1875 and, by 1878, 250 wells had been drilled. The United Pipe Line Co (1875) built a pipeline to transport the oil to refineries. Rte 17 (I-86) was built through Carrollton in 1985. A part of Allegany State Park occupies 11,114 acres (4,498 ha), about one-half of the town's area.

Bruce D. Fredrickson and Madelynn P. Fredrickson

car services. See TAXI AND CAR SERVICES.

Carter, Elliott (Cook) (*b* New York City, 11 Dec 1908). Composer. Carter studied composition at Harvard and in Paris with Nadia Boulanger. His early works, such as *Symphony No. 1* (1942) and *Holiday Overture* (1944), were strongly influenced by Igor Stravinsky, Paul Hindemith, and Aaron Copland. One of his later works in this vein, *The Minotaur* (1947), was commissioned by Lincoln Kirstein for George Balanchine's Ballet Society, the immediate forerunner of the New York City Ballet. Carter's first composition in a wholly original, personal style was *String Quartet No. 1* (1951). His modernist music is tremendously complex in its textures and rhythms, but also has energy and emotional power. His major scores include the *Double Concerto* (1961); *Concerto for Orchestra* (1969); *A Symphony of Three Orchestras* (1977); concertos for piano, violin, oboe, and clarinet; four more string quartets; and the vocal works *A Mirror on Which to Dwell* (1975) and *Syringa* (1978). Most recently Carter wrote his first symphony in over 50 years, *Symphonia* (1996), and his first opera, *What Next?* (1999).

Schiff, David. *The Music of Elliott Carter*, 2d ed. (Ithaca: Cornell Univ Press, 1998)

David Raymond

Carthage. Village (pop 3,721) in Wilna (Jefferson Co). Settled in 1798 and first called Long Falls, Carthage acquired a post office in 1816. St. James Church, Jefferson Co's first Roman Catholic congregation, was organized in 1819. The village was incorporated in 1841. Iron production, long an important industry, began in 1816; later products included mill machinery (1831), cotton cloth (1849), strawboard (1868), rakes and axes, leather, furniture, and pressed brick. It was served by the Carthage, Watertown and Sackets Harbor (1870) and Rome, Watertown and Ogdensburg (1871) Railroads. In the 1880s mills for pulp and paper became predominant. In 2003 Slack Chemical Co (1920) and Metropaper (2000) were the last remnants of Carthage's manufacturing sector; many residents commute to Fort Drum and Watertown.

Laura Lynne Scharer

cartography and mapping. Maps and other cartographic materials are critically important for understanding New York State. They do not simply mirror the landscape; they are tools that define and shape geographic reality. Maps guided the first explorers to New York, and each generation has produced its own maps to explore, analyze, and control the land and its people. They have been used to define the boundaries of the state and its political subdivisions. Property lines are recorded on maps, as are roads, electoral districts, and school districts. Maps are used to depict and evaluate farmlands, forests, mineral resources, demographic patterns, and other elements. Much of the way we conceive New York State—including its odd vaguely triangular shape with the long thin extension of Long Island jutting eastward—comes from our understanding of maps.

All cartographic materials (maps, atlases, globes, aerial photographs, and geographic data in digital form) are selective, symbolic, and stylized representations. Maps reflect the interests, biases, training, and abilities of the persons who make them. Because they are expensive to produce, they have usually served the interests of the rich and powerful. While mapmaking is in part a scientific endeavor, maps, like architecture and music, are cultural creations and cannot be fully understood outside their historical contexts. These observations should be kept in mind when considering maps of New York State. Early maps of New York Colony reflected the differing viewpoints, needs, and traditions of Native American, Dutch, French, and British mapmakers. Since the end of the colonial era, maps have been a product of the perceptions of successive generations of explorers, soldiers, scientists, land speculators, tourists, bureaucrats, and others.

Colonial Mapping, 1520–1783

New York's first mapmakers were its aboriginal inhabitants. Recent research has shown that many American Indian cultures made maps, some quite sophisticated. There are a number of records of maps being sketched out by Indians for the early explorers of what is now New York. In Harmen Meyndertsz van den Bogaert's "Narrative of a Journey into Mohawk and Oneida Country" (1634–35), we are told that the Oneida Indians made a map of their country for Dutch explorers using stones and grains of corn. Unfortunately, no Precontact or Contact period maps made by Indians in New York State still exist. However some early European maps include information derived from American Indians and sometimes reflect what was characterized as Indian ways of looking at the land. A spectacular example is the *Velasco Map,* which was procured for the king of Spain by his ambassador to England, Don Alonso de Velasco. It is an anonymous English manuscript map of the Northeast drawn around 1610 and shows recent discoveries by Henry Hudson, Samuel de Champlain, and others. This map depicts several features not yet seen by Europeans, including Lake Ontario, Lake Champlain, and the upper reaches of the Susquehanna River. These areas are colored in blue and accompanied by a note explaining that "all the blue is done by the relations of the Indians." As late as 1771, Guy Johnson's map of the country of the Six Nations credited information derived from "sketches of intelligent Indians."

We have to turn to European explorers for the earliest maps that show what is today New York State. The first European voyages to the area were made by French and Spanish explorers. The most important early explorations were Giovanni da Verrazano's voyage of 1524 to New York Bay and the Long Island coast, and Jacques Cartier's trip up the St. Lawrence River, which took him as far as what is now Montreal. Of the maps reflecting the knowledge acquired by these voyages, the most revealing is Giacomo di Gastaldi's map of New France, published in 1556. New York Bay is called Angoulême (Francis I's title before he became king), and Long Island is labeled Flora. An interesting feature is the depiction of the Hudson and St. Lawrence Rivers as adjoining, which may reflect the misinterpretation of information supplied to a European explorer by Native Americans, because no Europeans are known to have explored the Hudson River above New York Bay at this time. Although the two rivers do not join, in the early Contact period they were connected by a heavily used Indian route via Lake George, Lake Champlain, and the Richelieu River. Native American maps frequently show routes but do not distinguish between streams, paths, and portages. In this case the two rivers were largely connected by a water route that involved some short portages. Crude and distorted though it is, the Gastaldi map already shows a salient feature of New York State's geography—the easy access to the region's interior and to the continent beyond—which is

A Map of the Provinces of New-York and New-Yersey, with a Part of Pennsylvania and the Province of Quebec, from the Topographical Observations of C. J. Sauthier, 1777.

crucial in subsequent exploration, mapping, and settlement. Unfortunately for the French, they fell into a period of civil war shortly after the Gastaldi map was made and did not resume explorations in North America until the first decade of the 17th century. By that time the English and the Dutch were also on the scene, and a period of relatively rapid exploration and mapping took place, stimulated in part by a three-way rivalry.

Henry Hudson's rediscovery of what is now the Hudson River (1609) was one of the events to set off this period of exploration and mapping. Although Hudson was English, he was employed by the Dutch East India Co, and his discovery was followed by several privately sponsored fur-trading expeditions. Between 1611 and 1615 several Dutch sea captains, including Cornelis Hendricksen, Jan Cornelisz May, and Adriaen Block, explored the entire coastline between southern Maine and the Delaware River. Block is the best known, in part because of his circumnavigation of Long Island, discovery of the Connecticut River, and explorations elsewhere on the southern coast of New England. Block Island is named after him. The *Adriaen Block Chart* (1614) is actually a copy of a map similar to the *Velasco Chart* covering the entire Northeast. The *Adriaen Block Chart* was prepared by the Dutch cartographer Cornelis Doetsz, and later modified by Block to show his discoveries. It is the first map known to show Long Island as an island. Another important manuscript map produced at this time, known as "the second figurative map," records Hendricksen's explorations of the Hudson and Delaware Rivers and also shows the Mohawk River and includes information about the tribes living between the Hudson River and Chesapeake Bay that was gathered by a fur trader named Kleytjen, who made his way from the Dutch trading post at Fort Nassau [now Port of Albany] to the mouth of the Susquehanna River.

After this burst of activity, Dutch exploration, settlement, and mapping proceeded slowly, although the Dutch laid claim to a vast extent of territory. The first permanent settlers were sent to New Netherland by the Dutch West India Co in 1624, but as late as 1638 the population of the settlement was only about 1,000. The first printed maps of New Netherland were Johannes de Laet's *Nova Anglia, Novvum Belgium, et Virginia* (1630) and Willem Janszoon Blaeu's *Nova Belgica et Anglia Nova* (1635). These maps closely resembled the *Block Chart* and "the second figurative map," which were produced approximately 15 years previously. The Blaeu map is a thing of beauty, with its many drawings of Indians and native animals, and it illustrates the extensive boundaries claimed by the Dutch for New Netherland. Under Petrus Stuyvesant (1646–64), considerable efforts were made to bring in settlers, but even as late as 1664 New Netherland was inhabited by only about 9,000 people, of whom approximately 2,000 were English. At this time the Dutch colony came under increasing pressure from its much more populated English neighbors, and the Dutch were forced to concede much of Connecticut and eastern Long Island to the English.

The Nicolaes Visscher map of 1656 reveals much about the state of affairs toward the end of Dutch rule. By this time the Dutch had reasonably good knowledge of the geography of their domain. The major rivers and their tributaries are clearly shown; the Catskill Mountains and the Hudson Highlands are sketched in; and some fortifications and various Dutch and English towns are depicted. Boundaries are not shown, and, with the exceptions of Rensselaerswijck [now in Albany, Columbia, and Rensselaer Cos] and the ultimately unsuccessful Colonie van de Heer Nederhorst [now in northern New Jersey and Rockland Co], landholdings are not shown. Instead, numerous Indian villages and tribal names are given, which makes this map an important resource for students of Indians in the Northeast. The Visscher map shows the Dutch claims to control the entire region between the Delaware and Connecticut Rivers and applies Dutch names as far up the coast as Cape Cod. With its focus on navigation and on native trading partners, it is clearly the product of a trading empire.

While the Dutch were exploring southern New York, the French once again became active in investigating eastern North America. This time they were led by Samuel de Champlain, a great explorer and a skilled cartographer. In 1604–5 he explored and mapped the coast of New England as far as the southern shore of Cape Cod. In 1608 he founded Quebec City and in 1609 embarked on a campaign against the Iroquois, which led to his discovery of Lake Champlain. In 1615 another raid against the Iroquois took him to the vicinity of Oneida Lake. One of his lieutenants, Etienne Brûlé, visited the Susquehannock Indians and followed either the Susquehanna or the Delaware River as far as the Atlantic Coast.

After the fall of New Netherland in 1664, the French and the British, together with their Indian allies, were left to fight for European control of New York Colony. The maps made by these two nations show interesting contrasts between each of them and the Dutch. France and Holland were the two leading mapmaking countries of 17th-century Europe. The Dutch empire was based on sea power, and in the production of nautical charts they were without peer. The

French, like the Dutch, were interested in fur trading, but they were also using their armies to create a land-based empire. Under Louis XIV, French armies dominated Europe, and the French were the leading producers of military maps. In the New World the French continued their policy of aggressive expansion, furthered by the production of carefully drawn and often beautiful military maps.

A characteristic feature of New France was its strong missionary efforts among the Indians. The determined and partially successful attempts of the Jesuits to convert the Indians had no real parallel among the Dutch or the English. The Jesuit fathers were among the most educated men of Europe, and their skills included cartography. They were behind the many detailed maps of the Iroquois lands in northern and western New York, and because of their military explorations and the exploits of fur traders, the French had a better geographical knowledge of northern and western New York than the English had before the end of the French and Indian War.

The English brought with them a somewhat different set of priorities and cartographic traditions. English map publishing in the 17th century was, generally, inferior to that of the Dutch or the French. It was not until Henry Popple's *Map of the British Empire in America* (1733) that the British published a map that included a better depiction of New York Colony than the Visscher map. However, like the French, the British needed military maps, and from early on they produced a succession of detailed and carefully drawn maps of towns and strategic waterways. Most were produced by officers with continental backgrounds, because the nobles who dominated the British army regarded mapmaking and the other activities of the Royal Engineers as unsuitable for aristocrats. The list of British military mapmakers includes Wolfgang Römer, Samuel Holland, Claude-Joseph Sauthier, John Montresor, and J. F. W. Des Barres.

The most distinguishing characteristic of British colonial mapping was an abiding concern with delineating land ownership and boundaries. This preoccupation reveals itself at many levels. Large numbers of surveys of individual farms and estates were carried out, many of which can still be seen at the New York State Archives and at local county clerks' offices and historical societies. Surveyors from the British army were called in to survey the boundaries of large estates and to ascertain the borders between New York Colony and neighboring provinces. This attention to land ownership reflects the much greater size of the British colonial population than those of the Dutch and French, as well as the desire of landless Britons to become independent farmers and of those of some means to become landed gentry.

Sauthier's *Map of the Province of New-York* (1776) reveals this concern for marking ownership and boundaries. Even at the time of the Revolution, the settled areas of New York Colony had not progressed much beyond Long Island, the Hudson Valley, and the eastern Mohawk Valley. Strategic lines of communication with Canada via the Mohawk–Lake Oneida corridor and the Lake George–Lake Champlain corridor are shown as part of New York Colony but were still largely unsettled. Western and Central New York, which the British Crown ruled off limits for white settlers, is designated as "the territory of the Six Nations." The boundaries of New York Colony were still being determined. The long disputed boundary line between New York Colony and New Jersey is shown, and all of Vermont is designated as belonging to New York. Boundaries of counties and those of large estates in the Hudson Valley are carefully depicted.

The mapping of New York State reached a high point during the American Revolution. Because of New York's strategic location, the British conducted numerous surveys. A smaller number of maps were created by the Americans and their French allies. Military maps of this period are considered the treasures of many archives and libraries. Outstanding examples include Des Barres's map of British military operations around New York City in 1776, William Cumberland Wilkinson's maps of the Battle of Saratoga, and, from the American side, an anonymous *Map of Genl Sullivan's March from Easton to the Senaca and Cayuaga Countries.*

Mapping an Expanding State, 1783–1840

New York State's boundaries were still undetermined at the end of the Revolution, when most of its central and western regions were claimed by Massachusetts on the basis of that state's colonial charter. In 1786 Massachusetts gave up its jurisdictional claims to rule these lands in exchange for the right to sell them. New York reluctantly gave up its claim to the counties that now constitute Vermont in 1790. The boundary with Pennsylvania still had to be surveyed, and both Pennsylvania and Connecticut had claims to parts of modern New York. Finally, the status of the Iroquois lands remained undetermined. American Indian land claims were particularly troublesome for would-be developers. The Iroquois were no longer protected by British colonial policy and had largely ceased to be a military power by the end of the Revolution. Nevertheless, they still had title to much of Central and Western New York and were protected by a treaty with the federal government. The demand for freehold land among Yankees, Yorkers, and other Whites was high and growing, while, at the same time, New York and Massachusetts were short on money but long on land. Thus timely negotiations with the Iroquois, followed by the quick sale of land, provided the states with a way to raise money to pay off debts incurred during the Revolution. Between 1787 and 1794 huge swaths of northern, central, and western New York were sold to land speculators, including the Macomb Purchase, the Phelps and Gorham Purchase, and the 3.3 million-acre (1.3 million ha) Holland Land Purchase.

The success of these and other ventures depended in large part upon the work of surveyors and mapmakers. The man at the center of much of the cartographic activity during this period was Simeon DeWitt, surveyor general of New York from 1784 until his death in 1834. DeWitt

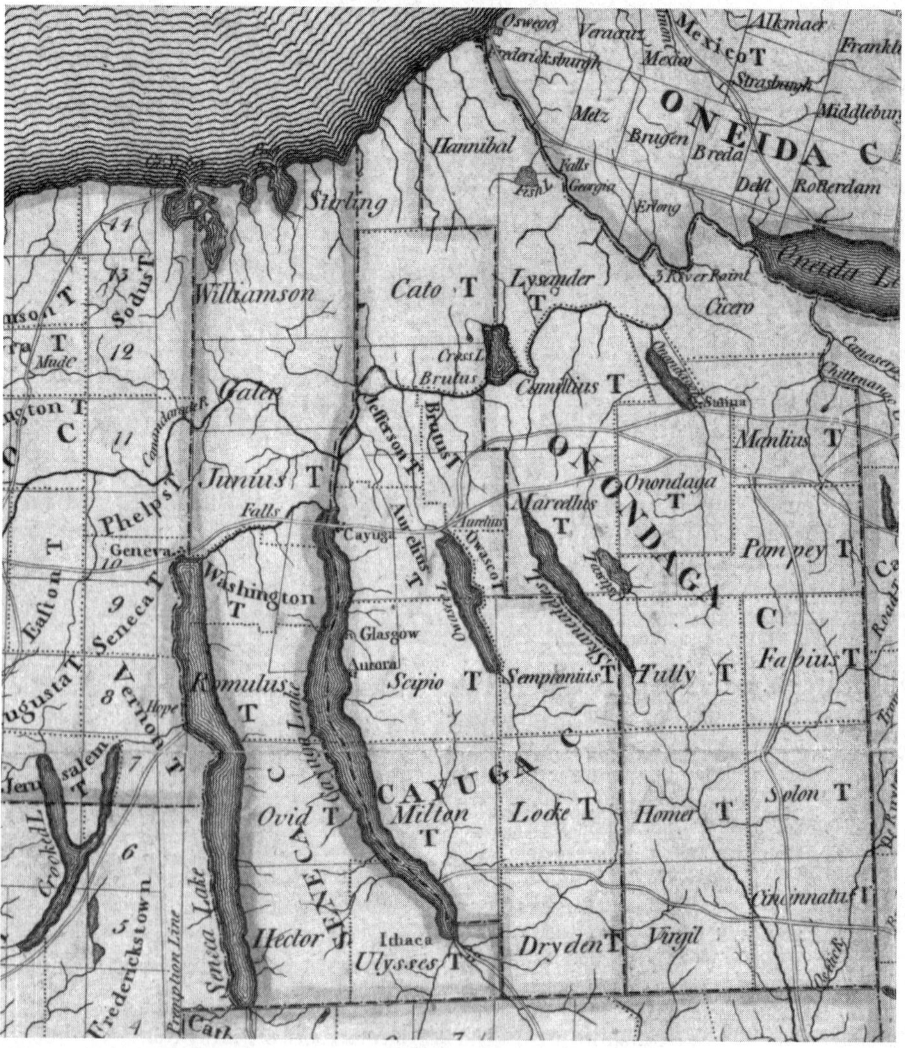

Detail of Central New York region from *Map of the State of New York*, Simeon DeWitt, 1804.

was one of the few American mapmakers who possessed technical skills comparable to those of professionally trained Europeans. He obtained his knowledge in the Continental army under the tutelage of Robert Erskine, who was the first geographer of the army and who had studied engineering at the University of Edinburgh. After Erskine's death in 1780, DeWitt succeeded him as geographer of the army.

DeWitt was a pioneer in a new type of mapping, which is often associated with the rectangular survey system used by the US government to allocate its western lands. During the colonial period, most land parcels were surveyed by so-called metes and bounds. This meant that individual grants of land were surveyed piecemeal by chain and compass; boundaries were often delineated by natural objects, such as streams, rocks, and trees. This system led to numerous lawsuits because of its liability to overlapping grants and uncertain boundaries. Under the rectangular system, huge areas of land were laid out in a grid of squares using compass and chain. These squares could be subdivided into smaller units, and the location of each lot could be defined precisely in relation to the grid as a whole. This system was well adapted to surveying large tracts of land at low cost and with reasonable accuracy.

Shortly after taking office in 1784, DeWitt was involved in surveying the boundary between New York and Pennsylvania and the townships for the New Military Tract in Central New York. The New Military Tract consisted of bounty lands set aside to pay soldiers of the Revolutionary War, and it was here that DeWitt first utilized a rectangular grid to lay out lands. At the same time, surveyors working in close association with DeWitt made maps of other areas, also mostly laid out in a rectangular pattern. Thus, Joseph Ellicott surveyed the lands belonging to the Holland Land Co, and Charles C. Brodhead made a map of the lands in northern New York known as Macomb Purchase (1792). DeWitt combined these and other materials to produce his remarkable map of New York State in 1802. It is far more detailed and accurate than any of its predecessors, and the general appearance of the state is strikingly modern. DeWitt's accomplishment is all the more extraordinary because it is not based on a systematic survey of the entire state; it is a work of compilation for which he brought together a number of surveys of varying quality into a reasonably coherent and accurate whole.

DeWitt was involved in many other projects. He made an important map of Albany in 1794 and later worked on surveying the route of the Erie Canal. He was one of the commissioners involved in laying out the street grid for the development of Manhattan known as the Commissioners' Plan (1811). In his final years he sponsored and published David H. Burr's *Atlas of the State of New York* (1830, although dated 1829). This was the first county atlas of the state and only the second such atlas produced in the country. A revised edition was published in 1839. Overall, Simeon DeWitt's mapping efforts captured a remarkable period of state expansion and growth.

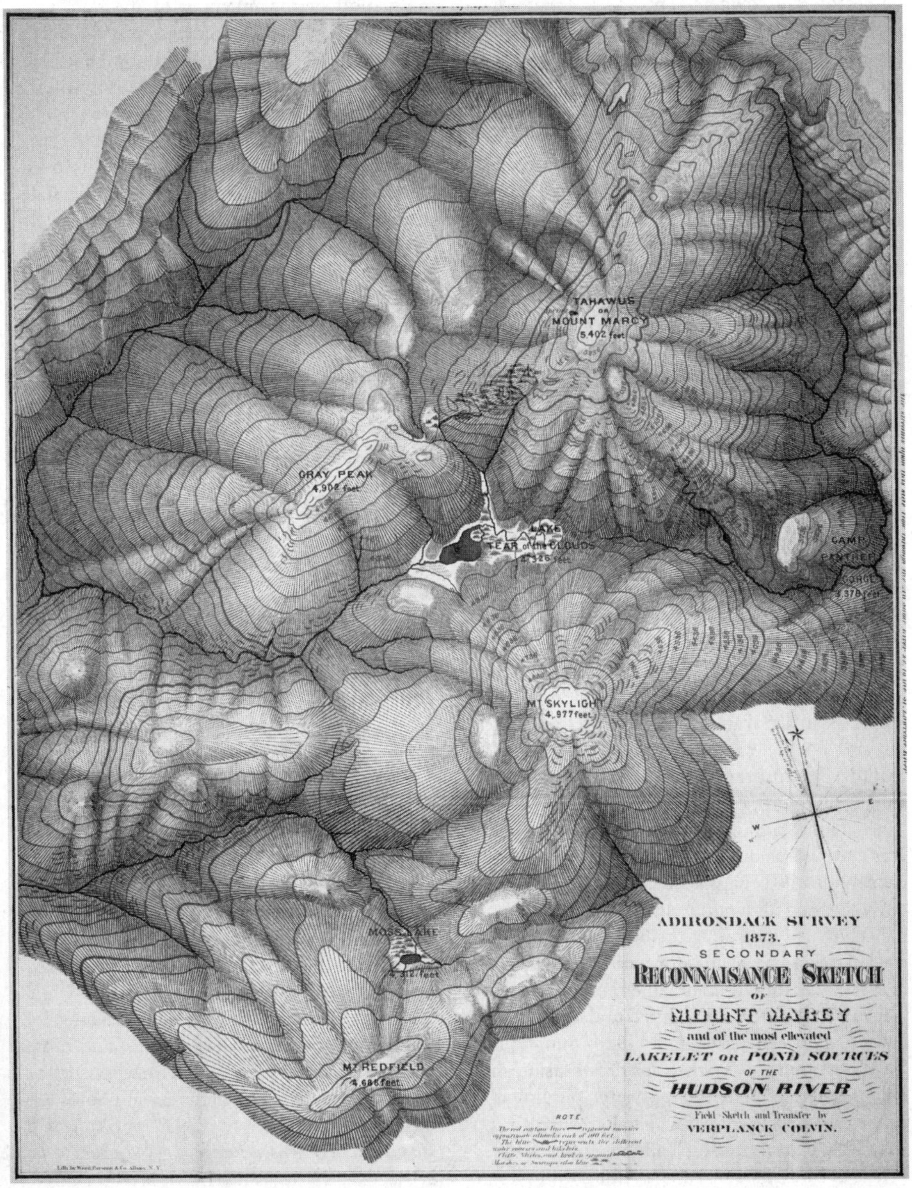

Elevation map of the High Peaks area from *Annual Report on the Progress of the Topographical Survey of the Adirondack Region of New York*, by Verplanck Colvin, 1883.

Scientific Mapping, 1830–1920

Although they were much superior to previous maps, the landmark works of DeWitt and Burr were not accurate enough to meet all needs, such as the delineation of property boundaries. Thus, in the first part of the 19th century a demand arose for more accurate "scientific mapping," an approach that is hard to define. European cartography had long been dominated by a set of conventions constituting the core of scientific mapping, such as the use of uniform scale, mathematical projections to represent the earth's curved surface on a flat sheet of paper, and longitude and latitude to pinpoint locations. The most accurate maps at the beginning of the 19th century were produced by trigonometric triangulation, which involved the determination of the longitude and latitude of key positions by astronomical observation, the laying out of painstakingly measured baselines, and the construction of a network of triangles from the baselines using optical instruments, such as theodolites. Using the principles of trigonometry, it was possible to define with considerable accuracy the location of any other specific place within the network of triangles. The techniques underlying triangulation were known to the British military surveyors in 18th-century America and to a few American surveyors, including Simeon DeWitt, but conducting such surveys was laborious and expensive and required considerable mathematical expertise on the part of the surveyors. Because of the huge area of the United States and the lack of sufficiently trained surveyors, it was, for a long time, impossible to carry out this type of surveying.

Scientific surveying in this country had its beginnings in 1807 when Pres Thomas Jefferson enticed the Swiss surveyor Ferdinand Hassler to head the newly created US Coast Survey. After many tribulations, Hassler began his survey near New York City in 1816, but it was not until the 1830s that extensive surveying was undertaken, and only in the 1840s were the first Coast Survey maps published. They covered Long Island, the New York City area, and the lower Hudson Valley. This constituted the extent of the scientific mapping of New York prior to the Civil War.

Starting in the 1850s, attempts were made to get the state legislature to subsidize a scientific survey of the state. Although these efforts were not immediately successful, they did help to stimulate the production of more detailed and accurate county maps. The improved county mapping eventually led in 1860 to the publication by John Homer French of a detailed map and gazetteer of New York. This map and the county maps upon which it was largely based superseded the Burr atlas, and revised editions of the French map were issued through the 1870s. Although not based on a triangular survey, the French map was unusually accurate and detailed for its time.

It was only after the Civil War that the state legislature was persuaded to subsidize systematic mapping activities. In 1872 Verplanck Colvin convinced the legislature to support his celebrated survey of the Adirondacks. Colvin used triangulation to produce greatly improved maps of this poorly surveyed region and introduced the use of contour lines to depict elevation, a technique that is now standard on modern topographic maps. The survey continued producing maps until the end of the 1890s, when its activities were merged into a new joint effort between the United States Geological Survey (USGS) and New York State to produce detailed topographic maps of the entire state. While Colvin was conducting his surveys in the Adirondacks, the state legislature in 1876 authorized another project to conduct a triangulation of the entire state. Conducted in cooperation with a federal survey of the Great Lakes, the project was completed in 1887. Although it did not directly lead to the production of topographic maps, it established a framework of fixed points and measured distances used in subsequent mapping endeavors. Finally in 1887 the state and federal governments reached an agreement to split the cost of producing detailed state topographic maps. The joint effort between the USGS and New York State marks the beginning of modern topographic mapping of the state. Between 1893 and 1930 the entire state was mapped at a uniform scale of 1:62,500 (1 mile to 1 inch). These maps set a new standard for accuracy and were sufficiently detailed to show individual structures in nonurban areas.

Although scientific mapping was mainly directed toward producing more accurate surveys, other scientists were involved in producing the first thematic maps. The first geological map of New York was published in 1842, and the first map showing the state's agricultural areas appeared in 1846. After 1900 the US Department of Agriculture began producing detailed soil maps. Still produced in modified form today, these soil surveys provide detailed information not only about soil conditions for farmers but also about other environmental factors.

Maps for Settlers, Business Owners, and Tourists, 1840–1920

While scientists were striving to make ever more accurate and detailed maps, commercial cartographers were looking for ways to profit from mapmaking. The period between 1840 and 1920 was a golden age for commercial map publishers. The growing population and prosperity of the state provided them with a market, and technological changes in map production (most notably lithography) made possible the publication of large numbers of inexpensive and colorful maps. Since the 1780s there had been a large enough market to sustain the publication of inexpensive maps and atlases for travelers, schools, and offices. Most of these early maps are unremarkable derivatives of the works of DeWitt and Burr. A notable exception is Christopher Colles's *Survey of the Roads of the United States of America* (1798). This effort, which was a commercial failure, included remarkably detailed route maps of the roads between New York City and Albany.

From the 1830s onward, the pace of publication of commercial maps increased rapidly. A growing and mobile population needed maps showing roads, canals, and railroads, as well as city plans to guide them around such metropolises as New York City and Buffalo. The most important publisher of these maps was New York City–based J. H. Colton and Co. Colton started out in 1833 by reprinting a map of New York State originally published by Burr and then went on to publish colorful and well-designed maps of the country and the world, many of which have become popular collectors' items. The Colton map company continued publishing until the early 1890s. The Chicago-based Rand McNally and Co rose in importance in the 1870s and has occupied a preeminent place in map publication into the early 21st century.

A new development in the production of county property maps occurred in the 1850s. These were initially large wall maps on a grand enough scale to show individual houses and the names of their owners. They were frequently embellished with inset town plans and illustrations of public buildings, individual businesses, and farms. The accuracy varied considerably. Not being publicly funded, their makers usually avoided extensive surveying; the maps were mainly compilations from secondary sources, sometimes supplemented by road measurements to locate individual buildings. Not all property owners were listed, and some of the maps contain many errors. They were often published by subscription, and subscribers paid to have their homes or an illustration of their business or farm put on the maps. In spite of their limitations, these maps are interesting pieces of Americana, and they are much used by genealogists and homeowners trying to determine when their houses were built and who occupied them.

After the Civil War, county maps were mostly published in atlas form, which allowed for the inclusion of much more information, and county atlases were quite popular. Compiled largely from real estate records, these atlases often included property boundaries as well as the names of homeowners. Between 1870 and 1920, most counties in New York were covered by one or more atlases. Like the earlier county maps, the atlases varied considerably in quality but are nonetheless invaluable sources of information. Fire insurance maps are an important variation of property maps. Most were published by the Sanborn Map Co, which was most active between 1890 and 1930. They are extremely detailed maps of urbanized areas, not only showing individual structures and floor plans but also indicating the building materials used in structures. Such information was important to fire insurance companies and is now invaluable to students of architectural and urban history. Between 1870 and 1920 numerous "bird's-eye views"—town maps drawn using an oblique aerial perspective—were published. These panoramic maps, which look like they were drawn from hot-air balloons, often show details of individual buildings. Along with photographs, they give us an excellent (if somewhat sanitized) view of towns in the late 19th and early 20th centuries. Many aerial views of towns in New York have been digitized by the Library of Congress and are available on the Internet.

From Triangulation to the Internet

In the 20th century, particularly its final decades, truly dramatic changes occurred in the ways maps were made and used. On the one hand, the impulse that led to the extensive production of property maps and atlases petered out in the early decades. On the other, commercial road maps, which first became widely available in the middle of the 19th century along with canal and railroad maps, received a boost from the popularity of the automobile. Between 1920 and 1960 vast numbers of road maps were printed and distributed for free by oil companies. For two generations these maps served as the primary source of geographic information for most New Yorkers. For those who preferred other modes of transportation, railroad and airline maps were also widely distributed. The inhabitants of New York City learned how to navigate their complex transit system with free subway maps.

Government mapping activities were unremarkable between 1920 and 1960. After the completion of the mapping of the state at a 1:62,000 scale in 1930, there was relatively little cartographic activity in New York by either federal or state government agencies for several decades. Topographic maps continued to be produced. Until 1928 the USGS worked with the New York State engineer and surveyor; from 1928 to 1970 the work continued with the State Department of Public Works. Approximately half of the cost of creating these maps was paid by the state. During and after World War II the federal government began replacing its 15-minute (1:62,000) scale maps with more detailed 7.5-minute maps at a scale of 1:24,000 or 1:25,000. The first of these maps were produced by the Army Map Service, and later ones were done by the USGS in conjunction with the state. These maps were infrequently updated, which was one of the reasons for the reorganization of mapping activities by New York State after 1965.

Starting in 1920s, high-altitude aerial photographs were taken of New York State. In 1923 the first aerial photographs taken at a uniform scale were completed in New York State; they covered the New York City metropolitan area. During the 1930s countywide aerial surveys were made for most of the state by the US Department of Agriculture. The first statewide aerial survey at a uniform scale was produced in 1967–68 by the commercial firm Lockwood, Bartlett, and Kessler. High-altitude aerial photographs are used to update topographic maps and soil surveys and are also popular with historians, archaeologists, and planners. They show types of information that do not appear on conventional paper maps (eg, vegetation and structures) and help to fill in the gaps for the years when detailed paper maps are not available. Black-and-white aerial photographs have been supplemented by color aerial photos, satellite images, and more exotic forms of remotely sensed imagery, such as side-looking radar. The older aerial photos are listed in the *Inventory of Aerial Photography and Other Remotely Sensed Imagery of New York State* (2001), which is published by the New York State Center for Geographic Information in Albany. Besides maintaining a reading room where many of them can be viewed, the agency has made recent editions of high-altitude color aerial photographs available on the Internet through the New York State GIS Clearinghouse.

There also was increased production of thematic maps, particularly demographic maps, in the 20th century. Governments have been using maps more frequently to analyze and present information on subjects such as public health, zoning, poverty, and voting patterns. Some of the earliest demographic maps were produced in the late 19th century by New York City to analyze the distribution of epidemic diseases. The production of zoning and other demographic maps, which was accentuated by the rise of big government after the New Deal, increased gradually until about 1970. Most of these maps were produced by local governments rather than by the state. The most ambitious statewide initiative along these lines was the Land Use and Natural Resource Inventory (LUNR) of New York State. This project was based on the analysis of aerial photographs and was conducted between 1968 and 1978 for the State Office of Planning Coordination by the Center for Aerial Photographic Studies at Cornell University. It produced a massive series of map overlays covering the entire state at a 1:24,000 scale. A few years later, the production of such maps was revolutionized by the introduction of geographic information systems (GIS).

Around 1970 the use of computers began to overturn established ways of producing maps. By the 21st century almost all maps are made with the aid of computers, and many require a computer to be displayed. At first computers were used primarily to simplify and speed up the revision of paper maps. The ability of computers to display statistical data by geographic area led to the production of a flood of demographic maps by local planning boards following the 1970 census. GIS began to be widely used in the 1980s to both create and view maps, making it easy to overlay various types of maps and to create maps from geographically coded statistical data, such as census information. GIS also facilitates combining conventional maps with other forms of spatial information, such as aerial photographs and satellite imagery, and makes it possible to mix and manipulate this information in unparalleled ways. Since 1967 New York State has become much more active in the production and distribution of cartographic information. The state's mapping activities were centralized that year in the Map Information Unit, which was part of the State Department of Transportation (DOT). The current series of topographic maps produced by the federal government is infrequently updated by the USGS, but the DOT has stepped in to produce a more frequently updated series of topographic maps based on the federal 1:24,000 series. The DOT also produces a series of planimetric maps, which show buildings but not topography, at the same 1:24,000 scale. Some of its planimetric maps were issued at an even more detailed (1:9,600) scale. Other paper products published by DOT include the *New York State Atlas* and individual county maps. In the early 21st century, this agency has taken the lead in making New York State maps, aerial photographs, and digital data available to the public via the Internet.

The New York State mapping program has been strongly affected by the reaction to the terrorist attack on the World Trade Center on 11 Sept 2001. The Map Information Unit (now New York State Center for Geographic Information) was transferred in 2003 to an agency known as the New York State Office of Cyber Security & Infrastructure Coordination, which has continued to distribute paper maps and has made increasing amounts of information available on the Internet through the GIS Clearinghouse. However, public access has been restricted from many maps and aerial photographs of areas deemed "sensitive."

The most recent, and for the ordinary map user probably the most important, of the technological innovations is the widespread availability of cartographic materials on the Internet, especially since the middle of the 1990s, and this trend is continuing in spite of the new security restrictions. Anyone with access to a computer and the Internet can draw upon a collection of maps that would be the envy of all but the largest libraries. These include detailed street maps, topographic and planimetric maps of the entire state, high-altitude aerial photographs (many in the form of geographically rectified orthophotoquads), and many historical maps. GIS-type demographic and environmental maps of individual neighborhoods can be created and displayed at sites sponsored by the US Bureau of the Census and the Environmental Protection Agency. Those with access to GIS software can download quantities of additional data, including land-use and census information, to create their own maps. The New York State GIS Clearinghouse, sponsored by the New York State Center for Geographic Information, and its affiliate, the Cornell University Geospatial Information Clearinghouse (CUGIR) are the leading sources of state GIS data. GIS information is being presented more frequently in forms that can be viewed and manipulated directly on the Internet, without the use of any special software. It is anticipated that even users with little experience will soon be able to examine any particular area by calling up and overlaying topographic maps, aerial photographs, thematic and demographic maps, soil maps, historical maps, and other type of cartographic data. Paper maps will continue to be produced, but even for the end user the future of cartography will be digital.

For other illustrations see MANHATTAN [NEW YORK COUNTY]; NEW YORK CITY.

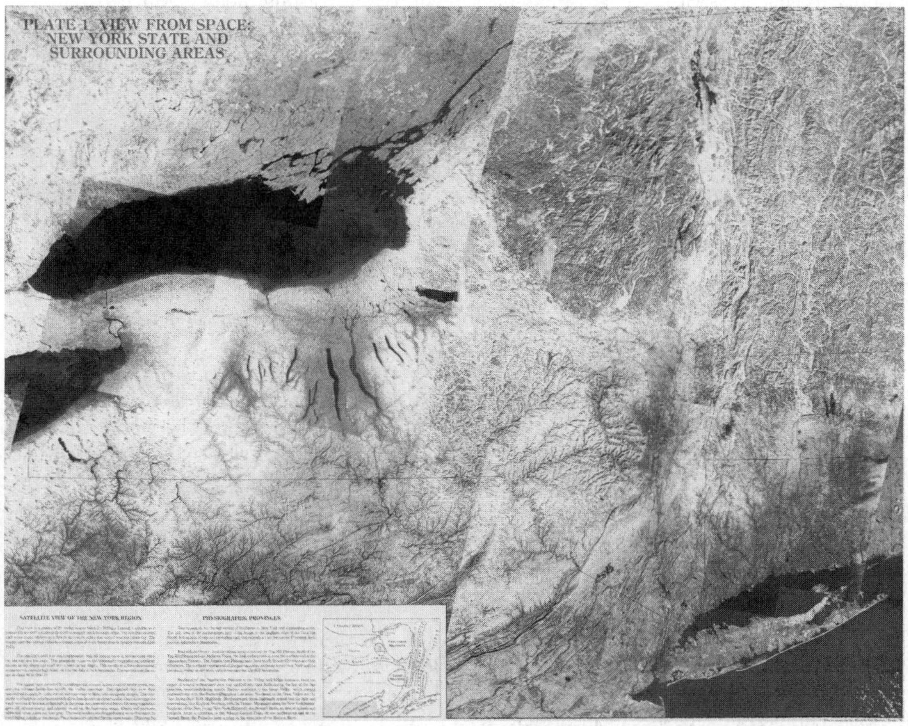

Satellite view of the New York region, 1990.

Allen, David Yehling. *Long Island Maps and Their Makers* (Mattituck, NY: Amereon House, 1997)

Bourcier, Paul G. *History in the Mapping: Four Centuries of Adirondack Cartography* (Blue Mountain Lake, NY: Adirondack Museum, 1986)

Cohen, Paul E., and Robert T. Augustyn. *Manhattan in Maps, 1527–1995* (New York: Rizzoli, 1997)

Colvin, Verplanck. *Report on the Adirondack and State Land Surveys of the Year 1884* (Albany: Weed, Parsons, 1884)

Cumming, William P. *British Maps of Colonial America* (Chicago: Univ of Chicago Press, 1974)

Mano, Jo Margaret. "Unmapping the Iroquois: New York State Cartography, 1792–1854." In *The Oneida Indian Journey: From New York to Wisconsin, 1784–1860*, ed. Laurence M. Hauptman and L. Gordon McLester III (Madison: Univ of Wisconsin Press, 1999)

New York State Department of Transportation. *Inventory of Aerial Photography and Other Remotely Sensed Imagery of New York State, 1968–83*, 3d ed (Albany: Author, 1995)

Rayback, Robert J., ed. *Richard's Atlas of New York State*, rev ed. (Phoenix, NY: F. E. Richards, 1965)

Reps, John W. *Views and Viewmakers of Urban America* (Columbia: Univ of Missouri Press, 1984)

Ristow, Walter W. *American Maps and Mapmakers: Commercial Cartography in the 19th Century* (Detroit: Wayne State Univ Press, 1985)

Wright, Albert Hazen. *A Check List of New York State County Maps Published 1779–1945* ([Ithaca?: Author?], 1965)

Wright, Albert Hazen, and Willard Waldo Ellis. *A Check List of the County Atlases of New York*, part 2 of *New York Historical Source Studies*. Studies in History No. 4 (Ithaca: A. H. Wright, 1943)

Wyckoff, William. *The Developer's Frontier: The Making of the Western New York Landscape* (New Haven, Conn: Yale Univ Press, 1988)

David Yehling Allen

Case, Theodore Willard (*b* Auburn, Cayuga Co, 12 Dec 1888; *d* Auburn, 14 May 1944). Inventor. An heir to the fortunes of several of Auburn's wealthiest families, Case began experimenting with sound and light while an undergraduate at Yale. He then returned to Auburn and built one of the country's finest research facilities, the Case Research Laboratory, in 1916. With chemist Earl I. Sponable, Case spent years experimenting with photoelectric and sound-on-film devices. His patents included the photosensitive Thalofide cell, which the US Navy used during World War I for signaling between ships, and the alkaline earth oxide (AEO) light, a helium-filled tube so sensitive it could modulate light and allow tiny lines of sound to be captured on film, and thus reproduced. Beginning in 1924 Case and Sponable demonstrated the viability of these innovations by making several of the world's earliest talking films. Theater entrepreneur William Fox acquired the technology in 1926. Case remained a partner in the Fox-Case Movietone Corp until 1929, when he sold all rights for $1.5 million. He continued his scientific investigation of the properties of light in later years. In 1936 Case donated his Auburn mansion to establish the Cayuga Museum of History and Art.

Cuddy, Michael J., Jr. "Theodore W. Case: Inventor of 'Talking Movies.'" In *Bicentennial Portraits: Noteworthy Sons and Daughters of Auburn, New York* (Auburn: Jacobs Press, 1993)

Scott W. Anderson

casinos. See GAMBLING AND GAMING.

casket and funeral industry. During the Dutch and the English colonial periods, most bodies were simply wrapped in sheets before burial. When a coffin was desired, cabinetmakers were often asked to provide them. It was a natural evolutionary path for some furniture makers to begin providing more than the mere box. In many towns in rural New York State, it was not unusual for the furniture store to be combined with the funeral parlor. In the early 21st century there are still examples of this with the H. S. Norton Furniture Store and Funeral Home in Sodus (Wayne Co). The livery trade also spawned its share of funeral directors, since a wagon was needed to cart the deceased. Services were generally simple and brief due to the body's impending decomposition. Refrigeration for corpse preservation was popular around the middle of the 19th century. This practice largely ended with the advent of modern embalming.

The Civil War was a catalyst for the development of funeral services. Embalming, heretofore not commonly practiced, found application on battlefields as grieving families sought to bring their sons home. New York City physician Auguste Renouard developed an injection embalming method in the 1890s, which is generally seen as the beginning of modern embalming science. Modern embalming presented the opportunity for longer and more elaborate funeral services. Enterprising undertakers, working previously from trade shops, began to build funeral homes. In June 1881 the National Funeral Directors Association hosted its first convention in Rochester.

Casket making advanced at the same time. Prior to 1865 most people were buried in simple wooden coffins that narrowed toward the feet, the "toe-pincher." After Pres Abraham Lincoln's funeral procession carried him in a rectangular casket, the style became popular. Soon many companies were providing caskets, made of both wood and sheet metal. In the late 19th and early 20th centuries, New York State had several important pioneers in the burgeoning casket industry. Will Chappell successfully consolidated three of the state's casket companies—Chappell, Chase and Maxwell in Oneida (Madison Co); Hamilton, Lemmon, Arnold in Allegany (Cattaraugus Co); and Stein Manufacturing in Rochester—to form the National Casket Co in Oneida. By 1910 National was the largest casket maker in the United States, with factories in Oneida, Rochester, and Long Island City (Queens Co). The company maintained its dominance throughout the first half of the 20th century. John Marsellus settled in Syracuse and founded the Marsellus Casket Co there in 1872, becoming a subsidiary in 1997 of Service Corp International, a Houston-based funeral services conglomerate, and remaining in operation until 2003. Thomas M. Taylor founded H. E. Taylor and Co in 1872 in New York City. His firm quickly rose to become America's largest funeral-supply provider. In 1830 Taylor's uncle, William A. Taylor, founded McGraw and Taylor in New York City. This firm is generally considered one of America's first organized coffin manufacturers, later changing its name to Brooklyn Burial Case Co. In the 20th century the growth of death benefits, especially after the federal Social Security Act of 1935, led to an expansion of the casket market. During and after World War II, metal caskets, less expensive to produce, were increasingly prominent, accounting for 40% of all caskets by 1957. By the early 21st century the casket-making industry had centralized in the Midwest, which provided a central location for better distribution. In 2003 New York State had approximately 2,000 funeral homes and 5 mortuary science colleges, including the Simmons Institute of Funeral Service in Syracuse and the American Academy McAllister Institute of Funeral Service in Manhattan.

See also CEMETERIES.

DeFort, Edward J. "Tracing the Development of Funeral Service," *The American Funeral Director* (Jan 2000)

Michael L. Beardsley and John D. Marsellus

Cassadaga [CASS-A-DAY-GAH]. Village (pop 676) in Stockton (Chautauqua Co). Settled in 1812 the village surrounds an outlet of Cassadaga Lakes. A cement plant opened in 1890, and a grape basket factory was built in 1894. Ice was harvested on the lake and shipped to surrounding cities by railroad. The village was incorporated in 1921. Best known for year-round recreation centered on the lake, it is the birthplace of tabloid celebrity and popular novelist Roxanne Pulitzer.

Michelle Henry

Castile [CAST-AISLE]. Town (pop 2,873) and village (1,051) in SE Wyoming Co. The site of the Genesee River Gorge, the town was the home of the Seneca author Mary Jemison until 1816 and location of the Gardeau Reservation from 1797 to 1826. European American settlement started in 1809, and the town was formed from Perry in 1821. Its sawmills produced lumber for the Rochester market. The Castile Plow Works manufactured plows in the mid–19th century. Castile was the site of the Greene Sanitarium (1849), operated by several generations of women physicians until after World War II. The Erie Railroad (1871) and Silver Lake Railroad (1872) served the town. The Silver Lake Institute (1873) was a Methodist camp meeting, later a Chautauqua, and is now a resort. Ice was cut on the lake until 1925. The Village of Castile incorporated in 1877. The DeWitt-Borg Mill produced silk in the mid–20th century. Letchworth State Park, which housed a prisoner of war camp during World War II, is partly in town, as is Silver Lake State Park. Dairy farms, along with potato and apple growing, remain important in the early 21st century. In 1855 a 60 ft (18 m) sea monster in Silver Lake, fabricated of coiled wire and rubber and inspired by an Indian legend, attracted large crowds until the hoax was revealed. The town was the birthplace of Frances Folsom Cleveland, wife of Grover Cleveland. The Wyoming Historical Pioneers Association picnic has been held in August since 1877. Castile is the site of the Elohim Bible Institute (1942).

cast-iron architecture. This mid–19th century mode of constructing multistory buildings with self-supporting iron facades involved prefabricated components that were molded to simulate carved stone. A plentiful natural resource in the state, iron was inexpensive by the early 19th century and began to be used architecturally. Iron columns could support great weight, were fire resistant, and allowed for larger windows to maximize natural light. In the 1830s New York City foundryman Jordan Mott produced iron column-and-lintel storefronts for conventional masonry buildings. The first iron bridge (1840) in the country spanned the Erie Canal at Frankfort (Herkimer Co). In 1848 James Bogardus constructed the first total iron facade when he renovated the Milhau Pharmacy in Lower Manhattan by adding an ornate facade composed entirely of cast-iron modules. Builders quickly adopted his iron-front techniques. Merchants and industrialists were able to built large fire-resistant structures that looked like grand Italian palazzi.

Cast-iron architecture flourished in commercial districts, especially in New York City, where the shimmering iron-and-glass Crystal Palace (1853; destroyed) symbolized the age. Among the outstanding iron fronts in Manhattan were Bogardus's Harper Building (1855); John P. Gaynor's Haughwout Building (1856); Stephen D. Hatch's Empire-style Gilsey Hotel (1869); and Richard Morris Hunt's Moorish-style Rensselaer Building (1872; destroyed). Fine cast-iron department stores were established along Broadway in the so-called Ladies Mile. Brooklyn had numerous iron-front structures clustered along Fulton St and in Williamsburg. Only a few, such as William Ditmars's Forman Building (1882), survived in the 21st century. The spacious iron-and-glass conservatory of the New York Botanical Garden in the Bronx was completed 1901.

Fine cast-iron buildings were built throughout the state. Albany's first iron front was Bogardus's Ransom Building (1857; destroyed). Daniel D. Badger erected an ornate iron front at 51 North Pearl St (*ca* 1862) and an all-iron storehouse at the Watervliet Arsenal (Albany Co) (1859), des-

Cast-iron storehouse at the Watervliet Arsenal, built in 1858.

ignated a National Historic Landmark in 1967. In Binghamton architect Isaac Perry built a four-story cast-iron office building (1876), which later became McLean's Department Store. Iron fronts were erected after fires destroyed old city centers: in Cooperstown (Otsego Co) the Iron-clad Building (1862) was built by Bogardus for George L. Bowne, and in Bath (Steuben Co) the Howell Building (1863) was designed by George Bartlett. Several cast-iron fronts were erected in Rochester; for example, the Second Empire–style Powers Building (*ca* 1881) by Andrew Jackson Warner, with its circular cast-iron interior staircase, and the seven-story factory (1882) designed by Louis P. Rogers for patent medicine king H. H. Warner. A cast-iron pavilion (1863) by Badger graces Magnesia Spring in Sharon Springs (Schoharie Co). Often cast-iron structures gave way to urban growth, such as Troy's Warren Building (1870) and Buffalo's seven-story Tucker Building (1887).

Changing taste and the advent of steel construction ended the era of cast-iron architecture by the late 1800s. After World War II many cast-iron structures were demolished during urban renewal efforts, but some are cherished as part of the local architectural legacy and have been restored. Some of the particularly notable structures are in the SoHo district in Manhattan, which has 139 cast-iron buildings and was designated a New York City Historic District in 1973.

Condit, Carl W. *American Building: Materials and Techniques* (Chicago: Univ of Chicago Press, 1968)
Gayle, Margot, and Edmund V. Gillon Jr. *Cast-Iron Architecture in New York: A Photographic Survey* (New York: Dover, 1974)

Carol Gayle and Margot Gayle

Castleton-on-Hudson. Village (pop 1,619) in Schodack (Rensselaer Co). Settled in 1792 on the site of Schotak, an important Mohican (Mahican) Indian village, Castleton quickly became an important river landing. The village incorporated in 1827. Brick manufacturing began *ca* 1825, and ice harvesting employed up to 1,000 people. The Hudson River Railroad (1851) helped foster the manufacture of postal cards (1856), straw wrapping paper (1863), binders' board (1888), and folding cartons (1907). Other industries included a piano action factory (1896) and the Anti-Corrosive Metal Products Co (1928). German immigrants (*ca* 1875) were soon joined by an influx of Dutch. In 2003 Hamilton Press was an important employer; Fort Orange Paper, successor to the 1856 mill, closed in 2002.

Kathryn T. Sheehan

Castorland. Village (pop 306) in Denmark (Lewis Co). Located in the Black River valley and named for a nearby settlement of French aristocrats (located in Lyonsdale), the village became a shipping depot on the Black River Canal (1851–1924) and, later, on the Rome, Watertown and Ogdensburg Railroad (1867). T. B. Basselin's huge sawmill and related operations (1883–1909) encouraged growth. In 1904 it became headquarters of Climax Manufacturing Co, a large producer of chicken incubators that later shifted to manufacturing cardboard boxes. The company removed to Lowville in the late 20th century, leaving only a warehouse in Castorland. The village incorporated in 1929.

Arthur Einhorn

Catharine. Town (pop 1,930) in SE Schuyler Co. Formed from the old town of Newtown (Tioga Co) in 1798, the area of the present town was settled a year later by Connecticut migrants. It was named after Catharine Montour, an 18th-century Seneca leader. Residents established the Catharine Library Association in 1817. Later in the 19th century, manufacturing included a tannery, a pump factory, shoe shops, and agricultural implements. The Kayuta Lake House was an established resort by the end of the Civil War. The Magee Trout Ponds (1871) encompassed nine built ponds and a fish hatchery. In 2002 land was still used primarily for farming. The 11,045-acre (4,470 ha) Connecticut Hill State Wildlife Management Area, partly in Catharine, is the largest such area in the state. The Lawrence Chapel (1881) at Cayuta Lake is a landmark.

Glenda Gephart

Cathedral of St. John the Divine. Cathedral church for the Episcopal Diocese of New York. Located in Morningside Heights at 112th St and Amsterdam Ave in New York City, it is the largest cathedral church in the world and seats 8,600. It is 601 feet (183.2 m) long, and its main vault is 124 feet (37.8 m) high. First planned in the 1870s with ground broken for it on 27 Dec 1892, it is indirectly owned by the Episcopal Church. Originally designed by the firm of George L. Heins and C. Grant La Farge, the sanctuary and choir are of a Romanesque style. After 1911 the building came under the direction of the firm of Ralph Adams Cram and Frank Ferguson, and the style was changed to French Gothic. The nave was completed in 1941. Work stopped on the building from 1941 to 1978, at first because of the war and later because of other needs. Based on its architectural preeminence and its location near Columbia University, it has been a center for artistic, social, and political events. A serious fire in the cathedral in late 2001 destroyed several historic tapestries.

Quirk, Howard E. *The Living Cathedral, St. John the Divine: A History and a Guide* (New York: Crossroads, 1993)

Robert Bruce Mullin

Catholic Charities. Network of independent and community-based Catholic agencies in New York State providing comprehensive charitable services. Their presence in the state began in the early 19th century when Catholics sought to aid children, the impoverished, and the vast number of Catholic immigrants arriving in New York City by providing shelter, care, and training. The Roman Catholic Orphan Asylum, the New York Catholic Protectory, the Society for Destitute Catholic Children, and other charities became popular because they gave Catholics the chance to fulfill their spiritual duty of aiding the less fortunate and a means through which their faith could be perpetuated. Though donations from private sources, including Catholic parishioners and philanthropists, were significant, Catholic charitable organizations and services proliferated in New York State because of late 19th-century state legislation permitting public funding of the state's private charities; the Children's Law (1875) provided for the care of needy children by individuals of the same religion as the child's parents. Catholic charities, especially those in New York City, also benefited from land grants provided by local governments.

In 1910 the National Conference of Catholic Charities (now Catholic Charities USA) formed to coordinate efforts nationally. The organization was incorporated by an act of the New York State legislature in 1917, and New York State's diocesan bishops assumed a more active role in administering the Catholic charities operating within their dioceses. Responding to calls for reform and the need to conform to state regulation, the dioceses opted to consolidate services, replace lay managers with clergy, and assemble a more professional staff. The earlier Association of Catholic Charities of New York, formed in 1902 by Catholic women, served as its organizational and structural prototype.

In the 20th century Catholic Charities altered its mission to meet the needs of New York State's changing population. As more Catholics entered the ranks of the middle class, Catholic Charities expanded to provide services to all individuals regardless of their religious, socioeconomic, ethnic, or racial background. In 1999 its 23,830 volunteers, paid staff, and board members addressed the needs of over 1.3 million people at a cost of over $800 million. Services include shelter and housing, food pantries and kitchens, adoption and foster care, pregnancy care, counseling, educational programs, daycare, employment services, and various outreach programs.

Brown, Dorothy M., and Elizabeth McKeown. *The Poor Belong to Us: Catholic Charities and American Welfare* (Cambridge, Mass: Harvard Univ Press, 1997)

John Marino

Catholic education. New York City, which remains a center of Catholic education in both the state and the nation, became the first Catholic diocese in the state in 1808, followed by Albany (1847), Buffalo (1847), Brooklyn (1853), Rochester (1868), Ogdensburg (1872), Syracuse (1886), and Rockville Centre (1957). The story of Catholic education in the state is an amalgamation of the histories of its eight dioceses.

Early Schools

In 1800 the Catholic community statewide numbered about 1,300 communicants, almost all of them in New York City. These Catholics achieved a certain measure of respect by operating St. Peter's Free School in Manhattan, the largest denominational school in the state, with an enrollment of 220. Although it was clearly sectarian, the school received a share of the state school fund to assist in paying expenses. The number of Catholics in the state grew rapidly over the next two decades. By 1820 the Catholic population had increased to 20,000, which included about 4,000 Catholic children. Only 700 of those children were enrolled in the four existing Catholic schools, all located in New York City.

The end of public funding in 1825 was a major blow. Public funds were allocated to the Public School Society (PSS), a private Protestant organization. To receive public funds from the PSS, schools had to agree to use the King James Bible, and Catholics refused to do so because of doctrinal differences. Without state subsidies, the modest growth of Catholic schooling came to a halt. By 1830 there were 35,000 Catholics in the state, but only five parish schools (all in New York City) for 7,000 children of school age. The appointment of John J. Hughes as bishop of New York in 1840 brought a new effort to obtain state funding for parish schools. But Hughes's combative style made a clash with city and state leaders over public and private education inevitable. In fact, Hughes's campaign for state funding for parish schools in 1842 received national attention in the press and is generally considered by historians to be a turning point in the Catholic Church's decision to establish parish schools in every diocese.

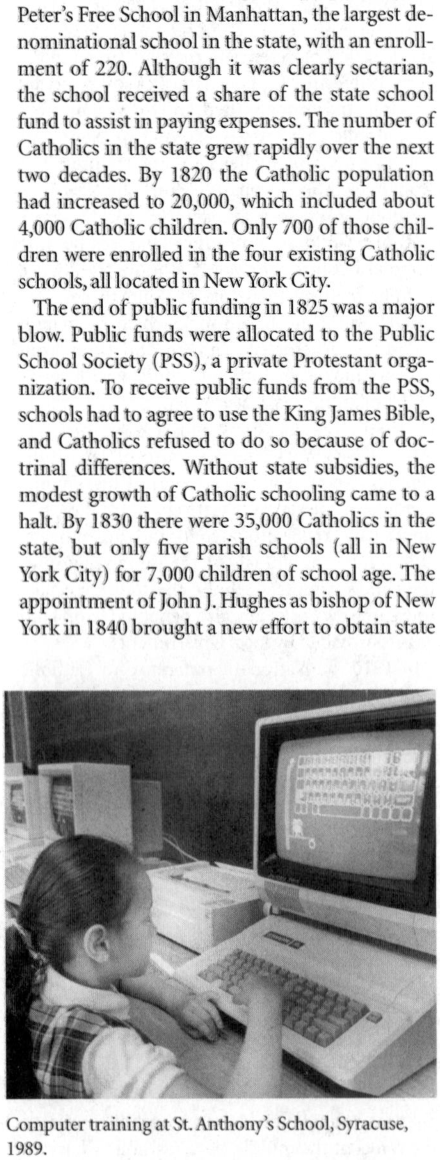

Computer training at St. Anthony's School, Syracuse, 1989.

By 1850 bitter confrontation over school funding no longer beset Catholic education. Without public financing, however, Catholic schools struggled to survive. In spite of the hierarchy's best efforts, there were only 18 Catholic schools in the state at midcentury: 12 in New York City and 3 in each of the new dioceses of Albany and Buffalo. They were far from adequate in meeting the needs of a statewide Catholic population that was estimated at 350,000. The importance of Catholic education in the mid–19th century should not be underestimated. Many parents, priests, and prelates believed that parochial schools were needed to protect the religious faith of Catholic children in a hostile, Protestant society. Although the Catholic curriculum focused for the most part on secular subjects, its social mission was to preserve the faith of future generations of communicants.

Catholic School Growth to 1900

The second half of the century heralded further population growth. Between 1850 and 1880, the number of Catholic immigrants increased sharply. As each group arrived, they built churches and schools with the blessing and encouragement of their bishops. By 1880 the number of dioceses had doubled, and the number of Catholic schools had increased to 210: 76 in New York City, 40 in Buffalo, 39 in Brooklyn, 25 in Albany, 22 in Rochester, and 8 in Ogdensburg, a rural diocese.

For the most part, the schools were privately supported. One notable option pioneered in New York State was the publicly funded Catholic school, a model that generated much controversy but educated few students. The unique structure, developed in Poughkeepsie, was created out of a financial crisis. In 1873 Rev Peter F. McSweeney threatened to close the local parish schools unless they were supported with public funds. Concerned about absorbing a 50% increase in the enrollment in its public schools, the local school board took over the parish schools and operated them for the next quarter century. Catholic nuns taught, but the curriculum was the same as that of the public schools except for an hour of religious instruction at the end of the school day. In 1895 the state school superintendent ordered the Poughkeepsie School Board to break the agreement or lose state aid. The decision was based on two grounds: the wearing of religious garb by the nuns who taught in the school, and the long-term rental of parish buildings for the purpose of public education. It underlined the incorporation of the so-called Blaine Amendment, which prohibited direct or indirect aid to educational institutions under the direction of a religious denomination, into the 1894 revision of the New York State Constitution.

Dissension and Stagnation

By 1900 the future of American Catholic education across the nation was uncertain, with various bishops divided on policy. The leader of the conservative faction was the archbishop of New York, Michael A. Corrigan. He concentrated on the means by which Catholics might obtain public funds for their schools and simultaneously retain Catholic teachings. He was joined in his cause by a number of conservative bishops from across the nation, among them Bernard J. McQuaid, the first bishop of Rochester and an outspoken supporter of Catholic education. McQuaid would consider no compromise with the public schools in his diocese and openly clashed with anyone who did not share his views.

In point of fact, the church was falling behind in the campaign to build enough schools to meet the needs of all the Catholic children in the state. By 1900 the number of Catholics in New York State had increased to nearly 2.3 million, but the number of schools had little more than doubled, with 190 schools in New York City, 73 in Buffalo, 65 in Brooklyn, 41 in Rochester, 38 in Albany, 16 in Ogdensburg, and 16 in the new Diocese of Syracuse. In response, Catholic administrators in the state sought to centralize diocesan school supervision. In an influential 1905 address, Edmund Gibbons, the Catholic superintendent of schools in Buffalo, argued that centralized supervision was necessary to facilitate communication among teachers in the diocese, to support the Americanization of ethnic schools, and most important, to convince skeptical Catholic parents of the uniform quality of parochial education. By 1920 every diocese in New York State had both a school board and a superintendent.

The Catholic population of New York State had increased to 3.3 million, and the number of Catholic schools was 765 in 1930. Although New York City had dominated Catholic education in the 19th century, by 1930 the percentage of Catholic schools in the New York Archdiocese had dropped to 30% of the state total. The other largest concentrations of Catholic schools were in Brooklyn (25%) and Buffalo (19%). Twenty years later, the Catholic population of New York State had grown to 4.2 million, an increase of 27% from 1930. The number of schools expanded more slowly, increasing by about 7%. New Catholic school building in the New York Archdiocese during the 1930s and 1940s was negligible, with the addition of only four new schools. The Diocese of Brooklyn increased the number of its schools by 10% and that of Buffalo by 11%. The remaining dioceses, however, had lower rates of growth.

The Heyday

The 1950s were boom times for Catholic education in the state and across the nation. The state's Catholic population had jumped to 5.6 million by 1960, an increase of 33%. Catholic educators struggled to respond to this growth and an unprecedented demand for Catholic schooling. The number of Catholic schools in the New York Archdiocese increased by 28% during the 1950s. Brooklyn grew too large to be a single diocese and was divided in 1957 with the creation of the Diocese of Rockville Centre (Nassau Co). There was an increase of 23% in the number of Catholic schools during the decade in these two dioceses. Buffalo had an increase of 20%; Syracuse, 55%; Rochester, 22%; and Ogdensburg, 37%. Typical of the problems arising from the demand for Catholic education were those faced by Francis Cardinal Spellman of the New York Archdiocese. During his tenure in the 1950s,

200 new elementary schools were constructed; nonetheless, by the end of the decade, there still was only one Catholic child in parochial school in his jurisdiction for every two such children in public schools. The situation would never get much better in either the city or the state.

Catholic Education on the Wane

The end of the 20th century presented no better news about Catholic education in New York State than that offered in the previous 40 years. One of the biggest changes in the years after Vatican II was in the composition of the teaching staff. For more than 125 years, Catholic schools in the state had been primarily staffed by women in religious orders. A sister-teacher in front of every class made these schools distinct. Following Vatican II, tens of thousands of nuns left their religious orders and their teaching positions, and within 20 years, most Catholic classrooms were staffed by lay teachers. Except for Rockville Centre, where the number of Catholic schools increased by 11%, the other dioceses suffered through double-digit declines in percentage as schools closed, with the Albany Diocese losing 40% of its Catholic schools between 1960 and 1980. The decline continued in the 1980s and 1990s. In fact, the continuing decline in the number of parish schools called into question the very survival of these institutions in the new century. Nevertheless, Catholic educators and a cadre of committed parents and priests across the state focused considerable time and energy in raising money for their schools and in increasing public awareness of the value of Catholic schools to their communities.

See also Higher education; New york city: education in new york city.

Curran, Robert E. *Michael Augustine Corrigan and the Shaping of Conservative Catholicism in America, 1878–1902* (New York: Ayer Press, 1978)

Kunkel, Norlene M. *Bishop Bernard J. McQuaid and Catholic Education* (New York: Garland Publishing, 1988)

Lannie, Vincent P. *Public Money and Parochial Education: Bishop Hughes, Governor Seward, and the New York School Controversy* (Cleveland: Press of Case Western Reserve Univ, 1968)

Leary, Mary Ancilla. *The History of Catholic Education in the Diocese of Albany* (Washington, DC: Catholic Univ of America Press, 1957)

Obidinski, Eugene. "Parochial School Foundations of Buffalo's Polania," *Urban Education* 18 (Jan 1984): 438–51

Ravitch, Diane, and Ronald K. Goodenow, eds. *Educating an Urban People: The New York City Experience* (New York: Teachers College Press, 1981)

Weisz, Howard. "Irish American Attitudes and the Americanization of the English Language Parochial School," *New York History* 53 (Apr 1972): 151–77

Timothy Walch

Catholics

Beginnings, 1609–1840

Catholicism constituted a relatively minor religious presence in colonial New York. A small band of French Jesuits began missionary labors among the Iroquois along the St. Lawrence River during the 1640s, but several, including Isaac Jogues and René Goupil, were martyred, and converts proved rare throughout the 17th century. Kateri Tekakwitha (1656–80), the orphaned daughter of a Mohawk chief, became the most famous Native American Catholic of her era. Her steadfast devotional commitments earned her a lasting place in Catholic cultural lore, and she was beatified by Pope John Paul II in 1980. Dutch and English colonial rulers proscribed Catholicism, excepting a brief respite (1664–88) under the Catholic proprietor (and later king) James, Duke of York that included the colony's only Catholic governor, Thomas Dongan (1682–87).

Following the American Revolution, Catholics began to establish an institutional presence in the state. New York City gradually emerged as a center of Catholic culture. Rome recognized this by establishing in 1808 the Diocese of New York, with ecclesiastical jurisdiction over the entire state and northern New Jersey. Still, only a few struggling congregations existed during the early years. St. Peter's Church on Barclay St incorporated in 1785, but New York City's Catholics did not open the doors of their second church, St. Patrick's on Mott St, until 1815. Progress was slow elsewhere in the state, with a few scattered congregations in Albany (1798), Utica (1817), and Rochester (1820). The diocese's administrative structure also remained rudimentary: New York did not receive a resident bishop until 1815. Anthony Kohlmann (1771–1836), the diocese's administrator from 1808 to 1815, defended the privacy of the confessional in 1812, successfully refusing to identify a thief in a nationally noted case that set a crucial precedent in civil law.

The situation began to change in the late 1820s as Irish, German, and French-speaking immigrants stimulated church expansion. Six new Catholic parishes appeared in New York City between 1825 and 1839, whereas congregations in northern and western New York State began sprouting up along the canal routes and railroad lines. Lay initiative fueled church growth, as communicants pressured the hierarchy for additional priests and services. Bishops relied heavily on such religious communities as the Redemptorists to minister to German congregations and the Sisters of Charity to staff schools and charitable enterprises. Francophone Canadians contributed significantly to the early 19th-century Catholic mix, dominating some smaller settlements in northern New York State, along the St. Regis and St. Lawrence Rivers, and constituting a substantial Catholic presence in such factory towns as Troy (Rensselaer Co) and Oswego. The church's increasingly immigrant character provoked a nativist reaction during the 1830s. Occasional acts of vandalism, a thriving anti-Catholic literature that bordered on the pornographic, and general political uneasiness concerning the existence of an impoverished foreign-born population became more common. These trends would intensify during the next several decades as Catholic growth exploded, as the church itself achieved greater political influence, and as ecclesiastical leaders adopted a more confrontational stance toward Protestants.

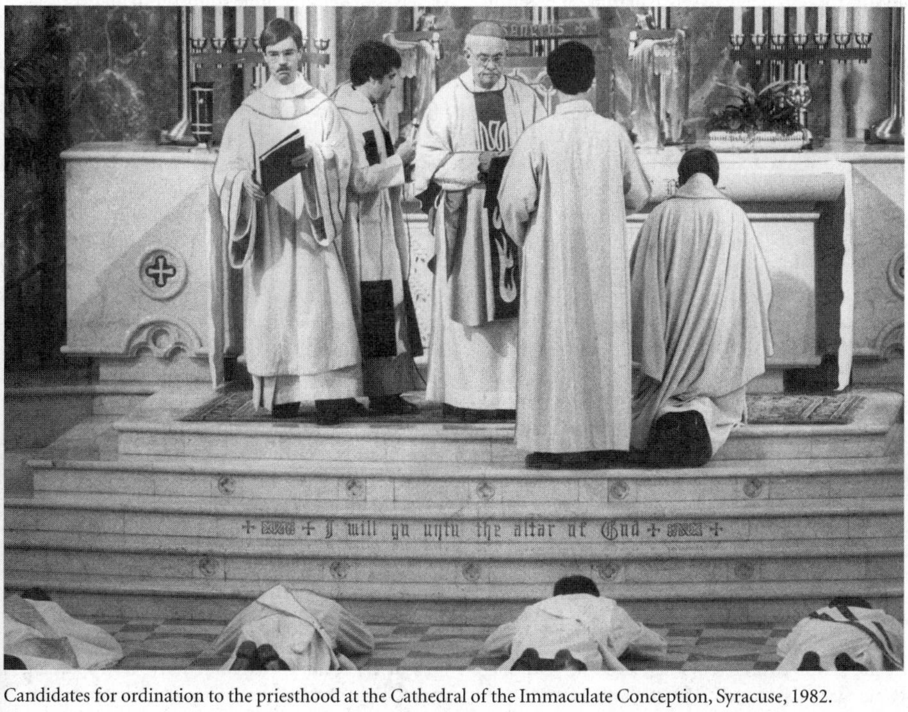

Candidates for ordination to the priesthood at the Cathedral of the Immaculate Conception, Syracuse, 1982.

The Institutional Church Matures, 1840–80

Postfamine Irish immigration and a steady influx of Germans from heavily Catholic areas helped to redefine the nature of New York Catholicism from 1840 to 1880. Urban centers, canal towns, and industrial villages all attracted large numbers of Catholic immigrant laborers. The denomination, now rapidly expanding, assumed a decidedly urban, working-class character. Rome established five dioceses within the state during this period, reflecting the new population patterns: Buffalo (1847), Albany (1847), Brooklyn (1853), Rochester (1868), and Ogdensburg (1872). After the church separated the Diocese of Syracuse from Albany in 1886, ecclesiastical jurisdictions in New York State remained essentially stable until 1957.

Bishop John J. Hughes (1797–1864) received episcopal authority over the Diocese of New York in 1842. (In 1850, reflecting its increased importance, it was elevated to an archdiocese.) Proud of both his Irish heritage and his humble roots, Hughes aggressively confronted New York City's growing nativist movement and became an eloquent spokesman for the urban immigrant laity. Initiating an organizational revolution within the church, he established scores of Catholic institutions within New York City. Following an unsuccessful political campaign in 1841 that sought state funding for parochial education, Hughes worked to create a separate and distinct Catholic educational system. He established a seminary (1840), colleges, including St. John's College (1841; now Fordham University), as well as selective schools for boys and girls, and parochial schools connected to individual parishes. Hughes even exhorted parishes to build schools before churches. He relied heavily on religious orders to staff and administer these institutions: by 1880, 17 religious communities of men and 22 communities of women labored in the diocese. Several religious communities established foundations within New York State. The Conventual Franciscan Friars (1859) and the Sisters of the Third Order of St. Francis (1860), for example, both operated motherhouses in Syracuse; the Jesuits and Christian Brothers played a major role in encouraging denominational education throughout the state; and the Redemptorists and Paulists provided revivalist missionary bands that traveled throughout the region.

Social service agencies also proliferated. St. Vincent de Paul Societies, fueled by lay contributions and offering poverty relief, remained an important feature of local parish life. Increasingly, however, dioceses and religious orders began sponsoring larger philanthropic and charitable enterprises. The New York Catholic Protectory (1863–1938) in Westchester Village [now Westchester Square, Bronx Co], which occupied 144 acres (58.3 ha), offers a good example, training and housing over 10,000 destitute and delinquent children during its first two decades; it relied on both state funding and private donations and was staffed by the Christian Brothers and the Sisters of Charity. Boys were instructed in skills including printing, shoemaking, tailoring, chair caning, and baseball manufacturing; girls learned machine sewing, hand knitting, and various household duties. Other institutions, typically staffed by religious orders, cared for the aged, the infirm, delinquents, prostitutes, and orphans. Some representative urban institutions from this period include St. Vincent's Hospital (1849), House of Mercy (1849), and New York Foundling Asylum (1869) in New York City; St. Vincent's Home for the Care and Instruction of Poor and Friendless Boys (1869) in Brooklyn; St. Joseph's Orphanage (1867–1938) in Rochester; and St. Joseph's Hospital (1869) in Syracuse.

Diocesan centralization and institutional consolidation sometimes produced conflict between priests and parishioners. Bishops and clerics often clashed with church trustees over pastoral assignments, financial allocations, property purchases, pew rents, building projects, and charitable expenditures. Hughes attempted to assert ecclesiastical control to end such controversies shortly after his appointment, demanding that all deeds to church property be turned over to the bishop and that lay trustees take a much more circumscribed role in parish governance. Dissent erupted throughout New York State, with especially acrimonious controversies occurring in Buffalo, Rochester, Troy, Oswego, and Utica. By the 1860s, however, Hughes's efforts led to an uneasy accommodation between lay initiative and priestly direction. Still, as the church hierarchy grew increasingly Irish and the laity became ever more diverse, the seeds of future conflict remained.

The Immigrant Church Diversifies, 1880–1920

Irish and German parishioners, along with their native-born progeny, continued to stimulate church growth after 1880, and the church expanded with a dramatic increase in immigration from southern and eastern Europe. Dioceses established ethnic-based parishes, and between 1880 and 1920, for example, the number of Catholic churches more than doubled in the Diocese of Brooklyn, which now boasted over 600,000 communicants and constituted the second largest Catholic population in the state behind the Diocese of New York. The number of parishes nearly doubled in the Dioceses of Albany, Syracuse, and Rochester, with Buffalo and Ogdensburg experiencing increases that exceeded 75%.

Utica offers a good example. Five Catholic churches existed in 1880, three organized along territorial lines and two catering to German speakers. By 1920 Utica had 14 churches, with 7 of the 9 new churches serving more recent ethnic arrivals: 2 Italian, 2 Polish, 1 Lithuanian, 1 Greek Melchite, and 1 Syrian Maronite. Nine churches maintained parochial schools, frequently administered by such European-based religious communities as the Felician Sisters (Polish) or the Franciscan Sisters (German). Each ethnic parish sought to preserve native languages and traditional customs of worship. Individual congregations carefully maintained their own physical facilities, created a network of social service agencies, and sponsored a panoply of lay organizations.

The ecclesiastical hierarchy remained divided on how best to administer the complex, sprawling, diverse institution that constituted American Catholicism. Some bishops, whom historians have termed "liberal," argued for greater immigrant assimilation into American life, the deemphasis of parochial schooling, an end to foreign language instruction, and more accommodation between Catholic and American institutional structures. Bishops Bernard J. McQuaid of Rochester and Michael A. Corrigan of New York, however, became national spokesmen for an alternative viewpoint. They cultivated Catholic distinctiveness, perpetuated nationality-based churches, and supported a distinctly Catholic subculture and school system, and their vision prevailed within most larger and ethnically diverse dioceses. As one key indicator, for example, 70% of the parishes in New York City maintained parochial schools in 1920, as did 64% in Buffalo and 56% in Rochester dioceses. By contrast Ogdensburg, the smallest and most rural diocese in the state and the one least affected by post-1880 immigration, reported a parochial school rate of less than 20%. The large urban ethnic church, with its parochial school and social service network, defined the public perception and institutional reality of American Catholicism.

The church continued to expand its numbers and influence. The US Bureau of the Census's *Religious Bodies: 1906* estimated that nearly 64% of the state's churchgoers belonged to Catholic congregations. (Such statistics, however, are somewhat arbitrary owing to the diverse ways in which denominations classify membership.) Catholics also began exercising significant political influence. Archbishop Corrigan forged important personal and institutional ties with Tammany Hall in New York City, obtaining substantial state funding for various child welfare endeavors. Catholic ethnic groups became integral to Democratic political machines in most major cities. Bishops proved less tolerant of alternative and radical viewpoints, as evidenced when Corrigan silenced and suspended Fr Edward McGlynn for his labor advocacy and support of Henry George's 1886 New York City mayoral campaign. Church leaders also spoke out more vehemently on such national social issues as birth control, welfare reform, sterilization legislation, and prohibition. More aggressive political activity heightened public influence and often produced tangible results. New York State would have the most restrictive divorce laws in the nation through the 1960s. The church received state appropriations to assist children in denominational childcare institutions, and priests earned the right to minister to Catholic children in public institutions during the late 19th century.

Diocesan institutions also grew more centralized and bureaucratized during this period. The Archdiocese of New York consolidated its social welfare programs under Associated Catholic Charities in 1920, and the state's other dioceses soon followed. Bishops established boards of education to coordinate curricula and to promote common standards throughout their parochial system. St. Joseph's Seminary in Dunwoodie (Westchester Co) and St. Bernard's Seminary in Rochester (1893) trained most priests in the state, replacing St. Joseph's Provincial Seminary in Troy (1864–96). Centralization often meant increased diocesan vigilance and control, as when Archbishop Corrigan suppressed the respected theological journal *New York Review* at Dunwoodie in 1908 and carefully rooted out modernists on the seminary faculty.

An American Catholic Church, 1920–65

A series of demographic shifts fundamentally altered American Catholicism between 1920 and 1965. Immigration restriction in the 1920s drastically limited Catholic migration from southern and eastern Europe, ultimately making it difficult to sustain many struggling nationality-based parishes. African Americans migrated north to such urban centers as Buffalo, Brooklyn, and Albany, which changed traditionally Catholic neighborhoods and often provoked a racist reaction. Heavy Puerto Rican migration into New York City presented new ministerial challenges in Manhattan and the Bronx, stimulating Francis Cardinal Spellman (1889–1967) to establish an active Spanish apostolate, recruit Spanish-speaking clergy, and attempt to integrate the newcomers into existing churches. Perhaps most significantly, Catholics experienced extraordinary economic and geographic mobility, especially following World War II. Second- and third-generation white ethnic groups took advantage of the cheap mortgages and GI Bill educational benefits, leaving old neighborhoods for the suburbs, moving into middle-class occupations, and attending college in greater numbers.

Church leaders responded by downplaying parochial distinctiveness and demonstrating their loyalty to broader American patriotic crusades and nationalistic movements, often becoming national cultural celebrities in the process. Cardinal Spellman, for example, aggressively backed Sen Joseph McCarthy's anticommunist campaigns during the 1950s and traveled the world supporting American troops in his position as military vicar. Fulton J. Sheen (1895–1979), a popular New York priest who subsequently served as bishop of Rochester, became one of the most familiar faces on network television with his *Life Is Worth Living* program during the 1950s. Sheen's genial common-sense advice and subtle explications of Catholic philosophy resonated well with an ecumenical national audience. The 1954 film *On The Waterfront* portrayed a priest modeled after New York's John Corridan (1911–84), who directed the Jesuit's Xavier Institute of Labor Relations in New York City and who fought racketeering and union corruption on the docks through his affiliation with the conservative Association of Catholic Trade Unionists. Some Catholic countercultural voices persisted. Dorothy Day (1897–1980) founded the *Catholic Worker* newspaper in 1933, dedicated to the notion of radical social justice based largely on papal labor encyclicals.

The church also launched massive building programs in the suburbs. The Diocese of Rockville Centre (Nassau Co), erected in 1957 to encompass Long Island's Nassau and Suffolk Cos, exemplifies this trend. Twenty-eight parishes had been established in these counties between 1948 and 1957, and eleven more were founded during the following decade, with almost 75% of parishes supporting parochial elementary schools. Baby boomer Catholics who settled these bedroom communities attempted to reconstruct the rich parish life they left behind in such places as Brooklyn and Queens. An aggressive high school building program produced such massive schools as Holy Trinity in Hicksville (Nassau Co) and Maria Regina in Uniondale (Nassau Co), and Catholic youth organizations and athletic leagues proliferated. Rockville Centre soon surpassed Buffalo as the third largest diocese in the state, behind only New York and Brooklyn. This consolidation of the Catholic secondary school network, coupled with such federal incentives as the GI Bill and the increasingly middle-class nature of the church, produced booming enrollments at Catholic colleges and universities. St. John's University became the largest Catholic university in the state, and growth completely transformed such institutions as St. Bonaventure University, Fordham University, Niagara University, Canisius College, Iona College, Siena College, Marist College, Manhattan College, St. Joseph's College, and St. John Fisher College. The early 1960s were an optimistic time for church leaders generally, as Catholics apparently had moved into the nation's social, economic, and political mainstream.

VATICAN II AND BEYOND, 1965–2000

The Second Vatican Council, which concluded its work in 1965, irrevocably altered Catholic parish life. The vernacular liturgy, broader lay participation in both the Mass and in parish affairs generally, a new ecumenical spirit, a greater emphasis on Scripture reading, and a commitment to confront constructively the modern world all translated into new programs and challenges for priests and parishioners. These changes coincided with unprecedented demographic difficulties for church leaders. A dramatic drop in priestly vocations, a steep decline in the number of women entering religious life, lagging weekly Mass attendance, and sharp internal disagreements over social priorities made the late 20th century an especially contentious and uncertain period.

Dioceses struggled to cope with dwindling urban ethnic congregations, declining school enrollments, and difficulties in staffing a vast institutional network owing to the shortage of priests and sisters. Mergers, consolidations, and closings defined the period. The Diocese of Albany, for example, boasted 209 parishes, 14 diocesan and private high schools, and 98 elementary schools in 1970. By 1990 those figures had decreased to 199 parishes, 5 high schools, and 44 elementary schools. Schools were consolidated in Syracuse, Binghamton, Utica, Rome, and Oswego, often over angry protests from local parishioners. Twenty-four churches in Buffalo have been closed or merged since the 1970s. When inner-city parishes remained open, as in New York City, bishops frequently assessed wealthier suburban churches to subsidize their urban ministries.

Political issues also exacerbated tensions. Episcopal leaders in such places as Buffalo and Brooklyn, committed to social justice and inner-city ministries, often confronted angry priests and parishioners alarmed by increasing African American populations in traditionally Catholic communities. Some priests, taking seriously the Vatican Council's call to confront the modern world, adopted controversial political stances. Daniel (1921–) and Philip (1923–2002) Berrigan, brother priests from Syracuse, angered conservative Catholics with their staunch public opposition to the Vietnam War. Other activists challenged the hierarchy over issues such as women's ordination, gay rights, contraception, racial justice, and homelessness. The right to life movement probably generated the most discord within church circles. New York's bishops took the lead in mobilizing protests against any changes to the state's restrictive abortion laws in 1967 and vehemently opposed the Supreme Court's *Roe v Wade* decision (1973) legalizing abortion. Intense lobbying, picketing of abortion clinics and Planned Parenthood offices, weekly Sunday sermons, and periodic prayer vigils all constituted part of the antiabortion political strategy.

John Cardinal O'Connor (1920–2000), who became archbishop of New York in 1984, often served as a lightning rod for issues that polarized clergy and laity. He criticized vice presidential candidate Geraldine A. Ferraro and Gov Mario M. Cuomo in 1984, arguing that Catholic politicians had a moral obligation to oppose public funding for abortion. O'Connor also vigorously fought efforts by New York City to compel the archdiocese to guarantee equal employment opportunities for homosexuals, opposed the participation of gay activists in the St. Patrick's Day parade, and remained a major traditionalist spokesman within the hierarchy concerning many sexual and social issues. He also, however, vigorously opposed capital punishment, personally worked in AIDS hospices, and fought conservative efforts to reform welfare in the 1990s, thus reflecting the complexity of Catholic teachings and the way in which they transcend traditional liberal/conservative distinctions.

As the 21st century dawned, the Catholic Church in New York had evolved from very humble beginnings into an incredibly complex institution. A remarkably heterogeneous laity varied widely in its class, ethnic, and social composition. Many issues remained controversial within the communion. Liberal activists during the 1980s and 1990s protested official church policies concerning homosexuality, birth control, women's ordination, and clerical celibacy. Conservatives, newly energized by the lengthy papacy of John Paul II, sought to reemphasize supernaturalism within Catholic teachings, and supported greater Roman authority over church life. The scandals concerning the sexual abuse of children by priests that started to surface in 2002 have threatened to divide clergy and laity further. Still, Catholics undeniably have exhibited a remarkable institutional loyalty, despite their internal disagreements over individual church teachings and political stances. According to the 2002 *Official Catholic Directory,* over 1,650 parishes in New York State ministered to a population that exceeded 7.8 million communicants, and Catholics worshiped in every corner of the state.

See also BIRTH CONTROL; DIVORCE; GERMANS; HEALTHCARE AND HOSPITALS; IRISH.

Becker, Martin Joseph. *A History of Catholic Life in the Diocese of Albany, 1609–1864* (New York: US Catholic Historical Society, 1975)

Curran, Robert Emmett. *Michael Augustine Corrigan and the Shaping of Conservative Catholicism in America, 1878–1902* (New York: Arno Press, 1978)

Dolan, Jay P. *The Immigrant Church: New York's Irish and German Catholics, 1815–1865* (Baltimore: Johns Hopkins Univ Press, 1975)

Leonard, Joan de Lourdes. *Richly Blessed: The Diocese of Rockville Centre, 1957–1990* (Rockville Centre, NY: Diocese of Rockville Centre, 1991)

McNamara, Robert F. *The Diocese of Rochester in America, 1868–1993* (Rochester: Diocese of Rochester, 1993)

O'Brien, David. *Faith and Friendship: Catholicism in the Diocese of Syracuse, 1886–1986* (Syracuse: Diocese of Syracuse, 1987)

Taylor, Mary Christine. *A History of the Foundations of Catholicism in Northern New York* (New York: US Catholic Historical Society, 1976)

Valaik, J. David. *Celebrating God's Life in Us: The Catholic Diocese of Buffalo, 1847–1997* (Buffalo: Heritage Press, 1997)

Peter J. Wosh

Catholic Worker. Lay religious movement. Founded by Dorothy Day and Peter Maurin in New York City in 1933, the movement seeks to realize Christian ideals of social justice and solidarity with the poor. *Catholic Worker,* the best-known product of the movement, includes radical reporting on social problems along with spiritual and political essays. By 1936 circulation had reached 150,000, and at the end of the 20th century the newspaper maintained a circulation of over 80,000. Members established "houses of hospitality" (urban hospices for the poor), rural farms, and retreats, in keeping with Maurin's ideal of a decentralized village economy. By 1940 the Catholic Worker had 29 branches, including houses in Buffalo, Rochester, and Troy (Rensselaer Co). In 1947 Maryfarm, the original farm, moved from Easton, Pa, to Newburgh (Orange Co) and closed in 1955. Other farms have been located in Pleasant Plains (1950–64) and Tivoli (1964–79) in Dutchess Co, and in Marlboro (1979–) in Ulster Co. The civil rights and peace movements helped to revive interest in this experiment in "applied Christianity." In the late 1960s and early 1970s, aspiring Catholic Workers established houses in Niagara Falls, Orwell (Oswego Co), Schenectady, and Syracuse. Later Jacques Travers founded the Arthur Sheehan House of Hospitality in Brooklyn (1977–90). Century's end found the Catholic Worker movement represented in Albany, Binghamton, Buffalo, Ithaca, Lacona, Marlboro, New York City, Niagara Falls, Orwell, Rochester, Syracuse, Utica, and Wyandanch. The Catholic Worker movement's commitment to social action and personal transformation influenced many activists, including Michael Harrington and Daniel and Philip Berrigan.

Piehl, Mel. *Breaking Bread: The Catholic Worker and the Origin of Catholic Radicalism in America* (Philadelphia: Temple Univ Press, 1982)

Phillip M. Runkel

Catlin. Town (pop 2,649) in NW Chemung Co. Settled about 1816, the town was formed from Catharine [now in Schuyler Co] in 1823. The Northern Central Railroad (1849; later Pennsylvania Railroad) and the Syracuse, Geneva and Corning Railroad (1877; later New York Central Railroad) served the town. Lumbering and agriculture, especially dairying and potato growing, sustained Catlin throughout most of the 20th century. Beginning in the 1950s, with a population increase, the town became increasingly residential; its residents work in Elmira, Horseheads, Big Flats, and Corning.

Heather A. Wade

Cato. Town (pop 2,744) and village (pop 601) in N central Cayuga Co. Settled in 1800, the town was formed in 1802 from Aurelius. The village, formerly a stop on the Southern Central Railroad (1869), was incorporated in 1880. Cigars and agricultural implements were produced during the second half of the 19th century. The town remains predominantly agricultural, although its population increased by one-third between 1960 and 2000. In 2003 many residents commuted to jobs in Syracuse, Auburn, Fulton, or Oswego or worked for the local school system, which served as the area's largest employer. Cross Lake on the town's eastern boundary is used for recreation.

David A. Dudley and Margaret Sweetman

Caton. Town (pop 2,097) in SE Steuben Co. Settled in 1819, the town was formed as Wormley in 1839 and had its name changed to Caton in 1840. Shingle making and lumbering were early sources of income, but the town became a dairying region, with maple sugar production as a sideline. In 2003 there were still a number of large dairy farms in Caton, but most residents worked in Corning or Elmira. Its school, centralized in 1957, was merged into the Corning district in 1982 and has been a facility for developmentally disabled adults since 1987.

Thomas Dimitroff

Catskill. Town (pop 11,849) and village (pop 4,392) in SE Greene Co. Settled by 1650 its population was Dutch and German. As Great Inbogt it was formed as a district of Albany Co in 1772 and became the Town of Catskill in 1788. Annexed to Ulster Co in 1798, it became an original town of Greene Co (1800). The village, the county seat, was surveyed near a river landing in 1773 and incorporated in 1806; it grew rapidly as an entrepôt for beef, potash, wheat, and timber from the backcountry and the Susquehanna region, attracting many New Englanders until, with the opening of the Erie Canal, its trade began to decline. Brickmaking and shipbuilding employed many. Textile mills at Leeds attracted Irish operatives from 1846 to 1882; Portland cement plants at Cementon opened in 1900 and drew a Croatian population. African Americans in the village were drawn by labor demands. The Rip Van Winkle Bridge (1935) connects the town with the east side of the Hudson River; the Thruway (1954) passes just west of the village. At the end of the 20th century an increasing number of residents were Albany-bound commuters, and the village also drew weekend homeowners from New York City. Important landmarks are the stone bridge at Leeds (1792) and the Thomas Cole House, where the artist lived from 1836 to 1848. The Catskill Game Farm has drawn tourists since 1933.

Field Horne

Catskill Mountain House. One of the most famous hotels in the United States during the 19th century, located in Hunter (Greene Co). It was built by a chartered stock company, the Catskill Mountain Association, on Pine Orchard near Kaaterskill Clove, an area that included North Lake, South Lake, and large rock platforms that protruded beyond the edge of the mountain. The Mountain House began as a small inn in 1823, added 50 rooms in 1825, and quickly became one of the most important tourist sights in the United States. Although designed in the Federal style, the hotel was remodeled with a Neoclassical facade embellished by 13 large columns and a 140 ft (42.7 m) porch facing the valley. Before the Civil War the Mountain House seemed perched on the very edge of civilization, accessible only by a sometimes frightening four-hour stage ride from the steamboat landing at Catskill (Greene Co).

The area benefited from the popularity of the American Romantic movement; the porch and ledge were a primary vantage point to view the sublimity of the landscape stretching a thousand feet below. The view was immortalized in James Fenimore Cooper's *The Pioneers* (1823), and the awe-inspiring sunrise in front of the hotel became one of the must-see attractions of the antebellum Fashionable Tour. The luxurious Mountain House was itself a principal attraction, its image widely reproduced in the form of lithographs by Currier and Ives; paintings by Thomas Cole, Jasper Francis Cropsey, and Sanford Robinson Gifford; and writers such as Washington Irving, William Cullen Bryant, and Nathaniel P. Willis. South Lake inspired Cole's *Lake with Dead Trees* (1825), essentially the first painting of the Hudson River school, and Cole also immortalized Kaaterskill Falls, the beautiful two-tiered waterfall 2 mi (3 km) from the Mountain House. Charles L. Beach (1807–1902), a wealthy local entrepreneur, leased the Mountain House in 1839 and bought it in 1845, contributing greatly to the flush times that lasted for the rest of the century.

By the 1880s the Catskill Mountains had been laced with railroads and new grand hotels. The narrow-gauge Catskill Mountain Railroad opened in 1883 from Catskill to Palenville (Greene Co), greatly reducing the travel time of Mountain House guests. In 1892 the Otis Elevating Railroad, a funicular, began operations, bringing guests directly to the resort. With the new ease of access, the Mountain House, although now offering more than 300 rooms, lost some of its luster and was no longer rough, remote, or inspirational. It remained, however, the oldest and most romantic and historic establishment in the Catskills and a shrine of summer pilgrimage. It slowly fell out of favor in the 20th century, the railroad stopped operating in 1918, and the resort itself closed in 1942. It lay in ever increasing ruins until the New York State Conservation Department, fearing a hazard to casual visitors, burned the remains in January 1963. The site is easily accessible and is still a favorite hiking and camping area.

A View of the Catskill Mountain House, by Sarah Cole, 1848.

Evers, Alf, et al. *Resorts of the Catskills* (New York: St. Martin's Press, 1979)

Van Zandt, Roland. *The Catskill Mountain House* (1966; repr Hensonville, NY: Black Dome Press, 1991)

Jon Sterngass

Catskills. An ecological, economic, and cultural region of southeastern New York State extending west from the Hudson River. In 1973 the New York State legislature officially defined the Catskill region to include Delaware, Greene, Otsego, Schoharie, Sullivan, and Ulster Cos, and the Towns of Berne, Coeymans, Knox, New Scotland, Rensselaerville, and Westerlo in Albany Co. At approximately 4 million acres (1.7 million ha), the region exceeds a more conservative definition that recognizes only the mountains of Greene Co west of the Town of Catskill; it also surpasses the boundaries of the Catskill Forest Preserve, established in 1885. The official definition more closely reflects interpretations that emerged with tourism expansion during the 19th and 20th centuries. In particular it includes Sullivan Co communities such as Liberty and Monticello, which appropriated the name Catskills to attract Jewish vacationers at the turn of the 20th century. Purists in Greene and Ulster Cos traditionally eschew this broader definition and assert that the "real" Catskills region is the mountainous area that attracted artists, writers, and the wealthy in the early years of tourism. The official definition also bucks the traditional understanding of the Catskills as a physical landscape dominated by the multiple peaks of an eroded plateau, since it encompasses many hill formations, such as the Shawangunk Mountains and Plattekill Mountains, which were traditionally excluded because of geological nonconformity.

Questions about the origin of the region's name also remain unresolved. Catskill is probably a combination of the Dutch words for cat and creek. From the beginning the name encountered resistance. After assuming rule over former Dutch territory in 1664, the English proposed Blue Mountains. About a century later, the Livingston family of Clermont [now in Columbia Co] suggested the name Lothian Hills in honor of their Scottish ancestors and Scotland's mountains. Both proposals failed. Finally, the Romantic movement offered Onteora, a name contrived by Indian expert Henry Rowe Schoolcraft from Iroquois terms for mountain and sky. Despite its lack of association with Indian tribes in the immediate area, the name Onteora fulfilled the public need to pay homage to American Indian culture. Onteora was popularized by Kingston (Ulster Co) poet Henry Abbey and by 19th-century guidebooks, but it never superseded the name Catskills.

Physical Geography

Popular conceptions of the Catskills are perhaps most strongly influenced by the region's physical geography. The ridges and valleys were formed by erosion of a portion of the Appalachian Mountain chain's Allegheny Plateau following its uplift to 6,000 feet (1,830 m) above present sea level approximately 300 million years ago. Erosion reduced the uplifted plateau to a carved peneplain of steep mountains. Summits range from a high of 4,180 feet (1,274 m) at Slide Mountain in Ulster Co to an average low of 2,700 ft (820 m) at Mill Brook Ridge in Hardenburgh (Ulster Co). Ninety-eight peaks exceed 3,000 feet (914 m), while only two exceed 4,000 ft (1,219 m). Mountains rise sharply from the west bank of the Hudson River in an area called the Eastern Catskills Escarpment and grade to the west. There are at least 10 recognizable ranges, including the Slide Mountain massif, the Dry Brook Ridge Range, and the Hunter Mountain Range. Only the Shawangunk Range in Ulster Co stands alone in geologic origin, being older and composed of limestone and quartz conglomerate.

Because the Allegheny Plateau was an inland seabed in the early Devonian period prior to its dramatic uplift, layers of shale, sandstone, and limestone dominate the region's subsurface geology. This sedimentary bedrock often underlies deposits of conglomerate and boulders left by retreating glaciers during the Pleistocene epoch (*ca* 1 million years BP). Despite the resultant rockiness of much Catskill soil, its fertility supports rich forests. Northern hardwood tree species such as sugar maple, yellow birch, and American beech dominate. Lowland areas also concentrate poplar, sycamore, and willow, while higher elevations concentrate hemlock, black cherry, and white birch. Less common species include balsam fir and red spruce at the highest summits, and hickory and white pine along the drier eastern escarpment. Prior to Europeans' arrival, elk, wolves, and panthers populated Catskill forests, but these animals are now locally extinct. Extant native fauna include the red fox and the black bear, which is the subject of regional folklore and festivals. Human beings are also present in great numbers, particularly during the summer months, when the average diurnal temperatures range from 70° to 85°F (21–29°C) compared to higher temperatures farther south. Winter temperatures vary. Lowland mid-Hudson Valley communities commonly experience diurnal January temperatures near 32°F (0°C), while northwest mountain communities are 3–7 degrees colder on average. Precipitation varies, too. Sullivan Co communities commonly have 45–50 inches (114–127 cm) of precipitation a year, while those near the Delaware River's headwaters in the northern Catskills see less total precipitation but up to 30 inches (76 cm) more snow.

Plentiful precipitation feeds numerous rivers and creeks in the region. Of the three major natural systems, the Hudson-Mohawk River watershed most strongly influenced historical economic trends and settlement. Eight tributaries in the region feed the Hudson, including Rondout, Esopus, and Catskill Creeks. Many of these tributaries contain waterfalls and rapids that generated power for early settlements and were tourist attractions during the 19th century. Portions of the Delaware and Susquehanna River systems also lie within the Catskills. The Delaware River rises near Stamford (Delaware Co). Its two branches flow roughly parallel in a southwest direction before converging at Hancock (Delaware Co) and continuing in a southeast direction. The Susquehanna rises at Otsego Lake in the western foothills of the region and remains at the periphery of the Catskills. Of the latter two river systems, only the Delaware has exerted significant influence on the region's topography because it is the source of three reservoirs completed between 1955 and 1967 to provide water for New York City. To the east, the Catskill Reservoir and Aqueduct system, constructed 1909–24, impounds water at the Ashokan Reservoir northwest of Kingston and at the Schoharie Reservoir in Gilboa (Schoharie Co).

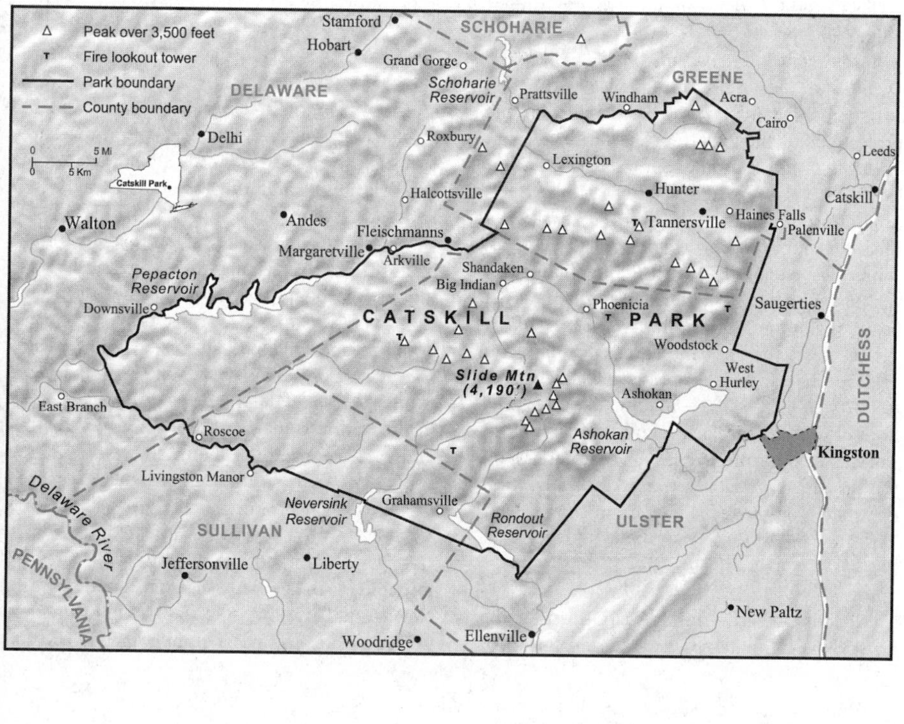

Settlement and Early Industries

The Catskills remained largely unsettled by Europeans during the Dutch period, although Algonquian-speaking Indians used the river valleys. The English colonial government provided four large land patents (Loonenburg, Coeymans, Catskill, and Hardenbergh) that drew settlers to the region beginning in 1664. At first, settlement remained scant, perhaps because of the steep slopes and rocky soil and concern about Indian attacks. Farmers who risked settlement cleared their fields with the labor of enslaved Africans, who made up 22% of the population of Greene and Columbia Cos in 1714. In 1763 settlement accelerated as British soldiers, relieved of service in the French and Indian War, were offered land grants in Catskill, Cairo, Durham, and Windham [now in Greene Co]. Still, as late as 1785, only a few German farmers populated the upland areas, and one present-day town, Denning (Ulster Co), was not settled until 1837. The general aversion to mountain habitation shifted in the coming decade as land-hungry New Englanders swarmed west and settled the Mountaintop of Greene Co, including Durham, Barbertown [now North Lexington], Jewett Heights, and Goshen [now Lexington]. Many built regionally distinctive "blockhouse" log cabins, characterized by an exterior of squared logs and dovetailed joints.

Settlers in the traditional Catskills region encompassing Greene Co and northern Ulster Co remained almost exclusively farmers and part-time craftspeople until the turn of the 19th century. In the uplands, farmers made some money from maple sugar and wool production, but market agriculture was concentrated in the river valley areas. From there, surpluses of wheat, corn, barley, and hay were routinely exported to New York City until 1825 when the Erie Canal opened up the Genesee Valley and subjected Catskill grain farmers to devastating competition. This turn of events prompted both westward emigration and a shift from grain to dairy and specialty crops. Butter, maple syrup, black spruce beer, and fruit poured out of the Catskills beginning around 1845. In 1855 farmers pastured 12,600 cows in the valleys of Greene Co, and they produced about 1.2 million pounds (544,000 kg) of butter for export. At the same time, commercial plum, pear, and apple orchards were on the rise in the fertile district stretching from Catskill to Kingston. Huckleberries were a particular specialty of the Shandaken (Ulster Co) mountain area. By the mid-1840s, huckleberry season prompted an annual migration of "Schoharies"—seasonal help of triracial heritage (white, black, and Native American)—to Greene and Ulster Cos. Pails and whiskey (said to cure rattlesnake bites) in hand, pickers scaled up to 5 miles (8 km) of steep Shandaken slopes to gather the berries that they sold each evening to dealers at Hudson River landings for shipment to New York City. By 1870 the huckleberry trade to New York City was well organized. Those with a stake in the industry were known to start fires in the hills surreptitiously to prompt a flourish of bushes on the burned-over land. Their actions conflicted with the nascent conservation movement's focus on forest preservation in the Catskill Mountains.

Farmers and berry pickers were only partially to blame for the deforestation that plagued the region by 1850. Extractive forest-based industries were the primary cause. Drawn by waterpower and the promise of timber profits, settlers of the northern Catskills established sawmills to produce lumber, staves, and potash as early as 1780. The potash industry boomed until 1825 and was superseded by tanneries, which relied heavily on hemlock bark for the production of tannin. Tanning began in Greene Co in 1792. As early as 1830, an unsustainable rate of hemlock bark peeling caused a massive tree die-off that, together with competition from western leather industries now linked to the east by the Erie Canal, was the death knell of the state's leather industry. The resultant emigration to Sullivan Co, Michigan, Ohio, and Indiana depopulated Hunter (Greene Co), Jewett, and other tannery villages. Still, in 1845, 32 tanneries remained in Greene Co alone. In addition, enough labor remained to support a strong lumber industry with over 100 sawmills in the peaks region. By 1840 Hunter was a production center for wooden items such as coffins, furniture, and farm implements. Within a decade Mountaintop farmers had begun to fill the demand for balsam Christmas trees in New York City, and by 1870 urban consumers demanded wooden souvenirs during their summer visits to the burgeoning mountain resorts. Chemicals distilled from hardwoods were a significant product of the Delaware and Willowemoc Valleys in Delaware and Sullivan Cos beginning in 1848; production ended after synthetics became widespread in the 1920s. The only industries that were not dependent upon forests were the numerous bluestone quarries near the Hudson River and brickmaking establishments along its shore.

Conservation

The imperiled status of Catskill Mountain forests was officially recognized in 1872 when the Commission of State Parks had the opportunity to recommend protecting those lands. Ironically, though, the commission ignored the Catskills region because of its poor ecological condition and chose to conserve land in the Adirondack Mountains instead. The focus on economically viable forests became apparent again in 1884 when a second commission dismissed Catskill forests on the grounds that they contained unprofitable tree stands and protected insignificant watersheds. The establishment of the Catskill Forest Preserve, initially 33,894 acres (13,716 ha), was mainly attributable to the efforts of Ulster Co politician Cornelius A. J. Hardenburgh. As an assemblyman he introduced a bill to transfer county-owned lands to the state to absolve the county of accrued tax debts and other obligations. On 20 Apr 1885 Hardenburgh unwittingly became a conservation pioneer when the bill's passage laid the foundations for the preserve. A provision added to the state constitution in 1894 dictated that all state forest preserve land remain forever wild.

The Catskill Park, containing a mixture of public and private land, was formed in 1904 with the establishment of its boundary, known as the Blue Line. State-owned land within the park remained forest preserve, subject to the protections of the 1894 forever wild provision. Regardless of the existence of private land within Catskill Park, it remains a controversial symbol of land-use rights in the region. The park set a precedent for state involvement in Catskill resource use, paving the way for land condemnation in support of reservoir development at the beginning of the 20th century. At the turn of the 21st century, the park measured 705,500 acres (285,506 ha) and encompassed 53% of Ulster Co, 27% of Greene Co, and sizable border portions of southeast Delaware and northeast Sullivan Cos. At this time, over 59% of the park's land was privately owned, illustrating the integration of public and private land use unique to the New York State Forest Preserve system.

Transportation and Tourism

The history of economic development in the Catskills is intimately tied to the evolution of transportation technology and corridors. From the earliest period of European settlement, the Catskill economy was geared toward New York City and Philadelphia markets. Turnpikes, notably the ones terminating at Catskill and Newburgh (Orange Co), drew backcountry products eastward across the hills and mountains by 1802. Until the completion of the Erie Canal in 1825, the region's privileged access to the Hudson River allowed it to develop into a grain, wood, and leather producer, and made river ports of Saugerties (Ulster Co), Kingston, and Catskill. Moreover, the efficiency of midcentury steamboat transport to New York City allowed the Catskills agricultural economy to rebuild around perishable products after the Erie Canal opened new markets that devastated Catskills grain production. Meanwhile, the Delaware and Hudson Canal made an important hub out of Kingston between 1828 and 1898. As the endpoint of the canal that brought coal from Pennsylvania, Kingston was also the starting point for coal shipment south to New York City.

Perhaps more revolutionary than the canals were the railroads that brought mass tourism to the Catskills starting in the 1880s. Tourism actually began during the 1820s, but it was concentrated in the northern mountains and generally only available to the leisure classes. The first hotel, the Catskill Mountain House, opened in Catskill in 1823; pioneering establishments in other parts of the region were J. B. Findlay's at White Lake (Sullivan Co) in 1846 and the Mountain Inn at Pine Hill (Ulster Co) in 1848. The region's tourism was characterized by inaccessibility and wilderness, images newly in vogue as a result of paintings by Thomas Cole, Asher B. Durand, Thomas Doughty, and John Frederick Kensett, and stories by James Fenimore Cooper (*The Pioneers*) and Washington Irving ("Rip Van Winkle"). Summering leisure classes of New York City, Boston, and Philadelphia joined intellectuals, artists, and politicians in laborious stagecoach rides into the mountain towns of Greene and Ulster Cos. There they enjoyed the picturesque Kaaterskill Falls and Plattekill and Stony Cloves in the Wall of Manitou (the eastern escarpment). Ironically, the hoteliers themselves sabotaged the coveted remoteness of their majestic resorts by introducing rail service in the early 1870s as a means of competing with each other. Proprietors of the Catskill Mountain House, Hotel Kaaterskill, Laurel House, and Overlook Mountain House supported and in some cases financed the Catskill Mountain, Stony Clove and Catskill Mountain, Kaaterskill, Otis Elevating, and Catskill and Tannersville Railroads.

The Ulster and Delaware Railroad operated from 1872 to 1954, all the while aggressively promoting the boarding business along its route from Kingston to Oneonta (Otsego Co). The boom in boardinghouses signaled this gradual transition from exclusivity. The small-scale accommodations that earned farm families extra income prior to the 1880s were considered second rate compared to mountain resort hotels and to the cottage communities like Onteora Park created near Tannersville (Greene Co) in 1887–89 to provide private retreats in parklike settings. Boardinghouses and rail travel were affordable for the working-class Irish and Jews of New York City. By 1890, 900 establishments helped create a summer population of 70,000 people in Greene Co, more than double its 31,000 winter population.

Ethnic diversity in tourism brought controversy. Boardinghouses tended to cater to Catholic, Protestant, or Jewish clienteles, as tourists gravitated toward their own communities. However, incidents of deliberate exclusion of Jews in the late 1870s stimulated a reaction. By 1900 Hunter and Tannersville and Griffins Corner [now Fleischmanns, Delaware Co] had established themselves as tolerant communities that attracted Jewish vacationers of Hungarian, German, Russian, and Polish descent. Meanwhile, entrepreneurs in Ulster and Sullivan Cos seized the opportunity to offer "Catskill vacations" to a growing number of American Jews. They built bungalow colonies and resort hotels in the Neversink and Rondout Valleys, beginning in the Fallsburg (Sullivan Co) vicinity in 1899. At that time, the Ontario and Western Railroad was the area's main transportation artery; it promoted the new resorts to enhance its own business. Because they were able to take advantage of the more extensive road and railroad system to the south, and because they solicited Jews, Sullivan Co hoteliers began draining tourism from the northern Catskills. The resort trade shifted further because of the relative ease with which Jewish hoteliers obtained financing during the Great Depression. The southern Catskills resort region, the borscht belt, was born; by 1935–40, the region's transition from gentile to Jewish resort was essentially complete. This resort business remained strong until the mid-1960s, when it began a steady decline.

New York City's demand for drinking water transformed the Catskills landscape beginning in 1907, when construction of Ashokan Reservoir began in Ulster Co. Five other reservoirs, scattered throughout the region, were placed in service by the time the system was complete in 1964. Initial impact included the loss of fertile valley farmland, destruction of communities, and reforestation of surrounding land. The long-term effect was the creation of greater scenic beauty, appealing to the region's tourists.

About the time Jewish summer boarding was reaching a dominant position in the region, a new sport was creating a winter season. Beginning in Shandaken in 1935, skiing became an attraction. By the 1960s half a dozen ski facilities were scattered throughout the mountains in Shandaken, Andes, Roxbury, Jefferson, Hunter, and Windham.

The automobile's lure drew Catskills tourists from the trains beginning in the World War I era. By 1920 the short lines serving Hunter and Cairo had discontinued passenger service; the main lines westward through Sullivan and Ulster Cos and into Delaware Co became freight-only in 1952 and 1954 respectively. This consumer shift in transportation created pressure on the state's highway system. One of the first roads to be improved for tourist traffic, the Rip Van Winkle Trail (Rte 23A), was built through Kaaterskill Clove in 1921. The pent-up demand of the war years released a huge volume on the roads after World War II and began the call for superhighways. The Thruway was the first to affect the region, completed in 1954 and linked to New York City in 1955. Rte 17 (I-86) was rebuilt from the Thruway into the heart of the Sullivan Co Catskills in 1959–60. The last of the region's superhighways, I-88 (1975–80), is more important as a commuter highway for residents in the northwestern fringe of the region than as a vacation artery, as it does not lead from a major city.

RECENT EVENTS

The Woodstock Festival, held in Bethel (Sullivan Co) in August 1969, was arguably the Catskills' most newsworthy event in the 20th century; even though there have been attempts to revive it on major anniversaries, its long-term impact has been small aside from enhanced name recognition. In the ensuing years, as the Jewish-oriented resorts faded in Sullivan Co and western Ulster Co, the major transformation was the ever increasing acquisition of property by urban residents; by 2000, for example, nonresidents owned as much as 70% of some parts of Delaware Co.

Population pressures along with increasingly stringent environmental regulations resulted in conflict following the 1990 promulgation of new rules to protect New York City's watershed in an effort to obviate a federally mandated filtration plant. Thirty-five towns in Delaware, Ulster, Sullivan, and Greene Cos formed the Coalition of Watershed Towns to fight the new regulations. In the following year more than 85% of the region's farmers became participants in the Watershed Agricultural Council. In 1996 the coalition, the state, and New York City signed a Memorandum of Agreement, which was perceived as a model for the preservation of watershed quality and of rural livelihoods.

As the 21st century dawned, the chief controversy involved the state provision for gambling casinos in Sullivan Co, perceived as a means of adapting huge, abandoned hotel buildings to new uses and of creating badly needed jobs. While favored by many because of the persistent unemployment problem in the region, the proposal was controversial because the Indian tribes that were to run the casinos were not local and because much of the profit, going to non-Indian management companies, would not remain in Sullivan Co and its environs.

See also BORSCHT BELT; GEOLOGY AND PLATE TECTONICS; TANNING INDUSTRY; TOURISM; WATER SUPPLY AND USE: NEW YORK CITY WATERSHED.

Adams, Arthur G. *The Catskills: An Illustrated Historical Guide with Gazetteer* (New York: Fordham Univ Press, 1990)

Evers, Alf. *The Catskills: From Wilderness to Woodstock* (Woodstock, NY: Overlook Press, 1982)

———. *In Catskill Country: Collected Essays on Mountain History, Life, and Lore* (Woodstock, NY: Overlook Press, 1995)

Horne, Field. *The Greene County Catskills: A History* (Hensonville, NY: Black Dome Press, 1994)

Van Valkenburgh, Norman J. *The Forest Preserve of New York State in the Adirondack and Catskill Mountains: A Short History* (Fleischmanns, NY: Purple Mountain Press, 1996)

Karen Nichols

Catskill Turnpike. See SUSQUEHANNA TURNPIKE.

Catt [née Lane], Carrie (Clinton) Chapman (*b* Ripon, Wisc, 9 Feb 1859; *d* New Rochelle, Westchester Co, 9 Mar 1947). Suffragist. The daughter of farmers, Carrie Lane attended Iowa State Agricultural College (now Iowa State University), where she organized debates on woman suffrage and earned a BS in 1880. She married Iowa newspaper editor Leo Chapman in 1885 and formed political equality clubs beginning in 1889 dedicated to the cause of woman suffrage in Iowa. After Leo Chapman's death in 1886, she married successful engineer George Catt in 1892, and the couple moved to Brooklyn. Carrie Chapman Catt recruited for the National American Woman Suffrage Association (NAWSA), founded in New York City two years earlier. A distinguished administrator and gifted public speaker, Catt's early speeches were often anti-immigrant as she abhorred the patriarchal traditions of the new arrivals. She became NAWSA president in 1900 and two years later established the International Woman Suffrage Alliance. Moving to Manhattan in 1903, she resigned her presidency of NAWSA the next year. In 1909 Catt helped launch the Woman Suffrage Party, and in 1914 she created the Empire State Campaign Committee and opened a New York City school to train volunteers in public speaking, suffrage history, and politics. Resuming the presidency of NAWSA in 1915, Catt remained the group's head through 1920, the year of final victory for woman suffrage. She moved to New Rochelle in 1919 and spent her later years working for international peace.

Van Voris, Jacqueline. *Carrie Chapman Catt: A Public Life* (New York: Feminist Press at the City Univ of New York, 1987)

Caryn E. Neumann

Cattaraugus. Village (pop 1,075) in New Albion (Cattaraugus Co). Settled in 1830, the community was platted when the Erie Railroad came through in 1851 and developed in response to it. Joseph Plumb (1791–1870), who owned most of the village land, was the 1844 candidate for lieutenant governor for the Liberty Party and an ardent abolitionist and temperance advocate. Dismayed by the carousing of railroad workers and others, he demanded that people purchasing his land refrain from selling alcoholic beverages or lose the property. A suit on this matter was litigated for many years before being decided in Plumb's favor by the State Court of Appeals in 1869. Among the industries that sustained Cattaraugus were C. Moench and Co's tannery (1865–1902), two furniture factories and a chair factory, a carriage works, the Common Sense Milk-Pan Factory (1873) and the Ten Eyck Edged Tool Co (1883–1908). The village incorporated in 1882. In 2003 employment is found at Setter-Stix (1940; candy sticks), Todco Division of Overhead Door Co (1953; custom laminating), and Chester-Jensen Manufacturing (1955; food-processing equipment). In the early 21st century Cattaraugus is noted for its Victorian charm and specialty shops.

Bruce D. Fredrickson and Madelynn P. Fredrickson

Cattaraugus County (1,310 mi²/3,393 km²; pop 83,955). Created in 1808 from Genesee Co and named for a Seneca word meaning "bad smelling banks," a reference to the odor of natural gas leaking from underground deposits in the area. Cattaraugus Co is divided into 2 cities (Olean and Salamanca), 32 towns that contain 13 incorporated villages, and all or part of 3 Seneca Indian reservations. Little Valley serves as county seat.

Elevations range from slightly above 600 ft (183 m) in the northwest corner where Cattaraugus Creek exits the county to 2,430 ft (741 m) at the Clare benchmark in the Town of Allegany.

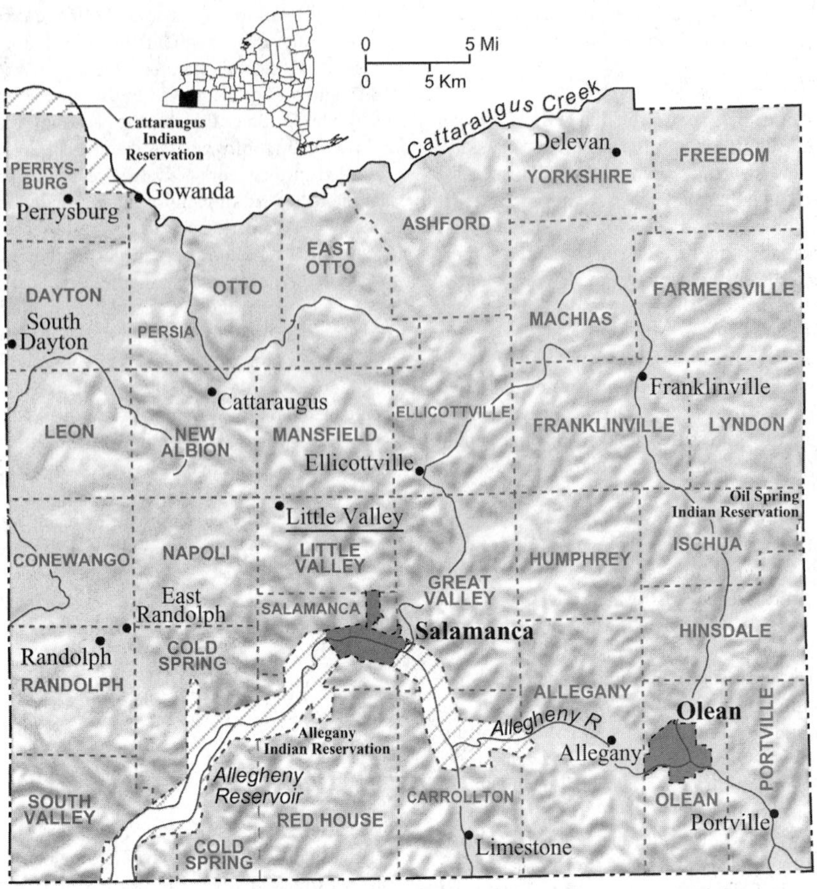

Cattaraugus Co lies within two subregions of the Appalachian Upland physiographic province: the rugged, steep-sided Allegheny Hills occupy the south-central portion, and the ice-sculpted, rolling Cattaraugus Hills cover the remainder. Lying primarily south of the sharply defined Allegheny River valley, the Allegheny Hills stand unique as the only unglaciated region in New York State. The Cattaraugus Hills are the remnants of a maturely dissected and glaciated plateau with modest slopes and elevations that decrease from south to north and east to west. Bedrock throughout consists nearly exclusively of Devonian shale and siltstone, intermixed with some sandstone. The exception is some Pennsylvanian and Mississippian conglomerate, sandstone, and shale in the immediate vicinity of the Pennsylvania border. Various Devonian sandstone formations in the county contain petroleum and natural gas deposits. High-grade, paraffin-based oil deposits were concentrated in the southeastern sector. First exploited in 1864, they are now largely depleted. A portion of the extensive Medina gas field underlies the county's western quarter, and two depleted fields currently serve as natural gas storage reservoirs. Glacial and postglacial deposition has significantly altered the routes of some major streams, including the Allegheny River that flowed northwest past Steamburg to the Conewango Valley to Gowanda before the Pleistocene. Three-quarters of the county is drained by the Allegheny River and its principal tributaries: Conewango, Ischua, and Great Valley Creeks. Most of the northern area lies within the Cattaraugus Creek–Lake Erie watershed. A small area in the northeast drains into the Genesee River via Caneadea Creek. Viable agricultural soils are generally concentrated in the county's northern half, especially the northeast. Elsewhere most soils hold limited potential for commercial agriculture.

Cattaraugus Co's climate is humid-continental. Mean January temperatures range from 20°F (-7°C) at Franklinville to an average of four degrees higher in the northwest. Winter lows can be expected to fall below 0°F (-18°C) every year, sometimes substantially so. Mean July temperatures range from 66°F (19°C) to a few degrees higher in the west and northwest. Daytime highs reach 90°F (32°C) at least a few times every summer. Average annual precipitation amounts range from 48 inches (122 cm) at Little Valley to 39 inches (99 cm) at Olean and less in the northeast. Seasonal snowfall amounts vary from 65 inches (165 cm) in the Allegheny River valley at Olean to 127 inches (323 cm) at Little Valley and still greater amounts in the northwest and the high country in the south. The primeval forest cover consisted of two communities. An Alleghenian hardwood community of beech, sugar maple, yellow birch, hemlock, white pine, and basswood, with scattered areas of oak and chestnut. Wetland forest of elm, hemlock, and black ash grew along the Allegheny River and Conewango Creek and a few other smaller creeks and streams. Approximately 70% of Cattaraugus Co is covered with forest, none of it virgin.

American Indians and Early Settlement

American Indian presence in the area dates back at least to the Indian mounds created by the Point Peninsula culture in the first millennium AD. White settlers found the mounds, primarily in the Town of Red House, but by the 1870s farmers had all but destroyed them by plowing. Archaeologists have excavated numerous Allegheny Valley Iroquoian sites dated from *ca* 900 to 1525. The reason for the abandonment of the region is not clear. The Seneca, whose homeland was in the Genesee Valley, were pushed westward during the Sullivan-Clinton campaign of 1779, and they sought refuge in valleys of the Allegheny, Cattaraugus, and Conewango. The Treaty of Big Tree (1797) between the US government and the Seneca created the county's three reservations: the Allegany Indian Reservation, wholly within Cattaraugus Co, the now uninhabited Oil Spring Indian Reservation, and the Cattaraugus Indian Reservation.

Cattaraugus Co was one of the last areas in New York to be settled by Whites, and its settlement patterns were similar to those in Ohio, Indiana, and Illinois. The preference of westbound travelers for the Buffalo and Great Lakes route was not a given. In the early 19th century, Cattaraugus Co experienced a small boom as immigrants used the Allegheny River to reach Ohio and the West. Speculators hoped that pioneers traveling west to Pittsburgh and southern Ohio, especially those from New England, would travel through Cattaraugus Co and decide to stay; they believed the Allegheny River would prove to be a natural transportation artery.

What became the Holland Land Co acquired the territory in 1792–93 and, after extinguishing Indian title at the Treaty of Big Tree in 1797, surveyed it into townships and lots in 1798–99. Even though the company had an office in Ellicottville, it had limited success in Cattaraugus Co. Many settlers who moved into New York State preferred the Genesee Valley's superior land and milder climate. New England farmers who had left hilly, rocky land were reluctant to settle on the similar Cattaraugus Co topography. The Allegheny River proved to be disappointing as a transportation artery; travel was seasonal because the river froze in winter and became too low for navigation in summer.

In 1803 Maj Adam Hoops purchased 20,000 acres (8,000 ha) from the Holland Land Co in the region that is now Allegany and Cattaraugus Cos. Hoops used his friendship with Federalist Party leader Alexander Hamilton, attorney for the company, to facilitate his purchase. The present county's first white settlement, aside from Quaker missionaries in Cold Spring (1798), was at Olean Point in 1804; Hoops named the village Hamilton after his friend, but it soon became known as Olean. Parts of the eastern half of the present county were settled in the five years that followed, but most initial settlements were made between 1810 and 1820.

Economic Development

During its early years the county developed the industries typically found in developing territory: gristmills, sawmills, and tanneries. In 1818 Olean acquired a newspaper, the *Allegany Mercury,* a critical step in economic advancement. Development came not so much from the Allegheny River or from oil found nearby but from the very forest that inhibited travel and farming. It provided much of the early capital for growth. The clearing of the forest gave residents commodities to sell to the outside world, including potash, charcoal, and lumber. A bit later, tanning and wood chemical manufacture drew upon forest resources. Lumbering opened the land for

CATTARAUGUS CO POPULATION CENSUS FIGURES

	White	Nonwhite	Total Population	Foreign-Born
1820	4,084	6	4,090	—
1830	16,703	21	16,724	33
1840	28,834	38	28,872	—
1850	38,848	102	38,950	4,639
1860	43,735	151	43,886	5,716
1870	43,745	164	43,909	5,665
1880	55,520	286	55,806	7,071
1890	60,606	260	60,866	7,986
1900	64,196	1,447	65,643	7,819
1910	64,572	1,347	65,919	7,357
1920	69,788	1,535	71,323	7,196
1930	70,955	1,443	72,398	6,194
1940	71,184	1,468	72,652	4,814
1950	76,585	1,316	77,901	3,851
1960	78,602	1,585	80,187	2,839
1970	79,714	1,952	81,666	1,770
1980	83,094	2,603	85,697	1,564
1990	81,093	3,141	84,234	1,173
2000	79,444	4,993	83,955	1,183

Notes: "Nonwhite" includes African Americans, Asians, American Indians, and Pacific Islanders and, for 2000, also the mixed race and other race categories. Through the 1960 census these figures primarily reflect the African American population. Foreign-born figures for 1820 and 1830 include only those not naturalized, and for 1930 and 1950, the foreign-born totals include Whites only. Other years include all foreign-born in the population.

agriculture, and its success spurred development by providing both reason and resources for better roads, canals, and ultimately railroads.

The building of the Erie Canal extinguished any hope that the Allegheny River would become a major transportation artery. Most travelers now crossed the northern part of the state with relative ease, and Buffalo became a boomtown. There was, as Joseph Ellicott said, a belief "that the Southern parts of this purchase are unfavorable to settlement." To encourage it, land was sold on credit to be paid over 10 years, but the rate of default was high and habitation remained thin. Nevertheless, Cattaraugus Co's population nearly tripled from 1825 to 1835, from 8,643 to 24,896. In 1835–36 the Holland Land Co sold its remaining land to Nicholas Devereux of Utica and his business partners.

Devereux and his associates represented a new type of speculator, more forward-looking than those of the Holland Land Co. They bought 417,978 acres (169,150 ha) in Allegany, Cattaraugus, and Wyoming Cos. The limited success of the Holland Land Co was apparent in the 90¢ an acre the buyers paid, a sum with the buying power of about $17 in 2000. Another contrast can be seen in the extent of improved acreage. In 1845 only 24% of the land in Cattaraugus and Allegany Cos was improved, while in Genesee, Orleans, Niagara, and Erie Cos, the figure was 44%. Devereux, however, with a broader vision for development than his predecessors, predicted that his planned village of Allegany would become a major commercial center at the junction of the Erie Railroad, the Genesee Valley Canal, and the Allegheny River.

Wheat culture was attempted in the early years, but soil and climate were inadequate. Grazing of cattle and sheep took over, with some butter and cheese making, and eventually dairying predominated. By 1874 cheese factories had largely supplanted butter making on the farm; Cattaraugus Co ranked 1st in the state in milk sent to factories but 16th in home butter production. Still later, condenseries were scattered around the county to process the raw milk. Ultimately, farmers shipped milk to New York City. In 1930 there were 3,999 farms, and it was thought that half of them shipped to the metropolis.

Besides farming, Cattaraugus Co residents continued to make use of the forests, producing lumber, cheeseboxes, shingles, barrels, and hemlock bark for tanneries. People had long noticed oil puddles around Cuba (Allegany Co), and the name Olean was an early allusion to oil reserves. A major step in the county's development followed the 1859 discovery of oil in Titusville, Pa. An oil boom spread north to the Bradford oil field and crossed the state line in 1864 when Carrollton became a boomtown, followed by Allegany in 1877. Olean and Bradford experienced prosperity transporting and refining oil, which provided the most substantial and prolonged period of economic growth for the area. From the 1880s to the late 1920s, Olean had massive oil storage facilities. At one point over 300 oil tanks surrounded the city. In 1881 Standard Oil connected Olean to New Jersey with a pipeline that functioned for over half a century.

Aside from oil, Cattaraugus Co's industrial sector was limited and dispersed throughout a number of towns. Many had tanneries and woodenware shops, making such items as handles and cheeseboxes. Chairs and other pieces of furniture were produced in Cattaraugus, Great Valley, and Salamanca. Foundries operated at various periods in East Randolph, Ischua, Olean, Otto, and Yorkshire; agricultural machinery and implements were made in Gowanda, Olean, Perrysburg, Randolph, and Yorkshire; and textile manufacturing was limited to woolen mills in East Randolph, Freedom, and Otto. Cutlery was a specialty of Little Valley, and edge tools were made in Cattaraugus. Other industrial products included milk pans (Cattaraugus and East Randolph), pumps (Gowanda), hats (Ischua), bricks (Ischua), washing machines (Little Valley), pottery (Olean), botanicals (Perrysburg), and glue (Persia). Many of these operations were relatively short-lived.

Lumber transport on the Allegheny River began in 1807, and 300 million board feet were shipped in 1834. Rafting continued until 1890. Westbound migrants, too, used the river; in the 1818 season over 3,000 boarded rafts at Olean. When the Erie Canal was completed in 1825, it reduced the Allegheny's usefulness by turning the tide of migrants toward northern Ohio, Indiana, Illinois, and Michigan. The Genesee Valley Canal, planned to link the upper Genesee Valley to the Erie system, was authorized in 1836 but did not reach Olean until 1857. In the meantime, the Erie Railroad was completed in 1851, providing the Southern Tier's long-sought transportation link east and west, and the Atlantic and Great Western (1860) provided a branch route to Jamestown and beyond. Salamanca became a railroad town, with repair shops and stockyards. The east-west lines were followed by others running south from Buffalo and Rochester: the Rochester and State Line (1878), the Buffalo, New York and Philadelphia (1872), and the Buffalo and Jamestown (1874–75) Railroads. In the 20th century they were joined by the short-lived Buffalo and Susquehanna (1906–16).

Religion, Education, and Culture

There was little organized religion in the county's early years, because the settlers were diverse and dispersed. Worship took place in a log barn in Hinsdale as early as 1807. A Congregational church organized in Franklinville by 1813, but in most of the county's towns, the first church wasn't formed until sometime between 1818 and 1831. Germans in Ashford and Olean, Welsh in Farmersville and Freedom, and Irish in Allegany and Carrollton were responsible for introducing their traditional church affiliations. In 1875 the county had 30 Methodist Episcopal congregations, 14 Baptist, 11 Roman Catholic (up from 4 in 1855), 7 Freewill Baptist and 7 Free Methodist, 6 Presbyterian, and 5 Congregational. Nicholas Devereux invited Franciscans to Allegany in 1855; by 1875 the Roman Catholic Church, serving both Irish and German immigrants, was the county's largest, with 4,045 members.

The first school was in a log cabin on the west side of Ischua Creek in 1809. Common schools were authorized by state legislation in 1812, and the Holland Land Co provided some school lots; by 1835 there were 202 common districts in the county. Olean Academy (1851) became a public high school under the Union Free School system in 1868. Rural schools centralized between 1931 (Randolph) and 1953 (Gowanda); in 2003 there are 11 central districts and 2 city districts. Randolph was briefly the home of the Eclectic Medical College (1848) before it moved to Syracuse. A longer-lived institution of higher education was Randolph Academy and Female Seminary (1850); in 1866 this teacher-training school was renamed Chamberlain Institute. During most of the 20th century, St. Bonaventure University (1858) was the county's only college until the creation of the Cattaraugus County Campus

POPULATIONS OF TOWNS AND CITIES, CATTARAUGUS CO

Town or City, Year Founded	1840	1880	1920	1960	2000
Allegany, 1831[a]	530	4,044	3,240	6,483	8,230
Ashford, 1824	1,469	1,813	1,379	1,490	2,223
Carrolltown, 1842	—	2,171	1,013	1,399	1,410
Coldspring, 1837	673	984	567	580	751
Conewango, 1823	1,317	1,299	931	1,162	1,732
Dayton, 1835	946	1,705	1,712	1,931	1,945
East Otto, 1854	—	1,251	915	701	1,105
Elko, 1890–1965	—	—	220	73	—
Ellicottville, 1820	1,084	1,949	1,766	1,968	1,738
Farmersville, 1821	1,294	1,128	999	721	1,028
Franklinville, 1812[b]	1,293	1,982	3,003	3,090	3,128
Freedom, 1820	1,831	1,312	1,016	1,059	2,493
Great Valley, 1818	852	1,859	1,336	1,408	2,145
Hinsdale, 1820	1,937	1,594	972	1,538	2,270
Humphrey, 1836	444	997	531	415	721
Ischua, 1846[c]	—	935	656	562	895
Leon, 1832	1,326	1,192	729	808	1,380
Little Valley, 1818	700	1,196	1,683	1,737	1,788
Lyndon, 1829[d]	628	831	567	406	661
Machias, 1827	1,085	1,545	1,431	1,390	2,482
Mansfield, 1830[e]	942	1,106	717	632	800
Napoli, 1823[f]	1,145	1,126	636	670	1,159
New Albion, 1830	1,016	1,732	2,053	1,981	2,068
Olean, 1808	638	6,575	1,316	2,268	2,029
Olean (city), 1893	—	—	20,506	21,868	15,347
Otto, 1823	2,133	1,111	773	715	831
Perrysburg, 1814[g]	1,660	1,376	1,150	1,857	1,771
Persia, 1835	892	1,370	2,194	2,756	2,512
Portville, 1837	462	2,400	2,164	3,321	3,952
Randolph, 1826	1,283	2,459	2,171	2,513	2,681
Red House, 1869	—	487	434	235	38
Salamanca, 1854[h]	—	3,498	361	432	544
Salamanca (city), 1913	—	—	9,276	8,480	6,097
South Valley, 1847	—	995	356	205	302
Yorkshire, 1820	1,292	1,784	1,524	2,012	4,210

[a]Burton until 1851.
[b]Ischua until 1824; erroneously identified as Hebe.
[c]Rice until 1855.
[d]Elgin 1857–58.
[e]Cecelius until 1831.
[f]Cold Spring until 1828.
[g]Perry until 1818.
[h]Bucktooth until 1862.

(1976) of Jamestown Community College, located in Olean. Olean Business Institute has provided technical education since 1961.

In the early 21st century the county has two dailies, the *Olean Times-Herald* (1860) and the *Salamanca Press* (1867), and a monthly, the *Randolph Register* (1865). There are two AM and two FM stations, the oldest being WHDL-AM (1929). Art venues include the Seneca Iroquois National Museum at Salamanca and the outdoor Griffis Sculpture Park (1966) in Ashford Hollow. Writer Arch Merrill (1894–1974) was a native of the county.

Politics

Although created in 1808 from Genesee Co, Cattaraugus Co could not complete its organization until it had 500 voters. It remained a part of Genesee Co until 1811 when the western part was attached to Niagara Co and the eastern part was attached to Allegany Co for administrative purposes. It began functioning independently in 1817, and in 1818 Ellicottville was designated the county seat. In 1820 a courthouse was built. The county seat remained at Ellicottville until 1868, when was moved to Little Valley to allow for rail access to the courts.

During and after the Civil War five of the county's towns, concentrated in the south, were Democratic strongholds, but by the 20th century Cattaraugus had become solidly Republican. Its greatest political triumph was the election of native Frank W. Higgins to the governorship in 1904. Until 1970 the county was governed by a board of supervisors representing the towns and cities. Responding to court mandate, it shifted to a board of legislators; the number of its members, 21 in 2003, was reduced to 17 effective at the 2004 election. Day-to-day business is managed by a county administrator, selected by the legislators.

The 20th Century

Other aspects of the economy flourished with the oil boom. In the 20th century Allegany was known for vegetable packing, Ashford for dried apples, Gowanda for glue, Franklinville and Little Valley for cutlery, and Limestone for nitroglycerine. Both Salamanca and Gowanda had large tanneries; furniture was made in Gowanda, Salamanca, and Portville; and food processing was done throughout the county.

A tourism and recreation industry developed, taking advantage of the natural beauty of the area. Allegany State Park (1921), the largest state park at 64,800 acres (26,224 ha), attracts visitors with its unusual topography. Allegheny Reservoir (1965), created to control flooding, enhanced the tourist potential of the Allegany Indian Reservation but was bitterly fought by the Seneca Nation, which lost much of its best land in the process. Ellicottville has a substantial ski industry because of Holimont and Holiday Valley ski areas. The Village of Cattaraugus attracts visitors with its Victorian charm, and Rainbow Lake in East Otto, Lime Lake in Machias, and Enchanted Lake in Napoli are resort areas.

Remnants of the oil industry survive in Cattaraugus Co. In 1937 Clark Bros merged with S. R. Dresser Manufacturing Co of Bradford to form a very successful company that made engines and pumps for the oil industry. Now Dresser Rand, a subsidiary of Ingersoll-Rand, it remains one of the major employers in Olean. In recent decades the oil business, centered in Allegany, Carrollton, and Dayton, has decreased. There remains a fair amount of oil in western New York State and Pennsylvania, but it is located in sand deposits, making drilling prohibitively costly.

Transportation continues to be problematic. Rte 17 (I-86) was rebuilt as a limited-access highway and completed in the county in stages between 1965 and 1985, while the northern part of Cattaraugus Co became more accessible to greater Buffalo with the completion of US 219 as far as Springville (Erie Co) in 1979. Nevertheless, Cattaraugus Co lacks easy access to city markets and employment. Besides Dresser Rand in Olean, other industries include Setter-Stix (candy sticks), Todco (custom laminating), and Chester-Jensen Manufacturing (food-processing equipment) in Allegany; Kendor Music Co in Delavan; Ontario Knife Co and Cattaraugus Container in Franklinville; Gowanda Electronics Corp (magnetic components) in Gowanda; Bush Industries (furniture) in Little Valley; Cooper Industries (electrical protection devices) and Olean Advanced Products (ceramic capacitors) in Olean; and Randolph Dimension Corp (furniture) and Metallic Ladder Manufacturing Co in Randolph. Many residents commute northward to the Buffalo area, especially from the northern towns.

Farming is widespread but much reduced from what it once was; in 1997 there were 946 farms covering 22.9% of the land area. An Amish community centered in Conewango and Leon has been present since 1949 and continues traditional farming practices, but the limited extent of good soils affects the potential for modern agriculture. Nevertheless, the economy is dominated by small farms and scattered industries.

The City of Salamanca is located on land leased from the Allegany Indian Reservation. Before the expiration of 99-year leases signed on favorable terms in 1892, there was much controversy in the county; the leases were eventually renewed with increases in the rent paid to the Seneca Nation of Indians. Another controversy, still active in 2003, began with state purchase of land in West Valley in 1961. It was leased to Nuclear Fuel Services for the dumping of radioactive waste and, starting in 1966, for reprocessing fuel. The tenant firm was responsible for many accidents and leaks, and the operation was shut down in 1972. The Department of Energy wants to bury the remaining waste, a position opposed by most area residents.

See also PETROLEUM AND NATURAL GAS INDUSTRY.

The settlement era is covered by Orsamus Turner, *Pioneer History of the Holland Land Purchase* (1849), compiled when many of the original settlers were living. There are four county histories: Franklin Ellis, *History of Cattaraugus County* (1879); William Adams, ed., *Historical Gazetteer and Biographical Memorial of Cattaraugus County* (1893); William J. Doty, *Historical Annals of Southwestern New York*, 3 vols (1940); and Michael C. Donovan, *Historical Review of Cattaraugus County* (?1959). Town histories that have been issued include Islay N. Bergreen and Thomas J. Schaeper, *Our Allegany Heritage, 1831–1981* (1981); *A Hundred Years and More of Cattaraugus-New Albion Happenings* (1979); Charles J. Shults, *History and Biographical History of the Township of Dayton* (1901); *The History of Dayton* (1985); I. R. Leonard, *Historical Sketches of the Village of Gowanda* (1898); Sally S. Pettengill, *History of Ischua* (1994); B. J. Dorsey, *History of the Town of Leon* (1958); *A History of the Town of Portville, 1805–1920* (1986); and Lila G. Cooper, *Hinsdale, My Home Town* (1999).

Phillip G. Payne

Cattaraugus Indian Reservation. It is one of three reservations of the Seneca Nation of Indians reserved from lands ceded at the Treaty of Big Tree on 16 Sept 1797. It comprises some 21,680 acres (8,774 ha) in Erie, Chautauqua, and Cattaraugus Cos. The reservation originally had a larger acreage, but several sales reduced its area. In 1802 Cattaraugus Reservation land was sold along the Lake Erie shoreline, and in 1826, 8 mi^2 (21 km^2) were sold. The Cattaraugus Reservation was one of those retained by provision of the so-called Compromise Treaty of 20 May 1842. The constitutional convention at which the Seneca republic, the Seneca Nation of Indians, was formed was at the Cattaraugus Reservation on 4 Dec 1848. A factor leading to the abolishing of the office of chief and to the adoption of a tripartite government was the corruption of the chief system, which allowed the land sales.

The Seneca of the Cattaraugus Reservation strongly supported those at the Allegany Indian Reservation in the tumultuous period in the 1950s and 1960s, when they fought, unsuccessfully, to stop the construction of the Kinzua Dam. In 1995 three Iroquois were killed on the reservation in an internecine fight over casino gambling, although both sides in this dispute subsequently muted their antagonism. Conflict with the State of New York over sovereignty issues has also led to protests and demonstrations on the New York State Thruway, which passes through the Cattaraugus Reservation.

Abler, Thomas S., and Elisabeth Tooker. "Seneca." In *Northeast*, ed. Bruce G. Trigger, vol 15 of *Handbook of North American Indians*, ed. William C. Sturtevant (Washington, DC: Smithsonian Institution, 1978)
Abrams, George H. J. *The Seneca People* (Phoenix, Ariz: Indian Tribal Series, 1976)

George H. J. Abrams

Cayuga. Village (pop 509) in Aurelius (Cayuga Co). Settled in 1788, its streets were platted in 1801. Courts were held at both Cayuga and Aurora until 1808. Cayuga was located on the State Road (1796), and in 1797 a company was chartered to build the Cayuga Long Bridge across Cayuga Lake. The 1.1 mi (1.8 km) bridge, twice rebuilt, served until it was abandoned in 1857, but Cayuga remained a transportation center with steamboat service to Ithaca (1820–1907). The Cayuga Branch of the Erie Canal (1832) and the Auburn and Rochester Railroad (1841; later New York Central) served the village, which was incorporated in 1857. It was the site of a malthouse (1866) and a marl manufactory (1877). In the early 21st century, significant enterprises were Benson Milling Co (1920), one of the nation's largest feed mills, and the Cayuga Wooden Boatworks (1991), which restores antique boats.

Cayuga and Seneca Canal. Connecting the two largest Finger Lakes to the Erie Canal, it runs 23 miles (37 km) from the Erie Canal at Montezuma (Cayuga Co) to the outlet at the northern end of Cayuga Lake to the outlet of Seneca Lake at Geneva (Ontario Co). Beginning in 1813 the Seneca Lock Navigation Co (SLNC) built locks and a small canal to carry boats around the cataracts at Seneca Falls. The first boat passed through the locks in 1818. In 1824 the state conducted surveys to determine the feasibility of finishing the work begun by SLNC and connecting the two lakes to the Erie Canal. By way of petition, business people pointed out that a canal of 20 miles (32 km) would connect 80 miles (129 km) of lake navigation to the canal system. From 1826 to 1828 the Cayuga and Seneca (C&S) Canal was built at a cost of $214,000. As part of the C&S system, the inlet at the southern end of Cayuga Lake was dredged in 1839 to allow boats improved access to Ithaca. In the 1850s stone locks replaced the original 11 wooden locks, and the canal was enlarged in the 1850s at a cost of $1,133,149. The improved transportation offered by the canal resulted in the rapid growth of many Central New York villages, such as Seneca Falls (Seneca Co), which grew from a population of 200 in 1824 to 4,000 in 1860. The closure of the Crooked Lake Canal (1877) and Chemung Canal (1878) and the growth of the railroads ended much of the canal traffic. The C&S was in danger of abandonment, but the large boat-building business in Ithaca and legal changes to its charter provided legal protection from closure. During the construction of the Barge Canal, the C&S was included in the canal system only after business people pointed out that a cement plant as well as large gypsum and salt deposits could be found along the shores of the two lakes. The C&S Barge Canal was constructed from 1911 to 1917 at a cost of $5,430,770. During construction a lower portion of Seneca Falls was lost by the construction of a dam, forming the so-called Van Cleef Lake. This lake destroyed a large portion of the village's waterpower and industrial center. Over 60 homes and 116 businesses were moved or destroyed during the construction. The C&S continues operation in the early 21st century.

Whitford, Noble E. *History of the Canal System of the State of New York* (Albany: Brandow Printing, 1906)
———. *History of the Barge Canal of New York State* (Albany: J. B. Lyon, 1922)

Michael Riley

Cayuga County (693 mi^2/1,795 km^2; pop 81,963). It was created in 1799 from part of Onondaga Co and named for the Cayuga Nation. All of Seneca and portions of Schuyler, Tompkins, Wayne, and Yates Cos were subsequently taken from the original Cayuga Co. The most recent boundary adjustment was made in 1828. The county is presently divided into 1 city, Auburn (the county seat), and 23 towns containing 9 incorporated villages. Elevations range from 245 feet (75 m) along the shores of Lake Ontario to over 1,840 feet (561 m) in the far southeast near the Cortland Co line. Cayuga Co straddles two landform provinces and was glaciated. The southern half lies within the Finger Lake Hills, the lowest of the Appalachian Upland subregions, and is characterized by deep, large, often U-shaped valleys trending north-south that are separated by slight to moderately rolling uplands. The three largest and deepest valleys each contain a Finger Lake: Cayuga, Owasco, and Skaneateles. The bedrock in the valleys is Upper Devonian shale, siltstone, and sandstone, except for a narrow band of limestone and dolostone. Strata dip gently southward. The county's northern half lies within the extensive but poorly drained drumlin field of the Erie-Ontario Lowland. In addition to areas of marsh, hundreds of drumlins, formed under retreating glacial ice, are scattered over the area. Bedrock is largely limestone and dolostone of Silurian age, except for a narrow band of Ordovician conglomerate along Lake Ontario. Aside from the northernmost quarter, which drains directly into Lake Ontario, the county lies within the watershed of the Seneca River, by far the largest stream in Cayuga. Other significant watercourses include Owasco Inlet, Owasco Lake Outlet, and Big Salmon Creek. Fine arable soils from glacial till are found throughout the county. In contrast, marginal lands are restricted to parts of the far southeast corner and to some of the wettest and steepest lands in the north.

Cayuga Co's climate is humid-continental. The mean July temperature along the shores of Cayuga Lake is 71°F (22°C), with daytime highs sometimes reaching into the 90s°F (32–37°C). The mean January temperature is 24°F (-4°C), although nighttime lows drop below 0°F (-18°C) on occasion. Temperatures are on average 3 degrees cooler in the higher elevations of the southeast. Lake Ontario moderates temperatures in the northern quarter, thereby delaying the arrival of the spring and fall seasons by a week or more. Annual precipitation ranges from 37 inches (94 cm) near the Cayuga and Ontario lakeshores to 42 inches (107 cm) along the eastern boundary. Seasonal snowfall typically ranges from 50 inches (127 cm) near Cayuga Lake to over 100 inches (254 cm) in parts of the north and in higher elevations of the south. Primeval forest cover varied. Central hardwood forests dominated by beech, sugar maple, and basswood covered most of the county. Oak-hickory forests occupied the eastern shores of Cayuga and Owasco Lakes, while an Alleghenian hardwood forest of beech, sugar maple, hemlock, white pine, and basswood blanketed the southeast corner. Swamp forest covered the wetlands along the Seneca River and elsewhere.

SETTLEMENT

Archaeological evidence found in Conquest indicates the earliest human activity in Cayuga Co to be paleo-age (11,000–12,000 BP). The county lies entirely within the ancestral homeland of the

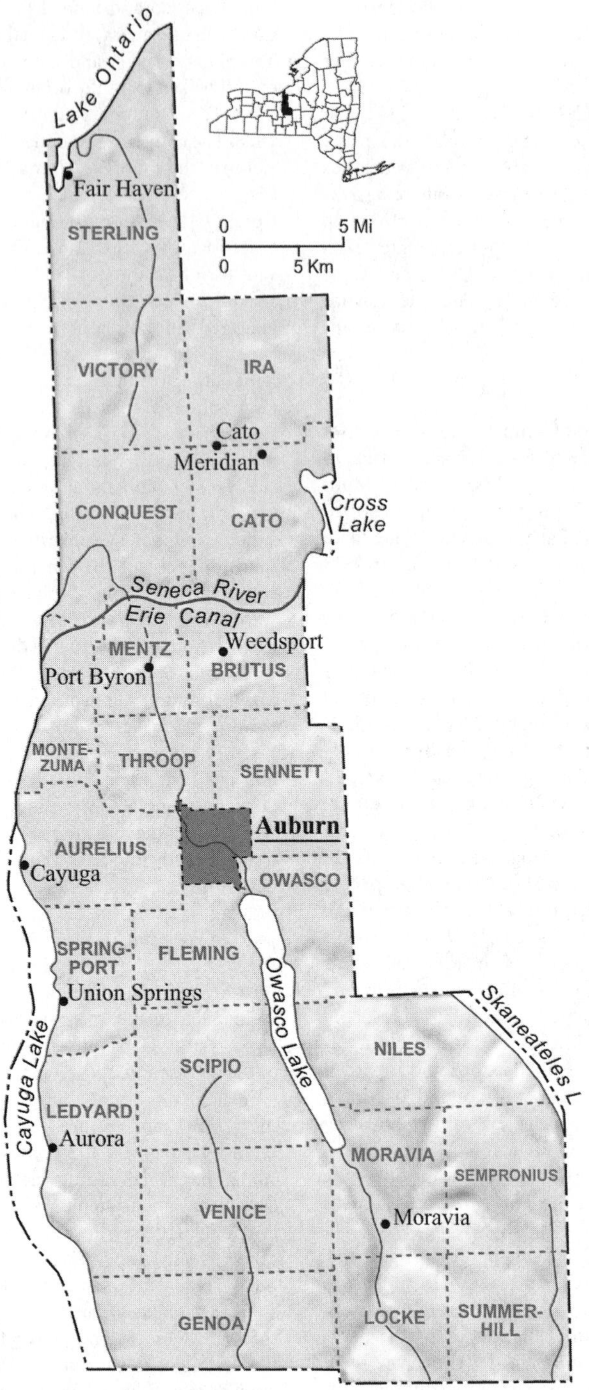

Cayuga, who migrated to central New York State from the lower Mississippi Valley in the 14th century and displaced Algonquian-speaking people who had inhabited the region in three periods beginning around 3,500 BC. The first Whites known to set foot in the area were fur traders from Albany and Jesuit missionaries from Canada; they were quickly driven out by the Iroquois.

At the time of the Revolutionary War, the Cayuga numbered around 1,000, most living in one of three villages east of Cayuga Lake. Their "castle," or primary village, was located in the Great Gully in Springport. The others were near Aurora and at Wasco, located within Auburn's city limits. Soldiers from the Sullivan-Clinton campaign of 1779 reported finding many acres of corn, beans, and squash surrounding these villages, along with substantial fruit orchards and gardens filled with a variety of vegetables. Having been driven from their homeland during the Revolutionary War, some Cayugas returned afterward, but in a sequence of treaties in 1789, 1795, and 1807 they ceded their territory within the present-day county to the state in exchange for cash and annuities. With the exception of the Cayuga Reservation, which encompassed what is now Springport and parts of Aurelius, Montezuma, and Ledyard, all the land that became Cayuga Co was part of the New Military Tract. Although intended for New York State's Revolutionary War veterans as compensation for their military service, most of the New Military Tract lands were settled by nonveterans.

The first permanent white settlers arrived in Aurelius in the 1780s. By 1800 Whites were actively breaking land in all parts of the county except the northernmost section and the Cayuga Marshes. Guided by the Genesee Road from the east and by north-south-trending valleys and Cayuga Lake from the south, settlers moved in from Connecticut, Massachusetts, the Hudson and Mohawk Valleys, and, to a lesser extent, New Jersey and Pennsylvania. Eastern New Yorkers, many of New England heritage, were especially dominant in the northern half. With some of the early settlers came a small number of enslaved African Americans, who were later manumitted. Most settled in Auburn on the west bank of the Owasco Lake Outlet. The population grew quickly largely because of an abundance of high-quality land and the early rise of industry. By 1810 the county contained an impressive number of upstart communities, including Aurora, Moravia, Montezuma, and Cayuga. The most promising was Auburn, where the Genesee Road crossed the Owasco Lake Outlet. A decade later Cayuga Co's population approached 40,000. In the decades that followed, important central places took root along the Erie Canal at Weedsport and Port Byron and further to the north as well. Immigrants, most notably Irish, Germans, English, and Scots, joined the stream of in-migrants. By 1850 the population was 55,458, including over 500 African Americans.

Economic Development

Industrial development came early. By 1800 four gristmills and one sawmill were in operation. Auburn quickly rose as the county's largest commercial center, a position made secure when the state routed the Genesee Road (1797) and Seneca Turnpike (1803) through the village. Until the statewide completion of the Erie Canal in 1825, most cross-state travelers passed through Auburn on their way to or from the famous 1.2 mi (1.9 km) long Cayuga Lake Bridge (1797–1857). Small manufacturing concerns developed in places with waterpower, such as Union Springs, New Hope, Montville, and Throopsville, but the Owasco Lake Outlet at Auburn became the foremost manufacturing site. Auburn Prison was built beside it in 1816 to take advantage of its power potential. By 1820 there were 92 sawmills, 47 gristmills, 43 distilleries, and 28 fulling mills operating across the county. A nail factory at Locke, two ironworks in Owasco, trip-hammers in Brutus and Locke, and a cotton and woolen factory at Union Springs were also present. Earlier there had been a saltworks at Montezuma. For all this industry, agriculture was the primary force in the economy, especially after the Erie Canal and cross-state railroads provided access to international markets. The Auburn Bank, the county's first, opened in 1817.

The Erie Canal altered the economic geography of Cayuga Co by moving the primary east-west transportation axis north and by helping create the villages of Weedsport and Port Byron. The Cayuga and Seneca Canal, opened in 1828, provided additional access to the communities on the two lakes. Auburn investors attempted to stay competitive by providing most of the funds for the Auburn and Syracuse Railroad, which opened in 1838. The Auburn and Rochester Railroad opened in 1841. The initiative proved short-lived when the Rochester and Syracuse Railroad, destined to become the main line of the New York Central, was built across the county in 1853 parallel to the canal and north of the older railroads. By 1850 there were over 4,000 farms encompassing nearly 400,000 acres (162,000 ha).

The production of winter wheat, corn, barley, and oats ranked well above the state average. The same was true for butter production.

Expanded rail service, agricultural adjustment, industrial growth, and increased ethnic diversity occurred in the last half of the 19th century into the 20th century. The Southern Central Railroad (1872; later Lehigh Valley) carried anthracite coal from Pennsylvania to Lake Ontario at Fair Haven, where it was transferred to lake shipping. Improved rail connections encouraged farmers to turn increasingly to fluid-milk production. Over the course of the 19th century Auburn grew to be an important manufacturing center. Its industries concentrated on shoes, wool and cotton textiles, tools, agricultural implements, and power plants. After the Civil War, they attracted substantial numbers of immigrants from Italy, Poland, Ukraine, and Russia.

CAYUGA CO POPULATION CENSUS FIGURES

	White	Nonwhite	Total Population	Foreign-Born
1800	15,799	72	15,871	—
1810	29,682	161	29,843	—
1820	38,658	239	38,897	211
1830	47,579	369	47,948	267
1840	49,903	435	50,338	—
1850	54,915	543	55,458	5,953
1860	55,316	451	55,767	7,503
1870	58,890	660	59,550	9,238
1880	64,384	697	65,081	9,353
1890	64,721	581	65,302	9,617
1900	65,532	702	66,234	8,519
1910	66,432	674	67,106	10,009
1920	64,638	583	65,221	9,508
1930	64,190	561	64,751	8,237
1940	64,804	704	65,508	6,699
1950	69,101	1,035	70,136	5,615
1960	72,555	1,387	73,942	4,751
1970	75,528	1,911	77,439	2,788
1980	77,157	2,737	79,894	2,460
1990	78,131	4,182	82,313	2,273
2000	76,501	5,462	81,963	1,856

Notes: "Nonwhite" includes African Americans, Asians, American Indians, and Pacific Islanders and, for 2000, also the mixed race and other race categories. Through the 1960 census these figures primarily reflect the African American population. Foreign-born figures for 1820 and 1830 include only those not naturalized, and for 1930 and 1950, the foreign-born totals include Whites only. Other years include all foreign-born in the population.

Religion, Education, and Culture

With its many New Englanders, Cayuga Co was home to many Presbyterian and Baptist churches. In 1855 Methodist congregations numbered 33, and there were 20 Baptist and 15 Presbyterian churches, as well as 4 Congregational bodies. Several Quaker settlements had created 7 meetings. After the canal era the Roman Catholic churches numbered 4. The Auburn Theological Seminary (1819–1939) was a center of New School Presbyterianism in the 19th century and of theological Modernism and anti-Fundamentalism in the 20th. Auburn is also home to the Harriet Tubman Thompson AMEZ Church, where the Underground Railroad heroine worshiped for many years. Modern school centralization began in 1926, when Sherwood Central School was established. Six centralized districts were created during the 1930s and one, Moravia, in the 1940s. Auburn City School District was extended beyond the city limits in 1956.

The cultural landscapes of Cayuga Co reflect its 19th-century prosperity and subsequent decline. Most of its homes were built before the 1940s and demonstrate the richness of 19th-century residential architecture. Auburn developed a vital cultural life around its many churches, hotels, theaters, opera houses, newspapers, and publishing companies. The first newspaper in the county was the *Levanna Gazette and Onondaga Advertiser* (1798). In the early 21st century, the *Auburn Citizen* is the daily paper, and the *Republican-Register* of Moravia provides weekly coverage of the southern part of the county. Important cultural institutions include the Cayuga Museum of History and Art (1936), the Schweinfurth Art Center (1981), and Cayuga Community College (1953).

Politics

Until 1971 Cayuga Co was governed by a board of supervisors made up of the elected supervisors of 23 towns and 10 city wards. This system was replaced by a county legislature of 21 elected legislators, 1 from each of the 21 districts, and a chair. The county has been home to a number of prominent politicians, including native son Pres Millard Fillmore, Secretaries of State William H. Seward and John Foster Dulles (and Dulles's brother Allen Welsh Dulles, one-time CIA director), New York governor Enos T. Throop, and Speaker of the House of Representatives Theodore M. Pomeroy. Other prominent residents included express company pioneers William G. Fargo and Henry Wells, anthropologist Lewis Henry Morgan, Gen Abner Doubleday, Mormon leader Brigham Young, and Underground Railroad conductor Harriet Tubman.

Recent History

Cayuga Co had 5,039 operating farms in 1900, and most were dairy farms producing fluid milk for urban markets. Fruit farming predominated in the towns close to Lake Ontario. The county's most important industries produced shoes, rope and twine, locomotive engines, power plants, and electrical and electronic components. At the beginning of the 20th century the population exceeded 66,000 residents, including 670 Blacks, 20 American Indians, and 8,500 foreign-born. The numbers remained much the same for the next 40 years. The Thruway opened across the county in 1954, near the route of the Erie Canal. During the last 60 years of the 20th century the total population increased by 25%, while minority populations grew by a dramatic 776%. In 2000 more than one-third of county residents lived in Auburn and more than one-half in the Auburn area. Rail service has shrunk back to the original two routes completed more than 150 years ago, one operated by CSX Transportation, the other by local carrier Finger Lakes Railway. In 1997 there were 846 operating farms. As the number of farms has declined, more marginal land has reverted to woodland. Inexpensive land, plenty of recreational opportunities, and some manufacturing development provide residents with a high quality of life. Industrial production reached $618,577,000 in 1997. In two rulings in 2000 and 2001, a federal judge awarded the Cayuga Nation of New York and the Seneca-Cayuga Nation of Oklahoma nearly $250 million to compensate for their loss of the Cayuga Reservation in what was deemed illegal sales in 1795 and 1802.

See also Architects and Architecture, Southern Tier (Western).

The standard history is Elliot G. Storke, *History of Cayuga County* (1879), with a limited update by Charles Itzin, *Back to Before: Anecdotes from the 20th Century in Cayuga County* (1999). Dorothy Wiggins edited two books covering districts in Scipio and Venice that presented detailed research of each farm: *History of Sherwood* (1988) and *History of the Poplar Ridge, NY, Area* (1994). Auburn's earliest published history is Henry Hall, *History of Auburn* (1869); recent works are Ward O'Hara, *Auburn* (1992) and *Auburn, NY: 200 Years of History, 1793–1993* (1993). Moravia has been chronicled in three books: two by James A. Wright, *Historical Sketches of the Town of Moravia from 1791 to 1873* (1874) and *Historical Sketches of the Town of Moravia from 1791 to 1918* (1918), and one by Leslie L. Luther, *Moravia and Its Past* (1966). While not footnoted, Raymond T. Sant, *Fair Haven Folks and Folklore* (1941) provides a detailed account. Also of interest is Judith L. Bellafaire, "Kith, Kin, and Community: Pioneer Networking in Cayuga Co, NY, 1800–1860" (PhD diss, Univ of Delaware, 1984) and Scott W. Anderson, "Entrepreneurs and Place: The Rise and Decline of Urban Communities in Central New York, 1848–1900," *New York History* 80 (1999): 245–78. The early *Collections of the Cayuga County Historical Society,* starting in 1879, contain some excellent scholarly articles.

Scott W. Anderson

Cayuga Heights. Village (pop 3,273) in Ithaca. Jared T. Newman and Charles H. Blood, who began development in 1901, sold many lots to faculty of nearby Cornell University. The village incorporated in 1915. In 1954 residents voted against annexation by the city and authorized an

POPULATIONS OF TOWNS AND CITIES, CAYUGA CO

Town or City, Year Founded	1800	1840	1880	1920	1960	2000
Auburn (city), 1848	—	5,626	21,924	36,192	35,249	28,574
Aurelius, 1789	3,312	2,645	1,954	1,277	2,600	2,936
Brutus, 1802	—	2,044	2,736	2,186	2,804	4,777
Cato, 1802	—	2,380	2,059	1,394	1,815	2,744
Conquest, 1821	—	1,911	1,661	1,044	1,170	1,925
Fleming, 1823	—	1,317	1,233	886	2,071	2,647
Genoa, 1789[a]	3,553	2,593	2,517	1,483	1,794	1,914
Ira, 1821	—	2,283	2,113	1,361	1,448	2,426
Ledyard, 1823	—	2,143	2,199	1,475	1,646	1,832
Locke, 1802	—	1,654	1,141	770	982	1,900
Mentz, 1802[b]	—	4,215	2,288	1,758	2,105	2,446
Montezuma, 1859	—	—	1,294	669	743	1,431
Moravia, 1833	—	2,010	2,699	2,066	2,406	4,040
Niles, 1833	—	2,234	1,875	1,076	943	1,208
Owasco, 1802	—	1,319	1,297	1,458	3,409	3,755
Scipio, 1794	3,147	2,255	2,093	1,218	1,143	1,537
Sempronius, 1799	875	1,304	1,138	575	548	893
Sennett, 1827	—	2,060	1,644	1,358	2,283	3,244
Springport, 1823	—	1,890	2,125	1,146	1,700	2,256
Sterling, 1812	—	2,533	3,034	2,039	2,495	3,432
Summer Hill, 1831[c]	—	1,446	1,028	539	667	1,098
Throop, 1859	—	—	1,188	958	1,559	1,824
Venice, 1823	—	2,105	1,889	1,215	1,203	1,286
Victory, 1821	—	2,371	1,952	1,078	1,159	1,838

Note: In 1800 Cayuga Co included the Towns of Ovid, Romulus, and Fayette [then Washington; now in Seneca Co] and the Town of Ulysses [now in Tompkins Co].

[a]Milton until 1808.

[b]Jefferson until 1808.

[c]Plato until 1832.

independent sewer system. At that time land area was increased considerably. Kendal at Ithaca, a life-care community, opened in 1994. Cayuga Heights is distinguished by its lofty location overlooking Cayuga Lake, its elegant and spacious properties, and its active volunteer fire department.

Jane Dieckmann

Cayuga Lake (66 mi²/171 km²). The second largest of the Finger Lakes after Seneca, Cayuga Lake flows 38 miles (61 km) from Ithaca to the Seneca River outlet at Mud Lock (Cayuga Co). With a mean width of 1.75 miles (2.82 km), the lake is 3.45 miles (5.55 km) at its widest point at Aurora (Cayuga Co), with a maximum depth of 435 feet (133 m) near King Ferry (Cayuga Co). It is deepest toward the south end, tapering to shallower depths at the marshy north end. Glacially formed deposits of salt and gypsum along the east shore are still extracted from mines extending several thousand feet inland and under the lake. The Cayuga Indians settled from AD 1400 around the north end of the lake. Between 1789 and 1807 they sold or ceded virtually all their land to New York State. In 1977 they launched legal measures to regain sovereignty of their traditional lands, but the issue is unresolved. The lake's eastern shoreline is the most industrialized, with salt and power production. Summer and year-round homes have dotted the east shoreline close to the rail line for 125 years. The south end, dominated by the City and Town of Ithaca and the Village and Town of Lansing (Tompkins Co), has the largest concentration of population and economic activity on the lake.

The north end of the lake connects to the Erie Canal via the Seneca River. In spite of marshy lands the lake has fared well economically, with favorable growing conditions, proximity to major east-west transportation routes, and recreational opportunities. No industrial activities or shoreline railway ever developed on the west shoreline, where picturesque landscapes anchored by public parks foster recreational homes and activities. Fourteen commercial vineyards, mainly on the west side, attract visitors and support local economic activity. Two coal-fired power-generating stations built in the 1950s by New York State Electric and Gas are found near Lake Ridge Point. A lake source cooling project to draw cold water from the lake bottom during the summer to help operate the air-cooling system at Cornell University campus was built in 1999, in spite of strong local opposition, and began operation in 2000. Fluctuating water levels, septic systems and municipal sewage (though treated), weeds, and runoff from agricultural lands have all created environmental pressures on the lake. The Cayuga Lake Watershed Restoration and Protection Plan (1999) proposes to address these and other issues.

Sisler, Carol U. *Cayuga Lake: Past, Present, and Future* (Ithaca: Enterprise Publishing, 1989)

Douglas B. McDonald

Cayuga Lake bridge. Series of wooden bridges built between 1799 and 1833 that carried the Seneca Turnpike (also known as the Genesee Road) over the northern tip of Cayuga Lake. Bypassing the Cayuga Marshes, the bridge, widely considered the longest in America when first completed, connected the communities of Cayuga (Cayuga Co) and West Cayuga [now Bridgeport, Seneca Co]. The Cayuga Bridge Co, incorporated by John Harris, Thomas Morris, Wilhelmus Mynderse, Charles Williamson, and Joseph Annin in 1797, built the first bridge between May 1799 and September 1800, financially supported by the Manhattan Co. The span was 1.2 miles (1.9 km) long and 22 feet (6.7 m) wide, enough to allow two Conestoga wagons to pass each other. The bridge was destroyed by winter ice in 1807–8. A shorter bridge had already been built in 1807 about 2 miles (3.2 km) to the north, to the consternation of East and West Cayuga villagers. Never very profitable, the shorter bridge was abandoned in 1840. A new long bridge was built at the original site in 1812–13; the engineering marvel attracted the interest of tourists and artists. Part of a major route of westward migration, the Cayuga Long Bridge, as it was also known, was popularly viewed as the dividing point between east and west. Many settlers of western New York State, Ohio, and Indiana passed over it, as did troops dispatched to the Niagara frontier during the War of 1812. The turnpike survived competition with the Erie Canal but not the railroads. Rebuilt a final time in 1833, the bridge was damaged by ice and made impassable in February 1857 and finally abandoned. The legislature chartered a new bridge company in 1858, but it never built a bridge, and ferry service resumed in 1860. The bridge's pilings can still be seen when the water level is low.

Wells, John W. *The Cayuga Bridge* (Ithaca: DeWitt Historical Society of Tompkins County, 1966)

Scott C. Monje

Cayuga Marshes. Historical name of the Montezuma Marsh, or Montezuma Wetlands, at the outlet and northern end of Cayuga Lake. Encompassing about 36,000 acres (14,600 ha) in Seneca, Wayne, and Cayuga Cos, the marshes are the remnant of what was a glacial lake approximately 12,400 years ago. Crossed by the Seneca and Clyde Rivers, the marsh played a role in the lore of the Cayuga Indians, who harvested abundant fish and waterfowl from it. Astride the natural transportation route from the Mohawk Valley and associated with mosquitoes, disease, and outlaws, the marsh was a significant barrier to westward movement. Many pioneers avoided it, traveling by ferry across the lake in the late 1700s and over the Cayuga Lake Bridge after 1800. Public works in the 19th century aimed at conquering the marsh. The Erie Canal cut through it, despite 6–12 inches (15–30 cm) of standing water, quicksand, and diseases that disabled thousands of workers (although reports of thousands dead from malaria were probably exaggerated), and a bridge carried the canal's towpath over the Seneca River. Engineers partially succeeded in draining the marsh by ditching around Jacks Reef, a rocky impediment to outward-flowing waters, and blasted the reef when enlarging the canal in the 1850s, draining thousands of acres of marshland.

The drainage in the 19th and early 20th centuries produced fertile mucklands used to grow peppermint, potatoes, onions, celery, and other crops. Van Rensselaer Richmond built a 31-arch stone aqueduct to lift the enlarged Erie Canal over the Seneca River, relocated the Clyde River, and built an embankment on a sunken timber raft for the New York Central Railroad. In the early 20th century, engineers returned the Barge Canal to river level by removing the aqueduct, straightening and deepening the rivers, and building a new dam and lock to control Cayuga Lake outflow.

In 1932 New York State bought 3,120 acres (1,263 ha) to create the Howland Island State Wildlife Management Area, which in 1991 became the 6,304-acre (2,551 ha) Northern Montezuma Wildlife Management Area (NMWMA). In 1938 the US government created the Montezuma Migratory Bird Refuge (now Montezuma National Wildlife Refuge; MNWR) on land it had acquired the previous year. The New York State Thruway intersected the marshes in the 1950s, but the wetlands are still visited annually by millions of migrating birds and remain an important feature of the area's natural environment. Facilities in the area include the Montezuma Wetlands Complex Research Institute, the Crusoe Conservation Center in the NMWMA, trails, and a visitors' center in the MNWR.

Watrous, Hilda R. *The County between the Lakes: A Public History of Seneca County, New York, 1876–1982* (Interlaken, NY: Heart of the Lakes Publishing, 1983)

Scott C. Monje

Cayuga Nation. An American Indian nation belonging to the Iroquois Confederacy. The original Five Nations of the Iroquois Confederacy consisted of the Cayuga and the Oneida as the "younger brothers" and the Seneca, Onondaga, and Mohawk as the "elder brothers." They hold 10 of the 50 hereditary chieftainships of the Confederacy. The *kaiohkhonon'*, or the Cayuga, are a relatively small nation and have longstanding linguistic and political ties to the more numerous Seneca, and through the end of the 18th century, they often allied with them in protecting the "western door" of the Confederacy. Of the original Five Nations of the Iroquois Confederacy, the Cayuga remain the most anonymous in terms of archaeological evidence, though unearthed tribal remains in the area surrounding Cayuga Lake date to 1300 BC.

Colonial and Revolutionary Period

By the 1660s, the period in which European contact commenced, the Cayuga had three villages near Cayuga Lake—Oiogouen, Thiokero, and Onontare—with an approximate population of 800 warriors and 1,500 people. The first Jesuit mission to the Cayuga was established in 1656 and reestablished by 1668. The English version of "Cayuga" derives from "Oiogouen," the town in which the mission was established. Starting in the 1630s, the Seneca and Cayuga were the major participants in wars that ranged on and off for 40 years with the linguistically related Susquehannock to their south in Pennsylvania. In a 1652 raid the Iroquois warriors reportedly carried between 500 and 600 captives back to their hometowns for adoption, execution, or exchange. In 1662 some Cayuga seeking refuge from further Susquehannock attacks removed to the northern shore of Lake Ontario. The Susquehannock war ended after the dispersed and diminished Susquehannock remnants finally accepted Five Nations sovereignty after 1675. Although closely allied with the Seneca, the Cayuga were autonomous enough to formulate their own foreign policy. In 1687 Cayuga diplomats maintained the peace and amicable relations when the French went to war with their Seneca neighbors. The Cayuga towns were spared from attack when Marquis de Denonville's column invaded Seneca country that same year. The Cayuga offered refuge to the fleeing Seneca. Again in 1687, 1693, and 1696, when the towns of other Iroquois nations were attacked, the Cayuga remained untouched. By signing the peace treaty that ended the fighting in 1701, most of the Cayuga remained neutral when the fighting between France and England resumed at the beginning of Queen Anne's War in 1702. Refusing to choose sides between the imperial European powers, the Cayuga instead turned their attention to trading with the Great Lakes and Ohio Valley Indian peoples and to warring with their traditional southern enemies, the Catawba, Saponi, and Cherokee.

Starting in the 1730s, there was a major migration of Cayuga to the Ohio Country, where they became part of the Mingo or Ohio Iroquois communities. This migration intensified after the American Revolution, when a number of Cayuga streamed into the Ohio Country around Sandusky Bay. The community, despite a preponderance of Cayuga, became known as the Senecas of Sandusky. The Ohio Iroquois lived independently of the central council fire of the Onondaga, and pursued their own interests.

From the late 17th century on, there was intermittent warfare between the Iroquois Confederacy and its southern enemies, primarily undertaken to find captives to add to their disease-depleted ranks. By the 1740s a peace was gradually achieved, with the Cayuga chiefs joining the other Six Nations sachems in urging their former adversaries to move further north and thus serve as a southern buffer against encroachment by the Pennsylvania settlers. As a small nation, the Cayuga were wise enough to welcome newcomers who would, in the words of Sir William Johnson, "strengthen their castle," in accordance with the Great Law, which held that any person or nation willing to be bound by that law shall find shelter under the Great White Pine Tree of Peace. The Saponi-Tutelo, Siouan groups of the Virginia-Carolina Piedmont, accepted the offer and began settling at Shamokin [now Sunbury, Pa] on the Susquehanna River beginning in earnest in the 1740s. The intrusion of settlers hastened their migration further northward until in 1753 they were adopted by the Cayuga. By 1771 Saponi-Tutelo peoples had established a series of towns south of Cayuga Lake to the Pennsylvania border. Other adoptions of some Nanticoke, Delaware, Conoy, and others also occurred in 1753.

During the French and Indian War, the Cayuga joined their Seneca allies on the French side. Recognizing the French defeat, most Cayuga made their peace with the British in 1760. The British failure to honor their promises angered the Cayuga to the point that many of them united with the Seneca in besieging the British Forts Pitt [now Pittsburgh] and Niagara [now in Porter, Niagara Co]. Unable to take either fort, the Cayuga and their allies formally made peace with the British at Fort Niagara in 1765.

With the outbreak of the American Revolution, the Confederacy officially declared its neutrality, which left individual nations and warriors to choose their own course of action. The Cayuga sided with the British. In 1779 Gen George Washington sent the Sullivan-Clinton expedition to lay waste to Iroquoia. All Cayuga settlements on the east and west banks of Cayuga Lake were destroyed, including Oiogouen, or Cayuga Town. The Cayuga joined the refugee stream to the vicinity of Fort Niagara in search of safety. After securing their families about the fort, Fish Carrier led a war party of Cayuga and adopted Tutelo-Saponi to wage war on the Americans.

1780s–1840s

After the peace settlement of 1783 formally ended the American Revolution, some of the displaced Cayuga settled at the predominantly Seneca Buffalo Creek Reservation [now in Erie Co]. Other Cayuga left New York State again to join their people already settled near Sandusky Bay in Ohio, eventually removing to Indian Territory in the 1830s and forming the Seneca-Cayuga tribe of Oklahoma. In 1783–84 loyalist Iroquois, including many Cayuga, began to settle in Joseph Brant's grant on both banks of the Grand River in Canada. Another body of Cayuga sought to reestablish themselves in the traditional homelands around Cayuga Lake. They were able to hold onto these lands until a rapid succession of dubious treaties with the State of New York in 1789, 1790, 1795, and 1807 left the Cayuga virtually landless in the state. Again the displaced Cayuga left for Grand River, Buffalo Creek, Cattaraugus, and Ohio. After the Buffalo Creek Reservation was ceded in 1842, most Cayuga in residence moved to the Seneca's Cattaraugus Indian Reservation [loc in Cattaraugus, Chautauqua, and Erie Cos].

Recent Cayuga History

Though landless, the Cayuga have retained a significant presence in New York State and have striven to regain their homeland. A prominent Cayuga chief and physician in the 1840s and 1850s, Peter Wilson, made the Cayuga case for land rights before a meeting of the New-York Historical Society. The 1890 census listed 183 enrolled Cayuga living in the state, the vast majority at the Cattaraugus Reservation. Longstanding legal actions to regain Cayuga land culminated in 1984 when the Cayuga Nation agreed to accept approximately 8,500 acres (3,440 ha) of land in Cayuga and Seneca Cos as a final settlement against the illegal taking of Cayuga land. However, the US Congress failed to pass enabling legislation to implement the settlement. In Syracuse in 2001 US District Judge Neal McCurn ordered New York State to pay the Cayuga $247.9 million for illegally acquiring tribal lands; the state appealed the decision.

By the early 21st century, there were three main groups of the Cayuga Nation. Though all population estimates must be used with extreme caution, the Seneca-Cayuga tribe of Oklahoma number about 600, and approximately 2,600 Cayuga live on the Grand River Reservation in Ontario. The enrolled Cayuga living in New York State number around 500 and live as guests on life estates, principally on the Seneca Cattaraugus Indian Reservation and elsewhere in Western New York.

See also Auburn.

Becker, Mary Druke. "Cayuga." In *Encyclopedia of North American Indians,* ed. Frederick E. Hoxie (Boston: Houghton Mifflin, 1996)
Halftown, Clint. "The Haudenosaunee Cayuga Nation Land Claim: Cayuga Nation v. New York," *Buffalo Law Review* 46 (1998): 1091–95
Starna, William A. "Cayuga." In *Native America in the 20th Century: An Encyclopedia,* ed. Mary B. Davis (New York: Garland Publishing, 1994)
Tower, Christopher B. "Cayuga." In *The Gale Encyclopedia of Native American Tribes,* ed. Sharon Malinowski and Anna Sheets (Detroit: Gale Research, 1998)
White, Marian, William E. Englebrecht, and Elisabeth Tooker. "Cayuga." In *Northeast,* ed. Bruce G. Trigger, vol 15 of *Handbook of North American Indians,* 20 vols, ed. William C. Sturtevant (Washington, DC: Smithsonian Institution, 1978)

Heriberto Dixon

Cayuta. Town (pop 545) in SE Schuyler Co. Cayuta Creek, a notable trout stream, flows through the town. Settled by migrants from Tioga Co, Pa, in 1798, the town was formed from Spencer (Tioga Co) in 1824. The first religious service was held in 1802, but there was no church until the Free Church was built in 1859. In 1860 there was a chair factory at Alpine. The main line of the Lehigh Valley Railroad (1892–1976) passed through Cayuta with two station stops. In 2003 Cayuta was the headquarters of Cotton-Hanlon, a timber sales and management company, and of Wagner Hardwoods, a lumber manufacturing facility. Some Cayuta residents commute to nearby cities.

Glenda Gephart

Cazenovia. Town (pop 6,481) and village (pop 2,614) in W Madison Co. Settled in 1793, it was named for the general agent of the Holland Land Co, Theophile Cazenove. The town was formed in 1795 from Paris and Whitestown (Oneida Co). Located on the Third Great Western Turnpike (1803–11), the village incorporated in 1810. In the 19th century Cazenovia produced paper, woolen cloth, ironwork, agricultural machinery, and town clocks. Two railroads were built through town in 1872. Cazenovia was favored by city dwellers for its large summer cottages, and after World War II it attracted Syracuse residents in particular, ultimately becoming an elegant commuter suburb. The village, which lies on the southeast end of Cazenovia Lake, has retained its historic streetscapes through diligent restoration and preservation efforts. Albany St is a National Historic District, and Lorenzo (1807–8), a Federal-style mansion at the foot of the lake, became a State Historic Site in 1968. The village is also the site of Cazenovia College (1824) and of Lincklaen House (1835), restored in 1916 as a fine small hotel. The town includes the 75-acre (30.4 ha) Stone Quarry Hill Art Park and Chittenango Falls, a spectacular 167 ft (50.9 m) cascade. The limestone ledges of the falls provide a home for the *Novisuccinea chittenangoensis* snail, a species unique to the location. Annual events include shows of antique Franklin and Reo automobiles, carriage driving exhibitions, and street festivals. Electronics manufacturing is based in Trush Industrial Park, east of the village.

William F. Helmer

Cazenovia College. Private college. Founded in 1824 as the Seminary of the Genesee Conference, of the Methodist Episcopal Church, in Cazenovia (Madison Co) and changing its name to the Cazenovia Seminary in 1873, the institution served for over a century as a preparatory school. One of the first coeducational prep schools in the nation, the seminary admitted women in its first year of operation and by 1841 had an anomalous all-female graduating class, but through its first half century only about 25% of its students were female. The depression in the 1930s hurt the school, which began offering junior college courses to men and women in 1934 and changed its name to Cazenovia Seminary Junior College in 1936. Since 1941 the school has been nonsectarian but is still closely connected to the Methodist Church. By fall 1941 the draft threatened to empty classrooms of young men, and in 1942 the seminary was converted into the Cazenovia Junior College for Women. It survived devastating fires in 1947 and 1959, and social and financial woes in the 1960s, and in 1974, deeply in debt to the Dormitory Authority, the board of trustees voted to close the school. Through the efforts of a group of Cazenovia townspeople, it stayed open. In 1983 the college once again admitted men and in 1988 gained baccalaureate status from New York State. In 2002, 86% of the college's approximately 700 full-time students hailed from New York State. Of that total 70% were female and 30% male.

Greene, J. R. *Generations of Excellence: An Illustrated History of Cazenovia Seminary and Cazenovia College, 1824 to the Present* (Syracuse, 2000)

John Robert Greene

CCC. See CIVILIAN CONSERVATION CORPS (CCC).

Cedarhurst. Village (pop 6,164) in Hempstead (Nassau Co). One of the Five Towns of Nassau Co, it originated as the Ocean Point station stop on the Rockaway Branch Railroad (1869). In 1871 landowner Thomas Marsh surveyed a village and began selling lots. A post office named Cedarhurst opened in 1886 at the Rockaway Hunting Club (1878), which before boundary changes covered most of the present village. The village incorporated in 1910 and had a population of 5,065 by 1930. With a large Jewish population, Cedarhurst attracted many Orthodox Jews in the late 20th century. By the early 21st century the village, with its upscale shopping district, had become the commercial hub of the Five Towns.

John A. Hewlett

Celler, Emmanuel (*b* Brooklyn, 6 May 1888; *d* Brooklyn, 15 Jan 1981). US congressman. After attending Columbia Law School, he passed the state bar in 1912 and entered into private practice while also active in local club politics. Elected to the US Congress from Brooklyn in 1922 as a liberal Democrat, Celler was a strong supporter of the New Deal in the 1930s and 1940s and in the 1950s was an opponent of the House Committee on Un-American Activities. He assumed the chairmanship of the Judiciary Committee in 1949 and from that post helped guide the passage of the federal Civil Rights Acts of 1957, 1960, and 1964. In Congress Celler led investigations of monopolistic business practices of firms in the television, steel, and insurance industries, as well as of major league baseball. In 1967 he chaired the House panel that recommended the imposition of penalties against Rep Adam Clayton Powell Jr for ethical breaches. After 50 years in Congress, Celler lost his 1972 bid for reelection in the Democratic primary to Elizabeth Holtzman and retired.

Celler, Emmanuel. *You Never Leave Brooklyn: The Autobiography of Emmanuel Celler* (New York: John Day, 1953)

Richard M. Flanagan

Celoron. Village (pop 1,295) in Ellicott (Chautauqua Co). A lakefront development begun in 1891, it was linked to Jamestown in 1893 by electric railroad. The trolley company created Celoron Park (1894–1962), named for Céloron de Blainville, who explored Chautauqua Lake in 1749. This amusement park included the 115 ft (35 m) Phoenix Wheel, an auditorium with two onion domes, a water toboggan slide, penny arcade, picnic grove, ball park, theater, and an extensive boardwalk among its many attractions. The village incorporated in 1896. In 1898 the Acme Colored Giants of Celoron played in an otherwise all-white minor league baseball league; they were among the last black athletes to play in organized baseball until 1946. Now a residential suburb of Jamestown, Celoron was the childhood home of Lucille Ball (1911–89).

Michelle Henry

cement industry. Cement comes in two primary varieties, natural and Portland cement, both of which are significant to New York State's industrial heritage. Natural cement is a hard, water-resistant mortar that results when certain varieties of limestone are burned at low temperatures, crushed into fine powder, and mixed with water. This material was known to numerous ancient cultures, then rediscovered by British engineers in the mid–18th century. In New York State, civil engineers building the Erie Canal locks sought a regional source of natural cement to limit chronic leakage. The first source was identified in 1818 near Fayetteville (Onondaga Co); farther west, natural cement from Williamsville (Erie Co) was instrumental in building canal locks at Lockport (Niagara Co) in 1824. Akron (Erie Co) also soon emerged as an important natural cement center. A cement works established in Rosendale (Ulster Co) in 1828 facilitated construction of the Delaware and Hudson Canal between Honesdale, Pa, and Kingston (Ulster Co). Rosendale's high-quality cement and proximity to New York City made it the leading natural cement producer in the country, accounting for nearly half of the nation's total over the course of the century and contributing to the growth of Kingston as a Hudson River port. Prominent 19th-century structures built with Rosendale cement in their foundations or supports include the US Capitol, Brooklyn Bridge, and Statue of Liberty.

The second variety, Portland cement, was patented in England in the 1820s but not produced in the United States until 1871. Named after the Isle of Portland, England, it is typically made from limestone and either clay, shale, or slate. The ingredients are crushed, mixed, and burned to form a material called clinker, which is then ground into cement powder. The American Portland cement industry developed in locations where the necessary ingredients could be found nearby, most notably in Lehigh Co, Pa. Portland cement weathers better and cures faster than natural cement and was eventually preferred for construction projects. In 1890 the new material made up less than 5% of the national market but eclipsed natural cement in volume a decade later and accounted for nearly the entire industry by 1905. Natural cement sites in New York State, such as Rosendale, were unsuitable for Portland cement production, and the industry focus shifted to Pennsylvania. Still, sizable Portland cement operations were established near Hudson, Catskill, Cementon, Ravena, Glens Falls, and Howes Cave, while several leading Pennsylvania firms established corporate offices in New York City. Rosendale, where cement production had ceased by 1920, enjoyed a modest midcentury recovery when it was found that Rosendale cement could act as a strengthening additive to Portland cement. By the 1970s, however, chemicals were found that performed this function less expensively. The passage of environmental laws in the United States and consolidation of the global cement industry beginning in the 1970s led to diminished production in New York State and the nation and to a heavy reliance on imports. In 2003, 1,000 people were employed at the four cement plants operating in New York, all with foreign parent ownership: Glens Falls Lehigh Cement in Glens Falls (Warren Co) and Cementon (Greene Co), Lafarge Cement in Ravena (Albany Co), and St. Lawrence Cement in Catskill (Greene Co). Combined, these plants produced 3 million tons (2.7 million MT) of Portland cement in 2000 with a value of $211 million, about 3% of the nation's total. Plans by St. Lawrence Cement to build a new plant near Hudson that would be the nation's largest were bitterly contested on environmental and aesthetic grounds in 2002.

Capiello, Dina. "A Division Set in Stone: Plan for Hudson Cement Plant Pits Newcomers against Tradition and Raises Environmental Worries," *Albany Times-Union,* 2 June 2002

Gilchrist, Ann. *Footsteps across Cement: A History of the Township of Rosendale, New York* (Lith Art, 1976)

Hadley, Earl J. *The Magic Powder: History of the Universal Atlas Cement Company and the Cement Industry* (New York: Putnam's, 1945)

US Geological Survey. *Minerals Yearbook: Area Reports: Domestic 2000* (Washington, DC: US Department of the Interior; Government Printing Office, 2003)

Francis P. Boscoe

cemeteries. Derived from the Greek word *koimeterion,* meaning sleeping chamber, burial places serve as repositories for New York State residents, but also as community memorials. They reveal evolving political, social, and cultural attitudes toward death. Cemeteries were established in New York Colony in the 1600s as simple grave sites, but by the 20th century they evolved into ornate memorial parks.

Colonial Graveyards and Family Plots

In the 1600s Europeans established burial places in secluded glens, on open fields, or along busy streets in villages. Burial places typically were small sites set aside by families, religious institutions, or municipalities and were accessible to mourners. During the 17th and 18th centuries, urban people typically were buried in their parish graveyard, while those living in the countryside had private family plots near a farmstead. Representative of an early city burial place was Trinity Church graveyard, which was established in 1697 in New York City. African Americans were barred from the Trinity Church graveyard and established their own cemetery, which was utilized from 1712 to *ca* 1795. The 5- to 6-acre (2 to 2.4 ha) plot was located in Lower Manhattan near the former Collect Pond and was referred to as the Negro Burial Ground. In Albany a few wealthy residents were buried beneath the Dutch Reformed Church, but most residents were buried in the public graveyard, where each parish and African Americans had their own section. Graves of the 17th and 18th centuries were marked by either wooden or stone markers and were oriented east to west since most colonists believed the deceased should face east at judgment. A variety of gravestone etchings evoked shifting religious and cultural ideas of the period, including death heads of the 17th century, soul effigies by the 18th century, and willow trees and urns after the Revolutionary War.

Rise of the Rural Cemetery

Two key issues changed both rural and urban cemetery patterns. First, as farms were sold or developed, new owners were not legally bound to honor old grave sites. Although they often did, eventually family graveyards went to ruin. Second, public health officials believed cemeteries in the immediate city environment were partly responsible for the miasmatic atmospheres, which they blamed for transmitting diseases. As early as 1822 New York City prohibited burials in densely settled neighborhoods after a devastating yellow fever epidemic. As a result rural cemeteries, a new type of burial place, were established on the outskirts of cities away from residential living. Rural cemeteries were garden sanctuaries and provided a counterpoint to harried urban life. Mount Auburn Cemetery (1831) outside Boston was the nation's first. Mount Hope Cemetery in Rochester (1838) and Green-Wood Cemetery in Brooklyn (1838) were the first rural cemeteries in New York State. Cemeteries also were considered parks. Green-Wood, for example, offered nature tours and bird-watching seminars, activities that have continued to the present, as exemplified by the 2002 Memorial Day concert.

By the 1830s most public cemeteries had associations to manage operations. In 1847 the state passed legislation allowing associations to incorporate. By the 1850s many cemeteries in the state were structured as nonprofit corporations and typically were managed by plot owners, although city governments operated some, like Rochester's Mount Hope. While most cemeteries served Protestants, the Catholics also organized cemeteries, such as Brooklyn's Calvary Cemetery (1848). People were encouraged to purchase large lots to serve generations of family members. Many families erected three-dimensional monuments, statues, and obelisks, which were decorated with symbols: an anchor meant hope, while a lily symbolized chastity. Plots were made ornate by elaborate ironwork fences. Founders viewed cemeteries as important institutions that would serve the state's culture and local historical societies, libraries, and other associations. By 1860, 37 rural cemeteries had been established throughout the state. Designers enveloped visitors in lush, naturalistic landscapes where trees and shrubs were clustered to produce vistas with shifting perspectives, encouraging people to contemplate the moral lessons of nature. By this time most 18th-century graveyards were excavated and remains were reinterred into larger public cemeteries but often in remote areas.

Stoneyards to Memorial Parks

Rural cemeteries never fully replaced churchyards or potters fields—burial places set aside for the indigent—and coexisted with a new generation of ethnic and religious cemeteries. By the late 19th century, communities established small burial places that imitated ones in Europe. These grounds were often a few minimally landscaped acres and were filled with large upright individual headstones. Gravestones were increasingly standardized models and were manufactured and shipped to local monument dealers, who etched names and dates. Some were ornamented with framed photographs of the deceased, such as those at Forest Hill Cemetery in Fredonia (Chautauqua Co).

Seven national cemeteries were established in the state, near camps or veterans' homes, beginning in the Civil War period, four of which were preexisting cemeteries: Cypress Hills in Brooklyn (1862); Albany Rural Cemetery, where the National Cemetery Administration has managed a plot for veterans since 1862; Woodlawn Cemetery (1874) in Elmira (Chemung Co), which was close to a Confederate prison camp and initially had more than 2,900 interments; and Bath's (Steuben Co) graveyard (1879) located near a home for disabled veterans. Three cemeteries were founded as national cemeteries, including Long Island National Cemetery (1936) in Farmingdale (Nassau Co), Calverton National Cemetery (1976) (Suffolk Co); and Gerald B. Solomon National Cemetery (1999) in Schuylerville (Saratoga Co).

In the early 20th century, cemeteries were criticized and called stoneyards because of the large number of markers. Critics argued that ostentatious monuments, such as the pyramid-shaped Longstreet mausoleum in Syracuse's Oakwood Cemetery, obscured the landscape. The concept of the grandiose cemetery declined by the 1910s, giving rise to the memorial park, designed to be more modern, accessible, and complementary to the landscape. In response to the popularity of suburbs, the memorial park was designed around open lawns. Individual graves were marked with flush-to-the-ground markers. Management erected features in each burial section that evoked collective identities, such as a statue of Christ, a Star of David, or an American eagle. Memorial parks also refined the use of mausoleums. In the 1870s cemeteries began constructing community mausoleums, where families or individuals could purchase one or more crypts. But the memorial park design made mausoleums more affordable for the middle class, and crypt burial continued into the 21st century. The first crypts were elaborate buildings decorated with stained-glass windows, statues, and marble. Ferncliff Mausoleum at Ferncliff Memorial Park (1927) in Hartsdale (Westchester Co) is an example. Ferncliff has over 8,000 crypts and 250 private family rooms. In the mid–20th century, mausoleums were redesigned as garden mausoleums with stacked crypts facing a small open courtyard.

Crisis and Continuity

Aggressive advertising led critics and state officials to worry that cemeteries were not serving the public's best interest. In 1949 New York State

Atty Gen Nathaniel Goldstein charged that cemetery operators had profited and defrauded bereaved people. An investigation ensued, unearthing unsavory hard-sell marketing practices and leading to legislation that regulated nonprofit cemetery associations. The State Cemetery Board, composed of the head of the Health Department, the secretary of state, and the attorney general, formed that year mainly to protect families from price gouging. The state's regulatory body, the Division of Cemeteries, was housed within the Department of State and has managed nonprofit cemeteries since the 1940s.

In the early 21st century, New Yorkers were ambivalent toward cemeteries. On the one hand cemeteries were less connected to hometowns and neighborhoods, and people were more willing to choose cremation. By 2000 roughly one of every five New Yorkers was cremated. On the other hand the majority of New Yorkers continue to inter their loved ones in the cemetery. They use laser engraved memorials, cremation gardens, stained-glass urns, and other innovative means to honor and memorialize their loved ones. In 2002 the State Cemetery Board met monthly and continued to oversee incorporated nonprofit cemeteries, while religious, municipal, and for-profit or family cemeteries were privately managed.

See also FOLK ART.

Jackson, Kenneth T., and Camilo Jose Vergara. *Silent Cities: The Evolution of the American Cemetery* (New York: Princeton Architectural Press, 1989)

Sloane, David Charles. *The Last Great Necessity: Cemeteries in American History* (Baltimore: Johns Hopkins Univ Press, 1991)

Wells, Robert V. *Facing the King of Terrors: Death and Society in an American Community, 1750–1990* (New York: Cambridge Univ Press, 2000)

David C. Sloane

census, federal. The US Constitution established a bicameral congress: a senate in which states have equal representation and a house of representatives in which seats are allocated to states on the basis of population. To implement this grand compromise, the framers required that a census be taken every 10 years. Because the Constitution leaves most of the details of the required actual enumeration to congressional discretion, the census has been an important source of conflict throughout American history.

History and Accessibility

In the original census of 1790 US marshals and hired assistants counted the number of persons in each household, noting the number of white male adults and children, white females, free Blacks, and slaves. While the first census simply counted the people in the nation, later ones included information on industry and social issues. Controversy over the accuracy of the 1840 census led to the creation of the first census office, the forerunner of the Census Bureau (established as a permanent agency in 1902), and to reforms that professionalized the enumeration. Meanwhile, the census added questions about education, income, nativity, household amenities, mining, agriculture, manufacturing, and other subjects of interest to policy makers and the public. The census also compiled data about race, although those categories have changed several times, most recently with the addition of a multiracial option in 2000. As of 2002 the Cen-

SELECTED SOCIOECONOMIC CHARACTERISTICS, 2000

	New York		United States	
Nativity and Place of Birth	*n*	%	*n*	%
Native	15,108,324	79.6	250,314,017	88.9
Born in United States	14,589,263	76.9	246,786,466	87.7
Resides in state of birth	12,384,940	65.3	168,729,388	60.0
Resides in different state	2,204,323	11.6	78,057,078	27.7
Born outside United States	519,061	2.7	3,527,551	1.3
Foreign-born	3,868,133	20.4	31,107,889	11.1
Naturalized citizen	1,783,744	9.4	12,542,626	4.5
Not a citizen	2,084,389	11.0	18,565,263	6.6
Entered 1990 to March 2000	1,561,609	8.2	13,178,276	4.7
N	18,976,457		281,421,906	
Race	*n*	%	*n*	%
One race	18,386,275	96.9	274,595,678	97.6
White	12,893,689	67.9	211,460,626	75.1
Black or African American	3,014,385	15.9	34,658,190	12.3
American Indian and Alaska Native	82,461	0.4	2,475,956	0.9
Asian	1,044,976	5.5	10,242,998	3.6
Asian Indian	251,724	1.3	1,678,765	0.6
Chinese	424,774	2.2	2,432,585	0.9
Filipino	81,681	0.4	1,850,314	0.7
Japanese	37,279	0.2	796,700	0.3
Korean	119,846	0.6	1,076,872	0.4
Vietnamese	23,818	0.1	1,122,528	0.4
Other Asian	105,854	0.6	1,285,234	0.5
Native Hawaiian and Other Pacific Islander	8,818	0.0	398,835	0.1
Native Hawaiian	1,684	0.0	140,652	0.0
Guamanian or Chamorro	1,931	0.0	58,240	0.0
Samoan	1,475	0.0	91,029	0.0
Other Pacific Islander	3,728	0.0	108,914	0.0
Some other race	1,341,946	7.1	15,359,073	5.5
Two or more races	590,182	3.1	6,826,228	2.4
N	18,976,457		281,421,906	
Hispanic or Latino and Race	*n*	%	*n*	%
Hispanic or Latino (of any race)	2,867,583	15.0	35,305,818	12.5
Mexican	260,889	1.4	20,640,711	7.3
Puerto Rican	1,050,293	5.5	3,406,178	1.2
Cuban	62,590	0.3	1,241,685	0.4
Other Hispanic or Latino	1,493,811	7.9	10,017,244	3.6
N	18,976,457		281,421,906	
Educational Attainment of Population 25 Years and Older	*n*	%	*n*	%
Less than 9th grade	1,005,805	8.0	13,755,477	7.5
9th to 12th grade, no diploma	1,620,519	12.9	21,960,148	12.1
High school graduate (includes equivalency)	3,480,768	27.8	52,168,981	28.6
Some college, no degree	2,103,404	16.8	38,351,595	21.0
Associate degree	898,828	7.2	11,512,833	6.3
Bachelor's degree	1,954,242	15.6	28,317,792	15.5
Graduate or professional degree	1,478,970	11.8	16,144,813	8.9
High school graduate or higher		79.1		80.4
Bachelor's degree or higher		27.4		24.4
N	12,542,536		182,211,639	
Employment Status of Population 16 Years and Older	*n*	%	*n*	%
In labor force	9,046,805	61.1	138,820,935	63.9
Civilian labor force	9,023,096	60.9	137,668,798	63.4
Employed	8,382,988	58.6	129,721,512	59.7
Unemployed	640,108	4.3	7,947,286	3.7
Armed forces	23,709	0.2	1,152,137	0.5
Not in labor force	5,759,107	38.9	78,347,142	36.1
N	14,805,912		217,168,077	

SELECTED SOCIOECONOMIC CHARACTERISTICS, 2000 (continued)

	New York		United States	
Occupation of Employed Civilian Population 16 Years and Older	*n*	%	*n*	%
Management, professional, related occupations	3,079,837	36.7	43,646,731	33.6
Service	1,389,202	16.6	19,276,947	14.9
Sales and office occupations	2,272,500	27.1	34,621,390	26.7
Farming, fishing, forestry	24,609	0.3	951,810	0.7
Construction, extraction, maintenance	633,091	7.6	12,256,138	9.4
Production, transportation, material moving	983,749	11.7	18,968,496	14.6
N	8,382,988		129,721,512	
Household Income in 1999	*n*	%	*n*	%
Less than $10,000	809,507	11.5	10,067,027	9.5
$10,000 to $14,999	453,320	6.4	6,657,228	6.3
$15,000 to $24,999	822,611	11.7	13,536,965	12.8
$25,000 to $34,999	807,043	11.4	13,519,242	12.8
$35,000 to $49,999	1,047,001	14.8	17,446,272	16.5
$50,000 to $74,999	1,297,712	18.4	20,540,604	19.5
$75,000 to $99,999	746,384	10.6	10,799,245	10.2
$100,000 to $149,999	639,525	9.1	8,147,826	7.7
$150,000 to $199,999	202,640	2.9	2,322,038	2.2
$200,000 or more	234,852	3.3	2,502,675	2.4
N	7,060,595		105,539,122	
Median household income ($)	43,393		41,994	

Family Poverty in 1999	New York	United States
Families below poverty level	535,935	6,620,945
% below poverty level	11.5	9.2
with related children under 18 years	418,591	5,155,866
% below poverty level	16.9	13.6
with related children under 5 years	198,252	2,562,263
% below poverty level	20.2	17.0
Families with female householder, no spouse present	294,906	3,315,916
% below poverty level	29.2	26.5
with related children under 18 years	257,263	2,940,459
% below poverty level	38.8	34.3
with related children under 5 years	115,454	1,401,493
% below poverty level	49.8	46.4

Source: US Census.

Compiled by Jacqueline Villarrubia-Mendoza

sus Bureau employed roughly 12,000 people in its headquarters and 12 regional offices; 860,000 people had been hired as temporary workers for the 2000 census.

Census data are available to the public through the National Archives, its regional centers, select depository libraries, and the Church of Latter-day Saints (LDS). However, full census information remains private for 72 years to protect sensitive personal information. The most recent one released for public viewing was the 1930 census, which was opened in 2002. The New York State Library in Albany has federal population census data available for on-site research from 1790 to 1930, excluding the 1890 census, which was almost entirely destroyed by fire in 1921. Indexes for each census provide assistance in locating desired information, and all the census documents may be viewed on microfilm, with only the 1790 census available on microfilm and in print. The State Library also has select information gathered from New York State's citizens through special schedules in the 19th century. For example, federal census takers asked questions about agriculture and mortality from 1850 to 1880, industry and manufactures in 1820 and from 1850 to 1880, and social statistics from 1850 to 1870. These special schedule data are accessible both at the archives and through interlibrary loan.

Challenges

Two early census controversies—the initial census clause that a slave would count as three-fifths of a person, which was eliminated after the Civil War, and the requirement that direct taxes be apportioned based on the census, which was effectively overturned by the 16th Amendment's authorization of federal income taxes—were resolved. Controversy over census-taking methods and reliability, however, has continually dogged the process. Although census inaccuracy was always recognized, studies beginning with the 1940 enumeration showed that Blacks and other minorities were disproportionately undercounted. The Supreme Court's reapportionment decisions made clear that the undercount could cost states like New York representation in Congress and urban areas like New York City seats in the state legislature. Moreover, the growth of federal programs distributing benefits on the basis of population meant that undercounted states and communities could lose money.

Nevertheless, the federal government refused to adjust the census for undercount until recently. This prompted many legal challenges to the accuracy of the census. The leading case was filed by New York City and New York State in 1980, which litigated for seven years in a fruitless effort to force the Census Bureau to make a statistical correction. New York City and New York State led a coalition of challengers who tried to force an adjustment of the 1990 census, but in 1996 the Supreme Court ruled that the federal government could not be compelled to correct the count.

Meanwhile, a different coalition challenged a planned adjustment of the 2000 census. New York City intervened in that litigation in support of the adjustment plan. In January 1999 the Supreme Court ruled that the Census Act forbids the use of adjusted data for allocating seats in the House of Representatives. The Court did not address the constitutionality of adjustment if the statute were amended, nor did it consider whether adjusted census data could be used for redrawing state and local legislative districts or distributing population-based federal money. Those issues remain open for further legal and political dispute. Despite the lingering questions surrounding the census, the growing popularity of genealogical research in New York and across the country has made public requests for and use of census data popular. In addition to traditional depositories, several large web sites offer access to census records.

Anderson, Margo J. *The American Census: A Social History* (New Haven, Conn: Yale Univ Press, 1988)
Cohen, Patricia Cline. *A Calculating People: The Spread of Numeracy in Early America* (Chicago: Univ of Chicago Press, 1982)
US Census Bureau, http://www.census.gov

Jonathan Entin

census, state. Between 1683 and 1771, nine complete and several partial censuses of the Province of New York were taken by sheriffs and justices of the peace, by order of the governor. The censuses compiled data on taxable households and total population for the provincial authorities and the Board of Trade in London. The Constitution of 1777 mandated a census of electors (adult males qualified to vote) every seven years. Electoral censuses were taken more or less regularly in 1790, 1795, 1801, 1807, 1814, and 1821. The latter two censuses also counted the total population and the number of men eligible to serve in the militia. The Constitution of 1821 required the secretary of state to supervise the taking of a census every 10 years on the fifth year of the decade. The state censuses of 1825, 1835, and 1845 recorded the name of the head of each household and counted the number of persons in various age groups. These censuses also collected other demographic data (eg, number of aliens, paupers, Blacks, "idiots") and economic data (eg, number of cows, horses, sheep, yards of home-woven cloth, sawmills, gristmills).

The accuracy of the data in these early state censuses is often dubious. Enumerators were local appointees who forwarded census schedules for towns and city wards to the county clerk, who sent the totaled figures to the secretary of state, who published them without verifying the data. In 1855 the legislature decided to gather more detailed data about the population, agriculture, and industry. To achieve this the secretary of state appointed the census enumerators statewide, which annoyed local officials and resulted in some inaccurate returns. The 1855 census was supervised by Franklin B. Hough, an accomplished historian and statistician. He compiled the statistical compendium, which contains a wealth of data about New York State's population and economy. Hough also supervised the 1865 census, but the industrial data were incomplete because business proprietors feared it might be used for taxation. The 1875 state census was compiled with the excellent quality controls used in the 1870 federal census.

A state census was not taken in 1885. Democratic governor David B. Hill preferred a simple, cheap enumeration of citizens and aliens for legislative reapportionment and vetoed two bills for a complete census that had been passed by the mainly Republican legislature. The counts taken in 1892, 1905, and 1915 recorded the names and characteristics of every resident of the state, but only population totals were published. In 1925 Florence E. S. Knapp of Syracuse, the secretary of state and the first woman in New York elected to statewide office, took personal charge of the census. She illegally hired about 150 people, mostly friends and relatives, for vague administrative duties, which most of them did not perform. The appropriation was exhausted and tabulating returns (using the new technology of punch cards) was suspended. An appointed secretary of state, Robert Moses, took office in early 1927. He informed Gov Alfred E. Smith of Knapp's apparent misconduct, and a Moreland Act commissioner exposed the full extent. She was indicted on numerous charges, finally convicted of grand larceny, and sentenced in May 1928 to 30 days in jail. Since this scandal New York State has relied on the federal census to reapportion the legislature and to plan its social programs. The constitutional requirement for a state census was repealed in 1931.

The first state to require a census, New York has compiled more data than any other. Statistical summaries of all of the state's censuses have been published. More than 750 folio volumes of manuscript census schedules dating between 1801 and 1905 were destroyed when the State Library burned in 1911. The 1915 and 1925 census schedules are available on microfilm, as are the county clerks' duplicate schedules for previous state censuses.

Douglas, Marilyn, and Melinda Yates. *New York State Census Records, 1790–1925.* New York State Library Bibliography Bulletin, no. 88 (Albany: NYS Education Department, 1981)

Dubester, Henry J. *State Censuses: An Annotated Bibliography of Censuses of Population Taken after the Year 1790 by States and Territories of the United States* (Washington, DC: Government Printing Office, 1948)

James D. Folts

Centereach. Locality (pop 27,285) in Brookhaven (Suffolk Co). During the 19th century residents cut cordwood and carried it to Stony Brook for shipment. Early residential development included the Agricultural City Co (1896) and Centereach Terrace (1937), but the area remained chiefly one of vegetable and fruit farming and poultry raising. The post office opened in 1916. After World War II development began in earnest, and the 1940 population of 628 soared to 6,700 by 1960. In the early 21st century Centereach is a suburban residential community.

Luise Weiss

Center Moriches. See MORICHES.

Centerport. Locality (pop 5,446) in Huntington (Suffolk Co). On a peninsula in Long Island Sound and settled in 1660, Centerport had Long Island's greatest concentration of mills in the 18th and 19th centuries. Its post office, established in 1831, was called Cow Harbour until renamed Centerport in 1835. After the Long Island Rail Road came through in 1868, Centerport became a summer resort. A boardinghouse, the Chalmers House (1879), became Mount Alvernia (1888), the first Catholic summer camp in the United States. Centerport's population increased after Huntington Beach (1927) was platted on the west side of the harbor. The 43-acre (17 ha) Vanderbilt Museum and Planetarium (1950), once the estate of William K. Vanderbilt II, lies on Little Neck peninsula overlooking Northport Harbor.

Robert C. Hughes

Centerville. Town (pop 762) in NW Allegany Co. Centerville was settled in 1808 by 18-year-old Joseph Maxson from Hartwick (Otsego Co). He bartered a new pair of shoes for an axe and started clearing land by himself. The town was formed from Pike (Wyoming Co) in 1819. A Welsh community settled in the southwest, forming Fairview Congregational Church (1840). Centerville became a dairying town and was served by the short-lived Buffalo and Susquehanna Railroad (1906–16). An Amish community settled in the mid-1970s and produces organic milk for the market. Reforestation in the 1930s created 1,344-acre (543.9 ha) Lost Nation, 1,569-acre (635 ha) Swift Hill, and 501-acre (202.7 ha) Cold Creek State Forests.

Central Asians. There are no precise numbers for immigrants from the region encompassing Mongolia, Xinjiang in western China, Afghanistan, and the former Soviet republics of Azerbaijan, Kazakstan, Kyrgyzstan, Tajikistan, Turkmenistan, and Uzbekistan. Central Asians, for the most part, live in New York City, especially Queens, and associate with larger immigrant communities based on shared religion or ethnicity. Most Central Asian Muslims are Sunni Muslims, but some Afghans are Shia. Mongolians are Buddhists, and Bukharans are Jewish. Many who came as political or religious refugees were engineers, doctors, or academics in their home countries but, because of the language barrier and different educational standards, have not been able to work in these fields.

Although 200 Pashtuns arrived in 1920, there was little immigration from Afghanistan or elsewhere in Central Asia before the 1970s. The Afghan population came largely during the 1980s, when 2,000–4,000 entered the United States annually, fleeing war and communism. An estimated 20,000 Afghans now live in an area of Flushing in Queens known as "Little Afghanistan." The relatively secular Afghan population in the United States grew more religious as the immigrant community rallied against the communist takeover of their homeland. After the 1989 Soviet withdrawal from Afghanistan, ethnic and tribal factionalism reemerged among Afghan Americans. Most speak Persian languages and mix with the larger and wealthier Iranian population but attend Sunni mosques. The Masjid Hazrat-I-Abubaker Sadiq, a $1.8 million marble edifice in Flushing, is the city's largest Afghan mosque, serving some 5,000 Pashtun, Tajik, and Uzbek members. Its religious and political positions have at times clashed with those of the smaller, mostly Pashtun, Sayed Jamal-ud-din mosque.

Although some war-weary exiles favored the Taliban's religious rule when it first came to power in Afghanistan in 1996, by 2001 the immigrant community was sharply divided and antiterror sentiment was strong. Since 11 Sept 2001 and the ensuing Afghan war, diaspora community organizations, such as the Afghanistan Council of the Asia Society (founded 1960), Afghan Community in America (1981), Afghanistan Peace Association (1989), School of Hope (2000), and Women for Afghan Women (2001), have been organizing against terrorism and promoting peace, democracy, and human rights. Publications include *Afghan Communicator* (1997) and *Voice of Peace* (1996). Afghans own and operate restaurant, retail, construction, taxi, and other businesses in Flushing, Jamaica, Manhattan, the Bronx, Huntington, Long Island City, Brooklyn, and elsewhere. By 1984 Afghan refugees ran 200 fried-chicken restaurants throughout the city, and they now dominate the pushcart business, with some 800 selling coffee and bagels. The Society of Afghan Engineers is an active professional organization. Community events include Inter-Afghan Youth Summits and celebrations of Afghanistan Independence Day and Afghan Heritage Day.

By the 1970s, central Queens was home to an enclave of Soviet Central Asian immigrants, a large new wave arriving in the 1980s. During the mid-1990s, some 3,000 people from Uzbekistan moved to the city every year. Uzbek cafés sprang up in Queens and continue to be community gathering places. Most of the Jews of Kazakstan, Kyrgyzstan, Tajikistan, Turkmenistan, and Uzbekistan, known as Bukharans, fled the collapsing post-Soviet economy in a mass exodus. Up to 50,000 settled in Rego Park in Queens, forming one of the largest such communities in the world; smaller groups settled in Queens in Forest Hills, Jamaica Estates, and Kew Gardens, and in Brooklyn. They own bakeries, restaurants, and other businesses; 108th Street from 67th Ave to 63rd Rd in Queens is known as Bukharan Broadway. Many who came before 1989 achieved success in the jewelry business. Later arrivals are generally poor and unassimilated. Others came via Israel. At first large extended families lived together in small apartments, but recent trends are toward smaller units in the same building complexes. Recently some have relocated to more southern states. Although intragroup social and economic relations remain close, their traditional association with Muslim cultures is waning as they mix with

Lubavitchers and other Orthodox Jews. Religious life is thriving, with several synagogues and an expanding yeshiva. Prominent Bukharan musicians settled in Queens, including Ilyas Malayev, Malika Kalontarova, and members of the Shashmaqam ensemble. There are weekly radio broadcasts in Russian and Farsi, and several community newspapers include *Druzhba (Friendship)* and the *Bukharian Times*. In addition to the Jewish population, an estimated 4,000 ethnic Uzbeks, 40% of the US total, live in the New York City area.

About 150 Turkestani families from Uzbekistan came in the 1950s and 1960s. The mostly Uzbek Turkestan Society of America (1958), Turkestan American Association, Uyghur American Association, and other New York City–based Turkestani or Uighur groups have actively protested Soviet and Chinese rule over their homelands. Azeri refugees came after World War II and again in the early 1990s; many settled around Brighton Beach in Brooklyn, gradually merging into the Russian Jewish community.

Ansary, Tamim. *West of Kabul, East of New York: An Afghan American Story* (New York: Farrar, Straus & Giroux, 2002)

Levin, Theodore. *The 100,000 Fools of God: Musical Travels in Central Asia (and Queens, New York)* (Bloomington: Indiana Univ Press, 1996)

Omidian, Patricia A. *Aging and Family in an Afghan Refugee Community* (New York: Garland Publishing, 1996)

Roden, Claudia. *The Book of Jewish Food: An Odyssey from Samarkand to New York* (New York: Knopf, 1996)

Grant Farr

Central Hudson Gas and Electric Corporation. Investor-owned electric and gas utility service supplying approximately 650,000 customers in the mid–Hudson Valley (Albany, Columbia, Dutchess, Greene, Orange, Putnam, Sullivan, and Ulster Cos). In 1900 William R. Beal, chair of the Consolidated Gas Co of New York, his son Thaddeus R. Beal, and New York City lawyer John L. Wilkie bought two companies that together provided 5,000 Newburgh (Orange Co) customers with gas and electricity. The two firms were then merged under the name Newburgh Light, Heat, and Power. Newburgh immediately expanded and acquired other existing companies in the region, including Poughkeepsie Light, Heat and Power (1901), Electric Light Co of New Paltz (1902), and Cornwall Electric Light and Power Co (1904). In 1927 the more than 60 companies assembled by Beale and Wilkie interests were consolidated and reorganized, becoming known as the Central Gas Co. They would produce water gas, used as a heating gas and for cooking in gas stoves until the 1950s, as well as steam and hydroelectric power. In 1951 the company converted from manufactured to natural gas and initiated its largest electrical generation project, the construction of what would eventually become four coal generating units at the Danskammer Plant in Newburgh and the Neversink Hydroelectric Plant in Grahamsville (Sullivan Co). Acquisitions continued through 1967, when Ellenville Electric Co became the last of more than 80 firms absorbed by the corporation. In 1987 the company completed Nine Mile Point Two Nuclear Plant, jointly owned with the Niagara Mohawk, New York State Electric and Gas, Long Island Lighting Co, and Rochester Gas and Electric, in Scriba (Oswego Co). In 1998, following the partial deregulation by the state of the electric and gas markets in New York State, company officers created an energy holding company called Central Hudson Enterprises (since 2000, CH Energy Group) as a parent company to the now subsidiary Central Hudson Gas and Electric Corp, which continued to provide electricity and gas. In 2001 CH Energy Group reported revenues of $729 million.

CH Energy. *The Central Hudson Century* (Poughkeepsie: CH Energy Group, 2001)

Jeffrey Kraus

Central Islip. Locality (pop 31,950) in Islip (Suffolk Co). The area was wooded when the Long Island Rail Road established Suffolk Station on Islip Ave in 1842. A post office by the same name opened in 1857. Both were changed to Central Islip in 1874. In 1905 the Branch Lunatic Asylum opened to relieve crowding at New York City institutions. After 1905 called the Central Islip State Hospital, it reached a peak of 10,000 patients in 1955 and closed in 1997. During its decline parts of the campus were redeveloped for the New York Institute of Technology, the Colahan Court Complex, and the Richard Meier–designed Federal Courthouse (2000), the largest structure on Long Island. In 2000 Central Islip's population was 27% black, and 36% of the total were of Latino ethnicity. Citibank Park is home to the Long Island Ducks baseball team and the Rough Riders soccer team.

Daria E. Merwin

Central Park (Manhattan). In 1853 state law established the projected park on an almost rural terrain of nearly 775 acres (314 ha), bounded by 59th St to the south, 106th St (now 110th St) to the north, and 5th and 8th Aves to the east and west. The modern park consists of 843 acres (341 ha). Between 1853 and 1856 numerous properties were condemned for park acquisition, with many city residents forced to relocate; most notable was Seneca Village, an African American settlement of approximately 1,600, near what is now West 82d St. The Board of Commissioners of Central Park, a governing body created by the state legislature, was authorized in 1857 and oversaw park planning and construction. The following year the Greensward Plan by Frederick Law Olmsted and Calvert Vaux won the board's design competition. It synthesized English pastoral style and a democratic social sensibility, mixed natural and formal areas, and included an innovative graded circulation system. By the early 1870s the park had largely taken shape, at an approximate cost of $16 million.

Two buildings predate the park: a state arsenal (since 1934 the headquarters of the City of New York/Parks and Recreation) and a blockhouse from the War of 1812. Other notable structures include the Metropolitan Museum of Art (begun 1881), Belvedere Castle (1873, since 1919 the weather station), Tavern on the Green (a sheepfold in 1871, a restaurant since 1934), and the Bandshell (1923). A zoo (begun 1859), two skating rinks (1950 and 1966), and a model-boat pond are popular attractions. Funds donated by former governor Herbert H. Lehman and his wife Edith Altschul Lehman helped build the children's zoo (1961) in the park. The Heckscher Playground (opened 1926) was the first of 19 park playgrounds, and the park's 50 sculptures include the beloved sled dog Balto (1925) and Alice in Wonderland (1959). Central gathering spots include Bethesda Fountain (1873) and the Great Lawn (1937), where concerts are held. In 1980 the Central Park Conservancy was founded to help restore, preserve, and maintain the park and has since helped the city rehabilitate most of its features; 23 years later 85% of the park's annual budget was provided by the Conservancy. The oldest major landscaped urban park in the United States, and the most heavily visited, at the start of the 21st century Central Park averages near 25 million visits per year.

See also ZOOS.

Miller, Sara Cedar. *Central Park: An American Masterpiece* (New York: Harry N. Abrams, 2003)

Rosenzweig, Roy, and Elizabeth Blackmar. *The Park and the People: A History of Central Park* (Ithaca: Cornell Univ Press, 1992)

Jonathan Kuhn

Central Square. Village (pop 1,646) in Hastings (Oswego Co). Settled in 1815 at the junction of the Old Salt Rd (US 11) and the road from Constantia to Fulton (Rte 49), and later the terminus of the state's first plank road (1846), it acquired stations on the Ontario and Western Railroad (1869) and the Rome, Watertown and Ogdensburg Railroad (1871). The village was incorporated in 1890. With easy access to I-81 (1961), some residents commute to Syracuse or other industrial cities nearby.

Barbara J. Dix

Central Terminal (Buffalo). At the outset of the 20th century, Buffalo needed a union station to consolidate the operations of 13 different railroads and to eliminate dangerous grade crossings. Numerous obstacles stalled the project, but in 1925 the New York Central Railroad agreed to construct a major station in the Fillmore District, east of downtown. The architects were noted railroad station designers Alfred Fellheimer and Steward Wagner. Central Terminal, which opened on 22 June 1929, was designed in an Art Deco style at a cost of $14 million. Though an average of 200 trains per day utilized Central Terminal in the years after its opening, after World War II there was a steady decline in railroad passenger traffic. This decline continued after the 1968 formation of Penn Central from the merger of New York Central and Pennsylvania Railroads. In 1976 Central Terminal was acquired by Conrail, the successor of Penn Central. Nearly demolished in the 1970s, passenger travel to the terminal ceased in 1979; the same year it was sold to an entrepreneur in July 1979 for $75,000. The City of Buffalo eventually acquired title to the building when property taxes had not been paid, and it was subsequently sold at auction with disastrous results: the new owner stripped the once elegant building of its interior Art Deco fixtures, and it was left open to vandals, who stole copper roof flashing for scrap value. The elements destroyed the building's interior finishes. After the building was sold once more with no success, it was placed on the State and National Registers of Historic Places in October 1984. Buffalo's most cherished landmark is now owned by a nonprofit corporation whose sole interest is to have the building preserved, sympa-

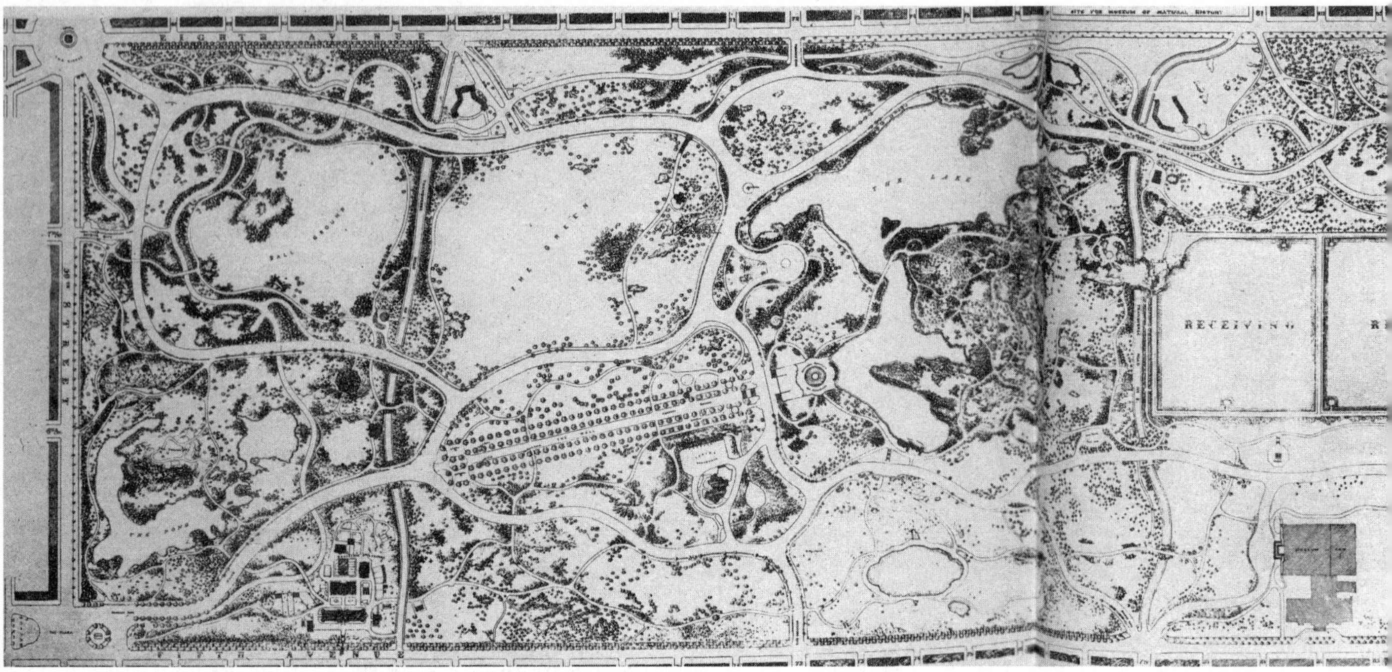

Greensward Plan for Central Park, by Frederick Law Olmsted and Calvert Vaux, 1858.

thetically restored, and used for a dignified purpose. Statewide attention was drawn to Central Terminal in 2003 when the Preservation League of New York State included the structure on its annual Seven to Save list.

Cousins, Garnet R. "Beacon at Mile 435.9–1: A Station Too Late, Too Far," *Trains: The Magazine of Railroading*, Sept 1985

———. "Beacon at Mile 435.9–2: Dedication to Dethronement," *Trains: The Magazine of Railroading*, Oct 1985

Michael J. Bosak

Centre Island. Village (pop 444) in Oyster Bay (Nassau Co). The village is on a peninsula formed 25,000 years ago by glacial action. Originally called Hog Island, it has been known as Centre Island since around 1840, at which time it was farmland with a brickyard located at its south end. The extension of the railroad to Oyster Bay in 1889 and the construction of a clubhouse and docks for the Seawanhaka Corinthian Yacht Club (1872) in 1892 spurred Centre Island's residential growth. During Prohibition rumrunners used several locations on Centre Island. The village incorporated in 1926 and is, with the exception of the yacht club, entirely residential.

Tom Kuehhas

Century Farms. In 1937 the New York State Agricultural Society began to identify farms that had been in the same family for at least 100 years. Through 2002 the society had honored 282 Century Farms, 36 of which were Bicentennial Farms. The Halsey-Organic Green Thumb Farm (1640) in Water Mill (Suffolk Co), and the Schoonmaker Farm (1680) near Accord (Ulster Co) are the oldest. The longevity of all these farms results from the tenacity and adaptability of their owners. The history of the Merckley-Bates Farm in Seward (Schoharie Co), in a county with six other Century Farms and two Bicentennial Farms, can speak to the history of all. German immigrants Frederick and Christian Merckley began farming in 1752, producing wool and flax on their 125 acres (51 ha). Later, hops became their main crop. When Spencer Bates married Mary Merckley, he emphasized dairying, purchasing the farm from his in-laws in 1884. In 2002 Richard Bates was the eighth generation of his family to work the farm, which had grown to 438 acres (177 ha). Dairying remained its focus, but the farm also produces corn, alfalfa, sorghum, forage soybeans, and hay.

Graves. Tammy, "250 Years of Farming and Counting for Bates Family," *My Shopper Business Review*, 21 Feb 2002

New York State Agricultural Society, http://www.nysagsociety.org

Peter Johnson and Dawn Johnson

ceramics and pottery

Redware

Over 2,500 years after early Woodland period American Indians began producing pottery in the region, colonial potters in New York first produced redware, a fragile, porous earthen body. The ubiquitous nature of its raw material ensured that redware would be the preferred medium for pioneer ceramists, whose pots, jugs, and tableware found a ready market within New York's early settlements. The first documented potter of the colonial period, Dirck Claesen of Manhattan (active *fl* 1655–86), made redware crocks and toys. He was followed by John and Thomas Campbell (?1759–96), whose products included roof tile and brightly slip-decorated pie plates. Fear of fire and congestion soon drove out Manhattan's potters, who followed expanding settlement into the east and north. The Dutch brothers Ewout and John Euwatse were active as early as 1686 in Bushwick (Kings Co), and a pottery (?1805–1905), which flourished under the Brown family beginning in 1863, was established at Huntington (Suffolk Co). The Middle Hudson region attracted many crafters, including Circleville's (Orange Co) David Mandeville (?1810–44), who was noted for his ovoid storage jars; Newburgh's (Orange Co) Selah Reeve (*fl* 1799–1822); and Quaker potters Amos Osborn (*fl* 1790–1814) and Joseph Shove (*fl* 1790–99), who made redware at Pawling (Dutchess Co) and Hudson (Columbia Co) respectively. Farther north Israel Seymour (*fl* 1809–52) of Troy (Rensselaer Co) made black glazed redware teapots in the 1820s, while Truman Wilcox (*fl* 1825–70) in the hamlet of Fortsville (Saratoga Co) and Charles Rood (*fl* 1811–28) in Hudson Falls (Washington Co) operated small local kilns. At Fort Edward (Washington Co) the Hilfinger family (1892–1942) ran one of the state's last redware factories. Despite its rugged terrain and sparse settlement, the North Country boasted a few potters, including Jeremiah Simmons (*ca* 1820) at Ticonderoga (Essex Co), William R. Edwards (?1840–72) of Essex (Essex Co), and James Bailey (*fl* 1810–20) of Plattsburgh.

Following the Revolutionary War new markets for potters opened in the Mohawk Valley and Central New York. Joshua Starr opened a shop at Cooperstown (Otsego Co) in 1792, maintaining his business through 1815 despite competition from Connecticut stoneware maker Jacob Fenton. Elija Cornell, father of Cornell University's founder, worked at DeRuyter (Madison Co) from 1824 until 1841, when, at his son Ezra's suggestion, he moved to Ithaca, where he carried on his trade until 1853. In Clinton (Oneida Co) John Betts Gregory (1810–29) made redware; a Gregory slip-decorated plate remains one of the earliest surviving examples of signed New York State redware. To the west Alvin Wilcox (*fl* 1825–62) of West Bloomfield (Ontario Co) systematically marked his pieces, though most redware manufacturers did not. Heber Kimball (?1820–33), who became a Mormon leader, operated a pottery in Mendon (Monroe Co), and the Gleason family and successors (?1829–1902) operated a redware factory in Morganville

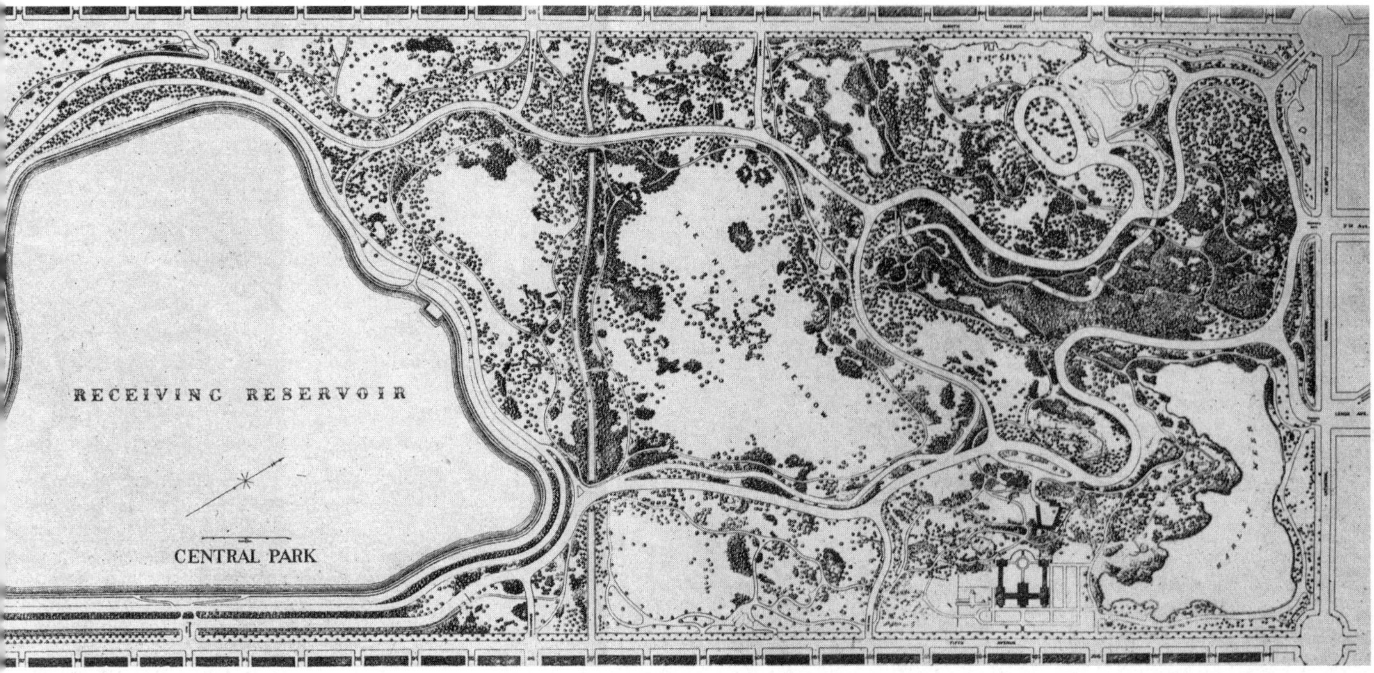

(Genesee Co). Like Wilcox they marked their pots. German potters in Western New York included Carl Mehwaldt (?1851–85) in Bergholz (Niagara Co), Lorenzo Johnson (?1850–87) of Newstead (Erie Co), and Mill Grove (Cattaraugus Co). On his redware Johnson imitated stoneware by using a blue decoration on a white glaze. By the 1870s most New York State redware makers were out of business as consumers came to prefer cheaper glass- and tinwares, which were favored for their durability, and because they lacked the unhealthy lead glazes found on redware vessels. The remaining redware potters produced flowerpots and tile.

STONEWARE

A strong, impervious ceramic body, stoneware had been made in Europe's Rhine Valley since at least the 16th century, and it was German crafters who introduced the ware to New York colonists. As with redware, the first known stoneware manufacturers in New York State operated in New York City. In the early 18th century, two Rhenish families, Crolius (1728–1849) and Remmey (?1735–1820), established themselves in what is now the City Hall area of Manhattan. They produced blue-decorated, salt-glazed stoneware pieces, including crocks, jugs, pots, and churns, many of which they marked, unlike redware producers. Other important early Manhattan makers included Thomas Commereau (*fl* 1797–1819); Washington Smith (?1833–61); William A. MacQuoid (1863–79), who often decorated his pieces in blue with animals, people, and amusing scenes; and the city's last stoneware maker, Francis Laufersweiler (?1876–89). In Suffolk Co the Huntington Pottery (?1805–1905) produced stoneware, while there were several early kilns in the mid–Hudson Valley. The Clark, Bell, and Machett families (?1810–67) made salt-glazed wares at Cornwall (Orange Co); and across the river, Poughkeepsie was home to dozens of potters from as early as 1797 until the Caire family factory, which occupied an entire city block, closed in 1896. Upriver there were kilns (?1844–54, 1868–70) in Hudson, but the major center was Athens (Greene Co), where Nathan Clark of Cornwall established a thriving pottery (1805–99). Clark is an important figure in New York State ceramic history, both because of his success and because, recognizing the Erie Canal's significance, he was the first to establish branch shops in Western New York.

In the early 1800s the Capital District succeeded Manhattan as the state's center of stoneware production. There were numerous manufactories in Albany, Troy, West Troy [now Watervliet, Albany Co], and Lansingburgh (Rensselaer Co). Among the better-known potters were Albany's pioneer, Paul Cushman (?1807–33); Troy's Israel Seymour (1809–52), who was followed by his son Walter until 1885; and West Troy's William E. Warner (*fl* 1835–71), who also owned potteries in New Jersey and Canada. Much of the Capital District's importance as a stoneware manufacturing center can be attributed to its location at the head of navigation on the Hudson River and as the eastern terminus of the Erie Canal. The bulky raw clay and finished product could be moved least expensively via water. Similarly the rise to prominence of Fort Edward, whose factories boasted an output exceeded only by those of Kings Co by the 1870s, is explained by its location on the Champlain Canal. Unlike the one- or two-person kilns of the early 1800s, the five businesses active in Fort Edward (?1858–92)—Satterlee and Mory; Haxstun, Ottman and Co; Ottman Bros and Co; Haxstun and Co; and G. S. Guy and Co—employed dozens and were capitalized in the tens of thousands.

Even before the Erie Canal was completed in 1825, stoneware makers were settling along the open sections to provide ceramics for settlers traveling west; Utica, Rochester, and Lyons (Wayne Co) became the most notable centers of production. Utica had nine firms in operation between 1823 and 1839, but overproduction and a national recession doomed all but one. White's Pottery (1838–1907), which was known as Central New York Pottery after 1870, became the dominant establishment in central and western New York State. White's was unique because it produced traditional wheel-thrown utilitarian ware and, from the 1880s until the factory closed, a line of molded decorative mugs, pitchers, and other ware. Syracuse's firms were located in Geddes (Onondaga Co), where William H. Farrar (?1840–72), once a partner at the US Pottery in Bennington, Vt, made stoneware in competition with the firm of Hubbel and Chesebro (1867–84). Apprentices of stoneware entrepreneur Nathan Clark of Athens established the potteries at Lyons and Rochester. In 1822 George G. Williams founded a shop at Lyons that remained open under other management until 1905. Another apprentice, John Burger, built a kiln at Rochester in 1839. The business remained in his family until it closed in 1890. Both firms produced high-quality stoneware vessels decorated in blue with elaborate floral compositions, deer, houses, birds, and human faces or figures. Samuel and James Hart, who began operating a pottery at Oswego Falls [now Fulton, Oswego Co] in 1832, also opened branch kilns. Like the other successful western kilns, it was located on a waterway, in this case the Oswego Canal. Samuel's sons maintained the business until it burned in 1892. James, however, removed in 1840 to Sherburne (Chenango Co) where he, his son, and grandson operated their own stoneware works through 1885. A third leg (1850–79) of the family dynasty was located at Ogdensburg (St. Lawrence Co). The most important stoneware factories in Western New York were located in Buffalo, where Godfrey Heiser and his brothers (?1835–56) operated a kiln with various associates. The following year the business was sold to Charles W. Braun, who ran it until 1896. By 1900 the New York State stoneware industry had diminished, as potters

Potter at work in his Buffalo shop, 1910.

fell victim to changing tastes and competition from highly mechanized potteries in the Midwest. However, because the ware is durable and so much bears a maker's mark, the industry is well documented and well represented within private and museum collections.

OTHER WARES

In contrast with New York State's redware and stoneware industries, scant evidence remains for the production of yellowware, a yellow-hued high-fired ceramic and Rockingham-glazed ware, which had a body splashed with a brown glaze. Documentary sources reveal that a handful of firms, including an early pottery established at Tivoli (Dutchess Co) in 1797, Syracuse's Manchester and Clark (?1868–70), Troy's Carpenter and Ball (*ca* 1885), and New York City's Morrison, Carr and Smith (?1855–88), produced yellowware. Two surviving vessels reveal that Otto Lewis (*ca* 1850) and Morrison's firm also manufactured Rockingham. Other New York State potters advertised "Rockingham" pots, but they proved to be stoneware vessels bearing an iridescent brown glaze. In contrast New York State in the late 19th century became a national center for the production of white earthenware, a fine-bodied high-fired ceramic. Syracuse China Co, founded in 1871 as the Onondaga Pottery Co, remains one of the nation's most important manufacturers of whiteware, which is best known for its use in modern tablewares. Other firms included the successful Buffalo Pottery (now Buffalo China Inc), which opened in 1901 and was famous for its highly decorative Deldare Ware, and the relatively short-lived Chittenango Pottery Co (Madison Co) (1897–?1920). Because it is difficult and expensive to make, few New York State potters undertook the production of porcelain, a translucent ceramic composed of kaolin, feldspar, ground flint, and sometimes burned bone. The potters that did were clustered in and around New York City. William Boch and his brothers of Greenpoint (Kings Co) went into business *ca* 1840; in 1861 Thomas Smith took over their firm, which became Union Porcelain Works, active until 1922. Charles Cartlidge's shop (1844–56) was a rival business in the same community. In Queens Co William Boch Jr (?1864–75) had a factory, and James Carr's New York City Pottery produced Parian (unglazed porcelain) in the 1870s. Outside of New York City, Syracuse China Co has remained New York State's major porcelain manufacturer.

20TH-CENTURY CERAMIC ART AND INDUSTRY

Not only significant for its ceramic tableware producers, New York State also became a center for art pottery and industrial ceramic production in the 20th century. Syracusan Adelaide Alsop Robineau (*fl* 1904–29), who created carved porcelain vessels taking hundreds of hours to produce, is regarded by some as one of America's finest potters. Other important crafters include Frederick Walrath of Rochester (?1904–20); Charles Volkmar, who had a kiln at Greenpoint (?1879–88); and Theophilus A. Brouwer Jr, whose Middle Lane Pottery operated at East Hampton and later Westhampton (Suffolk Co) from 1894 until the artist's death in 1932. Founded in 1900, the New York State School of Clay-Working and Ceramics (now SUNY College of Ceramics at Alfred University) remained the only school for ceramic art in the United States until 1930 and continues to produce and attract ceramic artists to Alfred (Allegany Co) in the early 21st century. Internationally recognized ceramic artists active in New York State at the start of the 21st century include Val Cushing (*b* 1931), William Parry (*b* 1918), Wayne Higby (*b* 1943), Andrea Gill (*b* 1948), and John Gill (*b* 1949), all of whom were educated or have taught at the SUNY College of Ceramics. Offering programs in ceramic engineering and materials science, its students also have pursued careers in the production of traditional and non-traditional ceramics, including tableware and industrial ceramics. Supported by the college and Alfred Technology Resources, which operates business incubators for ceramic, glass, and advanced material manufacturers in Alfred and Painted Post (Steuben Co), the Southern Tier and Central New York region became a center for industrial ceramic manufacturing and research in the late 20th century. The area is home to several companies, including two in Alfred, Vesuvius Hi-Tech Ceramics and Xylon Ceramic Materials, and one in Painted Post, Advanced Ceramics Inc, that produce a range of products, including decorative tile, filters, and machine components.

See also ARTS AND CRAFTS MOVEMENT; IROQUOIS ART.

Bensch, Christopher. *The Blue and the Gray: Oneida County Stoneware: Exhibition and Catalogue Essay* (Utica: Museum of Art, Munson-Williams-Proctor Institute, 1987)

Broderick, Warren F., and William Bouck. *Pottery Works: Potteries of New York State's Capital District and Upper Hudson Region* (Madison, NJ: Farleigh Dickinson Univ Press, 1995)

Case, Richard G. *Onondaga Pottery* (Syracuse: Everson Museum of Art, 1973)

Clement, Arthur W. *Our Pioneer Potters* (Brooklyn, 1947)

Emily Lowe Gallery. *Earth, Fire, and Salt: New York State Salt-Glazed Pottery* (Hempstead, NY: Hofstra Univ, 1983)

Ketchum, William C., Jr. *The Pottery of the State* (New York: Museum of American Folk Art, 1974)

———. *Potters and Potteries of New York State, 1650–1900*, 2d ed (Syracuse: Syracuse Univ Press, 1987)

———. *A Century of Ceramics in the Lower Hudson Valley, 1800–1900* (Scarsdale, NY: Scarsdale Historical Society, 1994)

Lukacs, George H. *Poughkeepsie Potters and the Plague* (Charleston, SC: Arcadia, 2001)

Perry, Barbara, ed. *American Ceramics: The Collection of Everson Museum of Art* (New York: Rizzoli, 1989)

Rochester Museum and Science Center. *Clay in The Hands of the Potter: An Exhibition of Pottery Manufactured in the Rochester and Genesee Valley Region c. 1793–1900* (Rochester: Rochester Museum and Science Center, 1974)

William C. Ketchum

cereal manufacturing. The modern breakfast cereal food industry was pioneered in Buffalo, which as a major center of the grain trade enjoyed a ready supply of ingredients, a skilled grain-handling workforce, and after 1896 cheap electrical power from Niagara Falls. Rolled oats, or oatmeal, was produced by the Hornby Oat Co from 1893. Despite introducing a popular early wheat flake named Force, Hornby struggled financially in the early 20th century; its oat business was continued by Hecker H-O from 1920 to 1960. In 1924 General Mills introduced Wheaties, which by 1942 became America's best-selling breakfast cereal. A large General Mills plant, built in 1940 and later heavily damaged by fire, has been rebuilt and continues to produce Cheerios, Wheaties, and Corn Kix. Although cereal manufacture in Buffalo has declined in recent decades, partly because of relatively high labor costs, other locations in the state have made contributions to the industry. The well-known product Shredded Wheat was invented in Watertown in the early 1890s, and in 1901 the Natural Food Co started production of Shredded Wheat in a Niagara Falls factory touted as the Palace of Light because of its very high and broad windows. The Shredded Wheat business was bought by the National Biscuit Co (now Nabisco) in 1928, with production at Niagara Falls continuing until 1995. Quaker Oats Co was making a similar product, called Muffets, in Depew (Erie Co) by 1927. In Penn Yan (Yates Co), the Birkett Mills Co produces Cream of Buckwheat cereal using a stone-grinding process, and Beech-Nut has produced baby cereals at a plant in Fort Plain (Montgomery Co) since 1931.

Bruce, Scott, and Bill Crawford. *Cerealizing America: The Unsweetened Story of American Breakfast Cereal* (Boston: Faber & Faber, 1995)

Henry H. Baxter

Cesnola, Luigi Palma di (*b* Rivarolo Canavese [now in Piedmont, Italy], 29 June 1832; *d* New York City, 3 Nov 1904). Soldier, diplomat, archaeologist, and museum administrator. After a career in the Sardinian army, Cesnola immigrated to the United States in 1858 and three years later opened a private military school at Broadway and 22d St in Manhattan. In a six-month period he trained over 700 students, many of whom went on to serve in the Civil War, in basic aspects of land warfare. In 1862 Cesnola closed his academy to accept an officer's commission in the New York State Volunteer Cavalry. He served with distinction in numerous campaigns and rose to the rank of colonel in the Union army. At war's end Pres Abraham Lincoln awarded Cesnola a brigadier generalship and appointed him American consul to Cyprus, where he served from 1865 to 1877. While in Cyprus, Cesnola became an amateur archaeologist, oversaw extensive excavations on the island, and amassed a 6,000-piece artifact collection, which he sold to New York City's Metropolitan Museum of Art (MMA). In 1879 he became MMA's first director and held that position for the next 25 years. In 1897 Cesnola received the congressional Medal of Honor for his service in the Civil War.

McFadden, Elizabeth. *The Glitter and the Gold: A Spirited Account of the Metropolitan Museum of Art's First Director, the Audacious and High-Handed Luigi Palma di Cesnola* (New York: Dial Press, 1971)

Nicholas P. Ciotola

Chabert de Joncaire family. {Chabert de Joncaire, Louis-Thomas (*b* Saint-Rémi de Provence, France, ?1670; *d* Fort Niagara [now in Porter, Niagara Co], 29 Jun 1739); Chabert de Joncaire, Philippe-Thomas (*b* Montreal, ?9 Jan 1707; *d* France, ?1766); Chabert de Joncaire, Daniel-Marie (*b* Repentigny, Canada, ?6 Jan 1714; *d* Detroit, ?5 July 1771)}. Military officers, interpreters, and French agents among the Iroquois Confederacy. For nearly 60 years, two generations of the Chabert de Joncaire family represented the interests of France among the Seneca Nation of the Iroquois Confederacy. Louis-Thomas traveled to Canada as a soldier in the late 1680s. Taken by the Seneca, he avoided a captive's death and was adopted by a people he came to know intimately. He was influential in negotiations leading to the 1701 treaty that ended the long wars between the French and the Iroquois. Operating first from Seneca country between the Finger Lakes and the Genesee River, Louis-Thomas eventually gained permission from the Seneca to build a trading house at the Niagara River portage in 1720 and prepared the way for establishment of Fort Niagara in 1726. He relinquished his position as principal agent for New France among the Iroquois Confederacy to his eldest son, Philippe-Thomas, in 1735 but continued his work among the Seneca and the peoples of the Ohio Valley until his death.

Louis-Thomas prepared two of his sons to follow in his footsteps. Both Philippe-Thomas and Daniel-Marie were sent as children to live among the Seneca. Their subsequent careers were closely associated, and English sources frequently confuse the two under the name Joncaire. Philippe resigned his post in favor of his brother in 1748 and shifted his activities to French efforts to control the Ohio Valley that ignited the French and Indian War. Returning to Seneca country by 1757, he was unable to repair deteriorating French prestige and fled to Fort Niagara in June 1759. After the post's surrender a little more than a month later, he was taken to New York City as a prisoner and eventually paroled to France in 1761.

His life also spent in Iroquois country, Daniel-Marie worked ceaselessly to keep the Seneca in the French interest. His efforts during the French and Indian War gained some active support from the Seneca between 1756 and 1758. Also present at the surrender of Fort Niagara in July 1759, he was exchanged to Canada that December. He helped raise Indian warriors for the defense of Montreal in 1760. Daniel went to France in 1761, where he found himself charged with financial corruption in what became known as the Affaire du Canada. He was convicted but received only a warning. In 1764 he went to England and Canada in an effort to restore his fortunes. Most of his claims were disallowed, and the British were reluctant to allow him to resume trade among the Indians. Sir Guy Carleton finally permitted him to go to Detroit in 1767, where he lived in meager circumstances until his death.

Dunnigan, Brian Leigh. *Siege—1759: The Campaign against Niagara*, rev ed. (Youngstown, NY: Old Fort Niagara Association, 1996)
Fauteux, Aegidius. *Les Chevaliers de Saint-Louis en Canada* (Montreal: Les Editions Dix, 1940)

Brian Leigh Dunnigan

Champ. Common name for legendary marine animals of Lake Champlain. Named after the waterway where they are reported to live, they are also called Champy or the Lake Champlain monsters and are said to resemble the Loch Ness monster of Scotland. In 1984 an analysis of sightings revealed the enigmatic animals averaged 26 feet (8 m) long, were dark in color, and had snakelike heads. Cryptozoologists, researchers who study secretive or mysterious animals, claim the lake supports a small breeding colony of these water creatures.

Sightings have been scattered across Lake Champlain, a 109 mi (175 km) long, 400 ft (122 m) deep freshwater body shared by the state of Vermont and province of Quebec. While there are several images purported to be of a Champ animal, such as the 1977 photograph taken by Sandra Mansi that was published in the *New York Times*, 30 June 1981, the most compelling evidence is from eyewitnesses. Three places on the lake have reported the most accounts: Port Henry (Essex Co), Plattsburgh (Clinton Co), and Rouses Point (Clinton Co). The first sighting was made in 1819 by a Port Henry citizen looking out on Bulwagga Bay; the large animal was dubbed the "Lake Champlain sea-serpent" by a *Plattsburgh Republican* reporter. Sightings were noted in the latter half of the 19th century. By the end of the 20th century over 300 reports had been documented.

Some dismiss the sightings as misinterpretations of either unique wave effects from passing watercraft, a floating log bobbing upon the lake surface, large fish such as the lake sturgeon *(Acipenser fulvescens)*, atmospheric refraction that creates an optical illusion, scuba divers, floating birds, or swimming animals like deer or dogs. For those who support the theory that Lake Champlain is home to unidentified animals there are several candidates. The three most cited are the plesiosaur, a marine reptile with a small head, long neck, large body, long tail, and four appendages, thought to have become extinct 60 to 70 million years ago; the zeuglodon, a snakelike primitive whale with a single pair of front appendages, believed to have become extinct 20 million years ago; and a seallike animal given the provisional scientific name *Megalotaria longicollis*.

Cryptozoologists have used a variety of strategies to prove Champ's existence, including shore and boat camera surveillance, sonar, and robotic cameras to search the lake bottom for a carcass. As of the early 21st century these mystery creatures remain elusive.

Zarzynski, Joseph W. *Champ: Beyond the Legend* (Port Henry, NY: Bannister Publications, 1984)

Joseph W. Zarzynski

Champion. Town (pop 4,361) in E central Jefferson Co. Settled in 1798, the town was formed from Mexico [now in Oswego Co] in 1800. It became a dairy region *ca* 1850, specializing in cheese production, and some of the earliest cooperative cheese factories were in this town. The Village of West Carthage was the town's manufacturing center. In 2003 most Champion residents commuted to Fort Drum and Watertown.

Laura Lynne Scharer

Champlain. Town (pop 5,791) and village (pop 1,173) in NE Clinton Co. The first permanent settler arrived in 1783 and was followed the next year by Canadian and Nova Scotian refugees. The town, bounded on the north by Canada and on the east by Lake Champlain, was formed from Plattsburgh in 1788. Armies tramped and fought here during the War of 1812. Its level land provided good farms for Yankees, Canadians, and Irish settlers. Established in 1848 the Northern Railroad (later Rutland Railroad) provided shipment to Boston, and in 1876 an alternate route between Plattsburgh and Montreal formed a junction with the Northern at Rouses Point. The opening of the Northway (1965) led to an expansion of trade with Canada. In the early 21st century two extensive international trade zones are near the highway, and Wyeth Pharmaceuticals (1934) has been an important employer.

Thomas A. Rumney

Champlain, Samuel de (*b* Brouage, France, ?1570; *d* Quebec, 25 Dec 1635). Explorer and governor of New France. Little is known of Champlain's early years, but in 1603 he accom-

Great Chazy River flooding Champlain, early 20th century.

panied a fur-trading expedition into the St. Lawrence River valley, eventually reaching the vicinity of what is today Montreal. Failed attempts elsewhere prompted him to establish a fur-trading post in 1608 at what is now Quebec City. That same year he convinced Henri IV to appoint him governor and establish a colony to advance the fur trade, to discover a passage to China, and to convert the natives to Christianity. An accomplished draftsman, Champlain explored and mapped northeastern North America. A trip south with Algonquin and Montagnais allies in 1609 took him through the lake he named for himself. This expedition led to a battle with the Mohawk near Ticonderoga [now in Essex Co]. Champlain killed several Indians, contributing to the French-Iroquois hostility that lasted into the 18th century. Shuttling between France and Canada over the next several years, Champlain married Hélène Boullé, aged 12, in December 1610 and received a large dowry. He surrendered Quebec to a British force in 1629 and spent the next three and a half years in France. He returned as governor in 1633 when the colony was returned to French control. His commercial and cartographic achievements helped France establish a foothold in eastern North America that lasted until 1763.

Morison, Samuel Eliot. *Samuel de Champlain: Father of New France* (Boston: Little, Brown, 1972)

Thomas A. Chambers

Champlain Canal. Canal that connects Lake Champlain at Whitehall (Washington Co) with the Erie Canal near Waterford (Saratoga Co). Built between 1817 and 1823, the 40 ft (12.2 m) wide by 4 ft (1.2 m) deep canal was capable of floating boats carrying 75 tons (68 MT). Its original cost of just over $920,000 included the 66 mi (106.2 km) canal and the original .5 mi (.8 km) water supply feeder at Fort Edward (Washington Co), but excluded the 1828–29 12 mi (19.3 km) water supply feeder from the Hudson River at Glens Falls (Warren Co) to the summit level of the canal, north of Fort Edward. There were 19 lift locks and four guard locks on the main line and 13 on the feeder, which allowed boats to make their way up to Glens Falls. The canal was enlarged a few times, once in 1860 to 50 feet (15.2 m) wide and 5 feet (1.5 m) deep and again in 1870 to 58 feet (17.7 m) wide and 7 feet (2.1 m) deep. The second enlargement was never completed. A third enlargement of 1896–98 to complete the 7 ft depth was also never completed, although by the early 1900s boats could carry 150–190 tons (136–172 MT). Between 1905 and 1918 it was finally enlarged to 123 feet (37.5 m) wide and 12 feet (3.7 m) deep as part of the state's Barge Canal program, which also included the Erie, Oswego, and Cayuga and Seneca Canals.

The canal once shipped iron ore and other products from the Adirondacks, including limestone, marble, and other building stone, and lumber, paper, and manufactured goods. In its last days as a commercial carrier, the canal was a means to transport petroleum products and jet fuel for the now abandoned Plattsburgh Air Force Base. Its peak toll years were 1866, 1867, and 1868. Annual tolls ranged from nearly $194,000 in 1866 to almost $200,000 in 1868; the canal's total revenue between 1821 and 1882 amounted to over $6.6 million. Between 1866 and 1892, annual tonnage exceeded 1 million in all years but 1873 and 1881. Peak years were 1872, 1883, and 1890, with 1.4 million tons (1.3 million MT) in 1883 and 1.5 million tons (1.4 million MT) in 1890. Part of the New York State Canal System, the Champlain Canal has 11 lift locks, with Lock 12 at Waterford serving as the 11th, and provides a connection north to the St. Lawrence Seaway and Montreal through Lake Champlain and the Chambly Canal in Canada. Although the Feeder Canal at Glens Falls is no longer navigable, an 8 mi (12.9 km) feeder trail runs along its shores between Glens Falls and Fort Edward, and there is talk of rejuvenating the waterway for pleasure boats. The Champlain Canal was listed on the National Register of Historic Places in 1976, and the Glens Falls Feeder Canal was listed in 1985.

Whitford, Noble E. *History of the Canal System of the State of New York* (Albany: Brandow Printing, 1906)

Thomas X. Grasso

Chandler, George Fletcher (*b* Clyde, Wayne Co, 13 Dec 1872; *d* Kingston, Ulster Co, 6 Nov 1964). Surgeon and organizer of New York State Police. Chandler went to grammar school in Portland, Oreg, before attending Ithaca High School and Syracuse University. In 1895 he graduated from the College of Physicians and Surgeons, Columbia University, and commenced practice at St. Vincent's Hospital in New York City. In 1901 he moved to Kingston, where he was staff surgeon and member of the board of managers at Kingston Hospital. Chandler served in the National Guard for many years. On 2 May 1917 Chandler accepted Gov Charles S. Whitman's offer of appointment as the first superintendent of New York State Police, with a mandate to create a police service for the state's rural regions. Chandler organized the new constabulary, bought horses, built training camps and barracks, and designed the uniform. In 1921 he founded a school for police officers at Troy (Rensselaer Co), now the New York State Police Academy in Albany. Chandler resigned in 1923 and returned to surgical practice at Kingston Hospital. He later served on the New York State Crime Commission under Govs Alfred E. Smith and Franklin D. Roosevelt.

"George Chandler, Police Aide, Dies," *New York Times*, 7 Nov 1964
Shelton, Pamela T. *History of the New York State Police, 1917–1987* ([New York State]: Trooper Foundation of the State of New York, 1987)

Ellen Sexton

Chappaqua. Locality (pop 9,468) in New Castle (Westchester Co). Settled *ca* 1730 by Quakers, the oldest documented building is the 1753 Friends Meeting House. The Harlem Railroad (1846) created a small trading hamlet. Horace Greeley (1811–72), editor of the *New York Tribune*, made it his summer home from 1853 to 1872. A shoe factory opened in 1874. The Saw Mill River Parkway, constructed to Chappaqua in 1934, enhanced automobile commuting and provided access to the *Readers' Digest* headquarters (1939). Intensive development followed World War II. In 1999 Hillary Rodham Clinton moved to Chappaqua to establish state residency for her successful US senatorial 2000 bid. It became the primary residence of her husband, Bill Clinton, at the conclusion of his presidential term in 2001.

charcoal industry. Charcoal is partially burned wood made up of nearly pure carbon. The art of charcoal burning was brought to New York State from Europe in the 1750s. Charcoal was burned throughout the state, but as forests were cleared the industry became concentrated in heavily forested areas. Charcoal burns at a higher temperature than wood and was formerly the only available fuel source for use in reduction processes, where combustion takes place at a high temperature with little oxygen. For this reason charcoal was the staple fuel used in the iron industry, with its centers in Troy (Rensselaer Co) and Millerton (Dutchess Co) and in the bloomery forges of the Adirondacks and foundries like the one at the Watervliet Arsenal (Albany Co). Charcoal was also vital to the glassblowing industry in such places as Durhamville (Oneida Co), Guilderland (Albany Co), and Sand Lake (Rensselaer Co). The resulting ash was useful in iron fluxing.

Most charcoal was burned in forest mounds made from stacks of vertical hardwood slabs, 30–40 feet (9–12 m) in diameter, with a tubelike space in the middle as a chimney. These mounds were covered with sod and burned over a one- to two-week period while watched by colliers. Often of German origin, colliers were known for their solitary woodland lifestyle and passed on the details of the burning process to future generations. By the mid–19th century some charcoal operations used large circular or conical kilns of brick, stone, or masonry. These larger operations supplied massive quantities of charcoal to New York State's iron furnaces until the burning of coked coal took its place in the second half of the 19th century. Charcoal was burned as a clean heating fuel into the 20th century and remains in use for outdoor cooking. A handful of colliers determined to preserve their nearly lost art, along with a few of the early kilns and burning sites, are all that remain of the industry at the start of the 21st century.

Myers, Frank Daniels, III. *The Wood Chemical Industry in the Delaware Valley.* Ontario and Western Railway Historical Society Publications, vol 1 (Middletown, NY: Prior King Press, 1986)

Rolando, Victor. *Two Hundred Years of Soot and Sweat: The History and Archaeology of Vermont's Iron, Charcoal, and Lime Industries* (Manchester: Vermont Archaeological Society, 1992)

Warren F. Broderick

Charismatics. Christians in traditional denominations who focus on experiencing the Holy Spirit and using spiritual gifts, like the gifts of healing and prophecy (1 Cor 12). The Charismatic movement, influenced by Pentecostalism, emerged during the 1950s and 1960s among Protestants and Roman Catholics. Charismatics differ from classical Pentecostals in their reliance on contemporary worship styles and a deemphasis on premillennial theology. Networks of Charismatics formed within and around denominations, and from its outset the movement has had both denominational and independent sectors. The movement was especially strong among Roman Catholics in Central New York. In the New York City area Harald Bredesen, the dynamic pastor of the First Reformed Church in Mount Vernon (Westchester Co), was an enthusiastic promoter of Charismatic Christianity. Charismatic congregations with classical Pentecostal roots include the Elim Bible Institute in Lima (Livingston Co) and the Brooklyn Tabernacle in Park Slope, perhaps the best-known New York City Charismatic congregation. In Brooklyn in 1958 David Wilkerson, an Assemblies of God pastor from Pennsylvania, established the hub for Teen Challenge, a ministry to gang members that has over 150 residential programs in 43 states and another 250 in 60 countries. Hundreds of Teen Challenge graduates work as evangelists and urban pastors. In 1987 Wilkerson established the Times Square Church, a thriving independent Charismatic congregation in Manhattan. His efforts remain a focal point for independent Charismatic renewal. As the Charismatic movement found its niche on the religious landscape, a new wave of renewal resulted in the formation of Vineyard churches, which built on the Charismatic foundation but did not feature speaking in tongues. Vineyard music has spread rapidly to become part of the praise repertoire of Charismatics everywhere.

Burguess, Stanley M. *The New International Dictionary of Pentecostal and Charismatic Movements* (Grand Rapids, Mich: Zondervan Publishing, 2002)

Cymbala, Jim. *Fresh Wind, Fresh Fire* (Grand Rapids, Mich: Zondervan Publishing, 1997)

Quebedeaux, Richard. *The New Charismatics II* (New York: Harper & Row, 1983)

Edith L. Blumhofer

charity organization societies. The nation's first comprehensive charity organization society was established in Buffalo in 1877 by the English-born Rev Stephen Humphreys Gurteen. It was modeled after the London Charity Organization (1869), which sought to coordinate that city's diverse and often inefficient and poorly organized charity organizations. New York City's Charity Organization Society (COS), founded by Josephine Shaw Lowell (1843–1905) in 1882, used charitable programs to enable direct supervision and social control in impoverished communities. Abhorring dependency and opposed to direct monetary assistance, Lowell created registries to ensure that beneficiaries did not receive relief from more than one agency. "Friendly visitors" from the COS instructed the poor on proper comportment and on how to seek employment. The society's Summer School of Philanthropy, established in 1898, was the first educational program for social work. It became the New York School of Social Work by 1919, then the Columbia University School of Social Work (1963). The COS also worked to publicize conditions in the city's overcrowded tenements and was instrumental in bringing about the 1901 Tenement House Act. In 1939 the society merged with the Association for Improving the Condition of the Poor (1843) to form the Community Service Society of New York, still active in 2002, providing emergency assistance, information about government programs and healthcare, and direct social services to families, as well as facilitating community development initiatives.

See also BUFFALO.

Waugh, Joan. *Unsentimental Reformer: The Life of Josephine Shaw Lowell* (Cambridge, Mass: Harvard Univ Press, 1997)

Milton Goldin

Charleston. Town (pop 1,292) in SE Montgomery Co. Settled before the Revolutionary War, the town was formed from Mohawk in 1793 by settlers of primarily English descent. At Burtonsville, site of the town's first mills (1785), a tannery (1817–63) and a woolen factory (1844) operated. Poor, rocky soil and conservative landlords inhibited development. After the Civil War much of its land was still leased to tenants by the Clarke family heirs; evicted tenants were known to burn down their houses and barns upon leaving. Later it became a productive dairying and hay-growing town. In the early 21st century Charleston remains predominantly agricultural. About 5,000 acres (2,000 ha) is public land in Rural Grove, Yatesville Falls, and Charleston State Forests.

James Crawford

Charlotte [SHAR-LOT]. Town (pop 1,713) in NE Chautauqua Co. Settled in 1809 the town formed in 1829 from Gerry. Several remnants of 14th- or 15th-century Indian villages, today known as Chautauqua phase sites, are in the town. Charlotte was the terminus of an early road from Canadaway [now Fredonia] and was served by the Dunkirk, Allegheny Valley and Pittsburgh Railroad (1871). Between 1990 and 2000 the population grew 12%. Kiln-dried lumber is a product in the early 21st century.

Michelle Henry

Charlotte County. See EXTINCT COUNTIES.

Charlton. Town (pop 3,954) in SW Saratoga Co. European settlers started arriving in 1770; a colony of Scots-Irish arrived in 1774 from Freehold, NJ, and Scots from Galloway came in 1775. The town was set off from Ballston in 1792. Having good soils, some underlain with limestone, it was a prosperous farming district. In the 1950s suburban houses were built in the southeast part of town. Charlton responded with the county's first planning board (1955), zoning board (1959), and historic district (1976). In the early 21st century, suburban residences coexist with a large agricultural district. The Charlton Industrial Farm School for Boys (1895–1938) was reestablished in 1955 as the Charlton School, serving young women.

Field Horne

Charter of Liberties and Privileges. For years many New York Colony settlers tenaciously advocated for a representative legislature, which had already been established in all other English colonies. In 1683 James, Duke of York, the colony's proprietor, finally assented to this pressure and instructed Gov Thomas Dongan to call an elected assembly for the colony. On 17 Oct 1683 the inaugural assembly convened with 18 delegates at Fort James in New York City. Influenced by ideas from the Magna Carta and the 1628 Petition of Rights, they drafted the Charter of Liberties and Privileges, which was designed to structure New York Colony's government and to protect the colonists' rights and freedoms. The charter placed the supreme legislative authority of the province "in a Governor, Council, and the people met in General Assembly." Thus under the charter no one was to be taxed without consent. Due process of the law, trial by a jury of peers, and religious freedom for Christians were among its other important provisions. After James granted his approval of the charter, but before it could be returned to New York Colony, he became king and subsequently changed his mind. In consultation with the Lords of Trade, he decided the charter was too liberal and disallowed it. Instead New York Colony would be ruled by royal prerogative. In 1691, in the wake of Leisler's Rebellion, the assembly once again revived the Charter of Liberties and Privileges in amended form. The government of William III disallowed the new charter six years later. Although the charter was revoked, some of its ideas influenced New York State's Constitution of 1777.

Lovejoy, David S. "Equality and Empire: The New York Charter of Libertyes, 1683," *William and Mary Quarterly,* 3d ser, 21 (Oct 1964): 493–515

Murrin, John. "The New York Charter of Liberties, 1683 and 1691." In *Roots of Republic: American Founding Documents Interpreted,* ed. Stephen L. Schechter, Richard B. Bernstein, and Donald S. Lutz (Madison, Wisc: Madison House, 1990)

Noah L. Gelfand

Chase, William Merritt (*b* Williamsburg [now Nineveh, Ind], 1 Nov 1849; *d* New York City, 25 Oct 1916). Painter and teacher. After studying art briefly in Indianapolis, Chase took classes at the National Academy of Design in New York City in 1869–70. He went to Europe in 1872, eventually settling in Munich, Germany, where he enrolled in the Royal Academy, and later spent time in Venice. In 1878 Chase returned to the United States and established a studio in the Tenth Street Studio Building in Manhattan. That fall he joined the faculty of the Art Students League in New York City. He later taught at the Brooklyn Art Association and the Pennsylvania Academy of Fine Arts. From 1885 until 1895 Chase served as the president of the Society of American Artists. He opened the Shinnecock Summer School of Art in 1891 in Southampton (Suffolk Co), where he taught each year until 1902. He founded the Chase School of Art (now Parsons School of Design) in 1896 in Manhattan, where he taught until 1907. In 1902 Chase joined the group of artists known as the Ten American Painters, who jointly exhibited their work outside the aegis of established art societies. Chase's works consisted of portraits, still lifes, and landscapes, including a number of scenes of Prospect Park in Brooklyn and Central Park in Manhattan. Some of his most famous students included Georgia O'Keeffe, Charles Sheeler, and Joseph Stella. Chase married Alice Gerson in 1886, and the couple had eight children.

Gallati, Barbara Dayer. *William Merritt Chase* (New York: Harry N. Abrams, in association with the National Museum of American Art, Smithsonian Institution, 1995)

Pisano, Ronald G. *William Merritt Chase* (New York: Watson-Guptill, 1986)

Alexandra Schein

Chateaugay [SHAT-A-GAY]. Town (pop 2,036) and village (pop 798) in NE Franklin Co. Settled in 1796, primarily by people from Vermont, the town was formed from Champlain (Clinton Co) in 1799. At first it encompassed all of what would become Franklin Co, as well as St. Armand (Essex Co). In 1812 the United States built a blockhouse here; Chateaugay was the site of a skirmish in 1813 and was invaded from Canada in the spring of 1814. The railroad came through in 1848, and the village was incorporated in 1868. Manufacturing included a creamery (1871), six starch factories, pulp mills (1892, 1895) and an excelsior mill (1902). In 2003 McCadam Cheese Co and Chateaugay Correctional Facility (1990) were the principal employers. Chateaugay Chasm, formed by the waters of the Chateaugay River, is a popular camping spot. One of the 12 Department of Environmental Conservation fish hatcheries is located in Chateaugay, raising various species of trout.

Thomas W. Perrin

Chatham. Town (pop 4,249) and village (pop 1,758) in N Columbia Co. Settled *ca* 1700 by Dutch and later joined by New England and Dutchess Co migrants, the town was formed from Canaan and Kinderhook in 1795. It was the site of many wool, cotton, and paper mills; other 19th-century products included plows, pumps, ironwork, thermometers, horse powers (treadmills on which a horse powers machinery), and shirts. Chatham developed into an important rail junction with the Albany and West Stockbridge (1841), Harlem (1852), and Harlem Extension (1869) Railroads, and more than 100 trains daily stopped in 1878, by which time Chatham's shipping facilities had made it a dairying town. Railroad work brought Irish and black families. The Berkshire Extension of the New York State Thruway (1957) and Taconic Parkway (1963) made Chatham a location of weekend homes for New York City residents. In the early 21st century, Sonoco-Crellin (plastic injection molding) employs 200. Chatham is the home of the Columbia County Fair (1852), the Old Chatham Hunt (1926), the Shaker Museum and Library (1950), and the Mac-Haydn Theatre (1969; summer stock). The Richardsonian Romanesque–style Union Station (1887) is listed on the National Register.

Chaumont [SHA-MO]. Village (pop 592) in Lyme (Jefferson Co). Settled in 1802, the village was named for its proprietor, James Le Ray Chaumont. Early industries included commercial fishing and boatbuilding; from 1816 to 1855 thousands of barrels of ciscoes (whitefish) were shipped annually from Chaumont. The village was incorporated in 1874. The large Rogers Bros seed house packed fancy peas and beans in the late 19th and early 20th centuries. In 2003 Chaumont serves tourists and summer residents who come for sailing, sportfishing, and duck hunting.

Laura Lynne Scharer

Chauncey, Isaac (*b* Black Rock, Conn, 20 Feb 1772; *d* Washington, DC, 27 Jan 1840). Naval officer. Chauncey grew up on the Connecticut shore, where he developed a liking for the sea and entered the Merchant Marine early, rising to command a ship by age 19. He entered the US Navy in 1798 as a lieutenant and served in the Quasi-War with France and in the Barbary War in North Africa before commanding the New York Navy Yard in Brooklyn from 1807 to 1812. Named naval commander on Lakes Ontario and Erie on 31 Aug 1812, Chauncey established his headquarters at Sackets Harbor (Jefferson Co) on 6 Oct 1812. Since 1809 Sackets Harbor had been the home port of *Oneida,* the only US warship on Lake Ontario prior to the War of 1812. Upon his arrival Chauncey purchased land for a navy yard and established a hospital and ropewalk, in addition to facilities to arm lake schooners and to construct warships, including the 20-gun corvette *Madison,* which was built in only 45 days. Sackets Harbor quickly became one of the busiest navy yards, with work begun on 11 warships, 8 of them completed before the end of the war. In November 1812 Chauncey's forces took temporary control of Lake Ontario by chasing HMS *Royal George* into Kingston Harbor and shelling the forts that protected the approaches to the British base. While supporting Maj Gen Henry Dearborn's attack on York [now Toronto] in April and May 1813, ships under Chauncey's command captured HMS *Duke of Gloucester* and burned the nearly completed sloop *Sir Isaac Brock* on the stocks. Chauncey then sailed westward to support Col Winfield Scott's 27 May 1813 capture of Fort George at the mouth of the Niagara River overlooking Lake Ontario and his 30 July 1813 attack on York. Chauncey was a capable administrator but cautious in battle, and he failed to force a decisive engagement with the British squadron commanded by James L. Yeo for the rest of the war. Chauncey thereafter commanded US forces in the Mediterranean (1816–18) and at the New York Navy Yard (1818–20, 1825–32).

Dudley, William S. "Commodore Isaac Chauncey and U.S. Joint Operations on Lake Ontario, 1813–14." In *New Interpretations in Naval History: Selected Papers from the Eighth Naval History Symposium,* ed. William B. Cogar (Annapolis, Md: Naval Institute Press, 1989)

Malcomson, Robert. *Lords of the Lake: The Naval War on Lake Ontario, 1812–1814* (Toronto: Robin Bass Studio, 1998)

James C. Bradford

Chautauqua. Town (pop 4,666) in SW Chautauqua Co. Settled in 1804 the town was formed in that year from Batavia (Genesee Co). It became, along with Pomfret, an original town of Chautauqua Co when the county was formed in 1811. It surrounds the north end of Chautauqua Lake and includes Chautauqua Institution (1874) and Mayville, the county seat. A prominent natural feature is Chautauqua Gorge on the Westfield town line, which exposes rocks and fossils 370 million years old. In the early 21st century, residents worked at the Ethan Allen furniture factory in Mayville until it closed in 2003 or commuted to other towns. A long-established Amish community near Mayville farms and sells handcrafts.

Michelle Henry

Chautauqua County (1,062 mi^2/2,751 km^2; pop 139,750). Set off from Genesee Co in 1808 as the westernmost county in the state, it remained attached to Niagara Co until 9 Feb 1811, when county government finally began functioning. Bounded on the south and west by Pennsylvania and on the northwest by Lake Erie, Chautauqua Co includes the cities of Jamestown and Dunkirk, part of the Cattaraugus Indian Reservation, and 27 towns containing 15 incorporated villages. Mayville, a planned village, serves as county seat. The county was named after its largest lake, which the Seneca called *Jad-dad-gwah.* The county lies in two physiographic provinces: the Erie-Ontario Lake Plain and the Appalachian Plateau. The former consists of a lowland, 2–6 miles (3–10 km) wide, extending along the shore of Lake Erie. Its elevation ranges from 572 feet (174 m) at the Lake Erie shore to about 850 feet (259 m) at the base of the adjoining plateau. The region is a former lake bed, hence local relief is confined primarily to a number of narrow ravines cut by streams. The upland region, sometimes referred to as the Cattaraugus Hills or the Allegheny Plateau, covers about 80% of the county and consists of rounded hills and wide ridgelines separated by a number of wide, flat-bottomed, steep-sided valleys containing slow-flowing streams. Most of the uplands lie between 1,600 and 1,800 feet (490 and 550 m), although the highest elevation, in the southeast

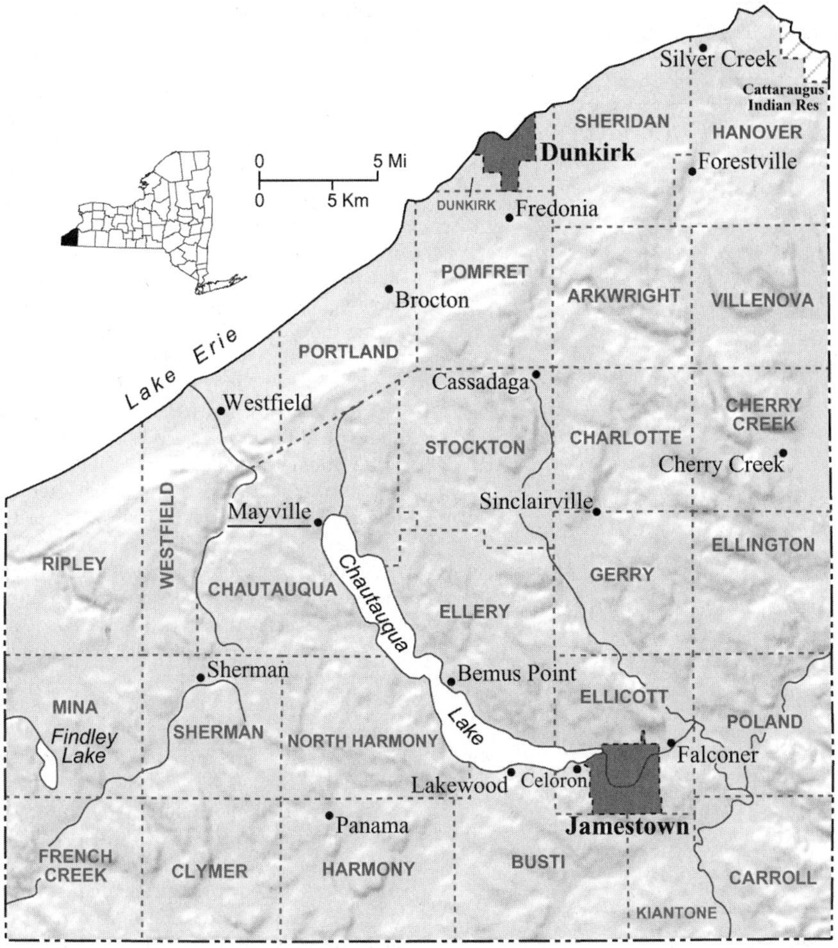

corner of the county, reaches 2,190 feet (668 m). The underlying bedrock throughout the county consists of various Upper Devonian shales that dip very gently to the south-southeast. The county was glaciated except for an approximately 2,000-acre (800 ha) area in the extreme southeast corner, which is part of the unglaciated Salamanca reentrant, where the topography is more rugged with flat-topped hills and V-shaped valleys.

The county's climate is humid-continental. July temperatures average 69°F (21°C), and daytime temperatures occasionally extend into the 90s°F (32–37°C). January temperatures average 29°F (-2°C); the lowest officially recorded temperature in the county was -11°F (-24°C) at Jamestown. Lake plain temperatures are moderated by Lake Erie and prevailing northwesterly winds. Lake effect precipitation is a major factor in seasonal snowfalls, which average about 100 inches (255 cm); the average in the high country around Sherman, however, is more than 150 inches (380 cm). The county lies within two of North America's primary watersheds. Streams of the lake plain and adjoining upland areas drain into the Lake Erie and St. Lawrence system. But most upland drainage, dominated by Chautauqua Lake and Cassadaga, Conewango, and French Creeks, flows southward into the Allegheny-Ohio-Mississippi system. Seventeen-mile (27 km) long Chautauqua Lake is the most prominent hydrologic feature within the county. Primeval forest cover varied. Central hardwood forests dominated by beech, sugar maple, basswood, and hemlock occupied the Erie Lake Plain, while Alleghenian hardwood communities of beech, sugar maple, hemlock, white pine, basswood, and, in some areas, oak and chestnut covered the Appalachian Plateau. Lake plain soils are almost uniformly of superior arable quality. In contrast, upland soils vary greatly in quality and are spotty in their distribution. Small areas of prime bottomland are interspersed with larger areas of farmland that is of medium, low, or no viability.

Settlement

The native occupation and use of Chautauqua Co is imperfectly understood. Evidence of an extensive village from the late Prehistoric period was excavated in Westfield beginning in 1927. Pottery, burial grounds, and tools speak to an established society. The Erie occupied territory south and east of Lake Erie; an Erie village was excavated at Ripley. They were supplanted by the Seneca in the 1650s. No Iroquois village has been uncovered in the county, but the Seneca used the land for hunting. René-Robert Cavelier de la Salle sailed along the Lake Erie shore in 1679, and subsequently the French established a portage between Lake Erie and the west end of Chautauqua Lake and the greater Allegheny River watershed that became known as the Portage Road (1739–58). Charles Le Moyne, second baron de Longueuil, used this route in 1739, and Céleron de Blainville and his troops traveled it in 1749 to reassert and formalize the French claim to the Ohio basin. In 1763 France ceded its western New York State land claims to Great Britain. The Seneca relinquished their claim to all but a small portion of the land in 1797 at the Treaty of Big Tree. That same year investor Robert Morris sold the land that would become the county to the Holland Land Co, a group of Dutch investors. Under the direction of Joseph Ellicott and Paul Busti, the Dutch company inventoried, subdivided, and began selling its extensive land holdings. As a consequence every deed in the county can be traced back to a Holland Land Co transaction. Company decisions played an integral role in shaping the county's physical structure, including village location and

CHAUTAUQUA CO POPULATION CENSUS FIGURES

	White	Nonwhite	Total Population	Foreign-Born
1820	12,555	13	12,568	—
1830	34,571	100	34,671	208
1840	47,851	124	47,975	—
1850	50,353	140	50,493	3,622
1860	58,217	205	58,422	8,172
1870	59,127	200	59,327	9,282
1880	65,178	164	65,342	10,818
1890	75,022	180	75,202	14,944
1900	88,124	190	88,314	17,549
1910	104,870	256	105,126	23,389
1920	114,984	364	115,348	23,104
1930	125,917	540	126,457	22,595
1940	123,098	482	123,580	17,141
1950	134,362	827	135,189	13,421
1960	143,906	1,471	145,377	9,500
1970	145,217	2,088	147,305	6,220
1980	142,928	3,997	146,925	4,594
1990	136,256	5,639	141,895	3,198
2000	131,416	8,334	139,750	2,643

Notes: "Nonwhite" includes African Americans, Asians, American Indians, and Pacific Islanders and, for 2000, also the mixed race and other race categories. Through the 1960 census these figures primarily reflect the African American population. Foreign-born figures for 1820 and 1830 include only those not naturalized, and for 1930 and 1950, the foreign-born totals include Whites only. Other years include all foreign-born in the population.

POPULATIONS OF TOWNS AND CITIES, CHAUTAUQUA CO

Town or City, Year Founded	1840	1880	1920	1960	2000
Arkwright, 1829	1,418	1,076	757	700	1,126
Busti, 1823	1,894	1,901	1,995	7,766	7,760
Carroll, 1825	1,649	1,718	1,761	2,661	3,635
Charlotte, 1829	1,428	1,667	1,173	1,323	1,713
Chautauqua, 1804	2,980	3,576	3,533	4,376	4,666
Cherry Creek, 1829	1,141	1,354	1,204	1,206	1,152
Clymer, 1821	909	1,455	1,205	1,377	1,501
Dunkirk, 1859	—	—	512	1,541	1,387
Dunkirk (city), 1880	—	7,248	19,336	18,205	13,131
Ellery, 1821	2,242	1,555	1,496	3,953	4,576
Ellicott, 1812	2,571	10,842	5,463	10,451	9,280
Ellington, 1824	1,725	1,602	1,061	1,314	1,639
French Creek, 1829	621	1,042	806	906	935
Gerry, 1812	1,288	1,175	993	1,468	2,054
Hanover, 1812	3,998	4,221	5,977	7,301	7,638
Harmony, 1816	3,340	3,455	1,443	1,797	2,339
Jamestown (city), 1886	—	—	38,917	41,818	31,730
Kiantone, 1853	—	513	623	1,254	1,385
Mina, 1824	871	1,102	903	1,188	1,176
North Harmony, 1919	—	—	1,235	2,132	2,521
Poland, 1832	1,087	1,539	1,308	2,036	2,467
Pomfret, 1808	4,566	4,551	7,973	11,459	14,703
Portland, 1813	2,136	2,014	3,140	3,605	5,502
Ripley, 1817	2,197	1,990	2,116	2,848	2,636
Sheridan, 1827	1,883	1,551	1,887	2,539	2,838
Sherman, 1832	1,099	1,558	1,467	1,511	1,553
Stockton, 1821	2,078	1,868	1,674	2,156	2,331
Villenova, 1823	1,655	1,446	961	969	1,121
Westfield, 1829	3,199	3,323	4,390	5,498	5,232

layout, the road system, and ultimately the shape and location of town boundaries.

The first European American settlement was made at the mouth of Cattaraugus Creek in 1796. In the years following many settlers migrated to the area from central and eastern New York State, although a large majority were native to New England, especially Vermont and Massachusetts; some moved north from Pennsylvania. Early settlement concentrated in areas bordering Lake Erie and Chautauqua Lake, districts that contained over 2,000 settlers by 1810. Settlement in the highlands of the southwest and east came later with less enthusiasm. By 1835 the influx of settlers had subsided, and the county's population fell just short of 35,000.

Economic Development

From the time of initial settlement, Lake Erie provided easy access to the Great Lakes basin. The waters of Chautauqua Lake, Chadakoin River, and Conewango Creek provided an avenue for passengers and freight, including central New York State salt, to Pittsburgh and beyond through perhaps 1819. By 1811 the Holland Land Co had helped create an impressive road network across the northern half of the county. The land office village of Mayville was particularly well served, with five roads extending north, west, east, and southeast. Turnpikes came later, and around midcentury several plank roads were built from the ports of Silver Creek, Dunkirk, and Westfield almost due south toward the Pennsylvania line. In 1851 the New York and Erie Railroad (later Erie Railroad) arrived in Dunkirk, thereby giving the area direct rail access to the Hudson River at Piermont (Rockland Co). The Buffalo and State Line Railroad (later New York Central) was completed along the lakeshore in 1853. Rail service reached Jamestown in 1860.

Despite the steady improvement in transportation, the market economy grew slowly, particularly among the interior towns. During the first half of the 19th century Chautauqua Co's farmers derived much of their income from the forests in the form of lumber and potash. Limited cash combined with land company efforts to collect delinquent payments led to rural unrest and destruction of the land office at Mayville in 1836. Forests remained important. In 1855 the county contained 184 sawmills and 25 tanneries, and ranked second in the state in maple sugar production. More conventional farm products included butter and cheese, and peaches were the dominant fruit crop. Although introduced in 1818 by Deacon Elijah Fay at Brocton, grape growing remained insignificant until the 1850s. By 1897, when Welch's Grape Juice Co relocated in Westfield, it was the center of the nation's largest grape-growing region. A small fishing industry grew up on Lake Erie's shores in Chautauqua Co during the 1800s. The county's first bank, the Chautauqua County Bank, was chartered in Jamestown in 1831. By midcentury the county had three woolen mills and a variety of wood product manufacturing facilities, including furniture factories, centered at Fredonia, Jamestown, and Westfield. The Erie Railroad established major shop facilities at Dunkirk, where the Brooks Locomotive Works set up in 1869. Jamestown's rise as a national center of furniture manufacture was closely tied to the abundance of local raw materials and the growth of the Swedish community, which began in 1849. The settlement of other ethnic groups was sometimes tied to particular facets of the local economy. The Irish came early and then later found work as railroad laborers; Poles were attracted to jobs at the Brooks Locomotive Works; and Italians came to work in Pennsylvania coalfields, later moving to Jamestown. Greeks and Albanians were less tied to particular industries. By century's end steel and textile mills were located in the county's two cities, and smaller towns had sawmills, creameries, paper mills, furniture factories, canning plants, and basket works.

Religion, Education, and Culture

Churches in Chautauqua Co reflect the three main streams of in-migrants. Protestant churches of various traditional denominations were founded by the early New England and Yorker settlers beginning in 1808. The first Catholic church was organized at Dunkirk in 1854. Lutheran churches in and around

View of Miller Bell Tower at the Chautauqua Institution.

Jamestown were founded by the Swedish community beginning in 1856. Chautauqua Co was also a center of Spiritualist activity. The Brocton Community, also known as Salem-on-Erie, was the home of Spiritualists led by Thomas Lake Harris from 1867 to 1881. A group of Spiritualists began holding camp meetings in the 1870s on a farm near the Village of Cassadaga. In 1879 they purchased land and established a community later named Lily Dale. Expanding over the years, it remains a vital center of Spiritualist thought and practice. Two Orthodox churches, one Greek and one Albanian, are located in Jamestown. Synagogues in Dunkirk and Jamestown appeared later, as did numerous independent evangelical churches across the county.

Three organizations that powerfully shaped late 19th-century America had their start in Chautauqua Co. The nation's first local chapter of the Patrons of Husbandry (Grange) was founded in Fredonia in 1868, becoming the first influential national farm organization. In late 1873 a group of Fredonia women held a prayer meeting against public drinking, which spawned the Woman's Christian Temperance Union, the first women's organization of truly national significance. In the summer of 1874 the first Chautauqua Assembly, a training venue for Sunday school teachers, was held on the grounds of a Methodist camp meeting at Fair Point on Chautauqua Lake. The Chautauqua Institution continues to draw well over 100,000 summer visitors annually to its offerings of entertainment, lectures, dance, and music.

Though schools were established before the 1812 and 1814 common school legislation, a lasting system arose in response to the 1814 law. The county's first secondary school, Fredonia Academy, opened to students in 1826. Others followed in Mayville (1834), Jamestown (1836), Dunkirk (1837), and Westfield (1837). Jamestown, Dunkirk, and Fredonia had their own union districts by the end of the 19th century; rural towns centralized between 1936 and 1956. In 2003, 16 central and 2 city school systems served the county. BOCES was chartered in 1954 to provide shared services to county schools, and in the early 21st century it is part of the Erie II-Chautauqua-Cattaraugus County BOCES. Higher education is provided by SUNY Fredonia, founded as Fredonia Normal School in 1868, and Jamestown Community College (1950), which was the first community college in the SUNY system. The Jamestown Business College dates from 1886.

Although short-lived circulating libraries existed earlier, and school district libraries began in 1838, the Sinclairville Library Association (1870) is the oldest in continuous operation. The first newspaper, the *Chautauqua Gazette* (1817), was published in Fredonia. *Jamestown Post-Journal* and *Dunkirk Observer* are published daily, and the *Westfield Republican* and *Chautauqua News* are issued weekly. The Arts Council for Chautauqua County (1972) serves the arts community from the Reg Lenna Civic Center in the renovated Palace Theater in Jamestown. The two SUNY colleges also offer musical, visual arts, and dramatic performances.

Perhaps the county's most famous native is Lucille Ball. An annual festival celebrates her career, and Jamestown, where she attended high school, has the Lucy Desi Museum. Among Chautauqua Co authors is Jean Webster (1876–1916), a native of Fredonia. Erastus Dow Palmer (1817–1904), who developed his career in Dunkirk from 1834 to 1849, was one of America's best-known sculptors of his generation. Other Chautauqua Co citizens of note include Jamestown native and naturalist Roger Tory Peterson and US Supreme Court Justice Robert H. Jackson (1892–1954). The rock band 10,000 Maniacs was organized and first performed in Chautauqua Co.

Politics

The county's governing body was for many years a board of supervisors elected from the towns, with the board's chair playing a dominant role in county politics. Beginning in 1856, under the influence of Reuben E. Fenton, a native son who became governor in 1864, the county evolved into and remained a Republican Party stronghold until the 1970s. Under state mandate a new charter was adopted calling for election of a county legislature in 1974. The reapportionment created the county's first ever Democratic majority. A county executive was elected in 1975. Overall Chautauqua Co is politically split, with Democratic majorities in the two cities and Republican majorities in the rural areas.

The 20th Century

In 1900 there were over 7,000 farms in Chautauqua Co, divided regionally between the fruit farms of the lake plain and the dairy farms of the uplands. By 1950 the number had dropped to 5,300 as the more marginal dairy operations were abandoned, a pattern that has continued into the 21st century. Chautauqua Co had a thriving manufacturing sector in the early 20th century. Dunkirk was the home of Atlas Crucible Steel, US Radiator Corp, and American Locomotive Co, as well as other smaller firms. Jamestown's industry included nearly 100 wood furniture factories. The 1957 completion of the New York State Thruway between Buffalo and the Pennsylvania state line west of Ripley gave the Lake Erie shore region early access to the nation's interstate highway network. Jamestown and other sections of the county were later linked to the high-speed automobile system via Rte 17 (I-86), completed between 1983 and 1996.

In 1997 Chautauqua Co had the highest number of farms (1,850) in the state. Leading goods were dairy products, fruit, cattle and calves, nursery and greenhouse products, and vegetables. Upland farms also produce about 15,000 gal (56,800 l) of maple syrup annually. The greatest change in the grape industry came with the introduction of mechanical harvesting equipment in 1968. Dunkirk and Jamestown remain the hubs of Chautauqua Co manufacturing, but much changed in the last half of the 20th century. Dunkirk's industrial base became less significant to the economy, and the number of wooden furniture factories in the county shrank to seven, only one of which was in Jamestown. In 2001 rail connections were provided by CSX Transportation and the Western New York and Pennsylvania Railroad. The county's population peaked at 147,305 in 1970, declining in each succeeding decade. In 2000 there were approximately 3,000 Blacks living in Chautauqua Co, about 2% of the population. The Latino population has increased, especially in Dunkirk, amounting to about 3.5% of the population.

See also Architects and architecture, Southern Tier (Western).

The first major county history, which concentrates on pioneer settlement, is Andrew W. Young, *History of Chautauqua County, N.Y.* (1875). Three others brought the story up to 1920, and William J. Doty, ed., *The Historic Annals of Southwestern New York* (1940), covers aspects of Chautauqua and two other counties to 1938. Two town histories of the early period are H. C. Taylor, *Historical Sketches of the Town of Portland* (1873) and Gilbert W. Hazeltine, *The Early History of the Town of Ellicott* (1887). Also useful is the promotional *Historical and Biographical Sketch of Cherry Creek* by Charles J. Shults (1900).

Two recent works were well conceived and include the 20th century: Ernest D. Leet, ed., *History of Chautauqua County, N.Y., 1938–1978* (1980) and B. Dolores Thompson, *Jamestown and Chautauqua County: An Illustrated History* (1984). An impressive study of Jamestown's largest ethnic group is M. Lorimer Moe, *Saga from the Hills: A History of the Swedes of Jamestown, N.Y.* (1983); it must, however, be used with care.

Pam Kirst

Chautauqua Institution. The Chautauqua Movement's roots are in evangelical Protestantism. Chautauqua's cofounders, the Illinois-based John Heyl Vincent (1832–1920), eventually a bishop in the Methodist Episcopal Church, and Lewis Miller (1829–99), a wealthy and active lay Methodist from Ohio, sought to create a new direction for the Sunday School Teacher's Assembly. Both had become suspicious of the emotionalism and superficiality of much of Methodist education, especially the camp meeting, and sought to create a new type of institution that would be decorous and more intellectually challenging. The Miller family had vacationed on the shores of Chautauqua Lake at Fair Point (Chautauqua Co), site of a Methodist camp meeting, and it seemed ideal. In 1874 Vincent and Miller held the first Chautauqua Assembly. They forbade preachers from proselytizing the guests and opened Fair Point to all comers and, in essence, transformed the Methodist camp meeting into a semipublic, ecumenical institute for the training of Sunday school teachers.

Early Years

The Chautauqua Assemblies proved remarkably popular. In the second year Pres Ulysses S. Grant paid a visit, firmly placing Chautauqua on the map. The Chautauqua Institution emerged as the country's pioneer in distance education and offered a range of courses, including Bible study, science, history, literature, and the arts. Its eight-week summer program gave visibility to Social Gospel–minded academics, politicians, preach-

Athenaeum Hotel at the Chautauqua Institution, designed by W. W. Carlin, opened in 1881.

ers, prohibitionists, and reformers. The Assembly's matrix of overlapping institutions comprised the degree-granting Chautauqua University (1883–92), renamed the Chautauqua System of Education (1892–98). William Rainey Harper was a leader of Chautauqua's educational efforts from 1883 to 1895, when the workload from his job as president of the University of Chicago forced him to step down as the principal of the Chautauqua System of Education. Chautauqua's ambitions to mimic a four-year college diploma program proved to be too expensive. In the 1880s hundreds of students enrolled and took courses during the summer sessions, but Chautauqua University was losing money, over $7,000 in 1888. A plan at that time to make Chautauqua the leader of the national university extension movement also fizzled.

But if the attempt to maintain an institution of higher education did not work, more informal education efforts were a great success. In 1878 Vincent inaugurated the Chautauqua Literary and Scientific Circle (CLSC), still the oldest continuous book club in the United States. Under the direction of Kate F. Kimball, the CLSC had enrolled approximately 275,000 people by 1914. At the book club's height in 1887, its enrollment of 18,000 far eclipsed that of the nation's largest universities. New York State residents were disproportionately represented in this number, making up 15% of CLSC enrollees in 1887. Between 80 and 90% of CLSC members nationwide were women, and the program offered a "college outlook" to thousands who, because of circumstance or gender, were denied entrance into traditional colleges. Students completing the four-year reading program received official, if symbolic, diplomas at elaborate commencement ceremonies. Criticized by some academic observers as superficial, the CLSC nonetheless provided opportunities mostly for white, Protestant, middle-class women to develop stronger public voices and organizational experience. Prominent suffragists, such as Susan B. Anthony and Rev Anna Howard Shaw, spoke frequently from Chautauqua's platform.

Growth and Development

Chautauqua, if at first glance rather out of the way, was in many ways well suited to become a major resort. It was in near proximity to the prosperous oil regions in northern Pennsylvania and to the new urbanization along the Great Lakes sparked by the Erie Canal. Entrepreneurs tapped into the tourist appeal of Chautauqua's lake and landscape. The Atlantic and Great Western Railroad had reached Jamestown (Chautauqua Co) in 1860. Railway extensions made the lake and its hotels accessible to legions of day-trippers from Buffalo and Rochester. Chautauqua's success lay in changing Anglo-American Protestant attitudes about leisure. Once viewed as licentious, leisure had emerged in many Protestant circles as a symbol of racial progress, bourgeois prosperity, and Christian civilization. Chautauqua's two founders embraced the summer vacation and turned it into an opportunity for cultural and spiritual renewal. The Chautauqua Assemblies welcomed vacationers and casual visitors because, as Vincent reasoned in 1886, they provided "financial support" for its "more radical work" and could perhaps be coaxed into enlightenment once inside the gates. The Chautauqua Institution's great innovation was to bring together leisure and self-culture—that is, the impulse to improve oneself through learning.

At first many of the attendees, true to Chautauqua's roots in the camp meeting tradition, stayed in converted tents or in relatively humble boardinghouses. At the turn of the 20th century accommodations became more elaborate. The Amphitheater, built in 1893 to replace the one erected in 1879, seats 5,000. A large, neoclassical, open-air classroom called the Hall of Philosophy (built in 1879, rebuilt in 1906) is now flanked by Victorian cottages. Chautauqua revealed its aspiration to compete with secular resorts when it unveiled the Athenaeum Hotel, with its Second Empire and Italianate flourishes, in 1881. In 1989 the grounds were designated a National Historic Landmark. In 1902, when the Chautauqua Lake Sunday School Assembly was formally reorganized as Chautauqua Institution, it had grown from its initial 50 acres (20 ha) to almost 200 (80 ha).

Chautauqua grew in other ways and soon became a national movement. Institutionally independent Chautauquas of all sorts proliferated. By 1900, 101 communities, often spurred by female CLSC members, had held assemblies patterned on the original Chautauqua. Though these were primarily in the Midwest, in New York State assemblies were held at Lake George village, Tully Lake Park, Point O'Woods, Findley Lake, and Binghamton. Catholics eager to emulate Chautauqua's success founded the Summer School on Lake Champlain in Plattsburgh in 1893. A Jewish Chautauqua Society was formed in the same year. Independent assemblies developed close ties with retail interests, boosters, interurban streetcar companies, and railroad executives, who saw them as profitable, yet moral, tourist attractions. The "circuit Chautauquas," which by 1904 proliferated in small towns, especially in the Midwest, used the Chautauqua name for commercial gain. These mobile Chautauquas were held under tents, colored brown to distinguish them from the white tents of the traveling circus. Using aggressive sales tactics, one-sided contracts, and a carefully orchestrated booking system, circuits hastened the decline of the independent assemblies. The circuit Chautauquas, a combination of vaudeville and lectures, flourished through the 1910s, although by the mid-1920s the rise of radio, movies, automobiles, and an expanded consumer culture signaled the end of their popularity in rural US regions. The last tent show, hit hard by the depression, folded in 1933. By then Chautauqua as a movement was over. The demise of the circuits allowed the Chautauqua Institution to reclaim its unique place in US culture.

The 20th Century

The founding generation, including Lewis Miller, William Rainey Harper, Kate Kimball, and John Heyl Vincent, had passed on by 1920. Also, young feminists early in the 20th century grew frustrated with Chautauqua's limitations, such as its preference for literary discussion over direct political action. Although many viewed the movement's intellectual model as outmoded and irrelevant and its middle-class northern Protestant, Republican, and Prohibitionist milieu dated, the original Assembly continued to flourish under Pres Arthur E. Bestor (1915–44). A series of 1920s expansions at mother Chautauqua, as the Chautauqua Institution was called, pushed it to the brink of bankruptcy in 1933, where it remained until 1936, when a gift from John D. Rockefeller Jr returned it to sound footing. Chautauqua was sustained by a commitment to create an informed citizenship in a modern democracy. Increasingly this was a secular commitment, shorn of religious coloration. Its service to the state was most apparent during World War I, when it hosted a Speaker's Training Camp to aid federal propaganda efforts. Competing perspectives on major social issues of the 20th century have found their way to the Chautauqua platform. From Ulysses S. Grant to Bill Clinton, nine men who have served as US president have visited the Chautauqua Institution. Probably the most famous address given at Chautauqua was on 14 Aug 1936, when Pres Franklin D. Roosevelt affirmed his commitment to keep the United States out of Europe's growing troubles in what is commonly known as his I Hate War speech.

Chautauqua remains committed to promoting the arts and humanities. Music has been a part of the program since the beginning, and the Chautauqua School of Music was founded in 1909. The New York Symphony Society, conducted by Walter Damrosch, first came in 1909 and appeared regularly until its 1928 merger with the New York Philharmonic. In 1929 the Chautauqua Symphony Orchestra had its first season. That same year the Chautauqua Opera had its first performances. The Chautauqua Dance Company was inaugurated in 1960. Chautauqua Institution's lectures, along with its orchestral, operatic, dance, and theater offerings, attract artists to the lake every summer, and attendance at scheduled public events reaches almost 150,000. Every year approximately 8,000 students attend the Chautauqua Summer Schools offering music, dance, and writing courses, among others. Its physical plant has grown to 750 acres (305 ha) from various land purchases that added hundreds of acres and a golf course to Chautauqua's holdings. The Chautauqua ideal lives on. State humanities councils stage summer educational programs under its name. Public television, elderhostels, and electronically based distance education programs owe much to the CLSC model for knowledge dissemination. At Chautauqua Lake, however, skyrocketing housing and ticket prices threaten to turn the institution into an establishment solely for the wealthy. The Chautauqua Institution, a nonprofit education institution governed by a 24-member board of trustees, owns most of the land inside the fence, sets the policies of the institution, elects officials, and runs the summer programs. What Chautauquans of the 21st century decide to do with their prosperity will help determine whether, in Martin E. Marty's words, "there is a future to the Chautauqua past."

Kett, Joseph F. *The Pursuit of Knowledge under Difficulties: From Self-Improvement to Adult Education in America, 1750–1990* (Stanford, Calif: Stanford Univ Press, 1994)

Marty, Martin E. "Popular Education in America Today: The Chautauqua Ideal," *Henry Ford Museum and Greenfield Village Herald* 13 (1984): 60–69

Morrison, Theodore. *Chautauqua: A Center for Education, Religion, and the Arts in America* (Chicago: Univ of Chicago Press, 1974)

Rieser, Andrew C. "Secularization Reconsidered: Chautauqua and the De-Christianization of Middle-Class Authority, 1880–1920." In *The Middling Sorts: Explorations in the History of the American Middle Class*, ed. Burton J. Bledstein and Robert D. Johnston (New York: Routledge, 2001)

———. *The Chautauqua Movement: Protestants, Progressives, and the Origins of Modern Liberalism, 1874–1920* (New York: Columbia Univ Press, 2003)
Trachtenberg, Alan. " 'We Study the Word and Works of God': Chautauqua and the Sacralization of Culture in America," *Henry Ford Museum and Greenfield Village Herald* 13 (1984): 3–11
Vincent, John Heyl. *The Chautauqua Movement* (Boston: Chautauqua Press, 1886)

Andrew C. Rieser

Chazy [SHAY-ZEE]. Town (pop 4,181) in NE Clinton Co. A French family settled in ?1763 under the Bedou seigneury (1752) but abandoned their farm during the Revolution. The area was resettled in 1783 by Canadian refugees and Yankees. Throughout town, which is bounded on the east by Lake Champlain, are houses built with local limestone during the first century of settlement. The town was formed in 1804 from Champlain. Farming, lumbering, and small ironworks were once the basis of the town's economy; dairying, apple growing, and maple sugar harvesting remain important in the early 21st century. The Chazy Central Rural School (1916) was the pioneer consolidated school in the United States. The Northway opened through Chazy in 1965. The Alice T. Miner Colonial Collection is a museum; the Miner Foundation runs an experimental farm, and the Miner Institute of SUNY Plattsburgh supports environmental education and research.

Sullivan, Nell Jane Barnett, and David Kendall Martin. *A History of the Town of Chazy* (Burlington, Vt: George Little Press, 1970)

Thomas A. Rumney

Cheektowaga. Town (pop 94,019) in W central Erie Co. Settled in 1808, the town was formed from Amherst in 1839 and developed into a supplier of farm produce to nearby Buffalo. Many Germans settled beginning in the 1820s and 1830s. The first railroad came through in 1851, and within ten years three others did as well. The New York Central and the Delaware, Lackawanna and Western Railroads later built freight yards, which provided employment. Late in the 19th century Poles and Italians joined the Germans. Cheektowaga grew dramatically from its 1920 population of about 11,923 to its 1970 peak of 117,000. Curtiss-Wright, Bell Aircraft, and Westinghouse had plants in Cheektowaga in the mid–20th century, but most residents commuted to jobs in Buffalo. In 1954 the New York State Thruway opened through town. Vic Weiss (1908–81), known as the Poor Man's Friend and originator of the Cheer for Cheektowaga campaign, served as the unofficial mayor of downtown Cheektowaga from the early 1960s until his death. It is the site of the Buffalo Niagara International Airport, and Villa Maria College (1961). The chapel of Our Lady Help of Christians (1853) is a pilgrimage site and is listed on the National Register.

Vicki Weiss

cheese. New or cured soft, semisoft, or hard dairy food made by curdling milk, with or without the addition of rennet, into solid curds, which are separated from liquid whey and pressed. A recognizable New York State cheese industry began in the early 1800s in Dutchess, Herkimer, Oneida, and Orange Cos. Herkimer Co cheese was available in Albany in 1808, and agents were buying Herkimer and Oneida Co cheeses by 1815. Agents or factors served as intermediaries between cheese makers and distant markets. Because of the agents, even the small and most isolated producers were guaranteed markets for their cheeses, and dairying became a viable full-time occupation. Most of the cheese produced on Central New York farms was marketed in New York City to grocers and produce dealers.

By the 1830s most farmers in eastern New York State had shifted away from wheat, unable to compete with western New York State yields, and turned to dairy. Eastern New York State's cool temperatures and water sources were ideal for dairying. Fields exhausted by tillage became profitable pastures. Agents and the state's extensive canal system were largely responsible for the expansion of farm cheese production in the first half of the 19th century. In 1834 more than 3,000 tons (2,700 MT) of cheese destined for domestic and foreign markets arrived in Albany over the Erie Canal. Commission houses, which sent agents to cheese-making districts and received and distributed the shipped cheeses, appeared after 1835. By 1840 much of the central and northern parts of New York State were also dedicated to dairying, and 10 years later half of the nation's cheese was being produced on state farms. Of the almost 19,500 tons (17,690 MT) of cheese produced in the state in 1855, more than 4,500 tons (4,080 MT) were produced in Herkimer Co, with 1,500 tons (1,360 MT) in Oneida Co, and substantial amounts in Jefferson, Erie, and Madison Cos. Almost all of this cheese was produced at home and was a significant financial contribution to the farm. At the time, this was typically the responsibility of women.

As cheese making became more important in farm life, farmhouses were altered. New designs placed the dairy near the main house, often with a sheltered passageway connecting the two buildings. Eventually, milk rooms were located just off the kitchen, or a section of the enlarged kitchen was devoted entirely to dairying. Traditional English barns were too small for the expanding home dairy and had an inefficient floor plan. Variations were designed that facilitated stabling, milking, feeding, storing feed, and removing manure.

The nation's first cheese factory was established in 1851 in Rome (Oneida Co) by Jesse Williams (1798–1864) and was devoted to making cheddar. By 1863 it was known as the Rome Cheese Manufacturing Association. For the first time, milk from several farms was combined at one location to be made into cheese by one operator. Under the factory system, uniform cheeses of excellent quality were produced less expensively. Once established, centralized cheese-making plants rapidly replaced home manufacture. In 1866 more than 500 cheese factories were in operation in New York State; by 1870 there were more than 1,000; and by 1875, 90% of the state's cheese was factory made. Entrepreneurs began distributing brand-name cheeses.

As methods of sanitation, refrigeration, and transportation improved in the late 19th century, fluid-milk shipments to urban areas became more profitable. Less milk was available at affordable prices to the cheese factories, and many local sites closed or consolidated into larger, corporate-owned factories. German immigrant Julius Wettstein launched the Monroe Cheese Co (Orange Co) in 1873 to make European-style cheese and Liederkranz cheese. The firm introduced a processed blend of natural cheeses under the brand name Velveeta around 1919 and employed up to 40 people before closing in 1926 and moving to Ohio. In 1872 A. L. and J. J. Reynolds established the Empire Cheese Co in South Edmeston (Otsego Co), one of the first cheese companies to produce Philadelphia Brand Cream Cheese in New York State. The factory was destroyed by fire in 1900. When the owners did not rebuild, local dairy farmers established the Phenix Cheese Corp, built a new factory, and continued marketing the cream cheese. In 1928 the company merged with Kraft and by 1930 the Kraft-Phenix Cheese Corp had captured 40% of the nation's cheese market. In 1971 Kraft moved cream cheese production to a new plant in Lowville (Lewis Co), and the South Edmeston plant was refitted to produce yogurt and cottage cheese. In 2002 the Kraft Foods Lowville plant was the biggest producer of soft-body cream cheese in the world, with a workforce of 350.

The McCadam Cheese Co in Heuvelton (St. Lawrence Co) was established in 1876 by William McCadam. In 1934 the manufacturing facility was reorganized and expanded to Chateaugay (Franklin Co). In 2003 it employed 200 workers and produced more than 20 types of cheeses, including cheddar, colby, brick, and monterey jack. Isaac and Joseph Breakstone opened a dairy store in New York City on the Lower East Side in 1882 and made cottage cheese, cream cheese, and sour cream, with manufacturing plants in Walton and Downsville (Delaware Co) by 1912. In 1928 Breakstone's was sold to National Dairy Products (now Kraft Foods) which continues to market Breakstone's cottage cheese and sour cream. The Colosse Cheese Factory (Oswego Co) was established in 1900 as the Mexico Farmers Cooperative by a group of dairy farmers to process their excess milk. Cheddar and wash curds were produced, and cream, once separated from the liquid whey, was sent to creameries to be made into butter.

There has been a resurgence in small, often organic, cheese factories and in those that manufacture goat and sheep milk cheese, such as Butternuts Valley Farms in Gilbertsville (Otsego Co) and Coach Dairy Goat Farm in Pine Plains (Dutchess Co). In 2001 the state produced 351,500 tons (318,875 MT) of cheese, excluding cottage cheese, and ranked third nationally in total cheese production, behind Wisconsin and California. New York State ranked first in the nation in cream, Neufchâtel, and cottage cheese production the same year. It is also known for its cheddar cheese and ranks seventh in production. In addition to McCadam, cheddar cheese makers include Lewis County Dairy Corp in New Bremen and Great Lakes Cheese in Adams (Jefferson Co). The New York State Museum of Cheese in Rome (Oneida Co) opened in 1988 and displays home and factory cheese-making implements and presents the history of cheese making in the state.

Durand, Loyal, Jr. "The Historical and Economic Geography of Dairying in the North Country of New York State," *Geographic Review* 57 (1967) 24–47
McMurry, Sally. *Transforming Rural Life: Dairying Families and Agricultural Change, 1820–1885* (Baltimore: Johns Hopkins Univ Press, 1995)
Stamm, Eunice R. *The History of Cheese Making in New York State* (Endicott, NY: Lewis Group, 1991)

Suzan D. Friedlander

Cheever, John (*b* Quincy, Mass, 27 May 1912; *d* Ossining, Westchester Co, 18 June 1982). Novelist and short story writer. Cheever was born into a secure middle-class existence, but that changed in 1928 when his father lost his job as a shoe salesman. He was drawn to writing from a young age. Dismissed from Thayer Academy in South Braintree, Mass, at age 17, he wrote a story based on the experience, "Expelled," which was accepted for the 1 Oct 1930 edition of the *New Republic.* Cheever moved to New York City in 1934 and supported himself with a variety of jobs while writing, selling stories to a number of magazines, especially the *New Yorker.* In 1934 he spent a brief period at Yaddo, the artists' retreat in Saratoga Springs. He continued writing throughout the 1930s and into the 1940s, married Mary Winternitz in 1941, and enlisted in the US Army in 1942, serving for four years. His first book, *The Way Some People Live,* a story collection, was published in 1943. In 1950 the Cheevers moved from Manhattan to Scarborough (Westchester Co), and he published his second story collection, *The Enormous Radio and Other Stories,* in 1953. Most of these pieces were set in New York City.

The Cheevers settled permanently in Crotonville (Westchester Co) in 1956. His first novel, *The Wapshot Chronicle,* appeared in 1957 and won the National Book Award. A sequel, *The Wapshot Scandal,* was published in 1964. Three more novels followed: *Bullet Park* (1969); *Falconer* (1977), set in prison, a background Cheever was familiar with through his teaching of creative writing at Sing Sing Prison in the mid-1970s; and *Oh What a Paradise It Seems* (1982), his final work. Cheever received the greatest critical acclaim for his short fiction. *The Stories of John Cheever* (1978) received the Pulitzer Prize. Most of his stories focus on affluent suburbanites whose material success cannot mitigate despair, boredom, marital discord, and the consequences of alcohol abuse. Cheever was well acquainted with the culture of suburbia, and he struggled with alcoholism for most of his adult life.

O'Hara, James Eugene. *John Cheever: A Study of the Short Fiction* (Boston: Twayne Publishers, 1989)

J. Justin Gustainis

chemical industry. In the mid-1700s New York Colony's potash industry, which made the strong alkali potassium carbonate from wood ash, grew and centralized at village works that purchased ashes from area farmers. Efforts were made to organize the tar industry, vital to shipping, through local monopolies and trading companies in order to improve the quality of the product (derived from coal or wood) and to demand higher premiums from the British government. The New York tanning industry developed through the partnering of numerous small-scale tanners that typically used hemlock bark as the main ingredient. Other chemicals from wood and coal were produced in New York State's mill and furnace industries.

Efficient Alkali Production

A cost- and labor-efficient method of producing a strong alkali was important to the expansion of the burgeoning chemical industry. By 1775 a Williamsburg (Kings Co) plant, later named the New York Quinine and Chemical Works, was producing potash as well as gunpowder and saltpeter, a component of gunpowder. After the war the plant added soap making, a process that uses potash to break down animal fats. William Partridge and Sons was established in Greenwich Village in 1798 to extract coloring from logwood. The New York Chemical Manufacturing Co, incorporated in 1823 by a group of New York City merchants, manufactured blue vitriol, alum, acids, drugs, dyes, and paints. The company competed with chemical manufacturers in Philadelphia and Britain, and had extensive sales in New England. However, the banking aspect of the New York Chemical Manufacturing Co eventually displaced the manufacturing component. Martin Kalbfleisch, a chemist and the firm's former manager, had begun producing paint pigments at a small plant in Harlem. In 1840 he moved his firm to Brooklyn, where, as the Brooklyn Chemical Works, its reputation was established in the manufacture of sulfuric acid as well as other sulfates, acids, minerals, and salts. (Kalbfleisch was later mayor of Brooklyn.) There were other developments in the field of chemistry in New York City at this time. The New York Chemical Convention, a meeting of industrial chemists, was held in New York City on 26 Oct 1831, and around 1840 in a small factory on Staten Island, Charles Goodyear spent a year developing the vulcanization process for rubber.

New York State's access to the Atlantic seaboard encouraged industrial development by making transportation costs relatively inexpensive, especially after the Erie Canal opened. Charles Pfizer and Co was established in Brooklyn in 1849 to meet the need for processing chemicals, such as tartaric acid, used in foods and pharmaceuticals as well as in chemical manufacturing. The chemical industry fueled the expansion of the textile industry as chemists developed new dyes. The H. Kohnstamm firm, established in Lower Manhattan in 1851, specialized in ultramarine. Foreign investment, particularly from German companies, contributed to the growth of the industry in New York State. In 1865 Bayer was established at a coal-tar dye plant in Albany. In 1879 the Schoellkopf family founded the Aniline and Chemical Works Co in Buffalo. Food production at all levels benefited from applied chemistry. Chemical works throughout the North grew from the manufacture of fertilizers by using sulfuric acid to reduce phosphate rock mined in the South. Kohnstamm introduced harmless food colors starting about 1880; previously, confectionary often had been tinted with dry paint. The Grasselli Dyestuffs Corp (later General Aniline Works), established in Greenbush [now Rensselaer] in 1882, and William Zinsser and Co, established at Hastings-on-Hudson (Westchester Co) in 1897, became important manufacturers of synthetic organic chemicals.

The New York State alkali industry expanded after William Cogswell, a mining engineer, and other Syracuse businessmen founded the Solvay Process Co in 1881. The Solvay process, developed by Ernest and Alfred Solvay of Belgium, was a continuous chemical process for the manufacture of sodium carbonate from a cold ammoniacal salt solution saturated with carbon dioxide. The precipitate could be heated to produce sodium carbonate, carbon dioxide, and ammonium chloride; slaked lime was used simultaneously to regenerate ammonia from the ammonium chloride. Cogswell had concluded that Syracuse was an ideal site because of its proximity to brine fields and limestone quarries. The Solvay brothers granted him a license and offered to invest in the company, providing one-third of the capital. After having secured additional financing, the Solvay Process Co of Syracuse started small-scale production of soda ash (anhydrous sodium carbonate) in 1884. By 1896 the plant had enlarged its production capacity to 500 tons (454 MT) daily, and by the turn of the century it was one of the largest manufacturers of soda ash in the United States. The electric furnace was used to smelt coke and lime to produce calcium carbide, which could be used to produce acetylene gas for heat and light. In 1898 the Union Carbide Co established a new plant at Niagara Falls for the manufacture of carbide.

New York State's contributions to research on plastics began in the mid–19th century. In Albany John Wesley Hyatt experimented with nitrocellulose and camphor, creating the synthetic plastic celluloid by 1869. Future plastics innovator Leo Baekeland, a Belgian immigrant, founded the Nepera Chemical Co in 1893 in Yonkers to manufacture his invention, the photographic paper Velox. In 1899 Baekeland sold the concern to George Eastman for $1 million and retired to work in his own private laboratory in Harmony Park (Westchester Co), where he studied the effects of temperature and pressure on phenol-formaldehyde liquid resin in the presence of hydrochloric acid. From Baekeland's autoclave came the moldable synthetic plastic Bakelite in 1907. Thermosets such as Bakelite harden by chemical reaction and cannot be softened and reshaped. Bakelite reached the market in 1909, when Baekeland set up the General Bakelite Co.

A laboratory for pure scientific research developed at General Electric's (GE's) manufacturing and administrative headquarters in Schenectady about 1900. W. Howard Wright, a former chemist at GE, started the Schenectady Varnish Co in 1906 to provide insulating varnish for GE. The company grew at a Schenectady site adjacent to the New York Central Railroad and expanded into production of enamel for electrical wires and cables.

Electrolytic Production

Some chemical reactions can take place only in the presence of an electrical current. The process requires a chamber, or cell, with an anode (positive charge) and cathode (negative charge) to conduct the electricity, and an electrolyte such as brine, a solution that conducts electricity and is broken down by it. When electricity is passed through brine, the salt (NaCl) and water (H_2O) that compose the brine are broken down. The sodium (Na) reacts with water to produce sodium hydroxide (NaOH), releasing the chlorine; some hydrogen gas is also released.

The mineral resources of the Niagara Falls area and the inexpensive hydroelectric power supplied by the falls attracted chemical manufacturers that used electrolysis to produce chlorine, caustic soda (sodium hydroxide), and hydrogen gas. Thomas T. Mathieson, a Virginia alkali manufacturer, secured the Castner electrolytic cell and began producing commercial bleaching powder at the Castner Electrolytic Alkali Co in

Niagara Falls in 1896. Elon Hooker, who had the Townsend cell, initiated similar operations at the Hooker Electrochemical Co in Niagara Falls in 1909.

The Electro Bleaching Gas Co, which had the technology to manufacture liquid chlorine, established a plant in Niagara Falls in 1909 and began production, introducing liquid chlorine to the textile industry that same year. In 1913 the company used liquid chlorine to sterilize water, and chlorination soon ensured the safety of most Americans' drinking water. Eastman Kodak of Rochester contributed to the industry through the development of chemicals used in photography. American markets were also attracting European investors to utilize their own technologies in several chemical plants in the United States. Roessler and Hasslacher of Germany applied the Castner process in its Niagara Electrochemical subsidiary in Niagara Falls to produce sodium and cyanides shortly before World War I; during the war, the company began producing hydrogen peroxide and perborates under the direction of the military.

The American chemical industry kept up with the World War I demand for sulfur, manufacturing sulfuric acid, mostly using pyrites and also by-products of zinc and copper smelting. The firm of Albright and Wilson from England invested in the Oldbury Electro-Chemical Co in Niagara Falls, producing phosphorus and sodium chlorate. Also in Niagara Falls, the Acheson firm was producing a form of silicon carbide known as Carborundum. In Syracuse, Solvay introduced an American market for benzene, toluene, and naphtha solvents from its coking furnace distillation units. After the United States entered the war in 1917, the stock of German firms was seized by the Office of Alien Property Custodian of the United States. Most industrial chemicals were directed toward the military effort on a priority basis, especially in the explosives and dyes industries, which produced poisonous gases. A government facility for the manufacture of mustard gas was erected on Zinsser's Hastings-on-Hudson (Westchester Co) site. To form National Aniline and Chemical Co in 1917, Schoellkopf combined a number of businesses, including W. Beckers Aniline and Chemical Works (Brooklyn), Standard Aniline Products (Wappingers Falls [Dutchess Co] and Newburgh [Orange Co]); and Century Colors Corp (New York City). National Aniline's manufacturing plant was in Buffalo, and the company had executive offices in New York City and branch offices in 11 other North American cities. In 1920 National Aniline merged through a share exchange with four other companies to create Allied Chemical and Dye Corp.

The Castner Electrolytic Alkali Co began to synthesize ammonia in 1923, greatly reducing the price of this product. Dr James Currie, a chemist working at Pfizer, developed a method for the production of citric acid through the mold fermentation of sugar. The United States produced enough citric acid to meet its needs by 1929, and Pfizer also began producing fumaric, gluconic, and itaconic acids. American Cyanamid, founded on the Ontario side of Niagara Falls by the Cornell-educated engineer Frank Washburn to produce calcium cyanamide fertilizer, began to produce cyanide and hydrocyanic acid. Acetylene, originally used for lighting and later for the manufacture of calcium cyanamide in the production of ammonia for fertilizers, became an important source of manufacturing chemical derivatives necessary to build new products and markets. During the 1920s research chemists began to experiment with its reactive properties for the purpose of producing other chemicals; for example, acetaldehyde, produced from acetylene, could be oxidized to acetic acid. These processes needed large amounts of inexpensive electricity to make them economically viable, and Niagara Falls again became a prime location for this effort. Roessler and Hasslacher established the Niacet Chemicals Corp in Niagara Falls to produce acetic acid, acetaldehyde, crotonaldehyde, and ethyl acetate. The acetylation of cellulose produced cellulose acetate, which could be turned into fibers and films. The E. I. Du Pont de Nemours (DuPont) site in Buffalo produced the world's first sheet of cellophane in 1924. Other synthetics emerged soon after; during the 1920s, the staff at the GE Research Laboratory at Schenectady explored polyesters as part of their work on insulation. In 1928 GE research produced glycerophthalic resins, which were used on automobiles in place of cellulose lacquers and required less time for application. Eastman Kodak products included hydroquinone and cellulose acetate by 1930.

Petrochemicals

The petrochemical industry is based around individual hydrocarbon compounds that are found in petroleum (crude oil) and natural gas, or derived by conversion processes. These intermediate compounds, such as butane, methane, propylene, ethylene, and benzene, include the basic components of polymers. Polymers are very large hydrocarbon molecules connected in chains; the interwoven polymer structure gives plastics their particular combination of strength and malleability. Union Carbide began marketing a number of petrochemical products, including polyvinyl acetate, polyvinyl butyral, and polyvinyl chloride (PVC) during the 1930s; in 1939 Union Carbide bought the Bakelite Corp. By the early 1940s B. F. Goodrich had several PVC facilities at Niagara Falls. As World War II approached, the need to develop a synthetic rubber intensified polymer research. In September 1940 Herman Mark, an Austrian refugee from the Nazi regime, came to the Polytechnic Institute of Brooklyn (now Polytechnic University) from the University of Vienna, where he had been engaged in polymer research. Mark continued his work under wartime contracts with the Office of Scientific Research and Development and started a world-renowned polymer chemistry program at Polytechnic that became the Institute of Polymer Research in 1947. Research in plastics at GE led to the creation of GE Silicones, with headquarters and main plant at Waterford (Saratoga Co), where production of resins and gums started in the late 1940s. In addition to industrial customers, GE Silicones supplied the military with silicone rubber for aircraft parts and reached the 1950s consumer with new car and furniture polishes. Participation in the synthetic rubber program brought American Cyanamid into polymers. Cyanamid bought the Formica Co and during the 1950s was producing and marketing Laminac, a polyester resin, and Creslan, a polyacrylonitrile.

W. R. Grace, a New York City–based conglomerate, acquired Davison Chemical Co and Dewey and Almy Chemical Co in 1954. Dewey and Almy had developed a synthetic rubber substitute, and Davison had brought out the Syloid line of silica products. Grace furthered public appreciation of the properties of linear polyethylene by providing technical assistance to the California toy company Wham-O Manufacturing in their development of the hula hoop, widely marketed in 1958. Grace introduced Cryovac plastic shrink film products starting in 1960 and delivered a number of construction products and a fluid cracking catalyst. Companies such as Union Carbide concentrated on commodity petrochemicals such as polyethylene, polyvinyl chloride, and polystyrene, which were turned into consumer products at other plants.

The abundance of inexpensive sources of petroleum continued until the 1973 oil embargo by the Organization of Petroleum Exporting Countries (OPEC), which disrupted supplies and increased prices dramatically. Other pressures came in the form of environmental action. In 1976 the US Congress passed the Toxic Substances Control Act to regulate the introduction of new chemicals and to review existing ones. That same year, the Resource Conservation and Recovery Act became law for the purpose of regulating toxic industrial wastes. Both programs have placed significant burdens on the American chemical industry by regulating its production and waste disposal practices. Further regulations came in 1980 with the creation of the Superfund program, which supervises the cleanup of contaminated sites, financed by taxes levied on the chemical and petroleum industries. This program can be linked directly to the Love Canal pollution crisis, which resulted from the early postwar dumping practices of Hooker Electrochemical in Niagara Falls. In the late 20th century many chemical firms divested themselves of the production units for commodity polymer chemicals, often selling them to energy companies.

Producing for a Global Market

Olin Chlor Alkali Products, a division of Olin Corp, which is descended from the Mathieson Chemical Corp that started the Castner Electrolytic Alkali Co, still maintains the Niagara Falls site, now 65 acres (26 ha) on Buffalo Ave. One of four successful Olin Chlor Alkali facilities in the United States at the beginning of the 21st century, this plant is still a major producer of chlorine and caustic soda as well as of sodium hypochlorite, hydrochloric acid, and hydrogen. Schenectady International, now an international corporation with 22 production sites and subsidiaries in 13 countries, maintains the sales of enamels and varnishes that gave the company its start as the Schenectady Varnish Co. Schenectady International is headquartered at Congress St in Schenectady, and its Chemical Division is located on Broadway. The company's other Schenectady Co sites are the Research Center in Niskayuna and the resin manufacturing plant in Rotterdam Junction. At the beginning of the 21st century, Schenectady International holds global status in the production of alkylphenols. With substantial extensions to its Waterford plant, GE was ranked fourth among US chemical producers in 2002 by *Chemical and Engineering News*.

Aftalion, Fred. *A History of the International Chemical Industry.* Trans Otto Theodor Benfey (Philadelphia: Univ of Pennsylvania Press, 1991)
Clark, Victor S. *The History of Manufactures in the United States,* 3 vols (New York: Peter Smith, 1949)
Coe, Jerome T. *Unlikely Victory: How General Electric Succeeded in the Chemical Industry* (New York: American Institute of Chemical Engineers, 2000)
Haber, L. F. *The Chemical Industry during the 19th Century: A Study of the Economic Aspect of Applied Chemistry in Europe and North America* (Toronto: Oxford Univ Press, 1958)
Haynes, Williams, and Edward L. Gordy, eds. *The Chemical Industry's Contribution to the Nation, 1635–1935* (New York: Chemical Markets, 1935)
Tullo, Alexander. "Top 50 Chemical Producers," *Chemical and Engineering News,* 12 May 2003
Wise, George. *Willis R. Whitney, General Electric, and the Origins of US Industrial Research* (New York: Columbia Univ Press, 1985)

Thomas Fletcher

Chemung. Town (pop 2,665) in SE Chemung Co. Settled *ca* 1785, the town was formed in 1788. It was served by the Erie Railroad (1849) and the Junction Canal (1854–71), which linked New York State's canal system to Pennsylvania's North Branch Canal. Pine lumber was a major product until about 1855, and broom corn and tobacco were cultivated after lumbering declined. Old Lowman Whiskey was a local product before Prohibition. Since 1951 the Chemung Speedrome has offered auto racing, and the town is the home of the Bodine racing family. Rte 17 (I-86) was completed across the town in 1970. The Chemung Spring Water Co bottles and ships its product regionally. Early 21st-century industry includes the manufacture of steel joists and girders.

Heather A. Wade

Chemung Canal. A 23 mi (37 km) canal from the outlet of Seneca Lake at Watkins Glen (Schuyler Co) south to Elmira. The New York State legislature authorized construction of the canal in April 1829 to connect the farming and mineral economy of the Seneca Lake region with the farming and coal economy of northeastern Pennsylvania. James Geddes, a notable canal engineer of the time who originally surveyed the canal route in 1812, was engaged to resurvey the construction path in 1825, and work began in the spring of 1830. To supply water to the canal, a dam was built in the Chemung River at Chimney Narrows near Corning (Steuben Co) for a separate 16 mi (26 km) canal feeder to Horseheads (Chemung Co). The canal was completed in May 1833 at a cost of $314,395, but a flood delayed navigation until October. The 53 locks on the main canal and its feeder were each 90 feet (27.4 m) long by 15 feet (4.6 m) wide and built of wood. The locks were troublesome and substantially smaller than other New York canal system locks. Between 1855 and 1858 the Chemung Canal was connected with the privately owned Junction Canal, which operated between Elmira and Athens, Pa. The joined canals enabled Pennsylvania to ship anthracite coal to Central New York and to the Great Lakes region. Flood damages, such as those at Gibson (Steuben Co) in 1871 and 1873, and railroad competition seriously eroded the viability of the Chemung Canal. The Junction Canal closed after the 1871 season. The Chemung Canal closed after the 1878 shipping season.

Whitford, Noble E., and Minnie M. Beal. *History of the Canal System of the State of New York, Together with Brief Histories of the Canals of the United States and Canada,* vol 1 (Albany: Bandow Printing, 1906)

F. Charles Petrillo

Chemung County (408 mi²/1,057 km²; pop 91,070). Created in 1836 from Tioga Co, its name is derived from a Delaware word meaning "big horn." In 1854 a portion of the county was taken to help form Schuyler Co. Chemung Co is subdivided into 1 city, Elmira (the county seat), and 11 towns that contain 5 incorporated villages. Elevation ranges from 775 feet (236.2 m) on the banks of the Chemung River, where it leaves the county, to 1,914 feet (583.4 m) north of Smith Corners in the Town of Catlin. Chemung Co straddles three subregions of the Appalachian Upland physiographic province, whose boundaries are defined by the Chemung Valley and the southern extension of the Seneca Lake trough. The county's eastern portion is part of the Susquehanna Hills, the northwestern third falls within the Finger Lake Hills subregion, and the area south of the Chemung Valley lies within the Cattaraugus Hills.

Topography is similar in all three. The land is heavily dissected by streams, and the higher rolling hills and ridges, ranging from 1,500 to 1,800 feet (460–550 m) in height, reflect the remnant surface of the pre-eroded plateau. Hill summits stand as much as 800 feet (245 m) above major valley floors, as exemplified by the Chemung Valley. Bedrock consists predominantly of Devonian shale and siltstone with minor concentrations of sandstone. There is evidence of continental glaciation throughout the county, beginning with rounded hilltops, steep-sided valley walls, and various sorts of unconsolidated debris deposits and including portions of the Valley Heads Moraine. Arguably most dramatic are the imposing Chemung Valley, which was widened and deepened by huge volumes of meltwater from the retreating glacier, and the new river channel cut west of Elmira when the ice front blocked the wide, preexisting river valley at Horseheads and forced the river to carve its present course farther south. The western headland of the massive isolated upland *(umlaufberg)* that resulted is the renowned Harris Hill. The Chemung River is part of the Susquehanna River watershed and drains most of the county. The exception is the Catharine Creek watershed, which empties into Seneca Lake and ultimately Lake Ontario. The Chemung River flooded frequently in the 20th century, and a flood that accompanied Hurricane Agnes on 22–23 June 1972 devastated Elmira and other regions of Chemung Co, forcing the evacuation of 15,000 residents. The better-quality soils are concentrated in the Chemung Valley and the eastern half of the Catharine Creek watershed. Upland soils are generally thin and sour and cannot support modern commercial agriculture.

Chemung Co's climate is humid-continental. Mean January temperatures range from 21°F (-6°C) in the northeast to 24°F (-4°C) at Elmira. Below 0°F (-18°C) temperatures are expected every winter. Mean July temperatures range from the high 68°F (20°C) in the northeast to 70°F (21°C) at Elmira. Daytime highs reach 90°F (32°C) at least a few times every summer. Average annual precipitation amounts range from 35 inches (89 cm) at Elmira to almost 40 inches (102 cm) in the northeast, while seasonal snowfall amounts vary from just under 40 inches (102 cm) in the southeast to approximately 60 in (152 cm) in the northeastern hills. Seasonal temperatures tend to be a degree or two colder and precipitation slightly greater in the up-country. The primeval forest cover consisted of two communities. Alleghenian hardwoods, primarily beech, sugar maple, hemlock, white pine, and basswood with scattered concentrations of oak and chestnut, predominated except in the major valleys, where a central hardwood forest dominated by beech, sugar maple, and basswood grew. Approximately 70% of Chemung Co is presently covered by second-, third-, or fourth-growth forest.

Native Inhabitants

A net sinker and distinctive projectile points found in the Chemung Valley indicate that American Indians may have inhabited the region

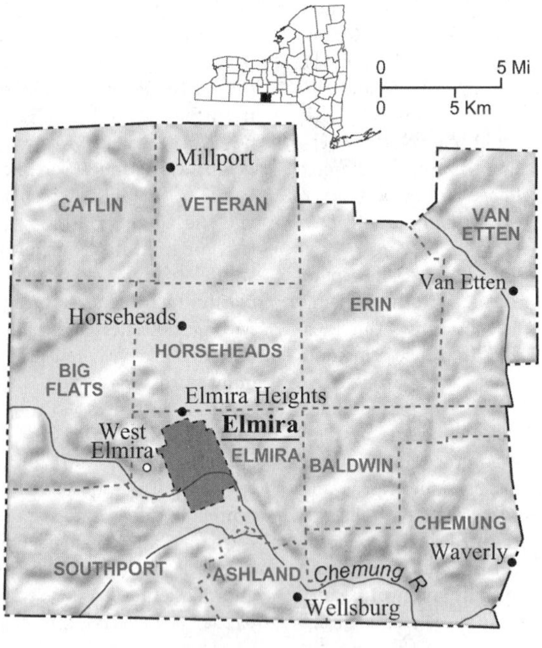

CHEMUNG CO POPULATION CENSUS FIGURES

	White	Nonwhite	Total Population	Foreign-Born
1840	20,619	113	20,732	—
1850	28,535	286	28,821	1,779
1860	26,345	572	26,917	2,853
1870	34,484	797	35,281	4,553
1880	42,098	967	43,065	5,118
1890	47,441	824	48,265	6,224
1900	53,152	911	54,063	6,411
1910	54,049	613	54,662	6,173
1920	65,244	628	65,872	5,928
1930	73,763	917	74,680	5,547
1940	72,516	1,202	73,718	4,286
1950	84,921	1,906	86,827	3,781
1960	96,069	2,637	98,706	3,380
1970	97,928	3,609	101,537	2,224
1980	92,636	5,020	97,656	2,443
1990	88,354	6,841	95,195	2,201
2000	82,840	8,230	91,070	1,972

Notes: "Nonwhite" includes African Americans, Asians, American Indians, and Pacific Islanders and, for 2000, also the mixed race and other race categories. Through the 1960 census these figures primarily reflect the African American population. For 1930 and 1950, the foreign-born totals include Whites only. Other years include all foreign-born in the population.

as much as 12,000 years ago. The variable climate and the river's propensity toward flooding deterred permanent settlement for many millennia. After AD 900 a horticulture-based settlement grew in the region; the inhabitants primarily cultivated corn, squash, and beans. The Andaste inhabited the region in the 15th and 16th centuries; the next long-term inhabitants were the Cayuga and Seneca Nations, which controlled the region beginning in the 17th century. By the mid–18th century, approximately 4,000 Seneca, Delaware, and Cayuga village dwellers developed an agrarian community and traded with distant European settlements.

In 1779 Gen George Washington dispatched brigades commanded by Gen John Sullivan and Gen James Clinton to join forces at the confluence of the Susquehanna and Chemung Rivers. The Sullivan-Clinton campaign, charged with eradicating Iroquois involvement in the war, encountered little resistance. The most serious battle occurred on 29 Aug 1779 at Newtown [now Elmira]. Almost all foodstuffs and the Iroquois villages in the Chemung Valley were destroyed in the days following the battle. After the war, the Seneca continued to inhabit the Chemung Valley as white settlers moved into the region. In June 1791 Chief Cornplanter and some 1,600 Iroquois gathered in the valley to meet with Pres Washington's envoy, Col Timothy Pickering, for discussions relative to Iroquois land rights specified in the Treaty of Fort Stanwix (1784). They negotiated the Treaty of Painted Post, which reinforced the promise of the US government to protect Iroquois prerogatives to sell or retain their lands. Most Native Americans left the Chemung Valley by 1809.

Settlement

Evidence does not support the theory that European exploration of the Chemung Valley preceded the Sullivan-Clinton campaign. Its veterans were among those who claimed land grants in the valley after the Revolution, and the first white settlement began in 1784. Before roads were built, the Susquehanna Valley was the principal route to the Chemung Valley. All of Chemung Co was contained in Chemung Township (1788), sold by the state through land commissioners, and in the Watkins and Flint Purchase (patented 1794), from whose proprietors land was sold. Ultimately the land was acquired by actual settlers who came primarily from New England, Orange Co, and Wilkes-Barre, Pa. Chemung Township contained nearly 1,000 inhabitants by 1791; the county had more than 20,000 residents by 1840. Each of the present towns in the Chemung Valley was settled in the 1780s, while Van Etten was settled in 1795 and Veteran in 1798. Hilly Baldwin, Erin, and Catlin were unoccupied until the middle 1810s. Enslaved and free African Americans were present by 1800. The county's African American population increased by 350% in the 1840s as hundreds of escaped slaves found freedom along with opportunities for education and employment. After 1850 Chemung Co became an important stop on the Underground Railroad as fugitive slaves fled to Canada via Elmira.

Transportation

Chemung Co sustained rapid economic growth especially between 1833 and 1864, spurred by the development of roads, the canal system, and railroads. A turnpike from Newtown to Seneca Lake was constructed between 1803 and 1807, and the area's first stagecoach route (1819) connected the county to Wilkes-Barre; the Plank Rd (1848) also provided direct access to the Pennsylvania state line. The Chemung Canal (1833–78) linked Chemung Co to the Great Lakes; the canal's feeder (1832) and Junction Canal (1856–71) linked the county to the Tioga River and the Pennsylvania coalfields respectively. A railway network, including the Erie (1849), the Chemung (1849; later Pennsylvania), the Utica, Ithaca and Elmira (1874–1938; later Lehigh Valley), the Syracuse, Geneva and Corning (1877; later New York Central), and the Delaware, Lackawanna and Western (1882), served most of the towns of Chemung Co.

The area's accessibility and its excellent transportation system resulted in the designation of Elmira as one of three federal rendezvous points in New York during the Civil War. More than 20,000 men from western New York State passed through the county en route to the front. The Elmira Prison Camp (1864–65) held more than 12,000 Confederate prisoners of war, who suffered from its unhealthy conditions. Nearly 3,000 Southern soldiers are buried at Woodlawn National Cemetery in Elmira. Military hospitals, police barracks, artillery ranges, and warehouses contributed to the economy.

Economic Development

Lumbering was the region's first industry; later mills, boatbuilding, and shipping sustained growing communities along the Chemung River. The canal created many jobs and enabled the transport of such goods as coal, lime, gypsum, and salt to distant markets. Early commercial agriculture focused on livestock raising, especially of cattle and sheep. The arrival of the Erie Railroad in 1851 prompted many farmers, especially in the uplands, to shift to butter and cheese production. Poultry farming also began to gain importance. Tobacco was introduced as a cash crop in the Big Flats/Horseheads area and expanded to nearly 2,000 acres (800 ha) by 1899 before sharply declining and then disappearing. Starting in the 1880s celery and other horticultural products became locally significant in the Elmira area. The diversity of economic interests represented in the county ensured prosperity, and the region's first bank, the Chemung Canal Bank, opened in 1833.

Chemung Co grew more rapidly after the Civil War than in any other era. Elmira Heights, Horseheads, and Big Flats became important industrial and commercial centers in the late 19th and early 20th centuries. Enterprises in Horseheads produced brick, agricultural implements, bridges, structural and architectural iron, woolen cloth, hardware, screen doors, and win-

Uno, mascot to Hose Company No. 1, Volunteer Firemen of Elmira, *ca* 1890.

POPULATIONS OF TOWNS AND CITIES, CHEMUNG CO

Town or City, Year Founded	1800	1840	1880	1920	1960	2000
Ashland, 1867	—	—	1,149	834	1,273	1,951
Baldwin, 1856	—	—	968	503	735	853
Big Flats, 1822	—	1,375	1,989	1,454	3,665	7,224
Catlin, 1823	—	1,119	1,450	737	1,831	2,649
Chemung, 1788	515	2,377	2,098	1,147	1,842	2,665
Elmira, 1792[a]	1,333	4,791	1,986	2,651	8,413	7,199
Elmira (city), 1864	—	—	20,541	45,393	46,517	30,940
Erin, 1822	—	1,441	1,562	761	1,175	2,054
Horseheads, 1854	—	—	3,449	6,809	17,808	19,561
Southport, 1822	—	2,101	3,619	3,084	11,433	11,185
Van Etten, 1854	—	—	1,991	1,028	1,285	1,518
Veteran, 1823	—	2,279	2,263	1,471	2,729	3,271

Notes: In 1800 the Towns of Chemung and Elmira were part of Tioga Co. In 1840 Chemung Co included the Towns of Catharine, Cayuta, and Dix [now in Schuyler Co].

[a]Newtown until 1808.

dows. Elmira manufacturers made glass, bridges, fire engines, typewriters, and automobile parts. Bridges, something of a Chemung Co specialty, were also made at Millport, until the 1880s, and in Elmira Heights, which also produced textiles, bicycles, furniture, and glass.

Throughout the 19th century, the English, Scots-Irish, Irish, and Germans were the dominant ethnic groups. Between 1880 and 1920, Jewish, Italian, and Polish immigrants arrived in large numbers. African Americans continued to migrate from the South, and by 1920 their population was triple its 1850 number. After 1910 Ukrainians, Russians, Czechoslovakians, and Hungarians immigrated to Chemung Co to seek work in its factories. Swedish and Finnish farmers settled in the northeastern area in the 1920s, as did Czech farmers in Veteran. The county's population expanded through the 1930s.

Religion, Education, and Culture

The earliest organized congregation in Chemung Co was the First Baptist Church of Wellsburg (1789). In 1855 Methodist churches were most numerous (13), with Baptist churches close behind (10). Two African American churches (1850, 1870), Temple B'nai Israel (1862), and Sts. Peter and Paul Roman Catholic Church (1849) were established in Elmira. Two Lutheran churches were organized by 1900, and Elmira had a Christian Science church by 1909. Later in the 20th century Ukrainian and Greek Orthodox churches served the county's Ukrainian population.

A school existed in the community of Newtown in the 1790s, and a system of common schools followed 1812 state legislation. The Elmira Academy (1840) began as a private school, but under state legislation it became Elmira Free Academy in 1859. Elmira Female College opened in 1855. In the late 19th century, business and technical schools such as Elmira School of Commerce and Warner Business School evolved into the Elmira Business Institute (1923). Between 1938 and 1953 the common schools were consolidated into large central districts; in 1957 the Elmira City School District swallowed all other school districts in the southern part of the county. In the early 21st century the county's school districts are Elmira, Elmira Heights, and Horseheads. The former Van Etten Central School District has become part of Spencer–Van Etten, administered in Tioga Co. Chemung Co joined with Tioga Co to form the Boards of Cooperative Educational Services (BOCES) in 1956; Schuyler Co joined it in 1968.

The first newspaper in the county was the *Telegraph,* published at Newtown in 1815. The *Elmira Gazette* (1828) has become the *Elmira Star-Gazette,* the county's daily newspaper. The first radio station, WESG, in the county started in 1932, and the *Star-Gazette's* radio station, WENY, hit the airwaves in 1939. In 1953 two television stations began to broadcast from Elmira, WTVE and WECT. In 2004 the county was served by 4 television and 11 radio stations.

Major recreation facilities include the Mark Twain State Park, Newtown Battlefield Reservation, Park Station (a county park; 1979), and Tanglewood Nature Center and Museum (2003). Sports complexes include Dunn Field (1921), Chemung Speedrome (1951), Elmira College's J. Ralph Murray Athletic Education Center (1973), and First Arena (2000). The Clemens Center for the Performing Arts (1999) attracts cultural performances to the region. *Mark Twain: The Musical!* (a Broadway-style show) was a major attraction from 1987 to 1995.

The Elmira Academy of Sciences (1858–?1920), housed at the Elmira Female College Observatory, was established to further astronomical and scientific studies in the community. The county's art and material culture are collected and exhibited by the Arnot Art Museum (1913) and the Chemung County Historical Society (1923). The John W. Jones Museum (2001) educates the public on the role of abolitionists in Chemung Co. Twenty-one sites, primarily in Elmira, Elmira Heights, and Horseheads, are listed on the National Register. The county operates its public library system through Elmira's Steele Memorial Library (1893). Big Flats Library, West Elmira Library, Horseheads Free Library, the Van Etten Reading Center, and the Bookmobile are its components.

Famous Chemung Co natives include director-producer Hal Roach (1892–1992); illustrator and cartoonist Eugene Zimmerman (1862–1935); Ernie Davis (1939–63), the first African American football player to win the Heisman Trophy; fashion designer Tommy Hilfiger (1951–); and astronaut Eileen Collins (1956–). Residents have included Mark Twain (Samuel L. Clemens, 1835–1910), radical feminist and author Crystal Eastman (1881–1928), and novelist Ellery Queen (Frederic Dannay, 1905–82).

Politics

In 1791 Newtown was the county seat of Tioga Co; when Chemung Co was created, Newtown retained that distinction. Chemung was administered by a board of supervisors until 1974, and in the early 21st century, it is governed by a legislature with a county executive. Until the late 19th century, a majority of its towns voted Democratic, but beginning in the 20th century it has been solidly Republican. The mid-19th-century debate over the abolition of slavery sparked many of the most heated political contests. An active community of communists, centered in Van Etten, flourished in the 1920s. Two past New York State governors had associations with Chemung Co: Lucius Robinson (1810–91) and David Bennett Hill (1843–1910), both Democrats. Other prominent politicians were J. Sloat Fassett (1853–1924), a Republican who served in the state senate for nine years and in the House of Representatives from 1905 to 1911, and Chancellor Carl T. Hayden (1941–), Regent for the Sixth Judicial District of the state (1990–2002).

The 20th Century

Known in the 19th century for its high-quality lumber, butter, leaf tobacco, and celery, Chemung Co's economy was transformed by fast-paced industrialization beginning around the turn of the 20th century. Dairy farming, almost exclusively whole-milk production, and field crops of hay and corn, continued to dominate agriculture, although chicken farming was important around Van Etten. Agriculture declined as the number of farms decreased from 1,280 in 1950 to 313 in 1997 and as most of the population went to work in factories in Elmira, Elmira Heights, and Horseheads. Two bridge companies operated in Chemung Co, as did renowned fire engine manufacturer American-LaFrance, several glass factories, textiles mills, steel mills, a bicycle factory, a box factory, and many other industries. Between 1930 and 1937 the Great Depression caused unemployment, business closings, and an increased need for private relief agencies like Catholic Charities (1930). Federal relief programs such as the Civilian Conservation Corps (CCC) were in place by 1933, providing forestry and construction jobs for residents. A massive project to eliminate at-grade railroad intersections throughout the county, funded by federal, state, and private sources, created many jobs between 1932 and 1937. The resulting railroad viaducts improved travel and significantly modernized the appearance of the urban core. A nationally known attraction developed during the 1930s: soaring and gliding. Begun in the Chemung Valley in 1930, it helped attract Schweizer Aircraft Corp (1938) and, in recent years, the National Soaring Museum (1969) and the National Warplane Museum (1983).

During World War II, Chemung Co industries were fitted as defense plants, and home-front workers aided in the war effort. The county boasted a model civil defense program that included scrap metal drives, blackout tests, and the state's first "incident" drills, recommended by the State Civil Protection Office to the War Council in 1943. The Big Flats Materials Center (1940) was transformed from a CCC camp and nursery into a federal conscientious objectors camp. The US Army Quartermaster Corps' Holding and Reconsignment Point was located in Horseheads, a prison for German prisoners of war was in Van Etten, and a facility for former Italian prisoners of war was in Horseheads. The Chemung Co Airport (1933; now Elmira-Corning Regional Airport) was designated a defense landing area during the war.

Residential construction in suburban Chemung Co increased in the years following World War II. The opening of the Arnot Mall in 1967 shifted commerce from downtown Elmira to Big Flats. The four-lane Southern Tier Expressway (Rte 17/I-86) was constructed in Chemung Co between 1945 and 1985, increasing accessibility to the region and reducing railroad traffic. Industries such as Corning Inc (1958) and Ann Page (1965–80s), a division of the A&P grocery chain, built facilities that were easily accessible from the new highway. The construction of a north-south arterial from Southport to Horseheads was approved in 1974; the project is continuing into the 21st century.

Products manufactured in Chemung Co in the early 21st century include glass containers, structural steel, rail vehicles, ceramics, software, nuclear instrumentation, and aircraft. Major employers are MT Picture Display (formerly Toshiba Display Services), Hardinge Inc, Anchor Glass Container Corp, Hilliard Corp, Kennedy Valve (a division of McWane), Schweizer Aircraft Corp, Cutler-Hammer Eaton Corp, and two state prisons (Elmira, 1876, and Southport, 1991). Major industrial and commercial centers include Airport Industrial Park (1995), Consumer Square (1992), and the Arnot Mall (1967), all located in Big Flats.

The standard county history is [Henry B. Peirce and D. Hamilton Hurd], *History of Tioga, Chemung, Tompkins, and Schuyler Counties* (1879). Others available are Ausborn Towner, *Our County and Its People: A History of the Valley and County of Chemung* (1892), and Thomas E. Byrne, ed., *Chemung County, 1890–1975* (1976). A visual approach was used by Amy H. Wilson and Peg Gallagher in *Chemung County: An Illustrated History* (1999). The *Chemung Historical Journal* has been issued quarterly since 1955. Town histories include *Big Flats, New York Sesquicentennial History, 1822–1972* (1972); Hebert A. Wisbey, ed., *Veteran, New York Sesquicentenial History, 1823–1973* (1973); and Sylvia Smith, *Town of Ashland* (1999), a pictorial review. Elmira's history is treated centrally in each of the countywide publications.

Heather A. Wade

Chenango. Town (pop 11,454) in central Broome Co. A late Woodland Algonquin village (AD 1000–1200) located on Castle Creek just west of its confluence with the Chenango River was later occupied by Iroquois, who remained a few years after European American settlement in 1787. The town was formed in 1791. Lumbering was the dominant early industry. The first sawmill began operation in 1788. The Salina and Chenango Turnpike (1806) terminated at Chenango, and the Syracuse, Binghamton and New York Railroad passed through town beginning in 1854. Until 1855 the City of Binghamton, then a village, was in Chenango. I-81 was completed through town in 1968. Much of the town is hilly and rural, with suburban and commercial development in the Chenango River valley.

Charles J. Browne

Chenango Canal. A lateral canal connecting the Susquehanna River at Binghamton with Utica on the Erie Canal, the Chenango Canal was completed in 1836 and opened in 1837, chiefly transporting coal, iron ore, manufactured goods, and farm products. The canal cost $2.3 million to build while bringing in $744,000 in tolls over its lifetime: a financial failure for New York State. Engineered by John B. Jervis, the canal ran 97 miles (156 km) with 114 locks, including 76 locks in 23 miles (37 km) in the steep northern section of the canal in Oneida and Madison Cos. Jervis designed an innovative system of feeders (combined length, 23 mi/37 km) and seven reservoirs in the Hamilton (Madison Co) area to ensure there would be enough water in the summit level of the canal. Communities grew along the canal's route. Villages such as Port Crane (Broome Co) and Bouckville (Madison Co) were named for their locations on the canal or for canal commissioners. The Chenango Canal brought coal to Utica, encouraging steam manufacturing in that city. Railroad competition and high maintenance costs closed the canal in 1878. The summit-level feeder system was retained as a water source for the enlarged Erie Canal and eventually the Barge Canal.

McFee, Michele A. *Limestone Locks and Overgrowth: The Rise and Descent of the Chenango Canal* (Fleischmanns, NY: Purple Mountain Press, 1993)

Michele A. McFee

Chenango County (898 mi^2/2,326 km^2; pop 51,401). It was created from Herkimer Co and Tioga Co in 1798; Sangerfield (Oneida Co) was taken off in 1804, and Madison Co was split off in 1806. The county is presently divided into the City of Norwich and 21 towns that contain 8 incorporated villages. Norwich serves as county seat. The entire county lies within the Susquehanna Hills subregion of the Appalachian Upland landform province. With very limited exceptions it is underlain with Devonian shales and shaley sandstones that readily fracture into flagstone, a fact reflected in numerous stone quarries scattered about the county. Local topography is dominated by blocks of steep-sided, round-topped hills that rise 300–600 feet (90–180 m) above the major valley floors and occupy the interfluves. Elevations range from slightly over 2,000 feet (610 m) above sea level in the Pharsalia State Wildlife Management Area to 890 feet (271 m) where the Chenango River exits the county in the far southwest corner. The entire county was glaciated, and it exhibits an assortment of remnant glacial features, including eskers, kame terraces, kettles, and deltas. More striking are the large glacial and meltwater-enlarged valleys, partially filled with deep layers of outwash material from the retreating glaciers. These valleys, which trend north-south, contain the county's best farmland.

Chenango Co's climate is humid-continental. Seasonal temperatures are remarkably uniform across the county, with elevation being the primary local influencing factor. Normal mean July temperatures are 68–69°F (20–21°C), with daytime highs at times exceeding 90°F (32°C). Corresponding mean January temperatures are 21–22°F (-6°C), and nighttime lows sometimes drop to 0°F (-18°C) or below. Seasonal snowfall ranges from about 100 inches (250 cm) in the high country near the county's western margins to 52 inches (130 cm) in the southern Chenango Valley. Total annual precipitation averages between 38 and 44 inches (97 to 112 cm), with the county's northeast quarter receiving the lowest amounts. Major rivers, including the Chenango, Otselic, and Susquehanna, flow southwest except the Unadilla, which serves as part of the county's eastern boundary and flows south. All but the extreme southeast corner falls within the greater Susquehanna watershed. There are sulfur springs in a number of towns; one, Pitcher Springs, was briefly a spa in the 1830s. The area's primeval forest was, with few exceptions, an Alleghenian hardwood community dominated by

Detail from *Chenango Packet*, by unidentified artist, 1850s, on Chenango Canal near Binghamton.

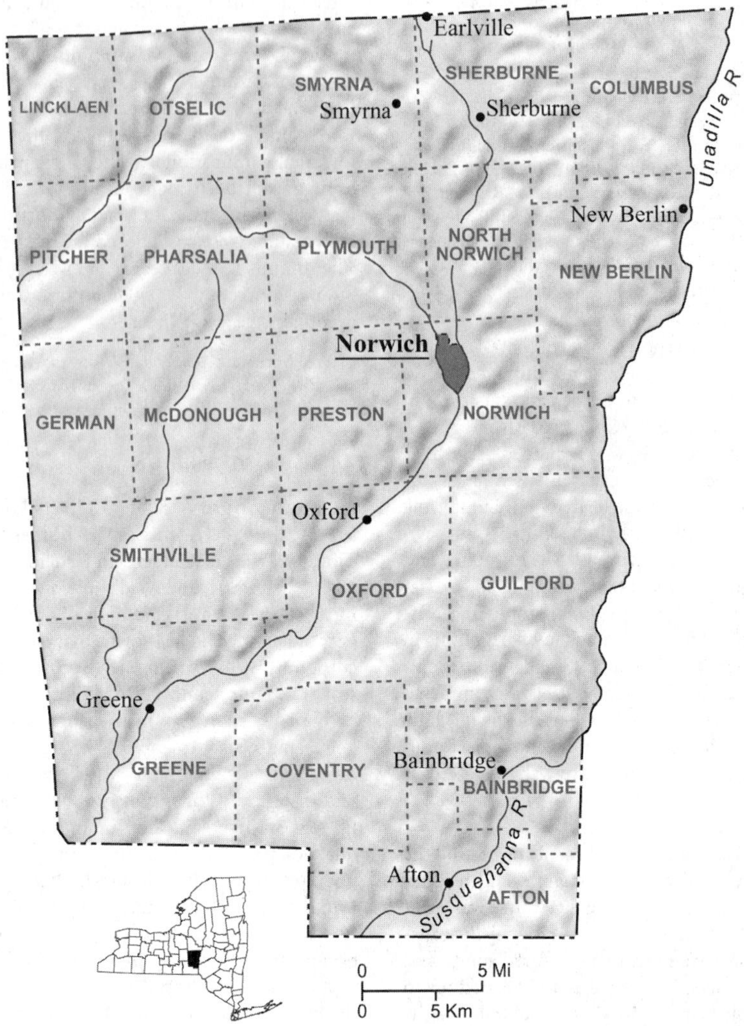

beech, sugar maple, hemlock, white pine, and basswood. All but the steepest of the upland slopes and isolated hilltops were cleared and farmed during the 19th century. Since then much of the less desirable farmland has reverted to second-growth woodland, which covers over 60% of the county.

Native Inhabitants

Archaeological evidence indicates at least two Paleo-Indian sites within Chenango Co that date from 10,000 to 12,000 years ago. Later the Oneida Nation established some settlements near what is now Afton and at Oxford while utilizing the rest of the area for fishing and hunting grounds. In 1741 the Tuscarora, who were leaving North Carolina, accepted an Oneida invitation to settle as their guests in the New Berlin and South New Berlin area. There were also Oneida settlements within the present county. The Treaty of Fort Stanwix (1768) established the Unadilla River as the western boundary of European settlement, thus designating what is now Chenango Co as Indian territory. The Indian population was devastated in two Revolutionary War campaigns. Col William Butler's party destroyed Indian villages along the Susquehanna in 1778; the next year Gen James Clinton led 1,800 men along the Susquehanna, destroying the Oneida villages near Afton. In the Revolution's aftermath the Oneida and Tuscarora were pressured to cede most of their lands in a sequence of treaties in 1784 and 1785 with the federal and state governments, including those of southern Chenango Co. This occurred even though they took a generally pro-Revolutionary stance during the war.

Settlement

The earliest European settlement is believed to have been in 1786, when Elnathan Bush and his family settled along the Susquehanna near Stowell's Island in what is now the Town of Afton. The state quickly sold the land it had acquired in the southern part of the county to individual settlers. By another treaty, concluded in 1788, the state acquired the northern part of Chenango along with much of present Madison Co and southern Oneida Co, dividing the entire tract into an area known as Chenango Twenty Townships, 11 of which lie within present-day Chenango Co.

Chenango Co settlers came predominantly from Connecticut, Massachusetts, Rhode Island, and eastern New York. Many were not averse to farming the poorer-quality hill land. In Bainbridge, the Vermont Sufferers received land grants from New York State in recognition of their loyalty in the face of Vermont's confiscation of their farms. A small colony of educated French refugees settled in Greene in 1792, but most left within a few years. The county's population, 21,000 in 1810, reached 40,000 by 1840, and remained relatively stable until 1870, when it began a protracted decline that lasted until 1950. The African American population was historically quite small, and few of those were enslaved. The minority population did not exceed 500, or approximately 1% of the county's total, until 1980. Aside from a single rural enclave south of Sherburne, Blacks resided in the larger villages, where they worked mostly as domestics, porters, and livery hands.

Economic Development

In early years, farmers produced wool, grain, beef, apples, and potatoes, shipping their produce south on the Chenango and Susquehanna Rivers or eastward along the turnpikes to Catskill [now in Greene Co] and Kingston (Ulster Co). Sawmills produced lumber for the Baltimore and Philadelphia markets. Potash was also produced. A rope-making business that began at South Otselic in 1816 subsequently expanded into fishing line, earning the settlement the title of Fishing Line Capital of the World. The immediate success of the Erie Canal (1825) prompted Chenango Co citizens to agitate for a branch canal, and the Chenango Canal was opened 12 years later and permitted industry to develop beyond the small shops serving local needs. Coal and iron ore were shipped in and finished products such as hammers and iron fencing were shipped to other areas. Hart Pottery in Sherburne imported clay from New Jersey and salt from Salina (Onondaga Co), sending finished stoneware to market. The canal also spurred the dairy industry beginning 1837–40, and farms in general increased in size and output. The first bank opened in Bainbridge in 1850. The Bank of Norwich followed in 1856, later became the National Bank of Norwich, and is now the National Bank and Trust Co (NBT), the county's largest.

The Albany and Susquehanna Railroad (later Delaware and Hudson) was chartered in 1851 but did not begin service along the Susquehanna Valley until 1867. Construction of the main line of the New York and Oswego Midland Railroad, later reorganized as the New York, Ontario and Western Railroad, began in Chenango Co in 1869 and was completed the following year, as was its New Berlin branch. The railroad made Norwich a division headquarters. Another branch was built west from Norwich into adjacent Cortland Co and beyond; due to limited economic potential, the Chenango Co section was soon abandoned. The Utica, Chenango and Susquehanna Valley Railroad (later Delaware, Lackawanna and Western) opened in 1870, providing the Chenango Valley communities with direct rail access to Utica and Binghamton and capturing enough of what had been barge traffic to doom the canal; it was abandoned in 1878. Rail transportation transformed established industries and helped create new ones. Regular train service proved instrumental, for instance, in the growth the dairy industry. By 1874 Chenango Co ranked first in the state in the number of cheese factories (48) and fourth in the domestic production of butter. Milk stations and creameries became important fixtures along the various rail lines. Bluestone was quarried at times in many towns. Quarries in Oxford and Norwich, for instance, shipped large quantities to New York City and Philadelphia for curbing. Other industries during this period were knitting mills at Norwich and Sherburne; during the 1880s about 600 Syro-Lebanese immigrants, drawn to work in the Ross Knitting Mill at Sher-

CHENANGO CO POPULATION CENSUS FIGURES

	White	Nonwhite	Total Population	Foreign-Born
1800	15,610	56	15,666	—
1810	21,615	89	21,704	—
1820	31,019	196	31,215	12
1830	36,969	269	37,238	1
1840	40,512	273	40,785	—
1850	40,047	264	40,311	970
1860	40,671	263	40,934	1,795
1870	40,259	305	40,564	2,779
1880	39,605	286	39,891	1,879
1890	37,474	302	37,776	1,876
1900	36,355	213	36,568	1,664
1910	35,378	197	35,575	1,815
1920	34,828	141	34,969	1,736
1930	34,495	170	34,665	1,760
1940	36,229	225	36,454	1,706
1950	38,947	191	39,138	1,553
1960	43,005	238	43,243	1,324
1970	46,010	358	46,368	900
1980	48,819	525	49,344	973
1990	50,911	857	51,768	821
2000	50,191	1,210	51,401	887

Notes: "Nonwhite" includes African Americans, Asians, American Indians, and Pacific Islanders and, for 2000, also the mixed race and other race categories. Through the 1960 census these figures primarily reflect the African American population. Foreign-born figures for 1820 and 1830 include only those not naturalized, and for 1930 and 1950, the foreign-born totals include Whites only. Other years include all foreign-born in the population.

burne, settled in the Sherburne Four Corners area. The county's best-known industry for nearly a century was Norwich Pharmacal Co (1885), manufacturer of aspirin, Pepto-Bismol, and Unguentine.

Religion, Education, and Culture

With settlers coming primarily from New England, the first church organizations were Presbyterian, at Jericho [now Bainbridge] in 1790, and Congregational, at Pharsalia in 1793, with Baptists, Methodists, and Episcopalians following soon after them. The Universalist Church attracted significant numbers during the early decades, but by 1950 they were all gone. Irish immigrants, drawn by canal construction, brought the Roman Catholic Church; the first congregation formed at Norwich 1854–55. Later, Italian Catholics moved into the county and found work on the railroads.

Oxford Academy was in operation before its 1794 charter date. Public schools came a few years later with the aid of state funding. Some schools in the larger villages became Union Free Schools beginning in the late 1860s. Modern school centralization started with Oxford in 1929; the last to centralize was Greene in 1941. Several central districts have since consolidated. The county is presently served by nine central school districts and one city school district. In 1969 SUNY Morrisville opened a branch campus at Norwich.

The county's first newspaper, the *Western Oracle,* began at Sherburne Four Corners around 1803. In the 19th century weekly newspapers were generally published at Norwich, Sherburne, New Berlin, and Oxford. In the early 21st century, weekly papers are published at Greene, New Berlin, Oxford, and Sherburne. The *Evening Sun,* a daily, is published in Norwich. In the 19th century the larger towns had opera houses or theaters that hosted lectures, concerts, and theatrical events. Of these, only the restored Earlville Opera House survives. The Chenango County Council on the Arts is housed in a renovated theater and gallery space in Norwich.

Politics

Political power broker Thurlow Weed lived in Norwich briefly (1818–20) and made strong political statements in his newspaper, the *Republican Agriculturalist.* The *Anti-Masonic Journal* was published at Norwich from 1826 to 1835. Chenango Co voters have a longstanding record of supporting Republican Party candidates. The county is governed by a board of supervisors consisting of one representative from each town and two from the City of Norwich. The supervisor's votes have been weighted according to population since 1969. Day-to-day operations of county government are overseen by the board chair, who is elected by the board.

Recent History

After decades of decline, the county's population began to increase in the 1940s and surpassed 50,000 in 1990, with the bulk of the growth associated with town in the Susquehanna and Chemung Valleys. The number of farms operating in Chenango Co declined steadily over the course of the 20th century, from 4,473 in 1900 to 2,689 in 1950 to 801 in 1997. The landscape changed as valley farms were consolidated and hilltop farms were abandoned. Viable commercial farming in the early 21st century is essentially restricted to the superior soils of the larger valleys. The state established the Pharsalia Game Preserve (now Pharsalia State Wildlife Management Area) in 1926 on land deemed better suited for forestry than for farming. During the depression, Civilian Conservation Corps camps at Sherburne and Pharsalia worked to reforest abandoned farmland across the county. By 1936 the state had acquired about 50,000 acres (20,200 ha) of land in Chenango Co for reforestation. The area has since grown to 73,000 acres (29,500 ha), or about 12.5% of the county's total area, as many people left farms during World War II for military service or civilian employment. The Sherburne State Game Farm (1909) operated until the early 1960s and then, through local initiative, was converted to the Rogers Environmental Education Center (1966). The county is also home to Bowman Lake and Hunts Pond State Parks, and the Otselic State Fish Hatchery.

Chenango Co lost many jobs in the second half of the 20th century as manufacturers like American Separator (Bainbridge), Craine Silo (Norwich), and Bennet-Ireland Foundry (Norwich) closed down or left the area. In the 1990s the county lost Procter and Gamble, successor to Norwich Pharmacal. After struggling with insolvency for 20-odd years, the Ontario and Western Railroad ceased operations in 1957. In the early 21st century, rail freight service is provided by the Canadian Pacific (formerly Delaware and Hudson) and the New York, Susquehanna and Western (formerly Delaware, Lackawanna and Western).

Some old firms remain; for example, the Raymond Corp of Greene, founded in 1840 as the Lyons Iron Works, manufactures forklift trucks. With the construction of I-88 through the southern part of the county in the 1970s, Afton and Bainbridge became bedroom communities for Binghamton and Oneonta. In recent decades tourism arose with the hope for prosperity by drawing visitors to historical, outdoor recreational, and hunting facilities around the county. There was also a modest number of new residents moving in from New York City to retire in the villages or to build homes in the surrounding countryside.

Prominent Chenango Co natives and residents include renowned "mountain man" Jedediah Strong Smith (1799–1831), born in Bainbridge; Mormon leaders Joseph Smith Jr, who lived in Afton in the late 1820s, and Brigham Young, who lived in Smyrna from 1804 to 1817; Norwich native Gail Borden Jr (1801–74), inventor of condensed milk; Otselic native George W. Ray (1844–1925), member of the House of Representatives (1883–85, 1891–1902); Harry Stack Sullivan (1892–1949), psychiatrist; Tompkins Harrison Matteson (1813–84), artist; and Norwich resident Warren E. Eaton (1888–1934), aviation pioneer.

Chenango has one of the earliest county histories, Hiram C. Clark, *History of Chenango County* (1850), which was followed by James H. Smith, *History of Chenango and Madison Counties* (1880). Most towns have been studied, and their histories began with Joel Hatch Jr, *Reminiscences, Anecdotes, and Statistics of . . . Sherburne* (1862). Edward Danforth, *Stones from the Walls of Jericho* (1987) provides an excellent topically organized history of Bainbridge up to recent years, and G. Herbert Entwistle Jr, "A History of New Berlin, NY, to 1907" (MA thesis, Colgate Univ, 1953), covers the first century.

Michele A. McFee

POPULATIONS OF TOWNS AND CITIES, CHENANGO CO

Town or City, Year Founded	1800	1840	1880	1920	1960	2000
Afton, 1857	—	—	2,248	1,840	2,245	2,977
Bainbridge, 1791[a]	939	3,324	1,924	2,009	3,177	3,401
Columbus, 1805	—	1,561	1,177	683	706	931
Coventry, 1806	—	1,681	1,317	733	859	1,589
German, 1806	—	965	664	365	253	378
Greene, 1798	655	3,462	3,378	2,917	4,624	5,729
Guilford, 1813[b]	—	2,827	2,441	1,818	2,368	3,046
Lincklaen, 1823	—	1,249	901	532	364	416
McDonough, 1816	—	1,369	1,298	765	639	870
New Berlin, 1807	—	3,086	2,572	2,104	2,633	2,803
North Norwich, 1849	—	—	964	619	1,096	1,966
Norwich, 1793	2,219	4,145	5,756	1,063	2,587	3,836
Norwich (city), 1915	—	—	—	8,268	9,175	7,355
Otselic, 1817	—	1,621	1,512	996	854	1,001
Oxford, 1793	1,405	3,179	3,035	2,871	3,457	3,992
Pharsalia, 1806[c]	—	1,213	1,147	553	515	542
Pitcher, 1827	—	1,562	1,075	609	650	848
Plymouth, 1806	—	1,625	1,302	885	1,004	2,049
Preston, 1806	—	1,117	909	618	753	928
Sherburne, 1795	1,282	2,791	3,128	2,820	3,338	3,979
Smithville, 1808	—	1,762	1,492	843	891	1,347
Smyrna, 1808[d]	—	2,246	1,651	1,058	1,055	1,418

Note: In 1800 Chenango Co included the Towns of Brookfield, Cazenovia, Hamilton, and DeRuyter [now in Madison Co] and the Town of Sangerfield [now in Oneida Co].

[a]Jericho until 1814.

[b]Eastern until 1817.

[c]Stonington until 1808.

[d]Stafford when formed; renamed same year.

Chenango Twenty Townships. Officially called the Governor's Twenty Towns, Governor's Purchase, or Clinton's Purchase, they are now in Oneida, Madison, and Chenango Cos. Part of lands acquired from the Oneida by the Treaty of Fort Schuyler (1788), its 484,000 acres (195,868 ha) were surveyed by Horace P. Schuyler into 20 numbered townships in 1789 and sold by auction to speculators. The speculators sold the land in smaller parcels to settlers, who were principally from southern New England. Settlement began in some of the towns as early as 1791, but others were not laid out until 1802. In some cases proprietors or agents were present, but in others purchasing was difficult and conducted over long distances. The new residents transplanted the cultural landscape of their native towns, such as village greens, to the region.

Darlington, James W. "Peopling the Post-Revolutionary New York Frontier," *New York History* 74 (Oct 1993): 341–81

Michele A. McFee

Cherry Creek. Town (pop 1,152) and village (pop 551) in NE Chautauqua Co. The town was settled in 1815 and formed from Ellington in 1829. In early years six kilns produced charcoal. Later barrels, cheese boxes, brooms, and ironwork were made. The Buffalo and Southwestern Railroad was built through town in 1875. The village incorporated in 1893. In 1900 the Cherry Creek Canning Co employed 175–200 in season. Cherry Creek is the site of Cockaigne Ski Area and of an Amish community begun around 1950. Dairy farming is its main industry, and Empire Livestock Market is an important component of the economy.

Joyce Chase

Cherry Grove and Fire Island Pines. Localities in Brookhaven (Suffolk Co) on Fire Island. They are notable for being among the earliest and most prominent gay and lesbian resort communities in the United States. In 1869 Archibald Perkinson purchased the land that would later form the basis of Cherry Grove, named after the indigenous wild cherry trees. The Perkinson Hotel (1880) became the isolated community's center; residents included fishers and several prosperous families. Becoming more accessible with the new highways on the Long Island mainland in the 1920s, Cherry Grove gradually became a resort for New York City's theatrical community, including a small number of gay men. The hurricane of 1938 was disastrous, destroying 65 of its 85 houses, but recovery was swift. Encouraged by proximity to the city, privacy, scenic beauty, and the freedoms the community offered during an era of rigid social and legal restrictions against homosexuals, Cherry Grove became a vibrant resort for gays and lesbians in the 1940s.

It attracted gifted artists and writers, including painter Paul Cadmus, poet W. H. Auden, and writer Truman Capote. Inspired by the rich cultural atmosphere, the Arts Project of Cherry Grove (1948) sponsored revues, chorus line numbers, and concerts for the surrounding community. By the 1950s almost all renters were gay, as were an increasing number of the property owners. A more ethnically and socially diverse group of men and women began to arrive in the 1960s and 1970s, drawn by word of mouth, publicity in the gay press, and job opportunities in the growing numbers of restaurants and bars. For many years the Cherry Grove Property Owners Association ran the only gay-controlled locality in the United States.

Cherry Grove has not always been a refuge from homophobia. Gay residents have faced verbal or physical abuse from neighboring Long Islanders, incidents not always reported by the local press. In the summer of 1953, Brookhaven police staged a series of raids, arresting men on charges ranging from perversion to indecent acts. Although police harassment largely abated after the 1969 Stonewall riots in New York City, periodic hostility to Cherry Grove and Fire Island Pines residents remains a concern.

Fire Island Pines lies immediately east of Cherry Grove. Developed in 1952 and known as the Pines to its residents, it became an increasingly gay enclave by the 1960s. Offering more privacy and space than Cherry Grove, the Pines also became a fashionable alternative to its neighbor. By the mid-1980s famous homeowners included Broadway star Tommy Tune and designer Calvin Klein.

Both communities suffered tragic losses with the spread of the AIDS epidemic in the 1980s and were at the forefront of fund-raising for AIDS awareness and treatment. In recent decades, rental and ownership statistics for lesbians in both communities have increased. Although since the 1970s other gay resorts have come to prominence, Cherry Grove and Fire Island Pines probably remain the best-known resorts for gays, lesbians, bisexuals, and transsexuals in the early 21st century.

Newton, Esther. *Cherry Grove, Fire Island: Sixty Years in America's First Gay and Lesbian Town* (Boston: Beacon Press, 1993)

Joshua Ruff

Cherry Valley. Town (pop 1,266) and village (pop 592) in NE Otsego Co. John Lindesay and others received a royal patent in 1738, and Scots-Irish families from Londonderry, NH, settled in the area in 1741. On 11 Nov 1778 British and Indian forces attacked, killing 32 civilians and taking others captive to Canada. Resettlement followed the war's end, and the town was formed in 1791 from Canajoharie (Montgomery Co). The village was the terminus of the First Great Western Turnpike (1799) and the starting point of others running westward; this stimulated commercial and cultural growth. The village, incorporated in 1812, was the site of an early post office (1794), academy (1796), and bank (1818). The Erie Canal (1825) and the New York Central Railroad (1853) diverted much traffic away from the village. Nationally known melodeons and parlor organs were produced in mid–19th century; limestone was quarried and ironwork was produced in the same era. Cherry Valley's economy declined rapidly after the Civil War, even though the town became the terminus of a railroad branch from Cobleskill in 1870. The Cherry Valley Turnpike, built in the 1920s as part of US 20, promoted tourism, but a 1954 rerouting bypassed the village. Agriculture, shifting from wheat to hops to dairy, has preserved a largely rural landscape; the 9,200-acre (3,723 ha) Lindesay Patent Rural Historic District was placed on the National Register in 1995. In the late 20th century, professionals and retirees sparked a modest revival in the village's commercial and cultural life. The hamlet of Salt Springville on the town's northern border hosts an annual music festival. Oakwood (1820s) is a quaint three-story house with square towers at each corner.

Hugh C. MacDougall

Cherry Valley raid. Revolutionary War engagement on 11 Nov 1778. Cherry Valley [now in Otsego Co] and other farming communities in Tryon Co were an important source of food for the Continental army, and British strategy in 1778 called for their destruction. A stockade built around the Cherry Valley church that year was named Fort Alden after Col Ichabod Alden, who commanded the nearly 300 men of the Seventh Massachusetts Regiment of the Continental army sent to Cherry Valley in July 1778 to protect the settlement. A message arrived on 6 November from Fort Stanwix [now Rome, Oneida Co] that an attack was imminent. Col Alden dismissed it and did not allow the settlers to move into the fort for protection. Alden and his officers were lodged in homes outside the fort. The approaching enemy consisted of approximately 700 men, almost half of whom were Iroquois (mostly Seneca), and the rest were from Butler's Rangers and the Eighth Regiment of Foot. Walter Butler, son of ranger commander John Butler, and the Mohawk Joseph Brant were among the leaders of the expedition. The attack came early on the morning of 11 November. Alden was quickly killed, and most of the officers either killed or captured. His remaining troops successfully defended the fort, but a contingent of Indians plundered and burned the village. Historical accounts differ, but some indicate a split within the Iroquois at Cherry Valley, with the Seneca primarily responsible for the destruction and Joseph Brant trying to protect the residents. Approximately 16 soldiers and more than 30 civilians, including women and children, were killed. Butler, Brant, and their men left with more than 70 captives but released most of the women and children within two days. A small force returned the next day to complete the destruction of the buildings outside the fort and to gather the livestock. The Cherry Valley raid and other attacks on the frontier settlements of New York State in 1778 prompted the Sullivan-Clinton campaign against the Iroquois in 1779. A monument to those killed in the raid was erected in 1878 in the Cherry Valley Cemetery.

Graymont, Barbara. *The Iroquois in the American Revolution* (Syracuse: Syracuse Univ Press, 1972)

Swiggett, Howard. *War Out of Niagara: Walter Butler and the Tory Rangers* (New York: Columbia Univ Press, 1933)

Christine Sternberg Patrick

Chesecock Patent. In 1702 a group of New York City residents and others fronted by Dr John Bridges purchased land in the present Orange and Rockland Cos from the native inhabitants. In 1707 Gov Edward Hyde, Viscount Cornbury, confirmed the purchase by awarding them the Chesecock Patent. It was surveyed by Charles Clinton *ca* 1740 and was settled gradually during the 18th century.

Ruth Piwonka

Chester. Town (pop 3, 614) in N central Warren Co. Settled in 1789, the town was formed from Thurman in 1799. Farming and sheep raising were replaced by tanning after 1835. The Joseph P. Leggett homestead served as a station on the Underground Railroad. Resorts developed *ca* 1900 at Friends, Loon, Mountain Spring, and Schroon Lakes. In the mid–20th century residents worked at an overalls factory, a glove factory, and a chipping mill; in 2003 the mill remained in operation as Northeastern Products Co. The Natural Stone Bridge and Caves at Pottersville is a tourist attraction. The Word of Life is a religious school and summer camp at Schroon Lake. Literary figure Jeanne Robert Foster and Irish painter John Butler Yeats are buried in Chestertown Rural Cemetery.

Marilyn J. Van Dyke

Chester. Town (pop 12,140) and village (pop 3,445) in central Orange Co. Settled in 1712, the town was formed in 1845 from Goshen, Warwick, Blooming Grove, and Monroe. The Erie Railroad came through in 1841, and local farmers began to ship their milk by rail in the following year. Chester was later a large and important producer of cream cheese. Muck farming began during the Civil War era, and beginning *ca* 1905 Italian farmers became dominant, using the rich soil to grow onions and other vegetables. The village, which is partly in Goshen, was incorporated in 1892. In the 20th century farming diversified to include poultry, and in the early 21st century muck farming remains important. The four-lane Rte 17 (I-86) opened in 1954. Sugar Loaf hamlet, where iron was mined in the 19th century, is an important tourist destination. Chester is the site of Goose Pond Mountain State Park and the birthplace of Hambletonian (1849–76), a famous trotting horse.

Rita Bahren

Chesterfield. Town (pop 2,409) in N Essex Co. Settled in 1792 it was formed from Willsboro in the same year. After settlement (?1806–7) Keeseville grew into an industrial village with iron and pulp industries. Port Kent on Lake Champlain was a busy lumber port but declined by 1885; it remains the landing for the Burlington, Vt, ferry. The Delaware and Hudson Railroad (1875) provided transportation for industrial products; the Northway (1967) provides excellent highway connections, both north and south, for commuters and tourists. In the early 21st century an industrial park housed four small industrial operations. The Ausable Chasm is partly in town. Elkanah Watson (1758–1842), agricultural reformer, lived at Port Kent from 1825 until his death.

Thomas A. Rumney

chestnut blight. See TREE DISEASES AND PESTS.

Chestnut Ridge. Village (pop 7,829) in Ramapo (Rockland Co). A group of Scots settled in the area, and a post office called Scotland served the area from 1827 to 1848. Later the area of the present village was known as South Spring Valley. The village incorporated in 1986 to control zoning. Near the Garden State Parkway Extension (1957) in the southern part of the village are several industrial parks. Education and sustainable agriculture were the original purposes of Threefold Community (1926), based on the ideas of Rudolf Steiner; it now includes the Green Meadow Waldorf School (1950), the Fellowship Community (1966, elder care), and Sunbridge College (1986). The Little Red Schoolhouse Museum (1890) is a local landmark. The Jerrahi Mosque (1990) is the American headquarters of the Jerrahi Order of Sufism.

Child [née Francis], **Lydia Maria** (*b* Medford, Mass, 11 Feb 1802; *d* Wayland, Mass, 20 Oct 1880). Abolitionist author and editor. Though most of her career was spent in her native Massachusetts, she lived with Quaker abolitionists Joseph and Mary Carpenter in New Rochelle (Westchester Co) in 1835–36 and again in 1847–49. In 1841 she moved to New York City to edit the *National Anti-Slavery Standard* and, aside from the time spent with the Carpenters, lived in Manhattan until 1850. While working in New York City, Child published several children's books and two volumes of *Letters from New York* (1843, 1845) based on a column begun in the *Standard*. She boarded with Quaker abolitionist Isaac Hopper and family in Manhattan, and after Hopper's death in 1852 wrote *Isaac T. Hopper: A True Life* (1853). Child also edited Rochester resident Harriet Jacobs's *Incidents in the Life of a Slave Girl* (1861).

Clifford, Deborah. *Crusader for Freedom: A Life of Lydia M. Child* (Boston: Beacon Press, 1992)

Karcher, Carolyn L. *The First Woman of the Republic: A Cultural Biography of Lydia M. Child* (Durham, NC: Duke Univ Press, 1994)

Christopher Densmore

child labor. With industrialization the problem of the employment of children in the workplace became widespread. By the late 19th century children would be employed in nearly every industry that employed adults, including rolling cigars, milling cloth, forging iron, and weaving carpets. Though factories were where the employment of children was most significant, they also worked on farms and in domestic service. Some lines of business were largely reserved for child workers, such as delivering messages, shining shoes, and selling newspapers. Employers saw children as a low-wage and generally pliant source of labor, and they became an important component of the state's factory labor force. For example, the Harmony mills in Cohoes (Albany Co) in 1886 employed 3,200 workers, of which 38% were under 16 years of age and 6% were 12 or younger. According to the 1880 US census approximately 50,000 of New York State's factory workers, or 4% of all industrial workers in the state, were younger than 16. Many school-age children worked rather than attended classes. In the city of Albany in 1880 only 39% of the approximate 35,500 children of school age attended the public schools. Many of these youngsters were ruthlessly exploited by their industrial employers; at the Harmony mills, for instance, child workers were routinely forced to work 12–16 hours per day. Working upward of 90 hours a week, children were also given some of the most dangerous tasks, such as getting underneath and in between swift moving looms.

Early Reform Initiatives

Such practices began to bring calls for change. One of the earliest state reformers was Charles Loring Brace, who in 1853 founded the Children's Aid Society. Based in New York City, Brace's organization sought to ameliorate the child labor problem by enrolling children in school. As a result of the efforts of Brace and others, in 1874 the state legislature enacted the Compulsory Education Law. This law required that all children from 8 to 14 years of age attend 14 weeks of school annually and that children could only work after receiving a certificate from school documenting their attendance. Few if any schools enforced the law, however, and it provided no extra funds for schools to inspect factories to ensure compliance. The labor movement also took up the cause of abolishing child labor, but its voice was somewhat muted since many working parents viewed their children's wages as essential to family survival.

New York State was in the vanguard of child reform efforts, which achieved another victory in 1886 when Gov David B. Hill signed the Factory Act into law on 18 May. The act barred all children 12 and younger from factory work (the ban was raised to 14 in 1889), required all working 13–16 year olds to have proof of age on file with their employer, and banned children from working 60 hours or more per week. However, only 2 state inspectors were hired to monitor compliance for the more than 43,000 manufacturing establishments that existed in the state. By 1896 the state inspection force had grown to 29, and 11 years later 51 inspectors were on the job. Not surprisingly these regulations had little effect. State inspectors reported in 1900 that children younger than 16 still constituted 4% of the workforce at factories inspected—the same percentage as in 1880. Further calls for reform came from the New York Child Labor Committee (NYCLC), formed in Manhattan in 1902. Composed largely of wealthy Protestant and Jewish reformers, the NYCLC dedicated itself to strengthening state labor protections for children. In 1903 the NYCLC sponsored several bills that were ratified with bipartisan support. The Finch-Hill Factory Act and the Finch-Hill Commercial Establishments Act made employers liable for children illegally employed by them and also limited children 16 or younger to working 9 hours or less per day. Others laws made school mandatory for children up to 14 years of age and required night school for all 14–16 year olds not in regular daytime school.

Reform and Structural Change

If these good intentions were not always backed up with enforcement, by 1920 there was a marked decrease in child labor. The 1920 US census reported the percentage of New York State's 10–14 year olds working in nonagricultural work to be less than one-third of what it had been two decades earlier. Increased agitation eventually resulted in more rigorous enforcement of child labor laws. The National Child Labor Committee, founded in New York City in 1904, brought national attention to the issue, especially through the remarkable photographs of Lewis Hine. Other laws that addressed child labor indirectly at best also played a crucial role. Workplace safety measures passed after the 1911 Triangle Shirtwaist Factory fire and the state's Workmen's Compensation Act of 1913 raised the cost and liability for child workers. Other changes to the structure of business were influential as well. Low-wage immigrants and African American migrants replaced children in some lines of work, such as shining shoes and selling newspapers. Automation and the telephone rendered other forms of child labor obsolete. The proponents of "scientific management," advocating the use of well-trained adults, scorned children because they had a reputation for sloppiness and unreliability. The Great Depression, the sweeping unionization drives of the 1930s, and tough federal laws provided the final push to end most forms of nonagricultural child labor in New York State.

Even after the rollback of such practices in industry, agriculture was notorious in its long-term exploitation of child workers. Although the 1903 Finch-Hill Factory Act applied to canneries, most of the state's canners got around the act by placing their initial vegetable processing in separate wooden sheds beside their plants, where youngsters did the initial unpacking and cleaning of vegetables. A 1912 investigation by the state legislature's Factory Investigating Commission (FIC) documented the notorious practice of the sheds and the wide-scale employment of children. In 1913 the FIC passed specific legislation barring the use of sheds, but later inquiries noted that even as late as the 1930s canners still openly violated the law. The use of children as field pickers on farms was also difficult to address. As late as 1937 the New York State Department of Labor had no legal authority over agriculture. Relying on a cheap and temporary workforce, many state farmers employed seasonal migrant workers—some as young as 9—to work from sunup to sundown to pick their crops. A 1939 probe by the NYCLC discovered that approximately 25% of all migrants at farms in Cortland, Genesee, Madison, Ontario, Seneca, Sullivan, and Ulster Cos were younger than 16. The problem grew worse during World War II and the immediate postwar period, when large numbers of underage southern black migrants were used as seasonal farm harvesters. More effective enforcement under the gubernatorial administrations of Thomas E. Dewey and W. Averell Harriman largely eliminated the problem by the late 1950s.

Although not as widespread as in the early 20th century, child labor continues to be a small but chronic problem in some sectors of state industry. Large numbers of children, primarily Asian and Latino migrants, constitute a significant aspect of the state's garment labor force, particularly in Manhattan's Chinatown and Brooklyn's Sunset Park. To help address this problem in 1996 Gov George E. Pataki signed into law a bill that forces all garment manufacturers to register with the state's Department of Labor and a "Hot Goods" bill that empowers the state attorney general to confiscate garments made by manufacturers who violate the labor law, including child labor infractions. Moreover to further increase awareness of garment trade abuses, in June 1997 the state assembly created the Subcommittee on Sweatshops, chaired by Assemblyman Felix W. Ortiz (D-Brooklyn).

Felt, Jeremy P. *Hostages of Fortune* (Syracuse: Syracuse Univ Press, 1965)
Nasaw, David. *Children of the City: At Work and Play* (New York: Oxford Univ Press, 1985)
New York Child Labor Committee. Papers. NYS Library, Albany
New York State. Department of Labor. *Migrant and Child Labor on New York State Farms, Summer 1947* (Albany: Author, 1948)

Tod M. Ottman

Children and Family Services, Office of. State agency created in 1998 that took over certain functions of the Department of Social Services and the Division for Youth, which were abolished by the 1997 New York State Welfare Reform Act. The office's responsibilities include foster care, adoption aid, preventative health services for children and families, and protective services for children and vulnerable adults. Many of these services trace their origin to the Children's Law of 1875, which succeeded in removing children from ineptly run poorhouses. The system of child welfare further improved in 1915 when mothers began to receive cash allowances and in 1922 when statewide children's courts were developed. The 1940 Social Welfare Law consolidated state authority and created the pattern of local responsibility for many social service functions. The office is also responsible for the services performed by the State Commission for the Blind and Visually Handicapped, established in 1913. The office's Native American Services unit is a liaison between local social service districts and tribal groups and Indian nations regarding the implementation of the Indian Child Welfare Act.

The services for troubled youth provided by the office were developed after World War II in response to a rise in juvenile delinquency. A temporary New York State Youth Commission was established in 1945 to study and make recommendations relating to the problems of youthful offenders and to provide local governments with financial and technical assistance for delinquency projects. This body was reorganized in 1956 as a permanent Youth Commission. Gov Nelson A. Rockefeller appointed a task force on youth and juvenile delinquency in 1959 to study state youth policy, resulting in the Division for Youth in 1960. The Youth Commission was renamed the Council on Youth and functioned as a consultative group to the division's director. The division assumed all the functions of the Youth Commission and was sanctioned to set up centers for the rehabilitation of delinquent youth. In 1971 youth-care facilities operated by the Department of Social Services were transferred to the custody of the Division for Youth and continue to be administered by the current office. The office's Division of Rehabilitative Services operates more than 40 juvenile residential facilities housing more than 2,000 youth remanded by family and criminal courts, providing guidance and financial aid to localities to develop and operate youth detention facilities and delinquency prevention programs. Headquartered in Albany, the agency employed 4,200 staff and oversaw a budget of $3.2 billion in 2003.

Richard Andress

Children's Aid Society. This child welfare institution formed in New York City in 1853 and was directed by one of its founders, Charles Loring Brace, until his death in 1890. Striving to improve working conditions and provide housing for children at risk, the society became famous for its orphan trains, which carried homeless children from New York City to Midwestern farm families who needed laborers. Between 120,000 and 150,000 children were placed in homes by the end of the program in 1929, after which the society's foster program was limited to placing children within New York State. In New York City, the society established industrial schools and, for working children, night schools and lodging houses. In the 50 years after 1953, participation in neighborhood centers increased, services to foster care providers and adoptive parents were expanded, Head Start schools and free breakfasts in schools were implemented, educational programs and dental and medical care were initiated. In 2001 the society offered more than 100 programs to 120,000 New York City children and their families in the areas of education, health, counseling, adoption, foster care, career readiness, arts and recreation, and emergency assistance.

See also CHILD LABOR.

Children's Aid Society: http://www.childrensaid society.org

O'Connor, Stephen. *Orphan Trains: The Story of Charles Loring Brace and the Children He Saved and Failed* (Boston: Houghton Mifflin, 2001)

Ruth Shackelford

child welfare. Network of services provided to poor, abused, and neglected children.

COLONIAL PERIOD

In the early colonial era, poor children with parents were usually supported in their own homes by the town, and orphaned children were placed in homes under terms of a written agreement called an indenture. Occasionally poor children were "boarded out" to a family paid to care for them. During the 18th century almshouses became popular, with New York City establishing the first publicly supported one in 1736. After the 1788 poor law authorizing all towns and cities to establish them, they spread throughout the state. In these overcrowded, unsanitary institutions, some children lived with people who were insane, senile, or suffering from incurable diseases, but most lived with at least one parent. An 1856 New York State study reported the appalling condition of children in almshouses and recommended that they be placed in orphanages instead, a shift in policy that reflected a change in attitude toward the poor. In the colonial era, poverty was seen as a misfortune that could befall anyone. By the 1850s its persistence led reformers to attribute it to a lack of morals that was apparently hereditary, given that the children in families receiving public relief often grew up to make their own claims on relief. To "save" children from this life, it was necessary to separate them from their parents' influence.

THE RISE OF THE ORPHANAGE

The first orphanage opened in New York State in 1806. Most orphanages were charitable institutions administered by sectarian religious groups (Protestant, Roman Catholic, and Jewish). There were few of them until after the Civil War, when 63 operated in New York State. Many of these privately run orphanages received financial support from the state until it was discontinued in 1872, and several institutions were in danger of closing for lack of funds. The state legislature then passed the Children's Act of 1875, requiring all children between the ages of 2 and 16 be removed from almshouses and placed in orphanages or other institutions, which then received a per capita fee from the appropriate locality. This locally based public support for private children's institutions became known as the New York System. By 1885 there were 204 orphanages in the state, some caring for more than 1,000 children.

Most orphanages in New York State were congregate institutions consisting of one building where children lived, worked, and went to school. Because of their emphasis on uniformity and discipline, orphanages came under attack in the late 19th century by philanthropists who believed that children belonged in families. The most famous of these was Charles Loring Brace, who headed the New York Children's Aid Society, which he helped establish in 1853. His efforts in support of family homes contributed to a new movement aimed at preserving needy families.

MOTHERS' PENSIONS AND AFDC

Mothers' pensions, first established in New York State in 1915, paid widowed mothers to care for their children in their own home; the laws were later expanded to include married women whose husbands were mentally or physically incapacitated or imprisoned. In 1920 New York State paid $2.8 million on such pensions. While they helped only a small fraction of needy families, they did help establish the standard of family-based care that led to the Aid to Families with Dependent Children (AFDC) program (then called Aid to Dependent Children), a federally funded, state-administered welfare system established under the Social Security Act of 1935. New laws guaranteed federal reimbursement of half of the amounts paid by states to support children who were deprived of parental support because of the absence of or physical or mental incapacity of one or both parents. AFDC also supported children in foster homes (earlier called boarding homes). In the 1940s the number of families in New York State receiving AFDC remained at around 25,000. In the 1950s the numbers began to increase as child welfare agencies became professional state agencies and federal social welfare dollars increased, with the number of families on AFDC rising from 69,000 to 256,000 during the 1960s. In the 1970s and 1980s, as the economy slipped deeper into recession, a number of federal and New York State initiatives attempted to reduce AFDC by funding preventative programs, such as daycare, housing, and drug treatment centers, and by forcing AFDC recipients to work or participate in training programs to avoid losing their benefits. Even with these attempts, welfare costs continued to rise in the 1990s.

ABUSED AND NEGLECTED CHILDREN

In the colonial era, parents were given wide discretion in child rearing, and discipline could be harsh, even cruel. A particularly heinous case of abuse of an 8-year-old girl in 1874 led New York State to enact laws making it a crime to abuse or neglect children. The New York Society for the Prevention of Cruelty to Children (NYSPCC), established in 1875, was granted powers of arrest and investigation to enforce the new laws. In 1880 it set up the first shelter for abused children and became a model for advocates of the protection of children. In 1973 New York State enacted the Child Protective Services Act, which required each county to establish a child protective service to receive and investigate reports of child abuse and mistreatment, to protect children from further abuse or mistreatment, and to provide rehabilitative services. The act also required that a statewide Central Register of Child Abuse and Maltreatment be established to track all cases of abuse or neglect. The register maintains a telephone hotline 24 hours a day, 7 days a week, where anyone can report child abuse or neglect.

RECENT DEVELOPMENTS

In 1996 Pres Bill Clinton signed the Personal Responsibility and Work Opportunity Reconciliation Act (PRWORA). Under the new system, the AFDC cash assistance program was eliminated, and states were allotted block grants for Temporary Assistance for Needy Families (TANF), which could be used to support whatever welfare programs the states chose. To qualify, states had to require TANF recipients to work at least 30 hours a week after two years of assistance or lose benefits and to set a lifetime limit of five years that families could receive TANF benefits. New York State adopted the provisions of PRWORA in the Welfare Reform Act of 1997. From 1995 to 2000, the number of recipients of TANF benefits in New York State dropped 45%, from 1,266,350 to 693,012. Of the 573,338 cases dropped in this period, 371,203, or 65%, came from New York City. This compares with a drop of 58% nationally, from 13.9 million to 5.7 million, over the same period.

Lindsey, Duncan. *The Welfare of Children* (New York: Oxford Univ Press, 1994)

O'Connor, Stephen. *The Story of Charles Loring Brace and the Children He Saved and Failed* (Boston: Houghton Mifflin, 2001)

Piven, Frances Fox, and Richard A. Cloward. *Regulating the Poor: The Functions of Public Welfare* (New York: Vintage Books, 1993)

Schneider, David M. *The History of Public Welfare in New York State, 1609–1866* (Chicago: Univ of Chicago Press, 1938)

Schneider, David M., and Albert Deutsch. *The History of Public Welfare in New York State, 1867–1940* (Montclair, NJ: Patterson Smith, 1969)

Ruth Shackelford

Chileans. See SOUTH AMERICANS.

Chili [CHY-LYE]. Town (pop 27,638) in SW Monroe Co. Permanent settlement commenced in 1792. German Americans from Pennsylvania and New Jersey settled some years later at South Chili. The town was formed from Riga in 1822. It was served by the Tonawanda Railroad (1837; later Buffalo and Rochester) and the Genesee Valley Canal (1840); ultimately four railroads crossed the town. Chili Seminary (1866) has evolved into Roberts Wesleyan College. Manufacturing included brickyards, a fertilizer plant, and the Standard Sewer Pipe Co (1902). The Greater Rochester International Airport is largely in the town. Chili's 1950 population of 5,283 more than doubled within a decade and continued to increase rapidly until the 1980s. Most of the suburban development is north of Black Creek, while the southern part of town is largely rural. Black Creek County Park offers trails through 1,500 acres (607 ha) of woods and wetland. The landmark Cobblestone Schoolhouse is a one-room school museum, and Chili Mills (1811) is listed on the National Register of Historic Places.

Carolyn Vacca

Chinese. The movement of Chinese into New York State in the 19th century was part of a much larger Chinese migration into various countries as many fled natural disasters, clan wars, and peasant rebellions. At the same time, Western powers imposed a series of unequal treaties on China, forcing it, among others, to pay heavy indemnities for lost wars. These crises exacerbated

Chinese immigrants arriving at the railroad depot in Ogdensburg, *ca* 1915.

the poverty of Chinese peasants. Meanwhile, the rapid development of capitalism created a huge demand for cheap labor in the United States and the European colonies in Southeast Asia, South Africa, and Latin America. Many Chinese peasants who survived the wars and disasters wanted to try their luck overseas.

Prior to the 1950s, Chinese immigrants and their descendants who made up the Chinese diaspora were primarily from two southeastern provinces in China, Guangdong (Canton), and Fujian. In the early 19th century, the burgeoning China trade hastened the rise of New York City as a leading port, and coupled with the trade, the coming and going of Chinese sailors led to the formation of New York City Chinatown, arguably the first Chinese American community. In the 1850s there were 150 Chinese living in New York City and only a few others statewide.

Most of the early Chinese population in New York State came from California. In 1842 Hong Kong, formerly part of Guangdong became a British colony, and between 1848 and 1851 more than 25,000 Cantonese immigrated to California on steamships that had begun traveling between San Francisco and Hong Kong. Attracted by the California gold rush and employment opportunities in building the transcontinental railroad in the 1860s, most Chinese immigrants settled in the western United States. But the industry and frugality of Chinese immigrants soon made them the targets of racial hostility: mob attacks and discriminatory laws, such as the Chinese Exclusion Act, beginning in 1882 and continuing into the early 20th century. These laws not only denied Chinese immigrants entry into the United States but also deprived them of the privileges to be naturalized as citizens and to send for their wives. To avoid the escalating racial discrimination, many Chinese moved east to larger cities in the 1880s. In 1880 the census counted 909 Chinese in New York State. By 1890 that count had reached 2,935. The actual number was probably much larger, however, because the census did not count many transient immigrants. Most early Chinese immigrants wished not to settle permanently in America but to return home with their earnings.

Community Life and Culture through World War II

Various forms of discrimination continued in New York State during the 19th and early 20th centuries, including negative stereotypes in newspapers and other publications, anti-coolie rallies organized by Tammany Hall in 1870, and several joint actions to restrict Chinese laundries during the 1890s. Many Chinese entered the United States across the Canadian border, both in the Buffalo/Niagara region and at the North County border. In the early 20th century, 621 Chinese were jailed in Port Henry (Essex Co) for violating the Exclusion Act in crossing that border. Plattsburgh (Clinton Co) and Massena (St. Lawrence Co) also had Chinese jails for such detentions. Unable to send for their wives, the Chinese remained effectively single, which kept vices such as prostitution and opium smoking alive for many decades.

Because of occupational discrimination, the Chinese could not find mainstream employment. From the 1880s to the 1960s, 80–90% of the Chinese in the state had concentrated in such service industries as restaurants and hand laundries. Early Chinese laundries were undoubtedly begun by those who had worked at New Jersey steam laundries and were discharged in the early 1880s. Most in New York State were either owned by one man or jointly owned by a few fellow townsmen or kinsmen. As a result, group loyalties between fellow townsmen and kinsmen outweighed class consciousness, and labor militancy remained low. New York Chinese were rarely part of the established American labor movement until the 1960s.

Denied permission to be naturalized as citizens, the Chinese for decades could not vote or participate in many of the institutions of society to redress their grievances. Some became political activists nonetheless. Journalist Wong Ching Foo moved to New York City in 1874 and in both English and Chinese language publications urged naturalized Chinese to take an active part in American politics. In 1915 a few hundred American-born Chinese in New York City organized the Chinese American Citizens Alliance to help members exercise their franchise. They made great, though unsuccessful, efforts to mobilize against the established order in Chinatown.

Chinese in New York State originally practiced an eclectic brand of religion, taking various elements from Buddhism, Taoism, and folk beliefs. The Christian Church of New York City began to proselytize the Chinese as early as the 1850s, and some Chinese churches were founded; the First Chinese Presbyterian Church of New York City, founded in 1868, was one of them. But because of their deep-rooted polytheism and sojourner mentality, few of the first-generation Chinese ever became Christians. Since the 1960s small groups of new immigrants from Taiwan and Hong Kong, along with some second-generation Chinese Americans, have founded congregations in New York State, such as the Christian Testimony Church on Long Island and the Rochester Chinese Christian Church, but the majority of the New York Chinese remain non-Christians.

Rendered politically and economically powerless by racism and without a unifying church to serve as a community center, New York City Chinese employed symbols and forms in their tradition for mutual help. People with the same family names, for example, formed surname associations, while those from the same counties in Guangdong formed district organizations. Such regional and kinship loyalties both united and divided the Chinese. Intergroup strife often arose from conflicting interests and was further complicated by the struggle between different secret societies known as Tongs. Turf wars between different Tongs were especially frequent from the late 1910s to the early 1930s, claiming dozens of casualties.

In New York City, an umbrella organization, the Consolidated Chinese Benevolent Association (CCBA), came into being out of the necessity to coordinate the interests of various organizations. Registered with the state government in 1890, the CCBA incorporated and had jurisdiction over all Chinese organizations within the boundaries of New York City until the late 1960s. Other important organizations included the Chinese Chamber of Commerce of New York (1903), the Chinese Hand Laundry Alliance of New York City (1933), and the Chinese Restaurant Association of New York (1934). For decades the New York branch of the Kuomintang (KMT) had joined hands with the CCBA to maintain the status quo of the Chinese community. The alliance, however, has been challenged by some leftist organizations in the New York Chinese community: the Chinese Anti-Imperialist Alliance in the late 1920s and early 1930s, the Chinese Hand Laundry Alliance from the 1930s to the 1950s, and the pro-mainland faction from the 1950s to the early 21st century. From the late 1920s to the mid-1930s, a group of Chinese leftists in New York City, mostly visiting students associated with the Communist Party USA, organized the Chinese Anti-Imperialist Alliance.

New York City Chinatown was long the center of social and cultural life for the nonprofessional Chinese in New York City. Because Chinese laundries and restaurants had to be scattered to be close to enough customers, most New York City Chinese had lived outside Chinatown, but on weekends, the enclave was a magnet, providing an opportunity to socialize and shop for the upcoming week. Even in 2002 most Chinese social organizations of New York City were located in Lower Manhattan. Over the years, Chinatown gradually expanded. In the late 19th century, it was bounded by Mott, Pell, and Doyers Sts; by the 1990s it had grown northward beyond Canal St into the former Little Italy, eastward to the bank of East River, and southward to City Hall. In 2000 New York City published nine Chinese newspapers, mostly in the Chinatown area, including *World Journal* (pro-Taiwan) and *China Daily* (pro-mainland).

Post-1945

World War II marked a watershed in the history of New York State Chinese. Factory work opened, and with the repeal of the Chinese Exclusion Act in 1943, increasing numbers of Chinese immigrated to the United States; more came as families, and more were naturalized as citizens. The Chinese community began to shift from being a bachelor's society to being a family community. After the Chinese civil war (1946–49), about 5,000 Chinese students previously sent by the KMT government became stranded in the United States, fearing persecution if they returned home. Many settled in New York State, boosting significantly the professional Chinese population in the state. Two, Zhenning Yang (SUNY Stony Brook) and Zhengdao Li (Columbia University), later became Nobel laureates in physics.

A more fundamental transformation of the Chinese community took place after the mid-1960s when the liberal 1965 Immigration Act passed Congress. Enjoying a larger quota than other countries, the Chinese now came by the tens of thousands each year from Hong Kong, Taiwan, northern China, Vietnam, and elsewhere. Many were professionals. The Civil Rights Movement for African Americans, and its Chinese American analogues, tore down the racial barriers impeding the Chinese community for decades. After World War II, second-generation Chinese Americans came of age, and increasing numbers of new immigrants became citizens. Consequently, more New York State Chinese became politically active. New York City Chinese founded radical organizations like the I Wor Kuen (1969) and the Basement Workshop (1971). However, for various reasons—including unfamiliarity with American political procedures, the often unfriendly attitude of poll workers, and Chinese tradition emphasizing modesty and nonaggressiveness—New York Chinese participation in electoral politics is still low in comparison with some other ethnic groups.

By the 1960s it had become easier for Chinese, especially professionals and second-generation Chinese Americans, to find mainstream employment. More and more established their homes outside of New York City. The number of Chinese in Long Island had grown to 10,500 by 1970 and to 17,934 by 1990. There were 627 Chinese living in the Rochester area in 1970 and 3,015 in 1990. A large part of the non-New York City Chinese were professionals working for major US companies and research institutes such as Eastman Kodak, Xerox Corp, Computer Associates, Symbol Technologies, and SUNY Stony Brook. Unlike the older immigrants, who organized themselves along the clan or district lines, the professional immigrants and second-generation Chinese who worked and lived outside of New York City formed various clubs and societies, such as the Chinese Center on Long Island (1960) and the Chinese Community Center of the Capital District of New York (1973), for entertainment and for educating their children in Chinese culture.

Although after the 1960s the Chinese population outside New York City increased rapidly, more than 80% are still concentrated in New York City because the majority of the post-1965 immigrants were laborers. Because of the language barrier and higher rents outside, most of them chose to settle in Manhattan Chinatown. Meanwhile, an ethnic enclave economy, marked especially by the rise of the Chinese garment industry in the 1960s, changed the economic profile of New York State Chinese. Realizing that the new immigrants were reluctant to live outside of Chinatown, employers located their clothing factories in the enclave to be close to their workers. When Manhattan Chinatown became saturated in the early 1980s, two new Chinese enclaves, one in Flushing (Queens Co) and the other in Sunset Park (Kings Co), emerged. In the 1990s the three Chinatowns together housed nearly half of New York State's Chinese population. The garment factories predominantly employed Chinese immigrant women, who often worked under sweatshop conditions, which nurtured labor militancy. During a general strike in 1982, almost all the 20,000 Chinese seamstresses walked off and forced their employers to compromise. Since the 1960s most of the Chinese garment workers have joined the International Ladies' Garment Workers' Union (now UNITE), and some restaurant workers have been affiliated with the AFL-CIO Hotel and Restaurant Employees and Bartenders Union.

New economic opportunities since World War II also changed the way in which the nonprofessional Chinese organized themselves. Because the garment factories and large restaurants hired dozens of workers, the immigrants from different regional and kinship backgrounds had a good opportunity to mix with each other. Gradually, their regional and kinship loyalties declined. The CCBA authority has been eroded by the services provided by new types of organizations, such as the Chinese-American Planning Council (1965). Relying on the city and state governments for funds, these new organizations attract more and more immigrants seeking employment information and other kinds of counseling. Since the late 1990s increasing numbers of Chinese clothing factories have moved out of Manhattan Chinatown primarily because of rising rents. Meanwhile, new Chinese garment factories and residential centers have emerged in Queens and Brooklyn.

The Chinese are a rapidly growing ethnic group in New York State. The Chinese population in the state had reached 424,774 by 2000, up from 1990's 285,332 and 1980's 147,250. Prominent New Yorkers of Chinese background include I. M. Pei, an internationally renowned architect based in New York City for decades; Charles Wang, founder, chair, and CEO of Computer Associates International, one of the world's largest software companies, based in Islandia (Suffolk Co); and New York City's Vera Wang, one of the world's more famous fashion designers.

See also ETHNIC PRESS.

Kwong, Peter. *Chinatown, New York: Labor and Politics, 1930–1950* (New York: Monthly Review Press, 1979)

———. *The New Chinatown* (New York: Hill & Wang, 1987)

Sung, Betty Lee. *The Adjustment Experience of Chinese Immigrant Children in New York City* (Staten Island: Center for Migration Studies, 1987)

Wang, Xinyang. *Surviving the City: The Chinese Immigrant Experience in New York, 1890–1970* (Lanham, Md: Rowman & Littlefield, 2001)

Xinyang Wang

Chittenango. Village (pop 4,855) in Sullivan (Madison Co). The waterpower of Chittenango Creek and a junction point of major roads, including the Genesee and Madison County Turnpikes, contributed to the settlement's early development. A manual labor school, the Polytechny (1825–37) reopened as Yates Polytechnic Institute (1853–71). The village incorporated in 1842. Nineteenth-century products included wool cloth (1824–66), cotton cloth (1869), and paper. The Chittenango Furnace manufactured an airtight stove for over 70 years, and the Merrell-Soule Canning Factory (1883–1947) processed local produce. The village's 1940 population of 885 grew rapidly with housing for World War II veterans' families. In the early 21st century, with no major industry in Chittenango, many residents find employment in Syracuse. The birthplace of L. Frank Baum (1856–1919), author of *The Wizard of Oz,* the village celebrates this distinction with an annual OzFest. The Chittenango Landing Canal Boat Museum exhibits the repair and dock facilities furnished by a sidecut waterway from the old Erie Canal route.

William F. Helmer

Choate, Joseph H(odges) (*b* Salem, Mass, 24 Jan 1832; *d* New York City, 14 May 1917). Attorney and diplomat. Educated at Harvard and Harvard Law School, Choate was admitted to the Massachusetts Bar in 1855 and moved to New York City in 1857. One of New York City's leading lawyers for many decades, he successfully overturned Gen Fitz-John Porter's Civil War era court-martial in 1886 and convinced the US Supreme Court of the unconstitutionality of the federal income tax in *Pollock v Farmer's Loan and Trust Co* (1895). As a so-called Swallowtail Republican, he opposed boss rule, supported commercial interests, and remained independent of party discipline. He helped launch Theodore Roosevelt's political career in 1880. Choate presided over the New York State Constitutional Convention of 1894 and successfully campaigned for its ratification by voters. From 1899 to 1905 he served as ambassador to Great Britain, and at the end of his life he promoted American support for the British cause in World War I. A well-known clubman and speaker, he was a founder and trustee of the American Museum of Natural History.

Strong, Theron. *Joseph H. Choate: New Englander, New Yorker, Lawyer, Ambassador* (New York: Dodd, Mead, 1917)

Jon Sterngass

cholera. Before 1832 this waterborne bacterial disease was not found in North America, but in that year it was introduced into the United States through New York State. As the world suffered from a cholera pandemic, North Americans hoped that the Atlantic Ocean would act as a protective barrier, but on 6 June 1832 cholera was reported among Irish immigrants at Montreal. Within days of its arrival, accounts from the Champlain Valley, Whitehall (Washington Co), and Mechanicville (Saratoga Co) confirmed its southerly progression. A second entry route into New York State was through the St. Lawrence River and the Great Lakes. It is also possible that cholera entered through New York City, but information of its presence was suppressed by local authorities. The disease was attributed to sinfulness, contagion, miasma, unchecked immigration, ethnicity, or race. Medical treatments in the 19th century included bleedings; ingestion of sometimes massive doses of quinine, camphor, morphine, and exotic teas; and application of mustard patches, leeches, turpentine, and cayenne peppers. None of these remedies proved effective.

New York State public health responses were comparatively primitive at first, but by 1832 they included state-mandated local health boards, establishment of simple welfare services, slum clearance programs, and food and drug regulations. The New York City Board of Health and its associated committees erected five temporary cholera hospitals at various locations. City streets that had accumulated several decades of excrement, dead animals, garbage, and other waste were cleaned and covered with tons of quicklime. The 1832 cholera epidemic dissipated in the early winter, but the disease reappeared several times during the remainder of the 19th century. In an 1849 epidemic similar health measures were instituted with a similar lack of success. After Robert Koch's 1883 discovery identifying the bacterial agent *(Vibrio cholerae)* that caused the disease, Hermann M. Biggs and T. Mitchell Prudden, working on behalf of the New York City Department of Health at the New York Quarantine Station at Staten Island, used cholera culture methods in 1887 to stop newly arrived immigrants who were infected with cholera from spreading the disease. Subsequent outbreaks in 1854, 1866, and 1892 occurred in such cities as Buffalo, Rochester, Utica, and Albany. It is estimated that more than 150,000 persons died nationally as a result of the 1832 and 1849 pandemics; 50,000 fatalities occurred in 1866.

Rosenberg, Charles E. *The Cholera Years: The United States in 1832, 1849, and 1866* (Chicago: Univ of Chicago Press, 1962)

G. William Beardslee

Christian Churches (Stone-Campbell movement and Christian Connexion). The conviction among 19th-century American Protestants that primitive, apostolic Christianity could be restored by following the New Testament as the sole authority spawned a number of enduring denominations. These included the three Stone-Campbell churches (Disciples of Christ, Churches of Christ, and Christian Churches/Churches of Christ), and the Christian Connexion, which merged with the Congregational Church in 1931.

Four independent groups were involved. The earliest arose in Virginia among the Methodists, led by James O'Kelly (1757–1826) in 1894. The second was the result of the work of Abner Jones (1772–1841) and Elias Smith (1769–1846) in Vermont and New Hampshire among the Baptists (1801). The third was spearheaded by Barton W. Stone (1772–1844) among the Presbyterians in Kentucky and Ohio after 1804. The fourth was led by Thomas Campbell (1763–1854) and his son Alexander (1788–1866), Northern Ireland–born Presbyterians living south of Pittsburgh after 1809 and later situated among the Baptists in Pennsylvania, West Virginia, and Ohio.

The Campbell and Stone churches began merging in 1832. Since the congregations in both cases were fiercely independent, the merger took place church by church in local communities. There were no Stone Christians in New York State in 1832, but there were a few from a Scottish Baptist, then Campbellian, background. The presence of churches from this merger was first noted in the latter half of the 1830s, and by 1860 a conservative estimate showed 5,000 New York members of what is now largely known as Christian Churches.

The O'Kelly, Jones/Smith, and Stone churches that did not enter the merger became known as the Christian Connexion after the Civil War. Although several of these churches amalgamated into the Stone-Campbell movement in Ohio and westward, fewer did so in New York. The Jones/Smith wing of the Christian Connexion was strong in Central New York. By 1823 it had 77 ministers in the state, and from 1820 to 1860 its key leaders lived in the Finger Lakes region, the most noted being Joseph Badger (1792–1852) and David Millard (1794–1873). The Jones/Smith churches differed from those of the Stone-Campbell movement in that they retained the emphasis of the Second Great Awakening upon a conversion experience and the hegemony of ordained ministers. The Stone-Campbell churches were more rationalistic, emphasizing baptism for the remission of sins, weekly communion, and independent congregations led by elders and deacons. The Christian Connexion established headquarters in Dayton, Ohio, after the Civil War. It merged with the Congregational Church in 1931, forming the Congregational-Christian Church, which became known as the United Church of Christ after a merger with the Evangelical and Reformed Church in 1957.

Toward the end of the 19th century, members of Protestant churches clashed over the social gospel, evolution, and biblical criticism. Those on the left rallied around the designation "modernism," and those on the right, "fundamentalism." Most Protestants remained in the middle. The Stone-Campbell churches were wracked by these same controversies. Modernists could be found especially among ministers trained at Yale and the University of Chicago. Those on the left in the Stone-Campbell movement came to be known as the Disciples of Christ (Christian Churches). They moved away from primitivist orientations and gradually embraced social concerns and progressivism in science, theology, and biblical studies. At the end of the 20th century Disciples members in New York State are mostly located in Western New York and metropolitan New York City. Their official report lists 62 churches and 7,818 members.

At the turn of the century Churches of Christ began to emerge from the Disciples of Christ and were designated a separate entity in the federal census of 1906. Leaders emphasized strict biblical interpretation, opposed mission societies and musical instruments in worship, and eschewed scientific and theological modernism. The oldest congregation in New York State with continuing existence was founded in Manhattan in 1920, with the numbers increasing after World War II, especially in Central and Western New York and Long Island. In the postwar years, an effort of the Churches of Christ to stimulate domestic missions was exemplified by "Exodus Bay Shore," which encouraged church members to move to Bay Shore (Suffolk Co) to further the work of the church. This church soon established its permanent base in West Islip. Black churches in the denomination were often at the forefront of the Civil Rights Movement. Franklin Florence, minister of a Church of Christ in Rochester, became the president of FIGHT (Freedom, Integration, God, Honor, Today), which challenged both government and private businesses in respect to their records on integration. The Churches of Christ, the largest of the Stone-Campbell heritage churches in the state and in the United States, now have 97 churches and 9,397 members in New York State.

In the 1930s the Christian Churches/Churches of Christ began to separate from the Disciples in New York. The focal points of the differences with the Disciples included the rejection of open church membership, evolutionism, and radical biblical criticism. For several years ministers in these churches, sometimes designated as Independent Christian Churches, were trained in Bible colleges rather than in liberal arts colleges to be followed by a seminary education, characteristic of the Disciples of Christ. These churches are the strongest in Central New York and metropolitan New York City. Christian Churches/Churches of Christ now comprise 58 churches and 4,285 members.

Hughes, Richard T. *Reviving the Ancient Faith: The Story of Churches of Christ in America* (Grand Rapids, Mich: Eerdmans Publishing, 1996)

McAllister, Lester G., and William E. Tucker. *Journey in Faith: A History of the Christian Church (Disciples of Christ)* (St. Louis: Bethany Press, 1975)

North, James B. *Union in Truth: An Interpretive History of the Restoration Movement* (Cincinnati: Standard Publishing, 1994)

Thomas H. Olbricht

Christian Science. Religious denomination. Mary Baker Eddy (1821–1910) founded the Church of Christ, Scientist, in Boston in 1879, based on the teachings of her book, *Science and Health* (1875). She claimed to have discovered the spiritual meaning underlying the Scriptures, including Jesus' scientific method of healing the sick and reforming the sinner. Between 1885 and 1891 four Christian Science Institutes were chartered in Manhattan, with another established in Brooklyn. In 1889 Eddy lectured in Manhattan's Steinway Hall to over 1,000 people. By this time churches were being formed in other large cities across the state, and by 1890 Christian Science academies and institutes had been established in Binghamton, Syracuse, and Buffalo.

Mary Baker Eddy sent several of her important students to New York City to establish Christian Science activities, and in 1887 First Church of Christ, Scientist, was established. Augusta Stetson, appointed pastor in 1888, also founded the New York Christian Science Institute in 1890. In 1891 Laura Lathrop organized Second Church of Christ, Scientist. At first meeting in public halls, congregations grew rapidly enough to support the building of two sizable edifices on Central Park West in 1901 and 1903. Stetson's First Church of Christ, Scientist, designed by prominent architects Carrère and Hastings, was the largest and most expensive branch church in the nation at the time, and smaller churches were built in towns and villages across the state. At the church's peak, Stetson had a group of 25 professional Christian Science practitioner-healers, and by 1908 the church's reading room greeted over 50,000 visitors a year. Stetson not only controlled her own students but was competitive with other teachers and even with Eddy, and amid great controversy she was excommunicated in 1909.

In the first two decades of the 20th century, churches with seating for over 1,000, many designed in a Neoclassical style, were being erected in Manhattan, Buffalo, and Rochester. Increasingly hostile criticisms were heard from traditional pulpits and the medical establishment. In 1912 Willis Vernon Cole, a Christian Science practitioner in New York City, was found guilty of practicing medicine without a license. In 1914 the Appellate Division of the Supreme Court of New York upheld the verdict, which was overturned in 1916 by the Court of Appeals. *People v Cole* was a nationally recognized case that secured the rights of Christian Scientists to practice their religion in New York State.

Though the Christian Science Church does not report membership statistics, available figures indicate that by 1890 the state had nearly 1,300 church members and more church services than any other state. By 1906 there were 51 churches with approximately 5,600 members, and in 1936, 157 churches were listed with possibly 15,000 members. By 1976 the number of churches had declined to 127 and by 2000 to 79, with congregations in larger cities consolidating their memberships and jointly maintaining public reading rooms for study and dissemination of denominational literature.

Gottschalk, Stephen. *The Emergence of Christian Science in American Religious Life* (Berkeley: Univ of California Press, 1973)

Ivey, Paul E. *Prayers in Stone: Christian Science Architecture in the United States, 1894–1930* (Urbana: Univ of Illinois Press, 1999)

Paul E. Ivey

Christmas Park. The first school to teach men and women to play Santa Claus was founded in 1937 by Charles W. Howard in Albion (Orleans Co). A longtime Santa at R. H. Macy in New York City, Howard started the school, known as Christmas Park from 1953, because the job performance of many Santas, from their appearances to their personalities and demeanors, disappointed him. In 1937 one student enrolled and paid $15 to attend the school. By the 1940s tuition was $40 per student, and class sizes grew steadily. In 1953 Howard converted his family farm into a holiday-themed amusement area, Christmas Park; the site soon became a major tourist attraction with a carousel, games, animals portraying reindeer, and human personnel portraying elves. He continued to teach Santa classes at his school at the park as well as throughout the nation and world. Howard and Ruth, his wife, ran the Albion school until his death in 1966. Sold in the late 1970s, Christmas Park moved to Midland, Mich, where the school operates as the Charles W. Howard Santa School.

Levy, Alan. "This to Be a Sophisticated Santa," *Saturday Evening Post,* 12 Dec 1964

Ronni Kent and Erin Bohen

Chrysler Building. Manhattan skyscraper. William H. Reynolds, a former New York State senator and real estate speculator, leased a building site on Lexington Ave between 42d and 43d Sts to construct an office tower that would be the tallest structure in the world, designed by architect William Van Alen. Reynolds's financial problems, however, allowed Walter P. Chrysler, founder of Chrysler Motors, to purchase the lease and Van Alen's plans in 1927. Chrysler worked with the architect to modify the original design, incorporating symbols of the auto industry, including projecting stainless steel eagle-headed gargoyles derived from Chrysler hood ornaments and winged decorations based on radiator caps. It is capped with a shining metal needle atop a succession of smaller stainless steel–clad arches. A decorative frieze of hubcaps is featured on the building's exterior, and the lobby ceiling contains an Art Deco mural by Edward Turnbull with the theme of modern transportation. Groundbreaking took place in September 1928, and the building opened in May 1930. The structure was briefly the world's tallest building, reaching 1,046 ft, 4.75 in (318.94 m) from the pavement to the top of its spire, until surpassed by the Empire State Building in 1931. The 68th and 69th floors originally were dedicated to the Cloud Club, an executive dining room, while the 71st floor was an observation deck open to the public. The space above this level, to the 77th floor, was not leased to commercial tenants but housed mechanical equipment and, at one time, broadcasting facilities for CBS Radio. In 1998 the building was acquired by Tishman Speyer Properties, which has faithfully renovated the structure's exterior and lobby. Still a dominant feature in the Midtown skyline, the Chrysler Building is a high point of American Art Deco.

The Chrysler Building (New York: Chrysler Tower Corp, 1930)

Curcio, Vincent. "The Chrysler Building." In *Chrysler: The Life and Times of an Automotive Genius* (New York: Oxford Univ Press, 2000)

Eric Wolf

Church, Frederic Edwin (*b* Hartford, Conn, 4 May 1826; *d* New York City, 7 Apr 1900). Landscape painter. As a youth Church studied with two Connecticut painters, Benjamin H. Coe and Alexander H. Emmons, before moving to Catskill (Greene Co) at 18 to become the first pupil of Thomas Cole from 1844 to 1846. Church adopted much of Cole's artistic philosophy and established a lifetime association with the Catskill region and the Cole family. Within three years of settling in New York City in 1846, Church's studio output of northeastern scenes and historical landscapes precociously gained him full membership in the National Academy of Design in Manhattan. Peripatetic by temperament, he traveled first through New England, then in 1853 to Colombia and Ecuador, where he was accompanied by future Atlantic Telegraph entrepreneur Cyrus W. Field. During their five-month trek they were guided by the writings of Prussian geographer Alexander von Humboldt, who had toured Latin America a half century earlier. In 1857 Church returned to Ecuador with a colleague, Louis-Rémy Mignot. These experiences were pivotal for Church. He became a broadly knowledgeable amateur scientist, and his self-confidence, artistic skill, and visual memory increased. After his marriage in 1860 to Isabel Mortimer Carnes (1836–99) of Dayton, Ohio, he enlarged a functioning farm near Hudson (Columbia Co) into a family homestead. He toured the Near East and Europe with his family between 1867 and 1869. From 1870 to 1876, and again between 1888 and 1891, he designed and supervised construction of a Persian-style mansion on a hilltop above his farm. From 1868 to 1880 Church painted a sequence of Mediterranean themes in which venerable architecture and ruins were the main components. Late in life, afflicted by rheumatism that curtailed his artistic output, he journeyed 15 times to Mexico, largely for reasons of health.

Church was the leading and most gifted second-generation Hudson River school artist. His celebrity peaked around 1860, when contemporaries on both sides of the Atlantic called him America's greatest artist and remarked on his grand New World subjects, which reached "from tropics to pole." His major studio works, all geographic in theme, operatic in scope, intimate in detail, and historic in their connotations, include *Niagara Falls* (1857), *The Heart of the Andes* (1859), *Twilight in the Wilderness* (1860), *The Icebergs* (1861), *Cotopaxi* (1862), *Niagara Falls, from the American Side* (1867), *Jerusalem* (1871), and *Syria by the Sea* (1873). His spirited oil studies and drawings, prized by connoisseurs during his lifetime, claim a modern following of their own. Now a state historic site, his house, which Isabel Church named Olana, and its 250-acre (101 ha) property have been a public park and museum since 1966.

Carr, Gerald L. *Frederic Edwin Church: Catalogue Raisonné of Works of Art at Olana State Historic Site* (New York: Cambridge Univ Press, 1994)

Huntington, David C. *The Landscapes of Frederick Edwin Church* (New York: George Braziller, 1966)

Kelly, Franklin. *Frederic Edwin Church and the National Landscape* (Washington, DC: Smithsonian Institution Press, 1988)

Gerald L. Carr

Church of Jesus Christ of Latter-Day Saints. See MORMONS (LATTER-DAY SAINTS).

Churchville. Village (pop 1,887) in Riga (Monroe Co). By 1814 Samuel Church owned two mills on Black Creek. The locality grew as a trading center for surrounding farms after the Tonawanda Railroad (1837; later New York Central) came through. It was the birthplace of temperance activist Frances Willard (1839–98). The village was incorporated in 1852. Industry included the Cummings and Turner Agricultural Implement Works. In the 1940s R. T. French shipped canaries across the nation from his large commercial aviary. Churchville is largely a residential community. Churchville Park (1928) covers 742 acres (300 ha) and includes a boat launch on Black Creek.

Carolyn Vacca

Cicero. Town (pop 27,982) in NE Onondaga Co. Settled in 1790, the town was formed in 1807 from Lysander. Many Cicero residents made a living producing barrels for the Syracuse salt industry after the Erie Canal (1820) allowed its expansion. Cicero was crossed by the first plank road in the United States (1846) and by the Syracuse Northern Railroad (1871). Along its Oneida Lake shore, resort hotels flourished beginning in the 1890s. One-third of the town's area is within the Cicero Swamp, much of which became state land in 1944, now Cicero Swamp State Wildlife Management Area. Improved roads (I-81, built 1954–57, and I-481, completed 1986) have encouraged rapid suburbanization, but in 2003 farmers continued grain and vegetable production. Paul de Lima Coffee Co (1916) employs 100 and remains in the de Lima family. The Log Frame House (*ca* 1840) and the Stone Arabia Schoolhouse (1854) are open seasonally.

Barbara J. Dunlap

Cincinnatus [SIN-SIN-AY-TUS]. Town (pop 1,051) in SE Cortland Co. Settled in 1795, the town was formed in 1804 from Solon. The Otselic River forms a valley with steep ridges on both sides. About 1870 Cincinnatus turned to producing butter and cheese. In the late 19th century the town was a large manufacturer of sleighs. The town made an unsuccessful attempt in the 1870s to acquire a rail line but succeeded in 1898; the line was abandoned in 1961. Agriculture remains the main industry, while Cincinnatus Central School is the largest employer.

Cathy A. Barber

circuses. The modern three-ring circus, with its high-wire acts, clowns, wild animal tamers, jugglers, acrobats, and horseback riders, has evolved in the United States from its beginnings at the turn of the 19th century in New York State. Englishman John Bill Ricketts, a superb horseman, demonstrated his skills and daring at the Greenwich Theater near the Battery in New York City in 1795, accompanied by a clown, tightrope walker, and other trick riders. An innkeeper in Somers (Westchester Co), Hachaliah Bailey, bought from a ship captain for $1,000 an African elephant he named Old Bet, which he exhibited from 1808 until 1816, when a farmer who thought the money spent on circuses was immoral shot and killed it. Nevertheless, the popularity of Bailey's touring menagerie in Westchester Co sparked an interest among residents in neighboring Putnam and Dutchess Cos, and the three-county area became known as the Cradle of the American Circus.

In 1816 Nathan A. Howes, born in Brewster (Putnam Co), organized a circus and menagerie with his brother Seth B. Howes and two men from Westchester Co, British immigrant Aaron Turner and George F. Bailey, Turner's son-in-law and the nephew of Hachaliah Bailey. Joshuah Purdy Brown of Somers invented the circus tent in 1825; Nathan Howes and Turner introduced the round top to circus audiences. Tents gave the circus owners mobility and lessened the need to rent buildings or sites in towns and cities, increasing the number of small circuses that traveled in caravans of horse-drawn wagons throughout New York. Turner introduced the street parade, which brought the performers, animals, curiosities, and calliopes through the town's main street in wagons to stir excitement before the shows opened. Bailey left Howes and Turner to run his own circus, featuring in its menagerie the first hippopotamus in the country. Seth Howes started his own circus in 1848, both in the United States and England, sometimes with partners. One of his contributions was using elaborately carved, ornate English wagons, which added to glamour and ostentation to the circus parades. James R. Raymond of Carmel (Putnam Co) brought new excitement to the traveling menagerie shows with the appearance of Isaac A. Van Amburgh as a lion tamer. Van Amburgh soon left to start his own troupe, and his name became synonymous with daring animal acts. In 1826 a 3,500-seat theater was built on Broome St in New York City as a venue for the Mount Pitt Circus; it was destroyed by fire in August 1829. Britain's Thomas Taplin Cooke built an amphitheater in the Bowery district of New York City in 1836 as a home for his show, Cooke's Olympic Circus. It too was destroyed by fire only six months later, but Cooke continued to tour the United States through 1840.

New York City–born Dan Rice was renowned as the King of American Clowns. His stars-and-stripes costume became the model for political cartoonist Thomas Nast's image of Uncle Sam. As an animal tamer, his specialties were pigs and mules, but he also had a tightrope-walking elephant and a rhinoceros in his shows. On 14 Jan 1835, several men gathered in Somers to form the Zoological Institute, which merged 13 menageries and three circuses. Also called the Flatfoot Party, it leased property at the Amphitheatre at 37 Bowery in New York City for its winter exhibitions until it went bankrupt in 1837. Many of its members founded new entertainment enterprises and continued to hold sway over the circus world for more than half a century.

Evolution

In 1854 there were four circuses operating in New York City in various arenas, but one of the city's big attractions, a precursor of the sideshows that became a tradition of the circus, was the American Museum of P. T. Barnum. A former circus man, Barnum turned to managing the museum from 1841 until it burned down in 1865. Full of curiosities and natural oddities, the museum was also home to many human spectacles, such as tiny Tom Thumb (Charles Stratton), various Siamese twins, and other people from around the world who attracted attention because of their physical anomalies. After the fire in 1865 and another to a second museum in 1868, Barnum retired. In 1870 he reentered the entertainment world to create P. T. Barnum's Grand Traveling Museum, Menagerie, Caravan and Circus with Dan Castello and William Cameron Coup. Six hundred horses were required to move the large show, which included a menagerie and curiosities that survived from his museum in New York City. In 1872, renamed P. T. Barnum's Great Traveling Exposition and World's Fair, it modernized its mode of transportation to 65 railroad cars. Barnum used two rings at the Hippodrome and made sideshows and street parades an integral part of the circus event. His partners withdrew in 1875, and he turned over the operation of his circus to George F. Bailey, one of the Flatfooters, from 1876 to 1880. In 1881 Barnum joined with James A. Bailey and James L. Hutchinson to form P. T. Barnum's Greatest Show on Earth, Howe's Great London Circus and Sanger's Royal British Menagerie. Touring in both England and the United States, the circus featured Jumbo, the white elephant, who died in 1885 in a railroad accident.

In 1889 the Barnum and Bailey Circus, which had added "The Greatest Show on Earth" to its name, had a train wreck near Potsdam (St. Lawrence Co) that killed many circus animals, including horses and camels. The 263 performers and 175 animals on tour with Barnum and Bailey in 1890 constituted the largest circus troupe ever. Barnum and Bailey was purchased by the Ringling Bros, their biggest circus rivals, originally from Baraboo, Wisc, in October 1907 for $410,000, but the two operated separately. In the first two decades of the 20th century, inventions modernized circus life: the power-driven stake driver, canvas spool wagon, motorized tractors, and portable bleacher seating. Charles T. Hunt of Kingston (Ulster Co) started the Hunt Bros Circus in 1892 and was one of the first to convert from horses to a motorized circus (1919–25) and to experiment with cooling tents (1937–39). Fire, always a risk in the wood and canvas structures housing circuses, hit the Barnum and Bailey big top tent in Schenectady on 21 May 1910, but no one was killed. In 1919, after a year of inactivity caused by the influenza epidemic, the Ringling Bros and Barnum and Bailey began appearing together in a troupe that required 100 railroad cars to transport them and their animals, including 55 elephants. In 1921 the American Circus Corp was formed to manage five competing circuses more efficiently and in 1930 bought one more. A powerful group, they were able to lease Madison Square Garden and to shut out the Barnum and Bailey Circus from performing there. In response, John Ringling bought the corporation for $1.7 million, thus ensuring the venue for his circus performances.

Recent Developments

As horse-drawn wagons had given way to railroad cars, by the 1930s and 1940s most circuses had become motorized, using tractors and semi-trailers to haul their equipment, personnel, and animals. The Ringling Bros and Barnum and Bailey Circus continued to open its spring season in New York City, although by 1956 the circus no longer used canvas tents as its big top. It still performs annually in Albany, Rochester, and New York City. In 2004 visitors saw the Big Apple Circus performing at the Lincoln Center, a modernized version of the one-ring circus under the big top, which debuted in New York City in 1977 in Battery Park, or enjoyed a traditional circus sideshow on Coney Island, with performers who ate fire, swallowed swords, charmed snakes, and twisted their bodies inside out in contortions. Also appearing in various locations throughout New York is the Universoul Circus, founded in 1994 by Cedric Walker, the first circus owned and operated by African Americans with traditional acts, featuring performers of African descent and a menagerie of circus animals under a big top tent. The Shrine Circus also runs shows in several cities in New York as a philanthropic venture of the Shriners, an organization affiliated with the Order of the Masons and benefactor to children's hospitals and burn centers.

Chindahl, George L. *A History of the Circus in America* (Caldwell, Idaho: Caxton Printers, 1959)

Verney, Peter. *Here Comes the Circus* (New York: Paddington Press, 1978)

Janet Daley

citizenship education. Because it has historically been the point of entry for a large proportion of the nation's immigrants, New York State has often been at the forefront of efforts to provide newcomers with the cultural and political knowledge and skills needed to participate in US society. Prior to the last quarter of the 20th century, these efforts reflected a dominant white, Protestant culture and were usually combined with efforts to promote English. In New York State such programs began at least as early as the mid–19th century, following the arrival of many Irish, German, and other immigrants. The rapid growth in the immigrant population was in part responsible for the rise of the nativist movement of the 1830s and 1840s and for calls for immigration restriction. Those willing to accept the newcomers were no less concerned with protecting American civic culture. They tried to reach the immigrant community through its children and employed the public schools, Sunday schools,

Children saluting the US flag in St. Lucy's churchyard, Syracuse, 1915.

and Protestant missionary organizations to reshape immigrant children into English-speaking Americans who embraced republican democracy. Citizenship education for immigrant children was a major motive for, and an important aspect of, urban public schools throughout the state in the 19th and 20th centuries.

The enormous stream of Italian, eastern European Jewish, and other immigrants to New York State from the 1880s until World War I was perceived by Americans of all political sympathies as a major problem. Again, some attempted to limit immigration, and others championed Americanization education. Starting in the late 1870s New York City's public schools provided adult classes in English in schools, ethnic clubs, and religious institutions. By the early 20th century the public schools expanded their well-attended English language lectures for adults to include lectures on US culture and citizenship in Italian and Yiddish. Programs in proper hygiene and nutrition were developed for the adult immigrant poor, and the "need" to instruct immigrant children in healthcare, the English language, playtime norms, and the rights and duties of American citizens shaped school curricula. The New York–New Jersey Committee of the North American Civic League for Immigrants (1908), organized by prominent citizens, promoted English language and civics education throughout the metropolitan region and worked with a wide array of ethnic and religious organizations to foster Americanization. The league followed immigrant workers to labor camps throughout the state; in Valhalla (Westchester Co) they assisted the Italian Immigrant Aid Society in organizing basic work-related English language instruction. The Rochester Board of Education created the Rochester Social Center Movement in 1907 to acculturate the city's immigrants, providing English and citizenship classes at five evening schools, while citizenship courses were offered to immigrants at Buffalo's newly opened Jewish Community Building in 1914.

During and after World War I, fear of immigrant "aliens" led to renewed attention to Americanization. Citizenship education became a weapon to defend mainstream culture from foreign influences. Americanization efforts were more intense and less sensitive to the cultural life of the immigrant, tying cultural conformity to political loyalty. Classes for working immigrant women, mixing scholastic instruction, cultural direction, and political conditioning, were organized in factories and community centers in New York City, Rochester, Syracuse, Watertown, Albany, and Saratoga Springs. New York State participated in federal efforts, led by the US Bureau of Naturalization, to educate immigrants. The bureau issued civics and language instruction texts such as "An Outline Course in Citizenship" (1916) and the *Federal Citizenship Textbook, Part I: English for American Citizenship* (1922). But immigration slowed to a trickle following the passage of highly restrictive immigration laws in 1921 and 1924, and interest in immigrant education evaporated.

The relaxation of federal immigration laws in the 1960s led to increased immigration to New York State and reawakened interest in citizenship education programs. Also, in the late 1980s, the federal government passed amnesty legislation enabling many long-term illegal immigrants to apply for legal residency. More than 170,000 illegal aliens living in New York State had applied by 1990. All "amnesty immigrants" were required to participate in civics classes and, for non-English speakers, English classes. These classes were offered statewide through the SUNY community college system, the branches of CUNY, community-based nonprofit agencies, public libraries, and New York City's Board of Education.

Brumberg, Stephan F. *Going to America, Going to School: The Jewish Immigrant Public School Encounter in Turn-of-the-Century New York City* (New York: Praeger, 1986)

Hartmann, Edward George. *The Movement to Americanize the Immigrant* (1948; repr New York: AMS Press, 1967)

Higham, John. *Send These to Me: Jews and Other Immigrants in Urban America* (New York: Atheneum, 1975)

McClymer, John F. "The Americanization Movement and the Education of the Foreign-Born Adult, 1914–25." In *American Education and the European Immigrant, 1840–1940,* ed. Bernard J. Weiss (Urbana: Univ of Illinois Press, 1982)

Stephan F. Brumberg

City Beautiful Movement. A progressive era urban reform drive based on the belief that a beautiful environment inspires and instills moral integrity, good citizenship, and community loyalty. In turn, living conditions of the urban poor would be improved and the economic and political investments of the burgeoning middle and upper classes protected. The 1893 Chicago World's Fair served as both model and inspiration for professional planners and civic leaders. The exposition incorporated the highly ordered formality of the Beaux Arts style from Paris, considered beautiful, dignified, and venerable, and an unmistakable departure from the physical conditions of US cities.

Supporters advocated for complete redesign and reconstruction of city centers, but the movement promoted less dramatic changes as well. Adding public art to the city landscape was achieved through the predominant use of Neoclassical architectural styles, which were highly embellished by decorative balustrades, brackets, cornices, and window and door detail. Public buildings, such as the 1895 Elmira City Hall (Chemung Co) and the 1906 Union Station in Utica, and private properties, such as the 1897 Graystone Hotel in Buffalo and the 1906 DeLamar House in New York City, contributed to this concept of civic art. The addition of fountains, sculpture, monuments, murals, mosaics, and the like also were encouraged. For example, the 1902 Watering Trough for Horses and Dogs in Binghamton, installed within the city's government center, was distinguished by classically inspired details. The 1903 Carrère and Hastings–designed Sheldon Exedra and Gaynor Memorial Sundial on the Cornell University campus in Ithaca included a semicircular marble seat framing a sundial and complemented the classicism of the surrounding academic buildings.

Many of these pieces were in urban spaces created or substantially revamped as part of the movement's emphasis on civic design. Some spaces increased in importance as social gathering places, such as Washington Square Park in Greenwich Village, originally a small neighborhood open space that took on significance with the addition of Stanford White's Washington Memorial Arch in 1892. Others were reinforced as community icons, such as Niagara Square in Buffalo, which was the pivot point in Joseph Ellicott's 1804 plan for the community and became a principal commemorative site with the installation of the 96 ft (29.3 m) McKinley Monument in 1907. And still others continued to serve commercial enterprises while emulating a newfound refinement and grandeur, like Clinton Square in Syracuse, which was the city's commercial hub on the Erie Canal that became the primary public ceremonial space with the addition of the 1910 Soldiers' and Sailors' Monument.

Municipal art and civic design often were supplemented by civic improvement, that is, routine and specialized forms of maintenance. The addition of trees and flower beds, removal of debris and scheduled street sweeping, and the installation of street lighting all added to the quality of urban life. The General Federation of Women' Clubs (1890) and the American League for Civic Improvement (1900) were just two of the national organizations that, through local chapters, championed such activities and, ultimately, gave rise to more formal community planning entities.

The movement also called for both social and political reforms to accompany sweeping physical change. Establishing settlement houses, purging government corruption, and regulating construction practices were necessary complements to the monumental building projects, public arts ventures, and grassroots initiatives. New York City was arguably at the forefront of the movement in the state. Efforts to reduce the influence of Tammany Hall epitomized a widespread interest in political reform. Additionally, enforcement of the Tenement House Act of 1901, particularly on the Lower East Side, illustrated a commitment to improving building conditions. Generally viewed as a short-lived period in American urban development (1893–*ca* 1910), the City Beautiful Movement failed despite isolated achievements in individual cities. The more significant lasting impact may be that it fueled an interest in comprehensive city planning.

Pregill, Philip, and Nancy Volkman. *Landscapes in History: Design and Planning in the Western Tradition* (New York: Van Nostrand Reinhold, 1993)
Schuyler, David. *The New Urban Landscape: The Redefinition of City Form in 19th-Century America* (Baltimore: Johns Hopkins Univ Press, 1986)
Wilson, William H. *The City Beautiful Movement* (Baltimore: Johns Hopkins Univ Press, 1989)

Christine Capella Peters

City College. The first public college in New York City and the first component of what became the City University of New York (CUNY). Established in 1847, the Free Academy on Lexington Ave and 23d St admitted its first class of 149 young men in January 1849. On 30 Apr 1866 the school became the College of the City of New York. In September 1907 it moved uptown to a greatly expanded campus with neo-Gothic buildings designed by George B. Post on St. Nicholas Heights, centered on Convent Ave and 138th St. The school provided higher education for high-achieving students who faced economic, religious, or ethnic discrimination elsewhere. A degree-granting evening session was established in 1910, when women began attending Extension Division courses. An outdoor amphitheater, substantially financed by Adolph Lewisohn, was built in 1915; dedicated as Lewisohn Stadium, it was the site of popular summer concerts until it closed in 1966. The school became the City College officially in 1929. By the 1940s women could attend the professional schools, and in September 1951 the college became formally coeducational. The School of Architecture, the School of Engineering, and the School of Biomedical Education are CUNY's strongest; there are also outstanding programs in biological and physical sciences and in psychology. Graduates include Upton Sinclair (1897), Edward G. Robinson (1914), Lewis Mumford (1918), A. Philip Randolph (1919), Jonas Salk (1934), Irving Kristol (1940), and Colin Powell (1958). City College has graduated eight Nobel laureates. In fall 2000 it enrolled 5,187 full-time and 2,968 part-time undergraduates, and 316 full-time and 2,584 part-time graduate students.

Roff, Sandra Shoiock, Anthony M. Cucchiara, and Barbara J. Dunlap. *From the Free Academy to CUNY: Illustrating Public Higher Education in New York City, 1847–1997* (New York: Fordham Univ Press, 2000)
Rudy, S. Willis. *The College of the City of New York: A History, 1847–1947* (New York: City College Press, 1949)

Pamela Cooper

city government. Cities are municipal corporations, chartered at local request in densely settled places to provide necessary or desired public services beyond those that counties or towns might offer under general laws. New York State has 62 cities, each with a unique charter obtained from the state legislature (or, before American independence, from the colonial authority). Twenty-two counties have no cities within their boundaries; Westchester Co, with the most cities, contains six. New Amsterdam [now New York City] was the first to be chartered, in 1653, with Albany following in 1686. The first city charter issued by the state legislature, and the first to be issued in the newly independent United States, was for Hudson (Columbia Co), in 1785. A total of 14 cities, including 5 of the state's 6 biggest in 2000, were chartered before the Civil War, although 2 of these, Brooklyn and Williamsburg (Kings Co), were absorbed in 1898 into greater New York City, as was Long Island City [now in Queens Co], established in 1870. More than half of New York State's cities were chartered between 1880 and 1920. The last city charter enacted by the legislature was Rye's (Westchester Co) in 1942. Attempts by localities to obtain city charters after 1950 either failed in the legislature or were vetoed by the governor as the state sought to avoid making the local government system even more complex and increasing its local assistance burden.

New York City, the nation's most populated city since 1790, had 8,008,278 residents in 2000. The total population of the state's cities excluding New York City in 2000 was 2,265,864. Cities in 2000 with populations greater than 100,000 besides New York City were Buffalo (292,648), Rochester (219,773), Yonkers (196,086), and Syracuse (147,306). Albany's population fell below 100,000 between 1990 and 2000 for the first time in over a century. More than half of the cities in the state had populations lower than 20,000. The state's smallest city, Sherrill (Oneida Co), was home for 3,147 New Yorkers in 2000. The fifth biggest government by budget in the United States, New York City employed 251,000 people in 2000 and spent $38.4 billion on operations and $4.8 billion on capital improvements. Sherrill's total spending was just under $4 million and revenues just over $4 million. Total revenue for all cities excluding New York City was $2.9 billion and total spending $3.1 billion. Primary sources of total revenues for cities other than New York City were property tax (23%), sales tax (17.8%), and state aid (16.9%). New York City was unusual in the diversity of its revenue base, which included a local income tax and a number of business taxes.

Growth and Change

Cities arose as centers of trade, commerce, and industry at critical junctures along New York State's major waterways and railways, the trade routes to the north and west. Between 1820 and 1840, Rochester, Buffalo, and Utica doubled and redoubled their populations. During the same time period, the cities of Kingston, Newburgh, Poughkeepsie, Hudson, Troy, West Troy [now Watervliet, Albany Co], and Cohoes became part of Hudson Valley's urban industrial network.

By 1860 almost two in five New Yorkers lived in cities. Fueled by immigration from abroad and migration from the countryside in response to the industrial revolution, New York State's cities continued to grow rapidly through the first decades the 20th century. The 1915 state census counted three-quarters of New Yorkers living in cities. At the same time, however, developments in transportation and new manufacturing techniques bred the beginnings of suburbanization, and by the 1920s suburbs on cities' borders were resisting the extension of urban boundaries. A state constitutional amendment passed in 1927 that barred the annexation of territory by cities without the consent of citizens in the jurisdictions to be annexed; it was sponsored by legislators from Westchester Co, on New York City's northern boundary.

Even before the onset of the Great Depression, New York State's cities were pressed to find funds to pay for infrastructure and service needs. Serious decline began in the 1960s. Most of the businesses and jobs that left the state left the cities, and many that remained followed or led white middle-class New Yorkers to the suburbs. In a vicious cycle, tax bases declined, urban infrastructure decayed, service quality dropped, and social conditions deteriorated. A special state aid program to cities was instituted in 1968, and emergency financial aid for the state's biggest cities was put in place in 1975. A massive fiscal crisis in New York City led to the 1975 creation of the Emergency Financial Control Board ("Emergency" was later dropped from the name) to oversee its affairs. A similar board was established for Yonkers in 1984 and Buffalo in 2003. Additional emergency state financial aid to certain cities was provided through the 1980s and 1990s.

Of 25 cities reviewed in 1996, half had experienced a change in bond rating since 1991, 4 to junk bond status. In the last part of the 20th century, residents of most cities in the state, many new immigrants and members of racial and ethnic minority groups, belonged to populations requiring high levels of services—the very old, the very young, the very poor, and the less educated. Although New York City and a number of southern New York State cities, including White Plains, New Rochelle, and Long Beach, bounced back financially in the 1990s and gained population, 44 cities, including 4 of the 6 biggest, declined in population between 1990 and 2000. Severe urban fiscal stress returned to most of the state's cities starting in 2001.

State Power and City Autonomy

Constitutional home rule in New York State seeks to be both a sword empowering cities and a shield protecting them from legislative intervention in their affairs. Article IX of the New York State Constitution protects localities' right to self-government, grants general and specific powers to them, authorizes the legislature to grant them additional powers (and places procedural limits on its capacity to remove these once they are given), and constrains the legislature from acting with regard to local matters. Constitutional provisions empowering localities to structure their own governments have been more effective than those empowering them to act and those limiting state intervention. Home rule notwithstanding, the state constitution and statutes direct, regulate, guide, or constrain cities in their taxing, spending, borrowing, personnel practices, and other substantive areas.

Although the current home-rule provisions of the New York State Constitution apply to all general-purpose local governments, they arose out of a century-long struggle by cities for greater autonomy from state government. Building upon precedent dating to medieval England, municipal corporations, self-governing and self-perpetuating (like all other corporations), were at first organized largely for economic purposes. Their charters protected their governance and operations from state intrusion, but cities could not alter their charters—only the sovereign or the legislature could. In the first decades of 19th century, an era of great pressure for democratization, cities sought charter changes from the legislature to augment their power. However, by inviting the state legislature into their affairs in this way, cities transformed their historic autonomous legal status and soon became the state's creatures. A rule of law articulated in an 1868 Iowa case by Judge John F. Dillon, and soon after enshrined in his treatise on local government, very narrowly limited cities' powers to those "expressly" granted by the legislature, "necessarily" or "fairly" implied, or "absolutely indispensable" to their governance. Even with regard to such core functions as public safety, the state government regularly found its way into city affairs. For example, in the late 19th century various special regional commissions were created by the legislature to control police and fire services in and around New York City. Such intervention was often motivated by partisan efforts to control jobs and other patronage. New York City government was a Democratic Party stronghold, while the Republicans often prevailed at the state level. The legislature did pass some general legislation applicable to cities in the 19th century, but there was no systematic approach to city government. The disparate needs of vastly different places justified particularism; in granting or changing charters, the legislature dealt with each city separately. Legislators with no political stake in the outcome deferred to local colleagues, leading to complexity and confusion.

Yet during the 19th century, cities in New York State did gain greater authority over their affairs in many areas. The 1821 Constitution provided for the filling of city offices by popular election; that of 1846 added that all local officials not selected in accord with constitutionally defined processes would be locally elected or appointed. Home-rule advocates sought additional state constitutional provisions that gave cities control over their forms of governance, carved out an autonomous sphere of action for city government, and limited state interference in city affairs. A New York State constitutional amendment adopted in 1874 prohibited local bills and required the legislature to act through general laws in some areas of concern to cities. A provision adopted 20 years later, at the 1894 Constitutional Convention, divided cities into three classes based upon size of population; more that 250,000 people, 50,000–250,000, and fewer than 50,000. Special legislation, defined as that which did not apply to all cities in a class concerning a city's property, affairs, and government, was made subject to suspensory veto by its mayor. If the mayor objected, the bill had to be re-passed to take effect. The 1923 home-rule amendment removed this provision and made a declaration of emergency by the governor a condition for special legislation and then required a two-thirds vote in each house. The current provision, adopted in 1963, allows passage by simple legislative majorities of a special law if requested by a locality, with a message of necessity from the governor and two-thirds vote required if there is no home-rule request. There is no provision for special legislation without a home-rule request for New York City.

The General Municipal Law dealing with the powers of and limits upon counties, cities, towns, and villages was passed in 1892. The first General City Law, adopted in 1900, gathered all provisions in force then applicable to cities. This law was extended in 1913 to give 23 broadly defined powers to cities and to empower each to "regulate, manage and control its property and local affairs." In 1917 city authority to regulate land use was added. An amendment adopted in 1923 gave constitutional basis to these provisions. Language added to the constitution in 1938 extended the affirmative power of the local legislature to act with regard to the locality's "property, affairs or government." The state constitutional provision in force in 2004 specified 10 areas subject to local action and, more generally, a locality's control over its property, affairs, or government.

In implementing home rule, the state government has been quite respectful of local prerogatives in some areas of policy, for example, land-use control and elementary and secondary education. Where the state government has wished to act, however, constitutional limits upon its entry into local affairs have often not been effective. The Court of Appeals, the state's highest court, has accepted laws as constitutional that are general in form but special in effect. For example, laws are frequently passed and upheld that apply to all cities with populations greater than 1 million; New York City is the only city in this general classification. Moreover, the court famously ruled in *Alder v Deegan* (1929) that special legislation on a "matter of State concern" is acceptable, even if local property, affairs, or government is affected, and it has defined "state concern" broadly. Professor Richard Briffault, the state's leading contemporary legal authority on home rule, has written that under this precedent the court has allowed the legislature to act unrestrictedly on such seemingly local matters as housing, local taxes, municipal sewers, planning and zoning, cultural institutions, and residential requirements for municipal civil servants. Additionally, state law may preempt local action when the two are found to conflict or when the state is determined to have "occupied the field." Thus, in a well-known case in 1962, *Wholesale Laundry Board of Trade, Inc v City of New York,* New York City was barred from effecting a higher minimum wage than the state's. This legal environment often makes cities hesitant to act on matters that are not clearly within their purview.

Second Class Cities laws were passed in 1906 and 1909 that sought to bring some uniformity to the charters of New York's middle-sized cities. The Home Rule Act of 1913 treated city charter–making powers more generally. The home-rule amendment of 1923, passed in a rare moment of Democratic control of both legislative houses and of the governorship, provided "Every city shall have the power to adopt and amend local laws not inconsistent with the Constitution and laws of the State relating to its property, affairs or government." The Home Rule Law passed to effect this provision gave cites the right to adopt or amend charters by local action, subject to popular referendum. Later a provision was added that allowed charter change by citizen initiative.

Forms of Government

Cities in New York State, like those across the nation, use three basic forms of government. All cities have councils, which vary in size from 3 (in Watervliet, including the mayor) to 51 (in New York City). Councils of 5–11 members are most common. Under the mayor-council form that prevailed in 45 cities in 2000, mayors are generally elected citywide and vested with executive authority. Council members are usually elected from wards, and the presiding officer of the council may be elected at large. Under the council-manager plan, used in 14 cities in New York State, council members are generally elected at large. The mayor, whose nonlegislative duties are largely ceremonial, presides over and votes as a member of the council; he or she may be elected at large with that title or selected to serve as mayor by the council from among their number. In council-manager cities, executive authority is vested in a professional manager appointed by and serving at the pleasure of the council. The commission form is used by three New York State cities, including its two smallest. Commissioners are elected to head the major departments of city government and sit together to constitute the city council. The mayor may be designated annually by the council, as in Sherrill, or elected to the title mayor and commissioner, which is the practice in Mechanicville (Saratoga Co) and Saratoga Springs.

The council-manager and commission forms of government, first advanced during the Progressive era, are often combined in the United States with nonpartisan local elections. These forms were less widely adopted in New York State and other areas of the Northeast where political parties were strongly established. With the exception of New Rochelle (Westchester Co), New York State's 15 largest cities have mayor-council systems. Many political scientists regard partisan systems with separately elected mayors as best suited to large municipalities with more heterogeneous populations. In response to changing local political and social conditions, cities regularly reconsider their governmental structure.

Cities' Relationship with Local Governments

The New York State Constitution provides for the transfer of functions between local governments and authorizes municipalities to do together what each is empowered to do individually. For example, seeking greater efficiency, Rochester transferred many functions to Monroe Co. In 2002 it also collaborated with Monroe Co in a number of areas, including emergency communications, public works equipment sharing, and police officer training. Other imperatives require city governments to work with local governments to serve their residents. Cities own and operate water and sewer systems and other facilities outside their boundaries by formal agreements with governments of host localities concerning access to services and tax liabilities. A barrier to more extensive collaboration between big cities and their municipal neighbors in southern New York State is suburban hostility, rooted in social and demographic differences between city and suburban populations. In 1995, for example, the mayor of the Village of Pelham (Westchester Co), in reaction to crime allegedly originating in Mount Vernon, proposed to tear down a footbridge linking the two localities. Certain structural arrangements facilitate city and county collaboration. New York City, which contains five counties, performs the functions of both city and county government. Across the state, boards of supervisors, made up of the elected supervisors of the towns within them and special supervisors elected to represent any cities they may contain, still govern 17 counties in New York State. For example, the City of Oneida selects 4 members of the 19-member Madison Co board. This system ensures the direct representation of city interests with the county government. In 1998 Joel Giambra was elected as comptroller in Buffalo and in 1999 as Erie Co executive, and has proposed that that city be dissolved and its functions entirely absorbed by Erie Co. Counties' interests at times require them to come into agreement with cities. Cities and counties may both levy a general sales tax under state law, but cities have prior claim to this revenue source. If a county wishes to levy a uniform countywide tax, it must come to agreement with the cities within it about the latters' share of the total revenue to be collected.

See also HOME RULE; STATE GOVERNMENT AND SERVICES.

Benjamin, Gerald, and Richard P. Nathan. *Regionalism and Realism: A Study of Governments in the Metropolitan New York Area* (Washington, DC: Brookings Institution Press, 2001)

Briffault, Richard. "Our Localism—Part I" and "Our Localism—Part II," *Columbia Law Review* 90 (Mar 1990)

———. "Local Government and the State Constitution: A Framework for Analysis." In *Decision '97: Constitutional Change in New York,* ed. Gerald Benjamin and Henrik N. Dullea (Albany: Rockefeller Institute Press, 1997)

New York State Constitutional Convention Committee. *Problems Relating to Home Rule and Local Government,* vol 11 of *Reports of the Constitutional Convention Committee* (Albany: Author, 1938)

New York State. Office of the Comptroller. *Special Report on Municipal Affairs, 2001,* 94th ed. (Albany: Author, 2002)

New York State. Secretary of State. Division of Local Government Services. *Local Government Handbook* (Albany: Office of the Secretary of State, 2001)

Gerald Benjamin

CITY UNIVERSITY OF NEW YORK (CUNY)

	Year Founded	Full-Time Students	Part-Time Students
Senior Colleges			
Baruch College[a]	1968	9,516	6,182
Brooklyn College	1930	7,046	7,993
City College of New York[b]	1847	5,503	5,552
Hunter College[c]	1870	10,406	9,605
John Jay College of Criminal Justice	1964	6,857	3,755
Lehman College[d]	1931	3,946	4,822
Medgar Evers College	1968	2,350	2,264
Queens College	1937	7,305	7,756
College of Staten Island[e]	1976	6,208	4,907
York College	1966	2,875	2,482
Community Colleges			
Borough of Manhattan Community College	1963	9,812	6,063
Bronx Community College	1957	4,475	2,453
Eugenio Maria de Hostos Community College[f]	1968	2,357	758
Kingsborough Community College	1963	7,426	7,375
La Guardia Community College[g]	1968	7,398	4,380
Queensborough Community College	1958	5,830	4,768
Technical Colleges			
New York City Technical College[h]	1946	7,426	3,602
Graduate Institutions			
Sophie Davis School of Biomedical Education/ City University Medical School	1973	294	7
City University School of Law at Queens College	1983	378	5
Graduate School and University Center	1961	3,095	472

Source: CUNY Facts and Figures, http://www.cuny.edu.

Note: Full- and part-time students are based on enrollment figures for fall 2000.

[a]Established as an independent college of CUNY in 1968. Before that it was the City College School of Business and Public Administration, formed in 1919; it was renamed for Bernard Baruch in 1953.

[b]Formed in 1847 as the Free Academy of New York and renamed in 1866.

[c]Formed in 1870 as the Female Normal and High School and renamed in 1914.

[d]Founded in 1931 as the Bronx campus of Hunter College. It was established in 1968 as an independent college of CUNY.

[e]Formed in 1976 through the union of Staten Island Community College (1955) and Richmond College (1965).

[f]Created by an act of the Board of Higher Education on 22 Apr 1968. A charter class of 623 students was admitted in Sept 1970.

[g]Enrolled its first class of students in 1971.

[h]Established in 1946 as the New York State Institute of Applied Arts and Sciences. It was renamed New York City Community College in 1953 and New York City Technical College in 1980.

City University of New York (CUNY). Founded in 1961 to combine the public colleges in New York City into a citywide system of public higher education, CUNY has grown to comprise 10 senior colleges, 6 community colleges, 3 graduate institutions, and a technical college. CUNY's origins date to the Free Academy of New York, a boys' school proposed by Townsend Harris and founded in 1847. Intended to serve both rich and poor, the academy educated the sons of lawyers, businessmen, porters, and laborers. After the state legislature granted the academy the authority to issue bachelor degrees, it was renamed the College of the City of New York in 1866. Shying away from more practical commercial studies, its curriculum emphasized training in mathematics and language, and featured one of the country's first science laboratory programs. Since its founding the college's population has reflected the city's changing demographics. By 1900 the sons of Jewish families who had emigrated from eastern Europe were becoming a significant part of the student body. In 1870 the municipally funded Female Normal and High School, whose curriculum initially focused on teacher training, opened to serve the city's young women. Authorized to grant degrees in 1888, the institution was renamed Hunter College in 1914.

Increased population and the creation of a system of high schools led to the need for more municipal colleges. In 1926 the Board of Higher Education replaced the boards of City College and Hunter College to facilitate expansion. Brooklyn College, the city's first coeducational public college, was established in 1930 and Queens College in 1937. Student bodies remained largely Jewish until around 1970. The New York State legislature reached new communities by authorizing the establishment of community colleges in 1948, and by 1958 they were established in Staten Island, the Bronx, and Queens.

In 1960 the Board of Higher Education followed the recommendation of its Committee to Look to the Future to expand the city's municipal college system and to institute doctoral studies. Gov Nelson A. Rockefeller in 1961 signed legislation establishing CUNY, which would be administered by a chancellor and a board of trustees. Doctoral studies began a year later, and the Graduate Center opened in Midtown Manhattan in 1965. Over the next decade, nine undergraduate campuses entered the CUNY system, many of them in underserved neighborhoods. Though the number of African Americans and Latinos in the university system remained low, the expansion during the 1950s and 1960s led to the enrollment of more students of Irish and Italian descent. But the growing demand for education outpaced the supply, and admissions became increasingly selective. When Albert Bowker became CUNY's chancellor in 1963, he confronted questions of access, particularly for underrepresented racial and ethnic groups. Efforts to ease admissions requirements proved inadequate, and in 1968 Bowker proposed that the top 100 graduates of each city high school be guaranteed admission to CUNY. The Board of Higher Education resolved to enroll all New York City high school graduates by 1975, and the state Board of Regents accepted this open admissions plan in 1969.

Widespread demonstrations on the campuses, sparked at City College and intensified by the state legislature's cut of $29 million of requested funding, led to citywide demands for representation of Black and Puerto Rican students at CUNY that was proportional to their numbers in the graduating classes of New York City's high schools. As a result of this conflict, and with support from faculty, alumni, and labor groups, the Board of Higher Education implemented a policy, effective in fall 1970, that guaranteed every graduate of a New York City high school a place at CUNY. Students with an 80 average or in the top 50% of their class were guaranteed admission to a four-year college, and other graduates were provided places in community colleges. Enrollment grew from about 19,000 to 35,000 between 1969 and 1970, and African American and Latino enrollments increased, most dramatically at City College. Remedial programs in math, reading, writing, and study skills were established to help new students.

Though substantial state aid to public higher education had been legally mandated since 1960, the legislation that created CUNY repealed the free tuition mandate, opening the way for the Board of Higher Education to charge tuition. Starting in the 1960s, annual rallies against tuition were held during state budget negotiations. In 1976, amidst a citywide financial crisis, tuition was imposed while faculty and staff were cut back. Enrollment dropped dramatically: about 29,000 freshmen entered CUNY in 1976, down 28% from the prior year. The state agreed to fund the four-year CUNY schools, while the city financed the two-year colleges. In 1979 a board of trustees that reflected the new alignment between city and state replaced the Board of Higher Education, with both governor and mayor appointing members.

Open admissions increased diversity, but it also contributed to the erosion of the elite academic status of City College and some other CUNY schools. In response, four-year colleges tightened admissions to the top third, not the top half, of each graduating class. The number of full-time faculty declined in the 1980s and 1990s because of reduced state and city appropriations, and tuition rose to replace those funds. In the late 1990s the Board of Trustees, over the opposition of student and faculty groups, renewed efforts to raise admissions standards and limit access by reducing remedial programs at senior colleges. Despite these concerns, in 2000 CUNY enrolled over 195,000 students in hundreds of degree programs, with another 150,000 in adult and continuing education classes. Students came from 145 countries with 115 native languages and mirrored the racial and ethnic diversity of the city; CUNY's student body was 32% black, 31% white, 25% Latino, and 12% Asian. In 2000 CUNY was the nation's largest urban university and its third largest public university.

Gordon, Sheila S. "The Transformation of the City University of New York, 1945–1970" (PhD diss, Columbia Univ, 1975)

Pardue, Duncan B., and Suzanne P. Ryder. *A Forty-Six Year Summary of the Board of Higher Education of the City of New York* (New York: Office of the Chairman of the Board of Higher Education, 1973)

Roff, Sandra Shoiock, Anthony M. Cucchiara, and Barbara Dunlap. *From the Free Academy to CUNY: Illustrating Public Higher Education in New York City, 1847–1997* (New York: Fordham Univ Press, 2000)

Traub, James. *City on a Hill: Testing the American Dream at City College* (Reading, Mass: Addison-Wesley, 1994)

Kenneth M. Gold

City Water Tunnel No. 3. New York City water distribution tunnel. It was designed to carry Delaware and Catskill Aqueducts' waters from a Yonkers reservoir to all the city's boroughs except Staten Island and to allow for inspection and repair of two earlier distribution tunnels that had been put into service in 1917 and 1936. Construction, first contemplated in the 1950s, began in 1970 but was suspended for several years during contractual and fiscal problems of the mid-1970s. As of 2001 completion was expected in 2020 at a cost of $6 billion, making it the largest capital construction project in the city's history. The first 13 mi (21 km) segment of the tunnel's planned 63 mi (101 km) length was opened in 1998, serving portions of the Bronx, Manhattan, and Queens. The concrete-lined segment has a maximum diameter of 24 feet (7 m) and runs as deep as 800 feet (244 m). In the first three decades of construction, 24 workers died in tunneling-related accidents.

Galusha, Diane. *Liquid Assets: A History of New York City's Water System* (Fleischmanns, NY: Purple Mountain Press, 1999)

Gerard T. Koeppel

civil defense. Seven months before Pearl Harbor, Pres Franklin D. Roosevelt created the Office of Civil Defense (OCD). First led by Mayor Fiorello La Guardia of New York City, the OCD involved thousands of volunteer New Yorkers during World War II in community services and as aircraft spotters or air-raid wardens. The beginning of the Cold War led to the Federal Civil Defense Act of 1950. The new Federal Civil Defense Agency directed a massive education effort, producing speakers, booklets, films, television shows, and media releases. Throughout New York State, schoolchildren were taught to get under their desks in "duck and cover" air-raid drills. In New York City the schools provided every student with a dog tag to identify dead or wounded children after nuclear war. The New York State Defense Emergency Act of 1951 defined state civil defense policy, gave city mayors and county officers leadership responsibility for civil defense, and established the State Civil Defense Commission.

From 1954 to 1961 a federal air-raid drill named Operation Alert was held once a year in scores of major cities. In New York State the failure to take cover for 15 minutes in subways or basements during the drill was punishable with a fine up to $500 and a year in jail. Informed scientists, pacifists, intellectuals, and thousands of ordinary citizens criticized civil defense as a dangerous government pretense that one could survive a nuclear war. Centered in New York City, the protest against Operation Alert began with the heavily publicized arrest of a small number of protesters during a 15 June 1955 demonstration. The 1959 resistance included protestors in Jamaica (Queens Co) and Haverstraw (Rockland Co). In defiance of the law thousands massed in City Hall Park in downtown New York City in 1960 and 1961, while hundreds of college students demonstrated on East Coast campuses, including Cornell University, Columbia University, and City College of New York.

Pres John F. Kennedy canceled the drill in 1962. He had supported civil defense primarily to prevent New York governor Nelson A. Rockefeller from using the issue to defeat him in the approaching 1964 presidential election. Gov Rockefeller had built both a fallout shelter in the governor's mansion and the largest bomb shelter in the country in downtown Albany, a $4 million underground complex programmed to hold 700 preselected state officials, business leaders, and professionals. His attempt to make fallout shelters mandatory in every home, business, and school in New York State at a cost of $100 million was defeated, but he did expedite a bill to provide aid to schools for bomb shelters. On 12 Feb 1962 hundreds of protesters came to Albany, most of them middle-class housewives and students who were also demanding a nuclear test ban and an end to school civil defense efforts. Both Rockefeller and Kennedy dropped their drive for civil defense. American civil defense continued for about 20 years as a poorly financed federal program.

Mayor Abe Beame initiated a task force for emergency preparedness that recommended in 1976 that New York City's Fallout Shelter Program be abandoned. The report cited aged and damaged supplies, incorrect signs and directions, and too few personnel to maintain the shelters. At that time there were about 61,500 shelters in New York City, but the report noted that the population could not expect assistance from the shelter program in the event of nuclear attack or natural disaster. In the early 1980s Pres Ronald Reagan announced a $4.2 billion program that called for evacuation from target areas instead of shelters. By the mid-1980s, however, New Yorkers, along with 90 million citizens in major cities in seven states, had formally refused any participation in nuclear crisis relocation. Through the 1990s the government continued its covert program to protect selected political and military elites in deep underground shelters.

In the early 21st century national and state emergency management agencies have focused

Mural depicting evolution of the civil service system, located in lobby of the Civil Service building, W. Averell Harriman State Office Campus, Albany, dedicated 1958.

their attention on preventing terrorist activities. The US Department of Homeland Security, created 24 Jan 2003, initiated Operation Liberty Shield, increasing security around nuclear and chemical plants and food supply and distribution locations as well as at airports, seaports, railways, and border crossings such as Buffalo/Fort Erie (Ont) and Lewiston (Niagara Co)/Queenston (Ont). Operation New York Shield, enacted by Gov George E. Pataki in March 2003, brought over 20 state agencies into the effort to improve security. National Guard troops were stationed at the Canadian border and at power plants; New York City subways and bridges were similarly protected.

Garrison, Dee. "Our Skirts Gave Them Courage: The Civil Defense Protest Movement in New York City, 1955–1961." In *Not June Cleaver: Women and Gender in Postwar America, 1945–1960*, ed. Joanne Meyerowitz (Philadelphia: Temple Univ Press, 1994)

Oakes, Guy. *The Imaginary War: Civil Defense and American Cold War Culture* (New York: Oxford Univ Pres, 1994)

Dee Garrison

Civilian Conservation Corps (CCC). Federal work-relief program (1933–42) established as part of the New Deal during the Great Depression. The CCC was created by the Emergency Conservation Work Act, which passed in March 1933 with the goal of providing work for unemployed single men ages 17–23. In 1937 it was formally recognized as a separate federal agency. The CCC's initial purpose was to employ men in environmental conservation work such as fighting soil erosion and replenishing timber resources. These men, commonly known collectively as Pres Franklin D. Roosevelt's Tree Army, were prepared for service by the US Army and transferred to work camps, where room and board, clothes and tools, educational services, and medical needs were provided. They received a monthly salary of $30, of which a mandatory $25 allotment was sent to their families at home.

More than 220,000 men were organized in roughly 130 camps around New York State. Among these camps were 13 solely for African Americans, although there were a few camps with a mixed-race population. There were also 12 camps for veterans. Members of the CCC worked on more than 1,000 projects in New York State, including the construction of roads, picnic and camping areas, cabins, trails, fire towers, beaches, and wildlife management areas. They also fought fires, erosion, floods, and insects; ran telephone and electric wires; planted trees; and assisted local communities with various natural disasters. Well-known CCC contributions to New York State parks remain evident, including improvements made at Paul Smiths, Tupper Lake, Lake Placid, Letchworth, Green Lakes, and Chenango Valley. All the camps were closed by July 1942. The New York State Civilian Conservation Corps Museum is located at Gilbert Lake State Park.

New York State Conservation Department. Civilian Conservation Corps Camp and Personnel Files, 1935–1942. New York State Archives, Albany

Salmond, John A. *The Civilian Conservation Corps, 1933–1942: A New Deal Case Study* (Durham, NC: Duke Univ Press, 1967)

Richard Ranieri

civil service. Created to discourage the spoils system of government. Appointments to non-policy-making positions are chosen from candidates who do best on a competitive examination open to all and impartially administered by a civil service commission.

Development

Through much of the 19th century, appointments to positions in the federal and New York State civil jurisdictions were generally made on the basis of political loyalty and association. Political leaders viewed public positions as rewards for the party faithful and as a source of financing, as it was common practice for party leaders to extract annual assessments from appointees in exchange for appointments. This so-called spoils system created terrible inefficiencies because of incompetence and corruption.

In the post–Civil War period, a progressive political movement developed whose goal was the outright reform of the political party system. The reformers were viewed as a direct and immediate threat to both Republican and Democratic Parties' bosses, who controlled federal patronage in their jurisdictions; threatened, for example, was Tammany Hall, the major Democratic Party institution in New York City and, through its base in the city, the dominant force in the party statewide. The reformers were a mix of reform politicians and establishment intellectuals from prestigious universities, the press, and journals of public opinion. They espoused support for the application of newly emerging scientific management principles to government administration, including competitive testing for public office.

The political movement to reform the spoils system was initiated by Republican president Rutherford B. Hayes, who in 1877 issued an executive order forbidding federal officeholders from taking part in political party management and protecting them from being assessed political contributions. The order was a broadside against the patronage operations at the federal government's largest revenue-collection post at the Port of New York and sparked conflict with US Senator Roscoe Conkling, a Republican from Utica and a chief dispenser of patronage in his state. Patronage and operations at the port were controlled by Conkling's chief political lieutenant, Port Collector Chester A. Arthur, and Conkling was outraged when Arthur was dismissed from this position.

Ironically, it was Arthur who, after becoming president following the assassination of James A. Garfield in 1881, would sign the national civil service Pendleton Act on 16 Jan 1883. The act set forth a program of competitive examinations for public office and prohibitions against political activity and assessments. The Civil Service Commission, composed of three appointees of whom no more than two could be from the same political party, was created to oversee the administration of the statute. Within weeks of the passage of the Pendleton Act, a young reform-minded New York State assemblyman from Manhattan, Theodore Roosevelt, sponsored a nearly identical version of the federal civil service law in the state legislature. Sensing the mood of the nation, New York State's Democratic governor, Grover Cleveland, immediately signed it into law on 4 May 1883. This act created the first state Civil Service Commission and appropriated funds to initiate a program of competitive examinations for state positions. The civil service program in New York State was significantly strengthened in 1894 when a constitutional convention incorporated a merit system standard in the state constitution.

Operation

The State Civil Service Commission determines the scope of the competitive examination program for thousands of state and local government positions. It also determines which positions may be filled based on political compatibility with the governor. This exempt category of appointees serves at the pleasure of the governor or local government officials and is intended to bring elected officials' policy perspective to the actual administration of state or local government. Historically, this category of positions has been no greater than 2% of the overall workforce.

In response to significant labor turmoil in the 1960s, the state legislature in 1967 enacted the Public Employees Fair Employment Act, which governs public sector labor relations. It created the administrative machinery that allows public employees the right to organize, be recognized, and collectively negotiate contract terms and conditions of employment for public employees. The Public Employment Relations Board is the state agency responsible for the oversight of this statute. Also in 1967 the legislature created the Governor's Office of Employee Relations, which is responsible for contract negotiations, contract administration, certain training and development functions, and the ongoing relationship between the governor and the labor organizations representing state employees. Thus, the New York State Civil Service Department and Commission are joined by two other state agencies in administering the state and local government employment systems. All public employers are also under the umbrella of numerous exacting federal and state labor laws that prohibit discrimination in such areas as age, disability, gender, and race.

The State Civil Service Commission has three members: the president of the commission, who is also the head of the Department of Civil Service, and two commissioners. By law, not more than two of the three can be of the same political party. Each serves a term of six years, and vacancies in the commission are filled by appointment by the governor, by and with the advice and consent of the senate, for the unexpired term. In 2003–4 the Department of Civil Service had a budget of more than $58 million and over 550 full-time equivalent staff positions.

Hoogenboom, Ari. *Outlawing the Spoils: A History of the Civil Service Reform Movement, 1865–1883* (Urbana: Univ of Illinois Press, 1961)
Jordan, David M. *Roscoe Conkling of New York: Voice in the Senate* (Ithaca: Cornell Univ Press, 1971)
New York State Department of Civil Service, http://www.cs.state.ny.us

Nicholas J. Vagianelis

Civil Service Employees' Association (CSEA). See Public employees unions.

Civil War. New York was the most populated state in the Union in 1860 and contributed more money and men to the war effort than any other between 1860 and 1865, despite a severely divided citizenry and a large number of opponents to the Republican national administration. Because much of its trade was with the South, many of the state's leaders were fearful of any disruption of the Union.

Election of 1860

At the time of the presidential election of 1860, New York State politics were considerably confused. By and large, downstate, including New York City, tended to be Democratic, while upstate, particularly the Burned-over District in Central and Western New York (largely settled by immigrants from New England), was Republican, but there was no unity within these parties. The Democrats were split into Hards, led by Daniel S. Dickinson of Binghamton, and Softs like Dean Richmond of Buffalo, Horatio Seymour of Utica, and Samuel J. Tilden of New York City. The Hards had been unwilling to permit the so-called Barnburners (supporters of Martin Van Buren) to return to the fold after the split of 1848; Hards were generally apologists for slavery and interested in maintaining good relations with the South. The Softs, often former Barnburners, had varying principles and disliked the abolitionists, although some of them later joined the Republicans. The regular Democratic organization upstate had long been the Albany Regency, closely allied to the New York Central and other railroads, but it was now in its decline. In New York City the Democrats were split between Tammany and Mozart Halls, the former the regular Democratic organization and the latter the creation of Mayor Fernando Wood, who had fallen out with the Tammany leaders. The Republicans divided into moderates, led by Thurlow Weed and William H. Seward, and radicals, represented by Horace Greeley, the editor of the *New York Tribune*, and determined former Free Soilers. The business community tended to divide between those interested in maintaining good relations with the South and those opposed to the spread of slavery. The state also contained a large number of immigrants, principally Irish Catholics and Germans. The Irish, concentrated in New York City, were generally attached to the Democratic Party and opposed any measure benefiting Blacks, whom they feared as possible competitors, while the Germans were divided by politics and religion.

Sheet music cover commemorating the death of Col Elmer E. Ellsworth, the first Union officer killed in the Civil War, 1861, of Mechanicville.

These divisions dated back to the 1850s and affected the state's influence upon the elections of 1860. Having lost the fight for delegates to the state Democratic convention in 1859, Mayor Wood seized the hall in Syracuse. The regulars, however, refused to be cast aside, resulting in two delegations that were sent to the Democratic National Convention at Charleston, SC, where the irregularly elected Wood delegates were excluded. The Softs won the support of the Hards by allegedly promising to back Dickinson for the presidential nomination. The New York State delegates then voted for the minority platform, espousing Stephen Douglas's program of popular sovereignty (the right of the inhabitants of a territory to decide whether or not to allow slavery there), instead of the majority platform, with its insistence on a federal slave code. However, they also backed the requirement for a two-thirds majority for a presidential nomination, even after southern seceders had withdrawn, thus rendering Douglas's nomination impossible. Unable to select a candidate by a two-thirds majority, the Charleston convention broke up but reassembled in June in Baltimore, where New Yorkers voted to refuse admission to the Charleston seceders. As such, the New York State delegation contributed to the formation of two Democratic tickets, one headed by Douglas, espousing popular sovereignty, and the other by Vice Pres John C. Breckinridge, favoring a federal slave code. The majority of New York delegates endorsed Douglas, but the seceding Breckinridge convention contained two delegates from New York State.

The New York State delegation to the Chicago Republican National Convention favored its native son, Sen William H. Seward, who two years earlier had spoken of an "irrepressible conflict" between North and South, thus gaining an undeserved reputation as a radical. His chief mentor was Thurlow Weed, known as the Dictator because of his decisive influence upon the state's Whig and Republican politics. However, his erstwhile supporter, Horace Greeley, had broken with Seward and his backer and now appeared as a representative of Oregon, determined to frustrate the ambitions of his former partner, which resulted in the nomination of Abraham Lincoln. Lincoln was known in the state chiefly as a result of his well-received speech on 27 Feb 1860 at the Cooper Institute (now Cooper Union for the Advancement of Science and Art) in Manhattan, where he had stressed the Republicans' conservative ideas but reasserted the constitutionality of outlawing slavery in the territories. Although many in New York State found his dress somewhat inappropriate and disliked his western twang, he had made a considerable impression on many, especially those who heard his address.

Because of the Democratic split, the Republicans' chances in the state (but not in New York City) were excellent, even though the opposition made an effort to combine the two Democratic tickets, as well as the former Whig John Bell's Constitutional Union Party, in a slate of 18 Douglas, 10 Bell, and 7 Breckinridge electors. After a spirited campaign in November, the Republicans carried the state by a vote of 362,646 to 312,510. They also reelected Gov Edwin D. Morgan, who had established a good record since first elected to that position in 1858. In addition, they captured the state legislature, which, after

Seward's appointment as US secretary of state, elected Republican Ira Harris to take his place in the US Senate. However, they lost the presidential race in New York City by about 30,000 votes.

The Republican victory did not imply a diminution of the widespread racism in the state. African American males could vote only if they met a property qualification of $250 and a three-year residence requirement, which was not applicable to white males, and in the election of 1860 an amendment to the constitution giving them equal suffrage rights was decisively defeated by a vote of 345,791 to 197,889, with an especially strong negative in New York City.

Secession Crisis

The election of Lincoln and the secession crisis that followed caused great consternation in New York City. The business community, which had contributed to the Democratic success in the city, was seriously worried about a possible war. At a meeting on 15 Dec 1860, some 2,000 representatives of this group adopted an address to the people of the South, assuring them of their sympathy and urging a peaceful solution, and selected delegates to deliver it. Mayor Wood, a determined, if allegedly corrupt, southern sympathizer, went so far as to suggest that the city secede and form a free trading port. Conservatives elected delegates to the Peace Convention about to meet in Washington, DC, and appointed commissions to confer with the South. Democrats were not the only ones who urged conciliatory measures. Preacher Henry Ward Beecher and Horace Greeley suggested a peaceful breakup of the Union, a policy characterized by the slogan Let the Erring Sisters Go. When Lincoln traveled through New York State on his way to Washington, his reception was cordial, but in New York City it was less enthusiastic.

The first contretemps between the state and the South occurred in January 1861, when the New York City police seized some 1,000 muskets aboard the steamer *Monticello* bound for Savannah, Ga. When the governor of Georgia commandeered New York ships in Savannah harbor, the muskets were released and the governor reversed his order. The city, if not the state, was in an appeasing mood. This divided attitude changed with the attack on Fort Sumter in South Carolina on 12 Apr 1861. For a moment party differences seemed to be forgotten. The governor and legislature responded immediately to Lincoln's call for 13,000 troops and money from the state, with Morgan ordering 17 regiments to gather at Albany, Elmira, and New York City, and with the legislature authorizing 30,000 troops for two years and appropriating $3 million. Private citizens lent the federal government $35 million in the first three months, and by September, 40 regiments had been raised, including a number of units of foreign-born soldiers. On 19 April the Seventh Regiment, feted by cheering crowds, marched through New York City to relieve Washington, DC, and on 20 April, a mass meeting at Union Square welcomed Maj Robert Anderson of Fort Sumter fame. A Union Defense Committee headed by John Adams Dix was organized to dispense a great number of funds for the war effort, and the business community loyally began to support the war.

At the same time, the many soldiers' aid societies, relief agencies, and ladies' aid groups had been working independently to provide supplies and goods for the soldiers in the field. An informal gathering of women from these various groups met New York City on 25 Apr 1861 to consolidate their efforts, which led to the establishment of the US Sanitary Commission on 9 June 1861. Divided into three departments, the commission's responsibilities to both Union soldiers and Confederate prisoners of war were general relief (delivering the food, clothing, quilts, medicine, and bandages contributed by the individual groups), preventative services (inspection of camps and hospitals, provision of education on sanitation), and special relief (creation of homes to provide for soldiers and veterans, and bureaus to assist soldiers and their families). The US Sanitary Commission helped to comfort the wounded and to take care of others. The 1864 establishment of Camp Chemung (Elmira Prison Camp) for Confederate prisoners of war, however, was widely criticized for its failure to provide adequate food stock, proper sewage, and adequate shelter to southern soldiers in frigid temperatures. Of the more than 12,000 soldiers held there, nearly one-fourth died of exposure, illness, and associated causes.

Renewed Party Struggle

The patriotic harmony did not last. Before long, Democratic newspapers, such as the *Albany Argus, New York World, Journal of Commerce, Day Book, Freeman's Journal,* and *Brooklyn Eagle,* constantly attacked the Lincoln administration and maintained a vigorous Democratic organization. The largely independent *New York Herald* often supported the papers. The Republicans, however, soon managed to make common cause with many War Democrats. Meeting in convention at Syracuse in September 1861, the People's Party nominated a slate that the Republicans endorsed, and the resulting Union Party was able to prevail in the fall, when it elected as attorney general the newly pro-war Dickinson. It also maintained control of the state legislature, which filled the New York quota of new recruits and authorized a bounty of $50 for each volunteer, but the opposition was not stilled. In 1862, following the Emancipation Proclamation, the Democrats, defeating Gen James Wadsworth, a radical Republican of Geneseo (Livingston Co), not only elected Seymour governor but also obtained half the seats in the assembly. They sent 17 Democrats, including Wood, against 14 Republicans, to the House of Representatives. However, in 1863 the Unionists were still able to elect former governor Morgan to the US Senate.

The Seymour Administration and the Draft Riots

Gov Seymour, a Democrat and determined opponent of the Lincoln administration, was nonetheless a patriot willing to support the war. When Lincoln sent him a letter suggesting close cooperation, however, he hesitated, not replying for several weeks and then rejecting closer contacts. Seymour's inaugural address was devoted to a reaffirmation of his loyalty to both the constitution of the state and of the United States. His annual message reaffirmed his criticism of such administration policies as the suspension of the writ of habeas corpus and interference with freedom of the press. In May 1863 he pointedly condemned the arrest of Clement L. Vallandigham, the Ohio Copperhead who had been seized after a speech defying Gen Ambrose Burnside's ban on disloyal addresses. A Democratic meeting in Albany on 16 May equally condemned the arrest, and Democratic activist Erastus Corning forwarded a decided protest to Lincoln, to which the latter sent a lengthy and fitting reply. Although the governor willingly sent troops to aid at the Battle of Gettysburg, on 4 July 1863 he delivered another stinging attack on the administration, particularly against the new conscription law.

The newly divided state legislature experienced great difficulty in passing legislation. Even the election of a Speaker caused trouble. After several unsuccessful ballots, the Republicans switched to a Democrat, Theophilus C. Callicot of Kings Co, who promised to sustain the administration's war effort and permit the election of a Republican senator. But before he was elected, the outraged Democrats, supported by rowdies from downstate, nearly caused a riot. In a dispute about the new national banking law, the legislature refused to extend a blanket permission to banks to join the system. When it passed a bill to extend voting rights to absentee soldiers, a measure that would have benefited the Republicans, the governor vetoed it, agreeing only to a constitutional amendment for the reform, which delayed it. A weak draft was finally enacted.

The main policy arousing the Democrats' ire was the new conscription law. Opposition to the draft was especially marked among the lower classes, often Irish immigrants, who not only opposed the administration because of their fear of black competition but also resented the provision enabling draftees to furnish a substitute for $300. Moreover, federal authorities were accused of not giving enough credit to the state for the troops already raised. Thus, after the draft started on 11 July 1863, a mob sacked the provost marshal's office on 3d Ave in New York City on 13 July, and for three days a serious riot engulfed the metropolis. An army officer attempting to control the crowd was lynched, the chief of police was severely mauled, and Blacks—victims of racism and immigrants' fear of competition—were mercilessly hunted, murdered, and mutilated. The latter were targeted for lynching in particular because of resistance to a war for abolition. In addition, houses of the rich, as well as the Brooks Bros clothing store, the *Tribune* building, and bars, hotels, and brothels were attacked, and the Colored Orphan Asylum on 5th Ave between 43d and 44th Sts was set aflame, but no children died in the fire. The governor arrived on the second day and attempted to calm the crowd by addressing them as "my friends," although only after sufficient troops were brought in were the mayor and the police able to restore order. Gen Dix, rather than Gen John Wool, assumed command of the troops in the department. The riots resulted in at least 119 lives and 300 wounded, as well as at least $1 million worth of property damage. Gov Seymour wanted Lincoln to stop the draft, but the president refused, and the process soon resumed.

The elections of 1863 were marked by a great effort of the Unionists to reverse the previous year's verdict. The War Department furloughed soldiers so they could go home and vote, the party brought in well-known governors and members of Congress to address the electorate, and the Unionists benefited from the strong reaction to the riots and the North's victories at Gettysburg and Vicksburg. They won the legislative elections by a 30,000-vote majority, and the new state legislature was able to pass the enabling legislation for the previously enacted absentee voting amendment. The reform passed after a referendum in March, so that soldiers were enabled to cast their ballots in 1864.

Election of 1864

During the presidential year of 1864, while the radical Republicans opposed the renomination of Lincoln, in January the Union Central Committee—the Republican Party now called itself the Union Party—endorsed him. The radicals then tried to postpone the meeting of the national convention, but they were outvoted, and in May the Syracuse state convention sent delegates to Baltimore in support of the president. Henry J. Raymond, the moderate editor of the *New York Times,* became national chairman, and although the delegation at first favored Dickinson for vice president, it finally acquiesced in the selection of Andrew Johnson. The radicals, however, were not satisfied. Having long supported Secretary of the Treasury Salmon P. Chase, they were perturbed by his resignation and made strenuous efforts to substitute another candidate for Lincoln, a movement in which Horace Greeley was especially active.

The Democratic National Convention met at the end of August in Chicago. August Belmont, the chairman of the New York Democratic Party and the New York State representative of the Rothschilds, called the convention to order, and upon Gov Seymour's refusal of the honor, George B. McClellan was nominated for president on a peace platform. Lincoln's chances seemed poor that month; he was criticized for his insistence on the abolition of slavery in any peace negotiations at a time when Greeley went to Niagara Falls to meet with southern representatives. However, the attempt to displace the president with another candidate was rendered nugatory after the capture of Atlanta in September and the subsequent victories in the Shenandoah Valley of Virginia. At the Syracuse Union Convention on 7 September, the Republicans nominated the radical Reuben E. Fenton of Chautauqua Co for governor. The Democrats, overriding Seymour's attempt to refuse renomination, saw him defeated in November. In the presidential race, the Union Party also won, carrying New York State by a vote of 368,736 to 361,987; Lincoln, who received fewer votes for president than Fenton's 369,557 for governor, finished with a majority of 6,749 votes. The state legislature, too, remained in Republican control and in early February 1865 became one of the first to ratify the 13th Amendment, abolishing slavery.

Because of intelligence that Confederate agents were going to come from Canada to burn various cities, Gen Benjamin F. Butler, who had ruled New Orleans with an iron hand, was commanded to move to New York City with troops to keep order. While there was no Confederate interference on election day, on 25 November the Confederates, who had previously been trying to commit sabotage in the city, made an effort to burn down a number of hotels in the metropolis. One of the perpetrators, Robert Kennedy, was caught and executed; the eight others escaped.

Col Henry A. Barnum from Onondaga Co, with the 149th New York Volunteers, 1864.

End of the War

The capture of Richmond, Va, on 2 Apr 1865 and the subsequent surrender of Gen Robert E. Lee at the Appomattox Court House in Virginia caused great celebrations throughout New York State. The streets were bedecked with flags, crowds sang "John Brown's Body" and other patriotic songs, and a 100-gun salute was fired at the foot of Wall St. The jubilation did not last long, however. The assassination of Lincoln plunged the state into deep gloom. On 24 April the funeral train carrying the president's remains arrived in the state and began its sad journey west. Crowds mourned at every station.

New York State's contribution to the war had been considerable: 448,000 men had been enlisted, 46,534 had become casualties, millions of dollars had been raised, and the individual New Yorkers distinguishing themselves were legion. They included Gouverneur Kemble Warren, Fitz-John Porter, Henry A. Barnum, John Adams Dix, James Wadsworth, John McAllister Schofield, Philip Kearney, George Stoneman, Henry W. Slocum, Darius N. Couch, Francis C. Barlow, Emory Upton, Daniel E. Sickles, and Abner Doubleday. William H. Seward served throughout the conflict as secretary of state, and Sens Morgan and Harris had distinguished careers in Congress. After his retirement, Gen Winfield Scott stayed at West Point (Orange Co), where Lincoln visited him in 1862.

The economy grew, and domestic commerce multiplied in volume, although foreign trade was barely able to hold its own. Railroads were built, especially the Atlantic and Great Western from Salamanca (Cattaraugus Co) to the West, and manufacturers gained war contracts. Workers fared less well because real wages fell and prices of necessities increased. After the war, the industrialization of the state continued. The New York City remained Democratic, while the rest of the state generally became Republican.

See also African Americans; Sculpture, public; United States colored troops; War memorials.

Brummer, Sidney D. *Political History of the State of New York during the Civil War* (New York: Columbia Univ Press, 1911)
Dell, Christopher. *Lincoln and the War Democrats* (Rutherford, NJ: Fairleigh Dickinson Univ Press, 1975)
Hesseltine, William B. *Lincoln and the War Governors* (New York: Knopf, 1955)
Holzer, Harold, ed. *The Union Preserved: A Guide to Civil War Records in the New York State Archives* (New York: Fordham Univ Press, 1999)
McKay, Ernest A. *The Civil War and New York City* (Syracuse: Syracuse Univ Press, 1990)
Migliore, Paul Renard. "The Business of Union: The New York Business Community and the Civil War" (PhD diss, Columbia Univ, 1975)
Mitchell, Stewart. *Horatio Seymour of New York* (Cambridge, Mass: Harvard Univ Press, 1938)
Phisterer, Frederick. *New York in the War of the Rebellion, 1861–1865,* 3d ed., 6 vols (Albany: J. B. Lyon, 1912)

Hans L. Trefousse

Civil War ethnic regiments. New York State fielded 23 ethnic regiments during the war, more than any other state. Many immigrants joined in the effort to demonstrate loyalty to their adopted country, others saw the military as an opportunity to better their economic situation, while still others were recruited by ethnic leaders seeking recognition of Old World nationalist causes. Irish and Germans, the two largest immigrant groups in New York State, provided the most men for service. The Irish Brigade originally consisted of the 63d, 69th, and 88th New York City regiments. Under the leadership of Brig Gen Thomas Francis Meagher, a former Irish revolutionary, members of the Irish Brigade won fame at Antietam, Md, and Fredericksburg, Va, for their bravery, carrying green regimental flags into battle. Over 4,000 men from the Irish Brigade were killed or wounded during the war. German regiments included recent immigrants, political exiles, and some nobility. Among the most famous were the 8th New York Infantry First German Rifles, commanded by Louis (Ludwig) Blenker, and the 46th New York Infantry Fremont Rifles, commanded by Rudolph von Rosa. The 20th New York Infantry United Turner Regiment was composed of members of turnvereins, sports clubs that promoted gymnastics, discipline, and German nationalism. The Highlanders were an established Scottish militia group who wore kilts and participated as the 79th New York Infantry. The 55th New York Volunteers Guards Lafayette, a predominantly French regiment, was too small to be federalized and received significant numbers from other groups before mustering. The most diverse of the ethnic regiments was the 39th New York Garibaldi Guard, led by Col Frederic D'Utassy. Members of its 10 companies spoke six different languages, with each company wearing distinctive uniforms. After numerous organizational and leadership problems, the 39th was captured at Harpers Ferry, WV, in 1862.

See also Poles.

Bilby, Joseph G. *The Irish Brigade in the Civil War: The 69th New York and Other Irish Regiments of the Army of the Potomac* (Conshohocken, Pa: Combined Publishing, 1998)
Burton, William L. *Melting Pot Soldiers: The Union's Ethnic Regiments* (New York: Fordham Univ Press, 1998)

Brett Michael Mills

Civil War Regiments. Congress authorized Pres Abraham Lincoln to call for state volunteers at the start of the Civil War in April 1861 because the 90-day service terms of state militia were too short to be effective. The US Army at that time numbered only about 13,000 regular troops, scattered along national frontiers. Although state forces were organized in a slapdash way, this system was the only means open to Lincoln for raising the soldiers he needed; the federal government had no power to compel military enrollment.

From 1861 to 1863 there were many ways of raising a regiment, the basic tactical unit of Civil War armies. The military was one of the traditional tracks to money and position, so there were plenty of recruiters eager to obtain an officer's position. In New York State an aspiring officer had to first obtain recruiting authority from Gov Edwin D. Morgan, Pres Lincoln, the secretary of war, or favored members of Congress. There was no coordination among these parties, however, and things quickly grew chaotic. Once he had authority to recruit, a would-be colonel still had to fill the ranks of his regiment with a sufficient number of males between 18 and 45. Regiments of New York Volunteers (NYV) were recruited locally from cities and counties within a single state senatorial district. After acceptance by the state, the unit was mustered into federal service. In part to control the recruiters' rivalries and the confusion over vague jurisdictions, Gov Morgan was commissioned a major general of US Volunteers on 28 Sept 1861 and put in command of the Military Department of New York.

The potential of a regimental commander had more to do with attracting enrollees than military competence. It was generally understood that his agents would be rewarded with officer's commissions in proportion to the number of men they brought into the unit. A second lieutenant's commission was granted to those recruiting at least 30 men, a first lieutenant's commission for at least 40 men, and a captain's commission for 83 or more men. Initially an infantry regiment of NYV was made up of 780 men, 10 companies of 77 men each plus 10 field and staff officers. This standard soon changed to 100-men companies, with a minimum of 844 and a maximum of 1,024 troops. The birth of a New York State regiment always included a ceremony during which it received one or both of its colors, the national and state flags. The New York flag was sometimes altered to reflect specific units, such as some regiments made up of Irish immigrants and American-born Irishmen born, who carried flags of green silk.

In 1861 and 1862 Gov Morgan and a staff of less than 20 men accomplished the remarkable task of raising a force that was 12 times the size of the prewar US Army. New York State sent 208 regiments into service, and more than 190,000 men left the state in the following units: the 1st NYV Engineer Regiment, the 1st–38th NYV Infantry Regiments (two-year enlistments; organized in 83 days, these had all left the state by 12 July 1861, including the 15th NYV Engineers), the 39th–165th, 169th, 170th, 173d–175th, and 185th NYV Regiments of Infantry (three-year enlistments, including the 50th NYV Engineers and the 1st NYV Marine Artillery), the 177th NYV Infantry Regiment (nine-month enlistment), 11 regiments of cavalry and the 1st NYV Mounted Rifles, 1 regiment of light artillery, 4 regiments of heavy artillery, and 18 infantry regiments of the New York National Guard. They left the state for 90-day terms of service, and 7 of these regiments were activated twice in two years. In addition 31 independent batteries of light artillery were raised. New Yorkers also joined the US Army, Navy, Marines, US Volunteers, and Veteran Reserve Corps, which increased the state's total enlistments to just over 255,000 during the first two years of the war.

In 1863 and 1864 fewer new units of volunteers were organized, and nearly all enlistees were sent as replacements to New York regiments already in the field. On 3 Mar 1863 Congress passed the Enrollment Act to enhance the federal government's ability to raise troops, strengthening the Federal Militia Act of 1862. The Enrollment Act gave the federal government power to raise and support armies without state assistance and would profoundly change the way in which regiments were brought together. The act called for involuntary conscription and had an ever-changing list of exemptions, including the possibility of a draftee paying $300 to commute his service or paying another individual to enlist in his place. In 1863, while he had the support of the state legislature, Gov Horatio Seymour did everything in his power to resist the draft and to oppose the Lincoln administration. Secretary of State William H. Seward aptly described Seymour's activities when he told a reporter that "confederate soldiers would cast in favor of Seymour if they could vote." Resistance to the draft in New York State culminated in the New York City draft riots of 13–17 July 1863, when over 100 people were killed and at least 50 buildings were destroyed by fire. It proved very difficult to conduct an effective draft. During the three drafts conducted in 1863–64, more than 440,000 names were drawn from New York State, but only 5,763 of these draftees donned uniforms, and another 17,617 furnished substitutes.

Even though there was resistance, New Yorkers nonetheless continued to step forward and enlist: more than 210,000 during 1863–64. Of these more than 54,000 left the state in the following new units: the 1st NYV Sharpshooters (three-year enlistments), the 168th NYV Infantry Regiment (nine-month enlistments), the 184th–189th NYV Infantry Regiments (one-year enlistments), the 176th, 178th, 179th, 7th Veteran, and 17th Veteran NYV Regiments of Infantry (three-year enlistments), 14 regiments of cavalry, 1 independent battery of light artillery, 4 regiments of heavy artillery, and 26 infantry regiments of the New York National Guard. They left the state for one-month terms of service during the Gettysburg campaign, and two regiments left the state for 100-day service during 1864. African American troops, not generally allowed to enlist before 1863, provided the 20th, 26th, and 31st Regiments of US Colored Troops. Only two new regiments, with approximately 2,000 men, left the state during 1865 for one-year terms of service into the 192d and 193d New York Volunteers.

Israel, Fred L. "New York's Citizen Soldiers," *New York History* 42 (Apr 1961): 145–56

Levine, Peter. "Draft Evasion in the North during the Civil War, 1863–1865," *Journal of American History* 67 (Mar 1981): 816–34

Lorello, Dan. *The Union Preserved: A Guide to Civil War Records in the New York State Archives* (New York: Fordham Univ Press, 1999)

Phisterer, Frederick. *New York in the War of the Rebellion, 1861 to 1865* (Albany: J. B. Lyon, 1912)

Benedict R. Maryniak

Clare. Town (pop 112) in S central St. Lawrence Co. Located entirely within the Adirondack Park, it was formed from Pierrepont in 1880. Historically logging and iron mining were important; in the early 21st century the economy is based on forestry and wages earned outside the town. Chief attractions are Lampson Falls on the Grass River, Twin Falls, and other falls and rapids on the South and Middle Branches of the Grass. Public access to these falls came with the state's purchase of land and conservation easements.

Richard E. Mooers

Clarence. Town (pop 26,123) in N Erie Co. Settled in 1799, the town was formed from Willink [now Aurora, Erie Co] in 1808. Mennonites settled in Clarence by 1829, when they built its first church. French Catholics and Bavarian Germans settled along Transit Rd in the 1830s, followed by Prussian Germans in the 1850s. The Canandaigua and Niagara Falls Railroad (later New York Central) crossed the town in 1853; the West Shore Railroad came through in 1884. In the Civil War era, Clarence was the county's leading poultry town, a large butter producer, and second to Newstead in wool production. Limestone was quarried at Shimerville beginning in 1875, and gypsum was mined from 1926 until 1982. Clarence's population doubled in the 1950s and doubled again between 1960 and 2000. In the early 21st century, Mennen-Greatbatch Electronics manufactured medical electronics. The brick Italianate J. Eshelman and Co Store (1872) at Clarence Center is listed on the National Register of Historic Places.

Nancy B. Mingus

Clarendon. Town (pop 3,392) in SE Orleans Co. Settled in 1811, the town was formed from Sweden (Monroe Co) in 1821. In the 19th century, limestone quarries and limekilns operated at Clarendon hamlet; Miller and Pettengill's cider and vinegar factory (1873–88) was a significant business. Muckland was drained in the 1910s and the 1930s for lettuce, onions, carrots, potatoes, and cabbage. The Clarendon Cheese Factory (1915–43) supplied a national market. The town's population increased during the 1990s by 25% due to an exurban influx from the Rochester metropolitan area. In the early 21st century, dairying and vegetables remain important, and Clarendon Cheesecakes and Hanson Aggregates are the major employers.

Susan Persia

Clark, Egbert Norman (*b* Milwaukee, 15 Aug 1872; *d* Utica, 16 Nov 1942). Artist and local historian. Clark became a commercial artist at an early age in Milwaukee and later worked in Chicago, New York City, and Columbus, Ohio, before moving to Utica around 1930. He developed an immense interest in Utica's rich, early history. Relying on his wife Lucy Dunn Clark's (1884–1945) research, he painted historical scenes of the city's growth for the Savings Bank of Utica periodical *Way to Wealth* in the 1930s and later for Clark's own publication *The Upstate Monthly* (1940–42). His initial murals were painted by commission of the Utica Mutual Insurance Co and the Hotel Utica. During the Great Depression, through the Public Works of Art Project (PWAP) of the Works Progress Administration, Clark created six murals for Thomas R. Proctor High School measuring 4 x 12 feet (1.2 x 3.7 m), portraying many important events of early commerce in Utica. Other smaller PWAP murals, 4 x 8 feet (1.2 x 2.4 m), have similar historic themes. Clark's numerous murals are considered by many to be his most important legacy as well as the best existing visual record of early Utica history. They are replete with detail, with the backgrounds filled with activity rather than scenery, reflecting the artist's confidence in the accuracy of his historic information. Despite his achievements as a muralist, Clark always considered himself an illustrator.

Cardarelli, Malio J. *Utica Preserved in Water and Oil: The Historic Paintings of Egbert Norman Clark* (New Hartford, NY: Author, 2001)

Malio J. Cardarelli

Clark, Myron H(olley) (*b* Naples, Ontario Co, 23 Oct 1806; *d* Canandaigua, Ontario Co, 23 Aug 1892). Governor. A businessman with an elementary school education, Clark held several local offices in Ontario Co and moved to Canandaigua while serving as county sheriff from 1837 to 1839. His fanatical support for prohibition made him popular, and he was elected president of Canandaigua in 1850 and 1851, representing it in the state senate from 1852 to 1854 as a Whig. In 1854 he played a key role in the passage of an alcohol prohibition bill modeled after the Maine Law of 1851, but Gov Horatio Seymour vetoed the measure. Nominated for governor in 1854 by a combination of antislavery and temperance reformers (groups that would soon become part of the developing Republican Party), Clark garnered only 33% of the vote in a four-way race including Gov Seymour and won election by only 309 votes of more than 469,000 of those cast. He signed a prohibitionary liquor bill in 1855, but eight months later the New York State Court of Appeals declared it unconstitutional in *Wynehamer v People* (1856). The Republican Party did not nominate Clark for a second term in 1856, although Pres Abraham Lincoln appointed him collector of internal revenue in 1862. Clark then lived in semiretirement in Canandaigua, emerging briefly in 1874 to accept the Prohibition Party's nomination for governor.

Booraem, Hendrik. *The Formation of the Republican Party in New York* (New York: New York Univ Press, 1983)
Milliken, Charles. *A History of Ontario County, New York, and Its People* (New York: Lewis Historical Publishing, 1911)

Jon Sterngass

Clarke, George (*b* Swainswick, England, ?1676; *d* Chester, England, 12 Jan 1760). Lieutenant governor. Clarke arrived in New York Colony on 23 July 1703 as deputy to his uncle, Auditor General William Blathwayt. Over the next 33 years he held a variety of appointed posts, including provincial secretary, judge of the appeals court, and provincial councilor. Clarke aggressively pursued Mohawk Valley land speculation, through which he parlayed the small income from his offices into a fortune. He became acting governor at the death of William Cosby on 10 Mar 1736 and after a brief challenge led by Rip van Dam received a royal commission as lieutenant governor on 30 Oct 1736. His negotiations with the Seneca in September 1737 forestalled French encroachment on Irondequoit [now in Monroe Co], and he successfully prodded the assembly into repairing Fort Oswego. He did nothing to stop the Negro Plot hysteria of 1741 but did commute the death sentences of 72 people. Replaced in 1743 by Gov George Clinton, Clarke returned to England, where he purchased an estate at Chester and was reportedly worth £100,000 at his death.

Katz, Stanley N. *Newcastle's New York: Anglo-American Politics, 1732–1753* (Cambridge, Mass: Belknap Press, 1968)

Daniel A. Piazza

Clark family. Philanthropists. Edward Clark (1811–82) created the family fortune. The son of small factory owners in Hudson (Columbia Co), Clark graduated from Williams College in 1830 and joined the New York State Bar in 1833. After practicing law in Poughkeepsie, in 1837 he entered a partnership with Ambrose L. Jordan, later New York State attorney general (1848–49), in New York City, marrying Jordan's daughter, Caroline, soon after. In 1851 Clark became a partner in the Singer Sewing Machine Co, founded one year earlier by the flamboyant former actor and innovative inventor Isaac Merrit Singer. Clark secured Singer's patent rights, saving the fledgling company from bankruptcy, and then directed the company's evolution from a handful of employees into the first successful US multinational company. A devout Protestant and publicity shy, Clark established the Edward Clark Benevolent Society to assist Singer employees financially. Beginning in 1854 he and Caroline maintained a residence in her birthplace of Cooperstown (Otsego Co). Clark also developed real estate and built many fine homes and apartment buildings in New York City, including the famed Dakota on Central Park West. On his death he left $25 million to his only surviving son and Cooperstown resident, Alfred Corning Clark (1844–1950). Three of Alfred's sons, Edward S. (1870–1933), Frederick (1880–1964), and Stephen C. (1882–1960), served as benefactors to and promoters of Cooperstown, building the 135-room Otesaga Hotel in 1909 and the Baseball Hall of Fame in 1939, as well as convincing the New York State Historical Association to place its headquarters there in the 1930s. A fourth son, Robert Sterling Clark (1877–1956), left his valuable art collection "away from" the town to the Sterling and Francine Clark Art Institute of Williamstown, Mass. At the beginning of the 21st century, the Clark family owns over 20% of the real estate in Cooperstown and controls in excess of $350 million. Seven Clark family foundations continue to benefit Cooperstown, and many Clarks reside there.

Birmingham, Stephen. *Life at the Dakota: New York's Most Unusual Address* (New York: Random House, 1979)
Bissell, Don. *The First Conglomerate: 145 Years of the Singer Sewing Machine Company* (Brunswick, Maine: Audenreed Press, 1999)

Don Bissell

Clarkson. Town (pop 6,072) in NW Monroe Co. Settled in ?1803, the town was formed from Murray (Orleans Co) in 1819. Clarkson Corners was the hub of activity in northwest Monroe Co until the Erie Canal was built through Brockport. The Clarkson Association, a Fourierist phalanx (a utopian socialist community), existed briefly (1844–45). In the 19th century Clarkson was a town of cereal, fruit, and general farming; in 1877 its largest business was the Ridge Road Creamery Co. George B. Selden (1846–1922) was awarded the first US automobile patent. Since the 1960s Clarkson has become increasingly suburbanized; its 1990 population of 4,517 increased 34% by 2000. The town is noted for its many cobblestone and brick buildings, including the Selden House (1819) and Clarkson Academy (*ca* 1855).

Nancy Martin

Clarkson University. Private university. Established in Potsdam (St. Lawrence Co) in 1896 as the Thomas S. Clarkson Memorial School of Technology to honor a local businessman who was killed in 1894 trying to save one of his workers, the school offered technical, normal, and liberal courses. Its name was changed twice, in 1913 to Thomas Clarkson College of Technology and in 1984 to Clarkson University. Clarkson offers undergraduate and graduate degrees in engineering, business, liberal arts, science, and physical therapy. In 2002 it enrolled more than 2,600 undergraduates and 350 graduates, and had a campus of 640 acres (259 ha) and nearly 50 structures.

Broughton, Bradford B. *A Clarkson Mosaic* (Potsdam, NY: Clarkson Univ, 1995)

Carl A. Westerdahl

Clarkstown. Town (pop 82,082) in E central Rockland Co. The town was named for Daniel DeClark, one of a group of investors who, in 1716, bought part of the Kakiat Patent. The town was formed from Haverstraw in 1791. The Dutch Factory (?1812) on the town's west boundary manufactured cotton at various periods but later made mosquito netting (1857) and brier pipes (1882). Ice was cut on Rockland Lake starting in 1831, and stone was quarried along the Hudson. In the late 19th century its farms shipped milk, apples, and garden produce. Clarkstown acquired two railroads in 1870, and the West Shore began operations in 1883. Dexter Press (1920), a postcard manufacturer, was located at West Nyack. Van Houten Fields (1937–45) was a back-to-the-land cooperative community near West Nyack founded by Ralph Borsodi. The Thruway (1955) opened Clarkstown to intensive suburbanization, and its population increased fourfold from 15,674 to 61,653 between 1950 and 1970. In the early 21st century Clarkstown is a commuter suburb, the site of the county's two largest shopping malls, in West Nyack and Nanuet, and of Hook Mountain, Nyack Beach, and Rockland Lake State Parks, which are contiguous.

Clarksville. Town (pop 1,146) in SW Allegany Co. Settled in 1822, the town was formed in 1835 from Cuba. Pine lumber was its first product followed by dairying, but in 1883 oil was struck, and in 1887 there were over 350 wells in town. A flooding system was used in the 1950s and resulted in an end to extraction. The Standard Oil Co pipeline (1880) crossed town from east to west. The Franciscans of St. Bonaventure operate the Mount Irenaeus retreat center at West Clarksville.

classical music, Albany and the Capital District. Although there had been classical music performed privately since the late 18th century, public concerts in Albany began after the arrival of many German immigrants in the 1840s. Between 1849 and 1897 the Capital District boasted the founding of 13 German singing societies established to promote interest in classical vocal music and to help unify the German community for musical purposes. One of the earliest large-scale concerts was a performance of Haydn's *The Creation,* with 150 soloists, in 1849. From the early 1840s to the 1870s concerts were held in local churches, the arsenal, parks, and, in the 1880s, the Leland Opera House and Harmanus Bleecker Hall. The singing society Cæcilia (1866) won the grand prize at Brooklyn Sängerfeste in 1885. Thirty men formed the Albany Musical Association (1867) and performed mostly at Tweddle Hall. Many of these organizations remained active into the 20th century. The Albany Philharmonic Society formed in 1884 to perform and promote musical instruction.

The tradition of vocal music has been maintained by a number of organizations. T. J. Bradley and Frank Sill Rogers founded the Mendelssohn Club (1909), an all-male chorus that often works with acclaimed soloists. The Octavo Singers, a notable amateur group, was founded in Schenectady in the 1930s with funds from the federal Works Progress Administration. Since 1970 the group's conductor has been George A. Moross. Capitol Hill Choral Society, founded in 1953 by conductor Judson Rand, is especially noted for its annual performance of Handel's *Messiah.* Albany Pro Musica (1981), founded by David Griggs-Janower, performs mostly a cappella works and records and commissions new choral works.

The Troy Chromatics Concerts series was formed in 1894 and since 1902 has presented internationally prominent soloists and instrumental groups at the acoustically renowned Troy Savings Bank Music Hall (1870). The Albany Symphony Orchestra (1931) was initially led by John Carabella, with concerts given at Philip Livingston Junior High School. In 1992 David Alan Miller became the orchestra's seventh conductor. The orchestra performs regularly, often with internationally prominent soloists, at Troy Savings Bank Music Hall, Canfield Casino in Saratoga Springs, and Albany's Palace Theater. Regularly performing works by past masters, the group also plays and records numerous pieces by 20th- and 21st-century American composers. A small ensemble from the orchestra, the Dogs of Desire, commissions and performs contemporary works. The Schenectady Symphony Orchestra (1934) performs at Proctor's Theater in Schenectady. Charles Schneider became its conductor in 1983. Chamber music is performed regularly at the Schenectady Museum, Union College music series, and the Friends of Chamber Music series, held at Emma Willard School in Troy. The Albany Records, founded in 1986 by Susan Bush and Peter Kermani, specializes in releases of contemporary American composers. Saratoga Performing Arts Center (SPAC) was founded in 1966 and hosts the Philadelphia Orchestra, the Saratoga Chamber Music Festival, and the Lake George Opera Festival each summer.

Paul Lamar

classical music, Buffalo. During its earliest years, Buffalo's musical activities mostly consisted of a variety of small wind band events. By 1838 the Handel and Haydn Society was headquartered at the music store of English immigrant James D. Sheppard, Buffalo's first classically trained musician. Buffalo became a regular tour stop for some of Europe's most celebrated soloists, the first of whom was the "Swedish Nightingale" Jenny Lind, who performed in 1851. The same year a former slave, Elizabeth Taylor Greenfield, who had moved to Buffalo, made her concert debut under sponsorship of the Buffalo Music Association. Known as the Black Swan, she went on to become the first African American to enjoy international acclaim as a concert singer. By the late 1860s Buffalo also had many ethnic singing societies, some of which presented German and Italian opera with piano accompaniment.

From 1882 to 1912 Buffalo was a tour venue for the well-known Theodore Thomas Orchestra. After the success of diverse local events such as the 1884 Buffalo Music Festival, the Buffalo Symphony Orchestra was founded in 1888 under conductor John Lund, who had been an assistant conductor at Manhattan's Metropolitan Opera. After 1897 the orchestra could not sustain financial support, but Buffalo became a regular venue for orchestras touring from Chicago, Boston, and New York, including appearances by Victor Herbert's Orchestra and the (John Philip) Sousa Band at the Pan-American Exposition in 1901. In 1922, under Dutch-born Arnold Cornelissen, another symphony orchestra was formed that, mostly on a part-time basis, employed many of the musicians who played in Buffalo's movie and vaudeville theaters. Again, without concerted community support the orchestra could not be sustained after 1929. The Buffalo Chamber Music Society, founded in 1924, has sponsored performances by leading chamber ensembles and soloists from around the world.

In the early 1930s interest was generated among civic and business leaders to form a professional orchestra. By late 1934, via the efforts of philanthropists Cameron Baird, Frederick Slee, and Samuel P. Capen, a conductor was recruited, European-trained Lajos Shuk, a cello virtuoso and director of the New York Civic Symphony. The Buffalo Philharmonic Orchestra Society was formed and a series of pops concerts was presented at the Elmwood Music Hall in the 1935–36 season. Through the leadership of Florence Wendt, the society's president, the orchestra was sustained through 1937, when support was received from the federal Works Progress Administration (WPA). Anticipating rapid artistic growth, the orchestra had added to the player roster and engaged Franco Autori as the orchestra's music director (1936–45). The city's need for a fine concert hall was fulfilled by a bequest from the estate of Buffalo clothier Edward L. Kleinhans and his wife Mary Seaton Kleinhans, with further assistance from the WPA. Designed by Eliel and Eero Saarinen and dedicated in 1940, Kleinhans Music Hall remains among the acoustical and architectural jewels of the United States. The main auditorium seats 2,839, and the Mary Seaton Room, a smaller chamber hall, seats up to 900.

In its new home the artistic level of the Buffalo Philharmonic Orchestra (BPO) rose dramatically. The podium of the orchestra was assigned to a string of prominent music directors, including the German émigré William Steinberg (1945–52) and his successor, Josef Krips (1954–63), both of whom excelled in the central European repertoire. When Lukas Foss (1963–70) became the music director, the orchestra's programming began to feature new music from the avant-garde, and the BPO made its first major recordings, television broadcasts, and national tours, including appearances at Carnegie Hall and Lincoln Center in New York City. Under Michael Tilson Thomas (1971–79), the spirit of adventurous programming continued, and he directed the orchestra in its celebrated recording of Gershwin overtures. Subsequent music directors have included Julius Rudel (1979–85), Semyon Bychkov (1985–89), and Maximiano Valdes (1989–98). With JoAnn Falletta (1998–), one of the first female music directors of a major American orchestra, the BPO has experienced an artistic renaissance and has recorded CDs on major labels, including issues devoted to American composers Frederick Shepherd Converse and Charles Tomlinson Griffes.

In 1974 Thomas also presided over the dedication of Artpark, the state theater at Lewiston

(Niagara Co), which, among other functions, was intended as the summer home of the BPO. The artistic helm of Artpark was assigned to Christopher Keene, who directed many opera productions there with the BPO through the late 1970s and early 1980s, often in collaboration with the City Opera of New York City and including the American premiere of Philip Glass's *Satyagraha* (1981). Another vital element in the history of classical music in Buffalo is SUNY Buffalo's Department of Music. Since its establishment in 1952, the department has attracted distinguished visiting faculty composers, including Paul Hindemith, Aaron Copland, Carlos Chavez, and Ned Rorem. A bequest from the Slee family has sponsored performances of Beethoven's complete quartet cycle every year since 1955 in Slee Concert Hall, a 670-seat auditorium with a full pipe organ. In 1964 department chair Allen Sapp and BPO music director Lukas Foss initiated the Center for the Creative and Performing Arts, beginning with 19 full-time, nonteaching appointments of extraordinary young composers and instrumentalists from around the world. While the requisite high level of state funding would prevail for just a few years, the center nonetheless maintained its Evenings for New Music series both in Buffalo and at Carnegie Hall for more than a decade, in addition to making two European tours in the early 1970s. In 1975 the June in Buffalo (JIB) festival for new music was initiated by Morton Feldman, a central figure in 20th-century composition who taught at SUNY Buffalo from 1972 to 1987. Since 1986 JIB has been directed by composer and SUNY Buffalo faculty member David Felder. During a hiatus of JIB, the North American New Music Festival (NANMF) was initiated at the university in 1983 by Yvar Mikhashoff and Jan Williams, who co-directed it through 1993.

Almquist, Sharon Grieggs. "A History of the State University of New York at Buffalo Music Department to 1968" (MA thesis, SUNY Buffalo, 1986)
Levine-Packer, Renee. "The Center for the Creative and Performing Arts in the State University of New York at Buffalo" (MA thesis, SUNY Buffalo, 2001)
Wolf, Mildred E. *History of Music in Buffalo 1820–45*, 3d ed. (Buffalo: Kleinhans Music Hall Management, 1953)

Edward Yadzinski

classical music, New York City. With Boston, New York City may be regarded as one of the two birthplaces for America's musical high culture. Nineteenth-century Boston was Brahmin and genteel: it cultivated a notable religious choral tradition. New York, by comparison, was heterogeneous and progressive: it passionately embraced opera and revered Richard Wagner.

The 19th Century

In the late 18th and early 19th centuries, opera in New York generally meant British and American ballad opera with spoken dialogue or bowdlerized versions of French and Italian works. The best known of these, *The Beggar's Opera* (1728) by English composer John Gay, first appeared in New York City in 1750. A turning point in the city's operatic history was the 1825–26 residency of Manuel García, a famous Spanish singer and pedagogue, with a company including the future Maria Malibran and a repertoire including Wolfgang Amadeus Mozart's *Don Giovanni* and four Gioacchino Rossini works. Assisting at these performances was Lorenzo Da Ponte, the librettist of *Don Giovanni* some 40 years earlier and a resident of the United States since 1805. The Academy of Music (1854) on 14th St and Irving Place centralized New York City opera to a degree. During its heyday it featured productions by warring impresarios, rival singers of international reputation, and raucously enthusiastic audiences. By the time opera moved uptown to the more fashionable and decorous Metropolitan Opera House (the Met) on Broadway and 39th St (1883), relative decorum prevailed. But the boxholders, who were also shareholders, could not call the tune. When French and Italian opera proved too expensive, they relinquished the house to a German language company for seven years, during which the operas of Wagner, transferred from the German language Stadttheater on the Bowery, reigned supreme. Anton Seidl presided in the pit, a world-class German ensemble was maintained, and the shareholders chafed. The Germans were expelled in 1891, after which German and French/Italian factions jostled for predominance. By 1900 a policy of giving operas in the original language—German, French, or Italian—had crystallized.

A landmark event in New York concert life was the American debut of Jenny Lind, the Swedish Nightingale, presented in 1850 by P. T. Barnum at Castle Garden in the Battery to a cheering audience of 5,000. A vogue for celebrity singers and instrumentalists ensued. Of the pianists, one of the most celebrated was American-born Louis Moreau Gottschalk, who gave 90 New York concerts in seven seasons beginning in 1853. Gottschalk mainly played his own music, a practice powerfully challenged and reformed by Russia's Anton Rubinstein, who in 1872 regaled New Yorkers with mighty doses of Bach, Beethoven, Chopin, and Schumann. Symphonic activity developed as well. The New York Philharmonic Society, begun as a musicians' cooperative in 1842, is the oldest American orchestra with a continuous existence into the early 21st century, but it by no means dominated New York's 19th-century concert life. The French conductor Louis Jullien appeared in 1853 with an orchestra of greater brilliance and polish; he also (more than the Philharmonic) gave American works, alongside such specialties as the "Fireman's Quadrille," with firemen and real flames. Theodore Thomas's summer seasons at Central Park Garden, comprising 1,127 concerts beginning in 1868, eclipsed all other symphonic efforts anywhere in the United States. At first, Thomas stressed light music; within a few seasons, full symphonies and concertos were performed as a matter of course. In 1877 Thomas became conductor of the Philharmonic, to be succeeded by Seidl in 1891. The rival New York Symphony, founded by Leopold Damrosch in 1878, was led by his son Walter beginning in 1885 and merged with the Philharmonic in 1928.

Of New York's concert composers, William Henry Fry, George Friedrich Bristow, and Anthony Philip Heinrich are among a notable antebellum generation. Fry was also the first music critic for a major American daily newspaper, Horace Greeley's *New York Tribune* (1852–64). While Boston's reigning critic, John Sullivan Dwight, ennobled Beethoven, Fry fulminated over the neglect of contemporary and American composers, not least himself. In 1853–54, supported by Bristow, he launched a vehement campaign against the Philharmonic's neglect of American music. Although Fry, Bristow, and Heinrich were not ignored in their time, their music swiftly disappeared after their deaths. Among the most famous of all 19th-century American composers was Edward MacDowell, Columbia University's first professor of music (1896–1904).

The 1890s were important for classical music in New York. Andrew Carnegie's new Music Hall opened at 7th Ave and 57th St in 1891; Peter Tchaikovsky, as guest of honor, was amazed to discover himself far better known in America than in Europe. Seidl, now the leading local symphonic conductor and still a presence at the Met, influentially championed the Music of the Future; probably nowhere in Europe were Wagner and Franz Liszt as frequently performed as at Seidl's summer concerts at Brooklyn's Brighton Beach, where he appeared 14 times a week with his own orchestra. New York City was the headquarters of the American Wagner movement, a distinctive meliorist variant on European Wagnerism. Meanwhile, the Met prospered, with stellar casts in three languages. The musical press, led by Henry Krehbiel of the *Tribune*, was abundant, intelligent, and progressive. The most celebrated musician of the decade was the Bohemian composer Antonín Dvořák, who directed the National Conservatory of Music on East 17th St from 1892 to 1895. Like Seidl and Krehbiel, Dvořák anticipated an American national school anchored by an indigenous canon of symphonies and operas. He attempted to point the way with his symphony *From the New World;* its Carnegie Hall premiere, led by Seidl with the Philharmonic on 16 Dec 1893, was a signature event.

The 20th Century

Following Dvořák's departure and Seidl's early death (1897), the push for an American repertoire diminished. Preoccupied with great orchestras, performers, and conductors, the New York scene grew less creative. In the course of the 20th century, the Met regularly presented glamorous vocal stars more often than any other opera house in the world. In particular, Enrico Caruso and Geraldine Farrar, members of the company during the first two decades of the 20th century, were cult figures. Oscar Hammerstein's Manhattan Opera (1906–10) was the most remarkable of numerous "opera for the people" ventures, offering new works and major artists to appreciative audiences before Hammerstein was bought off by the Met.

The first of the city's 20th-century celebrity conductors, Gustav Mahler, appeared at the Met (1908–10) and briefly presided over the reorganization of the Philharmonic as a permanent full-time orchestra (1909–11). Mahler was eclipsed by Arturo Toscanini, who—as conductor at the Met (1908–15), of the Philharmonic (1928–36), and finally of the NBC Symphony (1937–54), created especially for him—became the figurehead for classical music nationally. At the Met in 1910, Toscanini led a significant world premiere, that of Puccini's *The Girl of the Golden West.* But in contrast to Thomas, Dvořák, and Seidl, Toscanini in America concerned himself relatively little with contemporary or American culture; rather, he concentrated on the canonized European masters, beginning with Beethoven. Appraising the regime of his Philharmonic successor John Barbirolli, Virgil Thomson affirmed famously in the *New York Herald-Tribune* that the New York Philharmonic was "not a part of New York's intellectual life." But New York City was a mecca for stellar European performers, many of whom were refugees from war and revolution.

The Philharmonic acquired post-Toscanini glamor only in 1958, when Leonard Bernstein became the first American-born music director of a major American orchestra. Not since Thomas and Seidl did the Philharmonic enjoy the services of so popular and influential a music educator. Bernstein's legacies included widespread new appreciation for Gustav Mahler and Charles Ives; Bernstein the theater composer produced *On the Town* (1944), *Wonderful Town* (1953), and *West Side Story* (1957)—all visions of Manhattan. Bernstein's tenure, ending in 1969, also included the 1962 move to Lincoln Center's Philharmonic Hall (since 1973, Avery Fisher Hall) at Broadway and 66th St, an acoustically troubled facility several times revamped. The Met moved to Lincoln Center in 1966; James Levine, who in 1975 began his tenure as the company's artistic leader, mounted a belated push for 20th-century repertoire. New York's second opera company, the New York City Opera, was founded in 1943 and in 1966 moved from the City Center on West 55th St to its Lincoln Center home: the acoustically unsuitable New York State Theater, where it continued to emphasize American and contemporary works. Carnegie Hall, saved from the wrecking ball in 1960 by a campaign headed by the violinist Isaac Stern, maintained its status as a prestigious showcase for orchestras and recitalists.

Composers took a back seat to performers after World War I and were further marginalized by burgeoning popular music genres. The most prominent New York concert composer of the interwar decades was Aaron Copland, many of whose works evoke the energy or anomie of city life, and whose *Music for a Great City* (1964) explicitly depicts New York. On the fringes of classical music, George Gershwin bridged the high/low divide in such works as *Rhapsody in Blue,* presented at a legendary Paul Whiteman concert, An Experiment in Modern Music, at Aeolian Hall (12 Feb 1924). Among high modernists of the later 20th century, Elliott Carter, a lifetime New Yorker, was the preeminent figure. The "uptown" musical high culture of Carter and various university-affiliated composers was challenged by "downtown" minimalists. The latter included Philip Glass and Steve Reich, both sometime New York City residents whose most prominent New York showcase has been the Brooklyn Academy of Music, built in 1908 and revitalized in the late 1960s. John Cage, a leading avant-garde figure, made his home in New York City for half a century.

New York is also the American home of such music publishers as Boosey and Hawkes, Carl Fischer, C. F. Peters, and G. Schirmer, and of three leading music schools: the Juilliard School, founded in 1905 and a Lincoln Center constituent since 1968; the Manhattan School of Music, founded in 1917; and the Mannes College of Music, founded in 1916. For much of the 20th century the offices of Columbia Artists Management Inc (CAMI), on West 57th St, were considered the American headquarters for classical music, with Arthur Judson, as founder and head of CAMI (1930–48) and manager of the New York Philharmonic (1922–56), wielding more power than any other music businessperson. By 2000 CAMI's power had shrunk and so had classical music as a component of the city's cultural life.

Horowitz, Joseph. *Classical Music in the United States: A History* (New York: Norton, forthcoming)
Mayer, Martin. *The Met: 100 Years of Grand Opera* (New York: Simon & Schuster, 1983)
Shanet, Howard. *Philharmonic: A History of New York's Orchestra* (New York: Doubleday, 1975)

Joseph Horowitz

classical music, Rochester. Musical events were well integrated into Rochester society by the time of the city's incorporation in 1834. Band and vocal concerts were prominent, often taking place in meeting houses or rooms in local taverns. Among the earliest choral groups were the Rochester Academy of Music (1835) and the Mechanics Musical Association (1837). Notable music teachers included George Pryer and Henry Russell, the composer of "Woodman, Spare That Tree." As a reflection of the development of local musical interest and abilities, Rochester was the scene of "musical conventions" that featured teachers from Boston in 1843, 1845, 1848, and 1850.

Ole Bull, the Norwegian violinist, appeared in Rochester in 1844. Leopold de Meyer, one of Europe's most notable pianists, appeared in 1846, followed shortly by Austrian pianist, Henri Herz. Jenny Lind, the most famous soprano of her time, sang in Rochester in 1851, with tickets selling at the unheard of prices of $2, $3, and $5. Another famous soprano, Adelina Patti, appeared in 1852, only 9 years old at the time. Other performers included American pianist Louis Moreau Gottschalk and Swiss-born Sigismond Thalberg, the only pianist whom European audiences considered a possible rival to Franz Liszt. An early Rochester Philharmonic Orchestra was founded (1865-early 1880s), and international artists continued to appear in undiminished numbers. Corinthian Hall, on Exchange Place near the Reynolds Arcade, was the principal location of concerts until the late 19th century. Erected in 1849 at an impressive cost of $12,000, the hall had a seating capacity of about 1,600. Other local performing organizations founded in the later half of the 19th century included the Opera Club, the first Rochester Oratorio Society, the Mendelssohn Singing Society, and the Choral Union. A particularly important contribution was made by the Tuesday Musicale, founded in 1889. Established for the benefit of its own members, it soon developed a series of evening concerts for the general public and brought to Rochester a number of major international musicians.

The 20th Century

On 5 Feb 1900, the Dossenbach Orchestra presented its first concert under the direction of its founder, Hermann Dossenbach. Later renamed the Rochester Orchestra, it developed into the city's first professional symphony orchestra. From 1907 the orchestra's concerts and recitals by visiting international artists took place mainly at Convention Hall on Washington Square, originally built as the State Armory in 1870. Among local impresarios, James Furlong was perhaps the most prominent. The group enjoyed a successful existence until 1919, when it disbanded. In 1913 Dossenbach joined Alf Klingenberg in opening the Dossenbach-Klingenberg School of Music on Prince St. The following year Oscar Gariessen became a co-owner of the school, and its name was changed to the D. K. G. Institute of Musical Art, the initials reflecting the surnames of the three directors. This was the most serious effort to date in providing quality musical instruction in Rochester. In 1917 Klingenberg became the sole proprietor, and the following year George Eastman bought the property and the corporate rights, intending to present the school to the University of Rochester. This was accomplished in 1919, and Eastman committed himself to providing a new building and a municipal theater. In 1921 Eastman presented the new Eastman School of Music to the University of Rochester with an endowment. Since then, the school's faculty and alumni have included numerous musicians of national and international reputation. The adjoining Eastman Theatre opened in 1922, and it soon became the location of concerts and recitals by the leading musicians of the world, as well as the home of the newly organized Rochester Philharmonic Orchestra.

The Eastman Theatre Orchestra accompanied silent films in the Eastman Theatre in the early 1920s. Augmented by additional personnel, the orchestra began in 1923 to give orchestral concerts as the Rochester Philharmonic Orchestra. Its first concert was conducted by Arthur Alexander. Albert Coates and Eugene Goossens were among the earlier conductors of the orchestra, Goossens remaining until 1931. Other music directors have included Jose Iturbi (1936–44), Erich Leinsdorf (1947–56), Theodore Bloomfield (1958–63), Lászlo Somogyi (1964–69), David Zinman (1974–85), Mark Elder (1989–94), Robert Bernhardt (1995–98), and Christopher Seaman (1999–). The Rochester American Opera Co was founded in 1924 under the direction of Vladimir Rostig. Generously supported by George Eastman, it was composed entirely of American singers, with all performances in English, became an independent national company in 1927, and disbanded in 1929. Opera continued to flourish at the Eastman School, which sponsored a summer opera festival at Highland Park from 1952 to 1974.

The Rochester Philharmonic Orchestra and the Eastman School of Music continue to make major contributions to the city's rich concert life in the early 21st century. Also a vital part of the local musical scene are Opera Theatre of Rochester, founded in 1962 by Ruth Rosenberg, and the Rochester Chamber Orchestra, founded in 1964 by David Fetler, who remains its conductor in 2001. The Rochester Oratorio Society, founded in 1945 by Theodore Hollenbach, and Madrigalia, a chamber chorus founded in 1975 by Robert Dwelley, are both conducted by Roger Wilhelm in 2001. Concerts are held at the Eastman Theatre (capacity 3,094), the Eastman School of Music, principally in Kilbourn Hall (459), the Hochstein Performance Hall (857), Nazareth Arts Center (1,153), the Memorial Art Gallery (300), the Andrews B. Hale Auditorium (985), and in various churches throughout the city. Significant classical musicians raised in the

Rochester area include singers William Warfield and Renée Fleming, violinist David Hochstein, and composers David Diamond and Alec Wilder. Composers associated with the Eastman School of Music include Howard Hanson, R. Nathaniel Dett, Samuel Adler, Joseph Schwanter, and Christopher Rouse.

Klinzing, Ernestine. *Music in Rochester: A Century of Musical Progress, 1825–1925* (Rochester: Office of the City Historian, 1967)

Lenti, Vincent. *A History of the Eastman Theatre* (Rochester: Office of the City Historian, 1987)

Sabin, S.B. "A Retrospect of Music in Rochester." In *Home Builders,* vol 2 of *Centennial History of Rochester, New York* (Rochester: Rochester Historical Society, 1932)

Vincent Lenti

classical music, Syracuse. One of the first classical music performances documented in Syracuse is the 1851 appearance of Swedish soprano Jenny Lind. Ticket prices of $25 caused a small riot. Further interest in vocalism was demonstrated by the development of singing societies. The Syracuse Liederverein, still in existence, was founded in 1855 by members of an earlier saengerbund. Significant musical events include an 1872 visit from Russian pianist-composer Anton Rubinstein and an 1892 performance by pianist Ignace Jan Paderewski.

In 1890 the Civic Morning Musicals (CMM) was formed with an agenda of supporting performances by area residents and bringing in classical musicians of international renown. The group sponsored a Metropolitan Opera Orchestra visit in 1895, and the new century brought Victor Herbert and his Pittsburgh Orchestra. By 1907 there are accounts of a short-lived Syracuse Symphony Orchestra, conducted by Conrad Becker. CMM continued activities during the early 20th century, presenting the Boston and New York Symphonies, the Flonzaley Quartet, and pianist Josef Lhevinne. World War I caused cutbacks, but during interwar seasons tenor Roland Hayes, pianist Vladimir Horowitz, guitarist Andres Segovia, among others, came to perform. In this same period Syracuse Symphony was reconstituted, now under the baton of Vladimir Shavitch, a conductor who recorded for Victrola.

Despite the 1930s depression, CMM carried on, bringing singer Nelson Eddy, George Gershwin, and violinist Georges Enescu to Central New York. There was another activation of the Syracuse Symphony Orchestra, this time conducted by Andre Polah. During the next 40 years, CMM continued to sponsor performances by such groups and artists as the Vienna and New York Philharmonics, conductor Leopold Stokowski, sopranos Leontyne Price and Jeanette MacDonald, bass Ezio Pinza, and violinist Jascha Heifetz. Since 1980 CMM's main focus has been to facilitate performances by local musicians.

Founded in 1870, Syracuse University soon built Crouse College, a Gothic Revival building that includes a 1,000-seat auditorium. From its earliest days Syracuse University possessed a worthy music school, but it did not develop fully until the 1940s through 1960s with the efforts of such faculty members as composer Ernst Bacon, organist Arthur Poister, pianist George Mulfinger, composer and musicologist Howard Boatwright, soprano Helen Boatwright, composer Earl George, and pianist Frederick Marvin. Violinist Louis Kaufman, who premiered the violin concertos of Alban Berg and Arnold Schoenberg, joined the school in 1949 and formed a community organization, the Syracuse Friends of Chamber Music, the following year. Syracuse Friends became and remains the most important presenter of chamber music performances in the region.

In 1961, in another effort spearheaded by Kaufman, the current Syracuse Symphony Orchestra (SSO), led by conductor Karl Kritz, was founded. Kritz mentored several figures, including Calvin Custer, who became a conductor for the group and noted Pops arranger, as well as Henry Fogel, who piloted station WONO-FM, a now defunct but fondly remembered classical service that documented the early years of the orchestra. By 1971 contemporary music advocate Frederik Prausnitz was conductor, and in 1975 Christopher Keene succeeded him. Keene brought a new sense of excitement to the group, and the SSO recorded under him on several occasions. Shortly after the start of the Keene era, the orchestra moved to its present home, the Crouse Hinds Concert Theater of the John H. Mulroy Civic Center, a multipurpose facility that accommodates 2,117. In 1985 Kazuyoshi Akiyama became music director, succeeded by Fabio Mechetti in 1992, and Daniel Hege in 1999. The SSO operates two youth ensembles: the Syracuse Symphony Youth Orchestra and the Syracuse Symphony Youth String Orchestra. SSO concerts are broadcast over local classical station WCNY-FM, and under Hege the orchestra has resumed recording.

There has been a proliferation of performance organizations in the last four decades in the region. Starting as the Syracuse Symphony Opera Chorus in 1963, today's Syracuse Opera assumed its present name in 1984. Richard McKee has been artistic director since 1990. In the early 21st century Syracuse Opera produces three operas per season and employs the SSO in the pit. In 1971 the Society for New Music arrived. Headed by soprano Neva Pilgrim, the group offers about 25 performances per season and regularly commissions new works. Other organizations include the Syracuse Vocal Ensemble, founded in 1973, and the Syracuse Children's Chorus, organized in 1981. The Skaneateles Festival, founded in 1980, has proven to be an increasingly popular summer venue, featuring such performers as violinist Hilary Hahn, pianist Awadagin Pratt, and Syracuse natives Elliot Fisk and Andrew Russo.

George, Earl. *Civic Morning Musicals: Its First 100 Years* (Syracuse: Valley Press, 1990)

Chuck Klaus

Claverack [CLAW-VER-AK]. Town (pop 6,401) in central Columbia Co. Settled between 1650 and 1660 by the Dutch, Claverack was formed as a district in 1772 and recognized as a town in 1788. From 1786 to 1805 it served as the county seat; the courthouse, now a private residence, still stands. It was served by the Hudson and Berkshire (1838) and Harlem (1852) Railroads. Part of the Van Rensselaer Lower Manor, the town was the site of antirent unrest in the 1840s. Claverack was noted for the coeducational Claverack College and Hudson River Institute (1854–1902). The town's farmers, large hay producers for the New York City market, also grew rye straw for local papermaking, leading the state in rye production in 1855. Knitting mills, especially at Philmont, employed over 1,000 in 1892. The Taconic State Parkway reached Claverack in 1954. In 2003 Nova Pack employs 180 workers manufacturing plastic containers. The Double-Span Whipple Bowstring Truss Bridge (1870) is listed on the National Register.

Clay. Town (pop 58,805) in N Onondaga Co. The first settler arrived in 1793, and the town was formed from Cicero in 1827. Clay's first industry was barrel making for the shipment of salted fish. Tobacco and grain farming and peat harvesting occupied the town's flat land. The Rome, Watertown and Ogdensburg and the Syracuse Northern Railroads were completed in 1871 and crossed at Woodard. Flat land, I-481 access, and a public water supply have, since 1960, drawn the residential and commercial development that surrounds the 1,473-acre (596 ha) Clay Marsh State Wildlife Management Area and that make it the most populous town in Onondaga Co by a substantial margin. At the same time, farming continues in the town's north.

Barbara S. Rivette

Clayton. Town (pop 4,817) and village (pop 1,821) in NW Jefferson Co. First inhabited by lumber thieves, smugglers, and squatters by 1799, permanent settlement began in 1816. The town was formed from Lyme and Orleans in 1833; the village was incorporated in 1872. Shipbuilding (1832–*ca* 1895), the Frink Snowplow Co (1920–2000), and granite quarrying on Grindstone Island were important industries. Lumber was rafted down the St. Lawrence, and water lime was produced. Tourism, however, has dominated the town economically and culturally since resort hotels were built *ca* 1872 and it acquired service from the Clayton and Theresa Railroad (1873). The village is the site of the Antique Boat Museum (1964), the Handweaving Museum and Arts Center (1966), and the Thousand Islands Museum (1964).

Laura Lynne Scharer

Clayville. Village (pop 445) in Paris (Oneida Co). A manufacturing village in the Sauquoit Creek gorge, Clayville began as Paris Furnace, casting potash kettles and other hollowware starting in 1801. The Empire Woolen Co (?1843; later Utica Knitting) employed 230 workers in 1878 making fancy cassimeres. David J. Millard ran an agricultural implement works and produced swords during the Civil War. Railroad service was provided by the Utica, Chenango and Susquehanna Valley Railroad (1870). The village incorporated in 1887. Twentieth-century industries included Babbitt Harris Co (wire), Clayville Paper Mills (closed 1972), and Central Castings (closed 1975). Around 1950 Utica Forge and Tool took over the knitting mill building and produced jet blades. Homogenous Metals (nickel-based structural powder, 1979) and Clayville Ice Co were established businesses that moved to the village in the late 20th century.

Clean Pot. See KANATSIOHAREKE MOHAWK COMMUNITY.

***Clearwater* sloop.** A modern replica of the sloops that sailed the Hudson River in the 18th and 19th centuries. Since its construction at the Harvey Gamage Shipyard in South Bristol, Maine, in 1969, this 106 ft (32.3 m) wooden sailing vessel has carried approximately 20,000 people a year, primarily on the Hudson River, to educate them about the river's heritage and ecology. Activist and folksinger Pete Seeger is credited with introducing the idea of a sloop as an educational vehicle to the nascent Hudson River Sloop Restoration in 1966. The organization was renamed the Hudson River Sloop Clearwater three years later. Cyrus Hamlin of the Ocean Research Corp designed the sloop in 1968, using a painting of the sloop *Phillip R. Paulding* attributed to James E. Buttersworth (1817–94), a 1930s model kit of the sloop *Victorine*, and various 19th-century sources as guides. Some elements of the sloop's design did violate historical precedent in order to meet modern safety requirements.

The sloop has brought great visibility to Hudson River Sloop Clearwater's campaigns against river pollution, most notably the group's fight to spotlight the dumping of PCBs in the river by General Electric. The sloop is the best known of those associated with the Hudson River nonprofit environmental conservation movement; it has inspired other operational replicas. These include the *Woody Guthrie* (1978), operated by the Beacon Sloop Club (Dutchess Co), and the *Sojourner Truth* (1980), operated by Ferry Sloops, Inc of Yonkers. The Bronx Co–based Walkabout Clearwater organization displays a 7 ft (2.1 m) model of the *Clearwater* to promote river conservation during its folk concerts throughout the tri-state area. In 2003 the *Clearwater* sloop also provided sailing apprentice programs for adults and group charters. The sloop is moored each winter in Poughkeepsie, where Hudson River Sloop Clearwater's office is located.

Fontenoy, Paul E. *The Sloops of the Hudson River: A Historical and Design Survey* (Mystic, Conn: Mystic Seaport Museum, 1994)

Karen Nichols

Clermont. Originally known as *North River Steamboat* and later as *North River Steamboat of Clermont,* the world's first successful steam-powered vessel gained lasting fame under the name of part-owner Robert R. Livingston Jr's Columbia Co estate, Clermont. Naval engineer Robert Fulton designed the ship for New York City-to-Albany service on the Hudson River as part of a joint project funded by the wealthy Livingston. The 140 ft (42.7 m) by 16 ft (4.9 m) hull was built at Charles Browne's shipyard on Manhattan's East Side and fitted with a wood-fired steam engine built by the English firm Boulton and Watt. The vessel made a demonstration run from the Greenwich Village area of Manhattan's West Side on Monday, 17 Aug 1807, averaging almost 5 mph (8 kph) under steam and overnighting at Clermont before proceeding to Albany. The steamboat returned to New York City, carrying the first five paying passengers, at 4:00 PM Friday. Regularly scheduled commercial service began 4 Sept 1807, continuing until late November, when ice closed the river. Over that winter, the hull was expanded to provide more cabins with better berths as well as a dining area, and the spray-flinging paddle wheels were boxed. The renovated vessel operated until 1814, when replaced by larger, improved steamboats of the Fulton and Livingston company.

First Trip of Fulton's Steamboat to Albany, 1807; detail of a print by Samuel Hollyer, *ca* 1907.

Philip, Cynthia Owen. *Robert Fulton: A Biography* (New York: F. Watts, 1981)

Norman Brouwer

Clermont. Town (pop 1,726) in SW Columbia Co. Part of Livingston Manor, the area was settled in 1694 by the Dutch, who were later joined by Palatine Germans, the latter becoming the dominant group. A powder mill operated during the Revolution. Philip Livingston (1716–78), a signer of the Declaration of Independence, was a resident. Clermont formed as a district in 1787 and was recognized as a town in 1788. In 1791 it established a public school by state legislation, one of the first in New York. A post office opened in 1792. Merino sheep, introduced by Robert R. Livingston Jr in 1801, numbered 3,900 in 1820. Hay and rye were cash crops until *ca* 1910, but orchards (after 1870) and vineyards (after 1890) helped make it a fruit-growing town by the 1920s. Clermont (*ca* 1777), home of Chancellor Robert R. Livingston (1746–1813), is a state historic site; other National Register properties are Clermont Academy (1830), St. Luke's Church (1857), and Clarkson Chapel (1860).

Cleveland. Village (pop 758) in Constantia (Oswego Co). This settlement on Oneida Lake began around 1821–24. The first of two glassworks, employing many German glassblowers, was established in 1840 by Anthony Landgraff; glassmaking ended in 1912. The village incorporated in 1857 and acquired a station on the Ontario and Western Railroad in 1869. Edward "Ned" Sherman was elected in 1878 for a term as village president; he was one of the first African Americans to serve in an elective office in the state. Cleveland elected women to village offices as early as 1919.

Barbara J. Dix

Cleveland, (Stephen) Grover (*b* Caldwell, NJ, 18 Mar 1837; *d* Princeton, NJ, 24 June 1908). Governor and US president. Son of a Presbyterian clergyman, Cleveland grew up in Fayetteville (Onondaga Co) and Clinton (Oneida Co) before moving to Buffalo in 1855. He was admitted to the bar in 1859 and appointed assistant district attorney for Erie Co in 1863. When drafted that year, he avoided service by hiring a substitute, an action that, while legal, dogged him throughout his career. In 1870 he was elected sheriff of Erie Co, where, among his other duties, he twice served as hangman. After one term he returned to his more lucrative legal practice, where he remained until elected, with a large plurality, mayor of Buffalo in 1881. Acquiring a reputation as the "veto mayor," one who put civic advancement over partisan politics and expunged the city administration of corruption, he attracted the attention of reform-minded Democrats and was nominated and elected governor of New York State in 1882.

As governor Cleveland battled machine politics by breaking with Tammany Hall leader John Kelly and supporting civil service bills. His tenure was marked by legislation creating a bureau of labor statistics, abolishing the hiring-out of state prisoners, and reorganizing the militia. He continued his active and well-placed use of the veto. By 1884 he was a national figure and was nominated as the reform candidate for president to oppose the scandal-tainted James G. Blaine. The campaign was notoriously bitter, marked by Cleveland's admission that he accepted responsibility for an out-of-wedlock child in 1874 (though he always denied paternity). Blaine's inability to disavow a clergyman's remark that the Democrats were the party of "Rum, Romanism, and Rebellion" offended Catholics and helped Cleveland squeak through with a 2,000-vote victory in New York State, thereby ensuring him of his election. With the help of breakaway reform Republicans known as Mugwumps, Cleveland became the first Democratic president elected since 1856.

In his first term, he helped rebuild the navy, elevated the Department of Agriculture to cabinet status, and approved the Interstate Commerce Commission (1887). As a Democrat, he fought continually with the Republican-controlled Congress; his 414 vetoes during his first administration set a record. In 1886 he married Frances Folsom, his former ward and the daughter of his former Buffalo law partner. In 1887 he singled out a lower tariff as his main issue, but the position hurt him in the 1888 election, when he lost both New York State and the general election to Benjamin Harrison. Cleveland retired to New York City as a lawyer, but opposition to the McKinley Tariff of 1890 brought him a new political following. In 1892 he defeated Harrison, becoming the only US president to serve nonconsecutive terms. Cleveland's second term was not a success and earned him the title the Great Obstructionist because of his failure to act to relieve the nation's distress after the panic of 1893. More radical Democrats saw salvation in free coinage of silver, but Cleveland sided with conservative Republicans by supporting the gold standard and seeking to repeal the Sherman Silver Purchase Act. Despite his belief in limited government, Cleveland and his attorney general broke the Pullman strike through federal injunctions, the arrest of strike leader Eugene V. Debs, and the deployment of federal troops. In 1896 the populist wing of the Democratic Party took control and repudiated him by nominating William Jennings Bryan. After his second term, he moved with his wife and young family to Princeton, NJ. Throughout his career, Cleveland's independence and conscientiousness marked him as a man of courage and personal integrity.

Brodsky, Alyn. *Grover Cleveland: A Study in Character* (New York: St. Martin's Press, 2000)
Jeffers, Harry. *An Honest President: The Life and Presidencies of Grover Cleveland* (New York: William Morrow, 2000)
Welch, Richard. *The Presidencies of Grover Cleveland* (Lawrence: Univ Press of Kansas, 1988)

Jon Sterngass

Clifton. Town (pop 791) in S St. Lawrence Co. Located entirely within Adirondack Park, it was settled in 1866 under direction of the Clifton Iron Co and was formed from Pierrepont in 1868. Its initial population of 700 dropped to 85 in 1875. Extensive mining and furnace operations by several companies left Clifton, though heavily forested, with a huge, derelict mine and industrial complex adjacent to the state's Five Ponds Wilderness Hunting and Fishing Preserve. The Newton Falls Paper Mill (1896) was deactivated in 2001. South of Cranberry Lake, which was greatly enlarged by an 1867 dam to regulate water on the Oswegatchie River, the backcountry stretches southward for miles.

Richard E. Mooers

Clifton Park. Town (pop 32,995) in S Saratoga Co. Settled in 1672 along the Mohawk River, which forms part of its southern boundary, the town was set off from Halfmoon in 1828 as Clifton and received its present name in 1829. The Erie Canal (1823) ran along its southern edge. The town was chiefly agricultural, except for an important sand mine at Elnora providing sand to make iron foundry molds. Paved roads after World War I enabled residents to take jobs in Albany and Troy at General Electric (GE) and Watervliet Arsenal, while the remaining farms, especially potato and dairy, grew in size and value. The first of many subdivisions was Robert Van Patten's Country Club Acres (1956), but the town remained a farming district until the Northway was opened to Clifton Park in 1960. Population more than tripled in the 1960s from 4,512 to 14,867. Farming continues in the western part of town. The commercial district, centered on the Clifton Country Mall (1976, now Clifton Park Center) adjacent to Northway Exit 9, serves all of southern Saratoga Co.

Field Horne

Clifton Springs. Village (pop 2,223) in Manchester and Phelps (Ontario Co). As early as 1806 the first hotel was built to accommodate visitors to the sulfur springs. The Auburn and Rochester Railroad (1841) made the journey easier. The Water Cure (later Sanitarium) was built in 1850 and served 3,000 patients a year late in the century, with a new building completed in 1972, by which time the institution was called Clifton Springs Hospital and Clinic. The village incorporated in 1859. The Air Cure (1865–72) was another short-lived health institution. Two private schools, Clifton Springs Seminary (1868) and Foster School (1875), merged administratively in 1888 and were closed before the century ended. G. W. Lisk Co (1910) is an important employer, and restoration of the village in 1990 has created an attractive destination for tourists.

Marla A. Bennett

climate and weather. New York State's climate is formally classified as humid-continental, with severe winters, warm summers, and four distinct seasons. Most of the state is part of a broad band of temperate midlatitude climates that extends from the eastern Great Plains across the Great Lakes to the Atlantic seaboard. The extreme southern portions of the state, New York City, eastern Long Island, and the lower Hudson Valley, share some climate characteristics, notably milder winters and hotter summers, with the adjacent climate zone found in Mid-Atlantic and southern states. The North Country and the Adirondacks, in comparison, endure the bitter cold and heavy snowfalls typical of eastern Canada. This climate diversity and variability is a key feature of New York State and can produce great differences in temperature and precipitation over relatively short distances. For example, the average annual temperature of New York City, at about 55°F (13°C), is nearly 10°F (6°C) degrees warmer than Binghamton only 150 miles (241 km) away; similarly, Boonville (Oneida Co) receives more than two and a half times the annual snowfall of Little Falls (Herkimer Co) even though the communities are separated by only 46 miles (74 km).

Latitude, elevation, and proximity to large water areas (Lakes Erie and Ontario and the Atlantic Ocean) are the principal factors governing the state's climate. Prevailing westerly winds transport a succession of dry, cold air masses of Arctic origin across the state, where they interact with warm, humid, tropical air masses from the Mississippi Valley and the Gulf of Mexico and sometimes with maritime air masses formed over the North Atlantic Ocean. Being upwind of the state, Lakes Erie and Ontario have a pronounced effect on the upstate region's climate regime, and the warm Atlantic influences the climate of the lower Hudson Valley, Long Island, and New York City. Most of the year, the state is crossed by a series of storms called midlatitude cyclones, which originate in several locations, including Alberta, the Rocky Mountains, and the Gulf of Mexico. These storms are usually replaced on a regular basis by dry, cool, high-pressure cells in winter and often by hot and humid high-pressure cells in summer. Extratropical cyclones in the form of hurricanes often appear in late summer and fall, and no less severe coastal storms, called nor'easters, are a constant threat in the fall and winter months.

Winter can produce long periods of below-freezing temperatures with substantial snowfall and ice storms in areas such as the Adirondacks and North Country, while the lower Hudson Valley and Atlantic coastal counties experience much more benign conditions. For example, midwinter temperatures at Newcomb (Essex Co) average only 18°F (-8°C) and at Indian Lake (Hamilton Co) only 19°F (-7°C); average snowfall totals are 224 inches (569 cm) for Old Forge (Herkimer Co) and 278 inches (706 cm) for Hooker (Lewis Co). In comparison, midwinter average temperatures are about 37°F (3°C) at La Guardia Airport in Queens and a degree less in central Manhattan (Central Park), and Setauket (Suffolk Co) on Long Island's north shore records barely more than 13 inches (33 cm) of snowfall each year. Summer contrasts are less extreme since the differences in latitude and elevation are, in part, erased by the homogeneous nature of the hot and humid subtropical air masses that often blanket the entire state. July average temperatures are 64–76°F (18–24°C) with substantial amounts of convective precipitation (heavy showers, thunderstorms). The southern regions along the Atlantic coast can experience sustained periods of calm, muggy weather with daytime highs above 90°F (32°C) and relative humidity of 70% or more. In the winter months, westerly and northwesterly winds associated with cold high-pressure areas predominate; in the summer months, southerly and southwesterly flows are the rule. The strongest wind velocities, however, are often observed during coastal storms and are generally from the north or northeast. Central sections of the state and the lower Hudson Valley tend to record more hours of sunshine (eg, New York City has 58% of possible sunshine hours). In contrast, western portions of the state tend to record many more days with partial or total cloud cover (eg, an average of 208 days per year are cloud covered in Buffalo, 205 days in Syracuse).

Historical Climate

During the last major ice age (25,000–18,000 years ago), the surface temperatures in eastern North America were about 10°F cooler than at present, and the state's southern boundary coincided roughly with the southern extent of the Laurentide ice sheet. Since that time, air temperatures have climbed generally but sporadically upward through numerous periods of warming and cooling, (eg, warmer, 1895–1930; cooler, 1940–70; and warmer since 1980). The overall

Mean January Temperature
(in °F)

Mean July Temperature
(in °F)

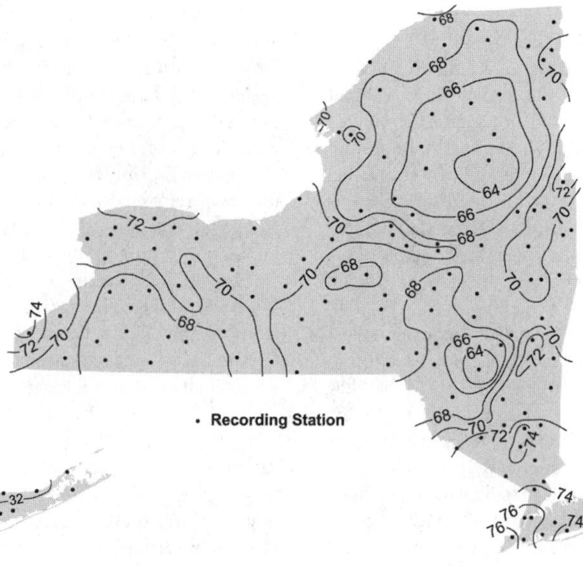

Average Annual Precipitation, 1971–2000
(in inches)

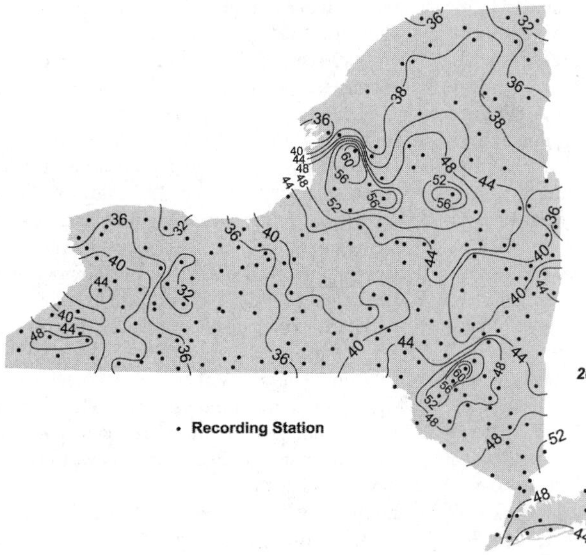

Average Seasonal Snowfall, 1971–2000
(in inches)

SOURCE: Data from NOAA, *Monthly Station Normals of Temperature, Precipitation, and Heating and Cooling Degree Days, 1971–2000* (Asheville, NC: Author).

warming trend for the state has been about 1°F (0.55°C) from 1855 to 1991, slightly more than the global average of 0.97°F (0.54°C). Annual average precipitation of 39 inches (99 cm) has increased at a rate of about 0.4 inch (1 cm) per decade between 1895 and 2001.

Climate Regions

The Adirondacks and Tug Hill. High in both elevation and latitude, Adirondack winters are cold and snowy, and summers are wet and cool. Average January temperatures are in the 15°F (-9°C) range with higher elevations several degrees cooler. Average July temperatures are in the order of 65°F (18°C), but average daily minimums of 50–54°F (10–12°C) can be found across the area's northern half. Precipitation is generous with 40–52 inches (102–32 cm) of precipitation and 120–200 inches (305–508 cm) of snowfall per year. Winter temperatures can and typically do plummet well below 0°F (-18°C) throughout the region. On 9 Feb 1934 the temperature dipped to -52°F (-47°C) at Stillwater Reservoir (Herkimer Co), the state's record low temperature. Monthly snowfalls of 24 inches (61 cm) and accumulations of 50 inches (127 cm) or more are common most winters. Hooker, at the northern end of the Tug Hill Plateau, has the greatest average snowfall in the state with 278 inches (706 cm). On 11–12 Jan 1997, the nearby Town of Montague (Lewis Co) received 77 inches (196 cm) of snow, an unofficial world record for a 24-hour period. The Tug Hill area in general receives the largest annual snowfalls of any location in the country east of the Rocky Mountains.

The St. Lawrence and Champlain Valleys. Similar to the Adirondacks in latitude but not in elevation, this region's winters are cold, but summer maximum temperatures can reach 90°F (32°C) because cloud cover is noticeably less than in the Adirondacks. Precipitation averages 32–36 inches (81–91 cm) annually; and the northeastern part of the region (Clinton and Essex Cos) experiences a "rain shadow" effect because the upland areas to the west interrupt the normal west-to-east flow of most storms, depleting them of their moisture before they reach the western slopes of the Champlain Valley. The results are lower levels of precipitation, fewer days with clouds, and more hours of sunshine. The North Country is particularly vulnerable to ice storms, which tend to occur in December and January when relatively warm air from the south or west overrides entrenched cold air in the lowland and valley areas, causing liquid precipitation to refreeze as it reaches the ground. During the 6–9 Jan 1998 ice storm, more than 1 million people in parts of New York, Vermont, Quebec, and Ontario were without power for over a week.

The Appalachian Upland. Consisting of the uplands in the Catskill Mountains, the Delaware, Helderberg, Susquehanna, and Cattaraugus Hills, and the Finger Lakes region, this region has cold, snowy winters and cool, frequently wet summers. January average temperatures range from 20° to 25°F (-7– -4°C); July means are 65–69°F (18–21°C). Total precipitation amounts are generally less than in the Adirondacks, ranging from 32 to 44 inches (81–112 cm) annually, but average snowfall amounts can be very high; for instance, parts of Chautaugua Co receive between 100 and 150 inches (254–381 cm) in a given year. These high amounts reflect lake effect–enhanced precipitation that occurs primarily in late fall and early winter in the lee of Lake Erie before the lake freezes over. Cold, westerly winds draw moisture from the lake surface, reach the shore area in an unstable condition, and drop large quantities of snow on the upland areas. Heavy snow squalls with rapid accumulations of up to 3 inches (7 cm) per hour can occur. Further east, the upland areas of Onondaga, Cortland, Chenango, Otsego, and Ulster Cos can receive annual snowfalls of 70–100 inches (179–254 cm) or more, and differences in snowfall between valley bottoms and nearby hilltops can be dramatic. The valley station at the City of Cortland averages 91 inches (231 cm) of snow annually, while the hilltop station at Tully–Heiberg Forest 15 miles (24 km) away receives 123 inches (312 cm). Summer temperatures are relatively low. The mean July daily maximum often ranges from 80° to 82°F (27–28°C) with abrupt temperature change commonly associated with change in elevation. Hurricanes, including Hazel and Carol (1954), Agnes (1972), Hugo (1989), and Alberto (1994) (some reducing to tropical storms), have tracked across this area causing considerable local flooding and property damage.

The Erie-Ontario Lowlands. Niagara, Erie, Orleans, Wayne, Oswego, and Monroe Cos share the severe winter weather found in the Appalachian Upland area of central and western New York State, but summers are somewhat dryer and warmer. July daily maximums are in the 80–84°F (27–29°C) range, precipitation averages 32–36 inches (81–91 cm) per year, and snowfall ranges from 40 to 80 inches (102–203 cm). Lake effect snowfall is a factor across this region; on average Buffalo receives about 96 inches (244 cm), Rochester about 100 inches (254 cm), and Syracuse about 121 inches (307 cm), but overall lowland amounts are less than those of nearby higher elevations. The area along the south shore of Lake Ontario (Niagara, Orleans, and Monroe Cos) is the driest part of the state, averaging less than 32 inches (81 cm) of annual precipitation, and the moderating effects of the slow-warming (and slow-cooling) lakes are particularly apparent in the spring and fall. The interior location of the City of Geneva (Ontario Co) allows daytime maximum temperatures in March, April, and May to rise quickly so that they are, on average, 1.7°F (0.93°C), 2.7°F (1.5°C), and 3.5°F (1.9°C) higher than those at the City of Oswego, where the cold lake waters retard the temperature increases considerably.

The Hudson and Mohawk Valleys. Sandwiched between the Adirondacks, the Taconic Mountains, and the Appalachian Upland are the elongated Hudson and Mohawk Valleys. These two lowlands are transitional regions in climatic terms, lying between the colder, upland climates to the north and the warmer coastal lowlands to the south. Mean January temperatures in the upper Hudson Valley can be quite cool, such as 8°F (-13°C) at Glens Falls (Warren Co), while 110 miles (177 km) south at Poughkeepsie the comparable measure stands at 25°F (-4°C). July means temperatures for the Mohawk Valley range from 70° to 73°F (21–23°C). Precipitation varies from 30 to 60 inches (76–152 cm) in the Hudson Valley and 70 to 90 inches (178–229 cm) in the Mohawk Valley. Lower elevation and higher solar radiation values produce a more benign climate in the lower Hudson Valley; nonetheless, the state's highest recorded temperature is held by the City of Troy (Rensselaer Co), at 108°F (42°C) on 22 July 1926.

The Atlantic Coastal Lowland. The hilly areas of the lower Hudson Valley, New York City, and eastern Long Island constitute a very distinctive climatic region. Winters are cool and wet with January averages of 29–32°F (-2–0°C). Annual precipitation ranges between 44 and 48 inches (112–22 cm); but annual snowfall is often considerably less than 40 inches (102 cm) in the region and less than 20 inches (51 cm) on Long Island. Summers are warm and humid with July daily maximums well above 90°F (32°C) and nighttime relative humidities in the "oppressive" range, above 70%. Higher levels of solar radiation and proximity to the ocean produce temperature regimes that are characteristic of the humid subtropical climates, a category very different from the rest of the state, and the coastal lowlands are properly grouped with the warmer climate zones of the southeastern United States. The ocean acts as a heat source in the summer months, bringing very hot and humid weather (New York City has up to 25 days a year with daytime temperatures over 90°F/32°C), a greater incidence of fog, and a higher risk of coastal storms and hurricanes than other parts of the state. There is about a 21% probability that in any given year a section of eastern Long Island will be struck by a hurricane. Slide Mountain (Ulster Co) is the wettest station in the state with 63 inches (161 cm) of precipitation every year.

Future Directions

Despite the current controversy over the nature and magnitude of global warming, there is general agreement that the midlatitude areas of North America, such as New York State, will continue to warm slowly over the next several decades, although existing estimates of the magnitude of Northern Hemisphere warming vary widely, from increases of about 4.5°F (2.5°C) to 14.5°F (8°C) by the year 2100. For the period 1895–2001, the state average temperature rose .1°F (.05°C) per decade and now stands at 45°F (7°C). The year 1998 was particularly warm, when the observed state average temperature rose to 49°F (9°C). Annual precipitation forecasts are more difficult to predict; the 1895–2001 trend showed an increase of 0.4 inch (1 cm) per decade with an average of 38.8 inches (98.55 cm) over the same time period. Assuming that these trends continue, there would likely be a rise in winter temperatures (both daily highs and lows), an overall increase in nighttime low temperatures for yearly values, a decrease in day-to-day temperature variation, and a possible increase in winter precipitation. Expected increases in snowfall for the lake effect areas of western New York State may be offset by higher average winter temperatures. Changes in the frequency and severity of coastal storms and hurricanes are difficult to forecast, but a general increase in both may occur.

See also WATER AND HYDROLOGY.

Bryant, Edward. *Climate Process and Change* (Cambridge, England: Cambridge Univ Press, 1997)
Carter, Douglas B. "Climate." In *Geography of New York State,* ed. J. H. Thompson (Syracuse: Syracuse Univ Press, 1977)
National Oceanic and Atmospheric Administration. *Monthly Station Normals of Temperature, Precipitation, and Heating and Cooling Degree Days, 1971–2000* (Asheville, NC: Author, 2002)
Northeast Regional Climate Center, Cornell University, http://www.nrcc.cornell.edu

C. G. Rose

Clinton. Town (pop 727) in NW Clinton Co. After settlement (1817–18) refugees from the Canadian Rebellion of 1837 added to its population. The town, bounded on the north by Canada, was formed from Ellenburg in 1845. The opening of the Northern Railroad (later Rutland Railroad) in 1850 facilitated extraction of its lumber resources, but with inadequate waterpower due to its level terrain, it never developed industries. In the early 21st century the economy is driven by dairy farming and lumbering.

Thomas A. Rumney

Clinton. Town (pop 4,010) in N central Dutchess Co. Part of the Great Nine Partners Patent (1697), it was first settled in the 1730s by Dutch and Palatines from elsewhere in the county along with New England and New York Quakers. It was formed as a town in 1788. The Dutchess County Peace Society (1871–90), organized by town resident Amanda Halstead Deyo, met here. The 1947 extension of the Taconic Parkway rendered the town more accessible. In the late 20th century it drew commuters working in the Poughkeepsie and Fishkill areas and weekend homeowners from New York City.

William P. McDermott, ed. *Clinton, Dutchess County, N.Y.: A History of a Town.* (Clinton Corners, NY: Town of Clinton Historical Society, 1987)

William P. McDermott

Clinton. Village (pop 1,952) in Kirkland (Oneida Co). Settled in 1787 it has long been associated with Hamilton College (1812), whose campus is a mile west of the village. Located on the Chenango Canal (1837–78), the village (incorporated in 1843) attracted numerous industries, including woolen manufacturing, brick making, and Clinton Canning (1892–1937). Two railroads, completed between 1866 and 1871, served the village. The Clinton Cider Mill (1926) is a landmark business. Important facilities include the Kirkland Art Center (1964) and the Clinton Arena (1948, rebuilt 1953), which was home to the Clinton Comets, a professional ice hockey team (1954–73). Statesman Elihu Root (1845–1937) was a native and graduate of the college, and Thomas Hastings (1784–1872), composer of the hymn tune "Rock of Ages," taught music and led a church choir.

Clinton, De Witt (*b* ?New Windsor, Orange Co, 2 Mar 1769; *d* Albany, 11 Feb 1828). Governor, and mayor of New York City.

Early Years

Son of James Clinton, a farmer, surveyor, and Revolutionary War general, and Mary De Witt, member of a New York Dutch family, Clinton attended Kingston Academy before enrolling in Columbia College in 1784. At Columbia he acquired an Enlightenment belief in progress through science and learning, which eschewed radical cleansing and emphasized dutiful and benevolent magistracy. To Clinton, to be liberal meant to foster human possibilities for development through knowledge; ignorance and the oppressive use of power denied those possibilities.

After graduating in 1786, he studied law in Samuel Jones's office. Wanting to provide the young lawyer with firsthand political experience, Gov George Clinton, De Witt Clinton's uncle, appointed him his private secretary in 1787. Like his uncle, Clinton was an Antifederalist: he opposed the strong national government outlined in the new US Constitution, arguing that it would enable an aristocracy to debase independent yeomen, whom he characterized as the bulwark of liberty. Yet he later worked to ease the Livingstons, one of New York State's great landed families, toward the Clintonian faction of the emerging Jeffersonian Republican Party. He shared George Clinton's caution toward revolutionary France but shared Livingston hostility to pro-British Federalists as a dangerous elite fostered by banking and commercial power.

Admitted to the bar in 1790, Clinton briefly continued to practice law after his uncle declined to stand for office in 1795. By then he had also begun to speculate in land and was managing over 600,000 acres (240,000 ha) in four states for his associates. In 1796 he married heiress Maria Franklin, a member of a Quaker family, who bore 10 children, 5 of whom survived their father. She brought significant wealth and landholdings to the marriage. Clinton became locked in ongoing litigation with Franklin executors, and the need for money contributed to his later eagerness to become New York City's mayor. A year after Maria's death in 1818, Clinton married Catherine Jones.

Clinton as Legislator and Mayor

After two unsuccessful runs for the New York State Assembly from New York City, he won a seat in 1797 and advanced to the New York State Senate the following year. He served as state senator until 1802, when he was elected to the US Senate. He resigned this senate seat the following autumn, though, when the Council of Appointment named him mayor of New York City, a post he held for almost ten years (1803–7, 1808–10, 1811–15). While mayor, Clinton sat in the state senate (1806–11) and served as lieutenant governor (1811–13). He would later be elected governor four times (1817, 1820, 1824, 1826).

Clinton first jostled with Aaron Burr for leadership of the state's Jeffersonian Republicans after 1800. Clinton joined Pres Thomas Jefferson in limiting the offices given to Burr's supporters in the state while serving on the Council of Appointment in 1801 and 1802. As a US senator, he

Bronze cast of De Witt Clinton, by Roman Bronze Works, 1940.

took the lead in promoting what would become the 12th Amendment to the US Constitution, closing a loophole in the presidential election process exploited by Burr in the 1800 campaign. When Clinton and his supporters escalated their press attacks on Burr, his supporter John Swartwout challenged Clinton to a duel. In their 1802 meeting Clinton left his opponent with nonfatal wounds when he put two bullets into Swartwout's leg before refusing to fire further. Although the Clinton-Livingston alliance had begun to fray, it held together long enough for Clinton and his partisans to defeat Burr's attempt to win the New York State governorship in 1804. Jefferson's denial of federal patronage and Clinton's control over the Bank of the Manhattan Co drove Burr to join with Federalists to develop the Merchants' Bank of New York City. Burr fell before Clinton's candidate, Morgan Lewis, the brother-in-law of Chancellor Robert R. Livingston (1746–1813). Meanwhile Clinton had blocked the incorporation of the Merchants' Bank and secured a New York City charter that enfranchised more Republican voters. Burr, perhaps aware that Clinton had practiced regularly with pistols, took out his wrath on Hamilton.

After 1804 Clinton battled the Livingston-backed faction led by Gov Morgan Lewis. Clinton had fostered Chancellor Livingston's steamboat monopoly and stood behind the chancellor's 1798 gubernatorial candidacy, but that did not stop the Livingstons from cutting into Clintonian patronage, and Clinton had no choice but to respond when Lewis successfully threw his weight behind the chartering of the Merchants' Bank, now favored by a coalition of Federalists, Burrites, and Lewisites. In spring 1805 Clinton won a seat in the New York State Senate, but his battle over the Merchants' Bank led him to lose the mayoralty in 1807. He backed Daniel D. Tompkins for governor that year, and Clinton regained the mayoralty in 1808 while maintaining his state senate seat. Concerned for the commercial health of New York City, he first opposed Jefferson's 1807 Embargo Act, but Tompkins differed and Clinton changed tack knowing that the governor's strong support for Jefferson's policies gave assurance that federal patronage would remain with the Tompkins-Clinton wing of New York State's Republican Party. Though supportive of this Jeffersonian policy, Clinton opposed Virginia's leadership again by supporting the futile effort to have Vice Pres George Clinton, and not Virginian James Madison, succeed Jefferson in the 1808 presidential election.

When the Federalists took over the 1810 state legislature, Clinton lost the mayor's office from February 1810 to February 1811. Still, Clinton won the lieutenant governorship in 1811. At a mid-September 1812 meeting in New York City, Federalist delegates from 11 states decided not to run a Federalist candidate and left an impression that Federalists could back Clinton for president. Gathering and proceeding secretively to mask their divisions and the overall weakness of their elite-centered party, they supported Clinton as the candidate who would restore peace with Great Britain and bring northern leadership sensitive to commercial interests to the White House. Failing to carry the key state of Pennsylvania, where he was often presented as the candidate who could best win the war, Clinton lost with 89 electoral votes to Madison's 128 in a contest in which the nation was largely divided along sectional lines. Although a New York State Republican caucus had initially nominated Clinton for the presidency, the following year the caucus declined to renominate him for lieutenant governor. Though some Republicans charged Clinton with a number of political sins—including courting Federalist leaders, muting his opposition to the incorporation of the Bank of America, and opposing a patriotic war—Federalist and Clintonian support kept him in the New York City mayor's office from February 1811 until March 1815.

As a state legislator, Clinton had cautiously supported the gradual emancipation act of 1799 and challenged Federalist governor John Jay's claim to the sole right to nominate appointees before the Council of Appointment. He insisted that senators, elected to the council by assemblymen, had the right to nominate. An 1801 constitutional convention agreed with Clinton. Supporting initiatives that favored merchants and immigrants while he was mayor, he pushed for the abolition of the test oath for Catholics and badgered the federal government for increased protection of the Port of New York. He led the attack on yellow fever as the presiding officer of New York City's Board of Health. Attempting to enhance the cultural and educational opportunities of New York City's residents, Clinton actively supported the Free School Society, the New York Academy of the Fine Arts (later American Academy of Fine Arts), and the New-York Historical Society.

Restorations to Power: Canals, Democracy, Businessmen, Taxes

Clinton's later success as New York State's governor turned on his forceful advocacy of a canal to run between Lake Erie and the Hudson River. Substantial state involvement in a canal had begun in 1808, when the legislature authorized Simeon DeWitt, the state's surveyor general and Clinton's cousin, to direct exploration of the two possible canal routes to the west: first, a line running from the Mohawk Valley to Oneida Lake then into Lake Ontario, supplemented perhaps by a canal around Niagara Falls; second, an excavated canal following an entirely inland route from the Hudson River near Albany to Lake Erie. Clinton helped to create the 1810 and 1811 commissions to explore the routes. Exploration convinced him that the inland route was feasible, but he failed to win national backing for the project, and in 1814 the state legislature repealed the commission's operative powers.

On 30 Dec 1815 supporters of the Erie Canal held a meeting in New York City, and Clinton prepared their memorial to the 1816 legislature. He argued that the Erie Canal would stimulate commerce throughout a state that "is both Atlantic and western," promising prosperity and subtly offering a united and more powerful North. The well-publicized memorial, along with Clinton's addresses as governor to the legislature and his appearances along the canal line, stamped the canal as his project. Though opponents ridiculed the project as "Clinton's Ditch" or "Clinton's Folly," the public support that it elicited brought about the 1816 act authorizing surveys for an Erie Canal and a canal routed northward to Lake Champlain. The second waterway ensured political support along the Vermont border. Under this law and the 1817 law authorizing the beginning of construction, the commission reemerged as an effective body, with Clinton as its leader.

When Gov Tompkins was elected vice president in 1816, the way to the governor's office lay open for Clinton. Nominated by a Republican caucus-convention in March 1817 and buoyed up politically by the popularity of the "Grand Canal," he won the governorship with little opposition and took office in July. The canal continued to be a central element of his political strength. Clinton, however, did little to allay growing opposition in eastern New York State, which feared that the canal would strengthen the economy and political weight of western New York at the expense of the city. While demanding state support of agricultural improvement, including a state board of agriculture, as well as demanding aid to manufacturing initiatives, he consistently emphasized the importance of internal markets and of the roads and canals that would develop those markets.

Clinton's commitment to internal improvements and his building of broad coalitions to advance his objectives increasingly placed him at odds with a faction of the Republicans known as the Bucktails. Their leader, Martin Van Buren, soon challenged Clinton's hold on the party. Seeking reelection in 1820, he faced his old ally, Tompkins, who was backed by the Bucktails. Clinton won a narrow victory, though the Bucktails now controlled both legislative houses. In 1821 a hostile Council of Appointment swept Clinton's appointees from office. He ran afoul of the legislature's call for a convention to revise New York's 1777 Constitution. The 1821 convention hammered out a new constitution that, along with other reforms, shortened the governor's term. Clinton's allies were squeezed off the supreme court; after a plebiscite approved the constitution, he declined to run in 1822.

Out of office, Clinton continued on the Canal Commission and fought back by raising doubts about Bucktail determination to support a harbor for the Erie Canal at Black Rock (Erie Co) rather than Buffalo Creek. Clinton, who in 1820 advocated the popular election of presidential electors on a general ticket, was able to align his cause with reform critics of the new constitution who lamented its failure to provide for the popular election of presidential electors and justices of the peace and who also wanted a still broader suffrage. He also built on the discontent of business interests threatened by a recent tax law and that wanted expansion of credit. Missteps by the Albany Regency–led Bucktails greatly assisted him as well: to dash hopes that Clinton might have had of leaping from political retirement to the presidency, they blocked a bill providing for the popular election of presidential electors, and then, in April, at the end of the 1824 session, they sought to unify their ranks and divide their opponents by throwing Clinton off the Canal Commission. Clinton won nomination for governor of the pro-reform People's Party and carried the office with a margin equal to almost 9% of the total vote. The People's men, a broadly based if loose fusion resting on support of John Quincy Adams for the presidency, Clintonians, and drawing strength from upstate banking and commercial interests, gained control of the assembly.

As governor, Clinton marked the official opening of the Erie Canal by pouring the waters of Lake Erie into New York Harbor while standing aboard the *Seneca Chief* on 4 Nov 1825. Inspired by his success Clinton advocated a more extensive canal system, professional training for teachers, and a state road built through the Southern Tier. These proposals did not get very far, but the political reforms advocated by the People's movement and embraced by Clinton succeeded. In his 1825 message to the legislature, Clinton repeated his recommendation that presidential electors be chosen on a general ticket, which favored his presidential aspirations. The legislature responded with a law that provided for election in congressional districts. Two other recommendations for political change led to amendments that were in place by 1826. One provided for the popular election of justices of the peace, and the other made age, residence, and citizenship the only qualifications for white male voters. In 1824, once his own slender presidential hopes had been dashed, Clinton openly threw his weight behind Andrew Jackson, who, like Clinton, drew on Irish Presbyterian heritage and opposed a meddlesome, misguided, and regionally dominated central government. Martin Van Buren, obliged to abandon his own candidate of 1824, William H. Crawford, switched to Jackson and engineered a rapprochement with Clinton. The truce was short-lived, for Van Buren ran a candidate against Clinton in the 1826 gubernatorial race, which Clinton narrowly won. The furor surrounding the September 1826 murder of William Morgan, ostensibly at the hands of Freemasons, consumed much time in Clinton's last term. He condemned the outrage, though as a state and national leader of Freemasonry since 1806, he was also a target of the incipient Antimasonic movement. Though his strength in New York State had eroded, he continued to consider himself a viable presidential candidate for the 1828 election. Overweight and in poor health, he died suddenly from heart failure in 1828.

Legacy

Clinton's legacy was manifold. Running for president as a Republican, he contested regional domination of the federal government, pitting most of the states north of Virginia against those south of it. Yet he also gave emphatic meaning to the unifying as well as the economic effects of transportation by overseeing the building of the longest inland lock canal. Clinton's persistent advocacy of cultural, social, and economic improvement under wise executive leadership suggested future uses of state power. It also triggered a creative response from Clinton's political opponents, who, in the early 1820s, carved out a philosophy of party that condemned personal ambition and emphasized loyalty to party and the collective formulation of party policy on the state and national level, all of which should serve to hold the nation together.

Cornog, Evan. *The Birth of Empire: DeWitt Clinton and the American Experience, 1769–1828* (New York: Oxford Univ Press, 1998)

Hanyan, Craig, with Mary Hanyan. *De Witt Clinton and the Rise of the People's Men* (Montreal: McGill-Queen's Univ Press, 1996)

Siry, Steven E. *De Witt Clinton and the American Political Economy: Sectionalism, Politics, and Republican Ideology, 1787–1828* (New York: Peter Lang, 1990)

Craig and Mary L. Hanyan

Clinton, George (*b* England, 1686; *d* England, 10 July 1761). Colonial governor. Clinton's appointment as governor on 3 July 1741 was arranged by an influential cousin. A career officer in the British Royal Navy and former governor of Newfoundland, Clinton sought the post to escape bankruptcy. After his arrival in New York on 20 Sep 1743, he chose Chief Justice James DeLancey as his adviser. Clinton had little political ability, and provincial politicians, including DeLancey, used his ineptitude to increase their own power. A rift soon developed between Clinton and DeLancey over support of King George's War (1744–48) that extended to the pro-DeLancey faction in the Colonial Assembly. In 1747 DeLancey managed to secure an appointment as lieutenant governor. At a conference in August 1746, Clinton tried to enlist the Iroquois in a campaign against the French. They declined, citing their 1701 treaties of neutrality. Notwithstanding this failure, Clinton appointed William Johnson to oversee Indian affairs, and Johnson was able to convince some Mohawks to participate. After the war Clinton made a futile attempt to chasten the pro-DeLancey assembly by repeatedly vetoing their appropriations bills. In response the assembly withheld Clinton's salary for two years, forcing him to relent. The last five years of his tenure were marked by border disputes between New York Colony, Massachusetts, and New Hampshire and by the July 1753 tenant riots at Livingston Manor [now in Columbia Co]. Clinton was replaced in October 1753 by Sir Danvers Osborne, who committed suicide shortly after arriving. Before Clinton left for England, his rival DeLancey took over as acting governor.

Katz, Stanley N. *Newcastle's New York: Anglo-American Politics, 1732–1753* (Cambridge, Mass: Belknap Press, 1968)

Daniel A. Piazza

Clinton, George (*b* Little Britain [now in Orange Co], 26 July 1739; *d* Washington, DC, 20 Apr 1812). US vice president, governor, and military officer.

Early Military and Political Career

After schooling from a private tutor as a young boy, Clinton left home in 1757 to serve on a privateer and then served as a subaltern in the militia in Canada during the French and Indian War. After the war he studied law with William Smith Jr in New York City. He returned to Ulster Co (the area is now in Orange Co), where he farmed and developed a successful law practice. Elected to the Colonial Assembly in 1768, he became associated with the anti-British Livingston faction. His marriage to Cornelia Tappen on 7 Feb 1770 strengthened his political position in heavily Dutch Ulster Co. Clinton was elected to the Second Continental Congress, but he left for military duty before signing the Declaration of Independence. In December 1775 the New York Provincial Congress commissioned him brigadier general in the militia and called on him to defend the Highlands of the Hudson River from British attack. He built two forts and stretched a giant chain across the river to keep the British forces in New York City from sailing northward. In March 1777 Congress commissioned him a brigadier general in the Continental army.

Under the new state constitution adopted in April 1777, Clinton ran for lieutenant governor and surprised everyone by not only winning that race but by being elected governor as well. Clinton resigned the lieutenant governor's position and his militia commission and was inaugurated governor in Kingston (Ulster Co) on 30 July 1777. Asked by George Washington to come back into the army to defend the forts at the Highlands, Clinton assumed command of 600 defenders while maintaining his role as governor. He defended the Highlands against an overwhelmingly large force in October 1777. The forts were lost but at a tremendous cost in enemy casualties. In 1780 Clinton led two militia raids on New York State's frontier, protecting settlers from bands of British regulars, loyalists, and Iroquois tribes who had raided western settlements for more than two years. On both occasions the raiders escaped with Clinton's troops in hot pursuit. Clinton's lobbying efforts with Congress and Gen Washington, as well as his own efforts to defend the frontier, did not go unnoticed by settlers and helped solidify trust and support for his administration.

Governor and Antifederalist Leader

Clinton served seven terms as governor (1777–95, 1801–4). Throughout the Revolution he advocated strengthening Congress, but after the war, when he and many other New Yorkers felt that Congress and their neighboring states endangered New York's interests, Clinton opposed most increases in congressional power. Many New Yorkers felt threatened by congressional demands calling for the annexation of western New York State to the national public domain, although that territory had been taken from Indians by Continental troops. Congress refused to allow New York's legislature to raise troops to occupy the British forts there, and in the spring of 1784 Massachusetts delegates to Congress further troubled New Yorkers when they announced that most of the disputed territory belonged to Massachusetts under the provisions of their colonial charter. In April 1784 New York Congressman Ephraim Paine wrote to the governor "that there is not the least Prospect of any Protection or assistance from Congress and that it is high time for our State to tak[e] the Same measures as though it was Surrounded with open and avowed Enemies."

Clinton pursued policies defending New York State from the increasing demands of outsiders. Called Clintonianism by his opponents, the governor's policies transformed New York and earned the state the nickname the Great Empire State. In 1784 the legislature enacted a state tariff that would serve as the foundation of state programs during the Confederation period. To combat the severe economic depression that ravaged the country, the legislature passed bounties on agricultural and manufactured goods and issued state paper money that was loaned to private individuals with real estate as collateral. The money, which could be used to pay taxes and private debt, would tide farmers over until the economy recovered. A large portion of the currency was also used to fund the interest and principal of the state's wartime debt and to purchase federal securities owned by New Yorkers. Through this program, New York became a net creditor of the United States by the end of the Confederation period. Clinton worked to keep the price per acre of state land low, thus encouraging sales. He also encouraged public education and internal improvements, especially the construction of roads and canals. Clinton did favor giving Congress more authority over commerce, which would increase commerce with all countries, but opposed the unconditional grant of an impost power to Congress and refused to compensate loyalists for their confiscated property. These policies stimulated the economy, and New York State recovered rapidly from the depression while most other states still suffered.

In 1787–88 Clinton led New York State's Antifederalists during the debate over the ratification of the US Constitution. His steadfast opposition to the unamended Constitution catapulted him onto the national scene as the most prominent Antifederal candidate for vice president in 1788–89. Alexander Hamilton strenuously opposed Clinton's postwar policies in New York State and lobbied against Clinton's candidacy. Clinton's antifederal conviction hurt his popularity within New York State after the Constitution was ratified in July 1788. After he ran unopposed for reelection as governor in 1786, his party lost control of both houses of the legislature in 1789, and Clinton barely defeated the Federalist candidate, Robert Yates, of Albany. In 1792 Clinton again won the governorship, defeating John Jay in a close, disputed election.

Vice President

Even with the narrow victories in New York State, in 1792 Clinton was chosen to oppose John Adams for the vice presidency. Overcoming a strong challenge from Aaron Burr, Clinton received the unanimous electoral votes of New York State but lost the election to Adams. He remained governor and later retired from public service, in 1795. He refused an offer to stand for vice president in 1796, but in spring 1800 Clinton was coaxed out of retirement to run for the state assembly from New York City. It was generally believed that the party that won the New York City assembly seats would control the New York State Assembly and that whoever controlled the assembly would determine the victor in the 1800 presidential election. Reluctantly, Clinton ran for the assembly and was elected. He halfheartedly sought the Republican vice presidential nomination in 1800; Burr tenaciously sought the nomination and won it. Clinton distrusted Burr and opposed his election, although Burr did win the vice presidency. When Burr prepared to run for governor of New York State in 1801, Clinton thwarted him by agreeing to run for governor. After winning the election he served as a figurehead for his nephew De Witt Clinton and then retired at the end of his term.

In 1804 Pres Thomas Jefferson asked Clinton to serve as his new vice president, preserving the important Virginia–New York State coalition that was crafted in the early 1790s. In February 1804 the Republican congressional caucus nominated Clinton for vice president. The 12th Amendment to the Constitution was adopted in June 1804, and Clinton became the first candidate officially to run for the position of vice president. In 1808 Clinton wanted to run for president, but the Republican congressional caucus nominated James Madison for president and Clinton for vice president. Clinton was reelected as vice president, this time serving under Madison. As vice president Clinton opposed the foreign and defense policies of both Jefferson and Madison. He favored strengthening coastal fortifications and enlarging the navy while opposing the implemented economic diplomacy that seemed to have no impact on France and Great Britain. Opposition clustered around Clinton, but he was too old and ill to provide effective leadership. On several occasions as president of the Senate, he cast a tie-breaking vote, most significantly on 20 Feb 1811 against rechartering the Bank of the United States. The first US vice president to die in office, Clinton was buried in the Congressional Cemetery, but his remains were moved to the Old Dutch Church in Kingston in 1908.

Kaminski, John P. *George Clinton: Yeoman Politician of the Young Republic* (Madison, Wisc: Madison House, 1993)

Spaulding, E. Wilder. *His Excellency George Clinton: Critic of the Constitution* (New York: Macmillan, 1938)

Young, Alfred F. *The Democratic Republicans of New York: The Origins, 1763–1797* (Chapel Hill: Univ of North Carolina Press, 1967)

John P. Kaminski

Clinton, Hillary Rodham (*b* Chicago, 26 Oct 1947). US senator and first lady. Hillary Rodham graduated from Wellesley College (1969) and Yale Law School (1973). In 1975 she married Yale classmate Bill Clinton and was a key policy and political adviser throughout his career as Arkansas governor and US president. She was an outspoken advocate for women's rights, universal healthcare, and other liberal causes during a time when women were taking on broader roles in business and public life. This caused her to become a controversial figure and a lightning rod for conservative critics. Clinton moved to Chappaqua (Westchester Co) in January 2000 and entered the race for a US Senate seat; the race received enormous publicity. After her likely Republican opponent, New York City mayor Rudolph Guiliani, was forced to drop out of the race because of health and personal problems, she defeated his replacement, Congressman Rick Lazio from Brightwaters (Suffolk Co), with 55% of the vote to his 43%. With her victory Clinton became the first former first lady elected to office and the first woman elected to the US Senate from New York State. In 2004 she was a member of the Senate Committee for Environment and Public Works, Committee for Health, Education, Labor, and Pensions, and Committee on Armed Services, and helped secure $21.4 billion in funds to assist cleanup and recovery at Ground Zero following the terrorist attacks of 11 Sept 2001. Clinton released a memoir, *Living History,* in June 2003.

For illustration see DEMOCRATIC PARTY.

Tomasky, Michael. *Hillary's Turn: Inside Her Improbable, Victorious Senate Campaign* (New York: Free Press, 2001)

Peter Slocum

Clinton, James (*b* Little Britain [now in Orange Co], 9 Aug 1733; *d* Little Britain, 22 Dec 1812). Continental army general. In his youth Clinton received private tutoring before entering the army. He served as a militia captain during the French and Indian War, represented Ulster Co in New York's First Provincial Congress in May 1775, and served as a colonel in the disastrous Canadian expedition later that year. Commissioned a brigadier general in the Continental army in 1776 and stationed in the Hudson Highlands, he oversaw the construction of Forts Montgomery and Clinton and served under his brother George's command in October 1777 when the Highlands were attacked by an overwhelming British force. He suffered a bayonet wound but escaped capture. From May through November 1779 he was second in command to Maj Gen John Sullivan in the campaign against the Iroquois led by Joseph Brant on the New York frontier. Although the expedition fought no major battles, it destroyed 40 Indian towns, their livestock, and most of their crops and orchards. This devastation temporarily stopped the marauding attacks on the frontier against rebellious colonists by the combined forces of the Iroquois and loyalists. In 1780 Clinton assumed command of the Northern Department of the army, headquartered in Albany, and led a brigade of over 1,100 men to Yorktown, Va, in 1781. He retired in protest when Congress passed over him for promotion despite his ranking status. In 1785 he served on the commission that settled the boundary dispute between New York State and Pennsylvania. In state politics, he was a Clintonian; on national issues he was an Antifederalist. In June and July 1788 he represented Ulster Co in the state convention, where he voted against the ratification of the Constitution. He served in the state senate from December 1788 through 1792. He was the father of De Witt Clinton.

John P. Kaminski

Clinton, Sir Henry (*b* Newfoundland, 16 Apr 1738; *d* Gibraltar, 23 Dec 1795). British army officer and son of a colonial governor of both New York and Newfoundland. As second in command of British forces in North America in 1776, Clinton pushed for aggressive operations against the revolutionaries and conceived the plan that resulted in British victory at Long Island in August 1776. He was knighted in 1777 and ordered to lead a force up the Hudson River to link up with Gen John Burgoyne's expedition marching south from Canada. Clinton captured the Hudson Highlands but could not prevent Burgoyne's surrender at Saratoga [now Stillwater, Saratoga Co]. Promoted to commander in chief in 1778, Clinton fought a tactical draw at the Battle of Monmouth in New Jersey on 28 June 1778. After his victory capturing Charleston, SC, in 1780, he continued the British occupation of New York City while the focus of operations shifted to the south. Through his aide-de-camp Maj John André, he negotiated with Benedict Arnold for the betrayal of West Point in 1780. Blamed for the British defeat at the Battle of Yorktown, he was replaced as commander in chief and returned to England in 1782.

Clinton, Sir Henry. *The American Rebellion: Sir Henry Clinton's Narrative of His Campaigns, 1775–82, with an Appendix of Original Documents.* Ed. William B. Willcox (New Haven: Yale Univ Press, 1954)

Ethan S. Rafuse

Clinton Correctional Facility. In 1845, at the site of an existing iron ore mine in Dannemora (Clinton Co), Clinton Prison for men opened. For 30 years, inmates worked in an unprofitable mining and iron manufacturing enterprise. After the mine closed in the 1870s, they made shoes, brushes, and other items for other New York State prisons and worked at road building and forestry projects. Inmates transferred to Clinton from other state facilities included those with discipline problems, drug addictions, or lengthy sentences, as well as inmates with tuberculosis, who might be helped by the climate and special hospital facilities. Electrocutions were performed at Clinton from 1895 to 1914, when a state law provided that any new death sentences handed down by the courts would be carried out at Sing Sing Prison (Westchester Co). Inmate disturbances in 1929, including one at Clinton that resulted in several deaths, led to extensive reform of the prison system, with emphasis on rehabilitative programs.

Clinton was the site of the Dannemora State Hospital for Insane Convicts, which opened in 1900. The hospital confined and cared for male inmates from state prisons, penitentiaries, and reformatories who were declared insane while serving sentences. In 1970 the current name of Clinton Correctional Facility was adopted for Clinton Prison, and in 1972 the Dannemora facility closed and inmates were transferred to Matteawan State Hospital in Fishkill (Dutchess Co). Clinton's innovative inmate programs include the Adirondack Correctional Treatment and Evaluation Center and the Clinton Annex. In 2003 Clinton Correctional Facility was the largest maximum security correctional institution in the state, confining 2,890 male inmates aged 16 years and older and employing a staff of 1,262.

"Clinton," *DOCS Today* (Jan 1999): 13–17

Clinton State Prison, Dannemora, NY: Its History, Purpose, Makeup, and Program (Albany: NYS Department of Correction, 1949)

Lewis, David. *From Newgate to Dannemora: The Rise of the Penitentiary in New York State, 1796–1848* (Ithaca: Cornell Univ Press, 1965)

Richard Andress

Clinton County (1,118 mi²/2,896 km²; pop 79,894). Located in extreme northeast New York State and named for then governor George Clinton, Clinton Co was formed from Washington Co in 1788. Although it once also encompassed parts of Essex, Franklin, and St. Lawrence Cos, its present boundaries were set in 1808. It is divided into 14 towns, the City of Plattsburgh (the county seat), and 4 incorporated villages. Its southwest quadrant lies within the Low Mountains subregion of the Adirondack physiographic province, where the highest elevations exceed 3,800 feet (1,160 m). The remainder of the county is part of the St. Lawrence–Champlain Lowland physiographic region. The eastern third of Clinton Co lies within the Champlain Lake Plain subregion; the remaining sector consists of the gently rolling to hilly terrain of the St. Lawrence Hills subregion. At 95 feet (29 m) the shore of Lake Champlain marks the lowest elevation. All parts of the county show evidence of glaciation. Underlying bedrock formations include Ordovician limestone in the area near Lake Champlain, Devonian sandstone in the north and the hilly areas, and gneiss-dominated metamorphic Precambrian rock in the Adirondack province. Aside from a limited area along the western margins, drainage flows east to Lake Champlain or to the Richleau River. The largest streams include the Ausable, Great and Little Chazy, and Saranac Rivers.

The climate is humid-continental; temperatures can exceed 90°F (32°C) in summer and drop below -30°F (-34°C) in winter. Normal mean January temperatures lie around 15°F (-9°C), and July temperatures are in the upper 60s°F (16–21°C). Because the county's eastern half is situated within the rain shadow of the Adirondacks, its average annual precipitation amounts include some of the lowest in the state. Figures range from 38 inches (97 cm) in the higher elevations to 30 inches (76 cm) along the lakeshore. Seasonal snowfall normals range from 56 to 71 inches (142–80 cm). With limited exception upland soils are nonarable, and lowland soils vary from highly productive agricultural loams, which helped attract initial settlement, to less productive soils, including some of no agricultural value. Spruce and fir dominated the primeval forest of the lowlands, while beech, sugar maple, and yellow birch interspersed with spruce and fir covered the higher elevations. Over 70% of Clinton Co is covered by forest, and approximately 40% lies within the Adirondack Park.

Settlement

Little is known about the pre-European peoples of the area. It is probable that the original people were Iroquoian. Some artifacts and traces of fishing and hunting camps have been found, but the area was lightly occupied when Europeans arrived in the early 1600s. The earliest European attempts to settle this area were made by the French beginning in the 1730s. Despite success elsewhere in the Champlain Valley, French efforts failed. After the French and Indian War farmers and sawyers from New England and Quebec settled small parcels of land on the west shore of Lake Champlain. A more ambitious settlement effort was made on a 30,000-acre (12,100 ha) tract that included the future site of Plattsburgh, by Charles von Vredenburgh, a retired German Swiss mercenary who had served with the British army in the region. His effort failed as well when his tenants and other settlers fled the area during the Revolution, and von Vredenburgh mysteriously disappeared. Some

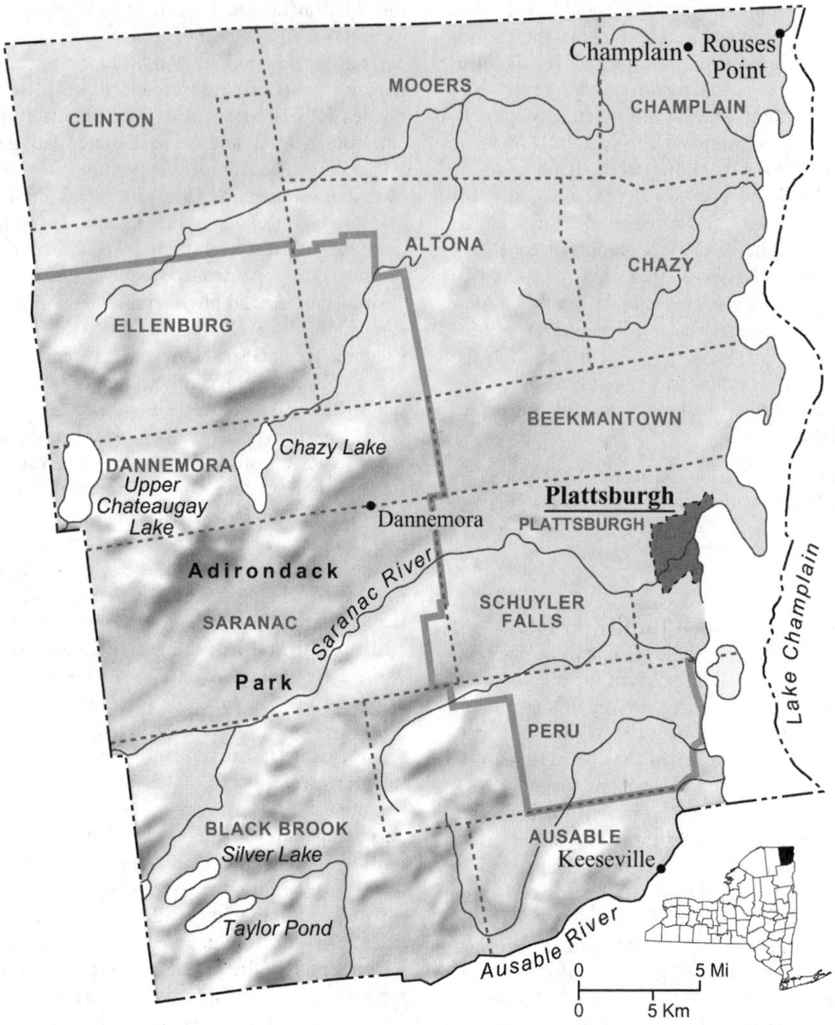

settlers reoccupied their lands when permanent settlement began immediately after the war, despite a continued British presence at Point au Fer in the Town of Champlain until 1796.

The land was initially divided into a number of patents and grants. The largest was a portion of the Old Military Tract in the western part of the county, intended for Revolutionary War veterans, but no grants were made, and the state ultimately sold the land to speculators. Other large tracts were the Canada and Nova Scotia Refugee Tract, set aside for Canadians and Nova Scotians who fought with the Americans during the Revolution, many in Moses Hazen's New York regiment; Beekman Patent; and Plattsburgh Old Patent, headed by Zephaniah Platt. Most settlers after 1783 came from New England, the Hudson Valley, and Quebec. Communities that developed on these grants after 1783 became the villages and larger settlements of the county. Besides Plattsburgh these include the farm centers of Champlain, Rouses Point, Ellenburg, and Chazy in the north, and Peru and Keeseville in the south. All were established during the 1790s. Overall, settlement advanced from east to west and north to south with the Adirondack country being the last occupied. Local residents found themselves once again in the path of marching armies during the War of 1812, particularly those in the Battle of Plattsburgh in September 1814, when outnumbered American forces turned back a major British invasion force.

Economic Development

Economic life during the 19th century was based at least as much on timber and mineral resources as on arable land. A mix of farming and lumbering occupied most early residents, and agriculture spread throughout the county. Before the Civil War, farming remained mixed, although disproportionately large amounts of fodder and oats were grown for draft animals working in the iron and lumber industries. Even though widespread, farming played a secondary role and supported other economic activities until the late 19th century, when dairying and apple growing became profitable because of fast, reliable rail service.

The transportation system of Clinton Co and its region both created industrial opportunities and was created by them. Almost all freight and passengers used Lake Champlain in the beginning. Before 1823 most trade moved toward Canada, but in that year the opening of the Champlain Canal, connecting the southern end of the lake with the Hudson River, redirected trade southward. The linkage fostered the development of iron and other industries in the Champlain Valley. Sailing canalboats, schooners, and steamboats plied the lake, making Plattsburgh, Port Jackson [now Valcour], Rouses Point, and other lakefront communities ports of call. Rough roads cut westward away from the lake. The Old State Rd (US 9) connected Albany with the Canadian border, and many plank roads built and maintained by the iron companies became the basis of today's highway network. Rail service began in 1850 with the opening of the Great Northern Railroad (later Rutland Railroad) connecting Rouses Point with Ogdensburg on the St. Lawrence. This was joined in 1855 by a line from Montreal, but the Delaware and Hudson Railroad did not complete the connection south from Plattsburgh to Albany until 1872. Two spurs later linked Au Sable Forks and Lyon Mountain to Plattsburgh.

For much of the 19th century, the primary industry centered around iron's mining, smelting, and fabrication. By 1815 bloomery furnaces and associated technologies had developed at power sites along the Ausable and Saranac Rivers. Using locally produced charcoal as fuel, these facilities manufactured bar and pig iron, wire, nails, horseshoes, and boilerplate. The cutting of fuel wood for either direct consumption or conversion to charcoal and its subsequent use in the iron industry arguably involved the largest segment of the workforce when considering full and seasonal labor. Small iron furnaces consumed over 100 acres (40 ha) of woodland annually. Large operations, such as Chateaugay Ore and Iron, covered 1,000–2,000 acres (400–800 ha).

A number of Clinton Co's central places grew up around the iron industry. Six miles (10 km) west of Keeseville on the Ausable, the company town of Clintonville was established by 1825, and six miles further upriver Au Sable Forks began in 1828. A string of iron-making hamlets developed along the Saranac River, including Cadyville, Clayburg, Plattsburgh, Saranac, and Redford (known also for glassmaking). Only Plattsburgh grew large enough to incorporate. Other settlements that coalesced around mines and ironworks, such as Irona, Black Brook, Peasleeville, and New Sweden, either disappeared or declined to rural residential communities after the 1880s as the iron operations closed. Dannemora grew up around a state prison built in 1845 directly atop an iron ore deposit so that the prisoners could mine and smelt the ore, thus paying the costs of prison operation. The experiment ended in 1877 after years of financial losses, but the prison continued, with the prisoners put to work on other jobs. Now known as the Clinton Correctional Facility, it remains a maximum security prison. In the region's more recent quest to create places of employment, Dannemora served as a model for other correctional institutions in Clinton Co at Altona and in adjoining counties.

Banking activities were slow to develop; between 1817 and 1856 five banks obtained state charters but all were short-lived. Plattsburgh-based First National and Vilas Banks, chartered in 1863 and 1881 respectively, survive in the early 21st century, although as branches of larger bank chains. Keeseville was served by the Essex County Bank from 1832 to 1862 and after 1870 by the Keeseville National Bank. The latter was absorbed by an external conglomerate in the 1990s, as was a bank in Champlain. The limited financial industry hindered development and was a factor in the economic downturns that plagued the county after the 1880s.

A substantial influx of Franco- and Anglophone Canadians and of Irish began in the 1840s; by 1870 a third of the population was foreign-born. There were also British, Germans, and others, but a Yankee-Yorker-Quebecois-

CLINTON CO POPULATION CENSUS FIGURES

	White	Nonwhite	Total Population	Foreign-Born
1790	1,581	33	1,614	—
1800[a]	8,395	121	8,516	—
1810	7,941	61	8,002	—
1820	11,972	98	12,070	961
1830	19,262	82	19,344	2,902
1840	28,071	86	28,157	—
1850	39,935	112	40,047	13,204
1860	45,607	128	45,735	12,627
1870	47,819	128	47,947	12,677
1880	50,710	187	50,897	10,605
1890	46,291	146	46,437	7,746
1900	47,278	152	47,430	6,117
1910	47,965	265	48,230	5,370
1920	43,672	226	43,898	4,018
1930	46,240	447	46,687	3,533
1940	53,258	748	54,006	3,038
1950	52,772	850	53,622	2,583
1960	69,962	2,760	72,722	3,275
1970	70,212	2,722	72,934	2,480
1980	76,991	3,759	80,750	3,377
1990	80,590	5,379	85,969	3,412
2000	74,562	5,332	79,894	3,628

Notes: "Nonwhite" includes African Americans, Asians, American Indians, and Pacific Islanders and, for 2000, also the mixed race and other race categories. Through the 1960 census these figures primarily reflect the African American population. Foreign-born figures for 1820 and 1830 include only those not naturalized, and for 1930 and 1950, the foreign-born totals include Whites only. Other years include all foreign-born in the population.

[a]Clinton-Essex.

Irish mix predominated through the latter half of the 19th and the early 20th centuries. There was a small but long-standing presence of African Americans, first brought as servants by French and British military personnel before 1783 and by American military personnel after 1800. The county had many active abolitionists, and it is believed there were Underground Railroad stations, particularly at Union, a Quaker settlement south of Peru. The highest number of Blacks recorded in the 19th century, in the 1880 census, was 187.

Religion, Education, and Culture

Most early settlers coming from New England and the Hudson Valley were Protestant, principally Presbyterian and later Methodist, and their congregations first met in homes being served by itinerant ministers. Catholic parishes developed later to serve Irish and Canadian immigrants; the first Catholic church was built in 1843 at Coopersville. Universalists were present by 1844, and Jewish residents organized a Plattsburgh congregation in 1861.

The first public school opened in 1786; by then other schools were already in place in private homes. School taxes were first collected in 1795. In 1811 Plattsburgh Academy, the first secondary school, opened. Both public and private (mainly Catholic) schools opened throughout the county during the 19th century. These evolved into consolidated central schools beginning in 1922, when the Chazy Central Rural School became the first consolidated rural school district in the state. In 2003 Clinton Co was served by six centralized school districts, one union free district, and the Plattsburgh City School District. Plattsburgh Normal School opened in 1890; the institution became part of SUNY in 1948 and since 2000 has been commonly known as Plattsburgh State University. Clinton Community College opened in 1969.

The first newspaper was the *Plattsburgh American Monitor* in 1807, but the first successful newspaper, the *Plattsburgh Republican* (1811), continues as the *Press-Republican*. Other newspapers, usually short-lived and always partisan, served Plattsburgh and the larger villages throughout the past two centuries. There are weeklies in Keeseville and Rouses Point. Broadcast media include radio station WMFF (1935) and television stations WIRI (1954; now WPTZ) and WCFE (1977), the public broadcasting station.

Politics

The county was Jeffersonian Republican and then Democratic, as the party evolved, from its earliest days to just before the Civil War. Subsequently the Lincoln Republicans became dominant. Prior to 1968 Clinton Co was governed by a 16-member board of supervisors with one supervisor from each town and two from the City of Plattsburgh. Since then a 10-member county legislature has governed, with each member having an equal vote. Since the 1960s the Republicans have been in the majority nearly two-thirds of the time. Daily county government operations are overseen by a county administrator appointed by the county legislature.

The 20th Century

Local farmers turned increasingly, and by 2000 almost exclusively, to dairy and apple production, while simultaneously retreating to the quality land in the county's east and north. By the 1890s the iron fabrication facilities had closed and many associated settlements abandoned, the consequence of a depressed market and strong competition from outside the region. One large iron company, J. and J. Rogers of Au Sable Forks, converted to papermaking in 1890 and operated until 1959. Iron ore continued to be mined near Lyon Mountain and at Standish west of Dannemora until 1966 by Republic Steel, but the ore was processed elsewhere. Forest industries remained a major element in the economy, but emphasis shifted to pulpwood. Forests also provided raw material to local sawmills such as the Prescott woodworking mill in Keeseville. Commercial quantities of firewood were also cut, as have been Christmas trees in more recent years. Other local industries included textile and clothing manufacture and machine tools. The Lozier Motor Co moved to Plattsburgh in 1900 to make marine engines but later produced cars for the wealthy and for auto racing. The plant closed in 1914, and the facility is used by Georgia-Pacific to produce a variety of paper products.

The primary road system was in place and paved by the mid-1920s, aside from the North-

POPULATIONS OF TOWNS AND CITIES, CLINTON CO

Town or City, Year Founded	1800	1840	1880	1920	1960	2000
Altona, 1857	—	—	3,570	1,911	1,750	3,160
AuSable, 1839	—	3,222	2,980	1,636	2,605	3,015
Beekmantown, 1820	—	2,769	2,644	1,590	2,538	5,326
Black Brook, 1839	—	1,064	3,365	1,822	1,595	1,660
Champlain, 1788	1,169	3,632	5,407	4,535	5,544	5,791
Chazy, 1804	—	3,584	3,147	2,607	3,386	4,181
Clinton, 1845	—	—	2,194	1,395	796	727
Dannemora, 1854	—	—	2,962	4,061	6,141	5,149
Ellenburg, 1830	—	1,171	3,162	2,475	1,945	1,812
Mooers, 1804	—	1,703	4,381	2,788	2,587	3,404
Peru, 1792	1,347	3,134	2,610	2,000	3,110	6,370
Plattsburgh, 1785	1,400	6,416	8,283	2,085	13,390	11,190
Plattsburgh (city), 1902	—	—	—	10,909	20,172	18,816
Saranac, 1824	—	1,462	4,552	2,684	4,006	4,165
Schuyler Falls, 1848	—	—	1,640	1,400	3,157	5,128

way (I-87), which was completed in 1967. Rail service was gradually cut back and after midcentury trackage eliminated. Nevertheless Plattsburgh remains an Amtrak stop. The Clinton County Airport opened in 1942 and provides commuter connections and private flights, but the road system carries most passengers and freight. Aside from abandoned iron hamlets, the settlement pattern created in the early 19th century remains. Most striking is the increased concentration of people and activities in and around Plattsburgh. With just over 30,000 people, the City and Town of Plattsburgh together constitute the county's largest community, containing 40% of the inhabitants and a larger percentage of the employment. The completion of the highway system and rising auto traffic after 1945 redirected commercial enterprises to the outskirts of settlements and, by the 1970s, to suburban shopping facilities around Plattsburgh.

After World War II the single most important addition to the county was the Plattsburgh Air Force Base (1956). A Strategic Air Command installation, it was a force for economic, social, and political change until its closure in 1995; empty, inconspicuous Atlas missile silos remain scattered around the county. The loss of over 7,000 personnel and their economic clout continues to be felt, and a major readjustment process with PARC (Plattsburgh Air Base Redevelopment Corp) is underway. In the 1990s a new wave of manufacturing operations opened at sites and in industrial parks around Plattsburgh, including the Bombardier Transportation subway car plant. A number of branches of Canadian firms have taken advantage of the international trade zone established west of Plattsburgh.

The county's population became more diverse as the 20th century progressed and with the opening of the air base, the expansion of the colleges, and the establishment of new industries like Wyeth-Ayerst Labs at Rouses Point. Even with the closing of the air base, many people have chosen to remain in the region. In 1977 the Mohawk claimed and occupied lands in the Town of Altona, calling the community Ganienkeh. Clinton Co meets the 21st century with its population base and economy somewhat uncertain. The region's focus remains on Plattsburgh, and strong social and economic connections with Canada, Vermont, and Albany continue. Environmentally, it is both beautiful and fragile.

See also ARCHITECTS AND ARCHITECTURE, ADIRONDACKS AND NORTH COUNTRY.

The standard county history is Duane H. Hurd, *History of Clinton and Franklin Counties, NY* (1880). While no updated volume has been written, Helen W. Allan et al's *Clinton County: A Pictorial History* (1988) covers both 19th and 20th centuries in illustrated format. There is one early town history with an interesting narrative style, *Old Keeseville Tales* (*ca* 1900), and a recent town history based on original research, Nell J. Sullivan and David Kendall Martin, *History of the Town of Chazy* (1970). Philip L. White, *Beekmantown, NY: Forest Frontier to Farm Community* (1979) is a scholarly study exploring that town's first half century, and David Kendall Martin, ed., *The Journal of William Gilliland* (1997) reproduces the writing of an influential early proprietor. The county's noteworthy architecture is well covered in Allan S. Everest, *Our North Country Heritage: Architecture Worth Saving in Clinton and Essex Counties* (1972).

Thomas A. Rumney

Clintonian Republicans. See DEMOCRATIC PARTY.

Clune, Henry W(illiam) (*b* Rochester, 8 Feb 1890; *d* Scottsville, Monroe Co, 7 Oct 1995). Journalist and historian. Born to a self-taught mining company treasurer and his wife, Clune grew up in Rochester and attended city schools through the eighth grade. He entered Phillips Academy in Andover, Mass, but left in 1910, after his first year, and joined the Rochester *Democrat and Chronicle* as an unpaid cub reporter. The following year he was placed on the payroll at $8 a week. As a member of what he called the "Downtown Boys," Clune began writing his "Seen and Heard" column in 1918. He married Olympic swimmer Charlotte Boyle in 1921 and moved to Scottsville six years later. Well known primarily in the Rochester area, he spent his life, with the exception of a few brief stints in New York City, Detroit, London, and Paris, chronicling the famous, notorious, and lowly happenings of his native city. Author of 14 books, including 6 novels and 1 volume of the Rivers of America series on the Genesee, he retired in 1969, writing into his second century. He published his autobiography, *The Rochester I Know*, in 1972 and continued writing occasional pieces for the newspaper and *Rochester History.*

Clune, Henry W. *The Rochester I Know* (Garden City, NY: Doubleday, 1972)

David Minor

Clyde. Village (pop 2,269) in Galen (Wayne Co). French traders built a blockhouse near the site of Clyde in the early 18th century. Two hamlets across the Clyde River from each other were settled in 1811 and 1818; the two merged and incorporated as Clyde in 1835. The Erie Canal (1822) and the New York Central Railroad (1853) provided transport for manufacturing, including a glassworks (1827–1915) that made window glass and, after 1864, bottles. In the 1880s Italian workers on the canal settled in the village, making up half its population by 1940. During World War II, there was a German prisoner of war camp in Clyde. A General Electric plant (1945–65) operated the first practical silicon-controlled rectifier in 1958. LSW Industries, a manufacturer of pallets and containers, was founded in 1971 by civil rights activists to provide jobs and training for the unskilled, especially migrant farmworkers. A grassroots movement to revitalize the downtown and to attract new industry began in 1996. In 2003 the largest employers were Parker Hannifin (machine parts) and Thomas Electronics (cathode ray tubes).

Scott C. Monje

Clymer. Town (pop 1,501) in SW Chautauqua Co. Settled in 1820 the town was formed in the same year from Chautauqua. The 1837 depression caused many of the original settlers to move west. Chautauqua Land Co proprietors offered special inducements to people from the Netherlands, who arrived in 1846. In 1953 thousands of tulips were planted, inaugurating Clymer's annual Dutch-themed Tulip Festival that takes place each May. Much of the town's dairy industry has been consolidated into fewer, larger farms, which remain family owned.

Suzanne Rhebergen

cobblestone architecture. Vernacular building technique most often associated with Monroe and surrounding counties but encountered throughout western New York State and the length of the Mohawk Valley, reaching to Albany. The technique spread north to Ontario and west to Wisconsin as New Yorkers migrated in those directions. Use of cobblestone masonry can be traced to England, but its expression in central New York State is entirely native. The preponderance of glacial and water-laid cobbles in the native soils and subsoils of the region inspired European settlers to use the material in construction. Water-rounded cobbles were the predominant material of choice, being more smoothly rounded than their glacially formed counterparts. Despite their similar appearance, cobblestone buildings were built using three different techniques. The earliest used cobbles as a veneer over a wood frame and is the rarest of the three, probably because of the fragility of the resulting wall. The schoolhouse at Albion (Orleans Co) is an example. More common was laying up walls entirely of cobbles. In later applications rubble stone walls were laid up and faced with a cobble veneer, yielding a stronger wall with more freedom in style. Different orientation, size, and colors of the stones selected allowed a wide range of decorative effects. Individual cobbles were accentuated by projecting them from the face of the wall and by using decorative mortar joints. Cut-stone quoins, lintels, and sills were typically used at critical parts of the structure and of a contrasting color. Reaching its peak of popularity between 1825 and 1860, cobblestone construction was most frequently used in Greek Revival–style buildings but was also used in Federal and Gothic Revival. Although primarily used in dwellings, the style is found as well in barns, silos, churches, schools, and commercial buildings. Albions Cobblestone Society works to preserve these structures.

Schmidt, Carl F. *Cobblestone Masonry* (Scottsville, NY: Author, 1966)

Shelgren, Olaf William, Cary Lattin, and Robert W. Frasch. *Cobblestone Landmarks of New York State* (Syracuse: Syracuse Univ Press, 1978)

Walter Richard Wheeler

Cobleskill [KO-BIL-SKIL]. Town (pop 6,407) and village (pop 4,533) in N central Schoharie Co. Dutch and Palatine farmers settled Cobleskill's flats by 1754 but were decimated by Tory and Indian raids during the Revolution. More settlers came after the war, however, and the town was established in 1797. An agricultural processing and manufacturing center from early in the 19th century, it benefited from the Albany and Susquehanna Railroad (1865; later Delaware and Hudson Railroad). The village was incorporated in 1868. Its center, including the Hotel Augustan (1874), was made a National Register Historic District in 1978. Empire Agricultural Works (1881) manufactured horse powers (treadmills on which a horse powers machinery), threshers, silos, and later, as Harder Manufacturing Co (1916), iceboxes and refrigerators until the 1960s. Quarrying and cement manufacture at Howes Cave continued from 1869 to 1986. In the early 21st century, dairy farming and light manufacturing predominate. The village hosts the county's Cobleskill Sunshine Fair (1876) and is home to SUNY Cobleskill (1916). I-88 opened through town in 1980, helping draw tourists to

Howe Caverns, Secret Caverns, and the Iroquois Indian Museum (1980). In 2003 the Cave House, a Victorian hotel, was studied for conversion into a museum of mining and geologic studies.

Peter Johnson and Dawn Johnson

Cochecton. Town (pop 3,052) in W Sullivan Co. Its name is from the Lenape word *cushetonk,* which is believed to mean "rock cliff washed by water." The first settlers, from the Connecticut-based Delaware Co in 1757, were driven out by the Lenape within six years. Resettled after the American Revolution, Cochecton became the western terminus of the Newburgh and Cochecton Turnpike (chartered 1801, completed 1809). The town formed from Bethel in 1828. Most of its early residents engaged in lumbering or tanning. The arrival of the Erie Railroad (1847) brought a surge in population. Lake Huntington became a resort popular with Germans. The crude oil pipeline (1880) operated by the National Transit Co, a division of Standard Oil, ran through the town; the remains of a large pump house still stands. Cochecton is largely agricultural although in summer the Delaware River makes it popular for recreation.

John Conway

Coeymans [KWEE-MUNS]. Town (pop 8,151) in SE Albany Co. Patented in 1673 by Barent Pieterse Coeymans and settled by him, the town was formed in 1791 from the extinct town of Watervliet [now Colonie]. In the Civil War era the town was a large producer of hay, shipped from its landing to the New York City market. Railroad service was provided by the Saratoga and Hudson River Railroad (1865; after 1883 West Shore Railroad). Molding sand, bluestone, and limestone were quarried; industrial enterprises included a hat factory, foundries, a paper mill (1847), a woolen factory (1870s), and a large brickyard (1885–1983). Albany city water is supplied by Alcove Reservoir (1926–32). Large icehouses stored ice cut on the Hudson, and in the 1930s some of these were converted for use in growing mushrooms. In the 1970s Fran Mushrooms employed 200 workers. The Atlantic Cement Co plant, the largest in North America, opened in 1962. Landmarks include the Ariaantje Coeymans House (1716) and the Civill Academy (1873; now Coeymans Civic Center).

Coffin, Henry Sloane (*b* New York City, 5 Jan 1877; *d* Lakeville, Conn, 25 Nov 1954). Presbyterian minister, educator, and author. Raised in New York City and educated at Yale, University of Edinburgh, Marburg University (Germany), and Union Theological Seminary in New York City, Coffin was ordained by the Presbyterian Church in 1900. He pastored the Bedford Park Presbyterian Church (1900–1905) and the Madison Avenue Presbyterian Church (1905–26), both in New York City. A nationally known preacher, liturgist, and ecumenist, Coffin was a key figure in the doctrinal disputes that divided the Presbyterian Church in the 1920s. Self-described as a liberal evangelical, Coffin believed that Presbyterian doctrine, to remain relevant, had to be adapted to the ideas of the time. He was president of Union Theological Seminary in New York City (1926–45) and moderator of the Presbyterian Church in the USA (1943–44). Coffin's books include *The Creed of Jesus* (1909), *Hymns of the Kingdom* (1910), *The Meaning of the Cross* (1931), and *God Confronts Man in History* (1947).

Niebuhr, Reinhold, ed. *This Ministry: The Contribution of Henry Sloane Coffin* (New York: Charles Scribner's Sons, 1945)

Noyes, Morgan Phelps. *Henry Sloane Coffin: The Man and His Ministry* (New York: Charles Scribner's Sons, 1964)

Wendy J. Deichmann Edwards

Cohocton. Town (pop 2,626) and village (pop 854) in NW Steuben Co. Settled in 1794, the town was formed from Bath and Dansville in 1812. The town's first big industry was lumbering, but the forests were fully cleared by the 1880s. Starting in the late 1840s, Germans from the Rhineland settled in town, and by 1880 the population was one-quarter German. Rail service was provided by the Buffalo and Cohocton Valley Railroad (1852), which was soon renamed the Buffalo, Corning, and New York Railroad and later assimilated into the Erie Railroad (1857), and the Delaware, Lackawanna and Western Railroad (1882). After the Civil War, potatoes, dairy products, and buckwheat became important crops. Cigars were manufactured from the 1870s to the 1890s. The village incorporated in 1891. In 1911 a creamery was established, later acquired by Pollio Cheese (a division of Kraft Foods), and closed in 1990. Other 20th-century employers included the Boggs Potato Grader Co at Atlanta (1918–early 1960s) and the Moore-Cottrell Subscription Agency at North Cohocton (1894–1982). Beginning in 1938 Cohocton drew potato growers from Long Island and Maine looking for cheaper land. Orson S. Fowler, phrenologist and popularizer of octagon houses, was born here in 1809. The annual Fall Foliage Festival has been held since 1976.

Virginia L. Wright and Jerry Wright

Cohoes. City (pop 15,521) in NE Albany Co. Located at the confluence of the Mohawk and Hudson Rivers, it is the site of the 78 ft (23.8 m) Cohoes Falls, admired by the earliest explorers. By tapping power from the falls, the Cohoes Manufacturing Co (1811–29) produced screws and cotton cloth. The Erie and Champlain Canals were both completed through Cohoes in 1823. The Cohoes Corp (1826) was formed to supply power and lease millsites; in 1832 one of the mills became the first to operate knitting machines by waterpower. Railroad service was provided by the Rensselaer and Saratoga (1835), Troy and Schenectady (1842), and Albany Northern (1853) Railroads. The Harmony Manufacturing Co mills (1837; cotton cloth) were the largest textile mills in the state. They attracted many women as operatives, beginning with Irish immigrants. A large influx of Francophone Canadians followed in the 1860s, and in the 1880s they were joined by Italians, Poles, Lithuanians, Russians, and Ukrainians. Cohoes incorporated as a village in 1848 and became a city in 1870. In the 19th century Cohoes manufacturing included knit goods, cotton cloth, strawboard and paper boxes, edge tools, knitting needles and machinery, soap, cement, and furniture. The vast majority of workers, however, produced textiles; in 1872 the Harmony mills alone employed 5,170, and the numerous knitting mills employed 2,503. Another 685 worked in iron industries, and only 394 in all other factories. The Harmony mills closed in 1932, but rayon products and knitted goods remained significant, with boats, fire hydrants, paper boxes, and wallpaper in smaller amounts. Much of Cohoes' heavy industry closed in the late 20th century, and the mill buildings were recycled for warehouses and small manufacturing plants. The Harmony Mills Historic District marks the largest extant textile mill complex in New York State. Other landmarks include the Van Schaick Mansion (*ca* 1735) and the Cohoes Music Hall (1874). An intact mastodon skeleton unearthed in Cohoes in 1866 is now in the lobby of the New York State Museum in Albany.

See also TEXTILE INDUSTRY.

Cohoes Mastodont. Remains of young male proboscidean excavated in Cohoes (Albany Co) in 1866, after a construction crew for the Harmony mills found an exceptionally large pothole in the shale near the Mohawk River. T. G. Younglove, a company official, wrote to James Hall of the State Cabinet of Natural History

Cohoes Falls along the Mohawk River.

(now New York State Museum) about the pothole's contents, which included the mandible of a large animal. Other parts of the skeleton were found nearby. Hall determined the remains to be those of an American mastodon *(Mammut americanum)* that had traveled on the post-glacial waters until it was caught in the eddy of the pothole. Mastodons lived in New York State during the end of the last Ice Age, about 14,000 years ago. The American mastodon could reach a height of about 10 feet (3 m) and was distinguished by the cone-shaped protrusions on its teeth, which allowed it to eat shrubs and tree bark as well as tender plants. Hall oversaw the excavation of the Cohoes Mastodont with the assistance of geologist Grove Karl Gilbert, who assembled and mounted the skeleton in Geological Hall. Its spinal column is 15 feet (4.6 m) in length; the skeleton is 8.4 feet (2.56 m) high at the shoulder with 4.5 ft (1.37 m) tusks. Carbon-14 tests of the specimen indicated that the animal had died 11,070 years ago. After its reconstruction in the 1990s, the Cohoes Mastodont returned in November 1997 to exhibit at the New York State Museum, where it stands in the lobby of the Cultural Education Center. A reproduction is displayed at the Cohoes Public Library.

Clarke, John M. *James Hall of Albany: Geologist and Paleontologist, 1811–1898* (1923; repr New York: Arno Press, 1978)

Pamela Cooper

Colchester. Town (pop 2,042) in SE Delaware Co. Settled ?1766 and resettled in 1783, the town was formed from Middletown in 1792. Rafting, lumbering, and farming supported its residents. The first acetate in the United States was produced by a Corbett factory in 1848. Later there were eight wood acid factories along the Beaver Kill and the East Branch of the Delaware River, the last of which closed in 1948. In the late 19th and early 20th centuries, summer boarders helped boost the economy. By 1912 Breakstone was manufacturing soft cheeses in Downsville. The construction of the Pepacton Reservoir (1955) brought prosperity to Downsville but inundated the hamlet of Pepacton. The Downsville covered bridge (1854) was restored in 2000. Good hunting and fishing in Colchester draw many visitors.

Dorothy Kubik

Cold Brook. Village (pop 336) in Russia (Herkimer Co). Cold Brook was settled in 1810 along the State Road (1806–8) from Johnstown to Sackets Harbor (Jefferson Co). After the Civil War it had a number of small factories making cheese boxes, sash and blinds, and button molds; several other important employers were located between the village and nearby Poland. The village was incorporated in 1903. The Cold Brook Feed Mill (1857) is listed on the National Register of Historic Places. The mill was the home of Grace Paull (1899–1990), author and illustrator of more than 100 books for children.

Susan R. Perkins

Colden. Town (pop 3,323) in S central Erie Co. Settled in 1810, the town was formed from Holland in 1827. Colden was served by the Buffalo, Rochester and Pittsburgh Railway (1878). Buffalo television stations built their transmission towers in town: WBEN (1952) and WKBW (1958). Farming, especially dairying, remains an important land use in the early 21st century. Ski Tamarack, established in the mid-1970s, has made Colden a popular winter destination.

Andrew C. Maines

Colden, Cadwallader (*b* Dunse, Scotland, 17 Feb 1689; *d* Flushing, Queens Co, 20 Sept 1776). Acting governor and scientist. Raised in Scotland where his father was a minister, Colden graduated from the University of Edinburgh in 1705. He then studied medicine in London and in 1710 emigrated to Philadelphia, where he both practiced medicine and became a merchant. Colden settled in New York Colony by 1718 and acquired an estate, Coldengham [now in Montgomery, Orange Co]. He had 11 children, including Jane (1724–60), a botanist who cataloged more than 300 species of plants in the lower Hudson Valley, and Cadwallader II (1722–97), a rising Ulster Co politician whose determined and very public loyalist position during the Revolutionary War ruined his career.

In 1720 the senior Colden was appointed the colony's first surveyor-general, was master in chancery, and had a seat in the provincial council, a position he held for more than 50 years (1721–75). Lured by Lewis Morris (1671–1746), Colden joined the Morris faction and became a leading figure in the party. The Morrisites had mainly middle-class supporters and were rivals of the James DeLancey–Adolph Philipse faction, largely supported by merchant elites. The Morrisites sought to relieve the middle class of certain taxes, protected artisans from imports, and offered subsidies to new businesses. During the 1740s the party began to fragment and a battle ensued between 1746 and 1750 over who held governmental authority. Colden, with Gov George Clinton (1743–53), held that the governor shared authority with the legislature; the DeLanceys claimed that the assembly alone held power. Colden's anti-DeLancey position thwarted him politically when DeLancey took office as governor (1753–55, 1758–60). When DeLancey died in 1760, Colden, as president of the council, asserted his royal prerogative as judge and took office as acting governor in 1760–61, serving as such again in 1763–65, 1769–70, and 1774–75. He challenged the merchant, lawyer-judge supporters of the DeLancey and newly formed Livingston factions, thinking that they had too much control in government, and granted an appeal to the defendant in an assault case, *Forsey v Cunningham* (1764), overriding and irking his rivals.

A royalist, he supported the notorious Stamp Act. During the related civil protest, in an attempt to quell public fervor, he had firearms at Fort George, located at the tip of Manhattan, aimed at the people of New York City. A mob continued protesting and burned his coach at Bowling Green and hanged two effigies, one of him and one of the devil. Afraid for his life, Colden took refuge on a British warship. In his third term as acting governor he sided with his DeLancey rivals to gain support. The Sons of Liberty published a pamphlet in 1769 denouncing policies that Colden and the assembly had established. When Gov William Tryon left seeking political advice in England in 1774, Colden again became acting governor and contended with New York City residents who objected to the Intolerable Acts with a tea party protest in April 1774. When the First Provincial Congress replaced the government, Colden fled to a family estate in British-occupied Flushing.

Politics aside, Colden was also a philosopher, historian, and botanist. He published many scientific papers, including *Plantae Coldenhamiae* (1742), one of the first studies of botany in the state; *The Principle of Action in Matter* (1751), a critique of Newtonian physics; and *The History of the Five Indian Nations* (1727), his most famous historical work.

See also SCIENTIFIC CULTURE (17TH–18TH CENTURIES).

Bonomi, Patricia. *A Factious People: Politics and Society in Colonial New York* (New York: Columbia Univ Press, 1971)
Hoermann, Alfred R. *Cadwallader Colden: A Figure of the American Enlightenment* (Westport, Conn: Greenwood, 2002)

Tricia A. Barbagallo

Colden, Jane (*b* New York City, 27 Mar 1724; *d* ?New York City, March 1760). Botanist. She was born to Cadwallader and Alice Colden, Scottish immigrants. Her father was the colony's surveyor-general and sat on the governor's council. When she was 4, her family moved to a Hudson Valley farm at Coldengham [now in Montgomery, Orange Co]. Living at her parent's home for most of her life, in her late 20s she took up the study of botany. Her father, who had a wide range of interests, taught her a new system of classifying plants, developed by the Swedish botanist Carl Linnaeus, that grouped plants according to their reproductive parts. Between 1752 and 1756 she examined and described more than 350 plants in the Hudson River valley. Many of these plants had been described by botanists in other colonies; her contribution was documenting their presence in New York. Several, however, were completely unknown, and thus her discoveries remain as significant contributions to the study of plant life in North America. Among these were the marsh Saint-John's-wort *(Triadenum virginicum/Hypericum virginicum)* and the goldthread *(Coptis trifolia)*. In 1756 her description of the Saint-John's-wort was published in the Scottish journal *Essays and Observations,* the first Linnean plant description published by a woman. She and her father corresponded with botanists around the world, including individuals in London, Edinburgh, and Leiden, Netherlands, and she sent them descriptions of other unusual plants, like the dwarf ginseng *Panax trifolius*). In 1757 Colden moved with her family to Flushing (Queens Co). While living there she met and in 1759 married a New York City doctor, William Farqhuar. She died the following year. Her botanical research materials are archived at the Natural History Museum in London.

Gronim, Sara Stidstone. "Ambiguous Empire: The Knowledge of the Natural World in British Colonial New York" (PhD diss, Rutgers Univ, 1999)

Sara Stidstone Gronim

Cold Spring. Village (pop 1,983) in Philipstown (Putnam Co). Sited strikingly on the Hudson River facing Storm King, Cold Spring grew up around the West Point Foundry (1817–1911), a producer of iron and brass, including the Parrott Gun, an accurate cannon used in the Civil War. During the war years the foundry employed as many as 600 men. The village incorporated in 1846 and was served by the Hudson River Railroad (later New York Central) beginning in 1849. Its location, surrounded by the Hudson Highlands, kept development at bay. In 1973 much of its wonderfully preserved historic fabric was incorporated into a historic district. In the last decades of the 20th century there was an increase in the village's prosperity because of an easy commute and tourism. The Foundry School Museum interprets village history.

Charlotte B. Eaton

Coldspring. Town (pop 751) in SW Cattaraugus Co. The town is divided by the Allegheny River and Allegany Indian Reservation. About one-third of Coldspring's area, 12,210 acres (4,941 ha), is within Allegany State Park (1921). In 1798 Quakers from Philadelphia became the first white settlers in Cattaraugus Co when they established an Indian school and mission farm on Seneca Indian Nation land. This passed through various forms until a Quaker boarding school for Indians was founded about 1848; it operated until 1938. The settlers found a dense forest of pine and hemlock; by 1822 there was a sawmill, and lumbering became Coldspring's principal industry. The town was formed from Napoli in 1837. The Atlantic and Great Western Railroad (1860; later Erie Railroad) provided transport. After the Civil War, dairying and raising hay, grain, and potatoes became important. The Trout Grove Fishery (1868) used 150 springs on a 14-acre (5.7 ha) tract to hatch trout; in 2003 it operated as the Randolph State Fish Hatchery. In 1965 the Town of Elko (1890) was dissolved and annexed to Coldspring. The same year the Kinzua Dam project created the Allegheny Reservoir, flooding portions of the Allegany Indian Reservation and State Park. Rte 17 (I-86) was built across the town in 1965–68.

Bruce D. Fredrickson and Madelynn P. Fredrickson

Cold Spring Harbor. Locality (pop 4,975) in Huntington (Suffolk Co). English settlers arrived in 1653. From 1799 to 1913 it was a US port of entry. In the early 19th century a woolen factory provided employment, and a whaling fleet operated from 1836 to 1862. The hamlet was later a summer resort. New York State established a fish hatchery in 1883, and the Cold Spring Harbor Laboratory, a leading molecular biology research center, opened its doors in 1890. An upper-middle-class community with a historic downtown of boutiques, it is the site of the Cold Spring Harbor Whaling Museum (1942).

Robert C. Hughes

Cold Spring Harbor Laboratory. The Brooklyn Institute of Arts and Sciences opened the facility at Cold Spring Harbor, in what is now Laurel Hollow (Nassau Co), as a marine biology station in 1890. Charles Davenport became director in 1898. With funding from the Carnegie Institution of Washington, DC, Davenport in 1904 established the Station for Experimental Evolution adjacent to the laboratory. Davenport later shifted attention to eugenics, the study of the controlled breeding of humans. By 1910, with financial support from the Carnegie Institution, Mary Williamson Averell Harriman, widow of railroad tycoon E. H. Harriman, and others, Davenport created the Eugenics Record Office. He sought to prove, by screening test subjects for various traits and family histories, how behavior was biological and could be enhanced or eliminated as need be. Eugenics as practiced in the United States was used as a model for similar practices in Nazi Germany in the 1930s and 1940s. The Eugenics Record Office was active until 1944.

Geneticist Milislav Demerec became the laboratory's director in 1941. Under his control Cold Spring Harbor became a leading center for genetic study and molecular biology. Breakthroughs were made in the study of viruses, the structure of genes, and DNA. In the 1950s geneticist Barbara McClintock studied the chromosomes of corn, work for which she received the Nobel Prize in 1983. James Watson, who co-discovered the structure of DNA and shared the Nobel Prize in 1962, became director in 1968 and focused research on the genetics of cancer. Throughout the 1960s and 1970s Cold Spring Harbor researchers did further study on recombinant DNA and RNA and on the structure of genes and how they work. In 1969 Al Hershey received the Nobel Prize for his discoveries on the genetic structure of viruses. The laboratory established the DNA Learning Center in 1988, a science center for educating the public about genetics, with teacher training workshops, student day camps, and field trips. Bruce Stillman became director in 1994, and Watson was named president and head of the laboratory's Human Genome Project, dedicated to mapping the entire sequence of human DNA and using that information to develop cures and treatments for genetically linked diseases. In 1998 the laboratory established the Watson School of Biological Sciences, a four-year PhD program.

See also EUGENICS; SCIENTIFIC CULTURE (19TH–21ST CENTURIES).

Cook-Deegan, Robert. *The Gene Wars: Science, Politics, and the Human Genome* (New York: Norton, 1994)

Kevles, Daniel. *In the Name of Eugenics: Genetics and the Uses of Human Heredity* (New York: Knopf, 1985)

Brian Regal

Cold War and McCarthyism. The Cold War, encompassing the period between World War II and the fall of the Soviet Union in 1991, ushered in a period of overt and covert anticommunism characterized by repression of radicals, domestic surveillance, and erosion of civil liberties.

Anticommunism and Suppression

Anticommunism came in many shades of opinion. Liberal anticommunism was espoused in journals such as *Commentary* and *Dissent,* leading publications of the so-called New York intellectuals, a loose group of writers combined in their opposition to Stalinism and the Communist Party (CP). The reactionary anticommunism of Joseph McCarthy also had many supporters in the state, among them the leaders of the Roman Catholic Church. Most varieties of anticommunism shared a commitment to curb and ultimately destroy left-wing politics and culture, which were particularly strong in New York State. The repression of the Cold War reached into the arts, local schools, newspapers, courts, government agencies, neighborhood organizations, churches, and homes, touching people in all walks of life. The state legislature, the New York State Police Non-Criminal Investigations Division, federal agents, and a number of right-wing organizations all participated in campaigns to ferret out radical influences in the state's society and culture. They especially targeted left-wing social, cultural, and political leaders. Vito Marcantonio, a strong Communist ally who represented East Harlem as a US congressman in 1934–36 and again in 1938–50, faced a united Republican, Democratic, and Liberal campaign against him in 1950 when he ran under the banner of the American Labor Party (ALP). His defeat ended his long political career and hastened the end of the ALP itself in 1954.

The numerous public hearings conducted by federal investigative agencies that often brought their deliberations to New York State constituted perhaps the most visible and effective catalysts fueling campaigns against New York's left-wing community. The House Un-American Activities Committee (HUAC), the Senate Permanent Investigating Subcommittee of the Senate Committee on Government Operations, and the Senate Internal Security Subcommittee probed social, cultural, and political institutions associated with the left. Their influence spread far beyond the Hollywood blacklist, which also affected New York actors, writers, and directors. The editor in chief of Little, Brown and Co was pressured to resign because of his failure to repudiate his left-wing associations. Communist authors and left-wing writers in New York City had difficulty publishing and printing their works. The extreme scrutiny of left-wing culture by the government is best illustrated by the FBI's stationing of a film crew across the street from a New York City bookstore that specialized in Marxist literature.

Private employers, professional organizations, and groups such as the John Birch Society, the Minutemen, the Veterans of Foreign Wars, the Daughters of the American Revolution, and the Catholic Church participated in one form or another of anticommunist and antileft campaigns; most rarely distinguished between communists, "fellow travelers," socialists, or even liberals. Corporations with government contracts, newspaper editors, and several professional organizations disassociated themselves from suspected communists by firing them or removing them from membership rolls. The *Knickerbocker News,* an Albany newspaper, fired reporter Janet Scott in 1953 for "gross misconduct," as she refused to answer questions posed to her by HUAC.

Many private fraternal and veterans organizations mounted surveillance of left-wing summer camps in the Catskills, led boycotts of businesses owned by radicals, like artist Rockwell Kent's Au Sable Forks (Essex Co) dairy farm, and harassed and blocked left-wing singers and actors from performing. Folksinger Pete Seeger, who had been a CP member from 1942 through 1950, faced an entertainment blacklist and frequent cancellations of his scheduled performances. In 1949, in Peekskill (Westchester Co), the famed Paul Robeson was prevented from singing when local right-wing veterans attacked concert attendees in what has come to be known as the Peekskill Riots. Anticommunist Catholic priests, bishops, and laity aggressively joined the campaigns against godless communists in schools, unions, and political organizations.

Antisubversive Legislation and Teachers

The Cold War also penetrated state government and public schools. State workers refusing to testify at various US congressional hearings held in the state in the 1940s and 1950s were removed from their jobs. Even before the late 1940s, the Ives Loyalty Oath Law (1934; also known as Ives Teacher Oath Law) required that state teachers and administrators and many private school teachers working in tax-exempted institutions affirm their loyalties to the state and federal constitutions in order to maintain employment. Additional legislation in 1939 permitted the removal of any educator verbally advocating the violent overthrow of lawful government. In public universities, this legislation soon led to a purge of dozens of radical faculty and was aided by the 1940–41 Rapp-Coudert Committee. A creation of the state legislature, this committee identified and interrogated suspected communists teaching at public schools, including state-funded colleges. It identified scores of red-tainted teachers and professors, including Jack D. Foner, a Baruch College professor. Foner was among the 60 New York City university faculty members who lost their jobs as a result of the Rapp-Coudert probe. He refused to testify before the committee and, along with his two brothers Moe and Philip Foner, was blacklisted. Similar purges of faculty took place in private colleges. During the height of the Cold War (1946 through the late 1950s), new laws reinforced previous antisubversive legislation. The Feinberg Law of 1949 required that the Board of Regents list seditious organizations and adopt rules to enforce more vigorously antiseditious acts already on the books. Hundreds of New York City teachers resigned or were dismissed as a result of this law. It was not until 1967 that the US Supreme Court, in *Keyishian v Board of Regents,* declared the state's teacher loyalty acts unconstitutional.

Legislation was not the only vehicle for eliminating left-wingers from the schools. Radical secondary school teachers throughout the state faced harassment and loss of employment for mere association with radicals. The son of a communist farmer in the Catskills region, for example, was hounded out of his teaching job in Hartsdale (Westchester Co) for no other reason than his father's notorious reputation. Others suffered similar fates. As recently released FBI records disclose, in 1951 J. Edgar Hoover initiated the "Responsibilities Program," designed to provide confidential information to state governors evaluating potential candidates for important state jobs. Between 1951 and 1955, however, the program was more often used to leak derogatory information on disloyal individuals being considered for all sorts of public employment. The program was soon expanded into a secret blacklist that affected 400 teachers and college professors.

Universities and Cold War Research

New York State's universities were also affected by the repressive atmosphere. In Ithaca, Cornell University political history doctoral student Lee Benson, undergraduate student and future economic historian Robert Fogel (later a Nobel Prize winner in economics), and several other campus CP members were under constant state police and FBI surveillance. Officials traced phone calls, opened and copied mail, and scrupulously monitored meetings. At Brooklyn College, liberal college president Harry Gideonse (1939–66) almost entirely eliminated the CP from the school by the early 1950s, demonstrating that even liberals could jump on the anticommunist bandwagon.

Beyond repression and harassment, the Cold War had another impact in the state's private and public universities: it reshaped research and scholarship. Young social scientists and humanists began to turn away from Marxist influences or disguised their political proclivities by adopting "Aesopian language," as Vladimir Lenin had called it years earlier, to express their radical ideas safely. Scientists working in the state's major universities began to engage in defense and Cold War–related research. Earth scientists and oceanographers working out of the Lamont-Doherty Earth Observatory of Columbia University, located along the Hudson River just north of New York City, concentrated their seismographic research on methods of measuring the size and extent of underground and underwater nuclear tests. Similarly, private research laboratories and firms, like General Electric, were drawn deeply into military contract work ranging from military nuclear research to developing complex electronic surveillance components.

Along with Cold War military research came a widespread phobia of military and scientific espionage, which increased with the development of nuclear weapons. Real and suspected nuclear spies were periodically arrested and bold headlines in the nation's papers increased the public's paranoia. In 1950 Klaus Fuchs, physicist and former Manhattan Project worker, was arrested and charged with espionage and passing secrets to the Soviet Union. This set off the labyrinthine search for a secret network of spies in the United States that eventually led to Ethel and Julius Rosenberg in New York. The conviction and execution of the Rosenbergs in New York in 1953 for treason marked the apogee of espionage paranoia in the United States and the level of distrust in government circles and intellectual communities.

Union and Labor Struggles

The Cold War severely fractured the state's labor movement. Many of the most volatile labor conflicts in the late 1940s and 1950s were waged not between workers and employers, but within and between unions. The passage of the Taft-Hartley Act in June of 1947, with its insistence on noncommunist affirmations from union leaders, led to numerous internal union rebellions and strongly fueled anticommunist currents within New York's unions. In New York City, Buffalo, Syracuse, Binghamton, Schenectady, and smaller communities throughout the state, major conflagrations took place between right- and left-wing unionists. The Congress of Industrial Organizations (CIO), after some debate, followed the lead of the Taft-Hartley Act and disqualified communists from leadership positions in 1949 and soon after that expelled 11 "communist-dominated" unions and one-fifth of its membership, a disproportionate number of whom worked in New York State. New York City's public teachers, organized by a radical left-wing union, fought an internal civil war leading to the formation of the Teacher's Guild, a right-wing alternative that later became the New York State United Federation of Teachers, led by avid anticommunist Albert Shanker. In Schenectady in 1954, after a bitter three-year battle, the International Union of Electrical Workers replaced Local 301 of the CIO-expelled left-wing United Electrical Workers Union. Similar conflagrations took place at the Remington Rand in the Tonawandas of Erie and Niagara Cos, in the Fulton Co tanneries of Gloversville and Johnstown, and throughout the state, ultimately affecting various CIO, the American Federation of Labor, and independent unions.

Polaris missile on display at the 1963 New York State Fair in Syracuse.

Epilogue

By the late 1960s the domestic manifestations of the Cold War began to subside. State Police surveillance continued until the early 1970s, focusing on many new left groups and the antiwar movement. The decline of the old left and the rise of an anti-Stalinist left changed the focus of concern of state and private officials. The finale demise of the Cold War came in 1991 with the fall and dismemberment of the Soviet Union.

Chamberlain, Lawrence H. *Loyalty and Legislative Action: A Survey of Activity by the New York State Legislature, 1919–1949* (Ithaca: Cornell Univ Press, 1951)
Schrecker, Ellen. *Many Are the Crimes: McCarthyism in America* (Princeton, NJ: Princeton Univ Press, 1998)

Gerald Zahavi

Cole, Thomas (*b* Bolton le Moors [now Bolton, England], 1 Feb 1801; *d* Catskill, Greene Co, 11 Feb 1848). Painter. He was an apprenticed engraver at 14, before the family's 1818 immigration to Philadelphia, where he continued in the engraving trade. The family moved to Steubenville, Ohio, where Cole became a wallpaper designer, portraitist, and landscape painter. He returned to Philadelphia in 1823 and studied exhibitions at the Pennsylvania Academy of Fine Arts before moving to New York City in 1825. He often ventured north to sketch the Catskills and would travel back to the city to paint large-scale landscapes. Cole's paintings depicted a wilderness where the human being was tiny and overwhelmed by the spirituality and vastness of nature. In 1826 Cole was a founder of the National Academy of Design. In the late 1820s Cole expanded his geographic scope to include romantic scenes near Lake George and Niagara Falls, and he produced historical landscapes and narrative sequences such as *The Garden of Eden.* In 1829 he traveled through England, France, and Italy and painted classical landscapes that incorporated religious and moral themes. He returned to New York City in 1832 and established his studio in Catskill, called Cedar Grove.

Cole's dramatic compositions, depicting nature and expressing moral and political opinion, were the crucial inspirations for the emerging Hudson River school of artists, of which he is considered founder. In the 1830s nature continued to be his subject, and he used his work to illustrate religious, political, and social themes. In 1836 Cole completed a five-part allegorical series, *The Course of Empire,* which illustrates the development and decline of a fictitious ancient empire, suggesting the possible corrosive effects of industrialization and democracy on US society. In 1842 Cole completed a second commissioned allegorical series, *The Voyage of Life,* depicting the journey of life with an unpredictable river and the guidance of an angel. In 1844 Cole traveled to Maine with his first student and later Hudson River school master Frederic Edwin Church. Cole also was an essayist, poet, writer, and theorist and was well known for his *Essay on American Scenery* (1835). Cole died after a brief illness. His friend and colleague, Asher B. Durand, memorialized Cole in *Kindred Spirits* (1849), a famous painting showing Cole and William Cullen Bryant mingling their artistic and literary sensibilities and communing with nature near Cole's favorite Hudson River spot, Kaaterskill Falls.

Powell, Earl. *Thomas Cole* (New York: Harry N. Abrams, 1990)
Truettner, William H., and Alan Wallach, eds. *Thomas Cole: Landscape into History* (New Haven, Conn: Yale Univ Press, 1994)

Nancy Knechtel

Colesville. Town (pop 5,441) in NE Broome Co. Several Tuscarora villages along the Susquehanna River were destroyed by James Clinton's troops in 1779. Resettled in 1785, the town was formed from Windsor in 1821. Much of the town was within the patent of Robert Harpur. In 1792 he sent a woman named Peggy Ludlow to superintend the building of a gristmill. Lumber was also produced in large quantities. Joseph Smith Jr, the Mormon prophet, lived on the Colesville farm of Joseph Knight Jr from 1826 to 1827, and members of the Knight family were among Smith's earliest converts. Sanitaria Springs was a water-cure resort from 1892 to about 1929. Farming continues in the 21st century with many other occupations.

Charles J. Browne

Colgate Rochester Divinity School. Theological school for the training of ministers and laypeople. It is the center of a cluster of institutions that includes Colgate Theological Seminary (1820), Rochester Theological Seminary (1850), Crozer Theological Seminary (1867), Baptist Missionary Training School (1881), and the affiliated Bexley Hall (1824) and St. Bernard's Institute (1892).

Colgate Theological Seminary was chartered in 1819 by Baptists in Hamilton (Madison Co). Originally the Theological Department of Hamilton Literary and Theological Institution (later Madison University, since 1888 Colgate University), instruction began in 1820. The seminary moved to Rochester in 1928. Rochester Theological Seminary was created out of the Theological Department in an urban/rural dispute in 1850. Some argued ministers were better trained in the urban setting and in a community less controlled by Baptists. Rochester Seminary was founded in connection with the University of Rochester, also originally a Baptist institution. It opened a German Department to meet the needs of the German Baptist community and became the leading Baptist seminary in the United States by 1900. Among its outstanding faculty were Augustus H. Strong and Walter Rauschenbusch. The campus, originally located at East Ave and Alexander St, was built with funds supplied in large part by John D. Rockefeller Sr. Colgate and Rochester seminaries merged in 1928, becoming Colgate Rochester Divinity School (CRDS) on a new campus.

From 1930 to 1970, the Divinity School developed a reputation as a liberal, ecumenical, socially concerned institution related to the American Baptist Convention. The Baptist Missionary Training School for women, in Chicago, relocated to Rochester in 1961. Bexley Hall, formerly the Episcopal theological school of Kenyon College in Gambier, Ohio, joined the Divinity School in 1968, and Crozer Theological Seminary in Upland, Pa, a Baptist school known for similar theological emphases, joined in 1970. The ecumenical cluster was completed in 1981 when Roman Catholic St. Bernard's Seminary moved to the campus as St. Bernard's Institute. All share a library and have a limited instructional relationship with the University of Rochester.

The Divinity Schools, as they are now designated, have often taken controversial positions. From its Rochester Seminary days, CRDS was known for social activism, which often placed it at odds with various evangelical traditions. Rauschenbusch developed his theological understanding of the social gospel while at Rochester and taught that all social institutions should be brought under the authority of God. Similarly, Pres Strong, in an early attempt to blend science and Scripture, accepted evolution as the means of best understanding the divine work in creation. In 1968 black students at the seminary staged a lockout of the seminary buildings to demonstrate the schools' perceived insensitivity to African American concerns. Also during the 1960s, theologian William Hamilton, W. N. Clarke Professor of Theology at CRDS, became well known for his involvement in the "Death of God" theological discussion. In the early 21st century, the Divinity Schools are thoroughly ecumenical, emphasizing clinical pastoral education, feminist traditions, African American thought, and social activism. Among outstanding faculty associated with Colgate Rochester, in addition to Strong and Rauschenbusch, are William Newton Clarke, Ezekiel G. Robinson, Conrad H. Moehlman, Winthrop S. Hudson, and James B. Ashbrook.

The institutional leadership in the Rochester Center for Theological Studies, as it is also known, is careful to recognize its predominant Baptist heritage. In 1955 Rochester's Samuel Colgate Baptist Historical Collection merged with the American Baptist Historical Society to form the world's largest collection of Baptist materials. The main seminary building includes the Gothic Samuel Colgate Memorial Chapel built in 1936. The current student body numbers 150.

Ewell, Glenn B. "Baptist Theological Education in New York State: A Genetic Survey," *Bulletin of Colgate Rochester Divinity School* 2 (Dec 1937)
Hopkins, Charles Howard. *The Rise of the Social Gospel in American Protestantism, 1865–1915* (New Haven, Conn: Yale Univ Press, 1940)

William H. Brackney

Colgate University. Private coeducational liberal arts college in Hamilton (Madison Co). The Baptist Educational Society of the State of New York established the Hamilton Literary and Theological Institute in May 1819 to train men for the ministry. It opened the following year, and the first nonministerial students were admitted in 1839. The name was changed to Madison University when it received a charter to grant baccalaureate degrees in 1846. Efforts from 1847 to 1850 to move the school to Rochester were defeated. It was renamed Colgate University in 1890 in deference to the Colgate family, whose members had served as trustees since 1823. In 1928 the theological seminary was removed from the institution and merged with the Rochester Theological Seminary to form the Colgate Rochester Divinity School in Rochester. Since then the university has been nondenominational. Colgate began accepting women in 1970. As of 2003 it offered 38 programs of study and enrolled 2,700 undergraduates on its 515-acre (208 ha) campus.

Howard D. Williams. *A History of Colgate University, 1819–1969* (New York: Van Nostrand Reinhold, 1969)

Sarah E. DeSanctis

College of Aeronautics. Private college. This urban 6-acre (2.4 ha) campus is adjacent to La Guardia Airport in Queens. Aviator Charles S. "Casey" Jones, George A. Vaughn Jr, and Lee D. Warrender founded the Casey Jones School of Aeronautics in 1932 to train technicians to design, build, and service aircraft and aircraft engines. The school later became known as the Academy of Aeronautics, and finally, in 1986, changed its name to the College of Aeronautics. In 1964 the school began to offer associate-level degrees. In 1969 it became accredited. The curriculum was revised, and the school offered its first bachelor's degree in 1996. By 2003 it offered eight BS degrees and two bachelor of technology degrees. Also offered are an associate degree in occupational studies, associates in applied science in six areas, and a certification program, Air Traffic Control–Collegiate Training Initiative (ATC-CTI). In 2003, 1,308 students attended the school.

Marianne Rahn-Erickson

College of Mount Saint Vincent. Founded in 1847 by the Sisters of Charity at 5th Ave and 105th St in Manhattan, the Academy of Mount Saint Vincent first served as an all-girl high school, moving to Riverdale [now in Bronx Co] in 1859. In 1910 the academy became the College of Mount Saint Vincent (CMSV) for women, with Archbishop of New York John Cardinal Farley as its first president. In 1964 CMSV formed a relationship with Manhattan College that allows students to cross-register for courses and that provides for some joint academic departments. In 1974 CMSV became coeducational and eventually introduced a master's degree program, first in nursing (1988) and then in education (1994). In 2002 it had 71 full-time faculty and 1,285 undergraduate and 169 graduate students. Corazon Cojuangco Aquino, president of the Philippines between 1986 and 1992, was a 1953 graduate.

Walsh, Marie De Lourdes. *The Sisters of Charity of New York, 1809–1959* (New York: Fordham Univ Press, 1960)

Jeffrey Kraus

College of New Rochelle. Private liberal arts college in Westchester Co. In 1897 the Order of St. Ursula founded the Ursuline Seminary for Girls in Leland Castle, a 1850s Gothic Revival mansion. In 1904 the order created the college, the first Catholic college for women in New York State. It offered courses in liberal arts and teacher training, as well as secretarial studies and home economics. In 1929 the seminary moved off-campus and became the North Avenue Ursuline School. In 1958 the property owned by the Convent Corp was transferred to the college, which now identifies itself as an independent institution of Catholic origin and heritage. Only the School of Arts and Sciences is restricted to women. In 1969 the college added the Graduate School, in 1972 the School of New Resources for adult learners, and in 1976 the School of Nursing. Courses are also taught at six other locations in New York City besides New Rochelle. In 2002 the college enrolled more than 7,000 students.

Schleifer, James T. *The College of New Rochelle: An Extraordinary Story* (Virginia Beach, Va: Donning, 1994)

Carl A. Westerdahl and Susan S. Clarke

College of Saint Rose. Private college. Founded by the Sisters of St. Joseph of Carondelet in 1920, the Roman Catholic, liberal arts college for women was named to honor St. Rose of Lima, the first saint from the Americas to be canonized. Located in Albany's residential Pine Hills neighborhood, its curriculum originally emphasized teacher education. The college added an evening division in 1946 and a graduate school in 1949. Fully coeducational since 1969, it became independent in 1970 when the sisters ceded administrative control to a board of trustees on which laypeople held the majority. Athletic teams, nicknamed the Golden Knights, compete in several NCAA Division II sports. In 2002, 39 bachelor's programs and 22 master's programs were offered to approximately 2,600 full-time undergraduates and 1,300 graduate students.

Manory, RoseMarie Schillaci. *Of Glory, of Praise: A 75-Year History of the College of Saint Rose* (Albany: College of St. Rose Press, 1994)

John Marino

College of Staten Island. Public college. By the 1950s Staten Island was the only borough in New York City without a municipal college. Community activism forwarded the creation of Staten Island Community College in 1955 at Sunnyside. Richmond College at St. George, providing the last two years for baccalaureate work, was inaugurated in 1965. These colleges were merged in 1976 to form the College of Staten Island (CSI). Physical consolidation followed in 1994 when CSI moved to the 204-acre (83 ha) former site of the Willowbrook State School for the Mentally Disabled in northwest Staten Island, making CSI the City University of New York's largest campus. Among research programs in the sciences are those conducted at the Astro Physical Observatory, and the college's performing arts center and art gallery are resources for the entire Staten Island community. In 2002 the college enrolled 10,616 undergraduate and 1,473 graduate students. In 2003 it offered nine associate degree programs, 38 bachelor's degree programs in the liberal arts and sciences and professional career preparations, and 12 master's degree programs and doctoral-level courses in five fields.

Roff, Sandra Shoiock, Anthony M. Cucchiara, and Barbara J. Dunlap. *From the Free Academy to CUNY: Illustrating Public Higher Education in New York City, 1847–1997* (New York: Fordham Univ Press, 2000)

Barbara J. Dunlap

Colles, Christopher (*b* Dublin, Ireland, 9 May 1739; *d* New York City, 4 Oct 1816). Engineer. After migrating to Philadelphia in 1771, Colles settled three years later in New York City, where he attempted to build its first public waterworks (1774–76), for which he designed one of the first American-made steam engines. The incomplete works were destroyed by the British during their wartime occupation. From 1784 to 1786 Colles promoted his plan to link Albany with Oswego on Lake Ontario via improvements of the Mohawk River and other watercourses. The ill-funded venture did not progress beyond initial surveys but was the first formal proposal for a water route between the Hudson River and Great Lakes. Colles's *Survey of the Roads of the United States of America* (1789), the first comprehensive atlas of American highways from Virginia to Albany, detailed routes to Albany on both sides of the Hudson. A New York City resident for most of his remaining years, Colles proposed and promoted numerous visionary projects, including a geographical atlas of the United States (1794), an above-ground timber canal connecting New York City and Philadelphia across New Jersey (1808), and a semaphore telegraph that may have operated briefly between New York City and Sandy Hook, NJ, during and after the War of 1812. Colles gained modest fame but little fortune from his projects and died impoverished.

Koeppel, Gerard T. *Water for Gotham: A History* (Princeton, NJ: Princeton Univ Press, 2000)

Gerard T. Koeppel

Collins. Town (pop 8,307) in S Erie Co. Settled between 1806 and 1809, the town was formed from Concord in 1821. Its first settler was part of a group of Pennsylvania Quakers who came to do mission work on the adjacent Cattaraugus Indian Reservation. In 1874 the western edge of town acquired service from the Buffalo and Jamestown Railroad (later Erie Railroad) and manufacturing developed, including Johnson Manufacturing Co (*ca* 1875–96; copperware). The town's first natural gas well was drilled at Zoar in 1888; drilling slacked off after 1955. Gowanda State Hospital (1898–1995) opened as a homeopathic institution and later became a psychiatric hospital. Its grounds are now the site of Collins (1982) and Gowanda (1994) Correctional Facilities. Collins's rich soil was ideal for growing small fruits and vegetables, processed at canneries in or near town, and for dairying. Twentieth-century employers included American Wire Tie Co (1935), National Sales System (1959), and gravel mines. In the early 21st century farming remains the predominant land use. The Zoar Valley State Multiple Use Area provides public access to the dramatic Zoar Valley Gorge on the Cattaraugus Creek.

Andrew C. Maines

Colman, Samuel (*b* Portland, Maine, 4 Mar 1832; *d* New York City, 26 Mar 1920). Artist and designer. Colman arrived in New York City as an adolescent and would live there, when not traveling, until 1882. By his early twenties he was exhibiting regularly at the National Academy of Design, and his place among the second-generation Hudson River school artists was secured with Hudson River views (*Looking North from Ossining*, 1867) and landscapes of New England and the Adirondacks. He traveled to Europe from 1860 to 1861 for new subject matter. Colman's painting *The Hill of the Alhambra* (1865) typifies his broadened interests, particularly in Orientalist motifs. He was a founder of the American Water-Color Society and its first president, serving from 1866 to 1870. In the 1870s Colman traveled to the American West and abroad. *The Moorish Mosque of Sidi Halou, Tlemcen, Algeria* (1875) was among his submissions to the Philadelphia Centennial Exposition in 1876.

In 1879 Colman joined Louis Tiffany, Candace Wheeler, and Lockwood de Forest in Associated Artists, the premier design firm of its time and a manifestation of the American version of the aesthetic movement. Colman planned the color schemes for the firm's projects and designed textiles and furniture for clients and for his own home in Newport, RI, where he resided after 1882. The partnership dissolved in 1883, but in 1890 Colman and Tiffany collaborated again on the interior and furnishings for Louisine and Henry O. Havemeyer's New York City mansion.

Throughout the 1880s Colman exhibited his textile designs, recycled his European and North African motifs into etchings, and attended to his extensive collection of paintings, prints, textiles, and ceramics, much of it Chinese and Japanese. He returned to New York City around 1900 and published his theories of art in *Nature's Harmonic Unity* (1912) and *Proportional Form* (1920).

Craven, Wayne. "Samuel Colman (1832–1920): Rediscovered Painter of Far-Away Places," *American Art Journal* (May 1976)

Flynn, Maribeth. *The Poetic Landscapes of Samuel Colman* (New York: Kennedy Galleries, 1999)

Maribeth Flynn

Colombians. Political turmoil and armed conflicts in the 1950s and early 1960s during the historical period known as La Violencia led to a significant exodus of Colombians to New York State. The first wave was mainly middle-class professionals and skilled workers in the printing industry. The more recent wave, however, was a predominantly working-class population with a visible professional and entrepreneurial element. Most came from Antioquía, Santa Fé de Bogotá, and Valle del Cauca. Immigrants are active in social, cultural, and political affairs through a number of cultural, professional, and entrepreneurial organizations, such as the Centro Cívico Colombiano, a nonprofit community organization founded in 1980, and Profesionales y Estudiantes Colombianos en el Exterior, founded in 1991. A milestone came in 1994 when Carlos Manzano was elected a Democratic state committee member, making him the first Colombian-born New York State official. Colombians in New York State celebrate their 20 July Independence Day with a cultural heritage festival in Queens. The 2000 census tallied the Colombian population in New York State at 111,727. It is mainly concentrated in Queens Co (66,192), specifically Jackson Heights, Jamaica, and Elmhurst, with a significant number in Nassau (7,576) and Suffolk Cos (7,125) as well as in Brooklyn (7,597), Manhattan (5,927), and Westchester Co (7,966).

Logan, John. "The New Latinos: Who They Are, Where They Are," http://mumford1.dyndns.org/cen2000/HispanicPop/HspReport/HspReportPage1.html

National Association of Hispanic Journalists. "Latinos in the United States," http://www.nahj.org/resourceguide/resourceguide.pdf

Ana Margarita Cervantes-Rodríguez and Michael C. English

colonial intellectual culture. The intellectual culture of the Colony of New York had a local distinctiveness that stemmed from its ethnic and religious diversity. During the 17th century, settlers to New Netherland and then New York Colony brought with them a popular culture common to ordinary people in northwestern Europe. In the early 18th century, a handful of elite residents practiced an erudite "high" culture. As the population grew and commercial and intellectual interactions with Europe and other colonies increased over the 18th century, more and more New Yorkers embraced a culture of refined gentility. Yet some of the concerns expressed through this new refinement were distinctively local, and popular culture did not disappear but was adapted to new political concerns.

17th-Century Culture

Settlers in New Netherland and, after 1664, New York Colony had origins throughout northwestern Europe, as well as a few from Mediterranean areas, although first Dutch and then English were the most commonly spoken languages. African slaves were brought into the colony beginning in the 1620s. Most of the free colonists were Protestant, although a group of Dutch Jewish families settled in New Amsterdam [now New York City] in 1654–55. Because of the Protestant emphasis on reading the Bible and because of the significant commercial orientation of the colony, many, if not most, colonists were literate. Schools to teach reading, arithmetic, and religious catechism were established in the 1630s in New Amsterdam, in the 1640s in Beverwijck [now Albany], and by the 1660s in Esopus [now Kingston, Ulster Co]. Colonists of Dutch origin celebrated holidays following the liturgical calendar, with the festive merriment that accompanied Shrove Tuesday, for example, followed by the solemnity of Ash Wednesday. Colonists also brought other holidays popular in Europe, such as May Day, and, after the English conquest, civic holidays, such as Pope's or Guy Fawkes Day, celebrated with bonfires and processions. Colonists brought pastimes like ninepin, ice-skating, and card playing, and socialized at church, taverns and inns, and local fairs.

The colony's first printer, William Bradford (1663–1756), moved to New York in 1693, setting up his print shop in New York City. He published New York's first almanac in 1694, a small pamphlet with monthly calendars, a page of medical guidelines, dates of local fairs, and a religious poem. Primarily Bradford printed government documents, but in 1725 he began to publish the colony's first weekly newspaper. It, too, was short and usually just printed news from Europe and local shipping schedules. Over the next several decades, however, several other printers moved to New York City and began printing their own almanacs and newspapers. Their almanacs were larger, with entertaining verses, agricultural advice, and currency and travel information. By the mid–18th century, their newspapers printed local as well as European news and had a page or two of local advertisements as well. They sold their publications throughout the colony and northern New Jersey. The first newspaper outside of New York City, the *Albany Gazette,* was established in 1771, but its span was brief.

18th-Century Culture

By the early 18th century, a small group of colonists and officials embraced a more erudite culture. Wealthy colonists like Lewis Morris (1671–1746) of Morrisania [now in Bronx Co] read classical literature, wrote poetry, and collected a library of nearly 3,000 volumes. Gov Robert Hunter (1710–19) wrote the colony's first play in 1714, a satire of local politics called *Androboros.* Gov William Burnet (1720–28) published a learned religious work in 1724 and the colony's surveyor general, Cadwallader Colden (1689–1776), wrote the colony's first historical study, *The History of the Five Indian Nations Depending upon the Province of New-York* (1727). A more modest colonist, Joseph Morgan, who briefly served as a minister to several churches in Westchester Co before moving to New Jersey, wrote the first novel published in New York colony in 1715, a religious allegory called *The History of the Kingdom of Basaruah.* These first efforts, however, had no immediate successors as the number of New Yorkers with the interest, leisure, and education to pursue these kinds of activities was small.

While more modest colonial New Yorkers did not produce much of this print, they were decisive in one of the most famous law cases of the period, the Zenger trial. In 1733 opponents of Gov William Cosby began publishing satirical commentary on his administration in John Peter Zenger's (1697–1746) newspaper. Cosby had Zenger charged with printing "seditious libel," seditious because, Cosby claimed, printing the criticisms undermined government authority. Under English law, the jury was not charged with judging whether the criticisms were valid or whether printing them was dangerous, but simply whether Zenger had in fact printed them. The jury, however, refused to limit itself to so narrow a role and refused to convict Zenger. By so doing, jury members insisted upon ordinary people's right to decide what kinds of political speech were acceptable within the colony. Thereafter, political satire was a potent weapon against unpopular officials in colonial New York.

Over the course of the 18th century the commercial and demographic expansion of the colony supported a wider variety of cultural activities. New York City's first coffeehouse opened in 1696 and as the population rose, more inns and taverns were established in communities from eastern Long Island to the Mohawk Valley. In New York City, men joined private clubs, like the Whig Club, for dining and conversation, and fraternal associations, like the St. Andrew's Society. Families hosted card parties, and public holidays were times for bonfires and balls, the most elegant of which was the annual Governor's Ball held on the king's birthday. Dutch families in the Hudson and Mohawk Valleys commissioned religious paintings and family portraits from local artists, such as Pieter Vanderlyn (1687–1778) of Kingston, and three generations of the Duyckinck family offered portraits for patrons in and around New York City. In Albany and elsewhere in the colony black New Yorkers celebrated Pinkster Day with a fair and the crowning of a "governor." Fairs in places like Jamaica (Queens Co) sometimes had exhibits of novel creatures like lions or monkeys, and itinerant showmen who traveled the seaports regularly set up their exhibits in New York City.

By the mid–18th century the culture of refined gentility that had become increasingly common among the middling and upper classes in Britain began to appear in colonial New York. By the 1740s booksellers in New York City advertised the novels, travel literature, essays, and advice manuals that were popular throughout Britain and its colonies. English-trained painters like John Wollaston did portraits of members of prominent families like Sir William Johnson, a Mohawk Valley Indian trader, and Cornelia Beekman Walton of a wealthy shipbuilding family in New York City. Theater companies regularly presented the latest English plays. Writing poetry to circulate among one's friends became fashionable, and occasionally such poems appeared in New York newspapers, although always under cognomens. On Long Island, Jupiter Hammon (1711–*ca* 1790), held as a slave by the Lloyd family in Queen's Village, in what is now Lloyd Harbor (Suffolk Co), became the first published African American author in North America. Wealthy families throughout the colony displayed their elegance through the purchase of fine silver, porcelain, home furnishings, and fashionable clothing. The colony's first public lending library, the New York Society Library, opened in New York City in 1754, taking over an early collection that had languished for want of management. Schools offering Latin and Greek, often in the homes of clergy, such as Chauncey Graham (1727–84) of Rumbout in what is now Fishkill (Dutchess Co), educated young men to be "gentlemen." By the 1770s girls could get a "lady's" education by attending schools teaching French, geography, dancing, and embroidery. In 1754 the colony's first college, King's College (now Columbia University), opened in New York City. Although its enrollment was always modest (never more than 30 students at a time), the curriculum laid a foundation for professions such as medicine, the law, and the ministry. The exposure to the classics and rhetoric at the college would give the sons of ambitious New York families a gentleman's polish.

Some of the most vigorous expressions of this culture of refinement were specifically addressed to New York Colony issues. In 1752 three young lawyers from New York City—William Livingston (1723–90), William Smith Jr (1728–93), and John Morin Scott (?1730–84)—began to publish a weekly journal of opinion, the *Independent Reflector,* modeled on British antecedents. The three men intended to expose what they deemed local religious and political abuses and to support local civil and religious rights, attacking in their essays the growth of luxury within the colony and the mismanagement of various governmental responsibilities. All three were Presbyterians and vigorously opposed claims to political and social dominance by members of the Anglican Church. The *Independent Reflector* was only one among a number of their publications. In 1747, for example, Livingston published a long poem *Philosophic Solitude; or, The Choice of a Rural Life,* which advocated a simple, contemplative life over the fashionable pursuits of the city. In 1757 Smith published the first general history of the colony, *The History of the Province of New York,* a volume strongly critical of local governance. While the form of all these works had British models, experiences within the colony itself shaped their content.

Tensions among religious beliefs, political power, and commercial experience were particularly strong in New York Colony. Newspapers and private letters registered both strong support for the benefits of being within the British Empire and a variety of criticisms over specific policies that some people experienced as unduly constraining. As a royal colony, New York was the focus of several initiatives intended to bind the colony closer to the British Empire after the French and Indian War. Colonial New Yorkers vigorously debated new British efforts to reform local currency, restrict land granting, and suppress smuggling, as well as the more famous revenue acts like the Stamp Act. By the mid-1760s middling artisans, shopkeepers, and laborers in New York City had adapted aspects of popular celebrations to political protest, as did tenants in the Hudson Valley resisting demands of landlords. In 1766 the efforts of Anglican clergymen in New York and New Jersey to requesting a bishop from Britain to oversee the Anglican Church in the colonies roused vehement opposition by non-Anglicans, who founded the Society of Dissenters in 1769. With a dozen distinct religious denominations active in the colony by the 1760s, many New Yorkers strongly resisted any moves toward domination by any one religious group. The disputes over currency and trade policy, over the relationship between church and state, and over political relations with Britain foreshadowed the divisions among New Yorkers during the American Revolution.

See also ART, NEW YORK CITY AREA.

Burrows, Edwin G., and Mike Wallace. *Gotham: A History of New York City to 1898* (New York: Oxford Univ Press, 1999)

Kammen, Michael. *Colonial New York: A History* (New York: Oxford Univ Press, 1996)

Merwick, Donna. *Death of a Notary: Conquest and Change in Colonial New York* (Ithaca: Cornell Univ Press, 1999)

Olson, Alison. "The Zenger Case Revisited: Satire, Sedition, and Political Debate in 18th Century America," *Early American Literature* 35 (2000): 223–45

Stuckey, Sterling. "African Spirituality and Cultural Practice in Colonial New York, 1700–1770." In *Inequality in Early America,* ed. Carla Gardina Pestana and Sharon V. Salinger (Hanover, NH: Univ Press of New England, 1999)

Tully, Alan. *Forming American Politics: Ideals, Interests, and Institutions in Colonial New York and Pennsylvania* (Baltimore: Johns Hopkins Univ Press, 1994)

Sara Stidstone Gronim

colonial New York

CONQUEST

Much of New York's early history was centered on the Port of New York and the Hudson River, from Henry Hudson's voyage to the Dutch West India Co's settlements to the August 1664 arrival of Col Richard Nicolls in the Narrows. Nicolls, sailing at the order of England's Charles II and in a time of peace with the Netherlands, was in command of a fleet of four warships carrying 300 English soldiers. England's North American settlements prior to that date were isolated and vulnerable, confined to New England and the Chesapeake. In between these areas was New Netherland, a vast territory that belonged to the Dutch West India Co. The determination of Charles II and his brother, James, Duke of York, was to seize this territory from the Dutch. If successful the English colonies would be joined and strengthened, both economically and militarily. Nicolls, approaching the capital city of New Amsterdam, demanded its surrender from its director general, Petrus Stuyvesant. With a small population, a fort in disrepair, few soldiers, and under pressure from the city's leading burghers, Stuyvesant yielded. The articles of capitulation were signed in New Amsterdam on 8 Sept 1664.

The territory conquered by Gov Nicolls (1664–67) was renamed New York in honor of the duke of York, who had been given the land by his brother even before Nicolls's fleet left England. The duke claimed all the land held by the Dutch, including what is now Long Island, New York City, and the broad Hudson River corridor to Albany, portions of Maine and New Hampshire, the islands from Cape Cod to Cape May (except for Block Island), and all land from the west bank of the Connecticut River to the Delaware River (or South River, to the Dutch). The Dutch had not settled the western part of Connecticut, and Nicolls in 1667 conceded that the disputed territory would remain under Connecticut's control. The duke himself had reduced the size of his territory by granting the area that would become New Jersey to John Lord Berkeley and Sir George Carteret. James eventually ceded the land on the west side of the Delaware River to the Quaker William Penn.

Although the area was large, the population was sparse, with less than 10,000 Europeans and Africans in the entire province. Ethnic diversity was the rule, even after the English conquest, with Dutch, English Puritans, Scots, Scots-Irish, Africans, French, Germans, Walloons, and Swedes. Several religious faiths were also represented, including Dutch Reformed, Congregational, Anabaptist, Presbyterian, Baptist, Quaker, Mennonite, Anglican, Roman Catholic, as well as Jewish. The duke promised religious freedom to the Protestant residents.

Nicolls, as governor, introduced English law, language, religion, culture, and mores. New York had traditionally enjoyed a thriving economy, with its major exports of furs, wheat, peas, beef, pork, fish, tobacco, wood products, horses, pitch, and tar going to Europe and the West Indies. At the duke's order, Nicolls instituted an authoritarian, nonrepresentative government in New York, without an assembly or town meetings. Francis Lovelace (1667–73) succeeded Nicolls as governor and continued his policies. The Dutch seized New York on 30 July 1673 during the Third Anglo-Dutch War (1672–74), a fleet arriving in the harbor when Lovelace was on his way to Connecticut. Upon return he found that his second in command, Capt John Manning, had surrendered the fort to the Dutch. Lovelace, Manning, and the garrison returned to England to face the duke, who was disconsolate at the loss of his territory and the loss of revenue. Within a year, however, the province would return to English control.

THE COVENANT CHAIN

New York's governors, like their Dutch predecessors, recognized the importance of maintaining good relations with the Five Nations of the Iroquois Confederacy (Mohawk, Oneida, Onondaga, Cayuga, and Seneca), whose territory spanned from the Mohawk Valley to the Niagara Frontier. The mutually beneficial arrangement brought economic and military advantages to each. The Iroquois served as a buffer between French Canada and New York. They expected and occasionally received military help from the English when the French threatened them. Having quickly become dependent on European trade goods, the Iroquois were determined to retain control of the fur supply by waging wars in the mid–17th century to eliminate rival Indian tribes. As a result of those wars, the Iroquois claimed hegemony over a vast territory that stretched from the Great Lakes to the Carolinas and as far west as the Mississippi River valley. The fur trade was as vital to New York's economy as it was to that of the Iroquois. To protect that trade, Edmund Andros (1674–80) granted Albany a monopoly on the buying and selling of furs. Andros was named governor by the duke after New York was re-

COLONIAL CENSUSES

County	White	Black	Total
1698			
Albany	1,453	23	1,476
Kings	1,721	296	2,017
New York	4,237	700	4,937
Orange	200	19	219
Queens	3,366	199	3,565
Richmond	654	73	727
Suffolk	2,121	558	2,679
Ulster and Dutchess	1,228	156	1,384
Westchester	917	146	1,063
Total	15,897	2,170	18,067
1703			
Albany	2,073	200	2,273
Kings	1,569	343	1,912
New York	3,745	630	4,375
Orange	235	33	268
Queens	3,968	424	4,392
Richmond	407	97	504
Suffolk	3,158	188	3,346
Ulster	1,504	145	1,649
Westchester	1,748	198	1,946
Total	18,407	2,258	20,665
1712 (partial)			
Kings	—	—	1,925
New York	4,866	975	5,841
Orange	385	53	438
Richmond	—	—	1,279
Suffolk	4,169	244	4,413
Westchester	2,485	333	2,818
1714 (partial)			
Albany	2,871	458	3,329
Dutchess	416	29	445
Ulster	1,787	333	2,120
1723			
Albany	5,693	808	6,501
Dutchess	1,040	43	1,083
Kings	1,774	444	2,218
New York	5,886	1,362	7,248
Orange	1,097	147	1,244
Queens	6,068	1,123	7,191
Richmond	1,251	255	1,506
Suffolk	5,266	975	6,241
Ulster	2,357	566	2,923
Westchester	3,961	448	4,409
Total	34,393	6,171	40,564
1731			
Albany	7,300	1,273	8,573
Dutchess	1,612	112	1,724
Kings	1,658	492	2,150
New York	7,045	1,577	8,622
Orange	1,785	184	1,969
Queens	6,731	1,264	7,995
Richmond	1,513	304	1,817
Suffolk	7,074	601	8,390[a]
Ulster	2,996	732	3,728
Westchester	5,341	692	6,033
Total	43,055	7,231	51,001
1737			
Albany	9,051	1,630	10,681
Dutchess	3,156	262	3,418
Kings	1,784	564	2,348
New York	8,945	1,719	10,664
Orange	2,547	293	2,840
Queens	7,748	1,311	9,059
Richmond	1,540	349	1,889
Suffolk	6,833	1,090	7,923
Ulster	3,998	872	4,870
Westchester	5,894	851	6,745
Total	51,496	8,941	60,437
1746			
Albany	—	—	—
Dutchess	8,306	500	8,806
Kings	1,686	645	2,331
New York	9,273	2,444	11,717
Orange	2,958	310	3,268
Queens	7,996	1,644	9,640
Richmond	1,691	382	2,073
Suffolk	7,855	1,399	9,254
Ulster	4,154	1,111	5,265
Westchester	8,563	672	9,235
Total	52,482	9,107	61,589
1749			
Albany	9,154	1,480	10,634
Dutchess	7,491	421	7,912
Kings	1,500	783	2,283
New York	10,926	2,368	13,294
Orange	3,874	360	4,234
Queens	6,617	1,323	7,940
Richmond	1,745	409	2,154
Suffolk	8,098	1,286	9,384
Ulster	3,804	1,006	4,810
Westchester	9,547	1,156	10,703
Total	62,756	10,592	73,348
1756			
Albany	14,805	2,619	17,424
Dutchess	13,298	859	14,157
Kings	1,862	845	2,707
New York	10,768	2,278	13,046
Orange	4,456	430	4,886
Queens	8,617	2,169	10,786
Richmond	1,667	465	2,132
Suffolk	9,245	1,045	10,290
Ulster	6,605	1,500	8,105
Westchester	11,919	1,338	13,257
Total	83,242	13,548	96,790
1771			
Albany	38,829	3,877	42,706
Cumberland	3,935	12	3,947
Dutchess	21,044	1,360	22,404
Gloucester	715	7	722
Kings	2,461	1,162	3,623
New York	18,726	3,137	21,863
Orange	9,430	662	10,092
Queens	8,744	2,236	10,980
Richmond	2,253	594	2,847
Suffolk	11,676	1,452	13,128
Ulster	11,996	1,954	13,950
Westchester	18,315	3,430	21,745
Total	148,124	19,883	168,007
1786 (State Census)			
Albany	67,670	4,690	72,360
Dutchess	30,991	1,645	32,636
Kings	2,669	1,317	3,986
Montgomery	14,652	405	15,057
New York	21,507	2,103	23,614[b]
Orange	13,204	858	14,062
Queens	10,901	2,183	13,084
Richmond	2,459	693	3,152
Suffolk	12,725	1,068	13,793
Ulster	19,473	2,662	22,143[c]
Washington	4,441	15	4,456
Westchester	19,304	1,250	20,554
Total	219,996	18,889	238,897

Sources: E. B. O'Callaghan, *Documentary History of the State of New York (DHSNY)* (1849); E. B. Greene and V. Harrington, *American Population before the Federal Census of 1790* (1932); *Census of the State of New York for 1855* (1857).

Notes: The totals have been recalculated and may differ from the totals published in *DHSNY.* Some additional partial censuses, noted in the records of the provincial council, are not included here.

[a]Total includes 715 Indians.

[b]Total includes 4 Indian taxpayers.

[c]Total includes 8 Indian taxpayers.

turned to England by the terms of the 9 Feb 1674 Treaty of Westminster that ended the Third Anglo-Dutch war. In addition to the Albany monopoly, Andros granted New York City a monopoly on the processing of wheat, thereby improving that city's economy. The governor further improved New York City's economy by ordering the construction of a covered market and an exchange, along with a mole, or pier, to protect shipping on the East River. With a liberal land policy, Andros attracted immigrants and increased New York's prosperity by welcoming English merchants into the community.

The most serious problem faced by Andros was to prevent the Iroquois from allying with the New England Indians who were fighting the English in King Philip's War (1675–76). At the same time the Chesapeake Indians were embroiled in a war against Virginia and Maryland. Andros and other English leaders feared a Pan-Indian uprising. When the Wampanoag chief, Philip (Metacom), and his allied New England Indians came close to Albany in the early winter of 1676, hoping to enlist the aid of the Mohawk, Andros persuaded the Mohawk to attack the enemy. The attack was so effective that the resistance of New England Indians fell apart in the summer of 1676, even before Philip was killed. In Albany during the spring and summer of 1677, under Andros's supervision, the Iroquois agreement with New York was extended to the New England and Chesapeake colonies through the Covenant Chain alliance. The Covenant Chain enabled the Iroquois and the English to live together peacefully, and it formed the basis for first English and then American land claims to New York State west of the Mohawk Valley and to the Ohio River and Mississippi River valleys. It similarly was beneficial to the Iroquois, who were able to

ROYAL AND ACTING GOVERNORS

	Service Began[a]
Richard Nicolls	Aug 1664
Francis Lovelace[b]	Aug 1668
Edmund Andros	Nov 1674
Anthony Brockholes, Acting Gov	Nov 1677
Sir Edmund Andros[c]	Aug 1678
Anthony Brockholes, Acting Gov	Jan 1681
Thomas Dongan	Aug 1682
Sir Edmund Andros	Aug 1688
Francis Nicholson, Lt Gov	Oct 1688
Jacob Leisler, Lt Gov[d]	June 1689
Henry Sloughter	Mar 1691
Richard Ingoldsby, Acting Gov	July 1691
Benjamin Fletcher	Aug 1692
Richard Coote, Earl of Bellomont	Apr 1698
John Nanfan, Lt Gov	May 1699
Richard Coote, Earl of Bellomont	July 1700
William Smith, eldest councillor present	Mar 1701
John Nanfan, Lt Gov	May 1701
Edward Hyde, Viscount Cornbury	May 1702
John Lord Lovelace, Baron of Hurley	Dec 1708
Peter Schuyler, Pres of Council	May 1709
Richard Ingoldsby, Lt Gov	May 1709
Peter Schuyler, Pres of Council	May 1709
Richard Ingoldsby, Lt Gov	June 1709
Gerardus Beekman, Pres of Council	Apr 1710
Robert Hunter	June 1710
Peter Schuyler, Pres of Council	July 1719
William Burnet	Sept 1720
John Montgomerie	Apr 1728
Rip van Dam, Pres of Council	July 1731
William Cosby	Aug 1732
George Clarke, Pres of Council	Mar 1736
George Clinton	Sept 1743
Sir Danvers Osborne[e]	Oct 1753
James DeLancey, Lt Gov	Oct 1753
Sir Charles Hardy	Sept 1755
James DeLancey, Lt Gov	June 1757
Cadwallader Colden, Pres of Council	Aug 1760
Robert Monckton	Oct 1761
Cadwallader Colden, Lt Gov	Nov 1761
Robert Monckton	June 1762
Cadwallader Colden, Lt Gov	June 1763
Sir Henry Moore	Nov 1765
Cadwallader Colden, Lt Gov	Sept 1769
John Murray, Earl of Dunmore	Oct 1770
William Tryon	July 1771
Cadwallader Colden, Lt Gov	Apr 1774
William Tryon	June 1775
James Robertson	May 1779
Andrew Elliot, Lt Gov	Apr 1783

Source: E. A. Werner, *Civil List and Constitutional History of the Colony and State of New York* (1888).

Notes: When a royal governor was absent from the colony or died, the lieutenant governor oversaw executive functions. A lieutenant governor might be a person with a royal commission for that office, a senior council member, or a commander of the regular armed forces. Names of royal governors appear in bold.

[a]Dates for royal governors, taken from colonial records, indicate arrival in the colony rather than appointment to office.

[b]Beginning in Aug 1673 English rule was disrupted for 14 months during the restoration of the colony to Dutch rule.

[c]Andros was knighted by Charles II during a visit to London on private affairs in early 1678.

[d]Leisler served as interim provincial chief executive beginning in June 1689 and became lieutenant governor in Dec 1689.

[e]Committed suicide 12 Oct 1753.

maintain much of their power and position intact for almost another century, or until the end of the French and Indian War. Thomas Dongan (1682–88), who succeeded Andros as governor, was equally committed to keeping the Iroquois allied to the English. The French resented the alliance, fearing that they would be cut off from the fur trade and that the Iroquois would help the English to destroy French Canada. The French decided to launch a series of preemptive attacks on the Onondaga and the Seneca, during which they took prisoners, destroyed stores of crops, and burned fields. Dongan, fearing that the entire Province of New York would be at risk if the Iroquois fell, renewed the Covenant Chain and promised the Iroquois protection. He remained in Albany during the winter of 1687–88 with several hundred troops.

Dongan was particularly interested in protecting outlying settlements. To encourage population growth in the Hudson River valley and elsewhere, Dongan built on the Dutch patroonship system, which awarded estates to any person who brought 50 people to New Netherland. Dongan confirmed the patent to Rensselaerswijck [now in Albany, Columbia, and Rensselaer Cos], the largest and only surviving patroonship, while awarding new manorial patents to Lloyd Neck [now in Suffolk Co], Livingston Manor [now in Columbia Co], Cassiltown [now in Richmond Co], and Bentley Manor [now in Richmond Co]. Landlords leased small plots to tenants, who paid rent and taxes, while manor lords paid no taxes at all on undeveloped land until 1753, when some of the more populous southern counties imposed a tax on all land. No similar taxation was imposed on manors in the more northern counties.

The duke permitted Dongan to call New York's first assembly for the purpose of guaranteeing permanent financial support of government. The assembly complied and passed the Charter of Liberties to ensure the rights of New Yorkers. The assembly met for three sessions and was then permanently dissolved. James disallowed the charter when he ascended to the throne as James II, following the 1685 death of his brother. In 1688 New York was added to the Dominion of New England, a newly created central government imposed on the New England colonies with headquarters in Boston and headed by former New York governor Sir Edmund Andros. Realizing it would be difficult to administer such a vast territory, Andros named his subordinate, Francis Nicholson as lieutenant governor of New York (1688–89).

The November 1688 Protestant overthrow of the Catholic James II's government in England by his son-in-law, William of Orange, led to the April 1689 overthrow of Andros's Dominion government in Boston. This, in turn, led to the June 1689 overthrow of Nicholson's government in New York by militia officer Jacob Leisler. Nicholson returned to England, and Leisler installed himself as acting governor (1689–91). After taking the throne William III was embroiled in the War of the League of Augsburg (1689–97) with France. The war, known as King William's War in North America, led to a devastating French and Indian raid on Schenectady on 9 Feb 1690, in which 60 people were killed and 27 taken captive; the community was burned to the ground. The French continued to attack the Iroquois throughout the war, leading them in

1701 to sign the Treaty of Neutrality with England and France. Leisler, who struggled to keep the French out of New York, also sought to rid New York of prominent Anglicans and Roman Catholics, imprisoning or exiling many of the prosperous merchants and landowners who had supported previous governors. The Leislerians were essentially Whigs who favored an orthodox Calvinism where the power for government came from the people. The anti-Leislerians, or Tories, favored a government with order imposed from above. Leisler's regime lasted until Sir Henry Sloughter, the new governor (1691), arrived in the spring of 1691. Sloughter immediately allied with the anti-Leislerians, who persuaded him to charge the leaders of the faction with treason. Both Leisler and his son-in-law, Jacob Milborne, were found guilty and sentenced to be executed, while the other men were eventually reprieved. The execution of the two men, along with the confiscation of Leislerians' land that followed, led to decades of bitterness between the two factions, as each sought to further its position by allying with succeeding royal governors.

Conflict and Concession

The new monarchs, William and Mary, authorized Sloughter to establish an assembly. The turn of the 18th century was marked by conflict, as the assembly tried to assert its power while reducing the governor's. The governor, who was not bound to call assemblies by any regular schedule and who could veto legislation and appoint judges "at pleasure," actually had more executive power than the post–Glorious Revolution English monarch. The number of assemblymen, which varied from 18 in 1692 to 31 in 1775, consisted of 27 members in 1752, 4 of whom were from New York City and 3 others were sent by the manors. According to an act passed in 1701, any adult white male worth £40 was eligible to vote. The assembly met once or twice a year in New York City, the provincial capital. The assembly's most important function was its control of raising and disbursing of funds. To receive their salaries and to pay for vital government expenditures, governors were often forced to make concessions to the assembly. While assembly members were elected, members of the upper legislative house, or council, which usually numbered 12, were appointed by the governor and approved by the monarch. By necessity the council was usually composed of the governor's allies and chief supporters, while those who failed to ally with the governor gravitated to the assembly, where they often formed a viable opposition party. When the 1691 assembly met in April, it promptly overturned the permanent revenue bill for support of government passed by the previous assembly. The 1691 assembly also adopted a new Charter of Liberties, which the home government disallowed, as it had the 1683 charter. New York remained one of only two colonies that lacked a charter or constitution, but New Yorkers believed they had certain rights and privileges, similar to those of other colonists, simply by virtue of tradition and custom.

Following Sloughter's death on 23 July 1691, Benjamin Fletcher was appointed governor (1692–97). A relative affluence was seen in New York, caused in part by a booming wartime economy and by Fletcher's tolerance of pirates, who brought goods and money to the province, thereby sparking the economy. In addition the establishment of new industries, such as sugar refining and shipbuilding, helped increase prosperity. Fletcher approved extravagant land grants for his allies, granting patents for the manors of Philipsburg, St. George, Sagtikos, Cortlandt, and Morrisania. Fletcher's excessive land grants, along with his support of piracy, his demands for bribes, and his acceptance of exorbitant fees, led the newly created Board of Trade and Plantations to oust him. He was replaced with Richard Coote, Earl of Bellomont (1698–1701), who enjoyed the support of a newly elected assembly. The assembly passed legislation against pirates and continued support of the government for six years. Bellomont complied with the assembly's advice to recall Fletcher's land grants. After Bellomont's death on 5 Mar 1701, Princess Anne's cousin, Edward Hyde, Viscount Cornbury, was named governor (1702–8). Lord Cornbury was notorious for his greed and heavy drinking. The assembly objected when he misappropriated funds slated for the colony's defense, using the money to build a pleasure palace for himself on Nutten, or Governors, Island off the coast of Manhattan. When news of Cornbury's actions reached England, along with reports that Cornbury had run up debts of over £8,000 to New York merchants, he was replaced with John Lord Lovelace, Baron of Hurley (1708–9), who arrived 18 Dec 1708. The assembly refused to raise the amount of the revenue, as Lovelace requested, and voted support for only one year.

Lovelace died in spring 1709 and was replaced by Robert Hunter (1710–19), appointed in New York by the Whig ministry. When that ministry fell and was succeeded by a Tory administration in June 1710, Hunter lost the backing of the home government. A competent governor much like Andros, Hunter was more flexible than his predecessor, but his administration was not as easy as he might have wished. He met immediate resistance from the assembly, which knew as well as he did that he lacked the support of the Tory government in London. The first confrontation came when the assembly refused to let the queen's receiver general handle the disbursement of the colony's funds, as Hunter had been directed. The assembly wanted its own representative to undertake this task. When Hunter refused, the merchant-dominated assembly simply refused to vote any funds at all, either for government expenses or for the governor's salary. During Hunter's tenure and those of his successors, the colony was split into factions with landowners opposing merchants. Hunter allied with the landowners, to the outrage of the merchant faction, which worked to achieve his recall from office. Hunter was able to quell merchant opposition by a combination of events in England and in New York. In 1714 Hunter permitted the assembly to select an agent to pay the colony's debts, a concession that reduced royal power. In return he received a five-year revenue to support his government. The next year, as news arrived of the Whig ascendancy in England after George I took the throne, Hunter called for new assembly elections and achieved a pro-administration, landowner majority in the assembly, in part by creating two new assembly seats. With this support Hunter reduced opposition, helped by a booming economy as New York merchants increased their overseas and coastal trade.

Hunter, who returned to England in 1719, exchanged offices with William Burnet (1720–28), controller of customs. On arrival Burnet, equally as competent as Hunter but lacking his tact, did not call for new assembly elections but kept in existence the agreeable landowner-dominated assembly elected during Hunter's tenure. The assembly proved its loyalty by voting another five-year revenue. The landowner faction that dominated the council and assembly on Burnet's arrival struggled for power against the merchant faction for much of colonial history. The landowners who dominated the political world were owners of large estates or related to the owners of these estates. Wealth came not only from the sale of wheat and other commodities but also from the leasing of land to tenant farmers, who paid rent to the owners. Merchants, primarily located in Albany and New York City, realized large profits from the trade in animal skins, wheat, timber, and other products. This trade was conducted with other British colonies in North America, with the West Indies, and with merchants in England. Although most members of the elite aligned with a faction, many landowners were engaged in trade and many merchants were also landowners. Still, most believed that one or the other faction best represented their interests and chose accordingly. During Burnet's tenure the merchant faction was alienated when he, determined to keep the full profits of the fur trade in New York, persuaded the assembly to pass a bill banning the highly lucrative Albany-Montreal trade with the French. Fur traders ignored the ban, while merchants complained bitterly to the first lord of the treasury, Robert Walpole, who listened sympathetically. Under Walpole's direction the ministry ordered the repeal of all assembly acts concerning the fur trade passed during Burnet's administration, thereby catering to mercantile interests at the expense of the royal prerogative. Burnet retained control of the landowner-dominated council but lost his influence over the assembly when several prominent merchants won seats in the elections of 1724 and 1725, with the latter assembly voting only a two-year support of the government.

Press, Placemen, and Politics

New Yorkers of all classes developed increasing political sophistication during Burnet's tenure in office and after, caused in part by the growing availability of printed material. By the 1730s New York had two newspapers: the *New-York Gazette* began publication in 1725, and the *New-York Weekly Journal* was established by the opposition in 1733 specifically to criticize the governor and his supporters. Newspaper reading became a habit for many New Yorkers, with 22 separate papers published between 1725 and 1776. New York's cultural horizons expanded during this period, partially due to the abundance of printed material, such as political and scientific essays, literary works, novels, plays, and histories.

The founding of an opposition press followed Burnet's transfer to the Massachusetts governorship to make room for one of George II's courtiers, John Montgomerie (1728–31). Named to the post as a reward for his past support of the king, Montgomerie had little interest in maintaining crown authority but instead followed a policy of appeasement toward the merchant faction. Chief Justice Lewis Morris (1671–1746), formerly Hunter's and Burnet's strongest ally, headed the landowner opposition. The now merchant-dominated assembly voted to reduce Morris's salary, an act that drew immediate protest from Morris's son, Councilor Lewis Morris (1698–1762). Montgomerie responded by suspending the younger Morris from his council seat. Fearful of alienating assembly supporters, Montgomerie overturned Burnet's ban on the Albany-Montreal trade and refused to erect or preside in prerogative courts, which sat without a jury, actions that the Morrisites saw as weakening the royal prerogative.

After Montgomerie's death William Cosby took office (1732–36). Related by marriage to Thomas Pelham-Holles, Duke of Newcastle, Cosby received the New York post as a personal favor from the duke to recoup his diminished fortune. Cosby allied with Montgomerie's merchant party, alienating the landowners. Cosby relieved Chief Justice Morris of his office, appointing in his place James DeLancey, son of the prosperous merchant Stephen DeLancey. James, educated in England and trained at the Inns of Court, was one of the ablest and shrewdest politicians of the colonial era. Morris and his faction launched a propaganda campaign against Cosby in the *New-York Weekly Journal,* printed by John Peter Zenger. The bulk of the population—the indigent and laboring poor, farmers, tenant farmers, mechanics, artisans, and small merchants—were receptive since they were already alienated from the governor by a severe economic depression. Although Cosby was not responsible for the depression, resentment was directed at him because he could not immediately solve the problem. The opposition mounted a vicious propaganda campaign against Cosby that culminated in the trial of printer John Peter Zenger for seditious libel. The jury, composed of Zenger's peers, refused to find the printer guilty, reasoning that the criticisms of Cosby printed in Zenger's paper were true. An account of the trial, published by Morris's ally James Alexander eventually helped to establish the principle that truth was a valid defense against libel. At Cosby's death the longest serving councilor, George Clarke, became acting governor (1736–43). It was during Clarke's administration that the 1741 New York City slave revolt broke out. New York City had the largest slave population of any northern city, with slaves constituting about 15% of the its population. When several fires started in New York City, including the burning of the fort on 18 Mar 1741, suspicion fell on slaves, who were presumably acting under the orders of Roman Catholics because England had been at war with Spain since 1739 in the War of Jenkins' Ear. Before the hysteria ran its course, 25 Whites and 160 Blacks were arrested. Of these, 18 Blacks and 4 Whites were hanged, 13 slaves were burned, and 72 were transported to a certain early death in the West Indies.

Factionalism

New York's economy boomed from 1744 to 1748 during King George's War (War of the Austrian Succession) and from 1756 to 1763 during the French and Indian War (Seven Years War) as a result of supplying and provisioning both American and English troops, although it slacked off between the wars. The newly found wealth led to the establishment of many businesses, the construction of roads, the expansion of poor relief, and attempts to control infectious and contagious diseases. The greatest changes in the province were wrought not by war but by factionalism, as two rival families, the Livingstons and the DeLanceys, vied for power, each seeking to ally with succeeding governors. Clarke's successor, Adm George Clinton (1743–53), immediately formed an alliance with Chief Justice James DeLancey, granting him lifetime tenure in that post. DeLancey soon controlled the council as well as the judiciary when Clinton appointed four of DeLancey's closest friends to the seven-member body. DeLancey's influence extended to the assembly, with his candidates dominating it in the five elections between 1743 and 1752. Through the influence of his brother-in-law, Adm Sir Peter Warren, DeLancey also received a commission as lieutenant governor.

DeLancey may have molded Clinton's negative attitude toward the Livingstons. Clinton suspected second manor lord Philip Livingston of selling weapons to the French enemy. Livingston, along with other landowners, had also threatened Indian relations when, in 1730, he bought the 8,000-acre (3,200 ha) Canajoharie tract [now in Montgomery Co] from three Mohawk Indians and then never made the promised token payment. Despite the 1701 Treaty of Neutrality, both powers tried to win the allegiance of the Iroquois in their frequent wars. The Five Nations, which became Six Nations in 1722 when the Oneida welcomed the southern Tuscarora to their territory, retained their power by playing one side against the other, but they usually united with the English. Despite their loyalty, by midcentury the Iroquois were forced by the 1744 Treaty of Lancaster to cede to the English large portions of territory in the Ohio and Mississippi Valleys. The treaty caused immediate alarm among the French, who also claimed that territory and who, in 1749, moved to claim it by burying lead plates asserting their ownership of the territory along the Ohio River.

After DeLancey broke with Clinton in 1746, the governor made futile attempts to gain control of the assembly until the ministry appointed a new governor, Sir Danvers Osborne, who arrived on 7 Oct 1753. Osborne met with the council on 11 October, when the latter, led by DeLancey, advised him it was impossible to expect the assembly to vote permanent support for government. In despair Osborne committed suicide the next day. Clinton, who had remained in New York to hand over the government to his successor, now saw his archenemy, DeLancey, assume office (1753–55, 1757–60).

Education was in the forefront during DeLancey's administration, and there was renewed concentration on learning at midcentury as the colony matured. Several primary schools opened throughout the province, and in 1754 the New York Society Library was established, the first public library in New York City. A determination to provide higher education, sadly needed in the province, caused religious issues about the separation of church and state to erupt during DeLancey's tenure. The plan was to establish an Anglican college, supported by public funds, on land held by Trinity Church. William Livingston, leader of the Livingston faction and brother of third manor lord Robert, argued that a church-controlled college should not be supported by public money. Much to Livingston's outrage, the assembly funded King's College (now Columbia University) when the new governor, Charles Hardy (1755–57), indicated his approval of the venture.

The battle over control of King's College was played against rising tensions between the British and the French. Realizing another war was likely, the ministry was concerned about securing the assistance of the Iroquois, who, angered by the theft of their land by speculators, were unwilling to ally with the English. The ministry instructed DeLancey to call an Indian conference at Albany in June 1754 for the purposes of defense and to redress Iroquois grievances. The Albany Congress, with 23 representatives from 7 colonies, suggested a plan of union for the 13 mainland colonies, a proposal subsequently rejected by every provincial assembly and by the home government as well. When the Congress failed to respond effectively to Iroquois complaints about ill treatment, the Iroquois promised only neutrality in the anticipated war. In fact all of the Six Nations did later ally with the English in the French and Indian War, assisting the English in significant victories at Fort Niagara and Crown Point. Their alle-

Marten Van Bergen's Hudson Valley farm in Leeds, overmantel painting attributed to John Heaten, *ca* 1733. The painting depicts a Dutch barn, hay barracks, and a cross section of the colony's population: Dutch families, indentured servants, black slaves, and American Indians.

giance to the English, formalized by the Covenant Chain, endured for nearly 100 years, ensuring the ultimate triumph of England over France in 1763. Despite their role in England's success, their loss of land continued. In 1768, with the Treaty of Fort Stanwix, the Iroquois were persuaded to yield large tracts of land in New York, Pennsylvania, and the Ohio River valley. Following Hardy's return to active duty, James DeLancey resumed his post as lieutenant governor until his death in 1760. Cadwallader Colden served as lieutenant governor (1760–61, 1763–65, 1769–70, 1774–75), while the leadership of the DeLancey faction passed to James's brother and son. Colden alienated both the Livingstons, who now controlled the assembly, and the DeLanceys, who controlled the council. The two families briefly worked together to thwart any legislative program advanced by the lieutenant governor. The Livingstons quickly allied with the new governor, Robert Monckton (1761–63), who returned to England in 1763, leaving Colden again in command of New York.

Toward Revolution

Following the conclusion of the French and Indian War, the British ministry sought to tighten colonial administration. The 1764 Sugar Act was part of this program. It was passed by Parliament because new sources of income were needed to support British troops in America. The Sugar Act, which barred the importation of cheaper French sugar, hurt the Livingston family, forcing the closing of the family's sugar refinery. The passage of that act and the 1765 Stamp Act put the colonies on a path toward revolution, but few colonists in 1765 favored separation from Great Britain. In New York neither the Livingstons nor the DeLanceys wanted the colonies to separate from Great Britain, nor did most other elite families. Members of the elite wanted to preserve the system that had brought them prominence and wealth. As events escalated, some New Yorkers, like the Livingstons, accommodated themselves to the revolutionary struggle. Others, like the DeLanceys, although equally outraged by Parliament, decided they wanted no part of the new society being created in America.

The Stamp Act, which taxed such items as legal documents, newspapers, and customs papers, was to go into effect 1 Nov 1765. Americans justified their objection to the act by insisting that only their own representative assemblies could tax them. In August 1765 irate colonists in Boston staged violent protest riots against the act. When news of riots reached New York, many polemicists, fearing mob violence, stopped writing inflammatory essays against the measure. Colden, also fearing violence, asked British commander in chief Gen Thomas Gage for additional troops and ammunition and turned the guns of New York City's Fort George from the harbor to the town. The day before the act was to go into effect, an irate mob, led by the Sons of Liberty, paraded through the streets and then burned an effigy of Colden, along with several of the governor's carriages. Colden wisely had taken refuge on a man-of-war in New York Harbor. The mob then marched on the fort, where Maj Thomas James was in command. James had earlier said he would cram the stamps down the throats of New Yorkers. The crowd remembered the threat and destroyed James's fine house. Colden remained on the ship until 4 November and returned to New York to barricade himself in the fort, where he remained until New York's new governor, Sir Henry Moore (1765–69), arrived on 13 November. Moore restored government and closed the port and the courts until the Stamp Act was repealed.

Rioting was not confined to New York City but in the spring of 1766 spread up the Hudson River valley, caused by questions of ownership of land in Dutchess, Westchester, and Albany Cos. The tenants on manors, knowing that manor lords' titles were uncertain, wanted to own their own land. Massachusetts claimed much of the same land and offered it to tenants at reasonable prices. When tenants bought the land they farmed from Massachusetts and then refused to pay rent to the lords, manor lords evicted them, but other tenants put the evicted tenants back on their land. Several leaders were jailed in May 1766, leading 500 farmers to march on New York City. Moore quickly dispersed the farmers, but rural rioting continued, particularly on Livingston Manor, where several hundred tenants threatened in June 1766 to kill third manor lord Robert Livingston. When the manor lords asked Gage for troops from the 28th Regiment, he obliged, leaving the tenants horrified by the brutality of the regulars. The tenant leaders were arrested, tried, and sentenced to death; they were saved from execution only by the king's pardon.

In 1767 the Livingstons lost the support of the Sons of Liberty by capitulating to Parliament's demands of compliance with the terms of the Quartering Act to supply British troops in New York. The displeasure of the Sons of Liberty was reflected at the polls during assembly elections that year. The Livingstons retained a majority, but DeLancey-backed candidates won three of the four influential New York City seats. The next year the DeLanceys won all four New York City seats, as well as a majority in the assembly, which they retained until the American Revolution. Colden took office again as lieutenant governor, following Moore's death on 11 Sept 1769. The new governor, John Murray, Earl of Dunmore (1770–71), arrived in October to be immediately confronted with rural unrest. Following the 1766 manor riots, many New York tenants had moved north to the Green Mountains [now in Vermont], claimed by New York. The area was also claimed by New Hampshire, which needed more territory to accommodate its expanding population. New Hampshire refused to heed a 1764 ruling by George III that the boundary of New York was the west side of the Connecticut River, making the Green Mountains part of New York. On the basis of the ruling, Colden granted land in the area to many members of New York's elite, who leased or sold the land in smaller parcels. When owners or tenants tried to establish themselves, they often found New Hampshire grantees in possession of the land. When Colden offered the New Hampshire patentees the opportunity to accept New York authority and pay New York's higher quit rents and fees to secure their title, they refused and attacked the New York patentees. The disorder escalated until the king in 1767 ordered New York to stop making grants in the disputed area. The ruling was ignored; over 2 million acres (800,000 ha) were granted by New York governors after the order, causing the violence to continue. The Vermont issue still raged when Dunmore was transferred to Virginia,

Dining room from the restored Van Cortlandt Manor House, Croton-on-Hudson.

replaced on 9 July 1771 by William Tryon (1771–79). The governor asked for help from Generals Frederick Haldimand and Thomas Gage in 1773 and again in 1774 to stop New Hampshire grantees from attacking New York tenants. The generals, who had more pressing concerns, refused, and the violence continued.

Tryon also had to deal with the aftermath of the 1774 Coercive Acts, which were greeted by disapproval in all colonies. The First Continental Congress, meeting in September 1774 in Philadelphia, recommended nonimportation and nonexportation to protest the acts. New York merchants, believing their best interests would be served by remaining part of the British mercantile empire, dominated the DeLancey assembly. Consequently the assembly, although appalled by the Coercive Acts and other British measures, could not support the recommendations of the Continental Congress. Instead the assembly sent petitions to the king and Parliament protesting the measures. The ministry rejected the petitions, saying the only function of a provincial assembly was to raise money. If any assembly failed in that function, it could be dissolved by the home government. By April 1775 New York was in the midst of an economic depression, which, along with the news of fighting at Lexington and Concord, Mass, helped to spark unrest. During the rioting that followed, the Sons of Liberty seized arms from City Hall, took the powder house, and closed New York City's port and customshouse, thereby effectively ensuring that New York would participate in the Continental Congress's trade boycott.

The Province of New York after April 1775 had two governments: the royal government under Tryon and a provincial congress of over 100 members. When Tryon returned to New York City on 15 June 1775 after a visit to England, he found he had no power to govern. When the Continental Congress ordered his arrest on 10 Oct 1775, he moved to the HMS *Dutchess of Gordon* in New York Harbor. On 18 Apr 1776 Tryon wrote the home government that the New York Assembly was dissolved. In the summer of 1776

Tryon sent a copy of the Declaration of Independence to England. New York's provincial congress accepted the declaration and called for the drafting of a state constitution and the election of a governor. In New York City the rejection of royal rule was confirmed on 9 July 1776, when the magnificent gilded equestrian statue of George III in Bowling Green, ordered from England only six years before by the assembly, was demolished by an unruly mob. Tryon remained on the man-of-war until Gen William Howe drove Washington's troops from New York City in the fall of 1776.

The onset of the war led many loyalists, including most of the DeLancey family, to leave America for Canada or England. Conversely many patriots, including most members of the Livingston family, fled from the city to more hospitable locations. In April 1777 a convention at Kingston (Ulster Co) voted to accept a new state constitution, and George Clinton was subsequently elected New York State's first governor. As patriots left the city, the center of revolutionary activity shifted to the hinterlands and to Albany. New York City remained in British hands during the war, with loyalists from nearby states sparking the city's economy and swelling its population to 33,000 in 1779. In addition to the civilians were British regulars, American loyalist militia, and American prisoners of war. The overcrowding was worsened because a devastating fire had swept the city on 21 Sept 1776, leveling over 1,000 buildings. A military government was established, which left Tryon with little actual power, although his successor as governor, Maj Gen James Robertson (1779–83) wielded greater authority. Military rule was ended under the governorship of Andrew Elliot, the last in a long line of British governors. The British occupation of the city lasted until the British commander in chief, Sir Guy Carleton, was satisfied that all loyalists wanting to leave New York City had left. Carleton then ordered the troops to depart. The end of British rule came on 25 Nov 1783, Evacuation Day, when the last British redcoat was seen boarding the last British ship in the harbor.

See also ANTI-SEMITISM; CAPITAL PUNISHMENT; CARTOGRAPHY AND MAPPING; CEMETERIES; COURTHOUSES; COURTS, STATE; FORESTRY; HUDSON RIVER FERRIES; LABOR; MENTAL HEALTH CARE; NEW YORK CITY: EDUCATION IN NEW YORK CITY; POLICING; PUBLIC HEALTH; RIOTS AND CIVIL DISTURBANCES.

Becker, Carl L. *The History of Political Parties in the Province of New York, 1760–1776* (1909; repr Madison: Univ of Wisconsin Press, 1960)

Bonomi, Patricia. *A Factious People: Politics and Society in Colonial New York* (New York: Columbia Univ Press, 1971)

Davis, T. J. *A Rumor of Revolt: The "Great Negro Plot" in Colonial New York* (New York: Free Press, 1985)

Fox, Dixon Ryan. *Yankees and Yorkers* (New York: New York Univ Press, 1940)

Jennings, Francis. *The Ambiguous Iroquois Empire: The Covenant Chain Confederation of Indian Tribes with the English Colonies* (New York: Norton, 1984)

———. *Empire of Fortune: Crowns, Colonies, and Tribes in the Seven Years' War in America* (New York: Norton, 1988)

Kammen, Michael. *Colonial New York* (1975; repr New York: Oxford Univ Press, 1996)

Katz, Stanley N. *Newcastle's New York: Anglo-American Politics, 1732–1753* (Cambridge, Mass: Belknap Press, 1968)

Kim, Sung Bok. *Landlord and Tenant in Colonial New York: Manorial Society, 1664–1775* (Chapel Hill: Univ of North Carolina Press, 1978)

Lustig, Mary Lou. *Privilege and Prerogative: New York's Provincial Elite: 1710–1776* (Madison, NJ: Fairleigh Dickinson Univ Press, 1995)

Merwick, Donna. *Possessing Albany, 1630–1710: The Dutch and English Experiences* (Cambridge, England: Cambridge Univ Press, 1990)

O'Callaghan, E. B. *Documents Relative to the Colonial History of New York,* 15 vols (Albany: Weed, Parsons, 1853–87)

Ritchie, Robert C. *The Duke's Province: A Study of New York Politics and Society, 1664–1691* (Chapel Hill: Univ of North Carolina Press, 1977)

Smith, William, Jr. *The History of the Province of New York.* Ed. Michael Kammen, 2 vols (Cambridge, Mass: Belknap Press, 1972)

Mary Lou Lustig

Colonie [COL-O-NEE]. Town (pop 79,258) and village (pop 7,916) in NE Albany Co. Colonie was settled as an agricultural "colony" of Rensselaerswijck in the 1640s. The earlier, now extinct, town (1791) and village (1804) named Colonie were absorbed by the City of Albany and the Town of Watervliet in 1815. The Town of Watervliet was renamed Colonie in 1895, and the name Watervliet was taken by the new city of that name in 1896. Colonie was the home of the Niskayuna Shaker settlement (1776–1938) founded by Mother Ann Lee, who is buried there. The town remained rural through the 1850s, leading the state in potato production in 1855, while Loudonville and other neighborhoods north of Albany became fashionable suburbs. At West Albany the railroads created a huge stockyard, and the Delaware and Hudson built a railyard adjacent to Watervliet. Settlement increased with the opening of interurban streetcar lines connecting Albany, Schenectady, and Troy by 1903, leading to the incorporation of the Villages of Colonie (1921) and Menands (1924). Suburbanization nearly tripled the population of the town between 1950 and 1990. It is the site of Albany International Airport (1928), Albany Rural Cemetery (1844), Siena College (1937), and several of the region's largest shopping malls.

Edward H. Knoblauch

Colton. Town (pop 1,453) in SE St. Lawrence Co. Settled in 1824, the town was formed in 1843 from Parishville. The Raquette River drops 200 feet (61 m) through Stone Valley below Colton hamlet; its water powered major 19th-century industries. Among them were a forge (1828–40) producing bar iron, a potato starch factory (1844), three gang sawmills (one with about 70 saws), a large tannery, two mills of the Raquette River Pulp Co (1893–1927), a cabinet factory, and a chair factory. A Niagara Mohawk hydroelectric project (1951–57) created a series of reservoirs and dams. The northern part of Colton, which includes the hamlets of Colton and South Colton, is outside the Adirondack Park; this area is the most populous and serves as a bedroom community for Canton and Potsdam. Inside the park, logging predominates. Sunday Rock, near the Adirondack Park boundary, marks the mythic transition between the relaxed Great South Woods and the workaday North Country. Colton was the home of Hamilton Ferry (1904–94), a noted storyteller, and is the home of Bill Smith (*b* 1936), also a storyteller and noted pack-basket maker. It was the hometown of banker and philanthropist A. Barton Hepburn (1846–1922). Higley Flow State Park (1968) is near South Colton.

Richard E. Mooers

Columbia. Town (pop 1,630) in SW Herkimer Co. Settled *ca* 1765 by Germans, the town was formed in 1812 from Warren. Its creeks flow both north and south, to the Mohawk and Susquehanna watersheds. Development was hindered by a lack of major roads, but railroad service came to Columbia in 1870. It was a farming town, with dairy predominating, especially cheese making. In the late 19th century limestone was quarried in the north part of town and burned in kilns; the product was shipped by railroad and canal. In the early 21st century most nonfarm residents commute to other places or work in service businesses. The Millers Mills Grange (1897) runs a community ice-cutting party on the millpond at Millers Mills hamlet and uses the ice for a summer ice cream festival.

James Crawford

Columbia County (636 mi^2/1,647 km^2; pop 63,094). Created in 1786 from Albany Co and named after Christopher Columbus, Columbia Co is subdivided into 18 towns that contain 4 incorporated villages and 1 city, Hudson, the county seat. Columbia Co forms a rhomboid and is situated between the Hudson River in the west and the Massachusetts border on the east. Elevations range from sea level on the Hudson River shore to 2,080 feet (634 m) on the slopes of Alander Mountain at the Massachusetts state line. The county lies within two major physiographic provinces. Its western half is part of the Hudson Valley subregion of the Hudson-Mohawk Lowlands and the eastern half in the Taconic Mountains subregion of the New England Upland. The valley of the Hudson broadens eastward across Columbia Co, and local relief is modest, ranging from approximately 100 feet (30 m) in the west to 250 feet (76 m) at the margins of the Taconics. Further east the land is significantly more broken and the relief greater as elevations rise from 400 to 1,000 ft (120 to 300 m) until the base of the higher Taconics is reached near the county's eastern margin and a more uniform and abrupt rise in elevation occurs. Bedrock throughout is Cambrian and early Ordovician in age except for one area of Devonian limestone just south of the City of Hudson. The bedrock is also folded, intensely in places. Aside from conglomerate in the far southwest corner, the mantle rock of the Hudson Valley section is predominantly slate. The Taconics—eroded remnants of faulted rock strata, tilted nearly vertical in many places, and pushed eastward during the Ordovician era—consist primarily of metamorphosed schist, phyllite, and slate. There are deposits of limestone and dolostone near the state line.

Columbia Co was glaciated throughout, most obviously in the lowlands, which contain the deep, dissected bottom sediments of prehistoric Lake Albany in the west and an old beach ridge farther east. A thin layer of glacial till covers the area beyond up to the margin of the mountains. The county lies within the Hudson River basin except for a small area drained by the Green River, which lies within the Housatonic River watershed. The prevailing stream flow is east to west, originating in the Taconic heights and ending at the Hudson, as exemplified by Claverack and Taghkanic Creeks and the circuitous, 40 mi (64 km) Roeliff Jansen Kill in the south and Kinderhook Creek, entering the county from Rensselaer Co in the north. The quality of the soils varies substantially. The best agricultural lands are formed from lacustrine deposits in the Hudson Valley region and the southern half of the Taconic Upland.

Columbia Co's climate is humid-continental. Mean January temperatures range from 21°F (-6°C) at Valatie in the north to 25°F (-4°C) at Hudson. Winter lows fall below 0°F (-18°C) a number of times every year. Mean July temperatures range from the high 60s°F (20°C) in the Taconic Mountains northeast of Copake to 73°F (23°C) at Hudson. Summer daytime highs reach 90°F (32°C) or higher every summer. Average annual precipitation varies upward from 40 inches (102 cm) in the north to 43 inches (109 cm) in the southeast. Seasonal snowfall totals range from 42 inches (107 cm) in the northwest to above 60 inches (152 cm) in the Taconics. Primeval forest cover consisted of two forest communities: Alleghenian hardwoods dominated by beech, sugar maple, hemlock, white pine, and basswood covered the eastern uplands, and a central hardwood community dominated by beech, sugar maple, and basswood, along with oak and chestnut, blanketed the rest. Second- and third-growth forest presently covers over 60% of Columbia Co.

American Indians and Early Settlement

Prior to white exploration and settlement, the area of Columbia Co was part of the territory of the Mohicans (Mahicans), an Algonquian-speaking group. The first European settlement was probably *ca* 1660; records of the purchase of land from the Indians by Jan Fransen van Hoesen at Claverack Landing [now Hudson] in 1662 refer to adjacent tracts already owned by Dutch men. Patents were granted in 1667 to van Hoesen's widow and to Abraham Staats at Kinderhook Landing [now Stuyvesant Landing]. Much of the county was settled under large patents. The southern third was Livingston Manor, purchased beginning in 1682 and patented as a manor in 1686. The middle third was patented in 1685 as Claverack, also called the Van Rensselaer Lower Manor. North of it was Kinderhook and a number of other small grants made in the late 17th century.

The western towns were settled by Dutch Americans before the end of the 17th century, including the present Hudson, Greenport, Stuyvesant, Stockport, Livingston, and Clermont on the river, and Claverack in the valley of Claverack Creek. Copake, in the valley of the Roeliff Jansen Kill and remote from the river, in 1685 was also settled by Dutch. In 1711 a large number of Palatine German refugees were resettled in four riverfront settlements in what is now the Town of Germantown. The colonial authorities imagined they would produce large quantities of turpentine, tar, and rosin for the British navy. Unfortunately, the Palatines had been promised freeholds in the Schoharie Valley, which, along with poor management and inadequate provisions, made them reluctant to work to produce naval stores. The industry was a failure.

Title to the eastern part of the county was disputed between New York and Massachusetts for many years. Because both the Hudson and the Connecticut had been perceived as the boundary between the colonies, landless settlers took advantage of the confusion. New Englanders pushed into Hillsdale around 1719 and into Austerlitz and Canaan around 1750. Dutch communities along the river moved eastward, to Taghkanic in 1714 and to Ancram, which had first been settled by Scots in 1741.

In 1751 conflict over disputed land came into the open. In the following year Livingston tenants in the eastern part of that manor petitioned Massachusetts for outright grants, and in 1754 Van Rensselaer tenants in Claverack claimed grants as well. The disputes by tenants continued for more than a century. New England squatters on "waste and unappropriated lands" in Canaan were vested in their land by a legislative act of 1791, but manor tenants continued the struggle through the antirent war of the 1840s.

Along with the Dutch and their diverse ethnic origins, the admixture of Palatines, Scots like the Livingstons and their Ancram settlers, New Englanders, and no fewer than 1,623 enslaved Africans in 1790 made Columbia Co culturally diverse by the time independence was won, although some of the western towns remained culturally Dutch for generations. Hudson, founded as a seaport, further added to the mix, initially with its New England Quaker proprietors.

Revolutionary War

Residents took both patriot and loyalist positions during the Revolution, and some attempted to straddle the fence. Many joined Albany Co residents in signing a pledge to support the patriot cause on 24 Feb 1775. Several residents served with distinction. Robert R. Livingston (1746–1813) of Clermont was a delegate to the Continental Congress and served on the committees that drafted the Declaration of Independence and the state constitution; he was the new nation's first secretary of foreign affairs (1781–83) under the Articles of Confederation. Col Henry Beekman Livingston (1750–1831) served on the fields of battle at Quebec, Saratoga, and Verplanck Point. The future county largely escaped the war's ravages, although a British force burned Clermont and Belvedere, two Livingston houses, in 1777.

Transportation

The Hudson provided easy access to the riverfront settlements, and the Kings Highway (now part of US 9) was authorized as early as 1703. A road was in use from the river at Oak Hill to Taghkanic by 1714, and gradually others linked the river with backcountry settlements. Turnpikes were the first significant improvement; five were built between 1799 and 1806, and radiated from Hudson like the spokes of a wheel. And in 1807, under the patronage of county resident Robert R. Livingston, the *Clermont* made the first successful voyage under steam between New York and Albany, ushering in the modern age of powered transportation and reliable schedules.

Columbia Co also made early use of railroads, the first being the Hudson and Berkshire (1838), which connected to Boston in 1841, and the Albany and West Stockbridge, completed in 1842; both were later part of the Boston and Albany. Two lines running parallel to the river, the Hudson River (1851) and the Harlem (1852) Railroads, were the most important, carrying the bulk of the passenger and freight traffic bound for New York City; the Harlem was largely responsible for the development of a thriving

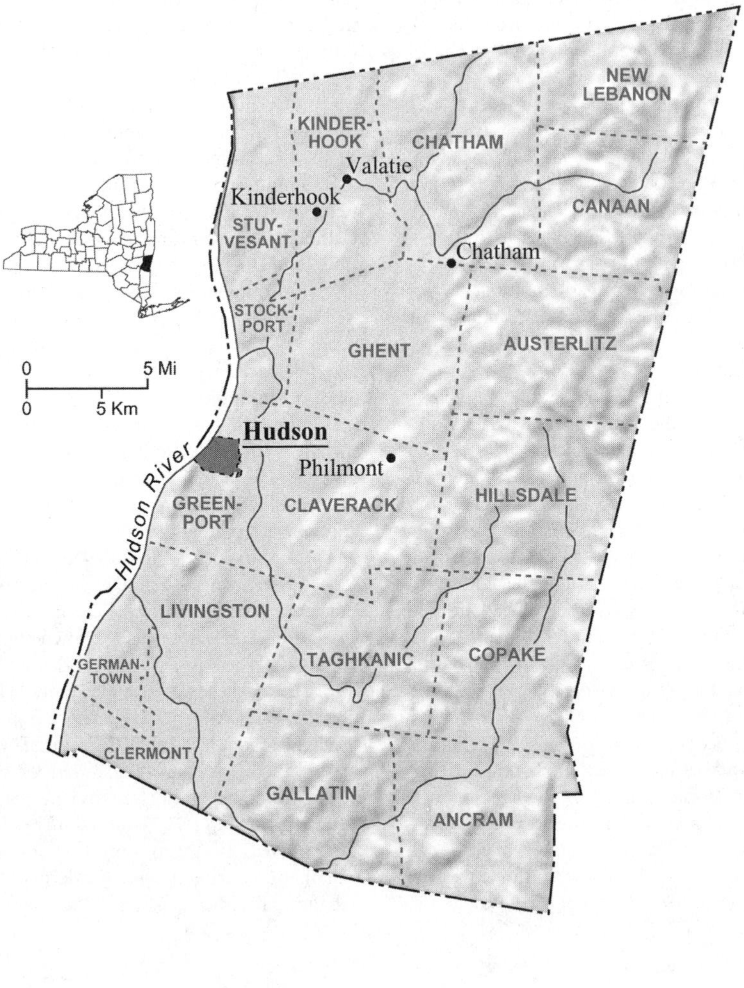

COLUMBIA CO POPULATION CENSUS FIGURES

	White	Nonwhite	Total Population	Foreign-Born
1790	26,054	1,678	27,732	—
1800	33,361	1,961	35,322	—
1810	30,661	1,729	32,390	—
1820	36,516	1,814	38,330	133
1830	38,325	1,582	39,907	392
1840	41,696	1,556	43,252	—
1850	41,761	1,312	43,073	3,573
1860	45,792	1,380	47,172	5,443
1870	45,730	1,314	47,044	5,859
1880	46,708	1,220	47,928	4,962
1890	45,089	1,083	46,172	5,331
1900	41,779	1,432	43,211	4,641
1910	42,545	1,113	43,658	6,075
1920	38,068	862	38,930	4,310
1930	40,538	1,079	41,617	4,617
1940	40,348	1,116	41,464	4,008
1950	42,107	1,075	43,182	4,037
1960	45,777	1,545	47,322	3,408
1970	49,594	1,925	51,519	2,526
1980	57,038	2,449	59,487	2,916
1990	59,919	3,063	62,982	2,580
2000	58,105	4,989	63,094	2,779

Notes: "Nonwhite" includes African Americans, Asians, American Indians, and Pacific Islanders and, for 2000, also the mixed race and other race categories. Through the 1960 census these figures primarily reflect the African American population. Foreign-born figures for 1820 and 1830 include only those not naturalized, and for 1930 and 1950, the foreign-born totals include Whites only. Other years include all foreign-born in the population.

dairy industry in the county's eastern half. The Harlem extended north from Chatham in 1869, and two east-west lines along the county's south boundary followed a few years later: the Poughkeepsie and Eastern (1872) and the Rhinebeck and Connecticut (1874), both later part of the Central New England. The county's last new railroad of any size, the Kinderhook and Hudson, was built in 1890.

Economic Development

In the 17th and 18th centuries, agriculture was the chief occupation of Columbia Co residents. Grain was shipped to New York City; in 1680 the boat carrying the Labadist missionaries took on grain at Claverack Landing to carry downriver. The earliest manufacturing, aside from the processing of farm and forest products, was the manufacture of bar iron and cast-iron goods at New York's first iron furnace in Ancram, begun in 1743. It used iron ore carried overland from Salisbury, Conn; but by the time of the Revolution iron was mined in Ancram, which continued throughout the 19th century. It was mined in Hillsdale (1833) and Livingston (1883) as well. Ancram also produced lead ore. The only other extractive industry of any size in Columbia Co was the quarrying of limestone, granite, and marble on Becraft's Mountain in the 19th century in Greenport, where cement was manufactured after 1902.

Hudson, settled in 1784 as a seaport, engaged in shipbuilding from its beginning, although trade occupied larger numbers of its residents. There and in the villages and hamlets throughout the county, manufacturing initially expanded in response to the 1807 Embargo. At first, iron goods and cotton and woolen cloth were produced. Hudson later had a large iron industry, and stoves were made in Stuyvesant. Farm tools and machinery were produced, including plows, grain cradles, mowing machines, and horse powers (treadmills on which a horse powered machinery). In the late 19th century, in addition to cotton and woolen cloth, ready-made clothing was produced, including hoop-skirts, hats, hosiery, and shirts, and several factories manufactured mill machinery. Paper, first produced at Stuyvesant Falls in 1801, became an important product (mostly straw paper made from rye straw). Other Columbia Co factories turned out bricks, gunpowder, linseed oil, patent medicines, thermometers, scales, needles, and silk thread.

Industry brought new populations. In the second quarter of the 19th century, Irish immigrants settled in various places where factory work was available; Hudson, which was 20% Irish-born in 1855, had the largest number, but they were present in many towns, and the county was more than 7% Irish at that time. African Americans came from outside the county in midcentury for railroad work in Chatham and Ghent. In the late 19th century, Italians, Poles, Hungarians, Jews, and Ukrainians moved to Hudson, and a group of Volga Germans found work in Stuyvesant about 1900.

Farming became more specialized during the 19th century. After Robert R. Livingston imported merino sheep in 1801, the breed became something of a craze, but after several decades interest declined. Hay for the stables of New York City was a big export of the county's western towns as it was easily shipped by water. The county's paper mills demanded rye straw, resulting in production that led the state in 1875. Dairying caught on among the more progressive farmers and those whose land was good for nothing but grazing. When the railroads, particularly the Harlem, provided fast shipment for fresh milk, dairying expanded rapidly. Finally, orchards (after 1870) and vineyards (after 1890) were planted in southwestern towns.

Columbia Co also developed a resort business at an early date. The Lebanon Springs were being used therapeutically in 1771, and a substantial hotel was erected in 1794 and became a minor resort. The Columbia White Sulphur Springs at Stottville were far less popular, but the area also had a resort hotel from 1855 to 1920. More lasting was the practice of summer boarding, which flourished once railroad lines, in this case the Harlem, reached the country districts. After the Civil War many of the eastern towns became favored boarding destinations, especially Hillsdale, Copake, and Canaan. Kinderhook Lake and Lake Charlotte [now Lake Taghkanic] were resorts during the same period, while Copake Lake developed as a cottage colony starting in 1908.

Religion, Education, and Culture

The first church, Dutch Reformed, organized at Kinderhook between 1677 and 1702. A Lutheran minister was with the Palatines at East Camp in 1711; four years later they petitioned the governor for permission to build a church at Kingsbury, with unknown results. Until the Revolution, Reformed and Lutheran churches dominated the western towns, while Presbyterian and Congregational bodies developed in the eastern towns as a result of New England settlement. Quakers arrived from Nantucket, Mass, and elsewhere to settle Hudson in 1784; the Shakers established two enduring communities in the county, Mount Lebanon (1787–1947) and Canaan (1813–97), each with several families, or groups. The first Roman Catholic Church, St. Mary's Hudson, formed in 1847 to serve Irish immigrants. In 1855 Columbia Co had 25 Methodist churches but, because of its Dutch and German roots, it also had a large number of Reformed (13) and Lutheran (7) churches. Its Catholic churches had already increased to three, and 20 years later there were seven. With a growing Catholic population, the same denominations were present in 2003. An exotic addition is the Abode of the Message (1974) in New Lebanon, a Sufi retreat at one of the former Shaker communities.

The earliest reference to a school is the one associated with the Kinderhook Reformed Church in 1702. The Palatines at Queensbury in Germantown had a school in 1711, and there was another at Linlithgo on Livingston Manor in 1722. The first school founded under the new state government, Washington Academy, was chartered at Clermont in 1777, and by special legislation Clermont began a town-supported public school in 1791. County residents made effective use of the funds provided by 1795 legislation and of the system developed in response to the 1812 school law. In 1877 Columbia Co had 180 school districts, of which 3 were Union Free School districts authorized by an 1853 law. Between 1928 and 1955 the county's districts consolidated into seven central school districts (Chatham, Germantown, Kinderhook, New Lebanon, Taconic Hills, and Ockawamick; the last two merged in 1971 as Taconic Hills) along with the Hudson City School District. In addition, the Berkshire Farm Union Free School District continues to serve the residents of Berkshire Farm for at-risk youth in Canaan; and Darrow School (1932), a college preparatory boarding school, occupies a former Shaker property in New Lebanon. Claverack College and Hudson River Institute (1854–1902) provided higher education, as does Columbia-Greene Community College (1969; present campus 1974).

Columbia Co's first newspaper was the *Hudson Gazette* (1785). In 2003 the daily paper was the *Hudson Register-Star,* and the *Chatham Courier* was a weekly. Four radio stations broadcasted from Hudson. Columbia Co has a number of important history museums. Olana, the home of painter Frederic Edwin Church, is perhaps the most spectacular, but others are also of high quality: Clermont (the Livingston home), the Martin Van Buren National Historic Site, the Shaker Museum and Library in Chatham, and the Mount Lebanon Shaker Village. Cultural life is fostered by such community institutions as Chatham's Mac-Haydn Theatre, Spencertown Academy, and North Pointe Cultural Arts Center in Kinderhook. Folk cultural expression has endured into the 21st century at West Taghkanic, where an indigenous basketry is still practiced by members of several families.

Edna St. Vincent Millay (1892–1950) was long an Austerlitz resident, and her home is now the Millay Colony for the Arts (1973). Other residents of national stature have included Samuel J. Tilden (1814–86), who received the majority popular vote for president in 1876, and Susan Bogert Warner (1819–85), a summer resident of Canaan, who wrote the best-sellers *The Wide, Wide World* (1850) and *Queechy* (1852).

POPULATIONS OF TOWNS AND CITIES, COLUMBIA CO

Town or City, Year Founded	1800	1840	1880	1920	1960	2000
Ancram, 1803[a]	—	1,770	1,602	1,015	1,080	1,513
Austerlitz, 1818	—	2,091	1,341	666	809	1,453
Canaan, 1772[b]	5,195	1,957	1,654	1,085	1,272	1,820
Chatham, 1795	3,716	3,662	4,574	2,705	3,402	4,249
Claverack, 1772[c]	4,414	3,056	4,347	3,747	4,989	6,401
Clermont, 1787	1,142	1,231	918	667	980	1,726
Copake, 1824	—	1,505	1,905	1,114	1,630	3,278
Gallatin, 1830	—	1,644	1,252	633	621	1,499
Germantown, 1775[d]	736	969	1,608	1,424	1,504	2,018
Ghent, 1818	—	2,558	2,953	2,451	3,485	5,276
Greenport, 1837	—	1,161	1,275	1,103	3,299	4,180
Hillsdale, 1782[e]	4,702	2,470	1,939	1,052	1,299	1,744
Hudson (city), 1785	3,664	5,672	8,670	11,745	11,075	7,524
Kinderhook, 1772[c]	4,348	3,512	4,200	2,935	4,185	8,296
Livingston, 1772[c]	7,405	2,190	2,060	1,339	1,770	3,424
New Lebanon, 1818	—	2,536	2,245	1,133	1,674	2,454
Stockport, 1833	—	1,815	1,980	1,909	2,025	2,933
Stuyvesant, 1823	—	1,779	2,097	1,541	1,496	2,188
Taghkanic, 1803[f]	—	1,674	1,308	666	727	1,118

[a]Gallatin until 1814.

[b]Formed as King's District; recognized as Town of Canaan 1788.

[c]Informally considered a district from before 1767; formed as district 1772; recognized as town 1788.

[d]Informally considered district of East Camp from before 1767; formed as German Camp District 1775; recognized as Town of Germantown 1788.

[e]Formed as district; recognized as town in 1788.

[f]Granger until 1814.

Politics

During the early national period, the county was usually but not always represented in Congress by a Federalist. Later Whigs and Democrats vied for the post, and since 1857 the county's representative in Congress has usually been Republican. During and after the Civil War, towns were more likely to vote Democratic than Republican; gradually the county became a Republican stronghold, with the smallest majorities in Hudson, Claverack, and Copake. Martin Van Buren (1782–1862), president of the United States between 1837 and 1841, was Columbia Co's most prominent politician and ranked among the great politicians of his era. His early experiences in the county provided him a mistrust of great landed estates and helped make him a committed advocate for the expansion of democratic rights. As leader of the Albany Regency beginning in 1817, he helped develop the institution of the modern political party. His Kinderhook home, Lindenwald, is open to the public and under management of the National Park Service. In the early 21st century, Columbia Co is governed by a board of supervisors, and each member is elected from a town or the City of Hudson. Since the 1970s their votes have been weighted in proportion to population. One member is elected chair and serves as the county's executive officer, receiving a modest salary.

Recent History

Columbia Co's farm sector remained central, with dairying an important component well into the late 20th century. In Ancram and Copake, the many dairy farms were the first in the United States to install bulk tanks, in 1948. In 1997 there were 464 farms in the county, producing dairy products, beef, corn, hay, alfalfa, orchard crops, and silage. The Berkshire Spur (1958) and the Taconic Parkway (1954, 1963) opened the area to second-home owners and increased tourism. Initially, the hamlets in the Town of Chatham were especially favored by summer residents, but in the 1980s Hudson began to attract similar interest, with its great architecture and easy rail access to New York City. Dealers of antiques set up business on Warren St, and art galleries, artisanal food, and other shops proliferated.

Despite the continuing decline in heavy industry, especially in textiles and paper, manufacturing continues at Schweitzer-Mauduit Corp (specialty papers) in Ancram; Sonoco-Crellin (plastic injection moldings) in Chatham; Nova Pack (plastic containers) in Claverack; Taconic Farms (laboratory animals) in Germantown; TCI (waste management), Smith Control Systems, and Doric Vault in Ghent; Kaz (electrical equipment), L. B. Furniture, and W. B. McGuire Co (millwork) in Hudson; American Bio Medica Corp in Kinderhook; and Ceramaseal in West Lebanon.

The limestone and cement industries in Greenport closed when St. Lawrence Cement purchased 1,200 acres (486 ha) of former quarry in the early 1970s. Proposing to replace its outdated Catskill plant, St. Lawrence drew up plans in the late 1990s for a large new cement plant on the site. The resulting controversy pitted hardworking native residents, who envisioned the potential jobs the plant would create, against wealthy weekend homeowners, who feared environmental and visual pollution. The issue remained in flux in 2003.

The basic history is Franklin Ellis, *History of Columbia County* (1878). Recent scholarship has produced two superb works, neither of them precisely a county history but both offering much updated information: Ruth Piwonka and Roderic H. Blackburn, *A Visible Heritage: Columbia County, NY: A History in Art and Architecture* (2000), and Peter Stott, *Looking for Work: The Industrial Archaeology of Columbia County* (forthcoming). Economic and social life in early Columbia Co has been interpreted in Martin Bruegel, *Farm, Shop, Landing: The Rise of a Market Society in the Hudson Valley, 1780–1860* (2002). The New England border is the subject of David J. Goodall, "New Light on the Border: New England Squatter Settlements in New York during the American Revolution" (PhD diss, SUNY Albany, 1984). Columbia Co towns and villages have been the subjects of more than the usual number of local studies. The pioneer works are Stephen B. Miller, *Historical Sketches of Hudson* (1862); Anna R. Bradbury, *History of the City of Hudson* (1908); and Edward A. Collier, *A History of Old Kinderhook* (1914). Among the bicentennial products, Walter V. Miller, *History of 18th-Century Germantown* (1976) stands out. A particularly engaging social history set in Ancram is Elinor Mettler, *The Fagan Sisters: A History of Life in a New York Country Village* (2000). Bruce E. Hall, *Diamond Street: The Story of the Little Town with the Big Red Light District* (1994) covers a colorful aspect of Hudson's history.

Columbia University in the City of New York. Private university. The oldest institution of higher learning in New York State was founded under a royal charter in 1754 as King's College. The original campus was located on lower Broadway on property ceded to it by Trinity Church but in 1760 moved to a new campus at Park Place. Among its earliest well-known students were John Jay (AB, 1764), Gouverneur Morris (AB, 1768), and Alexander Hamilton (1773–75). During the British occupation of Manhattan in the American Revolution instruction was suspended, but in 1784 the institution was reopened with the name Columbia College. The newly formed Board of Regents served as the trustees until 1787, when the college acquired its own board.

Into the middle of the 19th century Columbia had fewer than 175 students and retained ties to the Episcopal Church, which attenuated over time. With its move to a larger campus at 49th St and Madison Ave in 1857 the college began to develop into a modern and more secular university. During the presidency of Frederick A. P. Barnard (1864–89), the undergraduate curriculum that had been focused on classical languages and mathematics was expanded with electives. The law school (1858), a new affiliation in 1860 with the College of Physicians and Surgeons, and the School of Mines (1864) were the first of many professional schools founded in the late 19th and early 20th centuries. Columbia is also affiliated with Barnard College for Women (1889) and Teachers College (1898), which had been founded as New York College for the Training of Teachers in 1887. With the creation of graduate programs in political science, philosophy, and pure science between 1880 and 1892, Columbia emerged as one of the country's major centers for doctoral study. In 1896 the trustees changed the institution's corporate title to Columbia University and, formally, to Columbia University in the City of New York in 1912.

Under the leadership of Pres Seth Low (1890–1901), the university moved to its current site in Morningside Heights. Originally located between Broadway and Amsterdam Aves from 116th to 120th Sts, it has since spread over much of the surrounding area. Architect Charles Follen McKim designed the new campus. During the long presidency of Nicholas Murray Butler (1902–45), an unsuccessful candidate for the 1920 Republican presidential nomination, Columbia's leadership in the social and physical sciences rose to equal its prestige in the humanities. Columbia faculty, among them philosopher John Dewey, anthropologist Franz Boas, psychologist James McKeen Cattell, and historian Charles Beard, were among the leading national figures in a new approach to the social sciences that placed great emphasis on the role of social forces in shaping human history and thought. Notable scientists included pioneer geneticist Thomas Hunt Morgan and physicist Michael Pupin. Butler's often autocratic rule was highlighted when, in 1917, he dismissed Cattell for his defense of the rights of conscientious objectors. This in turn prompted the resignation of Beard. The first Great Books honors seminar was offered at Columbia College in 1919 and, along with the college's contemporary civilization sequence and humanities sequence introduced in the 1930s, became a model for undergraduate institutions across the country.

In the 1890s Butler promoted the development of a New York City high school system that provided strong academic preparation for college. By the 1910s this system was graduating many first- and second-generation immigrants, notably eastern European Jews. When the percentage of Jewish students reached about 40% in the early 1920s, the administration put in place a selective admissions policy that took applicants' religion into consideration, and the percentage of Jewish students rapidly dropped to 20%. The percentages of Jewish and Roman Catholic students continued to remain at lower levels throughout the interwar years. Public scrutiny of the selective admissions policy and the passage of the Fair Educational Practices Act in 1948 helped bring about a more diverse student body. The same year, Dwight D. Eisenhower became the first non-Anglican/Episcopalian president of the university, remaining until he was elected president of the United States in 1952. Leading faculty included English scholars Lionel Trilling and Mark Van Doren, sociologists Robert Merton, Paul Lazarsfeld, and C. Wright Mills, and historians Jacques Barzun and Richard Hofstadter. A number of the scientists who would be associated with the Manhattan Project taught at Columbia, among them Enrico Fermi, Harold Urey, and I. I. Rabi.

The decision by Columbia administrators in 1961 to build a gymnasium on a portion of Morningside Park, east of the campus, resulted in one of the most violent of the campus disturbances of the late 1960s. The groundbreaking for the gymnasium early in 1968 aroused opposition from both neighborhood residents and many in the Columbia community, and the university's participation in the research for the US Department of Defense's Institute for Defense Analysis had become a major issue for the antiwar Students for a Democratic Society. Students took over several campus buildings on 23 Apr 1968, where they remained until 30 April, when they were forcibly and violently removed by the New York City Police Department in what was widely described as a "police riot." Those turbulent events led to a thorough institutional self-examination, improved student life, greater concern for the surrounding community, and creation of a strong university senate with representation for all constituencies.

Since 1990 the university has expanded its undergraduate student body to about 4,000, substantially increased its endowments, and renovated several older buildings. In the early 21st century Columbia consists of *ca* 100 academic departments organized into 16 schools and colleges, and supports 105 institutes and centers. External research facilities include the Lamont-Doherty Earth Observatory in Palisades (Rockland Co), the Nevis Laboratory at Irvington (Westchester Co), and the Audubon Biomedical Science and Technology Park being developed near the Health and Biomedical Sciences campus in Washington Heights. Columbia College's first coeducational class was graduated in 1987. In fall 2002 a total of 23,422 students were enrolled across all programs.

See also BOTANICAL GARDENS; COLONIAL NEW YORK; HOME ECONOMICS; INTELLECTUAL EMIGRES; SCIENTIFIC CULTURE (19TH–21ST CENTURIES).

Columbia University. *The Rise of a University,* 2 vols (New York: Columbia Univ Press, 1937)

Dolkart, Andrew S. *Morningside Heights: A History of Its Architecture and Development* (New York: Columbia Univ Press, 1998)

Fact Finding Commission on Columbia Disturbances. *Crisis at Columbia: Report of the Fact-Finding Commission Appointed to Investigate the Disturbances at Columbia University in April and May 1968* (New York: Knopf, 1968)

McCaughy, Robert. *Stand Columbia: A History of Columbia University* (New York: Columbia Univ Press, 2003)

Wechsler, Harold S. *The Qualified Student: A History of Selective College Admission in America, 1870–1970* (New York: Wiley-Interscience, 1977)

Barbara J. Dunlap

Columbus. Town (pop 931) in NE Chenango Co. Settled in 1791, it was formed in 1805 from Brookfield (Madison Co) as the first place in the United States to be given the explorer's surname. After 1830 it was chiefly a dairy town, having eight cheese factories in 1880. The Columbus Community Church (1843) is on the National Register of Historic Places. By the late 20th century residents worked in town at Breakstone, a division of Kraft Foods, Golden Artist Paints, or commuted to work elsewhere. Unadilla Valley Sports Center draws as many as 10,000 spectators for weekends of motorcycle and truck racing.

Barbara B. Avery

Colve, Anthony (*fl* 17th century). Governor of New Netherland. Colve arrived in New York Harbor on 30 July 1673, during the third Anglo-Dutch War, as captain of the marines on the *Swaenenburgh* in the fleet of Dutch ships that restored the colony to Dutch rule. He served on the Council of War with fleet commanders Cornelis Evertsz the Youngest and Jacob Benckes, and was appointed governor general of the colony just before the commanders departed for the Netherlands. They left behind just a 40-gun warship and a frigate for defense, which meant the colony was vulnerable to attack by the English and the French. Based in New Orange [now New York City], Colve strengthened the colony's defenses, repaired Fort Willem Hendrick on Manhattan, and issued orders for the burgerwatch.

Despite threats from Massachusetts and Connecticut, much of Colve's administration had to do with appointing town governments, accepting oaths of allegiance, and dealing with requests and complaints from around the colony. Colve used the frigate to seize enemy ships, and he limited the number of ships going between New Orange and Willemstadt [now Albany], all of which had a negative impact on trade. Taxes had to be raised to meet the expenses of repairing the colony's fortifications. By May 1674 reports of peace had reached New Netherland, and Colve was formally instructed to turn the colony over to Edmund Andros in July. After trying to secure as many privileges for the Dutch as possible from Andros, Colve relieved the Court of New Orange of it oath of allegiance. On 10 Nov 1674 the colony was formally surrendered.

Schomette, Donald G., and Robert D. Haslach. *Raid on America: The Dutch Naval Campaign of 1672–1674* (Columbia: Univ of South Carolina Press, 1988)

Martha Dickinson Shattuck

Commack [CAH-MACK]. Locality (pop 36,367) in Smithtown and Huntington (Suffolk Co). The territory was purchased from the Matinecock Indians in 1656, and a settlement grew at the intersection of Jericho Turnpike and Townline Rd. Its post office opened in 1839. In the 19th century the Burr family bred and trained horses, including the great trotter Lady Suffolk (foaled 1833). The Long Island Motor Parkway (1908) passed through the hamlet. Extensive development followed World War II. The 7,500-seat

Long Island Arena (1959–96) was a landmark and home, until 1972, to the Long Island Ducks hockey club. Commack's major industry was the Lily-Tulip paper cup factory (1960–89). Commack is the site of the Long Island Telephone Pioneers Museum and was the childhood home of television personality Rosie O'Donnell (1962–).

Noel J. Gish

commercial banks. Depository institutions that accept deposits and make loans, primarily to businesses. Although a few of New York State's commercial banks were unchartered joint-stock companies, small partnerships, or sole proprietorships, most were chartered by the state or federal government. Banks chartered by foreign countries, and more recently banks chartered by other states, also operate within New York State.

Origins and Antebellum Development

In 1784 Alexander Hamilton helped New York City merchants to establish the country's second commercial bank, the Bank of New York. A national bank, the First Bank of the United States, was created in 1791 in Philadelphia to receive deposits, make loans, issue banknotes (bearer promissory notes made of engraved paper), and monitor banknotes issued by the states; a New York City branch opened in 1792. The same year the first New York State bank outside New York City, the Bank of Albany, was chartered, followed in 1793 by the Bank of Columbia at Hudson (Columbia Co). Early banks often found themselves embroiled in political controversies because the legislature had to approve each bank charter. Because banks were lucrative, legislators often withheld support for bank applications until the bankers paid bribes to individual legislators or "bonuses" into the state treasury. Many early banks were associated with political factions; for example, the Bank of New York was Hamiltonian Federalist. Aaron Burr played a key role in obtaining the 1799 charter of the Bank of the Manhattan Co, which was dominated by Republicans. Hamilton's attempt to establish the Merchants' Bank in New York City was rebuffed by the New York legislature, a factor in the growing feud between Burr and Hamilton. Other banks were chartered at this time, including the New-York State Bank of Albany (later the State Bank of Albany), chartered in 1803.

By 1804 New York State could boast seven banks with a total authorized capitalization of $5,380,000. Most were secure and profitable institutions. Bank assets included specie (gold or silver coins), the notes of other banks, government bonds, and, most important, short-term loans to businesses. Liabilities included checking deposits, equity capital, and banknotes. There was no standardized currency, and banknotes were the paper money of the early 19th century. The First Bank of the United States was intended to regulate the state banks' issuance of currency, but its charter expired in 1811 and was not renewed. As New York City's commerce grew, so did its number of banks. City Bank of New York was founded in 1812. The 1812 charter of the New York Manufacturing Co, a textile concern, provided for banking interactions and gave rise to Manufacturers Trust. The absence of a national bank led to inflation when US currency and banknotes could not be converted to specie.

Created in 1816 with much the same powers as the First Bank, the Second Bank of the United States agreed to pay its drafts in specie, placing it in competition with the state banks. Philadelphia financier Nicholas Biddle became president of the Second Bank in 1823. His policies maintained sound interregional currency but were perceived as slighting the West and the South as well as New York City business interests. Progenitors of some important New York banks were chartered in this era. In 1824 the New York Chemical Manufacturing Co started a bank that became the Chemical Bank of New York. The Commercial Bank of Albany was founded in 1825. By the end of that year, New York State was home to 43 incorporated banks, 27 of them located outside of New York City. Total authorized bank capital in the state in 1925 was over $30 million, and total commercial bank assets were in the neighborhood of $60 million.

In 1829 New York State passed a deposit insurance scheme setting up the Safety Fund, to which banks paid special taxes designed to cover banknote holders, and sometimes depositors, in case the bank failed. Other states soon adopted similar legislation. In July 1832 Pres Andrew Jackson vetoed a congressional bill that would have renewed the charter of the Second Bank of the United States. After reelection in November, Jackson began to remove federal deposits from the Second Bank, placing them in state-chartered banks. The demise of the Second Bank in 1836 confirmed the leadership of the New York banking industry. Eastern banks were most affected when exports to Britain fell in 1836, and the Bank of England tightened credit. Bank runs, large demands for payments that led to bank failures, increased, leading in late 1837 to a panic, widespread bank failures, and insufficiency of the Safety Fund to protect the creditors. New York State passed the Free Banking Act of 1838, which made entry into the commercial banking sector free from legislative interference; that is, a regulatory bureaucracy granted all bank applications that met certain criteria, including a minimum paid-in capital of $100,000. The Free Banking Act also mandated that commercial banks chartered under its terms secure their note issues with bonds and report annually to the comptroller. New York State had 35 banks in 1835 and 152 banks by 1846.

New York City attracted the large sums needed to finance export, import, and domestic trading patterns. Railroad investment, a significant force in the national economy, was also a factor in the expansion of banking. Banks throughout the country maintained deposits in New York City banks as part of correspondent banking relationships. The city's commercial banks accumulated large correspondent balances and loaned excess deposits to Wall St brokerage houses in the call loan market, in which the loans could be called in at any time. This helped finance the growth of the New York Stock and Exchange Board (after 1863 the New York Stock Exchange) by enhancing the liquidity and competitive advantage of New York City brokerage firms. To facilitate the interactions between banks, 52 banks (51 in New York City; 1 in Brooklyn) formed the New York Clearing House in 1853. Despite such measures, when areas of investment such as railroads became overextended, banks called in loans, investors sold securities, and the stock market fell, as in August 1857, precipitating the panic of 1857 and a two-year depression. The well-managed institutions survived; Chemical Bank continued to redeem its own notes in specie. By the end of the antebellum period, banks ranged in size from the Bank of Commerce in New York City, capitalized at $8.5 million, to small rural banks, such as the Commercial Bank of Clyde (Wayne Co), with a mere $25,000 in bank equity.

National Banking Era

Early in the Civil War, Treasury Secretary Salmon P. Chase began to finance the Union effort by selling US bonds and issuing "greenback" treasury notes, which were not redeemable in gold. At that time there were at least 7,000 varieties of banknotes in use throughout the United States. John Jay Knox, cashier of the Susquehanna Valley Bank in Binghamton, published a series of articles advocating the establishment of a national currency and a national banking system modeled on the New York State banking system. Knox's proposals helped inspire the National Currency Act of 1863 and the National Bank Act of 1864, which permitted the formation of nationally chartered banks. These banks had to invest in government securities that were deposited with the comptroller of the currency in exchange for national banknotes. The new laws not only provided a market for government bonds while introducing the national currency into wide circulation but also made New York City the reserve center of the country (joined by Chicago and St. Louis in 1887). By 1865 many New York State banks acquired national charters. National banks had to maintain a proportion of their reserves in central reserve and reserve city banks. National banks could earn the most interest in New York City banks, where the funds would be loaned out on the call loan market. By 1873 there were 321 national banks in New York State, and their assets totaled approximately $190 million, of which $150 million was in Manhattan-based banks. Twenty years later, New York State's 274 operational national banks had deposits of $326 million, far more than the $198 million deposited in state-chartered banks. Trust companies came to prominence in the 1870s, in part because they were free of the reserve requirements of commercial banks and could offer interest on deposits. Private commercial banks, of which the most prominent was J. P. Morgan and Co (founded in 1862), also played a prominent role in the nation's finances, especially after 1873, when the failure of the Philadelphia banking house of Jay Cooke gave J. P. Morgan and Co the lead in the distribution of government bonds.

Federal Reserve Board and New Deal Regulation

When the panic of 1907 began with the failure of the Knickerbocker Trust Co on 22 October, there was no central bank to contain the crisis. The important private bankers and Treasury Secretary George B. Cortelyou turned to the resources and influence of J. P. Morgan. Together they developed a plan to increase liquidity and so effectively stopped the panic in New York City that there was no ensuing depression. The panic of 1907 did, however, result in a widespread agreement on the necessity for a central bank. Although Wall St interests wanted a single central bank in New York City, the Federal Reserve Act of 1913 created a national system of 12 district banks. Paul Warburg, a Kuhn, Loeb and Co partner who helped design the Federal Reserve System, became vice chairman of the first Federal Reserve Board. Benjamin Strong, then president of Bankers Trust, accepted the governorship of the Federal Reserve Bank of New York (FRBNY). Strong and FRBNY became the dominant force in setting the policies of the Federal Reserve System.

New York State banks were increasingly reluctant to lend to farmers in the early 20th century, as agricultural communities faced low prices, high taxes, and insufficient labor. In 1914 State Banking Superintendent Eugene Lamb Richards started the Land Bank of the State of New York, which sold tax-free bonds to commercial banks, then loaned the funds to rural banks to use in making long-term loans such as mortgages. The Federal Farm Loan Bank passed by Congress in 1916 would be modeled on the program established by Richards for New York State. Most bankers in the state strongly supported British war efforts prior to the US entry into World War I in 1917. As a result of the war, New York City became the world's financial center, and by the end of 1918 the United States was the world's largest creditor nation by about $7 billion.

In the 1920s branch banking, which began as early the 1890s, become an important part of the banking business; by 1929 there were almost 600 branches in New York City. Commercial banks also opened investment trusts that enabled them to finance business development through offering securities. National City Bank of New York sold both bonds and stocks through National City Co; Chase National Bank had the same relationship with the Chase Securities Corp. New York State banks invested in real estate and participated in Wall St's call loan market. While the stock market brought a dramatic increase to the resources of upstate banks, the number of rural banks declined throughout the 1920s. Farmers had taken out mortgages to finance expansion during World War I, but farm prices fell further than nonfarm prices in the general depression of 1921, and the agricultural sector did not share in the 1922 recovery. As the value of farm property decreased, the bankruptcy rate among farmers increased, and New York State lost 33,389 farms between 1920 and 1930. Many small banks that had served their communities by making agricultural loans failed as a result of the contracting farm economy and the automobile, which gave local patrons access to larger banks in other municipalities.

The depression following the 1929 stock market crash led to a prolonged banking crisis. In late 1930 the Bank of the United States of New York collapsed, as did numerous agricultural banks. As the panics continued, the US Senate organized the investigative Banking and Currency Committee in 1931. National City Bank of New York was found to have produced about $20 billion in stocks and bonds, which it not only sold but also speculated in on the stock market. Charles E. Mitchell, National City Bank's president, resigned on 26 Feb 1933. Albert H. Wiggin, chairman of Chase National Bank, had anticipated the stock market crash; in July 1929 he had short-sold 42,000 shares of his own bank to realize a personal profit of millions. The Banking and Currency Committee collected enough information to facilitate stockholder suits against Wiggin and his colleagues. The investment trusts ceased operation, and their activities were prohibited by New Deal legislation.

Pres Franklin D. Roosevelt signed the Emergency Banking Relief Act on 9 Mar 1933. New York State's commercial banking sector was especially affected by the Glass-Steagall sections, which separated commercial banking activities from those of investment banking. Glass-Steagall prevented commercial banks from underwriting securities issues and investment banks from accepting retail deposits or making loans. As a result of Glass-Steagall, J. P. Morgan and Co split into a commercial bank of the same name and the Morgan Stanley investment bank. The Banking Act of 1933 also created the Federal Deposit Insurance Corp (FDIC), an insurance scheme designed to compensate depositors of insolvent banks. Regulation Q of the act set limits on interest rates for the time savings deposits of commercial banks. The probable impact of the act was to slow the growth of commercial banks compared to international competitors. Limitations on the expansion of the number and geographic scope of banks, epitomized in the 1927 McFadden Act that prohibited most interstate banking, also inhibited the growth of the major commercial banks.

Commercial banks had discovered consumer lending in the 1920s. National City Bank opened a consumer lending department as early as 1928. However, New Deal programs such as the Federal Housing Administration (FHA), created in 1934 to finance the construction and repair of private housing, really spurred the growth of the consumer market. One of the national pioneers in consumer banking was the Franklin National Bank of Franklin Square (Nassau Co), which opened in 1926. Under the leadership of Arthur Roth, Franklin National Bank introduced numerous innovations—savings accounts, parking lots, drive-in teller windows, and three-day turnaround for mortgage applications—to make banking seem friendlier and more approachable to consumers, especially female customers. In 1952 Franklin National Bank became the first bank to offer a credit card. By the late 1960s and early 1970s, most of the major banks offered their own version of credit cards, such as MasterCard and Visa, originally introduced under different names in 1968 and 1972, respectively. Automated teller machines (ATMs) were first offered in New York State by Chemical Bank in 1969 as a means to get quick cash. Citibank expanded ATM use as an alternative to regular teller transactions, and other commercial banks soon followed. Franklin National Bank, which played a major role in the suburban development of Long Island, was acquired by a sinister Italian financier in 1972 and shortly after went bankrupt in the largest commercial bank failure of its time.

Spurred in part by suburbanization and the burgeoning market for consumer loans, the larger banks undertook a series of mergers, expanding their number of branches. Although both endeavors were somewhat hampered by New Deal legislation, the larger banks reinforced and solidified their place in the state, national, and international economy. In 1955 Chase National, seeking a consumer and branch-banking outlet, merged with the Bank of the Manhattan Co. In the same year First National and National City merged to form First National City Bank of New York. J. P. Morgan and Co, seeking additional capital, merged with Guaranty Trust Co to form Morgan Guaranty Trust Co in 1959. Two years later Manufacturers Trust and the Hanover Bank formed Manufacturers Hanover. These mergers all involved New York City banks and branches, since they were unable to set up branches outside the five boroughs. After intense lobbying by the larger banks, New York State's Omnibus Banking Act of 1960 permitted New York City banks to expand into adjacent Nassau and Westchester Cos. Statewide banking networks became a reality with the 1971 banking bill that permitted statewide branch banking in stages, to be fully implemented by 1976. Facing a downstate challenge, the upstate banks formed their own banking networks. The First Trust and Deposit of Syracuse, National Commercial Bank of Syracuse, the National Bank of Homer (Cortland Co), and Oysterman's Bank and Trust of Sayville (Suffolk Co) formed the nucleus of the Key Bank group. The State Bank of Albany, Liberty Bank of Buffalo, Syracuse Savings Bank, Security Trust of Rochester, and the Hempstead Bank of Long Island (Nassau Co) formed a holding company that became Norstar Bancorp and later Fleet Bank. Chase Manhattan acquired Lincoln First Bank of Rochester in 1983, a major step toward developing a network that by 1984 encompassed over 300 branches across the state. If state law permitted more liberal branch banking, federal law started a trend to national banking, especially after the Bank Holding Company Act of 1968 permitted subsidiaries to offer consumer lending nationwide. Within a few years, all of the large commercial banks had become subsidiaries of holding companies.

The rise of interstate banking was one indication that the tight regulation characterizing commercial banking since the New Deal was beginning to slacken. Another indication came in 1961, when First National City Bank became the first bank to offer certificates of deposit (negotiable interest-bearing certificates) to major commercial customers, helping to create the so-called Eurodollar market outside the regulatory control of national governments. The rapid inflation and skyrocketing interest rates of the late 1970s and early 1980s brought about a liquidity crisis in many banks and widespread failures, especially among savings and loans institutions. In its aftermath many bankers pushed for greater deregulation, such as an end to Regulation Q, which was abolished in 1982.

The large New York City commercial banks had expanded overseas in the post–World War II period, developing significant presences in Europe, Asia, and Latin America. Loans from commercial banks became the most important source of financing for less-developed countries (LDCs) in the 1970s. A number of LDCs, most importantly Argentina, Brazil, Mexico, and Venezuela, slid into economic crisis during the 1980s and were unable to repay the interest, let alone the principle, on their debts. New York banks were forced to restructure the outstanding loans and to create reserves of billions of dollars to counter defaults. In 1987 Citicorp realized a $1.1 billion loss in earnings; Manufacturers, a $1.14 billion loss; Chase, an $895 million loss; and Chemical, an $853 million loss. The LDC crisis of the major commercial banks coincided with the savings and loan crisis. New York State recorded 20 failures between 1982 and 1990. By the mid-1990s New York State's commercial banks had regained profitability, largely by increasing the percentage of their revenues from fees, and regulatory procedures had been tightened.

The Glass-Steagall wall between commercial and investment banking was slowly chipped away. In 1990 Morgan Guaranty became the first bank holding company able to undertake some private corporate underwriting. The tendency to form large-scale "financial supermarkets" was well underway before the Riegle-Neal Interstate Banking and Branching Efficiency Act of 1994 ended almost all restrictions on interstate banking. Regulatory changes such as the Gramm-Leach-Bliley Act, which repealed Glass-Steagall in 1999, have created new opportunities for commercial banks. Financial services, including loans, deposits, brokerage, and insurance, are becoming increasingly integrated and national in scope.

In an effort to boost capital and better compete against Asian and European banks, US banks have engaged in extensive mergers since the late 1980s, leading to the disappearance of many of the most familiar names in banking. In 1988 the Bank of New York acquired Irving Trust in a hostile takeover, the largest bank merger up to that time. Retaining its name, Chemical Bank merged with Manufacturers Hanover in 1991. In 1996 Chase Manhattan merged with Chemical Bank. In 1998 Citicorp merged with the Travelers Group, a diversified financial company, to form Citigroup. In 2000 J. P. Morgan merged with Chase Manhattan to form J. P. Morgan Chase and Co. Foreign banks also purchased large New York City commercial banks for the first time during the 1980s and 1990s. The Hongkong and Shanghai Bank (HSBC) acquired a majority share in Marine Midland NA, a major commercial bank based in Buffalo, which eventually adopted the name HSBC Bank USA. In 1999 it acquired Republic New York Corp. That same year the venerable Bankers Trust was acquired by Deutsche Bank.

By the 1990s, in addition to raising funds with deposits, commercial banks regularly borrowed from domestic or foreign banks, issued commercial paper, and sold new types of equity capital. Also by the 1990s banks regularly sold loans instead of holding them to maturity as they had done in the past. Additionally banks began to engage extensively in fee-generating activities and to buy and sell financial derivatives, including forward, future, option, and swap contracts. In 2002 Citigroup and J. P. Morgan Chase were respectively the largest and second-largest banks in the United States, the Buffalo-based HSBC Bank USA was 11th, and Bank of New York was 15th.

Bodenhorn, Howard. *A History of Banking in Antebellum America: Financial Markets and Economic Development in an Era of Nation-Building* (New York: Cambridge Univ Press, 1999)

Fenstermaker, J. Van. *The Development of American Commercial Banking: 1782–1837* (Kent, Ohio: Kent State Univ, 1965)

Hubbard, J. T. W. *For Each, the Strength of All: A History of Banking in the State of New York* (New York: New York Univ Press, 1995)

Mishkin, Frederic. *The Economics of Money, Banking, and Financial Markets* (New York: Addison Wesley Longman, 1998)

Myers, Margaret. *New York Money Market: Origins and Development* (New York: Columbia Univ Press, 1931)

Wright, Robert E. *Origins of Commercial Banking in America, 1750–1800* (Madison, Wisc: Madison House, 2001)

———. *The Wealth of Nations Rediscovered: Integration and Expansion in American Financial Markets, 1780–1850* (New York: Cambridge Univ Press, 2002)

Commissioners for Detecting and Defeating Conspiracies. Revolutionary body established by New York State in September 1776 to identify and remove loyalist threats to its newly independent authority. Originally organized as a committee of six appointed by the Fourth Provincial Congress (its fluid membership included John Jay and other prominent individuals) and centrally located at the seat of state government, the commissioners mainly concerned themselves with overt tories and other people who might have actively aided the British or conspired to undermine the authority of the state's revolutionary leadership. After adopting the new state constitution in 1777, the legislature reorganized the commissioners in February 1778, and the new commission consisted of members sitting in separate boards in the various counties. The constitution authorized in each county a quorum of three or more commissioners to administer loyalty oaths, apprehend and confine suspicious persons, and, with the governor's approval, banish loyalists from the state. They also held the power to place suspects under recognizance and bond for good behavior. The most important and active board, in Albany Co, on which sat Jeremiah Van Rensselaer, regulated the actions of local slaves, tavern keepers, wives of banished tories, and religious dissenters such as the Shakers, whose pacifism and heterodoxy were seen as a threat to local political stability. The commissioners employed companies of Rangers raised exclusively to act as their police force and occasionally supplemented by local militia detachments. After receiving petitions complaining of the "Star Chamber Court of commissioners," New York State officially disbanded the commissioners on 27 Mar 1783, six months before the Revolutionary War officially ended with the signing of the Treaty of Paris.

Barck, Dorothy C., ed. "Minutes of the Committee and of the First Commission for Detecting and Defeating Conspiracy in the State of New York: December 11, 1776–September 23, 1778." In *Collections of the New-York Historical Society,* vols 57, 58 (New York, 1924)

Paltsits, Victor Hugo, ed. *Minutes of the Commissioners for Detecting and Defeating Conspiracies in the State of New York: Albany County Sessions, 1778–1781* (Albany: J. B. Lyon, 1909–1910; repr New York: Da Capo Press, 1972)

Sean M. O'Mara

Commissioners' Plan of 1811. One of the most significant and enduring human transformations of the Manhattan landscape, the plan established a rectilinear grid street pattern from what is now Houston St to 155th St. At the request of the Common Council, the New York State legislature established a commission in 1807 to design a plan to "lay out the leading streets and great avenues" of the emerging metropolis, which was then largely confined to the southern tip of Manhattan Island. The commission was composed of statesman Gouverneur Morris, Surveyor-General Simeon DeWitt, and lawyer John Rutherford, all members of old landowning families. The commissioners were to devise a street plan that would be "final and conclusive" and fulfill the Common Council's desire to reconstruct the Manhattan landscape so as "to unite regularity and order with the Public convenience and benefit, and in particular to promote the health of the city."

John Randel Jr was hired to survey the Manhattan landscape, and he created a series of maps depicting what came to be known as the Commissioners' Plan. The grid plan originally consisted of 12 parallel avenues and 155 cross streets, all numbered in consecutive order, thereby converting the area into a materialized coordinate system. There were also four smaller avenues east of 1st Ave labeled Aves A, B, C, and D. Well suited to surveyors' techniques of mapmaking, the grid plan laid the foundation for a standardized real estate market, while the numbering of its streets and avenues simplified the symbolic order of the cityscape. The grid was laid out on paper, presumably under the assumption that the existing topography would eventually be leveled and private property boundaries altered to make way for the homogenizing dictates of the grid. The plan included four small squares for neighborhood parks, open space for a reservoir, a centralized wholesale marketplace, and a "Parade" for military training purposes. The commissioners also sought to eliminate Broadway (its northern portion then called Bloomingdale Rd), because it did not conform to the linear logic of the grid. In 1811 the state legislature approved the plan. The grid was revised during its implementation, however, with the most conspicuous addition being Central Park, opened in 1859. Broadway was eventually exempted from the plan by legislation. Such alterations notwithstanding, the grid survived largely intact and continues to provide the spatial context for life in Manhattan.

Marcuse, Peter. "The Grid as City Plan: New York City and Laissez-Faire Planning in the 19th Century," *Planning Perspectives* 2 (Sept 1987): 287–310

Rose-Redwood, Reuben S. "Rationalizing the Landscape: Superimposing the Grid upon the Island of Manhattan" (MS thesis, Pennsylvania State Univ, 2002)

Spann, Edward K. "The Greatest Grid: The New York Plan of 1811." In *Two Centuries of American Planning,* ed. Daniel Schaffer (Baltimore: Johns Hopkins Univ Press, 1988)

Reuben Skye Rose-Redwood

Committee for Industrial Organization. See Labor.

Committee on Discrimination in Employment. Starting in 1935 state legislators tried to address, initially without success, the endemic discrimination in industrial employment faced by non-Protestants and racial and ethnic minorities. With the outbreak of World War II, discriminatory practices intensified in New York State, curtailing defense production levels. In response on 29 Mar 1941 Gov Herbert H. Lehman created the Committee on Discrimination in Employment, a temporary state agency dedicated to eradicating war plant discrimination. To aid the committee's work, three weeks later Lehman also signed the Mahoney Act into law, making employment discrimination on the basis of race, national origin, and religion illegal in defense industries. Initially the committee's chief weapon was publicity; the committee undertook school programs and aired radio shows endorsing racial harmony. Beginning in February 1942 the committee, through an investigatory staff, set out to enforce legal compliance of the Mahoney Act. Through an effective use of moral suasion, arbitration, and legal action, by war's end the committee had responded to more than 2,000 separate complaints of discrimination. Changes in New York State's race and labor policy accelerated following the 1942 election of Thomas E. Dewey as governor. With the change in administration, Alvin S. Johnson, the current head of the New School for Social Research, was appointed the committee's new chairman, and he dedicated himself to transforming the temporary wartime committee into a permanent state fair-employment agency. In the fall of 1944, Johnson and the state assembly majority leader, Republican Irving Ives, drafted the Ives-Quinn bill, which banned discrimination in employment and created the permanent State Commission against Discrimination (SCAD). Following establishment of SCAD on 1 July 1945, the Committee on Discrimination in Employment passed out of existence.

Ottman, Tod M. " 'Government That Has Both a Heart and a Head': The Growth of New York State Government during the World War II Era, 1930–1950" (PhD diss, SUNY Albany, 2001)

Tod M. Ottman

Committee on Open Government. New York State agency that oversees laws concerning the public's right to obtain government information. Its primary function involves offering advice regarding the Freedom of Information, Open Meetings, and Personal Privacy Protection Laws. Created in 1974 as the Committee on Public Access to Records, it reflected the state's involvement in the national movement toward greater government accountability, and New York State became the first to create an open government agency to monitor compliance with disclosure laws. Housed in the Department of State, the committee has five government representatives and six members of the public who serve without compensation. Four government members are ex officio and serve concurrently with the governor, and the fifth is an elected local government official designated by the governor. Four public members are appointed by the governor for four-year terms, and the remaining two are designated by the leaders of the senate and assembly, and serve until the expiration of the leaders' terms of office.

Led initially by Elie Abel, then dean of the Graduate School of Journalism at Columbia University, the committee recommended improvements to the state's Freedom of Information Law, which was replaced with a new law in 1978. The committee was also given the responsibility of overseeing the Open Meetings Law and in 1983, with its expanded role, was renamed the Committee on Open Government. In 1984 the committee was designated to implement the Personal Privacy Protection Law, which generally provides individuals with access to state agency records about themselves and limits the disclosure of those records. Its free services to the public, news media, and government officials include responses to an average of 8,000 telephone inquiries and the preparation of approximately 700 written opinions annually. Its opinions have been found to be persuasive, and courts frequently rely on them. Guides to open government laws and opinions prepared since 1993 are available on the agency's web site.

New York State. Department of State, Committee on Open Government, http://www.dos.state.ny.us/coog/coogwww.html
———. "Report to the Governor and the State Legislature." Albany, prepared annually

Robert J. Freeman

committees of correspondence and safety. State and local bodies created early in the Revolutionary War period, following precedents from the Puritan revolution in England and the uprisings against the Andros regime in New York and Massachusetts colonies in 1689. The committees of correspondence functioned to unite revolutionary thought and action through coordinated communication across borders, obtain intelligence, and direct public opinion; committees, or councils, of safety, did as well but primarily executed legislative directives, assisted military authorities, and enforced policies of the provincial congresses.

During major pre-Revolution crises in relations between New York Colony and British authorities, Whig leaders regularly instituted committees of correspondence. On 18 Oct 1764 the assembly authorized a committee to correspond during the house's recess with similar bodies in other colonies about Parliament's Sugar, Currency, and Stamp Acts. The Stamp Act crisis gave impetus to the creation of the Sons of Liberty, which in New York City on 4 Feb 1766 appointed a committee, under Secretary John Lamb, to correspond with like-minded associations elsewhere. After repeal of the Stamp Act, a new Colonial Assembly in December 1768 appointed another committee of correspondence. A public rally organized by the Sons of Liberty on 17 Dec 1773 during the crisis of the landing of the tea elected a standing committee of correspondence after reading letters from leaders of the tea protest in Boston and Philadelphia. Before the last Colonial Assembly adjourned in early May 1775, it appointed its final standing committee of correspondence. Patriots in communities across New York and other states also formed local committees of correspondence to maintain contact and coordinate the Revolutionary movement.

The First Provincial Congress created the New York Committee of Safety on 8 July 1775 to handle all official correspondence with the Continental Congress and other provincial and local committees. Additionally, it was responsible for examining suspected loyalists, coordinating military affairs, and ordering sessions of the Provincial Congress. It originally sat at New York City, but its members met in various Hudson River towns, including Fishkill (Dutchess Co) and Kingston (Ulster Co), after the British seized the city. The committee functioned until the state government assumed authority under the 1777 Constitution. County committees of safety were organized in 1774, and by 1776 they functioned as de facto local governments, managing municipal affairs and cooperating with the state's revolutionary leadership on war issues, especially the organization, outfitting, and financing of the militia. Like the New York Committee of Safety, the county committees were dissolved in 1778 when the New York State Assembly, acting under the new state constitution, confirmed the charters of cities and towns, allowing for legal local governments.

New York in the Revolution as Colony and State: A Compilation of Documents and Records from the Office of the State Comptroller (Albany: J. B. Lyon, 1904)
Sullivan, James, ed. *Minutes of the Albany Committee of Correspondence, 1775–1778* (Albany: Univ of the State of New York, 1923)

Sean M. O'Mara

communalism. See UTOPIAN AND INTENTIONAL COMMUNITIES.

communists. The history of New York State communists and communism dates to the 19th century, when secular and religious proponents of utopian socialism—such as social theorist Albert Brisbane and *New York Tribune* editor Horace Greeley (both influenced by Charles Fourier) and Oneida Community founder John Humphrey Noyes—proposed various schemes of communal property ownership. Most contemporary Americans and New Yorkers, however, equate communism with its modern Marxist manifestation inspired by the 19th-century writings of Karl Marx and Friedrich Engels. Twentieth-century communism found its most powerful domestic organizational proponent in the Communist Party, USA (CPUSA), which emerged in the wake of World War I and the worldwide revolutionary movement stimulated by the Russian Bolshevik revolution of 1917.

Party Formation

In 1919 American followers of Vladimir Illyich Lenin and the Third (Communist) International abandoned the Socialist Party to form two feuding revolutionary parties. The two tiny organizations reconciled in 1922 when, following a unity directive from the Third International (later known as the Comintern), they merged and formed the Workers (Communist) Party. In 1929 the organization changed its name to Communist Party, USA. The fledgling party hardly grew during its first decade; not only did it come under constant attack by overzealous government and private agents bent on eliminating all forms of domestic Bolshevism, but it continued to be engaged in fratricidal battles with other Marxist groups and internal dissidents.

Throughout the 20th century the CPUSA concentrated its organizational efforts on, and drew its membership from, immigrant and ethnic laborers steeped in socialist ideology and labor radicalism; most lived and worked in highly industrialized regions of the country. Because of its large immigrant population and its heavily industrial character, New York State soon became the center of the American communist movement. In 1927 the party relocated its national headquarters there from Chicago, its domestic birthplace, and later organized most of New York State's Communists into a separate organizational district, District #2 of the CPUSA. In New York City, where strong working-class communities had long existed, Communists were especially prominent and influential in a variety of trade union, cultural, and political organizations. They were dominant players in the city's Congress of Industrial Organization's (CIO's) central labor council and, in the 1940s and early 1950s, in New York State's American Labor Party, a state third party founded in 1936 to assist in the reelection of Pres Franklin D. Roosevelt (providing unionists and left-wingers

Communist Party headquarters draped with rally banners, Union Square, New York City. Photograph by Charles Rivers, 1941.

a non-Democratic line on which to vote for Roosevelt). They formed a number of nonparty auxiliary organizations, so-called front groups or mass organizations—unemployed councils, trade union leagues, civil rights organizations, cultural associations, and many others—established to broaden the base of support for party-backed causes. Whether actively pursuing racial equality, criminal justice reform, rent control, community revitalization, low bus and subway fares, or municipal health and welfare services, Communists (in alliance with other radical and liberal groups) helped forge New York City's unique liberal identity for six decades.

Regional Strongholds

The most active and highly concentrated enclaves of New York State Communists were located in New York City, where neighborhood party organizations, particularly in Harlem, Brooklyn, and the Bronx, flourished in the 1930s. Nevertheless, smaller but important local party organizations were active throughout the state. In Endicott (Broome Co) they emerged in 1919–20 from the numerous Socialist Party–affiliated language federation groups active among the numerous immigrant communities surrounding the vast Endicott Johnson Corp's shoe manufacturing and leather mills. Although these radical groups quickly died out during the post–World War I Red Scare, for a short period of time a substantial radical community sustained a modest movement that sponsored many social, cultural, and political events. Local communist picnics regularly drew large throngs (as undercover agents working for the New York State legislature regularly reported). Around Buffalo and Niagara Falls, where steel, railroad, shoe, textile, and metal manufacturing figured prominently in the local economy, party membership grew in the 1920s through the mid-1940s to such an extent that the party felt compelled to form a separate party district, District #4. Party membership in such industrial plants as Remington Rand in Tonawanda (Erie Co) and North Tonawanda (Niagara Co) and Buffalo's Republic Steel Corp, Bethlehem Steel, General Motors (Chevrolet Division), and Ford Motor Co helped foster a powerful industrial union movement in this region. Weaker but still locally important party organizations were established in other areas of the state, including Rochester, Syracuse, and Solvay (Onondaga Co), as well as in the North Country region around Ogdensburg (St. Lawrence Co) and near the seat of state government, in Albany. Smaller enclaves of Communist strength, such as existed within the Finnish colony of Spencer (Tioga Co), took root throughout the state. Still, the total numbers of New York State Communists rarely exceeded 20,000. The Communist Party's heyday came during the Great Depression, when national membership reached somewhere between 75,000 and 100,000 and when state party membership reached close to 40,000.

The Communist Party drew members and supporters from the state's industrial workforce (needle trades, electrical, textile, railroad, waterfront, chemical, metal, steel, fur and leather workers) and from its rural labor force (the state was a major dairy goods producer and exporter). Many CIO unions in New York State were built in the 1930s with active Communist involvement: the United Electrical Workers Union, the Fur and Leather Workers Union (with its openly Communist leader Ben Gold), the Transport Workers Union, the National Maritime Workers, and the United Retail and Wholesale Employees, among others. The party also attracted thousands of white-collar members and supporters, including state employees, professionals, teachers, service and welfare workers, and academics. A number of party organizations were located within the state's numerous college and university campuses: St. Lawrence, Syracuse, Columbia, City College, Cornell, Union, and many others. The most important and effective party organizations operated within highly industrial centers such as Schenectady, where Communist Party members were concentrated within and outside the city's General Electric plants. Many party members operated within industrial units, and others were active in community groups.

Regional and local Communist activists played important roles in shaping labor and political movements throughout the state. Clarence Carr, for example, a Fulton Co leather worker, was head of the local party organization in the 1930s–1950s and helped organize the county's 2,000 leather workers. He was also active among local dairy farmers and helped organize electrical workers in nearby Schenectady in the 1930s. Archie Wright, in Heuvelton (St. Lawrence Co), helped organize the Dairy Farmers Union (DFU), a left-wing union in the North Country that, in 1939, waged one of the largest and most successful milk strikes in the state's history. Concentrating on organizing the thousands of small farmers in rural New York State who had little political clout in negotiating with the major dairy cooperatives (such as the Dairymen's League Cooperative Association) and the three powerful corporations that dominated the New York State milk market (the United States Dairy Products Co, Borden Condensed Milk Co, and Sheffield Farms Milk Co), Wright and the Communist Party sought to rekindle New York State's long tradition of dairy farmer militancy. The DFU won a settlement and a price increase of 45% for its members, but its triumph was short-lived; effective use of anticommunist propaganda soon split the union and undermined its power, leading to the formation of a smaller and weaker organization known as the Farmers Union of the New York Milkshed (FUNY). Fred Briehl, who left the Socialist Party for the Communist Party after World War I, was active in Ulster, Dutchess, and Orange Cos organizing farmers. In the 1940s he headed the New York State Farm Commission of the CPUSA and was heavily engaged in agrarian work for the party.

Political and Social Contributions

While it is true that New York State communists failed to stimulate a national or a statewide revolutionary movement, their contributions to state social, political, economic, and cultural history remain important, if indirect. Their aggressive lobbying and protest tactics often permitted moderate social justice activists to achieve more modest political and economic goals. Particularly during the Great Depression years, when communists organized unemployed councils and joined liberals and socialists in lobbying for healthcare, minimum wage, and pension reforms, they contributed to the triumph of the federal New Deal, and of Gov Herbert H. Lehman's "Little New Deal" in New York State. Throughout its history, the CPUSA and its New

York State organization did more than focus on organizing industrial workers; it concentrated on a variety of social justice and political issues. It attempted to build an antifascist movement in 1936–39 by contributing arms, men, and financial resources to the Republican cause during the Spanish Civil War. It promoted the social, political, and economic rights and interests of African Americans, and through the International Labor Defense, the Civil Rights Congress, and a number of smaller and shorter-lived organizations, sought to defend them against racial injustice. In New York City, Communists focused on tenant rights and urban electoral reforms (proportional representation) and managed to draw a substantial following. They elected two members to the New York City Council: Peter Cacchione in 1941 and Ben Davis, an African American lawyer, in 1943. Statewide the party was extremely active in backing Henry A. Wallace's 1948 Progressive Party campaign. It advanced—imperfectly but ahead of its time—the social and economic rights of women; many communists or children of communists went on to help found the feminist movement of the 1960s. It promoted a strong United Nations and strongly advocated disarmament.

Suppression and Disillusion

Throughout CPUSA's history, many Americans viewed it with hostility and accused it of being un-American. Yet, in spite of being accused of taking stands overly sympathetic to the Soviet Union, American and New York State Communists rarely saw the interests of the Soviet Union as antithetical to their ideals and interests as Americans and as international revolutionaries. The party experienced its greatest growth in periods where it sought consciously to Americanize its identity, ideology, and goals, as seen from 1935 to 1939 during the so-called Popular Front period. The Hitler-Stalin Pact of August 1939 brought the party's period of greatest growth to an end, although after June 1941, with the Nazi attack on the Soviet Union, much of the Popular Front rhetoric and American patriotism resumed for the duration of the war. Despite turns in the party's ideology, most Americans continued to view communism and communists as un-American. This explains why the CPUSA was a constant target of repression, subversion, and infiltration by private organizations and by state and federal government agencies. Periodic vigilante attacks, such as occurred at a Paul Robeson concert in Peekskill (Westchester Co) in 1949, threatened the lives of party members and supporters. The FBI, from the 1920s to the 1990s, kept a close eye on CPUSA leaders and members, and on left-wing unions and various mass organizations identified with them. The New York State Police, through its Non-Criminal Investigations Unit, monitored the activities of Communists throughout the state between the late 1930s and the 1970s. The agency carefully documented Communists' everyday activities and maintained thousands of files on individuals and groups in almost every community in the state. State police agents collected license plate numbers, tapped phones, conducted surveillance of communist children's camps in the Catskill Mountains, monitored the activities of academics, stole and copied party documents, and intervened in the work lives of many individuals (sometimes leading to termination of employment). Although always justified on the basis of state and national security, such activities often violated US and New York State constitutional rights.

Ironically, while ostensibly representing itself as a revolutionary party, most of the CPUSA's members generally followed more gradualist and peaceful strategies for social and political transformation. If the 1953 executions of Julius and Ethel Rosenberg for treason in Sing Sing Prison in Ossining (Westchester Co) for many underlined the connection between the Communist Party and espionage, few CPUSA members participated in violent actions or domestic espionage. In the instances where they did, the conservative press and US congressional agencies suggested or asserted that such activities were far more typical than they really were. During the Cold War, lasting from 1946 until the demise of the Soviet Union in 1991, American and New York State Communists were generally viewed by the public as pariahs. During this long and complex period the CPUSA and associated organizations experienced a dramatic decline and a growing isolation from mainstream American culture. Communists lost much of the modest though significant power, prestige, and influence that they held in the 1930s and in the Grand Alliance years of World War II, when the Soviet Union was an integral part of an anti-Fascist alliance with the United States and Great Britain. Viable working-class alliances melted away, particularly after the party backed Wallace's presidential bid in 1948. The CIO purge of its left-led unions in 1949–50 ensured that Communists would play only a minor role in the future of the nation's and New York State's labor movement. The denunciation of Stalinism at the Soviet Union's 20th Communist Party Congress in 1956 led to a splintering of the American communist movement and marked its effective end as a significant political movement.

Despite the fervid talk of socialist revolution in the 1960s, most of the New Left had little forbearance for the CPUSA: it was too old, too rigid, and too authoritarian. The disintegration of the Soviet Union in 1991 led to the collapse of the CPUSA. At the 25th Convention of the CPUSA held in 1992, many New York State members abandoned the party, issued a "Declaration of Independence" accusing the national organization of excessive sectarianism and dogmatism, and soon afterward established an alternative, social democratic organization known as the Committees of Correspondence (CoC). In the early 21st century, many New York State and American communists grope for direction and leadership in a world that seemingly has no room for a revolutionary and socialist alternative to capitalism.

See also Labor; New York intellectuals; Popular front culture.

Isserman, Maurice. *Which Side Are You On? The American Communist Party During the Second World War* (Middletown, Conn: Wesleyan Univ Press, 1982)

Klehr, Harvey and John Earl Haynes. *The American Communist Movement: Storming Heaven Itself* (New York: Twayne Publishers, 1992)

Krieger, Thomas J. "The 1939 Dairy Farmers Union Milk Strike in Heuvelton and Canton, New York: The Story in Words and Pictures," *Journal for MultiMedia History* 1 (Fall 1998); see http://www.albany.edu/jmmh

Naison, Mark. *Communism in Harlem during the Depression* (Urbana: Univ of Illinois Press, 1983)

Zahavi, Gerald. " 'Communism Is No Bug-A-Boo': Communism and Left-Wing Unionism in Fulton County, New York, 1933–1950," *Labor History* 33 (Spring 1992)

———. "Passionate Commitments: Race, Sex, and Communism at Schenectady General Electric, 1932–1954," *Journal of American History* 83 (Sept 1996)

Gerald Zahavi

community colleges. In the early 20th century, as many western states embraced the two-year public college, New York State higher education officials made their opposition to this new institution clear. In 1921 August Downing, state commissioner of education, vowed that no junior college would be recognized by the state during his tenure, although the Packer Collegiate Institute in Brooklyn Heights had established a two-year program in 1919. With no state university and most higher education facilities in private hands, the New York State Board of Regents and the Education Department geared state policy to the benefit of private institutions. One of the central concerns of the private colleges was economic competition from new public colleges, particularly two-year institutions. By 1939 only nine junior colleges, all private, had been chartered by the Board of Regents. Among them were several colleges for women, including Sarah Lawrence Junior College (1926, Bronxville, Westchester Co), which would become a four-year program in 1931; Briarcliff Junior College (1933, Briarcliff Manor, Westchester Co); Bennett Junior College (1935, Millbrook, Dutchess Co); the coeducational Cazenovia Seminary (1934, Madison Co), and Seth Low Junior College (1928–38, Brooklyn), associated with Columbia University. The institutions in the junior college movement, as it was then known, in California and Texas, were publicly supported collegiate institutions offering the first two years of a standard baccalaureate program.

The Great Depression and World War II

In 1933 a number of "emergency" public junior colleges were established in New York State when the US government offered through its Federal Emergency Relief Administration (FERA) to fund a junior college in any state public school district. By 1934 more than 20 New York State school districts had accepted FERA's offer. At their peak, the FERA junior colleges in the state enrolled more than 3,000 students and enjoyed wide support, such as Rockland Junior College, sponsored by Nyack High School. Their central purpose was to provide new skills to the unemployed. The state's higher educational policy makers, however, always viewed the FERA colleges warily, seeing them as both an economic threat to the state's private colleges and, more importantly, as an unwarranted intrusion by the federal government into higher education, a policy realm that they felt should be left to state control. When federal funding for these junior colleges ended with FERA's reorganization into the National Recovery Administration, the Board of Regents seized the opportunity to deny alternative state sources of funding, despite the findings of a State Education Department survey in 1934 that per year an estimated 10,000 high school graduates in New York State wanted postsecondary education but could not pursue it because of the cost. By 1936 all of the FERA junior colleges in the state had closed.

Not until 1946 would New York State take its first, tentative steps toward a system of public junior colleges, or, as they were increasingly known, community colleges. That year a Board of Regents plan was implemented to establish five technical or vocational institutes in Binghamton, Buffalo, New York City, White Plains, and Utica. This did not mean that the state's education policy makers embraced public two-year colleges, however; the primary purpose was to help control what the Regents feared was a massive expansion by the federal government into higher education policy. This fear, grounded in the experience of the FERA colleges, proved correct in 1944 when the US Congress passed the GI Bill, establishing a massive grants program for war veterans to attend college. The Regents, again believing that they might lose control of higher education policy in New York State, set plans in motion in 1942 to cement state authority over such federal funding by establishing 20 state-directed institutes. Their move, however, proved impossible when Gov Thomas E. Dewey refused to support the proposed program because it was too expensive. By early 1946 the Regents scaled back the initiative from 20 to 5 institutes and, in a move designed to ensure that they would not threaten private colleges, prohibited them from offering programs in the arts and sciences. In April 1946 the state legislature and Gov Dewey not only adopted the revised plan but went further and limited enrollment, out of fiscal considerations, to 500 students per institute.

SUNY System

In a renewed effort to bring the community college to New York State, Gov Dewey created in 1946 the Temporary Commission on the Need for a State University after tremendous public pressure to establish a large state university. New York was the only state in the United States without one. Chaired by retired regent Owen D. Young, the commission was unable to agree on such an institution because many of the presidents of the state's private colleges were commission members. After two years of deliberation, in 1948 the Young Commission, as it was known, agreed to recommend converting the five institutes created two years earlier into locally sponsored community colleges and establishing an unspecified number of additional ones across the state. Sponsors could be a city, county, or some combination of school districts. In 1948 the state legislature and the governor approved the plan by creating the State University of New York (SUNY), with community colleges as one of its key elements and 11 state teachers colleges as another. The question of a large single state university was left unresolved. At first blush, the SUNY legislation appeared to have carefully balanced state and local interests in the formation of community colleges. It gave a community college's local sponsors, in consultation with state officials, considerable latitude in matters of personnel and academic programs. However, the structuring of the finances effectively limited the potential number and size of community colleges by shifting much of the cost onto sponsoring localities and students. Specifically, not only was a local sponsor required to underwrite at least half of a community college's capital costs, but student tuition was to provide a third of its operating revenue. The effect of the first provision was initially to restrict community colleges to those jurisdictions with a substantial and growing tax base.

A good illustration of the financial problems localities faced lies in Westchester Community College, formerly White Plains Institute. County officials had not been enthusiastic in assuming the costs of sponsorship, but increasingly impatient state representatives made it clear to them in 1953 that if the county did not assume sponsorship the highly successful school, which had grown significantly in its five years, would be closed. The county managed one critical concession from the state during the heated negotiations, a charge-back system to compensate it for enrolling noncounty students.

The Rockefeller Years and Rapid Growth

Despite the state's early efforts to constrain the number and size of SUNY community colleges, these institutions entered a period of sustained, even remarkable growth once their legal, financial, and supervisory framework was in place. Key to the growth were the rapid increase in high school graduation rates and the legislature's authorization in 1957 to allow liberal arts programs. By 1958 there were 11 community colleges in the SUNY system. During the long tenure of Gov Nelson A. Rockefeller, from 1959 to 1972, 19 more were established. New York State's community colleges quickly gained national recognition for innovative programs and services, such as Orange Community College, America's first higher education institution to introduce and popularize the associate degree in nursing, which it did in the early 1950s. No less significant, and largely through the advocacy of Dorothy Knoell, a senior staff member of SUNY's community college department in the 1960s, developmental programs gained acceptance as an essential component of the curriculum. In the 1950s New York City also established its own network of municipal community colleges. The New York City Community College (now the four-year New York City Technical College) in downtown Brooklyn, founded by the state in 1946, came under the auspices of New York City in 1953. It was joined by Bronx Community College in 1957 and Queensborough Community College in 1958. In the early 21st century, there are six community colleges in the City University of New York (CUNY) system.

Only since 1997 has enrollment in SUNY two-year colleges declined slightly. In part, this reflects broad demographic trends and will likely reverse itself as the number of high school graduates rebounds in the early 21st century. However, given that tuition in New York State was nearly twice the national average in 2000, future growth may be limited to contract training and similar programming. Many already find the costs of New York State's community colleges beyond their reach.

Since the 1980s the SUNY system has emerged as one of the nation's most respected and is widely recognized as a model of accessibility, program comprehensiveness, and responsible governance. Student enrollment, the principal measure of any system's strength, lends credence to this assessment: 98,937 full-time and 81,383 part-time students attended the state's 30 community colleges in 2000. But what makes the achievement particularly remarkable is not only that New York State was a relative latecomer to the community college movement but that its two-year colleges achieved their prominence despite a history of state government indifference and, at times, hostility.

Fields, Ralf R. *The Community College Movement* (New York: McGraw-Hill, 1962)

Fretwell, Elbert K. *Founding Public Junior Colleges* (New York: Bureau of Publications, Teachers College, Columbia Univ, 1954)

Kempton, Jamie. *Rockland Community College: The Early Years* (Virginia Beach, Va: Donning, 2000)

Knoell, Dorothy M. *Toward Educational Opportunity for All* (Albany: SUNY, 1966)

Witt, A., et al. *America's Community Colleges: The First Century* (Washington, DC: Community College Press, 1994)

Robert Pedersen

commutations. See Pardons, commutations, and reprieves.

commuter airlines. The industry was born out of the community of fixed base operators (FBOs), aviation entrepreneurs who owned a small airplane or two and provided various services like charter flights, surveys, flying instruction, or joyrides. Some operators discovered a demand for their services at regular times to the same destinations. Although they were not able to advertise these legally as scheduled passenger-carrying routes (under Civil Aeronautics Administration regulations), the local communities regarded them as such. One such service was Mid-Hudson Airlines, formed in the early 1950s by P. Ellsworth in Poughkeepsie. Quasi-scheduled service to the New York City airports started in 1955, mainly for employees of the local IBM plant. Ted Lafco purchased the airline in 1963 and sold it to Kingsley Morse in April 1966. On 1 July 1966 Morse changed the name to Command Airways and began to expand service to Albany, Binghamton, and other eastern cities, including Washington, DC, and Philadelphia. A public stock offering in October 1983 was followed by membership in the American Eagle group, and Command Airways was purchased by that group's parent, American Airlines, on 30 Sept 1988.

Several other commuter airlines started as FBOs. Empire State Airlines, founded by Ted Carpenter in 1953 at Syracuse as Flight Service, used a Lear jet rather than the standard small piston-engine aircraft. It served Binghamton, Elmira, Ithaca, Washington, DC, and New York City, and lasted two years. Starting in 1963 Montauk-Caribbean Airways provided local service on Long Island from its base at Montauk to East Hampton (Suffolk Co) and to the islands in Long Island Sound. It was taken over by Long Island Airways in 1985. Mac-Aire Aviation Corp, founded by Jim Keena, started service in March 1962 from Islip (Suffolk Co) to East Hampton, Connecticut points, and the New York City airports. Associated with American Airlines as part of the Metro Air Service, it ceased operations in 1968. Commuter Airlines, founded by Jerry Winston at Binghamton in 1964, operated to northeastern cities including Boston and Utica until 1982. Catskill Airways, founded by Steve Low at Oneonta (Otsego Co) in 1966, linked that city with La Guardia and John F. Kennedy International Airports (JFK). Mountain Airways, another pioneer of the commuter airlines linking small communities directly with New York City airports, flew from Saugerties (Ulster Co) in 1969 with services from Kingston (Ulster Co) and Newburgh (Orange Co) to JFK.

Between 1970 and 1990 no fewer than 30 commuter airlines were formed in New York State, although many lasted only a year or two. One exception was Empire Airlines, founded on 22 Sept 1975 at Utica as a division of Oneida County Aviation, with thrice-daily service to Syracuse. In May 1976 service to Boston replaced the Syracuse route. Under the direction of experienced US Navy and Aloha Airlines pilot Paul Quackenbush, a native of Herkimer, the network grew to include La Guardia and JFK. By the early 1980s Empire was the largest regional airline in the Northeast, serving 23 destinations, including Buffalo, Rochester, Syracuse, Utica, and Albany. In 1984 it carried more than 1 million passengers and was named Regional Airline of the Year by *Air Transport World* magazine. Empire appeared to have overstretched itself, however, and on 2 Oct 1985 a merger agreement with Piedmont Airlines of North Carolina was announced. Empire was the last of the commuter airlines based in New York State.

Davies, R. E. G. *Airlines of the United States since 1914* (1972; repr McLean, Va: Paladwr Press, 1998)

Davies, R. E. G., and I. E. Quastler. *Commuter Airlines of the United States* (Washington, DC: Smithsonian Institution Press, 1995)

R. E. G. Davies

comptroller. State government office. Established by statute as an appointment in 1797, it has since 1846 been a constitutionally based elective position. By the turn of the 21st century the New York State comptroller was vested with a combination of responsibilities that made the position among the most powerful in state government. As the state's chief fiscal officer and the head of the Comptroller's Office (designated in the constitution as the Department of Audit and Control), the comptroller is the state's principal auditor, controls payments of state funds, keeps the state's books, borrows for the state, invests for it (managing its cash), and reports on the state's fiscal condition. Additionally, as sole trustee of state and local government pension funds, which totaled $98.7 billion in December 2002, the comptroller is a key actor in world financial markets.

The constitution requires the comptroller to supervise the accounts of local governments and public authorities. A special office is maintained to oversee the finances and management of New York City. State and federal aid to local governments and local portions of shared taxes, such as the sales tax, are distributed by the comptroller. The comptroller establishes accounting and reporting standards for state agencies and local governments, maintains an extensive financial information base about local government, provides fiscal management training for local officials, conducts and oversees audits, gives legal advice to local governments and state agencies, and makes recommendations for the more efficient, effective use of public funds at the state and local levels.

In New York State's early history all tasks having to do with the receipt, management, and expenditure of funds fell to the comptroller, including "receiving taxes, monitoring banks, reviewing the books of canals, countersigning all checks, and preparing financial reports." In the mid–19th century the comptroller also supervised insurance company formation and oversaw prisons and charities. Also in the 19th century, the office was a stepping-stone to the governorship for William L. Marcy, Silas Wright, and Lucius Robinson. Millard Fillmore became vice president and then president of the United States after he served as New York State comptroller. Although several have sought it, the only 20th-century comptroller to win the governorship was Nathan L. Miller.

During the early 20th century, the state's first budgets were compiled in the Comptroller's Office. As new departments were created the office's functions narrowed. An amendment adopted in 1925 proscribed the legislature from giving the comptroller administrative duties beyond those allocated in the constitution to keep the audit function independent and distinct from executive branch operations. Morris Tremaine (1927–41) of Buffalo, a Democrat first elected in 1926 and six times thereafter (the last for a four-year term), was noted for exercising oversight of state and local finances in a manner that transcended partisanship. The state's longest serving comptroller, Arthur Levitt (1955–78) of New York City, also a Democrat, spoke out frequently and strongly against borrowing practices that bypassed constitutional referendum requirements for incurring full faith and credit debt. In doing so he developed a more public role for the office, based upon the centuries-long tradition of the comptroller acting as a force for fiscal probity in New York.

Succeeding comptrollers have built upon these efforts, commenting on state finances and management, provided early warning about localities in fiscal difficulty, and, as necessary, served on boards supervising their finances. In the recent history of the state, New Yorkers have shown an inclination to elect comptrollers for multiple terms. Just six men were elected comptroller between 1927 and 2002. The last of these, H. Carl McCall, (1993–2002), was the first African American to win statewide office in New York. The voters' predisposition for electing comptrollers from the major political party different from the governor during the second half of the 20th century reinforced the inherent tension between the role and responsibilities of the state's chief auditor and its chief executive. The modern New York State comptroller's outspoken advocacy for fiscal probity in state and local government resulted in public clashes not only with the governor but with prominent local leaders. Constitutional authority notwithstanding, for example, in 1997 McCall had to issue subpoenas and get a court order to overcome New York City Mayor Rudolph Guiliani's resistance to giving him access to records of some city agencies.

Galie, Peter. *Ordered Liberty: A Constitutional History of New York* (New York: Fordham Univ Press, 1996)

New York State. Office of the State Comptroller. *200th Anniversary Commemorative History: 1797–1997* (Albany: Author, 1998)

Gerald Benjamin

compulsory education. Legally mandated school attendance. The state's first compulsory education law (1874) required that all children aged 8–14 attend private, public, or home school for at least 14 weeks each year. The main arguments in favor of compelling education were that the health of a democracy relied upon an educated citizenry and that if the state provides schooling for this purpose, it must not be thwarted by parents, children, or employers. The State Superintendents of Public Instruction who served from 1861 through 1883 opposed such laws, viewing governmental compulsion as antagonistic to self-government.

Backed by Superintendent James E. Crooker, in 1894 the legislature passed a law requiring all children aged 8–16 to attend a private, public, or home school for varying durations dependent upon age. Superintendent Crooker argued that the child's long-term need for an education superseded a parent's right against compulsion. Between 1894 and 1902, 74,911 truant children and 2,206 uncooperative parents were arrested and prosecuted for failure to comply with the new statute. However, neither the 1874 nor the 1894 law had any visible impact on attendance or enrollment as both remained stable, at approximately 77% and 55% respectively throughout the last half of the 19th century and well into the 20th.

The current statute, Section 3205 of the Education Law, requires that "each minor from six to sixteen years of age shall attend upon full time instruction." Large districts may require attendance of unemployed youth to the age of 17. Home schooling is legal, but parents must provide instruction that is substantially equivalent in amount and quality to that provided by public schools. The provider must be a competent teacher, and parents must notify local school authorities and allow supervisory visits. Most New Yorkers voluntarily educated their children before being compelled to do so, and legal compulsion has had little or no impact on historical trends in enrollment and attendance.

Pugh, Thomas J. "Rural School Consolidation in New York State, 1795–1993" (PhD diss, Syracuse Univ, 1994)

Tyack, David, James Thomas, and Aaron Benavot. *Law and the Shaping of Public Education, 1785–1954* (Madison: Univ of Wisconsin Press, 1987)

Thomas J. Mauhs-Pugh

Comstock Laws. Federal and state antiobscenity laws named after Brooklyn resident Anthony Comstock (1844–1915). A pious Congregationalist, Comstock became incensed by saloons in his neighborhood violating the Sunday closing laws, and he became involved in antivice crusades. His targeting of free-love advocates led to the arrest in New York City of sisters Victoria Woodhull and Tennessee Claflin (1872) for printing that the Rev Henry Ward Beecher had committed adultery. In 1873 he spurred passage of the stringent federal Comstock Law, which prohibited the mailing of obscene materials, including information about contraception and abortion. Congress appointed Comstock as a special agent of the post office to make arrests. Two dozen states, including New York, adopted their own Comstock Laws. New York State's 1873 law "for the suppression of traffic in and circulation of obscene literature" was stricter than the federal law, prohibiting a person from selling, lending, or giving away obscene materials. By early 1874 Comstock had founded the New York Society for the Suppression of Vice (NYSSV), and an 1875 state law authorized agents of the NYSSV to make arrests under the state Comstock statute. Comstock crusaded against birth control and abortion and in one prominent case posed as a man who had impregnated his lover and then arrested New York City abortionist Madame Restell (Ann Trow Lohman) (1878) when she offered him abortifacients. She committed suicide before her trial started. Comstock's later years were in part consumed by the crusade against contraception advocates. In 1914 birth control advocate Margaret Sanger of New York City was arrested in a challenge to the federal Comstock Laws. These charges were dropped in 1916, but she was rearrested that same year and later convicted under the state's Comstock Law after opening the nation's first birth control clinic. Eviscerated through subsequent court decisions, the Comstock Laws were overturned by the Supreme Court in *Griswold v Connecticut* (1965) and repealed by Congress in 1971. The term Comstockery, coined by George Bernard Shaw in 1905, is still used to describe morality-based censorship efforts.

Beisel, Nicola. *Imperiled Innocents: Anthony Comstock and Family Reproduction in Victorian America* (Princeton, NJ: Princeton Univ Press, 1997)

Carolyn E. Cocca

Conable, Barber B(enjamin), Jr (*b* Warsaw, Wyoming Co, 2 Nov 1922; *d* Sarasota, Fla, 30 Nov 2003). Congressman and president of World Bank. Conable received his education in local schools and entered Cornell University, graduating in 1942. He enlisted in the US Marine Corps (USMC) Reserves, serving in the Pacific theater from 1942 to 1946. Conable returned to Cornell Law School and earned his LLB in 1948. He was reactivated during the Korean conflict and retired as colonel from USMC Reserves. He opened a law practice in Batavia (Genesee Co) in 1952. Becoming active in Republican politics, Conable was elected to the state senate and served from 1963 to 1964. In 1964 he was elected to Congress, serving 20 years and retiring as the ranking Republican on the House Ways and Means Committee. In 1986 Pres Ronald Reagan appointed him president of the World Bank. He retired in 1991 to Alexander (Genesee Co). In retirement Conable has remained active, serving as chairman of the National Committee on US-China Relations (1991–2001) and of the Executive Committee of the Board of Regents of the Smithsonian Institution (1993–2000).

Patrick Weissend

Concord. Town (pop 8,526) in S Erie Co. Settled in 1807, the town was formed from Willink [now Aurora, Erie Co] in 1812. By 1816 the first gristmill was built, taking advantage of Cattaraugus Creek; by 1860 a woolen factory, tannery, stone sawing mill, and furnace and machine shop were operating. Concord acquired rail service from the Buffalo, Rochester and Pittsburgh Railway (1878). The upgrading of US 219 as a four-lane highway was completed in 1979, improving Buffalo-bound commuting. In 2002 Concord's economy was based on agriculture, maple sugaring, and service industries. Kissing Bridge ski area, established around 1984, is a winter destination. Jack Yellen (1892–1991), composer of "Happy Days Are Here Again" and many other popular songs, was a Concord resident beginning in 1930.

Andrew C. Maines

Concordia College. Four-year, liberal arts institution located on a 33-acre (13 ha) campus in Bronxville (Westchester Co). The school was founded in 1881 in New York City as New York Progymnasium, a preparatory school for young men training to become Lutheran pastors. In 1894 it moved to Hawthorne (Westchester Co), and in 1905 was renamed Concordia-Gymnasium. In 1909 it moved to its present location, becoming Concordia Collegiate Institute in 1918. Accredited as a junior college in 1936, it became coeducational in 1939 and gained four-year accreditation and its present name in 1971. From 1992 it has functioned as part of the Concordia University system, a 10-institution network of US colleges and universities affiliated with the Lutheran Church–Missouri Synod. In 2002 it had an enrollment of 600 with 48 full-time faculty and offered more than 20 majors, awarding both associate and baccalaureate—BA, BS, and Bmus—degrees. In addition to serving the traditional student body of 18- to 22-year-olds, Concordia offers an accelerated degree for older adults and an English as a Second Language program. The Atlantic District of the Lutheran Church–Missouri Synod is headquartered on the campus.

Steinburg, Allan G. *We Will Remember: Concordia College, the First Century* (Bronxville, NY: Concordia College, 1981)

Jeffrey Kraus

Condolence Ceremony. An Iroquois ceremony that mourns deceased chiefs and installs new ones. In the ceremony the two moieties of the Iroquois, the Elder Brothers (Mohawk, Onondaga, and Seneca) and the Younger Brothers (Oneida, Cayuga, and later Tuscarora) perform reciprocal roles of "mourner" and "clear-minded." The clear-minded condole the mourners of the deceased chief, and his name is "requickened" in the person of the candidate in the name of 1 of the 50 hereditary chiefs of the Iroquois League. Of the founders there are 9 Mohawk, 14 Onondaga, 8 Seneca, 9 Oneida, and 10 Cayuga chiefs whose titles historically pass down in this manner.

The ceremonial rites begin with the procession of the clear-minded chanting the roll call of the 50 hereditary chiefs through the woods to the fire kindled by the welcoming mourners at the wood's edge. There the visitors chant the first part of the Requickening Address with the "three bare words" of requickening—translated "the wiping of the tears with a fawn skin," "removing of any obstruction from the ears," and "clearing the throat of choking grief"—which is sent back over the fire to the mourners, who reply in kind. Two warriors appointed by the clear-minded then escort the mourners into the longhouse to continue the ceremony with the recitation of ancient laws, and the clear-minded sing the six songs of requiem. The remaining 12 words of the Requickening Address are given by the clear-minded accompanied by wampum strings. The mourners reply with the six songs and the return of the wampum strings. The matron for the mourning side then presents the new chief for installation. This is followed by the charge to the new chief given by a clear-minded speaker. The Condolence Ceremony ends with a feast, which is followed by a social dance called "rubbing antlers."

In the postcontact period the Iroquois condoled European leaders and allies with an abridged Condolence Ceremony, termed the "Condolence Business" by Sir William Johnson, that consisted of a modified Requickening Address, wampum exchange, and exchange of gifts. For instance they condoled the French in Montreal two years after Comte de Frontenac's death (1698), and in July 1774 they condoled the English on the loss of Sir William Johnson and raised up Guy Johnson as his replacement. The Condolence Ceremony was in many ways the lynchpin of the Great Law of Peace of the Iroquois Confederacy, as it preserved the integrity of the league by eliminating blood feuds and any internal strife among member nations.

Fenton, William N. *The Great Law and the Longhouse* (Norman: Univ of Oklahoma Press, 1998)
Foley, Denis. "An Ethnohistoric and Ethnographic Analysis of the Iroquois from the Aboriginal Era to the Present Suburban Era" (PhD diss, SUNY Albany, 1975)
Hale, Horatio. *The Iroquois Book of Rites* (1883; repr Toronto: Univ of Toronto Press, 1965)
Shimony, Annemarie A. *Conservatism among the Iroquois at the Six Nations Reserve* (New Haven, Conn: Yale Univ Publications in Anthropology, 1961)

Denis Foley

Condon-Wadlin Act. Following a series of strikes by municipal employees, the New York State legislature enacted this law in 1947, which mandated the dismissal of any public employee who went on strike. It also required a three-year pay freeze for reinstated strikers and placed them on a five-year probation. Because of its draconian conditions the act was seldom invoked, and in 1963 the legislature passed an amendment that retained the prohibition against strikes but made other aspects of the law less oppressive. A final clause stated that the amendment would automatically be rescinded in 1965. That year the legislature passed a bill replacing Condon-Wadlin with a less punitive measure, but it was vetoed by Gov Nelson A. Rockefeller, leaving the 1947 law intact. A crippling strike by New York City transit workers in 1966 was settled without invoking Condon-Wadlin, and the more labor-friendly Public Employees' Fair Employment Act (the Taylor Law) replaced it in 1967.

Pauletti, James J., and Stuart R. Wolk. "The Condon-Wadlin Act: A Study in Legislative Futility," *New York State Bar Journal* 40 (Feb 1968): 86–93

Robert Allan Carter

Conesus [CON-EE-SHUS]. Town (pop 2,353) in E Livingston Co. Settled in 1793, the town was formed from Livonia and Groveland in 1821 as Freeport. It was renamed Bowersville in 1824 and Conesus in 1825. The Marrowback Hills, east of Hemlock Lake, rise to about 1,200 feet (370 m). The Buffalo Division of the Erie Railroad crossed the town in 1852–53. The Lakeshore House on Hemlock Lake drew resort business in the 1860s, and Hemlock and Conesus Lakes, which border the town east and west, became resorts in the 1920s. The site of the Roman Catholic Divine Word Seminary (1924–68) is now the Eagle Crest Vineyard, producing wines for liturgical use. The Turtle Stone Festival is an annual event celebrating the town's Indian and pioneer heritage. Conesus Inlet State Wildlife Management Area is in town.

Mary Jo Marks

Conesville. Town (pop 726) in SE Schoharie Co. Settled in 1764 by Dutch and Palatines from the lower Schoharie Valley who were joined by New Englanders after the Revolution, the town was formed from Broome and Durham (Greene Co) in 1836. Poor soils and mountainous Catskill terrain limited farming to a few areas and favored stock raising. A large part of the town is designated state forest, and many vacation homes have been built.

Peter Johnson and Dawn Johnson

Conewango [CON-A-WON-GO]. Town (pop 1,732) in W Cattaraugus Co. Settled in 1816, the town was formed in 1823 from Little Valley. A library was established in 1824, and a brickyard was started on Claw Creek in 1828. The town was crossed by the Atlantic and Great Western Railroad (1860; later part of Erie Railroad) and by the Erie Railroad (1875). With some of the county's best land, dairying became significant and supported five cheese factories. Amish farm families, who first settled in town in 1949, sustain a strong agricultural sector. Visitors come to observe the Amish way of life and to purchase their products.

Bruce D. Fredrickson and Madelynn P. Fredrickson

Coney Island. Resort on a peninsula, originally an island, in Brooklyn on the Atlantic Ocean. The beach seemed little more than valueless scrubland until sea bathing became popular in the 1800s, but the island remained a minor resort until improved steamboat service beginning in 1847 and railroad connections in the 1870s made it more accessible. In the 1880s and 1890s, three grand hotels, the Manhattan Beach (1877), Brighton Beach (1878), and Oriental (1880), on the eastern end of the island competed with three racetracks, Brighton Beach (1879), Sheepshead Bay (1886), and Gravesend (1886) and a vast amusement area in centrally located West Brighton. This area had a surreal skyline, dominated by a huge hotel shaped like an elephant and a 300 ft (91 m) tower, one of the largest structures in the United States when it was built in 1876, that oversaw the very public spectacles at the beach, dance hall, tavern, and promenade. Several hundred thousand urbanites visited on hot summer days, and the name Coney Island became nationally synonymous with an amusement area/beach resort, an appellation not entirely lost to this day.

The resort was, through 1894, part of the town of Gravesend (Kings Co), and Gravesend's political leaders had done much to boost its rise as a resort. In 1894 Gravesend was incorporated into Brooklyn, which in 1898 was in turn incorporated into New York City. None of these changes materially affected the status of the resort, which continued to grow, especially with the opening of three large amusement parks: Steeplechase (1897–1965), Luna Park (1903–44), and Dreamland (1904–11). Daily summer attendance often exceeded 1 million. With their glittering electric towers, re-created disasters, midget villages, freak shows, and mechanical rides, the amusement parks personified the new mass leisure and became a lightning rod for both the praise and condemnations of cultural analysts.

After World War I, new attractions, including the Wonder Wheel (1920), Cyclone (1927), and Parachute Jump (1939), all of which are still standing with landmark status, opened, but there was a growing sense that Coney Island was losing its cultural significance and distinctiveness. Much of its following began going to suburban amusement parks and more car-friendly beaches, trends exacerbated by racial changes in the area and the erection of high-rise housing projects in the 1960s. Nevertheless, the area continued to entice 5 million visitors a year throughout the 1980s and 1990s. Coney Island retains its ocean-front location, long boardwalk, and fine beach, and the possibility of a renaissance always remains. The construction of a minor league baseball stadium in 2001 may or may not signal a change in Coney's status.

See also AMUSEMENT PARKS; CAROUSELS.

Kasson, John. *Amusing the Million: Coney Island at the Turn of the Century* (New York: Hill & Wang, 1978)

Pilat, Oliver, and Jo Ranson. *Sodom by the Sea: An Affectionate History of Coney Island* (Garden City, NY: Doubleday, Doran, 1941)

Register, Woody. *The Kid of Coney Island: Fred Thompson and the Rise of American Amusements* (New York: Oxford Univ Press, 2001)

Sterngass, Jon. *First Resorts: Pursuing Pleasure at Saratoga Springs, Newport, and Coney Island* (Baltimore: Johns Hopkins Univ Press, 2001)

Jon Sterngass

Beach posing at Coney Island, 1897.

Congers [CON-GURRS]. Locality (pop 8,303) in Clarkstown (Rockland Co). Ice was cut on Rockland Lake from 1831 to 1926. The Knickerbocker Ice Co (incorporated 1855) came to dominate the industry locally. The West Shore Railroad (1883) built a station and named it Congers after a landowner, and in 1890 a post office was given the same name. The Boston Improvement Co (1889) divided 2,400 acres (971 ha) into 10,000 building lots intended as a summer resort, but the company failed, leaving land titles clouded for decades. It attracted German, Italian, and Bohemian residents. From 1,040 residents in 1950, it grew by 700% in the following half century. It is the site of 771-acre (312 ha) Rockland Lake State Park.

Congregationalists. Protestant Christians who organized churches characterized by congregational self-government, with local property ownership, lay leadership and calling of pastors, and relative freedom from denominational hierarchies on doctrinal and jurisdictional matters.

ROOTS AND REVIVALISM

In the 1620s and 1630s Calvinist Puritans migrated to New England under pressure from the Church of England. Their Congregationalist principles of church government were codified in the Cambridge Platform (Mass, 1648) and the Saybrook Platform (Conn, 1708). English settlers on Long Island who were part of this Puritan movement formed the first Congregational churches in colonial New York in the 1640s. In the 1790s and early 1800s families migrating from New England to the Mohawk Valley and Central and Western New York established Congregational churches. Congregationalists at this time were informally linked by voluntary societies devoted to mutual concerns such as social reform, home and foreign missions, and Sunday school work.

Congregationalism flourished in New York State after the Revolution during the religious revival commonly termed the Second Great Awakening led by New Divinity followers of Massachusetts pastor-theologian Jonathan Edwards. New School Presbyterian evangelist Charles Grandison Finney enjoyed great popularity among Congregationalists in the North Country and, after 1825, along the Erie Canal. At the 1827 New Lebanon Conference, evangelical Congregationalists from New England met with Finney and his Mohawk Valley colleagues to resolve disagreements over revival methods. Finney became a Congregationalist in 1836 when New England–born business leaders in New York City built Broadway Tabernacle for him to pastor. From the 1840s through the early 1900s new Congregational churches were formed in New York City and throughout the state, often including Pilgrim or Plymouth in their names, such as Henry Ward Beecher's Plymouth Church in Brooklyn.

Social Justice and Ethnic Diversity

Congregationalists of the antebellum period often supported social reform movements such as temperance and the abolition of slavery, sometimes participating in the Underground Railroad. Support for women's rights originated to some degree in the practice of female testimony and public prayer in the Finneyite revivals. The first woman ordained in an American denomination, Antoinette Brown (Antoinette Brown Blackwell after her 1856 marriage) was raised in this milieu and educated at Oberlin College (Ohio), where Finney was professor, graduating in 1850. In 1853 the Congregational Church of South Butler (Wayne Co) ordained her as pastor (without denominational approval), although she served only a year and then became a Unitarian. In the second half of the 19th century many Congregational churches and pastors embraced theological liberalism and the progressive Social Gospel movement. In the early 20th century, the denomination supported organized labor, education for African Americans, and international peace movements. In the 1950s and 1960s the church participated in the Civil Rights Movement and opposed the Vietnam War. Congregationalists also led the way in accepting women as ordained ministers.

While Congregationalism has had an overwhelmingly Yankee character, other ethnic groups established Congregational churches in certain parts of the state. Nineteenth-century Welsh immigrants with a strong tradition of piety and hymnody founded new churches, especially in and around Utica, and several black congregations were established in the New York City area. In the early 20th century, also around New York City, Armenian refugees formed a number of churches. Other New York City–area congregations—including those with members from Puerto Rico, Jamaica, China, Korea, the Philippines, and India—trace their origins to the denomination's foreign mission work.

Growth and Centralization

In 1801 the Congregational General Association of Connecticut entered into the Plan of Union with the Presbyterian Church to cooperate in founding new churches in New York State and on the western frontier, with the Connecticut Missionary Society sending at least 84 preachers into the state. The plan worked to Presbyterian advantage as many pastors, seeing the need for stronger regional organization, affiliated their congregations with presbyteries and created tensions that led to the plan's collapse in the 1830s.

Congregationalists organized formally at the state level in 1834 as the General Association of Congregational Churches, which held annual meetings, kept records, coordinated Sunday school and mission work, took responsibility for ministerial credentials, and after 1878 managed a fund for retired or needy pastors. Convinced that American Congregationalism was hindered in its growth by lack of a national body, the New York General Association invited delegates from 17 states to gather in 1852. This Albany Convention, which paved the way for a permanent national church body, officially ended the Plan of Union and initiated the funding of the American Congregational Union to build churches in the western states.

Denominational structures developed gradually from the mid–19th to the mid–20th centuries. The Christian Association, a denomination that shared Congregational concerns with local self-government and doctrinal independence, organized as the New York Christian Conference in 1818. Its national organization, the General Convention of the Christian Church, merged with the National Council of the Congregational Churches in 1931, forming the Congregational Christian Churches. German Evangelical churches were begun in Dansville (Livingston Co) in 1824 and Tonawanda (Erie Co) in 1830, with perhaps 125 more founded in the state over the next century, most densely from Buffalo to Rochester. Some of these affiliated with Lutheran synods, but others joined the Evangelical Synod of North America, which united with the (German) Reformed Church in the United States in 1934 to form the Evangelical and Reformed Church. This group joined with the Congregational Christian Churches in 1957, and in 1963 the state bodies combined as the New York Conference of the United Church of Christ (UCC). In 2001 the UCC reported 287 churches with almost 50,000 members in New York State, with another 40 churches identified as Congregational but not affiliated with the UCC. There is also an undetermined number of independent churches with Congregationalist roots.

Johnson, Curtis D. *Islands of Holiness: Rural Religion in Upstate New York, 1790–1860* (Ithaca: Cornell Univ Press, 1989)

Von Rohr, John. *The Shaping of American Congregationalism, 1620–1957* (Cleveland: Pilgrim Press, 1992)

Youngs, J. William T. *The Congregationalists* (New York: Greenwood Press, 1990)

Charles E. Hambrick-Stowe

Congress of Industrial Organizations (CIO). See Labor.

Conklin. Town (pop 5,940) in SE Broome Co. Settled in 1788, the town was formed from Chenango in 1824. In early years its lumber was floated down the Susquehanna River. Tanneries were also important. In 1844 the Turnbull Acid Works began distilling hardwood, the first such operation in the United States, and shifted to wood alcohol after 1885. A sugar beet factory operated until it burned in 1933. Eureka Tent Co and the Broome Corporate Park are located in the industrial corridor parallel to the river, railroad, and highway. The remainder of the town is rural and hilly.

Charles J. Browne

Conkling, Roscoe (*b* Albany, 30 Oct 1829; *d* New York City, 18 Apr 1888). US senator. His father, Alfred Conkling (1789–1874), Whig politician, onetime congressman, and federal judge for New York State, moved his family to Auburn (Cayuga Co) in 1839. After reading law, Roscoe Conkling joined the bar in 1850 and was named district attorney for Oneida Co the same year. In the mid-1850s he helped organize the Republican Party in New York State, although he crossed party lines in 1855 to marry Julia Seymour, the sister of the state's Democratic governor, Horatio Seymour. In 1858 he was elected mayor of Utica, a position he resigned from after his election to the House of Representatives in 1858. As a member of the House (1859–63; 1865–67) and the US Senate (1867–81), he was a strong supporter of Radical Reconstruction and black civil rights. African American US senator Blanche Bruce of Louisiana named his son after Conkling.

Conkling's good looks, dominating nature, unquestioned intelligence, scrupulous honesty, and brilliant oratory helped make him undisputed leader of the Republican Party in New York State. He controlled his party's patronage in the state, especially during Ulysses S. Grant's administration (1868–76). Conkling and Grant were extremely close, and Grant even offered Conkling the chief justice's position in the US Supreme Court, a position Conkling declined. At the deadlocked Republican National Convention of 1876, the exhausted delegates rejected both Conkling and James G. Blaine and instead nominated the relatively unknown Rutherford B. Hayes, whom Conkling did not enthusiastically support in the general election. In 1878 Hayes removed two Conkling protégés, Chester A. Arthur and Alonzo B. Cornell, from the management of the New York Customs House, the most lucrative patronage positions in the United States, over Conkling's outraged objections that his senatorial courtesy in patronage appointments had been disregarded. Conkling headed the third-term movement for Grant in 1880 and placed him in nomination at the national convention with one of his finest speeches. Although his Stalwart faction was unsuccessful, it did prevent the nomination of Blaine, Conkling's bitter personal enemy. Again the convention was forced to support a compromise candidate, this time James A. Garfield of Ohio. As a sop to the Stalwarts, Arthur was nominated for the vice presidency.

In the election of 1880, Conkling's power was at its acme; he was reelected by the legislature, another lieutenant, Thomas C. Platt, became the state's junior senator, and Cornell won the governorship. Conkling gave Garfield grudging support in the campaign, supposedly conditional on Conkling's right to senatorial courtesy. Pres Garfield, however, refused to grant Conkling control of patronage, and he further antagonized Conkling by making Blaine his secretary of state. When William H. Robertson, an anti-Conkling man, was appointed collector of the

Port of New York, Garfield trumped Conkling's objections by turning the patronage squabble into a constitutional issue about presidential prerogatives. When the senate refused to back him, Conkling resigned in protest on 14 May 1881, and Platt followed. To their surprise, the New York State legislature refused to reelect either one. Although Conkling could surely have revived his career, as Platt did, he returned to the practice of law in New York City; he even turned down an offer from Pres Arthur to become a US Supreme Court justice. Stubborn to the end, he refused to take a cab in the blizzard of 1888, plowing through enormous drifts until he collapsed at the entrance to his Gramercy Park townhouse. He died within the month.

Chidsey, Donald. *The Gentleman from New York: A Life of Roscoe Conkling* (New Haven, Conn: Yale Univ Press, 1935)

Conkling, Alfred Ronald. *The Life and Letters of Roscoe Conkling, Orator, Statesman, Advocate* (New York: Charles L. Webster, 1889)

Jordan, David. *Roscoe Conkling of New York: A Voice in the Senate* (Ithaca: Cornell Univ Press, 1971)

Jon Sterngass

Connecticut Gore. Land tract about 2 mi (4 km) wide and 220 mi (354 km) long along the New York State–Pennsylvania border from the Delaware River to the southwest corner of New York State. Connecticut's 1662 charter defined that colony's western boundary as the Pacific Ocean. Attempts to enforce the charter in the late 18th century led to land claims against Pennsylvania, which were unsuccessful, and to the establishment of the Connecticut Western Reserve (1786) in what is now northeastern Ohio. In 1795 speculators Jeremiah Halsey and Andrew Ward convinced the Connecticut legislature that the westward extension of Connecticut's northern border, where it overlapped New York State west of the Delaware River, also represented a legitimate land claim, because New York State had made formal claim to this land only four years earlier. In exchange for this land, Halsey and Ward agreed to complete the unfinished Connecticut statehouse. Halsey bought out his partner, formed the Connecticut Gore Land Co and began to issue deeds, despite New York State government protests. To secure a valid claim to its Western Reserve, Connecticut renounced jurisdiction over and claims to all other lands in 1800, thus giving up its claim to the Gore. The company soon folded.

Flick, Alexander C., ed. *History of the State of New York* (New York: Columbia Univ Press, 1934)

Livermore, Shaw. *Early American Land Companies: Their Influence on Corporate Development* (New York: Commonwealth Fund, 1939)

Francis P. Boscoe

Conquest. Town (pop 1,925) in NW Cayuga Co. Settled in 1800, the town was formed from Cato in 1821. Howland's Island in the Seneca River was settled in 1804 by 12 families of squatters who farmed until landowner Humphrey Howland ejected them around 1825. It is part of the approximately 3,600-acre (1,460 ha) Howland Island State Wildlife Management Area. In the late 19th century two factories manufactured wooden section pumps. In the late 20th century a significant number of Mennonite farm families settled.

Joni Lincoln

Conrail. Government-created corporation that controlled most of the rail trackage in New York State from 1976 to 1999. By the early 1970s most railroads operating in the Northeast were bankrupt, the largest being Penn Central, which lost over $1 million a day during the early 1970s. A 1973 act of Congress established US Railway Association, which the federal government used as a vehicle, three years later, to reorganize bankrupt carriers into Consolidated Railroad Corp, or Conrail. The corporation joined the former Penn Central, Erie Lackawanna, Lehigh Valley, Lehigh and Hudson River, Reading, and Central of New Jersey Railroads, as well as other small terminal lines. While its creation eliminated meaningful freight-rail competition for most markets in New York State, Conrail restored the financial health of most of its divisions. Helped by a revised regulatory climate, Conrail became profitable by selling or abandoning thousands of miles of track and rehabilitating what remained. The corporation kept and refurbished the former New York Central main line from Albany to Buffalo while downgrading or sending fewer and slower trains along the former Erie Lackawanna Southern Tier line through Binghamton and Elmira. Most Lehigh Valley lines in New York State and all Lehigh and Hudson River lines were abandoned. Conrail also escaped money-losing passenger operations by selling track and facilities to Amtrak and local commuter agencies. Conrail reported its first profits in 1981 and, in 1987, went public with the largest stock offering to that date. Conrail was the object of many failed takeover and merger attempts through the 1980s and early 1990s. In 1997 CSX Corp and Norfolk Southern Corp bought Conrail and divided most of its holdings. Conrail last operated as a major regional system 31 May 1999. The corporation, in much-reduced form, still handles local switching tasks in the metropolitan areas of Detroit, Philadelphia, and northern New Jersey.

Saunders, Richard. *The Railroad Mergers and the Coming of Conrail* (Westport, CT: Greenwood, 1978)

Wilner, Frank N. *Railroad Mergers: History, Analysis, Insight* (Omaha, Neb: Simmons-Boardman, 1997)

Jeff Schramm

conservatism. Political conservatism has been a vital force in New York State since the middle of the 20th century, despite the state's predominantly liberal sensibility. Conservatives encouraged a free-market economy, advocating reduced taxes and a limited role for government. Defense was the single exception, and a vigorous military was a necessary component in their anticommunist foreign policy. New York State conservatives published books and journals, and established organizations that bolstered the movement's intellectual foundation and public image, assisting in the rise of ideology nationally.

Opposing the New Deal and Postwar Renaissance

Opposition to Franklin D. Roosevelt's New Deal was a principal root of contemporary conservatism. In 1934 New York State business owners and politicians predominated among the organizers of the anti–New Deal Liberty League. The league's founders included former governor Nathan L. Miller, former senator James W. Wadsworth, and its most prominent Democratic spokesman, former governor Alfred E. Smith. When the debate over America's role in international events displaced domestic concerns at the end of the decade, Hamilton Fish, the congressman from Roosevelt's home district in Dutchess Co, emerged as one of the country's leading proponents of isolationism, often speaking on behalf of the America First Committee. Roosevelt made the congressman and two of his isolationist House colleagues infamous in the derisive chant of "Barton, Martin, and Fish." Like the organizers of the Liberty League before him, however, Fish's opposition to Roosevelt's policies never attracted significant political or intellectual support within the state. After World War II three distinct strands emerged in New York State's conservative intellectual community. Ludwig von Mises, an economics professor at New York University, expounded the ideology's libertarian strand in his 1949 book *Human Action,* which defended capitalism and a laissez-faire economy. The Foundation for Economic Education, begun in 1946 and based in Irvington (Westchester Co), disseminated Mises's work along with that of several other New York State economists who championed similar ideas. Leo Strauss, a professor at the New School for Social Research, promoted conservatism's traditionalist strand, extolling the wisdom of classical antiquity and warning of the dangers of relativism. In 1951 William F. Buckley Jr's *God and Man at Yale* argued for the critical role of religion in modern society and introduced the man who became New York State's most influential conservative. Finally, James Burnham, a philosophy professor at New York University, presented the anticommunist strand in his 1947 book *The Struggle for the World.* New York City's Francis Cardinal Spellman also emerged as one of the nation's leading anticommunist spokesmen during this period.

National Review

Although New York State conservatives produced an impressive body of work in the decade after World War II, their ideology remained outside the political and intellectual mainstream. In 1955 Buckley founded the conservative journal *National Review.* Preferring intellectual influence over mass acceptance, *National Review* helped integrate the three strands of conservatism into an intellectually defensible and coherent philosophy and redefined the public image of conservatism nationwide. Buckley banished the anti-Semitism that plagued the right before World War II, and *National Review's* unswerving anticommunism displaced any isolationist sentiment. Though his book *McCarthy and His Enemies* (1954) defended Joseph McCarthy for alerting the nation to the threat of communist infiltration while conceding a number of misjudgments, Buckley and the *National Review* later ostracized the John Birch Society and its conspiracy theories. Though the writings of New Yorker Ayn Rand appealed to some conservatives, others such as Whittaker Chambers found her writings to be didactic and antireligious. New York State conservatives also began organizing to influence public policy and politics. Conservative organizer Marvin Liebman founded and ran the Committee of One Million that opposed mainland China's entry into the United Nations. In 1960 Buckley helped establish Young Americans for Freedom, the organization for young conservatives committed to affecting national politics. In 1962 a group of disenchanted New York Republicans formed the Conservative Party to move the state Republican Party to the right. The Conservatives soon won some significant electoral victories, especially the referendum defeat of the New York City Police Civilian Review Board in 1966 and the 1970 election of James L. Buckley to the US Senate on the Conservative Party line.

Neoconservatism and Political Ascendancy

During the 1970s the New York City–based neoconservative movement emerged as a political force. Most neoconservatives began their adult lives on the left, often as socialists. By the 1970s finding liberalism deficient in waging the Cold War and in maintaining order domestically, they embraced conservatism albeit with reservations. Norman Podhoretz, editor of the journal *Commentary,* and Irving Kristol, editor of the *Public Interest,* were the most prominent of the group that also included New York State academics such as Gertrude Himmelfarb and Zbigniew Brzezinski. Despite policy differences between neoconservatives and the *National Review* conservatives, both groups united behind the candidacy of Ronald Reagan in 1980. Rep Jack Kemp also spoke for the supply-side economics that Reagan adopted as part of his successful campaign. Conservative think tanks, journals, and organizations prospered throughout the country, reducing the importance of New York State's conservative intellectuals. Meanwhile the ideologically dependable Sunbelt states produced the country's most prominent conservative politicians.

Although New York State conservatives had relinquished their central role in national conservatism by the 1990s, they continued to make intellectual contributions. *National Review* continued to publish, although William Buckley stepped down as editor in 1990. The Manhattan Institute, a prominent conservative think tank founded in 1978, sponsored scholars such as Abigail Thernstrom and David Frum. Demonstrating the continued relationship between intellectual and political conservatism, the institute provided many of the policy reforms implemented by New York City mayor Rudolph Giuliani in the 1990s. Founded in 1991 the Albany-based lobbying group Change-NY continued to advocate reduced state taxes and spending in 2001, focusing public attention on legislative and executive actions that failed to respect these goals.

See also Republican party.

Ehrman, John. *The Rise of Neoconservatism: Intellectuals and Foreign Affairs, 1945–1994* (New Haven, Conn: Yale Univ Press, 1995)

Hodgson, Godfrey. *The World Turned Right Side Up: A History of the Conservative Ascendancy in America* (Boston: Houghton Mifflin, 1996)

Judis, John B. *William F. Buckley, Jr.: Patron Saint of the Conservatives* (New York: Simon & Schuster, 1988)

Nash, George H. *The Conservative Intellectual Movement in America since 1945* (New York: Basic Books, 1976)

Timothy Sullivan

Conservative Party. State political party developed in the early 1960s when some conservative New York State Republicans grew disenchanted with what they perceived as the liberal policies of their party. Since state law required parties to choose statewide candidates through conventions rather than primaries, Gov Nelson A. Rockefeller's domination of the state Republican Party frustrated conservatives' attempts to influence it. New York State election law, however, provided minor parties with a unique source of leverage by permitting cross-endorsement of candidates. Using the New York State Liberal Party's relationship with the state's Democrats as a guide, conservatives began forming a new party in 1961, planning to cross-endorse ideologically acceptable candidates, almost always Republicans, and to run independent candidates when no acceptable alternative existed.

Kieran O'Doherty and J. Daniel Mahoney, brothers-in-law and Wall St lawyers, headed the effort to create the Conservative Party of New York State, which achieved official status when its 1962 gubernatorial candidate, Syracuse businessman David Jaquith, easily exceeded the state legal requirement of 50,000 votes. Mahoney was selected as the party's first state chairman (1962–86). Lacking significant financial backing, the party depended on the volunteer efforts of a large number of political novices. It also enjoyed the support of conservative journalists, many associated with the *National Review,* and a number of academics from around the state. The Conservative Party endorsed fiscal conservatism, limited government, and more aggressive cold war policies. Initially, however, even New York State Republicans who shared this ideological point of view shunned the new party. Change began in 1965 when William F. Buckley Jr accepted the Conservative Party's nomination for New York City mayor. The media attention surrounding Buckley's candidacy introduced the party to many voters. Buckley's 13% of the vote exceeded previous party efforts, and his campaign attracted the support of some middle-class Democrats. The party further strengthened its position the following year, when its gubernatorial candidate, Roberts Wesleyan College professor Paul L. Adams, drew more votes than the Liberal Party candidate, Franklin D. Roosevelt Jr. This secured Row C on the state ballot for the party, a development that Conservatives touted as demonstrating the party's staying power and legitimacy.

With the Conservative Party well established, more Republican candidates accepted the Conservative Party endorsement. The party achieved its greatest victory in 1970 with the election of its nominee for US Senate, James L. Buckley. With Rockefeller's resignation as governor in 1973, the state Republican Party began moving to the right, allowing Conservatives to strengthen their alliances with Republicans. In 1980 the Conservative Party helped Alfonse D'Amato defeat Sen Jacob Javits, the last major Republican liberal. Having achieved its initial goal of moving the Republican Party to the right, the Conservative Party recast its role as watchdog, prepared to revive independent challenges if necessary. Throughout the 1980s and 1990s, while the Conservative Party's backing of Republican candidates did not guarantee victory, its opposition made defeat almost inevitable. For example, in 1990, when Conservatives nominated Herbert London for governor, Republican nominee Pierre Rinfret almost finished third. In 1994 the Conservative Party provided the margin of victory for Republicans George E. Pataki and Dennis Vacco to become governor and attorney general, respectively.

From its 1963 membership of 10,329, the party grew to 107,372 by 1969 and to 165,610 by 2001. Party leaders deliberately limited efforts to draw registered members from other parties, as sympathetic voters, usually Republicans, could influence that party in primary elections. In 2001 the party drew its greatest strength from New York City suburbs, particularly Long Island's Nassau and Suffolk Cos, and from Queens and Staten Island.

See also United states senate.

Conservative Party of New York State. Papers. SUNY Albany Library, Albany

Spitzer, Robert J. "Third Parties in New York." In *Governing New York State,* 4th ed., ed. Jeffrey M. Stonecash (Albany: SUNY Press, 1994)

Timothy Sullivan

conservatories. Sharp competition and small endowments left a long history of defunct conservatories in New York City. These early schools were classes of applied instruction only. The Grand Conservatory of Music, directed by Ernst Eberhard, lasted from 1874 to 1914. New York Conservatory, New York College of Music, German Conservatory, Columbia Conservatory of Music, Mason-Thomas Conservatory, and William G. Vogt Conservatory all existed in New York City or Brooklyn before 1930.

In 1885 Jeannette Thurber founded the National Conservatory of Music, located at 128 East 17th St, modeled on the vocal instruction at the Paris Conservatory. The school was intended to encourage the growth of both indigenous American music and enrollment of African American students. From 1892 to 1895 Bohemian composer Antonín Dvořák was its director. The conservatory subsequently experienced financial difficulties and ceased operations in 1916. The Institute of Musical Art was founded by Frank Damrosch in 1905 and funded by James Loeb. In 1926 the institute merged with the Juilliard Graduate School and became the Juilliard School of Music. Renamed the Juilliard School it remained a premier conservatory in New York City at the beginning of the 21st century.

The Manhattan School of Music was founded in 1917 by pianist and philanthropist Janet D. Schenck, who directed the school from its founding until 1956. The school was located at 238 East 105th St until 1969, when it purchased the former uptown home of the Juilliard School at 120 and 130 Claremont Ave, near Broadway at 122d St. It is the largest private conservatory in the nation, with 850–900 students. The Mannes College of Music, at 157 East 74th St in New York City, was founded in 1916 by violinist and pianist David Mannes and Clara Damrosch Mannes. Their son, Leopold Damrosch Mannes, was director from 1940 to 1964. The school started offering degrees in 1953 and was the first school of music in the United States to offer a degree in early music performance. In 1984 the college moved to 150 West 85th St, and it affiliated with the New School for Social Research in 1989. Programs at Columbia University and New York University have ongoing ties with the city's major conservatories, and there are also music programs at Brooklyn College and Queens College.

The Eastman School of Music (1921), part of the University of Rochester, was founded by industrialist George Eastman. Led from 1924 to 1964 by composer Howard Hanson, the Eastman School became, and remains, one of the nation's leading conservatories. Syracuse University; SUNY colleges at Purchase, Stony Brook, and Binghamton; Cornell University; and Ithaca College, founded in 1892 as the Ithaca Conservatory of Music, all have respected programs. Morton Feldman, a central figure in avant-garde composition, taught in the SUNY Buffalo Music Department (1952), and the school is noted for its championing of new music. The graduate program in composition at Bard College in Annandale-on-Hudson (Dutchess Co) has a pronounced emphasis on avant-garde practice and interdisciplinary study.

Some of New York City's settlement schools, which offered musical training for underprivileged children, are still active. The Henry Street Settlement (1893), the Third Street Music School Settlement (1894) founded by Emilie Wagner, the Turtle Bay Music School (1925) founded by Eleanor Stanley White, and the Greenwich House Music School (1906) still offered music instruction into the 21st century. At the secondary school level, the High School of Music and Art and the High School of the Performing Arts combined in 1984 to form the Fiorello H. La Guardia High School. Harlem School of the Arts (1964) provides training in music and other arts from the primary to the preprofessional level to about 3,000 students, most of them African American or Latino. Rochester's Hochstein Music School (1920) provides intensive music and dance training to over 2,600 students at both primary and secondary levels.

Fitzpatrick, Edward John, Jr. "The Music Conservatory in America" (DMA diss, Boston Univ, 1963)

Gandre, James. "And Then There Were Seven: An Historical Case Study of the Seven Independent American Conservatories of Music That Survived the 20th Century" (EdD diss, Univ of Nebraska, Lincoln, 2001)

Andrea Olmstead

Consolidated Aircraft Corporation. Maj Reuben H. Fleet (1887–1975) formed the company in 1924. A native of Washington State, Fleet worked as a teacher, timber appraiser, and real estate agent before training as an Army Signal Corps pilot. He established Consolidated Aircraft after buying the assets of Gallaudet Aircraft Co of Greenwich, Conn, and purchasing designs from just closed General Motors subsidiary Dayton-Wright Corp. The new firm acquired the former plant of one of Glenn H. Curtiss's companies at 2050 Elmwood Ave in Buffalo. Consolidated soon developed PT-1 and PT-3 Husky biplanes and an experimental flying boat for the US military, plus 14 Commodore civil airliners for New York, Rio, and Buenos Aires Airline, of which Fleet was a partner. The airline also bought Fleetster monoplane transports, which featured the first commercial use of metal monocoque or single-shell fuselages. In 1929 Consolidated bought Thomas-Morse Aircraft Corp of Ithaca and built over 170 army observation planes in Buffalo. This same year Consolidated produced a new biplane, Fleet, selling 700 to US and foreign markets. A subsidiary, Fleet of Canada, established in 1930 in Fort Erie, Ont, built 700 additional Fleets. In 1931 Consolidated launched the P2Y; the company also acquired the design of Lockheed's Y1P-24 pursuit plane from defunct Detroit Aircraft Co and hired its designer, Robert J. Woods, who upgraded the design to create the P-25, P-30, and A-11 aircraft. In 1933 the firm purchased land near San Diego to access year-round open waters. In 1935 its PBY Catalina bomber won large navy orders, and Consolidated moved all operations west, leaving former vice president Larry Bell to form his own Bell Aircraft Corp in the Buffalo facility. Consolidated went on to produce large numbers of B-24 Liberators, PB2Y Coronados, and huge B-36 Peacemaker bombers.

Wagner, William. *Reuben Fleet and the Story of Consolidated Aircraft* (Fallbrook, Calif: Aero Publishers, 1976)

Richard Byron

Consolidated Edison (Con Edison). One of the nation's largest energy companies. The holding company's largest utility subsidiary, Consolidated Edison Co of New York, is regulated by the New York State Public Service Commission and provides electricity and gas to most of New York City and Westchester Co, and steam to Manhattan. Its other regulated subsidiary, Orange and Rockland Utilities, acquired in 1999, provides electricity and gas to a 1,300 mi^2 (3,370 km^2) area in Orange, Rockland, and Sullivan Cos, as well as to parts of Pennsylvania and New Jersey. Con Edison's four smaller, unregulated subsidiaries market energy and telecommunications development services.

Con Edison traces its origins to the New York Gas Light Co, established in 1823, the first company to provide manufactured gas service to Manhattan. Over the next six decades other gas lighting companies received franchises from the city, and periods of cutthroat competition alternated with cartel-like cooperation. In 1881 the city awarded franchises to Charles Brush's Brush Electric Light Co for a street lighting system using arc lamps and to Thomas Edison's Edison Electric Illuminating Co for incandescent lighting service. It did not take the gas companies long to respond. Six of New York City's major gas companies merged to form the Consolidated Gas Co of New York in 1884, but new gas and electric utilities continued to enter the market. Between 1899 and 1901, when utility consolidations were occurring in most major US cities, Consolidated Gas took control of most of its New York City competitors (except those serving Brooklyn), as well as most electric utilities, including the successors to the original Brush and Edison companies. Thereafter Consolidated Gas continued to purchase smaller local gas and electric companies as the opportunity arose. In 1936 the company formally changed its name to Consolidated Edison. Operating revenues increased from \$1.87 billion (in constant 2002 dollars) in 1939 to \$8.28 billion in 1979, but lean years followed in the energy industry, and by 1989 revenues had dipped somewhat, to \$8.05 billion. In 1998 Con Edison created its current holding company structure.

Although it is regulated, Con Edison has received frequent criticism. It has charged some of the highest rates in the country, and its Indian Point nuclear power facilities in Buchanan (Westchester Co) have been especially problematic. Indian Point Nuclear Power Plant 1, an experimental pressurized water reactor (PWR), began generating power in 1962 after many delays but had to be shut down permanently in 1974 following a steam leak that caused water to enter the reactor vessel. The 950 MW Indian Point 2 went operational in 1973, four years later than projected, and after numerous Nuclear Regulatory Commission citations and nearly continuous controversy, was sold with the defunct Indian Point 1 to Energy Nuclear in 2001. Indian Point 3 was sold to the New York Power Authority in 1975, before construction was completed (and the plant was later sold to Entergy Corp). Con Edison's transmission system has failed on a number of occasions, causing massive and lengthy blackouts, including ones in 1965, 1977, 1999, and 2003. Following substantial industry restructuring, the company enters an era in which New York State will see increased competition among energy providers. In 2001 Con Edison had total revenues of \$9.6 billion, 71% of which came from 3.4 million electricity customers, 15% from 1.2 million gas customers, 8% from the sale of other services, and 5% from 1,800 steam customers, mostly large commercial users and apartment houses. With the sale of its nuclear plants, Con Edison is left with less than 700 MW of generating capacity in two small plants in Manhattan and one in Brooklyn, along with some scattered gas turbines. As of 2002 the company had assets of about \$17 billion and employed approximately 14,000 people.

See also *Scenic Hudson Preservation Conference v Federal Power Commission*, 354 F 2d 608 (1965).

Collins, Frederick L. *Consolidated Gas Company of New York* (New York: Consolidated Gas, 1934)

Lurkis, Alexander. *The Power Brink: Con Edison, A Centennial of Electricity* (New York: Icare Press, 1982)

Pratt, Joseph A. *A Managerial History of Consolidated Edison, 1936–1981* (New York: Consolidated Edison, 1988)

William Hausman

Constable. Town (pop 1,428) in N Franklin Co. Settled in 1800, the town was formed from Harrison [now Malone] in 1807. Following political unrest in Canada in 1837, there was a substantial migration of Francophone Canadians to the town. Irish Fenians used Constable as a starting point for their abortive invasions of Canada in 1866 and 1870. In the 19th century the town had five starch mills. Market gardening (especially strawberries) and seed production were important beginning around 1900. In 2003 the basis of the economy was dairy farming. The hamlet of Trout River straddles the international border and at one time had a customhouse. The population increased by almost 19% between 1990 and 2000.

Thomas W. Perrin

Constable, William (Kerin) (*b* Dublin, Ireland, 1 Jan 1752; *d* New York City, 22 May 1803). Merchant and speculator. Constable was raised in Montreal and Schenectady, and was sent to Trinity College, Dublin, for his education. Before the Revolution he was in business at Schenectady. He served as an aide-de-camp to Marquis de Lafayette during the war. After moving to Philadelphia he settled in New York City in 1784 as a merchant, trading with the West Indies and Europe. When Indian lands in northern New York State were ceded to the state with the Treaty of Fort Stanwix (1789), the partnership of Constable, Daniel McCormick, and Alexander Macomb contracted to buy the Macomb Purchase: 3,607,175 acres (1,459,772 ha) of former Indian lands for 8 d (16¢) per acre. Constable's partners withdrew, leaving him as sole proprietor. He went abroad and sold large parcels to banking houses and private investors in France, England, and the Netherlands. Beginning in 1795 Constable sold land to settlers through agent Nathaniel Shaler in Constableville (Lewis Co). His son, William K. Jr, settled in Constableville.

Donald G. Tailby. "The Business Career of William Constable, a Merchant of Post-Revolutionary New York" (PhD diss, Rutgers Univ, 1961)

Emily Williams

Constableville. Village (pop 305) in West Turin (Lewis Co). Settled in 1796 it was named for proprietor William Constable. The village was incorporated in 1877 and fostered such industries as pump factories, cheese factories, a sash-and-blind mill, and a brewery. William Constable Jr's Georgian mansion (1810–19) has been a historic house museum since 1949. The village is a National Historic District that encompasses the Hotel Parquet (1796), St. Paul's Episcopal Church (1835), an octagon house (1856), and 48 houses predating 1857.

Emily Williams

Constantia. Town (pop 5,141) in SE Oswego Co. Settled in 1791 by a solitary Frenchman, the town, bounded on the south by Oneida Lake, was formed from Mexico in 1808. Iron furnace making and lumbering were early industries, and beginning in 1840 three glass factories operated at Bernhards Bay. Glassmaking ended in 1912. Trinity Episcopal Church (1831) is on the National Register of Historic Places. Three Mile Bay State Wildlife Management Area on Oneida Lake, the Oneida State Fish Hatchery, and Frenchman Island State Park are local attractions.

Barbara J. Dix

constitutions and constitutional conventions. The New York State Constitution, in addition to the constitutions of 12 other states, preceded the adoption of the US Constitution and was an influential precedent in its construction. The separate but parallel development of the state and national constitutions created a tradition of dual constitutionalism in the United States. State constitutions, like their national counterpart, establish the framework for governance, distribute and limit powers, and protect liberties. The New York State Constitution provides greater protection for certain individual rights than the national constitution and includes measures like the "forever wild" provision for the state's Adirondacks and Catskills (Art 14, § 31) that are not required by the national constitution.

Overview

New York has adopted four constitutions (1777, 1821, 1846, 1894) and convened eight constitutional conventions (1801, 1821, 1846, 1867, 1894, 1915, 1938, 1967). The Constitution of 1894, as revised in 1938, is the current document. In addition to the revisions adopted at the 1938 convention, over 225 amendments were added, resulting in a document of nearly 50,000 words, one of the longest state constitutions in the country. As of 2002 the constitution is divided into 20 articles: Article 1, the bill of rights; Article 2, suffrage; Articles 3, 4, 5, 6, 9, and 13, respectively, create a legislature, civil departments, judiciary, local government, and public officers. Articles addressing policy issues are Article 7, state finance; 8, local finance; 10, corporations; 11, education; 12, defense; 14, conservation; 15, canals; 16, taxation; 17, social welfare; and 18, housing. Article 19 concerns the amending process and, unlike the national process, is majoritarian and participatory. Amendments require passage by a majority vote of members elected to each house of the legislature, a second majority in the next regular legislative session following a general election of members of the assembly, and ratification by a majority of voters in a general election. The legislature can propose a constitutional convention subject to approval of that proposal by voters. The article also mandates that every 20 years the question of whether to hold a convention to revise and amend the constitution be submitted to the voters. Article 20 is a when-to-take-effect provision for implementing the constitution.

From Colony to Constitutional Republic: The Constitution of 1777

The roots of constitutional government in New York derived from English constitutional and common law. The state's first constitution was shaped by four conditions present in colonial New York: a heterogeneous society with an accompanying factional politics; a prominent and politically active elite whose power base derived from landed estates; a commitment to the idea of liberty as embodied in the common law, the Magna Carta, and various acts of the British Parliament; and the existence of written charters that functioned as instruments of government.

On 10 July 1776 the Fourth Provincial Congress renamed itself the Convention of Representatives of the State of New York. It was both a governing body and constituent assembly, and was the result of a special election called to grant the provincial assembly the mandate to form a new government by crafting a constitution defining its structure and powers. This election implicitly recognized a distinction between a constitutional convention and a legislative body, and affirmed the idea that a state constitution was superior to legislative enactments. The representatives, occupied with running the state and conducting a war, and subject to possible attack and capture by the British, met in March 1777 to draft the constitution. The convention was split between conservatives who wished minimal change and popular Whigs who wanted a more democratic document. John Jay, Robert R. Livingston Jr, and Gouverneur Morris held prominent roles in drafting the document, and they generally advocated traditionalist positions. Robert Yates, Charles DeWitt, and John Morin Scott were among those seeking a more democratic document. Compromises created an electorate consisting of 60% of the adult males and 70% of heads of families for the assembly, but only 29% of the adult males for the senate and governor. Free black males were permitted to vote and were subject to the same requirements established for white men.

The other central issue concerned the distribution of powers among the branches of government. A tripartite structure was established with a bicameral legislature. The governor would be elected directly by the people for a term of three years, granting an independence and stability unavailable in other states. He shared veto power with the Council of Revision, which consisted of the governor, the chancellor, and judges of the supreme court, whose veto could be overridden by two-thirds vote in both houses. The council could exercise this veto power to strike down unconstitutional as well as unwise legislation. Appointments would be made by a Council of Appointment consisting of the governor and four senators chosen by the assembly from each of the four senate districts. The judiciary was given a degree of independence, serving "during good behaviour." The Court of Impeachment and Correction of Errors, composed of the president of the senate, senators, the chancellor, and judges of the supreme court, was established to try impeachments and to correct errors on appeal from the supreme court or chancery. These institutions suggested that whatever their commitment to the doctrine of separation of powers, it did not prevent them from mingling various powers for specific purposes. Although no formal bill of rights was included there were provisions establishing the right of property owners to vote, religious freedom, and a right to trial by jury, a due process clause, a right to counsel, a conscientious objector provision for Quakers, and protection against bills of attainder. The constitution provided for the continuation of the common law, which afforded important protections. The religious liberty provision ended the tradition of multiple religious establishments in the state, thus defusing a potentially explosive church/state issue.

The constitution was approved at Kingston (Ulster Co) on 20 Apr 1777, marking the birth of New York State as a constitutional republic. It was a constitution written and adopted in the midst of a revolutionary war by a government literally on the run. In fewer than 7,000 words it embodied the ideas and institutions for which it was justly praised. The preamble incorporated the Declaration of Independence, and the executive article was to play a role in shaping the national executive office. Jay lamented that no clause abolishing slavery was included, and surprisingly, no means for amending the document was provided. The convention's decision to retain aspects of the colonial era governing process, like a strong executive, that had proven effective, along with the constitution's moderate character, led to a relatively smooth transition to the new constitutional government. These provisions and the institutional checks and balances implied in the Council of Revision and Council of Appointment foreshadowed and influenced the constitutional thinking that resulted in the US Constitution adopted in 1787.

The First Adjustments: The Constitutional Convention of 1801

The first constitutional convention in New York State—so defined because it was the first body elected by the people for the sole purpose of framing, revising, or amending the fundamental law—was the only one called for limited purposes. The convention was occasioned by a defect in the Council of Appointment and the expansion of the legislature. In the absence of any formal mechanism for amending the consti-

CONSTITUTIONAL CONVENTIONS IN NEW YORK STATE

	Duration	Power of Convention	Mode of Initiation	Vote on Convention Question	Number of Delegates (Dominant Party)	Convention President	Convention Proposals	Referendum on Convention Proposals
1777	10 July 1776–20 Apr 1777	Unlimited	Legislative	None	106[a]	—	First constitution	None (provisions adopted upon agreement of delegates)
1801	13 Oct 1801–27 Oct 1801	Limited	Legislative	None	107 (Dem-Rep)	Aaron Burr	Two amendments	None (provisions adopted upon agreement of delegates)
1821	28 Aug 1821–10 Nov 1821	Unlimited	Legislative	109,346-34,901	126 (Van Buren Rep)[b]	Daniel D. Tompkins	New constitution	Constitution adopted: 74,732-41,402
1846	1 June 1846–9 Oct 1846	Unlimited	Legislative	213,257-33,860	128 (Dem)	John Tracy	New constitution	Constitution adopted: 221,528-92,436
1867	4 June 1867–28 Feb 1868	Unlimited	Constitutional	352,854-256,364	160 (Rep)	William A. Wheeler	New constitution[c]	Constitution rejected: 223,935-290,456
1894	8 Apr 1894–29 Sept 1894	Unlimited	Constitutional	574,993-30,766	175[d] (Rep)	Joseph H. Choate	New constitution[e]	Constitution adopted: 410,697-327,402
1915	6 Apr 1915–4 Sept 1915	Unlimited	Legislative[f]	153,322-151,969	168 (Rep)	Elihu Root	New constitution	Constitution rejected: 400,423-910,462
1938	5 Apr 1938–25 Aug 1938	Unlimited	Constitutional	1,413,604-1,190,275	168 (Rep)	Frederick E. Crane	Nine proposals	Nine proposals submitted; six proposals adopted.
1967	4 Apr 1967–26 Sept 1967	Unlimited	Legislative	1,681,438-1,468,431	186 (Dem)	Anthony J. Travia	New constitution	Constitution rejected: 1,327,999-3,487,513

[a]There were 106 members of the Fourth Provincial Congress. A committee of 13 men was selected to draft the constitution; the core group who forged this first constitution consisted of Charles DeWitt, William Duer, John Jay, Robert R. Livingston Jr, Henry Wisner, Abraham Yates Jr, and Robert Yates.

[b]Includes several factions opposed to De Witt Clinton.

[c]The convention submitted a separate proposal on the judiciary that was approved by voters in 1869.

[d]Deaths and resignations brought the final number to 171.

[e]The convention submitted two separate proposals concerning apportionment and canals that were approved by the voters in 1894.

[f]This convention was called by the legislature in anticipation of the constitutionally mandated call scheduled for 1916.

tution, the legislature passed an act recommending a convention and calling for the selection of delegates. The convention, which met 13–27 Oct 1801, accomplished in two weeks what was, Aaron Burr acidly remarked, "the business of six hours." Rapid population growth had increased the number of state senators to 43. The convention fixed the number at 32 and set the assembly size at 100 with a maximum of 150. Senate seats were apportioned according to population, but one member of the assembly was guaranteed to each county regardless of population.

The second issue concerned the dispute over the power to nominate appointees to government positions. The governor claimed sole nominating power; the council claimed that power was shared. The convention decided the power was concurrent, thus placing effective control of nominations and appointments in the hands of the council and, in effect, the legislature. This both weakened the executive and accelerated the development of patronage. The convention did not submit its amendments to the electorate, believing its actions sufficient.

Participation and Property: The Constitutional Convention of 1821

The Convention of 1821 originated in the attempt by Tammany Hall's anti-Clintonian Republicans to destroy politically Gov De Witt Clinton. The more radical Republicans at the convention pushed for a one-year term for the governor, making it easier to override his veto. They succeeded in reducing the governor's term by one year, and the general restructuring of the state government by the convention convinced Clinton not to seek reelection in 1822. There were also, however, legitimate issues of constitutional reform. The state's population had increased from just over 190,000 in 1777 to over 1,300,000 in 1820 with the settlements occurring in the west and north. The suffrage, apportionment, and judicial provisions of the 1777 Constitution disadvantaged these new settlers. The Council of Appointment had become the chief vehicle for patronage, and the Council of Revision was perceived as an antidemocratic check on the will of the people.

In the absence of any constitutional provision for calling a convention the legislature had to decide. A dispute with the Council of Revision compelled the legislature to place the question before the people and to include a provision requiring ratification of convention proposals by the people prior to taking effect. This decision established the tradition in New York State of constitutional conventions as devices of the people and not of the legislature. The question of holding a convention was overwhelmingly approved 109,346 to 34,901. Strongest support came from Western New York and New York City.

The major battles occurred between Republican moderates led by Martin Van Buren and more radical Republicans led by Erastus Root. Of the 126 delegates, the vast majority belonged to Republican factions, and most victories went to the moderates. The convention debates over property qualifications for voting are considered among the great suffrage debates in American history. Delegates removed property qualifications for white males but simultaneously expanded the property qualification for African Americans, thus disenfranchising all but a handful of the state's 6,000 free adult black males.

The Council of Appointment was abolished, and the convention designated some offices elective, some appointed by local bodies, some by the legislature, and some by the governor. The Council of Revision, under attack as a violation of the separation of powers, antidemocratic, and partisan, was also eliminated. The replacement was modeled on the national presidency with the governor granted veto power that could be overridden by two-thirds of legislators present at the time of the vote, and the power to see that the laws were faithfully executed. The governor's term was reduced from three to two years with the power to adjourn the legislature eliminated.

The final major issue concerned the overburdened judiciary. A new system of circuit courts was instituted, members of the supreme court were dismissed, and a new supreme court was created, a partisan measure targeting the alleged partisanship of sitting judges. The convention added a provision requiring two-thirds of the legislature for passage of any bill appropriating money or property for local or private purposes, inaugurating a tradition of restricting legislative action that would continue throughout the 19th century. The canal policy of the state was constitutionalized. The 1821 convention devoted Article 7 to a bill of rights, drawing its provisions from the English Bill of Rights of 1689, the 1787 bill of rights adopted by the state legislature, and the federal bill of rights of 1791. Unique to the state constitution was a provision allowing conscientious objection to militia service to any member of a religious denomination. The convention also created a formal amending procedure for the constitution, authorizing amendment by majority of the legislature in one session and a two-thirds vote of the legislature in the subsequent session. Amendments would then require ratification by a majority vote of the electorate. In New York after 1821 voters could do what they could not do for the US Constitution: vote directly on whether to approve a constitutional amendment. The voters approved the proposed constitution by a vote of 74,732 to 41,402.

The Constitution of 1846: Canals, Commerce, and the Common Man

In 1826 the first amendments to the state constitution by formal constitutional procedure took place: universal white male suffrage was established (the 1821 Constitution had required payment of property taxes or personal taxes, performance of militia duty, or labor on public highways as conditions for exercising suffrage), and the office of justice of the peace was made elective. Other amendments made city mayors elective offices in New York City (1833) and then statewide (1839), and eliminated all property qualifications for holding public office (1845). Several other issues needed to be addressed. State indebtedness created by extensive public works programs, a system of land tenure that led to antirent riots, problems generated by special incorporation of private businesses, which granted corporate charters often including a variety of privileges such as exclusive franchises and the right of eminent domain, and a judiciary unequipped to cope with the rapid growth of the state were the major factors in the drive for a constitutional convention. The convention call was approved overwhelmingly. Delegates with legal backgrounds outnumbered farmers for the first time, reflecting the state's growing complexity and commercial character.

The convention swept away the quasi-feudal system of land ownership and provided the first extension of constitutional protection to local governments in New York State, providing for election of local officials and guaranteeing that all county offices, not otherwise provided for in the constitution, be chosen by electors of the respective counties or the board of supervisors. Delegates also constitutionalized debt structure for the canals and eliminated bank oligopolies by limiting legislative power to grant special charters. Practically all local offices would henceforth be elective. Senators' terms were reduced from four to two years, and members of the assembly would be elected from single-member districts according representation to small opinion clusters. The judiciary was made elective and reorganized. The Court of Appeals was created as the court of last resort, replacing the Court of Impeachment and Correction of Errors. The secretary of state, treasurer, attorney general, comptroller, canal supervisor, state engineer, and state prison inspector were made elective offices. Reflecting general disillusionment with the legislative branch, delegates added 22 restrictions on legislative power, including 2 remarkable provisions mandating popular referendums for issuance of long-term bonds and placing a limit of $1 million on the aggregate temporary debt of the state.

The convention devoted some attention to rights, incorporating provisions protecting against excessive fines or bail, cruel and unusual punishment, and unreasonable detention of witnesses. The capstone of the convention's determination to democratize the polity came with the addition of a new mode of initiating constitutional reform. Beginning in 1866 and every 20 years thereafter, and also at the recommendation of the legislature, the question "shall there be a convention to revise the constitution and amend the same?" would be submitted to the voters.

Only on the question of equal suffrage for black males did the delegates hesitate, submitting that question to the voters as a separate ballot proposition. The proposed constitution was approved overwhelmingly by a vote of 221,528 to 92,436, with the separate amendment on African American suffrage rejected by a similar margin. The constitution was essentially a new document with only 11 provisions unchanged. State and local offices were democratized, legislative power was restricted, and executive power was diffused, all in the name of grassroots democracy. For this reason the Constitution of 1846 has been called the "People's Constitution." The convention tripled the length of the document to approximately 20,400 words.

The First Failure: The Constitutional Convention of 1867

The convention of 1867 was the first to be triggered by the every-20-years provision, and it is the first state convention for which there is a verbatim record of debates and proceedings. The Republican Party garnered a majority of the delegates, and lawyers constituted the largest profession. The judiciary received the most attention with the changes adopted intended to reduce the accumulation of cases and to extend terms of judges from 8 to 14 years. These provisions were submitted separately to the voters and approved in 1869.

The issue of African American suffrage enmeshed the convention in the politics of race. Delegates proceeded cautiously, submitting an equal suffrage amendment as a separate item, which was defeated in 1869. The question of woman suffrage also was addressed. Delegates were aware of the 1848 Seneca Falls Convention, and a variety of proposals extending the franchise to women were proposed, but none received more than 24 votes. The delegates proposed significant reforms in other areas: senators would be elected to four-year staggered terms; more restrictions on the legislature were added; the governor's powers were strengthened; and a court of claims was founded. For the first time in a constitutional convention in New York State a committee on cities was created and a serious attempt was made to address the issue of home rule. Caught between the desire to root out corruption in the cities and the impulse toward local autonomy, the final recommendations did not provide much additional home rule. A search and seizure clause was included as were provisions for juries of less than 12 and for free common schools and a new article dealing with bribery of public officials.

Voters rejected the proposed constitution by a vote of 223,935 to 290,456. There is little agreement on the reasons for the failure, but fear of a vast scheme of centralized power, growing disenchantment with the policies of Republicans (who had controlled the convention), and voter rejection of African American suffrage were suggested. Efforts for reform continued and produced a new mode of constitutional revision, the Constitutional Commission. Commissions called by governors between the conventions of 1867 and 1894 made valuable recommendations regarding the legislature, the executive, the debt problems of the cities, and corruption. Many of the recommendations found their way into the constitution by way of legislatively proposed amendments. Constitutional commissions would play an important role in state constitutional reform.

The Constitution of 1894: Confronting a "New" New York

A loose alliance of independent Republicans and antimachine reformers set the tone for the convention, and four-fifths of the delegates were members of the legal profession. The convention incorporated the alterations to the judicial article recommended by the Judiciary Commission of 1890, adopted a "forever wild" state forest preserve in the Adirondacks, gave constitutional recognition and permanence to the University of the State of New York and provided some insulation for the Board of Regents from partisan politics, erected a merit-based civil service system, and made an explicit grant of home rule to cities and villages (for the first time in a New York State constitution). Measures regulating registration, authorizing voting machines, and establishing bipartisan election boards were attempts to reduce electoral fraud. The legislature was apportioned to ensure representation of all counties and to prevent New York City, with its large population, from dominating the body. The apportionment plan, emphasizing geography rather than population, privileged rural communities outside of New York City. Finally the convention established the present method of delegate selection for a constitutional convention, with 3 delegates elected from each senatorial district and 15 elected statewide.

A provision was added prohibiting aid, direct or indirect, to educational institutions under the direction of a religious denomination (often referred to as the Blaine Amendment after US Sen James G. Blaine, who had supported a similar amendment to the US Constitution). Delegates also guaranteed a right of action to recover in wrongful death cases, thus preventing the legislature from capping monetary damages. A woman suffrage amendment was reported to the floor of the convention and, after an extensive debate, rejected. The voters approved the new constitution, 410,697 to 327,402. As amended it is the state's constitution as of 2002.

The Constitutional Convention of 1915

The every-20-years clause would have required the convention question in 1916, a presidential election year. The legislature shifted the date to 1914 with the electorate approving a convention by the slimmest of margins. For a third time since the Civil War, Republicans gained a majority, electing Elihu Root convention president. Progressive era ideas of efficient and responsible government dominated. Delegates approved measures for executive reorganization and consolidation, the short ballot, and an executive budget. Delegates adopted three measures in the area of rights: an equal protection clause likely modeled on the Fourteenth Amendment, a separate amendment for voters on granting woman suffrage, and provision for defendants accused of minor crimes to waive their right to indictment by grand jury and jury trial.

Delegates had been influenced by the philosophies of expertise, efficiency, and economy, and the constitution reflected the ideas of reformers who extolled the virtues of the British parliamentary system, but the proposed constitution was rejected by 400,423 to 910,462. The manner of submission likely contributed to the defeat as voters were asked to approve everything or nothing. The document was one of the most far-reaching revisions of government structures ever undertaken by a constitutional convention in New York State. The powerful executive created by the document also proved too much for voters. Other factors included the limited time available for the ratification campaign and the inability of proponents to generate much emotional fervor for their reforms. Between 1917 and 1938, though, most of the measures proposed in 1915 were adopted through legislative amendment, including a woman suffrage amendment (1917), reorganization of the judiciary (1925), executive consolidation through the short ballot and gubernatorial appointment of many executive branch officers (1925), an executive budget (1927), and a four-year term for the governor (1937).

Constitutional Reform and the Depression: The Convention of 1938

The question of whether to hold a convention was placed on the ballot in 1936 and was approved by a margin of less than 250,000 votes. Less than half of those who voted in the governor's race cast a vote on the ballot proposition. For the fourth consecutive time Republicans secured a majority of delegates. Without a specific mandate or constitutional issues, few expected much from the convention. Yet social and economic issues could no longer be ignored in a depression. Delegates were compelled to reevaluate the role of government in society. Moreover labor was a more potent force in 1938 than it had been in 1915. The most striking features of the revised constitution were the inclusion of a "bill of rights for labor" and two new articles on care of the needy and housing, which recognized the state's responsibility for those needing support in the necessities of life. Following an enlightening debate on civil liberties, a protection against unreasonable search and seizure was added, but the convention rejected an amendment for an exclusionary rule that would bar the use of any evidence obtained in violation of the search and seizure clause. A provision prohibiting discrimination against an individual's civil rights based on race, color, or creed marked the first appearance of an equal protection clause in the state's constitution, one that included protection against private and state discrimination. The convention produced a new article on local finance consolidating various provisions on debt and taxing powers of local governments and created a new article on taxation. Delegates liberalized various restrictions placed on the legislature in the 19th century but simultaneously imposed additional limits on the use of state credit and on public authorities. Another clause prohibited a referendum on calling a convention during a national or state election year.

The convention submitted its proposals as nine separate amendments, thus allowing voters a choice, instead of submitting the entire revised constitution for a single vote. Voters approved six of the nine amendments, rejecting those generally viewed as the most partisan: proposals for barring use of proportional representation by local governments, for revising the apportionment formula, and for creating a new judicial district.

A Modern Constitution? The Constitutional Convention of 1967

New Yorkers amended the constitution 93 times between 1939 and 1966. These amendments, among others, created departments of commerce (1943) and motor vehicles (1959), accomplished court reorganization (1961), added a bill of rights for local government (1963), and established a lottery to support education (1966). In 1957 voters rejected the call for a convention. However, a series of US Supreme Court decisions declaring New York's legislative apportionment a violation of the national constitution precipitated a legislative call for a constitutional convention. The voters approved a convention in 1965. Democrats, with the help of Liberal Party votes, gained control of the convention.

Although the delegates did not mirror the state's population, they were the most diverse group elected to a constitutional convention in New York, including women, African Americans, Latinos, and people of Italian, Jewish, and Irish extraction. Two-thirds of the delegates were lawyers, with one-fourth of this number judges. The alliance of Democrats, Liberal Party delegates, and civic reformers produced a substantially revised document with far-reaching changes. Concerning rights, the ban on aid to sectarian schools was eliminated, and an exclusionary rule and a conservation bill of rights were incorporated. The state would assume the cost of welfare programs over a 10-year period as well as the cost of the statewide court system. The governor's pocket veto power was eliminated, but more flexibility in administering the executive branch was added. Apportionment, or redistricting, was removed from the legislature and transferred to a special commission. Provisions were added moving the state to provide free higher education and lowering the voting age to 18. The debt approval referendum requirement was removed.

The delegates produced a streamlined document with minimal restrictions designed for an activist state. No constitutional convention in New York State was more responsive to the needs of the cities, but its bold initiatives in the area of welfare, education, and community development were too much for the voters. Anthony J. Travia, the convention's president, submitted the changes to voters as an entire new constitution rather than in parts. That decision proved fatal. Sufficient opposition to many of the controversial provisions, combined with tepid support from reformers, resulted in a stunning defeat of 1,327,999 to 3,487,513.

Constitutional Developments: 1968–2002

The failure to pass significant constitutional revisions did not diminish the willingness to amend the document. Between 1968 and 2000, 47 amendments were adopted, including 8 related to the judiciary. They authorized centralized administration of the court system, completed a unified court system, and made major changes in the selection and removal of judges. Another 11 amendments concerned the perennial issue of debt and taxation limitations; nearly all loosened restrictions to allow state and local borrowing. The persistent attention to the judiciary and state and local finance is not surprising as nearly half of the present constitution is taken up by the three articles governing these subjects. In 1977 and 1997 voters rejected calls for a constitutional convention. In 1995 amendments addressing the state's questionable financial practices, particularly the use of "back door financing" schemes (using public authorities, lease agreements, or other such devices to avoid the constitutional prohibition against borrowing without a statewide referendum), were rejected by voters. Other constitutional issues confronting the state involved simplifying the court system and casino gambling.

The state constitution is an imperfect document generally acknowledged to be in need of reform, but use of the constitutional convention as a mechanism for change declined in the 20th century. Unlimited conventions create the fear of a Pandora's box, endangering provisions and providing opportunity to add what are perceived to be radical proposals. Well-financed and organized interest groups frequently see constitutional conventions as potential threats to their interests. Legislators dislike conventions because they have no formal role in the convention decisions and they may be the targets for reform. Groups proposing reform, in contrast, are usually less well financed and face voters who, in the absence of strong commitment, are likely to ignore the question or to vote no. Yet constitutional change continues. In 2001 voters approved an amendment that would eliminate gender-specific language in the document. Largely symbolic, the amendment reflects and extends New York's constitutional tradition of diversity and inclusion.

See also APPORTIONMENT AND DISTRICTING; BONDED INDEBTEDNESS; CITY GOVERNMENT; COURTS, STATE; US CONSTITUTION RATIFICATION.

Benjamin, Gerald, and Henrik N. Dullea, eds. *Decision 1997: Constitutional Change in New York* (Albany: Rockefeller Institute Press, 1997)

Carter, Nathaniel H., and William Stone. *Reports of the Proceedings and Debates of the Convention of 1821* (1821; repr New York: Da Capo Press, 1970)

Casais, John Anthony. "The New York State Constitutional Convention of 1821 and Its Aftermath" (PhD diss, Columbia Univ, 1967)

Croswell, Sherman, and Richard Sutton. *Debates and Proceedings in the New-York State Convention, for the Revision of the Constitution* (Albany: Argus Printers, 1846)

Dougherty, J. Hampton. *Constitutional History of the State of New York,* 2d ed. (New York: Neale Publishing, 1915)

Dullea, Henrik N. *Charter Revision in the Empire State: The Politics of New York's 1967 Convention* (New York: Rockefeller Institute Press, 1997)

Galie, Peter J. *The New York State Constitution: A Reference Guide* (New York: Greenwood Press, 1991)

———. *Ordered Liberty: A Constitutional History of New York* (New York: Fordham Univ Press, 1996)

Hindman, Wilbert L. "The New York State Constitutional Convention of 1938: The Constituent Process and Interest Activity" (PhD diss, Univ of Michigan, 1940)

Journal of the Convention of the State of New York, 1801 (Albany: John Barber, 1801)

Journal of the Provincial Congress, Provincial Convention, Committee of Safety and Council of Safety for the State of New York from 1775–1777, vol 1 (Albany: T. Weed, 1842)

League of Women Voters of New York. *Seeds of Failure: A Political Review of New York State's 1967 Constitutional Convention* (New York: Mt. Shiver Press, 1973)

Lincoln, Charles Z. *A Constitutional History of New York from the Beginning of the Colonial Period to 1905,* 5 vols (Rochester: Lawyers Cooperative Publishing Co, 1905)

Mason, Bernard. *The Road to Independence: The Revolutionary Movement in New York, 1773–1777* (Lexington: Univ of Kentucky Press, 1966)

Moss, Laura-Eve. "Democracy, Citizenship and Constitution-Making in New York, 1777–1894" (PhD diss, Univ of Connecticut, 1999)

Peterson, Merrill D., ed. *Democracy, Liberty, and Property: The State Constitutional Conventions of the 1820's* (New York: Bobbs-Merrill, 1966)

O'Rourke, Vernon, and Douglas Campbell, *Constitution-Making in a Democracy: Theory and Practice in New York State* (Baltimore: Johns Hopkins Univ Press, 1943)

Proceedings of the Constitutional Convention of the State of New York . . . 1967 (Albany: The Convention, 1968)

Report of the 1938 Constitutional Convention Committee, 12 vols (Albany: 1938)

Revised Record of the Constitutional Convention . . . 1894 (Albany: Argus, 1900)

Revised Record of the Constitutional Convention . . . 1915 (Albany: J. B. Lyons, 1916)

Revised Record of the Constitutional Convention . . . 1938 (Albany: J. B. Lyons, 1938)

Schick, Thomas. *The New York State Constitutional Convention of 1915 and the Modern State Governor* (New York: National Municipal League, 1978)

Shalala, Donna. *The City and the Constitution: The 1967 Convention's Response to the Urban Crisis* (New York: National Municipal League, 1972)

State Constitutional Conventions, Commissions and Amendments (Washington, DC: Congressional Information Service, 1988), microfiche

Underhill, Edward F., comp. *Proceedings and Debates of the Constitutional Convention of the State of New York, Held in 1867 and 1868, in the City of Albany,* 5 vols (Albany: Weed, Parsons, 1868)

Peter J. Galie

Consumer Protection Board. This state agency protects consumers' rights, investigates and resolves complaints about marketplace transactions, notifies the public about fraud or deceptive business practices, and educates on consumer issues in areas of healthcare, insurance, banking, housing, energy, utilities, and privacy protection. It also coordinates activities of consumer protection agencies. Lemon laws, credit reporting, telemarketing, as well as home improvement and construction scams fall within its scope. It also monitors prices for electric and natural gas services and guards citizen interests in the transition to competitive energy markets.

In 1955 Gov W. Averell Harriman appointed a consumer counsel with cabinet rank within his executive staff, making New York the first state to accord consumers direct representation in government. Protecting consumer interests and boosting consumer confidence were thought to promote a healthy economy. Early consumer protection efforts focused on limiting installment credit charges and battling fraud and misrepresentation. A law passed in 1956, with amendments in 1957 and 1958, protecting those buying goods and related services under installment sales plans. In 1957 a Bureau of Consumer Frauds and Protection within the Department of Law was established to prosecute businesses or individuals engaged in fraud.

In 1970 the New York State legislature created the Consumer Protection Board to conduct consumer investigations, research, and analysis; develop consumer education programs and materials; respond to individual complaints; and represent consumer interests before the Public Service Commission (PSC) and the Federal Energy Regulatory Commission. The board is made up of the chairperson of the PSC and agency heads of the Departments of Agriculture and Markets, Banking, Economic Development, Environmental Conservation, Health, Insurance, and State. The governor chooses its executive director. Among its primary divisions are the "Do Not Call" Telemarketing Law Investigation and Enforcement Unit, the Outreach and Education Unit, the Utility Intervention Unit, and the Consumer Assistance Unit, which operates a toll-free consumer complaint hot line. Headquarters are in Albany and other offices in New York City, Long Island, and Rochester. According to the 2004–5 budget, the board has 29 employees and will have a budget of about $3.4 million.

New York State Archives. "New York State Consumer Protection Board" (unpublished finding aid, 1981)

Christine Karpiak

continuing education. A network of services and providers addressing the educational needs of adults, including those who have dropped out of school or are either unemployed or underemployed. New York State began supervision of these programs in 1917 with the appointment of the first supervisor for immigrant education in the State Education Department's Division of Vocational and Extension Education. Individuals 16 years old or older received instruction in English, American history, civics, and other topics promoting good citizenship. In 1920 the legislature authorized establishing "good citizenship" instruction in community and workplace settings with a fixed level of compensation for teachers. A Bureau of Adult Education was established in 1928–29, and a 1945 law authorized state aid payments for courses approved by the State Education Department. Course offerings were broadened to include both vocational courses leading to employment and avocational courses for expanding personal interests and skills. Tradespeople and English as a Second Language (ESL) teachers assumed responsibility for these courses. In addition, conferences and institutes were conducted for teachers and administrators.

A number of reorganizations within the Education Department led in 1966 to the Bureau of General and Continuing Education being established within the Division of Continuing Education under the leadership of the assistant commissioner for Pupil Personnel Services and Continuing Education. In 1992 continuing education fell under the jurisdiction of the Education Department's Office of Workforce Preparation and Continuing Education, a subdivision of the Office of Elementary, Middle, Secondary, and Continuing Education.

Continuing education services are provided to more than 370,000 adults by a variety of organizations, including colleges, community-based groups, social services and other state agencies, libraries and cultural institutions, public school districts, and proprietary trade schools. Some programs offer academic opportunities, like the General Education Diploma (GED), while others promote career advancement and skills for employment. In 1998 the federal government passed laws to support workforce training (Workforce Investment Act) and family literacy education (Adult and Family Literacy Act). New York State continuing education services receive a portion of their funds from these federal programs, in addition to those allocated by the state legislature. The legislature also provides for coordination of job training and education to eliminate duplication and to strengthen accountability across New York State government agencies. Resources for continuing and adult education programs increased from $95 to $130 million between 1992 and 1999, and continue to grow with support from state and federal agencies, as well as business and industry.

See also CHAUTAUQUA INSTITUTION; EDUCATION DEPARTMENT AND UNIVERSITY OF THE STATE OF NEW YORK.

Adult Learning Services Council. *Adult Learning Services in New York State* (Albany: Allied Printing Trades Council, 1995)

Barbara Shay

contract law. Most of the North American colonies adopted the English legal system under which contract law, providing remedies in cases of unfulfilled promises between two or more individuals acting of their own free will, developed as "common law." This body of law arose from the successive decisions of judges. Through the 1890s legal precedents in the courts of different states varied enormously, with provisions of one state's contract law generally invalid in other states. But rapid US urbanization and industrialization during the 19th century created the need for more uniform legal remedies, and the New York State Court of Appeals—because of the eminence of its judges and the importance of the state as a center of commerce, finance, and immigration—helped to shape contract law throughout the nation.

From its establishment in 1846, the Court of Appeals worked to bring contract law closer to the changing realities of everyday life. New York was the first state to allow a person who was not a party to a contract but a potential beneficiary to bring suit to enforce the contract. In 1859 in *Lawrence v Fox* the court ruled that a creditor could recover a debtor's loan from a third party who had agreed to repay the loan. That case remains the foundation of modern third party beneficiary law. Following the 1878 founding of the American Bar Association (ABA), New York State's legislature was the nation's first to respond to the ABA call for a national commission to work for uniformity of common laws. After six more states responded positively, the first meeting of the Conference of State Boards of Commissioners on Promoting Uniformity of Law (from 1893, participants would become simply Commissioners on Uniform State Laws) took place in Saratoga Springs in 1892; contract law was one of the first issues discussed.

In 1923 Charles Evans Hughes (1862–1948), a future chief justice of the US Supreme Court, Elihu Root (1845–1937), former secretary of state, and other legal practitioners, judges, and law professors from across the nation incorporated the Philadelphia-based American Law Institute. Its purpose was to mold the different bodies of state case law into a single schedule of readily accessible rules. An early leader of the American Law Institute included New York State Court of Appeal judge Benjamin Cardozo (1870–1938). In 1917 Judge Cardozo wrote two important Court of Appeal opinions addressing the intent of contracting parties. In the first, *De Cicco v Schweitzer,* the court recognized the importance of "reliance"—essentially, trust—as a basis for contract enforcement, and in the second, *Wood v Lucy, Lady Duff Gordon,* the court decided that no contracting party can intend an unjust result and that a contract implies a reasonable-effort obligation to be fair or profitable to both contracting parties. Near the end of his career, Cardozo also participated in the American Law Institute's publication of *Restatement of Contracts* (1932), an explanation of various US common-law contracts, which furthered national uniformity of contract law.

At the end of World War II, the Commissioners on Uniform State Laws and the American Law Institute collaborated on the development of the Uniform Commercial Code (UCC) to regulate contracts dealing with commercial matters throughout the United States. A final draft of the UCC, prepared in 1952, met criticism from the Albany-headquartered New York State Law Revision Commission (created by the state's legislature in 1934), and the code was revised in 1958. In 1962 New York State adopted the UCC, which became effective in 1964.

A 1971 decision of the New York State Court of Appeals, *Austin Instrument Inc v Loral Corp,* is often cited as a case that modified the freewill doctrine of classical contract law and expanded the meaning of duress to include economic pressure. In this case a contractor recovered payments made under duress to a subcontractor who had refused to deliver specialized parts without a substantial increase in their price. During its first 100 years of participation in the Conference of State Boards of Commissioners on Promoting Uniformity of Law, New York has appointed 28 Commissioners on Uniform State Laws. Since 1892 it has adopted almost 70 of the 200 uniform laws approved by the commission.

Farnsworth, E. Allan. *Contracts,* 3d ed. (Aspen, Colo: Aspen Law & Business, 1999)

Maria Kiriakova

Cook, Maria (*b* Mendham, NJ, 2 Feb 1779; *d* Geneva, Ontario Co, 21 Dec 1835). Itinerant preacher. In 1811 at the annual meeting of the Western Association of Universalists in Bainbridge (Chenango Co), she was given an informal letter of fellowship as a "preacher of the Gospel." She thereafter preached in Central New York and stayed for several months at a Shaker community, possibly in Watervliet (Albany Co). While living at Pierstown (Otsego Co) around 1812, Cook was arrested on a dubious charge of vagrancy, and although jailed for several weeks she refused to acknowledge the authority of the local magistrate. She then moved to Geneva where several members of her family lived. In the 1820s Cook was reportedly interested in communal societies and resumed preaching shortly before her death. She was one of the first American women to be recognized as a preacher by a major denomination.

Semowich, Charles. "The Life and Ministry of Miss Maria Cook," *New York Folklore* 5 (1979): 146–49

Christopher Densmore

Cooke, Terence (*b* New York City, 1 Mar 1921; *d* New York City, 6 Oct 1983). Cardinal and archbishop. The son of Michael Cooke and Margaret Gannon Cooke, Terence Cooke was educated at St. Benedict's school and Cathedral College in New York City, and St. Joseph's Seminary in Yonkers. He was ordained a priest of the Archdiocese of New York on 1 Dec 1945. After serving in several parishes and the Youth Division of Catholic Charities, he became procurator, or chief financial officer, of St. Joseph's Seminary in 1954. He was named secretary to Francis Cardinal Spellman in 1957 and thereafter rose quickly in the local hierarchy, becoming chancellor (1961), vicar general, and auxiliary bishop (1965). Following Spellman's death he was appointed the seventh archbishop of New York on 8 Mar 1968 and military vicar for the armed forces on 4 Apr 1968. He was made a cardinal on 28 Apr 1969 by Pope Paul VI. Cooke presided over one of the major American archdioceses during a turbulent period in both church and state in the wake of Vatican Council II (1962–65), the Civil Rights Movement, and the Vietnam War. His administration was marked by careful financial management, a commitment to Catholic education, especially in the inner city, and preservation of the extensive network of Catholic social service institutions. In an era of increasing polarization in the American Catholic Church, Cooke preferred conciliation to confrontation. "He allows many flowers to grow," said one New York State priest in 1975, "even though he may not like them all." He died after a long battle with cancer.

Groeschel, Benedict J., and Terrence L. Weber. *Thy Will Be Done: A Spiritual Portrait of Terence Cardinal Cooke* (New York: Alba House, 1990)

Thomas J. Shelley

Cooper, James Fenimore (*b* Burlington, NJ, 15 Sept 1789; *d* Cooperstown, Otsego Co, 14 Sept 1851). Writer. The youngest surviving child of Quaker parents, Cooper grew up in Cooperstown, a post–Revolutionary War settlement founded by his father, William Cooper. Educated in Cooperstown and Albany, he matriculated at Yale in 1803 but was academically dismissed in 1805. To prepare for a naval career, in 1806 Cooper signed on as a sailor-before-the-mast traveling to England and Spain. In 1808 he enlisted in the navy and served on several vessels in New York State. Stationed at Lake Ontario, he worked to apprehend smugglers during the congressionally imposed trade embargo and later served as a recruitment officer in Manhattan. After his father's death in 1809 he took leave from the navy, formally resigning in 1811. The same year he married Susan Augusta DeLancey, daughter of a prominent New York State family, and moved to New Rochelle (Westchester Co). In 1813 the Coopers relocated to a farm on the western shore of Otsego Lake, near his childhood home. Financial difficulties fueled by a national depression, however, prompted Cooper to return to Westchester Co and build a farmhouse on DeLancey land in Scarsdale.

Reportedly in response to a challenge from his wife, Cooper wrote his first novel, *Precaution,* an imitation of popular English comedies of manners, in 1820. The publicity it garnered turned his attention to writing as a possible career. His second book, *The Spy* (1821), often considered the first American historical novel, was an instant international success. Set in Westchester Co during the Revolutionary War, the book draws on American history and the grandeur of New York's natural environment, two themes that would become hallmarks of Cooper's most celebrated works. Following that success, Cooper moved to New York City to be closer to the publishing market. In 1822 he founded the Bread and Cheese Club, a loose social circle including many prominent New York artists, entrepreneurs, military officers, and politicians. His next novel, *The Pioneers* (1823), sold 3,500 copies the day of its release, cementing Cooper's reputation as the preeminent American novelist of the day. A thinly disguised portrait of William Cooper's founding of Cooperstown, it is the first of the celebrated Leatherstocking series. Cooper tried to build on this success with his first sea novel, *The Pilot* (1824), and then another historical novel, *Lionel Lincoln* (1825), the first of a planned but later abandoned 13-novel sequence on the American Revolution. Cooper continued to write at a rapid pace, producing a book a year from 1825 to 1835. For the benefit of his children's education, he sailed to Europe in 1826 and traveled widely for the next seven years. On his return to America in 1833, he traveled to Philadelphia, Baltimore, and Washington before returning to Cooperstown in May 1836.

In total Cooper published 35 novels. A noteworthy travel writer, historian, and social critic, he also produced 13 volumes of nonfiction, in-

Cooper's Cave in Glens Falls, described in *The Last of the Mohicans.*

cluding the first history of the US Navy (1839). For all his commercial success as a novelist, Cooper was never able to free himself from financial difficulties. Continually involved in costly litigation and bad speculations, he subsisted at times barely ahead of his creditors. His reputation began to suffer from a lawsuit he brought against the citizens of Cooperstown in 1837 to stop them from using his family's land as a picnic ground. In 1838 Cooper wrote *The American Democrat* as a sustained defense of his position that social distinction was still possible in a democratic society, but he was reviled as an elitist after its publication. His *Homeward Bound* (1838) and *Home As Found* (1838), novels of the New York City elite, were attacked as antidemocratic; Cooper responded by suing reviewers for libel. The Littlepage novels, tracing a New York family for 100 years from the purchase of a land tract in the Mohawk Valley during the French and Indian War to the antirent riots of the 1840s, comprising *Satanstoe* (1845), *The Chainbearer* (1845), and *The Redskins* (1846), were disparaged as paeans for landholders' rights, further eroding his reputation. Cooper spent the late 1840s struggling to recoup losses from bad land investments. In 1849 he began to oversee the production of a standard edition of his works but abandoned the plan after 11 volumes. Cooper died while trying to complete a history of the New York City area, *The Towns of Manhattan.*

His most famous novels are the Leatherstocking Tales: *The Pioneers, The Last of the Mohicans* (1826), *The Prairie* (1827), *The Pathfinder* (1840), and *The Deerslayer* (1841). With the exception of *The Prairie,* the novels all deal with the complex colonial and Revolutionary histories of New York Colony, using the Otsego region as their central setting. With its warnings about the overconsumption of natural resources, the Leatherstocking series comprises some of the earliest American environmentalist fiction. The novels lovingly describe the beauties of New York State and contributed, along with the Hudson River school of painting, to the conception of the state as the most picturesque region in America.

See also AMERICAN INDIANS IN LITERATURE: NONINDIGENOUS AUTHORS.

Grossman, James. *James Fenimore Cooper: A Biographical and Critical Study* (1949; repr Stanford, Calif: Stanford Univ Press, 1967)

Long, Robert Emmet. *James Fenimore Cooper* (New York: Continuum, 1990)

Duncan Faherty

Cooper, Susan (Augusta) Fenimore (*b* Mamaroneck, Westchester Co, 17 Apr 1813; *d* Cooperstown, Otsego Co, 31 Dec 1894). Author. A daughter of James Fenimore Cooper and Susan De Lancey Cooper, she spent some of her childhood in Europe with her parents before she settled in Cooperstown in 1836. Cooper's first publication was a novel, *Elinor Wyllys; Or, The Young Folk at Longbridge* (1845). Better known is *Rural Hours* (1850; republished 1998), a version of her journal in which she argued for a balance between human progress and obligations to nature, while describing the seasons in Cooperstown. In *Mount Vernon: A Letter to the Children of America* (1859), she requested that children give their coins to preserve George Washington's home. Cooper edited three books of nature writing (1852–54) and wrote for almanacs and reference works. She also contributed to several journals, including *St. Nicholas,* which published her children's stories. "Small Family Memories," written in 1883, appeared in the first volume of *Correspondence of James Fenimore Cooper* (1922). Her writing conveys both her deep moral convictions and a sense of the beauty and serenity of the simple life in rural New York State in the mid–19th century.

Goodier, Susan. "Susan Fenimore Cooper." In *American Women Prose Writers: 1820–1870,* ed. Amy E. Hudock and Katharine Rodier (Detroit: Gale Publishing, 2001)

Johnson, Rochelle L., and Daniel Patterson, eds. *Susan Fenimore Cooper: New Essays on Rural Hours and Other Works* (Athens: Univ of Georgia Press, 2001)

Susan Goodier

Cooper, William (*b* Smithfield [now Somerton, Pa], 2 Dec 1754; *d* Albany, 22 Dec 1809). Land speculator and politician. Born into a poor family, Cooper was raised on a farm and at 19 left for New Jersey, where he married a wealthy Quaker's daughter, Elizabeth Fenimore. He became a wheelwright and in 1778 settled in Wellingborough [now Willingboro, NJ], where he commercially developed the hamlet he nicknamed Cooperstown. He moved to Burlington City, NJ, by 1782 and alienated Quaker philosophy by pursuing business, owning slaves, and selling liquor. Although he fathered 12 children, including novelist James Fenimore Cooper, he spent little time rearing them since he traveled to pursue land speculation. In 1785 he ventured to Otsego Lake to investigate 29,350 acres (11,878 ha). A year later, through suspicious means, Cooper acquired the sought after Otsego Patent. Although he had a partner, Andrew Craig, he saw this as a personal venture and hoped to create an ideal commercial village. Cooper sold land cheaply, was lenient with his terms, held mortgages, and marketed land to New Englanders. He fostered industry and potash production, and his community, though officially named Otsego Village, was referred to as Cooperstown. In 1790 his family joined him in Otsego and moved into his Manor House. They moved in 1799 into his new mansion, Otsego Hall. Cooper became county court judge (1791–99) and as a Federalist served two terms in Congress (1795–97, 1799–1801). He supported Jay's Treaty, partially out of friendship with John Jay, and the 1798 Alien and Sedition Acts. Cooper retired from politics in 1801. He died of natural causes after leaving a political meeting at Lewis's Tavern in Albany. (He was not murdered, as is widely believed.) In 1812 Otsego Village was reincorporated as Cooperstown (Otsego Co). His son James modeled the character Judge Marmaduke Temple in *The Pioneers* (1823) after his father. Cooper's heirs mismanaged his estate and lost his fortune by 1835.

Taylor, Alan. *William Cooper's Town: Power and Persuasion on the Frontier of the Early American Republic* (New York: Knopf, 1995)

Tricia A. Barbagallo

cooperative extension. Extension service in New York State began in Broome Co in 1911. Subsequently the federal Smith-Lever Act of 1914 made federal funds available for informal education in agriculture and home economics for people not attending college. Under the act the US Department of Agriculture and land grant universities provide educational services cooperatively through county-based associations. By 1918 every rural county in the state except Putnam and Hamilton were served. The land grant institution Cornell University has responsibility for program leadership and management. Initially the county-based educational specialists were called Farm Bureau, Home Bureau, and 4-H Club agents. Farm Bureau agents served men engaged in raising, marketing, or processing farm products; Home Bureau concentrated on homemaking and consumer education for women; and 4-H agents served rural youth with 4-H clubs.

In 1956 the County Extension Service Association replaced Farm and Home Bureaus, reflecting the legal separation of the Farm Bureau and cooperative extension in 1953 and the social obsolescence of gender-based representatives. Statewide in scope since 1975, cooperative extension addresses any topic that subject specialists based in Cornell's College of Agriculture and

Life Sciences or College of Human Ecology endorse. The programs offered by county associations and within New York City reflect local interests and financial support and include economic development, environmental management, and health and nutrition. Funding is approximately 14% federal, 30% state, and 30% local, the remainder being from grants, contracts, and other sources. In 2002 state funding was $35 million. New York State's county extension associations and regional groups employed 440 educational specialists and 807 support personnel in 2002. Cooperative extension is coordinated at the state level by Cornell's extension specialists, with guidance from a director of extension. County and New York City extension associations provide local coordination.

Smith, Ruby Green. *The People's Colleges: A History of the New York State Extension Service in Cornell University and the State, 1876–1948* (Ithaca: Cornell Univ Press, 1949)

Gould Colman

Cooperstown. Village (pop 2,032) in central Otsego Co. The village occupies the south shore of Otsego Lake at the source of the Susquehanna River. It lies within a 29,350-acre (11,878 ha) tract acquired in 1786 by William Cooper of Burlington, NJ. Cooper moved to the tract in 1787 and brought his family—including his son James, the future novelist—to his settlement in 1790. When Otsego Co was formed in 1791, Cooperstown became the county seat. The village was incorporated as the Village of Otsego in 1807 and reincorporated as Cooperstown in 1812. The village grew steadily in its early years. It had a number of small industries and a large publishing firm, H. and E. Phinney, which produced some 68,000 books and 200,000 almanacs. The site of New York State's first county fair, in 1817, Cooperstown was primarily a marketing center for the region's major agricultural industries, hop growing and dairy farming.

The village gradually became, to use James Fenimore Cooper's phrase, "a place of resort." The beauty of the lake and rural countryside and the altitude (1,194 ft/363.9 m above sea level) were components of cool and peaceful summers that attracted seasonal visitors, stimulated the construction of several large hotels, and brought several prominent families to Cooperstown and its environs. Edward Clark, creator of the Singer Sewing Machine Co, established a home in the village in 1856, thus initiating a profound and enduring relationship between the Clark family and the community. Cooperstown's social and economic character, including its charming isolation, was determined by its distance from major transportation routes. Not until 1869 was it served by a railroad and not until 1901 by an electric trolley line. In the opening decades of the 20th century, automobiles, buses, and trucks created a new and enduring system, but the village remained distant from major highways.

Cooperstown remained an agricultural marketing center, home to warehouses and a variety of food and service stores. It also had a cheese factory until 1926 and a major publisher, the Arthur H. Crist Co (1908–23), which published a variety of books and several magazines, including *American Motherhood, Table Talk,* and *Today's Housewife.* Its building eventually housed the village's last industry, the Cooperstown Manufacturing Co (1947–58), which employed as many as 60 garment workers.

At the beginning of the 21st century the village, maintained by zoning laws initiated in 1940, is still a place of salubrious resort. The Otesaga Hotel, built in 1909 by Edward S. Clark and his brother Stephen C. Clark, is a nationally known convention center. Cooperstown is also a retirement community. Most significant, however, is its role as a center of rural medicine. The Mary Imogene Bassett Hospital was built in 1918 by Edward S. Clark; several major additions, including a four-story outpatient clinic building, now make up a complex that, in 2000, admitted 7,947 patients, hosted 452,117 outpatient visits, and housed an internationally recognized research institute, all served by a staff of 2,047 with a payroll, in 2000, of $81,644,000. A pioneer in managed care, Bassett Hospital is now the central institution of Bassett Healthcare, a network of 20 hospitals and outpatient centers that serve a 10-county region.

Cooperstown is best known as the place where Abner Doubleday allegedly invented baseball in 1839. The village acquired the supposed site of the event in 1923, named it Doubleday Field, and in the 1930s, with the help of federal agencies, erected a small stadium on the site. Stephen C. Clark supported that project and espoused the idea of the National Baseball Museum and Hall of Fame, which were created in Cooperstown in 1935 and moved into a new building, provided by Clark, in 1938. The Fenimore Art Museum and the Farmers' Museum, which lie just outside the village, and the Baseball Hall of Fame have contributed to making Cooperstown the region's primary tourist destination.

Cooperstown's population reached its peak of 2,909 in 1930 and has declined steadily; in the early 21st century the population equals that of 1890. Parking problems, summer congestion, and the lure of malls have changed Cooperstown's Main St from a service street to a center for baseball memorabilia and restaurants. Many families now prefer to live in the village's rural environs; within the village, the number of houses used primarily as tourist accommodations has increased, and numerous houses are occupied by summer-only residents.

See also COOPER, JAMES FENIMORE; FOLKLORE AND FOLKLIFE STUDY.

Wendell Tripp

Cooper Union for the Advancement of Science and Art. Private professional college founded in 1859 by industrialist Peter Cooper on Cooper Square in the Lower East Side in Manhattan. Its building, designed by architect Frederick Peterson, is one of the oldest steel-framed buildings in the United States. It is the only private, full-scholarship college in the country dedicated exclusively to preparing students for art, architecture, and engineering professions. The school opened with free night classes in the applied sciences and architectural drawing for working class men and women, as well as day sessions in the Female School of Design for training in occupations such as photography, telegraphy, and shorthand. It awarded its first engineering degrees in 1886. Cooper also intended the school to be a civic forum. Many political and other leaders have spoken at the Great Hall, one of the oldest auditoriums in New York City; they include presidential candidate Abraham Lincoln in 1860, socialist Eugene Debs in 1894, and Pres Bill Clinton in 1993. Meetings at Cooper Union led to the founding of the American Red Cross and the NAACP. In 2001 the institution enrolled 870 undergraduate students, of which one-third were women.

Cooper Union for the Advancement of Science and Art, http://www.cooper.edu/

Krasnick, Phyllis D. "Peter Cooper and the Cooper Union for the Advancement of Science and Art" (PhD Diss, New York Univ, 1985)

Carl A. Westerdahl and Susan S. Clarke

Coote, Richard [Earl of Bellomont] (*b* Ireland, 1636; *d* New York, 5 Mar 1701). Colonial governor general. The eldest son of an Irish peer, he aligned himself with William of Orange during England's Glorious Revolution (1688–89). He was rewarded with the earldom of Bellomont after William was proclaimed king in 1689. Bellomont was appointed governor general of New York, Massachusetts, and New Hampshire, as well as captain general of the Connecticut, Rhode Island and Jersey Militias, on 18 June 1697. This broad prerogative was London's attempt to unite the northern provinces against New France. Bellomont's commission instructed him to enforce British navigation laws, which New York Colony had flouted for years by harboring foreign pirates. Before he left England, Bellomont formed a private company, outfitted a 30-gun frigate, and placed it under the command of William Kidd for the purpose of apprehending pirates. After turning to piracy himself, Kidd eventually returned to New York to explain his actions, but Bellomont had him arrested and sent to England where he was tried and hanged. New York tories falsely accused the governor general of conspiracy in Kidd's crime.

Bellomont arrived in New York on 2 Apr 1698 promising to mitigate the political and religious factionalism that had paralyzed the province since Jacob Leisler's rebellion 10 years earlier. His open contempt for his predecessor, Benjamin Fletcher, however, only exacerbated the situation. It enraged the anti-Leislerian, tory aristocrats favored by Fletcher, delighted the Leislerian Whigs, and perpetuated that feud. Bellomont purged Fletcher's friends from the governor's council and in 1699 convinced the assembly to revoke several of his large land grants to prominent tories in the Mohawk and Hudson River valleys. The governor general then assured the Mohawk that the confiscated land was once again theirs, even though the assembly had legislated that title reverted to the Crown. His duplicity stemmed from the understanding that friendly relations with the Iroquois were vital to the English cause in North America. Bellomont opposed the presence of French Jesuits in Iroquoia and encouraged the assembly to finance an English fort and trading post near Onondaga. Throughout his administration he desperately tried to keep the Iroquois from entering into peace negotiations with the French, but they sought a treaty with New France in 1701. His administration epitomized the difficulties royal governors faced in dealing with factions in New York Colony.

DePeyster, Frederic. *The Life and Administration of Richard, Earl of Bellomont* (New York: New-York Historical Society, 1879)

Trelease, Allen W. *Indian Affairs in Colonial New York: The 17th Century* (Ithaca: Cornell Univ Press, 1960)

Daniel A. Piazza

Copake. Town (pop 3,278) in SE Columbia Co. Settled under the Livingston family in 1685, Copake was linked to the river settlements by a road shown on the earliest (?1712) map. Its Dutch settlers were joined by Germans and New England migrants, and the town was formed in 1824 from Taghkanic. Rye, buckwheat, and peas were the chief crops until the Harlem Railroad (1852) made it a dairying town. Bash Bish Falls attracted tourists and boarders after the Civil War, and Copake Lake was developed as a resort beginning in 1908. Copake Iron Works (1845–1903) was an important industry at Copake Falls and provided work for Irish immigrants. By 1940 Copake was the county's second-ranking milk-producing town. In 1948 it became one of the first US localities served by bulk tanks, a technological change that led to a decrease in the number of farms. The population jumped 35% in the 1960s. It is the site of Camphill Village USA (1961), a facility for people with mental disorders, and Taconic State Park (1927).

Copeland, Royal S(amuel) (*b* Dexter, Mich, 7 Nov 1868; *d* Washington, DC, 17 June 1938). Physician and US senator. Born on a farm outside of Dexter, Copeland attended the Michigan State Normal School in Ypsilanti in 1886. He enrolled in the Homeopathic Medical College of the University of Michigan at Ann Arbor in 1887 and graduated in 1889. Copeland moved his family to New York City in 1908 to take a position as dean of the Flower Hospital Medical College. He also was a teacher and medical writer specializing in ophthalmology. A Republican mayor of Ann Arbor, Mich, Copeland became a Democrat in New York City, and in 1918 Mayor John F. Hylan appointed him the city's commissioner of public health. Copeland remained in that position until 1923 and is credited with decreasing infant mortality and increasing the consumption of milk in the city. In 1922 Alfred E. Smith and William Randolph Hearst secured for Copeland the state Democratic nomination for US senator. Appealing to more conservative voters outside of New York City, Copeland won and was reelected in 1928 and 1934. In office he opposed much of Pres Franklin D. Roosevelt's New Deal, concerned about the expansion of federal government power at the expense of state and local governments. Copeland was the Tammany candidate for mayor of New York City in 1937 but lost to Fiorello La Guardia, the Roosevelt administration's candidate. Copeland died shortly after successfully shepherding the Copeland-Lea Food, Drug, and Cosmetic Act of 1938 through the US Congress.

Potter, Raymond Joseph. "Royal Samuel Copeland, 1868–1938: A Physician in Politics" (PhD diss, Western Reserve Univ, 1967)

John David Rausch Jr

Copenhagen. Village (pop 865) in Denmark (Lewis Co). Originally Munger's Mills, it received its name in 1807 to honor the Danish city after its bombardment by a British fleet. In 1966 Mayor Urban Hansen of Copenhagen, Denmark, visited during a celebration linking the sister communities. Early industries included flour and lumber mills, tanneries, a rope factory, and textile mill, all powered by the Deer River. The village incorporated in 1869. The Copenhagen Band (1843) provided music at village events for a century. Today Copenhagen provides services to surrounding dairy farms and is the hub of a central school district.

Arthur Einhorn

Copiague [KOH-PEG]. Locality (pop 21,922) in Babylon (Suffolk Co). Located on the Great South Bay, it acquired a post office in 1903. Brinckerhoff Manor, a real estate development, was taken over in 1906 by John Campagnoli; he had attended the University of Bologna with Guglielmo Marconi and renamed the tract Marconiville. It attracted many Italian American residents. In the 1930s an attempt was made to create an American Venice with canals between building lots. Copiague's greatest population growth took place just after World War II; its 1940 population of 1,584 grew to 14,081 by 1960. It is the site of Bethel African Methodist Episcopal Church, founded in 1839.

Copland, Aaron (*b* Brooklyn, 14 Nov 1900; *d* New York City, 12 Dec 1990). Copland was raised in Brooklyn and graduated from Boys' High School before moving to Paris in 1920. He returned to New York City in 1924. As a fledgling modernist composer, he consciously pursued a sassy and optimistic American voice. His interest in jazz was especially manifest in *Music for the Theatre* (1925) and in the *Piano Concerto* (1926). The *Piano Variations* (1930)—brash, striving, streamlined "skyscraper" music—was a distinguished landmark in the evolution of the Copland style, with its characteristic evocation of big-city vigor and anomie. A second characteristic Copland mode, evoking the halcyon, preurban "West" of *Appalachian Spring* (1944), may be understood as an imagined antidote to urban chaos and decay. With Roger Sessions, Copland sponsored an important New York City new music series, the Copland-Sessions Concerts (1928–31). In the course of the 1930s, influenced by his friend Harold Clurman, he became a socially conscious leftist. His output now included the workers' song "Into the Streets May First" (which he later disowned as "the silliest thing I did") and a highly accessible children's opera, *The Second Hurricane* (1938). His appropriation of folksong in works such as *Billy the Kid* (1938) and *Rodeo* (1942) was, again, stimulated by a democratizing impulse. In wartime Copland's political outlook took the form of wholesome and declamatory patriotism, as in *A Lincoln Portrait* (1942) and *Fanfare for the Common Man* (1942).

Copland wrote eloquently of the challenge of mediating between democracy and art. His lectures for laypersons at the New School for Social Research between 1927 and 1937 generated the books *What to Listen for in Music* (1939) and *Our New Music* (1941). Copland's sense of utility and common touch also led him to score 10 films, beginning with *The City,* created for the 1939 New York World's Fair. Copland's final film score, for *Something Wild,* yielded *Music for a Great City* (1964), a portrait of New York City. A milder New York vignette is *Quiet City* (1939), drawn from incidental music to an Irwin Shaw play. In later years Copland became a well-known music educator on television and was increasingly active as a conductor. He led the New York Philharmonic 27 times.

Pollack, Howard. *Aaron Copland: The Life and Work of an Uncommon Man* (New York: Henry Holt, 1999)

Joseph Horowitz

Coram. Locality (pop 34,923) in Brookhaven (Suffolk Co). In 1780 Maj Benjamin Tallmadge burned 300 tons (270 MT) of hay stored in Coram that was to have fed British horses. Located at the junction of Brookhaven's main north-south and east-west routes, Coram was the seat of town government from 1790 to 1884 and acquired a post office in 1794. It was the site of the Sanitarium for Consumptives for children from 1905 to the late 1930s. In 1927 developers platted Gordon Heights, southeast of Coram, and sold building lots to African Americans from New York City. After 1960 the hamlet's population of 2,942 began expanding rapidly; by 2000 it was 8% Black, and 9% of its population were Latino. It is the site of the 66-acre (27 ha) Daniel R. Davis Sanctuary of the Nature Conservancy.

Suzanne Johnson

Corbin [née Cochran], Margaret (*b* Cumberland Co [now Franklin Co], Pa, 12 Nov 1751; *d* ?Highland Falls, Orange Co, ?1800). Soldier. One of several women associated with the legend of Molly Pitcher, Corbin may have been the first woman to be wounded on the battlefield fighting for American independence. She was orphaned at age 5 and raised by relatives, and she married John Corbin in 1772. When her husband enlisted to fight with the Continental forces, she accompanied him, probably as a nurse, cook, or washwoman for the troops. On 16 Nov 1776, after her husband was mortally wounded at Fort Washington in Upper Manhattan, she took over loading and firing his cannon until she herself was wounded by British fire. Surviving but losing the use of her arm, she became, on 6 July 1779, the first woman awarded a pension by Congress for her military service and disability. The following year she was part of the Invalid Regiment garrisoned at West Point (Orange Co). There is some uncertainty whether she was the person often referred to as "Captain Molly," who lived in that area for 20 years and earned a reputation as an eccentric woman who dressed in an artillery jacket and insisted on being saluted as an officer. In 1926 the Daughters of the American Revolution had the remains of "Captain Molly" exhumed and reinterred at West Point with full military honors.

Teipe, Emily J. "Will the Real Molly Pitcher Please Stand Up?" *Prologue: The Journal of the National Archives* 31 (1999): 118–26

Alison Duncan Hirsch

Corcraft. See PRISON INDUSTRY AND LABOR.

Corfu. Village (pop 795) in Pembroke (Genesee Co). Settled in 1807 as Long's Corners, the hamlet was on the main line of the New York Central Railroad (1852), and ensuing growth resulted in its 1868 incorporation. The cultivation of flowers, at first shipped by rail to wholesale markets throughout the United States, has been a leading industry. From 1883 to 1900, 26 greenhouses were built. Don Scott Florists (1893) is the oldest business in the village operated continuously by one family. The Colonial Days celebration is held annually in June.

Susan L. Conklin

Cori, Carl (Ferdinand) (*b* Prague, 5 Dec 1896; *d* Cambridge, Mass, 20 Oct 1984) and **Cori** [née

Radnitz], **Gerty (Theresa)** (*b* Prague, 15 Aug 1896; *d* St. Louis, 26 Oct 1957). Biochemists. Carl Cori came from a background of university professors on both sides of his family, and he met Gerty Radnitz at the German University of Prague. In the spring of 1920 they both graduated with medical degrees, and by summer they were married. In early 1922 Carl immigrated to the United States and joined the staff of the State Institute for the Study of Malignant Diseases (now Roswell Park Cancer Institute) in Buffalo as a biochemist. Gerty joined him half a year later as an assistant pathologist and later became an assistant biochemist. From 1922 to 1931 their scientific collaboration resulted in 91 publications on cancer research and the beginnings of their intense research on carbohydrate metabolism. In 1932 the Coris joined the staff at Washington University School of Medicine in St. Louis. In 1947 the Nobel Prize in physiology or medicine was awarded jointly to the Coris for their discovery of the course of the catalytic conversion of glycogen. Gerty Cori became the third woman, after Marie Curie and Irene Joliot Curie, and the first American woman to receive the Nobel Prize.

Edwin A. Mirand

Corinth [COR-INTH or CRINTH]. Town (pop 5,985) and village (pop 2,474) in N Saratoga Co. The town's east boundary is the Hudson River, and half of its area is contained in the Adirondack Park. First settlement was possibly in 1775 in the southeast corner. The town was set off from Hadley in 1818. Forest products overshadowed farming in early years. The village, originally called Jessup's Landing, incorporated under its present name in 1886. The Adirondack Railroad (built 1863–65) encouraged development of the Hudson River Pulp and Paper Co (1869), among the first mills producing paper from wood pulp. In 1898 it became part of International Paper, which sustained the community for over a century, closing in 2002. The village's other large employer was a Cluett Peabody and Co shirt factory (1899–1975). Land use is dominated by logging and vacation homes.

Field Horne

corn. From neolithic times American Indian women living on the land that is now New York State grew corn (Indian corn, or maize) and beans in small fields prepared by girdling and burning the trees, the ash dressing the soil. Dried kernels from the previous year's harvest were planted in squares. As the plants grew, soil was mounded up around the stalks. Corn quickly exhausts the soil, so native fields were regularly abandoned and new fields opened. European settlers learned the cultivation of corn indigenous to the Americas from native peoples of the northeast, and from the early 1600s, New York Colony farmers grew maize as their primary domestic grain crop. Corn, ground for meal for human consumption or used for fattening stock, was the staple crop of frontier farmers who continued traditional cultivation in squares interplanted with squash. Maize had several advantages over Old World grains; it grew easily in newly opened fields, rendered high yields, resisted disease and infestation, and could be left standing in the field long after maturity, allowing farmers to bring in other crops liable to spoil if not harvested at peak ripeness. Husking could wait until lulls in farmwork in late fall and early winter and was often done in communal bees.

Corn hybridizes easily, and by the early 1800s many varieties were known, with 8-row types predominating, although 12-row varieties were also reported. Kernels could be yellow, white, red, blue, or mixed. Flint and dent corns, used for animal feed and flour, were commonly grown throughout the region. Corn requires very dry storage conditions and from colonial days was stored in cribs separate from other grains. Usually small frame buildings, cribs had slatted sides that sometimes sloped inward toward a piered foundation.

With the rapid increase in wheat flour production in Western New York during the second quarter of the 19th century, cornmeal became less important. In 1855 New York State farmers produced 19.2 million bushels (676,589,000 l) of corn, with Onondaga and Cayuga Cos as the leading corn producers. Every county in the state grew corn, including New York Co, with 1,180 bushels (41,582 l). In the last quarter of the century, the development of silage, associated with dairy farming, returned corn culture to prominence. Silage, or fodder corn, is cut green, coarsely chopped, and stored in anaerobic conditions. Acres of standing corn were harvested using cutters powered by steam—traction engines perfected in the late 1800s.

Also late in the 19th century, the introduction of vertical wooden silos, replacing earlier stone-lined pits, allowed most farmers to add silage to their winter feed. Wooden silos were often built inside existing dairy barns. By the early 20th century, exterior octagonal and cylindrical types developed. The gambrel-roofed dairy barn flanked by cylindrical silos capped by metallic domed roofs became the iconic dairy farm of the first half of the 20th century. From the mid–20th century, wood stave silos were superseded by cylinders of ceramic block, concrete block, or riveted sheet metal in dairy farming areas. By the beginning of the 21st century, while vertical silos remained part of the landscape, many dairy farmers had begun to use either concrete-lined pits, very like early stone-lined silage pits, or enormous cylindrical plastic storage bags. The state's peak corn silage harvest was 77 million bushels (2,700 million l) in 1981. In 2000 New York State dairy farmers cut 500,000 acres (202,000 ha) to produce 7 million tons (6.4 million MT) of silage corn; an additional 480,000 acres (194,000 ha) of corn were grown to produce 47 million bushels (1,700 million l) of grain. Sweet corn for human consumption is only a small part of the state's corn production. In 2001, 33,400 harvested acres (13,520 ha) produced 3.8 million pounds (1.7 million kg) of sweet corn for the fresh market; another 29,200 acres (11,820 ha) produced 160,000 tons (145,150 MT) for processing.

Schlebecker, John T. *Whereby We Thrive: A History of American Farming, 1607–1972* (Ames: Iowa State Univ Press, 1975)

Jessie Ravage

Cornbury, Lord. See HYDE, EDWARD [VISCOUNT CORNBURY].

Cornell, Alonzo B(arton) (*b* Ithaca, 22 Jan 1832; *d* Ithaca, 15 Oct 1904). Governor. As a young man, Cornell worked in a variety of banking and telegraph management jobs before becoming director (1868–69) and vice president (1871–76) of the Western Union Telegraph Co, which was founded by his father, Ezra Cornell. A supporter of Roscoe Conkling, Alonzo Cornell received the plum patronage position of surveyor of customs for the Port of New York (1869–73), also serving as chairman of the Republican state central committee (1870–78). In 1873 he was elected to the state assembly, to which he was unanimously chosen Speaker. Pres Ulysses S. Grant, just before leaving office, appointed him to the lucrative position of naval officer in the New York Customs House. Pres Rutherford B. Hayes pressured him to resign in his attempt to wrest control of New York patronage from Conkling's forces, but Cornell refused and was removed in 1879. Conkling promptly engineered Cornell's nomination in the New York State gubernatorial race, which Cornell won easily. As governor (1880–83), he surprised his critics by modernizing state finances, making competent appointments, and liberally using the veto to combat what he viewed as extravagant legislation. By remaining neutral in the patronage fight between Conkling and James A. Garfield in 1881, Cornell contributed to Conkling's defeat in the legislature and was himself defeated for renomination as governor. He then wrote a biography of his father (1884), moved to New York City, and remained associated with Western Union.

Chadbourne, Paul A. *The Public Service of the State of New York during the Administration of Alonzo B. Cornell, Governor* (Boston: J. R. Osgood, 1882)

Mohr, James. *The Radical Republicans and Reform in New York during Reconstruction* (Ithaca: Cornell Univ Press, 1973)

Jon Sterngass

Cornell, Ezra (*b* Westchester Landing [now in Bronx Co], 11 Jan 1807; *d* Ithaca, 9 Dec 1874). Philanthropist and university founder. The eldest of 11 children, Cornell moved with his parents in 1819 to a Quaker settlement in DeRuyter (Madison Co), where his father operated a pottery. Ezra received scant schooling but exhibited a practical talent for carpentry and construction. In 1826 he set off to find employment and in 1828 arrived in Ithaca, where he worked as a carpenter, then as a journeyman mechanic. The next year he worked in a plaster mill. In 1831 he married Mary Ann Wood of Dryden (Tompkins Co). They had nine children, one of whom (Alonzo) became state governor. In 1841 Cornell traveled on behalf of the business community hoping to induce industries to resettle in Ithaca. While selling plows in Portland, Maine, in 1843 Cornell was introduced to the infant telegraph industry. He was deeply involved with the construction of telegraph lines, working with Samuel F. B. Morse until 1847; afterward he promoted, built, and managed telegraph lines. He was always financially overextended, often away from home, and, in 1855, quite ill. In 1856 the merger of a number of existing telegraph companies, including that of Cornell, created the Western Union Telegraph Co. Cornell, as a director, was soon a very wealthy man. He then set out to do "the most good" with his fortune. In 1862 he became president of the New York State Agricultural Society and trustee of the proposed New York State Agricultural College for Ovid (Seneca Co). He served two terms in the state assembly (1862–63), and in 1863 he proposed a free public library for the citizens of Tompkins Co, and it opened in 1866. Cornell was a state senator for two terms (1864–67), and he and Andrew Dickson White introduced a bill in the senate in 1865 to use the Morrill Land Grant Act script to establish a university, endowed by Cornell and to be located on his Ithaca farm. Until his death Cornell poured his energy and money into the university.

Cornell, Ezra. Papers. Cornell Univ Library, Ithaca
Dorf, Philip. *The Builder: A Biography of Ezra Cornell* (New York: Macmillan, 1952)

Carol Kammen

Cornell, Joseph (*b* Nyack, Rockland Co, 24 Dec 1903; *d* Queens, 29 Dec 1972). Sculptor and filmmaker. Cornell was raised by upper middle-class parents in Nyack. He attended Phillips Academy in Andover, Mass, from 1917 to 1921 but did not graduate. He moved to New York City in 1921 and took a sales position for the textile firm William Whitman Co, which he held for 10 years. In 1934 he became a designer at the Traphagen Commercial Textile Studio. He began his habitual "voyages" in Manhattan in the 1920s, collecting objects to later incorporate into his artwork of collages and box constructions. In 1929 he moved to a house at 37-08 Utopia Parkway, in Jamaica (Queens Co), where he later set up a studio in the basement. He lived there for the remainder of his life with his mother and brother. A self-taught artist, Cornell's early work shows the influence of surrealist Max Ernst, with whom he became friends. In 1932 he had a one-man exhibition at the Julien Levy Gallery in New York City. He made the first of his signature glass-covered box constructions, *Untitled (Soap Bubble Set)*, in 1936. The artist maintained over 150 subject dossiers, which he drew upon to create assemblages for exhibition. Among his favored themes were childhood, birds, science, art, ballet, theater, and movies. In his shadow box and dossier *Untitled (Penny Arcade Portrait of Lauren Bacall)* (1945–46) Cornell pays tribute to the actress. He made about 20 films, including *Rose Hobart* (1936) and *Nymphlight* (1957), the latter set in Manhattan's Bryant Park. Cornell is one of the most innovative and influential sculptors of the 20th century. Though in his private life largely a recluse, he mingled with the day's leading artists, including Pavel Tchelitchew, Willem de Kooning, Robert Motherwell, and Andy Warhol.

McShine, Kynaston, ed. *Joseph Cornell* (New York: Museum of Modern Art; Munich: Prestel, 1990)

Patricia Siska

Cornell University. Private land grant university in Ithaca. Under the 1862 Morrill Land Grant Act, federal land could be sold to finance the teaching of agricultural and mechanical subjects. In 1865, to initiate the university, Ezra Cornell provided the initial $500,000 to buy federal land script and donated his 300-acre (121 ha) Ithaca farm. Andrew Dickson White, a Yale College graduate who was a professor at the University of Michigan, drew up the plans for the university, melding the requirements of the Morrill act with a broadly conceived liberal arts curriculum. White also arranged for scholarships to be provided for the highest-ranking students in each legislative district. In March 1865 the state senate passed the university charter, by which the school was to be nonsectarian and open to every qualified person. The university opened on 7 Oct 1868 with 425 students.

Facilities for women were at first absent, though a few attended classes. In 1872 the trustees approved a measure encouraging women's enrollment. That fall 16 women registered. Women at Cornell were given equal access with men to all classes and facilities. After 1875 women were housed at Sage College. White served as the first president (1866–85), giving special attention to building a great library and creating America's first four-year architecture program (1871). Cornell offered students the option of selecting a course in agriculture, civil or mechanical engineering, classics, or an optional degree. From 1885 onward enrollment rose steadily. Pres Charles Kendall Adams (1885–92) created a law school (1887) and promoted extension activities, and Pres Jacob Gould Schurman (1892–1920) established the extension program (1894), which expanded the range of students and the type of courses offered. In 1894 the state assumed financial responsibility for the New York State College of Veterinary Medicine and in 1904 for the New York State College of Agriculture. Home economics began in 1900; the Department of Home Economics was established in 1907, growing into the New York State College of Human Ecology in 1969. Schurman also started the Graduate Department and divided the university into separate schools: Academic (Arts), Agriculture, Architecture, Veterinary, Engineering, and Law, which became a graduate program in 1925. The Cornell Medical School was founded in 1898 with programs in Ithaca and New York City; it affiliated with New York Hospital in 1912. During Schurman's presidency, in 1911 women were named to the faculty in the College of Agriculture, where they researched and taught nature study and home economics. In 1921 the American Hotel Association funded a course in hotel management within Home Economics. It became a department in 1922 and the School of Hotel Administration in 1950.

Under Pres Edmund Ezra Day (1937–49) the university supported military education for enrolled students and military personnel during World War II. In 1945 the state chartered the School of Industrial and Labor Relations at Cornell, while the university established the Laboratory of Nuclear Studies. The School of Business and Public Administration began in 1946. The state government created SUNY in 1948, and Cornell's state colleges were included in the system but defined as state-supported (not state-run) contract colleges. Pres James Perkins (1963–69) brought to campus a number of African American students whose presence at the university had always been minimal, although the first African American had graduated in 1890. A campus protest in 1969 led by some African American students took over Willard Straight Hall; they armed themselves when they felt threatened. This led to Perkins's resignation. He was succeeded by Dale Corson (1969–77), who guided the school through the national economic downturn of the 1970s.

Pres Frank H. T. Rhodes (1977–95) reorganized the administration and raised money for needed new facilities, especially for the sciences. The student population diversified even more with Asians, Hispanics, and larger numbers of international students. Pres Hunter Rawlings III (1995–2003) stressed the quality of undergraduate education and improved ties between students and faculty. Cornell is best known for its excellent interdisciplinary program in the biological sciences, its fine engineering school, the Theory Center, Veterinary Medicine, hotel school, and industrial and labor relations school. The campus, featuring gorges and distant lake views, is renowned for its beauty. Cornell's alma mater, beginning "Far above Cayuga's Waters," is one of the most familiar of all college songs. Its words were written by two undergraduates in the 1870s to the tune "Annie Lisle." Of the many novels set at Cornell, most loved is W. Bolingbroke Johnson's *The Widening Stain* (1942). Cornell's faculty has always been distinguished. On campus in 2002 are two Nobel Prize winners in low temperature physics (David Lee and

New York State College of Agriculture, Cornell University, 1923.

Robert Richardson), one in chemistry (Roald Hoffman), and Hans Bethe, a member of the Manhattan Project. A. R. Ammons, one of America's best-loved poets, made his home at Cornell for 30 years until his 2001 death. Cornell was also the home for 11 years of the novelist Vladimir Nabokov. In 2002 there were 13,725 undergraduates, 4,288 graduate students, and 1,562 in the professional schools, totaling 19,575 on the Ithaca campus and 650 in the medical school in New York City. The full-time faculty numbers 1,515. Cornell consists of the Ithaca campus, extension offices in every county, a teaching mission in New York City, a Geneva (Ontario Co) experiment station, a radiophysics facility in Arecibo, Puerto Rico, and medical school in New York City and Qatar.

See also ARCHITECTS AND ARCHITECTURE, SOUTHERN TIER (EASTERN); BOTANICAL GARDENS; GOLF; HOME ECONOMICS.

Becker, Carl L. *Cornell University: Founders and the Founding* (Ithaca: Cornell Univ Press, 1943)
Bishop, Morris. *A History of Cornell* (Ithaca: Cornell Univ Press, 1962)
Downs, Donald Alexander. *Cornell '69: Liberalism and the Crisis of the American University* (Ithaca: Cornell Univ Press, 1969)
Kammen, Carol. *Cornell University: A Short History* (Ithaca: Cornell Univ, 2003)
Parsons, Kermit C. *The Cornell Campus* (Ithaca: Cornell Univ Press, 1968)

Carol Kammen

Corning. Town (pop 6,426) and city (pop 10,842) in SE Steuben Co. Corning is located in the valley of the east-flowing Chemung River, which divides it into a Northside and a Southside. The town was settled in 1789; the first settlers of the present city purchased land in 1792. Sawmills proliferated as great rafts of locally cut timber were floated down the area's river system to Baltimore. In 1833 the Chemung and Feeder Canals (closed in 1878) connected the area via Seneca Lake to the Erie Canal and stimulated the local economy. The 1839 opening of the Corning and Blossburg Railroad (later New York Central) added coal from nearby Pennsylvania to the canal's freight. Erastus Corning of Albany was a founder of the Corning-Blossburg and, in 1835, had speculated on the area where the canal and railroad were to meet, purchasing the land that would become the City of Corning. It grew rapidly from 1839 to 1842, mostly with migrants from New England and Pennsylvania. South of the river the village incorporated in 1848, while Knoxville grew to the north. In 1851 the completion of the Erie Railroad placed Corning on the main line between New York City and Buffalo. In 1883 the Delaware, Lackawanna and Western Railroad did the same. Corning became a bustling railroad town and remained so well into the 20th century. It incorporated as a city in 1890, encompassing Knoxville, and since 1995 has had a city manager form of government.

Industrialization began in 1868 with the opening of the Corning Flint Glass Works (Corning Glass Works after 1875; Corning, Inc after 1989). This company's early and continuing commitment to research led to its tremendous growth, transforming it by 2002 into a world leader in fiber-optic cable and other related technologies. Corning's cut-glass industry also began in 1868, and its art-glass industry started in 1903, as the Steuben Glass Works, now a part of Corning, Inc, producing quality handcrafted glassware in 2002.

The Town of Corning formed as Painted Post in 1796 and took on its present name in 1852. It remained agricultural, with a particular focus on tobacco, until the 1920s and 1930s, when it transformed into a suburb containing many facilities related to Corning, Inc. In 1952 Rte 17 was rerouted along a railroad right-of-way as a four-lane highway; a bypass (now Rte 17/I-86) around the built-up area of the town was completed in 1995. Hurricane Agnes ravaged the city on 23 June 1972, causing the worst of many floods in Corning's history. Urban renewal, city planning, and Corning Glass Works' new directions introduced a postflood era in which the city changed, not only physically, but economically and culturally as well. Many of the changes were driven by Corning, Inc's replacement of much of its older and unionized manufacturing base with new high-technology facilities emphasizing state-of-the-art research and engineering. Due to reduced employment numbers, the city's population dropped from 17,085 in 1960 to 10,845 in 2000, but Corning, Inc remained the primary employer with more than 4,800 workers. In 2003 tourism was an important part of the economy with local attractions including the Corning Museum of Glass (established as Corning Glass Center, 1951), the Rockwell Museum of Western Art (established as Corning-Rockwell Museum, 1976), and the city's Market Street Historic District. Corning's educational institutions include Corning Community College (1958). The city was the birthplace of Margaret Sanger (1879–1966), the birth control activist.

See also ARCHITECTS AND ARCHITECTURE, SOUTHERN TIER (EASTERN).

Thomas Dimitroff

Corning, Erastus (*b* Norwich, Conn, 14 Dec 1794; *d* Albany, 9 Apr 1872). Entrepreneur and politician. A fall from his crib as a 2-year-old caused Corning to walk with crutches for the rest of his life. In 1805 his family moved to Chatham (Columbia Co), where he received an elementary education. He worked in his uncle's hardware business in Troy (Rensselaer Co) before moving to Albany in 1814 to clerk in another hardware firm. Corning married Harriet Weld in 1819 and by 1825 achieved partnership in the hardware company. In 1826 Corning founded Albany Nail Factory. He also began investing in banks, insurance companies, and railroads, and in 1833 became both vice president of New York's first railroad, Mohawk and Hudson, and president of the state's third line, Utica and Schenectady. A year later Corning was elected mayor of Albany as a Democrat, serving three one-year terms through 1837. Beginning in 1835 he speculated widely in New York State and midwestern land. In 1837 Erastus Corning renamed his nail factory Albany Iron Works and brought in John Winslow as partner. The firm manufactured railroad spikes, and business soared in the 1840s and 1850s because of railroad expansion. Across these same years Corning served two terms in the New York State Senate and became a principal stockholder of both Michigan Central and Canada's Great Western Railroads as well as president of a Michigan canal company. In 1852 he founded the Village [now City] and Town of Corning in the course of real estate ventures in Steuben Co. A year later he forged eight railroads between the Capital District and Buffalo into New York Central Railroad and was company president until 1864. Corning served in the US House of Representatives (1857–59, 1861–63). During the Civil War he won several government contracts for Albany Iron Works, including the manufacture of armor plate for USS *Monitor*. Corning's health began to fail by 1869. Only one of his five sons survived him, but two grandsons, Parker and Edwin Corning, were later active in New York State politics. Edwin's son, Erastus 2d, served as mayor of Albany from 1941 until his death in 1983.

Neu, Irene D. *Erastus Corning, Merchant and Financier, 1794–1872* (Ithaca: Cornell Univ Press, 1960)

F. Daniel Larkin

Corning, Erastus, 2d (*b* Albany, 7 Oct 1909; *d* Boston, Mass, 28 May 1983). Mayor of Albany. His father, Edwin Corning, was a businessman and politician who served as lieutenant governor of New York (1927–28) and as New York State Democratic Committee chair (1926–28). Erastus attended the Albany Academy (1917–22), Groton School (1922–28), and Yale University (1928–32). Returning to Albany in 1932, he established himself in insurance but before long entered into politics when he was elected as a delegate to the 1934 Democratic State Convention. In 1935 he was elected first to the state assembly and later to the state senate (1937–41). In 1941 he was chosen as the Democratic Party's candidate for mayor of Albany. Winning by a landslide, he became, at age 32, the youngest in Albany's history to hold the office. Following World War II, despite a movement of population and retail business from the nation's cities into its suburbs, the expansion of governmental operations kept unemployment relatively low in Albany.

In 1942 Thomas E. Dewey was elected New York State governor and soon after launched an investigation of Albany's Democratic organization, which was led by Daniel P. O'Connell. The effort failed to disclose any widespread corruption. Corning was drafted while Albany was under investigation and served in the US Army from 13 Apr 1944 to 18 Sep 1945. In 1946 he ran unsuccessfully as the Democratic candidate for lieutenant governor. During the 1960s Albany was the site of one of the largest government construction projects in American history, the Gov Nelson A. Rockefeller Empire State Plaza, a project Rockefeller himself envisioned. Corning

Friendly adversaries: Mayor Erastus Corning 2d *(left)* greets Gov Nelson A. Rockefeller, 1960.

overcame his initial hostility to the project and, as mayor, worked out its financing through Albany Co bonds. The most difficult mayoral election Corning faced was in 1973, when the Republican candidate, businessman Carl Touhey, came close to defeating him. When Democratic Party boss O'Connell died on 28 Feb 1977, Corning quickly assumed the chairmanship of the Albany Co Democratic organization, a position he held until his death. His 42-year tenure, from 1941 to 1983, was the longest of any city mayor in US history. The tallest building in the Empire State Plaza, also the tallest building in the state outside of the New York City metropolitan area, is the Erastus Corning Tower.

Grondahl, Paul. *Mayor Corning: Albany Icon, Albany Enigma* (Albany: Washington Park Press, 1997)

Steen, Ivan D. "Erastus Corning, 2d and Democratic Politics in Albany, New York, 1942–83." In *American Cities and Towns: Historical Perspectives,* ed. Joseph F. Rishel (Pittsburgh: Duquesne Univ Press, 1992)

Ivan D. Steen

Corning Inc. The glass manufacturing company known for more than a century as Corning Glass Works (Steuben Co) originated near Boston in 1851, when Amory Houghton, a wood and coal dealer, first invested in the Bay State Glass Co. A decade after founding the Union Glass Works in Somerville, Mass, in 1854, he shifted his interest to New York State when he and several partners, including his son Amory, purchased the Brooklyn Flint Glass Works, a firm established in 1823. Corning businessman Elias Hungerford, while seeking a manufacturer for his newly patented glass window blind in 1866, persuaded the Houghtons to bring their business to Corning if local investors could raise $50,000 for the venture. The offer of capital was appealing to the partners, who were also attracted to Corning because, unlike Brooklyn, it lacked an organized labor movement, resources were cheaper, and three railroads and the Chemung River provided access from the Great Lakes and the Atlantic Ocean. The Houghtons and their partners decided to move in May 1868, and Brooklyn Flint Glass Works became Corning Flint Glass Works. The equipment was shipped, and the factory, containing two furnaces with 8 and 10 pots, was erected next to the river at the foot of Walnut St. The fires were lit in October, and glassblowing soon became a popular local attraction. By November the company started issuing visitors' passes to residents eager to watch the crafters. By 1872 about 200 employees made a range of glass products, including table and druggists' wares, lighting glass, and blanks (uncut vessels) for cutting. After some initial financial problems, the partners restructured the firm in 1875 and incorporated it as Corning Glass Works.

During the late 19th and early 20th centuries, the production of blanks for cutting became more profitable as Corning's cutting industry also blossomed. John Hoare, whose shop cut the blanks produced by the Brooklyn Flint Glass Works, moved to Corning with some of his Brooklyn workers to start another branch of his glass-cutting business in 1868. He consolidated his business and brought the rest of his workers to Corning in 1873. By 1880 his foreman, Thomas G. Hawkes, had started a second cutting shop in Corning and in the 1890s, two more employees left to begin their own businesses. These companies purchased blanks from Corning Glass Works until its blank business was phased out around 1910. The proliferation of cutting shops in the area led Corning to be nicknamed the Crystal City. After the turn of the century, Corning Glass Works had more than 1,000 employees, and the various cutting shops employed nearly as many.

Corning's other early products included railway signal lenses, lantern globes, lightbulbs, thermometer tubing, and laboratory glassware. In 1879 Corning glassblowers blew the first lightbulb blanks for Thomas Edison, and by the later 1880s half of Corning's business consisted of lightbulbs. In the 1890s the company perfected a formula for copper ruby glass for red signal lights, which proved successful because the color was visible from long distances and the stable glassware did not break from the contrast of internal heat and external cold temperatures. Bulbs, railway signal lenses, and semaphores were the foundations of the company's prosperity for the next four decades. The firm increased production of these goods by expanding its melting facilities, and by 1905 Corning had 10 furnaces. It grew further when it entered the kitchenware industry with baking dishes made of heat-resistant glass. Pyrex, which was brought to market in 1915, became hugely successful, and eventually Corning added Pyrex stove-top cookware and in 1957 introduced a glass ceramic, Pyroceram, which was used for cooking and serving pieces as well as for rocket nose cones by the 1950s. In 1970 Corelle Livingware, a line of lightweight but durable dishes, was developed to compete with plastic dishware.

The company also researched and developed new manufacturing techniques and specialty glass products, many of which, like automobile windshields, television tubes, and fiberglass, were components of larger products. In 1913 a 187 ft (57 m) tower was erected at the west end of the factory to draw glass tubing upward. This breakthrough allowed a much faster rate of production than the horizontal hand method. At the same time, Corning initiated work to increase lightbulb production and perfected a semiautomatic bulb-blowing machine that could turn out over 400 bulbs an hour. In 1926 Corning developed the fully automatic ribbon machine, which produced bulbs from a continuous ribbon of molten glass; its successors eventually could produce 2,000 bulbs a minute. In 1934 Corning produced the 200 in (508 cm) mirror for the Mt. Palomar telescope; at the time of production, it was the largest piece of glass ever cast. Subsequent telescope projects included the production of glass for the Hubble telescope's mirror in 1990 and for the Japan National Large Telescope project in 1991.

During the 20th century, the company experienced changes that further affected its labor force and product line. In the 1940s the American Flint Glass Workers Union began representing Corning employees, and in the second half of the 20th century, the company expanded by buying other businesses and by engaging in joint ventures with other glass firms like Owens-Corning, Pittsburgh Corning, Dow-Corning, and Siecor. During the 1980s and 1990s, Corning pioneered the development of fiber optics for use in communication technology, including the Internet. In 1998 the company, known as Corning Inc since 1989, sold the division that made baking, cooking, and serving products to a Borden affiliate now known as World Kitchens. Corning Inc is no longer a glass company but rather a manufacturer of high-technology wares, some of which are glass. In addition to Corning's facilities, the company has plants in Canton (St. Lawrence Co), Oneonta (Otsego Co), and Rochester. Houghton family members continue to be principal stockholders, and James Houghton, great-great-grandson of founder Amory Houghton, became chairman and CEO in 1983, retiring in 1996 but returning to the company as nonexecutive chairman in 2001 and CEO in 2002. Though it thrived during the 1990s, a declining telecommunications market in 2001–2 led to profit losses and a reduction of its labor force. Revenues in 2001 were $6.2 billion. In 2002 Corning Inc employed 6,200 in the Corning area.

See also TECHNOLOGY.

Blaszczyk, Regina Lee. *Imagining Consumers: Design and Innovation from Wedgwood to Corning* (Baltimore: Johns Hopkins Univ Press, 2000)

Dyer, Davis, and Daniel Gross. *The Generations of Corning: The Life and Times of a Global Corporation* (Oxford: Oxford Univ Press, 2001)

Sinclaire, Estelle F., and Jane Shadel Spillman. *The Complete Cut and Engraved Glass of Corning* (1979; repr Syracuse: Syracuse Univ Press, 1997)

Jane Shadel Spillman

Corning Museum of Glass. Chartered by the Board of Regents as an educational institution, the museum was founded to commemorate the 100th anniversary of Corning Glass Works (now Corning, Inc). The museum opened in May 1951 in the Corning Glass Center on Centerway in Corning (Steuben Co). The Glass Center also housed the Hall of Science and Industry, showcasing technical glass displays, a community auditorium, and a new factory for Steuben Glass where visitors could watch crafters work. Eight years after a 1972 flood heavily damaged its collections, the museum moved into a new building attached to the Corning Glass Center. In 1996 the museum opened the Studio, a school for glassmaking, and in 2000 completed renovations that removed its library to a separate building and added the Glass Innovation Center, whose galleries highlight technical achievements in glassmaking. Corning's permanent collection includes almost 40,000 objects representing a broad range of glass production techniques and uses, both ancient and contemporary. Highlights include a portrait head of Amenhotep II (*ca* 1435 BC), a rare Roman cage cup (*ca* AD 300), the Wistar bottle (*ca* 1750–70), one of the earliest known pieces of American glass, and 20th-century windows, lighting, and sculpture by Emile Gallé, Louis Tiffany, Stanislav Libenský, and Dale Chihuly. Also displayed are Islamic, German, Bohemian, English, Venetian and *façon de Venise* glass. American glass objects include pieces from New York State's window and bottle glasshouses. The museum produces the annual *Journal of Glass Studies,* awards the Rakow Prize for Glass Scholarship, and sponsors the Rakow Commission, a new piece of glass art commissioned annually for the museum's collection. It also sponsors the New Glass Review, a juried competition for glass artists. The museum had approximately 300,000 visitors in 2001.

Charleston, Robert J., David Whitehouse, and Susanne K. Frantz. *Masterpieces of Glass: A World History from*

the Corning Museum of Glass, expanded ed. (New York: Abrams, 1990)
Whitehouse, David B. *The Corning Museum of Glass: A Decade of Glass Collecting, 1990–1999* (Corning, NY: Corning Museum of Glass, 2000)

Jane Shadel Spillman

Cornplanter [Gayantwaga; Kayenthwahkenh; O'Bail, John] (*b* Canawaugus [now Avon, Livingston Co], ?1736; *d* Cornplanter Grant, Pa, 18 Feb 1836). Seneca war chief. Son of a Seneca woman and Dutch trader John Abeel (O'Bail), Cornplanter had two siblings born to a Seneca father: a brother, Handsome Lake, the Seneca prophet, and a sister who became mother of Blacksnake, a Seneca political leader. Cornplanter was one of the Senecas who spoke for neutrality in the American Revolution but was reminded of his clan duty to support his clan brother in fighting with the British. He and the Seneca war chief Old Smoke (Sayenqueraghta) served as commanders for the Seneca and against the colonists during the Revolution. In the Battle of Wyoming Valley (1778) in Pennsylvania, Cornplanter was second in command of the Indians and one of the head warriors at Cherry Valley in 1778. Cornplanter, Joseph Brant, and Sayenqueraghta were the head war chiefs at Newtown [now in Chemung Co] in 1779, and commanded 265 Indians under Sir John Johnson in the Schoharie campaign (1780). It was after the Battle of Canajoharie in 1779 that Cornplanter learned that his father, John Abeel, had been taken captive and his house burned. He apologized and offered to take care of his father or return him to his white family. Abeel chose to return to his family.

Following the Revolution, Cornplanter worked to reconcile the Seneca with the Americans. He attended the treaty council of Fort Stanwix in 1784 where the American commissioners maintained that, while the whole of the Indian territory could be claimed as right of conquest, they were taking only a portion of the land. Under such pressure, large amounts of Seneca land were ceded to the new government. Because of his conciliatory posture at this council, Cornplanter became very unpopular with his people. Further involvement in efforts to alienate land from the Iroquois only worsened his image. In 1795 Pennsylvania awarded Cornplanter 750 acres [304 ha] along the Allegheny River, where he lived with his friends and family until his death. In 1964 anticipated flooding from the Kinzua Dam project on the Cornplanter Grant forced the removal of his grave to higher ground.

Abler, Thomas S. *Chainbreaker: The Revolutionary War Memoirs of Governor Blacksnake as Told to Benjamin Williams* (Lincoln: Univ of Nebraska Press, 1989)
Abler, Thomas S., and Elisabeth Tooker. "Seneca." In *Northeast,* ed. Bruce G. Trigger, vol 15 of *Handbook of North American Indians,* ed. William C. Sturtevant (Washington, DC: Smithsonian Institution, 1978)
Graymont, Barbara. *The Iroquois in the American Revolution* (Syracuse: Syracuse Univ Press, 1972)

Martha Symes

Cornplanter, Jesse J. [Hayonhwonhish] (*b* Cattaraugus Indian Reservation [loc in Erie, Chautauqua, and Cattaraugus Cos], 16 Sept 1889; *d* Tonawanda Indian Reservation [loc in Erie, Genesee, and Niagara Cos], 18 Mar 1957). Seneca artist, writer, and lecturer. His father, Edward Cornplanter, had worked with Arthur C. Parker, the Seneca anthropologist, on the Iroquois religion publication *The Code of Handsome Lake, The Seneca Prophet* (1913), for which Jesse provided the illustrations. Injured in a gas attack during his service in World War I, he suffered the effects for the rest of his life. From his youth, he was a careful student of Seneca traditions; his writings, including song texts and descriptions of ceremonies, are an important record of the cultural history of the Seneca. His letters to author Carl Carmer provided information that appeared in Carmer's *Listen for a Lonesome Drum* (1936). A talented carver, musician, and storyteller himself, Cornplanter achieved his greatest renown during the 1930s working for the Works Progress Administration's Seneca Arts Project as a lecturer and author of *Legends of the Longhouse* (1938). He recorded a number of tribal songs and remained a prolific correspondent in his later years. A major collection of his personal papers are housed at SUNY Geneseo. In the last decades of his life, Cornplanter made his home on the Tonawanda Indian Reservation.

Fenton, William N. " 'Aboriginally Yours,' Jesse J. Cornplanter, Hah-Yonh-Wonh-Ish, The Snipe." In *American Indian Intellectuals,* ed. Margot Liberty. Proceedings of the American Ethnological Society, 1976 (St. Paul, Minn: West Publishing, 1978)

George H. J. Abrams

Cornwall. Town (pop 12,307) in E Orange Co. Settled *ca* 1685, Cornwall was formed as a precinct in 1764 and recognized as the Town of New Cornwall in 1788; its name changed in 1797. Many of its settlers were Quakers. Nathaniel P. Willis (1806–67) built his home, Idlewild (1853), and began to popularize Cornwall with his writing. The town became a summer resort after the Civil War. Small fruits including grapes, strawberries, and raspberries were cultivated, and 19th-century products included wool and linen cloth, paper, and pianos. The largest industry was the Firth Carpet Co (1886–1962) at Firthcliffe. The town was served by the Ontario and Western (1873) and West Shore (1883) Railroads. The New York State Thruway (1954) opened up the western part of town to long-distance traffic and helped locate Star Expansion Industries (1954–98) at Mountainville. An important environmental protection case centering on Storm King between 1963 and 1980 is regarded by many as the birth of modern environmental activism. In the late 20th century Cornwall increasingly became a commuter town, with a growing Latino population (5% of the population in 2000). Landmarks include the Storm King Art Center (an outdoor sculpture park at Mountainville), the Museum of the Hudson Highlands and its Kenridge Farm, the Sands-Ring House, and part of Storm King State Park. The Storm King Highway (1916–22; now Rte 218), an engineering marvel, is listed on the National Register.

Janet Dempsey

Cornwall County. See EXTINCT COUNTIES.

Cornwall-on-Hudson. Village (pop 3,058) in Cornwall (Orange Co). Originating as a river landing where produce was shipped, it launched the Hudson River's first freight steamboat in 1828, but its shipping was largely eclipsed after the Erie Railroad began service to Goshen in 1841. By midcentury boardinghouses had opened, making it a summer resort; it was also the home of the famous four Ward brothers, Hank, Josh, Gilbert, and Ellis, champion oarsmen. Industry included Mead and Taft Builders, employing up to 500 workers; extensive brickyards at the landing; a woolen yarn mill; and a tannery. Cornwall-on-Hudson became the eastern terminus of the Ontario and Western Railroad (1873) and was also served by the West Shore (1883). In 1884 the three hamlets of Canterbury, Cornwall, and Cornwall Landing incorporated as the Village of Cornwall, whose name was changed to Cornwall-on-Hudson in 1978. A long controversy (1963–80) over siting a hydroelectric plant on Storm King Mountain ended with the village acquiring land for a riverfront park. Cornwall-on-Hudson is the site of the Storm King School (1867), New York Military Academy (1889), and Museum of the Hudson Highlands (1962).

Janet Dempsey

Correction, Commission of. Oversight body for all state and local correctional facilities. The commission advises the governor on policies and programs for improving the administration of the corrections system, establishes minimum standards for the state's corrections programs, and inspects facilities to ensure adherence to these standards. The 1894 state constitution and subsequent legislation provided for a State Commission of Prisons to visit and inspect all penal institutions in New York. In 1925–26 it was renamed the Commission of Correction and placed administratively within the new Department of Correction, whose head became the commission's chairperson. In 1973 the commission became an independent agency within the Executive Department because of widespread concern over its lack of independence from the Department of Correction despite its separate power of visitation and inspection. The commission functioned with part-time members until 1975, when a highly critical report issued by the State Commission of Investigation led to the appointment of three full-time commissioners and increased field staff. The three commissioners are appointed by the governor to five-year statutory terms with the advice and consent of the senate, with no commissioner serving more than two terms.

The commission has issued dozens of reports since the 1950s on such issues as local jail construction, inmate AIDS treatment, and early inmate release programs. Other reports are more specific, pertaining to investigations of deaths, escapes, and other events at individual facilities. Additionally, the commission's annual report provides detailed statistics on the inmate population and trends in corrections. Commissioners chair the Medical Review Board, which investigates deaths in correctional facilities and recommends improvements in the healthcare of inmates, and head the Citizen's Policy and Complaint Review Council, administering the inmate grievance process and coordinating public participation in oversight of local correctional facilities. These review bodies, as well as other commission initiatives, were established in the 1970s to deal with the dramatic increase in the state's inmate population. In 2002–3 the agency had a budget of $2.5 million and 36 full-time equivalent staff positions.

New York State Commission of Correction, http://www.scoc.state.ny.us

Richard Andress

Correctional Services, Department of. With a mission of keeping inmates in safe custody and offering them opportunities to improve their ability to avoid criminal doings when released, the department is responsible for the confinement of more than 70,000 inmates at 70 correctional facilities statewide. It and its predecessors have been in the forefront of numerous historical innovations, including the development of the Auburn (Cayuga Co) and Sing Sing (Dutchess Co) penitentiary systems, reformatory experiments at Elmira and Bedford Hills (Westchester Co), and recent boot camp, work release, drug treatment, and correctional alternate programs.

Since the state's first prison, Newgate, opened in 1797, the state has administered correctional institutions in various ways. Newgate was headed by a board of inspectors made up of various state officials, including the attorney general and several Supreme Court justices. As subsequent institutions opened, separate boards were also appointed. In 1847 a single elected board was given authority over all state prisons. When an 1873 investigation by the state comptroller found mismanagement in the state's prisons, the board was replaced with a single superintendent. A reorganization of state government in 1926 abolished this position and created a Department of Correction headed by a commissioner who was appointed by the governor, dividing the department into four functional divisions: administration, prison industries, parole, and probation. The new department also assumed the functions of the State Board of Charities relating to corrections. In 1930 the Division of Parole was transferred to the Executive Department. The modern Department of Correctional Services was established in 1970, consolidating the previous department, the State Commission of Correction, and the Division of Parole. In addition, all state institutions were designated as correctional facilities. In 1973 and 1977 respectively, the Commission of Correction and the Division of Parole were made independent agencies.

Reduction of the inmate population has been a constant concern of the department, particularly since World War II. During the 1960s, with rising crime, judicial backlogs, and prison overcrowding, the state revised the penal code for the first time since 1881. This gave more latitude to prison officials to determine length of inmate terms, which led to an increase in the number of inmates placed on probation. Despite this, prison population doubled between 1972 and 1983, largely the result of lengthy sentences imposed under new drug laws passed during the Rockefeller administration. From 1994 to 2000, the increase slowed, from 66,000 inmates to 70,000. This was accomplished during the Pataki administration's emphasis on a system that placed more nonviolent offenders in rehabilitative programs and increased the number of cells for violent offenders. Despite recent changes and programs, the image of the department remains tied to the state's response to the 1971 Attica uprising, which resulted in the death of 32 inmates and 11 prison employees, with broad criticism following the retaking of the prison by State Police and corrections officers.

The department's mission and budget have depended on fluctuating public perceptions of crime and punishment. Political priorities have shifted between punishment or rehabilitation and have determined resources allocated to each function. In 2003 the department employed a staff of 31,400 and had a budget of $2.2 billion.

McEleney, Barbara L. *Correctional Reform in New York: The Rockefeller Years and Beyond* (Lanham, Md: Univ Press of America, 1985)

New York State Department of Correctional Services, http://www.docs.state.ny.us

Richard Andress

Corrigan, Michael A(ugustine) (*b* Newark, NJ, 13 Aug 1839; *d* New York City, 5 May 1902). Roman Catholic archbishop of New York. The son of a wealthy grocer and real estate agent who had emigrated from Ireland, Corrigan attended private schools before entering Mount St. Mary's College in Emmitsburg, Md, in 1855. He graduated in 1859 and decided to study for the priesthood. After seminary training and ordination in Rome in 1863, Corrigan returned to New Jersey to teach at Seton Hall College, serving as president from 1868 to 1876. He became bishop of Newark in 1873. Corrigan was appointed as coadjutor archbishop of New York in 1880 and five years later as archbishop. Corrigan focused his energy on building schools, asylums, and churches to meet the needs of an archdiocese that included a substantial Irish and German middle class and a rapidly expanding group of poor eastern and southern European immigrants. During his 17-year tenure as archbishop, Corrigan established 89 elementary schools, 22 high schools and academies, and 18 schools for special needs students. Concerned about protecting and preserving the religious loyalty of his flock and Catholics across the nation, he became the national leader of the conservative faction of the American Catholic hierarchy. Corrigan's excommunication (subsequently rescinded) of Fr Edward McGlynn for his support of Henry George's 1886 mayoral campaign was the best known of his efforts to curtail liberal efforts to encourage Catholics to adopt American values, and he frequently complained to the Vatican about the growing tide of Americanism within the Church. He was gratified in 1899 when Pope Leo XIII issued *Testem Benevolentiae,* an encyclical condemning Americanism as heresy. Corrigan maintained order and stability within his sprawling archdiocese, but he tolerated no disloyalty or reform. He contracted pneumonia in April 1902 and died the next month.

Curran, Robert Emmett. *Michael Augustine Corrigan and the Shaping of Conservative Catholicism in America, 1878–1902* (New York: Arno Press, 1978)

DiGiovanni, Stephen. *Corrigan, the Vatican, and the Italian Immigrants* (Staten Island: Center for Migration Studies, 1990)

Timothy Walch

Cortland. City (pop 18,740) located in W Cortland Co. Settled in 1794 Cortland is situated on a broad plain with a hill in the center, from which seven valleys strike outward. The early nucleus of Port Watson on the Tioughnioga River was a trading center from which cattle and horses, maple sugar, pottery, whiskey, salt, and gypsum were shipped south to the Susquehanna River and Baltimore. The settlement became the seat of the county in 1810, was renamed Cortland in 1814, and incorporated as a village in 1853. The following year it became a station on the new railroad from Syracuse to Binghamton, and by 1898 rail lines extended in five directions from the village. The railroad stimulated industrial expansion, especially after the Civil War with the founding of two large wagon manufactories and the Wickwire Bros wire mill (1874–1971). An early women's school was the short-lived Cortland Village Female Seminary (1828–38), but the boys' Cortlandville Academy (1828–69) ceded its property to attract a state normal school, which opened in 1869 and grew into SUNY Cortland. Cortland was fertile ground for abolitionism, and African American Samuel Ringgold Ward held a pastorate there from 1846 to 1851. Irish immigrants arriving before the Civil War and Italians late in that century were joined by Ukrainian immigrants (1907–14) and Lebanese who relocated from Solon after 1898. In 1900 Cortland was chartered as a city; its industrial sector grew, largely because of larger firms' local plants. Despite improved access from the construction of I-81 in 1966, Cortland's manufacturing sector declined in the late 20th century. Smith Corona (1920) moved its manufacturing facility to a new plant constructed in Cortlandville in 1958 and shifted all production to Mexico in 1992; Brockway Motor Truck (1912) closed in 1977. The city's population decreased 5% between 1990 and 2000. But in the late 1990s industrial growth resumed, and in 2003 Cortland produced fishing line, hotel supplies, high-tech pumping components, television screen shields, camping equipment, steel products, cable, and chain.

See also ARCHITECTS AND ARCHITECTURE, SOUTHERN TIER (EASTERN).

Cathy A. Barber

Cortland County (503 mi^2/1,303 km^2; pop 48,599). Taken from the southern part of Onondaga Co in 1808 and named for Lt Gov Pierre Van Cortlandt. Cortland Co is divided into 15 towns, containing 3 incorporated villages, and the city of Cortland, which serves as the county seat. The county lies entirely within the Appalachian Upland physiographic province. Exposed bedrock consists of Devonian shales. Elevations range from 867 feet (264 m) above mean sea level along the shore of Skaneateles Lake in the county's extreme northwest corner to over 2,000 feet (610 m) in the Town of Virgil. The topography is dominated by moderate to steep hills that in places rise 700 feet (213 m) or more above the intervening valley floors. The largest and most prominent valleys trend north-south and are glacially scoured. All served as major meltwater channels, and consequently they contain deep deposits of outwash and alluvial material. The east and west branches of the Tioughnioga River occupy the most prominent of these impressive valleys. Their soils are superior and support highly viable agriculture. By comparison upland soils are thin, acidic, and not as productive.

Like most of Central New York the climate is humid-continental. Precipitation normally exceeds 39 inches (99 cm) annually. There is no dry season. Mean July temperatures are 69°F (21°C), but the daily high may exceed 90°F (32°C). January temperatures average 22°F (-6°C) but often drop below 0°F (-18°C). In higher elevations temperatures may be slightly lower. Average winter snow cover everywhere exceeds 50 inches (127 cm), with greater amounts in the higher elevations. Except for a limited area along the county's western margin lying within the greater Finger Lakes watershed, surface waters drain southward and empty into the Susquehanna. Aside from a few pockets of wetland, the primeval forest consisted of Alleghenian hardwoods, particularly maple, beech, and hemlock. In the early 21st century, forests cover most of the steeper slopes and hilltops.

Settlement

Prior to European settlement Cortland Co was claimed by the Onondaga Nation and used for hunting. Little settlement actually took place, and traces of occupation are limited to campgrounds in the Tioughnioga River valley, which served Indians as a north-south route. Cortland Co lands were originally surveyed as part of the New Military Tract. Although intended for Revolutionary War veterans, few came. Instead many early settlers migrated from Connecticut, Massachusetts, and Pennsylvania, and a substantial number from eastern New York State. Lying between the Ontario Lake Plain and the Susquehanna Valley, the area was settled comparatively late, and despite the construction of a state road in the early 1790s across the southern part of the county, travel was slow. Sometimes known as the Chaplin Road, it crossed through difficult terrain. Many of the early roads never advanced beyond planning stage, although in some cases trees were cleared.

The initial European settlement was at Homer in 1791. All but 2 of the county's 15 towns had settlers by 1797, and by 1804 there were residents in every part of the county. In general the more agriculturally promising lands were settled first. Though few Blacks took part in the early settlement efforts, an exception was Guinea-born Primus Grant, who bought a piece of New Military Tract land in Lapeer in 1799 and began clearing it; the parcel was long known as Guinea Farm. As late as 1810 the census counted only two nonwhite residents in the entire county.

Economic Development

By 1810 turnpikes began to appear. The most prominent was the Fourth Great Western Turnpike, known locally as the Albany Turnpike, which extended from Sherburne (Chenango Co) to its western terminus at Homer. From the confluence of its east and west branches (Port Watson) the Tioughnioga River was used to transport agricultural and forest products south to the Susquehanna and ultimately to Baltimore. Traffic included cattle, horses, maple sugar, whiskey, and gypsum. Compared to counties along the Erie Canal or subsequent branch canals, Cortland Co was isolated. Hence early manufacturing was largely limited to local consumption. Only at Homer was production directed to more distant markets. This included a short-lived cotton factory begun *ca* 1800 and the fabrication of nails, edge tools, and iron plows by 1825. Although the 1855 census reported that the county had 1 paper mill, 55 sawmills, and 13 tanneries, in addition to 288 tailors, 133 blacksmiths, 70 physicians, 41 lawyers, and 14 printers, the majority of residents earned their livelihood on one or another of the county's 4,835 farms that focused on mixed agriculture and produced butter, apples, flax, and maple sugar above the state's average per county.

In 1829 the legislature chartered the Salina and Port Watson Railroad to connect Syracuse and Cortland, but the line was never built. A quarter century passed before the Syracuse, Binghamton and New York Railroad (later the Delaware, Lackawanna and Western) was completed through the county in 1854. In 1872 an east-west rail line, subsequently part of the Lehigh Valley system, linked the Village of Cortland with Ithaca to the west and with points in Madison Co to the northeast. In 1898 a branchline was extended from Cortland to Cincinnatus. Early in the 20th century, Cortland was served by 14 train departures daily. The improved transport ties to the national economy prompted changes in local industry. Starting in 1863 cheese factories began springing up as growing numbers of farmers directed greater attention to dairy farming. Later emphasis shifted to fluid-milk production. From 1888 to 1966, at which point trucks became predominant, trains carried Cortland Co milk to New York City and other urban markets. Ready access to rail service was critical, and consequently the more isolated hill farms, already marginal, started to be abandoned.

The railroads also brought change to the county's larger villages, most notably Cortland, Homer, and Marathon, as new industries took hold. A number of local companies manufactured carriages, wagons, and sleighs after the Civil War. Other products included cheeseboxes, wire, farm implements, leather, corsets, furniture, and (after 1908 in Cortland and Homer) fishing line. Firms made transitions in a modernizing economy; the Brockway Wagon Co became a builder of trucks. With the limited and concentrated manufacturing, banking got a late start; two short-lived banks had both closed before the Civil War. Later Cortland had three in its central business district. With electronic banking, seven banks operated at 15 different sites early in the 21st century.

Immigration and Ethnicity

The county's population grew rapidly until about 1830, when it reached approximately 24,000, and then increased gradually, occasionally dipping, until 1920. Steadier growth resumed, fueled in part by industrial development in the City of Cortland. Since 1980 the population has been stable. The nonwhite population remained very small until the 1980s, after which it gradually increased to 3%. Moderate isolation combined with limited industrial jobs discouraged the heavy influx of immigrant settlement from the mid–19th through the early 20th centuries. Irish immigrants formed agricultural communities in both Solon and Truxton, where Roman Catholic churches were built in 1849 and 1854 respectively. A Lebanese community coalesced in Solon in 1898 but eventually gravitated toward Cortland, joining an earlier Italian and somewhat later (1907–14) Ukrainian influx. Cortland's Italian population, about 10% of the total, was largely employed in the wire mill.

Religion, Education, and Culture

Cortland Co in the 19th century demonstrated a remarkable uniformity of religious affiliation. In 1860 Presbyterian, Congregational, and Methodist churches were nearly equal in number, followed closely by Baptist churches. These four denominations accounted for 90% of the church congregations. The first Roman Catholic parishes were organized in mid–19th century. Toward the end of the 20th century, a larger variety of Protestant churches appeared, and many

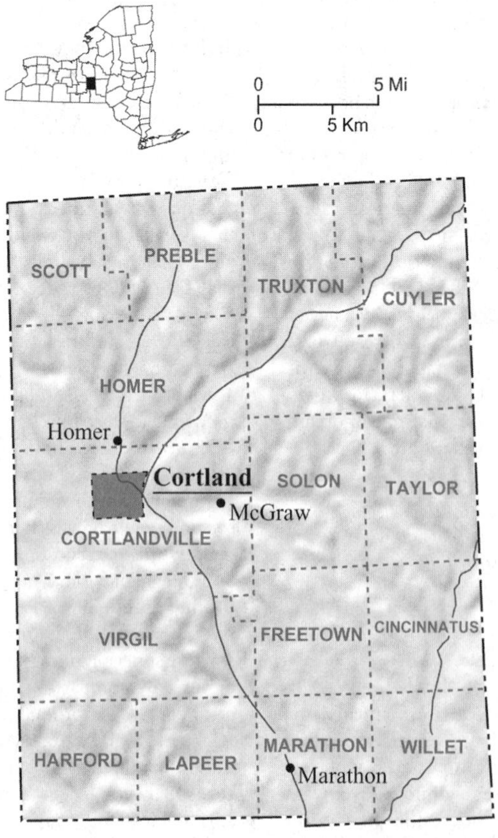

CORTLAND CO POPULATION CENSUS FIGURES

	White	Nonwhite	Total Population	Foreign-Born
1810	8,867	2	8,869	—
1820	16,456	51	16,507	21
1830	23,753	38	23,791	13
1840	24,561	46	24,607	—
1850	25,098	42	25,140	1,049
1860	26,278	16	26,294	1,666
1870	25,115	58	25,173	1,888
1880	25,732	93	25,825	1,735
1890	28,564	93	28,657	1,986
1900	27,494	82	27,576	1,523
1910	29,177	72	29,249	2,001
1920	29,567	58	29,625	2,016
1930	31,647	62	31,709	2,009
1940	33,602	66	33,668	1,861
1950	37,073	85	37,158	1,715
1960	41,022	91	41,113	1,673
1970	45,651	243	45,894	1,413
1980	48,133	687	48,820	1,398
1990	47,968	995	48,963	1,073
2000	47,115	1,484	48,599	1,081

Notes: "Nonwhite" includes African Americans, Asians, American Indians, and Pacific Islanders and, for 2000, also the mixed race and other race categories. Through the 1960 census these figures primarily reflect the African American population. Foreign-born figures for 1820 and 1830 include only those not naturalized, and for 1930 and 1950, the foreign-born totals include Whites only. Other years include all foreign-born in the population.

independent or fundamentalist groups have built on land surrounding the city.

In a few cases common schools preceded the 1812 state law that encouraged their establishment. Academies were chartered to provide secondary education in the larger communities, including Cortland Academy (1819) at Homer, Cortland Village Female Seminary (1828), Cortlandville Academy (1843) at Cortland, and Cincinnatus Academy (1858). Cortland High School was organized in the village in 1893. By mid–20th century the county was served by four centralized school districts and Cortland city district. Buses have been utilized to carry rural students to a central school facility located in a village or large hamlet.

Cortland Co was a stronghold of abolitionism, and with its location on a prevailing south-north transportation route, some residents assisted on the Underground Railroad. The Rev Samuel Ringgold Ward, who was born into slavery and escaped with his parents, was pastor at Cortland's Liberty Church from 1846 to 1851. The county's greatest experiment in abolition and equal rights was the New York Central College at McGraw (1849–61), a Baptist institution that emphasized manual labor, total abstinence, and antislavery sentiments. A coeducational institution, it not only accepted African Americans as students but also hired African American instructors, giving it the first integrated college faculty in the nation. Although short lived, the institution's closing prompted the Village of Cortland to submit a proposal to the legislature to secure the charter for a normal school. The effort succeeded, and the New York State Normal and Training School at Cortland opened to students in 1869. In 2003, as SUNY Cortland, it had an enrollment of over 6,200. Tompkins-Cortland Community College began operation in 1968 and moved to its campus in Tompkins Co in 1974. The college, popularly known as TC3, also operates a satellite site in Cortland and serves over 3,000 students.

The county's first newspaper was published in Homer in 1810. The primary newspaper in the early 21st century is the daily *Cortland Standard,* founded in 1877; one weekly is also published. Famous Cortland Co natives include Amelia Bloomer (1818–94) from Homer, a leader in the women's rights movement, and Francis B. Carpenter (1830–1900), a historical painter best known as the creator of *The Reading of the Emancipation Proclamation.* Elmer A. Sperry (1860–1930) developed the gyroscope and gyroscope compass, accumulating over 350 patents in his lifetime. Arguably the county's widest outside recognition has come from two books, both written by nonresidents. *David Harum* (1898) by Edward N. Westcott of Syracuse immortalized David Hannum (1823–92), a Homer horse trader known for his country speech and wisdom. Two Cortland Co residents were historical models for the protagonists of Theodore Dreiser's *An American Tragedy* (1925). Institutions in the county that present the fine and performing arts are Cortland Arts Council, Cortland Arts League, and Cortland Repertory Theatre. SUNY Cortland also has significant offerings in music, art, and drama that are enjoyed by the public.

Politics

The Republican Party grew progressively in strength from the 1850s and became the dominant political force throughout the county by 1900, a position it continued to hold a century later in some areas. In 1904 Cortland-born Alton B. Parker made an unsuccessful run for president on the Democratic ticket against New York City–born Republican Theodore Roosevelt; Parker failed to gain a majority in his native county. Solon native Nathan L. Miller (1868–1953) defeated Alfred E. Smith in the 1920 gubernatorial race. Following World War II and the expansion of SUNY Cortland came the growth of a more liberal population, particularly in the city. County government was from the beginning based on the town structure, and each town elected a supervisor to direct town affairs. Periodically the Board of Supervisors met at the county seat and transacted county business. The first major change came about with the Cortland city charter in 1899; multiple supervisors were elected from the more populous city. In 1975, following the growth of urban settlement beyond the city line, the county government was transformed into a county legislature with

POPULATIONS OF TOWNS AND CITIES, CORTLAND CO

Town or City, Year Founded	1800	1840	1880	1920	1960	2000
Cincinnatus, 1804	—	1,301	1,093	941	960	1,051
Cortland (city), 1900	—	—	—	13,294	19,181	18,740
Cortlandville, 1829	—	3,799	7,114	3,237	5,660	7,919
Cuyler, 1858	—	—	1,382	813	753	1,036
Freetown, 1818	—	950	844	485	542	789
Harford, 1845	—	—	1,034	553	635	920
Homer, 1794	612	3,572	3,691	3,554	5,751	6,363
Lapeer, 1845	—	—	757	423	459	686
Marathon, 1818[a]	—	1,063	1,700	1,296	1,696	2,189
Preble, 1808	—	1,247	1,138	678	991	1,582
Scott, 1815	—	1,332	980	625	600	1,193
Solon, 1798	370	2,311	842	498	549	1,108
Taylor, 1849	—	—	993	647	474	500
Truxton, 1808	—	3,658	1,550	920	907	1,225
Virgil, 1804	—	4,502	1,854	1,069	1,420	2,287
Willet, 1818	—	872	853	592	535	1,011

Note: In 1800, the Towns of Homer and Solon were in Onondaga Co.

[a]Harrison until 1827.

Popcorn peddler from Homer, 1860s.

members elected from districts in both the city and the towns. In 2003 there were 19 members, but only 5 came from election districts beyond the urbanized area.

The 20th Century

With much of the county's land hilly and isolated, and the railroad providing economic inducements to farming near its stations, less productive farms were abandoned beginning late in the 19th century. The rise of industrial methods of farming contributed to a sharp reduction in the number of farms. By the end of the 20th century only 3% of the households in the county were on farms. In 1920, 45% of the county's population lived in the City of Cortland, and this percentage held steady through 1960 but declined to 39% by 2000 because of increases in commuting and rural nonfarm residential patterns.

Manufacturing grew rapidly in Cortland Co during the first half of the century, led by the Wickwire Co. Other facilities included a number of branch plants of larger companies, such as Thompson Brothers boats (1924), Overhead Door Co (1929), Grumman Boats (1953), Trinity Equipment temperature indicating devices (1957), and Smith Corona Typewriter. Still others were locally owned: Brockway Motor Truck (1912), Cortland Line Co fishing line (*ca* 1915), Edlund Machinery drilling equipment (1918), and Cortland Corsets (1928). Many of these plants have since moved or ceased operation.

The 1967 completion of I-81 facilitated long-distance commuting to Syracuse and Binghamton. Factory closures—Wickwire Bros in 1971, Brockway Motor Truck in 1977, Smith Corona in 2001—began to affect adversely the county's industrial climate. In 2002 Cortland Co factories produce fishing line, aluminum canoes, television aperture masks, hotel products, filtration and separation products, machine tools, wooden pallets, and fire and emergency vehicles. Many Cortland Co farms continue to produce milk, which is shipped entirely by bulk tank trucks. While fewer farms produce milk, the number of dairy cows per herd continues to increase. By 2020 Cortland Co farms will be fewer but larger. Although most farms are family owned in the early 21st century, the future may see more corporate ownership.

Antiquarian writing on the settlement of Cortland Co began with Nathan Bouton, *Festive Gathering of the Early Settlers of the Town of Virgil* (1855), extended to all the towns by H. C. Goodwin, *Pioneer History: Or, Cortland County and the Border Wars of New York* (1859). Both benefited from the memories of early settlers. The standard county history, H. P. Smith, *History of Cortland County* (1885), included biographies and institutional and corporate histories. Promotional publications of the late 19th century often provide greater insight than the standard histories, such as D. Morris Kurtz, *Past and Present: A Historical and Descriptive Sketch of Cortland* (1883) and E. L. Welch's *"Grip's" Historical Souvenir of Cortland* (1899) and *"Grip's" Historical Souvenir of Marathon* (1901). The Cortland County Historical Society has published Louis M. Vanaria, ed., *From Many Roots: Immigrants and Ethnic Groups in the History of Cortland County, N.Y.* (1986), and a railroad history by Richard F. Palmer, *Rails through Cortland* (1991). The early period of church growth is examined in Curtis D. Johnson, *Islands of Holiness: Rural Religion in Upstate New York, 1790–1860* (1989).

Joseph W. Brownell

Cortlandt. Town (pop 38,467) in NE Westchester Co. The present town was settled under the jurisdiction of Cortlandt Manor, purchased from the Indians beginning in 1683, and two other smaller tracts purchased by others in 1685. In the colonial period it was the site of an iron furnace (*ca* 1750–*ca* 1770), and the colony's first paper mill moved from New York City in 1774 to a location near Annsville, burning three years later. Town meetings began in 1737, and the town was confirmed under state government in 1788. Croton Point, a large peninsula extending into the Hudson River, was the site of brickyards (1830–1915) and wine making (1827–73). The Annsville Wire Co (1833–83) was another important industry. The town benefited from good river transportation as well as the Hudson River Railroad (1849). A large Italian community came to construct the New Croton Dam, creating the Croton Reservoir (1904). Government facilities in town include the New York National Guard facility Camp Smith (1882) and the Franklin D. Roosevelt Veterans Administration Hospital (1950). Valeria Home (1921–37) was a convalescent and resort facility for middle-income people. In 2003, with excellent rail service to Manhattan, a large part of Cortlandt's residents were commuters. Landmarks include Old St. Peter's Church Van Cortlandtville (1767) and the Upper Van Cortlandt Manor House, now a nursing home. Composer Aaron Copland (1900–1990) was a resident for 30 years until his death.

Cortlandt Manor. Colonial estate in Westchester Co and headquarters of the Van Cortlandt family. Stephanus van Cortlandt (1643–1700) was the first to acquire the property. His position as New York City mayor and chief justice influenced Gov Edmund Andros to allow Van Cortlandt to purchase tracts from American Indians in 1677 along the Croton River. With the shortage of grain in the colony, Van Cortlandt invested in land to pursue agriculture but also for prestige. Gov Thomas Dongan granted him land near Haverstraw [now in Rockland Co] and Verplanck's Point (Westchester Co) in 1685, and Van Cortlandt continued to buy noncontiguous parcels in Westchester. Because he held political positions and acquired numerous patents, Gov Benjamin Fletcher designated Van Cortlandt's property a manor in 1697. Manor status connected all Van Cortlandt's tracts and gave him the title, Lord of the Manor. Cortlandt Manor included approximately 86,000 acres (34,800 ha) and extended from Anthony's Nose south to Teller's Point [now Croton Point, Westchester Co], and from the Hudson River east to the province border. After Stephanus van Cortlandt died his wife Gertrude Schuyler managed the family estate. In 1712 she oversaw 87 inhabitants. She died in 1723 and willed the manor to her ten children, who rarely instituted new leases.

By 1730 Philip Verplanck (1695–1771), who married into the Van Cortlandt family and controlled a manor estate, became the land agent for the family. He ordered a survey of the manor in 1734, and, according to a directive that Stephanus had established, the manor was partitioned into 40 tracts. Eight family estates were formed within the manor and individual Van Cortlandt family members sold or leased to farmers. Most estate owners had land agents to manage leases, ranging from 1 to a few years to 1 to 99 years. Landlords could evict tenants for not meeting lease obligations and protected property against squatters. Beginning in 1734 tenants were able to elect their own supervisor, treasurer, tax assessor, and tax collector. The manor grant of 1697 stipulated that the landlord could send a representative to the legislature, a privilege not exercised until 1734. Verplanck served in that capacity until 1768.

Philip (1683–1746), son of Stephanus, inherited land at the juncture of the Hudson and Croton Rivers, but lived in New York City and acted only as an absentee landlord. In the 1750s his son Pierre superseded Verplanck and took charge of manor lands. Pierre van Cortlandt built a mansion and integrated the manor for agriculture and commerce, making his land the most important crux of Cortlandt Manor. Emulating the success of Philipsburg Manor, Pierre was determined to create a similar enterprise. As tenant farmers produced crops they were processed in Van Cortlandt mills, and wheat was shipped to New York City from docks at Teller's Point. Because the manor contained ample wooded areas, sawmills were built along the Croton River. A ferry was established, and a ferryhouse provided lodging and food for travelers. While Pierre's estate prospered, John van Cortlandt's northeastern sector was in turmoil. Farmers had been anxious since Van Cortlandt tried to evict two tenants for delinquent rent and because he denied tenants their right to vote. Tenants rioted on 10 and 17 Apr 1766 and demanded to vote. Van Cortlandt farmers rallied Dutchess Co tenants, and on 29 April about 500 rioters attempted to burn Kingsbridge [now in Bronx Co] but were quelled by militia. A court decision against Van Cortlandt determined that 801 manor inhabitants were freeholders or that they were legal residents who owned enough property to qualify them to vote and serve as jurists.

During the Revolutionary War the manor straddled the so-called neutral ground. Patriots were in the majority and lived in the northern section, while those in the southern fluctuated between the American and British causes. Being at a location that might be easily overrun by British forces, Pierre abandoned his mansion. Other Van Cortlandt family members left their estates for safety, and tenants who remained were subjected to raids. After the state legislature passed the Township Act in 1788 the manor was divided into the Towns of Cortlandt, Yorktown, Stephentown [now Somers], Salem, and a portion of Poundridge. Following the close of the war, Pierre's son Philip returned to the manor house and restored it to its prewar condition. The home with its surrounding lands remained in Van Cortlandt hands for more than 100 years after Philip's death in 1831. The last descendants sold their property and contents in 1945.

In 1953 John D. Rockefeller Jr purchased the mansion and its surrounding 5 acres (2 ha). With the acquisition of an additional property, 11 acres (4 ha) were restored to their 18th-century condition. An additional 173 acres (70 ha), including marshlands, were being conserved. As of 2003 Historic Hudson Valley owned the property and operated a museum on the site.

See also MANOR SYSTEM.

Kim, Sung Bok. *Landlord and Tenant in Colonial New York: Manorial Society, 1664–1775* (Chapel Hill: Univ of North Carolina Press, 1978)

DeLancey, Edward Floyd. "The Origin and History of Manors in New York, and in the County of Westchester." In *History of Westchester County,* ed. J. Thomas Scharf (Philadelphia: 1886)

Jacob Judd

Cortlandville. Town (pop 7,919) in W Cortland Co. Settled in 1792 the town formed from Homer in 1829. Elkanah Watson began the survey of Port Watson in 1800 at the head of navigation on the Tioughnioga River. In the 19th century large quantities of lime were manufactured from marl taken from ponds at South Cortland. The City of Cortland was taken from the town in 1900, but in recent years some of its industrial enterprises have been located in the town, while agriculture remains important. In 1958 Smith Corona constructed its manufacturing facility in town, operating it until production moved to Mexico in 1992. In 2003 paving materials, electrical testing equipment, filters, tools, and lumber are made in Cortlandville. I-81 opened in 1966, providing improved road access. The town is the site of the federal Tunison Laboratory of Aquatic Science.

Cathy A. Barber

Cosby, William (*b* Queen's Co [now Laois Co], Ireland, *ca* 1690; *d* New York City, 10 Mar 1736). Royal governor of New York and New Jersey (1732–36). After rising to the rank of colonel of the Royal Irish Regiment of Foot, Cosby was appointed governor of Minorca (1717–27), where he was accused of appropriating a shipment of snuff from a Portuguese merchant. Tried in London, he was ordered to pay £10,000 in damages to the merchant. Faced with the need to replenish his fortune, Cosby successfully asked the duke of Newcastle for the governorship of New York and New Jersey after the 1731 death of John Montgomerie. On arrival in New York, Cosby, like Montgomerie, allied with the merchant faction, immediately embroiling himself in a controversy surrounding his claim to receive one-half the salary and fees collected by the acting governor Rip van Dam prior to Cosby's arrival. When Van Dam, backed by Chief Justice Lewis Morris, refused, Cosby dismissed Morris as chief justice. The opposition then launched a propaganda campaign against the governor, which resulted in the trial of printer John Peter Zenger for seditious libel. Cosby's attempts to deal with his New York opposition left him little time to govern New Jersey, where he called the assembly into existence on only one occasion.

Colden, Cadwallader. "History of Governor William Cosby's Administration as Governor of the Province of New York." In *Collections of the New-York Historical Society for the Year 1935.* Publication Fund Series, vol 68 (New York: New-York Historical Society, 1937)

Mary Lou Lustig

Costa Ricans. Prior to the 1980s, the US population of those originally from Central America was small; over 90% have arrived in the past 20 years. Costa Rica was among the least affected by the civil strife of the 1980s that generated large emigrations from other countries in the area, and few chose to immigrate to the United States. However, the 1980s and early 1990s brought economic hardship. Many saw emigrating as the only opportunity to move ahead socially. According to the 2000 census, there are approximately 8,655 foreign-born Costa Ricans living in New York State, most of whom tend to live in Brooklyn (2,638), Queens (1,451), and Suffolk Co (1,056). All celebrate their Independence Day of 15 September in social gatherings. The Costa Rican community in New York State is mainly composed of professionals, technicians, and students.

National Association of Hispanic Journalists. "Latinos in the United States," http://www.nahj.org/resourceguide/resourceguide.pdf

Ana Margarita Cervantes-Rodríguez and Michael C. English

Council of Appointment. Body given responsibility by the state's 1777 Constitution of selecting militia officers and all unelected public officials, from local justices of the peace to the chancellor of the Chancery Court. The council reflects the framers' efforts to provide a system of checks and balances. Article 23 of the constitution provided that the council would consist of the governor and four senators selected annually (for nonrenewable terms), one from each of the four senate districts. It did not, however, designate who was to nominate the appointees the council was to consider, leading to a minor constitutional crisis with the unforeseen emergence of political parties. After 17 years of Gov George Clinton controlling the council's appointments, in 1794 a Federalist majority on the council named Egbert Benson to the state supreme court. Five years later a Republican majority led by De Witt Clinton and Ambrose Spencer overwhelmed Federalist governor John Jay. The 1801 Constitutional Convention settled the matter, after the state supreme court and the legislature had declined to do so, by empowering all council members to make nominations. Throughout the council's existence its members were heavily lobbied, and the council may have served as a seedbed of the spoils system. The Council of Appointment was unanimously abolished by the Constitutional Convention of 1821, largely because it was recognized as an anachronism that controlled an ever increasing source of patronage.

Galie, Peter J. *Ordered Liberty: A Constitutional History of New York* (New York: Fordham Univ Press, 1996)

Lincoln, Charles Z. *The Constitutional History of New York from the Beginning of the Colonial Period to the Year 1905,* 5 vols (Rochester: Lawyers Cooperative Publishing, 1905)

Donald M. Roper

Council of Defense. Established 1 May 1917 to coordinate the war effort in New York State during World War I. Gov Charles S. Whitman headed the council, and many state governmental figures were also appointed to it, including the superintendent of public works and the commissioner of agriculture. Working closely with the Council of National Defense, New York's council helped with, among other efforts, recruiting for home defense, monitoring industrial and agricultural production, promoting the purchase of Liberty Loan bonds, orchestrating a public relations program to promote patriotism, and supervising aliens. Civil libertarians criticized the last two activities. The county was designated the basic organizing unit, and a seven-member home defense committee was formed in each of the state's 62 counties. There was an outpouring of community support for the war effort through the county home defense committees. The council was closed by law in March 1919; however, the efforts of its Bureau of Americanization were continued by the State Education Department. The council and the policies developed by it served as a model for New York State's response to World War II.

New York State Council of Defense. Records. New York State Archives, Albany

Christine Karpiak

Council of Revision. Body empowered by the state's 1777 Constitution to revise all bills "inconsistent with the spirit" of the constitution or "with the public good," subject to being overridden by a two-thirds legislative vote. The council's creation reflected the fear of repeating the unpopular obstructionism of royal governors and of the people acting through the legislature. Composed of the chancellor of the Chancery Court, supreme court members, and the governor, there was a degree of permanence to the council's membership since the judicial members served during "good behavior" to age 60—the council's originator, Chancellor Robert R. Livingston Jr, served 24 years—and the governors (of whom there were five over the council's 45-year history), although always present, wrote no opinions. The council vetoed only 169 of the 6,560 bills it reviewed, and the legislature overrode 51 of those vetoes, primarily between 1788 and 1800. Differences remained between the council and the legislature, however, and the long tenure of council members continued to rankle politicians, leading to the 1821 Constitutional Convention's replacement of the council with the seemingly safe gubernatorial veto. The council's value continues to be a subject of scholarly debate.

Prescott, Frank Williams, and Joseph F. Zimmerman. *Council of Revision and the Veto of Legislation in New York State: 1777–1822* (Albany: Graduate School of Public Affairs, SUNY at Albany, 1972)

Street, Alfred Billings. *The Council of Revision of the State of New York* (Albany: W. Gould, 1859)

Donald M. Roper

Council on Children and Families. Established in 1977 by executive order of Gov Hugh Carey and forming part of New York State's Executive Department, this body coordinates 13 health, education, and human service agencies serving the state's children and their families. In 2002 the council was made up of the heads of the following agencies: Office of Temporary and Disability Assistance, Office of Children and Family Services, New York State Department of Health, New York State Department of Labor, Office of the Advocate for Persons with Disabilities, Office for the Aging, Office of Alcoholism and Substance Abuse Services, Division of Criminal Justice Services, New York State Education Department, Office of Mental Health, Office of Mental Retardation and Developmental Disabilities, Division of Probation and Correctional Alternatives, and Commission on the Quality of Care for the Mentally Disabled. Through its New York State Touchstones program, the council sets goals, objectives, and outcome measures for use by member agencies in evaluating their programs. The council is also involved with other initiatives—the Head Start Collaboration Project and the Family Renaissance Consortium, among them—and publishes on child- and family-related issues. It is headquartered at 5 Empire State Plaza in Albany.

Jeffrey Kraus

counties, extinct. See EXTINCT COUNTIES.

Country Life Movement. Urban-led national rural reform movement, *ca* 1900–20, that promoted modernizing farm life and agricultural practices and initiating socioeconomic improvements to ensure future food supplies for the cities by keeping the younger generation on the farm. Movement leaders worked through an active press, formal agricultural educational institutions, youth clubs and school programs, and, after the passage of the federal Smith-Lever Act in 1914, county extension agents. The movement encompassed various viewpoints, from those of urbanites hoping to escape "back to the land" for a more satisfying life to scientific agronomists eager to apply industrial efficiency and economies of scale to farming. Its chief goals were to create an economically efficient, socially progressive, and politically stable agriculture to support America's emerging industrial economy. New York State efforts were centered at Cornell University under Liberty Hyde Bailey, dean of the College of Agriculture. Another important Country Lifer was John W. Spencer, a fruit grower in Cornwall (Orange Co) who organized numerous Junior Naturalist Clubs around the state.

The Country Life Movement applied the philosophy and methods of urban progressivism to the countryside. Proponents assumed that business innovation and the adoption of industrial efficiency would benefit farm families and contribute to the economic, social, and moral survival of the countryside. Initiatives included gathering sociological data through surveys and commissions, organizing farmers' cooperatives and associations, implementing rural church and road reforms, adopting social welfare measures, strengthening agricultural extension work to disseminate practical scientific information, promoting soil conservation and irrigation projects, and especially reforming rural schools, primarily through consolidation. Pres Theodore Roosevelt appointed the Country Life Commission in 1908 and named Bailey its chair. The commission's 1909 report recommended a nationalized extension service arising from the agricultural colleges, suggested a series of agricultural surveys, and asked Congress to establish a central agency to guide a campaign for rural progress. Bailey later elaborated on the local situation in *York State Rural Problems* (1913). The national movement split in 1919. Those emphasizing the idea that farming was a way of life formed the National Country Life Association, and those chiefly concerned with agricultural economics organized the American Farm Bureau Federation. Country Life organizations remained active into the early 1940s, but the movement faded after World War I. Actual results were limited because of rural self-defensiveness and resentment against the movement's urban and academic assumptions of superiority.

Bailey, Liberty Hyde. *The Country-Life Movement in the United States* (New York: Macmillan, 1911)
Bowers, William L. *The Country Life Movement in America, 1900–1920* (Port Washington, NY: Kennikat, 1974)
Danbom, David B. *The Resisted Revolution: Urban America and the Industrialization of Agriculture, 1900–1930* (Ames: Iowa State Univ Press, 1979)

Suzanne Etherington

county fairs. Multiday, multilayered rural public occasions designed to promote farming and to support local economies through education, exposition, competition, and recreation. Longtime Albany entrepreneur Elkanah Watson seized on the format of market fairs for selling livestock and agricultural produce in New Netherland and other American colonies in the 17th and 18th centuries as a rural public venue for sharing and inspiring improved agricultural and domestic methods and production. He devised plans for encouraging farmers to adopt improved breeds, crops, and agricultural methods after showing Spanish merino sheep on the town common of Pittsfield, Mass, in 1808. He persuaded other Berkshire Co gentlemen farmers to exhibit superior livestock at a cattle show in 1810. This led directly to the formation of the Berkshire Agricultural Society the following year, which sponsored its first county fair on 24 Sept 1811. The society offered premiums for livestock exhibited at the annual Pittsfield Fair, and eventually other prize categories were added, including crops and domestic manufactures.

After returning to Albany from Pittsfield in 1816, Watson promoted the creation of county agricultural societies that would sponsor annual fairs. The Berkshire System of agricultural organization and education soon evolved and spread across and beyond New York State. The first of the new societies in the state was the Otsego County Agricultural Society, which held its first fair at Cooperstown in October 1817. Jefferson Co followed suit in 1818, when it held the first of what would become the state's oldest continuous agricultural fair. Other counties soon joined the movement, including Erie (1819), Monroe (1823), and Genesee (1839). Early 19th-century county agricultural societies and fairs struggled with inconsistent financial backing, village and regional economic and political competition, rivalry from other fairs, difficult terrain for driving cattle, lack of farmer interest, and inclement weather.

In 1841 the New York State Agricultural Society successfully lobbied the state legislature for annual grants to the county agricultural societies for their fairs, as well as support for a state fair. By the 1860s, county fairs flourished across the state "for the instruction and inspiration of farmers, edification of the general public and innocent amusement of all." Most edifying were the demonstrations of patented agricultural machinery, tools, and implements, but no less important to contestants and spectators were the exhibits of livestock for dairy, meat, and motive power and displays of fruits, vegetables, grains, and flowers, as well as domestic manufactures such cloth spun and woven by hand, needlework, paintings, baked goods, and preserves. By the late 19th century, as separate breeder, horticultural, and trade societies evolved, county fairs tended to cater more to the educational, recreational, and nostalgic needs of increasingly urban fairgoers. In the early 20th century, lectures on nonagricultural topics—such as health and safety, rural electrification, forestry, insurance, finances, and environmental issues—appealed to a wider audience. County fairs became important venues for agricultural schools, 4-H, specialty breeder and grower organizations, the Farm Bureau, and Cooperative Extension programs, as well as for political figures and popular personalities.

Food and "innocent entertainment" have always been hallmarks of county fairs. Oysters, gingerbread, fruit, nuts, candy, ice cream, and cider were popular during the 1800s. Fried dough, blooming onions, hot dogs, cotton candy, and many varieties of sandwiches, fried delicacies, ethnic foods, and beverages were increasingly popular in the 20th century. Fair food fads, such as deep-fried Twinkies, come and go. The first spectacles to draw fairgoers—parades, plowing matches, and trials of working oxen—were superseded before the mid–19th century by horse racing, trotting contests, and, not without controversy, female equestrian events. After the Chicago's World Fair of 1893, midways with games of skill and chance, Ferris wheels and other rides, and sideshows became accepted and expected features at county fairs. Stock-car races and demolition derbies provided spectacle in the early 20th century.

The first county fairs occurred in temporary pens and tents on town commons and in local meeting houses. As support and popularity increased, sponsoring societies acquired accessible land for fairgrounds on which they built permanent structures, surrounded by tall board fences. Colorful, ornamented barns, stables and pens, ticket booths, grandstands, parking lots, bandstands, sanitary facilities, and exhibition halls appeared as fairs grew in the late 1800s and early 1900s. Carnival tents and booths and the characteristic oval horse track were located outside the fence in the mid-1800s. As these activities moved inside the fence, debates ensued concerning the balance of education and entertainment.

County fairs of the early 21st century compete with abundant entertainment diversions and face decreasing numbers of farms and farmers, changes in rural landscapes, and specialty agricultural exhibitions and trade shows. Most county fairs cater to audiences with fewer connections to rural life and agriculture. For the remaining agricultural participants, however, the institution remains an uplifting educational endeavor as envisioned by its founders. Entertainment is varied, and many fairs have special features, such as a balloon-blowing goat at the Delaware County Fair in Walton, rooster-crowing contests at the Franklin County Fair in Malone, and Farmer Olympics at the Saratoga County Fair in Ballston Spa. In 2002 an estimated 4.5 million attended the 50 or so county fairs in New York State and left an economic impact on surrounding communities of close to $50 million. The Erie County Fair in Hamburg, the largest county fair in the state, reported 1,013,110 visitors over 11 days.

Marti, Donald B. *Historical Directory of American Agricultural Fairs* (Westport, Conn: Greenwood, 1986)
Neely, Wayne Caldwell. *The Agricultural Fair* (New York: Columbia Univ Press, 1935)

Kathryn A. Boardman

county government. New York State is divided into 62 counties. Outside New York City, which contains five counties and four of the state's six most populated, Suffolk Co on Long Island was the most populated in the 2000 census, with 1,419,369 residents. Hamilton in the Adirondacks was the least populated, with 5,379 people. The largest in territory is St. Lawrence, larger than both Delaware and Rhode Island, with 2,686 mi^2 (6,957 km^2). New York Co, one of five counties within New York City, contained only 23 mi^2 (60 km^2). Rockland Co in the Hudson Valley, with 174 mi^2 (451 km2), was the smallest outside of New York City. The 57 counties outside of New York City operate as the workhorse local governments of the state. New York State county government revenues in 2000 (not including New York City) totaled $15.4 billion—38% more than the combined revenues of all other general-purpose local governments (cities, towns and villages) within the state, excluding New York City. Retail sales tax (22.7%) and real property tax (22%) provided about equal portions of county revenue with an additional 26.4% paid by the state (state and federal aid paid almost entirely through the state), mostly used to meet expenses mandated by the legislature. County government spending totaled just over $15 billion in 2000.

The services provided are vast and vary in detail from jurisdiction to jurisdiction. Counties are the state's principal partners in functions ranging from delivering health and mental health services and public assistance to less affluent New Yorkers to licensing drivers and their vehicles. Additionally county governments have maintained roads and bridges, supported community colleges, held and made available crucial public records, engaged in planning and economic development, ran nursing homes, operated jails and probation systems, paid for court facilities, disposed of solid waste, administered key elements of the property tax, served youth and senior citizens, supported the arts, engaged in consumer protection, provided police services, delivered public transportation, and even operated airports. Terrorist attacks on the United States and the transmission of anthrax through the mail in 2001 enhanced public awareness of county governments' responsibility for emergency preparedness and response, preventive healthcare, and public safety. Over half of total annual county government spending in New York State outside New York City was in five jurisdictions: Erie, Monroe, Nassau, Suffolk, and Westchester Cos. Each of these was among the largest local governments in size of budget in the United States. Nassau Co's operations alone cost over $2 billion annually. The governmental functions of the five counties within New York City are largely performed by the consolidated city government, which operates as both a city and a county. Its boroughs are city subunits with boundaries coterminous with county lines. Counties within New York City, however, do provide the organizational framework for the administration of justice. As is the case throughout the state, they are also the basis for political party organization and the administration of the electoral process.

County Formation

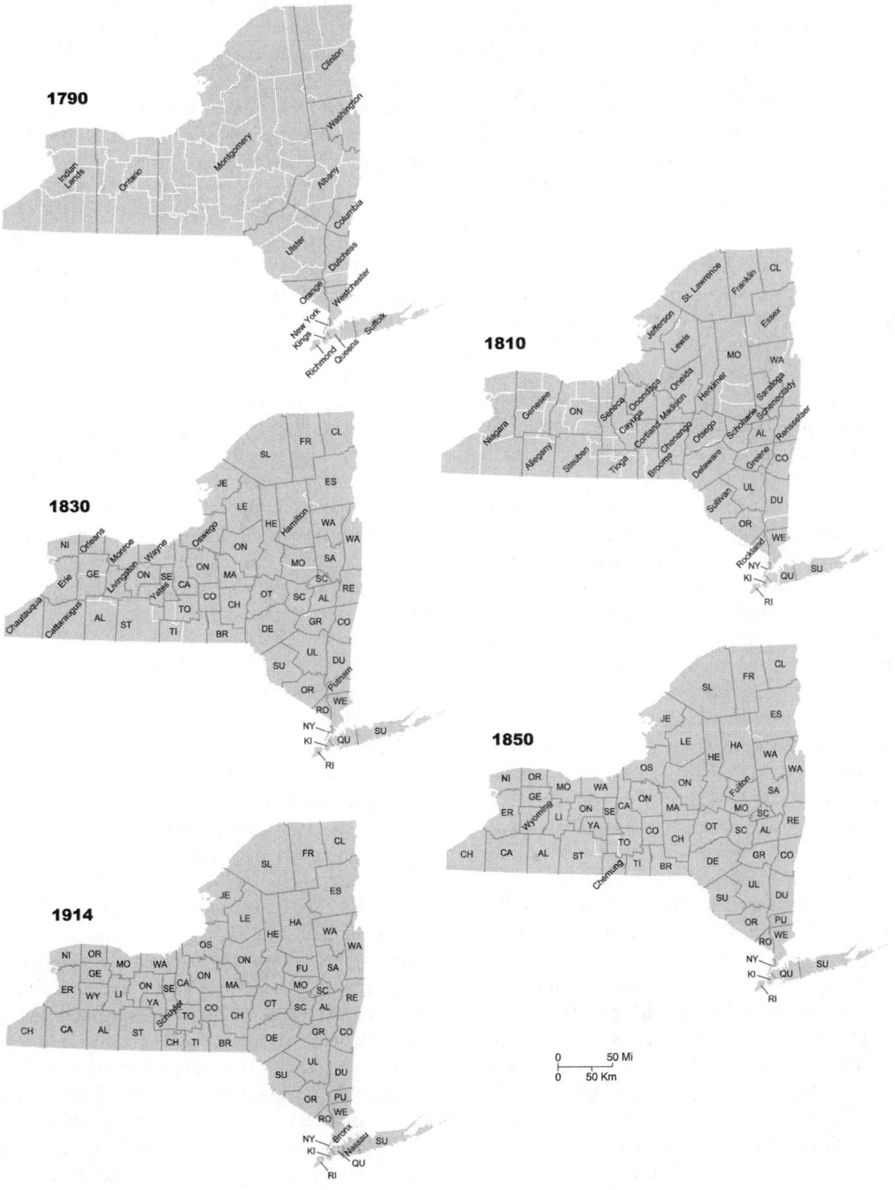

SOURCE: Data from W. Thorndale and W. Dollarhide, *Map Guide to the US Federal Censuses, 1790–1920* (1987).

Creation of Counties

Counties were created by the colonial (later state) government in New York for the decentralized delivery of essential services. They also provided the territorial basis for representation in the legislature. The 12 original counties were established in 1683, and 10 of them were within the current boundaries of New York State. The legislature's first general act relating to counties after independence, providing them the means to defray their "public and necessary charges," was passed in 1778. Counties were added by specific legislative actions as territory to the north and west was populated. For instance, in recommending the creation of Clinton Co in 1788, George Clinton wrote, "There is already a number of inhabitants in this quarter, and there is a prospect of speedy and considerable increase of the settlement; at present day they are within the jurisdiction of Washington Co, very remote from the seat of justice, and consequently the executive of the laws is most impracticable." Additionally, the establishment of new counties added opportunities for state and local office holding and patronage, and the location of public offices was a spur to the further development of the village or city chosen to be the county seat. Perhaps this is what the governor was implying when he added to his message to the legislature on the creation of Clinton Co, "Independent of the convenience of inhabitants, there are other reasons in favor of the measure, and which will no doubt occur to you in your deliberations on this measure."

After 1821 the new state constitution's population requirements for creating new counties and for maintaining the relative size of existing counties (linked to the fixed size of the state assembly) slowed their growth. New York State's counties numbered 60 by 1854. The portion of Queens Co not included in greater New York City became Nassau Co in 1899. The Bronx became the last county in 1914, conforming county organization for state purposes within the city to its charter-based borough structure. Proposals made by Gov Alfred E. Smith in the 1920s to reduce the number of counties to increase local government efficiency and to reduce costs failed to gain serious consideration in the face of entrenched local interests. In the 1990s there were proposals in the legislature to carve a Peconic county out of eastern Suffolk Co and to separate Richmond Co (Staten Island) from New York City. The first would have created an entirely new county; the second might have resulted in a new coterminous city/county government.

Evolution of County Government

From their early history, counties were governed by boards composed of the supervisors of their constituent towns and cities. The Colonial Assembly provided in 1703 that supervisors be locally elected. A 1777 state constitutional provision continued this colonial practice, thus confirming the supervisors' claim of democratic legitimacy and therefore of autonomy. These legislative actions established the basis for counties to evolve into something more than mere branch offices of the state government. Democratic underpinnings for county government were strengthened when the sheriff, clerk, and treasurer became elective offices with the adoption of the Constitution of 1821; election to fill the office of district attorney followed with the passage of the 1846 Constitution. Counties remained the basic building blocks of legislative apportionment until the mid-1960s. Within those counties entitled to more than one assembly seat by the state constitutional formula adopted in 1894, lines defining assembly districts were drawn by county boards. The 1962 US Supreme Court decision in *Baker v Carr,* establishing the one person–one vote standard for representation, diminished counties' importance for legislative districting but, because of greater democratization, gave additional weight to county structures as independent local governments rather than as subordinate state polities.

The adoption of the 1892 Consolidated County Law provided a general framework for the operation of county government. Under its provisions the Board of Supervisors, headed by a chair chosen by the members from among its own number, met annually. The board received and audited the reports of all countywide elected officials, including the treasurer (chief fiscal officer), the clerk (custodian of official record), the sheriff (in charge of the jail, with some law enforcement and civil duties), the district attorney (criminal prosecutor), several judges, one or more coroners, superintendents of the poor, and highway superintendents. Towns were required to certify their fiscal needs to the county. Based on its review, the board determined the level of county and town taxation and borrowing. Another important achievement of the 1892 law was to switch the compensation of county officials from a fee-based to a salary-based system, with the Board of Supervisors empowered to set salaries. Vestiges of the fee system remain in some counties for the compensation of the treasurer, in the role of public administrator of estates of people who die intestate. Additionally, this statute granted the board the authority to create towns, thereby allowing it to control the balance of power between cities and towns and among towns. During this time counties were also empowered to create school districts and review their fiscal needs. Thus, the Consolidated County Law is the root of the modern county's role in almost all jurisdictions (Westchester Co is an exception) as the guarantor of town and school district tax levies.

Charter Counties

At the turn of the 20th century, the same rapidly changing social and economic conditions that drove demands for home rule and reform for city government also resulted in efforts to achieve greater power and autonomy for counties. For more than a third of a century, reformers worked in vain for constitutional and statutory changes that would provide alternative governmental structures for suburban counties, reduce the number of countywide elected officials, introduce systematic budgeting, and establish a unifying executive authority in county government. In 1935 the state legislature passed the first county charter in New York State history; the people of Nassau Co approved it in a countywide referendum in 1936. J. Russel Sprague, a member of the Board of Supervisors and the county Republican leader, provided the critical political leadership for the adoption of the charter and then served under its provisions from 1938 to 1951 as Nassau's first county president (now executive). The first Nassau Co charter established a separation of powers system: the Board of Supervisors was retained to perform legislative functions while executive authority was vested in a county president, who prepared a budget and, with the advice and consent of the board, appointed most department heads. The audit function was placed in an elected comptroller. A countywide police department was created, and the office of sheriff was abolished. In 1937 the people of Westchester Co adopted the first county charter that employed the title "county executive" and established a county legislature in the place of the Board of Supervisors. It was approved by separate majorities in Yonkers, the county's other cities, and the area outside of cities in several referenda. Also in 1935 a County Home Rule Amendment to the state constitution was adopted, directing the legislature to provide for alternative forms of county government. In following actions 16 were offered in 4 separate laws. In 1937 only Monroe Co was able to muster the three separate majorities in a referendum on a charter to adopt one of these forms. Erie and Schenectady Cos tried and failed.

Under the leadership of Gov Thomas E. Dewey (1943–54) and Comptroller Frank C. Moore (later Dewey's lieutenant governor), the county law was recodified in 1950, and a revised Alternative County Government law passed, but no additional charter counties resulted. Suffolk Co became a charter county by special law in 1958. In 1959 counties were authorized by constitutional amendment and following statutory changes to devise their own forms of government. Erie Co immediately did so, and Oneida and Onondaga Cos followed in 1961. The passage of the constitutional Home Rule Amendment in 1963 extended full home rule to counties. Under its provisions Monroe Co adopted a new charter in 1965, and 12 additional jurisdictions became charter counties. Sullivan Co was the 20th and last to do so in 1993.

Almost all New York State counties containing major cities and those surrounding New York City operated under county charters in 2000. Most charter counties followed the separation of powers model, with executives elected for four-year terms and legislatures ranging in size from 9 members (Putnam Co) to 39 (Albany Co). Exceptions were Schenectady and Sullivan Cos with a county manager, Tompkins Co with an appointed administrator, and Herkimer Co with no provision in its charter for an executive.

Significant reforms occurred from the mid-1960s in counties still operating with boards of supervisors because of the one person–one vote decisions of the US Supreme Court. The traditional practice of equal voting power for supervisors, regardless of the population size of the towns or city wards each represented, clearly violated this principle. Some counties retained these boards but instituted weighted voting; others switched to legislatures. In 2000 there were 17 counties governed by boards of supervisors, with Saratoga Co the largest by population, with 181,276 people. Nassau Co, long the only charter county with a board of supervisors, switched to a legislature in 1996. County legislatures appointed administrators in 19 New York State counties without elected executives; of the remaining 18, 5 had managers; 13 continued to vest executive authority in the chair of the county legislature or board. The number of other countywide elected officials varies, depending upon local choice. Offices include county and family court judges, district attorney, treasurer, sheriff, county clerk and coroner.

The Dual Role of County Government

After more than three centuries of evolution, counties have come to serve simultaneously as semiautonomous, general-purpose local governments and as key service deliverers in New York State's decentralized state and local system. At times these two roles are mutually reinforcing, but often they conflict. County department heads are appointed by local elected officials but may be directly accountable by law to state agencies and often must conform to demanding state regulatory requirements. Counties adopt annual budgets by local legislative action, but taxation and borrowing are constitutionally limited, and spending, even locally raised revenue, is primarily to meet state, not local, priorities. For example, at the start of the 21st century, New York State's counties were required to pay about a third of the total state share of the costs of the federal Medicaid program from their own resources. The state constitution guarantees counties' democratic character (counties must have elected leadership) and provides their "sword" (prescribed duties and powers)and their "shield" (protections against state interference in local matters). Yet the New York State Court of Appeals, the state's high court, continues to regard counties as "creatures of the state" and to resolve most intergovernmental differences in favor of state, not county, government. Efforts to limit state legal, fiscal, and regulatory mandates on counties have had little effect. In New York the state and the counties may be partners in service of the people, but the counties remain decidedly the junior partners.

See also HOME RULE; STATE GOVERNMENT AND SERVICES.

Briffault, Richard. "Local Government and the State Constitution: A Framework for Analysis." In *Decision 1997: Constitutional Change in New York,* ed. Gerald Benjamin and Henrik N. Dullea (Albany: Rockefeller Institute Press, 1997)

Institute for Local Governance and Regional Growth. *State-County Relations in New York: Key Partnership Issues* (Buffalo: Author, 2000)

Liebschutz, David S., and Sarah F. Liebschutz. "Political Conflict and Intergovernmental Relations: Federal-State and State-Local Relations." In *Governing New York State,* 4th ed., ed. Jeffrey M. Stonecash (Albany: SUNY Press, 2001)

New York State Constitutional Convention Committee. *Problems Relating to Home Rule and Local Government,* vol 11 of *Reports of the Constitutional Convention Committee* (Albany: Author, 1938)

New York State. Office of the Comptroller. *Special Report on Municipal Affairs, 2001,* 4th ed (Albany: Author, 2002)

New York State. Secretary of State. Division of Local Government Services. *Local Government Handbook* (Albany: Office of the Secretary of State, 2001)

Gerald Benjamin

Court Administration, Office of. New York State agency created in 1977 to centralize management of the state's courts. In 1962 Article 6 of the New York State Constitution was amended to provide for a "unified court system for the state" to speed resolution of cases. But Democratic Party fears that Republican governor Nelson A. Rockefeller sought to control the judiciary through such a reorganization prevented the achievement of central management for another 15 years. In 1976 the New York State legislature enacted the Unified Court Budget Act, merging 120 separate court budgets into a single budget. A year later, with the support of Democratic governor Hugh Carey, the New York State Constitution was amended to allow the state to fund and administer all state and local courts. The chief judge of the Court of Appeals was designated chief judicial officer of the state court system and given the power to appoint a chief administrator for the courts—when the chief administrator is a judge, the title is chief administrative judge—subject to the approval of the Administrative Board of the Courts. The board consists of the four presiding judges of the Appellate Division of the New York State Supreme Court and the chief judge of the Court of Appeals, who serves as chair. The chief administrator directs the Office of Court Administration (OCA), which is responsible for management functions of the courts. The OCA's functions include overall responsibility for finances and personnel, encompassing labor negotiations with the court system's nonjudicial employees; preparation of the judiciary's budget; assignment of judges; provision of prospective juror lists to the 62 counties; serving as liaison with the legislature; maintenance of court libraries; education of judges; compilation and reporting of statistical data; general technical assistance to the courts; and planning and implementation of court improvement projects. In 1999 there were 1,230 judges and more than 16,000 nonjudicial personnel within the state court system. In 2000 the budget of the state court system surpassed $1.15 billion. Criticisms of the system remain; in a 1999 speech, Chief Judge Judith Kaye called New York State's present court structure "absurdly complex." The OCA is located in Albany, with additional offices in Binghamton and in Lower Manhattan.

New York State. Office of Court Administration. *Annual Report of the Chief Administrator of the Courts* (Albany: Office of Court Administration, 1979–)

Jeffrey Kraus

courthouses. As counties were established throughout the state during the colonial era, courthouses were gradually built in each county seat to provide a venue for legal proceedings. Until they were completed, court sessions were held elsewhere, in churches, schoolhouses, taverns, and residences. Often designed in the latest architectural style using the newest building methods, courthouses have historically been barometers of how important respective communities believed law and local government were.

EARLY BUILDINGS

Traditionally the largest and most important building in the community, the courthouse was prominently located on a public square or at an important crossroads. Many early courthouses initially housed the entire county government. Of those built in New York Colony before the Revolutionary War, only one still operates as such: the Fulton County Courthouse in Johnstown. Attributed to architect Samuel Fuller, it was built in 1772–73 for Sir William Johnson. Now a single room, it was originally subdivided into the main courtroom and several spaces for use by the jury and attorneys, reflecting British law practices. Two others from the 18th century, the old Columbia County Courthouse in Claverack (1788) and the old Westchester County Courthouse in Bedford (1790), have survived but are no longer used as courthouses.

Despite some variation in architectural styles, the courthouse became an easily recognized building type in the early 19th century, usually with the main facade having a portico supported by columns and a dome or cupola, often containing a bell. The first floor usually housed offices and meeting rooms and the second the courtroom. Many were designed as monumental Greek Revival buildings, including the Yates County Courthouse in Penn Yan (1835), the Cayuga County Courthouse in Auburn (1836), and the Chenango County Courthouse in Norwich (1837).

Until the canal and railroad systems were developed, building materials were restricted to what could be found locally, usually masonry, either locally burned brick or native stone, such as limestone. After the middle of the 19th century, however, materials such as brick, iron, sheet metal, and slate were available throughout the state. These materials contributed not only to building permanence but to fire resistance, an important consideration in protecting records. Later in the century some of the first iron framing in New York State was used in courthouses.

FROM THE MID–19TH CENTURY

The earlier courthouses were built by skilled masons, many of whom had previously worked on building canals in the state, and pattern books of sophisticated architectural details that could be replicated by local builders were important sources for courthouse design. As architecture developed as a profession, however, counties called on architects rather than local builders to design courthouses. Many of these buildings did not follow the typical Greek Revival design. Some distinctive examples include the Chemung County Courthouse in Elmira (1862) by Horatio Nelson White, the old Washington County Courthouse in Salem (1869) by Marcus F. Cummings, the Herkimer County Courthouse in Herkimer (1873) by A. J. Lathrop, and the Otsego County Courthouse in Cooperstown (1880) by Archimedes Russell. No doubt the state's most notorious is the Tweed Courthouse of old New York Co, a marble building with a Corinthian portico designed by architects John Kellum and Leopold Eidlitz and built between 1861 and 1881. Its spiraling cost of over $13 million and irregular financing helped lead to the downfall of the Tweed Ring in 1871.

During the late 19th and early 20th centuries, monumental Classical Revival structures were built using the latest construction technologies, especially in the more urbanized and industrialized counties. The Rensselaer County Courthouse in Troy (1898), designed by the prominent local firm M. F. Cummings and Sons, was constructed of granite and other fire-resistant materials in a dignified but not opulent manner. Another Neoclassical courthouse of note was in Nassau Co, where the county supervisors chose a radical new construction technology: reinforced concrete. The old Nassau County Courthouse (1901) in Mineola is now one of the oldest remaining concrete public buildings in the United States. Its replacement, also in Mineola, opened in 1940 and was built by the Works Progress Administration (later Work Projects Administration) and featured Art Deco elements, including a series of decorative panels along the main facade's top entablature. Cass Gilbert's federal courthouse (1936) at Foley Square in Lower Manhattan was the most massive of the Classic Revival courthouses in the state.

RECENT TRENDS

Unlike their predecessors, modern courthouses generally accommodate only judicial functions, following the requirements of New York State's Unified Court System (1962), which combined local and state courts into a single system. Although its requirements for judicial facilities are stringent for security and functional reasons, many historic courthouses have recently been restored for continued court use. Because of the quality of courthouses' original design and construction, as well as their association with local history, both government officials and the public often prefer restoring historic courthouses to building new ones. Examples of historic courthouses restored to meet modern court requirements include those of Ontario Co in

Canandaigua (1858), Otsego Co in Cooperstown (1880), and Rensselaer Co in Troy (1898). Other buildings have been restored to serve alternate purposes; the Tweed Courthouse, now used by the New York City Department of Education, is one of these. Courthouses continue to be built, but since the mid–20th century governments have often been reluctant to spend money on civic buildings, which is reflected in the lower architectural and construction expectations for many recently constructed courthouses. An exception is Richard Meier's federal building and US courthouse in Islip (Suffolk Co), built in 2000 with an award-winning design that avoided the traditional classical courthouse style.

Historical Society of the Courts of the State of New York, http://www.courts.state.ny.us/history

Johnson, Herbert Alan, and Ralph K. Andrist. *Historic Courthouses of New York State: 18th- and 19th-Century Halls of Justice across the Empire State* (New York: Columbia University Press, 1977)

New York State Court Facilities Task Force. *Survey of Court Facilities in New York State* (Albany: NYS Office of Court Administration, 1981)

John G. Waite and Jennifer R. Breslin

courts, federal. The US Constitution authorized a federal court system, and the initial framework was outlined by the Judiciary Act of 1789. The US Supreme Court met for the first time on 2 Feb 1790 at the old Royal Exchange in New York City. The first chief justice was native New Yorker John Jay. The Court met only a few times during its tenure in New York State and heard no cases, dealing instead with attorneys' admission to its bar and other administrative matters before following the nation's capital to Philadelphia in 1790. Federal district and circuit courts remained in the state. The US Constitution and federal statutes determine which cases are adjudicated in federal courts, and there is some overlap in jurisdiction between federal and state courts. The bulk of cases heard in federal courts are those involving the US government, its programs, federal laws, or cases involving litigants of different legal jurisdictions, such as citizens from different states.

District Courts

The first federal court to convene after ratification of the US Constitution was the District Court of New York, which commenced meeting at the old Royal Exchange on 3 Nov 1789. From 1791 to 1812 federal courts met in the city at Federal Hall. Among the federal courts, district courts had exclusive jurisdiction in admiralty cases; the District Court of New York was heavily occupied with maritime cases, including a number of prize cases determining the owners of ships seized during hostilities off coastal waters during the Napoleonic era. The court also had jurisdiction over minor crimes and in its first decades gained authority to hear patent (1790) and bankruptcy (1820) cases. To handle a heavy caseload, a second judge was authorized for the district in 1812, the first time two judges served in one district. In 1814 the District of New York was split into Northern and Southern Districts.

The Southern District began to hear more cases than any other district in the nation, and its docket became more varied, including patent and copyright infringement matters after the Civil War and noteworthy cases concerning economic regulation, bankruptcy, and civil liberties

Judge Learned Hand in 1924, the year he was appointed to the Court of Appeals for the Second Circuit.

in the 20th century. It was the venue of the well-publicized Cold War era trials of Alger Hiss (1949), Eugene Dennis (1949), and Julius and Ethel Rosenberg (1951), many of the notable insider trading cases in the 1980s, and the terrorism trials of the people indicted in the February 1993 bombing of the World Trade Center and the August 1998 bombing of the American embassies in Kenya and Tanzania. Two courthouses (500 Pearl St, 40 Centre St) and the district clerk's office are located near Foley Square in Lower Manhattan, with another courthouse in White Plains (Westchester Co). The district's 28 justiceships in 2001 were the most of any district court in the country.

In 1865 Congress divided the Southern District and created the Eastern District with jurisdiction over Long Island and Richmond Co. In its early years the Eastern District handled many personal injury cases arising from tugboat and ferry accidents. Later, patent and bankruptcy became staples, and, like all federal courts in New York State during Prohibition, its judges spent considerable time preventing illegal sales of alcohol and shutting down speakeasies. The *Schechter* "sick chicken" case was first litigated in the Eastern District in 1934, and organized crime boss John Gotti was tried and convicted there of murder and racketeering in 1992. The Eastern District, with 15 judgeships in the early 21st century, has two courthouses, one in Brooklyn, where the clerk's office is located, and the other in Central Islip (Suffolk Co).

The Northern District was created in 1814 to handle increases in litigation caused by the movement of people to the northern and western parts of the state, and held court in Utica, Canandaigua (Ontario Co), and Salem (Washington Co). It heard a number of patent cases in the late 19th century and handled the prosecution of liquor bootleggers from Canada during Prohibition. In 1935 gangster Dutch Schultz was tried and acquitted for income tax evasion. The Northern District's five judges hear cases at Fort Drum and in Albany, Binghamton, Plattsburgh, Utica, and Syracuse, also the location of the clerk's office.

The Western District was created from the Northern District in 1900 and given jurisdiction over the state's 17 westernmost counties. One of the first duties of the new district judge was to administer the oath of office to Theodore Roosevelt following the 1901 assassination of Pres William McKinley in Buffalo. In addition to an increasing load of commercial and bankruptcy cases, it also deals with customs and immigration cases and the enforcement of federal environmental laws against chemical industries in the Niagara River region. Western District judges also heard cases stemming from the 1971 rebellion at the Attica Correctional Facility. Like the neighboring Northern District, which has handled land claim cases of the Oneida and Cayuga Indians, the Western District has handled litigation related to the Seneca and Tuscarora reservations in its jurisdiction. The Western District of New York, with four judges at the start of the 21st century, holds court in Rochester and Buffalo, where the clerk's office is located.

Second Circuit of the US Court of Appeals

Federal circuit courts also date to 1789, when three circuits were established; New York State became part of the Eastern Circuit. In the Judiciary Acts of 1801 and 1802, additional circuits were created and all circuits assigned numbers. New York State, along with Vermont and Connecticut, was placed in the Second Circuit. As trial courts, the circuits were intended to handle most federal criminal cases, disputes between residents of different states, and all civil suits brought by the federal government. Trial jurisdiction of the circuit courts initially included major crimes, with minor crimes being heard in district courts. An 1842 law gave circuit and district courts concurrent jurisdiction over non-capital crimes, although in practice the circuit and district courts often handled different types of cases. Among notable cases in this era was the 1861 trial and conviction of Nathaniel Gordon, in which the circuit court for the Second Circuit became the only federal court to sentence a slave trader to death for piracy; Gordon was hanged in New York City in February 1862.

The circuit courts also had appellate jurisdiction for district court cases. This role was limited, however, because there was no independent staff of judges for the circuit courts. District court judges and Supreme Court justices had the additional duty of riding circuit to hear cases, and district court judges could not hear appeals on cases they had already judged. It was not until 1869 that Congress provided for the appointment of separate judges to staff the circuit courts. Change came in 1891 with creation of the Circuit Courts of Appeal (now US Courts of Appeals). The original circuit courts were relieved of their appellate duties that year, and they were abolished in 1911, with their remaining trial duties given to the district courts.

The Second Circuit of the Court of Appeals is known for its procedural innovations, such as its three-judge panel exchanging memorandums before voting on a case, and has been instrumental in shaping the US Supreme Court's jurisprudence in many areas of the law. In 2001 the Second Circuit had 13 judgeships, and its pri-

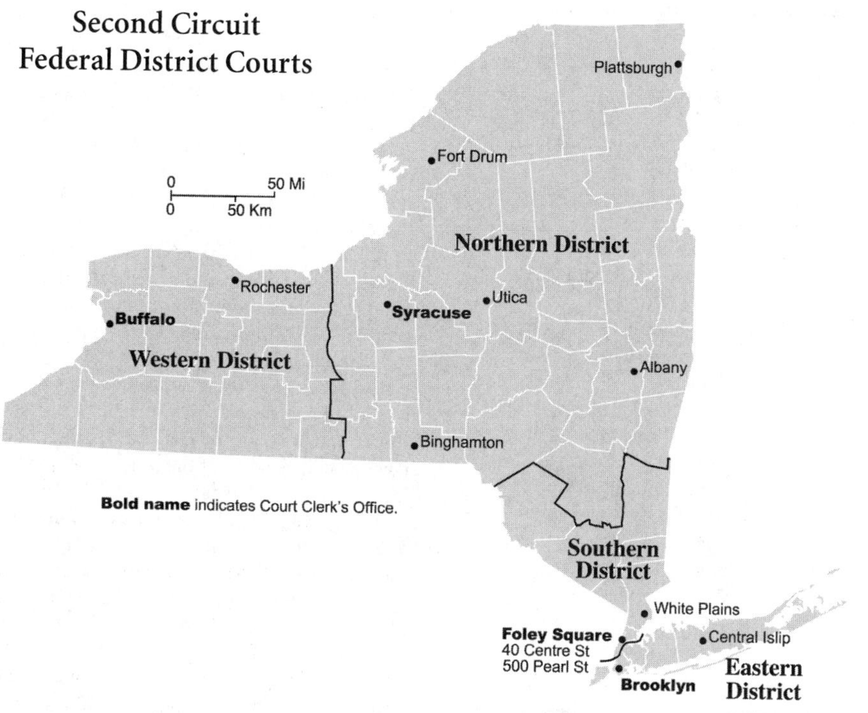

mary courts were at the US Courthouse at Foley Square, although cases were also heard in Albany, Rochester, Syracuse, and Utica, as well as at locations in Vermont and Connecticut. For the year ending 30 Sept 2001, the court's 4,519 cases included criminal cases (16%), US prisoner petitions (7%), other US civil cases (7%), private prisoner petitions (20%), other private civil cases (34%), bankruptcy cases (2%), administrative appeals (6%), and original proceedings (8%).

Specialized Courts

Two types of specialized federal courts also function in the state. The four federal judicial districts in New York State each have bankruptcy courts, which trace their history to the late 19th century. For decades federal district courts relied on referees in bankruptcy and channeled bankruptcy cases to the referees, who served as the initial hearing officers. A 1973 law changed referees' status to that of bankruptcy judges, and a 1978 law created a separate US Bankruptcy Court—with its own judges and full jurisdiction—in each federal district. After this arrangement was ruled unconstitutional in 1983, jurisdiction in bankruptcy cases was invested in the federal district courts; bankruptcy cases are automatically referred to the bankruptcy courts, but the district courts can pull back any cases they want to hear directly. By the late 20th century the Southern District's Bankruptcy Court developed into an important business court for the nation, with many major corporate bankruptcy proceedings, such as those involving Texaco (1987) and Enron (2001), begun there even though the businesses were centered elsewhere. Additionally the US Court of International Trade, successor to the US Customs Court, is based in Manhattan. The court is authorized to decide civil cases against the United States or its agents that relate to international trade law. The court can hear cases nationwide and abroad.

Carp, Robert A. *Policymaking and Politics in the Federal District Courts* (Knoxville: Univ of Tennessee Press, 1983)

Lyles, Kevin L. *The Gatekeepers: Federal District Courts in the Political Process* (Westport, Conn: Praeger, 1997)

Morris, Jeffrey Brandon. *Federal Justice in the Second Circuit: A History of the United States Courts in New York, Connecticut, and Vermont, 1787 to 1987* (New York: Second Circuit Historical Committee, 1987)

Surrency, Erwin C. *History of the Federal Courts*, 2d ed. (Dobbs Ferry, NY: Oceana Publications, 2002)

United States Courts in the Second Circuit: A Collection of History Lectures Delivered by Judges of the Second Circuit (New York: Federal Bar Council Foundation, 1992)

Timothy P. Gordinier

courts, state. New York State's modern court system is built on a complex foundation that dates to the colony's earliest European settlement.

Dutch Colonial Courts

The laws of New Netherland were the laws of the province of Holland. Compiled in 1580, they comprised customary and statute laws, established privileges and usage, canon law, and Roman law. Reflecting the varied sources, the jurisprudence was called Roman-Dutch law by the mid–17th century. The municipal laws of Amsterdam also governed New Netherland. Any laws and ordinances related to the colony had to be approved by the Dutch West India Co (WIC).

The director and council, appointed by the WIC, governed the colony; they were the criminal court, court of last appeal, Surrogate Court, and Court of Admiralty. The director and council also provided judicial and administrative oversight of the settlements until they reached sufficient size to be granted their own courts. Villages were governed by local inferior courts of justice, which had both administrative and judicial responsibilities. The *schout,* appointed by the director and council, was president of the court, sheriff, and prosecuting attorney. As president he had one vote, as did each of the *schepenen* (magistrates), but when prosecuting a case he could not vote. The *schepenen* were chosen by the director and council from a double number of names submitted by the local court. New Amsterdam's municipal court was established in 1653; as a municipality, New Amsterdam also had two burgomasters, or mayors.

British Colonial Courts

After installation of the proprietary government of New York in 1664, the common and statute law of England became the law of the colony, as supplemented by laws enacted by the governor or, after 1683, the Colonial Assembly. Under the charter from King Charles II to his brother James, Duke of York, the governor of New York appointed officials, promulgated laws, and established courts. By the Duke's Laws of 1665, Gov Richard Nicolls continued the existing local courts and appointed new court officers. The Dutch-dominated mayor's court of New York City began to use juries but adopted other common-law procedure only reluctantly. Courts of Sessions, conducted by justices of the peace, were established for the English-speaking areas of Long Island, Staten Island, and Westchester and, after 1674, for the rest of the colony.

New York's early superior courts bore names of specialized English courts but had broader jurisdiction. The highest court under the Laws of 1665 was the Court of Assizes. The governor presided over annual and special sessions in New York City, assisted by council members and local magistrates. The Court of Assizes tried major civil and criminal cases and heard appeals from local courts. In 1683, at the direction of Gov Thomas Dongan, New York's first elected assembly replaced the Court of Assizes with a traveling Court of Oyer and Terminer. The new court's two judges held at least one trial term a year in each of New York's newly established counties; the Court of Sessions in each county met more frequently. The Court of Chancery, headed by the governor, functioned as the court of equity and the court of last resort. After 1686 the governor also supervised the probate of wills and administration of estates in what was called the Prerogative Court. Routine probate business was carried out by appointed Surrogates and by the county and city courts. Elements of Dutch inheritance law protecting widows' property rights persisted until the 18th century.

In 1688 King James II made New York part of the Dominion of New England, a multicolony conglomeration governed from Boston. Following the Glorious Revolution in England, Capt Jacob Leisler in 1689 seized control of New York's government in the name of the new sovereigns, King William and Queen Mary. When Gov Henry Sloughter arrived in 1691, he ordered the arrest of Leisler and his associates, then called an assembly and directed it to reestablish the court system. The governor approved a law creating the Supreme Court of Judicature, which replaced the Court of Oyer and Terminer. The new court had all the civil, criminal, and appellate jurisdiction of England's central common-law courts. A litigant could bring one of the common-law actions to recover a debt, damages, or the possession of real or personal property or its value. One could also obtain a special-purpose writ, such as mandamus, to compel a public officer or a corporation to perform a mandated act or to review such acts, or habeas corpus, to inquire into the cause of detention of an individual. The Judiciary Act of 1691 continued the Court of Chancery, the governor serving as chancellor. The court was not fully operational until 1704, and for decades

CHIEF JUDGES OF THE COURT OF APPEALS AFTER 1898

Name	Dates of Service	Residence
Alton B. Parker	1898–5 Aug 1904	Kingston (Ulster Co)
Edgar M. Cullen	2 Sept 1904–13	Brooklyn
Willard Bartlett	1914–16	Brooklyn
Frank H. Hiscock	1917–27	Syracuse
Benjamin N. Cardozo	1928–7 Mar 1932	New York City
Cuthbert W. Pound	8 Mar 1932–Dec 1934	Lockport (Niagara Co)
Frederick E. Crane	1935–39	Brooklyn
Irving Lehman	1940–21 Sept 1945	New York City
John T. Loughran	28 Sept 1945–31 Mar 1953	Kingston (Ulster Co)
Edmund H. Lewis	22 Apr 1953–54	Syracuse
Albert Conway	1955–59	Brooklyn
Charles S. Desmond	1960–66	Eden (Erie Co)
Stanley H. Fuld	1967–73	New York City
Charles D. Breitel	1974–78	New York City
Lawrence H. Cooke	19 Apr 1979–84	Monticello (Sullivan)
Sol Wachtler	28 May 1985–11 Nov 1992	Manhasset (Nassau Co)
Richard D. Simons, acting	17 Nov 1992–22 Mar 1993	Rome (Oneida Co)
Judith S. Kaye	23 Mar 1993–	New York City

Source: New York Red Book.

Note: If only years of service are given, the term ran from January through December.

after that the governor's opponents disputed his right to set up the court without the assembly's approval. Equity jurisdiction was useful, especially for the propertied class. The Court of Chancery had powers to grant equitable relief in commercial disputes; to appoint and supervise trustees for the property of persons needing judicial protection, such as orphans and widows; to foreclose mortgages; and to assist the common-law courts by issuing subpoenas, injunctions, and other special orders.

The Judiciary Act of 1691 also continued the county Courts of Sessions for criminal prosecutions only and established county Courts of Common Pleas for civil suits. The bench of a county court was a panel of three justices of the peace and had considerable administrative responsibilities. The city courts of New York and Albany, established by charters granted in 1686, were continued. Justices of the peace were empowered to try small suits for amounts up to 40s (after 1754, £5). The assembly renewed the 1691 Judiciary Act periodically but in 1698 refused to do so. Thereafter, until the American Revolution, the royal governors issued ordinances continuing the province's higher courts, and the assembly passed a few acts relating to lower courts. The governor appointed judges and justices of the peace. Starting in 1678 the governors appointed a judge of the Court of Admiralty, which had general jurisdiction in maritime cases, including prize vessels and cargoes taken in wartime. The State Court of Admiralty operated briefly, but its jurisdiction passed to the federal courts in 1789.

The three (after 1758, four) justices of the Supreme Court of Judicature traveled on circuit to preside over civil and criminal trials in the counties. Court documents were filed by the court clerk in New York City. The full Supreme Court met four times a year to hear arguments on motions and points of law raised during trial, to review lower court proceedings, and to try felony cases arising in the city. In civil cases appeals might be taken to the governor and council if the case involved more than £100 or to the king and his Privy Council if more than £300; such appeals were few. Civil court documents now closely imitated those used by the English common-law courts—writs (orders to a sheriff) and pleadings (formal statements of a plaintiff's demand and defendant's response)—but court procedure was much simpler than in England. By the 1750s the Supreme Court handled several thousand cases yearly, mostly suits for debts. Most cases never went to trial but were settled by the parties, conceded by the defendant, sent to referees, or simply dropped; thus commercial relations were expedited, while judicial oversight was retained.

Like the civil courts, the criminal justice system was cumbersome and not entirely effective. Justices of the peace had little or no training in the law. Suspects often avoided or resisted arrest by a sheriff or constable. Felony prosecutions resulted in convictions only about half the time, more often in law-abiding Suffolk Co and less often in raucous New York City and in remote Albany Co. In 1732 the assembly permitted justices of the peace or city magistrates to dispose of minor criminal cases without a jury if no bail was given. Nevertheless, criminal caseloads in the county and city courts grew alarmingly during the troubled 1750s and 1760s, and judges increasingly sentenced convicted thieves to flogging, branding, or hanging.

Courts under the Constitutions of 1777 and 1821

In Revolutionary War era New York the regular courts were suspended from 1776 to 1778, and special committees exercised judicial powers. The state's first constitution, adopted in 1777, declared that the common and statute law of England and the laws of the colony in force in 1775 should "continue the law of this State." The colonial trial courts were continued largely unchanged except that an appointed chancellor, instead of the governor, headed the Court of Chancery. In place of the governor and council, the constitution established a new court of last resort, the Court for the Trial of Impeachments and Correction of Errors, which heard appeals from the Supreme Court and the Court of Chancery and tried any state officer impeached by the assembly (none were during the court's 70-year history). The Court of Errors (as it became known) was a cumbersome body composed of the chancellor, the Supreme Court justices, and the entire senate. The court's procedure resembled that of the senate, and the court's deliberations and decisions were often politicized. All judges and justices of the peace in the state from 1777 through 1822 were appointed by the Council of Appointment.

New York's trial court system was slowly expanded. Each new county had its Courts of Common Pleas and of General Sessions; each new town, its justices of the peace. City and village charters established courts of limited jurisdiction. In 1787 the Surrogate's Court was established in each county to prove wills, oversee the settlement of estates, and appoint guardians for orphans and widows. The state-level Court of Probates exercised certain functions until 1823. Supreme Court terms for argument of legal points and review of lower court judgments were held in New York City and later also in Albany (starting 1797), Utica (1820), and Rochester (1841). For the convenience of attorneys filing papers, Supreme Court clerk's offices were located in New York City, Albany, Utica, and Geneva (Ontario Co). Until 1823 the five Supreme Court justices traveled on circuit to hold trial terms in each county. The chancellor held terms of the Court of Chancery, sometimes in his own home as the court used no juries (except in contested divorce proceedings).

The 1821 Constitution, effective in 1823, changed the method of selecting judges, who were now appointed by the governor with consent of the senate; justices of the peace were made elective in 1827. This constitution somewhat increased the capacity of the higher trial courts by dividing the state into eight judicial circuits, or districts. In each one an appointed circuit judge traveled to county courthouses to try Supreme Court civil cases and to hold Courts of Oyer and Terminer for felony cases. The same judges also presided over Courts of Equity to handle most cases formerly heard by the chancellor, who now heard appeals and cases involving parties in more than one circuit or from outside the state. After 1830 the circuit judges or separately appointed judges were designated vice chancellors; the Courts of Equity were abolished. The Supreme Court's three justices now heard only motions or appeals from the common-law trial courts. These structural changes failed to accommodate a huge increase in civil court business during the 1820s and 1830s. Complaints about case backlogs mounted, and the legislature considered proposals for court reform.

Courts under the Constitutions of 1846 and 1894

The state's 1846 Constitution, effective the following year, restructured the higher trial courts and the appellate courts. The Court of Chancery was abolished and its equity jurisdiction given to the Supreme Court, which became a trial court of general jurisdiction, where any case might be adjudicated, either in an original proceeding or by transfer or appeal from a lower court. The bench of the Supreme Court was expanded from

11 to 33 justices. The court continued to hold trial terms in each county, and the county clerks were made custodians of the resulting records. The Supreme Court exercised its appellate jurisdiction in general terms held in each of eight judicial districts. The general terms were reduced to four in 1870 and increased to five in 1884. The Court of Errors was abolished in 1847 and succeeded by the Court of Appeals as the state's court of last resort. The court sat in Albany and was composed of elected judges, augmented during the periods 1847–69 and 1900–1921 by designated Supreme Court justices. The County Court, with limited civil and extensive criminal jurisdiction, replaced the old Court of Common Pleas and Court of General Sessions (except in New York Co, where those two courts were continued until 1896 and 1962, respectively).

The Constitution of 1846 made almost all judicial offices elective, from judges of the Court of Appeals down to police justices in cities and villages; an exception was lower criminal court justices in New York City, who to the present are appointed by the mayor. The framers of the new constitution intended that the elective judiciary should be directly responsible to the sovereign people and thereby help check any excesses by the legislature. However, court jobs throughout the state were often dispensed as political rewards. Civil service status was extended to nonjudicial positions in 1962.

Common-law procedure during the early 19th century was burdened by archaic, prolix language and pointless legal fictions, as reformer Henry D. Sedgwick pointed out in 1822. After 1839 David Dudley Field, a New York City lawyer, campaigned relentlessly for procedural reform and codification of the law. The 1846 Constitution required the legislature to appoint three commissioners (among them was Field) to draft a code of civil procedure. A simple, short code enacted in 1848–49 recognized just one form of civil action, in place of about a dozen common-law actions, abolished all the intricacies of common-law pleading, and expanded the right to appeal in civil cases. The "Field Code" was imitated by some 30 other states. However, the revised New York Code of Civil Procedure enacted in 1876–80 contained several thousand sections, prompting much criticism from legal reformers. A code of criminal court procedure and a penal code (specifying penalties for classes of crimes) were adopted in 1881, over 30 years after they were first proposed. Appellate review of criminal court judgments was significantly expanded. The new Civil Practice Act enacted in 1920 simplified civil court procedure, notably by authorizing pretrial discovery of evidence without a judicial order, though its changes tended to favor creditors and commercial interests.

The Constitution of 1894, effective in 1896, reorganized the state's inefficient, redundant system of higher courts. Abolished were the circuit courts and Courts of Oyer and Terminer, antique names for trial courts (civil and criminal) held by Supreme Court justices. The superior civil courts in New York City, Brooklyn, and Buffalo, each holding trial terms and a general term for appealed cases, were merged into the Supreme Court. The general terms of the Supreme Court were replaced by an Appellate Division organized in four multicounty judicial departments, with court facilities in Manhattan, Brooklyn, Albany, and Rochester. Justices of the Appellate Division were designated by the governor from among the Supreme Court justices in each department. Appellate Terms were organized in the first and second departments to hear appeals from the lower trial courts in New York City and the suburban counties. Elsewhere in the state the county courts continue to hear appeals from local courts. As a branch of the Supreme Court, the Appellate Division received very broad authority to review trial court proceedings and determinations, both legal and factual, and to dispense justice as required. The Appellate Division has also been authorized to hear appeals from administrative determinations of state agencies, such as the Workers' Compensation Board.

The 1894 Constitution also explicitly stated the jurisdiction of the Court of Appeals, with the intent of limiting its caseload. For decades the court had been overburdened with routine cases, because various statutes permitted appeal of almost any legal point and even questions of fact raised in the general (appellate) terms of the Supreme Court and of the superior city courts of New York, Brooklyn, and Buffalo (the general terms sometimes handed down conflicting decisions). The Commission of Appeals (1869–75) and a second division of the Court of Appeals (1889–92) eliminated large case backlogs only temporarily. The 1894 Constitution essentially limited the jurisdiction of the Court of Appeals to questions of law after final determinations by the Appellate Division. In addition the Court of Appeals reviewed the facts and the law in all cases in which the defendant was sentenced to death, as it had done since 1887. A 1917 statute and a 1925 constitutional amendment empowered the Court of Appeals to review new findings of fact in the first-level appellate review of civil cases in certain circumstances. By 1985 all appeals were by permission of the Court of Appeals or the Appellate Division, except for constitutional issues in civil cases and capital cases.

Development of Specialized Courts

The Court of Claims developed in the decades around 1900 to adjudicate private claims against the state and counterclaims by the state. Traditionally the sovereign state was immune from lawsuits; the legislature decided claims against the state at its discretion. In 1817, however, the legislature designated, and later constituted as a board, canal appraisers to decide the numerous claims arising from the taking of lands and waters for the construction and operation of the Erie Canal. An 1875 constitutional amendment barred the legislature from determining private claims, which was prone to many abuses. The State Board of Audit was empowered to settle contract claims against the state. In 1883 the Board of Claims took over the functions of the two earlier boards. Renamed the Court of Claims in 1897 (and again called the Board of Claims between 1911 and 1915), the court received jurisdiction over claims arising out of state contracts and public works; in 1929, torts committed by any state officer or employee; and, in 1996, state violations of certain civil rights. Court of Claims judges are appointed by the governor with consent of the senate. The court is organized into eight districts, though it may sit in any county in the state.

Specialized courts dealing with juvenile and family matters were established during the early 20th century, though provisions for juveniles had accumulated gradually during the 19th century. Judges could commit juvenile delinquents under age 16 to state-financed houses of refuge in New York City (established in 1824) and in Rochester (1849). After 1892 children charged with crimes could be tried separately from adults, and after 1909 they could not be sentenced as adults, except for the most serious felonies. Between 1901 and 1910 children's courts were set up as branches of city criminal courts in Buffalo, New York City, Rochester, and Syracuse. Implementing a constitutional amendment of 1921, a separate children's court was set up in each county and in New York City (in the latter the Children's Court established in 1924 became a branch of the new Domestic Relations Court in 1933). The Children's Court received jurisdiction over delinquent, neglected, and disabled children under age 16. Hearings were informal and private; criminal court procedure and, after 1932, due process safeguards were largely eliminated. Probation officers, physicians, and social workers were supposed to provide the judge with guidance in deciding the case for the benefit of the child. In most counties the county judge presided over the Children's Court, and probation officers were few.

A major report on children and families in the New York City courts, sponsored by the city bar association in 1954, found severe understaffing and fragmented jurisdiction. The report recommended that there be a single court with jurisdiction in all matters involving children and families, a goal partly realized in the Family Court established statewide in 1962. The new court had jurisdiction, some of it still shared with other courts, over juvenile delinquents, other minors under age 16 "in need of supervision," and cases involving child abuse and neglect, family assault, support, paternity, custody, and adoption. The Supreme Court has retained exclusive jurisdiction over divorce and other marital proceedings.

Movement toward a Unified Court System

Supreme Court caseloads rose steadily after about 1900. A 1905 constitutional amendment authorized the legislature to increase the number of justices according to census population. By the early 1930s negligence lawsuits—the majority arising from automobile accidents—made up 60–70% of the Supreme Court's caseload, and marital proceedings much of the rest; the proportion of debt cases, predominant during the 19th century, had greatly declined. Typical case backlogs were about two years in New York City, one year elsewhere. Both civil and criminal caseloads grew steadily after World War II, and case delays in some courts, most of them in the New York City area, got much worse. The judicial assignment system was inflexible. After 1902 Supreme Court justices could be assigned outside their judicial district, but only if they consented. In 1954 temporary reassignments of judges among different courts was authorized in New York City, which at that point had 190 trial court facilities. In 1956 the Temporary Commission on the Courts, chaired by Harrison Tweed, recommended mergers of most trial courts and a centralized administration for New York State's vast, fragmented court system. Various political and judicial interest groups blocked these proposals. However, as recommended by the Tweed

NEW YORK STATE UNIFIED COURT SYSTEM

Court (date established)	Composition	Jurisdiction	Appeals to
Court of Appeals (1847)	7 judges serving 14-year terms; nominated by Commission on Judicial Nomination, then appointed by governor with consent of senate	Appeals from Supreme Court Appellate Division; appeals of death sentences or substantial constitutional issues directly from trial courts	US Supreme Court (issues involving US Constitution or federal law)
Court for Trial of Impeachments (1847)	Judges of Court of Appeals and members of senate	Trial of state officers who have been impeached by assembly for "willful and corrupt misconduct"	—
Supreme Court Appellate Division, First through Fourth Departments (1896)	24 justices serving 5-year terms permanently authorized, plus additional justices designated temporarily; designated by governor from elected Supreme Court justices in each department	Appeals from Supreme Court Appellate Term (First and Second Departments); from county-level courts (Third and Fourth Departments); and in limited circumstances from executive agency determinations (eg, Public Service Commission, Workers' Compensation Board); also admission and discipline of attorneys	Court of Appeals
Supreme Court, Appellate Term, established in First and Second Departments (1896)	3–5 justices authorized in each department; designated by chief administrator of the courts from elected Supreme Court justices, with approval of presiding justice of the department	Appeals from New York City Civil Court and Criminal Court (First and Second Departments); and from county, district, city, town, and village courts (Second Department outside New York City)	Supreme Court, Appellate Division
Supreme Court (1691)	12 judicial districts; 323 justices authorized; justices nominated by political party judicial conventions in each district and elected for 14-year terms	General jurisdiction in original proceedings; court usually hears cases outside jurisdiction of other courts (eg, suits for more than $25,000; divorce and other marital proceedings); in New York City all felonies and certain misdemeanors are prosecuted in Supreme Court; in other counties felonies are prosecuted either in County Court or Supreme Court	Supreme Court, Appellate Division
Court of Claims (1883)	22 judges appointed by governor with consent of the senate for 9-year terms; some Court of Claims judges are assigned to other courts	Claims against the state and certain state-created entities (eg, CUNY, New York Power Authority)	Supreme Court, Appellate Division
County Court (1847) (in counties outside New York City)	1 or more judges elected for 10-year terms; County Court judges in smaller counties may also serve as Family Court judge and/or as surrogate	Limited civil jurisdiction (suits up to $25,000); criminal jurisdiction (felonies); appeals from city, town, village courts (Third and Fourth Departments only)	Supreme Court Appellate Term; appeals in felony cases go to the Appellate Division (Second Department); Supreme Court Appellate Division (Third and Fourth Departments)
Surrogate's Court (1787)	1 or more surrogates in each county; elected for 10-year terms (14-year terms in New York City)	Probate of wills; administration of estates; guardianship for property of minors; adoption of minors	Supreme Court, Appellate Division
Family Court (1962)	1 or more judges elected for 10-year terms in each county outside New York City; 47 judges of the New York City Family Court are authorized and nominated by the Mayor's Advisory Committee on the Judiciary and appointed by mayor for 10-year terms	Juvenile delinquents and other minors under age 16 "in need of supervision"; crimes or offenses within families; guardianship and custody of minors; support of dependents; paternity determinations; foster care placements; adoption of minors	Supreme Court, Appellate Division
New York City Civil Court (1962)	131 judges authorized; elected for 10-year terms; Civil Court administrative judge appoints judges of New York City Housing Court	Limited civil jurisdiction (suits up to $25,000); small claims part (suits up to $3,000); housing part (landlord-tenant matters and housing code violations)	Supreme Court, Appellate Term (First or Second Department)
New York City Criminal Court (1962)	107 judges authorized; nominated by Mayor's Advisory Committee on the Judiciary and appointed by mayor for 10-year terms	Limited criminal jurisdiction (misdemeanors, felony arraignments, preliminary hearings); violations; traffic infractions (a noncourt administrative agency handles traffic infractions and parking violations)	Supreme Court, Appellate Term (First or Second Department)
City Courts (outside New York City)	1–12 judges, varying by size of city; full-time judges elected for 10-year terms and part-time judges for 6-year terms	Limited civil jurisdiction (suits up to $15,000; some courts have small claims parts for suits up to $3,000); limited criminal jurisdiction (misdemeanors, felony arraignments, preliminary hearings); violations; traffic infractions (in Buffalo and Rochester noncourt administrative agencies handle traffic infractions and parking violations)	Supreme Court, Appellate Term (Second Department); County Court (Third and Fourth Departments)

NEW YORK STATE UNIFIED COURT SYSTEM (continued)

Court (date established)	Composition	Jurisdiction	Appeals to
District Court (Nassau Co, 1939; western Suffolk Co, 1964)	Judges elected by districts for 6-year terms	Limited civil jurisdiction (suits up to $15,000; small claims up to $3,000); limited criminal jurisdiction (misdemeanors, felony arraignments, and preliminary hearings); violations; traffic infractions (noncourt administrative agencies handle traffic infractions and parking violations)	Supreme Court, Appellate Term (Second Department)
Town and Village Justice Courts (except in Nassau Co and western Suffolk Co; some villages elsewhere do not have their own justice courts)	Justices elected for 4-year terms	Limited civil jurisdiction (suits up to $3,000); limited criminal jurisdiction (misdemeanors, felony arraignments, preliminary hearings); violations; traffic infractions	Supreme Court, Appellate Term (First and Second Departments); County Court (Third and Fourth Departments)

Note: A 1961 constitutional amendment providing a new judiciary article for the state constitution established the Unified Court System comprising all trial and appeals courts.

Compiled by James D. Folts

Commission, the legislature in 1955 established the Judicial Conference, an oversight and advisory group of appellate and trial court judges that replaced a judicial council dating from 1934.

In the late 1950s the Judicial Conference proposed and the Rockefeller administration promoted a new judiciary article for the state constitution, approved in 1961. The article established the statewide Unified Court System and reorganized some of the trial courts. Effective in 1962, Family Court replaced the Domestic Relations Court in New York City and the Children's Court in each county outside the city. The Court of General Sessions in Manhattan and the County Courts in the other four boroughs were merged into the Supreme Court. Two levels of lower civil and criminal courts in the city were replaced by two new courts, the Civil Court and the Criminal Court of New York City. Supreme Court justices and other trial court judges could be assigned to other locations and even to other courts to help reduce case backlogs. The presiding justices of the four departments of the Supreme Court Appellate Division were still responsible for most details of court administration and for disciplining local court justices. However, after 1974 a chief administrator of the courts (or chief administrative judge) coordinated statewide court operations through the Office of Court Administration.

Constitutional amendments proposed by a legislative commission, promoted by Hugh Carey's administration and approved by voters in 1977, made major changes in judicial administration. The reforms were prompted by the growing need for more efficient court operations, by the unseemly, and unusual, contested elections for Court of Appeals judgeships in 1973 and 1974, and by the lack of an effective disciplinary mechanism for the judiciary (the Court on the Judiciary, set up in 1947, was mostly inactive). The 1977 amendments established a commission to nominate Court of Appeals judges, who would then be appointed by the governor with consent of the senate, and continued the Commission on Judicial Conduct established by a 1975 amendment. The commission has actively used its power to investigate and discipline or retire judges and justices charged with misconduct or incapacity. The constitution still empowers the legislature to remove judges by impeachment and trial or by joint resolution of both houses or of the senate alone, but such proceedings are rare. The 1977 reorganization formally transferred responsibility for administering statewide court operations to the chief administrator, who is appointed by the chief judge of the Court of Appeals. Appointed administrative judges manage court operations throughout the state. Starting in 1978 the state took over the costs of operating all the trial courts except the town and village justice courts, but not the substantial costs of local court facilities. In 1987 a court facilities fund was established to help defray construction and renovation costs.

Between the 1960s and the 1980s the legislature almost completely recodified the state's laws and rules for court procedure. The Civil Practice Law and Rules, effective in 1963, replaced the Civil Practice Act of 1920 and its associated court rules. The 1967 Penal Law and 1971 Criminal Procedure Law were the first comprehensive revisions of those laws since 1881. The new Family Court, the Surrogate's Courts, the New York City lower courts, the city courts elsewhere in the state, the district courts in suburban Long Island, and the town and village justice courts all received updated, initially uniform statutes that eliminated a multitude of special or local provisions. Uniform court rules took effect in all courts statewide in 1986. One of these rules established an "individual assignment system," which has a single judge handling most or all phases of a case to ensure familiarity with the facts and the issues.

Since 1962 various proposals to reorganize and consolidate further have had little success. District courts replaced town courts in Nassau Co in 1939 and western Suffolk Co in 1964, but the state still has 3 or 4 superior courts in each county, 61 city courts besides the New York City civil and criminal courts, and about 2,200 town and village justices. Three new Supreme Court judicial districts were formed in the New York City metropolitan area between 1948 and 1981. A proposed fifth department of the Appellate Division would reduce caseloads in the busy Second Department. The many advocates of a merger of the County Court, Family Court, Surrogate's Court, and Court of Claims into the Supreme Court assert that it would facilitate judicial assignments, enhance the status of juvenile and family justice, and simplify access to judicial remedies now provided by different courts.

New York State has developed mechanisms for quicker, easier resolution of disputes. The Civil Practice Act of 1920 provided for compulsory arbitration of business and labor contracts outside of the court system. A 1934 statute authorized uncomplicated "small claims" litigation in the New York City Municipal Court, later extended to other city courts and the district courts. Compulsory arbitration of smaller suits was adopted in many county and local courts starting in 1978. The state made grants to nonprofit organizations after 1981 to run community dispute resolution centers providing conciliation, mediation, and arbitration services, and these centers operate in every county. Starting in 1985 experienced attorneys served as hearing examiners in Family Court to help manage the huge volume of child and spousal support cases. The Commercial Division of the Supreme Court, created to expedite complex business litigation, has operated in several large urban and suburban counties since 1995.

The Supreme Court experienced moderate increases in its civil business after the 1960s. After much controversy, no-fault automobile insurance was adopted in 1974, easing the load of tort litigation. The criminal and family courts experienced major increases in caseloads. Even though New York City felony caseloads decreased by nearly half during the 1990s, the total in 2001 was still nearly two-thirds more than that of the late 1970s. Felony caseloads outside of the city nearly doubled after the 1970s and dropped off only slightly after 1999. Close to half of all criminal cases by the late 1990s were drug related. Misdemeanor cases in the New York City Criminal Court increased dramatically starting in the mid-1990s because of a "get-tough" policy on petty crime. The state's busiest court is the Family Court; spousal support and child custody are the most numerous cases. Since 1962 juvenile justice has been increasingly formalized, with court-assigned lawyers and reinstituted due process rights. Acts of 1976 and 1978 recriminalized violent offenses committed by persons aged 13–15. Most Family Court proceedings were opened to the public starting in 1997. The huge criminal and family court caseloads have overburdened judges, court-appointed attorneys, probation officers, social agencies, and court facilities. Several innovative programs have been set up within the existing court system to expedite justice and to address intractable social problems: drug treatment courts routing nonviolent drug addicts to treatment programs, integrated domestic violence courts, and community courts serving three New York City neighborhoods.

New York State's court system had just over 4 million new case filings in 2001. The Unified Court System's operations budget for 2002–3 was $1.32 billion; its personnel included over 1,200 state-paid judges, 2,200 town and village justices, and nearly 15,000 nonjudicial employees. Despite several major reorganizations over the past two centuries, New York's system of multilevel, special-purpose, and locally and regionally organized courts is the most complex of any state. A constitutional amendment consolidating the trial courts remains an announced goal of the state's political and judicial leaders. However, centralized court administration and programs of alternative dispute resolution and expedited criminal justice are already reshaping New York's judicial system in the early 21st century.

Bergan, Francis. *The History of the New York Court of Appeals, 1847–1932* (New York: Columbia Univ Press, 1985)

Botler, Jill P., et al. "The Appellate Division of the Supreme Court of New York: An Empirical Study of Its Powers and Functions as an Intermediate State Court," *Fordham Law Review* 47 (1979): 929–85

Chester, Alden, with E. Melvin Williams. *Courts and Lawyers of New York: A History, 1609–1925,* 4 vols (New York: American Historical Society, 1925)

Christoph, Peter R., and Florence A. Christoph, eds. *Records of the Court of Assizes for the Colony of New York, 1665–1682* (Baltimore: Genealogical Publishing, 1983)

Folts, James D. *"Duely and Constantly Kept": A History of the New York Supreme Court, 1691–1847 and an Inventory of Its Records (Albany, Utica, and Geneva Offices), 1797–1847* (Albany: NYS Court of Appeals and NYS Archives and Records Administration, 1991)

Gellhorn, Walter. *Children and Families in the Courts of New York City* (New York: Dodd, Mead, 1954)

Gibson, Ellen M., and William H. Manz. *New York Legal Research Guide,* 2d ed. (Buffalo: William S. Hein, 1998)

Goebel, Julius, Jr, and T. Raymond Naughton. *Law Enforcement in Colonial New York: A Study in Criminal Procedure (1664–1776)* (1944; repr Montclair, NJ: Patterson Smith, 1970)

Greenberg, Douglas. *Crime and Law Enforcement in the Colony of New York, 1691–1776* (Ithaca: Cornell Univ Press, 1976)

Hershkowitz, Leo, and Milton M. Klein, eds. *Courts and Law in Early New York: Selected Essays* (Port Washington, NY: Kennikat, 1978)

Johnson, Herbert A. *Essays on New York Colonial Legal History* (Westport, Conn: Greenwood, 1981)

Johnson, Herbert A., and Ralph K. Andrist. *Historic Courthouses of New York State: 18th and 19th Century Halls of Justice across the Empire State* (New York: Columbia Univ Press, 1977)

MacCrate, Robert, James D. Hopkins, and Maurice Rosenberg. *Appellate Justice in New York* (Chicago: American Judicature Society, 1982)

McNamara, John J., Jr. "The Court of Claims: Its Development and Present Role in the Unified Court System," *St. John's Law Review* 40 (1965): 1–49

Nelson, William E. *The Legalist Reformation: Law, Politics, and Ideology in New York, 1920–1980* (Chapel Hill: Univ of North Carolina Press, 2001)

New York State Bar Association. *The Courts of New York: A Guide to Court Procedures, with a Glossary of Legal Terms* (Albany: Author, 2000)

New York State. Court of Appeals. *"There Shall Be a Court of Appeals . . .": 150th Anniversary of the Court of Appeals of the State of New York* (Albany: Author, 1997)

Rosen, Deborah A. *Courts and Commerce: Gender, Law, and the Market Economy in Colonial New York* (Columbus: Ohio State Univ Press, 1997)

James D. Folts

Covenant Chain. Alliance and treaty system between the Iroquois and English. From 1677 to 1777 the Iroquois and their allies met almost annually in Albany with the English from colonial New York and other English colonies to renew the terms of the alliance.

Alliances among the Iroquois

The Covenant Chain grew out of the governing practices of the Iroquois Confederacy and diplomatic relations between the Europeans and American Indians living in New York. Government among the tribes of the Iroquois Confederacy was an extension of their clan system. Links were forged with other tribes in the confederacy through a series of real and fictive kinship ties. There was no governing body permanently in session overseeing affairs. When coordinated village, tribal, or confederacy action was needed, the clan system provided the needed mechanism for joint action. Group decisions were made in councils and reached by consensus. Wampum strings and belts served to record and confirm what was said and done, and speeches at councils were laden with rich metaphors. When one tribe, or group within a tribe, no longer wished to adhere to some course of action, it was free to do as it wished. For these reasons, alliances—a form of group decision making—needed to be carefully monitored. The terms of alliance and the duties of each party needed to be repeated and reaffirmed; any breaches needed to be explained and amends made for them.

The Iroquois extended this same process to their dealings with tribes outside of their confederacy. Each new partner was given a kinship term (brother, uncle, father, nephew) to designate the nature of the relationship to the Iroquois, and periodic councils were held to renew and reaffirm the alliance. When Europeans intruded into Iroquoia, the Iroquois followed the same process with them, and European negotiators quickly learned the protocols of councils and adapted to the Iroquois way. Accustomed to formal written treaties, Europeans tried to follow their own protocols and kept extensive written records of meetings between the Iroquois and Dutch, French, and English traders, missionaries, and government officials. But Europeans learned to view matters in Iroquois terms and soon were involved in the series of at least annual negotiations to work out trade relationships and military alliances. Although Europeans may have come to North America with ethnocentric notions of their superiority, of their "right" to native land, and of natives as "subjects" of European crowns, the actions of the Dutch and English governments of New Netherland and New York Colony belie that arrogance. Their participation in alliances with the Iroquois showed that they viewed the Iroquois as nations with rights to negotiate treaties.

Evolution of the Covenant Chain

The term Covenant Chain entered the written record around 1677, shortly after the English had regained control of New York from the Dutch. Prior to that date, the Iroquois had made treaties with Dutch traders and officials but had not used the term. At a council in 1659 between the Mohawk and Dutch, official reference was made to a 1643 treaty in which the Mohawk claimed that they had metaphorically bound themselves to the Dutch by an "iron chain." By the late 1670s the term Covenant Chain was increasingly used to convey that sense of alliance. At meetings in Albany and various Iroquois villages, participants renewed alliances, claiming that they came to "polish" the chain. In later Iroquois oral traditions, Iroquois leaders expressed how their relationships with Europeans grew in significance by describing how their alliances had gone from one bound by "rope" to one linked by a "chain of silver."

Over time the Iroquois became increasingly linked to New York, seeking guns, ammunition, and even military support for their wars against the French and French native allies. When Iroquois aspirations, military or otherwise, in areas controlled by other English colonies led to difficulties, the Iroquois used their English allies in New York to help resolve matters. New York officials, in turn, sought to use their connection with the Iroquois to promote their trade and imperial ambitions at the expense of other colonies. Thus the Covenant Chain alliance grew to include more and more tribes and colonies, all trying to use the mediation process promoted by the alliance to achieve their own ends. No one group ever controlled the Covenant Chain, and preeminence within it varied across time. As the aims of the various groups came into sharper opposition during the 18th century, the Covenant Chain became less useful as a means to reach accord. Alliances were not renewed, amends were not made for deaths incurred in sporadic raids, and with the increasing encroachments of the English onto Iroquois claimed lands, the Iroquois became less willing to trust their partners. Gen Maj John Sullivan's raid into Iroquoia in 1779 only confirmed how badly the Covenant Chain alliance had been sundered.

See also Colonial New York.

Jennings, Francis. "The Constitutional Evolution of the Covenant Chain," *American Philosophical Society Proceedings* 115 (Apr 1971): 88–96

———. *The Ambiguous Iroquois Empire: The Covenant Chain Confederation of Indian Tribes with English Colonies, from Its Beginnings to the Lancaster Treaty of 1744* (New York: Norton, 1984)

———, ed. *The History and Culture of Iroquois Diplomacy* (Syracuse: Syracuse Univ Press, 1985)

Richter, Daniel K., and James H. Merrell, eds. *Beyond the Covenant Chain: The Iroquois and Their Neighbors in Indian North America, 1600–1800* (Syracuse: Syracuse Univ Press, 1987)

José António Brandão

Cove Neck. Village (pop 300) in Oyster Bay (Nassau Co). In 1885 future president Theodore

Roosevelt built his home, Sagamore Hill, on Cove Neck; it served as the summer White House from 1901 to 1908 and is now a National Historic Site. Composed of about a dozen estates, Cove Neck incorporated as a village in 1927. It remains an estate community. In 2002 it was home to computer magnate Charles Wang and tennis star John McEnroe.

Richard A. Winsche

Coventry. Town (pop 1,589) in S central Chenango Co. Residents of Coventry, Conn, settled the area in 1785, and the town was formed from Greene in 1806. One of the highest towns in the county, it is located on a ridge dividing the watersheds of the Chenango River to the northwest and the Susquehanna River to the southeast. Its chief industry was dairying, and after the Civil War it had a number of cheese and butter factories. In the early 21st century, some residents participate in small agricultural enterprises such as beef cattle, herbs, and maple syrup, while others commute to jobs in Bainbridge, Afton, and Greene.

Michele A. McFee

covered bridges. With origins in European antiquity, these all-wood structures of heavy timbers, weather protected by siding and roofing, were once numerous in New York State, peaking at about 250 in the mid–19th century. Salmon Wheat's 1807 span across the Neversink River at what became Bridgeville (Sullivan Co) was the first bridge in the state known to have been weather protected when built. Theodore Burr of Oxford (Chenango Co) erected the first timber arches over the Hudson, Mohawk, Delaware, and Susquehanna Rivers, and his first covered bridge was completed in 1811. Later promoters designed and patented various trusses (beams that form the bridge's framework), such as the Town Lattice (1820) and Long (1830). The advent of railroads saw acceptance of the Howe truss (1840), used until wood was replaced by iron. The erection of sturdy wooden bridges at major river crossings

Covered bridge in Allegany State Park.

HISTORIC COVERED BRIDGES

Name (Year Built)	Locality (County)	Truss Type	Length[a] ft/m
Beaverkill (1865)	Livingston Manor (Sullivan)	Town lattice	98/29.9
Bendo (1860)	Roscoe (Sullivan)	Town lattice	48/14.6
Blenheim (1855)[b]	North Blenheim (Schoharie)	Long and center arch	210/64
Buskirk (1857)	Buskirk (Rensselaer) and White Creek (Washington)	Howe	164/50
Lower Shavertown (1877)	Hancock (Delaware)	Town lattice	32/9.8
Copeland (1879)[b]	Edinburg (Saratoga)	Queenpost	29/8.8
Downsville (1854)	Downsville (Delaware)	Long and queenpost	174/53
Eagleville (1858)	Eagleville (Washington)	Town lattice	101/30.8
Fitch's (1870)	Delhi (Delaware)	Town lattice	100/30.5
Forge (1906)[b]	Hardenburgh (Ulster)	Kingpost	27/8.2
Grants Mills (1902)[b]	Hardenburgh (Ulster)	Town lattice	66/20.1
Halls Mills (1912)[b]	Claryville (Sullivan)	Town lattice	130/39.6
Hamden (1859)	Hamden (Delaware)	Long	128/39
Hyde Hall (1823)[b]	East Springfield (Otsego)	Burr arch	53/16.2
Jay (1857)[b]	Jay (Essex)	Howe	175/53.3
Newfield (1853)	Newfield (Tompkins)	Town lattice with arch	115/35.1
Ashokan-Turnwood (1898)[b]	Olivebridge (Ulster)	Town lattice	62/18.9
Perrine's (1844)[b]	Esopus and Rosendale (Ulster)	Burr arch	154/46.9
Rexleigh (1847)	Rexleigh (Washington)	Howe	107/32.6
Salisbury Center (1875)	Salisbury Center (Herkimer)	Burr arch	50/15.2
Shushan (1858)[b]	Shushan (Washington)	Town lattice	161/49.1
Tappan (1906)	Hardenburgh (Ulster)	Kingpost	43/13.1
Tuscarora Club (1870)[b]	Margaretville (Delaware)	Stringer span	38/11.6
Van Tran Flat (1860)	Livingston Manor (Sullivan)	Town lattice with arch	117/35.7

Sources: R. L. Berfield, *Covered Bridges of New York State* (2003); New York State Covered Bridge Society, http://www.nycoveredbridges.org.

[a]From abutment to abutment.

[b]Closed to automobile traffic as of 2002.

led to their sites becoming arteries of commerce and trade. The distribution of these bridges generally followed population trends and the influence of individual erectors on local bridge builders. In 2002 New York State had 24 authentic covered wooden bridges, and in recent years there has been avid interest by hobbyists and historic preservationists. Hyde Hall in East Springfield (Otsego Co) is the state's oldest (1823) covered bridge, and Blenheim in North Blenheim (Schoharie Co) is the longest single-span covered bridge in the world at 210 feet (64 m).

Allen, Richard Sanders. *Covered Bridges of the Northeast*, 2d rev ed. (Brattleboro, Vt: Stephen Greene Press, 1983)

———. *Old North Country Bridges* (Utica: North Country Books, 1983)

Berfield, Rick L. *Covered Bridges of New York State: A Guide* (Syracuse: Syracuse Univ Press, 2003)

Richard Sanders Allen

Covert. Town (pop 2,227) in SE Seneca Co. Settled ?1796, the town was formed from Ovid in 1817. In the late 19th century, five flagstone quarries operated in the southeast part of town. Rail shipment was provided by the Geneva and Ithaca Railroad, later Lehigh Valley (1873–1960s). In the early 21st century Covert was largely agricultural. There were several vineyards, and grain corn was raised for the dairy industry. A part of Finger Lakes National Forest is located in Covert, as is the privately owned Deere Haven Farm Museum.

Lisa Compton

Covington [KAHV-ING-TON]. Town (pop 1,357) in NE Wyoming Co. Settled in 1806, the town was formed from Perry and Le Roy (Genesee Co) in 1817. An influx of Irish immigrants came by 1860. The Fiero diamond-toothed cultivator was produced briefly at Peoria in the 19th century, and the Pearl Salt Co was in operation from 1886 to 1899. The Rochester and State Line Railroad came through in 1877. The town's orchards were wiped out by the 1934 freeze. In the early 21st century, farming is concentrated in dairy with some wheat, corn, and vegetable crops. Markin Tubing (1974) and D and M Precision (1996, tool and die makers) are local employers. Other workers commute to Rochester and elsewhere. The Crossman Bridge (1879), a Pratt truss bridge, is a local landmark.

Coxsackie [COOK-SOCK-Y]. Town (pop 8,884) and village (pop 2,895) in NE Greene Co. The Pieter Bronck House (1663) is the site of one of the earliest settlements and remains an important landmark. Coxsackie was formed as a district of Albany Co in 1772 and became a town in 1788. The village site developed as a river landing after the Revolution but did not incorporate until 1867. Brickmaking and foundries provided extensive employment in the 19th century. American Valve (1901–86) and various metal manufacturing thrived in the 20th century. The ice trade began in 1828 with a shipment to New York City, expanded until 1873, and then declined due to refrigeration and was extinct by 1950. Many of the icehouses became mushroom-growing factories in the 1920s. In 1935 a juvenile prison (now Coxsackie Correctional Facility) was built west of the village and was joined by Greene Correctional Facility in 1984. A Thruway interchange added in 1971 has aided industrial expansion, including a United Stationers warehouse.

Field Horne

Coxsackie Correctional Facility. The New York State Vocational Institution at Coxsackie (Greene Co) opened in March 1935. Its first inmates were males aged 16–19 transferred from the famed New York House of Refuge in Manhattan, which had closed. Coxsackie continued the House of Refuge's reformatory tradition, providing inmates convicted of minor crimes with a program of both academic and vocational education. Inmate age limits were gradually raised to 21 and then eliminated altogether. Coxsackie was initially built without walls; surrounded by open farmland, its ivy-covered dormitories and classrooms made the institution feel more like a school than a prison. Ambitious offerings enabled inmates to learn mechanics, machine shop, printing, agriculture, and other trades. Since the 1950s, however, Coxsackie has come to look more like a prison, as cellblocks, razor-ribbon fences, and other security measures were installed to meet a growing population. The institution was renamed the Coxsackie Correctional Facility in 1970 and designated a maximum security prison for male felons. Inmate disturbances in 1972, 1977, and 1987 reflected the changes in the institution's population. In the early 21st century, however, broad educational and counseling opportunities remain available to its 1,057 inmates, who, as a group, are younger than those in other facilities statewide. Nearly one-quarter of all inmates are under the age of 21 and nearly two-thirds under 30. Coxsackie's staff numbered 544 in 2003.

"Coxsackie," *DOCS Today* (May 2001): 12–15, 21

Richard Andress

Crane, (Harold) Hart (*b* Garrettsville, Ohio, 21 July 1899; *d* at sea, Atlantic Ocean, 27 Apr 1932). Poet. Crane was raised in Cleveland. His parents had an unhappy marriage and divorced in 1917, a year after their only son departed for New York City. Crane was determined to be a disciplined poet despite a turbulent personal life, occasioned in part by his homosexuality. In 1926 he published *White Buildings,* containing the complex lyric poems "For the Marriage of Faustus and Helen," "Voyages," and "Chaplinesque," among others, all preparations for his long, polyphonic *The Bridge* of 1930. This ode, Crane's most famous poem, ventured to do for modernist America what Walt Whitman's *Song of Myself* tried to do for mid-19th-century America: to provide a "bridge" over the dark waters of nihilism, the idea that life has no meaning, through the myths of America's landscapes. *The Bridge* takes Brooklyn Bridge as its central image, detailing other New York City scenes as well as the Indian past of the Adirondacks, and then moves outward to encompass all American landscapes and mythologies. His troubled life, which ended in an apparent suicide at sea near Cuba, found some resolution in his art, where he dramatized the modern world's longing for spiritual meaning, found only intermittently, in Crane's view, in cultural mythologies that rise and fall.

Unterecker, John. *Voyager: A Life of Hart Crane* (New York: Farrar, Straus & Giroux, 1969)

Eugene Paul Nassar

Crane, Stephen (*b* Newark, NJ, 1 Nov 1871; *d* Badenweiler, Germany, 5 June 1900). Author. The youngest of 14 children, Crane was raised in a Methodist household. From 1878 to 1883 he lived in Port Jervis (Orange Co). He attended Claverack College and Hudson River Institute (Columbia Co), becoming captain in the school's cadet corps from 1888 to 1890. After unsuccessful semesters at Lafayette College in Pennsylvania in 1890 and Syracuse University in 1891, he abandoned formal education, but while at Syracuse he may have begun a story about a prostitute that eventually became his first novel. After briefly contributing local New Jersey news, outdoor sketches, and tales of Sullivan Co to the *New York Tribune,* in August 1892 he moved to New York City, joining its semibohemian subculture of actors, artists, and medical students, and beginning studies of tenement life. These experiences intensified the depiction in his first novel, *Maggie: A Girl of the Streets* (1893), of the brutality and self-delusion of the Bowery. Unable to find a publisher for the novel, Crane borrowed money to issue it himself under the name Johnston Smith. Crane became an instant celebrity when *The Red Badge of Courage,* his synthesis of Civil War memoirs and histories, was published as a newspaper serial in 1894 and as a novel the following year. The main protagonists, the fictional 304th New York State Volunteers, were based in part on reminiscences of Civil War veterans Crane knew in Port Jervis. His writings also include a collection of poems entitled *The Black Riders* (1895); *George's Mother* (1896), a companion Bowery study; and such stories as "The Open Boat" (1897), based on his experience surviving rough seas in a small dinghy after his boat sank en route to Cuba, "The Bride Comes to Yellow Sky" (1897), and "The Blue Hotel" (1897). His defense of a New York City prostitute against police harassment made him unwelcome in the city thereafter. He covered the Greco-Turkish War for the *New York Journal,* then left Greece in June 1897 to take up residence in England. In 1898 Crane went to Cuba to cover the Spanish-American War, first for the *New York World* and then for the *New York Journal.* He revisited New York City briefly in December of that year then returned to England in January 1899. Crane died of tuberculosis in a German sanitorium. His brief writing career produced work of stylistic distinction, capturing the physical and emotional brutality underlying civilized modern life and making him a pioneering literary naturalist.

Stephen Crane at Syracuse University in baseball uniform, 1891.

Stallman, R. W. *Stephen Crane: A Biography* (New York: G. Braziller, 1968)
Wertheim, Stanley, and Paul Sorrentino. *The Crane Log: A Documentary Life of Stephen Crane, 1871–1900* (New York: G. K. Hall, 1994)

David J. Nordloh

Crapsey, Adelaide (*b* Brooklyn, 9 Sept 1878; *d* Rochester, 8 Oct 1914). Poet. Crapsey moved with her family to Rochester in 1879 and attended public schools, a Wisconsin boarding school, and Vassar College, from which she graduated with honors in 1901. In the decade that followed she taught in several states and in Europe, and studied archaeology in Rome (1904–5). In 1911 she accepted a position at Smith College (Northampton, Mass) as an instructor in poetics. There she invented and perfected the cinquain, an original verse form in five lines and 22 syllables, its brevity much like the haiku. Chronic fatigue and ill health were diagnosed as tuberculin meningitis, and she went to a Saranac Lake (Franklin and Essex Cos) nursing home where she wrote most of the poetry in *Verse.* Published posthumously in 1922 it earned her immediate acclaim.

Alkalay-Gut, Karen. *Alone in the Dawn: The Life of Adelaide Crapsey* (Athens: Univ of Georgia Press, 1988)
Butscher, Edward. *Adelaide Crapsey* (Boston: Twayne Publishers, 1979)

Pam Kirst

Crapsey, Algernon Sidney (*b* Fairmount, Ohio, 28 June 1847; *d* Rochester, 31 Dec 1927). Episcopal priest and controversialist. Crapsey had little formal schooling as a child but found employment beginning at age 11 in various business offices in Ohio, Washington, DC, and then New York City in the mid-1860s, where he joined the Episcopal Church and entered its ministry. He attended St. Stephens College (now Bard College) in Annandale-on-Hudson (Dutchess Co), then returned to New York City, where he graduated from General Theological Seminary in 1872, was ordained in 1873, and served on the staff of Trinity Church from 1872 to 1879. He then accepted a call from St. Andrew's Church in Rochester. Crapsey had a successful ministry there and involved the church in a number of ministries of social outreach. He was associated with Walter Rauschenbusch, a leader of the Social Gospel movement, in the People's Sunday Evening Hour, a program aimed at nonchurchgoers. His fame, or notoriety, came late in his ministry when he became attracted to some of the more radical theories of late-19th-century biblical scholars. A series of lectures delivered in 1905 and published the same year as *Religion and*

Politics challenged traditional teachings concerning the virgin birth of Jesus. He was charged and convicted of heresy in 1906. Refusing to recant his position, he was deposed from the priesthood. The case attracted great attention and was one of a series of liberal-conservative clashes within American Protestantism. Crapsey continued to write and speak on religious topics until his death, claiming in his later years to be a "pantheistic humanist."

Crapsey, Algernon Sidney. *The Last of the Heretics* (New York: Knopf, 1924)

Robert Bruce Mullin

Crater, Joseph. See JOSEPH CRATER DISAPPEARANCE.

Crawford. Town (pop 7,875) in NW Orange Co. The town was formed from Montgomery in 1823. Served by the Middletown and Crawford Railroad (1871), it became a dairy region, producing and shipping butter and milk. Its main hamlet, Pine Bush, grew up on the Shawangunk Kill and on an important plank road. While less affected than towns to the east by suburbanization, Crawford had its population increase 23% in the 1990s with the growth of commuting, and it has an increasing Latino population. In the early 21st century the town has dairy and horse farms, and it is the site of the First US Army Communications Facility. Rte 302 is designated a National Scenic Highway.

cream cheese. A cheese derived from pasteurized cow's milk, easy to spread and with a slightly tart but mild flavor. The cheese was invented in 1872 by William A. Lawrence at his cheese factory in Chester (Orange Co). Lawrence, who was trying to imitate the French cheese Neufchâtel by adding cream to cow's milk, called his product "Philadelphia cream cheese" because he shipped it to Philadelphia, Pa, for packaging and shipping. Dairies in Philadelphia (Jefferson Co) labeled their cream cheese similarly in the 1880s. The Empire Cheese Co (later Phenix Cheese Corp) of South Edmeston (Otsego Co) acquired the legal right to produce Philadelphia Brand Cream Cheese in 1885. Jewish immigrants in New York State took a liking to cream cheese, especially on bagels. In 1928 the Kraft Cheese Co of Chicago (now part of Kraft Foods) acquired the Phenix Cheese Corp and began marketing the cheese on a nationwide basis. In New York City, Lithuanian-born merchants Isaac and Joseph Breakstone had first established a dairy store at 135 Madison St on the Lower East Side in 1882 and had begun a wholesale butter business by 1886 at 29 Jay St in Brooklyn under the name of the Breakstone Bros. The company eventually purchased a dairy in Downsville (Delaware Co) and in the early 1920s began manufacturing cream cheese, particularly for kosher dairy restaurants. They too were eventually bought out by Kraft Foods. By the 1930s the distribution of cream cheese had greatly expanded, partly a result of the dramatic increase in the consumption of bagels and cheesecake (in which cream cheese is a central ingredient). In New York City, several restaurants became famous for cheesecake, most notably Lindy's in Manhattan's Times Square. Jewish cooks also found that cream cheese was useful in making blintzes, a kind of crepe first popular in eastern Europe, and rugelach, filled pastries. In response to changing American tastes, flavored cream cheeses were developed in the early 1960s, and low-fat varieties, in which the cream cheese is whipped to infuse air, were available by the 1980s.

Cooper, John. *Eat and Be Satisfied: A Social History of Jewish Food* (Northvale, NJ: Jason Aronson, 1993)

Donna L. Halper

creameries. Sites of dairy processing, milk and cream bottling, and, especially, butter making. Centralized creameries became practical with the introduction of the continuous cream separator, developed in Sweden by Carl Patrick de Laval in 1878. This device quickly and easily separated cream from milk and made centralized cream collection and butter production economically feasible. By the late 1880s creameries appeared along northern and northwestern New York State railroad lines, providing farmers with local cash markets for their milk and cream. Creameries were owned and operated by the New York, Ontario, and Western Railroad and the Delaware and Hudson. In 1914 the former operated 15 creameries along its line from the New Jersey border to Lake Ontario. It also provided access to creameries located on other railroads, including the Unadilla Valley Railroad and the Delaware and Northern Railroad, and in New York City. Other major creameries in the state at the time were operated by the Borden, Sheffield Farms (whose first New York State creamery was built in 1890 in Hobart in Delaware Co), and Breakstone companies. Many creameries were built by the railroad companies and rented or sold to operators.

By the 1920s many small creameries could not compete with the high prices paid for fluid milk in urban markets. The rise in trucking from the 1920s through the 1940s encouraged creamery consolidation, and many small sites closed. Bulk-milk handling was introduced in the late 1940s, further consolidating operations; milk cans were obsolete by the 1960s. Creameries and dairy farms that did not invest in the new machinery redirected their efforts or closed. In the 21st century plants that process milk and dairy products are referred to as fluid-milk processing plants or manufactured dairy product plants, with the designation based on the primary activity at the plant. In 2003 New York State was home to 27 fluid-milk processing plants and 58 manufactured dairy products plants.

Durand, Loyal, Jr. "The Historical and Economic Geography of Dairying in the North Country of New York State," *Geographic Review* 57 (1967): 24–47

Suzan D. Friedlander

credit agencies. Specialized businesses that gather and distribute commercial and financial information. There are two main types: credit-reporting agencies and credit-rating agencies. The former supplies businesses with information on the reliability of potential suppliers and customers. For example, companies planning to order and pay for supplies require assurance of timely delivery, and companies shipping goods on credit to distant customers need to know if and when they will receive payment. Credit-rating agencies rate—in terms of quality—the securities and other financial instruments issued by corporate enterprises and by governments. In the case of bonds and other debt instruments, the quality rating indicates the likelihood of default or nonpayment of the debt's interest or principal when due.

Since the early 19th century New York City has served as the leading commercial, financial, and information center in the United States. Both credit-reporting and credit-rating agencies appeared first in New York City and then spread nationally and internationally. In 1841 New York City dry goods and silk merchant—and prominent abolitionist—Lewis Tappan founded the first credit-reporting agency, the Mercantile Agency, which employed a network of agents to gather information on the business standing and creditworthiness of companies all across the United States and sold this information to subscribers. In 1859 the Mercantile Agency became R. G. Dun and Co. Dun's subscribers included wholesalers, importers, manufacturers, banks, and insurance companies. By 1900 its reports covered more than a million businesses. John Bradstreet had founded a similar enterprise in Cincinnati in 1849, and the two companies merged in 1933 to form Dun and Bradstreet (D&B), headquartered in New York City. At the beginning of the 21st century, D&B ranks as perhaps the world's foremost credit-reporting and commercial information enterprise.

Financial journalist John Moody founded the first credit-rating agency in New York City in 1909. He produced ratings of railroad bonds, the nation's largest class of securities, to guide the rapidly expanding class of US investors seeking such information. Poor's, founded in 1860 by Henry Varnum Poor to provide information on the operations and finances of railroad companies, entered the credit-rating business in 1916. In 1941 Poor's merged with Standard Statistics, another New York City–based information and ratings company, to form Standard and Poors (S&P). In 1966 New York City–headquartered publishing giant McGraw-Hill bought S&P, which at the beginning of the 21st century remains a subsidiary of McGraw-Hill.

Credit reporting and credit rating have natural affinities, a fact recognized in 1962 when D&B acquired Moody's Investors Service, the credit-rating agency founded by John Moody. The two credit agencies continued to operate as independent organizations, though united under one corporate roof. In 2000 Moody's regained its independence as a separate company. Moody's and S&P, both headquartered in New York City, are the world's largest credit-rating agencies, with extensive international presence.

Norris, James D. *R. G. Dun & Co* (Westport, Conn: Greenwood Press, 1978)

Richard Sylla

Crèvecoeur, J. Hector St. John de [Michel-Guillaume Jean de] (*b* Caen, France, 31 Jan 1735; *d* Sarcelles, France, 12 Nov 1813). Writer. Born into minor nobility and receiving a broad Jesuit education at the Collège Royal de Bourbon, Crèvecoeur mapped French territories in Canada during the 1750s, serving as a lieutenant in the French and Indian War. Wounded in the 1759 British siege of Quebec, he resigned his commission and went to New York City. Over the next decade he traveled widely through the colonies trading, surveying, and joining exploration expeditions as far west as St. Louis.

Crèvecoeur became an official resident of New York Colony in 1765. After residing for a time in Ulster Co, he married Mehitabel Tippett in 1769. He purchased 120 acres (49 ha) of land not far from the Hudson River in what is now Blooming Grove (Orange Co). After draining a large swamp, he built his Pine Hill Farm on the site. Life on the farm inspired him to write the 1782 classic *Letters from an American Farmer.* (Frequently taken as nonfiction, these epistolary essays addressed to a European correspondent are actually a thinly disguised work of fiction set in Pennsylvania.) He cultivated his land and developed friendships with Hudson Valley neighbors including natural scientist and historian Cadwallader Colden, educated merchant William Seton, and Huguenot pastor Jean Pierre Têtard. His prosperous and peaceful life was suddenly shattered by the outbreak of the Revolutionary War. Although Crèvecoeur was sympathetic to the tories, his loyalties were deeply divided. He fled to New York City in 1779, intending to return to France. Suspected of spying, he was held in prison, and his manuscripts were confiscated by British authorities. After the Revolution *Letters from an American Farmer* was published in London, where it was an immediate popular success among English reformers and Romantic radicals, contributing to the utopian notion of the American frontier spirit. The *Letters* are a seminal statement of American ideals and remain highly influential today. In them, Crèvecoeur makes the case for the superiority of American freedom and wide-open economic opportunity over the oppressive European system of nobility, land tenure, and taxation. His famous question—"What, then, is the American, this new man?"—is answered in "Letter III" by one of the earliest expositions of a distinctive American cultural identity.

Crèvecoeur's comprehensive report for the French government on American geography, commerce, and the struggle for independence led to his 1783 appointment as consul to New York, New Jersey, and Connecticut for Louis XVI. He returned to New York State to find his farm burned down by Indians, his wife murdered, and his children missing. After recovering the surviving family members, he settled in New York City. As French consul, Crèvecoeur encouraged trade, promoted scientific and cultural exchange, and in 1785 helped found the state's first Catholic church, St. Peter's on Barclay St in Manhattan. He also sponsored agricultural improvements and published articles on practical aspects of farming in American newspapers under the pseudonym Agricola (Latin for farmer). He was elected to the American Philosophical Society in 1789. Crèvecoeur returned to France in 1790 and spent the rest of his life there. Settling in Normandy, far from the upheavals of the French Revolution, he wrote *Voyage dans la Haute Pennsylvanie et dans l'Etat de New York* (Travels in Upper Pennsylvania and New York State) (1801). Other manuscripts, including *Sketches of 18th-Century America* (1925), were published after his death.

Allen, Gay Wilson, and Roger Asselineau. *St. John de Crèvecoeur: The Life of an American Farmer* (New York: Viking, 1987)

Crèvecoeur, J. Hector St. John de. *Letters from an American Farmer.* Ed. Susan Manning (New York: Oxford Univ Press, 1999)

Susan Manning

crew. See ROWING AND CREW.

cricket. The English game of cricket was the first team sport in the United States. Introduced in the British colonies in North America during the 1700s, its modern era dates from the 1830s, when English-born merchants, professionals, diplomats, military officers, and factory workers founded clubs in several towns and cities in the United States. Although several cricket teams from Albany, Schenectady, and Troy (Rensselaer Co) played matches in 1837, the St. George Cricket Club of Manhattan, founded in 1838, claimed to be the first regular outfit in the United States governed by rules and regulations. In 1844 it faced a new rival, the New York Cricket Club. A dispute over a hotly contested match embittered relations between the St. George and New York clubs during the late 1850s, as the former became the leading cricket organization in the New York City metropolitan region and one of the most prestigious clubs in the nation. During the mid-1800s the Dragon Slayers of St. George helped to arrange international contests that matched select teams from the United States, Canada, and England.

Although baseball surpassed cricket as the national pastime in the 1850s and 1860s, the English sport remained popular after the Civil War among English immigrants and some upper-class, native-born sportsmen in the New York City metropolitan area and elsewhere in the state. The golden age of American cricket began in the 1880s and lasted until World War I, but during that era Philadelphia elevens eclipsed teams from New York City. However, the English game did not die out completely in New York State, as transplanted British businessmen, professionals, and skilled craftsmen continued to pitch their wickets on public and private grounds. Between 1837 and 1914, 243 cricket clubs competed in New York State, including 6 each in Albany and Buffalo, 7 in Syracuse, 8 in Troy, and 138 in New York City (counting those from all five boroughs). During the early 20th century and especially after World War I, cricket suffered a severe decline in the United States, but during the late 1900s a new wave of immigrants from British Commonwealth countries revived the sport's fortunes in America, including the greater New York City metropolitan area. Cricket's fate in New York State and throughout the nation depended on English- and Australian-born residents and especially Asian, West Indian, and other immigrants whose countries had once been colonies in the British Empire. In the 1990s several of these ethnic groups (especially West Indians) were active in the greater New York City metropolitan region and other urban areas of the state, fielding cricket elevens that played on grounds in public parks.

Kirsch, George B. *The Creation of American Team Sports: Baseball and Cricket, 1838–72* (Urbana: Univ of Illinois Press, 1989)

Melville, Tom. *The Tented Field: A History of Cricket in America* (Bowling Green, Ohio: Bowling Green State Univ Popular Press, 1998)

George B. Kirsch

crime. Crime and fear of crime have long been potent shapers of New York State life and politics, particularly in urban settings. Murder, assault, robbery, rape, drunkenness, and prostitution were common crimes under the Dutch and English in New York Colony, with their frequency often tied to fluctuations in economic prosperity. Concerns about crime often take the form of worries about disorder, whether arising from civil disturbances and riots, particular areas of a city, specific occupations or pastimes, or certain classes in society. The waterfronts in New York City and Albany were loci of crime, with many young transients without deep social ties. So too, and for similar reasons, the large military presence in the colony was a potential source of criminal activity and a worry to sober colonists. But perhaps the greatest fear was of organized attacks on persons and property. On the frontier there were fears of attacks by the French and Indians, as in the bloody attack on Schenectady in 1690. In urban areas the greatest fear was of slave revolts such as the New York City revolt of 1712. In 1742 the "Negro Plot" in New York City resulted in the execution of 30 Blacks and 4 Whites for thefts, arsons, and robberies, and alleged plans to foment widespread insurrectionary violence. Antagonism between landlords and tenant farmers frequently flared into violence. In 1763 and again in 1766, military force quelled tenant uprisings in Livingston Manor and in the northeastern sector of Cortlandt Manor. These tensions were not resolved until the 1840s, when the antirent war on the upper Hudson Valley manors was the occasion of widespread civil disobedience. Mob violence could also have a more ambiguous aspect, covertly or actively courted by the supposed upholders of order, as was the case with much of the mob violence associated with the Stamp Act and the other civil disturbances during the 1760s and 1770s.

The 19th and Early 20th Centuries

After independence in 1783, the threat of insurrectionary violence largely ebbed, while concerns with the problems of murder, robbery, prostitution, and other forms of criminal activity remained high. The rise of the penny press in the 1830s helped create new interest in sensational crimes, such as the extensively covered trial after the 1836 murder of the New York City prostitute Helen Jewitt. These problems were not limited to New York City. The areas around the Erie Canal had many of the same problems as the waterfront and Tenderloin districts in New York City. Sensational murders such as the disappearance in Rochester in 1855 of Emma Moore and the discovery of her body beneath the ice two months later was avidly covered in local newspapers. Perhaps no sensational crime in 19th-century America was as extensively covered as the kidnapping and presumed murder at the hands of Freemasons of William Morgan of Batavia (Genesee Co) in 1826. His disappearance sparked the rise of the Antimasonic movement and helped create a major shift in the nation's party politics.

During the 19th century and into the 20th century, concerns about various types of crime followed fairly predictable cycles of sensational news reports, calls for change, attacks on those responsible for public safety, and get-tough campaigns by the police and prosecutors, all resulting in a temporary decline in crime until public interest waned and the cycle began anew. Newly arriving ethnic minorities, especially Irish and German immigrants, were often associated with criminal activity. Reformers associated crime in the state with a variety of urban problems, especially prostitution, gambling, and excessive alcoholic consumption, and decried the prevalence of crime in certain neighborhoods like the waterfront and the Tenderloin, or slum areas like the notorious Five Points in mid-19th-century Manhattan, a center of the new Irish immigrants. Irish immigrant resentment of the city's Protestant elite, anti-black racism, and bleak poverty, all accentuated by the pressures of the Civil War, led to the convulsive draft riot of July 1863, during which over 100 people were killed in New York City. The riot would shape public opinion and response for decades. Concerns about gangs and organized crime have long fueled public debate about the source of crime. Organized crime has often been associated with ethnic groups: the Irish in the mid–19th century, the Jews and Italians in the early 20th century, and African Americans, Chinese, and Russians in recent decades.

For many reformers, lax enforcement or even protection of crime by politicians was at the heart of the crime problem. From the Tweed Ring of the 1860s and 1870s until its demise a century later, Tammany Hall, the powerful Democratic machine in Manhattan, was accused, both fairly and unfairly, of being a source of corruption and criminal activity in New York City. State politics have often been shaped by corruption scandals. During an investigation of New York City's Police Department (NYPD), the state legislature's Lexow Committee (1894–95) found links between organized crime and Tammany Hall. Theodore Roosevelt, president of the police board in 1895, promised to clean up the city and the NYPD and used public attention to crime as a springboard to higher office. The Seabury Investigations (1930–32) uncovered the corruption of New York City mayor Jimmy Walker and forced his resignation, greatly aiding Fiorello La Guardia's bid to become mayor in 1933. Thomas E. Dewey's success in prosecuting organized crime in Manhattan between 1931 and 1942 enabled him to win election as district attorney for New York Co, a stepping stone to his career as three-term state governor.

Crime after 1960

Crime and the perception of a criminal crisis grew after World War II, especially after 1960, the roots of which are extremely complex. Perhaps the most prominent cause was the increased use and abuse of drugs, especially heroin, which flooded New York City and urban areas after World War II. The increase in illegal drug use created a criminal subculture of those who supplied the drugs and addicts willing to commit crimes to feed their habit. In the 1950s and 1960s there was a heightened concern about juvenile delinquency, sparked by some sensational crimes and much media attention. The declining industrial base of cities made steady employment often difficult to find and led to a deterioration in social services.

In the 1950s and 1960s, the movement of large numbers of middle-class urban residents to the suburbs and the mass migration of southern Blacks and Puerto Ricans to New York State's urban areas created a social context in which discussion of crime often had a racial component, and the newcomers were often seen, fairly or unfairly, as the cause of the increase in crime. The situation was exacerbated by the often strained relations between the police and minorities. If the police and their supporters felt they were doing a dangerous job in difficult circumstances, many minorities felt that the police were biased against them, regularly engaged in unnecessary brutality in subduing potential suspects, and were more interested in the crimes against Whites than in addressing the crime problems in minority areas. A series of urban disturbances erupted in cities across the nation. Those taking place in Rochester (1964), Harlem (1964, 1965), Troy (1966), and Albany, Buffalo, and Syracuse (1967), and a particularly devastating and deadly riot in Newark, NJ (1967), adjacent to the New York City metropolitan area, were defining events in the perception of urban crime. For many the riots served to reinforce negative perceptions, either of the nature of urban crime or of the attitudes of the police toward minorities. In the late 1960s, in the wake of the riots, the further exodus of Whites to the suburbs, and the economic decay of the inner cities, crime rates soared.

A few sensational and highly reported crimes served as a focus of media and political attention. In 1964 Kitty Genovese, a 28-year-old woman, was stabbed to death in the middle-class neighborhood of Forest Hills in Queens; neighbors listened to her screams but did not alert the police or intervene. The case helped create an image of a cloistered city that had ceded control of the streets to the criminals. Fear of random violence intensified the furor around the murders of David Berkowitz, popularly known as Son of Sam, who shot six people and wounded seven others between 1976 and 1978, and left New York City residents terrorized until his arrest. Many of the victims were young couples in relatively secluded lovers' lanes. Arthur Shawcross, known as the Genesee River Killer because of his habit of dumping the victims' bodies in the Genesee River near Rochester, was convicted of killing 10 women between 1988 and 1991.

Parents began fearing for their children's safety after the disappearance of 6-year-old Etan Patz, who was last seen walking to the bus stop two blocks from his home in the SoHo neighborhood in New York City on 25 May 1979. The disappearance of Patz began the modern missing-child movement, and Pres Ronald Reagan declared 25 May National Missing Children's Day in 1980. One of the most publicized cases was that of 4-year-old Kali Poulton, who was abducted from her Pittsford (Monroe Co) home in 1994. Her killer confessed in 1996. Well-publicized incidents, such as the attack of Trisha Meili as she jogged through Central Park on 19 Apr 1989, heightened the fear of attack by strangers. Known only as the "Central Park Jogger" until 2003, Meili was raped and severely beaten. Many of the most publicized cases had a racial component. A group of white youths killed Michael Griffith, a young black man, by chasing him onto a busy highway in the Howard Beach section of Queens in 1986. Another gang of white youths killed young black Yusuf Hawkins, mistaking him for someone else in the Bensonhurst neighborhood of Brooklyn in 1989. Mobs of African Americans angry about the police handling of an automobile accident that claimed the life of Gavin Cato, an African American youth, attacked their Hasidic Jewish neighbors in the Crown Heights neighborhood in Brooklyn in 1991. The attack resulted in the death of Yankel Rosenbaum from knife wounds. The bizarre case of Tawana Brawley, a 15-year-old black teenager from Wappingers Falls (Dutchess Co), who reported she had been sexually abused by six white men, including police officers, in November of 1987, roiled the state for several years. A grand jury found no evidence of the assault.

Crime Rates and Politics

The rise in crime profoundly affected politics. Renewed investigations of police corruption, notably the Knapp Commission probe (1970–72) and the Mollen Commission investigation (1992–93), found widespread police misconduct in New York City. Candidates for mayor of New York City like Mario Procaccino (1969) used a rhetoric of toughness on crime. This law-and-order approach was central to the appeal of Ed Koch, three-term New York City mayor (1977–89). Gov Nelson A. Rockefeller convinced

Beauties of Street-Car Travel in New York, drawn by C. S. Reinhart, from a sketch by M. Woolf, late 19th century.

PROPERTY CRIMES, 1965–2000

	Burglary		Larceny-Theft		Motor Vehicle Theft		Total	
	New York City	Whole State	New York City	Whole State	New York City	Whole State	New York City	Whole State
1965	51,072	183,443	115,782	253,353	34,726	58,452	201,580	495,248
1966	120,903	196,127	163,683	286,409	44,914	64,368	329,500	546,904
1967	150,245	219,157	182,151	314,472	58,169	83,775	390,565	617,404
1968	173,559	250,918	216,245	375,143	77,448	104,877	467,252	730,938
1969	171,393	248,477	190,540	367,463	85,796	115,400	447,729	731,340
1970	181,694	267,474	193,005	386,553	94,835	125,674	469,534	779,701
1971	181,331	273,704	187,232	388,612	96,624	127,658	465,187	789,974
1972	148,046	239,886	134,664	321,096	75,865	105,081	358,575	666,063
1973	149,311	246,246	127,500	320,307	82,731	112,328	359,542	678,881
1974	158,321	271,824	163,157	390,357	73,731	104,095	395,209	766,276
1975	177,032	301,996	188,832	447,740	83,201	116,274	449,065	866,010
1976	195,243	318,919	232,069	516,328	96,682	133,504	523,994	968,751
1977	178,907	309,735	214,838	498,653	94,420	133,669	488,165	942,057
1978	164,447	292,956	200,110	466,516	83,112	119,264	447,669	878,736
1979	178,162	308,302	220,813	500,589	89,748	124,343	488,723	933,234
1980	210,703	360,925	249,421	535,783	100,478	133,041	560,602	1,029,749
1981	205,825	350,422	258,369	539,486	104,706	136,849	568,900	1,026,757
1982	172,794	295,245	264,400	534,244	107,430	137,880	544,624	967,369
1983	143,698	249,115	253,801	504,346	92,725	127,861	490,224	881,322
1984	128,687	222,956	250,759	488,621	88,478	115,392	467,924	826,969
1985	124,838	219,633	262,051	502,276	79,426	106,537	466,315	828,446
1986	124,382	217,010	281,713	519,570	85,853	113,247	491,948	849,827
1987	123,412	216,826	289,126	539,175	95,654	125,329	508,192	881,330
1988	127,148	218,060	308,479	560,887	119,940	153,898	555,567	932,845
1989	121,322	211,130	287,749	544,459	133,861	171,007	542,932	926,596
1990	119,937	208,813	268,620	536,012	147,123	187,591	535,680	932,416
1991	112,015	204,499	256,473	531,681	139,977	181,287	508,465	917,467
1992	103,476	193,548	236,169	495,708	126,959	168,922	466,604	858,178
1993	99,207	181,709	235,132	481,166	112,464	151,949	446,803	814,824
1994	88,370	164,650	209,808	452,322	95,420	128,873	393,598	745,845
1995	73,879	146,562	180,949	425,184	72,679	102,596	327,507	674,342
1996	61,270	129,828	162,246	399,522	60,379	89,900	283,895	619,250
1997	54,099	118,306	157,039	386,435	51,893	79,697	263,031	584,438
1998	46,185	104,821	147,018	363,295	44,056	68,171	237,259	536,287
1999	40,469	93,217	140,370	338,118	39,693	58,261	220,532	489,596
2000	37,112	87,946	139,664	340,901	35,847	54,231	212,623	483,078

Source: FBI Uniform Crime Reports.

the state legislature to enact the nation's harshest laws against drug possession and selling. These laws, passed in 1973 and popularly known as the Rockefeller Drug Laws, require mandatory prison sentences for anyone caught in possession of or in the act of selling narcotics. Sentence length is determined by the amount of the controlled substance. In 1994, during his campaign for governor, George E. Pataki pledged to reinstate the death penalty. He did so in 1995, shortly after his election to office. Rudolph Giuliani earned a worldwide reputation as a crime fighter by imposing a zero tolerance crackdown on quality-of-life offenses while he was the mayor of New York City (1994–2001).

Certain horrible events also led to stiffer punishments for criminals. The murder of a young husband who acted as a Good Samaritan and intervened to stop harassment on a Manhattan subway train in 1965 led to the establishment of the New York State Crime Victim's Compensation Fund (now New York State Crime Victims Board). After a deeply troubled adolescent killed a man over a minor dispute in 1977, the state legislature enacted procedures to enable district attorneys to put certain defendants between the ages of 13 and 15 on trial in adult court if they faced serious murder, rape, or robbery charges. The 1997 murder of college student Jenna Grieshaber in Albany by a man who had just been released on parole after serving two-thirds of his sentence led the legislature to pass Jenna's Law in 1998 requiring first-time felons to serve at least six-sevenths of their sentences before becoming eligible for parole. Kendra Webdale was pushed in front of a subway train in Manhattan in 1999 by a mentally ill man. Her murder led to the passage of Kendra's Law, which compels certain mental patients deemed to be dangerous to take their medication in supervised settings or else lose their freedom and undergo involuntary hospitalization.

High rates of crime seemed an inescapable fact of life in New York State in the 1970s and 1980s. The crack cocaine epidemic of the late 1980s directly fueled a crime wave. In 1990, 2,605 people—an all time high—were murdered in the state (2,245, over 86%, were in New York City). However, during the 1990s, New York City's murder rate underwent a remarkable decline and dropped by more than 70%. The factors most often credited for the decrease in crimes during the 1990s include more effective policing strategies like team policing and aggressive street policing. Other reasons often cited are tougher laws leading to greater numbers of offenders in jails and prisons, along with an improving economy and a slowing of the crack epidemic. Some believe the youth culture is becoming less violent, pointing to an increase in college entrance rates for teenagers and young adults, along with a rejection of lifestyles revolving around drugs, guns, gangs, and lawbreaking as self-destructive modes of adolescent rebellion. After declines for several years, the decreases leveled off in most cities in the early 21st century, and some cities, such as Rochester, experienced an increase in the murder rate.

Cohen, Patricia Cline. *The Murder of Helen Jewitt: The Life and Death of a Prostitute in 19th-Century New York* (New York: Knopf, 1998)

Greenberg, Douglas. *Crime and Law Enforcement in the Colony of New York, 1691–1776* (Ithaca: Cornell Univ Press, 1976)

Jacob, James. *Gotham Unbound: How New York City Was Liberated from the Grip of Organized Crime* (New York: New York Univ Press, 1999)

Karmen, Andrew. *New York Murder Mystery: The True Story behind the Crime Crash of the 1990s* (New York: New York Univ Press, 2000)

Sloat, Warren. *A Battle for the Soul of New York: Reverend Charles Parkhurst's Crusade against Police Corruption, Vice, and Tammany Hall, 1892–1895* (New York: Cooper Square Press, 2003)

Peter Eisenstadt, Charles Lindner, and Andrew Karmen

Crime Victims Board. State agency providing direct support services, financial relief, and advocacy for victims of crime. Through a network of community-based programs, the board funds local organizations specializing in helping victims and provides contacts to similar county or regional agencies. The legislature created the Crime Victims Compensation Board in 1966 to provide assistance and care for crime victims. In 1981 that mission was expanded to include grant funding to municipal and nonprofit community-based organizations to better meet the immediate needs of victims. The following year the name was changed to Crime Victims Board. Placed within the Executive Department, the board comprises five governor appointees (three of whom must have been licensed to practice law in New York State for a minimum of five years) serving for seven-year terms.

The federal Victims of Crime Act of 1984 provided additional funds to victim-support agencies. Originally, three priority categories of victims were identified: child abuse, spousal abuse, and sexual assault. A fourth was added, violent crime. Those who are eligible may receive reimbursement for crime-related expenses, including compensation for medical, counseling, or funeral expenses or loss of essential personal property, earnings, or support; services of a domestic violence shelter; expenses for securing or cleaning up a crime scene; and attorney fees and transportation costs for court appearances or representation before the Crime Victims Board. A victim who acts as a Good Samaritan by attempting to prevent a crime, lawfully apprehend a perpetrator, or assist police in making an arrest may recover the cost of damaged, lost, or destroyed property.

The board also advises victims and witnesses of their rights in the criminal justice system and helps fund the Victim Information Notification

VIOLENT CRIMES, 1965–2000

	Murder and Nonnegligent Manslaughter		Forcible Rape		Aggravated Assault		Robbery		Total	
	New York City	Whole State	New York City	Whole State	New York City	Whole State	New York City	Whole State	New York City	Whole State
1965	681	836	1,154	2,320	16,325	27,464	8,904	28,182	27,064	58,802
1966	734	882	1,761	2,439	23,205	29,142	23,539	30,098	49,239	62,561
1967	809	996	1,905	2,665	24,828	31,261	35,934	40,202	63,476	75,124
1968	976	1,185	1,840	2,527	28,515	34,946	54,405	59,857	85,736	98,515
1969	1,116	1,324	2,120	2,902	29,717	36,890	59,152	64,754	92,105	105,870
1970	1,201	1,444	2,141	2,875	31,255	39,145	74,102	81,149	108,699	124,613
1971	1,513	1,823	2,415	3,225	33,865	42,318	88,994	97,682	126,787	145,048
1972	1,757	2,026	3,271	4,199	37,130	45,926	78,202	86,391	120,360	138,542
1973	1,740	2,040	3,735	4,852	38,148	47,781	72,750	80,795	116,373	135,468
1974	1,607	1,919	4,054	5,240	41,068	51,454	77,940	86,814	124,669	145,427
1975	1,690	1,996	3,866	5,099	43,481	54,593	83,190	93,499	132,227	155,187
1976	1,647	1,969	3,400	4,663	42,948	54,638	86,183	95,718	134,178	156,988
1977	1,553	1,919	3,899	5,272	42,056	57,193	74,404	84,703	121,912	149,087
1978	1,503	1,820	3,882	5,168	43,271	58,484	74,028	83,785	122,684	149,257
1979	1,733	2,092	3,875	5,394	44,203	60,949	82,572	93,471	132,383	161,906
1980	1,812	2,228	3,711	5,405	43,476	60,329	100,550	112,273	149,549	180,235
1981	1,826	2,166	3,862	5,479	43,783	60,189	107,475	120,344	156,946	188,178
1982	1,668	2,013	3,547	5,159	42,784	59,818	95,944	107,843	143,943	174,833
1983	1,622	1,958	3,662	5,296	43,326	59,452	84,243	94,783	132,853	161,489
1984	1,450	1,786	3,829	5,599	47,472	64,872	79,540	89,900	132,291	162,157
1985	1,384	1,683	3,880	5,706	50,356	68,270	79,532	89,706	135,152	165,365
1986	1,582	1,907	3,536	5,415	57,306	76,528	80,827	91,360	143,251	175,210
1987	1,672	2,016	3,507	5,537	64,244	82,417	78,890	89,721	148,313	179,691
1988	1,896	2,244	3,412	5,479	71,030	91,239	86,578	97,434	162,916	196,396
1989	1,905	2,246	3,254	5,242	70,951	91,571	93,377	103,983	169,487	203,042
1990	2,245	2,605	3,126	5,368	68,891	92,105	100,280	112,380	174,542	212,458
1991	2,154	2,571	2,892	5,085	66,832	90,186	98,512	112,342	170,390	210,184
1992	1,995	2,397	2,815	5,152	63,529	87,608	91,239	108,154	159,578	203,311
1993	1,946	2,420	2,818	5,008	62,778	85,802	86,001	102,122	153,543	195,352
1994	1,561	2,016	2,666	4,700	59,755	82,100	72,540	86,617	136,522	175,433
1995	1,177	1,550	2,317	4,290	51,251	74,351	59,278	72,492	114,023	152,683
1996	983	1,353	2,332	4,174	45,673	64,857	49,672	61,822	98,660	132,206
1997	770	1,093	2,157	4,075	45,218	63,628	44,708	56,094	92,853	124,890
1998	633	924	2,046	3,843	43,853	62,023	39,359	49,125	85,891	115,915
1999	664	903	1,702	3,563	40,488	58,860	36,091	43,821	78,945	107,147
2000	673	952	1,630	3,530	40,880	60,090	32,562	40,539	75,745	105,111

Source: FBI Uniform Crime Reports.

Everyday (VINE) program run by the State Department of Correctional Services. In 1999, under special grant, the board created an outreach program through the New York State Police to hire trained victim advocates for underserved areas. As of 2003 there were over 170 funded programs. The board has offices in Albany, Buffalo, and Brooklyn, assists an average of 30,000 victims annually, provides a toll-free hot line for victim assistance, and funds more than 200 local victim-assistance programs throughout the state. According to the 2003–4 budget, the board employs 103 workers and has a budget of approximately $6.1 million.

New York State Archives. "New York State Crime Victims Board" (unpublished finding aid, 1981)

Christine Karpiak

criminal justice. New York State's criminal justice system has three parts: courts, law enforcement, and corrections. The first state constitution, ratified in 1777, established a court system based largely on the colonial model. The Constitution of 1846 established the Supreme Court, the Court of Appeals, and county courts. The Constitution of 1894, which became effective in 1896, consolidated the courts, created an Appellate Division of the Supreme Court, and increased the number of justices in the latter. Although the state constitution has undergone numerous changes during the 20th century, it is the 1894 Constitution under which the criminal justice system continues to operate at the start of the 21st century. The state established its first comprehensive penal code in 1881, after administering justice for more than a century under numerous individual offense-specific statutes. This code was revised in 1909 and then again in the 1960s. The present code has been in effect since 1967.

Article VI of the New York State Constitution, approved in 1961, defines the state's Unified Court System, which includes the New York State Court of Appeals, Supreme Court, Court of Claims, County Court, Surrogate's Court, and Family Court (established in 1962 for juvenile offenders). The highest of these is the Court of Appeals, which is the court of last resort for decisions on legal questions. Cases before it generally come from decisions of the Supreme Court, which usually has original jurisdiction over criminal cases and is the trial court for criminal matters. The Appellate Division reviews felony convictions from the Supreme Court and acts of delinquency from Family Court. The Appellate Term of the Supreme Court has original jurisdiction over misdemeanors. The Appellate Division and Term are thus intermediate appellate courts. Recent innovations to the system include such specialized courts as the Midtown Community Court (1993) in Manhattan and the Mental Health Court (1999) in Brooklyn. These primarily handle recurring nonviolent cases, such as substance abuse, and relieve the case burden of the higher-level criminal courts.

Law Enforcement

Local law enforcement comes under Article IX of the New York State Constitution, which provides home rule for local governments. This means that each jurisdiction has the right to establish its own police department, policies, and procedures. The state also provides for a number of special jurisdiction police agencies, such as county sheriffs and state, park, railroad, and reservoir police.

In 1845 New York City created the nation's first modern police force, the first chief of which was an appointed politician, George W. Matseller. Before then law enforcement had been handled by marshals, constables, and watchmen working on a fee-for-service basis rather than for regular wages. In 2003 the New York City Police Department was, with more than 40,000 uniformed officers and support staff, the nation's largest municipal police department. Under Mayor Rudolph Giuliani, a new crime-control model was forged in 1994 that focused on quality-of-life issues in the city and new managerial techniques emphasizing the statistical analysis of crime, and, perhaps most important, holding senior police managers accountable for local crime. The crime rate decreased 44% between 1994 and 1997, prompting the Federal Bureau of Investigation to characterize New York City as one of the safest cities in the United States. Other municipalities in the state, just as other cities in the nation, have attempted to model their police department policies on those of New York City, and funding has been provided. The key to success in this and similar crime-control programs is implementation. Although many jurisdictions pay lip service to new managerial techniques, the crime rates in major New York cities other than New York City have not shown the same dramatic results.

There were 55 elected sheriffs in New York State in 2003 providing police services to unincorporated localities, operating county jails, maintaining security in county courts, serving civil and criminal processes, and helping local police in criminal investigations. Large sheriff's offices, such as Erie Co's of 285 employees, have significant and active investigative and narcotics and intelligence bureaus, as well as fledgling computer crime units. Sheriffs generally have police jurisdiction countywide, even in cities that maintain local police forces, with the exception of New York City. The New York State Police, founded in 1917, had more than 5,000 troopers at the start of the 21st century, the largest such force in the country. Its officers focus on patrolling the state's highways but also investigate violent crime and drug trafficking. A full-service police agency, the State Police maintain fingerprint and other databases, assist local law enforcement agencies, and provide direct police services statewide.

Correctional Facilities

New York State pioneered the creation of the penitentiary in the United States. The State Prison of the City of New York, better known as Newgate Prison, was established in Manhattan's Greenwich Village in 1797. In 1817, because it was already overcrowded, a second penitentiary was opened, the Auburn Prison (Cayuga Co), with the discipline of solitary confinement at night and on weekends, and silent congregate work during the day. Pennsylvania, by contrast, housed its prisoners in solitary confinement at all times. Sing Sing Prison [now in Ossining, Westchester Co] was built about a decade after Auburn Prison, using the latter's convict labor. Ten years later the state built a wing at Sing Sing for female prisoners, but the first women's prison did not open until 1893, at Auburn. In 1876 the state established the nation's first adult reformatory for offenders aged 18–30 at Elmira. This facility was based on the Progressive era's goal of reform and rehabilitation as an alternative to punishment. The Constitution of 1894 provided for a New York State Commission of Prisons responsible for inspecting penal institutions. In 1925–26 the Department of Correction was created to oversee all correctional facilities throughout the state. In 2003 the state prison system held nearly 70,000 inmates, 97% of whom were male, in 70 facilities. Whites accounted for 18%, Blacks for 51%, and Latinos for 30% of the prison population. A system of jails exists in each of the state's 62 counties. Jails usually house those awaiting trial and offenders with short-term sentences. New York City's jail colony on Rikers Island consists of 10 jails with a capacity for about 16,000 inmates; the second-largest system, Erie Co's, has a holding center in Buffalo and a correctional facility in Alden, with a total capacity for 1,750.

All counties in New York and all boroughs in New York City have family courts with jurisdiction over juvenile offenses. Those guilty of juvenile offenses receive indeterminate sentences and are housed in juvenile detention centers, such as the secure co-ed facility for 24 in Albany or the co-ed group care facility for 8 in Canandaigua (Ontario Co). The largest such center is the Bridges Juvenile Center in the Bronx, which holds 141 in secure detention. In 1978 the state legislature passed a stringent juvenile offender law in response to a notorious double robbery/murder committed that same year on a New York City subway by a juvenile who came under the more lenient jurisdiction of the Family Court. Under this 1978 law, juveniles as young as 13 years old who have committed violent offenses can be diverted to the adult criminal justice system.

Both probation and parole arose from the reform movements of the late 19th century. Reformers believed they could rehabilitate offenders through a variety of services aimed at reintegration into the community. Probation is still the first recourse for operating a large, overcrowded criminal justice system. New York State's Division of Probation and Correctional Alternatives, first created in 1901 and now headquartered in Albany, supervises the majority of convicted offenders in the state. In most jurisdictions, convicted cases usually result in a probationary sentence; statewide there were about 197,000 probationers in 2001. New York City's Probation Department, which supervises approximately 90,000 adult probationers and nearly 4,000 juvenile offenders each year, is second only to Los Angeles in its size. Each probation officer averages an unmanageable caseload of about 200 adults and 84 juveniles monthly.

Probation is a practical necessity. Parole, although created with the best benevolent intentions, is politically controversial and has never operated properly. By the end of the 1990s, parole had been effectively abolished throughout New York State for violent offenders. The state's 1995 Sentencing Reform Act eliminated parole for repeat violent felons and indeterminate sentences for second-time felony/first-time violent felony offenders. In 1998 Jenna's Law was enacted, named for Jenna Grieshaber, who was murdered the previous year in Albany by a violent felon on parole. Spurred by the public's outrage, the state legislature passed the law in a rare special session called primarily to enact it. Jenna's Law mandates determinate sentences without parole for violent felony offenders and requires them to serve at least six-sevenths of their sentence before release. The increasing use of victims at sentencing and parole hearings has also reduced chances for parole.

As a result of sentencing reform and truth-in-sentencing for time served initiatives, New York State ranks among the top for average percentage of time a convicted offender serves. New York ranked fourth nationally in 1999 in mean time served and eighth in percentage of sentence served. To give more voice to victims during the judicial process, the legislature has passed several amendments to Penal Law, Criminal Procedure Law, and Family Court Law. The changes required the following: assessment of victim impact in presentence investigation report (1982); written impact statement to parole board (1985); written impact statement in Family Court (1986); written impact statement included in presentence investigation report (1991); victim impact statement at sentencing (1992); oral victim impact statement to the Parole Board (1993).

At the beginning of the 21st century, Albany had the highest crime rate of any county outside of New York City, and Lewis Co had the lowest. Incarceration rates for the state have decreased, but not nearly as much as the crime rates, from a high of 73,960 in correctional institutions in 1999 to 67,535 in 2001. There is no clear-cut consensus among scholars on the causes of the decline. Still, the number of prisoners in 2002 was roughly the same as in 1994, when the crime rate began its decline. Sentences are longer and harsher, and most amenities have been removed from the prisons. Combined with the recent alterations in the parole system, New York State has increasingly moved toward stressing greater punishment for offenders.

See also Capital punishment; Policing.

Cohn, Ellen G., and Karel Jurst-Swanger. *Criminal Justice in New York Today* (Upper Saddle River, NJ: Prentice-Hall, 2001)

Jones-Brown, Delores, with Elsie Chandler and Susan Decker. *Criminal Justice in New York* (Boston: Allyn & Bacon, 2000)

Scott, Henry W. *The Courts of the State of New York: Their History, Development, and Jurisdiction* (Union, NJ: Lawbook Exchange, 2001)

Larry E. Sullivan

Criminal Justice Services, Division of. Body advising the governor on programs to improve the effectiveness of the state's criminal justice system. The division collects and analyzes statewide crime data, conducts research on criminal justice issues, administers federal and state grants, and provides training and advice to the state law enforcement and prosecution agencies. It is composed of five program bureaus: Office of Justice Information Services, Office of Public Safety, Office of Strategic Planning, Office of Legal Services and Forensic Services, and Office of Administration. The division's commissioner also serves as the state's director of criminal justice, overseeing policy development for all criminal justice programs in the state.

In 1893 the State Prison Department became one of the first in the country to use the French Bertillon system to help solve the perpetual problem of identifying repeat offenders among the prison population. The Bureau of Identification was established within the Prison Department in 1896 and represents the beginning of the modern Division of Criminal Justice Services. By 1900 the bureau had developed an enormous collection of Bertillon data, gathering information on thousands of criminals in New York, other states, and Canada. At the same time, bureau staff began to examine and modify British fingerprinting methods for American prisons and at the 1904 St. Louis World's Fair gave the country's first public demonstration of the use of fingerprinting in criminal identification. In 1913 fingerprinting was officially adopted for use in New York State prisons. The bureau in 1928 expanded into the Division of Identification within the new Department of Correction, continuing as a leader in improving criminal identification methods. As early as 1937 it pioneered the use of automated fingerprint search machines. The American System of Fingerprint Classification, developed in New York State, was a standard in the field until it was superseded in the 1990s by automated Fingerprint Identification Systems.

In 1962 the division was absorbed into the New York State Identification and Intelligence System (NYSIIS). The present division was established in 1972, within the Executive Department, joining the NYSIIS, Office of Local Government's Division for Local Police, and Office of Planning Service's Division of Criminal Justice. Legislation in the 1990s added to the division's varied functions, making it responsible for maintaining new statewide information resources, including a DNA databank with the State Police, a sex offender registry, and a clearinghouse of missing and exploited children. In 2002–3 the agency, headquartered in Albany, had a budget of approximately $220 million and 740 full-time equivalent staff positions.

Harling, Michael. "Origins of the New York State Bureau of Identification," http://www.correctionhistory.org/html/chronicl/dcjs/html/nyidbur0.html

New York State Division of Criminal Justice Services, http://criminaljustice.state.ny.us

Richard Andress

Croatians. Ethnic group whose members primarily come from Croatia, Bosnia, and other regions of the former Yugoslavia. Croatian settlement in New York State occurred in three broad waves. Although some Croats resided in the state by the 1790s, the first major influx took place from the late 1870s to 1914, caused by economic need resulting partly from Croatia's political subjugation by Austria-Hungary. Until World War II, Croats in New York State formed a minor portion of the Croatian population in the United States. The size and relative importance of the New York community increased during the second wave of immigration, from 1945 to the early 1980s, which was motivated by political persecution in Communist Yugoslavia and continued economic privation. Instability and wars in the former Yugoslavia produced the third wave of immigration, from the late 1980s to the late 1990s. Males predominated among the pre–World War II immigrants, who generally had little education and performed unskilled dock or industrial work. The better-educated, post–World War II immigrants included more women and children. In the latter 20th and early 21st centuries, many Croatians worked in construction and restaurant businesses in New York City, both as owners and employees. College-educated Croatians were doctors, lawyers, teachers, and other professionals.

Fraternal and social organizations have formed an important part of Croatian life in the state. The earliest include the Croatian-American Benevolent Society, founded in New York City in 1880, and Zora (Dawn), founded in Lackawanna (Erie Co) in 1902. Most of these locally significant organizations drew members from a single Croatian town or island. National organizations also established lodges in New York State. The Croatian Fraternal Union maintains chapters in Cementon, Gloversville, Buffalo and nearby Lackawanna, Niagara Falls, Oakfield, and New York City. Churches have also played an important role. Croats are generally Roman Catholics. The Croatian language parishes of Sts. Cyril and Methodius, established in New York City in 1913, and Our Lady of Bistrica, established in Lackawanna in 1917, continue to serve their communities. Since 1971 a Croatian-speaking apostolate, or mission, has functioned within an English language parish in Astoria (Queens Co). Numerous Croatian language newspapers have been published in New York City, including *Narodni list* (1898–1922), *Svijet* (1908–56), *Hrvatski list i Danica hrvatska* (1922–44), *Novi list* (?1948–?1954), and *Croatian American Times* (1999–). Editors and publishers have included such community leaders as *Narodni list*'s Frank Zotti and *Svijet*'s Don Niko Grskovic. Since the late 1930s locally broadcast Croatian language radio programs have reached audiences in the New York City area, and the *Journal of Croatian Studies*, an English language scholarly journal based in New York City, has appeared annually since 1960.

The Croatian community in New York State has struggled with political divisions caused by differing positions on events in Croatia. For much of the 20th century these included splits between pro- and anti-Yugoslavs and pro- and anti-Communists. In New York City, Croatian Communist sympathizers generated support for Yugoslav partisans during World War II, while Croatian nationalists agitated for Croatian independence during the 1970s and early 1980s, with certain extreme nationalists launching terror attacks on New York–based Yugoslav institutions and pro-Yugoslav Croats. But the 1991–95 wars in Croatia and Bosnia-Herzegovina erased these differences as Croatians in New York State focused on war relief efforts. The US Census of 2000 recorded 19,886 Croats living in the state, with over half of this number concentrated in Queens, New York, and Nassau Cos. Croatians who have made important contributions to New York State include New York Metropolitan Opera singer Zinka Milanov, sculptor Ivan Mestrovic, and New York Yankee Roger Maris.

Kraljic, Frances. *Croatian Migration to and from the United States, 1900–1914* (Palo Alto, Calif: Ragusan Press, 1978)

Prpic, George J. *The Croatian Immigrants in America* (New York: Philosophical Library, 1971)

John P. Kraljic

Croghan. Town (pop 3,161) and village (pop 865) in NE Lewis Co. First settled briefly in 1794 by French refugees and in 1798 by Germans and Swiss, it was permanently settled in 1824. Several immigrant companies of Alsatian, German, and Swiss farmers arrived *ca* 1830. Many of them were Mennonites; other German speakers formed a Catholic congregation around 1832, building the Church of St. Vincent de Paul in 1843–44, which remained in active use in 2003. The town was formed in 1841 from Watson and Diana. It is mostly bottomland, ideal for farming. Early industries included tanning and lumbering; the Beaver River Lumber Co (1890) employed 400 in 1895. With the first pulp mill in 1881, the hamlet of Beaver Falls became a major paper manufacturing center, notable producers being the J. P. Lewis Co/Interface Solutions (1894), Beaverite (1927), and Latex Fiber Industries (1932), all of which ceased production before 2002. Beginning in 1906 they were served by the Lowville and Beaver River Railroad. The village, which lies in the Towns of Croghan and New Bremen, incorporated in 1906. United Block Mill (1918–61) manufactured bowling pins. Croghan is the home of folk artist Veronica Terrillion, the American Maple Museum, and the Railway Historical Society of Northern New York. A maple festival is celebrated in May, and a lumberjack festival in June. Croghan bologna, a kielbasa-like sausage, is a famed local product. In 2003 the Croghan Island Mill, a water-powered sawmill, remained in service.

Arthur Einhorn

Croghan bologna. This ring sausage is most popular in the North Country, though a mail-order business is building wider recognition. Made from a Swiss recipe, it was brought to the United States by Frederick Hunziger, who mixed the bologna by hand, using garlic, beef, and pork raised entirely by his family. In 1888 Hunziger and his brother-in-law founded the Croghan Meat Market. Driving a horse-drawn paneled truck, Hunziger made a circuit of the local communities and lumber camps to sell his products. John Michael Campany, the owner in 2002, is the third generation of his family to run the market, located in Croghan (Lewis Co). The building has expanded to encompass the smokehouses that in Hunziger's day stood in the backyard, but otherwise the operation remains much the same. The bologna is made according to Hunziger's original recipe, and the beef still comes from the butcher's own farm.

Lynn Ekfelt

Croker, Richard (*b* Blackrock, Ireland, 24 Nov 1841; *d* Glencairn, Ireland, 29 Apr 1922). Political leader. After immigrating to the United States in 1846, Croker became a machinist, boxed in amateur fights, and cultivated a following as a Fourth Avenue Tunnel Gang leader in New York City. Later as a Tammany Hall Democrat, he was elected alderman (1869) and coroner (1873, 1876), and was appointed fire commissioner (1883) even though he was tried for murder in 1874. When John Kelly retired in 1886, he served as Tammany boss and maintained the position until 1902. As boss he acquired wealth and shaped city politics through patronage. Mayoral candidates Abram S. Hewitt (1886), Hugh J. Grant (1888, 1890), and Thomas F. Gilroy (1892) were all Democrats with strong Tammany ties at the time of their elections. Croker also served as city chamberlain (1889–90). He retired from politics and returned to his English and Irish estates following the defeat of his 1901 mayoral candidate. He regularly vacationed in West Palm Beach, Fla, and was active in horse racing.

Hammack, David C. *Power and Society: Greater New York at the Turn of the Century* (New York: Russell Sage Foundation, 1982)
Stoddard, Lothrop. *Master of Manhattan, the Life of Richard Croker* (New York: Longmans, Green, 1931)

John Marino

Crooked Lake Canal. Canal connecting Penn Yan (Yates Co) at the north end of Keuka Lake with Dresden (Yates Co) to the east on Seneca Lake, allowing for communication with the Erie Canal at Montezuma (Cayuga Co) through the Cayuga and Seneca Canal. Built in 1831–33 the canal was 8 miles (12.9 km) long and cost $157,000 to complete, with 27 lift locks and one guard lock at Penn Yan to overcome an elevation difference of 277 feet (84.4 m). Close to the original measures of the Erie Canal (40 ft x 4 ft/12.2 m x 1.2 m), Crooked Lake Canal had a 42 ft (12.8 m) surface width and a 4 ft (1.2 m) depth, allowing for a capacity of 70–76 tons (64–69 MT) per boat. Although the canal carried farm products, grain, and some lumber, it never achieved its anticipated volume, and traffic stopped in 1875; it was officially abandoned 4 June 1877. While only a small portion of one lock remains, Friends of the Finger Lakes Outlet maintains the Keuka Lake Outlet Trail along the canal's original route.

Whitford, Noble E. *History of the Canal System of the State of New York* (Albany: Brandow Printing, 1906)

Thomas X. Grasso

Cropsey, Jasper Francis (*b* Rossville, Richmond Co, 18 Feb 1823; *d* Hastings-on-Hudson, Westchester Co, 22 June 1900). Artist and architect. The son of farmers, Cropsey took up drawing as a child. At 14 he was apprenticed to architect Joseph Trench in New York City. By 1842 he opened his own office and practiced architecture periodically throughout his life, often to supplement his income as a painter. Cropsey was strongly influenced by the work of Thomas Cole and Asher B. Durand, and he became a prominent painter of the Hudson River school. Cropsey worked in a series of studios in New York City. He is best known for his brilliantly colored autumn landscapes, such as the acclaimed *Autumn on the Hudson River* (1860), as well as literary themes and allegorical cycles. Cropsey embraced the movement's meticulous detail, and his work reflected a deep Christian faith through its use of moralizing themes. He turned increasingly to watercolor in his later years. In 1867 Cropsey began work on a 29-room summer home named Aladdin in Warwick (Orange Co). Upkeep of Aladdin proved costly, however, and in 1885 he moved to a cottage he called Ever Rest in Hastings-on-Hudson, where he remained until his death. His legacy is preserved at Ever Rest by the Newington-Cropsey Foundation.

Newington-Cropsey Foundation, http://www.newingtoncropsey.com
Talbot, William S. *Jasper F. Cropsey, 1823–1900* (New York: Garland Publishing, 1977)

Kimberly A. Orcutt

Crosby, Enoch (*b* Harwich, Mass, 4 Jan 1750; *d* Carmel, Putnam Co, 26 June 1835). Revolutionary War spy. Crosby's family moved to Dutchess Co in 1753, and he was apprenticed to a shoemaker at age 16, becoming one himself in Danbury, Conn. In 1775 he enlisted and fought against the British on Lake Champlain and in Canada. Setting out to reenlist in August or September 1776, he fell in with a tory who discussed a secret rendezvous of a loyalist company. Crosby reported this to John Jay and the Commission for Detecting and Defeating Conspiracies at Fishkill (Dutchess Co), which enlisted him as a spy. For 9 months, until May 1777, Crosby posed as a tory in the lower and mid-Hudson Valley and passed intelligence to American authorities. In 1779 he reenlisted in the Fourth New York Regiment and later transferred to the Second, in which he served as a sergeant until November 1780. Harvey Birch, the hero of James Fenimore Cooper's *The Spy* (1821), strongly resembled Crosby, a resemblance noted in Crosby's memoir. Although the novelist had never heard of Crosby, John Jay had told Cooper of the exploits of an unnamed spy. Crosby retired to a farm he had acquired in 1782 and served as a town supervisor, justice of the peace, and church deacon in North East (Putnam Co).

Barnum, H. L. *Spy Unmasked; or, Memoirs of Enoch Crosby, Alias Harvey Birch . . .* (New York: J. & J. Harper, 1828)
Deane, James E. "Enoch Crosby Not a Myth." *Magazine of American History* 18 (July 1887): 73–75

Brad L. Utter

cross-endorsement. The provision of New York State election law, also known as fusion, that permits a party's candidate for office to accept the nomination for that same office from one or more additional parties. A cross-endorsed candidate appears on the ballot line of each of those parties. Each party's vote is counted separately, then added together for the candidate's overall vote total. Cross-endorsement promotes the state's robust third party tradition by allowing voters to support a minor party without fear of wasting a vote. Its first statewide use was in New York's 1854 gubernatorial race, and in the late 19th century it was used to challenge the power of New York City's Tammany Hall. With the turn of the century, cross-endorsement helped elect New York City mayors Seth Low (1901) and Fiorello La Guardia (1933). After World War II, ideologically focused minor parties selectively offered and withheld their cross-endorsement. The Liberal Party used this strategy to sway the Democrats, and the Conservative Party formed with the explicit purpose of using cross-endorsement to influence Republican positions. Minor parties' use of cross-endorsement has been effective enough that both major parties periodically complain of the "tail wag-ging the dog." This sentiment has produced temporary county bans on cross-endorsement, but the state legislature has consistently refused to prohibit the practice. Various forms of cross-endorsement were common nationally in the late 19th century, but most states had prohibited it by the onset of World War I. While nine states allowed cross-endorsement in 2002, it played a significant role only in New York State politics.

Scarrow, Howard A. *Parties, Elections, and Representation in the State of New York* (New York: New York Univ Press, 1983)
Spitzer, Robert J. "Multiparty Politics in New York." In *Multiparty Politics in America*, ed. Paul S. Herrnson and John C. Green (Lanham, Md: Rowman & Littlefield, 1997)

Timothy Sullivan

Croswell, Edwin (*b* Catskill, Greene Co, 29 May 1797; *d* Princeton, NJ, 13 June 1871). Newspaper editor and political leader. Croswell went to work on his father's *Catskill Recorder* at age 14 and by 1823 had become coeditor of the semiweekly *Albany Argus*. In 1824, the year he married Catharine Adams of Catskill, he became sole editor of the *Argus*, which he began issuing as a daily. Croswell helped to formulate and promulgate Albany Regency policies, guiding many Bucktail Republican and, later, Democratic newspapers. New York State printer for over 20 years, he served as a director of the Canal Bank of Albany from 1829 until its failure (except for the year beginning July 1840) and invested in the American Land Co and the Mohawk and Hudson Railroad, among other ventures. In the late 1830s he began to part from antibank Democrats who endorsed Pres Martin Van Buren's Independent Treasury and who insisted that the state restrain public spending on internal improvements. Attempting to straddle the gap between the Barnburners and Hunkers of the Democratic Party, he came under increasing Barnburner attack, which forced him further into the Hunker camp. Croswell opposed Van Buren's Free-Soil candidacy in 1848 and vainly attempted to avoid a legislative investigation when the Canal Bank failed in 1848. He then departed from the *Argus* and in 1854 moved to New York City, becoming a partner to George Law of the US Mail Steamship Co. Remaining marginally active in politics, Croswell attended the 1860 Democratic National Convention. After suffering a stroke in 1870, he moved to Princeton, NJ, and was cared for by his daughter.

Manning, Richard H. "Herald of the Albany Regency: Edwin Croswell and the *Albany Argus*, 1823–1854" (PhD diss, Miami Univ, 1983)

Craig and Mary L. Hanyan

Croton-on-Hudson. Village (pop 7,606) in Cortlandt (Westchester Co). The Hudson River Railroad station (1849) became a nucleus for commercial growth, and the village incorporated in 1898. The Harmon development, begun about 1906 by Clifford B. Harmon (1868–1915), was intended as a "colony of cultured people" with its own railroad station, which became Croton-Harmon in the late 20th century. In 1932 the village annexed Harmon as well as Mount Airy (a retreat for freethinkers and intellectuals) and part of the river hamlet of Oscawana. The railroad developed an electric and steam terminal in 1913; Metro-North and Amtrak remain major employers. After World War II increasing numbers of commuters drove to Harmon station; the large municipal parking lot dates from 1954. US 9 was rebuilt as a six-lane highway, cutting off the village's neighborhoods from the riverfront, in 1964. In the early 21st century, the old village retains much historic character. It is the site of Van Cortlandt Manor Restoration.

Carl Oechsner

Croton Reservoir and Aqueduct. This first public water supply for New York City ended its reliance on inadequate and polluted wells. The project was conceived in 1832, authorized by the state legislature in 1834, and approved by New

Croton Aqueduct, 1830, print by Samuel Hollyer, *ca* 1903.

York City voters in 1835. From a 375 mi² (971 km²) watershed in Putnam and Westchester Cos, smaller rivers and streams fed Croton River, which met the Hudson River at Croton-on-Hudson (Westchester Co). Supervised by state-appointed water commissioners, Chief Engineer David B. Douglass surveyed Croton and laid out the aqueduct's route between 1833 and 1836. John B. Jervis detailed the engineering plans and oversaw construction from 1836 to 1842. From Jervis's pioneering 50 ft (15 m) high dam on lower Croton River, which created the 500 million gal (1.9 billion l) Croton Reservoir, the aqueduct stretched 40.5 miles (65.2 km)—through Westchester Co, across the Harlem River, and south along Manhattan—to a distributing reservoir in open country 1 mile (1.6 km) north of the city's limits, at what is now the site of the New York Public Library. The unpressurized brick and masonry conduit was roughly 7 feet 6 inches (2.3 m) wide and 8 feet 6 inches (2.6 m) high. Most of the aqueduct was laid at or near ground level, except several miles of tunneling, high embankments, and raised arches such as those of High Bridge over the Harlem River. Croton Aqueduct opened in 1842 and helped prevent further outbreaks of waterborne disease such as the 1832 cholera epidemic as well as further devastating fires such as the Great Fire of 1835. By the mid-1880s, daily water use rose beyond the aqueduct's capacity of 90 million gallons (341 million l), and work began on New Croton Aqueduct, a 31 mi (50 km) pressurized tunnel, three times the size of the old aqueduct, that ran entirely underground along roughly the same course. Completed in 1893 New Croton was the world's longest and largest tunnel. The 240 ft (73 m) high New Croton Dam, the largest masonry dam in the world when opened in 1905, increased the capacity of Croton Reservoir to 19 billion gallons (71.9 billion l), creating a 9 mi (14 m) long "lake" on lower Croton River and submerging Jervis's original dam. As the Catskill and Delaware Aqueduct systems came into service during the 20th century, Old Croton was cut back and closed in 1955; it was designated a National Historic Landmark in 1992. New Croton continues to supply 10% of the city's water into the 21st century.

See also SANITATION AND SEWAGE.

Koeppel, Gerard T. *Water for Gotham: A History* (Princeton, NJ: Princeton Univ Press, 2000)

Gerard T. Koeppel

Crown Point. In 1734 the French approved plans for the construction of a substantial stone fortress on the western shore of Lake Champlain at Crown Point [now in Essex Co]. Named after a French minister, Fort St. Frédéric eventually included a four-story fortified citadel, a barracks, a chapel, and several other structures. The French used the outpost as a staging point for raids against the British during King George's War (1744–48). British and provincial expeditions were organized to capture the fort during the French and Indian War (1754–63), including one by Sir William Johnson, who for several reasons did not attack Fort St. Frédéric after his victory at the Battle of Lake George in September 1755. Maj Gen James Abercromby led 15,000 men to take Forts Carillon [now Fort Ticonderoga, Essex Co] and St. Frédéric in 1758, but his troops were defeated on 8 July by a smaller force of about 3,500 under the Marquis de Montcalm at Fort Carillon. The following year, outnumbered by British forces led by Maj Gen Jeffery Amherst, Brig Gen François-Charles de Bourlamaque evacuated Forts Carillon and St. Frédéric after blowing up a portion of each fortification.

Amherst began construction of a new fort at Crown Point that would become the largest military fortification built by the British in North America in the 18th century. Designed for approximately 4,000 troops, the main pentagon-shaped fort encompassed over 6 acres (2 ha). In addition to the stone fortress, three stone barracks, a guardhouse, armory, storehouses, three redoubts, a 10-acre (4 ha) garden, and a small village were on the grounds. The Crown Point fortress was never fully completed, and in the years leading up to the American Revolution, the lightly garrisoned fort began to deteriorate. A fire in 1773 set off an explosion in the powder magazine and severely damaged the barracks.

Crown Point and Ticonderoga were captured by the Americans in May 1775. The artillery pieces seized from the two forts were transported over land for George Washington to use in his siege of Boston the following year. Crown Point otherwise played a minor role in the Revolution and was abandoned by the Americans in late 1776 upon the approach of British forces under Gen Guy Carleton. In 1910 the ruins of the Crown Point fortress and Fort St. Frédéric became the property of New York State, which administers the land as a state historic site.

Bellico, Russell P. *Sails and Steam in the Mountains: A Maritime and Military History of Lake George and Lake Champlain,* 2d ed. (Fleischmanns, NY: Purple Mountain Press, 2001)

Coolidge, Guy Omeron. *The French Occupation of the Champlain Valley from 1609 to 1759* (Fleischmanns, NY: Purple Mountain Press, 1999)

Russell P. Bellico

Crown Point. Town (pop 2,119) in SE Essex Co. Named Crown Point by 1690, it became the site of a French settlement surrounding Fort St. Frédéric (1731), which was replaced by an English fort in 1759; this fort was abandoned after the Revolution. The town was formed in 1788, but within present town limits it was resettled *ca* 1800 by squatters from New England and patented by speculators in 1805, who then sold lots to the squatters. Lumber and iron industries were stimulated by the opening of the Champlain Canal (1823). The Penfield and Hammond families developed extensive iron mines and factories in the mid–19th century; at Hammondville miners included Swedish immigrants. The mines and most industry closed by World War I, resulting in a 70% population decrease between 1880 and 1920. The Crown Point State Historic Site and the Penfield Homestead Museum are in town.

Thomas A. Rumney

Crucible Materials Corporation. Specialty steel manufacturer. The Sanderson Bros and Co of Sheffield, England, established a plant in Syracuse in 1876 by purchasing the former Sweet's ironworks on the city's industrial west side, adjacent to the Erie Canal and two major railroad lines. The North American market used steel for woodworking tools, gun parts, and cutting blades on agricultural equipment. In 1900 Sanderson merged with 12 other American steel firms to form Crucible Steel Co of America, a name taken from the graphite and clay pots that held the steel's unprocessed components while they were melted in a 2,900°F (1,600°C) furnace. The crucibles were then removed, and up to 100 pounds (45 kg) of molten steel was individually poured into ingot molds by a "teemer."

Sanderson's executive at Syracuse, C. Herbert Halcomb, became Crucible's first president, but he left Crucible in 1902 to form a new tool steel company, Halcomb Steel, in the nearby Town of Geddes (Onondaga Co). In 1906 Halcomb Steel installed and operated the first electric, arc-fired steelmaking furnace in the United States, developed by Paul Heroult of France. This technology revolutionized the production of high-grade specialty steel. Crucible acquired Halcomb Steel in 1911, and by 1930 the crucible technique was made obsolete by the arc-fired furnace. In 1947 the two operations were consolidated at the Geddes site. Colt Industries acquired Crucible in 1968, and local management purchased the company in 1985. It has been called Crucible Materials Corp since then, and its operations are headquartered at the Specialty Metals Division plant site in Geddes. Crucible's Service Centers Division, based in Camillus (Onondaga Co), oversees its national inventory distribution.

The Specialty Metals Division struggled in the 1980s and early 1990s with foreign competition and attaining satisfactory contracts with unionized workers, but it remains a major Syracuse area employer. The Geddes factory is an industrial landmark of 65 acres (26 ha), seen annually by thousands of visitors to the adjacent New York State Fairgrounds. Ongoing technological improvements and a $25 million expansion in 2000 helped maintain the plant's reputation as a center for tool steel production. Its varied products are employed for medical equipment, automobile parts, injection molding machinery, and aerospace technology. Its pioneering electric arc furnace, used until 1929, was transferred to the Smithsonian Institution in the 1970s. Crucible employs approximately 560 workers in New York State.

Crucible Specialty Metals, http://www.crucible.com
Schramm, Henry W., and William F. Roseboom. "Crucible Specialty Metals Division of Colt Industries." In *Syracuse from Salt to Satellite* (Woodland Hills, Calif: Windsor Publications, 1979)

Dennis J. Connors

Cruger, Henry, Jr (*b* New York City, 22 Nov 1739; *d* New York City, 24 Apr 1827). Member of Parliament and New York State senator. The son of merchant Henry Cruger and Elizabeth Harris, Henry Jr belonged to a prominent transatlantic family. After briefly studying at King's College (now Columbia University), he began working in 1757 at the mercantile house of Henry Cruger and Co in Bristol, England, to learn the family's business operations. In 1765 Henry was elected to the Bristol Common Council, a position he held until 1790. The harm that the Stamp Act (1765) did to his personal finances persuaded him to abandon the political conservatism of his New York City relatives and to embrace the radical movement in Bristol. Cruger consequently supported John Wilkes, annual parliaments, and the right of voters to instruct their representatives. In 1774 he won a seat in Parliament. Although many of his American relatives were loyalists, and he realized that the colonies needed to make concessions, events pushed Cruger closer to the American Whigs. In his first speech before Parliament, he criticized it for worsening the breach between Britain and its colonies. In 1776 he faulted the ministry for abandoning British sympathizers in the Colony of New York. In 1777 he supported the repeal of the Declaratory Act (1766), and by 1780 he favored American independence. Defeated for reelection in 1780, he became Bristol's mayor in 1781. In 1784 Cruger returned to Parliament as a supporter of William Pitt, parliamentary reform, and British-American trade. In 1789 his financial predicament led him, in vain, to seek a consular appointment in the United States. Cruger nonetheless returned to New York State in 1790 and was elected as a Federalist to the New York State senate in 1792. Despite his financial difficulties, he was able to retire from politics and business, marry for a third time in 1799, and father four more children.

Underdown, P. T. "Henry Cruger and Edmund Burke: Colleagues and Rivals at the Bristol Election of 1774," *William and Mary Quarterly* 15 (January 1958): 14–34
Van Schaack, Henry Cruger. *Henry Cruger: The Colleague of Edmund Burke in the British Parliament; a Paper Read before the New-York Historical Society, January 4th, 1859* (New York: C. B. Richardson, 1859)

Joseph S. Tiedemann

CSEA. See PUBLIC EMPLOYEES UNIONS.

CSX Corporation. Based in Richmond, Va, its subsidiaries CSX Transportation and CSX Intermodal operate railroads and other rail facilities in New York State. CSX Corp was formed in 1980 by the merger of Chessie System and Family Lines System, each the product of many prior mergers. Chessie held Chesapeake and Ohio, Baltimore and Ohio, and Western Maryland Railroads while Family Lines principally owned Louisville and Nashville, and Seaboard Coast Line Railroads. After the 1980 merger of the two systems, the CSX rail network covered the Southeast and Midwest but not New York State. Until 1986 CSX-owned railroads retained their individual names though were centrally controlled. That year newly created subsidiary CSX Transportation began to operate all these railroads under the CSX name. CSX, Norfolk Southern, and Conrail were the three principal railroads east of the Mississippi River for most of the 1980s and 1990s. In 1997 after long, involved, often unfriendly negotiations, CSX and Norfolk Southern purchased Conrail and divided the Conrail properties. CSX received 42% of Conrail, which included most New York State lines, though not Erie Lackawanna's Southern Tier route through Binghamton and Elmira, which went to Norfolk Southern. New York Central's main line from Albany to Buffalo became CSX Transportation's main line. A secondary CSX line extends north from Syracuse to Montreal. CSX Transportation runs a large classification yard at Selkirk (Albany Co) and facilities in Syracuse, Rochester, and Buffalo. CSX Intermodal, which handles rail-to-truck and rail-to-ship transfers, runs facilities in Syracuse and Buffalo. Conrail's breakup returned freight-rail competition to the Ports of New York and New Jersey, both served by Norfolk Southern and CSX.

CSX Corp, "Rail Heritage," http://www.csxt.com/index.cfm?fuseaction=history.heritage
Wilner, Frank N. *Railroad Mergers: History, Analysis, Insight* (Omaha: Simmons-Boardman, 1997)

Jeff Schramm

Cuba. Town (pop 3,392) and village (pop 1,633) in W central Allegany Co. The Oil Spring Indian Reservation [loc in Allegany and Cattaraugus Cos] abuts the town. The spring for which it is named was first observed by Europeans in 1627. Settled in 1812, the town was formed in 1822 from Friendship. The Erie Railroad (1851) and Genesee Valley Canal (1856–78) both crossed the town, and the Oil Creek Reservoir (1858), now Cuba Lake, was created to feed the canal's summit level and became an important resort. A short-lived resort at Greenwood Springs (1845) later became a water cure. The village incorporated in 1850. In the Civil War era Cuba had two tanneries and a foundry. After the war it became a dairying town and claimed in the 1890s to be the third-largest market for cheese in the state. D. B. Whipple's imported Holstein-Friesian cow Pieterje II (calved 1877) set a world record by producing 30,318 pounds (13,752 kg) of milk in one year. W. A. Bates Manufacturing Co (1886) was a large concern producing tin-lined butter tubs as well as oilcans. Rte 17 (I-86) made the town more accessible when completed in 1974. In 2003 Empire Cheese employed 120 workers to produce American cheese, and Acme Electric Corp, maker of power conversion equipment, employed 200. An Amish community continues the town's agricultural traditions. The South Street Historic District in the village is composed of 47 buildings.

See also ARCHITECTS AND ARCHITECTURE, SOUTHERN TIER (EASTERN).

Cubans. Cubans have immigrated to New York State and New York City for almost 200 years, for both political and economic reasons. One of the earliest prominent émigrés was Fr Felix Varela, born in Havana in 1788 and forced into exile in 1824. An advocate of Cuban republicanism and abolitionism, he became a leader of the small Spanish-speaking community in New York City and in the Catholic Church, as well as vicar general of the New York Diocese in 1837. He was a defender of the largely immigrant church against the nativists and remained eloquent on religious and American and Cuban political topics for many decades until his retirement in 1850. Like him, many of the Cubans who migrated during this period were male, educated, from the middle and upper classes, and interested in ending Spanish control. In 1868 Cuban rebels declared war on Spanish authorities. The 10-year Grito de Yara war ensued, causing massive economic destruction and leading a cross section of Cuba's population, from professionals and entrepreneurs to working-class people, to immigrate to New York City during the 1870s. There Calixto García and other rebel leaders organized a second attempt to expel the Spanish, the Guerra Chiquita (Little War), in 1879–80. This campaign adversely affected the tobacco industry, causing some cigar manufacturers to move their operations to New York State, which in turn attracted a large number of Cuban economic refugees. By 1894 there were approximately 1,000 cigar factories in New York City, many employing Cuban immigrants, who typically lived in boardinghouses in the Yorkville and Chelsea neighborhoods.

The high concentration of Cubans made New York a natural stronghold of Cuban nationalist activism. Women played an important political role through associations such as the Liga de Hijas de Cuba (League of Daughters of Cuba), founded in 1869 by Emilia Casanova de Villaverde. In 1880 the Cuban revolutionary leader José Martí, having been exiled by the Spanish colonial government, arrived in New York City, which would be his home for much of the next 15 years. He founded the Cuban Revolutionary Party (Partido Revolucionario Cubano, or PRC) in 1892, and within a few years it evolved into the most important exile organization devoted to Cuban independence. The first issue of the PRC's newspaper *Patria* was published in 1892. Exile leaders in New York City formed a junta with the goal of gaining US support for another armed uprising, and in 1895 the revolutionaries launched what would become the Cuban Revolution. PRC leader Tomás Estrada Palma found a staunch ally in Assistant Secretary of the Navy Theodore Roosevelt. In

April 1898 the United States intervened in Cuba, and by August the Spanish military was defeated. Roosevelt, whose role in the American victory gave him a high public profile, was elected governor of New York later the same year. With the United States in control of Cuba, American policy toward the Cuban independence movement shifted substantially. Estrada Palma, a supporter of the US occupation, dissolved the PRC after the war and went on to become the Republic of Cuba's first president (1902–6).

Post-1898 Migration

While Cuban immigration to New York State declined somewhat during the early 20th century, a steady stream flowed into the city from the late 1930s to the mid-1950s. Many found work in the garment industry. The Florida cigar industry experienced an economic crisis in the 1930s, and large numbers of working-class Cubans migrated to New York State in search of better jobs. Many had Afro-Cuban ancestry and were highly represented in the leather and shoe industry. In 1932 Cuban exiles in New York City convened another group to overthrow the authoritarian government of Gerardo Machado; the turmoil surrounding his flight the following year sent additional waves of Cubans to New York State.

New York City thus became the epicenter of the Cuban community in the United States during the 1940s and 1950s. Numerous political organizations and cultural clubs were created, and many Cubans moved to East Harlem, living there with other Latino migrants from Puerto Rico and Central and South America. New York City was also the incubator of the Cuban musical influence on American popular culture. In the 1940s Cuban musicians like Mario Bauzá, Machito, and Chano Pozo merged their Caribbean rhythms and percussion instruments with the bebop jazz of Dizzy Gillespie and others, creating what became known as Afro-Cuban or Latin jazz. New York City–based bands imported the mambo dance craze from Cuba in the 1950s, selling millions of records and making a permanent stylistic contribution to American jazz. At the same time, bandleader Desi Arnaz brought a Cuban American presence into the nation's living rooms as the real-life and television husband of Lucille Ball. *I Love Lucy,* with Ball and Arnaz as a Manhattan couple, was the nation's most popular show for much of the 1950s.

The Castro Years

The bulk of Cuban immigration to New York State occurred after the revolution of 1959, in which Fidel Castro overthrew Pres Fulgencio Batista. Castro came to New York City in 1960 to speak at the United Nations, choosing to stay in Hotel Theresa in Harlem rather than in one of the downtown hotels. Within a few years he established diplomatic ties with Moscow, severed relations with Washington, and declared himself a Marxist-Leninist. Before the Bay of Pigs invasion (1961) and the Cuban Missile Crisis (1962) brought travel between the countries to a halt, large numbers of Cubans, especially the wealthy and well educated, came to New York State. Castro's announcement in 1965 that those with relatives in the United States would be permitted to leave generated another mass exodus of Cuba's upper and middle classes, regarded by the US government as refugees fleeing a communist regime and, as such, eligible for assistance under the Cuban Refugee Program (1961) and later the Cuban Adjustment Act (1966). New York City's Cuban population soared from 28,567 in 1960 to 63,043 in 1970. Castro again allowed unrestricted emigration in 1980, and more than 125,000 made their way to the United States in a "boat lift" from the port of Mariel. Unlike their predecessors, the "Marielitos" were mainly poor and unskilled and relatively few settled in New York State. The number of Cubans in New York City had dropped to 42,286 by 1990 and to 39,731 by 2000 but is still the highest concentration of Cuban Americans outside Miami. The state as a whole was home to approximately 69,590 Cubans in 2000.

See also LATIN MUSIC.

Mirabal, Nancy Raquel. "No War but the One We Must Fight For: The Emergence of an Antillean Nation and Community in New York City, 1860–1901." In *Mambo Montage: The Latinization of New York,* ed. Agustín Laó-Montes and Arlene Dávila (New York: Columbia Univ Press, 2001)

Pérez, Louis A., Jr. *Cuba: Between Reform and Revolution,* 2d ed. (New York: Oxford Univ Press, 1995)

Poyo, Gerald E. *With All, and for the Good of All: The Emergence of Popular Nationalism in the Cuban Communities of the United States, 1848–1898* (Durham, NC: Duke Univ Press, 1989)

Nancy Raquel Mirabal

Cuffee, Paul (*b* Suffolk Co, 1757; *d* ?Hampton Bays, Suffolk Co, 1812). Shinnecock preacher. He followed in the tradition of his grandfather, Peter John, who was an ordained minister in the Congregational Church and who established Christian mission churches on the Shinnecock and Poospatuck Reservations [loc in Suffolk Co]. Cuffee led a dissolute life as a young man until he underwent an emotional conversion. He served Indian congregations at Shinnecock, Montauk (Suffolk Co), and Poospatuck. Unlike many white missionaries, he was sensitive to Indian aboriginal religious traditions, encouraging Indians to continue their traditional observation of a spring celebration in a Christian form called June Meeting. This soon became a popular and widely attended event that drew Indians from all over Long Island to the Poospatuck and Shinnecock Reservations. Cuffee's work was highly regarded by the Presbyterian Church, which provided him with a yearly salary of $80. He was ordained in 1790 by a council of ministers from Connecticut. An accomplished orator, Cuffee regularly drew an attentive congregation and was involved in the evangelical movement that flourished after the Great Awakening in New England. He is buried under a stone monument erected by the New York Missionary Society in a small plot of land between Hampton Bays and the Shinnecock Canal.

Eells, Earnest Edward. "Indian Missions on Long Island." In *The History and Archaeology of the Montauk,* ed. Gaynell Stone (Stony Brook, NY: Suffolk County Archaeological Association, 1993)

John A. Strong

Culinary Institute of America. Private college. Located in Hyde Park (Dutchess Co), the Culinary Institute of America (CIA) is the nation's oldest extant culinary school. It is also the world's only residential degree-granting college dedicated exclusively to culinary and baking and pastry arts education. Founded by Frances Roth and Katharine Angell in New Haven, Conn, in 1946, it provided training to veterans of World War II. CIA's first class comprised 49 men and 1 woman with 3 faculty members. The CIA purchased the former Jesuit seminary site at St. Andrew-on-Hudson in 1970 and relocated there in 1972. Between 1972 and 2001 the college added four residence halls and buildings for continuing education, nutrition, baking and pastry, Italian cuisine, and student recreation. Its Conrad N. Hilton Library houses one of the largest collections of culinary publications in the country. The CIA began conferring associate degrees in 1972 and has offered baccalaureate programs in culinary and baking and pastry arts management since 1994. The school enrolls 2,100 students in its degree programs and 6,000 in its continuing education programs. Its first public restaurant opened in 1973, and facilities have expanded to include four campus restaurants and a bakery café, which all serve as classrooms. With 200,000 annual visitors, the CIA contributes an estimated $20 million to the local economy alone.

The Professional Chef/The Culinary Institute of America, 7th ed. (New York: John Wiley & Sons, 2002)

Ruhlman, Michael. *The Making of a Chef: Mastering Heat at the Culinary Institute of America* (New York: Henry Holt, 1997)

Jeff Levine

Cumberland County. See EXTINCT COUNTIES.

CUNY. See CITY UNIVERSITY OF NEW YORK (CUNY).

Cuomo, Mario M(atthew) (*b* South Jamaica, Queens Co, 15 June 1932). Governor. Born to an immigrant Italian family, Cuomo received his law degree from St. John's University in 1956, afterward serving as confidential legal assistant to State Court of Appeals judge Adrian P. Burke. Cuomo came to public attention while an attorney in private practice when he mediated a public housing dispute in Queens, about which he wrote in his *Forest Hills Diary* (1974). He failed in a quest for the Democratic nomination for mayor of New York City in 1977, served as the appointed secretary of state from 1975 to 1978, and was elected lieutenant governor in tandem with Hugh Carey in 1978.

In 1982 Cuomo became the first Italian American governor of New York State, his first independently won elective office. In defeating Republican Lewis Lehrman, Cuomo drew his greatest support from New York City. In 1986 he was reelected by a wide majority and in 1990 by a lesser margin in a three-way race. Employing the powerful image of the "Family of New York," Cuomo in his first inaugural address communicated inclusiveness, seeking to calm the partisan and interbranch tensions that marked Gov Carey's final year. This message was reinforced by his appointment of upstate Republican Richard D. Simons to the Court of the Appeals. He later appointed the state's first African American, the first two women (including the chief judge, Judith Kaye), and the first Latino Court of Appeals judges. The new governor worked to balance the budget by cutting spending and raising taxes in equal proportions to fill the fiscal gap he inherited and through this strategy achieved timely budgets in his early years in office.

In an era during which government was la-

Gov Mario M. Cuomo, 1990.

beled as the problem, Cuomo insisted on the value of the compassionate use of governmental power to achieve social change. Among the achievements in social policy during his tenure were publicly financed healthcare programs for low-income children and pregnant women and an emphasis on job training for welfare recipients that anticipated later innovations in national policy. Cuomo's politically costly, principled stand against the death penalty (the legislature passed and he vetoed it for each of his 12 years in office) was a defining element of his governorship, as was his willingness to speak out on such complex questions as the conflicting obligations of a believing Roman Catholic leader in American public life.

Extremely intelligent and an enormously hard worker with a hands-on approach to government, Cuomo was criticized for not trusting others outside a small circle, for not delegating, for lacking priorities, and, in the end, for failing to use the full extent of his powers to reach goals he so eloquently defined. His advocate's style in political exchange was often considered abrasive. Cuomo sought but failed to achieve a state takeover of Medicaid funding and public financing of elections, although the legislature did enact enhanced ethical standards for New York State's elected officials during his tenure. He encouraged a state constitutional convention to achieve reform, but this effort also fell short.

Divided partisan control of the state legislature for his entire tenure and Republican dominance of the national executive branch for much of it provided a difficult political context for Cuomo's governorship. Co-partisans across the nation expected the state's Republican senate to provide roadblocks to Cuomo's presidential prospects, and resources available from Washington to meet social needs were limited. Federal tax cuts in the mid-1980s threatened many states' own income tax bases, requiring New York State's governor to (successfully) lead them in a collective effort to protect these.

Cuomo was regarded as one of the most powerful political orators of his time. In arguing for "only the government we need, but all the government we need," he offered a Democratic alternative to the vision advanced by Pres Ronald Reagan. His televised keynote address at the 1984 Democratic National Convention helped make him a serious contender for the presidency in 1988 and 1992, although after months of public Hamlet-like vacillation he backed away on both occasions, giving the nominating address for Bill Clinton's candidacy in 1992. After Clinton was elected, Cuomo declined a proposed nomination to a US Supreme Court seat.

In 1994 Cuomo was defeated by Republican George E. Pataki, then a little-known Hudson Valley state senator. Persistently high crime rates, welfare dependency, and state and local taxes, combined with loss of upstate manufacturing and economic growth in New York State that lagged behind the nation's all led to Cuomo's loss. The longest-serving Democratic governor to date in the state's history, Cuomo returned after his three terms to the private practice of law and became a nationally prominent speaker and commentator on public affairs.

Chartock, Alan. *Me and Mario: Conversations in Candor* (New York: Barricade Books, 1995)

Cuomo, Mario Matthew. *Diaries of Mario M. Cuomo: The Campaign for Governor* (New York: Random House, 1984)

———. *More Than Words: The Speeches of Mario Cuomo* (New York: St. Martin's Press, 1993)

McElvaine, Robert S. *Mario Cuomo: A Biography* (New York: Scribner's, 1988)

New York State. Governor. *Public Papers of Mario M. Cuomo, 1983–1991,* 9 vols (Albany: State of New York, 1987–94)

Gerald Benjamin

curling. A winter sport of Scottish origins brought to New York State by immigrants from the British Isles. Players scribed circles on frozen lakes and ponds, swept the snow from the ice with brooms, and slid stones, wooden or metal blocks with handles, toward the target. The earliest recorded match in the state was held at Clark Mills (Oneida Co) in 1832 by Scottish and English textile workers. The Utica Curling Club formed in 1868, and other clubs began in the late 19th century in New York City, Albany, Ogdensburg (St. Lawrence Co), and Buffalo. Rules for the sport were established for American curling on 26 June 1867 when delegates met in New York City to form the Grand National Curling Club. The Utica club moved to an indoor site in 1891, though refrigeration was limited to leaving windows open on cold days. The club acquired an ice plant in 1925. Women entered the sport after World War II; in Utica, for instance, women were first allowed to curl in 1947. Curling now has men's, women's, mixed, and junior leagues. Modern curling facilities with ice-making equipment allow the games to go on from October until April each year. Clubs vary in size from two to six sheets (one sheet measures 146 ft x 14 ft 2 in) with a public viewing area and locker rooms. Curling competitions, called bonspiels, are arranged among clubs. In the early 21st century there were New York State member-owned curling clubs in Utica, Schenectady (1907), Rochester (1960), and Albany, and curling clubs that rented ice as needed in Amherst (Erie Co), Lake Placid (Essex Co) and at the St. Andrews Country Club in Hastings-on-Hudson (Westchester Co). There are approximately 1,000 curlers in New York State.

1999–2000 Directory and Media Guide (Stevens Point, Wisc: US Curling Association, 1999)

Utica Curling Club, http://www5.uticacurling.org:8000

Peggy Rotton

Curtiss, Glenn H(ammond) (*b* Hammondsport, Steuben Co, 21 May 1878; *d* Buffalo, 23 July 1930). Motorcycle and aeronautics innovator and entrepreneur. After his father's death, Curtiss moved with his mother to Rochester, where he completed the eighth grade. As a teenager he worked for Eastman Co (now Eastman Kodak Co) and Western Union in Rochester and competed in bicycle races. At age 19 Curtiss married Lena Pearl Neff and opened a bicycle shop in Hammondsport. In 1901–2 he began experiments with the design and manufacture of motorcycles, continually improving the power-to-weight ratio of the new gasoline engines, and in 1904 supplied a lightweight Curtiss motorcycle engine for the nation's first successful dirigible, piloted by Thomas S. Baldwin.

In January 1907 Curtiss's motorcycle business and racing career climaxed at Ormond Beach, Fla, where he rode the world's first V-8-engine motorcycle at 136 mph (219 kph), breaking every existing mile speed record. Later that year Curtiss joined Alexander Graham Bell and others in the Aerial Experiment Association, and in 1908 the group built four biplanes at Curtiss's Hammondsport works, a striking feat since none of the men had ever seen an airplane. While *Red Wing* and *White Wing* were quickly wrecked, *White Wing* originated tricycle landing gear and the first ailerons (movable wing flaps) on a US aircraft. Curtiss piloted a third model, *June Bug,* in the nation's first exhibition flight on 4 July 1908, winning *Scientific American*'s trophy for an unassisted takeoff followed by a .6 mi (1 km) straightaway flight. Curtiss also helped Thomas Baldwin create the SC-1 dirigible, the first US government aircraft. The association's *Silver Dart* featured the first water-cooled airplane engine and in 1909 made the first flight in Canada. The association dissolved that year, and Curtiss began manufacturing and exhibiting aircraft on his own, despite patent infringement lawsuits filed by the Wright brothers. Curtiss made the first US airplane sales in 1909 and also set a world air speed record at Rheims, France. In 1910 he completed the first flight from Albany to New York City, and a year later he produced a practical float plane, which became the first US Navy aircraft. Curtiss also earned US pilot's license no. 1 in 1911. His attention to infrastructure—flying fields, flying schools, exhibition companies—hastened development of the aircraft business. In 1912 Curtiss developed the flying boat and in 1913, with substantial help from English engineer B. D. Thomas, developed the JN or Jenny, which became the main training plane for the United States, Canada, and Great Britain during World War I. The war prompted production of over 7,000 Jennies. Curtiss opened a vast factory in Buffalo, with other sites and licensees across the country.

In 1917 he relinquished controlling interest in the company but continued to serve as chairman of the board and established a subsidiary, Curtiss Engineering Corp, in Garden City (Nassau Co). There, among other projects, he oversaw design of the NC class flying boats, one of which made the first Atlantic aerial crossing in 1919. A multimillionaire by the 1920s, Curtiss was involved in developing several Florida cities. He also ventured into automotive design, creating the Curtiss Aerocar, a streamlined fifth-wheel travel trailer. Curtiss died suddenly from a pulmonary embolism after an emergency appendectomy and was buried in Urbana (Steuben Co).

House, Kirk W. *Hell Rider to King of the Air: Glenn Curtiss's Life of Innovation* (Warrendale, Pa: SAE International, 2003)

Mitchell, Charles R., and Kirk W. House. *Glenn H. Curtiss, Aviation Pioneer* (Charleston, SC: Arcadia, 2001)

Roseberry, C. R. *Glenn H. Curtiss: Pioneer of Flight* (Garden City, NY: Doubleday, 1972)

Kirk W. House

Curtiss-Wright Corporation. Aeronautics manufacturer. At one time the largest US corporation after General Motors, Curtiss-Wright grew from two bicycle shops: Glenn H. Curtiss's works in Hammondsport (Steuben Co) and the Wright brothers' similar business in Dayton, Ohio. On entering the motorcycle business, Curtiss incorporated as G. H. Curtiss Manufacturing Co. Following a disastrous merger with Augustus Herring (1909–10), Curtiss formed three new companies: Curtiss Aeroplane Co (airframes), Curtiss Motor Co (engines and motorcycles), and Curtiss Exhibition Co (air shows). The group, which successfully fended off lawsuits from Herring and the Wright brothers, quickly became the largest US manufacturer of aeronautics. At the beginning of World War I, Curtiss ceased motorcycle production, established a Canadian subsidiary, and built a vast factory in Buffalo.

In 1916 Curtiss sold controlling interests in all four companies to William Morris Imbrie and Co, which created Curtiss Aeroplane and Motor Co. Curtiss Aeroplane made more acquisitions, licensed other manufacturers to produce Curtiss aircraft, and established the subsidiary Curtiss Engineering Corp in Garden City (Nassau Co). Military aircraft production, mostly JN (Jenny) training planes and flying boats for submarine patrol, surpassed 18,000 during the war, but shrinking demand after the war brought Curtiss near bankruptcy. Vice Pres Clement M. Keys bought a controlling interest in 1920, and over the next decade Curtiss fighters became mainstays of the army and navy. Civil aviation slowly grew, with a burst of development following Charles Lindbergh's 1927 flight to Paris.

Wright Co incorporated in 1909 with headquarters in New York City and manufacturing around Dayton, Ohio. Like Curtiss, the firm restructured several times during its early years, in part suffering from Pres Orville Wright's attachment to outdated design. After a partnership with Glenn L. Martin ended in 1919, new leadership decided to manufacture engines only. Acquiring Lawrance Aero Engine Co in 1923, Wright gained patents to a powerful air-cooled radial engine that, with ongoing development, led the industry for 30 years.

Keys and Richard Hoyt, chairman of Wright, arranged a merger, absorbing several smaller firms at the same time and establishing a new headquarters in New York City's Rockefeller Center. But the depression blighted a promising start. Slashing airport and flying service operations, the firm concentrated on engines, its most profitable division, and airframes. The new Curtiss-Wright also depended on a small military business, which included the export of outdated aircraft. At the start of World War II, Curtiss-Wright was the only American firm poised for mass production, and the company's production of P-36 and P-40 fighters expanded rapidly. Other significant wartime aircraft were the C-46 cargo plane and SB2C dive-bomber. Over 22,000 people worked for wartime Curtiss-Wright in Buffalo.

After 1945 shareholder profit taking aggravated postwar shrinkage, and the overextended company fell behind in jet and engine design. By 1947 only 3 of the 19 wartime plants remained, all outside New York State. During the 1950s the firm diversified into plastics, electronics, and other areas. During the 1960s Curtiss-Wright expanded into the field of nuclear technology by acquiring Target Rock Corp of East Farmingdale (Suffolk Co), a manufacturer of valves for nuclear submarines. In this same decade the Wankel rotary engine and some new vertical takeoff and landing projects were unsuccessful, along with attempts to acquire other corporations. In the 1990s Curtiss-Wright, headquartered in Lyndhurst, NJ, employed 2,400 people in eight countries. Main businesses included shot peening to improve metal durability in aircraft, aerospace control components and systems, including mechanisms used on the Space Shuttle, component overhaul and repair services, leakless valves for nuclear and nonnuclear applications, and rescue tools.

Eltscher, Louis R., and Edward M. Young. *Curtiss-Wright: Greatness and Decline* (New York: Twayne Publishers, 1998)

House, Kirk W. *Hell-Rider to King of the Air: Glenn Curtiss's Life of Innovation* (Warrendale, Pa: SAE International, 2003)

Kirk W. House

Cusick, Cornelius C. (*b* Tuscarora Indian Reservation [loc in Erie Co], 2 Aug 1835; *d* 2 Jan 1904). Tuscarora soldier. The son of a Baptist minister, Cusick was 1 of 23 Tuscaroras to enlist in the Union army, continuing the tradition of his people's service in America's wars, which included his grandfather, Nicholas Kaghnatsho (Cusick), who fought with patriots during the American Revolution. He helped recruit 17 of the 25 Iroquois enlistees in Company D of the 132d New York State Volunteer Infantry, known because of Cusick's leadership as the Tuscarora Company. In December 1862 he was sent to the New Bern area of North Carolina, from where, 150 years earlier, the Tuscarora had been forced to flee. Cited for heroism three times in 1864, he made the military his career. In 1866 he received a commission as a lieutenant in the regular army, first in the 13th US Infantry and later in the 31st US Infantry. As an officer on the trans-Mississippi frontier he rose to the rank of captain, serving in many engagements, fighting Red Cloud's warriors in 1867 and 1868, and participating in the Sioux War of 1876–77. He retired from military service in 1892 and received full military honors at his funeral at Old Fort Niagara, only a few miles from his birthplace.

Hauptman, Laurence M. *The Iroquois in the Civil War: From Battlefield to Reservation* (Syracuse: Syracuse Univ Press, 1993)

Laurence M. Hauptman

Cusick, Nicholas [Kaghnatsho, Nicholas] (*b* ?Oneida territory [now Madison and Oneida Cos], ?1760; *d* Tuscarora Indian Reservation [loc in Niagara Co], 29 Oct 1840). Tuscarora leader. He supported the American cause in the Revolutionary War. In 1777 he enlisted as a private in the Indian Rangers under Caughnawaga Mohawk lieutenant colonel Louis Cook (Atayataghronghta) and participated in the Battle of Saratoga. In 1779 he received a commission from Congress as a lieutenant in the Indian Rangers and served throughout the war. He was an active Christian and a firm friend of missionary Samuel Kirkland. Cusick served as interpreter for the Tuscaroras who attended John Sergeant Jr's church at New Stockbridge [now Stockbridge, Madison Co], where he was also a deacon. Between 1800 and 1805, Cusick traveled intermittently to Tuscarora Village (as the reservation in Niagara Co was known) to be interpreter for the missionary Elkanah Holmes. In 1806 he moved with his family permanently to the Tuscarora Reservation, at which the Tuscarora Congregational Church was formally organized in July of that year. Cusick and two other leading men were chosen and ordained as ruling elders of the church. He was literate in English and continued to serve as church interpreter until 1828. With other Tuscarora chiefs he made trips to North Carolina to collect lease money for the lands his people had left behind when they migrated north. Cusick was a signer in 1794 of the Treaty of Canandaigua and, in the same year, of the treaty between the Oneida, Tuscarora, and Stockbridge. Four decades later he signed the Treaty of Buffalo Creek (1838). In his later years he became a Baptist after his son, James N. Cusick, organized a Baptist church on the reservation in the late 1830s.

Jones, Electa F. *Stockbridge Past and Present; or, Records of an Old Mission Station* (Springfield, Mass: S. Bowles, 1854)

Kappler, Charles J., comp. *Indian Affairs: Laws and Treaties*, 5 vols (Washington, DC: Government Printing Office, 1904–41)

Barbara Graymont

cutlery industry. There are four principal types of cutlery: tableware, knives, scissors, and razors. Traditionally cutlery makers were specialists, centered in particular locations, such as Solingen, Germany, and Sheffield, England. By the mid–19th century many Sheffield cutlers were immigrating to New England, and by the 1870s these workers were settling in New York State. By 1900 there were dozens of small firms clustered in four areas: Cattaraugus Co, the Rome-Syracuse area, Orange and Ulster Cos, and New York City. In the early 21st century, New York State remains a major cutlery producer. Oneida Ltd near Rome (Oneida Co), Camillus Cutlery (Onondaga Co), Utica Cutlery, and Whitney Point Knives and Books (Broome Co) are Central New York's largest manufacturers. Alcas in Olean and Ontario Knife in Franklinville, both in Cattaraugus Co, continue the Southern Tier's tradition of cutlery making, and Village Cutlery Plus in Scottsville (Monroe Co) is active in Western New York. In the eastern part of the state, Drue Sanders in Albany, Warren Cutlery Corp in Rhinebeck (Dutchess Co), Imperial Schrade in Ellenville (Ulster Co), Max Ams in Mount Vernon (Westchester Co), and D. W. Haber and Son (Bronx Co) are all manufacturers of cutlery. The largest company in the state, Oneida Ltd, grew out of the Oneida Community, the well-known utopian religious community. It had sales of $516 million and 4,800 employees in 2001.

Hinsworth, Joseph B. *The Story of Cutlery: From Flint to Stainless Steel* (London: Benn, 1953)

Jack Westbrook

Cuyler. Town (pop 1,036) in NE Cortland Co. Settled in 1794 the town formed from Truxton in 1858. Dairying became increasingly important, and the first cheese factory was built in 1864; railroad service, beginning in 1872, allowed easy shipment of dairy products. Dairying remains present, but the railroad station is now a museum. Cuyler's population increased 22% between 1990 and 2000.

Cathy A. Barber

Czechs. Before the creation of Czechoslovakia in 1919, Czech-speaking immigrants were usually listed as Bohemians, a category that included German speakers. Colonial era immigrants from Bohemia include Augustine Hermann (1621–86) and Frederick Philipse (1676–1720). The bulk of clearly Czech-speaking immigrants came in the second half of the 19th century, driven by economic hardship. In the late 19th century two Czech neighborhoods emerged, one on the Upper East Side in Manhattan and the other in Astoria (Queens Co). A Czech agrarian community was founded in 1855 in Bohemia (Suffolk Co). By 1900 an estimated 17,000 Czechs and their descendants lived in New York State. Of these about 15,000 lived in New York City, and the remainder resided in farming communities in Suffolk, Rockland, and Cayuga Cos.

Czechs usually came as families, and the majority were Roman Catholic, with Protestant, Jewish, and free-thinking minorities. Czechs, especially women and girls, found a niche in the cigar-making factories in New York City. In 1882 the United Cigar Makers published a Czech language monthly, *Pravda* (Truth). Czechs dominated the New York pearl-button industry in the 1890s and also entered the professions, becoming piano makers, furriers, brewers, lawyers, teachers, painters, sculptors, instrumental musicians, and composers, as well as ballet masters for the Metropolitan Opera. In Manhattan the National Hall was built on East 73d St in 1896, which today has landmark status, while the John Hus Church, affiliated with the Presbyterian Church, included a settlement house providing social services for Czech newcomers. In Astoria the still extant Bohemian Citizens Benevolent Society was founded in 1892, and its Bohemian Hall and Garden were built in 1910 on 24th Ave. Three gymnastic organizations were created—the Sokol (Falcon), the Delnicky Americky Sokol (American Workers's Falcon), and the Catholic Orel (Eagle)—all combining physical fitness with dedication to Czech cultural and national goals.

When the Hapsburg empire collapsed during World War I, Czech immigrants and their children supported the Czechoslovak National Council of America and the creation of independent Czechoslovakia. A huge rally at Carnegie Hall on 15 Sept 1918 was attended by Thomas Masaryk, the future president of Czechoslovakia, whose wife, Charlotte Garrigue Masaryk, was a native of Brooklyn. During World War I the community collected for war relief. After both the Communist coup of February 1948 and the Soviet invasion of Czechoslovakia in August 1968, Czech refugees moved to New York State, including Alice Masaryk, daughter of the president, and filmmaker Milos Forman. They were helped by the American Fund for Czechoslovak Relief, set up in 1948 in New York. Within the Czech American community, tensions existed between older immigrants, who tended toward the Democratic Party, and the political refugees, who tended to be strongly Republican. These tensions were transcended by a common interest in Czech heritage and support for the new Czech Republic created in 1993 after the Communist regime had ended and Slovakia became independent.

As reported by the 2000 US Census, more than 90,000 people in New York State reported Czech or Czechoslovakian birth or ancestry. In New York City there are still active Sokol branches and a branch of the Czechoslovak Society of Arts and Sciences. The Citizens Benevolent Society of Astoria provides Czech language instruction and hosts the annual Czech and Slovak Memorial Weekend Festival at its Bohemian Hall. In September 2000 the president of the Czech Republic, Vaclav Havel, planted a linden tree as a symbol of Czech-American friendship. The biweekly *Americke Listy* is published in Glen Cove (Nassau Co). The Czech government has purchased the old National Hall in Manhattan and plans to house the consulate general, a Czech cultural center, and a home for Czech American associations there in 2004. A number of Czechs made an impact on the classical music scene in New York State, such as Antonín Dvořák, who led the National Conservatory of Music from 1892 to 1895, Metropolitan Opera soprano Jarmila Novotna, and in more recent decades pianist Rudolf Firkušný and Cornell University composer Karel Husa.

Chada, Joseph. *The Czechs in the United States* ([Washington, DC]: Czechoslovak Society of Arts and Sciences [SVU] Press, 1981)

Rechcigl, Miloslav, Jr. *Czech Settlements and Communities in the US* ([Washington, DC]: Czechoslovak Society of Arts and Sciences [SVU] Press, 1999)

Barbara Reinfeld

Czolgosz, Leon F. (*b* Detroit, 1873; *d* Auburn, Cayuga Co, 29 Oct 1901). Assassin. The son of Polish immigrants and a manual laborer throughout his life, Czolgosz achieved worldwide infamy when he traveled to Buffalo and shot Pres William McKinley during a public reception at the Pan-American Exposition's Temple of Music on 6 Sept 1901. Czolgosz was immediately apprehended and jailed. After initially giving his name as Fred Nieman ("no one" in German), Czolgosz stated that socialist literature and the teachings of anarchist Emma Goldman had inspired his actions, but he denied having any accomplices. Two days after McKinley's death on 14 Sept 1901, Czolgosz was charged with first-degree murder. His trial began in Buffalo on 23 September, and his defense was handled by two court-appointed attorneys who called no witnesses. The jury returned a guilty verdict the next afternoon. Sentenced to death, Czolgosz died in the electric chair at Auburn Prison. In assassinating McKinley, Czolgosz precipitated a nationwide crackdown on anarchists and other radicals, though he had little connection to any organized anarchist group. New York State passed laws restricting the activities of radicals, and federal immigration laws were amended to exclude those perceived as threats.

Johns, A. Wesley. *The Man Who Shot McKinley* (South Brunswick, NJ: A. S. Barnes, 1970)

Lenora M. Henson

D

Daemen College. Private, nonsectarian, liberal arts college in Amherst (Erie Co). Founded in 1947 as Rosary Hill College by the Sisters of St. Francis of Penance and Christian Charity, it was originally a women-only college but became coeducational in 1971. The name changed to Daemen College in 1976 when it became nonsectarian. Daemen offers baccalaureate and master's degrees in many disciplines at its 35-acre (14 ha) campus just northwest of Buffalo. In 2002, 75% of its approximately 1,900 students was female.

Daemen College, http://www.daemen.edu

David W. Sawicki

dairy industry. Before the development of railroads, dairy farmers were largely restricted to the production of cheese and butter. The vast majority of farmers in 19th-century New York State worked small, semisubsistence farms, producing a diversified selection of crops. This often included dairy products. By 1850 New York State was the nation's leading dairy producer, accounting for almost half of the total cheese production in the United States; St. Lawrence Co alone produced more butter than 17 states combined. Farmers in the St. Lawrence, Black, and Mohawk River valleys in particular developed a reputation for producing cheese and butter of excellent quality.

From Semisubsistence to Dairy Farming

By the mid–19th century, few New York State farmers produced fluid milk as a cash crop. The extension of rail service into the Hudson Valley changed all this. In 1842 Philo Gregory, a farmer who lived near Chester (Orange Co), took part in a daring experiment. Thomas Selleck, stationmaster on the New York and Erie Railroad, proposed that Gregory and other farmers ship fresh "country" milk to New York City via the Erie line. The few cans of milk that Gregory shipped in an unrefrigerated baggage car became the first upstate milk ever sold in New York City. In 1842 trains carried an average of 45 cans daily to the city. By 1843 the number had increased to 275 cans and by 1844 to 420 cans per day. The first regular milk train began operation in 1847, and service was extended to Port Jervis (Orange Co) in 1868. One beneficial aspect of upstate milk was the improvement of New York City's milk supply. For years the growing urban population had been forced to consume "swill" milk, produced within the city by cows fed brewer's waste. Not surprisingly swill milk was poor in both nutrition and appearance. Historians believe that many children died annually from drinking contaminated milk. In addition to improving the quality of milk, the development of a milk market in the Hudson Valley engendered profound changes in farmers' lives. As semisubsistence farmers, their daily rhythms varied according to the dictates of the seasons or their particular needs. The new type of farmer—the dairy farmer—had to deliver the milk according to the railroad schedule. And as farmers added more cows, they became less self-sufficient. As part of this transition, for example, cheese production shifted from farm to factory. Once the domain of wives and daughters, cheese was increasingly produced after 1850 at the more than 1,500 cheese factories constructed across New York State by century's end.

Perhaps the greatest change for farmers occurred when they surrendered control of the marketing and sale of their milk to urban dealers or their agents. In contrast to the face-to-face dealings farmers experienced in their local communities, dairy farmers sold milk by contract. In these new contractual relationships, the milk dealers often had greater financial resources, better legal advice, and a greater familiarity with the workings of such a large-scale market. The key question was whether any group of farmers or dealers could dictate prices in the New York City "milkshed," a term referring to the flow of milk from New York State farmers to the New York City market. From 1842 to 1870, the Hudson Valley milk market was largely a free and unmanipulated market. The large number of dealers and agents gave dairy farmers the option of avoiding those dealers who offered low prices. In 1882, however, a number of larger dealers, assisted by a small group of Wall St financiers, established the Milk Exchange for the purposes of setting, or fixing, wholesale milk prices. Hudson Valley dairy farmers fought back in 1883. Assisted by Erie Railroad executives, the Erie Mutual Milk Producers' Association organized an 11-day strike that became known as the Orange County Milk War. During the boycott, the movement's "spilling committees," which dumped the milk of nonstriking farmers, severely curtailed deliveries to New York City; many urban consumers were unable to buy more than a single pint of milk. On 24 Mar 1883 farmers ended the strike when they agreed with dealers who were not part of the Milk Exchange on an acceptable price. From 1884 to the turn of the century, the milk business was transformed by increased mergers and consolidations among dealers. Two new milk companies, the Borden Condensed Milk Co and the Sheffield Farms-Slawson-Decker Co, gained significant market share. Borden's and Sheffield Farms would dominate the New York City market after the reorganized Consolidated Milk Exchange dissolved in 1913, following years of farmer lawsuits alleging restraint of trade, and similar patterns of consolidation occurred in other New York State cities.

Butter churn made in Fort Edward, late 19th century.

Between 1884 and 1916, the state initiated regulation of the dairy industry, focusing first on developing sanitary standards for the production and manufacture of milk products. In 1884 New York State created the Dairy Commission (which became the Department of Agriculture in 1893) to "prevent deception and adulteration of dairy products." By 1896 the state required all milk dealers to have permits, and by 1906 most farms, processing plants, and manufacturing plants were regularly inspected. The next advance in sanitary regulation occurred in 1911 when the state required most milk to be pasteurized to eliminate pathogens. Pasteurization hastened the consolidation of the milk industry because the higher cost of stricter sanitary standards forced thousands of small milk peddlers out of business, and they were replaced by large companies that instituted the system of home milk delivery. State policy makers also sought to introduce the latest business and scientific methods to farmers, with the goals of raising rural income and keeping young people, who were increasingly drawn to urban areas and industrial work, on the farm. Legislators organized a system of agricultural colleges and created the Department of Food and Markets in 1914, which had as one of its responsibilities the creation of farmer cooperatives. The department's first commissioner was John J. Dillon of Orange Co, the outspoken editor of *Rural New Yorker* and critic of the New York City milk dealers. Dillon used his newfound powers to help organize one of the largest milk strikes in state history in 1916. With as many as 100,000 farmers participating, Dillon and the leaders of the Dairymen's League, a revitalized cooperative, forced Borden's and other major metropolitan dealers to recognize the league and pay higher prices to member farmers.

Changes in the Dairy Industry, 1920–30

Despite occasional unrest, by the 1920s dairy production and marketing was one of the state's major industries. With increased population, sanitary regulations, and advances in transportation, the New York City milkshed had been expanded. To the north the milkshed reached the St. Lawrence River valley, and from the west milk flowed into New York City from Central New York and the western Southern Tier counties. Similar arrangements were in place by this time around Rochester, Syracuse, and Buffalo. Demand for dairy products increased in the 1920s as the economy improved. In fact demand for milk reached the point where industry analysts questioned whether the milk supply would be adequate in certain seasons. In 1919 the Dairymen's League attempted another, but less successful, milk strike without the support of John J. Dillon, who had lost his position in state government shortly after the 1916 strike. In reaction a

INVENTORY OF CATTLE BY COUNTY, 1 JAN 2002

County	All Cattle and Calves	Milk Cows	Beef Cattle
Albany	8,000	2,000	1,700
Allegany	34,000	13,500	2,800
Broome	16,000	7,500	1,400
Cattaraugus	39,000	19,000	2,600
Cayuga	55,000	27,000	2,100
Chautauqua	47,000	22,000	2,500
Chemung	8,000	3,000	800
Chenango	44,000	20,000	2,000
Clinton	36,000	20,000	600
Columbia	20,000	10,000	1,000
Cortland	27,000	14,000	1,200
Delaware	32,000	14,500	2,000
Dutchess	10,000	2,500	1,400
Erie	26,000	14,000	1,200
Essex	6,300	3,000	500
Franklin	34,000	19,000	900
Fulton	7,000	2,600	500
Genesee	38,000	19,000	900
Greene	4,000	1,000	600
Hamilton[a]	—	—	—
Herkimer	31,000	16,000	500
Jefferson	63,000	35,000	3,300
Lewis	53,000	28,500	500
Livingston	40,000	19,000	1,700
Madison	41,000	22,500	1,200
Monroe	7,000	2,500	800
Montgomery	29,000	15,500	1,100
Niagara	18,000	7,500	1,700
Oneida	48,000	23,000	1,400
Onondaga	33,000	17,500	800
Ontario	31,000	16,000	1,300
Orange	16,000	8,000	800
Orleans	10,000	3,500	1,700
Oswego	15,000	4,500	1,800
Otsego	36,000	17,500	2,100
Putnam[a]	—	—	—
Rensselaer	16,000	9,500	1,800
Rockland[a]	—	—	—
Saratoga	16,000	7,500	1,300
Schenectady	1,500	800	500
Schoharie	19,000	7,500	2,100
Schuyler	8,000	3,000	600
Seneca	16,000	6,000	1,600
St. Lawrence	75,000	35,500	3,500
Steuben	54,000	21,000	5,300
Sullivan	10,000	4,500	700
Tioga	18,000	9,000	1,500
Tompkins	18,000	10,000	1,300
Ulster	3,000	600	1,000
Warren[a]	—	—	—
Washington	49,000	23,000	1,200
Wayne	16,000	6,500	1,500
Westchester[a]	—	—	—
Wyoming	87,000	50,000	1,900
Yates	20,000	10,000	1,300
Other Counties	1,200	500	500
State Total	1,390,000	675,000	75,000

Source: New York State Department of Agriculture and Markets, Agricultural Statistics Service.

Note: No figures available for Bronx, Kings, Nassau, New York, Queens, Richmond, or Suffolk Cos.

[a]Included in "Other Counties."

Compiled by Hannah M. Springer

new board of directors transformed the league from a politicized cooperative into a profit-oriented marketing association by building farmer-owned milk plants and distribution networks. To critics like Dillon, the reorganized league, now known as the Dairymen's League Cooperative Association (DLCA), might be forced to cut prices paid to league farmers when they entered into direct competition with corporate milk dealers.

For farmers, milk dealers, and policy makers, the key question in the 1920s was how to rationalize production across such a large and complex market. There were two milk markets in New York State: one market was for fluid milk, which was highly perishable and subject to more stringent sanitary requirements; the second was for manufactured products such as cheese and butter. Another dilemma was that milk production varied by season. Cows produced more milk during the spring "flush" when forage was plentiful but less in winter when they were in the barn. The handlers' biggest problem, therefore, was to maintain a steady supply of fluid milk in the face of both market and seasonal uncertainties. The largest milk dealers had to maintain excess fluid-milk capacity of roughly 20% (known as "surplus" fluid milk) to meet consumer demand when farm production declined seasonally.

In 1922 representatives of the largest milk dealers joined forces with leaders of the largest cooperatives to ensure an adequate supply of surplus milk and to make the market more predictable. The specific marketing innovations used were known as classified pricing and pooling. Under the former, when farmers signed a contract with the DLCA, for example, they were guaranteed a set price of milk for one year. Farmers were paid a "blend," or average price, which represented the percentage of their milk that went into either fluid milk (Class I) or manufactured products (Class II). With pooling, the league determined the blend price by pooling its receipts, deducting expenses, and dividing what was left among its member farmers. The blend price was also subject to modification based on a farm's location, which affected transportation costs, and the milk's butterfat content.

YEARS OF CONFLICT, 1930–45

Following a period of relative price stability, wholesale milk prices fell sharply during the depression. Causes for this rapid decline included decreased demand, overproduction, and cutthroat competition among fluid-milk dealers in New York City. Although many farmers tried to weather the price collapse, others fought back. In late March 1933, 1,000 members of the newly organized Western New York Milk Producers Association (WNYMPA) voted to declare a milk "holiday" unless the DLCA agreed to pay them a flat rate of 4.5¢ per quart. When their demands were not met, the association called a strike that quickly evolved into a war between the league and independent dairy farmers who belonged to smaller cooperatives or sold their milk to the many smaller dealers or local cheese plants. Independent dairy farmers supported state price controls in the 1930s as a way to challenge the large dealers' domination of the state's largest markets. Much of their anger stemmed from smoldering resentment over classified pricing and pooling. From the dealers' perspective, farmers benefited from classified pricing and

A "spilling committee" of milk producers emptying milk into the streets of Goshen, from *Frank Leslie's Illustrated Newspaper,* 31 Mar 1883.

pooling because their markets were guaranteed. In fact a DLCA slogan read, No League Producer Is Ever without a Market. According to the independents, however, classified pricing and pooling delivered greater benefits to the dealers and their allies. Pooling gave the dealers greater control over milk production because once farmers signed pooled contracts, they were obligated to a certain cooperative or handler for one year, making it difficult to negotiate a better deal or to strike. Many of the independents' complaints, moreover, focused on the close relations between the large dealers and cooperatives such as the DLCA or Sheffield Farms, which were considered nothing more than company unions. After three days of violent picketing in April 1933 in Central New York, the state legislature authorized the creation of the Milk Control Board with broad regulatory power to fix prices. Within a few days, the board quickly set retail and farm prices. The DLCA in particular came under fire in the early 1930s because it paid the lowest prices in the milkshed because of its considerable investment in processing plants and distribution networks. A more violent strike by the WNYMPA in Boonville (Oneida Co) in June 1933 attracted national attention. The Dairy Farmers Union (DFU), founded by Archie Wright in 1936, sought to organize farmers into one unified movement, made alliances with other groups, such as consumers and organized labor, and worked to construct alternatives to the corporate-dominated milk market.

In 1939 the DFU organized the most successful milk strike in New York State history after another crisis in the dairy industry. This crisis had its origins in 1938, when the US Congress passed a law regulating wholesale milk prices on a state-by-state basis, which was called the market order system. The system in New York State, however, did not survive its first legal challenge and was struck down in US District Court because it discriminated in favor of DLCA, Borden's, and Sheffield Farms. (The law was eventually upheld by the US Supreme Court and in modified form remains in effect in the early 21st century.) After the law was initially thrown out, the largest milk dealers cut both farm and retail milk prices, prompting the DFU to vote for a strike. Under the skilled leadership of Pres Archie Wright, a socialist and former member of the Industrial Workers of the World (IWW), the DFU was able to dry up the flow of milk into New York City and upstate cities in August 1939. Wright sought to avoid many of the problems associated with previous New York State milk strikes, and local DFU strike committees closely supervised picketing to avoid violence. In addition Wright urged farmers to divert their milk to local creameries or cheese factories rather than to dump it, which enabled them to hold out longer against the better-financed dealers. Wright, a supporter of the Congress for Industrial Organizations (CIO), also sought alliances with organized labor, which proved invaluable during the 15-day 1939 milk strike. This strike was eventually settled with help from New York City mayor Fiorello La Guardia, who negotiated an agreement between the DFU and New York City dealers at a conference in Queens. A sweeping victory for the DFU, the agreement brought farmers a 45% increase in milk prices. In response, however, the milk dealers immediately began a well-financed Red-baiting campaign to discredit Wright and the DFU that by 1942 split the union and rendered it politically ineffective. During World War II dairy farmer unrest abated as milk prices and demand for milk products increased because of the war effort.

Dairy Farming in the Postwar Era

After the war policy changes and technological innovations transformed American dairy farming. For policy makers the immediate concern was the potential for renewed overproduction. American farmers were becoming increasingly productive because of three overlapping technological innovations. New mechanization brought bulk milk tanks and tank trucks, pipeline milkers, silo unloaders, and mechanized gutter (barn) cleaners to dairy farms; botanical science brought new disease- and drought-resistant hybrid plant varieties; and agricultural chemistry developed pesticides, herbicides, and more effective petrochemical fertilizers. Policy makers engineered a shift from price supports and subsidies, such as the New Deal's market order system, to more market-oriented policies, such as federally subsidized research to increase milk production and export loan guarantees. The result was a transformation in the structure of American agriculture. Average farm size increased nationally, while farm prices and income, in constant dollars, fell throughout the postwar period; in only two years between 1954 and 1984, for example, did net farm income exceed the 1954 level. In the dairy sector, farms grew larger and were more productive; production per cow nearly doubled between 1954 and 1974. In New York State the number of dairy farms declined throughout the postwar era, from 71,765 in 1954 to 8,732 in 1997. While the total number of cows in New York declined, the average number of cows per farm more than doubled between 1954 and 1987. The end result was larger, more technologically sophisticated, and more productive dairy farms. By the 1990s, while small family farms (the state average was 69 cows per farm) still accounted for a bare majority of the milk produced, large dairy farms (250 or more cows) produced an increasing market share. It is only a matter of time, analysts predict, before the small family farmer will disappear in the dairy sector.

Policy and technological changes also transformed the sale and distribution of milk in the postwar era. By the 1970s the time-honored tradition of the milkman and home delivery gave way to grocery and convenience store milk sales, while the number of milk dealers and milk plants across the state continued to shrink. Throughout this period policy makers placed strict limits on the number of milk licenses granted to process and distribute milk out of concern for market stability and the potential for out-of-state and international competition.

The waning number of dairy farms has led farmers, milk dealers, and policy makers to confront problems caused by the decline in milk usage and the need to maintain the stability of milk prices. In the marketplace, farmers shifted

DAIRY PRODUCTION IN NEW YORK STATE, 1930–2000

	Milk		Butter		Cheese	
Year	million lb	million kg	thousand lb	thousand kg	thousand lb	thousand kg
1930	7,068	3,206.0	—	—	—	—
1940	7,658	3,473.6	—	—	—	—
1950	8,853	4,015.7	—	—	—	—
1960	10,171	4,613.5	—	—	—	—
1970	10,341	4,690.6	51,196	23,222.1	158,317	71,811.3
1980	10,974	4,977.7	47,035	21,334.7	319,579	144,958.5
1990	11,067	5,019.9	20,296	9,206.1	507,229	230,075.0
2000	11,921	5,407.3	21,819	9,896.9	728,305	330,353.3

Source: National Agricultural Statistics Service, Agricultural Statistics Data Base, http://www.nass.usda.gov:81/ipedb/.

Notes: No figures available for butter and cheese production before 1970. In 2002 New York State was the nation's 3d leading producer of milk; Wyoming Co led the state in production, and New York State cows produced 12,200 million pounds (5,533.8 million kg) of milk, valued at $1.56 billion.

Compiled by Hannah M. Springer

production to low-fat dairy products, appealing to health-conscious consumers, although demand for cheese increased substantially after the introduction of policies such as federally funded school lunches. Politically the key was to keep farmers on the land. In 1991, faced with economic conditions reminiscent of the 1930s, New York dairy farmers again pushed for a milk strike. That year wholesale milk prices fell by 29% while production costs skyrocketed. Although the state legislature enacted an emergency price increase for farmers, organizers from New York and Pennsylvania connected to the National Farmer's Organization (NFO) called for a milk strike beginning 1 October. Although the strike never occurred, a few hundred farmers dumped milk to express dissatisfaction and to generate media coverage. On 20 Sept 1991 farmers from 20 states (including New York) and Canada voted to postpone the strike because of dwindling support.

In the state legislature, battles over chronically low milk prices have been fought over the Northeastern Interstate Dairy Compact, a regional pricing structure where farmers in participating states are paid prices above those set by state market orders. Farmers have also had to adjust to a changing federal regulatory environment and are increasingly suspicious of government intervention. Some members of Congress have called for the abolition of the milk market order system altogether. The prevailing trends in the New York dairy industry in the 21st century continue toward fewer, larger, more productive dairy farms, and toward continued technological innovation. Biotechnology, including growth hormones, gene insertion, and embryo transfer, stands as the current "revolution" confronting an ever decreasing number of New York State dairy farmers (7,200 in 2001). Nevertheless dairy is still a major industry in New York State and, despite its problems, will continue to be in the future. In 1999 cash receipts from the sale of milk totaled $1.74 billion, while milk production was at 1.2 billion pounds (544,310,400 kg) and cheese production (excluding cottage cheese) totaled 682 million pounds (309,349,800 kg), both all-time records in New York history.

See also AGRICULTURAL IMPLEMENT MANUFACTURE; CHEESE.

Gates, Paul W. *The Farmer's Age: Agriculture, 1815–1860* (New York: Harper Torchbooks, 1960)

Kriger, Thomas J. "Syndicalism and Spilled Milk: The Origins of Dairy Farmer Activism in New York State, 1936–41," *Labor History* 38 (Spring–Summer 1997): 266–86

———. "A Very Unusual Partnership: The Consumer-Farmer Milk Cooperative in New York City, 1938–1971," *New York History* 80 (July 1999): 305–32

New York State. Senate, Legislative Commission on Dairy Industry Development, *Review of Dairy Regulations* (Albany: NYS Senate, 1988)

Thomas J. Kriger

Dairylea. See DAIRYMEN'S LEAGUE.

Dairymen's League (Dairylea). A farmer-owned agricultural marketing and service organization established in 1907 by dairy farmers who hoped to increase their bargaining power and to obtain fair pricing and a guaranteed market for their milk. The Orange County Pomona Grange organized dairymen, and producers from that county and neighboring counties met in Middletown (Orange Co) to discuss a new association. One of the country's first cooperatives, the Dairymen's League, primarily a bargaining association, served as liaison between dairy producers and urban wholesalers. The cooperative became active in 1910 when its combined membership owned 50,000 cows. A strike called by the league in October 1916 ended successfully for its members when urban dealers agreed to meet set prices after just two weeks. League membership increased from 15,000 when the strike began to more than 22,400 when it ended.

Following a less successful strike in 1919, the league reorganized in 1921 as the Dairymen's League Cooperative Association (DLCA), a merchandising association, and introduced the brand name Dairylea for its products in 1923. By the mid-1920s, the DCLA was the largest fluid-milk operating and marketing cooperative in the country, serving more than 100,000 member farms. Its Healthy Milk campaign was in part responsible for increased milk consumption beginning in the 1920s. In 1969 the DCLA changed its name to Dairylea Cooperative to better identify the cooperative with its products. Dairylea products were produced until 1988, when the cooperative sold its commercial interests and reorganized, returning to its original interest in milk marketing. In 1999 Dairylea formed Dairy Marketing Services with Dairy Farmers of America's Northeast Council to manage the raw-milk sale and distribution of both groups. In 2001 Dairylea Cooperative was the largest raw-milk marketer in the Northeast. Nearly 2,750,000 tons (2,494,800 MT) of milk were marketed in 2001; annual sales reached $1 billion. Based in Syracuse, the cooperative also provides services such as insurance, loans, and business consulting, and had more than $10 million invested in agricultural businesses in the Northeast in 2002.

Selitzer, Ralph. *The Dairy Industry in America* (New York: Magazines for Industry, 1976)

Suzan D. Friedlander

D'Amato, Alfonse M(arcello) (*b* Brooklyn, 1 Aug 1937). US senator. The son of Italian immigrant parents, D'Amato was raised in Island Park (Nassau Co). He graduated from Chaminade High School in Mineola (Nassau Co) (1955), Syracuse University (1959), and Syracuse University School of Law (1961). After admittance to the New York State Bar in 1962, D'Amato practiced law for three years before becoming public administrator in Nassau Co (1965–68). He held a number of positions in the Town of Hempstead (Nassau Co): tax assessor (1969–71), town supervisor (1971–77), and presiding supervisor (1977–80). He also served as vice chairman of the Nassau Co Board of Supervisors (1977–80).

In 1980 D'Amato was elected to the US Senate, upsetting ailing incumbent Jacob K. Javits in the Republican primary. During his three-term Senate career (1981–99), D'Amato was active in foreign affairs and was a forceful critic of federal banking regulations and high taxes. Known for his ability to meet the needs of his constituents, D'Amato earned the nickname Senator Pothole and proved adept at bringing federal dollars to the state. A power broker in New York State politics, he was a key figure in the rise of Gov George E. Pataki. Together with state Republican chairman Bill Powers, D'Amato led a highly effective state Republican effort until the 1990s. A prolific fund-raiser, he served as chairman of the National Republican Senatorial Campaign Committee from 1995 to 1997. He was defeated in 1998 by Democratic Rep Charles Schumer for a fourth Senate term. In 1998 D'Amato founded his own corporate consulting business, Strategies, in Washington, DC, which was later relocated to New York City. The federal courthouse in Central Islip (Suffolk Co) was named in his honor in 2003.

D'Amato, Alfonse. *Power, Pasta, and Politics* (New York: Hyperion, 1995)

J. Brooks Flippen

Damer, Annie (*b* Stratford [now in Ont], 30 Nov 1858; *d* New York City, 9 Aug 1915). Nurse. In 1885 she graduated from the New York City Training School, connected with Bellevue Hospital. She was a private duty and public health nurse, a pioneer in establishing tuberculosis nursing in New York State, and a leader in nursing organizations. From 1893 to 1898 she was a public health nurse for the Charity Association of Buffalo. In 1898 she went to Bellevue Hospital, where she organized visiting nurses to teach dispensary patients how to control the spread of tuberculosis. From 1901 to 1911 she supervised Echo Hill Farm in Yorktown Heights (Westchester Co), a convalescent home for children. She served as the president of the Buffalo Nurses Association (1900–1), the New York State Nurses Association (1904–6), the Nurses Associated Alumnae (now the American Nurses Association), and the New York State Board of Nurse Examiners (1908–10). She was the only Nurses Associated Alumnae president to serve two nonconsecutive terms (1901–2, 1905–9). In 1910 Damer was thrown from a carriage and was disabled for the remaining years of her life.

Julie M. Pavri

Damnation of Theron Ware, The. This Harold Frederic novel, published in 1896 (under the title *Illumination* in England), is the author's finest achievement. The book incorporates the surface realism of Frederic's earlier New York State novels with the depth of vision of Nathaniel Hawthorne and Henry James. Its setting, the fictional city of Octavius, resembles Frederic's hometown of Utica, and Frederic's family could find familiar characters and places in the book. Yet the problems Theron Ware, a naive, young Methodist minister, confronts are not local but universal.

Theron has been transferred to Octavius from a successful if improvident assignment with a sophisticated congregation, not realizing that his elders have sent him there to chasten him. But the barren, mean-spirited fundamentalism of his new church awakens him rudely, and in his disillusionment he turns to three new, interesting acquaintances. His traditional biblical thinking is challenged by the scriptural scholarship of a Catholic priest, Fr Forbes (based on Frederic's friend Fr Edward A. Terry). One of Forbes's parishioners, the beautiful, rich, and talented Celia Madden, offers seductive aestheticism as a substitute for Theron's wavering faith, and this in turn is derided by the third member of the priest's party, the scientist Dr Ledsmar. Dazzled and befuddled by these encounters, Theron falls victim to an itinerant debt raiser, Sr Soulsby. A marvelous creation, she makes an art of fakery, convincing him that honesty and sincerity are only disguises for self-interest: the means to an end, not the end itself. With new eyes, Theron sees Forbes as a fraud and Celia as a trophy to be won away from him. In the ensuing confrontation, Theron's new friends are alienated, his calling is destroyed, his crippled marriage is barely salvaged, and his innocence is lost.

The Damnation of Theron Ware was a best-seller, particularly well received by the new generation of New York City writers, who hailed it as a literary landmark. It also gained the admiration of some of the most prominent authors of the following generation, such as Sinclair Lewis and F. Scott Fitzgerald. Although the novel has been in print continuously since its first appearance and has seen periodic revivals of interest, it has never found the place it deserves in the American literary canon.

Raleigh, John Henry. *"The Damnation of Theron Ware," American Literature* 30 (1958): 210–27

Stanton Garner

dams and reservoirs. Many of the earliest dams in New York State were built in the late 18th century to create navigational shortcuts on the Mohawk River. Oxbows were eliminated by damming their ends, which forced the river to scour and enlarge a path cut between them. Throughout the 19th century dams made possible the state's extensive Barge Canal System by diverting and impounding water for use in the dug-out channels. With waterpower becoming an important component of industrial development in the 1830s, the Cohoes Co obtained the right to use the Mohawk River and create a waterpower complex in the vicinity of Cohoes (Albany Co); a wooden dam completed across the Mohawk in 1831–32 diverted water to canals, which fed factory waterwheels, thus enabling this small village to grow into an industrial center. Otherwise useful dams sometimes had unintentional and harmful impacts. As early as the mid–19th century, it was observed that extensive mill dam construction on the lower Salmon River in Oswego Co kept native Lake Ontario Atlantic salmon from moving to their upriver spawning grounds. This was one of the factors that led to the extinction of this subspecies by the end of the century.

In the late 19th century New Yorkers first began to propose using dams and reservoirs for flood control by storing water when there was an excess and releasing it when there was need. Aside from water management, many of these lakes became recreational and state park sites as well. While the Stillwater (Herkimer Co, originally flooded in 1876) and the Allegheny (Cattaraugus Co, originally flooded in 1965) Reservoirs are typical of these areas, the 215 ft (65.5 m) high Mt. Morris Dam (Livingston Co), completed by the US Army Corps of Engineers in 1952, and the lake it created, which lies within Letchworth State Park, are the most memorable. Located on the Genesee River, the dam is the largest concrete dam in the United States east of the Mississippi River, and it alone may have prevented $1 billion in damages since 1952 given that, historically, the Genesee was prone to flooding. Even as dams and reservoirs have provided drinking water for great numbers of New Yorkers, they also have displaced others and removed some towns and valuable farmland from the state's economy. Meeting the water needs of New York City has had the greatest impact in these respect. The watershed system developed for it is immense and began with the Croton River Dam (Westchester Co) of 1842 and spread westward by the early 20th century to dams on branches of the Delaware River.

Methods and materials of dam construction in New York State have varied over time, and the type of dam used has depended on local conditions and materials. Timber and earth-filled dams tended to be short-lived and were replaced with dams made of stone. Gravity dams, held in place by their sheer mass, were built of earth or stone. Concrete was being used when the massive dam and powerhouse for the St. Lawrence Power Co were built at Massena (St. Lawrence Co) in the late 1890s. It was the state's first large-scale hydroelectric installation and ushered in an era when most new large dams would produce electricity. By the end of the 20th century it was estimated that New York State had as many as 6,000 dams. Pointing to unused dams and those in bad condition, environmental activists such as New York Rivers United have urged for their removal, believing that without them ecosystems, aquatic life, and recreational possibilities might be restored and improved.

See also ST. LAWRENCE SEAWAY.

Blake, Nelson M. *Water for the Cities: A History of the Urban Water Supply Problem in the United States* (Syracuse: Syracuse Univ Press, 1956)

William E. Worthington Jr

Danby. Town (pop 3,007) in S central Tompkins Co. Settled in 1795, the town was formed from Spencer (Tioga Co) in 1811 and annexed to Tompkins Co in 1823. The Ithaca and Owego Turnpike (1810) was used to ship local grain, lumber, salt, plaster, and livestock to Philadelphia and Baltimore. Beginning in 1871 Danby was served by the Ithaca and Athens Railroad (later Lehigh Valley Railroad). Many Finns took up farms near South Danby in the 1910s. A Civilian Conservation Corps camp (1933–39) was responsible for reforestation of 7,259 acres (2,938 ha) in what is now Danby State Forest. Native W. Grant Egbert founded the Ithaca Conservatory of Music (now Ithaca College) in 1892. In 1962 Danby resident Wilson Greatbatch (1919–) invented the implantable heart pacemaker. In the 1970s Danby was famous for its communes, including Yea God!, Birch Hill, and Dawes Hill. The Danby Dish, an 84 ft (25.6 m) radio telescope, was used by Cornell University from 1966 to 1974. Stork H and E Turbo Blading (1976) employed 88 in 2003, manufacturing and serving turbine blades. Many residents work in Ithaca.

Jane Dieckmann

dance. See BALLET; FOLK DANCE; MODERN DANCE; TAP DANCE; and individual performers.

Danes. Danes were present in New Netherland, often as indentured servants or members of ship crews. By the 1670s there were as many as 100 Danes in New York City, where they were active in the city's small Lutheran community. The largest wave of Danish immigrants came in the second half of the 19th century in response to a crisis in Danish agriculture. Most only passed through New York on their way to the Midwest, although by the turn of the 20th century, 8,746 Danish immigrants lived in New York State. Working as crafters and laborers, and in the naval trades, nearly half of the 6,078 in New York City were in the Scandinavian neighborhood of Bay Ridge in Brooklyn, where they founded the Danish Seamen Church (1879) and Our Savior Danish Lutheran Church (1883). The main fraternal and cultural societies were branches of the Danish Brotherhood (1866) and the Dania Society (1886), the main organ the weekly *Nordlyset* (Northern Light, 1891–1953). Several hundred Danish-born lived in Chautauqua, Yates, and Rensselaer Cos by 1900, working often as farmers or in related occupations such as butter and cheese making. In Yates Co Danes began arriving in the 1870s and concentrated in the communities of Penn Yan, Benton, Milo, and Torrey. Immigration from prosperous Denmark has been very slight since World War I. The specifically Danish Lutheran synods have closed: the Danish Evangelical Lutheran Church (1872) in 1962 and the United Danish Lutheran Church (1884) in 1960.

In 2000, 38,000 in New York State claimed Danish ancestry. A few lodges of the Danish Brotherhood remain, such as in Troy (Rensselaer Co). There is the Danish Home for the Aged in Croton-on-Hudson (Westchester Co), the Danish Seamen's Church in Brooklyn, and the Danish-American Society (1959) in Manhattan. Jacob Riis was born in Ribe, Denmark, in 1849, before moving to the United States in 1870 to become a journalist and reformer and the author of *How the Other Half Lives* (1890). Lauritz Melchior, born in Copenhagen in 1890, was the leading dramatic tenor at the Metropolitan Opera House from 1926 to 1950.

Chittenden, Varick A. *The Danes of Yates County* (Penn Yan, NY: Yates County Arts Council, 1985)
Mussari, Mark. *The Danish Americans* (New York: Chelsea House, 1988)

Thomas Reimer

Dannemora. Town (pop 5,144) and village (pop 4,129) in W Clinton Co. Settled in 1836, it acquired an iron mine in 1842. When the town was formed in 1854 from Beekmantown, it was named for a mining town in Sweden. Clinton Prison was built atop an iron deposit in 1845; prisoners mined ore and fabricated nails until 1878. Mining and logging were supported by a plank road and a railroad (1879–80) to Plattsburgh. Mining at Lyon Mountain began in the late 1860s and was extensive by the 1880s; in 1939 new owner Republic Steel expanded the operation, closing in 1971 due to the high cost of extraction. The Village of Dannemora, partly in the Town of Saranac, was incorporated in 1901. The 2,700-inmate maximum security prison (now Clinton Correctional Facility) is the largest employer in town.

Thomas A. Rumney

Dannon Company. Yogurt manufacturer. In 1919 Spaniard Isaac Carasso perfected the first industrial manufacturing process for yogurt and opened a small business in Barcelona, Spain, called Danone (Little Daniel) after his son. In

1942 Daniel Carasso immigrated to the United States and established Dannon Milk Products, the first American yogurt company, in the Bronx. Two hundred half-pint, returnable glass jars of yogurt were produced per day and sold in the New York City area primarily to local immigrants and health-conscious consumers. Carasso formed a partnership with businessman Joe Metzger and his son Juan in 1943 and moved the factory to Long Island City (Queens Co). In 1947 Dannon added strawberry preserves to the bottom of the container to balance yogurt's health-food reputation and natural sour taste. This sweetened product became very popular and led to the financial success of the company. Carasso sold his interest to the Metzgers in 1948 and returned to Spain to manage Danone, the family's original business.

Dannon moved to a larger facility in Long Island City in 1950, and five years later production reached 160,000 cups of yogurt per day. In 1959 the company produced over 50% of the yogurt made in the United States and was sold to Chicago-based Beatrice Foods. Automation had increased production, but the basic method of converting milk into yogurt remained almost unchanged. A Paris firm, Boussois Souchon Neuvesel (later Danone Group) merged with Danone in 1973 and eight years later bought Dannon from Beatrice, changing the company's name to the Dannon Co. The company moved its headquarters to White Plains (Westchester Co) in 1986 and to its present location in Tarrytown (Westchester Co) in 1993. In 2001 Dannon was the top-selling yogurt worldwide with plants in Ohio, Texas, and Utah, and produced 3 million cups of yogurt per day. The workforce at Tarrytown in 2002 was 140.

Halasz, Robert. "Dannon Co, Inc." In *International Directory of Company Histories,* vol 14, ed. Paula Kepos (Detroit: St. James Press, 1993)

Suzan D. Friedlander

Dansville. Town (pop 1,977) in NW Steuben Co. The town was founded in 1796, but the area of the present town was not settled until 1804. In 1822 Livingston Co annexed the part of town in which the village of Dansville lies. In 1832 the Marsh Ditch was dug through the Town of Dansville, draining the mucklands and providing fine flat fields for cultivation. Stony Brook tumbles over a glacial moraine into a glen to form several waterfalls in Stony Brook State Park (1928). During the 1930s a federal Civilian Conservation Corps camp was established, and park trails were blazed and park facilities built. Truck farming remained important in 2003, and potatoes were grown on the hills.

Virginia L. Wright and Jerry Wright

Dansville. Village (pop. 4,832) in North Dansville (Livingston Co). Settled in 1795, it had excellent waterpower resources on Canaseraga and Mill Creeks and was the site of the first paper mill in Western New York (1810). By 1836 Dansville was producing paper, flour, iron, cloth, leather, and lumber in large quantities, shipping them after 1844 on a spur linking it with the Genesee Valley Canal. The village incorporated in 1845 and was the center of an important nursery region starting in 1851. Our Home Hygenic Institute opened as a mineral springwater cure in 1858, becoming a resort hotel in 1883 and then Bernarr Macfadden's Physical Culture Hotel (1929–56); it continued under other ownership until 1971. The Erie and Genesee Valley Railroad came to the village in 1872, and the main line of the Delaware, Lackawanna and Western was completed in 1881. Clara Barton was a resident from 1876 to 1886 and formed the first local chapter of the American Red Cross in 1881. The Foster Wheeler Energy Corp (1900–2003) manufactured steam power equipment. I-390 opened in 1979. The village is the home of the Dogwood Festival (1967) and New York State Festival of Balloons.

Mary Jo Marks

Danube. Town (pop 1,098) in SE Herkimer Co. Settled *ca* 1730 by Palatines, it was frequently the site of an important Mohawk village or "castle" and, later, of the Indian Castle Church, a mission, established in 1769–70 under Sir William Johnson's patronage. Gen Nicholas Herkimer, ill-fated commander of the colonial militia, built his home overlooking the Mohawk River in the 1750s; the *ca* 1762 house is a state historic site. The town was formed in 1817 from Minden (Montgomery Co). In the 19th century Danube was predominantly agricultural, with an emphasis on dairying. Danube was served by the West Shore Railroad from 1883 to 1966 and, since 1954, by the New York State Thruway, with an exit and arterial in Danube serving Little Falls. In the early 21st century land use remains predominantly agricultural.

James Crawford

Darien. Town (pop 3,061) in SW Genesee Co. Settled in 1803 the town formed from Pembroke in 1832. Darien Lakes State Park (1970), a 1,846-acre (747 ha) hilly woodland, provides camping, hiking, hunting, and picnicking. Six Flags Darien Lake (1964) is the largest combination theme park and family entertainment resort in the state. Dairy and truck farming and small businesses are the other economic supports for this community. A state historical marker honoring Mina C. Griswold, believed to be the first female Rural Free Delivery carrier (1902–15) in the United States, was dedicated in 1998.

Susan L. Conklin

Davenport. Town (pop 2,774) in N Delaware Co. Settled by the mid-1780s, the town was formed from Maryland (Otsego Co) and Kortright in 1817. It occupies the valley of the Charlotte River. English, German, and Scottish settlers used the plentiful water supply for grist- and sawmills. Tanneries and factories produced leather, shoes, woolen cloth, grain cradles, and rakes. By 2003 agriculture was limited to four farms, and others had been subdivided for permanent and seasonal homes. Numerous small businesses have sprung up along Rte 23 (Charlotte Turnpike, 1834), which connects Davenport with Oneonta and I-88. An automated lumber mill employs 45 workers.

Dorothy Kubik

Davis, Alexander Jackson (*b* New York City, 24 July 1803; *d* Orange, NJ, 14 Jan 1892). Architect. Raised in Newark, NJ, Utica, and Auburn (Cayuga Co), Davis resolved to become a professional artist but moved into architecture by drawing buildings while employed by a lithographer. Unlike the typical architect-builder of his era, he approached design as an art form, and although he experimented with many styles he is best known for his interpretation of the Gothic Revival. In 1829 he launched his career with the successful completion of James A. Hillhouse's New Haven (Oswego Co) residence. Another early success was William Paulding's Knoll (1838–42) at Tarrytown (Westchester Co), later enlarged (1864–67) as Lyndhurst, a prime example of Gothic Revival. To Montgomery Place in Annandale-on-Hudson (Dutchess Co), initially a Federal-style house when it was built in 1804–5, he added Gothic Revival additions in the 1840s and 1860s.

Classic examples of his Italianate style include a Georgian-style house (1830) near Poughkeepsie, to which he added wings and a four-story tower (1851–52), and Grace Hill, or Litchfield Villa (1854–56) in Brooklyn [now in Prospect Park]. Davis worked with Ithiel Town in the Greek Revival style between 1829 and 1835, designing, among other buildings, the US Customs House (1833–42; now Federal Hall) and the New York University Chapel (1835–37) in New York City. From 1839 to 1850, he collaborated with Andrew Jackson Downing, popularizing the picturesque house in America. Other New York State buildings Davis designed include Cannon Place (1832–35) in Troy (Rensselaer Co), the Robert C. Johnson House (1834) in Owego (Tioga Co) (both much altered from their original state), several buildings on the Robert Donaldson estate (1836–51, only one extant) in Annandale-on-Hudson, the Henry Delamater House (1844; now Beekman Arms) in Rhinebeck (Dutchess Co), the Oliver Bronson House (1839, 1849; also known as Plumb-Bronson House) in Hudson (Columbia Co), the John Alsop King Jr house (1853–57) in Kings Point (Nassau Co), and the John Munn house (1854–55; now Rutger House for Adults) in Utica. The Civil War interrupted his career and his practice never fully recovered, although he continued working into the late 1870s.

For illustration see ARCHITECTS AND ARCHITECTURE, MID-HUDSON.

Peck, Amelia. *Alexander Jackson Davis, American Architect, 1803–1892* (New York: Rizzoli, 1992)

Vicki Weiss

Davis, Andrew Jackson (*b* Blooming Grove, Orange Co, 11 Aug 1826; *d* Boston, 13 Jan 1910). Spiritualist and author. Raised near Poughkeepsie, Davis became attracted to mesmerism and healing. His trance lectures, published in 1847 as *The Principles of Nature, Her Divine Revelations, and a Voice to Mankind,* combined mesmerism with the doctrines of Swedish mystic Emanuel Swedenborg and French utopian Charles Fourier. The séances of the Fox sisters in western New York State inspired Davis to become one of the leading theoreticians of Spiritualism, a philosophy he developed in his five-volume *Great Harmonia* (1850–55). After a brief marriage (1848–53) to Catherine DeWolfe Dodge, Davis in 1855 married women's rights activist Mary Fenn Love and lived in New York City, promoting Spiritualism, alternative healing methods that included medical diagnosis through clairvoyance, and children's education. Distaste for sensational séances alienated Davis from the Spiritualist movement, and in 1878 he formed the short-lived First Harmonial Society of New

York. He divorced Mary in 1884 and married Della E. Markham in 1885. In 1886 he moved to Boston, where he practiced alternative medicine until his death.

Delp, Robert W. "Andrew Jackson Davis and Spiritualism." In *Pseudo-Science and Society in 19th-Century America,* ed. Arthur A. Wrobel (Lexington: Univ of Kentucky Press, 1987)

Bret E. Carroll

Davis, Ernie [Ernest Randolph] (*b* New Salem, Pa, 14 Dec 1939; *d* Cleveland, 18 May 1963). Football player. A three-sport standout at Elmira Free Academy (Chemung Co), Davis accepted a football scholarship to Syracuse University in 1958. A year later the "Elmira Express" led his team to an 11–0 record and the national championship. Davis dominated his sport, wearing the same No. 44 made famous at Syracuse by Jim Brown. Sometimes playing defensive back or kicking extra points, Davis excelled as a running back, breaking the school's major rushing records. After running for 823 yds and 12 touchdowns during his senior season in 1961, Davis became the first African American to win the Heisman Trophy, presented annually to the top college player in the nation. The top pick in the 1962 National Football League draft, Davis signed with the Cleveland Browns. Davis was diagnosed with leukemia that summer though and never played a professional game. He died 16 months later. The College Football Hall of Fame inducted Davis in 1979.

Gallagher, Robert C. *Ernie Davis: The Elmira Express* (Silver Spring, Md: Bartleby Press, 1983)

Scott Pitoniak

Dorothy Day. Photograph by Vivian Cherry, 1955.

Day. Town (pop 920) in NW Saratoga Co. The first settler came from Vermont in 1797. Day town was formed from Hadley and Edinburg in 1819 as Concord. Day was chosen in 1827. The town's mountainous territory, entirely within the Adirondack Park, was productive chiefly for logging, tanneries, and small woodenware works, except for the Sacandaga River valley that bisected the town and was occupied by farms. It was flooded in 1930 to create Great Sacandaga Lake, opening Day to limited summer cottage development that, with lumbering, sustains its economy in the early 21st century.

Field Horne

nie Davis at Syracuse University.

Day, Dorothy (May) (*b* Brooklyn, Kings Co, 8 Nov 1897; *d* New York City, 29 Nov 1980). Social and religious activist. The daughter of a newspaper reporter, she was raised in Chicago but returned to New York City with her family in 1916. During the 1920s she worked as a reporter and editor on several socialist dailies, including the *New York Call* and the *Liberator.* After an abortion, marriage and divorce, the publication of an autobiographical novel, and the birth of her daughter out of wedlock, Day was received into the Roman Catholic Church in December 1927. On May Day 1933 she and French mystic Peter Maurin published the first issue of the *Catholic Worker,* which sold for one cent. The Catholic Worker movement—at once personalist, anarchist, communitarian, pacifist, and radical—was committed to carrying out Christian ideals by housing the homeless and feeding the hungry. Day and her followers were dedicated to a threefold program that included "houses of hospitality" (hospices for the poor and homeless), discussions with workers about Catholic social teaching, and back-to-the-land communal farms inspired by English Catholic agrarians G. K. Chesterton and Eric Gill. A pacifist in both world wars, Day led protests against the civilian defense air-raid drills from 1955 to 1960. Her activism continued into the 1960s and 1970s with her opposition to the Vietnam War, advocacy for civil rights, and support of migrant farmers. On 16 Mar 2000 the Vatican agreed to begin the process of considering Day for sainthood.

Day, Dorothy. *Loaves and Fishes* (New York: Harper & Row, 1963)

Mark S. Massa

Dayton. Town (pop 1,945) in NW Cattaraugus Co. Settled in 1810, the town was formed from Perrysburg in 1835. With only modest water power, manufacturing expanded after steam power became available, and forest products were processed, including shingles, staves, heading, sashes, and doors. The first cheese factory for the developing dairy industry opened in 1865. The Erie Railroad (1851) and the Buffalo and Southwestern Railroad (1875; later part of Erie Railroad) intersected at Dayton hamlet, which grew after the tracks were laid. Many gas wells were drilled in town beginning in 1982, and some oil wells were still producing in 2003.

Bruce D. Fredrickson and Madelynn P. Fredrickson

DDT (dichlorodiphenyltrichloroethane). One of a host of synthetic pesticides that emerged during the 1940s, DDT and other chlorinated hydrocarbons were heralded as saviors in World War II because their use protected US soldiers from insect-borne diseases like malaria. After the war DDT powder was used liberally throughout New York State and the nation—dusted in children's beds and sprayed from planes onto agricultural crops, forests, and cities—to eradicate a variety of insects, some quite harmless. During the 1940s and 1950s, tons of DDT powder entered the state's ecosystem as the US pesticide industry grew rapidly. While DDT successfully killed pests, it was harmful to the environment, in particular to fish, birds, and a range of mammals, including humans. Nature writer Rachel Carson issued one of the earliest warnings of pesticide hazards in her influential *Silent Spring* (1962). Though labeled alarmist by industry voices, her book started the groundswell of the modern environmental movement. In 1966 residents of Brookhaven (Suffolk Co) and scientists from Brookhaven National Laboratory and SUNY Stony Brook formed Brookhaven Town Natural Resources Committee (BTNRC), called the Environmental Defense Fund beginning in 1967, to address a wide range of environmental issues. Because of widespread use of DDT throughout Suffolk Co, the problem of this substance soon became the group's most prominent issue, and in May 1966 BTNRC joined Patchogue (Suffolk Co) lawyer Victor Yannacone's class-action suit against the Suffolk County Mosquito Control Commission regarding a DDT-associated fish kill in Yaphank Lake. This partnership between scientists and lawyers, which sought to end spraying, won a major victory later that year when New York State Supreme Court judge Jack Stanislaw signed a temporary injunction blocking the spraying. Suffolk Co became the nation's first county to ban DDT. The breakthrough ruling led to a state ban of DDT in 1970, followed by a national ban two years later.

Gottlieb, Robert. *Forcing the Spring: The Transformation of the American Environmental Movement* (Washington, DC: Island Press, 1993)

Lear, Linda. *Rachel Carson: Witness for Nature* (New York: Henry Holt, 1997)

Michael Egan

deafness. Deaf persons in New York State have been prominent in deaf educational issues and in building the institutional framework for independent deaf life.

Education

New York State was one of the most important arenas for the prolonged debate between oral and signed approaches to deaf education. Founded in New York City in 1818, the New York Institution for the Instruction of the Deaf and Dumb was the second school for the deaf in the United States and in 1833 the first to adopt the use of American Sign Language (ASL) as the primary language of instruction. Harvey Prindle Peet, the school's principal from 1830 to 1866, was a leader in the adoption of ASL and author of a widely used textbook. Under Peet's direction, the institution took a strong stand against oral education. The school's reputation for academic excellence grew in 1853, when it established what it called a "High Class," a forerunner of Gallaudet University (1864) in providing postsecondary education for the deaf. Commonly known as Fanwood from its location in Washington Heights in Upper Manhattan, the school has been located in White Plains (Westchester Co) since 1938 and after several name changes is now known as New York School for the Deaf.

The oral method of deaf education, which prohibits the use of sign language and teaches solely through speech and speechreading, also has its roots in New York State. The oldest school for the deaf in the United States using that method is the New York Institution for the Improved Instruction of Deaf Mutes. It was organized through the efforts of a German Jewish couple, Hannah and Isaac Rosenfeld, who, in searching for a way to educate their deaf daughter Carrie, hired teacher Bernard Englesmann from Vienna, Austria, in 1864 to establish the school in New York City. Now known as the Lexington School and located in Jackson Heights in Queens, its focus on oral instruction spawned many imitators in the state and elsewhere. The Rochester School for the Deaf was founded as the Western New York Institution for Deaf-Mutes in 1876 and introduced a system of deaf education in 1878 that became known as the Rochester Method. It was an English-only system, combining spoken, written, and finger-spelled English to teach deaf children. Finger spelling was the only form of gestural communication allowed in the classroom. The system never spread to other schools but was used in Rochester until the 1970s. The school acquired its present name in 1919. The Central New York School for the Deaf in Rome (Oneida Co) was founded by Alphonso Johnson, a deaf person, in 1875. Since 1963 it has been known as the New York State School for the Deaf and is the only such state-operated school in the state. Other important educational institutions include St. Mary's School for the Deaf in Buffalo and St. Joseph's School for the Deaf in the Bronx. During the 1970s and 1980s, most former oralist schools adopted mixed methods of instruction. Many adopted Total Communication, which permits the use of any methodology that promotes the education of the child, including ASL. In 1989 the Cleary School for the Deaf in Nesconset (Suffolk Co) adopted a bilingual/bicultural approach known as bi-bi, adopting ASL as the language of instruction, the only school in the state to use this approach. The National Technical Institute for the Deaf (NTID), part of the Rochester Institute of Technology, is the premier American technical college for the deaf and hard of hearing.

Institutions

The Central Asylum for the Instruction of the Deaf and Dumb was in Canajoharie (Montgomery Co) from 1823 to 1836, when the state-sponsored school was merged into the New York City school. A consequence of the location of the school was that the *Canajoharie Radii*, a weekly newspaper, became one of the first newspapers for the deaf in the United States, when it was acquired in 1837 by Levi S. Backus, who became the first deaf editor of a newspaper in the country. He had the masthead of the *Radii* printed in finger spelling. As Canajoharie's paper, the *Radii* contained regular features and articles, although Backus added a column consisting of news of special interest to the deaf community. In 1844 he convinced the New York State legislature to give him funds to mail the *Radii* to "educated deaf people" across the state. Around 1870 the *Radii* was acquired by another deaf man, Henry C. Rider. In 1871 he transformed the *Radii* into the *Deaf-Mutes' Journal* (1875). Rider later founded the Northern New York School for the Deaf in Malone (Franklin Co) in 1884. The New York Institution for the Instruction of the Deaf took over the *Journal* around 1878. Edwin A. Hodgson, the school's printing instructor, served as editor from 1880 until 1931. The *Journal* ceased publication in 1951. *The Mute and the Blind* (1859–64), a newspaper that promoted the educational cause of African American deaf and blind children, was founded by Platt Henry Skinner, a blind man, in Niagara Falls in 1859. Skinner and his wife ran a school in Niagara City.

Prominent deaf organizations in the state include the Empire State Association of Deaf-Mutes, established in 1865, making it one of the oldest state organizations. Committed to advancing the interests of the deaf community, it was in 2002 an affiliate of the National Association of the Deaf. On 17 Apr 1887 former students of the Lexington School formed the Deaf-Mutes' Union League and quickly gained a large membership. An early example of a flourishing deaf club, it serves as an example of the way even oral education served—despite its emphasis on integration with the hearing population and suspicion of deaf institutional life—to bind deaf people closer together.

The earliest church in the United States with a deaf congregation, founded for a deaf constituency, was St. Ann's Episcopal Church, founded in 1852 by Thomas Gallaudet (1822–1902), the son of Thomas Hopkins Gallaudet, a cofounder of the first school for the deaf in the United States, the American School for the Deaf, in Hartford, Conn. The younger Gallaudet was ordained a priest in the Episcopal Church in 1851 and immediately began ministering to the deaf community of New York City. All services were conducted in sign language. The church also welcomed blind members and members of all races equally. Gallaudet encouraged all the hearing members of the parish to learn sign language and worked with some of the first American deaf men to receive holy orders, including Rev Henry Syle (1846–1890; ordained 1883), the first deaf American to be ordained, and Rev Job Turner (1820–1903; ordained 1891). As the 21st century opens, St. Ann's continues its ministry to the deaf at 209 East 16th St in New York City.

There have been a number of significant deaf writers in New York State, beginning with the sentimental poet James Nack (1809–79). A native of New York City, his works include *The Legend of the Rocks and Other Poems.* Albert Ballin (1861–1932), also a native of New York City, published *The Deaf Mute Howls* (1930), in which he proposed that sign language be universally taught so that all barriers between the deaf and the hearing would disappear. Robert Panara (1920–), a New York City native and professor at NTID, was a founder of the modern deaf poetry movement, which promoted the creation of original poetry in ASL. His 1984 collaboration with poet Allen Ginsberg became known as the Deaf-Beat Summit. Thomas Coughlin, a native of Malone (Franklin Co), became in 1977 the first deaf American ordained a Roman Catholic priest.

Buchanan, Robert M. *Illusions of Equality: Deaf Americans in School and Factory, 1850–1950* (Washington, DC: Gallaudet Univ Press, 1999)

Edwards, Rebecca A. R. "Words Made Flesh: 19th-Century Deaf Education and the Growth of Deaf Culture" (PhD diss, Univ of Rochester, 1997)

Gannon, Jack. *Deaf Heritage: A Narrative History of Deaf America* (Silver Spring, Md: National Association of the Deaf, 1981)

Van Cleve, John Vickrey, and Barry A. Crouch. *A Place of Their Own: Creating the Deaf Community in America* (Washington, DC: Gallaudet Univ Press, 1989)

R. A. R. Edwards

Deale County. See Extinct counties.

debt. See Bonded indebtedness; Moral obligation debt.

DEC. See Environmental conservation, department of.

Decatur. Town (pop 410) in E Otsego Co. Settled ?1790, the town was formed from Worcester in 1808. A hilly and sandy town, its population peaked at 1,110 in 1830 and decreased to 254 in 1960. Reforestation efforts created Maple Valley, Decatur, and Bear Swamp State Forests. Modest population growth since 1960 was probably due o road access to Worcester; all but two workers in 2000 commuted outside town. Decatur was the birthplace of Lewis E. Waterman (1837–1900), inventor of the first practical fountain pen.

Hugh C. MacDougall

Declaration of Independence. In July 1776 New York was the last American colony to declare independence from Britain. New York Whigs were mildly receptive to independence, but many Whigs sought reconciliation or worked to delay independence. New York eventually declared for independence because the public, influenced by pro-independence propaganda and Britain's harsh political and military policies, demanded it. Whig leaders yielded to the public will, although fearing the consequences of a failed rebellion. The independence movement gained momentum on 10 May 1776 when the Continental Congress recommended the establishment of new governments in colonies lacking sufficient governments. On 4 June 1776 New York City's Committee of Mechanics requested that the Third Provincial Congress instruct the colony's Continental Congress delegates to pursue independence. The Provincial Congress responded that the committee had no business making this request; only the Continental Congress could declare for independence, and it had not done so. The Provincial Congress would not presume to instruct the colony's delegates. Three days later Virginia delegate Richard Henry Lee moved that the Continental Congress declare for independence. On 8 June New York's delegates—William Floyd, Francis Lewis, Robert R. Livingston, and Henry Wisner—wrote the Provincial Congress for instructions. On 11 June the Continental Congress appointed a committee of five (Livingston included) to draft a declaration of independence.

In response to the colony's congressional delegates, the Provincial Congress, on John Jay's motion, resolved unanimously on 11 June that New Yorkers had given neither the Provincial Congress nor the colony's congressional delegates the authority to declare New York independent. It asked the voters to give the congress the power to do what was best for the colony and at the upcoming elections for Provincial Congress delegates to inform them on "the great question of independency." In accordance with these resolutions, two Albany Co localities, King's District [now Canaan, Columbia Co] and Spencer-Town [now in Columbia Co], instructed their Provincial Congress delegates to support independence. On 28 June the Continental Congress's committee on a declaration of independence presented a draft. Exactly what role committee member Livingston played is unknown. On 1 July Congress resumed debate on Lee's 10 May motion. The next day New York's delegates (John Alsop, George Clinton, William Floyd, Francis Lewis, and Henry Wisner) wrote the Provincial Congress for instructions because every colony was about to adopt independence. This congress never responded since it adjourned on 30 June, never to reconvene.

The Continental Congress, with New York abstaining, voted unanimously for independence on 2 July. The declaration was revised until 4 July, when the congress voted a last time on independence, and New York again abstained. Two days later the president of the Continental Congress, John Hancock, wrote New York and other states, enclosing the printed declaration and asking for it to be proclaimed. On 9 July the Fourth Provincial Congress read the 2 July letter of the colony's congressional delegates and the enclosed declaration. It adopted resolutions that authorized the state's congressional delegates to adopt all measures they thought "conducive to the happiness and welfare of the United States of America," approved and supported the declaration, and ordered the printing and distribution of 500 copies of the declaration with these resolutions. It lamented that "cruel necessity" made independence "unavoidable." On 11 July the Provincial Congress informed the Continental Congress that New York accepted independence even before receiving official news. Beginning on 2 August the New York delegates to the Continental Congress—William Floyd, Philip Livingston, Francis Lewis, and Lewis Morris, in that order—signed the engrossed declaration.

Maier, Pauline. *American Scripture: Making the Declaration of Independence* (New York: Knopf, 1977)
Mason, Bernard. *The Road to Independence: The Revolutionary Movement in New York, 1773–1777* (Lexington: Univ of Kentucky Press, 1966)
Wall, Alexander J. "New York and the Declaration of Independence," *New-York Historical Society Quarterly Bulletin* 10 (July 1926): 43–51

Gaspare J. Saladino

deeds and recording of deeds. Deeds conveying real property took their modern legal forms and began to be almost universally recorded in public offices in the decades around 1800. In New Netherland, starting in the 1630s, deeds were recorded either by the provincial secretary or an official notary. The English government established by the duke of York in 1664 confirmed Dutch deeds. The Duke's Laws of 1665 required that deeds and mortgages be in writing and recorded both by a local court clerk and by the provincial secretary. When New York Colony was divided into counties in 1683, county clerks assumed the primary responsibility for recording real property conveyances. After the Duke's Laws were superseded in 1691, uncertainty prevailed about the recording requirements for the English forms of deeds. "Bargain and sale" deeds were usually recorded, as required by an English statute of 1535. However, the deed of "lease and release" was exempt and thus frequently used, avoiding the trouble and expense of recording. In 1767 the governor and council declared that "there is no law which compels the recording of deeds," but the recording of mortgages was required by a 1753 statute. Unrecorded deeds were often lost, which complicates research on early land ownership.

Strong recording statutes were first enacted to confirm the numerous land transfers occurring as a result of the Revolutionary War. Starting in 1780 the county clerks had to record abstracts of sales of loyalists' lands confiscated by the commissioners of forfeitures. A 1794 statute required the recording of deeds in the New Military Tract of Central New York because of the "many frauds" in buying and selling lands granted to individuals holding land bounty rights issued to New York veterans of the Continental army. The recording requirement was extended to other new counties in western and northern parts of the state beginning in 1798 and to all counties in 1823. A register's office was established in New York City in 1813 to record deeds and mortgages; it now operates in all boroughs except Staten Island. In all other counties (except Westchester, which has a county register of deeds) the county clerk's office continues as the recording office for real property transfers.

Attorneys developed the modern warranty deed (an absolute conveyance, warranting the title to be free of liens or other encumbrances) and quitclaim deed (conveying the seller's own title and interest in property) after statutes of 1788 effectively abolished most remnants of feudal tenure in the state's real property law. That process was confirmed and completed by the Revised Statutes of 1827–28, effective 1830, which abolished several little used common-law forms of real property conveyance. Deeds still contained much legalese, inherited from the common law; an 1890 statute authorized use of a short form of a deed to save expense in recording.

Fowler, Robert L. *History of the Law of Real Property in New York* (New York: Baker, Voorhis, 1895)

James D. Folts

deer, white-tailed [*Odocoileus virginianus*]. One of two species of deer native to New York State, with the other being the moose (*Alces alces*). The name derives from the white underside of the tail, raised when the deer is alarmed or in flight. During the summer and fall, male deer, or bucks, grow antlers that are discarded after the breeding season. Female deer, or does, give birth to a fawn, or more commonly twin fawns, after a 207-day gestation period; the offspring typically reach reproductive maturity during their second year. Deer vary greatly in size, in part depending upon diet; bucks may weigh over 200 pounds (90 kg). Their range extends throughout the state.

Deer were widely hunted prior to European contact by native peoples, and European settlers continued and expanded this practice. Subsistence and commercial hunting during the 1800s nearly resulted in the extirpation of the species, but beginning in 1886 progressive regulation of hunting seasons led to recovery and then to tremendous growth in numbers. In 2001 the deer population in the state was roughly 1 million and continued to expand. Unchecked, this population could grow by 30% per year. Since the early 1900s, with natural predators such as the mountain lion and the gray wolf either exterminated or greatly reduced in numbers, sport hunting has been the primary cause of deer mor-

White-tailed deer.

tality. At the beginning of the 21st century, hunting was the most economical method of deer population control, and during the 2000 season hunters killed approximately 295,000 deer. But the number of hunters has declined for reasons related to demographics and changes in societal attitudes toward hunting. With the ratio of hunters to deer now dramatically altered, hunting regulations are under review.

Growth of urban and suburban areas has increased the forest-edge environments favored by deer, but hunting plays a minimal role in urban and suburban communities. In 2001 collisions with automobiles caused the majority of deer deaths in such areas. In addition to the hazards of deer-automobile collisions, deer have damaged crops, gardens, and ornamental plants. Deer ticks also serve as the primary vector for Lyme disease, a particular problem on Long Island and in the lower Hudson Valley. Urban and suburban deer populations have soared because of low mortality, high levels of fecundity, and readily available food sources. With chemical contraceptives generally unsatisfactory, other forms of intervention, including lethal means, have been increasingly accepted.

Heuser, Ken. *The Whitetail Deer Guide* (New York: Holt, Rinehart & Winston, 1972)

Brad Coon

Deerfield. Town (pop 3,906) in E central Oneida Co. A part of Deerfield that was annexed by Utica in 1891 and 1916 was first settled in 1773; the present town was settled at North Gage *ca* 1800. The town was formed from Schuyler (Herkimer Co) in 1798. Dairy farming was important in the 19th century, giving rise to cheese factories; fluid-milk production succeeded cheese in the 20th century. Suburbanization of the southern part of town, whose vegetable farms had supplied Utica, began in 1936. The Horatio Mall (1971) was later transformed into the Fleet Bank Operations Center, the town's largest business in 2002. Deerfield is in part a suburb of Utica, though the northern part is still a farming district.

Deer Park. Locality (pop 28,316) in Babylon (Suffolk Co). Located on Long Island's pine and oak barrens, the Long Island Rail Road (1842) made possible its development beginning about 1853; a post office was established in 1873. Deer Park was the site of a brickworks, of dahlia growing on a large scale (*ca* 1900), and of the Golden Pickle Works (1902). Edgewood State Hospital (1938–69) began as a tuberculosis sanatorium and was converted for mental health services. Dahlia growing was still a large industry in the 1950s when Deer Park's population began to expand rapidly. Housing development began in 1952; the locality's 1954 population of 3,570 grew to 10,750 in 1960 and reached 16,000 a year later. Industry was attracted to provide employment, including Fairchild Engine and Airplane Corp (1956), whose site had become a shopping mall by 2003, and smaller enterprises in Western Suffolk Industrial Park (1963). Deer Park was the birthplace of Rodney Dangerfield (1921–2004). New York State controls the 644-acre (261 ha) Edgewood Oak Brush Plains State Preserve. A persistent claim that Pres John Quincy Adams was a summer resident is unsupported by historical evidence.

Deerpark. Town (pop 7,858) in W Orange Co. The area was settled *ca* 1690 and raided in 1778 and 1779 by tories and Indians under Col Joseph Brant. The town was formed from Minisink (Orange Co) and Mamakating [now in Sullivan Co] in 1798 and later served by the Delaware and Hudson Canal (1828–98) and the Ontario and Western Railroad (1871–1957). Timber, bluestone, dairy, and farm produce were the chief products, and timber from areas north was sent down the Delaware River on large timber rafts from the late 1700s to the early 1900s. D. W. Griffith made 22 silent films in Deerpark between 1909 and 1915, including *Birth of a Nation* (1915). In the late 20th century the 1960 population of 2,777 nearly tripled. In 2003 the largest employers were Summit Research Laboratories, makers of aluminum chlorhydrate for deodorants and water purification, and C and D Technologies. Part of Mongaup Valley State Wildlife Management Area lies in town. Cuddebackville, a former canal hamlet, is the site of the Neversink Valley Area Museum, which interprets the canal and offers canalboat rides.

Peter Osborne

Deferiet [DE-FER-EE-ET]. Village (pop 309) in Wilna (Jefferson Co). Founded in 1900 by the St. Regis Paper Co for mill employees, primarily Polish and Italian immigrants, it acquired a post office in 1901 and was incorporated in 1921. The village was named for Madame Jenika de Feriet, a Frenchwoman who came to the area in the early 1800s and owned the land on which the village was built. In 1953 the company sold the houses to residents. The company merged with Champion International in 1984. The mill became the Deferiet Paper Co in 1999 and has operated as Newtech of New York since 2001.

Laura Lynne Scharer

Deganawidah. See IROQUOIS CONFEDERACY; IROQUOIS GOVERNMENT AND RELIGION.

deindustrialization. The industrial sector of the New York State economy radically shrank in the second half of the 20th century. Throughout this period state government responded with a variety of new programs to reverse this trend, but by the start of the 21st century these initiatives for the most part had failed. The programs were unable to overcome the forces of regionalization and globalization. The migration of industry out of New York State has been painful for many areas of the state. Factory closures have resulted in the loss of high-paying unionized jobs as well as in declines in new industrial job creation, phenomena particularly detrimental to immigrants and to people without a college degree. Plant shutdowns have also meant losses in local property tax revenues, a falloff in revenue that many communities have found difficult to replace.

THE GREAT DEPRESSION

Many early signs of deindustrialization in the state appeared, however, in the first half of the 20th century, during the depression. In 1935, in an effort to help defray relief costs, Gov Herbert H. Lehman greatly expanded the state's tax power. He enacted for the first time in state history a tax on unincorporated businesses, at 4% of profits. Taxes on the profits of incorporated businesses were raised from 4.5% to 6%. New York State's tax initiatives were significant, particularly the unincorporated business tax, fc they were undertaken at a time when there wa virtually no tax burden levied by the federal other state governments on the average busines This action by state government brought a chc rus of complaints from business. The presence c these business taxes in New York State would re main a long-term and powerful inducement fc manufacturers to leave the state.

Other factors were also instrumental in the ir dustrial flight out of New York during the de pression. Since the state had long been a hotbe of labor activism, by the depression many of th state's factories were either already unionize or were undergoing fights over unionizatio Moreover, as part of New York's "Little Ne Deal," the state had by the mid-1930s perhap the most pro-labor regulations in the natio After the enactment of the Social Security Act c 1935, it had the highest workers' compensatio fees of any state, and they were in part paid b employers. Hence by the mid-1930s many ir dustrial firms began to leave. A 1940 study un dertaken by the *New York Times* concluded tha 5,582 New York State businesses had relocated t New Jersey—a state that had no business taxe weaker unions, and few labor regulations—be tween 1936 and 1939. Connecticut, another sta without a business tax, also attracted large num bers of Empire State manufacturers; in 193 160 large New York State manufacturers per manently relocated to Connecticut, includin numerous units of General Electric Co (GE) Schenectady. Both New Jersey and Connecticu created during the depression their own govern mental agencies, such as the Connecticut Devel opment Commission, to entice principally Ne York State manufacturers to relocate to thei states.

In the late 1930s and early 1940s the Join Legislative Committee on Industrial and La bor Conditions, a state commission chaire by assembly majority leader Irving M. Ive (R-Chenango Co), studied the problem of de industrialization and made numerous polic recommendations to make the state mor amenable to business. One of the committee initiatives was a failed attempt to reduce busi ness taxes. During this same period the sta comptroller, Morris Tremaine (1926–38), an the state tax commissioner, Mark Grave (1923–31; 1933–42), both Democrats, also ar gued publicly for a reduction in state busine taxes to help retain manufacturers. Gov Lehma refused to consider such proposals.

EARLY EFFORTS

The first serious efforts to address the issue o deindustrialization by state government bega during the administration of Gov Thomas E Dewey (1942–54). During World War II Dewe laid plans for the construction of the New Yor State Thruway, a massive limited-access stat highway network. Begun in 1946 and complete 10 years later, the roadway linked the state's far flung industrial centers together. Dewey envi sioned the Thruway as a grand public work project that would aid state industry like the Eri Canal had done in the 19th century. Upon th Thruway's opening, New York was one of the fev states in the nation to have such an extensiv road system. The New York State Department o Commerce was created upon the urging of th Joint Legislative Committee on Industrial an

Labor Conditions in 1944. The major objective of this agency was to aid the business environment by either helping existing New York plants modernize or attracting new factories. The department undertook statistical surveys and recommended new legislation to increase industrial growth, but its main work came in publicity. With an annual advertising budget of near $1 million in the late 1940s, the department ran thousands of print advertisements in business periodicals, filmstrips in movie theaters, and radio spots trumpeting the advantages of placing manufacturing facilities in New York State. Promoting the fledgling aviation industry was a special effort of the department. In regard to taxes, however, despite pressure from the business community, Gov Dewey made no substantive, long-term effort to reduce them.

Top of the World

Even though there were disadvantages for industrial production in New York, the state remained the nation's leading manufacturer well into the 1950s. In 1952 the state was responsible for 12% of the nation's entire manufacturing work. In that year, of the state's 2,045,000 manufacturing jobs, 59% (1,213,000) were concentrated in New York City and Nassau, Suffolk, Westchester, and Rockland Cos. The remaining 41% (832,000) were spread throughout the rest of the state, and nearly half were concentrated in the cities and environs of Buffalo, Rochester, and Syracuse. The state's four leading manufacturing sectors in 1952 were garments, printing, metal fabrication, and nonelectrical machinery. However, New York's manufacturers produced almost every conceivable product—the state held a near monopoly on the production of the nation's leather hand gloves, with manufacturing based in Fulton Co—and nearly one in three New Yorkers was employed in a factory. New York State was the national leader in manufacturing until 1957, when US industrial plants increasingly began to concentrate first in the South and West and then later overseas.

Although concerns stemmed back to the depression about industry migrating out of New York and although state manufacturing jobs relative to the national sector had been shrinking since 1958, most New Yorkers did not express significant alarm about the problem until the late 1960s. Between 1958 and 1969 the number of US manufacturing jobs had grown significantly (21%, or over 4 million), while New York State manufacturing positions had remained essentially flat, rising a minuscule .3%, or 4,000 jobs. The industries in New York State that experienced actual job declines between 1960 and 1974 were in the garment trades, food processing, leather, and printing (88% of the job losses in these four sectors occurred exclusively in New York City). A good portion of the garment industry's lesser-skilled positions were lost to advances in technology; moreover many garment manufacturers migrated to the South. Most of the New York manufacturers that had moved out of state, however, did not go South; rather they relocated to adjoining states. Between 1961 and 1973 more than half of the manufacturing jobs went to New Jersey, Connecticut, or Pennsylvania (39%, 11%, and 8% respectively); only 12% were relocated to the South during this time.

Because the problem of deindustrialization did not seem serious to many until the late 1960s the administration of Gov Nelson A. Rockefeller (1958–73) did little to arrest a deteriorating manufacturing climate. Many critics have pointed to the Rockefeller years as a critical time when the actions and inactions of the governor precipitated the state's industrial decline. Between 1959 and 1973 the state legislature took 18 separate actions to increase business, personal income, sales, and other taxes. The top personal income tax rate rose from 10% to 15%. Moreover the state budget during the Rockefeller years and the total debt of the state's public authorities each quadrupled. Between 1966 and 1976, 22 of the largest corporations in the United States relocated their headquarters out of state, principally to New Jersey and Connecticut. These firms included Xerox Corp (1969), Ingersoll-Rand Co (1972), GE (1974), and Union Carbide Corp (1976). The lack of a personal income tax in New Jersey and Connecticut was a prime push out as business executives sought to maximize their income. (New Jersey did not enact a tax on personal income until 1976, and Connecticut held off until 1991.) Besides executives of large corporations, high-income earners who owned their own manufacturing firms were also leaving the state and taking their firms with them.

The 1970s

In the 1970s New York State's industrial sector rapidly deteriorated. Between 1970 and 1978, despite high unemployment, stagflation, and rising oil prices, jobs in US manufacturing grew by 5%, but the state's industrial job base contracted significantly, by 16%, from 1,761,000 positions to 1,483,000. Overall the nation's manufacturing jobs located in New York State fell from 9% to 7%. The falloff in industrial employment was greatest in New York City and Nassau, Suffolk, Westchester, and Rockland Cos. In 1952, 59% of state manufacturing positions were concentrated in this region, but by 1978 only 53% were, with the remaining 47% located throughout the rest of the state. However, because of the strength of the metropolitan's region service sector, deindustrialization hit the state outside of the New York metropolitan hardest. Communities like Schenectady were devastated; GE cut its workforce in that city from 20,000 to 8,500 from 1954 to 1965.

In the first half of the 20th century high taxes, strong unions, and numerous labor regulations spurred large numbers of New York's manufacturers to relocate to other states, but the second half of the century was characterized by other incentives enticing industrial leaders to quit not only New York but the United States altogether. Locations for factories overseas, particularly in Southeast Asia, South America, and Africa, increasingly became available as advances in communications, transportation, and international finance arose. These areas of the world had distinctive advantages for manufacturers that New York State could not match, including a pliant labor force, extremely low wages, and in many cases no environmental regulation. In response to a renewed environmental movement, in 1970 New York State created the Department of Environmental Conservation, an agency whose responsibilities included regulating industrial pollution. For many manufacturers that had long dumped their industrial wastes with little or no state oversight, adherence to new environmental laws was not worth the cost of staying in New York State. The Anaconda Wire and Cable Co of Hastings-on-Hudson (Westchester Co), for example, was a factory notorious throughout the mid–20th century for discharging metal filings, waste oils, and PCBs into the Hudson River. After a successful 1971 lawsuit by the federal government that found Anaconda in violation of federal antidumping laws, the company rather than comply boarded up its Hastings facility in 1975, resulting in the loss of hundreds of jobs. In 2003 Anaconda was owned by BICC Cables Corp, a United Kingdom industrial conglomerate with wire and cable production based in the developing world.

With the decline in high-paying, unionized manufacturing jobs, New York State's per capita personal income fell during the 1970s from 113% to 109% of the US average. New York, moreover, was the only state to have a net loss of jobs during the 1970s. Responding to the economic malaise, Gov Hugh Carey (1974–82) approved a series of tax cuts on business and personal income in 1977–79 and 1981, a total reduction package of $2.7 billion. It was the first comprehensive and sustained tax reduction program in state history. Moreover Carey also held the state budget below the rate of inflation and sought to spur the state's economy in directions beyond manufacturing, viewing the loss of older industries as irreversible. In Manhattan he provided start-up funding in 1979 to build what later became known as the Jacob K. Javits Convention Center. Also in 1979 he gave state backing to the construction of the Carrier Dome, a large sports arena in Syracuse that helped revitalize that city's downtown. In the final years of his tenure, Carey, through a mix of public and private funds, spurred the initial redevelopment of Manhattan's Times Square, a district that boomed in the 1990s with a new business service industry that came to symbolize the state's economic rebirth.

Recent Conditions

Despite the efforts of state government to revitalize industry, by 2000 New York State's share of national manufacturing jobs had fallen to 5% and only 1 in 10 New Yorkers was working in a factory. In 2000 one-quarter of the state's industrial employment was located in Long Island, New York City, and the lower Hudson Valley. Long Island, once heavily dependent on the aerospace industry with firms like Fairchild Republic, Grumman Corp (from 1994, Northrop Grumman Corp), and Sperry Rand (from 1986, Unisys Corp) that employed tens of thousands of workers, suffered significantly as US defense spending steadily fell after the Korean War. In the 1980s and 1990s all three firms shuttered most of their facilities on Long Island. However, in New York City, employment in the finance, legal, and banking industry sectors compensated for the loss of industrial jobs in the overall metro region. In Sleepy Hollow (Westchester Co), General Motor Corp's (GM's) oldest US automobile plant (1904) was closed in 1996. (It was the last facility in the state to make complete cars.) The closure of this plant indicated the inability of large traditional manufacturers in the later 20th century to remain in the lower Hudson Valley, a region that had become a wealthy suburb with a robust set of environmental values, high real estate taxes, and significant energy costs.

In the Capital District GE still has a presence in

the 21st century at Schenectady, operating the world's largest turbine plant and employing 5,000 workers as recently as 1998. Yet this workforce is a shell of its former self as more than 40,000 worked at GE's Schenectady facilities during World War II. In 2000, 8% of the state's manufacturing jobs were located in the Capital District. Similar downsizing has occurred in the Mohawk Valley, an area once known as the state's industrial heartland. In the late 1960s GE operated a series of facilities in Utica, making electronic equipment for the US Defense Department, but closed these facilities in 1991, with a dreadful impact on the community. In central New York State, manufacturing has been hit hard by downsizing, but the area still contains significant facilities. In the 1980s and 1990s International Business Machines Corp (IBM) cut its workforce in and around Endicott (Broome Co), the company's birthplace, from 12,000 to 5,000. Endicott Johnson, once an employer of almost 20,000 in the Susquehanna Valley during the 1930s, experienced painful contractions starting in the 1960s and had exited the state entirely by 1998. Smith Corona Typewriter, America's last typewriter maker, employed 4,200 at its height of production in Cortland in 1979 but quit the state in 1994 and moved to Mexico. Despite significant plant closures and consolidations, in 2000 the Mohawk Valley and central New York State contained 30% of the state's manufacturing jobs.

Some manufacturing areas in western New York State have remained comparatively strong despite setbacks. Rochester and its environs are home to the renowned photographic, optics, and office equipment manufacturers of Eastman Kodak Co, Bausch and Lomb, and Xerox. Kodak, the world's largest photographic equipment and film manufacturer, employed at its height 60,200 workers in Rochester in 1980, 21% of that city's workforce. However, competition forced the photographic giant to reduce its Rochester presence and by 1999 only 24,600 Kodak employees were based there. Nevertheless the high-technology character of the Rochester area industries has remained strong, and at the opening of the 21st century many optics makers have formed partnerships with the University of Rochester and other area schools to nurture new cutting-edge firms. The same cannot be said for the Buffalo/Niagara region. Once home to traditional industries like the primary-metals giant Bethlehem Steel Co, the aviation conglomerate Bell Aircraft, and the automobile behemoth GM, huge employment cutbacks started in the region in the late 1960s and eventually shattered the local economy. Spread throughout Erie Co, Bell Aircraft employed nearly 50,000 workers during World War II, but after the firm was acquired by Lockheed-Martin in 1966, almost all of Bell's Buffalo area plants were closed over the next three decades. Bethlehem's massive steel facilities in Lackawanna (Erie Co) once formed one of the world's largest steel centers, employing 21,500 workers at its peak of production in 1966, and symbolized the industrial might of the region. Foreign competition and the relocation of the domestic automobile industry to the American South and to Mexico, however, forced Bethlehem by 1983 to close most of the facilities; in 2002 fewer than 500 were employed, and in 2003 Bethlehem sold the facility. At the start of the 21st century, automobile parts production remains a major Buffalo/Niagara region industry, although in 1985 windshield wiper manufacturer Trico Products Corp laid off 1,800 employees, closed two of its three plants, and relocated most of its operations to Texas and Mexico. In 2000 Western New York claimed a 20% share of the state's manufacturing employment.

New State Initiatives

Initiatives by state government in recent decades to make New York more attractive for industrial production have been moderately successful. Starting in 1985 under Gov Mario M. Cuomo (1982–94)—when the top marginal rate stood at 9.5%—the state began to reduce steadily its personal income tax. This policy continued under Gov George E. Pataki (1994–), and by 1997 the top rate was 6.85%, where it remained until being raised to 7.7% for the 2003 tax year. Other initiatives under the Pataki administration included the Build Now–NY (1998) and Semi-NY (1998) programs, which are operated by the Governor's Office of Regulatory Reform and the Empire State Development Corp (successor of the Department of Commerce). Beyond offering tax incentives and other types of state aid to private firms, these offices provide an expedited regulatory process for the construction of new industrial plants. Efforts by the state to attract high-tech manufacturing, particularly semiconductor research and production, have received the greatest emphasis. After a $660 million state incentive package, in 2002 IBM opened the Hudson Valley Research Park in East Fishkill (Dutchess Co), a $2.5 billion facility (the largest private industrial investment in state history) to produce semiconductors, employing 200; upward of 1,000 employees may work at the site by the mid-2000s. In 2003 the research consortium of International Sematech, consisting of firms such as IBM, Intel Corp, Motorola, and Royal Philips Electronics of the Netherlands, finalized plans for the construction of a massive $400 million semiconductor research facility centered at the University at Albany. It is hoped that this facility will spur growth of the semiconductor sector in New York State. Illustrating the increasing importance of computer and electronic manufacturing to the overall health of New York State industrial production, as of 1997 this sector ranked second (86,243) in the total number of people employed in the state's factories (785,891), just behind the number working in garments (91,516).

See also Carpet industry; General electric (GE).

Benjamin, Gerald, and Robert H. Connery. *Rockefeller of New York: Executive Power in the State House* (Ithaca: Cornell Univ Press, 1979)

Kramer, Daniel C. *The Days of Wine and Roses Are Over: Governor Hugh Carey and New York State* (Lanham, Md: Univ Press of America, 1997)

McClelland, Peter, and Alan Madgovitz. *Crisis in the Making: The Political Economy of New York State since 1945* (New York: Cambridge Univ Press, 1981)

Rubin, Bernard. *Public Relations and the Empire State: A Case Study of New York State Administration, 1943–1954* (New Brunswick, NJ: Rutgers Univ Press, 1958)

Schoolman, Morton, and Alvin Magid. *Reindustrializing New York State: Strategies, Implications, Challenges* (Albany: SUNY Press, 1986)

Smith, Richard Norton. *Thomas E. Dewey and His Times* (New York: Simon & Schuster, 1982)

Thomas, Alexander R. *In Gotham's Shadow: Globalization and Community Change in Central New York* (Albany: SUNY Press, 2003)

De Kalb. Town (pop 2,213) in W central St. Lawrence Co. De Kalb was settled in 1803 under direction of its proprietor, Judge William Cooper of Cooperstown (Otsego Co); the town was formed in 1806 from Oswegatchie. Lead ore (galena) was mined in the 19th century. De Kalb had a small community of Welsh miners, and Welsh celebrations were held annually until the late 20th century at Richville; the Welsh Society remains active. De Kalb was served by two railroads: the Potsdam and Watertown (1854) and the Ogdensburg branches (1862) of the Rome, Watertown and Ogdensburg. Agricultural in character, it was the site of St. Lawrence Co's first cheese factory at Richville Station (1863). De Kalb has a growing Swartzentruber Amish community.

Richard E. Mooers

DeKay, James E(llsworth) (*b* Lisbon, Portugal, 1792; *d* Oyster Bay, Nassau Co, 21 Nov 1851). Naturalist and physician. Son of an American sea captain, DeKay graduated from Yale and earned a medical degree at Edinburgh. In 1818 he returned to New York City where he became an associate of such literary figures as James Fenimore Cooper. DeKay showed far more interest in zoology, especially in reptiles and amphibians, than in medicine. He served as editor (1819–30) and librarian (1826–27) of New York City's Lyceum of Natural History, and in 1831–32 he visited Turkey, studying the Asiatic cholera. DeKay headed the zoology section of the New York Geological and Natural History Survey, which produced the book *Zoology of New-York or, The New York Fauna* (1842–44). The archetype of the 19th-century gentleman-scholar, DeKay died at his Oyster Bay home, The Locusts, and was buried in St. George's churchyard, Hempstead (Nassau Co). Also called the little brown snake, DeKay's snake *(Storeria dekayi)* is named for him.

Welch, Richard F. "James Ellsworth DeKay, Oyster Bay Naturalist," *Long Island Forum* 59 (Spring 1996): 30–39; (Summer 1996): 29–37

Richard F. Welch

de Kooning, Willem (*b* Rotterdam, Netherlands, 24 Apr 1904; *d* East Hampton, Suffolk Co, 19 Mar 1997). Artist. The son of a beverage distributor and a café owner, de Kooning left school in 1916. After apprenticing with a commercial art firm, he took courses at the Rotterdam Academy of the Fine Arts and Techniques between 1917 and 1924. In 1926 he journeyed to the United States as a stowaway. Traveling up the East Coast, de Kooning settled in Manhattan the following year and befriended artists including Stuart Davis, David Smith, Jackson Pollock, and Franz Kline, visited galleries, and worked odd jobs to support himself. De Kooning began painting full-time in 1936 after being released from the mural division of the Works Progress Administration for not being a US citizen. In 1948 he had his first solo exhibition at the Egan Gallery in New York City featuring his black-and-white abstractions, and also exhibited for the first time in the Annual Exhibition of Contemporary American Painting at the Whitney Museum of American Art. That year de Kooning also met art criti

Thomas Hess, who would become an early supporter, and began visiting East Hampton, a haven for abstract expressionists. By 1950 he had established an international reputation as a leading artist in the New York school.

De Kooning was best known for his large-scale, abstract expressionist paintings such as *Excavation* (1950) and his *Woman* series from the 1950s. He became a US citizen in 1962 and the following year moved from New York City to East Hampton. The landscape of East Hampton was reflected in a series of large abstractions that he painted in the mid-1970s. De Kooning continued to paint into his 80s. His work can be viewed at the Solomon R. Guggenheim Museum, Museum of Modern Art, Metropolitan Museum of Art, and the Whitney Museum of American Art in New York City; the Albright-Knox Art Gallery in Buffalo; and the Neuberger Museum of Art in Purchase (Westchester Co).

Yard, Sally. *Willem de Kooning* (New York: Rizzoli, 1997)

Tracy Schpero Fitzpatrick

DeLancey, James (*b* New York City, 27 Nov 1703; *d* New York City, 30 July 1760). Chief justice and acting governor. Born into a wealthy and political family, DeLancey was educated in London. He returned to New York City and in 1725 was admitted to the bar. Through his marriage in 1728 to Anne Heathcote, he established connections with English officials, which augmented his influence and made him a major force in politics. He was the leader of a powerful political faction, referred to as the DeLanceys. His supporters were Episcopalian merchants and rivals of the Livingstons, who were land barons and Presbyterians. DeLancey was appointed to the provincial council in 1729 and to the New York Supreme Court in 1731. Gov William Cosby promoted him to chief justice in 1733 in part, some thought, so DeLancey could preside over the libel trial (1734–35) of John Peter Zenger, printer of the *New-York Weekly Journal*. Although DeLancey pressed for conviction, the jury acquitted Zenger. Because many saw his appointment as a political maneuver to convict Zenger, DeLancey lost political favor.

Despite the trial and because he was intelligent and had deep-rooted political connections, DeLancey maintained influence over the assembly and provincial council. He introduced issues that opposed and challenged Gov George Clinton (1686–1761), which created an intense rivalry as the two vied for control of the colony. In 1747 and against Clinton's efforts, DeLancey secured the commission of lieutenant governor. In 1753 he became acting governor after Clinton's replacement, Sir Danvers Osborne, committed suicide. During his term he aimed to ease tensions between the colony and England. In 1754 he presided over the Albany Congress and signed a charter to establish King's College (now Columbia University) despite a vocal Presbyterian opposition that wanted a nondenominational rather than an Anglican institution. He served as lieutenant governor (1755–77) under Gov Charles Hardy and as acting governor (1757–60) until his death.

See also COLONIAL NEW YORK.

Bonomi, Patricia U. *A Factious People: Politics and Society in Colonial New York* (New York: Columbia Univ Press, 1971)

Launitz-Schürer, Leopold, Jr. "Whig-Loyalists: The DeLanceys of New York," *New-York Historical Society Quarterly* 56 (1972): 179–98

Mark G. Spencer

DeLancey, Oliver (*b* New York City, 16 Sept 1718; *d* Beverley, England, 27 Oct 1785). Politician and loyalist. Born into a prominent Huguenot family, DeLancey learned the family mercantile business and in 1742 secretly married Phila Franks, who was Jewish. He was an army commander during the French and Indian War. A rival of the Clintons, DeLancey was popular with many of the city's lower classes. He was a New York City alderman (1754–57), an assembly representative (1756–61), and a New York City Common Council member (1760). After his brother James died in 1760, he became head of the DeLancey faction. During the Revolutionary War he sided with the British and was appointed brigadier general. He financed and organized the largest regiment in the colony, called DeLancey's Brigade, a three-battalion unit of 1,500 volunteers from Westchester and Suffolk Cos, New York City, and Connecticut. His Third Battalion defended New York City and Long Island posts, and was involved in skirmishes in Westchester and on Long Island. In 1777 patriots destroyed his mansion located near today's Greenwich Village in New York City. After the war he moved to England, where he lived on his military pension.

Launitz-Schürer, Leopold, Jr. "Whig-Loyalists: The DeLanceys of New York," *New-York Historical Society Quarterly* 56 (1972): 179–98

Mark G. Spencer

DeLancey family. Colonial political family. The first American DeLancey was Stephen, or Etienne (1663–1741), a Huguenot refugee born in France, who emigrated to New York City in 1686 after the revocation of the Edict of Nantes and became one of the most influential merchants in the colony. Along with Adolph Philipse he spearheaded a political group known as the merchant party, or the Philipse-DeLancey coalition, which opposed the landed party led by the Morris and Livingston families. Stephen DeLancey married into the Van Cortlandt family, and his daughter's marriage to Peter Warren consolidated political connections to both England and the province. A member of the Colonial Assembly for 24 years, where he dominated politics and was active in regulating trade duties, Stephen lost a 1737 election and afterward became less active politically. His sons, however, took over the helm.

James (1703–60) became one of the most influential figures in colonial politics, serving as chief justice from 1733 to 1760 and overseeing the 1754 Albany Congress, and his position as justice allowed him to judge cases related to trade and land titles, major and often controversial issues. James garnered support for his party in New York City, Westchester, Albany, Schenectady, and Rensselaerswijck; other counties supported the Livingston-Morris faction. James's brother Peter (1705–70) established mills in Westchester Co and served as an assemblyman (1750–68), earning family support outside New York City.

Oliver (1718–85) led the family after the death of his brother James in 1760 but not for long. He mainly ran the DeLancey mercantile firm but also was assemblyman (1756–61), New York City alderman (1754–57), and council member (1760–75), and he created an alliance of merchant and radical interests and supported colonial rights. But in 1775 he abandoned the patriot cause, and organized and funded DeLancey's Brigade, a loyalist militia. Other DeLanceys were also tied to the loyalist movement. These included James's son James (1732–1800), who authored the Colonial Assembly's 1775 grievances to the Crown and Parliament and, when those were rejected, went to England to plea the colonial cause. He did not, however, advocate secession from England. His New York City property was confiscated, and he remained in England. After the Revolution he became a primary advocate for loyalist property rights. Another James (1747–1804), the son of Peter, founded the Westchester Refugees, a notorious loyalist regiment known as DeLancey's Cowboys. They raided cattle and captured patriots, who they exchanged for loyalist prisoners.

Oliver's children included Stephen (1740–98), who became the governor of Tobago. Stephen's son, Sir William DeLancey (1781–1815), served as quartermaster general to the Duke of Wellington and died at Waterloo. The DeLancey estates confiscated during the Revolutionary War were among the largest in New York City, approximately 120 blocks, ranging from the Bowery to the East River, and from Stanton to Division Sts. One family legacy is Delancey St, a major thoroughfare on Manhattan's Lower East Side.

Bonomi, Patricia U. *A Factious People: Politics and Society in Colonial New York* (New York: Columbia Univ Press, 1971)

Launitz-Schurer, Leopold S., Jr. "Whig-Loyalists: The DeLanceys of New York," *New-York Historical Society Quarterly* 56 (July 1972): 179–98

Jennifer Steenshorne

Delanson. Village (pop 385) in Duanesburg (Schenectady Co). The Albany and Susquehanna Railroad (1863) established Quaker Street Depot at the present Delanson. The Delaware and Hudson Railroad leased the line and, in 1873, built the Schenectady and Duanesburgh Railroad with a junction at Quaker Street Depot, with turntable and roundhouse. It became an important hay shipping point and acquired a sawmill and creamery. The village name is an acronym created in 1891 from DELaware ANd hudSON. The post office opened in 1892. From about 1900 to 1929 Delanson was the site of a huge railroad coaling station. In the early 21st century the village, which incorporated in 1921, is a bedroom community for the Capital District.

Ellen McHale

Delany sisters {Delany, Sadie [Sarah Louise] (*b* Raleigh, NC, 19 Sept 1889; *d* Mount Vernon, Westchester Co, 25 Jan 1999); Delany, Bessie [Annie Elizabeth] (*b* Raleigh, NC, 3 Sept 1891; *d* Mount Vernon, 25 Sept 1995)}. Both raised in North Carolina, these two sisters later moved to New York State. Sadie Delany moved to Harlem in 1916 and after earning a two-year degree from the Pratt Institute went onto Columbia University, graduating in 1920 with a BS. Taking a teaching job at a local elementary school, Sadie received a master's degree from Columbia in 1925 and transferred to Theodore Roosevelt High School in the Bronx five years later to teach science, thereby becoming New York City's first black teacher of high school domestic science. Bessie Delany followed her sister to Columbia, graduating with a dentistry degree in 1923. After becoming the second African American woman to receive a state dentistry license, Bessie opened a Harlem dental practice, which she operated for over 20 years. After World War II the sisters moved together to Bronx Co, and in 1956 they relocated to Mount Vernon. The Delanys rose to prominence in 1993 when they coauthored the memoir *Having Our Say: The Delany Sisters' First 100 Years.* In this best-seller they recalled the pervasive racism and sexism they faced as black female professionals and described how they overcame these obstacles through faith, hard work, and persistence. Striking an instant chord with readers, *Having Our Say* eventually sold over 1 million copies.

Delany, Sarah L., and A. Elizabeth Delany. *Having Our Say: The Delany Sisters' First 100 Years* (New York: Kodansha International, 1993)

Floris Barnett Cash

Delaware. Town (pop 2,719) in W Sullivan Co. The town was formed from Cochecton in 1869. The Erie Railroad was built through the present town in 1847 and brought tourists. Kenoza Lake, a resort formerly known as Pike Pond, was renamed in 1890 after a poem by John Greenleaf Whittier. The *Sullivan County Democrat* (1891) is published by descendants of its founder. Villa Roma, a successful resort and conference center, was established in the mid-1940s. Farming and tourism dominate the economy; the hamlet of Callicoon promotes itself aggressively to visitors as "Callicoon on the Delaware."

John Conway

Delaware. See MUNSEE.

Delaware and Hudson Canal. One of the early canals built to bring anthracite coal to New York City and other urban centers. Four Wurts brothers of Philadelphia owned coal-bearing land in the Lackawanna Valley of Pennsylvania, around what is now Carbondale. Unable to market their anthracite successfully at home, they joined forces with New York City investors who had formed the Delaware and Hudson Canal Co (D&H) in 1823. The two groups cooperated uneasily to complete a navigation system in 1828. Geography necessitated an indirect route. The 108 mi (174 km) canal, with 108 locks, began in Honesdale, Pa, followed the Lackawaxen River, crossed the Delaware River, ran along the Delaware to Port Jervis (Orange Co), and turned overland to Rondout, the port for Kingston (Ulster Co). From there the cargo was transferred, or later towed, down the Hudson River to New York City or New England. In addition to coal, the canal hauled New York State products: lumber, slate, bluestone, and natural cement from around Rosendale (Ulster Co). Towns prospered along its route in both New York State and Pennsylvania.

Although the D&H was the most important privately owned canal in New York State, it could not have been completed without state government assistance through stock subscriptions. This funding was used largely to construct a gravity railway from the head of navigation at Honesdale to the mines. Completed in 1829, this system moved railcars by means of horses and cables powered by steam engines and gravity. The total length of railway and canal was almost 125 miles (201 km). The D&H was an innovative company open to new technology. It bought steam locomotives in England for use on the gravity railway, although this experiment proved unsuccessful. During the 1830s the D&H was a leader in promoting the development of steamboats able to burn anthracite fuel. As one of the largest private companies in existence in the 1820s, the D&H pioneered many aspects of corporate management.

During a period of crisis, John Wurts became president of the company in 1831 and served until 1858. Wurts presided over a series of continual conflicts, including those involving Delaware River rafters, rival canals, real and proposed railroads, opposition in the state legislatures, and problems raising capital. The company weathered national economic depression in the late 1830s and various technical problems, and on occasion added to its own troubles by selling inferior coal. Efforts to expand into new coal-producing regions led to a prolonged and ruinous conflict with a supposed ally, the Pennsylvania Coal Co, in the 1850s. Also in the 1850s the D&H began evolving into a coal and railroad enterprise, which still exists as a railroad company. The canal was allowed to slip into obsolescence, and the last coal boat traveled down it in November 1898. That same year the canal was sold to Samuel Coykendall, president of the Cornell Steamboat Co. Immediately after the sale a new entity was formed, the Delaware Valley and Kingston Railroad, to build a railroad over much of the canal route. The New York, Ontario, and Western Railroad then purchased the canal from Summitville (Sullivan Co) eastward and used a portion of its route for its Kingston branch, opened in 1902.

Lowenthal, Larry. *From the Coalfields to the Hudson: A History of the Delaware and Hudson Canal* (Fleischmanns, NY: Purple Mountain Press, 1997)
Sanderson, Dorothy H. *The Delaware and Hudson Canalway: Carrying Coals to Rondout,* 2d ed. (Ellenville, NY: Rondout Valley Publishing, 1974)
Wakefield, Manville B. *Coal Boats to Tidewater: The Story of the Delaware and Hudson Canal* (1965; repr Fleischmanns, NY: Purple Mountain Press, 1992)

Larry Lowenthal

Delaware and Hudson Railroad. The railway began as the Delaware and Hudson Canal Co (D&H), chartered 23 Apr 1823 to build a canal to transport the company's coal from Honesdale, Pa, to the Hudson Valley at Kingston (Ulster Co). On 8 Aug 1829 the D&H operated the first steam locomotive in America, the Stourbridge Lion, on its 16 mi (26 km) gravity railroad built to carry coal from the mines at present Carbondale, Pa, to Honesdale. The locomotive proved unsuccessful for regular use, however, because of its excessive weight for the existing track structure. As railroad technology developed during the 1840s and 1850s, the D&H expanded its delivery of coal by building tracks connecting its mines near Carbondale to existing railroads and obtained rights to build and operate railroads in New York State and Pennsylvania. In 1870 the company leased the 6 ft (1.8 m)-gauge Albany and Susquehanna Railroad between Binghamton and Albany. The following year it leased the Rensselaer and Saratoga Railroad in the area north of Albany and by 1875 completed a line to Canada along the west side of Lake Champlain north of Whitehall (Washington Co). The canal, having become technologically outdated, was sold to the Cornell Steamboat Co in 1898, and the word Canal dropped from its corporate title.

The D&H expanded around the turn of the century, operating steamboats and hotels on Lake George and Lake Champlain, iron mines in the Adirondacks, electric interurban and street railways in the Capital District, and apple orchards and lime kilns north of Plattsburgh; it

Delaware and Hudson Building, Albany, designed by Marcus T. Reynolds, built 1912–18. It now houses SUNY administrative offices.

extended its coal mines in Pennsylvania. The D&H became one of the financially strongest and technologically advanced railroads for its size, which was less than 1,000 miles (1,609 km) in the United States under the leadership of company president Leonor F. Loree (1907–38), paying dividends through World War I and the early depression years. Loree improved the company's infrastructure with new bridges, track, and signal systems, and added new and rebuilt locomotives and cars. Business was expanded into streetcar lines, Adirondack iron mines, and Wall St investments.

Prior to and during World War II, the use of coal in industry and home heating declined, and moving merchandise, such as newsprint and forest products from Canada and manufactured goods and raw materials to and from New England, became the railroad's primary endeavor. Several marginal branchlines were abandoned, and most local passenger service was eliminated in the mid-1950s. The expanded use of trucks and cars on improved highways and industrial migration south after World War II gradually eroded rail traffic in the Northeast, and railroad mergers and abandonments became necessary for survival. In 1968, faced with the threat of the newly merged giant Penn Central Transportation Co, the D&H and the Erie Lackawanna Railroad (EL) joined Norfolk and Western's holding company Dereco in hopes of maintaining adequate traffic. It returned to independence in 1972 when EL went bankrupt. The formation of Conrail in 1976 forced the D&H to double the size of its system to 1,400 miles (2,253 km) by acquiring running rights over existing railroads in southern New York and in other states to reach beyond the boundaries of the Conrail territory to maintain its traffic base. Although expensive, this move was necessary to survive as an independent railroad, and losses were inevitable with dwindling traffic. Guilford Transportation Industries (GTI) purchased the D&H in 1984, hoping to incorporate it into a long proposed New England system, but after extended labor trouble GTI placed the railroad into bankruptcy in 1988. The Canadian Pacific Railway purchased the D&H in January 1991, and it became part of that company's St. Lawrence and Hudson subsidiary in 1996. The 177-year existence of the oldest continuously operated transportation enterprise in the country disappeared on 1 Dec 2000, when Canadian Pacific obtained authority from New York State and Pennsylvania to eliminate the name and operate the trackage as Canadian Pacific Railway.

Delaware and Hudson Co. *Century of Progress, History of the Delaware and Hudson Company, 1823–1923* (Albany: J. B. Lyon, 1925)

Shaughnessy, Jim. *Delaware and Hudson* (1967; repr Syracuse Univ Press, 1997)

Jim Shaughnessy

Delaware County (1,446 mi²/3,745 km²; pop 48,055). It was created from Otsego and Ulster Cos in 1797 and named for the river whose headwaters are contained within its territory. Area was subsequently gained from Ulster (1801) and Otsego (1817) but lost to Greene (1801), Ulster (1812), and Otsego (1822). Delaware Co is presently divided into 19 towns that contain 10 incorporated villages. The Village of Delhi serves as county seat. Elevations range from 820 ft (250 m), where the Delaware River exits the county in the far south, to over 3,520 ft (1,073 m), at the summit of Bearpen Mountain on the Greene Co line. The entire county lies within one or another of three major subregions of the Appalachian Upland. The eastern and central parts lie in the Catskill Mountain subregion. Here summit elevations decrease from around 3,000 ft (910 m) in the east to 2,500 ft (760 m) or less in the center. Simultaneously the valleys increase in number and width, thereby creating a more open topography. The Delaware Hills occupy areas south of the Beaver Kill and west of the Catskills and are noticeably lower, and the valleys more gently sloped. Closer to the northwest border, the Delaware Hills merge almost imperceptibly into the Susquehanna Hills, a subregion of similar topography whose extent is here defined by the Susquehanna River watershed divide.

Aside from the northeast corner of the Town of Roxbury, where waters drain north via Schoharie Creek into the Mohawk River, surface drainage is southward throughout the county. Major streams include the Susquehanna, which flows parallel to but just beyond the county's northwest border, the west and east branches of the Delaware, and the Beaver Kill. Dams on the branches of the Delaware near Downsville and Deposit create Pepacton and Cannonsville Reservoirs respectively, by far the largest water bodies in the county. Both are major components of New York City's water supply system. Farther downstream the Delaware serves as the county boundary from the Village of Deposit to the Sullivan Co line. The best agricultural soils are almost all in the larger valley bottoms in the northern half of the county. Moderately productive soils occur on some of the adjoining hillsides and tops.

Delaware Co's climate is humid-continental. Mean annual July temperatures range from about 64°F (18°C) in the higher Catskills to 68°F (20°C) at Walton. Summertime highs reach 90°F (32°C) or above a few times every summer in the hill country to the south and west, and more so in the lower elevations. Conversely they are uncommon in the higher eastern elevations. Mean January temperatures hover close to 21°F (-6°C) throughout the county's lower elevations. Higher areas are, on average, a degree or two colder. Temperatures drop below 0°F (-18°C) every winter, sometimes by a substantial margin. Precipitation is spread quite evenly throughout the year. Totals range from about 40 inches (102 cm) in the north to nearly 47 inches (119 cm) at Walton. Seasonal snowfall ranges from 96 inches (244 cm) at Walton to only 55 inches (140 cm) at Arkville in the far northeast. Approximately 90% of the county's primeval forest cover was an Adirondack hardwood community dominated by beech, sugar maple, yellow birch, hemlock, and white pine. The remaining 10% consisted of small isolated patches of Alleghenian hardwood and central hardwood forest, along with some wetland forest. At the present time approximately three-fourths of Delaware Co is covered by second- or third-growth forest. Most of the area east of the Delaware River's east branch and north of the Beaver Kill is within the Catskill Park.

American Indians and Early Settlement

There is little archaeological evidence of American Indian occupation in Delaware Co. The area was used on a seasonal basis by the Munsee, an Alquonquian-speaking people, with temporary settlements along the Delaware River. In 1769 traveler Richard Smith visited a permanent settlement called Cookose in what is now the Town of Deposit, noting his purchase of a pair of moccasins.

Delaware Co was made available for settlement under the colonial system of land patents. The county's south was part of the Hardenbergh Patent (1708), for which boundary disputes were

DELAWARE CO POPULATION CENSUS FIGURES

	White	Nonwhite	Total Population	Foreign-Born
1800	10,182	46	10,228	—
1810	20,171	132	20,303	—
1820	26,449	138	26,587	558
1830	32,821	203	33,024	474
1840	35,206	190	35,396	—
1850	39,633	201	39,834	3,236
1860	42,279	186	42,465	3,247
1870	42,740	232	42,972	3,469
1880	42,493	228	42,721	2,521
1890	45,232	264	45,496	2,689
1900	46,203	210	46,413	2,227
1910	45,349	226	45,575	2,077
1920	42,630	144	42,774	2,085
1930	41,040	123	41,163	1,976
1940	40,878	111	40,989	1,867
1950	44,319	101	44,420	2,126
1960	43,341	199	43,540	1,707
1970	44,314	404	44,718	1,443
1980	46,206	618	46,824	1,534
1990	46,535	690	47,225	1,308
2000	46,346	1,709	48,055	1,648

Notes: "Nonwhite" includes African Americans, Asians, American Indians, and Pacific Islanders and, for 2000, also the mixed race and other race categories. Through the 1960 census these figures primarily reflect the African American population. Foreign-born figures for 1820 and 1830 include only those not naturalized, and for 1930 and 1950, the foreign-born totals include Whites only. Other years include all foreign-born in the population.

settled by the Treaty of Fort Stanwix (1768). Along the Susquehanna River, the Wallace and Sir William Johnson patents covered the valley, while more than a dozen small patents, surveyed to run from the south boundaries of the Wallace and Johnson patents to the East Branch Delaware, were granted mostly in 1770. Patentees often chose to lease rather than to sell land to settlers.

By 1763 a band of Dutch Americans from Hurley (Ulster Co) settled in what became Middletown. Colchester was settled in 1766 and Sidney in 1770. In 1771 Col John Harper and others moved to what is now Harpersfield, with some subsequently moving down the West Branch Delaware. By 1774 seven of the county's present towns had white inhabitants. Although the area that was to become Delaware Co was sparsely settled at the time of the American Revolution, both tories and patriots were active. In August 1775 a meeting of patriots in Harpersfield was held to form a vigilance committee. In the summer of 1777, fearing attack by Native Americans supporting the British, most of the inhabitants of Harpersfield relocated to Schoharie Co or Cherry Valley (Otsego Co). After the Revolution settlement resumed, and between 1785 and 1797 the rest of the county was occupied. The population of the future Delaware Co was only 2,745 according to the 1790 census but had grown to 10,228 by 1800. The 1800 census included only 16 slaves, 5 of them owned by a single family, and 29 free Blacks; in 1855 the number had grown to 151 Blacks.

Delaware Co settlers were primarily from eastern New York and New England; Dutch and Palatine Germans moved over the mountains from Ulster Co. After the Revolution, Scots settled in Kortright, Andes, Bovina, and Delhi; Scottish-born people amounted to 3.4% of the population in 1855, while Irish immigrants, who arrived somewhat later, were present in the same numbers in that year. Smaller numbers of Germans came to Hancock and Davenport, and a few French settled in Hancock. In 1855 more than 84% of county residents were born in New York State. Immigrants from Italy came to the county to work on the railroads. Nicholas Launt (Landi) from Chiaramonte, Italy, immigrated to the United States and got a job on the Ontario and Western Railroad, encouraging others from his village to come to Walton beginning in 1882; it became the county's largest Italian community.

Antirent Agitation

In 1839 the heirs of Stephen Van Rensselaer began to collect back rents from tenants in several counties, including Delaware. Farmers organized antirent societies to resist the collections. The antirent actions culminated when Undersheriff Osman Steele attempted to evict Moses Earle from his farm in Andes on 7 Aug 1845 and was shot and killed by someone in the crowd. The county was declared to be in a state of insurrection, and 300 troops arrived to maintain order. Indicted for crimes including murder, robbery, rioting, and appearing armed and disguised were 242 antirenters; 84 were convicted, 12 others pled guilty to manslaughter, and 2 were convicted of murder. The trial was presided over by Judge Amasa J. Parker, who was clearly in favor of the landlords. After convictions, the jurors petitioned the governor for clemency, and in 1847 Gov John Young pardoned all of the antirent prisoners. The antirent wars also had an effect on local politics; an Antirent Party elected delegates to the constitutional convention, county supervisors, and a district attorney, and nominated a successful candidate to unseat Judge Parker.

Transportation

Turnpikes were the earliest transportation improvement. The Susquehanna Turnpike Road Co completed its highway, familiarly known as the Catskill Turnpike, from Catskill (Greene Co) to Unadilla (Otsego Co) by 1802. In 1835 ground was broken for the Erie Railroad at Deposit. It was thought that the most difficult part of the line's construction would be from Deposit to Callicoon (Sullivan Co), so that stretch was constructed first; the line was in service in 1849. The U&D opened to Grand Gorge in 1872 and was extended to Oneonta (Otsego Co) in 1900. The New York, Ontario and Western Railroad was put in service in 1872, crossing the county with a short branch to Delhi. The Delaware and Northern Railroad provided service along the East Branch of the Delaware from 1905 to 1942, with a line to Andes.

Economic Development

Much of Delaware Co's early industrial growth was related to the abundant natural resources. Because of the network of streams feeding both branches of the Delaware River, the harvesting of timber became a major industry; logs were sent to Pennsylvania and New Jersey markets in the form of large rafts. The first successful Delaware River raft trip to Philadelphia was in 1764, and as late as 1875, 3,000 rafts were sent downriver. Another forest product was hemlock bark, used in the tanning industry. In the mid–19th century, tanneries were built in the eastern part of the county and later spread to the valley of the East Branch. Wood chemicals were something of a Delaware Co specialty. Acetate was first produced at Corbettsville in 1848, and the first acid factory began producing chemicals from hardwood at Keeryville in 1878. Acid factories were concentrated in Hancock, Andes, and Tompkins, but closed with the depletion of forests and the development of synthetics in the early 20th century.

Despite the county's historic reliance on agriculture, the rocky hillsides made farming difficult and led some residents to describe their farmland as "two stones for every dirt." The earliest farmers relied on diverse products including wool, butter, maple syrup, and apples. By 1855 farmers shifted to dairy products as their primary cash crop, producing more than 4 million pounds (1.8 million kg) of butter and more than 61,000 pounds (27,700 kg) of cheese. The advent of the railroads made it possible to ship fluid milk, primarily to the New York City market. By 1878 the Ulster and Delaware Railroad (U&D) built platforms to receive the milk cans, and farmers soon concentrated on milk rather than butter. The nation's first milk pasteurization as part of commercial milk processing was performed at Bloomville's Sheffield Creamery in 1893. The relationship between farmers and those buying their products was sometimes difficult. The county was a center of the militant Dairy Farmers Union. During a 1939 strike farmers in the Town of Andes picketed and dumped milk. In the 20th century, poultry and cauliflower were also important. As late as 1950, 581 cauliflower growers shipped their produce from Margaretville, but the crop disappeared soon afterward.

Other industries served the farming community. The 1855 census enumerated 24 tanneries, 26 gristmills, 31 blacksmith shops, and 224 sawmills. In the late 19th century, bluestone quarries began to ship stone by rail to cities for use in sidewalks and buildings. In a few larger communities, factories produced goods for sale. Walton Novelty Works (1876–1930s), Sidney Silk Mill (1893–1906), Munn Piano Factory (1901–20) in Walton, and Cortland Cart and Carriage Co in Sidney were the most notable manufacturers.

Beginning with rail service in 1872, railroad companies produced summer vacation guides, and the eastern end of the county began to host growing numbers of tourists attracted to farms and boardinghouses that offered fresh eggs, milk, and country air. The Grand Hotel opened on the Delaware Co–Ulster Co border in 1881, and in Stamford Dr Stephen E. Churchill built two large hotels: Churchill Hall (1883) and the Rexmere (1898). Roxbury, Margaretville, and Griffin's Corners [now Fleischmanns] also became resorts. The last of the grand hotels closed in the 1960s.

POPULATIONS OF TOWNS, DELAWARE CO

Town, Year Founded	1800	1840	1880	1920	1960	2000
Andes, 1819	—	2,176	2,639	1,922	1,274	1,356
Bovina, 1820	—	1,403	1,022	858	594	664
Colchester, 1792	1,207	1,567	2,941	2,849	1,920	2,042
Davenport, 1817	—	2,052	1,939	1,313	1,261	2,774
Delhi, 1798	820	2,554	2,941	2,721	3,398	4,629
Deposit, 1880	—	—	1,714	1,415	1,560	1,687
Franklin, 1792	1,390	3,025	2,907	2,132	2,133	2,621
Hamden, 1825[a]	—	1,469	1,496	1,248	1,108	1,280
Hancock, 1806	—	1,026	3,238	4,122	3,907	3,449
Harpersfield, 1788	1,007	1,708	1,420	1,184	1,193	1,603
Kortright, 1793	1,513	2,441	1,730	1,559	1,073	1,633
Masonville, 1811	—	1,420	1,673	878	1,030	1,405
Meredith, 1800	213	1,640	1,563	1,394	1,112	1,588
Middletown, 1789	1,064	2,608	2,977	3,522	3,310	4,051
Roxbury, 1799	936	3,013	2,344	2,258	2,238	2,509
Sidney, 1801	—	1,732	2,461	4,133	7,110	6,109
Stamford, 1792	924	1,681	1,638	2,104	2,103	1,943
Tompkins, 1806[b]	—	2,035	2,534	1,737	1,463	1,105
Walton, 1797	1,154	1,846	3,544	5,425	5,753	5,607

[a]Hampden until 1826.

[b]Pinefield until 1808.

Religion, Education, and Culture

Settlers brought their religious traditions from eastern New York and New England. Presbyterian churches were established at Kortright (1774) and Harpersfield (1787), and St. Peter's Episcopal Church was formed at Hobart in 1794. In 1855 Presbyterian churches numbered 23, and Congregational churches numbered 10, together outnumbering the 28 Methodist churches. The first Roman Catholic church was established at Hancock in 1851. The county's only synagogue, B'nai Israel, was incorporated at Fleischmanns in 1918, reflecting a booming summer community; funds for the synagogue were raised by the Jewish Farmers Association. Beginning in the late 20th century, Delaware Co began to attract believers from other religions, including believers of Buddhism and Islam, who founded rural retreats.

For the 19th and much of the 20th centuries, Delaware Co's educational efforts were centered around the common school districts that operated one-room schools; the last was Trout Creek District No. 6 in Tompkins, which closed in 1968. Several academies provided higher education. Franklin's Delaware Literary Institute (1835) educated both men and women; it became a Union Free School in 1902 and operated a century later as the Franklin Central School District. Abraham L. Kellogg, who became a state Supreme Court justice, attended a one-room school near Treadwell and the Delaware Literary Institute. Kellogg's commitment to the best education possible for children of his hometown was responsible for the first central school in the county, formed at Treadwell in 1927; its new building was dedicated in 1929 as the A. L. Kellogg School. It merged with the Delhi Central School District in 1967, but the multimillion-dollar Kellogg Fund continues to support the A. L. Kellogg Elementary School as well as other Delhi school district improvements. Most centralization was completed in the 1930s, except for Sidney (1941) and Walton (1949), but a number of common school districts in Tompkins remained independent as late as 1958. In 2003, 13 central school districts served the county's students.

Elizabeth and Amelia McDonald, daughters of a Delhi farming couple, worked with others to lobby the state for a two-year college at Delhi dedicated to agriculture. In 1913 the legislature authorized it on the site of the old Delaware Academy; it opened in 1915 with a student population of nine young men, and in 1921 women were admitted. The college offered courses such as agriculture, teacher training, and veterinary science. It is a sign of the changing nature of the county that the college (now State University College of Technology at Delhi) no longer offers agriculture courses, and its first four-year degree is in hospitality management.

Over time, the county's culture has been most strongly expressed through its folk arts. Traditional fiddlers played at barn dances and house parties, and storytellers recounted tales of rafters like Boney Quillen and other tales of hunting and fishing. Visual artists used the materials around them to create baskets and to carve wood and stone. Women took the everyday work of making quilts and turned it into an art form, often through quilt groups, which are still popular. In the mid–19th century, three men of Scottish descent, John Holmes, Asahel Amora Phelps, and John Benjamin Phelps, wove dozens of intricately patterned bedcovers now known as the Delhi Coverlets. Delhi-born Candace Wheeler (1827–1923) founded the Society for Decorative Arts in New York City in 1877. In partnership with Louis C. Tiffany and others in 1879, she established the Associated Artists, an interior design firm that decorated Mark Twain's Hartford home and parts of the White House. Wheeler also headed an all-woman firm specializing in needlework and printed textiles. In 1893 she helped design the decoration of Woman's Building at the World's Columbian Exposition.

The county's two most famous sons were born in Roxbury within a year of each other and attended the same one-room schoolhouse. Both men loved and studied the natural environment, although they used this knowledge in very different ways. Jay Gould (1836–92) wrote the first history of Delaware Co and worked as a surveyor; he eventually entered the railroad business, becoming one of the nation's best-known (and often, one of the most reviled) railroad financiers of the late 19th century. John Burroughs (1837–1921) was a leading and much beloved nature writer at the turn of the 20th century and the author of *Wake Robin* and many other books celebrating the sense of place in the Catskills and Hudson Valley. His writings earned him the friendship of leaders such as Theodore Roosevelt, Henry Ford, and Harvey Firestone. In the late 20th century, the county was enriched by the arrival of visual artists, performers, writers, and others as both full- and part-time residents. At the same time, local arts organizations blossomed, including the West Kortright Centre and the Roxbury Arts Group.

The first newspaper published in county was the *Delhi Delaware Gazette* (1819–1915). In 2003 the county was served by *Margaretville Catskill Mountain News* (1894), still owned by its founding family, as well as the *Walton Reporter,* the *Hancock Herald,* the *Deposit Courier,* the *Sidney Tri-Town News,* and the *Delaware County Times* (1978). One of the earliest printed references to baseball is in the *Delaware Gazette,* where in 1825 nine Hamden residents issued a challenge to the county's other towns to play the game of "Bass-ball" for $1 per game.

Recent History

The number of farms has steadily declined: 5,449 farms in 1875, 3,956 in 1930, and 3,234 in 1950. In 1997 Delaware Co had 717 farms, with 183,667 acres (74,327 ha) in farming, 19.8% of the total area. Dairy products represented 78% of the product value, followed by cattle and calves, hay and silage, nursery and greenhouse products, and vegetables. The average age of a farm operator in 1998 was 54.4 years, reflecting the movement of young people away from farming.

Construction of the Pepacton Reservoir began

in 1947 to provide water to New York City. More than 18 miles (29 km) long and located on the East Branch of the Delaware River in the towns of Colchester, Andes, and Middletown, the reservoir flooded four communities and displaced 974 residents before its 1954 opening. The 16 mi (26 km) Cannonsville Reservoir on the West Branch in Deposit and Tompkins was constructed from 1955 to 1967. Put in service in 1965, it displaced five small communities, from which there was little organized resistance, but some individuals carried out limited acts of vandalism. Although the reservoirs brought boom construction times to the county, New York City's condemnation of homes, villages, and farmland left a bitter legacy. In 1990 New York City's Department of Environmental Protection issued much tougher rules to protect the watershed in an effort to avoid a federally mandated water filtration plant. All of the towns in the Catskill watershed—eventually 35—joined together as the Coalition of Watershed Towns to fight the new regulations. In 1991 kitchen-table diplomacy convinced more than 85% of the farmers in the region to participate in the Watershed Agricultural Council; in 1996, New York City, New York State, and the Coalition of Watershed Towns formally signed a Memorandum of Agreement forming the Catskill Watershed Corp, a national model for the preservation of both watershed and the livelihood of those who live in the region.

The county has only two short stretches of four-lane highway. I-88 was completed across the northern edge of Sidney in 1976, and Rte 17 (I-86) runs across Colchester, Hancock and Deposit. The ease of travel to New York City, Binghamton, and Albany on these two roads has noticeably reduced the county's isolation. In some towns in the early 21st century, second-home owners from outside the county make up as much as 70% of landowners, and Delaware Co is attracting greater numbers of retirees. The tourism industry promotes outdoor activities such as hiking, biking, and fishing. Ski Plattekill operates in Roxbury, Bobcat Ski Center is in Andes, and Scotch Valley Ski Area of Jefferson is just outside Stamford. The Catskill Scenic Trail is an 18 mi (29 km) stretch of converted railbed from Grand Gorge to Bloomville. Hanford Mills Museum in East Meredith features a working, 150-year-old waterpowered sawmill, gristmill, and blacksmith shop.

In the early 21st century, manufacturing firms employ more than 4,000 people in the county. The Scintilla Co of Sidney began manufacturing a Swiss-invented magneto for airplanes in 1926. It produced the magneto used on Lindbergh's successful flight over the Atlantic in 1927; later purchased by Bendix, the plant reached its peak during World War II, when it employed more than 8,600 people. The company is now Amphenol. Calendar manufacturer Keith Clark moved to Sidney in 1946 and became At-A-Glance, the world's largest manufacturer of calendars. Other large employers are DMV International Nutritionals and Ultra Dairy in Delhi; Norbord Industries (medium density fireboard [MDF] panels), Deposit Computer Services, and Courier Printing in Deposit; Tyco Health Care/Mallinckrodt in Hobart; and two Kraft dairy plants in Walton.

The first book about Delaware Co was written by a young man soon to become a famous financier: Jay Gould, *History of Delaware County* (1856). It was followed by the standard work, *History of Delaware County* (1880), and the two-volume work by David Murray, ed., *Delaware County, NY: History of the Century, 1797–1897*, 2 vols (1898). They have been updated by Douglas DeNatale, *Two Stones for Every Dirt: The Story of Delaware Co* (1987). There have been a number of town and village histories, including Diane Galusha, *As the River Runs: A History of Halcottville* (1990); Elma H. Mitchell, *History of East Meredith* (1993); Bernice Graham Telian, *200 Years of Rolling Suns: Meredith Township, 1800–2000* (2000); Irma Mae Griffin and Caroline Evelyn More, *History of the Town of Roxbury* (1953); Irma Mae Griffin, *History of the Town of Roxbury* (1974); Isabelle Adams Swantek and Elisabeth Post, *The Valley We Love: Township* (1980) (Township is a community in the Town of Stamford); *The Story of Walton, 1785–1975* (1975); and Frank and Helen Lane, *Walton Yesteryears* (1985). A book of considerable significance to the history of the county's southern towns is Frank D. Myers III, *The Wood Chemical Industry in the Delaware Valley* (1986).

Linda Norris

Delaware, Lackawanna and Western Railroad. Famed as the "Road of Anthracite," this railroad originated in the mid–19th century to serve the coalfields of eastern Pennsylvania; it included several early short lines, the oldest being the Ithaca and Owego Railroad (1828). Following the Civil War, mergers, leases, and new-line construction made the Delaware, Lackawanna and Western (DL&W) an important trunk line. From the early 1900s its crack mainline trains, including the celebrated Phoebe Snow, carried large numbers of passengers between Hoboken, NJ, and Buffalo; its fast freights hauled carloads of high-grade merchandise over the same route. But anthracite ("stone coal"), which DL&W carried in quantity beginning in the 1880s, continued to generate the largest portion of the line's tonnage. In the early 20th century, company earnings were so strong that its Board of Managers regularly voted extra dividends. During the Great Depression of the 1930s, DL&W avoided bankruptcy despite damaged earnings. Increased business during World War II energized the carrier, allowing it to enter the postwar era with improved equipment, including diesel locomotives, which produced sizable savings. In the mid-1950s a substantial decline in anthracite traffic and increased competition from trucks and automobiles caused hardship for the line. Company earnings declined sharply, and DL&W soon faced expenses associated with weather damage in the Poconos, a bridge replacement over the Hackensack River, and increased costs of operating its northern New Jersey commuter service. Beginning in the mid-1950s DL&W and longtime rival Erie Railroad began sharing their physical plants. After the elimination of duplicate freight facilities at Binghamton and Elmira and other successful joint ventures, the railroads' executives decided on a corporate marriage, which took place 17 Oct 1960. The new company, Erie Lackawanna Railroad, was headquartered in Cleveland, Ohio. Conrail acquired most of its assets in 1976.

Casey, Robert J., and W. A. S. Douglas. *The Lackawanna Story: The First Hundred Years of the Delaware, Lackawanna and Western Railroad* (New York: McGraw-Hill, 1951)

H. Roger Grant

Delaware River (140 mi/225 km). The longest free-flowing river in the United States east of the Mississippi. The Delaware runs 330 miles (531 km) from its source at the confluence of its east and west branches near Hancock (Delaware Co) to the Delaware Bay, forming part of the boundary between New York State and Pennsylvania. Cutting a passage through what is now known as the Delaware Water Gap, postglacial waters continued to flow along the edge of the Piedmont before swerving eventually to the east and carving an outlet to the Atlantic Ocean. In 1609 explorer Henry Hudson came upon a waterway at what is now Delaware Bay, which he named the Sudyt River and which would later be called the Delaware. The Dutch used it as a primary route through the southern part of New Netherland, and a vibrant beaver trade followed from New Netherland south to a trading post established in 1635 at present-day Philadelphia. The Delaware Aqueduct, built in 1848 by engineer John Roebling, who also designed the Brooklyn Bridge, is the oldest existing wire suspension bridge in the United States and joins Lackawaxen, Pa, with Minisink Ford (Sullivan Co). Begun in 1847, the suspension aqueduct was a canal built above the Delaware River to ease congestion of Delaware and Hudson Canal traffic and river timber rafting. Locks on the aqueduct raised or lowered the boats from the canal level to the aqueduct. The aqueduct operated until the canal closed in 1898 and was then converted to a highway bridge, designated part of the Delaware and Hudson Canal National Historic Landmark in 1968.

By the beginning of the 20th century, the Upper Delaware had become well known as a recreational area, accommodating campers and canoeists. In 1978 the National Park Service designated 73.4 miles (118.1 km) of the Upper Delaware along the New York State and Pennsylvania border as part of the National Wild and Scenic Rivers System. This portion, from Hancock to Deerpark (Orange Co), serves as a natural passage through the terrain and is significant as a recreational area, offering scenic beauty as well as a prized trout fishery. The second section of the river, below Port Jervis (Orange Co), is navigable and is designated a Wild and Scenic River for 40 miles (64.4 km). The lower portion of the river flows through Delaware Bay to the ocean.

The Delaware River basin encompasses 13,539 mi^2 (35,066 km^2) and is fed by 216 tributaries, draining 2,362 mi^2 (6,118 km^2) in New York State. Although it drains less than 1% of the total continental US land area, 17 million people depend on the basin for both drinking and industrial-use water. Three reservoirs on the river's tributaries provide nearly half of New York City's water supply. In 1961 the Delaware River Basin Compact was formed among the states of New York, New Jersey, Pennsylvania, Delaware, and the federal government. The agreement established the Delaware River Basin Commission, a planning, development, and regulatory agency for the basin.

Tyler, David Budlong. *The Bay and River, Delaware: A Pictorial History* (Cambridge, Md: Cornell Maritime Press, 1955)

Veronica A. Weigand

Delevan. Village (pop 1,089) in Yorkshire (Cattaraugus Co). Settled in 1821 and called Coonville, it had a post office named Delavan from 1838 to 1852, when it was renamed Yorkshire Center. Growth was promoted by the Buffalo, New York and Philadelphia Railroad (1872; later Pennsylvania Railroad). Cheese boxes and shingles were products in the late 1870s; wooden type was manufactured by the Empire Type Foundry (1893). Named Delevan starting in 1892, the village incorporated in 1915. The Merrill Soule Milk Plant (1922) was sold to Borden's. In the middle of the 20th century, Delevan was a favorite training spot for wrestlers and boxers. The Kendor Music Co, publisher of student-level stage band music, markets internationally.

Bruce D. Fredrickson and Madelynn P. Fredrickson

Delhi [DEL-HI]. Town (pop 4,629) and village (pop 2,583) in central Delaware Co. Settled *ca* 1785, the town was formed from Middletown, Kortright, and Walton in 1798. The village, incorporated in 1821, serves as the county seat and was the site of the antirent trials in 1845. During the 19th century Delhi was at various times the site of brick making, the Delaware Woolen Factory Co (1824-after 1900), a tannery (1809–35), and an iron foundry. The Ontario and Western Railroad (1872) encouraged dairy production, which remained predominant into the mid–20th century. The town is home to SUNY Delhi (1948) and the Delaware County Historical Association. DMV International Nutritionals and Ultra Dairy, both at Fraser, provide employment. Fitch's Bridge (1870) is one of three covered bridges in public use in the county. Lafayette B. Mendel (1872–1935), a Delhi native, is credited with first hypothesizing the existence of vitamins in 1911.

Dorothy Kubik

Delmar. Locality (pop 8,292) in Bethlehem (Albany Co). A turnpike hotel opened by Nathaniel Adams in 1836 resulted in the name Adamsville. The Albany and Susquehanna Railroad came through in 1863, and its station made the place a potential residence for Albany entrepreneurs. A post office named Adams Station opened in 1868 and was renamed Delmar in 1885. In the 1910s suburban development began, advanced by the construction in 1928 of a viaduct carrying Delaware Ave over the Normans Kill. In 1940 its population was 2,992. Development accelerated after World War II and was augmented by Delaware Plaza, a shopping center, in the early 1960s. It remains a close-in commuter suburb for downtown Albany workers.

De Mille, Agnes (*b* New York City, 18 Sept 1905; *d* New York City, 7 Oct 1993). Choreographer, dancer, and author. De Mille's grandfather and father and her uncle, the famous director Cecil B. De Mille, were all successful writers and actors in the theater. Her family moved in 1915 to Los Angeles, where she studied dance at the Denishawn School. Returning to New York City in 1927, she performed solo recitals to excellent reviews. In 1932 she moved to England, where she studied at Madame Marie Rambert's Ballet Club and worked with Antony Tudor and Frederick Ashton. In 1939 De Mille got her break when she was invited to join the American Ballet Theatre's (ABT's) inaugural season and created her first ballet, *Black Ritual* (1940), one of the first ballets to use black dancers.

De Mille was one of the most innovative contributors to American musical theater, choreographing *Oklahoma!* (1943), *Carousel* (1945), *Brigadoon* (1947), *Gentlemen Prefer Blondes* (1949), and *The Girl in Pink Tights* (1954). *Oklahoma!* was a particularly groundbreaking endeavor, as it integrated choreographed numbers with the plot in a way that had not been done before. De Mille had a long association with ABT and was instrumental in bringing Tudor to the company. Her ballet *Rodeo* (1942), choreographed for the Ballets Russes de Monte Carlo, became part of her ABT repertoire, which also included *Tally-Ho* (1944), *The Rib of Eve* (1956), *A Rose for Miss Emily* (1970), and her last work, *The Other* (1992). She received a Capezio Dance Award for choreography in 1966, the Handel Medallion (1976), and in 1980 was a Kennedy Center honoree. She was also a prolific author, writing a number of autobiographies and dance books, including *To A Young Dancer* (1962) and *American Dances* (1984).

Easton, Carol. *No Intermissions: The Life of Agnes de Mille* (New York: Da Capo Press, 1996)

Anya Peterson Royce

Democratic Party. It is the longest enduring of the state's political organizations and has provided leaders and formulated policies since the 1790s.

Origins

In the 1790s artisans in New York City formed Democratic-Republican Societies modeled on similar clubs in Revolutionary France. Determined to preserve the ideals of the American and French Revolutions, these clubs discussed current political issues, including Secretary of the Treasury Alexander Hamilton's policies of friendship with England, promotion of manufacturing, funding of the national debt, and creation of a national bank. Fearing that such measures would encourage aristocracy and endanger the republic, the clubs argued the merits of a politics that allowed the elevation of all classes, not just those enjoying governmental favor. They urged democratic political reforms and limits on the powers of government, especially the national government because it was far removed from the citizenry. Even after the original Democratic-Republican Societies declined, these ideals of popular participation, limited government, and states' rights shaped the rhetoric of Democratic-Republican elites as they contested with Federalists for power in the state.

In a competitive political environment prospective leaders of the group, also known as Republicans or Jeffersonian Republicans in the early 1800s, needed organized support. But existing republican theory equated party with selfish combinations aimed at self-enrichment rather than the public good. While an Aaron Burr or De Witt Clinton might seek to utilize an existing organization like Tammany Hall to win elections, their factional followings remained largely personal and subject to sudden changes as competitors contested their claims to leadership. Martin Van Buren, leader of the Bucktail faction of Republicans, broke the impasse in the 1820s by creating the rationale for modern political parties. Conceiving of conflict as inevitable rather than avoidable, he argued that citizens were best served by disciplined political parties that found their legitimacy in conforming to the popular will. By 1828 a newly organized Democratic Party held conventions, selected candidates, enforced discipline through patronage, and used the party press to address policy issues. Popular electioneering techniques helped voters develop lasting partisan identities, which reduced electoral volatility.

Antebellum Growth

In 1836 Van Buren reached the pinnacle of his remarkable political career with his election to the presidency. With better initial organization than their opponents, Van Buren's Democrats controlled both legislature and governorship before the panic of 1837. Not until 1834 did Antimasons and National Republicans coalesce into the Whig Party, the Democrats' principal opponent until the 1850s. The Democrats' emphasis on limited government made it most attractive to ethnoreligious minorities such as Irish Catholics, the largest immigrant group in the state. Limited government signified for them a commitment to protect the autonomy of white men (but not white women or African Americans) from legislation seeking to impose a common set of cultural values, such as temperance or Sunday observance, on society. The Democrats also appealed to those who feared they (usually urban workers or subsistence farmers) would not benefit from the state's transition to a competitive commercial economy. The party was necessarily a broad coalition, however, and in the legislature its representatives often bowed to local pressures in favoring canal extensions or promotion of local corporations, which theoretically the party opposed. By "balancing" their political slates with candidates of diverse opinions and the judicious use of patronage, the Democrats sought to avoid disruption.

In 1835 dissatisfied Democrats remained after a nominating convention in Tammany Hall at which their concerns had been ignored. They formed an equal rights faction, dubbed Locofocos by their opponents. The group opposed banks, corporations, and the accumulation of state debt to make transportation improvements. The onset of depression in 1837 cost the Democrats control of the legislature and governorship and heightened intraparty disputes. In 1841 the Locofoco faction, now designated Radicals, or Barnburners, and including such leaders as Michael Hoffman, Silas Wright, and Samuel Young, gained control of the legislature. They proposed to suspend work on the canals, which the Whigs had continued despite the depression, and to levy taxes to reduce the state debt. Conservatives, or Hunkers, who included Edwin Croswell, Daniel S. Dickinson, Horatio Seymour, and William C. Bouck, began cooperating with Whigs to support the canals. The factions also differed over slavery, with the Barnburners opposing its extension, and over nativism, with the Barnburners more leery of the party's dependence on Irish immigrants.

Factionalism and Civil War

Even though the Constitutional Convention of 1846 intended to iron out differences over the state's role in the economy, Pres James K. Polk's apparent favoring of the Hunker faction and the reemergence of the slavery extension issue in the form of the Wilmot Proviso during the Mexican War exacerbated factional differences. In 1848, unable to secure satisfaction at the national convention, the Barnburners bolted to join with political abolitionists and antislavery Whigs in the new Free Soil Party, which chose Martin Van Buren as its unsuccessful presidential candidate.

Barnburners did not plan to languish in a third party, however. Underway was a battle to define the Democratic Party that would last a decade and significantly reshape it. By 1849, having proved that their support was essential to control both New York State and the presidency, Barnburners sought to return to the Democrats. Some Hunkers, dubbed Softs, including Horatio Seymour and William L. Marcy, welcomed them, while Hards, led by Dickinson, insisted they be punished. Complicating any permanent reunion were the continuation of the slavery and temperance issues, the collapse of the Whig Party, and the emergence in its stead by the mid-1850s of two new parties, the nativist American Party and the antislavery extension Republicans. Over the course of the decade the Democrats seldom mustered a unified state ticket, and many former supporters wandered into and out of the new party offerings. By 1860 the Republicans, appealing to dominant evangelical Protestant and middle-class cultural groups, had established themselves as the Democrats' chief opponents. Many former Barnburners joined the new party, and the Democrats lost much of their support in western and northern New York State.

Continuing immigration kept the Democrats competitive in the state and capable of winning the governorship for Horatio Seymour in 1862 during the Civil War despite Abraham Lincoln's presidential victory in 1860. Wedding themselves to strict construction of the US Constitution, the party supported the war against the Confederacy and condemned measures such as the draft and suspension of habeas corpus as abuses of power. The bloody draft riots in New York City in 1863 helped discredit a faction of Peace Democrats but signaled the growth of a restive working class, attuned to issues of race and class.

Gilded Age and Progressive Era

Because Republicans more easily controlled the malapportioned legislature, Democrats continued to prefer localized solutions to their constituents' problems. The postwar era's boss rule in New York City was under a succession of Tammany chieftains: William M. "Boss" Tweed, "Honest John" Kelly, and Richard Croker. Bosses yoked together diverse groups by doling out favors such as municipal contracts to elites and jobs and Sunday outings to the working class. Tammany was not without competitors, such as Irving Hall and its Swallowtail faction, but despite the internecine conflict, New York State's electoral importance in a closely divided nation guaranteed such Democratic leaders as Horatio Seymour, Samuel J. Tilden, and Grover Cleveland as presidential candidates and in other important positions. No faction, however, dealt satisfactorily with the massive dislocations accompanying the state's industrialization, urbanization, and influx of immigrants.

The closest to a statewide Democratic boss during the Gilded Age was Gov David B. Hill, who used patronage to align party organizations across the state in the late 1880s. Grover Cleveland, who favored civil service reform, opposed Hill. The resultant squabble over the state ticket at the time of a national depression (1894) led to a Republican landslide. When the national party in 1896 turned to Nebraska for a presidential candidate (William Jennings Bryan) and a platform pledged to basing the money supply on silver (which had little appeal in New York State's commercially based economy), the party imploded. Goldbugs ran John M. Palmer nationally in opposition to Bryan, Democratic organizers failed to organize, and the party in New York State experienced permanent losses among most groups except Irish Catholics.

While the Republicans emerged as the majority party in the state, Democratic leaders argued over strategy. Hoping to appeal to growing numbers of eastern European Jews and other new immigrant groups in New York City and to well-organized groups like labor unions and women suffragists, as well as to fend off socialists, some Tammanyites (eg, Charles F. Murphy, Robert F. Wagner Sr, Alfred E. Smith) experimented with new issues such as labor laws, thus broadening and redefining reform to include more than just elite concerns. Other Democrats sought alliances with political independents or with the Progressive wing of the Republicans. Taking advantage of Republican divisions, the party elected several governors: John Alden Dix, William Sulzer, and Martin H. Glynn. Although intraparty wrangling continued and Sulzer was impeached and removed from office when he lost the support of Tammany, the party was slowly learning to respond to pressure groups, many of which were skeptical of all politicians. After the tragedy of the Triangle Shirtwaist Factory fire, younger leaders became more convinced that active regulation of working conditions by government was a better choice than the limited government so admired for the past century. In 1918, with Gov Al Smith's election, the party was moving into a new era. —*PFF*

Party Evolution in the 20th Century: An Overview

Al Smith's gubernatorial tenure (1919–20, 1923–28) established the modern, strong executive model for the state's governors. Smith was a crucial figure in the creation of the contemporary Democratic Party in the state: liberal, progressive, and oriented toward New York City. (The two most influential Democratic governors in the half century before Smith's election were the upstate conservatives Cleveland and Hill.) The Democrats controlled the governorship for 20 consecutive years, between 1923 and 1942. Both Franklin D. Roosevelt and Herbert H. Lehman, who followed Smith in office, endorsed and in many ways expanded his policies. Roosevelt's response to the depression, both in Albany and, after 1933, in Washington, DC, cemented the identification of the state's Democratic Party with an expansive view of the role of government as an agent for social welfare. However, conservative New York Democrats were still very much in evidence. One notable example was US senator Royal S. Copeland (1923–38), an opponent of the New Deal.

The growing power of the state's governor created an alternative center of power to Tammany Hall in the Democratic Party. While Smith had good relations with Tammany Hall, Roosevelt and Lehman did not; both supported Fiorello La Guardia, the very liberal Republican-Fusion mayor of New York City (1933–45), against the Tammany candidates. Disputes between regulars and reformers were a standard feature of Democratic primaries, especially in New York City, until the Tammany organization was reduced to a fraction of its former influence in the 1960s.

After World War II New York government remained the model of an activist, progressive state government, providing an ever expanding range of services even as Republicans held the governor's office for all but four years between 1943 and 1974 and controlled the state legislature for much of this time. (Democrat W. Averell Harriman served a term as governor from 1955 to 1958.) Democrats came to lead statewide voter enrollments and had a majority in the senate in 1965 and prevailed in the assembly between 1965 and 1968. The party also dominated local politics for much of this time in New York City, Albany, and Buffalo.

Ironically, Democrats won the governorship and control of the assembly in 1974, at a time when the postwar liberal consensus was beginning to fade. Govs Hugh Carey (1975–82) and Mario M. Cuomo (1983–94) remained committed to progressive social policies even though they governed in increasingly conservative times. Although constrained by fiscal crisis, Carey did much to improve conditions in state mental health facilities. Cuomo supported a range of social initiatives and successfully resisted the imposition of the death penalty in the state. The Democrats have retained control of the state assembly since 1975, and from that time the Speaker, invariably a Democrat from New York City, has emerged as one of the most powerful politicians in the state. The party expanded its margin over Republicans among registered voters and also had considerable success in elections for the other statewide elective offices of comptroller and attorney general.

Party Organization

Development of the party during this period is best understood from an examination of three categories: the party as an organization focused on winning elections, as a locus of political identification for voters, and as an instrument for organizing government to implement policy. By the early 20th century political parties had been transformed from private to quasi-public organizations. The statutory adoption of the secret ballot (1890) and indirect primary (1898) required that parties be defined in law, with their organizational structures specified, their processes for leadership selection democratized, and their membership systematically identified. Additionally, the state's two major political parties had been given constitutional responsibility (1894) for managing state and local elections.

Despite such Progressive era reforms, party leaders at the county level remained the dominant force in state politics in the early part of the 20th century by continuing to control nomination and election to legislative, judicial, local, and the then more numerous statewide elected offices and the patronage these positions commanded. For example, Charles F. Murphy, leader of New York City's Tammany Hall machine, used his dominance of the party in the first two decades of the century to advance the careers of Gov Smith and Sen Wagner and to end that of Gov Sulzer. Murphy's principal intraparty adversary was the reformer Thomas Mott Osborne of Auburn (Cayuga Co). The contest between machine and reform Democrats for control of the party organization, manifest in the Murphy/Osborne rivalry, was a theme in nominating politics and party leadership fights for much of the century.

The strength of party leaders in state politics declined with constitutionally required direct popular election of US senators (1913), reduction in the number of statewide elected officers, and concentration of governmental power, especially the appointing power, in the hands of the governor (1927). By the 1930s party leaders were far more dependent upon, than directive of, the Democratic governors Roosevelt and Lehman. With the development of New Deal programs, urban party organizations were displaced as primary sources of social support for immigrant and working-class city dwellers. In the post–World War II era, city populations transformed. New urban dwellers, many of whom were members of racial and ethnic minorities, remained predisposed to the Democratic Party, but demographic change and population mobility engendered intraparty conflict and disrupted established political bases. Meanwhile, second- and third-generation voters (many owning suburban homes) evinced a diminished willingness to provide automatic, consistent support for Democratic Party candidates. Finally, advances in communication technology (television, public opinion polling, direct marketing, and the Internet) allowed candidates to reach voters without reliance on party organizations.

Although the O'Connell organization in Albany persisted for years, the defeat in 1961 of Carmine DeSapio, Tammany's last great boss, in his attempt to block the renomination and reelection of Robert F. Wagner Jr as mayor of New York City, was symbolic of the diminished importance of the classic Democratic Party urban machine in state politics. At the end of the century, county Democratic organizations remained important for the nomination and election of local and judicial candidates, but their importance diminished vastly for statewide races and for legislative elections. The state's modern Democratic Party organization, like those in many other states, evolved into a political service organization for the party's candidates, professionally staffed and closely linked to the national party and at the center of a network of organizations supportive of Democratic candidates and programs.

The Voters

In 1920, the first year for which systematic statewide data were found, enrolled Republicans in New York State outnumbered Democrats by a ratio of about two to one. The Republican Party lost its plurality advantage among enrolled New York voters in 1930, the early days of the Great Depression. This was a time when the national electorate expanded and shifted, as political scientists say, from the "normal Republican" majority (created with the economic depression of 1896) to a "normal Democratic" majority. A rough balance in state voter enrollment between the two major parties was restored in the early 1940s and persisted for about two decades. The Democratic advantage returned in 1960 and continued to grow for four decades, even after the national electorate became more Republican. The number of enrolled Democrats in New York State exceeded the number of enrolled Republicans by almost 2 million in 2000. The disjunction between the partisan majorities in the state and those in the nation is a clue to the declining importance of the state and its elected leaders in national politics in the later portion of the 20th century.

The upstate-downstate split, with New York City the locus of Democratic Party strength and suburbs and rural areas strongly Republican, remained a defining metaphor in state politics over the century. Over the decades Democratic strength among enrolled voters grew in suburbs and rural areas. In 1920 enrolled Democrats outnumbered Republicans only in Bronx, Queens, and Richmond Cos in New York City. In fact, in that year there were over 100,000 more Republicans than Democrats in New York City, even though city Democrats were 57.6% of all Democrats in the state. In contrast, in 2000 enrolled Democrats in the city outnumbered enrolled Republicans by a ratio of five to one but constituted a slightly smaller portion (53%) of all party enrollees in the state.

At the turn of the 21st century, in addition to New York City, Albany and Erie Cos were centers of Democratic strength. Six other counties had more Democrats than Republicans: Westchester, Rockland, Niagara, Schenectady, Sullivan, and Tompkins. Partisan divisions were close in four other counties: Chautauqua, Clinton, Montgomery, and Monroe.

Democratic Party adherents were disproportionately drawn from less affluent, working-class backgrounds. At the beginning of the 20th century the state's urban Irish Catholic immigrant population was at the core of party strength. Especially after the onset of the Great Depression, the party added Jewish arrivals from central and eastern Europe and then African Americans migrating northward. Still later it attracted voters of Puerto Rican background and others of Latino origin. Although many Italian Americans became Democrats, many provided a core constituency of the state Republican Party, especially in suburban and rural areas. Organizationally, Democrats drew consistent support from labor unions and groups with liberal positions on social, economic, and environmental policy questions.

Electoral Success

Success in statewide elections in the 20th century was evenly shared by candidates of the two major parties. Of the 26 presidential elections, the Democratic and Republican Parties each won 13 in New York State. Reflecting the state's partisan balance, Democratic success was more common in the second half of the century. Between 1960 and 2000 the party prevailed in 8 of 11 presidential contests. Of the 32 elections for US senator between 1914 and 2000, Democrats prevailed in 18. They filled both US Senate seats from New York State between 1927 and 1946. The state was not again represented by two Democrats in the senate until 1999, when Charles Schumer joined Daniel Patrick Moynihan in that body. State governors were Democrats for half of the century's years. The party dominated the governorship for all but two years from 1919 through 1942, and then again from 1975 through 1994. Cuomo, elected to three four-year terms, was the longest serving Democratic governor in the century. Lehman served 10 years, and Smith and Carey 8 years each.

Apportionment and districting provisions created by a Republican majority in the state's 1894 Constitutional Convention assured that the legislature was "constitutionally Republican." After the US Supreme Court overturned most of these provisions in the mid-1960s, artful gerrymandering resulted in a state senate that remained a Republican bastion. Democrats controlled the senate for only 14 years in the 20th century and only one year (1965) since the end of World War II. Their control of the state assembly held from 1965 to 1968. In the "Watergate election" of 1974, the party achieved dominance in the assembly for the rest of the century. Gerrymandering was again a factor. Previously during the century there had been Democratic assembly majorities for only six years: 1913, 1935, and the four-year span in the 1960s. For only two years in the century (1913 and 1935) did Democrats simultaneously hold the governorship and the senate and assembly majorities, and thus fully control state government.

Into the 21st Century

By many measures New York began the 20th century as a Republican state and ended it as a Democratic state. All seven statewide officers elected in 1900 were Republican, as were both houses of the state legislature and 19 of 32 Congress members. At the start of the 21st century, the state assembly was Democratic, as were the independently elected state comptroller and attorney general, both of the state's US senators, and 19 of 31 of its members in the US House of Representatives. There were, however, important exceptions: the governor was Republican, as was the majority in the state senate.

In the early 21st century the state remains one of the most liberal in the nation, an identification confirmed in 2000 by the election of Hillary Rodham Clinton to the US Senate. In increasingly conservative times, the Democrats have had both successes and failures. Since 1994 a fairly conservative Republican, George E. Pataki, has been elected as governor three times. In 2002 he defeated Democratic candidate H. Carl McCall, the state's first African American major party candidate for governor, who received only 34% of the vote in a three-way election. In 2003 the state had 5,125,534 voters enrolled as Democrats, and they outnumbered enrolled Republicans five to three. The Democratic Party held

Sen Hillary Rodham Clinton.

this numerical advantage even though, over the course of the 20th century, the party had weakened (and transformed in function) as an organization and diminished in its command of enrolled Democrats' loyalty. —*GB*

See also ANTIRENT MOVEMENT; APPORTIONMENT AND DISTRICTING; CIVIL WAR; ITALIANS; LABOR; LIBERALISM; UNITED STATES HOUSE OF REPRESENTATIVES; UNITED STATES SENATE.

Bass, Herbert J. *"I Am a Democrat": The Political Career of David Bennett Hill* (Syracuse: Syracuse Univ Press, 1961)

Benson, Lee. *The Concept of Jacksonian Democracy* (Princeton, NJ: Princeton Univ Press, 1961)

Brewer, Mark D., and Jeffrey M. Stonecash. "Political Parties and Elections." In *Governing New York State*, 4th ed., ed. Jeffrey M. Stonecash (Albany: SUNY Press, 2001)

Finan, Christopher M. *Alfred E. Smith: The Happy Warrior* (New York: Hill & Wang, 2002)

Flynn, Edward J. *You're the Boss* (New York: Viking Press, 1947)

Moscow, Warren. *Politics in the Empire State* (New York: Knopf, 1948)

Mushkat, Jerome. *The Reconstruction of the New York Democracy, 1861–1874* (East Brunswick, NJ: Associated Univ Presses, 1981)

Scarrow, Howard. *Parties, Elections, and Representation in the State of New York* (New York: New York Univ Press, 1983)

Wesser, Robert F. *A Response to Progressivism: The Democratic Party and New York Politics, 1902–1918* (New York: New York Univ Press, 1986)

Young, Alfred F. *The Democratic Republicans of New York* (Chapel Hill: Univ of North Carolina Press, 1967)

Gerald Benjamin, Phyllis F. Field

Democratic-Republican societies. Beginning in 1793 societies under this or similar names organized in nearly every state to protest Federalist policies. Seven societies were formed in New York State. The first groups were in Ulster Co, a center for Antifederalists. The Republican Society of Ulster County was organized in Montgomery [now in Orange Co] in 1793, and the Democratic Society of Shawangunk formed a year later. In Columbia Co, a well-known center for tenant farmer activism, a group was founded in 1794 and was known mostly as the Democratic Society of Canaan. The Democratic Society of the City of New York (1794) became a catalyst for similar groups that formed in the city. Antifederalists took over the Tammany Society of New York City, previously a benevolent society during the 1790s. The short-lived Juvenile Republican Society of New York City formed in 1795, and smaller, less influential societies formed in Kings, Ontario, and Suffolk Cos.

Officers of the Democratic-Republican societies were largely merchants, elites, and the middling sort, and members were mostly artisans, farmers, and laborers. The Democratic Society of the City of New York met monthly, but other societies met less regularly. Initially societies were patriotic groups, and organizers modeled activities on democratic principles established by the Sons of Liberty. Platforms and agendas had regional variations, but all members believed in freedom of the press, religion, and speech and detested policies established by elite government leaders that made the upper class wealthier. Canaan's society based its agenda on groups in New York City and Vermont and in 1796 boasted a civil liberties campaign reminiscent of the Revolutionary War era. Ulster's societies followed the New York City group but instituted a separate agenda suggesting prisoners should be reformed instead of serving lengthy sentences. Ulster and New York City groups promoted the mechanic and crafts trades, worked to formalize public education, and funded public and charity schools.

The societies supported Thomas Jefferson and the French Revolution and opposed aristocratic government, class favoritism, and the pro-British position that Federalists such as Alexander Hamilton adopted. Their views were disseminated by, among others, Thomas Greenleaf, printer of New York City's *New-York Journal and Patriotic Register* and the *Argus*. He frequently published essays and pamphlets for the Ulster and New York City groups. Societies began to decline in 1798 due to internal factionalism, and most were defunct by the time Jefferson took office as president in 1801, except for the Tammany Society, which remained a dominant force in Democratic politics in New York City for the next century and a half.

Foner, Philip, ed. *The Democratic-Republican Societies, 1790–1800: A Documentary Sourcebook of Constitutions, Declarations, Addresses, Resolutions, and Toasts* (Westport, Conn: Greenwood, 1976)

Young, Alfred F. *The Democratic Republicans of New York: The Origins, 1763–1797* (Chapel Hill: Univ of North Carolina Press, 1967)

Mark G. Spencer

Demorest [née Curtis], **Ellen** (*b* Schuylerville, Saratoga Co, 15 Nov 1824; *d* New York City, 10 Aug 1898). Patternmaker. Curtis graduated from Schuylerville Academy and opened her first millinery shop in Saratoga Springs in 1842. She worked for one year in Troy (Rensselaer Co), finally settling in Brooklyn. On 15 Apr 1858 Curtis married William Demorest and moved to Philadelphia, where she invented mass production of accurate paper patterns for dressmaking. The Demorests moved back to New York City and in 1860 launched *Mme Demorest's Mirror of Fashions*, which included a paper dressmaking pattern in each issue, and she opened the Emporium of Fashions, serving New York City elite. Demorest introduced new designs in hoopskirts and corsets and also ventured into the cosmetics industry. She became interested in social issues and helped to form the Woman's Tea Co, which helped women get into the tea business. A cofounder of the New York City women's club Sorosis (1868), she served as treasurer of the New York Medical College for Women and chaired the Welcome Lodging House for Women and Children. Demorest's patternmaking business began to decline in the early 1880s. Ready-to-wear designs and the failure to patent her patterns allowed competition to damage her business, and she retired in 1887.

Ross, Ishbel. *Crusades and Crinolines: The Life and Times of Ellen Curtis Demorest and William Jennings Demorest* (New York: Harper & Row, 1963)

Walsh, Margaret. "The Democratization of Fashion: The Emergence of the Women's Dress Pattern Industry," *Journal of American History* 66 (1979): 299–313

Kerry Delaney

Denmark. Town (pop 2,747) in NW Lewis Co. Settled in 1800, the town was formed in 1807 from Harrisburg. Early products included cloth (beginning in 1807), a rope factory (1832–*ca* 1860), cheese boxes, hoops, and steel plows. Products were shipped on the Black River Canal (1851) or the Black River and Utica Railroad (1872). Along the Deer River are 2,000 acres (810 ha) of flats, and dairy farming remained important in 2003. Large stands of sugar maple continue to supply syrup as a side crop. High Falls (160 ft/49 m) is a natural landmark. The privately owned Freedom Wright Tavern was the site of an 1804 meeting that petitioned the legislature to set off Lewis and Jefferson Cos from Oneida Co.

Arthur Einhorn

Denning. Town (pop 516) in W Ulster Co. Settled when a sawmill was built at Dewittville, just north of what is now Claryville (Sullivan Co), in 1827, the town was formed in 1849 from Shandaken. Its chief industries were lumbering, tanning, and wooden goods, and in 1880 it had three tray mills, a turning mill, and at Ladleton a ladle factory. Located in the Catskill Park, its wilderness is ideal for outdoor sports; a number of sportsmen's clubs acquired tracts in the late 19th century. Denning's most important institution is the 6,500-acre (2,630 ha) Frost Valley YMCA Camp (1956).

Ruth Piwonka

Denonville, Marquis de [Brisay, Jacques-René de] (*b* Denonville, France, 10 Dec 1637; *d* Denonville, 22 Sept 1710). Denonville's appointment as governor general of New France in 1685 followed a humiliating peace made by his predecessor with the Iroquois Confederacy after a failed attack against them in 1684. Denonville had to restore French prestige and counter Iroquois and English attempts to control the fur trade. He brought military reinforcements to New France when he took office, which he used in the summer of 1687 to invade the country of the Seneca nation of the Iroquois Confederacy. He landed near Irondequoit Bay [now in Monroe Co] and attacked and burned several settlements, principally the village at Ganondagan [now Victor, Ontario Co]. Large quantities of crops and stores of corn were also destroyed at nearby Fort Hill. Before returning to Montreal, he established Fort Denonville, which lasted only a year at the mouth of the Niagara River. Denonville's expedition did not end the threat to Canada from the Iroquois; by September 1687 they attacked settlements in the vicinity of Montreal. Denonville was recalled to France in 1689 for military service in Europe. The Ganondagan site was formally dedicated a New York State Historic Site on 14 July 1987, the 300th anniversary of its destruction.

Eccles, W. J. *Canada under Louis XIV* (Toronto: McClelland & Stewart, 1978)

Brian Leigh Dunnigan

dentistry. In early New York dental care was largely ineffective; extractions and denture making were the main stocks in trade. Although wigmaker James Mills offered his dental care services via a 1735 New York City newspaper advertisement, the first full-time professional dentist in New York, Robert Woofendale, did not arrive from England until 1766. New York City dentist John Greenwood is remembered for his dental services to George Washington. Richard

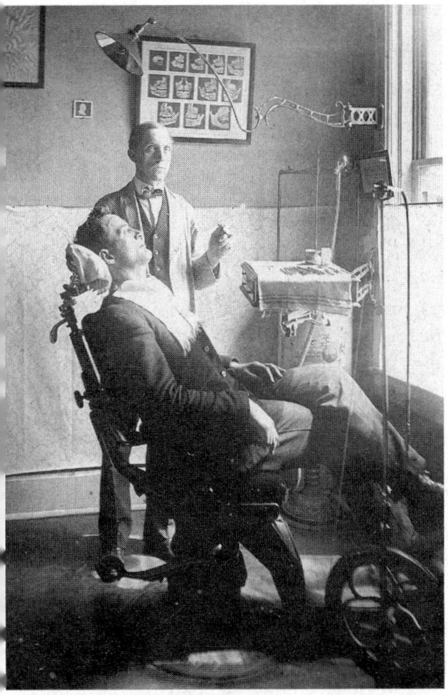

Dr Austin practices dentistry on patient Wesley Stour of Kendrew Corners, 1907.

Cortland Skinner, during 45 years of practice starting in 1790, established the New York Dispensary and the Hospital and Alms House of New York City, the first hospital dental clinic and the first free dental clinic in the United States. In 1834 Solyman Brown and Eleazer Parmly created the Society of Surgeon Dentists of the City and State of New York. This, the world's first dental organization, was superseded in 1840 by the American Society of Dental Surgeons. In New York City in 1839 Horace Hayden, Brown, and Parmly started the world's first dental journal, the *American Journal of Dental Science.* In 1859 the dental organizations that had formed in the United States met at Niagara Falls and established the American Dental Association. New York was the first state to create a qualifying board of censors in 1868, which in 1896 came under the aegis of the New York State Board of Regents, eventually evolving into the State Board of Dental Examiners.

The state's first dental school, Amos Westcott's New York College of Dental Surgery, opened in Syracuse in 1852 but closed in 1855 after a fire. A school operating under the same charter, the New York State College of Dental Surgery, opened in New York City in 1879, merging in 1923 with the Dental School of Columbia University (1918). The New York College of Dentistry was founded in New York City in 1865, becoming the College of Dentistry of New York University in 1925. In 1892 the University of Buffalo established its School of Dentistry. SUNY Stony Brook established a dental school in 1962. In 1916 Hunter College and the Eastman Dental Dispensary in Rochester became the first schools in the state to offer programs for dental hygienists.

Many scientific advances in dentistry were made in New York State. Sanford C. Barnum of Monticello (Sullivan Co) invented the rubber dam, which made a dry and clean operative field possible. The Buffalo Dental Manufacturing Co, founded in 1880, was a pioneer in its field. In 1945 H. Trendley Dean, a public health dentist, showed the public health value of fluorides in a famous controlled study in Newburgh (Orange Co) and Kingston (Ulster Co). In 1930 the Rockefeller Foundation established a program in dental research at the University of Rochester School of Medicine and Dentistry. An early fellow, Basil G. Bibby, discovered how fluorides alter the character of dental enamel to make it resistant to decay. At Rochester's Eastman Dental Center in 1967, Michael G. Buonocore created the sealant technique useful for cavity inhibition for children, revolutionized restorative dental methods, and made possible new dental aesthetic procedures.

McCluggage, R. W. *A History of the American Dental Association, 1859–1959* (Chicago: American Dental Association, 1959)

Ring, M. E. *Dentistry: An Illustrated History* (New York: Harry N. Abrams, 1985)

Frederick J. Halik

department stores. New York State was a seedbed for the development of the department store. Several of the world's first department stores, including A. T. Stewart's, Macy's, Arnold Constable, and Lord and Taylor, originated in New York City, and more than 50 stores were founded in New York State. Department stores were the first mass-retailing (high-volume, low markup) institutions in the United States, preceding mail order houses, chain stores, and supermarkets. They were typically large and ornately decorated, primarily organized into dry goods departments, and were usually staffed with hundreds of female clerks (and mainly catered to female customers). They generally were upscale (although some catered to people of moderate incomes), advertised heavily, encouraged browsing, discouraged haggling over prices, and offered free wrapping, delivery, and other services.

The Pioneers, 1842–1914

Several of New York City's leading department store founders got their start in small specialty shops in Lower Manhattan during the 1820s. The typical retail shop was small, poorly lit, and usually cold in the winter and hot in the summer. Goods were neither displayed attractively nor labeled with prices. A. T. Stewart entered dry goods retailing on lower Broadway in Manhattan in 1823. His landmark Marble Palace, which opened in 1848, and Iron Palace, in 1862, defined the pattern for the industry. Aaron Arnold opened his first dry goods shop nearby in 1825. After he joined with James M. Constable in 1842 to form Arnold Constable and Co, the two men opened their own Marble House at Canal, Howard, and Mercer Sts in 1857. They followed with a cast-iron emporium at Broadway and 19th St in 1869. The original Lord and Taylor opened in New York City's Bowery district in 1826. With several moves northward up Manhattan, the store grew and added white marble facades, glass-domed rotundas, and other hallmarks of the early department store era. Another pioneer with modest origins in the 1820s was English immigrant George A. Hearn Jr, the founder of what became James S. Hearn and Sons. Following his original shop in 1827, Hearn partnered with Aaron Arnold and subsequently opened his own store on Broadway near Canal St in 1842.

By the 1850s New York City featured a glamorous retail district along a five-block strip of Broadway (traversing Canal, Grand, Broome, Prince, and Houston Sts) that included the emporiums of Arnold, Constable, Lord and Taylor, and Hearn's, as well as elegant specialty shops such as Tiffany and Co and Brooks Brothers. The geography of Manhattan retailing began another shift northward with the arrival of R. H. Macy in 1858, with his first New York store, R. H. Macy's, at 6th Ave and 14th St. This opened a retail region between 14th and 23d Sts, a stretch that became known as Ladies' Mile. James McCreery and Co, which began farther south in 1850, opened a new store at 23d St in 1895. Benjamin Altman opened the first B. Altman and Co at 3d Ave and 8th St in 1865, followed by a Palace of Trade at 6th Ave and 19th St in 1876, where a fleet of luxury carriages delivered parcels to upscale customers. One of the last major players to enter this district, Paul J. Bonwit, opened a luxury department store at 6th Ave and 18th St in 1895. Two years later he took on Edmund D. Teller as a partner in the soon renamed Bonwit Teller.

From the 1870s to the turn of the century, New York City's department stores began to become more economically and geographically diverse. In 1879 Albert Best and James A. Smith founded the Lilliputian Bazaar, an infant clothing store, on 6th Ave and 12th St. Best and Co opened a more moderately priced department store farther uptown. Lyman and Joseph Bloomingdale opened their first store on 3d Ave in 1872 targeting thrifty middle-class shoppers. At the other end of the price spectrum was the likes of Henri Bendel Inc, which began in 1890 as a hat store on East 9th St catering to New York's social elite. By the late 19th century many of the largest department stores were owned by German Jewish families. The Straus brothers, Nathan and Isidor, acquired Macy's in 1888 and in 1902 moved the store to 34th St and Broadway. In 1893 the Straus family purchased Wechsler and Abraham on Fulton St in downtown Brooklyn, founded by Abraham Abraham and Joseph Wechsler in 1865, renaming the store Abraham and Straus. In 1910 the Gimbel brothers opened their department store at 34th St, one block from Macy's, with which they had an intense rivalry until Gimbel's closed in 1986.

Many stores followed Macy's and Gimbel's to Midtown Manhattan, with the upscale emporiums along 5th Ave between 34th and 42d Sts, and the cheaper class of trade along 14th St. In 1902 Andrew Saks opened his first Manhattan store on 34th St, while Franklin Simon opened the first women's fashion store on 38th St at 5th Ave. Two years later Lane Bryant (born Lena Himmelstein in Lithuania) launched what would become a maternity and larger-size women's clothing empire at West 38th St. In 1911 Bonwit Teller opened a store at 5th Ave and 38th St, and in 1914 Bergdorf Goodman (founded as Bergdorf and Voight, a furrier and tailor shop, in 1901), B. Altman, and Arnold Constable opened ornate new stores in Midtown Manhattan. In Jamaica (Queens Co), the first Gertz stationery store opened in 1911. They opened a five-story store in 1933 and grew into a major New York City area department store chain.

The Interwar Years: Prosperity, Depression, and Merger

New York City department store expansions and new ventures slowed during World War I, then surged during the prosperous 1920s. Two trends defined the interwar decades for them. Those that survived became department store chains, and several began to expand outward from urban centers such as Manhattan—with their high rents, congestion, and relatively limited parking—to suburbanized regions of New Jersey and Long Island. Both trends were driven in large measure by the state's growing dependence on automobiles. In 1929 major department store chains were responsible for 15.3% of the state's total department store sales; by 1954 they would account for 65.5%. At the same time, the number of stores fell from 4,221 to 2,761. The interwar decades also ushered in a wave of consolidations that would continue for decades. Gimbel's expanded its retail base upscale with the 1923 purchase of Saks Fifth Avenue. Bonwit Teller was acquired by Atlas Corp in 1934. B. Altman began its Long Island expansion in Manhasset (Nassau Co). Arnold Constable sold to Isaac Liberman in the 1920s and opened several new stores in New Jersey and Long Island, and Best opened a branch store in Garden City (Nassau Co) in 1929.

Before the late 1930s, only a tiny percentage of department store clerks belonged to unions, many of them in small shops rather than urban department stores. In May 1937, the same month that the Retail Employees of America (REA) was formed, Hearn's was unionized. Gimbel's and Bloomingdale's followed in 1938. But walkouts, such as the one-month strike at Gimbel's in mid-1941 over a 40-hour workweek, were rare. High turnover among department store workers, frequent management crackdowns, and resistance on the part of some union leaders to organizing saleswomen kept department store union membership at only around 5%.

Postwar Suburbanization and Nationalization

After World War II department store sales surged and migration from urban centers to suburbs intensified. Along with restaurants, movie theaters, and branch banks, department stores became a common feature of the suburban landscape, especially its proliferating shopping malls, where they served to "anchor" scores of smaller, specialty shops. New discount department stores proliferated. Alexander's, a leading discount store, opened on New York City's 3d Ave in 1928, had nine branch stores in New York City and its suburbs by the 1970s. Frieda Mueller Loehmann founded a discount designer store that bore her name in Brooklyn in 1920. She and her family diversified into other discount high fashion lines and expanded first locally and then into 16 states. E. J. Korvette's, founded by Eugene Ferkauf in 1948, was perhaps the most successful of the new metropolitan area discounters. Many of the state's leading department store firms lost their New York City identity as they went out of business, were merged into giant conglomerates, or expanded into the sunbelt or other regions of the country. By 1977 Macy's operated 76 branches, 60 of them outside of New York State. Many of the New York City department store chains bore the names of their 19th-century founders, but few were controlled by the heirs of their founders, and many were incorporated into larger companies. Federated Department Stores was founded in Columbus, Ohio, in 1929, the year it acquired Abraham and Straus. It subsequently acquired Bloomingdale's and, in 1994, Macy's. Saks Fifth Avenue remains independent and currently operates 60 stores in 24 states.

As some chains expanded, many of the old-time department stores failed. McCreery failed in 1954, and Hearn closed its doors the following year. In the 1970s the closings included Arnold Constable's parent company, which failed in 1975, Gimbel's in 1986, and B. Altman in 1989. The large postwar discounters also fell on hard times. E. J. Korvette's closed in 1981 and Alexander's in 1992. In the early 21st century, some of the famous names in department stores in New York City remain but many more have closed, and the great shopping emporiums of the 19th and 20th centuries play a diminished role in the retail commerce of the city.

Department Stores outside of New York City

Department stores also flourished outside of New York City. Burke, Fitzsimons and Hone and Co developed the first department store in Rochester in the late 1850s, followed by the opening of Sibley, Lindsay and Curr in 1868. Sibley's became Rochester's largest department store and, following a fire in 1904 (which destroyed a large portion of the downtown Buell block and the store itself), encouraged the opening of two other major department stores after the reconstruction. E. W. Edwards (a Syracuse department store) and Benjamin Forman opened a ready-to-wear clothing store, and J. C. McCurdy (of Philadelphia) expanded its store on Elm St (south side of Main St), making downtown a retail shopping district. Main and Clinton Sts eventually became home to six major department stores, including Sibley's, which closed downtown in 1990, and McCurdy's, which closed in 1994. In 1876 Buffalo's Adam and Meldrum formed a partnership and a department store and in 1892 became Adam Meldrum and Anderson (AM and A's), remaining in downtown Buffalo on Main St for nearly 100 years before closing in 1990. Other Main St Buffalo stores included Hens and Kelly Co, established in 1892 and eventually bought out by Twin Fair in 1978 (all stores closed in 1981); Flint and Kent, located on Main St between Huron and Chippewa Sts; and William Hengerer and Co, formed in 1895 from Barnes, Hengerer and Co. They all eventually were closed by the 1990s. John G. Sattler, a real estate tycoon, founded Sattler's Department Store at 998 Broadway (known as "good ol' 998" in its well-known 1955 commercial jingle) in 1889 and by 1950 was the largest department store in Buffalo. Other locations included stores in Amherst and West Seneca (Erie Co); all stores were closed in the late 1970s.

Sibley's downtown Syracuse store, 1988.

Dey Bros and Co, founded in Elmira in 1877, was opened in Syracuse in 1883 by Robert Dey and his brothers on South Salina St. It was one of the leading dry goods firms in Central New York and Syracuse's largest department store until its closure in the 1990s. In the 1970s Dey's merged with the Addis Co, primarily a bridal and women's shop, to become Addis and Dey's and was the primary place to shop for bridal gowns. Charles E. Chappell started his own dry goods business as Chappell and Tuttle in Baldwinsville (Onondaga Co) in 1887. The store expanded to Fulton in 1890 where it was initially known as C. E. Chappell Co. In 1895 Chappell further expanded into the larger Syracuse market with a partnership with Francis E. Bacon, opening a store in the 200 block of South Salina St. By then all the major department stores in Syracuse were within two blocks of each other. In 1910 Bacon relocated, but a new partner (William Dyer) bought out his interest in 1912, and the store was renamed Chappell-Dyer Co. Chappell bought out Dyer in 1924, and it became E. E. Chappell and Sons. Chappell's opened its first "suburban" store in the Eastwood section of Syracuse in 1951. Its first true suburban plaza store opened in the Northern Lights shopping plaza in 1956 in the Town of Salina. It closed its downtown store in 1974 and concentrated in malls and plazas in Central New York communities; its remaining stores were purchased by Bon-Ton in 1994.

In Troy, William H. Frear, who initially made his money running a dry goods store out of the Cannon building, constructed the marble building that bears his name on the corner of Fulton and 3d in 1897. The Frear building was converted into offices in the 1980s following its failure as a retail center in the 1970s. Troy was also home to Stanley's Department Store (1927–89) and Peerless and Denby's, which also maintained Albany locations. Founded in 1867 at 75 North Pearl St, B. Lodge and Co was the oldest department store in Albany and one of the oldest in the state. Binghamton was home to downtown stores Fowler Dick and Walker, which opened in 1881 and included a store in Auburn (Cayuga Co), Sisson Bros and Weldon, McLean's, and Drazen's.

The Hildreth Department Store opened in Southampton (Suffolk Co) in 1842, initially selling a variety of grocery items, housewares, cigars, hardware, and sewing supplies. In 2003 Hildreth's includes a "bath shop," children's section, furniture showroom, and a separate patio and clearance center. It is one of the few remaining family-owned early department stores. Swezey's, with five locations on Long Island, closed in 2003 after 110 years of business. Other Long Island stores included Hartman's, family-owned and operated Chwatsky's, and Mid-Island. Few, if any, of the department stores in the larger cities in the state remain open, their role largely replaced by suburban chain stores such as Kaufmans and Wal-Mart.

Fogelson, Robert M. *Downtown: Its Rise and Fall, 1880–1950* (New Haven, Conn: Yale Univ Press, 2001)

Hendrickson, Robert. *The Grand Emporiums: The Illustrated History of America's Great Department Stores* (New York: Stein & Day, 1979)

Hower, Ralph M. "Urban Retailing 100 Years Ago," *Bulletin of the Business Historical Society* 12 (Dec 1938): 91–101

Pasdermadjian, Hrant. *The Department Store: Its Origins, Evolution, and Economics* (London: Newman Books, 1954)

Ziskind, Minna P. "Citizenship, Consumerism, and Gender: A Study of District 65, 1945–1960" (PhD diss, Univ of Pennsylvania, 2001)

Amybeth Gregory and David B. Sicilia

Depew. Village (pop 16,629) in Cheektowaga and Lancaster (Erie Co). In March 1892 New York Central Railroad officials announced that the company would build new repair shops in Cheektowaga, along with a community for workers similar to Pullman, Ill, but one in which occupants would own their homes. Although the plan was not fully realized, the community was named for Chauncey M. Depew, president of the railroad. When, in 1894, it reached a population of 1,500, it incorporated as a village. By 1900 the repair shops employed 1,000, and nine other firms, all railroad or metals related, employed nearly 1,000 more. Depew's railroad heritage continues as the site of an Amtrak station serving Buffalo's eastern suburbs.

Vicki Weiss

Depew, Chauncey M(itchell) (*b* Peekskill, Westchester Co, 23 Apr 1834; *d* New York City, 5 Apr 1928). Railroad executive, attorney, and politician. As a boy Depew studied privately with a tutor and later was formally educated at Peekskill Military Academy (Westchester Co) and Yale University (1856), where he became an active member of the Republican Party. He read law and was admitted to the New York Bar in 1858. Depew served in the state assembly from 1862 to 1863, when he was elected as New York's secretary of state. He began a lengthy, successful railroad career in 1866 when he became attorney and lobbyist for Cornelius Vanderbilt's railroads, positions he held for 20 years. In 1871 he married Elise Hegeman and had one son. Depew became president of the New York Central Railroad in 1885, a job he held until 1899. Never closely involved in railroad operations, Depew instead used his skills as a likable and popular speaker to improve the public image of the Vanderbilt railroads. Nationally known for his avocation of public speaking, for several decades he spent three to five nights a week as an entertaining and informative after-dinner speaker, usually at the close of trade association meetings in New York City. Depew also contributed significantly as a writer and editor. He was a serious candidate for the Republican Party presidential nomination in 1888, but he withdrew due to western Republican opposition and turned down Pres Benjamin Harrison's offer to appoint him secretary of state. He served two terms in the US Senate from 1899 to 1911. Influential in Senate foreign affairs, Depew never had the impact on national politics that his prominence suggested. Until his death he practiced law, presided over the board of the New York Central, and served on the board of several other corporations.

Depew, Chauncey Mitchell. *My Memories of 80 Years* (New York: Scribner's, 1922)

Yeager, Willard Hayes. *Chauncey Mitchell Depew, the Orator* (Washington, DC: George Washington Univ Press, 1934)

E. Dale Odom

De Peyster [DE-POY-STER]. Town (pop 936) in W St. Lawrence Co. Settled in 1802, the town was formed in 1825 from De Kalb and Oswegatchie. The Rome, Watertown and Ogdensburg Railroad came through in 1854. Largely agricultural, De Peyster has some of the county's best farmland on its limestone uplands, along with extensive forested tracts, especially on wetlands. Black Lake forms much of its northern border. De Peyster is home to a growing Swartzentruber Amish community, which came from Holmes Co, Ohio, in 1974. The octagonal wood town hall is listed on the National Register of Historic Places.

Richard E. Mooers

Deposit. Town (pop 1,687) and village (pop 1,699) in SW Delaware Co. Settled in 1789, the town was formed in 1880 from Tompkins. The village, incorporated in 1811, is partly in Sanford (Broome Co). Situated on the West Branch of the Delaware River, Deposit became a lumbering and rafting center. Plentiful supplies of bluestone were quarried. The Erie Railroad (1848) brought industry, including creameries, acid factories, and a cut-glass factory; later products included sleds, snow shovels, buttons, and gloves. In the early 1900s summer boarders boosted the economy. Writer Zane Gray and illustrator N. C. Wyeth lived in Deposit and were connected with locally published *Outing* magazine (1903–9). Deposit lost business when the Cannonsville Reservoir (1966) inundated nearby farms and hamlets. Lumbering and quarrying continue in the early 21st century. Other employers include Norbord Industries (1990; medium density fiberboard [MDF] panels), Deposit Computer Services (1985), and Courier Printing. MDF panels were first manufactured at Cel-O-Tex Corp (now Norbord) in 1966. The annual Lumberjack Festival celebrates the town's history.

Dorothy Kubik

Dering Harbor. Village (pop 13) in Shelter Island (Suffolk Co). The Manhanset House, a four-story, 300-room resort hotel, opened in 1874. After it burned in 1910, the Island Realty Co was formed and developed the hotel's environs. The village incorporated in 1916 to ensure that water and other services would be continued. The 1890 Manhanset House Chapel was moved to the village center in 1924 and is now a museum. The 200-acre (81 ha) village consists of 33 houses, which are mostly second homes, and a village hall.

Natalie A. Naylor

DeRuyter [DE-RIDE-ER]. Town (pop 1,532) and village (pop 531) in SW Madison Co. Settled in 1793, the town was formed from Cazenovia in 1798. The village was incorporated in 1833. In 1860 DeRuyter had two large tanneries, an oil mill, a furnace, and a cabinet factory. It was served by the Utica, Ithaca and Elmira Railroad (1877; later Lehigh Valley Railroad). DeRuyter Reservoir (1863) was created as an Erie Canal feeder. For many years the village provided the winter quarters for the Sig. Sautelle Circus, which traveled by wagons, canalboats, and railroad cars. DeRuyter Textile, the town's only factory, closed in 2003. Several dairy farms still operate, but most residents commute to Syracuse or Cortland. The DeRuyter Fair (1908) and its opening day event, the Tromptown Runs, are annual events.

William F. Helmer

DeSapio, Carmine (Gerard) (*b* New York City, 10 Dec 1908; *d* New York City, 27 July 2004). Political leader. DeSapio, like Fiorello La Guardia, was a product of the dynamic community of Italian immigrants that dominated the cultural and political life of Greenwich Village at the end of the 19th century and the beginning of the 20th century. Elected chair of the New York County Democratic Committee in 1949, the charismatic DeSapio struggled to revive the influence of Tammany Hall. He played a key role in the elections of Mayor Robert F. Wagner Jr in 1953 and of Gov W. Averell Harriman in 1954, and served as secretary of state during Harriman's term as governor. With Nelson A. Rockefeller's defeat of Harriman in 1958, DeSapio's influence began to wane. A reform faction organized by Wagner, Eleanor Roosevelt, and Herbert H. Lehman ousted DeSapio from his post as county chairman in 1961. He mounted comeback campaigns for district leadership in 1963 and 1965 but was defeated in primary elections in each case by Ed Koch. By the middle of the decade, the new leaders of the city's Democrats were happy to see the last vestiges of the Tammany phenomenon slip into irreversible obscurity. DeSapio was convicted of conspiring to bribe former city water commissioner J. L. Marcus in December 1969 and was released from federal prison three years later after completing his sentence. For the remainder of his life DeSapio avoided politics.

Moscow, Warren. *Last of the Big Time Bosses* (New York: Stein & Day, 1971)

William S. Helmer

de tawl [*de taal*]. The descendants of the original settlers of New Netherland continued to speak the Dutch language for many generations after the English takeover. They referred to their language as *de tawl*, which is a quasi-phonetic rendering of Dutch *de taal* (the language). Because *de tawl* was a minority language, its speakers were under intense pressure to conform to the patterns of English, the majority language, especially in vocabulary acquisition. An example of this is evident in a legal certificate issued in 1716 stating that the undersigned had been present in the court at Albany when a case was tried: "Deese sertiefieseeren dat wy . . . geweest syn int coert huis der stat Albany sijnde in open coert waer een actie getryt wiert. . ." Besides the English loanwords for "certify" and "court," the verb "to try" was also restructured in the form of a Dutch past participle, *getryt*. In addition to numerous English loanwords, especially those associated with English cultural institutions, *de tawl* was characterized by divergent forms of phonology, morphology, and syntax, which developed from the long separation from the Netherlands. Such divergent forms spread because of the lack of reinforcement of standardizing developments occurring in the Netherlands. By the end of the 18th century, *de tawl* had diverged so much from the Dutch of the homeland that it was practically a different language. As *de tawl* became increasingly relegated to use in the home during the 18th century and into the 19th century in isolated, rural areas, contact with the outside world gradually became associated with English, the common language of the people who were shaping the future of this new country called America. Today remnants of *de tawl* survive in a handful of words and phrases used mostly by speakers of American English in the Hudson, Mohawk, and Schoharie Valleys, and in Bergen Co, NJ. Old-timers especially will be immediately familiar with words such as "winklehawk," a right-angle tear in a garment, derived from the Dutch *winkelhaak*, a carpenter's square.

Bachman, Van Cleef. "What Is Low Dutch?" *de Halve Maen* 57 (Fall 1983): 14–17, 23–24

Buccini, Anthony F. "The Dialectal Origins of New Netherland Dutch." In *The Berkeley Conference on Dutch Linguistics*, ed. Thomas F. Shannon and John Snapper (Lanham, Md: Univ Press of America, 1995)

Gehring, Charles T. "The Dutch Language in Colonial New York: An Investigation of a Language in Decline and Its Relationship to Social Change" (PhD diss, Indiana Univ, 1973)

Charles T. Gehring

Dett, R(obert) Nathaniel (*b* Drummondville [now Niagara Falls, Ont], 11 Oct 1882; *d* Battle Creek, Mich, 2 Oct 1943). Musician and composer. Dett moved with his family to Buffalo at age 11. He studied at the Oliver Willis Halstead Conservatory in Lockport (Niagara Co) and graduated from Oberlin College in Ohio in 1908, later studying at many different conservatories and colleges, including a stint with Nadia Boulanger in Paris in 1929. Dett taught at several southern colleges, was director of music at Hampton Institute (1913–31) in Virginia, and was president of the National Association of Negro Musicians (1924–26). He moved to Rochester in 1932 and received an honorary master's degree from the Eastman School of Music in Rochester. The leading African American classical composer of his generation, Dett's works include five piano suites such as *In the Bottoms* (1913), numerous settings of Negro spirituals, and several large-scale choral works.

Simpson, Anne Key. *Follow Me: The Life and Music of R. Nathaniel Dett* (Metuchen, NJ: Scarecrow Press, 1993)

Vincent Lenti

developmental disabilities. See MENTAL RETARDATION AND DEVELOPMENTAL DISABILITIES.

De Vries, David Pietersz (*b* La Rochelle, France, ?1592; *bur* Hoorn, Netherlands, 13 Sept 1655). Captain and author. Although born in La Rochelle, where his father had settled in 1584, De Vries, who lived in Holland after age 4, came from an old Hoorn family. From 1618 to 1638 De Vries made seven voyages, one each to the Mediterranean, Newfoundland, La Rochelle, and the East Indies, and three to America. The voyages are described in his book, *Short Historical and Journal-Notes of Various Voyages Performed in the Four Quarters of the Globe*, published in Alkmaar, Netherlands, in 1655. In 1630 De Vries became a partner in a patroonship called Swanendael, which was established on the west side of Delaware Bay in 1631. The small settlement was destroyed by Indians. In 1632 De Vries made his first trip to New Netherland, where he visited the site of the ill-fated colony's ruins before sailing to New Amsterdam. The rights to Swanendael were sold back to the West India Co soon afterward. After falling out with the partners on his return to Holland in 1634, he made a second voyage to the Americas from 1634 to 1636. According to his journal it was during this trip, on 13 Aug 1636, that he applied to director Wouter van Twiller, who had the authority to grant him the patroonship of Staten Island. From 1638 to 1643 De Vries, financially supported by Amsterdam merchants, tried to make this venture a success. Due to Kieft's War, the settlement on Staten Island was destroyed in 1641 by the Raritan Indians. De Vries also founded a plantation called Vriessendael on the west side of the Hudson River, some distance north of Pavonia [now Jersey City, NJ]. After the massacre of the Indians at Pavonia by the Dutch in February 1643 (an action taken against De Vries's advice), Vriessendael was attacked as part of the general retaliation by the Indians. De Vries, blaming Kieft for his misfortunes, returned to Hoorn in 1644 a disappointed man. His book, published 11 years later, contains several important details on the early history of New Netherland.

De Vries, David Pietersz. *Korte historiael ende journaels aenteykeninge van verscheyden voyagiens in de vier deelen des wereldts-ronde, als Europa, Africa, Asia, ende Amerika gedaen*. Ed. H. T. Colenbrander. Werken Linschoten-Vereeniging 3. The Hague: Martinus Nijhoff, 1911)

Jacobs, Jaap. *Een zegenrijk gewest: Nieuw-Nederland in de zeventiende eeuw* (Amsterdam: Prometheus/Bert Bakker, 1999)

Jameson, J. Franklin, ed. "From the *Korte historiael ende journaels aenteyckeninge*, by David Pietersz de Vries, 1633–1643 (1655)." In *Narratives of New Netherland, 1609–1664* (1909; repr New York: Barnes & Noble, 1967)

McKew Parr, Charles. *The Voyages of David de Vries, Navigator and Adventurer* (New York: Crowell, 1969)

Murphy, Henry C., trans. and ed. *David Pietersz de Vries. Voyages from Holland to America, A.D. 1632 to 1644* (New York, 1857)

Jaap Jacobs

Dewey, John (*b* Burlington, Vt, 20 Oct 1859; *d* New York City, 1 June 1952). Philosopher. After receiving his PhD from Johns Hopkins University (1884), Dewey taught philosophy at the University of Michigan (1884–88, 1889–94), the University of Minnesota (1888–89), and the University of Chicago (1894–1904). He moved to the faculty of Columbia University in 1904, where he would remain for the rest of his career. Dewey was a reformer and innovator in primary and secondary education. His ideal of progressive education was to instill good habits, not to drill facts. He founded the Laboratory School at the University of Chicago in 1896 to test, refine, and promote his educational theories and continued this work at Columbia. Dewey's optimism about the possibility of human progress characterized his entire life and work. He encouraged exploiting experience to produce change and fostering intelligence to ensure that the change would be for the better. His philosophy, generally known as instrumentalism, claimed that reason can always shape the data of experience into a tool to try to achieve a human end.

Dewey was one of the foremost liberal thinkers of his time and a leader in numerous progressive causes. His opposition to the Red Scare after World War I led him to support the founding of the New School for Social Research (1919) and the American Civil Liberties Union (1920). Long interested in socialism, he was an opponent of communism, and in 1937 he chaired a commission that investigated and defended Leon

Trotsky's accusations against Joseph Stalin's tyranny in the Soviet Union. Dewey wrote 40 books and over 700 articles. Among the best known are *Democracy and Education* (1916), *Experience and Nature* (1925), and *The Quest for Certainty* (1929). He retired from Columbia in 1930 but continued to teach as emeritus professor until 1939 and to write and lecture until just before his death.

Ryan, Alan. *John Dewey and the High Tide of American Liberalism* (New York: Norton, 1995)
Westbrook, Robert B. *John Dewey and American Democracy* (Ithaca: Cornell Univ Press, 1991)

Dewey, Melvil(le Louis Kossuth) (*b* Adams Center, Jefferson Co, 10 Dec 1851; *d* Lake Placid, Fla, 26 Dec 1931). Librarian and educator. Raised in Adams Center and Oneida (Madison Co), where he attended a Baptist seminary, Dewey graduated from Amherst College in Massachusetts in 1874. At Amherst Dewey became interested in more efficient communication through shorthand, simplified spelling, and metric measurements. In May 1873 he presented the Amherst College Library Committee with a decimal scheme for structuring collections of books. After graduating in 1874, Dewey became Amherst College's assistant librarian, managing and reorganizing the Amherst library until 1876. In 1876 he published *A Classification and Subject Index for Cataloging and Arranging Books and Pamphlets in a Library,* the Dewey Decimal Classification, which became widely adopted. After moving to Boston he organized the 6 Oct 1876 conference that initiated the American Library Association (ALA) and also helped found the Spelling Reform Association and the Metric Bureau that same year. Founder of the *Library Journal* in 1876, Dewey served as editor until 1881.

Dewey was named chief librarian of Columbia College in New York City in 1883. In an era when few vocational opportunities were open to women, Dewey hired seven women to library positions. He started the nation's first library school, the School of Library Economy at Columbia College, in 1887; the inaugural class of 20 students included 17 women. The school was transferred to Albany as the New York State Library School in 1889 after Dewey was appointed state librarian as well as secretary to the Board of Regents. While secretary, Dewey instituted standards for secondary and higher curricula, entrance examinations for medical students, and the examination and licensing of teachers. As state librarian he organized the New York Library Association and set up programs in the hope of establishing a continuing education system based on public libraries. Under Dewey's presidency in 1893, the ALA presentation at the Chicago World's Fair included a model library that became a bibliographic guide and forerunner of such publications as *Booklist.*

He and his wife Annie opened the Lake Placid Club, a private resort with a paid membership, in 1894. He left his position as Board of Regents secretary in 1900. Public knowledge of the restrictive nature of his club—African Americans, Jews, and other ethnic minorities were excluded as members—and Dewey's inappropriate behavior toward several women librarians forced Dewey to resign as state librarian in 1905. His wife died in 1922, and he married Emily Beal in 1924. In 1927 he opened a resort in Florida, where he died in 1931.

See also LIBRARIES.

Stevenson, Gordon, and Judith Kramer, eds. *Melvil Dewey: The Man and the Classification* (Albany: Forest Press, 1983)
Wiegand, Wayne. *Irrepressible Reformer: A Biography of Melvil Dewey* (Chicago: American Library Association, 1996)

Pamela Cooper

Dewey, Thomas E(dmund) (*b* Owosso, Mich, 24 Mar 1902; *d* Bal Harbour, Fla, 16 Mar 1971). Governor and presidential candidate. Raised in rural Michigan where his father was a postmaster, Dewey worked his way through the University of Michigan, graduating in 1923. He moved to New York City that same year to pursue an opera singing career under the tutelage of Percy Rector Stephens, the famous singing coach. But lacking sufficient talent, Dewey enrolled in Columbia Law School instead, earning his LLB in 1925.

PROSECUTOR

Dewey achieved national prominence during the 1930s when, as a prosecutor, he presided over a series of sensational organized crime trials in New York City. As an assistant US attorney for the Southern District of New York (1931–33), Dewey convicted Mafia boss Waxy Gordon on 1 Dec 1933 for racketeering. Building on this success, on 1 July 1935 Dewey was appointed by Democratic governor Herbert H. Lehman as a New York State special prosecutor (1935–37). Charged with breaking organized crime's hold over New York City, for the next two years Dewey convicted 72 of the 73 persons he brought to trial, including on 7 June 1936 the notorious Charles "Lucky" Luciano for prostitution and extortion. By 1937 Dewey's exploits against the underworld transformed him into a national figure, which Dewey parlayed into his election as Manhattan district attorney (1937–41). Capitalizing on his stardom Dewey sought the New York State governorship in 1938 but lost by a mere 64,000 votes. In 1940 he also made an unsuccessful bid, at just 38 years of age, for the presidential nomination at the Republican National Convention. With Dewey's prosecutorial record, most New Yorkers saw his eventual election as governor preordained, and on 3 Nov 1942 Dewey was elected to that office by a near record margin of more than 647,000 votes. He would hold the governor's chair for three consecutive terms (1942–54).

GOVERNOR

As governor, Dewey was the seminal figure in the Republican Party's postwar embrace of liberal republicanism. In the face of the New Deal's tremendous popularity, Dewey abandoned the party's traditional antistatism, moving it toward a more politically viable progressive conservatism. In Albany Dewey not only continued the social welfare policies initiated by his Democratic predecessors but also strengthened these policies for a postwar age. Yet these programs appealed to conservatives because Dewey grounded them in a sound fiscal basis. As a result Dewey's fiscally responsible liberalism made him tremendously popular with New York State voters. Nationally Dewey's liberal republicanism greatly influenced Presidents Dwight D. Eisenhower and Richard M. Nixon (Dewey served as a close political mentor to both men). Liberal republicanism remained the party's dominant political orientation until the election of Ronald Reagan as president in 1980. Dewey modernized

Gov Thomas E. Dewey with his family and dog at home in the governor's mansion.

many traditional Democratic programs during his tenure as governor, such as doubling state aid to localities for primary and secondary education, and tripling state aid to the poor and to mental health programs; he also expanded workers' compensation and unemployment insurance. As governor Dewey pioneered whole new policies for New York State. On 12 Mar 1945 he signed into law the Ives-Quinn bill, which outlawed racial and religious discrimination in employment, making New York the first state in the nation to have such legislation. In 1946 Dewey authorized the construction of a massive limited-access state highway system that became the New York State Thruway, renamed in 1964 in honor of the governor. On 4 Apr 1948 Dewey signed a law creating the State University of New York (SUNY) system. New York was the last state to have a public university, but in 2002 SUNY was the largest state university system in the United States.

Presidential Candidate

Dewey's record of success in New York State, however, did not extend nationally. He lost his party's presidential nominee bid twice (1944, 1948). Dewey appeared aloof to many in public. His popularity was built instead on his analytical mind. His public persona led Alice Roosevelt Longworth to describe him as the little man on a wedding cake. In his 1944 bid for the presidency against Franklin D. Roosevelt, Dewey at first resisted his party's nomination. He believed it was impossible to defeat Roosevelt with the nation engaged in global war. Dewey relented, however, when he feared that his refusal to run would compromise his chances of securing the 1948 nomination. On 8 Nov 1944 Pres Roosevelt won, as Dewey anticipated.

Expectations in 1948 were different, and early opinion polls assured a crushing Dewey victory. On 24 June 1948, at the Republican National Convention, Dewey captured the nomination on the third ballot. Once nominated, the governor and his advisors assumed that the election was already won because of a large lead in the polls and mistakenly adopted a campaign strategy that stressed broad political themes rather than specific policy recommendations. This approach, however, evidently led many Americans to feel that the governor was avoiding the issues. In response, Pres Harry S. Truman ran an aggressive and negative campaign. On 2 Nov 1948 the president won by a narrow margin in perhaps the greatest political upset in American history.

After 1948

Dewey slowly receded from the state and national spotlight after 1948. Although he wanted to retire from politics by 1950, state and national Republicans, fearful of the party losing its most prominent figure, persuaded Dewey to seek another term as governor. In 1950 Dewey was elected to a third and final gubernatorial term. At the 1952 Republican National Convention, Dewey played a critical role in securing the presidential and vice presidential nominations for Dwight D. Eisenhower and Richard M. Nixon. On 7 Sept 1954 Dewey announced his decision to retire from public life at the end of his gubernatorial term for a corporate law practice in New York City. He became a partner at Dewey Ballentine, where he practiced law from 1955 until his death. He spent much of his free time in his summer home and farm at Pawling (Dutchess Co). When Pres Nixon in 1968 offered Dewey the federal positions of chief justice of the Supreme Court or the secretary of state, the former governor declined. A father of liberal republicanism, Dewey was a vital figure in the postwar resurgence of the Republican Party.

See also Community colleges; New York State Thruway; State University of New York (SUNY).

Beyer, Barry K. *Thomas E. Dewey, 1937–1947: A Study in Political Leadership* (New York: Garland, 1979)
Smith, Richard Norton. *Thomas E. Dewey and His Times* (New York: Simon & Schuster, 1982)
Stolberg, Mary M. *Fighting Organized Crime: Politics, Justice, and the Legacy of Thomas E. Dewey* (Boston: Northeastern Univ Press, 1995)

Tod M. Ottman

DeWitt. Town (pop 24,071) in E central Onondaga Co. The first settler arrived in 1789, and the town was formed from Manlius in 1835. The Jamesville Iron and Woolen Factory (1809) was the first heavy industry; gypsum was quarried beginning in 1811–12, and water lime (cement) was produced beginning in 1818–19. In the early 21st century, the town's hilly southern section is the site of a 3,000-acre (1,214 ha) limestone quarry. In DeWitt's southwest corner a meromictic lake, in which bottom and surface waters do not mix, is the centerpiece of Clark Reservation State Park. The central part of town is a residential suburb, beginning in the 1920s, with shopping centers built after World War II. On the industrialized northern plain is CSX Railroad's Intermodal Rail Center, begun in 1872 as a division point and repair yard of the New York Central Railroad, along with such corporate offices as Bristol-Myers Squibb, Carrier, Inficon, and New Process Gear. Northern DeWitt is also the site of Syracuse Hancock International Airport (1949) and some crop farms and nurseries along with the Thruway (1954).

Barbara S. Rivette

DeWitt, Simeon (*b* Wawarsing, Ulster Co, 25 Dec 1756; *d* Ithaca, 3 Dec 1834). Surveyor and cartographer. DeWitt was the sixth of Dr Andries DeWitt and Jannetje Vernooy's 14 children. He received his early education from a local minister, went on to Queen's College (now Rutgers University) in New Brunswick, NJ, and was awarded a BA in 1776 and an MA in 1788. He enlisted in the Continental army in 1777 and was present at Gen John Burgoyne's surrender later that year. Trained in surveying by his uncle, Brig Gen James Clinton, DeWitt was appointed assistant to the army's geographer, Col Robert Erskine in June 1778. After Erskine's death, DeWitt became geographer to the United States in December 1780. Erskine, DeWitt, and a handful of surveyors produced over 250 sketches and maps during the Revolutionary War.

On 13 May 1784 DeWitt was appointed surveyor-general of New York State, a post he held until his death. Required by law to maintain his office in Albany, DeWitt moved there after his appointment and later mapped the city in 1794. Directed by the commissioners of the Land Office, he was authorized to determine land boundaries and to survey, map, and sell state lands. DeWitt was involved in many of the negotiations and treaties that New York State made with the Iroquois for their territory. During 1786–87 he served as a New York–Pennsylvania boundary commissioner. From 1789 to 1791 he directed the surveying of the New Military Tract in Central New York, compiling the data to create a map copyrighted in 1793. This sheet was redrawn and incorporated in his six-sheet 1802 New York State map, which was presented to the governors of all the other states, and a smaller 1804 version. These maps provided examples in their elegant and spare symbolization, as well as the techniques employed in their creation, for other US mapmakers. They provided templates for a new American school of cartography, which differed from European antecedents. After 1802 he became more involved with overseeing the state's developing roads and canals. DeWitt was one of three commissioners who designed the gridiron street pattern for the expansion of New York City in 1807 and an original Erie Canal commissioner (1810–15), directing surveys from 1808. He also supervised the production of David H. Burr's 1829 *New York State Atlas.*

DeWitt had a lifelong commitment to education and science, with interests in geography, meteorology, astronomy, and agronomy. Serving as a regent of the University of the State of New York from 1798 until his death, he became vice chancellor in 1817 and chancellor in 1829. A member of the American Philosophical Society from 1790, he authored "Observations on the Eclipse of the Sun, June 16, 1806, at Albany." In 1791 he was a founding member, and in 1813 became president, of the Society for the Promotion of Agriculture, Arts and Manufactures, incorporated in 1793, the precursor of the Albany Institute. He founded and planned the development of Ithaca and stayed there when his duties permitted, managing his properties through several agents. DeWitt married three times: Elizabeth Lynott (*b* 3 Jan 1767; *d* 13 Dec 1793) in 1789; Jane Varick Hardenbergh (*b* 18 May 1760; *d* 10 Apr 1808) in 1799, by whom he had two children; and Susan Linn (*b* 30 Oct 1778; *d* 5 May 1824) in 1810, with whom he had four children.

See also Cartography and mapping.

Heidt, William, Jr. *Simeon DeWitt: Founder of Ithaca* (Ithaca: DeWitt Historical Society of Tompkins County, 1968)
Mano, Jo Margaret. "Unmapping the Iroquois: New York State Cartography, 1792–1845." In *The Oneida Indian Journey,* ed. Laurence M. Hauptman and L. Gordon McLester III (Madison: Univ of Wisconsin Press, 1999)
Ristow, Walter W. "Simeon DeWitt, Pioneer Cartographer." In *American Maps and Mapmakers* (Detroit: Wayne State Univ Press, 1985)

Jo Margaret Mano

DeWitt Clinton. The first locomotive owned by and operated on a New York State railroad. In 1831 Mohawk and Hudson Railroad, then under construction between Albany and Schenectady, contracted with West Point Foundry in New York City to build the 6,200 lb (2,812 kg) engine for $3,200. DeWitt Clinton was designed to burn anthracite coal and to operate at 30 mph (48 kph), pulling three to five cars on level track. Copper tubes 6 feet (1.8 m) long by 2.5 inches (6.35 cm) in diameter passed heat from the firebox through the boiler's water, creating steam that drove two inclined cylinders, each 5.5 inches (13.97 cm) in diameter with a stroke of 16 inches

The First Railroad Train on the Mohawk and Hudson Road, Edward Lamson Henry, 1892–93.

(40.6 cm). Connecting rods from the cylinders transferred power to four iron-rimmed wooden drive wheels, supported by wrought-iron spokes connected to cast-iron hubs. Tests in 1831 revealed problems, including DeWitt Clinton's inability to burn coal. Converted to burn wood and otherwise patched up, the locomotive made its first official run 9 Aug 1831 and continued in service that year. Following more problems in 1832, a new boiler was installed and other repairs performed, but chief engineer John B. Jervis had lost faith in the engine. DeWitt Clinton was withdrawn from use at the end of 1833 and disposed of in April 1835.

Larkin, F. Daniel. *Pioneer American Railroads: The Mohawk and Hudson and the Saratoga and Schenectady* (Fleischmanns, NY: Purple Mountain Press, 1995)

F. Daniel Larkin

Dexter. Village (pop 1,120) in Brownville (Jefferson Co). Dexter, settled in 1811 as Fish Island, was the site of little used locks of the Black River Navigation Co (1810). It acquired a post office in 1838. A woolen factory opened in 1837, and Dexter, which incorporated in 1855, was a textile mill village until the 1880s. At that time the dams were rebuilt and the textile mills were replaced by paper mills: the Dexter Sulphite Pulp and Paper Co (1887–late 1950s) and the Frontenac Paper Co (1889–1949). In 1975 the empty sulfite mill was converted for use by smaller companies such as the Venus Manufacturing Corp (1987; swimwear). Sportfishing was extremely popular until snagging was prohibited in the Black River in 1990; although reduced, fishing remains important.

Laura Lynne Scharer

Deyo [née Halstead], **(Julia) Amanda** (*b* Clinton, Dutchess Co, 24 Oct 1838; *d* Glen Cove, Nassau Co, 1 Nov 1917). Minister and peace activist. Halstead was educated in Clinton and attended the Poughkeepsie Female Collegiate Institute. After graduating in 1855 she taught school in Clinton, where she met Charles Deyo and married 24 Oct 1857. They lived in Lloyd (Ulster Co) and Pleasant Valley (Dutchess Co) before returning to Clinton by the mid-1860s. Raised a Quaker, Deyo was a strong opponent of war and in 1871 became the secretary of the Dutchess County Peace Society, an organization affiliated with the Universal Peace Union. Deyo became an ordained Universalist minister in September 1885. She held the pastorate at Poughkeepsie's Universalist Church in 1886 and at the Universalist Church in Oxford (Chenango Co) in 1888, where she organized the Oxford Peace Society. In June 1889 Deyo was a representative at the Universalist Peace Conference in Paris. Upon her return she continued to speak and preach on issues of peace, temperance, women and minority rights, and the use of arbitration in dispute resolution. Deyo retired from the ministry in 1903 and moved throughout New York State, living in Glen Cove, Highland (Ulster Co), and a Shaker community in New Lebanon (Columbia Co). She returned to Glen Cove in 1906.

McDermott, William P. "The Rev. Amanda Halstead Deyo (1838–1917): A Chrononarrative of a Preacher of Peace," *Hudson Valley Regional Review* 8 (Mar 1991): 1–21

Kerry Delaney

dialects. See SPEECH AND DIALECTS.

Diamond, David (*b* Rochester, 9 July 1915). Composer. Diamond studied at the Cleveland Institute of Music (1927–29), with Bernard Rogers at the Eastman School of Music (1930–34), and with Roger Sessions at the New Music and Dalcroze Institute in New York City (1934–36). He spent two summers (1937–38) at the American Conservatory in Fontainebleau, France and studied with Nadia Boulanger. Diamond taught composition at the Metropolitan Music School in New York City (1950) before being appointed Fulbright professor at the University of Rome (1951–52). He then settled in Florence, returning in 1961 and 1963 to teach as the Slee professor at the University of Buffalo, returning permanently to the United States in 1965. He was professor of composition at the Manhattan School of Music (1967–68), visiting professor at the University of Colorado (1970), and composer-in-residence at the American Academy in Rome (1971–72). Diamond also taught at the Juilliard School of Music in New York City (1973–97). He maintains a residence in Rochester. Among Diamond's many awards are three Guggenheim Memorial Grants and the Paderewski Prize. A prolific composer, he has written music for ballet, film, radio, opera, and music comedy, as well as symphonies, concertos, vocal and choral works, song cycles, piano works, and chamber music, including string quartets. A master of orchestration, he has generally adhered to classical forms and procedures. One of his notable works is *Rounds for String Orchestra* (1944).

Kimberling, Victoria J. *David Diamond: A Bio-Bibliography* (Metuchen, NJ: Scarecrow Press, 1987)

Vincent Lenti

Diamond, Legs [Jack] (*b* Philadelphia, 1896; *d* Albany, 17 Dec 1931). Gangster and bootlegger. The young Jack Diamond was a petty thief who earned the nickname Legs for his ability to outrun pursuing police. Moving to Brooklyn after the death of his mother in 1913, he soon became involved in gang activities. Drafted into the army in 1918, he deserted and subsequently served time in the disciplinary barracks at Leavenworth, Kans, in 1919–20. He then began his Prohibition bootlegging career by hijacking illegal shipments of beer and liquor from Canada into the United States. Diamond also dealt in drugs and stolen jewels. Under the tutelage of crime lords "Little Augie" Orgen and Arnold Rothstein, he rose through the ranks of the New York City mob. He started a Manhattan speakeasy, the Hotsy Totsy Club, and had enemies killed in its backrooms. In 1924 Diamond was the target of a gangland shooting; several other attempts followed, earning him a reputation as the "clay pigeon of the underworld." To avoid such attacks he relocated to the Catskill Mountain hamlet of Acra (Greene Co) in 1930, taking with him both his wife, Alice, and his mistress, the showgirl Kiki Roberts. Nevertheless, he was eventually shot and killed in a hideaway in the Center Square neighborhood of Albany, perhaps on orders from his longtime rival Dutch Schultz. Diamond's violent and flamboyant life was the basis of Budd Boetticher's film *The Rise and Fall of Legs Diamond* (1960) and William Kennedy's novel *Legs* (1975).

Levine, Gary. *Jack "Legs" Diamond: Anatomy of a Gangster* (Fleischmanns, NY: Purple Mountain Press, 1995)

Martin Stahl

Diana. Town (pop 1,661) in NE Lewis Co. Settled before 1818, the town was formed from Watson in 1830. It was named for the Greek goddess of the hunt by Joseph Bonaparte, former king of Naples and Spain; he arrived in 1828 and built a cabin on the shore of what became known as Lake Bonaparte. Poor soil hinders farming, but important industries have included forest products, iron making, and mining, especially at the Carbola Chemical Co mine (1906; talc), operated in 2003 by Suzorite Mineral Products. The 1941 expansion of Pine Camp (now Fort Drum) displaced many residents. Work is found in Diana in the talc mine and wood products industries and in St. Lawrence Co at paper mills and mining operations. The Rose Grotto, a geological wonder composed of calcite and rhombohedron crystal specimens, was found in Diana caverns in 1906; a part of it is in the collection of the New York State Museum. Lake Bonaparte is the location of many private camps.

Arthur Einhorn

Dickinson. Town (pop 5,335) in Broome Co. The Iroquois settlement of Otsiningo was the site of a 1756 conference at which Sir William Johnson's Iroquois allies urged peace upon the Delaware and Shawnee; it was destroyed *ca* 1779. The site of Dickinson was settled by European Americans around 1786. The town was formed from Binghamton when that town was divided because of the city's expansion in 1890. Suburban development accelerated around 1912 with the opening of Prospect Terrace. Poles and Slovaks formed communities and built churches. Dickinson has been home to Broome Community College (1946) since 1956 and to Cutler Botanic Gardens. The annual Otsiningo Powwow (1976) is held in June at Otsiningo County Park.

Charles J. Browne

Dickinson. Town (pop 739) in W Franklin Co. Settled in 1810, principally by people from Vermont, the town was formed from Harrison [now Malone] in 1808. Within the present bounds of Dickinson the first settlement was in 1810. The railroad came through in 1883, primarily to facilitate lumbering. In addition to lumbering, maple sugaring, and starch factories, there was a tannery, a "rossing" (de-barking) mill, and, briefly from 1911, a mica factory, all at St. Regis Falls.

Thomas W. Perrin

Dickinson, Daniel S(tevens) (*b* Goshen, Conn, 11 Sept 1800; *d* New York City, 12 Apr 1866). US senator. Nicknamed Scripture Dick because of his penchant for biblical quotations, Dickinson studied law and practiced in Guilford (Chenango Co) before moving to Binghamton in 1831. A controversial prosouthern Democrat and Hunker leader, he served as a state senator (1837–41) and played a key role in stimulating economic development after the panic of 1837, especially by chartering state banks and constructing the Erie Railroad through Binghamton. Following one term as lieutenant governor (1842–44), Dickinson became a US senator (1844–51) and gained national prominence by helping forge the Compromise of 1850. Denied reappointment, he spent the next decade at the center of party factionalism over issues connected to slavery's expansion. Dickinson led the Hards, a faction who opposed compromising with antislavery Democrats. Dickinson placed nation over partisanship during the Civil War, supported Pres Abraham Lincoln's administration, and became New York State's attorney general in 1861 on the pro-war People's ticket. After failing to gain the vice presidential nomination at the 1864 Union convention, he received the post of US district attorney for New York State's Southern District, which Dickinson held until his death.

Alexander, DeAlva Stanwood. *A Political History of the State of New York*, 4 vols (1906; repr Port Washington, NY: I. J. Friedman, 1969)
Dickinson, John R., ed. *The Speeches, Correspondence, Etc. of the Late Daniel S. Dickinson of New York*, 2 vols (New York: Putnam's, 1867)

Jerome Mushkat

DiFranco, Ani (*b* Buffalo, 23 Sept 1970). Singer-songwriter. Ani DiFranco was exposed to folk music at an early age by musicians who stayed with her family when performing in Buffalo. She learned acoustic guitar at age 9, began writing autobiographical songs at 14, and graduated from Buffalo's Visual and Performing Arts High School two years later. Enthusiastic word of mouth led to concerts in coffeehouses and colleges throughout the Northeast. In 1989 DiFranco relocated temporarily to New York City, where she attended the New School for Social Research. The following year she recorded a self-titled and self-released debut album, thereafter refusing offers from major labels and choosing to focus on live performance instead of radio or video airplay to build an audience. Early albums in a "punk folk" style were sparsely produced solo undertakings. Lesbians and bisexual women connected with her unflinching exploration of sexuality. Touring drummer Andy Stochansky and several guests appeared on *Out of Range* (1994) and other releases leading up to the harder-edged *Dilate* (1996). The 1997 live album *Living in Clip* documents the humor, outspoken politics, and onstage intimacy of DiFranco's performances in ever larger venues. Over the next several years, with a five-piece band, she further explored the strains of funk, jazz, and spoken-word poetry that had always informed her music. By 2002 she had produced 13 albums, a video documentary, 2 collaborations with singer and storyteller Utah Phillips, and several other projects. In 1999 DiFranco's Righteous Babe Records began releasing albums by an eclectic roster of other artists. In 2002 the label's Righteous Babe Foundation supported grassroots cultural and political endeavors nationwide. DiFranco and her company have supported the preservation of historic buildings in Buffalo and have worked to provide resources for underfunded public school art programs in the city.

"How a Righteous Babe Saved Her Hometown: Folk Singer's Success Lifts Buffalo, Too," *New York Times*, 16 Feb 1998
Hutchinson, Lydia. "Ani DiFranco: The Little Folksinger," *Performing Songwriter*, June 1999

Ronald Ehmke

DiMaggio, Joe [Joseph Paul] (*b* Martinez, Calif, 25 Nov 1914; *d* Hollywood, Fla, 8 Mar 1999). Professional baseball player. Raised in San Francisco, Joe DiMaggio signed with the minor league San Francisco Seals in 1932. Four years later he debuted in the majors with the New York Yankees. DiMaggio's entire career (1936–42, 1946–51) was spent with the team, interrupted only by military service during World War II. In 1941 Joltin' Joe set a remarkable baseball record by hitting safely in 56 consecutive games. DiMaggio won American League Most Valuable Player honors three times (1939, 1941, 1947). During his tenure the Yankees won 10 pennants and 9 World Series championships. A player of unmatched grace and elegance, DiMaggio was elected to the Baseball Hall of Fame in 1955. A short-lived marriage to Marilyn Monroe (1954) enhanced DiMaggio's star status, which also served him well as an advertising spokesman. Though protective of his privacy, DiMaggio remained a beloved public figure for half a century after ending his baseball career.

Pepe, Phil. *The Yankees: An Authorized History of the New York Yankees*, 3d ed. (Dallas: Taylor Publishing, 1998)
Whittingham, Richard, ed. *The Di Maggio Albums: Selections from Public and Private Collections Celebrating the Baseball Career of Joe Di Maggio*, 2 vols (New York: Putnam's, 1989)

diners. Originally conceived as a simple lunch cart in Providence, RI, in 1872, diners evolved into portable sit-down restaurants by the early 1900s. New York State is credited with significant milestones in the history, architecture, and development of the American diner. Westchester Co became a center of diner manufacture during the early 20th century thanks to New Rochelle's Patrick Tierney. He set up 38 movable lunch cars in busy areas, served light fare—coffee, pies, and sandwiches—and offered 24-hour service. With his success Tierney transformed his eateries into an industry that influenced American roadside culture. He and sons Edward and Edgar built hundreds of lunch wagons until 1927. The DeRaffele Manufacturing Co, established in 1933, continues to build diners in New Rochelle. Other builders included Ward and Dickinson in Silver Creek (Chautauqua Co) and the Orleans Manufacturing Co in Albion, which built the stunning Highland Park Diner in Rochester.

Diners in New York State exemplify the history of this unique architectural form. One of the oldest examples is the 1923 O'Mahony make, a lunch car found at the Palace Lunch in Gloversville (Fulton Co). Palace Lunch retains much of its original interior, such as marble counter and ceramic tile floors and walls. After the mid-1930s architects introduced the Streamline Moderne design to accommodate growing business, to introduce booth service, and to attract female customers. An example of this type is found at the Cutchogue Diner (Suffolk Co), which has shiny, easy-to-clean porcelain, enamel, and stainless steel surfaces. Immediately following World War II, the diner entered its golden age as elaborate, streamlined, and modular designs were built to attract families. Examples from this period are the Empire Diner in Herkimer and Doc's Little Gem Diner in Syracuse. After the development of highways diners began offering home-cooked meals, which became the main fare.

The Taconic Parkway serves as a type of postwar diner museum. Beginning in 1952, gas station operator Burton Coons had success with a diner he moved to Red Hook (Dutchess Co) on US 9. He added diners at successive junctions in Columbia Co in Martindale, Philmont, and Chatham; he had five diners along the parkway in the 1950s. His diner Silk City 5113 (now Historic Village Diner) in Red Hook was listed on the National Register of Historic Places in 1988 since it is a distinctive example of early 20th-century roadside architecture.

Diners declined in the 1960s after the rise of fast food and self-service eateries. Builders shed the streamlined architecture to construct colonial- and Mediterranean-influenced restaurants, as seen at the Thornwood Coach (Westchester Co). Mediterranean or Greek family-owned diners are dominant features on the New York landscape and are found in Buffalo, Albany, and Syracuse. In the early 1990s the nostalgia and pop culture craze revived the American diner. The retro-styled Latham Circle (Albany Co) and Dutchess Co's Eveready in Hyde Park and 84 Diner in Fishkill exemplify this reinterpretation. Though some debate the definition of the word, most agree a diner is fundamentally a prefabricated food service facility (with counter service) hauled to its intended location. In 2003 New York State had between 450 and 500 diners.

Anderson, Will. *Mid-Atlantic Roadside Delights* (Portland, Maine: Will Anderson & Sons Publishing, 1991)

Gutman, Richard J. S. *American Diner Then and Now* (Baltimore: Johns Hopkins Univ Press, 2000)

Randy Garbin

distance learning. The Chautauqua Institution, created in 1874 as a venue for summer lectures on educational topics, pioneered distance learning in New York State. From 1883 to 1891 it added a winter correspondence component to its popular summer program; completion of all course work resulted in a state-recognized college degree. Cornell University also organized a correspondence university in 1883, but those doors never opened. Later, in the first decades of the 20th century, it did add correspondence learning to its extension program. But overall correspondence learning would decline in the first half of the 20th century. During the 1920s and 1930s, the federal government granted radio licenses to a number of the state's educational institutions, but none offered any college-level credit courses that attracted students.

In the 1950s television broadcasting added sound and sight to distance learning. Stations across the state, including WNET in New York City and WMHT and WRGB in Schenectady, began broadcasting college lectures, mostly in the early morning hours. In the 1970s and 1980s the Public Broadcasting System (PBS) and the 1981-launched Corporation for Public Broadcasting-Annenberg School of Communications Project also developed prime-time telecourses such as Carl Sagan's *Cosmos* and Juan Williams's *Eyes on the Prize*, followed in 1990 by Ken Burns's *Civil War*.

SUNY Empire State College, founded in 1971, was the nation's first college specifically created to reach students unable to attend conventional courses. In 1979 it set up the Center for Distance Learning (CDL) to offer instruction to both off-premises students via new technologies and to on-premises students enrolled in local units statewide. CDL provided print-based courses and employed telephone tutorials. The center soon brought computer technology into distance learning; one approach was the short-lived computer conferencing system called CAUCUS. In 1991–95 SUNY operated the SUNY by Satellite Program (SUNYSAT), which provided interactive televised courses statewide. Enrolled students traveled to selected sites where audio hookups allowed them to ask questions on air.

Beginning in the mid-1990s, advances in computer technology, the emerging Internet in particular, enhanced interactive distance learning and resulted in the full integration of web-based courses into SUNY's curriculum. Empire State College was one of the founding institutions of the SUNY Learning Network (SLN), established in 1995. It functions as SUNY's on-line education arm, offering undergraduate and graduate courses to both degree and nondegree students through 53 member campuses. From a handful of enrollments in its first year of operation, SLN's course registrations topped 25,800 in 2001. The state's many private colleges and universities—Syracuse University, Columbia University, New School University, Skidmore College, Rensselaer Polytechnic Institute, and Rochester Institute of Technology, among others—also offer distance-learning programs. At the secondary level, some examples of these programs are at Stillwater Middle and High School (Saratoga Co), Liverpool Central Schools (Onondaga Co), and Broome-Tioga BOCES.

Distance learning is becoming an increasingly popular way for New York State residents to gain nonacademic learning and job-related skills; both public institutions and specialized proprietary schools offer such courses, often termed e-learning. Examples include the New York Public Library, the National Tax Training School in Monsey (Rockland Co), and Sessions.edu in New York City, which offers courses in design.

Bonnabeau, Richard F. *The Promise Continues: Empire State College, the First 25 Years* (Virginia Beach, Va: Donning, 1996)

Reimer, Thomas. *Trends in Virtual Education in the United States: A Snapshot of the Transformation of Distance Education* (Albany: NYS Education Department, 2001)

Rosenberg, Marc J. *e-learning: Strategies for Delivering Knowledge in the Digital Age* (New York: McGraw-Hill, 2001)

Paul Trela

districting. See APPORTIONMENT AND DISTRICTING.

divorce. During the colonial period divorces were rare in New York Colony and only available by special action of the royal governor or provincial assembly. After the American Revolution, most states transferred the venue for divorce actions to the courts and adopted a wide range of grounds for divorce, such as desertion, imprisonment, drunkenness, neglect, and cruelty. But New York State's 1787 law, drafted by a legislative committee chaired by Assemblyman Alexander Hamilton, allowed divorce only upon proof of adultery. The law also barred the adulterous spouse from ever remarrying and allowed the innocent partner to remarry "as if the party convicted was actually dead." These stark terms reflect the cultural understanding that divorce was a form of social death, to be certified only upon the most dire circumstances. Given the difficulty of obtaining divorces in the colonial period, however, the new law in effect expanded access to divorce. The act was aimed both to administer divorce through the courts and to punish adultery by prohibiting the remarriage of the guilty spouse (during the lifetime of the innocent partner). Although the bill readily passed the assembly and senate, the Council of Revision vetoed the bill, reasoning that unless adulterous spouses could be permanently sequestered, the ban on remarriage was likely to result in immoral and illegal liaisons. Nevertheless, state legislators passed the statute over the council's veto, favoring its strong condemnation of adultery.

In 1813 the state legislature permitted courts to grant legal separations to wives in cases of cruelty and abandonment. In these circumstances, the court could decree as to child custody and property, but the parties remained legally married. Eleven years later, judicial separation was made available to husbands on the same basis. In 1827 the legislature crafted an annulment statute. Further efforts to broaden New York State's divorce law were not successful.

The Political Power of the Catholic Church

Despite popular fervor for more liberal methods to undo marriage ties, opposition in the 20th century from conservative legislators and the powerful Roman Catholic Church continued to doom any effort to reform the state's restrictive law. In the first third of the 20th century, some Democratic legislators from the New York City area attempted without success to reform the divorce law. But the Democratic leadership, even when it controlled the legislature, considered the issue too controversial, given the dependence of the party upon the urban Catholic vote. After 1933 some Republican legislators made similar efforts, but a divided Republican Party could not propel the reforms over the opposition of most Democrats. Catholic leaders organized effective opposition, which doomed all efforts to liberalize divorce. In 1948–49, in response to calls for divorce liberalization from Protestant and Jewish sources, Monsignor Robert E. McCormick, presiding judge of the Roman Catholic Archdiocesan Tribunal of New York, called upon the legislature to ban divorce entirely, referring to the movement to broaden access to divorce as "a menace to society."

Circumventing Strict Divorce Laws

The tight legal lid on divorce led to a busy market in fraudulent uncontested matrimonial actions. New Yorkers seeking to dissolve their marital bonds typically enacted a hotel fable: they arranged for the husband to be caught in the act of sitting beside a scantily clad woman when the wife, a process server, and a private detective armed with a flash camera burst into the hotel room. The woman in bed was usually hired by the couple to play her prescribed role in the hotel and later in the courtroom. The farcical nature of this fraud was well documented by a series that ran in the *New York Daily Mirror* in 1934, "I Was the 'Unknown Blonde' in 100 New York Divorces!" A 1951 grand jury concluded that "widespread fraud, perjury, collusion and connivance pervade matrimonial actions[,] exude a stench and perpetuate a scandal."

Migratory divorce was another option; Nevada achieved fame as a haven for New York State residents, who could establish a domicile in that state in 42 days and return with a valid divorce decree. In 1962 Gov Nelson A. Rockefeller's first wife, Mary Todhunter Rockefeller, became one such divorcée. Legal annulments were another alternative. Marriages could be annulled on the basis of misrepresentations about virtually any aspect of the conjugal relationship. By the end of World War II, New York State provided over 150 grounds for annulment, and its courts were issuing one-third of all legal annulments in the United States. In 1950 in many counties in the state annulments outnumbered divorces.

No-Fault Divorce Arrives

That Gov Rockefeller had been easily reelected in 1962, despite his divorce and remarriage, signaled a seismic shift in New York State's cultural and political ground. The 1966 Divorce Reform Law greatly expanded the divorce law, specifying adultery, cruelty, abandonment, confinement in prison, and living apart for two years as grounds for divorce. The Catholic Church, in the wake of the progressive Second Vatican Council (1962–65), did not actively lobby against the divorce legislation, husbanding its resources instead to oppose changes to the abortion law. Sen Robert F. Kennedy, a prominent Catholic, announced his support for the bill. The Divorce Reform Law was adopted in the assembly by a vote of 157 to 7, and in the senate by a margin of 64 to 1.

Reacting to the ease of obtaining divorces on traditional fault grounds, 1960s divorce reformers throughout the country tried to eliminate fault grounds, often replacing them with a standard of "irreconcilable differences." Consistent with the tenor of therapeutic divorce reform throughout the nation, New York State's law also contained a mandatory and elaborate mechanism for counseling divorce-minded spouses in the hope of effecting reconciliation. This procedure was abolished by the state legislature in 1973 because of its expense and ineffectiveness. The Divorce Reform Law took effect on 1 Sept 1967, and its impact could be seen immediately: the 4,073 New York State divorces granted in 1966–67 grew to 18,180 in 1968–69. In 1994, the last year state rankings were tallied, New York had the fifth lowest divorce rate in the United States. The state's contemporary no-fault divorce law is more restrictive than most, requiring that a divorce filing be preceded by a one-year period of living apart pursuant to a judicial separation or a written, notarized agreement resolving all property and spousal support issues. Perhaps because of these more exacting requirements, New York State residents frequently continue to rely on fault grounds when they seek the dissolution of their marriages.

Alimony and Property Division

Alimony, the traditional requirement that ex-husbands support their ex-wives, existed largely in the realm of illusory obligation (not legally binding) until recent times. The first New York State alimony statute dates from 1813 and authorizes a court order compelling the husband "to provide a suitable allowance to the [wife] for her support as to the said court shall seem reasonable and just, having regard to the circumstances of the parties." Alimony provisions were rarely effective, however, due to a combination of poverty and the paucity of enforcement mechanisms. Moreover, the gender bias of the law is most evident in alimony determinations: a husband could commit adultery many times over, and a court would still fix his financial obligation based on his income. A wife guilty of one indiscretion would forever lose all right to any support from her husband. Moreover, even if awarded and collected, alimony ceased upon the death of the paying spouse or the remarriage of the wife. As for property division, until quite recently a court could only divide jointly titled property, which, since almost all property was traditionally titled solely in the husband's name, meant that wives frequently received disproportionately fewer of the assets of the marriage at its end.

In 1980 New York State's legislature enacted the Equitable Distribution Law, which required divorce courts to divide all marital property "equitably" between the parties. In the same year alimony was replaced with "maintenance" payments, which were to be calculated to preserve the parties' standard of living during the marriage and to provide for the recipient's "reasonable needs." Although the Equitable Distribution Law left open the possibility that marital fault might be considered in dividing the parties' property, the decision of New York State's highest court in *O'Brien v O'Brien* (1985) held that fault could not be considered in property division "[e]xcept in egregious cases which shock the conscience of the court."

Child Custody and Support

Eighteenth-century English jurist Sir William Blackstone decreed that the father had a natural right to his children, while the mother was "entitled to no power [over her children], but only to reverence and respect." Early American law reflected English antecedents. A father always prevailed in a custody dispute, unless he had abused, abandoned, or neglected the child. During the first third of the 19th century, courts began considering the welfare of the child as a counterweight to the natural rights of the father.

By the 20th century courts routinely awarded mothers custody of their children. But the maternal preference standard yielded in the latter third of the 20th century to an assessment of the best interests of the child. A landmark child custody case in New York State Family Court, *State ex rel Watts v Watts* (1973), held that the presumption that a mother's inherent right to custody violated the due process clause of the 14th Amendment to the US Constitution. Despite the law's formal gender equality, however, a 1993 report on the New York State Child Support Standards Act Evaluation Project showed that mothers in New York State were awarded sole custody of their children during divorce 93% of the time. Child custody decisions require the awarding of either sole or joint custody, with the latter divided into joint legal or joint physical custody. A parent receiving sole custody of a child has the right and obligation to care for, control, and make all necessary decisions about that child. Noncustodial parents have a legal right to visitation, allowing them to spend time with their child. Gradually the law is recognizing the pervasiveness of alternative family forms, awarding custodial and visitation rights to grandparents and stepparents, as well as increasingly to those whose deep relationship with the child qualifies them as "equitable" or "de facto" parents.

Contemporary New York custody standards focus on the quality of the home environment and the parental guidance the custodial parent provides for the child. New York State courts traditionally fixed the amount of support owed by fathers to their minor children, based on the parent's "means and station in life." In 2002 both parents were held liable for child support, to the extent of their respective financial resources. Whether the parents were ever married to each other is irrelevant to the determination of their child support obligations.

Basch, Norma. *Framing American Divorce: From the Revolutionary Generation to the Victorians* (Berkeley: Univ of California Press, 1999)

Blake, Nelson Manfred. *The Road to Reno: A History of Divorce in the United States* (Westport, Conn: Greenwood, 1962)

DiFonzo, J. Herbie. *Beneath the Fault Line: The Popular and Legal Culture of Divorce in 20th-Century America* (Charlottesville: Univ Press of Virginia, 1997)

Jacobson, Paul H. *American Marriage and Divorce* (New York: Rinehart, 1959)

O'Neill, William. *Divorce in the Progressive Era* (New Haven, Conn: Yale Univ Press, 1974)

J. Herbie DiFonzo

Dix. Town (pop 4,197) in S Schuyler Co. Settled in 1797–98, the town was formed from Tioga Co's Catlin [now in Chemung Co] in 1835. Dix established a town poorhouse in 1875; three years later it had nine residents. The town was served by the Syracuse, Geneva and Corning Railroad (1877). Watkins Glen State Park, Watkins Glen International raceway, and most of the Village of Watkins Glen are located in the town. Cargill manufactures food-grade salt at its salt brine extraction plant.

Glenda Gephart

Dix, John Adams (*b* Boscawen, NH, 24 July 1798; *d* New York City, 21 Apr 1879). Governor, US senator, and secretary of the treasury. At 14 Dix joined the army and served in the War of 1812, rising to the rank of major. After leaving the army in 1828, he moved to Cooperstown (Otsego Co) and soon became a leading member of the Albany Regency, the powerful political faction headed by Martin Van Buren. Dix served as New York State's secretary of state from 1833 to 1839, overseeing the creation of the New York State Geological and Natural History Survey. In 1844, after Silas Wright resigned his US Senate seat to enter New York State's gubernatorial election, the state legislature chose Dix to replace him. A supporter of the free soil Wilmot Proviso, in 1848 Dix ran a futile campaign for governor on the Free Soil ticket and as a result lost his bid to return to the senate in 1849.

He moved to New York City in 1849 and became active in railroad finance, serving briefly as president of the Union Pacific (1862) and Erie (1872) Railroads. Unlike most New York State free soilers, he returned to the Democratic Party and served as US secretary of the treasury in the early months of 1861, earning a reputation as a staunch Unionist with his famous order to a New Orleans treasury officer to shoot anyone who tried to lower the American flag. He became a leading War Democrat and in 1861 a major general in the army. In Maryland he tried to find the middle ground, arresting secessionists but returning refugees from slavery. In August 1863 Dix played a key role in supervising the draft in New York City following the bloody riots the previous month. After the war he supported Andrew Johnson and was appointed minister to France (1866–69). In 1872, at the age of 74, he was easily elected governor of New York State but in 1874 the effects of the panic of 1873 led to his defeat for reelection by Samuel J. Tilden.

Dix, Morgan, ed. *Memoirs of John Adams Dix,* 2 vols (New York: Harper & Bros, 1883)
Lichterman, Martin. "John Adams Dix, 1798–1879" (PhD diss, Columbia Univ, 1952)

Jon Sterngass

Dix, John Alden (*b* Glens Falls, Warren Co, 25 Dec 1860; *d* New York City, 9 Apr 1928). Governor. From a wealthy family, Dix attended Cornell University, graduating in 1883. After college he became a lumber merchant, paper manufacturer, banker, and dealer in marble in Washington and Albany Cos. A strong conservationist, he had a tree planted for every tree he had cut down on his forestlands. Long active in the Democratic Party, and in 1910 the state party chairman, Dix was chosen that year as his party's gubernatorial nominee with the support of Charles F. Murphy, the leader of Tammany Hall, who was looking for a moderate reformer to head the ticket. Though often thought of as a lackluster, one-term governor, Dix's administration accomplished much: a law providing for direct primaries; the creation of the State Conservation Commission; and, after the horrible Triangle Shirtwaist fire of 1911, the one-day-of-rest-in-seven law limiting the working hours of women and children and several laws mandating improved sanitary and safety conditions in factories. However, in trying to balance the concerns of the reformers and Tammany Hall, Dix alienated both factions, leading Murphy to block successfully Dix's renomination for governor. After leaving the Executive Mansion in 1912, he returned to the lumber and paper business and spent his last years in Santa Barbara, Calif.

Wesser, Robert. *A Response to Progressivism: The Democratic Party and New York Politics, 1902–1918* (New York: New York Univ Press, 1986)

Daniel C. Kramer

Dix Hills. Locality (pop 26,024) in Huntington (Suffolk Co). A Secatogue Indian, Dick Pechagan, sold the land to the Town of Huntington in 1700, giving the locality its name. In the early 20th century it was the site of large estates and was crossed by the Long Island Motor Parkway (1908). The Northern State Parkway (1949–52) and the Long Island Expressway (1963) opened Dix Hills for extensive development in the postwar era. It is the site of the 34-acre (14 ha) campus of Five Towns College (1992).

Robert C. Hughes

DMV. See MOTOR VEHICLES, DEPARTMENT OF.

Dobbs Ferry. Village (pop 10,622) in Greenburgh (Westchester Co). Settled by tenant farmers of Philipsburgh Manor, the locality was the site of a ferry operated by the Dobbs family beginning *ca* 1730. In 1830 lots were surveyed under the name of Livingston's Landing, and growth of its trade followed the creation of Piermont (1832) across the river. It acquired a station on the Hudson River Railroad (1849) and began to attract owners of riverfront estates. Its only large factory was the Hudson River Brewing Co. The village incorporated in 1873 as Greenburgh, but its name was restored to Dobbs Ferry in 1875. Irish settled in Dobbs Ferry in the mid–19th century, followed by Italians *ca* 1890–1910. A suburban village, it acquired its first large apartment house in 1927. Dobbs Ferry is the site of Masters School (1877), Children's Village (1901), and Mercy College (1961). Zion Episcopal Church (1834), where Washington Irving served as a vestryman, is a landmark.

Henry Steiner

Doctorow, E(dgar) L(aurence) (*b* New York City, 6 Jan 1931). Writer. Raised in New York City, Doctorow's father owned a music store in the Bronx and his mother was a pianist. He attended the Bronx High School of Science, received his BA at Kenyon College in Ohio (1952), and returned home for graduate work at Columbia University. Doctorow worked as a script reader for Columbia Pictures (1956–59) and as a book editor at New American Library (1959–64) and Dial Press (1964–69). His early works include *Welcome to Hard Times* (1960), a Western, and *Big as Life* (1966), a science fiction–based satire set in New York City. *The Book of Daniel* (1971), a thinly disguised account of the trial of Julius and Ethel Rosenberg, earned him attention as a major novelist and was nominated for a National Book Award. *Ragtime* (1975) is perhaps Doctorow's most important novel, and it won the National Book Critics Award. Set in New York City and New Rochelle (Westchester Co) in the pre–World War I years, it interweaves the lives of real and fictional characters. The book was adapted into a film (1981), featuring Jimmy Cagney in his last screen role, and a Broadway musical (1989). *Loon Lake* (1980), set in the Adirondacks, was a departure for Doctorow. In 1982 he joined the faculty at New York University, where he holds the Glucksman Chair in American Letters. He was designated New York State Author for 1989–91 by the New York State Writers Institute. Doctorow returned to New York City for the setting of *Billy Bathgate* (1989), which is about a naive young man who falls in with notorious gangster Dutch Schultz. Doctorow's most recent novel is *City of God* (2000). He lives in New York City and Sag Harbor (Suffolk Co).

Levine, Paul. *E. L. Doctorow* (New York: Methuen, 1985)
Williams, John. *Fiction as False Document: The Reception of E. L. Doctorow in the Postmodern Age* (New York: Camden House, 1996)

J. Justin Gustainis

Dolgeville. Village (pop 2,166) in Manheim (Herkimer Co) and Oppenheim (Fulton Co). Located on East Canada Creek, it was settled around 1795 and was known as Brockett's Bridge, its business centering on a tannery (1832–72). In 1874 German immigrant Alfred Dolge (1848–1922) began development of an industrial complex, making felt for piano hammers (1874), sounding boards (1875), slippers (1881), piano cases (1886), and autoharps (1893). He recruited fellow Germans in large numbers and introduced socialist principles, including a pension plan (1876), life insurance, and his "Earning Sharing" system (1890), an early profit-sharing plan. In 1882 the post office was renamed Dolgeville. The village incorporated in 1891, and the Little Falls and Dolgeville Railroad arrived in 1892, but in 1898 Dolge went bankrupt and left the village. In 1894 the Daniel Green Co, footwear makers, acquired Dolge's felt footwear factory. It was the village's principal employer throughout the 20th century, but it closed in 2001, leaving only Rawlings' Adirondack Bat factory. Harold "Prince Hal" Schumacher (1910–93), pitcher for the New York Giants (1931–42, 1946), was raised in Dolgeville and returned to become an executive at Adirondack Bat after his Major League career.

James Crawford

Dominican College. Private liberal arts college. The Catholic Dominican Sisters of Blauvelt founded Dominican Junior College in 1952 on a 14-acre (6 ha) campus in Blauvelt (Rockland Co). As more buildings were added, the main office moved next door to the original building, and in doing so the address changed from Blauvelt to the adjacent Orangeburg. Its first mission was to provide teacher training for religious women, but by 1957 the school opened its doors to lay students. In 1959 it became chartered to offer bachelor of arts and bachelor of science degrees and changed its name to Dominican College. The first coeducational freshman class entered in 1967. Master's programs began in 1994. Dominican emphasizes programs for full-time working adults to complete their education. In 1980 it began offering a weekend college format, and in 1990 accelerated evening programs were added. In 2004 both bachelor's and master's degrees could be obtained through these programs as well as in traditional day and evening classes. The college offers associate in arts, bachelor of arts, bachelor of science, bachelor of science in education and nursing, master of science, and master of science in education degrees. In 2003 approximately 1,800 students attended Dominican.

Marianne Rahn-Erickson

Dominicans. Dominicans have lived in New York State since the late 19th century. As a result of increasing US involvement in the economic and political life of the Dominican Republic, many business owners, politicians, and intellectuals found their way to various cities in the state. Pedro Henríquez Ureña (1884–1946), who would become a renowned Hispanist and philologist, and his brothers were sent to study in New York City in February 1901. Buffalo was home to feminist educator Mercedes Mota (1880–1964). By 1915 Dominican writers, scholars, and entrepreneurs occupied a prominent position in New York City–based Spanish language publishing. With the American occupation of the Dominican Republic from 1916 to 1924, contact between Dominicans and the United States increased. Well-known Dominicans in the state during the first half of the 20th century include film star María Montéz

(?1912–51) and diplomat and international playboy Porfirio Rubirosa (1909–65). After 1930, during the three-decade iron-fisted dictatorship of Rafael Leónidas Trujillo (1891–1961), a swarm of exiles headed for New York City despite restrictions on immigration, and a significant Dominican population arose during the 1950s. With the assassination of Trujillo, the American invasion of 1965, new US immigration laws the same year, and a declining Dominican economy, conditions ripened for a massive exodus from the Dominican Republic.

Since 1965 the migratory flow has remained uninterrupted. By 1989 the Dominican Republic ranked seventh among countries of origin for migrants to the United States. Dominicans entering the mainland between 1991 and 2000 far exceeded the number for any previous decade. During the 1990s Dominicans were the fastest growing ethnic minority in New York City because of unabated migration from the Dominican Republic and a high rate of reproduction. They had the highest birth rate in the city from 1990 to 1996, with 77,853 births (8.6% of the city's total). Dominicans constitute some 7% of the city's population, and Dominican children formed one of the largest ethnic groups in the public schools (10% of the student body) in 2003. By 1998 Dominicans made up the largest segment of the Hispanic and Caribbean student population on 5 of the 21 campuses of the City University of New York (CUNY) and were the second or third largest segment on at least 6 others. The Dominican Studies Institute at CUNY, established in 1994, represents a milestone of recognition by the city.

People who trace their ancestry to the Dominican Republic are, after Puerto Ricans, the second largest Latino subgroup in New York State. The 2000 US census initially identified 406,806 Dominicans in New York City and 48,255 elsewhere in the state; the statewide total of 455,061 constituted over half the total reported for the United States. Because of official undercounting attributed to ambiguously worded census questions, in June 2001 the Census Bureau issued a revised estimate of 532,793 Dominicans in New York City. Given the presence of undocumented immigrants, the actual number may be higher. In September 2001 the Lewis Mumford Center for Comparative Urban and Regional Research at SUNY Albany estimated the Dominican population to be 1,121,257 in the United States and 652,347 in New York State, up from 366,625 in the state in 1990.

The majority lives in New York City. In addition, many members of metropolitan New Jersey's large Dominican community work in New York City. The Mumford Center estimates there are 30,394 Dominicans in Nassau and Suffolk Cos, dispersed but with concentrations in various towns including Babylon and Riverhead (Suffolk Co). Dominicans are found, according to the center's rankings, in the areas of Rochester (2,416), Albany/Schenectady/Troy (1,792), Newburgh (1,695), Buffalo/Niagara Falls (1,367), Dutchess Co (1,345), Syracuse (955), Utica/Rome (829), Binghamton (386), Jamestown (240), Glens Falls (228), and Elmira (190). More than other Latino group, Dominicans are highly clustered in certain neighborhoods of New York City. Manhattan has the greatest proportion, with over 40%, then the Bronx, with over 25%. Nearly 60% of Dominicans in the United States live in the Upper Manhattan neighborhood of Washington Heights, where community leaders have emerged and been elected to school boards and other public offices. Dominican neighborhoods are also heavily concentrated in Manhattan's Lower East Side and Manhattan Valley on the Upper West Side, in the South Bronx, in Queens (Jackson Heights and Corona, with much smaller groups in Sunnyside and Woodside), and in Greenpoint, Brooklyn. In the 1990s a trend began for Dominicans to spread beyond their ethnic enclaves.

Although large numbers eventually return to their homeland, since the 1980s foreign-born Dominican adults have led all other immigrant communities in rate of naturalization. Many men are employed in factories, healthcare, and the hospitality and service industries, and women are especially found in the garment industry. The city's thousands of Dominican-owned businesses include car services, clothing stores, real estate companies, travel agencies, and bodegas; as many as one-third of Manhattan's grocery stores are owned by Dominicans. Income lags behind nearly all other immigrant groups. The percentage of high school graduates is relatively low and unemployment is high, although the number of professionals is increasing.

Dominicans are highly active in political organizations and civic life. The first voluntary ethnic association was formed in 1962. Early associations were controlled mainly by elite professionals in the community. The number of organizations increased gradually, accelerating from the mid-1970s to the mid-1980s, when more than 125 such groups existed throughout the city. Many associations are broadly based and include members of the working class, among them the Association of Clubs, the Dominican Political Front, the Dominican Women's Caucus, and La Unión de Jóvenes Dominicanos (The Dominican Youth Union). Recently formed groups for the growing number of professionals include the Dominican-American Professional Alliance and Dominicans 2000. In 1992 Guillermo Linares became the first Dominican in the United States to win public office when he was elected to the City Council from the 10th District, which included Inwood in Upper Manhattan. The annual Dominican Day Parade, held in Manhattan in August, is a major political and social event, and control over it is often contested by various community groups. The November 2001 crash of American Airlines Flight 587 en route from John F. Kennedy International Airport to Santo Domingo, which killed 265 people (primarily Dominicans), was an occasion for the expression of collective grief on the part of the state's Dominican community.

Dominicans are mostly Catholics who may simultaneously follow African-descended religious practices. Many Dominican homes contain small shrines paying homage to Catholic saints, especially the Virgin of Altagracia, the patron saint of the Dominican people. Meanwhile, the accoutrements that decorate the small altars (flowers, lighted candles, food, water, rum, and other earthly goods) frequently recall the trappings of Santería and other African-descended Caribbean religions. New York City churches serving Dominican congregations include the Church of the Incarnation on St. Nicholas Blvd in Washington Heights and St. Theresa's in Woodside. Dominican culture is increasingly visible in the life of the city, with merengue music and novels in English by Julia Alvarez (*b* 1950) and other authors growing steadily in popularity. Dominicans are served by various New York City–based Spanish language publications, and newspapers published in the Dominican Republic such as *El Nacional* and *El Tiempo* can be found at newsstands throughout the city.

Fischkin, Barbara. *Muddy Cup: A Dominican Family Comes of Age in a New America* (New York: Scribner's, 1997)

Hernández, Ramona, and Francisco Rivera-Batiz. *Dominican New Yorkers: A Socioeconomic Profile, 1997* (New York: CUNY Dominican Studies Institute, 1997)

Pessar, Patricia. "Dominicans: Forging an Ethnic Community in New York." In *Beyond Black and White*, ed. Maxine Seller and Lois Weiss (New York: SUNY Press, 1997)

Ricourt, Milagros. *Power from the Margins: The Incorporation of Dominicans in New York City* (New York: Routledge, 2002)

Torres-Saillant, Silvio, and Ramona Hernández. *The Dominican Americans* (Westport, Conn: Greenwood, 1998)

Silvio Torres-Saillant

Dongan, Thomas (*b* Castletown, Ireland, 1634; *d* St. Pancras, England, 14 Dec 1715). Colonial governor. Inheriting his family's Catholicism and loyalty to the house of Stuart, Dongan followed the Stuarts into French exile during the Cromwellian Interregnum (1649–60) and became a colonel in Louis XIV's army. On 30 Sept 1682 he was appointed governor of New York by James, Duke of York. He arrived on 25 Aug 1683 and summoned the province's first elected assembly, which met for only two years. James II ultimately vetoed its most famous act, the Charter of Liberties and Privileges.

Dongan intervened in 1684 when Gov Gen Joseph-Antoine de La Barre of New France threatened retaliation against the Iroquois for a raid on Fort St. Louis [now Peoria, Ill]. He asserted English sovereignty over the Iroquois Confederacy and forbade them, as subjects of the Crown, to negotiate a settlement with a foreign power. This was the first time an English governor had described New York's relationship with the Iroquois in those terms. It infuriated neutralist Iroquois, who reminded Dongan that they were allies of the English, not subjects. La Barre's invasion fell apart because of an epidemic among his troops, but three years later the Marquis de Denonville destroyed several Seneca villages, including Ganondagan [now Victor, Ontario Co]. After provisioning the stricken Indian settlements, Dongan was able to press more successfully his claims of sovereignty over them.

In an attempt to open trade with the western Indians, Dongan licensed trapping expeditions as far west as Michilimackinac [now in Mich]. He settled New York Colony's early boundary disputes with Pennsylvania and Connecticut and secured permanent charters for the cities of New York and Albany. In August 1688 James II replaced Dongan with Sir Edmund Andros, who brought New York into the short-lived Dominion of New England. Dongan retired to his estate on Staten Island as perhaps the most able and energetic of New York's colonial governors. In 1691 his Catholicism and French connections made him a suspect in a mythical plot to hand New York Colony over to the French. Maligned in the colony he had worked tirelessly to improve, Dongan returned to England and later became earl of Limerick.

See also COLONIAL NEW YORK.

Kennedy, John Harold. *Thomas Dongan, Governor of New York, 1682–1688* (1930; repr New York: AMS Press, 1974)

Trelease, Allen W. *Indian Affairs in Colonial New York: The 17th Century* (Ithaca: Cornell Univ Press, 1960)

Daniel A. Piazza

Donohue, Mary O('Connor) (*b* Troy, Rensselaer Co, 22 Mar 1947). Lieutenant governor. Donohue attended the College of New Rochelle, graduating in 1968, and spent the next 10 years as a teacher in the Albany area, during which time she obtained a master's degree from Russell Sage College. While attending Albany Law School, from which she graduated in 1983, she clerked for the US attorney in Albany and was a staff member to Sen Joseph L. Bruno. From 1983 to 1992 she practiced law in Albany and Troy and served, from 1990 to 1992, as assistant county attorney for Rensselaer Co. She was subsequently elected Rensselaer Co district attorney (1992) and justice to the New York State Supreme Court (1996) from the Third Judicial District. Donohue was elected lieutenant governor in 1998 and reelected in 2002, both times on a Republican ticket headed by Gov George E. Pataki. Donohue's duties have included chairing task forces on school violence, small business, and quality communities.

Jon Lines

Donovan, William J(oseph) (*b* Buffalo, 1 Jan 1883; *d* Washington, DC, 8 Feb 1959). Lawyer, soldier, and intelligence officer. A prominent Buffalo state attorney who joined the New York National Guard in 1911, Donovan, during World War I, commanded the First Battalion of the 69th "Fighting Irish" Infantry Regiment of the National Guard and earned the nickname Wild Bill for his rigorous training methods. After the war Donovan bolstered a successful legal and political career in Washington, DC, and New York City. In 1941 he became coordinator of information, a position created to gather intelligence information during World War II. Replaced by the Office of Strategic Services in 1942, the strong intelligence organization created by Donovan became the blueprint for the CIA. As a national hero of both world wars, Donovan became the first person to receive the four highest US military decorations.

Brown, Anthony Cave. *The Last Hero: Wild Bill Donovan* (New York: Times Books, 1982)

Bernadette Zbicki Heiney

doo wop music. See ROCK MUSIC.

Dormitory Authority of the State of New York. Established in 1944 to finance construction of dormitories at state colleges, the authority in its first four years was unable to fulfill its mission because of a dispute between the state Board of Regents and Gov Thomas E. Dewey. The Regents backed a massive expansion of the state's subsidies to private colleges, while Dewey sought to enlarge the public higher education system. The governor eventually won, creating in 1948 the State University of New York (SUNY). Therefore in 1949 the Dormitory Authority sold its first $10 million bond issue to the New York State Employees' Retirement System. Originally financing facilities for the state teachers colleges and SUNY, the authority expanded its mission in 1960 to fund dormitory projects at private universities and to finance the expansion of facilities at the City University of New York. In 1972 the authority started financing projects at local community colleges and moved to building other types of public facilities unrelated to education. During this same period it also became active in the management of building projects and in the early 21st century supervises construction sites from architectural planning to actual construction for public and nonprofit higher education, healthcare, and other public and nonprofit facilities. The largest expansion of the authority occurred in 1995 when it absorbed the functions of the Medical Care Facilities Finance Agency, which issued bonds for the construction of healthcare facilities, and of the Facilities Development Corp, which built mental hygiene facilities. Although originally created to finance the construction of facilities for higher education, in the 1990s the largest part of the authority's new debt was for medical facilities. An 11-member board of directors governs the authority. Five of these positions are appointed by the governor, four are ex officio, one is named by the Speaker of the assembly and one by the majority leader of the senate. As of 2001 the authority was one of the largest and most frequent issuers of tax-exempt bonds in the United States. For 30 Sept 2001 the authority's total outstanding bonded debt stood at $28.5 billion.

Dormitory Authority of the State of New York. *Annual Reports* (Albany: Author)

Thomas A. Birkland

Doubleday, Abner (*b* Ballston Spa, Saratoga Co, 26 June 1819; *d* Mendham, NJ, 26 Jan 1893). Army officer and baseball legend. One of four children born to Ulysses F. Doubleday, newspaper publisher-editor and congressman, and Hester Donnelly Doubleday, he attended private schools in Auburn (Cayuga Co), where he lived during his youth, and Cooperstown (Otsego Co). Graduating from the Cooperstown Classical and Military Academy in 1838, he was appointed to the US Military Academy at West Point (Orange Co) and graduated in 1842. Eventually attaining the rank of major general (1862) in the volunteer army and of colonel (1867) in the regular army, Doubleday saw combat service in the Mexican War and the Civil War, where he distinguished himself at the Battle of Gettysburg. After retiring in 1873 he wrote two books and several articles that bolstered his military reputation. He also was active in New York City's Theosophical Society, becoming its president in 1880 and remaining on its board until 1886.

Despite his military achievements, Doubleday is best remembered as the alleged inventor of baseball in Cooperstown in 1839. This theory, promulgated by Organized Baseball's Mills Commission in 1907, relied on a letter from onetime Cooperstown resident Abner Graves, who claimed that Doubleday rationalized a raucous game of town ball by diagramming a baseball diamond and assigning fixed positions, 11 players to a side. Despite the overwhelming evidence of baseball's gradual evolution from English rounders and other kindred games, many Americans wished to believe that its national pastime was of purely native origin. Baseball embraced the Doubleday story, rendered attractive by its attachment to a personage whose youth and military heroics evoked small town/rural nostalgia and patriotism. The establishment of the Baseball Hall of Fame in Cooperstown in 1939 attests to the power of the Doubleday myth. Doubleday Fields in Cooperstown and at West Point were also dedicated in his honor in 1939.

Doubleday, Abner. Files. National Baseball Hall of Fame Library, Cooperstown, NY

Salvatore, Victor. "The Man Who Didn't Invent Baseball," *American Heritage* 34 (June–July 1983): 65–67

William M. Simons

Douglass [Bailey], Frederick (*b* Talbot Co, Md, Feb 1818; *d* Washington, DC, 20 Feb 1895). Reformer, writer, and newspaper editor. The son of Harriet Bailey, an enslaved woman, and an unknown white man, he grew up as Frederick Bailey on Maryland's eastern shore. One of six children, he lived with his family on tobacco planter Col Edward Lloyd's plantation, though they were owned by one of Lloyd's white managers, Aaron Anthony. He was moved to Baltimore, where he lived with Hugh and Sophia Auld, relatives of Anthony's daughter Lucretia and her husband Thomas Auld, in 1826. He returned to Lloyd's plantation in 1827, when he became the property of Thomas Auld and was formally separated from his family, save for one sister, Eliza. Sent again to Hugh and Sophia Auld, he remained in Baltimore for nearly six years, during which time he secretly mastered reading and writing.

FREEDOM

In 1833 Douglass was moved to Thomas Auld's plantation in St. Michaels, Md, and then back to Baltimore, where he was hired out as a laborer. There he encountered Baltimore's vibrant free black community and connected with a broader world of antislavery thought and action. In September 1838, using the free papers of a black sailor, and relying on a complex network of boats and trains, he fled to New York City, where he stayed with black abolitionist David Ruggles.

Frederick Douglass, daguerreotype, *ca* 1841–45.

Anna Murray, a free domestic servant he met in Baltimore, soon joined him. The couple married before departing for New Bedford, Mass. Soon after arriving, he adopted the last name Douglass, a name suggested by Nathan Johnson, a Quaker who first assisted the newlyweds in New Bedford.

Douglass worked at jobs from sawing wood to shoveling coal and became active within New Bedford's antislavery community. A subscriber to William Lloyd Garrison's antislavery newspaper the *Liberator,* Douglass attended antislavery gatherings and made his public speaking debut in 1841. His ability to recount eloquently and passionately his personal experiences in slavery earned him the esteem of fellow abolitionists, including Garrison, who observed that he could see in Douglass a whole new future for the antislavery movement, "for here was a slave—ay, a slave" denouncing bondage. "I never hated slavery so intensely as at that moment," Garrison declared. Douglass quickly became a leading abolitionist himself. As an agent for Garrison's American Anti-Slavery Society and a leader in the black convention movement, Douglass packed churches and lecture halls throughout New England, New York State, and Great Britain in the 1840s. He visited Rochester for the first time in August 1842 and in 1843 attended a convention at Buffalo, where he opposed the publication of Henry Highland Garnet's call for enslaved Blacks to rise up, physically if need be, against their masters, thinking such a move tactically unwise. Douglass's 1845 autobiography, *Narrative of the Life of Frederick Douglass,* which took readers onto the plantation and inside the mind of the enslaved, sold 5,000 copies in its first year; he later wrote more elaborate versions of his autobiography, *My Bondage and My Freedom* (1855) and *The Life and Times of Frederick Douglass* (1881). Fearing that Douglass's master would try to recapture the well-known activist, British and American abolitionists raised funds to pay off Thomas Auld, who received about $1,250 for Douglass's final freedom in 1846.

ROCHESTER

In 1847 Douglass returned from a 15-month trip to Scotland and England and announced plans to move to Rochester, then a hotbed of reform, to begin publishing the *North Star* (later *Frederick Douglass' Paper*), a newspaper dedicated not only to abolitionism but also to providing information to free Blacks throughout the nation. With funds raised from his trip abroad and with the support of friends, including Rochester's Amy and Isaac Post, the newspaper was inaugurated in December 1847. He moved his family into a house at 4 Alexander St in 1848. While living in Rochester and touring western and central New York State, Douglass encountered a thriving network of reformers, political abolitionists, and women's rights activists. He attended the Free Soil Party Convention in Buffalo in 1848, eventually endorsed the Free Soil Party in the *North Star,* and was the Liberty Party candidate for New York's secretary of state in 1855. He maintained a strong bond with Liberty Party leader Gerrit Smith of Peterboro (Madison Co) in the 1850s. The move to Rochester and his support and friendship with political abolitionists like Smith signaled a break with Garrison and other moral suasionists. Douglass supported women's rights activists by signing the Declaration of Sentiments and calling for voting rights for both women and Blacks at the Seneca Falls Convention (Seneca Co) in 1848. According to Elizabeth Cady Stanton, it was through Douglass's efforts that the resolution calling for women's right to vote received support among convention attendees.

Continuing with his speaking engagements throughout the 1850s, he delivered his famous July 5th address to the Rochester Ladies' Anti-Slavery Society at Corinthian Hall in 1852. In a speech that proclaimed the constitution an antislavery document, Douglass reminded attendees that the July 4th holiday celebrated the political freedom of only some of the country's residents. He declared that July 4th "is your holiday, not mine." Douglass welcomed his fellow black activists to Rochester in 1853 for a convention, at which he opposed colonizationists by claiming that America was as much a homeland for Blacks as it was for Whites. An active supporter of the Underground Railroad, Douglass and his family sheltered freedom seekers at their farm, which was purchased around 1852. The farm was on a hill on St. Paul Rd (later South Ave), 2 mi (3 km) south of Rochester's center, and housed Douglass's family, which now included five children: Rosetta, Lewis Henry, Frederick Jr, Charles Redmond, and Annie.

In 1859, the same year he began issuing *Douglass' Monthly,* Douglass was fingered as a conspirator in John Brown's failed raid on Harpers Ferry [now in W Va]. Fearing arrest, Douglass left Rochester for Canada and then traveled to England on a preplanned speaking tour. After returning to Rochester in 1860, Douglass turned from agitator to organizer. At the beginning of the Civil War, Douglass led the black abolitionist charge, urging Pres Abraham Lincoln to attack slavery and not just to restore the Union. Despite concern for Lincoln's interest in colonizing Blacks overseas, Douglass called African Americans to fight, and he actively recruited for the first black regiment formed in the North, the Massachusetts 54th. Douglass continued his activism after the war ended and in 1866 joined a group of black leaders meeting with Pres Andrew Johnson to protest the passage of discriminatory black codes in southern states. He became a leading advocate for the Republican Party and fought for passage of the 15th Amendment, which gave black men the vote. He also returned to journalism, as a sponsor of the *New Era* and later as editor of its successor, the *New National Era* in 1870.

WASHINGTON, DC

Based in Washington, DC, the newspaper brought Douglass to the nation's capital, and his family followed after their Rochester farm burned in 1872. After he stopped publishing his newspaper in 1874, he served as the Freedman's Savings and Trust Co president (1874) and later as US marshal of the District of Columbia (1877–81). In 1882 Anna Douglass died, and two years later Douglass married Helen Pitts, a white woman from a Honeoye (Ontario Co) abolitionist family; she worked as a clerk in Douglass's Washington, DC, office while he was serving as recorder of deeds (1881–86). Douglass's second marriage and his close associations with other white women, including reformer Julia Griffiths and German émigré Ottilie Assing, reaped criticism from both black and white contemporaries. Appointed diplomat to Haiti (1889–91), his last great protest action came just a few years afterward, when he spoke against the horrific rise in southern lynchings in the 1890s. He viewed the renewed racial violence and disfranchisement as affronts to African Americans everywhere, past as well as present, who died for their country and for the cause of liberty.

Douglass died in 1895 at his Washington, DC, home. He laid in state at Rochester's City Hall (now Irving Place) and was buried in Mount Hope Cemetery. A monument to him was erected on Central Ave in Rochester in 1899 and was moved to Highland Park in 1941.

Diedrich, Maria. *Love across Color Lines: Ottilie Assing and Frederick Douglass* (New York: Hill & Wang, 1999)

Douglass, Frederick. *The Life and Writings of Frederick Douglass,* 5 vols. Ed. Philip S. Foner (New York: International Publishers, 1950–75)

———. *The Frederick Douglass Papers: Speeches, Debates and Interviews,* 5 vols. Ed. John W. Blassingame (New Haven, Conn: Yale Univ Press, 1979–92)

———. *Autobiographies.* Ed. Henry Louis Gates Jr (New York: Library of America, 1994)

McFeely, William S. *Frederick Douglass* (New York: Simon & Schuster, 1991)

Stauffer, John. *The Black Hearts of Men: Radical Abolitionists and the Transformation of Race* (Cambridge, Mass: Harvard Univ Press, 2002)

Stephens, George E. *A Voice of Thunder: The Civil War Letters of George E. Stephens.* Ed. Donald Yacovone (Urbana: Univ of Illinois Press, 1997)

Richard Newman

Dove, Arthur G(arfield) (*b* Canandaigua, Ontario Co, 2 Aug 1880; *d* New York City, 23 Nov 1946). Painter. After graduating from Cornell University in 1903, Dove moved to New York City to work as a commercial illustrator and painter, drawing for many leading magazines. He left in 1908 to study painting in Paris, where he was exposed to the work of Henri Matisse, whose use of vivid color and decorative patterning influenced his own style. Dove returned to New York City in 1909 and met Alfred Stieglitz, the influential photographer and gallery owner, who encouraged Dove to experiment with abstract art. Dove divided his time over the next decade between Westport, Conn, and New York City, where he associated with a group of young painters tied together by Stieglitz, including Georgia O'Keeffe. He was one of the earliest American abstract painters; along with Wassily Kandinsky and Manierre Dawson, Dove is credited with creating the first abstract paintings in 1910. He experimented with assemblage techniques, sometimes relying on mixed media to create collage-like images. Although natural forms inspired much of his work, he moved to more geometric and abstract images in his later art. Much of his work was based on locations within New York State, including his abstract, stylized landscapes of Geneva (Ontario Co). He also captured images of the Long Island Sound, where he painted while living aboard a sailboat moored at Halesite (Suffolk Co) from 1924 to 1933. In 1933 dire economic straits and the need to settle his mother's estate forced Dove to return to his family's home in Geneva, but in 1938 he mustered the fiscal resources to move back to Long Island with his second wife, artist Helen "Reds" Torr. The couple purchased a one-room cottage in Centerport (Suffolk Co). Becoming seriously ill from pneumonia, he never fully regained his health and remained there until his death, the eight-year span representing the most productive period of his life. In 1988 the Heckscher Museum of Art acquired the couple's home, which will be restored to house the Newsday Center for Dove/Torr Studies and an archive containing much of Dove's personal tools, his art library, and sketches.

Morgan, Ann L. *Arthur Dove: Life and Work, with a Catalogue Raisonné* (Newark: Univ of Delaware Press, 1984)

Jennifer Steenshorne

Dover. Town (pop 8,565) in E Dutchess Co. Part of the Beekman Patent (1697) and the Oblong (1731), it was first settled by New York Dutch in the 1720s and later by New Englanders. The town was formed from Pawling in 1807. The Harlem Railroad (1849) opened the New York City fluid-milk market, making Dover an important dairying region; otherwise it had some small iron mines and marble quarries. The Harlem Valley State Hospital (1924–94) was a leading psychiatric facility and the town's major employer for many years. Since the 1960s stations on the Metro-North Railroad have drawn commuters from a wide region in Dutchess Co and adjacent Connecticut. Native-born John H. Ketcham (1832–1906) attained the rank of major general during the Civil War and subsequently served in Congress (1865–1906). Historian Benson J. Lossing (1813–91) was also a resident.

William P. McDermott

Dowling College. Private liberal arts college in Oakdale (Suffolk Co). In 1955 Adelphi College (now Adelphi University) initiated extension programs in public schools in Sayville, Riverhead, and Port Jefferson (Suffolk Co), and in 1959 created Adelphi-Suffolk College in Sayville. In 1961 it bought Idle Hour, William K. Vanderbilt's former estate in Oakdale, and held the first classes on the new campus in January 1963. The institution became independent in 1968 and took the name Dowling College. It offers undergraduate and graduate degrees in liberal arts, business, and education, but is best known for its aviation-related programs. In 2002 it enrolled more than 6,900 students at its main campus in Oakdale and its Brookhaven Center branch in Shirley (Suffolk Co).

Thierfelder, William Richard, III. *Dowling College: A Collection of Personal Remembrances, 1955–1989* (Oakdale, NY: Dowling College, 1990)

Yayin Chu-Reimer

Downing, Andrew Jackson (*b* Newburgh, Orange Co, 31 Oct 1815; *d* Yonkers, 28 July 1852). Landscape gardener and architect. After attending Montgomery Academy (Orange Co), Downing joined his brother Charles in managing the nursery their father had established in Newburgh. In 1838 Andrew married Caroline De Windt, daughter of a prominent family from Fishkill Landing [now Beacon, Dutchess Co] and they lived at Highland Gardens, a Gothic Revival villa Downing built in 1839 near his birthplace. Downing authored several highly influential pattern books in the 1840s and became a contributing editor of the *Horticulturist* in 1846. His focus expanded from horticulture to landscape design to architecture, and his adaptations of English cottage and Gothic Revival villa designs emphasized domestic convenience and discouraged ostentatious size and ornamentation as contrary to egalitarian republican ideals. By the time *The Architecture of Country Houses* was published in 1850, Downing was middle-class America's recognized arbiter of taste in housing, furnishings, interior design, and landscaping. Associations with Alexander Jackson Davis, Calvert Vaux (whom Downing met while traveling in Europe), and Frederick Law Olmsted placed him at the center of change in mid-19th-century material culture. In collaboration with Davis and later with Vaux, Downing enjoyed architectural and landscape design commissions from wealthy Hudson Valley landowners, including Robert Donaldson and Matthew Vassar. Pres Millard Fillmore commissioned Downing to landscape the Public Grounds (including what is now the Mall) in Washington, DC. Traveling aboard the steamboat *Henry Clay* to the capital for a supervisory visit, Downing was killed when the steamship caught fire and ran aground near Yonkers. He is buried in Cedar Hill Cemetery in Newburgh.

Downing, Andrew Jackson. *The Architecture of Country Houses* (1850; repr New York: Dover, 1969)
Schuyler, David. *Apostle of Taste: Andrew Jackson Downing, 1815–1852* (Baltimore: Johns Hopkins Univ Press, 1996)

Ronald J. Burch

downstate. See UPSTATE AND DOWNSTATE.

downtown music. Term used to describe a musical style composed primarily in Lower Manhattan since the early 1950s. The movement is characterized by an experimental ethos that frequently cuts across disciplinary divisions and seeks to break down barriers between art and everyday life. Downtown music is generally performed by nonstandard ensembles, and composers often perform their own music. The finished artistic product is not the musical score but the performance itself, lessening the absolute need for a musical score in the traditional sense.

John Cage (1912–92), whose compositional process incorporated chance operations, altered instruments, long silences, and unconventional sounds, was the major figure in the emergence of a downtown music scene, a movement perhaps initiated with the 29 Aug 1952 premiere in Woodstock (Ulster Co) of *4'33"*, in which the performer sits silently for the duration of the piece. Another major figure was Morton Feldman (1926–87), whose scores left precise choices of pitch up to the performers. He taught at SUNY Buffalo from 1973 until his death, bringing a "downtown" aesthetic to that campus. His later works include a string quartet that runs approximately six hours. In the early 1950s dance composer Lucia Dlugoszewski (1934–2000) performed primarily on invented instruments, including her own "timbre piano" and later on the many percussion instruments made for her by sculptor Ralph Dorazio.

In the 1960s the downtown scene came to include multimedia and performance art, microtonal and nonpitched instruments, often homemade, and a variety of improvisational and compositional styles. In 1961 conceptual artist Yoko Ono offered her loft for performances, which were sometimes led by composers La Monte Young (1935–) and Richard Maxfield (1927–2000). These often featured artists associated with the downtown Fluxus movement, founded around 1960 by George Maciunas (1931–78) as a revival of the Dada movement. Scores by Fluxus composers often simply and sometimes cryptically described an action to be performed. Young's *Composition 1960 #10* consists simply of the instruction: "Draw a straight line and follow it." Young, noted for his composition with tones held for long durations, was among those who pioneered the minimalist movement in music, which emerged downtown and included composers Terry Riley (1935–), Philip Glass (1937–), and Steve Reich (1936–). Much minimalist music was repetitively structured, with recurring phrases changing gradually over time.

The freedom of the scene was formative for multimedia artists like Meredith Monk (1943–), a composer, dancer, singer, choreographer, and filmmaker who emerged in the late 1960s. Laurie Anderson's (1947–) performances in the early 1970s included playing violin on a block of ice in skates until the ice melted. She went on to national celebrity, blending music with dance, poetry, comedy, animation, and video. Monk and Anderson were among the early performers at the Kitchen, founded in 1971 in the unused kitchen of the Mercer Arts Center, which launched numerous multimedia artists and has become a well-known institution, now on West 19th St. The Knitting Factory, a club founded in 1987 on Houston St, became the key venue for a distinctive community of musicians that included Fred Frith (1949–), Tom Cora (1944–98), Ikue Mori, and John Zorn (1953–), and that merged avant-garde compositional practices and pop, jazz, and punk styles with free and structured improvisation. The center of a growing scene, the club moved to a larger building on Leonard St, expanding to encompass several emerging musical threads, including avant-garde ethnic music, a resurgence of free jazz, and electronic music.

Gann, Kyle. *American Music in the 20th Century* (New York: Schirmer Books, 1997)

Olivia Mattis

draft riots. The mob actions during the week of 13 July 1863 originated in protest against federal conscription. The draft focused antiwar and antiabolitionist opposition to Pres Abraham Lincoln's Republican administration and unleashed class and racial hatred leading to acts of violence in New York City. Smaller outbreaks occurred in nearby Brooklyn and Jamaica (Queens Co), as well as in Troy (Rensselaer Co).

The Conscription Act of March 1863, the first federal military draft, aroused opposition especially through its exemptions by commutation (payment of $300) and substitution (finding someone else to enlist), which created resentment among those who could not afford them. The first lottery drawing of draftees occurred quietly on Saturday, 11 July, at the Ninth District Provost Marshall Office at 3d Ave and 47th St in Manhattan. The violence began on Monday, 13 July, when a company of firemen, angry that one of their men had been drafted on Saturday, set fire to that office. Firemen had been exempt from service in the state militia. Crowds gathered around the city and attacked police stations, the Eighth District Provost Marshall Office, and the 21st Street Armory at 2d Ave. Rioters and police battled for control of the armory, and after

Depiction of the burning of the Colored Orphan Asylum at 5th Ave and 43d St on 13 July 1863 during the New York City draft riot; detail from the *Illustrated London News,* 15 Aug.

seizing it, some rioters locked themselves in on an upper floor, where they burned to death when other rioters set fire to the building. Another mob looted and burned the Colored Orphan Asylum at 5th Ave and 43d St. Police held the crowd at bay while asylum staff led the orphans to safety out the 44th St exit. This assault continued for several days, with mobs lynching Blacks or hanging their corpses after murdering and mutilating them. Some were drowned. On Monday there were also attacks on police and federal officials, prominent Republicans, and their houses. Rioters tore up streetcar tracks and tore down telegraph lines. A mob attacked the offices of the *New York Tribune,* a proabolitionist newspaper edited by Horace Greeley. Fearing a similar attack, the editor of the *New York Times* obtained three Gatling guns from federal authorities and mounted one on its roof and two others in its business offices.

On Tuesday and Wednesday there was more looting than political rioting, although some mobs tore up railroad tracks, attacked ferries, and tried to burn bridges and the gasworks. The armed employees of Lord and Taylor held off a crowd of looters, but another mob sacked Brooks Brothers. Police and the few military units not sent to the battle at Gettysburg began to organize against the rioters. The rioters in Troy behaved similarly to their New York City counterparts. On Tuesday mobs attacked the *Troy Times,* destroyed a black church, and freed prisoners from jail. As requested, five regiments of New York State and other units arrived in New York City on Wednesday night and Thursday morning and fought rioters, broke up their barricades, occupied factories and other strategic spots, and seized weapons and stolen goods. Militia from Albany entered Troy in a show of force on Wednesday, and the riots there ended. By Friday the riots in New York City were over.

Many elected officials took a conciliatory approach toward the rioters. In a speech at City Hall on Tuesday morning, Gov Horatio Seymour promised to make money available to draftees who could not afford the commutation fee. On Wednesday the New York City Common Council passed a resolution appropriating $2.5 million to pay $300 to each draftee who could not afford commutation or to anyone willing to volunteer. Mayor George Opdyke vetoed it.

Many groups participated in the riots, but recent Irish immigrants stood out. As working poor they resented the exemption clauses in the act and feared competition from African Americans. The hiring of black strikebreakers by shipping companies enraged longshoremen. Lincoln's Emancipation Proclamation moved demagogues to raise the specter of freed Blacks moving to the North to work for lower wages than Whites received.

Contemporary accounts claimed that hundreds or thousands of rioters were killed and thousands more were wounded. Recent scholarship has lowered the body count to a total of about 100–150, including several dozen rioters, one or two dozen Blacks, eight soldiers, and three policemen, although the precise number remains uncertain. Property damage amounted to about $1.5 million. Of the 450 arrested, 80 were tried and 67 convicted, many receiving light sentences. The New York City draft riots remain the single bloodiest episode of urban violence and rioting in American history. The draft resumed that August without incident, but the rioting that convulsed the city in July 1863 was long remembered by those on both sides.

For other illustrations, see LYNCHING.

Bernstein, Iver. *The New York City Draft Riots* (New York: Oxford Univ Press, 1990)
Fort, Milton George. *Abraham Lincoln and the Fifth Column* (New York: Collier Books, 1962)
Headley, Joel Tyler. *The Great Riots of New York, 1712–1873* (New York: E. B. Treat, 1873)
McKay, Ernest A. *The Civil War and New York City* (Syracuse: Syracuse Univ Press, 1990)

David Chenkin

Draper, Andrew S(loan) (*b* Westford, Otsego Co, 21 June 1848; *d* Albany, 27 Apr 1913). Commissioner of education. Starting in a one-room school, Draper graduated from Albany Academy, taught there for a year, then spent a second year teaching in Otsego Co. He graduated from Albany Law School in 1871 and married Abbie Lyon in 1872. Draper served on Albany's Board of Public Instruction from 1879 to 1881, was elected to the state assembly in 1881, and became a federal judge in 1885. As state superintendent of public instruction (1886–92) he advocated compulsory education, emphasized teacher training, and created noncompulsory state examinations for teachers. Named president of the University of Illinois in 1894, Draper left that position in 1904 to become New York State's first commissioner of education. An opponent of local control of schools, he unified the K–12 school system, worked to consolidate schools and districts, established a statewide teacher retirement system, and led in the funding and design of the State Education Building. Draper's book *American Education* appeared in 1909, and he continued as commissioner until his death.

See also HIGHER EDUCATION.

Horner, Harlan Hoyt. *The Life and Work of Andrew Sloan Draper* (1934; repr Urbana: Univ of Illinois Press, 1981)

Thomas J. Mauhs-Pugh

Dreiser, (Hermann) Theodore (*b* Terre Haute, Ind, 27 Aug 1871; *d* Hollywood, Calif, 28 Dec 1945). Author. The 12th of 13 children of German-speaking parents, he was born two years after a factory fire had crippled his father and reduced the family to poverty and transience. Leaving home after high school, Dreiser spent several years in Chicago as a common laborer, attended Indiana University (1889–90), and returned to Chicago, eventually finding a job as a newspaper reporter. Similar positions in St. Louis, Toledo, Cleveland, and Pittsburgh brought Dreiser in 1894 to New York City, which would be for the next 40 years the center of his intellectual life. After a brief stint as a reporter for the *New York World,* he edited the magazine *Ev'ry Month.* His first novel, *Sister Carrie* (1900), a fictionalized account of the experience of one of his sisters, tells the story of a woman whose success in the glitter of the city is not deterred by her living without moral qualm with two different men. When the publisher virtually suppressed the book, Dreiser suffered a physical and emotional collapse, but by 1904 he had embarked on a series of increasingly successful editorships of family magazines. His next novel, *Jennie Gerhardt* (1911), also based on a family experience, established him critically as the foremost literary naturalist. His Trilogy of Desire comprised three novels that drew on the life of transportation magnate Charles Tyson Yerkes: *The Financier* (1912), *The Titan* (1914), and *The Stoic* (1947). *The "Genius"* (1915), the most autobiographical of his novels and arguably the weakest, was banned by the New York Society for the Suppression of Vice and not reissued until 1923. He wrote works of reminiscence, including *The Color of a Great City* (1923), a miscellany of sketches of New York City at the turn of the century; philosophical speculation; two volumes of a projected autobiographical, "A History of Myself"; and collections of biographical sketches, stories, poems, and plays. Dreiser spent four years writing in California before returning to New York City in 1923.

In 1925, after almost three years of concentrated research and writing and with a visit to the sites of the original events, he published the two-volume *An American Tragedy.* Based on a 1906 Herkimer Co trial involving a young man's murder of his pregnant working-class girlfriend to clear his way to a wealthier socialite, the book was an impressive critical and popular success. From 1928 to 1931 Dreiser built a home, Iroki, in Mount Kisco (Westchester Co). His outspokenness on matters of social and economic inequality led Dreiser to visit Russia in late 1927 as a guest of the Soviet government. He focused on American conditions in *Tragic America* (1931), an outgrowth of his investigative visit to a coal miners' strike in Harlan, Ky, and in *America Is Worth Saving* (1941). Five months before he died he applied for membership to the Communist Party.

Lingeman, Richard. *Theodore Dreiser: At the Gates of the City, 1871–1907* (New York: Putnam's, 1986)

———. *Theodore Dreiser: An American Journey, 1908–1945* (New York: Putnam's, 1990)

Swanberg, W. A. *Dreiser* (New York: Scribner's, 1965)

David J. Nordloh

Dresden. Town (pop 677) in N Washington Co. Settled at the foot of South Bay around 1784, the town was formed from Putnam in 1822 as South Bay but was immediately renamed Dresden. It is located on the peninsula between Lakes Champlain and George. The Delaware and Hudson Railroad came through in 1875. Dresden was not a good farming town because most of its land away from Lake Champlain is rugged, but lumbering and harvesting of hemlock bark were important. Graphite, iron, and flint were mined. In the late 19th century cottages were built at Huletts Landing on its Lake George shore. In the early 21st century, it is primarily a vacation destination. The town is located entirely within Adirondack Park; Black Mountain (2,650 ft/808 m) overlooks Lake George.

R. Paul McCarty

Dresden. Village (pop 307) in Torrey (Yates Co). Surveyed in 1814, it became a steamboat landing and the eastern terminus of the Crooked Lake Canal (1833–77), and developed sawmills, gristmills, a boatyard, dry dock, and woolen factory. The village incorporated in 1867. The birthplace of orator and agnostic Robert Green Ingersoll (1833–99) is a museum. Since 1939 power has been generated by the coal-fired Greenidge Plant, and since 1962 the US Navy has operated the Naval Underwater Systems Center of the New London Laboratory on Seneca Lake from a former marina in the village.

Gwen Chamberlain

Drew, Daniel (*b* Carmel [now in Putnam Co], 29 July 1797; *d* New York City, 18 Sept 1879). Entrepreneur and financier. Drew left his family's farm in Carmel to serve in the War of 1812 as a paid substitute for a wealthy draftee. A horse trader and cattle drover after the war, he settled in New York City in 1829 and operated Bull's Head Tavern. Five years later Drew established the Hudson River People's Line, which owned two of the world's largest and most opulent steamboats, *Isaac Newton* and *New World,* and competed with Cornelius Vanderbilt's boats. Drew also ran lines on Long Island Sound and Lake Champlain. In 1844 he formed the investment firm Drew, Robinson and Co, which dissolved in the early 1850s. Drew became a director of Erie Railroad in 1857, and his operations with the railroad stock often pitted him against Vanderbilt. Drew built Methodist churches near his boyhood home and funded Drew Theological Seminary (now Drew University) in Madison, NJ. In 1870 former allies Jay Gould and Jim Fisk manipulated Erie stock, costing Drew millions of dollars. He went bankrupt in 1876, living his last years in his son's New York City home. Drew, a prototype of the "Robber Baron" and a coarse, shrewd upstate horse trader who triumphed in downstate finance, is widely—if perhaps apocryphally—credited with coining the term "watered stock" from the practice, familiar to him as a drover, of watering cattle just prior to a sale.

Browder, Clifford. *The Money Game in Old New York: Daniel Drew and His Times* (Lexington: Univ Press of Kentucky, 1986)

Arthur G. Adams

drug addiction and treatment. The evolution of treatment and prevention strategies has been strongly influenced by the degree to which alcohol and drug addiction has been seen as a curable disease rather than a moral failing. In the 19th and early 20th centuries drug addiction was widely seen as a disease, and treatment consisted of clinical techniques for detoxification and practical prescriptions for diet, exercise, "occupation[s] of an absorbing kind," and proprietary remedies (hypnotics, purgatives, or diluted forms of the drug such as laudanum or paregoric). White women maintained on opiates (morphine and heroin) by physicians represented the majority of the addicted population in the 19th and early 20th centuries. Opening in 1864, the New York State Inebriate Asylum in Binghamton, supported through alcohol-related tax revenues, was the first state-run, specialized treatment facility. One of the first facilities devoted solely to drug addiction, the Brooklyn Home for Habitues, opened in 1891. The first professional association for treatment providers, the American Association for the Study and Cure of Inebriety (AASCI), was founded in 1870 at the New York City YMCA. In 1910 the New York Board of Inebriety set up New York City Hospital and Industrial Colony in Warwick (Orange Co).

The Progressive Era

The New York State legislature enacted the Boylan Act (1914), an antinarcotics bill covering opiates, codeine, and chloral hydrate that provided for commitment of addicts to institutions licensed by the State Lunacy Commission and allowed physicians to prescribe narcotics after physical examination and verification. Narcotics prescriptions could not be refilled, and hypodermic syringes required prescriptions. Later that year the federal Harrison Antinarcotic Act was passed, and states like New York could not allow physicians the degree of autonomy to prescribe narcotics permitted under Boylan. According to David Courtwright, 9 out of 10 American heroin addicts were living within 180 miles (290 km) of Manhattan by 1920, and treatment capacity was inadequate to meet demand resulting from the Boylan and Harrison Acts. The US Supreme Court decisions in *United States v Jin Fuey Moy* (1916) and *Webb v United States* (1919) made medical maintenance illegal, rendering physicians reluctant to treat addicts for fear of prosecution. New York State created the Department of Narcotic Drug Control in February 1918, and from April 1919 through January 1920, the New York City Clinic, operated by the City of New York Department of Health and administered by the state, served 7,464 addicts.

Critics of maintenance clinics, particularly Harry J. Anslinger, a former US Treasury agent who headed the Federal Bureau of Narcotics (FBN; forerunner of Drug Enforcement Administration) from 1930 to 1962, used the administrative failures that ultimately forced the closure of the New York City Clinic to bolster their position that maintenance would not work. By 1925 it was clear that addiction researchers and clinicians could not identify physiological markers to distinguish addicts from nonaddicts. In this climate, criminalization proponents asserted the view that drug abuse was a voluntary, criminal act best met by law enforcement. Institutions founded on the notion that addiction was a curable medical condition declined. In the 1910s and 1920s policy makers explored a variety of directions, ranging from detoxification and maintenance clinics in 44 cities across the nation to heightened law enforcement. By 1923 all the clinics had closed because of the lack of public support, legal constraints on operation, and the stigmatization of their clientele.

The opportunity for systematic study of addiction was lost with the abrupt closure of the clinics and the decay of the treatment infrastructure. Physicians emerged from the Progressive era knowing less about addiction and treatment than they had prior to it. Popular culture of the 1920s depicted physicians as nefarious purveyors of dope, and the United States was widely depicted as a "drugged nation." Such concerns arose again in the 1940s after the federal Marihuana Tax Act (1937) went into effect. In response to federal "scare tactics," New York City mayor Fiorello La Guardia commissioned a scientific study that rebutted exaggerated claims about the negative effects of marijuana (1944). During World War II, the FBN stockpiled opiates and effectively kept them off the streets. The first signs of the postwar emergence came in the late 1940s, and the epicenter was located squarely within New York City.

Postwar Heroin Epidemic

Warnings that a frightening wave of narcotics addiction was about to engulf New York City youth spurred officials to action after war's end. A series of *New York World-Telegram and Sun* articles by Edward Mowery about heroin use in Harlem appeared in spring 1950. During that year, the New York City Police Department increased its number of drug enforcement officers from 18 to more than 50. The first televised congressional hearings before the US Senate Crime Investigating Committee and the Subcommittee to Investigate Juvenile Delinquency, stimulated intense fervor among an estimated 20 to 30 million viewers. Chaired by Sen Estes Kefauver, a Democrat from Tennessee, the hearings lasted from May 1950 to August 1951. Mention of teenage drug addiction aided the 2 Nov 1951 passage of the federal Boggs Act, which mandated the first minimum sentences for drug offenders. New York State legislative hearings on teenage narcotic addiction held by Atty Gen Nathaniel Goldstein in the summer of 1951 in Buffalo and Albany, because of "suspicion that right here in New York City [there] was a great incidence of narcotic addiction, especially amongst girls," helped establish justification for the first state institution dedicated to the treatment and rehabilitation of drug addicts at Westfield State Farm (now Bedford Hills Correctional Facility) in Westchester Co. At the US Public Health Service narcotics hospital in Lexington, Ky, teenage youth admissions increased from 52 in 1948 to 440 in 1950, with more than half of them from New York City.

New York City and State became a locus for addiction and public discussion about it throughout the 1950s. Groups included New York City mayor Vincent R. Impellitteri's committee, the New York City Welfare Council Committee on the Use of Narcotics among Teenage Youth with representatives from 58 organizations, and, most prominently, the Committee on Public Health Relations of the prestigious New York Academy of Medicine, which held conferences titled Drug Addiction among Adolescents in 1951 and 1952. The academy's recommendation to reestablish maintenance clinics contradicted the direction of federal drug policy. In response, the FBN arranged for a congressional inquiry later resulting in the federal Narcotics Control Act (1956), which stiffened the mandatory minimum sentencing leveled by the Boggs Act. The act galvanized a joint effort to humanize the drug addict by the American Bar Association and the American Medical Association, resulting in their report *Drug Addiction: Crime or Disease?* (1961). In the 1950s animosity escalated between law enforcement and a fragile alliance of legal experts, scientists, and physicians committed to humanitarian treatment, research, and a public health paradigm.

A team headed by Isidor Chein at the Research Center for Human Relations at New York University conducted the classic addiction research of the 1950s. Their social-psychiatric study of heroin use among adolescents in three boroughs of New York City between 1949 and 1954 was published as *The Road to H* (1964). Considered definitive for decades, the study criticized federal drug policy for exaggerating the scope of the drug addiction problem, a view shared by many treatment professionals who worked directly with drug users.

The 1950s epidemic was followed by the resurgence of interest in drug use and experimentation in the 1960s. New York State passed a short-lived civil commitment law under Gov Nelson A. Rockefeller in the 1960s following the US Supreme Court ruling in *Robinson v California* (1962), which held that addiction could not be considered a crime any more than having a common cold could be criminalized. Responsibility for administering civil commitment fell to the New York State Department of Mental Hygiene (DMH) in 1962, when the legislature moved responsibility for addiction services from the State Health Department (where it had resided since the 1930s) to a narcotics unit within DMH. In 1973 Gov Rockefeller pressed the New York State legislature to adopt strict penalties for drug crimes, establishing mandatory prison sentences of 15 years to life for persons convicted of possessing more than 4 oz (113 g) or selling more than 2 oz (57 g), of cocaine or heroin. The Rockefeller Drug Laws, as they have been known since then, have remained relatively unchanged despite periodic attempts at legislative reform.

State Institutions

The Department of Mental Hygiene housed the Bureau of Alcoholism and the alcoholism rehabilitation units (ARU) in the early 1960s. The first ARU, established in 1962, was C. K. Post at Central Islip Psychiatric Center, later moved to Pilgrim Psychiatric Center (Suffolk Co). Still operating in 2004, these units, numbering 13 statewide including those in New York City, Middletown (Delaware Co), Rochester, and Buffalo, were redesignated addiction treatment centers after consolidation of the divisions of alcoholism and substance abuse. New York State's civil commitment laws created a new agency in 1967 called the Narcotic Addiction Control Commission for treatment and rehabilitation of narcotics addicts who were certified as "civil" or "criminal" depending on their legal status. In 1973 its mission and name were changed to the Drug Abuse Control Commission, and in 1975 it became the Office of Drug Abuse Services. In 1978 the Office of Alcoholism and Substance Abuse was created. These two agencies merged in 1992, yielding the current Office of Alcoholism and Substance Abuse Services (OASAS) and following the nationwide trend toward a unified approach.

Treatment and Prevention

Since the 1950s, community-based programs have provided the bulk of New York State's treatment and prevention services. Hospitals, including Albert Einstein College of Medicine in the Bronx, St. Peter's in Albany, and Yonkers General Hospital, developed detoxification and inpatient treatment to address acute symptoms. Community-based agencies developed crisis services and residential rehabilitation programs where alcoholics could receive nonacute detoxification and treatment. Following the 1963 start of Daytop Village in Staten Island, therapeutic communities developed in the 1960s as long-term residential treatment centers, including Phoenix House in New York City, Hope House in Albany, Ithaca Alpha House, and Veritas Villa in Kerhonkson (Ulster Co). At New York City's Rockefeller University in 1963 Vincent Dole and Marie Nyswander developed pilot studies on methadone maintenance as a treatment for opiate addicts. Additionally, halfway houses and supportive-living programs were established to help people move into society after their treatment.

Prevention services emerged to counter the scare tactics of 1960s antidrug rhetoric. There was optimism in the late 1970s that accurate information could influence users and inform more effective prevention and treatment strategies. In the 1980s social skills—including self-awareness, communication, and refusal techniques—began to be taught in response to rising substance abuse among adolescents. Also in the 1980s communities became increasingly involved in prevention, including pressures to stop distribution at the neighborhood level. New York State raised the drinking age from 18 to 19 in 1982 and to 21 in 1985. Comprehensive strategies emerged in the 1990s as New York State led the nation in coordinating drug/alcohol and HIV/AIDS prevention. As the new century dawned a risk and protective factor framework that focused on science-based or evidence-based approaches to prevention was incorporated into programs. Prevention strategies targeted community, school-based, and individual/peer factors to reduce risk and to enhance protection for healthy behavior.

Statewide advocacy organizations played a significant role in the professionalization of the addiction field during the 1970s. The New York State Association of Substance Abuse Providers and the New York State Association of Prevention Professionals emerged in the 1980s as the voice of community-based and school-based service providers. The New York Federation of Alcoholism Counselors and the New York State Council on Alcohol Dependence and Abuse surfaced as major advocates for the alcoholism field. In the early 1990s the Unified Alcoholism Constituency of New York State was formed. Upon consolidation of the state agencies, advocacy organizations joined to create the New York Association of Alcoholism and Substance Abuse Providers in 1996. The treatment system in 2002 served close to 120,000 clients on any given day in more than 1,200 clinic sites throughout New York State.

See also Crime.

Acker, Caroline. *Creating the American Junkie: Addiction Research in the Classic Era of Narcotic Control* (Baltimore: Johns Hopkins Univ Press, 2002)

Campbell, Nancy D. *Using Women: Gender, Drug Policy, and Social Justice* (New York: Routledge, 2000)

Courtwright, David T. *Dark Paradise: A History of Opiate Addiction in America* (Cambridge, Mass: Harvard Univ Press, 2001)

Goldstein, Nathaniel L. *Narcotics: A Growing Problem, A Public Challenge, A Plan for Action.* Report to the Legislature Pursuant to Chapter 528 of the Laws of 1951, 175th Session, No. 3 (Albany, 1952)

Musto, David F. *The American Disease: Origins of Narcotic Control Policy,* 3d ed. (New York: Oxford Univ Press, 1999)

Terry, Charles, and Mildred Pellens. *The Opium Problem* (1928; repr Montclair, NJ: Patterson Smith, 1970)

White, William L. *Slaying the Dragon: The History of Addiction Treatment and Recovery in America* (Bloomington, Ill: Lighthouse Institute, 1998)

John J. Coppola and Nancy D. Campbell

drumlins. Small hills formed during glaciation exhibiting a form often compared to an inverted spoon, whereby the steeper, wider portion faces up-ice and the gently sloping pointed end faces down-ice. The orientation of drumlins is frequently used to reconstruct flow paths of Pleistocene ice sheets. Drumlins usually form in clusters and exist in several areas of New York State. One of the most significant is the swarm of over 10,000 drumlins that extend from west of Syracuse to beyond Rochester on the Erie-Ontario Lowland. These drumlins average 2,000 feet (610 m) in length, 1,000 feet (305 m) in width, and 50–80 feet (15–24 m) in height.

The mechanisms of drumlin formation are controversial but appear to vary from location to location. In the southeastern and northeastern parts of the state many rock drumlins exist; bedrock creates an obstacle to ice flow, allowing the accumulation of sediment in its lee. The large Central New York field, however, consists of unconsolidated sediment, which has been interpreted in a variety of ways. One theory holds that erosion and the reworking of sediment from catastrophic meltwater released under the retreating ice sheet create networks of channels that isolate erosional remnants. Other theories invoke processes of subglacial deformation resulting from varying resistance, grain size distribution, and hydrological properties of the sediment. Some of the sediment or till therefore can form a rigid, coherent core that modifies less competent material as it flows around this obstacle. The more rigid core subsequently allows the accretion of till, thus enlarging the drumlin form. Recent studies from Chimney Bluffs State Park (Wayne Co) on the Lake Ontario shoreline suggest that subglacial deformation is the more likely mechanism of formation in that region.

Isachsen, Yngvar W., et al, eds. *Geology of New York: A Simplified Account,* 2d ed. (Albany: NYS Museum, 2000)

Susan Millar

Drums Along the Mohawk. Historical novel by Walter D. Edmonds. Published in 1936, the book tells the story of the American War of Independence from the point of view of the white settlers of the Mohawk Valley, the upper reaches of which were wilderness and frontier. Edmonds deliberately eschews grand figures and events, focusing instead on the everyday life of the valley's farmers. While he is painstakingly true to the historical facts, the novel's core characters—Gilbert and Lana Martin, Sarah McKlennar, Joe Boleo, John Weaver—are imagined ones. Beginning in 1776 and ending in 1781, with a postscript from 1784, the book's chronology is that of the war, although for much of this time the valley folk see their local conflicts in isolation from it. In the Mohawk Valley the pro-Revolutionary settlers fight not to create the United States of America but to preserve their lives and property from loyalist forces and their Indian allies. Catastrophic events are rendered as personal tragedies: when the Martins's home is raided in 1776 soon after their marriage, they lose not only their emerging livelihood but their unborn baby; when Mrs McKlennar's house turns to ashes, so does her life; when John Weaver returns from the Sullivan-Clinton expedition against the Indians in 1779, he does not exult in a strategic victory but grieves over the Indian orchards and fields having been laid waste. Though Edmonds's basic sympathies clearly lie with the pro-Revolutionary settlers, various episodes and passages show them extending to the loyalists and the Indians as well. *Drums Along the Mohawk,* as a best-seller and a novel perennially assigned in the state's high schools, has substantially shaped the popular view of the region's pioneer period. Unfortunately the 1939 film directed by John Ford, starring Henry Fonda and Claudette Colbert, abandons the historical complexity of the original for the mythic simplification of an all-American Western.

Countryman, Edward. "John Ford's *Drums Along the Mohawk:* The Making of an American Myth," *Radical History Review* 24 (Fall 1980): 93–112

Frank Bergmann

Drych. See *Y Drych [The Mirror].*

Dryden. Town (pop 13,532) and village (pop 1,832) in SE Tompkins Co. Settled in 1797 along the state-built Bridle Road (1795), the town was formed from Ulysses in 1803. In the 19th century Dryden produced lumber, leather, and woolen cloth. The Dryden Springs House (1845) became a sanatorium (1862–*ca* 1900) under Dr Samantha S. Nivison (1833–1906). The village was incorporated in 1857. Always off the main routes, Dryden finally acquired service from three rail lines (1870–72). In 1974 Tompkins-Cortland Community College ("TC3"; founded 1968) relocated from Groton. In 2003 about 12% of its land remained in agriculture, producing milk, livestock, grain, and hay. Small industries included Vendapin LLC (1976; vending machines), Sturges Electronics (1978; cables and harnesses), and Avinet (1987; field biology equipment). The brick, octagonal Eight Square School (1827) has been restored as a museum.

Margaret D. Costello

Duane. Town (pop 159) in central Franklin Co. Settled in 1825, the town was formed in 1828 from Malone. Iron mining and a forge were active from 1828 to 1849, and a furnace operated 1838–?1846. In 1883 an attempt was made to grow hops and 100 acres (40 ha) were planted, but it ended in failure. Duane continues to depend on forest industries. It is the site of the Meacham Lake State Campground. Duane's population had declined to a low of 95 in 1960 but had increased 60% by 2000.

Thomas W. Perrin

Duane, James (*b* New York City, 6 Feb 1733; *d* Duanesburg [now in Schenectady Co], 1 Feb 1797). Politician. Duane studied law and was admitted to the bar in 1754 and clerked for the Court of Chancery (1762). After inheriting thousands of acres from relatives he founded the settlement of Duanesburg in 1765. He held numerous public offices, including attorney general (1767), boundary commissioner (1768, 1784), Indian commissioner (1774), and delegate in the Third and Fourth Provincial Congress (1775–76). A cautious supporter of American independence, he opposed the Sons of Liberty yet served on the Committee of Correspondence. He served in the Continental Congress (1774–83), was state senator (1782–85, 1788–90) and was the mayor of New York City (1784–89). Politically a Federalist by the 1780s, he favored adoption of the US Constitution as a delegate to the state ratifying convention (1788). Duane served as US district judge for New York City (1789–94).

Alexander, Edward P. *A Revolutionary Conservative: James Duane of New York* (New York: Columbia Univ Press, 1938)

Chris Brooks

Duanesburg. Town (pop 5,808) in SW Schenectady Co. The town was patented in 1765 to James Duane (1733–97), who immediately settled it with 20 Pennsylvania German tenant families. Quaker Street hamlet was settled soon after 1780 by Quakers. In 1793 Duane dammed Mariaville Creek for waterpower, creating Mariaville Lake and a prosperous mill village where handles, axe heads, cheese, and molding were made in the 19th century. The town was served by the Albany and Susquehanna Railroad (1863; later Delaware and Hudson). I-88 was constructed across town in 1980. In the early 21st century, Mariaville Lake provides seasonal recreation, and most town residents work elsewhere in the Capital District.

Ellen McHale

Dubinsky [Dobnievski], **David** (*b* Brest-Litovsk [now Brest, Belarus], 22 Feb 1892; *d* New York City, 17 Sept 1982). Labor leader. He immigrated to New York City in 1911 and like many Jewish immigrants found work in the garment industry. He joined Local 10 of the International Ladies' Garment Workers' Union (ILGWU) and quickly rose to the leadership. In 1921 he became the local's agent or manager. In 1922 he was elected vice president of the ILGWU, in 1929 secretary-treasurer, and in 1932 president. Dubinsky originally was a moderate socialist who had supported the US entry into World War I, and within the ILGWU he was a leader of the socialists in their victorious struggle with the communists. He left the Socialist Party in 1928 and thereafter was a liberal Democrat and a strong supporter of Pres Franklin D. Roosevelt. Dubinsky supported industrial unionism, used the labor legislation of the early New Deal to organize further his industry, and supported industrial unions elsewhere. When the American Federation of Labor (AFL) resisted, he joined with John L. Lewis and formed the Committee for Industrial Organization (CIO) in 1935. When Lewis separated the CIO from the AFL, Dubinsky opposed and refused to follow. In 1937, when the AFL finally expelled the CIO unions, Dubinsky took the ILGWU out in protest. It remained independent until 1940, when it rejoined the AFL. In 1936 he helped found the American Labor Party (ALP) as a vehicle to support FDR and to find a local alternative to Tammany Hall, which was hostile to pro-labor New Deal actions. When the ALP and the Communist Party became close in 1944, he resigned and helped found an alternative, the Liberal Party. He became a liberal-labor spokesman in American politics. Though active in New York State politics, he was slow to support civil rights actions, to recognize the transformation of his industry, and to recruit new ethnic groups into the union, especially African Americans and Puerto Ricans. He was a vocal supporter of the AFL's strongly anti-Communist foreign policy initiatives after World War II. He retired from union activities in 1966.

Danish, Max. *The World of David Dubinsky* (Cleveland: World Publishing, 1957)
Dubinsky, David, with A. H. Raskin. *David Dubinsky: A Life with Labor* (New York: Simon & Schuster, 1977)

Richard A. Greenwald

ducks. See Long Island Ducks.

Dudley Observatory. The initial vision for the observatory, built on a hill in north Albany between 1852 and 1856, came from scientists Joseph Henry, Alexander Dallas Bache, Benjamin Peirce, and Benjamin Gould. Gould served as its first director. Its origins also lay in the public interest in science and learning as a means of cultural enlightenment, moral development, and civic pride. Albany elites, including banker Thomas W. Olcott and physician James Armsby, oversaw the fund-raising campaign. The initial cost of the building and instruments was $17,000. In addition an endowment of $50,000 was created from local subscriptions and a gift by Blandina Dudley, widow of Sen Charles Dudley. Dudley's philanthropy would eventually total $105,000. Conflict between the local and scientific backers of the observatory led to the removal of Gould as director in 1858–59. In 1873 the observatory merged with the Albany College of Pharmacy, Albany Medical College, Albany Law School, and Union College in Schenectady to form a consortium called Union University, with the president of Union College serving as chancellor. Director Lewis Boss (1876–1911) oversaw the building of a second observatory in Albany in 1893. The original observatory and property were given to the City of Albany as part of the exchange for the land on Lake Ave where the second observatory was built. Upon his father's death Benjamin Boss became director of the observatory (1912–56), completing his father's lifework, *General Catalogue of 33,342 Stars* (1937), and writing a history of the observatory. The observatory was also responsible for publishing the *Astronomical Journal* from 1909 to 1941. Curtis L. Hemenway was the last director (1956–76) of a working observatory. He made Dudley the center of the study of micrometeorites, and under his direction the observatory operated a 100 ft (30.5 m) radio telescope installed in 1973 in Bolton Landing (Warren Co) on land leased from SUNY Albany. Operation of the telescope was gradually discontinued in the 1980s as the Dudley Observatory changed its mission and experienced a decline in funding. In the early 1990s the radio telescope was dismantled, and the land was returned to SUNY Albany. In 1976 Dudley ceased functioning as a working observatory and established itself as an educational foundation sponsoring research awards in astronomy and the history of astronomy and fostering educational activities in the Albany region. The organization is located at Union College.

Boss, Benjamin. *History of the Dudley Observatory, 1852–1956* (Albany: Dudley Observatory, 1968)
Dudley Observatory, http://www.dudleyobservatory.org
James, Mary Ann. *Elites in Conflict: The Antebellum Clash over the Dudley Observatory* (New Brunswick, NJ: Rutgers Univ Press, 1987)

Timothy W. Kneeland

due process. See RIGHTS.

Duer, William (*b* Devonshire, England, 18 Mar 1743; *d* New York City, 7 May 1799). Entrepreneur and politician. Educated in England at Eton College, Duer served in the British army and pursed commercial activities in India and the West Indies before immigrating to New York Colony in 1768. He settled at Fort Miller [now in Washington Co] and established several mills. In 1772 he was appointed county judge and served in the New York Provincial Congress (1776–77). During the Revolutionary War he continued in business but began a more active political career, serving on a committee that drafted the state's first constitution, on the committee of safety, and in the state senate (1777). He moved to Fishkill (Orange Co), was a delegate in Congress (1777–78), and moved to New York City (1783), where he helped to established the Bank of New York. Duer was a state assemblyman (1786) and managed bonds, land, and stock as assistant secretary of the US Treasury (1789–90). An active speculator in the nascent New York City securities market, his poor investments and the failure of his real estate speculation through the Scioto Co helped precipitate the city's first financial panic. Duer was imprisoned for debt in 1792 and died in jail.

Jones, Robert Francis. *The King of the Alley: William Duer, Politician, Entrepreneur, and Speculator, 1768–99* (Philadelphia: American Philosophical Society, 1992)

Mark G. Spencer

Duke of York. See JAMES, DUKE OF YORK AND ALBANY.

Duke's County. See EXTINCT COUNTIES.

Duke's Laws. The earliest English legal code for New York Colony and the basis for much of current New York State law. The code's name refers to James, Duke of York, the colony's proprietor, and the term is applied to both the original laws of 1665 and the amendments up to 1690. In preparing the original draft, Gov Richard Nicolls consulted the laws of Massachusetts Bay, New Haven, Maryland, and Virginia, but the wording in the 1665 Duke's Laws is generally more terse and almost certainly the work of provincial secretary Matthias Nicolls, a lawyer.

Gov Nicolls met at Hempstead [now in Nassau Co] on 10 March with elected representatives from the 17 English towns of Long Island and Westchester to discuss the proposed laws. Nicolls had not prepared tax laws before the meeting and offered the delegates their choice from other colonies' laws, including Connecticut's (which he had received en route). The delegates proposed changes and additions, and many were accepted. However, their principal request, that towns elect their own magistrates, was rejected because James, Duke of York, had instructed the governor to appoint magistrates. The duke approved the laws on 4 Nov 1667.

The Duke's Laws were at first intended only for the English communities of Long Island and Westchester, but copies were later sent to the court in New Castle, Del, and to the court for Nantucket and Martha's Vineyard [both now in Massachusetts], all then part of the duke's domains. Few of the early manuscripts have survived, and no one copy includes all the amendments. New York State in its 1894 publication of colonial laws used the text of the copy received by East Hampton on 4 July 1665, with variations in the earlier Roslyn (Hempstead) copy noted. The New-York Historical Society used another copy in its collections for an 1811 edition.

Christoph, Peter R., ed. *Administrative Papers of Governors Richard Nicolls and Francis Lovelace, 1664–1673* (Baltimore: Genealogical Publications, 1980)
The Colonial Laws of New York from the Year 1664 to the Revolution, vol 1 (Albany: J. B. Lyon, 1894)
Pennypacker, Morton. *The Duke's Laws: Their Antecedents, Implications, and Importance* (New York: New York Univ School of Law, 1944)

Peter R. Christoph

Dulles, John Foster (*b* Washington, DC, 25 Feb 1888; *d* Washington, DC, 24 May 1959). Diplomat, US senator, and secretary of state. Dulles was raised in Watertown, where his father, Rev Allen Macy Dulles, served as pastor of the First Presbyterian Church. Dulles graduated from Princeton University (1908) and attended the Sorbonne in Paris (1909). He completed his studies at George Washington University Law School and joined the New York City firm of Sullivan and Cromwell in 1911 as an expert in international law, remaining associated with the firm until 1948.

His public service began as counsel to the 1919 Paris Peace Conference. In subsequent years he served as an adviser at several international conferences, including the 1945 San Francisco Conference that created the United Nations (UN). Dulles served as a delegate to the UN General Assembly (1946, 1947, 1950) and as a member of the New York State Banking Board (1946–49). On 7 July 1949 Republican governor Thomas E. Dewey appointed Dulles to the US Senate. He was defeated for this seat in a special election four months later by former Democratic governor Herbert H. Lehman. On 21 Jan 1953 newly elected Pres Dwight D. Eisenhower appointed him secretary of state. A fervent anticommunist, Secretary Dulles stressed collective security and helped create the Southeast Asia Treaty Organization and the Central Treaty Organization alliance in the Middle East. He moved quickly to defuse the 1956 Suez crisis but remained a critic of Egyptian president Gamal Abdel Nasser. He supported the Chinese Nationalist defense of the islands of Matsu and Quemoy, and the presidency of Ngo Dinh Diem in South Vietnam. He resigned from office a month before his death. His brother, Allen Welsh Dulles, was director of the CIA from 1953 to 1961.

Immerman, Richard, ed. *John Foster Dulles and the Diplomacy of the Cold War* (Princeton, NJ: Princeton Univ Press, 1990)

J. Brooks Flippen

Dundee. Village (pop 1,690) in Starkey (Yates Co). Permanent settlement started around 1807. Dundee grew up around the waterpower on Big Stream, which supported sawmills and gristmills as well as several foundries beginning in 1835, one of which produced the Dundee chilled plow. The village, which incorporated in 1848, supported grain elevators, fruit barrel and basket production, and fruit drying and shipping on the Northern Central Railway (1851). Dundee was the premier US market for kiln-dried black raspberries at the end of the 19th century and developed into a food-processing center in the 20th century. The Dundee Grape Juice Co (1940) became Seneca Foods and was closed by new owner Northland Cranberries in 2002.

Gwen Chamberlain

Dunkirk. Town (pop 1,387) and city (pop 13,131) in N Chautauqua Co. After settlement in 1805 a nearby harbor attracted the Dunkirk Association to subdivide for a village in 1817. The village incorporated in 1837, just before the business failures of that period slowed its growth. The town was formed from Pomfret in 1859, and the city was incorporated in 1880. Industrial development was due largely to the railroads. The Erie (1851); the Buffalo and State Line (1852), which later became New York Central; and the Dunkirk, Allegheny Valley and Pittsburgh (1871) Railroads met at Dunkirk village, where the Erie maintained large shops until 1869. The Brooks Locomotive Works (1869) employed up to 1,000 and was succeeded (1901) by American Locomotive Co (ACLO), which employed 4,500 in 1921; in 1928 it shifted to other products. Other heavy industry included Atlas Crucible

Steel, US Radiator Corp (1891), Merrill Silk Mills, and the Van Raalte Co. Workers were drawn from Polish (after 1870) and Italian (after 1888) immigrants. A coal-fired Niagara Mohawk steam station was placed in service on the lakeshore in 1950, and the company became the largest taxpayer in the city; it was sold in 1999 to NRG Energy. The New York State Thruway was completed through Dunkirk in 1957. The city's population declined by almost 30% between 1960 and 2000. In the 1970s urban renewal razed about 70 structures, replacing them with public buildings. Suburban retail development has taken place near the Thruway and Rte 60. In 2000 almost 20% of the city's population consisted of ethnic and racial minorities, predominantly Latino. Dunkirk is the site of the Chautauqua County Fairgrounds, where the Dunkirk Historical Society maintains a railroad exhibition. Since 1967 the groundhog Dunkirk Dave has been a competitor with Pennsylvania's Punxsutawney Phil for weather prognostication. Early 21st century plans for harbor development include an interpretive center on Lake Erie history.

Michelle Henry

Dunlap, William (*b* Perth Amboy, NJ, 19 Feb 1766; *d* New York City, 28 Sept 1839). Playwright and author. The son of a former British officer and merchant with loyalist sympathies, Dunlap moved with his parents to British-occupied New York City during the American Revolution. Ultimately siding with the patriot cause, he left his parents and became an itinerant portraitist whose sitters included George Washington. In 1784 he was sent by his father to study painting with Benjamin West in London; intimidated by West, he spent more time in theaters than painting. He returned to New York City three years later and launched a career as a playwright with *The Father* (1789), which solidified his ambitions. He cultivated intellectual interests as a member of New York City's Philological Society and the Friendly Club. Following his father's death in 1791, Dunlap freed his family's slaves, turned his business over to his brothers-in-law, and in 1796 purchased a quarter interest in the Old American Co, a professional acting troupe. In 1798 he opened the New Theatre (later Park Theatre), where he rapidly turned out original works and translated popular European plays. Critics generally considered his Revolutionary War drama *André* (1798) his best work, though it failed on stage. In 1805 Dunlap went bankrupt and later turned to painting and writing. His publications included a short-lived magazine, the *Monthly Recorder* (1813), and a biography of his old friend Charles Brockden Brown (1815). Active in literary circles throughout his life, Dunlap formed friendships with writers James Fenimore Cooper and Washington Irving, among others. In 1826 he helped found the National Academy of Design in New York City. Before he died he published a history of the American stage (1832), a history text on New York State for schoolchildren (1837), and a larger two-volume work on the state from colonization to the adoption of the US Constitution (1839); the second volume was published in 1840, after his death. Despite Dunlap's hard work and congenial nature, which helped promote art and literature in New York State for more than half a century, his career was never a personal financial success.

Coad, Oral Sumner. *William Dunlap: A Study of His Life and Works and of His Place in Contemporary Culture* (New York: Dunlap Society, 1917)

Bryan Waterman

DuPont. In 1920 the E. I. DuPont Co, headquartered in Wilmington, Del, bought the former Philadelphia Rubber Co building and property in Buffalo and established a subsidiary, the DuPont Fibersilk Co, with Leonard A. Yerkes as president. Under his direction, a new plant was built on 90 acres (36 ha) near Buffalo and began producing silk-like fiber in 1921. The subsidiary firm's name became the DuPont Rayon Co in 1925 after the fiber was renamed; production of rayon was discontinued in 1955. In 1924 DuPont opened the first cellophane manufacturing plant in the United States in Buffalo, at a site adjacent to its rayon plant. As the demand grew, a second plant was built, and cellophane continued to be produced in Buffalo until 1986. Yerkes retired in 1945, and the complex was renamed the Yerkes Works in his honor. Facilities were expanded with a polyvinyl chloride film plant in 1961 and synthetic marble surfacing material and nylon shutters factories in 1968. In 1992 DuPont's Tedlar Business Center relocated to the Yerkes site from the company's headquarters. The Yerkes Works' principal products in 2002 are its Corian solid surfaces and Tedlar polyvinyl chloride film.

Dutton, William S. *DuPont: The First 140 Years* (New York: Scribner's, 1942)
DuPont, http://www.dupont.com

Joseph Golombek Jr

Durand, Asher B(rown) (*b* Jefferson Village [now Maplewood, NJ], 21 Aug 1796; *d* Jefferson Village, 17 Sept 1886). Painter and engraver. Durand displayed an early talent for engraving and was apprenticed to the New Jersey engraver Peter Maverick in 1812. By 1817 Durand had joined with Maverick to open a New York City branch of his business. Maverick's professional jealousy over a prominent commission would end the partnership in 1820. That commission from the artist, John Trumbull, for an engraving of his *Declaration of Independence* established Durand as the country's leading engraver. Into the 1830s he worked steadily on fine art projects, such as the National Portrait Gallery of Distinguished Americans, and an engraving of John Vanderlyn's *Ariadne* (1835), considered his highest achievement in that medium. Durand also took

In the Woods, by Asher B. Durand, 1855.

on more pedestrian commissions, with banknotes making up a large part of his work.

The engraver turned increasingly to painting with the support of New York art patron Luman Reed. A founder of the Hudson River school, Durand moved from portraiture to landscape subjects and, in middle age, emerged as a leader of the genre. He returned from an 1840–41 European sojourn at the height of his powers and in the ensuing decades painted some of his best-known works, including *Kindred Spirits* (1849), a memorial to painter Thomas Cole depicting him and William Cullen Bryant on a precipice overlooking Kaaterskill Clove in Greene Co. In 1855 Durand's "Letters on Landscape Painting" were published in the art journal *The Crayon* and represent the most formal statement of the philosophy of the Hudson River school. In them he advocated a highly detailed and finished style, suggesting that rather than studying with a teacher, artists should enroll in the "Studio of Nature." This period was also marked by Durand's presidency of the National Academy of Design (1845–61). During the summers between 1837 and 1880 he explored the natural settings around the Catskills, Lake George, and the Adirondacks, searching out subjects for his brush. Durand remained active as a painter into his 80s.

Durand, John. *The Life and Times of A. B. Durand* (1894; repr Temecula, Calif: Reprint Services, 1993)
Lawall, David Barnard. *Asher B. Durand: A Documentary Catalogue of the Narrative and Landscape Paintings* (New York: Garland Publishing, 1978)

Kimberly A. Orcutt

Durham. Town (pop 2,592) in NW Greene Co. Initial settlement occurred by 1774, but the permanent settlers were from Connecticut beginning in 1782. The town was formed from Coxsackie in 1790 as Freehold, which became Durham in 1805. Catskill Creek flows through the town, and its valley was an important route to the Schoharie Valley. Other parts of town are rough and hilly, but successful farming continues in sections. Beginning in the 1920s the town, especially East Durham, became a large Irish summer resort and is the site of the Irish-American Heritage Museum. Since 1946 Stiefel Laboratories at Oak Hill has manufactured medical soaps.

Field Horne

Durham boats. Flat-bottomed riverboats. In 1798 the Western Inland Lock Navigation Co removed the last of the portages and other obstructions along the water route between Albany and Oswego. Small boats could then be replaced by the long, narrow rivercraft known as the Durham boat. Its prototype was the mid–18th century iron ore boat of the Delaware River and noted for its use in Gen George Washington's crossing of the Delaware on Christmas Eve 1776. Before the end of the century Durham boats became common in New York State. About 60 feet (18 m) long and 8 feet wide (2 m), they had a cargo capacity up to 12 tons (11 MT) and were poled in shallow waters by men who walked along cleated boards that ran the length of the gunwales. In deep water they were rowed and occasionally sailed. They were steered with a 28 ft long (9 m) sweep at the stern. Their straight, parallel sides suited them to the early canals of New York State. During the initial construction and use of the Erie Canal, Durham boats navigated the combined river and canal systems but were mostly replaced by larger boats by 1825.

Schultz, Christian. *Travels on an Inland Voyage* (1810; repr Ridgewood, NJ: Gregg Press, 1968)

Philip L. Lord Jr

Duryea, Perry B(elmont), Jr (*b* Montauk, Suffolk Co, 18 Oct 1921; *d* Southampton, Suffolk Co, 11 Jan 2004). Speaker of the assembly. Raised in a family active in Republican Party politics, Duryea graduated from Colgate University in 1942. After a stint during World War II in the US Navy's Air Transport Service, he took over the family's lobster distribution business. He was elected to the New York State Assembly in 1960 from Suffolk Co and became minority leader in 1966. He became Speaker in 1969 and held this post until 1975, when the assembly fell into Democratic hands. He provided crucial support in 1970 for a measure liberalizing the state's abortion law, and in another unpopular stance in 1975 he garnered the necessary Republican support for a tax increase that was a condition of federal aid to New York City. In response to legislative complaints that Republican governor Nelson A. Rockefeller exercised too much influence in policy making, Duryea increased the assembly's muscle through staff increases and larger committee budgets. Armed with more clout, the assembly under Duryea now challenged Rockefeller, including forcing tax and spending cuts in the governor's 1972 budget. Some saw Rockefeller's hand behind a 1973 indictment of Duryea, later dropped, for a relatively minor violation of the campaign law, which nonetheless likely undermined his chances to secure the 1974 Republican gubernatorial nomination. Duryea served as the assembly's minority leader from 1975 to 1978 before losing the race for governor in 1978 against Democrat Hugh Carey. Duryea was viewed as a political moderate who was conservative on finance issues but a liberal on social and environmental concerns. He retired from the assembly at the end of 1978, returning to his family's business in Montauk.

Benjamin, Gerald, and Robert Nakamura, eds. *The Modern New York State Legislature: Redressing the Balance* (Albany: Rockefeller Institute of Government, 1991)

Daniel C. Kramer

Duryee's Zouaves. See FIFTH NEW YORK INFANTRY REGIMENT.

Dutch. The ethnic Dutch are now scattered across New York State, although the greatest concentration is in the Dutch areas of the 17th and 18th centuries: Manhattan, Long Island, the upper and lower Hudson Valley, and the Hackensack, Ramapo, Mohawk, and Schoharie Valleys. Millions of New Yorkers and other Americans have Dutch ancestry largely because of the 17th-century Dutch colony of New Netherland.

Immigration Trends

Emigration from the Netherlands to New York Colony stopped after the English takeover in 1664. The activities of the Holland Land Co, formed by Dutch bankers in 1792, opened several million acres of land in western New York State to settlers, a significant number of whom were Dutch or part Dutch. Another influx began about 1846, generated by both religion and economic conditions. A third wave arrived in the World War II period, and many settled in New York City and the metropolitan region.

Although the Netherlands continued to have a large Roman Catholic population after the Reformation, the Dutch who came to America in the 17th century were Protestant, mostly Reformed, but some were Lutheran. The Reformed Dutch Church was the only officially recognized church in New Netherland, and it continued to grow after the English takeover in 1664. From the 17th century throughout the 19th, it was the central cultural institution wherever the Dutch settled. The marked persistence of Dutchness in New York can be traced to the devotion of the church and its members to the Dutch language and the theology and traditions of the denomination. Gradually, as use of Dutch declined in the pulpits of New York State over the decades from the 1760s to the 1830s, the language declined into dialects. In the lower Hudson Valley, "Jersey Dutch" was spoken in some strongholds of the old Dutch settlements into the 20th century, as was the dialect known as de tawl *(de taal,* the language) in the Mohawk Valley. Population growth and ethnic attachment is suggested by membership in the Reformed Dutch Church, which in 1850 was 110,275, a figure more than 10 times the estimated population of 6,000–10,000 for all of New Netherland in 1664.

Settlement

A discussion of Dutch ethnicity in New York State must recognize a threefold curiosity. First, the population of New Netherland was only about 50% Dutch. Second, the Dutch had widely varying folk customs, traditions, and linguistic heritages, so that there was no single Dutch national culture in New York Colony in the 17th century. Third, many, regardless of ethnic or national background and often with no firsthand experience of the Netherlands, had simply opted for the umbrella of ethnic Dutchness.

Those who adopted the Dutch culture seem to have done so in part because of the appeal of values traditionally associated with the Netherlands—tolerance, freedom of conscience, entre-

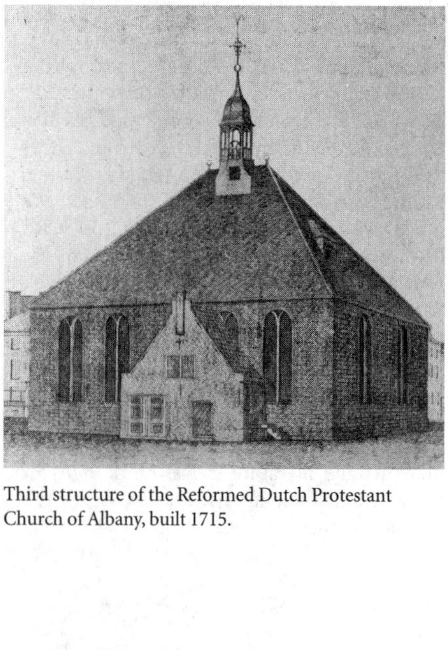

Third structure of the Reformed Dutch Protestant Church of Albany, built 1715.

Funeral spoons for Abraham Lansing (*d* 4 Oct 1899) and infant Stephen Van Rensselaer IV (*d* 4 Sept 1787). Giving funeral spoons to commemorate the dead was a custom among New Yorkers of Dutch ancestry from the 17th into the early 20th century.

The Reformed Church appears to have been over time the single most influential factor in helping the Dutch maintain their ethnic identity. The devotion of Dutch Americans to the theological ideas and religious customs of the 17th-century Reformation Netherlands proved potent enough to color not only the religious culture of New York State and New Jersey but also social life, educational institutions, marrying patterns, and child-rearing practices for two centuries and more. The persistence of Dutch cultural patterns was made possible by 17th-century patterns of land tenure that created tightly knit communities.

A progressive element in the Reformed Church's leadership and in the community it served argued for the greater involvement of its clergy and laity in the missionary, Sunday school, ecumenical, benevolent, and moral reform movements of the 19th century. The Dutch were instrumental in forming and administering many such organizations in New York City and State, including temperance, Sabbatarian, and abolition societies. It was this progressive element that understood that the continuing influence of the old Dutch ways was not always salutary, especially in rural areas. By the middle of the 18th century, and certainly in the 19th, the Dutch were admired for their industry, independence, and patriotism on the one hand but also derided, by Yankee observers in particular, for their insularity, parochialism, conservatism, thrifty ways, rural manners, dress, language, architecture, and eating habits on the other. They were also lampooned in the popular press and literature for these traits. In 1809, on the 200th anniversary of Henry Hudson's voyage up the river named for him, Washington Irving's burlesque, *Knickerbocker's History of New York,* caricatured the Dutch as bumbling buffoons blithely mismanaging their own colony. Although the stereotype stuck, it is easily refuted by the contributions of the Dutch as a charter group and "founding nation" to the institutions, laws, customs, history, culture, landscape, and demographics of New York State.

A new stage that helped erase such stereotypes began in the mid–19th century with John Lathrop Motley's best-selling *Rise of the Dutch Republic* and continued into the 20th century with various accounts asserting Dutch history and culture as being as formative as British history and culture. Works such as *The Puritan in Holland, England, and America* (1893) and *Brave Little Holland and What She Taught Us* (1894) claimed Dutch ideals and institutions such as free public education, freedom of religion, freedom of the press, and the secret ballot to be the source of these institutions in America, views that the public came to embrace. Acceptance rehabilitated the image of the Dutch, while inspiring an enthusiasm—called Holland Mania, which flourished from 1880 to 1920—for all things Dutch, from art to architecture, antiques

Maple and walnut kas, *ca* 1780. People of Dutch descent in New Netherland and New York Colony made these heavy cupboards.

preneurial spirit, economic justice, and civic concord—as well as Dutch law, educational system, treatment of women, and what was often referred to as the "purity" of the Reformed Dutch Church.

After the English takeover of New Netherland, the relationship between the Reformed Church and the local government or civil community, which had been one of mutual cooperation and interaction, changed. The Dutch were suddenly relieved of official accountability. English civil and ecclesiastical authorities were now responsible for law, order, and the moral health of the community. Dutch culture and institutions did not disappear as suddenly as Dutch officialdom, however. They persisted and are still discernable today in language, material culture, and ideas.

Nevertheless, many Dutch and Dutch sympathizers, finding their expectations for progress and prosperity different in New York Colony after the change in administration, remained aloof from the mainstream culture evolving in British North America. Some made or strengthened connections to the new ruling class, honed their English language skills, continued to compete for local and provincial offices and for advantage on the commercial front, married exogamously, and, in the 18th century, even affiliated themselves with the Anglican or Presbyterian churches. But many also moved out of Manhattan to establish new communities in the lower Hudson Valley and other river valleys in the area, where they prospered and Dutch ethnicity persevered into the early 20th century. It prospered as well, nurtured by Reformed clergy and laity determined to honor their religious roots and to remain somewhat apart from developments around them.

to advertising, and home furnishings to women's fashions.

Cultural Life

The Dutch legacy survives in both the material culture and what may be called the spiritual culture of New York State. On the material side, it survives in church architecture, in hundreds of houses in "Dutch colonial" style, in Dutch barns and smokehouses, and in artifacts and paintings preserved in museums, historical societies, and historical houses. In language it survives in such words as *anchor, ballast, caboose, cambric, cranky, duffel, easel, landscape, scow, sloop, spook, stoop, stove, wagon,* and *yacht*. It survives in literature in the works Anne Grant, James Fenimore Cooper, Washington Irving, and Irving's brother-in-law, James Kirke Paulding, and Charles Fenno Hoffman, Herman Melville, and Walt Whitman, among others. From buckwheat cakes to doughnuts, from cole slaw to crullers, from sleighs, skates, and golf to the thimble and the saw mill, linen underclothes, and soap, Dutch ingenuity caused even the Connecticut Yankee to admire any clever invention with the backhanded compliment, "it sure beats the Dutch." And Santa Claus has his Dutch progenitor in Sinte Klaas (St. Nicholas).

Dutch influence persists in New York State in the presence of the Reformed Dutch Church (now Reformed Church in America). It also continues in several educational institutions historically associated with the denomination, including Union College in Schenectady and Rutgers University and the New Brunswick Theological Seminary in New Jersey. Ethnic Dutch have figured prominently in US and New York State history. Three US presidents (Martin Van Buren, Theodore Roosevelt, and Franklin D. Roosevelt) were of New York State Dutch descent. All three were also governors of the state.

In the early 21st century, ethnic Dutch live throughout New York State. Originally farmers and craftspeople, traders and merchants, they work in all sectors of the economy. Even the most recent immigrants are thoroughly assimilated. Conversely, the denomination originally associated with the Dutch has a congregation of many ethnic backgrounds. In New York State alone, 11 languages are used in the Reformed Church of America.

Several historical societies, established in the patriotic flush of the centennial in 1876, are still active, including the Holland Society of New York, the Society of Daughters of Holland Dames, the Netherland Club of New York, and the Dutch Settlers Society of Albany. The Netherland-America Foundation, with headquarters in New York City, promotes Dutch culture and educational exchanges, the New Netherland Project, based in Albany, has been translating the administrative papers and official correspondence of New Netherland and publishing the results on a regular basis since the mid-1970s. A Dutch Heritage Day was established by Congress in 1996 and is observed annually on 16 November.

See also Architects and architecture, mid-Hudson; Schenectady; Troy; Yonkers.

Blackburn, Roderick H., and Ruth Piwonka. *Remembrance of Patria: Dutch Arts and Culture in Colonial America, 1609–1776* (Albany: Albany Institute of History & Art, 1988)

Cohen, David Steven. *The Dutch-American Farm* (New York: New York Univ Press, 1992)

De Jong, Gerald F. *The Dutch in America* (Boston: Twayne Publishers, 1975)

Fabend, Firth Haring. *A Dutch Family in the Middle Colonies, 1660–1800* (New Brunswick, NJ: Rutgers Univ Press, 1991)

———. *Zion on the Hudson: Dutch New York and New Jersey in the Age of Revivals* (New Brunswick, NJ: Rutgers Univ Press, 2000)

Kenney, Alice P. *Stubborn for Liberty: The Dutch in New York* (Syracuse: Syracuse Univ Press, 1975)

Meeske, Harrison. *The Hudson Valley Dutch and Their Houses* (Fleischmanns, NY: Purple Mountain Press, 1998)

Schulte Nordholt, Jan Willem. *The Dutch Republic and American Independence* (Chapel Hill: Univ of North Carolina Press, 1982)

Stott, Annette. *Holland Mania: The Unknown Dutch Period in American Art and Culture* (Woodstock, NY: Overlook Press, 1998)

Swierenga, Robert P., ed. *The Dutch in America: Immigration, Settlement, and Cultural Change* (New Brunswick, NJ: Rutgers Univ Press, 1985)

Firth Haring Fabend

Dutch American folklife. Washington Irving shaped the popular impression of Dutch American folkways. His short stories "The Legend of Sleepy Hollow" and "Rip Van Winkle" from his 1819–20 collection *The Sketch-Book* have been widely misunderstood to be authentic sources of Dutch American folklore rather than imaginative creations based on German and other European written sources. While little survives of the Dutch American oral tradition, it can be reconstructed from local histories and historical descriptions.

Language

The spoken language of Dutch in New York and New Jersey was itself part of Dutch American folklore. Numerous languages were spoken in New Netherland due to the diverse origins of its population, but Dutch was dominant by virtue of being the official language of the Dutch Reformed Church and the Dutch West India Co. After the English conquest in 1664, English gradually replaced Dutch as the official language of business and government, but Dutch continued to be spoken in the church and home. By the 19th century, two distinct spoken dialects of Dutch had developed: Jersey Dutch in Bergen Co, NJ, and Hudson-Mohawk Dutch in the upper Hudson and Mohawk River valleys of New York. There also seems to have been a variant of Dutch spoken by the African Dutch, both slaves and free Blacks who were culturally Dutch. By the early 19th century, these dialects diverged from Dutch as spoken in the Netherlands, as loanwords and syntax were borrowed from Algonquian and Iroquoian Indian languages and from English.

Music, Dance, and Song

The same creolization is evident in Dutch American folk music and dance. In the 1780s a Scottish physician named Alexander Coventry, living in Hudson (Columbia Co), mentioned in his diary that the Dutch farmers sang songs both in Dutch and English. He wrote that they were fond of dancing reels, a dance tradition borrowed from the British Isles. Coventry cited an outing with Jeremiah Van Rensselaer and the latter's two sisters during which he "had the pleasure of hearing the young ladies sing a number of songs, of which several were Scottish."

Notwithstanding these cultural borrowings, a Dutch folksong tradition survived into the 19th century, especially in the rural areas of New York State. In 1907 Ulster Co local historian Benjamin Myer Brink transcribed and translated one such song titled "De Pruttelarij Voorman" ("The Grumbling Wagoner"). The song describes a wagoner who complains about taking various people to the "fair" *(kermis),* including "old curmudgeons" *(oude mannen),* "old maids" *(oude dochters),* and "old lords" *(oude heeren).* But when he picks up "young women" *(jonge dochters),* he changes his tune. The song was known in America and the Netherlands.

There was also a rich tradition of children's folklore. The most common example was a Dutch nursery rhyme known as *Trip a Trop a Troontjes.*

Trip a trop a troontjes,
De varkens in de boontjes.
De koetjes in de klaver,
De paarden in de haver.
De eenjes in de water-plas,
De kalf in de larger grass.
So grott mij klijne popetjje was.

Trip a trop a troontjes,
The pigs are in the beans.
The cows are in the clover,
The horses in the oats.
The ducks are in the pond,
The calf is in the long grass.
So big my little baby was.

This nursery rhyme was collected in Flatbush in Brooklyn in 1887, in Ulster Co in 1905, and in Bergen Co, NJ, in the 1950s. Also collected in South Africa, it has been traced back to the Netherlands.

Holidays

Distinctive Dutch American customs were associated with the yearly calendar. Pentecost, or Whitsunday, was known as Pinkster among the Dutch. The religious basis for the holiday was to commemorate the appearance of the Holy Ghost to the apostles after Christ's crucifixion. However, in its folk manifestation it became a springtime carnival celebration. In 1786 Alexander Coventry described Pinkster as follows: "It is all frolicking to-day with the Dutch and Negro. This is a holy day, Whitsunday, called among the Dutch 'Pinkster,' and they have eggs boiled in all sorts of colors, and eggs cooked in every way, and everybody must eat all the eggs he can. And the frolicking is still kept up among the young folks, so that little else is done to-day but eat eggs and be jolly."

In the early 19th century, Blacks in Albany and the countryside nearby would gather on Pinkster Hill under the leadership of a slave known as King Charles. He would lead the Guinea dance, dressed in the uniform of a British soldier. The dances were described as "the original Congo dances as danced in their native Africa" accompanied by eel-pot drums. Similar celebrations were held in New York City in the early 19th century. From contemporary descriptions it seems that Pinkster had become a celebration similar to carnival in New Orleans, the Caribbean, and South America, which fused African cultural survivals with European Christian traditions. By 1874, according to local Long Island historian Gabriel Furman, "poor *Pinckster* has lost its rank among the festivals, and is only kept by the negroes; with them, however, especially on the west end of this island, it is still much of a holiday."

FOOD CULTURE

Dutch American foodways demonstrated a similar fusion of cultural traditions. The Dutch adopted from American Indians a cornmeal porridge known by the Algonquian word *sappaen.* Rather than mix the cornmeal with water, as the Native Americans did, the Dutch mixed it with milk. In the 1740s the Swedish traveler Peter Kalm described it as follows: "In the evening they [the Dutch] made a porridge of corn, poured it as customary into a dish, made a large hole in the center into which they poured fresh milk, but more often buttermilk. They ate it taking half a spoonful of porridge and half of milk. As they ordinarily took more milk than porridge, the milk in the dish was soon consumed. Then more milk was poured in. This was their supper." According to an 1884 source, the Dutch in the Schoharie Valley continued to consume a "Mush and Milk Dish for their evening meal, which they call 'Mush Sapahn.' "

In conclusion, Dutch American folklife was very different than Washington Irving's depiction of Dutch American manners and customs in "The Legend of Sleepy Hollow" as "fixed, while the great torrent of migration and improvement, which is making such incessant changes in other parts of this restless country, sweeps them by." Unlike Irving's comic stereotype, Dutch American folklife constituted a dynamic and changing regional subculture within a predominantly English-speaking nation.

See also MID-ATLANTIC REGION; ST. NICHOLAS.

Brink, Benjamin Myer. *The Early History of Saugerties, 1660–1825* (Kingston, NY: R. W. Anderson & Sons, 1902)

Cohen, David Steven. "Folklore and Folklife." In *The Dutch-American Farm.* The American Social Experience Series (New York: New York Univ Press, 1992)

———. "Afro-Dutch Folklore and Folklife." In *Folk Legacies Revisited* (New Brunswick, NJ: Rutgers Univ Press, 1995)

Coventry, Alexander. Diary, July 1782–August 1789. New York State Library, Albany

Furman, Gabriel. *Antiquities of Long Island* (New York: J. W. Bouton, 1874)

Kalm, Peter. *Travels in North America,* 2 vols, ed. Adolph B. Benson (New York: Wilson-Erickson, 1937)

Rodes, Sara Puryear. "Washington Irving's Use of Traditional Folklore," *Southern Folklore Quarterly* 19 (1956): 143–53

Van Loon, L. G. *Crumbs from an Old Dutch Closet: The Dutch Dialect of Old New York* (The Hague, Netherlands: Martinus Nijhoff, 1938)

David Steven Cohen

Dutch barn. The most commonly erected barn in colonial New York, it is most noted for its distinctive boxlike appearance. America's first distinct barn form, it is also known as the New World Dutch barn or the Dutch American barn, and was introduced into New York with the arrival of the Dutch in 1614. Made exclusively of wood, a Dutch barn is almost square, generally 40–50 feet (12–15 m) long per side, and has a steep gable roof and low outer walls. The barn is supported by a unique H-shaped structural frame that is set back within the building. In contrast, frames of English-style barns extend directly to the outer walls. Other distinctive features of the Dutch barn include large double doors centered on each of the gable ends; the doors of English barns are placed on the sides. When the double doors of the Dutch barn are opened a large central area is created, providing an ideal place to thresh wheat, which, grown as a crop for export, was New York's principal crop during the 18th century. Erected in large numbers, these barns followed Dutch settlement and were concentrated in the valleys of the Hudson, Mohawk, and Schoharie Rivers. Many colonial observers, including the famous naturalist Peter Kalm, noted the distinctive appearance and size of the colony's Dutch barns. After 1830 English barns came to predominate, as this ethnic group supplanted the Dutch.

Regional variations exist within New York State's Dutch barns, with buildings north of Ulster Co primarily made of pine—reflecting the dominant wood of that region—and barns in Ulster Co and south made near exclusively of oak. Moreover many of the design features of the state's Dutch barns can be traced to similar barns present in distinct areas of the Netherlands, particularly the Drenthe and Brabant regions. Since the 1960s public awareness has helped preserve the Dutch barn as one of the most identifiable colonial artifacts left in New York State's rural countryside. In 1985 the Dutch Barn Preservation Society, of Altamont (Albany Co), was founded; the society sponsors tours and raises funds for preservation. In 2002 approximately 510 Dutch barns remained in 29 of New York State's counties. Columbia Co is home to the largest number with 25, followed by Rockland Co with 11, and 6 barns apiece in Fulton, Greene, Nassau, and Rensselaer Cos. Many restored Dutch barns were open to the public in 2002, including at Salt Springville, the Old Stone Fort Museum in Schoharie, the Altamont Fairgrounds, the Bronck Museum in Coxsackie, the Slate Museum in Granville, the Philipsburgh Manor in Sleepy Hollow, and at the Bethpage Historic Village.

Fitchen, John. *The New World Dutch Barn: The Evolution, Forms, and Structure of a Disappearing Icon,* 2d ed. (Syracuse: Syracuse Univ Press, 2001)

Tod M. Ottman

Dutch elm disease. See TREE DISEASES AND PESTS.

Dutchess County (810 mi^2/2,098 km^2; pop 280,150). Created in 1683 as one of New York's original 12 counties, it was named after Mary Beatrice d'Este, Duchess of York, the wife of New York Colony's proprietor, James, Duke of York. In 1812 the southern quarter was separated to form Putnam Co. The county lies immediately east of the Hudson River, and the state line with Connecticut serves as its eastern boundary. It is divided into 20 towns containing 8 incorporated villages and 2 cities, Beacon and Poughkeepsie (the county seat). Elevations range from the sea-level flats and marshes along the Hudson to 2,311 feet (704 m) at the summit of Brace Mountain in the county's far northeast corner. Physiographically, Dutchess Co is divided between the Hudson Valley subregion of the Hudson-Mohawk Lowlands in the west and the Taconic Mountains subregion of the New England Upland in the east. The Taconic Mountains consist of an assortment of individual high points and ridges that occupy approximately half the county from southwest to northeast. Summit elevations tend to increase to the south and east, with the highest points exceeding 1,300 feet (400 m). These are the remains of highly deformed and folded metamorphic rock thrust westward during the Ordovician era and consist primarily of schist, phyllite, and granite. A band of slate, with some schist, extends along the region's western margin. The bedrock of the Hudson Lowlands is more highly erodible shale, siltstone, and sandstone; but even here bluffs 100–200 ft (30–60 m) high overlook the Hudson River and its very narrow floodplain. Associated hills are well rounded and exhibit variations in relief of 25–300 feet (8–90 m). The southeastern boundary with Putnam Co bisects the northernmost ridge of the Hudson Highlands, here more than 1,200 feet (365 m) in height. The county's rugged topography is further broken by three troughlike valleys. Two run

Dutch barn anchor beam. New World Dutch Barn Survey 2000.

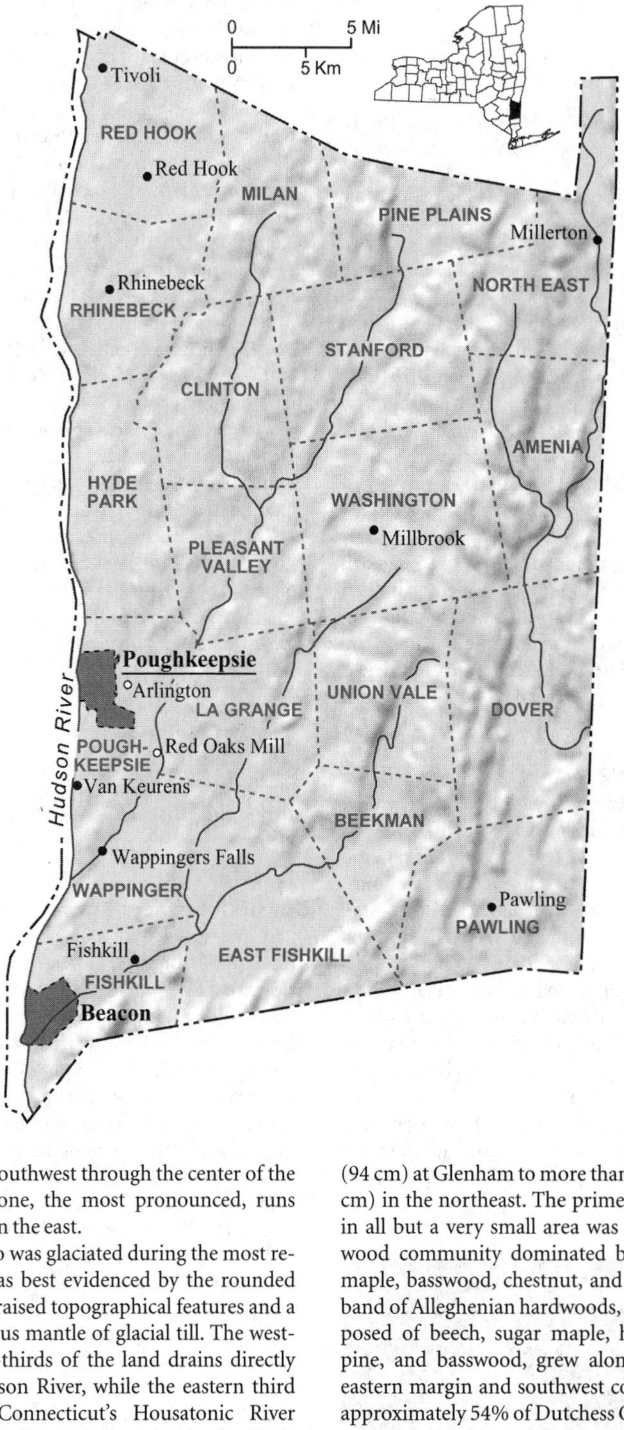

northeast to southwest through the center of the county, and one, the most pronounced, runs north-south in the east.

Dutchess Co was glaciated during the most recent ice age, as best evidenced by the rounded outline of its raised topographical features and a near ubiquitous mantle of glacial till. The westernmost two-thirds of the land drains directly into the Hudson River, while the eastern third lies within Connecticut's Housatonic River watershed. The largest tributaries to the Hudson are Wappinger Creek and Fishkill Creek. Tenmile River is the principal tributary of the Housatonic. The county's extreme southeast corner is within the Croton River watershed. Soils capable of supporting modern agriculture are limited to numerous but small and scattered lowland areas, with a noticeable concentration in the northeast quarter.

Dutchess Co's climate is humid-continental. Mean January temperatures range from 23°F (-5°C) in the northeast to 27°F (-3°C) at Glenham in the southwest. Winter lows can fall below 0°F (-18°C). Mean July temperatures range from 69°F (21°C) at Millbrook to 74°F (23°C) in the south, with daytime highs sometimes reaching 90°F (32°C) or higher. Average annual precipitation ranges from 43 inches (109 cm) in the northeast to 50 inches (127 cm) in the far south. Seasonal snowfall amounts vary from 37 inches (94 cm) at Glenham to more than 60 inches (152 cm) in the northeast. The primeval forest cover in all but a very small area was a central hardwood community dominated by beech, sugar maple, basswood, chestnut, and oak. A narrow band of Alleghenian hardwoods, primarily composed of beech, sugar maple, hemlock, white pine, and basswood, grew along the county's eastern margin and southwest corner. Presently approximately 54% of Dutchess Co is covered by second or third growth forest.

American Indians and Early Settlement

Two Algonquian-speaking Indian nations referred to locally as the Wappinger and the Mohican (Mahican) occupied the southern and northern parts of the county, respectively. Living in small family groupings, they sustained themselves on crops of corn, squash, and beans, and supplemented their diet by hunting in nearby forests. After European contact, disease and out-migration greatly thinned their ranks. In 1740 several family groups joined the Moravians, a Christian missionary settlement at Shekomeko, but fled to Pennsylvania with the Moravians after the provincial government expelled the religious group. A few Indians remained in the county until the mid–19th century.

Beginning in 1683 New York governors, attempting to encourage settlement, awarded separate tracts of land to two men, Henry Beekman Sr and Pieter Schuyler, and three partnerships, the Great Nine Partners, the Little Nine Partners, and Rombout Patents. The tracts ranged approximately from 22,000 acres (8,900 ha) to 160,000 acres (65,000 ha). Several smaller patents were also awarded, three of which encompassed land now known as the City of Poughkeepsie. Dutchess Co, initially thought by the Dutch and later by their English successors to be too hilly to cultivate, was slow to develop. By 1714 it was occupied by fewer than 50 families, most of whom were farmers of Dutch origin, from Ulster, Albany, and New York Cos. An infusion of German Palatines, abruptly discharged in 1712 from a failed naval stores venture at Livingston Manor, accounted for more than one-third of the county's 129 families by 1718. Approximately half of the population lived as tenants in the vicinity of Fishkill, Poughkeepsie, and Rhinebeck until 1740. Beginning that year, land in the Great Nine Partners Patent, an unoccupied tract of one-third of the county's acreage, was subdivided for sale as small farms. Drawn by this opportunity, families migrated from crowded New England and from the lower counties of New York. With this influx Dutchess became New York's second most populous county by 1756. The ethnic composition gradually changed, and by 1775 two-thirds of its nearly 4,000 families were of English origin. Agricultural products, principally grain received as rent from tenants, were shipped by water to New York City from the three fledgling commercial centers of Fishkill, Poughkeepsie, and Rhinebeck.

African Americans

Enslaved African Americans accompanied the first settlers to Dutchess Co. During the 1780s slaves were found in 12% of the county's households and accounted for an estimated 6% of the population. Of approximately 1,300 slaves present at the start of the American Revolution, three of every four were in Fishkill, Poughkeepsie, and Rhinebeck. Typically one or two slaves were found in slave-owning households; in the wealthiest households the number was closer to five. Though serving primarily as household servants and farm laborers, slaves were also used by merchants in grain mills and sawmills as well as for dock work and road maintenance. Less than 10% of Africans were free during the colonial period. Manumissions after the American Revolution freed some slaves, but in 1790 there were still approximately 1,750 slaves in the county. By 1820 one-third of the African American population remained enslaved. Freed finally by New York State law in 1827, the Dutchess Co's African American population declined to under 3% after 1875. Post–World War II migration gradually increased their presence to 8% in 1990. Since 1840 the largest concentrations of African Americans have been in Fishkill and Poughkeepsie. Prominent African Americans include Gaius Bolin, president of the Dutchess County Bar Association in 1945, and his daughter Jane, who in 1939 became the first female African American judge in the United States.

Revolutionary and Early National Period

Resistance to England was supported initially by two of every three people in 1775. Except for two brief skirmishes in 1776, there was no organized resistance to the American Revolution, though the sentiment of dissent continued and resulted in an occasional arrest. Throughout the war Fishkill served as a significant supply depot, winter camp, and hospital for the Continental army. In October 1777 British naval vessels raided three Dutchess Co localities, Poughkeepsie, Rhinebeck, and Red Hook. Cannon fire and a small number of troops destroyed or damaged a few storehouses, mills, small boats, and homes. Dutchess Co sites served as the state capital during this early period. Representatives met at Fishkill from August 1776 to February 1777 to create the State of New York. After Kingston (Ulster Co) was burned in October, Poughkeepsie served as the state capital intermittently after 15 Jan 1778, until Albany was so designated in 1798. In 1788 Poughkeepsie was the site of the New York State convention for the ratification of the US Constitution. Dutchess Co representatives were all Antifederalists, though a majority eventually voted in favor of a federal government.

DUTCHESS CO POPULATION CENSUS FIGURES

	White	Nonwhite	Total Population	Foreign-Born
1790	42,970	2,296	45,266	0
1800	45,235	2,540	47,775	0
1810	48,977	2,386	51,363[a]	0
1820	44,158	2,457	46,615	248
1830	48,440	2,486	50,926	592
1840	50,128	2,270	52,398	0
1850	57,022	1,970	58,992	7,387
1860	62,890	2,051	64,941	9,822
1870	71,926	2,115	74,041	12,103
1880	77,068	2,116	79,184	11,671
1890	76,191	1,688	77,879	12,053
1900	79,424	2,246	81,670	12,093
1910	85,279	2,382	87,661	13,460
1920	89,508	2,239	91,747	12,504
1930	102,250	3,212	105,462	15,341
1940	116,239	4,303	120,542	15,595
1950	131,167	5,614	136,781	14,956
1960	165,748	10,260	176,008	15,139
1970	206,202	16,093	222,295	14,575
1980	221,833	23,222	245,055	17,167
1990	229,506	29,956	259,462	18,019
2000	234,385	45,765	280,150	23,600

Notes: "Nonwhite" includes African Americans, Asians, American Indians, and Pacific Islanders and, for 2000, also the mixed race and other race categories. Through the 1960 census these figures primarily reflect the African American population. Foreign-born figures for 1820 and 1830 include only those not naturalized, and for 1930 and 1950, the foreign-born totals include Whites only. Other years include all foreign-born in the population.

[a]Recalculated; 51,434 printed in 1810 census.

Transportation

The Hudson River was the principal passenger and freight transportation artery from the time of the county's first settlement until late in the 19th century. An increasing demand for surplus agricultural products prompted the construction of turnpikes in the first two decades of the 19th century. Also, in 1821 and 1826, consideration was given to the construction of a canal from Sharon, Conn, through Dutchess Co to the Hudson River in lower Westchester Co, but no action was taken. Local businesses in 1832 obtained a charter to construct a railroad from Poughkeepsie to the Connecticut state line. After a survey had been done and funds had been raised, the plan was abandoned in 1836. In 1850 both the New York and Harlem Railroad and the Hudson River Railroad were constructed from New York City to Albany on the eastern and western boundaries of the county, respectively. Farmers in the eastern part benefited most. Seizing the opportunity to export fluid milk to New York City, many of them switched from mixed farming to dairy production. In 1868 and 1872 two locally financed intracounty railroads were constructed to the Connecticut state line in the southeastern corner of the county. The Dutchess and Columbia Railroad originated in Fishkill, and the Poughkeepsie and Eastern Railroad originated in Poughkeepsie. The scenic Taconic Parkway, constructed between 1929 and 1963, afforded residents easy access to New York City and Albany. The Metro-North Railroad serves as a commuter line to New York City.

Religion, Education, and Culture

Colonial Dutch, English, and German settlers brought their Protestant religious practices to Dutchess Co. Quakers had a strong presence until the Hicksite schism of the mid–19th century. The influx of Irish and German immigrants made Roman Catholicism the county's largest denomination by the 1870s, while Jewish worshipers were few until the 20th century. By the early 21st century there were over 200 religious congregations. In 1776 two printers escaping the British in New York City established Dutchess Co's first newspapers. The *Poughkeepsie Journal* is the only survivor of the numerous daily papers. Although small collections of books were accessible to the average resident in several towns in the early 1800s, formal library facilities did not become available until midcentury. The forerunner of the Adriance Memorial Library, established in Poughkeepsie in 1841, was among the earliest tax-supported libraries in the country. Beyond the ubiquitous one-room schools, small private schools, such as the Amenia Seminary, the Poughkeepsie Female Academy, and the Poughkeepsie Collegiate School, were established during the second and third quarters of the 19th century to provide education for boys and girls from economically successful families. By the mid–19th century, colleges in Poughkeepsie, such as Vassar College and the Eastman National Business College (1860–1933), grew swiftly, attracting students nationally and internationally. In the latter half of the 20th century, new facilities were built at Bard and Vassar Colleges, and the Culinary Institute of America, Dutchess Community College, and Marist College were established.

Economic Development

The family farm was central to the county's economy during the 19th century. Agricultural acreage accounted for 75% of the improvable land by 1840. Population growth in rural towns had by that time almost reached its height. The rate of growth was quite slow during the remainder of the century, and in some decades there was no growth or population declined. Primarily a semisubsistence enterprise during the early 1700s, farms became involved in market production, exporting butter, meat, wool, and a variety of other agricultural commodities to New York City in the 1790s. Confronted with increasing competition from western farmers, Dutchess Co farmers gradually changed the array of products they marketed with production of fluid milk becoming necessary for survival by 1875. In the early 20th century, milk was the county's single most important agricultural product.

During the first quarter of the 19th century, industry was limited to mills for grain, timber, and fabric and to the manufacture of consumer products for the farm communities. Poughkeepsie briefly had a silk thread industry, and several whaling companies were based in the county. Also during this period newly established textile mills at Glenham and Matteawan [now Beacon] in the Town of Fishkill employed more than 100 men, women, and children. By 1850 the Matteawan mill employed over 600 persons. Beginning in the second quarter of the 19th century, industrial growth was evident along the Hudson River, particularly in Poughkeepsie and Fishkill. Raw materials such as iron ore, produced in the Towns of Beekman, Dover, North East, and Union Vale, were sent to furnaces in the Towns of Poughkeepsie and Fishkill. Heavy machinery and spring mattresses were manufactured in Poughkeepsie, and bricks, pottery, springs, chairs, doors, blinds, mattresses, soap, and candle manufacturing took place elsewhere in the county. Cotton and woolen clothing and shoes were also factory produced. Overalls made by the Sweet-Orr Co in the Town of Wappinger achieved national prominence, as did the Smith Brothers Cough Drop Co and the Vassar Brothers Brewery, both in Poughkeepsie. The Poughkeepsie Savings Bank (1831) and the Bank of

POPULATIONS OF TOWNS AND CITIES, DUTCHESS CO

Town or City, Year Founded	1800	1840	1880	1920	1960	2000
Amenia, 1762[a]	2,978	2,179	2,697	1,831	7,546	4,048
Beacon (city), 1913	—	—	—	10,996	13,922	13,808
Beekman, 1737[a]	3,756	1,400	1,578	844	3,326	13,652[b]
Clinton, 1786	5,208	1,830	1,640	1,198	1,639	4,010
Dover, 1807	—	2,000	2,281	1,710	8,776	8,565
East Fishkill, 1849	—	—	2,574	1,944	4,778	25,589
Fishkill, 1737[a]	6,168	10,437	10,732	2,095	7,083	20,258
Hyde Park, 1821	—	2,364	2,873	2,880	12,681	20,851
La Grange, 1821[c]	—	1,851	1,745	1,132	6,079	14,928
Milan, 1818	—	1,725	1,275	704	944	2,359[b]
North East, 1737[a]	3,252	1,385	2,181	1,922	2,489	3,002
Pawling, 1769[a]	4,269	1,571	2,006	1,955	3,938	7,521
Pine Plains, 1823	—	1,334	1,352	1,252	1,608	2,569
Pleasant Valley, 1821	—	2,219	1,785	1,160	4,046	9,066
Poughkeepsie, 1737[a]	3,246	10,006	4,628	10,519	32,164	42,777
Poughkeepsie (city), 1854	—	—	20,207	35,000	38,330	29,871
Red Hook, 1812	—	2,829	4,471	3,218	6,023	10,408
Rhinebeck, 1737[a]	4,022	2,659	1,569	2,770	4,612	7,762
Stanford, 1793	2,344	2,278	2,092	1,368	1,614	3,544
Union Vale, 1827	—	1,498	1,407	987	1,138	4,546
Wappinger, 1875	—	—	4,961	3,467	9,577	26,274
Washington, 1788	2,666	2,833	2,797	2,795	3,695	4,742

Note: In 1800 Dutchess Co included the Towns of Carmel, Kent [then Frederick], Patterson [then Franklin], Philipstown, and Southeast [now in Putnam Co].

[a]Formed as a precinct; recognized as a town 1788.

[b]Because of an error in counting prison population, the Census Bureau originally reported the 2000 population of the Town of Beekman to be 11,452 and the Town of Milan to be 4,559.

[c]Freedom until 1828.

Fishkill (1850) funded small business enterprises and provided mortgages for farmers and home buyers. Iron ore mining in several eastern towns, a marble works in Dover, a cotton mill in Pleasant Valley, flour mills in several towns, cigar manufacturers, and similar small enterprises exported their products. From 1901 to 1912 the Lane Motor Vehicle Co in Poughkeepsie manufactured steam automobiles.

Politics

A board of town supervisors administered county government from 1717 until 1968. The principal elected official, a town supervisor, represented each town at the annual meeting of the County Board of Supervisors. A chair elected from that body became the chief executive officer, and meetings were held at the chair's discretion. The number of supervisors, at first only 3, grew as municipalities were created until there were 27 members by 1967. As a result of a countywide referendum, government was changed in 1968 to a county executive, elected every four years, and county representatives from 37 county districts, elected every two years. Thereafter the number was reduced first to 35 and, in 2001, to 25 legislators. Elected mayors administer the cities of Beacon and Poughkeepsie and several villages. Dutchess Co has voted Republican in most elections since the 1850s. Its most famous son, however, is Democrat Franklin D. Roosevelt, who in six victorious races for governor and president carried his home county only once (1930). More popular locally and nationally in her later years was Eleanor Roosevelt. Franklin Roosevelt's Dutchess Co neighbor, Henry Morgenthau Jr, served as US secretary of the treasury (1933–44). Among the strongest congressional opponents of Roosevelt's New Deal was another county neighbor, Hamilton Fish (1921–45). His son, Hamilton Fish Jr, represented Dutchess Co in the House of Representatives (1969–95). Pawling resident Thomas E. Dewey, governor of New York (1943–55), was a twice-defeated candidate for US president, in 1944—running against fellow Dutchess Co resident FDR!—and again in 1948.

Recent History

Suburban development and the collapse of dairy farming were the most significant changes in Dutchess Co after World War II. At the close of the 20th century, of the more than 1,500 dairy farms that existed 100 years ago, fewer than 75 have survived, and most of them are in the northeastern corner of the county. Newer agricultural pursuits include wineries, vegetable and fruit production, horse breeding and boarding, Christmas tree farms, and nurseries. Open land reforested to an 18th-century appearance defines much of the terrain in the north and east. Transportation improvements include three new bridges across the Hudson River after 1930. IBM, with plants in Poughkeepsie and East Fishkill, became the world's largest producer of computers during the third quarter of the 20th century. Concurrent with this growth was suburban development, particularly between Poughkeepsie and Fishkill. Accommodating newly arriving families was the development of suburban shopping malls, the first of which appeared in 1958. Subsequently the Cities of Beacon and Poughkeepsie, formerly the county's principal retail centers, experienced sharp declines. Since 1975 blue- and white-collar employment has also declined. During the 1990s several major factories closed, relocated, or downsized, including IBM, Texaco, and DeLaval Separator Co, while county banks consolidated. Patient capacity has sharply dropped at the Hudson River Psychiatric Center, the county's one remaining state-supported psychiatric hospital. In contrast, the prison populations at Green Haven and Fishkill Correctional Facilities have grown. Suburbanization continues as families seeking less expensive housing, lower taxes, better schools, and "country living" migrate from New York City and Westchester Co to the southern parts of Dutchess, commuting to higher-paying jobs closer to the city. Demand for additional housing and its consequent use of open land, particularly in the southern part of the county, has raised concerns among town officials about their towns' futures. Similarly, school boards confronted with new students in already fully utilized school buildings are struggling to add classroom space and to maintain reasonable taxes. County officials are promoting small business development, employment in the service sector, and tourism.

Prominent and important Dutchess Co residents include Revolutionary War hero Egbert Benson (1746–1833), historian Benson J. Lossing (1813–91), birth control advocate Margaret Sanger (1879–1966), broadcaster Lowell Thomas (1892–1981), and folksinger Pete Seeger (1919–). Franklin D. Roosevelt's presidential library and home and Eleanor Roosevelt's cottage and furniture factory are designated National Historic Sites, as are the Vanderbilt Mansion and Montgomery Place. The latter was the home of Gen Richard Montgomery's wife Janet (1743–1828), granddaughter of Robert Livingston of Livingston Manor.

Dutchess Co does not have the single stand-out centennial era publication that most New York State counties do. Three early sources are Philip H. Smith, *General History of Duchess [sic] County* (1877); James H. Smith, *History of Dutchess County* (1882); and Frank Hasbrouck, *History of Dutchess County* (1909). Its historiography since that time, however, has been extensive and of high quality. The *Dutchess County* volume in the American Guides series (1937; repr 1975) contains a great deal of useful material. Henry N. McCracken, *Old Dutchess Forever! The Story of an American County* (1956) is a rarity as a literary work based on good research. Staughton Lynd, *Anti-Federalism in Dutchess County* (1962) is an important, if dated, political history. In more recent years, *Transformation of an American County: Dutchess County, NY, 1683–1983* (1986) is a collection of essays by scholars for its tercentenary.

Beginning with Edmund Platt, *The Eagle's History of Poughkeepsie* (1905), the county seat has received considerable attention, most recently in the excellent work of Clyde Griffen and Sally Griffen, *Natives and Newcomers: The Ordering of Opposition in Mid-19th-Century Poughkeepsie* (1978) and Clyde Griffen, *New Perspectives on Poughkeepsie's Past* (1987). Pioneer town histories include Newton Reed, *Early History of Amenia* (1875); Isaac Huntting, *History of Little Nine Partners* (1897); and Warren H. Wilson, *Quaker Hill: A Sociological Study* (1907). In recent years a number of good community histories have been published, including Richard C. Wiles, *Tivoli Revisited: A Social History* (1981) and Sari B. Tietjen, *Rhinebeck: Portrait of a Town* (1990).

Frank J. Doherty, *Settlers of the Beekman Patent,* issued in multiple volumes beginning in 1990, reconstructs the entire population of that part of the county. Michael E. Groth, "Forging Freedom in the Mid-Hudson Valley: The End of Slavery and the Formation of a Free African-American Community in Dutchess County" (PhD diss, SUNY Binghamton, 1994) explores the once significant rural black population.

William P. McDermott

Dutch literature. Dutch prose pertaining to New Netherland began close on the heels of the earliest Dutch presence in that area. The first writings depended on firsthand accounts and became part of histories, geographies, and periodicals, such as Emanuel van Meteren's *History of the Netherlanders* (*Historie der Neder-landscher ende haerder Naburen Oorlogen ende Geschiedenissen,* 1611), Johannes De Laet's *New World* (*Nieuwe Wereldt,* 1625, 1630), and Nicolaes van Wassenaer's biannual *Historical Relation* (*Historisch Verhael,* 1624–30), which directly addressed itself to possible immigrants. Some were official documents, such as the Dutch West In-dia Co's (WIC's) regulations and instructions (1624–26), or books and pamphlets that argued for or against the colony or sought to promote emigration. Although practical purposes motivated the latter, these books and pamphlets reveal their authors' belletristic aspirations. Adriaen van der Donck, lawyer, author, and landowner, wrote his *Representation of New Netherland,* or *Remonstrance* (*Vertoogh van Nieu-Neder-Land*) for publication in the Netherlands in 1650. This pamphlet sharply criticizes WIC policies in New Netherland but also looks toward a promising future as encouragement for would-be settlers. More descriptive and encouraging, and less critical, is Van der Donck's *Description of New Netherland* (*Beschrijvinge van Nieuw-Nederlant,* 1655), the first book about early New York. Its simple prose enriched with allusions to art and the classics, the *Description* has ample detail regarding agricultural practices, indigenous population, and native plant and animal life, and ends with a dialogue on the advantages of New Netherland.

Extant New Netherland journals share a simple, chronological structure. Harmen Meyndertsz van den Bogaert's journal calmly relates the difficulties of his 1634–35 trade mission to the Mohawk and Oneida undertaken from his post at Fort Orange. Mariner and patroonship partner David Pietersz de Vries used his diaries from 1633 to 1643 and the accounts of others to compose his *Short History* (*Korte Historiael,* 1655). The tone is practical, self-confident, and sharply critical of Directors Wouter van Twiller and Willem Kieft. In 1679–80 Jasper Danckaerts and a companion traveled through former New Netherland and surroundings to find a location for a Labadist community. Landscape, villages, individuals, and situations are astutely observed and vividly related in Danckaerts's journal.

Correspondence pertaining to administration, business, and church reveal the variety of personalities in charge of the affairs of New Netherland. Letters from the clergy, for example, not only report on the condition of the church but also relate incidents that clearly illustrate the interactions with those of other faiths and different origins. The letters between Jeremias van Rensselaer, his wife Maria, and their correspondents consist of detailed discussions about the affairs of the patroonship of Rensselaerswijck and about Indian relations and family matters.

Poetry writing was a common pastime among the well educated of the 17th century. Selections from the works of three New Netherland poets have been transcribed and translated, albeit not flawlessly. The merchant Jacob Steendam, known as a poet before he arrived in New Netherland around 1650, left New Amsterdam in 1663. His "The Praise of New Netherland" ("'t Lof van Nuw-Nederland") is the region's earliest epic poem in its emphasis on the subject's dignity, its use of the four elements, and its grand inventory of actual flora and fauna. Biblical and devotional references, a plea for gratitude to God, and a prayer for peace convey the poet's Christian faith. His "Complaint of New Amsterdam" ("Klagt van Nieuw-Amsterdam") combines praise and censure in personifying the town as the thriving daughter of a careless mother. Its conclusion proposes emigration for their mutual benefit. Emigration is also the purpose of Steendam's "spurring" verses, included with Pieter Cornelisz Plockhoy's *Short and Clear Design (Kort en Klaer Ontwerp,* 1662), a plan for settlement in the Delaware.

Henricus Selyns served as minister of the Dutch Reformed Church in New Netherland from 1660 to 1664 and again from 1682 to his death in 1701. His occasional poems are purely celebratory, such as "Nuptial Song" ("Bruydlofts-Liedt"), or temper the joyful event with mourning and admonition, as in "Bridal Torch" ("Bruydloft Toorts"); several are mostly secular and often playful. Similar distinctions mark his epitaphs; some are religious in nature, while others, notably that for Petrus Stuyvesant, derive humor from wordplay.

Nicasius de Sille, an inhabitant of New Utrecht [now in Kings Co], was a councillor and administrator during Stuyvesant's tenure. "The Earth Speaks to Its Cultivators" ("Het Aerdryck spreeckt tot seyne opqueckers") remarkably presents the Dutch settler as a "new Adam," who readies the land for cultivation and honors it by naming it [New] Utrecht. De Sille's use of this figure implies that God has granted humankind a second opportunity in the New World, where one finds not a new Eden, however, but a wilderness that can only be brought to fruition by one's labor.

Prose and poetry in the Dutch language continued to be written in the area of former New Netherland as long as it remained viable but was largely out of public view. However, the custom to import books from the Netherlands continued well into the 19th century. These were mainly histories, biographies, religious material, and works by the great authors of the Dutch Golden Age, especially those by Jacob Cats (1577–1660). His verses remained part of the Hudson Valley's oral tradition until the early 20th century. That tradition's tales and legends live on, notably in the works of some of New York's early 19th-century authors.

See also ST. NICHOLAS.

Funk, Elisabeth Paling. "De Literatuur van Nieuw-Nederland," *De Nieuwe Taalgids: Tijdschrift voor Neerlandici* 85 (Sept 1992): 383–95

Jameson, J. Franklin, ed. *Narratives of New Netherland, 1609–1664* (1909; repr Bowie, Md: Heritage Books, 1990)

Murphy, Henry C. *Anthology of New Netherland; or, Translations from the Early Dutch Poets of New York with Memoirs of Their Lives* (Port Washington, NY: I. J. Friedman, 1969)

Van den Bogaert, Harmen Meyndertsz. *A Journey into Mohawk and Oneida Country, 1634–1635: The Journal of Harmen Meyndertsz van den Bogaert.* Trans and ed. Charles T. Gehring and William A. Starna (Syracuse: Syracuse Univ Press, 1988)

Van Laer, A. J. F., trans and ed. *Documents Relating to New Netherland, 1624–1626, in the Henry E. Huntington Library* (San Marino, Calif: Huntington Library and Art Gallery, 1924)

Elisabeth Paling Funk

Dutch restoration. The return of New York Colony to Dutch rule during the Third Anglo-Dutch War (1672–74). On 30 July 1673 Cornelis Evertsz the Youngest and Jacob Benckes, commanders of a 21-sail Dutch squadron, anchored off Fort James on Manhattan and demanded the fort's surrender.

The Dutch had not intended to take New York. Evertsz was sailing for the Netherlands province of Zeeland, with secret instructions to raid areas in South America, the Caribbean, Virginia, New York, and Newfoundland. Off Martinique he joined forces with Benckes, who was sailing for Amsterdam. Following a successful raid of English tobacco ships along the Chesapeake, they stopped at Sandy Hook, NJ, for fresh water, and several Dutchmen from Long Island and Staten Island came aboard and complained of their treatment by the English. Of more interest was their report that Gov Francis Lovelace was out of town, the fort was poorly garrisoned, and its munitions were in disrepair. After confirmation of the information, the commanders decided to try to capture New York City.

Evertsz and Benckes sent a trumpeter to the fort announcing that they commanded ships of war of the States General of the Netherlands and the Prince of Orange and calling for the English surrender. Capt John Manning, in charge of the fort during Lovelace's absence, stalled surrendering because he hoped—in vain—to get reinforcements from Long Island. Only a handful from Manhattan offered help. When the last request to surrender was ignored, Evertsz fired two warning shots and then a broadside into the fort, while Capt Anthony Colve and 600 marines went ashore and marched to the fort, which finally surrendered.

Evertsz, Benckes, and Colve quickly established a council of war, renamed the fort for Willem Hendrick, and gave the city the name New Orange. Some initial looting was quickly and permanently stopped, and the fort was garrisoned. Gov Lovelace returned from Connecticut and surrendered on 2 August. He, Manning, and the English garrison were sent back to England. The commanders worked quickly to put a Dutch government in control, and Colve was appointed military governor general pro tem over the colony. His commission covered the New York territory that had been under Dutch rule prior to 1664, plus all of Long Island. By 17 August the commanders had established a provisional government in the Dutch form for New Orange and called on the community to make nominations for *schout* (chief law enforcement officer) and *schepenen* (magistrates) for the city's municipal government.

As part of the effort to retake the whole colony, now returned to its original name of New Netherland, a ship was sent to Albany on 2 August to demand its surrender. The town was renamed Willemstadt and the fort's name was changed to Fort Nassau [now Port of Albany]. Kingston, renamed Swanenberg, also surrendered. Released from their oath of allegiance to England, the towns of New Jersey, Staten Island, Long Island, and Delaware agreed to come under Dutch rule and take on Dutch forms of government. An order for confiscation of English property was made but was mostly confined to property belonging to the Duke of York and his officers.

Evertsz and Benckes left in September, with the majority of the fleet, to complete their original orders. Before departing they made Colve's appointment as governor permanent and left a 40-gun warship and a frigate for defense. The court of New Orange, fearing its weakened position would encourage attack from the English colonies to the north and south and the French in Canada, sent a letter to the States General to request reinforcements. The ship carrying the letter and the commanders' report of the reconquest was captured by the English and the letters thrown overboard to avoid getting into enemy hands. An oral report, however, was made to the admiralty board in Amsterdam and then passed on to a surprised States General. They appointed a new governor on 15 Dec 1673. Four days later the Dutch government offered the return of New Netherland in peace treaty discussions with England.

The Peace of Westminster was completed in February 1674, and in April the States General ordered Colve to restore the colony to the English governor, Edmund Andros; by June, Colve was already restoring confiscated property to the English; and the formal orders were sent in July. Colve absolved the court of Fort Orange of its allegiance to the States General and the Prince of Orange on 9 November, formally surrendering New Netherland to Andros the following day.

Ritchie, Robert C. *The Duke's Province: A Study of New York Politics and Society, 1664–1691* (Chapel Hill: Univ of North Carolina Press, 1977)

Schomette, Donald G., and Robert D. Haslach. *Raid on America: The Dutch Naval Campaign of 1672–1674* (Columbia: Univ of South Carolina Press, 1988)

Martha Dickinson Shattuck

Dutch West India Company. On 3 June 1621 the States General of the United Provinces of the Netherlands approved the charter of the West India Company (WIC), the date coinciding with the end of the Twelve Years' Truce in the war of independence from Spain. The company was formed to carry on the war with Spain in the Atlantic theater of operations and to eliminate the cutthroat competition between Dutch trading companies that had been raging in the various trading zones. As a monopoly WIC would embrace all competing parties as shareholders in a venture that would benefit all equally. The company was modeled after the highly successful Dutch East India Company (VOC). The latter was chartered in 1602, and its trading monopoly extended from the Cape of Good Hope in Africa eastward to the Strait of Magellan. It had the power to raise its own armies and navies, make alliances with local sovereigns within its jurisdiction, and, if necessary, make war and conclude peace in defense of its interests. Company shares were traded on the Amsterdam stock exchange, and investors represented all walks of life.

The WIC was formed in the VOC's image as a joint-stock venture with a trading monopoly from the Cape of Good Hope westward to the outer reaches of New Guinea in the Pacific. It was divided into five chambers at Amsterdam, Zeeland, Maes, Noorderquartier, and Groningen-Friesland. The financial obligation of each chamber determined the proportion of directors on the governing board. As the largest investor, Amsterdam sent 8, followed by Zeeland with 4, the other three chambers with 2 each, and the States General with 1, for a total of 19. The Amsterdam chamber was responsible for managing the WIC's interests in New Netherland. The WIC reached its zenith in 1628 when Piet Hein captured the Spanish silver fleet. This sudden wealth encouraged the directors to renew efforts to gain a foothold in Brazil, a preoccupation that would consume WIC's resources until 1654, when the Portuguese regained control of their possessions. In 1674 the WIC was reorganized and most of its nonfinancial records were discarded. The WIC limped along on subsidies from the government, always in the shadow of its successful and wealthy sister company, the VOC, until it was dissolved in 1791.

Bachman, Van Cleaf. *Peltries or Plantations: The Economic Policies of the Dutch West India Company in New Netherland, 1623–1639* (Baltimore: Johns Hopkins Press, 1969)

Heijer, Henk den. *De Geschiedenis van de WIC* (Zutphen, Netherlands, 1994)

Charles T. Gehring

Dylan, Bob [Zimmerman, Robert] (*b* Duluth, Minn, 24 May 1941). Songwriter and singer. Robert Zimmerman grew up in Hibbing, Minn, and attended the University of Minnesota in Minneapolis. Immersing himself in the folk revival, he adopted the name Bob Dylan and in 1961 moved to Greenwich Village, where he met his idol Woody Guthrie and became a fixture at such folk clubs as Gerde's Folk City, quickly attracting attention from the local folk community as well as music critic Robert Shelton. Dylan's record contract with Columbia was arranged by producer John Hammond. His first few albums, such as *The Freewheeling Bob Dylan* (1963), placed him squarely in the tradition of left-wing protest music through songs like "Blowin' in the Wind," though he would soon move to more personal lyrics. In 1964 he appeared at the Newport Folk Festival, where he performed raucous music backed by a full electric band, heralding a pair of albums that established his national fame as a rock songwriter. During this period he began to spend more time in Woodstock (Ulster Co), a small town that served as a refuge for New York City musicians. In 1966 Dylan went into seclusion after suffering injuries from a motorcycle accident, emerging in 1968 with a turn toward more traditional folk and country music. During the period of seclusion he recorded many traditional-style songs with the Band that were later released as *The Basement Tapes* (1975). Since the 1970s he has gone through a number of style changes with varying degrees of critical success.

Heylin, Clinton. *Bob Dylan: Behind the Shades Revisited* (New York: William Morrow, 2001)

Jake Besterman

Butter lamb by Malczewski Poultry Co.

Dyngus Day. A Polish American holiday observed on Easter Monday. In 19th-century Poland on this day young men chased and swatted young women with pussy willow branches or, alternatively, doused them with water or perfume. On the following day the women took revenge. When Poles immigrated to the United States in the late 19th and early 20th centuries, they brought the Dyngus Day custom. In New York State the whipping and water dousing were observed in Polish American neighborhoods until approximately 1960; in 1962 the holiday was revived in Buffalo by the Chopin Singing Society in a new form: a party featuring Easter foods blessed by a priest, speeches by politicians, and polka music. Since then, the Dyngus Day party custom has spread to Syracuse and other cities in the northeastern United States. Among the characteristic Polish foods is the butter lamb, sculpted of butter to represent the paschal lamb, with a red resurrection banner, signifying Christ's victory over death. Today in Polish American communities, the butter lamb is generally purchased from a local grocery store or, less often, is made at home.

Silverman, Deborah Anders. *Polish-American Folklore* (Urbana: Univ of Illinois Press, 2000)

Deborah Anders Silverman

D'Youville College. Private, nonprofit, liberal arts college. Founded in the early 1900s on Buffalo's west side as a women's school by the Grey Nuns, it is named for St. Marguerite D'Youville, founder of the Canadian order. It was the first college in the Buffalo area to offer baccalaureate degrees to women. D'Youville was chartered by New York State in 1908 and became coeducational in 1971. Early in the 21st century, the college continues affiliation with the Grey Nuns and offers baccalaureate and master's degree programs to its approximately 2,000 students, with a 3 to 1 female to male ratio. It has one of the largest four-year private college nursing programs in the United States.

D'Youville College, http://www.dyc.edu

David W. Sawicki

E

Eagle. Town (pop 1,194) in S central Wyoming Co. Settled in 1808, the town was formed from Pike in 1823. In the 1840s the town produced and shipped a large quantity of black cherry lumber. After the Civil War, cheese and apples became the dominant products. The Rochester and State Line Railroad came through in 1878. The Bliss Manufacturing Co (1892–1935), originally an iron foundry, later made woodenware. Farming consists of a small number of large dairy farms, with some potatoes and Christmas trees also grown. Residents who do not work on the farms commute to other towns in the county and to Buffalo.

Earlville. Village (pop 791) in Sherburne (Chenango Co) and Hamilton (Madison Co). Its post office opened in 1821 as Forks and became Earlville in 1835. It became a port on the Chenango Canal (1837–78) and was later served by three railroad lines. Tanning and leather finishing were industries beginning in 1851. In the early 21st century Earlville is the headquarters of USA-GLAD (1982), a 24-hour Internet-based gift service. The Earlville Opera House (1890) was restored beginning in 1971 and is a cultural center for the region. The Carpenter Gothic Grace Episcopal Church (1877) is now the Quincy Square Museum. Earlville's historic district (1982) includes 165 properties.

earthquakes. Several hundred earthquakes occur in New York State each year, and 5–10 of these are of sufficient magnitude to be felt. Earthquakes are vibrations produced by the release of energy that accompanies slippage of rock along fractures in the earth's crust, and the focus of an earthquake is the point of slippage. Earthquakes in New York State originate from a few to 12.5 miles (20.1 km) underground. Active tectonic plate margins such as on the West Coast of the United States produce most earthquakes. The Atlantic coast is considered a passive margin. However, the northern border of New York State falls within the seismically active St. Lawrence Valley, and the Ramapo Fault Zone travels through Westchester Co and into New Jersey. Some New York State earthquakes that occur outside these zones may be due to the rebounding of the earth's crust from the weight of glaciers of the Ice Age that ended only 10,000 years ago. New York State ranks third in earthquake activity among states east of the Mississippi River. Significant earthquakes that occurred at Attica (Wyoming Co) on 12 Aug 1929, at Massena Center (St. Lawrence Co) on 5 Sept 1944, and at Newcomb (Essex Co) on 7 Oct 1983 may be related to fractures along the St. Lawrence Valley floor. The 1944 Massena Center event, with an intensity of VIII, was the most destructive earthquake recorded in the state. It was felt over an area of about 175,000 mi^2 (453,000 km^2), as far south as Virginia, as far west as Michigan, and as far north and east as James Bay and New Brunswick in Canada. It caused severe damage in Massena, breaking residential waterlines and interrupting electrical service for 90 minutes. Effects on buildings included broken windows, fallen ceilings, and cracked and buckled walls. No deaths were attributed to the event, and only two individuals received minor injuries.

In the New York City area the greatest seismic risk is presented by the Ramapo Fault, which has produced numerous small earthquakes, indicating the potential for a larger event. While Manhattan was built over hard metamorphosed rock, areas of landfill and the sand of Long Island might act as a fluid during a major earthquake, causing building collapse. During the 10 Aug 1884 earthquake at Rockaway Beach in Queens, the largest recorded seismic event in the metropolitan area, some buildings on southwestern barrier islands settled into the sand. The increased infrastructure and population in the area would produce greater destruction should such an event recur. Awareness of earthquake risk in the metropolitan area resulted in the introduction of seismic provisions to the New York City building code in 1995. At the beginning of the 21st century Cornell University, in collaboration with Rensselaer Poly-

MAJOR EARTHQUAKES IN NEW YORK STATE

Date	Place	Intensity[a]	Magnitude[b]	Damage
18 Dec 1737	New York City	VI	5.2[c]	Bells rang, several chimneys fell
12 Mar 1853	Lowville (Lewis Co)	VI	4.8[c]	Machinery knocked down
23 Oct 1857	Buffalo	VI	4.6[c]	Bells rang, crockery broke
18 Dec 1867	Canton (St. Lawrence Co)	VI	4.8[c]	Sleepers awakened
11 Dec 1874	Tarrytown (Westchester Co)	VI	4.8[c]	Bricks fell from chimneys in Irvington, crockery broke in Tarrytown
10 Aug 1884	Rockaway Beach (Queens Co)	VI	5.2[c]	Chimneys and bricks fell, walls cracked
28 May 1897	Dannemora (Clinton Co)	VI	—	No damage reported
3 Feb 1916	Schenectady	VI	—	Windows broken, people thrown out of bed
18 Mar 1928	Saranac Lake (Franklin/Essex Co)	VI	4.5[c]	Some broken crockery and small objects reported in Saranac Lake and Malone
12 Aug 1929	Attica (Wyoming Co)	VII	5.2	Chimneys fell, brick buildings damaged, Attica Prison walls damaged, wells went dry
20 Apr 1931	Warrensburg (Warren Co)	VII	4.5	Chimneys fell, church spire twisted
15 Apr 1934	Dannemora (Clinton Co)	VI	4.5	Houses shifted
5 Sep 1944	Cornwall, Ont–Massena (St. Lawrence Co)	VIII	6.0	Nearly all chimneys fell, buildings damaged, $20 million damage
9 Sep 1944	Cornwall, Ont–Massena (St. Lawrence Co)	V	4.5	Chimneys fell, houses damaged
1 Jan 1966	Attica (Wyoming Co)	VI	4.6	Chimneys and walls damaged
13 Jun 1967	Attica (Wyoming Co)	V	4.4	Chimneys and walls damaged
9 Jun 1975	Altona (Clinton Co)	—	4.2	Chimneys and fireplaces cracked
7 Oct 1983	Newcomb (Essex Co)	VI	5.1	Tombstones rotated, chimneys cracked
19 Oct 1985	Ardsley (Westchester Co)	V	4.0	Windows broken, walls damaged
20 Apr 2002	Au Sable Forks (Clinton/Essex Co)	—	5.0	Some damage to roads, bridges, chimneys, and water mains

Sources: G. N. Nottis, *Epicenters of Northeastern United States and Southeastern Canada, Onshore and Offshore: Time Period 1534–1980* (1983); New York State Geological Survey, http://www.nysm.nysed.gov/geosige.html.

Note: Only earthquakes with a registered magnitude of 4.0 or more or intensity of V or more are included.

[a]Modified Mercalli scale, a measure of the effects of an earthquake at a particular place on humans, structures, and/or the land itself.

[b]Richter magnitude.

[c]Estimated.

technic Institute, became part of a national network of earthquake testing and research sites.

Isachsen, Yngvar W., et al, eds. *Geology of New York: A Simplified Account,* 2d ed. (Albany: New York State Museum, 2000)

Pamela Cooper

East Aurora. Village (pop 6,673) in Aurora (Erie Co). Two hamlets, Aurora to the east and Willink to the west, were little more than a mile apart; a post office named Willink opened in 1814. Aurora incorporated as Auroraville in 1836; Willink incorporated in 1849. In 1850 the west village's post office became West Aurora, and the east village's became East Aurora. West Aurora post office became Willink in 1854. In 1874 the Village of Willink, which incorporated both portions of the community, was renamed East Aurora. In the 1860s it was the site of the Aurora Woolen Mills and the Eagle Furnace, a producer of agricultural implements. Influenced by the arts and crafts movement and the work of William Morris, Elbert Hubbard (1856–1915) formed the Roycroft community (1895–1938) in the village. In the 20th century East Aurora became headquarters of Fisher-Price (1930); the plant moved out in the early 1980s, but the offices remained. In the early 21st century the village's Roycroft heritage draws many tourists.

Andrew C. Maines

East Bloomfield. Town (pop 3,258) in NW Ontario Co. It was purchased and settled in 1789 by a company from Sheffield, Mass. Bloomfield was formed in 1795, ceded Victor and Mendon (Monroe Co) in 1812, and was divided into East and West Bloomfield in 1833. The Chapin orchard, planted about 1800, developed the Northern Spy, Early Joe (1843), and Melon (1845) apples. The town had small factories, including one in 1876 that produced "sowers" for farmers. It was also the county's leading hop-growing town. Oakmount Sanitarium (1911–39) is believed to have been New York State's first county tuberculosis hospital. L. W. Bennett and Sons (1928–98) was the largest mink and silver-fox ranch east of the Mississippi River. Grain, hay, and dairy farming continues. Crosman manufactures recreational equipment. The New York Steam Engine Association (1960) runs an annual exposition in August.

Marla A. Bennett

Eastchester. Town (pop 31,318) in S Westchester Co. The town is bounded on the west by the Bronx River and on the east by the Hutchinson River. Originally encompassing Mount Vernon and eastern Bronx Co, Eastchester was first occupied in 1642 by New England exile Anne Hutchinson, whose settlement [now in Bronx Co] was exterminated by Indians during Kieft's War in 1643. Under English rule, 10 families from Fairfield Co, Conn, founded the town in 1664; town minutes have survived from 1671. In 1844 the Harlem Railroad provided transportation for the Village of Tuckahoe marble quarries, aiding their expansion and drawing Irish and Italian immigrants until their 1930 close. Lawrence Park (1890) created a distinctive residential community in the Village of Bronxville. The population of the town's two villages has remained nearly stable since the 1920s, but with growth in the unincorporated sections of the town, Eastchester's population more than tripled between 1920 and 1960.

Richard Forliano

Easter, Luke [Luscious] (*b* Jonestown, Miss, 4 Aug 1915; *d* Euclid, Ohio, 29 Mar 1979). Baseball player. After spending the early years of his baseball career with the Cincinnati Crescents and Homestead Grays (Pittsburgh) in the Negro Leagues, Easter spent six seasons (1949–54) with the Cleveland Indians. He hit 86 home runs from 1950 to 1952, but injuries ended Easter's major league career. He continued to play with several minor league teams, including the International League's Buffalo Bisons (1956–59) and Rochester Red Wings (1959–64). Easter was renowned for his mammoth home runs, his rapport with fans, and his charity work. The Bisons, wanting to let younger men play, released Easter despite his 113 home runs in only three seasons. That decision met with public outcry in Buffalo, and the Red Wings quickly signed Easter. Though he hit just 67 home runs in six seasons with Rochester, Easter became one of the most popular players in franchise history and remained with the team as a coach once his playing days were through at age 49. He returned to Cleveland, working to make aircraft parts and becoming a union steward. In 1969 Easter was hired as a part-time hitting coach with the Cleveland Indians. Later working as a union steward for the Aircraft Workers Alliance, he was shot and killed after cashing paychecks for his union workers. Easter's legend lives on in Buffalo and Rochester—both the Bisons and Red Wings retired his number.

Karst, Gene, and Martin J. Jones, Jr. *Who's Who in Professional Baseball* (New Rochelle, NY: Arlington House, 1973)
Peary, Danny. *Cult Baseball Players: The Greats, the Flakes, the Weird, and the Wonderful* (New York: Simon & Schuster, 1990)
Pitoniak, Scott. "The Legend of Luke," *Rochester Democrat and Chronicle,* 12 Apr 1998

Scott Pitoniak

Eastern Air Lines. It grew out of Pitcairn Aviation and Florida Airways, carrying airmail between New York City, Atlanta, and Miami in the late 1920s. After being sold to North American Aviation Corp in 1930, Eastern (known at this point as Eastern Air Transport) became a General Motors (GM) subsidiary in 1933. Despite controlling air traffic between New York City and Florida, the airline failed to prosper because of a lack of managerial focus and government encroachment on airmail operations on which all airlines depended. In 1934 Edward V. "Eddie" Rickenbacker, a founder of Florida Airways, became general manager of Eastern Air Lines (as it became known in that year) and put the company in healthy condition. Aided by investors including Laurance S. Rockefeller, Rickenbacker organized a buyout from GM in 1938 and became president and chief executive officer. In 1940 Eastern moved its New York City headquarters to Rockefeller Center from the General Motors Building. By 1941 the airline was among the nation's largest and most profitable and had moved its main northern terminal from Newark International Airport to La Guardia Airport in Queens.

Eastern gave valuable service to the Air Transport Command in World War II, and Rickenbacker performed special missions for the War Department, including one that left him floating on a raft in the Pacific Ocean for three weeks. Rickenbacker's business judgment began to deteriorate from his ordeals. After he returned to Eastern in 1943 the airline added new cities to its route system and briefly flourished, but its fortunes declined as the Civil Aeronautics Board (CAB) allowed competition in markets that Eastern had once monopolized. By absorbing Colonial Airlines in a 1956 merger, Eastern acquired several New York State destinations, including Albany, Binghamton, and Syracuse. In the 1950s and early 1960s the company suffered from strikes, passenger complaints, and poor relations between Rickenbacker and the CAB. In 1963 Rickenbacker was forced to retire, and Floyd D. Hall, a former TWA (Transcontinental and Western Air) executive, took over but could not completely resolve Eastern's chronic problems. In the late 1970s former astronaut Frank Borman restored Eastern to profitability, but its malaise continued, partly because of labor problems, after airlines were deregulated in 1978. Acquired by corporate raider Frank Lorenzo in 1986, Eastern declined rapidly and went into Chapter 11 bankruptcy on 9 Mar 1989. It passed out of existence in 1991.

Lewis, W. David. "Eastern Air Lines." In *The Airline Industry,* ed. William M. Leary (New York: Facts on File, 1992)
Serling, Robert J. *From the Captain to the Colonel: An Informal History of Eastern Airlines* (New York: Dial Press, 1980)

W. David Lewis

East Farmingdale. See FARMINGDALE.

East Fishkill. Town (pop 25,589) in S central Dutchess Co. Part of the Rombout Patent (1685), it attracted Dutch settlers before 1720. It was formed from Fishkill in 1849. Its largest settlement, Hopewell Junction, developed at the junction of two railroads, the Dutchess and Columbia (1869) and the New York and New England (1881). The Taconic Parkway (1940) preceded construction of Green Haven Correctional Facility (1949) and a major IBM manufacturing facility (1963). I-84 opened in 1969. Suburban development resulted in a 535% growth rate from 1960 to 2000. East Fishkill was the home of Henry Morgenthau Jr, US secretary of the treasury (1934–45).

William P. McDermott

East Greenbush. Town (pop 15,560) in W Rensselaer Co. Settled ?1628–29, the town was formed from Greenbush in 1855 as Clinton with a name change to East Greenbush in 1858. Former French diplomat Edmund C. Genet (Citizen Genet; 1763–1834) was a resident from 1810 until his death. The Boston and Albany Turnpike (now US 20) played a significant role during the War of 1812, when more than 4,000 troops were stationed at a cantonment (1812–31) at what is now Hampton Manor. Early suburbs arose along trolley lines (1895–1925), and the completion of I-90 in 1976, which created a fast commuting route to Albany, encouraged further growth. Until Sterling-Winthrop Research Institute (*ca* 1950; now SUNY Albany's East Campus) closed in 1993, it was the town's most important employer.

Kathryn T. Sheehan

East Hampton. Town (pop 19,719) and village (pop 1,334) in SE Suffolk Co. The town was founded in 1648 by settlers from New England and Southampton. By 1666 they had developed a government vested in a board of trustees that exists into the 21st century. Driven by the export of animals, especially whale products, to the West Indies and elsewhere, the town experienced a period of heightened economic activity and affluence from 1670 to 1720. With the decline of offshore whaling it became a backwater characterized by farming and maritime pursuits. In the 1870s wealthy vacationers, especially artists, discovered East Hampton. The village was incorporated in 1921. Since World War II the town has had a vibrant cultural scene increasingly dominated by media and entertainment personalities; the village's Guild Hall, a museum, presents high-caliber art exhibitions. The town contains the localities of Amagansett, Springs, and Montauk, as well as four state parks and the Amagansett National Wildlife Refuge.

See also ARCHITECTS AND ARCHITECTURE, LONG ISLAND (NASSAU AND SUFFOLK COUNTIES).

Richard F. Welch

East Hills. Village (pop 6,842) in North Hempstead and Oyster Bay (Nassau Co). From 1898 to 1938, 600 acres (243 ha) were included in Harbor Hill, the estate of Clarence Mackay. Located on the highest point in Nassau Co, its mansion, gatehouse, and water tower were designed by Stanford White; the mansion was demolished around 1947, but the gatehouse and water tower remain. Part of the greater Roslyn area, the village was incorporated in 1931, with a population of 343 in 1940. Major residential growth followed World War II, including Abraham Levitt and Sons' Strathmore (?1948), and businesses developed along Glen Cove Rd and Northern Blvd. In 2000 the US government purchased the 50-acre (20 ha) Roslyn Air National Guard Station to create a village park.

Myrna Sloam

East Islip. Locality (pop 14,078) in Islip (Suffolk Co). The territory was acquired by William Nicoll with a 1683 patent; after the Revolutionary War land was sold to repay debts. The economy centered on farming and fishing, with some boat building and lumbering. The South Side Rail Road (1869) brought wealthy New York City residents who established summer estates on the bay. The post office opened in 1890. The 1,500-acre (600 ha) George E. Taylor estate, site of the original Nicoll house, was acquired through the efforts of Robert Moses and became Heckscher State Park (1929). East Islip's population, 2,834 in 1950, began to grow rapidly, and had more than doubled to 6,681 by 1970.

Daria E. Merwin

Eastman, George (*b* Waterville, Oneida Co, 12 July 1854; *d* Rochester, 14 Mar 1932). Entrepreneur and philanthropist. The youngest of George and Maria Eastman's three children, he transformed photography from a cumbersome professional skill into a hobby for everyone. In 1860 the family moved from Waterville to Rochester, where the father had operated an innovative business school since 1842. The elder George Eastman died in 1862, and the younger dropped out of school in 1868 to help support his mother and invalid sister. His first jobs were with insurance offices, where he rose from office boy to policy writer. In 1871 he went to work for the Rochester Savings Bank and appeared to be on track for a successful banking career. Beginning in 1877, however, the amateur photographer set about simplifying the complex wet-plate collodion process for his own purposes. While Eastman kept his day job at the bank until late 1881, he spent his nights in his mother's kitchen, experimenting with a gelatin emulsion formula taken from an article in the *British Journal of Photography.* Plates coated with this emulsion remained sensitive after they dried and so could be exposed at leisure. In April 1880 Eastman leased the third floor of a building in downtown Rochester and began to manufacture dry plates and paper for sale. He continued his experiments, hoping to find an alternative to the heavy and inflexible glass plates then in use. From 1882 to 1900 Eastman invented and refined the transparent roll film and light, handheld cameras upon which his success as a supplier for amateur photography would be built. In 1884 the Eastman Dry Plate and Film Co manufactured roll holders and rolls of paper-backed film. The original Kodak camera was introduced in 1888, and transparent, flexible film the following year. With demand growing, Eastman began building the Kodak Park film manufacturing plant in Rochester in 1890. The business was renamed Eastman Kodak Co in 1892.

Eastman relied heavily on marketing. He invented the word Kodak for his prototype handheld camera and coined the slogan "You push the button, we do the rest" in 1888. In 1893 he introduced the Kodak Girl, whose style of clothes and the camera she carried changed each year as she enticed women and girls to take up photography. The first ads were written by Eastman himself. In 1892 he hired an advertising manager but retained tight control of Kodak marketing concepts and slogans. Eastman's success was based in part on his own inventions but had even more to do with his ability to recruit employees with technical skills, to outmaneuver his competitors, and to raise capital. The late 1890s brought unexpected markets for film in the new industries of X-ray and motion picture photography. The photographic products business was highly competitive, but Eastman was able to win dominance in the United States, Great Britain, and Europe in less than 20 years. In 1898 he refinanced his whole enterprise in London, bypassing investment bankers and netting a personal profit of $1 million, which he shared with company employees. He would later introduce wage dividends, stock options, savings and loan institutions, and benefit and pension plans.

With the turn of the 20th century, Eastman shifted from active and intensely applied years to years of relative leisure and travel, from amassing great wealth to distributing it, and from building a business and the factories to support it to building institutions that served people in more humanistic ways: through music, medicine and dentistry, the liberal arts, and racial advancement. Two hitherto struggling institutions, the University of Rochester and the Massachusetts Institute of Technology, benefited from his donations, as did two historically black colleges, Tuskegee Normal and Industrial Institute (now Tuskegee University) in Alabama and Hampton Institute (now Hampton University) in Virginia. The University of Rochester gained a medical and dental school, a teaching hospital, a school of music, and an enormous concert hall. By the end of his life, Eastman had distributed at least $100 million to various institutions. He established the Community Chest of Rochester and the Rochester Bureau of Municipal Research (now Center for Governmental Research). He gave many buildings to Rochester educational and charitable organizations and two parcels of land for Cobbs Hill and Durand-Eastman Parks in Rochester. Eastman remained at the helm of the company he founded until 1925, when he retired to become chairman of the board. Thereafter he spent time hunting, fishing, and camping; it was said his goal was to take two six-month vacations a year. Eastman's predominant characteristic had been enthusiasm for life, and when health problems dampened that enthusiasm the industrialist ended his life with a pistol. His suicide note read, "My work is done. Why wait?" His home at 900 East Ave in Rochester and its contents plus residual estate, valued at $51 million, were bequeathed to the University of Rochester and his art collection to the university's Memorial Art Gallery.

Ackerman, Carl. *George Eastman* (Boston: Houghton Mifflin, 1930)

Brayer, Elizabeth. *George Eastman: A Biography* (Baltimore: Johns Hopkins Univ Press, 1996)

Jenkins, Reese. *Images and Enterprise: Technology and the American Photographic Industry, 1839–1925* (Baltimore: Johns Hopkins Univ Press, 1975)

Elizabeth Brayer

Eastman Dental Center. Dental clinics in Rochester offering inexpensive care to the poor date back to the free dental dispensaries at City Hospital from 1892 to 1894, at the Rochester Public Health Association in 1905, and at a school-based clinic from 1910 to 1917. Aided by a substantial donation from George Eastman in 1915, the Rochester Dental Dispensary opened at 800 Main St on 15 Oct 1917, charging 5¢ per session. Preparation for the opening had begun in 1916 when Harvey J. Burkhart became director of the dispensary and the new Rochester Dental Dispensary School for Dental Hygienists. This, the first licensed school for dental hygienists in the state, trained women to work at the clinic. In 1918 over 40,000 children visited the dental office, and a year later the dispensary began a tonsil-adenoid clinic that would run until World War II. In 1941 the dispensary was renamed the Eastman Dental Dispensary, in posthumous honor of its major benefactor, who had given it more than $3 million. Dr Basil G. Bibby, who became the dispensary's director in 1947, placed increasing emphasis on specialized education for dentists and research, and in 1952 the state sanctioned a master's degree program to be offered by the dispensary, in cooperation with the University of Rochester. Renamed the Eastman Dental Center in 1964, its headquarters were moved in 1978 to grounds adjacent to the Strong Memorial Hospital of the University of Rochester. The dental center merged with the university in 1997.

Burkhart, Harvey J. "Rochester Dental Dispensery," *Journal of the American Dental Association* 13 (1926): 1027–37

Hudson, Nathaniel C. "The Eastman Dental Center:

50 Years of Service," *Journal of the American Dental Association* 76 (1968): 533–40

Ruth DuMont

Eastman Kodak Company. Photographic products manufacturer. In 1879 George Eastman, a Rochester bank clerk, developed a successful dry-plate photographic process. The next year he formed the Eastman Dry Plate Co in Rochester. In 1882 Eastman's six employees produced cameras, dry plates, and photographic paper. Incorporating his firm in 1884, Eastman introduced four years later a simpler camera with an invented name, Kodak, which was loaded with another firm invention—paper-backed roll film; this was the beginning of snapshot photography.

Business at Eastman's firm boomed, and the company quickly became the leading photographic equipment manufacturer in the world. In 1891 the company relocated to a site north of downtown Rochester in Greece (Monroe Co). Known as Kodak Park, by the turn of the century this industrial complex consisted of 30 buildings, serving as the firm's manufacturing center; around this time Kodak also opened a manufacturing complex in Harrow, England. In 1892 the firm was reorganized as the Eastman Kodak Co, which it has been known as ever since. The success of Kodak accelerated when Thomas Edison choose Kodak film for his Kinetoscope motion picture machine, which, following the opening of America's first movie theater in 1895, marked a vast new market. The invention of X-rays in 1896 also created new opportunities. Despite photography's growth in popularity, due to its expense it was still a niche hobby. Kodak's Brownie, a handheld camera released in 1900, revolutionized photography. The Brownie was small, with a two-piece lens, and was simple to use. Marketed to adults and children it sold for just one dollar. At its low price the Brownie transformed photography from a luxury affordable only by the rich to a pastime of the masses. In 1913 Eastman founded the first industrial research center devoted exclusively to the study of photography at Kodak Park.

During this same time, Kodak, fearing that the keys to its success, including its patent and film formula secrets, might escape to rival firms, sought to cultivate the loyalty of its workers through a unique benefits program, including reading and recreation rooms and lavish dining halls at Kodak Park. Moreover, Eastman paid his workers well above industry standards, and in 1899 he gave a special bonus in excess of $78,000 to Kodak's 3,000 workers—a substantial sum in that period. In 1912 he standardized this profit-sharing plan, with all employees receiving an annual "divvy" tied to the firm's stock dividend. By 1929 the firm employed 24,000, 80% of whom worked in Monroe Co, making up one-fifth of the City of Rochester's workforce. During the 1920s the firm accelerated its employee benefit plan to include retirement annuities and its own realty association.

Midcentury

Kodak entered the 1930s with its leading market position unchallenged. In the previous decade the firm had introduced an array of new products, including the world's first home-movie camera in 1923 and five years later 16-mm Kodacolor film, making color home movies a reality. As a result of continuous profits at the firm, under Pres Frank W. Lovejoy (1934–41) the company's benefits remained, and no labor troubles occurred throughout the Great Depression, although there were modest layoffs. During World War II almost all of Kodak's products were dedicated to the war effort, including Kodacolor film for consumer cameras, which was ready for market in 1942 but expropriated for military use. Between 1940 and 1944 the Kodak Park workforce surged from 19,000 to 31,000. As a result of Kodak's vaunted benefits program, a 1946–47 effort by the United Electrical, Radio, and Machine Workers of America to organize firm workers was unsuccessful; this was the only significant labor drive the company ever faced. In 1950 Kodak installed its giant Colorama in Grand Central Terminal in New York City. A three-panel screen that depicted changing sets of color photographs, Colorama was viewed by millions each year and was a tremendous advertising success for the company.

However, Kodak also faced postwar challenges. The photography giant's dominance in the film market had long raised antitrust concerns. Kodak enjoyed a near monopoly on the production of film stock (movie film constituted 16% of firm revenues by 1939), and up through the 1950s Kodak controlled 80% of the domestic film market and 90% of the color film market (after 1946), resulting in higher consumer prices. In 1911 the US Department of Justice initiated an antitrust lawsuit alleging that Kodak monopolized the trade of photographic goods by signing exclusive contracts with paper manufacturers, by purchasing competing businesses, and by imposing fixed prices. In 1921 Kodak settled the case by entering a consent decree with the US government in which the firm agreed to sell some manufacturing assets and eliminate fixed pricing. After similar Justice Department suits against Kodak in 1947 and 1954—the first charging Kodak with controlling color cinematography through signing exclusive agreements with Technicolor, and the second alleging that the Rochester giant restrained the consumer photofinishing trade by including photofinishing costs in its color film prices—Kodak again signed consent decrees agreeing to share patents and film formulas with rivals. None of these legal actions reduced Kodak's market dominance or lowered prices.

Fall from Dominance

Under firm presidents Albert Chapman (1952–60), William S. Vaughn (1960–67), and Louis K. Eilers (1967–70), Kodak experienced tremendous success. By the 1950s employment had surged to 73,000 workers, and net earnings hit $50 million in 1953 and then doubled to $100 million just four years later. In 1959 Kodak released its first high-speed color film, Ektachrome, and debuted in 1963 its easy-to-use Instamatic camera that made photography ubiquitous. In 1980 net sales hit $10 billion, and global firm employment crested at 136,500 workers (60,200 worked in Rochester, making up 21% of the city's labor force). However, by the early 1970s serious competitors to Kodak emerged. In 1972 the Massachusetts-based Polaroid Corp released its Land Camera, the world's first instant camera with automatic ejecting, self-developing prints; sales of Polaroid's camera surged. Kodak responded with its own instant camera in 1976. Polaroid immediately filed a patent infringement lawsuit, which Polaroid won after 10 years, locking Kodak out of the instant market. In 1982 Kodak released its Disc Camera to help counter the Polaroid threat, but sales were disappointing.

The more serious cause for concern for Kodak came from the Fuji Film Co, which by the 1970s offered consumer films that were priced 20% cheaper than Kodak's. By 1993 the Japanese-based Fuji had captured almost one-sixth of the US film market. As a result Kodak was forced to lay off 23,000 workers between 1983 and 1990. By 1993 Kodak employment in Rochester fell to 36,800 (12% of the city's workforce). Between 1991 and 1995 Kodak let go an additional 20,300 employees.

Kodak also faced environmental problems. Investigations by the New York State Department of Environmental Conservation and federal agencies revealed in 1988 that the groundwater at Kodak Park was contaminated with methylene chloride, a suspected carcinogen used to make film. In 1990 and 1994 Kodak settled legal cases with the New York State and US governments, paid $7 million in fines, and agreed to clean up Kodak Park.

However, there have also been bright spots in the company's recent history, including Kodak's release of its first digital camera for professional photographers (1991) and the world's first point-and-shoot digital camera for the broader consumer market (1997). In 2003, with traditional film sales declining dramatically, the company announced its decision to move aggressively into the digital market and to cut its investment in film. To accommodate the shift, in January 2004 Kodak announced a plan to reduce its workforce by 23% over the next three years. The cuts would include 4,500 jobs based in Rochester. In 2004 the company employed about 64,000 people worldwide and 21,000 in Rochester. Kodak Park, which consisted of 160 manufacturing buildings on 2,200 acres (890 ha), remained the firm's production center. Its net sales were $13.3 billion in 2003.

Collins, Douglas. *The Story of Kodak* (New York: Abrams, 1990)

Jacoby, Sanford M. *Modern Manors: Welfare Capitalism since the New Deal* (Princeton, NJ: Princeton Univ Press, 1997)

Swasy, Alecia. *Changing Focus: Kodak and the Battle to Save a Great American Company* (New York: Random House, 1997)

Tod M. Ottman

Eastman School of Music. In 1918 industrialist George Eastman proposed the establishment of a large school of music within the University of Rochester. He purchased a small Rochester conservatory, the Institute of Musical Art (est 1913), and in 1919 bought land and gave $3.5 million to build the Eastman School of Music (1921) and the Eastman Theatre. Between 1920 and his death in 1932, Eastman donated $20 million to the school. The Eastman School of Music has two concert facilities, the 3,094-seat Eastman Theatre and the recital hall Kilbourn Hall. In 1921, its opening year, 104 degree and certificate seekers enrolled. Noted composer Howard Hanson, the school's director (1924–64), helped shape it into one of the leading conservatories in the nation. Hanson championed the music of young American composers and in 1930 inaugurated the First Festival of American Music, which continued until 1971. The festival included a wide range of compositional styles, as did Eastman's extensive publishing and recording program. Notable student ensembles include the Eastman Philharmonia and the Eastman Wind Ensemble, both featured in a famous series of recordings on Mercury Records, the new music groups Musica Nova and Ossia, the baroque ensemble Collegium Musicum, and the Eastman Jazz Ensemble. In 2001 the undergraduate and graduate students totaled about 800.

See also CLASSICAL MUSIC, ROCHESTER.

Lenti, Vincent A. "The Eastman School of Music." In *Rochester History*, vol 58 (Rochester: Rochester Public Library, 1996)

Andrea Olmstead

East Massapequa. See MASSAPEQUA.

East Meadow. Locality (pop 37,461) in Hempstead (Nassau Co). European American settlers grazed their cattle on East Meadow. Beginning in the 1650s a few scattered farms were located on the edge of the plains, which were held by the town in common until 1869. Landmarks in East Meadow at the end of the 19th century included Sarah and Peter Barnum's 2,500-acre (1,000 ha) dairy farm and Alva (Mrs O. H. P.) Belmont's Brookholt estate. The population grew rapidly after World War II, increasing from 3,145 in 1940 to 46,000 by 1960. The county established the 930-acre (376 ha) Eisenhower Park in 1944, which in 2002 has golf courses, an aquatic center, playing fields, and picnic areas. Mitchel Manor military housing, the Nassau University Medical Center, and the Nassau County Jail are also located in East Meadow, which is otherwise primarily a residential community.

Natalie A. Naylor

East Moriches. See MORICHES.

East Nassau. Village (pop 571) in Nassau (Rensselaer Co). In 1997 residents of the hamlets of East Nassau, Brainard, and Hoag Corners became concerned about quarrying by the Lane Construction Co in their vicinity and felt the town board was disinterested in their position. A petition to incorporate as a village was denied by Supervisor William Knight but was approved on appeal to the state supreme court. The village incorporated in 1998. While Brainard was a manufacturing hamlet in the mid- to late 19th century with the Nassau Cotton Mills and J. D. Tompkins' straw wrapping mills, the new village's residents commute to work elsewhere in the vicinity.

Field Horne

East Northport. See NORTHPORT.

Easton. Town (pop 2,259) in SW Washington Co. A part of the Saratoga Patent (1684), it was the site of Fort Saraghtoga (1709–45), just south of the Batten Kill's mouth. Settled by Dutch Americans after the French and Indian War, it received an influx of Quakers beginning in 1773, Rhode Island Baptists, and some 17 former sea captains from Martha's Vineyard, Mass, and Nantucket, Mass, during and after the American Revolution. The Friends Meeting House was the site of a 1777 visit by hostile Indians who, curious at the behavior of the silent meeting, entered and sat quietly until its conclusion, leaving without inflicting harm. The town was formed in 1789 from Saratoga and Stillwater, which was in Albany Co at the time, and was annexed to Washington Co in 1791. Manufacturing was concentrated along the Batten Kill in Greenwich and Galesville [now Middle Falls], but elsewhere the town was agricultural. Scandinavian, Russian, and Polish farmers settled in the decades preceding World War I. In 2003 much of Easton's land was occupied by large farms. Fort Miller Co produced concrete components for engineering projects. Easton is the site of Willard Mountain ski area (1957) and of the Washington County Fair, held every August.

R. Paul McCarty

East Otto. Town (pop 1,105) in N Cattaraugus Co. Settled in 1816, the town was formed from Otto in 1854. The first settlers arrived in 1816 and cleared the forest for agriculture, raising potatoes, corn, apples, oats, and hay, and producing butter and cheese. An apple factory operated in the late 19th century. In 2003 agriculture remains the predominant land use. Rainbow Lake is a four-season vacation resort, and a part of Griffis Sculpture Park extends across the border from Ashford.

Bruce D. Fredrickson and Madelynn P. Fredrickson

East Patchogue. See PATCHOGUE.

East Randolph. Village (pop 630) in Randolph and Conewango (Cattaraugus Co). Settled in 1825, the village was bypassed by the railroad, which came through Randolph in 1860. Industries included a woolen factory; the Pease and Swan Foundry (1828–*ca* 1835); the Randolph Steam Engine Co (1857), which also produced mill machinery, the Eagle mower, and beginning 1873 oil-drilling engines; the East Randolph Tannery (1872); and Willard and Hammond's milk pan factory (1873). The village incorporated in 1881. In the early 21st century, residents work in Randolph or commute to the Jamestown area.

Bruce D. Fredrickson and Madelynn P. Fredrickson

East River (16 mi/26 km). This saltwater estuary separates Brooklyn and Queens from Manhattan and the Bronx. It meets the Harlem River, another estuary, about 8.5 miles (13.7 km) above the southern tip of Manhattan Island. The river contains three islands: Roosevelt, Wards, and Randalls. In the 18th and 19th centuries, hundreds of daily ferry crossings transported New Yorkers between Brooklyn and Manhattan. These rides were largely discontinued with the construction between 1883 and 1909 of four major bridges connecting Manhattan with Queens and Brooklyn: the Brooklyn Bridge, Williamsburg, Queensboro, and Manhattan Bridges. Four later bridges—Hell Gate (1917), Triborough (1936), Bronx-Whitestone (1939), and Throgs Neck (1961)—cross the East River as well. In addition, there are two vehicular tunnels, the Queens-Midtown Tunnel (1940) and the Brooklyn-Battery Tunnel (1950), and 1 Long Island Rail Road and 10 subway tunnels. Manhattan's South St near the southern end of the river functioned as the city's and state's greatest port from immediately after the Revolutionary War through the boom years of the Erie Canal. South St became known as the "Street of Ships." Decline set in after the 1860s, however, as New York City outgrew its East River port and as commercial activity moved west to the Hudson. In 1967 South Street Seaport Museum, offering tours of historic ships, opened at South and Fulton Sts, followed in the 1970s and 1980s by lively retail development of the old port area.

McCullough, David, G. *The Great Bridge: The Epic Story of the Building of the Brooklyn Bridge* (New York: Simon & Schuster, 1973)

Leonard Benardo

East Rochester. Town and village (pop 6,650) in E Monroe Co. The Merchants Despatch Transportation Co constructed railroad car shops in 1896, with workers' housing, thus spawning the first planned suburb of Rochester. A Despatch post office was opened in 1897. In 1902 the Foster-Armstrong Piano Co (later American Piano) moved from Rochester and built a large complex. The village was incorporated in 1906 as East Rochester. In the 1910s businesswoman and engineer Kate Gleason (1865–1933) began Concrest, a community of poured-concrete houses. Her golf course, the present site of Gleason Estates, gave village native Robert Trent Jones (1906–2000) his early experiences as caddy and golfer. Other industries included Brainerd Brass (1899–1998), Ontario Grain Drill Co (1900–61), Pierce Oil Co (1902–70s), Lawless Bros Paper Mill (1926–65), Northway Trailer Car Co (*ca* 1915–27), Crossman Seed Co (1927), and Nance's Mustard (1950–70s). East Rochester's population peaked in 1920 at 8,152. The car shops closed in 1970, and the piano factory closed in 1985 and was transformed into a retail facility called Piano Works Mall. In 1981 East Rochester became a coterminal town and village. In the early 21st century the town/village has struggled with its transition from industrial suburb to commercial and residential community, and has tried to increase ownership and revitalize its downtown.

Carolyn Vacca

East Rockaway. Village (pop 10,414) in Hempstead (Nassau Co). Settled by the English in the 1640s and known as Near Rockaway, the village grew around a tidewater gristmill (1688) and became a flourishing seaport, with packets carrying produce and oysters to city markets. Oystering and shipbuilding were also lucrative businesses. Growth slowed when the railroad (1867) drew business to what is now Lynbrook and effectively ended water commerce. The same year the name East Rockaway was adopted. The village was incorporated in 1900. During the 1920s and 1930s East Rockaway went through a new stage of growth as summer residents and commuters built houses. In the early 21st century the bayside community remained residential.

Georgina Martorella

East Setauket. See SETAUKET.

East Shoreham. See SHOREHAM.

East Syracuse. Village (pop 3,178) in DeWitt (Onondaga Co). In 1872 the New York Central Railroad established its freight yards, roundhouses, and shops at this point, midway between

Albany and Buffalo. A community grew up around it, naming a post office established in 1876 East Syracuse and incorporating as a village in 1881. The population reached 1,009 in 1880 and 2,331 in 1890. In 2003 East Syracuse was still a rail freight center: CSX Railroad's mostly automated Intermodal Rail Center handles 67 million tons (61 MT) of freight annually. The village, an inner suburb of Syracuse, is the site of drug research and production by Bristol-Myers Squibb.

Barbara S. Rivette

East Williston. Village (pop 2,503) in North Hempstead (Nassau Co). Located on the northern edge of the Hempstead Plains, it was originally called the North Side and became known as Williston after the Willis family, prominent early residents. An East Williston post office was established in 1879 and a railroad station in the following year. After the Civil War, brickmaking, windmill construction, and carriage building became important trades; the East Williston Road Cart, patented in 1891 by Henry M. Willis, was known for its strength, stability and speed. Incorporated in 1926, East Williston experienced suburban growth in the 1930s through the 1950s. In the early 21st century, it is an upscale residential community.

Georgina Martorella

Eaton. Town (pop 4,826) in central Madison Co. Settled in 1792–93, the town was formed from Hamilton in 1807. It was located on the Third Great Western Turnpike (1803–11) and later on the Ontario and Western Railroad (1870). Its farmers raised cattle, sheep, and grain until *ca* 1850, when dairying assumed dominance; the first cheese factory in Madison Co opened in Eaton in 1861. Eaton hamlet was the site of the Eaton Woolen Manufacturing Co (1817–45) and of Wood, Taber and Morse (1859; stationary, portable, and four-wheel chain drive steam engines for farm and mill use); West Eaton had Monitor Mills and Eureka Mills, making woolen cloth; and Eagleville was the home of Dwight, Graham and Co (1869; agricultural steam engines). Other products of the town included augers, leather, and distilled liquor. In the early 21st century the major employer is SUNY Morrisville. Beginning in 1841 Emily Chubbuck (1817–54), writing under the name Fanny Forester, achieved a substantial, though transient, popularity with her domestic tales.

William F. Helmer

Eaton, Amos (*b* Chatham [now in Columbia Co], 17 May 1776; *d* Troy, Rensselaer Co, 10 May 1842). Scientist and educator. Eaton was the son of farmers and at the age of 14 was sent to live with an uncle, Russell Beebe, a blacksmith in Duanesburg [now in Schenectady Co] who taught him the basics of surveying and instrument making. He made a private study of the classics with tutors and then entered Williams College in Williamstown, Mass, in 1795, graduating in 1799. Deciding on a legal career, in 1800 he began reading law in New York City under New York State Atty Gen Josiah O. Hoffman. That same year he published *Art without Science,* a surveying manual. He passed the state bar exam in 1802 and opened a practice in Catskill (Greene Co), engaging in land speculation while continuing his interest in science. Involved in a questionable land deal, Eaton was convicted of forgery on 26 Aug 1811 and given a life sentence in Newgate Prison in Manhattan's Greenwich Village. While incarcerated he studied geology and tutored the prison agent's son, John Torrey, in botany. Torrey would become New York State botanist in 1836. On 17 Nov 1815 Gov Daniel D. Tompkins granted Eaton a pardon conditional on his leaving the state. Relocating in New Haven, Conn, Eaton began studying natural history under professors Eli Ives and Benjamin Silliman of Yale College. Two years later he was exonerated by Gov De Witt Clinton, who became Eaton's first patron. Eaton then returned to Williams College, earning his MA and teaching mineralogy and botany.

Eaton published *A Manual of Botany for the Northern States* (1817), which would go into eight editions, and in 1818 he published *An Index to the Geology of the Northern States.* He moved to Troy in 1819. Eaton lectured on botany, chemistry, and geology throughout New England and the Hudson Valley from 1817 to 1824. In 1820 under the patronage of Stephen Van Rensselaer of Troy, the wealthy patroon of Rensselaerswijck [now in Albany, Columbia, and Rensselaer Cos], Eaton began a survey of Albany and Rensselaer Cos. Publication of his geologic profile of the region between Boston and south central New York State led to his 1824 report on the geology of the future Erie Canal route. Van Rensselaer, admiring Eaton's theories of scientific education, backed him in founding the Rensselaer School (now Rensselaer Polytechnic Institute) in 1824. Eaton led 24 students on a field and survey trip, the first of its kind in the United States, in 1826. Embarking on 2 May, the group, including entomologist Asa Fitch and the governor's son George Clinton, traveled the length of the Erie Canal, arriving back in Troy on 20 June. In 1836 the New York State Geological and Natural History Survey was founded, largely based on Eaton's works. He continued working at the Rensselaer School until his death. Although not known as a farseeing theorist, Eaton was one of the pioneers of North American geology, combining a keen sense of observation with robust enthusiasm to popularize the study of the natural sciences.

McAllister, Ethel M. *Amos Eaton, Scientist and Educator 1776–1842* (Philadelphia: Univ of Pennsylvania Press; London: Oxford Univ Press, 1941)

David Minor

Ebenezer Society. Religious communal society. The name, from 1 Samuel 7:12, signifies "Hitherto hath the Lord helped us." It was the first American settlement of the Community of True Inspiration, a German Radical Pietist group, established in 1843 six miles (10 km) southeast of Buffalo. The Inspirationists arranged to purchase 5,000 acres (2,023 ha) from the Ogden Land Company. The tract had been part of the Seneca tribe's Buffalo Creek Reservation, and neither the company nor the US Senate had been forthright in dealing with the Seneca on the land transfer. Consequently the Germans began to arrive while the Seneca still held title to the land and were living on it, leading to tensions that were not resolved until 1846, by which time the last of the Seneca departed and over 700 Inspirationists had settled on the property. The members formally adopted community of goods in 1846 for both religious and practical reasons. Incorporation under state law as a religious association occurred the same year. Ebenezer consisted of four villages as well as two satellites in Canada West [now Ont]. The society prospered through agriculture and woolen manufacturing, but facing a land shortage as their numbers increased, the entire population relocated to Iowa between 1855 and 1862 as the Amana Society. Many Inspirationist buildings survive in the vicinity of West Seneca (Erie Co).

Shambaugh, Bertha M. H. *Amana That Was and Amana That Is* (Iowa City: State Historical Society of Iowa, 1932)

Jonathan G. Andelson

eclecticism. See ALTERNATIVE MEDICINE.

Ecuadoreans. Political and economic instability in Ecuador has increased immigration to New York State since the mid-1960s. Ecuadorean immigrants come from a cross section of society in terms of social classes, but they are predominantly middle class. Coming largely from the areas of Guayaquil, Cuenca, and Quito, Ecuadoreans have tended to settle in New York City, with the majority living in Queens in the Jackson Heights, Jamaica, and Woodhaven neighborhoods. Increasing numbers also settled in Port Chester (Westchester Co) at the end of the 20th century. According to the US census, foreign-born Ecuadoreans in New York State numbered 139,226 in 2000. Of the 113,916 living in New York City, 66,643 (59%) resided in Queens. Elsewhere in the metropolitan area, 10,963 lived in Westchester Co, 6,097 in Suffolk Co, and 3,967 in Nassau Co. Ecuadoreans have established extensive social networks and associations within their New York State communities, such as the Ecuadorean American Association, which was founded in 1932. The Comité Civico Ecuatoriano, a not-for-profit organization, is dedicated to helping Ecuadorean immigrants adapt to their new environment by providing English language classes. The majority of Ecuadoreans are Roman Catholic, and one of their most important holidays is the Dia de los Difuntos, which is commemorated as All Souls' Day on 2 November. The largest patriotic celebration, Independence Day, is celebrated on 10 August. *Ecuador News* is a weekly publication with national distribution. Radio broadcasts, such as *Radio Delgado* and *Radio Sucre,* are other important information outlets for the growing Ecuadorean community.

Consulate of Ecuador of New York. "National Plan for Ecuadorians Abroad," http://www.consulecuadornewyork.com/ing/comunidad/htm/plan_nal/plan_nal.htm

Logan, John. "The New Latinos: Who They Are, Where They Are," http://www.hccwpa.org/Census_and_Data/HCC_New_Latino2.htm

Ana Margarita Cervantes-Rodríguez and Deborah Woeckner Saavedra

Eddy, Thomas (*b* Philadelphia, 5 Sept 1758; *d* New York City, 16 Sept 1827). Quaker reformer. A loyalist during the American Revolution, Eddy moved to New York City in 1779, where he built a fortune at first through services to the occupying British public debt. Eddy's philanthropic interests included free schools, opposition to slavery, humane treatment of the insane and

American Indians, and prison reform. His involvement in the Free School Society helped establish public education in New York State. From 1793 to 1823 he was one of the governors of New York Hospital. He worked with De Witt Clinton on the construction of the Erie Canal and lobbied the New York State legislature to provide funds for the project. He served as inspector for New York City's Newgate prison, wrote *An Account of the State Prison or Penitentiary House in the City of New-York* (1801), and played a central role in the creation of the House of Refuge in New York City, the nation's first juvenile reformatory in 1825. He helped to found the American Bible Society and the New York Bible Society, and he was an outspoken critic of Elias Hicks, denouncing him as anti-Christian, though Eddy died before the Hicksite-Orthodox separation of 1827–28.

Barbour, Hugh, et al. *Quaker Crosscurrents: 300 Years of Friends in the New York Yearly Meetings* (Syracuse: Syracuse Univ Press, 1995)

Knapp, Samuel L. *The Life of Thomas Eddy* (New York: Conner & Cooke, 1834)

Thomas D. Hamm

Eden. Town (pop 8,076) in SW Erie Co. Settled in 1808, the town was formed from Willink [now Aurora, Erie Co] in 1812. Germans and Alsatians settled in Eden in the 1830s, organizing a Catholic church in 1834; by the end of the Civil War, Schweickhardt's Brewery was an important institution but closed in 1896. Agriculture, especially truck farming, was prosperous, and the Eden Center Preserving Co processed farm products. The Buffalo and Jamestown Railroad (later Erie Railroad) came through in 1874. Eden is home to the Original American Kazoo Co (1916), the only metal kazoo factory in the world. In the early 21st century, the town is a farming community. The Eden Corn Festival (1969) is held annually. The iron-truss bridge (1911) at Clarksburg is a local landmark.

Andrew C. Maines

Edinburg. Town (pop 1,384) in NW Saratoga Co. Settled in 1787 the town was formed from Providence in 1801 as Northfield; the present name was chosen in 1808. Its land is not good for farming, and it was sustained by lumbering, tanneries, and woodenware works. Lucien DeGolia patented a combination washboard (wood and zinc) here in 1867. Flooding of the Sacandaga River valley, which bisected the town, created Great Sacandaga Lake in 1930 and opened the town for summer cottage use. Much of the reforested land is owned by pulp and paper companies. The town is completely within the Adirondack Park. The Copeland Bridge (1879)—a covered bridge over Beecher Creek—and the 3,150 ft (960 m) Batchellerville Bridge over Great Sacandaga Lake are the town's landmarks.

Field Horne

Edison, Thomas Alva (*b* Milan, Ohio, 11 Feb 1847; *d* West Orange, NJ, 18 Oct 1931). Inventor and manufacturer. Born into a family of modest means, Edison was largely self-educated. Working as an itinerant telegrapher from 1863 to 1868 he was introduced to the world of big business and invention. In 1869 he went to New York City and sold his inventive and design services to Gold and Stock Reporting Telegraph Co, makers of stock tickers, giving him the resources to begin inventing full time. After selling the rights of some inventions to Western Union, Edison moved to Newark, NJ, opened the first of several invention and manufacturing operations, and from 1870 through 1876 designed equipment, mostly for the telegraph industry, obtained patents, and manufactured his products. He married Mary G. Stilwell in 1871, and the couple had three children. In 1876 Edison relocated to Menlo Park, NJ, where he and his team developed an electrical lighting system.

Edison moved to New York City in 1881 to oversee operation of the Edison Electric Co on Fifth Ave. While living in Gramercy Park, he built, for that time, the world's largest central power station at Pearl St in New York City. Eighteen months after the death of his wife in 1884, he married Mina Miller, and they had three children. In 1886 the Edison Machine Works moved from New York City to Schenectady. Machine Works was consolidated with other Edison companies in 1889 to create Edison General Electric Co. Edison Electric merged with Thomson-Houston Electric Co in 1892 and formed General Electric Co, with headquarters in Schenectady. Edison built an estate in West Orange and in 1887 erected a sizable research park nearby, where he perfected the phonograph, developed a rudimentary motion picture camera, and created the alkaline storage battery. After the turn of the century, Edison spent less time inventing and became a popular symbol for science in the United States. During World War I he served as president of the Naval Consulting Board from 1915 until 1921.

See also CAPITAL PUNISHMENT.

Baldwin, Neil. *Edison: Inventing the Century* (New York: Hyperion, 1995)

Jenkins, Reese V., ed. *The Papers of Thomas A. Edison*, vols 1–4 (Baltimore: Johns Hopkins Univ Press, 1989–98)

Josephson, Matthew. *Edison: A Biography* (1959; repr New York: John Wiley & Sons, 1992)

Millard, Andre. *Edison and the Business of Innovation* (Baltimore: Johns Hopkins Univ Press, 1990)

Timothy W. Kneeland

Edmeston. Town (pop 1,824) in W Otsego Co. British army officers and brothers Capt William Edmeston and Lt Robert Edmeston received a 10,000-acre (4,000 ha) patent (1770) on the Unadilla River, which was guarded during the American Revolution by their retainer, Sgt Percifer Carr. In the early 1790s it was resettled from New England; the town was formed from Burlington in 1808. Population peaked at 2,087 in 1830. In 1889 it became the terminus of an Ontario and Western Railroad branchline from New Berlin (Chenango Co). Edmeston is headquarters of New York Central Mutual Fire Insurance Co (1899); another large employer is Bishop Printing. Pathfinder Village (1980; successor to the Otsego School [1922]) is an internationally known institution for children and adults with Down's syndrome.

Hugh C. MacDougall

Edmonds, Francis William (*b* Hudson, Columbia Co, 22 Nov 1806; *d* Bronxville, Westchester Co, 7 Feb 1863). Artist and banker. In 1822 Edmonds served as underclerk in a New York City bank, in 1823 worked at the city's Tradesman's Bank, in 1826 took evening classes at the Antique School of the National Academy of Design, and in 1830 put his art career on hold to become cashier of the Hudson River Bank in Hudson. In 1832 he returned to banking in New York City, resumed his painting by mid-decade, and in 1839 took a position with Mechanics' Bank. After his wife's death in 1840 Edmonds sought refuge in Europe, where he studied the old masters. His style was influenced by 17th-century Dutch genre scenes, although his subjects often reflected local culture with humor. James Kirke Paulding's novel *The Dutchman's Fireside* (1831), about a Hudson Valley family, inspired Edmonds's *The Bashful Cousin* (?1841–42). In 1855 Edmonds resigned from Mechanics' Bank after being accused of embezzling funds, a charge that later proved false. Edmonds retreated to Crow's Nest, his Bronxville estate, and continued painting.

Clark, H. Nichols B. *Francis W. Edmonds: American Master in the Dutch Tradition* (Washington, DC: Smithsonian Institution Press for the Amon Carter Museum, 1988)

Kathryn Clippinger Kosto

Edmonds, Walter D(umaux) (*b* Boonville, Oneida Co, 15 July 1903; *d* Concord, Mass, 24 Jan 1998). Author. Edmonds was born on his family's summer property, Northlands, on the Black River, and became strongly attached to this home despite spending most of the year in New York City, where his father was a patent lawyer. At Harvard, from which he would graduate in 1926, he was a student of writing teacher Charles Townsend Copeland and edited and contributed to the *Harvard Advocate*. His early work dealt largely with the Revolutionary history of New York and with the Erie Canal. *Rome Haul* (1929), *Erie Water* (1933), *Drums Along the Mohawk* (1936), and *In the Hands of the Senecas* (1947) are representative novels; *Mostly Canallers* (1934) is a major collection of short stories. Edmonds also chronicled country and city life in New York State in the 19th and 20th centuries; *The Big Barn* (1930), *Chad Hanna* (1940), *Young Ames* (1942), and *The Boyds of Black River* (1953) are fine examples. *Drums Along the Mohawk, Chad Hanna,* and *Rome Haul* (under the title *The Farmer Takes a Wife*) were all made into movies starring Henry Fonda.

Edmonds wrote many books for younger readers, among them *The Matchlock Gun* (1941), which won a Newbery Medal; *Two Logs Crossing* (1943); *Hound Dog Moses and the Promised Land* (1954); *Time to Go House* (1969); and *Bert Breen's Barn* (1975), a National Book Award winner. He also wrote some nonfiction, including a history of the Oneida Community, *The First Hundred Years* (1948). *The South African Quirt* (1985) and *Tales My Father Never Told* (1995) are autobiographical. In all his works, Edmonds celebrates the common folk who are the backbone of American democracy. He does so with painstaking historical accuracy, a deft understanding of human nature, a great love of animals and the outdoors, and well-tempered language that delights in the folksy and the humorous. For many years Edmonds made his home in Cambridge, Mass, but he also retained possession of Northlands until 1976. Twice married, he made his final home in Concord, Mass.

Wyld, Lionel D. *Walter D. Edmonds, Storyteller* (Syracuse: Syracuse Univ Press, 1982)

Frank Bergmann

education. See ACADEMIES; BILINGUAL EDUCATION; (CATHOLIC EDUCATION); CITIZENSHIP EDUCATION; COMPULSORY EDUCATION; CONTINUING EDUCATION; DISTANCE LEARNING; HIGHER EDUCATION; JEWISH EDUCATION; MEDICAL EDUCATION; PUBLIC EDUCATION; RELEASED TIME; RURAL EDUCATION; TEACHER TRAINING AND CERTIFICATION; THEOLOGICAL EDUCATION.

educational testing. See REGENTS EXAMINATIONS AND STATE TESTING.

Education Department and University of the State of New York. The University of the State of New York was established by the state constitution as a public corporation governed by a Board of Regents. The 16 Regents (1 from each judicial district and 4 at large) are elected for five-year terms by a majority vote of the legislature in joint session. Regents receive expenses but no salaries. The board elects a chancellor as its presiding officer and appoints the commissioner of education as chief administrative officer of the State Education Department and president of the university. The university comprises all incorporated educational institutions in the state. The Board of Regents is the only state board of education that oversees all types and levels of educational organizations: preschool programs, public and private elementary and secondary schools, postsecondary institutions (granting and not granting degrees), and nonacademic institutions of learning such as libraries, museums, and historical societies. The Education Department's functions are classified by five major program areas: elementary, middle, secondary, and continuing education; vocational and educational services for individuals with disabilities (preschool through adult); higher education, including teacher certification; professional licensing, registration, and discipline; and cultural education, embracing the State Library, State Museum, State Archives, and public and educational television.

ORIGINS AND EARLY RESPONSIBILITIES OF THE BOARD OF REGENTS

The Board of Regents was created by statute in 1784 to serve as trustees of Columbia College and of other colleges and academies incorporated thereafter. In 1787 the legislature altered and broadened the responsibilities of the Regents, empowering them to "visit and inspect all the colleges, academies, and schools" in the state, award academic degrees, and act as a corporation. Colleges and academies now had their own trustees, but the Regents were given the power to incorporate those institutions, to obtain annual reports from them, and to distribute financial aid to academies from the state's Literature Fund. Until the mid–19th century, the state legislature continued to incorporate some academies by special acts. The Regents strengthened educational standards by requiring use of "preliminary" examinations for entry into secondary schools (1865) and "academic" examinations for high school courses (1877) and by publishing syllabi. Issuance of Regents' high school diplomas was authorized in 1889. During the 1890s the Regents consolidated their control over secondary education through programs to inspect and register high schools. The range of institutions overseen by the Regents was gradually widened. The legislature made the Regents trustees of the State Library (1844) and the State Museum (1845), and the Regents obtained legislation in 1889 and 1892 authorizing them to incorporate and supervise libraries, museums, and other nonprofit educational institutions, as well as correspondence schools.

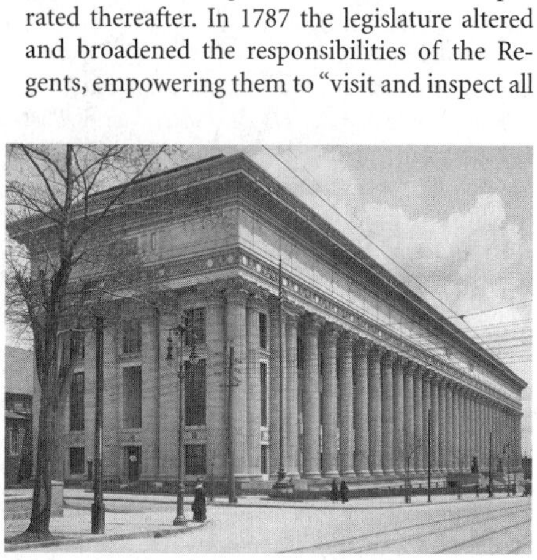

New York State Education Department building in Albany, designed by Palmer and Hornbostel, built 1908–12.

The statewide system of public elementary schools was established by the Common School Law of 1812. An appointed superintendent of common schools allocated and distributed aid to school districts from the Common School Fund (1805), advised school district trustees, and reviewed their statistical reports. After 1821 the secretary of state served as superintendent, although a deputy performed most of the office's functions. In 1854 the legislature created the Department of Public Instruction, headed by a superintendent elected jointly by the senate and assembly for a three-year renewable term. The new superintendent's local agents were the commissioners of schools (one or more elected in each county), who licensed teachers, inspected schools, and sent reports to Albany. They began to issue course outlines for elementary schools in the 1880s, and in 1896 the Department of Public Instruction prepared an official syllabus for statewide use.

During the 19th century the Regents had a vague authority to oversee all schools, but their primary responsibility was secondary education—private academies and public high schools—and higher education. Administrative confusion arose after midcentury, because the superintendent of public instruction had oversight of secondary schools operated by city and union free school districts, while the Regents supervised secondary school academic programs. Both the superintendent and the Regents distributed financial aid to schools. The legislature and the Constitutional Conventions of 1867 and 1894 rejected repeated proposals to unify elementary, secondary, and higher education under one administration. During the 1890s the superintendents of public instruction lobbied to get control of secondary education, even as the university expanded its programs and influence under Melvil Dewey, secretary of the Board of Regents. In 1899 a special commission named by Gov Theodore Roosevelt proposed a new, unified department of education. After much legislative wrangling, a unification bill supported by Gov Benjamin B. Odell Jr became law in 1904, establishing the State Education Department as the administrative embodiment of the University of the State of New York.

DEVELOPMENT OF THE STATE EDUCATION DEPARTMENT

The new department and its commissioner, Andrew S. Draper, continued the educational initiatives of the late 19th century. The Education Department, housed in an imposing building opened in Albany in 1912, became known for its authoritarian attitude toward the "field." The department scrutinized the statistical reports and Regents examination papers sent to Albany. Department inspectors regularly visited high schools, libraries, colleges, and special schools for students with disabilities. Most attention was given to high schools in smaller communities; the school systems of cities and larger villages operated with considerable autonomy under their own superintendents. The department had few experts on elementary education until the later 1930s, and the imbalance in favor of secondary education persisted into the 1950s. The Regents' Inquiry into the Character and Cost of Public Education (1935–38) found that the department had many internal inefficiencies and a "dictatorial" attitude toward local school authorities; the department's services were partially reorganized in response.

Despite its problems, the Education Department presided over remarkable improvements in public education during the 1920s and 1930s. State aid to rural and city school districts more than doubled; thousands of rural school districts were consolidated and their one-room schoolhouses closed; and standards for teacher education and certification were elevated. Starting in the late 1920s, the department promoted what was termed "child-centered" or "progressive" education, and the "social studies" became the centerpiece of the secondary school curriculum.

STANDARDIZATION OF CURRICULUM AND TESTING

During the 1950s schools faced rapidly rising enrollments because of the postwar Baby Boom. The department issued new school building standards favoring one-story, sprawling structures instead of multistory, compact buildings. The building boom was accompanied by a slower strengthening of the public school curriculum and pupil assessment programs. Since

COMMISSIONERS OF EDUCATION

Commissioner	Tenure
Andrew S. Draper	1904–13
John H. Finley	1913–21
Frank P. Graves	1921–40
Ernest E. Cole	1940–42
George D. Stoddard	1942–45
Francis T. Spaulding	1946–50
Lewis A. Wilson	1950–55
James E. Allen Jr	1955–69
Ewald Nyquist	1969–77
Gordon M. Ambach	1977–87
Thomas Sobol	1987–95
Richard P. Mills	1995–

Compiled by James D. Folts

1906 high schools had been authorized to issue a local diploma to students who had not passed Regents exams. State requirements for the local high school diploma were not very stringent. Not until 1934 did the Regents adopt rules for basic and elective courses in secondary schools, and integrated course sequences for grades K–12 were developed only in the 1950s. The secondary school science curriculum was revised in the late 1940s, after a generation of relative neglect, but science was not required to be taught in elementary schools until 1958, in response to Soviet successes in space technology. Since the 1920s the Education Department had promoted use of national standardized tests to measure pupil achievement, and it started issuing its own reading and math progress tests in 1940. Declining student test scores became a statewide concern in the later 1960s. After 1965 the department's Pupil Evaluation Program (PEP) tests measured basic skills in grades three, six, and nine, and basic competency tests were required of high school students starting in 1978.

Higher Education

The Regents continue to oversee higher education. Registration of courses of study in colleges, universities, and professional schools began in 1897. For-profit proprietary schools were required to be licensed starting in 1910. The Regents were given broad authority to regulate professional education and conduct, enabling New York State to lead the nation in the movement to improve standards for the health professions. The Regents were empowered to license physicians (1890), dentists (1895), nurses (1903), pharmacists (1910), and many other legally recognized professions (totaling 44 in 2003, comprising about 645,000 professionals registered). Each profession has its own state board, examinations, licenses, registers, and formal disciplinary process for misconduct. The Education Department's Office of Teaching administers the teacher certification program (there are more than 200,000 certified teachers and other education professionals working in the state). The Board of Regents is the only state board of education that accredits postsecondary degree-granting institutions, an activity in which the Education Department cooperates with private accrediting groups. The Regents issue periodic master plans for higher education, and they also sponsor reviews of doctoral programs. This much publicized activity, begun in 1973, has resulted in the closing of many weak programs.

The Regents have also started innovative programs for adults wanting college-level education. Starting in 1963 the Regents College Examinations gave degree credits for noncollege learning. The Regents External Degrees were first granted in 1972, and that program was institutionalized as the independent Regents College (now Excelsior College) in 1984. However, the Regents did not lead in developing the state university system. Between 1927 and 1944, the Education Department supervised the long-established state teachers colleges and normal schools; the specialized contract state colleges at Cornell, Syracuse, and Alfred Universities; and the state schools of agriculture and technology. In 1948 those institutions became part of the State University of New York (SUNY), established nominally within the Education Department. The Regents had opposed a publicly funded state university system and would have preferred putting more resources into private colleges (through the Regents Scholarship program) and expanding the state-run agricultural and technical institutes. SUNY became fully independent of the Regents in 1961.

Vocational Education Programs

Regents' curricula and exams for industrial and domestic arts courses began to appear in the 1890s. After 1908 state aid was provided for vocational education in city and village school districts; federal aid started in 1917. Enrollments in vocational courses soared, and by the 1930s all the state's largest cities had night schools, trade schools, and industrial and technical high schools. The many new central rural school districts offered academic and some vocational courses, and as a result of the broader programs, by 1940 nearly half of public school pupils graduated from high school. High school equivalency (General Education Diploma [GED]) exams for adults began to be offered in 1947.

The rise of community colleges and the expansion of the SUNY agricultural and technical institutes during the 1950s and 1960s increased opportunities for postsecondary vocational education. After 1967 the regional Boards of Cooperative Educational Services (BOCES), first authorized by a 1948 law, began building and operating vocational education centers for high school students living outside large cities. The Education Department approves BOCES programs, distributes federal aid for vocational education, and administers various adult literacy, job training, and high school equivalency testing programs.

Special Education Programs

State support for deaf and blind children in private institutions dates to the 1830s and continues today. The New York State School for the Blind at Batavia (Genesee Co) opened in 1868 and has been operated by the department since 1919; the School for the Deaf at Rome (Oneida Co), founded in 1875, has been state run since 1963. The strong school attendance law of 1894 brought many children with disabilities into the classroom for the first time. A 1917 law required larger school districts to identify children with physical or mental handicaps and to provide special classes or place the children in private schools. By the 1930s the state had hundreds of special school classes for children with disabilities.

The policy of separation slowly began to shift toward one of inclusion. BOCES began offering special education programs in 1967. State aid for education of handicapped children, abolished in 1962, was restored in 1974 (some federal aid had been available since 1967). A Regents' statement of 1973 recommended "mainstreaming" children with handicapping conditions whenever possible. Since 1975 federal law has required that all children with disabilities receive a "free, appropriate education in the least restrictive environment." In New York State, school districts have been made fully responsible for identifying and educating all children with disabilities, in either public or special schools. During the 1990s new Education Department rules promoted the shifting of children with special education needs from special classes or schools into regular classrooms.

School Integration Controversies

Following the 1954 US Supreme Court decision in *Brown v Board of Education*, which declared that racially segregated schools are inherently unequal, the Education Department launched a campaign to integrate New York State's large school systems. In the late 1950s the department encouraged school districts to achieve "racial balance," but de facto segregation continued to increase; by 1960 a majority of the pupils in 307 elementary schools in New York City and 59 schools elsewhere were black. In 1963 Commissioner James E. Allen Jr directed every school district to eliminate racial imbalance. Eventually he ordered the Buffalo district and several suburban districts near New York City to integrate their schools. Integration proceeded slowly in New York City, where experimental community school districts and citywide teachers' strikes caused immense controversy in 1967–68. In response, the legislature divided the city into community school districts to operate elementary and middle schools and retained the citywide Board of Education; a chancellor appointed by the board administered the vast system. Commissioner Ewald Nyquist ordered several more urban districts to integrate their schools. Political sentiment had turned against mandatory busing of pupils, however, and the Regents fired Nyquist in 1976.

Recent Trends

Since the late 1960s the Education Department has allocated special state and federal aid to all school districts having significant numbers of underperforming students. The department has gradually raised standards for all elementary, middle, and secondary school students. The Regents Action Plan of 1984 required high school graduates to demonstrate competency in several basic subjects and directed school districts to publish pupil performance data for each school building; schools could have their registration reviewed or revoked for unsatisfactory performance. The New Compact for Learning (1991) adopted a policy of statewide goals for schools, challenging programs for all students, and cooperation by schools, families, and communities. Starting in 1994 schools were required to involve teachers and parents in planning and decision making. After 1996 the less demanding competency exams were phased out, and the Regents examinations became the state's standard exams for all high school students. This decision helped intensify public debate on the goals of testing and public education overall.

The University of the State of New York and the Education Department are sometimes called the fourth branch of state government because the Regents and the commission are not gubernatorial appointees and because state operating aid to elementary, middle, and secondary schools—$21.4 billion in 2003–4—was huge. Each year the final amount of school aid is a matter of intense, nonpublic negotiation between the Governor's Office and legislative leaders. In 2003 the New York Court of Appeals ordered the legislature and the executive branch to reform state aid formulas as they apply to the New York City school district to provide a sound, basic high school education. The Education Department itself is a midsized agency, with about 3,150 employees in 2003. About 12% of its annual operating expenses ($380 million) comes from the state's general fund; most of the rest comes from special revenue funds (federal aid, fees for services such as professional registration and teacher certification, and other state-imposed fees).

See also COMMUNITY COLLEGES.

Abbott, Frank C. *Government Policy and Higher Education: A Study of the Regents of the University of the State of New York, 1784–1949* (Ithaca: Cornell Univ Press, 1958)

Corey, Albert B., Hugh M. Flick, and Frederick A. Morse, comps. *The Regents of the University of the State of New York, 1784–1959* (Albany: Univ of the State of New York, 1959)

Detlefsen, Bruce B. *A Popular History of the Origins of the Regents of the University of the State of New York* (Albany: NYS Education Department, 1975)

Folts, James D. *History of the University of the State of New York and the State Education Department, 1784–1996* (Albany: NYS Education Department, 1996)

Horner, Harlan H., ed. *Education in New York State, 1784–1954* (Albany: NYS Education Department, 1954)

Hough, Franklin B., comp. *Historical and Statistical Record of the University of the State of New York during the Century from 1784 to 1884* (Albany: Weed, Parsons, 1885)

New York State. Education Department. *Annual Report*, 1904/05–1955/56 (Albany: Author, 1905–58

James D. Folts

Edwards. Town (pop 1,148) and village (pop 465) in S central St Lawrence Co. Settled in 1812, the town was formed in 1827 from Fowler, and an influx of Scottish immigrants came to the northeast area of town in 1819. Located in the Adirondack foothills, its farms are limited to the Elm Creek valley, which is rimmed by hard-rock hills. An early industry was the bog iron furnace (1830) at what is now Talcville. The Gouverneur and Oswegatchie Railroad began service in 1897. Mining was the town's lifeblood: talc (1878) at Talcville and zinc (1903–81) at Edwards hamlet. The village, incorporated in 1893, retains Victorian charm despite economic decline and population loss. The Romanesque Revival Town Hall (1896), built of Potsdam sandstone and Gouverneur marble, is a landmark. The 4,316-acre (1,747 ha) Wolf Lake State Forest is in town.

Richard E. Mooers

egg cream. Despite the name, this legendary New York City soda fountain drink contains neither eggs nor cream. The origin of the term remains mysterious, but it possibly originated and certainly was popularized in the early 1890s by Louis Auster, a Jewish immigrant who owned a chain of five candy stores in Brooklyn that reportedly served 3,000 egg creams a day. Auster never revealed his recipe, but other soda fountains eventually copied and began serving the concoction. Moisha Zamrowsky, owner of Moisha's Luncheonette, is credited with importing the egg cream to Manhattan's Lower East Side in the 1920s.

The classic egg cream contains milk, seltzer water (preferably from a siphon or seltzer bottle), and vanilla or chocolate syrup. Authentic chocolate egg creams are made with Fox's U-Bet Chocolate-Flavored Syrup from Brooklyn. Lightly salted pretzel rods and whipped cream are sometimes included. Mango and raspberry egg creams have been reported in recent years but are not taken seriously by traditionalists. Although less common than in decades past, when almost every candy store and deli served them, egg creams are still found on many neighborhood menus. They remain one of the most evocative and nostalgic of all New York City foods.

Nancy Groce

Elba. Town (pop 2,439) and village (pop 696) in N Genesee Co. The town was formed from Batavia in 1820 after the area's settlement in 1801, and the village was incorporated in 1884. Woolen cloth manufacturing provided employment after the Civil War, as did the Tornado Windmill Co (1874) and the Elba Food Products Co (1915). Elba has over 2,500 acres (1,012 ha) of mucklands, made usable by the draining of the Oak Orchard Swamp by a stock company in 1915; the mucklands are used to produce vegetables, especially onions and potatoes. Elba, called the Onion Capital of the World, has two of the nation's 100 largest vegetable farms. Drawn by railroad work, Italians came to Elba, went to work in the mucklands, and became landowning farmers themselves. A landmark is the cobblestone Quaker Meeting House (1836).

Susan L. Conklin

Elbridge. Town (pop 6,091) and village (pop 1,103) in W central Onondaga Co. Settled in 1793, the town was formed in 1829 from Camillus and crossed by both the Erie Canal (1820) and the Rochester and Syracuse Railroad (1851; later New York Central). The village incorporated in 1848. Manufacturing in the 19th century included chairs (from *ca* 1850), bedsteads (1859), gloves and mittens, strawboard (1865–1917), pails, wheelbarrows, and pearl barley. The Elbridge Electric Manufacturing Co (1889–1913) produced magnetos and windshield wipers. The Amphion Player Piano Co was another distinctive industry until it closed in 1909. The north part of town is crossed by the New York State Thruway (1954). In the early 21st century the largest employers are Jordan-Elbridge Central School district and Tessy Plastics (1973), which had some 400 employees locally in 2003.

Barbara S. Rivette

election law. The complex structure of New York State's election laws is controversial. To critics, the laws represent all that is bad about politics, yet to others they embody a commitment to a democratic process. They are regularly characterized as arcane, designed to stifle the emergence of new ideas and competing candidates. Their defenders characterize them as precise rules for political process. Each law in force at the start of the 21st century was legislated in response to a perceived abuse of that process. Registration laws, for example, were established in the mid–19th century to deal with the claims that Tammany Hall in New York City was getting votes from those ineligible to vote. An 1890 law and 1894 constitutional revision mandated a secret ballot and allowed voting machines in response to claims that voters were being coerced to submit color-coded ballots that party leaders could see. The primary, in which voters select a candidate, was created in 1890 because of concerns that party bosses controlled candidates. Abuses, alleged or in fact, in turn led to reform: changes that largely consisted of precise specification of the rules of the process and public announcement of those rules.

Election law is a product of statutes enacted by the state legislature and court rulings. The 1894 Constitution was one of the first documents to specify many of these requirements. It established bipartisan county Boards of Elections as government entities to manage the election process. Comprehensive updates to the law were enacted in 1949 and 1976, and continual enactments modify it. There are also regular legal challenges to existing administrative practices and interpretations leading to equally regular court rulings that modify existing practices. Election law is a product of the cumulative effect of these developments. While ongoing incremental changes are fairly common, in New York State there have been eras when major changes were a central concern.

PARTICIPATION

Election law defines, among many other things, who is eligible to vote and the date by which a person must register to qualify for a particular election. It provides precise rules about how the validity of a registration can be challenged and when a registrant can be eliminated, or purged, from the rolls. It specifies how a voter chooses to enroll, or chooses a party, after registering to vote. Enrollment is crucial to political parties because it gives them an idea of their electoral base. It is also crucial to voters because only those enrolled in a party may vote in the party's primary. Not all elections are covered by the state election law. Votes on school board budgets and members, for example, are conducted by school districts with far looser practices. For almost all elections and voter situations, however, there are clear rules and court judgments about what one must do to participate. In general, the rules are intended to reduce arbitrary decisions by local officials about who can participate.

In the mid-1800s registration and voting were loosely managed by city governments, and there were complaints that the Tammany Hall was illegally mobilizing immigrants to vote. State requirements for a registry of voters date to an 1840 law that was repealed two years later. Several other registry laws were enacted and amended from the 1850s through the 1890s. Most affected registry lists in New York City and Brooklyn, although some also applied to cities and villages statewide. An 1866 law required potential voters in New York City and Brooklyn to appear in person before the registry board to qualify to vote. The state's general registration law of 1890 mandated personal registration in all cities, with registry lists based on the previous election used elsewhere in the state. These rules were adopted to prevent partisan officials from encouraging some to register and vote, while discouraging others. Registrants had to choose (enroll in) a party when they registered until 1957, when a registrant won a suit to void the requirement. Since then the percentage choosing not to enroll has increased greatly.

CANDIDATE ACCESS

There are also rules for how candidates get on the ballot. The general principle of these laws was established in 1880 out of concern that party bosses were controlling candidates. The law specifies practices candidates and parties must follow in nominating candidates but also grants some autonomy for how parties organize their nomination process. The rules that draw the most attention are those requiring a minimum of signatures on a candidate's petition. The law indicates how petitions must be written, what the form must look like, how a registrant's signature must appear, and how the petitions must be certified. If the process is not done as specified, an opposing candidate can challenge the petition; invalid signatures can be discounted or whole pages can be eliminated. If enough signatures are disqualified, a candidate may not have the required minimum and may not qualify for the ballot, a possibility that leads to controversies about ballot access. These petition rules were established to prevent fraud in signature gathering and to ensure that a candidate could demonstrate adequate support among enrolled registrants. Some critics maintain that the complexity of the rules favors the established parties.

Receiving and Counting Votes

Equally detailed and complex are the rules about how voting is conducted, which votes are counted, how they are counted, and how they can be challenged. Election law states when polling places must be open and limits the ability of candidates or their advocates to get within a certain distance of the polling site on election day. The law specifies that a voter list be present at the polls and that each person sign in to vote. There are poll watchers from each major party to observe the process to make sure no rules are bent. There are also precise rules about how votes must be counted, including the handling, counting, and challenging of mailed-in absentee ballots.

All of these specifics are again a direct reflection of past cases where there were doubts about the fairness of the process. The Gilded Age was particularly important for changes in the election law in New York State. Prior to that voting was done by voters dropping a ballot in a box for one party or another. There was little secrecy because the ballots generally had different colors, and party poll watchers could see a voter's ballot. Objections to this practice led to the adoption during the 1890s of a ballot with all offices and candidates on one sheet, on which a voter could mark choices, fold the ballot, and drop it unseen into a box. Voting machines came into use in 1892.

Boards of Election

The administration of the election law is largely in the hands of boards of election. The law provides that each county and the state have a board. The local boards manage all aspects of registration and voting. Local candidates file their campaign finance reports at the county level, and candidates for state offices file with the state board. To ensure that board administration does not reflect the views of a locally dominant party, the board is administered by two commissioners, one from each major party, and no decisions can be made without the approval of both. Finally, the law provides for the creation of third (minor) parties through a process requiring that signatures be gathered and submitted for review. Third parties must follow the same practices as other parties in nominating their candidates.

Impact

The precision and demands of these rules have led to criticism. Groups such as NYPIRG (New York Public Interest Research Group) and many newspaper editors argue that the rules hinder people who wish to run for office. The primary criticism has been that the strict rules about signatures on petitions make it difficult for challengers, who likely are not experts in the law and who must rely on volunteers. Assessing the effects of these rules is not simple, however. For the democratic process to be fair, the rules of participation must be known by all and applied equally to all. The statutes that have been enacted over time serve multiple purposes. The requirement about signatures, for example, is an attempt to reduce fraud. While the rules are much criticized, they are a response to past problems. If the rules have a bias, it is to keep the role of political parties paramount in the electoral process.

McKinney's Consolidated Laws of New York Annotated. Election Law (Bk 17) (St. Paul, Minn: West Publishing, 1998)
New York Public Interest Research Group, http://www.nypirg.org/goodgov
New York State Board of Elections, http://www.elections.state.ny.us
Spitzer, Robert. "Third Parties in New York." In *Governing New York,* 4th ed., ed. Jeffrey M. Stonecash (Albany: SUNY Press, 2001)

Jeffrey M. Stonecash

elections. See Cross-endorsement; Election law; Gubernatorial elections; Presidential elections; Primary elections; United States Senate.

Elections, State Board of. Bipartisan agency established in 1974 as part of New York State's Executive Department to administer and enforce the state's election law. Prior to its creation, election administration had been left to the 57 county boards and the New York City board, and their different interpretations of the election law had produced inconsistent voter registration and voting procedures throughout the state. Since 1974 local boards remain responsible for the day-to-day supervision of the electoral process, but they receive guidance from a central board that issues opinions on election law. Employees of the State Board of Elections visit, inspect, and investigate local boards of elections; prepare standard forms for use by local officials; and encourage voter participation. The state board has subpoena power, can bring judicial proceedings in the courts, and can refer complaints to district attorneys. It regulates limitation and disclosure of the campaign finances of candidates for state offices and investigates complaints under the Fair Campaign Code, adopted by the board in 1975 to govern campaign practices. The state board is also responsible for overseeing the implementation of the 1993 National Voter Registration Act. The governor selects the board's four commissioners from lists submitted separately by chairpersons of the state Democratic and Republican Parties and jointly by party leaders of the two legislative houses. The governor appoints the four to serve in two-year, staggered terms; the commissioners are evenly divided between the two political parties—thus far, always the Democratic and Republican Parties—whose gubernatorial candidates received the most votes in the most recent election. In addition to the four-member board, there is a staff headed by an executive director and deputy executive director, who cannot be of the same political party.

New York State. Board of Elections. *Annual Report* (Albany: State Board of Elections, 1974)

Jeffrey Kraus

elective offices, statewide. Over its history New York State has had as few as 2 and as many as 10 offices filled by statewide election. At the start of the 21st century there are four: governor, lieutenant governor, attorney general, and comptroller. Only the lieutenant governor is not independently elected; a 1953 constitutional amendment mandated a single ballot to cover the governor and lieutenant governor. These offices have been filled concurrently since 1894. A 1937 constitutional amendment made the tenure four years, with election in even nonpresidential years and no limit on reeligibility. New York has fewer statewide elected officials than most states.

The governor and lieutenant governor have been elected offices since independence. The offices of comptroller and attorney general were first filled by appointment, initially by a Council of Appointment and then, after the 1821 Constitution was adopted, by the legislature. They became elective under the Constitution of 1846, as did the offices of secretary of state, treasurer, canal commissioner, state engineer and surveyor, state prison inspector, and Court of Appeals judge. The reliance in the "people's constitution" of 1846 to fill numerous statewide offices by election reflects both the full flowering of Jacksonian democracy and a decline in confidence in the state legislature as an instrument of democratic governance. One rationale for this practice was that officials whose function it was to ensure the probity of the governor and legislature, like the comptroller, should be kept independent of both by making them directly answerable to the sovereign people. Another was that those who were charged with taking or restricting the liberty of others, such as the attorney general, judges, and prison managers, needed to be kept under special scrutiny by the electorate. A third was that those responsible for large governmental investments crucial to the economic well-being of the state, like canals and internal improvements, were best kept directly accountable through election.

Efforts to "shorten the ballot" began immediately after the Civil War with proposals by the 1867 Constitutional Convention that the governor appoint the board of prison inspectors and a superintendent of public works, with responsibilities for canal administration and the duties of the state engineer and surveyor consolidated. Although these failed at the polls, proposals by the 1872 Constitutional Commission that gubernatorially appointed superintendents of public works and prisons replace the statewide elected canal commissioners and prison inspectors became law in 1876.

During the early 20th century, Progressive era reformers sought to re-create state government on the corporate model, with the governor as chief executive and executive branch departments headed by his or her appointees account-

PUBLIC OFFICERS ELECTED STATEWIDE

Officer	Years Elective	Term
State Officers		
Governor	1777–present	3 years (1777–1821)
		2 years (1822–75)
		3 years (1876–94)
		2 years (1895–1937)
		4 years (1938–present)
Lieutenant Governor	1777–present	(same as governor)
Attorney General	1847–present	2 years (1847–1937)
		4 years (1938–present)
Comptroller	1847–present	2 years (1847–1937)
		4 years (1938–present)
Court of Appeals Judges	1847–1977	8 years (1847–69)
		14 years (1870–1977)
Secretary of State	1847–1925	2 years
State Canal Commissioners	1847–76	3 years
State Engineer and Surveyor	1847–1925	2 years
State Prison Inspectors	1847–76	3 years
Treasurer	1847–1925	2 years
Federal Officers		
Electors for US President and Vice President	1832[a]–present	—[b]
US Representative[c]	1874–76	2 years
	1882–84	
	1932–44	
US Senator	1914–present	6 years

Sources: M. J. Dubin, *United States Congressional Elections, 1788–1997* (1998) and P. J. Galie, *Ordered Liberty: A Constitutional History of New York* (1996).

[a]Through the 1824 presidential election, electors from New York State were chosen by the state legislature. Electors were chosen by popular vote on a district basis in 1828 and by popular vote on a statewide basis beginning in 1832.

[b]Electors fulfill their obligations of service by voting for president and vice president and certifying their ballots. No term is served.

[c]In 1872 and 1882 New York State voters elected one at-large delegate to the House of Representatives. In 1932, 1934, 1936, 1938, 1940, and 1942 they elected two at-large delegates to the House of Representatives.

Compiled by Laura-Eve Moss

able to the people through the governor. The reduction in the number of statewide elected offices also promised to diminish the power of the state's political party bosses, who controlled nomination to them and in this way gained access to the patronage that nourished a disciplined party system. The constitution proposed by the 1915 convention would have abolished the office of state engineer and surveyor and converted the secretary of state and treasurer to appointive status. These proposals failed at the polls, but amendments making the three offices appointive were signed into law by Gov Alfred E. Smith in 1925.

Policy disputes between the governor and attorney general, and the absence in the latter office of significant criminal justice responsibilities, occasionally led to suggestions (never seriously pursued) that the attorney general position be made appointive. During the mid-1970s the growth of highly partisan elections for positions on the state's highest court resulted in a 1977 amendment that switched selection of judges of the Court of Appeals from election to appointment by the governor (after nomination by a 12-person Commission on Judicial Nominations and with advice and consent by the senate).

New Yorkers have also elected a handful of federal officers on a statewide rather than district basis. These include, from 1832, electors for the US president and vice president. (Prior to that, presidential electors were chosen by the state legislators or by voters on a district basis.) Questions about congressional apportionment have led three times to the creation of at-large seats in the US House of Representatives: single seats filled in 1872 and 1882, and two seats filled in every congressional election between 1932 and 1942. Since the 17th Amendment to the US Constitution was adopted in 1913, voters also directly elect two US senators.

Benjamin, Gerald. *The Governor and the Attorney General in New York* (Albany: Rockefeller Institute, 1986)
Galie, Peter J. *Ordered Liberty: A Constitutional History of New York* (New York: Fordham Univ Press, 1996)

Gerald Benjamin

electoral college. Established by the US Constitution, the electoral college meets separately in all 50 states and the District of Columbia every four years following the November presidential election. The electors meet on the first Monday after the second Wednesday of December. After casting their votes, they sign and forward the certificates of ascertainment and vote to the archivist of the United States. Each state's electors equal the number of its US senators and representatives. Legislative disagreement over how to select electors caused New York State to miss the first electoral college of 1789. In 1792 the electors met at the courthouse in Poughkeepsie and between 1796 and 1808 in Hudson (Columbia Co). From 1812 onward, the electors have gathered at the State House in Albany. The state legislature selected electors for the first few presidential elections (1792–1824), resulting in the divided electoral votes of 1808 and 1824. The state used district selection in 1828, also leading to a split vote. Since the adoption of the winner-take-all system in 1832, New York State has not divided its electoral vote among different candidates. There is no state law compelling electors to vote according to their pledge, but the state has never had a true "faithless elector." In 1824, though, two of the six electors originally supporting Henry Clay for president instead cast their ballots for Andrew Jackson and William H. Crawford. Political party competition was so weak at the time that the legislature did not provide clear instructions to electors.

Each state political party committee selects a slate of individuals who will serve as electors if the party's presidential ticket wins the popular vote of the state. In November voters choose a party's electors rather than vote directly for the president and vice president. Electors are usually party loyalists and leaders, although representatives of associations and financial contributors have also served. Horace Greeley, founder and editor of the *New York Tribune* and a leader of the Republican Party, was an elector in 1864. Frederick Douglass, active in the Republican Party, voted at the 1872 meeting and was the first African American to serve as a New York State elector. No women served as electors in the state until 1921, when Ruth B. Pratt, Sadie Koenig, C. Mathilde Schaefer, and Elizabeth D. Miller, wife of Gov Nathan L. Miller, cast ballots. The US Constitution provides that "no Senator or Representative, or person holding an office of trust or profit under the United States, shall be appointed an elector," and the New York City Charter forbids city officials from serving as electors. Since the meeting of 1913, the state's electors have often given their $15 stipends and mileage reimbursements to charity.

New York State Archives. "Viewing the Electoral College through Historical Records," http://www.archives.nysed.gov

Gary Bugh

electric companies. See MUNICIPALLY OWNED ELECTRIC COMPANIES; POWER AND LIGHTING; and individual companies.

Elizabethtown. Town (pop 1,315) in E Essex Co. Settled in 1792, the town was formed from Crown Point in 1798. Elizabethtown hamlet became the county seat in 1807, and an arsenal was sited there in 1812. Ore and peat beds, forges, and lumbering drove the economy in the 19th century; beginning about 1873 hotels were built to accommodate summer visitors. The hamlet was an incorporated village from 1875 to 1979. Its 21st-century economy is based on outdoor recreation and tourism, facilitated by Northway (1967) access, and on county and state government functions. It is the site of the Adirondack Center Museum.

Thomas A. Rumney

Ellenburg. Town (pop 1,812) in NW Clinton Co. Permanent settlement began in 1803 but was retarded by cross-border raids until after the War of 1812. The town, bounded on the north by Canada, formed from Mooers in 1830. Most settlers made a living by farming on the favored northern tracts or by lumbering in the hilly south. Established in 1850, the Northern Railroad (later Rutland Railroad) helped stimulate construction of an immense tannery (1851), the town's first starch factory (1853), which processed local potatoes, and later many butter factories. Early in the 21st century, Ellenburg is rural, with dairy farms and some forestry; many residents work in Plattsburgh, at the border crossings, or in the nearby prisons.

Thomas A. Rumney

Ellenville. Village (pop 4,130) in Wawarsing (Ulster Co). Its post office was named Ellensville in 1823 and changed to the current spelling in 1844. It began to thrive when the Delaware and Hudson Canal (1828–98) was completed. Chief industries were the Ellenville Glass Co (1837–*ca* 1895), maker of demijohns, Ellenville Tannery (1838), a foundry, and a pottery (*ca* 1830–1905). The village was incorporated in 1856. The Ontario and Western Railroad reached Ellenville in 1871 and was extended north to Kingston in 1902. Jews were residents by 1855, and after 1900 Ellenville became the center of a popular Jewish boarding house and hotel district. The Ulster Knife Co (1872) became Imperial Schrade and employed 450 in 2003; a similar number was employed by Hydro Aluminum NA (extrusions). In 2003 Ellenville's population was 12% black, and 28% of the total were of Latino ethnicity. The Ellenville Museum exhibits the world's earliest production automobile, an 1888 DeDion. A landmark is the *Boy with the Boot* fountain (1890s).

Ruth Piwonka

Ellery. Town (pop 4,576) in central Chautauqua Co. Settled in 1806 the town was formed in 1821 from Chautauqua. It is the eastern terminus of the Bemus Point–Stow Ferry, in existence since 1811, and of the Chautauqua County Veterans Memorial Bridge (1982) carrying Rte 17 (I-86) across the narrows of Chautauqua Lake. Midway Park (1898), originally a trolley company amusement park, and Long Point State Park are located in town. Ellery's economy is based on recreation and tourism, but farming and the production of maple sugar continue.

Michelle Henry

Ellicott. Town (pop 9,280) in SE Chautauqua Co. Settled in 1806 the town was formed from Pomfret in 1812. In the earliest days flatboats were constructed at Levant to transport lumber and salt to Pittsburgh and New Orleans. The Fluvanna House (1836) on the lake is said to have later become the first resort hotel in the county when people escaping a Buffalo cholera outbreak stayed there in 1849. Until 1886 what became the City of Jamestown was the business center of the town. Jamestown continues to draw workers and shoppers, but Ellicott has its own industrial and commercial areas in addition to farms and residential areas. The Duquesne (1903–6) and Birmingham (1921–22) automobiles were made in town. Ellicott's population increased 45% in the 1920s and doubled between 1920 and 1960. Rte 17 (I-86) was opened through town between 1971 and 1973. Ellicott is the site of Chautauqua County Airport (1931), served by Chautauqua Airlines (1974). Industries include Valeo Engine Cooling, Bush Industries, and others located in Mason Industrial Park.

Karen E. Livsey

Ellicott, Joseph (*b* Bucks Co, Pa, 1 Nov 1760; *d* New York City, 19 Aug 1826). Land agent and developer. In 1774 Ellicott moved with his family to a homestead along the Patapsco River in Maryland, where he was exposed to the rigors of land development on the frontier. He learned surveying from his brother Andrew, working with him on the planning of Washington, DC, beginning in 1791. In 1797 Joseph Ellicott was placed in charge of the general survey of the Holland Land Purchase, a tract of nearly 3.3 million acres (1.3 million ha). From 1797 to 1799 Ellicott and his team surveyed the entire tract, dividing it into a grid of townships and taking careful field notes concerning trees and vegetation, information useful to prospective settlers.

In 1800 Ellicott became resident-agent for the Holland Land Purchase and was charged with the sale and development of the Holland Land Co's western New York State lands. Ellicott used company funds to survey farms and to build the economic infrastructure that settlement required: roads, stores, mills, and taverns. In particular he platted the Cities of Buffalo and Batavia [now in Genesee Co]. An advocate for the Erie Canal, Ellicott served as a state canal commissioner beginning in 1816. His sales strategy accepted the likelihood that many of the first settlers would default and move on and that their land would therefore be sold to others. The strategy led to conflict because the value of the first settlers' improvements did not keep pace with their cumulative debt to the company, and in 1819 Ellicott's policy of compounding interest at the time contracts were renewed sparked a debt crisis for the settlers. The Holland Land Co asked for his resignation in 1821. Ellicott's last eight years were marked by severe bouts of melancholia. He entered the Bloomingdale Asylum in New York City, where he committed suicide by hanging.

Brooks, Charles E. *Frontier Settlement and Market Revolution: The Holland Land Purchase* (Ithaca: Cornell Univ Press, 1996)

Chazanof, William. *Joseph Ellicott and the Holland Land Company: The Opening of Western New York* (Syracuse: Syracuse Univ Press, 1970)

Charles E. Brooks

Ellicottville. Town (pop 1,738) and village (pop 472) in central Cattaraugus Co. Settled in 1815, the town was formed from the old town of Ischua [now Franklinville] in 1820. The site of the village was laid out by the Holland Land Co, which opened an office there in 1818, and is named after Joseph Ellicott (1760–1826), longtime resident-agent of the company. The town became the county seat in 1817, and a courthouse was built in 1820. These two factors led to rapid growth. The village was incorporated in 1837. The courthouse was moved to Little Valley in 1868 to be on the railroad, but in 1878 railroads from Rochester and Buffalo were completed to Ellicottville, which had become a logging and mill village surrounded by dairying and stock raising. Mid-20th-century factories produced shoe blocks, baskets, and condensed milk. In 2003 Ellicottville is an important tourist destination, drawing over 650,000 visitors a year to Holiday Valley and Holimont, both ski facilities. Other attractions include the Nannen Arboretum and the Ellicottville Brewing Co, a microbrewery. The hamlet of Plato is on the border with East Otto.

Bruce D. Fredrickson and Madelynn P. Fredrickson

Ellington. Town (pop 1,639) in SE Chautauqua Co. Settled in 1814 the town was formed in 1824 from Gerry. Its Yankee settlers created a typical New England green in the center hamlet, also called Ellington. The Ellington Academy (1852) became a union free school in 1871. For many years Ellington was noted for its excellent dairy products, including butter and cheese; four cheese factories were in operation in 1901. A sawmill, a number of dairy farms, and work in Jamestown provide livelihoods in the early 21st century.

Michelle Henry

Ellington, Duke. See JAZZ.

Elliott, Charles Loring (*b* Scipio, Cayuga Co, 12 Oct 1812; *d* Albany, 25 Aug 1868). Portraitist. Elliot was trained in his father's Syracuse architectural firm and studied drafting at an art academy in Onondaga Hollow (Onondaga Co) in 1827. He abandoned architecture and moved to New York City in 1829 to pursue painting. A year later Elliot returned to Central New York, where he worked as a portraitist. In 1839 he established a studio in New York City, exhibited his work, and formed an important affiliation with leading portraitist Henry Inman. Elliott was elected to the National Academy of Design in 1846. His painterly technique and use of shadow and light created vivid images that captured the essence of his subjects, including artist William Sidney Mount (*ca* 1850) and photographer Matthew Brady (?1857). During the Civil War Elliott accepted a number of important commissions and moved to Albany, where he completed *Erastus Corning I* (1864). Considered one of America's best portraitists, Elliott produced nearly 700 works.

Bolton, Theodore. "Charles Loring Elliott: An Account of His Life and Work" and "A Catalogue of the Portraits Painted by Charles Loring Elliott," *Art Quarterly* 5 (Winter 1942): 59–96

Mary Alice Mackay

Ellis, David M(aldwyn) (*b* Utica, 14 Oct 1914; *d* Delmar, Albany Co, 13 Apr 1999). Historian. The son of Welsh immigrants, Ellis grew up in Utica, graduated from Hamilton College in 1938, earned a PhD from Cornell University in 1942, and taught at Hamilton from 1946 until 1980. Ellis was a social and economic historian who focused on the development of New York State, especially its regional and ethnic diversity. He wrote a score of seminal articles and numerous monographs and textbooks, including the award-winning *Landlords and Farmers in the Hudson-Mohawk Region, 1790–1850* (1946), *A Short History of New York State* (1957; revised

1967), and *New York: State and City* (1979). In the latter, he explored the ongoing economic and cultural divide between New York City and the rest of the state. Ellis's work combined scholarly integrity and interpretive insight with a highly readable style. He became the preeminent authority of his era on New York State history and remains a central figure in the state's historiography.

"Ellis, David Maldwyn." In *Encyclopedia of American Agricultural History,* Edward L. Schapsmeier and Frederick H. Schapsmeier (Westport, Conn: Greenwood, 1975)

Frank K. Lorenz

Ellisburg. Town (pop 3,541) and village (pop 269) in SW Jefferson Co. The town is rich in American Indian archaeological sites. Early French explorers Samuel de Champlain (1615), Joseph-Antoine de La Barre (1684), and Fr François-Xavier de Charlevoix (1721) all visited. Lyman Ellis, for whom the town was named, became its first settler in 1797. He founded the village in 1799, and the town was formed from Mexico [now in Oswego Co] in 1803. During the War of 1812 Ellisburg was the site of the Battle of Sandy Creek and the "Carrying of the Cable" in which a 5 ton (4.5 MT) rope needed for a nearly completed ship was hand-carried from Sandy Creek (Oswego Co) to Sackets Harbor (Jefferson Co). The town was served by the Rome, Watertown and Ogdensburg (1851) and the short-lived Sackets Harbor and Ellisburgh (1853–62) Railroads. Residents' primary occupations have been general farming, stock raising, and, after 1850, dairying. In 1865 the town produced the fifth-largest quantity of cheese in the state. Other products included agricultural implements (1833) and furniture (1857). Since World War II the number of farms has declined, but dairy farming remains strong. I-81 was opened through town in 1961, and many people in both town and village commute. Ellisburg was the home of regionalist author Marietta Holley (1836–1926). It is the site of Southwick Beach State Park and several large state wildlife management areas.

Laura Lynne Scharer

Ellis Island. Situated in upper New York Bay about 1 mile (1.6 km) southwest of Manhattan Island and 1,350 feet (410 m) east of the New Jersey shore, Ellis Island served as the main immigrant processing station for the United States between 1892 and 1954. Named for butcher Samuel Ellis, who owned it during the 1770s and 1780s, the island then passed to New York State and in 1808 to the federal government. Between 1855 and 1890 as many as 8 million immigrants entered New York City through Castle Garden (now Castle Clinton), an immigration facility located in Battery Park at the southern tip of Manhattan. By the mid-1880s immigration rates had increased substantially, rendering the Castle Garden facility inadequate. In 1890 the federal government began construction of a new immigrant processing station on Ellis Island, and it opened two years later. In June 1897 this station was destroyed by fire and immediately replaced by a second center. Between 1892 and 1954 an estimated 17 million persons entered the United States through Ellis Island, and landfill extended the 3-acre (1.2 ha) body to 24 acres (9.7 ha). The

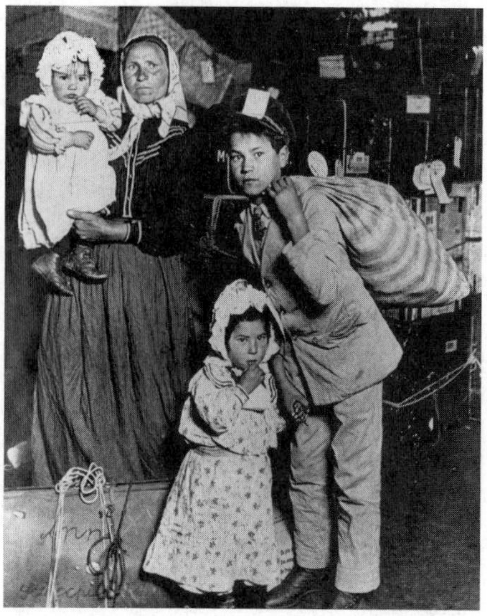

Immigrants at Ellis Island. Photograph by Lewis Hine, 1905.

majority of immigrants who came during this period hailed from eastern and southern European countries such as Russia, Poland, and Italy.

Upon arrival in New York City, immigrants disembarked at the Hudson or East River piers and passed through customs. First- and second-class passengers were processed on board the ships and then allowed to enter the United States immediately. Third-class or steerage passengers took ferries to Ellis Island, where they underwent a series of inspections and examinations designed to keep out unhealthy and undesirable immigrants. In the first stage of the screening process, doctors examined the new arrivals to identify physical disabilities, mental illness, or contagious and infectious diseases such as trachoma, tuberculosis, and leprosy. Those diagnosed with such disorders were quarantined or in some cases sent back to their native countries. After passing the medical examinations, immigrants proceeded to the registration division, where they were interrogated and registered in the facility record books. By 1903 a crude political test barred anarchists from entry as well. If papers were in order and further examinations deemed unnecessary, an immigrant could pass through the station in as little time as several hours. Others had to remain in the facility for days before finally being granted passage to the American mainland. In a single workday Ellis Island officials could process over 5,000 immigrants.

In the 1920s the federal government passed a series of acts that restricted immigration to the United States and therefore lessened the importance of Ellis Island. By the 1930s immigration inspectors had begun to inspect and process immigrants on arriving ships rather than on Ellis Island, and the facility was used only for holding detained immigrants, often political refugees, and potential deportees. In 1954 the federal government closed the facility and transferred its activities to offices in Manhattan. In 1965 Ellis Island became part of the Statue of Liberty National Monument and 11 years later was opened to sightseers by the National Park Service. After renovation in the 1980s funded by the National Park Service and private donations, the complex reopened in 1990 as Ellis Island Immigration Museum. In 1993 New Jersey sued New York State for jurisdiction over the popular site. In 1998 the US Supreme Court ruled that New Jersey owned the island's landfilled areas but that New York State retained jurisdiction over the original 3 acres.

Coan, Peter Morton. *Ellis Island Interviews: In Their Own Words* (New York: Facts on File, 1997)
Yans-McLaughlin, Virginia, and Marjorie Lightman. *Ellis Island and the Peopling of America: The Official Guide* (New York: New Press, 1997)

Nicholas P. Ciotola

Ellison, Ralph (Waldo) (*b* Oklahoma City, Okla, 1 Mar 1914; *d* New York City, 16 Apr 1994). Writer. Ellison's mother encouraged both him and his brother to become educated professionals, and he attended college at Alabama's Tuskegee Institute on a scholarship from 1933 to 1936. An accomplished trumpet player, he especially loved jazz and planned for a career in music but while in college was attracted to literature, particularly the works of Ernest Hemingway and T. S. Eliot. In 1936 Ellison traveled to New York City, home to numerous jazz musicians he admired. Although unable to find work in the music industry, he did meet two prominent black authors, Langston Hughes and Richard Wright, both taking an interest in him and encouraging him to become a writer. After securing a job with the Federal Writers' Project in 1936, Ellison stayed in New York City and began research on the black experience in urban America. His earliest published works were literary reviews and short stories, most of which appeared in *New Masses,* a left-wing magazine. He became managing editor of the *Negro Quarterly* in 1942 and later a reporter for the *New York Post,* for which he covered the Harlem race riot in 1943. He is best known for his 1952 novel *Invisible Man,* which depicts the dichotomy between the democratic idealism of the United States and its racially biased reality. Ellison won the National Book Award in 1953 for the book, which is widely regarded as one of the most significant and influential American novels of the second half of the 20th century. Ellison's essays were collected in *Shadow and Act* (1964) and *Going to the Territory* (1986). A theme running through his work is his firm belief that African American culture had influenced and was an integral part of American culture. Ellison was the Albert Schweitzer Professor of the Humanities at New York University from 1970 to 1980. His long-awaited second novel was not completed during his lifetime; a version under the title of *Juneteenth* was released five years after his death by his long-time friend and literary executor John Callahan. In late April 2003 a bronze sculpture honoring Ellison was unveiled across the street from his home on Riverside Drive.

Jackson, Lawrence. *Ralph Ellison: Emergence of Genius* (New York: John Wiley & Sons, 2002)

Donna L. Halper

Ellsworth's Avengers. See 44TH NEW YORK VOLUNTEER INFANTRY.

Elma. Town (pop 11,304) in central Erie Co. Elma was originally part of Buffalo Creek Reservation. Two years after the 1826 Treaty of Buffalo Creek a small number of white settlers arrived. The final sale of the reservation in 1842 opened the entire area for settlement. The Buffalo and Aurora Plank Road (1849) aided residents carrying lumber to city markets. The first Catholic place of worship, Mother Freiburg Chapel (1854–70), was a 10 x 14 ft (3.1 x 4.3 m) structure built by a German immigrant woman and her neighbors. The town was formed from Lancaster and Aurora in 1856. The arrival of the Buffalo, New York and Philadelphia Railroad (1867; later Pennsylvania Railroad) provided easy transportation of produce. Rte 400, rebuilt as a four-lane highway in 1966–68, made commuting to Buffalo convenient. Although many residents commute, in 2003 Motorola employed 741 in Elma, manufacturing automobile electronics, and Moog employed 1,958, producing electronic instruments.

Andrew C. Maines

Elmira. Town (pop 7,199) and city (pop 30,940) in central Chemung Co. Located on the Chemung River, the town was formed from Chemung in 1792 as Newtown, and its name was changed in 1808. The village was incorporated in 1815 as Newtown and renamed Elmira in 1828. Local tradition holds that the name was derived from a mother whose frequent and piercing calls for her daughter became attached to the settlement. The city was formed in 1864 from Elmira and Southport.

Elmira businesses such as the Tioga Coal, Iron, Mining, and Manufacturing (1828), the embryonic Chemung and Ithaca Railroad (1837), and Chemung County Mutual Insurance (1838) invested in transportation improvements in the region. The port of the Chemung Canal (1833–78), near the center of Elmira, linked Elmira to the Erie Canal via Seneca Lake and led to boatbuilding and shipping. The Junction Canal (1854–71) provided access to the coalfields of northern Pennsylvania. With the rise of the railroad after 1850, canal use declined. Elmira, served by the Erie (1849), Chemung (1849), and the Williamsport and Elmira (1854), thrived as a railway hub. By 1860 Elmira's chief industrial products were woolen cloth, iron, axes, and barrels.

The Underground Railroad passed through Elmira, aided by stationmaster John W. Jones (1817–1900), a former slave who had arrived in the city in 1844. It is estimated that Jones and other area abolitionists provided safe passage through Elmira for more than 800 runaway slaves in the 1850s. Elmira Female College (now Elmira College) opened in 1855, the first women's college to confer degrees equal to those received by men.

Elmira's central location and excellent transportation system led it to be named one of three military depots in the state during the Civil War. In 1864 one of the military barracks in Elmira was transformed into the Elmira Prison Camp, which held 12,000 Confederate prisoners; 2,963 men died there and were buried in what is now Woodlawn National Cemetery. In 1870 Samuel L. Clemens (Mark Twain; 1835–1910) married Elmira native Olivia Louise Langdon. The Clemens family summered at Quarry Farm in Elmira throughout the 1870s and 1880s; Clemens's in-laws built an octagonal study in 1874 for him, where he wrote *The Prince and the Pauper* (1881), *The Adventures of Huckleberry Finn* (1885), and other famous works. The Langdon family gave Quarry Farm to Elmira College in 1982. It houses visiting Twain scholars through the Center for Mark Twain Studies (1983).

Between 1865 and 1900 the city's population increased from about 12,300 to 35,600. Elmira expanded south of the Chemung River in 1890, annexing part of Southport. Businesses crowded Elmira's downtown, and large factories like Elmira Iron and Steel Rolling Mill (1869), LaFrance Manufacturing (1873; fire engines), American Bridge (1889), and Thatcher Glass (1912) attracted Irish, Jewish, Italian, and Polish immigrants from 1880 to 1920. Public transportation began in 1871 with horse-drawn streetcars between Horseheads and Elmira, replaced by electric cars from 1890 to 1939. Additional rail lines—the Northern Central (1866; later Pennsylvania), Lehigh Valley (1874), and Delaware, Lackawanna and Western (1882)—served Elmira into the 20th century. The New York State Reformatory (1876; now Elmira Correctional Facility) pioneered methods of reform using a rewards system, indeterminate sentencing, and a points-based parole system. The Gleason Health Resort, a private hospital on Watercure Hill, operated from 1852 to 1959. In 1862 the Elmira Board of Health was established, followed by the Elmira Surgical Institute (1872) and two hospitals that survive into the 21st century, the Arnot Ogden Medical Center (1888) and St. Joseph's Hospital (1908). Eldridge Park (purchased by the city in 1889) and Rorick's Glen (?1900), with its summer theater (1901) and amusement park, provided diversions for Elmira residents. The 250-room Mark Twain Hotel was completed in 1929, shortly before the stock market crashed.

In December 1931, hard hit by economic depression, the city became insolvent and failed to pay its employees. In the fall of 1932 enrollment at Elmira College dropped by 50%, and by 1933 many Elmira businesses closed. In 1935 area residents rallied to form Elmira Industries and bought the idle Willys-Morrow factory, which they transferred to the Precision Tool Co (1936), later a division of Remington Rand (office machines). In 1936, 79 factories in Elmira employed 10,000 workers. A massive project to eliminate at-grade railroad crossings in Chemung Co, started in 1932, transformed the look of downtown Elmira, notably with a 1,600 ft (488 m) concrete railroad viaduct (1934).

During World War II Elmira's homefront activities included wartime production at the Elmira Foundry (1916), Remington Rand (1937) and Ward LaFrance plants. Elmira was the first city in New York State to have incident practices and blackout drills; in 1943 the State Civil Protection office declared Elmira's civil defense to be a model for other War Councils across the state to follow. Industry in Elmira boomed after the war. Remington Rand's plant on Elmira's south side was, with 6,600 workers, the world's largest office equipment plant in 1957, but employment declined after 1960, and the plant was sold to Westinghouse Electric Corp in 1973.

Urban renewal brought the demolition of slum areas beginning in 1967 and the construction of 200 modern housing units in Elmira and its environs, including high-rise apartment towers for elderly residents. A Hurricane Agnes flood on 22–23 June 1972 devastated Elmira, forcing nearly half its population to evacuate. Federal and state governments contributed to combined urban renewal and disaster relief efforts, leaving 40% of Elmira's commercial space demolished. By 2000 the city's population, 82% white and 13% black, with 3% of the total Latino, had declined 62% from its 1950 peak of 49,716.

By the mid-1990s plans to revitalize downtown Elmira included a new, large civic center, First Arena (2000) on Main Street. The Keeney Theatre (1925) was expanded to become the Clemens Center for the Performing Arts in 1999. In 2003 Elmira's largest employers included Kennedy Valve, the Hilliard Corp (auto parts), F. M. Howell and Co (medical packaging), Motor Components, and Trayer Products (truck suspensions).

The Chemung Canal Bank Building (1833), Chemung County Courthouse Complex, Elmira Civic Historic District, Elmira Coca-Cola Bottling Co Works (1940), Elmira College's old campus, F. M. Howell and Co (1883), Near Westside Historic District, Park Church (1871), and Quarry Farm, among other properties, are listed on the National Register.

See also ARCHITECTS AND ARCHITECTURE, SOUTHERN TIER (EASTERN).

Heather A. Wade

Mark Twain's study, Elmira.

Elmira College. Private, liberal arts college. Originally chartered in 1852 as Auburn Female University in Cayuga Co, the institution was established largely through the efforts of the Rev Samuel Robbins Brown and his associates, most notably Simeon Benjamin, a wealthy Elmira businessman. In 1853 Benjamin moved the university to Elmira, and in 1855 its charter was amended and the name changed to Elmira Female College. The original mission was to offer education to women in a nondenominational setting, and Elmira was the first US college to grant baccalaureate degrees to women. Men were first admitted in 1969. The college is the location of the Center for Mark Twain Studies, the nearby summer home of the author, donated to the college in 1983 by his descendants. In 2002 Elmira is the only college in the United States that required student internships and community service as a prerequisite to graduation. Enrollment in 2002 was 1,179.

Barber, William Charles. *Elmira College, the First 100 Years* (New York: McGraw-Hill, 1955)

Mary Anne Hansen

Elmira Correctional Facility. Opened in 1876 as the New York State Reformatory at Elmira, it was the first adult reformatory in America and one of the country's most influential penal institutions. Its program descended directly from the Irish prison mark system and from reforms put forward at the groundbreaking 1870 Congress on Penitentiary and Reformatory Discipline. The reformatory's reputation was synonymous with that of its first superintendent, Zebulon Reed Brockway. Under Brockway, Elmira instituted programs based for the first time on individual treatment, indeterminate sentences, and closely supervised parole. Inmates, aged 16–30 earned their way out of the institution by passing through an elaborate grading system based on behavior, education, military training, and skills learned in its workshops and iron foundry.

Elmira's promotion and promise, however, did not match its reality. Investigations in the 1890s uncovered widespread mismanagement, brutality, and corruption. By 1900 Brockway's reputation was tarnished, and he was forced to resign. Elmira's new managers refined its direction, emphasizing classification, custody, and treatment over rehabilitation. Dr Frank Christian, who worked for 39 years at Elmira, first as physician and then as superintendent from 1917 to 1939, undertook numerous new initiatives. A psychological laboratory created at the institution found large numbers of feeble-minded "defective" inmates who could not be reformed and who needed special custody. These inmates subsequently were transferred to Elmira's sister institution, the Eastern New York Reformatory at Napanoch (Ulster Co).

In 1945 an innovative reception center was opened on the reformatory grounds, further enhancing Elmira's classification program. This separate center tested and made placement recommendations for all male inmates aged 16–21 entering the state's correctional system. In 1970 it merged with the reformatory, creating the Elmira Correctional and Reception Center. During the 1990s the institution no longer concentrated on younger offenders because they were sent to several new facilities for those 21 and under. Known as the Elmira Correctional Facility since 1970, in 2003 the maximum security institution held approximately 1,800 male inmates.

Brockway, Zebulon R. *Fifty Years of Prison Service: An Autobiography* (1912; repr Montclair, NJ: Patterson Smith, 1969)
"Elmira," *DOCS Today* 7 (Oct 1998): 14–17

Richard Andress

Elmira Heights. Village (pop 4,170) in Horseheads and Elmira (Chemung Co). The area was farmland until 1890, when an investment company, the Elmira Industrial Association, acquired about 500 acres (200 ha) with the intention of attracting industries. Beginning in October 1892, 2,160 lots were sold by lottery at $200 each, and on 24 Oct 1893 a lottery was held to assign specific lots to subscribers. Manufacturers of textiles, glass, bridges, furniture, bicycles, cigars, plows, and ladders set up shop in Elmira Heights. The factories attracted immigrants, including a number of Ukrainians. The area was known as the Elmira Industrial Association Grounds until the village incorporated under the name Elmira Heights in 1896. In the early 21st century the village is both residential and industrial; products include glass containers, rail vehicles, wood and metal patterns, carbide tools, sheet metal, and corrugated packaging. Pierce's Restaurant (1894) is a local landmark, and the Elmira Heights Village Hall (1896) is listed on the National Register of Historic Places.

Heather A. Wade

Elmira Prison Camp. A Civil War prison on 40 acres (16.2 ha) along the Chemung River near Elmira. It had been a former Union training and deployment camp, and on 15 May 1864 the empty barracks were designated as accommodations for the overflow of captured Confederate soldiers. The site was used in this capacity for 14 months. Initial modifications included a 16 ft (4.9 m) fence with a raised walkway for guards and 35 two-story barracks, with unsealed roofs and floors, as well as a camp bakery. Detainees began arriving in July 1864. By August, although the facility was designed for 5,000 men, it held nearly 10,000. Confederates quartered at Elmira endured such physical and mental anguish that survivors entitled it Hellmira.

Intentional cruelty complicated the overpopulation and incompetent management. Administrators responded to reports of severe conditions at Confederate prison camps by issuing punitive rations of only bread and water for months. Prisoners lacked clothing and blankets and were subject to voyeurism by civilians on specially constructed viewing platforms. Clothes and gifts sent from the South were withheld or sold by camp officials. The federal government evaded or rejected requests for medical supplies for Elmira's tent hospital, and prison commanders often refused inspection by US Sanitary Commission representatives. Human waste and garbage were dumped into a small pond within the camp, contributing to an intractable stench as well as increased incidence of diarrhea, scurvy, and smallpox. Disease and malnutrition combined with the winter cold resulted in a death rate of 25 per day in December 1864. After the Confederacy's surrender in April 1865, Elmira's prisoners received improved treatment until the last inmate left in September. Of the 12,000 Confederates imprisoned, almost 25% perished; the facility's death rate was double the average of Northern prison camps.

Hesseltine, William B. *Civil War Prisons* (Kent, Ohio: Kent State Univ Press, 1994)
Holmes, Clayton W. *Elmira Prison Camp: A History of the Military Prison at Elmira, NY, July 6, 1864 to July 10, 1865* (New York: G. P. Putman's Sons, 1912)

Nathan R. Meyer

Elmont. Locality (pop 32,657) in Hempstead (Nassau Co). Elmont was part of Foster's Meadow, a tract of land on the Hempstead Plains given to Christopher and Thomas Foster to pasture sheep and cattle (1647). The name Elmont was chosen for its post office in 1882. In 1905 the building of Belmont Park spurred growth, including the Wollkoftown neighborhood intended for Jewish immigrants who wished to move out of New York City (1907). International aviation contests were held at the horse track, and in 1918 the nation's first scheduled airmail service was inaugurated from Belmont Park to Washington, DC. Largely residential, Elmont experienced considerable postwar growth, its population increasing from 8,957 in 1940 to 30,138 in 1960; after decline and stasis, it again grew in the 1990s at a 14% rate. Elmont is one of the most ethnically diverse communities on Long Island; in 2000 its population was 35% African American and 9% Asian, primarily Asian Indian. People of Latino ethnicity constituted 14%.

Georgina Martorella

Elmsford. Village (pop 4,676) in Greenburgh (Westchester Co). Known as Storms Bridge and Halls Corners before a post office named Elmsford opened in 1866, the community centered on farming. It grew slowly until the railroad, what became the Putnam Division of the New York Central (1880–1958), brought commerce, industry, and commuters. The village incorporated in 1910. A modern crossroads, it is now served by the Saw Mill River Parkway (1930), the Cross Westchester Expressway (I-287, 1960), and the Sprain Brook Parkway (southward, 1969; northward, 1980). Elmsford has diversified manufacturing including machinery, electronics, and fire-safety equipment, along with wholesale distribution centers and office parks. In 2000 the population was 20.3% black and approximately 23.3% of Latino ethnicity.

Scott C. Monje

Elwood. Locality (pop 10,916) in Huntington (Suffolk Co). Originally known as Upper or North Dix Hills, Elwood had its own post office from 1870 to 1902. In 1950 its population was only 300, but rapid development began shortly afterward. An Elwood station of the East Northport post office opened in 1963. It is the site of the 102-acre (41 ha) Berkeley Jackson County Park.

Robert C. Hughes

Emancipation Day. Free Blacks in New York State regularly hailed landmarks in the evolution of the freedom of enslaved Africans and African Americans worldwide, both as great events in themselves and as foretokenings of the final liberation of all in bondage. The end of the legal slave trade to the United States on 1 Jan 1808 was celebrated with meetings and orations in New York City for a number of years. Orators, such as William Hamilton in 1815, rejoiced that "the slave trade, that cursed viper that fed on Africa's vitals, is swept away." On 4 July 1827 slavery was abolished in New York State, and it was celebrated in every black community in the state on 5 July; celebrants chose that day to protest Independence Day celebrations commemorating freedom when many Blacks remained enslaved. In New York City on 5 July, black organizations of the city held a festive march past City Hall, and in Rochester the Declaration of Independence was read and businessman and abolitionist Austin Steward spoke in Johnson's Square (now Washington Square Park). The day also was acknowledged in black churches. Nathaniel Paul, pastor of the First African Baptist Society of Albany, preached that he looked forward to that time "when it shall no longer be said that in a land of freemen there are men in bondage." Frederick Douglass's famous oration to the Rochester Ladies' Anti-Slavery Society on 5 July 1852 acknowledged the precedents of the day.

The abolition of slavery in the British Empire on 1 Aug 1834 was another day celebrated by antebellum Blacks in the state by rallies, orations, and dinners. Large gatherings assembled in New York City, where more than 3,000 people attended an 1837 event at which abolitionists Lewis Tappan and Theodore S. Wright spoke. In Rochester around 2,000 people attended an 1848 celebration, which featured processions, speeches, dinners, dancing, and the firing of cannon. Crowds turned out in Buffalo and smaller communities such as Canandaigua (Ontario Co) for similar celebrations held during the decades leading up to the Civil War. After Abraham Lincoln issued the Emancipation Proclamation on 22 Sept 1862, making all southern slaves free on 1 Jan 1863, celebrants commemorated emancipation on various days. Some, such as those assembled in Poughkeepsie and Hudson (Columbia Co) in 1868, chose a September celebration, while others, such as those gathered at Elmira in 1880 and Lockport (Niagara Co) in 1884, continued to celebrate in August. At a 22 Sept 1898 gathering in New York City, organizers blamed poor attendance at the event on disagreements over which date was most appropriate.

Celebrations on different days continued into the 20th century. Rev Martin Luther King Jr spoke in New York City at the New York State Civil War Centennial Commission's 100th anniversary celebration of the Emancipation Proclamation on 12 Sept 1962, criticizing the slow pace of the nation's fight against racial injustice and touting the proclamation as one of its most important declarations. A national celebration on 22 Sept 1962 in Washington, DC, featured speeches by Judge Thurgood Marshall of New York City and New York governor Nelson A. Rockefeller, who brought a preliminary draft (penned in Lincoln's hand) of the document held by the New York State Library. In 2004 Gov George E. Pataki signed legislation making Juneteenth a holiday; it celebrates 19 June 1865, the day the news of emancipation reached the enslaved of Texas, finally bringing an end to slavery in the entire United States.

"Colored Folk Celebrate: The Issuance of the Emancipation Proclamation Is Commemorated," *New York Times*, 23 Sept 1898

Gellman, David N., and David Quigley, eds. *Jim Crow New York: A Documentary History of Race and Citizenship, 1777–1877* (New York: New York Univ Press, 2003)

Rael, Patrick. *Black Identity and Black Protest in the Antebellum North* (Chapel Hill: Univ of North Carolina Press, 2002)

Hadley Kruczek-Aaron and Peter Eisenstadt

Embargo of 1807–9. A moratorium on all American trade with foreign countries imposed by Pres Thomas Jefferson and Congress in December 1807 to pressure the British and French into respecting American neutrality during the Napoleonic Wars. In the congressional debate on the embargo, New York State's delegation split seven to six in favor, reflecting the deep divisions in the state. Seven Republicans voted in favor, with the two Federalists in the delegation and four Republicans opposed. From its inception New Yorkers resisted the embargo. Almost 300 ships lay at anchor in New York Harbor when news of it arrived on 25 Dec 1807. Shipowners sent word to the vessels to leave port, and several dozen sailed partly laden, with half of their crews, and without government clearance papers. Revenue cutters and gunboats chased several vessels out to sea while crowds gathered on the wharves to cheer the violators of the embargo, which quickly devastated New York City's economy. By late January 1808, 40 mercantile houses had gone bankrupt. Unemployed sailors organized the first public protest and requested relief or jobs. The New York City Common Council provided relief funds to sailors who took up employment at the Brooklyn Navy Yard for the duration of the embargo. The city voted funds to hire unemployed mechanics and laborers in temporary municipal jobs, planting trees and cleaning vacant lots. By February 1808, more than 5,000 people found shelter in the city's almshouse or received daily rations. The state legislature appropriated $100,000 for jobs building fortifications around New York City. The embargo also had a negative impact on farmers, especially those who sold part or all of their crop for export, leading to a decline in commodity prices and land values. To placate them, the state passed legislation giving out about $450,000 in loans to farmers suffering specifically from the embargo.

In violation of the embargo, smuggling took place from Lake Champlain to Buffalo. Inhabitants of the Champlain Valley smuggled potash, lumber, and agricultural produce to Canada; the islands and channels at the north end of the lake provided the avenues. Responding to appeals for help from customs officials, Pres Jefferson authorized the use of troops and on 19 Apr 1808 proclaimed the Champlain Valley in a state of insurrection. Initially state militia was authorized to deal with the smuggling, but federal troops were activated by the end of 1808. Three companies were sent to Plattsburgh, Salem, and Champlain, and others to Oswegatchie [now Ogdensburg, St. Lawrence Co], Sackets Harbor, and Oswego. Along the shores of Lake Ontario, a civil war erupted between local residents and customs officers. An armed mob of 60 attacked the customhouse at Oswego in August 1808. Secretary of the Treasury Albert Gallatin advised Jefferson to declare Oswego also in a state of insurrection. Fearing the political ramifications, Gov Daniel D. Tompkins advised against it but dispatched additional militia. At Sackets Harbor 60 men armed with axes and pikes threatened the militia, and citizens refused to sell food to the militia. Farmers in the Hudson Valley sold their grain to smugglers who shipped the goods north from Albany by wagon, and Canadian merchants went to Albany to facilitate the smuggling. In March 1809 Jefferson removed the Plattsburgh customs collector Malcolm Woolsey for his collaboration with smugglers.

The volume of Canadian-American trade also increased along the Niagara Frontier. Buffalo and Canandaigua (Ontario Co) emerged as way stations for smuggling as British and Canadian merchants crossed the border to buy produce, potash, beef, and cattle. New Yorkers resorted to smuggling because of the sharp decline in agricultural prices and the economic distress of the state's farmers that led to a significant increase in foreclosures. In early 1809 James Maury, the first American consul in Liverpool, England, reported that 80% of illegal American ships in his district came from New York State and New Jersey.

In spite of their reservations, all the major Republican factions rallied behind the embargo during the 1808 campaign, holding public meetings to mobilize support and public enthusiasm for the law. Gov Tompkins opened the campaign with an anti-British, pro-embargo, pro-Jefferson speech to the legislature. Federalist leaders Oliver Wolcott, Gouverneur Morris, Rufus King, and others met to discuss campaign strategy in early March 1808 and decided to use the embargo to regain their lost political power. Federalists appealed to farmers hurt by lower agricultural prices and to the urban residents the embargo left unemployed. After the election Federalist seats in the assembly jumped from 24 to 47 and in Congress from 2 to 8 seats.

Faced with opposition to the embargo at home and its minor impact on the economies of France and England, Pres Jefferson asked Congress to lift the embargo just before leaving office in March 1809. The Republicans regained control of the assembly in 1810, but it took New York City until 1825 to regain the value of the city's exports to their pre-embargo level.

Casey, Richard P. "North Country Nemesis: The Potash Rebellion and the Embargo of 1807–1809," *New-York Historical Society Quarterly* 64 (Jan 1980): 31–49

Harrington, Virginia. "New York and the Embargo of 1807," *Quarterly Journal of the New York Historical Association* 8 (Apr 1927): 143–51

Irwin, Ray Watkins. "Governor Tompkins and the Embargo, 1807–1809," *New York History* 22 (July 1941): 311–20

Strum, Harvey J. "Impact of the Embargo on New York Politics," *Journal of Historical Studies* 5 (Spring 1982): 20–39

Harvey Strum

Emergency Management Office. See STATE EMERGENCY MANAGEMENT OFFICE (SEMO).

emery. A naturally occurring abrasive that is a mixture of corundum or aluminum oxide (Al_2O_3) and magnetite or iron oxide (Fe_3O_4). Found in limestone and shale, emery deposits are thick at the center, tapering toward the perimeter. Emery has been quarried from the Cortlandt series in Westchester Co since colonial times. At the end of the 19th century, the New York Emery Co at Peekskill was still based around the Cortlandt series, and deposits near that community and Croton supported the DeLuca Emery Mine, DiRubbio and Ellis, the Howard Emery Co, and Scalzo and Pisani. At mid–20th century the yield from the Peekskill and Croton deposits accounted for all of the natural emery production in the United States. Formerly used to polish glass, teeth, and fingernails and to prevent skids on floors and stairs, emery has been largely replaced by synthetic materials, but it is still used by machinists and lapidaries. The last commercial emery mine near Peekskill closed in 1989.

New York State Department of Commerce. *The Mineral Industries of New York State* (Albany: Division of Commerce and Industry, 1950)

John J. Chiment and Victoria J. Chiment

eminent domain. The power that governments possess to take private property, for just compensation, for public purposes. The principle that individuals should be protected against arbitrary government "takings" found its earliest expression in England's Magna Carta (1215) and was reiterated in the Fifth Amendment of the US Constitution, which states that no person shall "be deprived of life, liberty, or property, without due process of law; nor shall private property be taken for public use, without just compensation." It appears that the Dutch colonial government of New Amsterdam [now New York City] observed the principles of just compensation as early as the 1650s. New York State's first constitution (1777) did not contain a statement of eminent domain. This was not unusual; only the constitutions of Massachusetts, Vermont, and the Northwest Territory contained them before 1800. The principle was defended on natural law grounds. New York State chancellor James Kent in *Gardner v Village of Newburgh* (1816) ruled that a landowner must be compensated when the village diverted a stream and reduced the amount of water available to him. As Kent put it in his *Commentaries on American Law* (1826–30), this principle was "founded on natural equity, and is laid down by jurists as an acknowledged principle of universal law." New York State's 1821 Constitution contained an explicit "takings" clause.

The power of eminent domain often was delegated to private enterprises engaged in the construction of roads, canals, or other public improvements. In *Bloodgood v Mohawk and Hudson Railroad Co* (1837) the railroad was given eminent domain power to construct a railroad for public use and had to compensate property owners for land it took. However, through the 19th century the principles of public use and just compensation mitigated the redistributive effects of the process. The protection of property rights eroded after 1900, driven by progressive and New Deal liberalism, and the New York State courts widened the range of takings that were regarded as serving public purposes, such as low-income housing, parking, museums, and historic preservation. The New York State Court of Appeals, in *New York City Housing Authority v Muller* (1936), allowed condemnation of a blighted area to build low-income public housing. New York City's great postwar urban renewal projects, many spearheaded by Robert Moses, made sweeping use of eminent domain. In 1963 the state accepted the condemnation of a delicatessen (*Courtesy Sandwich Shop v Port of New York Authority* [1963]) so that commuters could more conveniently reach the World Trade Center, then under construction in Lower Manhattan. In recent decades there has been a backlash against the wholesale use of eminent domain to condemn neighborhoods, but in the view of many observers, New York State remains one of the states most unfriendly to property rights.

Stoebuck, William B. "A General Theory of Eminent Domain," *Washington Law Review* 47 (1972): 553–608

Paul Moreno

Emma Willard School. Private girls secondary boarding and day school in Troy (Rensselaer Co). In 1814 Emma Hart Willard opened the Middlebury Female Seminary in Middlebury, Vt, in an effort to provide girls with opportunities for academic study similar to those available to young men. In 1819 the school was relocated to Waterford (Saratoga Co). After Willard was refused funding from the New York State legislature, she prepared to close the school for lack of capital. However, it was rescued in 1821 by a $4,000 grant from the City of Troy, and Willard moved the school there. That year the Troy Female Seminary opened its doors to 90 students. The seminary's early educational philosophy sought to reconcile traditional perceptions of women's roles with serious academics. Throughout the 19th century girls studied mathematics, chemistry, physics, and philosophy, as well as traditional female disciplines such as drawing, painting, penmanship, and music. Many of the seminary's graduates became teachers, and some established new institutions modeled after the school. Willard herself provided scholarships for girls who promised to become educators. In 1895, 25 years after its founder's death, the seminary's name was changed to the Emma Willard School. A gift from alumna Margaret Olivia Slocum Sage enabled the school to become permanently endowed in 1910. The school was then moved from downtown Troy to a new campus on Pawling Ave, atop Mt Ida, and the old campus later became part of Russell Sage College. The school's notable alumnae include Elizabeth Cady Stanton and Jane Fonda. At the turn of the 21st century, the Emma Willard School enrolled approximately 100 day students and 200 boarding students in a college preparatory curriculum.

Emma Willard School, http://www.emmawillard.org
Lay, Clemewell, and Anne Wellington. *Emma Willard Plan of Education* (Troy, NY: Emma Willard School, 1961)

Erin Melissa Silverman

Emmons, Ebenezer (*b* Middlefield, Mass, 16 May 1799; *d* Brunswick Co, NC, 1 Oct 1863). Geologist. He studied geology at and graduated from Williams College in Williamstown, Mass (1818) and Rensselaer School (now Rensselaer Polytechnic Institute) (1826). He also took a course at Berkshire Medical Institution and later gained financial independence by practicing and teaching obstetrics. In 1836 Emmons joined the New York State Geological and Natural History Survey based at Albany; he also served as professor of chemistry at Albany Medical College (1838–52). While engaging in research for the state survey, Emmons named the Adirondacks after an Iroquoian term. His discoveries in New York State led Emmons to develop the Taconic System, a nomenclature for identifying geological formations. He held the position of New York State agriculturalist from 1843 to 1849 but lost standing in American science when colleagues vehemently attacked his Taconic System in the 1850s. He accepted an appointment as state geologist of North Carolina in 1851. Emmons's mineral collection was given to the New York State Museum by Erastus Corning in 1870.

Merrill, George P. *The First 100 Years of American Geology* (1924; repr New York: Hafner, 1969)
Schneer, Cecil J. "Ebenezer Emmons and the Foundations of American Geology," *Isis* 60 (1969): 439–50

Adam Bostanci

Empire State. Although the term has been attributed to New York State for almost 200 years, its origin and originator remain a mystery. The earliest reference to New York State associated with the word "empire" is in a letter from George Washington to Mayor James Duane of New York City on 10 Apr 1785. Replying to Duane's letter informing him that he had been given the freedom of the city, Washington referred to New York City as "at present the Seat of the Empire." Legend has it that Washington, on a tour with Gov George Clinton after the war, observed the Bronx River valley and commented: "Surely this is the seat of the Empire," but this cannot be verified from any source. Another undocumented story states that while traveling in 1790, the general viewed the Mohawk River corridor and commented that it was a major gateway to the West and hence a "Pathway to Empire."

The term Empire State first appeared in print in the 19th century. An editorial in the *New-York Spectator* on 8 Jan 1822 claimed that New York's growing resources "appear like those of a mighty and flourishing empire." The first use of the term in a publication appears to be in the R. L. Christopher's *Empire State Book of Practical Forms* (1849), a compilation of legal forms for the use of business owners, farmers, merchants, and others. In 1871 Mrs. S. S. Colt wrote and published a travel book titled *The Tourist's Guide through the Empire State,* and within the next 15 years, a number of books used the phrase in its titles. In 1890 a bank opened in New York City with the name Empire State, and six years later it built the Empire State Building at 640 Broadway. In 1891 the New York Central Railroad introduced its fast train between New York City and Buffalo and called it the Empire State Express. By then the term was in common use.

Dixon Ryan Fox, in the 1940 Work Projects Administration guide *New York: A Guide to the Empire State,* could do no better than to introduce his subject with the bemused comment: " 'The Empire State'—it would gratify the people of New York if they could discover who first dared that spacious adjective." No one since has improved on that explanation of the origin of the term. Paul Eldridge, in his 1957 *Crown of Empire: The Story of New York State,* has perhaps had the last word on the subject in his observation: "Who was the merry wag who crowned the State . . .

[as the Empire State]? New York would certainly raise a monument to his memory, but he made his grandiose gesture and vanished forever."

Klein, Milton M., ed. *The Empire State: A History of New York* (Ithaca: Cornell Univ Press, 2001)

Milton M. Klein

Empire State Building. With a height of 1,250 ft (381 m), this landmark New York City skyscraper became the tallest building in the world, surpassing the Chrysler Building, upon its completion in 1931. That distinction lasted until construction of the World Trade Center in New York City in the early 1970s. The 102-story building has 85 floors of office space beneath the famous Art Deco mast; there is an observatory on the 86th floor open to the public. The building takes up an entire city block, from 33d to 34th Sts on 5th Ave. The steel mast atop the building was originally conceived of as a mooring post for dirigibles, but this proved impractical because of strong wind conditions at that altitude. Instead the mast became a base for broadcasting antennas and continues to be used for that purpose. Financier John J. Raskob commissioned the building as a speculative venture. Former governor Alfred E. Smith was chairman of the building corporation. The principal architect was William Lamb of Shreve, Lamb, and Harmon. Construction began in March 1930, and the building was completed in May 1931 at a cost of $45 million. The project coincided with the beginning of the Great Depression, though, and Raskob had trouble leasing this vast amount of new office space for many years. The building has been immortalized in a wide range of artistic media, including Lewis Hine's heroic photographs documenting its construction and the 1933 classic horror film *King Kong*. The Empire State Building remains among the most famous and iconic skyscrapers in the world. After the terrorist attack on the World Trade Center 11 Sept 2001, the Empire State Building is, tragically, once again the tallest building in New York State.

Northwest view of the Empire State Building in 1932.

Tauranac, John. *The Empire State Building: The Making of a Landmark* (New York: Scribner's, 1995)

Eric Wolf

Empire State Development. Collective name for the New York State Department of Economic Development and the Empire State Development Corp. An executive branch agency, Empire State Development (ESD) was formed in 1995 when the Urban Development Corp (established in 1968 to generate industrial, commercial, and civic development in distressed urban areas) consolidated with the Department of Economic Development (established 1987 to create and coordinate statewide economic policy), the Job Development Authority (established 1962 to provide loans and loan guarantees to help businesses expand or build facilities in New York State), and the Science and Technology Foundation (established 1963 to provide financial assistance and technical service to technology-based businesses). The agency advocates for a healthy business environment and provides assistance and service to businesses to encourage economic investment and prosperity. It is also responsible for the I♥NY tourism program and for overseeing the administration of New York State's 71 Empire Zones (EZs), where businesses can receive special tax incentives, designed to increase investment, create jobs, and encourage economic growth. The program began in 1986 as the Economic Development Zones Program and was renamed Empire Zones in 2001. At first limited to economically depressed areas, they were subsequently expanded. ESD's additional programs include financing, training, export assistance, infrastructure improvements, government contract procurement, community revitalization, and assistance to minority- and women-owned businesses. The agency also provides assistance to targeted industrial sectors and regional waterfront planning and development. ESD is co-headquartered in Albany and Manhattan and maintains 10 regional offices statewide. It also operates a network of international offices to attract foreign investment and to assist New York State–based companies with international ventures.

ESD played a visible role in rebuilding efforts following the World Trade Center disaster of 11 Sept 2001. Such activities included administering federal funds for tax concessions to area businesses and issuing tax-exempt Liberty Bonds to renovate and rebuild commercial, residential, and public utility properties. The agency was also given responsibility, with the New York City Economic Development Corp, for managing a $250 million WTC Disaster Recovery Loan Program for businesses and nonprofit organizations that had suffered economic injury or physical damage as a result of the attack, as well as a $700 million federal community development block grant. ESD created a subsidiary, the Lower Manhattan Development Corp (LMDC), to act as the lead state agency in the rebuilding effort.

The agency had in 2003 an annual operating budget of $236 million and 241 staff, with leadership provided by nine directors, including the state superintendent of banks, the chair of the New York State Science and Technology Foundation, and seven others, who are appointed by the governor with the consent of the senate. Two of the members serve at the pleasure of the governor, and the other five serve four-year terms. The governor designates the chair who also serves as the agency's commissioner. ESD's activities have been criticized by those who believe that its redevelopment efforts are ineffective or tied into politics. The agency was also responsible, as of March 2003, for more than $5.7 billion in outstanding debt in Urban Development Corp bonds and $50.9 million in outstanding Job Development Authority debt.

See also DEINDUSTRIALIZATION; LIBERALISM.

Braslow, Laura. *Pay to Play? Campaign Contributions to Governor Pataki and Funds from the Empire State Development Corporation* (Albany: Public Policy and Education Fund, 2002)

New York State. Office of the State Comptroller. *State of New York: Empire State Development Corporation: Administration of Selected Projects Funded through the Regional Economic Development Partnership Program.* Report 96-S-39 (Albany: Author, 1999)

———. *Empire State Development: Performance of Job Development Programs.* Report 98-S-7 (Albany: Author, 2000)

New York State. Senate. *Money for Nothing: The High Cost and Low Success Rate of Business Subsidies in New York,* State Senator Franz S. Leichter; Jonathan Bowles, Research Director (Albany: Author, 1998)

Jeffrey Kraus

Empire State Express. One of the world's earliest high-speed, long-distance passenger trains. Empire State Express linked New York City and Buffalo, beginning regular daily service on 7 Dec 1891. A flagship of the New York Central and Hudson River Railroad (later New York Central Railroad), the train's 436 mi (702 km) daylight run took just over seven hours. On 10 May 1893 Charles Hogan drove Locomotive 999, an American-type engine with four leading wheels and four driving wheels, at full throttle near Batavia (Genesee Co) and claimed a new speed record of 112.5 mph (181.05 kph). This never confirmed speed inspired a two-cent stamp issued as part of the Pan-American Exposition Series in 1901. In its first 50 years, Empire State Express made 40,000 one-way trips without injury to any passenger. On 7 Dec 1941, the train's 50th anniversary as well as Pearl Harbor Day, New York Central introduced a new, streamlined Empire State Express, sheathed in fluted stainless steel. The Hudson locomotive with four leading wheels, six driving wheels, and four trailing wheels drew cars produced by Philadelphia's Edward G. Budd Mfg Co using its patented "Shotwelding" method; Paul Cret designed the car interiors. Besides passenger coaches the train featured parlor cars, two diners, and a tavern-lounge observation car. A New York–Buffalo train continued to operate under the name Empire State Express until 1999 when Amtrak, which had acquired the New York Central route, dropped individual names for trains serving New York State.

Klein, Aaron E. *The History of the New York Central System* (New York: Bonanza Books, 1985)

Karl Zimmermann

Empire State Federation of Women's Clubs. A coalition of various New York State–based black women's clubs. Alice Wiley Seay formed

Empire State Express at Hudson.

the federation at a settlement house in Harlem, the White Rose Home, in 1908. Initially the federation had two primary goals: to provide financial assistance for Harriet Tubman, the elderly abolitionist who lived in Auburn (Cayuga Co), and to create programs to assist young African American women. After Tubman's death in 1913, the federation expanded its programs for women by endowing educational scholarship funds and in 1933 forming the Empire State Association of Youth Clubs, an ancillary club for black girls. To achieve its goals the state-based federation also worked closely with national African American organizations, including the NAACP. By World War II the federation expanded its mission to heightening the awareness of the state's Blacks on political and public policy issues. In the postwar period the federation helped shape state educational policy in Albany by lobbying the State Education Department to incorporate African American history into the state curriculum; the federation was also critical of the state government's use of lottery funds to help finance school budgets. In 2002 the federation consisted of 12 active clubs in four regions of New York State (Albany, Buffalo, Westchester Co, and Middle Hudson).

Empire State Federation of Women's Clubs. Papers. SUNY Albany Library, Albany

Floris Barnett Cash

Empire State Games. A statewide amateur sports competition conducted annually since 1978 by New York State's Office of Parks, Recreation, and Historic Preservation. The 1976 Olympic Games in Montreal inspired Louis Wolfe, an attorney in Plattsburgh, to begin the Empire State Games (ESG), intended to encourage athletic competition among New York State residents and to improve amateur athletics throughout the state. The inaugural summer meet began on 16 Aug 1978 with a torch-lighting ceremony at Syracuse University's Archbold Stadium attended by 4,500 athletes, both youth and adult, representing 21 sports. The selection of athletes begins with free tryouts that attract as many as 30,000 participants. Competing in either open or scholastic categories, athletes represent one of six geographic regions: Adirondack, Central, Hudson Valley, Long Island, New York, and Western. Basketball and lacrosse (introduced in 1984) became popular spectator events. The summer games were held in Syracuse through 1984 and in Buffalo through 1986. Although the winter games, created in 1981, remain at Lake Placid (Essex Co) to ensure the availability of certain specialized facilities, men's ice hockey has been held in the summer since the inception of the games. Competition among areas of the state led to the games being hosted by Ithaca, Rochester, Albany, Long Island, Binghamton, and Utica. The summer 2002 ESG were held in Syracuse and Cortland, with 32 sports and more than 7,000 participants in scholastic, open, and masters' division competitions. Additional facilities are needed for the annual Empire State Senior Games (for athletes over 50 years old) and the Empire State Games for the Physically Challenged. The first state to present such a program of amateur athletic competition, New York State provided a model that 45 other states had emulated by the beginning of the 21st century. Among the better-known athletes who competed at the ESG are Brooklyn-born boxer Mike Tyson and Olympic gold medalists Jeff Blatnick of Clifton Park (Saratoga Co), who won in Greco-Roman wrestling in 1984, and Diann Roffe-Steinrotter of Potsdam (St. Lawrence Co), who won the super giant slalom in 1994.

New York State Empire State Games, http://www.empirestategames.org
"Wolfe's Brainstorm Became Blueprint for a Nation," *Rochester Democrat and Chronicle*, 1 Aug 1993

John Moriello

Empire State Plaza, Governor Nelson A. Rockefeller. New York State's office and cultural complex constructed in 1962–78 in Albany, immediately to the south of the Capitol Building.

Background

The idea for this large governmental complex is usually credited to Gov Nelson A. Rockefeller and dated to the 1959 visit of Queen Juliana of the Netherlands to Albany, when the self-conscious governor made special arrangements so that the queen would pass through as little of the city as possible. Yet the state's offices had been located in downtown Albany since 1797, and even before completion of the Capitol Building in 1900, city planners had advocated removal of surrounding residential districts. New York State architects, beginning with Franklin B. Ware in the 1900s, had also pushed for park spaces and additional office buildings in the vicinity of the Capitol Building. After the razing of the neighborhood to its west and completion of the New York State Education Building in 1912, architect Marcus T. Reynolds suggested a new state office building on State St as a third "anchor" to the area's emerging formal public space. It was not built, but portions of his proposal were ultimately integrated into the plaza design.

The creation of the W. Averell Harriman State Office Campus on the outskirts of Albany in 1957 and the subsequent removal of thousands of state workers had a devastating effect on the city's downtown economy. Thus the economic concerns of Mayor Erastus Corning 2d meshed neatly with the newly inaugurated Gov Rockefeller's aspirations in 1958 for his new home, which, beyond any anxiety caused by Queen Juliana's comments, were rooted in a desire to create an urban monument rivaling his father's Rockefeller Center in New York City. Rockefeller was responsible for much of the plaza's conceptual design, and Wallace K. Harrison, one of the Rockefeller Center architects, was selected as chief architect.

Site and Description

Creating a site for the plaza and its access roads, beginning in the mid-1960s, meant destroying nearly 40 blocks of the city's historic core and a substantial portion of Albany's Italian neighborhood, and displacing almost 9,000 people. The governor courted popular support for the demolition by misrepresenting the target area as a slum. Journalistic interest in the plight of the soon-to-be-evicted "slum-dwellers" led *Albany Times-Union* reporter William Kennedy to con-

Construction of the Egg at Empire State Plaza. Photograph by William Bergan, 1975.

duct extensive interviews. After a preservation movement was organized in Albany by 1974, plans for leveling the neighborhood between Swan St and Washington Park were abandoned.

The 1965–78 construction of the plaza involved removing 9 million feet (2.7 million m) of blue clay. The complex has 10 buildings constructed on and around an 11th structure known as the Platform Building, a quarter mi (.4 km) wide by a half mi (.8 km) long structure housing the Concourse and a parking garage. The roof of the Platform Building serves as a grand plaza and features trees, reflecting pools, and monumental sculpture. The central reflecting pool was the world's largest edge-supported body of water. The concept of the Platform Building is said to have been inspired by the Dalai Lama's palace at Lhasa in Tibet.

The Mayor Erastus Corning 2d Tower (1973) measures 589 feet (179.5 m) and is the tallest structure in the state outside New York City. Four structures known as the Agency Buildings (1974) rise to the west of the reflecting pools. Built using taproot construction, their floors are cantilevered from central cores, which also house circulation systems and mechanical equipment. Another building on the plaza is the Center for the Performing Arts (1975), nicknamed the Egg, one of the largest free-form concrete structures ever attempted. The Cultural Education Center—home of the New York State Library, New York State Archives, New York State Museum, and New York State Education Department—was completed in 1977. Marble revetment covers most plaza buildings except the Platform Building, which is sheathed with Llenroc stone (a type of sedimentary stone quarried near Cornell), and the concrete Egg. Total cost of the complex is reported to have exceeded $2 billion.

Context and Assessment

In keeping with Reynolds's suggestions of 1919, the Legislative Office Building (1972) follows the general volumetric form, height, and cornice lines of the 1912 State Education Building. The Legislative Office Building and Justice Building (1972) frame a south-to-north view of the Capitol, the northern end of the project's major axis. The southern end of this axis is anchored by the Cultural Education Center. A memorial arch in honor of the Emancipation Proclamation, which would have dramatically framed a view of the Catskill Mountains, was originally planned for this location.

The abrupt cliff face that confronts visitors arriving from the east is said to have been intended to evoke the Helderberg Escarpment, visible to the southwest. Two "waterfalls" flank four tunnels, reminiscent of caves in the escarpment. In one subtle effect, the one-story restaurant pavilion and a curving wall located between the Corning Tower and the Egg frame a pair of hills that form the visual terminus of the view east down State St from the Capitol Building's steps.

Art critic Robert Hughes characterized the various buildings of the Empire State Plaza as reminiscent of the public monuments built in Fascist Italy and as presenting "an architecture of coercion." This assessment, while overly general, does capture something of the spirit of the plaza's intimidating monumentality. That said, the quality of the design varies widely. The Harrison-designed elements of the plaza are generally the most successful, with detailing and proportions evocative of a quiet, if gigantic, neoclassicism. The buildings designed by other firms, which include the Legislative Office Building (James, Meadows, and Howard), the Justice Building (Sargent Webster Crenshaw and Folley) and the Swan Street Building (Carson, Lundine, and Shaw), are less successful. All are neoclassical pavilions of abstract form but with exaggerated postmodern details. Harrison adopted a similar "mannerist" approach to his design of the Cultural Education Center. From the plaza's inception, artworks were envisioned as integral parts of the public environment. The plaza art collection is the subject of two monographs (1987, 2002).

Abrams, Jonathan K., ed. *Empire State Plaza: A Design for the Future* (Albany: Office of General Services, 1976)

Bleecker, Samuel E. *The Politics of Architecture: A Perspective on Nelson A. Rockefeller* (New York: Routledge, 1981)

Fickies, Robert H. *Building Stones of the Empire State Plaza* (Albany: NYS Education Department, 1986)

Lowry, Glenn D., and Dennis R. Anderson. *The Governor Nelson A. Rockefeller Empire State Plaza Art Collection and Plaza Memorials* (New York: Rizzoli, 2002)

Newhouse, Victoria. *Wallace K. Harrison, Architect* (New York: Rizzoli, 1989)

Walter Richard Wheeler

Employee Relations, Governor's Office of.

On 16 Aug 1967 Gov Nelson A. Rockefeller announced a new special committee to represent the governor in all negotiations held in accordance with the 1967 Public Employees' Fair Employment Act (the Taylor Law). In 1968 an Office of Employee Relations in the executive branch replaced the committee, and in 1969 the legislature enacted a law granting the office a statutory basis. The governor appoints a director of employee relations to act as agent in negotiating, implementing, and administering collective bargaining agreements with representatives of state employees. The office also has the power to direct heads of executive agencies to take any actions necessary to implement binding agreements negotiated under the Taylor Law. Although the law has never been amended, the office's responsibilities have been expanded to include oversight of salaries and working conditions for management and confidential employees, benefits and training for all state employees, and workforce planning. In 1983 two executive orders gave the office the responsibility of formulating state policies in the areas of sexual harassment and sexual orientation discrimination in state workplaces. Several unsuccessful attempts have been made to combine the Department of Civil Service, the Civil Service Commission, and the Governor's Office of Employee Relations into a department of personnel services and a merit protection board. The office is located in Albany and in 2003–4 employed 62.

New York State Governor's Office of Employee Relations, http://www.goer.state.ny.us

Robert Allan Carter

Endicott. Village (pop 13,038) in Union (Broome Co). In 1900 streets were laid out by the Endicott Johnson Co, which completed its first Endicott factory in 1901. The company constructed well-built homes for sale to employees at low cost. Endicott grew rapidly and incorporated in 1906, and in 1921 it merged with the older village of Union (1871). Italians, Slovaks, Poles, and Russians were drawn by employment and generous company benefits. In 1916 the company voluntarily adopted the eight-hour day; four years later employees built the "Square Deal" arch to commemorate the good management-labor relationship. It remains a landmark at the entrance to the village. Union Forging Co (1883–1995) and Endicott Forging Co (1915–2001) were other significant employers. International Time Recording Co built an Endicott plant in 1906, evolving into IBM by 1924. Population peaked in 1950 at 20,050. After a new plant opened outside the village in 1968, Endicott Johnson's factories and tanneries closed, followed by warehousing and distribution facilities; the last vestige left in 1999. The Cider Mill Playhouse is in Endicott, as is the annual B.C. Open PGA tournament at En-Joie Golf Course, named after the comic strip by village native Johnny Hart.

See also IBM.

Charles J. Browne

Endicott Johnson Corporation. Boot and shoe manufacturer. The company that became Endicott Johnson (EJ) grew out of a family-owned firm, the Lester Bros and Co, founded in 1854 in Binghamton by two East Haddam, Conn, transplants, Horace N. Lester and his brother George W. Lester. The firm grew modestly in the late 19th century. When Horace Lester died in 1882, George Lester took over the running of the company. In 1890 financial difficulties led Lester to sell the firm to a shoe manufacturer from Massachusetts, Henry B. Endicott. By this time the company had relocated to the newly established industrial village of Lester-Shire [now Johnson City, Broome Co]. In 1892 Endicott, who had reorganized and renamed the firm the Lestershire Manufacturing Co, selected Massachusetts-born George F. Johnson, the firm's former assistant superintendent, as the new general manager. Endicott remained an absentee owner and investor in the company. Eight years later, after years of buying into the firm and accumulating over $80,000 in equity, Johnson received from Endicott a substantial loan, allowing him to pay the latter $222,000 for half-interest in the firm. By 1902 the junior partner had repaid his loan, and the firm formally changed its name to the Endicott Johnson Co.

As a general manager and partner, Johnson, whose attitude toward labor was influenced by his early affiliation with Massachusetts socialism, began to introduce a number of labor-management innovations that soon came to differentiate EJ from many other firms. EJ's Square Deal policies (as they came to be known) sought to cultivate benevolent employer-employee and factory-community relationships. To foster worker loyalty, Johnson and other partners, including his two brothers, tried to inculcate in the firm's workers a proprietary attitude toward their company. The company's profit-sharing plan, or "bonus plan," was designed primarily to create a feeling of responsibility in the workers by transforming individual material self-interest into a collective interest. Soon, with the public incorporation of the company in 1919 and Johnson's rise to the presidency of the firm, the Endicott Johnson Corp began to transform its inchoate paternalistic practices into what historians have called welfare capitalism, a system and philosophy of corporate management that views the corporation as the guarantor of economic and social security of workers. As a system EJ's welfare capitalism included home-building loans and low mortgage rates for employees, company pensions, recreational and athletic facilities, employee medical care (which included company-run hospitals and clinics, tubercular sanatoriums on Seneca Lake, and dozens of doctors and healthcare specialists) as well as extensive community services, and donations to churches and numerous civic organizations.

Johnson relinquished control of the company in 1930, handing over the reigns to his son George W. Johnson, though he remained board chairman until 1937. He left a legacy that stretched for miles along New York State's Susquehanna River valley, from Binghamton in the east to Owego (Tioga Co) in the west—a string of factories and tanneries employing close to 20,000 workers. At its acme EJ was America's fifth largest manufacturer of boots and shoes, and one of the most vertically integrated firms in the industry. The company expanded into tanning as well as retail sales, in its heyday owning hundreds of retail shoe stores throughout the nation. Johnson lived for another decade, long enough to see unions make temporary inroads into his once union-free firm, and died in 1948. In the decades that followed George F. Johnson's death, internal mismanagement and aggressive foreign competition undermined EJ's economic health. In the 1960s the company suffered dramatic reverses of fortune. New chief executive officers were recruited from outside the firm. The firm was transformed from an integrated manufacturer and retailer into mainly a merchandiser. In 1981 EJ was purchased by a subsidiary of Hanson PLC, a London-based syndicate, but EJ's troubles continued. In 1996 George Newman and Co bought the 75-store chain, the remains of a vast manufacturing and retail empire, from Millennium Chemicals, Inc, a spin-off of Hanson, Plc. In 1999 with sales and profits dipping, George Newman and Co filed for bankruptcy protection. At the time EJ employed 326 workers at its headquarters and remaining five dozen Father and Son stores.

Inglis, William. *George F. Johnson and His Industrial Democracy* (New York: Huntington Press, 1935)
Zahavi, Gerald. *Workers, Managers, and Welfare Capitalism: The Shoemakers and Tanners of Endicott Johnson, 1890–1950* (Urbana: Univ of Illinois Press, 1988)

Gerald Zahavi

Endwell. Locality (pop 11,706) in Union (Broome Co). Endwell grew from Hooper, which had a post office from 1853 to 1897. The Carmel Grove Methodist camp meeting operated here from 1872 to 1914. Endwell's post office opened in 1921. Upscale suburban developments now surround the commercial center. Washingtonian Hall (1799) and the Amos Patterson Museum are landmarks, as is the Binghamton Country Club (1889). Amphenol Interconnect Products Corp operates a cable assembly plant in Endwell.

Charles J. Browne

energy. See MUNICIPALLY OWNED ELECTRIC COMPANIES; NUCLEAR POWER; PETROLEUM AND NATURAL GAS INDUSTRY; POWER AND LIGHTING.

Energy Research and Development Authority. Established in 1975 in response to energy shortages and high prices, the authority finances and promotes energy-related research and development. An important part of the authority's work is the staff support it lends to the development of the state energy plan developed by the State Energy Planning Board. The authority and the US Department of Energy co-manage the Western New York Nuclear Service Center in West Valley (Cattaraugus Co). Opened in 1961 by New York State, this facility was the nation's only center to reprocess used nuclear fuel into new fuel. Nuclear Fuel Services, the private operator between 1966 and 1972, abandoned the site because of debts and mounting environmental problems. In the face of continual protests by local residents, the US government and the authority took joint control of the site; the Department of Energy pays 90% of the cleanup cost, which through 1998 was almost $1 billion, but a far higher amount is anticipated.

In 2002 the authority was a national leader in energy efficiency and alternative energy research and development, including fuel-cell research and new forms of decentralized power generation. The authority issued $4.6 billion in bonds to fund pollution control projects. A 13-member board appointed by the governor and confirmed by the senate governs the authority. Its work is funded by annual assessments on electric utilities, voluntary contributions from the New York Power Authority, and federal funds. Total revenues in 1999–2000 were $25 million.

New York State Energy Research and Development Authority. *Annual Reports* (Albany: Author)
Peterson, Thomas V. *Linked Arms: A Rural Community Resists Nuclear Waste* (Albany: SUNY Press, 2002)

Thomas A. Birkland

Enfield. Town (pop 3,369) in W Tompkins Co. Settled in 1804, the town was formed from Ulysses in 1821. The Enfield Falls Hotel (1830s) accommodated visitors to Lucifer Falls (115 ft/ 35 m) in Enfield Glen, now part of Robert H. Treman State Park. The turbine mill (1838) in the park has a horizontal waterwheel and is open for visitors. Enfield was the site of a Civilian Conservation Corps camp (1933–41). Population reached 2,340 in 1840, declined to 939 in 1930, then doubled between 1960 and 2000. In 2003 some residents farm, while many commute to jobs in Ithaca.

Jane Dieckmann

***Engel v Vitale*, 370 US 421 (1962).** School prayer case. In 1951 New York State's Board of Regents composed a 22-word nondenominational religious invocation to be read aloud in public schools at the discretion of the school district. After the Union Free School District of New Hyde Park (Nassau Co) adopted its recitation following the morning flag salute in 1958, several parents, including Stephen I. Engel, challenged the prayer, bringing a case against the members of the Board of Education, including board president William J. Vitale. Between 1959 and 1961 three New York courts upheld the practice so long as no pupil was compelled to join in the prayer over their own or their parents' objections. The Supreme Court held by a vote of 6–1 that the prayer was unconstitutional under any circumstances. Justice Hugo L. Black ruled that "it is no part of the business of government to compose official prayers for any group of the American people." Neither the prayer's denominational neutrality nor its "voluntariness" shielded it from being a violation of the Establishment Clause of the First Amendment to the US Constitution. This was in keeping with a number of Court precedents that the First Amendment is violated not only when government endorses a particular faith but when it favors religion generally. Though civil libertarians praised the decision, many felt it indicated that the Court had gone beyond neutrality and demonstrated hostility toward religion.

Hall, H. Glen. "Freedom of Worship: State and Federal Guarantees," *New York State Bar Journal* 63 (Sept–Oct 1991): 18–24, 54

Timothy P. Gordinier

English. Unlike most other immigrants and their descendants, the English are not significantly concentrated in specific areas of America, in part because theirs was the common language and in part because they were quick to intermarry. Reliable counts are impossible because of this situation and because there was little distinguishing among the English, the Welsh, and the Scots, and, to a lesser degree, the Irish. Nearly 20% of the US population in 2000 has a British heritage. The English in New York State are fairly representative of the country.

SETTLEMENT

The earliest English immigrants were a small, transient, but significant minority in Dutch New Netherland. During the 1630s and 1640s, English men and women fleeing religious intolerance in England or Puritan New England arrived in New Netherland. They included a group led by Quaker minister John Throckmorton, as well as Puritan Anne Hutchinson, who was banished from Massachusetts Bay Colony for religious heresy. New Netherlanders invited the English to settle within their territory at Hempstead (1644), Gravesend (1645), Flushing (1645), Mespath/Middleburgh (1652), and Jamaica (1656) on Long Island and at Vreedlant (1656) in what is modern Bronx or Westchester Cos. English settlements were also created outside of the ambit of New Netherland on eastern Long Island: Southampton and Southold (1640), East Hampton (1648), Smithtown (1650), Huntington (1653), and Brookhaven (1655).

After New Netherland came under English control in 1664, the population of New York Colony was still more diverse and less English than that of any other English colony, yet the English filled a disproportionate number of political offices, professions, and lucrative occupations. By 1680 the English constituted less than 20% of New York City's population, 40% of the taxable population, and nearly 50% of the wealthiest merchants. During the 18th century more English, predominantly single men, arrived, and New York Colony assumed a distinctly English character, even though only about 5% of England's emigrants chose it as a destination. Most English immigrants to New York Colony came not from London but from various provincial areas, especially Yorkshire; farmers predominated, but there were many rural crafters, skilled and unskilled laborers, and merchants. By this time English immigration was also more familial. Most appear not to have been poor but enterprising and ambitious, seeking better opportunities in America, as were the English who arrived in later years.

English immigrants established important institutions such as King's College in 1754 (now Columbia University), many of the first newspapers, and St. George's Society in 1770, which catered to the elite of English society in the colony and aided the arrival of their poorer compatriots. By 1776 about half of the white population in New York State had English ancestry, and most followed English cultural trends. The state's aristocracy modeled itself after the English nobility, and its trade and labor systems were patterned on England's. Once the English language, legal system, institutions, and customs predominated, English immigrants found a familiar environment. They did not need to form separate ethnic enclaves and could easily participate in social and civic affairs. During the War of 1812 and other episodes of tension between Britain and America, while English immigrants were not always trusted, they were generally welcomed and seen not so much as true foreigners as "cousins." Because England was the world's leading trading and industrial nation in the late 18th and the 19th centuries and because Americans still looked to England for intellectual and cultural leadership, English immigrants continued to be overrepresented in political, financial, scientific, literary, and artistic communities. New York City's first mayor, Thomas Willet, was an English immigrant. English immigrant Calvert Vaux, who with Frederick Law Olmsted designed Central Park and Brooklyn's Prospect Park, was one of many who brought English tastes and designs for gardens and other public spaces. English immigrants Richard Upjohn, known for his Gothic Revival–style buildings, Thomas Adams, Jacob Wrey Mould, and others became famous architects in New York City.

MIGRATION PATTERNS

English immigration occurred throughout the 19th century, but three waves of immigrants can be identified, most of them clearly informed, responding more to American opportunities than to bad conditions in England. The first, from the late 1840s through the mid-1850s, brought mostly farmers and people who intended to farm. With them came building trades workers, skilled craft workers, and some industrial workers, who could earn wages twice or even thrice those in England. Many young single women also came to work as domestic servants for New York's growing middle and upper classes. The second and third waves, from the end of the Civil War to the early 1870s and from the 1880s to the panic of 1893, included more unskilled laborers and fewer farmers. Throughout the century there was a fairly small but important class of industrial workers whose skills and experience helped build the state's iron, steel, and textile mills. In the 1860s skilled English weavers, spinners, and ironworkers (puddlers and molders) were attracted to the mills of Troy (Rensselaer Co) and Cohoes (Albany Co) by the higher wages and positions of authority offered. Some were "birds of passage," seasonal migrants regu-

St. Peter's Church. Depiction of the Episcopal Church in Albany as it appeared in 1800, by James Eights, *ca* 1850.

larly moving back and forth across the Atlantic. Proximity to the main American port made this relatively easy.

Although the immigrants were for the most part economically motivated, sometimes America's greater political freedom and social mobility were factors, as was religion. The first Shakers, Mother Ann Lee and her first followers, arrived in New York from England in the 1770s. From the late 18th century through the 19th, probably a sizable majority of English immigrants to the state were nonconformists, primarily Methodists, but some were Quakers, Congregationalists, and Mormons. Nonconformists were more likely to migrate because biases and restrictions against them, which lingered into the early 19th century, weakened their attachment to England. More significant, networks of communication between British and American Methodists channeled English Methodists to New York State. Ontario Co was especially popular for immigrant weavers and farmers from Norfolk, while Wayne Co attracted farmers from southeastern England, particularly Sussex, Kent, and the London area. Yorkshire immigrants were common throughout the state. Immigrants from the Isle of Man, including some successful carpenters and builders, clustered in Albany. By the 1860s there were sizable clusters of English on Manhattan, especially on the West Side. Many immigrants sent encouragement and advice to facilitate the migration of friends and family, and some even prearranged their accommodation and employment. The clusters soon dissipated as the English assimilated.

Agriculture and Industry

Until the Civil War, agriculture probably drew most of the state's English immigrants. Here they could buy land for the cost of renting it for a few years in England, and there was enough agricultural variety to appeal to English farmers and farm laborers of various backgrounds. Still, there were adjustments necessary to prosper in New York State. In England, land was scarce and expensive, and labor was abundant and cheap. In America the opposite was true, thus their labor-intensive methods had to be abandoned in favor of more land-intensive methods. The English brought valuable knowledge and experience in animal breeding and drainage. John Lyth, for example, was an apprenticed earthenware maker from Stafford who became a master drainage tile maker in York before immigrating in 1850. After setting up a company in Buffalo, he toured the state to promote his tiles and to teach techniques that raised productivity and allowed the exploitation of rich, wetter soils.

Coming from the world's first industrial nation and most developed economy, English immigrants to New York State included unusually high proportions of skilled people. Engineers, building trades workers, toolmakers, machinists, and other skilled crafters were common. New York's textiles industries were especially indebted to English immigrants. One particularly influential immigrant weaver was William Broadhead, who left Yorkshire in 1843 to settle in Chautauqua Co. After building a textile mill patterned after one he had studied in England, Broadhead eventually owned nine factories, employed 800 operatives, and helped establish railways, shipping companies, and water- and gasworks in the southwestern part of the state. Another Yorkshire weaver, Charles Bailey, came to New York State in 1857 to set up Jacquard looms in Little Falls (Herkimer Co) and established one of the state's largest knitting companies. British carriage makers also excelled. William Morrell left Yorkshire in 1869 and used the skills he had acquired in England to run a large carriage-making company in Ontario Co.

English industrial workers brought experience in labor organization and helped lead New York State's early labor movement. New York City's Working Men's Party was formed in 1829 under the leadership of Fanny Wright and other English immigrants, and the arrival of English Chartists in the late 1840s also brought vitality to the state's labor movement. By midcentury there were about 100,000 English immigrants in New York State (102,286 in 1855). The vast majority of English in New York State saw slavery as a betrayal of America's ideals and a violation of God's law. Some were abolitionist leaders, such as John Pierce, who arrived from Yorkshire in 1826 to farm in Wayne Co. When war came, the English were among the first to enlist and had the highest participation rate of all immigrants, and the war aided their becoming American. The English showed a strong preference for the Whig and Republican Parties.

The 20th Century

English immigration declined in the 20th century, in part because of opportunities to emigrate to other British colonies. New York City continued to attract English theatrical talent, including icons like Charlie Chaplin, Cary Grant, and many others before they proceeded to Hollywood. During World War II many English people were evacuated to New York City for safety, and some stayed. More came after the war as "war brides" of American soldiers. New York City's artistic and publishing circles drew English immigrants, including W. H. Auden, Sir Rudolph Bing, John Lennon, and Tina Brown. Also, a significant number of professionals and technicians settled in New York State after the war, as British taxes became too burdensome. New York State's universities, laboratories, and flourishing entertainment industries received a heavy share of their talent from England. Over the course of the 20th century, immigrants from England had an increasingly diverse ethnic background, including, in the first half of the century, a large Jewish component (including London-born New York City mayor Abe Beame) and, in recent decades, a substantial number with Caribbean and South Asian ancestry. In 1950 there were 400,000 British immigrants in New York, and more than 1.14 million New Yorkers claimed English ancestry in the 2000 census.

See also Architects and architecture, Long Island (Nassau and Suffolk counties); New Netherland.

Berthoff, Rowland T. *British Immigrants in Industrial America, 1790–1950* (New York: Russell & Russell, 1953)

Burrows, Edwin G., and Mike Wallace. *Gotham: A History of New York City to 1898* (New York: Oxford Univ Press, 1999)

Erickson, Charlotte. *Invisible Immigrants: The Adaptation of English and Scottish Immigrants in 19th-Century America* (Coral Gables, Fla: Univ of Miami Press, 1972)

———. *Leaving England: Essays on British Emigration in the 19th Century* (Ithaca: Cornell Univ Press, 1994)

Goodfriend, Joyce D. *Before the Melting Pot: Society and Culture in Colonial New York City, 1664–1730* (Princeton, NJ: Princeton Univ Press, 1992)

Van Vugt, William E. *Britain to America: The Mid-19th Century Immigrants to the United States* (Champaign and Urbana: Univ of Illinois Press, 1999)

William E. Van Vugt

Entenmann's. Founded in 1898 by German immigrant William Entenmann, the company originated as a home-delivery bakery in the Brooklyn neighborhood of Flatbush. Entenmann moved the business to Bay Shore (Suffolk Co) in the early 1900s, eventually turning its operations over to his son and grandsons. Home deliveries were phased out and wholesale distribution phased in during the 1950s. An Entenmann's facility built in Bay Shore in 1961 was the largest fresh cake bakery in the United States and one of the largest in the world, and remains the company's headquarters. Since 1978 the Entenmann's brand has been owned by a series of food and consumer product conglomerates. The company, which employs over 2,000 people in its main factory in Bay Shore, remains a leading national brand of fresh bakery-style cakes and pastries.

Alexandra Schein

Environmental Conservation, Department of. The New York State Forest Commission was created in 1885 in response to widespread concern about the state's water supply, then threatened by deforestation caused by fires and illegal cutting. The commission was charged with control of the Adirondack Forest Preserve and with responsibility for tree planting and fire prevention in all state forests. It also had a mandate to promote forestry education as well as to determine the nature and extent of forests in New York State. In 1888 the state legislature authorized the commission to establish parks for the propagation of deer and other game in the Catskills. The Forest Commission's activities disappointed many; their enforcement of forest laws was almost nonexistent, and widespread cutting occurred on forest preserve lands. In 1892 the Adirondack Park was established, and in 1895 a now famous clause was added to the state constitution prohibiting all cutting on state-owned lands within the park, mandating that such lands "be forever kept as wild forest lands."

Also in 1895 the Forest Commission joined with a state fisheries commission to form the Fisheries, Game and Forest Commission, which assumed the duties of propagation and distribution of food and game fish and enforcement of laws protecting fish and game, in addition to attending to forest duties. In 1900, along with a change in name to Forest, Fish and Game Commission, the commission expanded forest fire protection and in 1902 established the first tree nursery at Lake Clear in the Adirondacks to supply seedlings for planting on state-owned burned sites and wastelands. The commission ventured into disease control in 1909 with active work against white pine blister rust.

In 1911 the state legislature, with strong support from Gov John Alden Dix, created the New York State Conservation Commission, which combined the duties of the Forest, Fish and Game Commission, the Water Supply Commission, and the Forest Purchasing Board. In its initial year the Conservation Commission—

organized into three divisions, Fish and Game, Lands and Forests, and Inland Waters—was overseeing 1.6 million acres (647,000 ha) of forest preserve, 6 tree nurseries, and a fish-stocking program handling 1 billion fish. In 1926 the Conservation Commission became the Conservation Department with five divisions: Fish and Game; Lands and Forests; Parks; Saratoga Springs; and Water Power and Control. With the 1946 addition of a division of Conservation Education (publishers of *New York State Conservationist* magazine), this department remained in place until 1970.

The 1931 Hewitt amendment to the state constitution (and subsequent enabling legislation) authorized the purchase of 2 million acres (809,000 ha) of land in blocks of at least 500 acres (202 ha) within 11 years and required that the land be reforested. Throughout the 1930s, purchase of abandoned farmlands and replanting of old fields with seedlings grown in the state-run nurseries became major activities of the Conservation Department. Although the economic depression of the 1930s reduced funding, the tree-planting program used labor from the federally funded Civilian Conservation Corps throughout New York State.

Recreational activities on forest preserve lands in the Adirondacks and Catskills grew substantially during the 1920s and 1930s with the advent of the automobile. The public desired campsites and trails. In a controversial decision of the 1930s, the State Court of Appeals ruled that, despite the state constitution's forever wild clause, campsites could be developed as long as they did not remove timber to a material degree. This requirement tended to limit campers to more open areas and thereby lessened the danger of forest fires.

In 1946, to address concerns about the management of private forestlands, the state legislature passed the Forest Practice Act, which authorized the Conservation Department to provide free technical assistance to private forest owners. In return, such owners agreed to follow certain minimum forestry practices in timber harvests and forest protection. This voluntary program was enacted partly to forestall any federal action regulating private lands. The Conservation Department's Division of Lands and Forests consolidated its field operations in 1946 into 15 forest districts, and the Division of Fish and Game (now the Division of Fish and Wildlife) operated from 9 regional offices, often located separately from forest district offices.

In 1970 greater population pressure on natural resources and new environmental concerns led to formation of the Department of Environmental Conservation (DEC), which took over activities of the Conservation Department as well as those of the Water Resources Commission, Air Pollution Board, Pesticides Control Board, and Natural Beauty Commission, and the environmental activities of other state agencies. At the same time, DEC ceded management of all state parks to the newly created Office of Parks and Recreation (now Office of Parks, Recreation, and Historic Preservation). The DEC's orientation shifted somewhat, away from the immediate stewardship of natural resources to a broad environmental perspective. In part, this shift is reflected in the DEC's changed role in the Adirondacks after creation of the Adirondack Park Agency in 1971. The DEC developed a working relationship with the new agency to handle the often controversial management of the Adirondack Forest Preserve and the Adirondack region.

At the beginning of the 21st century, the DEC has three main functions: natural resource management; environmental quality and protection; and promotion of public health, safety, and recreation. The Divisions of Lands and Forests, Fish and Wildlife, Marine Resources, and Mineral Resources address natural resources issues. The Divisions of Air Resources, Environmental Remediation, Pollution Prevention, Solid and Hazardous Materials, and Water deal with environmental quality and protection. DEC officers and forest rangers operate out of the Public Protection Division, and a special services unit maintains such services as recreation, education, and permit processing. The department employs about 4,000 persons. There are nine regional offices as well as a central office in Albany.

See also BIRDS; FISH; FISH HATCHERIES; POLLUTION; STATE HISTORIC PARKS, SITES, AND HERITAGE AREAS; STATE PARKS.

Canham, Hugh O. *Forest Management Programs of the Department of Environmental Conservation.* New York State Forest Resources Assessment Report No 18 (Albany: NYS Department of Environmental Conservation, 1982)

Terrie, Philip G. *Contested Terrain: A New History of Nature and People in the Adirondacks* (Blue Mountain Lake, NY: Adirondack Museum; Syracuse: Syracuse Univ Press, 1997)

Hugh O. Canham

environmentalism. Advocacy for the safeguarding of pure water, clean air, undisturbed land, and wild animals. New Yorkers' attitudes toward the environment have changed dramatically over the last 200 years, with these changes affecting the management of natural resources and pollution control.

Environmental Values

When most New Yorkers lived in rural areas and viewed the natural world as a frequent adversary in their own battles for survival, nature was respected but not valued for its own sake. This situation changed under the impact of the Romantic movement, which taught many to aestheticize nature. The novels of James Fenimore Cooper, published after 1820, portrayed heroic trappers and Native Americans in the wilds of colonial New York, and beginning in the 1830s, Thomas Cole and other painters of the Hudson River school emphasized the beauty of wild landscapes in the Hudson River valley. This new appreciation of nature was often tied to the conviction that fetid air and water caused disease and, conversely, that pure air and water could slow or halt the spread of infectious diseases. Nature was thought to be inherently health giving and needed to be preserved.

For urban dwellers nature increasingly became both an abstraction and an alternative—something to escape to—especially in the hot summer months. In 1836 Manhattan-born journalist Charles Fenno Hoffman published "Wild Scenes near Home; or, Hints for a Summer Tourist," probably the first travel article about the Adirondacks. In 1858 Ralph Waldo Emerson's poem "The Adirondacs" memorialized his trip to the Philosophers' Camp, a getaway for wealthy and prominent men established by Albany artist William J. Stillman at Follensby Pond (Franklin Co). In 1871 Catskills farmer and writer John Burroughs began to publish essays on the sanctity of nature that quickly made him a celebrity spokesman for this belief.

After the Civil War there was a growing belief that unbridled economic development and personal greed were destroying nature and its denizens. One of the first manifestations of this new sensibility was a concern for animals. In 1866 former diplomat and Manhattan resident

John Burroughs with grandchild at his retreat, Slabsides, near West Park, *ca* 1920.

Henry Bergh organized the American Society for the Prevention of Cruelty to Animals (ASPCA) and drafted its "Declaration of the Rights of Animals." Bergh also wrote and, in 1866, won passage of a law forbidding cruelty to animals (domestic and wild) from the New York State legislature. Columbia University lecturer George Perkins Marsh made a crucial contribution to environmental awareness in *Man and Nature* (1864), which argued that any society's long-term health depended on the protection of its forests and water supplies. This argument was embraced and promoted by preservationists like Verplanck Colvin, the wealthy Albany native who produced the first maps and detailed descriptions of many of the Adirondack peaks in the 1870s and 1880s. Other wealthy New York City residents founded two of America's first conservation organizations: the National Audubon Society (1886) and the Association for the Protection of the Adirondacks (1901). European-trained forester Bernhard Fernow founded a forestry department at Cornell University in 1898, and following its closure in 1903—after objections to Fernow's experiments with clear-cutting—the state established the College of Forestry at Syracuse University (now SUNY College of Environmental Science and Forestry) in 1911.

For most of the 20th century, environmental thinking was dominated by the "conservation" movement, which favored scientific control of natural resources to maximize sustained yields. Two New Yorkers led this movement in its early days. One was Theodore Roosevelt, who had made his first trip to Paul Smith's Hotel in Franklin Co's north woods in 1871. In his journal of that summer, the 12-year-old Roosevelt wrote of falling asleep as his father read aloud from Cooper's *Last of the Mohicans* by the light of a campfire. The other leader was a New York City financier's son, Gifford Pinchot, whose first published book was a forestry manual called *The Adirondack Spruce* (1898). Pinchot managed New York State's natural resources under Gov Theodore Roosevelt and then served as secretary of the interior under Pres Theodore Roosevelt. During Roosevelt's presidency, scientific land management became the official US government policy, and the number of acres under federal control increased from about 46 million acres (18.6 million ha) to more than 150 million acres (60.7 million ha).

In the 1920s the drive to protect nature gained momentum when middle-class New Yorkers began to tour the countryside in their automobiles. Outdoor recreation and the preservation of natural areas were linked in the minds of such middle-class explorers as famed birdwatcher Roger Tory Peterson, who moved from Jamestown (Chautauqua Co) to New York City in his teens, becoming a member of the Bronx County Bird Club in the late 1920s. Robert Moses's work as chair of the State Council of Parks aided automobile tourism significantly. Beginning in 1927, Moses developed parks across the state for camping and recreation. He also built a system of bridges and limited-access parkways facilitating travel from New York City to Long Island, New Jersey, Westchester Co, and central and northern New York State. In 1928 the Adirondack Mountain Club (ADK), founded six years earlier by hiking enthusiasts, endorsed a policy of environmental advocacy in three areas: conservation, recreation, and education. During the 1930s Bob Marshall and other ADK members began to lobby the federal government to preserve wilderness areas. In the 1940s and 1950s, the club and other groups scored several antidevelopment victories in the courts. Yet environmental activism remained largely restricted to sporting clubs until the 1960s and 1970s, when environmental concerns became part of the mainstream.

The 1962 serialized publication of Rachel Carson's *Silent Spring* in the *New Yorker* magazine heightened the concern over the environment, and in subsequent years, data and arguments relating to environmental pollution were widely disseminated. Between 1965 and 1972 ADK memberships tripled, and between 1968 and 1978 memberships in the National Audubon Society increased from 88,000 to 388,000. On the first Earth Day (22 Apr 1970), Gov Nelson A. Rockefeller signed legislation establishing the New York State Department of Environmental Conservation (DEC), a vast new consolidation of state agencies charged with coordinating and strengthening all aspects of natural resource protection and pollution control. Between 1970 and 2000 the new environmentalism swayed the thinking and actions of many public employees and elected officials.

At the beginning of the 21st century, scientists continue to amass evidence that human activities are permanently changing nature on a global scale. New York State—as the home of more than 100 nongovernmental organizations dedicated to environmental protection as well as of the United Nations—is a locus of environmental thinking and action. But to the vast majority of New Yorkers environmental issues are intensely local, exemplified by the successful campaign to prevent construction of a nuclear power plant on Cayuga Lake from 1967 to 1969, the successful 1999–2002 struggle to prevent the opening of a regional dump near Harrisville (Lewis Co), and the ongoing cleanup of Love Canal and other toxic waste sites in Erie and Niagara Cos. Every corner of the state now boasts an environmental organization, and officials in even the most rural towns must consider the environmental impacts of their actions.

Natural Resources

The 1859 opening of Central Park in New York City marked an important victory for the idea that cities required pastoral areas for the health and well-being of their residents. By the 1860s railroad lines also allowed wealthy New Yorkers to swim in Lake George or climb the peaks of the Adirondacks. These early ecotourists showed little concern over rapid consumption of the state's natural resources by loggers and hunters. Indeed many visitors took part in these activities. George Bird Grinnell, founder of the National Audubon Society, was the affluent publisher of a New York City–based hunting magazine, and the major North Country landowners who founded the Association for the Protection of the Adirondacks often drew substantial revenues from logging.

New York State led the nation in the production of lumber in 1850, but overcutting and fires caused it to drop to 4th place in 1880 and to 17th place in 1900. Political support for efforts to control timber cutting, regulate game hunting, and protect water sources came from scientists and the growing ranks of tourists, physicians, and others who valued the therapeutic aspects of wild nature. Support was also found among those having an economic interest in protection. A *New York Times* editorial of 9 Aug 1864 suggested that a planned rail link from Saratoga Springs to North Creek (Warren Co) might turn the Adirondack region into a suburb of New York City and exhorted readers to "form combinations" to buy Adirondack mountain land for parks, "owned in common." At this time, the Board of Commissioners of the Land Office, established to sell the state's excess property, was the only state agency that dealt with natural resources. The state regularly reclaimed land for unpaid taxes, but its first purchase of land did not occur until 1866. Most tax-delinquent land in the North Country had been abandoned after logging for choice species such as white pine was completed. As logging accelerated, more lands were left to the state.

In the 1870s private clubs began to buy huge tracts of scenic, North Country land. These purchases raised the concern that wilderness recreation might soon be a pastime only for the rich. Also in the 1870s unregulated private land uses created significant public nuisances. In 1872 and other years, cinders from wood-fired railroad engines ignited accumulated brush from recently logged lands, causing huge fires. White-tailed deer, bear, and beaver were being exterminated in all but the most remote areas. A drought cycle that peaked in 1883 created the popular impression that fires and erosion were drying up the land, as George Perkins Marsh had warned in *Man and Nature*. In 1872 the state created the Commission of State Parks and asked commission members to evaluate the idea of a large public park in the north woods.

Concern over the state's water supplies drove the creation of the Adirondack Forest Preserve. In the mid–19th century, Erie Canal freight traffic was a key reason for New York State's dominance of the North American economy. Without enough fresh water to float barges through the canal, New York City's economy would falter, as it did briefly when water levels dropped dangerously in 1883. Still more important was clean drinking water for the expanding metropolis. Since 1842 Manhattan had drawn water via aqueducts from the Croton River. New York City's leaders entertained long-range plans to look farther north for water. Yet neighboring cities depended on increasingly uncertain sources. As a result of the water issue, the Chamber of Commerce of the State of New York joined nature tourists, naturalists, and physicians in support of an Adirondack park. In 1883 Chamber of Commerce president Morris Jesup, an ardent naturalist and social reformer who was also president of the American Museum of Natural History in New York City, proposed that New York State use its power of eminent domain to set aside 4 million acres (1.6 million ha) as a forest preserve. Responding to popular pressure, Gov David B. Hill signed the New York State Forest Preserve, which included the Adirondack and Catskill Preserves, into law on 15 May 1885. Another campaign resulted in the March 1883 passage of the Niagara Reservation Act, which created a park containing the American side of Niagara Falls and 912 surrounding acres (369 ha). The park was the second in the nation purchased by a state to protect scenery.

The creation of the New York State Forest Preserve and what became Niagara Reservation State Park represented the first real victories for the state's environmental movement. These acts, in particular the preserve law, established precedents for public goals—in this case, protection of water, soil, and timber resources—to override private property rights. Although the original preserve measure was relatively toothless and lacked enforcement provisions, slowly the state began to put teeth into it. In 1892 the legislature appropriated $25,000 for land acquisition, and Gov Hill directed the state's Forest Commission (founded 1885) to draw suggested boundaries of an Adirondack park. Two years later Gov Roswell P. Flower signed the Adirondack Park Enabling Act, placing 2.8 million acres (1.1 million ha)—of which 551,000 acres (222,980 ha) were owned by the state—within the commission's mapped Blue Line. That year at the state constitutional convention the famous forever wild clause was adopted. This held that on state land within the New York State Forest Preserve not only logging but also removal of dead timber or creation of dams (which flooded preserve land) were prohibited. The clause did not refer to privately owned lands within the Blue Line, and the state would not address activity on these properties until 1973.

In 1945 Paul Schaefer and other wilderness advocates learned of plans to build a system of dams that would flood thousands of acres in Adirondack forests. Via Friends of the Forest Preserve, founded that year, they opposed the plan through local meetings, court challenges, and skillful use of media coverage. By the time the plan was defeated in 1955, Schaefer and his supporters had established the template for future environmental crusades. Meanwhile New York State's public land acreage continued to increase through most of the 20th century. Between 1938 and 1941 the federal government purchased 16,000 acres (6,480 ha) of rock ridge and pasture between Seneca and Cayuga Lakes, creating the Finger Lakes National Forest. Other federal purchases created 13 wildlife refuges in New York State, encompassing 28,000 acres (11,330 ha). In addition the state claimed more than 700,000 acres (283,280 ha) in abandoned or purchased land for state forests outside the Adirondacks and Catskills.

Within the Adirondacks continued development on private land threatened the park's wilderness character. In 1973 the Adirondack Park Agency (APA), founded two years earlier, created a regional zoning plan that assigned an acceptable level of development to every park acre. In 1990 the APA attempted to strengthen zoning regulations to increase environmental safeguards, but local opposition coalesced to protect the property rights of park landowners, and the new zoning proposal was defeated, leaving the old zoning regulation in effect.

The controversy encouraged state leaders to protect critical natural areas by purchasing them outright rather than by attempting to regulate private use. New York State voters endorsed this approach by passing Environmental Quality Bond Acts allocating money for land purchases in 1986 and 1996. Since 1992 the DEC has submitted an annual Open Space Plan that targets parcels for acquisition. Private groups such as the Nature Conservancy (founded in 1951 and headquartered in Arlington, Va) and over 80 local land trusts own additional New York State preserves. In 2003 the Nature Conservancy alone owned 277,000 acres (112,100 ha) in New York State.

Pollution Control

The rapid expansion of urban populations in the 19th century and persistent urban poverty created continuing public health problems. In 1892, as an outbreak of cholera threatened Manhattan, the city's Common Council established the Division of Pathology, Bacteriology, and Disinfection, under the direction of Dr Hermann M. Biggs. He dispatched teams to scrub the homes of cholera patients and to treat or burn their clothes and bedding. His staff also disinfected 39,000 tenements. As a result, the epidemic took only nine lives in Manhattan. This public health triumph launched an era of municipal leadership in preventative medicine, including the first real efforts to protect the quality of urban air and water. Biggs later claimed more successes against diphtheria, typhoid, and tuberculosis. Outbreaks of disease also drove the development of municipal water and sewer systems in rapidly growing upstate cities. These were typically expensive and difficult undertakings. In 1852, in the wake of an epidemic, Rochester authorized construction of a 16 mi (26 km) aqueduct from Hemlock Lake; it did not operate until 1876. Eventually the city bought and condemned all shoreline properties on Hemlock and Canadice Lakes to reduce contaminants in municipal water.

While New York State began regulating municipal drinking water in 1904, efforts to control water pollution from sewage began in 1935 with the establishment of a federal commission to regulate discharges into the waters around New York Harbor. Yet sewage treatment plants were often inadequate until 1965, when the state's Pure Waters Bond Act released $300 million for sewage treatment. The first state agency to control air pollution was formed in 1957, but the prime cause of air pollution, the automobile, did not come under regulation until 1970, with passage of the federal Clean Air Act.

The modern field of environmental law was born on 29 Dec 1965, when New York State's Second Circuit Court of Appeals ruled that the citizens' group Scenic Hudson Preservation Conference had legal standing to sue Consolidated Edison Co to halt its construction of a new facility at Storm King Mountain. Leaders of Scenic Hudson later founded the New York City–headquartered Natural Resources Defense Council, which would claim over 400,000 members in 2000. In 1966 Patchogue (Suffolk Co) resident and lawyer Victor Yannacone sued the Suffolk County Mosquito Control Commission to prevent it from further use of dichlordiphenyltrichloroethane (DDT). His lawsuit initiated the group Environmental Defense, which would have more than 300,000 dues-paying members in 2000. These and other environmental groups received crucial early support from the Rockefeller Foundation, Ford Foundation, and other New York State–based charitable funds.

During the 1970s new federal and state laws increased the DEC's power, with employment at the agency jumping from 2,140 in 1970 to 4,000 in 2000. The agency's successes included a 1992 law requiring all municipalities to have separation programs for recycling solid waste. The state banned DDT in 1970 and began regulating many other pesticides in 1987. Meanwhile scientists at Cornell University and elsewhere have explored ways of controlling agricultural pests with fewer or no synthetic chemicals.

On 10 Aug 1977 the *Niagara Gazette* published the first front-page story on Love Canal, a Niagara Falls neighborhood poisoned by wastes from an abandoned plant of Hooker Chemical Co. Love Canal became a national symbol for the problem of toxic waste disposal and spurred establishment of the state's federally mandated program for hazardous waste control in 1978. Federal and state legislation of the 1980s—beginning with the 1980 Comprehensive Environmental Response, Compensation, and Liability Act, also labeled Superfund—targeted 80 of the state's toxic waste sites for cleanup. By 2000 cleanup efforts were ongoing at many sites. New York State passed 11 clean water bills in the 1970s and 12 more in the 1980s. In 1997, after years of negotiation, New York City signed an agreement with several dozen towns in the Catskills and Hudson River valley that protected the watersheds that produce the city's drinking water.

Since 1970 there has been measurable progress in cleaning up New York State's environment, but much remains to be done. For example, since the late 1970s scientists have identified acidic rainwater as a source of damage to wildlife and forests in the Adirondacks. Particles released by power plant smokestacks in the Midwest have been identified as one of its major causes. At the beginning of the 21st century, New York State remains powerless to regulate the plants in neighboring states, where utilities producing the pollution label the scientific research inconclusive. Environmental cleanup efforts often proceed slowly; they require many different groups to make complex agreements, and scientific evidence regarding environmental problems is often subject to dispute.

See also Wetlands.

Nash, Roderick. *Wilderness and the American Mind* (New Haven, Conn: Yale Univ Press, 1973)

———. *The Rights of Nature: A History of Environmental Ethics* (Madison: Univ of Wisconsin Press, 1989)

Talbot, Allan R. *Power along the Hudson: The Storm King Case and the Birth of Environmentalism* (New York: Dutton, 1972)

Terrie, Philip G. *Contested Terrain: A New History of Nature and People in the Adirondacks* (Syracuse: Syracuse Univ Press, 1997)

Brad Edmondson

environmental law. Laws to protect the environment in New York stretch back into colonial times. At common law, certain types of rights to natural resources, such as the right to navigate in tidal waters, inhere in the sovereign as the representative for the people, and the sovereign is without power to deprive the public of these rights. At the same time, the sovereign has the right and the duty to preserve the resource when intensive use puts the resource at risk. Thus, in 1698, the royal governor, Richard Coote, Earl of Bellomont, imposed restrictions on the cutting of white pine, which was needed for ship's spars. After the Revolutionary War, the delegates to the Constitutional Convention of 1777 affirmed that the common law of England, as it existed on 20 Apr 1777, would still serve as the basic law of the land, as it does to this day.

Early Historical Development

The conservation movement took root early in New York State, drawing strength from public appreciation and consumption of the art of the Hudson River school of painters and the writings of novelists and travelers enamored of the state's natural beauty. Prior to the American Civil War, the movement had relatively little impact on the development of the law, but this changed soon after the conflict ended. The wartime economy was succeeded by a period of rapid expansion of population, technology, and leisure, all of which imposed new burdens on the state's resources and on the protections those resources were afforded by the common law. The New York State Court of Appeals in *Morgan v King* (1866) extended the ancient right of the public to resort to navigable tidal waterways to freshwater, nontidal streams that were "navigable in fact." This holding was a boon to the logging industry, which then could use Adirondack rivers for log driving without regard to the demands of riparian landowners for compensation. The conservation movement was also making significant progress in the postwar period. Only two years after *Morgan v King,* legislation created the Fisheries Commission, the state's first environmental agency, to study the impact of logging on fish and water supplies. In 1883 legislation provided for the creation of the Niagara Reservation for the preservation of the scenic beauty of the falls. When the land acquisitions were made two years later, New York earned the distinction of having created the first state park in the nation.

Preserves and Parks

In 1885 the state legislature created the Adirondack Forest Preserve and the Catskill Forest Preserve, consisting of state lands in and around the two mountainous regions. Article 14 of the Constitution of 1894 prohibited the state from transferring forest preserve land and from removing timber. In 1892 the state had established the Adirondack Park and in 1904 the Catskill Park. By 1912 each of the two parks had been defined by a "blue line," and all public and private lands within the line were deemed to be "within" the park. The Adirondack Park Agency was established in 1971 with extensive powers to regulate development on private land. There is no comparable Catskill agency. State land outside of the blue line but within one of the forest preserve counties can be and often is part of the constitutionally protected forest preserve, while state land within the blue line, if obtained by the state for nonpreservation purposes, can be and sometimes is not a part of the forest preserve. Examples would be the Lake George battleground and the bed of Lake George itself. In 1993 the state provided for the creation in eastern Long Island of a third region of New York State subject to special restrictions, the Central Pine Barrens in Suffolk Co. A management plan adopted two years later created a "core preservation area" and a "compatible growth area" for pine barrens in the Towns of Brookhaven, Southampton, and Riverhead. Although this area is sometimes referred to as the Pine Barrens Preserve, state lands within it are not subject to constitutional protection because Suffolk Co is not one of the forest preserve counties.

Contemporary Environmentalism

In 1962 Consolidated Edison (Con Edison) of New York announced plans to build a hydroelectric plant in the Hudson Highlands behind Storm King Mountain (Orange Co). The announcement touched off a controversy that ended with Con Edison's surrender of its federal license in 1980. In the intervening years, a revolution in environmental protection had taken place in the US Congress, the courts, and the statehouses across the country. In the Storm King litigation, *Scenic Hudson Preservation Conference v Federal Power Commission* (1965), the Second Circuit Court of Appeals had determined that activists who, while having no economic interest at stake, had legal standing to challenge agency action on the ground that environmental values were inadequately considered. In 1970 Pres Richard M. Nixon created the Environmental Protection Agency and Gov Nelson A. Rockefeller transformed the Conservation Department into the Department of Environmental Conservation (DEC), a new agency that absorbed many functions of the Health Department while relinquishing many of its former functions to the Office of Parks and Recreation (now Office of Parks, Recreation, and Historic Preservation). For the next three decades, environmental law was kept in a state of constant ferment by the issuance of new laws, regulations, and agency and court determinations. Only in the last decade of the 20th century did the process of creation give way to consolidation and retrenchment.

Types of Environmental Law

The constitutional relationship between the states and the federal government has given rise to a situation in which the two frequently cooperate but sometimes compete in the area of environmental law. The major regulatory programs relating to air and water pollution are federal, but New York State implements them under state statutes and regulations that must, at a minimum, be as strict in terms of environmental protection as the models developed at the federal level. These programs typically forbid "discharge" or "release" of contaminants above de minimis thresholds within the state by any person without a DEC permit. The actions of DEC itself, along with all other state and municipal agencies, boards, and authorities, are restrained by the State Environmental Quality Review Act (SEQRA), enacted in 1975. This statute requires that any action of a government body, including issuing a permit to a private party, must be supported by a "hard look" at the environmental impacts. When coupled with the proliferation of permit requirements in many previously unregulated areas, SEQRA can have and has had an enormous indirect impact on private behavior. It not only adds an additional layer of review to a proposed project but also provides that the cost of any required review be borne by the applicant and not the government.

The scopes of independent federal and state environmental programs often overlap, but they also can dovetail in fortuitous ways. In the latter category are Superfund-type statutes applicable in New York State that impose strict liability on property owners (which may, in certain cases, include the parent corporation, successor entities, officers, directors, or shareholders) of contaminated locations, as well as other parties bearing some relationship to the contamination. On the federal level, the Comprehensive Environmental Response, Compensation and Liability Act of 1980 addresses releases of "hazardous substances," a term that includes a wide range of elements, compounds, and mixtures but excludes petroleum. Article 12 of New York's Navigation Law, adopted in 1977, three years before the federal statute, addresses discharges of petroleum.

The wetlands protection programs of the two governments often overlap. The program implemented under the much amended 1977 federal Clean Water Act, which began as the federal Water Pollution Control Act of 1972, operates under an expansive definition of "navigable waters," while the program implemented under the State Freshwater Wetlands Act of 1975 operates by reference to filed maps showing wetlands above a certain minimum size. Thus, a property may be deemed a federal wetland but not appear on the relevant state map. In its regulation of mapped wetlands, as in its regulation of surface mining, the state government involves itself in the area of land-use regulation, which is typically the province of local governments in New York. The resulting tension between local and state control in these areas has often given rise to litigation and attempts to harmonize the relationship through legislative and regulatory reform. A similar phenomenon has occurred in the area of siting of nuclear and hydroelectric power-generating plants, with respect to which federal authority generally displaces state authority. Another area of controversy involves "transboundary" pollution, particularly relating to emissions of air pollution in other states leading to the occurrence of ground-level ozone and acid rain in New York State. The state has been at the forefront of efforts to reduce air pollution and has aggressively promoted the development of newer, cleaner technologies through its agencies and authorities, particularly the New York Power Authority and the New York Energy Research and Development Authority.

Cronin, John, and Robert F. Kennedy Jr. *The River Keepers: Two Activists Fight to Reclaim Our Environment as a Basic Human Right* (New York: Scribner's, 1977)
Helmer, William S. "Blue Line Fever: An Introduction to New York's Forest Law," *One on One* 18 (Spring/Summer 1997): 9–12
Talbot, Allan R. *Power along the Hudson: The Storm King Case and the Birth of Environmentalism* (New York: Dutton, 1972)
Ward, Robert B. *New York State Government: What It Does, How It Works* (Albany: Rockefeller Institute Press, 2002)

William S. Helmer

Ephratah [EE-FRAY-TAH]. Town (pop 1,693) in S central Fulton Co. Settled *ca* 1720 by Palatine Germans, the town was formed from Palatine (Montgomery Co) in 1827. Much of the town is plateau land and not good for farming, but in the 19th century cheese was an important product, along with lumber. Industries in Ephratah hamlet (platted in 1803) over time included a tannery, a cheese factory, and paper, woolen, and knitting mills; other products manufactured were straw cardboard and gloves. A number of residents grew ginseng, which was dried at two locations of the Adirondack Ginseng Co at Garoga. In the early 21st century farming continues in the southernmost part of town, and the Amish community in Palatine has spread into Ephratah.

Three sites on the National Register of Historic Places are in Ephratah, both large Mohawk villages thought to date from the late 16th century. Saltsman's Hotel, built in the second quarter of the 19th century, is a landmark restaurant.

James Crawford

episcopacy controversy. Colonial political and religious issue. Anglican priests and some in the laity had long advocated the appointment of a bishop for the North American colonies to perform such essential functions as ordination, confirmation, and consecration of new churches. The movement was given particular impetus from a convention of Anglican clergy in New Jersey in 1766, which sent petitions to Anglican prelates in England to support the movement. Responding to dissenter charges that an American bishop presaged tithes, church courts, and enforced religious conformity, Anglicans asserted that an American bishop would exercise no political power. Skeptical dissenters, such as New York City lawyer and prominent Presbyterian layman William Livingston, expressed fears that a political bishop was being foisted on the colonies in the guise of a benign clergyman. He expressed his opposition in a series of powerful essays titled "The American Whig," which appeared in the *New-York Gazette* between 14 Mar 1768 and 15 May 1769. Anglican clergymen responded with their own column, "A Whip for the Whig," and this prompted a further Presbyterian response, probably by William Livingston, "A Kick for the Whipper." The Whig series was reproduced in Boston and Philadelphia papers, and the issue spilled over into the assembly elections of 1768 and 1769 in New York City and in the province. The DeLancey faction supported the Anglican position, while the Livingston faction secured support from dissenters. Although the Livingstons were defeated in both the city and provincial elections, the demand for a bishop lost appeal at home and from the ministry in London, and no American bishop was ever appointed before the Revolution. Nevertheless, the ferment created by this issue, linked with the fears of taxes, currency restrictions, and troop quartering, helped to increase New Yorkers' fears of Great Britain and to propel them into the American revolutionary movement. No bishop of the Church of England was consecrated in what became the United States until after the Revolution.

Bridenbaugh, Carl. *Mitre and Sceptre: Transatlantic Faith, Ideas, Personalities, and Politics, 1689–1775* (New York, Oxford Univ, 1962)

Cross, Arthur L. *The Anglican Episcopate and the American Colonies* (New York: Longmans, Green, 1902)

Milton M. Klein

Episcopalians. They are an offshoot of the Church of England, part of the worldwide Anglican communion. Like other Anglicans, Episcopalians understand their church as standing between Roman Catholicism and Protestantism. Governed by episcopal polity (bishops), with a set liturgy *(Book of Common Prayer)*, they employ much formal religious ceremony. Because of the Episcopal Church's long history, close connections with England, and the social prominence of many of its members, it has had a far more important role in the history of New York than its current modest numbers might suggest.

Early History

Though individual English settlers probably made private use of the *Book of Common Prayer* during the era of Dutch rule, the public presence of Episcopal worship began with the English occupation of New Amsterdam. Anglican services apparently began with Nicholas Van Rensselaer, the chaplain of Gov Richard Nicolls at Fort Amsterdam. The first recorded stipend for an Anglican minister is from 1674. Since Anglicanism was the established religion of England, many royal governors attempted to move it to a quasi-established status in the colony. Worship was regularized under Gov Edmund Andros in 1686, and during this decade there were unsuccessful attempts to enforce uniform Anglican worship on the colony. In 1693 Gov Benjamin Fletcher convinced the Provincial Assembly to pass the Ministries Act, providing public support for a "sufficient Protestant minister" in the counties of New York, Richmond, Westchester, and Queens. Although Fletcher intended to establish Anglicanism, the vagueness of the act's language frustrated his attempt. Of far greater importance was the founding of Trinity Church in 1697 and its receipt of the Queen's Farm, a 62-acre (25 ha) plot stretching from Fulton to Christopher Sts, in 1705. Trinity would serve as the mother church of New York Episcopal churches. Other early churches include St. Peter's in Albany (1708).

The association of New York Anglicans with the royal government continued in the 18th century. Anglican missionaries early in the century worked to convert the Iroquois Confederacy, motivated not only by religious factors but by hopes that an anglicized Iroquois could serve as

Church of Our Savior, also known as the Floating Church, located at the foot of Pike St on the East River, New York City, 1895.

a buffer between New York settlers and French opponents, who often attacked them with their Indian allies. These missions were particularly successful among the Mohawk, and in 1712 a chapel was built at Fort Hunter [now in Montgomery Co] on the Mohawk River. Anglicans were also active in establishing King's College (now Columbia University) in Manhattan. In 1754 Trinity Church provided the land on the condition that the president of the college be an Anglican (as remained the case until 1948) and that the *Book of Common Prayer* be used in its chapel. During the 1760s Anglicans championed the establishment of an episcopate for the colonies, and its clergy, on the whole, were strong defenders of the imperial cause. Lay members were far less univocal, and indeed three of the four New York signers of the Declaration of Independence were Anglicans. The partisan divisions at King's College, where 80% of the clerical faculty and just over 50% of the students were loyalists, may fairly represent the larger picture of New York Anglicanism. In 1775 there were 26 Anglican congregations in the colony.

The war had a devastating effect on New York Episcopalians. The British occupation of New York City for much of the war made it a haven for Anglican loyalists. The British withdrawal in 1783 following the Treaty of Paris included large numbers of Anglican clergy and laity, which began a transformation of Anglicanism in the state. Pro-patriot Whig Episcopalians wrested control of Trinity Church and elected Samuel Provoost as rector. He was elected bishop of the newly organized Protestant Episcopal Church in the State of New York in 1786 and was consecrated in 1787. In 1796 the Committee of the Protestant Episcopal Church for Propagating the Gospel in the State of New York was founded to send out missionaries and assist in planting churches throughout the state, especially among the growing upstate population.

The 19th Century

There was new vitality in the early 19th century among the state's Episcopalians. Much came from the energy infused by John Henry Hobart (1775–1830). Hobart, who became assistant bishop in 1811 and bishop in 1816, traveled extensively around the state. During his episcopacy, church growth in the region between Utica and Buffalo was three times faster than population growth. Hobart was also influential in founding institutions of learning. The General Theological Seminary in New York City (1817) was the first theological seminary in the Episcopal Church, and Geneva College (1822; now Hobart and William Smith Colleges) was an early center of upstate learning. In 1838 a separate diocese of Western New York was established to accommodate rapid growth. Eventually, additional dioceses were created for Long Island (1868), Albany (1869), Central New York (1869), and Rochester (1931).

During the mid–19th century many New York Episcopalians were affected by the Oxford Movement, or the Anglo-Catholic revival in Anglicanism. Controversial at the time, the revival introduced Neo-Gothic architecture, elaborations in worship, and renewed attention to monasteries, sisterhoods, and deaconesses. High Church and Low Church divisions would continue to roil the New York State Episcopal Church for many decades. The revival also coincided with an increased ministry to growing urban industrial areas, and large numbers of urban missions were established. During the 19th century the Episcopal Church became home to a small but important part of the African American community. Churches such as St. Philip's in Harlem became centers for leading African American families.

The 20th Century

In the late 19th and early 20th centuries, a spirit of anglophilism increased the church's importance. Several private schools were begun, and many impressive church buildings were constructed. New York Episcopalians increasingly focused on affairs of the larger world. Many, including William Rainsford and R. Heber Newton, became advocates of urban reform and proponents of the Social Gospel movement. During both world wars Episcopalians were strong advocates for the Allied cause. Samuel Shoemaker, rector of Calvary Church in Manhattan (1925–52), was an advocate of the Oxford Group with its concern for the conversion of the individual and the training of the individual's will as the basis for society's moral regeneration, and was a major influence on the founding of Alcoholics Anonymous. William Thomas Manning, Episcopal bishop of New York from 1921 to 1946, was a doughty High Church conservative who strictly upheld Episcopal doctrine. After World War II Episcopalians strongly participated in the struggle for the rights of racial minorities, and 20th-century Caribbean immigration increased the role of the Episcopal Church in the black community, especially after 1965. In the second half of the 20th century Episcopalians grappled with the same social and cultural changes many other groups faced: the growth of suburbanization and its effect on inner cities, the loss of privileged status by older Protestant religious groups, and changing attitudes toward race, gender, and sexuality. Women were first ordained in the Episcopal Church in 1976. At the start of the 21st century, church membership was just over 200,000.

Burrows, G. Sherman. *The Diocese of Western New York, 1897–1931* (Buffalo: Diocese of Western New York, 1935)

Galpin, William Freeman. *The Diocese of Central New York: The Huntington Years* (Boonville, NY: Willard Press, 1968)

Lindsley, James Elliot. *This Planted Vine: A Narrative History of the Episcopal Diocese of New York* (New York: Harper & Row, 1984)

Robert Bruce Mullin

equestrian sports. Sporting activity involving horses, usually with riders. Horse showing in New York State started in the early 1800s as scattered classes at cattle and agricultural shows. The classes were usually limited to stallions and mares of saddle and light draft type, and the horses were presented in hand and judged on their conformation. The only performance classes at these early fairs were plowing contests. The state's first modern horse show was the inaugural National Horse Show (1883), held at Madison Square Garden. Its organizers sought to provide a proving ground for a variety of horses, including practical workaday horses, which were ignored by other societies that catered to racehorses. The show included classes for hunters, jumpers, saddle horses, ponies, draft horses, high school dressage horses, driving horses, coaching teams, cobs, ladies' mounts, fire horses, and police horses. Considered too important to cancel during World War II, it was held at Madison Square Garden almost every fall (1883–1988, 1996–2001) until 2002, when it moved to the Palm Beach Polo Equestrian Club in Wellington, Fla.

Other important New York State shows include the Hampton Classic (Bridgehampton, Suffolk Co), which dates to the early 20th century, when it was known as the Southampton Horse Show, and Saratoga Festival of Dressage, held since 1990. The American Horse Shows Association (AHSA), formed in New York City as the Association of American Horse Shows to ensure clean and fair equestrian competition, has governed these competitions and others nationwide since 1917. When the US Cavalry turned international equestrian competition over to civilians in 1936, the AHSA became the US representative to the International Equestrian Federation, the governing body for the Olympics and other international competitions. The AHSA (renamed US Equestrian in 2003) was headquartered in New York City until 1998.

Hunter/jumper and dressage shows make up only a fraction of the equestrian sports held in New York State. By the turn of the 21st century, competitions evolving out of the work of western ranch horses, such as cutting, reining, and team penning, were popular, as were carriage driving events and long-distance competitions like endurance racing and competitive trail riding. Combined training events, wherein horse and rider must complete a dressage test, a cross-country jumping course, and a show jumping course, were also popular. The New York State Fair and most county fairs host horse shows with classes for a variety of horses, and competitions for disabled riders are held throughout the state. New York State also hosts hundreds of shows catering to specific breeds, with quarter horses, Appaloosas, pintos, Arabians, Morgans, saddlebreds, and miniature horses among the most numerous.

Equine Journal (1998–)

Northeast Equine Journal (1988–98)

Elizabeth Redkey

Erie Canal

Origins

The roots of the Erie Canal lie in New York State's unique geography, which creates a network of natural waterways and lowlands offering low-level passage between the Atlantic seaboard and the Great Lakes basin. About 50 miles (80 km) north of New York City's deepwater harbor, the southerly flowing Hudson River cuts through the Highlands segment of the 1,500 mi (2,410 km) Appalachian barrier. About 100 miles (161 km) farther north (roughly 10 mi/16 km upstream of Albany), the Mohawk joins the Hudson and extends 100 miles west to the Oneida Carrying Place, across which is the headwater of Wood Creek. This small steam leads to Oneida Lake and then to the Oneida River, which joins the Oswego and Seneca Rivers at Three-River Point. The Oswego flows north to Lake Ontario; the Seneca provides passage to the larger Finger Lakes to the west and south. The corridor's strategic importance was recognized first by American Indians and then by European

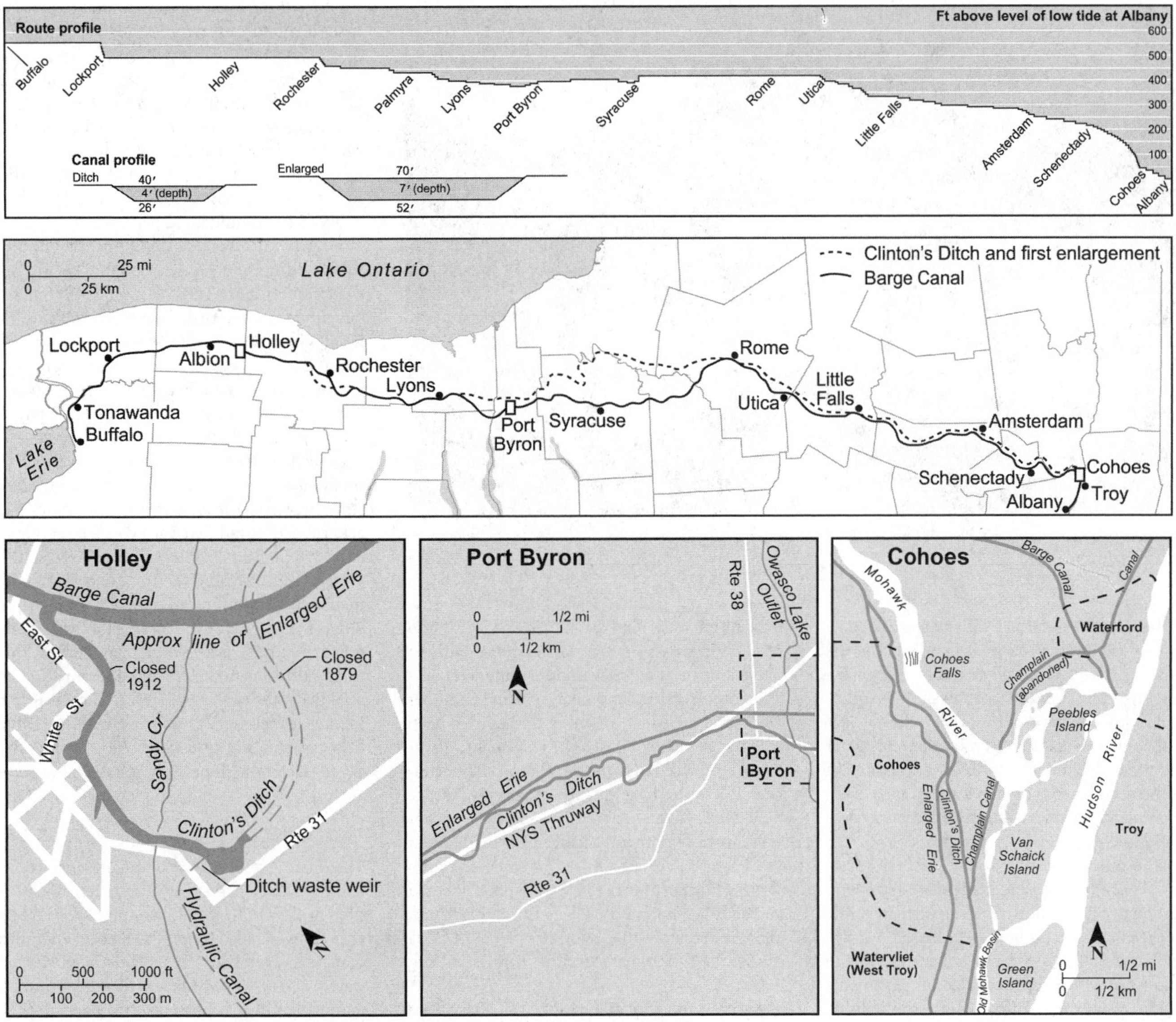

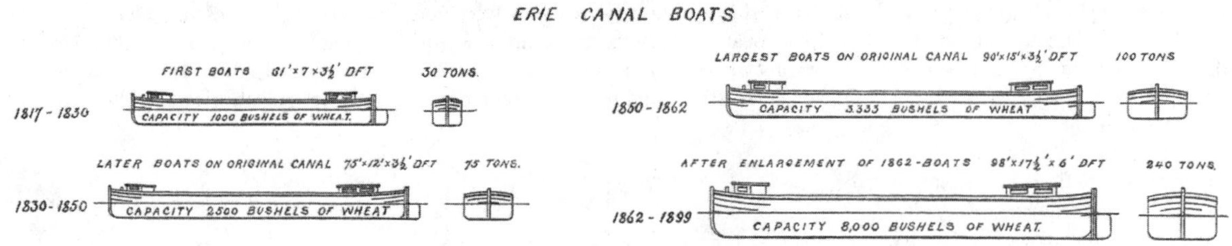

SOURCE: Drawings of Erie Canal boats from *Report of the Committee on Canals of New York State* (1900), following p 56.

travelers in the 17th century. The establishment of a French presence in the Niagara Frontier in the late 17th century was countered by an English trading post at Oswego in 1727. Military campaigns during the colonial wars and the American Revolution highlighted the significance of the corridor. Water transport set a standard rarely matched by wagons and stages, tied to primitive roads. In 1783 George Washington stood at the eastern end of Oneida Lake, saw the potential of this corridor and hoped others would see the same.

There were several false starts to improve the water route. Irish immigrant and engineer Christopher Colles called upon the state legislature in 1785 to create better navigation on the Mohawk. In 1792 the semiprivate Western Inland Lock Navigation Co was incorporated by the legislature. With substantial support from the state, the company undertook construction of three independent canals to bypass hindrances in the natural waterway at Little Falls (Herkimer Co), German Flatts (Herkimer Co), and Rome (Oneida Co). Elsewhere wing dams deepened water flow to a foot or more at shoals in the Mohawk. A series of meanders in Wood Creek were cut off, thereby shortening the route. Deeper draft and longer vessels could now make the Schenectady-Oswego route more dependably. By the beginning of the 19th century, the company had made the water route from the Hudson to Oswego more efficient.

These improvements proved insufficient to draw the attention of the growing population of Central and Western New York that wanted a commercial link to the seaboard. Between 1800 and 1810 the number of residents between Schenectady and the Niagara Frontier increased from 95,000 to 226,000, and substantial numbers looked north to the St. Lawrence River area and Montreal as the convenient market. Others turned south to the Susquehanna and the rising port of Baltimore. The War of 1812 highlighted the deficiencies with the central route. Military campaigns that revolved around the state's northern and western borders depended on the timely delivery of requisite supplies, and those deliveries proved arduous and expensive despite the navigational improvements. Cohoes Falls on the Mohawk north of Albany was a major impediment that forced traffic to take an overland

Canalboats crossing the aqueduct over the Genesee River in Rochester, early 20th century.

trek between tidewater at Albany and Schenectady. A different approach was needed. The use of natural waterways was gradually recognized as being inherently flawed given inadequate technology for controlling water flows. Seasonal- and storm-induced variations in water conditions remained a constant nuisance if not threat to boaters of larger and heavier craft. A completely artificial, regulated channel was viewed as the only viable solution.

The resources available to the Western Inland Lock Navigation Co were inadequate. Even with additional state support, funding was constantly insufficient to accomplish its chartered goals. The Company's most important success was to demonstrate that significant accomplishments would require the resources and accountability of a totally public enterprise. A state or federal public works effort seemed justified, indeed necessary, if New York State was to connect the seaboard with the interior. Efforts to gain federal support proved futile. The canal would be built from New York State funds.

Finally, the War of 1812 solidified the realization that a commercial, political, and potential military competitor would remain in Canada. Even before the war, commercial interests in central and western New York State eyed the economic advantages of Montreal. Albany and Washington understood, as did parties on the frontier, that political allegiance could easily follow commercial connections. To strengthen the union, the proposed inland waterway must be an "Erie" canal across the state to Lake Erie rather than a connector to Lake Ontario that might funnel commerce to the north. That commerce was becoming significant as Central and Western New York began growing out of its frontier economy. Further, the evidence was clear that the Old Northwest would need an outlet for the products of its fertile lands.

The molding of the new approach began with Jesse Hawley, a grain merchant from Geneva (Ontario Co). He provided the most visible and remarkable prediction of a completely inland canal. Close on the heels of his 1807–8 newspaper essays was the first of a series of state legislative enactments that led the way to the Erie's final authorization in 1817. The 1808 legislation resulted in surveys by James Geddes of both an Ontario route to Oswego and a completely inland route. A critical moment came in December 1808 when Geddes discovered that the deep Irondequoit Valley east of the Genesee River could be crossed in a manner that would permit Lake Erie water to supply the canal as far east as the Seneca River. A perhaps no less significant political development occurred in 1810, when the state established a board of canal commissioners. Support for the Erie Canal had reached to nearly all points on the political spectrum, enough so to draw the attention of De Witt Clinton, at the time a state senator from New York City.

The movement for a canal appears to have been rapid and assured, but to supporters at the time, it appeared in constant jeopardy. In December 1815 advocates for the canal met in New York City. Clinton's famous memorial came from that meeting. His strong and reasoned arguments in support of the canal sparked a flood of petitions to the legislature from across the state. Supporters of the canal bill (in a simplification of a complex political situation) mainly were Clintonians who backed the political ambitions of De Witt Clinton, along with members of the Federalist Party. The majority Jeffersonian Republicans tended to be split on the issue, but in the end enough of their ranks were brought behind the bill by belated supporter and influential party member Martin Van Buren. Still, voices of caution, if not opposition, held up final legislative approval for construction until April 1817. Opponents tended to be centered in New York City and the Hudson Valley. It is ironic that the city was so solidly opposed because once it was completed, few, if any, communities in the state benefited more than New York City. The threat of new taxation to pay for the project seemed to drive the opposition.

The act of 15 April 1817 that authorized the building of the Erie Canal and Champlain Canal (the latter from the Hudson to Lake Champlain) also created a fund to pay for construction managed by a board called the Commissioners of the Canal Fund. The fund was to be derived from an increased duty on salt, a tax on steamboat passengers, proceeds from certain lotteries, duties on auction sales, grants of land and other donations, and a tax on land located within 25 miles (40 km) of the two canals. Tolls collected as soon as each canal section was opened also would help pay the cost of construction. In addition, the fund commissioners could issue canal bonds against state credit of up to $400,000 per year.

The First Canal

The planning for what popularly was called Clinton's Ditch had already been extensive by the time of the 1817 groundbreaking. Repeated but even more detailed surveys created an alignment that was essentially independent of natural waterways. It would remain dependent on the natural landscape, however, for water and the mechanisms to deliver it. The channel of the canal, the first of three generations of Erie Canal, amounted to what one 20th-century historian has called a "wet dish rag" across the state. Just 4 feet (1.2 m) deep, its 28 ft (8.5 m) wide flat

Clinton Square in Syracuse, early 20th century.

Entering the Lock, by Edward Lamson Henry, 1899.

bottom angled up to a 40 ft (12.2 m) maximum width at the waterline. A towing path was established along one bank to accommodate the horse or mule teams that pulled canal craft along the Erie's 363 miles (584 km). Ground was formally broken for the "Great Western Canal" near Rome on 4 July 1817. The canal opened from Rome to Utica on 19 Oct 1819 and was extended to Syracuse on 4 July 1820. Work proceeded in both directions. Eastward, the canal was opened to Little Falls by 1821, to Schenectady by 1822, and to Albany by 1823. The westward excavations were also underway. The Montezuma Marshes, difficult to cross because of quicksand, were reached in 1822, and on 1 Oct 1823, a boat traveled the canal from Rochester to Albany. The western parts were then completed to Brockport (Monroe Co) and then to Lockport (Niagara Co) by the end of 1824. The Buffalo to Lockport section along with the latter town's famous lock complex were completed the following year. The full extent of the Erie Canal opened on 26 Oct 1825 with much fanfare, including what became known as the "Wedding of the Waters." Clinton led a delegation of dignitaries in escorting barrels of Lake Erie water from Buffalo to New York Harbor.

Management of the water supply for the Erie Canal is perhaps its greatest but most overlooked engineering achievement. Lake Erie was a natural source of water. To use it, the canal's water level had to be kept lower than the lake, driving the decision to cut through miles of hard rock at the top of the Niagara Escarpment to Lockport. Lake Erie water flowed east down a slight decline, filling the canal's prism as far as the Seneca River, roughly 160 miles (260 km). In the eastern third of the state, the Mohawk River was the primary water supply. In central New York State, the terrain demanded two summit levels, high sections on the canal where water emptied to the east and west via locks. Each required its own constant source of dependable water. The short Jordan Summit, west of Syracuse, was fed from creeks and lakes to the south. The Rome Summit was maintained by tapping several north-flowing streams and the Mohawk River. The latter was special because of its remarkable length, from Frankfort (Herkimer Co) to near Syracuse. This level terrain would thus be free of expensive and time-consuming locks. Shortened by the mid-19th-century enlargement, Rome Summit remains as part of the present-day Erie Canal.

Aqueducts, locks, and other engineering structures were soon recognized as marvels of the day. The first generation of Erie Canal aqueducts was one of two ways that the Erie crossed intersecting rivers or creeks. These arched stone bridges carried the Erie's channel over, and independent of, such wide waterways as the Mohawk and Genesee Rivers and numerous smaller creeks. At some locations, however, engineers opted to cross these rivers and creeks at grade. For instance, when boats came to the Schoharie Creek crossing, they entered through guard locks into the dammed-up, slack-water channel of the creek. Teams of horses or mules accompanied the boats alongside on a bridge. The slack-water approach was used at a handful of locations, all proving difficult to maintain and all replaced by aqueducts with the first enlargement.

Locks raised and lowered boats nearly 700 feet (210 m) to compensate for terrain changes as the canal made the over 560 ft (170 m) descent from Lake Erie to tidewater. These 83 single-chambered locks of hewn stone with wooden gates made the canal work. For the boater, there was a downside. The 90 x 15 ft (27.4 x 4.6 m) dimensions restricted what could go through. Each lock, depending on the expertise or attitude of the lock operator, consumed precious time as boaters crossed the state during the summer season. If one lock failed, traffic halted until repairs were completed. These complications were worse where the terrain demanded clusters of locks, such as the combined locks at Lockport, which became the most famous of the Erie's engineering achievements. To scale the ridge of the Niagara Escarpment, Nathan Roberts designed a paired flight of five combined locks. Nowhere else on the original canal were locks doubled. If one of the five locks on one side broke, the other side could still move boats. The Cohoes Falls at the eastern end of the Mohawk created the need for multiple clusters of locks, slowing the passage of boats. Although the first enlargement of the canal reduced the number of locks from 23 to 18, the Cohoes stretch remained wearing and frustrating. During the end-of-season rush to get harvests to tidewater and market, the 10 mi (16 km) Cohoes stretch could take more than a day of the usual seven-day trip across the state.

Enlargement

Initial efforts toward the first enlargement began with the recognition that the locks were the bottlenecks of the system. In 1833 the canal commissioners recommended doubling the locks east of Syracuse, the busiest portion of the waterway. Two years later and before any doubling occurred, authorization came for a more aggressive approach. The first enlargement aimed to increase the width of the channel to 70 feet (21.3 m) and the depth to 7 feet (2.1 m), and to double a new generation of larger locks whose new dimensions would be 110 x 18 feet (33.5 x 5.5 m).

The first enlargement was launched in the midst of the strong economic situation of the early 1830s. A dramatic pause occurred in the depressed 1840s because of the Stop and Tax Law of 1842. The gusto of the first enlargement's early years began to stagger as the nation entered a severe economic depression. The bust of the late 1830s left the state with an unprecedented debt and disappearing revenues. The debt from enlargement bonds frightened enough politicians, primarily Democratic ones, into retrenchment. Overnight, contractors were told to stop work, including that on nearly completed structures, for fear that the state would default. The contemporary Whig philosophy of greater pump priming by continuing with the enlargement with its employment and improvement of the economic infrastructure was placed on hold. A few years later, work was authorized to complete a few partially built structures, such as the Schoharie Aqueduct. Travelers along the canal in the mid-1840s would have seen a sorry situation as they observed abandoned work on enlarged locks and aqueducts and, in contrast, failing first-generation structures. The work halt lasted from 1842 through 1847, when the new state Constitution of 1846 authorized construction to recommence. The first enlargement was declared completed by New York State in 1862, although some work continued for at least another decade.

Though generally following an east-to-west program, the first enlargement did target certain first-generation structures most in need of replacement. One was the Genesee River Aqueduct in Rochester, which had been built, as had several other nearby canal structures, with a type of sandstone that disintegrated upon exposure to air. New York State's abundant supply of good-quality limestone was now exclusively used. Even the humble channel of the Erie grew stronger with the first enlargement. As originally constructed, the Erie hugged many of the hillsides across the state. The technique was cost effective since the hill served as one of the two banks. Additionally, a serpentine course was followed to avoid the expensive construction of locks or deep land cuts or high embankments. Improved engineering tactics and better resources meant that many of the curves in the first Erie Canal could be eliminated, reducing the total length of the Erie from 363 miles (584 km) to just over 350 miles (563 km). That reduction could mean another entire and profitable transit during the navigation season. These changes were not always well received at the local level. A community such as Pilgrimport (Wayne Co) was left several miles from the new alignment, having grown up at the northern end of one of the many abandoned loops of the first Erie Canal as it negotiated the drumlin fields west of Syracuse. Likewise, the commercial interests of Port Byron (Cayuga Co) fought a decade-long losing battle with the state over the relocation of the Enlarged Erie to the north of the village. In contrast, the petitions of Rome residents were satisfied when the enlargement passed through that village; the original canal bypassed the community, with the effect of slowing its growth.

Builders of the Canal

The engineering experiences from the construction of the first Erie Canal made these midcentury improvements possible. The engineers of the Erie Canal learned largely by doing and learned so well that the canal would later be designated as "America's First School of Engineering." Benjamin Wright (1770–1842), the Erie's first chief engineer and sometimes called the Father of American Civil Engineering, began as a land surveyor. His expertise was sought by states, companies, canals, and railroads after the Erie proved successful. The former Canastota (Madison Co) schoolteacher Nathan Roberts (1776–1852), besides designing the Lockport locks on the original canal, worked on the enlargement as well. He built canals and railroads across the United States. John B. Jervis (1795–1885) of Rome began under Wright and later gained fame on the privately built Delaware and Hudson Canal and some of the nation's first railroads. Canvass White (1790–1834) had traveled to England in 1817 to study its canals and then worked on the Erie Canal. White's discovery in Central New York of a particular type of limestone essential to make hydraulic cement, which hardened under water, was instrumental to the success of the Erie's structures. Union College graduate Squire Whipple (1804–88) assisted with surveys on the Erie. His studies and designs of bridges for the canal set the standards nationally for such engineering work. The Whipple bridges, whether of wood or iron, were notable landmarks on the canal.

The roster of contributors to the construction and rebuilding of the Erie Canal is lengthy. Throughout the canal's history, the actual work was accomplished by private contractors hired by the state. Many remained committed to canal work in New York State and nearby regions. For the first Erie, contractors were predominantly farmers and merchants along the Erie's route. They found and employed the laborers who figured so much in canal folklore. One of the first comments about this workforce came in early 1819, when the canal commissioners announced that "three-fourths of all the laborers were born among us." Although most lived along the canal route, some came from New York City and from adjoining states. The composition shifted dramatically to foreign immigrants as the easy work of the beginning was replaced with such labor-intensive projects like the Lockport locks and the Montezuma Marshes. The number of workers exceeded what local farms could provide. Certainly by the time of the first enlargement, the cliché of the Irish building the Erie Canal rang true. Census schedules from the period document large camps of Irish canal workers who had been in the county for only a month or two. Other nationalities, such as Francophone Canadians and Germans, were also represented. Often thousands of laborers toiled on canal construction for between 75¢ and $1.25 a day. Rates were based upon skill. The length of the work year depended mainly on the weather and the coming of winter.

Boom Times

By 1833 there were over 1,600 canalboats registered with the state. Custom designed to the Erie's dimensions, these horse- or mule-pulled boats were nearly all geared toward cargo rather than people, even though the image of the passenger-carrying packet boat still dominates canal folklore. Annual revenues from the Erie doubled from $492,000 in 1825 to over $1 million in 1831, reaching $2 million in 1844 and $3 million only three years later. By 1832 the sum of tolls exceeded the $7.5 million cost of canal construction. The tolls had an additional benefit for the state. Structured around weight and type of cargo, the toll schedule design was frequently altered by state officials to promote New York interests. Over $120 million was collected before tolls were abolished in 1882, which was almost double the cost of building, maintaining, and enlarging the Erie in the 19th century.

By the mid-1830s, the volume and type of cargo on the Erie Canal pointed to even greater traffic in the future. The canal made markets and connections among them profitable. Syracuse salt now more easily found its way to midwestern markets, and production soared. Grain from the recently settled Midwest began to funnel onto the Erie at Buffalo. Communities prospered, or remade themselves, as canal ports along the Albany-to-Buffalo axis. Port Byron changed its name from Bucksville in 1824 in recognition of canal-induced prosperity. The Erie Canal itself was a destination for numerous tourists before the railroad pulled away such traffic. The canal offered unprecedented convenient and predictable access for the business, immigrant, and tourist traveler.

The Erie Canal was the catalyst for boom economies, especially where it touched unique combinations of geographic assets. Rochester and Buffalo went from hamlet, or in the case of Lockport from forest, to thriving urban center. In a waterpowered economy, the great falls of the Genesee at Rochester was sought early on to help process the grains and lumber from the fertile valley to the south. Lockport had an artificial waterfall brought to its doorstep by the Erie's surplus water as it reached the escarpment from Lake Erie. And Buffalo was the western terminus of the Erie Canal and, more important, the location where cargo was transferred between canalboats and lake vessels. In the 1830s Buffalo real estate values soared.

Population along the canal route increased dramatically between 1820 and 1840. During those years New York State's population increased by 77%, to nearly 2.5 million people, and New York City nearly doubled the state's rate of growth with a population of almost 313,000 by 1840. Cities along the Erie Canal, however, did much better; 1820–40 rates of increase included Albany's 167%, Utica's 330%, Syracuse's 507%, Buffalo's 769%, and Rochester's 1,244%. Albany in 1840 was the 9th largest city in the United States, with Buffalo, Rochester, Troy, and Utica all among the top 30. Rural communities prospered also, especially those within a half-day's wagon ride of the canal. Farmers became much more market oriented, and many exhibited their newly found prosperity by erecting new farmhouses in the popular Greek Revival style. Some prospered far more than others, thereby increasing economic diversity and, less directly, social stratification and tension.

With travelers moving along the Erie corridor and population increasing, the waterway carried ideas and movements, as reflected, for example, in religion and reform. Charles Grandison Finney, the great revivalist of the pre–Civil War era, used the canal to spread his message, helping Central and Western New York earn the sobriquet of the Burned-over District. One crusade that took root along the Erie corridor was abolitionism. Aided by the preaching of Finney and others and by the settlement of New Englanders along the canal route, the drive to free slaves developed into a potent social force in many canal towns and adjoining countrysides, especially between Utica and Buffalo. While numbers are elusive, evidence indicates that some fugitive slaves used the canal as part of their route to Canada along the Underground Railroad.

Impact

The Erie Canal was hailed from all quarters as a remarkable success. Sectionalism within New York State that had nearly condemned the canal's original construction now cast a new light. Nearly every corner of the state was infected with "canal fever" from the Erie's accomplishments. Lateral canals from the northern and southern regions to connect to the Erie were demanded; soon the construction of many of them was underway, with the expectation that they would join the Champlain Canal (completed in 1823) as economic feeders to the state's main line. Planning for these additions began with the 1825 "Grand Canal" Act. The Oswego Canal, reestablishing the colonial trade route, was completed in 1828. The state's Cayuga and Seneca Canal, completed the same year, improved upon the work of the 1813 Seneca Lock Navigation Co. Between 1833 and 1855 six more lateral canals were in operation, although based upon weaker economic and technological foundations. They included the Chemung, Crooked Lake, Oneida Lake, Chenango, Genesee Valley, and Black River Canals. While most would be abandoned by New York State in 1878, the first three remain in operation in the early 21st century as part of the New York State Canal System. This canal network created unprecedented possibilities and growth for communities at Binghamton, Ithaca, Elmira, Boonville (Oneida Co), and other towns miles away from the Erie.

The Erie Canal clearly influenced areas beyond New York State. The same canal fever that plunged New York State into an unmatched public works program led to extensive canal construction elsewhere, not all wisely undertaken and none as successful. Ohio imitated New York State's efforts. De Witt Clinton himself dug the first shovel of dirt for Ohio in the same year that the Erie was completed. Ohio's citizens, like those in Indiana and Illinois, saw in the Erie a model of unprecedented growth. Pennsylvania and Virginia, in trying to match the Erie's access to the interior, also learned too late that the Erie Canal benefited from a unique topography and was the right economic tool at exactly the right time. The most successful of the competitors was the nearest. In direct response to the Erie's capture of midwestern trade, construction began on the Welland Canal in 1825 to connect Lakes Erie and Ontario across Upper Canada [now Ont]. These strategic initiatives point to the Erie's greatest national significance. It almost single-handedly established the commercial and thus political connections that tied the Midwest to the Northeast. The Erie was opportune. In the early 19th century, the regional linkages were still being forged, and the Erie shaped them.

By the late 19th century, although volume continued to increase, competition from the railroads had seriously eroded the centrality of the Erie Canal to the national economy. The canal had been competing with railroads since the early 1830s. The competition did not become serious until 20 years later, when single lines crossed the state from the Hudson River to Lake Erie. The New York and Erie Railroad was opened in 1851 between the lower Hudson Valley and Lake Erie. Two years later the New York Central was organized, combining eight short lines between Albany and Buffalo. Even then the canal held its own until about 1870, when the railroads began to capture noticeable amounts of the canal's mainstay: low-value, bulk goods traffic. In an effort to remain competitive, all canal tolls were abolished in 1883. The lateral canals were not nearly as competitive, and several were closed in 1878. That same year the Canal Commission was abolished; in its place, the state superintendent of public works was charged with repair, navigation, improvement, and construction of canals. Improvement and construction were to be done in consultation with the state engineer and surveyor. The superintendent also had membership on the Canal Board.

The Barge Canal

The Barge Canal was the Erie's last great rebuilding. It was preceded by the failed efforts of the 1895 improvement. The late 1890s work was a final attempt to enhance the working of the Enlarged Erie by increasing its depth to 9 feet (2.7 m) and raising its bridges for greater vertical clearance. By 1898, with only two-thirds of the work completed, the $9 million original appropriation had been expended and work on the second enlargement came to a halt. The 1895 improvement demonstrated the need for a more radical redesign of the Erie. In 1903 the people of New York State authorized bonding for such a new approach, to be called the Barge Canal. The building of the canal continued to attract newcomers to the region. At Lockport, for instance, a community of African Americans was brought in by the contractor for the skilled but dangerous tunneling work required for the new Barge locks. Elsewhere, Irish workers were replaced by Italians and other southern Europeans.

Keg used by Gov De Witt Clinton in the "Wedding of the Waters," the opening ceremony of the Erie Canal, on 26 Oct 1825, during which he poured water from Lake Erie into the Atlantic Ocean.

Completed in 1918, the new Barge Canal System included the Erie, Champlain, Oswego, and Cayuga and Seneca Canals. It is the system in operation in the early 21st century. The redesign as the Barge Canal was conceived as a contrast to an even more dramatic rebuilding. One proposal at the time was for a ship canal that would have required more costly deeper and wider channels to enable oceangoing vessels to transit between the seaboard and the Great Lakes. Economically, barges were felt to make more sense. As had happened during the century before, goods would be transferred between barges and lake vessels at Buffalo and larger freighters in New York Harbor.

The Barge Canal was revolutionary in other ways. It left the Erie's 19th-century artificial channel and returned traffic where possible to natural, now canalized waterways such as the Mohawk, Oneida, and Seneca Rivers. A byproduct of that change was the setting of new eastern and western ends of the main line. No longer did the canal enter tidewater at Albany; rather, the eastern end was established at Waterford (Saratoga Co). At the western end, Tonawanda (Erie Co) replaced Buffalo as the terminus. The entrances to both ends were controlled by locks operated by the federal Army Corps of Engineers, based at Troy (Rensselaer Co) and Black Rock (now Buffalo). Instead of using technology based on cut stone and animal power, the engineers turned to the new tools offered by concrete and electricity to build and operate structures. Mules no longer were needed to pull boats back and forth across the state. Steam-powered tugs and self-propelled barges defined the character of this next generation.

Yet the Barge Canal remained true to one of the principles that had guided the Erie from the beginning: that New York State government had a duty to maintain and protect its economic infrastructure. The designers of the Barge Canal eyed the privately operated railroads as competitors if not threats to a level playing field of economic interests. The state-operated canals have provided a publicly owned transport infrastructure through the strategic east-west transportation corridor across the upstate region. It was a principle that was restated in the mid-1930s when the state, with the assistance of the federal government, deepened the Erie between Waterford and Oswego to 14 feet (4.3 m).

The Barge Canal never matched the capacity of 10 million tons (9 million MT) that its designers had envisioned. Some felt that the canal suffered when the federal government assumed control of its operation at the end of World War I. Railroad interests dominated that takeover and perhaps hampered its development. Peak annual tonnage for the Barge Canal System did not come until the mid-1950s, and the figures fell well below those of the 19th-century Erie. The completion of the St. Lawrence Seaway in the late 1950s removed grain and other commodities that had been an essential part of Barge Canal tonnage. Pipelines took over the transport of fuel oil. The last petroleum shipments ceased with the end of the Cold War and with the closures of Griffiss AFB at Rome and Plattsburgh AFB. The *Day Peckinpaugh,* the first vessel specifically designed for the Barge Canal, became the last regularly scheduled industrial commercial vessel on the system. It hauled its last load of cement to Rome from Oswego in 1994. New York State's four large canals—the Erie, Oswego, Champlain, and Cayuga and Seneca Canals—total roughly 450 miles (725 km) of waterway. They still connect the Hudson with Lakes Erie, Ontario, and Champlain, and with the two largest Finger Lakes, Cayuga and Seneca. Commercial traffic on the canals presently consists of a few tour and dinner boats. Most current traffic is of privately owned pleasure craft.

In 1992 the state legislature transferred authority for the operation of the canals from the Department of Transportation to the New York State Thruway Authority and its subsidiary, the New York State Canal Corporation. The Barge Canal System was renamed the New York State Canal System, and its four canals reverted to their original names. The legislature also created the Canal Recreationway Commission, signaling future directions for the waterways. The Canal Recreationway Plan, completed in 1995, set forth three basic goals: preserve the best of the past, enhance recreational activities, and encourage appropriate economic development. Trails for hiking and cycling have been built along major portions of abandoned sections of the old Erie Canal as well as adjacent to sections of the modern Erie. A number of canal landings are under construction that are similar to the one at Fairport (Monroe Co), where shops, restaurants, and boat rentals offer tourists diverse recreational opportunities. Marinas are being improved and constructed to accommodate the needs of boaters. How successful the effort to make the Barge Canal System into a major tourist and recreation attraction remains to be determined. Soon after the formal completion of the Barge Canal in 1918, its premier engineer, Frank Williams, stated that he "did not expect the canal ever to be entirely completed." It will always be a work in progress as it adjusts to the needs and visions of New York State and its residents.

See also BONDED INDEBTEDNESS.

Edmonds, Walter D. *Rome Haul* (1929; repr Syracuse: Syracuse Univ Press, 1987)
Garrity, Richard G. *Canal Boatman: My Life on Upstate Waterways* (Syracuse: Syracuse Univ Press, 1977)
Larkin, F. Daniel. *A Short History of New York State Canals* (Fleischmanns, NY: Purple Mountain Press, 1998)
Larkin, F. Daniel, Julie Daniels, and Jean West, eds. *Erie Canal: New York's Gift to the Nation: A Document-Based Teacher Resource* (Peterborough, NH, 2001)
McFee, Michele. *A Long Haul: A History of the New York State Barge Canal* (Fleischmanns, NY: Purple Mountain Press, 1998)
O'Malley, Charles T. *Low Bridges and High Water on the New York State Barge Canal* (Ellenton, Fla: Diamond Mohawk Publishing, 1991)
Shaw, Ronald E. *Erie Water West: A History of the Erie Canal, 1792–1854* (Lexington: Univ of Kentucky Press, 1966)
———. *Canals for a New Nation: The Canal Era in the United States, 1790–1860* (Lexington: Univ of Kentucky Press, 1990)
Sheriff, Carol. *The Artificial River: The Erie Canal and the Paradox of Progress, 1817–1862* (New York: Hill & Wang, 1996)
Whitford, Noble E. *History of the Canal System of the State of New York,* 2 vols (Albany: Brandow Printing, 1906)
———. *History of the Barge Canal of New York State* (Albany: J. B. Lyon, 1922)
Wyld, Lionel D. *Low Bridge! Folklore and the Erie Canal* (Syracuse: Syracuse Univ Press, 1962)

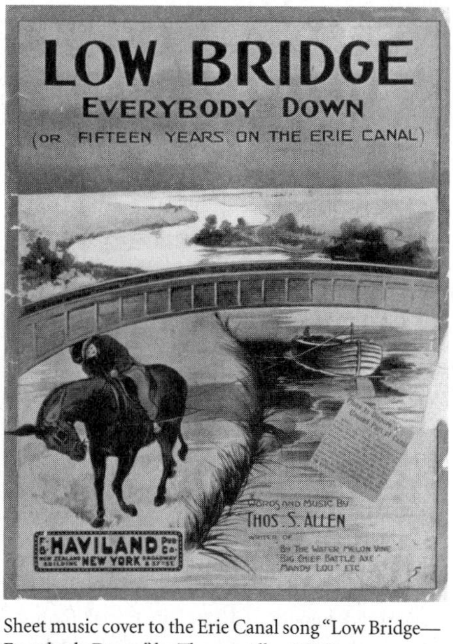

Sheet music cover to the Erie Canal song "Low Bridge—Everybody Down," by Thomas Allen, 1913.

Erie Canal in folklore and the arts. The builders of the Erie Canal were well aware of the symbolic significance of their creation. The opening on 26 Oct 1825 was announced by the roar of gunfire. Placed 10 miles (16 km) apart, the cannons fired sequentially upon the sound of the nearest cannon, covering the 363 mi (584 km) distance from Buffalo to New York City in less than 90 minutes. Gov De Witt Clinton boarded the *Seneca Chief,* part of a small flotilla of boats that made the initial trip on the canal. Named after the Iroquois nation whose dispossession from most of Western New York made the building of the canal possible, the boat completed the journey in nine days. Foxes, wolves, and raccoons were kept onboard to symbolize the state's frontier. In the cabin of the *Seneca Chief* was a painting by George Catlin, depicting Clinton in a Roman toga opening the canal locks, encouraged by his peers, Hercules and Neptune. When Clinton's party entered New York Harbor, the Grand Canal Celebration reached its climax. The *Seneca Chief* was met by a small fleet of boats, and Clinton poured a keg of Lake Erie water into New York Harbor, effecting the "Wedding of the Waters." Other participants added the water of other rivers, including the Nile and the Amazon. The Erie Canal was hailed as one of humankind's greatest works of art, and the Grand Canal Celebration was remembered in paintings, lithographs, wallpaper, commemorative medals, fine ceramic vases, and engraved silver, and numerous original airs and odes were composed. Charles Gilfert composed "The Grand Canal March." S. Woodworth's "The Meeting of the Waters of Hudson and Erie" added new lyrics to a popular Thomas Moore ballad. Since 1825 the celebration of the Erie Canal has continued in various media; in painting, music, theater, and literature.

The *Day Peckinpaugh,* built in 1921 for use on the Barge Canal.

FOLKLORE

By the time of the gala opening, boatmen ("canallers" or "canawlers") were already plying opened sections of the canal. "Clinton's Ditch" was dug at first by Yankee settlers under contract and later worked primarily by Irish immigrants, celebrated in the ballad "Paddy on the Canal," which appeared in 1853. The "jigger-boss" distributed whiskey to the workers as often as 16 times a day, and the improved "Brainard Barrow," contrived by Jeremiah Brainard of Rome (Oneida Co), made earth hauling a bit easier. Workers sang as they cut through the marshlands:

We are digging the ditch through the mire;
Through the mud and the slime and the mire,
  by heck!
And the mud is our principal hire;
Up our pants, in our shirts, down our neck,
  by heck!
We are digging the ditch through the gravel;
So the people and freight can travel.

Boat captains were often also owners, and cooks were, frequently, their wives. Other crew included steersmen and drivers (hoggies). Although romanticized in songs like the merry "I Was a Boatsman's Boy," canal life was difficult, and canallers were often disdained. This taunt was one of many that were hollered from bridges: "Hoggie on the towpath / Five cents a day / Picking up horse-balls / To eat along the way!" Low bridges, if unexpected, could cause serious injury, and a common vaudeville motif in the region had a highfalutin society type drop instinctively when "low bridge" was shouted, exposing the person's origins.

Fights often took place at locks as boats vied for position, and some captains hired steersmen for their fighting ability. By the 1880s the side-cut area of Watervliet (Albany Co) was known as the Barbary Coast of the East, with bars including the Black Rag and the Tub of Blood. The best-known product of this environment was Watervliet bar owner Paddy Ryan, born in County Tipperary, Ireland, who became heavyweight champion of the world after defeating the English champion Joe Goss in 1880 in an 87-round bare-knuckle fight.

Dog and cock fighting were common entertainments, but milder amusements like caterpillar racing also were pursued during long eventless stretches like the "Long Level" from Frankfort (Herkimer Co) to Salina (Onondaga Co), almost 70 miles (113 km) without a lock. Dining was austere, and several ballads complain of meal after meal of Black Rock pork, apparently a generic term originating with the preserved meat sold at Elijah Leonard's grocery in Black Rock (Erie Co) around 1840. Cooks, typically the only women on the canal, were sometimes described as attractive, but others reputedly had breath that could open locks, according to the ballads.

From the 1830s, advertisements for (Dr George W.) Merchant's Gargling Oil, based in Lockport (Niagara Co), could be seen on barns and walls for the length of the canal. Actually a liniment, it came in one version for mules and horses and another for people. Some barges attempted to edify canal culture: a floating museum with wax figures, paintings, and natural history specimens set forth in the canal's earliest years. Other educational schemes were more blatantly commercial. In the 1880s Oakes Anderson traveled the canal, charging admission to see a 65 ft (19.8 m) embalmed whale and a professional lecturer. Anderson's enterprise appeared, modified, in a 1932 story by Walter D. Edmonds, apparently passed down as a tale.

In general, these tales were fairly implausible. A driver named McCarthy, a recurring figure, had his mules run away, and he dragged his barge for miles, not noticing when it hit a rock and sank. The state legislature purportedly granted him $500 for deepening the canal by 4 feet (1.2 m) from Pittsford (Monroe Co) to Rochester. McCarthy also trained his mules to walk single file on a rope, saving the trouble of dropping a gangway to the shore. Numerous other tales appeared. There was the case of a squash, which, when its roots touched the canal water, grew rapidly to enormous proportions and drained the canal for 10 miles (16 km), leaving numerous barges "mudlarked." Giant Lake Erie sturgeon were known to tow barges for many miles down the canal at alarming speeds. Boats that became lost in fog were occasionally sidetracked as far as Lake Ontario. In one complex scheme, Erie Sal, a legendary redhead, put her fiery hair in the water, causing fish to leap up in a fright. John Darling, a Paul Bunyan–like figure, maneuvered his barge under them before they fell, catching hundreds.

Canallers were superstitious, and many kept a new broom on the bow of the boat to fend off witches, a practice borrowed from the Pennsylvania Dutch. The swamps around Rome were thought to harbor ghosts, but some were fabricated for the occasion. In initiation rites for new workers, Irish drivers would use their powers to conjure up pagan spirits, while accomplices lurked in the dark, making increasingly terrifying noises as white shapes intermittently appeared just beyond the firelight.

Passed from person to person, most canal songs are hard to date and exist in many versions. One of the best known is "The Raging Canal," which wryly tells of mighty storms and huge waves endangering masts and rigging. In its common version, it begins

> We were forty miles from Albany,
> Forget it I never shall
> What a terrible storm we had one night
> On the E-Ri-E Canal.
>
> Of the E-Ri-E was a-rising,
> The gin was getting low;
> And I scarcely think we'll get a drink
> Till we get to Buffalo.

In fact, the canal was around 4 feet deep for much of its length, with sunken boats and cargo posing more danger than any high seas peril; at least two variants, "The Danger Ballad" and "The E-RI-E Canal," complain of being run aground on Lackawanna coal. Canallers, especially captains, did sometimes play the part, though, with daily costumes that mimicked the garb of ocean-going seamen.

The Weighlock Building (Syracuse), by Newton A. Wells, 1886.

The best known Erie Canal song is undoubtedly Thomas Allen's 1913 "Low Bridge, Everybody Down; or 15 Years on the Erie Canal." Written at a time when the enlarged canal, renamed the New York State Barge Canal in 1918, was making towpaths and low bridges memories from the past, the song looked back nostalgically on the days when mule power was a prime means of locomotion. The song retained key elements of Erie Canal folklore: the dedicated laborers (in this case the song's narrator and his beloved mule, Sal), the tough Irish canallers ("once a man named Mike McGinnty tried to put it over Sal / Now he's way down at the bottom of the Erie Canal"), and the hard work conditions ("I eat my meals with Sal each day / I eat beef and she eats hay"). Allen was an obscure Tin Pan Alley composer, and his song "Low Bridge" perhaps drew on earlier songs, such as Edward Harrigan's 1885 "Oh, Dat Low Bridge," but it was Allen's version that entered American folklore. It was even sung by the cavalry as John Wayne led them out to fight the Apaches in *Rio Grande* (1950.) The final stanza was prophetic.

> You'll soon hear them sing all about my gal
> Fifteen years on the Erie Canal. . . .
> Oh, every band will play it soon,
> Darned fool words and darned fool tune;
> You'll hear it sung everywhere you go
> From Mexico to Buffalo.

The Arts

Although the canal transformed economic life in much of Western New York and created several new urban centers, it did so without the noise and commotion of the railroad, and it was often portrayed as a more or less natural feature in a romanticized pastoral setting. James Eights, an artist for the canal's geological survey, painted several watercolors before the canal's official opening, concentrating on bridges and engineered features. Early paintings include folk artist Mary Keys's *Lockport on the Erie Canal* (1832) and British painter George Harvey's *Pittsford on the Erie Canal* (*ca* 1840). Thomas Cole's *Genesee Scenery* (*ca* 1846–47) was painted at the invitation of Canal Commissioner Samuel Ruggles to document the spectacular scenery that was to be altered by the proposed Genesee Valley Canal, and Albert Bierstadt sketched the Erie Canal in oil around 1860. Several works by Edward Lamson Henry depict the Erie Canal in the late 19th century.

Erie Canal Literature and Theater

William Dunlap's three-act comedy, *A Trip to Niagara* was the first play to deal directly with the canal and was initially staged in New York City in 1828. The play discloses differing attitudes to the work of the canal. The heroine, Amelia, opines that everyone "must admire this great patriotic work—the union of the inland seas with the Atlantic Ocean." Her brother, Wentworth, is somewhat more jaundiced, "To be dragged along a muddy ditch, hour after hour, in constant fear of lifting your head above your knees for fear of having it knock'd off your shoulders by a bridge!" Sam Patch, the daredevil who jumped off waterfalls along the route of the Erie Canal before being bested by the High Falls of the Genesee River near the Rochester viaduct in 1829, inspired a rash of literature, including *Sam Patch; or, The Daring Yankee* (1830). In James Kirke Paulding's *Book of Saint Nicholas* (1836), young Dutch readers learned of the wonders of the canal, which convinced St. Nicholas not to abandon New Yorkers of Dutch descent. Jacob Abbott's *Marco Paul's Travels and Adventures in Pursuit of Knowledge on the Erie Canal* (1843) is a well-known children's book. In Edward N. Westcott's *David Harum* (1899), one of the best-known regional novels of its era, the title character is an eccentric banker who had worked on the Erie Canal until he was 21.

The most famous Erie Canal novel remains Walter D. Edmonds's *Rome Haul* (1929). Dan Harrow comes off the farm to work on the canal, finding employment on the *Searsy Sal.* When the captain dies of cholera, a common canal ailment, Harrow takes over. He hires—and falls in love with—a cook by the name of Molly Larkins. Not really a canaller, he goes back to farming while Larkins stays with the canal. The story, reworked, appeared as the film *The Farmer Takes a Wife* (1934), starring Henry Fonda. In 1953 Buffalo-raised composer Harold Arlen and lyricist Dorothy Fields turned the film into a musical of the same name, starring Betty Grable as a cook on a canalboat (though the décolletage of her outfits differed from 19th-century models) and Dale Robertson. The score included several canal-related songs, including "Can You Spell Schenectady?" Edmonds's *Mostly Canallers* (1925) was a collection of episodes, many of them canal based. Samuel Hopkins Adams's family heritage included many involved with the canal, which provided the basis for his *Grandfather Stories* (1955), although *Canal Town* (1944), which depicted Palmyra (Wayne Co) in the 1820s, was Adams's main contribution to the literature of the Erie Canal.

Cook, Patricia. "The Erie Canal: American History through Folklore," *New York Folklore* 5 (1979)

Harlow, Alvin. *Old Towpaths: The Story of the American Canal Era* (1926; repr, frwd Frank B. Thomson, Port Washington, NY: Kennikat Press, 1954)

Thompson, Harold W. *Body, Boots, and Britches* (New York: J. B. Lippincott, 1939)

Willis, Alan Scot. *Everyday Life on the Erie Canal: A Social History Sketch for the Erie Canal Museum* (Syracuse: Erie Canal Museum, 1997)

Wyld, Lionel. *Low Bridge! Folklore and the Erie Canal* (Syracuse: Syracuse Univ Press, 1962)

———. *Boaters and Broomsticks: Tales and Historical Lore of the Erie Canal* (Utica: North Country Books, 1986)

Alan Scot Willis

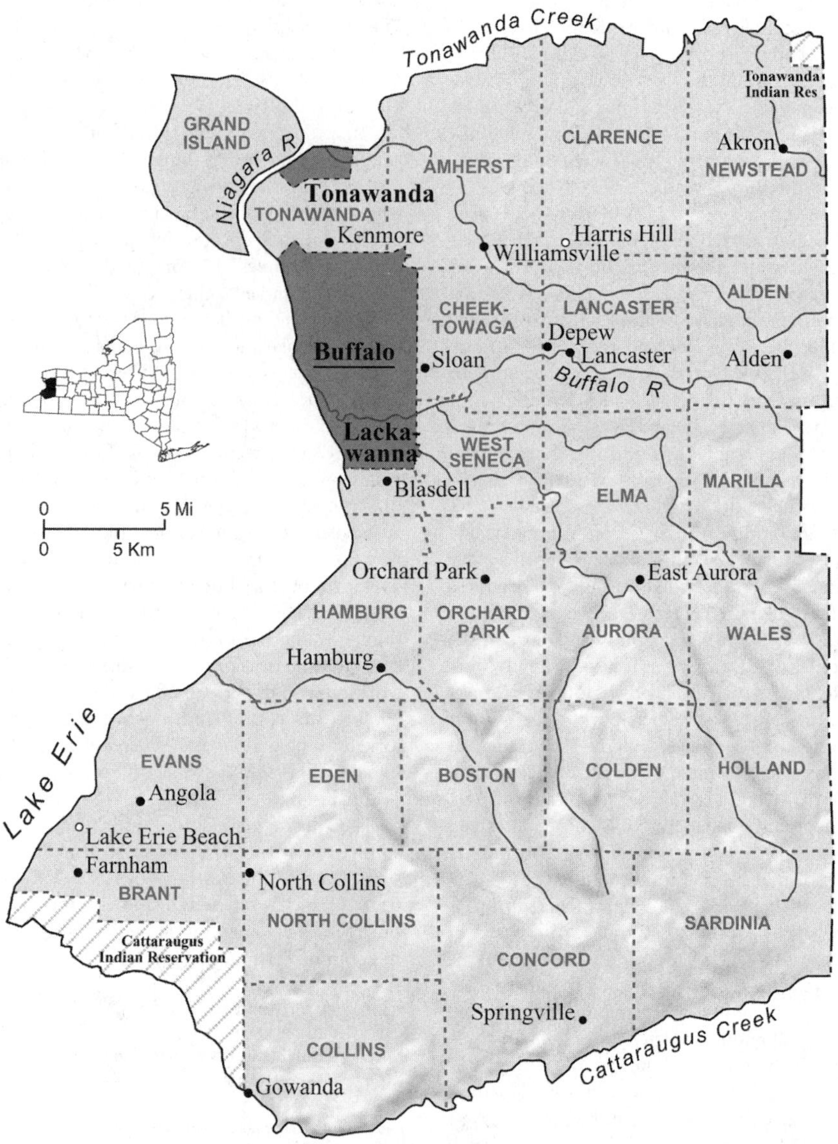

Erie County (1,044 mi²/2,704 km²; pop 950,265). Created in 1821 from Niagara Co and named after the Erie people who once occupied the area, Erie Co is subdivided into 3 cities—Buffalo, Lackawanna, and Tonawanda—and 25 towns that contain 15 incorporated villages and portions of the Tonawanda and Cattaraugus Indian Reservations. Buffalo serves as the county seat. Elevations in the county range between 569 feet (173 m) along the Lake Erie shore to over 1,940 feet (591 m) at the summit of Sardinia Hill about 6 miles (10 km) northeast of Springville in the county's southeast corner. Erie Co falls within two major physiographic provinces. The northern half and a narrow band of country that runs along Lake Erie to the county's southern border are the Southern Ontario Plain and Erie Lake Plain subregions of the Erie-Ontario Lowland. Here the country increases from gently rolling to rolling moving inland and south. The remainder of the county is part of the Cattaraugus Hills subregion of the Appalachian Upland, where generally round-shouldered, flat-topped hills rise 300–600 feet (90–180 m) above valley streams. Aside from a 5–7 mi (8–11 km) wide band of Silurian-age shale and dolomite along the northern border that includes Grand Island, bedrock consists of Devonian-age materials (mostly sandstones and shales). The exception is a narrow band of limestone that extends from Akron in the east to the lakeshore at Buffalo. Beds dip gently to the southwest. Erie Co is underlain by extensive natural gas fields associated with Lower Silurian Medina sandstone. A number of the depleted gas fields have been converted into natural gas storage reservoirs. The Zoar Field, located east of Gowanda, was established in 1916 and is the first such underground storage facility in the nation.

Most landforms reflect evidence of continental glaciation. Glacial lake waters covered the lowland portion of the county, as evidenced by the lacustrine deposits across the area and a prominent beach ridge that extends from Arden to North Collins. A mantle of till covers the upland country. Erie Co is drained by northwesterly- to westerly-flowing streams, most of which empty into Lake Erie. The exception is Ellicott Creek, the main drainage channel north of Buffalo, which empties into the Niagara River. Erie Co has scattered patches of highly fertile soil able to support modern commercial agriculture, most extensively in the southwest.

Erie Co's climate is humid-continental. Mean January temperatures range from 22°F (-6°C) near Colden in the south-central region to 25°F (-4°C) at Buffalo. Below 0°F (-18°C) temperatures are part of every winter. Mean July temperatures range from 67°F (19°C) near Wales to 71°F (22°C) in the north. Westerly winds off Lake Erie moderate summer temperatures, thus making daytime highs of 90°F (32°C) or more less frequent than areas farther east. Mean annual precipitation totals range from about 37 inches (94 cm) in the northeast to approximately 48 inches (122 cm) in the south-central part of the county. Mean seasonal snowfall totals vary from about 80 inches (203 cm) in the northeast to over 155 inches (394 cm) in higher elevations in the south-central hills. The dramatically higher snowfalls experienced in some of the more elevated areas reflect lake effect conditions. The primeval forest cover was made up of four forest communities. Central hardwood forest, consisting primarily of beech, sugar maple, basswood, and hemlock closer to the lakeshore, covered the northwestern portion of Erie Co. An Alleghenian hardwood community dominated by beech, sugar maple, hemlock, white pine, basswood, and in places oak and chestnut blanketed the rest of the county except for a narrow band of wetland forest along Tonawanda Creek.

Native Inhabitants

Immediately before the Contact period, the area was inhabited by the Neutral, who had villages on both sides of the Niagara River, on Grand Island, and at the mouth of Eighteenmile Creek. The Erie, meaning "People of the Cat," lived along the lake. Between the 1630s and 1670s, the Seneca expanded their influence into the area, defeating (and later absorbing) the Neutral in 1651 and the Erie in 1657. The Seneca used the area for temporary hunting and fishing camps and established a village that dealt with the French and then the English presence at Fort Niagara [now in Porter, Niagara Co]. The Sullivan-Clinton campaign of 1779 drove many Senecas westward from the Genesee Valley to the Niagara Frontier. At the Treaty of Big Tree in 1797, Seneca territory in the area was reduced to the Cattaraugus, Tonawanda, and Buffalo Creek Reservations, along with a claim to Grand Island. In the 1838 Treaty of Buffalo Creek the Seneca lost almost all of their remaining land in New York State, but they were able to reacquire the Cattaraugus Reservation (1842) and a reduced Tonawanda Reservation (1856). The Buffalo Creek Reservation was divided between Buffalo, West Seneca, and Elma and within 30 years had 100,000 non-Indian inhabitants. In addition to the Cattaraugus and Tonawanda Reservations, Americans Indians lived in Brant, Collins, Elma, Newstead, and West Seneca, and they continue to be a significant presence on Buffalo's West Side and in Black Rock. In 2000 Buffalo had a American Indian population of 2,250, and Erie Co's population of 5,755 was the highest in the state outside of New York City.

Settlement

In 1788 much of western New York State was sold by Massachusetts to investors Oliver Phelps and Nathaniel Gorham, who failed to complete the purchase; they sold their contract in 1790 to Robert Morris. He, too, failed, and the land was sold in 1792–93 to the Holland Land Co, a corporation of Dutch investors. Its American agent, surveyor Joseph Ellicott, established a system of 15 north-south ranges divided into townships roughly 6 mi^2 (16 km^2). Buyers arrived as early as 1800 to purchase land. In 1804 Ellicott designed the radial street plan of Buffalo, which is largely intact today. By 1839 all Holland Land Co lots had been sold to domestic buyers.

Significant battles of the War of 1812 were fought in Erie Co, including the July 1813 Battle of Black Rock, in which the British destroyed shipyards and naval supplies. A militia led by Gen Peter B. Porter forced the British back to Canada. In retaliation for the American burning of Newark [now Niagara-on-the-Lake, Ont], the British invaded on 18 Dec 1813, burning the settlements along the Niagara River from Tonawanda to Buffalo. Few settlers stayed to fight; most fled inland to Amherst and Clarence.

Transportation

Lake navigation began in 1679 when René-Robert Cavalier de la Salle launched the *Griffon,* the first major vessel to sail the upper Great Lakes. Steamship travel on Lake Erie commenced with the *Walk-in-the-Water* in 1818. Many early roads followed Indian trails. During the planning process for the Erie Canal, Buffalo was in fierce competition with Black Rock to become its western terminus. Judge Samuel Wilkeson organized the dredging of Buffalo Creek [now Buffalo River] to create a viable harbor, winning the designation. The canal brought explosive population growth and spurred the creation of an intricate network of canal slips and basins along the Buffalo River and harbor, transforming the city into a major inland port. The canal between Tonawanda and Buffalo was abandoned prior to World War I and filled in for highway use. The opening of the St. Lawrence Seaway in 1959 diverted almost all Great Lakes shipping from the Port of Buffalo and was the beginning of the end of freight on the canal, which continues to serve pleasure craft. By 2002 Buffalo's largely abandoned industrial waterfront was reinventing itself as a recreational destination, and there were plans to excavate the paved-over street network, canal slips, and building foundations of the city's famed 19th-century canal district.

Augmenting and later supplanting canal-based commerce was the first railroad, the Attica and Buffalo, which opened in 1842. It was followed by several trunk lines, including the Erie (1853), the Lehigh Valley (1876), and the Delaware, Lackawanna and Western (1882). The New York Central was created in 1853 by a consolidation of a number of existing shorter lines. The Pennsylvania Railroad was also created from earlier lines that served the city. Buffalo became a rail hub second only to Chicago. Beginning in 1860 an interurban streetcar system connected city and suburb, declining after World I. Private, experimental airfields led the way to commercial aviation when a municipal airport was opened in Cheektowaga in 1926, which in turn attracted Curtiss-Wright, Irving Air Chute, and Bell Aircraft factories.

Economic Development

Prior to the completion of the Erie Canal in 1825, most economic activity was agricultural: clearing land, growing crops, raising cattle, and building saw- and gristmills. After the canal opened, factories and mills concentrated around the Buffalo harbor. Nineteenth-century urban enterprises included slaughterhouses, tanneries, soap factories, lumberyards, and breweries, or involved furniture making, shipbuilding, flour milling, ironworking, garment making, shoemaking, tool and machinery manufacturing, and railroads. In certain villages, such as Akron, Angola, and Springville, similar enterprises operated on a smaller scale. Elsewhere, farmers milked cows, raised sheep and poultry, and tended orchards. In 1900 Erie Co had 7,929 farms (the third highest number in the state) on 571,084 acres (231,110 ha).

Drawn by inexpensive hydroelectric power from Niagara Falls, 20th-century industries included steel, chemicals, ceramics, automobiles and automotive parts, and aircraft. Along with Buffalo, the suburban industrial cities and villages (Blasdell, Cheektowaga, Depew, Hamburg, Lackawanna, and Tonawanda) were sustained by heavy industry. Production peaked with defense contracts during World War II and declined in the 1960s, with most of the manufacturers closing or relocating. Surviving heavy industry includes automotive plants in Tonawanda and Hamburg. Buffalo remains an important flour-

ERIE CO POPULATION CENSUS FIGURES

	White	Nonwhite	Total Population	Foreign-Born
1830	35,476	243	35,719	1,773
1840	61,857	608	62,465	—
1850	100,168	825	100,993	37,473
1860	141,093	878	141,971	54,904
1870	177,841	858	178,699	60,907
1880	218,757	1,127	219,884	65,378
1890	321,717	1,264	322,981	103,453
1900	430,516	3,170	433,686	119,470
1910	525,675	3,310	528,985	144,231
1920	628,330	6,358	634,688	148,713
1930	743,754	18,654	762,408	148,692
1940	776,403	21,974	798,377	119,598
1950	856,212	43,026	899,238	97,900
1960	985,443	79,245	1,064,688	90,144
1970	1,006,843	106,648	1,113,491	69,640
1980	893,195	122,277	1,015,472	56,357
1990	832,129	136,403	968,532	42,950
2000	780,942	169,323	950,265	42,886

Notes: "Nonwhite" includes African Americans, Asians, American Indians, and Pacific Islanders and, for 2000, also the mixed race and other race categories. Through the 1960 census these figures primarily reflect the African American population. Foreign-born figures for 1830 include only those not naturalized, and for 1930 and 1950, the foreign-born totals include Whites only. Other years include all foreign-born in the population.

POPULATIONS OF TOWNS AND CITIES, ERIE CO

Town or City, Year Founded	1840	1880	1920	1960	2000
Alden, 1823	1,984	2,534	2,433	7,615	10,470
Amherst, 1818	2,451	4,519	6,286	62,837	116,510
Aurora, 1804[a]	2,908	2,723	5,312	12,888	13,996
Black Rock, 1839–53[b]	3,625	—	—	—	—
Boston, 1817	1,745	1,617	1,325	5,106	7,897
Brant, 1839	1,088	1,527	1,830	2,290	1,906
Buffalo (city), 1832	18,213	155,134	506,775	532,759	292,648
Cheektowaga, 1839	1,137	2,327	11,923	84,056	94,019
Clarence, 1808	2,271	3,495	2,660	13,267	26,123
Colden, 1827	1,088	1,464	1,259	2,384	3,323
Collins, 1821	4,257	2,371	4,061	6,984	8,307
Concord, 1812	3,021	3,400	4,223	6,452	8,526
Eden, 1812	2,174	2,363	2,352	6,630	8,076
Elma, 1857	—	2,555	1,966	7,468	11,304
Evans, 1821	1,807	2,610	3,468	12,078	17,594
Grand Island, 1852	—	1,156	728	9,607	18,621
Hamburg, 1812	3,727	3,234	8,656	41,288	56,259
Holland, 1818	1,242	1,720	1,410	2,304	3,603
Lackawanna (city), 1909	—	—	17,918	29,564	19,064
Lancaster, 1833	2,083	3,944	13,172	25,605	39,019
Marilla, 1853	—	1,825	1,237	2,252	5,709
Newstead, 1804[c]	2,653	3,570	4,043	5,825	8,404
North Collins, 1852[d]	—	1,856	2,271	3,805	3,376
Orchard Park, 1850[e]	—	2,409	3,120	15,876	27,637
Sardinia, 1821	1,743	1,767	1,518	2,145	2,692
Tonawanda, 1836	1,261	4,909	5,505	105,032	78,155
Tonawanda (city), 1903	—	—	10,068	21,561	16,136
Wales, 1818	1,987	1,392	985	1,910	2,960
West Seneca, 1851[f]	—	3,463	7,062	33,644	45,920

[a]Willink until 1818.

[b]Incorporated as village 1837; formed as town 1839; annexed to City of Buffalo 1853.

[c]Erie until 1831.

[d]Shirley until 1853.

[e]Ellicott until 1852, then East Hamburg until 1934.

[f]Seneca until 1852.

milling center; for much of the 20th century it led the world in flour production. Major employers include food processors, service industries, light manufacturing, electronics, printing, healthcare, and government.

Immigration and Ethnicity

Native-born settlers from New England were the first to move to Erie Co, and the first significant European immigrants were Germans, who began arriving in the 1820s, followed by another wave in the 1840s. Like New Englanders, Germans settled in both city and country, contributing large numbers to almost every town, becoming farmers, brewers, and manufacturers. Irish famine immigrants began arriving in the 1840s; they concentrated in South Buffalo and labored in the flour mills and grain elevators or worked in canal-related business.

African American settlement began with Joseph Hodge, a trapper, trader, and interpreter who lived on Cattaraugus Creek *ca* 1792. Concentrated on Buffalo's East Side, the black community remained small but urban throughout the 19th century. In 1816 Buffalo had 16 Blacks, of whom 9 were slaves. By the Civil War, the black community numbered 500. Many were freed and fugitive slaves, attracted to Buffalo by its ample employment opportunities and strategic position on an international border as part of the Underground Railroad. They worked largely in service occupations, but some were skilled tradespeople and professionals. African Americans established churches, cultural organizations, social welfare agencies, and advocacy groups, and were prominent in abolitionist and civil rights causes. During the early 20th century, African Americans from the South migrated to Buffalo and Lackawanna in search of factory employment, swelling the population to about 9,000 out of a county population of 528,985 in 1910. Notable African Americans include civil rights activist Mary Burnett Talbert, author and abolitionist William Wells Brown, and Rev J. Edward Nash, for 61 years pastor of the Michigan Avenue Baptist Church.

Immigration peaked in the mid–19th century: in 1855 over 50% of the county population of 132,321 was foreign-born. Poles came in the 1870s and populated Buffalo's East Side, Black Rock, and Cheektowaga, working in slaughterhouses, steel mills, and on the railroads; they formed the county's largest ethnic minority. Italians began arriving in the 1880s, settling on the Buffalo waterfront and in Brant and Lancaster, laboring on farms and in canneries. Puerto Ricans arrived in the 1950s, settling on Buffalo's West Side and working in the southern towns as seasonal farm labor. A second wave of eastern Europeans immigrated to Buffalo after World War II and during the Cold War.

Smaller ethnic enclaves include an early French settlement in Clarence; eastern Europeans of all nationalities in Lackawanna, Tonawanda, and Lancaster; and Greeks in Lackawanna. By the end of the 20th century, immigrants included Mexicans, Cubans, East Indians, Pakistanis, Yemenites, Vietnamese, Chinese, Serbs and Croatians, Russians, Ukrainians, Arabs, Somalians, Nigerians, Tibetans, and Lebanese.

Religion, Education, and Culture

Using "gospel" lots supplied by the Holland Land Co, Episcopalians, Baptists, Presbyterians, Congregationalists, and Quakers established the first churches and meeting houses, followed by Methodists, Lutherans, and Roman Catholics. Southern Erie Co experienced the fiery Protestant revivalism of the antebellum period, spawning abolitionist and temperance activism. A Mennonite community, one of three in New York State prior to World War II, settled in Clarence in 1829. Eastern European Jews arrived in the 1830s, settling on Buffalo's East Side and later migrating to North Buffalo and Amherst. In 1843 the German immigrant Community of True Inspiration settled Ebenezer in West Seneca but eventually moved west. In 1855 Erie Co had 28 Methodist and 27 Baptist churches, but also 26 Roman Catholic churches, the most of any county in the state. With continuing German immigration, the 9 Lutheran churches of 1855 tripled to 27 in 1875, while Catholic and Methodist churches numbered 40 and 39, respectively. In 2003 the Roman Catholic diocese has more parishes in Erie Co than any other denomination.

Common schools were established soon after settlement. In the mid–19th century, secondary private, parochial, trade, and business academies developed to meet the expanding educational needs of a commercial and industrial city. The Union Free School law of 1853 authorized public high schools, and some were established in the larger communities during the second half of the 19th century. Consolidation of common school districts began with Holland Central School District in 1931 and was largely complete by 1956. In 2003 Erie Co included 19 central districts, 7 union free school districts, and city school districts in Buffalo, Tonawanda, and Lackawanna.

SUNY Buffalo began as the Medical Department of the University of Buffalo in 1846. The university transformed the former Erie County Hospital grounds into a city campus in the 1920s and built a suburban Amherst campus in the 1970s. In 1871 New York State opened a normal school, now SUNY Buffalo State. Other colleges include Canisius College (1870) in Buffalo, Daemen College (1947) in Amherst, Villa Maria College (1961) in Cheektowaga, and Hilbert College (1969) in Hamburg. Erie Community College (1946) and Bryant and Stratton Business College (1854) each have three campuses in both city and suburban locations.

The Erie County Agricultural Society (1820) operates the annual Erie County Fair, one of the largest county fairs in the nation. The Roycroft community in East Aurora was the nation's most influential center of the arts and crafts movement. The City of Buffalo has rich offerings in

Johnson's Cottage. Depiction of home of Ebenezer Johnson, Buffalo's first mayor, by William J. Wilgus, 1833.

museums, music, and the performing arts. The daily *Buffalo News* (1880) is the county's paper of record; the weekly *Springville Journal* (1870) serves the southern part of the county. Commercial broadcasting began in 1922 with a short-lived Buffalo radio station, WWT, immediately followed by WGR-AM, which remained in operation in 2003. George "Hound Dog" Lorenz (1920–72), with WKBW in Buffalo, was one of the first radio disc jockeys to broadcast rhythm and blues and rock and roll. WBEN (now WIVB), Buffalo's first television station, began broadcasting in 1948.

Politics

Buffalo, with its preponderance of population and tax revenues, dominated county politics until World War I, sending Millard Fillmore and Grover Cleveland to the White House. The postwar urban exodus brought growing power and obligations to county government, and consolidations of health, welfare, and library services occurred. A revised county charter enabled the election of the first county executive, Edward A. Rath, in 1960. The Erie County Board of Supervisors operated until 1967, when it was replaced by 20 elected county legislators. For decades, voting patterns were along ethnic lines: Germans and Italians usually supported Republicans, and Irish and Poles usually supported Democrats. At the end of the 20th century, the split was geographic and class based: Buffalo was heavily Democratic, and the suburbs were heavily Republican.

Recent History

The creation of a superhighway network was one of the first of the dramatic changes to follow World War II. It began with the Thruway link from Buffalo to Niagara Falls in 1951 and with the Thruway eastward in 1954; the Thruway westward was completed in 1957. Two other highways later became limited-access roads: US 219 (1968–79) and Rte 400 (1967–68).

Suburban expansion and urban decline characterized Erie Co at the end of the 20th century. While agriculture has remained important in large expanses of the south, southwest, and, to a limited extent, northeast, the number of farms has dropped precipitously, from 4,611 farms on 376,353 acres (152,305 ha) in 1950 to 973 farms on 143,234 acres (57,965 ha) in 1997. Dairy products, grain, vegetables, and fruit are the leading farm products. In 1900 80% of the county's population lived in Buffalo and was served by the city government. In 2000 over two-thirds of its population was dispersed outside Buffalo under 45 municipal governments. The resulting duplication of services required high taxes. Suburban relocations of Buffalo-based companies, often induced by tax incentives offered by the county's five competing industrial development agencies, achieved little net economic gain for the county.

While towns and villages grew, the Cities of Buffalo, Lackawanna, and Tonawanda were hampered by state laws restricting annexation. They lost jobs and residents. In 2001 the Town of Amherst surpassed Buffalo in assessed real estate value. The county's population peaked at 1,113,491 in 1970 and had dropped to 950,265 by 2000. In spite of population loss, land consumption and new construction continued, resulting in abandoned residential and commercial properties not only in the cities but also in the suburbs. A growing understanding of the costliness of suburban sprawl led to the 1999 election of County Executive Joel Giambra, who ran a "regionalism" campaign. Few consolidated government services have been achieved at this writing.

See also Airports; Motor vehicle industry; Suburbanization.

Orsamus Turner, *Pioneer History of the Holland Patent* (1849) is indispensable for the settlement period. The standard work is Crisfield Johnson, *Centennial History of Erie County* (1876); another work is Truman C. White Jr, *Our County and Its People: A Descriptive History of Erie County* (1898). In the late 20th century, the Buffalo and Erie County Historical Society published two important books: Walter S. Dunn Jr, ed., *History of Erie County 1870–1970* (1971) and Scott Eberle and Joseph A. Grande, *Second Looks: A Pictorial History of Buffalo and Erie County* (1987). Erasmus Briggs, *History of the Original Town of Concord* (1883), although dated, gives thorough coverage to the early history of that town and those formed from it (Collins, North Collins, and Sardinia). Other early community histories are Warren Jackman, *History of the Town of Elma* (1901) and Frederick S. Parkhurst, *History of Kenmore* (1926). A series of town histories in eight-page, standard-format pamphlets was issued by the Buffalo and Erie County Historical Society in 1971; with various authors, the titles begin with *A History of the Town of.* Among the modern histories are *The History of Lackawanna* (1976) and Joseph A. Grande, *Glancing Back: A Pictorial History of Amherst* (2000). Not currently published but a source of useful articles is the journal *Niagara Frontier* (1953–79).

Cynthia Van Ness

Erie disaster. A wooden side-wheel steamer commissioned in 1836 and owned by the Reed Line of Erie, Pa, *Erie* operated from Buffalo to Milwaukee and Chicago during the heyday of immigration into the Great Lakes states, which occurred largely between 1825 and 1845. At 176 feet (53.6 m) and 497 tons (451 MT), it was one of the larger and more popular packets at the time. En route to Lake Michigan on 9 Aug 1841 the *Erie* caught fire off Silver Creek (Chautauqua Co), some 25 mi (40 km) west of Buffalo, where it burned to the waterline and sank in Lake Erie. A nearby steamer saved 29 people, but 175 were lost. For many years it remained the worst disaster on Great Lakes waters. The fire was blamed on turpentine and paint stored on board. The tragedy was widely publicized and dampened passenger steamship travel for a time but ultimately resulted in safety requirements for American passenger vessels, such as life preservers and fire pumps.

Heyl, Erik. *Early American Steamers*, vol 2 (Buffalo: Erik Heyl, 1956)

C. Patrick Labadie

Erie Indians. The Erie, an Iroquoian-speaking group culturally similar to the Five Nations and the Huron and Neutral Confederacies, lived along the southern shore of the lake that now bears their name in Pennsylvania and western New York State. They were known to the Huron as the "people of the cat" or "people of the panther." Little more is known about the tribe. No European visit was ever recorded, and what the Jesuits in Canada learned about them came by way of the Huron and the Five Nations. Like many of the Iroquoian communities in the Great Lakes region, the Erie came under attack by the westernmost of the Five Nations. Huron refugees, who themselves had found shelter and protection among the Erie after their own villages had been destroyed, encouraged the Erie to attack the Iroquois. The Erie captured and eventually killed the Onondaga chief Annereaes. After ensuing feuds and raids in June 1654, Seneca, Cayuga, Onondaga, and Oneida united to fight the Erie, with 1,200 Onondaga and 700 Mohawk. Several villages were burned, captives taken, and considerable damage done, but the Erie apparently remained a powerful foe. In 1655 and 1656 the Onondaga still stood guard, fearing that the Erie would invade their territory. Only in 1656 did the tide of the war change. There is no evidence describing the nature of the fighting that year, but the Five Nations clearly emerged victorious and the defeated Eries were dispersed. Many of the Seneca villages west of the Genesee River included a sizable Erie component in their populations. By the end of the 1650s, like the Neutral and the Wenro, the Erie had become victims of the Five Nations' mourning war tradition, in which defeated enemies were either executed, to assuage the grief of a distraught kinsman or kinswoman, or adopted into Iroquoian village communities to make up for population lost to warfare and disease.

White, Marian. "Erie." In *Northeast,* ed. Bruce G. Trigger, vol 15 of *Handbook of North American Indians* (Washington, DC: Smithsonian Institution, 1978)

Michael Leroy Oberg

Erie Lackawanna Railroad. Freight and passenger carrier created by the 1960 merger of two former competitors, the 2,313 mi (3,722 km) Erie Railroad, headquartered in Cleveland, Ohio, and the 940 mi (1,513 km) Delaware, Lackawanna and Western Railroad (DL&W), based in New York City. Erie owned a main line between Jersey City, NJ, through New York State's Southern Tier to Chicago; DL&W connected Hoboken, NJ, with Buffalo. The two railroads had entered station- and track-sharing agreements in the mid-1950s, and by the late 1950s, as both carriers experienced financial reversals, their managements agreed to merger talks. The corporate marriage occurred 17 Oct 1960, and the 3,188 mi (5,131 km) Erie-Lackawanna Railroad (EL)—the hyphen would be dropped in 1963—made its debut. After a shaky start, the merged company achieved some success. By 1963 savings amounted to about $21 million annually rather than the $13 million initially predicted. The same year the company's Board of Directors named William "Bill" White, former president of both DL&W and New York Central and subsequently chief executive officer of Delaware and Hudson, as its chairman. White streamlined operations and for a time oversaw an economic upturn, but he and associates concluded that the firm could not operate alone. The era of railroad "mega-mergers," which would produce Penn Central (Conrail), CSX, and Norfolk Southern, was beginning. Poorer railroads like EL needed partners. By 1967 financial conditions had deteriorated at EL, and the Interstate Commerce Commission pressured Norfolk and Western (N&W) to take charge of it. This control became effective 1 Apr 1968 and lasted until 1972, when Hurricane Agnes devastated large parts of the railroad in New York and Pennsylvania, forcing EL into bankruptcy, and N&W withdrew. In 1976 EL became a perfect candidate to enter Conrail, which was designed to absorb several bankrupt northeastern carriers. Assets not conveyed to Conrail were administrated by Erie Lackawanna Inc, which settled EL's debts before disbanding in 1992.

Grant, H. Roger. *Erie Lackawanna: Death of an American Railroad, 1938–1992* (Stanford, Calif: Stanford Univ Press, 1994)

H. Roger Grant

Erie-Ontario Lowland. A low-lying plain extending from east of Lake Ontario along its southern shore to the Niagara Frontier. The lowlands are underlain by shales and sandstones of the Paleozoic age. Only local minor deformation is evident; the bedrock sequences dip very gently to the south-southwest, resulting in younger rocks preserved to the south. Glacial erosion and deposition are the cause of the most significant landscape features of the lowland, evident in deposits of drift up to several hundred feet thick, extensive drumlin fields west of Syracuse, and widespread kame and kettle topography. The region was completely inundated by the Laurentide ice sheet at the maximum glacial extent during the Pleistocene some 22,000 years ago. During deglaciation glacial Lake Iroquois was impounded south of present-day Lake Ontario. Shoreline features of the ancient lake are evident east of Rochester on Ridge Rd, which is built along a relict beach barrier system. As deglaciation continued, the outlet for Lake Iroquois switched to the St. Lawrence Valley, resulting in a lowering of lake levels, eventually approaching those of modern Lake Ontario. Following complete ice retreat, the region experienced slight rising due to the removal of the ice burden, greatest to the north of Lake Ontario. Many of the river valleys along the south shore have been submerged, causing cliff erosion and retreat, exemplified dramatically at Chimney Bluffs State Park (Wayne Co).

See also CLIMATE AND WEATHER.

Isachsen, Yngvar W., et al, eds. *Geology of New York: A Simplified Account,* 2d ed. (Albany: NYS Museum, 2000)

Susan Millar

Erie Railroad. New York and Erie Railroad, core of the future Erie, opened in 1851 between the New York State communities of Piermont (Rockland Co) and Dunkirk (Chautauqua Co), connecting the Hudson River with Lake Erie. Built to a 6 ft (1.8 m) gauge and running 447 miles (719 km), New York and Erie rightfully claimed the title of longest railway in the world for a few years, also winning the accolade of "the Work of the Age." Sixteen 100 ft (30.5 m) bluestone arches make up the grand and beautiful Starrucca Viaduct near Susquehanna, Pa, that was the basis for this honor. From its earliest days, however, problems plagued the railroad, particularly the two terminals. Piermont abutted a desolate marsh, and Dunkirk, another hamlet, lacked a developed harbor. The railroad, according to a popular adage, "ran from Nowhere-in-Particular to Nowhere-at-All." The company improved its geographic position, gaining access to Jersey City, NJ, by 1853 and to Buffalo soon afterward. But in 1859 it fell into receivership, partly as a result of stock manipulations by one of the directors, Daniel Drew. Over the next decade Drew, Jay Gould, Jim Fisk, and Cornelius Vanderbilt—in shifting alliances—struggled for control of the company, reestablished as Erie Railway in 1864. Alternate watering and dumping of stock in their "Erie War" sullied the company's reputation and gave rise to the company nickname, "Scarlet Woman of Wall Street." From 1867 to 1872 Jay Gould directed the company and markedly improved its financial position. Reorganized in 1878 as the New York, Lake Erie and Western Railroad, the firm then boasted modernized rail and rolling stock, standardized track gauges, and an expanded, albeit patchwork system that included a 998 mi (1,606 km) main line between Jersey City and Chicago. But the depression of the 1890s forced another bankruptcy, and in 1895 New York, Lake Erie and Western became Erie Railroad Co.

By the early 20th century, J. P. Morgan and Co controlled Erie Railroad, a relationship that resulted in substantial upgrading of routes and equipment, including a major line relocation in the state's Southern Tier. Beginning in 1923 the Van Sweringen brothers, Oris P. and Mantis J., emerging rail titans from Cleveland, began to buy large blocks of Erie stock, but on two occasions (1926 and 1929), the federal Interstate Commerce Commission denied their Chesapeake and Ohio Railroad control of Erie Railroad. The Great Depression caused disarray in the Sweringen empire, resulting in another receivership. In 1941 the company emerged from court protection and prospered from heavy wartime rail traffic. After the conflict, dieselization, two-way radios, and other new technologies augured well for the company's future. But competition from motor vehicle transport and heavy debt obligations prompted Erie's management to seek first cooperation and then merger with Delaware, Lackawanna and Western (DL&W), its old rival for New York City to Buffalo traffic. On 17 Oct 1960 Erie united with DL&W and became Erie Lackawanna Railroad, headquartered in Cleveland.

Grant, H. Roger. *Erie Lackawanna: Death of an American Railroad, 1938–1992* (Stanford, Calif: Stanford Univ Press, 1994)
Hungerford, Edward. *Men of Erie* (New York: Random House, 1946)
Klein, Maury. *The Life and Legend of Jay Gould* (Baltimore: Johns Hopkins Univ Press, 1986)

H. Roger Grant

Erin. Town (pop 2,054) in NE Chemung Co. Settled *ca* 1815, the town was formed from Chemung in 1822. The town's first industry was lumber, and after 1865 the central hamlet of Erin grew up around a successful steam sawmill. The Utica, Ithaca and Elmira Railroad (1874–1938; later Lehigh Valley Railroad), served the town. At the end of the 19th century, tanning, chair making, and basket making employed some of its residents. Poultry and dairy farms anchored the town until farming declined in the 20th century; some former farmland was reforested beginning in 1931. In the early 21st century residents worked in industries in Elmira and Horseheads.

Heather A. Wade

Erlanger, A(braham) L(incoln) (*b* Buffalo, 4 May 1860; *d* New York City, 7 Mar 1930). Theatrical booking agent and producer. Erlanger's family moved to Cleveland when he was a youth, and after little formal education he worked in a local theater and later an opera house. Arriving in New York City in 1886, Erlanger became a successful advance agent for an acting tour. Two years later he joined with Marc Klaw, a lawyer friend, to purchase a small theatrical booking agency. In 1895 Klaw and Erlanger, with five theatrical businessmen, formed an association, soon called the Theatrical Syndicate, which became a dominant force in legitimate theater and vaudeville. The group pooled clients and the theaters they owned or controlled and created a powerful and efficient means of scheduling performances in New York and in other major cities. The syndicate, which controlled almost 700 theaters across the country by 1907, operated until about 1916. Klaw and Erlanger remained the dominant booking agency until 1919, when their partnership dissolved. Erlanger continued to manage and produce, and in 1927–28 he built the Erlanger Theater (now St. James Theater) at 246 West 44th St.

Bordman, Gerald. *American Theater: A Chronicle of Comedy and Drama, 1869–1914* (New York: Oxford Univ Press, 1994)

James R. Belpedio

Erwin. Town (pop 7,227) in SE Steuben Co. William Harris, a trader with the region's native peoples, settled in 1787. Twelve years later Col Arthur Erwin, a land speculator, purchased the area's land from Phelps and Gorham. The town was formed in 1826 from Painted Post. Lumbering was an important industry in the early 19th century. Timber floated down the Canisteo and Tioga Rivers to markets in Baltimore, and Erwin lumber was later transported by the Chemung and Feeder Canals (1833–78). One of the many machine shops established to repair the sawmills evolved into the Ingersoll-Sergeant Drill Co (1897), which became the Ingersoll-Rand Co (1899) and, since 1987, Dresser Rand (a subsidiary of Ingersoll-Rand). In 2003 Dresser Rand employed 800 in Erwin. Between 1990 and 2000 Erwin was the fastest-growing part of Steuben Co because of the expansion of the Corning facilities. Corning's Sullivan Research Park is in town, as are several of its high-tech production facilities.

Thomas Dimitroff

Esopus [EE-SO-PUS]. Town (pop 9,331) in E Ulster Co. Settled in the 1650s, it was formed from Kingston in 1811. Its diverse industries were dispersed among its many hamlets. Products included brick, cement, cotton and woolen cloth, army blankets and carpets, pressed-coal brick, boats, and dynamite. In addition, limestone was quarried, ice was cut on the Hudson, and shad fishing continued until the mid-1930s. Port Ewen, platted in 1851 by the Pennsylvania Coal Co, was an important coal depot until 1865. The town started rail service in 1883 with the West Shore. In the 20th century, Hercules at Port Ewen manufactured explosives detonators, employing 1,000 during World War II. The Hutterian Society of Brothers (now Hutterian Brethren) established two communities: Woodcrest (1954) near Rifton and Maple Ridge (1985) at Ulster Park. Some fruit growing continues near the river. The town is the site of the Esopus Meadows Environmental Center and of Slabsides, the John Burroughs home.

Ruth Piwonka

Esopus Indians. A group of Munsee-speaking communities whose homeland stretched from the west bank of the Hudson River between the Hudson Highlands and the Catskill Mountains. Their name probably derives from the Munsee word for river. In 1609, at the beginning of European settlement, 1,000–2,000 may have lived within the Esopus homeland. Later colonial records affirm that most of the major Esopus towns were along the broad flats bordering the lower reaches of the Esopus and Rondout Rivers in a region the Esopus called Atkarkarton, in and around Kingston (Ulster Co). Colonists documented other communities at Waranawankong in the hinterlands beyond Kingston, around Waoraneck along the lower Wallkill River, in Rondout Valley settlements at Kerhonkson, Mamakating, Napanoch, and Wawarsing (Ulster Co), and at Moodna Creek (Orange Co). The Esopus also maintained hunting camps in nearby Catskill, Shawangunk, and Hudson Highland valleys, along the upper Delaware Valley at Lackawaxen and Cochecton in Pennsylvania, and at the Delaware Co locations of Cookhouse, or Owltown [now Deposit], Pepacton [now Pepacton Reservoir], and Papakating [now Margaretville].

White settlement in Esopus lands had started by 1652, with a few settlers from Beverwijck [now Albany] who established a farming community named Wiltwijck in 1661. Conflicts with settlers, known as the Esopus Wars, compelled the Esopus to sign a treaty giving up their most productive lands on 15 May 1664. Determined to prevent more conflicts, Gov Richard Nicolls negotiated a lasting treaty of friendship with Esopus sachems at Kingston on 7 Oct 1665. Treaty terms included a pledge that Esopus leaders annually meet with English authorities to adjudicate disputes and renew friendship. Records preserve proceedings of 23 of these meetings held between 1665 and 1777. This pledge helped maintain an enduring friendship with the English that survived several land disputes and more than a few assaults and murders. Forced to sell off most of their traditional homeland by 1746, many Esopus moved elsewhere. Small numbers settled in Christian Indian mission towns in Schaghticoke, Conn, Stockbridge, Mass, and Bethlehem, Pa, in the 1730s and 1740s.

Many Esopus lived among other displaced Indians at Oquaga [now Windsor, Broome Co] and nearby Indian towns under Iroquois control along the north branch of the Susquehanna River when the Revolutionary War broke out in 1776. Maintaining loyalty, confirmed by more than a century of treaty affirmations, Esopus warriors fought alongside their English allies. Many served as guides and spies for war parties raiding the Ulster and Tryon Cos' frontiers. Most Esopus, with other British Indian allies, took refuge behind the protecting walls of the British bastion of Fort Niagara (now in Porter, Niagara Co) after 1778 and subsequently joined Iroquois expatriates resettling in Canada at the Six Nations Reserve. Many Esopus living at Six Nations gradually moved to the present Munceytown, Ont, area in the early 1800s. Others moved farther west, ultimately joining Delaware communities that today are in Wisconsin, Kansas, and Oklahoma.

Hauptman, Laurence M., and Jack Campisi, eds. *Neighbors and Intruders: An Ethnohistorical Exploration of the Indians of Hudson's River.* National Museum of Man Mercury Series, Canadian Ethnology Service, Paper 39 (Ottawa, Ont: National Museums of Canada, 1978)

Ruttenber, Edward Manning. *History of the Indian Tribes of Hudson's River* (Albany: J. Munsell, 1872)

Scott, Kenneth, and Charles E. Baker "Renewals of Governor Nicolls' Treaty of 1665 with the Esopus Indians at Kingston, NY," *New-York Historical Quarterly* 37 (1953): 251–72

Robert S. Grumet

Esopus Wars. Two violent conflicts embroiling Esopus Indians and Dutch settlers in the mid-Hudson Valley between 1659 and 1664. Contention first arose after Dutch settlers began building farms near the most fertile lands at Esopus [now in Ulster Co] in 1652. Made uneasy by the outbreak of the Peach War in September 1655, most settlers moved from the area, returning only after hostilities wound down. Reacting to the settlers' request for military help in May 1658, Director General Petrus Stuyvesant ordered that the settlers be relocated behind palisades; 25 soldiers remained for defense. He also asked that the Indians sell the land under the settlement. The settlement, which would be called Wiltwijck [now Kingston, Ulster Co] when chartered on 2 May 1661, commanded the strategic place where the Esopus and Wallkill Rivers flowed into the Hudson.

On reports of 500 Indians gathering around the settlement, Stuyvesant returned in October. He added to the garrison, leaving Ensign Dirk Smit in charge with instructions not to provoke the Indians. At a meeting with the Indians, Stuyvesant demanded land to compensate for Dutch expenses. The Indians gave the present of land as a sign of peace and asked for presents in return. Things remained quiet until May 1659, when the Indians complained that they had not yet received the presents. Finally, on 20 September some drunken Indians, carousing outside the palisades, shot a gun into the air. A few nervous settlers took the matter into their own hands and shot and killed one Indian and captured another, thus precipitating Indian retaliation and war. A reported 500 Esopus warriors laid siege to the town for the next three weeks and destroyed outlying farmland. Counterattacks mounted by Dutch soldiers aided by militiamen and 25 Indian auxiliaries from Long Island managed to kill or capture a number of Esopus. The Dutch murdered several captives, including the prominent elder sachem Preumaken; 11 others were sent to the Dutch West Indies colony of Curaçao as hostages. Pressured to make peace by Iroquois and Susquehannock leaders and Mohican (Mahican), Wappinger, Hackensack, and other Indian intermediaries, Esopus sachems signed a treaty ending hostilities on 15 July 1660. Treaty terms required that the Esopus free all captives and surrender their most productive lands around the settlement.

Although the treaty ended the fighting, it did not end the tensions. Nor did tensions end with Stuyvesant's order to return 2 of the 10 surviving Indian hostages at Curaçao in April 1661 and his promise to repatriate the remainder. A year later, a much resented Dutch expansion into the broad fertile planting flats west of Wiltwijck, christened Nieuwe Dorp, "New Village" [now Hurley, Ulster Co], during the summer of 1662 threatened the Esopus with the loss of their last best planting lands. War began again on 10 June 1663 when Esopus warriors surprised Nieuwe Dorp planters in their fields, destroyed their town, broke into Wiltwijck, and burned most of it before being driven out. Esopus warriors killed 20 settlers and took 47 prisoners. A force of 165 soldiers, militiamen, enslaved Africans, and 45 Long Island Indians led by Ensign Martin Cregier arrived in late July. Guided by a ransomed prisoner to a point some 30 miles (48 km) southwest of Wiltwijck, Cregier's force found and burned two Indian forts, more than 200 acres (81 ha) of standing corn, and much of their stored provisions. On 5 Sept 1663 another force led by Cregier surprised and destroyed a new Esopus fort about 10 miles (16 km) farther inland. This time, the Dutch managed to kill or capture more than 30 Indians (including a number of visiting Minisinks) and liberate 23 captives at a cost of 3 dead and 6 wounded. Fighting wound down as lengthy diplomatic efforts undertaken by Hackensack sachem Oratam and other Indian intermediaries during the winter of 1663–64 ultimately brought the combatants back to the negotiating table. Meeting with Stuyvesant and representatives from all of the major Indian nations along the Hudson Valley at Wiltwijck on 15 May 1664, Esopus sachems finally agreed to end resistance. Treaty terms required that they surrender their best lands and move farther into the interior.

Fried, Marc B. *The Early History of Kingston and Ulster County, NY* (Marbletown, NY: Ulster County Historical Society, 1975)

O'Callaghan, Edmund Burke, ed. "Journal of the Esopus War, by Captain Martin Cregier." In *Documents Relating to the Colonial History of the State of New York*, ed. Berthold Fernow (Albany: Weed, Parsons, 1881)

Trelease, Allen W. *Indian Affairs in Colonial New York: The 17th Century* (Ithaca: Cornell Univ Press, 1960)

Robert S. Grumet

Esperance. Town (pop 2,043) and village (pop 380) in NE Schoharie Co. In 1717 Palatine Germans settled Kniskern's Dorf along Schoharie Creek in the southern portion of the town. A bridge on the First Great Western Turnpike (1793), a main route to the west, was the nucleus for the hamlet of Schoharie Bridge, which was surveyed into lots in 1803, acquired a post office in 1809, and was incorporated as Esperance in 1818. The town was formed from Schoharie in 1846. The village was a prosperous manufacturing and trading center, producing paper (1809–68), leather, boots, ironwork, clothing, and hats. The railroad from Albany began operating in 1863. Later (*ca* 1885–1905) bluestone was quarried. An impressive limestone ridge, rising just west of the village, provides fertile soil for dairy farming and corn and other crops. The 200-acre (81 ha) George Landis Arboretum (1950) is a living collection of woody plants.

Peter Johnson and Dawn Johnson

espionage. The business of spying in New York State dates back at least to one of the best-known and least-successful spies of the American Revolution, American captain Nathan Hale, who operated within New York City and Long Island observing British military operations, was captured in Manhattan by the British, and was executed in 1776. British forces also received a setback during the Revolution when British major John André, who was conveying documents that indicated American brigadier general Benedict Arnold had agreed to surrender the fortress at West Point (Orange Co) to the British for £20,000, was captured in September 1780 by an American patrol in Tarrytown (Westchester Co). André was later hanged in Tappan [now in Rockland Co]. Upon hearing of André's capture Arnold fled to British-occupied New York City, making his name a byword for treason. There was little espionage in New York State in the 19th century, save the unsuccessful efforts of some Confederate spies to start a general conflagration in Manhattan in November 1864.

Espionage activities greatly accelerated in the 20th century. During World War I German agents, headed by Franz von Tintelen, made some efforts in New York City at sabotage. The massive explosion at the railroad terminal on Black Tom Island in Upper New York Bay on 30 July 1916 is widely attributed to German sabotage. Tintelen set up a front organization called Labor's National Peace Council, intending to encourage strikes among local longshoreman, but accomplished little. There was also a rise in American espionage when Herbert O. Yardley set up MI-8, a cryptanalysis organization based in Manhattan. Working for the US Army and State Department, Yardley's team (informally known as the American Black Chamber) broke the codes of at least 17 foreign countries between World War I and 1929, including those of France, Japan, and the Soviet Union. German efforts at espionage and sabotage within New York State restarted during World War II, activities treated in the well-known film *The House on 92d Street* (1945). In June 1942, four Nazi agents were landed from the submarine U-202 onto a beach near Amagansett (Suffolk Co); armed with explosives, they intended to blow up aircraft plants on Long Island, but the plot failed when one of the agents divulged the mission to US authorities. The American spy agency during World War II, the Office of Strategic Services (forerunner of the Central Intelligence Agency), was headed by the Buffalo-born William J. Donovan, the 1932 Republican candidate for New York State governor.

Arguably the most successful espionage undertaken by a foreign government within New York State was by the Soviet Union. Starting in the 1930s, a variety of Soviet intelligence agencies including the GRU (Main Intelligence Administration/Glavnoye Razvedyvatelnoye Upravlenie) engaged in military and industrial espionage centered in New York City. Operating from safe houses like 17 Gay St in Manhattan, the chiefs of GRU operations in the United States, Aleksander Ulanovsky (up to 1933) and thereafter Valentin Markin, directed a series of spies who stole documents that were microfilmed at Gay St and then transported abroad. Much of this information was of limited value. Soviet agents during this period operated with impunity because US counterintelligence was almost nonexistent. Activities by the underground section of the Communist Party, USA, overseen after 1933 by the New York City–based Hungarian Josef Peters, were more successful. Peters directed the Ware Group, which consisted of at least eight American-born policy makers working principally at the US Department of Agriculture in Washington, DC. Documents stolen by the Ware Group were first brought by couriers like Whittaker Chambers, raised in Lynbrook (Nassau Co) and later a famous defector, to Peters in New York City. One of the most successful operations by Peters was a document-production ring based at the New York Public Library in Manhattan that helped collect information to acquire approximately 100 US passports illegally per month during the late 1930s for Soviet agents. Chambers in 1948 accused Alger Hiss of being a member of the Ware Group, leading eventually to Hiss's conviction for perjury in 1950 at the US Courthouse at Foley Square in Lower Manhattan. In 1951 Julius and Ethel Rosenberg of New York City were also tried at the same venue. Charged by the US government with having passed atomic secrets to the Soviets, the Rosenbergs were found guilty and executed at Sing Sing Prison in Ossining (Westchester Co) in 1953. The presence of the United Nations (UN) in Manhattan since 1950 has ensured that New York State remains a fertile ground for espionage. Former US ambassador to the UN Daniel Patrick Moynihan claimed in *A Dangerous Place* (1978) that all member nations use their diplomatic mission as a base for at least some form of clandestine activity.

Shevenchenko, Arkady. *Breaking With Moscow* (New York: Knopf, 1985)

Tanenhaus, Sam. *Whittaker Chambers: A Biography* (New York: Random House, 1997)

Essex. Town (pop 713) in E Essex Co. It was included in an unsettled 1737 French seigneury; part was included in William Gilliland's grant (1765) and was settled under him in 1784, but reverted to the state after his 1796 death. The town formed in 1805 from Willsboro. Lumbering supplied the markets in Montreal and Quebec until the Champlain Canal (1823) facilitated shipping to Albany. Small iron mines and forges and a vigorous boat-building business continued through the 19th century. In recent years the town has developed tourism and outdoor recreational facilities. It is the site of Crater Club (1914), a private summer resort residential park, and of the landing for the Charlotte, Vt, ferry. Essex hamlet and the octagonal schoolhouse on the Bouquet River are on the National Register of Historic Places.

Thomas A. Rumney

Essex County (2,160 mi²/5,594 km², pop 38,851). Bounded on the east by Lake Champlain, Essex Co is composed of 18 towns, containing two incorporated villages and parts of two others. The county lies completely within the Adirondack Park and the Adirondack Mountain physiographic region. The hamlet of Elizabethtown is the county seat. The shore of Lake Champlain is the lowest elevation at 95 ft (29 m). Most of the Adirondack High Peaks, including New York State's highest point, Mt Marcy (5,334 ft/1,626 m), lie within the county's western half. Bedrock consists of various igneous and metamorphic rocks—largely gneiss, quartzite, and feldspar—with some limestone along the eastern margins. As numerous remnant features attest, the entire county was glaciated.

Essex Co's climate is humid-continental. Normal mean January temperatures range from 13 to 16°F (-11 to -9°C) with extremes falling below -30°F (-34°C). Mild summers average between 64 and 69°F (18 to 21°C) but occasionally exceed 90°F (32°C). Precipitation ranges from over 42 inches (107 cm) in the high peaks region to under 30 inches (76 cm) along Lake Champlain. Snowfall varies from 69 inches (175 cm) at Elizabethtown to 124 inches (315 cm) at Ray Brook. The county lies largely within the Lake Champlain and Hudson River watersheds, and its primary streams are the Ausable, Boquet, Schroon, and Hudson. Aside from the highest elevations, which lie above the tree line and have never supported tree growth, red spruce, balsam, and fir dominated the county's primeval forest in the higher western region, and beech and sugar maple dominated Adirondack and Alleghenian hardwood communities; stands of white pine, spruce, and fir were interspersed elsewhere. While most of these timberlands have been harvested at least once, isolated pockets of old-growth forest remain. Forests cover 90% of the county today. Shallow, sour soils confine economically viable agriculture to a few small areas near Lake Champlain.

Settlement

Before European contact in the 1600s, the area was very lightly used by Indians, probably Iroquois, but possibly also by the Algonquin, who lived east of Lake Champlain. There is, however, no evidence of significant native settlement in the county. Indeed, other than some temporary campsites, there seems to have been no one living in the county when Europeans arrived. The first European contact was with Samuel de Champlain and three other Frenchmen who joined Algonquins in a battle against the Mohawk in 1609 near Ticonderoga. Early French settlements, primarily of discharged soldiers and petty merchants, developed around the military posts at Crown Point and Ticonderoga, but all were abandoned in 1759. In 1765 William Gilliland was granted lands by the British Crown near the later settlements of Westport, Willsboro, and Essex. His estate was settled by over 200 tenants but was abandoned during the Revolution. Smaller grants to veterans were made along the lakeshore, but these too were abandoned as armies and marauders moved back and forth across the area, focusing particular attention on forts at Ticonderoga and Crown Point until John Burgoyne's defeat in the autumn of 1777, after which there was minimal conflict in the area. After the Revolution, newcomers from New England, attracted by land and timber resources, resettled the Champlain shore at Essex, Westport, and Willsboro. After 1795 small settlements formed in the interior towns of Jay, North Elba, and Wilmington, but much of land was too steep, rocky, wet, or isolated to support permanent settlement.

Economic Development

Essex Co was formed from Clinton Co in 1798, by which time migrants from New England and the Hudson Valley were clearing farms. Initially farming, potash production, and lumbering were the main economic activities, but soon extensive iron deposits of high quality were discovered and developed. Iron ore had been known to exist in the territory before the Revolution, because William Skene, proprietor of a large estate at the southern tip of Lake Champlain, had mined it in what became Moriah. These ores were used during the Revolution to make iron for Benedict Arnold's fleet. Most of the county's villages and hamlets had mines, ore pits, forges, furnaces, or rolling mills at some point during the 19th century. Early in the century, Adirondac (1832–56), New Russia, Westport, Willsboro, and Essex became major producers of iron ore, metal, and fabricated products such as nails, horseshoes, plates, billets, chains, and anchors, followed in later years by Mineville, Moriah, Crown Point, and Port Henry. Once the Champlain Canal opened in 1823, these products were shipped throughout the Northeast and Midwest. The Delaware and Hudson Railroad, completed along the lakeshore in 1875, provided speedier freight service. By the 1890s many of the smaller iron operations had closed down, but those at Mineville and Moriah continued to mine ores for refining elsewhere until 1971, when Republic Steel ceased operations. Lead ore (galena) and graphite were mined near Ticonderoga, the latter providing the "lead" for Ticonderoga pencils and other products (1818–1921).

After the settlement period, during which land clearance supplied lumber and raw material for large quantities of potash, lumbering stabilized until after the Civil War. At that time a regional paper industry centered at Ticonderoga began exploiting second-growth poplar and other trees. It expanded just as the smaller ironworks began closing. In 2003 International Paper Co still operated a large paper mill there. Throughout these cycles of the iron and lumber industries, farming remained a stable, unspectacular, common activity; dairying and apple growing were the norm by the end of the 19th century. While mining and heavy manufacturing began soon after settlement, banking started late and at few locations. The Essex County Bank operated at Keeseville from 1832 to 1862, followed in 1870 by the Keeseville National Bank and the First National Bank of Port Henry. In the early 21st century, most banking is with branches of banks headquartered elsewhere.

One of the county's most lasting businesses, tourism, originated just before the Civil War. At first a hardy few braved the wilderness for fishing, hunting, canoeing, and hiking, with the help of local guides. Tourism grew to become a major economic force by the 1880s, when large resort hotels opened, improved roads and railway connections made travel more pleasant, and advertising promoted growth. Merchants and hotel keepers in the hamlet of North Elba [now Lake Placid] were especially successful in this business and helped turn an empty wilderness landscape into a vacation land. By the first decade of the 20th century tourism expanded into a year-round business as resort owners offered their visitors the traditional snowshoes, sleds, skates, and good food, but also skiing, bobsledding, and other winter sports. By the late 1920s winter recreation had become a major economic factor in Essex Co. Under the leadership of Dr Godfrey Dewey, a successful bid was made to host the 1932 Winter Olympics. New York State largely financed the construction of many of the original venues for the 1932 Games, including Mt Van Hoevenberg bobsled run, various ski jumps, and Olympic Stadium. The winter sports and tourism industry continued to expand in the decades that followed, and a second successful Winter Olympics bid was made. The 1980 games brought an even larger crowd of athletes, officials, and spectators to the county, again backed financially by the state and organized by the Olympic Regional Development Authority. Winter tourism remains a major part of the county's economy and landscape in the early 21st century. In summer and fall, hiking, fishing, hunting, and camping attract many thousands of visitors annually.

Religion, Education, and Culture

For much of the early settlement period beginning in the 1760s, most settlers came from New England and the Hudson Valley. This pattern is demonstrated by the development of churches. Congregational and Baptist groups from New England tended to organize first, followed by Methodist, Episcopal, Presbyterian, and Universalist congregations generally after 1830. Early

ESSEX CO POPULATION CENSUS FIGURES

	White	Nonwhite	Total Population	Foreign-Born
1810	9,474	3	9,477	—
1820	12,780	31	12,811	189
1830	19,227	60	19,287	590
1840	23,556	78	23,634	—
1850	31,098	50	31,148	2,912
1860	28,091	123	28,214	4,391
1870	28,962	80	29,042	4,633
1880	34,392	123	34,515	5,047
1890	32,927	125	33,052	3,820
1900	30,641	66	30,707	2,384
1910	33,373	85	33,458	3,848
1920	31,829	42	31,871	2,577
1930	33,864	95	33,959	2,251
1940	34,089	89	34,178	1,632
1950	34,947	139	35,086	1,557
1960	35,138	162	35,300	1,178
1970	34,486	145	34,631	913
1980	35,857	319	36,176	958
1990	35,632	1,520	37,152	1,296
2000	36,848	2,003	38,851	1,310

Notes: "Nonwhite" includes African Americans, Asians, American Indians, and Pacific Islanders and, for 2000, also the mixed race and other race categories. Through the 1960 census these figures primarily reflect the African American population. Foreign-born figures for 1820 and 1830 include only those not naturalized, and for 1930 and 1950, the foreign-born totals include Whites only. Other years include all foreign-born in the population.

French settlers were served by traveling priests. Roman Catholic parishes were founded after the 1840s, when significant numbers of Irish Catholics settled in the county; Francophone Canadian parishes followed a decade or more later. After the Civil War, immigration reflected the ups and downs of the iron industries of Moriah, Port Henry, and Crown Point. Through the 1920s new ethnic groups came into Essex Co, including Poles, Hungarians, Swedes, Italians, and Portuguese, forming lasting communities.

In 1845 a unique settlement was created in North Elba. Abolitionist Gerrit Smith offered land to African American families, including some former slaves, to aid them in qualifying to vote. In 1849 abolitionist John Brown joined this community, known as Timbucto. Brown bought land, raised sheep, and served as the colony's leader. The colony did not succeed, however, as the colonists were unable to adjust to the unfamiliar surroundings, a lack of economic support, and the long, cold winters. After his 1859 execution for the Harpers Ferry [now in W Va] raid, Brown was interred on his North Elba farm.

The earliest schools in the county began before 1800, when women taught the rudiments of writing and ciphering in homes. District or one-room schools began to appear after 1800 in the settlements of Willsboro, Elizabethtown, Chesterfield, Essex, Lewis, and Moriah. Academies were founded in Keeseville (1835) and Ticonderoga (1851). Union schools were organized first in Westport in 1860 and then in Elizabethtown, Port Henry, Essex, and Ticonderoga by 1871. High school courses were offered in Port Henry in 1866, but in most of the larger villages high schools were created in the early 20th century. Today the county is served by 11 centralized school districts. A branch of North Country Community College opened at Ticonderoga in 1979.

The first newspaper was published about 1810 at Elizabethtown. Continuing in print are the *Essex County Republican* (1839), a weekly in Keeseville, *Ticonderoga Sentinel* (1873), and *Port Henry Herald* (1873). Radio stations date from 1952 at Ticonderoga (WIPS) and 1962 at Lake Placid (WIRD). A classical station (WCLX) began broadcasting at Westport in 1998. Essex Co, with a long tradition of supporting the Republican Party, is governed by an 18-member board of supervisors, one representing each town. In 1992 the day-to-day government operations were turned over to a county manager.

Recent History

Essex Co passed through a series of economic cycles during the 20th century. The most important industries of the 19th century declined or disappeared. Only the International Paper plant at Ticonderoga and a small number of timber cutters remain of the once strong timber industry; the iron industry has pulled out completely. Extensive deposits of titanium were first exploited in 1941 at Tahawus in the west. Opened in conjunction with a rail line extending from the D&H railhead at North River, it was the largest titanium mine in the nation until its closure in 1989. In 2003, aside from sand and gravel, the only mine operating in the county was at Willsboro, producing wollastonite. In Essex Co, as throughout northern New York, the declining dairy industry has been replaced by recreational and tourist businesses and by the development of second homes. The Northway, completed through the county in 1967, provides a scenic access and an easier drive for tourists and second-home owners.

The prospects of Essex Co remain mixed, particularly with the current restrictions on development, specifically on type of construction, residential density, and land use, mandated by the Adirondack Park Agency (1971). These have limited the recreation and economic growth potential of villages and hamlets, and the state occasionally takes over private lands, thereby reducing tax rolls. No significant urban development or related sprawl is anticipated, and further expansion of resort developments is restricted. Residents often rail against this perceived control by "outsiders," but they also acknowledge some of the benefits, such as state protection of the environment, state-financed sports facilities, and state employment. While details may change over time, it is likely that the Essex Co of future will retain many of its current characteristics. The conditions do not attract many newcomers, and the lack of abundant, well-paying jobs is often cited by the youth as

POPULATIONS OF TOWNS, ESSEX CO

Town, Year Founded	1800	1840	1880	1920	1960	2000
Chesterfield, 1802	—	2,716	2,752	1,538	2,003	2,409
Crown Point, 1788	941	2,212	4,287	1,413	1,685	2,119
Elizabethtown, 1798	899	1,061	1,363	1,042	1,328	1,315
Essex, 1805	—	1,681	1,462	1,025	880	713
Jay, 1798	601	2,258	2,443	2,226	2,257	2,306
Keene, 1808	—	730	910	1,032	726	1,063
Lewis, 1805	—	1,505	1,774	739	803	1,200
Minerva, 1817	—	455	1,162	610	700	796
Moriah, 1808	—	2,595	7,379	6,626	5,837	4,879
Newcomb, 1828	—	74	237	313	1,187	481
North Elba, 1849	—	—	480	4,343	6,005	8,661
North Hudson, 1848	—	—	693	397	220	266
St. Armand, 1844	—	—	452	727	868	1,321
Schroon, 1804	—	1,660	1,731	852	1,220	1,759
Ticonderoga, 1804	—	2,169	3,304	5,267	5,617	5,167
Westport, 1815	—	1,932	1,737	1,492	1,565	1,362
Willsboro, 1788	1,716	1,658	1,450	1,684	1,716	1,903
Wilmington, 1821[a]	—	928	899	545	683	1,131

[a]Dansville until 1822.

reason for leaving the area. For better or worse, the wide swings from boom to bust that once plagued the area are gone. Aside from Lake Placid, which has attempted unsuccessfully to secure a city charter, Essex County remains rural, with a scattering of small, often picturesque villages, hamlets, farms, and clearings tucked in the massive Adirondack forests. In the early 21st century it is even a bit difficult to imagine that this largely unoccupied, untamed, and undeveloped landscape was once a place of mining, smelting, and clear-cut logging.

See also ARCHITECTS AND ARCHITECTURE, ADIRONDACKS AND NORTH COUNTRY; ART, ADIRONDACKS AND NORTH COUNTRY.

The two county histories are Winslow C. Watson, *The Military and Civil History of the County of Essex, N.Y.* (1869) and H. P. Smith, *History of Essex County, N.Y.* (1885); Watson does not devote chapters to the towns. Early town histories include George Levi Brown, *Pleasant Valley: A History of Elizabethtown* (1905) and Caroline H. Royce, *Bessboro: A History of Willsboro, Essex County, N.Y.* (1904). Arthur W. Masten, *The Story of Adirondac* (1923) discusses that early iron-working community based on primary sources. Two recent scholarly books are Richard Plunz, ed., *Two Adirondack Hamlets in History: Keene and Keene Valley* (1999) and Valerie Rosenquist, *The Iron Ore Eaters: A Portrait of the Mining Community of Moriah, N.Y.* (1990), based on sociological methods and oral history. The architectural assets of the county are described in Allan S. Everest, *Our North Country Heritage: Architecture Worth Saving in Clinton and Essex Counties* (1972). Another book of interest covers a typical private club: Edith Pilcher, *Up the Lake Road: The First 100 Years of the Adirondack Mountain Reserve* (1987).

Thomas A. Rumney

estate villages. Nassau Co villages incorporated in the 1910s through 1930s. As Nassau Co's population exploded in the early part of the 20th century (doubling in the 1920s) local property taxes increased at a similar pace to help support construction of new schools, lighting, and roads. In reaction, many of Nassau Co's wealthy estate owners incorporated their properties as villages to avoid the new levies, hence the term estate villages. One of the earliest estate villages was Saddle Rock, incorporating in 1911. It included the estate of Louise Eldridge and had about 50 inhabitants at the time of its incorporation; all residents were employees of Eldridge and lived on the estate. Eighteen villages incorporated in Nassau Co before 1920, and at least five were estate villages. Beyond giving local residents the ability to minimize taxes, village incorporation empowered residents with the ability to zone, which was a powerful tool to slow or manage growth. Of the 63 villages within Nassau Co, 39 were incorporated between 1924 and 1932. A condition of the 1938 Nassau Co charter was that any village created thereafter could not zone because town zoning prevailed, effectively halting new village incorporations. Only one village has been created in Nassau Co since, Atlantic Beach in 1961.

Sobin, Dennis P. *Dynamics of Community Change: The Case of Long Island's Declining Gold Coast* (Port Washington, NY: I. J. Friedman, 1968)

Estonians. Part of Sweden from 1561 to 1700 and of Russia from 1700 to 1918, Estonia sent its earliest emigrants to what became New York State in the mid–17th century; they arrived together with groups of Swedes. But the first significant Estonian emigration to the United States developed during the 1890s after the czarist government increased its program of Russifying ethnic and religious minorities. Precise numbers are difficult to obtain because until 1922 US records often inaccurately classified Estonians as Russians, Swedes, or Finns. Perhaps 200,000 Estonians had entered the United States by 1920. In 1896 the Estonian-Latvian Lutheran missionary Hans Rebane arrived in New York State to organize congregations under the auspices of his church's Missouri Synod. Rev Rebane was active mainly in New York City and in Yonkers, where most Estonian immigrants settled to work in area factories and later in the building trades; he founded the first Estonian newspaper, the *Estonian-American Courier* (1897–1911). But Estonian anticlericalism, stemming from perceived German control of the Lutheran Church in the homeland, hampered Rebane's efforts to organize urban Estonian communities. The arrival of socialists and radicals after the 1905 Russian Revolution intensified anticlerical feelings. After the 1917 Russian Revolutions, a leftist-nationalist schism in Estonian political life plunged Estonian American organizations into disarray until 1929 and led to the creation of the largely nationalist Estonian Educational Society. At the same time, left-wing Estonian groups merged into mainstream American trade union and socialist movements.

The arrival of thousands of Estonians in the United States—perhaps 10% of Estonia's population—following the Soviet reoccupation of 1944 and the close of World War II further bolstered the nationalist orientation. In 1952 the Estonian American National Council was formed in New York City to represent Estonian interests at the national level. The Lutheran Church predominated in Estonian religious life in New York State, and by the 1950s Estonian congregations served major urban centers such as Buffalo, the Mid-Hudson region, Long Island, and the Capital District, where an Estonian Association school and Girl Guide troop operated by 1949. Most Estonians who settled in New York State chose to lead urban lives, entering professional work in increasing numbers. Exceptions were Estonian residents of several small mining communities in Essex Co, established in the early 1900s and vanished by the 1960s.

By 1960, 6,002 first- and second-generation Estonians lived in New York State. During the 1960s and 1970s, much of New York City's Estonian population moved to suburbs on Long Island and in New Jersey. In the latter 20th century, Estonian American assimilation, intermarriage, and entrance into the middle class were rapid. On the US Census of 2000, 2,892 New York State residents claimed one or more Estonian ancestors. Of these, close to half lived in New York City or Nassau Co, with small communities in Buffalo, Syracuse, Albany-Schenectady, and Middle Island (Suffolk Co). Many of New York City's ethnically conscious Estonians attend the Immanuel and Gustavus Adolphus Lutheran Churches in Manhattan.

Parming, Tõnu. "Estonians." In *Harvard Encyclopedia of American Ethnic Groups*, ed. Stephan Thernstrom (Cambridge, Mass: Belknap Press of Harvard Univ Press, 1980)

Pennar, Jaan, Tõnu Parming, and P. Peter Rebane, eds. *The Estonians in America, 1627–1975: A Chronology and Fact Book*. Ethnic Chronology Series, no. 17 (Dobbs Ferry, NY: Oceana Publications, 1975)

Martin Fedor Ziac

Ethical Culture Society. Devoted to a secular humanist vision of a universal spirituality grounded in moral deeds ("Deed above Creed"), the New York Society for Ethical Culture was founded in 1876 in New York City by Felix Adler (1851–1933), a Reform rabbi who had renounced traditional Jewish ideas and institutions. Originally conceived as a Sunday lecture movement, early meetings were held in Carnegie Hall and later in the Fieldston School in the Riverdale section of the Bronx.

Intended to provide a spiritual and educational complement to rising labor and social justice movements, the society attracted mostly upper-class Jews and Christians. Early activities included a free kindergarten for poor laborers' children (1878), the first in the eastern United States, and a medical service that later developed into the Visiting Nurse Service. The society also started a grammar and upper school in 1890, eventually known as the Ethical Culture School, which moved in 1904 to a new building on Central Park West, which would become the society's headquarters. Ethical societies were formed in other US cities, and the American Ethical Union was founded in New York City in 1889 to coordinate national efforts. By the end of the 19th century, membership figures reached a plateau, remaining under 700 for decades.

Led by Adler, his wife, Felicia, and prominent liberal thinkers such as John Lovejoy Elliot, the society also started camps, libraries, clubs, and job services and was active in housing reform and civil liberties issues. It expanded to Brooklyn in 1905, building a grand meeting house (1922), and to other areas of the state, especially Westchester Co and Long Island, by the 1950s. Since Adler's death in 1933, the society has expanded and redefined its activities. Led by Algernon Black (1932) and Jerome Nathanson (1940), among others, society members, many of them graduates of the society's schools, have been instrumental in local, national, and international causes devoted to human rights and the environment. In 1944 Black organized the interracial, international Encampment for Citizenship, whose campers were, in the camp's early years, invited each summer to Hyde Park (Dutchess Co) by Eleanor Roosevelt and educated in the ideas and practices of liberal democracy. The society's activities turned increasingly international, with the founding of the International Humanist and Ethical Union in 1952.

Radest, Howard. *Toward Common Ground: The Story of the Ethical Societies in the United States* (New York: Ungar, 1969)

Jonathan Gill

Ethics Commission. The state agency that interprets and enforces the ethics provisions for executive branch officers and employees, including public benefit corporations and public authorities, SUNY and CUNY, and major political party chairs. It provides advice through opinions, conducts training, investigates potential violations, and assesses monetary penalties of up to $10,000 for certain violations. It reviews annual financial disclosure statements from required filers. The commission was created by the Ethics in Government Act of 1987 following scandals involving New York City government officials and legislative impasse on the nature of ethics reform. The act strengthened Public Officers Law, Section 73, which restricts certain business and professional activities of state officers and employees (eg, regarding gifts and postemployment activities) and imposed a new financial disclosure filing requirement on policy makers and higher-paid employees. The Code of Ethics in Section 74 remained unchanged, but the commission was authorized to interpret it and investigate potential violations.

The commission, with headquarters in Albany, has five members appointed by the governor, one of whom is nominated by the state comptroller and one by the attorney general. Of the three direct gubernatorial appointees, no more than two members may belong to the same political party and at least two members shall not be public officers or employees, or hold any public office. No member shall be a political party officeholder or be employed as a lobbyist. The governor names the chair. Members serve staggered five-year terms and receive no compensation except reimbursement for necessary expenses. The commission's 2002 budget of $1,939,000 and staff of 20 have remained fairly constant throughout its history.

ethnic press. Newspapers for distinct ethnocultural groups have a long history in New York State. By the 19th century Germans, Irish, and African Americans were publishing newspapers in considerable numbers; Poles, Italians, and Jews were doing the same by the early 20th century. Since the 1960s other groups have dominated the publishing of ethnic newspapers, among them Latinos, Chinese, and Koreans.

Dutch and French

The Dutch in New Netherland and New York Colony did not publish any Dutch language newspapers. There remains the tantalizing possibility, though, that a newsletter called *de Nieu Nederlanse Marcurius* (New Netherland mercury) appeared in New Netherland; there are two references to it in 1663 letters written by Jeremias van Rensselaer. No copies are extant, however, and as there were no printing presses in New Netherland, it is not clear if this serial was ever actually published. This possibility aside, the first ethnic newspapers in New York State were published in New York City by French émigrés from Saint Domingue [now Haiti] and revolutionary France. They published the semiweekly *Journal des Révolutions de la Partie Française de Saint-Domingue* (Journal of the revolutions in the French part of Saint Domingue) in 1793 and the thrice-weekly *Gazette Française et Américaine* (French and American gazette; 1795–99), shortened in 1796 to *Gazette Française.* The French language press in the state remained small. The main papers were the *Courrier des Etats-Unis* (Mail from the United States; 1828–1937), initially a weekly and then a daily from 1851 to 1932, and the daily *Le Messager Franco-Américain* (The Franco-American messenger; 1860–83). North of the city were several French Canadian weeklies such as *Le Phare des Lacs* (The lighthouse of the lakes; 1859–?1884) in Watertown and *La Patrie Nouvelle* (1875–90) in Cohoes (Albany Co). In 1943 the weekly *France-Amérique* was established in New York City, and it is now a monthly owned by the Paris daily *Le Figaro.*

British and Irish

Irish American papers in the state were generally published in New York City as weeklies; English-speaking Irish could read the mainstream press for daily news. The first Irish paper was the *Shamrock, or Hibernian Chronicle* (1810–24), published in Manhattan by Edward Gillespie. Although Irish Gaelic was still spoken by many immigrants, the Irish press was in English from the beginning, with occasional Gaelic words. The *Shamrock* was succeeded by the *Globe and Emerald* (1824–27) and the *Truth Teller* (1825–55). The first outright Catholic weekly was the *Catholic Register* (1839), followed by the *Freeman's Journal* (1840), named for a Dublin paper. These two publications merged as the *New York Freeman's Journal and Catholic Register* (1841–1917), which was sold in 1842 to the local diocese. In 1848 Thomas D'Arcy McGee, a veteran of that year's Irish uprising against England, published the first radical nationalist weekly, the *Nation* (1848–49). He also published the *American Celt* (1849–57), first in Boston, in 1852 in Buffalo, and after 1853 in New York City. Moderate nationalist papers were the *Irish Citizen* (1867–72) and the *Irish-American* (1849–1915); the latter was the largest Irish American paper in New York City in the 1870s and 1880s until being surpassed by Patrick Ford's pro-labor *Irish World and American Industrial Liberator* (1870–1951). There were also small radical nationalist weeklies, such as the Fenian *Irish People* (1866–73) and the *Gaelic American* (1903–51). The *Irish Advocate* was founded in 1893, and the *Irish Echo* was established in 1928. Both are still published, selling about 150,000 copies together in 2002.

Among immigrants from the British Isles, the Welsh created a strong ethnic press in New York State, with over 30 titles. The most important of these was the weekly *Y Drych Americanaidd* (The American mirror), also known as *Y Drych* (The Mirror), founded in 1851 in New York City. The paper was moved to Utica in 1861, and during the 1940s it became an English language monthly, which is now published out of state. Other groups from Great Britain created few newspapers, but one example is the New York City weekly the *Scotsman* (1869–86).

African American

African American papers were generally weeklies, as people read the mainstream press for daily news. *Freedom's Journal* (1827–29), published in New York City by John B. Russwurm and Presbyterian minister Samuel E. Cornish, was the first regularly published African American newspaper in the United States. In Central New York, Congregationalist minister Samuel Ringgold Ward published the *True American* (1847–48) in Cortlandville (Cortland Co), then the *Impartial Citizen* (1849–51) in Syracuse and, after 1850, in Boston. In Rochester, Frederick Douglass published the *North Star* (1847–51) and *Frederick Douglass' Paper* (1851–60). Douglass edited or published a larger number of newspapers and magazines before moving to Washington, DC, in 1867. After the Civil War, the number of African American papers grew, especially in New York City; these included the influential weekly *Age* (1880–1952). In 1909 James H. Anderson founded the still published *Amsterdam News.* Marcus Garvey, the founder of the separatist Universal Negro Improvement Association, published several papers, such as the *Negro World* (1918–33). The struggle for civil rights fostered new militant weeklies such as the *People's Voice* (1942–47), edited by future congressman Adam Clayton Powell Jr. Other African American newspapers include the *New York Voice* (1959), *Big Red News* (1975), *City Sun* (1985), and *Daily Challenge* (1972), one of the few African American dailies nationwide. In 2001 the *Daily Challenge* sold 80,000 copies per day; the *Amsterdam News, Big Red News, New York Voice,* and *City Sun* together sold 127,500 copies per week.

Other papers were published outside of the New York City area. Among these were the weekly (and sometimes daily) *Buffalo Star* (1932–61) and the weekly *Buffalo Criterion* (1925–73) and *Buffalo Challenger* (1962–79). Publications in Rochester include the bimonthly *Rochester Voice* (1934–96), in 1967 renamed *Frederick Douglass' Voice,* and the flourishing monthly *about . . . time* (1972). Syracuse had two short-lived publications in the late 1960s, the *Challenger* and *Around the Town.* In Albany there is the monthly *New York Sojourner-Herald* (1994) and in Newburgh (Orange Co) the weekly *Hudson Valley Black Press* (1983).

Spanish Language

Spanish language newspapers have been published mainly in New York City. The first such newspaper was the weekly *El Mensangero Semanal de Nueva York* (The weekly messenger from New York; 1828–31). Early papers were strongly political, such as the weekly *La Verdad* (The truth; 1848–?1860), which advocated the annexation of Cuba as a slave state; *El Mulato* (The mulatto; 1854–?1860), which opposed it; and *Patria* (1892–?1898), for Cuban exiles. Spanish immigrants founded socialist weeklies such as *El Despertar* (The awakening; 1891–1912) and *España Libre* (Free Spain; 1939–77). Cultural magazines include the weeklies *La Revista Ilustrada de Nueva York* (The illustrated magazine from New York; 1882–?1893), nicknamed the Spanish *Harper's Magazine,* and *El Gráfico* (The drawer; 1916–18, 1926–31), and the monthly *Artes y Letras* (Arts and letters; 1933–45) by the feminist Josefina Silva de Cintrón. In 1913 José Campubrí founded the weekly *La Prensa* (The press), since 1918 a daily. In 1948 the rival daily *El Diario de Nueva York* (The New York diary) was founded by Porfirio Domenici. In 1963 these two papers merged as *El Diario–La Prensa,* which was sold in 1981 to Gannett Co, in 1989 to the investor group El Diario Associates, and in 2003 to the Canadian Knight-Patton Media Corp. In 1980 an affiliate of the Unification Church founded the daily *Noticias del Mundo,* and in 1998 *Newsday* established the daily *Hoy.* In 2002 the combined daily circulation of these papers was 165,000. There are also Spanish language weeklies such as *El Tiempo de New York* (1963), *Impacto Latin News* (1967), and *La Voz Hispana* (1974). An example of the few Spanish language papers published outside of New York City is the Buffalo socialist monthly *La Hacienda* (1905).

German

The wide array of religious, social, and professional backgrounds of German immigrants fostered a diverse German press during the 19th and 20th centuries. New York City was the center of German language publishing, but German newspapers existed in 34 localities across the state. In 1914 there were 12 German dailies, 46 weeklies, and 12 monthlies. Most titles varied somewhat over time.

In New York City the German-English *German Correspondent* appeared irregularly in 1820 and 1821. Established in the following decades were weeklies such as the *Allgemeine Deutsche Zeitung* (General German newspaper; 1835–?1840), the *New Yorker Demokrat* (1845–76), and the still existing *New Yorker Staats-Zeitung* (1834). The latter, a daily from 1854 to 1975, sold 60,000 copies daily in the 1870s and 1880s. Other Manhattan-based dailies were the *New Yorker Deutsches Journal* (German journal; 1890–1918), owned by William Randolph Hearst under varying titles such as *Morgen-Journal* (Morning journal), and the Republican *New Yorker Herold* (1880–1919). There were also smaller papers such as the *Brooklyn Freie Presse* (Free press; 1864–1918), daily after 1873; the weekly *Morrisania Volksfreund* (People's friend; 1880–?1900) in the Bronx; and *Der Deutsche Staten Islander* (1867–1909).

Special-interest newspapers, usually weeklies, included *Plattdütsche Post* (Lowland German post; 1883–1960s) for North Germans, *Schwäbisches Wochenblatt* (Swabian weekly paper; 1877–1944) for emigrants from Swabia, and the business weekly *New Yorker Handels-Zeitung* (Trade newspaper; 1855–1917). Among labor newspapers were the weeklies *Die Republik der Arbeiter* (Workers' republic; 1850–55); *Arbeiter-Zeitung* (Workers' newspaper; 1873–75), organ of the First International; and *Arbeiter-Stimme* (Workers' voice; 1874–78), of the Workingmen's Party. Other labor publications were the daily *New Yorker Volks-Zeitung* (New Yorker people's newspaper; 1878–1932), which became the weekly *Neue Volks-Zeitung* (New people's newspaper; 1932–49), and anarchist publications such as the weekly *Freiheit* (Freedom; 1879–1910), by Johann Most.

Outside of New York City, before 1914, there were several weekly newspapers that became dailies for a period. These include the *Albany Freie Blätter* (1852–1913) and the *Albany Herold* (1869–1913), which merged as the weekly *Albany Herold-Freie Blätter* (1913–20); the *Rochester Abendpost* (Rochester evening mail; 1851–1967); and the *Rochester Volksblatt* (Rochester people's paper; 1854–1900). In Buffalo at least 89 titles were published in German from 1837 to 1982, notably the *Buffalo Demokrat* (1837–1918), first a weekly, then a daily paper; the daily Catholic *Buffalo Volksfreund* (People's friend; 1868–1982), a weekly after 1935; and the labor weekly *Buffaloer Arbeiter-Zeitung* (Workers' newspaper; 1887–1918). Other important weeklies were published in Troy (Rensselaer Co), Schenectady, Syracuse, Utica, Lockport (Niagara Co), Yonkers, Hicksville (Nassau Co), Bardonia (Rockland Co), Kingston (Ulster Co), Poughkeepsie, Amsterdam (Montgomery Co), Auburn (Cayuga Co), and Tonawanda (Erie Co).

After World War II the German language press declined sharply. By 1982 only the *New Yorker Staats-Zeitung und Herold* and the *Aufbau* (Construction) remained, the latter founded in 1934 by Jewish refugees and a bilingual semimonthly in the early 21st century. In 1990 the *New Yorker Staats-Zeitung* dropped "Herold" from its masthead and in 2001 moved its editorial offices to Sarasota, Fla.

Yiddish and Jewish

The first Yiddish newspaper in the state was the short-lived weekly *Di Yidishe Tsaytung* (The Yiddish newspaper) founded in 1870 by Kasriel H. Sarasohn. After the pogroms of 1881, Yiddish-speaking immigrants from Poland and Russia streamed to New York City. Highly literate and split into various political factions, they supported a large number of newspapers, and by 1915 five Yiddish dailies had combined circulation of 525,000. Sarasohn in 1885 had created the first daily, *Yidishes Tageblat* (Jewish daily news), which was bought in 1928 by the *Morgen Zhurnal* (Morning journal; 1901–53) and published as *Morgen Zhurnal-Yidishes Tageblat.* Other dailies included *Teglicher Herold* (Daily herald; 1891–1904) and two successors, *Die Wahrheit* (The truth; 1904–19) and the liberal Zionist *Der Tog* (The day; 1914–72). In 1953 *Der Tog* bought the *Morgen Zhurnal.*

There was also a strong Yiddish labor press in New York City, beginning with the *Di Naye Tsayt* (New times) by Abraham Cahan in summer 1886, the anarchist *Fraye Arbeter Shtime* (Free workers' voice; 1890–1977), and the socialist *Di Arbayter Tsaytung* (Worker's newspaper; 1890) by Louis Miller and Abraham Cahan, which became the daily *Das Abend-Blatt* (The evening paper; 1894–1902). In 1897 Cahan and Miller founded, with the support of the German American labor daily *New Yorker Volks-Zeitung,* the daily *Forverts* (Forward). By 1915, with 153,000 copies sold daily, it was the largest Yiddish daily in the United States. In 1983 *Forverts* became a weekly and introduced an English supplement, which in 1990 became the separate weekly *Forward.* A Russian edition was launched in 1995.

There was little publishing in Yiddish outside of New York City. In 2002 the Yiddish edition of *Forverts* sold only 6,500 copies, but the bilingual weeklies for Orthodox and Hasidic readers, *Der Yid* and *Algemeiner Journal* (1972), sold close to 300,000 copies nationwide. The New York City Yiddish press has been replaced by English language publications such as the weeklies *Jewish Press* (1961), *Jewish Herald* (1986), *Jewish Week* (1970), and the *Reporter.* In 2002 there were a few small publications outside of the New York City area, either weeklies or biweeklies, including the *Jewish Review* (1918) in Buffalo, the *Jewish Ledger* (1924) in Rochester, the *Jewish World* (1965) in Albany, the *Jewish Observer* (1971) in DeWitt (Onondaga Co), and the *Wyoming Valley Jewish Reporter* in Vestal (Broome Co).

Italian

In New York City the first Italian paper was the weekly *L'Eco D'Italia* (Echo from Italy; 1850–96), published by Francesco Secchi di Casala; it appeared as a daily after 1881. Other dailies include *Il Progresso Italo-Americano* (Italian-American progress; 1879–1988) and *L'Araldo Italiano* (Italian herald; 1889–1921). More to the political left were *Il Proletario* (The proletarian, 1896–1946), *La Guitizia* (Justice; 1919–?1975), and the anarchist *Il Martello* (The hammer; 1916–46). By the mid-1920s *Il Progresso* had become the leading paper, with a daily circulation of 400,000 in the late 1930s. The *Corriere Italiano* (Italian mail; 1898–1950s) in Buffalo became the state's first Italian newspaper outside the New York City area. Important newspapers north of New York City included the weeklies *Gazzetta di Syracuse* (Syracuse gazette; 1906–?1952); *La Lotta* (The struggle; 1901) in Albany; *Corriere* (Mail; 1903) and the *Record* (1925–32) in Schenectady; *Corriere di Rochester* (Rochester mail; 1905); and *Cronaca Illustrata* (Illustrated chronicle; 1915) in Mount Vernon (Westchester Co). The Italian language press declined after the 1940s. *Il Progresso* closed in 1988. Several of its editors, led by Andrea Mantineo, then founded the daily *America Oggi* (America today) in Westwood, NJ. That paper sold 65,000 copies daily in 2002.

Polish

The weekly *Echo z Polski,* published in New York City around 1863, was the state's first Polish language newspaper. Others included the labor weekly *Robotnik* (Worker; 1896–1967), renamed in 1917 *Robotnik Polski* (Polish worker), and the dailies *New Yorksky Dennik* (New York daily; 1913–62), *Nowy Swiat* (Polish morning world; 1919–71), and *Nowy Dziennik* (Polish daily news; 1971), which sold 39,000 copies daily in 2002. Outside of the metropolitan area, there were Polish community newspapers in Buffalo, such as the labor weekly *Glos Wolny* (Free voice; 1887–93), the influential *Polak w Ameryce* (The Pole in America; 1887–1919), a daily after 1895, by Rev Jan Pitass; and *Dziennik dla Wszystkich* (Everybody's daily; 1907–57). The *Polish-American Journal* (1911) is now an English language monthly. Several papers were also published in smaller Polish communities, such as the *Gazeta Tygodniowa* (Weekly gazette; 1908–?1943) in Schenectady.

Asian

Newspapers published for Asian immigrants flourish in the early 21st century. Although a short-lived Chinese weekly, the *Mei hua shin pao* (Chinese American), was published in New York City in 1883, Asian language newspapers in the state were negligible until the 1970s. Contemporary Chinese, Japanese, and Korean newspapers are often branch editions of a newspaper in the country of origin, transmitted electronically to be published locally. In 2002 there were seven Chinese dailies in New York City: *Hua mei jih pao* (China tribune; 1943); *Lian he ri bao* (United journal; 1952); *Qiao Bao* (China press; 1990); *Shi jie ri bao* (World journal; 1976); *Ming-Pao News,* the East Coast editions of a Taiwanese and a Hong Kong newspaper chain; and the East Coast editions of the Los Angeles dailies *Chung kuo jih pao* (China daily) and *Mei-chou Hua chiao jih pao* (Chinese free daily news). These papers sold together 315,000 copies daily in the New York City area in 2002. Published for the Japanese business community since the mid-1980s are weekly editions of the Tokyo dailies *Asahi Shimbun, Nikkan San Shimbun* and *Yomiuri Shimbun* (the latter daily since 2001). There are also three Korean dailies: *Chosun Ilbo* (Korean daily times; 1983); *Segye Times* (1981), by the Unification Church; and the New York edition of the Korean daily *Hankook Ilbo* (Korean times). In 1975 the state had no newspapers published in a language of India, but in 2002 there were eight such weeklies.

OTHER ETHNIC NEWSPAPERS

The American Indians of New York State also created newspapers, beginning with *Ne Jaguhnigoagesgwathah* (The mental elevator; 1841–50), which was published irregularly in English and Seneca at the Buffalo Creek Reservation [now in Erie Co] and the Cattaraugus Indian Reservation [loc in Cattaraugus, Chautauqua, and Erie Cos]. Since 1969 the quarterly *Akwesasne Notes* has been published, mainly in English, by the Mohawk Nation in Rooseveltown (St. Lawrence Co).

Many immigrant groups that came from Europe and the Middle East in smaller numbers after the late 19th century also supported newspapers, usually in New York City, such as the Arabic weekly *Al-Hoda* (The guide; 1898–1992); the Hungarian *Amerikai Magyar Nepszava* (Hungarian American people's voice; 1899–1969); the Czech *New Yorske Listy* (New York herald; 1886–1966), a daily from 1886 to 1923; and the Russian weeklies *Znamia* (The banner; 1889–90) and *Novyi Mir* (New world; 1911–38). The Greek dailies *Proini* (Morning; 1976) and *Ethnikos Keryx* (National herald; 1915) are still published in the early 21st century, as is *Novoe Russkoe Slovo* (New Russian word), founded in 1910 as the weekly *Russkoe Slovo,* a daily since 1913; sales were strong (55,000 copies) in 2002 because of the recent immigration of Russian-speaking Jews to New York City. Other languages in which daily newspapers were at one time published in New York City include Carpatho-Russian, Croatian, Hebrew, Serbian, Slovak, Slovenian, and Ukrainian, while weeklies were published notably in Swedish, Lithuanian, Latvian and Finnish.

Several weeklies cater to immigrants from the Caribbean: *Haiti-Observateur* (1971), *Haiti-Progrés* (1983) in Haitian Creole, *Haitian Times* (2000) for those from Haiti, with a focus on the English-speaking second generation, and the *New York Carib News* for English-speaking African immigrants from the West Indies.

In New York City there were about 140 ethnic publications in 1920. This number was 65 in 1990 but increased to 189 by 2001. In general, European American media are moribund; only the Jewish press has succeeded in creating a large number of ethnic papers in English to replace the Yiddish press. Yet supported by post-1965 immigrants from Asia and Latin America, the ethnic press remains a powerful economic and intellectual force in New York State.

Arndt, Karl, and May E. Olson. *The German Language Press of the Americas,* 3 vols (Pullach, Germany: Verlag Dokumentation, 1974)

Gale Directory of Publications and Broadcast Media, 137th ed. (Detroit: Gale Research, 2002)

Hoerder, Dirk, ed. *The Immigrant Labor Press in North America, 1840s–1970s: An Annotated Bibliography,* 3 vols (Westport, Conn: Greenwood, 1987)

Joyce, William L. *Editors and Ethnicity: A History of the Irish-America Press, 1848–1883* (New York: Arno Press 1976)

Kanellos, Nicolás, and Helvetia Martell. *Hispanic Periodicals in the United States, Origins to 1960: A Brief History and Comprehensive Bibliography* (Houston: Arte Público Press, 2000)

Karlowich, Robert A. *We Fall and Rise: Russian Language Newspapers in New York City, 1889–1914* (Metuchen, NJ: Scarecrow Press, 1991)

Miller, Sally, ed. *The Ethnic Press in the United States: A Historical Analysis and Handbook* (Westport, Conn: Greenwood, 1987)

Moss, Jordan, and Abby Scher. *Small Papers, Powerful Voices: New York City's Ethnic and Community Newspapers* (New York: Independent Newspaper Association, 2001)

Scher, Abby, Anna Gutierrez, and Daniel Lang. *Many Voices, One City: The IPA Guide to the Ethnic Press of New York City,* 2d ed. (New York: Independent Press Association 2002)

Soltes, Mordecai. *The Yiddish Press: An Americanizing Agency,* 2d ed. (New York: Columbia Univ Press, 1950)

Wolseley, Roland E. *The Black Press, USA,* 2d ed (Ames: Iowa State Univ Press, 1990)

Wynar, Lubomyr, and Anna T. Wynar. *Encyclopedic Directory of Ethnic Newspapers and Periodicals in the United States,* 2d ed. (Littleton, Colo: Libraries Unlimited, 1976)

Thomas Reimer

eugenics. The theory of eugenics emerged in the late 19th century largely from the work of the English polymath Francis Galton, who coined the term "eugenics" in 1869 and argued that society would be best served if only the "fittest" individuals were to produce the most offspring. The eugenics movement was a product of the Progressive era, and its ideas were received enthusiastically in the United States. New York State and its residents were at the center of the movement during its most active years (1910–35). Among the movement's most famous icons is *The Jukes* (1877), a study of a New York State family that Richard Dugdale, an Englishman who had immigrated to New York City in the early 1860s, discovered while acting as a prison inspector in several counties. Dugdale reported that the Jukes (a pseudonym) were a large, poor, rural, white, multigenerational family in Ulster Co of over 700 drunkards, prostitutes, minor criminals, and general riffraff. He published the book to demonstrate the remarkably high social costs—expense of jailing, maintenance in an almshouse, public drunkenness, inadequate support of children—generated by a single family. (Recent research has emphasized that "the Jukes" actually included dozens of families and a number of the community's well-respected members.) Although Dugdale characterized the family as having "hereditary pauperism," he did not forcefully argue that they should not reproduce. *The Jukes* engendered many similar family studies, most written just before World War I. Greatly influenced by the rediscovery of the laws of genetic inheritance, the later monographs unequivocally embraced the claim that people with mental retardation were often the unusually fecund parents of children with the same condition. This thesis appeared in many high school biology books in the 1920s.

Charles Davenport, a Harvard-educated biologist and Long Island resident who founded the Station for Experimental Evolution at Cold Spring Harbor (Suffolk Co), gave the eugenics movement early scientific legitimacy as he zealously applied new theories to problems in human genetics. Davenport convinced wealthy New York City residents, especially Mary Williamson Averell Harriman, the widow of railroad magnate E. H. Harriman, to donate substantial funds to create in 1910 the Eugenics Record Office (ERO) at Cold Spring Harbor; for a short time the Rockefellers modestly supported the enterprise. Several famous eugenics works were written by those closely associated with or on the staff of the ERO, such as Arthur Estabrook and Florence Danielson.

In 1910 Davenport recruited Harry Hamilton Laughlin, a schoolteacher from Missouri, to direct the ERO. For more than two decades, Laughlin, an ardent eugenicist and indefatigable worker, made the ERO the most important force in advocating eugenic public policies in the United States. He drafted model state legislation for involuntary sterilization of people with mental retardation, testified in the landmark lawsuit *Buck v Bell* (1927) that decided the constitutionality of those laws, and was a key expert witness before Congress, testifying in favor of an immigration bill that created a quota system sharply skewed by ethnic background. By the 1920s Davenport pulled back from a staunchly pro-eugenics position, and as the years passed he became embarrassed by much of Laughlin's work. Without Davenport's support, the Carnegie Institute, a major contributor to Cold Spring Harbor, was reluctant to support Laughlin, who was forced into retirement in 1939.

In 1918 several patrician residents of New York City, including the attorney Madison Grant, established the eugenically oriented Galton Society, which was the forerunner of the much larger American Eugenics Society (AES), founded in 1922 and incorporated in 1926. The AES attracted many socially and intellectually prominent New Yorkers and helped to legitimize eugenic ideas in debates over social welfare throughout the nation. Among its leaders was anthropologist Henry Fairfield Osborn, director of the American Museum of Natural History. The AES, which often met at the museum, grew out of the Second International Congress of Eugenics held there in 1921. The society flourished in the 1920s but quieted during the Great Depression. The organizers read as a "who's who" of the American eugenics movement. During the second half of the 20th century, the AES evolved into an organization that focused on limiting population growth.

At the state level the major goal of eugenicists was curbing reproduction by the "unfit." This reached its apotheosis in the involuntary sterilization laws, which were eventually enacted in about 30 states. The New York State sterilization law was passed by an overwhelming majority of the legislature in 1912 but was not implemented with nearly the zeal that was evident elsewhere. In 1918 it was struck down by a state court as an unconstitutional violation of the equal protection clause. Interestingly, Davenport and other leading New York eugenicists, such as Bleeker Van Wagenen, were at best lukewarm in their support of the law; Davenport did not think there was sufficient evidence to judge if any particular person was retarded due to a genetic disorder. Only a few dozen persons were ever sterilized pursuant to the law, and almost all were mentally ill women for whom doctors argued that hysterectomies would help control behavior. In the years just after World War II, several New Yorkers, especially the geneticist Theodosious Dobzhansky of Columbia University, were among the most ardent critics of eugenics. By the 1950s it was clear that conditions such as mental retardation were far more complex than had been envisioned by Davenport's early genetic theories and that eugenic programs could have no significant impact of the success or failures of the next generation. Eugenic ideas still surface occasionally, especially from conservative organizations that support population control.

Kevles, Daniel. *In the Name of Eugenics* (New York: Knopf, 1985)
Ludmerer, Kenneth. *Genetics and American Society* (Baltimore: Johns Hopkins Univ Press, 1972)
Reilly, Philip R. *The Surgical Solution: A History of Involuntary Sterilization in the United States* (Baltimore: Johns Hopkins Univ Press, 1991)

Philip R. Reilly

Evacuation Day. Lapsed holiday. On 25 Nov 1783 occupying British forces and loyalists departed New York City after seven years of occupation, and George Washington made his triumphal return to the city. When the British colors at Fort George were hauled down, a boisterous 10-day celebration followed, and for more than a century New Yorkers observed November 25 with parades and patriotic events as the end of the Revolutionary War. The centennial in 1883 was one of the great civic celebrations of the 19th century in New York City, rivaling the nation's centennial on 4 July 1876. Approximately 200,000 citizens took part, with Pres Chester A. Arthur presiding, braving a torrential downpour. Following the centennial, observance dropped off dramatically. One of the last recorded was in 1916 when 60 members of the Old Guard, a veterans' group, held a rally around a flagpole at the Battery. The demise of observing the event is clearly tied to both the decline of anti-British sentiment with the onset of World War I and its proximity to Thanksgiving. After World War I the holiday was formally observed only once, in 1983, its bicentennial year, at Fraunces Tavern in New York City.

Riker, James. *Evacuation Day, 1783, Its Many Stirring Events: With Recollections of Capt. John Van Arsdale* (New York: 1883)

Leonard Benardo

Evans. Town (pop 17,594) in SW Erie Co. On Lake Erie and settled in 1804, the town was formed from Eden in 1821. The Buffalo and State Line Railroad (1852) was the first of three parallel lines running through town. The New York State Thruway crossed Evans in 1957. In the early 21st century it is a town of dairy and corn farms. The New Era Cap Co at Derby employed 904 workers (2003) to produce sports caps. Graycliff (1926–27), the summer home of Darwin and Isabel Martin designed by Frank Lloyd Wright, is listed on the National Register of Historic Places and is open to the public. Evans was the birthplace of Willis Haviland Carrier (1876–1950), who invented modern air-conditioning in 1902.

Andrew C. Maines

Subway passengers in New York City. Photograph by Walker Evans, 1938. All rights reserved, The Metropolitan Museum of Art.

Evans, Walker (*b* St. Louis, ?3 Nov 1903; *d* New Haven, Conn, 10 Apr 1975). Photographer. Intending to become a writer, Evans entered Williams College (Williamstown, Mass) in 1922 to study literature but left a year later for Manhattan, where he subsisted on odd jobs. In 1926 he lived in Paris, studying French literature and civilization. Shortly after his return to New York City in 1927 Evans turned seriously to photography. From 1927 to 1929 he focused on the city's streets, people, and buildings, often in an abstracting style influenced by European modernism. Three of his photographs of the Brooklyn Bridge were published in 1930 in Hart Crane's *The Bridge*. Also that year Evans became proficient with large-format cameras and developed the aloof, frontal approach to his subjects that characterizes his mature oeuvre. He began a record of American Victorian architecture in 1931, resulting in a 1933 solo photography exhibition at the Museum of Modern Art in New York City. He took his first assignment with *Fortune* magazine in 1934 and from 1935 to 1937 worked for the federal Resettlement Administration, which was later called the Farm Security Administration (FSA), documenting the depression. On leave from the FSA in 1936, Evans collaborated with writer James Agee on a photo-essay for *Fortune* describing the conditions of three sharecropping families in Alabama. The article was rejected, but Evans and Agee turned the material into the book *Let Us Now Praise Famous Men* (1941). By the late 1930s Evans was considered the leading documentary photographer of his generation. In 1938 his Museum of Modern Art exhibition and its accompanying publication, *American Photographs,* enjoyed tremendous acclaim. Over the next several years Evans used a concealed camera to photograph passengers on New York City subways. The series was published a quarter-century later as *Many Are Called* (1966). Evans was special photographic editor at *Fortune* from 1948 to 1965 and was on the faculty of the Yale School of Art and Architecture from 1964 to 1972. He was named a fellow of the American Academy of Arts and Letters in 1968. A retrospective of his work was held in 1971 at the Museum of Modern Art in New York City.

Evans, Walker. *American Photographs,* 50th anniversary ed. (New York: Museum of Modern Art, 1988)
Mellow, James. *Walker Evans* (New York: Basic Books, 1999)

Amy Kurlander

Evans Mills. Village (pop 605) in Le Ray (Jefferson Co). Settled in 1804 at the confluence of Pleasant and West Creeks, the village took its name from saw- and gristmills built by founder Ethni Evans. A post office opened in 1823, and in the following year Charles Grandison Finney arrived, newly ordained, and is credited with the religious conversion of most of the residents. With the arrival of the Potsdam and Watertown Railroad (1854; later Rome, Watertown and Ogdensburg), Evans Mills became an important shipping point for the town's agricultural products. The village was incorporated in 1874. As a result of Pine Camp expansion in 1941, the village is at the edge of the military base. The Fort Drum expansion in the 1980s brought new development: new homes and military housing, new stores and service businesses, new jobs and opportunities.

Laura Lynne Scharer

Evarts, William M(axwell) (*b* Boston, Mass, 6 Feb 1818; *d* New York City, 28 Feb 1901). US attorney general, secretary of state, and senator. After graduating from Yale University and Harvard Law School, Evarts moved to New York City, was admitted to the New York Bar in 1841, and soon became one of the city's leading lawyers. Following passage of the Kansas-Nebraska Act (1854), he played a key role in organizing the New York State Republican Party and chaired the state delegation to the 1860 Republican convention, in which he supported William H. Seward. In 1868 Evarts's 14-hour summation contributed to Pres Andrew Johnson's acquittal in impeachment hearings, for which he was rewarded with an appointment as US attorney general (1868–69). From that office he ended the treason trial against Jefferson Davis and defended the right of Congress to issue greenbacks in the Legal Tender cases. He was the first president of the New York Bar Association (1870), serving as such for nine years. In 1875 he was the principal defense lawyer in

Henry Ward Beecher's adultery trial. In 1877, as Republican counsel before the electoral commission, he successfully argued Rutherford B. Hayes's presidential claim, and served Hayes as secretary of state (1877–81). In this position he worked for a Central American canal under US control and was an influential advisor on domestic affairs, advocating the end of Reconstruction and railroad regulation. Within the New York State Republican Party, he was a leader of opposition to Roscoe Conkling. He served as US senator from New York State (1885–91) and spent his last years quietly in New York City.

Barrows, Chester. *William M. Evarts: Lawyer, Diplomat, Statesman* (Chapel Hill: Univ of North Carolina Press, 1941)

Dyer, Brainerd. *The Public Career of William M. Evarts* (1933; repr New York: Da Capo Press, 1969)

Jon Sterngass

Eve, Arthur O(wen) (*b* New York City, 23 Mar 1933). Democratic assemblyman. Raised in Manhattan, Eve attended West Virginia State College in Institute but in 1953 withdrew due to financial pressures, found work in Buffalo, attended Erie Community College, and gained his degree in 1957. An unsuccessful candidate for the New York State Senate in 1965, Eve was elected to the New York State Assembly in 1966 from a Buffalo district and remained in the assembly through 2002. During the 1971 uprising at Attica Correctional Facility (Wyoming Co), he led a committee attempting to resolve the conflict and later condemned Gov Nelson A. Rockefeller for how he handled it. In 1977 Eve won the Democratic nomination for mayor of Buffalo, becoming the first African American to win a Democratic mayoral primary in the state, although he lost in the general election. He became deputy speaker of the state assembly in 1979, holding this post until he retired. In the assembly Eve advocated aid to disadvantaged students, minority businesses, and the elderly and funds for housing rehabilitation. Shortly before his retirement, Eve founded Buffalo-based Freedom, Justice and Hope, a foundation addressing public policy issues.

"Eve Begins a New Era: Veteran Lawmaker Says Goodbye to Public Office," *Buffalo News*, 7 Dec 2002

Jeffrey Kraus

Everson Museum of Art. Initially the Syracuse Museum of Fine Art, established in 1896 by George Fisk Comfort, the founder and dean of Syracuse University's College of Fine Arts and a cofounder of the Metropolitan Museum of Art in New York City. Comfort believed that an art museum should serve as an educational tool within the community, and to this end he launched America's first museum educational program. The museum was originally housed in the Onondaga Savings Bank in downtown Syracuse. In 1906 it relocated to the Syracuse Public Library. Four years later, on Comfort's death, Fernando Carter was named museum director. Carter focused on acquiring American art and ceramics, and organized exhibitions of local artists. One of his major acquisitions, in 1916, was a 31-piece porcelain collection by Adelaide Alsop Robineau, Syracuse's celebrated ceramist. The museum named its third director, Anna Wetherill Olmsted, on Carter's death in 1931. Olmsted added community outreach programs and began a series of ceramic exhibitions that earned the museum international notice. In 1937 the museum relocated to James St near downtown Syracuse.

In 1968, on moving into its present home at 401 Harrison St, a new building and the first of its type designed by architect I. M. Pei, it was renamed the Everson Museum of Art for local art patron and philanthropist Helen S. Everson. In subsequent years its directors added collections of video art, ethnic art, and photography. Milton Avery, Helen Frankenthaler, Morris Louis, John Marin, Jackson Pollock, Frederic Remington, Gilbert Stuart, and Andrew Wyeth are among the artists featured in the museum's permanent collection. Its ceramic and video art collections are among the most significant in the nation. The museum attracts approximately 100,000 visitors annually.

Everson Museum of Art, http://www.everson.org

Perry, Barbara A. *American Art Pottery: From the Collection of Everson Museum of Art* (New York: Harry N. Abrams, 1997)

Excelsior. See STATE SEAL AND STATE FLAG.

Excelsior College. Private college based in Albany. Originally part of the SUNY system, the school opened as the Regents External Degree Program (1971), awarding associate's and bachelor's degrees to students demonstrating college-level learning acquired through conventional college course work, college-level proficiency examinations, and evaluated courses taken from the military, government, and industry. The school functions through home-based and distance-learning courses. Renamed Regents College in 1984, then Excelsior College in 1998 after becoming a private institution, the school offers degrees in 30 undergraduate programs, including business, liberal arts, and nursing, with more limited master's programs. In 2001 undergraduate enrollment stood at 17,886.

Nolan, Donald J. *Regents College: The Early Years* (Virginia Beach: Donning, 1998)

Paul Trela

executive branch. As Alexander Hamilton, one of New York State's delegates to the US Constitutional Convention of 1787, observed, "Energy in the executive is a leading character in the definition of good government." Although Hamilton focused on the executive branch of the national government, his observation has long been apt for the executive branch of the New York State government. From the early 20th century in particular, New York State's governors have vigorously assumed the challenges of organizing and administering the executive branch.

EVOLUTION AND STRUCTURE

By the beginning of the 20th century, the executive branch had grown into a massive entity. At the time the 1915 Constitutional Convention convened, there were 169 separate departments, bureaus, commissions, boards, and committees—many with overlapping functions. One goal was to streamline all of them into 17 departments, which could be grouped into three categories: those headed by the separately elected attorney general and comptroller, those whose duties included administrative as well as some judicial or legislative powers (such as education or the Public Service Commission), and those that served as purely executive agencies (such as the Division of the Budget).

EXECUTIVE BRANCH DEPARTMENTS, 2003

- Agriculture and Markets
- Audit and Control (Comptroller's Office)
- Banking
- Civil Service
- Correctional Services
- Empire State Development
- Education
- Environmental Conservation
- Executive (headed by the governor)
- Family Assistance
- Health
- Insurance
- Labor
- Law (Attorney General's Office)
- Mental Hygiene
- Motor Vehicles
- Public Service
- State
- Taxation and Finance

Although voters rejected the whole of the revised constitution, in the 1920s Gov Alfred E. Smith spearheaded executive branch reforms similar to those proposed. The executive branch of the early 21st century took shape following a 1925 constitutional amendment permitting a maximum of 20 departments, one of which, the Executive Department (formally, since 1961, the Executive Offices of the Governor), the governor heads. In terms of formal powers, the office of governor is one of the strongest in the nation. It derives its muscle from broad appointment authority, an executive budget system, the item veto on appropriation bills, and the absence of limitation on number of terms served. Many of these powers were incorporated as amendments to the state constitution in the 1920s and 1930s.

While the formal powers of the office of the governor are strong, they are not absolute. Seventeen departments report directly to the governor, and their heads are appointed by him or her, subject to the advice and consent of the senate. Three departments, Law, Education, and Audit and Control, derive authority from independent sources. The State Education Department, the administrative agency to the Board of Regents, whose members are elected by the state legislature, is not directly responsible to the governor; the commissioner of the Education Department is appointed by the Board of Regents. The Law Department and the Audit and Control Department are headed by the independently elected attorney general and comptroller, respectively. Thus while the governor does not exercise direct control over all executive functions, these three departments are subject to the same budget process as other executive agencies.

Unlike the presidential model, in which the only elected officials are the president and vice president, a plural executive presents special challenges. For the governor, this means working with officials who claim their own statewide, political constituency. The nature of the relationship between the governor and each of the three department heads depends on institutional powers, personal style, and political ambitions. From time to time, disputes surface publicly. For example, Gov George E. Pataki proposed to abolish the Board of Regents and streamline the Department of Education shortly after he took office in 1995. The legislature failed to act on the proposal, but Pataki's initiative reflected his and his predecessors' frustration at not being able to manage directly this large executive branch agency.

The comptroller's extensive auditing power derives from the state constitution, and the role of sole trustee of the state's huge common retirement fund derives from statutes. Recent governors have welcomed the comptroller's agreement with revenue estimates in the executive budget proposals. However, the independent standing of the comptroller in the executive branch is ever present, as felt, for example, in the comptroller's choices of state agencies for audit.

The attorney general, the state's chief legal officer, represents state officials and agencies in numerous lawsuits each year. Yet disagreements over the role of the attorney general as the executive's lawyer date at least to the administration of Gov W. Averell Harriman during the 1950s. One of the most publicized disputes occurred in 1984, when Attorney General Robert Abrams refused the request of Gov Mario M. Cuomo to prepare a legal defense of a sports-betting proposal.

Although potential for conflict exists, the executive branch is conspicuous for the wide range of occupational skills represented and services rendered. State employees vary from police officers, professors in the SUNY system, and highway engineers, to psychologists, physicians, and health-care aides at state developmental institutions. In many policy areas, New York State provides services that are not offered by the governments of most other states. It spends more per capita for mental health patients; it provides more extensive Medicaid services; and it supports more research in such health-related areas as alcoholism and communicable diseases. The state's regulatory functions are also extensive, ranging from such issues as permit requirements and business development and expansion to inspection of children's camps.

Some agencies receive substantial funding from the federal government, while others charge fees to offset the costs of providing services. Regardless of financing source, each agency is subject to the executive budget process, bound by the restrictions of civil service regulations, influenced by periodic public employee union negotiations with state management, and subject to audit processes from the state comptroller's Department of Audit and Control.

Wielding Executive Power

In the 20th century, particularly since the constitutional convention in 1938, the New York State government provided an increasing number of services to its citizens and residents. Although the number of executive branch departments is restricted to 20 by the state constitution, governors have not been fettered by this limitation and have expanded the duties of some departments, restructured others, and created new, sometimes nontraditional, agencies to meet the state's needs. Notably, Gov Nelson A. Rockefeller reshaped and enlarged the executive branch in the 1960s and 1970s. When he believed new agencies were needed to handle public programs, he created them. When new programs were developed, he enlarged existing agencies and opened new offices throughout the state. When traditional agencies were deemed inappropriate to handle new challenges, Rockefeller turned to public authorities. All of these actions added to the governor's authority and prestige within the governmental system. Rockefeller managed to stay within the constitutional limitations by creating offices, divisions, and boards to serve similar purposes as executive departments.

When he took office as governor, Rockefeller's priorities were to improve rail transportation and increase New York State's electric power resources. To circumvent the Public Service Commission, part of the Department of Public Service, which he viewed as unsympathetic to his goals, he encouraged the State Power Authority to promote electric power development. In addition, he sponsored legislation creating the State Office for Atomic Development to pursue nuclear research and nuclear industry. The Metropolitan Transportation Authority (MTA) in New York City and transportation authorities in the Niagara Frontier, the Rochester area, Syracuse, and Albany-Troy-Schenectady, as well as other areas were also established. All were exempted from Public Service Commission regulation.

Gov Hugh Carey continued creating new agencies, reorganizing the administration of mental health in 1978, for example, after public revelations about shocking conditions at Willowbrook, a major state facility serving the mentally retarded. The Department of Mental Hygiene, which Carey characterized early in his administration as "in disarray," was divided into an Office of Mental Health (with responsibility for operating an increasing number of state psychiatric hospitals), an Office of Mental Retardation and Developmental Disabilities (with responsibility for operating a growing number of mental retardation facilities), and an Office of Alcoholism and Substance Abuse (OASA). OASA, in turn, was divided into separate alcoholism and substance abuse divisions. In 1991–92 Gov Cuomo, Carey's successor, reconsolidated these two divisions into a single office in response to pressures for budgetary savings.

External forces have also stimulated changes in the executive branch. Welfare reform, in the Personal Responsibility and Work Opportunity Reconciliation Act (PRWORA) enacted by Congress in 1996, set the stage for New York State to restructure the social welfare function. Article 17 of the New York State Constitution asserts the state's affirmative responsibility to provide aid, care, and support of the needy. Until 1997 the executive agency charged with provision of such services was the Department of Social Services. This department, representing nearly 40% of total state appropriations in 1995–96, was responsible for income transfer (Aid to Families with Dependent Children, Home Relief, and Supplemental Security Income), Medicaid, and other social services.

As part of the New York State Welfare Reform Act of 1997, the state legislature approved abolishment of the Department of Social Services and its replacement with a new Department of Family Services (DFS). DFS is essentially a shell superstructure housing two agencies: the Office of Temporary and Disability Assistance and the Office of Children and Family Services. Part of the restructuring included several major program reassignments: Medicaid was shifted to the Department of Health, welfare employment programs to the Department of Labor, and child support enforcement to the Department of Taxation and Finance. Some of these functional reassignments had been under consideration in prior administrations, and the federal welfare reform provided an external rationale for dismantling the Department of Social Services.

Public Authorities

Public authorities, entities responsible to their boards of directors rather than to the governor, are also loosely grouped within the executive branch. Created by governors and legislatures to escape requirements on procurement, personnel, and budgets that restrain other state agencies, public authorities are typically formed to focus on single policy areas, such as housing and transportation, or to manage large projects or services that are regional or metropolitan in nature. As public sector agencies, public authorities have the power of eminent domain and the ability to issue tax-exempt bonds to finance their activities and to set fees and charges for their services.

Public authorities proliferated during the Rockefeller years. Rockefeller resorted to authorities to undertake urban renewal projects and build housing, transportation networks, and medical and other facilities. In many cases authorities were created only after voters had rejected multimillion and multibillion dollar bond issues for these very purposes. As of 2003 there were 31 major debt-issuing New York State public authorities, including MTA, with revenues of $7.1 billion, and the Port Authority of New York and New Jersey, with revenues of $2.9 billion.

The independence of several of the public authorities created during the Rockefeller years was curtailed in the late 1970s after the default of the large, heavily financed Urban Development Corp (UDC), a development authority. Gov Carey saw potential for economic recovery and housing development in the agency, and his key advisors developed a financial rescue plan for the UDC that incorporated executive and budgetary control under closer legislative oversight. These measures were subsequently extended to some other New York State public authorities. In 2004 Gov Pataki proposed an initiative to tighten Executive Department control over public authorities.

Central Control Agencies

Four control agencies—the Division of the Budget, the Department of Civil Service, the Governor's Office of Employee Relations, and the Department of Audit and Control—are paramount to operations in all executive branch agencies. The Civil Service Department has responsibility for maintaining the merit system of personnel selection and promotion; the Governor's Office of Employee Relations, for conducting negotiations with unions representing more than 90% of the state's workforce; and the Department of Audit and Control, for audits both before and after disbursement of state funds.

Of these central control agencies, the Division of the Budget is widely acknowledged to be at the very center of executive branch operations, with the director of the budget recognized as one of the most powerful and influential persons within the executive branch. Created by constitutional amendment in 1927, the division was strengthened greatly during both the Dewey and Rockefeller administrations. The division plays a key role in developing agency budgets for inclusion in the executive budget and in ensuring that agencies spend funds allocated to them consistent with the purposes of each allocation. At any moment during a fiscal year, the division is working on three budget cycles: the year just passed, the current year, and the following year.

THE MODERN EXECUTIVE BRANCH

At the start of the 21st century, the executive branch of the New York State government engages in activities more wide ranging than those of most states. New York State's executive branch is distinguished from other states by its size and scope of functions. In 2000 the state government employed 250,000 full-time equivalent persons, roughly 90% of them in executive (as opposed to legislative or judicial) branch agencies. New York State, the third largest state in population in 2000 behind California and Texas, also ranked third in the actual number of state employees. In relative terms, state government employee figures, the equivalent of 132 to every 10,000 New Yorkers, were well below the ratio of 145 per 10,000 for all states in 2000. In contrast, local government employment in New York State at 487 per 10,000 was well above the national ratio of 391 per 10,000. This disparity between state and local government employment ratios is, in large part, a reflection of services mandated by the state government to be carried out by local governments; notable among these are educational services, with teachers being employed by local school districts. The largest single group of state workers, more than 35,000 in 2000, is employed in the Department of Correctional Services, which operates the nation's third largest state prison system comprising about 70 correctional facilities throughout the state that house inmates serving one year or more.

Axelrod, Donald. *Shadow Government: The Hidden World of Public Authorities and How They Control $1 Trillion of Your Money* (New York: John Wiley, 1992)
Benjamin, Gerald, and T. Norman Hurd. *Rockefeller in Retrospect: The Governor's New York Legacy* (Albany: Rockefeller Institute Press, 1984)
———. *Making Experience Count: Managing Modern New York in the Carey Era* (Albany: Rockefeller Institute Press, 1985)
Caro, Robert A. *The Power Broker: Robert Moses and the Fall of New York* (New York: Vintage Books, 1974)
Galie, Peter J. *Ordered Liberty: A Constitutional History of New York* (New York: Fordham Univ Press, 1996)
Liebschutz, Sarah F. *New York Politics and Government: Competition and Compassion* (Lincoln: Univ of Nebraska Press, 1998)
Stonecash, Jeffrey M., ed. *Governing New York State*, 4th ed. (Albany: SUNY Press, 2001)
Ward, Robert B. *New York State Government: What It Does, How It Works* (Albany: Rockefeller Institute Press, 2002)
Zimmerman, Joseph F. *The Government and Politics of New York State* (New York: New York Univ Press, 1981)

Sarah F. Liebschutz

Executive Department. Historically the term refers to a department of New York State government whose components are under the direct supervision of the governor. Although reference to the "Executive Department" was removed from the constitution in 1961 and replaced by the "Executive Offices of the Governor," there continues to be mention of the Executive Department in official documents, and the term is widely used informally within the state government. In 2003 the Executive Offices included 30 divisions, commissions, boards, and offices, ranging from those with responsibility for the general management and administration of government to those with clearly programmatic missions and constituencies.

The rationale for this somewhat eclectic grouping of agencies lies in the reorganization of state government engineered by Alfred E. Smith, Charles Evans Hughes, and their allies in the years from 1924 to 1928. One of the aims of this landmark structural reform was to consolidate the approximately 180 individual departments, bureaus, commissions, boards, and offices into 16–18 departments, rendering the heads of these departments directly answerable to the governor.

To prevent the creation of agencies outside the new framework, a constitutional amendment approved in 1927 limited and enumerated the number of executive branch departments to 18. One of these was the Executive Department, a group of divisions directly responsible to the governor as "head of the department." These divisions had either defined duties affecting the entire state government or responsibilities generally recognized in the United States as belonging to a chief executive. In the first category were the Division of the Budget, the Division of Standards and Purchase, and the Division of State Police. In the second, because the governor was commander of the state militia, the Division of Military and Naval Affairs also fell within departmental jurisdiction, as did the parole of persons incarcerated within the state's correctional institutions, transferred to the Executive Department from the Department of Correction in 1930. As originally enacted in 1926, the reorganization included an additional agency in the Executive Department, a division of interdepartmental relations. Its functions included reconciling differences among departments with overlapping responsibilities and promoting the joint use of state property. It proved stillborn; an amendment to the reorganization statute abolished the division early in the 1927 session.

What had not been foreseen in the original structure was the impact of events leading the state to take on significant responsibilities that had no obvious home in the departmental structure defined in the constitution. For instance, the end of Prohibition in 1933 created a need for a body of laws and rules regulating the manufacture, import, distribution, sale, and consumption of alcoholic beverages. Legislation assigned these regulatory responsibilities to a new agency, the Division of Alcoholic Beverage Control, which was placed in the Executive Department. Similarly, during the Great Depression, New York was among the first states to follow the federal government's lead with a counterpart low-rent housing construction program of its own. A small research agency had emerged in the 1920s as the Bureau of Housing in the Department of Public Works. In 1932 it was transferred to the Department of State and retitled Division of Housing. In 1938, anticipating the approval of Article 18 of the state constitution (the "housing amendment"), the division, complete with vastly enhanced responsibilities, was transferred to the Executive Department to administer the state's new public housing program. As agencies have emerged in the ensuing decades to deal with problems not foreseen at the time of the 1926 reorganization, they have often been placed in the Executive Offices of the Governor either for greater "visibility" or for want of a more logical organizational home. Among them are the Council on the Arts, the Office for the Aging, and the Advocate for Persons with Disabilities. Recent additions in this group are the Office for Technology and the Office of the Inspector General. In 2003 the 30 agencies making up the Executive Offices included nearly 19,000 positions, with a budget, from all funds, of $6.3 billion.

Galie, Peter J. *The New York State Constitution: A Reference Guide* (New York: Greenwood, 1991)
New York State. Division of the Budget. *The Executive Budget in New York State: A Half-Century Perspective.* Ed. Robert P. Kerker (Albany: Author, 1981)

Robert P. Kerker

Executive Offices of the Governor. See EXECUTIVE DEPARTMENT.

Exeter. Town (pop 954) in NW Otsego Co. Settled before the American Revolution by members of the Tunnicliff, Schuyler, and Herkimer families on the 43,000-acre (17,400 ha) Schuyler Patent (1755), it was resettled by New Englanders in 1789. The town was formed from Richfield in 1799. The Old Stone Church (1839–40) and the stone Herkimer House (*ca* 1840) are landmarks in the principal hamlet of Schuyler Lake near the outlet of Canadarago Lake, a part of which is in the town. Agriculture remained the predominant land use in 2003.

Hugh C. MacDougall

exotic species. Plants, animals, or fungi that have gained access to areas where they did not occur historically. Introduced by human activity, either directly or through habitat alteration, many have a severe impact upon the ecosystems they have entered.

Almost one-third of the wild plants in New York State are exotic weeds, originating in neighboring states or on other continents. Though few are noxious, about 40 species pose considerable environmental threats, and future control may be important. They have found their way into a variety of local plant communities, damaging them by competing for space, light, nutrients, and water, and by altering the balance of soil microorganisms. Some exotics cause direct economic losses by spreading onto farms and into orchards. Some of the more problematic exotic, invasive plant species in the state are oriental bittersweet *(Celastrus orbiculatus)*, a vine that may shade out entire forests; purple loosestrife *(Lythrum salicaria)*, a tall, showy garden plant that invades wetlands and destroys other marsh vegetation; and water chestnut *(Trapa natans)*, a floating plant that can take over estuaries and reservoirs, completely shading out aquatic habitat and severely altering it. Trees may pose invasive threats as well. Norway maple *(Acer platanoides)* is a weedy tree that has spread in the New York City metropolitan area.

Numerous game animals have been purposely introduced to supplement the fishing and hunting potential of certain areas of the state. Both the gray partridge *(Perdix perdix)* from Czechoslovakia [now Czech Republic and Slovakia] and the ring-necked pheasant *(Phasianus colchicus)* from Asia were successfully introduced for hunting from the late 1800s to the early 1900s. By the beginning of the 21st century, the gray partridge was limited to a few localities in northern New York State, but the ring-necked pheasant was common on farmland across the state.

Some species were introduced intentionally for absurd reasons, often with disastrous consequences. In 1890, 100 European starlings *(Sturnus vulgaris)* were released in Central Park to provide the city with all the species of birds mentioned in Shakespeare's plays. European starlings are now the most abundant bird in the state and chase native eastern bluebirds *(Sialia sialis)* from potential nest sites. Some invasive animal species arrived on their own, though typically aided by human-caused changes in the landscape. By hunting the wolf (*Canis* spp) to extinction by the end of the 1800s, New Yorkers prepared the way for the invasion in the 1940s and 1950s of its cousin and close competitor, the coyote *(Canis latrans)*, native to the western United States. Fallow farmland across the state also helped welcome this prairie animal and gave it the chance to adapt and invade New York State forests as well.

Species native to one part of New York State may be exotic in other parts, a fact best illustrated by reference to the state's aquatic life. Unlike their terrestrial counterparts, many freshwater species are restricted to a drainage or group of neighboring drainages. Most cannot survive on land and thus are unable to move between drainages except as a result of relatively rare natural events. Their presence in a new drainage almost always depends on human intervention; this was the case with the spread of the black basses, two species of which are native to drainages in Western New York. Although their mode of arrival is not clearly documented, since the 1830s largemouth and smallmouth bass *(Micropterus salmoides* and *M dolomieui)* have flourished as exotics in the Hudson and Delaware drainages; both species often function as invasives as well. At the beginning of the 21st century, exotic species form an important part of every freshwater system in the state; in some they dominate.

The introduction of nonnative species is a form of biological roulette, since consequences are rarely possible to predict with accuracy. The cost of this dangerous game can be high: millions of dollars have been spent in New York State and elsewhere in North America to clean the exotic European zebra mussels *(Dreissena polymorpha* and *D bugensis)* from clogged pipes of municipalities and industries. They cause problems in the state's major rivers, such as the Hudson and Mohawk, and in its lakes, such as the Finger Lakes, Great Lakes, Oneida Lake, and Lake Champlain. Likewise, the establishment of thick weed beds of Eurasian milfoil *(Myriophyllum spicatum)* and water chestnut have negatively affected recreational activities and caused a decline in waterfront property values along the Mohawk River, on Saratoga Lake, and on Lakes George and Champlain. The Norway rat *(Rattus norvegicus)*, pigeon (*Columba* spp), and starling have negatively affected the state's municipalities and rural areas alike. Though macroscopic plants and animals are the most visible exotics, some of the most destructive species established in the state have been pathogenic microbes, such as the European fungus *(Ophiostoma ulmi)* that arrived *ca* 1930 and eliminated the American elm tree *(Ulmus americana)*.

See also FISH; WILDFLOWERS.

Invasive Plant Council of New York State, http://www.ipcnys.org

Levine, Emanuel, ed. *Bull's Birds of New York State* (Ithaca: Cornell Univ Press, 1998)

Roland W. Kays, Robert A. Daniels, Richard S. Mitchell, Daniel P. Molloy, and Clifford A. Siegfried

Experiment. Pioneer locomotive of the Mohawk and Hudson Railroad (M&HRR) that ran between Albany and Schenectady. John B. Jervis, engineer in charge of constructing the M&HRR line, designed the 7-ton (6.4 MT) engine built in 1832 by West Point Foundry in New York City for $4,600. Experiment relied on contemporary power-generating machinery: its white oak frame supported a round, multitubular boiler plus an anthracite coal-burning furnace, or firebox, measuring 5 feet (1.5 m) long by 34 inches (86.4 cm) wide. The purpose and arrangement of the locomotive's wheels, however, marked a radical change from the four-wheel, English-style engines then in use. Experiment was built with two drive wheels at the rear of the engine, but instead of the usual two additional drive wheels supporting the front of the locomotive, it had a truck, attached by a strong iron rod, with four nondriving wheels. Friction rollers, or bearings, enabled the truck to swivel, allowing the truck wheels, 33 inches (83.8 cm) in diameter, to follow track curves easily. During an August 1832 test run, David Matthew drove Experiment at 80 mph (128.8 kph) on straight and level track, likely a land speed record. The key to Experiment's success was simplicity of design. While Jervis did not invent the movable railroad truck, he was the first to apply the technology to locomotives. Engine builders quickly adopted Experiment's 4–2–0 wheel arrangement, notably Matthias Baldwin, whose E. L. Miller locomotive followed the Jervis plan. From 1835 to 1842, almost all locomotives were built as 4–2–0s, or Jervis types. In 1846 Walter McQueen, M&HRR's master mechanic, rebuilt Experiment to a new 4–4–0 design. It continued in service for many years with few problems.

Larkin, F. Daniel. *Pioneer American Railroads: The Mohawk and Hudson and the Saratoga and Schenectady* (Fleischmanns, NY: Purple Mountain Press, 1995)

F. Daniel Larkin

exploration. The first people to explore what is now New York State were ice age hunters, who followed the retreating glaciers approximately 12,000 years ago. Archaeology has documented the evidence of subsequent occupation. Long before Christopher Columbus, American Indians had established a complex network of paths and water routes for hunting, trade, and warfare. The first documented accounts were by European explorers in the 16th century. It is possible that Vikings arrived here centuries earlier, but no widely accepted evidence has been uncovered to confirm this.

Early European Voyages

There is some belief that European fishermen or explorers touched on the shores of New York as early as 1500, but nothing definite is known. The first known European voyage to New York was that of Italian explorer Giovanni da Verrazano in 1524. Sailing under the French flag, Verrazano entered what is now New York Harbor and coasted along the south shore of Long Island. His discoveries are documented in maps and in a written account of his voyage. In the same decade Esteban Gómez, a Portugese explorer sailing for Spain, also may have seen the Atlantic coast of New York, but because written accounts of his voyage have not survived, his actual route is uncertain. This was the case for several other explorers in the 16th century. Jacques Cartier made important discoveries between 1534 and 1543 in a series of voyages up the St. Lawrence River. He did not reach New York but made it as far as a Huron village at the site of what is now Montreal, where he established a French claim to the St. Lawrence River valley, the northern gateway to New York.

Colonial Exploration

Largely because of political conditions in Europe, there was little follow-up to the discoveries of Verrazano and Cartier until the early 17th century, when exploration was resumed and carried forward with much more lasting results. The period of Dutch exploration opened with Henry Hudson sailing up the Hudson River in 1607. Hudson was an English navigator sailing for the Dutch East India Co, and his voyage made known the course of the Hudson River between what are now New York City and Albany and was followed quickly by Dutch fur traders and explorers. In three different voyages from 1611 to 1614, Adriaen Block circumnavigated Long Island and explored both sides of Long Island Sound. In 1615–16 Cornelis Hendricksen explored the lower Delaware River. From information on maps produced by Block and Hendricksen, we know that between 1610 and 1616 other fur traders were active on the western Mohawk River and the upper reaches of the Delaware River. Dutch explorations beyond these posts were minor. Their first trading post on the upper Hudson River was Fort Nassau (1614–17), approximately .8 mile (1.2 km) south of what is now Albany, where the Dutch West India Co established Fort Orange in 1624. At least one trip was made to the interior of New Netherland. In 1634–35 Harmen Meyndertsz van den Bogaert traveled to the headwaters of the Mohawk River to counter the French effort to establish trade with the Oneida. The Dutch were aware of the route between Fort Orange and Montreal via Lake Champlain and the Richelieu River, but there is no evidence that they traveled it.

The French were more enterprising. Under Samuel de Champlain they reestablished themselves in the St. Lawrence River valley in 1603. Like the Dutch they were also interested in the fur trade, which got them entangled in supporting Algonquin and Huron Indians against their traditional Iroquois enemies. The ensuing wars brought French troops repeatedly into northern and western New York. The first took place in 1609 when Champlain and his Indian allies paddled up the Richelieu River into Lake Champlain and fought a successful battle at the south end of the lake, near what is now Ticonderoga (Essex Co). One of Champlain's assistants, Etienne Brûlé, was sent on a mission at about the same

Detail of "Defeat of the Iroquois," from *Les voyages du sieur de Champlain Xaintongeois, capitaine ordinaire pour le roy,* by Samuel de Champlain, 1613.

time to make contact with the Susquehannock, the enemy of the Iroquois to the south. In the course of this journey, he reached the Atlantic coast by traveling down either the Delaware or Susquehanna River. The French war with the Iroquois dragged on for decades and led to other expeditions into New York. In 1666 the French staged raids on Mohawk villages along the Mohawk River west of Schenectady. These raids followed the route from Lake Champlain to the Hudson River and then to the Mohawk River. Careful maps of the entire corridor were produced as a consequence.

Jesuit missionaries were active in New York starting in the 1640s and made important contributions to the geographical knowledge of this area. Fr Isaac Jogues traversed the area between Lake Champlain and the Mohawk River in 1642 and 1646. In 1654 Fr Simon Le Moyne explored the upper St. Lawrence River, the east shore of Lake Ontario, and the Oswego River. René-Robert Cavalier de la Salle explored the territory of the Senecas, south of Irondequoit Bay [now in Monroe Co] in 1669. In 1678 he established Fort Conti at the mouth of the Niagara River [now in Porter, Niagara Co], at the site that would later become Fort Niagara. He also built a ship above Niagara Falls, the *Griffon,* for use in exploring the Great Lakes. In 1683 a member of La Salle's party, Fr Louis Hennepin, published the first description of Niagara Falls by a European. The 17th-century French explorations in New York are summarized on Guillaume de L'Isle's 1718 map of Louisiana and the Mississippi River.

After the English took over New Netherland in 1664, explorations of the northern and western regions were stimulated by rivalry with the French, and the English worked systematically to improve their knowledge of the area. In 1685 Gov Thomas Dongan sent out a trading and exploring expedition headed by Johannes Roseboom of Albany. He ventured along Lake Ontario, portaged around Niagara Falls, and eventually paddled through Lake Erie as far as Lake Huron. A few years later, Col Wolfgang Römer of the English army ventured into the territory controlled by the Iroquois, and in 1700 he produced a map of western New York.

Final Frontiers

By 1700 most of the major discoveries had been made. Further exploration was mainly a matter of filling in details. After the close of the French and Indian War in 1763 and the reduced military threat, a gradually expanding population promoted the settlement and surveying of such areas as the Susquehanna River valley and the lands around Lake Champlain.

The work of surveyors was supplemented by the observations of scientists, including John Bartram and Peter Kalm. Bartram was a Pennsylvania botanist whose travels included a 1743 journey up the Susquehanna River, through the Onondaga territory to Oswego. He was accompanied on this trip by Lewis Evans, who in 1755 published his *Map of the Middle British Colonies in America.* Kalm was a Swedish naturalist who wrote an account of his trip through the Lake Champlain corridor to Niagara Falls in 1749.

The final phase of exploration in New York took place within about 20 years after the Revolutionary War and the reduction of most of the Iroquois Confederacy territory. Large tracts of land were surveyed and opened up to settlement. In 1784 Simeon DeWitt was appointed surveyor-general of New York State, and much of this work was conducted under his direction. A map of northern New York State was made in 1792 by Charles C. Brodhead. The lands west of the Genesee River, purchased by the Holland Land Co in 1795, were surveyed under the direction of Joseph Ellicott. By 1810 New York had passed the frontier stage of development, and only a few pockets remained partially unknown to white settlers in areas such as the Adirondacks. These blank spots were filled in by 19th century scientists such as Ebenezer Emmons, who led the first ascent of Mt Marcy (Essex Co) in 1837 and Verplanck Colvin, superintendent of the Adirondack survey from 1872 to 1900 and a leading voice for the creation of Adirondack Park.

Bogaert, Harmen Meyndertsz van den. *A Journey into Mohawk and Oneida Country, 1634–1635: The Journal of Harmen Meyndertsz van den Bogaert.* Trans and ed. Charles T. Gehring and William A. Starna (Syracuse: Syracuse Univ Press, 1988)

Crouse, Nellis M. *Contributions of the Canadian Jesuits to the Geographical Knowledge of New France, 1632–1675* (Ithaca: Cornell Publications, 1924)

Cumming, William P. *The Exploration of North America, 1630–1776* (New York: Putnam's, 1974)

Johnson, Adrian Miles. *America Explored: A Cartographical History of the Exploration of North America* (New York: Viking Press, 1974)

Wroth, Lawrence C. *The Voyages of Giovanni da Verrazano, 1524–1528* (New Haven, Conn: Yale Univ Press, 1970)

David Yehling Allen

extinct counties. When King Charles II granted land to James, Duke of York in 1664, establishing the Province of New York, its territory comprised the former New Netherland colony, which consisted of most of what became eastern New York State below the Adirondack region, as well as the present New Jersey and parts of Connecticut, Delaware, and southeastern Pennsylvania. It also included most of what is now the state of Maine and the islands of Massachusetts.

In 1664 the shire of Yorkshire was organized. Like Yorkshire in England, it was divided into an East, West, and North Riding. The East Riding was the eastern end of Long Island, the West Riding was the middle section of Long Island (now parts of Suffolk, Nassau, and Queens Cos) and Staten Island, and the North Riding included parts of the present Queens, Kings, Bronx, and Westchester Cos. Manhattan Island was not part of Yorkshire. The other pre-1683 jurisdictions were in Delaware and southeastern Pennsylvania. During the 1673–74 return of New York Colony to Dutch control, three courts were established: New Amstel, Whorekill (sometimes bowdlerized to Hoarkill), and Upland. After 1674 these became English counties; the first two were renamed, respectively, New Castle and Deale. In 1680 St. Jones Co was formed from parts of Deale and New Castle. In 1681 and 1682 all of this territory was transferred to the control of Pennsylvania.

New York's modern county system was instituted in 1683, when the newly formed Colonial Assembly established 12 counties. Yorkshire was replaced by Kings, Queens, Richmond, Westchester, and Suffolk counties. Manhattan became New York Co. Four other counties were formed in the Hudson Valley: Albany, Orange, Ulster, and Dutchess. Cornwall Co comprised much of what is now coastal and central Maine.

It was eliminated in 1686 when it became part of the short-lived Dominion of New England. Dukes Co included Martha's Vineyard, Nantucket, and the Elizabeth Islands. Massachusetts took control of these islands in 1691. Much later, in 1777, two counties covering areas in present Vermont were eliminated upon that state's independence. Cumberland Co had been formed in 1766 in southeastern Vermont and Gloucester Co in 1770 in northeastern Vermont.

In 1784 two New York counties, formed in 1772 and bearing names of unpopular colonial figures, were changed to honor Revolutionary War heroes. Tryon Co, named for Gov William Tryon, was renamed Montgomery Co after the late general Richard Montgomery, and Charlotte Co, named for Queen Charlotte, wife of King George III, was renamed Washington Co. The older county names from 1683, however, all with names referring to James, Duke of York and his family, did not prove similarly bothersome and were retained.

Long, John H., ed, *New York: Atlas of Historical County Boundaries* (New York: Simon & Schuster, 1993)

Ritchie, Robert C. *The Duke's Province: A Study of New York Politics and Society, 1664–1691* (Chapel Hill: Univ of North Carolina Press, 1977)

Francis P. Boscoe

E-Z Pass. The state's first automated toll-collecting system began in August 1993 on the New York State Thruway at the Spring Valley (Rockland Co) barrier. An electronic tag attached to a vehicle is scanned at the tollbooth, letting motorists drive through at 5 mph (8 kph) without stopping; the toll is electronically subtracted from the motorist's prepaid E-Z Pass account. Dedicated lanes can handle 900 cars an hour, compared to 400 for automated coin machines and 250 for cash booths. The original toll system was developed by Dallas-based Amtech Corp. E-Z Pass was introduced in New York City in 1995. The system was installed on the entire New York State Thruway by February 1997. By March 1997 the Triborough Bridge and Tunnel Authority had issued 570,000 tags, and E-Z Pass was being used on the Verrazano-Narrows, Marine Parkway, Cross Bay, Throgs Neck, Bronx-Whitestone, Henry Hudson, and Triborough Bridges and the Brooklyn-Battery and Queens-Midtown Tunnels. As of 2002, the East Coast E-Z Pass network covered seven states, from Maine to West Virginia, with more than 6 million participating motorists. E-Z Pass is administered by the Regional Consortium, consisting of area transportation agencies, including the Port Authority of New York and New Jersey.

E-Z Pass New York Service Center, http://www.e-zpassny.com

F

Fabius. Town (pop 1,974) and village (pop 355) in SE Onondaga Co. Settled in 1794, the town formed from Pompey in 1798. The Skaneateles-Hamilton Turnpike (now Rte 80) was built in 1816. After the Syracuse and Binghamton Railroad opened in 1854, the town's dairy products became marketable, and in 1868 Fabius led the state in dairy production and had two agricultural tool factories. Toward the end of the 19th century poultry raising and ginseng grew in importance. The village incorporated in 1880. Highland Park (now Highland Forest) opened in 1932. Researchers at the 733-acre (297 ha) Agway Farm Research Center (1967–99) studied dairy nutrition and farm systems. Agriculture remains important. The 1,468-acre (594 ha) Labrador Hollow State Unique Area (1978), similar to a high mountain bog, is located in a glacier valley. The highest point in Onondaga Co (2,060 ft/628 m) is in Fabius.

Marla A. Bennett and William Casey

Factory Investigating Commission. The horrific Triangle Shirtwaist fire of 1911 in New York City brought into focus the need to reform working conditions and to implement more effective safety codes within the state. Reformers like Frances Perkins pressured Tammany boss Charles F. Murphy and his allies Alfred E. Smith, speaker of the state assembly, and Robert F. Wagner Sr, state senate majority leader. On 30 June 1911 Gov John Alden Dix signed the bill creating the New York State Factory Investigating Commission. Led by Wagner and Smith the 12-member commission traveled the state taking testimony and visiting sweatshops and factories. Between 1911 and 1914 the commission made 63 recommendations, 56 of which became law. The commission started its work by focusing on fire safety and building codes, and by 1912 it moved to issues of child labor and women's work. It recommended legislation to protect women from the excesses of industrial work, but these laws mainly restricted the employment of women. By 1913 the commission called for unemployment insurance as well as minimum wage and maximum hour laws for all workers. Many of the laws enacted at the behest of the Factory Investigating Commission became models for legislation elsewhere in the United States. These included mandating the installation of automatic sprinklers in buildings seven stories or higher, establishing standards for lighting and ventilation, and limiting the work of women in factories to a 54-hour week. In 1914 a coalition of upstate Democrats and Republicans gained control of the state legislature and ended the commission.

Photograph taken to document the work of the Factory Investigating Commission, *ca* 1911–12.

Boris, Eileen. *Home to Work: Motherhood and the Politics of Industrial Homework in the United States* (New York: Cambridge Univ Press, 1994)

Wesser, Robert F. *A Response to Progressivism: The Democratic Party and New York Politics, 1902–1918* (New York: New York Univ Press, 1986)

Richard A. Greenwald

Fadden, (Edgar) Ray(mond) [Aren Akweks; Tehanetorens] (*b* Franklin, Franklin Co, 23 Aug 1910). Educator, author, and advocate for Native Americans. Beginning in the mid-1930s, Fadden taught science in the Indian schools on the Tuscarora Indian Reservation and Akwesasne (St. Regis Indian Reservation). A passionate teacher and defender of the Indian's place in American history, he championed the pivotal role of the Iroquois Confederacy in the creation of the United States. Deploring the negative representation of Indians in most history books and the lack of cultural input afforded Indian students in the public schools, he began publishing charts and pamphlets that focused on Iroquois culture, history, biography, legend, and contributions to modern world society. He founded the Akwesasne Mohawk Counselor Organization *ca* 1940, a scoutlike organization whose mission was to train young Indians for counselor work in summer camps, where accurate information about Indian life could be taught. For many years in the 1930s and 1940s he served as secretary for the Indian Defense League of America, founded by Chief Clinton Rickard (Tuscarora) and was also closely associated with Arthur C. Parker (Seneca), founder of the Rochester Museum and Science Center. During the 1930s and 1940s Fadden traveled widely in the Northeast with groups of young Indians, taking them to famous historic sites in Indian history and visiting other Indian communities. In 1954 he established the Six Nations Indian Museum, one of the first Indian-owned museums in the country, at Onchiota (Franklin Co). Fadden has long emphasized the need to conserve and respect nature and its wildlife in a world of diminishing resources. In 1972 the New York State Council on the Arts honored him at a banquet in the Whitney Museum. Married to a Mohawk and adopted into the Mohawk Nation at Akwesasne, Fadden was first given the name Aren Akweks (Far Eagle) and later Tehanetorens (He Splits the Wood). His son, John, a renowned artist, and his grandsons operate the museum and carry on his work.

Clyne, Patricia Edwards. "Ray Fadden: Sachem of Onchiota," *Adirondack Life* (Summer 1975): 9–12

George-Kanentiio, Doug. "Fadden: Teacher, Friend to Iroquois," *Syracuse Herald American*, 20 June 1993

Fagan, Garth (*b* Kingston, Jamaica, 3 May 1940). Dancer and choreographer. Fagan, whose father was a teacher, grew up in Jamaica, where he trained and performed with Ivy Baxter and the Jamaica National Dance Theater while in his teens. At age 20 he moved to Detroit to study psychology at Wayne State University. He became choreographer/principal soloist with the Dance Theater of Detroit and Detroit Contemporary Dance Co as well as head of the All-City Dance Co. Fagan studied in New York City with José Limón, Martha Graham, Alvin Ailey, and Mary Hinkson, and in 1969 began teaching dance at SUNY Brockport. He also became an instructor at Rochester's Educational Opportunity Center, a SUNY affiliate, where he prepared disadvantaged youth for college. Part of this groundwork included dance training, and his charges became the initial members of the dance company he established in 1970, The Bottom of the Bucket, But . . . Dance Theatre, so named because its members lacked classical training and were from inner-city Rochester. By 1990 the company became known as Garth Fagan Dance.

Fagan's style of choreography is a union of ballet, modern dance, and Afro-Caribbean influences. In 1993 he collaborated with composer-trumpeter Wynton Marsalis and sculptor Martin Puryear on *Griot New York*, a modern ballet that spotlights New York City's multiculturalism. In 1999 he choreographed *Ellington's Elation*, commissioned to celebrate the New York City Ballet's 50th anniversary and Duke Ellington's 100th birthday. Fagan was cited as a Fulbright 50th Anniversary Distinguished Fellow in 1996. Two years later, he won a Tony Award for his choreography of *The Lion King*. Fagan is one of the late 20th and early 21st centuries' most innovative and acclaimed modern dance choreographers. In 2003 his dance company remained based in Rochester, conducted ongoing community dance classes, and performed an active schedule.

"A Distinct Style in Odd Shapes and Lightning Leaps and Turns," *New York Times*, 1 Nov 2001

Thorpe, Edward. *Black Dance* (Woodstock, NY: Overlook Press, 1990)

Fairchild Aviation Corporation. Established in 1925 by Sherman Fairchild, the company began production in East Farmingdale (Suffolk Co) the following year. It specialized in large, single-engine monoplanes geared to photographic work. In 1928 Fairchild laid out a flying field at its facilities. Adm William Byrd flew a Fairchild FC-2 named the *Stars and Stripes* on his 1929 and 1934 Antarctic expeditions. Although the corporation had opened a new factory building in 1928, it relocated to Maryland in 1931. The firm's Ranger Aircraft Engine Division continued operations in Farmingdale until 1945. In 1965 Fairchild Industries bought the Republic Aviation Corp, which operated on Fairchild's old Farmingdale site. In the following year Republic Airport (Suffolk Co), the 1928 Fairchild flying field, opened to the public; it has become Long Island's premier general aviation airport. Fairchild Republic's last major project was the close-ground support A-10 *Warthog*. Production at East Farmingdale ended in 1987, and the

Fairchild Aviation conducted extensive aerial photographic surveys of New York State's major cities. In this 1948 photograph of Albany, the Alfred E. Smith Building is in the center. The area to the right later was leveled to make way for the Empire State Plaza.

land was sold in 1988, becoming a shopping mall.

Stoff, Joshua. *The Aerospace Heritage of Long Island* (Interlaken, NY: Heart of the Lakes Publishing, 1989)

Richard F. Welch

Fairfield. Town (pop 1,607) in central Herkimer Co. Settled *ca* 1770 by Germans from the Mohawk Valley, the town was formed from Norway in 1796. Fairfield Academy, at Fairfield hamlet, operated under various names from 1802 to 1901. The College of Physicians and Surgeons of the Western District of New York (1812–41) was the first medical school in the state outside of New York City. In the 19th century Fairfield was a major cheese-making town, easily ranking first in New York State in 1855 and again in 1865, when it produced 1,731,534 pounds (785,410 kg). An Amish community was present from 1979 to *ca* 2000. In the early 21st century, Fairfield is a residential town for people working in Mohawk Valley towns. Trinity Episcopal Church (1807) is listed on the National Register.

Susan R. Perkins

Fair Haven. Village (pop 884) in Sterling (Cayuga Co). Situated on Little Sodus Bay, a natural harbor on Lake Ontario (improved 1854–77), the locality was called Little Sodus until the name Fair Haven was adopted in 1852. By 1859 hotels and cottages began to appear, and the area became a resort. After becoming the northern terminus for the Southern Central Railroad in 1869, Fair Haven became a coal depot for lake shipment. The Lake Ontario Shore Railroad came a few years later. A lighthouse was built in 1872 and a second one in 1877. The village incorporated in 1880. The Lehigh Valley Railroad took over the Southern Central in 1888 and operated the line through 1953. Fair Haven remains a vacation and recreation area, and the western part of the 862-acre (349 ha) Fair Haven Beach State Park is within the village.

Erwin Fineout

Fairmount. Locality (pop 10,795) in Camillus (Onondaga Co). The settlement took its name from the progressive farm of James Geddes (1763–1838) and his son, George (1809–83). The locality was the site of the New York State Farm Colonies (1883–1971) for developmentally disabled children and its successor, the Fairmount Children's Center (1969–96). Building lots platted in the 1890s were undeveloped until the 1920s but filled in only after World War II. Extensive shopping facilities followed.

Barbara S. Rivette

Fairport. Village (pop 5,740) in Perinton (Monroe Co). Created when the Erie Canal came through in 1822, Fairport became a manufacturing village (incorporated in 1867) and was a station on the New York Central Railroad (1853) and the West Shore Railroad (1882). Products made in the 19th century included agricultural implements, candy, patent medicines, extracts and perfumes, vinegar, sashes and blinds, and boxes, but dominant were the baking soda produced by the DeLand Co (1852–?1904) and the cans manufactured by American Can Co (1908–93) and its predecessors, dating back to the Cobb Preserving Co (1851). In 1912 Fairport Vinegar Works developed Certo, a pectin from apples for use in making jellies. Sold to General Foods in 1928, the factory left the village in 1946. A Rochester suburb, the village owns and operates an electric plant. It retains a box factory and has developed tourism based on the Erie Canal.

Carolyn Vacca

Fairview. Locality (pop 5,421) in Poughkeepsie. A suburb of Poughkeepsie, a large part of its territory is occupied by institutions: Hudson River Psychiatric Center (1871), St. Francis Hospital (1914), Children's Home of Poughkeepsie (1922), Marist College (1929), and Dutchess Community College (1958). It was the site of Woodcliff Pleasure Park (?1925–?41) and the Fiat Automobile Works (1910–17), and later Western Printing and Lithography Co. Marist College expansion, a shopping mall, and additional housing have taken their places.

William P. McDermott

Falckner, Justus (*b* Langenreindorf [now in Germany], 22 Nov 1672; *d* New York City, 1723). Lutheran clergyman. Falckner, son of a Lutheran pastor, was educated at Halle University (Germany). In 1700 he moved to Germantown, Pa, with German immigrants. In 1703 he took over parishes in the Albany area and in Manhattan that were poorly organized, had decrepit buildings, and were reduced by defections to Dutch Reformed and Anglican congregations. Falckner, ordained in the same year, revived the congregations and also began preaching in Athens [now in Greene Co] and Hackensack, NJ. He learned to preach in Dutch, the lingua franca of a polyglot flock composed of Dutch, High Germans, Swedes, Danes, Norwegians, Poles, Lithuanians, and Transylvanians. Reaffirming confessional Lutheranism in the face of Reformed hostility, Falckner wrote a defense, *Grondlycke Onderricht* (Fundamental Instruction), in 1708. In 1719 he added congregations in Germantown [now in Columbia Co], Newburgh (Orange Co), and Rhinebeck (Dutchess Co) to his responsibilities. Falckner was the first Lutheran pastor ordained in America and a transitional figure who rallied immigrant Lutherans amidst pluralism.

Nelson, Clifford E. *The Lutherans in North America* (Philadelphia: Fortress Press, 1980)

Robert F. Scholz

Falconer. Village (pop 2,540) in Ellicott (Chautauqua Co). Edward Work settled in 1807 and built the first sawmill on the Chadakoin River in 1808. Falconer post office was established in 1874. The W. T. Falconer Manufacturing Co (1888), which made beekeepers' supplies, was Falconer's first major industry. Later washing machines, novelties, textiles, millwork, worsted, sash and doors, and auto parts were made in the village, which incorporated in 1891. In the 1950s it became the site of metal furniture factories. In 2002, 10 factories were in operation, including SKF Bearings.

Michelle Henry

Fall River Line. Steamship company that provided overnight freight and passenger service from New York City via Newport, RI, to Fall River, Mass, along a 175 mi (282 km) East River–Long Island Sound–Narragansett Bay route. Thomas Borden of Fall River founded the line in 1846 as Bay State Steamboat Co. Old Colony Railroad acquired its interest in 1863, creating Boston, Newport and New York Steamboat Co. In 1869 Jim Fisk gained control of the company, dubbing it Fall River Line, a name that endured in the public mind despite later changes. Principal eastbound freight was baled raw cotton, and westbound freight featured finished textiles. Top-quality service included comfortable staterooms and lounges, fine food, and entertainment. Jay Gould became president of the line in 1872 and in 1874 sold it to Old Colony once again, which built two of the company's most famous ships, *Pilgrim* (1883) and *Puritan* (1889). In 1893 New York, New Haven and Hartford Railroad acquired the line through a long-term lease. It continued to operate some of the largest and most luxurious steamers on the East Coast, all side-wheelers capable of 18 mph (29 kph), including *Priscilla* (1894) and *Commonwealth* (1907). The latter slept 1,500 passengers, was 440 feet (134.1 m) long and 52 feet (15.9 m) wide and had five boilers producing 8,500 horsepower. The opening in 1916 of Cape Cod Canal, which provided a more direct water route, and the opening in 1917 of the Hell Gate Bridge, which allowed direct sleeping-car service between New York City and Boston, cut into service. Fall River Line service ceased altogether after a labor dispute in 1937.

Hilton, George W. *The Night Boat* (Berkeley, Calif: Howell–North Books, 1968)

McAdam, Roger Williams. *Floating Palaces: New England to New York on the Old Fall River Line* (Providence, RI: Mowbray, 1972)

Arthur G. Adams

Fallsburg. Town (pop 12,234) in E Sullivan Co. Dutch settlers are believed to have lived in the area before the American Revolution, but the town was resettled in 1789. It had excellent waterpower and in 1818 was reached by a branch turnpike. The town was formed in 1826 from Thompson and Neversink. Lumbering was followed by paper mills and, beginning 1831, tanneries. Production peaked during the heavy demand for leather during the Civil War but disappeared *ca* 1870. The Ontario and Western Railroad provided passenger service through town beginning in 1872 and opened the town as a resort; in 1878 the railroad published the first of its annual *Summer Homes* brochures. Beginning in 1899 some resorts catered to Jews. The noted Hotel Flagler (?1872) changed to Jewish ownership in 1908 and was rebuilt 1919–20; it was the county's premier resort until the 1930s. Other Jews came to farm through the efforts of the Jewish Agricultural Society (1900). The *kuchalayn* ("cook yourself") business peaked in the years after World War II, and the resort business as a whole declined after 1965. In 2003 the 322-room Hotel Raleigh (1902) was the only famous resort still in operation. Some old resorts were converted to Hasidic use, while several others became Siddha meditation ashrams. The largest employers are Woodbourne (1935) and Sullivan (1985) Correctional Facilities.

John Conway

Family Assistance, Department of. New York State social service agency in operation since January 1998 that serves needy families through two main units: the Office of Children and Family Services (OCFS) and the Office of Temporary and Disability Assistance (OTDA).

The origins of the Department of Family Assistance (DFA) reach back to the state's first supervisory body concerned with social welfare, the Board of Commissioners of Public Charities (1867). This board of 8 governor-appointed members visited public almshouses and all charitable institutions receiving state aid. Renamed the State Board of Charities in 1873 and enlarged to 11 members, the body continued to address problems of the institutionalized poor, including inmates of insane asylums and reformatories. In 1896 the board grew to 12 members and extended its supervision to dispensaries and fact-finding missions, and provided some oversight of the "outdoor [poor] relief" provided by most localities since the early 1800s. In 1926 the board became the executive arm of a larger Department of Charities, which lost all association with mental health and correctional facilities. In 1929 the State Board of Charities became the Board of Social Welfare (with 15 members serving five-year terms), and the Department of Charities became the Department of Social Welfare (from 1967 to 1997 it was called Department of Social Services). The board chose a commissioner of public welfare, continued to regulate institutions, and created state and local welfare policy. Removed from the Department of Social Services and established in the Executive Department in 1971, the board ceded to the governor the power to name the social services commissioner. Following the replacement in 1996 of the national welfare program (Aid to Families with Dependent Children) with the Temporary Assistance for Needy Families (TANF) program, the New York State legislature enacted the State Welfare Reform Act of 1997, reorganizing the state's social service agencies and creating the DFA.

Through its OCFS unit, formed by merging the Division for Youth (1960–98) with family and child programs once administered by the Department of Social Services, the DFA oversees foster care, adoption, child protective services, preventative services for children and families, and services for pregnant adolescents, the blind, and vulnerable adults. In 2002 the OCFS operated 48 juvenile residential and day facilities for court-remanded youths under 16 and coordinated the state response to American Indian needs, on and off reservations. County social services departments and nonprofit community groups administer most OCFS programs. In 2002 the Rensselaer-headquartered OCFS had a $3.3 billion budget—40% state funded and 60% federally funded—and a staff of 4,441.

Through its OTDA unit, the DFA delivers temporary assistance via the TANF-funded Family Assistance (FA) program, which aids, for a limit of 60 months, families with children. The state-funded Safety Net Assistance (SNA) aids individuals and families who have exhausted their 60-month grants. These programs are administered through 57 county welfare agencies and, in New York City, through the city's Human Resources Administration. In addition the OTDA provides access to food stamps, Medicaid, housing for the homeless, and other "transitional" benefits and seeks to help TANF recipients find and hold jobs and avoid out-of-wedlock births. The OTDA also delivers Supplemental Security Income (SSI), or federal disability assistance, and collects child support. Further, it coordinates city and state job training, medical screening, language instruction, and citizenship services—funded at $45 million in state and federal monies in 2002—to aid documented refugees and immigrant families.

In 2001–2, with a budget of $4.4 billion and a staff of 2,511, the Albany-headquartered OTDA served 655,280 FA and SNA recipients, 1,317,034 food stamp recipients, and 624,971 SSI recipients, and it collected $1.3 billion in child support. The terrorist attacks of 11 Sept 2001 caused the OTDA to relocate two Manhattan facilities, 80 Maiden Lane and 22 Cortlandt St, and to approve New York City's $3.8 million Food Stamp Disaster Relief Program, benefiting 33,000; the OTDA also ran the Governor's World Trade Center Relief Fund, which received over $61 million in donations.

Bernstein, Nina. *The Lost Children of Wilder: The Epic Struggle to Change Foster Care* (New York: Pantheon, 2001)

White, Julie Anne. *Democracy, Justice, and the Welfare State: Reconstructing Public Care* (University Park: Pennsylvania State Univ Press, 2000)

Jeffrey Kraus

Fargo, William G(eorge) (*b* Pompey, Onondaga Co, 20 May 1818; *d* Buffalo, 3 Aug 1881). Entrepreneur and businessman. A mail carrier as a youth, Fargo became an agent for the express firm Pomeroy and Co in Buffalo in 1843. The following year he, Henry Wells, and Daniel Dunning founded Wells and Co, the first express company to offer service west of Buffalo. Mergers with competing lines led to the formation of the American Express Co in 1850, with Fargo as secretary. In 1852 Wells, Fargo and Co was created to provide express service to California. Fargo also helped form Butterfield Overland Mail Co, a stage line connecting Missouri and California, in 1857. A Democrat, he served two terms as mayor of Buffalo from 1862 to 1865 but was defeated in a run for the state senate in 1871. He was president of Wells Fargo from 1870 to 1872 and of American Express from 1868 until his death. The Northern Pacific Railroad, which Fargo had helped finance, named the town of Fargo, ND, after him in 1871.

American National Biography, sv "Fargo, William George"

Martin Stahl

Farley, James A(loysius) (*b* Grassy Point, Rockland Co, 30 May 1888; *d* New York City, 9 June 1976). Democratic Party leader. The son of Irish immigrants, Farley became a bookkeeper at a Rockland Co gypsum mining and processing firm. He began his political career when he won the post of town clerk of Stony Point (Rockland Co) in 1912. He moved to the New York State Assembly from Rockland Co in 1922, serving one term, and later was chair of the New York State Athletic Commission (1925–33). Farley's rise to prominence came through his association with Franklin D. Roosevelt, playing an important role in Roosevelt's winning the governorship in 1928 and 1930. As chair of the state Democratic Party (1930–44) he was known to have memorized almost every state party operative's name, down to the lowest precinct worker. Farley managed Roosevelt's presidential campaigns of 1932 and 1936, and was postmaster general in his cabinet (1933–40). He backed Herbert H. Lehman's election as governor in 1932 and reluctantly helped organize the American Labor Party in 1936, a state third party that channeled additional votes to Lehman and Roosevelt. However, Farley openly broke with Roosevelt in 1940 when the president sought a third term. Some observers felt that Farley wanted the nomination himself. Farley and Roosevelt backed different candidates in the 1942 gubernatorial race, and while Farley's candidate, John J. Bennett, won the nomination, he ran and lost in the general election without Roosevelt's backing. In 1944 Farley resigned from the state Democratic Party chairmanship and spent the rest of his life as head of the Coca Cola Export Corp. In 1965 he briefly returned to politics to lead Abe Beame's unsuccessful campaign for mayor of New York City. Many consider Farley as the most significant state Democratic organization figure of the 20th century.

Farley, James A. *Behind the Ballots: The Personal History of a Politician* (New York: Harcourt, Brace, 1938)

Daniel C. Kramer

Farley, John M(urphy) (*b* Newton-Hamilton, Ireland, 20 Apr 1842; *d* New York City, 17 Sept 1918). Roman Catholic cardinal. After a youth spent in Ireland, Farley emigrated to New York City in 1864 and enrolled in St. John's College (now Fordham University). A year later he transferred to the Catholic theological seminary at Troy (Rensselaer Co), and the following year to the North American College in Rome, where he was ordained on 11 June 1870. He returned to the New York City area that year and ministered in St. Peter's parish on Staten Island for two years. In 1872 he became secretary to Archbishop John McCloskey, a post he held for 12 years. Between 1884 and 1902 Farley served as pastor of St. Gabriel's parish in Manhattan, vicar general of the archdiocese, president of the Catholic school board, and auxiliary bishop. He became archbishop of New York in September 1902 and cardinal in 1911. Farley made Catholic education a hallmark of his administration, adding 50 parish schools to the archdiocese during the first eight years of his tenure. He was committed to higher education and scholarship, as reflected in his opening of Cathedral College in Brooklyn and his sponsorship of the *Catholic Encyclopedia.*

Cohalan, Florence D. *A Popular History of the Archdiocese of New York* (Yonkers: US Catholic Historical Society, 1983)
Thornton, Francis B. *Our American Princes: The Story of the Seventeen American Cardinals* (New York: Putnam's, 1963)

Timothy Walch

Farmer's Brother [Honayawas] (*b ca* 1725; *d ca* 1815). Seneca war chief and diplomat. A warrior and leader, he was among those who agreed in September 1776 to abandon the official Iroquois Confederacy policy of neutrality and to support the British. During the Revolutionary War, he took part in numerous battles, including Wyoming Valley in Pennsylvania in 1778 and Schoharie Valley in 1780. During the War of 1812 he fought for the United States. Present during various important treaty negotiations, he and other Seneca leaders accepted a life annuity in exchange for their support of the Treaty of Big Tree in 1797. He and the famous Seneca orator Red Jacket resisted the educational efforts of missionaries. His 1798 speech, which accompanied the gift of a 2 mi (3 km) plot of land to Horatio Jones, a former white captive, commemorated Seneca gratitude for Jones's services as interpreter.

Wallace, Anthony F. C. *The Death and Rebirth of the Seneca* (New York: Knopf, 1970)

George H. J. Abrams

farmers' markets. New York farmers carried produce and drove livestock to centrally located fairs and markets along the upper and lower Hudson River as early as the late 17th century. In 1693 a weekly market was established at Westchester [now in Bronx Co], along with an annual fair to meet alternately at Westchester and Rye (Westchester Co). The Rochester Public Market, established in 1905, is owned and operated by the City of Rochester and is one of the few original market structures in the state. It began as a wholesale produce and grocery distribution point but started retail sales after World War I as a way to combat inflation. In 2002 the market had 230 outside covered vending spaces and 68 indoor heated ones, was open throughout the year, and attracted more than 1.5 million shoppers annually. The Central New York Regional Market in Syracuse, established in the 1930s, is open from May through November, is operated by a public authority, and is the largest market in the state, serving 300 farmer-growers in 2001 at its 61-acre (24.7 ha) site north of downtown Syracuse. An $8.5 million renovation was completed in 2003. Greenmarket, founded in 1976 by Barry Benepe, organizes and manages open-air farmers' markets throughout New York City. The first opened at 59th St and 2d Ave, with stated goals of bringing high-quality produce to New York City, protecting the viability of local small farms, and strengthening the community by forging bonds among farmers, consumers, and local residents. It is a program in the Council on the Environment of New York City, a privately funded organization in the Office of the Mayor. In 2001 the market had 25 locations in Manhattan, Brooklyn, Queens, Bronx, and Staten Island, with close to 175 farmers and food producers participating.

The number of farmers' markets in New York State has risen dramatically since the 1970s. Public interest in the environment, neighboring farms, and living "closer to nature" played a role, as did the desire to know more about one's food source. Also since the late 1970s, the markets have been supported by federal programs. The Farmers' Market Nutrition Program, established in 1988 by the US Department of Agriculture, educates consumers and provides those eligible with coupons to patronize local farmers' markets. Ten markets in New York City were in the pilot project, and 41 were involved by 2001. The Farmers' Market Grant Program of the New York State Department of Agriculture and Markets provides up to $25,000 in matching funds annually to municipalities for building and rehabilitating farmers' markets in the state. The New York State Farmers' Direct Marketing Association (1993) and the Farmers' Market Federation of New York (1998) are dedicated to increasing the overall profitability of small farm operations. In recent decades traditional enterprises such as grain and dairy have become less profitable for small farms. Farmers' markets enable producers to establish new businesses in specialty crops or value-added products such as jams and baked goods. The markets support local agriculture, make fresh produce and specialty products available to community residents, and aid in the economic redevelopment of their areas. In 2001 there were an estimated 250 markets in New York State representing approximately 1,000 farmers.

Gottlieb, Robert. *Environmentalism Unbound: Exploring New Pathways for Change* (Cambridge, Mass: MIT Press, 2001)

Suzan D. Friedlander

Farmers' Museum. History museum in Cooperstown (Otsego Co) chartered by the New York State Board of Regents in 1942. Its 5,000-piece collection was dedicated on 4 July 1942 to commemorate the 125th anniversary of the state's first county fair, held there in 1817. Its sole exhibit building, the Main Barn of Fenimore Farm, opened to the public in 1943. Concerned with industrial influences on rural life, inspired to preserve democratic ideals during World War II, and emulating Henry Ford's Greenfield Village outdoor museum (1929) in Dearborn, Mich, and Scandinavian folk parks, its founders created the Farmers' Museum as an educational tribute to New York State pioneers. Cooperstown philanthropist Stephen C. Clark Sr, grandson of Edward Clark, a partner in the Singer Sewing Machine Co, had purchased an initial collection of trade, farming, and domestic tools from the estate of William B. Sprague, founder and president of the Early American Industries Association. Cooperative arrangements with the Otsego County Historical Society and the New York State Historical Association brought and restored old shops, barns, and houses to the site to recreate a *ca* 1845 historic area in which working artisans practiced their trades. It is one of the earliest examples of a successful crafts program of interpretation. Other interpreters also staffed the structures, furnished with period pieces and artifacts. The Main Barn displays were updated during the 1950s. *The Farmers' Year* exhibit—which organized tools in contexts of their use and of the seasonal work cycle of central New York State, illustrated by graphics and documented with almanac sections and diary quotes—was a revolutionary approach copied widely by other museums.

In the 1950s the museum also pioneered hands-on exhibits, providing visitors the oppor-

Blacksmith's shop at the Farmers' Museum.

tunity to experience processes such as building a trapper's cabin, boiling maple syrup, and, since the 1990s, harvesting hops. In the late 1990s the museum acquired another nine historic structures and built three more, including a Seneca log house. Known regionally and internationally, the museum remains a popular tourist destination; a resource for historic agriculture, trades, and domestic arts; a classroom for elementary and secondary students; and a laboratory for the Cooperstown Graduate Program in History Museum Studies. In 2003, 71,300 visitors toured the museum's 26 buildings and 23,000 artifacts.

Kulik, Gary. *Growth and Change: The Farmers' Museum 1999 Annual Report* (Cooperstown, NY: Farmers' Museum, 2000)

Kathryn A. Boardman

Farmersville. Town (pop 1,028) in NE Cattaraugus Co. Settled permanently in 1817, the town was formed from the old town of Ischua [now Franklinville] in 1821. A Welsh community began forming about 1851 and organized the Welsh Congregational Church of Siloam (1856). Railroads from Buffalo (1872) and Rochester (1878) provided service. In the early 21st century, agriculture remained the predominant land use; the only industry is gravel mining. In 1989 land in town was designated for a landfill for areas as distant as Canada and New York City. Residents opposed the plan, and the matter remained unresolved in 2003. The Farmersville Field Days and the Summer Festival take place in July. At the watershed between the Allegheny and Genesee Rivers and Cattaraugus Creek, water from Farmersville flows to both the Gulf of St. Lawrence and the Gulf of Mexico.

Bruce D. Fredrickson and Madelynn P. Fredrickson

Farmingdale {Farmingdale, village (pop 8,399) in Oyster Bay, Nassau Co; East Farmingdale, locality (pop 5,400) in Babylon, Suffolk Co; South Farmingdale, locality (pop 15,061) in Oyster Bay}. The area's first settler was Thomas Powell (1687), who negotiated the Bethpage Purchase (1695) with native representatives of the Massapequa, Matinecock, and Secatogue tribes. In the early 19th century the settlement, composed of eight farms, was known as Hardscrabble. The Long Island Rail Road named a station here Farmingdale in 1841; building lots were surveyed, and a post office was established in 1845. Farmingdale, though largely agricultural, had a brickyard and six pickle factories later in the 19th century. The village incorporated in 1904. The New York State School of Agriculture on Long Island (now SUNY Farmingdale) opened in 1916 in East Farmingdale. Industrial development followed World War I, especially aircraft factories: the Lawrence Sperry Airplane Co (1917–23) in Farmingdale and (1921) South Farmingdale; Kirkham (1932–40), then Liberty (1940–58) in South Farmingdale; Fairchild (1927–52), de Seversky (1931–38), and Republic (1938–87), all in East Farmingdale. The population surged in the 1950s and 1960s. The Farmingdale railroad station (1896) is listed on the National Register of Historic Places. East Farmingdale is the site of Republic Airport, a large shopping center, and many cemeteries.

William J. Johnston

Farmington. Town (pop 10,585) in N Ontario Co. Settled in 1789 almost entirely by Quakers from Adams, Mass, it was formed as a town in 1796. The Quakers briefly operated a manual labor school beginning in 1838. The Auburn and Rochester Railroad came through the southwest corner of town in 1841. Farmington remained chiefly agricultural until after it acquired a New York State Thruway exit in 1948. Suburbanization accelerated as Rochester's suburbs and highway network grew outward. Many residents commute to Rochester. Finger Lakes Racetrack (1962) hosts thoroughbred racing.

Marla A. Bennett

Farmingville. Locality (pop 16,458) in Brookhaven (Suffolk Co). The Farmingville Reunion is an annual picnic started in 1885 at a schoolhouse built *ca* 1850; for many years the gathering was a reunion for the school's former pupils. The area began to develop after World War II, acquiring a post office in 1950. Since the early 1970s it has had a significant Portuguese population and in the 1990s became a daily meeting point for as many as 1,500 Mexican day laborers. A brutal attack on two laborers in 2000 and the firebombing of a Mexican immigrant family's home in 2003 are believed to be actions of an anti-immigrant movement that enjoyed open support from some politicans, police, and members of the fire station where the group held meetings. Bald Hill, at 334 feet (101.8 m), was the site of the Bald Hill Ski Bowl (1965–80) and is the location of the Bald Hill Cultural Center and of the Suffolk County Vietnam Veterans Memorial (1991). In 2000, 8% of its population was of Latino ethnicity.

farmsteads. Agriculture was a dominant industry in New York State from earliest European settlement until well into the 20th century, and it remains important. The farmstead is made up of a number of buildings and different plots of land often separated by stone walls, tree lines, or fences. The principal buildings are the farmhouse and barn and often a smaller, hired-hand's house, with numerous specialized smaller outbuildings supporting the operation. The farmland is generally divided into crop and pasture lands, wood lots, orchards, and meadows. Interior farm roads connect the fields.

The farmstead is divided into work centers, where specific tasks are performed. The farmhouse, kitchen dooryard, and, traditionally, the garden were the center of domestic functions. The barn and barnyard were the center of farmwork. Outbuildings were positioned in relation to their role within the two spheres. Farmsteads evolved as animal husbandry and the agricultural economy changed. Outbuildings varied by region and function, with specialized buildings being constructed to accommodate the production of milk, hops, maple syrup, tobacco, and other agricultural products. As the predominant agricultural activity on a farm evolved, so did the complex of buildings on the farmstead. Replaced structures were typically put to new use. Log cabins became livestock shelters when a house was built. Sometimes expansion took the form of an addition. Over time the farmstead took on a complex but logical arrangement, one that took environmental and convenience factors into account. The principal barn was often sited to block the house from winter winds. Chicken coops were oriented for southern exposure. The barnyard was positioned where it was not directly upwind from the house. New Englanders often attached buildings together.

Farmhouses

The farmhouse serves as the family dwelling and center of farm operations. From the simplest beginnings, often a crudely built log cabin, the farmhouse has followed the economic prosperity of the farm and reflected the architectural trends of the times. For example, the tens of thousands of Greek Revival–style farmhouses built across upstate areas in the decades following the opening of the Erie Canal are reflective of the newly found prosperity. Farmhouse interiors of the 17th and 18th centuries were simple, with little differentiation made in the use of space. As farmers prospered, however, the farmhouse was enlarged and embellished. Additions were at times made for commercial reasons. In the latter half of the 19th century, many farm families in the Catskill region of Greene, Ulster, and Delaware Cos began to take in summer boarders. The more ambitious increased accommodations by building a rear or side addition and perhaps a wrap-around porch.

In many 19th-century farmhouses the kitchen was located in a wing or ell and included more than one room. It was the heart of the home, where the family gathered and entertained, sharing space with domestic help. It was also the center of domestic production, especially cooking and food preservation—butter churning, cheese making, and canning. Until after the Civil War, most butter and cheese production in New York State took place at home. As the number of farms declined during the 20th century, the number of abandoned farmhouses has not kept pace. Some have succumbed to the elements, but others remain the home of former farm families, and still others, most notably the more prominent, are taken over by urban folk wanting a more rural lifestyle.

Barns

In colonial and early 19th-century New York State, a pioneer farmer's building efforts, after erecting a crude log shelter for the family, shifted to building a barn. Initially a crude log affair, the early barn was soon replaced by a substantial and carefully built barn that took far more time and effort to construct than the first. The barn was the primary tool and largest investment, after the land, on which the family's livelihood depended. It followed one of several cultural traditions. Virtually all were timber framed. Early Dutch, Palatine German, some Huguenot farmers, and many of their descendants built a New World version of the Dutch barn: a broad, often nearly square structure, with a low-pitched, gable roof. Aside from the Schoharie Valley, where one set of primary doors was the rule, large, hinged, double doors were normally centered in both gable ends. The eave or drip sides of the barns swept low, sometimes ending only 10–12 feet (3–4 m) above the ground. The building sometimes lacked a foundation. Instead sills resting on large stones held the vertical support beams. Dry stone foundations were also common. The principal supports were spaced along the building's central aisle that doubled as a thrashing floor. Granaries, fodder, tools, workspace, and perhaps some livestock pens filled the side bays. Exterior

Left: A New York State farmstead soon after settlement, *ca* 1810. *Right:* Late the following summer, the farm begins to take shape, with a log house, a fenced garden, free-ranging livestock, and field clearing.

Left: The farm is well established after a decade, with a large house addition, a three-bay barn, an orchard, a sawmill on the stream, and a road. *Right:* A generation later the farm is a financial success. There is an imposing sawn-timber house, an expanded outbuilding complex, an enlarged mill, a distant farm village, and a railroad. From *The Pioneer Period of Western New York,* Chipman Turner, 1880.

walls were covered with horizontal planks. Few Dutch barns were built after the 1830s. It is estimated that 600–700 exist in New York State early in the 21st century.

A far smaller number of settlers from southeast Pennsylvania erected large, imposing barns with basements that housed livestock. Wooden upper stories were often cantilevered to extend beyond the foundation on the structure's long barnyard side. Known as a forebay, this provided sheltered exterior space for workers and animals. Protected by a gable roof, wide, double doors were placed on the eave-side opposite the forebay and accessible from an earthen ramp if the barn was not built into a natural slope. Siding was vertical. Typically referred to as a Pennsylvania or forebay barn, these were the largest barns built by early settlers in New York State and the only ones designed to house animals.

The third and unquestionably most common barn built by early settlers was the English three-bay thrashing barn. Early versions were typically about 30 x 40 feet (9 x 12 m). As farm production and crop storage needs increased, sizes increased to roughly 34 x 48 feet (10 x 15 m). These gable-roofed buildings had no basement and were sheathed in vertical siding. Some of the principal vertical beams were placed along exterior walls, which sometimes made them vulnerable to rot. Large, hinged, double doors were placed in the center of each eave-side; a wagon could be driven through, and grain could be thrashed and winnowed in the central aisle by opening both sets of doors and allowing the wind to blow. The side bays were used for storage, workspace, and livestock. At least 50,000 and perhaps as many as 100,000 English threshing barns were built in the state by 1850.

By mid–19th century the English threshing barns were modified in response to farm expansion and agricultural change. As crop production increased, more storage space was needed and thousands of major additions were built, often so well matched to the original that they are nearly impossible to detect. Farmers turning to dairying jacked their barn up and installed a full foundation and basement, where the dairy herd could be milked and housed. Where possible the basement was cut into a hillside, permitting entry at two levels. Regional variations in barn design began to appear. In Delaware Co farmers began building so-called high-bridgeway or overshot barns along high hillsides. They featured a ramp and bridge that allowed hay wagons direct access to the third story. In Lewis Co traditional three-bay English barns with basements were reoriented so that the doors were located in the gable ends.

Farm machinery and new technology also prompted changes in barn design. Hay was traditionally stored loose in the barn's haymow, a demanding job done entirely by hand. During the 1850s the horse-powered hay fork mounted on a track directly under the barn's ridge board was introduced, making the work of hay storage substantially easier. Existing barns were often modified to accommodate the new technology, and new barns were built taller with enlarged hay storage capacities, developments that permitted dairy herd expansion. By the late 1800s these efforts resulted in the introduction of the gambrel roof, which provided 50% more loft storage space. Many farmers had the gable roof of their old barn removed and replaced with a gambrel, increasing loft capacity by 50%. This desire to free the loft area of cross bracing and to increase storage capacity led to a number of locally designed roof truss systems. David Jennings of Lyons (Wayne Co) patented a system in 1879 that opened the loft area and proved highly successful in New York State and the eastern Midwest. As the supply of heavy timber stock declined, barn builders turned to plank trusses. John T. Wells Sr of Scottsville (Monroe Co) was awarded such a patent in 1889. Wells built nearly 200 gambrel roof barns across the state, most in Western New York and nearly all identified by a "lazy W" window lintel signature design feature high in the end. By then improved sawmill technology facilitated efficient clapboard production, and for the first time horizontal siding became the standard. Other barn builders incorporated signature features also. The Raymer brothers of Wayne Co placed round windows above their barns' main doors. During this period the need for improved ventilation was recognized, and many builders used a distinctive cupola design to mark their work.

There were more design changes in the 20th

century. The Gothic arch roof dairy barn built with laminated timbers and a large number of basement windows reached its height in popularity during the 1940s. Hay-handling technology affected barn architecture once more with the introduction of field baling in the 1930s. By the end of the 1950s loose hay storage was a thing of the past and so was the need for voluminous hay storage space. The more recent development of large round bailing technology has eliminated the need for interior hay storage. Low-profile pole barns were first introduced in the late 1940s and have grown to be the standard design at the beginning of the 21st century. Hoop barns consisting of bent metal ribs, with a tough synthetic fabric stretched over them, is the most recent design.

Specialty Barns and Silos

Most farmsteads contained secondary barns, the most common of which was the horse barn. By the middle of the 19th century every prosperous farm had one. Its main entrance was typically at the gable end. Two stories high but smaller than the primary barn, horse barns frequently displayed some architectural detailing, a feature typically missing on other agricultural buildings. As the 19th century advanced and competition from various sections of the country increased, more New York State farmers turned to specialty crop production, requiring special buildings to process and store the crop. Although distinct in appearance, tobacco, apple, teasel, and hop barns all functioned as drying barns. The first three were distinguished by a series of hinged sidewall panels that could be opened and closed. Hop barns stood out for their steep pyramidal or conic roof, or in some cases a brick chimney associated with the kiln where the hop flowers were dried before bailing. Other specialty barns included potato, cabbage, and poultry barns. During the 1930s many farmers switched from dairy to chicken farming and "chickenized" their dairy barns, an adjustment evidenced by the large number of windows added to the structures' upper stories.

The latter 1800s brought another significant architectural addition to New York State dairy farms: the silo. Designed to store chopped corn or silage in an anaerobic atmosphere that preserved nutrients, early silos were often square and directly attached to the interior or exterior of the dairy barn. The square shape proved inefficient and was soon replaced by a cylinder, initially made of wood staves bound by wire rods and a conical roof. Wooden versions were later replaced by sheet metal or, more often, interlocking cement or glazed ceramic block silos with significantly larger storage capacity. Fiberglass silos usually colored dark blue first appeared in the late 1940s. By the 1970s much less conspicuous trench silos were replacing above-ground structures. Even more recently, mass storage has been replaced by round cylinders of compressed silage wrapped in white plastic sheeting, sometimes called marshmallows, that can be stored outdoors wherever convenient.

Outbuildings

Individual farmsteads have varying numbers of additional outbuildings depending on the size of the farm and its focus. Outbuildings can be divided into two distinct types: domestic outbuildings and farm outbuildings. Historically, domestic outbuildings were closely associated with the farmhouse and its functions. They most commonly included the privy (outhouse), woodshed, springhouse, smokehouse, summer kitchen, and icehouse. All were close to the rear of the farmhouse and the kitchen door. Although many of these outbuildings remain today, modern technology has made them unnecessary. The privy was the ubiquitous domestic outbuilding on all farmsteads. Nearly always close to the rear of the house, they contained the outdoor toilet. Some privies were about the size of a telephone booth, but others were quite grand, architecturally matched to the farmhouse, and could accommodate several occupants at a time, with lower seating for the children.

The smokehouse was a small building used to process meat. A smoldering fire was built in a recess in the center of the floor, and fresh meat would hang from hooks above the fire to be cured. Unlike other domestic outbuildings, the icehouse was deliberately built in the shade but as near as possible to where the ice would be used. It was frequently built into the ground and insulated with sawdust. These buildings had no windows, and the door, sometimes unusually tall, was normally located on the north side.

The springhouse was built over or adjacent to a running spring, and the water was channeled into troughs along the interior walls that served as cooling basins for dairy products. Farm outbuildings vary according to the type of farm and crop but most include a carriage house or garage and a machinery shed. Many general farming operations feature varied animal shelters suited to mixed husbandry. These often include chicken coops, pigpens, and sheep barns. Outbuildings for produce storage include corncribs, granaries, apple barns, and root cellars. Department of Health regulations adopted in 1915 required the separation of milk storage from the milking parlor, leading to the construction of milk houses on dairy farms throughout the state. Typically one story, many were cement block structures attached directly to the cow barn.

Fink, Daniel. *Barns of the Genesee Country, 1790–1915* (Geneseo, NY: James Brunner, 1987)

Fitchen, John. *The New World Dutch Barn,* 2d ed. (Syracuse: Syracuse Univ Press, 2001)

Grow, Lawrence. *Country Architecture* (Pittstown, NJ: Main Street Press, 1985)

Hedrick, U. P. *A History of Agriculture in the State of New York* (New York: Hill & Wang, 1966)

Leffingwell, Randy. *The American Barn* (Osceola, Wisc: MBI Publishing, 1997)

McMurry, Sally Ann. *Families and Farmhouses in 19th-Century America: Vernacular Design and Social Change* (New York: Oxford Univ Press, 1988)

Tomlan, Michael A. *Tinged with Gold: Hop Culture in the United States* (Athens: Univ of Georgia Press, 1992)

Cynthia Carrington Carter

Farnham. Village (pop 322) in Brant (Erie Co). Farnham grew as a result of the Buffalo and State Line Railroad (1852) and was named for Leroy Farnham, its first merchant. A post office opened in 1855, and the village was incorporated in 1892. The Erie Preserving Co plant (1876–99) processed the region's agricultural produce. In the early 21st century Farnham continues to serve its surrounding farms.

Andrew C. Maines

Fasanella, Ralph (*b* Brooklyn, 7 Sept 1914; *d* Yonkers, 16 Dec 1997). Folk artist. His parents were Italian immigrants; Fasanella's mother was a buttonhole maker and active in left-wing politics, and his father delivered ice. He spent his childhood in a tenement on Sullivan St in Greenwich Village and received little formal education. In the late 1930s he joined the Abraham Lincoln Brigade and fought against the fascists in the Spanish Civil War. On his return to Greenwich Village, Fasanella became active as a union organizer with the Congress of Industrial Organizations from 1940 to 1945. He began painting in 1944, when a co-worker suggested he take up art as therapy for severe finger pain. In 1948 he had his first solo show at ACA Galleries in Manhattan.

Fasanella worked in near anonymity until 30 Oct 1972, when he was featured in *New York Magazine,* which named him "the best primitive painter since Grandma Moses." Subsequently, his work was included in one-man and group shows featuring urban/folk art. Fasanella's paintings are vibrant and intricately detailed, his subject matter often reflecting everyday life in New York City, from Yankee Stadium ballgames to the S. Klein department store on Union Square and the San Gennaro festival in Little Italy, subway rush hours to workers in union halls and the garment district. His paintings can be viewed at the Ellis Island Immigration Museum, the Museum of American Folk Art, and the 53d and 5th Ave subway station in New York City, and at the Baseball Hall of Fame in Cooperstown (Otsego Co). He lived in his later years in Ardsley (Westchester Co).

D'Ambrosio, Paul S. *Ralph Fasanella's America* (Cooperstown, NY: Fenimore Art Museum, 2001)

Fashionable Tour. The experience of traveling between, viewing, and residing at several antebellum resorts and tourist sites, many in New York State, and usually the province of a self-styled elite, or "fashionable" set. The itinerary encompassed the scenery of the Rhine-like Hudson River, the glamour of Saratoga Springs and Ballston Spa (Saratoga Co), the technology of the Erie Canal, and the sublimity of Niagara Falls. Lesser exotic attractions included inmates at Auburn Prison, cadets drilling at West Point, the unusual dancing at the Watervliet Shaker settlement, and the newly discovered Trenton Falls (Oneida Co). There were also detours to New Hampshire's White Mountains, Boston, Lowell, Mass, and even Montreal. The tour was especially popular with southerners escaping the heat and sickness of the plantation in summer and English travelers eager for a look at the country. More than 200 travel accounts by British visitors to the United States were published between 1816 and 1860.

The Fashionable Tour derived from English precedents, especially the Grand Tour of continental Europe and the cult of romantic scenery, but also benefited from the rapid development of transportation systems in America, especially steamboats, the Erie Canal, and railroads. The railroad from Schenectady to Ballston Spa and Saratoga, completed in 1833, was one of the first in the United States. *The Traveller's Directory through the United States* (1814) by John Melish may have been the earliest American tourist guide, but it was Gideon Davison's pocket-sized guide, *The Fashionable Tour; or, A Trip to the Springs, Niagara, Quebeck, and Boston, in the Summer of 1821,* that helped initiate the craze. Davison's work went through 10 editions by 1840, and Theodore Dwight Jr's *The Northern Traveler; Containing the Routes to Niagara, Quebec, and The Springs* (1825) went through 7 by 1841. John Disturnell, Henry Gilpin, Orville Luther Holley, Horatio Gates Spafford, William and Charles Peck, Wellington Williams, George Temple, Robert Vandewater, and Samuel De Veaux also wrote antebellum guidebooks for this route, all touting New York tourist sites.

The era's literature and art, such as Washington Irving's *Sketch Book* (1819), James Fenimore Cooper's *Last of the Mohicans* (1826), and Thomas Cole's painting trips into the Catskills (1825), helped popularize the Fashionable Tour. The smashing success of the Catskill Mountain House (1823) led many entrepreneurs to replace inns with hotels and to speculate in local improvements. Tourists in search of the picturesque and the sublime, and perhaps social status as well, roamed the Northeast, and traveling became not only socially acceptable but desirable as an end in itself. In this way, the Fashionable Tour offered the experience of travel to a larger, more inclusive, group of tourists, and led to the development of the first commercialized tourist industries, especially hotels, in the United States. It also turned New York State into a tourist attraction in its own right and aided its economic development in the early 19th century.

Brown, Dona. *Inventing New England: Regional Tourism in the 19th Century* (Washington, DC: Smithsonian Institution Press, 1995)

Haydon, Roger, ed. *Upstate Travels: British Views of 19th-Century New York* (Syracuse: Syracuse Univ Press, 1982)

Sears, John. *Sacred Places: American Tourist Attractions in the 19th Century* (New York: Oxford Univ Press, 1989)

Jon Sterngass

fashion industry. New York City's role as a fashion capital of the world dates to the late 19th century. Prior to that, Americans had relied largely on Europe for their style of dress.

Rise of Ready-to-Wear Clothing

The industrial revolution of the late 18th and early 19th centuries allowed textiles to be manufactured far more cheaply and quickly than ever before, paving the way for ready-to-wear clothing. The first such enterprises in New York City were small-scale, appearing as early as 1805 and suppling sailors with inexpensive, basic clothing. By the early 1830s most tailors kept a stock of ready-to-wear garments for men, which were often sold to the large immigrant labor force. The men's industry began in earnest in the 1850s after the sewing machine allowed for fast and cheap mass production. Little capital was needed to produce ready-to-wear aside from the purchase of fabric, and clothing factories were built in New York City, Albany, and Rochester. Some firms were quite sizable, such as Brooks Brothers in New York City, which had 78 employees on the premises and more than 1,500 outside workers by the 1840s.

Women's ready-to-wear clothing developed during the 1850s with the production of loose wraps and outerwear. By 1860 there were 15 manufacturers of ladies' ready-to-wear cloaks and mantillas in New York City. These garments were not tailored closely to the figure and were far simpler to produce than ladies' dresses, which required a precise fit. Ellen Curtis Demorest, a native of Schuylerville (Saratoga Co) who moved to New York City, brought an improvement to home sewing in the late 1850s with sized paper dress patterns. It would be several decades, however, before one-piece dresses were mass manufactured.

Innovations in Women's Styles

Through the mid–19th century Europe continued to dictate fashion trends, particularly Paris for women and London for men. The first significant American women's fashion magazine, *Godey's Lady's Book,* was published from 1830 to 1898, first in Boston and then in Philadelphia. It described the latest European fashions but also offered less ornate modifications for the more independent and active US woman. In 1846 the magazine began to include fashion plates titled "Godey's Paris Fashions Americanized."

In 1851 an early American innovation in women's fashion was created by Elizabeth Smith Miller. This fashion, made up of a knee-length skirt worn over full-styled trousers, was attributed to Amelia Bloomer of Seneca Falls (Seneca Co) after her appearance in the costume. Bloomers, as they came to be known, were not very popular and were considered fashionable among women in the Northeast and West for only about three years.

Additional changes came after the Civil War because the increasing numbers of women entering the work force wanted and needed more practical garments than the cumbersome hoopskirts and petticoats of earlier years. The street suit—a matched skirt and jacket, with an overcoat for poor weather—became popular, as did the shirtwaist, or blouse, to be worn with a skirt and jacket. By matching different shirtwaists with only one skirt, a woman was able to create a variety of outfits on a small budget. The tailored suit and shirtwaist combination, also known as the tailor-made, formed the foundation for the women's ready-to-wear industry. This costume was readily available for purchase by the 1890s from department stores, smaller establishments, and mail-order catalogs. In the early 1900s Manhattan artist Charles Dana Gibson created the Gibson girl, an athletic young beauty in straw hat and shirtwaist ensemble. She became the ideal that many American women aspired to and reinforced the popularity of the shirtwaist and skirt. By the early 20th century New York State, and particularly New York City, were home to a well-established and highly respected women's ready-to-wear industry; its dress industry alone was valued at $900 million in 1929. Rochester, with such firms as Hickey-Freeman, had a substantial niche in the high end men's ready-to-wear industry as well.

Rise of the American Look

At the turn of the 20th century American clothing designs received little attention. American fashions were typically given false French labels or department store or manufacturer labels instead of the names of their designers. American fashion began to draw more attention following a 1912 *New York Times* contest for the top three designs for afternoon dress, evening dress, and hat. The contest sparked much discussion about the condition of the industry. After the contest magazines ran advertisements celebrating and promoting American designs, and New York City manufacturers began to receive more recognition.

With the absence of French fashion influence during World War I, New York City retailers began to rely increasingly on American designs. One of the first influential and practical of these was the "little silk dress" by E. M. A. Steinmetz, a fashion artist and designer for Stein and Blaine. The Steinmetz gown, created soon after World War I, was the first simple all-day dress, made of silk instead of wool, with a fairly short skirt that reached only to the top of the boot. It became, along with the suit, a staple of American women's fashion, with later printed variations in rayon and silk.

An important fashion innovation of this time was the brassiere, which offered a simplicity and comfort that went well with the many changes occurring in women's clothing during the first part of the 1900s. Corset alternatives appeared in the late 19th century, but the first brassiere to be patented was created by Mary Phelps Jacob, a New York socialite, in 1913. She later sold the patent for $1,500 to the Warner Bros Corset Co of Bridgeport, Conn, which made more than $15 million from the garment over the next 30 years.

Sportswear became an acknowledged clothing genre in the late 1920s and early 1930s with such designers as Clare Potter and William Bloom. Designs were frequently made up of separates, stressed simplicity and ease, and were particularly suited to the increasingly versatile roles women played. Other prominent New York City designers of the 1930s include Muriel King, Germaine Monteil, A. Beller, Louise Barnes Gallagher, and Helen Cookman.

Production of many designs was linked to the garment district, an area created around 1920 when members of the growing fashion industry left their locations in Lower Manhattan and moved to an area centered on 7th Ave (although ranging between 5th and 8th Aves), from 28th to 41st Sts. The area became a center of wholesale and retail businesses in textiles, trimmings, furs, millinery, costume jewelry, accessories, and production and sewing tools. Most prominent, however, are the fabric shops.

Although the industry flourished through the 1930s, it faced new challenges and legal restrictions in the 1940s. Women's designs tended to be trim with slim silhouettes, narrow skirts, and unique detailing added to create interest. Regulations for men's clothing permitted only single-breasted two-piece suits and no vests. Garment details that used extra fabric, such as pleats, cuffs, sashes, and hoods, were banned. Rayon gabardine commonly replaced wool, and the use of leather, rubber, and metal was restricted. Designers responded creatively. Claire McCardell, an early sportswear designer, fashioned garments with brass hooks and fasteners and created such practical clothes as evening dresses with matching aprons for hostesses who gave home-cooked dinner parties. When a lack of heating oil left houses cold, Mainbocher, who ran New York City's most exclusive couture house, designed evening sweaters for women. Most designers used cap sleeves, which saved fabric, and created garments that fastened with only two buttons. Sydney Wragge was a notable designer of separates. Other important New York City designers of this time include Tina Leser, Charles James, Jo Copeland, Nettie Rosenstein, Norman Norell, and Tom Brigance.

After the war, designers abandoned austere simplicity and experimented with luxuriously full-skirted gowns, leg o' mutton sleeves, and extra detailing. The so-called New Look, created by Christian Dior in Paris in 1947, signaled a return to more traditional women's styles that included higher heels, longer and fuller skirts, corsets, pointed bras, and fitted bodices. Some New York City designers associated with the New Look were Ceil Chapman and Anne Fogarty. At the same time, designers began to use standardized sizing for women's clothes, a practice started by the War Production Board that eliminated the need for multiple fittings and made belts unnecessary on every ready-made garment. In 1957 American adaptations of Christian Dior's "sack" dress became popular but gave way to the sheath silhouette of the 1960s. Important designers of the 1950s include Anne Klein and Bonnie Cashin.

From the 1960s

Popular at the start of the 1960s were the boxy pastel-colored suits and undecorated shift dresses worn by Jacqueline Kennedy. These garments were created by designers like Donald Brooks, who studied at Parsons School of Design, and Oleg Cassini, who had established a very successful ready-to-wear company in New York City in 1950. Other notable styles emerged over the course of the decade, including ornamental evening clothes, baby-doll dresses, bell-bottoms, miniskirts, ethnic looks, clothes printed with or inspired by Op and Pop art, and denim jeans. Boutiques in Greenwich Village and Midtown Manhattan between 2d and 6th Aves, once mainly outlets for 7th Ave ready-to-wear, became laboratories for creativity and featured original styles made by in-house designers and artists. Freedom of expression and the idea that "anything goes" was reflected even in underwear, which included bikini underwear for both women and men and the "no bra" bra. Betsey Johnson, who began her career in a New York City boutique in 1965, became immensely popular. Geoffrey Beene started his own label during the 1960s as well, and Bill Blass became a favorite among American designers.

Focus shifted in the 1970s to natural fabrics in more subdued patterns and softer silhouettes, and fashions became simpler and more casual, with a renewed interest in separates and career wear. Women took to wearing pants for all occasions, often to show their rejection of the new midiskirts and their mini counterparts, and also to exercise their power, at least symbolically, in a masculine world. Designers started to make feminine versions of men's tailored clothing. Calvin Klein and Ralph Lauren, among others, adapted men's wear almost directly for women, and the most important wardrobe piece of the decade became the blazer. Because of the simplification of clothing and a decrease in competition based on innovation, designers began to focus on their image rather than on their designs. Labels previously attached on the insides of garments were moved to the outside as logos, and initials on clothes became common. Designers also increased their advertising and sought celebrity status in an effort to improve sales and make themselves known. By the end of the decade the man-tailored fashions for women became much more defined, and a new style emerged for scaling the ladder of success, characterized by the preppy look: a skirt suit, blouse, and low heels. Perry Ellis led this change in fashion. Other important designers of the 1970s included Halston and Diane von Furstenberg, whose 1972 wrap dress sold over 300,000 models.

During the 1980s power dressing became the fashion, with bold styles in boxy silhouettes; more was better, and styles were dramatic and decorative. One of the era's notable designers was Donna Karan, known for her separates made to give women an edge in the world of business. In 1983 Fashion Week was organized by the group Seventh on Sixth. An annual September event, it is a time of frenzied activity with fashion shows held in huge tents in Bryant Park and in various theaters and studios around Manhattan. Fashion buyers, photographers, writers, celebrities, socialites, and many others attend the shows, which are broadcast daily on cable television networks. Much of the innovation in the decade, however, involved style of business rather than style of clothing. Many designers became increasingly focused on advertising to sell not only clothes but also coordinating accessories, perfumes, and cosmetics.

During the 1990s there was a shift from power dressing to office casual, involving khakis, jeans, and knit tops or shirts for both men and women. Many looks of the past were revived, including platform heels, bell-bottoms, miniskirts, and sheath dresses. Women selected clothes in virtually every color, and there was a return to feminine prettiness in the form of silky lingerie slip dresses, camisole tops, and wide-legged trousers. Underwear pieces like slips, bustiers, and bras became acceptable as outerwear, and many women took to wearing skimpy garments that exposed their bodies. Important designers of this time include Tommy Hilfiger, Isaac Mizrahi, and Michael Kors. There was also the rise of African American street styles as the immense popularity of rap and hip hop music spawned fashions that many found salable. Such companies as FUBU, Phat Farm, Pure Playaz, and UB Tuff offered clothes that appealed to the hip hop culture. In 2000 New York City had more than 5,000 fashion showrooms and fashion industry sales of $14 billion.

New York City is also home to the Fashion Institute of Technology (FIT), founded in 1944, and the Parsons School of Design, founded in 1896 and part of what is now the New School University since 1970. Several significant fashion publications have offices in New York, including *Women's Wear Daily* (*WWD;* 1910), *Harper's Bazaar* (1867), and *Vogue* (1892). The Costume Institute at the Metropolitan Museum of Art houses over 75,000 costumes and accessories and is rivaled by the extensive collection of the Museum at FIT.

Ewing, Elizabeth. *History of 20th Century Fashion,* rev ed. (Totowa, NJ: Barnes & Noble Books, 1986)
Martin, Richard. *American Ingenuity: Sportswear, 1930s–1970s* (New York: Metropolitan Museum of Art, 1998)
Milbank, Caroline Rennolds. *New York Fashion: The Evolution of American Style* (New York: Harry N. Abrams, 1989)
Steele, Valerie. *Fifty Years of Fashion: New Look to Now* (New Haven, Conn: Yale Univ Press, 1997)
Wilcox, R. Turner. *Five Centuries of American Costume* (New York: Charles Scribner's Sons, 1963)

Hannah M. Springer

Fashion Institute of Technology (FIT). Public college established by the Educational Foundation for the Fashion Industries in Manhattan in 1944. The original school, tuition free when it opened, had only 100 students and held classes in the top two floors of the Central High School for Needle Trades (now High School of Fashion Industries) on 24th St between 7th and 8th Aves. Liberal arts courses and two majors were offered: design, including programs in apparel, textiles, and millinery, and scientific management. In 1951 FIT joined the SUNY system and became the second community college in the system authorized to award the AAS degree. In 1959 it moved to 27th St and 7th Ave, on the periphery of New York City's garment district, and by 1963 enrolled 4,000 students. The Museum at FIT, founded in 1967, holds one of the world's largest collections of costumes and textiles. During the late 1970s the college began to offer bachelor's and master's programs. In 1994 the Annette Green Fragrance Foundation Studio was opened for study in fragrance development, the first of its kind on a college campus. Famous former students include Norma Kamali and Calvin Klein. In 2002 FIT offered 31 majors and enrolled nearly 11,000 full- and part-time students from nearly all the states and more than 50 foreign countries.

Hannah M. Springer

Father Divine [Baker, George, Jr] (*b* Rockville, Md, May 1879; *d* Merion, Pa, 10 Sept 1965). Religious leader. The child of former slaves, George Baker moved to Baltimore around 1900 after a childhood spent in rural Maryland. In Baltimore he worshiped and often preached in the city's independent storefront churches and began a career as an itinerant preacher. After a ministry in Georgia and other southern states, in 1917 he moved to Brooklyn where he adopted a new name, Reverend Major Jealous Divine, or more commonly Father Divine. Drawing on the combined income of his followers, in 1919 he purchased a house in Sayville (Suffolk Co), which became the headquarters of Father Divine's Peace Mission Movement. His adherents met regularly at his home to receive spiritual advice, to share in lavish banquets, and to seek their pastor's help in obtaining jobs. The local residents—almost exclusively white—were at first relatively tolerant of the black religious movement in their midst, but as both the numbers attending the services and the interracial appeal of Father Divine increased, local harassment mounted and culminated in his 1932 conviction for disturbing the peace and creating a public nuisance. The presiding State Supreme Court judge Lewis J. Smith died of a heart attack four days after rendering his harsh one-year sentence. ("I hated to do it," was Father Divine's perhaps apocryphal response.) This apparent act of providence gave his movement much national publicity. The Peace Mission moved to Harlem in 1933 and augmented its evangelical outreach, first with the *Spoken Word* (1934–37) and then with the weekly paper *New Day.* Father Divine's distinctive theology, derived from a number of Christian and New Thought sources, encouraged his disciples to believe that he was God and that his message was one of personal and collective uplift. With a network of missions and groceries offering low-cost meals, Father Divine soon acquired a wide following in New York City and other cities. Racial equality was the most important secular cause of the integrated Peace Mission Movement, and Father Divine encouraged his disciples to transcend the given categories of racial thought and to view the concepts of White and Negro as concessions to "negative thought." Starting in 1935 some members of the Peace Mission purchased farms and land in Kingston, Saugerties, Samsonville, and other localities in Ulster Co, creating their Promised Land, which provided summer excursions, vacations, and food for Peace Mission followers in the city. The centerpiece of Father Divine's Ulster Co holdings was Krum Elbow, a Hudson River estate in Highland purchased in 1938 that attracted much attention for its proximity to Franklin Roosevelt's estate at Hyde Park (Dutchess Co). Father Divine's influence and movement waned in the 1940s, and the center of the movement moved to the Philadelphia area, where the Peace Mission Movement continues in reduced circumstances.

Burnham, Kenneth E. *God Comes to America: Father Divine and the Peace Mission Movement* (Boston: Lambeth Press, 1979)

Fauset, Arthur H. *Black Gods of the Metropolis: Negro Religious Cults of the Urban North* (1944; repr Philadelphia: Univ of Pennsylvania Press, 1971)

Harris, Sara, and Harriet Crittenden. *Father Divine: Holy Husband* (Garden City, NY: Doubleday, 1953)

Parker, Robert A. *The Incredible Messiah: The Deification of Father Divine* (Boston: Little, Brown, 1937)

Watts, Jill. *God, Harlem U.S.A.: The Father Divine Story* (Berkeley: Univ of California Press, 1992)

Weisbrot, Robert. *Father Divine and the Struggle for Racial Equality* (Urbana: Univ of Illinois Press, 1983)

Henry Warner Bowden

Fayette. Town (pop 3,643) in central Seneca Co. Part of the town was included in the Cayuga Reservation ceded by the Cayuga between 1789 and 1807. Settled in 1789, the town was formed from Romulus in 1800 as Washington. The name was changed in 1808. A substantial group of Pennsylvania Germans migrated to Fayette in the first quarter of the 19th century. The Church of Latter-day Saints was organized at Peter Whitmer's farm in Fayette on 6 Apr 1830. Founder Joseph Smith Jr and converts migrated west the following year. John Johnston pioneered the use of agricultural drain tile in 1835, and the Mike Weaver Drain Tile Museum is housed in Johnston's home. Mennonite farmers from Pennsylvania established a community in town in 1976. Hogs, dairy, and grain are the farm products in the early 21st century. Rose Hill Mansion (1839) is a National Historic Landmark.

Lisa Compton

Fayetteville. Village (pop 4,190) in Manlius (Onondaga Co). Settled in 1791, the village was incorporated in 1844. The Ledyard Canal, which diverted Limestone Creek through the village and powered 12 waterwheels, was built with local financing in 1845. Cement had been manufactured locally since 1818. With waterpower from the new canal, several large establishments were built to process lime, plaster, water lime, gypsum, and cement. Grain cradle, paper, pearl barley, sash and blind, and knife factories flourished in the 19th century. Precision Castings (later Accurate Die Castings, 1915–1990s) was a dominant industry, while McIntyre Paper Co (1855), B. H. Tracy Lumber Co (1909), and L. and J. G. Stickley Furniture Co (1908) remained important in 2003. The village acquired railroad service in 1870. By 1920, with the development of the Collincroft neighborhood, it was becoming a Syracuse suburb, a process which accelerated in the 1950s.

See also STICKLEY FURNITURE.

Marla A. Bennett

Federal Art Project. One of several programs initiated during the Great Depression with the dual goals of providing public funding for the arts and of assisting unemployed artists. Artists were paid slightly less than the "prevailing" wage based on the assumption that if they could find work elsewhere they would leave the program.

In May 1935 Pres Franklin D. Roosevelt established the Works Progress Administration (WPA) to provide government jobs for unemployed workers in a variety of professions. In addition to construction projects for numerous public buildings, parks, and roadways, the WPA developed assistance programs for impoverished artists, writers, musicians, and actors. To qualify for employment for one of the WPA cultural projects, individuals had to prove that they were destitute and that they were or had been trained or working as an artist. Because the qualification was based on need rather than on talent, the quality of the art produced under the Federal Art Project (FAP) varied greatly. The art itself was for public buildings constructed specifically by WPA workers.

Almost half of the works of art commissioned by the FAP in New York State were murals and sculptures for schools, libraries, and other public buildings. Post office paintings, often considered part of the WPA project, were commissioned under a separate program administered by the Treasury Department. Although public murals were never commissioned on such large scale either before or after the Great Depression, this type of art did have several predecessors in the 1920s and early 1930s. Most often cited by scholars are the murals painted by Mexican artists such as José Clemente Orozco and Diego Rivera. Other sources of the FAP artworks, in terms of style and subject matter, were American regional artists such as Grant Wood, Thomas Hart Benton, and Paul Sample. In Buffalo, WPA murals include works by Pascal Scime for the Buffalo and Erie County Historical Museum, the 106th Artillery Armory, Buffalo Zoo, and Barker Central High School (Niagara Co), and by Raphael Beck and William Rowe for several WPA-built schools. Ernest Smith, a Seneca Indian, completed a mural based on Iroquois religious themes at the Rochester Museum and Science Center, and Carl W. Peters did several murals at Rochester schools.

The program was controversial at times. In 1940 three murals at the administration building of Floyd Bennett Municipal Airport in Brooklyn determined to be communist propaganda by civic and patriotic groups were removed and destroyed; the artist, August Henkel, was dismissed from the FAP. The WPA/FAP also hired photographers and writers to document the project as it evolved. Essays written for this project were published in *Art for the Millions* (1973), which provides excellent source materials for scholars. In addition to photographs recording WPA programs, some photographers, such as Dorothea Lange, were allowed to photograph general living conditions during this era.

The Index of American Design was an equally significant FAP undertaking, in which about 200 artists produced drawings of early American and colonial decorative arts and architecture. Artists were also hired to create art in their studios for installation in public buildings. In Utica seven artists produced a series of dioramas portraying the early history of Central New York. The models were given to the Oneida County Historical Society, housed in 1942 in the Utica Public Library, and are now at the Utica Children's Museum of History, Natural History, Science, and Technology. Productions of traveling performances of theater and music were also funded by the WPA, using unemployed performing artists from urban areas, particularly New York City, for shows in smaller cities and rural areas. The art programs funded during the Great Depression mark a commitment from the federal government on a scale not since replicated. Congress abolished funds to the FAP effective 1 Jan 1940 but permitted funds on contracts awarded prior to that date to be spent provided the works were completed before 1 Jan 1942. The WPA ceased to exist on 30 June 1943.

McKinzie, Richard. *The New Deal for Artists* (Princeton, NJ: Princeton Univ Press, 1973)

O'Connor, Francis V., ed. *Art for the Millions* (Boston: New York Graphic Society, 1973)

James Crawford

Federal Dance Project. Employment program for dancers that first existed within the federal Works Progress Administration's (WPA) Federal Theatre Project (FTP), founded in August 1935. After lobbying by New York City modern dancers—in particular choreographer Helen Tamiris, chair of the Manhattan-headquartered American Dance Association (1936)—the Federal Dance Project (FDP) was launched as a separate entity on 30 Jan 1936, with units in New York City, Chicago, Los Angeles, and Philadelphia. Congress awarded the New York City FDP $150,000 to mount eight productions in six months and to pay for 185 dancers, 3 musical directors, technical and staff support, costumes, and sets. With 90% of the budget mandated for payroll, most productions utilized large casts and sparse production elements. Many New York City FDP employees, like Tamiris, were political liberals or radicals. Following budget cuts, the FDP merged back into the FTP in October 1937, where it functioned with a reduced number of dancers until the FTP's demise, engineered by congressional conservatives, in June 1939.

The FDP gave modern dance a new level of public exposure, and acclaimed modern dance works sprang from its stages, such as Tamiris's *Salut au Monde* (1936), based on Walt Whitman's poem of the same name; *How Long, Brethren?* (1937), scored with protest songs performed by the Federal Theatre Negro Chorus; Spanish Civil War–referenced *Adelante* (1939); Charles Seidman's *Candide* (1936); and Doris Humphrey's *With My Red Fires* (1939). Other notable choreographers of the New York City unit were Felicia Sorel, Gluck-Sandor, Nadia Chilkovsky, Don Oscar Becque, Lily Mehlman, and Roger Pryor Dodge. Black choreographer Momodu Johnson and the actors and dancers of the largely segregated African American company at Harlem's Lafayette Theatre created *Bassa Moona* (1936), which portrayed images of Nigerian life. Supervisors of the dance project were Don Oscar Becque (1936), Lincoln Kirstein (1936–37), and Stephen Karnot (1937–39).

O'Connor, John, and Lorraine Brown, eds. *Free, Adult, Uncensored: The Living History of the Federal Theatre Project* (Washington, DC: New Republic Books, 1978)

Robin Lakes

Federalist Papers. In response to an effective early campaign against the newly proposed US Constitution, Alexander Hamilton and John Jay agreed to write a series of newspaper essays to explain why the Constitution should be ratified. Hamilton introduced the essays entitled "The Federalist" and signed "Publius" on 27 Oct 1787. Eventually 85 essays were published in four New York City newspapers: the *Independent Journal,* the *New York Packet,* the *Daily Advertiser,* and the *New York Journal.* The series was also published in two volumes in March and May 1788. "The Federalist" extolled the benefits of union, pointed out the weaknesses of the Articles of Confederation, justified provisions of the Constitution, and explained the omission of a bill of rights and the prohibition of a religious test for officeholding. The essays rarely mentioned opposition writers and did not resort to personal attacks. Jay authored essays 2 through 5 but became ill and withdrew (although he later wrote essay 64), and James Madison joined the enterprise. The identity of the authors was at first unknown, although it soon became widely suspected that Hamilton and Madison were primary contributors. The authorship of 69 essays is certain. Hamilton wrote 50; Madison, 14; and Jay, 5. The most recent scholarship suggests that Madison, sometimes with the help of Hamilton, wrote the remaining essays. Hamilton's essays often emphasized the importance of an energetic federal government, whereas Madison's essays stressed the checks placed on that government in the form of free and frequent elections, the separation of powers, and the healthy tension created by the division of power between the states and the federal government.

"The Federalist" was by far the longest series of essays on the Constitution. When other supporters of the Constitution slowed their efforts after January 1788, "Publius" continued unabated. Though widely acclaimed, "The Federalist" had little immediate impact because New Yorkers elected a large majority of Antifederalists to their state ratifying convention. "Publius," however, succeeded beyond the authors' expectations; arguments they espoused became the standard Federalist explanations in the public debate over ratification. Since the adoption of the Constitution, the essays have been raised to a unique status as the most authoritative source in understanding the original intent of the framers. As such, the *Federalist Papers* are recognized as America's most important contribution to political theory.

See also US CONSTITUTION RATIFICATION.

Cooke, Jacob E., ed. *The Federalist* (Middletown, Conn: Wesleyan Univ Press, 1961)
Engeman, Thomas S., Edward J. Erler, and Thomas B. Hofeller, eds., *The Federalist Concordance* (Chicago: Univ of Chicago Press, 1980)

John P. Kaminski

Federalist Party. Federalist political ideology emphasized the importance of an ordered and structured social system that supported programs directly benefiting particular segments of society (creditors, merchants, and manufacturers) while indirectly benefiting the whole. Federalist ideology had its roots in the colonial period, grew in the 1770s and 1780s among those individuals who wanted a stronger central government at the expense of the states, and then fully emerged as an official, consolidated political force during the 1790s.

Party Foundation

One of the first two political parties to form in the United States, the Federalist Party drew its name from the group that supported ratification of the Constitution during the late 1780s. Early Federalist leaders in New York State included Alexander Hamilton, John Jay, Robert R. Livingston, Philip Schuyler, and John Sloss Hobart. During the 1790s most supporters of the Constitution became members of the Federalist Party, and most opponents of the Constitution became Democratic-Republicans, although there were some exceptions. In 1789 New York Federalists won control of both houses of the state legislature and selected Antifederalist Robert Yates (associate justice of the New York State Supreme Court) as their candidate to oppose the reelection of Gov George Clinton. Yates was narrowly defeated, but New York Federalists led by Hamilton successfully defeated Clinton's bid for the vice presidency in 1789.

Federalist New Yorkers played a significant role in the national government during George Washington's presidency. Schuyler and Rufus King became New York's first US senators in 1789, Hamilton became secretary of the treasury, and Jay served as chief justice of the United States. When the Livingstons received no federal patronage, many of them, led by Chancellor Robert R. Livingston, abandoned the Federalist Party in favor of the new coalition formed by Gov Clinton. This coalition maneuvered in the state legislature to defeat Schuyler's reelection to the US Senate in 1791, replacing him with Aaron Burr.

The prosperity and peace provided by the Washington administration, a gradual loss of popularity of Gov Clinton caused by scandals in granting public lands to his supporters, and the economic panic of 1792 allowed New York Federalists to gain strength. With the population of the state expanding, especially with large numbers of immigrants from New England, who settled in the western counties of the state, Federalists sensed their chance to defeat Gov Clinton's bid for a sixth term. They nominated US Chief Justice Jay as their gubernatorial candidate in 1792. Jay received a majority of the votes, but the ballots in three counties were disallowed for voting and reporting irregularities, and Clinton was declared victorious. Jay graciously accepted defeat, but Federalists bitterly denounced this political skulduggery and stridently opposed the governor throughout his three-year term. By 1794 political lines were clearly drawn between Federalists and the consolidated opposition, the Democratic-Republicans. In 1795 Federalists elected Jay governor of New York State while he was negotiating the Jay Treaty in England. Congressional debate over that treaty further factionalized politics and illustrated the important role that New Yorkers played in the development of the national political parties during the 1790s.

Federalist Power in the Late 1790s

Foreign affairs dominated the politics of the late 1790s. European belligerents persisted in violating American shipping rights. Federalists wanted closer economic ties with Britain and supported the British in their war with France, but Democratic-Republicans backed the French. Neither party particularly cared for Pres Washington's policy of neutrality, but both sides abided by it.

Domestically, Federalists advocated the same policies pursued by Clintonians after the war with one significant variation: the Clintonians wanted power and programs to originate from state governments, whereas Federalists favored similar programs initiated by the new federal government. Treasury Secretary Hamilton advocated and New York Federalists supported the federal government's funding of its debt and the federal assumption of the wartime debt of the states. This policy greatly favored New York because the state had funded its own debt since 1786 and had purchased many of the federal securities owned by New Yorkers. New York was thus a creditor of the federal government, and Hamilton's fiscal policies provided the state with substantial annual revenue from the interest and principal due on federal securities. Federalists also favored the continuation of bounties on select agricultural commodities and manufactured goods. This part of Hamilton's program was not implemented but continued on the state level. Federalists also advocated the chartering of state banks to benefit merchants and serve as a profitable investment for the wealthy.

Although Federalists benefited from New York State's policy of granting land to speculators at a low price, they publicly condemned Gov Clinton for favoritism among his supporters. Both Federalists and Clintonians advocated public support for education (common schools first received state support in 1795), fortifications, internal improvements such as new canals and roads, and the reform of the state's penal code. Federalists opposed a liberalization of bankruptcy and insolvency laws as well as efforts to abolish the tenant law system on the vast manorial estates of the Hudson Valley. After the initial public condemnation of the Jay Treaty in 1795, the US Senate confirmed it and relations with Britain moderated. In 1797 the Federalist-controlled New York State legislature ousted Aaron Burr from the US Senate and replaced him with Philip Schuyler. By 1798 relations with France worsened, and the United States found itself in an undeclared naval war with its former ally. The passage and vigorous enforcement of the Alien and Sedition Acts in 1798 and the creation of a large provisional army with Alexander Hamilton second in command behind the elderly George Washington furthered Federalist power and created fear among Republicans throughout the country. Federalists, more than their opponents, supported the manumission of slaves and finally were successful in 1799 in obtaining an act for the gradual emancipation of slaves in New York State.

Fall of the Party

After the presidential election of 1796, the Federalist Party split. Alexander Hamilton, who personally and politically despised Pres John Adams, sought to undermine the president and replace him with Thomas Pinckney of South Carolina in the election of 1800. Other New York Federalists, however, including Gov Jay, supported the president and his efforts to avert war with France. This division slowly led to the defeat of the Federalist Party. In the bitterly fought election of 1800, Republican Thomas Jefferson defeated a nationally divided Federalist Party to win the presidency. Crucial to Jefferson's victory was the Republican victory in the New York State legislative elections in May 1800, ensuring Jefferson all of the state's electoral votes. With its loss of the national executive and state legislature, the Federalist Party lost much of the influence it had held in New York State in the 1790s. Hamilton proposed that the lame-duck Federalist-controlled legislature be called into special session to adopt a district method of electing electors, one previously advocated by De Witt Clinton but rejected by the legislature. Gov Jay rejected the proposal as too partisan, thus dooming Pres Adams's reelection. Stephen Van Rensselaer, who had been Jay's lieutenant governor, lost the 1801 gubernatorial election to George Clinton. With Jefferson at the height of his popularity in 1804, Clinton was chosen to be vice president. The divided New York State Federalist Party had no chance of electing one of its own to replace Clinton and chose Aaron Burr to oppose Republican Chief Justice Morgan Lewis in the 1804 gubernatorial election. Hamilton campaigned against Burr, handing Lewis the election. Federalists also lost control of the New York City Council that year, never to regain it.

When Alexander Hamilton and Philip Schuyler died in 1804, Federalists lost their two most important leaders. Although Rufus King, Stephen Van Rensselaer, and Jonas Platt assumed leadership, the party did not have support of a majority in statewide elections after Gov Jay's resignation in 1801; only individual Federalists were still elected locally in certain sections of the state, including Albany, Rensselaer, and Columbia Cos and in certain New York City wards. The party was no longer a force throughout the state, although it did soon experience a brief resurgence.

Attempted Recovery

With New Yorkers upset with Jefferson's embargo policy and the resulting economic depression, Federalists gained strength in the legislative elections of 1808, but their presidential hopes were dashed when James Madison and George Clinton defeated South Carolinian Charles Cotesworth Pinckney and Rufus King. Federalists gained control of the assembly in 1809 and made serious inroads in the state senate. They again captured the Council of Appointment and replaced 6,000 Republicans with Federalists. In 1810 Clintonian Republicans successfully elected Daniel D. Tompkins as governor over Federalist Jonas Platt. Continuing to exploit the unpopularity of the Republicans' foreign policy, Federalists won control of the legislature in 1812, 1813, and 1814, largely through the adroit efforts of local branches of the Washington Benevolent Society. Disgusted with Madison's presidency, Federalists supported antagonist De Witt Clinton for president in 1812. With the successful conclusion of the War of 1812, Gov Tompkins was reelected in 1816 and became vice president under James Monroe in 1817. De Witt Clinton was elected governor in 1817 with 95% of the vote, and the Federalist Party was dead.

See also Clinton, de Witt; War of 1812.

Fox, Dixon Ryan. *The Decline of Aristocracy in the Politics of New York, 1801–1840* (New York: Harper Torchbooks, 1965)

Kaminski, John P. *George Clinton: Yeoman Politician of the Young Republic* (Madison, Wisc: Madison House, 1993)

Livermore, Shaw, Jr. *The Twilight of Federalism* (Princeton, NJ: Princeton Univ Press, 1962)

Young, Alfred F. *The Democratic-Republicans of New York: The Origins, 1763–1797* (Chapel Hill: Univ of North Carolina Press, 1967)

John P. Kaminski

Federal Reserve Bank of New York. It is the Second District bank created by the Federal Reserve Act of 1913, which established a national system of 12 district banks. The Federal Reserve Bank of New York (FRBNY; also known as New York Fed) opened at 62 Cedar St in Manhattan in November 1914 and moved to 33 Liberty St in June 1924. Unique among the reserve banks, the FRBNY implements monetary policy by buying and selling US Treasury securities in the open market and intervenes in the foreign exchange market when necessary to stabilize conditions. In 1916 the FRBNY began acting as a gold depository for foreign countries; it now plays a pivotal role in international banking, storing gold and securities and holding accounts for international organizations as well as for foreign governments and overseas central banks. It also supplies currency and services to the major New York commercial banks that make loans to foreign governments. The largest of the reserve banks in assets and banking activity, the FRBNY has a branch office in Buffalo and regional offices in Utica and East Rutherford, NJ.

Bruchey, Stuart. *Enterprise: The Dynamic Economy of a Free People* (Cambridge, Mass: Harvard Univ Press, 1990)

Pamela Cooper

federal-state relations. See State government and services.

Federal Theatre Project. Performing arts division of the depression era Works Progress Administration (WPA), the federal agency that provided work for the unemployed. As part of the effort to match unemployed individuals with jobs congruent with their training and experience, WPA chief Harry Hopkins launched the Federal Theatre Project (FTP) on 27 Aug 1935, appointing Vassar College theater professor and playwright Hallie Flanagan as director. Charged with creating free, adult, uncensored theater, the FTP operated in 32 states before its closure 30 June 1939. New York City served as the national hub for the organization, and FTP productions were also staged in Syracuse, Buffalo, Yonkers, White Plains, Cedarhurst, and Roslyn. New York State's FTP presented 22,671 performances, employed 5,843 theater artists and technicians at its height, tallied over 14 million people in total attendance, and expended more than $24 million for labor and nonlabor costs.

New Deal political philosophy, or even more radical views, infused the project, along with the reexamination of the American economy, social structure, and values being catalyzed by the depression. The FTP struggled to find an identity for itself among the myriad roles it played. It represented not only the beginnings of a national theater but also a relief agency for performing artists, a laboratory for experimental productions, a conduit for social change, and a vehicle for the democratization of art through federal sponsorship. Decisions made by Flanagan and other project artists during their FTP years reveal a desire to meet all of those goals.

FTP repertory in New York State ranged from populist programming such as puppet theater, vaudeville, and pageants to innovative productions of both new and classic plays. The New York City unit also produced children's theater, musicals, radio dramas, German and Yiddish productions, and, under the leadership of the unit's chief playwright Arthur Arent, theatrical docudramas known as "living newspapers," which merged fact-based scripts on topical problems with multimedia staging.

The FTP launched Orson Welles's directing career, and director John Houseman participated in numerous productions. The antirealist aesthetics many FTP directors favored were conjoined with creative freedom from box office pressures, large casts, long rehearsal periods, and minimal budgets favoring stark, abstract sets. This led to the creation of arresting new productions, among them Welles's *Tragical History of Dr. Faustus* (1937), with talking puppets, masks, bold costumes, and magical entrances and exits, Houseman and Welles's *The Cradle Will Rock* (1937), and Marc Blitzstein's musical courtroom drama dealing with labor organizing. The New York City FTP's unit housed at the Lafayette Theatre in Harlem employed both black and white artists as playwrights and directors. Its repertory included *Turpentine* (1936), a drama of black labor camps in the South, and *Haiti* (1938), which examined issues of race and power. At the Lafayette, Welles directed a 1936 production of *Macbeth* set in a Caribbean jungle and featuring aspects of voodoo culture.

From its inception, differences of artistic taste and political viewpoint among FTP personnel and struggles with government censorship caused internal turmoil. But external assault from Congress's House Committee on Un-American Activities led to the cutoff of FTP funding on 30 June 1939.

Fraden, Rena. *Blueprints for a Black Federal Theatre, 1935–1939* (New York: Cambridge Univ Press, 1994)

O'Connor, John, and Lorraine Brown, eds. *Free, Adult, Uncensored: The Living History of the Federal Theatre Project* (Washington, DC: New Republic Books, 1978)

Robin Lakes

Federal Writers' Project. Work relief program and one of the New Deal arts programs under the Works Progress Administration (WPA) for unemployed writers, federally funded and administered from 1935 to 1939, then under state auspices until 1943. The Federal Writers' Project (FWP) produced local and oral histories, ethnographies, and state guides. Each state and territory had its own office. New York State had two projects, one for New York City, because of its large number of writers, and another for the rest of the state.

Harry Hopkins, appointed by Pres Franklin D. Roosevelt to head the program, was determined to establish one for white-collar workers, especially writers. Henry Alsberg, national FWP director, had been a lawyer, journalist, and diplomat. Robert West Howard, a former journalist on the *Syracuse Herald,* became assistant state director of the New York State project and toured the state by car to compile material for its guide. Howard eventually joined the *New York Post.* His successor, Paul Corey, a short story writer, proved especially talented. Falsely accused of being a Communist, Corey cleared himself during an investigation and then resigned from the project.

The experiences of Howard and Corey demonstrate the main obstacles to the work of the FWP. Staff turnover was high because competent writers found jobs outside the FWP, delaying publication of the guidebooks, especially in New York City. Political feuds between Communist and other left-wing factions became a significant problem, provoking a 1938 congressional investigation by the Committee on Un-American Activities. In 1940 the WPA suspended about 15 FWP employees suspected of Communist Party membership. The FWP ended on 30 June 1943.

The best-known FWP publications are the American Guide Series to the 48 states and Alaska, including *New York: A Guide to the Empire State* (1940) and New York City's *New York Panorama* (1938) and *New York City Guide* (1939). The state guide contains a description of the cities and towns. The city guides are complementary: *Panorama* consists of 26 essays on various topics and the Baedeker-like *Guide* describes each section of each of the five boroughs as well as general points of interest.

FWP authors in the New York State project also wrote separate guides to individual counties and cities: *Dutchess County* (1937), *Rochester and Monroe County* (1937), and *Warren County: A History and Guide* (1942). One contribution from the New York City office, *American Wild Life* (1940), had sold 22,000 copies by November 1941. *Changing New York* (1939) contains text accompanying Berenice Abbott's photographs of New York City skyscrapers. The Living Lore unit, consisting of some two dozen writers, collected folklore among New York City's many national groups. The Yiddish Writers Group produced *The Jewish Landsmanschafften of New York* (1938) and *Jewish Families and Family Circles in New York* (1939), both in Yiddish. The state project initiated the first serious attempt to create an encyclopedia of New York State. Project members compiled a gazetteer, versions of which exist in manuscript form in the New York State Archives. Funding, however, ran out before the project could be completed.

Many prominent writers as well as those about to earn their literary reputation participated in the FWP, especially in the New York City project: Conrad Aiken, Maxwell Bodenheim, Edward Dahlberg, Ralph Ellison, Philip Rahv, Harold Rosenberg, Anzia Yezierska. John Cheever was an editorial assistant on the *New York City Guide,* and Richard Wright was also a staff member. Winning first prize for his book of short stories, *Uncle Tom's Children* (1938), in a contest for FWP authors marked the beginning of Wright's career as a writer.

Bascom, Lionel C., ed. *A Renaissance in Harlem: Lost Essays of the WPA, by Ralph Ellison, Dorothy West, and Other Voices of a Generation* (New York: Amistad Press, 2001)

Mangione, Jerre. *The Dream and the Deal: The Federal Writers' Project, 1935–1943* (New York: Avon Books, 1972)

Penkower, Monty Noam. *The Federal Writers' Project: A Study in Government Patronage of the Arts* (Urbana: Univ of Illinois Press, 1977)

David Chenkin

Feiner v New York, 340 US 315 (1951). A First Amendment case about the right to free speech and the responsibility of law enforcement to maintain order. Leftist Syracuse University student Irving Feiner was arrested 8 Mar 1949 for disorderly conduct after being asked three times by police to stop addressing a small crowd of Blacks and Whites near the corner of South McBride and Harrison Sts in Syracuse. His speech, which included criticism of the state of race relations and derogatory comments about public officials (eg, calling Pres Harry S. Truman "a bum") normally would have fallen within constitutional limits. However, police were concerned that the crowd he was addressing was somewhat restless, and an onlooker threatened to silence Feiner if they did not ask him to stop. The US Supreme Court upheld Feiner's conviction in a 6–3 vote, holding that his arrest had been a reasonable measure motivated by a concern to preserve order, not the officers' disapproval of the opinions expressed. Expelled from Syracuse University, Feiner served his 30-day jail term in 1951.

Sullivan, Kathleen M., and Gerald Gunther. *First Amendment Law* (New York: Foundation Press, 1999)

Timothy P. Gordinier

feminism. See WOMEN'S RIGHTS AND FEMINISM.

Fenian Brotherhood. In 1858 Irish exile John O'Mahony, with the help of Michael Doheny and James Stephens, mobilized complex strands of an Irish nationalist tradition and Great Famine memory to found a New York City–based revolutionary, secret, oath-bound society dedicated to ending British rule in Ireland, by force if necessary. Soon identified as the Fenian Brotherhood, commemorating a mythological Gaelic band of warriors called the Fianna, the society claimed a New York City membership of 50,000 by the early 1860s. The several thousand Fenians serving on the Union side during the Civil War returned to New York State prepared to mobilize for the Irish cause. Leaders clashed with Ireland's parallel organization, the Irish Republican Brotherhood (IRB), over tactics and goals, but lectures, fairs, prominent functions, a women's auxiliary, and endorsement by city politicians seeking Irish votes led to the movement's rapid expansion across New York State and the country. Fenian Senate president William R. Roberts proposed and carried the majority in favor of an invasion of Canada in the mid-1860s (with O'Mahony opposing). The goal was to generate Anglo-American conflict. They also aimed to create leverage against British authority in Ireland. This seemed ambitious at best, but support from Civil War veterans of the 155th and 164th New York Infantry, and especially the 63d, 69th, and 88th regiments, propelled the idea.

An O'Mahony counterplan to capture British-administered Campobello Island off Maine backfired, and Fenian secretary of war Brig Gen Thomas W. Sweeney and Col John O'Neill, in May 1866, marshaled approximately 800 Fenians toward Potsdam Junction (St. Lawrence Co) and Malone (Franklin Co), and a contingent of Western New York supporters to Buffalo, to mount a Canadian invasion. Sweeney's grandiose plans to capture railroad, canal, and roadway links faltered because of inadequate military resources, but O'Neill prevailed against Canadian volunteer forces at the Battle of Ridgeway in Canada West [now Ont]. Disorganization ensued as forces from the USS *Michigan* on Lake Erie detained some Fenian contingents, and other battalions dispersed. The invasion dissipated when Pres Andrew Johnson and Secretary of State William H. Seward condemned the attack based on American law. In general, the failure dismantled any surviving coherency within the Fenian structure.

During the 1870s proposed attacks on the British navy using the submarine *Fenian Ram* foundered as the last vestiges of the movement folded into Clan na Gael. Established in 1867, Clan na Gael took up the Fenian cause, establishing a secret, revolutionary organization in the same manner as its predecessor. Clan na Gael, however, was governed by a seven-member Revolutionary Directory involving the Clan executive, the IRB Supreme Council, and ex-Fenians outside the United States. This society preserved immigrant connection, funding, and supplies for the Irish nationalist cause well into 20th century, paving the way for other agencies of Irish Republican support. NORAID (Irish Northern Aid), for instance, mobilized during the Northern Ireland "troubles" of the late 1960s and 1970s.

D'Arcy, William. *The Fenian Movement in the United States: 1858–1886* (New York: Russell & Russell, 1947)

O'Broin, Leon. *Fenian Fever: An Anglo-American Dilemma* (New York: New York Univ Press, 1971)

Rafferty, Oliver "Fenianism in North America in the 1860s: The Problems for Church and State," *History* 84 (Apr 1999): 257–77

Mary C. Kelly

Fenner. Town (pop 1,680) in central Madison Co. Originally part of the Oneida Indian Nation Reservation, the area was settled *ca* 1795, and the town formed from Smithfield and Cazenovia in 1823. Chittenango Falls State Park lies on the town's western border and contains one of the town's two waterfalls; the other, Perryville Falls, lie on the northern border. One of the state's largest wind farms occupies a site off Oxbow Rd to the northeast; placed in operation in 2000, its 20 windmills generate 30 MW of electricity. While Fenner remains to some extent a dairy farming town, many residents commute to Syracuse or Utica.

William F. Helmer

Fenton. Town (pop 6,909) in NE Broome Co. Settled in 1788, the town was formed in 1855 from Chenango as Port Crane and changed its name to Fenton in 1867. The Chenango Canal operated through town from 1837 to 1876. Lumbering was eventually succeeded by dairy farming. Link Flight Simulation operated a facility in Fenton from 1941 to 1996, developing flight training simulators. In the early 21st century the town remains chiefly rural, with farming in decline. It has some small industries and the Defense Logistics Agency Depot (1942). By 1978, I-88 was completed through town. Chenango Valley State Park, developed by the Civilian Conservation Corps and the Public Works Administration, contains two glacial kettle lakes.

Charles J. Browne

Fenton, Reuben E(aton) (*b* Carroll, Chautauqua Co, 4 July 1819; *d* Jamestown, Chautauqua Co, 25 Aug 1885). Governor, US representative, and US senator. Educated in local schools, Fenton taught for two years at Jamestown Academy while reading law. He took control of his father's store in Frewsburg (Chautauqua Co) after the 1837 panic, and later business ventures, including land and lumber speculation, led to considerable wealth. Elected to the House of Representatives as a Free Soil Democrat in 1852, Fenton lost the seat to a Know-Nothing candidate in 1854. That same year Fenton became involved with the new antislavery Republican Party. In 1855 he chaired the party's first New York State convention and a year later was a delegate to its first national nominating convention. Fenton returned to Congress in 1857 as a Republican, serving until his 1864 election as governor. Programs implemented during Fenton's four years in office included creating both a professional fire department for New York City and the State Board of Charities to inspect state hospitals, asylums, and homes; using federal land grant funds to establish Cornell University; and raising teacher standards, establishing additional normal schools for teachers, and making public education free. He then was elected to a term in the US Senate (1869–75). Fenton spent most of his last 10 years in Jamestown as director and then president of the First National Bank, and in 1878 he chaired the US commission to the International Monetary Conference in Paris.

Mohr, James C. *The Radical Republicans and Reform in New York during Reconstruction* (Ithaca: Cornell Univ Press, 1973)

Gregory P. Rabb

Fenton, William N(elson) (*b* New Rochelle, Westchester Co, 15 Dec 1908). Anthropologist and ethnohistorian. A graduate of Dartmouth College (1931), Fenton received his PhD from Yale College in 1937. After starting his career as a community worker with the Tonawanda Seneca (1935–37), he later became senior ethnologist at the Smithsonian Institution's Bureau of American Ethnology (1943–51), executive secretary for anthropology and psychology at the National Research Council (1952–54), and director of the New York State Museum (1954–68). He later served as professor of anthropology at SUNY Albany (1968–94). Fenton's scholarly publications include *An Outline of Seneca Ceremonies at Cold Spring Longhouse* (1936), *The False Faces of the Iroquois* (1987), *The Great Law of the Longhouse: A Political History of the Iroquois Confederacy* (1998), and *The Little Water Medicine Society of the Senecas* (2002). One of the founders of the discipline of ethnohistory, he cofounded the annual Conference on Iroquois Research, which began in 1945.

Denis Foley

Fernow, Bernhard Eduard (*b* Inowrazlaw, Prussia [now Poland], 7 Jan 1851; *d* Toronto, 6 Feb 1923). Forester and educator. Educated in Germany at Hanover's Munden Forestry Academy and at the University of Königsberg in law studies, in 1876 Fernow became engaged to US citizen Olivia Reynolds and immigrated to the United States. Within two years he took a position as manager of Pennsylvania woodlands that supplied charcoal to foundries owned by New York City industrialists Peter Cooper and Abram S. Hewitt. Fernow married Olivia in 1879; the couple had five children. His own observations and a prepublication reading of Charles Sargent's 1884 *Report on the Forests of North America,* warning of forest decline, spurred Fernow to help establish the American Forestry Congress (since 1992, American Forests) in 1882.

He favored government legislation to rein in exploiters of forestland but also opposed moves to turn vast tracts into nonproductive parks. He wrote the Adirondack Forest Preserve bill in 1885 and advised the Adirondack League Club on its forest holdings. From 1886 to 1898, he served as chief of the US Division of Forestry, helping to craft the federal Forest Reserve Act of 1891 and the Forest Management Act of 1897, measures that established the national forest system. From 1898 to 1903, Fernow directed the New York State College of Forestry at Cornell University, the country's first professional forestry school. There, he founded *Forestry Quarterly* (from 1916, *Journal of Forestry*) in 1902, serving as editor until 1922, and also wrote *Economics of Forestry* (1902). The college closed in 1903 due to conflicts with neighboring Adirondack landholders, and Fernow moved on to organize forestry programs at Pennsylvania State College and the University of Toronto. He published *A Brief History of Forestry* in 1913.

Lewis, James G. "The Pinchot Family and the Battle to Establish American Forestry," *Pennsylvania History* 66 (Spring 1999): 143–65
Rodgers, Andrew, III. *Bernhard Eduard Fernow: A Story of North American Forestry* (Princeton, NJ: Princeton Univ Press, 1951)
Steen, Harold K. *The US Forest Service: A History* (Seattle: Univ of Washington Press, 1976)

James G. Lewis

Ferraro, Geraldine A(nne) (*b* Newburgh, Orange Co, 26 Aug 1935). US representative and first major-party woman candidate for the vice presidency. Daughter of Italian immigrant Dominick Ferraro and Antonetta Ferraro, from 1944 Geraldine lived in the Bronx with her widowed mother, a seamstress. After graduation from the Tarrytown (Westchester Co) Marymount School in 1952, she attended Marymount Manhattan College and then, while working as a teacher, Fordham University Law School. In 1960 she married real estate developer John Zaccaro and was admitted to the bar the next year. In 1974–78 active Democrat Ferraro, now mother of three children, served as a Queens Co assistant district attorney, and in 1978–84, as US representative from New York's Ninth District. In 1984, following her selection as first woman chair of the Democratic platform committee, she was nominated as Walter Mondale's running mate. Her husband's financial dealings became a campaign issue; Mondale and Ferraro were defeated by Republican incumbents Ronald Reagan and George H. W. Bush. Between unsuccessful senatorial bids in 1992 and 1998, Ferraro was US ambassador to the United Nations Human Rights Commission (1994–96).

Breslin, Rosemary, and Joshua Hammer. *Gerry: A Woman Making History* (New York: Pinnacle Books, 1984)
Ferraro, Geraldine, with Catherine Whitney. *Framing a Life: A Family Memoir* (New York: Scribner's, 1998)

Jeffrey Kraus

ferries. See FINGER LAKES FERRIES; HUDSON RIVER FERRIES; LAKE CHAMPLAIN FERRIES; LONG ISLAND FERRIES.

Field, David Dudley (*b* Haddam, Conn, 13 Feb 1805; *d* New York City, 13 Apr 1894). Attorney and legal reformer. Field studied law in Albany, moved to New York City in 1825, was admitted to the bar in 1828, and soon had a large and profitable practice. He began working for legal reform in 1837, a cause that consumed much of the rest of his life. In 1847 he convinced the New York State legislature to create commissions to prepare codes of court practice and procedure. He became a leader of the Practice Commission after being appointed to it in 1848, and his proposals greatly simplified rules of procedure and merged the courts of law and equity. He argued several significant Reconstruction cases before the US Supreme Court, including *Ex parte Milligan* (1866), *Ex parte McCardle* (1868–69), and *United States v Cruikshank* (1876), usually supporting restrictions on federal or state authority even if minority rights were imperiled. He enjoyed taking on high-profile and challenging cases in New York State, often at cost to his reputation, serving as counsel for Jay Gould and Jim Fisk in the Erie Railroad litigation in 1869 and later defending William M. "Boss" Tweed. In 1881, after much political wrangling, Field's code of criminal procedure and his penal code became law in New York State. His civil code was never adopted in the state but did become the basis for the reform of civil law procedure throughout the United States and Great Britain.

Field, Henry. *The Life of David Dudley Field* (New York: Charles Scribner's Sons, 1898)
Reppy, Alison, ed. *David Dudley Field: Centenary Essays Celebrating 100 Years of Legal Reform* (1949; repr Buffalo: William S. Hein, 2000)
Subrin, Stephen. "David Dudley Field and the Field Code: A Historical Analysis of an Earlier Procedural Vision," *Law and History Review* 6 (1988): 311–73

Jon Sterngass

Fifth New York Infantry Regiment (Duryee's Zouaves). Organized as a two-year unit to fight in the Civil War, the unit was formed on 12 Apr 1861 and chose Col Abram Duryee, an experienced militia officer, as its commander. Recruitment followed a preference for educated and physically imposing men. The regiment included former soldiers, college graduates, law students, and businessmen; more than 80% of its members were born in America. The Fifth New York's Zouave uniform reflected a French military style inspired by Berber forces. The ensemble included baggy red trousers, white leggings, a short dark-blue jacket, and a tasseled red fez. Col Duryee drilled his 848 men at Fort Schuyler [now in Bronx Co]. The regiment left New York City 24 May 1861, was transported to Fortress Monroe on the Virginia peninsula, and on 10 June 1861 took part in an early skirmish of the war at Big Bethel, Va, where Priv George Tiebout became the regiment's first fatality. After Duryee's promotion to brigade command, Lt Col Gouverneur Kemble Warren assumed command and moved the regiment to an eight-month stint of garrison duty in Baltimore.

The Fifth was attached to Brig Gen George Sykes's division of regulars. Under the command of Lt Col Hiram Duryea, the regiment took part in the Peninsular Campaign, suffering significant casualties at the battle of Gaines' Mill on 27 June 1862; of 450 men who entered the fight, 162 fell. In mid-August 1862, the regiment took part in the Second Bull Run. After Duryea was sent home with malaria, command fell to Capt Cleveland Winslow. The Fifth went into the battle with 500 men and suffered 326 casualties in less than eight minutes. The regiment later fought at Chancellorsville, Va, and was mustered out on 14 May 1863 with one of the finest records of the war. Warren was promoted to major general in 1863, played a major role in the Union victory at Gettysburg, and later commanded the Second and Fifth Corps of the Army of the Potomac.

McAfee, Michael J. *Zouaves: The First and the Bravest* (Gettysburg, Pa: Thomas Publications, 1991)

Brett Michael Mills

figure skating. Derived from the practice of skating basic patterns or figures on ice, the sport was introduced to New York State by the mid-1700s. The Central Park Lake, which opened in 1858, became the center of the sport in the Northeast. It was the primary venue for the New York Skating Club, formed in 1860, which patented a new type of skate in 1862, and claimed Jackson Haines as an early member. According to some accounts, Haines was born in Troy. He originated the sit spin and the classic spiral and invented the attached blade. Trained in ballet, Haines demonstrated fluid movement and interpretation in figure skating and brought the waltz, mazurka, and quadrille to the ice. In the mid-1860s he moved to Europe, where he inspired and helped create modern figure skating. Irving Brokaw of New York City, who had studied the sport in Europe, was a moving force behind the establishment of the US championships, first held in 1914.

The Skating Club of New York (SCNY), organized in 1863, the Sno Birds of Lake Placid (Essex Co), organized in 1920, and the Beaver Dam Skating Club of New York of Locust Valley (Nassau Co) were among the seven clubs that founded the United States Figure Skating Association (USFSA) on 31 Mar 1921. New York City native Beatrix Loughran, who won the Olympic figure skating silver medal in 1924 and bronze in 1928, was a member of the SCNY, as was Sherwin Badger, with whom Loughran won the pairs silver in 1932. Lake Placid drew attention to figure skating in 1932 as site of the Winter Olympics and attracted Gustav Lussi to set up a summer training camp. Dick Button started training with Lussi in 1942. Button created the flying camel spin in 1947 and won the Olympic gold medal in figure skating in 1948 and 1952. Carol Heiss of Ozone Park (Queens Co) was a SCNY champion who went on to win the Olympic silver in 1956 and the gold in 1960. Dorothy Hamill of Connecticut belonged to the SCNY when she won the Olympic gold in 1976. Other Olympians who represented the SCNY included Elaine Zayak and pairs skaters Calla Urbanski and Rocky Marval, and Kyoko Ina, partnered with John Zimmerman. SCNY member Sarah Hughes of Great Neck (Nassau Co) won the 2002 Olympic gold medal in figure skating.

Copley-Graves, Lynn. *Figure Skating History: The Evolution of Dance on Ice* (Columbus, Ohio: Platoro Press, 1992)

Milton, Steve. *Skate: 100 Years of Figure Skating* (London: Robert Hale, 1996)

Pamela Cooper

Filipinos. Filipinos began to settle in the United States after the Philippine Islands became an American colony in 1898. By 1920, a small number of Filipinos lived in New York State, and most were farmworkers who had worked their way from the West Coast. In New York City, they often worked as dishwashers and bussers while living in boardinghouses in Brooklyn. Some opened restaurants and small stores. Several artists were part of this community, including Manuel Rey Isip, Venancio Igarta, and Bruna Pascua Seril, who in 1943 founded the still operating Philippine Dance Company of New York. After World War II and Philippine independence, wealthier families sent their children to study in the United States. Corazon Cojuangco, a 1953 graduate of the College of Mount Saint Vincent in the Bronx, was elected president of the Philippines in 1986 under her married name, Corazon Aquino.

After immigration laws changed in 1965, larger numbers of Filipinos moved to New York State. Many were professionals, especially physicians, nurses, and medical technologists recruited through H-1 preference visas by short-staffed hospitals and nursing homes. Among them also were engineers, accountants, lawyers, and teachers, especially for Catholic schools. Many Filipino intellectuals fled to the United States after Pres Ferdinand Marcos, elected in 1965, established authoritarian rule in the Philippines (1971–86). A number of them formed anti-Marcos groups based in New York State.

Because higher education in the Philippines is taught in English, most Filipino immigrants already possess a high level of fluency in the English language before their arrival. This has greatly facilitated their adjustment to life in the state. In 1990 about 50,000 people of Filipino origin lived in New York State; ten years later, more than 86,000 did. Although Filipino professionals, especially physicians and nurses, can be found in many cities in the state, most still live in the New York City area, notably Woodside, Flushing, and Hollis (Queens Co), with smaller numbers in Staten Island and Brooklyn.

With the exception of the Iglesia ni Cristo, a Filipino Protestant group with a church in Uniondale (Nassau Co), the overwhelming majority of Filipinos are Catholic. The Filipino community has been served since 1972 by the weekly newspaper *Filipino Reporter,* based in New York City, and by Radio Pinoy, based in Nutley, NJ. The community supports professional associations such as the Philippine Nurses Association of New York and the Filipino American Medical Society; social clubs such as FAMILI (Filipino Americans in Long Island) in Holbrook (Suffolk Co); advocacy groups such as the Coalition for the Advancement of Filipino Women in New Hyde Park (Nassau Co) and the Philippine American Senior Citizens of Rockland County; fraternal groups such as the Knights of Rizal; and a branch of the Filipino American National Historical Society. Many Filipino associations in New York State have joined the National Federation of Filipino American Associations, founded in 1997. Americans of Filipino ancestry who have left their mark on New York State include Libertito Pelayo, the founder of the *Filipino Reporter* and a community activist; Manuel Rodriguez Sr, a multifaceted visual artist; Lea Salonga, a Broadway stage actress; and Loida Nicolas Lewis, an activist and businesswoman.

Alejandro, Reynaldo G., and Eva Florentino. *The Filipino Americans in New York* (New York: Filipino American National Historical Society, 1998)

Reynaldo Gamboa Alejandro

Fillmore, Millard (*b* Locke Township [now Summer Hill, Cayuga Co], 7 Jan 1800; *d* Buffalo, 8 Mar 1874). US president. His parents, Nathaniel Fillmore and Phoebe Millard Fillmore, were poor tenant farmers. Fillmore was self-educated and eventually read law while clerking for a local attorney. Moving with his family to Buffalo, Fillmore was admitted to the bar in 1823 and thereafter established a law practice in nearby East Aurora (Erie Co), becoming one of the village's leading citizens. He married Abigail Powers, born in Saratoga Co, in 1826. The Antimasonic Party elected Fillmore to the state assembly, where he served three terms before declining renomination in 1831 because of his move back to Buffalo. He was elected to the House of Representatives in 1832, and though not accepting renomination in 1834, he was politically active in the Whig Party's formation. Fillmore was re-elected to Congress in 1836, 1838, and 1840. He took a lead role in espousing the Whig position for high, protective tariff rates and a national bank, which led to his becoming chair of the Ways and Means Committee. He declined renomination in 1842.

In 1844 Fillmore captured the Whig nomination for governor of New York State but was defeated by Democrat Silas Wright. Meanwhile a growing split within the state's Whig Party favored the more strongly antislavery bloc, led by former governor William H. Seward, which was larger than Fillmore's conservative faction. Seward's group monopolized the more important political nominations, though Fillmore did successfully run for state comptroller in 1847. At the 1848 Whig convention where Gen Zachary Taylor, considered a Seward confidant, was nominated for US president, party leaders hoped to maintain the support of both factions by selecting Fillmore for the vice presidential slot. Fillmore became vice president in March 1849, though the ensuing struggle with Seward's faction over New York State's patronage appointments indicated that Fillmore wielded little clout.

Upon Taylor's sudden death on 9 July 1850, Fillmore became president. He took office amidst controversy surrounding the spread of slavery to the other new territories acquired in the Mexican War. Fillmore quickly replaced Taylor's cabinet with more conservative Whigs who favored appeasing the South, and he lobbied for passage of a Whig compromise bill that would enhance enforcement of the Fugitive Slave Act and that did not rule out the spread of slavery into some of the territory acquired in the Mexican War. When the so-called Compromise of 1850 passed Congress, Fillmore claimed it to be the "final settlement" of the slavery issue. But Fillmore's replacement of Taylor's cabinet officers exacerbated factionalism within the Whig Party and doomed his already slim chances of winning its nomination in 1852. He returned to Buffalo in March 1853.

The Know-Nothings, whose nativist agenda opposed immigrant and Catholic political influence, wanted Fillmore to be their presidential candidate in 1856, and in February the American Party (as the Know-Nothings' political organization became known) selected Fillmore as its nominee. Though Fillmore had never expressed public support for their nativist program, the early Know-Nothing agenda also included patriotism and national unity, and Fillmore's devotion to the Union made him seem an ideal candidate. But Fillmore carried only Maryland and won just 22% of the vote in the three-way race. After his defeat he devoted himself to philanthropic work, partly because of his marriage to Caroline Carmichael McIntosh, a wealthy Albany widow, in 1858. His first wife had died in 1853. Among his many civic activities, he was a founder of the University of Buffalo (1846) and served as the school's first chancellor, and he also helped establish the Buffalo Historical Society (1862), serving as that organization's first president. Fillmore suffered a stroke in February 1874 and died soon after. The Millard Fillmore House in East Aurora is a National Historic Landmark, and a replica of his birthplace stands a few miles from the original site, in Fillmore Glen State Park.

Fillmore, Millard. *The Millard Fillmore Papers,* 2 vols. Ed. Frank H. Severance (Buffalo: Buffalo Historical Society, 1907)

Rayback, Robert J. *Millard Fillmore: Biography of a President* (1959; repr Norwalk, Conn: Easton Press, 1986)

Smith, Elbert B. *The Presidencies of Zachary Taylor and Millard Fillmore* (Lawrence: Univ Press of Kansas, 1988)

Tyler Anbinder

film, avant-garde. Experimental cinema. In New York State the form dates from short films shot in New York City in the mid-1890s by former Edison employees, including Charles E. Chinnock and Woodville Latham. *Manhatta* (1921), a city symphony montage directed by Charles Sheeler and Paul Strand, was the first avant-garde release. Experimental films by Maya Deren, such as *Meshes of the Afternoon* (1943), were influenced by European surrealism and anticipated the underground films of the 1950s and 1960s. Stan Brakhage, perhaps the most influential avant-garde filmmaker, came to New York City in 1954. In some 300 short 16-mm films (*Dog Star Man,* 1961–64; *The Act of Seeing with One's Own Eyes,* 1971), his visual explorations of the effects of light, color, hue, shape, and dimension were both narrative and abstract. The central figure in the avant-garde of the 1960s was Jonas Mekas, who made a series of "diary films," including *Diaries, Notes, and Sketches* (1968). An émigré from Lithuania who arrived in New York City in 1950, he founded the journal *Film Culture* (1955), reviewed films for the *Village Voice,* and cofounded Anthology Film Archives (1970). In *Tom, Tom, the Piper's Son* (1969), Ken Jacobs deconstructed a 1905 short film into abstract visuals and optical microstructures. Jacobs taught at SUNY Binghamton and founded the Millennium Film Workshop in Manhattan in 1966.

Many films took film itself as a subject, either in visual abstraction or in the use of cinema verité techniques, as in Jim McBride's *David Holzman's Diary* (1967). In *Film in Which There Appear Sprocket Holes, Edge Lettering, Dirt Particles and etc.* (1967), George Landow used found footage and visually explored the materials of the medium. In *Still* (1971), Ernie Gehr trained his camera on a section of Lexington Ave, closely observing trees, traffic, and the comings and goings in a small diner. Harry Smith's experimental animation techniques of drawing directly on celluloid and using cutouts (*Heaven and Earth Magic,* 1962) influenced the psychedelic light shows of the 1960s. Among the many visual, conceptual, and performance artists exploring the film medium were Carolee Schneeman (*Fuses,* 1967) and Yoko Ono (*Fly,* 1970). Underground films by Ron Rice (*The Flower Thief,* 1960), George and Mike Kuchar (*Hold Me While I'm Naked,* 1966), and others featured bizarre sexual extravaganzas, openly gay themes, and occult symbols. Jack Smith's *Flaming Creatures* (1963) was perhaps the most influential underground film of its time. A visionary set of orgiastic mock-Hollywood tableaux shot on the roof of an abandoned movie theater, it was banned as pornographic by the state.

Andy Warhol made his first films in 1963. Visitors to his Factory on Union Square in Manhattan were automatically filmed in 15-minute stationary portraits (*Screen Tests,* 1964–66). Warhol experimented with real time and long durations in such films as *Sleep* (1963), a six-and-a-half-hour film of poet John Giorno sleeping, and the eight-hour *Empire* (1964), a study of the lights of the Empire State Building. Warhol made more than 10 films featuring the iconic Edie Sedgwick, including *Poor Little Rich Girl* (1965), using out of focus cinematography and portraiture. In 1966 the underground movement drew national attention with *The Chelsea Girls,* Warhol's groundbreaking split-screen collage; projectionists chose when to alternate between two parallel soundtracks. Paul Morrissey's exploitation trilogy, *Flesh* (1968), *Trash* (1970), and *Heat* (1972), combined performance art with narrative. Warhol's Factory turned out hundreds of films before he withdrew them from distribution in 1972.

In the 1970s Yvonne Rainer and a number of minority filmmakers revitalized avant-garde film. They were followed by a new generation of film producers in the 1980s, with super-8 film and video prominently in use. Digital video technology in the 21st century has made filmmaking a more accessible medium for artists to explore. Independent filmmakers' organizations, such as the Film-Makers' Cooperative, have been centers for the avant-garde film community, and many short film festivals are held in Manhattan and Brooklyn every year. Matthew Barney's elaborate *Cremaster* cycle of film and art (1994–2002) had a complete installation at the Guggenheim Museum in 2003. Early 21st-century avant-garde filmmakers include Mary Filippo, Holly Fisher, Courtney Hoskins, Jim Jennings, Jeanne Liotta, and Julie Murray.

Gidal, Peter. *Andy Warhol: Films and Paintings: The Factory Years* (New York: Da Capo Press, 2000)

Hoberman, J. *On Jack Smith's "Flaming Creatures" (and other Secret-Flix of Cinemaroc)* (New York: Granary Books, 2001)

James, David E., ed. *To Free the Cinema: Jonas Mekas and the New York Underground* (Princeton, NJ: Princeton Univ Press, 1992)

Rees, A. L. *A History of Experimental Film and Video* (London: British Film Institute, 1999)

Sitney, P. Adams. *Visionary Film: The American Avant-Garde in the 20th Century,* 3d ed. (New York: Oxford Univ Press, 2002)

Stuart Smyth and Kevin Smyth

film, silent. In 1889 the Eastman Dry Plate and Film Co (now Eastman Kodak) in Rochester released the first commercially available transparent roll film, which in 1891 made Thomas Edison's motion picture camera possible. Motion pictures were first shown publicly in the United States in New York City in 1896, and soon the city became the center of American production.

Early Industry Structure

Although Edison built a primitive studio called the Black Maria in 1893 in West Orange, NJ, in 1901 he built a studio in the Bronx to be near writers, actors, set designers, and costumers. His rivals first improvised by building sets on rooftops where they could get the strong light needed for the slow film stock of the time and not be bothered by onlookers. Hampered by wind, clouds, and temperature, these pioneer firms soon constructed indoor studios in Manhattan, Brooklyn, and Staten Island. Among the most significant early firms were Biograph, founded in 1896 and headquartered at a lighted studio at 11 East 14th St until 1913, when it moved to Upper Manhattan, and Vitagraph, founded in 1896–97 and filming in Brooklyn, often outdoors. Edison sued Biograph for patent infringement, one of many such cases, but in 1907 the courts rejected the claim. The intense litigation about patents ended in 1908 when firms including Biograph, Vitagraph, and Edison agreed to pool their patents to join together in the Motion Pictures Patents Co, commonly known as the Trust. Its effort to monopolize the shooting, production, distribution, and exhibition of all films failed, even before this effort was ruled to be a trust in restraint of trade. There was almost immediate opposition to this monopoly, and so-called illegal firms quickly sprang up. To escape legal harassment and attacks by company operatives who would find out where a crew was filming and smash the cameras, many of these companies, known as independents, left the closely watched New York City area. By 1920 most of the independents moved their operations to California, as had the "legal" firm of Biograph in 1910. Other independent firms such as Thanhouser had facilities in New Rochelle (Westchester Co). Kalem (K-L-M), set up by George Kleine, Samuel Long, and Frank Marion, had its headquarters in New York City, where it alternated production with its other facilities in

Film still from *The Capture of Fort Ticonderoga,* filmed on location by the Edison Moving Picture Co, 1911.

Florida and California. Unlike the Trust, which was committed to one- and occasionally two-reel films and opposed longer features, many of the independents believed the future lay in feature production. By 1916 most of the founding members of the Trust went out of business or had to merge.

The next generation of New York City film companies would have greater staying power. William Fox formed an exchange called the Greater New York Film Rental Co in 1907 and led a fight against the Trust, eventually winning a court decision. By 1914 he began producing films at a small studio in Staten Island, then moved to Manhattan, and in 1916 shifted some production to California, where he initiated an ambitious program of westerns. By 1917 Fox was releasing about 70 features a year. Among his most famous stars was Theda Bara. Adolph Zukor, who also started as a theater owner, bought the rights to Sarah Bernhardt's feature-length French production *Queen Elizabeth* in 1912 and made a fortune. Zukor, believing that the future of the movies lay in feature films, created his production firm, Famous Players, and opened his first studio in a converted warehouse on West 26th St in 1912. The next year he engaged the popular screen actress Mary Pickford at $500 a week. New York City had the advantage of also being close to famous Broadway stars, such as James O'Neill, who in 1913 starred in *The Count of Monte Cristo.* Another stage figure, Maurice Costello, was engaged by Vitagraph. Soon after, in 1916, Zukor went into partnership with the Jesse L. Lasky Feature Play Co, located in Hollywood, and formed Famous Players–Lasky, which took over the Paramount distributing company and ultimately became known as Paramount Pictures by 1935. Zukor's purchase of theaters in 1919 was financed by a $10 million line of credit achieved by Wall St contacts. The company opened a studio in Astoria (Queens Co) in 1920; it also had a studio in Hollywood. Another important producer was Carl Laemmle, who formed Independent Motion Picture Co in 1909. In 1912 his firm was renamed Universal Studios. Although production was in New York City at this time, in 1915 he purchased a large area of land on the north side of Hollywood, which became a filmmaking complex known as Universal City. The Warner brothers (Jack, Sam, Harold, and Albert) made their first major success in 1918 with *My Four Years in Germany,* with its battle scenes filmed at the US Army's Camp Upton (Suffolk Co). The following year they moved to Hollywood, and in 1923 they formed the firm Warner Bros.

When pioneering director D. W. Griffith left Biograph in the fall of 1913, he independently produced and directed two features at studios hastily set up on 29th St and by the beginning of 1914 went to California. In 1919 he returned to New York State and built studios in Mamaroneck (Westchester Co) at Orienta Point where he produced several films, among them *Way Down East* (1920) and *Orphans of the Storm* (1921). By 1924 Griffith ran out of money, lost his studio, then shot three features for Zukor at Astoria in 1925–26. Thereafter, he again went to California but returned to New York, where he shot his last film, a low-budget talkie called *The Struggle* (1931) at Audio Cinema, the old Edison studio at 198th St and Decatur Ave in the Bronx. He also used many city locations.

By the early 1920s most production was done in the Los Angeles area, but the financial center of the industry remained in New York City. Most studios had their corporate headquarters in New York, including Loew's (the parent of MGM), Zukor (then with Famous Players–Lasky, ultimately the head of Paramount), Fox, Warner Bros, and later Columbia. All major films were premiered in New York City, where the trade press—such as *Moving Picture World, Exhibitor's Trade Review, New York Dramatic Mirror*—and the major magazines were located.

Films Made in New York State

New York State was used for location shoots during the silent film era, with city streets, Central Park, Coney Island, and New York Harbor often appearing. For village scenes, Fort Lee, NJ, just across the Hudson River from Manhattan by ferry, was often employed by Biograph, as was the hamlet of Cuddebackville (Orange Co). Other companies (Reliance, Vitagraph, Mary Pickford, Fine Arts Film, and D. W. Griffith) used various locations in the state; among them were Ausable Chasm in *The Great Leap* (1914), Van Cortlandt Park in *The Battle Cry of Peace* (1915), Yonkers and Sharkey's gym in Manhattan in *His Picture in the Papers* (1916), Long Island in *Less Than the Dust* (1916), Saratoga in *The Whip* (1917), New York Harbor in *Regeneration* (1917), and Somers in *America* (1924).

The area near Ithaca was used in dozens of films made by various companies from 1912 to 1920, often using nearby geologic features for "cliff-hangers," with stars including Pearl White, Irene Castle, and Oliver Hardy in some of his earliest roles. Ithaca and the other locations mentioned earlier were usually used during the warmer months, except for snow scenes. Theodore and Leopold Wharton, however, had a year-round studio at Renwick Park [now Stewart Park] and produced 69 films.

Animation

New York City became the birthplace of modern animation when 19th-century developments in the art combined with the burgeoning entertainment and newspaper businesses flourishing around the turn of the 20th century. James Stuart Blackton was born in England but began his cartooning career at Joseph Pulitzer's *New York World* in 1896. A founder of the Vitagraph, Blackton specialized in the "trick film," in which various camera techniques such as stop motion, dissolves, and multiple exposures were used to create the illusion of "magic." In 1900 he produced a precursor of the animated film, *The Enchanted Drawing,* under license for Edison. Blackton produced the first true animated film, *Humorous Phases of a Funny Face,* in 1906, pioneering stop-frame animation using chalk drawings and cutouts.

Winsor McCay, famed for his *New York Herald* comic strip "Little Nemo in Slumberland" (1905–11), was renowned as one of the greatest animation artists. He crafted the thousands of individual drawings needed for the new animated films and spent four years making the 4,000 hand-painted images with India ink on rice paper used in the 1911 animated version of "Little Nemo." *Gertie the Dinosaur,* released in 1914, was one of the most influential early animations, and the character of Gertie was incorporated into McCay's ongoing vaudeville act. He adopted the new cel technology in his controversial 1918 project *The Sinking of the Lusitania.* He continued making animated films until 1921.

Craftsmanship like McCay's could not be sustained in an industry demanding more and more films with a quicker turn-around time. Animation studios became viable by using a variety of assembly line techniques. Raoul Barre opened his innovative studio in 1913 across the street from Fordham University in the Bronx and developed the peg system of registering drawings. J. R. Bray created a character named Col Heeza Liar and a studio full of outstanding talent. His first animated film was *The Artist's Dream* in 1913. In Bray's studio Earl Hurd patented the clear cel animation process in 1914.

Max Fleischer also worked for Bray. Along with his brothers Dave and Joe, Fleischer developed and patented the rotoscope, which helped produce realistic animation. The Fleischer brothers developed the first *Out of the Inkwell* series, for Bray, which featured Koko the Clown. In 1921 they broke from Bray's studio and established their Out of the Inkwell Films in Manhattan. The Pat Sullivan Studio on West 63d St in Manhattan was home to Otto Mesmer, creator of the wildly successful Felix the Cat, who appeared in his first film, *Feline Follies* in 1919 and who bridged the silent and sound eras.

Theaters

Amusement parlors of the late 19th century gave way to penny arcades that featured rows of "peep show" machines boasting lurid content to attract the patronage of young men and boys but in reality showing fairly tame content. In 1903 Mitchell Mark built New York's first penny arcade, located on 125th St in Harlem. Soon Adolph Zukor, Morris Kohn, and William Fox, among others, located new arcades on busy downtown shopping streets around the city. Known variously as automats or automatic vaudeville emporiums, they included not only peep shows but other, more family-oriented entertainment, including a variety of coin-operated machines and tests of skill. Although successful, the novelty of these venues soon wore off; the public's clamor for moving pictures, however, did not. By 1904 arcade owners had plenty of profits, projection technology was improving, and movies were getting better.

To enable more people to see more movies, the nickelodeon was born. The state's first nickelodeon (the Bijou Dream) was built by Harry Davis in 1906 in Rochester. By the end of that year, nickelodeons could be found in every borough of New York City, as well as in Oswego and Troy (Rensselaer Co). Initially, nickelodeons were makeshift affairs, often adjacent to the arcades, in a storefront or tenement with the windows papered over and a piece of canvas hung as a screen. The crowd was packed in on folding chairs, and the air was fetid and hot. Outside, street-front barkers hailed customers with megaphones. Because these storefront locations were considered common shows instead of theaters, licensing fees were minimal ($25 a year instead of $500) and stringent building codes did not apply. The venues were inexpensive to capitalize and provided a viable entrée into small business ownership for many recent immigrants. Wealthier entrepreneurs, including Zukor and Marcus Loew, built more elaborate nickel theaters. Two hundred common show "nickelets" were licensed within New York City in 1906 alone. By 1911 there were 450, as well as 290 larger movie theaters. The nickelodeons appealed to a wide range of people, including immigrants who did not need to understand English to enjoy the show. The public took full advantage of "the nickel madness" for inexpensive social outings. It was claimed that daily attendance in 1906 was 200,000–500,000. Blacks were almost universally not welcome as customers; lawsuits were filed against theater owners around the country, including New York State, but to little avail. Blacks were, however, the subjects of many films. Along with Jews, the Irish, and other ethnic minorities, they were the subject of unrestrained racial and ethnic caricatures.

Other genres included westerns, melodramas, and short adaptations of classic literature. While promoters claimed exposure to the picture shows enlightened the masses, detractors pointed to increasing safety and moral hazards and to the general low quality of the entertainment. Laws passed in 1911 requiring stiffer fire and building codes made it less profitable to operate small storefront nickelodeons, and the era of larger, more elaborate movie palaces arrived.

Many of the first giant movie theaters were built in New York City, including the 3,300-seat Strand (1914), the Capitol (1919), the Paramount (1926), and the opulent 5,900-seat Roxy (1927). One of the last was Radio City Music Hall (1932), seating 6,200. All but the last have been demolished. The major theater chains were also centered in the city and had rapidly expanded by the late 1920s. These included Paramount, Fox, and Loew's theaters, with venues in Manhattan as well as the outer boroughs. Loew's had the Valencia in Queens and the Paradise in the Bronx. Other cities in the state had their own movie palaces: Rochester had the Eastman Theatre and Syracuse, the Landmark Theatre, both originally built for silent films. In New York State a censorship board was instituted in 1921–22, which has proved to be a remarkable resource; in its archives are copies of scripts and the cuts that were ordered. The American Museum of the Moving Image (1988), located on the site of Zukor's Astoria studio, has the nation's largest collection of cinema artifacts, including many from the silent era. The International Museum of Photography and Film (1947) at the George Eastman House in Rochester has an immense archive of silent films and an ongoing preservation program.

Brown, Gene, ed. *New York Times Encyclopedia of Film*, 13 vols (New York: Times Books, 1984)
Everson, William K. *American Silent Film* (New York: Oxford Univ Press, 1978)
Findler, Joel. *The Hollywood Story* (New York: Crown Publishers, 1988)
Ramsaye, Terry. *A Million and One Nights* (1921; repr New York: Touchstone, 1986)
Smith, Albert. *Two Reels and a Crank* (Garden City, NY: Doubleday, 1952)
Zukor, Adolph, and Dale Kramer. *The Public Is Never Wrong* (New York: Putnam's, 1953)

Arthur Lennig

film, sound

The Early Sound Era

Sound film projection systems were exhibited in New York City by Thomas Edison and others from the 1910s. Warner Bros experimented with synchronized sound at their Vitagraph Studios in Midwood, Brooklyn, acquiring the Vitaphone sound-on-disc system developed by Western Electric and Bell Telephone Laboratories in 1925. The first synchronous sound feature, Alan Crosland's *Don Juan*, premiered on 6 Aug 1926 at Warner's Theatre in Manhattan. It was filmed at the Manhattan Opera House and featured the New York Philharmonic on the Vitaphone, with sound effects. By the mid-1920s, several studios had moved operations to California to take advantage of bright light and clear weather. Warner Bros moved to Hollywood and premiered Crosland's *The Jazz Singer,* starring Al Jolson, on 6 Oct 1927. The mostly silent film was partly shot on location, on Manhattan's Lower East Side and on Broadway. It featured songs and, for the first time in a widely distributed commercial release, bits of dialogue (ad-libbed by Jolson). The film's sensational nationwide success spelled the demise of the silent era. *The Lights of Broadway* (1928) by Warner Bros was the first "talkie" feature with synchronized dialogue integrated throughout. Sound film often utilized indoor sound stages, and for a time New York City was again a center for film production. Paramount's studio in Astoria, Queens, produced the feature-length *The Letter* (1929) and a newsreel series.

By 1937 nearly all mainstream feature production was located in Hollywood. Promotional efforts by Mayor Fiorello La Guardia in 1939 failed to draw studio productions back, though short sequences were still produced for Hollywood. Several notable films with all-black casts were produced in the city, including *Moon over Harlem* (1939) and *Murder on Lenox Avenue* (1941). Yiddish productions based in New York City included *Dem Khazns Zundl* (*The Cantor's Son,* 1937). New York City remained a principal source of creative talent for the industry and a favorite setting for narrative films. The musicals of the *Broadway Melody* series were hit movies in 1929, 1936, 1938, and 1940. *King Kong* (1933) used a model of the Empire State Building in one of the most imitated scenes in cinema history. During the depression, tales of the Lower East Side such as *She Done Him Wrong* (1933), *Hallelujah, I'm a Bum* (1933), *Dead End* (1937), and *Angels with Dirty Faces* (1938) were popular. Other films with distinctive New York settings included *Mr. Deeds Goes to Town* (1936), *Ziegfeld Girl* (1941), *Yankee Doodle Dandy* (1942), *Coney Island* (1943), *The Clock* (1945), and *A Tree Grows in Brooklyn* (1945).

Postwar Narrative Films

A 1938 federal suit forcing Paramount to screen independent features in its theater chain, changes in tax law, and an influx of skilled technicians from the emerging television industry led to both an upsurge in independent filmmaking and the return of major studio productions after the war. *The Lost Weekend* (1945), *The House on 92nd Street* (1945), *The Naked City* (1948), *The Quiet One* (1948), *On the Town* (1949), and *Sweet Smell of Success* (1957) used extensive location shooting in Manhattan and were unmistakably influenced by documentary innovations. RKO Pictures built a studio in Manhattan, and several studios were revived in the 1950s–1960s, including Biograph Co in the Bronx (*A Face in the Crowd,* 1957) and Famous Players-Lasky studios, later renamed the Production Center (*12 Angry Men,* 1957; *The Producers,* 1967). After Mayor John Lindsay established the Mayor's Office of Film, Theater, and Broadcasting in 1966, 366 films were made in the next eight years. Many films had memorable New York City settings, including *All About Eve* (1950), *Lullaby of Broadway* (1951), *Rear Window* (1954), *Marty* (1955), *Blackboard Jungle* (1955), *The Apartment* (1960), *Breakfast at Tiffany's* (1961), *West Side Story* (1961), *Rosemary's Baby* (1968), and *Midnight Cowboy* (1969). Among the independent filmmakers of the period were John Cassavetes and Shirley Clarke.

Since 1970

Many independent-minded directors dedicated to New York City subjects emerged from the New

York University film school (1965), including Martin Scorsese (*Mean Streets,* 1973; *Taxi Driver,* 1976; *After Hours,* 1985; *Goodfellas,* 1990; *Gangs of New York,* 2002). Woody Allen (*Annie Hall,* 1977; *Manhattan,* 1979; *Broadway Danny Rose,* 1984; *Bullets over Broadway,* 1994) and Sidney Lumet (*Serpico,* 1973; *Dog Day Afternoon,* 1975) also became known for their vibrant portrayals of the city's atmosphere. The Filmways Studio in Harlem was used for *The Godfather* (1971), which was shot in 120 locations throughout the city. Gritty urban dramas predominated in the 1970s. Gordon Parks's *Shaft* (1971), shot on location in Harlem, helped establish the blaxploitation genre, which provided black actors with new opportunities in the industry. Other films shot on location included *The French Connection* (1971), *Next Stop, Greenwich Village* (1976), and *Saturday Night Fever* (1977).

By the late 1970s most of the studios refurbished in previous decades had closed. In 1975 the renovated 14-acre (6 ha) Astoria Studios reopened on Paramount's old site, housing the first major studio production in New York City since the silent era (*The Wiz,* 1978) and was renamed Kaufman Astoria Studios in 1982. Silvercup Studios, established in 1983 in a converted bread factory in Queens, was used for over 40 films. The Chelsea Piers complex at 23d St on the Hudson houses Silver Screen Studios (1988), Manhattan's largest center of film and television production in 2003. Location shooting in the 1980s included *Fame* (1980), *Escape from New York* (1981), *Fort Apache, the Bronx* (1981), *Wild Style* (1982), *Ghostbusters* (1984), *Desperately Seeking Susan* (1985), *Prizzi's Honor* (1985), *Wall Street* (1987), *Crossing Delancey* (1988), and *New York Stories* (1989).

In 1989, 143 features were shot, but a 1990–91 labor dispute caused the major studios to boycott the city, bringing studio productions to a halt. Unions formed the East Coast Council, enabling independent directors to negotiate wage deferments with workers. When the boycott ended there was a huge wave of growth; by 1999 the industry accounted for 50,000 jobs and $850 million per year in local spending. With new encouragement from city government, independent producers and distributors such as Miramax, Gramercy, October, and Fine Line set up operations in or near the Tribeca Film Center (1989), a production, screening, and editing complex established by actor Robert De Niro and producer Jane Rosenthal. New York University graduate Spike Lee has made numerous films with vivid New York City settings, including *Do the Right Thing* (1989), *Malcolm X* (1992), *Crooklyn* (1994), *Summer of Sam* (1999), and *25th Hour* (2002), which features scenes shot on the streets of Manhattan in the days immediately following 11 Sept 2001. Other films shot on location since 1990 include *Carlito's Way* (1993), *The Brothers McMullen* (1995), *Smoke* (1995), *As Good as It Gets* (1997), *Donnie Brasco* (1997), *You've Got Mail* (1998), and *Spider-Man* (2002). The line between independents and studio productions has blurred in recent years. MGM acquired United Artists in 1981 and moved it to New York to be near the city's independent directors, and Sony Pictures Classics (1992) pursued a similar strategy. Universal Studios purchased October Films, and Disney absorbed Miramax. In 1995, 175 features were filmed in New York City.

Many young filmmakers got their start through cooperatives, at the independent production house Shooting Gallery (1991–2001), and at film schools at New York University and Columbia. In 2002 the mayor's office listed 28 production facilities available for rent. Foundation work on Steiner Studios began in 2001; the 15-acre (6 ha) site at the Brooklyn Navy Yard will be the largest production facility outside Hollywood; of the six studios being built, one will be 42,000 ft^2 (3902 m^2). Studio City is planned to be a 15-story, 700,000 ft^2 (65,032 m^2) film and television studio between 44th and 45th Sts on 11th Ave in Manhattan. The Kaufman Astoria Studios also have expansion plans. The city is home to numerous major film festivals, including the New York Film Festival and the Tribeca Film Festival.

Outside New York City

The filmmaking industry outside New York City has been mostly confined to location shooting, including *Niagara* (1953); *The Way We Were* (1973), partly filmed in Ballston Spa (Saratoga Co) and at Union College in Schenectady; *The Cotton Club* (1984), filmed in Albany; *Ironweed* (1986), shot in Albany and Troy (Rensselaer Co); and Scorcese's *Age of Innocence* (1993), with some filming in Albany's Washington Park. *Billy Bathgate* (1991), *The Horse Whisperer* (1998), and *Seabiscuit* (2003) were filmed in Saratoga Co.

Documentary Film

Manhattan's Fox Film Corp began Fox Movietone News in 1927. Depression era Fox and Paramount newsreels were made with entertainment in mind, and in 1930 the Workers Film and Photo League formed in New York City to document protests, hunger marches, strikes, evictions, and "Hoovervilles" (shantytowns) absent from upbeat studio newsreels. League members Ralph Steiner, Paul Strand, and Leo Hurwitz were recruited as cameramen for Pare Lorentz's pioneering *Plow That Broke the Plains* (1936), scored by Virgil Thomson. Members also formed the Frontier Film Group, which produced social documentaries in the late 1930s and early 1940s. Willard Van Dyke directed over 50 documentaries, including *The City,* an urban planning film made with Steiner for the 1939 World's Fair, which used experimental montage techniques and an Aaron Copland score to evoke the rush of city life. In 1942 the Army Signal Corps bought the Astoria studio and turned it into the Army Pictorial Center, which produced military and medical training films. James Agee and Helen Levitt's lyrical short film *In the Street* (1952) used a hidden camera to document everyday life in Spanish Harlem. New York Newsreel made radical films (eg, *Columbia Revolt,* 1968). Michael Wadleigh's *Woodstock* (1970), filmed at the 1969 rock festival in Bethel (Sullivan Co), remains one of the highest grossing documentaries ever made. Documentary directors associated with New York include cinematographers Alexander Hammid and Boris Kaufman, Lionel Rogosin (*On the Bowery,* 1956), Frederick Wiseman (*Hospital,* 1970), Albert and David Maysles (*Grey Gardens,* 1976), and D. A. Pennebaker (*Moon over Broadway,* 1997). Notable New York documentaries since 1990 include *Paris Is Burning* (1990); *Brother's Keeper* (1992), filmed in Munnsville (Madison Co); *A Great Day in Harlem* (1995); *9/11* (2002), by Jules and Gedeon Naudet; and *Capturing the Friedmans* (2003). The New York Documentary Center (1997) holds regular screenings.

Barnouw, Erik. *Documentary: A History of the Non-Fiction Film,* 2d rev ed. (New York: Oxford Univ Press, 1993)

Katz, Chuck. *Manhattan on Film: Walking Tours of Hollywood's Fabled Front Lot* (New York: Limelight Editions, 2000)

Levy, Emanuel. *Cinema of Outsiders: The Rise of American Independent Film* (New York: New York Univ Press, 1999)

Lippy, Tod, ed. *Projections 11: New York Film-Makers on Film-Making* (New York: Farrar, Straus & Giroux, 2000)

Sanders, James. *Celluloid Skyline: New York and the Movies* (New York: Knopf, 2001)

Stuart Smyth and Kevin Smyth

Financial Control Board (FCB). In the spring of 1975 the market for New York City bonds and notes closed because City Hall had been spending more than it could afford. To avert bankruptcy and help reassure investors that the city would meet its obligations, New York State created the New York City Emergency Financial Control Board (now FCB) in September 1975. Members of the board include the governor, the mayor of New York City, the state and city comptrollers, and three individuals appointed by the governor with the consent of the New York State Senate. At first FCB had the power to force New York City to cut its spending by rejecting the city's budgets and multiyear financial plans, but FCB always lacked the ability to target specific budgetary items for reduction or modification. Under the leadership of Gov Hugh Carey and the board's executive director Stephen Berger (1976–77), FCB compelled City Hall to reduce its budgets, resulting in the dismissal of approximately 30,000 people in the city's workforce from 1975 to 1978. The FCB also had the authority to reject contracts that the city had signed with municipal unions; it used this authority to ensure that from 1975 to 1978 city employees received only minimal cost of living adjustments (COLAs) in their salaries. The COLAs had to be funded through productivity savings. These cutbacks pleased important political figures in Washington, DC, including US Senate Banking Committee chairman William Proxmire, a Democrat from Wisconsin, and US Treasury Secretary William Simon. Most city labor figures, such as Victor Gotbaum, head of the city's largest municipal union, accepted the FCB's actions as necessary. In 1986, with the city in the black, the FCB voted to surrender its general power to revise budgets, although this will be restored if the city ends a fiscal year with a deficit of $100 million or more. The board is scheduled to shut its doors in 2008.

Kramer, Daniel C. *The Days of Wine and Roses Are Over: Governor Hugh Carey and New York State* (Lanham, Md: Univ Press of America, 1997)

Daniel C. Kramer

Fine. Town (pop 1,622) in S St. Lawrence Co. First occupied in 1823 and settled permanently in 1834, the town was formed in 1844 from Russell and Pierrepont. A distinctive early industry was the Spencer and Anderson oar factory (1858). After the Carthage and Adirondack Railroad (1889) began service, paper mills provided employment, as did an iron mine (1889; intermittent under various names to 1978). Wanakena was a planned hamlet (1902) created by a lumber company and since 1912 has been the site of the Ranger School of the SUNY College of Environmental Science and Forestry. The town's population declined in the late 20th century with the loss of industry, but there has been some influx of retirees. Town life centers on Star Lake hamlet, site of the central school, a small hospital, and retail trade. The 171 ft (52.1 m) Wanakena Suspension Footbridge (*ca* 1902) and the Fine Town Hall (*ca* 1885) are listed on the National Register.

Richard E. Mooers

Finger Lakes. A series of 11 elongated, glacially formed lakes in central and western New York State and the region associated with them. Development is dispersed among a number of small and moderate-sized cities and villages, with none dominant.

GEOLOGIC ORIGINS AND DESCRIPTION

As the Ice Age glacial front proceeded from the Ontario Lake Plain, it encountered the north-facing escarpment of the Appalachian Upland, which was cut by a series of preexisting stream valleys running roughly in the same direction as the ice flow. The advancing ice was concentrated into the valleys, which it then scoured and deepened, in some cases by 1,000 feet (305 m) or more. Some of the valleys, because the scouring was so deep or because of damming by glacial deposits, formed lakes as the glacier receded. Keuka and the lakes to its west reflect more closely the orientation of the original streams; Seneca and the lakes to its east mimic the direction of the ice flow. Onondaga Creek, south of Syracuse, occupies a similarly formed valley that did not become a lake. A recessional moraine deposited to the south of the lakes functions as a divide between the Lake Ontario and Susquehanna River drainage systems.

The four smaller western lakes (Conesus, Hemlock, Canadice, and Honeoye) flow into the Genesee River system, and the other seven (Canandaigua, Keuka, Seneca, Cayuga, Owasco, Skaneateles, and Otisco) flow into the Oswego system. They are all north-south oriented and have a long, narrow finger-like shape, except Keuka (historically known as Crooked Lake), which is Y shaped, with an 812 ft (247.5 m) bluff dividing the north half into two branches. Cayuga is the longest (38 mi/61.2 km) of the Finger Lakes and has the lowest elevation. With Keuka flowing into Seneca and Seneca into Cayuga, the latter acts as a reservoir for floodwaters. Seneca (618 ft/188.4 m) and Cayuga (435 ft/132.6 m) are among the deepest lakes in the eastern United States, and Taughannock Falls (215 ft/65.5 m) in Tompkins Co, where Taughannock Creek enters the Cayuga Lake valley, is one of the highest waterfalls east of the Rockies. The climate is warmer in both summer and winter than in the higher plateaus to the south, and there is less snow than on the Ontario Lake Plain. The summer is relatively dry, and the region's annual water surplus is among the lowest in the state. Still, the climate favors horticulture, and the slopes overlooking the lakes are especially well suited for grapes. The region's native vegetation consists of oak and northern hardwood forests.

HISTORY AND LAND USE

Traditionally home to the Iroquois, the Finger Lakes were made known to Easterners by the troops of the Sullivan-Clinton campaign (1779). Western New York State's earliest settlement centers—Auburn (Cayuga Co), Ithaca, Geneva (Ontario Co), and Canandaigua (Ontario Co)—are in the region, and settler streams from both the south and the east intermingled, as symbolized by the Village of Penn Yan (Yates Co), home to both Pennsylvanians and Yankees. In the 19th century the region became a center of reform; abolitionist political leader William H. Seward came from Auburn, and Seneca Falls hosted the nation's first women's rights convention in 1848. The opening of the Erie Canal in 1825 shifted major settlement and development northward, but the canal system also extended into the Finger Lakes region. The Cayuga and Seneca Canal (1828) joined the Erie Canal to both of those lakes, allowing the region's farmers to market their wheat. The Crooked Lake Canal (1833–77), joining Keuka to Seneca, brought more farmers into the system. The Chemung Canal (1833–78), connecting Seneca Lake with the Chemung River and the extensive Pennsylvania canal system, created an outlet for Pennsylvania coal all the way to the Erie Canal. Canal barges were bundled together and towed across the lakes by steamboat. The canal system faded with the expansion of railroads through the area, although the Cayuga and Seneca and a portion of the Chemung continue to be used for recreation.

As the western New York State wheat economy faded in the second half of the 19th century, local farmers shifted to dairying, dairy-related crops, grapes, and, for a time, teasels. The Finger Lakes wine industry began on Keuka Lake about midcentury and later spread to Canandaigua, Seneca, and Cayuga Lakes. A handful of wineries survived Prohibition by producing juices, jellies, and sacramental wines. Boutique wineries, often growing higher-quality European vinifera grapes, proliferated after 1976. Manufacturing also rose in the 19th century, with firms such as Goulds Pumps (Seneca Co) and Corning (Steuben Co) still operating.

The recreation industry dates from at least 1816, when the first excursion boat was launched on Skaneateles Lake. Throughout the region are numerous vacation homes, boating and fishing facilities, excursion boats and trains, state parks (six of them featuring scenic glens and waterfalls), a federal wildlife refuge, and the state's only national forest. Other economic activities include hog raising (often by Mennonites), food processing, and salt mining. The New York State Agricultural Experiment Station and a biotechnology business incubator are in Geneva, and an infotonics business incubator is in Canandaigua. Among the region's educational institutions are Cornell University and Hobart and William Smith Colleges, home of the Finger Lakes Institute. Ongoing environmental problems include nonpoint source pollution, caused by runoff traveling over and through polluted soil, and the spread of invasive species, such as zebra mussels, lampreys, and Eurasian milfoil, which entered through the canal system. A variety of public and private organizations seek to maintain the quality of the lakes, which supply drinking water for communities as distant as Rochester and Syracuse.

See also FINNS.

Engeln, O. D. von. *The Finger Lakes Region: Its Origin and Nature* (1961; repr Ithaca: Cornell Univ Press, 1988)
Merrill, Arch. *Slim Fingers Beckon* (1951; repr Interlaken, NY: Heart of the Lakes Publishing, 1991)
Thompson, John H., ed. *Geography of New York State* (Syracuse: Syracuse Univ Press, 1977)

Scott C. Monje

Finger Lakes ferries. The Finger Lakes are a series of long, narrow, north-south-oriented lakes in central and western New York State. The longest, Cayuga Lake, stretching 38 miles (61.2 km) and connecting to an extensive marsh in the north, intersected the main pioneer routes connecting Albany with the western part of the state. The first ferry of record on the Finger Lakes was established in 1788 by John Harris, whose grandfather had founded Harris Ferry [now Harrisburg, Pa]. It crossed northern Cayuga Lake at the Genesee Rd. Service ended in September 1800 with the opening of the Cayuga Lake Bridge, because the bridge company's charter prohibited any ferry service within three miles of the bridge. The state reauthorized ferry service in 1808 when the bridge collapsed, on other occasions when the bridge was in disrepair, and again in 1858 after the bridge had been abandoned. By then, however, much of the region's long-distance traffic moved by barge or rail.

Speed and reliability improved as the ferries' source of power evolved from oars and sails, to horses on treadmills, to steam engines. The first steamboat on the Finger Lakes, the *Enterprise* (1820), was subsidized by the Village of Newburgh (Orange Co) to make the Newburgh-Catskill Turnpike more competitive with the Albany-based roads. It received passengers from the stage in Ithaca, at the south end of Cayuga Lake, and delivered them to the Seneca Turnpike stage at the Cayuga Lake Bridge. Railroads later replaced the stages, but the Ithaca-to-Cayuga ferry route was used until 1907. The longest-surviving ferry crossing on Cayuga ran between Northville [now King Ferry, Cayuga Co] and Kidders (Seneca Co) from 1825 to 1913. In all, the state issued 18 ferry licenses on Cayuga Lake between 1808 and 1866.

Seneca Lake's first ferry, the *Goodwin*, was built by John Goodwin in 1805, received a charter in 1810, and served until 1897. It crossed between North Hector [now Valois, Schuyler Co] and Starkey (Yates Co). The state also chartered ferries between Lancaster [now Willard, Seneca Co] and Dresden (Yates Co) in 1825 and between Peach Orchard Point (Schuyler Co) and Big Stream (Yates Co) in 1829. An unchartered ferry ran out of Lodi Landing (Seneca Co). Later in the 19th century, steamboats ran the length of the lake, between Geneva (Ontario Co) and Watkins Glen (Schuyler Co), crisscrossing the lake to make stops along the way. Other lakes also had locally significant ferries, including service on Keuka Lake, which began as early as 1803, between Keuka and Gibson Landing (Steuben Co).

Later steamboats cruised many of the lakes for excursions as well as passenger service. Ferries began to decline in the late 1800s, however, as faster railroads bypassing the lakes competed for passengers and for contracts to carry the mail. Most ferry services had ended by the 1920s, but private operators still offer excursion and dinner cruises on several of the Finger Lakes.

Inshaw, Charles C., "Steamboating on the Finger Lakes," *New York History* (July 1942): 307–14
Sisler, Carol U. *Seneca Lake: Past, Present, and Future* (Ithaca: Enterprise Publishing, 1995)
———. *Cayuga Lake: Past, Present, and Future* (1989; repr Ithaca: DeWitt Historical Society of Tompkins County, 1999)

Scott C. Monje

Finger Lakes National Forest. New York State's only national forest and one of the smallest in the country. It is administered jointly with the Green Mountain National Forest, with headquarters in Rutland, Vt. The 16,032-acre (6,488 ha) complex lies on a ridge between Seneca and Cayuga Lakes in Seneca and Schuyler Cos. The federal government purchased marginal farmlands in the area starting in 1938. The Soil Conservation Service managed them, planted conifers to stabilize the soil, and instituted a grazing program, which continues on 5,000 acres (2,023 ha). The land was transferred to the US Forest Service (Department of Agriculture) in 1954 for multiple-use management. In 1982 the Forest Service proposed selling off the land, but in response to public demand for continued federal ownership and public access, Congress in 1985 established the Finger Lakes National Forest (initially called the Hector Ranger District of the Green Mountain National Forest). Between 1999 and 2001 the Forest Service considered opening the forest to oil and gas development but decided against it after public protests. Deer, beaver, fox, cattle, and a variety of birds roam the forest freely. The forest also has camping facilities, blueberry patches, and snowmobile, hiking, riding, and cross-country trails.

Green Mountain and Finger Lakes National Forests, http://www.fs.fed.us/r9/gmfl

Watrous, Hilda R. *The Country between the Lakes: A Public History of Seneca County, 1876–1982* (Waterloo, NY: Seneca County Board of Supervisors, 1982)

Scott C. Monje

Finney, Charles Grandison (*b* Warren, Conn, 29 Aug 1792; *d* Oberlin, Ohio, 16 Aug 1875). Evangelist, pastor, professor of theology, and college president. Finney grew up in Hanover [now Kirkland, Oneida Co], where his parents Sylvester and Rebecca Rice Finney settled in 1794. In 1808 the family moved to Henderson (Jefferson Co). He was educated in common schools and at Warren Academy in Connecticut. He taught in New Jersey (1814–18), later returning to Jefferson Co and serving as a law clerk in Adams. Aloof from religion even as music director of the Presbyterian Church, in October 1821 Finney experienced a dramatic conversion and left law for ministry. After study with his pastor, George W. Gale, the St. Lawrence Presbytery licensed him to preach in December 1823. In March 1824 the Female Missionary Society of the Western District of New York commissioned Finney as an evangelist. Ordained on 1 July 1824, Finney married Lydia Root Andrews in October, and they had six children.

Finney drew emotional North Country crowds with his powerful, direct preaching. As the Erie Canal opened in 1825 he moved to Oneida Co, where, in league with New School Presbyterian pastors, he ignited revival in Utica, Rome, and other Mohawk Valley cities. In 1826 he preached from Auburn (Cayuga Co) to Troy (Rensselaer Co), attracting national attention. Old School Presbyterian and New England Congregational critics objected to such new measures as prayer for sinners by name, immediate conversion, and female testimony. In July 1827 Lyman Beecher organized a conference of New England and Mohawk Valley clergy at New Lebanon (Columbia Co) that resulted in the vindication of the Finneyite revivals.

Finney preached in eastern cities, including Wilmington, Del, and Philadelphia and in 1829 at a Free Presbyterian Church in New York City. From September 1830 to June 1831 in Rochester, Finney led his most influential revival with protracted meetings, a call to temperance, and the use of the anxious seat, an area in the front of the congregation where penitent seekers awaited individual prayer with the preacher. After his 1831–32 Boston campaign, Arthur and Lewis Tappan and other philanthropists established him as pastor in New York City at the Chatham Street Chapel, linking revivalism and the antislavery movement. In 1835 Finney published *Sermons on Various Subjects* and *Lectures on Revivals of Religion.* With Presbyterian heresy charges looming, in 1836 Finney joined the Congregational denomination while patrons built his Broadway Tabernacle in New York City. Meanwhile, Tappan money founded Oberlin College, which called Finney as professor of theology with the intent that he divide his time between Ohio and New York City. He resigned from Broadway Tabernacle, however, settling in Oberlin, where he served as professor (1835–75), pastor (1837–72), and college president (1851–65).

At Oberlin, Finney borrowed from Wesleyan ideas, developing the doctrine of holiness or "entire sanctification," which sparked further controversy when he used the term "perfection" to describe the sanctified life of complete obedience to God. He also launched evangelistic campaigns each winter, often in New York State. After his wife's death, he married Rochester widow Elizabeth Ford Atkinson, a long-time friend and supporter, with whom he undertook two preaching tours of Great Britain. At age 73, after Elizabeth's death, he married Rebecca Allen Rayl, who assisted in writing his memoirs. Acknowledged as a creator of the modern urban revival, Finney influenced later evangelists from Dwight L. Moody to Billy Graham.

See also ABOLITIONISM; BURNED-OVER DISTRICT; CONGREGATIONALISTS; PRESBYTERIANS.

Finney, Charles G. *The Memoirs of Charles G. Finney.* Eds. Garth M. Rosell and Richard A. G. Dupuis (Grand Rapids, Mich: Zondervan, 1989)

Hambrick-Stowe, Charles E. *Charles G. Finney and the Spirit of American Evangelicalism* (Grand Rapids, Mich: Eerdmans Publishing, 1996)

Charles E. Hambrick-Stowe

Finns. After New Sweden was established along the Delaware River in 1638, the first Finns settled in the Dutch colony of New Netherland. The settlers included passengers from a Swedish ship seized by the Dutch and seamen from other ships. Official records also identify settlers with birthplaces in Finland and label more than one court defendant as "the Finn." Later, when Finland had become a Russian duchy, Finnish sailors left its merchant ships to work in New York State during the Crimean War of 1854–56.

Modern immigration from Finland got underway during the American Civil War. For about the next 30 years, most Finnish newcomers entered the country through New York State. In 1887 G. A. Grönlund established the Scandinavian and Finlanders Emigrant Co. He sold tickets until the depression of 1893 reduced immigration. Other Finnish entrepreneurs operated rooming houses and saloons for the newcomers. By 1900 New York State had 4,048 foreign-born Finns, ranking fourth in the United States. More than 92% lived in New York City, largely in the Finntown section of Sunset Park in Brooklyn and Harlem in Manhattan. The Finland Seamen's Missionary Society inaugurated mission stations in 1887, and four years later its first clergyman, Emil Panelius, helped establish the Brooklyn Evangelical Lutheran Church. In 1890 Brooklyn got a Finnish working people's society, later named the Finnish Aid Society Imatra, that erected a hall. In 1893 the Finnish American Publishing Co started the newspaper *Siirtolainen* (The Emigrant), and other Finns published the short-lived first workingman's newspaper in 1900.

Between 1900 and the immediate aftermath of World War I, new Finnish immigrants arrived in the state. By 1920 New York City was home to 82% of the state's 12,504 foreign-born Finns. Women found employment in domestic service, outnumbering men, who often worked as carpenters. These newcomers supported religion, temperance, and other causes. They also helped to start the *New Yorkin Uutiset* (New York News) in 1906, recruiting the utopianist editor Matti Kurikka. In Brooklyn and Harlem there were large numbers of Finnish socialists, the latter organizing the Finnish Workers Educational Association that acquired the Fifth Avenue Hall. In the 1920s the Finnish immigrant population in New York State increased by almost 40% to 17,444. The overwhelming number of Finns in New York State lived in New York City and environs, while only 14% resided in rural areas. Finns classified as farm residents totaled 4%, most of whom had worked elsewhere before acquiring hill farms.

Between the two world wars the Finnish communities were in their heyday. Brooklyn Finns were noted for their cooperative apartment buildings, while upstate farmers organized the Spencer Co-operative Society in May 1928. The co-op was established to help local Finns purchase goods on a larger scale and to find markets for the farm goods they produced. The first store opened with a limited line of groceries, feed, fertilizer, and hardware items, and all business was conducted in Finnish. By 1953 members totaled 750, with sales of $2.8 million; in 1995 the co-op was liquidated.

Finnish immigration to the Finger Lakes region began in 1910 in Tompkins, Chemung, and Tioga Cos. Nationally, Finns were seeking to leave the mines and factories of the Midwest to find agricultural properties, and within the next four decades upward of 500 Finnish landowners arrived in the Finger Lakes, with the most significant influx occurring between 1916 and 1920. The Finns established chicken farming and strong community organizations. Most organizations recruited the children of immigrants. The post–World War I debate on communism divided socialist ranks, and the left-oriented Finnish Workers Federation established the Labor Temple in Harlem. The economic depression of the 1930s weakened institutional life, as the *New Yorkin Uutiset* and Labor Temple lost ownership of their buildings. In 1938 all the major organizations cooperated, in spite of their ideological divisions, to celebrate the 300th anniversary of the establishment of New Sweden. During the Russo-Finnish War of 1939–40, most groups sent relief to Finland.

By 1940 the immigrant era was fading. The number of foreign-born Finns in the state had decreased in the 1930s, and in the 1940s and 1950s the Finnish American population became much less based in New York City than before.

In 1960 New York City Finns numbered 4,637, slightly less than half the state's total. This aging immigrant base and the second generation totaled 9,803 in 1950, not a large enough population to sustain the earlier pace of Finnish institutional life. Their descendants intermarried with other ethnic groups so that by 1980 almost 60% claimed at least two ancestor groups. The number of people claiming any degree of Finnish ancestry decreased from 23,475 in 1980 to 21,288 in 1990. Harlem Finns sold the Fifth Avenue Hall, and Brooklyn Finns subsequently did the same with Imatra Hall. The *New Yorkin Uutiset* lasted until the 1990s. On the 2000 US census, 16,833 New York State residents claimed Finnish ancestry.

Ekman, Katri, Corinne Olli, and John B. Olli, eds. *A History of Finnish American Organizations in Greater New York, 1891–1976* (New York: Greater New York Finnish Bicentennial Planning Committee, 1976)
Hoglund, A.William. *Finnish Immigrants in America, 1880–1920* (Madison: Univ of Wisconsin Press, 1960)

A. William Hoglund

Steam engine built by the American Fire Engine Co, Seneca Falls, 1901, and used by the Elmira and Albany fire departments.

firefighting. In New Netherland and colonial New York, fire was a constant and serious threat. Almost all buildings of the period were constructed out of wood, and many were covered by highly combustible thatched roofs and had poorly ventilated hearths. In New Amsterdam in 1648 the first fire ordinances restricted the construction of wooden chimneys; that same year Gov Petrus Stuyvesant appointed that city's first four fire wardens. The Dutch and the English established codes throughout the colony for the maintenance of chimneys and required households to keep fire buckets. Many of these codes were backed with enforcement powers, such as in Lansingburgh [now in Rensselaer Co], whereby local inspectors in the late 18th century could shutter buildings until chimneys had been properly swept of soot. The threat of fire in the colonial period, however, remained ominous. In 1690 the stockaded settlement of Schenectady was destroyed by fire following a raid by French troops and their American Indian allies, killing 60.

Firefighters in Elmira, 1888.

Evolution

One of the earliest volunteer fire departments in the state was organized in Albany in 1731. In that year New York City purchased two fire engines from London to be operated by citizens in case of fire; the trucks were taken over by a volunteer fire company, provided for by the Colonial Assembly in 1737. Incendiary burning was also a serious cause for concern. The infamous New York City "Negro Plot" of 1741, which led to the execution of 30 Blacks and 4 Whites, hinged on an alleged arson conspiracy. Whether the incident was the result of a genuine slave conspiracy or reflected the paranoid imagination of city residents is still debated by historians. A suspicious fire that started days after the British army occupied New York City in 1776 burned approximately 500 buildings, or one-third of the city. In 1786 the New York City Common Council passed an ordinance creating a new department of 300 volunteers divided among 15 engine companies and 2 hook-and-ladder companies; this organization was known as the Fire Department of the City of New York (FDNY).

Volunteer fire companies were distinctive institutions. In addition to fighting fires, they were venues for socializing and meeting influential persons. Many joined New York City's department as a means of social or political advancement. The best-known example is William M. Tweed, who used his captainship of the Americus Engine Co in Lower Manhattan as a platform to become boss of Tammany Hall in the 1860s. Volunteer fire companies were, in many circles, also notorious for incompetence and lack of discipline. In Utica in the early 19th century, rivalries between volunteer fire companies commonly led to brawls as competing groups fought to see which would have the privilege of extinguishing the conflagration. Efforts were made to transform volunteer fire companies into career departments, which were often opposed by volunteers. In Schenectady, even though the city had acquired a paid force in 1899 to replace its volunteers and two years later had formed a training school for its career firefighters, the last volunteer company was not disbanded until 1960 because of the political influence of the volunteers.

In some localities the connection between volunteer fire companies and fighting fires was purely nominal. The volunteer fire department in the wealthy New York City suburb of Mount Vernon (Westchester Co), founded in 1855, was primarily a privileged social club. Membership was exclusive, and funds were raised through privately sponsored clambakes and fairs. Not until 1895 did Mount Vernon's volunteers receive any comprehensive training to fight fires. In New York City the volunteers objected to horse-drawn trucks, introduced in 1832, and steam engines, introduced in 1858.

New York City built eight fire towers in 1845, connecting them by telegraph in 1851. The volunteer fire department ended on 1 Aug 1865, when New York City and Brooklyn were included in the Metropolitan Fire Department, established by the state legislature. This new career department was divided into 34 engine and 12 ladder companies, protecting Manhattan as far north as 87th St. In 1868, through the influence of Tweed, New York City regained control of the department, though the career organization remained. Other innovations included the installment of fire alarm boxes throughout the city starting in 1870. The shift to a career fire department took longer for the northern reaches of Manhattan and for the City of Brooklyn. Staten Island did not have paid firefighters until 1913. Indeed, there were still 10 active volunteer fire companies, though formally unrecognized, in four of New York City's five boroughs in 2001.

Other cities in the state had patterns similar to New York City and replaced their volunteer fire departments with full- or part-time career forces during the 19th century. Buffalo organized its first volunteer fire company in 1817, four years after British troops had set most of the village ablaze during the War of 1812. The city bought its first hand fire engine in 1824 and acquired its first steam fire engine in 1859. A career fire de-

MAJOR FIRES IN NEW YORK STATE

Date	Location	Description
8 Feb 1690	Schenectady	Fire set by French troops and Native Americans following raid destroys village, killing 60
18 Mar 1741	New York City	Fort George partly destroyed by fire; charges of arson conspiracy (the "Negro Plot") result in 34 executions
21 Sept 1776	New York City	Series of fires destroy one-third of Manhattan after British troops occupy city; known as the Great Fire of 1776
30 Dec 1813	Buffalo	Fire set by British troops following raid destroys village, killing approximately 40
5 Dec 1819	Rochester	*Gazette* newspaper building burns; first major fire fought by Rochester volunteer firemen
16 Mar 1834	Syracuse	21 buildings burn along Erie Canal
16–17 Dec 1835	New York City	Lower Manhattan burns in massive fire on bitterly cold day; destroys 20 square blocks; known as the Great Fire of 1835; disaster leads to the bankruptcy of 23 state insurance firms
20 Aug 1841	Syracuse	Explosion and subsequent fire at explosives warehouse on East Willow St kills 26 volunteer firemen; most firemen lost in the state until 11 Sept 2001
19 July 1845	New York City	Lower Manhattan burns in a massive fire, killing 30; known as the Great Fire of 1845
5 Oct 1858	New York City	Fire destroys Crystal Palace
10 May 1862	Troy (Rensselaer Co)	Massive fire consumes nearly one-half of city, killing 5; 17 square blocks destroyed; Troy takes 10 years to rebuild
5 Dec 1876	Brooklyn	Fire in Conway's Theater kills 296; prompts city law requiring theater exit inspections
7 Dec 1880	Buffalo	Fire at M. H. Birge and Sons wallpaper factory on Perry St kills 10
12 July 1885	Albany	Fire at Boardman and Gray piano factory on North Pearl St kills 3 firemen
19 Dec 1892	Albany	Fire at Fort Orange Milling Co on Columbia Street Pier kills 4 firemen
14 June 1904	New York City	Fire onboard the SS *General Slocum* in East River kills 1,021; greatest loss of life in the state from fire until 11 Sept 2001
25 Mar 1911	New York City	Fire at Triangle Shirtwaist Factory on Washington St kills 146; prompts the creation of the Office of the State Fire Marshall and a sweeping array of new state fire regulations
29 Mar 1911	Albany	New York State Capitol partially destroyed by fire; major collections of the state's colonial and 19th century documents lost
29 July 1913	Binghamton	Fire at Binghamton Clothing Co factory kills 60; prompts new state standards for exits in buildings
1 Aug 1932	New York City	Fire at Ritz Hotel kills 7 firemen
13 June 1934	Jamestown (Chautauqua Co)	Fire at Richfield Refinery kills 4 firemen
3 Aug 1939	Syracuse	Fire and structure collapse on Genesee St kills 8 firemen
28 July 1945	New York City	Airplane crashes into Empire State Building; crash and subsequent fire kills 14
31 Mar 1954	Cheektowaga (Erie Co)	Fire at Cleveland Hill Elementary School kills 15; prompts new state standards in building safety code
19 Dec 1960	Brooklyn	Fire onboard USS *Constellation* at New York Naval Shipyard kills 50
25 July 1962	Berlin (Rensselaer Co)	Fire sparked by vehicular accident of a propane tanker kills 10
17 Oct 1966	New York City	Fire at building on 23d St kills 12 firemen
5 Apr 1967	Cayuga Heights (Tompkins Co)	Fire at Cornell University dormitory kills 9; prompts annual state inspections of all college dormitories
10 Feb 1973	Staten Island	Explosion and subsequent fire at Liquid Natural Gas Storage facility kills 40
30 June 1974	Port Chester (Westchester Co)	Fire at Gulliver's Discotheque kills 24
24 Oct 1976	Bronx	Fire at Puerto Rican Social Club kills 25
9 Apr 1978	Syracuse	Fire at 701 University Ave kills 4 firemen
16 Nov 1978	Greece (Monroe Co)	Fire at Holiday Inn kills 10
4 Dec 1980	Harrison (Westchester Co)	Fire at Stouffer's Inn kills 26; prompts the New York State Uniform Fire Prevention and Building Code
5 Feb 1981	Binghamton	Fire at the State Office Building leaves PCB contamination that takes 12 years to clean up
13 Mar 1990	North Blenheim (Schoharie Co)	Fire from the rupture of the Texas Eastern propane pipeline kills 2
25 Mar 1990	Bronx	Fire at Happy Land Social Club kills 87
26 Feb 1993	New York City	Explosion and fire set of by a truck bomb at World Trade Center kills 6
11 Sept 2001	New York City	Explosion, fire, and structure collapse set off by the collision of 2 highjacked airliners into the World Trade Center kills 2,795 including 343 firefighters and 87 police officers; greatest loss of life caused by fire in state history

Compiled by Frederick S. Richards

partment was formed in 1880. Rochester purchased its first fire truck in 1818 and its first steam engine in 1861. Its volunteer companies disbanded about the same time, and by 1863 it had a paid force of 50 men. Utica organized its first volunteer force, consisting of 25 men, in 1805, instituted a nightly fire patrol four years later, and both hired a paid force and installed a fire telegraph system throughout the city in 1874. In 1939 the Schenectady Fire Department was perhaps the first department in the state to install in its trucks a two-way radio system, provided by locally based General Electric. Other cities in the state, however, lagged behind. Although nearly half of Troy (Rensselaer Co) was obliterated by a massive fire in 1862, the community did not hire a career force until 1893 because of the opposition of local volunteer companies. In Plattsburgh, where the business district had been completely reduced to ashes in 1849 and again in 1867, city officials did not deploy a paid force until 1913.

The life of a paid 19th-century fireman was not easy. Departments were organized with military discipline including captains and lieutenants. Firemen were obliged to live in the firehouse, more or less full-time and in New York City were on call for up to 147 hours a week. Because Irish immigrants were active in the early volunteer departments, they became prominent in the paid force. By one account, of the approximately 1,000 firemen in the FDNY in 1888, more than 25% had been born in Ireland and over 75% were of Irish descent. With the advent of civil service protection in the late 19th century, higher ranks in the fire department were available by competitive examination, and firemen of Irish descent rose in the departmental ranks.

Comprehensive fire regulation began in the 19th century (New York City required tenements to have fire escapes as early as 1850), and it dramatically increased in the 20th century. No doubt the most far-reaching governmental action on the state level transpired after the 1911 Triangle Shirtwaist Factory fire in New York City, leading to the creation of the Office of the State Fire Marshal (1911), a new office within the State Department of Labor. State fire marshals inspected tens of thousands of buildings and could order the demolition of dilapidated structures; investigated incendiary fires, arresting arsonists; and required the installation of additional exits, fire escapes, and fire protection devices in nearly all public and private buildings. The 1913 fire in the Binghamton Clothing Co, killing 60, added impetus to the fire marshal's push for better exit requirements. The work of the state fire marshal became the foundation of many National Fire Protection Association standards, including the Life Safety Code. Similar offices were established nationwide, and New York State was looked to for leadership.

Fire departments continued to grow rapidly over the course of the 20th century. In New York City the number of firefighters grew from approximately 5,000 to almost 15,000 by 1970. In 1917 New York City firefighters established a union, the Uniformed Firemen's Association, for the first time and gained the right to work shifts, cutting their workweek to 84 hours. The 84-hour week remained common throughout New York State until 1958, when a new state law forced paid departments to reduce hours. In Albany the average workweek for firefighters fell from 84 to 56 hours between 1958 and 1962, but it was not until 1974 that they enjoyed a 40-hour week. Pay, however, both historically and in the contemporary period, has remained notoriously low for career firefighters throughout the state.

The Irish continued to dominate the fire departments in most large cities, and other groups, especially other Catholic ethnicities, joined the paid departments in large numbers. However, minorities and women faced great challenges in being accepted into the profession. African Americans faced unrelenting harassment. The first African American joined the FDNY in 1898. Wesley Williams, who became the third Black in the fire department, joined in 1919, and eight years later he became the first black officer in the department. In 1982 the first woman joined the department. There has been some progress in recent decades, but at the turn of the 21st century racial and ethnic minorities made up only 6–8 % of the FDNY, with only several dozen women as firefighters.

Contemporary Firefighting

In New York State in 2001 there were four types of organizational structures that facilitated fire protection. There were 61 city-sanctioned fire departments, 385 village fire companies under the control of village trustees, 810 fire districts administered by elected fire commissioners, and 415 town fire protection districts where towns or villages are served jointly through contracts with nonprofit incorporated fire departments. Since the 1960s an increasing number of fire departments have elected to provide emergency medical services (EMS), and by the start of the 21st century most departmental responses are EMS calls. The experience of the Albany Fire Department is typical within the state, with 76% of all calls received in 2001 being EMS calls.

The state legislature and Gov Hugh Carey in 1979 created, within the Department of State, the position of state fire administrator and the Office of Fire Prevention and Control. That office carries out the Statewide Mobilization and Mutual Aid Plan, firefighter and code enforcement official certification, fire investigation training and technical assistance, fire- and burn-reporting data collection, tracking of firefighter deaths, hazardous materials response training and technical assistance, urban search and rescue, and fire grants administration. It also inspects 12,000 universities, colleges, and public buildings, and operates the training centers of the New York State Frederick L. Warder Academy of Fire Science in Montour Falls (Schuyler Co) and Camp Smith in Cortlandt (Westchester Co). It also oversees approximately 40 outreach training programs across the state. Unlike the former state fire marshal, this office has only limited enforcement powers.

Other state agencies that lend support to firefighters include the Department of Labor, which enforces regulations mandated by the federal Occupational Safety and Health Administration (OSHA) for career and volunteer fire departments. Other supportive agencies include the Department of Health, the Forest and Fire Management Division of the Department of Environmental Conservation, and the Workers' Compensation Board. In 2001 the state had 109,946 active volunteer firefighters, 19,312 career firefighters, and 1,293 paid, on-call fire service personnel. Of the 1,786 municipal fire departments in New York State, 1,693 were full volunteer departments and the remaining 93 were partly or full career departments. Altogether municipal departments in 2001 responded to 736,465 calls, 67% (or 493,432) of them were handled by career departments in urban areas. Three institutions, the New York State Museum in Albany, the American Museum of Firefighting in Hudson (Columbia Co), and the New York City Fire Museum in Manhattan, hold extensive collections of historical memorabilia and original equipment, and offer continually changing exhibits and lectures on the history and evolution of firefighting in New York State.

In 1998 Gov George E. Pataki and other dignitaries dedicated the New York State Fallen Firefighters Memorial at the Empire State Plaza in Albany. In the fall of 2002, 359 names were added to the memorial. Of those, 343 were firefighters who had perished in the destruction of the World Trade Center on 11 Sept 2001. A total of 2,241 New York State firefighters have lost their lives in the line of duty since 1811.

See also September 11th, 2001: ephemera of September 11th.

Abriel, Warren. *Albany Fire Department, 1867–1967: 100 Years of Paid Service* (Albany: Argus-Greenwood, 1967)

———. *30 Years of Smoke, Heat, and Hell* (Hicksville, NY: Exposition Press, 1976)

Costello, Augustine E. *Our Firemen: A History of the New York Fire Department from 1609 to 1887* (New York: Knickerbocker Press, 1887)

Golway, Terry. *So Others Might Live: A History of New York's Bravest—The FDNY from 1700 to the Present* (New York: Basic Books, 2002)

Radzinsky, Charles L. *100 Years of Service, 1872–1972, Firemen's Association of the State of New York* (Rensselaer, NY: Centennial Committee, Firemen's Association of the State of New York, 1972)

Utica Fire Department: Souvenir History (Utica: Metzler Printing, 1925)

Fire Island. Locality (pop 310) in Brookhaven and Islip (Suffolk Co). A 32 mi (52 km) barrier island off the south shore of Long Island between the Atlantic Ocean and Great South Bay, Fire Island is reached by ferry service and by roads through Robert Moses State Park at its west end and Smith Point County Park at its east. Prior to the 1850s few people lived on or visited Fire Island, with the occasional exceptions of transient fishers, eccentrics, and criminals, so-called wreckers who according to persistent legend lured ships to their doom on the rocks. South Shore farmers used it for abundant salt hay and cattle grazing. In the 19th century Fire Island was the site of 10 US lifesaving stations and, after 1915, of 2 Coast Guard stations. Located at the approach to New York Harbor, Fire Island was important in protecting commerce, and the lighthouse built in 1826 was replaced by an improved one in 1858. At 168 feet (51.2 m), this beacon remains a regional icon because of preservationists' advocacy and efforts in the 1980s in support of restoration.

The development of Fire Island as a summer resort began with an influx of wealthy New York City residents in the mid–19th century. Just east of the lighthouse, the Surf Hotel (1856–92) accommodated 1,500 guests and attracted political and cultural figures such as writer Herman Melville. The first seasonal community, Point O' Woods, was developed in 1894. Eventually the island became the site of 18 small communities heavily populated during the summer season. These communities differ in their composition. After World War II Cherry Grove and Fire Island Pines became well known as gay communities, while Ocean Beach and Saltaire attracted upper-middle-class second-home owners.

The development of Fire Island as a resort has led to many environmental issues. The devastating hurricane of 1938, which took four lives and destroyed 265 houses, was a reminder of the barrier island's fragility. Repeated efforts to build an automobile road on it have been thwarted, and much of the island remains restricted to foot and bicycle traffic. After the 1938 hurricane Robert Moses proposed a limited-access extension of Ocean Parkway to connect Fire Island to Long Island's South Shore. Initially blocked because of World War II and development priorities in the 1950s, Moses raised the issue again in 1960. A coalition of Fire Island homeowners rose up in a successful grassroots campaign, and the road was never built.

A 1959 effort saved Sunken Forest, a sea-level wood with a unique ecosystem, from development. In 1964 it became a part of the Fire Island National Seashore (1964), the staff of which has worked in concert with the island communities on dune preservation through the cultivation of sea grasses and strict rules regarding beach access.

Joshua Ruff

fireworks industry. New York State has a long history of both using and manufacturing fireworks. In the late 17th century, revelers in the New York Colony celebrated the birthday of England's King William III with fireworks. From the 1760s into the 19th century fireworks by Italian pyrotechnicians were on show in the Vauxhall pleasure gardens on Bowery Rd in Manhattan. Pyrotechnic re-creations of historical events, with titles such as the Burning of Moscow and the Bombardment of Alexandria, were long popular in the late 19th century at permanent amphitheaters on Staten Island, Manhattan Beach, and Brighton Beach. Fireworks have also marked civil celebrations, most notably a huge show for the opening of the Brooklyn Bridge in May 1883. Major displays accompanied celebrations of the nation's bicentennial in 1976, the centenary of the Statue of Liberty in 1986, and the millennium. Fireworks have provided entertainment at political rallies, sports events, and carnivals, and as movie special effects.

Since the 1930s the fireworks industry in New York State has been dominated by Italian family-owned businesses that began producing fireworks for Italian festivals and the Fourth of July on an informal basis and have since organized into larger-scale companies. Fireworks by Grucci in Brookhaven (Suffolk Co) had its roots in Bari, Italy, in 1850 with pyrotechnician Angelo Lanzetta, great-great-grandfather to Felix Grucci Sr. Lanzetta emigrated to Elmont [now in Nassau Co] in 1870 to set up his fireworks business. Grucci entered the business in 1923, and the firm moved to Bellport (Suffolk Co) in 1929. After assisting the War Department by simulating atom bombs in the 1940s, the Gruccis gained renown for their pyrotechnic shows. The company developed stringless shells in 1954, which improved safety by eliminating the falling, burning fragments of conventional twine-wrapped shells. In 1979 the Gruccis won the gold medal for the United States at the Monte Carlo International Fireworks competition. The company pioneered the use of computers in 1986 to choreograph, preview, and set off fireworks, beginning with the Statue of Liberty centennial that year. Alonzo Fireworks in Mechanicville (Saratoga Co) was founded in 1939 by Alfred Alonzo. The company manufactures and displays fireworks and produces pyrotechnic components for many other US manufacturers. Alonzo provided displays for the 2000 Summer Olympics in Sydney, Australia, and the 1999 Paul McCartney World Tour. A more recent company is Bay Fireworks Co, which was established by former Wall St traders Bob Yale and Charlie Rappa; it has operated from Huntington Station (Suffolk Co) since 1985. In 2000 the industry employed a core of 500 to 600 persons, but employment varies according to season. More than a dozen companies that manufacture and display fireworks in the state interact through two nationwide industry bodies, the National Fireworks Association and the American Pyrotechnics Association.

The possession, sale, and use of fireworks by individual consumers is outlawed by New York State Penal Law Section 270, in effect since 1909. The law defines fireworks as any blank cartridge, blank cartridge pistol, or toy cannon in which explosives are used; firecrackers, sparklers, or other explosives of like construction are also included. Display fireworks are also regulated, requiring a minimum of $5,000 insurance, safe storage, and a license supplied by local authorities at least five days before a performance. The national Consumer Product Safety Commission, the Bureau of Alcohol, Tobacco and Firearms, and the US Department of Transportation regulate fireworks, in combination with the superintendent of the New York State Police Department. A large illegal trade in fireworks is known to operate, and from 1996 to 1998 the New York State Police Department confiscated some 40,000 cases of illegal fireworks. One of the worst accidents in the state occurred 4 Nov 1902, when William Randolph Hearst, proprietor of the *New-York Journal*, arranged a display at Madison Square Garden to celebrate his election to Congress. A mortar tipped over and 10,000 shells blew up, killing 17 people and injuring 100. Since 1995 New York City Police and Fire Departments have operated a task force to combat the trafficking of illegal fireworks. Before the crackdown illegal fireworks caused some 1,000 fires and 50 injuries every year in the city. Since then the number of fires in the city has declined to fewer than 200 and injuries to half a dozen or so per year. In New York State 42 people suffered injuries serious enough to be hospitalized in 1998, compared to 56 in 1997 and 113 in 1996.

Boorsch, Suzanne. *Fireworks! Four Centuries of Pyrotechnics in Prints and Drawings.* Catalog of exhibition at the Metropolitan Museum of Art, July to September 2000 (New York: Metropolitan Museum of Art, 2000)

Brock, Alan St. Hill. *A History of Fireworks* (London: George G. Harrap, 1949)

Plimpton, George. *Fireworks: A History and Celebration* (Garden City, NY: Doubleday, 1984)

Simon R. E. Werrett

First International. See INTERNATIONAL WORKINGMEN'S ASSOCIATION (IWA).

first ladies. Many wives of presidents of the United States have had ties to New York State. Martha Dandridge Custis Washington (1731–1802) created the role of first lady in New York City, the first capital of the United States, from the house on Cherry St that served as both her family's home and the president's office.

Native New Yorkers

Several women born in New York State served as the nation's first lady. Elizabeth Kortright Monroe (1768–1830) was born in New York City and married Virginian James Monroe at the age of 17 at Trinity Episcopal Church in New York City. Hannah Hoes Van Buren (1783–1819), born in Kinderhook (Columbia Co), died before her husband assumed office. Julia Gardiner Tyler (1820–89) was born on Gardiner's Island (Suffolk Co), grew up in East Hampton (Suffolk Co), and was later educated at Madame N. D. Chagaray's Institute on Houston St in Manhattan. Abigail Powers Fillmore (1798–1853), born in Stillwater (Saratoga Co), lived in Buffalo and Albany with her husband Millard Fillmore before he was elected to the vice presidency in 1849 and then became president after the death of Zachary Taylor the following year. An avid reader and former schoolteacher, she worked before and after her marriage in 1826 and created the first White House library with a special appropriation from Congress. Frances "Frankie" Folsom Cleveland (1864–1947), born in Buffalo, became immensely popular at age 21 as the youngest of all first ladies and the first to be married at the White House. She had known Grover Cleveland, her father's law partner, since she was an infant. The couple married in 1886 after her graduation from Wells College in Aurora (Cayuga Co), and following his electoral defeat in 1888 they moved to New York City, where their first child was born.

Eleanor Roosevelt (1884–1962) was born in New York City and lived with her grandmother in Tivoli (Dutchess Co) after the death of her parents in 1894. After attending school in England, she married Franklin D. Roosevelt in 1905. Residing in New York State until her husband's election to the presidency in 1932, she was active in state and national politics. Eleanor maintained residences in Greenwich Village and at Val-Kill in Hyde Park (Dutchess Co), the latter now a museum.

Jacqueline Lee Bouvier Kennedy Onassis (1929–94) was born in East Hampton and lived in New York City until the age of 13. She attended Vassar College in Poughkeepsie and as first lady became an international celebrity noted for her personal style and command of languages. The White House was renovated under her direction, and she inspired the image of Camelot, a mix of youth and culture that was associated with her husband's brief time in office. When Pres John F. Kennedy was assassinated in 1963, she moved back to New York City where she lived both before her marriage to Aristotle Onassis in 1968 and again after his death in 1975. She worked as an editor for Viking and Doubleday. Nancy Davis Reagan (1923–) lived in New York City until age 6 and then returned during the 1940s to pursue an acting career on Broadway. Barbara Pierce Bush (1925–) was born and grew up in Rye (Westchester Co).

Other Connections

Several other first ladies also have notable ties to New York State, in many cases linked to their own family connections or to their husbands' careers. Anna Tuthill Symmes Harrison

(1775–1864) spent much of her childhood on Long Island with her maternal grandparents. She attended the Clinton Academy in East Hampton and later boarding school in New York City before she married William Henry Harrison in 1795. Julia Dent Grant (1826–1902) and her husband moved to a townhouse on 66th St just off 5th Ave in New York City after leaving the White House in 1877 and later to the cottage at Mount McGregor (Saratoga Co) where he died. She is buried alongside her husband in Grant's Tomb on Riverside Dr in Manhattan. Ellen Lewis Herndon Arthur (1837–80) lived in New York City from the mid-1850s, where she met and married Chester Arthur. She died before her husband assumed office.

Edith Kermit Carow Roosevelt (1861–1948) was born in Connecticut but grew up on Union Square in New York City as the neighbor of Theodore Roosevelt and best friend of his younger sister Corinne. After the death of his first wife, Roosevelt married Edith in 1886, and they raised their family in New York City and their summer home, Sagamore Hill, near Oyster Bay (Nassau Co). In 1901 Edith became first lady when Pres William McKinley was assassinated, and she moved their six children into the White House. Under her supervision, the executive mansion was renovated in 1902, and the living quarters were separated from the presidential offices in a new West Wing. Lou Henry Hoover (1874–1944) spent part of her time in an apartment at the Waldorf Towers in New York City after her husband left office.

Of first ladies since World War II, Mamie Geneva Doud Eisenhower (1896–1979) moved to New York City with her husband Dwight D. Eisenhower when he served as president of Columbia University from 1948 to 1951. Betty Bloomer Ford (1918–) lived in the Chelsea neighborhood of Manhattan in the late 1930s to train with the Martha Graham dance troupe and worked as a Powers model. Patricia Ryan Nixon (1912–93) moved to New York City while her husband worked as a corporate lawyer in the mid-1960s and again to be near their daughters in the early 1980s. Rosalynn Smith Carter (1927–) moved to Schenectady in 1952 so that her husband Jimmy could study nuclear physics at Union College, but he was called back to run his family peanut farm in Georgia in 1953. Hillary Rodham Clinton moved to Chappaqua (Westchester Co) in January 2000 and won a US Senate seat from New York State later that year, becoming the first first lady elected to office and the first woman elected to the US Senate from New York State.

Gould, Lewis L., ed. *American First Ladies: Their Lives and Legacy,* 2d ed. (New York: Routledge, 2001)

Klapthor, Margaret Brown, and Allida M. Black. *The First Ladies of the United States of America* (Washington, DC: White House Historical Association, 2001)

Susan Ingalls Lewis

Firthcliffe. Locality (pop 4,970) in Cornwall (Orange Co). Originally called West Cornwall, it grew around Broadhead Woolen Mills (1869), which were sold to the Firth Carpet Co in 1886. Firth brought skilled workers from England and Scotland and by 1900 employed 350. The hamlet was served by the Ontario and Western Railroad (1883) and changed its name to Firthcliffe in 1898. The carpet mill closed in 1962. Firthcliffe's population increased at the end of the 20th century as building lots developed around it.

American shad.

fish. New York State claims representatives from 3 classes, 33 orders, and 123 families of these chordates, characterized by possession of a cranium, medial fins, and gills, and with most also possessing paired fins and vertebrae. There are 159 freshwater or estuarine forms, which dwell primarily in streams and lakes, and 305 marine species, which spend their lives in saltwater. There are also 10 diadromous species, which are either anadromous (spawning in freshwater but spending most of their lives in the ocean) or catadromous (spawning in saltwater but spending most of their lives in streams).

The dominant freshwater group is minnows, or *Cyprinidae* (49 species). Other important freshwater groups are suckers, or *Catostomidae* (12 species); trout, or *Salmonidae* (17 species); sunfish, or *Centrarchidae* (14 species); and perch, or *Percidae* (21 species). The diadromous species include important commercial or sport fish and feature some landlocked populations that do not migrate between salt- and freshwater. Atlantic salmon *(Salmo salar),* an anadromous species in part of its range, is regarded as a freshwater form in New York State, with all populations presumed landlocked. The state's anadromous fish include Atlantic sturgeon *(Acipenser oxyrynchus),* American shad *(Alosa sapidissima),* alewife *(Alosa pseudoharengus),* and striped bass *(Morone saxatilis).* American eel *(Anguilla rostrata)* is the only catadromous fish in the state. Major marine groups include cod, or *Gadidae* (11 species); jacks, or *Carangidae* (21 species); drums, or *Sciaenidae* (10 species), and mackerel, or *Scombridae* (16 species).

The freshwater fish fauna of New York State is more diverse than that of all New England states combined but less diverse than that of a typical Mississippi River drainage state. One reason for the high freshwater diversity is that New York State is drained by five major river systems. The distribution of freshwater organisms, unlike that of terrestrial organisms, is often limited to a single river system or group of neighboring river systems, and most fish disperse naturally between drainages only under rare geological or meteorological events. Diversity varies by drainage, with the St. Lawrence River system the state's richest, and the Delaware and Susquehanna Rivers systems, represented only by the rivers' headwaters, claims the fewest species. New York State's greatest centers of fish diversity are the low-elevation tributaries and main channels of the Allegheny and St. Lawrence Rivers systems and Lakes Ontario and Erie. The state's diversity of marine fish is high but typical of northern states.

The study of fish has ranked as an important intellectual pursuit of New Yorkers for two centuries. The earliest publications are by Samuel Latham Mitchill, Columbia College chair of natural history and US senator, who wrote on fish in the 1810s and 1820s. De Witt Clinton (1769–1828) also published on the state's fish, even describing and naming a new species, the spottail shiner, or *Notropis hudsonius.* Physician, diplomat, and early member of Troy's Lyceum of Natural History James E. DeKay published a monographic treatment on fish in his *Zoology of New York State* (1842), as did physician and US Bureau of Fisheries biologist Tarleton Bean in

Brown trout.

Fishes of New York (1903). During the late 1920s and 1930s, the New York State Department of Conservation intensively sampled watersheds, with results published in a series of annual reports authored by the department's biologist, John R. Greeley, and others. From 1980 to 1985 SUNY's Robert G. Werner and American Museum of Natural History's C. Lavett Smith published compendia on the fish of the state.

During the last 200 years, few New York State species have become extinct; it is believed that blue pike *(Sander vitreum glacum)* is extinct. Other species, though not extinct, have been extirpated from New York State waters. Examples are bloater *(Coregonus hoyi)*, paddlefish *(Polyodon spathula)*, and gilt darter *(Percina evides)*. The causes of these losses range from habitat degradation via deforestation or pollution, habitat alteration via draining of wetlands or dam construction, and changes in land use resulting from urbanization, overfishing, and introduction of exotic species.

The New York State Department of Environmental Conservation (DEC) identifies several of the state's protected species as "endangered," "threatened," or "species of special concern." These are all rare species, either confined to a small range within a single drainage, such as the bluebreast darter *(Etheostoma camurum)*, or found in low numbers in several drainages, such as the round whitefish *(Prosopium cylindraceum)*. Most rare fish are found in the Allegheny or St. Lawrence River systems. Since 1967 both New York State and the federal government have listed the anadromous shortnose sturgeon as endangered. The DEC sets seasons and catch limits to protect game fish.

Few species are exotic, that is, native to a region outside New York State. Only 14 species have been introduced into the state from Eurasia or North America's Pacific slope, and not all are established. These species were introduced to enhance the sportfishery (brown trout *[Salmo trutta]* and rainbow trout *[Oncorynchus mykiss]*) or to develop a commercial fishery (common carp *[Cyprinus carpio]*), or they came via bait fish escapes (rudd *[Scardinius erythrophthalmus]*) or other accidental releases (oriental weatherfish *[Misgurnus anguillicaudatus]*). Although few New York State species are extralimital or out-of-state exotics, many species are exotic to specific drainages. For example largemouth and smallmouth bass *(Micropterus salmoides* and *Micropterus dolomieu)* are native to the western drainages of New York State but exotic in the systems of the Hudson and Delaware Rivers.

Briggs, P. T., and J. R. Waldman. "Annotated List of Fishes Reported from the Marine Waters of New York," *Northeastern Naturalist* 9 (Spring 2002): 47–80

Smith, C. L. *Inland Fishes of New York State* (Albany: NYS Department of Environmental Conservation, 1985)

Werner, Robert G. *Freshwater Fishes of New York State: A Field Guide* (Syracuse: Syracuse Univ Press, 1980)

Robert A. Daniels

Fish, Hamilton (*b* New York City, 3 Aug 1808; *d* Garrison, Putnam Co, 7 Sept 1893). Governor, US senator, and secretary of state. Born into an elite family and son of Nicholas Fish and Elizabeth Stuyvesant, Hamilton Fish graduated from Columbia College in 1827 and was admitted to the bar in 1830. An ardent Whig, he served New York State as a member of the House of Representatives (1843–45) from New York City, lieutenant governor (1847–48), governor (1849–50), and US senator (1851–57). Only mildly opposed to slavery, Fish deplored the disintegration of the Whig Party and lost national standing because he belatedly and only reluctantly joined the Republicans. Although he supported Abraham Lincoln in 1860, he advocated compromise with the South right up to the beginning of hostilities in 1861. He held only minor positions during the Civil War. Although Fish was friendly with Pres Ulysses S. Grant, his appointment by Grant to succeed Elihu Washburne as secretary of state in 1869 came as a complete surprise. Fish accepted reluctantly and expected to serve briefly, but remained through both Grant administrations. His greatest achievement, the Treaty of Washington (1871), led to the settlement of the *Alabama* claims and several other disputes with Great Britain. Fish carefully negotiated difficult issues with Spain, pressing Grant not to recognize the belligerency of Cuba and successfully obtaining reparations in the *Virginius* affair (1873). He supported American expansion into the Caribbean but did not expend much effort on Grant's unsuccessful project to annex the Dominican Republic. Fish retired from national political life after Grant's presidency but remained prominent in civic activities in New York State and served as president of the Society of the Cincinnati, the Union League Club, and the New-York Historical Society. The one-time congressman was the progenitor of a unique political dynasty. His son, grandson, and great-grandson, all named Hamilton Fish, served as representatives from New York State in the US Congress.

Cook, Adrian. *The Alabama Claims: American Politics and Anglo-American Relations, 1865–1872* (Ithaca: Cornell Univ Press, 1975)

Corning, Amos. *Hamilton Fish* (New York: Lanmere, 1918)

Nevins, Allan. *Hamilton Fish: The Inner History of the Grant Administration,* 2 vols (New York: Dodd, Mead, 1936)

Jon Sterngass

Fish Carrier [Hojiagede] (*b* ?Canoga [now Fayette, Seneca Co], *ca* 1740; *d* Grand River Reservation [loc in Ont], 1807). Cayuga leader. Little is known about his early life. After the 1779 Sullivan-Clinton campaign destroyed Iroquois villages and crops in Central New York, Fish Carrier, a war chief, led a war party of Cayugas and Tutelos, their adopted brethren who fought at many of the major battles on the British side, including the Wyoming Valley Raid of 1778, the Battle of Newtown in 1779, and the invasion of the Canajahorie area in 1780. After the Revolution Fish Carrier, living at the Seneca's Buffalo Creek Reservation [now in Erie Co], was the principal leader of the Cayuga in the treaties with the federal and state governments over the next two decades, but he was often opposed by a Cayuga-Saponi minority that had returned to the Cayuga Lake area. Probably sometime around 1807, Fish Carrier relocated to Grand River, where a sizable contingent of Cayugas following Joseph Brant had already settled. Fish Carrier's name is still remembered by his descendants at Grand River.

Fenton, William N. *The Great Law and the Longhouse: A Political History of the Iroquois Confederacy* (Norman: Univ of Oklahoma Press, 1998)

Graymont, Barbara. *The Iroquois in the American Revolution* (Syracuse: Syracuse Univ Press, 1972)

Heriberto Dixon

Fisher-Price. Toy company founded in East Aurora (Erie Co) in 1930 by Herman G. Fisher, Irving L. Price, and Helen M. Schelle, with financing of $100,000 arranged by Elbert Hubbard II. The initial toy line was small, featuring pull toys. Materials included ponderosa pine and steel decorated with laminated lithographs and pieced together by hand. The labor force consisted of a dozen or so assembly line workers with occasional piecework in the local community. In 1932 Fisher gained controlling interest in the firm. During World War II Fisher-Price altered its facilities to produce war materials, and from 1943 through 1945 the company halted toy production. After the war Fisher-Price expanded, moving from quarters on Church St to a larger and more modern plant on Girard St. The company began using plastics in its manufacturing and added another production facility in nearby Holland (Erie Co).

Major changes occurred after Fisher retired as president in 1966. Quaker Oats Co of Chicago purchased the company in 1969. A third manufacturing plant was opened in Medina (Orleans Co) in 1970. Two years later production facilities were opened in Texas and Mexico, and product lines including juvenile toys and soft goods were added. In 1977 the world headquarters of Fisher-Price was built in East Aurora alongside the Girard St plant, but the number of production workers there declined throughout the 1970s and 1980s. Production in East Aurora and Holland ceased in 1990. In 1999 the production plant became the site of the Toy Town Museum and a Fisher-Price retail store. Reflecting the global economy of the 1990s, Quaker Oats first spun off Fisher-Price in 1991, and it was traded for the first time on the New York Stock Exchange. In November 1993 the California-based Mattel Co bought Fisher-Price for $1.2 billion, and over the next seven years all of US Fisher-Price production facilities were closed, and operations relocated to Europe, Asia, and Latin America.

Murray, John J., and Bruce R. Fox. *Fisher-Price, 1931–1963: A Historical, Rarity, and Value Guide* (Florence, Ala: Books Americana, 1991)

Timothy W. Kneeland

Fishers Island. Locality (pop 289) in Southold (Suffolk Co). The island, which lies just off the Connecticut coast and 12 miles (19 km) from Long Island's North Fork, was purchased in 1644 from the Pequot Indians by John Winthrop Jr, who used it to graze sheep and cattle; in 1668 Gov Richard Nicholls awarded it a manor charter. Its ownership was disputed by Connecticut and New York until a joint commission decided in favor of New York in 1879. The Winthrop family held the island until 1863, when they sold it to Robert R. Fox. After his death in 1871, the Fox family developed lots for large summer cottages and for the Lyles Beach Hotel. It acquired a post office in 1881. The unsold portion of the island was sold to brothers Edmund and Walton Ferguson in 1889; their holdings were incorporated in 1918 as Fishers Island Farms, and many stately homes were built in the 1920s and 1930s. In the early 21st century the island remains an exclusive summer enclave with a small permanent population at its west end. A lighthouse was built off the island's coast, on North Dumpling Island, in 1848.

Antonia Booth

fish hatcheries. Facilities where fish eggs are cultivated and raised until they reach a variety of sizes suitable for release in natural waters. Early efforts to propagate fish artificially in New York State focused on restocking fisheries already sorely depleted by the effects of early 19th-century industry and agriculture. Dams and canals also damaged the fish stock, especially anadromous species that migrate between salt and fresh waters. Overfishing was rampant. Later industrial pollution, urbanization, and the introduction of non-native species further compromised the state's waterways.

Hatcheries often maintain a brood stock of adult fish from which to get eggs for propagation. Eggs and milt can also be "milked" or "stripped" from wild fish netted in waters around the state. This generally means gently squeezing adult fish to release the eggs or milt, then returning the fish to the water unharmed. The gametes are taken to the hatchery and mixed together under specific conditions. Fertilized eggs develop into "sac fry" in hatching jars and are then transferred to rearing units until they reach "fingerling" size, 3–5 in (8–13 cm) long. Most fingerlings are stocked in the spring, but yearlings of some species can be released in the autumn. Fry can be shipped either in plastic bags filled with oxygenated water or in larger, oxygenated tanks mounted on trucks. Fingerlings are transferred by hand to tanks on the stocking trucks.

The oldest fish hatchery in New York State (and in the United States) is the Caledonia State Fish Hatchery in Livingston Co. It opened in 1864, founded by Seth Green (1817–88), "the father of fish culture," who had been artificially propagating brook trout since 1837. By 1870 the Caledonia hatchery was being run by the state. Green introduced rainbow trout to New York from California in 1874 and also worked on increasing shad production. He operated a shad hatchery on the Hudson in the 1870s and is credited with boosting supplies of shad in the Hudson and other northeastern rivers. Appointed fish commissioner for New York State in 1868, a year later Green became the state's first superintendent of fish culture. Fred Mather began to hatch various species at his farm in Honeoye Falls (Monroe Co) in 1868. He was also active in the propagation of shad in several states. He successfully hatched salmon in Roslyn [now in Nassau Co] for release in the Hudson River. In 1883 he imported brown trout eggs from Germany and was appointed superintendent of the state's Fish Commission Station at Cold Spring Harbor (Suffolk Co), which produced hatches of lobster, cod, and other marine animals. Private citizens rapidly took up the practice of aquaculture, and in 1870 the American Fish Culturists' Association was formed in New York City. Its members experimented with feeding, breeding, and restocking techniques, control of fish diseases, successfully advocated for international removal of obstacles impeding fish migration, and lobbied Congress to create the US Commission of Fish and Fisheries (1871).

In time a number of fish hatcheries, both private and state, would be established in New York State. In 2003 the New York State Department of Environmental Conservation (DEC) operated 12 hatcheries and one fish pathology laboratory, which produced about 900,000–1,000,000 pounds (408,000–454,000 kg) of fish. That stock replenished over 1,200 public streams, rivers, ponds, and lakes in 57 counties. The fish were used primarily for recreational purposes, but hatcheries also restored native species to their original habitats.

In 2003 a number of DEC hatcheries were producing a variety of brown, rainbow, and brook trout: Caledonia, Bath (1893; Steuben Co), Chateaugay (1925; Franklin Co), Rome (1932; Oneida Co), Randolph (1933; Cattaraugus Co), Van Hornesville (1935; Herkimer Co), and Catskill (1948; Sullivan Co). Varieties of salmon, including Atlantic, coho, and chinook, were raised at hatcheries at Adirondack (1885; Franklin Co) and Salmon River (1980; Oswego Co). The Oneida (1897; Oswego Co) and Chautauqua (1943) hatcheries raised walleye. The South Otselic State Fish Hatchery (1932; Chenango Co) raised tiger muskellunge. Unusual species such as heritage strain brook trout, paddlefish, pure strain muskellunge, splake, temiscamie, and lake sturgeon were also cultivated at a few sites. The Rome Fish Disease Control Center (Rome Lab) conducted research and diagnostics, with a special focus on the parasite that causes whirling disease. All DEC hatcheries are open to the public at specified days and hours throughout the year. In 2003 there were 40 privately run hatcheries licensed to operate. The hatchery at Cold Spring Harbor, established in 1883, became a nonprofit aquatic education center specializing in freshwater ecosystems in the 1980s.

McClane, A. J., ed. *McClane's Standard Fishing Encyclopedia* (New York: Holt, Rinehart & Winston, 1965)
McPhee, John. *The Founding Fish* (New York: Farrar, Straus & Giroux, 2002)
New York State Department of Environmental Conservation. "New York State's Fish Hatcheries," http://www.dec.state.ny.us/website/dfwmr/fish/foe4chat.html

Marianne Rahn-Erickson

fishing, commercial. Harvesting seafood from the Atlantic Ocean, Long Island Sound, Raritan Bay, the Great Lakes, and the Hudson River remains important to the economy of New York State. Onondaga, Oneida, and Huron Indians fished the St. Lawrence River and Great Lakes using hooks, harpoons, spears, and seine nets. North Country Native Americans regularly caught salmon, eels, smelt, herring, brill, whitefish, pike, carp, sturgeon, and bass. Algonquian-speaking people on Long Island and environs lived on substantial reserves of shellfish, which also supplied wampum, the basis of colonial currency. To survive through winters, Native Americans throughout the state salted and dried their catch.

Dutch and English farmers in the 17th century supplemented their income by fishing with a variety of nets, including haul seine nets similar to those used by Native Americans that were pulled ashore by groups of men or horses. A typical seine catch brought in 8–10 bu (282–352 l) of fish. Cod, mackerel, and bluefish were the most frequent takes. Fishers used spears to catch eels in winter. Menhaden, also known as moss bunkers, were caught in great nets, infamous for their stench, and valued as fertilizer by farmers. Whaling started in the 1670s with drift whales that became stranded on Long Island's ocean beaches and later gave way to ocean whaling in the late 1700s. Whaling boats left from New York City and Cold Spring Harbor (Suffolk Co). From 1815 to 1825 a fleet of 60 whaling ships made Sag Harbor (Suffolk Co) both extremely wealthy and a preeminent port community. African Americans and Native Americans were often engaged as harpooners and occasionally became first mates or captains on whaling boats. The whaling industry survived into the 1870s, ending when kerosene replaced whale oil as fuel. Oysters from Raritan Bay, Long Island Sound, and the Great South Bay of Long Island were harvested with long tongs from the early 1700s until the 1860s, when dredging began. Unlike fish, oysters were able to survive long sea transport to New England and New York City markets. Most fish sold at the Fulton Fish Market, a wholesale fish em-

Clam diggers in Peconic Bay, Long Island. Photograph by Lionel Green, *ca* 1930.

porium that opened in 1822 on the East River in New York City, were from the immediate area. Fishers depended upon steamboats or large wagons to transport the catch to market until the emergence of refrigerated railroad cars around 1880. Commercial fishing for shad, bluefish, and striped bass also thrived on the Hudson River in the 19th century. The Hudson was the breeding ground for many of the varieties of fish caught in Long Island Sound and the Atlantic, and a lack of limits soon led to declines.

By the early 20th century, commercial fishing was suffering from the impacts of pollution and overharvesting. Fishers on Long Island also found their access to waters limited by the growth of country estates on waterfront property, which was especially troubling to oyster harvesters, who were also beginning to contend with the depletion of oyster beds due to overfishing and silt runoff from erosion. Ocean fishing was challenged by a 1924 legislative effort, when conservationists (citing a decreasing population of striped bass) pushed to prohibit dragging or trawling in state waters. The motion was defeated. The hurricane of 1938 decimated the fishing business off eastern Long Island until after World War II. Sea lampreys from the Atlantic Ocean traveled up the Erie Canal to Lake Ontario, where they destroyed a large part of the trout and whitefish populations by the 1940s. The government's use of DDT and pesticides in the 1940s and 1950s decreased catches on both the Great Lakes and the Atlantic Coast. PCB contamination in the Hudson River led to a state-imposed ban of commercial fishing in the Hudson in 1976. Subsequent local, state, and federal regulations, plus the efforts of conservationists, have greatly improved the water quality, and marine life has been steadily returning.

The number of resident commercial fishing licenses declined from 1,265 in 1994 to 746 in 1999. Although many fishers have left the occupation, including the majority of baymen who harvested shellfish along Long Island shores, the business in New York State continues apace with contemporary demands for fresh seafood. Many species, such as the striped bass, have had a revival in numbers in recent years. In 1999 commercial fishing was a $76 million enterprise; professional fishers that year took 27 million lobsters, 1.8 million summer flounders, and 1.6 million tuna. Yellow perch were the most important New York State catch on the Great Lakes. By the early 21st century New York State's major fishing ports were Shinnecock Bay and Montauk (Suffolk Co). The Shinnecock fleet comprises mostly otter-type trawlers, which catch squid and whiting by towing conical nets through the water. Longline vessels, which employ long lines of baited hooks, lobster boats, clam dredge vessels, and gillnetters are also based at Shinnecock. The Montauk fleet comprises trawlers for catching whiting, flounder, and squid; longline vessels for tilefish, tuna, swordfish, and shark; and lobster boats, as well as some commercial hook and line fishing.

Matthiessen, Peter. *Men's Lives: The Surfmen and Baymen of the South Fork* (New York: Random House, 1986)

Recht, Michael. "The Role of Fishing in the Iroquois Economy, 1600–1792," *New York History* 86 (Jan 1995): 5–30

Smith, Lavett C., ed. *Fisheries Research in the Hudson River* (Albany: SUNY Press, 1988)

Joshua Ruff

fishing, fly. See FLY FISHING.

fishing, recreational (freshwater). New York State hosts at least 165 species of freshwater fish in about 63,000 miles (101,400 km) of streams and rivers and over 18,000 lakes and ponds. Trout, salmon, bass, pickerel, walleye, pike, muskellunge, sturgeon, shad, various panfish, and several imported species have long attracted anglers.

ORIGINS AND REGIONS

For much of the state's history, it has been difficult to separate clearly recreational angling from fishing for subsistence, a pleasurable necessity of rural life. New York City residents made Long Island a center for trout fishing by the late colonial period. British army officers were seen fly fishing at the mouth of the Saranac River in the 1780s, and Oneida Lake was noted for fishing by the 1790s.

Though there is no single birthplace for American fly fishing, Catskill trout streams such as the Beaver Kill, Willowemoc Creek, and Neversink River were early centers. Anglers arrived by stagecoach and horse in the early 1800s, and railroads dramatically increased their numbers by midcentury. This had a huge impact on fish populations. Anglers fished aggressively for quantity, and a party of four traveling home with over 1,700 brook trout was notable but not unique. Private clubs were established on many of the best streams, and James Spencer Van Cleef, who would write the state's first general fish and game laws in 1895, saw these clubs as the only hope of preserving trout populations.

Fishing in the Catskills and Adirondacks was heavily promoted by the *American Turf Register* (1829–44) and William Trotter Porter's *Spirit of the Times* (1831–61). Ausable River and Saranac and Raquette Lakes were favorite Adirondack fishing spots before the Civil War, and the publication of William H. H. Murray's *Adventures in the Wilderness* (1869), combined with improved transportation, sparked a rush of sportsmen. Other publicity during the 19th century came from writers including George LaBranche, Thaddeus Norris, Edward R. Hewitt, and George Washington Bethune, and John J. Brown, a New York City tackle dealer, produced *The American Angler's Guide* in 1845, the first book-length fishing guide published in the United States. Writers and anglers Ray Bergman, Art Flick, and Lee Wulff continued this promotion in the 20th century.

Countless other locations provide excellent angling opportunities. The bass, pike, and muskellunge fishing of the Cape Vincent–Thousand Islands area was known by the 1840s. Oneida Lake is one of the best walleye lakes in the nation, the Batten Kill is a noted trout stream, and the Niagara River is an excellent bass, walleye, and muskellunge fishery. Chautauqua Lake is known for muskellunge, the Finger Lakes for lake trout, and Otsego Lake for lake whitefish, known as "Otsego bass." Many of the state's small rivers, creeks, ponds, and lakes are filled with trout, bass, and panfish.

HUMAN IMPACT AND INTERVENTION

Settlement, urbanization, and industrialization have affected the state's fishery throughout its history. In the 19th century logging and the clearing of land had negative impacts, and milldams cut off trout and salmon from spawning grounds. One remedy was propagation and stocking. In 1864 Seth Green established one of the first fish hatcheries in the nation in Caledo-

Fresh trout, Upper Saranac Lake, 1870s.

nia (Livingston Co), and the state Fisheries Commission (1868) helped expand and establish hatcheries statewide. Green imported rainbow trout from California, which were released statewide in 1878, and by 1881 the state was stocking over 1 million per year. As tourism increased, railroads saw healthy fisheries as crucial to their success, and conductors would stop express trains at streams to release baby trout.

In 1883 Fred Mather imported brown trout eggs from Germany to Cold Spring Harbor (Suffolk Co) and sent many of them to Green's hatchery. Brown trout were hardier than native species, but these "cannibals" also ate baby brook trout and quickly became the dominant trout species. Other attempts to alter fish populations were disastrous. In the Adirondacks newly introduced bass devoured baby trout in huge numbers, and when yellow perch were introduced, they ate both trout and bass. By the 1950s there were four times as many yellow perch as trout in the Adirondacks. Many ponds have been "reclaimed," where the fish are killed off and the ponds are restocked with trout. The salmonid program, started in 1968, has been more successful. Pacific salmon and steelhead trout were introduced to Lakes Erie and Ontario, and these new species, which grew to over 40 pounds (18 kg), created a substantial sportfishing industry in the region. The program also reestablished lake trout and landlocked salmon, which had nearly disappeared from many waters. In 1983 the state began stocking Atlantic salmon in Lake Ontario, where once plentiful stocks had been wiped out by overfishing, dams, and development by the beginning of the 20th century. At the beginning of the 21st century a dozen hatcheries produce several million fish annually, largely trout but also muskellunge, walleye, and salmon.

The expansion of New York City's water supply also had a huge impact, and the creation of the Ashokan Reservoir (1912) permanently altered the Catskill fishery. When the Barge Canal (1918) and the St. Lawrence Seaway (1959) were constructed, exotic species such as sea lampreys and zebra mussels entered state waters and have done considerable harm to native fish populations, particularly in the Great Lakes.

Fishing has been further hurt by PCB and mercury contamination. Fish from more than 70 bodies of water in New York State contain contaminant levels that exceed federal standards, and pollution from chemicals and pesticides has led to state health advisories and curtailed fishing on some waters. Acid rain, caused by industrial emissions, has impoverished the biology of many Adirondack ponds and lakes.

REGULATION

Declining fish populations in the early 19th century led to statewide restrictions on the use of seine nets in 1813, and in 1857 the state legislature restricted sportfishing to hook and line only. In 1895 the Fisheries Commission merged with related groups to form the Fisheries, Game and Forest Commission, which evolved to become the Department of Environmental Conservation in 1970.

By the 1880s some counties had established catch-and-release laws to protect threatened waters. New York was among the first states to designate "no-kill" waters in an effort to offer anglers quality experiences with large, wary fish. Over 1,300 miles (2,090 km) of state-owned trout waters are designated as fishing areas. To fund fishery protection efforts, fishing licenses were required for men 16 and older in 1925 and for women beginning in 1949. In the 1999–2000 season, 868,015 fishing licenses were issued to state residents and 173,636 to nonresidents. The state continues in various efforts to help problem fisheries recover, and angling and related tourism play a crucial role in the state's economy.

Hammond, S. H. *Wild Northern Scenes* (1857; repr Harrison, NY: Harbor Hill Books, 1979)
Jamieson, Paul, ed. *The Adirondack Reader* (Lake George, NY: Adirondack Mountain Club, 1982)
Schullery, Paul. *American Fly Fishing: A History* (New York: Nick Lyons Books, 1987)

John C. Pitarresi

fishing, recreational (saltwater). New York State's salt waters have provided sustenance for inhabitants for thousands of years, ever since the earliest American Indians made fish a staple of their diet. The Hudson River estuary, the Atlantic Ocean, the Long Island Sound, and the bays and brackish lagoons along Long Island's South Shore all gained fame for recreational fishing during colonial times. Anglers sought striped bass, bluefish, weakfish, porgies, flounder, and even sharks. During the 19th century sportswriters Henry William Herbert (1807–58) and Genio C. Scott (1809–79) helped popularize the New York City area for wealthy individuals with time on their hands.

After 1850 increased transportation linkages and leisure time converged to make oceanic sportfishing accessible to a wider range of people. Steamboats took people to offshore Atlantic fishing grounds that extended from Long Island to New Jersey, at times transporting more than 3,000 passengers at once. Sports clubs, such as the South Side Sportsmen's Club in Oakdale (Suffolk Co), blossomed around New York City. Fishing enthusiasts were able to reach Southampton (Suffolk Co) by train after 1870 and were often met by enterprising local baymen who served as guides. Montauk, at the eastern end of Suffolk Co, became a major fishing center; in 1900, a record 76 lb (34.5 kg) striped bass was caught near the Montauk Point Lighthouse. The expansion of the subway to south Brooklyn increased the popularity of Sheepshead Bay as a destination for city anglers. Boat chartering began in the 1920s as commercial fishers diversified and marketed the ability of taking small groups to go "where the big ones were." Pres Herbert Hoover was one early client of eastern Long Island boat charter services. Anglers left from Freeport on the south shore of Nassau Co to catch 200–400 lb (90–180 kg) tuna. Boat chartering declined after the devastating hurricane of 1938 and amateur recreational anglers began purchasing their own powerboats after World War II. Private boats troll for striped bass and bluefish off Long Island's North Shore, where there is little accessibility for casting. On the South Shore large stretches of beach are open to surf casting, mainly for stripers and blues.

Fishing boat with catch off Long Island, *ca* 1925.

Pollution and overfishing led to a gradual decline in the quality of fishing in many state salt waters, especially New York Harbor. Striped bass were protected by state legislation in 1983. Major restrictions in industrial and sewage pollution, as well as careful limitations on takes, led to a fishing renaissance in the 1990s. At the beginning of the 21st century the number of New York State resident applications for noncommercial marine fishing licenses average approximately 1,700 per year. The top three fish caught in state salt waters are summer flounder, bluefish, and striped bass, the last having made a strong comeback after near extinction.

Matthiessen, Peter. *Men's Lives: The Surfmen and Baymen of the South Fork* (New York: Vintage Books, 1988)
Zeisel, William. *A History of Recreational Fishing on the Hudson River from Colonial Times to 1920* (New York: Institute for Research in History, 1988)

Joshua Ruff

Fishkill. Town (pop 20,258) and village (pop 1,735) in SW Dutchess Co. Part of the Rombout Patent (1685), it was settled by Dutch families *ca* 1710. Fishkill Landing [now Beacon] was a principal Hudson River port for Dutchess Co farm produce headed for New York City. During the Revolution it served as a supply depot and, briefly, as the provincial capital (1776–77). The town was formed in 1788, and the village incorporated in 1899. In the 19th century manufacturing, especially textiles, bricks, and shoes, became important at Fishkill Landing. It was a junction for the Hudson River (1849) and Dutchess and Columbia (1869) Railroads; later rail connections with New England (1881) made it a conduit for coal shipments to New England factories. It is the site of the Texaco Research Center, Downstate and Fishkill Correctional Facilities, and a minor league baseball stadium.

William P. McDermott

Fitch, Asa (*b* Salem, Washington Co, 24 Feb 1809; *d* Salem, 8 Apr 1879). Entomologist and agriculturist. Fitch grew up in rural Salem, where his father, a former US congressman from New York State (1811–13), was a doctor and judge. He received his early education at Washington Academy in Salem and entered the Rensselaer School (now Rensselaer Polytechnic Institute) in 1826, where he studied zoology and entomology. He graduated in 1827 and studied at Rutgers Medical College in New York City and the Vermont

Academy of Medicine in Castleton, where he received an MD in 1829. Abandoning a medical career in Stillwater (Saratoga Co), Fitch returned to Salem in 1838 and became active in the Washington County Agricultural Society in 1841. He turned to the study of insects, especially crop pests such as wheat and Hessian flies, publishing articles in the *American Quarterly Journal of Agriculture and Science* (1845–46) and *Transactions of the New York Agricultural Society* (1846–72) as well as various farm publications. Writing in a style accessible to both farmers and scientists, he acquired a reputation for thoroughness, which in 1854 led to his appointment by the New York State Agricultural Society as the state's first entomologist, a post he held for 18 years. He single-handedly created the field of economic entomology by classifying plant pests according to the crops they attacked, and his contributions to the field were internationally recognized, placing New York State in the forefront of the nation's food production with the use of imported natural pest controls.

Barnes, Jeffrey K. "Asa Fitch and the Emergence of American Entomology, with an Entomological Bibliography and a Catalog of Taxonomic Names and Type Specimens," *New York State Museum Bulletin* 461 (1988): 1–120

David Minor

Fitch Crèche. One of the nation's first child daycare facilities, it was established in 1881 by Maria M. Love (1840–1931) at the behest of Buffalo's Charity Organization Society (1877). Buffalo native and New York City philanthropist Benjamin Fitch (1802–82) supplied both the house, a once fashionable brick mansion at 159 Swan St in Buffalo, and funds for the project, which was designed to serve poor working mothers. The term crèche, or "cradle school," derived from a French model opened near Paris in 1844. The project's aim was to keep 40 to 50 children aged from 1 month to 6 years safe, fed, washed, and amused from 6:45 AM to 6:00–7:00 PM for a 5¢ daily fee. A matron and three nurses, assisted by a cook and a laundress, also instructed attendees in health, good habits, and socialization. The facility soon operated at full capacity and gained national fame through articles in publications such as *Harper's New Monthly Magazine* (1885), sparking development of similar institutions elsewhere. From its first years, the staff also supplied such services as home visitation, vocational training for poor women, and placement of ill mothers and children in convalescent homes. In 1884 Fitch Crèche established Buffalo's first kindergarten, and from 1890 its on-site Training School for Nursery Maids served as a model for other such schools in the United States and abroad. From 1894 the facility provided afterschool care for children up to 8 years of age. The Fitch Crèche survived until the 1933 exhaustion of its endowment. Despite efforts of landmark preservationists, the Fitch Crèche building was demolished in June 1996.

Little, Karen Berner. *Maria M. Love: The Life and Legacy of a Social Work Pioneer* (Buffalo: Western Heritage Institute, 1994)

Maria Kiriakova

Fitzgerald, F. Scott. See GREAT GATSBY, THE.

Five Towns. An area in southwestern Hempstead (Nassau Co) bordering Queens Co, at the eastern end of the Rockaway Peninsula. The name is something of a misnomer, because the area comprises not towns but the Villages of Lawrence and Cedarhurst and the three unincorporated localities of Hewlett, Woodmere, and Inwood. It also includes the Villages of Hewlett Harbor, Hewlett Bay Park, Hewlett Neck, Woodsburgh, and the locality of Meadowmere Park. Development began after the Rockaway Branch Railroad (1869) began transporting visitors to Rockaway Beach, with station stops at Hewletts [now Hewlett], Woodsburgh [now Woodmere], Ocean Point [now Cedarhurst], and Lawrence, places that were collectively called the Branch after the rail line. Developers subdivided farms so that summer visitors, attracted by the seashore and rapid rail service, could build homes. The Five Towns designation came into use when the Five Towns Community Chest began in 1931. In the early 21st century, the majority of residents are Jewish. The gracious old homes and more modest newer neighborhoods are organized into two school districts and are served by two weekly newspapers.

John A. Hewlett

Five Towns College. Private college in Dix Hills (Suffolk Co). Chartered in 1972, the college began classes in Merrick (Nassau Co) in 1974, although it had planned to locate in the Five Towns area of southwestern Nassau Co. Originally it was a two-year college offering associate degrees in liberal arts, music technology, and business. Growing from its initial enrollment of 88 students, the institution relocated to Seaford (Nassau Co) in 1980 and became a four-year college in 1988. It moved to its present location in 1992 but retained its original name. The most popular programs are in music, including audio-recording technology, music business, music education, composition, and performance. The college offers associate, bachelor's, and master's degrees in more than 30 programs of study. Its Dix Hills Center for the Performing Arts presents cultural events for the surrounding community. In 2002 the first dormitories were opened and enrollment numbered 963 students, 65% men and 35% women.

Five Towns College, http://www.fivetowns.edu/

Natalie A. Naylor

Flagg, Azariah C(utting) (*b* Orwell, Vt, 28 Nov 1790; *d* New York City, 24 Nov 1873). Government official and political leader. Trained as a printer in Burlington, Vt, he moved to Plattsburgh, where he brought out the *Republican* (1811–26) and served as the Bank of Plattsburgh's director (1820–25). In 1814 he married Phoebe Maria Coe. A legislative leader for the Albany Regency in the 1823 assembly, he strove to sidetrack the popular election of presidential electors and maneuvered to remove De Witt Clinton as New York State canal commissioner. As New York's secretary of state (1826–33), he opposed rechartering the Bank of the United States, attended the first Democratic National Convention in 1832, and contributed to the *Albany Argus.* While state comptroller (1834–39, 1842–47), he worked to reduce public spending by fostering the 1842 Stop and Tax Law, which levied a new tax on all taxable property, halted public works, and directed canal revenues toward payment of the state's debts. Edged out as head of the Hudson River Railroad in 1849 and resigning as the Mohawk Valley Railroad president in 1852, he ran for comptroller of New York City as a fiscal conservative and was elected in November 1852. After leaving office in 1859 his sight failed. A Barnburner who had reluctantly embraced Free Soil in 1848, Flagg opposed the Kansas-Nebraska Act and shifted quietly toward the Republican Party.

Cole, Donald B. *Martin Van Buren and the American Political System* (Princeton, NJ: Princeton Univ Press, 1984)

Craig and Mary L. Hanyan

Flanagan [née Ferguson], **Hallie (Mae)** (*b* Redfield, S Dak, 27 Aug ?1889; *d* Old Tappan, NJ, 23 July 1969). Educator and director of Federal Theatre Project. A graduate of Grinnell College in Iowa (1911), she first taught high school but returned to Grinnell as an English instructor following the death of her husband in 1919. In 1922 Flanagan became the director of Grinnell's Colonial Theater. She then studied theater at Harvard/Radcliffe through 1924 and began to teach at Vassar College in Poughkeepsie in 1925. She traveled to Europe and the Soviet Union on a Guggenheim Fellowship in 1926–27 and founded Vassar Experimental Theater in 1928, producing Euripides' *Hippolytus,* performed in the original Greek, and contemporary drama, including *Can You Hear Their Voices?,* which she wrote in 1931 with Margaret Clifford based on a story by Whittaker Chambers about a 1930 drought in the South.

Pres Franklin D. Roosevelt named her to run the Federal Theatre Project (1935–39), initiated as part of the Works Progress Administration. It employed about 12,000 actors in 158 theaters nationwide and produced new and classic plays, as well as introducing a theater of social reform called "living newspapers," which presented facts about issues of the day to audiences. An early example was *Triple-A Plowed Under,* a living newspaper on agriculture in America. The Federal Theatre Project also produced Kurt Weill's first American musical, *Johnny Johnson,* and John Houseman and Orson Welles produced and directed an all-black version of *Macbeth* and Marc Blitzstein's *The Cradle Will Rock,* an agitprop musical that the government closed on the eve of its opening. In 1938 the House Committee on Un-American Activities accused Flanagan of communist tendencies, and Congress voted to end the Federal Theatre Project in 1939. Flanagan returned to Vassar and published *Arena* (1940), an account of her work with the Federal Theatre. In 1942 she accepted a deanship at Smith College in Northampton, Mass (1942–46), and created a theater department, where she taught until the early 1950s. *Dynamo,* a memoir recounting her years at Vassar, was published in 1943. In 1947 she wrote a play about the atomic age, $E=mc^2$, using elements of the living newspaper that had originated with the Federal Theatre Project.

Bentley, Joanne. *Hallie Flanagan: A Life in the American Theatre* (New York: Knopf, 1988)

Joan Morris

flax *[Linum usitatissimum].* An annual plant that grows 18–30 inches (46–76 cm) tall and bears blue flowers. Flax is typically planted in April, harvested during late summer, and cultivated to produce linen and linseed. The flax stalk has a thin bark and a woody core composed of fibers, which are bound together by a gluelike substance called mucilage. Europeans introduced flax agriculture and processing techniques in the colony during the 17th century. Early flax farms were small and located in Westchester and Ulster Cos or on Long Island. Scots-Irish immigrants helped develop the industry because they knew how to spin flax fiber. Several processes were necessary to separate the long fibers, called line flax, from the short fibers, called tow, making linen production labor intensive. Line fibers were spun into yarns and woven into towels and fabric for bedding and clothing. Tow was used to make yarns for rope and sack cloth.

In reaction to the Stamp Act, the Society for the Promotion of Arts, Agriculture and Economy was established in New York City in the 1760s, encouraged linen manufacture, and established grades of flax, making textile production more professional. Flaxseeds were pressed into cakes for fodder and milled to produce linseed oil, an essential ingredient in paint and varnishes. As early as 1748 seeds and oil were exported to Ireland because Ireland's flax produced low-quality seed. From 1790 to 1794 the average annual exports of flaxseed to Ireland from New York and New England were 241,000 bushels (8,492,600 l). Production increased in the early 1800s when flax became industrialized. Cultivation centered in Central New York, and by 1855 it was grown in 52 counties statewide. The largest and most productive farms were in Rensselaer, Washington, and Montgomery Cos. In 1865 flax agriculture peaked with 23,874 acres (9,661.5 ha) under cultivation in the state. Beginning in the 1870s it declined sharply in the face of competition from southern cotton growers and western farmers who could cultivate the crop more inexpensively. In 1909 only 58 acres (23.5 ha) were cultivated in New York State. By 2003 most US flax was grown in the Dakotas.

See also IRISH.

Bishop, J. Leander. *American Manufactures from 1608 to 1860* (Philadelphia: Edward Young, 1868)
Coons, Martha. "Preindustrial Linen-Making: The Process." In *Linen Making in New England, 1640–1860* (North Andover, Mass: Merrimack Valley Textile Museum, 1980)
Hedrick, U. P. *A History of Agriculture in the State of New York* ([Albany]: Printed for NYS Agriculture Society, 1933)

Gwendolyn L. Miner

Fleischmanns. Village (pop 351) in Middletown (Delaware Co). The village was incorporated in 1913 from the hamlets of Griffin Corners and Fleischmanns. A typical farm hamlet, Griffin Corners had acquired a post office in 1851. The Ulster and Delaware Railroad (1870) opened the area for summer boarders. In 1883 Charles F. Fleischmann (1834–97), founder of Fleischmann Yeast Co, built the Schloss, a luxurious summer home west of Griffin Corners. Near his cottage, a Fleischmanns post office opened in 1888. Resort growth followed, and by 1910 the area had 18 large hotels and 4,200 beds. By the time the railroad failed in 1963 the hotels had been abandoned; many burned. In recent years second-home owners have replaced summer visitors.

Dorothy Kubik

Fleming. Town (pop 2,647) in central Cayuga Co. Settled in 1790, the town was formed from Aurelius in 1823. Located on the west shore of Owasco Lake, Fleming had several resorts, including the Four Mile House, a hotel and picnic ground from the late 1840s until 1899, and Lakeside Park, a trolley-line amusement park that closed in 1966. The Southern Central Railroad reached town in 1870. Fleming was the home of the abolitionist Harriet Tubman in her latter decades (*d* 1913), during which she operated a home for indigent Blacks. Beginning *ca* 1960 the northern part of town adjacent to Auburn suburbanized. In 2002 crop farming continued in the western part of Fleming, along with several dairy farms of over 1,000 head each.

Sheila Tucker

Fleming, Renée (*b* Indiana, Pa, 14 Feb 1959). Soprano singer. Fleming grew up in and around Rochester, where her parents were high school voice teachers. She moved to Churchville (Monroe Co) as a teenager and earned a bachelor of music degree at SUNY Potsdam (1981) and a master's degree from the Eastman School of Music in Rochester (1983). After additional study at the Juilliard American Opera Center in New York City (1983–84), she studied in Frankfurt, Germany (1984–85) as a Fulbright scholar. In 1986 Fleming made her debut at Landestheater in Salzburg, Austria, as Konstanze in Mozart's *Abduction from the Seraglio.* She debuted with the New York City Opera in 1989 as Mimi in Puccini's *La Bohème* and in 1991 created the role of Rosina in John Corigliano's *Ghosts of Versailles* at the Metropolitan Opera. Her first solo album was released in 1996. One of the leading lyric sopranos of her generation, she performs throughout the world.

Scott, Paula Pyzik. "Renée Fleming." In *Contemporary Musicians: Profiles of the People in Music,* ed. Luann Brennan, vol 24 (Farmington Hills, Mich: Gale Group, 1999)

Vincent Lenti

Flemish Bastard [**Canaqueese; Dutch Bastard; Smits, Jan; Smith, John**] (*fl* 1650–87). Mohawk chief. Son of a Mohawk mother and a Dutch father, the man most often known as the Flemish Bastard became a Mohawk leader and a negotiator for the Mohawk in their relations with the Dutch, English, and French. He joined the Dutch in an attempt to get prisoners returned from the Esopus Indians in 1663. In July 1666 he led the Mohawk in a successful peace mission to the French that stopped their invasion of Mohawk country. During the years 1666–67, he was used as a courier in the negotiations between the governors of New France and New York and the Albany magistrates concerning the peace negotiations with the Mohawk. Together with his followers, he moved to the vicinity of Quebec after the Iroquois-French peace treaty of 1667. He is last mentioned in a 1687 document as having participated in a French-Indian expedition against the Seneca.

Richter, Daniel K. *The Ordeal of the Longhouse: The Peoples of the Iroquois League in the Era of European Colonization* (Chapel Hill: Univ of North Carolina Press, 1992)

Mark Meuwese

Flick, Alexander (Clarence) (*b* Galion, Ohio, 16 Aug 1869; *d* Santa Rosa, Fla, 30 July 1942). Historian and educator. Flick received his BA in 1894 from Otterbein College in Ohio and then was a fellow in history at Columbia University in 1895–96, when he left to join the faculty at Syracuse University. He received his MA (1897) and PhD (1901) from Columbia. Although a professor of European history at Syracuse (1899–1923), Flick was a pioneer in the serious historical study of New York State. In 1923 he became state historian and director of the Department of Archives and History of the New York State Department of Education. Important projects during his 16-year tenure included a new emphasis on local history, commemorating the sesquicentennial anniversary of the American Revolution, and establishing historical markers with information supplied by county historians. His books with New York State themes include *Loyalism in New York during the American Revolution* (1901), *American Revolution in New York* (1926), and a biography of Samuel J. Tilden (1939). He was editor of *New York History* (1924–39). Probably his most important work was the 10-volume *History of the State of New York* (1933–37), which he edited. It was the first attempt at a comprehensive scholarly overview of the states history.

"Alexander C. Flick, State Ex-Aide, 72," *New York Times,* 31 July 1942
Meany, Joseph F., Jr. "New York: The State of History," http://www.nysm.nysed.gov/services/meanydoc.html
Winslow, Edmund J. "Local Historians in New York State," http://www.nysm.nysed.gov/services/winslowdoc.html

John R. Deitrick

Flint, Austin (*b* Petersham, Mass, 20 Oct 1812; *d* New York City, 13 Mar 1886). Physician. After attending Amherst and Harvard Colleges, he received his MD from Harvard College in 1833. He practiced medicine in Boston and Northampton, Mass, and then moved to Buffalo in 1844. In 1846 he founded the *Buffalo Medical Journal* and, with Millard Fillmore, James Platt White, and Frank Hastings Hamilton, cofounded the University of Buffalo, which initially consisted only of the Medical Department. He taught at Buffalo (1846–52), Geneva Medical College (Ontario Co) (1847–49), and University of Louisville in Kentucky (1852–56). From 1856 to 1859 he again taught at the University of Buffalo and served as president of the Buffalo Medical Society. In 1859 he moved to New York City. He became a leader in heart research and in 1862 discovered a cardiac disorder that came to be called the "Austin Flint murmur." He earned lasting fame with the publication of clinical books and articles, including his *Treatise on the Principle and Practice of Medicine* (1866), a classic medical textbook. Flint was professor of pathology at Long Island College Hospital in Brooklyn from 1861 to 1868, professor of clinical medicine at Bellevue Hospital Medical College from 1861 to 1886 in Manhattan, and president of the American Medical Association (1884–85).

Batt, Ronald Elmer. "Flint, Austin." In *Dictionary of American Medical Biography* (Westport, Conn: Greenwood, 1984)

Eric v. d. Luft

Flood of 1972. See HURRICANE AGNES/FLOOD OF 1972.

flora and vegetation. The contemporary flora of New York State, while mostly a subset of the flora of temperate and boreal parts of North America, encompasses all species of terrestrial and aquatic plants growing outside cultivation within the state. Many species within the state are naturalized from other regions such as Eurasia. The term "vegetation" concerns associations of plants and groups of species that have similar ecological tolerances to environmental factors such as climate, topography, soil characteristics, and water availability. Plant associations are recognizable, quantifiable, and mappable at large or small scales.

Floras

The plant life of New York State is described in books or other sources called floras; the first comprehensive flora was written by John Torrey and published in 1846 and 1847. It treated only spore-producing plants, such as ferns and other groups, and seed-producing plants, such as conifers and flowering plants. Other plants contained within the state's flora—and cataloged in flora treatises—are mosses, liverworts, hornworts, and algae of terrestrial, freshwater, and marine species. Fungi and lichens have been included in floras as well, although they have a closer evolutionary connection to animals than to plants.

Although no comprehensive flora lists and describes New York State species in all these organism groups, Richard Mitchell and Gordon Tucker's *Revised Checklist of New York State Plants* (1997) tallies 3,603 pteridophytes, such as club and spike mosses, quillworts, horsetails, and adder's-tongue, and other ferns, such as gymnosperms, conifers, and angiosperms. Of these, 35%, or 1,117 species, are nonnative plants. Another 324 ephemeral species of flowering plants did not become naturalized, that is, capable of reproducing in the wild. The coverage of the *Revised Checklist* is identical to that of Torrey's early compendium in which 1,452 species, including 161 nonnative species, were listed. But during the 150 years separating the publication of the two works, New York State's flora became better known, and the number of naturalized species increased sevenfold.

Geographic Occurrence of State Flora

New York State's indigenous plants assembled within its boundaries rather recently, within the last 23,000 years or less, as glacial ice disappeared at the close of the Pleistocene. Only small parts of Allegany and Cattaraugus Cos in Western New York and seaward portions of Long and Staten Islands are unglaciated. The first plants to inhabit deglaciated terrain, arctic and alpine species of bryophytes and flowering plants, migrated in part from these areas. In the absence of trees, these plants produced tundra-like landscapes that lasted until 14,000 years ago. Forest trees began with white spruce and jack pine and were followed by balsam fir and tamarack and then by white pine, hemlock, and various broadleaf deciduous trees, such as maples, birches, oaks, hickories, American chestnut, and American beech. They migrated from their glacial refuges and replaced the tundra plants. This occurred in an order that was remarkably consistent from place to place across the state. Descendants of some of the first tundra plant inhabitants did not all move northward as the ice retreated and climate changed. Some remained isolated on Adirondack summits and on gorge walls in this region and elsewhere in the state, disjunct from the arctic and subarctic regions where they more characteristically occur.

Flora history and the influence of climate and soils on plant distribution allow the flora treatises of New York State to be divided into groups of species sharing patterns of geographic occurrence: plants of the coastal plain; arctic-alpine and boreal or northern species, which have southernmost stations in New York State; prairie plants, found on dry, thin soils in the state's northwestern counties and occasionally elsewhere; and special-habitat species disjunct from the Atlantic coast but that grow, for example, in Onondaga Lake's inland marshes. Bedrock soil and glacial drift are variously calcareous or acidic in different parts of the state, and floras of distinctive composition correlate with such soil patterns. Thin, dry soil associated with limestone flatrock pavements in Jefferson Co, for example, harbors mixtures of species more typical of boreal, calcareous peatland and western grassland regions. Richard Mitchell and Charles Sheviak's *Rare Plants of New York* (1981) provides descriptions and illustrations of most conspicuous plant rarities in the state, and the New York Natural Heritage Program, headquartered in Albany in 2003, maintains information about rare plants, many examples of which grow in the state.

Vegetation

During the colonial period at the onset of European settlement much of future New York State was covered by forest of varying composition, reflecting the associations of different forest trees and herbs in regions with similar environmental characteristics. Interspersed with forest lands were areas of wetland, exposed bedrock, and fields of Native American crops (corn, beans, squash). As European American agriculture took hold and expanded along the coast and then inland, much forest was cut and the land turned into cultivated fields and pastures. Deforestation steadily increased until it peaked at 80% or more in some counties by 1880, when farm abandonment began to accelerate as farmers moved to richer, more easily cultivated lands beyond New York State. Reforestation of unused agricultural land has continued, and at the beginning of the 21st century, over 62% of New York State is forest again, despite population growth and increased housing development.

Ecologists such as William L. Bray (*The Development of the Vegetation of New York State,* 1930), E. Lucy Braun (*Deciduous Forests of Eastern North America,* 1950), and August W. Küchler (*Potential Natural Vegetation of the Conterminous United States,* 1964) have mapped the state's vegetation. While the types of vegetation recognized by these individuals vary, their maps are similar. The Hudson River valley, Erie-Ontario Lake Plain, and the valleys of the Allegheny and Susquehanna Rivers of the Southern Tier contain beech-maple and oak-hickory associations. Much of the Allegheny Plateau is white pine-hemlock-northern hardwood forest, as is the perimeter surrounding the Adirondack Mountain core. Higher elevations in the Adirondacks support red spruce-balsam fir forest, as do upper slopes of the Catskill Mountains and the Tug Hill and Rensselaer Plateaus. The state's vegetation varies latitudinally and longitudinally and with altitude, which can be seen along Veterans Memorial Highway on Whiteface Mountain (Essex Co) and elsewhere in the Adirondack and Catskill high peaks. As one travels upward, low-elevation, mixed conifer-hardwood forest gives way to red spruce-balsam fir, which yields to balsam fir and then to treeless, alpine expanses. Dwarf forests of conifers, mostly balsam fir, occur at the transition between forest and alpine tundra. Beneath such areas of krummholz, or dwarf, twisted trees are found herbs more typical of lower elevations. New York State's smaller-scale vegetation types are described in Carol Reschke's *Ecological Communities of New York State.*

Important examples of wetland vegetation were found throughout the state at the start of the 21st century. Large areas of peatland occur in the Adirondack region and in the Erie-Ontario Lowland, where many wetlands have been drained to support truck farms on black muck soil. Peat—unoxidized plant remains—has accumulated in kettle-hole bogs in many state locations and as large expanses of fen in the Adirondacks. Fen ground cover consists mainly of sphagnum moss, 50 species of which are known to occur in New York State, the greatest number for any state in the eastern United States. Fens contain disjunct boreal species. Wetlands not sequestering peat deposits, such as swamps (with trees) and marshes (without trees), are common landscape elements in areas of impeded drainage.

See also Wetlands; Wildflowers.

Miller, Norton G., and Richard S. Mitchell. "Tracking the Mosses and Vascular Plants of New York (1836–1994)." In *Our Living Resources,* ed. E. T. LaRoe et al (Washington DC: US Department of the Interior, National Biological Service, 1995)

Mitchell, Richard S., and Charles J. Sheviak. *Rare Plants of New York.* Museum Bulletin 445 (Albany: NYS Museum, 1981)

Mitchell, Richard S., and Gordon C. Tucker. *Revised Checklist of New York State Plants.* Museum Bulletin 490 (Albany: NYS Museum, 1997)

Reschke, Carol. *Ecological Communities of New York State* (Latham, NY: New York Natural Heritage Program, NYS Department of Environmental Conservation, 1990)

Norton G. Miller

Floral Park. Village (pop 15,967) in Hempstead and North Hempstead (Nassau Co). Louis Siebrecht began flower cultivation in the area in 1869, but it was John Lewis Childs (1856–1921) who made Floral Park famous with his large mail-order seed company named for himself; his first catalog was issued in 1875. A post office named East Hinsdale opened in 1877; after a brief change to Floral, it was renamed Floral Park in 1887. The village incorporated in 1908. Flowers were grown until the 1920s, but in that decade its population surged 400% to 10,016, pushing out the farms. A few garden apartments and some additional houses were built after World War II, but by 1950 the development of the comfortable middle-class village was virtually complete.

Richard A. Winsche

Florence. Town (pop 1,086) in NW Oneida Co. Settled in 1801 the town was formed from Camden in 1805. Many Irish immigrants arrived in the 1830s, and St. Mary's Roman Catholic Church opened in 1845. Located in the Tug Hill Plateau, the land was never good for farming, and in the 20th century over 11,000 acres (4,450 ha) of marginal farms were purchased by New York State for reforestation. The population roughly doubled between 1960 and 2000. The City of Oneida draws drinking water from Florence Creek. In 2002 the town had three dairy farms; other residents worked at Spinks Lumber Co or commuted to Williamstown (Oswego Co), Camden, or to Harden Furniture in McConnellsville.

Florida. Town (pop 2,731) in SE Montgomery Co. Because the present town was one of the sites of the most eastern Mohawk castle, or village, French Catholic, Dutch Reformed, and Anglican missionaries came in the late 17th and early 18th centuries. Fort Hunter (1711) was the site of Queen Anne's Chapel (1712), and a permanent settlement surrounded it. Sir William Johnson opened a store on the Mohawk River in 1738. The town was formed from the extinct town of Mohawk in 1793 and was served by the Erie Canal beginning in 1825. In 1841 a large aqueduct over the Schoharie Creek at Fort Hunter replaced earlier guard locks. Area farms have always been productive, and the town remains predominantly agricultural in the early 21st century. The Florida exit on the New York State Thruway opened in 1954, spurring modest growth. A large Target distribution center opened in 2004. Fort Hunter is the locale of the Schoharie Crossing State Historic Site.

James Crawford

Florida. Village (pop 2,571) in Warwick (Orange Co). The present village originated as two hamlets, Florida, along a main street, and Randallville, around mills and a piano factory on Quaker Creek. Adjacent to Warwick's Black Dirt region, where German and Polish farmers settled after the Civil War, it became a market village for the rich vegetable farms. In 1946 the village was incorporated, encompassing both hamlets. In the early 21st century Florida residents produce vegetables and aerospace ceramics. It was the birthplace of statesman William H. Seward (1801–72) and is the home of Jimmy Sturr, who has won 13 Grammys for polka band music recordings.

Gary Allen Randall

flour milling. Flour and grain milling in what is now New York State has evolved from a household industry using Stone Age methods to one in which modern, scientifically designed mills are operated primarily by a handful of large corporations.

Colonial Period

Before the arrival of Europeans, Indians produced a nutritious if impure whole grain cornmeal by manually crushing corn between two stone surfaces. European settlers introduced wheat and other Old World grains, as well as the millstone method of size reduction. The millstones were powered by animals, wind, or falling or moving water, including tidal flows. Because of limited transportation facilities, most mills were small and processed locally grown grain, with the product also consumed locally. The milling operations in New Netherland, particularly on Manhattan and Nutten Island (now Governors Island), were an exception. The abundance of wheat grown on and around the island resulted in a surplus of flour and an export trade, mainly with the Caribbean islands. Problems with quality control resulted in a Dutch decree that all export flour be bolted (sifted to remove impurities) in Manhattan. This monopoly on bolting operations was continued by the English until 1694, after which the uneven quality of flour once again resulted in a loss of trade, and by 1750 New York Colony had lost its long-standing leadership in the industry. As settlers moved inland local mills appeared in most communities.

The 19th Century

The 19th century was a period of major changes in milling technology. Delaware native Oliver Evans (1755–1819) devised methods for mill automation that increased production and product quality while reducing labor requirements. Around 1810 Evans developed high-pressure steam engines that freed mills from dependence on wind and waterpower. By the end of the century steam-powered mills in New York State exceeded waterpowered ones in total capacity but not in number. The middlings purifier, introduced *ca* 1865, efficiently separated bran and other impurities from the flour. A milling system known as gradual reduction, wherein grain passed over a series of disk-shaped millstones or cylindrical roller mills, was developed about this time. The roller mill produced a finer flour with less energy and rapidly replaced stones in the late 1870s and early 1880s.

The New York State Census of 1835 listed 2,031 flour and gristmills statewide. An industry center emerged at Rochester because of the abundant supply of Genesee Valley wheat, waterpower from the falls on the Genesee River, and cheap freight shipping on the Erie Canal. Rochester's pre-canal population of 2,500 reached 14,400 in 1835, when the city had 21 working mills, including the large operations of Thomas Kempshall, Hervey Ely, E. H. S. Mumford, and Emerson and Graves. By 1840 Rochester was the nation's "Flour City," with a milling capacity of over 1.6 million bushels (56.4 million l), climbing to 2.3 million bushels (81 million l) in 1847. Although there were several years in the 1850s with low wheat yields and increased competition from other states, in 1860 the city's population stood at more than 48,000.

The second Welland Canal (1845), which carried vessels up to 750 tons (680 MT), created a route to New York City by way of Oswego that was for a time competitive with the main Erie Canal line from Buffalo. The Oswego Canal and Oswego River waterpower resulted in a number of grain elevators and flour mills locating there. These activities peaked during the Civil War but declined precipitously thereafter. Other 19th-century milling centers included the Albany area, Buffalo, Lockport, Niagara Falls, and Ithaca.

By the end of the 19th century small, water-powered mills were disappearing quickly. With the exception of some large independent mills in New York City, such as the 22,000 cwt (997,900 kg) capacity Hecker Jones Jewell mill, flour milling was consolidating into large operations, usually near the sources of grain production in the Midwest. This consolidation led to a number of strikes in the 1890s and the beginnings of workforce organization in the industry.

Since 1900

The pace of technical innovation slowed in the 20th century, but important developments included the use of pneumatic conveying, which allowed better control of product quality while improving dust control, mill cleanliness, and safety. Notable too was the shipping of flour in bulk, instead of bags, to consumers such as large bakeries. Relative technological stability did not slow industry consolidation, however, and there were major changes in mill concentrations. Milling in New York City declined because its location was no longer ideal and capacity nationwide was more than needed; the city's largest mill, then owned by the Standard Milling Co, closed in 1922. Soon after the turn of the century Buffalo rose to prominence because of its location as the Great Lakes transshipment point for the railroads and the Erie Canal, cheap electric power from Niagara Falls, and the institution of special milling-in-transit freight rates, which encouraged the milling of midwestern grain in Buffalo. Canadian wheat was also shipped to Buffalo for milling and the flour returned to Canada. By 1930 Buffalo was the largest flour-milling center in the world. In 1950 it had seven mills, with a combined daily capacity of 100,000 cwt (4.5 million kg). However, further changes in freight rates and transportation patterns led to decline of the industry in Buffalo. In the 1970s, 5,000 cwt (226,800 kg) "forward" mills were built in Albany and Hudson (Columbia Co) to bring milling operations closer to the points of use. By 1995 Buffalo had lost its position as the US leader in flour production, and in 2003 it had only two mills, with a combined capacity of 32,000 cwt (1.5 million kg).

With fewer and larger employers dominating, labor groups likewise strove to integrate. After decades of sporadic efforts, a number of federal unions combined in 1936 to form the National Council of Grain Processors, which became the American Federation of Grain Millers (AFGM) in 1948. A nationwide strike in 1954 had a big impact on several Buffalo mills. Labor actions, however, were unable to prevent the aggressive merging, downsizing, and decentralization that has characterized the industry since the 1960s, resulting in fewer jobs and union members. In 1998 the AFGM merged with another union to form the Bakery, Confectionery, Tobacco Workers and Grain Millers International Union. By 2001 there were only 21 operating mills in New York State. Remaining large mills include those of ConAgra and General Mills (Buffalo), Archer Daniels Midland (Buffalo and Hudson), and Cargill (Albany). Mills utilizing waterpower and millstones have nearly disappeared, exceptions being buckwheat manufacturer Birkett Mills Co in Penn Yan (Yates Co) and New Hope Mills (Cayuga Co). Others in this category are mostly noncommercial historic restorations, such as The Mill at Philipsburg Manor in Tarrytown (Westchester Co).

See also Rochester (city).

Albion, Robert Greenhalgh. *The Rise of New York Port, 1815–1860* (1939; repr New York: Scribner's, 1970)
Bullis, Harry A. *Buffalo: Its Flour Milling Heritage* (New York: Newcomen Society of England, American Branch, 1948)
Steen, Herman. *Flour Milling in America* (Minneapolis: T. S. Dennison, 1963)

Henry H. Baxter

Flower, Roswell P(ettibone) (*b* Theresa, Jefferson Co, 7 Aug 1835; *d* Eastport, Suffolk Co, 12 May 1899). Governor and businessman. Flower worked on his family's farm during his youth and graduated from Theresa High School in 1851. He taught for a few years before becoming the Watertown deputy postmaster (1854–60). In 1859 Flower married Sarah M. Woodruff of Watertown; the couple had three children. He ran a jewelry business until 1869, when he moved to New York City to manage the multimillion-dollar estate of his brother-in-law Henry Keep. Flower increased his own wealth through banking and investments. Active with Democratic Party committees, Flower was elected to Congress three times and served from 1881 to 1883 and 1889 to 1891. During the latter period he called for lower tariff rates and lobbied, unsuccessfully, for locating a world's fair in New York State. Elected governor in November 1891, Flower signed the bill creating the Adirondack Park and approved laws for revision of state statutes. During the 1893 depression he provided employment by approving contracts for canal improvements, but he favored a government that exercised only limited powers. Faced with repercussions from the depression, corruption scandals involving the Democratic Party, and declining support from the Tammany political machine, Flower did not seek reelection in 1894. He held stock in numerous corporations, including Brooklyn Rapid Transit, and his philanthropy included donations to churches in Theresa, Watertown, and New York City; to Cornell University's veterinary school; and to construction of Manhattan's Flower Free Surgical Hospital. The Roswell P. Flower Memorial Library in Watertown was dedicated in his honor in 1904.

McSeveney, Samuel T. *The Politics of Depression: Political Behavior in the Northeast, 1893–1896* (New York: Oxford Univ Press, 1972)

Laura-Eve Moss

Flower Hill. Village (pop 4,500) in North Hempstead (Nassau Co). Shipping magnate Carlos Munson gave 15 acres (6 ha) to the Sisters of the Franciscan Missionaries of Mary in 1920 to be a home for children with cardiac diseases; it developed into St. Francis Hospital (1954), an institutional pioneer in open-heart surgery. Other former Munson property has become Elderfields Historic Preserve (Nassau Co). Developed in the 1920s the Village of Flower Hill was incorporated in 1931. The North Hempstead Country Club, with its 18-hole golf course, is the largest landowner in the village. The Sands-Willets House, built between 1715 and 1735, is on the National Register of Historic Places. There is a small commercial strip on Northern Blvd; otherwise the village is composed of substantial homes.

Joan Gay Kent

Floyd. Town (pop 3,869) in central Oneida Co. The town was formed from Steuben in 1796 after settlement of the area in 1790. Many Welsh immigrants settled in the northern part of town. A dairy economy developed after the first cheese factory began operating in 1862. The town's population declined in the early 20th century, dipping to 663 in 1920, but thereafter more than tripled by 1950 to 2,234 as workers from Rome and Utica built homes in town. On 12 Aug 1960 the first intercontinental voice message by satellite was received from Trinidad at the US Air Force's Floyd Annex, which closed in 1982. Most residents in 2003 work in Utica and Rome.

Flushing Remonstrance. A petition, dated 27 Dec 1657, protesting an ordinance by Director General Petrus Stuyvesant and his council against the harboring of Quakers in New Netherland. In the 1650s the disciples of a new sect, the Society of Friends, or Quakers, which believed that God could be apprehended without ministers, churches, or creeds, began to appear on Long Island. Alarmed at the spread of Quaker missionary efforts, which seemed to threaten the social order, and influenced by the complaints of Dutch Reformed Dominies Samuel Drisius and Johannes Megapolensis, Stuyvesant and his council passed an ordinance on 1 Feb 1656 against the holding of conventicles. In defiance of this ordinance, Henry Townsend of Rustdorp [now Jamaica, Queens Co], who had recently moved from Vlissingen [now Flushing, Queens Co], was fined for holding meetings at his house. This was followed by a proclamation by Stuyvesant forbidding the harboring of Quakers. In response to the proclamation, Vlissingen town clerk Edward Hart wrote the remonstrance, which was signed by 28 fellow townsmen as well as by Henry Townsend and his son John of Rustdorp. Citing the "freedom from molestation" clause of the 1645 Vlissingen town charter granted by Dutch West India Co director Willem Kieft and the "fundamental law of the States General" of the Dutch Republic (possibly a reference to Art 13 of the 1579 Union of Utrecht, which guaranteed freedom in religion), the petitioners protested, "we can not condemn them [Quakers]" nor "punish, banish or persecute them." As a result of their action, Stuyvesant charged that the town had violated the orders and placards of the director general and his council. Stuyvesant, after reading the remonstrance, had Vlissingen sheriff Tobias Feake, who had delivered the document, immediately arrested. He and his council then called two other Vlissingen magistrates, William Noble and Edward Farrington, who had signed the remonstrance, and had them arrested. Edward Hart was also summoned for examination and then sent to prison. Under this pressure the signatories recanted the document. The Flushing Remonstrance thereafter remained largely forgotten until early national historians resurrected it as a precursor to the First Amendment of the US Constitution. In 1911 the document, which is preserved in the New York State Archives in Albany, was badly damaged in the New York State Library fire.

Corwin, Edward T., ed. *Ecclesiastical Records, State of New York,* vol 1 (Albany: J. B. Lyon, 1901)
DiRiggi, Mildred Murphy. "Quakerism on Long Island: The First Fifty Years, 1657–1707" (PhD diss, SUNY Stony Brook, 1994)

David William Voorhees

fly fishing. European settlers brought the sport to America before the Revolution. Fly fishing is distinguished by unique tackle with a long rod, heavy line, and lighter leader, which delivers a lure made of fur, feathers, or synthetic materials meant to approximate an insect such as the mayfly or other food sources such as bait fish. Early fly fishing venues were Long Island's coastal trout rivers and streams. Anglers later went to the Beaver Kill, Willowemoc Creek, and Esopus Creek in the Catskills, and to the Adirondacks. Rochester and Buffalo residents traveled to the upper Genesee River and its tributaries. With the support of wealthy sportsmen such as Robert Barnwell Roosevelt, Seth Green of Caledonia (Livingston Co), and Fred Mather of Cold Spring Harbor (Suffolk Co), hatcheries were established to replenish fish and fisheries compromised by overfishing and pollution. In 1883 Mather became the first American to breed brown trout for stocking streams too warm or polluted for brook trout.

By the late 19th century the Catskills were the center of American fly fishing innovation, a position that has in large part been retained. While brook trout tend to favor bright, attractor flies, brown trout are difficult to catch and require flies more imitative of stream insects. In the 1870s Sara McBride from Mumford (Monroe Co) offered a systematic classification of fly patterns. Theodore Gordon developed the new, more natural fly patterns essential for catching brown trout, which he tested on Catskill streams starting in the 1890s. Edward R. Hewitt and Preston Jennings in the mid–20th century and Lee Wulff and Francis Betters in the late 20th century developed dry fly patterns such as the Bivisible, Variant, and Ausable Wulff to float in turbulent mountain streams. In the 1940s Art Flick of West Kill (Greene Co) developed a systematic schedule of mayfly emergences and his own matching fly patterns. In the 1960s and 1970s, Robert Boyle and Eric Leiser developed hatching charts and fly patterns for stone flies, aquatic insects sometimes favored by trout over mayflies. Harry and Elsie Darbee and Walt and Winnie Dette helped pass down Gordon's fly-tying style to modern flytiers. Major rod-building companies flourished in the Catskill foothills. Through tournament casting and teaching at her school in Lewbeach (Sullivan Co), Joan Salvato Wulff has made fly fishing a more accessible sport.

The Catskill Fly Fishing Center and Museum (1978) in Livingston Manor (Sullivan Co) is a major source of information on the sport. All fly fishers in New York must have a license unless they fish marine waters or meet special criteria. Throughout the state there are waters restricted to artificial lures or catch-and-release fishing, regulation that tends to favor fly fishers. Fly fishers are increasingly beginning to cast in saltwater—the Hudson River as far north as Troy (Rensselaer Co), New York Harbor, and the waters around Long Island—and Paul Dixon of East Hampton (Suffolk Co) has been instrumental in developing the technique of sight fishing for striped bass.

Francis, Austin M. *Catskill Rivers: Birthplace of American Fly Fishing* (New York: Lyons Press, 1983)
Schullery, Paul. *American Fly Fishing: An Illustrated History* (Piscataway, NJ: Winchester Press, 1999)
Van Put, Ed, ed. *The Beaverkill: The History of a River and Its People* (New York: Lyons & Burford, 1996)

John Rowen

folk art. Along with New England and Virginia, the Colony of New York became a center of vernacular artistic activity in the late 17th and early 18th centuries. Many Dutch and English settlers were successful landowners and merchants in the Hudson Valley and New York City, and enjoyed material comforts such as silver, furniture, and paintings. Portraiture thrived in the large colonial communities, including New York City and Albany, through the work of artists Pieter

Vanderlyn, John Watson, John Heaten, Abraham Delanoy, John Durand, and many anonymous painters. Four members of the Duyckinck family were also prominent: Evert I (1621–1702), Gerrit (1660–?1712), Gerardus (1695–1746), and Evert III (?1677–1727). These artists' work varies considerably in expression of the subjects and the alternating use of conventional landscape background elements derived from engraved and printed sources and naturalistic landscape backgrounds. They are also important social records. For instance, the Van Bergen Overmantel attributed to John Heaten (*fl* 1700–45) presents a document of life in Leeds [now in Greene Co] about 1730. Against a background of the Hudson River, the painting shows a Dutch-style house and farm buildings, a wagon, and a population including indentured servants, black slaves, and American Indians. The overmantel is part of the Fenimore Art Museum's collection in Cooperstown (Otsego Co). Biblical paintings, coats-of-arms, and decorative paintings were also produced for Dutch and English patrons.

The 18th and 19th Centuries

The development of inland New York State after the Revolution and the success of the Erie Canal supported a merchant middle class encouraging industry and art. Typical of the folk artists of the period was Ezra Ames (1768–1836), based in the Albany area, who was at the height of his career during the first three decades of the 19th century. Ames was likely an influence on Ammi Phillips (1788–1865), who began a 50-year career as an itinerant portrait painter covering New York State, Connecticut, and Massachusetts. In New York State, Phillips traveled extensively, painting portraits of residents in Rensselaer, Columbia, Dutchess, and other neighboring counties. He lived in Troy (Rensselaer Co) during his first marriage and later settled in Dutchess Co. Phillips began painting in 1811 and continued into the 1860s. His style evolved throughout his career, but he is known for his fine facial delineations, set poses, and sensitivity to details of lace or coiffure. Other significant figures included Henry Walton (1804–65) of Ithaca, Sheldon Peck (1797–1868) of Jordan (Onondaga Co), and Asahel Powers (1813–43) of Clinton and Franklin Cos; Peck and Powers were originally from Vermont. Late 19th-century folk painters included Joseph H. Hidley (1830–72) of Poestenkill (Rensselaer Co) and, at the end of century, Fritz G. Vogt (1841–1900), who rendered approximately 200 meticulously detailed architectural portraits of homes, farms, and local businesses in the Mohawk Valley. While men outnumbered women as artisan painters, several women were professional artists. Mary Ann Willson (*fl* 1810–25) lived on a farm in Greenville (Greene Co), and her boldly designed, spare, idiosyncratic watercolors on paper include a notable series on the parable of the Prodigal Son. Deborah Goldsmith (1808–36) of North Brookfield (Madison Co) painted portraits and miniatures to help support her family before her marriage to George Addison Throop. Susan Waters (1823–1900) of Binghamton painted portraits in the small towns of the state's Southern Tier.

New York State artists also painted works related to the sea and sailing. New York City twins James (1815–97) and John Bard (1815–56) painted several hundred Hudson River paddle

Sunflower pattern quilt, by Mary Totten, first quarter of 19th century.

steamboats, towboats, and other vessels. They worked together for 20 years. James successfully continued alone after the death of his brother. Initially a landscape and then a marine painter, Thomas Chambers left a body of colorful canvases that included romantic views of the Hudson River with architectural views of imaginary castles. Born in England and a Boston resident from 1843–51, Chambers lived between New York City and Albany on and off from 1834 to 1866. Painters of the Erie Canal included Mary Keys (*Lockport on the Erie Canal,* 1832) and Terence J. Kennedy.

Religious enthusiasm inspired vernacular artists in New York State fueled by the evangelism of the Second Great Awakening of the first half of the 19th century. Notable among the state's folk arts are exquisitely crafted wood objects, textiles, and drawings by members of the Watervliet (Albany Co) and Mount Lebanon (Columbia Co) Shaker communities. *View of the Church Family* (1838) by David A. Buckingham is a schematic drawing of the Watervliet Shaker community depicting both the built and natural environments. Shaker drawings from the Mount Lebanon community feature emblematic doves, crowns, and trumpets interspersed with text inscriptions. Respect for hand labor, orderliness, usefulness, and harmony of the sacred and secular worlds resulted in finely crafted material culture objects such as furniture and textiles. During the middle of the 19th century, distinctive quilts were made in other communitarian societies, such as the Oneida Community (Madison Co) and the Mennonites in southwestern New York State. An outstanding textile inspired by religion is the Pieties Quilt (1848) of Maria Cadman Hubbard of Troy, filled with pious sayings and homilies appliquéd and pieced in red on a white cotton ground.

There is a distinct regional folk art form of family records made in New York State between the 1780s and the 1840s. Family registers of births, marriage, and baptismal certificates ensured permanent records for farmers and merchants proud of their identity in the new Republic. William Murray (1756–1828) and other artisan painters who worked in the Mohawk Valley accepted commissions to make watercolor and ink family registers, which were richly embellished with decorative detail and clear text and which transcended their utilitarian purpose. Murray and other artists, including Henry Moyer, lived in an area populated by Germans and were influenced by European *fraktur,* a style of utilitarian decorative watercolor drawing. Decorated and painted home furnishings such as chests were characteristic in German communities in the Hudson, Mohawk, and Schoharie Valleys.

Folk textiles from New York State include fancy embroidered schoolgirl samplers and mourning pictures, braided and hooked rugs, blankets, and an array of quilts and distinguished woven coverlets. Women often supplied homespun woolen yarn to professional weavers, who made coverlets outside the home. Master weavers James Alexander (1770–1870) and Archibald Davidson (*fl* 1833–48) trained in the British Isles and made distinguished coverlets in New York State, often with the name of the client and the date woven into the fabric.

The 20th Century

By the mid–20th century, nostalgia for a fast disappearing rural environment motivated Eagle Bridge (Rensselaer Co) resident, Grandma Moses (Anna Mary Robertson; 1860–1961) to recall an idyllic past through her paintings. Morris Hirshfield (1872–1946) of Brooklyn, a retired slipper manufacturer, painted patterned, finely textured, stylized canvases of people, especially women, and animals. The paintings of Harry Lieberman (1876–1983) link his eastern European past with his secularized Jewish life in America. Vestie Davis (1903–78) captured metropolitan New York with vignettes of crowds at Coney Island and City Hall. Through the second half of the 20th century, social themes and concerns for the laborer stoked the creative fire of former garage mechanic and labor union organizer Ralph Fasanella (1914–97), who recorded precise details of urban life, primarily that in New York City and Westchester Co, where he lived. Likewise, Malcah Zeldis (1931–) of Manhattan captured the rhythmic pulse of New York City. Her works also emphasize her concern for civil and human rights, and peaceful solutions to world problems.

Among contemporary self-taught artists is Aaron Birnbaum (1895–1998), who started to paint his memories and views on life at age 70 after his wife died. Ray Hamilton (1920–96), who took part in the art program at Hospital Audiences in New York City, painted works that often referred to his early life on a farm in South Carolina. Inez Nathaniel Walker (1911–90) started her patterned, colored drawings, mostly of women, at the Bedford Hills Correctional Facility, where she was briefly imprisoned for killing a man who abused her. Although most of her work was done while in prison, she did continue after her release. Freddie Brice (1920–) painted large animals, room interiors, watches, and clocks, and was introduced to painting at a day program at a Brooklyn psychiatric center. Bernard Goodman (1910–2003) of New York City began to paint his energetic, crowded, colorful works at age 80. The people in Goodman's paintings seem to be from many different parts of the world. Ray Materson (1954–) uses readily available thread unraveled from socks to embroider his miniature pictures. Art making relieved his boredom and helped him pay for a legal defense to obtain his release from prison. Max Romain (1930–), a former hotel bell captain and security guard, began to paint after he retired in 1988. His works are deeply rooted in the spirituality of his Haitian heritage. Ionel Talpazan (1956–), obsessed with space travel, sells works through a New York gallery and on the street. Philip Travers's (1914–) narrative drawings combine text and image with main characters from Lewis Carroll's *Alice in Wonderland* and popular images of King Tut. Mary Whitfield's (1947–) strongest works depict the struggle of African Americans, and David Zeldis's (1952–) delicate pencil-on-paper works belie the inner psychological turmoil he experiences.

Sculpture and Decorative Arts

Gravestones are America's earliest sculptural forms, and Trinity churchyard in Lower Manhattan has several carved stones by the prolific Elizabeth, NJ, stonecutter Ebenezer Price (*b* 1729). His regionally distinctive carvings, which take the forms of soul effigies (benign angels), floral decorations, and shell motifs, are less menacing than earlier New England stone carvings of skulls, death masks, and hourglasses. Price's stones are in cemeteries as far north as Albany. Among New York Colony's most distinctive stylists were Thomas Brown, John Zuricher, and Henry Osbourne, who favored Dutch floral motifs, such as tulips. Stylish tin document boxes, containers, and trays were painted by Ann Butler at the Butler family's shop at Brandy Hill in Greenville, which was active from 1824 to about 1855. Her work exemplifies the artisan trades of 18th- and 19th-century New York. Art by commission or for its own sake was created by Asa Ames (1824–51) of Erie Co. He sculpted wood portraits and created, among other works, a polychromed phrenological bust portrait of a young girl.

Weathervanes proliferated throughout the United States. New York City factory weathervane makers included J. W. Fiske and Co and J. L. Mott Iron Works. The tobacconist shop figure in the form of an American Indian was the most common in the mass of trade and advertising figures that dotted city streets from the last quarter of the 19th century to the beginning of the 20th. Samuel Anderson Robb (1851–1928), from a ship-carving family, headed a shop in New York City that sold many types of trade and advertising figures, including cigar store Indians, sport figures, and likenesses of Punch, a Turk, and Sir Walter Raleigh.

More recent sculptors include Ted Ludwiczak (1927–), a carver of monumental heads into the stones at his house on the banks of the Hudson River, in Haverstraw (Rockland Co), and Mary Shelley (1950–), from Ithaca, who worked as a sign painter and now carves and paints topical bas-reliefs in series such as cows, diners, and water scenes. Joseph Schoell (1907–92), a retired tinsmith and plumber from Long Island, made fanciful tin lawn ornaments for his summer house in Margaretville (Ulster Co). His subjects included the space shuttle *Columbia,* the *Starship Enterprise,* and Disneyland castles. Sulton Rogers (1922–2003), born in Mississippi, lived in Syracuse and whittled caricatures of people and tableaux. Veronica Terrillion's (1908–2003) sculpture garden in Indian River (Lewis Co) is inhabited by life-size human and animal cement forms, several in religious settings. Structural steel worker, Joseph A. Furey's (1906–90) apartment in Park Slope in Brooklyn was a dense mosaic of shells, lima beans, painted cardboard cutouts, and mirrors. Scores of unidentified artists also create distinctive works, including decoys, carnival figures, game boards, signs, decorative carvings, and other three-dimensional objects. The work of folk sculptors and artists has been strengthened by the diverse ethnic backgrounds of the artists. Konstantinos Pilarinos (1940–), a Greek immigrant and traditional orthodox Byzantine icon woodcarver, participated in the Smithsonian Folklife Festival's Master of Building Arts program in 2001. Pysanky, or Ukrainian egg painting, still survives in New York City as a folk art. Sculptors Saturnino Portuondo "Pucho" Odio (1928–) and Gregorio Marzan (1906–97) of New York City's East Harlem, chose subjects as diverse as animals, angels, and the Statue of Liberty, and used materials as varied as wood, plastic, and recycled Elmer's glue caps.

For another illustration see Colonial New York.

Black, Mary C. "Limners of the Upper Hudson Valley" In *American Painting to 1776: A Reappraisal.* Winterthur Conference Report 1971 (Charlottesville: Univ Press of Virginia, 1971)

Black, Mary C., and Jean Lipman. *American Folk Painting* (New York: Bramhall House, 1987)

Blackburn, Roderic H., and Ruth Piwonka. *Remembrance of Patria: Dutch Arts and Culture in Colonial America, 1609–1776* (Albany: Albany Institute of History & Art, 1988)

Lipman, Jean, Elizabeth V. Warren, and Robert Charles Bishop. *Young America: A Folk-Art History* (New York: Hudson Hills Press/Museum of American Folk Art, 1986)

Rosenak, Chuck, and Jan Rosenak. *Museum of American Folk Art Encyclopedia of 20th-Century American Folk Art and Artists* (New York: Abbeville Press, 1990)

Sellen, Betty-Carol, with Cynthia J. Johanson. *Outsider, Self Taught, and Folk Art Annotated Bibliography: Publications and Films of the 20th Century* (Jefferson, NC: McFarland, 2002)

Lee Kogan

folk ballads. The origins of old-time music in New York State rest in the unaccompanied ballads that were brought to the state in the late 18th and early 19th centuries by European settlers. With the opening of the west by the building of the Erie Canal in 1825, English, Scottish, and Irish workers brought their folkways. In Anglo-Celtic customs, folk ballads are realized in several forms and stem from an older English or Irish singing tradition. The so-called Child Ballads, those collected by Francis James Child and published in 1882 as *The English and Scottish Popular Ballads,* are regarded as the foundation for the English ballad tradition and have been gathered in New York State by such collectors as Emelyn Gardner (Schoharie Co, 1912–18), Edith Cutting (Essex Co, 1930s), Marjorie Lansing Porter (Essex and Clinton Cos, 1940s), and Kenneth S. Goldstein (Washington Co, 1970s). These ballads—such as "Butcher's Boy," "Lord Lovell," "Barbara Allen," and "In the Garden"—were performed or recited within a family setting.

Folk ballads in New York State were also found within the 19th- and early 20th-century occupational setting. Work such as lumbering, canal building, farming, and hop picking supported a rich singing tradition. Perhaps no occupation that gave rise to more songs than that of lumbering in the northern woods of the state. The isolation and hard work of the lumbermen provided an environment for both vocal and instrumental music, and such songs as "Lumberman's Alphabet" (early 19th century) and "The Jam on Gerry's Rock" (*ca* 1860) remain well known. Tragedies on the work site as well as within communities often gave rise to narratives, which were frequently printed in 19th-century news sources and then entered the oral tradition by way of song. "Murder in Cohoes," "Shipwreck on Lake Champlain," and "Mary Wyatt," the latter a

19th-century murder ballad from Berlin (Rensselaer Co), are native New York ballads.

In the 20th century, with the rise of the commercial recording industry and mass media entertainment, folk ballads ceased to be part of popular entertainment. The impact of radio has been profound. Although topical compositions, stage and music hall tunes, and Tin Pan Alley songs entered singers' repertoires, local songwriting saw a decline. With the folk revival in the 1960s and onward, local singers began to be once again noticed. Songs by the late Sara Cleveland of Brant Lake (Warren Co) were recorded by folksong collectors Sandy and Caroline Paton and Kenneth Goldstein in Hudson Falls (Washington Co) from 1966 to 1969. Cleveland's recordings include "Ballads and Songs of the Upper Hudson Valley" (1968). During the 1960s the songs of Lawrence Older of Middle Grove (Saratoga Co) were recorded by folklorists Vaughn and George Ward of Rexford (Schenectady Co) and include "Adirondack Songs, Ballads and Fiddle Tunes" (1964). Folklorist Bob Bethke of the University of Delaware recorded several Adirondack singers in St. Lawrence Co during his collecting in the 1970s. While not commonplace, folk ballads can still be heard within community settings. Collections exist at Traditional Arts of Upstate New York in Canton (St. Lawrence Co) and SUNY Albany's Special Collections.

Bethke, Robert. *Adirondack Voices: Woodsmen and Woods Lore* (Urbana: Univ of Illinois Press, 1981)

Ellen McHale

folk dance. Participatory ethnic dance forms, including northern and eastern European, clog, Scandinavian, Israeli, English, Scottish, Irish, and other international dance forms, as well as American contra dances. In the opening decade of the 20th century, New York City's Elizabeth Burchenal traveled to northern Europe and encouraged leaders of the English revival, most notably the pioneering folklorist Cecil Sharp, to help spread what was soon embraced as a European American dance tradition: traditional sword and morris dancing, and the English country dance.

Middle-class reformers embraced folk dancing as an alternative to radical working-class political and recreational culture and to dancing in unchaperoned music halls. Settlement house residents in Buffalo, Rochester, and New York City taught "native" dances as a way to give immigrant children pride in their ethnic cultures and taught English country dances, seen as a European American tradition, to help them assimilate. Children did maypole and morris dancing in Van Cortlandt Park in the Bronx as early as 1909, and by the mid-1920s the Girls' Branch of the Public Schools Athletic League was leading upward of 5,000 children through annual maypole dances and various northern European folk dances in Central Park's Sheep Meadow. In 1915 Sharp established what remains the oldest folk dance group in the nation, the US branch of the English Folk Dance Society (now Country Dance and Song Society). Founded in New York City, it moved to Northampton, Mass, in 1987. In 1916 Burchenal formed the Folk Dance Association of America in New York City. Manhattan's Seventh Regiment Armory hosted the first folk dance Spring Festival in 1926. Held annually until World War II, the festivals grew in size and splendor. In 1929, 368 dancers in 25 different groups participated. In the 1930s radical ethnic politics incorporated folk dance. Adults would gather at Folk Dance House (?1948–67) on West 16th St, one of the nation's leading folk dance venues, run by Michael and Mary Ann Herman, while many of their children were taught the same dances at left-wing, overnight children's camps in the Catskills.

Although cold war hostility to left-wing cultural activities led to a closing of most of the left-wing camps, the same anticommunism led many eastern Europeans to champion their national folk dances, especially in the immigrant urban centers of New York City and Buffalo. A less political folk revival in the postwar era employed a broader definition of "folk" that incorporated ballroom or social dance and focused on country western squares and contra dance as American folk dance. In the 1960s international dance experienced a revival on college campuses. The Brooklyn-based Folk Dance Association (1970) published several national directories and magazines, and their web site remained a key resource in 2003.

Folk dance in the late 20th century gained a broader base as folklorists expanded the term to include all vernacular urban, rural, social, and ritual dances. The earlier emphasis on political content was replaced with a focus on recreation and exercise. The Ethnic Arts Center on Varick St in Manhattan, formed in 1968, renamed itself in 1998 the Center for Traditional Music and Dance, and in 2002 it sponsored a rich program of ethnic, roots, and traditional performance troupes. Meanwhile country and social dance has continued to flourish across New York State. Fiddle and Dance in Ashokan (Ulster Co) remains a center for contra and western squares in summer dance camps for adults and families, and folk dance groups continue to dance in every part of the state in every tradition.

Folk Dance Association, http://www.folkdancing.org
Graff, Ellen. *Stepping Left: Dance and Politics in New York City, 1928–1942* (Durham, NC: Duke Univ Press, 1997)
Tomko, Linda J. *Dancing Class: Gender, Ethnicity, and Social Divides in American Dance, 1890–1920* (Bloomington: Indiana Univ Press, 1999)

Daniel J. Walkowitz

folklore and folklife study. Efforts to collect, preserve, and present the state's folklore and folklife have been active since the late 19th century. Organizations and institutions in New York State have contributed significantly to a national movement to identify the traditions composing American culture. Folklore generally refers to cultural expressions learned by word of mouth, imitation, demonstration, and custom, often emphasizing songs, tales, legends, and speech. Folklife usually refers to the integrated customs of regional, ethnic, religious, and occupational communities, and emphasizes social and material traditions such as crafts, architecture, food, ritual, and festival.

Origins and Pioneers

Wide public notice of regional lore dates to the fiction of Washington Irving (1783–1859), James Fenimore Cooper (1789–1851), and James Kirke Paulding (1778–1860). Taking notice of their use of legends and customs from frontier days, antiquarians such as John Fanning Watson recorded "traditionary lore" from elderly New York City residents who recalled local legends from the colonial period, which he published in *Historic Tales of the Olden Time, Containing Olden Time Researches and Reminiscences of New York City* (1832). After 1846, when "folklore" was coined in England and spread to the United States, formal studies and organizations began to appear. When the American Folklore Society (AFS) formed in 1888, almost a quarter of its members were from the state, and its officers included residents Franz Boas of the magazine *Science,* Thomas Frederick Crane of Cornell University in Ithaca, and H. Carrington Bolton, retired chemistry professor from Trinity College in Hartford, Conn. A New York branch of the AFS formed in February 1893 with Bolton (1843–1903) as president. Franz Boas's internationally prominent teaching of folklore and editing of the *Journal of American Folklore* (1888) at Columbia University helped establish New York City as a center for folklore scholarship, though most folklorists in the city were not working with local materials. One exception was Stewart Culin (1858–1929) of the Brooklyn Museum (president of the AFS in 1897), who explored topics such as city boys' street games, Chinese secret societies, and Italian marionette theater. Influenced by Culin, Allen Eaton of the Russell Sage Foundation in New York City installed influential exhibitions of immigrant folk arts that traveled throughout the state in 1919. The publication (1932) and exhibitions, *Immigrant Gifts to American Life,* emphasized the contributions of immigrants to American culture at a time when restrictions on immigration were being debated.

Educated at Columbia by Boas, Martha Beckwith (1871–1959) held the first chair of folklore in the United States at Vassar College in Poughkeepsie (1920). She established a folklore foundation at the college, which fostered local research including collections of folksongs in Dutchess Co. Teaching at Wayne State University in Detroit, Emelyn Gardner (1872–1967) returned to her native Central New York to collect folklore beginning in 1912 and published *Folklore from the Schoharie Hills* (1937). During the 1930s and 1940s more collectors were attracted to rural New York to recover folktales and folksongs and to understand them as part of regional American culture. Harold Thompson (1891–1963) drew together many such collections to form *Body, Boots and Britches: Folktales, Ballads and Speech from Country New York* (1939). An extension of earlier attention to folksongs and ballads of the southern Appalachians was the collection of the British American legacy in the Catskills and Adirondacks. Camp Woodland in Phoenicia (Ulster Co) was a summer institution for city children that promoted the collection and performance of mountain song and dance. A monumental collection that came out of this period is *Folk Songs of the Catskills* (1982) by Norman Cazden, Herbert Haufrecht, and Norman Studer. A significant regional-occupational collection in the Adirondacks gathered from 1970 to 1977 is Robert Bethke's *Adirondack Voices: Woodsmen and Woods Lore* (1981). Work in urban, occupational, and ethnic folklore was most pronounced in the Living Lore program of the Federal Writers' Project in New

York City during the late 1930s, directed by Benjamin A. Botkin (1901–75). Inspired by this effort Botkin published an anthology entitled *New York City Folklore* (1956).

After World War II: New Trends

Originally affiliated with the New York State Historical Association, the New York Folklore Society was founded in 1944 with a populist orientation. The journal *New York Folklore Quarterly* was launched in 1945 with association director Louis C. Jones (1908–90) as editor. Indicative of the regional split in conceptualizing folklore, society meetings typically alternated between Cooperstown (Otsego Co) and New York City. In 1947 Jones organized the annual Seminars on American Culture during the summer at the association's headquarters in Cooperstown that featured courses for college credit in folklore and folklife. Influenced by the European folk museum movement, which he applied to the interpretation at the Farmers' Museum in Cooperstown, he envisioned a graduate program with an emphasis on fieldwork, history museum interpretation, and material culture research. In 1965 the Cooperstown Graduate Program, offering a master's degree in American folk culture, were launched in cooperation with the New York State Historical Association and SUNY Oneonta (Otsego Co). Between 1965 and the end of the folk culture program in 1979, student-collected materials composed the Archive of New York State Folklife at the New York State Historical Association in Cooperstown. In 2002 folklore and folklife research could be pursued through various university programs and archives and through English, history, anthropology, sociology, American studies, ethnic studies, and performance studies departments. Folklore as a minor or concentration could be taken at Brooklyn College, at SUNY campuses at Binghamton, Fredonia, Potsdam, and Albany, and at New York University, which also has a major in folk art studies.

There are several public programs in folk arts at the state, regional, county, and local levels. The Folk Arts Program at the New York State Council on the Arts (NYSCA) in New York City was founded in 1985 and by 2000 provided funding for over 70 nonprofit organizations. Among prominent public organizations are City Lore and the Institute for African American Folk Culture in New York City, Long Island Traditions in Port Washington, Traditional Arts of Upstate New York in Canton, and Hallockville Museum Farm and Folklife Center in Riverhead. Many local arts councils feature folk arts programs including those in Schoharie, Queens, Genesee-Orleans, Capital Region, and Greater Rochester. They typically offer exhibitions, school programs, folk arts apprenticeships, publications, and festivals. In the 21st century these organizations have created folk arts forums with the encouragement of the NYSCA and the New York Folklore Society. In 1999 the society, one of the largest state folklore groups nationally, set up headquarters in Schenectady and expanded its services to include technical assistance programs and folk archives inventories and standards.

Popularizing and Applying Folklore and Folklife

New York folklorists have been especially active in popularizing and applying folklore and folklife in the public sector, in connecting folk art, material culture, and the study of everyday life to local and regional history, and in understanding emergent urban and ethnic traditions. With public intellectuals such as Thompson, Botkin, and Jones encouraging the collection and popular presentation of folklore to return to common people an awareness of their own traditions, many New York folklore organizations from the 1940s to the 1960s had a reputation among state societies for a populist agenda. They supported "applied folklore" in the form of productions aimed at children, organization of folk festivals, literary retellings of field-collected folklore, and revivals of folk performances. Richard Dorson (1916–82), a New York City native, singled out the work of New York State folklorists for public criticism as director of Indiana University's Folklore Institute. He loudly chided them for distorting the authenticity and social meaning of folklore from the field and for demeaning the scholarly role of the folklorist. Debates between Dorson and the New York folklorists peppered AFS meetings and spilled over into the popular press. At issue was the image that should be projected for folklore in public and academic settings. In answer to the criticism, the New York Folklore Society took an academic turn during the 1970s with the publication of a scholarly journal, *New York Folklore,* which replaced the *Quarterly* in 1975. The bicentennial celebration of American independence in 1976, however, nurtured the growth of many grassroots programs that sought to connect folklore and folklife to a search for subcultural identity in a spreading mass culture. Academically trained folklorists became active in many folk arts programs in the public sector. With this movement public and applied folklore (terms that its practitioners preferred to "popularized") became theorized by folklorists, such as NYSCA Folk Arts Program director Robert Baron, as community cultural empowerment, identity performance building, and cultural diversity promotion. The New York State Folklore Society reemphasized its founding populist orientation in 2000, transforming its scholarly journal *New York Folklore* into a magazine format, retitled *Voices.*

The Folklife Movement

The folklife movement in the United States gained momentum after World War II, especially in Pennsylvania and New York. While folklore had largely been defined as oral tradition, folklife emphasized the persistence of communities that were bound by tradition and often overlooked in histories based on great figures and events. Folklife study reminded Americans of the significance of traditions to historic ways of life and of the self-esteem and sense of belonging they brought. It recorded examples of regional, ethnic, occupational, and religious communities that had not capitulated to pressures of assimilation and modernization. It examined the adaptation and hybridization of cultural forms brought to New York State from New England and Europe. An early focus of inland settlement, the state became especially important in the understanding of regional formation and diffusion of cultural forms westward. The New York State Historical Association complex in Cooperstown includes the Farmers' Museum, an outdoor "folk" museum that re-creates a crossroads village from the early 19th century, the Fenimore Art Museum with its folk art collection, and the Cooperstown Graduate Program, and is often credited with advancing the folklife movement in the United States. Cooperstown-based studies of the integration of crafts, architecture, food, and clothing in the daily life of Central New York State communities inspired many similar fieldwork-based projects throughout the state at local historical societies and museums.

Emergent Urban and Ethnic Traditions

The assumption that folklore persists longest in rural, isolated areas received a challenge as early as the 1890s from folklorists investigating traditions in New York City. While studies at that time focused on "survivals" or "transplants" of folklore from other places to New York City, after the 1930s attention turned increasingly to the effects of the urban environment on the emergence of adapted or new traditions. Whether it is the street and sidewalk games, crime victim stories, or urban legends of alligators in the sewers, New York City residents share a variety of lore connecting them to neighborhoods, boroughs, and the city. Ethnic and religious diversity and intercultural connections drew attention from scholars investigating the emergence of traditions in urban settings. For example, both the distinct and shared folklore and folklife of the city's Chinese, Jewish, Italian, African, Greek, Puerto Rican, and Syrian communities have been documented. City Lore, founded in 1986, has been particularly active in documenting ethnic traditions as well as occupational groups like taxi drivers and subway workers, and has documented the spontaneous shrines in New York City after the 11 Sept 2001 attack on the World Trade Center. Folklore research is less prevalent, but nonetheless significant, in other cities. The New York Folklore Society, for example, has published special issues of *New York Folklore* and *Voices* on the ethnic traditions of Buffalo and Utica, and folk arts organizations are devoted to the cities of Rochester and Binghamton. The 2001 Smithsonian Folklife Festival in Washington, DC featured New York City traditions, highlighting a city rather than a state or region for the first time.

See also Erie Canal in Folklore and the Arts; Mid-Atlantic Region; St. Nicholas.

Bronner, Simon J. *Following Tradition: Folklore in the Discourse of American Culture* (Logan: Utah State Univ Press, 1998)

Dargan, Amanda, and Steven Zeitlin. *City Play* (New Brunswick, NJ: Rutgers Univ Press, 1990)

Jones, Louis C. *Three Eyes on the Past: Exploring New York Folk Life* (Syracuse: Syracuse Univ Press, 1982)

Suter, John, ed. *Working with Folk Materials in New York State* (Ithaca: New York Folklore Society, 1994)

Zygas, Egle, ed. *Proceedings of the 50th Anniversary Fall Conference* (Ithaca: New York Folklore Society, 1995)

Simon J. Bronner

folk magic. See Magic, folk.

folk music revival. Scholarly interest in traditional Anglo-American and African American folk music began in the early decades of the 20th century, but the flowering of performance by traditional and urban musicians, with commercial appeal as well as radical political connections, took off in New York City in the 1930s.

Beginnings

One pioneer was Aunt Molly Jackson, who connected an earthy folk style to the developing communist left. The wife of a Kentucky coal miner and composer of "Ragged Hungry Blues," she moved to New York City in 1931 and soon appeared at local political rallies, recorded for Columbia Records, and settled on the Lower East Side before relocating to the West Coast in 1943. She was one influence on a group of radical composers, including Charles Seeger, Marc Blitzstein, and Aaron Copland, who organized the New York City–based Composers Collective (1932–36) and began to use folk-style songs as an organizing tool. Folk music collectors and promoters John Lomax and his son Alan recorded Lead Belly (Huddie Ledbetter) in Louisiana's Angola Penitentiary in 1933. On 1 Jan 1935 they brought him for a concert to New York City, where he lived until his death in 1949. In late 1938 John Hammond's Carnegie Hall concert Spirituals to Swing featured jazz and blues performers, including Big Bill Broonzy and Sonny Terry. Greenwich Village clubs, such as Barney Josephson's Cafe Society and Max Gordon's Village Vanguard, featured Josh White, Lead Belly, and other folk acts. Woody Guthrie arrived in New York City in March 1940 for a Grapes of Wrath Evening at the Forrest Theater, where he joined Aunt Molly Jackson, Alan Lomax and his sister Bess, Burl Ives, the Golden Gate Quartet (a black gospel ensemble), Margot Mayo's square dance troupe, and a very young Pete Seeger. Alan Lomax brought folk performers before a national radio audience with his *American School of the Air* (1939–41) and *Back Where I Come From* in 1940. At the same time, radio personality and ethnomusicologist Henrietta Yurchenco had a local program on city-owned WNYC.

The Almanac Singers and the Weavers

In late 1940 Pete Seeger met Lee Hays and his roommate Millard Lampell. They moved to Greenwich Village and founded Almanac House, a 12th St loft. The stage was set in 1941 for the organization of the Almanac Singers, a group that performed both topical and traditional songs, drawing upon the growing market for folk music, particularly among the city's political left. The fluctuating group would also include Bess Hawes, Agnes "Sis" Cunningham, Josh White, Woody Guthrie, and various others. Sunday afternoon gatherings attracted the city's growing folk crowd. The Almanac Singers' first recordings, in March 1941, bitterly opposed American preparation for World War II; subsequent recordings, after the German invasion of the Soviet Union and the attack on Pearl Harbor, praised the war effort and the fight against fascism. The group recorded and toured until war work ended their performing. Pete Seeger returned to New York City from army duty in late 1945 and immediately organized People's Songs, a loose group of performers who mixed leftist politics and a love of folk music. Publishing a bulletin and forming a national organization, it was involved with Henry Wallace's Progressive Party presidential campaign of 1948. People's Songs ended the following year, and Seeger joined with Lee Hays, Ronnie Gilbert, and Fred Hellerman to form the Weavers in 1948. Their short but spectacular success (1950–52) demonstrated that folk music had a large national as well as local audience. Meanwhile Oscar Brand had launched his *Folk Song Festival* on WNYC in late 1945, featuring local and national talent, which as of 2002 remained on the air.

While Seeger's career during the 1950s was hampered by political blacklisting because of his connection with Communist Party activities and the 1948 Wallace campaign, he performed on college campuses and in summer camps. The latter served to introduce thousands of young campers to traditional and contemporary folk songs. Norman Studer organized the progressive, integrated Camp Woodland in Phoenicia (Ulster Co) in 1940, which featured Seeger and local Catskills performers whose songs were collected and later published. Folk music flourished at other camps, such as Wo-Chi-Ca (Workers' Children's Camp) in Port Murray, NJ, Kinderland at Sylvan Lake (Dutchess Co), and Unity near Wingdale (Dutchess Co). Folk fans could also listen to Seeger and other performers on records, mostly from companies based in New York City, particularly Folkways Records. Moses "Moe" Asch had begun recording in 1939. For the next four decades, his labels, Asch, Disc, and finally Folkways Records, emerging in 1949, would record and circulate a remarkably eclectic store of music, including that by Woody Guthrie, Lead Belly, and Pete Seeger. Jac Holzman, raised in New York City, started Elektra Records in Greenwich Village in 1952 and quickly released numerous folk albums (the company moved to California in the mid-1960s). Maynard and Seymour Solomon launched Vanguard Records in the city in 1950 as a classical label but soon added folk performers. They issued the influential Weavers' 1955 Carnegie Hall concert album and featured Joan Baez in the 1960s. New York City became the center of folk recording through the 1950s and 1960s.

The 1960s Village Folk Scene

In 1950 *Sing Out!* magazine was launched in New York City by People's Artists. Irwin Silber shortly became the editor. Although *Sing Out!* struggled through the 1950s, it emerged in the early 1960s to play an instrumental role in the developing revival. The magazine moved out of state in 1982. Lee Hoffman launched *Caravan* in 1957, a small, national folk magazine based in Greenwich Village. In 1959 Billy Faier became editor as Hoffman created the short-lived and more locally focused *Gardyloo.* These folk magazines joined a growing number of clubs and coffeehouses in Greenwich Village that featured folk music. Israel G. "Izzy" Young in 1957 opened the Folklore Center on MacDougal St, which served as a vital meeting place and concert venue. After producing folk concerts at Town Hall and Carnegie Hall, Art D'Lugoff opened the Village Gate in early 1958, featuring jazz, folk, and comic acts until its closing in the early 1990s. Gerde's Folk City (1960) and the Bitter End (1961) were two of many folk establishments that appeared. Around the corner during the summer months, artists, including Theodore Bikel, Phil Ochs, Dave Van Ronk, and John Cohen, and fans would gather on Sundays around the fountain in Washington Square Park to pick and sing, a ritual initiated following World War II that reached its peak of popularity during the 1960s.

Throughout the decade New York City, particularly Greenwich Village, played a central role in shaping and promoting folk music. Bob Dylan arrived from Minnesota in early 1961 and connected with Dave Van Ronk and other seasoned performers. Dylan's original compositions appeared in the first issue of *Broadside* magazine in February 1962. Published by Sis Cunningham and her husband Gordon Friesen, *Broadside* quickly became the prime outlet for the increasing number of singer-songwriters, including Pete Seeger, Tom Paxton, Phil Ochs, Malvina Reynolds, and Janis Ian. *Broadside* gave voice to various protest movements, publishing songs of peace, civil rights, the environment, and the women's movement until 1988. In 1961 Izzy Young, Ralph Rinzler, and John Cohen formed the Friends of Old Time Music in Greenwich Village, which sponsored concerts for the blues and old-time musicians who were being rediscovered and brought north, influencing a new generation of musicians to carry on their traditions. Other folk performers included Peter, Paul, and Mary; Peter LaFarge; Eric Andersen; and Len Chandler. The complex New York City music scene, promoted by *New York Times* music critic Robert Shelton, gave shape and scope to the 1960s developing national craze for folk music. Folk clubs and activities spread throughout the state, such as Caffè Lena in Saratoga Springs and the folk festival at Grossinger's Hotel in Liberty (Sullivan Co) in the Catskills. Every college town had a local folk spot either on or off campus.

Recent Decades

The folk music revival peaked in 1964–65. With the arrival of the Beatles in 1964 and the turn toward folk rock by Dylan and others at mid-decade, folk music began to decline in popularity in New York City and nationally. As clubs turned to rock, Izzy Young initiated a series of concerts in the Folklore Center, relocated on 6th Ave, until its closing in 1973. Folk music survived the next three decades with new and old performers alike, although the number of venues became increasingly limited. Folk concerts at Carnegie Hall, however, continued to attract a full house with artists such as Arlo Guthrie, Pete Seeger, and Judy Collins. *Fast Folk*, a series of concerts and a magazine/record (1982–96), carried on the *Broadside* tradition of promoting fledgling singer-songwriters. As the 20th century ended, folk music remained very much alive in New York City and throughout the state, increasingly including a wide range of ethnic styles.

See also Old-time music; Rock music; Woodstock festival.

Cohen, Ronald D. *Rainbow Quest: The Folk Music Revival and American Society, 1940–1970* (Amherst: Univ of Massachusetts Press, 2002)

Cohen, Ronald D., and Jeff Place. *The Best of "Broadside," 1962–1988: Anthems of the American Underground from the Pages of "Broadside" Magazine* (Smithsonian Folkways Recordings SFW CD40130, 2000)

Cohen, Ronald D., and Dave Samuelson. *Songs for Political Action: Folk Music, Topical Songs, and the American Left, 1926–1953* (Bear Family Records BCD 15720, 1996)

Hajdu, David. *Positively 4th Street: The Lives and Times of Joan Baez, Bob Dylan, Mimi Baez Fariña and Richard Fariña* (New York: Farrar, Straus & Giroux, 2001)

Woliver, Robbie. *Bringing It All Back Home: 25 Years of American Music at Folk City* (New York: Pantheon, 1986)

Ronald D. Cohen

Fonda. Village (pop 810) in Mohawk (Montgomery Co). In the late 18th century a community grew to take advantage of the waterpower of Cayadutta Creek; a cotton mill (1811) operated briefly, followed by a woolen mill, a satinet factory (1825–43), a threshing machine factory, and other industries. A post office established in 1806 as Caughnawaga was renamed in 1836, when the community became the county seat and a stop on the Utica and Schenectady Railroad (later New York Central). Local investors formed the Fonda Land Association to develop the new railroad town. The village was incorporated in 1850. The Fonda, Johnstown and Gloversville Railroad (1870) brought industrial and farm products to Fonda for transshipment and carried passengers bound for Adirondack resorts. The Fonda Glove Lining Co (1902) was one of the longer-lived industries; others included a knitting mill, paper mill, flour mill, cheese factory, and broom factory. In the early 21st century Keymark Corp/Kasson and Keller (1946) is Montgomery Co's largest manufacturer, with 655 workers in 2003. Fonda is the site of the Montgomery County Fairgrounds (1864).

James Crawford

football. During the academic year 1875–76, students at Columbia University took up a rugby-like game that had become popular at New England colleges. Columbia joined Harvard, Yale, and Princeton on 23 Nov 1876 to organize the Intercollegiate Football Association, accept standard rugby rules, and begin a series of Thanksgiving Day contests.

Establishment of Collegiate and Scholastic Football

Starting in 1880 the Thanksgiving Day game was held in New York City, either at the Polo Grounds or at Manhattan Field. This contest eventually earned tens of thousands of dollars, and attendance soared from 5,000 at the inaugural game to nearly 40,000 by 1893. Syracuse organized an intercollegiate football team in 1889, and Colgate began a team the following year. West Point cadet Dennis M. Michie suggested a football game between Army and Navy; the rivalry was first played out on the West Point Parade Ground on 29 Nov 1890. Newspapers attracted millions to follow football. Merchants placed banners in store windows, civic leaders held rallies, and fans with no connection to colleges waved pennants and celebrated big games.

By the turn of the century, Cornell nearly matched the strength of Harvard and Yale, and Columbia helped initiate recruiting and scholarships. Most colleges in the state fielded powerful teams, and schools secretly offered stipends, tuition, and board to achieve gridiron success. Escalating violence in the game also served to discredit football. In autumn 1905 there were 20 football fatalities across the nation, 18 of them high school students, and 1 a factory worker on a scrub team. The 25 Nov 1905 death of 19-year-old Union College student Harold Moore, who received a fatal head injury in a contest against New York University (NYU), served as the catalyst for football reform. Columbia temporarily eliminated its football program, and national politicians and college administrators called to disband or reform the sport. At a 28 Dec 1905 meeting in Manhattan, officials from over 60 colleges agreed to create the Intercollegiate Athletic Association, with West Point's Palmer Pierce as president, to protect the integrity of the game and the schools and to set new rules to open the game. The new organization became the National Collegiate Athletic Association in 1910.

At this time college football began supplying professional teams. Canandaigua Academy halfback Henry McDonald played for the Rochester Jeffersons from 1911 through 1917; he was one of the first African American professional players. Cornell was the country's top college football team in 1921, and contests between New York City high schools such as Erasmus Hall and Manual Training or De Witt Clinton and High School of Commerce attracted up to 40,000 fans by the 1920s. Even in places where crowds did not approach those figures, the game transcended many other civic concerns.

Development of Professional Football

Most small towns and neighborhoods within larger cities fielded amateur and semi-pro teams made up of those who simply wanted to play football after work. Although originating in the early 20th century as amateur teams, the Jefferson Avenue squad from Rochester and the Stapleton Football Club of Staten Island began hiring salaried players as the drive to beat rival neighborhood teams or clubs from nearby small towns grew; the teams went on to become two of the most successful semi-pro teams in the state. Professional football derived from this practice as well as from organized professional teams.

Some semi-pro games drew up to 10,000 supporters, and some teams, including the

PROFESSIONAL FOOTBALL TEAMS IN NEW YORK STATE

Dates	Team Name/Name Variants	League
Buffalo		
1920–23	Buffalo All-Americans/	National Football League
1924–25	Buffalo Bisons	National Football League
1926	Buffalo Rangers	National Football League
1927, 1929	Buffalo Bisons	National Football League
1946	Buffalo Bisons/	All-American Football Conference
1947–49	Buffalo Bills	All-American Football Conference
1960–69	Buffalo Bills	American Football League
1970–	Buffalo Bills	National Football League
New York City		
1921	Brickley's Giants (New York)	National Football League
1925	New York Giants	National Football League
1926	Brooklyn Horsemen[a]	American Football League
1926	Brooklyn Lions[a]	National Football League
1926	New York Yankees	American Football League
1927–28	New York Yankees	National Football League
1929–32	Staten Island Stapletons	National Football League
1930–43	Brooklyn Dodgers/	National Football League
1944	Brooklyn Tigers	National Football League
1936	Brooklyn Tigers	American Football League
1936–37	New York Yankees	American Football League
1940	New York Yankees	American Football League
1941	New York Americans	American Football League
1946–48	New York Yankees	All-American Football Conference
1946–48	Brooklyn Dodgers	All-American Football Conference
1949	Brooklyn–New York Yankees	All-American Football Conference
1949	New York Bulldogs	National Football League
1950–51	New York Yanks	National Football League
1960–62	New York Titans	American Football League
1963–69	New York Jets	American Football League
1970–	New York Jets	National Football League
1974	New York Stars	World Football League
Rochester		
1920–25	Rochester Jeffersons	National Football League
1936–37	Rochester Tigers	American Football League
Syracuse		
1921	Syracuse Pros	National Football League
1936	Syracuse/Rochester Braves	American Football League
Tonawanda (Erie Co)		
1921	Kardex	National Football League

Source: T. Maher and B. Gill, eds., *Pro Football Encyclopedia* (1997).

Note: For its first two years (1920–21), the NFL was called the American Professional Football Association.

[a]The Brooklyn Horsemen and Brooklyn Lions merged during the 1926 season and played the remainder of their games as the Brooklion Horsemen.

Compiled by Pamela Cooper

Stapleton Football Club and the Jefferson Avenue squad, achieved so much on-field success that local competition became scarce. Fans tired of lopsided wins, and attendance dropped. To reinvigorate community interest, these clubs looked for other professional teams to play in a national league. Regional champions, including the Rochester Jeffersons and the Buffalo All-Americans, joined the newly formed American Professional Football Association (APFA) in 1920. The Tonawanda Kardex, Syracuse Pros, and New York Brickley's Giants joined the next year but were gone from the league when the APFA changed its name to the National Football League (NFL) in 1922.

Tim Mara's New York Football Giants, created in 1925, helped win over the New York City market for professional football. Losing a considerable amount of money near the end of the first season, Mara, a wealthy bookmaker, nearly disbanded the team. He changed his mind after witnessing over 60,000 customers at the Polo Grounds to see University of Illinois superstar Harold "Red" Grange, who had signed with the Chicago Bears, in action against the Giants on 6 Dec 1925. The Giants lost, but the fans went away happy. In 1929 quarterback Benny Friedman came to the Giants through Mara's purchase of the Detroit Wolverines. Friedman brought the Giants to second place in the NFL and received $10,000 compensation for the 1929 season; most players received between $100 and $150 per game. Friedman played for the Giants from 1929 through 1931 and then for the Brooklyn Dodgers in 1932 and 1933, when he retired to coach football at the City College of New York.

Promoter C. C. Pyle started the American Football League (AFL) with eight teams, including his New York Yankees, in 1926. The league failed at the end of the season, and the New York Yankees moved to the NFL but lasted only two seasons, 1927 and 1928. The renamed Staten Island Stapletons joined the NFL in 1929. Many of these teams had a difficult time. The Rochester Jeffersons only drew a few hundred supporters each game, while Rochester's semi-pro Oxfords and Scalpers, who fielded local talent and played local opponents, attracted as many as 8,000 paying customers. Even in Buffalo, with its successful All-Americans, interest in semi-pro clubs surpassed the NFL.

In the 1940s the All-American Football Conference (AAFC), which functioned from 1946 through 1948, ended discrimination against African Americans that had pervaded professional football since 1934. The AAFC signed African Americans Buddy Young to the New York Yankees and Elmore Harris to the Brooklyn Dodgers in 1947. Emlen Tunnel played for the New York Giants from 1949 through 1958 and became the first African American elected to the professional football Hall of Fame in 1967.

Significant College Teams

New Yorkers also focused on their great school players and teams. Columbia's Sid Luckman, NYU's Ken Strong, Fordham's Seven Blocks of Granite, and Army's Chris "Red" Cagle led their colleges to gridiron glory. In a game that culminated Columbia's 1933 fairy-tale season, Coach Lou Little's notorious double-spin play, KF-79, led to the only score in Columbia's upset victory over Stanford in the 1934 Rose Bowl. Cornell's two-time All-American end, Jerome "Brud" Holland, born in Auburn (Cayuga Co), was one of the most famous African American players of the 1930s. During this period black players also faced discrimination at the college level. In 1929 NYU player David Myers was left off the team when it played West Virginia Wesleyan and Georgia. Syracuse's Wilmeth Sidat-Singh did not play in a game at Maryland in 1937, and NYU refused to allow African American Leonard Bates to play against certain opponents, such as the University of Missouri, in 1940.

Unsurpassed in New York State football are Earl H. "Red" Blaik's Army teams. Blaik's club won the national title in 1944 and 1945 and narrowly missed another in 1946. Only Notre Dame, in a 0–0 tie, stopped Army's "Touchdown Twins," backs Felix A. "Doc" Blanchard and Glenn W. Davis; each won a Heisman Trophy. In 1947 Columbia stunned the nation by defeating Army, ending its 32-game unbeaten streak. Over the next 10 seasons, Blaik fielded 5 more Army squads that were ranked among the top 10. In the late 1940s no New York State high school team was more successful than the Aquinas Institute of Rochester, known as the "Little Notre Dame of the East." Coach Harry Wright's Aquinas Institute averaged 18,000 fans per game and earned recognition as the nation's best by defeating squads from as far away as Michigan and Texas. Since the 1950s Syracuse University has dominated New York college football, winning a national title in 1959 with Heisman-winner Ernie Davis; Syracuse has appeared in 13 bowl games since 1957. Cornell's Ed Marinaro in 1970 led the nation in rushing and in 1971 earned another rushing title, a scoring title, and United Press Internal's (UPI's) award as college player of the year while finishing a close second for the Heisman Trophy.

National Status

Professional football was less popular than the college game until the 1950s, when television launched the NFL ahead of all other sports in terms of revenue and interest. Rule changes made professional football more exciting, and a liberal but controlled policy toward televising contests created large and passionate followings. The 1958 NFL championship game at Yankee Stadium between the Giants and Baltimore Colts, watched by 40 million Americans, demonstrated the unique partnership that television and the NFL had forged and the seemingly unlimited potential for even greater popularity and prosperity. A strong rival league, the American Football League (AFL), was formed in 1960, and the NFL expanded in a race to claim lucrative markets. Communities wanting franchises, such as Buffalo, supported and followed hometown teams. The fan base and television dollars were large enough to support both leagues and many new cities and promised more growth. Since the inception of the NFL, the five boroughs of New York City as well as Buffalo, Syracuse, Rochester, and Tonawanda have fielded 17 NFL franchises.

Two years after Joe Namath's flamboyant style and bold guarantee of victory for his AFL New York Jets against the heavily favored Colts in Super Bowl III helped secure professional football's place at the top of the hierarchy of American sports. The AFL and NFL merged in 1970 under the aegis of the NFL, and the media began dubbing professional football the new national pastime. The three New York State teams in the NFL have had considerable success. The Buffalo Bills earned two AFL championships (1964, 1965) and an unprecedented four consecutive Super Bowl appearances (1991, 1992, 1993, 1994) but without a victory. The Jets stunned the sports world in Super Bowl III (1969), and the Giants added to their storied history with two Super Bowl wins (1987, 1991) in three appearances.

Coenen, Craig. "Little Cities That Led Them: Urban Responses to National Football League Franchises" (PhD diss, Lehigh University, 2001)

Oriard, Michael. *Reading Football: How the Popular Press Created an American Spectacle* (Chapel Hill: Univ of North Carolina Press, 1993)

Smith, Ronald A. *Sports and Freedom: The Rise of Big-Time College Athletics* (New York: Oxford Univ Press, 1988)

Waterson, John Sayle. *College Football: History, Spectacle, Controversy* (Baltimore: Johns Hopkins Univ Press, 2000)

Craig Richard Coenen

Fordham University. Private university. It was founded in 1841 as St. John's College by Bishop John J. Hughes in Fordham Manor [now in Bronx Co]. The first president was Rev John McCloskey, later the first cardinal archbishop of New York. In 1846, the year the college received its state charter and held its first graduation, Hughes transferred it to the Society of Jesus. Augustus J. Thébaud was the first Jesuit president. A diocesan seminary remained on campus until 1860. The School of Law was opened in 1905, and the college changed its name to Fordham University in 1907. Schools of Education, Sociology and Social Service, and Graduate Arts and Sciences were added in 1916, and a business school in 1920. The university's baseball (1859), football (1883), track (1900), basketball (1902), and other athletic programs have a long history. Frankie Frisch (1919), nicknamed the Fordham Flash, had a Hall of Fame career as a baseball player, and from 1935 to 1937 the football team achieved national success with a line known as the Seven Blocks of Granite that included the future coach, Vince Lombardi (1937). In 1955 the university became part of the project to develop Lincoln Center in Manhattan, and during the 1960s the Manhattan-based colleges and schools moved to their new Lincoln Center campus. In 1962 Fordham inaugurated a chapter of Phi Beta Kappa. Thomas More College, an undergraduate college for women, was established in 1964 and merged with Fordham's undergraduate program in 1974. In 1969 the Graduate Institute of Religion and Religious Education was created and the board of trustees enlarged to include a majority of nonclergy. From its opening the school welcomed non-Catholics and in 2002 had 12,916 full-time equivalent students and more than 140 academic programs. In July 2002 Fordham linked a women's college, Marymount, in Tarrytown (Westchester Co) into its undergraduate programs. Distinguished alumni include Cardinals John M. Farley (1867) and Francis Spellman (1911), both archbishops of New York, and New York State governors Martin H. Glynn (1894) and Malcolm Wilson (1933).

Hennessy, Thomas C., ed. *Fordham: The Early Years* (Bronx: Fordham Univ Press, 1998)

Thomas C. Hennessy, SJ

Forestburgh. Town (pop 833) in S Sullivan Co. Settled before the Revolutionary War, the town was formed from Mamakating and Thompson in 1837. It was site of the majestic Mongaup Falls, an 80 ft (24.4 m) three-tiered waterfall, which, prior to its destruction in 1922–23 to form power company reservoirs, was the primary tourist attraction in Sullivan Co. Lumbering and tanning were succeeded by the quarrying of flagstone and curbstone. William Howe Crane and other wealthy men formed the Hartwood Park Association in the 1870s. Author Stephen Crane spent time in his youth on his brother Edmund's land adjacent to the 6,000 ac (2,428 ha) Hartwood Park, and his *Sullivan County Sketches* (1891), while minor, inaugurated his career as a writer of fiction. In contrast, Merriewold Park (1889) was an artists' retreat founded by economist Henry George; a famous resident was Dr Jokichi Takamine (1854–1922), a Japanese American scientist who synthesized adrenaline. Pioneering motion picture director D. W. Griffith made dozens of movies in town between 1909 and 1911, developing such techniques as the fade-out, the close-up, and on-location filming. Forestburgh, which is still heavily wooded, has the smallest population of any town in the county.

John Conway

forest fires. Such fires, primarily human caused, have occurred in New York State since the first human settlement. The topography, weather, and tree species growing in the state all combine to make the area less prone to large fires than the western United States. But there have been large fires in New York State's history. Since 1885 statewide responsibility for forest fire control has rested with the New York State Department of Environmental Conservation and its predecessors. Prior to this date there was little coordinated effort to control forest fires and no accurate record of these conflagrations, though a 1743 law, passed by New York's provincial assembly, authorized any person discovering a fire to obtain all necessary assistance to extinguish it.

Three early years stand out for occurrences of devastating fires, mainly in the Adirondacks and Catskills: in 1899, 79,000 acres (32,000 ha) burned; in 1903, 464,000 acres (188,000 ha); and in 1908, 368,000 acres (149,000 ha). Sparks from railroad locomotives often started early fires; farmers burning brush to clear fields, and campers and hunters leaving unattended fires added to the problem. Another contributor was timber harvesting in the Adirondacks, which concentrated mainly on spruce, fir, and pine: softwoods whose tree parts that were left behind by loggers were very flammable. Dry summers increased the fire danger. Reportedly ash and cinders from fires of these years fell in Albany, and in September 1908 great smoke clouds hung over New York City.

After the 1908 fires the state moved to institute a system of fire control. Forest rangers were hired with fire control as their primary duty. Antiburning laws and requirements to cut softwood tops down to a 3 in (7.6 cm) diameter were established by the state legislature and state governmental agencies for the Adirondacks and Catskills. New federal legislation also provided for fire control throughout the rest of the state, with the federal Weeks Act of 1911 and Clark-McNary Act of 1925 supplying funds for state fire control. By 1910 there were 20 fire observation towers throughout New York State for smoke detection. New towers were added each year with early wooden ones gradually replaced by steel towers; by the 1950s approximately 110 towers were in seasonal use. These structures were concentrated in the Adirondacks and Catskills, with some scattered elsewhere in the state in heavily forested areas.

Fire tower in the Adirondack Mountains.

Following these measures, fire occurrence in the state generally declined, though summers with very hot weather and low rainfall continued to increase the risk of major fires. In 1930 dry weather was a factor in over 2,000 fires, with Gov Franklin D. Roosevelt closing wooded areas to all uses for several days both in the spring and fall. On 25 Nov 1950 a major hurricane blew down trees on 400,000 acres (162,000 ha) in the Adirondacks, and in a unique precedent the state legislature set aside the prohibition on tree cutting in the Forest Preserve to authorize salvage of the downed timber, which threatened to become a fire hazard. But in the summer of 1953, a campfire in Hamilton Co's inaccessible Cold River area east of Long Lake sparked a 250-acre (100 ha) fire.

At the beginning of the 21st century, fires annually burn between 2,000 (800 ha) and 7,000 acres (2,800 ha) of New York State forest, depending on weather conditions. Since the 1970s airplanes have replaced fire observation towers for detection. Major fire danger areas are the eastern Adirondacks with its heavy cover of white pine, the western side of the lower Hudson Valley in Orange and Rockland Cos with its thin rocky soils and generally low summer rainfall, and the pitch pine areas of Long Island's eastern Suffolk Co.

Curth, L. C. *The Forest Rangers: A History of the New York State Forest Ranger Force* (Albany: NYS Department of Environmental Conservation, 1987)

Hugh O. Canham

Forestport. Town (pop 1,692) in NE Oneida Co. Settled in 1795, the town was formed in 1869 from Remsen. The Black River Canal feeder (1848–1922) brought Irish immigrants to the region. Employment was also available in a large tannery and in lumbering, but farming was never significant. White Lake and Otter Lake grew into Adirondack resorts reached by the Mohawk and Malone Railroad (1892); the Otter Lake Hotel was in business from 1893 to 1946. In 1897–98 deliberate breaks in the feeder made by residents created plenty of employment in repairs. A village of Forestport was incorporated from 1903 to 1937. In the late 20th century Oneida Pink Granite Co quarried stone near White Lake. In 2002 Hansen Quarry shipped stone, and Rome Specialty Co manufactured fishing tackle, but many residents commute to Utica and Rome. The summer population is triple the year-round number. In December the Snowmobile Shootout takes place at Woodgate. The northern section of Forestport is the only portion of Oneida Co within the Adirondack Park.

forestry. New York State has been a pioneer in the management of forested land together with associated waters and wasteland. Forests have productive, protective, and social functions. Modern forestry's prime goal is promoting timber harvests, but the science has evolved parallel with the movement to conserve natural resources. New York State's professional foresters work to conserve soil, water, and wildlife and to maintain public recreation sites in wilderness areas.

Early Efforts

Conservation of American forests began during the colonial period. In 1691, to secure a steady supply of timber for ships and masts, William and Mary of England granted a new charter to the Massachusetts Bay Colony reserving trees for the use of the Royal Navy. Certain trees were marked with the Crown's symbol, the "broad arrow," and could be cut or removed only under royal license. Within a few years, this law was extended to the Province of New York and other colonies. In 1772 New York Colony made an additional attempt, one of only a few in the state's history, to limit the size of harvested trees: its assembly passed an act ordering that firewood not be cut from pine trees under 6 inches (15 cm) in diameter or from other trees under 4 inches (10 cm).

In 1820 Gov De Witt Clinton asked the state legislature to halt the sale of state lands in the mountains to protect watersheds vital to the operation of the Erie Canal. Logging stripped the land of trees, which led to soil erosion; soil washed down into rivers, clogged waterways, and jeopardized the navigability of the canal. The legislature voted to protect the watersheds and the canal, and their timely action to limit logging ultimately benefited the state's lumber industry. New York State became a leader in the national lumber trade from the 1820s through the 1890s.

In the post–Civil War era, concern slowly shifted from guarding watersheds to eliminating forest fires, waste, and the destruction of timber. In 1871 the state began paying taxes to local governments for tracts abandoned by lumbermen, and the public domain grew from 17,000 acres (6,880 ha) to over 500,000 acres (202,340 ha) by 1885. In 1873 the *Report of the Commissioner of State Parks* called for protection of the forest, but the state took no action. Ten years later the state

Primeval Forest Cover

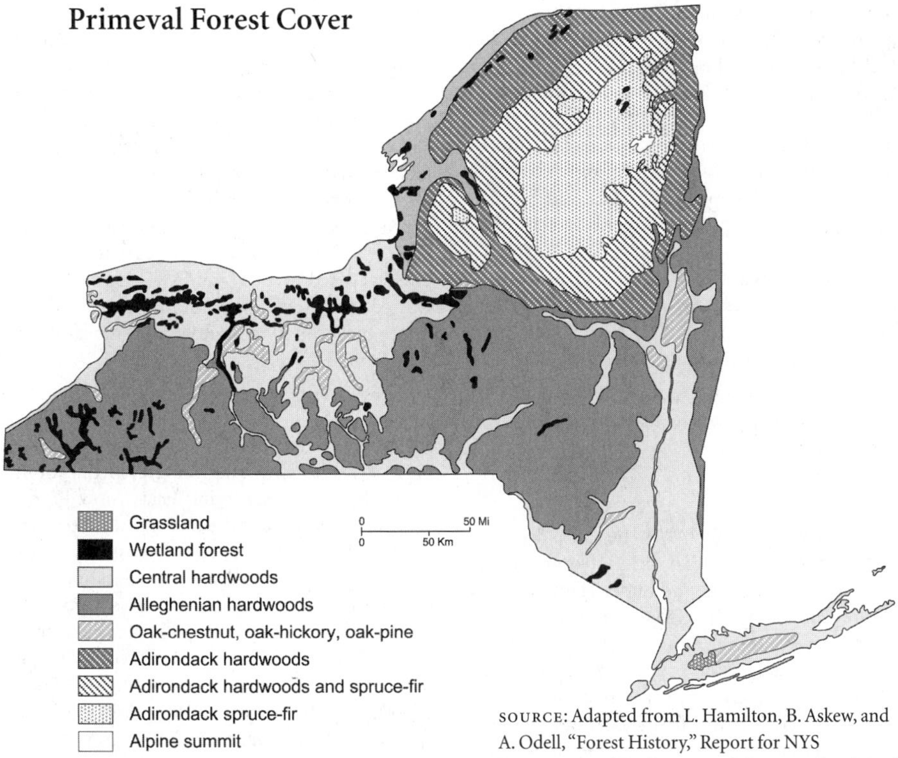

SOURCE: Adapted from L. Hamilton, B. Askew, and A. Odell, "Forest History," Report for NYS Department of Environmental Conservation (1980).

enacted a law forbidding further sale of state-owned lands.

In 1884 the state legislature appointed the Sargent Commission to investigate forest preservation, and a year later, on the commission's recommendation, New York State established the first state forest, which included the Adirondack and Catskill Forest Preserves. The law creating it—drafted by Bernhard Fernow, chief of the US Division of Forestry (predecessor of the US Forest Service)—also urged that forestry be taught in the state's public schools and colleges and that circulars on the proper care of private forests be distributed to the public. Also in 1884, the state legislature created the Forest Commission to oversee custody of the lands and appointed a forest ranger service to police the woods and prevent fires.

Scientific Management

Scientific foresters like Fernow opposed passage of the 1894 forever wild amendment to the state's constitution, which made it illegal to cut timber for any reason on state-owned land. In 1897 the state legislature created the Forest Preserve Board, authorizing it to acquire additional land within the Adirondack Park. Yet the following year the state legislature asserted the necessity for scientific forestry management by establishing the New York State College of Forestry at Cornell University to train scientific foresters and appointing Fernow as dean. The state purchased a 30,000-acre (12,100 ha) forest near Tupper Lake for the school to serve as a demonstration forest. When Fernow moved his lumber operations too close to the school's influential neighbors in 1900, they protested to Gov Benjamin B. Odell Jr. After much wrangling, the school was shut down in 1903. In 1911, the same year the Forest, Fish and Game Commission became the Department of Conservation, a new state forestry school opened at Syracuse University, but the 1903–11 closure of Cornell's College of Forestry had dealt scientific forestry management a significant setback in the state. In the early 1900s the US Division of Forestry designed sustained-yield lumbering plans for several New York State landowners, although few were fully implemented. On state land, preservation remained paramount, limiting foresters' efforts to manage public land through harvesting of trees, as the state continued to expand the Adirondack and Catskill Forest Preserves by buying abandoned farmlands.

Focus on Reforestation

New York State's continued focus on preservation led to the Reforestation Law of 1929 and the Hewitt amendment of 1931; both measures authorized the Department of Conservation to acquire land by gift or purchase for reforestation areas outside the Adirondack and Catskill Forest Preserves. Such reforestation areas, consisting of not less than 500 acres (202 ha) of contiguous land, were to be devoted in perpetuity to "reforestation and the establishment and maintenance thereon of forests for watershed protection, the production of timber, and for recreation and kindred purposes." Any timber production was limited to cutting for forest health only. The areas became the nuclei of New York's present state forest systems outside the Adirondack and Catskill Preserves.

In 1930 the Department of Conservation established forest districts and began the tasks of further land acquisition and reforestation. With depression era forestry budgets reduced, the Civilian Conservation Corps supplied federally funded labor; jobless young men, many from the state's urban areas, planted millions of trees and undertook a range of other projects, including road and trail building, campground and park construction, erosion control, watershed restoration, and forest protection. These activities ushered in a new era of public forestry and provided the basis for the Conservation Department's activities after World War II. Under New York State's Forest Practice Act of 1946, the state was divided into 15 administrative districts, with fire protection expanded to cover 22 million acres (8.9 million ha). Conservation Department foresters also began providing free, on-site technical assistance to private owners of forests. In 1970 the department was renamed the Department of Environmental Conservation (DEC).

As of 1998, 62% of the state, or over 18.6 million acres (7.5 million ha), was forested. Of this land, 3 million acres (1.2 million ha) are protected as forever wild lands, about 1 million acres (405,000 ha) are state forest and wildlife management lands used for timber production and outdoor sports, and 1 million are owned by industrial interests. At the beginning of the 21st century, the DEC's Bureau of Public Lands oversees all forestry activities on New York State's 750,000 acres (304,000 ha) of public land.

Forest Cover, 1978

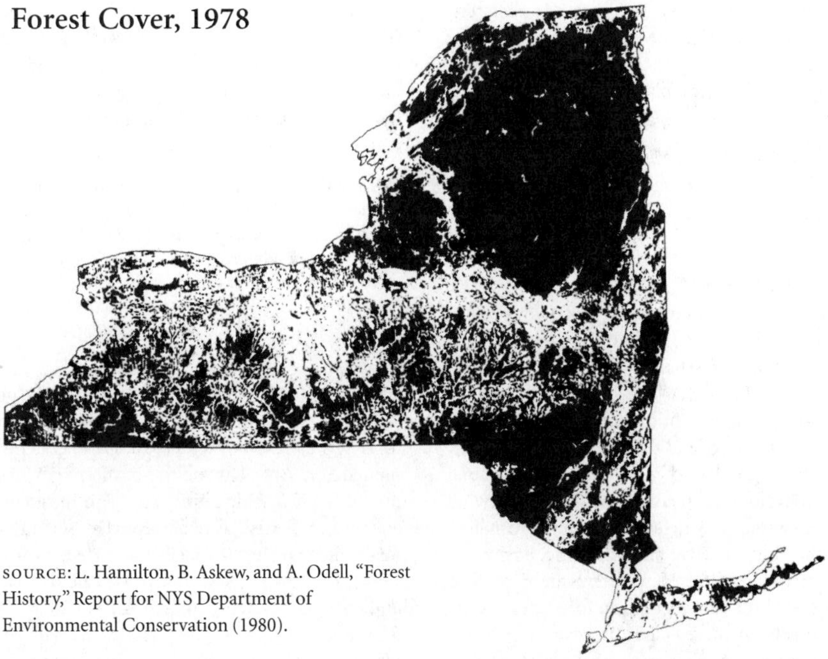

SOURCE: L. Hamilton, B. Askew, and A. Odell, "Forest History," Report for NYS Department of Environmental Conservation (1980).

See also FLORA AND VEGETATION; LUMBER AND TIMBER PRODUCTS.

Cox, Thomas R., Robert S. Maxwell, Phillip D. Thomas, and Joseph J. Malone. *This Well-Wooded Land: Americans and Their Forests from Colonial Times to the Present* (Lincoln: Univ of Nebraska Press, 1985)
McMartin, Barbara. *The Great Forest of the Adirondacks* (Utica: North Country Books, 1994)
Robbins, William G. *American Forestry: A History of National, State, and Private Cooperation* (Lincoln: Univ of Nebraska Press, 1985)
Rodgers, Andrew D., III. *Bernhard Eduard Fernow: A Story of North American Forestry* (Princeton, NJ: Princeton Univ Press, 1951)

James G. Lewis

Forestville. Village (pop 770) in Hanover (Chautauqua Co). In 1808 Jehiel Moore built a sawmill at the falls on Walnut Creek. Originally called Walnut Falls, its post office was established as Forestville in 1823. In the 1830s and 1840s the locality was a drovers' stop. The village incorporated in 1849, and it became a station on two railroads in 1851–52. Grapes, small fruits, and vegetables have been important area crops, packed by a number of companies from 1890 until 1956. The Forestville Apple Festival is held on the first weekend of October.

Mildred L. Becker

forever wild. This clause, ratified in 1894 and now Article 14, Section 1 of the New York State Constitution, requires that state forest preserves "shall be forever kept as wild forest lands." Applying primarily to lands in the Adirondacks and the Catskills, this constitutional mandate was originally intended to end logging in the two regions, which was seen by many as environmentally damaging. Timber companies openly ignored the clause until Gov Theodore Roosevelt enforced this policy in 1898. In 2002 the forever wild clause is interpreted as preventing a wide range of development, not just logging, in these protected lands. The clause applies to over 3 million acres (1.2 million ha) and gives these lands greater protection than the US national parks have. The lands are protected because to develop these preserves, the state constitution must be amended, which requires the approval of two consecutive legislatures and a referendum. The clause is at the heart of contemporary debate over the role of the wilderness and the conflicting demands placed on these lands by different segments of New York State society.

Terrie, Philip C. *Forever Wild: A Cultural History of the Wilderness in the Adirondacks* (Syracuse: Syracuse Univ Press, 1994)

Thomas A. Birkland

Forman, Joshua (*b* Pleasant Valley, Dutchess Co, 6 Sept 1777; *d* Rutherfordton, NC, 4 Aug 1848). Erie Canal promoter and founder of Syracuse. A 1798 graduate of Schenectady's Union College, Forman established a legal practice in 1800 at Onondaga Hollow (Onondaga Co), then a near wilderness. He rose to prominence as a lawyer, county judge, landowner, mill and mineral works developer, and civic benefactor. Following 1807 newspaper articles suggesting a canal to link the Hudson River and Lake Erie, Forman, a new member of the New York State Assembly, introduced the first legislation for such a waterway in 1808. A survey later that year by engineer James Geddes confirmed a possible route, but funding questions and the War of 1812 postponed planning for nearly a decade. In 1819 Forman moved to the future site of downtown Syracuse, a swampy location alongside Onondaga Lake, where he laid out land he owned in town lots. Forman led successful efforts to drain the area and in 1825 represented the community at the opening celebrations for the Erie Canal, which passed through Syracuse. In 1829 he devised a plan to secure bank deposits, enacted that year as New York State's Safety Fund Act. At the time a resident of New Jersey, Forman moved shortly thereafter to North Carolina, where he speculated in land.

Shaw, Ronald E. *Erie Water West: A History of the Erie Canal, 1792–1854* (1966; repr Lexington: Univ Press of Kentucky, 1990)

Gerard T. Koeppel

Fort Amsterdam. Dutch West India Co fort, located at the southern end of Manhattan Island and now the site of the Alexander Hamilton US Custom House at 1 Bowling Green. Fill from excavations for building and subway construction has since separated the original location of the fort from the waterfront by the creation of Battery Park. The fort was first staked out in 1626 after the purchase of Manhattan and the arrival of the surveyor and engineer Cryn Fredericksz. The original plans to construct a large five-star fort, enclosing both public buildings and private dwellings, were abandoned in favor of a more modest design of a fort with four points. The natural defenses of the island and lack of labor probably contributed to the reduction in size. Construction was completed in 1633 under the administration of Director Wouter van Twiller. During the New Netherland period (1624–64, 1673–74) conditions at the fort varied from one under repair and being faced with stone to one described as "a molehill or a tottering wall." Located within the fort was the Reformed Church, barracks for soldiers, the director's and secretary's houses, and a prison. After Director General Petrus Stuyvesant surrendered the fort to an English naval force in September 1664, Fort Amsterdam was renamed Fort James after James, Duke of York and Albany, brother of King Charles II. From then on the fort assumed the name of the reigning sovereign: Willem Hendrick (during the Dutch restoration of 1673–74), James (after King James II), followed by the successive English monarchs: William, Anne, and George.

Gehring, Charles T., trans and ed. *New Netherland Documents, Council Minutes, 1651–1656*, vols 5 and 6 (Syracuse: Syracuse Univ Press, 1983, 1992)
Jameson, J. Franklin, ed. *Narratives of New Netherland, 1609–1664* (New York: Charles Scribner's Sons: New York, 1909)

Charles T. Gehring

Fort Ann. Town (pop 6,417) and village (pop 471) in NW Washington Co. The third of three forts in the present town (1690, 1709, 1711) was named Fort Ann. During the Battle of Fort Ann on 8 July 1777, which hindered John Burgoyne's advance, a British officer reported seeing the Stars and Stripes (officially adopted 14 June 1777). The town was formed as Westfield in 1786 and changed its name to Fort Ann in 1808. The Champlain Canal (1819) made the village a place of commerce, and it was incorporated in 1820. The railroad (later Delaware and Hudson Railroad) came through in 1848. Near Mount Hope, iron was mined (1825–77), and a furnace (1826) produced pig iron; a forge (1828) at West Fort Ann made anchors and chains. At Kane's Falls was another foundry, along with a woolen factory that processed California wool and a glass factory. The town is divided into rugged Adirondack wilderness in the west to Lake George and flat farmland in the east. It is the site of Great Meadow (1911) and Washington (1985) Correctional Facilities at Comstock, whose inmates make up a substantial percentage of the town's population.

R. Paul McCarty

Fort Bull. During the French and Indian War (1754–63), the British built several fortifications along the Oneida Carrying Place [now Rome, Oneida Co] to protect the important supply line from the Mohawk Valley to their post at Oswego. Fort Bull, a wood palisade surrounding four buildings built during the winter of 1755–56, guarded the western terminus of this portage at Wood Creek. The French considered it a threat to their control of Lake Ontario, and by March 1756 an expedition to attack the portage was underway. Lt Joseph-Gaspard Chaussegros de Léry left Fort La Présentation [now Ogdensburg, St. Lawrence Co] with approximately 350 French regulars, provincial troops, and Indian allies and proceeded overland. The exact route is unknown, but they possibly followed what are now the Indian and Black Rivers, attacking and burning Fort Bull on the morning of 27 March and destroying 16 bateaux loaded with supplies destined for Oswego. Approximately 60 British soldiers were killed and another 35 taken prisoner. A small relief party sent from Fort Williams on the eastern end of the carry was quickly overtaken, after which the French returned to Fort La Présentation. Within two months the British were building a new fort at Wood Creek. After the French captured Oswego in August 1756, the British destroyed all of their posts at the Oneida Carrying Place and withdrew to the Mohawk Valley.

Hagerty, Gilbert. *Massacre at Fort Bull: The de Léry Expedition against Oneida Carry, 1756* (Providence, RI: Mowbray, 1971)

Douglas J. Pippin

Fort Clinton. See FORT MONTGOMERY AND FORT CLINTON.

Fort Corchaug and Fort Massapeag. Built at Cutchogue (Suffolk Co) and Massapequa [now in Nassau Co], respectively, by American Indian peoples and in active use from the 1630s to the 1650s. Archaeological studies of the forts show them to be roughly square, palisaded, with corner bastions indicating European influence. Fort Corchaug is 210 x 160 feet (64 x 49 m), and construction was probably directed by Europeans. Massapeag measured approximately 100 x 100 feet (30 x 30 m), and construction may have been directed by the Dutch. Both forts were sites of wampum production and a place of refuge, although no evidence of defense has been recovered. The forts are two of the seven fortified places on Long Island from this period, the largest number of forts recorded for any area in the Northeast. The others were located in Suffolk

Co at Montauk (Old Fort at Fresh Pond and New Fort on the height by Fort Pond, noted in 1661 in *East Hampton Town Records*), on Shelter Island (probably at Sachem's Neck), and two in the Shinnecock area. Excavations have uncovered slight remains of the second Montauk fort, which is the only one to appear on any colonial maps; Old Fort has not been located. The Shelter Island and Shinnecock forts are mentioned in documents but have not been found. Native habitation and/or burial sites are located near the excavated sites.

Stone, Gaynell, ed. *Native Forts of the Long Island Sound Area* (Stony Brook, NY: Suffolk County Archaeological Association, 2002)

Gaynell Stone

Fort Covington. Town (pop 1,645) in N Franklin Co. Settled by Francophone Canadians *ca* 1796 and first called French Mills, the town was renamed for Brig Gen Leonard Covington, who was mortally wounded at Chrysler's Farm (Morrisburg, Ont) during the ill-fated invasion of Canada in 1813. An unfinished blockhouse was occupied by American forces from 1812 to 1814. Akwesasne (St. Regis Indian Reservation) ceded a square mile in 1816 that was surveyed in streets two years later, becoming a market locality. The town was formed in 1817 from Constable. Fort Covington is located at the head of navigation on the Salmon River; steamboats ran from here to Dundee, Que, and manufactured goods could be shipped easily. Woolen factories operated *ca* 1828–1917 as well as a foundry and various woodenware manufactories. The Grand Trunk Railroad came through in 1883. Agriculture was the predominant land use in 2003.

Thomas W. Perrin

Fort Drum. Military base in Jefferson and Lewis Cos. In 1908 Brig Gen Frederick Dent Grant, son of Ulysses S. Grant, conducted training with 8,000 New York National Guard troops and 2,000 regular army troops on an area suggested by the Watertown Chamber of Commerce, about 10,000 acres (4,050 ha) along the Black River. The War Department bought the land in 1909, leasing additional parcels for peacetime maneuvers during the 1930s. The permanent training site became known as Pine Camp. The area was selected for further expansion during the mobilizations for World War II, and by mid-1941 more than 75,000 acres (30,350 ha) were added to the camp. The cantonment area consisted of 240 barracks with 84 mess halls, 144 warehouses and storehouses, 27 officers' barracks, 22 headquarters, 99 recreational buildings, and some buildings for guardhouses and a hospital. The 45th Infantry Division, the 5th Armored Division, and Gen George Patton's 4th Armored Division prepared for war at Pine Camp, where the sandy and lightly treed terrain was excellent for armored and mechanized training. Lying about 9 miles (14 km) northeast of Watertown, the installation was renamed Camp Drum in 1951 for Lt Gen Hugh A. Drum, commander of the First Army during World War II. The area's northern climate made it a suitable location for training troops for the Korean War; since then, it has remained a major training site for Army National Guard and Army Reserve forces from the northeastern areas of the county. The facility became Fort Drum in 1974, when the US Army stationed a permanent presence there. On 3 Dec 1984 the first troops of the 10th Light Infantry Division arrived at Fort Drum; redesignated the 10th Mountain Division (Light Infantry), the unit was officially activated on 13 Feb 1985. Significant construction projects, such as the Inclement Weather Weapons Training Facility, continue into the 21st century. Fort Drum remains an important training center for the Army Reserve and the New York National Guard.

Michael J. Stenzel

Fort Edward. Construction began under Maj Gen Phineas Lyman in 1755 during the French and Indian War on the site of two previous works—Fort Nicholson (1709) and Fort Lydius (1731–45)—at an important portage on the upper Hudson River in what is now Washington Co. The new fort was named Edward by William Johnson after the Battle of Lake George in September 1755 to honor a son of King George II. Following a large fire, military engineers James Montresor and Henry Gordon supervised renovations during the summers of 1756 and 1757. A four-bastioned defensive work built primarily of earth and timber on the eastern bank of the river, the fort shielded Albany from the French to the north. It also served as the concentration point for Maj Gen Jeffery Amherst's forces in capturing the forts at Ticonderoga and Crown Point [now in Essex Co] in 1759. It fell into disuse following the defeat of the French and was abandoned by the British in 1766, although its remains were occupied briefly by both the Americans and the British during the 1777 Saratoga campaign during the Revolutionary War. The Town and Village of Fort Edward developed around the site, which is on the National Register of Historic Places.

Hill, William H. *Old Fort Edward Before 1800: An Account of the Historic Ground Now Occupied by the Village of Fort Edward, New York* (Fort Edward, NY, 1929)

Alexander V. Campbell

Fort Edward. Town (pop 5,892) and village (pop 3,141) in W central Washington Co. Located on the Hudson River, the principal north-south route during the colonial period, it was the site of Fort Nicholson (1709), a small stockade that was soon abandoned. A trading post (1731) was later absorbed into large fortifications called Fort Edward (1755); permanent settlers followed in ?1762. Jane McCrea was murdered in Fort Edward in 1777, on the eve of John Burgoyne's invasion, inciting sympathy for the American cause. The town was formed from Argyle in 1818. Although cloth and lumber were produced before the Champlain Canal opened in 1819 and paper was made as early as 1832, the railroad (1848; later Delaware and Hudson Railroad) stimulated paper (1853), iron (1854), and stoneware (1858) manufacturing. The village incorporated in 1849 and was the site of Fort Edward Institute (1854–1910), a boarding school. In 1940 half the village's workers were employed at the International Paper Co mill (1898–1942). Reopened under new ownership in 1945, the mill was operated by Irving Tissue Co in 2003. Other industries were General Electric (1942) and Decora (1945–2002). In 1993 the county offices were relocated from Salem and Hudson Falls to the Town of Fort Edward. The Old Fort House (1772) is a museum.

R. Paul McCarty

fortifications. American Indian defensible villages, protected by circular or oval palisades, probably appeared between 1100 and 1300 and represent an early form of fortification in the area. Between 1300 and 1500 Iroquois peoples constructed double-walled villages with palisades. In the 16th century these villages became larger and better fortified, and were sited on defensible terrain. Constructed from larger diameter poles, the palisades sometimes were triple-walled with reinforcing bark infill. The Huron, Erie, and Algonquian-speaking Indians in the lower Hudson Valley established similar fortified villages during this period. Observations of the Iroquois by 17th-century Dutch and

Winter training exercises at Fort Drum, 1978.

French explorers noted interlocking timbers, zigzag entrances, and walls 9–30 feet (2.7–9.1 m) high.

Colonial Period

The few principal forts of the colonial period were based on the designs of the French military engineer Sébastien le Prestre de Vauban (1633–1707), emphasizing a low silhouette with masonry walls obscured by outlying sloping earthworks. Bastioned fortifications surrounded by parallel counterscarps, or outer walls, gave many colonial forts in North America a star-shaped appearance. Temporary forts built during various military campaigns, mostly British movements north into New France, were often blockhouses with palisades at strategic points, typically a day's march apart for supply routes. Community defenses such as blockhouses and palisaded buildings also increased, and numerous forts appeared where villages had been established along the Mohawk River at the entrances to major tributaries.

The Dutch West India Co built Fort Nassau in 1614 on an island in the Hudson River near what is now Albany. The wooden redoubt, an outwork without defensive flanks, was subject to frequent flooding and was abandoned in 1617. In 1624 Fort Orange was built on the west bank of the Hudson River three-quarters of a mile (1.6 km) north of Fort Nassau. Built of logs, Fort Orange was a focal point for the fur trade in New Netherland and became a source of contention for Mohawks and Mohicans (Mahicans) competing for manufactured trade goods. To guard their settlement on Manhattan, the Dutch built Fort Amsterdam, a stone fortification with bastions, at the island's southern tip in 1626.

The French venturing south from Canada for exploration and trade with Indians built simple palisaded encampments on major water routes. Such forts appeared as trading camps or debarkation points on Lake Champlain's southern end in the early 1660s and along the Niagara River. With open hostilities between the British and the French in the late 17th and through the mid-18th centuries, forts were established at the terminals of major portage sites. The French built Fort Niagara [now in Porter, Niagara Co] in 1726 on the Niagara River at Lake Ontario on the site of two previous French forts. Originally a stockade around a stone structure, it was enlarged with earthworks and barracks around 1756–57. The French also built Fort Little Niagara [now in Niagara Falls] above the falls and forts at the bottom and top of the Niagara Escarpment. In the Lake Champlain corridor, French forts were usually built of stone. Fort St. Frédéric was built in 1734 in what is now Essex Co and included a barracks, chapel, and fortified tower, surrounded by limestone walls. Fort Carillon was built from 1755 to 1757, also in what is now Essex Co, and had wooden palisade walls filled with earth and faced with stone. By 1759 the British held these forts, the first destroyed and a new larger fort built nearby as Crown Point, the last renamed Ticonderoga.

When the English took control of New Netherland from the Dutch in 1664, the settlements that spread north and west had community blockhouses and fortified farmhouses. Albany grew in size and was completely enclosed by a gated stockade. In 1676 Fort Frederick replaced Fort Orange. Schenectady was another settlement surrounded by a stockade with a blockhouse. Renamed and rebuilt several times, Fort Amsterdam was known as Fort George after 1714 and was used until 1790. In response to the French construction of Fort Niagara, the British built Fort Oswego in 1727 on the Onondaga River [now Oswego River] at Lake Ontario. British-built forts were typically constructed of stockade timbers and earthen embankments. The French and Indian War (1754–63) prompted new fortifications along British trade routes in New York. The portage between Wood Creek and the Mohawk River [now Rome, Oneida Co] became the location of Forts Craven, Williams, Bull, and Newport in 1755. That same year Fort George and Fort Ontario were added near Fort Oswego. By August 1756 the French destroyed or captured all of these forts. In 1758 the British refortified much of the route from the headwaters of the Mohawk River to Oswego. The greatest effort was put into Fort Stanwix [now Rome], built by British general John Stanwix. In the vicinity of Lake Champlain and Lake George, the British built several forts to guard the water route north. Many were built and rebuilt at the same location throughout the colonial period, including Fort Anne [now Fort Ann, Washington Co], Fort William Henry [now in Lake George, Warren Co], and Fort Edward [now in Washington Co].

Revolutionary War Fortifications

During the Revolutionary War (1775–83) the British retained control of Lake Ontario and the St. Lawrence Valley. After 1776 they also occupied New York City and the lower Hudson Valley. Fortifications in the Hudson Highlands and Lake Champlain areas changed hands several times during the war. Albany and the Mohawk Valley remained under Continental control, despite two invasions and numerous raids by the British and their allies.

Many fortifications built during the French and Indian War were still in use, but without the threat of French encroachment, they had been neglected or were poorly garrisoned. New field fortifications were constructed by Continental troops to defend against British attacks. Typically these were individual redoubts connected with earthen curtain walls, hastily constructed with materials at hand. The Battle of Long Island and subsequent actions around New York City from June to November 1776 created a number of such fortifications. After the Continental forces' defeat or withdrawal, the British maintained many of them, and they guarded the British occupation of New York City for the duration of the war.

In 1776 American forces built Fort Montgomery (Orange Co) and Fort Clinton [now in Rockland Co] on the north and south banks of Popolopen Creek with the first chaining of the Hudson River. British forces destroyed both in October 1777. That same month, but farther north, Continental troops were building the field fortifications and redoubts at Bemis Heights [now in Saratoga Co] that eventually led to victory at Saratoga [now Schuylerville, Saratoga Co], blocking the southern advance of Gen John Burgoyne's invasion. The American occupation and reconstruction of Fort Stanwix, which they renamed Fort Schuyler, was partly responsible for halting the advance of British general Barry St. Leger in August 1777 on his way to meet up with Gen Burgoyne. The following year several batteries, two stone fortifications, and a second great chain across the Hudson River were installed at West Point (Orange Co) to defend the Hudson Highlands; they were responsible for holding the British to the south for the duration of the war. In 1780 British general Henry Clinton attempted to take West Point with the help of the American commander at that post. Gen Benedict Arnold's treason was uncovered when Clinton's aide, Maj John André, was caught with plans to West Point and hanged as a spy.

The fortifications of villages and portage points on major navigable waterways remained in use during the Revolutionary War. Communities fortified stone churches and other major masonry buildings with palisades, earthen fieldworks, blockhouses, and barracks for defense when needed. Many throughout the Mohawk Valley, such as the Dutch Reformed Church in Schoharie [now in Schoharie Co], came under attack from loyalists, Indians, and British regulars during the war. The British retained possession of Fort Niagara, Fort Oswego, and Fort Oswegatchie [now Ogdensburg, St. Lawrence Co] until 1796, when they relinquished control in compliance with the Jay Treaty of 1794.

War of 1812

As the British harassed American shipping and impressed American sailors in the early 1800s, relations with Great Britain deteriorated, and concerns for the protection of New York City increased. Major coastal fortifications were built at the entrances and within the harbor. Planned by Jonathan Williams, who served during the war as brigadier general of the New York Militia, they included Castle Williams on Governors Island, Castle Clinton at the Battery, Fort Gibson on Ellis Island, and Fort Wood on Bedloe's Island [now Liberty Island].

Both the American and Canadian sides of the Niagara River were refortified from Fort Niagara to Buffalo during the war. State arsenals of stone, surrounded by palisades, were constructed at Buffalo, Plattsburgh, New York City, Cherry Valley, Rome, Watervliet, and Whitehall to provide weapons and ammunition for the state militia. To protect shipbuilding, navy yards were encircled by numerous redoubt-type structures connected by fieldworks. Fort Tompkins at the Sackets Harbor naval shipyard in Jefferson Co played a role in protecting American troops and the New York Militia in the Battle of Sackets Harbor on 29 May 1813. The following spring the British raided supplies held at Fort Ontario, destined for Sackets Harbor, after the Americans briefly tried restoring the neglected fort. During the Battle of Plattsburgh on 11 Sept 1814, British troops attacked Forts Scott, Brown, and Moreau until they withdrew following the American naval victory on Plattsburgh Bay that same day. In response to the American burning of Newark [now Niagara-on-the-Lake, Ont] in December 1813, the British captured Fort Niagara on 19 December and burned Lewiston (Niagara Co), Buffalo, and most structures on the American side of the Niagara River. They held the fort for the duration of the war.

1815–World War I

During the period 1815–1914 there were major improvements to the coastal fortifications in New York Harbor, such as Fort Hamilton, constructed between 1825 and 1831 in southwestern

Kings Co. To defend New York City from the possibility of warships coming through Long Island Sound, Fort Schuyler was built from 1833 to 1838 on a peninsula in what is now northeastern Bronx Co, and Fort Totten was begun in 1862 in northeastern Queens Co on the East River across from Fort Schuyler. Joseph Gilbert Totten, an 1805 graduate of West Point, was pivotal in planning and constructing seacoast defenses. West Point graduate engineer Capt Robert E. Lee supervised improvements on many New York Harbor forts during the 1840s, such as Fort Hamilton, as well as improvements to Fort Niagara and Fort Ontario, which were used during the Civil War for Confederate prisoners of war. New York State was a major contributor of regiments to the Civil War, and temporary mobilization camps were some of the significant efforts in this period. Permanent camps or barracks had been developed at Fort Porter in Buffalo, Fort Niagara, and Fort Ontario. Madison Barracks and Plattsburgh Barracks replaced the battle forts at Sackets Harbor and Plattsburgh. New York State armories, built in the late 1800s, were often designed to resemble castles but still had many features to make them defendable. They became models for armories in other states.

The Spanish-American War of 1898 caused an extensive upgrading of the coastal fortifications around New York Harbor, and new coastal fortifications were developed at Long Island's eastern tip and on islands covering the entrances into Long Island Sound, such as Fort Michie on Great Gull Island. Additional mobilization and training camps were established on Long Island. These coastal forts were typically spread over a large area and had a cantonment. The gun batteries were named and consisted of a mix of 12 in. mortars and 6 and 3 in. guns.

The 20th and 21st Centuries

During the 20th century the concept of fortifications changed radically, from heavily fortified walls to cantonment areas with widely dispersed batteries constructed of concrete with earthen embankments to hide the positions. The changes were initially driven by the firepower of the more modern naval ships, but by midcentury the dispersion was dictated by airpower. Starting about 1915 aviation became an integral part of military planning, and one of the earliest airfields was Hazelhurst (Nassau Co) on the Hempstead Plains in 1915. Some harbor control posts had trenches and barbed wire, with minefields protecting underground buildings. Training camps and mobilization sites had cantonment areas with vast training grounds for modern mechanized armies and long-range weapons training.

After the United States declared war with Germany on 6 Apr 1917, a system of 16 training camps, located throughout the nation, was mandated. Located 60 miles (96.6 km) east of New York City on Long Island, Camp Upton was one of them; its specifications included 10 miles (16.1 km) of paved roads and 1,400 buildings, including barracks, stables, a hospital, a laundry, administration buildings, and accommodations for carrier pigeons. There were no substantial changes to fortifications in New York during World War I. Most major installations at Fort Niagara, Fort Ontario, Madison Barracks, and Plattsburgh Barracks remained in use, and additional training and mobilization camps were established as needed. The coastal defenses remained in use around New York Harbor and on the outer reaches of Long Island. Because of no perceived threat, these defenses were not expanded; the major concern was sabotage.

The coastal defenses began to be upgraded in the 1920s with larger guns of 12 and 10 inches on disappearing carriages, and parapets offered the gun crews protection during reloading. The installations in New York Harbor had their guns removed, and although these old coastal forts remained in use as headquarters and training posts, they no longer had direct fire defensive roles. With the larger guns farther out, a number of small rapid-firing guns were added near the harbor entrances to stop small high-speed assault boats. Created about 1917, Fort Tilden on the Rockaway Peninsula of Queens in 1941 had 16 in. guns added in coordination with similar batteries in New Jersey. A new 16 in. gun post, Camp Hero, was added at Montauk (Suffolk Co) in 1941. Army airfields throughout the state were expanded during this period.

Going into World War II, Pine Camp was developed in Jefferson and Lewis Cos about 9 miles (15 km) northeast of Watertown and expanded as a major training site for the new mechanized armies. An additional 75,000 acres (30,350 ha) and hundreds of buildings were added, accommodating the training of the 4th and 5th Armored Divisions and 45th Infantry Division. Renamed Camp Drum in 1951, it remained a major training site through the Korean War. Other major installations started in the early 1940s were the Sampson Naval Training Station in Seneca Co on the east shore of Seneca Lake, nearby Seneca Army Depot in Romulus (Seneca Co) and Griffiss Air Force Base adjacent to Rome. After World War II most minor training camps around old forts and barracks were gradually closed. The increased use of strategic airpower to strike behind the lines at sites of industrial and political significance rendered coastal defenses obsolete as a first line of defense. The coastal artillery posts closed, and their defensive missions were taken over by larger inland air interceptor bases such as Niagara Falls and Hancock Field, with Stewart Air Force Base as the Northeast Sector Headquarters. At this time New York State had some of its first offensive bases with strategic bomber units at Rome (Griffiss AFB) and Plattsburgh. Air bases far inland, with fast interceptors to meet the threat offshore, had become the defensive plan. Camp Drum was redesignated Fort Drum in 1974 and remained a major reserve training site, and West Point remained the army's Military Academy.

New York's fortifications moved into the missile age with the Nike Hercules program from 1958 to 1974. These missiles guarded defense plants on eastern Long Island, New York City, and the Buffalo–Niagara Falls area. Typically these were control centers with radar and missile batteries, sometimes miles apart. There were five to seven such installations often 10–15 miles (16–24 km) apart surrounding a defensive area. New York State had an Atlas F Intercontinental Ballistic Missile Squadron with 14 missile silos around the Plattsburgh AFB from 1961 to 1965. The standard had become wide dispersion and underground missile silos designed to withstand overpressure of 1,000–5,000 pounds per square inch (psi) (70–350 kg/cm^2). Bomarc surface-to-air cruise missiles along with fighter interceptors, centrally controlled from an air defense electronic air surveillance and weapons control facility at Hancock Field, were at Niagara Falls and Suffolk Co from 1961 to 1969. The end of the Cold War in 1991 meant the closing of missile, interceptor, and strategic bomber bases, as well as depots and naval ports. The New York Air National Guard continues to use many bases for air transport, air rescue missions, and a fighter wing. Fort Drum remains in use as home of the 10th Mountain Division.

The American Revolution in New York (Albany: Division of Archives and History, 1926)

Bliven, Bruce, Jr. *Under the Guns: New York, 1775–1776* (New York: Harper & Row, 1972)

Diamant, Lincoln. *Chaining the Hudson: The Fight for the River in the American Revolution* (New York: Kensington Publishing, 1989)

Everest, Allan S. *The War of 1812 in the Champlain Valley* (Syracuse: Syracuse Univ Press, 1981)

Hamilton, Edward P. *The French and Indian Wars: The Story of Battles and Forts in the Wilderness* (Garden City, NY: Doubleday, 1962)

Howard, Robert West. *Thundergate: The Forts of Niagara* (Englewood Cliffs, NJ: Prentice-Hall, 1968)

Lonnquest, John C., and David F. Winkler, *To Defend and Deter: The Legacy of the US Cold War Missile Program.* Special Report 97/01 (Champaign, Ill: US Army Construction Engineering Research Laboratory, 1996)

Roberts, Robert B. *Encyclopedia of Historic Forts: The Military, Pioneer, and Trading Posts of the United States* (New York: Macmillan, 1988)

Starbuck, David R. *The Great Warpath: British Military Sites from Albany to Crown Point* (London: Univ Press of England, 1999)

Vrooman, John J. *Forts and Firesides of the Mohawk Country, New York* (Johnstown, NY: Baronet Litho, 1951)

Michael J. Stenzel

Fort Johnson. Home of Sir William Johnson in what is now Montgomery Co. Johnson arrived in the Mohawk Valley in 1738, charged with overseeing the estate of his uncle, Adm Peter Warren, at the confluence of the Mohawk and Schoharie Rivers. Within a decade he amassed considerable property of his own along the Mohawk River north of his uncle's estate. The home he built at this site in 1749 became known as Fort Johnson because of the fortifications it provided for the surrounding community. It served, while he lived there, as a site for Indian treaty councils and as a center for colonists working his land and using his mills and store. In 1763 he moved to the Georgian-style Johnson Hall in what is now Johnstown (Fulton Co), and his son John moved into Fort Johnson. In 1776 the property was confiscated by New York State after John Johnson fled to Canada to avoid arrest for his loyalist sympathies. It then passed through several owners until the early 20th century, when the Montgomery County Historical Society acquired it and opened it to the public.

Hamilton, Milton W. *Sir William Johnson: Colonial American, 1715–1763* (Port Washington, NY: Kennikat, 1976)

Timothy J. Shannon

Fort Johnson. Village (pop 491) in Amsterdam (Montgomery Co). Sir William Johnson bought land in 1747 and built his stone house, now a museum called Old Fort Johnson, in 1749; it was the site of important treaty negotiations with the Iroquois. Crossed by the Utica and Schenectady Railroad (1836), the locality acquired a post office named Akin in 1882, which was renamed Fort Johnson in 1912. The A. V. Morris and Sons Knitting Mill (1887) employed as many as 150 workers. The village was incorporated in 1909 and remains small and residential, with some service business in the early 21st century. Old Fort Johnson has an elegant 18th-century privy, and the house itself is considered one of the finest Georgian houses in America.

James Crawford

Fort Lévis. Built in 1759 by the French on Isle Royale [now Chimney Island], 3 miles (5 km) northeast of Fort La Presentation [now Ogdensburg, St Lawrence Co], the fort was to protect the western approaches of the St. Lawrence River. It was named for François Gaston, Duc de Lévis, the commander of French forces in Canada. Hastily constructed of earth and timber, the asymmetric polygon was surrounded by a moat approximately 30 feet (9 m) wide and 12 feet (4 m) deep. On 18 Aug 1760 a British force of 10,000 men led by Maj Gen Jeffery Amherst encircled the island stronghold and began an eight-day siege. Led by garrison commander Capt Pierre Pouchot, the defenders were able to resist one amphibious assault on 23 August but were forced to surrender two days later following a sustained artillery bombardment. Amherst renamed the fort William Augustus in honor of King George II's son and proceeded downriver to capture Montreal on 8 Sept 1760. The fort was abandoned by the British in 1766.

Pouchot, Pierre. *Memoirs on the Late War in North America between France and England.* Trans Michael Cardy, ed. Brian Leigh Dunnigan (Youngstown, NY: Old Fort Niagara Association, 1994)

Alexander V. Campbell

Fort Massapeag. See FORT CORCHAUG AND FORT MASSAPEAG.

Fort Montgomery and Fort Clinton. In late February 1776, along the west bank of the Hudson River at the mouth of Popolopen Creek in Orange Co, Capt William Smith laid out Fort Montgomery for the Continental army. Six months later, Lt Thomas Machin supervised the building of Fort Clinton in what is now Rockland Co on a hill just south of the creek. In October 1777 British lieutenant general Sir Henry Clinton planned a diversion to draw off American forces opposing Lt Gen John Burgoyne's expedition into New York State from Canada. Clinton led a naval armada bearing 3,000 soldiers up the Hudson River to the vicinity of Stony Point [now in Rockland Co]. Landing some soldiers on the eastern bank of the river on the night of 5 October, Clinton landed the majority of his troops the following morning on the western bank at Stony Point. This deception fooled Maj Gen Israel Putnam, the American commander at Peekskill (Westchester Co), who expected to engage the British with his 1,500 troops. Clinton led 2,100 men, including loyalists, Hessians, and regulars, in an attack against the landward approaches of Forts Montgomery and Clinton. American brigadier general George Clinton, the newly elected governor of New York, and his brother, Brig Gen James Clinton, both distant cousins of the British general commanding the attack against them, had to defend the two forts with a garrison of fewer than 700 men. The posts fell to overwhelming British attack by nightfall. Approximately 70 Americans were killed, 40 wounded, and 240 captured. The Americans nonetheless exacted a substantial price, killing 40 and wounding 150 of their attackers.

Although British forces won the battle, the engagement disrupted Sir Henry Clinton's timetable, complicating attempts to relieve Burgoyne's trapped army. One of the American obstacles to halt the British advance was an enormous iron chain on wooden rafts stretched across the Hudson River near Fort Montgomery. The chain proved to be only a minor delay, however, and after the battle Clinton sent 1,600 men north, eventually burning Kingston (Ulster Co) before receiving news of Burgoyne's surrender at Saratoga. Returning to New York City by the end of October 1777, the British abandoned the Hudson Highlands. The remnants of Fort Montgomery became a New York State historic site on 6 Oct 2002, the 225th anniversary of the battle.

Carr, William H., and Richard J. Koke. *Twin Forts of the Popolopen: Forts Clinton and Montgomery, New York, 1775–1777* (Bear Mountain, NY: Commissioners of the Palisades Interstate Park; American Scenic and Historic Preservation Society, 1937)
Diamant, Lincoln. *Chaining the Hudson: The Fight for the River in the American Revolution* (New York: Carol Publishing Group, 1994)

James M. Johnson

Fort Niagara. Strategic fortification at the mouth of the Niagara River at Lake Ontario, on what is now the US side. The French were the first Europeans to occupy this site. Two early fortifications were briefly occupied, Fort Conti, built by the explorer René-Robert Cavelier de la Salle in 1679, and Fort Denonville, built by the Marquis de Denonville in 1687. A permanent fort with a defensible stone house and stockade was built in 1726. In building it the French took control of the portage around Niagara Falls and secured communications across Canada, the upper Great Lakes, and Louisiana. From that time until the end of the War of 1812, Fort Niagara would dominate military affairs in western New York State.

The fort was central to the conflict on Lake Ontario during the French and Indian War and served as a base for French raids against the British frontier. Capt Pierre Pouchot completely rebuilt the fortifications in 1755–57 to their existing form. Bordered by the lake to the north and river to the west, the fort's defenses comprised earthen walls, half-bastions, ditches, and outer works facing inland, designed in the style of French military engineer Sébastien le Prestre de Vauban. The British and their Iroquois allies besieged Fort Niagara for 19 days in July 1759, and Pouchot surrendered his garrison on 25 July. During the American Revolution the fort was crucial to the British defense of the Great Lakes region. Fort Niagara was a haven for loyalist and Iroquois refugees and a base from which raids were launched against the frontiers of New York and Pennsylvania. The Treaty of Paris of 1783 placed Fort Niagara in US territory, but the British retained control until the Jay Treaty of 1794 enabled its peaceful transfer to the United States on 10 Aug 1796.

Fort Niagara thereafter faced British fortifications on the Canadian side of the Niagara River and was on the front lines of the War of 1812. It was the base for a US invasion of Canada in May 1813 but was in turn captured by a surprise British assault on the night of 19 Dec 1813 and not returned to US control until 22 May 1815. The fort lost much of its strategic importance during the 1820s, when the Erie and Welland Canals diverted traffic from the Niagara portage. A garrison remained, however, and the fortifications were modernized during periods of border tension in the 1840s and 1860s.

By the end of the Civil War, Fort Niagara was obsolete and subsequent expansion occurred outside the historic walls. From the early 1870s through the 1940s hundreds of buildings even-

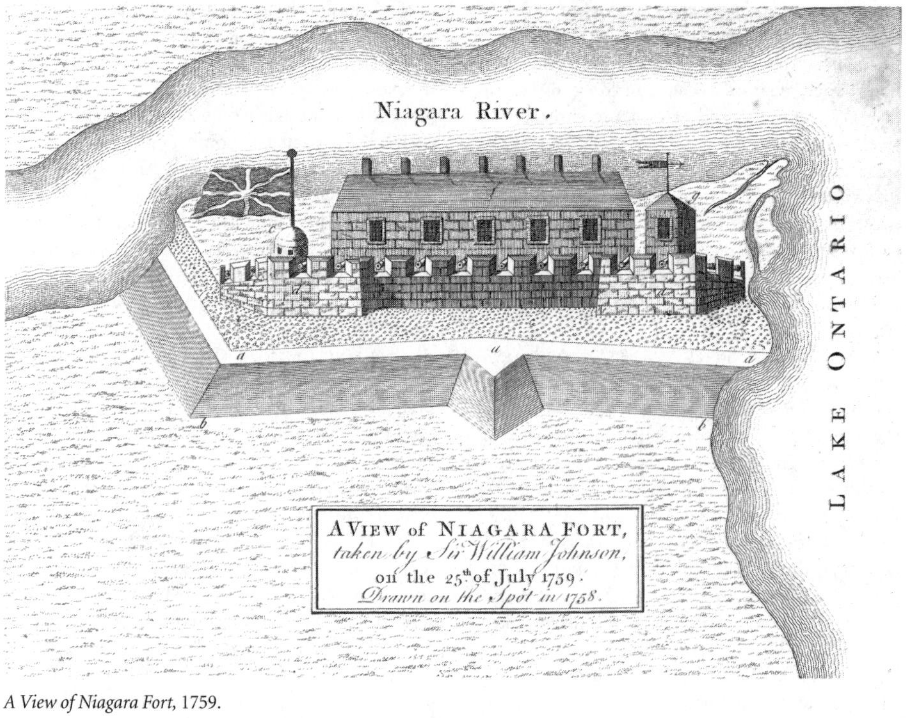

A View of Niagara Fort, 1759.

tually occupied an extensive military reserve around the old fort. Fort Niagara was a training camp during World War I, an induction center and prisoner of war compound during World War II, and an anti-aircraft defense headquarters during the Cold War. The historic defensive works and buildings of the fort were restored between 1926 and 1934 in a cooperative effort between the US Army and the Old Fort Niagara Association. The army closed the post in 1963 and transferred it to New York State. The fort is a National Historic Landmark and a New York State Historic Site.

Dunnigan, Brian Leigh, and Patricia Kay Scott. *Old Fort Niagara in Three Centuries: A History of Its Development* (Youngstown, NY: Old Fort Niagara Association, 1991)

Brian Leigh Dunnigan

Fort Ontario. Fortification and settlement at the mouth of the Oswego River, in what is now the City of Oswego. Many names were used for the 18th-century forts on the site. The first permanent European settlement was a palisaded British trading post established in 1722. Within a few years, furs sent from Oswego made up approximately two-thirds of the volume traded in Albany. This post was followed by a stone fortification on the west bank of the river in 1727 in response to the French construction of Fort Niagara [now in Porter, Niagara Co] at the mouth of the Niagara River in 1726. Known as Fort Oswego, parts of the same fortification were also known as Fort Burnet and Fort Pepperell. It was the only British outpost on the Great Lakes until the French and Indian War (1754–63). The French referred to the fort, and Oswego in general, as Chouaguen.

Maj Gen William Shirley ordered the construction of two additional earthwork fortifications at Oswego in 1755 in preparation of an attack on Fort Niagara that was eventually abandoned. Fort George was sometimes known as Fort Rascal or the West Fort and was located on a hill about half a mile southwest of Fort Oswego. Its construction was never finished. Situated on high ground east of the river, Fort Ontario was also called the Fort of the Six Nations or the East Fort. Viewed as a threat to Fort Niagara, the Oswego fortifications were attacked and destroyed by French forces under the Marquis de Montcalm in August 1756. For several years the British left no permanent garrison at Oswego, but it became a staging area for several large campaigns. It was the launching point for Col John Bradstreet's attack and capture of Fort Frontenac [now Kingston, Ont] in August 1758. Brig Gen John Prideaux and Sir William Johnson assembled their forces at Oswego before capturing Fort Niagara in July 1759. They assigned a small garrison to Fort Ontario, under Brig Gen Thomas Gage, directed to make repairs to the fort. Maj Gen Jeffery Amherst left Oswego in August 1760 in a campaign to take Montreal that led to the French surrender of New France. The British victory and subsequent claim to the Ohio Country ignited Pontiac's War in 1763. Three years later Pontiac capitulated to English authority and signed a treaty at Oswego, negotiated by Sir William Johnson.

At the start of the Revolutionary War, Fort Ontario was mostly deserted but resumed its role as a staging point for military campaigns when Gen Barry St. Leger assembled his combined British, German, provincial, and Indian forces in the summer of 1777 to launch the western component of Gen John Burgoyne's invasion of New York. The British did not make an effort to refortify Fort Ontario until 1782, when Maj John Ross arrived on 15 April with about 500 troops from the British post at Carleton Island [now in Jefferson Co]. The last action of the war in New York took place at Fort Ontario in February 1783. Leading troops from New York and Rhode Island, Col Marinus Willett attempted a surprise attack of the fort but withdrew when discovered at the last minute. During this expedition, news arrived in New York that Great Britain and America agreed to an end of hostilities. The British occupied Fort Ontario until 1796, when they turned it over to the United States in compliance with Jay's Treaty.

American troops were forced to evacuate Fort Ontario during the War of 1812. On 6 May 1814 a British squadron under the command of Sir James Yeo briefly captured the fort and seized a large quantity of stores destined for the American shipyard at Sackets Harbor (Jefferson Co). The US Army kept a small garrison at Fort Ontario for the rest of the 19th century. The post gradually expanded beyond the fort to the adjacent property during this time. From 1863 to 1871 the army reinforced the fort's exterior with stone walls and replaced several interior buildings. The post was expanded substantially from 1903–5 through the 1940s. In the 20th century it served primarily as a training center and during World War I as a hospital. Troop capacity after 1905 increased from approximately 500 to 5,000 by World War II. At that time there were 125 buildings on the post.

Circumventing US immigration law in August 1944, Pres Franklin D. Roosevelt arranged for 982 Jewish refugees to stay at Fort Ontario as his "guests." Because of their uncertain immigration status, they were confined behind barbed wire and allowed to leave only with permission for short periods. The camp remained occupied until January 1946, by which time most refugees were allowed to stay in the United States. Later that year, the federal government transferred Fort Ontario, by then too small to meet the needs of the army, to New York State. It became a state historic site in 1951. Today it is restored and interpreted to reflect the period immediately following the Civil War. A museum dedicated to the Holocaust refugees is also located at the fort.

Anderson, Fred. *Crucible of War: The Seven Years' War and the Fate of Empire in British North America, 1754–1766* (New York: Vintage Books, 2000)
Gruber, Ruth. *Haven: The Dramatic Story of 1,000 World War II Refugees and How They Came to America*, rev ed (New York: Random House, 2000)
Scott, Stuart D., and Patricia Kay Scott. *Fort Ontario Archaeology* (East Amherst, NY: NYS Office of Parks, Recreation, and Historic Preservation, 1984)

Douglas J. Pippin

Fort Ontario Emergency Refugee Shelter. A temporary camp established in August 1944 at Oswego to house war refugees, primarily Jews. Early in 1944 John Pehle, director of the War Refugee Board (WRB), and Josiah DuBois Jr, its counsel, urged Pres Franklin D. Roosevelt to establish temporary havens, or "free ports," for Jewish refugees. Simultaneously the Emergency Committee to Save the Jewish People of Europe dramatized the need for rescue. Many prominent Americans, including former Gov Alfred E. Smith, Syracuse University chancellor William P. Tolley, and *New York Post* columnist Samuel Grafton, endorsed the idea of temporary havens. Roosevelt announced on 9 June 1944 that the United States would admit 1,000 refugees. As a concession to immigration restrictionists in Congress, the refugees would not be considered immigrants and were to return to Europe after the war. Some in Congress denounced even this limited gesture.

The group, selected by WRB and War Relocation Authority (WRA) officials from among 3,000 applicants, left Naples, Italy, on 21 July 1944 aboard the troopship *Henry Gibbins.* Of the 982 refugees, 874 were Jewish, 73 Roman Catholic, 28 Greek Orthodox, and 7 Protestant. Most of the refugees came from Poland, Austria, Germany, and Czechoslovakia. They disembarked in Hoboken, NJ, on 4 August and arrived the following day at Fort Ontario, a former US Army training camp whose relatively remote location, it was thought, would help deflect criticism from anti-immigrationists. The WRA ran the shelter and Joseph H. Smart served as settlement director. A barbwire fence surrounded the camp, and guards prevented the refugees from leaving without permission. They were allowed out to visit Oswego for six hours at a time, or to harvest crops, where they worked alongside German prisoners of war. Jewish organizations in Syracuse, Oswego, Utica, Rochester, and Buffalo organized a committee that cooperated with voluntary agencies like the Catholic Refugee Service to provide educational, recreational, and cultural assistance. Refugee children attended Oswego's public and parochial schools.

Soon after their arrival, the refugees formed a Freedom Committee to appeal for their release. In May 1945, following Roosevelt's death, Smart resigned as director to organize the Friends of the Fort Ontario Guest Refugees and to lobby for their freedom. New York representative Samuel Dickstein, who chaired the House Committee on Immigration and Naturalization, held a subcommittee hearing on the refugee issue in Oswego on 25–26 June 1945, but it had little impact on antirefugee sentiment in Congress. The uncertainty over their status, the forced confinement, and the war's end led 69 refugees to return to Europe. The others continued to wait for Pres Harry S. Truman to act. In December 1945 he issued a directive allowing the Fort Ontario refugees to apply for admission to the United States under existing quotas. Government representatives processed the refugees in January 1946, and after applying from Niagara Falls, Ont, they reentered the United States as legal immigrants, most within a few weeks. Fort Ontario closed on 28 Feb 1946.

In 1985 the New York State Museum in Albany presented an exhibit on the Fort Ontario refugees. As early as 1989 Oswego mayor John Sullivan organized support for a museum commemorating the refugee shelter; these plans were finally realized when the Safe Haven Museum and Education Center, occupying what had been the shelter's administration building, was dedicated on 6 Oct 2002. A traveling exhibition, sponsored by the Holocaust Museum and Study Center in Spring Valley (Rockland Co), was launched in the fall of 2003. The refugees' experience has been the basis of several documentaries, a television miniseries, and a musical.

Baron, Lawrence. "Haven from the Holocaust: Oswego, NY, 1944–1946," *New York History* 64 (Jan 1983): 4–34

Gruber, Ruth. *Haven: The Dramatic Story of 1,000 World War II Refugees and How They Came to America,* rev ed. (New York: Random House, 2000)

Lowenstein, Sharon R. *Token Refuge: The Story of the Jewish Refugee Shelter at Oswego, 1944–1946* (Bloomington: Indiana Univ Press, 1986)

Harvey Strum

Fort Orange. The fort was built by the Dutch West India Co in 1624 on the low, flat west bank of the Hudson River at a location in what is now within the City of Albany. It was small (intended to replace old Fort Nassau) was surrounded on three sides by a wide moat open on the east side to the river. Fort Orange became a major fur trading center, within which the company built its headquarters and houses for soldiers during the 1630s. A major flood in 1648 almost washed it away, and Director General Petrus Stuyvesant immediately attempted to rebuild the fort with stone, allowing private individuals to build houses inside its walls. He also established a new town, Beverwijck, north of Fort Orange in 1652. With the threat of war with England, construction included a new guardhouse and courtroom in the fort. Continued flooding, notably in 1654 and 1661, further damaged the fort despite rebuilding efforts and by 1663 Fort Orange was nearly defenseless. In 1664 the English arrived and took New Netherland, occupying Fort Orange and Beverwijck, renaming them Fort Albany and Albany, respectively. During the Dutch reoccupation in 1673–74, Fort Albany was renamed Fort Nassau, but when the English returned in 1674 they restored the name Fort Albany. In 1675 they decided to abandon the fort and the next year built a new Fort Albany on the hill above Albany.

In 1766 the visible ruins in the pasture south of Albany measured 140 ft (42.7 m) long, north to south along the river, and 125 feet (38.1 m) deep. Archaeological excavations at the site, now under I-787, in 1970–71 uncovered an area within the east curtain wall of the fort extending south to the south moat and curtain wall. It consists of nearly 2,700 ft^2 (250 m^2) of the original fort, in a space 170 feet (51.8 m) long north to south, 10 feet (3.1 m) wide at the north end, and 30 feet (9.1 m) wide at the south. There was evidence of the wood-lined cellars of three houses, the brick foundation of a probable guardhouse from the 1624 fort near the entrance, with the adjacent remains of the hard-packed main entrance path and a stone ravelin built in 1648 to protect the south curtain wall from attack. Many objects from these excavations are on display at Fort Crailo State Historic Site.

Fisher, Charles L., ed. *People, Places, and Material Things: Historical Archaeology of Albany, New York* (Albany: NYS Museum, 2003)

Huey, Paul R. "Aspects of Continuity and Change in Colonial Dutch Material Culture at Fort Orange, 1624–1664" (PhD diss, Univ of Pennsylvania, 1988)

Paul R. Huey

Fort Orange, 1635, by L. F. Tantillo, 1993.

Fort Plain. Village (pop 2,288) in Canajoharie and Minden (Montgomery Co). Gov George Clarke, who built a stone house in 1738, is believed to have been the first European settler. When Fort Rensselaer was built a half mile northwest, the community grew to a small cluster of houses on Otsquago Creek by 1776 and garrisoned as many as 400 soldiers, including those under Col Marinus Willett, who fought in the Burning of the Valleys campaign (1780). It became an Erie Canal port in 1822, drawing trade from the country to the south, and incorporated as a village in 1832. Late 19th-century products included furniture (1852), springs and axles (1874–94), and textiles (1892). Railroad service was provided by the West Shore (1883). In the 20th century Fort Plain Furniture (1882–1932) made high-quality reproduction furniture, mostly in Classical Revival styles. Textile mills operated until Johnstown Knitting closed in 2002, leaving a small Beech-Nut baby cereal plant as the sole industry. The New York State Thruway cut through the village in 1954 but, without an exit, failed to promote growth. In the early 21st century Fort Plain is mostly a service-based village.

James Crawford

Fort Salonga. Locality (pop 9,634) in Smithtown and Huntington (Suffolk Co). It is named for the British Fort Slongo built during the Revolutionary War, the successful American raid of which in 1781 forestalled the British fleet from leaving New York City to reinforce Gen Charles Cornwallis at Yorktown, Va. Brick was manufactured in the late 19th century. Fort Salonga became a site for large estates and had its own post office from 1893 to 1924. Beginning in 1911 Booker T. Washington spent several summers there. It is the site of Sunken Meadow State Park. Most of the estates were subdivided in the mid–20th century.

Robert C. Hughes

Fort Schuyler. See FORT STANWIX.

Fort Stanwix. Located in what is now Rome (Oneida Co) at the strategic Oneida Carrying Place, between the Mohawk River and Wood Creek, the British fortified this portage several times during the French and Indian War (1754–63) to protect the supply line to their post at Oswego. A substantial earthwork with a moat and palisade, it was built in 1758 and named after its first commander, Brig Gen John Stanwix. Despite a French attack on the portage two years earlier, no military action took place at the fort during the war, after which it was abandoned.

By 1777 the fort was occupied by Continental army troops and renamed Fort Schuyler, after Maj Gen Philip Schuyler. It was repaired and rebuilt under the command of Col Peter Gansevoort. That summer, combined British, provincial, German, and Indian forces under Gen Barry St. Leger marched from Oswego for Albany as the western component of Gen John Burgoyne's invasion of New York. On 3 Aug 1777 they began a siege of the fort. Tryon Co militia en route to support Fort Schuyler, under the command of Gen Nicholas Herkimer, were ambushed on 6 August at the Battle of Oriskany, about 5 miles (8 km) east of the fort. While the British and their Indian allies fought this engagement, Lt Col Marinus Willett left the fort and raided their encampments as a diversion, capturing or destroying most of their supplies. This loss contributed to the Indians eventually abandoning the campaign. The end of the siege followed a deception, planned by Gen Benedict Arnold, that convinced the attackers an overwhelming army of Continental troops was already on its way to defend the fort. St. Leger and his forces hastily abandoned the siege on 22 Aug 1777. No further military action took place at the fort, which was partly destroyed by fire in 1781 and then abandoned. After the war, the name Fort Schuyler was generally not used, and the fort reverted to its previous name.

Fort Stanwix was the site of several significant treaty conferences. In 1768 Sir William Johnson, the British superintendent of Indian affairs, led negotiations to establish a boundary line to limit westward colonial expansion, and in 1784 at the second Treaty of Fort Stanwix, the Iroquois Confederacy ceded their claim to land in the Ohio Country.

As the settlement that is now Rome evolved, almost all traces of the fort disappeared, but in 1935 it nonetheless became Fort Stanwix National Monument. As first the city then the federal government acquired title to the site from 1965 to 1973, about 70 buildings were removed in preparation for the fort's reconstruction. Archaeological excavations from 1970 to 1972 recovered thousands of artifacts and the original position of the fort. The rebuilt Fort Stanwix opened to the public in 1976. In 2004 construction began on a new visitors' center and adjacent museum.

Hanson, Lee, and Dick Ping Hsu. *Casemates and Cannonballs: Archaeological Investigations at Fort Stanwix, Rome, New York* (Washington, DC: National Park Service, 1975)
Lowenthal, Larry. *Marinus Willett: Defender of the Northern Frontier* (Fleischmanns, NY: Purple Mountain Press, 2000)
Watt, Gavin K. *Rebellion in the Mohawk Valley: The St. Leger Expedition of 1777* (Tonawanda, NY: Dundurn Press, 2002)

Douglas J. Pippin

Fort Ticonderoga. Eighteenth-century fortress in what is now Essex Co that defended a critical pass on Lake Champlain, sometimes known as the Gibraltar of North America. In 1755 the French began construction on a fortification they named Fort Carillon to protect the strategic southern gateway into New France during the French and Indian War. From here in the summer of 1757, French troops under the Marquis de Montcalm launched a devastating attack on the British at Fort William Henry at the southern end of Lake George [now in Warren Co]. A year later, on 8 Jul 1758, Montcalm led a successful defense of Fort Carillon even though his troops were outnumbered five to one by the British and had approximately 3,000 combined casualties. In 1759, under the command of Maj Gen Jeffery Amherst, the British successfully laid siege. In response, the French blew up the powder magazine on 26 July and evacuated the fort. Amherst renamed it for the Mohawk name of the area, Ticonderoga, "the place between the great waters." The British repaired and garrisoned the four-bastioned fort, replacing the French-built wooden ramparts with stone walls.

The fort was captured by Col Ethan Allen and the Green Mountain Boys from the New Hampshire Grants [now Vermont] and Col Benedict Arnold in command of Massachusetts militia on 10 May 1775, three weeks after the Battles at Lexington and Concord and the start of the American Revolution. Only a small number of British troops guarded the fort. From this post the Continental Army launched the ill-fated invasion of Canada in August 1775 under the command of Brig Gen Richard Montgomery. The supply of cannon and gunpowder taken at the fort were a needed prize to support Gen George Washington in Boston. In December 1775 Col Henry Knox arrived at the fort and began preparations to haul 59 cannons, and supplies, from the fort across New York and Massachusetts. By early March 1776 the guns were in place south of Boston on Dorchester Heights, and on 17 Mar 1776 the British withdrew to Halifax, NS. A British invasion of the Champlain Valley under Sir Guy Carleton in the fall of 1776 routed the American flotilla at the Battle of Valcour Island and briefly occupied Crown Point [now in Essex Co], approximately 12 miles (19 km) north of Ticonderoga. Carleton's forces laid siege to Ticonderoga but returned to Canada by early November because of the onset of winter and because the American forces there outnumbered his own by more than two to one. The British returned the following year under the command of Lt Gen John Burgoyne and forced the American evacuation of Fort Ticonderoga on 5 Jul 1777. American generals Arthur St. Clair and Philip Schuyler were court-martialed for having given up fort without firing a shot in defense, but both were later acquitted. After Burgoyne's surrender at Saratoga [now Schuylerville, Saratoga Co] on 17 Oct 1777, the British garrison destroyed the fort in a series of explosions and withdrew in November 1777.

Fund-raising clambake for the preservation of Fort Ticonderoga, 2 Sept 1908.

The US Congress turned the fort over to New York State in 1785. In 1802 the state transferred the "Garrison Grounds" to Columbia College in New York City and Union College in Schenectady. In 1820 the colleges sold the site to William Ferris Pell, who began preserving the ruins, the earliest attempt at historic preservation in the United States. In 1826 Pell built a hotel, the Pavilion, on the shore of Lake Champlain to meet the needs of tourists who traveled to view the ruins of the fort and the scenery of the Adirondacks. Numerous 19th-century artists and writers recorded their visits to the fort. In 1908 Pell's great-grandson Stephen H. P. Pell launched the reconstruction of the fort. Pres William H. Taft celebrated the opening of the restored fort and museum in July 1909. In 1931 Stephen Pell established the not-for-profit Fort Ticonderoga Association, which today manages the fort, its museum collections, and 2,000 acres (810 ha) of surrounding land, which receive about 100,000 visitors a year. The fort was designated a National Historic Landmark in 1960.

For another illustration see HISTORIC PRESERVATION AND RESTORATION.

Hamilton, Edward P. *Fort Ticonderoga: Key to a Continent* (1964; repr Ticonderoga, NY: Fort Ticonderoga Association, 1995)

Nicholas Westbrook

Fort Washington. Revolutionary War fortification. Under the direction of engineer Rufus Putnam, construction began on a field of solid granite along the Hudson River at the highest point on Manhattan (268 ft/81.7 m) in June 1776. The 4-acre (1.6 ha) pentagonal fort, however, was poorly designed and hastily built, no match for Gen William Howe's army as it moved up the Hudson River after the British victory on Long Island in August 1776. Because it was the last American-held position in Manhattan, Gen George Washington initially agreed with Gens Nathanael Greene and Israel Putnam to hold the fort. By the time Washington decided to evacuate the position, however, it was too late to save the garrison. Provided with plans of the fort by an American defector, Howe captured Fort Washington and its 2,800-man garrison on 16 Nov 1776, leaving about 150 Americans killed or wounded. Watching from across the Hudson River at Fort Lee, NJ, Washington was unable to assist his troops. The fort, renamed Knyphausen after a German general serving under Howe, remained in British control for the rest of the war. The area of the fort is now in the neighborhood of Washington Heights.

Roberts, Robert B. *New York's Forts in the Revolution* (Cranbury, NJ: Associated Univ Presses, 1980)

Ethan S. Rafuse

Fort William Henry. Located at the southern end of Lake George, it was the first English fort on the Richelieu River watershed and the site of a siege and bloody aftermath immortalized in James Fenimore Cooper's *The Last of the Mohicans* (1826). In the course of the French and Indian War, British-American forces led by Sir William Johnson withstood attack by a French, Canadian, and Indian force led by Jean-Armand Dieskau in the Battle of Lake George in September 1755. Johnson's men immediately built Fort William Henry, named for the 12-year-old son of the Prince of Wales at the time, to defend their newly completed wagon road connecting Lake George with Fort Edward on the Hudson River. Fort William Henry was also to serve as a base from which to attack the French. Capt William Eyre, an engineer with the British regulars, oversaw the New England soldiers who built the sturdy, four-bastion fort within two months. Pine logs faced the exterior and interior and cross-braced the 30 ft (9.1 m) thick sand walls, topped with parapets. These 15 ft (4.6 m) high walls were filled with the earth excavated from a 30 ft wide defensive ditch surrounding three sides of the fort. The lake's steep bank controlled access on the north side.

In March 1757 Capt Eyre's garrison of 474 British regulars and rangers foiled a surprise attack by 1,500 well-outfitted French, Canadians, and Indians. On 3 Aug 1757 Marquis de Montcalm's army of nearly 8,000, including approximately 1,800 Indians from 33 tribes, attacked more systematically. The siege was an efficient combination of regular and irregular warfare. For three days, while the French established their first battery, Indian allies isolated the fort and harassed an entrenched camp containing most of the garrison's recently arrived reinforcements. By August 7 two French batteries pounded the outgunned defenders. The fort suffered little damage, but constant bombardment killed dozens, exhausted the sleepless garrison, and disabled several of the cannons. At the same time, other cannon exploded from metal fatigue.

With no further reinforcements expected and a third French battery ready to open fire, on August 9 the defenders, commanded by Lt Col George Munro, surrendered. They agreed to return all prisoners held in North America and not to fight the French or their allies for 18 months; released prisoners were allowed to keep their arms and personal effects and to march south to Fort Edward. But this arrangement ignored French recruitment promises—of scalps, prisoners, and booty—made to France's Indian allies. In the morning Indians killed 17 wounded remaining in the fort and attacked the departing column, demanding packs, guns, money, and clothes. Any who resisted were killed, as were some who fled in panic. Escapees spread tales of a massive slaughter that endured in Cooper's novel and in subsequent dramatizations. In fact, 1,600 warriors attacked a column of more than 2,300 people, leaving 70 evacuees confirmed killed, about 300 taken captive, and another 105 missing. It was a limited attack, not a massacre. But European and Indian martial values had collided. The Indian allies resented French protection of their enemies and would never return in comparable numbers to defend New France.

Montcalm leveled Fort William Henry's walls with explosives and withdrew from the most advanced position the French had gained on this frontier. The English used the incident to rally troops, to deny the honors of war to defeated French garrisons, and to justify a series of anti-Indian measures that helped to provoke Pontiac's War (1763–65). After archaeological investigation, a version of the fort was reconstructed on the site in 1953, and a museum now operates there.

Steele, Ian K. *Betrayals: Fort William Henry and the "Massacre"* (New York: Oxford Univ Press, 1990)

Ian K. Steele

44th New York Volunteer Infantry Regiment (Ellsworth's Avengers). Formed between August and October 1861 in response to the death of Col Elmer E. Ellsworth, the first Union officer killed in the Civil War. The recruitment plan was to have each town and ward in New York State select one man and raise funds to equip him for service. Attached to the Union Fifth Corps, the 44th New York participated in many of the major battles of the war, beginning with the Peninsular Campaign of April–July 1862, in which it suffered heavy losses from battle and disease. After losing half of its remaining force at Second Bull Run (29 Aug–1 Sept 1862), the regiment, reduced to fewer than 100 of its original 1,023 men, was reinforced by companies from Yates and Albany Cos. Its most famous service was helping defend Little Round Top at the Battle of Gettysburg on 2 July 1863. The 44th was mustered out on 18 Oct 1864. Its total losses were 192 killed, 120 dead of disease, 524 wounded, and 113 captured.

Nash, Eugene A. *A History of the 44th Regiment, New York Volunteer Infantry, in the Civil War, 1861–1865* (Chicago: R. R. Donnelley & Sons, 1911)

Christopher Hunter

Fosdick, Harry Emerson (*b* Buffalo, 24 May 1878; *d* Bronxville, Westchester Co, 5 Oct 1969). Baptist minister. After a religious conversion at age 7 left him with a sense of call to full-time Christian service, Fosdick was educated at Colgate University in Hamilton (Madison Co) and at Union Theological Seminary and Columbia University in New York City. Two of Fosdick's primary mentors were William Newton Clarke, a theologian at Colgate, and Walter Rauschenbusch, a church historian and social activist at Rochester Theological Seminary. While at Union, he experienced severe depression and was treated in a sanatorium. In 1904 Fosdick became pastor of the First Baptist Church of Montclair, NJ. In 1908 he became a part-time lecturer at Union Theological Seminary and a full-time professor in 1915. Fosdick traveled widely as a speaker and published several devotional books, which sold in the millions, including *The Meaning of Prayer* (1915). A vocal advocate for American intervention in World War I, Fosdick enlisted and served briefly in France in 1918. Horrified by this war experience, he became an ardent and lifelong pacifist.

In late 1918 Fosdick crossed denominational boundaries, joining the pastoral staff at First Presbyterian Church in New York City, a prestigious congregation. In 1927 he began two decades of radio preaching on the *National Vespers Hour.* That same year his sermon "Shall the Fundamentalists Win?" won him national attention and much criticism among Presbyterian churches. Conservative Presbyterians attacked him and demanded that he subscribe to the *Westminster Confession of Faith,* which he refused to do. With the backing of his close personal friend, John D. Rockefeller Jr, Fosdick went to serve Park Avenue Baptist Church, a congregation in transition. The next years were spent creating an interdenominational congregation, the Riverside Church, whose impressive edifice was dedicated in 1931 in Manhattan's Morningside Heights. Fosdick became one of the leading pulpit orators in the United States until his retirement in 1946 and an outstanding popular spokesman for modernist theology. In retirement he edited the massive work *Great Voices of the Reformation* and completed his best-selling autobiography, *The Living of These Days* (1956). He was also active in a neighborhood action group in Morningside Heights to preserve the character of the community as an attractive cultural and residential area. Fosdick's publications, which often touched upon social and political issues, include *As I See Religion* (1932), *A Guide to Understanding the Bible* (1938), *On Being a Real Person* (1943), and his autobiography. He also authored the popular hymn "God of Grace and God of Glory."

Fosdick, Harry E. *The Living of These Days: An Autobiography* (New York: Harper & Row, 1956)
Miller, Robert M. *Harry Emerson Fosdick: Preacher, Pastor, Prophet* (New York: Oxford Univ Press, 1985)

William H. Brackney

fossils. See ANCIENT LIFE.

Foster, Henry A(llen) (*b* Hartford, Conn, 7 May 1800; *d* Rome, Oneida Co, 12 May 1889). US representative and senator. As a boy, Foster moved with his family to Cazenovia (Madison Co), where he received a common school education. After admission to the bar in 1822, he practiced law in Oneida Co over the next two decades, when not occupied with political office. In 1829–30 he served as supervisor of Rome and in 1831–34 as a New York State senator, joining an ascendant group of Democrats known as the Albany Regency. In 1839 he was elected to the House of Representatives and then returned to the New York State Senate again in 1841–44. When fellow Democrat Silas Wright resigned his US Senate seat to become governor of New York, Foster was appointed to fill his place in 1844–45. In 1863 Gov Horatio Seymour appointed Foster a Supreme Court judge in New York State's Fifth District, a position he held until 1869. He also had served before the Civil War as vice president of the American Colonization Society, a body that sought to repatriate Blacks to Africa.

American Biographical Index (New York: K. G. Saur, 1993)

Ronni Kent and Stacey Coburn

Foster, Nat(haniel) (*b* Hinsdale, NH, 30 June 1766; *d* Ava, Oneida Co, 16 Mar 1841). Adirondack trapper, hunter, and frontiersman. Foster first settled near Johnstown [now in Fulton Co] on the estate of deceased Sir William Johnson. He is said to have used the name Leatherstocking 26 years before a character of that name appeared in James Fenimore Cooper's novel *The Pioneers.* Foster is also thought to have been the inspiration for Cooper's Natty Bumppo character. After his marriage in 1790, Foster moved to Salisbury (Herkimer Co), where he lived as a hunter and trapper for 30 years and attributed his success as a hunter to a "double-shotter" gun with a single barrel but two locks. In 1832 he rented land in the Brown's Tract area near Old Forge (Herkimer Co). Here his reputation as an "Indian killer" caught up with him, and he was arrested and tried for killing a Native American hunter named Blue-Eyed Pete Waters in 1834 but found not guilty.

Beetle, David H. *Up Old Forge Way* (1948; repr Lakemont, NY: North County Books, 1972)
Thompson, Harold W. *Body, Boots and Britches: Folktales, Ballads, and Speech from Country New York* (1940; repr Syracuse: Syracuse Univ Press, 1979)

Dick Case

Fourierists. Communitarian reform movement based on the theories of French utopian socialist Charles Fourier (1772–1837). Fourier's followers in New York State, also known as Associationists, promoted his theories as the answer to all of the problems of industrializing society, a comprehensive reform that would ensure economic stability and bring human society in line with Fourier's description of the divine plan. A significant source of Fourierism's appeal for Americans lay in the prospect of economic security to be found in model communities. In the ideal future that Fourier called Harmony, people would live in communities called phalanxes. In each phalanx approximately 2,000 people would live and work in a huge, luxurious building called a phalanstery, which would house the community's workshops, apartments, and meeting rooms. While the full benefits of such cooperative living could be achieved only in Harmony, building model phalanxes could hasten the coming of this utopia.

EARLY GROUPS AND PUBLICATIONS

Albert Brisbane (1809–90), born in Batavia (Genesee Co), encountered Fourier's ideas while a student in Europe in the 1830s and imported them to the United States. A tireless and central promoter of the Fourierist idea, he translated and summarized Fourier's theories under the title *The Social Destiny of Man* in 1840 and started several short-lived Fourierist journals. Brisbane founded the Fourier Association of the City of New York in 1842, which became the nucleus of the Fourierist movement in the United States. Among its members were editor and reformer Horace Greeley, who allowed Brisbane to write a regular column in Greeley's *New York Tribune* from March 1842 to September 1843. It was reprinted outside New York City in Greeley's *New York Weekly Tribune*, enabling Brisbane to reach a mass audience. Later journals, the *Phalanx* (1843–45) and the *Harbinger* (1845–49), edited by Brisbane and his associates, continued to win new adherents to the movement.

FOURIERIST COMMUNITIES

Brisbane's plans for building Fourierist communities appealed to a wide range of working-class and middle-class men and women. In the mid-1840s, the Fourierist movement boasted tens of thousands of adherents. Many formed local clubs, and some spawned model phalanxes. In many ways New York State was at the center of the Fourierist movement in the United States. No state had more urban Fourierist clubs, or "unions," which outside New York City included organizations in Rochester, Syracuse, Seneca Falls, Poughkeepsie, Albany, King Ferry, Oneida, Utica, and Westmoreland. And no state had more phalanxes. Of the 24 established between 1843 and 1846, 7 were in New York State. These stretched from the North Country and the Adirondacks—the Jefferson County Industrial Association at Cold Creek and the Morehouse Union (Piseco, Hamilton Co)—to the Mixville Association (Allegany Co) in the Southern Tier. The remainder were, broadly speaking, in the greater Rochester area: Clarkson Association (Monroe Co), Bloomfield Union Association (North Bloomfield, Ontario Co), Ontario Union (Manchester, Ontario Co), and the Sodus Bay Phalanx (Wayne Co). In addition, there was an earlier Ontario phalanx at Rochester that split into the communities at Sodus Bay and Clarkson, and an abortive phalanx at Rush (Monroe Co). The Rochester area phalanxes, in addition to the community at Mixville, formed the American Industrial Union in 1844. This, the only effort at cooperation among phalanxes in the United States, was intended to aid the economic viability of these communities and to provide practical advice on implementing Fourier's theories.

Most phalanxes originated with small groups of enthusiasts who had read Brisbane's books or his columns in the *New York Tribune* or both. For instance, urban mechanics from Albany, Brooklyn, and New York City were instrumental in establishing the Morehouse Union (1843–44). In many cases these enthusiasts set up arrangements resembling joint-stock corporations, in which both residents and outside investors held shares. Phalanxes tended to be racially and ethnically homogeneous, but native northerners of Anglo-American descent made up the vast majority of members. The Fourierists were diverse in terms of occupation and religion. Professionals and white-collar workers of the emerging middle class worked side by side with artisans, manual laborers, and farmers. Overwhelmingly Protestant, Fourierists ranged from evangelical to liberal, and many phalanxes suffered battles over such issues as Sabbath observance. Financially, Fourierists tended to overcommit themselves, buying large tracts of undeveloped land and finding themselves unable to meet large mortgage payments. Most communities lasted only a year or two before succumbing to financial and political stress. At the communities' peak, the number of members ranged from 420 at Clarkson and 400 at Jefferson County to 150 at North Bloomfield. All New York State phalanxes were dissolved by 1846.

INFLUENCE

The impact of the Fourierist movement extended beyond the brief experiments in cooperative living represented by the phalanxes. At times the Fourierist circle in New York City included health reformer Mary Gove Nichols, Swedenborgian Henry James Sr, abolitionist editor Lydia Maria Child, minister William Henry Channing, and anarchist and reformer Stephen Pearl Andrews. Fourierism was an inspiration to later efforts at creating alternative communities. Oneida Perfectionist John Humphrey Noyes claimed Fourierism as a precursor of his own community, and Andrews was a cofounder of Modern Times, an anarchist community on Long Island. Nichols and Andrews were two of the leading defenders of free love in New York City in the 1850s, another movement with roots in Fourierist thinking about the sexes. The literary transcendentalists were profoundly influenced by Fourierism, and the movement had an impact on other antebellum reform movements, including those for women's rights, social and economic change, land reform, and workers' cooperatives. Fourierist ideas also influenced notions of social harmony and cooperation in urban planning and housing. Frederick Law Olmsted, a sometime proponent of Fourierist ideas, incorporated a commitment to interclass mingling and social interdependence into his plans for New York City's Central Park and Brooklyn's Prospect Park. In 1881 Philip G. Hubert, raised in a Fourierist family, created one of New York City's distinctive housing forms, the cooperative apartment house, perhaps a distant cousin of the phalanstery.

Beecher, Jonathan. *Charles Fourier: The Visionary and His World* (Berkeley: Univ of Calif Press, 1986)
Bestor, Arthur E., Jr. *American Phalanxes: A Study of Fourierist Socialism in the United States with Special Reference to the Movement in Western New York* (1938; repr Ann Arbor, Mich: Univ Microfilms, 1977)
Guarneri, Carl J. *The Utopian Alternative: Fourierism in 19th-Century America* (Ithaca: Cornell Univ Press, 1991)

Kathryn Tomasek

Four Indian Kings. Peter Schuyler and Francis Nicholson took the Mohawk Indians Tejonihokarawa, his brother Cenelitonoro (John), Sagayonguaroughton (Brant, the grandfather of Joseph Brant), and a Mohican (Mahican) man to London to meet Queen Anne in 1710. Capt Abraham Schuyler was brought along as interpreter. Schuyler's and Nicholson's purpose for the trip was to gain support for another assault on New France, and they wished to emphasize the importance of their Indian allies. Tejonihokarawa's agenda was to appeal to the queen for aid in fighting the French and for Anglican missionaries.

Queen Anne ordered the construction of a fort at the mouth of Schoharie Creek, along with a chapel and a house for two missionaries. She had the Indians' request for missionaries sent to the Society for the Propagation of the Gospel and also arranged for the Mohawk to receive a six-piece silver communion set. It was later divided between Mohawks who fled to Niagara and the Bay of Quinte during the American Revolution. A matching set originally intended for the Onondaga remains at St. Peter's Episcopal Church in Albany. There were other gifts as well, including Bibles, prayer books, and related items.

The Indians stayed in London long enough to become popular celebrities. Crowds followed them and songs were written about them. Enterprising publishers made quick money selling pamphlets that reported all kinds of false information about the Indians and America. All four sat for the Dutch artist John Verelst, and the portraits are in the Public Archives of Canada. Each is shown with a wolf, bear, or turtle behind him to indicate his clan. They were lionized at an array of public events, but no one thought to make a careful record of their reactions to what had to have been a strong dose of culture shock. They sailed home on the *Dragon*, reaching Boston on 15 July 1710.

Bolus, Malvina. "Four Kings Came to Dinner with Their Honours," *Beaver* (Autumn 1973): 4–11
Garratt, John G., and Bruce Robinson. *The Four Indian Kings* (Ottawa: Public Archives of Canada, 1985)

Dean R. Snow

Fowler. Town (pop 2,180) in SW St. Lawrence Co. Settled in 1807, Fowler was formed in 1816 from Rossie and Russell. A group of French settlers arrived in the 1830s. Early industries included the Fullerville Iron Works (1833), red hematite mining at Little York (1833), a woolen factory active during the Civil War era, and talc mining at Hailesboro beginning 1878. Mining by Zinc Corp of America near Sylvia Lake and by Gouverneur Talc Co at Balmat, while it has decreased, remains important to the economy, as does dairy farming. Expansion of nearby Fort Drum led to a population increase in the 1980s.

Richard E. Mooers

Fowler, Bud [Jackson, John W.] (*b* Fort Plain, Montgomery Co, 16 Mar 1858; *d* Frankfort, Herkimer Co, 26 Feb 1913). Baseball pioneer.

The Four Indian Kings, drawn by Bernard Lens Jr, engraved by Bernard Lens Sr, 1710.

The son of barber John Jackson and Mary Lansing Jackson, both free Blacks, he grew up in Cooperstown (Otsego Co), where he attended public school and discovered a passion for baseball. Likely the first black professional baseball player, he debuted in minor league baseball in 1878 with Lynn, Mass, of the International Association and subsequently affiliated with 19 teams in 12 leagues, including Binghamton of the International League in 1887, before playing his last season of Organized Baseball with Lansing of the Michigan State League in 1895. Fowler had the longest Organized Baseball career of any African American in the 19th century. Despite his modest size (5 ft 7 in [170 cm], 155 lb [70.3]) and facing ubiquitous racism, he attained a .308 batting average, scored 455 runs, and stole 190 bases in 465 recorded games. A skilled and versatile fielder, he could fill any position, although he typically played second base. His career in Organized Baseball cut short and his ascent to the major leagues curtailed by discrimination, Fowler barnstormed with American and Canadian independent teams from the mid-1870s to the early 1900s and played for, managed, and promoted all-black franchises. Buried in an unmarked grave in Frankfort, Fowler was celebrated on 25 July 1987 when the Society for American Baseball Research dedicated a memorial stone at his grave.

Peterson, Robert. *Only the Ball Was White: A History of Legendary Black Players and All-Black Professional Teams* (1970; repr New York: Gramercy Books, 1999)

William M. Simons

Fowler [née Folger], **Lydia** (*b* Nantucket, Mass, 5 May 1822; *d* London, 26 Jan 1879). Physician. She showed early interest and talent in mathematics and astronomy. In 1844 she married phrenologist Lorenzo Niles Fowler. In that same year she, her husband, his brother Orson S. Fowler, and Samuel R. Wells founded in New York City the publishing house of Fowler and Wells to promote phrenology, hydropathy, and other medical novelties. Between 1845 and 1849 she published works for children on hygiene, physiology, and astronomy while also lecturing to women on these topics. In 1849 she enrolled in the eclectic Central Medical College in Syracuse. The college moved to Rochester in 1850, and when Fowler graduated in June 1850, she became the second woman in the United States to earn a medical degree. As professor of midwifery, gynecology, and pediatrics there (1851–52), she was the first woman on the faculty of a US medical school. Fowler practiced medicine in New York City (1852–60) and then moved to Europe. After returning to New York City to serve as an instructor at New York Hygeio-Therapeutic College in 1862, she and her husband settled in London. She continued to lecture and write while in Europe.

Stern, Madeleine B. *Heads and Headlines: The Phrenological Fowlers* (Norman: Univ of Oklahoma Press, 1971)

Eric v. d. Luft

Fowler, Orson S(quire) (*b* Cohocton, Steuben Co, 11 Oct 1809; *d* Sharon Station, Conn, 18 Aug 1887). Phrenologist and author. Raised in the Southern Tier, Fowler was educated in Massachusetts, first at the Ashfield Academy and later at Amherst College, where his interest in phrenology (the study of skull shapes to determine intellect and character) was stimulated by his close friend and classmate, Henry Ward Beecher. After graduation in 1834, he moved with his brother Lorenzo Niles Fowler to New York City, where they had offices at 135 Nassau St. Their *Phrenology Proved, Illustrated, and Applied* (1836) went through 30 editions. They also ran a successful mail order business, sending out materials, such as *The Self-Instructor in Phrenology and Physiology,* and doing character readings for a fee, based on daguerreotypes that customers sent them. From 1838 to 1842, he and Lorenzo published the *American Phrenological Journal* until 1911. He was a partner from 1842 to 1854 with his brother-in-law Samuel R. Wells in the publishing firm of Fowler and Wells, the leading publisher of phrenological material in the United States. Fowler also inspired the building boom of octagon houses in the 1850s, particularly through the publication of *A Home for All; or, The Gravel Wall and Octagon Mode of Building* (1848), in which he argued that the octagonal design was ideal for creating comfortable, affordable living space that was equally satisfactory for all economic classes. He built himself a five-story, 60-room octagonal house in Fishkill (Dutchess Co), to which he moved in 1846. In 1863 Fowler moved to Massachusetts and remained active as an author and lecturer. Twenty years later, he moved to Sharon (Schoharie Co), where he resided for the remainder of his life. He and his brother Lorenzo popularized phrenology and became synonymous with it as a viable alternative medicine in the mid–19th century.

Stern, Madeline. *Heads and Headlines: The Phrenological Fowlers* (Norman: Univ of Oklahoma Press, 1971)

John R. Deitrick

Fox sisters {Fox, (Ann) Leah (*b* ?Rockland Co, ?1818; *d* New York City, 1 Nov 1890); Fox, Margaret (*b* near Bath [now in Ont], ?1833; *d* Brooklyn, 8 Mar 1893); Fox, Kate [Catherine] (*b* near Bath [now in Ont], ?1839; *d* New York City, 2 July 1892)}. Spiritualist mediums. As teenagers steeped in supernatural folklore, the Fox sisters claimed to hear knockings at their farmhouse in Hydesville (Wayne Co) in 1848. The response of the sounds to specific questions convinced their family and others in the area that they were caused by a human spirit. Their parents sent Kate and Margaret to live with their sister Leah (?1818–90) in Rochester, but the phenomena continued. A group of abolitionist ex-Quakers there accepted the spirit origin of the knockings and gathered to seek religious truth through the girls' mediumship. Belief in spirit communication combined with interest in mesmeric trance and the ideas of 18th-century mystic Emanuel Swedenborg to produce Spiritualism.

Demonstrations in Rochester in 1849 and at P. T. Barnum's hotel in New York City in 1850, coupled with favorable coverage in the *New York Tribune,* made the Fox sisters and the "Rochester rappings" a national sensation. Kate and Margaret traveled during the early 1850s to Buffalo, Pittsburgh, Cincinnati, and Washington, DC, while Leah remained in New York City and attracted prominent social reformers to her séances.

The sisters slipped from public prominence by the mid-1850s as writing and speaking mediumship displaced the rappings. Margaret converted to Roman Catholicism, practicing mediumship only occasionally afterward, and slipped into alcoholism. Leah, already married twice by her own account, married wealthy Spiritualist Daniel Underhill in 1858. She remained a medium but offered only private nonprofit consultations. Kate, also an alchoholic, moved to a curative facility in New York City where she began offering séances in 1869. In 1871 she went to England to give demonstrations and married Spiritualist Henry D. Jencken in 1872. Margaret joined them in 1876. Jencken died five years later, and the sisters returned to New York City in 1885. In 1888 Margaret, with Kate by her side, announced that Spiritualism was a deception that had begun with crackings of their toe joints and had been exploited for profit by Leah. Spiritualists attributed the exposé to Margaret's alcoholism. Margaret disavowed it the following year, and Kate resumed her séances in New York City.

Isaacs, Ernest. "The Fox Sisters and American Spiritualism." In *The Occult in America: New Historical Perspectives,* ed. Howard Kerr and Charles L. Crow (Urbana: Univ of Illinois Press, 1983)

Bret E. Carroll

Leah, Margaret, and Kate Fox.

Frankfort. Town (pop 7,478) and village (pop 2,537) in SW Herkimer Co. White settlement started prior to the French and Indian War, and the town was formed from German Flatts in 1796. Because natural waterpower was limited, it was only after 1821 and the coming of the Erie Canal that a mixed economy developed. Industries included a woolen factory (1807–9, with gaps), a paper mill, and canalboat building; surrounding farms produced dairy products, especially cheese. Matches were manufactured beginning in 1844, and the factory employed as many as 300 workers; that enterprise merged with nine other companies under the control of the Diamond Match Co and, in 1893, moved to Oswego. The village was incorporated in 1863. In the late 19th century, Frankfort was the site of the Balloon Farm, the home of the husband and wife balloonists, Carl and Carlotta Myers. The West Shore Railroad (1883) initially located its shops in Frankfort, but, after merging with the New York Central, they were moved to Depew (Erie Co). Many foreign-born workers brought by the railroad, especially Italians, remained in Frankfort. The New York State Thruway opened a nearby Mohawk exit in 1954. In the early 21st century, Union Tools and Fyberdyne Optics each employ about 100 people. Many residents commute to jobs elsewhere in the Utica area.

James Crawford

Franklin. Town (pop 2,621) and village (pop 402) in NW Delaware Co. Settled in 1785, the town was formed from Harpersfield in 1793. In the early 19th century, Franklin was a state leader in producing wool for New England factories. Shipment of dairy products began as early as 1825. The village, laid out in 1827 along the Susquehanna Turnpike (1802), was incorporated in 1836. It was the site of Delaware Literary Institute (1835–1922). The decline of agriculture in the late 20th century resulted in the closing of auxiliary businesses, but a few farms have survived and are served by Catskill Tractor. In Treadwell hamlet, Barlow's General Store has operated continuously since 1841; it was still in business in 2003. The village is on the National Register of Historic Places and contains many examples of 19th-century architecture.

Dorothy Kubik

Franklin. Town (pop 1,197) in E Franklin Co. Settled in 1827 with construction of a forge and sawmill, the town was formed from Bellmont in 1836. At Franklin Falls, connected to Port Kent (Essex Co) by a plank road, was a large sawmilling operation. At Vermontville a foundry produced plows, cultivators, and scrapers from 1861 to *ca* 1889. The resort business began with the Loon Lake House (1879), which later added a cottage colony. Stony Wold Sanitarium (1903) was a New York City charity; students at the Adirondack-Florida School (1903–49) at Onchiota divided their school year between the Adirondacks and Florida. The Six Nations Indian Museum at Onchiota is open during the summer months.

Thomas W. Perrin

Franklin Automobile Company. Syracuse car manufacturer. Die manufacturer Herbert H. Franklin was president of the H. H. Franklin Manufacturing Co, which first produced automobiles in 1902. The Franklin Automobile Co was a subsidiary company, organized to sell the cars. Designed by John Wilkinson through 1922, Franklin cars were unique in the American market during their final decades, as Franklin was the last company to utilize an air-cooled engine. Early Franklins were visually distinctive with sloping hoods confirming the lack of radiators beneath, although later models resembled the water-cooled competition. Other Franklin characteristics for many models included wooden frames and full-elliptical springs. Overproduction of the 1929 model may have doomed the company and its expensive cars. Despite the introduction of a cheaper Olympic model in October 1932, production figures sank in the depression, and the bankrupt company was sold at auction in 1934. Air-Cooled Motors acquired the Franklin name and its patents and trademarks but produced engines rather than cars at Liverpool (Onondaga Co). In terms of production numbers, Franklin was the most successful New York State–based automobile builder, turning out more than 150,000 cars from 1902 to 1934. Its legacy remains in the Franklin Program of Transportation and Distribution Management at Syracuse University's School of Management and in the H. H. Franklin Club, founded by a group of enthusiasts in 1951. The club hosts a yearly Franklin Trek in Cazenovia (Madison Co).

Kimes, Beverly Rae. *Standard Catalog of American Cars, 1805–1942,* 3d ed. (Iola, Wisc: Krause Publications, 1996)
Powell, Sinclair. *The Franklin Automobile Company* (Warrendale, Pa: Society of Automotive Engineers, 1999)

Geoffrey N. Stein

Franklin County (1,632 mi^2/4,227 km^2; pop 51,134). Created in 1808 from Clinton Co, it was named in honor of Benjamin Franklin. A small portion was annexed to Essex Co in 1822. It is divided into 19 towns, and Akwesasne (St. Regis Indian Reservation) occupies the extreme northwest corner. The county contains six incorporated villages, and Malone is the county seat. The county's northern third is within the St. Lawrence Lowland landform region; the remainder is within the Adirondack Upland, including a portion of the high peaks region in the far southeast. Overall the moderate relief in the north gives way to increasingly rugged higher country in the south. Elevations range from 160 feet (49 m) on the banks of the St. Lawrence River to the summit of Seward Mountain at 4,347 feet (1,325 m). Bedrock formations are igneous and metamorphic in the Adirondack Province. These give way to sandstone and then limestone near the Canadian border. Evidence of glaciation is present throughout, and much of the area is poorly drained as a result. Water flows generally north via the Raquette, St. Regis, Salmon, and Chateaugay Rivers and east via the Saranac. There is a large swarm of naturally occurring lakes and ponds in the south. Upper Saranac Lake is the largest. With limited exception the highland soils are nonarable, while those of the north range from very productive tills, which helped direct initial white settlement, to tills of no agricultural value.

Franklin Co's climate is humid-continental. Mean July temperatures range from 70°F (21°C) in the north to 65°F (18°C) in the south, although annual daytime highs over 90°F (32°C) can occur at all but the highest elevations. Comparable mean January temperatures are 16 to 18°F (-9 to -8°C). On rare occasion Saranac Lake records the nation's coldest temperature for a day, Alaska included. Average annual precipitation ranges from less than 32 inches (81 cm) in the north to over 40 inches (102 cm) in the south. Annual snowfall ranges from 60 inches (152 cm) in the extreme northwest to more than 160 inches (406 cm) in the high peaks of the southeast. Primeval forest consisted of beech, sugar maple, yellow birch, hemlock, and white pine in the north. This community gave way to a spruce-fir-dominated mix in the higher elevations of the south. Over 80% of Franklin Co is presently forest covered. The southern two-thirds of the county lies within the Adirondack Park.

American Indians and Early Settlement

Archaeological evidence suggests that the area was first occupied approximately 7,000 years ago. Before European settlement, the area was partially occupied by Iroquoian peoples in scattered settlements sometime after 1200. In 1760 the Jesuit mission of St. Regis was established, and it was incorporated into the federal reservation system when the latter was established in the 1850s. Alexander Macomb's purchase (1791) included the western two-thirds of what became Franklin Co. The remaining third was part of the Old Military Tract. The first permanent European settlers arrived and began purchasing land in northern Franklin Co in 1796. Many migrated from hardscrabble hill farms in western Vermont for the more fertile soils and level lands of the St. Lawrence Valley frontier. By 1800 there were at least 92 families living in the newly created Town of Chateaugay, then part of Clinton Co, on lands originally part of the Old Military Tract. During the next two decades many more Vermonters pushed the settlement frontier west across the county onto Great Tract 1 of the Macomb Purchase and south to the margins of the arable land to create part of a larger region that became known as New Vermont. Francophone Canadians settled in Fort Covington at the same time Vermonters were settling in Chateaugay. After the unsuccessful Canadian revolt (1837–40), the Canadians came in greater numbers. The Irish began arriving *ca* 1825 via Montreal.

Within a few years of the county's creation, geography and war with Great Britain (1812–15) placed the settlements in a vulnerable position. A shared border with Canada made the county a potential invasion route and exposed it to raids by British forces; a constant fear of attack characterized the war years. In October 1813 over 400 casualties from the Battle of Chrysler's Farm north of Cornwall, Ont, poured into Ma-lone. The village's facilities were overwhelmed, and many public buildings became temporary hospitals for the wounded. Government supplies arrived to support the recovering soldiers, but when the army moved on in early February 1814, the stores that were left made the community an attractive military target, and later that month the British raided and ransacked the village. Franklin Co people repeatedly petitioned state and federal governments for protection but to no avail. Settlement of the county's southern two-thirds came later with the expansion of forest industries and the rise of the tourist industry after the building of a "primitive hotel" by Paul Smith in 1859 on the shore of Lower St. Regis Lake.

Economic Development

The cessation of hostilities permitted Franklin Co to grow in population and to expand its economic base. Subsistence agriculture was central in the northern towns. Surpluses were marketed locally or in nearby Ontario. Grist- and sawmills were built. Other early industry included charcoal-fueled iron forges and furnaces. The first was at Westville (*ca* 1810); other ironworks operated at various times in Bellmont, Burke, Duane, Fort Covington, and Franklin. At Malone a woolen mill (1825) and a cotton mill (1828) were built alongside the omnipresent sawmills. In 1855 the manufacturing census reported 85 sawmills, 6 tanneries, and 4 shingle factories in the county. Around 1844 the first of several local mills began converting portions of the potato crop into starch, an industry that remained profitable until after 1900.

Despite the intervening international border, the relative ease of water transport and proximity to the St. Lawrence River encouraged farmers and business owners to establish economic links with Canada, particularly Montreal, early on. Lumber and potash were the principal products. Steamboat service did not extend beyond Fort Covington and Hogansburg in the extreme northwest; thus early transport was overland. The main roads were the Northwest Bay Rd from Lake Champlain to Hopkinton in St. Lawrence Co (1810) and the Hopkinton and Port Kent Turnpike (funded in 1827). Efforts to gain railroad connections began in 1836, but service did not materialize until 1850 with the completion of the Ogdensburg and Lake Champlain Railroad (later Rutland Railroad). Other rail connections came considerably later. The New York Central Railroad's Adirondack line opened in 1883 and the Adirondack and St. Lawrence (later New York Central Ottawa Division) in 1892. Both ran north from Tupper Lake and opened up large tracts to timber harvest and helped sustain the fledgling resort industry.

By the third quarter of the century, more than 500,000 acres (202,000 ha) were under cultivation to produce tons of sugar beets, hay, buckwheat, corn, oats, and rye. Hops, a distinctive specialty crop, were introduced around midcentury and extensively grown in Bangor, Constable, Duane, and Malone. In 1880, 253 growers cultivated 918 acres (372 ha) in Malone alone, but production faded soon after. The dairy industry, the backbone of the agricultural economy, began with the railroad. In 1851 refrigerated car service was introduced to carry locally produced butter to Boston markets. In 1869 the county's first creamery opened in Malone, and by 1875 over 5,000 cows produced milk "sent to the factory." By the turn of the century the dairy industry dominated county agriculture.

Starting around 1850 logging became the central economic activity in the southern two-thirds

FRANKLIN CO POPULATION CENSUS FIGURES

	White	Nonwhite	Total Population	Foreign-Born
1810	2,614	3	2,617	—
1820	4,439	0	4,439	195
1830	11,288	24	11,312	825
1840	16,515	3	16,518	—
1850	25,040	62	25,102	7,965
1860	30,818	19	30,837	7,793
1870	30,244	27	30,271	6,950
1880	32,351	39	32,390	6,161
1890	38,050	60	38,110	6,324
1900	41,492	1,361	42,853	6,033
1910	44,246	1,471	45,717	7,163
1920	42,418	1,123	43,541	5,608
1930	44,534	1,160	45,694	4,559
1940	42,865	1,421	44,286	3,225
1950	43,233	1,597	44,830	2,923
1960	42,958	1,784	44,742	2,581
1970	42,167	1,764	43,931	1,967
1980	42,640	2,289	44,929	1,856
1990	42,117	4,423	46,540	1,910
2000	42,970	8,164	51,134	1,905

Notes: "Nonwhite" includes African Americans, Asians, American Indians, and Pacific Islanders and, for 2000, also the mixed race and other race categories. Through the 1960 census these figures primarily reflect the African American population. Foreign-born figures for 1820 and 1830 include only those not naturalized, and for 1930 and 1950, the foreign-born totals include Whites only. Other years include all foreign-born in the population.

of the county. Large stands of timber were cut through the summer and fall, skidded to collection points over the winter, and sent down the rivers in the spring freshets. Other forest products included charcoal and potash. Where access and waterpower merged, sawmills were built. The smaller mills spawned hamlets in the wilderness that became ghost towns once the surrounding forest was cleared. Saranac Lake and Tupper Lake alone became substantial villages in the southern part of the county. In addition to sawmills, wood provided the raw material for several local industries. Ambitious entrepreneur Samuel C. Wead (1805–76), previously instrumental in founding the Bank of Malone (1851), established a paper mill at Malone in 1872. A pulp mill began operations there in 1878 and one at Chateaugay in 1892. At Tupper Lake two large rossing mills for pulpwood began operating in 1898–99, and the Oval Wood Dish Co followed in 1917 and began mass-producing woodenware.

The forest industries attracted immigrant and minority laborers. Many loggers were Francophone Canadian or Native American men who worked in the forests for most of their lives. The various mills drew many Irish and Francophone Canadian workers, as did railroad construction. By 1875 more than 20% of the county's population was foreign-born, with the greatest diversity in Malone, where 18% of the residents were Canadian, largely Francophone.

The Adirondack wilderness attracted tourists despite its being despoiled by forestry practices. The Banner House at Chateaugay Lake is the oldest resort hotel, dating from its utilitarian establishment in 1816. The first hotel at Saranac Lake was built in 1849. Famous early hostelries include Paul Smith's (1859), Saranac Inn (1864), Mount Morris House at Moody (1868), and Loon Lake House (1879). Private cottages and parks followed by the end of the century, most notably the vast William Rockefeller tract at Bay Pond (1896) and the patrician enclave at Upper St. Regis. Dr Edward Livingston Trudeau discovered the benefits of mountain air and a strict regimen for tubercular patients, establishing his Adirondack Cottage Sanitarium (later the Trudeau Sanatorium) near Saranac Lake in 1884. Other sanatoriums followed there and in Brighton, creating an economic engine for southeast Franklin Co, which ended with the closure of the Trudeau facility in 1954, following the successful application of new antibiotics. The Trudeau Institute, a research facility for immunology and infectious diseases, opened in Saranac Lake in 1964.

Religion, Education, and Culture

Early settlers were primarily Protestant and established a number of Congregational, Methodist, and Baptist congregations beginning with the Congregational church at Malone in 1807. By 1850 there were two Baptist, six Congregational, and four Methodist congregations in the county, but by then the influx of immigrants and the establishment of four Catholic parishes had begun to alter significantly the religious landscape. By the 1880s the largest congregations were Catholic, and in some communities they were split along ethnic lines. Malone had both French and Irish Catholic churches. The Catholic churches also provided education; by the turn of the 20th century a number of parishes operated schools.

Franklin Co's current public school districts evolved out of the early common school system that began in 1799 at Chateaugay. There were concurrently several private academies offering secondary education. Harrison Academy opened in 1806 and was chartered as Malone Academy in 1831, the same year Fort Covington Academy opened. By the end of the 19th century, population growth prompted the construction of over 175 separate school buildings with almost 400 teachers and 9,000 students. Beginning in the 1920s and the advent of better roads, school buses, and state funding incentives, the widely dispersed system began to centralize. In the third quarter of the 20th century, another series of school consolidations reduced the number of districts to seven. Higher education is available at Paul Smith's College, which was established in 1937, and North Country Community College, which opened in 1969.

The county's first newspaper was the *Franklin Telegraph,* published in Malone starting in 1820. Of a dozen 19th-century newspapers, half survived into the 20th century and two into the 21st century, the *Malone Evening Telegram* and the *Adirondack Daily Enterprise* in Saranac Lake. In addition WNBZ-AM and WSLK-FM broadcast from Saranac Lake. Public libraries are fixtures in the larger villages, and the entire county is served by the Clinton, Essex, and Franklin Free Library System.

Politics

The first local elections were held in 1822. Early Federalist and Whig dominance preceded a Democrat ascendancy in the 1840s and 1850s. The Republican Party dominated for the remainder of the 19th century but not to the exclusion of the Democrats, who drew much support from the Irish and Francophone Canadian segments of the population. National prominence was gained when Malone native son William A. Wheeler served as the nation's vice president during the Rutherford B. Hayes administration. There was a more even split, with about 20% of the voters identifying themselves as independent, in the 20th century. The traditional board of supervisors form of county government was disbanded by court order and replaced by a seven-member legislature in 1970.

The 20th Century

The 20th century brought tremendous change to all sectors of Franklin Co's economy. In 1900 farmers still worked the 500,000 acres (202,000 ha) reported in the 1875 state census. The already paramount dairy industry rose further in importance, stimulated by the opening of a condensery in 1904 and daily milk train service in 1908. The latter made it possible to send fluid milk to distant markets like Boston and New York City. Traditional mixed-farming operations disappeared. At the start of the 20th century, dairying was complemented primarily by oat, hay, vegetable, and potato production, all well adapted to Franklin Co soil and climate. In 1918 the county had the highest yield per acre of potatoes in New York State. By 1930 roughly 30,000 cows were producing on 3,000 farms. The depression hit dairy farmers very hard. Demand decreased and prices declined, putting enormous pressure on them. Tucked away in a politically less influential part of the state, Franklin Co farmers lacked the kind of political or financial clout to demand state government's attention.

POPULATIONS OF TOWNS, FRANKLIN CO

Town, Year Founded	1800	1840	1880	1920	1960	2000
Altamont, 1890	—	—	—	4,927	6,546	6,137
Bangor, 1812	—	1,289	2,440	1,927	1,896	2,147
Bellmont, 1833	—	472	2,098	1,552	1,088	1,423
Bombay, 1833	—	1,446	1,644	1,251	1,103	1,192
Brandon, 1828	—	531	815	728	369	542
Brighton, 1858	—	—	267	684	1,092	1,682
Burke, 1844	—	—	2,161	1,578	1,475	1,359
Chateaugay, 1799[a]	443	2,824	2,828	2,856	2,176	2,036
Constable, 1807	—	1,122	1,532	1,100	1,153	1,428
Dickinson, 1808	—	1,005	2,329	1,312	857	739
Duane, 1828	—	324	285	209	95	159
Fort Covington, 1817	—	2,094	2,424	1,966	1,905	1,645
Franklin, 1836	—	192	1,184	1,280	695	1,197
Harrietstown, 1841	—	—	533	4,797	5,664	5,575
Malone, 1805[b]	—	3,229	7,909	10,830	11,997	14,981
Moira, 1828	—	962	2,254	2,264	2,362	2,857
Santa Clara, 1888	—	—	—	541	158	395
Waverly, 1880	—	—	—	1,695	1,050	1,118
Westville, 1829	—	1,028	1,687	1,028	1,287	1,823

[a]In 1800 the Town of Chateaugay was in Clinton Co.

[b]Harrison until 1808, then Ezraville until 1812.

Desperate to make themselves heard, many joined the Dairy Farmers Union (DFU) and participated in the 1939 milk strike. Despite the efforts of the DFU, the economic problems of the depression had a significant impact on Franklin Co's dairy industry and farming. Between 1920 and 2000, the number of acres devoted to agriculture decreased from 500,000 (202,000 ha) to less than 250,000 (101,000 ha). The number of farms declined from 3,000 in 1900 to 575 in 1998. Yet, through hard work and modernization efforts, the industry has persisted and in some ways grown. Although there are fewer acres in production, yields are higher per acre. In the early 21st century, most of the cropland in the county is planted in corn and hay. Dairy farms have survived, though there are fewer cows in production.

In the postwar period the industrial sector reoriented as well. Fabric, clothing, and paper mills closed; iron mining is gone. The forest products industries that were the mainstay of the Saranac Lake and Tupper Lake regions have retrenched, and the wood-processing factories have closed. Recreation and tourism have moved to the forefront of southern Franklin Co's economy. Winter sports play a key role. Saranac Lake inaugurated its Winter Carnival in 1898; Tupper Lake opened downhill ski facilities in 1960, which have since fallen on hard times. In the north, agriculture exists side by side with three state prison facilities built near Malone in the 1980s and 1990s and a drug treatment facility at Chateaugay. All were established for economic reasons. Renewed efforts to attract low-impact manufacturing firms have also been undertaken.

Despite this economic upheaval, Franklin Co's population has remained remarkably stable over time. The 19th-century growth trend culminated in a population of almost 43,000 in 1900, after which it hovered between 43,000 and 45,000 until the 1980s, when further growth occurred. The most dramatic change in the 20th century took place in its last decade, when the county experienced a net population gain of almost 5,000 (roughly 11%), largely a consequence of expanded prison populations and related job growth.

The standard history of Franklin Co is Duane Hamilton Hurd, *History of Clinton and Franklin Counties* (1880), updated by Frederick J. Seaver, *Historical Sketches of Franklin County* (1918). Despite their small populations, a number of towns and localities have good published histories, especially Tupper Lake: Louis J. Simmons, *Mostly Spruce and Hemlock* (1976). Morton Cross Finch, *History of Ragged Lake* (1934), and Floy S. Hyde, *Water over the Dam at Mountain View in the Adirondacks* (1970) chronicle small places in depth. Although intended for a popular audience, Robert Taylor, *Saranac: America's Magic Mountain* (1986) was written with attention to sources. The architectural heritage of the county is well covered in Robert McGowan, *Architecture from the Adirondack Foothills* (1977).

Susan M. Ouellette

Franklin D. Roosevelt Presidential Library and Museum. The nation's first presidential library was the idea of Franklin D. Roosevelt, who sought to preserve his papers and those of his wife, Eleanor, and their contemporaries. He also provided for a museum, housed within the library, to educate the public about the Roosevelt years. The library is situated on 16 acres (6.5 ha) of Roosevelt's family estate in Hyde Park (Dutchess Co). Built in 1939–40 with $376,000 in private funds, the museum opened on 30 June 1941. Roosevelt took a personal interest in the library's Dutch colonial architectural design and played a large part in arranging the original exhibits drawn from his personal collection of naval ship models, prints, and presidential gifts. Through documents, photographs, memorabilia, and multimedia technology, the exhibits explore the lives of Franklin and Eleanor Roosevelt and the turbulent period of the nation's history from the Great Depression through World War II. The library's research room, which opened 1 May 1946, houses more than 17 million pages of documents, audiovisual materials, museum objects, and books, including Roosevelt's personal collection of 14,000 volumes. The library serves 600 scholars who visit the research room each year and 125,000 museum visitors. The library's web site, with an ever growing collection of digitized documents and photographs, reaches nearly 250,000 people every month. Educational programs at the library include student activities, lectures, special exhibits, and public events. In donating his papers to the library, Roosevelt established the precedent for public ownership of presidential papers, which became federal law through the Presidential Records Act of 1978. His library was a model for the Presidential Libraries Act of 1955. The presidential libraries system administers the library through the National Archives and Records Administration. The library is assisted and supported in its work by the Franklin and Eleanor Roosevelt Institute, a private foundation, and works in partnership with the National Park Service, which administers the adjoining Franklin D. Roosevelt National Historic Site.

Franklin D. Roosevelt Library and Digital Archives, http://www.fdrlibrary.marist.edu

Ward, Geoffrey. "Future Historians Will Curse as Well as Praise Me," *Smithsonian* (Dec 1989): 58–69

Lynn A. Bassanese

Franklin Square. Locality (pop 29,342) in Hempstead (Nassau Co). Used as grazing land for sheep and consisting of a few scattered farms, the community was known first as Trimming Square and then as Washington Square. German immigrant farmers settled in the area in the 1850s; by the 1870s it was known as Franklin Square, the name given to the post office in 1923. An attempt to incorporate Franklin Square as a village in 1929 was unsuccessful. The Franklin Square National Bank (1926–74; later Franklin National Bank), an innovative institution, built the first outdoor banking facility (1941) and issued the country's first revolving bank credit card (1951). After World War II a real estate boom made Franklin Square one of the fastest-growing communities on Long Island, growing from 5,765 in 1940 to 32,483 in 1960.

Georgina Martorella

Franklinville. Town (pop 3,128) and village (pop 1,855) in E central Cattaraugus Co. Settled in 1806, the town was formed as Ischua in 1812; the name was changed to Franklinville in 1824. The Buffalo, New York and Philadelphia Railroad (later Pennsylvania Railroad) came through in 1872. It became chiefly a dairying town; there was some crop farming, served by Franklinville Canning Co (1882). The village incorporated in 1874. In the early 21st century, Ontario Knife Co and Cattaraugus Container are employers. Tourists are drawn by the village's Victorian character; Park Square is a National Register historic district, and the Miner's Cabin, a Queen Anne house built by a successful Klondike miner, is a museum operated by the Ischua Valley Historical Society. The Western New York Maple Festival (1962) is held in April.

Bruce D. Fredrickson and Madelynn P. Fredrickson

Fraser [née Loguen], **Sarah Marinda** (*b* Syracuse, 29 Jan 1850; *d* Washington, DC, 9 Apr 1933). Physician. The daughter of abolitionist Jermain Wesley Loguen and Caroline Storum, she decided to become a physician in 1873. Upon receiving her MD from the Syracuse University College of Medicine in 1876, she became the second African American woman physician in New York State and the fourth in the nation. After interning in Philadelphia and Boston, she opened a private practice in Washington, DC, in 1879; friend Frederick Douglass nailed up her shingle. In 1882 in Syracuse she married Charles Fraser, a friend of Douglass, then moved with him to the Dominican Republic and became that country's first woman physician. Her husband died in 1894, and she returned to Syracuse in 1901 with her daughter, Gregoria, who attended the fine arts program at Syracuse University. In 1907 Fraser and her daughter settled in Washington, DC.

Luft, Eric v. d. "Sarah Loguen Fraser, MD (1850 to 1933): The Fourth African-American Woman Physician," *Journal of the National Medical Association* 92 (Mar 2000): 149–53

Eric v. d. Luft

fraternal organizations. The Freemasons organized the first fraternal societies in colonial New York. There was a lodge in New York City by 1730 and lodges in Albany, Johnstown [now in Fulton Co], Poughkeepsie, and Schenectady by the late 1700s. Freemasonry spread rapidly thereafter, with some 480 lodges in the state by 1827. The Antimasonic movement of the 1820s and 1830s slowed the growth of Freemasonry, but it continued to prosper as perhaps the most influential of fraternal organizations.

Early Fraternalism

The Freemasons had many rivals and imitators. In 1771 the Society of St. Tamina was founded in Annapolis, Md, as a patriotic, fraternal, and charitable society. Soon Tammany societies were founded in several cities, such as in New York City in 1786, where it became a long-lasting political force. The first college fraternity in the United States, Phi Beta Kappa, which had Masonic-like secret initiation rites, was founded at the College of William and Mary in Williamsburg, Va, in 1776. It slowly spread to New England, and in 1817 a chapter was founded at Union College in Schenectady. Between 1825 and 1827, Union College students founded the "Union Triad" of Kappa Alpha, Sigma Phi, and Delta Phi to compete with Phi Beta Kappa. These soon spread to other campuses in and out of New York State and inspired the creation of more student fraternities.

Fraternal organizations had long provided support to needy members but on an ad hoc, discretionary basis. In newer organizations, fraternal orders paid set benefits to members with a common bond, whether social, regional, professional, philosophical, religious, or ethnic, as was done in England. A lodge affiliated with the English Independent Order of Odd Fellows (IOOF) was founded in Brooklyn in 1822 and spread statewide, with the Daughters of Rebekah for women added in 1851. The Improved Order of Red Men, founded in 1834 in Baltimore and using Indian paraphernalia yet barring Indian members, formed lodges ("wigwams") in the state. To identify members from other areas and give decorum to lodge meetings, these societies adopted Freemasonic-styled handshakes, rituals, and ranks with peculiar titles. A number of ethnic societies were founded in New York City: St. Andrew's Society (1756) for Scots, Friendly Sons of St. Patrick (1784) and Ancient Order of Hibernians (1836) for Irish, St. George's Society for English (1786), and German Society of New York (1784). To accommodate the largest non-English speaking group, the Freemasons, IOOF, and Red Men also chartered German-speaking lodges. New York City Germans also founded the German Order of the Sons of Hermann (1840) and the German Order of the Harugari (1847), which soon spread nationwide. In New York City German Jews founded the International Order of B'nai Brith (1843), United Order of True Sisters (1846), Independent Order of Free Sons of Israel (1849), and Order of B'rith Abraham (1859). In the 1840s branches of nativist and prohibitionist fraternal societies were also founded in the state.

Post–Civil War

The era between the Civil War and the Great Depression was the golden age of fraternal societies. A few older-type societies—social clubs with ad hoc benefits—were still founded, such as the Knights of Pythias (1864) in Washington, DC, and the Benevolent and Protective Order of Elks (1868), originally the Jolly Corks, a New York City drinking club for actors. The Grand Army of the Republic (1866) was a veteran's society with fraternal characteristics. The greatest growth came from societies that offered life insurance. The Ancient Order of United Workmen, founded in 1868, was the first fraternal benefit society to do so. By 1907 there were an estimated 150 fraternal insurance orders in the United States, such as Royal Arcanum, founded in 1877 in Boston, plus local societies. Fraternal societies also began to contract with doctors to have members treated for a flat fee and opened retirement homes and orphanages. Would-be Robin Hoods could join the Ancient Order of Foresters, the breakaway Foresters of America, or the Catholic Order of Foresters. In addition, many of the new fraternal organizations had increasingly extravagant pageantry. The United Ancient Order of Druids offered Celtic robes; the United Order of Pilgrim Fathers, high Puritan hats. Perhaps the most popular costumes were ersatz Arabic, the standard garb for the Freemason's Ancient Arabic Order of Nobles of the Mystic Shrine (Shriners), the IOOF's Ancient Order of Samaritans, and the Knights of Pythias's Dramatic Order Knights of Khorassan.

Because almost all fraternal societies had a strict color bar, African Americans created parallel organizations, such as Prince Hall Masonry and the Grand United Order of Odd Fellows, with 2,000 members in Manhattan and Brooklyn by 1848, and after the Civil War the Knights of Pythias; the Order of Forestry, with six courts in New York City in the 1890s; and the Improved Benevolent and Protective Order of Elks. Ethnic organizations continued to proliferate. Germans founded many local Krankenunterstützungsvereine (sickness support societies), also called Landsmannschaften if membership was based on origin in a region or town. Yiddish-speaking eastern European Jews in New York City founded hundreds of such societies, such as the Grodno Sick Support Society for immigrants from the city of Grodno [now in Belarus]. Francophone Canadians, Italians, Slovaks, Hungarians, Chinese, and other ethnic and immigrant groups also had their own societies. Catholics created their own fraternal organizations, local parish sodalities, and the Catholic Mutual Benefit Association (1876), the Catholic Benevolent Legion (1881), and the successful Knights of Columbus (1882). Two New York City–based societies supported the socialist movement, the Workmen's Benefit Fund/Arbeiterkrankenkasse (1884) for German workers and the Workmen's Circle/Arbeiterring (1892) for eastern European Jews.

By the end of the 19th century, cities in New York State had a dense net of fraternal lodges. In Rochester, for example, the 1896 *City Directory* listed for its 144,000 inhabitants 211 fraternal lodges, not including union locals with fraternal characteristics. By 1907 fraternal societies in New York State reported 724,000 members, including multiple memberships. The largest society was the Masons, followed by IOOF, Royal Arcanum, and Grand Army of the Republic. The main Anglo-American societies, later joined by ethnic societies, formed in 1886 the National Fraternal Congress as a trade organization and to fight attempts by commercial insurance companies and medical organizations, which opposed the "lodge doctor" as a threat to their incomes, to hamper fraternal societies through legislative measures.

Decline and Consolidation

After the Great Depression, the number and membership of fraternal societies declined. The depression cost them investments and dues-paying members, the New Deal's social insurance made them less needed, and new regulations subjected them to the same costly regulatory requirements as commercial insurance providers. Medical societies succeeded in suppressing lodge doctors. New forms of socializing undercut their appeal, as did the end of immigration. In 2002, 48 fraternal societies still provided insurance in the state, regulated by the New York State Insurance Department. They had 294,000 members, with nearly two-thirds belonging to the Knights of Columbus (110,000) and Thrivent Lutheran (66,000). The other societies were small, such as the Workmen's Benefit Fund, now in Hicksville (Nassau Co), with 4,139 members in the state, and the Workmen's Circle, with 6,270 New York State members. Societies focusing on philanthropy have fared better. There are still about 136,000 Freemasons and 22,000 Knights of Pythias in the state, and ethnic fraternal societies such as the Schenectady Hungarian Benevolent Society and the Sons of Italy are social clubs rather than insurance providers.

See also Irish.

Beito, David T. *From Mutual Aid to the Welfare State: Fraternal Societies and Social Services, 1890–1967* (Chapel Hill: Univ of North Carolina Press 2000)

Ferguson, Charles Wright. *50 Million Brothers: A Panorama of American Lodges and Clubs* (New York: Farrar & Rinehart, 1937)

Greenberg, Brian. "Worker and Community: Fraternal Orders in Albany, New York, 1845–1885," *Maryland Historian* 8 (1977): 38–53

Schmidt, Alvin J. *Fraternal Organizations* (Westport, Conn: Greenwood, 1980)

Soyer, Daniel. *Jewish Immigrant Associations and American Identity in New York, 1880–1939* (Cambridge, Mass: Harvard Univ Press 1997)

Thomas Reimer

Frederic, Harold (Henry) (*b* Utica, 19 Aug 1856; *d* Kenley, England, 19 Oct 1898). Author and journalist. His father, a railroad employee, died when Harold was quite young, and his mother worked tirelessly to support the family. Harold Frederic graduated from the Utica Advanced School in 1871 and within a few years was established in journalism. In 1880 he assumed the editorship of the *Utica Daily Observer* and in 1882 was made editor of the *Albany Evening Journal*. A Democrat on a Republican paper, he resigned, or was fired, in 1884 for supporting Grover Cleveland for governor. This brought him national recognition and offers to edit major newspapers; he accepted the position of London correspondent for the *New York Times*. His weekly cables of world news, reprinted in other American newspapers, helped elevate the *Times* to a paper of international stature. Reporting on affairs in Europe, Frederic developed special interest in two oppressed groups, the Russian Jews and the Irish.

He gained a reputation as a raconteur, and his friends could hardly have been surprised when, in 1887, he published a realistic novel, *Seth's Brother's Wife*, set in the fictional locale of Tecumseh, Dearborn Co (a thin disguise for Utica). It was followed in 1890 by *The Lawton Girl*, which features some of the same characters, and *In the Valley*, set in the Mohawk Valley during the American Revolution. Among his other works were a number of Civil War stories based on memories of his Utica childhood and several Irish stories, including a novel, *The Return of the O'Mahony* (1892). He also published two nonfiction works, *The Young Emperor, William II of Germany* (1891) and *The New Exodus* (1892), a study of anti-Semitism in czarist Russia. But none of these prepared readers for *The Damnation of Theron Ware* (1896), which, although bearing a superficial resemblance to his other Mohawk Valley novels, many regard as one of the major American literary achievements of its age.

Although Frederic had married Grace Williams of Utica in 1877 and they had four living children, he fell in love with another American woman, Kate Lyon, and established her in the London suburb of Surrey. Their courtship presumably was the inspiration for the novel *March Hares* (1896). She had three children with him, and their home welcomed such literary lights as Stephen Crane, while his wife was all but abandoned in London. Frederic continued writing and published *Gloria Mundi*, a novel of the British aristocracy, in 1898. He was finishing another groundbreaking novel, *The Market-Place*, when his heart began to fail. This strong and ominous, though little remembered, book pointed to the coming era of demagogues and dictators. Cooperating neither with physicians, whom he did not trust, nor with Kate's Christian Science healer, he died before the novel's publication in 1899. He left both families in dire need, with his acquaintances divided over which family they should aid. The rift worsened when Frederic's legitimate family accused Kate and the healer of killing him by failing to provide him with medical care. The subsequent trial was a scandal on both sides of the Atlantic, and although the accused were acquitted, Frederic's reputation was badly tarnished. That damage and his background as a journalist prevented him from receiving the recognition as an author that he deserved. He stands with James Fenimore Cooper as a premier chronicler of life in Central New York.

Bennett, Bridget. *The Damnation of Harold Frederic: His Lives and Works* (Syracuse: Syracuse Univ Press, 1997)

Garner, Stanton. *Harold Frederic*. University of Minnesota Pamphlets on American Writers, no 83 (Minneapolis: Univ of Minnesota Press, 1969)

Myers, Robert M. *Reluctant Expatriate: The Life of Harold Frederic*. Contributions to the Study of World Literature, no 59 (Westport, Conn: Greenwood Press, 1995)

Stanton Garner

Fredonia. Village (pop 10,706) in Pomfret (Chautauqua Co). Settled in 1804 Fredonia had the first natural gas well in the United States (1821) and put the gas to use for street lighting in the same year, the first community in the world to do so. Fredonia Academy (1824) began a tradition of education that was continued by the Fredonia Normal School (1867; now SUNY Fredonia). The village incorporated in 1829. It was a large producer of bulk and packaged seeds beginning in 1834. Fredonia was the birthplace of the Patrons of Husbandry (Grange) in 1868 and the Woman's Christian Temperance Union (WCTU) in 1873. Fredonia's downtown retains its historic charm with significant features, including the Barker Common, Barker Library and Museum, and the Fredonia Opera House (1891). The Red Wing Co (*ca* 1900) began by processing grape jelly and expanded to become a large food processing plant known for peanut butter; it was sold in 1999 to Carriage House Cos.

See also ARCHITECTS AND ARCHITECTURE, SOUTHERN TIER (WESTERN); POWER AND LIGHTING.

Michelle Henry

Freedom. Town (pop 2,493) in NE Cattaraugus Co. Settled in 1811, the town was formed from the old town of Ischua [now Franklinville] in 1820. A group of some 30 Mormon converts from the Crystal Lake vicinity moved to Ohio in 1835. Beginning around 1841 a Welsh community formed, in part by migration from Oneida Co. The Hayden Mill at Sandusky (*ca* 1830) began producing yarn in 1869 and flannel in 1871; the town also had a carriage factory (1867). The Rochester and State Line Railroad came through in 1878. Freedom was also crossed by the short-lived Buffalo and Susquehanna (1906–16). In the early 21st century agriculture remains the predominant land use, with some gravel mining. The Freedom Raceway features stock cars in spring and summer. Daniel Frederick Bakeman (1759–1869), veteran of the New York Militia and the last surviving Revolutionary War soldier, died and was buried in Freedom. His 1782 marriage to Susan Brewer (1758–1863) lasted 81 years. Author Arch Merrill (1894–1974) was a native.

Bruce D. Fredrickson and Madelynn P. Fredrickson

Freeman, William. See WILLIAM FREEMAN CASE.

Freemasons. Members of the Free and Accepted Masons, America's oldest fraternal order. Freemasonry evolved from English stonemasons' guilds. Colonists brought Freemasonry and its Enlightenment ideals to the United States, where the order took root firmly in the early 18th century. By the American Revolution, lodges operated in New York City, Poughkeepsie, Albany, Schenectady, and Johnstown. Freemasons also met in traveling military lodges established during the French and Indian War and the Revolution. The Atholl or Provincial Grand Lodge of New York, located in New York City and established in 1781, became the precursor of today's Grand Lodge of New York. In 1787, under the leadership of the state's first chancellor, Robert R. Livingston, New York Freemasons declared their independence from English Masonry.

Freemasonry spread rapidly as New York expanded westward, with additional lodges established throughout the state's interior. The post-Revolutionary order particularly attracted upwardly mobile young men, with Freemasons frequently elected or appointed to political office, taking a role in public ceremonies such as the opening of the Erie Canal, and among the founders of community voluntary organizations. By 1827 some 480 New York lodges housed over 20,000 Masons.

Freemasons faced troubled times, however, after the September 1826 disappearance of William Morgan, a Mason planning to publish the fraternity's secrets. Allegations that Morgan had been murdered by Masons led to a brief but explosive Antimasonic movement and political party. By 1833 only 48 lodges and 1,500 Masons remained active in New York State. Freemasons never again played as prominent a public role as they had, but Antimasonry faded and new lodges began to be established by midcentury. Steady growth followed, with over 83,000 Freemasons in New York State by 1876 and a peak membership of 346,413 in 1929.

In 2003, 628 New York State blue lodges served 64,932 Freemasons. Two concordant bodies, the Scottish Rite and the York Rite, also operated in New York State, along with related organizations, such as the Shrine, the Order of the Eastern Star, the Order of DeMolay for Boys, and the Order of the Rainbow for Girls. Masonic benevolence led to establishment of a home and hospital for needy members and their families in Utica and of the Foundation for Medical Research and Human Welfare in 1947. The Livingston Masonic Library and Museum in New York City houses one of the largest Masonic research collections in the United States. Prominent New York Masons have included Robert R. Livingston, De Witt Clinton, Stephen Van Renssalaer, John Jacob Astor, Theodore and Franklin D. Roosevelt, Herbert H. Lehman, Fiorello La Guardia, Thomas E. Dewey, Irving Berlin, and George M. Cohan.

Since the mid–19th century immigrants in cities such as Albany, Buffalo, and New York have established ethnic lodges under the aegis of the Grand Lodge, conducting rituals in their native languages. Manhattan's Ninth District, for example, completed its own German Masonic Temple in 1880. By contrast, Prince Hall Freemasonry is an independent, parallel organization that has attracted prominent African American New Yorkers such as Duke Ellington, Revs Adam Clayton Powell Sr and Jr, and Arthur A. Schomburg. Free Blacks formed Boyer Lodge in Manhattan in 1812 and established their first Grand Lodge in 1845. In 2002 there were 72 regular lodges, 3 military lodges, and 9 "foreign" lodges (in the Bahamas, Barbados, and Guyana) within New York Prince Hall Masonry. The New York

State Grand Lodge created the Committee on Unity in 1988 and granted full recognition to Prince Hall Masonry on 7 May 2001, and the latter reciprocated.

See also ANTIMASONRY.

Ross, Peter. *A Standard History of Freemasonry in the State of New York,* 2 vols (New York: Lewis Publishing, 1899)

Singer, Herbert T., and Ossian Lang. *New York Freemasonry: A Bicentennial History, 1781–1981* (New York: Grand Lodge of Free and Accepted Masons of the State of New York, 1981)

Kathleen Smith Kutolowski

Freeport. Village (pop 43,783) in Hempstead (Nassau Co). Bordering on the South Shore, it was settled in 1659 and known as Raynortown. The post office (1853) took the name Freeport; the South Side Rail Road (now Long Island Rail Road) made it a station stop in 1867. An important oyster depot after the Civil War, the village incorporated in 1892. It had a number of shipyards from after World War I until *ca* 1990. Freeport grew quickly because of good rail service and proximity to New York City; it had 20,410 residents by 1940. It received a measure of notoriety in the 1920s as one of the Long Island strongholds of the Ku Klux Klan. Nevertheless, African Americans moved in substantial numbers to the Bennington Park neighborhood in the center of the village in the decades before World War II, and in larger numbers after the war. Although racial tensions persisted in the 1950s and 1960s, at first centered on a low-income housing project completed in 1959 and, subsequently, on the movement of black families into formerly all-white neighborhoods, strong civic associations helped keep Freeport integrated. This process was aided by the village's independent, broad-based political parties, such as the Village Party, which was in power for most of the 1960s. In 2000 Freeport's population was approximately 43% white. The Nautical Mile waterfront has fishing boats and boat dealers, casino boats, fish stores, and seafood restaurants. Bandleader Guy Lombardo was a long-time resident.

Lynda R. Day

Free Soil Party. Political party that arose from the controversy over the expansion of slavery. Lasting from 1847 to 1854, it originated in and drew its greatest strength from New York State. In 1847 the New York State Democratic convention did not endorse the Wilmot Proviso, an act that would have banned slavery in any territory won in the Mexican War. Almost half the delegates, known as Barnburners, walked out after denouncing the national platform. Lewis Cass, the Democratic Party's 1848 presidential nominee, supported popular sovereignty for determining the status of slavery in US territories—a system allowing residents in each territory to decide the issue themselves. This stance repulsed many New York State Democrats and encouraged them to join forces with antislavery Whigs and several former abolitionist Liberty Party members to organize the Free Soil Party, which was formalized during the summer of 1848 at conventions in Utica and Buffalo. The group included prominent New York State politicians Samuel J. Tilden, John Van Buren, Preston King, and James Wadsworth, who nominated Martin Van Buren for the presidency on the Free Soil ticket in 1848. This new party garnered 10% of the national vote. Van Buren received 120,497 votes in New York State, 41% of the Free Soil Party total, outpolling Cass. Electoral successes included former Democrat Preston King, who served two terms as a Free Soil congressman between 1849 and 1853.

The party downplayed abolitionism and avoided the moral problems implicit in slavery. Members emphasized instead the threat slavery would pose to free white labor and northern businessmen in the new western territories. Although William Lloyd Garrison derided the party as "white manism," the new approach appealed to many moderate opponents of slavery. The 1848 platform pledged to promote internal improvements, work for a homestead law, pay the public debt, and support moderate tariffs for revenue only. When the Compromise of 1850 neutralized the slavery issue, most Barnburners returned to the Democratic Party, and the Free Soil Party became dominated by vehement antislavery voters. The national party ran John Hale for president in 1852, but he received less than 5% of the vote in New York State. After enormous outrage over the Kansas-Nebraska Act of 1854, the remains of the Free Soil Party helped form the Republican Party.

Blue, Frederick. *The Free Soilers: Third Party Politics, 1848–1854* (Urbana: Univ of Illinois Press, 1973)

Mayfield, John. *Rehearsal for Republicanism: Free Soil and the Politics of Antislavery* (Port Washington, NY: Kennikat, 1980)

Jon Sterngass

free speech. New York State's longstanding role as the center of the national media and as a home for various strains of dissenting politics has ensured its courts a prominent role in defining the limits of free speech in a democratic society. Although the state's constitution since 1821 has mirrored the protection afforded by the First Amendment of the US Constitution, the right to free speech has been bitterly contested throughout the history of the state.

Questions of censorship and freedom of the press have dominated much of the state's history. Nearly half the prosecutions under the federal Alien and Sedition Acts of 1798 originated in New York State. In *People v Croswell* (1804) the state's highest court upheld a conviction for alleged libel of Pres Thomas Jefferson, although agreeing with Alexander Hamilton's argument on behalf of his client that established truth as a defense against libel. During the Civil War the Lincoln administration prohibited certain opposition newspapers, such as the *Journal of Commerce* and the *New York News,* from being distributed through the mail, a decision applauded by pro-war newspapers such as the *New York Times* and *New York Herald.* Freedom of the press fared better in 1892, when the legislature repealed a gag order prohibiting journalists from giving detailed accounts of executions carried out via electric chair. The provision had been included in the 1888 state law mandating use of the new device.

In the 20th century New York State newspapers and publishers continued to be at the forefront of free press cases. In *New York Times v Sullivan* (1964), an outrageously partisan libel case that came close to bankrupting its main targets (civil rights groups in Alabama), the US Supreme Court established a stiffer libel standard for public figures, who had to show that individuals accused of printing falsehoods about them had acted in reckless disregard of the truth. The press has been given even greater protection from libel suits by the State Court of Appeals. In the Pentagon Papers case, *New York Times v United States* (1971), the Supreme Court removed a prior restraint against the newspaper for publishing classified military documents.

Controversy over freedom of expression, particularly when social upheaval is the perceived consequence, also has a long history in New York State. In 1836 the zeal of the abolitionist movement in the state prompted Gov William L. Marcy to call for measures restricting the distribution of antislavery literature, though they were not adopted. The mailing of "obscene materials," including information on contraception and abortion, was prohibited in the Comstock Law passed by Congress in 1873 at the prompting of Anthony Comstock, a leader of the New York Society for the Suppression of Vice. New York State followed suit and adopted its own "baby" Comstock Law. During the early 20th century, the growth of socialist and anarchist ideologies led to many restrictions on speech rights. In 1902, prompted by Pres William McKinley's assassination in Buffalo at the hands of self-described anarchist Leon F. Czolgosz, New York State passed legislation outlawing "criminal anarchy." This law, the first of its kind in the country, not only made it an offense to espouse the overthrow of the government by violence, force, or any other unlawful means, but also made it illegal to belong to any organization that espoused such views. Despite its passage, New York State remained a national center of anarchism and anarchist publications.

Congress's enactment of the Espionage Act of 1917 contributed to many more disputes in the state over speech rights and society's right to preserve domestic order and security, especially during World War I and the postwar Red Scare. In *Masses Publishing Co v Patten* (1917), Judge Learned Hand, then on the US Southern District court, blocked the US postmaster from refusing to distribute "subversive" journals. Hand adopted an expansive view of speech protection, one that comes very close to the contemporary standard that requires spoken or written words to be an "imminent incitement" to illegal acts before such expression can be punished or suppressed. On appeal the US Second Circuit reversed Hand, and for many years thereafter judges were deferential to government interests, not individual speech liberties. In Red Scare era free speech cases like *Abrams v New York* (1919) and *Gitlow v New York* (1925), involving left-wing pamphleteers, the US Supreme Court addressed the issues of what constituted protected speech and unlawful incitement and upheld the convictions of individuals for distributing or simply publishing revolutionary leaflets. In the wake of such cases, New York City became a center for defending freedom of speech, particularly after the founding of the American Civil Liberties Union in 1920. The Syracuse-based case *Feiner v New York* (1951) raised the question of what should be done when protected speech evokes a hostile reaction from an audience and the Supreme Court rules in favor of restricting speech as necessary to maintain order. In *Schenck v Pro-Choice Network of Western New*

York (1997) the Supreme Court addressed a lower court injunction prohibiting the right of antiabortion demonstrators to protest in certain areas outside clinics. While the Court upheld "fixed buffer zones" around doorways, driveways, and driveway entrances as necessary to ensure safe entrance for employees and patients, it struck down other "floating buffer zones" as burdening more speech than was necessary to serve these interests.

Since the mid–20th century, the Supreme Court has ruled on several other types of free speech cases emanating from New York State. Dealing with religious freedom, the Court in *Kunz v New York* (1951) reversed a conviction for violating a New York City ordinance that required permits before individuals could worship in public. In the first flag-burning case to reach the Court, *Street v New York* (1969), the Court chose to decide the case on narrower grounds and overturned Sidney Street's conviction on the basis that he had been arrested simply for speaking contemptuous words against the flag. In *Buckley v Valeo* (1976), the Supreme Court addressed campaign finance when US senator James Buckley of New York and others successfully challenged campaign reform laws limiting the amount of personal expenditures one could make in political contests as a violation of free speech. The case remains central to controversies over campaign finance reform. In cases involving victim rights, *Simon and Schuster v New York State Crime Victims Board* (1991) invalidated New York State's "Son of Sam" law, which had placed earnings from a criminal's literary or other artistic endeavors into an escrow account to compensate victims. And in *Shea v Reno* (1996), the Southern District of New York heard a challenge to the Communications Decency Act, a statute that tried to prohibit obscene and indecent material from being transmitted over the Internet. The case ultimately was heard by the Supreme Court, which invalidated parts of the act for infringing upon protected speech.

Curtis, Michael Kent. "The Curious History of Attempts to Suppress Antislavery Speech, Press, and Petition in 1835–37," *Northwestern University Law Review* 89 (Spring 1995): 785–870

Forkosch, Morris D. "Freedom of the Press: Croswell's Case," *Fordham Law Review* 33 (Mar 1965): 415–48

Jasper, Margaret C. *The Law of Speech and the First Amendment* (Dobbs Ferry, NY: Oceana Publications, 1999)

Sullivan, Kathleen M., and Gerald Gunther. *First Amendment Law* (New York: Foundation Press, 1999)

Timothy P. Gordinier

Freethought. A tradition of religious skepticism rooted in the Deist philosophy of the 18th-century Enlightenment. It posited an orderly universe created by a rational god who had set its laws into motion and then left it to run on its own. By the middle of the century Deism was widespread among the English upper classes and was introduced to America through publications and by British officers serving in the colonies. Revolutionary leaders, including Thomas Paine and Ethan Allen, espoused Deist beliefs, which seemed to support their radical ideas of secular democracy. In 1794, two years before Paine's *Age of Reason* appeared, a former Presbyterian minister named Elihu Palmer established a Deistical society in New York City. Soon Deist groups spread throughout the state, from Newburgh (Orange Co) to Rochester and Wheatland (Genesee Co). Palmer published a series of weeklies, such as the *Prospect: View of the Moral World* (1803–5), which included a series of anti-Christian articles written by Paine when he returned to New York in 1804, but Christians energized by the Second Great Awakening largely suppressed public expressions of Deism for the next two decades.

The first Thomas Paine birthday celebration in New York City in 1825 was so successful that its organizers founded a newspaper, the *Correspondent* (1827–29), and established a popular lecture series. Soon the movement was bolstered by the arrival of English radicals Frances Wright and Robert Dale Owen. After experimenting with a utopian communist colony in New Harmony, Ind, Wright and Owen moved to New York City and resumed publishing their weekly newspaper, *Free Enquirer* (1829–35), formerly known as the *New Harmony Gazette* (1825–29). Popular as lecturers, they soon opened a Hall of Science to promote their socialist and Freethought doctrines. Wright then toured the state, drawing large audiences along the Hudson River and Erie Canal. Although the hall closed soon after Wright sailed back to England in 1832, Freethinkers continued to lecture to large audiences at Tammany Hall and other venues through the rest of the decade, and New York City was their national center. The *Free Enquirer* was followed by the *Beacon* from 1836 to 1846. Organizations in the city included the Moral Philanthropists of Tammany Hall, and groups developed in Rochester, Pultneyville, Corning, Flint Creek, and Penn Yan by 1845. All contributed delegates to the national Convention of Infidels held in New York City that May.

Freethought had a long tradition in Germany, and immigrants arriving in the 1840s and 1850s formed numerous congregations and organizations. Led by figures like Samuel Ludvigh, Philipp Merkle, Rudolph Dulon, and Friedrich A. Sorge, they played a dominant role in many German American communities and were probably more numerous and influential than their English-speaking counterparts in mid-19th-century America. Felix Adler, the founder of the Ethical Culture Society in Manhattan (1876) and a prominent leader of the third wave of the Freethought movement nationwide, inherited this tradition.

The publication of Charles Darwin's *Origin of Species* (1859) seemed to put the weight of science behind Freethought. After the Civil War a relatively conservative alliance of liberal Unitarians, progressive Universalists, radical Quakers, Reform Jews, Spiritualists, and nonbelievers formed the Free Religious Association in Boston in 1867 to promote evolutionism, secularism, and the ideas of liberal religion generally. More radical Freethinkers formed their own base in New York City, where the weekly *Truth Seeker* (1873–), the leading freethinker, agnostic, and atheist journal for many decades and an early defender of family planning efforts, was based until 1964. By 1876 the radicals had founded the National Liberal League (later American Secular Union), which promoted local affiliates like the Nineteenth Century Club of New York and the Schenectady Freethought and Rationalist Association. In 1877, 2,500 of the most radical freethinkers, agnostics, and atheists formed the New York State Freethinkers' Association at a convention in Wolcott (Wayne Co) to operate as a militant auxiliary to the league.

Campaigning against Sunday closings proposed for Manhattan's Central Park and Metropolitan Museum of Art and an amendment to the US Constitution making explicit mention of God and declaring the United States a Christian Nation provided energy to these organizations. The increasingly secular nature of late 19th- and 20th-century America seems to have kept them from attracting large numbers of members. Other issues appeared to be more pressing to many potential recruits, and most who abandoned traditional religion saw little need to join Freethinker organizations. Millions of freethinking Americans have called themselves agnostics or atheists and joined women's rights, peace, labor, socialist, or anarchist campaigns in this period, but only a few thousand joined the Ethical Culture Society, the American Secular Union, the Freethinkers of America, or the American Association for the Advancement of Atheism (all based in New York City). The Ethical Culture Society, the Council for Secular Humanism in Amherst (Erie Co), the Spiritualists of Lily Dale (Chautauqua Co), and the New York State section of American Atheists all maintain an active presence in New York State, but none of them attract the membership of more than a tiny fraction of the state's large population of individuals whose beliefs would place them among the ranks of traditional Freethinkers.

Post, Albert. *Popular Freethought in America, 1825–1850* (New York: Columbia Univ Press, 1943)

Turner, James. *Without God, Without Creed: The Origins of Unbelief in America* (Baltimore: Johns Hopkins Univ Press, 1985)

Warren, Sidney. *American Freethought, 1860–1914* (New York: Columbia Univ Press, 1943)

Stan Nadel

Freetown. Town (pop 789) in S central Cortland Co. The area was settled in 1795, and the town formed in 1818 from Cincinnatus. The land is hilly and lies on a ridge between the Tioughnioga and Otselic Rivers. In the late 19th century its agriculture increasingly emphasized dairying, which remains the largest land use.

Cathy A. Barber

Freeville. Village (pop 505) in Dryden (Tompkins Co). Settled in 1798, Freeville became a junction of three railroads: the Utica, Ithaca and Elmira (1871), the Southern Central (1871), and the Ontario and Western (1872). A factory manufactured window glass for cathedral use from 1886 to 1890. The village incorporated in 1887. George Junior Republic (1895) was developed to teach citizenship and responsibility to at-risk boys on 1,200 acres (486 ha), and in 2003 it had more than 250 "citizens." Since 1897 the village has been the site of a campground of the Central New York Spiritualist Association.

Jane Dieckmann

Freihofer Baking Company. Commercial bakery. Brothers William and Charles Freihofer established the Freihofer Vienna Baking Co in Camden, NJ, in 1899. By 1913 it became the Charles A. Freihofer Baking Co, and neighborhood bakeries were established in New Paltz (Ulster Co), Albany, Schenectady, and Troy

(Rensselaer Co). Horse-drawn wagons home delivered Freihofer's bread, cakes, and coffee. In the 1930s trucks were used, and the last horses were retired in 1966. Children waited for hot rolls handed out off the truck or at the bakery's back door. Freihofer's products were stocked in grocery stores, and in 1972 home delivery ended. Freihofer's sponsored the children's television program *Freddie Freihofer Show* (1949–66), featuring BreadTime Stories. Host Jim Fisk was famous for Squiggles, cartoons he drew from children's scribbles. The company organized the Freihofer's Run for Life (1979), a 10 km road race in Albany, which was renamed the Freihofer's Run for Women in 1981. It became an international competition and one of the largest races in the United States. In 2001, 3,500 registered for either the Freihofer's Run for Women, Kids' Run, or Community Walk. Freihofer's was purchased in 1987 by General Foods for $115 million. Later that year Kraft Foods acquired General Foods and sold Freihofer's for $865 million to CPC International Inc/Bestfoods Baking Co of New Jersey. Bestfoods oversaw bakeries on Long Island, in the Hudson Valley, and in Albany. They created 17 Freihofer's Outlet Stores and established new markets in Rochester and Central New York. In 2001 Freihofer's was best known for its bread and chocolate chip cookies, and was acquired by George Weston Bakeries of Toronto. In 2001 Freihofer's was headquartered in Bay Shore (Suffolk Co), had a sales volume of $162 million, and sold to 11 states.

Freihofer Baking Company. Business Records. Temple Univ Archives, Pennsylvania

Rittner, Don. "Saying Goodbye to Freihofer," www.themesh.com

Tricia A. Barbagallo

Fremont. Town (pop 964) in NW Steuben Co. Settled in 1812, the town was formed in 1854 from Hornellsville, Dansville, Wayland, and Howard. Its land supported timber production and later dairy farming and Christmas tree farming. The 110 million gal (416 million l) Hornell Water Department reservoir was established in the town in 1910. In the early 21st century, dairy and potato farming are the primary industries. An annual Old Home Day has been celebrated since 1919.

Virginia L. Wright and Jerry Wright

Fremont. Town (pop 1,391) in NW Sullivan Co. First settled before the Revolutionary War along the Delaware River, it was populated by German and Swiss immigrants in the 1840s; the town was formed from Callicoon in 1851. Despite its location on the Erie Railroad (1847), tanning and lumbering were its chief industries, because of land too rough for tillage. The Long Eddy Hydraulic and Manufacturing Co (1867) attempted to dam the Delaware for industrial purposes and created Douglas, an incorporated village (1867–73), but both dam and city incorporation attempts were abandoned. Wood acid and other hardwood distillates were produced at Long Eddy, Fernwood, and Acidalia, where the first acid factory in Sullivan Co was built in 1878. Other products were apple crates, bluestone, and chinchillas. In the early 21st century the town is lightly populated and has no significant industry.

John Conway

French. Most French immigrants to colonial New York were Huguenots, Protestants who fled from religious persecution at home and assimilated into the Dutch and English communities of the Hudson Valley. Others included J. Hector St. John de Crèvecoeur, author of *Letters from an American Farmer* (1782), which was based in part on his experiences as a farmer in Pine Hill (Orange Co). In the 1790s two streams of French refugees arrived: planters fleeing the great slave revolt in St. Domingue [now Haiti] and royalists fleeing the French Revolution. In what is now Greene (Chenango Co), royalist refugees created a short-lived settlement (1792–96), which was visited by the celebrated diplomat (then in exile) Charles Maurice de Talleyrand-Périgord. In 1792 other royalists founded the Companie de New York to create a settlement called Castorland on 630,000 acres (254,952 ha) in what is now Jefferson Co; it soon failed. After a diplomatically controversial career, the first ambassador of the French Republic to the United States, Citizen Genet, married a daughter of New York State governor George Clinton and settled in East Greenbush (Rensselaer Co). After 1815 Bonapartist refugees arrived, including James Le Ray Chaumont, who founded Le Raysville (Jefferson Co) as a haven for former soldiers of the Napoleonic armies. Since then, the number of French immigrants to New York State has been small but steady.

North of New York City, French immigrant workers and farmers often joined Francophone Canadian parishes, but professionals, because of the sharp difference in social status, generally preferred to join English-speaking congregations. French middle-class immigrants commonly assimilated quickly and sustained few ethnic associations. Among them is the still existing Masonic lodge Clémente Amitié (1857) in Manhattan. Influential cultural associations in New York City were the Alliance Française (1894) and the Institut Français (1911), which merged in 1971 to form the French Institute–Alliance Française. In 1924 the Comité Central des Sociétés Françaises de New York (since 1997, Committee of French-Speaking Societies) was founded. Most of its 46 member societies in 2003 were professional associations, including those of chefs, lawyers, and bankers. The weekly newspaper *France-Amérique* is published in New York City by the French daily newspaper *Le Figaro,* and the French-American School of New York is located in Mamaroneck (Westchester Co). In the 20th century small-scale French immigration to the United States continued, including a number of Jewish refugees during and after World War II. In 2000 about 21,000 people born in France lived in New York State, while 400,000 claimed French ancestry, many of whom are probably of Francophone Canadian ancestry.

See also ARCHITECTS AND ARCHITECTURE, ADIRONDACKS AND NORTH COUNTRY.

Pula, James S. *The French in America, 1488–1974* (Dobbs Ferry, NY: Oceana Publications, 1975)

Thomas Reimer

French, John Homer (*b* Batavia, Genesee Co, 7 July 1824; *d* Rochester, 23 Dec 1888). Author. French was educated at Cary Collegiate Seminary (Genesee Co) and Clarence Academy (Erie Co), and taught math in Alabama and Stafford (Genesee Co) and Seneca Castle (Ontario Co). At 21 he revised a frequently used textbook, *Adam's Arithmetic.* In 1856 he moved to Syracuse, where he became superintendent of schools in 1865. He designed and patented a folding desk and a folding globe in 1860, and became Dr French that year when the University of Iowa conferred him with a doctor of law degree. In 1869 he published his own math book, known as *French's Arithmetic.* He traveled throughout the county instructing teachers on methodology as a member of the teachers institutes for the State Education Department.

Although nationally celebrated as a pedagogue, French was best known for compiling the *Gazetteer of the State of New York* (1860). He began work in 1856 under the direction of Robert Pearsall Smith, and produced the first comprehensive map of the state that included lakes, roads, canals, railroads, and town and county boundaries—unique information for the period. French oversaw a staff of 60 people who edited surveys, facts, and statistics on geography, history, agriculture, and topography. He produced a state map and others on geography, land patents, and meteorology. The *Gazetteer* was privately funded and cost $94,000 to produce. The 769-page volume sold for $10. Upon his death, French was buried in Syracuse's Oakwood Cemetery. The *Gazetteer*, an indispensable reference work on New York State, is still widely used almost a century and a half after its publication.

French, Mary Elizabeth Washburn, comp. *In Memoriam, John Homer French* (?1889)

Ristow, Walter W. "The French-Smith Map and Gazetteer of New York State," *Quarterly Journal of the Library of Congress* 36 (1979): 68–89

Stephanie Barrett

French and Indian War. The North American component of the Seven Years War (1756–63) and the last in a series of military conflicts in North America between France and Great Britain, and their respective colonial and Indian allies. New York's geographic location made it a strategic center for the British war effort.

Outbreak of Hostilities

Great Britain did not formally declare war against France until 1756, but fighting began in North America in 1754. New York officials were apprehensive about the French presence on their colony's frontier, but it was Virginia that sent provincial troops under Lt Col George Washington to remove the French from Fort Duquesne [now Pittsburgh]. The expedition failed after Washington's surrender at the Battle of Great Meadows on 3 July 1754. Later that year Gen Edward Braddock was appointed commander in chief of the British army in North America, with instructions to remove the French from British-claimed territory.

The Albany Congress of June–July 1754 mended New York Colony's deteriorating relations with the Iroquois Confederacy but failed to achieve greater intercolonial cooperation against French encroachment. The British had a small garrison on Lake Ontario at Oswego, but the French controlled most traffic on that lake and Lake Erie, and therefore access to the interior of the continent and the lucrative fur trade. The French and their Indian allies also commanded the Lake George–Lake Champlain corridor between Albany and Montreal, another important trade route. When Indians burned farms near Hoosick Falls [now in Rensselaer Co] in August 1754, Gov James DeLancey ordered the Albany stockade and blockhouses repaired and the local militia to a state of readiness. Two of the four New York Independent Companies normally garrisoned in New York City had been sent to assist Virginia in the spring of 1754, but DeLancey assigned most of the remaining troops to Albany, Schenectady, Fort Hunter [now in Montgomery Co], and Fort Oswego.

Military Campaigns

The British planned three army expeditions for 1755. Braddock undertook another campaign to remove the French from Fort Duquesne, but his forces were defeated at Battle of the Monongahela on 9 July 1755. Braddock's death in that battle left Massachusetts governor William Shirley in command, who was appointed to lead an attack against Fort Niagara [now in Porter, Niagara Co]. Commissioned major general of provincial troops, William Johnson commanded an expedition against Fort St. Frédéric at Crown Point [now in Essex Co].

Shirley's army departed Albany in summer 1755. He led provincial, British, and Indian troops, as well as civilian workmen. Most arrived in Oswego by late summer; some were assigned to build Forts Bull and Williams to guard the Oneida Carrying Place on Wood Creek. Shirley made several defensive improvements at Oswego, including the construction of Forts George and Ontario, and constructed the first British fleet on the Great Lakes. They did not advance against Fort Niagara because of supply problems.

Provincial troops from New York and New England met at Albany to serve in Johnson's expedition against Fort St. Frédéric in summer 1755. Bateaux and wagons transported the soldiers and supplies to the Carrying Place on the Hudson River, where some troops stayed to construct Fort Lyman, later renamed Fort Edward [now in Washington Co]. More than 2,000 soldiers marched to the southern end of Lake George, where they met Mohawks led by Chief Hendrick (Theyanoguin) and other Iroquois. At the Battle of Lake George on 8 Sept 1755, Johnson's army defeated French and Indian forces under Baron Jean-Armand Dieskau, but the expedition did not continue against Fort St. Frédéric. Some provincial troops remained at Lake George to build and garrison Fort William Henry [now in Lake George, Warren Co], while the French constructed Fort Carillon at Ticonderoga [now in Essex Co]. Johnson was awarded a baronetcy for his victory.

The campaigns of 1755 revealed numerous problems that would challenge a series of commanders in chief of the British forces. The Colonial Assembly at first allocated money reluctantly for wartime expenses. The quartering of British soldiers was expensive and potentially a threat to civil liberties. New York Colony officials constructed barracks at Albany, Schenectady, and New York City only when pressured and quartered troops in private homes only when threatened with force. New Yorkers were often unwilling to serve in provincial regiments, and recruits from other colonies, especially Connecticut, were needed to complete New York's assigned quotas. Provincial troops enlisted each year for a specific campaign under a designated provincial officer and often refused to serve under regular British officers, submit to British military discipline, or extend their time of service into the winter. Wartime profiteering raised prices sharply for food, wagons, horses, and other military supplies, and New York merchants continued their prewar patterns of trade with French colonies.

The British suffered several defeats in New York Colony from 1756 to 1757. Under the new command of Gen John Campbell, Earl of Loudoun, the British army in New York expanded its deployment of Roberts' Rangers and reorganized its transport and supply system. The British government adopted new policies that included generous reimbursement of colonial expenses, increased allocation of regular troops, and more favorable conditions for service in provincial regiments. Improvements came too slowly, however. A French raid led by Lt Joseph-Gaspard Chaussegros de Léry destroyed Fort Bull on 27 Mar 1756. British forces at Oswego surrendered to the Marquis de Montcalm on 14 August; the survivors were imprisoned at Montreal. The following year Lt Col George Munro surrendered Fort William Henry to Montcalm on 9 August, after which France's Indian allies killed or captured more than 500 British regulars, provincial troops, and camp followers.

In early July 1758, the new commander, Gen James Abercromby led an army of British regulars, provincials, and Iroquois allies in an unsuccessful attack against Fort Carillon, where Montcalm prevailed against a much larger British force at the Battle of Ticonderoga. Brig Gen John Stanwix reestablished a British presence at the head of the Mohawk Valley with the construction of Fort Stanwix [now Rome, Oneida Co] at the Oneida Carrying Place. In August 1758 Lt Col John Bradstreet led an expedition across Lake Ontario from Oswego and captured Fort Frontenac [now Kingston, Ont] at the head of the St. Lawrence River.

British victories continued in 1759 under the next commander in chief, Gen Jeffery Amherst. In June 1759 he led New England and New Jersey provincials and British regulars against Forts Carillon and St. Frédéric. The expedition paused at the southern end of Lake George to construct Fort George and to build ships and rafts for the advance northward. The French retreated in late July after destroying both of their forts, which Amherst replaced with Forts Ticonderoga and Crown Point. In late June 1759 New York provincials and British regulars under Brig Gen John Prideaux met Iroquois allies under Sir William Johnson at Oswego. Leaving Brig Gen Thomas Gage to direct the rebuilding of Fort Ontario, Prideaux commanded the siege of Fort Niagara until his death in battle, when Johnson assumed command. Capt Pierre Pouchot surrendered the fort on 25 July. The British captured the City of Quebec two months later on 18 September after the Battle of Quebec.

In 1760 Amherst directed a three-pronged attack on the French at Montreal. Brig Gen James Murray approached from Quebec. Brig Gen William Haviland led an army of New York Independent Companies, New England regiments, and Stockbridge Indians northward along the Lake Champlain corridor and the Richelieu River, forcing the French troops under Louis-Antoine de Bougainville to abandon a series of intervening forts and retreat toward Montreal. After crossing Lake Ontario from Oswego, Amherst led British regulars, Iroquois Indians, and provincial regiments from New York, Connecticut, and New Jersey down the St. Lawrence River to capture Fort Lévis, near Oswegatchie [now Ogdensburg, St. Lawrence Co], before joining the other two armies on the outskirts of Montreal in early September 1760. The governor general of Canada, Pierre de Rigaud, Marquis de Vaudreuil, surrendered Canada on 8 September. Although the fighting against the French in North America ended in 1760, the New York Independent Companies participated in one last campaign in 1762. They sailed from New York City with British regulars and joined the successful siege of Spanish forces at Havana, Cuba.

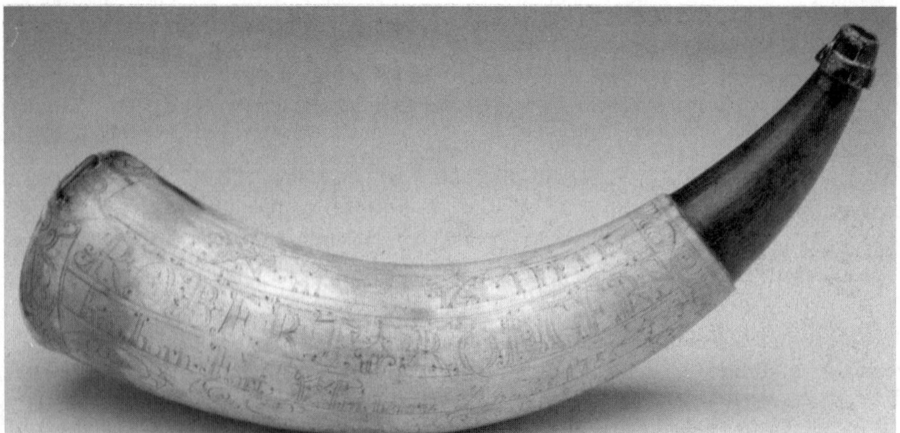

Powder horn used by Capt Robert Rogers at Fort William Henry, 1756.

Impact of the War

Hundreds of New York colonists enlisted in provincial and regular regiments, and even larger numbers of New England and New Jersey provincial regiments and British regulars participated in campaigns in New York. Some New York colonists served in the British navy, often by impressment, while others joined the many privateers that operated out of New York City's harbors. Laborers and craftsmen joined military expeditions to build fortifications, roads, and boats. The majority of the Iroquois Confederacy remained neutral during the first years of the war, but as British victories increased, the Iroquois participated more actively as British allies. Great Britain's victory meant that the Iroquois could no longer use the French-British rivalry to their advantage in negotiations with New York officials.

Under the Treaty of Paris effective 10 Feb 1763, France relinquished its territory east of the Mississippi River to Great Britain. New imperial policies designed to pay for war debts and increased administrative costs and to control Great Britain's enlarged empire led to conflict with the colonists and eventually to the American Revolution.

Anderson, Fred. *Crucible of War: The Seven Years' War and the Fate of Empire in British North America, 1754–1766* (New York: Vintage Books, 2000)

Gipson, Lawrence Henry. *The British Empire before the American Revolution*, rev ed. (New York: Knopf, 1958)

Jennings, Francis. *Empire of Fortune: Crowns, Colonies, and Tribes in the Seven Years War in America* (New York: Norton, 1988)

Pargellis, Stanley M., ed. *Military Affairs in North America, 1748–1765* (1936; repr Hamden, Conn: Archon Books, 1969)

Sullivan, James, et al, eds. *The Papers of Sir William Johnson*, 14 vols (Albany: Univ of the State of New York, 1921–65)

Christine Sternberg Patrick

French Creek. Town (pop 935) in SW Chautauqua Co. Settled in 1812 the town formed in 1829 from Clymer. Although the town is a dairy farming community, the French Creek Preserve has become a recreational destination. Designated as one of the "Last Great Places" by the Nature Conservancy, French Creek contains a biologically diverse riverine system with 12 rare species, primarily fish and mussels. The town is also the site of Peek'n Peak ski and golf resort (1964).

Michelle Henry

Fresh Air Fund. A not-for-profit program with headquarters in New York City giving city children access to country homes in the summertime. The fund was founded in 1877 by Willard Parsons, a minister born in Franklin (Delaware Co) who began his career working with tenement families at the Mayflower Mission in Brooklyn. From there he was assigned to a rural parish in Sherman, Pa. Struck by the difference in health between the tenement children and the rural children, Parsons urged his new parishioners to host some of the more sickly youths from the city mission. During that first summer 60 children spent two weeks or more on farms in southern New York and northern Pennsylvania. In the summer of 1878, the number of participating children increased to 1,000.

Like similar programs in other cities across the country, the New York Fresh Air Fund also offers free camping experiences to children of low-income families, maintaining five separate summer camps at a 3,000-acre (1,200 ha) site in Fishkill (Dutchess Co). The New York City program is unique in its family hosting aspect, with three-quarters of the children who participate taking their vacations in private homes. Since 1877 more than 1,700,000 city children have visited volunteer host families. The program's initial success was attributed to the great public transportation system of the late 19th century and to the single-family dairy farms surrounding New York City. Early in the 21st century, children ride on chartered buses to 300 Friendly Towns from Maine to Virginia and are as likely to stay in suburban houses as on farms. The fund has always had the support of New York City newspapers in its effort to procure donations, beginning with the *Brooklyn Union* until 1883, the *New York Tribune* and *Herald-Tribune* until 1967, and the *New York Times* since 1967.

Fresh Air Fund, http://www.freshair.org

Parsons, Willard. "The Story of the Fresh Air Fund." In *The Poor in Great Cities: Their Problems and What Is Being Done to Solve Them* (London: K. Paul, Trench, Trubner, 1896)

Wright, Lawrence. *City Children, Country Summer* (New York: Scribner's, 1979)

Deborah Schwabach

Fried, Manny [Emanuel] (*b* Brooklyn, 1 Mar 1913). Actor, writer, and labor activist. One of nine children, Fried grew up in a house on Genesee St in Buffalo. During the 1930s, he acted and danced in 13 Broadway plays and joined the Communist Party. In 1939 he returned to Buffalo to direct the short-lived Contemporary Theater. As war loomed, the theater closed, and he went to work at the Cheektowaga (Erie Co) Curtiss-Wright aircraft plant, where he helped the United Auto Workers organize the facility. He joined the United Electrical, Radio, and Machine Workers of America (UE) as an organizer in 1941. Although he left the Communist Party after his service in World War II, he remained active in the UE until 1955, which was expelled from the Congress of Industrial Organizations in 1949 for its pro-Communist sympathies. Fried twice appeared before the House Committee on un-American Activities (1954, 1964). Blacklisted from union work, he sold insurance from 1956 until 1971, received a PhD in English literature from SUNY Buffalo in 1974, and afterward pursued a career as a teacher and writer. His works include *The Dodo Bird* (1967), set in a blue-collar bar in Buffalo, a volume of short fiction, *Meshugah and Other Stories* (1982), and two autobiographical novels, *Big Ben Hood* (1987) and *The Un-American* (1992).

Autodidact Project, http://www.autodidactproject.org/other/mfried

Joseph Golombek Jr

Friendly Club. Founded in New York City in 1793–94, primarily by young graduates of Yale College. The club met privately each Saturday in members' homes to discuss current issues and common reading. With members drawn from the full range of professions, the club both idealized general knowledge and promoted a disciplinary division of intellectual labor. Many of its members achieved great prominence: the poet and doctor Elihu Hubbard Smith edited the first anthology of American poems and with fellow doctors Edward Miller and Samuel Latham Mitchill founded the first American medical journal, *Medical Repository;* Mitchill was elected to both the US Congress and US Senate; James Kent became a state judge and a nationally prominent jurist; William Dunlap became a playwright and opened the New Theatre (later Park Theatre); and Charles Brockden Brown became a novelist and published the *Monthly Magazine.* Together they promoted one another's careers and New York City as a major American intellectual center. Much of their public activity was consumed by their advocacy of sanitary reform in response to the city's recurring outbreaks of yellow fever in 1795 and 1798 in particular. The club crumbled following Smith's death of yellow fever in 1798 and internal disagreements over the politically contentious 1800 election of Thomas Jefferson. Because many club members later rose to such prominence, the group achieved almost mythological status in 19th-century histories of New York City. Many contemporary scholars regard the club as an unsurpassed model of early American intellectual association.

Waterman, Bryan. "The Friendly Club of New York City: Industries of Knowledge in the Early Republic" (PhD diss, Boston Univ, 2000)

Bryan Waterman

Friendship. Town (pop 1,927) in central Allegany Co. Settled around 1805, the town was formed in 1815 from Caneadea. The Erie Railroad (1851) was followed by a short-lived narrow-gauge line and the Pittsburg, Shawmut and Northern (1903–46). Baxter University of Music was an important presence for decades starting in 1853. Friendship was also the home base of the Gorton Minstrels. The Latta Bros manufactured bicycles from 1870 to 1900. In 1881 an oil refinery began operations. Other than dairy farming, important 20th-century employers were Macler Industries (1897; originally Drake Manufacturing Co), a foundry, and Guenther Hosiery Co (1921). In the early 21st century Friendship Dairies (1937) employs 180 workers by manufacturing cottage cheese. Rte 17 (I-86) was completed in town in 1974. Sidney Rigdon (1793–1876), a Mormon leader who contended unsuccessfully with Brigham Young for the presidency after the death of Joseph Smith Jr, was excommunicated and from 1847 on lived the rest of his life in town. A landmark, the Octagon House (1842), was moved in 1978 to Genesee Country Village. The 2,343-acre (948.2 ha) Coyle Hill State Forest is mostly in town.

Frontenac (et de Palluau), Comte de [Buade, Louis de] (*b* Saint-Germain-en-Laye, France, 22 May 1622; *d* Quebec, 28 Nov 1698). Governor of New France. Born into a prominent family, with King Louis XIII as his godfather, Buade had a long military career in France and was appointed governor of New France in 1672. Frontenac scorned Canada's civil officials, jailed dissenting colonists, and quarreled with the Catholic hierarchy. His efforts to extend French influence into the Ohio Valley put him at odds with the Iroquois Confederacy and ran counter to minister Jean-Baptiste Colbert's vision of a compact colony centered on the St. Lawrence River. He was recalled to France in 1682.

His two successors were ineffective in putting down the Iroquois threat to New France, and Frontenac was reappointed to his former post in 1689. His return to Canada coincided with the outbreak of King William's War, during which his strategy was to neutralize the Iroquois and weaken the English with a series of attacks on New York Colony and New England. A February 1690 attack on Schenectady destroyed the settlement and heightened New Yorkers' dissatisfaction with Jacob Leisler's provisional government. In 1693 Frontenac's forces attacked Mohawk villages in what is now Montgomery

Co and were pursued by militia under Albany mayor Pieter Schuyler and New York governor Benjamin Fletcher. Frontenac personally led more than 2,000 French troops, Canadian militia, and allied Indian warriors on an attack against the main villages of the Onondaga and the Oneida in August 1696. The Peace of Rijswijk ended the war a year later, and the Iroquois confederacy agreed to a treaty of peace with New France in 1701. In his final years and once again in defiance of Louis XIV, Frontenac encouraged the expansion of the fur trade when the French economy had difficulty absorbing the supply. Frontenac's death relieved the king from having to remove him as governor a second time.

Eccles, William J. *Frontenac, the Courtier Governor* (Toronto: McClelland & Stewart, 1959)

Daniel A. Piazza

frozen food industry. While a fur trader in the Labrador region of Newfoundland in the 1910s, Brooklyn native Clarence Birdseye witnessed fish freezing as soon as they were pulled from icy water and exposed to frigid air. He discovered that these fish tasted better than cold-packed or slow-frozen fish and worked to develop methods for quantity production. In 1923 Birdseye established the first freezing company in New York State, Birdseye Seafoods, in New York City, with $20,000. Here, packages of food were floated in vats of chilled brine until they were frozen. In 1924 Birdseye introduced the parallel belt system, a controlled, quick-freezing method, where packaged food was rolled between cold, brine-sprayed steel belts. The same year he organized the General Seafoods Corp in Gloucester, Mass. In 1929 the Postum Co (now Kraft General Foods) paid $22 million for a controlling interest in his company, adopted the name General Foods, and established "Birds Eye" as a trademark name. By 1933 Birds Eye's New York City headquarters on Park Ave was the acknowledged frozen food information center. Second to Birds Eye was the New York State–based Honor Brand, sold in ?1939 to Stokely–Van Camp.

During World War II most canned foods were rationed to the war front, increasing demand for frozen foods on the home front and causing the industry in general to claim that "frozen foods will win the war." The nation's first frozen food store, Frostar Frozen Food Center, chartered in 1944 in White Plains (Westchester Co), opened, and W. L. Maxson Co of New York City developed the first commercially frozen meal. During the war it was Maxson who developed the idea of heating frozen cooked foods in airplanes ferrying troops overseas, and later the first frozen dinners on commercial flights known as Sky-Plates, available in markets as Strato-Meals. Loretto Foods, established in 1948 in Olean (Cattaraugus Co), was one of the first frozen soup packers in the United States. In the 1950s, ethnic lines, such as Zion Kosher Meat in New York City and Temple Frosted Foods in Brooklyn, and specialty items, such as deep-dish pies from Orchard Hill Farms in Redhook (Dutchess Co), were introduced.

In 1951 the New York Canned Goods Packers Association (1885) changed its name to the New York State Canners and Freezers Association (now Associated New York State Food Processors). Based in Spencerport (Monroe Co), it became the first state or regional food-processing organization to include frozen food processors. Small processing plants were once located near harvest sites and water sources throughout the state. By the 1950s and 1960s improvements in transportation and mechanization led to fewer but larger plants located farther away from harvest sites. In 1998 the annual production value of processed vegetables in New York State was nearly $50 million. Birds Eye was acquired by Agrilink Foods of Rochester in 1998, and in 2003 the company changed its name to Birds Eye Foods. In 2003 the firm had sales of $1 billion and was the largest processor in the state, with five plants that freeze or repack frozen vegetables. Other processing plants include Boekhout Farms of Ontario (Wayne Co), frozen apple slices; Columbia County Fruit Processors of Germantown, cranberries; and the Western New York Cherry Producers Cooperative in Burt (Niagara Co), frozen tart cherries. In 2001 New York State was seventh in the nation in processed vegetables, which included canned and frozen.

Williams, Edwin William. *Frozen Foods: Biography of an Industry* (Boston: Cahners Publishing, 1963)

Suzan D. Friedlander

fruit farming. New York State's fruit production is concentrated near large bodies of water that provide both a source for irrigation and moderate temperatures, which favor growth and reduce the risk of spring frosts. Lands around Lake Erie, the Finger Lakes, and Long Island are noted for grape production, while those near Lake Ontario, Lake Champlain, and the Hudson River valley are recognized for tree fruits. Unlike grapes and tree fruits, which are sold mostly through wholesale markets and processors, most berries are sold fresh from the farm directly to customers. Berry production can therefore be found around most cities and villages in New York State, especially near the population centers of Syracuse, Buffalo, Rochester, Albany, and Binghamton.

American Indians harvested vast quantities of berries from wild stands and may have burned some tracts of land to enhance fruit production. Throughout the 17th and 18th centuries, European settlers brought with them fruit not found in North America, including apples, pears, peaches, cherries, and currants, and began to plant them in home orchards. Native fruits such as raspberries, strawberries, gooseberries, and grapes were hybridized with European strains to improve their hardiness and resistance to disease. But because of the abundance of blueberries, cranberries, blackberries, elderberries, and other wild fruits in the northeastern United States, significant breeding and cultivating did not occur until the mid-1800s, after the country had begun to urbanize.

In 1771 Prince's Nursery in Flushing (Queens Co) was the first nursery in the country to feature fruit, such as berries, and grafted trees in its catalog. In 1889 New York State established the nation's first publicly funded fruit-breeding program at the Agricultural Experiment Station in Geneva (Ontario Co). This led to the release of many varieties of apples, grapes, raspberries, and strawberries, and formed the foundation of a strong fruit industry. Processors built plants, particularly in Western New York, and made apple juice, cider, sauce, and vinegar, and grape juice. In 1896 Dr. Welch's Grape Juice (now Welch Foods) moved its plant from New Jersey to Watkins Glen (Schuyler Co) and the following year relocated to Westfield (Chautauqua Co). Technology developed at Cornell University in the 1940s and 1950s allowed producers to store apples in top condition for many months, making local apples available year-round. However, as fruit production expanded into western states and to other countries with lower labor costs and less expensive land, several large processors relocated in the mid-1900s and New York State's market share began to decline.

In the 18th century apple orchards were well established in the Hudson and Mohawk Valleys. In 2001 New York State growers produced 412,000 tons (373,800 MT) of apples, ranking them second in the nation behind those of Washington State. The leading variety was McIntosh, accounting for 18% of total production. Other important varieties were Empire, Delicious, Golden Delicious, Cortland, Ida Red, Crispin, Jonagold, and Rome. The Geneva station developed several, including Cortland (1898), Macoun (1932), Empire (1966), and Jonagold (1968). In 2001 Wayne Co, with 17,000 acres (6,900 ha) in orchards, was the leading producer of apples in New York State. The same year the state ranked third in tart cherry production and fourth in pear production. In 2003 farmers in Wayne Co, also the state's leading cherry producer, suffered severe losses when an April ice storm destroyed an estimated 85% of the county's sour cherry trees.

Wild, native grapes are found throughout the state, but do not, as European settlers discovered, make good wine. French Huguenots established a vineyard and winery in the Hudson River valley near New Paltz (Ulster Co) in 1677. Rev William Bostwick started one of the earliest vineyards in Western New York at Hammondsport (Steuben Co) in about 1830. By the mid-1800s growers had worked out some of the production problems with European grapes, and small wineries were becoming successful around New York City and the Hudson River valley. Once the native Concord variety was found in Massachusetts in 1852, however, grape growing in New York State expanded significantly. The hardy and disease-resistant Concord could be eaten fresh and made into juice. By 1907 New York State was producing 4 million gallons (15 million l) of wine from hybrid and native grapes like Concord, as well as juice and champagne. Most of the production was along Lake Erie. In 2002 Concord grapes accounted for two-thirds of the total grape production. Most of the grapes grown in the rest of the state are made into wine. The Finger Lakes and Long Island regions have acquired national reputations for high-quality wine made from French American hybrids and *vinifera* grapes. State growers deliver about 150,000 tons (136,000 MT) of grapes to wineries and processing plants each year, ranking them third in production nationally. Table grapes make up only a very small component of the state's grape industry. Seedless varieties developed at the Geneva station, such as Himrod (1952), Canadice (1962), and Einset (1985), are grown throughout the state to supplement farm markets. In 2001 the value of the state's tree fruit and grape production was $189 million.

Berries are widely grown since they are very perishable and are mostly sold directly to the consumer through farmers' markets, roadside stands, or pick-your-own operations. Their perishability and a lack of farm labor has constrained expansion into large-scale processing. The leading strawberry variety in the northeastern United States is Jewel, developed at the Geneva station in 1985. In 2001 strawberry production in the state was valued at $7 million, raspberries at $1.9 million, and blueberries at $1.7 million.

Hedrick, U. P. *The Small Fruits of New York* (Albany: J. B. Lyon, 1925)
2001 Annual Fruit Report (Albany: NYS Department of Agriculture and Markets)

Marvin Pritts

Fulton. City (pop 11,855) in central Oswego Co. Settled in 1793 at rapids in the Oswego River, Fulton grew under the influence of the Oswego Canal (completed 1828) and became a major industrial center with a number of large gristmills. Among other manufactories, woolen mills made uniforms for soldiers from the Civil War through World War II. The City of Fulton was formed in 1902 from the Villages of Fulton (1835) and Oswego Falls (1847). Hunter Arms (1890), Oswego Falls Pulp and Paper Co (1886), Olympic Silk Mills (1928), machine works, flour mills, and several food-processing plants provided full employment for workers, including many people from Ukraine. In the 1930s Fulton was nicknamed "The City the Depression Missed," and by 1960 it was the most industrialized city in Oswego Co, with Nestlé's chocolate factory (1900), Armstrong Cork (1860), and Sealright (1917), which coated cardboard dairy cartons, employing more than half the total number of county factory workers. After 1960 loss of jobs resulted in population decline and economic stress. Urban renewal destroyed much of Fulton's eastside business district, but many parts of the city's built environment—including outstanding examples of churches and schools, as well as the post office and public library—still reflect Fulton's earlier prosperity. When Nestlé's chocolate factory closed in 2003, Fulton lost 487 jobs. Several major industries remained, however, including Black Clawson (coating equipment for paper and plastic), Agrilink (frozen foods), Interface Solutions (floor backing and gaskets), and Humataki, the successor to Sealright.

Judith Wellman and Mary Ellen Ross

Fulton. Town (pop 1,495) in central Schoharie Co. Settled in 1716 by Palatines, the town was formed from Middleburgh in 1828. It was the home of Timothy Murphy (*d* 1818), a hero of the Revolution, and William C. Bouck (1786–1859), governor of New York State (1843–44). A peculiar landform, Vroman's Nose, rises 1,230 feet (375 m) above the valley. The rich, alluvial soil of the Schoharie floodplain supports many prosperous dairy, vegetable, and fruit farms. General Electric tested the first successful smoke-screen generator for military use in Fulton on 24 June 1942. Camp Summit (1961), a forestry-oriented minimum security prison, was converted in 1988 to the Summit Shock Correctional Facility, a military-style camp for young men at risk. Max V. Shaul State Park is in town.

Peter Johnson and Dawn Johnson

Fulton, Robert (*b* Little Britain [now Fulton Township, Pa], 14 Nov 1765; *d* New York City, 23 Feb 1815). Inventor of first successful steamboat. The son of Scots-Irish immigrants, Fulton trained with a Philadelphia jeweler before becoming an independent painter *ca* 1785. Traveling to England, he exhibited at the Royal Academy (1791–93) and worked on canal design and construction. His *Treatise on the Improvement of Canal Navigation* (1796) won him fame as a civil engineer, and in 1797 he moved to France to experiment with submarines. There he met former New York State chancellor Robert R. Livingston, who held the exclusive right to operate steamboats (then purely experimental vessels) in his home state. An 1802, after a hiatus of several years during which Fulton worked on naval mines, agreement between the two men led to the New York City-built *North River Steamboat* (often called *Clermont*), completed in 1807. This craft made a trial run to Albany that August and, after improvements were made, began regular service between New York City and Albany the next year. Also in 1808, Fulton married his partner's cousin, Harriet Livingston. Within five years, the Fulton-Livingston partnership controlled steamboats throughout the East and Midwest. But Robert Livingston's death in 1813 spurred challenges to both the New York State monopoly and the company's patents (1809, 1811) on the steamboat. While embroiled in these battles, Fulton died of pneumonia.

Sale, Kirkpatrick. *The Fire of His Genius: Robert Fulton and the American Dream* (New York: Free Press, 2001)

Norman Brouwer

Fulton County (496 mi^2/1,285 km^2; pop 55,073). It was created from Montgomery Co in 1838 and named in honor of Robert Fulton, inventor of the steamboat. Territory was surrendered to Hamilton Co in 1860. Fulton Co is presently divided into 2 cities, Gloversville and Johnstown, and 10 towns that contain 3 entire incorporated villages and part of another. Johnstown serves as county seat. Elevations range from 455 feet (139 m), where Cayadutta Creek exits the county southwest of Johnstown, to over 2,780 feet (847 m) at the summit of Pigeon Mountain just south of the Hamilton Co line in the Town of Bleecker.

Fulton Co lies within two major physiographic provinces. Two subregions of the Adirondack Upland province, the Adirondack Low Mountains and the Western Adirondack Hills, occupy approximately two-thirds of the county. The low mountain region extends south as an inverted triangle as far as Gloversville. Local relief varies from 1,000 feet (300 m) in the north to 200–300 feet (60–90 m) along the southern margins. Local relief in Adirondack Hills in the western portion of the county is similar, but the slopes are noticeably gentler, creating a rolling topography with few distinct hill forms. The bedrock in the Adirondack portion consists of metamorphosed sedimentary rock, including marble, quartzite, and gneiss, all metamorphosed during the Grenville orogeny of the middle Proterozoic age and much more recently uplifted. The county's remaining third lies within the Mohawk Valley subregion of the Hudson-Mohawk Lowland physiographic province. Elevations range from 700 to 1,000 feet (200–300 m) in the more rolling east and are 200 feet (60 m) higher in the more hilly southwest. Bedrock is of late Cambrian- and, further south, Ordovician-age limestones and shales. Glaciation is evident throughout by till and alluvial sediments laid down during the Wisconsonian glaciation. These materials impeded the southward flow of the Sacandaga River, diverting it to its present eastern course. As a consequence, most surface waters in the eastern half of the county drain east to the Hudson. The western half lies within the watershed of the Mohawk River, the primary streams being the Caroga, Cayadutta, East Canada, and Sprite Creeks. The dam creating Sacandaga Reservoir (also known as Great Sacandaga Lake), by far the largest water body in the county, was completed in 1930 to alleviate flooding on the Hudson. Soils in northern Fulton Co are not considered viable for modern agriculture. The limited amount of good arable land in the south is located immediately to the east of Gloversville and Johnstown.

The climate of Fulton Co is humid-continental with warm summers. As measured in Gloversville, average January and July temperatures are

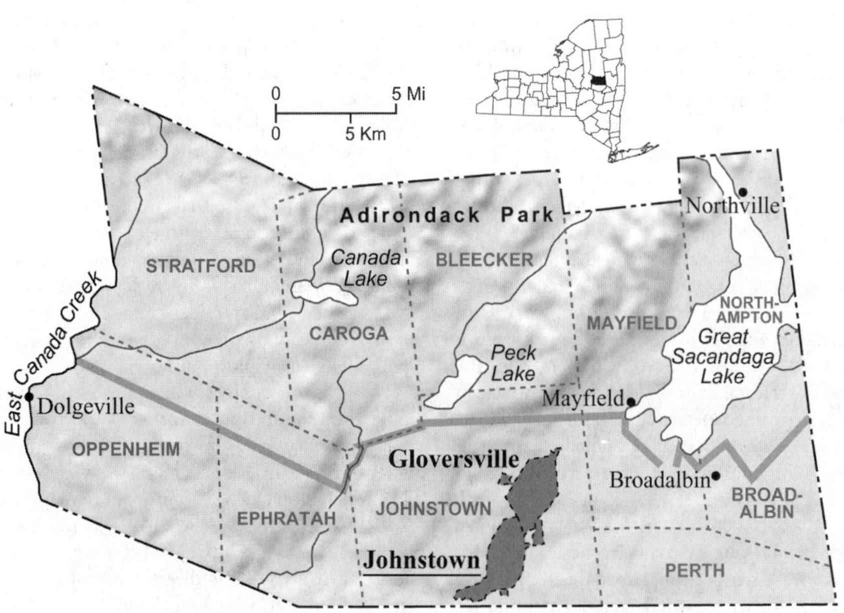

19°F (-7°C) and 69°F (21°C), respectively. Lows fall below 0°F (-18°C) frequently during the winter, while daytime highs reach 90°F (32°C) or above in the lower elevations a few times in most summers. Monthly precipitation normals are quite consistent throughout the year. Mean annual precipitation is between 44 and 47 inches (112–19 cm) with higher amounts in the west and north. Seasonal snowfall averages 77 inches (1956 cm) at both Northville and Broadalbin, and is typically over 100 inches (254 cm) in the higher elevations of the north. Aside from the county's extreme southern margins, primeval forest cover consisted of an Adirondack hardwood community dominated by beech, sugar maple, yellow birch, hemlock, and white pine in the lower elevations and intermixed with red spruce, balsam fir, and paper birch in the higher north. An Alleghenian hardwood forest dominated by beech, sugar maple, hemlock, white pine, and basswood covered the southernmost parts. At the present time over 75% of Fulton Co is forest covered, virtually all of it second or third growth. The northern half lies within the Adirondack Park Blue Line.

FULTON CO POPULATION CENSUS FIGURES

	White	Nonwhite	Total Population	Foreign-Born
1840	17,935	114	18,049	—
1850	20,069	102	20,171	1,421
1860	23,977	185	24,162	2,239
1870	26,835	229	27,064	2,515
1880	30,707	278	30,985	2,931
1890	37,364	286	37,650	3,984
1900	42,476	366	42,842	4,945
1910	44,210	324	44,534	6,568
1920	44,612	315	44,927	6,314
1930	46,291	269	46,560	5,955
1940	48,335	262	48,597	5,319
1950	50,706	315	51,021	4,329
1960	50,947	357	51,304	3,297
1970	52,150	487	52,637	2,187
1980	54,369	784	55,153	1,829
1990	52,905	1,286	54,191	1,210
2000	52,863	2,210	55,073	1,070

Notes: "Nonwhite" includes African Americans, Asians, American Indians, and Pacific Islanders and, for 2000, also the mixed race and other race categories. Through the 1960 census these figures primarily reflect the African American population. For 1930 and 1950, the foreign-born totals include Whites only. Other years include all foreign-born in the population.

American Indians and Early Settlement

Fulton Co was part of the homeland of the Mohawk Nation. Its northern reaches were used chiefly for hunting, but archaeological evidence demonstrates that the valley land in the south was the site of some permanent villages. Three excavations near Ephratah, all dating from the late 16th century, bear witness to significant populations. One contains the remains of three sets of three longhouses; each of the other two had at least five. One longhouse was 315 feet (96 m) in length. Mohawk villages during the Contact period were closer to the Mohawk River.

Purchases authorized by the British colonial government from the Mohawk, some of questionable legitimacy, began with the Kayaderosseras Patent (1708), although it remained unoccupied and in dispute until 1771; it included a part of Perth and Amsterdam. The Stone Arabia Patent (1723) was partly in Johnstown and Ephratah, and white settlement began when some Palatine Germans began clearing land in the present Ephratah; about 1750 Palatines settled in Oppenheim as well. Between 1735 and 1770, some 16 other patents were granted by the provincial government within the present county, the most important of which was Sir William Johnson's Kingsborough Patent (1753). Made superintendent of Indian affairs for the Northern Department in 1756, Johnson approached the development of his tract with a feudal vision. He began settling tenants, mostly English, Scots, and Irish immigrants, on his lands in Johnstown and Mayfield about 1760; he platted Johnstown, a market town under his patronage, in 1763. He began settling tenants in Broadalbin and Perth about 1770 and was able to secure the creation of Tryon Co (named for the royal governor), with its seat at Johnstown, in 1772. He immediately erected a fine courthouse and jail, both of which remained standing in 2003. With conflict on the western frontier in 1774, a large council was held at Johnson Hall, drawing over 600 Indians from many nations. After the Revolutionary War, the loyalist Mohawks were removed to Canada, ending native presence for over two centuries. The more remote towns of Fulton Co were settled later. Caroga was settled around 1783, but its growth did not begin until 1790, while rugged Stratford and Bleecker were occupied about 1800 during the westward migration from New England.

Revolutionary War

Sir William Johnson died immediately after the large council in the summer of 1774, and his proprietary role was assumed by his son John. The Committee of Safety for Tryon Co met at the start of hostilities (1 June 1775), but John Johnson and his relatives, notably his cousin and brother-in-law Guy Johnson, were steadfastly loyal and quite hostile to patriot sympathizers. Guy left soon after for Montreal, where he served as a British agent to the loyalist Indians; John followed in May 1776.

Meanwhile, a significant part of the population of Tryon Co, which included settlements in present-day Montgomery, Otsego, Herkimer, and Fulton Cos, supported the patriot cause; the Tryon Co Militia under Gen Nicholas Herkimer fought bravely at Oriskany. The region's worst losses occurred during the war's last full year. On 21 May 1780 Sir John Johnson led a raid on Johnstown; and on 25 Oct 1780 a force under Col Marinus Willett routed another British raiding party at Johnson Hall. In December 1780 the Tryon Co supervisors reported the statistics: 700 buildings were burned, 613 residents went over to the enemy, 354 residents abandoned their homes and property, 197 lives were lost, and 121 people were taken into captivity.

The Johnson family's holdings were forfeited after the war, and on 2 Apr 1784 the county's name was changed from Tryon to Montgomery, after Gen Richard Montgomery, who lost his life in an assault on Quebec. Johnstown remained its county seat until 1836, when it was moved to Fonda (Montgomery Co). The increased distance to court was the direct cause of the creation of Fulton Co two years later.

Transportation

Sir William Johnson's patent was centered 5 miles (8 km) north of the Mohawk River, so Fulton Co did not benefit from water transport. Roads from the river provided access to the settlements. Johnstown was on a state military road from Albany to Sackets Harbor (Jefferson Co) during the War of 1812; its route westward through Ephratah and Oppenheim benefited those isolated towns. Perhaps because the territory had been so dependent upon short roads to the Mohawk, it was little involved in the turnpike-building business.

Most transportation improvements were a short distance away in the Mohawk Valley. The Erie Canal was finished through the valley in 1822 and connected it to the Hudson in 1823. In 1826 residents of the county, like those of many other regions in the state, called a meeting to request a canal through the area: from the Erie to the Sacandaga, or even to the distant Raquette or Grass Rivers. Nothing came of it. In 1836 the Utica and Schenectady Railroad (later part of New York Central) was completed along the north side of the canal and the Mohawk River. It was not until 1870 that a branchline, the Fonda, Johnstown and Gloversville (FJ&G), connected Fonda to Fulton Co's population centers. Another line, the Gloversville and Northville, linked those communities in 1875 and was sold to the FJ&G in 1881. Johnstown, Gloversville, and Kingsboro were connected by a street railway in 1874, which was electrified around 1892. The county's final rail link was the FJ&G branch to Broadalbin (1895).

Economic Development

The first industries were forest related. Lumbering and tanning provided cash incomes to households practicing subsistence farming. The best-known firm and one of the largest was established just after the Civil War: the Wheeler-

POPULATIONS OF TOWNS AND CITIES, FULTON CO

Town or City, Year Founded	1800	1840	1880	1920	1960	2000
Bleeker, 1831	—	346	1,046	389	245	573
Broadalbin, 1793	1,133	2,738	2,175	1,949	2,945	5,066
Caroga, 1842	—	—	855	332	568	1,407
Ephratah, 1827	—	2,009	2,157	1,038	1,237	1,693
Gloversville (city), 1890	—	—	—	22,075	21,741	15,413
Johnstown, 1793	3,932	5,409	16,626	1,948	5,120	7,166
Johnstown (city), 1895	—	—	—	10,908	10,390	8,511
Mayfield, 1793	876	2,615	2,231	1,866	3,613	6,432
Northampton, 1799	990	1,526	2,069	2,191	2,033	2,760
Oppenheim, 1808	—	2,169	1,845	1,182	1,223	1,774
Perth, 1838	—	737	915	596	1,768	3,638
Stratford, 1805	—	500	1,066	453	421	640

Note: In 1800 the Towns of Broadalbin, Johnstown, Mayfield, and Northampton were in Montgomery Co.

Claflin Co (1865) operated a sawmill at Pine Lake and a large tannery elsewhere in Caroga. The tannery closed in 1888, but many sawmills in the area continued for some years. Paper manufacturing began in Broadalbin at the Scotland Paper Mills (1828–77) and was also carried out in Ephratah and Mayfield; much of the product was strawboard for boxes. A limited amount of metalworking took place, producing saws and files, steel traps, and metal bindings. Woodenware was made in Mayfield. But most of Fulton Co's manufacturing was of leather, gloves, and mittens, or industries supporting those trades.

Tourism developed after the Civil War, initially with the Canada Lake House (1868) and cottages nearby (1880s) and summer boarders at Northville. With the railroad in 1875, Sacandaga Park was created across the river from Northville and was resurveyed and expanded in 1898. Tourism remained at the county's margins, separate from its industrial cities and farming towns.

Tanning and Glove Making

Throughout the 19th and 20th centuries, economy was dominated by tanning and glove manufacturing. Unlike tanning in other regions of New York State, this was not hemlock bark tanning of cowhides for shoes and boots, but deerskin tanning using other organic materials, and manufacturing into gloves and clothing. It began with the first glove and mitten shops in Johnstown in 1808 and in what became Gloversville in 1810.

At first, the same shops that tanned the leather made the finished product, but by the 1840s the two trades were separate but remained connected. They developed into a vertically integrated business with a full panoply of supporting industries, and local producers were marketing gloves as far away as the West Coast. Sewing machines were introduced in 1851 and became a necessity because of the labor demands of the Civil War; dies for cutting gloves were introduced about the same time and, beginning in 1857, were manufactured in Gloversville. Glue, a side product, was made starting in 1868, and the same waste from hides led to the development of Johnstown's Knox Gelatine Co (1890).

The first few generations of tanners and glove makers were New Englanders or British immigrants, but there was a large ethnic presence in the industry. Nathan Littauer, a German Jewish immigrant, began manufacturing gloves in 1866. He employed some other German Jews, but it was after the relatively liberal era in the Russian Empire ended in 1881 that many skilled workers, fleeing oppression, immigrated to Fulton Co. Their numbers peaked about 1900, when many of the factories were Jewish owned.

Shops ranged from family-run businesses in homes to large factories with 500 employees, such as Littauer Bros Glove Co and Daniel Hays Glove Co. With expansion, Johnstown and Gloversville became the center of the US glove industry but on different scales. In 1890 Gloversville had twice as many shops as Johnstown, and their average size was larger. Outlying factories and shops were located in Mayfield, Broadalbin, Northville, and Ephratah. The trade dominated the county: in 1905, 82.4% of its wage earners worked in gloves or leather, and in 1909 there were no fewer than 12,950 glove workers. So great was the concentration of glove making in Johnstown and Gloversville that, in 1900, Fulton Co produced 57% of all gloves made in the nation. Manufacture of the cheaper grades of gloves moved west around that year, and the county came to specialize in men's fine leather dress gloves. In the continuing search for skilled workers for what remained a craft rather than an industrial operation, glove shops attracted Slovaks, Italians, and Irish to Johnstown and Germans, Jews, and Italians to Gloversville.

Other, related business developed: the manufacturing of glove-making machines (1893), a knitting mill (1893), and silk mills. Straw paper boxes for packaging and shipping were made locally beginning in 1889. The zenith of the glove business was reached about 1890 and continued into the first decade of the new century. In 1904 there was a strike/lockout, constructed in an open shop, leaving the International Table Cutters Union powerless, and union strength declined thereafter. Another strike by the cutters, protesting the lack of a wage increase since 1904, took place in 1914–15; mediation failed to gain concessions from the manufacturers. Another strike/lockout followed, but this, too, ended with workers conceding.

As late as 1929, 138 of the nation's 257 substantial glove manufacturers were located in Fulton Co. People were satisfied with the good living that the glove business afforded. Johnstown and Gloversville had high rates of homeownership, and residents' children attended college in substantial numbers. The depression led to a rise in union membership, but the industry spread work around, so people were generally underemployed rather than unemployed. There was a complacency to the Fulton Co glove industry that was to prove costly. Business actively discouraged any broadening of the industrial base, and the glove manufacturers were highly conservative, tending not to adjust to changing technology or markets. Crucial parts of the glove-making process were difficult to mechanize and required cheap labor. With the restriction of immigration in the 1920s, new arrivals willing to work hard for low starting wages were no longer available. Around 1938 owners began to contract work out of the country, initially to Puerto Rico.

For generations, the seasonal nature of the work and the consequent limits on shop space had been compensated for by "homework," in which workers, mostly women, took gloves home to stitch. Under union demands, the New York State Department of Labor began to restrict homework in 1941. World War II brought government contracts, but the war's end was followed by higher unemployment. Many factors were conspiring against the industry, including seasonality, high costs, high wages, and competition from overseas. Tannery workers called a strike in 1949–50, with Communist participation, that resulted in 7,000 of the county's 9,000 workers being out of work. Even after the strike ended, 5,615 remained out of work. The industry's ultimate decline had begun, and it became precipitous in the 1960s.

Religion, Education, and Culture

Sir William Johnson, an Anglo-Irishman, was a strong Anglican, and he founded St. John's Church soon after he platted Johnstown in 1763; its second building was erected in 1771. A colony of Roman Catholics from the Scottish Highlands settled on Johnson's land in 1773 and were accompanied by a priest, Fr Peter McKenna, but most moved in the spring of 1776 to Glengarry in Canada. Following the Irish immigration in the mid–19th century, Catholic missions were established, growing into two parishes before 1855. In that year, Fulton Co had 38 churches, 9 of them Presbyterian, reflecting the Scottish settlement, and 4 Reformed, reflecting the Palatine diffusion from the Mohawk Valley. Methodist congregations were most numerous at 11. Gloversville's German Jewish Littauer family arrived in 1855 and attracted other Jews, especially after Russian Empire persecution resumed in 1881. Their synagogue, Knesseth Israel, formed in 1891 and constructed a building in 1906.

Sir William Johnson provided education in 1771 when he secured a teacher by advertising in New York City and Philadelphia newspapers. A long list of the school's students has survived, showing that it was heavily patronized. Johnstown Academy incorporated in 1794 and erected a building in 1796, offering higher branches of learning. In 1800 a school of slab wood was built in the present Gloversville. The countywide system of publicly supported common schools followed legislation of 1812 and 1814.

Gloversville Union Seminary was founded in 1855, but by that time, public support for high schools was possible because of the Union Free School legislation of 1853. The seminary was purchased by the new Gloversville Union Free School District in 1868, and Johnstown Academy became the foundation of the Johnstown district in the following year. Union Free School districts were formed elsewhere in the county (Northville, Broadalbin, and Mayfield) in the 1890s.

Centralization of rural schools began with Northville and Stratford in 1928, and there were six central districts in the county by 1939. Johnstown and Gloversville city districts enlarged in 1958 by absorbing most of the remaining common schools in the county, and shortly afterward the Stratford Central School merged into Oppenheim-Ephratah and the Mayfield Central School merged into Northville. In 2004 Fulton Co was served by four central schools, two city schools, and the Wheelerville Union Free School in Caroga. Higher education is provided by Fulton-Montgomery Community College, just beyond the county line. The Tryon School for Boys (1966) at West Perth educates at-risk youth; its counterpart for girls dates from 1974.

The county's first newspaper was the *Johnstown Gazette* (1796). Through two centuries, Johnstown and Gloversville were the sites of most of the county's newspapers. The only paper published in 2003 was the *Leader Herald* (1955), created from a merger and headquartered in Gloversville. Fulton Co's first radio station, WENT-AM (1944) at Gloversville, was still broadcasting in 2003, as were WIZR-AM and WSRD-FM (both 1968) at Johnstown.

Caroga was the home of a small summer colony of artists, illustrators, and celebrities in the early 1900s. The Colonial Little Theatre has been in operation since 1946, and the Fulton County Arts Council was founded in 1975. Additional live performances and arts events are promised by the ongoing restoration of the 1916 Glove Theater in Gloversville. The most important museum is Johnson Hall State Historic Site, the restored 1763 home of Sir William Johnson. Robert W. Chambers (1865–1933) of Broadalbin was a popular writer, and movie magnate Samuel Goldwyn (1879–1974) was a Gloversville native.

Politics

Fulton Co is governed by a Board of Supervisors that, since the incorporation of its two cities, has consisted of members from each town and each city ward. By a law passed in 1969, weighted voting was imposed. For a period of years in the last quarter of the 20th century, a county administrator was employed as the executive officer, but in 2003 day-to-day operations were handled by the chair of the board, who is elected annually.

Although the county was and is largely Republican, the Town of Bleecker was overwhelmingly Democratic during and after the Civil War, and Northampton somewhat less so. By the time of the depression, those towns were Republican like the rest of the county. Some Democratic strength is found in the City of Gloversville, but a native son, Lucius N. Littauer (1859–1944), scion to the founder of the glove-making firm, was a leader of the Republican Party in New York State, served five terms in Congress (1897–1907), and was Fulton Co's most prominent philanthropist.

Recent History

Agriculture, never favored by Fulton Co's soil or topography, declined dramatically in the early 20th century. The 1930 filling of the Great Sacandaga Lake in the northeastern towns inundated some of its best farmland. By 1950 there were only 830 farms, about one-third the 1900 number. In 1997 only 176 farms remained on 34,291 acres (13,877 ha), 10.8% of the county's area. Fulton Co ranks as one of the least-farmed counties in the state. Outside the New York City metropolitan area, it has the smallest percentage of land in farms except for Hamilton, Warren, and Sullivan Cos. Still, the Model Dairy Farm near Gloversville and the waterpowered Eagle Mills (cider) near Broadalbin not only survive but draw substantial numbers of visitors for education and enjoyment. Tourism is growing and is concentrated around Sacandaga, Canada, and Caroga Lakes.

The population changed little in the 20th century; an exception was the Ukrainian community, peripheral to a much larger one in Amsterdam, which settled at Union Mills in Broadalbin soon after World War II. In recent years, Amish farmers have spilled over the county line into Ephratah from their original 1986 settlement in Palatine (Montgomery Co). The county has attracted no substantial immigrant group since the Slovak and Italian immigration before World War II.

In the early 1960s the chemical tanning of cowhide briefly revived the leather industry, but in 2003 only 12 tanneries remained, chiefly coloring and finishing and much of that contracted abroad. By 2003 glove making was nearly gone. Joseph P. Conroy Co remained in business, along with two or three small, specialized shops; most of their work, too, was performed in factories overseas, either owned by local firms or contracted by them. These locations have migrated since 1938 from Puerto Rico to the Philippines, Korea, Japan, Indonesia, and India.

Fulton Co fought against this trend with considerable success in the last decades of the 20th century. In 1987 Gov Mario M. Cuomo selected Gloversville as one of the state's first Economic Development Zones (now Empire Zones). At the time, the county faced 18% unemployment, which was seventh highest in the nation. In the 16 years through 2003, the county's Economic Development Corp has managed business expansion that brought 24 new businesses and created 2,000 new jobs. Three industrial parks are the sites of most of the new business: Johnstown Industrial Park, Crossroads Industrial Park, and Crossroads Business Park.

In 2003 the county's largest employers were outside the manufacturing sector: Lexington Center (1,200; services for people with disabilities), county government (830), and Nathan Littauer Hospital (800). The diversification in many new firms in many sectors, each employing a moderate number of workers, is an answer to the leather monoculture whose decline nearly destroyed the county's two cities in the late 20th century. Of particular note was the 2000 construction of an 850,000 ft^2 (79,000 m^2) Wal-Mart Northeast Region Food Distribution Center, which created over 700 jobs. The largest manufacturers in 2003 were Nelson A. Taylor Co (300; canvas goods) and School House Companies (250; pallets).

The first historical work to cover Fulton Co and surrounding territory was William W. Campbell, *Annals of Tryon County* (1831). The standard histories are *History of Montgomery and Fulton Counties* (1878) and Washington Frothingham, *History of Fulton County* (1892). There have been a number of town histories, including an exemplary one by Barbara McMartin, *Caroga: The Town Recalls Its Past* (1976). Also good are *Our Todays and Yesterdays in the Town of Ephratah* (1976) and Sylvia Zierak, *Perth: Memories and Reflections* (1976). Three pictorial histories, all by Kenneth B. Shaw, have useful information: *Broadalbin, Then and Now: A Pictorial History* (1973), *Bleecker, Mayfield, Perth: A Pictorial History* (1974), and *Northampton, Then and Now: A Pictorial History* (1975). The extraordinary history of Gloversville's Jewish community is treated by Herbert M. Engel, *Shtetl in the Adirondacks* (1991). Scholarly and annotated, Barbara McMartin, *The Glove Cities* (1999), treats tanning and glove making in Gloversville and Johnstown in detail. Few counties have the kind of documentation of their earliest years that is provided by *The Papers of Sir William Johnson*, 14 vols (1921–65).

Field Horne

Fultonville. Village (pop 710) in Glen (Montgomery Co). A small community developed in the late 18th century around a tavern owned by John Starin (1754–1832). The first bridge across the Mohawk at this point was built after 1810, and the community grew rapidly after becoming a port on the Erie Canal in 1825. A post office opened in 1832, and the village was incorporated in 1848. Manufacturing included William B. Wemple's Sons foundry (1845), Wemple and Yates Steam Furnace (1853), Starin Silk Fabric Co, and Myers and Parker (brooms and brushes). John H. Starin (1825–1909), grandson of John Starin and Fultonville businessman, built a large transportation empire in New York City that included tugboats, ferries, and a steamboat line. The West Shore Railroad came through in 1883 and the New York State Thruway in 1954. The major 20th-century industries were small, specialized textile mills and the White Mop Wringer Co (1904–2003; commercial cleaning equipment).

James Crawford

Fundamentalists. Protestants who emphasize revivalism, missionary work, and the literal truth of the Bible, including its apocalyptic prophecies. In the late 19th century, revival preachers like D. L. Moody called for sinners to be converted, and the Bible Conference movement spread the doctrine of premillennial dispensationalism, which predicted increasingly evil times before the Second Coming of Christ. Arno C. Gaebelein, pastor of the Allen Street Memorial Methodist Church in New York City, sparked interest in Bible prophecies through his magazine *Our Hope,* founded in 1894. Leaders in the Holiness movement, such as A. B. Simpson of New York City, taught converted Christians to seek an experience of "consecration," which would enable them to overcome sin and devote their lives to Christian service. Simpson founded the Missionary Training Institute in New York City in 1882 (now Nyack College and Alliance Seminary) and the Christian and Missionary Alliance, also in Nyack (Rockland Co), in 1897. In response to evolution and modernist theology, theological conservatives published a 12-volume collection of essays entitled *The Fundamentals* between 1910 and 1915, giving rise to the Fundamentalist label.

John Roach Straton, pastor of Calvary Baptist Church in New York City from 1918 to 1929, became well known for his criticism of the vices rampant in New York City and for his public debates with modernist theologians. He founded the Fundamentalist League of Greater New York in 1922. During the early 1920s Fundamentalists like Straton tried to root out modernism from the northern Baptist and Presbyterian denominations. An opponent, Harry Emerson Fosdick of First Presbyterian Church in New York City, called for tolerance of diverse theological views in his famous 1922 sermon, "Shall the Fundamentalists Win?" In the wake of the 1925 Scopes trial over evolution, the visibility of the Fundamentalists waned nationally, and some withdrew to form their own alliances, such as the Independent Fundamentalist Churches of America, the Orthodox Presbyterian Church, and the Baptist Bible Union.

During the 1930s Fundamentalists focused on building networks that included Bible colleges, churches, publications, and radio programs. William Ward Ayer, pastor of Calvary Baptist Church from 1936 to 1949, had a weekly radio broadcast with an audience of 250,000. During World War II a new generation of Fundamentalists launched youth rallies that gained national attention. Hundreds of young Christians attended Jack Wyrtzen's weekly Word of Life meetings, which were broadcast live from New York City on radio station WHN starting in 1941. Wyrtzen's 1944 Victory Rally drew 20,000 to the city's Madison Square Garden. This new breed of conservative Christians called themselves evangelicals and began to cooperate more with other Christian groups, as seen in Billy Graham's 1957 Evangelistic Crusade in New York City sponsored by the New York Council of Churches. Since the 1950s conservative churches have grown steadily, outpacing their liberal and modernist rivals. Fundamentalists and evangelicals have made a dramatic impact on the spread of Christianity throughout the world, with most American missionaries since World War II coming from these groups.

Carpenter, Joel A. *Revive Us Again: The Reawakening of American Fundamentalism* (New York: Oxford Univ Press, 1997)

Marsden, George. *Fundamentalism and American Culture: The Shaping of American Evangelism, 1870–1925* (New York: Oxford Univ Press, 1980)

Thomas E. Bergler

funeral industry. See Casket and funeral industry.

Furchgott, Robert F(rancis) (*b* Charleston, SC, 4 June 1916). Pharmacologist. He received a BS in chemistry from the University of North Carolina at Chapel Hill in 1937 and a PhD in biochemistry from Northwestern University in Chicago in 1940. He held positions at Cornell University Medical College (1940–49) and at Washington University in St. Louis (1949–56). In 1956 he became chairman of the new Department of Pharmacology at SUNY Downstate Medical Center; in 1982 he resigned as chair but continued as distinguished professor emeritus. He has continued to conduct research at SUNY Downstate and has been adjunct professor of pharmacology at the University of Miami School of Medicine since 1989. In 1998 he was awarded the Nobel Prize in physiology or medicine, along with Louis J. Ignarro and Ferid Murad of Los Angeles, for discoveries concerning nitric oxide as a signaling molecule in the cardiovascular system. Furchgott is SUNY Downstate's first Nobel Laureate and the first Nobel Laureate within the SUNY system to have conducted his research on a SUNY campus. He is the recipient of numerous awards and honors, including the 1996 Albert Lasker Award for Basic Medical Research.

Watson, Ellen. "Downstate's Nobel Laureate Dr. Robert F. Furchgott," *Science and Health* 1 (1999): 3–9

Jack E. Termine

furniture making. New York State furniture of the colonial period is quite distinctive. Generous proportions and bold lines echo the state's Dutch heritage. Furniture of the late 17th and early 18th centuries was often made of gumwood or pine, the latter painted and typically decorated with fruit and floral designs. Pewterbanks (cupboards to hold earthenware) and kasten (large storage cabinets) were made by Dutch settlers in the Hudson Valley. These and other items such as blanket chests featured bold moldings or uniquely Dutch carved decoration. Maple Queen Anne–style chairs (often painted), called Hudson Valley or Dutch chairs, were popular from about 1730 to 1820. Much of the furniture favored by early New Yorkers was imported from Boston, including Cromwellian chairs covered with turkey work (tufted knot stitch) or leather upholstery, and William and Mary–style leather-covered chairs with Spanish feet and a shaped back, called Boston chairs.

Sidechair made in the Hudson Valley, *ca* 1790.

The formal furniture of the Queen Anne and Chippendale periods adheres closely to English cabinetmaking designs. New York City furniture of this era is defined by the square claw and ball foot, club feet on the rear legs of chairs, the bracket foot on the back of case pieces, carved and pierced splats (the central back supports on chairs), ornamental gadrooning, simple bold lines, and heavy proportions. Two of New York City's leading cabinetmakers were Samuel Prince and his former apprentice Thomas Burling. During the Federal period, New York City surpassed Philadelphia in high-style cabinetmaking. Spade feet, Prince of Wales plumes, case pieces with hollow-center, serpentine-outlined skirts and French feet, and certain types of decorative inlay identify New York City furniture of this period. A popular New York City chair in the Sheraton style was a square-back chair with Gothic arches, turned columns, and tapered and often reeded legs terminating in spade feet; the firm of Slover and Taylor made several variants.

Duncan Phyfe and His Peers

The high point of New York State cabinetmaking was achieved in the 19th century. Duncan Phyfe (1768–1854), perhaps the best-known cabinetmaker of early 19th-century New York State, came to Albany from Scotland in 1784. Around 1790 he moved to New York City, where he opened his famous cabinetmaking shop in 1795. Phyfe's interpretations of English Regency forms inspired many rivals. One well-known competitor, French immigrant Charles-Honoré Lannuier (1779–1819), arrived in 1803 and specialized in veneered pieces in the Sheraton and French Empire styles. Michael Allison (1773–1855), a neighbor of Duncan Phyfe, was one of the most skilled, prolific, and long-lived cabinetmakers of the Federal period. Allison's name appeared in the New York City directories from 1800 to 1847. Throughout his long career, he was able to adapt to changes in furniture styles.

During the 1830s an even greater massiveness began to dominate Empire furniture design in New York City. Crisply carved palmetto posts, cornucopias, acanthus leaves, and hairy paw feet were replaced by plain undecorated surfaces and scroll supports distinctly influenced by the design of the French restoration period. Joseph Meeks and Sons (1829–35) was one of the most important cabinetmaking firms to disseminate this last phase of Classicism in America. Meeks worked in the late Empire and late Classical styles, with projecting columns in the French manner and an extraordinary use of S and C scrolls of all forms. In later years the Victorian firm of J. and J. W. Meeks (1836–60), owned by the sons of Joseph Meeks, would compete with that of John Henry Belter (1804–63), a German immigrant who had apprenticed in Stuttgart, Germany. Belter became the leading cabinetmaker of the mid–19th century. His laminated Rococo Revival furniture made a huge impact on the industry, and his name became synonymous with the style. Belter's workmanship was unrivaled; his business was so successful that he built a five-story factory in New York City in the 1850s and changed his occupational title from cabinetmaker to cabinet manufacturer.

By the mid–19th century New York City was the leader in American furniture style and remained so for the rest of the century. Elsewhere in New York State, country cabinetmakers gave their own interpretations to the more formal styles popularized by New York City cabinetmakers. Besides the usual mahogany veneers used in Federal and Empire furniture, they often worked in figured maple. Elijah Galusha (1804–71) was born in Shaftsbury, Vt. In 1825 he came to Troy (Rensselaer Co), where he apprenticed under H. M. Smith. By 1828 Galusha had his own shop on River St, where he became Troy's master cabinetmaker, the quality of his workmanship approaching that of Belter. He was an exacting craftsman who made both fashionable and plain furniture in all the styles that were in vogue, although the Rococo Revival was his best. Galusha's furniture can be identified by a distinctive carved, open rose or shell motif. In addition to the larger New York City cabinetmaking firms, his mid-19th-century competitors included Robert Green of Troy and William Randell and John Meads Jr of Albany. After Galusha retired in 1869, his former apprentice, J. Crawford Green, took over and with Marcus Waterman continued to run the cabinetmaking shop for over three decades.

During the Victorian period, a time of revivals and specialized furniture forms, there was a striving toward elegance, comfort, and physical ease. Country furniture of this period, although not as intricately carved as more formal examples, was painted with complex designs. One of New York City's most celebrated cabinetmakers of the Victorian period was Jacque Alexander Roux (1813–86). He was born in the French Alps and immigrated to New York City, where he opened his furniture shop in 1837. Roux and Co produced furniture in rosewood, oak, black walnut, and ebony. In the 1850s the firm also sold black and gilt furniture manufactured in Paris by Roux's brother Frederick, who was briefly a partner in the New York City company in 1847 and 1848. Roux made some of America's most important furniture in the Rococo and Renaissance Revival styles. His son, Alexander J. Roux, continued the business until 1898.

Victorian Furniture Making

The application of steam power between 1835 and 1850 led to the development of a new system of woodworking machines in the United States. After the mid–19th century, even more complicated forms in wood were produced at lower cost, with an accuracy unattainable by hand. Late Victorian furniture design in New York City was influenced by machine age aesthetics. The city's chief proponent of this style was George Hunzinger (1835–99), whose family-operated cabinetmaking shop was in business from 1866 until the 1920s. Hunzinger's chairs were carved with boltlike connections; although stationary, they appear as if they could fold or be set in motion. Gustave (1830–98) and Christian Herter (1840–83), half-brothers who immigrated from Stuttgart, became the favorite furniture makers and leading interior decorators of the wealthy industrialist class that arose in the latter half of the 19th century. Their opulent designs, drawing on a variety of sources including historic English and Japanese styles, were highly influential throughout the furniture industry.

Shaker furniture, although made during the same period as the elaborate designs of Roux and Hunzinger, expresses the simplicity and functionalism of the Shakers' religious philosophy. The furniture of the Shaker villages at Watervliet (Albany Co) and New Lebanon (Columbia Co) was typical of eastern Shaker furniture, and that of Groveland (Livingston Co) was closer to Victorian style and resembled the furniture of western and southern Shaker communities. In the 1890s the public began to tire of machine-made Victorian furniture, and the Arts and Crafts movement grew in response. The trendsetters of this new style were Gustav Stickley (1858–1942) of Eastwood (Onondaga Co) and Elbert Hubbard (1856–1915) of East Aurora (Erie Co). Hubbard's Roycroft Print Shop started making Mission-style furniture in 1903, generally of oak and entirely hand tooled. Echoing the Shaker principles of a half century earlier, Arts and Crafts furniture moved toward natural forms, simple lines, and an emphasis on artisanry in sharp contrast with Victorian styles and machine-made products.

The 20th Century

Mass production replaced artisanship as the standard in the furniture industry. Art Deco design, which reached its most monumental expression in the architecture of New York City skyscrapers, was at a peak of popularity in the 1920s and 1930s. The signature materials of Art Deco furniture were Bakelite and chrome. Walter Van Nessen (1889–1943), who opened a studio in New York City in 1923, was an outstanding designer known for his metal lamps and fixtures in the aerodynamic style called Streamline. Donald Deskey (1894–1989) was another influential modernist designer associated with the Art Deco movement. New York City was a center for modern architects and designers creating radically innovative, functional, often minimalist furniture designs for industrial manufacturers, particularly from the 1940s to the 1970s. Hallmarks of midcentury modernism include angular lines and abstract forms; ovoid, teardrop, and kidney shapes; plastic and acrylic materials; and solid colors in bright pastel shades. Prominent modern industrial furniture designers who worked in New York City include Gilbert Rohde (1894–1944), Isamu Noguchi (1904–88), Edward Wormley (1907–95), George Nelson (1908–86), Erwine (1909–) and Estelle Laverne (1915–98), Vladimir Kagan (1927–), and Karim Rashid (1960–). Furniture artist Wendell Castle (1932–) of Scottsville (Monroe Co), who teaches at the Rochester Institute of Technology's School for American Crafts, creates unique postmodern sculptural tables and chairs of wood, fiberglass, and metal echoing the forms of the Arts and Crafts movement.

See also Arts and crafts movement; Stickley furniture.

Comstock, Helen. *American Furniture* (New York: Viking Press, 1962)

Otto, Celia Jackson. *American Furniture of the 19th Century* (New York: Viking Press, 1965)

Scherer, John L. *New York Furniture at the New York State Museum* (Alexandria, Va: Highland House Publishers, 1984)

John L. Scherer

fur trade. The mid–16th century marked the beginning of dramatic alterations in pre-Contact Indian lifeways in the region that became the colony of New York. Over the next two centuries, New York achieved status as a vital crossroads in the North American fur trade. The use of two key communication routes, the Hudson River–Lake Champlain corridor and the Mohawk River–Lake Ontario corridor, enabled Indians, the Dutch, and the English to emerge as central players in an economic network that linked North American forests with the fashions of Western Europe.

Origins and Dutch Trade to 1664

Europeans fishing in the Gulf of St. Lawrence in the 16th century began trading for furs as an economic sideline. By the 1570s the Mohawk were competing with Algonquian-speaking peoples for access to the goods brought annually by the French to the St. Lawrence River valley. Direct trade between Europeans and Indians in what is now New York State began in September 1609 with the arrival of Henry Hudson's *Half Moon (Halve Maen)* in the river that now bears his name. Indians were eager to trade for manufactured goods; the ready supply of beaver pelts in North America and their scarcity in Europe made the fur trade a primary vehicle of European colonization. Beaver pelts yielded the finest quality felt for hats deemed fashionable by wealthy Europeans.

The Dutch used their experience with overseas shipping and joint-stock capital enterprise to exploit the fur trade of the Hudson River valley. Between 1614 and 1618, when its patent expired, the New Netherland Co arranged annual spring voyages to Fort Nassau on Castle Island in the Hudson River near what is now Albany. The Dutch West India Co (WIC), chartered in 1621 and given a trade monopoly in New Netherland, established the trading post of Fort Orange [now Albany] in 1624. Its restrictive economic policies, however, which stayed in force until trade reforms in 1638, failed to discourage Dutch immigration to America. The fur trade remained the basis of the New Netherland economy until the British took over in 1664.

Mohawk, Mohican (Mahican), and northern Algonquian-speaking peoples all sought to dominate the Hudson River valley fur trade through direct exchange with the Dutch at Fort Orange. From 1624 to 1635, the additional Mohawk River valley trade enabled WIC representatives to buy almost 90,000 pelts, predominantly beaver, from Indians. Valued at roughly eight guilders apiece, beaver pelts were both currency and commodity. After 1624 the Dutch traded cloth and metal implements for marine shell harvested by Indians in Long Island Sound and used to produce wampum. It became prized for its ceremonial value and use in intercultural diplomacy and was traded for pelts brought to Fort Orange.

The profitability of the early fur trade encouraged both illegal practices among the colonists and overhunting by the Indians. Alcohol and firearms had become part of the fur trade by 1640, despite ordinances against selling either to the Indians. After restrictions on private trading were eliminated in 1640, smuggling, violence, and a boom-and-bust cycle came to characterize the region's fur trade economy. Exports from Beverwijck [now Albany], named for the beaver trade, peaked in 1657 at nearly 38,000 pelts. The WIC's inability to control private traders and Amsterdam's failure to reinvest fur trade profits in New Netherland contributed to England's takeover of the colony in 1664.

American Indians

By the end of the Dutch period, the impact of the fur trade on local Indians was evident. Before the 1650s Indian involvement with it dovetailed with traditional activities. Beavers taken during the regular fall hunting season provided meat, clothing, and valuable pelts to exchange. After local beaver populations were reduced or decimated, Iroquois and Algonquian-speaking peoples became intermediaries in trade between the colonists and other Indians or supplemented their hunting with raids or warfare against trade rivals. The Iroquois "Beaver Wars" of the mid–17th century are a classic example of the phenomenon, with firearm-bearing Iroquois hunters ranging as far west as what is now Wisconsin in their search for furs and captives to replace tribe members lost to European disease epidemics.

Although they performed the bulk of the labor in the fur trade, Indians did not reap long-term benefits from their involvement. Historians have debated the extent to which Indians were influenced by profit motives in the fur trade, but it is clear that they adapted quickly to European business norms. Indians bargained skillfully and imposed specific economic demands on their Dutch and English trading partners, even as they became increasingly locked into a system in which Europeans controlled both the supply of commodities and the prices of furs required to obtain those commodities. This relationship forced the reorientation of indigenous practices toward market-based hunting of furs. Some Iroquois turned to wage labor after 1720. The Seneca had a monopoly to carry furs and trade goods for the French along the Niagara River while the Oneida did the same for traders en route to and from Oswego and the head of the Mohawk River [now Rome, Oneida Co]. By the 18th century, social effects on American Indians included abandonment of traditional craft skills, skewed patterns of traditional gendered labor division, alterations in leadership structures, and increased entanglement in European colonial conflicts.

English Period, 1664–1776

The geopolitical influence of the fur trade increased dramatically during English control of colonial New York, even as its relative economic significance declined with respect to other commodities. English colonial officials sought to optimize the economic benefits of the fur trade and the relationships it sustained with powerful American Indian allies. New Yorkers proved reluctant, however, to alter basic patterns of exchange established under the Dutch prior to 1664.

By 1670 increased competition with New France for the Great Lakes fur trade led English officials in New York to correct abuses against native traders that characterized the latter phase of the Dutch regime. Between 1686 and 1725, the majority of New York's fur trade was conducted at Albany in designated public areas and under specific commercial regulations, but still through Dutch traders. Albany thus became a key listening post for Anglo–American Indian relations in North America. Its dependence on the fur trade however, still led its mercantile community to engage in business practices that many English governors of the colony deemed illegal.

The overall volume of the New York fur trade had declined to approximately 15,000 pelts per year by 1699, owing to considerable fluctuations in supply caused by military conflict. After the conclusion of King William's War in 1697, private Dutch traders from Albany sought a rapprochement with their French counterparts in Montreal. Seeking better-quality northern pelts, the Albany merchants employed Mohawk couriers from the Kahnawake community near Montreal to carry lower-priced, English trade goods to French traders. As this trade crossed imperial boundaries and contributed to a de facto neutrality between New York Colony and New France, both French and English officials condemned the practice. Efforts to eliminate the "illegal fur trade" by Gov William Burnet from 1722 to 1725 were ultimately overturned by the English Parliament in 1729 on the strength of lobbying from New York City wholesalers of Indian goods. Iroquois nations participated in this north-south trade until the conquest of Canada in 1760.

The English established a permanent trading post at Oswego in 1727 to compete with the French post at Fort Niagara [now in Porter, Niagara Co] constructed the previous year. This represented the final phase of New York's colonial fur trade. By 1725 traders at Oswego supplied 67% of all peltry at Albany, while direct trade accounted for 17% and smuggled furs from Canada represented 15% of the volume. Despite the advantages conveyed by Oswego's proximity to the trapping grounds, its establishment led to increased transportation costs and to the involvement of greater numbers of white traders. Rampant abuses inflicted upon Indians by these traders led to greater regulation of the fur trade at Oswego.

Furs accounted for an estimated 25% of New York's exports to England between 1700 and the 1720s, but this proportion declined to 16% after 1750 and to 2% by 1775. Yet even as furs declined in absolute economic significance, intercolonial wars and provincial expansion westward kept the attention of authorities focused on the fur trade as they endeavored to regulate the efforts of ambitious colonists to place their own interests ahead of imperial objectives. After 1763 the steady northwestward movement in trapping relocated the competitive advantage in the fur trade away from Albany toward Montreal, whose traders had better access to the interior via the Ottawa River. The elimination of intercolonial regulatory provisions for the fur trade in 1768, the transfer of Detroit and Michilimackinac [now in Michigan] to the jurisdiction of Quebec in 1774, and the outbreak of the American Revolution a year later brought an effective end to the fur trade in New York. Following the war, the fur trade moved farther into western territories, but dealers based in New York like Peter Smith and John Jacob Astor made millions of dollars trading western furs to Europe and Asia.

Conclusion

The fur trade retained significance in New York for far longer than it did in many other colonies because of its excellent riverine communications linking the Atlantic and the continental interior. New York's fur trade consisted primarily of the transfer of peltry and trade goods procured or manufactured elsewhere. The trade provided the initial rationale for Dutch settlement of the Hudson River valley and sustained their presence until 1664. Although the fur trade represented a primary factor contributing to the subjugation of the region's native peoples over the long term, the profits greatly enhanced their political and diplomatic stature during the colonial era. In no other British colony were native peoples part of a diplomatic relationship to the degree of the Iroquois Confederacy of New York, who attained a decisive role in Anglo-French affairs on the basis of their role in the fur trade. As the trade in furs yielded to agriculturally oriented settler expansion in New York after 1760, non-natives increasingly came to view native peoples as obstacles to civil progress.

Brandão, José A. *"Your Fyre Shall Burn No More:" Iroquois Policy toward New France and Its Native Allies to 1701* (Lincoln: Univ of Nebraska Press, 1997)
Burke, Thomas E. *Mohawk Frontier: The Dutch Community of Schenectady, New York, 1661–1710* (Ithaca: Cornell University Press, 1991)
Engelbrecht, William. *Iroquoia: The Development of a Native World* (Syracuse: Syracuse Univ Press, 2003)
Kammen, Michael. *Colonial New York: A History* (New York: Scribner's, 1975)
Matson, Cathy D. *Merchants and Empire: Trading in Colonial New York* (Baltimore: Johns Hopkins Univ Press, 1998)
Norton, Thomas E. *The Fur Trade in Colonial New York, 1686–1776* (Madison: Univ of Wisconsin Press, 1974)
Richter, Daniel K. *The Ordeal of the Longhouse: The Peoples of the Iroquois League in the Era of European Colonization* (Chapel Hill: Univ of North Carolina Press, 1992)
Rink, Oliver A. *Holland on the Hudson: An Economic and Social History of Dutch New York* (Ithaca: Cornell Univ Press, 1986)

Jon Parmenter

F. X. Matt Brewing Company. Founded as the West End Brewery in Utica in 1888, it employed 12 workers and produced 4,000 barrels of beer in its first year of production. A cofounder, German immigrant Francis Xavier (F. X.) Matt, became treasurer in 1891 and president in 1905, a position he would hold until 1951. During Prohibition the firm stayed active by making a range of alternative products, including soft drinks, fruit beverages, and malt tonics. With the end of Prohibition in April 1933, West End Brewery, along with four other Utica breweries, resumed beer production. Walter Matt, son of Francis Xavier, became president in 1951. Under his leadership the company undertook both an extensive plant modernization and a successful advertising campaign featuring the "Schultz and Dooley" talking beer steins. By 1960 West End was the last brewery operating in Utica, with an annual production of more than 500,000 barrels. In 1980 the brewery was renamed F. X. Matt Brewing Co in honor of its longtime leader. Although it continued to produce its main brands of Matt's and Utica Club, the company began in the early 1990s to focus on a new line of beers sold under the name of Saranac, including Saranac Adirondack Amber and Saranac Black Forest. The company also manufactures soft drinks, such as Saranac Root Beer and Orange Cream. In 2004 it was still owned and operated by the Matt family.

Van Wieren, Dale. *American Breweries II* (West Point, Pa: Eastern Coast Brewiana Association, 1995)

Martin Stack

G

Gaebelein, Arno C(lemens) (*b* Thuringia [now in Germany], 27 Aug 1861; *d* Mount Vernon, Westchester Co, 25 Dec 1945). Fundamentalist editor and missionary to Jews. In 1879 Gaebelein emigrated from Germany to Lawrence, Mass, where he worked in a mill and attended a German Methodist church. From 1881 to 1891 he was pastor in several German Methodist churches in Manhattan, Connecticut, Maryland, and New Jersey. Influenced by a converted Jewish parishioner, Gaebelein became a student of Jewish culture and Hebrew and began his mission as an evangelist to Jews on the Lower East Side of Manhattan. He founded the Hope of Israel Mission, which distributed food, medical supplies, and Christian literature, including his own journal, *Our Hope* (1894), which was also published in Yiddish *(Tiqweth Israel)* and German *(Unsere Hoffnur)*. In 1899 Gaebelein left the Methodist Church because of its theological liberalism and resigned from the Hope of Israel Mission because he no longer believed that converted Jews should keep the Law or observe Jewish ways of life. After 1900 Gaebelein became a leading advocate of dispensationalism, which interpreted current events as apocalyptic precursors to the Second Coming of Christ, but he disagreed with those who set the date prophetically. He was a consulting editor for the dispensationalist *Scofield Reference Bible* (1909), wrote more than 40 books, and was a popular lecturer. In the 1930s *Our Hope* warned readers about the Nazis' genocidal intentions, but Gaebelein also believed that "apostate Jews" were behind organized crime, the New Deal, and an international communist conspiracy. He was editor of *Our Hope* until his death; the journal continued publication until 1958.

Rausch, David A. *Arno C. Gaebelein, 1861–1945: Irenic Fundamentalist and Scholar* (New York: Edwin Mellen Press, 1983)

Timothy P. Weber

GAF Corporation. Photographic and diversified products manufacturer. In 1842 Edward Anthony (1819–88) opened one of America's first photographic supply houses, E. Anthony Co, in Manhattan. In the 1850s Anthony expanded his firm into the manufacture of cameras, lenses, and plates, and turned the firm into the largest photographic retailer and manufacturer in the world. In 1902 the firm acquired the Scovill and Adams Co, another Manhattan photographic manufacturer, and relocated its production facilities and headquarters to Binghamton. In 1907 the firm was renamed Ansco Co. After several decades of a losing battle in the photographic products industry to Eastman Kodak Co, in 1928 the firm was sold to the Agfa Film Organization, a subsidiary of I. G. Farben, the German chemical conglomerate, creating Agfa-Ansco Corp. The German firm poured $4 million into Agfa-Ansco in the 1930s, enlarged the Binghamton workforce from 500 to 3,000, creating one of the world's most modern film and camera production centers, and aggressively competed with Kodak. In 1939 I. G. Farben, to distance Agfa-Ansco from the Nazi regime, reorganized Agfa-Ansco and many of its other US holdings into a single, newly created holding company, General Aniline and Film Corp. This new firm, based in Binghamton, consisted of three divisions: the film and camera maker Agfa-Ansco (now Ansco), the General Aniline Works, a chemical producer with facilities including a 95-acre (38 ha) dye plant in the City of Rensselaer that employed 500 workers, and Ozalid, a pioneering document duplicating equipment maker centered in Johnson City (Broome Co).

Because of its ties to Farben, after America's introduction into World War II General Aniline and Film was seized by the US Treasury in 1942 and handed over to a government-appointed Alien Property Custodian. The largest company acquired by the US government during the war, General Aniline and Film relocated its headquarters to New York City and dedicated its production to the US military. After 1945 US congressmen from New York State pressured the government to relinquish the firm. A quick divestiture proved impossible when legal action ensued over the legality of the seizure. In the 1950s General Aniline and Film, employing 8,000, made record profits with its chemical unit controlling 20% of the national dye market, its Ansco division holding 15% of the consumer film business and a leader in color film (it released the first high-speed color film in 1955, beating Kodak by four years), and its Ozalid division making perhaps the world's most sophisticated office duplicators. But as the legal case dragged on, the government's appointed directors failed to meet new market challenges. Not until 1965 were the legal issues resolved, enabling the government to relinquish control and the firm to go public. Renamed GAF Corp in 1967, the company entered the building materials business by acquiring Ruberoid Co. Continually losing market share in its older businesses, between 1977 and 1980 GAF exited the photography sector. In 1978 it also sold most of its chemical assets, including the Rensselaer plant, to BASF Group, a German chemical firm. By the early 1980s GAF no longer had a presence in New York State.

Jenkins, Reese V. *Images and Enterprise: Technology and the American Photographic Industry, 1839 to 1925* (Baltimore: Johns Hopkins Univ Press, 1975)
Marder, William, and Estelle Marder. *Anthony, the Man, the Company, the Cameras: An American Photographic Pioneer: 140 Year History of a Company from Anthony to Ansco to GAF.* Ed. Robert G. Duncan (Plantation, Fla: Pine Ridge Publishing, 1982)

Tod M. Ottman

Gage, Matilda (Electa) Joslyn (*b* Cicero, Onondaga Co, 24 Mar 1826; *d* Chicago, Ill, 18 Mar 1898). Suffragist and reformer. She was the daughter of educated, abolitionist parents, and her childhood home was a station on the Underground Railroad. After schooling in De Peyster (St. Lawrence Co) and Hamilton (Madison Co), she sought entry, without success, to Geneva Medical College. In 1845 she married dry goods store owner Henry Gage. The couple would live in Syracuse, Manlius, and Fayetteville (Onondaga Co) and have four children. Drawn to many reform causes, Gage first spoke on woman suffrage at the 1852 Syracuse National Women's Rights Convention, eventually joining Elizabeth Cady Stanton and Susan B. Anthony as leaders of the suffrage movement's more radical wing. She wrote *Woman as Inventor* (1870), detailing women's unsung scientific and technical work and became president of the National Woman Suffrage Association (NWSA; founded in 1869) in 1872 as well as of the New York State Woman Suffrage Association. She published Syracuse-based *National Citizen and Ballot Box* (1878–81) and coedited, with Stanton and Anthony, three volumes of the *History of Woman Suffrage* (1876–86).

In 1890, as Anthony, with Stanton's support, formed the National American Woman Suffrage Association (NAWSA) (which merged suffrage elements with conservative Woman's Christian Temperance Union women), Gage separated from her former allies and formed the radical National Woman's Liberal Union (NWLU). This group, which included labor leaders, prison reformers, and anarchists, assailed Christian theology as oppressive to women. Gage expressed her boldest views in *Woman, Church, and State* (1893) and in contributions to the Stanton-edited *Woman's Bible* (1895–98). Adopted into the Mohawk Nation's Wolf Clan in 1893, she voted with the Mohawk Council of Matrons while still disenfranchised by the United States. Her disagreement with Anthony and her views on religion largely erased Gage from women's movement history until the 1970s. Some claim that her son-in-law, L. Frank Baum, portrayed aspects of Gage's personality in the dynamic female characters of his *Wonderful Wizard of Oz* (1900).

Wagner, Sally Roesch. *Matilda Joslyn Gage: She Who Holds the Sky* (Aberdeen, SD: Sky Carrier Press, 1998)

Susan Goodier

Gage, Thomas (*b* Highmeadow, England, ?1720; *d* London 2 Apr 1787). British general. After service in Europe and Scotland, he arrived in America as a lieutenant colonel at the beginning of the French and Indian War, in which he led the advance guard at Edward Braddock's defeat in 1755, took part in the failed attempt to relieve Fort Oswego in 1756, and was at the failed attack on Ticonderoga in 1758. Also in 1758 Gage raised a light infantry regiment, the 80th, an experiment in adapting regular troops to North American conditions by rigorous training in frontier warfare. He was raised in rank to brigadier general and given local command of troops and garrisons in northern New York. Gage married Margaret Kemble, an heiress from New Jersey. In 1760 he commanded the rearguard of Gen Jeffery Amherst's conquest of Canada and was appointed military governor of Montreal. With Amherst's return to England in 1763 at the end of the French and Indian War, Gage was appointed commander in chief of all British land forces in the American colonies. Headquartered in New York City, he was careful in his dealings with Americans unhappy about British attempts to tax and more closely govern the colonies. In 1765 when trouble was brewing over the Stamp Act, Gage strengthened the garrison of Fort George on the southern tip of Manhattan but also warned Lt Gov Cadwallader Colden that without civil authorization the military could do nothing. Neither Colden nor any other magistrate dared to call for military aid as protesters roamed the city, and Gage stayed in his large double house on Broad St while his soldiers stayed in the fort. Unlike the situation in Boston, where British soldiers "massacred" several townspeople in 1770, Gage kept civil-military relations fairly cool in New York. In 1766, when the civil government asked for help against land rioters in Albany and Dutchess Cos, he allowed his troops to be used against American civilians. In 1773 he returned to England on leave, and when he returned it was as governor of Massachusetts, with a large military force and orders to suppress rebellion in Boston. He failed and was recalled in 1775. His wife's sympathy for the American cause may best explain his relative popularity in New York and his final failure in New England.

Alden, John R. *General Gage in America* (Baton Rouge: Louisiana State Univ Press, 1948)

Shy, John. "Thomas Gage: Weak Link of Empire." In *George Washington's Opponents,* ed. George Billias (New York: William Morrow, 1969)

John Shy

Gaines. Town (pop 3,740) in N central Orleans Co. Settled in 1807, the town was formed from Ridgeway in 1816. Located on the Ridge Rd, it was crossed by the Erie Canal (1824). Largely a farming town, Gaines produced wheat and fruit. In the early 21st century, farming continues, while some residents commute to jobs in Rochester or other cities in the region. A recent addition to the agricultural base is Intergrow Greenhouses, a 15-acre (6 ha) hydroponics tomato business. The Cobblestone Society (1960) preserves and interprets a number of fine examples of cobblestone construction.

Gainesville. Town (pop 2,333) and village (pop 304) in SE Wyoming Co. Settled in 1805, it was formed from Warsaw in 1814 as Hebe and changed to Gainesville in 1816. Sandstone was mined at Rock Glen in the 19th century. The first railroad, the Rochester and State Line, came through in 1877. At the end of the 19th century, the Warsaw Bluestone Co quarried in Gainesville. The village incorporated in 1902. The town's farms primarily produced milk and potatoes in 2002. The Gainesville Seminary at one time had Belva Ann Lockwood (1830–1917), lawyer and suffragist, on its faculty.

Galen. Town (pop 4,439) in SE Wayne Co. Part of the New Military Tract, the town was named after the ancient Greek physician; it was settled in 1800. The town was taken from Junius (Seneca Co) in 1812. Crossed by the Erie Canal (1822) and the New York Central Railroad (1853), Galen has fertile mucklands, producing potatoes and onions. It is the home of the Galen Marsh State Wildlife Management Area. At Lock Berlin a county park incorporates an Erie Canal lock.

Scott C. Monje

Gallatin. Town (pop 1,499) in S Columbia Co. Settled probably in the 1740s, the town was formed from Ancram in 1830. A poor upland, it was never good farming country, but a plow factory and foundry operated at Spaulding Furnace from *ca* 1843 to *ca* 1910. Rail service came in 1874 with the Rhinebeck and Connecticut, and Silvernails became the line's junction with the Poughkeepsie and Connecticut in 1889. Lake Charlotte [now Lake Taghkanic] was a resort by the end of the 19th century, becoming part of Lake Taghkanic State Park in 1929. With access provided by the Taconic State Parkway (1954), the population grew 267% between 1960 and 1990.

Galway. Town (pop 3,589) and village (pop 214) in W Saratoga Co. The area was settled in 1774 by ten families from Galloway, Scotland; the name was corrupted to Galway. A colony from Elizabeth, NJ, came after the Revolution. The town was formed from Ballston in 1792, and its economy has been primarily agricultural. In the 19th century waterpower was tapped for small-scale enterprises including several potteries, a foundry (1847–1926), a distillery, and a vinegar works. In 1855 the Chuctenunda Creek, in the west part of town, was dammed to provide reliable waterpower for the mills in Amsterdam (Montgomery Co), creating Galway Lake, which is surrounded by a large summer colony. A part of the Kenneth A. Kesselring Site of Knolls Atomic Power Laboratory is in the town. The village, a half-mile square centered on a four-corners settlement, incorporated in 1838. The town was the birthplace of Joseph Henry (1797–1878), founder of the Smithsonian Institution.

Field Horne

gambling and gaming. Laws limiting or prohibiting certain forms of gambling were passed in the colonial period by both the Dutch and the English but did little to limit the prevalence of gambling activities at taverns, horse races, cockfights, and other venues. Lotteries, both legal and illegal, were a common game of chance in New York Colony, and the first lottery control law was passed in 1721, but lotteries persisted until the New York State Constitution of 1821 banned them statewide. In the first half of the 19th century, gambling dens became more and more common in New York City, Buffalo, and other large cities of the state. For many reformers, gambling was part of the unholy trinity of urban vices, along with alcohol and prostitution, that required remediation. All three were widely blamed on lax oversight and official corruption. In 1851 Horace Greeley founded the New York Association for the Suppression of Gambling, which Greeley and reformed gambler Jonathan Green headed and which led to the passage of the state Green Law of 1851. Fines and imprisonment were mandated for those who kept gaming establishments, exhibited gaming devices, or encouraged others to visit a gambling house. The law proved remarkably ineffective. If anything, in making it imperative that gambling establishments obtain official connivance to operate, it enhanced already close ties between gamblers and local politicians, especially among members of Manhattan's Tammany Hall. An example of this symbiosis can be found in the career of John "Old Smoke" Morrissey, an ex-prizefighter, a US congressman (1866–70), and a state senator (1875–78) who helped turn Saratoga Springs into perhaps the nation's best-known gambling and racetrack resort.

Reformers continued to provide evidence of the ties between gambling and political corruption. The much publicized Lexow Committee (1894–95) of the state legislature found that the New York City Police Department (NYPD) extorted monthly payments from lottery and poolroom operators in exchange for protection from arrest. This attention in part spurred the 1894 New York State Constitutional Convention to adopt a ban on "pool-selling, book-making, or any other kind of gambling." The state legislature, more cautious than the constitutional convention, tried to mitigate the constitutional ban in the Percy-Gray Act of 1895, which permitted licensed gambling at racetracks, but the climate for any sort of legal gambling remained extremely uncertain, a situation reinforced by the Agnew-Hart Bill of 1908, which largely eliminated racetrack betting. In 1913 racetracks successfully opened with a modified form of on-track bookmaking, which persisted until 1934 when the antibetting law was repealed. Bookmaking was again made illegal in 1940 after New York State voters had approved a constitutional amendment permitting pari-mutuel betting.

Organized crime became more involved in gambling in the 1920s, with figures such as Arnold Rothstein, Meyer Lansky, and Dutch Schultz achieving considerable notoriety. The numbers game came to prominence at this time and was thought to bring in $100 million a year in New York City alone. With the impetus from leaders such as Mayor Fiorello La Guardia and Special State Prosecutor Thomas E. Dewey, reform efforts in the mid- to late 1930s were at times impressive but always ephemeral. After some major prosecutions of underworld figures and corrupt public officials in New York State, an investigation of organized crime by US senator Estes Kefauver (D-Tenn) in 1950 revealed that the governments of New York City and New York State were still heavily influenced by organized crime. The Kefauver Committee found that in Saratoga Springs the superintendent of the New York State Police, John A. Gaffney, openly tolerated casino gambling. Illegal gambling was also tolerated at Hudson (Columbia Co), where a vibrant prostitution trade also thrived.

The New York State Crime Commission was subsequently created by Gov Dewey in 1951 to look at gambling and organized crime throughout the state. That commission prompted the creation, in 1958, of the New York Temporary Commission of Investigation. This commission found, in its examination of a statewide police raid of over 100 bookie establishments, a gambling network that spread through Buffalo, Rochester, Syracuse, Utica, Albany, and smaller communities, with contacts and gambling associates throughout the United States, Canada, and Cuba. New state antigambling laws enacted in 1960, 1962, and 1965 under Gov Nelson A. Rockefeller provided for tougher penalties and greater ease in prosecution, but proved to be ineffective. The 1972 findings of New York City's Knapp Commission into the excesses of the NYPD revealed that the links between gambling and the city's corrupt police officers were commonplace.

Persistent illegal gambling and the public corruption associated with it precipitated a movement in New York State toward legalizing but regulating certain forms of gambling. In 1970 the state legislature instituted off-track betting (OTB) as a way to raise additional revenue and to combat organized crime. In 2001, $780 million was wagered at New York State's 10 thoroughbred and harness racetracks and $2 billion through the state's six OTB corporations. Combined, live, and simulcast wagering netted state and local governments $148 million in 2001. In 1995 the law was amended to allow the broadcast of New York State races on television, with a subsequent explosion of off-track telephone betting. While off-track wagering may have increased revenues, it has hurt profits at the tracks and may be siphoning money from sales tax revenues. Organized crime bookmakers focus on the multibillion dollar sports betting industry, which is insulated from legal competition. Another New York State foray into relegalization was instituted in 1957 with a state constitutional amendment permitting bingo. Another major push into legalized gambling came in 1967 with the implementation of the New York Lottery, with some of the proceeds going to education. Since that time legal lotteries have expanded tremendously in type and frequency of drawing, and in 2001 the state legislature permitted New Yorkers to buy tickets in the state for the interstate Powerball lottery.

Legalized gambling also spread when the US Supreme Court decision in *California v Cabazon Bar Mission Indians* (1987) gave American Indian tribes the authority to conduct gaming activities on reservations. Since this decision Indian gaming in the state has been a by-product of federal law, judicial interpretation, traditional tribal sovereignty, and political battles over the legalized gambling industry. As of 2002, three Iroquois nations operated gambling facilities in the state. The Seneca ran bingo games in Cattaraugus and Allegheny Cos, the Oneida had a casino resort in Verona (Oneida Co), and the Mohawk opened a casino and a bingo palace in Hogansburg (Franklin Co). The Seneca also opened a casino in Niagara Falls in December 2002 and have others in the planning stages in western New York State.

See also SARATOGA SPRINGS; THOROUGHBRED RACING.

Asbury, Herbert. *Sucker's Progress: An Informal History of Gambling in America from the Colonies to Canfield* (New York: Dodd, Mead, 1938)

Chafetz, Henry. *Play the Devil: A History of Gambling in the United States from 1492 to 1955* (New York: Clarkson N. Potter, 1960)

Cornell Law School. *The Development of the Law of Gambling, 1776–1976* (Washington, DC: Government Printing Office, 1977)

Ezell, John Samuel. *Fortune's Merry Wheel: The Lottery in America* (Cambridge, Mass: Harvard Univ Press, 1960)

Stolberg, Mary M. *Fighting Organized Crime: Politics, Justice, and the Legacy of Thomas E. Dewey* (Boston: Northeastern Univ Press, 1995)

Don Liddick

gangs. See URBAN GANGS.

Ganienkeh [Kanyekehaka]. The name for the Mohawk in their language, meaning "people of the flint place." Ganienkeh broadly refers to the territory the Mohawk Indians controlled prior to European contact, in what is today the Mohawk Valley and the northern reaches of New York State. On 13 May 1974, a traditionalist faction of the Mohawk at Akwesasne (St. Regis Indian Reservation) occupied a 612-acre (248 ha) site of a former girls camp at Moss Lake in Herkimer Co, claiming it was part of the historic Mohawk homeland that had been illegally taken from them. Relations with local residents were fairly tense, and sporadic incidents of shooting culminated in October 1974, when the residents of Ganienkeh, in what they claimed was defensive retaliation, injured two persons with shotgun fire, including a girl aged 9. When the New York State Police attempted to assert their jurisdiction over the settlement, the Grand Council of the Six Nations claimed it was a violation of the 1794 Treaty of Canandaigua. In May 1977, after several years of controversy, the residents of Ganienkeh agreed to move to a 698-acre (282 ha) site in the Miner Lake area at Altona (Clinton Co). They also received access to 5,000 acres (2,023 ha) of state forest land. In Altona, too, they faced local opposition, especially after the Indians barricaded an access road to Miner Lake. Subsequently the state closed the road. A suit brought by an Altona Citizens Committee was dismissed. Ganienkeh was envisioned as a utopian collective community, an effort to establish what they called the "Independent North American Indian State of Ganienkeh." The community has endured, but economic self-sufficiency was not achieved, and its population has dwindled.

Landsman, Gail H. *Sovereignty and Symbol: Indian-White Conflict at Ganienkeh* (Albuquerque: Univ of New Mexico Press, 1988)

Ute Ferrier

Gannett, Frank E(arnest) (*b* Bristol, Ontario Co, 15 Sept 1876; *d* Rochester, 3 Dec 1957). Newspaper publisher. Born to poverty, Gannett and his tenant-farmer parents moved constantly, living in numerous towns in Central and Western New York when Gannett was a boy. In 1885 the family moved to Bolivar (Allegany Co), where Gannett's parents took up running a hotel and Gannett graduated high school, winning a scholarship to Cornell University in 1894. At Cornell, Gannett worked for the school newspaper, the *Ithaca Journal,* and for the *Syracuse Herald,* showing great promise as a reporter. He graduated from Cornell in 1898 and in the following year traveled to the Philippines to become secretary to the head of the Philippine Commission in Manila.

He returned to the United States in 1900 and for the next five years worked as an editor for newspapers in Ithaca, New York City, and Pittsburgh. In 1906 he purchased half of the *Elmira Gazette* on credit; the following year he bought the *Gazette*'s crosstown rival, the *Elmira Star,* and than merged the newspapers to form the *Star-Gazette.* Exhibiting shrewd business instincts, in the 1910s and 1920s Gannett bought numerous New York State newspapers to build a chain of papers that became Gannett Co in 1923. Many of the newspapers he acquired were in the same city or town, and he would merge them to lower costs and increase circulation. In 1918 Gannett moved to Rochester, where he lived and where Gannett Co was based until his death. In Rochester, that same year, he bought two newspapers, the *Times* and the *Union and Advertiser,* and merged them to create the *Times-Union.* By the time of his death Gannett Co comprised 22 newspapers, 4 radio stations, and 3 television stations. At least 17 of the newspapers were in New York State, including papers in Albany, Rochester, Utica, Elmira, Ithaca, Binghamton, Newburgh, Olean, Ogdensburg, Malone, Saratoga Springs, Massena, and Niagara Falls. Enjoying robust circulation, Gannett Co was a financial success, much of which stemmed from Gannett's emphasis on integrity in reporting and from his granting to each newspaper within the group editorial independence, allowing each editor to tailor content to fit local taste. Only Rochester's *Times-Union* was edited by Gannett himself.

Gannett took a great interest in politics, and even though his newspapers were editorially independent, as head of one of the largest media empires in the nation, Gannett was seen as a powerful shaper of public opinion. Hence he was endlessly courted by politicians and was a prominent political figure. Although a Republican, Gannett was an early supporter of Pres Franklin D. Roosevelt. He turned against Roosevelt during the president's second term, however, and founded in 1937 the National Committee to Uphold Constitutional Government, which thwarted numerous New Deal initiatives. Gannett was also influential in state politics. Prominent state Republicans, at times, molded their positions or the party platform to gain Gannett's backing. In 1936 Gannett sought but failed to capture the Republican gubernatorial nomination and four years later coordinated with assembly Republicans an effective campaign against the fiscal policies of Gov Herbert H. Lehman. In 1940 Gannett also made a failed bid for the Republican presidential nomination. But he was also unpredictable, causing many Republicans to dislike him; in 1948–49 Gannett alienated the state Republican leadership when he tried unsuccessfully to derail the efforts of Gov Thomas E. Dewey in passing the necessary legislation to create the SUNY system.

In 2002 Gannett Co, based in McLean, Va, was an international media conglomerate and within the United States consisted of 22 television stations and 100 daily newspapers, including its flagship newspaper *USA Today,* and was the largest newspaper group in the United States in terms of daily circulation.

Polenberg, Richard. *Frank E. Gannett: A Progressive Publisher in Politics* (Rochester: Gannett Foundation, 1987)

Tod M. Ottman

Ganondagan State Historic Site. Only New York State Historic Site with an American Indian theme. Located in Victor (Ontario Co) and comprising 523 acres (212 ha), Ganondagan was the capital of the Seneca Nation in the mid–17th century. The name translates as "a town situated on a hill surrounded by the substance of white," a reference to white blossoms appearing there when the site was first occupied. A visitor to Ganondagan in 1677 reported seeing 150 bark longhouses in the town. The Seneca refer to Ganondagan as the Town of Peace because its history is identified with Jikhonsaseh, the woman who, according to tradition, was the first person to accept the message of peace brought by the Peacemaker who unified the nations of the Iroquois Confederacy. Competition between the English and the French over control of the fur trade led to an attack on Ganondagan and three other Seneca towns by the French in July 1687. Under the command of the Marquis de Denonville, more than 3,200 men assembled at Irondequoit Bay and traveled overland to the town. Seneca warriors were in the country of the Miami, south of Lake Michigan, when the French arrived. Approximately 500 elderly men, boys, and some women ambushed the attackers, halting their advance long enough for the women and children to escape. Failing to annihilate the Seneca, the French burned an estimated 1.2 million bushels (42.3 million l) of corn and destroyed the settlement. Beginning with the efforts of Seneca archaeologist Arthur C. Parker and local historian J. Sheldon Fisher in the 1940s, the site was eventually secured. Ganondagan was officially dedicated on 14 July 1987, the 300th anniversary of its destruction. In addition to a visitor center, the site has three hiking trails and a reconstructed longhouse measuring 20 x 20 x 65 feet (6 x 6 x 20 m).

Ganondagan State Historic Site, http://www.ganondagan.org

G. Peter Jemison

Gansevoort, Peter (*b* Albany, July 1749; *d* Albany, 2 July 1812). Military officer. Born into a prominent Dutch family, Gansevoort obtained a commission as major in the Second New York Regiment in June 1775. His first service was in the failed invasion of Canada later that year, and his most distinguished achievement was in August 1777 as colonel of the Third New York. In command at Fort Stanwix [now Rome, Oneida Co], he withstood a siege by a British force under Barry St. Leger, part of Gen John Burgoyne's invasion. This repulse contributed to Burgoyne's eventual defeat and made Gansevoort the "Hero of Fort Stanwix." In 1779 he participated in the Sullivan-Clinton expedition, which was intended to punish the Iroquois who had supported the British. When the New York regiments were consolidated in January 1781, Gansevoort became brigadier general of militia forces in the region north and east of Albany. After the war, he and other members of his family established a mill community in 1784 that became Gansevoort [now in Saratoga Co]. In addition to his military activity, Gansevoort received income from his lumber mills, gristmills, and other family businesses, a brewery among them. He remained active in the militia and at his death was a general in the regular army in command of the Northern Department, which made up one-third of the entire army.

Kenney, Alice P. *The Gansevoorts of Albany: Dutch Participants in the Upper Hudson Valley* (Syracuse: Syracuse Univ Press, 1969)

Lowenthal, Larry. *Marinus Willett: Defender of the Northern Frontier* (Fleischmanns, NY: Purple Mountain Press, 2000)

Larry Lowenthal

Garacontie [Daniel] (*b* ?; *d* Onondaga Nation Territory, ?1677–78). Onondaga leader. Although not an Iroquois League chief, Garacontie rose to prominence in the 1650s, becoming an influential leader. He promoted peaceful relations with New France to circumvent the Albany trade monopoly and to free warriors to fight against the Susquehannock and Erie Nations. By preventing the torture of French captives and deflecting Iroquois raids away from Quebec, Garacontie won the trust of French officials. He sponsored the Jesuit mission of Sainte Marie de Gannentaha at Onondaga [now Liverpool, Onondaga Co] in 1656 and used his status with the French to enhance his prestige. Arousing sharp opposition when he adopted Christianity and renounced traditional Iroquois ceremonies and customs, Garacontie was baptized in 1670 and took the Christian name Daniel after his godfather, governor of New France Daniel Remy de Courcelle. He died of disease in the winter of 1677–78 and received a Christian burial. Although Garancontie's pro-French policies divided the Onondaga, he always sought to secure Iroquois interests.

Webb, Stephen Saunders. *1676: The End of American Independence* (New York: Knopf, 1984)

James Paxton

garbage plate. A legendary concoction first served at Nick Tahou Hots at 320 W Main St in Rochester. The classic garbage plate is composed of a cheeseburger or two "hots" (hot dogs, no buns) placed on a bed of home fries, macaroni salad, and baked beans, topped off with special-recipe Tahou sauce and slices of Italian bread and butter. Alexander Tahou, a Greek immigrant who sought to provide hearty, nourishing meals for a reasonable price to the hungry, created it in the 1930s. College students began calling it the garbage plate in the early 1980s. The restaurant has been in the Tahou family since 1918 and managed by Alexander's son Nick and grandson Alex. Its present location is slightly west of the original site where I-490 now crosses West Main. So successful has the trademark garbage plate been that other Rochester-area restaurants have created counterparts, such as the trash plate, but none has achieved the status of the original Tahou. Part of the original's success lies in the ambience of Tahou's, which approximates street theater at its best, dispensing with social class distinctions and encouraging all to intermingle on an equal basis.

"More Than Sauce Is Spicy at Nick's," *Rochester Democrat and Chronicle,* 22 Oct 1973

Nancy Martin

Gardeau Reservation. In 1797, at the Treaty of Big Tree, the US government recognized Gardeau as a Seneca reservation. The tract, which contained 28 mi^2 (73 km^2), or 17,927 acres (7,255 ha), was in an area that the Seneca had occupied since they conquered the Wenro Indians in the first half of the 17th century. The reservation, half in the southwest part of what is now the Town of Mount Morris (Livingston Co) and half in the present-day Town of Castile (Wyoming Co), ran along both sides of the Genesee River. Gardeau (Ga-da-oh or Kau-tau in Seneca) means "down and up" and suggests valley, hillside, or bluff. From 1797 onward it was also known as the White Woman's Reservation, in reference to Mary Jemison, a famous white captive adopted by the Seneca, who with 48 others (mostly family members) occupied the reservation. In two federal treaties (1823, 1826), neither of which were ever formally ratified by the federal government, the Seneca were dispossessed of their lands at Gardeau, largely through pressure brought by agents of the Ogden Land Co.

Doty, Lockwood L. *History of Livingston County, New York,* 2d ed., 2 vols (Jackson, Mich.: W. J. Van Deusen, 1905)

Hauptman, Laurence M. *Conspiracy of Interests: Iroquois Dispossession and the Rise of New York State* (Syracuse: Syracuse Univ Press, 1999)

Laurence M. Hauptman

Garden City. Village (pop 21,672) in Hempstead (Nassau Co). Conceived by A. T. Stewart (1803–76), who in 1869 purchased the Hempstead Plains (7,170 acres/2,900 ha) and began development, it had the curious feature that land could only be rented, a policy continued until 1893. Settlement of Stewart's estate resulted in the creation of the Garden City Co that built model homes and, later, sold lots, providing all services and setting the rules. In 1919 the village incorporated under the Community Agreement, a unique governmental form under which four property-owner associations rotate management of the village.

In 1910 Doubleday, Page and Co established Country Life Press. Doubleday remained an employer in the village until its 1988 closure. In 1917–18 the village hosted Camp Mills, a troop assembly depot during World War I, and since 1929 it has been the home of Adelphi University. Garden City is known as the "Cradle of Aviation": the first airmail flight in the United States started from the village, as did Charles Lindbergh's first transatlantic flight (1927). It was also the home of the Curtiss engineering plant (1917–31). The population expanded from 7,180 in 1930 to 23,837 in 1960, and it has been mostly stable since then. In the 1950s Franklin Ave became a high-quality suburban shopping district. The glory of Garden City is its cathedral; completed in 1885 it is the seat of the Episcopal bishop of Long Island. The present Garden City Hotel (1983) is the fourth such structure on its site, the first having opened in 1874. Garden City has become a village predominantly of upper-middle-class residents in single-family houses.

Vincent F. Seyfried

Garden City Park. Locality (pop 7,554) in North Hempstead (Nassau Co). Originally known as North Hempstead, this was the site of the Queens Co courthouse built in 1786. It was renamed Garden City Park in 1873 by Benjamin W. Hitchcock, a real estate promoter, in order to benefit from publicity being given to neighboring Garden City. Development began in the 1920s, but the major portion of the middle-class community was built after World War II, peaking in population in 1960. In 2000 Garden City Park was 20.5% Asian, many of whom were from India.

Richard A. Winsche

gardening. See HORTICULTURE.

Gardiner. Town (pop 5,238) in S central Ulster Co. Settled by the Dutch and Huguenots, the town was formed in 1853 from New Paltz, Rochester, and Shawangunk. A tannery operated beginning *ca* 1830 through most of the 19th century. The Wallkill Valley Railroad came through in 1869. Gardiner has remained an agricultural town, especially a fruit-growing one, but it experienced considerable residential growth in the last decade of the 20th century. Landmarks include Locust Lawn (1814), which is open seasonally, and the working Tuthill Grist Mill (1788).

Ruth Piwonka

Gardiner, Lion (*b* England, ?1599; *d* East Hampton, Suffolk Co, 1663). Land proprietor. After serving as an engineer in the Low Countries for the Prince of Orange, Gardiner was recruited in 1635 by Puritan ministers Hugh Peter and John Davenport to build a fort at what would become Saybrook, Conn. During the 1636 Pequot War, Gardiner became an ally of the Montaukett, rivals of the Pequot, thus keeping peace for the fledgling settlement. In 1639 Gardiner purchased from the Montaukett an island between Long Island's North and South Forks. Moving there, he created the first permanent English settlement in what would become New York State. Originally called the Isle of Wight, it became known as Gardiners Island. In 1653 Gardiner moved to East Hampton and took part in town government and economic development. In 1659, having negotiated the return of Wyandanch's daughter from mainland Indian kidnappers, he was given a tract of land that, once sold to Richard Smith, became Smithtown (Suffolk Co).

Gardiner, Curtiss C. *Lion Gardiner and His Descendants* (St Louis: A. Whipple, 1890)

Wunderlich, Roger. "Lion Gardiner: Long Island's Founding Father," *Long Island Historical Journal* 10 (1998): 172–85

Jennifer Steenshorne

Gardiners Island (3,000 acres/1,214 ha). Located in Gardiners Bay between Long Island's North and South Forks, it is 7.5 x 3 mi (12.07 x 4.83 km). In 1639 Lion Gardiner purchased the island, then called Manchonake, from the Montauk tribe and initially called it the Isle of Wight. It was the first English settlement in what became New York State, and a carpenter's shed built there in 1639 is the state's oldest wood-frame structure. The royal patent, granted to Gardiner by Charles I on 10 Mar 1639–40, gave him the "right to possess the land forever." A new patent was issued by Gov Richard Nicolls in 1665. The island was established as a manor in 1686 and annexed to East Hampton in 1688 for town government purposes. In 1699 Capt William Kidd left part of his treasure with John Gardiner, and although that was later turned over to colonial authorities, treasure hunters have sought booty on the island ever since. During both the American Revolution and the War of 1812, British fleets lay at anchor in Gardiners Bay and plundered the island for cattle and other provisions. Most proprietors lived on the island for long periods, but starting in 1920 the land was leased to other parties as a hunting preserve. Due to debt and inheritance taxes, the island was sold in 1937 to a Gardiner cousin. Since the 1980s it has been the subject of a title dispute between two descendants. Central to the conflict is the future use of the land, each side accusing the other of wishing to sell or develop it. Gardiners Island is, as the dispute highlights, an important wildlife preserve. Its grasslands and tidal wetlands are home to the largest colony of nesting osprey in New York State as well as to other endangered birds. It also has the largest stand of white oak in the Northeast.

Gardiner, Curtiss C. *Lion Gardiner and His Descendants* (St. Louis: A. Whipple, 1890)

Jennifer Steenshorne

Gardner, Emelyn Elizabeth (*b* Laurens, Otsego Co, 1 July 1872; *d* Los Angeles, 15 Oct 1967). Folklorist and educator. Born into a Quaker family, Gardner attended the New York State Normal School at Oneonta and graduated in 1894. Her first teaching position was in Cobleskill (Schoharie Co), where she began to collect the folklore of the region. After obtaining a BA from the University of Chicago in 1902, Gardner collected the folklore (stories, songs, ballads, legends, riddles, counting-out rhymes, and superstitions) of Schoharie Co from 1912 to 1918. The information became the material for Gardner's graduate thesis at the University of Michigan in 1915 and was published as *Folklore from the Schoharie Hills* in 1937. Gardner's work followed the literary and historic-geographic approaches to folklore of the time and was an expedition to locate surviving forms of older European folklore. It remains the only document of its kind relating to the folklore of that county and is important as a model for collecting folklore from a specific geographic region. After graduating from the University of Michigan, Gardner taught folklore and children's literature at Wayne University (now Wayne State University) in Michigan from 1918 until her retirement in 1942. She inspired her students to collect the folklore of their own communities and established the Wayne State Archives in 1939. After her retirement she moved to California.

Friedman, Albert. Frwd. *Ballads and Songs of Southern Michigan,* ed. Emelyn Gardner (1939; repr Hatboro, Pa: Folklore Associates, 1967)

Gardner, Emelyn. *Folklore from the Schoharie Hills* (Ann Arbor: Univ of Michigan Press, 1937)

Ellen McHale

Gardner, John (Champlin) (*b* Batavia, Genesee Co, 21 July 1933; *d* near Susquehanna, Pa, 14 Sept 1982). Writer. His mother a teacher and his father a farmer, Gardner spent his childhood near Batavia, graduating from Batavia High School and receiving his BA from Washington University in St. Louis in 1955. He became a Woodrow Wilson Fellow at Iowa State University, where he earned his MA (1956) and a PhD (1958) in classical and medieval literature. He then began teaching at university-level schools, including Oberlin, in Ohio, and Southern Illinois University, writing the first drafts of his novels, editing journals, and establishing his reputation as a writer.

Several of Gardner's novels are set in his home state. *The Sunlight Dialogues* (1972) offers a detailed portrait of Batavia while chronicling the conflict between the town's police chief and a mysterious drifter. *Nickel Mountain* (1973), set in the Catskills, follows the union of a middle-aged man and the 16-year-old girl he marries. Gardner also translated Old and Middle English writings, and wrote a biographical study of Chaucer. In addition, he was a poet (*Jason and Medeia,* 1973), a distinguished critic (*On Moral Fiction,* 1978), and short-story writer (*The Art of Living and Other Stories,* 1981). In his provocative *On Moral Fiction,* Gardner harshly critiqued contemporary fiction, alleging that too many writers were focusing on trends, novelty, and ideology rather than on enduring human values, values that characterize Gardner's best fiction. Gardner lived briefly in Cambridge (Washington Co) in 1976 and taught at Skidmore College in Saratoga Springs. From 1978 until his death in a motorcycle accident, he was director of SUNY Binghamton's Creative Writing Program, which he founded.

Howell, John M. *Understanding John Gardner* (Columbia: Univ of South Carolina Press, 1993)

Thornton, Susan. *On Broken Glass: Loving and Losing John Gardner* (New York: Carroll & Graf Publishers, 2000)

garment industry. For much of the 19th and 20th centuries, New York State was the world center of the garment industry. Although the state's core of production was in New York City, substantial garment manufacturing was present in other areas of the state, notably Rochester and Troy (Rensselaer Co).

Early Industry

The rise of a garment industry in New York State was tied to the rapid decline in home garment manufacture between the American Revolution and the early 1800s. As late as 1791 Alexander Hamilton noted in his "Report on Manufactures" that four-fifths of clothing in the United States was homemade. Married women and their daughters or traveling seamstresses or tailors who would visit farms made most garments of homespun wool. The remaining garments were destined for wealthy urban residents and were often manufactured in Europe. By the 1840s, with the rise of national markets facilitated by the growth of turnpikes and canals and the emergence of the New England textile industry, New York City had become a cosmopolitan center of fashion. The rising demand for intricate women's clothing featuring fur linings, ostrich feathers, silk, satin, and multicolored ribbons helped encourage the rise of a custom industry in which female tailors and dressmakers manufactured garments to order. These early garment workers and designers relied heavily on fabrics and fashions imported from Europe.

While the custom trade depended on middle- and upper-class consumers, another industry was emerging that created clothing for workers, sailors, and slaves. This cheap, rough "slopwork" was the first example of presized, ready-made clothing produced in New York State. As early as 1805 small slopshops dotted the New York City waterfront, making inexpensive pants, shirts, and jackets for visiting sailors. The War of 1812 expanded the market for slopwork to include military uniforms. In the 1820s and 1830s low-cost clothing was produced and destined for southern slaves. The opening of the Erie Canal in 1825 positioned New York City manufacturers to take advantage of growing markets statewide and in the Midwest and West for such products as dungarees, flannel drawers, overalls, and calico shirts. By 1860 two-thirds of ready-made garments produced in New York City entered the southern market.

Small- and medium-scale garment shops emerged throughout New York State. The 1855 state census listed 124 men's hat and cap manufacturers in New York State, 73 of which were outside Manhattan. The millinery industry was far more decentralized; of the 151 shops in the state, Oneida Co had the most at 15 and Manhattan had 12. Statewide, immigrants dominated the garment industry. In 1855, 96% of the state's tailors and 67% of its dressmakers were foreign-born, principally German and Irish. Regional concentrations of garment manufacturing outside of New York City also emerged during this period. As early as 1834 Rochester—a city that later became one of the four principal centers of the garment industry in the United States—had more than 20 independent tailors making and selling clothing. By 1860 Rochester had 42 shops that employed more than 1,500 workers, almost half of whom were women. After the invention of the detachable cloth shirt collar in Troy (which allowed individuals to launder shirts less frequently) by Hannah Lord Montague in 1827, detachable collars quickly became a rage and transformed Troy into the nation's center for collar production. Montague, with her husband and another partner, opened their own firm, Montague and Granger, in Troy in 1834, and another collar maker, Independence Starks, opened in that city in 1835. These plants were small, with the initial cutting of the cloth done in the shop, followed by the sewing of the collars by local women at home; final boxing and shipping were done in the Troy shops.

The antebellum ready-made industry operated on an enduring model of inside and outside production. Small numbers of skilled artisans and journeymen worked in inside shops directly owned by manufacturers, while most of the unskilled work, such as the assembling of precut lots or bundles of garments, was done in workers' homes, where children were often put to work, or in cramped outside shops or "sweatshops." In New York City such shops were housed in tenements and were owned by contractors or subcontractors. Brooks Brothers, a large men's clothing retailer and manufacturer in Manhattan, employed only 78 inside workers by the 1840s, while passing on the costs of rent, fuel, and needles to numerous outside contractors who employed 1,500 workers. Lewis and Hanford, another Manhattan retailer and manufacturer, was similar, directly employing 75 workers while shifting most of the production to outside contractors who employed 4,000. Wages were notoriously low for the outworkers, and hours were long. Their work was often solitary, and there was little recourse to forms of collective action. Garment outwork did, however, provide jobs for women, notably widows. By 1860 garment manufacture was the single largest source of women's employment in New York City.

The introduction of the sewing machine in the 1850s over time led to significant changes in the structure of garment manufacturing. In Troy, Gardner and White introduced the first steam-powered sewing machines in 1852. The machines greatly increased the speed of work and scale of production and lowered labor costs. In Troy the outwork of hand sewing diminished as large factories arose in the new "Collar City," which housed hundreds of machines and consolidated all aspects of collar making under one roof. The collar work process involved a series of tasks with sets of workers dedicated to each aspect of production, from initial cutting to packaging. By 1860 the collar factories in Troy, which also made men's shirts and detachable cuffs, employed 3,700, most of whom were Irish women.

The Gilded Age

New York State's garment industry grew rapidly in the decades after the Civil War, strengthened by an expanding national market and the influx of enormous numbers of immigrant workers. By the end of the 19th century the state's garment industry contained 4,204 shops and over 90,000 workers, making the industry the largest in the state in terms of the number of establishments, the number of employees, and the dollar value of production.

Rochester became a national leader in the ready-made men's clothing industry. Originally centered in numerous small firms, its garment industry consolidated into a handful of large companies in the latter half of the 19th century by spurning the use of subcontractors. These big firms included Michaels, Stern and Co, L. Adler Bros and Co, and Stein, Bloch and Co. Owned by German Jews, these manufacturers used new technologies and accessed capital markets. The Rochester firms opened large factories, which by 1891 employed more than 5,000, mostly Polish and Russian Jews. Increasingly Rochester concentrated on high-end men's wear, and in 1899 the Hickey-Freeman Co was founded, which later became Rochester's best-known firm. In 1912 Hickey-Freeman opened at that time perhaps America's most modern garment factory, which eight years later employed more than 1,700 workers.

The collar, cuff, and shirt industry in Troy experienced even more significant growth. Like Rochester, with access to capital markets plus a large Irish immigrant workforce, the garment manufacturers of Troy erected enormous factories. Located in what became known as the Collar Shop District, these facilities encompassed an area spanning seven square blocks of Troy's Hudson River waterfront and employed more than 14,000 workers by 1890. Women made up 85% of the city's garment workforce, and almost 50% of the working women of Troy labored in the garment trade. In total 22 firms in Troy produced 90% of all the detachable collars and cuffs sold in the United States by 1890. Native Protestants owned most of these firms, and some of the more prominent firms were Cluett, Peabody and Co, United Shirt and Collar Co, and Earl and Wilson. These manufacturers sold their products directly through their own chain stores and held some of America's most popular trademarks, such as the cloverleaf lettering of Corliss Bros and the English bulldog of William Barker.

New York City rapidly developed and established itself as the nation's leader in garment manufacturing, particularly in ready-made women's wear. German Jews dominated the industry in the city in the early years after the Civil War. But starting in the 1880s new groups of Jews arrived, this time from Russia and eastern Europe. Their arrival spurred the industry's growth, and by 1897, 75% of the city's garment workers were Jewish. Although manufacturers in other parts of the state built large factories, the city's garment shops remained small scale. New York City's garment manufacturers consisted of thousands of contractors and subcontractors who operated little shops employing on average less than a dozen workers each. Moreover the employment of women in the city's garment trade fell sharply as male workers increased, with women becoming restricted to the lowest-paying, least-skilled tasks. Jews would remain, until 1920, the majority in New York City's garment-making crafts, most prominently of women's cloaks, shirtwaists, and dresses, transforming the Lower East Side of Manhattan into the center of the city's growing garment industry. By the end of the 19th century, 64% of the nation's women's wear, by dollar value, was produced in New York City, with the city serving as America's most significant center of overall garment production.

The physical conditions within many of the state's garment manufactories, particularly in the small New York City shops, were egregious. Some later immigrants became proprietors, leading to the proliferation of small shops. With little money to open a small shop, these owners were often as poor as their employees. But the persistence of small-shop production perpetuated the abuses present in the inside/outside model of production, where workers toiled for low wages and long hours in dangerous and cramped quarters.

With mixed results, workers responded to these problems with collective action. Irish workers founded the first continuously organized women's union in the United States in Troy, the Collar Laundry Union, in 1864, which successfully struck for a 25% wage increase in February and March of that year. Two more strikes occurred in Troy in the late 1860s and another two job actions in the 1880s; all were for higher wages and were generally successful. Among the state's garment industry regions, labor relations in Troy were perhaps the best, likely a result of high salaries paid by local manufacturers. Although hours were long and unsafe conditions were common in the factories, many of Troy's female collar workers received wages in 1869 that were twice the national average of working women and almost as much as men. Labor relations were not as good in Rochester, where manufacturers pressed workers in the garment factories to work at high speeds and for long hours, leading to poor safety conditions. A group of Rochester cutters did organize under the Knights of Labor in 1888, and the union won a pay increase that same year. In 1891 the Rochester Clothier's Exchange, a business organization formed to counter the labor threat, successfully crushed the union. Although the United Garment Workers (UGW), a national men's wear workers union affiliated with the American Federation of Labor (AFL), organized in Rochester in 1893, a strike for improved wages two years later failed.

Collective efforts by garment workers in New York City perhaps faced the most difficulty. Small groups in a sweatshop could not organize as effectively as workers at a big Troy factory, where large groups could meet and plan. But small clusters of Jewish garment workers did organize and launch citywide strikes in 1883, 1885, 1890, and 1894 in the hope of bettering conditions. Despite the fervor of these early strikes, these actions achieved little; the social scientist Jesse Pope noted after a 1902 visit to the Lower East Side that many garment shops had no ventilation and were dangerously overcrowded. The terrible fires at the Triangle Shirtwaist Co in Manhattan that killed 146 workers in 1911 and at the Binghamton Clothing Co in which 60 perished in 1913 became symbols for these deplorable conditions.

The 20th Century

During the early 20th century widespread unionization of the garment workforce remedied many of the problems within New York State garment manufacturing. Unionization drove up wages, improved shop-floor condi-

Striking garment workers in Rochester. Photograph by Albert R. Stone, 1913.

tions, and provided long-term economic stability for the industry. In 1900 Jewish garment workers founded under the aegis of the AFL the International Ladies' Garment Workers' Union (ILGWU). Initially the ILGWU in New York State grew slowly. However, two strikes on Manhattan's Lower East Side—the 1909 "Uprising of 20,000" led by women shirtwaist makers, and the "Great Upheaval" of 1910 organized by male cloak makers—greatly strengthened the ILGWU and led to its widespread organization of New York City's garment workers. Facing an organized workforce, the city's leading garment makers signed with the ILGWU in 1910 what become known as the Protocol of Peace. This agreement provided better wages, work hours, and paid holidays for workers; but the protocol was perhaps more helpful to manufacturers. Unlike Rochester and Troy, where a small number of large manufacturers easily set local industry standards, the New York City garment trade was still primarily characterized by a contract system consisting of thousands of small producers. In effect, with all these producers competing against each other and all embracing differing practices, chaos reigned. Thus the introduction of the ILGWU into New York City's garment trade provided a desperately needed structure to stabilize conditions and ensure profitability.

A prolonged and violent strike in Rochester in 1913 led to the decline of the UGW and to the rise of the more militant Amalgamated Clothing Workers of America (ACW). In 1919 all of the workers at four of Rochester's five principal makers, including Hickey-Freeman and Stein-Bloch Co—with management's cooperation—organized under the ACW. Louis Kirstein, an executive at the Boston-based retailer Filene's (a main buyer in Rochester) brokered this agreement. The introduction of the ACW in Rochester brought better wages and shop-floor conditions for workers and stabilized labor costs for manufacturers.

With labor peace, New York State's garment industry reached its height during the two decades before World War II. Rochester was the first to peak during World War I when defense orders for uniforms pushed its clothiers to employ just over 10,000; the garment workforce slipped to 9,000 after the Armistice but stabilized at that figure until the 1950s. Troy hit its height of employment in the early 1920s when its collar manufacturers crested at 26, with nearly 16,000 workers. However, as the decade wore on clothing tastes changed, with men beginning to prefer softer attached collars, an ominous development for Troy. In the years immediately before and after World War I much of New York City's garment industry relocated from the Lower East Side to the garment district on Manhattan's 7th Ave, just south of Times Square. During this same period, women permanently eclipsed men as the majority in ILGWU membership in New York City. By 1925, 78% of the nation's ready-made women's wear, by product value, was produced in New York City, an all-time high. But in the late 1920s many city garment manufacturers began to move out of state, principally to rural areas in the Northeast and the South. New production demands were perhaps the most significant push out of the city, as department stores required ever larger orders that could not be filled in cramped urban quarters. Other factors were the city's high labor costs and the state government's enactment of America's most strenuous labor and workplace safety regulations during the first few decades of the 20th century. Illustrating the shift statewide, in 1919, 58% of the nation's garment workforce was based in New York State, but only 36% of the workforce was there by 1948.

Although the overall size of the New York State garment industry continued to slip, the years immediately following World War II were still healthy for the industry. New York City, spurred by innovative designers like Bill Blass, Chuck Howard, Anne Klein, Pembroke Squires, and John Weitz, became the postwar center for American fashion. By the early 1960s, 70% of the nation's high-end fashion trade, in dollar value, was produced in New York City. In Rochester, Bond Stores opened in 1948 what became for a time the largest garment factory in the world, employing 3,000. Overall Rochester's garment workforce continued to decline, falling to 7,900 workers by 1960, but the city's firms—particularly Hickey-Freeman—continued to retain their strong hold over the high-priced men's suit market.

Other changes occurred in the state garment trade. In 1920 Italians surpassed Jews as the majority in the trade in Rochester and New York City, and large numbers of African Americans and Puerto Ricans began to take garment jobs, particularly in New York City. Minority employment accelerated after World War II and by the 1960s Blacks and Latinos made up the majority of women's garment workers in New York City. This new influx brought racial tensions as minorities were generally restricted to less-skilled, lower-paying positions while most of their white co-workers held higher-skilled, better-paying jobs. Whites also controlled the leadership of the garment unions, and these leaders initially did little to organize minority workers. In the late 1940s the ILGWU did begin to organize black and Puerto Rican workers, and by 1952 these workers constituted 23% of ILGWU membership in New York City. The ILGWU leadership itself, however, still remained largely white, and in 1962 the State Commission on Human Rights concluded that the union had denied a member a leadership position because that person was black.

Compounding the problems of racial barriers for black and Latino garment workers, the state garment industry overall continued to shrink in the postwar period. By 1980 New York State's share of the total number of US garment jobs had fallen to 13% (170,000), from 36% (424,000) in 1948. Moreover, to keep remaining jobs, state garment workers had to make wage concessions. In 1950 garment workers in New York City received on average 10¢ per hour more than the average city manufacturing worker; by 1965 the gap reversed, with the city manufacturing worker averaging 22¢ more. Even with wage concessions, the state's garment industry continued to relocate overseas, lured by lower wages, the near absence of safety and workplace regulations, and weak or nonexistent unions. In Troy, although the detachable cuff and collar factories had been driven out of business through changing tastes, by 1962 only six shirtmakers remained in the city; eight years later most were gone. As early as the 1930s, Puerto Rico emerged as a center of garment production for children's clothes. During the Cold War US foreign policy encouraged the movement of garment manufactures to the Caribbean in an effort to combat communism. As a result the share of clothing sales in the United States attributable to imports rose from 4% in 1961 to 31% in 1976. Also emerging as garment production centers during this period were China, Hong Kong, Mexico, South Korea, and Taiwan. By 1995 over 60% of garments sold in the United States were manufactured abroad.

New York State, however, remains a significant center of garment production. Although state garment employment has fallen precipitously, 105,000 garment jobs remained in New York

City as of 1987, with the garment trade still the city's largest manufacturing sector. After the 1965 repeal of restrictive federal immigration laws, large numbers of ethnic Chinese immigrated to the United States, and 25,000 of them worked in the city's garment trades by 1980. Unfortunately sweatshops have reappeared in Manhattan's Chinatown as well as in Queens Co and Sunset Park in Brooklyn—all areas with high Asian immigrant populations. Like their predecessors a century earlier, these immigrant garment workers generally labor without the benefits of union contracts. By 1989 the ILGWU's membership in New York City had fallen to 70,000 members. A 1990s survey of garment shops in New York City found that 63% had wage and hour violations. The ILGWU and ACW, which had seen their ranks shrink dramatically in the 1980s and 1990s, merged in 1995 to form the Union of Needletrades, Industrial and Textile Employees (UNITE). Despite the continuing significance of New York City as a center of fashion, including designers such as Liz Claiborne, Donna Karan, Calvin Klein, and Ralph Lauren, the garment industry in New York State has continued to wane early in the 21st century.

See also DEINDUSTRIALIZATION; JEWS AND JUDAISM; LABOR.

Adler, Robert. *The Rise and Decline of the Men's Clothing Industry of Rochester, New York* (Rochester: Porter Associates, 1987)

Bao, Xiaolan. *Holding Up More Than Half the Sky: Chinese Women Garment Workers in New York City, 1948–92* (Urbana: Univ of Illinois Press, 2001)

Fraser, Steven. *Labor Will Rule: Sidney Hillman and the Rise of American Labor* (Ithaca: Cornell Univ Press, 1991)

Freeman, Joshua B. *Working Class New York: Life and Labor since World War II* (New York: New Press, 2000)

Gamber, Wendy. *The Female Economy: The Millinery and Dressmaking Trades, 1860–1930* (Urbana: Univ of Illinois Press, 1997)

Green, Nancy. *Ready-to-Wear and Ready-to-Work: A Century of Industry and Immigrants in Paris and New York* (Durham, NC: Duke Univ Press, 1997)

McKelvey, Blake. "The Men's Clothing Industry in Rochester History," *Rochester History* 22 (July 1960): 1–32

Pope, Jesse. *The Clothing Industry in New York* (Columbia: Univ of Missouri, 1905)

Turbin, Carole. *Working Women of Collar City: Gender, Class, Community in Troy, New York, 1864–86* (Urbana: Univ of Illinois Press, 1992)

Daniel E. Bender

garnet. Found extensively in large areas of New York State, garnets are silicate minerals with a general chemical formula of $A_3B_2(SiO_4)_3$, where A is calcium, magnesium, iron, or manganese and B is aluminum, chromium, iron, or titanium. Major high-quality deposits of garnet, especially in the Adirondack Mountains and the Hudson Highlands, led the United States to become the world's earliest processor. Gore Mountain mine at North Creek (Warren Co) was founded in 1878 and commercially developed in 1882 by the Barton Mines Corp. Bigelow Mountain, Casey Mountain, Keeseville, North River, and Thirteenth Lake were briefly mined locations in the Adirondack Mountains. The US and Canadian garnet market was divided in the early part of the 20th century between Barton Mines Corp and North River Garnet Co. The two companies merged in 1928.

Garnet became the official New York State gem in May 1969. The Gore Mountain mine closed in 1983, and Ruby Mountain, near North Creek, replaced it as a source for garnet mining. The North Creek area has yielded crystals up to 3.3 feet (1 m). Although gem-quality stones are occasionally found, garnets are used primarily in industry. As an abrasive, garnet is considered superior to silica because it does not produce dangerous dust. It is also used for water jet cutting and in the petroleum industry to clean drill pipes and well casings. Because it is relatively inert, garnet is used in water filtering systems.

At the beginning of the 21st century, New York State is one of the three industrial garnet-producing states. In 2003 three companies in New York State mined and processed garnets as primary product or by-product: Barton Mines in North Creek (its mines contain the largest domestic source of garnet), NYCO Minerals in Willsboro (Essex Co), and Patterson Materials in Wingdale (Dutchess Co).

For illustration see MINING AND MINERAL INDUSTRY.

Isachsen, Yngvar W., et al, eds. *Geology of New York: A Simplified Account,* 2d ed (Albany: NYS Museum, 2000)

Marian Lupulescu

Garnet, Henry Highland (*b* New Market, Md, 23 Dec 1815; *d* Monrovia, Liberia, 13 Feb 1882). Abolitionist. Born to enslaved parents, Garnet survived a breathtaking escape to freedom in 1824 when his father moved the family to New York City under the pretext of attending a neighbor's burial. There Garnet attended the African Free School and at an early age experienced the activities of the city's vibrant free black community: parades, lectures, and celebrations of African heritage and community solidarity. With black schoolmates Alexander Crummell and Thomas Sidney, Garnet studied at the Noyes Academy in New Hampshire, where white mobs forced them to flee. He was a student of Beriah Green at the Oneida Institute in Whitesboro (Oneida Co). Having completed his schooling by 1839, Garnet moved to Troy (Rensselaer Co), lectured for the American Anti-Slavery Society, and canvassed statewide for Liberty Party candidates. Ordained by the Troy Presbytery in 1842, he pastored at Liberty Street Presbyterian Church; he also taught at a school in Troy, served as an agent for the *Colored American,* and copublished the *National Watchman* in Troy during the 1840s before moving to Geneva (Ontario Co).

One of the most outspoken black abolitionists, Garnet is renowned for his 1843 speech to the National Convention of Free Colored Persons in Buffalo. Eventually published in 1848, Garnet's speech challenged the enslaved population of the South to demand freedom from their masters, even if this entailed violence. An advocate of militant tactics, Garnet believed that black abolitionists had to control the antislavery struggle. Disillusioned with America's refusal to confront slavery and racial injustice more directly, by the 1850s Garnet favored voluntary emigration. After traveling to England and Jamaica, he started the African Civilization Society in 1858 and began preaching at the Shiloh Presbyterian Church in New York City. During the Civil War Garnet helped recruit black troops and continued to preach, lecture against slavery, and publish pamphlets. In later years he became active in the Republican Party and was made US minister to Liberia in 1881.

Garnet, Henry Highland. *Walker's Appeal, Together with Garnet's Address to the Slaves of America* (New York: J. H. Tobitt, 1848)

Stuckey, Sterling. *Going through the Storm: The Influence of African American Art in History* (New York: Oxford Univ Press, 1994)

Richard Newman

Garvey, Marcus (*b* St. Ann's Bay, Jamaica, 17 Aug 1887; *d* London, 10 June 1940). Black nationalist. Garvey grew up in Jamaica, leaving school at age 14 to work as a printer's apprentice. In 1910 he traveled through Central America and in 1912 moved to London, England. Two years later he returned to Kingston, Jamaica, and founded the Universal Negro Improvement Association (UNIA) to promote racial advancement. Settling in New York City in 1916, Garvey established a new headquarters in Harlem. He proposed that Blacks rebuild a separate and self-sufficient African civilization. To encourage black enterprise and to provide transportation to Africa, Garvey launched the Black Star Line shipping company in 1919. Professing to be a Roman Catholic, Garvey nonetheless fostered the creation of an African Orthodox church and helped prepare a catechism for the new denomination.

After World War I, Garvey and his movement saw phenomenal success, claiming hundreds of chapters and millions of adherents around the world. Wearing a military uniform, Garvey led enormous parades sponsored by UNIA in New York City in the early 1920s and held UNIA conventions at Madison Square Garden. Despite his early successes, the various enterprises he launched were often poorly managed. Convicted of mail fraud in connection with the sale of Black Star stock in 1923, he was incarcerated two years later in federal prison in Atlanta. Pres Calvin Coolidge commuted the sentence in 1927, and Garvey was deported to Jamaica. Although the initial vogue of Garveyism had passed, he continued to advocate his ideas to a worldwide audience. He moved to London in 1935, where he spent the last years of his life. Garvey's movement and ideas were an inspiration for black nationalists in the United States, the Caribbean, and Africa.

Hill, Robert A., ed. *The Marcus Garvey and Universal Negro Improvement Association Papers,* 8 vols (Berkeley: Univ of California Press, 1983–91)

William S. Helmer

gas. See PETROLEUM AND NATURAL GAS INDUSTRY; POWER AND LIGHTING.

Gates. Town (pop 29,275) in central Monroe Co. Settled in 1800, the town was formed in 1802 as Northampton. The name was changed to Gates in 1813. The Tonawanda Railroad (later New York Central Railroad) came through in 1837; later the Rochester and State Line Railroad (incorporated 1867) crossed it. The loss of half its area to Greece in 1822 and nine annexations by Rochester between 1834 and 1950) radically altered its landscape. Harris Seed (1879), once the largest mail order company in the nation, and Dolomite Products are early ventures that continue in the 21st century. The town's population increased rapidly after World War II, doubling from 1950 to 1963 and again by 2000. Two expressways (now I-390 and I-490) were completed in 1964. The Italian heritage of one-third of its residents is reflected in Gates's cultural life and bakeries. Wegmans Food Markets, based in Gates, was Monroe Co's second largest employer in 2002.

Carolyn Vacca

Gates, Horatio (*b* ?Old Malden, England, ?April 1728; *d* New York City, 10 Apr 1806). American general. After a successful military career in England, Gates continued his service in Nova Scotia in 1749 and moved to New York City in 1755. During the French and Indian War he served as captain of a provincial company, was injured near Fort Duquesne [now Pittsburgh], returned to England, left the army in 1772, and moved to Virginia. Siding with the patriots, Gates was commissioned a brigadier general of the Continental army in June 1775 and promoted to major general in 1776, taking command of Fort Ticonderoga (Essex Co). Gates won lasting fame for his strategy during the Battle of Saratoga (1777), where he defeated British forces led by Gen John Burgoyne. Considered a monumental achievement, the victory was a major turning point for the American cause. In 1777 Gates was appointed president of the Board of War and in 1780 commanded the Southern Department. He served as George Washington's deputy (1782–83) at Newburgh (Orange Co) and encouraged John Armstrong Jr to write his Newburgh Addresses. Following the death of his wife, Gates married the wealthy Mary Vallance in 1786 and four years later settled in New York City. As a Republican he was elected to the New York State Assembly and served one term, 1800–1801.

Nelson, Paul David. *General Horatio Gates: A Biography* (Baton Rouge: Louisiana State Univ Press, 1976)

Mark G. Spencer

gays. See LESBIANS, GAYS, BISEXUALS, AND TRANSGENDERED PEOPLE.

Geddes. Town (pop 17,740) in Onondaga Co on the west shore of Onondaga Lake. Settled in 1794 and formed from the Town of Salina in 1848, it occupies the western half of the former Onondaga Salt Springs Reservation. The village was incorporated in 1832 and annexed by Syracuse in 1886. The early economy centered around salt manufacturing and farming. The original Erie Canal passed through the town. The Auburn and Syracuse Railroad (1836), later part of the original New York Central, was the first of three rail lines serving Geddes by 1853. W. H. Farrar established a stoneware pottery in 1841, relocated in the Village of Geddes in 1857, which subsequently became Syracuse China Co. In 1884 the Solvay Process Co (later Allied Corp) began producing alkali products and quickly became the town's largest employer. Crucible Specialty Metals, the town's largest employer in the early 21st century, was established in 1902 and used the nation's first electric arc-fired, steelmaking furnace. The first permanent mental health facility run by New York State, the New York State Asylum for Idiots (later Syracuse Developmental Center), opened in the village in 1854. In 1872 the first of several resort hotels opened along the west shore of Onondaga Lake, near the mouth of Ninemile Creek. The nearby Smith farm became the New York State Fair Grounds in 1890. Built during the 1960s, I-690 parallels the lakeshore. Suburban development, begun in the 1920s, now covers most of the town.

Thomas E. Darlington

Geddes, James (*b* near Carlisle, Pa, 22 July 1763; *d* Camillus, Onondaga Co, 19 Aug 1838). Engineer and surveyor. Son of a Pennsylvania farmer, Geddes studied law and surveying and traveled in Tennessee and Kentucky before coming to Central New York. After seeing salt being made on the shores of Onondaga Lake in 1793, he formed the first company for boiling Onondaga salt commercially. Geddes settled first near his saltworks on the southwest shore of Onondaga Lake in July 1794, bringing with him salt-boiling equipment. At the time part of the Onondaga Salt Springs Reservation, the area became known as Geddes (Onondaga Co) in 1848 and in 1886 was annexed to the west end of Syracuse. In 1798 he bought a 2,000-acre (809 ha) estate, Fairmount, in adjacent Marcellus [now Camillus], to which he moved after marrying in 1799.

His greatest impact, however, would be not as a businessman but as a surveyor and engineer for major transportation projects. Geddes was able to look at thick, trackless forests or dense swamps and visualize successful routes for roads and canals. With this skill he was able to map the Genesee St and mill site (1804) and the Oswego Canal (1808–9) with detailed surveys of difficult points. Geddes was involved with the Erie Canal continuously from 1807, when he began searching for a route, through its completion in 1825, having been named chief engineer for the entire project in 1816. Asked for advice on all New York State canal routes and construction, Geddes submitted regular reports to the canal commissioners. In the 1820s he did similar work for canals in Ohio, Maine, and Pennsylvania. He also held various public offices, including justice of the peace (1800) and Onondaga County court judge (1812), served in the US House of Representatives in 1813–15, and was elected to the New York State Assembly in 1804 and 1822.

Barbara S. Rivette

Gehrig, (Henry) Lou(is) (*b* New York, 19 Jun 1903; *d* Riverdale, 2 Jun 1941). Professional baseball player. The son of German immigrants, Lou Gehrig played both football and baseball at Columbia University. He played baseball with the New York Yankees for 17 seasons (1923–39), much of the first two years for their Hartford, Conn, farm team. On 1 June 1925 first baseman Gehrig began a record that stood until 1995 of playing in 2,130 consecutive games. This streak of the "Iron Horse" ended on 2 May 1939 when an ailing Gehrig removed himself from the lineup. Soon after he was diagnosed with amyotrophic lateral sclerosis, a disease of the central nervous system now commonly called Lou Gehrig's disease. On 4 July 1939 during Lou Gehrig Appreciation Day, he told the Yankee Stadium capacity crowd, "Today I consider myself the luckiest man on the face of the earth." By special election Gehrig was named to the Baseball Hall of Fame that same year. A two-time American League Most Valuable Player (1927, 1936), he ended his career with a .340 batting average, 493 home runs, and 1,995 runs batted in. Gehrig held an honorary position as a New York City parole commissioner after retiring.

Lou Gehrig playing baseball at Columbia University in 1923.

Robinson, Ray. *Iron Horse: Lou Gehrig in His Time* (New York: Norton, 1990)

genealogy. Genealogical data have been created and preserved since earliest times in New York State in oral tradition; grave markers; church and synagogue records; deeds, wills, tax rolls, military rolls, censuses, and other government records; newspapers; and city directories. Much genealogical documentation has been lost, however, in the State Library fire of 1911 and in other disasters, and by deliberate but shortsighted destruction of public and private records. Biographical and genealogical data on New Yorkers were first published extensively in the town, city, county, and regional histories that appeared between the 1850s and the 1920s. The New York Genealogical and Biographical Society, established in New York City in 1869, has collected and published voluminous genealogical data on families that immigrated to New Netherland and colonial New York, and, in recent decades, on New Yorkers of all origins and time periods. Patriotic and hereditary societies, such as the Holland Society of New York (1885) and the New York State organizations of the Sons of the American Revolution (1890), Daughters of the American Revolution (1891), and Sons of Union Veterans of the Civil War (1881), require that prospective members supply documented proof of their lineage.

During the 20th century many public libraries in the state built collections of family and community histories and genealogical source materials. The largest collections are at the New York Public Library in Manhattan, the Queens Borough Public Library, the State Library in Albany, the Onondaga County Public Library in Syracuse, the Rochester Public Library, and the Buffalo and Erie County Public Library. The public libraries in Poughkeepsie, Utica, Elmira, Watertown, and other cities hold good regional collections. After the 1960s many genealogical societies were organized across the state, numbering about 60 in 2003. The Western New York Genealogical Society, the Central New York Genealogical Society, and the Jewish Genealogical Society in New York City have significant publication programs. The Genealogical Society of Utah, run by the Church of Jesus Christ of Latter-day Saints (LDS), holds more than 56,000 microfilm rolls of New York State genealogical source documents. The largest branch LDS library is in Manhattan. Since the mid-1990s genealogical research has been facilitated by libraries' and archives' web sites and by commercially sponsored sites like NYGenWeb.

Guzik, Estelle M., ed. *Genealogical Resources in New York* (1989; repr New York: Jewish Genealogical Society, 2003)

Schweitzer, George K. *New York Genealogical Research* (Knoxville, Tenn: Author, 1995)

James D. Folts

General Electric (GE). One of the most successful and diversified corporations in the world dating back to the early 1890s, it was headquartered for most of the 20th century in New York State: in New York City from 1892 to 1894, in Schenectady (the site of its largest plant) from 1894 to 1956, and again in New York City from 1956 to 1974. Since 1974 it has been headquartered in Fairfield, Conn.

Corporate leaders of Edison General Electric of Schenectady and the Thomson-Houston Electric Co of Lynn, Mass, joined—backed by J. P. Morgan and various Boston financiers—to form the General Electric Co in 1892, becoming a pioneer in industrial research under Charles P. Steinmetz and Willis R. Whitney and establishing the first corporate research laboratory in the country in 1900. In its first three decades, under the leadership of Charles A. Coffin (1892–1913) and Edwin W. Rice (1913–22), GE concentrated on manufacturing lamps, motors, and power generation hardware and was centrally involved in the electricity revolution sweeping the nation.

Swope and Young

With the arrival of Gerard Swope as president and Owen D. Young as board chairman in 1922 GE's management began to develop and promote sophisticated corporatist notions of labor-management cooperation, aimed at encouraging labor loyalty and ensuring job stability. Swope and Young (both serving 1922–40 and 1942–45), as industrial statesmen, elaborated advanced views on the social responsibilities of capital and vastly enlarged GE's economic mission and ambitions. Swope, a former Hull House volunteer and architect of the famous 1931 Swope Plan (anticipating the federal National Industrial Recovery Act of 1933), and Young, a strong advocate of corporate liberalism, made a powerful and effective team. Their vision of cooperative corporatism led to an expansion of GE's employee welfare practices: recreational programs, compensation enhancements, employee representation plans, paid vacations, pensions, and improvements in job security. Under their leadership, GE also dramatically increased its product lines by aggressively expanding into the consumer appliance business, manufacturing refrigerators, irons, radios, washers, sewing machines, clocks, and more. The firm tapped the talents of advertising executive Bruce Barton and began a vigorous media campaign to launch its new electrical appliances. Popular magazines of the 1920s were filled with advertisements promoting the virtues of electricity as well as the advantages of the latest, and most modern, GE consumer products. Success in consumer product manufacturing and merchandising led to dramatic expansion of the firm in the 1920s. By the late 1920s, it was operating more than four dozen manufacturing works, located mainly in New England and the Mid-Atlantic states. The Great Depression slowed corporate growth, but production during World War II and advantageous financial arrangements with the US Defense Commission encouraged extensive, new, federally subsidized plant construction during the conflict. The escalation of military spending during the Cold War and the rise of a postwar consumerist revolution fueled yet another spurt of GE expansion in the decades from the 1940s through the 1960s.

The Irony of Expansion

The firm's midcentury expansion was also nourished and shaped by a new management style and philosophy closely associated with GE president Ralph J. Cordiner (1950–58): decentralization. Already implemented by other firms across the nation, including DuPont and General Motors decades earlier, decentralization meant rearranging managerial hierarchies, giving corporate departments more autonomy, and encouraging manufacturing units to act as quasi-independent firms. Top management retained responsibility for charting long-term growth and concentrated on broad strategic planning. Moving manufacturing divisions from one locale to another soon became a major element in the firm's new policy. Behind decentralization and managerial restructuring were important demographic, economic, and labor considerations influencing management thinking: shifting population and markets in the postwar era, the lure of advantageous tax opportunities and low-cost facilities, and a desire to flee heavily unionized regions. In the 1950s these factors motivated GE managers to pursue plant expansion in rural areas of New England and the Mid-Atlantic states, the South, the West, and Puerto Rico. By 1961 GE had 170 plants operating in the United States, located in 134 cities and dozens of states, including Georgia, Texas, New Mexico, Oregon, and California.

Many old plant communities, however, suffered considerably from these changes, particularly those in New York State. Schenectady, for example, with more than 40,000 GE employees during the peak of production in the 1940s, had long been a flagship plant of the corporation. The firm's heavily unionized labor force—first organized by the United Electrical, Radio, and Machine Workers of America (UE) in the late 1930s and then represented by the International Union of Electrical Workers (IUE) after 1954—experienced a dramatic decline as a result of the firm's decentralization and restructuring. Blue-collar employment in Schenectady plummeted from 20,000 to 8,500 between 1954 and 1965. Manufacturing departments long based there were moved to communities in Virginia, Indiana, Maryland, Vermont, and California. These moves, further exacerbated by GE's overseas expansion and the farming out of formerly in-house work to subcontractors, devastated Schenectady and led to its economic decline. After years of shifting divisions and operations out of the city, employment at GE's facilities there stood at around 4,700 in 2001. Utica experienced a similar fate: in the late 1960s more than 10,000 workers were employed at the local GE works manufacturing radar and electronic equipment for the US military, but in 1991 the plant closed. By 2002 GE employed only 13,300 workers in New York State.

A Global Conglomerate

Ironically, the downsizing of GE's New York State operations was the flip side of a corporate success story. Under the leadership of chief executive officers Fred J. Borch (1963–72), Reginald J. Jones (1972–81), John (Jack) F. Welch Jr (1981–2001), and Jeffrey R. Immelt (2001–), in the last four decades GE has undergone the most dramatic corporate sea change in its history. It has increased its net worth by acquiring hundreds of new subsidiaries worldwide. Its profits ($13.7 billion in 2001) and earnings ($125.9 billion in 2001) have grown impressively. It has become a truly global corporation with extensive operations in South America, Europe, Asia, and Africa. Furthermore, its activities are no longer adequately represented by its name. Originally a concern that focused on lighting, turbine, and consumer electrical product manufacturing, GE is now a diverse service, research, and manufacturing firm. Under Welch it moved from deriving 85% of its revenues from the sale of products to only 30%. Around 70% of its 2001 revenues came from a variety of service functions, such as personal and corporate financing, aircraft leasing, insurance, real estate, and entertainment (it owns NBC and several other media outlets), and more than 40% were from overseas operations. Although it has deep historical and financial connections to New York State, as well as obligations in the form of dredging and environmental cleanup costs associated with former PCB discharges into the upper Hudson River, GE is in the early 21st century a quintessentially global corporation, operating in more than 100 countries with over 300,000 employees in 2002.

See also Chemical industry; Pollution; World war II.

Hammond, John Winthrop. *Men and Volts: The Story of General Electric* (New York: J. B. Lippincott, 1941)

Schatz, Ronald W. *The Electrical Workers: A History of Labor at General Electric and Westinghouse, 1923–60* (Urbana: Univ of Illinois Press, 1983)

Zahavi, Gerald. "Passionate Commitments: Race, Sex, and Communism at Schenectady General Electric, 1932–1954," *Journal of American History* 83 (Sept 1996): 514–48

Gerald Zahavi

General Electric Global Research Center. One of the largest corporate research laboratories in the world, this facility is based in Niskayuna (Schenectady Co). It is the global headquarters of General Electric's (GE's) worldwide research division, and additional sites are located in Bangalore, India, Munich, Germany, and Shanghai. Originally established through the efforts of GE's chief consulting engineer and most famous scientist, German-born Charles P. Steinmetz, the laboratory became the nation's first science-based corporate industrial research laboratory, influenced by semi-independent research laboratories operated by German chemical, drug, and electrical companies. Opened in 1900, its mission—unlike that of industrial testing, engineering, and standardizing laboratories established by many firms in the 1870s–1900s—was expansive and ambitious. The scientists and engineers were free to probe the fundamental science behind existing and new technologies and not be narrowly confined to pursuing market-driven product development or refinement.

Steinmetz and his corporate backers believed that good science would ultimately produce good products.

The laboratory's first director was Willis R. Whitney (1900–1932), recruited from the Massachusetts Institute of Technology, as were many other early scientists and engineers. Under Whitney the laboratory made important contributions to lighting, x-rays, and electronics. By the end of Whitney's tenure the laboratory had grown to more than 500 employees, and research and development had become a critical element in forging GE's corporate success. The next director, William D. Coolidge (1932–46), continued to broaden the work of the institution and to make his own contributions in the fields of lighting and x-rays. Under Coolidge the laboratory charted new research paths into military technology, engineered materials, and high-energy physics. After World War II the laboratory, under C. Guy Suits (1946–65), became a major innovator in the development of artificial diamonds, translucent ceramics, plastics, and solid-state electronic devices.

In 1965 GE's Advanced Technology Laboratories (originally founded in 1895 as the General Engineering Laboratory) and GE Research Laboratory merged to form GE's Corporate Research and Development Center (CRD). Renamed the General Electric Global Research Center in 2002, as of 2003 it was organized around a dozen multidisciplinary and semi-autonomous laboratories, including Ceramics, Characterization and Environmental Technology, Information Technology, and Manufacturing and Business Process laboratories. Major corporate changes made at GE during the last decades of the 20th century resulted in a more aggressive management emphasis on profits and marketing and a more focused approach to product development. These changes limited somewhat Global Research Center scientists' autonomy and freedom to pursue promising scientific research. Research and development continued not only in the traditional realms of metals, plastics, and lighting but also in capital services, software development, electronic marketing, industrial electronics, medical diagnostic technologies, and quality control and productivity measurement.

The GE Global Research Center has attracted many world-class and Nobel Prize–winning scientists, including Willis R. Whitney and Irving Langmuir, the first American industrial scientist to win a Nobel Prize (1932), as well as William D. Coolidge, Albert Hull, and Ivar Giaever (who shared the 1973 Nobel Prize in physics for his contributions to understanding superconductivity). The center has generated more than 20,000 patents—263 in 2001 alone—in many scientific and product areas. In 2002 GE's Global Research Center in Niskayuna employed more than 1,600 individuals, including 1,100 scientists, engineers, and technicians.

Wise, George. *Willis R. Whitney, General Electric, and the Origins of U.S. Industrial Research* (New York: Columbia Univ Press, 1985)

Gerald Zahavi

Book on the *General Slocum* disaster, 1904.

General Slocum. The German immigrant congregation of St. Mark's Evangelical Lutheran Church, East 6th St, Manhattan, chartered the steamer *General Slocum* for its 17th annual Sunday School picnic on 15 June 1904. Some 1,300 members and friends of the church boarded the boat on the East River to sail to Long Island Sound. Within an hour the vessel had caught fire in the Hell Gate section of the river and burned on North Brother Island with the loss of some 1,200 lives. Investigation by the US Steamboat Inspection Service (USSIS) revealed that life jackets and fire hoses fell apart with age, lifeboats had been wired in place, and the crew had never had a fire drill. Capt William Van Schaick was indicted for negligence, not holding fire drills, and not training the crew. Sentenced to 10 years at Sing Sing Prison starting in 1908, he served three and a half years before Pres William H. Taft pardoned him in 1911. After the tragedy Pres Theodore Roosevelt ordered reorganization of the USSIS, dismissal of inspectors involved with the *General Slocum*, and recommendations for changes in the laws for passenger vessels. The accident was the largest inland waters, peacetime disaster in the nation's history and the largest fire fatality in New York City until loss of the World Trade Center towers in 2001.

O'Donnell, Edward T. *Ship Ablaze: The Tragedy of the Steamboat General Slocum* (New York: Broadway Books, 2003)

Rust, Claude. *The Burning of the General Slocum* (New York: Elsevier/Nelson Books, 1981)

Francis J. Duffy

General Theological Seminary. Episcopal seminary. Founded in 1817, General is the oldest theological seminary in the Episcopal Church, and the only one sponsored by the church's general convention. Except for a brief sojourn in New Haven, Conn (1820–22), it has been located in Manhattan and since 1827 in Chelsea on land donated by Clement Clarke Moore, its first professor of biblical language. Its original campus consisted of two stone buildings in Gothic style, one of which, the West Building (1835), still stands. By the late 1830s it engendered much opposition over its support for the Oxford Movement's attempt to reclaim Anglicanism's Catholic heritage, and it never recovered its early preeminence. The seminary was reorganized and expanded under the deanship of Eugene A. Hoffman (1879–1902) and largely rebuilt in an English collegiate Gothic style, with the Chapel of the Good Shepherd (1887) a particularly distinguished example. In addition to first theological degrees, the seminary has offered doctoral degrees since 1881. In 1926 a tutorial system was established both to encourage advanced theological study and to supplement regular teaching. Since 1971 women have been admitted, and there were 179 students in 2002. The seminary houses the St. Mark's Library, arguably the finest theological library in the Episcopal Church. In addition to possessing over 240,000 volumes, it boasts a large collection of Latin bibles and of 16th- and 17th-century English theology. The seminary also operates a Center for Jewish-Christian Studies (1986) and a Center for Christian Spirituality (1976).

Dawley, Powel Mills. *The Story of the General Theological Seminary: A Sesquicentennial History, 1817–1967* (New York: Oxford Univ Press, 1967)

Robert Bruce Mullin

Genesee. Town (pop 1,803) in SW Allegany Co. Settled in 1818, the town was formed in 1830 from Cuba. A mountainous town, it was still producing lumber in 1860. Drilling for oil and gas began in 1877. It received rail service beginning in 1881 from several lines, notably the Pittsburg, Shawmut and Northern (1903–46). Manufacturing included a washing machine factory at Little Genesee and the Ceres Glass Factory (*ca* 1900). Little Rock City, on a high hill a little northeast of the center of town, consists of boulders that appear from a distance to be a collection of houses. The Ink Bottle House is a two-tier octagon house built in the late 1860s.

Genesee Country. Name used in the last quarter of the 18th century for the land west of a line drawn north from Elmira to Utica. With the creation of Ontario Co in 1789, the phrase became associated with the greater Genesee River valley, which was the homeland of the Senecas. The word Genesee is believed to derive from a Senecan word for "gentle valley," referring to the Genesee River, which crosses New York State from the Pennsylvania border to Lake Ontario. The Sullivan-Clinton campaign of 1779 destroyed many of the Seneca settlements in the area but alerted the soldiers to its agricultural promise. After the Revolutionary War, the Seneca remained in the river valley on six small reservations that were eliminated by treaty in 1826.

Genesee Country was settled by people from Connecticut, Massachusetts, Pennsylvania, and eastern New York, some of them veterans of the Revolution who had participated in the Sullivan-Clinton campaign. Early settlers were enthusiastic about the potential of the area but faced epidemics of malaria-type fevers that were so severe that the region became known for the Genesee Fever, spread by mosquitoes that bred in stagnant wetlands and shallow millponds. Carl Carmer's 1941 novel *Genesee Fever* not only described the affliction but also wryly dubbed the hunger for land by the early settlers the Genesee Fever. In 1802 the state legislature created Genesee Co; it was formed from the western section of Ontario Co and extended west from the Genesee River to Lake Erie and south to the Pennsylvania border. The eastern part of old Genesee Country became the Finger Lakes region. The Genesee Country Village and Museum, located in Mumford (Monroe Co) and the state's largest living history museum, depicts life in the region during the 19th century.

Doty, Lockwood R. *History of the Genesee Country,* vol 1 (Chicago: S. J. Clarke Publishing, 1925)

McKelvey, Blake. *A Bibliographical Guide to the Genesee Country and Western New York* (Rochester: Rochester Public Library, 1965)

Lynne Belluscio

Genesee County (501 mi^2/1,298 km^2; pop 60,370). Formed from Ontario Co on 30 Mar 1802, Genesee Co is divided into 13 towns with 6 incorporated villages and 1 city. Part of the Tonawanda Indian Reservation is located in the northwest corner of the county. Situated midway between the Rochester and Buffalo urban areas, the region is rural except for Batavia, the county seat. The county straddles Erie-Ontario Lowland and Appalachian Plateau landform regions. Its northern half is part of the southern Ontario plain, and the remainder lies within the Cattaraugus Hills subregion of the Appalachian Province. The land surface tilts generally northward and is slightly to moderately rolling with stronger relief in the south. Elevation ranges from approximately 570 feet (174 m) in the northeast along Black Creek to over 1,420 feet (433 m) in the Town of Bethany. Bedrock consists of Devonian shales, sandstones, and limestones. The latter is minable and outcrops in a band extending east-west across the middle of the county. Because Genesee Co is covered by a mantle of glacially deposited material of variable character, the soils vary in quality but, with limited exceptions, strongly support viable agriculture.

The climate is humid-continental. Mean January temperatures fall in the mid-20s°F (-4°C), although nighttime lows near 0°F (-18°C) are not unusual. Mean July temperatures range from the high 60s°F to the low 70s°F (20–22°C), the difference largely the result of elevation. Daytime highs above 90°F (32°C) are not unusual. There is no dry season. Average annual snowfall exceeds 83 inches (211 cm). At least 30 inches (76 cm) of precipitation are expected annually throughout the county, with marginally higher amounts in the southwest. Drainage conditions vary. The western two-thirds of Genesee Co are within the Tonawanda Creek watershed, and the area's streams flow into Lake Erie. The eastern one-third is drained by Oatka and Black Creeks, both tributaries of the Genesee River. The northern reaches of the Genesee Co are poorly drained, which is reflected in substantial peat muck deposits. Except for the northern margins and a few pockets of wetland elsewhere that supported a swamp forest community, the county's primeval forest was dominated by beech, sugar maple, and basswood.

American Indians and Early Settlement

Chipped-stone spear points and mastodon bones have been found on a Byron farm. These items and a notable flint quarry at Divers Lake in Alabama provide evidence that humans were present beginning 11,000 BP. At the time of contact the Seneca occupied the area that would become Genesee Co. Their presence included a council fire site at the elbow of Tonawanda Creek, the present location of Batavia, although their settlement area was essentially east of the Genesee River, where their fields and orchards were located. Trails developed by the First Nations were later adopted by European settlers and remain in use as Rtes 5, 33, 63, and 98. Despite Senecas' crippling defeat in the Revolutionary War, they continued to claim ownership of their tribal lands until, at the Treaty of Big Tree (1797), they relinquished control of most tribal lands in Genesee Co. The exception was a sizable area in the northwest quarter, which was set aside as a major part of the Tonawanda Indian Reservation. After several treaties it was reduced to its present size in 1857.

Concurrently, Massachusetts, in accordance with the Hartford Convention of 1786, initiated efforts to sell the land that is Genesee Co to a group of New England investors led by Oliver Phelps and Nathaniel Gorham and, when that effort failed, to Robert Morris. In 1792 Morris, in turn, sold the western portion of his vast tract, including approximately the western two-thirds of Genesee Co, to a group of Dutch bankers. Four years later the Holland Land Co, through its chief surveyor and resident land agent Joseph Ellicott, proceeded to subdivide and inventory its purchase. Batavia, named in honor of the short-lived Dutch republic and located at a strategic fork in the Buffalo Rd, was selected as the company's regional headquarters. Land sales began in November 1800. The eastern one-third of the county, also once owned by Morris, was subdivided and sold under the auspices of several land companies.

Permanent European settlement began in Le Roy in 1797. Prior to 1815 most farms had fewer than 20–25 acres (8–10 ha) of cleared land. By 1825, 25% of the county was improved land and by 1845, 58%. A modest but varied African American community was established early in the settlement process. The 1820 federal census lists 33 slaves and 83 free Blacks living in the county; in 1836–37, 3 people born in Africa were residents of the County Home.

As the century progressed support for the Underground Railroad took root, especially in the county's eastern towns, where the "Covington Route" ran from Covington (Wyoming Co) through Pavilion and East Bethany to Le Roy, and from Le Roy it passed Morganville and Horseshoe Lake to Elba, and thence to the Niagara River and Canada. Along with churches came other institutions, such as fraternal organizations. The county's first Masonic lodge was established at Batavia in 1811. Undoubtedly the most sensational event in the early history of Genesee Co was the abduction and murder in 1826 of Batavia resident William Morgan after he published a book divulging the secrets of Freemasonry. The crime sparked an Antimasonic movement that swept the country in the following years.

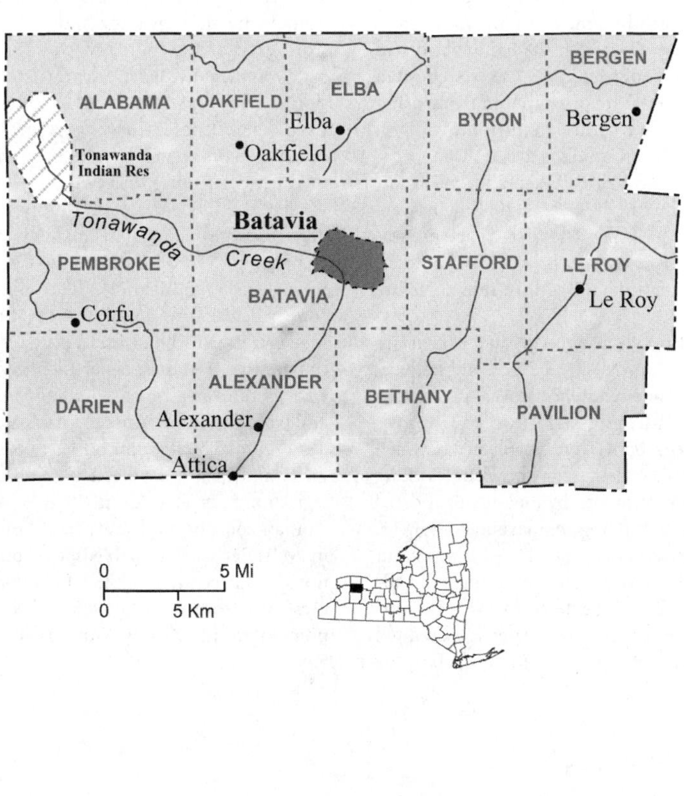

Economic Development

Genesee Co's economy has centered around agriculture following an initial period of clearance, which produced marketable ash from burning forest trees. In 1813, 68 asheries produced 178 tons (161 MT) of potash. The production of potash and pearl ash soon gave way to winter wheat as more lands were cleared and broken and as farmers took advantage of the growing fame of Genesee flour and the expanding transportation infrastructure that, through the influence and aid of the Holland Land Co, focused on Batavia. Although the Erie Canal did not pass through the county, its farmers carried their crop to the canal at Brockport (Monroe Co) or Albion or Medina (Orleans Co). In 1855 the state census reported over 41,000 acres (16,600 ha) of winter wheat being grown in Genesee Co, third in the region after Livingston and Monroe Cos. In that year there were seven large flour mills operating in the county, four at Le Roy, two at Batavia, and one, the most productive by far, at Stafford. In 1855 the county also had 4 sash and blind manufactories, 7 plaster mills, 9 tanneries, and 46 sawmills. By that time wheat production in western New York State was in decline because of expanding production in the Midwest. Rather than abandon agriculture, Genesee Co farmers began to turn

GENESEE CO POPULATION CENSUS FIGURES

	White	Nonwhite	Total Population	Foreign-Born
1810	12,563	25	12,588	—
1820	57,948	145	58,093	147
1830	52,055	92	52,147	344
1840	59,472	115	59,587	—
1850	28,411	77	28,488	2,874
1860	32,105	84	32,189	6,223
1870	31,453	153	31,606	5,833
1880	32,652	154	32,806	5,694
1890	33,135	130	33,265	5,797
1900	34,053	508	34,561	5,379
1910	37,010	605	37,615	6,910
1920	37,422	554	37,976	5,676
1930	43,709	759	44,468	5,777
1940	43,627	854	44,481	4,438
1950	46,729	855	47,584	3,684
1960	52,753	1,241	53,994	2,862
1970	57,029	1,693	58,722	2,109
1980	57,414	1,986	59,400	1,741
1990	57,762	2,298	60,060	1,201
2000	57,167	3,203	60,370	1,305

Notes: "Nonwhite" includes African Americans, Asians, American Indians, and Pacific Islanders and, for 2000, also the mixed race and other race categories. Through the 1960 census these figures primarily reflect the African American population. Foreign-born figures for 1820 and 1830 include only those not naturalized, and for 1930 and 1950, the foreign-born totals include Whites only. Other years include all foreign-born in the population.

their attention to dairy farming and corn production. Conversion of marshland in the northern parts of the county into productive muckland between 1913 and 1915 immediately resulted in rich crops of lettuce, onions, carrots, potatoes, turnips, beets, celery, and spinach. Italians came to work the new farmland on shares, but within a few years many of the families became landowners in the muck.

The county acquired rail service in 1836 when the Tonawanda Railroad opened between Bergen and Rochester; it provided service to Batavia in the following year. That line was extended to Attica in 1842, the same year the Attica and Buffalo opened. In 1853 Batavia resident Dean Richmond used his political influence to help secure the consolidation of seven short railroads into the New York Central to compete successfully for western traffic with the Erie and Pennsylvania Central lines to the south. This consolidated line passed through the center of the county. Other railroads followed and, by the end of the century, the main lines of the Delaware, Lackawanna and Western, the New York, Lake Erie and Western, and the Lehigh Valley, along with the busy Buffalo Division of the Erie and the West Shore Division of the New York Central, all passed through the county. In 1893 New York Central Locomotive 999 broke the world's land speed record on a run from Batavia to Buffalo.

Improved transportation brought more manufacturing activity to the larger communities. By the 1890s Batavia was home to Massey Harris farm machinery, the Baker Gun Co, Wiard Plow Works, and the E. N. Rowell box factory. Le Roy was the place of origin of Jell-O and manufactured it from 1897 to 1964. All these firms remained in operation well into the 20th century. This industrial growth provided local and migrant labor with a variety of opportunities, drawing Irish, British, German, and Italian immigrants. The first bank opened in 1829 at Batavia.

Religion, Education, and Culture

Churches were prominent among the county's early institutions, and an Episcopal service, the county's first, was held at Le Roy in 1802. The leading denominations were Baptist, Methodist, and Presbyterian, and many congregations were active in the evangelical outpouring of the middle decades of the 19th century in western New York State, which became commonly known as the Burned-over District. In 2000 the county had 54 Protestant congregations. The first Roman Catholic parishes were organized in Batavia and Le Roy in 1849 in response to the influx of Irish immigrants. More Catholic parishes were organized with the arrival of Italian and Polish immigrants in the early 1900s. In 2000 there were nine Catholic parishes. The first synagogue was dedicated in 1912 in Batavia. In 2000 the Rochester Zen Center built a Buddhist retreat facility in Stafford.

The first schoolhouses west of the Genesee River were built in 1801 in Le Roy and Batavia, and the first frame schoolhouse was constructed in Le Roy in 1804. In the majority of the county's towns, district schools were established between 1811 and 1814. A desire for knowledge among adults was demonstrated by the organization of libraries, the first being in Alexander in 1811. Female seminaries were established throughout the county by the 1840s. In Le Roy, Ingham Collegiate Institute was chartered in 1852. Becoming a university by an 1857 charter, it is credited with being the first university for women in the country, operating until 1891. The New York State School of the Blind (1868) still operated its Batavia campus in 2003. Between 1936 and 1957 central school districts were formed, laying the foundation of Genesee Co's present educational system of one city school district and seven central school districts. Genesee Community College (1966) in Batavia is the only college in the county and offers liberal arts and professional skills programs.

The first newspaper published in the county was the *Genesee Intelligencer* at Batavia in 1807. There have been newspapers printed in a number of towns, but the *Batavia Daily News* has been issued continuously since 1878. The Dillinger Opera House (1874) provided stage entertainment in Batavia until it burned in 1935. The first moving picture theater opened in 1906 in Batavia, and a theater in Le Roy began showing films in the mid-1920s. Competition from larger theaters located in neighboring suburbs and the availability of rental movies have made it difficult for these theaters to remain profitable. In 2001 Batavia's Mancuso Theater (1948) closed its doors, leaving only multiple cinemas in the Genesee Country Mall and one in downtown Le Roy.

Batavia's Dwyer Stadium is home to the oldest franchise in baseball's New York–Pennsylvania League, known until 1967 as the PONY League. Professional baseball started in 1939 with a team named the Clippers. Poor attendance and financial problems led to the surrender of the franchise in 1953. After two years Batavia reentered the PONY League. In 1998 the team's name was changed to the Muckdogs. It is an affiliate of the Philadelphia Phillies. Batavia Downs Racetrack (1940–98) pioneered nighttime harness racing in the United States; racing resumed in 2002. There are two radio stations in the county, both in Batavia: WBTA-AM/WXOX-FM, broadcasting since 1941, and WGCC-FM, since 1985, at the community college.

Politics

County government began in 1803 with the completion of the first courthouse and the appointment of county officials. Under the first state constitution all county officials were appointed by the governor and by one senator from each of the four districts into which the state was then divided. Under the 1821 Constitution sheriffs and county clerks were elected by the people. Genesee Co was governed by a board of supervisors, which after 1932 consisted of 19 members: 1 from each town and 1 from each ward of the City of Batavia. County government grew as a result of state mandate and social changes. In 1968 the county was divided into nine legislative districts. The nine-member county legislature appointed the first county manager in 1981; this official oversees and coordinates the 28 county departments. The county also operates an airport, a nursing home, forests, and parklands, and provides financial support to a museum. The Republican Party is in the majority and wins most elections. The first female legislator was elected in 1978 and the first woman chair of the county board of legislators in 2001. Barber B. Conable Jr, the county's most noted 20th-century politician, was a US congressman from 1965 to 1985 and then was appointed president of the World Bank, retiring in 1991.

POPULATIONS OF TOWNS AND CITIES, GENESEE CO

Town or City, Year Founded	1840	1880	1920	1960	2000
Alabama, 1826[a]	1,798	1,975	1,530	1,931	1,881
Alexander, 1812	2,242	1,608	1,287	1,987	2,451
Batavia, 1802	4,219	7,516	1,752	4,325	5,915
Batavia (city), 1915	—	—	13,541	18,210	16,256
Bergen, 1812	1,832	2,002	1,497	1,996	3,182
Bethany, 1812	2,286	1,671	1,196	1,569	1,760
Byron, 1820	1,907	1,754	1,273	1,589	2,493
Darien, 1832	2,406	2,046	1,617	2,357	3,061
Elba, 1820	3,161	1,968	1,394	2,260	2,439
Le Roy, 1812[b]	4,323	4,469	5,510	6,779	7,790
Oakfield, 1842	—	1,495	2,438	3,388	3,203
Pavilion, 1841	—	1,649	1,337	1,721	2,467
Pembroke, 1812	1,970	2,845	2,202	3,451	4,530
Stafford, 1820	2,561	1,808	1,057	2,005	2,409

Note: In 1840 Genesee Co included the Towns of Arcade [then China], Attica, Bennington, Castile, Covington, Gainesville, Java, Middlebury, Orangeville, Perry, Sheldon, Warsaw, and Wethersfield [now in Wyoming Co].

[a]Gerrysville until 1828.

[b]Bellona until 1813.

Recent History

There were significant changes in Genesee Co's economy, along with substantial population growth and adjustment, in the second half of the 20th century. Agriculture remains the foundation, with $110 million in sales, 1,500 farmworkers, and 1,275 people employed in agriculture-related manufacturing, according to figures of Cornell Cooperative Extension. Over 53% of the county's area, including 7,000 acres (2,830 ha) of highly productive muckland, is classified as farmland, the highest percentage in the state. Genesee Co ranks third in the state for agricultural sales per farm. Dairying is the largest sector of the farm economy, followed by vegetables (it has 3 of the top 100 vegetable farms in the United States), grain, hogs, and sheep. Small family farms are being replaced with commercial farm operations. Muckland agriculture has long been tied to migrant labor. The Farm Security Administration opened the county's first migratory farm labor camp in 1942, recruiting workers from New York City and southern states. In 1943 Jamaican migrant workers arrived to ease the critical labor shortage. In 1953 the Genesee Co Migrant Committee was established to improve the welfare of these workers.

Sylvania Electric opened a plant in Batavia in 1953 and became one of the county's largest employers, with 2,000 workers, but moved to North Carolina in 1976. The large industrial firms mentioned previously all ceased their local operations by 1981. At the beginning of the 21st century, hundreds of small businesses are scattered throughout Genesee Co. Manufacturing companies with the highest number of employees are Lapp Insulator Co (Le Roy; 350 workers), O-at-ka Milk Products (Batavia; 320), Graham Corp pumps (Batavia; 280), P. W. Minor and Son Inc shoes (Batavia; 250), and Chapin Manufacturing sprayers and dusters (Batavia; 225). County government was the leading employer (811 workers) followed by the United Memorial Medical Center (706) and the Batavia school system (440).

Development of natural resources and recreational opportunities has encouraged the growth of tourism. Genesee County Forest and Park in Bethany began in 1915 and covers more than 400 acres (160 ha). It was designated the state's first county forest in 1935. The 2,000-acre (810 ha) Bergen Swamp was dedicated as a National Natural Landmark in 1965. Darien Lake Fun Country, started in 1976 as a camping facility, has grown into New York State's largest theme park and entertainment complex. Renamed Six Flags Darien Lake in 1998, it now features more than 100 rides, including one of the tallest and fastest roller coasters in North America.

Highway construction has brought substantial change. The New York State Thruway was completed across the county in 1954, with exits at Le Roy and Batavia; a Pembroke exit was added in 1971. The Rochester arterial (I-490) connected with the Thruway at Le Roy when it opened in 1966. These high-speed highways and an efficient conventional road system encouraged residents of the eastern towns to seek employment, entertainment, and shopping in Rochester, while the western towns turned to Buffalo. Much cut back, rail service is presently provided by CSX, Norfolk Southern, and two short lines. Railroad passenger service ended in 1971.

Improved transportation has influenced demographic patterns as well. Between 1940 and 1970 the county experienced a 31% increase, and since 1970 population has continued to increase but at somewhat under 1% per decade. Much of the growth was tied to suburban development associated with the expanding range of commuters to Rochester and Buffalo. The largest increase in the 1990s was in Pembroke, which grew nearly 14%. Many Genesee Co residents seek employment in Monroe or Erie Cos, and most use the facilities of those metropolitan areas for television, cinema, sports events, and major shopping needs. By 2000 the African American population had grown to 1,284, 82% of whom resided in Batavia.

In the early 21st century the foundation of the countywide water system, coupled with "Smart Growth" policies, is expected to aid in industrial development while protecting farmland and preventing urban sprawl. County government is to coordinate with local municipalities to improve technology and shared services in an effort to combat unfunded federal and state mandates that have been identified as major constraints on the county's economic future.

The standard county history is F. W. Beers, ed., *Gazetteer and Biographical Record of Genesee County, NY, 1788–1890* (1890), which emphasizes individual pioneer biographies. Far better, though unannotated, is Mary McCulley, ed., *History of Genesee County, NY, 1890–1982* (1985). A volume of countywide significance is *The Architectural Heritage of Genesee County, NY* (1988). Most of the limited number of town histories are recent pictorial books or are derivative of the older works. For Batavia there is a very early work, William Seaver, *A Historical Sketch of the Village of Batavia* (1849), and a recent volume, Ruth M. McEvoy, *History of the City of Batavia* (1993). J. L. Broughton's *The Pavilion Community of New York State, 1800–1941* (1942) is a good history. An excellent recent history is Scott Benz, *Town of Elba History* (1995).

Susan L. Conklin

Genesee Falls. Town (pop 460) in SE Wyoming Co. Settled in 1804, the town was formed from Pike and Portage (Livingston Co) in 1846. It is the site of the Genesee River Falls. The Genesee Valley Canal, constructed from 1836 to 1856, passed through town, closing in 1878. William P. Letchworth of Buffalo purchased a part of the Genesee River Gorge in town around 1860. He also purchased Letchworth State Park, which he gave to the state in 1907, including the Genesee Falls Inn (1872; restored 1972); Lauterbrunnen, a Swiss chalet (?1876); the Iroquois Council House, formerly at Caneadea Reservation [now in Allegany Co] and rebuilt by Letchworth; the cabin of Mary Jemison's daughter; and the Letchworth Park Museum (1912). Bluestone was formerly quarried in the southeastern part of town.

Genesee River (159 mi/256 km). It begins at Gold in Potter Co, Pa, about 15 miles (24 km) south of the New York State border, and flows north to Lake Ontario, draining 2,463 mi^2 (6,379 km^2). Prior to the advance of the Wisconsinan ice sheet, a preglacial river flowed north as a tributary to the great river Ontarian [now in the area of Lake Ontario]. The geology and geomorphology of the Genesee River valley influenced the region's development. The depth and composition of glacial deposits and the more recent fluvial deposits are the basis for the valley's agricultural wealth and fame, while the river's flow powered significant early industry.

Early History

The Seneca Nation hunted and fished the Genesee River valley, making scattered camps along the river but establishing few villages because of swamps and rattlesnakes. In 1615 Etienne Brûlé became the first European to enter the Genesee Valley, traveling with Samuel de Champlain, who was searching for the water route to the Pacific. He probably crossed the river in present Livingston Co. Half a century later Jesuit priest Jacques Frémin (1628–91) arrived to minister to the Iroquois. In 1779 Gen John Sullivan led an expedition to rout the Iroquois from the valley, burning all the Seneca villages he encountered. After the 1788 Phelps and Gorham Purchase ac-

Lower falls of the Genesee River in Rochester, *ca* 1911.

quired much of this land from the Seneca, the valley was opened to settlement. At the Treaty of Big Tree in 1797, the Seneca retained six reservations along the Genesee River, but these were taken from them in the Treaty of Buffalo Creek in 1826.

Attracted by the fertile soil, waterpower and lake access provided by the north-flowing river, pioneers moved westward to the Genesee Country following the state road to Avon (Livingston Co) or along the Ridge Rd closer to the lake. Tethered to the waterpower of the Genesee, six settlements hugged its banks at what is now Rochester. Charlotte [now in Monroe Co] began as a port in 1805, providing access to Lake Ontario and international trade. South of Rochester, settlers were clearing forest and using tree species as a quality indicator, acquiring new land. Sugar maple and basswood were thought, for example, to identify the best soil for grains. Most New England farmers assumed the Genesee Flats, the area extending north from the river's gorge near Mount Morris (Livingston Co), to be poor quality land because it was largely open grassland rather than forest; such areas, at the time, were thought to be infertile. The vegetation cover, however, was the result of periodic burning and the annual flooding of the river, which left rich alluvial deposits over an area 4 miles (6 km) wide and 20 miles (32 km) long. Other factors helped make the Genesee Valley north of Mount Morris favorable to agriculture. The growing season was significantly longer: 177 days on average near the Lake Ontario shore, compared to 108 days near the Pennsylvania border.

Wheat was well suited to the soils in the northern half of the valley and yielded the best return. Upon the opening of the Erie Canal, land under cultivation tripled in Monroe Co and doubled in Livingston and Genesee Cos between 1822 and 1825. Much of the wheat grown north of Mount Morris was sent by river raft or, after 1840, by canalboat on the Genesee Valley Canal to mills at Rochester, which became known as the Flour City by the 1830s. Wheat production began to decline in select locations after a wheat blight (1846–48) devastated crops; harvesting and flour milling both moved west. Natural resources of the Genesee River Valley, tapped since the 19th century, include salt, gypsum, building stone, and lumber. In 2002 commercial activities included cattle raising, dairying, crop production, lumbering, and salt mining. The settlers in the south half of the valley shipped goods to Pennsylvania on the Susquehanna or Allegheny Rivers, in part because the Genesee was not navigable above Mount Morris.

Floods

Settlers learned the river's habits over time. Every spring it ran high and fast, fed by snowmelt and rain. Serious floods occurred in Rochester in 1785, 1865, 1894, twice in 1902, 1913, and twice again in 1916. The flood of 1865 was the most serious, prompting the city's first flood control study, focusing on the entire watershed. The river was again studied between 1889 and 1893 for flood control and for water supply potential to the Erie Canal. In 1898 the state granted the Genesee River Co a license to build a dam at Portageville (Wyoming Co), despite the lobbying efforts of William P. Letchworth, whose 1,000-acre (405 ha) estate included the gorge and falls near Portageville. Plans for the dam died when the company was unable to bring together enough investors, but they were revived three years later. Letchworth, in further attempts to prevent the project, deeded his property to the state in 1907 for use as a public park. A 1907–10 study included flood control and power development and identified two potential sites (one by Portageville and one by Mount Morris) for a multipurpose reservoir. In 1911 the New York State Water Supply Commission voted against the Portageville dam. Flood-control efforts in 1916–17 included retaining walls and deepening the riverbed within the city. Flooding recurred in 1936. In response the Army Corps of Engineers determined that a concrete gravity dam should be built 4 miles (6 km) upstream from Mount Morris. Stretching 1,028 feet (313 m) across the valley floor, the dam was placed in service in 1951. Kept empty under normal conditions, the entire reservoir is contained within the river's 17 mi (27 km) natural gorge between Mount Morris and Portageville. For the first time the 25,000 acres (10,120 ha) of fertile farmland that constitute the Genesee Valley Flats between Mount Morris and Rochester were protected against annual flooding. The dam has saved millions of dollars in lost crops, bridge and highway replacement and repairs, and individual property damage.

Pollution

For generations, industrial and household wastes were dumped into the river and carried downstream to Lake Ontario. Runoff from roads and farms also fouled the river. As Rochester grew, its waste became a major burden. An east-side trunk sewer was built in 1891, which emptied untreated effluent into the river. By 1920 municipal treatment plants were in operation, and attention turned to the industrial wastes dumped untreated into the river. The depression and World War II interrupted efforts, but by the 1950s old tunnels and overflows were breaking down. Planning studies revealed development potential of fishing and tourism if remediation was successful. In the 1960s and 1970s stricter federal pollution laws were put into place, and major industries led the cleanup. Quality of life became an important community issue as complaints about water and beach pollution were raised. The Monroe Co Pure Waters Agency was created in the late 1960s to build and upgrade sewage systems countywide. Stricter pollution controls south of the city improved waters and nearly ended dumping. In the early 21st century, water quality is much improved. Recreational uses of the Genesee include boating, kayaking, canoeing, camping, hiking, fishing, and hunting, particularly in the southern upriver region. A salmon-fishing derby is held annually in Rochester. The Erie Canal crosses the river at grade in Rochester's Genesee Valley Park. Hiking is particularly popular in the riverside parklands and the Genesee Valley Greenway, which runs along the old Genesee Valley Canal towpath, connecting Rochester with the Allegheny River at Olean (Allegany Co).

Clune, Henry W. *The Genesee* (New York: Holt, Rinehart & Winston, 1963)

Fisher, Edwin A. *Report on Flood Conditions on the Genesee River* (Rochester: City of Rochester, 1937)

McNall, Neil Adam. *An Agricultural History of the*

Genesee Valley (Philadelphia: Univ of Pennsylvania Press, 1952)
Rosenberg-Naparsteck, Ruth, and Edward P. Curtis, Jr. *Runnin' Crazy: A Portrait of the Genesee River* (Virginia Beach, Va: Donning, 1996)

Ruth Rosenberg-Naparsteck

Genesee Road. State-authorized highway. By legislation of 22 Mar 1794, New York State dictated that a public road be built through the New Military Tract, starting at Fort Schuyler [now Utica] and going westerly in a "nearly straight line" to the ferry at Cayuga (Cayuga Co) and on to the Genesee River. The route passed through the present communities of Oneida, Manlius, Onondaga Valley, Skaneateles, Auburn, Seneca Falls, Geneva, following roughly the present Rtes 5, 173, and 5 again, and ending at Canandaigua. In some places it is now called Seneca Turnpike and in others Genesee St.

Hills, creeks, and rivers forced road builders to deviate from the straight line, and in some places they were able to use Indian trails and old military roads. The result was the first improved road west of Albany, a cleared path more than 20 feet (6 m) wide, ditched, and topped with gravel that aimed at no more than a 7.3% grade. Traffic was heavy; 80–100 horses were sometimes stabled at one stop, with the overflow huddled under trees or oiled cloth. Gazetteer writers hailed the state's investment in public works, noting that other states had only narrow tracks, river fords, and rutted trails.

Three state lotteries were authorized in 1797 to pay for the project, and approval was given for the route to extend to the western border of the state. The same year the Cayuga Bridge Co formed. The bridge, more than 1 mile (1.6 km) long, was completed in 1800 and became essential to all-weather travel. Also in 1800 the legislature authorized the private investors of the Seneca Road Co to take over construction of the unfinished project; following the same general route, that road was called the Seneca Turnpike.

In 1806 a north branch was approved beginning at Chittenango (Madison Co), and it ran through Fayetteville, Geddes, and Elbridge (Onondaga Co), passed north of Auburn (Cayuga Co), and rejoined the original road at Seneca Falls (Seneca Co). In Onondaga Co this branch provided access for commercial traffic to and from the saltworks and, later, Syracuse. Heavy wagons with wide tires, which packed the surface, were such a help with maintenance that tolls were reduced for iron tires over four inches (10 cm) wide, and eventually those over five inches (13 cm) were free.

The Cayuga Bridge was destroyed in 1808 by high water, and a new bridge had to be built, at a large financial investment, 2 miles (3 km) north of the first location. The consequent traffic detours were also costly in both time and energy. By 1845 portions of the road began to revert to public ownership or were converted to plank roads by private companies. The Seneca Road Co was dissolved in 1852. Some of the plank road companies sold their rights-of-way to electric railroad lines beginning *ca* 1880. In some places the former locations of turnpike tollgates were used to mark the fare structure for the trolleys and for the buses that succeeded them.

Barbara S. Rivette

Genesee Valley Canal. Canal connecting Mill Grove (Cattaraugus Co) on the Allegheny River with the Erie Canal at Rochester. The original 117 miles (188.3 km) of the canal between Rochester and Olean (Cattaraugus Co) were constructed between 1837 and 1856, with the final 7 mi (11.3 km) portion reaching Mill Grove in 1861. At a cost of nearly $5.7 million, the canal included 112 locks over 1,127 vertical feet (343.5 m). Its surface width of 42 feet (12.8 m) and depth of 4 feet (1.2 m) could accommodate boats carrying freights of 70–76 tons (63–69 MT). The highest summit-level canal in the world, it soared to its peak elevation between Cuba (Allegany Co) and Hinsdale (Cattaraugus Co) at 1,489 feet (453.9 m) above sea level. The steepest gradient was from Sonyea (Livingston Co), south of Mount Morris (Livingston Co), through Nunda (Livingston Co) to Portageville (Wyoming Co), where the canal had to bypass the Genesee River Gorge and waterfalls in what is now Letchworth State Park in Wyoming Co. Here 50 locks in as little as 12 miles (19.3 km) overcame 530 feet (161.5 m) in elevation. From Portageville south to the summit at Cuba, the canal used another 37 locks in 34 miles (54.7 km) to overcome an additional 357 feet (108.8 m).

The canal shipped the lumber and sawed timber that fueled Rochester's furniture, boatbuilding, and barrel-making industries. In addition, blue sandstone was loaded from quarries south of Portageville, and the flats of the Genesee north of Sonyea supplied wheat and grain for the city's numerous flour and grist mills, helping make Rochester the Flour City. However, the canal never fully met its expectations, and after years of troublesome maintenance problems it was abandoned in 1878. Eventually the Pennsylvania Railroad occupied almost all of the right-of-way. As of 2003 the Genesee Valley Greenway, a rail/canal trail, covered the 90 mi (144.8 km) route of the canal through five counties between Rochester and Cuba; 52 miles (83.7 km) were open to the public.

Whitford, Noble E. *History of the Canal System of the State of New York* (Albany: Brandow Printing, 1906)

Thomas X. Grasso

Geneseo. Town (pop 9,654) and village (pop 7,579) in central Livingston Co. A center of Seneca settlement in the Genesee Valley, it was originally known as Big Tree and was the site of the 1797 Treaty of Big Tree. The first white settler came in 1788; James and William Wadsworth followed in 1790 and amassed vast landholdings, some of which are still owned by James Wadsworth's descendants. The brothers sold and leased farms to settlers from Connecticut and Pennsylvania in the fertile flats of the Genesee River, the town's western border, and wheat became an important product. The town was formed in 1791 and is the county seat; the village was incorporated in 1832. The Avon, Geneseo and Mount Morris Railroad opened in Geneseo in 1859. The Genesee Valley Hunt, the second oldest foxhunt in the nation, was established in 1876 by W. Austin Wadsworth. Geneseo Normal School opened in 1871 and became SUNY Geneseo in 1948; its enrollment (5,497 in 2002) swells the village population during session. I-390 (1980) has made Geneseo more accessible to Rochester, and its population more than doubled between 1960 and 2000. National Register listings in town include the Wadsworth residence, The Homestead (*ca* 1804), the 308-structure Main Street Historic District, and the Wadsworth Fort Site, an Iroquois earthwork of *ca* AD 1400–1500.

Joyce Rapp

Geneva. Town (pop 3,307) and city (pop 13,617) in NE Ontario Co. Settlement on the site of the Seneca village of Kanadesaga at the foot of Seneca Lake began in 1786. Under Pulteney Associates, English capitalists, Geneva was platted in 1793 and became the headquarters of the New York Genesee Land Co, which promoted Geneva and the surrounding region to potential settlers in New Jersey, Pennsylvania, Maryland, and Virginia. Settlers of Geneva brought wealth and enslaved workers, some of whom became part of a cohesive African American community. In 1796 the residents established Geneva Academy, forerunner of Geneva College (1822; now Hobart College). The state road from Utica to Avon was completed through Geneva in 1797. The village, then located in the Town of Seneca, was incorporated in 1806, and the town of Geneva was taken from Seneca in 1872. The village became a city in 1897.

Geneva became a powerful commercial center for the region at an early date. Despite relatively limited waterpower, Geneva built a diverse manufacturing sector, of which Ontario Glass Manufacturing Co (1810–30) was an early example. During its first years when transportation was difficult, the region's wheat and fruit crops were made marketable by distilling them into whiskey and brandy. The Cayuga and Seneca Canal, begun as a private endeavor in 1813, was rebuilt under state auspices between 1826 and 1828 and connected Geneva to the Erie Canal system. In 1841 the Auburn and Rochester Railroad linked Geneva to Rochester and Syracuse. In 1873 the Geneva and Ithaca Railroad (Lehigh Valley after 1876) opened.

Beginning in the mid–19th century, Geneva became an important center of nurseries and agricultural innovation. The first major nursery was in operation before 1840. John Johnston developed the use of drainage tile to increase yields per acre in 1835. Thomas D. Burrall invented a multitude of farm implements, later manufactured and sold by the E. J. Burrall Manufacturing Co. The Geneva Nursery of W. and T. Smith (1846) achieved notable success with fruit trees and expanded to ornamental specimens on some 400 acres (160 ha). And the New York State Agricultural Experiment Station (1882) opened just west of the village.

With the advent of electrical power, Geneva expanded its industrial base. Major firms included US Radiator Corp (1868–1962), Standard Optical Co (1873–1969), Phillips and Clark Stove Co (1885–1951), Patent Cereals Co (1888–1962), Geneva Preserving Co (1889–1953), Geneva Wagon Co (1891–1938), Vance Boiler Works (1897; now Vance Metal Fabricators), American Can Co (1901–89), and Geneva Cutlery Co (1902–62). Its labor force was diverse: the first Irish Catholics came in the 1820s, but with industrial expansion Italians came to Geneva starting in 1895 and Syrians starting in 1899. The city acquired a second college when William Smith College, a coordinate college for women affiliated with Hobart, opened in 1906.

Canal and rail transport industries declined in the 1940s and 1950s. Associated industrial de-

Hobart College, 1873.

cline was partially offset by commercial activity generated by the nearby Sampson Naval Training Station (1942–46, 1950–56), which housed as many as 40,000 servicemen for training during two wars. Motor vehicle congestion prompted the construction of a lakefront bypass (1953), which effectively destroyed the outdated manufacturing district but opened the vicinity to public and private development, and provided the stimulus for downtown revitalization. Replacing lost manufacturing jobs were service jobs: in 2000, 22% of workers were in that sector. Leading employers in 2003 were Finger Lakes Regional Health System, the colleges, and the experiment station. Notable landmarks are Belhurst Castle (1885), Smith Opera House (1894), and Geneva-on-the-Lake (1910).

Marla A. Bennett

Geneva Experiment Station. A research facility in the City of Geneva (Ontario and Seneca Cos) and the Towns of Geneva and Seneca (Ontario Co), it is part of the New York State College of Agriculture and Life Sciences at Cornell University. The New York State Agricultural Experiment Station was established by an act of 26 June 1880 and began operating on 1 Mar 1882 at the western edge of the Town of Geneva. The station's scientists concentrated research efforts on the dairy industry, horticultural practices, and the evaluation of varieties of vegetable and field crops. In 1887 the program was broadened to include studies on beef cattle and swine and the evaluation of fruit varieties. During this period the station also continued its active role in the state's agricultural law-enforcement program. Manufacturers of agricultural products were opposed to scholarly scrutiny of their products and, in 1890, they campaigned to have it moved to Cornell. The controversy ended under the governorship of Roswell P. Flower (1892–94).

The station became part of Cornell University in 1923 and expanded its research to include studies in the fields of bacteriology, dairy science, fruit horticulture, chemistry, plant diseases, and insect and mite species. At the end of World War II all animal research moved to the Cornell campus, and the Geneva Experiment Station became solely a horticultural research institute. Since 1950 it has been the center for research in the state on the production, protection, and utilization of fruit and vegetable crops. In Geneva over 1,730 acres (700 ha) of land are devoted to research on crop production, protection, and processing, utilizing classical techniques and biotechnology on test plots, orchards, and vineyards. The station has two outlying facilities in Highland (Ulster Co) and Fredonia (Chautauqua Co).

In 2003 its budget was approximately $26 million, about half of which was SUNY funding channeled through the College of Agriculture, one of New York State's contract colleges. The station's financial base is increasingly augmented by funds from foundations, industry, grower and food-processor organizations, and individuals. It employs 300 staff (46 of them professors) as well as many graduate students, conducting research on 230 different projects in a complex of 20 major buildings, greenhouses, and ancillary structures. The Plant Genetic Resources Unit maintains the US collection of germ plasm of apple, cold-hardy grapes, tart cherry, and vegetable crops, which is used to develop new and improved varieties. The station is also the headquarters for New York State's Integrated Pest Management Program. In 2002 Gov George E. Pataki announced plans for the 74-acre (30 ha) Cornell Agriculture and Food Technology Park adjacent to the experiment station. The groundbreaking took place in the fall of 2003.

Chapman, P. J., and E. H. Glass. *The First 100 Years of the New York State Agricultural Experiment Station at Geneva, NY, 1882–1982* (Ithaca: Cornell Univ Press, 1999)

Marla A. Bennett

Genoa [JEN-OH-AH]. Town (pop 1,914) in SW Cayuga Co. Settled in 1791, the town, much larger at that time, was formed in 1789 as Milton. Its name was changed to Genoa in 1808. The King Ferry across Cayuga Lake operated until 1913. Genoa hamlet was the site of Stevens Thrasher Works (?1838–78) until it burned and was rebuilt in Auburn. The Lehigh Valley Railroad (1872–1950) provided service along the lakeshore, and other shorter-lived railroads served the eastern part of town. From 1964 to 1968 Genoa farmers devoted thousands of acres to sugar beet production. The experiment failed due to processing problems. Genoa's economy is based on wine making, dairying, poultry, and cash crops, including snap beans, sweet corn, hay, and cereal grains. Since 1988 Ithaca Gun Co, a shotgun manufacturer, has operated at King Ferry.

geography. See GEOLOGY AND PLATE TECTONICS; LANDFORMS; see also individual counties.

geology and plate tectonics. New York State has an array of geological features typical of a continent-sized land mass. Its geological heritage is particularly extensive in terms of the great age span of its rocks, the variety of geological features, and the long period of scientific research that it has received.

GEOLOGICAL SUBDIVISIONS

The ancient basement exposed in the interior of continents is the shield. Shields are dominated by metamorphic rocks (rocks resulting from the change of older rocks by heat, pressure, and fluids during deep burial) produced during ancient mountain building and have not been subjected to more recent mountain building. On top of the geologically stable shield are sedimentary rocks (older rock fragments or materials produced biologically, as fossil-rich limestones, or chemically, as salt deposits) that have not been folded, faulted, or metamorphosed by mountain building. These sedimentary rocks that commonly lie closer to the margins of continents are the craton.

New York State can be broadly divided into three geological regions. The first is the ancient shield and overlying sedimentary rocks of the craton. The Adirondack Mountains are part of the Canadian Shield. The craton includes the sedimentary rocks that overlie the Adirondack basement and extend into Ontario, Quebec, and the Lake Champlain valley and that underlie all areas south of the Adirondacks and west of the Hudson–Wallkill River valley. The craton south of the Mohawk–Lake Ontario Lowlands lies at the north end of the Allegheny Plateau, an upland east of the Appalachians that extends to Alabama and into the Midwest. Because of repeated episodes of folding and faulting by orogenic (mountain-building) processes, the craton changes east of the Wallkill–Hudson–Lake Champlain Lowlands into the Appalachian Mountain belt of easternmost New York State. This second geological region of the state features New England–type geology. In this area, Adirondack-type basement was uplifted on faults (Hudson Highlands), and deepwater, continent-margin rocks of the Taconic slate belt were pushed into New York from their original position in the Connecticut River valley region. The state's third geological region is coastal New York. The southern end of the New England Appalachians is covered by relatively young, flat-lying coastal plain rocks deposited during the "Age of Dinosaurs," 225–65 million years ago (mya). Similar coastal plain rocks extend south from Long Island and southeast Staten Island to Florida and along the Gulf of Mexico.

Most New York State bedrock, with exception of the Adirondack, Taconic, Catskill, and Westchester-Manhattan area highlands, is mantled by late and postglacial sediments that are

EON	ERA	GEOLOGIC PERIOD AND AGE IN MILLIONS OF YEARS		MAJOR GEOLOGIC EVENTS
PHANEROZOIC (time of abundant fossils)	Cenozoic	Quaternary		Latest "Ice Age" sediments cover New York State, ice terminus on Long Island
			2	"Ice Age" begins
		Tertiary		No rocks or fossils in New York
			65	
	Mesozoic	Cretaceous		Sandstones and shales of Staten and Long Islands (Garvies Point Preserve)
			138	
		Jurassic		Atlantic Ocean forms, sands deposited offshore of New York
			195	
		Triassic		Pangaea supercontinent breakup, palisades injected into sedimentary rocks
			225	
	Paleozoic	Permian		Glaciation of southern Africa and South America
			280	
		Carboniferous		Coal deposits of eastern United States, sandstones of Allegany State Park area
			345	Collision with west Africa, Appalachians rise
		Devonian		Collision with Avalon, Acadian Mountains rise, Catskill delta forms
				Ash from Maine volcanoes laid down in tropical sea deposits of New York
			418	
		Silurian		Important salt deposits in New York
				Marine rocks and fossils of Niagara Falls
			440	Seas limited to western New York, African glaciation
		Ordovician		Muds and sands deposited across New York
				Taconic mountain building, volcanic arc pushes slate belt into eastern New York
			489	Tropical limestone deposition across New York and Laurentian continent
		Cambrian		Seas cover New York State
				Shallow seas flood Dutchess Co
				Earliest mudrocks of Taconic slate belt
				Rensselaer plateau rocks laid down on continental slope
			543	
PRECAMBRIAN			600	Origin of Iapetus Ocean east of New York with Rodinia supercontinent breakup
			1,000	Adirondack and Hudson Highlands rock forms 40 km (25 mi) underground with collision with Amazon heartland (Grenville Mountain building)
			1,300	Ancient volcanic and sedimentary rocks of Adirondack and Hudson Highlands laid down
			4,600	Origin of solar system and earth

rarely more than 20,000 years old. The black–dark gray colors of most of the state's soils reflect a relatively recent origin following the northern retreat of continental ice sheets. From central Pennsylvania and further south, soils are red.

The State as a Plate Tectonics Laboratory

Understanding New York State's historic development requires an appreciation of how its geology was shaped by plate tectonics. Plate tectonics theory sees the earth as a dynamic planet, with the distribution of oceans, continents, and mountains continually defined by processes that originate deep in the planet. Plate tectonics is based on the recognition that the earth's surface is broken into huge plates, which may have continents on them. Plates move relative to each other as a consequence of a slow convective movement of deep, hot rock with a plastic consistency. Pairs of convection cells rise under the middle of the Atlantic and diverge east and west about 60 miles (100 km) below the seafloor. The seafloor is stretched, broken, and liquid rock is injected into cracks along submarine mountains that mark the boundary between plates. The distance between New York State and Europe increases 2 inches (5 cm) per year from convection currents beneath the floor of the Atlantic Ocean. Spreading centers (rifts) also develop under continents and break them apart.

If plates move away from each other, they must collide on their far sides with more distant plates. Major mountain chains result from continent-continent collisions when the lithosphere (the brittle crust of the earth and underlying rock) of two continents is greatly thickened and deformed during collision. The subcontinent that contains modern India has traveled from the southern hemisphere to collide with South Asia; that collision is now uplifting the Himalayas. Western North America shows a different type of collision, with the continental lithosphere overriding the higher-density oceanic lithosphere of the Pacific plate. The Pacific plate is forced under the Americas plate. A belt of very deep ocean (a trench) appears above the subduction zone. Explosive volcanoes (the Pacific "ring of fire") develop near the edge of the overriding plate as the subducting plate melts, and low-density liquid rock rises to the surface.

A result of seafloor spreading and plate movement is the ultimate coalescence of all continents into a supercontinent. Supercontinents appear with a period of about 600 million years through geologic time and then fragment into many small continents. The geologic history of New York State includes two intervals when this region was part of a supercontinent (first Rodinia, then much later Pangaea) and two periods of continent fragmentation.

Vestiges of Rodinia: Adirondacks and Hudson Highlands

The Adirondack Mountains are a massif (an uplifted area of old rock). Unlike the Appalachians or Rockies, the Adirondacks are not an elongate mountain belt but are a circular dome caused by the upwarping of continent basement and erosion of overlying younger rocks. The Adirondacks are largely composed of such metamorphic rocks as gneiss (feldspar-, quartz-, and mica-rich rocks with minerals segregated into layers) and minor marble (metamorphosed limestone). These rocks are composed of minerals formed at temperatures and pressures associated with burial to 19–25 miles (30–40 km). Such depths of burial are produced in Himalayan-type continent-continent collisions where one continent overrides another. The Adirondacks are a small outcrop area of the Grenville orogen (mountain belt). Grenville rocks extend for 3,100 miles (5,000 km) underground from the eastern United States to Mexico and from northern Lake Huron across Ontario to Labrador, southern Greenland, and areas now separated from North America. All of these areas show a date of 1,100 mya determined by radiometric dating of microscopic zircon crystals produced during metamorphism and mountain building. Anorthosite, an unusual light-colored rock composed largely of the feldspar anorthite, underlies large areas of the Adirondack High Peaks and may have been injected as liquid rock early in the Grenville orogeny. Gore Mountain garnet, formed with anorthosite metamorphism, is the state mineral.

Older dates of 1,300 mya are known on zircons in metamorphosed volcanic rocks in the Adirondacks. These dates indicate the time of volcanism and, likely, the age of such associated metamorphosed sedimentary rocks as quartzites (metamorphosed sandstones) and marbles. Marble-rich intervals in the Adirondacks indicate deposition of tropical limestones 1,300 mya. Marble is less resistant to erosion than gneiss and forms valleys; the Fulton Chain of Lakes Lowland is a marble belt.

Reconstructing the Grenville orogeny is difficult; it is unclear what continents collided *ca* 1,100 mya. Old, rounded zircons in Adirondack metasedimentary rocks have 2,700 mya ages. This is the age of mountain building in the Superior orogen of the northern Midwest and Ontario, and these zircons were eroded from old rock in the heartland of ancestral North America. In 2002 reworked zircons with 2,075 mya and 1,500 mya ages were reported in Grenville rock in Harriman State Park. Rocks formed 2,000 and 1,500 mya are best known in the northern Amazon Basin. These data suggest that Amazonian rocks were eroded to supply the zircons; it is possible that the southwestern Hudson Highlands lay near a collision zone between ancestral North America and a continent that included much of South America. This collision may have produced the Grenville orogeny and the rocks of the Adirondacks and Hudson Highlands. The Grenville orogeny was an early stage in the assembly of the supercontinent Rodinia. No record of the next 550 million years is known in this region, but this time included erosion of the Grenville mountains and the removal of 19–25 miles (30–40 km) of Grenville rock down to about its present level. It is unknown where the sediment eroded from the Adirondack Mountains and Hudson Highlands in the Grenville belt was deposited.

Breakup of Rodinia

Rodinia began to break apart somewhat before 550 mya in the latest Precambrian, slightly be-

Generalized Bedrock Geology

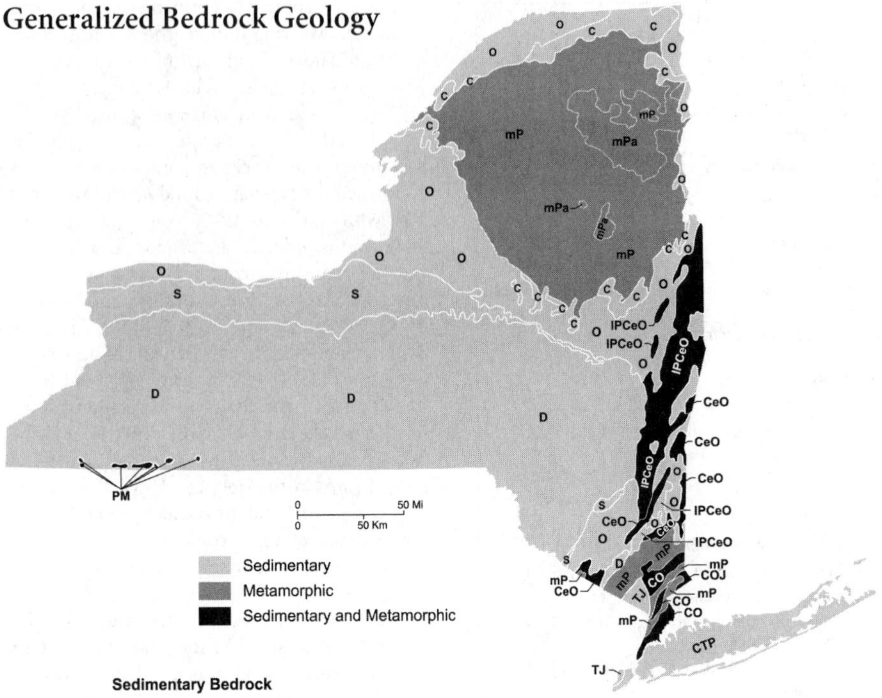

Sedimentary Bedrock

CTP	Cretaceous, Tertiary, Pleistocene: unconsolidated
TJ	Triassic, Jurassic: conglomerates, red sandstones, red shales, diabase
PM	Pennsylvanian, Mississippian: conglomerates, sandstones, shales
D	Devonian: limestones, shales, sandstones, dolostones
S	Silurian: limestones, shales, sandstones, dolostones, salt, gypsum, hematite
O	Ordovician: limestones, shales, sandstones, dolostones
C	Cambrian: limestones, shales, sandstones, dolostones

Metamorphic Bedrock

mP	Middle Proterozoic: gneisses, quartzites, marles
mPa	Middle Proterozoic: anorthositic rocks

Sedimentary and Metamorphic Bedrock

CeO	Cambrian, early Ordovician: sandstone dolostone
CO	Cambrian, Ordovician: quartzites, dolostones, marbles, schists, gneisses
IPCeO	Late Proterozoic, Cambrian, early Ordovician: sandstones, shales, slates, graywackes

SOURCE: Adapted from New York State Geological Survey, *Generalized Bedrock Geology of New York* (map) (1986).

fore the origin of modern animal groups in the Cambrian period (543–489 mya). Basalts (volcanic rocks rich in iron-magnesium silicates) of 550 mya flowed from spreading centers into marine sediments in southern Quebec and northern Vermont. These rocks and similar basalts and sedimentary rocks north of Grafton Lakes State Park in Rensselaer Co record continent breakup and the origin of the Iapetus Ocean east of New York State.

Features expected of continent breakup, such as broken edges having a zigzag outline with the fractures meeting at about 120°, are recorded in the New York State region. One fracture zone trends southwest, approximately parallel to the northern margin of the Appalachians and the St. Lawrence River in Quebec. This "active arm" is replaced at a 120° angle by a second arm that runs south from Montreal and somewhat east of the Lake Champlain–Hudson Lowlands to New York City. The less active "failed arm" of this rift system runs northwest of Montreal to Ottawa. Another 120° angle in the fracture system in the New York City region made the new continent margin angle west into Pennsylvania.

This configuration of rifts formed the New York Promontory at the edge of the new continent of Laurentia (ancestral North America). Promontories tend to remain as high areas along the edge of continents, which means that the thickness of Paleozoic marine rocks laid down across New York State is thinner than that in the Pennsylvania Reentrant. Continent breakup is not along a single fracture, and many smaller fractures parallel the major rifts. For example, smaller fractures roughly parallel to the Lake Champlain–Hudson Lowlands define the north-northeast trend of many eastern Adirondack features such as Long, Indian, Schroon, and Brant Lakes; Lake George; upper West and East Branches of the Ausable River; and stretches of the Northway where it runs along valleys. Old fractures contain shattered rock, and erosion by the last continental glaciation scoured them to form the modern Adirondack topography. Fractures are zones of weakness, and the abundance of small earthquakes on a line from Ottawa, Ont (on the failed arm), along the eastern Adirondacks and Hudson Valley to New York City likely reflects these *ca* 550 mya fractures.

Tropical Seas in Eastern Laurentia

Sea-level rise brought shallow marine waters across Dutchess Co relatively early in the Cambrian (543–489 mya); they completely covered New York State by the end of the period. Cambrian shoreline sandstones overlie the Grenville at Stissing Mountain in Dutchess Co, Skene Mountain in Washington Co, Ausable Chasm in Clinton Co, and Chateaugay Chasm in Franklin Co. Overlying deposits that range high into the younger Ordovician period (489–438 mya) are dominated by limestones (calcium carbonate rock often changed into the calcium-magnesium carbonate rock dolostone). Evaporite minerals (halite and gypsum) and mud cracks in parts of the Upper Cambrian–Lower Ordovician in the Mohawk Valley and Middle Ordovician on Isle La Motte in Lake Champlain, and coral reefs in the lower Upper Ordovician at Plattsburgh indicate tropical conditions. New York State and eastern Laurentia were rotated 90° clockwise from their modern position and lay 35° south of the equator. These limestones are present as far south as New York City, where the rock succession includes the Grenville (Yonkers and Fordham Gneisses), the Lower Cambrian Lowerre Quartzite, and Cambrian-Ordovician Inwood Marble. The latter easily eroded unit forms the beds of the lower Hudson, East, and Harlem Rivers.

Collision and Rise of the Taconic Mountains

Mountain-building intervals in eastern New York State record events that led to growth of the supercontinent Pangaea. The first was the collision of eastern Laurentia with a volcanic island arc that extended from western Newfoundland to Alabama in the late Ordovician (450 mya). This collision, the Taconic orogeny, produced the Taconic Range of eastern New York and western New England, which was first proposed on the basis of geologic relationships in the Taconic Range and foothills of eastern New York State. Volcanic ashes, now claylike beds up to 4 inches (10 cm) thick in Upper Ordovician limestones of the Mohawk Valley and Saratoga areas, are the first evidence for proximity of the volcanic arc. During the Taconic collision, deep-water sandstones and mudrocks deposited on the Laurentian margin were pushed into eastern New York State in front of the volcanic arc. These overthrust rocks comprise the slate-rich Taconic hills of Washington and Dutchess Cos and are much more highly metamorphosed in Westchester Co. Further south, the highly metamorphosed Taconic overthrust forms the Manhattan Schist in Central Park.

The Taconic orogeny ended Ordovician shallow-water limestone deposition. East of Syracuse, the weight of the Taconic overthrust depressed the earth's crust. This deepwater trough was filled with black shales, seen in cuts on the New York State Thruway from Amsterdam (Montgomery Co) to Herkimer, and overlying sands and muds, like those seen in the Mohawk River cliffs downstream of Schenectady. These sands and muds were eroded from the Taconic Mountains. Vertical movement of up to 1,310 feet (400 m) took place along old basement fractures late in the Taconic orogeny. Local uplifts of hard Grenville and Upper Cambrian rock define the canyons and "narrows" along the Mohawk River at Hoffmans (Schenectady Co), Randall (Montgomery Co), and Little Falls (Herkimer Co).

The Ordovician period ended as the retreating seas deposited shallow-marine sandstones across the state. Sandstones of this type make up the Tug Hill Plateau, a giant mesa of flat-lying rocks between the Black River valley to the east and the Lake Ontario Lowlands on the west and southwest. The triangular plateau is a topographically high remnant of harder rock that was isolated by erosion before the Ice Age. Downward erosion by the Black River, which runs north-south, and the Mohawk River, which runs west-east, cut through the hard sandstone cap of the plateau and isolated the area as a high-standing region. The latest Ordovician deposits are very shallow-marine to subaerial (land deposited) red shales and sandstones exposed along Lake Ontario from Rochester to the lower Niagara River. The retreat of the seashore west of New York State at the end of the Ordovician was due in part to infilling by the apron of sediment eroded from the Taconic Mountains. In addition, water evaporated from the ocean accumulated as ice caps in South America and northern Africa, then at the South Pole, and caused the global sea level to fall.

New Tropical Seas

Glacial melting early in the Silurian (438–418 mya) led to sea-level rise. Shorelines advanced eastward only gradually, as the state east of Syracuse remained uplifted after the Taconic orogeny. Eastern highlands that continued to be eroded are indicated by the gravels and coarse sandstones of the Upper Silurian in the Shawangunk Mountains in southeast New York State. (Mohonk Mountain House in Ulster Co, is nestled in this rock.) Fossiliferous early Silurian rocks occur west of Syracuse and include the Rochester Shale, with its more than 200 species of marine fossils.

The resistant caprock of Niagara Falls was formed of coral reef-bearing limestones consisting originally of calcium carbonate, now largely changed to dolostone. They comprise the Lockport Group, visible in the Niagara Escarpment that extends from Hamilton, Ont, to Medina (Orleans Co). Continuing sea-level rise drove shorelines east to Newburgh (Orange Co) and Hudson (Columbia Co) by the end of the Silurian, but this rise was so slow that the seas became shallow and very salty. Thus, most late Silurian rocks in the state are sparsely fossiliferous. Significant deposits of salt (used primarily for road salt) and gypsum (used for wallboard and plaster) are Upper Silurian and were early mined south of Syracuse. Dating to the late 1880s, the Retsof mine in Livingston Co was the largest underground mine in the world by 1994, when groundwater started to flood it following a roof collapse. Salt production continued in the unflooded parts of the mine until 1996, when it was closed. Salt, gypsum, and thin-bedded dolostone and shale mean that the Upper Silurian does not resist erosion and is poorly exposed west of Syracuse, where it forms a lowland crossed by the old Erie and modern New York State Barge Canals.

Acadian Mountain Building and the Catskill Delta

The Acadian orogeny, the second mountain-building episode in the Appalachians, occurred during the Devonian period (418–362 mya). In the latest Silurian, a subduction zone developed off eastern Laurentia. The Iapetus Ocean seafloor was subducted, and volcanoes developed on the Laurentian margin. This subduction seems to have pulled the east Laurentian margin down, with the result that Lower Devonian marine rocks occur only east of Syracuse. Fossiliferous Lower Devonian limestones form the Helderberg Escarpment south of Albany and extend south to Port Jervis (Orange Co). Thin volcanic ashes in the Lower Devonian (seen as clay seams in road cuts on US 20 just west of Sharon Springs in Schoharie Co) are known to have come from volcanoes in central Maine. The end of the early Devonian featured a sudden deepening, recorded by the nearly nonfossiliferous, low-oxygen environments of the black Esopus Shale from the Helderbergs to Port Jervis. This first mountain-building pulse was followed by quiescence in the early Middle Devonian, when New York was covered by a shallow tropical sea extending from the present Hudson River to Lake Erie and beyond. The sea-level rise brought reef-bearing limestones across the state and into the Midwest; these marine deposits are the Onondaga Limestone, the last major tropical limestone in New York State. Buffalo is built on the Onondaga Limestone, which is also visible in road cuts on the Thruway just north of Catskill (Greene Co). A major pulse of the Acadian orogeny ended Onondaga Limestone deposition by downwarping eastern New York State and depositing a blanket of mud, called the Marcellus Formation, across the state.

The Iapetus Ocean closed with the collision of eastern Laurentia and the Avalon microcontinent. Avalon, once a New Zealand–sized land mass, is recognized by similarity in the rocks and fossils from Rhode Island to northern Nova Scotia and eastern Newfoundland and includes modern Wales, England, and Belgium. As the west margin of Avalon approximately corresponds to the north-south trend of the lower Connecticut River, projection of this trend south suggests that the deep bedrock of eastern Long Island is Avalonian and not part of ancestral North America.

The Peekskill Granite was another result of the Acadian orogeny. It appeared in the Devonian as liquid rock punched through the Hudson Highlands of southeastern New York and formed a circular mass almost 10 miles (16 km) in diameter. However, the primary evidence of the Acadian orogeny is a broad, thick apron of sedimentary rocks termed the "Catskill delta." Sands and muds deposited by Devonian rivers of the Catskill delta now form a thickness of 2,800 feet (850 m) of rock in eastern New York, where the youngest sandstones and conglomerates comprise the Catskill High Peaks. These rocks include subaerial, lacustrine, and river deposits with earth's oldest forests preserved in Middle Devonian shale and sandstone at Gilboa (Schoharie Co). Further west, marine deposition continued, and the gray limy shales of the Hamilton Group yield diverse marine fossils from the northern Finger Lakes to the Lake Erie bluffs. Rising and falling sea levels and intervals of greater and lesser sediment drove shorelines east and west across the state through the later Devonian. By the end of the Devonian, shallow seas were limited to westernmost New York State.

Formation of Pangaea

The Allegheny orogeny was the last Appalachian mountain-building episode. It featured the collision of the west African margin of the Gondwana continent with eastern Laurentia in the final stage of formation of the supercontinent Pangaea in the later Carboniferous (362–286 mya) and Permian (286–245 mya) periods. Unfortunately, Carboniferous rocks are limited and Permian rocks absent in New York State; thus local sedimentary rocks provide little data on this orogeny. The bedrock east of Syracuse provides indirect evidence of the Allegheny orogeny. Compositions of the clay mineral illite and the baking of carbon-based biologic remains to graphite in eastern New York indicate high burial temperatures. Because rocks get hotter with depth, the data indicate the Catskills were once buried by 4 miles (6 km) of rock. Deep burial "baked" all of the petroleum in eastern New York State to graphite and limited any hydrocarbons to natural gas. Future sources of petroleum will probably continue to be in Silurian-Devonian sandstones and carbonates in the western parts of the state, which have yielded oil since the late 1800s. Some features traditionally assigned to the older Acadian orogeny may be referable to the Allegheny orogeny. For example, a major fault that trends north-northeast and south-southwest from Cornwall (Orange Co) uplifted the Grenville rock of the Hudson Highlands against the Middle Devonian in southern Orange Co and could be an effect of the Allegheny orogeny.

Origin of the Atlantic

Pangaea did not last very long. Continent fragmentation began in the New York State region in the later part of the Triassic period (245–201 mya). Rifting of Pangaea led to the origin of the Atlantic Ocean in the Jurassic period (201–144 mya). The 120° angle formed by the New York Bight (the edge of the continental shelf south of Long Island) and seen in the trend of the southern Massachusetts–New Jersey shoreline reflects two of the active arms of the rift system along which west Africa broke away from eastern North America. Roughly parallel to the southwest arm is the Ramapo-Canopus fault, which runs southwest from Peekskill (Westchester Co) to Suffern (Rockland Co). The small area east of the fault and west of the Hudson River in Rockland Co dropped down and received a thickness of 20,000 feet (6,000 m) of Upper Triassic and Lower Jurassic sand, mud, and gravel eroded from the Hudson Highlands. These subaerial sedimentary rocks have yielded dinosaur tracks at Blauvelt (Rockland Co) and continue into New Jersey in the Newark Basin. They are similar to rocks deposited in the Connecticut River valley, the failed arm along this spreading system that extends under eastern Long Island.

The creation of the Palisades was one result of the breakup of Pangaea. Stretching of the earth's crust and development of the Ramapo-Canopus fault allowed the release of basaltic molten rock, which moved laterally in the Triassic-Jurassic sediments as a subhorizontal injection called a sill. As it cooled, the rock shrank and fractured into the six-sided columns that are now exposed as the Palisades cliff on the western bank of the Hudson River. The Palisades sill is 390–980 feet (120–300 m) thick and over 40 miles (65 km) long; it extends from Staten Island to High Tor in Haverstraw (Rockland Co). The second effect of the continental breakup was the uplifting of the region that underwent rifting, as it was underlain by less dense molten rock. This meant that the dinosaurs at Blauvelt wandered around in a highland valley that was probably arid. In addition, large areas lateral to the rift were elevated and eroded. It is possible that much of the rock laid down during the Allegheny orogeny across New York was eroded at this time.

With further spreading along fractures that defined the New York Bight, ocean waters entered the rift, and the Atlantic Ocean was born. Initially, the edges of the New York Bight were elevated because of the heat of their rocks. With time they cooled, became denser, and subsided. This subsidence allowed Jurassic and Cretaceous (144–65 mya) shorelines to creep northward, reaching Staten Island and Long Island by the later Cretaceous. These Cretaceous red shales and sandstones are now easily accessible only along the shore at Garvies Point Preserve on northwestern Long Island. Latest Cretaceous and Cenozoic era (65 mya–) rocks occur underwater south of Long Island but can be seen east of the state at Gay Head Cliffs on Martha's Vineyard, Mass.

An odd rock type appeared in Ithaca during the Cretaceous: small vertical veins of kimberlite (a black igneous rock derived from the mantle of the earth) that fill fractures in Late Devonian sandstone. Diamonds are mined from kimberlite in South Africa and elsewhere, but none have been found in Ithaca. The Ithaca kimberlite may reflect development of a hot spot, a giant plume of molten rock that moved upward through the earth's crust, comparable to the source of the volcanic rock in Hawaii and Yellowstone Park. Hot spots remain relatively fixed and leave a track of volcanoes as the plate moves above them. The Ithaca kimberlites may be the earliest expression of a plume recorded by a line of younger volcanic vents. These vents underlie Montreal, continue northeast along the St. Lawrence River, then run south along the Connecticut River valley until they run offshore (and underwater) as the New England Sea Mounts and terminate at Bermuda. Movement of this region above a plume during the Cretaceous (and with heating and doming of the crust along the track of the plume) may explain the doming of the Adirondacks and the erosion of thousands of feet of sedimentary rocks that once covered it.

Pleistocene Epoch

The Pleistocene epoch is often informally called the Ice Age, a two-million-year-long interval that featured four main intervals of global cold and glacial ice advance in North America with intervening warm (or interglacial) times. For the last 10,000 years, Earth has been in an interglacial interval. The sculpting of the state's landscape by continental glaciations during this epoch complicated research on the older rocks by burying much of the state under late and postglacial deposits. All of the state, with exception of the Salamanca reentrant in the Allegany State Park area, was covered by the last advance of continental glaciers. The Salamanca reentrant was a notch in the roughly east-west-trending south margin of the continental ice cap. It was bounded by two ice tongues that did not overrun the relatively high Allegany State Park region. Scours and scratches made by ice-transported rock fragments on the highest Adirondack peaks record the thickness of the ice cap. Depression of the northern Lake Champlain and St. Lawrence Valley by about 540 feet (165 m) under the weight of the ice further demonstrates its thickness. With so much water trapped in ice on land, sea levels were about 330 feet (100 m) lower. The remains of many of the first humans and animals to return to the New York State region are probably submerged along the old Ice Age shoreline well south of Long Island.

Most of the major highlands, rivers, and lowlands of New York State existed prior to the Ice Age and were only modified by glaciation and with the melting of the ice cap. The Finger Lakes were river valleys that flowed south but were scoured out to great depths by glacial ice and then had their north ends dammed with sediment derived from the melting of the ice sheet. The Niagara, Mohawk, and Hudson are old rivers that also existed before glaciation. The soft Triassic and Jurassic rocks of the lower Hudson below Peekskill were deeply eroded almost 1,000 feet (300 m) below sea level by a tongue of glacial ice. This wide area of the Hudson is the modern Tappan Zee. With the melting of the ice sheets, huge amounts of water from the Great Lakes drained through the Niagara River and began erosion of Niagara Gorge and Niagara Falls. This meltwater filled Lake Iroquois (the ancestor of Lake Ontario), which overflowed near Rome (Oneida Co) into the Mohawk River. This enormous amount of water cut the deep water gaps, such as the Noses, in the Mohawk Valley and formed Cohoes Falls on the Albany-Saratoga county line at the confluence with the Hudson River.

Further downstream, the raging meltwaters of the Hudson River deeply eroded the softer Upper Ordovician sandstones and shales just east of the hard rocks of the Taconic overthrust and laid down a thick blanket of sediment in the Tappan Zee. With low sea level just at the end of the Ice Age, the sand- and mud-charged waters of the Hudson River cut a deep valley across the exposed continental shelf. The Hudson River discharged sediment into the deep waters of the Atlantic through the Hudson canyon on the continental slope. With the final melting of the ice sheets, sea level rose to fill the Tappan Zee and the old river lowland that is now Long Island Sound.

See also ANCIENT LIFE.

Fisher, Donald W. *Bedrock Geology of the Central Mohawk Valley, New York* (Albany: NYS Museum, Map and Chart 33, 1980)

Isachsen, Yngvar W., et al, eds. *Geology of New York: A Simplified Account,* 2d ed (Albany: NYS Museum, 2000)

Landing, Ed, ed. *The Canadian Paleontology and Biostratigraphy Seminar, Albany, New York* (Albany: NYS Museum, 1987)

Rogers, William B., et al. *New York State Geological Highway Map* (Albany: NYS Museum, 1990)

Tesmer, Irving H., ed. *Colossal Cataract: The Geologic History of Niagara Falls* (Albany: SUNY Press, 1981)

Van Diver, Bradford B. *Roadside Geology of New York* (Missoula, Mont: Mountain Press Publishing, 1985)

Ed Landing

George, Henry (*b* Philadelphia, 2 Sept 1839; *d* New York City, 29 Oct 1897). Social reformer, writer, and labor activist. Essentially self-taught, he moved to California as a young man and in 1861 married Annie Fox. After living in poverty for several years, he became a reporter at the *San Francisco Times* and in 1868 wrote a piece for the *Overland Monthly* critiquing the unequal nature of economic gains under modern capitalism. A visit to New York City in 1868 served as a catalyst for George's concerns about the gap between rich and poor. In 1879 he published *Progress and Poverty,* which argued that the distribution of America's wealth could be improved by deriving all government revenues from a single tax on the value of land minus any improvements, such as construction or landscaping, made to it. In 1880 he relocated to New York City and a year later published *The Irish Land Question,* arguing that a combination of the single-tax concept and land reform could most effectively redress the exploitation of Irish tenants by British landlords. The book's popularity in Ireland and within the Irish American community took George to the British Isles in 1881–82 as a special correspondent for the New York City paper *Irish World and Industrial Liberator.* He published *Social Problems* in 1883 and *Protection or Free Trade* in 1886.

The Central Labor Union asked George to run for mayor of New York City in 1886 as the candidate of the Independent Labor Party. Although a coalition of labor, socialist, German, Irish, and Jewish groups rallied to George, he lost to Tammany Hall's candidate Abram S. Hewitt. George then established a weekly newspaper, the *Standard* (1887–92), and ran for New York secretary of state in 1887 with the United Labor Party. However, his active support of Social Gospel Catholics like Fr Edward McGlynn, who wished to apply Christian ethics to societal problems, led both socialists and nonactivist Irish Catholics to abandon George, and he was again defeated. George further alienated his Irish base with *The Condition of Labor* (1891), which attacked Pope Leo XIII's encyclical on labor. During George's last 10 years he promoted single-tax clubs and free trade in the United States, Europe, and Australia. In 1897 he campaigned a second time for mayor of New York City on a platform of tax reform, municipal ownership, and economic justice, but he suffered a stroke five days before the election and died the next morning. Perhaps as many as 100,000 New Yorkers viewed his funeral bier or participated in the funeral procession; the occasion was described as the most remarkable expression of public grief since Lincoln's death.

Barker, Charles. *Henry George* (New York: Oxford Univ Press, 1955)

Cord, Steven. *Henry George: Dreamer or Realist?* (Philadelphia: Univ of Pennsylvania Press, 1965)

Rose, Edward. *Henry George* (New York: Twayne Publishers, 1968)

Harvey Strum

George, Samuel (*b* Buffalo Creek Reservation [now in Erie Co], ?1795; *d* Onondaga Indian Reservation [loc in Onondaga Co], 24 Sept 1873). Onondaga leader and chief. George came to prominence during the War of 1812 as a courier, serving the American army along the Buffalo-to-Albany corridor. A thin, sinewy man, his long-distance running prowess was legendary. From the end of the war until the early 1840s, George remained on the Buffalo Creek Reservation, rising in prominence at Iroquois Confederacy councils, but moved later in the decade with his wife and five children to the Onondaga Reservation in Central New York. In 1850 he became a chief, taking the name Hononwirehdonh (the Great Wolf), the hereditary keeper of the wampum held by a member of the Wolf Clan of the Onondaga Nation, a title he held until his death more than 20 years later. In this capacity, his responsibilities were to foster consensus and to pacify diverse elements among the Six Nations. George tried to preserve Iroquois traditions and opposed amalgamation into the broader American culture. As the Iroquois Confederacy's leading spokesman during and after the Civil War, George conferred with Washington and Albany officials. He met with Pres Abraham Lincoln in 1864 and expressed Iroquois support for the Union cause, but protested efforts to recruit underage Iroquois youth into service. After the war he corresponded with Gov John T. Hoffman, objecting to timber stripping on the Onondaga Reservation. In the last years of his life, he was well known as an Indian medicine man and storyteller. George kept his Iroquoian faith and language, accepting Handsome Lake's ideas for embracing traditional ceremonials and rejecting the alienation of Indian lands. But George's flexible brand of conservatism, which had allowed him to serve in the War of 1812, also led him to permit missionaries and schools to operate at Onondaga. He lived his final years in a small-frame, single-story house just northeast of the Onondaga Council House, about a quarter mile from the center of the reservation.

Hauptman, Laurence M. "Samuel George (1795–1873): A Study of Onondaga Indian Conservatism," *New York History* 70 (Jan 1989): 5–22

———. *The Iroquois in the Civil War: From Battlefield to Reservation* (Syracuse: Syracuse Univ Press, 1993)

Laurence M. Hauptman

George Eastman House, International Museum of Photography and Film. Located at 900 East Ave in Rochester in the former home of George Eastman, founder of Eastman Kodak Co. The 50-room mansion, built between 1902 and 1905, was the residence for University of Rochester presidents from Eastman's death in 1932 until 1946, when plans were made to establish a private not-for-profit museum to accommodate two photographic collections previously housed at Kodak facilities in Rochester. The museum opened in 1949 with Oscar N. Solbert of Kodak as director and Beaumont Newhall as curator. James Card, a collector and historian of film, opened the Motion Picture Department in 1950, when the Dryden Theatre was built. In 1951 groundbreaking traveling exhibits were initiated.

The museum's holdings comprise over 400,000 photographs representing more than 8,000 photographers; 23,000 film titles, including the original negatives to such classics as *Gone with the Wind* and *The Wizard of Oz;* 5 million film stills; and the world's largest photographic technology collection, opened in 1949, featuring 25,000 pieces and including a rare 1839 Giroux daguerreotype camera. Named a National Historic Landmark in 1966, Eastman House is also a leader in film preservation and photograph conservation; the transfer of unstable and flammable nitrate films to acetate is an ongoing project. A complete restoration of the first-floor public rooms in the 1980s brought the residence back to its 1932 appearance. A new archive facility was added in 1989, and in 1999 the George Eastman Archive and Study Center was established to give researchers access to Eastman's correspondence, photographs, motion picture collection, and other memorabilia and research materials. The museum has a full-time staff of over 70 and receives more than 170,000 visitors per year.

A Collective Endeavor: The First 50 Years of George Eastman House (Rochester: George Eastman House, 1999)

Elizabeth Brayer

George Junior Republic. Private institution founded in 1895 for delinquent and underprivileged youths by William Reuben George (1866–1936), a New York City businessman. George Junior Republic (GJR) evolved from a fresh air camp that George established around 1890 in Freeville (Tompkins Co). GJR was coeducational, with predominantly city youths ranging in age from 12 to 21. George was a vigorous advocate for teaching youth responsibility and self-reliance by imitating adult society. Approximately 100–150 residents, called "citizens," participated in all aspects of society; they elected their own officials, made their own laws, and enforced those laws through a court. The school had its own currency and economic enterprises, including a farm, trade shops, and bakery, that offered citizens employment. The motto of the republic was Nothing without Labor—youths were not forced to work but were required to pay for room, board, and clothing. Education also played a role. GJR enjoyed the support of educators and prominent New York State social reformers such as Theodore Roosevelt, Jacob Riis, and Andrew Carnegie. The school's distinctive model was used to establish similar junior republics in seven states. Beginning in the early 1980s, the program was restructured to serve as a more traditional residential treatment center for emotionally disturbed adolescents, although emphasis is still placed on work experience. These changes followed trends within the therapeutic community, where the challenges of working with juveniles have become more substantial and require greater supervision of residents. Since 1991 the program has served only boys aged 13–16. In 2002, 150 youths resided at GJR. The agency also maintains the George Junior Republic Union Free School District on its campus, a 12-month academic program for its youths.

Holl, Jack M. *Juvenile Reform in the Progressive Era: William R. George and the Junior Republic Movement* (Ithaca: Cornell Univ Press, 1971)

Katherine B. Killoran

Georgetown. Town (pop 946) in S Madison Co. Settled in 1804, the town was formed from DeRuyter in 1815 and named for George Washington. On Muller Hill, a wealthy refugee from Napoleon's France who called himself Louis Anathe Muller built a large house *ca* 1810 but returned to France in 1816. His real identity is unknown. At Georgetown hamlet, spiritualist Timothy Brown (1815–75) built a house in "wedding-cake" style that he used for spiritualist meetings. The disembodied voices heard at the Spirit House later proved to be a human hoax. The town was served by the Syracuse and Chenango Valley Railroad (1872–1937). Potatoes were an important crop in the late 19th century, the town had a tannery from 1859 to *ca* 1880, and stoves were manufactured at Georgetown Station in the 1870s. Beginning in 1927 seed potatoes were an important export. In 2003 five farms continued to ship milk, but most residents worked in Syracuse, Cortland, Norwich, or Hamilton.

William F. Helmer

George Washington Bridge. Steel-cable suspension bridge spanning the Hudson River between Fort Lee, NJ, and Manhattan at 179th St, built by the Port of New York Authority (now Port Authority of New York and New Jersey). The chief engineer, responsible for selling the idea of the bridge to the public as well as for design and execution of the structure, was Swiss émigré Othmar H. Ammann. Architect Cass Gilbert contributed to the design and planned stone-sheathed steel towers for the structure. Depression era cost cutting left the space-frame towers uncovered, an omission that enhanced the aesthetic merit of the bridge in the eyes of many. Built between 1927 and 1931 at a cost of $59 million, George Washington Bridge had four lanes plus pedestrian sidewalks, and its span of 3,500 feet (1,076 m) doubled the previous record for a suspension bridge. The addition of a second, lower deck in 1959–62, part of the original plan, added 6 more lanes to the by then 8-lane structure, creating 14 lanes of vehicular traffic, with bicycles limited to the upper-level walkways. On the construction of connecting highways, such as the Cross Bronx Expressway in the 1960s, the bridge became part of New York City's "northern bypass," providing the Hudson River crossing for the US 1 and I-95 highway corridor along the east coast. Direct ramps connect the Manhattan end of the bridge to George Washington Bridge Bus Station, opened in 1963, which has direct passageways to the New York City subway. Since 1970, tolls are collected eastbound only. In 2000 average weekday traffic volume was 153,461 vehicles.

Doig, Jameson. *Empire on the Hudson: Entrepreneurial Vision and Political Power at the Port of New York Authority* (New York: Columbia Univ Press, 2000)

Reier, Sharon. *Bridges of New York* (New York: Quadrant Press, 1977)

Thomas R. Flagg

German. Town (pop 378) in W Chenango Co. Settled in 1796, the town was formed in 1806 from DeRuyter. It became a dairying town in the 19th century and in 1854 produced 451,433 pounds (204,766 kg) of butter, the second-largest quantity of any town in the state. By 1930, however, much of the land was no longer productive. Between 1933 and 1941 New York State purchased more than 6,000 acres (2,400 ha), creating Five Streams and Red Brook State Forests. Beginning in the 1960s the town's beauty attracted commuters who work in Norwich, Syracuse, Cortland, and Binghamton.

Dale C. Storms

German American Bund. Pro-Nazi organization active in New York State, especially in New York City, from 1933 to 1942. In 1933 Germany's Nazi Party (NSDAP) permitted Heinz Spanknöbel, a four-year US resident and Nazi activist, to launch a nationwide movement among German Americans. In July of that year Spanknöbel and his followers used coercion and the evidence of NSDAP support to form the Friends of the New Germany (otherwise known as the Bund), headquartered in New York City. Spanknöbel's attempts in the following months to bully New

York City business and political leaders sparked bad publicity, and he returned to Germany. A 1934 congressional investigation of the society caused the NSDAP to sever its direct links, but membership continued to grow. The Bund infiltrated German societies throughout the country, and in the mid-1930s swastika flags and Nazi salutes appeared in German Day festivals across New York State.

On 29 Mar 1936 naturalized US citizen Fritz Kuhn, a former chemist, reconstituted the society as the Amerikadeutscher Volksbund at a gathering in Buffalo. The charismatic Kuhn led the Bund from its New York City headquarters during its most prosperous period, 1936–39. Chapters of the group emerged in over 45 states with a total membership of near 25,000. By 1937 there were Bund chapters in 22 cities and towns in New York State, and up to 40% of its national membership came from New York City. Bund members worked to imbue Americans of German descent with a consciousness of their German race, blood, and culture, also calling on them to prepare for a coming civil war instigated by Jews and communists. In Manhattan, however, Bund members remained a small minority of the German American community. The organization operated saloons and to attract crowds offered free beer and promises of aid for the unemployed. Major chapters had youth groups, uniformed guards, and German dating services. Bund camps, such as Siegfried in Yaphank (Suffolk Co) and Tanglewood in East Aurora (Erie Co), served as indoctrination centers and as grounds for uniformed drills.

New York's Jewish community as well as some labor leaders, ministers, and politicians had long assailed the state's Nazis as un-American and subversive. Regardless, Kuhn continued to claim personal ties with Hitler, and provoking wide public disapproval in 1937, the Schenectady Bund chapter produced a pamphlet lauding Nazi contributions to the United States. In Syracuse in 1938, a crowd smashed windshields and slashed tires of cars outside a Bund rally. A 1939 fight between American veterans and uniformed Bundists in an American Legion Hall in Buffalo ended with the arrests of Bund leaders. In New York City Mayor Fiorello La Guardia worked with District Attorney Thomas E. Dewey to indict leading Nazis on a variety of charges. In 1939 a New York State court convicted Kuhn of embezzling the society's funds, and the Bund began to disintegrate. In Buffalo the Spring Garden Association became an outlet for former Bundists, and in Troy (Rensselaer Co) members continued to meet secretly. But by the time of the 1941 attack on Pearl Harbor, Kuhn was in jail, the Bund was bankrupt, and hundreds of former Bundists were in internment centers. In 1942 the last of Kuhn's successors in New York City, George Froboese, committed suicide.

Diamond, Sander A. *The Nazi Movement in the United States 1924–1941* (Ithaca: Cornell Univ Press, 1974)
Holian, Timothy. *The German-Americans and World War II: An Ethnic Experience* (New York: Peter Lang, 1996)

Andrew P. Yox

German Flatts. Town (pop 13,629) in S central Herkimer Co. Palatine Germans settled in the area *ca* 1725 on a tract north of the Mohawk River but saw their settlements destroyed in 1757 during French and Indian War hostilities. When the town was being formed in 1788, Surveyor-General Simeon DeWitt made a clerical error and misapplied the name German Flatts to what had been Kingsland District (1772) on the south side of the Mohawk rather than to the original tract north of it. The town was the site of a 1795 canal to improve navigation on the Mohawk built by Western Inland Lock Navigation Co and, with the opening of the Erie Canal in 1821, grew more rapidly. Dairy products and hops were the chief farm products in the mid–19th century. The West Shore Railroad (1883) and the New York State Thruway (1954) both passed through town. In the World War II era, dairying, poultry, strawberries, and vegetables were the chief products outside the Villages of Ilion and Mohawk. In the early 21st century German Flatts remains chiefly agricultural.

James Crawford

Germans. The history of German-speaking people in New York State reaches back to the earliest days of the colony of New Netherland. Early passenger lists record numerous immigrants from Muenster, Westphalia, and other German states in the vicinity of the Netherlands. Peter Minuit, the first director of New Netherland, was born in Wessel in the German state of Cleves. Between 1708 and 1710, the still tiny German population of New York Colony was given a significant boost as a result of the arrival of several thousand refugees from the religious and political strife (notably the Thirty Years War) that wracked Germany in the 17th and 18th centuries. Known as the Palatines, these refugees came from central western and southern German states, as well as from Switzerland, and not just from the German state of Rhineland Palatinate, as the name suggests.

The first group of 55 Palatines arrived in New York City in 1708 and soon established themselves in the Hudson River valley at what would become Newburgh (Orange Co). The second, much larger wave of Palatines arrived in 1710, adding 40% to New York City's population. Approximately 350 remained in New York City, but the bulk of them, nearly 2,000, moved to Dutchess, Ulster, and Albany Cos. Some Palatines remained in the Hudson Valley and either became tenants on the Livingston Manor [now in Columbia Co] or settled in Rhinebeck (Dutchess Co). Another contingent went southward to New York City and Hackensack, NJ, and still others moved northward to the Schoharie Valley in 1713.

The Schoharie Palatines soon found themselves in difficulty, as speculators in Albany advanced better claims to the group's newly acquired lands and ordered the Palatines either to lease, purchase, or leave the property. This resulted in a final dispersal of these Palatines in two principal directions. One stream migrated southward along the Schoharie and Susquehanna Rivers to Pennsylvania between 1717 and 1723, while the other group settled a number of communities, like German Flatts (Herkimer Co) and Palatine Bridge (Montgomery Co), in the frontier wilds of the lower and central Mohawk Valley in 1722–25. Led by the prosperous German farmer Nicholas Herkimer, the Palatines played a decisive role in preventing the Mohawk Valley from falling to the British in 1777.

Well-known German immigrants of this period include John Peter Zenger, an early New York newspaper publisher who was arrested and tried for libel by the English government for criticizing the governor of New York Colony. His trial and acquittal in 1735 became a landmark in the development of the doctrine of the freedom of the press. In 1783 John Jacob Astor immigrated to America from Germany and formed the American Fur Co along with numerous real estate ventures. By the time of his death in 1848, he was one of the richest men in America, leaving $20 million.

A Flood of Newcomers, 1815–1890

Migration from continental Europe diminished significantly between the time of the American Revolution and the end of the Napoleonic Wars in 1815. German immigration to New York State began to rise rapidly in the 1830s. Because of increasing land pressure, bad harvests, political upheaval, and urban unemployment from the importation of manufactured goods, the Germans became the second largest immigrant group in the state during the 19th century. By

The Great Sangerfest at the music hall in Buffalo, 1883.

the early 1880s only Berlin and Vienna had more residents of German parentage than New York City. Approximately 256,252 Germans had emigrated from the states of Prussia, Bavaria, Baden, Hesse, Nassau, and Würtemberg by 1860, with 2,438 from Austria. In New York City and Kings Co, German settlement centered in three neighborhoods: Kleindeutschland (Little Germany), located to the east of the Bowery in what later became known as the Lower East Side; Yorkville, on Manhattan's Upper East Side; and Williamsburg in Brooklyn. There were 316,882 German immigrants (excluding 3,928 Austrians and 7,911 German-speaking Swiss) in New York State in 1870, although the number of German-speaking people has been estimated to have been as high as 700,000 by 1870. New York State's German immigrant population was highly urbanized, with 78% of those in New York residing in the state's eight largest cities in 1890. Nearly half (210,723) resided in New York City, while much of the remainder lived in Brooklyn (94,798), Buffalo (42,660), Rochester (17,330), Syracuse (8,412), Albany (7,605), Utica (4,092), and Troy (2,107).

Growth of German Religious Life

While language and nationalism were generally powerful sources of group cohesion among German Americans (particularly beginning in the late 19th century), strong homeland regionalism and differences in religion were sometimes divisive factors among them. By the mid–19th century the German American community comprised Catholics (typically from southern Germany and Austria), Lutherans, German Reformed (Calvinist), Moravians, and Jews. Although this mix did not historically have harmonious relations in Germany, in New York State they often found common cause in the effort to preserve German language and culture. Cooperation between the Lutheran and Reformed Churches increased over the course of the 19th century, and Christian Germans generally interacted positively with German Jews, who often were leaders in German communal institutions. There were exceptions to this generally ecumenical trend among German Americans, as the anti-Catholic American Party enjoyed widespread support among German Protestants in mid-19th-century New York City, and some German Catholics in the metropolitan area denounced Martin Luther on the 400th anniversary of his birth in 1883.

Lutheran religious life in New York State began in the 17th century. Johann Gutwasser became the first Lutheran minister in the Dutch colony in 1656, although the freedom of non-Reformed churches to worship openly in New Netherland was limited. With the influx of the Palatine Germans, the New York Colony Lutheran community was given new life, new pastors, and a new ethnic composition. The Lutheran community grew considerably as a result of mass German immigration after 1815, and dozens of congregations were established in localities west of the Hudson in the middle decades of the 19th century. The decisive shift toward the use of English as the primary or sole language for religious services took place in the early 20th century, largely as a result of the decline of the immigrant population and the outburst of anti-German sentiment during World War I.

Saint Nicholas Church, established in Lower Manhattan in 1833, became the center of the first specifically German Catholic parish in New York State. By the mid-1830s German-speaking Catholic priests began visiting smaller German communities in parts of the state west of the Hudson River. The Rev Johann Raffeiner, born in Austria and founder of New York City's Saint Nicholas Church, was active in these early efforts to minister to German-speaking Catholics throughout the state and helped organize German parishes in numerous locations along the route of the Erie Canal. He also served as vicar general of the New York and Brooklyn Dioceses. In the 1840s and 1850s German Catholic parishes were established in the New York City area, Buffalo, Rochester, Syracuse, Utica, and Albany, as well as in some smaller settlements. By the 1870s there were 51 German Catholic parishes, 96 German-speaking priests, and 45 German parish schools in New York State.

German immigration to New York also included a large contingent of Jews. In 1820 there was only one synagogue in New York City, but by 1860 there were 27, and congregations had also been established in other urban centers across the state, with many adopting Reform Judaism by 1880. Anti-Semitic sentiment was relatively rare among non-Jewish Germans, and some German Jews, like Rochester's Rabbi Max Landsberg, were prominent as leaders of German communities.

Community Organizations, Business Life, and Politics

Germans were renowned for being prolific founders of voluntary associations. In each German community by the late 19th century one could find an array of German mutual aid societies, many established by and catering to immigrants from the particular states of Germany, and by 1914 there were 251 such *landsmannschaftliche Vereine* in the state. Working-class and socialist organizations were also common, particularly in the second half of the 19th century. Other characteristically German organizations included rifle clubs, the Odd Fellows, and fraternal societies like the Order of the Harugari and the Druids. By 1870 there were some 277 German American lodges of various types in New York State, and by 1914 there were 103 rifle clubs. By the time of the First World War there were also 258 choral music societies, known as *Gesangvereine.*

The *Turnverein* was another characteristically German social institution that could be found in communities. The Turner movement promoted the cultivation of physically sound German youth through gymnastic exercise, and it was dedicated to republicanism, national unity, and the extension of human freedom. By the late 1850s Turners in New York and other northern states had started to gravitate toward the antislavery movement, and many were among the first volunteers for the Union army at the outbreak of the Civil War. Socialism also influenced the movement, especially in the generation following the arrival of refugees from the unsuccessful German revolutions of 1848–49. These ideological aspects of the Turner movement eventually died out in the decades after the Civil War, and most *Turnvereine* in New York State became more exclusively dedicated to social camaraderie and exercise by 1900.

In the field of business, German immigrants had become the preeminent brewers in the state by the post–Civil War period. The Hellgate Brewery, established by George Ehret in New York City in 1866, was the largest in the United States by 1879, at which point German brewers were also prominent in the rest of the state. By the 1890s over 600,000 barrels of beer were being brewed in Buffalo, and one-half of this was produced by the Gerhard Lang Brewery, the second largest brewery in New York State. The F. X. Matt Brewing Co, founded by a Bavarian immigrant in Utica in 1888, is the last of the state's old family-owned German breweries. German craftsmen also made a mark in the production of musical instruments in New York State. Steinway and Sons, founded in Manhattan in 1853 by Henry Engelhard Steinway (Steinweg), was well known for its innovative artisanship, which helped define the modern standard of quality piano building. Today Steinway and Sons crafts approximately 5,000 pianos worldwide each year.

German immigrants also made their mark in what were the high-tech fields of their day, most notably in optics, chemical synthetics, and electrical engineering. In Rochester, John Jacob Bausch and Henry Lomb established the Bausch and Lomb Co, which by the 1880s had become the leading optical company in the United States. Jacob F. and Hugo Schoellkopf, sons of a prosperous German tanner in Buffalo, studied chemistry in German universities in the 1870s and 1880s and returned to Buffalo to establish companies that became the largest American producers of artificial dyes and of chemicals used in the manufacture of explosives. Charles P. Steinmetz, an inventor and electrical engineer, emigrated from Germany in 1889 and settled in Schenectady, where he worked for General Electric Co (GE). His research contributed significantly to both the prosperity of GE and the adoption of electricity as the principal source of power and light in industrial settings.

German Jews in New York City and Rochester became leading entrepreneurs in the garment industry. They also were prominent in the retail trade, especially in the ownership of department stores in New York City, including R. H. Macy, Gimbel's, Bloomingdale's, and Saks Fifth Avenue. German Jews also became investment bankers. Among the firms they founded in the mid- to late 19th century were J. and W. Seligman; Goldman Sachs; Lehman Bros; and Kuhn, Loeb and Co. Under the leadership of Jacob Schiff, Kuhn, Loeb challenged J. P. Morgan for preeminence in investment banking at the turn of the 20th century.

Some German Americans also became important in politics. August Belmont, of German Jewish background, was a banker who served as national chairman of the Democratic Party from 1860 to 1872. William Sulzer served briefly as governor in 1913 before being impeached, largely because of his break with Tammany Hall. Perhaps the most notable New York politician of German parentage was Robert F. Wagner Sr, a German immigrant from the Yorkville neighborhood of Manhattan. A leading New Dealer, he served in the US Senate from 1927 to 1949. His son and namesake served three terms as mayor of New York City from 1954 to 1965. Morgenthau was another multigenerational political family: Henry Morgenthau Sr, a German Jewish immigrant who was a businessman, finance chairman of the Democratic National

Committee, and ambassador to Turkey (1913–16); his son, Henry Morgenthau Jr, secretary of the treasury throughout the presidency of Franklin D. Roosevelt; and Henry Jr's son, Robert Morgenthau, first elected district attorney of New York Co in 1974, a position he still held in 2004.

Decline of German Immigration, 1890–1940

Economic reorganization and growth, along with political unity, had transformed Germany into one of the leading industrial powers of the world by 1900. This gave younger Germans fewer incentives to leave their homeland, and between 1890 and 1910 the German immigrant population of New York State dropped by approximately 60,000, bringing it to 436,874. By 1940 it was 316,844, a decrease of 36% since 1890, with much of the loss occurring in communities outside of New York City.

While the number of German immigrants in New York City was bolstered during the interwar years (1918–39) by the arrival of the 95,000 refugees from the economic and political disorder in Germany, few of these post–World War I German immigrants chose to settle in the rest of the state. The German immigrant populations of Albany, Utica, Syracuse, and Buffalo consequently declined 68–78% in the half century between 1890 and 1940, and only Rochester's German community seems to have experienced the slower rate of numerical decline that prevailed in New York City.

World War I had a devastating effect on the state's shrinking but still vibrant German immigrant community. Between 1914 and 1917 the debate in the United States over the European war pitted many German-speaking immigrants and their children against an America that increasingly considered imperial Germany a threat to its values and vital interests. German speakers were looked upon with great suspicion for their attempts to defend Germany and Austria-Hungary against American and Allied criticism. In a number of school districts throughout the state, German language instruction was abolished in 1918 in the belief that all things German were expressions of a fundamentally antidemocratic and warlike culture. Many businesses with the word "German" in their title were pressured to change their names. The German-American Bank in Buffalo was renamed the Liberty Bank; the Germania Life Insurance Co in New York City became known as Guardian Life Insurance Co. Many German American social organizations ceased their activities and died out altogether. Before the war there were 12 daily, 46 weekly, and 12 monthly newspapers throughout New York State, but many stopped publication between 1917 and 1919 as large numbers of readers canceled subscriptions for fear that they might seem sympathetic to the German cause. Many other German American newspapers saw subscriptions plummet but managed to stay in publication until the 1920s and early 1930s.

In the 1930s the rise of Adolf Hitler and of the German-American Nazi Party, also known as the Bund, again placed the German American community in an uncomfortable position. Although racist ideas were beginning to make headway among nationalists in Germany around 1900, anti-Semitism did not become an explosive force in modern Germany until the World War I era. By that time, German immigration to New York State had long since slowed to a trickle. During the 1920s, however, New York experienced an influx of young German immigrants, predominantly skilled workers, many of whom brought with them the bitterness born of German defeat in World War I and the anti-Semitic, hypernationalist ideas that would lead to the rise of the Nazis in Germany. German American enthusiasm for the Nazis was therefore most prominent in the 1930s in a handful of New York communities in which there was a high demand for skilled labor, notably New York City and Rochester. Although the great bulk of German Americans throughout New York State kept their distance from the Bund, the US declaration of war on Germany in 1941 compounded the damage done by the World War I. Many of the German American institutions that had survived the First World War ceased to function, and public German American cultural events were curtailed in many communities for some time.

The victory of the Nazis in Germany after 1933 led to an influx of refugees, including Henry Kissinger, whose family, like many German Jews escaping Nazism, settled in Washington Heights in Manhattan in 1938. German intellectuals, notably Jews and Socialists ejected by the Nazis from their teaching posts in German universities, went into exile in New York City. Many joined the University in Exile at the New School for Social Research in Manhattan, where their talents became the foundation of the New School's graduate programs.

After World War II many German Americans joined the postwar movement to the suburbs and one-time German neighborhoods in cities throughout the state went into decline; most disappeared altogether, but there was still some German flavor in the Astoria neighborhood of Queens and in the sprinkling of *Gesangvereine* and German American clubs throughout the state in the early years of the 21st century. A total of 2,122,620 New York State residents (approximately 11% of the state population) reported in the 2000 census that they were of German ancestry; another 95,837 identified themselves as being of Austrian ancestry.

See also Ethnic press; Labor; Rochester; Socialists.

Arndt, Karl John Richard, and May E. Olson. *German-American Newspapers and Periodicals, 1732–1955: History and Biography* (Heidelberg, Germany: Quelle & Meyer, 1961)

Diamond, Sander A. *The Nazi Movement in the United States, 1924–1941* (Ithaca: Cornell Univ Press, 1974)

Gerber, David A. "Modernity in the Service of Tradition: Catholic Lay Trustees in Buffalo's St. Louis Church and the Transformation of European Communal Traditions, 1829–1855," *Journal of Social History* 15 (Summer 1982): 655–84

Goldman, Mark. *High Hopes: The Rise and Decline of Buffalo* (Albany: SUNY Press, 1983)

Knittle, Walter Allen. *Early 18th-Century Palatine Emigration: A British Government Redemptioner Project to Manufacture Naval Stores* (Philadelphia: Dorrance, 1937)

Krohn, Claus-Dieter. *Intellectuals in Exile: Refugee Scholars and the New School for Social Research* (Amherst: Univ of Massachusetts Press, 1987)

McKelvey, Blake. *Rochester: The Flower City, 1855–1890* (Cambridge, Mass: Harvard Univ Press, 1949)

Nadel, Stanley. *Little Germany: Ethnicity, Religion, and Class in New York City, 1845–1880* (Urbana: Univ of Illinois Press, 1990)

Nelson, E. Clifford, et al. *The Lutherans in North America* (Philadelphia: Fortress Press, 1975)

Roeber, A. G. *Palatines, Liberty, and Property: German Lutherans in Colonial America* (Baltimore: Johns Hopkins Univ Press, 1993)

Philip A. Bean

Germantown. Town (pop 2,018) in SW Columbia Co. In 1710 Gov Robert Hunter purchased, for the Crown, 6,000 acres (2,430 ha) of Livingston Manor for a Palatine German colony, which was projected to produce turpentine, tar, and rosin for the Royal Navy. By the following year 342 families were settled in four riverfront villages. The industries were unsuccessful, but many families remained and in 1725 patented their settlement, which became known as East Camp. Formed as German Camp District in 1775, Germantown was recognized as a town in 1788. Because of the lack of natural waterpower, residents concentrated on agriculture, especially hay for the New York City market and later fruit. Fishing, particularly shad, and ice harvesting also proved profitable. The Hudson River Railroad (1851) made it possible to build wealthy residents' estates along the river and for summer boarders to arrive. Fruit growing remains significant in the early 21st century; Taconic Farms (1991) was the second-largest breeder of laboratory animals in the United States in 2003. The German Reformed Sanctity Church Parsonage (1746) is listed on the National Register.

Gerry [GEAR-EE]. Town (2,054) in E Chautauqua Co. Settled in 1810, the town formed from Pomfret in 1812. Civil War brigadier general John McAllister Schofield (1831–1906) was a native of Gerry. The Strong Veneer Mill operated from 1893 to 1918. A western rodeo, begun in 1945 and sponsored by the Gerry Volunteer Fire Department, is the longest-running rodeo east of the Mississippi.

Jean Bedient

Gershwin, George [Gershvin, Jacob] (*b* Brooklyn, 26 Sept 1898; *d* Beverly Hills, Calif, 11 July 1937) and **Gershwin, Ira** [Gershvin, Israel] (*b* Manhattan, 6 Dec 1896; *d* Beverly Hills, 17 Aug 1983). Composer-lyricist team. George Gershwin left high school in 1914 to work as a pianist and song plugger in Tin Pan Alley and soon was writing and selling his own songs. His first hit was "Swanee" (1919) with lyrics by Irving Caesar and was popularized by Al Jolson. By 1918 he had collaborated with his brother as lyricist for "The Real American Folk Song [Is a Rag]" (1918), a modest success, and the brothers soon contributed songs to the revues in *George White's Scandals* (1921–24), which in the 1922 edition included a miniature jazz opera set in Harlem, *Blue Monday (135th Street)*. Gershwin's wish to compose in larger forms was spectacularly realized on 12 Feb 1924 at Manhattan's Aeolian Hall, when his *Rhapsody in Blue* premiered at bandleader Paul Whiteman's concert "An Experiment in Modern Music," an effort to combine jazz and classical forms. An immediate sensation, it led to other major classical compositions such as the *Piano Concerto in F* (1925), premiered by the New York Philharmonic, and the tone poem *An American in Paris* (1928), premiered by the New York Symphony Society. His successful Broadway scores included *Lady, Be Good!* (1924), *Oh, Kay!* (1926), *Strike Up the Band* (1927), *Funny*

Face (1927), and *Girl Crazy* (1930), which introduced classic songs like "Fascinating Rhythm," "Someone to Watch Over Me," " 'S Wonderful," "I Got Rhythm," and "Embraceable You." A satirical political operetta, *Of Thee I Sing*, written with George S. Kaufman, became the first musical to win the Pulitzer Prize in drama (1932). *Let 'Em Eat Cake* (1933) was more satirical but less successful. Gershwin's melodic genius and serious musical ambitions came together in the opera *Porgy and Bess* (1935), which had lyrics written by DuBose Heyward and Ira and was based on Heyward's play. Its initial 124-performance run on Broadway with an all-black cast was not a commercial success, and *Porgy and Bess* was indifferently received by most theater and music critics. Revivals after Gershwin's death established *Porgy and Bess* not only as the source of popular standard songs like "Summertime" and "It Ain't Necessarily So" but also as a powerfully dramatic opera.

The Gershwins moved to Hollywood in 1936, writing scores for several film musicals, including *Shall We Dance?* (1937) and *A Damsel in Distress* (1937), both with Fred Astaire. After a short period of declining health, George Gershwin died during a brain tumor operation. Ira remained in California and wrote lyrics for three more Broadway musicals: *Lady in the Dark* (1941) and *The Firebrand of Florence* (1945) with Kurt Weill, and *Park Avenue* with Arthur Schwartz (1946). Ira wrote lyrics for Harold Arlen's music for the film *A Star Is Born* (1954) and wrote *Lyrics on Several Occasions* (1959), a collection of his best lyrics with witty and enlightening comments. For many, George Gershwin's music has become a quintessential sound of New York City during the jazz age.

Jablonski, Edward. *Gershwin* (New York: Doubleday, 1987)

Rosenberg, Deena. *Fascinating Rhythm: The Collaboration of George and Ira Gershwin* (New York: Dutton, 1991)

David Raymond

Ghent. Town (pop 5,276) in central Columbia Co. Settled *ca* 1740 by Dutch and Germans, the town was formed in 1818 from Chatham, Claverack, and Kinderhook. Farm products included hay, grown for sale after railroad shipment became available, and rye, of which the town was the second-largest producer in the state in 1855. Ghent was served by the Hudson and Berkshire (1838) and Harlem (1852) Railroads; the latter created Ghent hamlet, and Irish and black workers found employment on the railroad. Manufacturing included woolen cloth, straw paper, and scales. The Taconic State Parkway (1963) improved access. Ghent is the site of the Columbia County Airport and Commerce Center. Manufacturers in town include TCI (electrical industry waste management), Smith Control Systems, and Doric Vault (burial vaults). Ghent was the site of the Columbia County Poorhouse from 1829 to 1955 and of the Columbia County Fair since 1852.

Gibbons, Edmund (*b* White Plains, Westchester Co, 16 Sept 1868; *d* Albany, 19 June 1964). Bishop. The son of James Gibbons and Joanna Ray Gibbons, Edmund Gibbons was raised in Albany and educated at Christian Brothers Academy, Niagara University, and the North American College, Rome, where he was ordained a priest of the Diocese of Buffalo on 27 May 1893. After serving as a parish priest and superintendent of parochial schools in the Diocese of Buffalo, Gibbons was appointed the sixth bishop of Albany on 10 Feb 1919 and consecrated on 25 Mar 1919. During his 35 years as bishop, the Catholic population of the diocese grew by more than 50%, to over 300,000, and the number of diocesan priests increased from 225 to 316. Gibbons was instrumental in expanding the number of Catholic elementary schools, establishing a diocesan high school system, and founding a college seminary, Mater Christi Seminary in Albany. He also encouraged the growth of the College of Saint Rose and Siena College. Gibbons resigned as bishop of Albany on 10 Nov 1954 and was named the titular bishop of Verbe. He died at age 95, then the oldest bishop in the world.

Gibbons, Edmund. Papers. Archives of the Diocese of Albany

Thomas J. Shelley

***Gibbons v Ogden*, 22 US (9 Wheat) 1 (1824).** Supreme Court case involving the commerce clause of the US Constitution (Art 1, § 8). The decision upheld congressional control of interstate commerce.

Origins of the Case

The rise of steam travel excited New York State business operators and farmers eager for more cost-efficient methods of transportation. In 1798 Robert R. Livingston Jr, one of the state's leading political figures and landowners, secured a monopoly from the New York State legislature to operate steamboats in state waters. Livingston's attempts to build a workable steamboat failed until he met scientist and inventor Robert Fulton in Paris around 1802. The two men established a partnership and on 17 Aug 1807 their prototype vessel, the *North River Steamboat* (often called *Clermont*), successfully navigated the Hudson River from New York City to Albany. The same year Livingston secured new monopoly rights from the state legislature for himself and Fulton.

Competition from rival steamboat companies soon threatened the Fulton-Livingston monopoly. Fulton and Livingston fought off competition from individuals such as Albany businessman James Van Ingen and Aaron Ogden, a lawyer, statesman, and former governor of New Jersey, by securing injunctions against them in state court. After losing several such legal battles, Ogden bought a license to operate steamboats in New York State from Fulton's and Livingston's steamboat company. In 1818 Ogden brought suit in New York State court against Thomas Gibbons, a Georgia businessman and former partner, for operating a rival steamboat service between New York City and New Jersey. Gibbons argued in court that he held a federally granted coasting license that superseded state law. But Chancellor James Kent, chief justice of the New York Court of Chancery, ruled against Gibbons (*Gibbons v Ogden*, 1820). Kent argued that Gibbons's license merely designated his ships as American vessels and did not infringe upon state control of trade. Gibbons defied the decision and appealed his case to the New York State Court for the Correction of Errors in 1820 and the US Supreme Court in 1821.

Supreme Court Decision

After considerable delay, the Supreme Court heard the case of *Gibbons v Ogden* on 4 Feb 1824. Sen Daniel Webster of Massachusetts and Attorney General William Wirt represented Gibbons. Webster and Wirt argued that according to the commerce clause of the US Constitution, only Congress could regulate trade between states. Gibbons's license granted by Congress under the Federal Coasting Act of 1793 gave him the right to navigate freely the waters of any state. To leave interstate trade in local hands risked legal chaos and civil war. Former New York State attorneys general Thomas Oakley and Thomas Emmet spoke for Ogden. They insisted that both Congress and the states shared concurrent power over interstate commerce. But New York State retained exclusive power over commerce within its borders and could thus grant monopolies as it saw fit. State action in this case was valid because it did not interfere with any congressional regulation of commerce. Because Fulton's and Livingston's steamboat had brought social and economic benefits to New York State, ending the monopoly would undercut progress.

The Supreme Court rendered a unanimous ruling on 2 Mar 1824. Chief Justice John Marshall stated that the New York State steamboat monopoly grant was unconstitutional. He argued that "commerce" consisted of any commercial intercourse between states and that Congress alone could regulate interstate trade under the commerce clause. But since Marshall merely held that Gibbons's federal coasting license took precedence over Ogden's state license, he left open the possibility for future state regulation. In contrast, Justice William Johnson argued in a concurring opinion that the commerce clause itself was all that was needed to invalidate the Fulton-Livingston monopoly.

Repercussions

The *Gibbons* decision held profound significance for New York State. With the destruction of the Fulton-Livingston monopoly, a rising class of entrepreneurs, steamboat owners, merchants, and farmers now stood to benefit from unrestricted trade. The general public also enjoyed lower transportation costs and increased service from steamboat companies. Local companies emerged as New York City continued to grow as the country's most important commercial center. Northern newspapers supported *Gibbons v Ogden*, but some leading southerners worried that giving Congress control of interstate commerce could hurt the interstate slave trade. Former president Thomas Jefferson attacked the *Gibbons* decision as harmful to agricultural interests and states' rights. Chancellor Kent avoided embarrassment by stating that his earlier rulings had been overturned only on a technical interpretation of the federal coasting law.

Because Marshall's decision in *Gibbons v Ogden* left many issues unclear, the question of state versus federal control of commerce continued to appear before the Supreme Court. The Marshall court went on to uphold federal control of interstate trade in *Brown v Maryland* (1827) but limited it in *Wilson v Blackbird Creek Marsh Co* (1829). From the 1830s to the

1860s the Taney court routinely supported state regulation of controversial issues such as immigration, slavery, alcohol, and unemployment compensation. In later years the Supreme Court cited *Gibbons v Ogden* both to expand federal control of interstate commerce in *Wabash Railway v Illinois* (1886) and *Swift v United States* (1905) and to strike down such power in *A. L. A. Schechter Poultry Corp v United States* (1935) and *United States v Butler* (1936). The *Gibbons* decision also served as a precedent for cases involving segregation, wage and labor standards, and gun control.

Baxter, Maurice G. *The Steamboat Monopoly: Gibbons v Ogden, 1824* (New York: Knopf, 1972)
White, G. Edward. *The Marshall Court and Cultural Change, 1815–1835* (New York: Macmillan, 1988)

Thomas H. Cox

Gibson, Althea (*b* Silver, SC, 25 Aug 1927; *d* Orange, NJ, 28 Sept 2003). Tennis and golf player. Gibson moved with her family to Harlem in 1930 and began taking tennis lessons at Harlem's Cosmopolitan Club in 1941. She advanced quickly, winning the American Tennis Association National Junior Championships in 1944 and 1945 and moving to Wilmington, NC, to continue training in 1946. Gibson joined the US Lawn Tennis Association in 1950 and received an invitation to play in the US Nationals at Forest Hills (Queens Co), becoming the first African American to play there. She graduated from Florida A&M University in 1953. Her win at the French Open three years later made her the first black athlete to claim a major tennis championship. She was also the first Black to win at Wimbledon, where she claimed five titles (singles, 1957, 1958; doubles, 1956–58), and at the US Nationals, where she claimed three titles (singles, 1957, 1958; mixed doubles, 1957). In 1957 and 1958 Gibson was honored as Woman Athlete of the Year by the Associated Press. After tennis, which lacked a professional tour at the time, Gibson took up golf, starting on the Ladies Professional Golf Association (LPGA) tour in 1964 and retiring in 1971. She was inducted into the National Lawn Tennis Hall of Fame and the International Women's Sports Hall of Fame. The Althea Gibson Foundation helps urban youth learn to play tennis.

Biracree, Tom. *Althea Gibson* (New York: Chelsea House, 1989)

Leslie Heaphy

Gilbertsville. Village (pop 375) in Butternuts (Otsego Co). Settled in 1787, the village developed as a stage stop on a Catskill Turnpike spur in the 1820s and incorporated in 1896. The village center, placed on the National Register of Historic Places in 1982, includes the Gilbertsville Academy and Collegiate Institution (Greek Revival, 1839; operated as a school from 1840 to 1935), the Presbyterian Church (1882–84), the Tudor Revival Gilbert Block (1893–95) and Major's Inn (1895), and the Gilbertsville Free Library building (1818), rebuilt in 1888 to serve as the first free library in the county.

Hugh C. MacDougall

Gilboa. Town (pop 1,215) in S Schoharie Co. Settled in 1764, the town was the site of many mills and small factories making leather, barrels, bricks, and ironwork, as well as of the Gilboa Cotton Mills (*ca* 1840–69). Formed from Blenheim and Broome in 1848, the town was the most populous in the county in 1850, boasting 3,024 residents and leading in butter production. Manufacturing declined soon after, and population dropped sharply. In 1926 Gilboa Dam was built on Schoharie Creek, creating the Schoharie Reservoir, the northernmost source of New York City's water supply. Gilboa hamlet was condemned during construction. In the early 21st century vacation homes are scattered throughout the town, and a number of dairy farms still operate.

Fossil stump being removed from Riverside Quarry in Gilboa, 1920s.

Peter Johnson and Dawn Johnson

Ginsburg, Ruth (Joan) Bader (*b* Flatbush, Kings Co, 15 Mar 1933). US Supreme Court justice. A graduate of James Madison High School in Brooklyn (1950), she earned a BA at Cornell University (1954), married classmate Martin D. Ginsburg soon after graduation, studied at Harvard Law School, and transferred to Columbia Law School (1958) when her husband accepted a job in New York City. Although she earned top honors and had been elected to the law review at both institutions, she was unable to find a job with a New York City law firm because of her gender. Instead she clerked in the US District Court, Southern District of New York, from 1959 to 1961. In 1972 she became the first female tenured faculty member at Columbia Law School and in June 1980 was sworn in as justice of the US Court of Appeals for the District of Columbia. Ginsburg maintained a moderate stance and generally adhered to a policy of judicial restraint. A firm defender of a woman's right to abortion, she objected to the grounds on which *Roe v Wade* (1973) had been decided, maintaining that the fundamental issue was not privacy but equal protection under the law. In June 1993 Pres Bill Clinton nominated Ginsburg to the Supreme Court; she was confirmed on a Senate vote of 97 to 3 and sworn in on 10 Aug 1993. As associate justice, Ginsburg has generally taken liberal to centrist positions. She was awarded the American Bar Association's Thurgood Marshall Award in 1999.

Profile of Justice Ginsburg from the Supreme Court Historical Society, http://www.supremecourthistory.org/justice/ginsburg.htm
United States Congress. Senate. Committee on the Judiciary. *Nomination of Ruth Bader Ginsburg, to Be Associate Judge of the Supreme Court of the United States* (Washington, DC: Government Printing Office, 1994)

Veronica F. Towers

ginseng ***[Panax quinquefolium].*** A herbaceous, perennial, woodland plant native to New York State. It grows in shade in moist well-drained forest soils and is a valuable medicinal herb. Ginseng grew in all regions of the state with the exception of Long Island, but overharvesting considerably diminished the supply by the late 19th century. American ginseng resembled Asian ginseng *(Panax ginseng)*, which was widely prescribed in Chinese medicine to prevent disease. The Iroquois used ginseng root, or *garangtoging,* for stomach disorders. Sir William Johnson exported ginseng in 1751, but it was John Jacob Astor who developed a significant export market. After the China trade opened in 1784 Astor bought ginseng in Albany, Schenectady, and Fort Stanwix [now Rome, Oneida Co] and shipped it to China. His first shipment netted a profit of $55,000 and was one of the cornerstones of his fortune. In 1890 George Stanton of Apulia Station (Onondaga Co) was the first person to commercially grow American ginseng under artificial shade. Stanton formed a ginseng association in the 1880s that exists now as the Empire State Ginseng Growers Association and has approximately 170 members and a headquarters in Cooperstown (Otsego Co).

In 1977 the state's ginseng was protected under a federal conservation program for wild plants. In 1988 the state established ginseng harvest season as 1 September–30 November. In 1989 the State Department of Environmental Conservation considered ginseng exploitably vulnerable, meaning its growth and harvesting are likely to become threatened if not routinely evaluated. In 1995 approximately 2,000 pounds (900 kg) of forest-grown ginseng root, worth more than $1 million, was harvested during the season. In 2002 up to 100 acres (40 ha) of ginseng were cultivated in approximately 30 counties, including Greene, Onondaga, and Fulton. Cornell University's Department of Natural Resources and Cornell Cooperative Extension support new ginseng cultivation efforts. In 2002 the state's ginseng industry either grown, harvested wild, or exported was worth $50 million.

Beyfuss, Robert. *The Practical Guide to Growing Ginseng* (Cairo, NY: Cornell Cooperative Extension Greene County, 1999)

Robert Beyfuss

***Gitlow v New York,* 268 US 652 (1925).** Free speech case stemming from the 8 Nov 1919 arrest of Benjamin Gitlow, one of the organizers of the Communist Labor Party and an ex-assemblyman from the Bronx, and James "Big Jim" Larkin, an Irish labor leader. New York City police detained them for violating a state law, the first of its kind in the nation, making it a crime to advocate "anarchy." That July, Gitlow had been involved in publishing a manifesto for the National Council of the Left Wing of the Socialist Party in that group's paper, the *Revolutionary Age.* The indictment alleged that the manifesto's discussion of how socialism could be established through strikes and other means was in fact a call for the overthrow of the government by force and violence. Defended by attorney Clarence Darrow, Gitlow lost every state court appeal. In a 7–2 vote the US Supreme Court upheld his conviction, declaring his activities unprotected speech. Justice Oliver Wendell Holmes dissented, arguing that Gitlow's actions had not presented an imminent threat to peace and order. Ironically, while Gitlow lost his case, the Court held for the first time that the 14th Amendment protected speech liberties from being abridged by the states. It was also the first time the Court upheld a conviction for "seditious incitement" in peacetime. In 1920 Gitlow had been sentenced in state court to serve 5–10 years at Sing Sing Prison. He was in and out of prison while the case was on appeal, serving three years of the sentence before being pardoned by Gov Alfred E. Smith in December 1925. In the late 1920s Gitlow became disenchanted with Stalin's leadership and later became prominent in anticommunist circles.

Novak, David. "Political Justice during the Red Scare: The Trial of Benjamin Gitlow." In *American Political Trials,* rev ed, ed. Michal Belknap (Freeport, Conn: Greenwood, 1994)

Timothy P. Gordinier

Giuliani, Rudolph (William) (*b* Brooklyn, 28 May 1944). New York City mayor. Raised in Brooklyn and Garden City (Nassau Co) by working-class parents, Giuliani attended Manhattan College, graduating in 1965. He once considered the priesthood but became a lawyer, earning a JD from New York University in 1968. In 1970 he became a lawyer at the office of the US Attorney for the Southern District of New York (SDNY). Excelling at SDNY, Giuliani moved on to various other posts at the US Department of Justice, and in 1983 he was appointed US attorney for SDNY. As chief prosecutor he garnered numerous high-profile courtroom victories in the mid- to late 1980s, including the convictions of Ivan Boesky for insider trading, Congressman Mario Biaggi for racketeering, and Leona Helmsley for tax evasion. In 1989 Giuliani ran for New York City mayor as a Republican, losing to Democratic Manhattan Borough president David Dinkins by a very narrow margin. He won the rematch four years later, inheriting a city beset with high levels of crime and the perception that it was unmanageable. On crime he quickly directed the police to employ new tactics, including the compilation of crime statistics at the precinct level and the vigorous enforcement of minor offenses. Between 1993 and 2000 the number of murders fell 65%, and total crime fell 57%. Giuliani also made significant improvements in city services. He combined the housing and transit police forces with the police department to create greater efficiency, established the Administration for Children's Services to provide better public protections to needy children, and created the Office of Emergency Management to help the city respond to disasters. In 1997 Giuliani was easily reelected for a second term as mayor. By the late 1990s many viewed the city as transformed, with booming tourism, a population surge to a record 8 million, and flourishing cultural life. Giuliani's strong, often combative, personality was one of the keys to his success. To his supporters he was a tough man who took on difficult tasks; his critics saw him as bullying and uninterested in dialogue. Several incidents between police and minorities, including the assault and brutalization of Abner Louima and the shooting of Amadou Diallo, led to accusations that the mayor's crime reduction efforts unfairly targeted African Americans, Latinos, and other minorities. In 2000 Giuliani started a high-profile bid for the US Senate in New York State against Hillary Rodham Clinton, but he aborted the challenge when revelations surfaced about his marital infidelity and health problems.

Few observers had anything but praise for his handling of the aftermath of the terrorist attack of 11 Sept 2001. Giuliani directed a massive recovery to find survivors and reassured a stunned city through daily television press conferences that it would overcome this immense tragedy. Unable to run again due to a two-term limit provision within the city charter, Giuliani left office in 2001 with a national following and prestige unprecedented for a New York City mayor.

See also SEPTEMBER 11TH, 2001.

Kirtzman, Andrew. *Rudy Giuliani: Emperor of the City* (New York: Morrow, 2000)

Thomas A. Birkland

glass

EARLY INDUSTRY

Although Dutch colonists brought flat glass for windows, as well as bottles and drinking glasses, to New Netherland, at least two glassmakers, Everett Duycking, a glass painter and stainer (possibly a stained-glass window maker), and Johannes Smedes, are recorded as residing in the colony in the mid–17th century. Several Manhattan glasshouses are listed in the 1732 census, but none lasted for long; one is thought to have been started in Brooklyn in 1754. Manhattan's Glasshouse Co of New York (1752–67) was the most successful. During this period three other window glass manufacturers—at Woodstock (Ulster Co) (?1752–*ca* 1785), Peterboro (Madison Co) (*ca* 1795–1813), and Hamilton [now Guilderland, Albany Co] (1785–?1815)—opened to serve northern settlements. The glass industry in New York State, however, remained small during the 18th century because British policies discouraged glassmaking by colonists. The end of British rule stimulated the glass industry, and it blossomed as increasing numbers of New Yorkers desired glass windows and glass bottles, which were used for a variety of household necessities from medicines to ink. New York State's glassmakers produced fewer drinking glasses, as glass tableware was a luxury generally reserved for the rich, who preferred English or continental European glasses and serving ware.

POST-1800 WINDOW AND BOTTLE GLASS

Several window and bottle glass manufacturers responded to consumer demand in newly settled regions of northern, central, and western New York State. Forests in these regions provided ample fuel for the wood-fired furnaces used in the glasshouses, and the Hudson and Mohawk Rivers and the Erie Canal provided ready transportation to market. The popularity of mineral and soda waters at places like Saratoga Springs and Ballston Spa (Saratoga Co) increased the demand for bottles in the state, as did the presence of manufacturers of bitters and patent medicines in several upstate towns. A new glasshouse was built in Peterboro around 1810 and produced window glass until 1830, and the Rensselaer Glass Factory in Rensselaer Village [now Sand Lake, Rensselaer Co] operated from 1806 until 1853, when it relocated to Durhamville (Oneida Co) and continued operating until 1890. The Utica Glass Works and the Oneida Glass Works both made window glass in the Utica area from 1809 until 1836; the Mount Vernon Glass Co operated in Vernon (Oneida Co) from 1810 to 1845 and then in Saratoga from 1846 to 1890; and the Ontario Glass Manufactory made window glass in Geneva (Ontario Co) from 1810 until at least 1847. In Ulster Co the Woodstock Glass Manufactory revived glassmaking from 1810 until 1836, as did the Ulster Glass Manufactory from around 1813 until about 1855. The Dunbarton Glass Works (Oneida Co) opened around 1825 and made window glass until 1895. Almost all of these were window glass factories, but the Mount Vernon Glass Co made bottles and tableware of all types. The Clyde Glass Works (Wayne Co) made window glass from 1827 until 1889 and added a second furnace in 1864 for the manufacture of bottles, fruit jars, and novelties until 1922; the Redford Crown Glass Works (Clinton Co) operated from 1830 until 1851; the Redwood Glass Works near Watertown made window glass from 1833 until after 1877; and the Cleveland Glass Works (Oswego Co) was open from 1840 until about 1905, as were two others in the area. Bottles were made in Ellenville (Ulster Co) from 1836 until 1896, in Lancaster (Erie Co) from 1849 until 1908, and in Lockport (Niagara Co) from 1840 until *ca* 1900.

In the 19th century window glass was manufactured completely by hand, with workers blowing large flat circles of glass, once called crowns, or long cylinders. The crowns were annealed (heated then cooled in a slow, controlled manner to prevent breakage), before they were cut into small panes; the cylinders were split lengthwise and flattened, which permitted a larger pane size but resulted in an uneven surface. The panes were then sorted by size and shipped to retailers in large cities and in the local area. Bottle glassmaking was also a handcraft, although the individual bottles were blown into molds that gave them shape and decoration. Most mid-19th-century bottle and window glass factories employed 40–50 people and had only one furnace. In the 1870s many firms increased the number of employees to 80 or more but continued to use one furnace. The increase in labor meant that the glasshouses worked around the clock in two shifts. Technological innovation played a role in the increased size of glassworks after 1870. The Anglo-American Glass Co began operating the first continuous tank furnace in the United States in 1879 at its Poughkeepsie bottle glassworks. Because raw materials were fed continuously into the tank to melt, making the supply of molten glass constant, use of the tank (rather than individual pots) eliminated any downtime for workers who had to wait for the glass to come to the right temperature and consistency.

Although the factories all made utilitarian glass, workers were allowed to make objects of their own choosing after they fulfilled their daily quotas. Many made gifts for their families or objects to sell locally, and consequently a number of pitchers, bowls, and other glasses were also made in these factories in the mid–19th century. Many of the glassmakers were immigrants from Bohemia [now in the Czech Republic] and Germany, and the glassware often reflected the influence of German traditions. Experienced European glassblowers had easily found work in the United States at a higher wage than at home. By the 1840s many American-born apprentices had become glassblowers as well. Many were itinerant, and influences from New Jersey and New England glasswork tableware designs often showed up in the offhand ware they made in New York factories. As factory automation developed in the late 19th century, however, and as coal and natural gas succeeded wood as the cheapest fuel, most of the factories in the northern, central, and western parts of the state closed. Window and bottle glass production mostly moved westward, although a few glasshouses modernized and remained in the state.

POST-1800 GLASSMAKING

One national center of glass tableware production was New York City, where the New York Glass Works was established at 47th St in 1820. The factory, making table and decorative glass, was successful until 1840. One of its founding partners, John L. Gilliland, left in 1823 to start the Brooklyn Flint Glass Works. This firm operated under several owners until 1868, when Amory Houghton and his partners moved the company to Corning (Steuben Co), where in 1875 it became Corning Glass Works (now Corning Inc). The New York Glass Works and the Brooklyn Flint Glass Works won prizes for their table glass, and Gilliland was commended at the Crystal Palace Exhibition in London in 1851. By mid–19th century, several other firms operated in Manhattan and Brooklyn, both melting glass and decorating it. Christian Dorflinger started three glasshouses in Brooklyn at midcentury before moving to Pennsylvania. Corning Glass Works was the first in the state to produce pressed glass serving ware with its production of Pyrex, a glass baking ware first marketed in 1915.

The cutting and other decoration of glassware was usually done in a separate workshop. Manhattan and Brooklyn were centers for glass decoration from the early 19th century and had several crafters and firms cutting and engraving glass, of which Manhattan's Stouvenel workshop was probably the largest. Louis C. Tiffany in 1885 founded the Tiffany Glass Co, which produced critically acclaimed stained-glass windows, glass vessels, and lamps. L. Straus and Sons began in the late 19th century importing cut glass but eventually ran a large glass decorating company in New York City that employed more than 100 people; it remained in business as a retailer under several partnerships until the 1970s. By 1905 Corning was also a center for luxury glassmaking, with two glass factories and five large cutting shops as well as many smaller ones. Steuben Glass Works made art glass, and Corning Glass Works specialized in the production of industrial and technical products. Unlike the 19th-century window and glasshouses that closed due to fuel shortages, luxury glass producers increased production at the end of the century because much of their work was glass decoration, for which the cost of fuel was less important. Luxury tableware production suffered during World War I and the Great Depression, and consequently most glass companies closed by the mid–20th century. In the last quarter of the 20th century, however, as interest in blown glass increased, a number of individual crafters and small firms started making art glass in New York State once again.

In the late 20th century, industrial applications of glass, notably in fiberglass and fiber optics, greatly contributed to Corning Inc's success, and the Southern Tier and Central New York became centers for industrial glass production. Major industrial glass firms of the region during this period included Corning Inc, Toshiba Display Devices in Horseheads (Chemung Co), and Imaging and Sensing Technology Corp in Horseheads. Since 1992 new manufacturers have been attracted to the region by Alfred Technology Resources, a nonprofit group established by SUNY College of Ceramics at Alfred University and Corning Inc to provide technical and business support to producers of glass, ceramic, and other advanced materials. It runs business incubation centers at Alfred (Allegany Co) and Painted Post (Steuben Co).

Davis, Pearce. *The Development of the American Glass Industry* (Cambridge, Mass: Harvard Univ Press, 1949)

McKearin, George S., and Helen McKearin. *American Glass* (1948; repr New York: Bonanza Books, 1989; distributed by Crown Publishers)

McKearin, Helen, and Kenneth M. Wilson. *American Bottles and Flasks and Their Ancestry* (New York: Crown Publishers, 1978)

Spillman, Jane Shadel, and Susanne K. Frantz. *Masterpieces of American Glass: The Corning Museum of Glass, the Toledo Museum of Art, Lillian Nassau Ltd.* (New York: Crown Publishers, 1990)

Jane Shadel Spillman

Gleason, Kate (*b* Rochester, 25 Nov 1865; *d* Rochester, 9 Jan 1933). Banker and designer. Gleason was raised and educated in Rochester, where she attended school and assisted her father, William Gleason, as a bookkeeper in his tool shop. She entered Cornell University in 1884 but departed within the year to return to her father's business. In 1890 the Gleason Tool Co was incorporated, and she became the secretary-treasurer, working there through 1913. On 1 Jan 1914 she became the receiver in bankruptcy for another machine tool firm and in one year paid off the company's debt and turned a profit. In 1917 Gleason became the first woman president of a national bank, the First National Bank of East Rochester, while its president was on duty in World War I. She held this position for three years. During her presidency she became interested in housing and experimented with concrete houses, which were fireproof and economical, in Rochester and later in California and South Carolina. Gleason later spent much of her time at a castle she rebuilt in France and at an estate in Beaufort, SC.

Leavitt, Judith A. *American Women Managers and Administrators* (Westport, Conn: Greenwood, 1985)

Kerry Delaney

Glen. Town (pop 2,222) in S central Montgomery Co. Sometimes the site of the Mohawk village of Ossernenon, the area is the birthplace of Kateri Tekakwitha (1656–80) and the locale of Jesuit martyrdom. White settlement began *ca* 1725, but the town was not formed until 1823, from Charleston, and was named for Jacob S. Glen. Many settlers were Palatine Germans, although Sir William Johnson settled 16 Irish families southwest of Fort Hunter *ca* 1740, many of whom returned to Ireland. Glen became a farming town, and in the early 21st century most of its land remains in agriculture. The town is the site of the National Shrine of North American Martyrs (1885) at Auriesville, a major tourist attraction that includes a massive coliseum (1931).

James Crawford

Glen Cove. City (pop 26,622) in N central Nassau Co. Settled by Europeans in 1668, it was first called Musketa Cove. Its first post office was called Moscheto Cove. Steamboat service began in 1829, opening it as a summer resort, and residents changed its name to Glen Cove in 1834. Pottery clay was mined in the 19th century, and the Duryea Corn Starch Factory (1859–?1900) employed hundreds, processing the corn of Long Island farms. In 1918 the city was incorporated. It contains both estates and middle-income neighborhoods, and it has long-established Italian and black neighborhoods. The Russian United Nations delegation is housed in a Glen Cove estate. In 2000 Glen Cove's racial composition was about 80% white, 6.4% black, and 4.2% Asian. In addition 20% of the population was of Latino ethnicity. Pall Corp and Photocircuits were major employers in the early 21st century. Glen Cove is the site of the 62-acre (25 ha) Garvies Point Museum and Preserve, which interprets geology and Native American archaeology, the Holocaust Memorial and Educational Center, and the Webb Institute of Naval Architecture.

Richard F. Welch

Glen Head. Locality (pop 4,625) in Oyster Bay (Nassau Co). Originally known as Cedar Swamp, it acquired a post office by that name in 1830; it was renamed Greenvale in 1866 and became Glen Head in 1874 to conform to the existing name of the railroad station stop (1864). After the Civil War it housed workers from the Glen Cove starch factory and had a brickyard and a boatbuilding industry. Later it attracted Norwegian and Polish immigrants. The community grew rapidly between 1945 and 1960 and acquired a large Italian population.

Richard A. Winsche

Glen Island Casino. Dance hall in a boat harbor clubhouse on Long Island Sound, off New Rochelle (Westchester Co). Glen Island, a chain of five small islands connected by causeways and later by landfill, was a resort for workers from New York City in the late 19th century, when proprietor John Henry Starin brought daytrippers to the islands by ferry in great numbers. The casino's heyday corresponded to the swing era, from about 1933 to 1946. Bands were hired at low wages for long residencies, generally all summer, with the incentive of regular nationwide radio broadcasts, which made stars of several previously obscure bands and their leaders. Among those who played at the casino were Glen Gray and the Casa Loma Orchestra (1933); the Dorsey Bros Orchestra (1935), during which engagement Tommy and Jimmy Dorsey quarreled bitterly and broke up their band; and the Glenn Miller Orchestra (1939). About the turn of the 21st century, the venue ceased presenting live music and began operating as a catering hall and restaurant managed by Continental Hosts Co.

Stanton, John. "Glen Island, Cradle of the Big Band," *On the Sound* (Sept 1971): 70–76

Weigold, Marilyn. "Disney World on the Sound: John Starin's Glen Island," *Westchester Historian* 77 (Spring, Summer 2001): 36–45, 83–91

Elliott S. Hurwitt

Glen Park. Village (pop 487) in Brownville and Pamelia (Jefferson Co). Founded in 1881 by the C. R. Remington Paper and Pulp Mill, Glen Park was the site of three paper mills by 1887. Incorporated in 1893, the village had its own post office from 1896 to 1925. The International Brotherhood of Papermakers struck the mills in 1920. Already in trouble, the mills never recovered, and the last one closed in 1926. The Watertown and Brownville Street Railway (1888–1931) ran the popular Glen Park amusement park (1891–904). The village's most important economic force is Glen Park Hydro (1987), an electric plant. Most residents work in Watertown.

Laura Lynne Scharer

Glens Falls. City (pop 14,354) in Warren Co. Located at a 60 ft (18.3 m) waterfall where the Hudson River emerges from the Adirondack foothills, Glens Falls was historically the largest industrial center in the southeast Adirondack region. The falls were included in the Queensbury Patent of 1762, whose patentees sold out the next year to a Quaker colony from Dutchess Co, one of whom, Abraham Wing (1721–95), built a sawmill and a gristmill at the falls. The settlement was twice burned during the American Revolution. Originally called Wing's Falls, it was renamed Glens Falls after John Glen, another mill owner, who came in 1788. A bridge across the Hudson was built in 1792, and about three years later Pearl Village was surveyed, that name alternating with Glens Falls until the post office was established in 1807. The village was incorporated in 1839.

Industrial Growth

Early production centered on resource extraction. The Feeder Canal (1832–1928) connecting with the Champlain Canal led to expanded industrial development of the waterpower at the falls and commercial exploitation of resources, particularly lumber and limestone. At about the time the Feeder was constructed, Abraham Wing III organized a system of log booms and sluices to control timber being driven on Schroon and Hudson Rivers to Glens Falls. By 1849, with the introduction of the "Big Boom," logs were halted above the falls, and those of the various lumber companies were sorted, tallied, and directed to the sawmills, where they were milled for the Albany and Troy lumber markets. Limestone and black marble were quarried nearby and were shipped via the Feeder. Some limestone was burned, using sawmill refuse as fuel, to produce lime for shipment; the Jointa Lime Co (1851) was an important firm. Glens Falls industries were also served, though at a late date, by the Delaware and Hudson Railroad (1869). The Glens Falls Co (1832), composed of New York City capitalists, gradually acquired all the mills on the Warren Co side of the falls, before selling to Finch Pruyn and Co in 1865. With the hardwood running out, that firm built a large paper mill in 1902.

Paper mill machinery was another development of the late 19th century; as late as 1967 the Swedish firm Kamyr entered the American market with its Glens Falls facility, which in 2003 was owned by Andritz Co. With the introduction of municipal water supply in 1873, the clothing industry set up shop; Glens Falls Shirt Co (1876) was the first and Joseph Fowler Shirt and Collar the largest. These industries drew large numbers of workers. By 1837 there was a significant Francophone Canadian population in the village, joined by immigrants from Ireland. Later immigration from Germany and Italy added to diversity. From 1870 to 1900, the population of Glens Falls almost tripled, from 4,500 to 12,613.

Glens Falls entrepreneurs invested capital in other profitable businesses, particularly banking and insurance. Glens Falls Dividend Mutual Insurance Co (1849) became Glens Falls Insurance Co (1864), a stock company. It employed almost 1,000 people locally until it was absorbed by Continental Insurance Co in 1970, which built an impressive skycraper (1973). Continental left the city in 1985. Entrepreneurs also financed the building of the Spier Falls Dam (1903), upstream on the Hudson, then the largest hydroelectric dam in the world. By the early 20th century Glens Falls was the richest and most populous village in New York State and in 1908 voted for a city charter.

Education and Culture

The Academy (1813–*ca* 1840), privately chartered, was contemporary with and supplemental to the development of common schools under the Law of 1812. It was followed by the long-lived Glens Falls Academy (1841–1937). The village's common schools formed a Union Free School District in 1881, opening a public high school in 1888. Also important were two Roman Catholic parish schools, St. Alphonsus School (1873), which was primarily for Francophone Canadians, and St. Mary's Academy (1883); they merged in 1991. In the early decades of the 20th century civic-minded business leaders contributed parks, the Crandall Library (1892) and Glens Falls Hospital (1900) to the community. In 1952 Louis and Charlotte Hyde founded the Hyde Collection Trust, which opened the Hyde Collection Art Museum in 1964. The daily newspaper, the *Post-Star,* was joined in the late 20th century by a vigorous independent weekly, the *Chronicle.*

Recent History

During World War II, Glens Falls was prosperous and busy. *Look* magazine ran a series of articles on Glens Falls in 1944, designating it as "Hometown, USA" and depicting it as a "typical" American small city contributing to the war effort. The city reached its peak population of 19,610 in 1950, the year the last spring log drive on the Hudson took place. Afterward local industries slowly declined, and financial services businesses lost local ownership and many local jobs. The Northway bypassed Glens Falls in 1961, ending traffic jams but also its favored position as the gateway to Adirondack resorts. Downtown Glens Falls, once the largest retail market between Montreal and Albany, lost its shops and theaters to shopping centers north of the city. In part to counter this decline, the Glens Falls Civic Center opened in 1978, presenting sporting events and entertainment. While the population of the city has declined over the past half century, the surrounding metropolitan region, including the neighboring Towns of Queensbury, Moreau (Saratoga Co), and Kingsbury and Fort Edward (Washington Co), has grown, with over 70,000 inhabitants in the 2000 census.

At the turn of the 21st century, community efforts were showing signs of success in returning activity to the downtown. Several of the city's historic industry sectors were still large employers. Finch Pruyn employed 745 workers in 2002, manufacturing pulp and paper, Native Textiles (210 workers) made tricot, and Glens Falls Lehigh Cement Co (130 workers) was the successor to the early limekilns. Newer sectors were medical devices (Boston Scientific, 675 workers) and packaging material (Pactiv, 155 workers). The city's most famous native is Charles Evans Hughes (1862–1948), the 1916 Republican presidential candidate. Other famous natives were Charles Reed Bishop (1822–1915), husband of Princess Bernice Pauahi of Hawaii, and Robert Porter Patterson (1891–1952), secretary of war under Pres Harry S. Truman. The city's greatest landmark is its falls. This attraction has not been exploited for tourism since its earliest years;

Hudson River flowing through Glens Falls, 1875.

Cooper's Cave, commemorated in James Fenimore Cooper's *The Last of the Mohicans* (1826), has been closed to visitors since 1961.

See also ART, ALBANY AND THE CAPITAL DISTRICT, UPPER HUDSON, AND MOHAWK VALLEY.

Bridging the Years: Glens Falls, NY, 1763–1978 (Glens Falls, NY: Glens Falls Historical Association, 1978)
Brown, William H., ed. *History of Warren County* (Glens Falls, NY: Warren County, 1963)
Hyde, Louis F. *History of Glens Falls, NY, and Its Settlement* (Glens Falls, NY: Author, 1936)

Edward H. Knoblauch

Glenville. Town (pop 28,183) in N Schenectady Co. The area was first settled by the Dutch around 1658. In 1748 a Canadian Indian raiding party ambushed 40 Schenectady militiamen at Beukendaal. The town was formed from Schenectady in 1820. A woolen factory operated at High Mills in the 1860s, and brooms were made from locally grown broom corn in two Scotia factories and elsewhere along the river, an industry that declined after 1900. In the early 20th century vegetables were grown for urban markets. The town's population doubled with suburban development in the 1920s and grew again after the opening of Scotia Naval Depot (1943; now an industrial zone) and Mayfair Shopping Center (1952). Glenville is home to the Schenectady County Airport (1927) and the 109th Airlift Wing at the Stratton Air National Guard Base (1950). The Empire State Aerosciences Museum (1984) is an attraction.

Stephanie Przybylek and Christopher Hunter

Glickman, Marty [Martin Irving] (*b* the Bronx, 14 Aug 1917; *d* New York City, 3 Jan 2001). Athlete and sportscaster. The son of Romanian immigrants, Glickman grew up mostly in Brooklyn and attended James Madison High School, where he broke New York City and New York State track records in the 100-yard dash and played varsity football. When a group of Jewish alumni seeking to support a Jewish athlete on campus offered to pay his tuition, Glickman enrolled at Syracuse University in 1935. He continued to excel at track and football, winning a berth on the 1936 US Olympic 4 x 100 m relay team slated to race in Berlin. He never competed, however, because the American coaches benched both him and his teammate Samuel Stoller, probably because they were Jewish.

Glickman returned to Syracuse, where he continued to succeed in athletics and began a career at WSYR as a radio broadcaster in 1937. After graduating in 1939 he returned to New York City, eventually becoming a leading voice of New York City sports. He is best remembered for his knowledgeable and animated play-by-play radio announcing of New York Knicks basketball (1946–67), New York Giants football (1948–71), and New York Jets football (1973–78, 1988–92), although he announced on radio and television for more than 20 different professional and amateur sports, including harness racing from Yonkers Raceway, New York Americans' National Hockey League hockey, Madison Square Garden track and field meets, and Brooklyn Dodgers' baseball pre- and postgame shows. Credited with creating the "verbal geography" of basketball—he coined the phrases "top of the key" and "swisshhh"—he was hired by media companies, including NBC, to train basketball and football commentators later in his career. On 8 Nov 1972 he was play-by-play announcer for HBO's first program, a New York Rangers–Vancouver Canucks hockey game. Apologizing for its 1936 mistake, the US Olympic Committee awarded Glickman the first Douglas MacArthur Award for service to the Olympic community in 1998.

Glickman, Marty, with Stan Isaacs. *The Fastest Kid on the Block: The Marty Glickman Story* (Syracuse: Syracuse Univ Press, 1996)

David Marc

gliding. See SOARING AND GLIDING.

Glimmerglass Opera. Operatic repertory company in Cooperstown (Otsego Co). Glimmerglass Opera began in the summer of 1975 with a performance of Giacomo Puccini's *La Bohème* at Cooperstown High School. The interest of local opera lovers led to steady growth artistically and financially. The Alice Busch Theater, a beautiful 912-seat structure designed by Hugh Hardy, was built for the company in 1987 on the shore of Otsego Lake. Glimmerglass was James Fenimore Cooper's name for the lake.

Started as a volunteer operation, Glimmerglass Opera stages four productions each summer; the 2000 season had a total attendance of 38,000. The company is highly regarded for presentations of 20th-century opera, innovative productions of standards like *Fidelio* and *La Traviata*, and its emphasis on Baroque works, particularly Monteverdi and Handel. Glimmerglass has presented such rarely performed operas as Hector Berlioz's *Beatrice and Benedict*, Richard Strauss's *Intermezzo*, and Benjamin Britten's *Paul Bunyan*; it also gave the first performances of William Schuman's *A Question of Taste* (1989), David Carlson's *Midnight Angel* (1993), and the trilogy *Central Park* (1999), which was broadcast nationally on PBS. *Central Park*, like several other recent Glimmerglass stagings, was a coproduction with the New York City Opera. The Young American Artists Program gives talented young singers opportunities to perform in productions and recitals.

Glimmerglass Opera, http://www.glimmerglass.org

David Raymond

glove industry. See FULTON COUNTY.

Gloversville. City (pop 15,413) in central Fulton Co. The area was settled by Scottish and Irish tenants of Sir William Johnson's Kingsborough (1753) and Mayfield (1770) patents. Deerskin was tanned for leather as early as 1803, and the first glove shop began production in 1810. Plentiful water and hemlock bark supplied the tanneries. The glove industry grew rapidly, and in 1829 the new post office was named for it. The village was incorporated in 1851. A post–Civil War boom, during which Gloversville dominated the US market for men's fine leather dress gloves, attracted immigrant laborers from Germany, England, Scandinavia, Poland, and Italy, many of them skilled glove makers. By 1890 the village's population reached 25,000, and it was incorporated as a city. In the 1890s nearly 100 glove and mitten factories produced 3 million pairs annually. Allied industries included tanning, the manufacture of glove-cutting machines, and paper-box making for the glove industry. The German-Jewish Littauer family arrived in 1855 and became successful business and civic leaders. A large Eastern European Jewish population came to Gloversville, forming a congregation in 1891. By 1914, 500 of the city's 1,765 cutters were Russian Jewish by birth. The four largest glove shops, all owned by German Jews, employed 1,344. During the interwar period the city boasted that "Gloversville Gloves America." After World War II imports increased, as did the practice of sending work overseas. Local jobs were lost, and around 1950, due to the greater capital required by larger, import-based firms, Gloversville's glove business began to decline. By the early 21st century the leather and glove businesses only barely survived. A number of firms assembled offshore production for sale, and some leather finishers also remained in business. Downtown revitalization includes efforts to restore the Glove Theater (1916). Famous sons are Lucius N. Littauer (1859–1944), whose philanthropy created much of the fabric of the 20th-century city, and movie magnate Samuel Goldwyn (1879–1974), who apprenticed as a glove maker.

Glynn, Martin H(enry) (*b* Kinderhook, Columbia Co, 27 Sept 1871; *d* Albany, 14 Dec 1924). Governor, newspaper editor, and publisher. The son of Irish immigrants, Glynn attended public school in Kinderhook and graduated from Fordham University in 1894. Moving to Albany, he became a reporter for the *Albany Times-Union* in 1896, becoming an editor-publisher by 1902 and a prominent voice in the state Democratic Party. While serving in the US Congress (1899–1901), he championed the rights of labor, political reform, and religious tolerance. Distinguishing himself as state comptroller from 1906 to 1908, Glynn was elected lieutenant governor in 1912. He succeeded William Sulzer as governor in 1913 after Sulzer was impeached and removed from office. As governor, Glynn again promoted his reform program, including workers' compensation and statewide primaries, but he lacked a commanding executive leadership and in 1914 lost a bid for another term. With his impressive oratorical skills, Glynn won the role of temporary chairman of the Democratic National Convention in 1916 and an appointment to the Federal Industrial Commission (1919–20). While in Europe in 1921, Glynn helped facilitate negotiations between British and Irish leaders that would result in the Irish Free State.

Lizzi, Dominick C. *Governor Martin H. Glynn: Forgotten Hero* (Valatie, NY: Valatie Press, 1994)

Wesley G. Balla

Gold Coast. A popular name for the area of great estates on the North Shore of Long Island between Great Neck (Nassau Co) and Centerport (Suffolk Co). In the late 19th century the North Shore was an ideal place for the era's plutocrats to build their sprawling estates, with ample rolling land, bluffs, beaches, and easy access to New York City via the Long Island Rail Road. Thomas Clapham's granite villa (1868) in Roslyn Harbor (Nassau Co), designed by architect Jacob Wrey Mould, was among the earliest of the grand houses on the North Shore. Clapham had been drawn to Roslyn Harbor by excellent sailing in Long Island's sheltered bays and coves. Outdoor sports became fashionable, and golf, yacht, tennis, and polo clubs sprang up along the

Clarence Mackey mansion in Roslyn, designed by McKim, Mead and White, 1902.

length of the Gold Coast. Members built estates near their clubs with mansions designed by the country's leading architectural firms, including McKim, Mead and White; Delano and Aldrich; and Peabody, Wilson and Brown. Between the Civil War and World War II, about 975 great estates, as identified by the Society for the Preservation of Long Island Antiquities (SPLIA), were created in the present Nassau and Suffolk Cos; about half were in the Gold Coast region. Many featured tennis courts, swimming pools, and guest quarters; private golf courses and polo fields were not uncommon. Long docks for oceangoing yachts, such as J. P. Morgan's 300 ft (91 m) *Corsair,* extended into the Sound. By the early 20th century the North Shore was being called the Gold Coast by the press in recognition of its concentration of wealthy residents and their lavish lifestyles. Memorable depictions of the Gold Coast during its 1920s heyday include the mansion of nouveau riche Jay Gatsby in the fictional locality of East Egg in F. Scott Fitzgerald's *The Great Gatsby* (1925) and the lavish party disrupted by "Captain Spaulding, the African Explorer" in the Marx Brothers' film *Animal Crackers* (1930). A later depiction is in the film *Sabrina* (1954), starring Humphrey Bogart and Audrey Hepburn.

But after the boom came the bust. It took a lot of money and servants to run Gold Coast establishments. By the 1930s taxes and depression-era financial reverses began to take their toll. Many country houses were boarded up and abandoned. With the onset of World War II, the labor supply dried up as men and women went off to war. After 1945 many estates were sold to developers, who tore down the mansions to make way for middle-class housing. But there is still a lot of the Gold Coast around. According to the 2000 median home sale price, the 15 wealthiest localities on Long Island were on the Gold Coast. More than half of the mansions in SPLIA's survey survive, with many residential and others in public use. Among the latter are the former homes of Walter P. Chrysler (United States Merchant Marine Academy, Kings Point); Childs Frick (Nassau County Museum of Art, Roslyn); John S. Phipps (Old Westbury Gardens); Daniel and Florence Guggenheim (Sands Point Village Club); as well as Coe Hall in the Planting Fields Arboretum State Historic Park (Oyster Bay). Landmark commissions in the Towns of North Hempstead, Oyster Bay, and Huntington, and the Villages of Sands Point, Kings Point, Roslyn, and Flower Hill are charged with preservation mandates.

McKay, Robert B., Anthony Baker, and Carol A. Traynor, eds. *Long Island Country Houses and Their Architects* (New York: Norton, 1997)

Joan Gay Kent

Golden Gloves. Amateur boxing tournament. In the spring of 1927 the *New York Daily News* held a Golden Gloves tournament for local boxers in Madison Square Garden, modeled on a tournament sponsored by the *Chicago Tribune* in 1923. In early 1928 *Daily News* sports editor Paul Gallico and *Tribune* sports editor Arch Ward decided on an intercity competition, and the winners of the New York tournament met the winners of the Chicago tournament for the first time on 24 Mar 1928. In 1930 the tournament became national. Winners who went on to fame as professional boxers include Sugar Ray Robinson, Gus Lesnevich, Floyd Patterson, Rocky Marciano, Tony Zale, Barney Ross, Joe Louis, Ezzard Charles, Muhammad Ali (then known as Cassius Clay), José Torres, Mark Breland, and Riddick Bowe. Women first competed at the Golden Gloves in New York City on 7 Apr 1995. Tournament finals are held annually in April at Madison Square Garden, and the *Daily News* remained the sponsor through the early 21st century.

New York Daily News Archives, New York

Bill Gallo

Goldman, Emma (*b* Kovno, Russia [now Kaunas, Lithuania], 27 June 1869; *d* Toronto, 14 May 1940). Political and social radical. The daughter of Jewish shopkeepers, Emma Goldman moved with her family in 1881 to St. Petersburg, where she was exposed to new revolutionary movements. Immigrating to the United States in 1885, Goldman settled in Rochester, where she sewed overcoats in a factory and married another Russian immigrant, Jacob Kersner. Soon Goldman, in part influenced by the anarchists charged with the 1886 bombing at Chicago's Haymarket Square, embraced radical politics and left Kersner to join a New York City circle of anarchists. By 1889 she was active in the anarchist movement as a Yiddish speaker and writer. Goldman held that all forms of government relied upon violence; she called for a new social order based on liberty, unrestricted by laws. In 1892 she aided Alexander Berkman following his assassination attempt on Henry Clay Frick, chairman of the Carnegie Steel Co, though this assistance remained unknown until publication of her memoirs, *Living My Life,* in 1931. Sentenced to New York City's Blackwell's Island [now Roosevelt Island] Penitentiary in 1893 for inciting a riot in Manhattan's Union Square, Goldman spent her prison time learning English and training as a nurse. Released in 1894 she began to speak against organized religion and conventional sexual morality throughout the nation. She viewed the institution of marriage as a prison for most women. Alone among American anarchists, Goldman expressed sympathy for Leon F. Czolgosz following his 1901 assassination of Pres William McKinley, although she stopped short of endorsing political violence. Suspected of complicity in McKinley's death, Goldman narrowly escaped jail. A prolific writer, she penned *Anarchism and Other Essays* (1911) and *The Social Significance of the Modern Drama* (1914), and published an anarchist magazine, *Mother Earth* (1906–19), from her Greenwich Village apartment. In 1916 "Red Emma" received a prison term for distributing birth control literature in Queens Co, and in 1919 she was deported to the Soviet Union as an alien radical. Unimpressed by the Soviet Union, which she left in 1921, she spent the rest of her life in Europe and Canada, save for a three-month visit to the United States in 1934, which included reunions and speaking engagements in Rochester and New York City.

Emma Goldman. Photograph by Carl Van Vechten, 1934.

Paneled brandywine bowl by Albany silversmith Jacob C. Ten Eyck, *ca* 1730–50.

Chalberg, John. *Emma Goldman: American Individualist* (New York: Harper Collins, 1991)
Goldman, Emma. *Living My Life* (1931; repr New York: Da Capo Press, 1970)

Caryn E. Neumann

goldsmithing and silversmithing. Of some 70 gold- and silversmiths active in New York Colony from 1675 to 1750, 59 worked in New York City. A majority had Dutch ancestry, such as Jurian Blanck Jr (*bap* 1645–*ca* 1714), and Huguenots, such as Bartholomew Le Roux (*ca* 1665–1713), accounted for about a quarter. These silversmiths produced flatware and domestic and liturgical objects generally following English fashion. Distinct to New York Colony were forms such as the brandywine bowl, the syllabub cup, and the gadrooned capstan trencher saltcellar, ornamented with repoussé chasing, engraving, cut-card work, and cast appliqués. From 1755 to 1775, silversmiths, including Manhattan's Myer Myers (1723–95), the most prominent colonial Jewish metalworker, and New York City–trained and Southampton (Suffolk Co)–based Elias Pelletreau (1726–1810), adopted elements of the International Rococo style, inspired partly by the work of Swiss-born Daniel Christian Fueter (active in Manhattan 1754–69).

Gold- and silversmithing persisted as an artisan craft in Manhattan and Albany into the 19th century. Utica housed three silversmiths by 1800. Other craftsmen, such as Nicholas Bogert (1776–1843) of Saint Andrew's [now Montgomery, Orange Co], settled in rural communities to produce goods for both local and metropolitan markets. In the mid-19th century, manufacturing silversmiths began to employ machine-assisted techniques and larger workforces. Firms such as Manhattan's William Gale (1799–1867) and various partners, his rivals Wood and Hughes, and Syracuse's J. Seymour and Co (active 1857–95) gradually displaced small artisan shops. Simultaneously, New York manufacturing and retail silversmiths won international recognition, first at London's 1851 Crystal Palace exhibition. The 1878 Paris Universal Exposition awarded Tiffany and Co's Japanesque wares, manufactured under the direction of Edward Chandler Moore (1827–91), a grand prize.

Tiffany and Co, Wilcox and Evertsen, and George W. Shiebler Co retained New York City showrooms in the 1890s but relocated their plants outside Manhattan, to Newark, NJ, Meriden, Conn, and Brooklyn, respectively. Alvin Manufacturing Co (later Alvin Silver Co) moved operations from Irvington, NJ, to Sag Harbor (Suffolk Co) in 1895 and later functioned as a division of Gorham after 1928. Crafts colonies like Elverhoj, which moved to Milton-on-Hudson, near Poughkeepsie, in 1912, and individuals including Danish-born Peer Smed (1878–1943) and German-born Peter Müller-Munk (1904–67; active in Manhattan for several years, beginning in 1926) continued handcraft production of precious metalwork in the early 20th century. Designer Marie Zimmermann (1878–1972), trained at Manhattan's Art Students League, won national renown for modernist tableware and jewelry designs in the mid-1920s. Wartime restrictions stopped industrial production of silverware in 1942. Occupational therapy programs, such as that operated by the War Veterans Art Center at Manhattan's Museum of Modern Art between 1944 and 1948, introduced silversmithing to many veterans. Silversmith Margret Craver (1907–) directed precious metal refiner and supplier Handy and Harman's New York City–based Hospital Service Program 1944–46 and then initiated the firm's not-for-profit Crafts Service Department. She organized a series of five summer workshops for metalsmithing instructors between 1947 and 1951 at the Rhode Island School of Design, generating films and booklets covering various techniques. Among those participating was Earl Pardon of Skidmore College.

New training programs and exhibit venues promoted gold- and silversmithing within New York State after World War II. The School for American Craftsmen (SAC, now Crafts), which began in Hanover, NH, in association with Dartmouth College, relocated in July 1946 to Alfred University and joined the Rochester Institute of Technology in 1950, with John Prip, a New York City native, as head of jewelry and silversmithing. Prip and Ronald Hayes Pearson (1924–96), who was trained at Elverhoj and SAC, helped found Rochester's innovative, artisan-managed crafts gallery Studio One (1953). Today, Manhattan's Crafts Students League and the 92nd Street Y, like arts organizations statewide, offer avocational courses in metalsmithing. University coursework in metalsmithing is offered at SUNY New Paltz, the Fashion Institute of Technology, and Skidmore College, as well as at SAC.

Braznell, W. Scott. "The Early Career of Ronald Hayes Pearson and the Post–World War II Revival of American Silversmithing and Jewelrymaking," *Winterthur Portfolio* 34 (Winter 1999): 185–213
Waters, Deborah Dependahl, ed. *Elegant Plate: Three Centuries of Precious Metals in New York City* (New York: Museum of the City of New York, 2000)

Deborah Dependahl Waters

Goler, George W(ashington) (*b* Brooklyn, 24 Aug 1864; *d* Rochester, 18 Sept 1940). Health officer. Goler was educated in the Brooklyn public schools and in 1884 moved to Rochester. He received his MD from the University of Buffalo in 1889 and became assistant physician at the Infants Summer Hospital (now Crestwood Children's Center) in Charlotte (Monroe Co) in 1891. In 1892 he became health inspector for the Rochester Board of Health and in 1896 was promoted to health officer. He established municipal milk stations in 1897 to provide pasteurized milk to infants and children, reducing the death toll of children aged 0–5 from 7,451 in 1887–96 to 4,965 in 1897–1906. In 1904 he instituted municipal prenatal clinics and established the Rochester Municipal Hospital for Infectious Diseases. Goler was tireless and outspoken in his crusade for proper sanitation, and he made enemies of many for whom that proved expensive or inconvenient. In 1932 he resigned, complaining that interference by ward politicians had created an intolerable situation for him and his department. Goler lectured on preventive medicine at the Medical School of the University of Rochester and was a prolific writer on health-related topics.

See also PUBLIC HEALTH.

Rosenberg-Naparsteck, Ruth. "Life and Death in 19th Century Rochester," *Rochester History* 45 (Jan, Apr 1983): 3–11

Joann Minor

golf. The St. Andrew's Golf Club in Yonkers is believed by many to be the first golf course in the United States. John Reid had clubs shipped to him from his native Scotland, and on 12 Feb 1888, he and a few friends played a few holes on a triangular three-hole course constructed across the street from his home.

Early Golf Courses

Golf courses were built and clubs formed soon after Reid started St. Andrew's. America's first sporting community was built by Pierre Lorillard in Tuxedo Park (Orange Co) in the late 1880s, and golf was offered there in 1889. The Champlain Hotel Golf Course (now Bluff Point Golf Resort) was built in Plattsburgh in 1890, and two years later the Shinnecock Hills Golf Club was established in Southampton (Suffolk Co) and quickly became the social center of the region. Golf was popular with the women of Shinnecock, who had their own nine-hole course. Beatrix Hoyt of Shinnecock Hills became a teenage sports star by winning three consecutive US Women's Amateurs in the late 1890s. Shinnecock Hills and St. Andrew's were two of

Golfing at West Point, *ca* 1906.

the five founding clubs of the United States Golf Association (USGA) in 1894. The first authentic public golf course in the United States was Van Cortlandt Park, which opened in 1895 in what is now the Bronx. The course, built by New York City at the suggestion of the wealthy residents of Riverdale, was quickly dominated by the city's working class golfers.

The Metropolitan Golf Association (MGA), which now reaches into the Hudson Valley, was founded in 1897 and is now based in Elmsford (Westchester Co). The Hudson River Golf Association, established in 1902, complemented the MGA, extending golf associations deeper into the state. Robert White, the golf pro at Wykagyl Country Club in New Rochelle (Westchester Co), was instrumental in the organization of the Professional Golfers' Association of America (PGA) in 1916. The PGA held its first championship at Siwanoy Country Club in Bronxville (Westchester Co) later that year. The New York State Golf Association, organized in 1923, is now based in Syracuse.

Early 20th-Century Golfers

At the turn of the 20th century, Garden City Golf Club in Garden City (Nassau Co) was one of the landmark courses in the United States. Garden City's Walter Travis, an Australian who moved to the United States as a child, took up golf at age 34 and later won five US Amateurs. He spent his entire golf career living on Long Island and had a great rivalry with Jerry Travers, who grew up in Oyster Bay (Nassau Co). Travers won four US Amateurs and a US Open. Their most famous match took place at the 1908 US Amateur at Garden City, when Travis failed to escape a deep bunker on the 18th green that he had built a few years earlier. Travis used a center-shafted putter to become the first American to win the British Amateur in 1904. General Electric engineer Arthur F. Knight began designing and building the putter in Schenectady, in 1901. He patented the design in 1903, and Travis's victory with the putter the next year made it a commercial success.

The 1911 US Amateur at the Apawamis Club in Rye (Westchester Co) had a dramatic and controversial conclusion. British amateur Harold Hilton waltzed through to the finals, where the pro-American gallery had its moment when Fred Herreshoff closed a huge gap to force extra holes. Hilton won on the 37th hole when his seemingly errant approach shot bounced off a rock (henceforth called Hilton's Rock) and onto the green for a winning par. The debate raged for years about whether he played the shot intentionally to the right or just got a lucky bounce. Another miracle shot came from Bobby Jones at the 1923 US Open at Inwood Country Club (Nassau Co); Jones won his first major tournament after surviving a collapse at the end of the fourth round and a back-and-forth play-off round with Scot Bobby Cruickshank. The winning blow was a remarkable 190 yd (174 m) mid-iron from the rough over a wide lagoon to the final green, a shot *Golf Magazine* called the "Shot of the Century."

Two New York State natives became golf stars during the 1920s: Walter Hagen of Rochester and Gene Sarazen of Harrison (Westchester Co). Hagen won his first PGA Championship at Inwood in 1921 and won four more titles between 1924 and 1927. Sarazen was the only man to challenge Hagen during his streak of dominance. In 1922 Sarazen beat Hagen in the first World's Championship, played at the Westchester Country Club; in 1923 at Pelham (Westchester Co), Sarazen won on the second play-off hole, hitting a wedge shot from deep rough close to the hole. Sarazen also won the 1932 US Open held at Fresh Meadow in Great Neck (Nassau Co).

New York State women were also atop golf's hierarchy in the 1920s. Marion Hollins won the US Women's Amateur in 1921 and went on to found the Women's National Golf and Tennis Club. Her supremacy among the women was challenged by Helen "Billie" Hicks, who won the 1931 US Women's Amateur at the Country Club of Buffalo and then became America's first female golf professional four years later. Hicks also played on the first American Curtis Cup team.

The state's most prominent family of golfers, the seven Turnesa brothers from Elmsford (Westchester Co), enjoyed prominence from the 1920s into the 1950s. Joe Turnesa was second to Walter Hagen in the 1927 PGA, Mike Turnesa was second to Sam Snead in the 1942 PGA and to Ben Hogan in the 1948 PGA, and Jim Turnesa won the PGA in 1952. Perhaps the best of the brothers was Willie, the only one to remain an amateur. Willie won the 1939 and 1940 US Amateur and 1948 British Amateur and was a successful Walker Cup player and captain.

Golf since World War II

The depression and World War II had a debilitating effect on golf throughout the country, but golf grew in popularity in the lower Catskills in the postwar era. Outstanding courses constructed in 1957 at the Concord Resort and Golf Club and in Liberty at Kiamesha Lake (Sullivan Co) were followed by the Monster at the Concord, regarded by many professionals as the toughest in the country after its completion in 1964. Oak Hill Country Club in Rochester grew in prominence after the war as well, hosting the 1949 US Amateur as well as the 1956 and 1968 US Opens. In 1968 Lee Trevino won his first professional tournament in the US Open at Oak Hill, becoming the first golfer to shoot four consecutive sub-70 rounds in the US Open. Among other championships, Oak Hill hosted the 1995 Ryder Cup and the 2002 PGA Championship. Several male New York State golfers had success on the professional tour at the end of the 20th century. Jeff Sluman, born in Rochester, won the 1988 PGA Championship as well as 5 other tour events; Wayne Levi, who was born in Little Falls (Herkimer Co), has 12 tour wins. Joey Sindelar, a resident of Horseheads (Chemung Co), won 6 times on tour, and Mike Hulbert, born in Elmira, has 3 tour wins.

Among professional women golfers, Betsy Rawls and Susie Maxwell both won a pair of US Women's Opens in the state, one each at Winged Foot Golf Club in Mamaroneck (Westchester Co) and the Country Club of Rochester, Rawls in the 1950s, Maxwell in the 1970s. Rawls's victory at Winged Foot in 1957 came at the expense of Jackie Pung, who had won the tournament but was disqualified for signing an incorrect scorecard. Carol Mann, a native of Buffalo, had 38 wins on the Ladies Professional Golf Association (LPGA) Tour, including the 1965 US Women's Open, and has been elected to the LPGA Hall of Fame. Dottie Pepper of Saratoga Springs won the New York State Women's Amateur and Girls' Amateur Championships in 1981 and has gone on to a successful career on the LPGA Tour, with 15 victories, including 2 majors—the Nabisco Dinah Shore in 1992 and 1999. In 1995 she reached the $3 million mark in earnings faster than any woman had done so. Wykagyl Country Club has a long history with the LPGA Tour, hosting the Girl Talk Classic, Golden Lights, Chrysler-Plymouth Tournament of Champions, Master Card International, and, since 1990, the JAL Big Apple Classic.

Notable Courses and Designers

Many of the golfers in New York State have had the opportunity to play on courses created by the sport's top designers. Charles Blair Macdonald, who was born in Niagara Falls, Ont, and educated in Scotland, was influential in the formation of the USGA and won the first US Amateur in 1895. Macdonald moved to Long Island in 1900 and devoted several years to the development of the National Golf Links of America in Southampton. He introduced British elements of course design, imitating hole design and features, hoping to elevate American golf course architecture. The course opened to rave reviews in 1911, as did his subsequent course on Lido Beach (Nassau Co), a course that was reclaimed from marshland between the Atlantic Ocean and the Reynolds Channel. During the 1920s

MAJOR GOLF CHAMPIONSHIPS HELD IN NEW YORK STATE

Year	Course and Location	Winner
US Open		
1896	Shinnecock Hills Golf Club, Southampton (Suffolk Co)	James Foulis
1902	Garden City Golf Club, Garden City (Nassau Co)	Laurie Auchterlonie
1912	Country Club of Buffalo	John McDermott
1923	Inwood Country Club, Hempstead (Nassau Co)	Bobby Jones
1929	Winged Foot Golf Club, Mamaroneck (Westchester Co)	Bobby Jones
1932	Fresh Meadow Country Club, Flushing (Queens Co)	Gene Sarazen
1956	Oak Hill Country Club, Rochester	Cary Middlecoff
1959	Winged Foot	Billy Casper
1968	Oak Hill	Lee Trevino
1974	Winged Foot	Hale Irwin
1984	Winged Foot	Fuzzy Zoeller
1986	Shinnecock Hills	Ray Floyd
1989	Oak Hill	Curtis Strange
1995	Shinnecock Hills	Corey Pavin
2002	Bethpage State Park, Farmingdale (Nassau Co)	Tiger Woods
PGA Championship		
1916	Siwanoy Country Club, Bronxville (Westchester Co)	Jim Barnes
1919	Engineers Country Club, Roslyn (Nassau Co)	Jim Barnes
1921	Inwood	Walter Hagen
1923	Pelham Golf Club, Pelham Manor (Westchester Co)	Gene Sarazen
1926	Salisbury Golf Links, Westbury (Cayuga Co)	Walter Hagen
1930	Fresh Meadow	Tommy Armour
1939	Pomonok Country Club, Flushing (Queens Co)	Henry Picard
1980	Oak Hill	Jack Nicklaus
1997	Winged Foot	Davis Love III
2003	Oak Hill	Shaun Micheel
US Women's Open		
1953	Country Club of Rochester	Betsy Rawls
1957	Winged Foot	Betsy Rawls
1972	Winged Foot	Susie Maxwell Berning
1973	Country Club of Rochester	Susie Maxwell Berning
Senior Open		
1980	Winged Foot	Robert De Vicenzo
1984	Oak Hill	Miller Barber
US Amateur		
1896	Shinnecock Hills	H. J. Whigham
1900	Garden City	Walter Travis
1903	Nassau Country Club, Glen Cove (Nassau Co)	Walter Travis
1908	Garden City	Jerry Travers
1911	Apawamis Club, Rye (Westchester Co)	Harold Hilton
1913	Garden City	Jerry Travers
1920	Engineers	Charles Evans Sr
1936	Garden City	John Fischer
1940	Winged Foot	Richard Chapman
1949	Oak Hill	Charles Coe
1998	Oak Hill	Hank Kuehne
Women's Amateur		
1895	Meadow Brook Club, Hempstead [now in Nassau Co]	Mrs. C. S. Brown
1898	Ardsley Club, Ardsley-on-Hudson (Westchester Co)	Beatrix Hoyt
1900	Shinnecock Hills	Frances Griscom
1914	Nassau	Kate Harley
1923	Westchester-Biltmore Country Club, Rye (Westchester Co)	Edith Cummings
1927	Cherry Valley Club, Garden City (Nassau Co)	Miriam Burns Horn
1931	Country Club of Buffalo	Helen Hicks
1962	Country Club of Rochester	JoAnne Gunderson

Compiled by William Quirin

National and Lido were widely regarded as two of the three best courses in the United States. Macdonald also was involved with the design of the course at Sleepy Hollow Country Club in Westchester Co and the courses at Piping Rock Club and the Creek Club, both on Long Island's North Shore. Piping Rock was a focal point of 1920s social activity, and the Creek was conceived as a quiet refuge for select Piping Rock members.

A. W. Tillinghast designed courses at three future US Open venues in New York State during the early 1920s. He designed the East and West courses at Winged Foot and the course at Fresh Meadow. In 1934 Tillinghast designed the Black Course at Bethpage State Park, his last New York State design. Like the other courses at Bethpage, it suffered through periods of neglect but rose from the weeds in splendor to host the 2002 US Open, the showcase for Tiger Woods's first major victory in New York State.

Cornell University has played an important role in golf's evolution. Cornell was one of the first universities to introduce a program of study in the late 1920s for prospective club managers. The program grew out the hotel management program. Robert Trent Jones designed his own major in golf course architecture at Cornell that prepared him for an illustrious career designing golf courses worldwide. Among his best courses in New York State are those at Albany Country Club, Crag Burn Golf Club in East Aurora (Erie Co), the Tuxedo Club in Tuxedo Park (Orange Co), and Wiltwyck Golf Club in Kingston (Ulster Co). Anglebrook Golf Club in Lincolndale (Westchester Co) was the last course in his portfolio.

Saratoga National in Saratoga Springs, Trump National in Briarcliff Manor (Westchester Co), Hudson National in Croton-on-Hudson (Westchester Co), and Manhattan Woods in West Nyack (Rockland Co) all may soon appear in the national rankings. In 2003 New York State had 886 golf courses (9- and 18-hole courses), of which 11 were nationally or internationally ranked; 447 courses were public, 235 were private, 164 were semiprivate, 39 were part of resort complexes, and 1 was designated for military use.

Lonnstrom, Douglas. *A History of Golf in New York's Capital Region* (Slingerlands, NY: CML Press, 1998)
Martin, J. Peter. *Adirondack Golf Courses: Past and Present* (Lake Placid, NY: Adirondack Golf, 1987)
McCarthy John F. *The Beauty of Golf in New York State* (Auburn, NY: Summerfield House, 1989)
Quirin, William. *Golf Clubs of the MGA* (Elmsford, NY: Golf Magazine Properties, 1997)
———. *America's Linksland* (Chelsea, Mich: Sleeping Bear Press, 2002)
The Women's Metropolitan Golf Association, 1899–1999 (Virginia Beach, Va: Q Publishing, 1999)

William Quirin

Gompers, Samuel (*b* London, 27 Jan 1850; *d* San Antonio, 13 Dec 1924). Labor leader. Gompers attended the Jewish Free School in London for 4 years, leaving at age 10 for an apprenticeship in cigar making. The family immigrated to the United States in 1863, initially settling on Manhattan's Lower East Side. A cigar maker, Gompers increasingly became active in labor issues, organizing the United Cigarmakers in 1873, which joined two years later as a local of the Cigar Makers International Union. He was chairman of the union's constitutional committee and together with national officials helped establish workers' benefits, such as sick relief and unemployment compensation, as well as a centralized union structure. In 1881 Gompers helped organize the Federation of Organized Trades and Labor Unions to lobby Congress and state legislatures for laws to benefit labor. The federation had little influence, however. In 1886 Gompers was a leading architect in the founding of the American Federation of Labor (AFL). Elected as AFL president in 1886, he held this position almost continuously until his death. He ran the union for many years from his Manhattan home, and the AFL reflected his labor philosophy of focusing on immediate economic interests such as collective bargaining and legislative issues affecting workers while rejecting broad political or social solutions.

Gompers, Samuel. *Seventy Years of Life and Labor: An Autobiography.* Ed. Nick Salvatore (Ithaca: ILR Press, 1984)

John Cashman

Goodell, Charles E(llsworth) (*b* Jamestown, Chautauqua Co, 16 Mar 1926; *d* Washington, DC, 21 Jan 1987). Raised in Jamestown, Goodell graduated from Williams College in Williamstown, Mass, before serving in the navy during World War II. He then earned degrees in government and law at Yale University before joining the air force during the Korean conflict. A congressional liaison for the Department of Justice in 1954, Goodell returned to Jamestown the following year to begin his law practice. Local Republicans tapped him to run for Congress in a 1959 special election. Winning a House seat, Goodell aligned himself with Republican moderates. In 1965 he joined a group of Republican members of Congress known as the "Young Turks" who helped Gerald R. Ford become House minority leader. After Sen Robert F. Kennedy's assassination in 1968, Gov Nelson A. Rockefeller appointed Goodell to serve out Kennedy's term. In the Senate, Goodell was a prominent critic of Pres Richard M. Nixon's conduct of the Vietnam War, and the administration actively opposed him in his 1970 campaign to win a full Senate term. Defeated by a conservative third party candidate, Goodell resumed practicing law in New York City and Washington, DC. He also served in the Ford administration, first as an informal advisor to the president and then as chairman of the Clemency Review Board (1974–75), which reviewed applications by war resisters hoping to return to the United States. He chaired DGA International, a lobbying firm, from 1974 until his death.

Goodell, Charles E. Papers. New York City Public Library
———. *Political Prisoners in America* (New York: Random House, 1973)

Timothy Sullivan

Goodell, William (*b* Coventry, Chenango Co, 25 Oct 1792; *d* Janesville, Wisc, 14 Feb 1878). Editor, reformer, and political abolitionist. Following a career in business, Goodell became editor of a New York City temperance paper in 1830 and organized the New York City Anti-Slavery Society and the American Anti-Slavery Society (AAS) in 1833. After editing the AAS's periodical, the *Emancipator,* in New York City (1833–35) and the New York State Anti-Slavery Society's paper, the *Friend of Man,* in Utica (1836–42), he became the unordained pastor (1843–52) of a nonsectarian abolitionist church that he established in Honeoye (Ontario Co). A Liberty Party founder, Goodell led a Liberty Party faction that refused to join the Free Soil Party at an 1847 meeting held in Macedon Lock (Wayne Co). In the 1850s and 1860s, he edited the paper of this Liberty faction, the *Radical Abolitionist* (later *Principia*), in New York City. He became the party's nominee for president (1852) and its candidate for New York State governor (1860). In 1865 Goodell moved out of New York State, going first to Connecticut and then to Wisconsin. Goodell helped organize the Prohibition Party in 1869.

Strong, Douglas M. *Perfectionist Politics: Abolitionism and the Religious Tensions of American Democracy* (Syracuse: Syracuse Univ Press, 1999)

Douglas M. Strong

good-government reform. Political reform movement that sought to reduce bossism and corruption in politics beginning in the 1870s and reaching its zenith before World War I. New York State perhaps had the greatest number of good-government organizations in the nation. Membership, centered in cities, drew mostly from the business community and the medical, legal, and kindred professions. By 1894 active good-government associations included a significant number of these nonpartisan municipal organizations. In Buffalo, for example, specific reform groups included the Citizen's Association, the Commission Government Association, the Corrupt Practices Association, and the Referendum League. Albany had the Citizens Association, and in Troy (Rensselaer Co), a Committee of Public Safety was formed, chiefly to ensure an honest ballot.

An early victory for these reformers was New York State's adoption in 1890 of an official ballot to be used in general elections, prepared at public expense, which lent to greater secrecy in voting. In 1894 reformers, including New York City's Joseph H. Choate and Elihu Root Jr, gained another victory when numerous proposals to ensure honest elections, which Choate and Root had sponsored, were adopted at the 1894 Constitutional Convention. They included the introduction of voting machines, the creation of bipartisan election boards, and personal registration for voting. In 1912 the newly established Municipal Government Association of New York State presented its agenda to the New York Conference of Mayors, which included nonpartisan municipal elections, centralized authority in municipal government through a strong mayor-council or commission structure (adding the city manager plan in 1913), and merit selection of civil servants. The City of Brooklyn adopted a "strong-mayor" charter in 1881, and New York City did the same in 1898, with a number of cities across the state emulating them.

In New York City the prestigious City Club of New York was founded in 1892 to promote honesty and efficiency in city government, and two years later the club played a key role in electing anti-Tammany candidate William L. Strong (Republican) as mayor. In 1901 another anti-Tammany candidate, Seth Low, was elected mayor, principally through the help of the reformist Citizens Union of the City of New York (1897). In Rochester, reformer Joseph T. Alling started a good-government movement in the mid-1890s to challenge George W. Aldridge, the local Republican boss. The positions Aldridge held, chairman of the city's executive board, mayor, and state superintendent of public works, made him the chief distributor of patronage and ensured his dominance over city and Monroe Co government. Alling's efforts resulted in a two-term electoral victory for his mayoral candidate, Democrat George E. Warner (1896–1900). Warner's victory enabled Rochester reformers to depoliticize the public school system, get a charter for the city, and empower the mayor to make appointments.

By the mid-1890s good-government reformers were labeled disparagingly by their critics as "goo-goos." Many party regulars thought the goo-goos to be dilettantes, who did not understand how patronage created a system of mutual obligation crucial for the success of the party system. Tammany politico George Washington Plunkitt famously said in 1905 that reformers were "morning glories" who looked lovely in the morning but soon withered because they did not have a network of committed supporters. Beginning in the early 1900s the established parties were increasingly forced to accommodate the demands of reformers to maintain their electoral viability. Democrat Thomas Mott Osborne of Auburn (Cayuga Co), a reformer, organized a state conference in Saratoga Springs in 1909 that created the Democratic League of New York State to rid the party of bossism beyond New York City. The pressure became so intense that by 1910 Tammany boss Charles F. Murphy and the Democratic gubernatorial candidate Alfred E. Smith felt that there was no other political choice but to adopt a party platform of social reform.

McCormick, Richard L. *From Realignment to Reform: Political Change in New York State, 1893–1910* (Ithaca: Cornell Univ Press, 1981)

Bernard Hirschhorn

Good Peter [Agwerondongwas] (*b* Oquaga [now Windsor and Colesville, Broome Co], *ca* 1715; *d* 1792). Oneida leader. Taught by the missionaries to read and write English, in 1748 Good Peter converted to Christianity and soon began preaching in Oquaga and often spoke out for temperance. Starting in the mid-1760s, Good Peter was a deacon to Samuel Kirkland, the Presbyterian missionary to the Oneida, gaining a reputation for eloquence and the sobriquet "Peter the Priest." He served the American cause during the Revolutionary War as an emissary and was imprisoned by the British at Fort Niagara [now in Porter, Niagara Co]. After the losses of Oneida land following the Treaty of Fort Schuyler (1788), he thought himself betrayed by Kirkland and tricked by Gov George Clinton. In the early 1790s Good Peter educated Timothy Pickering, George Washington's commissioner to the Six Nations on Iroquoian mores and beliefs, which played a vital role in Pickering's dealings and treaty making with the Iroquois in 1794.

Hauptman, Laurence, and L. Gordon McLester, eds. *The Oneida Indian Journey: From New York to Wisconsin, 1784–1860* (Madison, Wisc: Univ of Wisconsin Press, 1999)
Pilkington, Walter, ed. *The Journals of Samuel Kirkland* (Clinton, NY: Hamilton College, 1980)

Thelma C. McLester

Good Roads Movement. Beginning in the 1880s the Good Roads Movement, led by the League of American Wheelmen (LAW), sought the betterment of poorly drained and graded earthen roads. Proponents favored the introduction of professional engineering and new types of equipment to produce and maintain durable rural highways less affected by adverse weather conditions. They also strove to add road-building responsibilities to state and county governments and to have private citizens pay taxes instead of providing labor for road work. In New York State, Issac B. Potter of the LAW, whose watchword was "there is no more common interest than the common roads," was instrumental in organizing the New York Road Improvement Association in 1888. Another organization, the State League for Good Roads, spent the 1890s distributing literature and lobbying to convince the public that improved roads were to everyone's benefit. The Fuller-Plank Act, passed by the state legislature in 1898, allowed counties to adopt a money taxation system. That same year the Higbie-Armstrong Act created a system of county highways, with construction costs paid 50% by the state, 35% by the counties, and 15% by towns or abutting landowners. Town roads also benefited from state funding and specifications. The federal government became involved in road construction with the 1893 establishment of the Office of Road Inquiry to survey and advise on road construction. The first federally supervised demonstration highway in the United States was built at Geneva (Ontario Co) in 1896 and 1897 with local funding and donated labor and equipment.

Opposition to the Good Roads Movement came initially from agricultural property owners, who feared an increased tax burden. By the early 20th century, however, farmers became proponents of highway improvement. Railroads, which had earlier campaigned for road improvements to funnel agricultural traffic to rail stations, in the 1910s withdrew their support as plans for an interurban road network arose. With the waning of the LAW in the 1900s, other road improvement advocates came to the fore, namely motorists and automobile manufacturers.

Mason, Philip P. "The League of American Wheelmen and the Good-Roads Movement, 1880–1905" (PhD diss, Univ of Michigan, 1957)

Geoffrey N. Stein

Gorham. Town (pop 3,776) in SE Ontario Co. Settled in 1789, the town was formed as Easton in 1796. It was renamed Lincoln in 1806 and became Gorham in 1807. Level in the north and hilly in the south, its southwestern part is called Vine Valley for its grape crop. An early thrashing machine was manufactured by John Stowits in 1835. Cottage City, where the first summer cottage was built in 1878, became a steamboat landing. Much of Gorham's Canandaigua Lake shoreline was divided into narrow lots before 1911. Crystal Beach, a resort colony, was surveyed in 1929 but never developed. The annual Pageant of Bands has been held since 1960.

Marla A. Bennett

Gorky, Arshile [Adoian, Vosdanig Manoog] (*b* Khorkom [now in Turkey], 15 Apr 1904; *d* Sherman, Conn, 21 July 1948). Painter. He fled his native country at age 16 after his mother's death during the Turkish persecution of Armenians. He arrived in the United States in 1920 and settled in New York City in 1924. Shortly thereafter he took on the pseudonym Arshile Gorky, claiming to be related to the radical Russian writer Maxim Gorky. The artist essentially taught himself through visiting museums and art galleries. He studied at the Grand Central School of Art but quickly advanced from student to teacher and continued to be affiliated with the school for much of his career. In the late 1920s and early 1930s, Gorky began to paint cubist still lifes. He painted poignant portraits of his family, including two versions of *The Artist and His Mother* (1926–29), inspired by a 1912 photograph, and from 1932 to 1934 worked on a series of abstract black-and-white drawings, *Nighttime, Enigma, Nostalgia.* From 1935 until 1941 he painted abstract murals (no longer extant) on the theme of aviation for the Works Progress Administration's Federal Art Project for the 1939–40 New York World's Fair. In the early 1940s Gorky's dealer, Julien Levy, introduced him to Surrealists such as Roberto Matta Echaurren and André Breton, who had recently arrived in New York City, and Gorky adapted their theories and designs. In this period he created many of the works for which he is most renowned. These abstractions combine memories of his Armenian childhood with surrealist fantasies, resulting in evocative, imaginary landscapes such as *Garden in Sochi* (1941) and *The Liver Is the Cock's Comb* (1944). Gorky's experiments with abstraction had a great impact on the development of New York school artists. In 1945 Levy presented Gorky's work in a one-man show, the success of which allowed the artist to work without financial worries for the first time. A series of devastating disasters began the next year. Gorky and his family had moved to Sherman in September 1945, and in January 1946 a fire in his studio there destroyed many of his drawings and paintings. In March 1946 he had an operation related to cancer. In June 1948 a car accident fractured his neck and paralyzed his painting arm, and the next month his wife and two daughters left him. A few days later an extremely depressed Gorky committed suicide in his studio.

Jordan, Jim M., and Robert Goldwater. *The Paintings of Arshile Gorky: A Critical Catalogue* (New York: New York Univ Press, 1982)
Spender, Matthew. *From a High Place: A Life of Arshile Gorky* (Berkeley: Univ of California Press, 2000)

Dana Pilson

Goshen. Town (pop 12,913) and village (pop 5,676) in central Orange Co. Settled between 1703 and 1714, Goshen formed as a precinct in 1714, although its records date only to 1722. It became the half-shire town for Orange Co in 1727. Recognized as a town in 1788, it was named the county seat in 1798. The village, which had been platted in 1721, was incorporated in 1809 and again in 1843. Goshen was the center of a rich dairy district producing famed Goshen butter, but the Erie Railroad (1841) encouraged a shift to fluid milk. In 1838 the Historic Track, a harness-racing facility that operates in the summer months, was founded in the village. Goshen industries included cut-glass production along with the Newbury Foundry (1896) and the Coates-Goshen Manufacturing Co (1908; automobiles). The Drowned Lands in the town's southwest corner were reclaimed beginning *ca* 1835; after 1910 Polish farmers made it an important truck-farming district. First- and second-generation Dutch farmers and traders founded Goshen Christian Reformed Church (1934) and Goshen Christian School (1948). The four-lane Rte 17 (I-86) was built 1951–55, making Goshen more accessible by automobile, and in the early 21st century, it has many commuters. The town's 1960 population essentially doubled by 1990. In 2000 the racial composition of the town was 89% white and 7% African American; 7% were of Latino. The village has many remarkable historic buildings, including the Richard Upjohn–designed St. John's Episcopal Church (1855), with Tiffany windows and a Cass Gilbert altar; the Greek Revival courthouse (1841); and the Goshen Inn (1912). Goshen is the site of the Harness Racing Museum and Hall of Fame (1951).

Goshen Historic Track. North America's oldest active harness track. Opening in 1838 in an effort to stop Goshen (Orange Co) townsfolk from racing their horses down Main St, the racetrack was converted from an informal circus ring to a one-third mile oval in 1854, to a one-half mile rectangular track in 1858, and to a one-half mile oval in 1873. In 1911 the track became part of trotting's Grand Circuit, and in 1966 the National Park Service designated it a National Historic Landmark. The last private owner, E. Roland Harriman, died in 1978, leaving a will stipulating that the property be used for recreational and cultural purposes, but not for pari-mutuel betting. In 1979 the Harriman Foundation transferred ownership to the nonprofit Goshen Historic Track Inc, which conducts races without the benefit of pari-mutuel profits and hosts concerts, fairs, and other community events. In the mid-1980s, an all-weather surface of crushed stone replaced the old clay oval, permitting year-round use as a training facility.

Sharts, Elizabeth. *Cradle of the Trotter: Goshen in the History of the American Turf* (Goshen, NY: Book Mill, 1946)

Elizabeth Redkey

gospel and school lands. In 1781, late in the Revolutionary War, the state legislature passed a law intended to raise two regiments of troops for frontier service. In appropriating land bounties to those who served, it described townships to be surveyed, specifying that 500 acres (202 ha) be set aside for the support of the gospel and 360 acres (146 ha) for the use of schools. In subsequent acts, the policy was continued with varying acreage. In 1784 the legislature created the Commissioners of the Land Office with the power to execute these promises. In the Chenango Twenty Townships, the allocation was 250 acres (101 ha) for each purpose, but the lots themselves were sold and the Canastota Tract in Sullivan and Lenox (Madison Co) were given in their place in 1805–8; the proceeds were then divided among the towns. In the St. Lawrence Ten Towns, schools and the gospel shared 1 mi^2 (3 km^2), and an identical tract was designated for the Literature Fund, a statewide school fund. In addition, some private land developers made gifts of land in towns they owned. With the 1814 common school funding law, education received permanent state support, and in 1823 the legislature designated all public land not appropriated to the Common School Fund. As late as 1859 the state still held 49,581 acres (20,065 ha) for this purpose.

"Gospel and School Lots." In *The Constitutional History of New York,* 5 vols, Charles Z. Lincoln (Rochester: Lawyers Cooperative Publishing, 1906)

"Lands." In *Gazetteer of the State of New York,* John Homer French (Syracuse: R. Pearsall Smith, 1860)

Gould, Jay [Jason] (*b* Roxbury, Delaware Co, 27 May 1836; *d* New York City, 2 Dec 1892). Entrepreneur and speculator. Gould spent his youth on his family's farm and attended local academies. His capacity for hard physical and mental labor was matched by an uncanny business insight that manifested itself in early adolescence. By the age of 17 Gould had become a successful surveyor. Two years later he wrote and published a history of Delaware Co. After establishing a tannery in a village named Gouldsboro in the mountains of Pennsylvania, he moved to New York City in 1860, achieving notable successes as a speculator in the volatile wartime securities market. In 1867, with Daniel Drew and Jim Fisk as allies, he became embroiled in a celebrated battle against Cornelius Vanderbilt for control of the Erie Railroad. Removed as a director of the Erie in 1872, Gould then channeled his energies into the financing and construction of the great transcontinental rail lines. In 1878 he established himself as a Hudson Valley squire at Irvington (Westchester Co), where he purchased Lyndhurst, a Gothic Revival mansion designed by Alexander Jackson Davis. From 1879 to 1883 Gould owned the *New York World* newspaper. In 1881 he gained control of the Western Union Telegraph Co and by 1886 had full ownership of the New York Elevated Railroad Co. At his death he left a fortune, conservatively estimated at $77 million.

Klein, Maury. *The Life and Legend of Jay Gould* (Baltimore: John Hopkins Univ Press, 1986)

William S. Helmer

Goulds Pumps. In 1848 Seabury S. Gould, proprietor of a dry goods shop in Seneca Falls (Seneca Co), purchased an interest in that town's pump manufacturing firm of Downs, Mynderse and Co at Green and Ovid Sts. In 1849 the first all-iron pumps were cast by the company, and they proved vastly superior to the all-wood pumps of that time. Iron pumps came into great demand in the late 19th century, when water-filling stations at train stops (previously relying on windmills to pump water) now needed all-metal steam-powered pumps to meet the demands of transcontinental rail service. A new factory was built in 1855 between the Seneca Canal and the Seneca River. In 1869 the firm became the Goulds Manufacturing Co with Gould as president. Construction of an industrial complex covering 70 acres (28 ha) began in 1898. Norman Gould, grandson of the founder, served as president from 1908 to 1964. In 1926 the name was changed to Goulds Pumps, Inc. During World War II Goulds became a major supplier of pumps to the military, especially the US Navy. The company merged with ITT Industries in 1997. Corporate headquarters are in Seneca Falls.

Connell, Coleman. *The Goulds Pumps Story, 1848–1998: A Century and One-Half "Doing It Right"* (1998)

Madelynn P. Fredrickson

Gouverneur [GUV-A-NOOR]. Town (pop 7,418) and village (pop 4,263) in SW St. Lawrence Co. The town was settled in 1805 by a group of settlers who walked from the head of Lake George in seven days guided by a compass. It formed in 1810 from Oswegatchie; the village was incorporated in 1850. The Rome, Watertown and Ogdensburg Railroad initiated service in 1854. Important industries have included lumber, wood pulp and paper, talc mining (1876), marble quarrying (*ca* 1880–1941), and, in the 20th century, silk hosiery and lace. In the early 21st century Gouverneur is the business center of western St. Lawrence Co, with mining (zinc, talc, marble), construction trades, and structural steel. It lies within commuting distance of Fort Drum (Jefferson Co). Other employers include the headquarters of the regional Kinney Drugs (1903) chain and the Gouverneur Correctional Facility (1990). Dairy farming continues in the town. Gouverneur native Edward J. Noble (1882–1958) developed the Life Saver Candy Co and founded the ABC network. A giant Life Savers pack was placed in a village park in 1987. Gouverneur is the site of the St. Lawrence County Fair (1859).

Richard E. Mooers

government. See CITY GOVERNMENT; COUNTY GOVERNMENT; LOCAL GOVERNMENT JURISDICTIONS; STATE GOVERNMENT AND SERVICES; TOWN GOVERNMENT; VILLAGE GOVERNMENT.

governor. A strong governorship is a New York State historic legacy. In 1777 the state's first governor, unlike those of the other original states, was elected popularly rather than by legislature for three years instead of one, with no limit on succession. The powers of the governorship were consolidated in accord with the progressive model by reforms championed in the early 20th century by Gov Charles Evans Hughes (1907–10), a Republican, and Gov Alfred E. Smith (1919–20, 1923–28), a Democrat.

Gubernatorial power is derived not only from state constitutional provisions. Added strength may flow from a perceived mandate, based on the size of the governor's election victory. After election, governors inherit their party's leadership, another extraconstitutional source of support. Partly because it is the focal point of media attention, the governorship in the popular mind *is* the state government. In the absence of a major crisis or scandal, this gives advantage to the governor within the state political system. With opinion polling now a regular feature of public life, the measured ebb and flow of popular perceptions of gubernatorial performance also affects executive power. New York City's status as a world financial, media, and cultural center also elevates the visibility of the New York State governorship and enriches the pool of skilled people upon whom the governor may call for help. The presidential aspirations and prospects of the governor, a constant in modern New York State politics, has a similar impact. Governors also bring particular personal strengths that combine in unique ways with the formal and informal powers of the office. Gov De Witt Clinton (1817–22, 1825–28), steeped in New York City's intellectual and cultural life, had the connections of a deeply entrenched political family. Gov Grover Cleveland (1883–84) was known for his personal probity and work ethic. Gov Nelson A. Rockefeller (1959–73) brought a world-renowned name, great private wealth, and personal charisma. Gov Hugh Carey (1975–82) had a quick wit and great political courage in the face of crisis.

The institutional governorship has four key staff offices with distinctive but overlapping duties at its center. These are headed by the secretary to the governor, the counsel to the governor, and the director of state operations, all located in the Executive Chamber and staffed at the governor's discretion, and the budget director, who heads a division largely staffed by career professionals. The secretary is principally responsible for policy development. The counsel prepares and tracks legislation and manages the governor's legislative program. The director of state operations is charged with pursing gubernatorial priorities in program implementation. The budget director leads in developing the central policy document in state government and putting it into effect. The importance of some staff positions is linked to the personal relationship between those who hold them and the governor. For example, early in the George E. Pataki administration (1995–) the political and policymaking role of the governor's communications director became significantly more important. Other key staffers coordinate the gubernatorial appointment process and work in Washington, DC, to guard New York State's interests.

In any governorship the role of the lieutenant governor, elected but not necessarily nominated with the governor, depends on political compatibility and a trusting personal relationship. Stan Lundine was a key figure in Mario M. Cuomo's administration (1983–94); Betsy McCaughey Ross was isolated in Pataki's first administration. Some governors have been comfortable having a chief of staff; others have favored a less hierarchical system. Generally, if there was a chief of staff, it was the secretary to the governor. Without such an arrangement, interpersonal chemistry combines with political and fiscal circumstance to affect who within the Executive Chamber will have the most power and influence. Although appointed by the governor and sometimes organized in subcabinets, department and agency heads are not usually considered a part of the institutional governorship. New York State's constitution limits the number of state departments to 20. This has led to including, artificially, many

Gov George Clinton.

operating agencies, offices, and bureaus in a single Executive Department. Most of these cannot rightly be considered part of the institutional governorship, but some are, for example, the state inspector general, the Governor's Office of Employee Relations, and the Governor's Office of Regulatory Reform.

"Great men are not drawn to small office," Nelson A. Rockefeller observed in 1967. The governorship "comprises a substantial grant of authority. And because our governors possess this authority," he continued, "we have enjoyed leadership that has established New York as a pioneering, innovative, and eminently successful state." Several of New York State's chief executives, including Hughes, Smith, Herbert H. Lehman, Thomas E. Dewey, and Rockefeller, can be considered among the leading American governors of the 20th century.

As the 21st century began, the formal powers of the New York State governor were among the strongest in the nation. The governor is elected for four years with no limit on reelection, and all governors but one, W. Averell Harriman (1954–58), elected since the adoption of the four-year term in 1938 have served two terms or more. The state constitution directs the governor to deliver an annual state-of-the-state message and empowers him or her to prepare and present an executive budget. With these powers the chief executive defines the state's policy agenda annually. The veto and item veto powers give the governor a final say over legislation and, because gubernatorial negatives in New York State are rarely overridden, ensures the executive serious negotiating power over bill contents. The direction that the governor "take care that the laws are faithfully executed" and the power to appoint most department heads, subject to advice and consent of the state senate, ensures control of policy implementation. Exceptions are the Department of Education, headed by the legislatively elected Board of Regents, and the Departments of Law and Audit and Control, headed respectively by the attorney general and comptroller, New York's two other independently elected statewide officials. The governor may grant reprieves, commutations, and pardons after criminal conviction. Only in the lack of unilateral authority to reorganize the executive branch is New York State's governor less formally powerful than many other state governors.

See also GUBERNATORIAL ELECTIONS; MORELAND ACT INVESTIGATIONS.

Benjamin, Gerald, and Robert C. Lawton. "New York's Governorship: Back to the Future?" In *Governing New York State,* 4th ed., ed. Jeffrey M. Stonecash (Albany: SUNY Press, 2001)

Beyle, Thad. "Governors: The Middlemen and Women in Our Political System." In *Politics in the American States: A Comparative Analysis,* 6th ed., ed. Virginia Gray and Herbert Jacob (Washington, DC: Congressional Quarterly Press, 1996)

Leibschutz, Sarah F. "The New York Governorship." In *New York Politics and Government,* ed. Sarah F. Leibschutz, et al (Lincoln: Univ of Nebraska Press, 1998)

Gerald Benjamin

GOVERNORS OF NEW YORK STATE

	Dates of Service	Residence
George Clinton (RW, DR, JR)[a]	July 1777–95, 1801–4	Little Britain (Ulster Co)
John Jay (F)	1795–1801	New York City
Morgan Lewis (JR)	1804–7	Rhinebeck (Dutchess Co)
Daniel D. Tompkins (JR)[b]	1807–24 Feb 1817	Tompkinsville (Richmond Co)
John Tayler (JR)[c]	24 Feb 1817–1 July 1817	Albany
De Witt Clinton (CR)	1 July 1817–22[d]; 1825–11 Feb 1828	New York City
Joseph C. Yates (VBR)	1823–24	Schenectady
Nathaniel Pitcher (JD)	11 Feb–31 Dec 1828	Sandy Hill (Washington Co)
Martin Van Buren (JD)	1 Jan–12 Mar 1829	Kinderhook (Columbia Co)
Enos T. Throop (JD)[e]	12 Mar 1829–31 Dec 1832	Auburn (Cayuga Co)
William L. Marcy (JD)	1833–38	Troy (Rensselaer Co)
William H. Seward (W)	1839–42	Auburn (Cayuga Co)
William C. Bouck (D)	1843–44	Fultonham (Schoharie Co)
Silas Wright (D)	1845–46	Canton (St. Lawrence Co)
John Young (W)	1847–48	Geneseo (Livingston Co)
Hamilton Fish (W)	1849–50	New York City
Washington Hunt (W)	1851–52	Lockport (Niagara Co)
Horatio Seymour (D)	1853–54, 1863–64	Deerfield (Oneida Co)
Myron Clark (FR)	1855–56	Canandaigua (Ontario Co)
John A. King (R)	1857–58	Queens
Edwin D. Morgan (R)	1859–62	New York City
Reuben E. Fenton (U)	1865–68	Frewsburg (Chautauqua Co)
John T. Hoffman (D)	1869–72	New York City
John Adams Dix (R)	1873–74	New York City
Samuel J. Tilden (D)	1875–76	New York City
Lucius Robinson (D)	1877–79	Elmira
Alonzo B. Cornell (R)	1880–82	New York City
Grover Cleveland (D)[f]	1883–84	Buffalo
David B. Hill (D)[g]	1885–91	Elmira
Roswell P. Flower (D)	1892–94	New York City
Levi P. Morton (R)	1895–96	Rhinecliff (Dutchess Co)
Frank S. Black (R)	1897–98	Troy (Rensselaer)
Theodore Roosevelt (R)	1899–1900	Oyster Bay (Nassau Co)
Benjamin B. Odell Jr (R)	1901–4	Newburgh (Orange Co)
Frank W. Higgins (R)	1905–6	Olean (Cattaraugus Co)
Charles Evans Hughes (R)[h]	1907–6 Oct 1910	New York City
Horace White (R)[i]	6 Oct–31 Dec 1910	Syracuse
John Alden Dix (D)	1911–12	Thompson (Sullivan Co)
William Sulzer (D)	1 Jan–17 Oct 1913	New York City
Martin H. Glynn (D)[j]	17 Oct 1913–31 Dec 1914	Albany
Charles S. Whitman (R)	1915–18	New York City

Governors Island. Known to local Indians as Pagganck, land of plentiful nuts, and known in the 17th century as Nutten Island. In the early 21st century it encompasses 172 acres (70 ha), half of which is landfill from city subway tunnels, and lies about half a mile south of Manhattan Island. In 1624 Nutten Island was the original center of government of New Netherland and the first settlement in the area of New York Bay. With the purchase of Manhattan Island from the Indians in 1626, government operations and most settlers were transferred to the larger island. Nutten Island was formally purchased from the Indians in 1637, and its structures included a wind-powered sawmill recorded on the 1639 Vingboons map. After Edward Hyde, Viscount Cornbury, built a residence on the island in the early 18th century, it became known as Governors Island. In the colonial period, it was also a garrison and a quarantine site for Palatine refugees.

The federal government acquired Governors Island from New York State in 1800 for use in defending New York City. Three early 19th-century fortifications still stand: Fort Jay, completed 1808; Castle Williams, completed 1811; and the Half-Moon Battery, completed 1812 and later remodeled and renamed the South Battery Officers Club. During the Civil War the island was a Union army depot and prison for captured Confederates. Federal boats left Governors Island to seize German ships and sailors in New York Harbor in the first American action of World War I, when the island served as a depot, and as a training and embarkation center. It also served as headquarters for the eastern theater of operations from 21 Dec 1941 until 9 Sept 1943 during World War II. It was the Coast Guard's largest base from 1966 to 1997, when the island's population rose to 5,000. Six of its buildings are protected by the New York City Landmarks Preservation Commission; 20 acres (8 ha), including Fort Jay and Castle Williams, are a national monument. In November 2002 New York State reacquired the island from the federal government. New York City and New York State have equal representation on the board of the Governors Island Preservation and Education Corp, responsible for the development and administration of the island. In 2003 the Governors Island National Monument was established.

Seitz, Sharon, and Stuart Miller. *The Other Islands of New York City: A Historical Companion* (Woodstock, Vt: Countryman Press, 1996)

Richard E. Mooney

GOVERNORS OF NEW YORK STATE (continued)

	Dates of Service	Residence
Alfred E. Smith (D)	1919–20; 1923–28	New York City
Nathan L. Miller (R)	1921–22	Syracuse
Franklin D. Roosevelt (D)	1929–32	Hyde Park (Dutchess Co)
Herbert H. Lehman (D)[k]	1933–3 Dec 1942	New York City
Charles Poletti (D)[l]	3–31 Dec 1942	New York City
Thomas E. Dewey (R)	1943–54	New York City
W. Averell Harriman (D)	1955–58	Harriman (Orange Co)
Nelson A. Rockefeller (R)[m]	1959–73	Tarrytown (Westchester Co)
Malcolm Wilson (R)[n]	1973–74	Yonkers
Hugh Carey (D)	1975–82	Brooklyn
Mario M. Cuomo (D)	1983–94	Queens
George E. Pataki (R)	1995–	Garrison (Putnam Co)

Source: New York Red Book.

Abbreviations: CR: Clintonian Republican; D: Democrat; DR: Democratic-Republican; F: Federalist; FR: Fusion Republican; JD: Jacksonian Democrat; JR: Jeffersonian Republican; R: Republican; RW: Revolutionary Whig; U: Union; VBR: Van Buren Republican; W: Whig.

[a]The Constitution of 1777 did not specify the time when the governor would enter on the duties of his office. Gov George Clinton was declared elected 9 July. A 1778 law provided that the governor and lieutenant governor would be elected in April and take office on the first Monday in July. A 1787 law changed the day for taking office to 1 July.

[b]Resigned 24 Feb 1817 to assume the office of vice president.

[c]Assumed the position upon the resignation of Gov Tompkins, although he never took the oath of office.

[d]The Constitution of 1821 provided that the governor and lieutenant governor would be elected in November and in 1823 and thereafter would take office on 1 Jan.

[e]Lieutenant governor; became governor upon the resignation of Martin Van Buren, 12 Mar 1829; elected Nov 1830 for a full term.

[f]Elected president of the United States in 1884; resigned the office of governor 6 Jan 1885.

[g]Lieutenant governor; became governor upon the resignation of Grover Cleveland, 6 Jan 1885; elected 6 Nov 1885 for a full term and reelected 6 Nov 1888.

[h]Resigned 6 Oct 1910 to be associate justice of US Supreme Court.

[i]Lieutenant governor; became governor upon the resignation of Charles Evans Hughes.

[j]Succeeded William Sulzer, who was removed from office 17 Oct 1913.

[k]Resigned 3 Dec 1942 to become director of the US State Department's Foreign Relief and Rehabilitation Operations.

[l]Lieutenant governor; became governor upon the resignation of Herbert H. Lehman.

[m]Resigned 18 Dec 1973 to serve as chairman of National Commission on Water Quality and National Commission on Critical Choices for America.

[n]Lieutenant governor; became governor upon the resignation of Nelson A. Rockefeller.

Gowanda. Village (pop 2,842) in Persia (Cattaraugus Co) and Collins (Erie Co). Settled in 1816, it acquired a post office called West Lodi in 1830, which became Persia in 1831 and Gowanda in 1848 when the village was incorporated. In the 19th century Gowanda had a variety of enterprises, including mills, a tannery, Gowanda Preserving Co (1882), Gowanda Agricultural Works (1885), pump factory, woodenware factories, and breweries. The Buffalo and Jamestown Railroad (later Erie Railroad) came through in 1874; in 2003 the New York and Lake Erie Railroad offered excursions. A historic district is composed of five commercial buildings built in 1925–26. Gowanda Electronics Corp (1963) supplies high-performance magnetic components to electronics manufacturers. Annual events include Pioneer Days in May and the Harley Happening, a benefit for the restoration of the Hollywood Theater, in June.

Bruce D. Fredrickson and Madelynn P. Fredrickson

grade crossings. See RAILROAD GRADE CROSSINGS.

Grafton. Town (pop 1,987) in central Rensselaer Co. Settled ?1779 by New Englanders, the town was formed in 1807 from Troy and Petersburgh. A high, rugged area with 25 ponds, it was never good farming country. Wood, charcoal, and tanbark were produced for the Troy market, "brush blocks" and handles were produced for the Lansingburgh brush factories, mineral paint was made at Quackenkill, and shirtmaking was a cottage industry that involved 300 families. In the late 19th century, summer boarding became a source of income, and the *Troy Times*'s Fresh Air Home (1887) opened at East Grafton. Babcock Lake developed as a summer colony starting in 1925. Grafton was the subject of the book *Small Town* (1946) by resident Granville Hicks, a noted literary critic. Grafton Lakes State Park (1971), whose water bodies were formerly part of the Troy water supply, encompasses 2,357 acres (954 ha). Gravel mining and lumbering remain important industries, but many residents commute to the Capital District.

Kathryn T. Sheehan

Graham [née Marshall], **Isabella** (*b* Lanarkshire, Scotland, 29 July 1742; *d* New York City, 27 July 1814). Teacher and charitable worker. After marrying Dr John Graham in 1765 and accompanying him to Canada and Antigua, Isabella Graham returned to Scotland with their five children upon his death in 1773. Moving to New York City in 1789, she opened a well-regarded girls school that enjoyed the patronage of the city's leading political and mercantile families. Graham, a Presbyterian, taught her own evangelical version of Republican Motherhood, elevating piety and useful labor over mere worldly accomplishment. With daughter Joanna, son-in-law Divie Bethune, and a transatlantic network of evangelicals, she promoted missionary fundraising, tract distribution, and religious education. With Joanna and other women, including Elizabeth Bayley Seton, she founded the Society for the Relief of Poor Widows with Small Children in 1797. As late as 1812, at age 70, she agreed to head up a women's auxiliary for a magdalen society. After her death Graham achieved a kind of sainthood, her exemplary life held up as a model of evangelical womanhood and her published life story reprinted in numerous editions.

Benson, Mary Sumner. "Isabella Marshall Graham." In *Notable American Women* (Cambridge, Mass: Harvard Univ Press, 1971)

[Bethune, Joanna Graham]. *The Power of Faith, Exemplified in the Life and Writings of the Late Mrs. Isabella Graham,* 2d ed. (New York: American Tract Society, 1843)

Bethune, Joanna. *The Unpublished Letters and Correspondence of Mrs. Isabella Graham, from the Year 1767 to 1814; Exhibiting Her Religious Character in the Different Relations of Life* (New York: John S. Taylor, 1838)

Anne M. Boylan

Graham, Martha (*b* Allegheny, Pa, 11 May 1893; *d* New York City, 1 Apr 1991). Modern dance pioneer. Martha Graham's strict but devoted father was a psychiatrist of Scots-Irish descent; her mother claimed Plymouth, Mass, pioneer Miles Standish as an ancestor. In 1908 the family, which included Graham's two younger sisters, moved to Santa Barbara, Calif. In 1911 Graham attended a Los Angeles concert of Ruth St. Denis, whose exotic dancing inspired Graham to imagine a future for herself as a dancer. After her father's death Graham enrolled at Denishawn, the California school founded by St. Denis and her husband Ted Shawn, and in 1921 joined a New York City tour organized by Shawn. Graham spent several years with the Greenwich Village Follies before being hired in 1925 as co-director of the Eastman School of Music in Rochester, where she began to develop a dance training mode based on a system of contractions and releases.

From 1926 Graham offered classes and prepared concerts in New York City. She taught at the Neighborhood Playhouse and at the studio she opened in Carnegie Hall, establishing the roots of what became the Graham School and Comp. Graham began producing dances of artistic substance at a time of mostly superficial work in the medium. Her work explored universal themes and psychological issues through powerful, theatrical storytelling, with choreography often featuring bold, expressive movements of the body different from the dances of St. Denis. She collaborated with her music director and lover, Louis Horst, who influenced Graham to work with the era's leading composers to create new scores for her dances. Her approach also eliminated unnecessary or distracting ornamentation in stage settings and costumes. Some dances focused on a female figure at the center of a heroic saga, such as *Letter to the World* (1940). Graham expanded the all-female company in 1938 to incorporate male performers and in 1944 developed her celebrated *Appalachian Spring* as a gift to dancer Erick Hawkins, an emerging force in the company. Graham and Hawkins, who starred together with Merce Cunningham in this production, married in 1948, separating a year later. While mainstream critics of the 1920s and 1930s had attacked Graham's productions, critics of the 1940s showered praise on *Appalachian Spring,* and in 1958, when 64-year-old Graham premiered her first full evening-length dance drama *Clytemnestra,* the work received worldwide recognition as one of the great choreographic contributions to modern theater.

In the 1970s and 1980s, when she was no longer choreographing for herself, Graham's style changed. Works such as *Acts of Light* (1980) revealed a new emphasis on technical virtuosity. Her descent into alcoholism and an increasingly cloistered existence in later life possibly reveal the personal price she paid for her dedication to dance. She died before the completion of *Maple Leaf Rag* (1991). Graham entered her field, above all, to perform—not to create dance technique or to become a great choreographer. But her legacy included the hundreds of works she choreographed, the many students she trained, and her tremendous influence on the century's art, theater, and dance.

For illustration see DANCE, MODERN.

DeMille, Agnes. *Martha: The Life and Work of Martha Graham* (1956; repr New York: Vintage Books, 1992)
Graham, Martha. *Blood Memory* (New York: Doubleday, 1991)

Susan A. Lee

grain elevators. In 1842 Joseph Dart built the first storage and transfer grain elevator in Buffalo, eliminating a serious bottleneck in the transshipment of grain from boats on Lake Erie to boats on the Erie Canal. Dart's 55,000 bu (1.9 million l) elevator, designed on principles devised by engineer Oliver Evans, was powered by a high-pressure steam engine and included a "marine leg," with metal buckets attached to a conveyor belt that could be lowered into a ship's hold to raise the grain. Soon grain became the principal commodity handled on the canal. By 1862 there were 20 elevators lining Buffalo Creek [now Buffalo River], with a total capacity of over 4 million bushels (141 million l). The overall grain traffic at Buffalo during this period increased from around 2 million bushels (70 million l) to 55 million bushels (1.9 billion l). Work at the grain elevators was under the control of powerful bosses, who also owned boardinghouses where grain shovelers, or "scoopers," resided and saloons where they ran up large tabs. By keeping the mainly Irish laborers in their debt, the bosses enforced control over an essentially captive workforce. In 1899 the Buffalo grain shovelers went on strike to protest this "saloon system," resulting in vastly improved working conditions and recognition of their union.

Some elevators were floating and thus mobile. Beginning in 1844 merchant elevators in Oswego supplied the Erie Canal from Lake Ontario, while some on the Hudson and East Rivers, like Cargill's 12 million bu (4.2 million hl) elevator in Albany and the giant wooden Dows' Stores elevator in Brooklyn (built in 1879–81 and replaced in 1922 by a state-funded elevator at nearby Gowanus Bay), transferred grain to ocean vessels. The grain export trade from New York reached well over 300 million bushels (10.6 billion l) per year in the mid-1940s but ended in 1959 with the completion of the St. Lawrence Seaway, which permitted traffic to bypass the state altogether. Captive elevators, which supply a particular grain mill, also played a role in Buffalo's flour-milling industry. A notable example is the General Mills 4.9 million bu (172 million l) elevator, which still serves the company's nearby flour and cereal mills.

See also ARCHITECTS AND ARCHITECTURE, BUFFALO AND THE NIAGARA FRONTIER; PORT OF BUFFALO.

Baxter, Henry H. *Grain Elevators* ([Buffalo]: Buffalo & Erie County Historical Society, 1980)

Henry H. Baxter

Grain elevators at Buffalo harbor, *ca* 1890.

Grainger, Percy (Aldridge) (*b* Brighton, Australia, 8 July 1882; *d* White Plains, Westchester Co, 20 Feb 1961). Composer, pianist, and conductor. The only son of John Grainger, architect of Australian bridges, and Rose Aldridge, daughter of an Adelaide hotelkeeper, he was born George Percy Grainger. But after Rose separated from her husband in 1891, she changed her son's name to include her own. Grainger debuted as a concert pianist in Melbourne in 1894, continuing his studies in Frankfurt, Germany, a year later. From 1901 to 1914 he and Rose lived in London, where he performed and published compositions, many of which reflected his interest in collecting and transcribing English folksongs, such as *Country Gardens* (1919) and *Lincolnshire Posy* (1937). In New York he gave a solo concert at Manhattan's Aeolian Hall in 1915 before serving in the US Army band during World War I. In 1921 he bought a home in White Plains, where he would live for the rest of his life, first with Rose and, from 1928, with his wife, Swedish poet Ella Strom. A vegetarian and exercise enthusiast, he designed and wore unusual clothing, including grass skirts; he also advocated reforming the English language by eliminating Latin-root words. In 1932–33 Grainger headed New York University's Music Department. From the 1950s he composed music for his invented instrument, the Free Music machine, precursor of the electronic synthesizer. After Grainger's death, his house at 7 Cromwell Place became the headquarters of the International Percy Grainger Society, dedicated to preserving his musical legacy, and was named to the National Register of Historic Places. In 2002 Australian director Peter Duncan completed a film, *Passion,* on the composer's life.

Gillies, Malcolm, and David Pear. *A Portrait of Percy Grainger* (Rochester: Univ of Rochester Press, 2002)

Marilyn E. Weigold

grain milling. See FLOUR MILLING.

Granby. Town (pop 7,009) in SW Oswego Co. Settled in 1792 the town was formed from Hannibal in 1818. Located on the west bank of the Oswego River, the town had adequate waterpower, especially at Oswego Falls [now in City of Fulton]. The Syracuse and Oswego Railroad (1848) passed through town and encouraged woolen factories in the Civil War era. When Southern produce became unavailable during the war, tobacco was raised for a time. In the late 19th century it became a dairy town but also produced potatoes and strawberries on the upland and lettuce and onions on the muckland. Many residents work in the City of Fulton and elsewhere.

Barbara J. Dix

Sheet music commemorating the Grand Army of the Republic, 1889.

Grand Army of the Republic (GAR). National Civil War veteran's organization. Founded in April 1866 in Decatur, Ill, by Union army surgeon Benjamin F. Stephenson and William J. Rutledge, the GAR limited membership to Union army veterans and represented their needs, aligning itself with the Republican Party. In Albany it requested legislation to provide burial expenses and headstones for indigent honorably discharged veterans. As membership increased, peaking at 490,000 nationwide in 1890, its political influence grew, culminating with passage of the 1890 Dependent Pension Act providing federal assistance to needy veterans. Toward the end of the century, the GAR promoted patriotism through parades, encampments, and war memorials. New York City's Lafayette and Hamilton Posts donated flags to local schools; other posts urged singing of the "Star-Spangled Banner" and reciting of the "Pledge of Allegiance." Beginning about 1893 the Lafayette Post encouraged the public schools to introduce military drills, a plan endorsed by the *New York Tribune* in 1894. About 20,000 students participated in drill in 1895, despite the governor's veto of a legislative bill providing for the addition of military training to the public school curriculum. Much of this was a reaction to the new influx of immigrants and later to the Spanish-American War. In this effort, the GAR together with others groups sought to indoctrinate new arrivals and children as loyal Americans. The GAR also lobbied to establish Flag Day, which was nationally recognized in 1916. Over time, 676 GAR posts were established in New York State. In 1937 the state legislature named New York's portion of US 6, between the Connecticut border near Brewster (Putnam Co) and Port Jervis (Orange Co) via the Bear Mountain Bridge, the Grand Army of the Republic Highway. Victor (Ontario Co) native James A. Hard (1841–1953), the last surviving Civil War veteran in the state, was the state's final GAR department commander.

Beath, Robert Burns. *History of the Grand Army of the Republic* (New York: Bryan and Taylor, 1889)
McConnell, Stuart. *Glorious Contentment: The Grand Army of the Republic, 1865–1900* (Chapel Hill: Univ of North Carolina Press, 1992)

Martin Bannan

Grand Central Terminal. Manhattan rail terminal at 42d St and Park Ave. Grand Central Terminal succeeded other rail facilities on the same site. In 1869 Cornelius Vanderbilt began constructing a new station to serve his rail lines running to New York City, including New York and Harlem Railroad and New York Central and Hudson River Railroad (later New York Central Railroad). Vanderbilt's Grand Central Depot opened at the corner of 4th Ave (now Park Ave) and 42d St on 9 Oct 1871. It featured an L-shaped red brick building with five mansard-roofed towers surrounding a vaulted iron and glass train shed that held 12 tracks. At 652 feet (199 m) long and almost 100 feet (30 m) high, the shed became a popular tourist site. The facility handled 85 trains a day in its first year; by 1900 traffic had grown to 300 per day.

Renovations in 1898 added three new stories of offices to the brick structure, now renamed Grand Central Station. But within a year New York Central's chief engineer, William J. Wilgus, was urging the use of electric power to move trains inside and near the station to eliminate the need for above-ground track. By 1902 Wilgus designed two tiers of underground track, an upper-level loop for long-distance expresses and a lower-level loop for suburban trains, with most of the ground above left free for development. His plan also called for links to three subway lines and to the 3d Ave elevated line. Charles Reed of Reed and Stem in St. Paul, Minn, planned ramps to lead passengers smoothly from sidewalk to trains and subways, and Whitney Warren of Warren and Wetmore in Manhattan designed the building's Beaux Arts architecture. Excavation began in the summer of 1903, and tunnel work eventually extended over 40 acres (16 ha) between 42d and 50th Sts. The new complex, Grand Central Terminal, cost $80 million and opened 1 Feb 1913. It showcased the Main Concourse—275 feet (84 m) long, 120 feet (37 m) wide, and 125 feet (38 m) high—with its sky-blue ceiling painted in gold with Paul Helleu's design of the constellations (inexplicably rendered backward) featuring 2,500 stars, 60 lit by electric light. The south facade holds Jules-Alexis Coutan's sculpture group of Mercury, Hercules, and Minerva. The lower-level Oyster Bar, with ceiling vaults of Italian tile, also opened in 1913. The Commodore Vanderbilt and Biltmore Hotels, with direct links to Grand Central, were built above the underground tracks, as were the New York Central Building (now the Helmsley Building) and the Waldorf-Astoria Hotel on Park Ave.

The terminal's design accommodated growing traffic, serving 88,500 persons per day in 1919 and 111,040 in 1921. In 1947, the facility's busiest year, 65 million passengers rode 520 daily trains using the station's 67 tracks. But declining numbers in the 1960s threatened Grand Central with demolition or disfigurement. The New York City Landmarks Preservation Commission in 1967 named the terminal a landmark. In 1978 a US Supreme Court decision upheld the law authorizing Grand Central's protected status. Also that year the Metropolitan Transportation Authority (MTA) took over operations from owner Penn Central Railroad. In 1983 the MTA established the Metro-North Commuter Railroad, running three suburban lines. A $197 million restoration program, launched in 1989, repaired stone and plaster, cleaned away grime, and removed commercial signs from the terminal. At the same time many shops and restaurants returned. In 1991 Amtrak shifted long-distance trains to nearby Penn Station, making Grand Central a commuter hub. The following year MTA acquired a 110-year lease on the terminal from Penn Central Co, the holding company of the long-defunct rail line. In 2000 half a million people passed through Grand Central Terminal daily.

Grand Central Depot, New York City, from *Harper's Weekly*, 3 Feb 1872.

Belle, John, and Maxinne R. Leighton. *Grand Central: Gateway to a Million Lives* (New York: Norton, 2000)
Schlichtling, Kurt C. *Grand Central Terminal: Railroads, Engineering, and Architecture in New York City* (Baltimore: Johns Hopkins Univ Press, 2001)

Karl Zimmermann

Grand Island. Town (pop 18,621) in NW Erie Co. In the mid–17th century the Seneca Nation, moving westward, defeated and dispersed the Neutral Nation, which had lived on Grand Island, the largest island in the Niagara River. New York State acquired it from the Seneca in 1815 for $1,000 plus $500 in annuities. In 1819 the Joint Mixed Boundary Commission awarded possession of the disputed island to the United States. Squatters had arrived in 1817, set up an independent government, and engaged in lumbering; they were expelled in 1819 by the US Army, which burned 70 houses. In 1825 Maj Mordecai M. Noah from New York City planned a Jewish homeland called Ararat on Grand Island but found no support and gave up. Grand Island became a lumbering and fruit- and grain-farming town, and the East Boston Co (1833) ran a sawmill at Whitehaven and manufactured ships' timber. The town was formed from Tonawanda in 1852. In the late 19th century private clubs and hotels were built, including the Bedell House (1877), open until 1935, and the McComb House (1887). During Prohibition, Grand Island was a locale of rumrunning. The opening of bridges in 1935 connecting the island to Tonawanda and to Canada resulted in population growth in communities such as Sandy Beach (1937) and Grandyle Village (1942). From 1,055 residents in 1940, the population soared to 9,607 in 1960. The Niagara Extension of the Thruway crossed the island in 1959. In 2003 it was the site of Martin's Fantasy Island, an amusement park, and of Buckhorn Island and Beaver Island State Parks. The Seneca Indians' suit, contesting ownership of Grand Island and holding that it was taken from their ancestors unjustly, is being adjudicated in federal court.

Andrew C. Maines

Grand View-on-Hudson. Village (pop 284) in Orangetown (Rockland Co). Its steep grades impeded farming, but its brownstone quarries shipped stone to New York City in the 19th and early 20th centuries. It acquired a station on the Nyack and Northern Railroad (1870–1966) and became a summer resort. Most of the 100 houses in the modern village were built before 1900. In that year Grandview incorporated, but in 1918 the eastern portion of that village below the railroad reincorporated under the present name, leaving the western portion unincorporated. It is entirely residential.

Grange. National farmers' organization and fraternal order formally called the Order of the Patrons of Husbandry, founded on 4 Dec 1867 in Washington, DC, by one-time Minnesota farmer Oliver Hudson Kelley and seven others, including Francis M. McDowell, a Wayne (Steuben Co) pomologist who was an early financier of the association. After corresponding with A. S. Moss of Fredonia (Chautauqua Co), Kelley established New York State's first Grange chapter, in Fredonia, in April 1868, and it was one of the first permanent chapters in the nation. The number of local Granges in New York State grew from 2 in 1870 to 354 in 1875, with a total membership of 11,723.

The organization's goals included improving the intellectual attainments of the farm family, financially protecting the rural community through cooperative purchasing and selling, and increasing farmers' political power. The Grange aimed at educating the farm family in politics and finance along with modern agricultural practices. At the insistence of Kelley's niece Caroline Hall, the Grange was open equally to women, and the organization early supported woman suffrage. It also emphasized educational programs aimed at helping farmers operate more efficient businesses and create homes that fostered intellectual as well as physical interests. Beginning in the late 19th century, the Grange was instrumental in organizing purchasing cooperatives and mutual insurance companies for farmers, including the Cooperative Grange League Federation Exchange (now Agway), which was established in Ithaca in 1920.

The number of chapters in the state grew to about 600 in 1935, with multiple chapters in nearly every county. In 1956 the National Grange met in Rochester. By 1974 only 273 Granges remained active in the state, but the number grew to 323 in 2001, with another 48 active Junior Granges, for a total membership of around 13,000. State headquarters were in Cortland. The New York State Grange at the beginning of the 21st century emphasizes family farms and continues to advocate for families, initiate community action, facilitate leadership development, and convey rural and community needs to legislators and policy makers. Its bipartisan, grassroots political activism rests on local Grange chapters, and it perpetuates itself through various youth programs that work to develop leadership skills among its young members.

Alexander, L. Ray, and Leonard L. Allen. *100-Year History of the New York State Grange* (Washington, DC: National Grange, 1973)

Suzanne Etherington

Granger. Town (pop 577) in N Allegany Co. Settled in 1816, the town was formed from Grove in 1838 as West Grove; it was renamed Granger in 1839. Sheep raising was succeeded by dairying; in the 1830–50 period, the braiding of palm-leaf hats was a home industry. In 2003 three large dairy farms ship milk, while many residents commute, some as far as Rochester; good hunting attracts recreational enthusiasts. Granger is the site of the 1,395-acre (565 ha) English Hill State Forest.

Granger, Gideon (*b* Suffield, Conn, 19 July 1767; *d* Canandaigua, Ontario Co, 31 Dec 1822). US postmaster general. Admitted to the bar in 1789, Granger served seven years in Connecticut's lower house between 1792 and 1801. At first a Federalist, he became an ally of Thomas Jefferson, who appointed him US postmaster general in 1801. Granger held this position for the next 13 years and successfully expanded the size of the postal service. In the spring of 1814, however, Pres James Madison forced his resignation over internal politics. Granger then moved to Whitestown (Oneida Co), where he resumed his law career and built a grand mansion in Canandaigua in 1815 from which he could manage the many land tracts he had acquired in the west. A supporter of De Witt Clinton, he enthusiastically boosted the Erie Canal, speculated in real estate in Rochester, and supported the state's commercial expansion. Granger served in the New York State Senate in 1820–21 and started a nasty political debate (ultimately unsuccessful) when he proposed to have the state buy out the Holland Land Co and resell its extensive landholdings in western New York State on the open market. His son Francis Granger (1792–1868) was the unsuccessful National Republican (Antimasonic) candidate for governor of New York State (1830, 1832), Whig congressman (1835–37, 1839–41, 1841–43), and, although only briefly, US postmaster general (1841).

Hamlin, Arthur. *Gideon Granger* (Canandaigua, NY: Granger Homestead Society, 1982)
White, Leonard. *The Jeffersonians: A Study in Administrative History, 1801–1828* (New York: Macmillan, 1951)

Jon Sterngass

Grant [née MacVicar], **Anne** (*b* Glasgow, Scotland, 21 Feb 1755; *d* Edinburgh, 7 Nov 1838). Diarist. In 1758 MacVicar and her mother traveled to America, where MacVicar's father, a British soldier, had been sent a year earlier to fight in the French and Indian War. The family lived in the Dutch settlement of Claverack outside of Albany and moved to Clarendon [now in Vermont] in 1765. During her time in Albany, MacVicar became acquainted with Margaretta Schuyler, wife of Philip Schuyler, and spent much time at the Schuyler home, the Flatts. Mrs Schuyler's attitudes toward culture, society, America, and learning had a great impact on MacVicar's later work. The family returned to Scotland in 1768, and MacVicar began publishing letters and poetry. She married James Grant in 1779 and used her writings to support her eight children after his death in 1801. Grant's *Memoirs of an American Lady* (1808) was largely a tribute to Mrs Schuyler. She portrayed pre–Revolutionary War America as a place of harmony among Europeans, Native Americans, and slaves, celebrating the "aristocratic families" of Dutch Albany: the Schuylers, Van Rensselaers, and Van Cortlandts. A tory supporter, Grant depicted the Revolution as bringing discord and war to a peaceful society.

Grant, Anne. *Memoirs of an American Lady; With Sketches of Manners and Scenes in America, as They Existed Previous to the Revolution, with Unpublished Letters and a Memoir of Mrs. Grant by James Grant Wilson* (1808; repr Manchester, NH: Ayer, 1977)

Kerry Delaney

Granville. Town (pop 6,456) and village (pop 2,644) in Washington Co. Settled *ca* 1770, the town was formed in 1786. The village tried to incorporate in 1849 but did not succeed until 1885. A railroad (1852, later Delaware and Hudson Railroad) made it possible to ship Granville's slate; quarrying began about 1853, and that year Welsh immigrants began arriving for work in an area that became known as the slate valley. They were later joined by Ruthenians (from the present Slovakia), Italians, and Poles. Other products included textiles, ironwork, paper, paint, and cough syrup. Granville's farms raised sheep, grew potatoes, and engaged in dairying. Since the depression the village's largest employer has been Telescope Folding Furniture Co (1921). Attractions include the Pember Museum of Natural History (1908) and the Slate Valley Museum (1994). Ethnic consciousness has survived into the early 21st century with occasional Welsh *eisteddfodau* (singing festivals, first held in 1886) and the Ruthenians' Byzantine-rite St. Peter and St. Paul Church (1902).

See also WELSH.

R. Paul McCarty

grapes. Over 40 grape varieties, divided into three major categories, are grown in New York State. Native varieties, also known as *Vitis labrusca,* have been grown commercially since the 1830s around Lake Erie, the Finger Lakes, and the Hudson Valley. Concord and Niagara are common examples. They are processed into both juice and wine. Interspecific hybrid varieties, or French hybrids, are hybrids of several American *Vitis* species and European *Vitis vinifera.* Examples are Baco Noir, Aurore, and Seyval Blanc, first grown in the 1940s around the Finger Lakes. *V. vinifera* varieties have been grown commercially around the Finger Lakes since the 1960s. White Riesling, Chardonnay, Merlot, Cabernet Franc, and Pinot Noir are the most common varieties grown in New York State.

There are four major production regions in the state, all in areas where winter, spring, and fall temperatures are moderated by large bodies of water. In 2001 the Lake Erie District, including Chatauqua, Erie, and Niagara Cos, had 19,741 acres (7,989 ha) of grapes, 95% of which were Concord and Niagara grapes used for juice production. Juice manufacture dates back to 1896, when Thomas Welch moved his unfermented juice production facility from New Jersey to Watkins Glen (Schuyler Co) and the following year to Westfield (Chautauqua Co). Wine production started in the 1860s in the Finger Lakes region. In 2001 the area had 7,856 acres (3,179 ha) of grapes planted on the slopes surrounding Keuka, Canandaigua, Seneca, and Cayuga Lakes. About 90% of the 40,000 tons (36,287 MT) produced in the Finger Lakes are for wine, and the region manufactures wine from a diverse assemblage of over 30 native *V. labrusca* (65% of acreage), French hybrid (25%), and *V. vinifera* (10%) varieties. The Hudson River valley produces largely native and hybrid grapes, and is the home of Brotherhood Winery (1839) in Washingtonville (Orange Co), the oldest commercial winery in continuous operation in the United States. Suffolk Co on Long Island is the newest wine region, all *V. vinifera,* with production beginning in the late 1970s. In 2001 the Hudson Valley and Long Island had 2,540 acres (1,028 ha) of vineyards.

The Farm Winery Act, passed by the state legislature in 1976, has spurred recent growth in the number of wineries from 19 at that time to 160 in 2002. The act simplified licensing procedures for wineries and allowed farmers to produce and sell on their premises. Bulk wine production at five major wineries existing at that time has been consolidated through mergers into Canandaigua Wine Co, a subsidiary of Constellation Brands. In 2001 New York State had 31,745 acres (12,847 ha) of vineyards on 926 farms and was ranked third nationally in production with 150,000 tons (136,078 MT). Two-thirds is processed into juice and one-third into wine. *V. labrusca* varieties make up 83% of the New York State grape acreage, French hybrid varieties 9%, and *V. vinifera* varieties 7%.

Cattell, H., H. L. Stauffer, and L. S. Miller. *Wines of the East,* 3 vols (Lancaster, Pa: L & H Photojournalism, 1978)

Timothy Martinson

Greatbatch, Wilson (*b* Buffalo, 6 Sept 1919). Medical inventor. He grew up in West Seneca (Erie Co) and served in the navy during World War II. After receiving a BS in electrical engineering from Cornell University in 1950, he moved to Clarence (Erie Co) and taught at the University of Buffalo, where he obtained his MA in 1957. He developed his first successful internal pacemaker in 1958, patented it in 1960, and licensed it to Medtronic. Holding more than 240 patents, his further research ranged from medical electronics to genetics and space travel. He founded numerous companies to pursue his interests. Wilson Greatbatch Ltd (1960), which went public in 2000 as Wilson Greatbatch Technologies, manufactures most of the world's pacemaker batteries.

Greatbatch, Wilson. *The Making of the Pacemaker: Celebrating a Lifesaving Invention* (Amherst, NY: Prometheus Books, 2000)

Carl A. Westerdahl and Susan S. Clarke

Great Carry. See ONEIDA CARRYING PLACE.

Great Fire of 1776. Shortly after midnight on the morning of 21 Sept 1776, six days after the British army had occupied New York City following the Battle of Long Island, a fire broke out at Whitehall Slip on the East River in Lower Manhattan. Fanned by wind, flames sped up the Battery, over Broadway, and eventually destroyed nearly every building west of Broadway as far north as Beaver St, at the edge of the grounds of King's College (now Columbia University), then in Lower Manhattan. Total losses included 493 houses, Trinity Church, and other outbuildings. The cause of the fire is unknown. The British accused departing rebels—more accurately, lingering saboteurs—of arson, and there were reports of people being arrested or shot during the fire for hindering attempts to put it out. Gen George Washington and the Continental Congress had ordered that no harm be done to the city as it was being abandoned, but a lone rebel or small group could have started the blaze. The British would continue investigating the cause until 1783, with no conclusive results. The destruction created a severe housing shortage for the New Yorkers who remained during the British occupation and the many loyalist refugees from other parts of the United States. The war prevented any significant reconstruction from taking place, so the aftereffects of the Great Fire shaped the city that Washington reoccupied peacefully in 1783. Builders took advantage of the open area to construct new, larger houses on wider streets, and these, plus a location away from the center of commerce on the East River, made the west side of Broadway the fashionable part of town. Reconstruction took time, however, and a visitor in 1787 noted that the fire's destruction was still clearly noticeable. The rebuilding of Trinity Church, for example, was not even begun until 1788 and not completed until 1790. By 1800 the area had been completely rebuilt.

Schecter, Barnet. *The Battle for New York: The City at the Heart of the American Revolution* (New York: Walker, 2002)

Rohit T. Aggarwala

Great Gatsby, The. Novel by F. Scott Fitzgerald (1896–1940). Published in 1925, the story follows bootlegger Jay Gatsby's tragic attempt to recapture the love of the beautiful Daisy Buchanan. Its underlying theme is the failure of material success to bring emotional fulfillment, a perennial comment on the nature of the American dream. Narrated by the impressionable Nick Carraway, readers meet Daisy's brutish husband Tom, his crass mistress Myrtle, her sad husband Wilson, Gatsby's shady partner Meyer Wolfsheim, and the alluring Jordan Baker.

The action moves between Long Island and Manhattan. Gatsby and Nick live on West Egg, probably Great Neck (Nassau Co), and the Buchanans reside across the bay in East Egg, probably Manhasset (Nassau Co). Fitzgerald luxuriates on the grand homes and stunning scenery of the Gold Coast of the North Shore of Long Island, showing the enormous wealth and decadence of the 1920s. This affluent area contrasts sharply with "the valley of ashes," the Corona Dumps area in Flushing (Queens Co), where Myrtle and her husband live (this area was redeveloped into the 1939 World's Fair site). Many plot elements unfold in Manhattan. Tom takes Nick, who works on Wall St, to a party uptown in Washington Heights. Later Nick glimpses Gatsby's criminal life at a lunch with Meyer in a busy 42d St restaurant. A pivotal scene in which Gatsby confronts Tom about Daisy takes place in a suite at the Plaza Hotel on 59th St. Nick and Jordan experience a romantic interlude in a carriage beside Central Park, while Nick has introspective moments strolling along Fifth Ave. The novel has been filmed at least four times (1926, 1949, 1974, 2001), and John Harbison's opera *The Great Gatsby* premiered at the Metropolitan Opera in 1999.

A native of St. Paul, Minn, Fitzgerald attended Princeton University and lived in New York City after World War I. While working at an advertising agency, he lived at 200 Claremont Ave in Morningside Heights in New York City. After publishing *This Side of Paradise* in 1920, Fitzgerald and his wife Zelda Sayre moved into the Biltmore Hotel on East 43d St before moving to France in 1924.

Bruccoli, Matthew Joseph. *Some Sort of Epic Grandeur: The Life of F. Scott Fitzgerald,* 2d rev ed. (Columbia: Univ of South Carolina Press, 2002)
O'Meara, Lauraleigh. *Lost City: Fitzgerald's New York* (New York: Routledge, 2002)

Anthony L. Dunlap

Great Gull Island. See LITTLE GULL AND GREAT GULL ISLANDS.

Great Lakes shipbuilding. Regular New York State shipbuilding for the Great Lakes began in the first decade of the 1800s. Asa Stanard and his apprentice and brother-in-law Benjamin Bidwell built a schooner at Cambria [now Lewiston, Niagara Co] for the merchants of Black Rock [now in Erie Co]. The first American steamer and the first to go into service above Niagara Falls on the upper Great Lakes, *Walk-in-the-Water,* departed Black Rock on 23 Aug 1818. The second American steamer on the lakes, *Sophia,* was launched at Sackets Harbor (Jefferson Co) the same year. In November 1831 the 142 ft (43.3 m) steamer *United States* was launched at Ogdensburg (St. Lawrence Co) and was one of the first steamers on the Great Lakes to have two engines.

By the 1850s passenger traffic and immigrant trade justified the construction of a large fleet of first-class passenger steamers. In 1852 *Crescent*

City and *Queen of the West* at 324 ft (98.8 m) were built, and in 1853 *Plymouth Rock* at 336 ft (102.4 m) and *Western World* at 347 ft (105.8 m) were constructed. In 1854 there were seven shipyards in Buffalo, and in 1855, 38 ships were built. The first iron propeller on the lakes and the first iron ship to be built completely in the lakes region was *Merchant.* Its iron plates were manufactured at Black Rock, and it was launched at the yard of David Bell at Buffalo in 1862. In 1871 the iron hull steamers *India, China,* and *Japan* were built by the King Iron Works in Buffalo, and the yard that had been operated by Bidwell and Banta was taken over by the newly formed Union Dry Dock Co. The first vessel built by the new organization was the 216 ft (65.8 m) wood package freighter *William M. Tweed.* In 1882 the firm built its first iron vessel. The company constructed a total of 91 vessels, including freighters, barges, tugs, canalboats, tankers, and survey vessels between 1871 and 1898. In 1896 Union Dry Dock and the adjacent R. J. Mills merged and in 1899 reorganized as the Buffalo Dry Dock Co. In the next few years it built tugs, barges, bulk carriers, and the passenger excursion steamers *Americana* (1908) and *Canadiana* (1910). The yard that had been leased and operated by American Ship Building Co in Cleveland was officially transferred to that firm in 1910.

With World War I and the demand for oceangoing steamers, the Buffalo yard and other Great Lakes yards constructed the Laker class of ocean freighters and turned out 11 of them. During World War II the industry in Buffalo built a variety of smaller craft for the military—six tugs for the US Navy, four US Army tugs, and various landing craft—and converted two passenger vessels, *Seeandbee* and *Greater Buffalo,* into the aircraft training carriers *Wolverine* and *Sable* for the US Navy in 1942. By 1962 shipbuilding work in this field had declined to the point where the American Ship Building Co closed the Buffalo yard, the last remaining one in the area.

Institute of Great Lakes Research. *American Ship Building Company and Predecessors: 1867–1920* (Bowling Green, Ohio: Bowling Green Univ, 1988)

Wright, Richard J. *Fresh Water Whales* (Kent, Ohio: Kent State Univ Press, 1970)

Walter C. Cowles

Great Lakes shipping lines and watercraft. Steamboats were introduced on Lake Ontario at Sackets Harbor (Jefferson Co) in 1816 and on the upper Great Lakes at Black Rock [now in Erie Co] the following year, in both cases financed by syndicates of local businessmen. The 135 ft (41.2 m) *Walk-in-the-Water,* built at Black Rock in 1818, was the first steam vessel on the upper Great Lakes. Dozens of others, ranging from 150 feet (46 m) to almost 300 feet (91 m) in length, were built at Buffalo between the 1820s and 1840s to accommodate the immigrant trade after the Erie Canal opened in 1825. Numerous partners, or "subscribers," owned most of these vessels because they were much more costly than contemporary canalboats or sailing craft. No real transportation lines were formed, however, until almost 1840.

Earliest Fleets

The first fleets were called combinations, loosely organized groups of independently owned steamboats cooperatively serving specific routes or timetables and sharing the proceeds. In 1831 a steamboat combination with six ships offered daily sailings from each end of Lake Erie. Five years later a combination of 20 steamers was organized to provide departures daily from Buffalo for Sandusky, Ohio, and Detroit. These exerted a powerful influence over the economies of the cities they served. In the mid-1840s several railroads were begun from Lake Erie ports westward into Ohio and Michigan. Depending on passengers and freight coming out of Buffalo, the railroads built their own ships to compete with the combinations for the immigrant traffic. The Michigan Central Railroad began running steamers out of Buffalo on its Lake Erie North Shore Line in 1848, and the Michigan Southern and Northern Indiana followed suit in 1852. The North Shore Line built two 350 ft (107 m) "palace steamers," and the Michigan Southern Line three similar vessels. The financial panic of 1857 forced them all into retirement.

Palatial side-wheel steamers dominated the lucrative passenger trade on Lake Erie. Forty of these lavish vessels were built for the Great Lakes trade between 1844 and 1856, mostly at Buffalo shipyards. But sailing craft and the more utilitarian "propellers" driven by John Ericsson's newly introduced propeller-wheels garnered most of the freight traffic. The earliest propellers were built at Oswego between 1841 and 1845 to exploit the Erie Canal trade, and Sylvester Doolittle of Oswego employed six of them to form his New York, Oswego and Chicago Line. The fleet was composed of vessels small enough to pass through the 150 ft (45 m) locks of the Welland Canal, enabling them to connect Lake Ontario's Erie Canal ports with the upper Great Lakes. The venture proved highly successful. The Northern Transportation Co was organized at Ogdensburg (St. Lawrence Co) in 1851 by businessmen John Crawford and Philo Chamberlain to serve the Northern Railroad of New York and to connect it with port cities around the Great Lakes. The fleet had 20 canal-sized propellers, forming lines from Ogdensburg down the St. Lawrence River to Montreal and to American ports on Lakes Michigan and Superior. The company went bankrupt in 1876 in the face of competition from larger, more efficient bulk freight ships in the grain and flour trades.

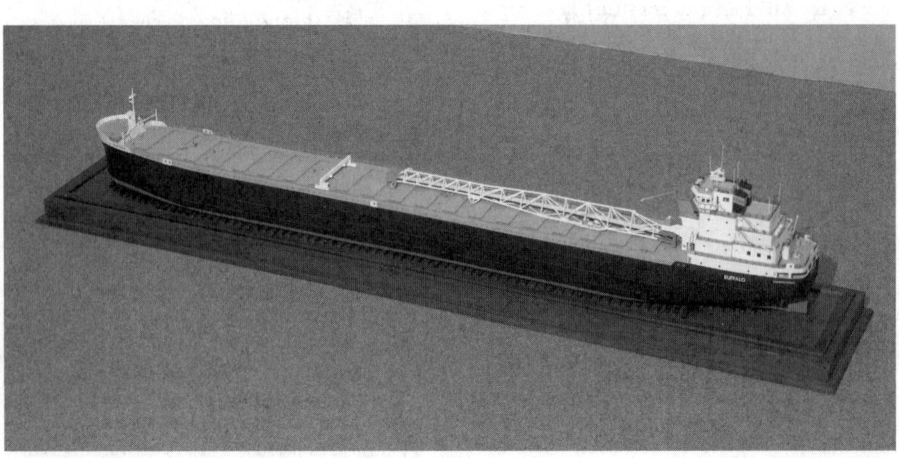

Scale model of the American Steamship Co's M/V *Buffalo,* which was launched in September 1978.

Shipping Lines Heyday

All of the immigrant traffic and manufactured goods intended for the Midwest passed through the Erie Canal, while the agricultural commodities, timber, and minerals mined in the Great Lakes states were funneled through Buffalo's docks and grain elevators bound for coastal markets. During the first half of the 19th century, a time characterized by phenomenal population growth, the movement of passengers and package freight into the lakes far surpassed the tonnage of agricultural commodities shipped back East. Most of the early Great Lakes steamboat fleets were extensions of canalboat lines and railroads originating in New York City and serving Buffalo and were largely financed by New York City capital. Because Buffalo was the western terminus for the Erie Canal, it served as the center of Great Lakes shipbuilding and waterborne commerce from 1825 until the Civil War began.

The New York Central Railroad and Hudson River Railroad formed the Western Transportation Co in the late 1830s. Its original fleet consisted of 200 canalboats, but before 1840 the line had extended its services westward from Buffalo using several chartered Great Lakes steamers. In 1851 it began building its own propeller-vessels to link Buffalo with Milwaukee and Chicago. In following years it operated from 8 to as many as 20 vessels, all 200 ft (61 m) "upper lakes" ships too large to navigate Welland Canal's locks to Lake Ontario and the St. Lawrence River. The company incorporated at Buffalo in 1855, reorganized in 1883 as Western Transit Co, and served the Great Lakes until it went out of business in 1915. The New York and Erie Railroad Line ships carried passengers and freight from Dunkirk (Chautauqua Co) on Lake Erie to Erie, Pa, Cleveland, Sandusky, Ohio, and Detroit. In 1858 the eastern terminus was relocated from Dunkirk to Buffalo. The line was incorporated on 4 Feb 1869 as the Union Steamboat Co with Jay Gould of New York City as president; the fleet was liquidated in 1915 after new federal antitrust laws were enacted. The Panama Canal Act, passed by Congress in 1912, forced American railroads to divest of wholly owned passenger and package freight steamboat lines. Afterward, most lines reorganized to form independent businesses competing directly with the railroads for freight trade.

The Lake Navigation Co was organized at Buffalo in April 1856 by various ship owners to fight the monopolistic influence of contemporary railroad fleets. The company was capitalized at $1 million, with H. C. Walker of Buffalo as president. It was the largest fleet on the Great Lakes, with 5 steam tugs and 62 sailing craft. That company was dissolved on 2 Feb 1858 in the face of the 1857 financial panic. The American Transportation Co (ATC) was incorporated at Buffalo in 1854 with Rufus C. Palmer of Buffalo as president. Within a year its fleet was running eight steamers between Buffalo and Chicago. At the end of the 1859 season, however, it also liquidated. ATC officers James C. and Edwin T. Evans of Buffalo bought several of the propellers from the defunct fleet in 1859 and formed the Buffalo and Lake Michigan Propeller Line to connect with the New York Central Railroad. It incorporated in April 1873 as the Erie and Western Transportation Co's popular Anchor Line, which operated successfully to ports on Lakes Michigan and Superior until it was broken up by federal antitrust legislation in 1915.

During this period the first large iron vessel was built on the Great Lakes, the 190 ft (58 m) propeller *Merchant,* built in 1862 by the David Bell Iron Works at Buffalo. The ship routinely hauled greater payloads than its wooden contemporaries and earned a fortune for its owners. The 250 ft (76 m) *Philadelphia* followed in 1868, and between 1871 and 1873 Buffalo's King Iron Works produced the iron steamers *India, China, Japan, Alaska, Cuba, Java, Scotia,* and *Russia,* all large propellers. Wood was used for shipbuilding purposes until 1900, but iron and steel gradually supplanted it after the success demonstrated by these early Buffalo-built craft. As late as 1885 only 10% of new ships were iron or steel; by 1895 the proportion had grown to 60% and by 1905 to 100%. Buffalo shipyards dominated the iron shipbuilding industry on the Great Lakes until the middle 1880s, when shipyards in Detroit and Cleveland assumed the lead.

Later Shipping Lines

By the Gilded Age, Buffalo had lost its dominance among Great Lakes ports. Railroads completed after the Civil War also diverted a substantial share of the remaining immigrant traffic past Buffalo. With its extensive grain-milling capacity and the demands of the hungry Lackawanna (Erie Co) steel mills, the port's emphasis shifted to the receipt of bulk cargoes. Although Buffalo remained one of the most important ports in the nation well into the 20th century, it was no longer the "Queen City of the Great Lakes." As the immigrant-based passenger trade waned, New York State lines that depended on that traffic reorganized in the 1870s to carry package freight and bulk cargoes. George Hall and Co established a coal business at Ogdensburg in the mid-1870s and purchased several tugs, sailing craft, and small steamers to serve the business during the following decades, operating through several subsidiary firms in the United States and Canada. In 1922 the company disposed of its US holdings. The Lake Superior Transit Co chartered vessels from several competing firms to run from Buffalo to ports on Lake Superior, incorporating in 1878 and running 21 vessels until 1892. The Delaware, Lackawanna and Western Railroad began running package freight steamers on the Great Lakes in the early 1880s when it incorporated the Lackawanna Transportation Co at Buffalo, known informally as the Red Star Line. It started with two chartered vessels but began building its own ships in 1887, eventually operating a fleet of 10 modern steel craft before closing down in 1907.

James J. Hill's Northern Steamship Co was incorporated at Buffalo in 1888 with $1.5 million in stock, largely owned by Hill's Great Northern Railroad. The firm built six steel package freighters in 1889 and then added the palatial passenger liners *North West* and *North Land* in 1893–94. The Mutual Transit Co, organized by the Great Northern and Northern Pacific Railroads, acquired all of the freighters in 1903, and this fleet operated until 1915.

Increasingly, the steamship traffic on the Great Lakes was in specialized bulk freight ships that carried low-value commodities in very large quantities. The first bulk freighters were small single-decked vessels built to carry lumber. They were introduced in 1865 and 1866, measuring about 120 feet (37 m) long and carrying 300–500 tons (272–454 MT) of forest products such as lumber, railroad ties, shingles, or square timber; predictably, most were built in Michigan and Wisconsin, where the lumber industry was centered. Bulk freighters also towed barges laden with cargo, minimizing crew requirements and maximizing payloads. The "consort barges" they towed were often the stripped hulks of old steamers and sailing ships. Larger double-decked bulk freighters were introduced around 1870 for the grain and iron ore trades. These ships commonly measured 200 feet (61 m) long and carried up to 1,200 tons (1,090 MT) of cargo; they also towed barges with similar loads. Technological and economic improvements occurred in water transport in the 1880s. Deeper channels and harbors, provided at the expense of the federal government, allowed for larger ships. Improved shipbuilding methods enabled shipyards at Buffalo, Cleveland, and Detroit to build bulk freighters 250 feet (76 m) long and longer. The change from wood to iron shipbuilding during the 1880s (and to steel soon afterward) caused the average vessel to grow from 250 to 350 feet (76 to 107 m) and from 1,500 to 3,500 tons (1,361 to 3,175 MT), and a shipbuilding boom resulted in some 350 new ships, almost exclusively bulk freighters. Several very large fleets, such as the US Steel Corp with 112 ships, were organized between 1895 and 1900 to transport bulk iron ore, coal, and grain across the Great Lakes. Between 1895 and the advent of World War I, no fewer than 470 steel ships were built, and the carrying capacity of the largest vessels grew from 4,500 to more than 15,000 tons (4,080 to 13,600 MT).

Great Lakes waterborne transportation evolved between 1880 and the 1920s to accommodate bulk grain, coal, limestone, iron ore, and petroleum, almost to the exclusion of other commodities. A few passenger and package freight fleets survived until World War II, but the nation's expanding network of state and federal highways put an end to both by 1960. Only a dozen highly efficient and high-volume bulk freight shipping lines, which ran fewer than a total of 100 technically sophisticated ships, remained on the Great Lakes as the 20th century drew to a close; the vessels themselves were very large, running 730–1,000 feet (223–305 m) in length and carrying 30,000–65,000 tons (27,200–59,000 MT) of cargo. Another unique factor of the 20th century was the appearance of foreign-flag ocean ships made possible by the completion of the St. Lawrence Seaway system, which connected the Great Lakes with the Atlantic Ocean by way of the St. Lawrence River, in 1959.

In 1902 Horace S. Wilkinson and W. W. Brown of Buffalo began organizing a fleet of bulk freighters and during the next two years had 10 modern steel ships built. In 1911 they incorporated the Great Lakes Steamship Co with headquarters at Oswego, operating 21 vessels; the company was dissolved in 1957. The Great Lakes Transit Corp was organized at Buffalo in 1915 with 32 package freight vessels and three passenger craft, all acquired from railroads that had been forced by federal antitrust laws to divest of their steamship lines. All but two vessels in the fleet were requisitioned by the US government's War Shipping Administration between 1942 and 1945; the remainder were sold off and the company liquidated. John J. Boland and Adam E. Cornelius incorporated the American Steamship Co at Buffalo in 1907. At times the company managed as many as 50 vessels in the Great Lakes dry bulk trades. GATX Capital Corp of Chicago acquired the firm in 1973. American Steamship Co of Williamsville (Erie Co) still operated as a subsidiary of GATX in 2002 and was the only remaining Great Lakes steamship fleet based in New York State.

American Steamship Co, http://www.americansteamship.com

Dunn, Walter S., Jr. *History of Erie County, 1870–1970* (Buffalo: Buffalo and Erie County Historical Society, 1971)

Mansfield, J. B. *History of the Great Lakes* (Chicago: J. H. Beers, 1899)

Odle, Thomas D. "The American Grain Trade of the Great Lakes, 1825–1873" (PhD diss, Univ of Michigan, 1951)

Rae, James David. "The Great Lakes Commodity Trade, 1850 to 1900" (PhD diss, Purdue Univ, 1967)

C. Patrick Labadie

Great Neck {Great Neck, village (pop 9,538) in North Hempstead, Nassau Co; Great Neck Estates, village (pop 2,756) in North Hempstead; Great Neck Plaza, village (pop 6,433) in North Hempstead}. English and Dutch settlers arrived in the 1640s and corrupted the Matinecock name for the area, *Menhaden-Ock,* to Madnan's Neck. By the 1670s it was called Great Neck. The area's farms supplied New York City with flour, hay, cattle, and apples. The railroad came in 1866. In the 1870s the area developed into an elite resort and later into an estate area. Great Neck, Great Neck Estates, and Great Neck Plaza, along with the villages of Kings Point, Saddle Rock, and Russell Gardens, and the localities of Kensington, Thomaston, Saddle Rock, Harbor Hills, Great Neck Gardens, and University Gardens are located on either the Great Neck peninsula or the main body of Long Island immediately to the south. Great Neck incorporated in 1922. In the early 21st century it is predominantly Jewish, with over a dozen synagogues and mostly single-family homes. Iranian Jews have clustered in Great Neck since the late 1970s. Great Neck Estates was the property of the Thorne family until the early 20th century, when it was developed; incorporated in 1911, it is an area of single-family houses on streets laid out to resemble an English village. Zelda and F. Scott Fitzgerald lived in Great Neck Estates from 1922 to 1924 and were among many luminaries to enjoy its vibrant social life. The area of Great Neck Plaza was, in the late 19th century, the property of William R. Grace, entrepreneur and mayor of New York City. Incorporated in 1930,

Great Neck Plaza is the location of the Great Neck station of the Long Island Rail Road. The three-story Grace (1914) and Thomaston (1926) commercial buildings are on the National Register. There are some single-family homes, but most residents of the Plaza live in rental apartments or cooperatives, and over 40% are over age 55. The autumn Street Festival and Antique Auto Festival draw more than 35,000 visitors annually. All three villages are affluent residential suburbs with a substantial Jewish population but with increasing ethnic diversity.

Laura E. Mann

Great Nine Partners Patent. Land patent of approximately 160,000 acres (64,750 ha) in Dutchess Co comprising the Towns of Clinton, Pleasant Valley, Stanford, Washington, Hyde Park, Amenia, and a small part of North East. It was granted by Gov Benjamin Fletcher in 1697 to Caleb Heathcote, member of the governor's council, Augustine Graham, surveyor general of the province, and seven other New York City speculators. The patent languished until 1730 when it was divided into nine parts. Settlement began 1734 with sales to migrants from other Dutchess Co settlements, from elsewhere in New York Colony, and from Connecticut and Massachusetts. By the time of the American Revolution its population was the largest of any division of Dutchess Co.

McDermott, William P. "The Nine Partners and Their Land." In *Clinton, Dutchess County, NY: A History of a Town,* ed. William P. McDermott (Clinton Corners, NY: Town of Clinton Historical Society, 1987)

William P. McDermott

Great Sacandaga Lake (42 mi²/109 km²). Reservoir formed by construction of the Conklingville Dam (Saratoga Co) on the Sacandaga River, completed in 1930 by the Hudson River Regulating District. The reservoir was created in response to Hudson River flooding at the turn of the century, which affected many localities, including Albany. Although the Great Sacandaga Lake (until the 1960s the Great Sacandaga Reservoir) lies within the boundaries of the Adirondack Park, it is not on Forest Preserve land. It is the largest reservoir in the state with a total storage capacity of 37.73 billion ft³ (1.07 billion m³) and 125 miles (201 km) of shoreline. The Black River Regulating District (1919) and the Hudson River Regulating District (1922) were combined by the New York State legislature to create the Hudson River–Black River Regulating District in 1959, which has oversight responsibility for Great Sacandaga Lake. Recreational use is an important benefit, as well as improved navigation and a sanitary domestic water supply.

Board of Hudson River–Black River Regulating District, http://www.hrbrrd.com/history.htm

Veronica A. Weigand

Great Valley. Town (pop 2,145) in central Cattaraugus Co. Settled in 1812, the town was formed from Olean in 1818, and its southwest corner abuts Seneca Nation territory. Lumbering became the chief industry, with logs and shingles rafted down the Allegheny as far as the Ohio River, and some woodenware factories produced chairs and handles; the forests were exhausted by the 1870s. The Erie (1851) and Rochester and State Line (1878) Railroads served the town. Stock raising and dairying succeeded lumbering; the first cheese factory was built in 1858. In the early 21st century two huge antique complexes, Bear Hollow Antique Co-op and Green Gable Village, attract visitors to Great Valley. The "breathing well," located off Bear Hollow Rd, is an oddity scientists have been unable to explain. Dug *ca* 1840, it was dry, but people found that air passes both up and down; some believe it acts as a barometer. A thousand canoes, boats, and kayaks take part each spring in the Great Valley Fireman's Regatta on Great Valley Creek.

Bruce D. Fredrickson and Madelynn P. Fredrickson

Great Western Turnpikes. Five turnpikes of the same name, built between 1799 and 1814. They opened the center of New York State to settlement and provided a means for shipping farm produce to Albany, New York City, and New England markets. All were authorized by the New York State legislature and financed by private investors. Tolls provided funds for maintenance and repayment to stockholders. The routes, in some cases, paralleled older and poorly maintained public roads.

The first of the Great Western Turnpikes (1799) was authorized to run from the former Town of Watervliet [now Colonie, Albany Co] through Sloansville (Schoharie Co) to Cherry Valley (Otsego Co), roughly the path of US 20. In 1802 it was extended eastward into Albany along the present Western Ave as far as Quail St. The second (1801) began at Cherry Valley and passed through Cooperstown and Edmeston (Otsego Co) to a terminus at Sherburne (Chenango Co); Rtes 166 and 80 follow part of the old road. The third (1803) also began at Cherry Valley and passed through Richfield Springs (Otsego Co), Bridgewater and Sangerfield (Oneida Co), Morrisville and Cazenovia (Madison Co), to Manlius (Onondaga Co), where it joined the Seneca Turnpike. The modern US 20 and Rte 92 follow the route. The fourth (1805) began with a bridge over the Chenango River at Sherburne and passed through DeRuyter (Madison Co) to Homer (Cortland Co), following the present path of Rtes 80, 26, and 13. The fifth (1814) began at Homer and was authorized to reach Genoa (Cayuga Co) on the east shore of Cayuga Lake but apparently was never built west of Locke (Cortland Co).

In the system's early years, traffic was intense. One winter 1,200 sleighs passed through Albany, most headed for the Genesee Valley, on the turnpikes. Legislation provided that turnpikes would become free public roads if not maintained or when formally abandoned by the investors. This began to happen when the Erie Canal took away much of the passenger traffic and especially so after 1840, when the railroads began to carry livestock, ending the role of the drover in driving cattle, sheep, and turkeys. Between 1844 and 1850, several sections of the turnpikes were converted to plank roads, and they continued collecting tolls. The Third Great Western Turnpike, also called the Cherry Valley, was the most profitable of the five and operated the longest, dissolving in 1859. Dividends ranged from 5% to 7% annually. It was 70 mi (113 km) long, cost $95,000 to build, and had seven tollgates. Inns and taverns along the route provided food and shelter for travelers.

The turnpikes were abandoned or sold in sections, and parts continued to operate until after 1900. The turnpike name continues in public use because US 20 was designated the Cherry Valley Turnpike across New York State after it was rebuilt for automobile traffic in 1926; many local roads and streets use the early turnpike names as well.

Barbara S. Rivette

Greece. Town (pop 94,141) in NW Monroe Co. White settlement commenced within the town's present limits in 1806; Greece was formed from Gates in 1822. In 1829 early Irish settlement resulted in the founding of the St. Ambrose's Church (now Church of the Mother of the Seven Sorrows), one of the first Roman Catholic churches in a rural location in the state. The Rome, Watertown and Ogdensburg Railroad came through in 1875, but it was the electric railroad (1889–1925) that made the town's beaches accessible as resorts, though its best-known beach area and business center, Charlotte, was annexed by Rochester in 1890. Eastman Kodak first built a plant in Greece in 1890, but Rochester annexed Kodak Park in 1916. By midcentury other Kodak facilities had been developed in the present town, along with housing developments for Kodak workers. The presence of Kodak fueled a rapid increase in Greece's population from 3,350 in 1920 to 25,508 in 1950. Through rapid suburbanization during the next decade, the population almost doubled to 48,670 by 1960 and continued to increase sharply through the 1980s. In 1997 a program was introduced that offered tax incentives to businesses that built or enlarged in specific sections in an effort to provide an economic boost to aging areas and to limit expansion of the overdeveloped Ridge Rd corridor. The Braddock Bay State Wildlife Management Area is in Greece, and in 2002, 10 areas of environmentally sensitive land were earmarked for retention as open space.

Carolyn Vacca

Greek Orthodox churches. See ORTHODOX CHURCHES.

Greeks. The first wave of Greek immigration to New York State and the United States as a whole occurred in the late 19th century. The first Greek Orthodox Church in the northeastern United States, Holy Trinity, was founded in Manhattan in 1892. Two years later *Atlantis,* a Greek language newspaper serving immigrants throughout the nation, began publication in Manhattan; it published daily from 1905 to 1972. By 1913, 32,200 Greeks lived in New York State with 20,000 concentrated in New York City. Initially they worked at menial jobs, but by 1910 many succeeded as small business owners. They established confectionery stores, florists, luncheonettes, restaurants, shoe-shine parlors, fruit stores, and wholesale produce enterprises that propelled them into the middle class in one generation. Greek immigrants soon supported a second Manhattan-based daily Greek language newspaper, *National Herald* (1915–), and in 1922 the Greek Orthodox Archdiocese of North and South America was established and headquartered in Manhattan. This same year Greek Americans founded the American Hellenic Educational Progressive Association (AHEPA) in Atlanta—originally to counter attacks by the Ku Klux Klan and later to represent the community on many issues affecting the new immigrants—

with chapters soon springing up in New York State.

A second wave of Greek immigration came after World War II. These arrivals moved in large numbers to Astoria (Queens Co) and transformed the economy and ambience of this New York City neighborhood, to create a robust new community there by the 1960s. Archbishop Demetrios Iakovos headed the Greek Orthodox Archdiocese of America from 1959 to 1997. During Archbishop Iakovos's tenure, the church launched its own widely read monthly newspaper, *Orthodox Observer* (1971), available in both Greek and English language editions. In 1972 George Douris founded the Astoria-based Hellenic American Neighborhood Action Committee (HANAC) to provide social services for post–World War II Greek immigrants. Additional newspapers commenced publication to serve the expanded community: biweekly English language *Hellenic Times* (1973–) headquartered in Manhattan, and daily Greek language *Proini* (1976–2001) and its weekly English language edition, *Greek American* (1986–2001) headquartered in Astoria. The 2000 US Census cited 159,763 people in New York State of Greek ancestry. Of these, 45,257 lived in Queens Co, 20,864 in Nassau Co, and 18,419 in Suffolk Co. Well-known Greek New Yorkers include the New York City–born opera star Maria Callas, actors Olympia Dukakis and Telly Savalas, entrepreneurs Dr T. Roy Vagelos of Merck Inc and Peter Peterson of Blackstone Group, and presidential advisor George Stephanopoulos.

See also ORTHODOX CHURCHES.

Saloutos, Theodore. *The Greeks in the United States* (Cambridge, Mass: Harvard Univ Press, 1964)

Scourby, Alice. *The Greek Americans* (Boston: Twayne Publishers, 1984)

Alice Scourby

Greeley, Horace (*b* Amherst, NH, 3 Feb 1811; *d* Pleasantville, Westchester Co, 29 Nov 1872). Journalist and politician. Greeley displayed a passion for learning from his earliest years, teaching himself to read by age 3. Largely self-taught, he became an apprentice to printer Amos Bliss at the *Northern Spectator* in East Poultney, Vt, in 1826. The paper failed in 1830, and the following year Greeley moved to New York City, where he found employment at several newspapers and dailies. He began to contribute articles to the papers and soon garnered a reputation in the city's press circles. Greeley's literary talents, along with his knowledge of printing, allowed him to found his own weekly literary journal, the *New-Yorker*, in 1834. Cheaper than most periodicals of its kind, the *New-Yorker* attained a circulation of more than 9,000 by 1837.

William H. Seward and Thurlow Weed encouraged Greeley to launch another weekly publication, the *Jeffersonian*, which served as the organ of the Whig Party in 1838–39. Its successor, the *Log Cabin*, began publication in May 1840, and a year later Greeley merged it with the *New-Yorker* to form the *New York Weekly Tribune*. Also in 1841, he founded a Whig penny daily, the *New York Tribune*, which quickly became one of the leading newspapers in the city, setting a new standard in American journalism by eschewing sensational stories in favor of items with moral content and intellectual appeal. The paper reflected Greeley's nationalism by championing a protective tariff, social and educational improvements, and a stable currency, while denouncing slavery. Greeley had political ambitions and ran for office in several elections, successful only once, in 1848, as a one-term Whig member of the US House of Representatives. He popularized editor John Soule's advice, "Go west, young man, go west," and traveled to California, writing about his trip in dispatches to the *Tribune*, which were published as *An Overland Journey*. Another of his trips, to the London World's Fair in 1851, led to a book, *Glances at Europe*.

Although dedicated to emancipation for slaves, Greeley also believed in the importance of maintaining the Union. Once war was started, he supported the North but also urged Pres Abraham Lincoln to engage in peace talks in July 1864. Nevertheless, the managing editor of the *Tribune*, Charles A. Dana, made the paper famous for its headline, "Forward to Richmond!" After the war, Greeley tended to side with the radical Republicans and endorsed the 14th and 15th Amendments. Initially a supporter of Pres Ulysses S. Grant, Greeley cooled toward the war hero because of the corruption of the first Grant administration. He ran against Grant on a combined Liberal Republican/Democratic ticket in 1872, and Greeley's critics attacked his ambivalent positions about the war and Grant and his shifting of party allegiances. The campaign was emotionally and physically draining. Greeley's wife died just one week before the election, and after Grant soundly defeated him, Greeley himself died only a month later.

Van Deusen, Glyndon G. *Horace Greeley: 19th-Century Crusader* (1953; repr Philadelphia: Univ of Pennsylvania Press, 1967)

Ryan Staude

Green, Andrew Haswell (*b* Worcester, Mass, 6 Oct 1820; *d* New York City, 13 Nov 1903). Lawyer and public official. Raised in Massachusetts, Green moved to New York City, where he studied law under Samuel J. Tilden and later became his partner, assisting in the indictment procedures (1871) against William M. "Boss" Tweed and other members of Tammany Hall who had defrauded the city. Green dedicated most of his life to public service and was a member of the New York City Board of Education (1855–61) and president and comptroller of the Central Park Commission (1857–71), where he worked with landscape architects Frederick Law Olmsted and Calvert Vaux. Credited with the development of several other city parks, including Riverside, Morningside, and Fort Washington, Green was also a board member for the Niagara State Preserve (1885; now Niagara Reservation State Park), the first state park in New York State, and is credited with consolidating the Lenox and Astor Foundations into the New York Public Library (1895), using a bequest left by Tilden.

He is best remembered for his critical role as an advocate for a consolidated New York City. In 1868 he proposed that the New York City region be placed "under one municipal authority," contending that the different local governments in the metropolitan area stymied development. He spent the next three decades championing his proposal to combine the City of New York and the cities and towns of Kings, Richmond, Queens, and lower Westchester Co into one municipality. In 1895 he was president of the Consolidation Inquiry Committee that drafted the plan for the consolidation of greater New York, which established the current five-borough city in 1898. Green was shot and killed in front of his Manhattan home by a deranged man who mistook him for someone else.

Foord, John. *The Life and Public Services of Andrew Haswell Green* (Garden City, NY: Doubleday, Page, 1913)

Jeffrey Kraus

Green, Beriah (*b* Preston, Conn, 24 Mar 1795; *d* Whitesboro, Oneida Co, 4 May 1874). Abolitionist and educator. Raised in New England where his family farmed and made furniture, Beriah Green trained for the ministry at Middlebury College in Vermont and Andover Seminary in Massachusetts. Ordained in 1822 he served the Congregational churches in Brandon, Vt, and Kennebunk, Me. In 1830 Green went to Hudson, Ohio, where he taught sacred literature at Western Reserve College. When students and faculty began discussing the immediate emancipation of slaves as called for by William Lloyd Garrison, Green used the chapel pulpit to condemn slaveholders and supporters of African colonization. Opposition from the school's conservative trustees caused Green to accept in 1833 the presidency of the Oneida Institute of Science and Industry in Whitesboro. Green radicalized the school, which had been chartered to educate recruits from the revivals of Charles Grandison Finney. He enrolled African American students, reformed the curriculum, and preached abolitionism. In his abolitionist career Green presided over the constituting convention of the American Anti-Slavery Society (1833), authored theological and exegetical essays, and supported the Liberty Party and its program of immediate emancipation.

After the demise of the Oneida Institute in 1844, Green developed a political philosophy based on his theories of "righteous government" in which wise leaders would replace participatory democracy where voters elected politicians who failed to end slavery. Breaking away from the Garrisonians, Green helped spearhead political abolitionism. He continued to preach, and his collected writings appeared in 1860 as *Sermons and Other Discourses with Brief Biographical Hints*. Green married twice. He had two children with his first wife, Marcia Deming, who died in 1826. Later that year he married Daraxa Foote and they had seven children. A temperance advocate, Green was speaking before Whitesboro's Board of Excise against the granting of a liquor license when he died in 1874. Though many of Green's former abolitionist associates failed to embrace his antidemocratic notions, they admired his scholarly writings and contributions to education reform; African Americans held Green in highest esteem for his radical humanitarian spirit.

See also ABOLITIONISM.

Sernett, Milton C. *Abolition's Axe: Beriah Green, Oneida Institute, and the Black Freedom Struggle* (Syracuse: Syracuse Univ Press, 1986)

Milton C. Sernett

Green, Shields (*b* ?1836; *d* Charles Town [now in W Va], 16 Dec 1859). Militant abolitionist. It was rumored that Green, a slave from Charleston,

SC, was of African royalty since he called himself Emperor. He escaped to Canada in 1856 and often worked in Rochester as a servant and waiter in Frederick Douglass's home. Green met John Brown in 1858 while visiting Douglass. Impressed with Green's fortitude and passionate stance against slavery, Brown convinced Green to participate in a large-scale slave revolt in the South involving the seizure of a US arsenal. On the night of 16 Oct 1859, Green and 20 compatriots raided Harpers Ferry [now in W Va] and took control of the arsenal. Robert E. Lee's troops suppressed the raid, capturing Green in the engine house. He was tried, convicted, then hanged for being a conspirator.

Renehan, Edward. *The Secret Six: The True Tale of the Men Who Conspired with John Brown* (New York: Crown Publishers, 1995)

Glenn Reynolds

Greenburgh. Town (pop 86,764) in SW Westchester Co. Greenburgh's riverfront on the Hudson was settled at the end of the 17th century by Dutch farmers, and English settled its eastern side in the second quarter of the 18th century. Both were tenants of Philipsburg Manor (1693). Part of the Neutral Ground during the Revolutionary War, it was the site of part of the Battle of White Plains (1776) and of a six-week encampment (1781) by the French forces under Comte de Rochambeau and American troops under Gen George Washington. Maj John André, carrying the plans to West Point for the British, was intercepted at Tarrytown in 1780. Philipse land, which had been devastated by the war, was sold by the state in 1785 as a result of the loyalist position of Frederick Philipse III and became freehold farms. Greenburgh was formed in 1788. Tarrytown developed in the 1780s as a river landing from which farm produce was shipped to New York City. The Harlem (1844) and Hudson River (1849) Railroads, running along east and west edges of Greenburgh, opened it up for suburban residences, particularly in the four river hamlets (Tarrytown, Irvington, Dobbs Ferry, Hastings-on-Hudson). Manufacturing followed in the second half of the 19th century, chiefly on the shore near the railroad. While improved roads date from the construction of Central Park Ave (1871), the Putnam Division of the New York Central (1880–1958) was more influential in the town's central area until the Westchester Co parkway system completed the Greenburgh sections of the Bronx River (1929) and Saw Mill River (1930) Parkways, encouraging residential development. Further growth followed World War II, facilitated by the Thruway (1955) and the Sprain Brook Parkway (1969). Industrial sites on the river were gradually given up in the late 20th century, and manufacturing, warehousing, and office functions are now concentrated north and west of Elmsford, while both White Plains Rd (commonly known as Tarrytown Rd) and Central Park Ave are major highway shopping districts. Greenburgh is the site of several social welfare agencies, including New York School for the Deaf, Graham School, and Children's Village, as well as three colleges: Marymount (1907), Mercy (1961), and Westchester County Community (1946; Greenburgh campus 1957).

Frank S. Jazzo

Greene. Town (pop 5,729) and village (pop 1,701) in SW Chenango Co. The Chenango River runs southwest through the center of the town. It was first settled in 1792, when a colony of upper-class French refugees from the French Revolution arrived, but most left within five years. The town was formed from Union [now in Broome Co] and Jericho [now Bainbridge] in 1798. The village, which incorporated in 1842, was laid out in 1806 on the Susquehanna and Bath Turnpike, an important east-west link between Bainbridge and Bath (Steuben Co). After 1837 the Chenango Canal passed through town, giving rise to groceries, warehouses, and hotels. Manufacturing included a foundry and machine shop (1840), still operating as the Raymond Corp; a woolen mill; a knife factory; and the Page Seed Co after 1896, which continues to market seeds worldwide. The Greene Railroad (1870) to Chenango Forks encouraged the establishment of a cheese factory and, later, a fluid-milk station. A large poultry operation at Genegantslet began in 1866 and was freezing poultry by 1878. From 1930 to 1950 poultry production was dominant in town, but high feed costs and the cold climate eventually moved it south. With increasing awareness of historic preservation, the Sherwood, a 1913 hotel, was reopened in 1988, helping to develop tourism. Many residents commute to jobs in the Binghamton region.

Michele A. McFee

Greene County (654 mi²/1,694 km²; pop 48,195). Formed from Albany and Ulster Cos in 1800 and named after Revolutionary War general Nathanael Greene, the county lies immediately west of the Hudson River and is divided into 14 towns that contain five incorporated villages. The Village of Catskill is the county seat. Greene Co straddles two physiographic regions: the Appalachian Plateau and the Hudson Valley portion of the Ridge and Valley Province. Its eastern margins fall within the Hudson Valley and comprise two distinct subregions that parallel the river: a relatively flat terrace that borders and overlooks the river and a range of low hills, 300–500 feet (90–150 m), known as the Kalkberg, whose bedrock is Ordovician, comprising various, relatively soft limestones, shales, siltstones, and sandstones. The plateau extends over more than 85% of the county and consists of two distinct subregions: the Catskill Mountains and the Helderberg Hills. The latter, known locally as the Hoogeberg, is an area of distinct, rounded hills that rise 800–1,000 feet (240–300 m) above the base and extend from the county's northern border south to the Catskills. Known colloquially as the Mountaintop, the Catskills rise abruptly as an escarpment nearly 2,000 feet (610 m) above the Hudson Valley and cover the southwestern part of the county. Overall, elevations range from sea level at the Hudson River to 4,025 feet (1,227 m) at the summit of Hunter Mountain. The bedrock is flat-lying limestone, shale, and sandstone of Devonian age. Continental ice sheets covered the entire county, smoothing and sculpting the terrain and depositing a substantial mantle of till. Mountain glaciers further shaped the Catskills. All but the extreme southwest corner of Greene Co lies within the greater Hudson River watershed, which includes the Hudson River, north-flowing Schoharie Creek, which drains most of the Mountaintop, southeast-flowing Catskill Creek, and its principal tributary, Kaaterskill Creek. Aside from some lands in the Hudson Valley and other limited areas, Greene Co soils are generally poor and best suited for grass-based agriculture.

Greene Co's climate is humid-continental. Mean July temperature is 70°F (21°C), slightly lower in the mountains and higher in the Hudson Valley. Daytime highs in the 90s°F (30s°C) are not unusual. Mean January temperature is less than 22°F (-6°C), somewhat lower in the mountains. Winter lows sometimes fall below 0°F (-18°C). Annual precipitation totals vary substantially, from 60 inches (152 cm) in the higher elevations in the southwest to 36 inches (91 cm) in the extreme northeast. Snowfall patterns also vary with elevation. Over 130 inches (330 cm) are expected in the higher Catskills, but only about 50 inches (127 cm) are anticipated near the Hudson. Primeval forest cover varied. Central hardwood forests, dominated by beech, sugar maple, and basswood along with some oak and chestnut, covered the Hudson Valley. Catskill forests consisted primarily of beech, sugar maple, yellow birch, hemlock, and white pine, augmented in places with spruce and fir. The Helderberg Hills were covered with beech, sugar maple, hemlock, white pine, and basswood. Roughly 80% of the county was covered by forest in 2000, and ap-

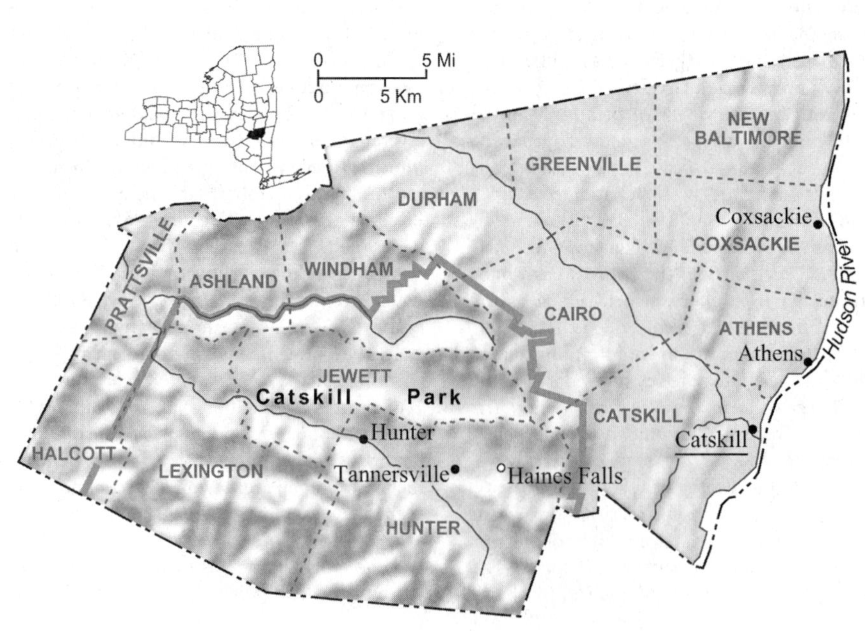

proximately 70,000 acres (28,000 ha) in south-central Greene Co lie within the Catskill Park.

American Indians and Early Settlement

Archaeological findings in Athens suggest that Greene Co was inhabited 12,500 years ago by seminomadic hunters. From about 500 BC on, Woodland peoples established villages along creeks and raised crops that included squash, maize, and tobacco. Village sites have been excavated at Four Mile Point in the Town of Coxsackie and at Lotus and Van Orden Points below Catskill. Flint artifacts have been found along Catskill and Coxsackie Creeks and Batavia Kill, and burial sites at Greenville and Leeds. The Flint Mine Hill, a National Register site, produced high-quality flint cores for at least 1,000 years. After European contact the Kattskill Indians, a Mohican (Mahican) group, occupied the eastern watershed of the Catskills from Saugerties [now in Ulster Co] to the lower reaches of the Coeymans Patent. With European encroachment on their lands, the Kattskill lost tribal identity and dispersed; some moved east to join the Stockbridge-Munsee Band of Mohicans, others migrated west, ultimately settling in Wisconsin.

The proximity of fertile land to the Hudson encouraged the earliest European settlers and patentees to secure title from the native inhabitants. The first settlement in what is now Greene Co is believed to have been along the banks of Catskill Creek in the late 1640s. One of the first settlers, Jan Jansen van Bremen, received a patent for land there in 1653. Pieter Bronck acquired his patent in 1662 at Coxsackie, to which he moved the following year; his dwelling forms part of the oldest surviving house in the state outside of the New York City area. Loonenburg Patent (1667), Coeymans Patent (1673), and Catskill Patent (1680) followed, opening much of the lowlands to settlement. Later officers and enlisted men of the French and Indian War received land patents of varying size. Altogether 71 patents were recorded for land in what is now Greene Co. The largest was about 140,000 acres (56,700 ha) of the 2 million-acre (809,000 ha) Hardenbergh Patent (1708). Colonial settlers were chiefly Dutch, Palatine German, and English migrants from other parts of the Hudson Valley. The earliest African Americans came as slaves at the time of initial European settlement. Most worked alongside their owners in the household or on the farm. In 1800 there were 520 slaves and 59 free Blacks in Greene Co. Some took Dutch surnames such as Van Slyke, Bronk, and Hotaling. A second group of African American men came in the decade following the Civil Was to work as laborers in the brickyards and elsewhere.

The Revolutionary War brought dissension and unrest. Resident loyalists were required to surrender their guns and were put under careful watch, and all eligible male residents were required to enroll in the companies making up the 11th Regiment of Albany Co Militia. Settlers on the western fringes of settlement abandoned their farms in fear of British-led raiding parties. Spared most ravages of the war, the area provided food, clothing, forage, and firewood for the war effort, including the military hospital at Albany. The end of the Revolution brought a large influx of New Englanders. Aside from John Hunter's holdings in the Hardenbergh Patent, which were leased to tenants, the land grants were quickly sold as freeholds or subdivided by inheritance. Rapid growth stalled after 1810 only to resume a decade later. But by 1830 Greene Co's population stood just shy of 30,000, a number that remained relatively stable for the next 140 years.

GREENE CO POPULATION CENSUS FIGURES

	White	Nonwhite	Total Population	Foreign-Born
1800	12,005	579	12,584	—
1810	18,798	738	19,536	—
1820	22,225	771	22,996	81
1830	28,531	994	29,525	182
1840	29,553	893	30,446	—
1850	32,231	895	33,126	2,049
1860	31,111	819	31,930	2,190
1870	31,203	629	31,832	2,486
1880	31,966	729	32,695	1,994
1890	30,942	656	31,598	1,862
1900	30,670	808	31,478	2,067
1910	29,699	515	30,214	2,579
1920	25,403	393	25,796	2,037
1930	25,308	500	25,808	2,448
1940	27,194	732	27,926	2,556
1950	27,859	886	28,745	2,941
1960	30,455	917	31,372	2,524
1970	32,118	1,018	33,136	2,569
1980	39,259	1,602	40,861	3,079
1990	41,583	3,156	44,739	2,894
2000	43,740	4,455	48,195	3,064

Notes: "Nonwhite" includes African Americans, Asians, American Indians, and Pacific Islanders and, for 2000, also the mixed race and other race categories. Through the 1960 census these figures primarily reflect the African American population. Foreign-born figures for 1820 and 1830 include only those not naturalized, and for 1930 and 1950, the foreign-born totals include Whites only. Other years include all foreign-born in the population.

Economic Development

Greene Co's economy has long been tied to the easy and inexpensive means of transport provided by the Hudson River. Fur trapping was important in the 17th century. Commercial agriculture developed during the 1700s with the sale of wheat, hay, and buckwheat. Saw, grist, and other mills also date from the colonial period. A tannery was established in 1750 at Athens. An abundance of waterpower encouraged other early manufacturing, including paper, combs, hats, bells and other iron goods, and stoneware. Each river town had one or more busy landings. Away from the river, all towns were linked by a road, unofficially known as the King's Highway, that extended from northern New Jersey to Albany. Athens, Catskill, and Coxsackie had horse and later steam ferry service across the Hudson. Access to the county's interior improved beginning in 1802 when the Susquehanna Turnpike joined Catskill with Wattles Ferry [now Unadilla, Otsego Co]. Other toll roads linked Hudson River ports with Mountaintop settlements and industry, most notably tanning. The Mountaintop's first tannery was established at Lexington in 1792, and larger ones followed in the Town of Hunter beginning in 1817. The largest was at Prattsville in 1824. The tanneries operated until the local supply of hemlock bark was exhausted. Other large manufacturers of the period included flour mills at Leeds and Red Falls, woolen mills at Prattsville, metal foundries at Oak Hill, a wrapping paper factory in the Town of Cairo, and a stoneware pottery at Athens. Beginning about 1820 Greene Co quarries and clay deposits began supplying bluestone, limestone, and bricks for buildings and pavement in New York City and Hudson Valley communities. By 1830 Coxsackie had over 20 brickyards. To secure Catskill's trade hinterland, the Canajoharie and Catskill Railroad was proposed and a line constructed between Catskill and southwest Albany Co before the effort was abandoned in 1841. The Hudson River fostered two major industries. Shipbuilding was done at Catskill by 1784 but, more important, at Athens and New Baltimore, where it continued until after World War I. Ice was first cut commercially in 1828. The region's tourist industry began in 1823 when the renowned Catskill Mountain House opened in the Town of Hunter. The county's first banks were the Catskill Bank (1813) and the Tanners Bank (1831), both at Catskill. The Coxsackie Bank was founded in 1851. By midcentury Irish famine refugees were living and working in the county as domestics and as common laborers.

There was substantial industrial expansion and subsequent decline in the second half of the 19th century and in the early 20th century. By the 1870s the woolen mills at Leeds had 700 workers and used 2,500 pounds (1,134 kg) of wool daily; a decade later they closed. The ice industry expanded dramatically in the mid-1870s, but refrigeration sent it into decline by 1920. Cement production began at Cementon and Alsen in 1900. Many Hudson Valley farmers turned to apple and pear production in what was otherwise an increasingly marginalized local farm economy. Railroad construction was revived in 1864 with a line connecting Athens and Schenectady, but through rail service arrived only in

POPULATIONS OF TOWNS, GREENE CO

Town, Year Founded	1800	1840	1880	1920	1960	2000
Ashland, 1848	—	—	899	560	548	752
Athens, 1815	—	2,387	3,065	2,361	2,804	3,991
Cairo, 1803[a]	—	2,862	2,287	1,487	2,825	6,355
Catskill, 1772[b]	2,408	5,339	8,311	7,670	9,906	11,849
Coxsackie, 1772[c]	4,676	3,539	4,009	2,994	4,794	8,884
Durham, 1790[d]	3,812	2,813	2,173	1,211	1,313	2,592
Greenville, 1803[e]	—	2,338	2,043	1,362	1,879	3,316
Halcott, 1851	—	—	396	272	193	193
Hunter, 1813[f]	—	2,019	1,882	2,309	1,799	2,721
Jewett, 1849	—	—	1,075	883	562	970
Lexington, 1813[g]	—	2,813	1,356	1,075	698	830
New Baltimore, 1811	—	2,306	2,620	1,536	1,972	3,417
Prattsville, 1833	—	1,613	1,118	830	790	665
Windham, 1798	1,688	2,417	1,461	1,246	1,289	1,660

[a]Canton until 1808.

[b]Informally considered a district from before 1767; formed as Great Inbogt District 1772; recognized as Town of Catskill 1788.

[c]Informally considered a district from before 1767; formed as district 1772; recognized as town 1788.

[d]Freehold until 1805.

[e]Greenfield until 1808, then Freehold until 1809.

[f]Greenland until 1814.

[g]Formed as New Goshen; renamed same year.

1883 when the West Shore linked the Hudson River towns with areas to the south. In the early 1880s some narrow-gauge lines were built to improve access to the Mountaintop and thus promote expansion of summer resort business. In the 1890s a cable railroad was added. The strategy worked: by 1907 tourist accommodations in the Town of Hunter alone exceeded 6,500. Simultaneously, an influx of various ethnic groups and a growing demand for privacy spawned five private residential resorts in the Town of Hunter between 1887 and 1889. As the period wore on clientele changed, and various ethnic groups began to establish distinct enclaves. In the 1890s, for example, Hunter and Tannersville became popular Jewish resorts. Other ethnic resort islands included Irish at Leeds, East Durham, and South Cairo; Italians at Cairo; and Scandinavians at Round Top.

The automobile fostered further change as the county's road system was improved and resort areas elsewhere in the country became more easily accessible. Partly in response all narrow-gauge rail lines permanently ceased operations in 1918. In 1900 there were over 2,700 farms in the county, averaging 123 acres (49.8 ha), but the agricultural economy languished, forcing farmers to search for income alternatives. More took in summer boarders. When Christmas trees became an American household custom, Mountaintop farmers began harvesting balsam fir. Elsewhere farmers attempted to specialize in dairying, aided by nearby creameries and improved refrigeration.

Religion, Education, and Culture

The earliest churches were organized by Dutch and Palatine German settlers. The first was erected by the Loonenburg [now Athens] Lutheran congregation in 1704. The Reformed Low Dutch Churches of Kattskill and Kocks-Hacky formed in 1732. The oldest standing church building is the Leeds Reformed Church, built of local stone in 1818. Methodism spread rapidly after the Revolution because of the efforts of circuit missionaries. The first Presbyterian and Baptist churches were formed at Greenville in 1793 and the first Episcopal church at Catskill in 1795. Irish immigration resulted in Roman Catholic parishes being established at Hunter (1836–37), Coxsackie (1845), Ashland, and Catskill (1853). At Hunter and Tannersville, four synagogues serving Jewish vacationers and year-round residents were formed between 1899 and 1909, later merging into two. Academies were founded at Catskill (1793), Greenville (1815), and Prattsville (1842). As the county's economic conditions improved prior to the outbreak of the Civil War, seminaries or collegiate institutes provided higher education to both sexes. The first public high school was in Catskill (1861). Centralization of Greene Co's schools took place between 1930 and 1961, and six school districts exist in the early 21st century. Since 1969 the county has also been served by SUNY's Columbia-Greene Community College, located in Hudson (Columbia Co).

The county's first newspaper, the *Catskill Packet,* began publication in 1792. Later called the *Recorder,* it represented a Democratic viewpoint. The *Catskill Messenger* (later *Catskill Examiner*) became the voice of the more conservative Whig and then Republican Parties. The papers merged in the 1930s. The *Catskill Daily Mail* (1901) continues the tradition, along with five weeklies. Libraries date from at least 1808, but the first free library was founded at Catskill in 1893. Nineteenth-century cultural offerings were often fostered by social clubs and presented by traveling troupes at local opera houses in Athens, Catskill, Coxsackie, and Greenville. One of the most famous people associated with Greene Co is landscape painter and founder of the Hudson River school of painters Thomas Cole (1801–48), who married Catskill native Maria Barton and made that village his permanent home. In the late 20th century, Greene Co experienced a burgeoning of arts groups, the most important being the Greene County Council on the Arts, with galleries at Catskill and Windham. Others include the Lexington Center for the Performing Arts, Altamura Center for Arts and Cultures at Round Top, and Shakespeare on the Hudson.

Politics

Politics in Greene Co was dominated in the early 19th century by the Federalists and later by the Democrats. Abraham Lincoln failed to carry the county in his two elections, and the Democratic majority continued until the mid–20th century. A shift after World War II began when some popular officials changed parties and got re-elected as Republicans. The county was thereafter a Republican stronghold, although some Democratic gains were evident in local Mountaintop elections in the late 1990s. The county government consisted of a board of supervisors elected by their towns until 1969 when a county legislature of 13 elected representatives was formed. Each representative is elected by the citizens of one or more towns, depending upon population. Government is administered by a county administrator.

Recent History

Greene Co's population remained relatively stable from 1850 until 1910. With abandonment of hill farms in the 1910s the population decreased 15%, and despite steady post–World War II growth, it was not until 1970 that the 1850 figure was exceeded. Since 1970 the population has increased 45%. Most African Americans reside in Catskill and Coxsackie; each village has a long-established black community and church. Since the end of World War II, change and revitalization efforts mark Greene Co's landscape. The construction of the New York State Thruway (1953–54) brought improved highway access and economic change, as evidenced by the warehouse facilities near the highway interchanges at Coxsackie and New Baltimore. In 2002 there were fewer than 250 active farms in the county, down from 1,300 in 1950. Ukrainian Americans began purchasing second homes in Jewett and Lexington in 1951 and within 10 years built the spectacular Church of St. John the Baptist. As the 21st century begins, these and other previously established ethnic enclaves have largely dissolved. Most resort hotels and boardinghouses are gone; some have been taken over by religious organizations. Second-home and condominium construction is apparent in various parts of the county. The largest development is Sleepy Hollow Lake (1971) in Athens. Skiing, first enjoyed locally in 1927, has become economically significant. The large ski areas at Hunter (1960) and Windham (1963) draw day use and weekend vacationers, and are large employers. A ski school was inaugurated at Hunter in 2002, providing an another attraction.

In addition to ski areas and Coxsackie and Greene Correctional Facilities, large employers included Stiefel Laboratories (350 workers) at Durham, Dynabil Industries (titanium prod-

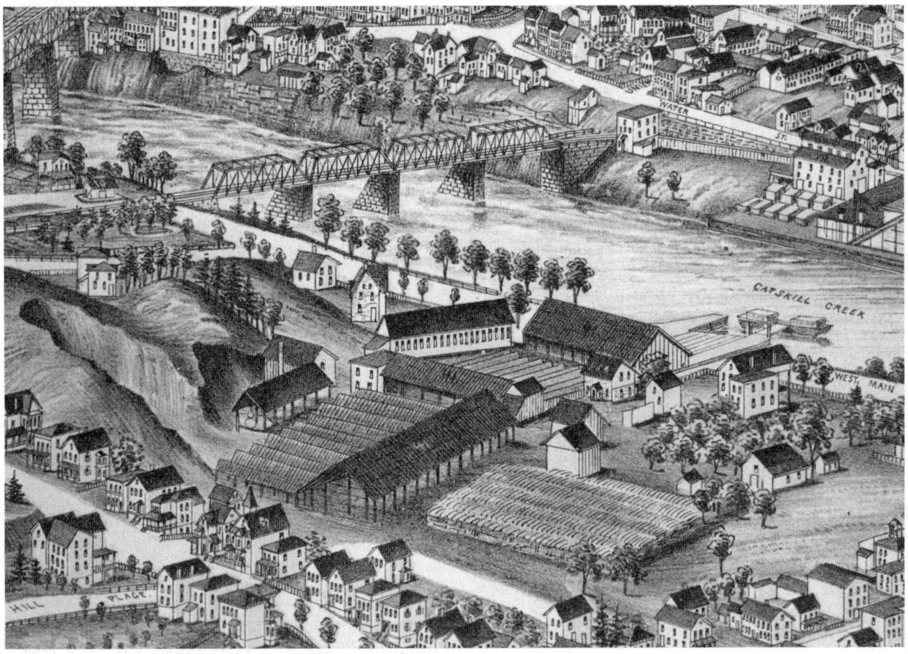

Panoramic view of Catskill, 1889.

ucts; 140 workers) at Coxsackie, and United Stationers (warehousing; 150 workers) also at Coxsackie. The river landings at Catskill, Athens, Coxsackie, and New Baltimore have been reconstructed for better utilization of the Hudson River and its shoreline. With the installation of municipal sewage treatment plants, the river has become a major recreational resource. The New Baltimore Conservancy and the Catskill Center for Conservation and Development, among others, have worked to improve and facilitate public use of Greene Co's natural environment.

At the beginning of the 21st century, the county was taking steps to diversify the economy to balance the long-established tourism sector. It invested in acquiring and building the infrastructure for the 200-acre (81 ha) Greene Business and Technology Park in Coxsackie; the first facility, a warehouse for Save-A-Lot (groceries), opened in 2003. The county has also turned its attention to the resources of the Village of Catskill, planning a new county office building, developing a farmers' market and recreational space at Catskill Point, and encouraging historic preservation efforts. The Athens Generating Plant, a facility of National Energy Group, came on-line in 2003 after a protracted debate and provides power at a reduced rate.

The standard histories are J. B. Beers, ed., *History of Greene County* (1884), which includes town histories, and Field Horne, *The Greene County Catskills: A History* (1994), which treats the county's history comprehensively and includes a thorough bibliography. The physical nature of the county is well covered in *Soil Survey of Greene County, New York* (1993) by the US Department of Agriculture, Soil Conservation Service. There are a number of town and village histories; for Coxsackie, see Raymond Beecher, *Under Three Flags* (1991). An excellent scholarly article discussing the 19th-century economy of one town is Richard C. Wiles, "Windham," *Hudson Valley Regional Review* 2 (1985): 54–72. Two of the residential parks have been chronicled by John A. MacGahan, *Twilight Park: The First 100 Years* (1988), and Christine G. McKay, et al, *There's a Place Up in the Mountains: A Centennial History of Elka Park* (1989). Black Dome Press in Hensonville has an ongoing publishing program that releases local documents and memoirs; an example is Philip duBois, *A Catskill Boyhood* (1992).

Raymond Beecher

Greenfield. Town (pop 7,362) in central Saratoga Co. Permanent settlement commenced in 1786, and the town was formed from Saratoga and Milton in 1793. Despite much infertile and mountainous land, farming predominated. A good site on Kayaderosseras Creek at Middle Grove was utilized for an early paper mill beginning in 1836. Bottles for Congress Spring water were made at Mount Pleasant (1846–66), and the Empire Graphite Co mined near Porter Corners from ?1903 until just after World War II. The first housing development in town was in 1966. Stewart's Ice Cream Co is the town's largest business. In the early 21st century, many residents commute to Saratoga Springs or larger cities to the south. The town's landmarks include Lester Park and Petrified Sea Gardens, where preserves of 500-million-year-old stromatolites *(Cryptozoon proliferum halli),* the remaining colonies of blue-green algae, are found. Lifelong resident Lawrence Older (1912–82) was a tradition-bearer of ballads and the Adirondack fiddle repertoire.

Field Horne

Green Haven Correctional Facility. A maximum security prison for men located in Stormville (Dutchess Co). The last of New York State's "Big Houses," its origins date from the 1920s, when the state conceived huge prisons to stem the tide of Prohibition era crime. Four of these institutions, including Attica (Wyoming Co) and Wallkill (Ulster Co), were built in the early 1930s, but more were needed as the number of inmates essentially doubled. Green Haven was built between 1939 and 1941, on a plan similar to Attica's, with 30 ft (9.1 m) walls and multitiered cellblocks surrounding enormous exercise yards. The US entry into World War II delayed the prison's opening, with the federal government leasing the property and using it as disciplinary barracks for deserters and problem soldiers during the war. Green Haven finally opened as a state prison in October 1949. After several decades of gradual growth, it reached capacity of about 2,200 inmates in the early 1980s.

Green Haven has from the beginning housed a large number of older violent felons with lengthy sentences. During the 1970s, corruption, mismanagement, and high turnover of staff led to a dramatic increase in inmate disturbances and a number of well-publicized escapes. Subsequent investigations resulted in numerous personnel changes and tighter security procedures. Since the 1980s Green Haven has become a prison of choice among the state's long-term inmates because its location, only 80 miles (129 km) north of New York City, allows many of them to be nearer their families. In addition, inmates are attracted to an honor program that allows special privileges including more spacious cellblocks and lenient visitation rights. The prison has developed extensive academic and vocational education offerings, as well as work opportunities in textiles, furniture construction, automotive repair, and farming. Also available are special counseling and treatment programs for substance abuse, aggression, and other problems. Since the 1990s the facility has maintained a special unit for physically disabled inmates and an Office of Mental Health psychiatric unit. Although Green Haven replaced Sing Sing (Dutchess Co) as the location for state executions in 1969, no execution had been performed there as of 2003. Green Haven's death house now consists of two cells with outdoor recreation areas, a visiting room, a viewing room for witnesses, and the execution room with the gurney. In 2003 inmates numbered *ca* 2,105 and staff, 831.

"Green Haven," *DOCS Today* 10 (Sept 2001): 12–16

Walinsky, Adam. *Corruption and Abuses in the Correctional System: The Green Haven Correctional Facility* (New York: , NYS Temporary Commission of Investigation, 1981)

Richard Andress

Green Island. Town (pop 2,278) and village (pop 2,278) in NE Albany Co. The coterminal municipality consists of Green Island, between the Hudson River and the sixth sprout (branch) of the Mohawk, along with Center and McGill Islands. The Rensselaer and Saratoga Railroad crossed the main island in 1835 and built its repair shops in 1840, but it was the Troy and Schenectady Railroad (1842) that fostered real growth. The Green Island Malleable Iron Works set up shop in 1852, and the Eaton and Gilbert Car Works, manufacturer of railroad cars, relocated from Troy the next year. The village incorporated in 1853. After the Civil War Green Island had two railroad car works and four foundries, and attracted many Francophone Canadian workers. In 1896 the town was formed from the extinct town of Watervliet [now Colonie]. As late as 1976, eight factories employed 2,200 workers, most notably Ford Motor Co (1923). It closed as deindustrialization affected the economy in the last decades of the century, but in 2003 Lydall Manning Paper Co, Zac Machine Tool and Die, and Honeywell remain industrial employers. Also in that year Sealy Mattress opened a plant employing 460 workers and Silhouette (eyewear) opened its North American corporate headquarters in the village. Congressman Michael McNulty, the third generation of his family to be active in politics, is a Green Island resident.

Greenlawn. Locality (pop 13,286) in Huntington (Suffolk Co). Originally common pastureland known as Oldfields, the name was changed when the Long Island Rail Road arrived in 1868, and it acquired a post office in 1872. In the 19th century it was known for its pickle works. Samuel Ballton (1838–1917), an escaped slave and Civil War veteran from Virginia who later became a real estate developer, earned the title "Pickle King" from his huge production of cucumbers. Home economist Christine Frederick (1883–1970) was a resident from 1912. The pickle industry was wiped out by a 1920s blight, but sauerkraut production continued until the 1940s. Suburban subdivision began in earnest in the 1950s. BAE Systems (1957; defense systems) employed 700 workers in 2003. The Greenlawn Pickle Festival (1977) is an autumn event.

Robert C. Hughes

Green Party. Political party. Active from the late 1980s, the party achieved four-year permanent status on the ballot in New York State after the statewide elections of 1998. Its strategy to achieve the requisite 50,000 votes was to nominate 88-year-old Al Lewis, famous for playing the role of Grandpa in the 1960s television series *The Munsters,* for governor. Adhering to the national Green Party's 10 values, the New York State platform stressed environmental, liberal social, and pro-worker issues. Specific Green legislative efforts in the state include the repeal of the Rockefeller Drug Laws, an increase in minimum wage, establishment of a living wage, and the expansion of housing subsidies and welfare. There are, in addition to the established party, numerous regional groups that operate as local, often issue-oriented, environmental organizations that are considered "Greens" on the basis of their adherence to the Green Party platform. Despite low enrollment the New York State Green Party presidential candidate Ralph Nader polled 244,030 votes in the state in 2000. Low turnout in 2002 cost the party its automatic slot on New York State ballots. Enrollment in 2003 was just over 36,000, with most members concentrated near urban areas, one-third in New York City.

Green Party of New York State, http://www.gpnys.org/
Sifry, Micah L. *Spoiling for a Fight: Third-Party Politics in America* (New York: Routledge, 2002)

John Evers

Greenport. Town (pop 4,180) in W Columbia Co. The town was formed in 1837 from Hudson so that its farmers would not have to pay taxes for city services. Limestone, granite, and shell marble were quarried on Becraft's Mountain in the 19th century; the short-line Jones Mountain Railroad (1889) served the quarries, which attracted some Italian quarrymen. The same part of town began cement production in 1902; in 2003 St. Lawrence Cement's plan to build a large plant was the focus of intense debate. Greenport began growing when, in 1920, suburban development adjacent to Hudson was initiated; in the following year an industrial tract opened. Greenport's US 9 developed as Hudson's highway retail district beginning with Simmons Hudson Plaza Shopping Center (1962). The town is the site of Columbia-Greene Community College (1969; Greenport campus, 1974), Olana State Historic Site (1870–72; home of painter Frederic Edwin Church), the Rip Van Winkle Bridge (1935), the oddly shaped Turtle House, and Rogers Island State Wildlife Management Area. Mt Merino's summit is the country's northernmost locale of cactus.

Greenport. Village (pop 2,048) in Southold (Suffolk Co). Settled from New England in the mid-17th century, the area was known as Sterling after the royal grantee, William Alexander, Lord Stirling. Greenport became a center of trade with the West Indies and a major whaling port from the 1790s. Main St was platted in 1827, and the original post office, called Farms (1824), was renamed Greenport in 1832. The village was incorporated in 1838. It became the terminus of the Long Island Rail Road in 1844 and thus an important steamboat landing en route to Boston. When whaling ended, *ca* 1860, menhaden fishing became important; later, around 1900, Greenport oysters became famous. Shipyards built and repaired commercial fishing boats, coastal schooners, and pleasure craft. At the Beebe-McLellan yard, lifesaving boats were the main product (1879–1918). During both World Wars the yards built minesweepers and landing craft for the US Navy. Always a magnet for actors and writers, Greenport has revitalized its waterfront in recent decades. It is the site of the Railroad Museum of Long Island (one of two branches) and of the East End Seaport Museum, and the Maritime Festival is held annually in September. Mitchell Park, which features a restored 1920s carousel, hosts dances and concerts.

Antonia Booth and Thomas Monsell

Greenville. Locality (pop 8,648) in Greenburgh (Westchester Co). Its identity was shaped by the Greenville Community Reformed Church (1842) and Greenville School District No. 10 (1858), but especially by the Edgemont Estates development (1910), which gave the area its other commonly used name, Edgemont. In 1871 growth was stimulated by the construction of Central Park Ave (Rte 100), now a major retail corridor. Suburban development accelerated after World War II. Greenville is the site of the Greenburgh Nature Center and Museum. Asians, residents since the 1970s, made up 19.75% of the population in 2000, with Japanese representing 7.7%.

Scott C. Monje

Greenville. Town (pop 3,316) in NE Greene Co. While first settled in 1750 and patented and resettled, in part, in 1764 by Augustine Prevost, most settlers arrived after the Revolution from Connecticut, Massachusetts, and Dutchess Co. Formed as Greenfield in 1803, its name was changed to Freehold in 1808 and to Greenville in 1809. It was chiefly agricultural, with no industry and very few boardinghouses, until guest farms became an important local business after World War I and declined in the last quarter of the 20th century. A few farms remain, but the town is chiefly rural residential, with many residents commuting to Albany.

Field Horne

Greenville. Town (pop 3,800) in W Orange Co. Settled in the early 18th century, the town was formed in 1853 from Minisink. The Shawangunk Mountains form its western border. Greenville became a farming district, chiefly in dairy; in 1860 it had five creameries, as well as a cider mill and a hat factory. In 1966 and 1970, I-84 was completed across the town. Greenville's 1960 population of 890 more than quadrupled by 2000. Farming continues, with some dairies along with beef, horse, and crop farms.

Greenwich [GREEN-WITCH]. Town (pop 4,896) and village (pop 1,902) in W Washington Co. Settled 1763–64, the town was formed from Argyle in 1803. It is bounded on the south by the Batten Kill, which provided waterpower for mills at a string of dams along its length, producing cloth, paper, plows, woodworking machinery, lumber, plaster, and cement. It had one of the state's early cotton factories (1804). The village, first called Whipple City, was incorporated in 1809 as Union Village and changed its name to Greenwich in 1867. It extends into the Town of Easton. Rail service was provided by the Greenwich and Johnsonville Railroad (1870), part of which survives as the Batten Kill Railroad (1994). Bald Mountain, a hamlet, was devoted to the production of lime. Irish workers at Dunbarton Flax Mill (1880–1952), a branch of a firm at Gilford, Ireland, manufactured linen thread; its employees helped form the Greenwich Cricket Club (1880–88). In the early 21st century, many residents commuted to Saratoga Springs and the Capital District, but Toy Works in Middle Falls and Phantom Laboratories (prosthetic devices) and the Hollingsworth and Vose paper mill in Center Falls and Clarks Mills continued the manufacturing sector. Battenville and Center Falls were home to Susan B. Anthony (1820–1906) from 1826 to 1845.

R. Paul McCarty

Greenwich Village. Lower Manhattan neighborhood whose borders run from 14th St south to Houston St and from the Hudson River east to 4th Ave. After the English conquest of New Amsterdam in 1664, the area developed into a country hamlet known as Greenwich. For the next 150 years, it retained its sleepy nature, a bucolic suburb over 2 miles (3 km) from the developed area of New York City. It was dotted with farms and estates, many serving as summer retreats for the city's elite. In 1789 the city bought half of the current site of Washington Square Park to produce a potter's field, the northwest corner of which was the site of a public gallows. During this time Greenwich Village was a refuge for wealthy residents, and the severe yellow fever epidemic of 1822 led to a major influx of city residents, many staying on once the outbreak had subsided. The population quadrupled from 1825 to 1840, transforming it into a more vibrant, residential district. The burial ground was converted to a military parade ground, the area of Washington Square was built up extensively with row houses, and lower 5th Ave experienced a surge in real estate development.

The upper-class residences built around Washington Square Park were the most fashionable homes in the city. Built in brick Federal style and later Greek Revival, these homes made up a pure residential district and were an early example of separating home from work. While west and north of Washington Square housed the more affluent residents, the south was a working-class community. One-quarter of New York City's black residents lived in an area known as Little Africa around Bleecker and MacDougal Sts. This district housed the first black newspaper in the country, *Freedom's Journal* (1827–29), and the first black theater, the African Grove (1821–23) on Mercer St.

Around the turn of the 20th century, new immigrants, especially Italians, came to the neighborhood. The area had some factories, and in 1911 the fire at the Triangle Shirtwaist Factory on Washington and Greene Sts that took the lives of 146 females (mostly immigrant women and girls) had a catalyzing effect on the labor movement and working conditions generally. In the first decades of the 20th century, because of its comparative isolation, historic flavor, and cheap rents, Greenwich Village found itself populated and frequented by a growing community of artists and intellectuals, often with avant-garde, left-leaning political orientations. It became home to noteworthy radicals such as Max Eastman, editor of the *Masses,* a monthly socialist magazine published from 1911 to 1917, and John Reed, who also worked for the magazine, and early feminists including Ida Raugh and Crystal Eastman. In the fine arts, the Ashcan school, including Robert Henri, John Sloan, and William Glackens, with its signature style of heavy realism focusing on the grittier details of everyday life, had its first show at the Macbeth Gallery in Greenwich Village in 1908. In literature, resident writers included Theodore Dreiser, Sherwood Anderson, Marianne Moore, John Dos Passos, and Hart Crane.

During the 1940s and 1950s Greenwich Village was again the site of influential artistic movements. Many of the resident abstract impressionist painters included Robert Motherwell, Jackson Pollock, Robert Rauschenberg, and Mark Rothko. Greenwich Village became, with Harlem and the 52d St area, a beacon for jazz. In the 1950s it was the center of the beat movement in poetry alongside the growth of coffeehouses, galleries, and theaters where poetry readings and "happenings" were a nightly occurrence. By the early 1960s the folk movement was in full bloom, especially on MacDougal St, with Bob Dylan as a rising force. The modern gay rights movement was born in Greenwich Village following the June 1969 Stonewall riots when police raided the Stonewall Inn, a gay bar on Christopher St. The patrons fought back, barricaded the police in the bar, and protested their treatment by the officers. The protests lasted for three days and began a highly visible effort at political mobilization for the gay community. Each year, the Gay Pride Parade culminates in Greenwich Village during the last weekend in June to commemorate Stonewall. Greenwich Village continues to have a high concentration of gay residents.

The Greenwich Village community has also worked to preserve the integrity of the neighborhood. A plan to build a four-lane sunken highway through Washington Square Park was defeated in 1958 because of strong community opposition. In 1969 came the designation of the Greenwich Village Historic District, which encompasses approximately one-third of the neighborhood. Since then, the historic district has protected more than 2,000 buildings from potential destruction. With the increase in the desirability of the area, escalating rents and housing prices caused many, especially artists, to leave, a large number taking up residence farther east of Broadway, in the area that became known as the East Village. Greenwich Village has become in the last several decades one of the most exclusive parts of Manhattan.

See also FOLK MUSIC REVIVAL; THEATER, NEW YORK CITY.

Miller, Terry. *Greenwich Village and How It Got That Way* (New York: Crown Publishers, 1990)

Stonehill, Judith. *Greenwich Village: A Guide to America's Legendary Left Bank* (New York: Universe Publishing, 2002)

Wetzsteon, Ross. *Republic of Dreams: Greenwich Village, the American Bohemia, 1910–1960* (New York: Simon & Schuster, 2002)

Leonard Benardo

Greenwood. Town (pop 849) in SW Steuben Co. Settled in 1821, the town was formed in 1827 from Troupsburg and Canisteo. Irish Catholics settled in the 1830s. The first natural gas well in New York State was established here *ca* 1870, abandoned, then reestablished in 1904 and 1934. The New York and Pennsylvania Railroad served Greenwood on its route from Genesee, Pa, to Canisteo (1896–1935). In the early 21st century the Greenwood public school system is the major employer. The highest point on a New York State highway, 2,306 ft (702.9 m), is on Rte 417 at West Greenwood.

Virginia L. Wright and Jerry Wright

Greenwood Lake. Village (pop 3,411) in Warwick (Orange Co). Located on Orange Co's largest lake, it developed as a resort following construction of its first hotel in 1874. A steamboat on the lake provided passenger service, as did the New York and Greenwood Lake Railroad (1876–1930s). Greenwood Lake post office opened in 1876. In the 1890s land at the lake's north end was platted, and cottages were constructed. The village was incorporated in 1924. It remains a center of both summer and winter recreation.

Greig [GREG]. Town (pop 1,365) in SE Lewis Co. Settled in the 1790s by French refugees, the town was formed from Watson in 1828 as Brantingham and renamed in 1832. In addition to sawmills and a tannery (1849), Greig was home to wooden toy and piano sounding-board production; two paper mills (1887–95) were short-lived. Brantingham and other lakes are the sites of many private camps, and the Brantingham Inn (1876–1966) was a resort hotel. After World War I large numbers of Hungarian and Polish immigrants arrived; the Hungarian American Citizens League was formed in Greig in 1924 and continued through the 1950s. Hungarian Americans remain a large part of the population, which has doubled since World War II.

Arthur Einhorn

gridlock. A term coined in the early 1970s by Sam Schwartz and Roy Cottam, traffic engineers in the New York City Department of Traffic, to describe traffic conditions grinding to a halt in the rectangular grid pattern of Manhattan streets. This ominous term was used between these engineers for a decade before it was formally introduced into the public vocabulary. The word made it into the public lexicon during the New York City transit strike of 1980, when reporters learned that traffic engineers were worried about gridlock and started using the term in the newspapers and on the airwaves. The word was an instant hit. It has evolved to mean any large-scale traffic jam and to describe any type of stalemate, "legislative gridlock" and "economic gridlock" being but two examples.

See also NEW YORK CITY REGIONAL TRANSPORTATION.

Samuel I. Schwartz

Griffes, Charles Tomlinson (*b* Elmira, 17 Sept 1884; *d* New York City, 8 Apr 1920). Composer, pianist, teacher. Griffes was tutored in music, art, literature, manners, dress, and grammar by Mary Selena Broughton, a piano teacher at Elmira College. When he graduated from high school in 1903, he set off for Berlin to study piano and composition until 1907 with teachers such as Engelbert Humperdinck. Griffes performed occasionally and taught piano and harmony to a handful of students. When he returned to the United States, he became director of music at the Hackley School in Tarrytown (Westchester Co), where he taught piano, directed a choir, performed recitals, and accompanied church services, and he spent every spare moment in New York City promoting his music. He frequented several homosexual meeting places in the city and developed a relationship with a city policeman. He explored German Romanticism in his early works and French Impressionism in works between 1911 and 1916. Moving beyond these models he began to cultivate a more personal style, which employed "near-atonality," oriental idioms, and scales of his own creation. During his short career Griffes produced a small body of beautiful and haunting works, including songs for voice and piano in English, German, French, and Javanese/Sundanese. He wrote *Three Poems of Fiona MacLeod;* works for piano including *The White Peacock* and his *Sonata;* a few orchestral compositions, most of them based on his piano works, such as *The Pleasure-Dome of Kubla Khan;* theater pieces including *The Kairn of Koridwen;* and a string quartet based on Indian themes. In *Three Preludes for Piano,* his last works completed before he died of complications from influenza, Griffes arrived at an austere succinctness of means and expression.

Anderson, Donna K. *Charles T. Griffes: A Life in Music* (Washington, DC: Smithsonian Institution Press, 1993)

Donna K. Anderson

Griffiss Air Force Base (AFB). The Rome Air Depot (Oneida Co) began operations in August 1941 and in 1948 was renamed for Lt Col Townsend E. Griffiss of Buffalo, the first American flyer to die over Europe during World War II. The base served as the Air Materiel Command (AMC; later Air Force Logistical Command), until 1951. That year Watson Laboratories, renamed the Rome Air Development Center and later the Rome Laboratory, moved to the base, which from 1951 to 1954 served as the Air Research and Development Command and from 1954 to 1968 as the AMC again. Headquarters Ground Electronics Engineering Installation

Agency, stationed at Griffiss in 1958, became the host command, responsible for the facilities for the assigned units, in 1968. Combat units have included the 1st Interceptor Group (1950–51), the 4727th Air Defense Group (1957–59), and the 49th Fighter Squadron (1959–87). Beginning in 1959 Griffiss was also home to the 4039th Strategic Wing, redesignated the 416th Bombardment Wing in 1963. The 416th, which became host in 1970, was charged with part of the Northeast American Air Defense Sector (NEADS) mission, maintaining the Strategic Air Command (SAC) around-the-clock flight by B-52s with the potential to carry nuclear weapons. Both air refueling tankers and heavy bombers were based at Griffiss. Beginning in 1983 it was Headquarters 24th North American Air Defense Region. The base comprised 2,488 acres (1007 ha) in the northeastern section of Rome and engaged 7,000 civilian and military personnel to maintain operations when closure was recommended in 1993; the New York Air National Guard assumed the NEADS mission. Except for Rome Laboratory, all other Air Force units were relocated, and Griffiss AFB officially closed in 1998. At the beginning of the 21st century the site houses Griffiss Business and Technology Park and employs 3,700.

Yenne, Bill. *SAC: A Primer of Modern Strategic Airpower* (Novato, Calif: Presidio Press, 1985)

Michael J. Stenzel

Griffith, D(avid Lewelyn) W(ark) (*b* near Crestwood, Ky, 22 Jan 1875; *d* Los Angeles, 23 July 1948). Film producer and director. The son of an impoverished Confederate colonel, Griffith became an actor in 1896, touring under several stage names and moving to New York City in June 1906, where he wrote an unsuccessful play. In 1907 he began acting for the Biograph Co and the following year directed his first film, *The Adventures of Dollie.* Over the next five years, he became the company's principal director and made close to 500 films, almost all of them one reel (6–14 minutes), the standard length of the period.

His superior work was immediately recognized, particularly for his varied camera placements and imaginative editing. He either initiated or perfected conventions later adopted by the industry—fade-ins, fade-outs, close-ups, and the last-minute ride-to-the-rescue—and was one of the primary creators of the language of the cinema. Some films were made on location in New York City streets, in Central Park, and across the Hudson River in Fort Lee, NJ. In the summers of 1909 and 1910 he traveled to Cuddebackville (Orange Co) for its country settings. The difficulty of shooting exteriors in winter prompted him in 1911 to take his actors and technicians to Los Angeles, where he could build large exterior sets lit by sunlight. Each year he returned to New York for the warmer seasons.

After leaving Biograph in the fall of 1913, he made two feature films at a studio at 29th St and, back in California, made his most famous and controversial film, *The Birth of a Nation,* which premiered at the Liberty Theater on 42d St in 1915. Returning west, he produced and directed seven additional features, including the extraordinarily lavish landmark *Intolerance* (1916). He then went independent and in 1919 purchased the Flagler Mansion at Orienta Point in Mamaroneck (Westchester Co). There he erected a large studio and filmed portions of *Way Down East* (1919), *Orphans of the Storm* (1921), which used an extensive reconstruction of 18th-century Paris, and several other films. The Revolutionary War epic *America* (1923) was shot partially in nearby Somers (Westchester Co). In 1919 Griffith founded United Artists with Charlie Chaplin, Douglas Fairbanks, and Mary Pickford. United Artists was initially intended to be a distribution, not a production, company.

By 1924 Griffith's independent studio failed, and in 1925–26 he joined Paramount at its Astoria (Queens Co) studios, using many Suffolk Co locations in *Sally of the Sawdust* (1925) and making two other films. In 1927 he returned to California and sold his voting rights in United Artists; he later became a contract director for the company and directed four more films for it. His final film was an independent production, *The Struggle* (1931), a study of alcoholism. For his interiors he used studios at 175th St and, unusual for this time, shot dialogue scenes on actual city streets in the Bronx. Griffith continued to live in hotels in Manhattan until 1934, when he returned to Kentucky. From the mid-1940s until his death he lived in Hollywood.

Henderson, Robert M. *D. W. Griffith: His Life and Work* (New York: Oxford Univ Press, 1972)
Schickel, Richard. *D. W. Griffith* (New York: Simon & Schuster, 1984)

Arthur Lennig

Groton. Town (pop 5,794) and village (pop 2,470) in NE Tompkins Co. Settled in 1797, the town was formed from the southern half of Locke (Cayuga Co) in 1817 as Division, and the name changed to Groton in 1818. Products in the 19th century included carriages, ironwork, and agricultural implements. The village incorporated in 1860, acquiring a railroad station on the Southern Central in 1870. The Groton Iron Bridge Co (1877–1901) was famed for metal-truss bridges. Typewriter manufacture began in the 1890s, and L. C. Smith Co (1896) became Smith Corona in 1926 and employed over 1,000 in the 1930s. As Smith-Corona-Marchant (1958) it left the village in 1983. Tompkins-Cortland Community College operated in town from 1968 to 1974 before moving to Dryden. Many Groton residents commute to Ithaca and Cortland. The early 20th-century photographs of Verne Morton (1868–1945) at the DeWitt Historical Society in Ithaca document the agricultural, technological, and social changes of the area. Welthea Marsh of Groton is thought to have been the first woman bank president in the United States (1896).

Jane Dieckmann

Grove. Town (pop 533) in NE Allegany Co. Settled in 1818, the town was formed from Nunda [now in Livingston Co] in 1827 as Church Tract; the name was changed in 1828. The Buffalo Division of the Erie Railroad came through in 1852. Grove was also served by the Pittsburg, Shawmut and Northern (1903–46). Germans in the west part of town formed a German evangelical church in 1856. Farming included dairying and stock breeding. In the early 21st century, Swain Ski Center is an attraction. A portion of Rattlesnake Hill State Wildlife Management Area lies within Grove's boundaries.

Groveland. Town (pop 3,853) in central Livingston Co. A village called Williamsburgh was settled in 1792 by German immigrants under Charles Williamson, who organized a fair and races in 1793, but that colony broke up a few years later. The town was formed from Sparta (Ontario Co) in 1812, and three railroads were built through it between 1868 and 1891. Sonyea was the site of a Shaker community from 1837 to 1894, which then became the Craig Colony (1896–1968), a state facility for people with epilepsy and, later, for those with developmental disabilities. The site became Groveland Correctional Facility in 1982 and was joined by Livingston Correctional Facility in 1991. Inmates made up 62% of the town's population in 2000. I-390 opened through town in 1979. American Rock Salt Co (1997) opened a mine at Hampton Corners in 2001, served by a new (2000) spur of the Genesee and Wyoming Railroad. The town's flats are excellent for crops and grazing, and farming is central to its economy.

Mary Jo Marks

Grumman, Roy [Leroy Randle] (*b* Huntington, Suffolk Co, 4 Jan 1895; *d* Manhasset, Nassau Co, 4 Oct 1982). Aeronautical engineer and aviation executive. Grumman, whose family owned a carriage shop in Huntington, decided on an aviation career at an early age. He attended Huntington High School and in 1916 graduated from Cornell University with a degree in mechanical engineering. He continued his education at Columbia University and, as a member of the Naval Reserve during World War I, studied airplane inspection and aeronautical engineering at the Massachusetts Institute of Technology. Trained as a naval aviator, Grumman was a flight instructor at the Naval Air Training Station in Pensacola, Fla in 1918 and the following year was transferred to the Naval Aircraft Factory in Philadelphia, where he became a test pilot and project engineer. In 1920 Grumman went to work for a small New York City aircraft manufacturer, Loening Aeronautical Engineering Corp, as a test pilot and plant manager. He left Loening in 1929 to start his own company, the Grumman Aircraft Engineering Corp, which opened 2 Jan 1930 in Baldwin (Nassau Co). In 1931 the company secured a contract from the US Navy to produce the first of an unbroken line of Grumman navy aircraft that extended to the end of the century. The company settled in Bethpage (Nassau Co) in 1937 and became one of Long Island's major employers. Grumman resigned as company president in 1946 but continued to take an active role as chairman of the board until 1966. He remained a board member until 1972 and held the honorary title of board chairman until his death.

Thruelsen, Richard. *The Grumman Story* (New York: Praeger, 1976)

Louis R. Eltscher

Grumman Corporation. See NORTHROP GRUMMAN CORPORATION.

Gualillo, Nicholas Demi (*b* Utica, 19 Apr 1903; *d* Franklin, NC, 1 May 1990). Violinist, composer, and conductor. He studied music at the New England Conservatory of Music in Boston and in 1938 received his master's degree from

Syracuse University. In 1928 Gualillo married the soprano Meta Dinger. They settled in Utica, where he frequently performed as a violinist and operated his own music studio. That same year he became the first conductor of the Warner Bros Stanley Theater Symphony Orchestra and in 1933 established the Utica Symphonic Orchestra to provide work for unemployed musicians. From 1935 to 1940 he was co-conductor of the New Utica Orchestra and in 1939 became the first student at Syracuse University to earn a doctoral degree in music. He was appointed conductor of the Syracuse Symphony Orchestra in 1940, when it was under the auspices of the Work Projects Administration. Gualillo was founder and director of the Syracuse Conservatory of Music, the Syracuse Philharmonic Orchestra, the Syracuse Inter-City Opera, and the Manhattan Grand Opera Cos. He composed at least 60 works of music, including symphonies, songs, transcriptions, and one opera, which premiered in New York City in 1977. In 1984 Gualillo was selected for the *International Who's Who in Music.*

Cardarelli, Malio J. *Classical Music in Utica, New York—A History—Featuring Nicholas D. Gualillo* (New Hartford, NY: Author, 2000)

Malio J. Cardarelli

Guatemalans. The Guatemalan presence in New York State is the creation of a migration wave that began in the early 1970s as a result of political violence in Guatemala. People also left in search of economic opportunities, with men migrating first, followed by wives and families. They initially settled in New York City, but by the 1990s there were significant populations in Westchester Co and smaller groups in urban areas statewide. By that time 50% of Guatemalan New Yorkers had English proficiency. About 25% had attained the equivalent of an eighth-grade education, and 43% had a high school degree or some college education. Less than 2% of the state's Guatemalans had resorted to any form of state or federal assistance. Most households contained two, three, or more workers. Guatemalans held a large array of jobs, most commonly working as aides, cooks, janitors, gardeners, machine operators, truck drivers, construction workers, carpenters, or painters, or labored in textile production or assembly work in garment-producing shops, particularly in New York City. Many also worked in the service sector in private households. Most Guatemalans in New York State are Roman Catholics, though perhaps 20–30% belong to evangelical Protestant churches, reflecting the religious breakdown in Guatemala. In 1994 the Roman Catholic Church of the Presentation in Queens acquired an image of Christ of Esquipulas, a national Guatemalan religious symbol. In New York City, Guatemalans gather on 15 September to celebrate the independence of Guatemala. The national musical instrument, the marimba, is played on this and other festive occasions. The 2000 US Census recorded 29,074 Guatemalan residents in New York State, 15,212 of them living in New York City (largely in Queens Co); other sources suggest that the numbers may be higher.

Loucky, James, and Marilyn M. Moors, eds. *The Mayan Diaspora: Guatemalan Roots, New American Lives* (Philadelphia: Temple Univ Press, 2000)

Liliana R. Goldín

gubernatorial elections. The governor is the most visible public official in New York State, and elections for the office receive extensive public attention. They are important to state politics for two reasons. First, they provide an arena for debating the public policy directions the state should take. Second, the constitution grants the executive considerable power over forming the budget and executing state policy. The policy debate during the elections continues to be shaped by the regional political fault lines within the state.

Gubernatorial elections in New York State have since the 1820s generally not been won by wide margins. When the state was split on vital issues, such as the expansion of slavery, the conduct of the Civil War, or the role of Tammany Hall, gubernatorial votes were close. Horatio Seymour, a two-term governor of the state, lost to opponents in 1850 and 1854 by margins, respectively, of 262 and 309 votes. Since the 1850s Democrats and Republicans have vied for office. Of the 31 men elected governor between 1856 and 2002, 16 have been Republicans and 15, Democrats. The battleground has generally been geographic, with the Democrats controlling New York City and the Republicans, much of the rest of the state. This pattern emerged in the 1850s and 1860s and continues at the start of the 21st century. Frank S. Black, in 1896, was the last Republican candidate to win a majority of the votes from New York City.

The Simple Upstate-Downstate Era

Modern-day New York City was created in 1898 when the state legislature merged five counties. New York City has generally been more Democratic and liberal, and the remainder of the state has been conservative and Republican. These regional bases were central to the appeals and electoral bases of the political parties. For much of the 20th century gubernatorial elections were shaped by the dominance of New York City as a source of votes. Only one city in the nation, New York City, had contributed such a high percentage of one state's votes. From 1900 through the mid-1970s, New York City constituted at least 40% of all votes in the state (Fig 1). The gubernatorial elections of 1918 and into the 1920s involving Alfred E. Smith, a Democrat from New York City, had a major impact on the partisan loyalties of the city. New York City varied between roughly 45% and 55% Democratic until Smith, a liberal Democrat by standards of that era, made a strong appeal to the ethnic Whites and the working class that dominated the city. His appeals were successful, and he mobilized many new voters into the political process, shifting Democratic support into the range of 70%. The city has continued to vote predominantly Democratic.

The gubernatorial elections of Smith's era were held every two years. As governor, Smith led an effort to enhance the power of the governor's office, which resulted in the creation of the executive budget, implemented in 1927; it is submitted by the governor and must be voted upon before the legislature can create its own budget. The executive budget gave the governor significantly greater power over most state agencies and hence state policy. The term of office was increased to four years beginning in 1938.

Because of New York City's size, beginning in the 1920s Republican candidates had to appeal to New York City voters to have a chance to win the gubernatorial election. From the 1920s through the 1990s the only Republicans who won were those who received approximately 40% or more of the New York City vote. Republican candidates have almost always done well outside New York City (Fig 2, page 680). Crucial is the variation in success within New York City. The cases of relatively high percentages within New York City coincide with Republican victories. Republicans who ran as conservatives were not successful. In contrast, victorious Republican gubernatorial candidates Thomas E. Dewey (1942, 1946, 1950) and Nelson A. Rockefeller (1958, 1962, 1966, 1970) were relatively liberal for Republicans. This pushed the policy debate in New York State more to the liberal side, which was particularly significant in the 1960s. Gov Rockefeller was willing to support significant tax increases to fund more state programs. Taxes and state spending, which had been close to the national average for decades, rose well above the national average. These higher levels of taxation and spending on many programs (eg, Medicaid) have continued into the 21st century, resulting in the state having one of the highest state and local tax burdens in the nation.

Diminished Influence of New York City?

The 1994 gubernatorial election between Democratic incumbent Mario M. Cuomo and Republi-

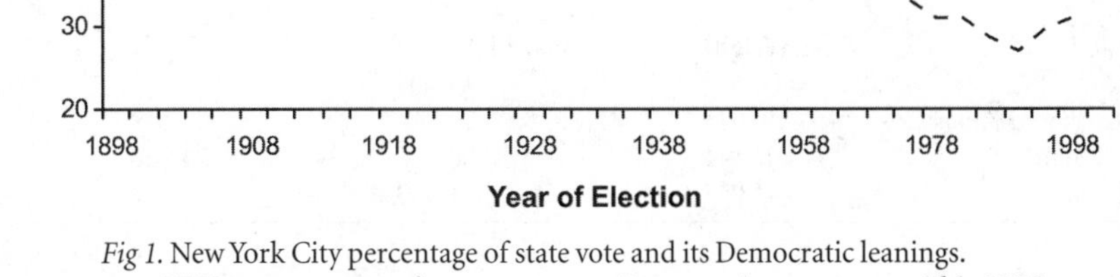

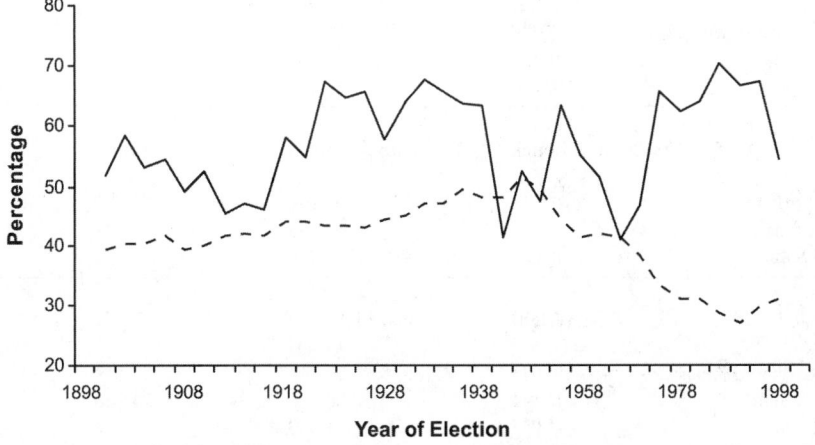

Fig 1. New York City percentage of state vote and its Democratic leanings.
– – – NYC as percentage of state vote; —— Democratic percentage within NYC.

GUBERNATORIAL ELECTIONS

1824	**De Witt Clinton**	Samuel Young	Total
	(Clinton Rep)	(Van Buren Rep)	
New York and Kings Cos	5,921	5,103	11,024
Rest of State	97,763	82,934	180,697
Total State	103,684	88,037	191,721

1826	**De Witt Clinton**	William B. Rochester	Total
	(Clinton Rep)	(Van Buren Rep)	
New York and Kings Cos	6,296	4,891	11,187
Rest of State	93,512	91,189	184,701
Total State	99,808	96,080	195,888

1828	**Martin Van Buren**	Smith Thompson	Solomon Southwick	Total
	(Jackson Dem)	(Nat Rep)	(Antimason)	
New York and Kings Cos	16,550	10,642	141	27,333
Rest of State	120,245	95,773	33,194	249,212
Total State	136,795	106,415	33,335	276,545

1830	**Enos T. Throop**	Francis Granger	Total
	(Jackson Dem)	(Nat Rep)	
New York and Kings Cos	12,019	8,457	20,476
Rest of State	116,928	112,210	229,138
Total State	128,947	120,667	249,614

1832	**William L. Marcy**	Francis Granger	Total
	(Jackson Dem)	(Nat Rep)	
New York and Kings Cos	19,584	13,868	33,452
Rest of State	146,826	142,804	289,630
Total State	166,410	156,672	323,082

1834	**William L. Marcy**	William H. Seward	Total
	(Dem)	(Whig)	
New York and Kings Cos	21,055	18,185	39,240
Rest of State	160,845	150,823	311,668
Total State	181,900	169,008	350,908

1836	**William L. Marcy**	Jesse Buel	Total
	(Dem)	(Whig)	
New York and Kings Cos	18,879	17,835	36,714
Rest of State	147,339	118,818	266,157
Total State	166,218	136,653	302,871

1838	William L. Marcy	**William H. Seward**	Total
	(Dem)	(Whig)	
New York and Kings Cos	21,892	22,647	44,539
Rest of State	160,569	170,235	330,804
Total State	182,461	192,882	375,343

1840	William C. Bouck	**William H. Seward**	Other	Total
	(Dem)	(Whig)		
New York and Kings Cos	25,488	23,247	206	48,941
Rest of State	191,238	198,764	2,455	392,457
Total State	216,726	222,011	2,661	441,398

1842	**William C. Bouck**	Luther Bradish	Other	Total
	(Dem)	(Whig)		
New York and Kings Cos	25,742	23,299	127	49,168
Rest of State	182,320	162,790	7,137	352,247
Total State	208,062	186,089	7,264	401,415

1844	**Silas Wright**	Millard Fillmore	Other	Total
	(Dem)	(Whig)		
New York and Kings Cos	33,943	30,844	149	64,936
Rest of State	207,144	200,216	14,988	422,348
Total State	241,087	231,060	15,137	487,284

GUBERNATORIAL ELECTIONS (continued)

1846	Silas Wright (Dem)	**John Young** (Whig)			Total
New York and Kings Cos	27,513	21,760			49,273
Rest of State	164,848	175,867			340,715
Total State	192,361	197,627			389,988

1848	Reuben Hyde Walworth (Dem)	**Hamilton Fish** (Whig)	John Dix (Free Soil)		Total
New York and Kings Cos	23,709	35,182	5,894		64,785
Rest of State	90,748	183,098	117,466		391,312
Total State	114,457	218,280	123,360		456,097

1850	Horatio Seymour (Dem)	**Washington Hunt** (Whig Antirent)	Other		Total
New York and Kings Cos	27,642	27,076	6		54,724
Rest of State	186,710	187,538	3,410		377,658
Total State	214,352	214,614	3,416		432,382

1852	**Horatio Seymour** (Dem)	Washington Hunt (Whig)	Other		Total
New York and Kings Cos	43,041	34,797	246		78,084
Rest of State	221,080	206,728	19,415		447,223
Total State	264,121	241,525	19,661		525,307

1854	Daniel Ullman (American)	**Myron H. Clark** (Fusion Rep)	Horatio Seymour (Soft Dem)	Greene C. Bronson (Hard Dem)	Total
New York and Kings Cos	23,581	17,520	35,385	6,226	82,712
Rest of State	98,701	139,284	121,110	27,624	386,719
Total State	122,282	156,804	156,495	33,850	469,431

1856	Amasa J. Parker (Dem)	**John A. King** (Rep)	Erastus Brooks (Amer)		Total
New York and Kings Cos	55,671	22,018	30,200		107,889
Rest of State	142,945	242,382	100,670		485,997
Total State	198,616	264,400	130,870		593,886

1858	Amasa J. Parker (Dem)	**Edwin D. Morgan** (Rep)	Lorenzo Burrows (Amer)	Other	Total
New York and Kings Cos	54,575	29,772	9,999	123	94,469
Rest of State	175,754	218,096	51,138	5,323	450,311
Total State	230,329	247,868	61,137	5,446	544,780

1860	William Kelly (Dem)	**Edwin D. Morgan** (Rep)	James T. Brady (Breckinridge Dem)		Total
New York and Kings Cos	72,017	50,005	7,837		129,859
Rest of State	222,786	307,997	12,004		542,787
Total State	294,803	358,002	19,841		672,646

1862	**Horatio Seymour** (Dem)	James S. Wadsworth (Union)[a]			Total
New York and Kings Cos	73,866	35,458			109,324
Rest of State	232,783	260,439			493,222
Total State	306,649	295,897			602,546

1864	Horatio Seymour (Dem)	**Reuben E. Fenton** (Union)[a]			Total
New York and Kings Cos	99,200	57,055			156,255
Rest of State	262,064	312,502			574,566
Total State	361,264	369,557			730,821

1866	John T. Hoffman (Dem)	**Reuben E. Fenton** (Union)[a]			Total
New York and Kings Cos	109,843	53,126			162,969
Rest of State	242,683	313,189			555,872
Total State	352,526	366,315			718,841

continued on page 674

GUBERNATORIAL ELECTIONS (continued)

1868	**John T. Hoffman** (Dem)	John A. Griswold (Rep)	Total
New York and Kings Cos	153,941	69,521	223,462
Rest of State	285,360	341,834	627,194
Total State	439,301	411,355	850,656

1870	**John T. Hoffman** (Dem)	Stewart L. Woodford (Rep)	Total
New York and Kings Cos	122,996	57,850	180,846
Rest of State	276,556	308,586	585,142
Total State	399,552	366,436	765,988

1872	**John Adams Dix** (Rep)	Francis Kernan (Lib Rep)	Total
New York and Kings Cos	92,361	113,689	206,050
Rest of State	353,492	278,581	632,073
Total State[b]	445,853	392,270	838,123

1874	**Samuel J. Tilden** (Dem)	John Adams Dix (Rep)	Other	Total
New York and Kings Cos	127,245	71,719	904	199,868
Rest of State	289,146	294,355	11,590	595,091
Total State	416,391	366,074	12,494	794,959

1876	**Lucius Robinson** (Dem)	Edwin D. Morgan (Rep)	Other	Total
New York and Kings Cos	166,792	99,909	795	267,496
Rest of State	353,039	389,462	4,913	747,414
Total State	519,831	489,371	5,708	1,014,910

1879[c]	Lucius Robinson (Dem)	**Alonzo B. Cornell** (Rep)	John Kelly (Tammany Dem)	Other	Total
New York and Kings Cos	104,944	79,138	48,835	4,408	237,325
Rest of State	270,846	339,429	28,731	25,204	664,210
Total State	375,790	418,567	77,566	29,612	901,535

1882	**Grover Cleveland** (Dem)	Charles J. Folger (Rep)	Other	Total
New York and Kings Cos	190,550	73,933	5,652	270,135
Rest of State	344,768	267,531	33,105	645,404
Total State	535,318	341,464	38,757	915,539

1885	**David B. Hill** (Dem)	Ira Davenport (Rep)	Other	Total
New York and Kings Cos	181,009	123,291	3,454	307,754
Rest of State	320,456	367,040	30,989	718,485
Total State	501,465	490,331	34,443	1,026,239

1888	**David B. Hill** (Dem)	Warner Miller (Rep)	Other	Total
New York and Kings Cos	251,386	168,099	5,541	425,026
Rest of State	399,078	463,204	28,365	890,647
Total State	650,464	631,303	33,906	1,315,673

1891	**Roswell P. Flower** (Dem)	J. Sloat Fassett (Rep)	Other	Total
New York and Kings Cos	228,752	153,170	9,943	391,865
Rest of State	354,141	381,786	35,061	770,988
Total State	582,893	534,956	45,004	1,162,853

1894	David B. Hill (Dem)	**Levi P. Morton** (Rep)	Other	Total
New York and Kings Cos	198,044	211,186	38,194	447,424
Rest of State	319,666	462,632	45,949	828,247
Total State	517,710	673,818	84,143	1,275,671

GUBERNATORIAL ELECTIONS (continued)

1896	Wilbur E. Porter (Dem/People's)	**Frank S. Black** (Rep)	Other	Total
New York and Kings Cos	221,737	250,635	34,401	506,773
Rest of State	352,787	536,881	37,605	927,273
Total State	574,524	787,516	72,006	1,434,046

1898	Augustus Van Wyck (Dem)	**Theodore Roosevelt** (Rep)	Other	Total
New York and Kings Cos	275,002	195,952	18,799	489,753
Rest of State	368,919	465,755	34,763	869,437
Total State	643,921	661,707	53,562	1,359,190

1900	John B. Stanchfield (Dem)	**Benjamin B. Odell Jr** (Rep)	Other	Total
NYC	316,393	272,130	21,612	610,135
Downstate Suburban	31,298	41,264	2,589	75,151
Upstate Urban	95,294	116,546	10,865	222,705
Upstate Nonurban	250,748	374,919	22,862	648,529
Total State	693,733	804,859	57,928	1,556,520

1902	Bird S. Coler (Dem/Greater NY Dem)	**Benjamin B. Odell Jr** (Rep)	Other	Total
NYC	327,132	204,499	29,516	561,147
Downstate Suburban	31,542	34,883	2,541	68,966
Upstate Urban	82,448	102,753	11,999	197,200
Upstate Nonurban	215,225	323,015	24,246	562,486
Total State	656,347	665,150	68,302	1,389,799

1904	D. Cady Herrick (Dem)	**Frank W. Higgins** (Rep)	Other	Total
NYC	348,493	268,362	38,503	655,358
Downstate Suburban	36,512	45,495	2,903	84,910
Upstate Urban	96,631	122,934	11,234	230,799
Upstate Nonurban	251,068	376,473	27,299	654,840
Total State	732,704	813,264	79,939	1,625,907

1906	William Randolph Hearst (Dem)	**Charles Evans Hughes** (Rep)	Other	Total
NYC	338,530	261,463	20,951	620,944
Downstate Suburban	30,845	44,835	3,957	79,637
Upstate Urban	92,162	113,150	10,413	215,725
Upstate Nonurban	211,731	329,554	34,628	575,913
Total State	673,268	749,002	69,949	1,492,219

1908	Lewis Stuyvesant Chanler (Dem)	**Charles Evans Hughes** (Rep)	Clarence J. Shearn (Ind League)	Other	Total
NYC	321,290	261,386	34,023	34,714	651,413
Downstate Suburban	36,342	51,881	2,688	3,035	93,946
Upstate Urban	113,602	127,793	1,403	8,079	250,877
Upstate Nonurban	263,955	363,591	5,098	24,976	657,620
Total State	735,189	804,651	43,212	70,804	1,653,856

1910	**John Alden Dix** (Dem)	Henry L. Stimson (Rep)	John J. Hopper (Ind League)	Other	Total
NYC	302,989	197,727	39,883	35,340	575,939
Downstate Suburban	41,432	40,016	2,362	2,428	86,238
Upstate Urban	98,750	105,110	1,608	12,872	218,340
Upstate Nonurban	246,529	279,446	4,617	34,140	564,732
Total State	689,700	622,299	48,470	84,780	1,445,249

1912	**William Sulzer** (Dem)	Job E. Hedges (Rep)	Oscar S. Straus (Nat Prog)	Other	Total
NYC	304,000	111,630	194,479	61,997	672,106
Downstate Suburban	38,546	27,342	27,970	2,756	96,614
Upstate Urban	89,437	76,515	59,762	20,633	246,347
Upstate Nonurban	217,576	228,618	110,972	39,439	596,605
Total State	649,559	444,105	393,183	124,825	1,611,672

continued on page 676

GUBERNATORIAL ELECTIONS (continued)

1914	Martin H. Glynn (Dem/Ind League/No Party)	**Charles S. Whitman** (Rep)	William Sulzer (Proh/Amer/No Party)	Other	Total
NYC	292,076	238,245	30,435	60,525	621,281
Downstate Suburban	33,010	48,003	5,870	6,983	93,866
Upstate Urban	71,105	130,388	11,511	24,087	237,091
Upstate Nonurban	145,078	270,065	78,454	41,040	534,637
Total State	541,269	686,701	126,270	132,635	1,486,875

1916	Samuel Seabury (Dem)	**Charles S. Whitman** (Rep/Nat Prog/Ind League)	Algernon Lee (Soc)	Other	Total
NYC	326,199	305,890	38,518	42,701	713,308
Downstate Suburban	40,967	62,946	1,180	5,620	110,713
Upstate Urban	98,566	145,048	5,196	21,212	270,022
Upstate Nonurban	221,130	336,136	7,666	56,793	621,725
Total State	686,862	850,020	52,560	126,326	1,715,768

1918	**Alfred E. Smith** (Dem)	Charles S. Whitman (Rep/Proh/No Party)	Charles W. Ervin (Soc)	Other	Total
NYC	559,284	290,708	86,384	25,061	961,437
Downstate Suburban	59,106	77,117	3,619	5,140	144,982
Upstate Urban	128,584	175,530	19,874	13,751	337,739
Upstate Nonurban	262,962	451,739	11,828	22,283	748,812
Total State	1,009,936	995,094	121,705	66,235	2,192,970

1920	Alfred E. Smith (Dem)	**Nathan L. Miller** (Rep)	Joseph D. Cannon (Soc)	Other	Total
NYC	709,604	389,729	99,130	98,647	1,297,110
Downstate Suburban	80,133	112,856	6,439	14,450	213,878
Upstate Urban	167,660	238,064	27,115	25,338	458,177
Upstate Nonurban	304,355	595,229	27,120	66,716	993,420
Total State	1,261,752	1,335,878	159,804	205,151	2,962,585

1922	**Alfred E. Smith** (Dem)	Nathan L. Miller (Rep)	Edward F. Cassidy (Soc)	Other	Total
NYC	756,283	277,073	57,218	30,960	1,121,534
Downstate Suburban	86,746	88,813	5,973	6,379	187,911
Upstate Urban	206,888	178,140	20,680	13,312	419,020
Upstate Nonurban	347,740	467,699	16,073	28,984	860,496
Total State	1,397,657	1,011,725	99,944	79,635	2,588,961

1924	**Alfred E. Smith** (Dem)	Theodore Roosevelt, Jr (Rep)	Other	Total
NYC	936,941	417,975	89,672	1,444,588
Downstate Suburban	103,508	149,193	17,490	270,191
Upstate Urban	224,058	272,803	42,856	539,717
Upstate Nonurban	362,604	678,581	59,944	1,101,129
Total State	1,627,111	1,518,552	209,962	3,355,625

1926	**Alfred E. Smith** (Dem)	Odgen L. Mills (Rep)	Other	Total
NYC	839,656	355,630	81,630	1,276,916
Downstate Suburban	104,920	128,694	10,482	244,096
Upstate Urban	233,329	238,287	30,181	501,797
Upstate Nonurban	345,908	553,526	55,657	955,091
Total State	1,523,813	1,276,137	177,950	2,977,900

1928	**Franklin D. Roosevelt** (Dem)	Albert Ottinger (Rep)	Other	Total
NYC	1,135,217	728,712	99,345	1,963,274
Downstate Suburban	170,342	215,534	17,448	403,324
Upstate Urban	329,065	353,645	37,475	720,185
Upstate Nonurban	495,614	806,739	67,361	1,369,714
Total State	2,130,238	2,104,630	221,629	4,456,497

GUBERNATORIAL ELECTIONS (continued)

1930	**Franklin D. Roosevelt** (Dem)	Charles H. Tuttle (Rep)	Robert P. Carroll (Law Pres)	Other	Total
NYC	926,815	369,598	9,039	138,814	1,444,266
Downstate Suburban	138,261	138,712	8,590	11,971	297,534
Upstate Urban	276,973	181,720	42,595	25,095	526,383
Upstate Nonurban	428,293	355,311	130,442	38,053	952,099
Total State	1,770,342	1,045,341	190,666	213,933	3,220,282

1932	**Herbert H. Lehman** (Dem)	William J. Donovan (Rep)	Other	Total
NYC	1,531,165	541,321	182,783	2,255,269
Downstate Suburban	219,257	233,713	22,957	475,927
Upstate Urban	374,491	322,229	49,541	746,261
Upstate Nonurban	534,606	714,817	89,174	1,338,597
Total State	2,659,519	1,812,080	344,455	4,816,054

1934	**Herbert H. Lehman** (Dem)	Robert Moses (Rep)	Other	Total
NYC	1,210,515	406,559	226,647	1,843,721
Downstate Suburban	180,467	177,396	23,246	381,109
Upstate Urban	361,346	248,125	36,376	645,847
Upstate Nonurban	449,401	561,559	55,562	1,066,522
Total State	2,201,729	1,393,638	341,832	3,937,199

1936	**Herbert H. Lehman** (Dem/Amer Labor/No Party)	William F. Bleakley (Rep)	Other	Total
NYC	1,803,429	874,087	145,675	2,823,191
Downstate Suburban	214,897	322,501	20,405	557,803
Upstate Urban	411,587	397,003	35,451	844,041
Upstate Nonurban	540,682	856,513	67,863	1,465,058
Total State	2,970,595	2,450,104	269,394	5,690,093

1938	**Herbert H. Lehman** (Dem/Amer Labor)	Thomas E. Dewey (Rep/Ind Prog)	Other	Total
NYC	1,468,010	786,641	59,677	2,314,328
Downstate Suburban	168,008	313,943	7,269	489,220
Upstate Urban	334,202	407,956	13,449	755,607
Upstate Nonurban	421,066	818,352	23,058	1,262,476
Total State	2,391,286	2,326,892	103,453	4,821,631

1942	John J. Bennett Jr. (Dem)	**Thomas E. Dewey** (Rep)	Dean Alfange (Amer Labor)	Other	Total
NYC	822,961	737,653	346,557	90,383	1,997,554
Downstate Suburban	114,546	295,665	15,689	5,786	431,686
Upstate Urban	252,908	400,582	17,097	11,745	682,332
Upstate Nonurban	310,624	714,646	24,283	15,950	1,065,503
Total State	1,501,039	2,148,546	403,626	123,864	4,177,075

1946	James M. Mead (Dem/Amer Labor/Lib)	**Thomas E. Dewey** (Rep)	Other	Total
NYC	1,367,255	1,182,270	49,112	2,598,637
Downstate Suburban	125,060	409,968	7,397	542,425
Upstate Urban	298,468	446,036	10,564	755,068
Upstate Nonurban	347,699	787,359	15,612	1,150,670
Total State	2,138,482	2,825,633	82,685	5,046,800

1950	Walter A. Lynch (Dem/Lib)	**Thomas E. Dewey** (Rep)	John T. McManus (Amer Labor)	Other	Total
NYC	1,278,029	1,119,450	176,202	131,557	2,705,238
Downstate Suburban	196,369	434,763	11,634	11,051	653,817
Upstate Urban	358,962	431,875	13,866	17,843	822,546
Upstate Nonurban	413,495	833,435	20,264	24,255	1,291,449
Total State	2,246,855	2,819,523	221,966	184,706[d]	5,473,050[d]

continued on page 678

GUBERNATORIAL ELECTIONS (continued)

1954	**W. Averell Harriman**	Irving M. Ives	Other	Total
	George B. DeLuca	J. Raymond McGovern		
	(Dem/Lib)	(Rep)		
NYC	1,464,119	765,464	78,935	2,308,518
Downstate Suburban	278,013	511,873	13,229	803,115
Upstate Urban	375,682	448,951	15,613	840,246
Upstate Nonurban	442,924	823,325	23,049	1,289,298
Total State	2,560,738	2,549,613	130,826	5,241,177

1958	W. Averell Harriman	**Nelson A. Rockefeller**	Other	Total
	George B. DeLuca	Malcolm Wilson		
	(Dem/Lib)	(Rep)		
NYC	1,321,768	1,011,814	59,585	2,393,167
Downstate Suburban	362,961	684,728	16,002	1,063,691
Upstate Urban	400,384	520,084	15,915	936,383
Upstate Nonurban	468,782	910,303	23,155	1,402,240
Total State	2,553,895	3,126,929	114,657	5,795,481

1962	Robert M. Morgenthau	**Nelson A. Rockefeller**	Other	Total
	John J. Burns	Malcolm Wilson		
	(Dem/Lib)	(Rep)		
NYC	1,279,912	1,078,293	123,644	2,481,849
Downstate Suburban	363,209	706,471	58,880	1,128,560
Upstate Urban	438,825	450,780	45,949	935,554
Upstate Nonurban	470,472	846,043	59,025	1,375,540
Total State	2,552,418	3,081,587	287,498	5,921,503

1966	Frank D. O'Connor	**Nelson A. Rockefeller**	Franklin D. Roosevelt Jr	Paul L. Adams	Other	Total
	Howard J. Samuels	Malcolm Wilson	Donald S. Harrington	Kieran O'Doherty		
	(Dem)	(Rep)	(Lib)	(Cons)		
NYC	1,034,012	964,364	218,740	234,590	80,531	2,532,237
Downstate Suburban	357,388	653,373	90,320	143,104	22,497	1,266,682
Upstate Urban	421,303	377,295	77,006	60,657	18,119	954,380
Upstate Nonurban	485,660	695,594	121,168	71,672	32,185	1,406,279
Total State	2,298,363	2,690,626	507,234	510,023	153,332	6,159,578

1970	Arthur J. Goldberg	**Nelson A. Rockefeller**	Paul L. Adams	Other	Total
	Basil A. Paterson	Malcolm Wilson	Edward F. Leonard		
	(Dem/Lib)	(Rep/Civil Service Ind)	(Cons)		
NYC	1,099,892	1,083,351	106,777	69,208	2,359,228
Downstate Suburban	437,388	774,598	122,814	24,113	1,358,913
Upstate Urban	414,629	454,447	87,985	24,354	981,415
Upstate Nonurban	469,517	839,036	104,938	37,430	1,450,921
Total State	2,421,426	3,151,432	422,514	155,105	6,150,477

1974	**Hugh Carey**	Malcolm Wilson	Other	Total
	Mary Anne Krupsak	Ralph Caso		
	(Dem/Lib)	(Rep/Cons)		
NYC	1,216,736	525,721	103,848	1,846,305
Downstate Suburban	633,499	612,003	62,441	1,307,943
Upstate Urban	502,593	372,817	52,621	928,031
Upstate Nonurban	675,675	709,126	76,574	1,461,375
Total State	3,028,503	2,219,667	295,484	5,543,654

1978	**Hugh Carey**	Perry B. Duryea Jr	Other	Total
	Mario M. Cuomo	Bruce Caputo		
	(Dem/Lib)	(Rep/Cons)		
NYC	952,754	447,486	126,334	1,526,574
Downstate Suburban	526,547	606,395	69,811	1,202,753
Upstate Urban	394,327	373,567	62,145	830,039
Upstate Nonurban	555,644	728,956	85,460	1,370,060
Total State	2,429,272	2,156,404	343,750	4,929,426

GUBERNATORIAL ELECTIONS (continued)

1982	**Mario M. Cuomo**	Lewis Lehrman	Other	Total
	Alfred B. DelBello	James L. Emery		
	(Dem/Lib)	(Rep/Cons/Statewide Ind)		
NYC	1,079,840	503,878	102,213	1,685,931
Downstate Suburban	598,870	644,218	55,703	1,298,791
Upstate Urban	447,450	451,699	37,149	936,298
Upstate Nonurban	549,053	895,032	72,262	1,516,347
Total State	2,675,213	2,494,827	267,327	5,437,367

1986	**Mario M. Cuomo**	Andrew P. O'Rourke	Denis Dillon	Other	Total
	Stan Lundine	Michael Kavanagh	Thomas Droleskey		
	(Dem/Lib)	(Rep/Cons)	(RTL)		
NYC	908,434	252,371	25,418	102,619	1,288,842
Downstate Suburban	612,414	369,723	55,544	32,951	1,070,632
Upstate Urban	544,363	227,849	20,127	29,026	821,365
Upstate Nonurban	709,834	514,025	29,738	47,283	1,300,880
Total State	2,775,045	1,363,968	130,827	211,879	4,481,719

1990	**Mario M. Cuomo**	Pierre Rinfret	Herbert London	Other	Total
	Stan Lundine	George Yancey Jr	Anthony Diperna		
	(Dem/Lib)	(Rep)	(Cons)		
NYC	775,944	118,047	134,750	131,537	1,160,278
Downstate Suburban	484,154	249,750	181,328	96,555	1,011,787
Upstate Urban	392,911	134,475	181,921	67,283	776,590
Upstate Nonurban	504,078	363,676	329,615	144,237	1,341,606
Total State	2,157,087	865,948	827,614	439,612	4,290,261

1994	Mario M. Cuomo	**George E. Pataki**	Thomas Golisano	Other	Total
	Stan Lundine	Betsy McCaughey Ross	Dominick Fusco		
	(Dem/Lib)	(Rep/Cons/Tax Cut Now)	(Ind Fusion)		
NYC	1,060,063	423,007	16,516	76,574	1,576,160
Downstate Suburban	530,234	664,104	24,415	42,155	1,260,908
Upstate Urban	348,322	442,568	82,686	32,141	905,717
Upstate Nonurban	426,285	1,009,023	93,873	53,357	1,582,538
Total State	2,364,904	2,538,702	217,490	204,227	5,325,323

1998	Peter F. Vallone	**George E. Pataki**	B. Thomas Golisano	Other	Total
	Sandra Frankel	Mary O. Donohue	Laureen Oliver		
	(Dem/Wrkg Fam)	(Rep/Cons)	(Ind)		
NYC	835,660	464,094	34,624	200,383	1,534,761
Downstate Suburban	328,126	707,903	52,189	87,205	1,175,423
Upstate Urban	186,680	439,118	139,461	71,693	836,952
Upstate Nonurban	219,851	960,876	137,782	120,287	1,438,796
Total State	1,570,317	2,571,991	364,056	479,568	4,985,932

2002	H. Carl McCall	**George E. Pataki**	B. Thomas Golisano	Other	Total
	Dennis Mehiel	Mary O. Donohue			
	(Dem/Wrkg Fam)	(Rep/Cons)	(Ind)		
NYC	732,176	533,564	73,562	75,793	1,415,095
Downstate Suburban	286,794	635,500	117,818	51,231	1,091,343
Upstate Urban	228,552	331,985	201,229	38,511	800,277
Upstate Nonurban	286,542	761,206	261,407	75,098	1,384,253
Total State	1,534,064	2,262,255	654,016	240,633	4,690,968

Sources: ICPSR Election Returns for New York; *New York Red Book; Manual for the Use of the Legislature of the State of New York;* New York State Board of Elections.

Note: Winners' names appear in bold. Regional designations are as follows: NYC: Bronx, Kings (Brooklyn), New York (Manhattan), Richmond (Staten Island), Queens Cos; Downstate Suburban: Nassau, Rockland, Suffolk, Westchester Cos; Upstate Urban: Albany, Erie, Monroe, Onondaga Cos; Upstate Nonurban: remainder of cos.

[a]The Republican candidate ran under the Union Party ticket.

[b]The ICPSR data do not add correctly and do not agree with the totals in the Legislative Manual.

[c]There is a 2-vote discrepancy between the printed whole number of votes and the actual sum of the votes for each candidate in Essex County. There is also an 8-vote discrepancy between the printed vote total for the Greenback Party candidate and the actual sum of his votes in each county.

[d]There is a 2-vote discrepancy between these totals and those reported in the Legislative Manual.

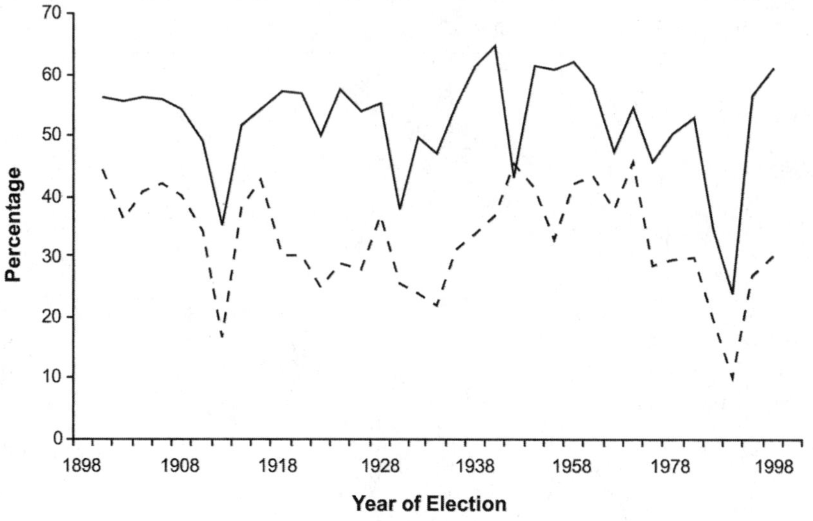

Fig 2. Republican success by region, 1990–98.
– – – percentage within NYC; —— percentage outside NYC.

can challenger George E. Pataki suggested that Republicans may not have to appeal to New York City votes for electoral success. New York City's percentage of the vote in gubernatorial elections has declined in recent decades from an average of nearly 50% from the 1930s through the early 1950s, to about 40% from the mid-1950s to the mid-1960s, and to approximately 30% from the mid-1970s into the early 21st century. With New York City's electoral weight diminishing, a Republican gubernatorial candidate could make a conservative argument, lose badly in New York City, and still win, as Pataki did in 1994; he drew only 27% of the New York City vote. By many accounts, Pataki's 1994 victory was the beginning of an end to the dominance of New York City and liberals over the state fiscal agenda. Pataki was able, helped by economic growth in the 1990s, to advocate and enact significant tax cuts. It must be noted that Pataki was more liberal than many of his Republican peers on issues such as abortion and seeking the support of labor unions. Still, by the end of the 20th century the ability of New York City to affect gubernatorial campaigns and state policy appeared to be on the wane.

Erosion of Republican Strength Outside New York City

As regularly happens in politics, just as a new pattern is perceived, further change occurs and creates new uncertainties. The presumption of Republicans, after a century of evidence, is that areas outside New York City, where the party has almost always won 50–60% of the vote, will remain solidly Republican. There are two reasons to wonder if that pattern will persist. First, Republican enrollment began to drop in many upstate counties at the end of the 20th century. Once overwhelmingly Republican counties are edging toward greater balance in party enrollment. In counties like Chenango, Herkimer, and Onondaga, Republicans were almost 70% of all registrants in the 1950s, but by 2003 were less than 40%. Party enrollment often has a significant impact on voting, and Republicans can no longer count on high Republican enrollments to generate support for them upstate. Second, the election of Hillary Rodham Clinton to the US Senate from New York State in 2000 and her success in running almost even with her opponent Rick Lazio outside New York City genuinely surprised Republicans. Many of them believed that a Democrat like Clinton, with relatively high negative ratings in opinion polls, would not be able to do well outside New York City. The ability of a Democrat to do well upstate created doubt about what Republican stance (conservative or much more moderate) would be most successful outside New York City. With the declining importance of the Democratic vote in New York City and the shift in Republican allegiance elsewhere in the state, the trends in future gubernatorial campaigns are unclear.

Benjamin, Gerald, and Robert C. Lawton. "New York's Governorship: Back to the Future?" In *Governing New York State,* 4th ed., ed. Jeffrey M. Stonecash (Albany: SUNY Press, 2001)
Liebschutz, Sarah F. "The New York Governorship." In *New York Politics and Government,* eds. Sarah F. Liebschutz, et al (Lincoln: Univ of Nebraska Press, 1998)
Stonecash, Jeffrey M., and Amy Widestrom. "Political Parties and Elections." In *Governing New York State,* 5th ed., ed. Robert F. Pecorella and Jeffrey M. Stonecash (Albany: SUNY Press, 2005)

Jeffrey M. Stonecash

Guilderland. Town (pop 32,688) in N Albany Co. In 1792 a glass factory was built on the Hunger Kill, and soon afterward woolen mills were built on the Normans Kill, but these enterprises collapsed after the War of 1812, and the town was agricultural through the 19th century. At the glass factory a community named Hamilton was platted around 1796. Colonie, which formed in 1803 from the extinct town of Watervliet [now Guilderland], established a post office in 1815. Nineteenth-century products also included hats, ironwork, woolen cloth, and oilcloth. Watervliet Reservoir was created in 1917. The population remained below 10,000 until after World War II, when the town grew rapidly as a bedroom suburb of Albany. The Schenectady Army Depot that opened in 1941 near Guilderland Center became the Northeastern Industrial Park. Guilderland was the birthplace of ethnologist Henry Rowe Schoolcraft (1793–1864) and is the site of Stuyvesant Plaza (1964), a portion of Crossgates Mall, and a part of the SUNY Albany campus. National Register landmarks include the Mynderse-Frederick House (1802) and the Gothic Revival Schoolcraft House (1840s), both town owned.

George Wise

Guilford. Town (pop 3,046) in E Chenango Co. Settled *ca* 1790, the town, bounded on the east by the Unadilla River, was formed from Oxford in 1813 as Eastern; the name was changed to Guilford in 1817. The first organ made west of the Hudson River was assembled in Guilford around 1819. Guilford Creek, an outlet of Guilford Lake, falls 140 feet (43 m) in the hamlet of Guilford. It powered 19th-century mills, a foundry and machine shop, and furniture, cheese box, and butter tub manufactories. A creamery was established at Rockdale in 1865. Businesses began to close after the Ontario and Western Railroad discontinued service in 1957. At the beginning of the 21st century, Guilford is a bedroom community, and most residents work in Norwich, Oxford, and Bainbridge (Chenango Co), and Sidney (Delaware Co).

Michele A. McFee

gun control. Attempts to control the trade in guns in New York dates back to the Dutch colonial period. The Dutch prohibited the sale of firearms to American Indians, but this largely ended with the arrival of Gov Willem Kieft in 1638, and initiatives by the colony were undermined by merchants who found such sales lucrative. The English continued efforts to prohibit the sale of guns to Indians after the English took control of the colony, adding further prohibitions on the possession of firearms by slaves, indentured servants, Catholics, and suspicious foreigners. The colonial government reserved the right to seize firearms in private hands. It occasionally exercised this power in times of political or military crisis, most notably during the French and Indian War, when the government was desperate to acquire every possible firearm for the defense of the colony. The government also kept track of the location of firearms within its territory.

The American Revolution did not change this pattern of legislation. Loyalists, Indians, and even the uncommitted were disarmed by the state. Local patriots routinely disarmed those suspected of loyalty to the Crown, and the state set up a commission for expropriation of loyalist property. The Oneida were systematically disarmed and then attacked. Other Iroquois tribes that did not offer resistance were also disarmed. The state's reserved sovereignty continued to allow the government authority to appropriate privately held firearms at its discretion, a power that persisted through the Civil War. The only significant change in New York State gun control came in the early 19th century, which coincided with an increase in the number of gun makers and private gun ownership. It was also during the first decade of the 19th century that New York State passed its first hunting laws. Most significant were the limitations on hunting certain animals in specific seasons. Hunters were also required to acquire licenses from local sheriffs or constables. Public fears of the misuse of firearms extended to the police, who were not allowed to carry guns. New York City police first carried guns in 1857, in violation of local ordinances. Public opposition to the police carrying firearms

Gunsmith and police department headquarters, New York City. Photograph by Berenice Abbott, 1937.

ended with the violent New York City draft riots of July 1863, when a civilian crowd opened fire on police for the first time.

After the Civil War, as guns became cheaper, smaller, and easier to use, a strenuous debate filled the newspapers over the potential threat of guns to public safety. The state's Concealed Weapons Act of 1866 failed to include pistols. In their first major lobbying effort, New York City's police persuaded the legislature in 1877 to add handguns to the list of proscribed weapons, though an infraction was treated as a misdemeanor. The debate persisted over the next 30 years, and calls for gun control had no necessary relation to political position, as both liberals and conservatives perceived a need for safety.

In 1911 the legislature passed the Sullivan Act, which served as a model for legislation throughout the United States. This act required permits for the purchase of pistols and the carrying of concealed weapons and prohibited the possession of firearms by resident aliens and minors. Police hailed the Sullivan Act as a great success and rigorously enforced it, especially in New York City. It may in fact have been selectively enforced against minorities. Critics doubted that it had any impact on the homicide rate. There was little opposition to the Sullivan Act until the late 1920s, when rural legislators attempted to weaken its enforcement mechanism as too burdensome. In 1932 the legislature passed the Hanley-Fake Bill, which would have terminated enforcement of gun control laws in New York by superseding the Sullivan Act. Gov Franklin D. Roosevelt vetoed the law as a threat to public safety, calling for federal regulation. Later, as president, Roosevelt signed into law the National Firearms Acts of 1934 and 1938.

In the years since World War II, New York has maintained some of the strictest gun regulations in the United States by continuing to require permits for the purchase of handguns. In the 1980s New York City police discovered that the majority of weapons used in the commission of a crime came from outside the state. Proponents of gun control argued for federal regulation to halt the flow of firearms from other states into New York State, whereas opponents insisted that the presence of so many guns indicated the futility of gun control. New York State's courts have consistently upheld the constitutionality of gun control legislation. Most decisions upheld the state's authority to delimit the uses of firearms, finding that the possession of a gun is a privilege and not a right. In 1976 the New York Supreme Court, Appellate Division, ruled in *Guida v Dier* that the Second Amendment does not grant an individual the right to carry pistols or other readily concealable weapons. At the end of the 20th century, frustrated by the failure of the legislature and Congress to pass further gun regulation, a number of cities turned to the courts to regulate firearms; many local variations in regulations exist. Westchester Co requires that applicants complete a firearms safety course before being issued a license. District attorneys joined lawsuits against gun manufacturers, claiming that cities were bearing the cost of firearms-related damages. In the early years of the 21st century, gun control in New York State deviates little from the framework established by the Sullivan Act in 1911, except by greater specificity and fervent public debate.

Bellesiles, Michael A. *Arming America: The Origins of a National Gun Culture* (New York: Knopf, 2000)
Davidson, Osha Gray. *Under Fire: The NRA and the Battle for Gun Control* (New York: Henry Holt, 1993)
Kennett, Lee, and James L. Anderson. *The Gun in America: The Origins of a National Dilemma* (Westport, Conn: Greenwood, 1975)

Michael A. Bellesiles

guns and ordnance. In the mid–17th century Dutch settlers in the Hudson River valley developed the Hudson River fowler, a long-barreled flintlock that served both hunting and military purposes. Early New York State gun-making concerns were mostly individual artisans such as Covert Barent, who opened a gun-making shop in New Amsterdam in 1646.

Gun Making in the 19th Century

By the early 19th century gun making flourished in Herkimer and Oneida Cos, areas with local ironworks and charcoal burners and sandstone for grinding and finishing. The forge and blacksmith shop that equipped the Remington farm in Herkimer Co, near what is now the Village of Ilion, gave a start to one of the earliest large-scale American gun manufacturers. Around 1816 Eliphalet Remington crafted his first barrel by smelting ore and scrap iron in his father's furnace and welding the metal sheet around a rod. He brought the barrel to the Utica shop of gunsmith Morgan James, who reamed and rifled it, smoothing the bore inside and then cutting it with shallow grooves to cause the bullet to spin. James fitted it with a flintlock for igniting the charge; Remington added the wooden stock. After local farmers admired the gun, Remington began filling orders for neighbors, at first making only barrels in his father's forge, where an adjacent dam provided waterpower for the grindstones to finish the product. As business grew Remington rifled the barrels and fitted the locks himself. In 1821 a section of the Erie Canal was dug within four miles (6 km) of the Remington concern, and Remington began using barge transportation to reach customers as far as New England. In 1828 the foundry moved to 100 acres (40 ha) of land in Ilion close to the canal. Production continued to rely on New York State resources, such as nearby stands of timber and iron from the mines at Clinton (Oneida Co).

Anticipating the Mexican War (1846–48), the US government ordered breech-loading carbines invented by William Jenks, who came to Remington when the company took on the project in 1845. Remington also received special machinery for reproducing the new design, which incorporated drilled, cast-steel barrels, an advance in gun making. With the delivery of these carbines to the US Navy, Remington became famous for precision drilling. During the 1850s the factory designed and produced the Beals and Rider revolvers. The company E. Remington and Sons was created in 1856 by Eliphalet and his sons, Philo, Samuel, and Eliphalet Jr.

Other well-known 19th-century New York State gun makers included Nelson Lewis, George Ferris, and Horace Warner in Syracuse. Ezra Ripley of Troy (Rensselaer Co) developed the revolving battery gun, an early machine gun that had some limited service during the Civil War but was complicated to operate and subject to frequent malfunction. William Billinghurst's Requa Battery could fire seven volleys of .50 caliber rounds from 25 barrels. The Billinghurst Co of Rochester began producing the new weapon in 1861, and it was used during the Civil War as a defensive weapon. At the West Point Iron and Cannon Foundry in 1861 Capt Robert Parker Parrott invented a process in which big guns were cast around a hollow core, allowing them to cool from the inside, and then bound with red-hot bands that shrank into place. The process strengthened the breech, permitting the use of greater explosive power to propel the shells.

Union demands for arms during the Civil War meant round-the-clock production, which sometimes had almost every man and boy in Ilion working at the Remington factory. The company installed steam power at the Ilion works and expanded to a temporary annex at Utica. E. Remington and Sons grossed almost $3 million for arms delivered to the Union army. The company hired John Rider to develop a breech-loading rifle, which became so successful it replaced the muzzle-loading variety. Although the end of the Civil War meant a reduction in employees and production, Remington sold breech-loaded rifles to Sweden, Denmark, Holland, France, Spain, Greece, Egypt, and Cuba.

When the Franco-Prussian War broke out in 1870, the French ordered large quantities of Remington guns and employed Samuel Remington as their agent for all arms purchases made in the United States; he placed over $11 million in orders during 1870–71. The company became a major international supplier in the 1870s, selling arms on three continents and engaging in large-scale manufacture of cartridges for small arms. Remington manufactured the James P. Lee military rifle, a bolt-action gun that was the forerunner of the modern military rifle, and introduced a rapid-fire naval gun that presaged the machine gun. At the height of the 1870s activity, Remington employed about 1,850 workers and produced 1,400 rifles and 200 revolvers per day. The armory had a 10-hour workday, and employment was organized on the contract system; the heads of departments were contractors who bid for jobs and hired their own crews. It benefited everyone on the crews if a contractor or worker found a faster or more efficient way to perform a task.

Sport shooting increased in popularity throughout the 19th century, and target shooting was advanced as a humane alternative to the slaughter of pigeons. Upon receiving a charter by the State of New York, the National Rifle Association (NRA) was officially founded in New York City on 17 Nov 1871. The NRA encouraged the learning of marksmanship on a scientific basis. Target rifles were developed with special features to enhance accuracy, including heavy barrels, telescopic sights, and precise loading mechanisms. Remington produced the Creedmoor long-range rifle, which American riflemen used in international competitions held in the 1870s at the NRA's Creedmoor range in Queens Co.

In the late 1870s Remington faced financial setbacks, some because of ill-advised and poorly performing holdings outside New York State. The Remington armory employed only 300–400 men in 1877 and went bankrupt in 1886. In 1888 Marcellus Hartley, a cofounder of Schuyler, Hartley, and Graham, a New York City sporting-goods firm, bought Remington Arms. Business continued to decline, however, and the Remington workweek was cut to three and a half days in 1893. Innovation and diversification could not compensate for financial setbacks; both the Egyptian and Mexican governments defaulted on their bills, and overall international orders declined. A US government contract for 100,000 guns brought Remington Arms back to prosperity during the Spanish-American War (1898).

The government armories of the United States produced small arms by hand well into the 19th century. As breech-loading cannon replaced muzzle-loading cannon, the increasingly complicated manufacture of big guns led to the establishment of five national ordnance factories. Watervliet Arsenal (Albany Co), founded in 1813 to produce ammunition and ancillary equipment for the US Army during the War of 1812, underwent modifications starting in October 1887 to produce heavy ordnance. During the 1890s Arthur Savage organized Savage Arms in Utica to manufacture his own invention, a hammerless lever-action rifle that fired smokeless powder. The Model 99 was priced to be accessible to the average sports hunter and quickly gained a good reputation for deer hunting. The Savage inventory expanded into a variety of rifles, pistols, and ammunition.

The Gun Business in the 20th Century

Remington acquired Union Metallic Cartridge Co of Bridgeport, Conn, in 1912. Before the United States entered World War I, Remington Arms supplied England and France with rifles. Savage Arms had the rights to produce the Lewis machine gun and gave up its sporting arms manufacture to supply the British army with thousands of weapons starting in 1915. In 1916 Savage merged with the Driggs-Seabury Ordnance Co, creating a major industrial entity in Utica. After the United States entered World War I in 1917, Remington employed between 11,000 and 15,000 workers, many of them women.

Savage was reorganized as Savage Arms Corp after the war and merged in 1920 with the J. Stevens Arms and Tool Co of Chicopee, Mass, to market an extensive range of sporting arms. In Rochester the Crosman family began manufacturing a .22 caliber air rifle in 1923. Crosman remained a small company concentrating on air guns, which used compressed air rather than powder to propel bullets, and on accessories. The gun business declined during the Great Depression and large corporations acquired many small arms companies. Remington's Ilion plant cut back to 300 workers. In 1933 a major interest in Remington was bought by DuPont, a US manufacturer of gunpowder and explosives.

Both Remington and Savage were awarded large US government contracts during World War II, and both received government recognition for excellence. Remington employed over 9,000 workers on three shifts, seven days a week. After the war, Remington reduced its workforce to about 1,500 and shifted part of its production to sporting rifles and shotguns. The company streamlined production by producing parts that were simpler in design and interchangeable among models. Owning a controlling interest in the company since the 1930s, DuPont bought the company's remaining shares in 1980. In the 1980s Remington introduced computer-aided equipment in its manufacturing process.

New types of sporting guns were developed in the 1980s. Air rifle shooting became an Olympic event in 1984, and Crosman manufactured air rifles to Olympic specifications. Remington manufactured deer rifles with components of Kevlar, a synthetic that is lighter in weight and stronger than steel. During the 1990s the possibility of government restrictions on the sale and manufacture of guns and ammunition caused a rebound effect, increasing sales as enthusiasts acquired guns and ammunition in preparation for limited availability.

In 1993 DuPont sold Remington to the Manhattan investment firm Clayton, Dubilier and Rice. Savage Arms is owned by a Texas-based investment group. In 1997 private ordnance and accessories manufacturers in New York State employed fewer than 2,000 workers.

See also World war i.

Clarke, T. Wood. *Utica: For a Century and a Half* (Utica: Widtman Press, 1952)

Hatch, Alden. *Remington Arms in American History* (New York: Rinehart, 1956)

Schulz, Warren E. *Ilion: The Town Remington Made* (Hicksville, NY: Exposition Press, 1977)

Serven, James E. *200 Years of American Firearms* (Chicago: Follett, 1975)

Watervliet Arsenal. *A History of the Watervliet Arsenal, 1813–1968* (Watervliet, NY: Author, 1969)

Pamela Cooper

Guyanese. Until the 1960s Guyanese relocation to the United States consisted of a small number of students, merchants, and professionals. After the relaxation of immigration laws in 1965, political unrest at home and a weak economy led to a steady immigration to New York State. As reported by the 1980 US Census, 32,000 Guyanese-born lived in the state, 76,000 in 1990, and over 109,000 in 2000. About half have their roots in India, the others in Africa. A small group is of Chinese ancestry. With children and undocumented aliens, the number of Guyanese in New York State is estimated by community activists at up to 300,000. About four-fifths of Indo-Guyanese are Hindu and one-fifth are Muslim. African Guyanese are mostly Methodist, Anglican, and Catholic. Antagonistic in Guyana, the two groups have few common organizations and tend to live apart, with African Guyanese blending into the West Indian community. Educated Guyanese have entered technical and educational fields. The majority, however, work in stores and factories, and most live in the New York City area. Guyanese communities can be found in Queens in Richmond Hill, nicknamed Little Guyana, which is mainly Indo-Guyanese, and in Brooklyn and the Bronx. In an effort to strengthen its economic base, Schenectady has sponsored efforts to increase its Indo-Guyanese population. In 2002 over 1,000 resided in the city. The Indo-Guyanese community has created a variety of informal support networks and religious institutions, generally apart from organizations for people from India. Guyanese of Hindu faith support over 40 *mandirs* (places of worship) in the New York City area, the largest being Sewa Ashram Sangh.

Roopnarine, Lomarsh. "Indo-Guyanese Migration: From Plantation to Metropolis," *Immigrants and Minorities* 20 (July 2001): 1–25

Lomarsh Roopnarine

Gypsies. Term used to cover several distinct ethnic groups (some writers prefer the term Roma), including Travelers, Rom, Romnichels, and Ludar, each with its own history, language, and culture. There are no reliable population figures for any of these groups. Gypsies have lived and traveled throughout New York State, providing goods and services that might not be permanently supported by any single community. Almost all of these groups followed flexible, peripatetic occupations through the first third of the 20th century. Traveling has decreased since the middle of the 20th century, and the various groups live in scattered patterns and nonlocalized networks.

Gypsy camps were a source of fascination and fear in rural areas. In the 19th century mock coronations attracted customers to Romnichel camps, and in the 20th century Rom weddings drew crowds. Peripatetic groups in rural areas were subject to expulsion by local or county authorities. In cities, opposition to their presence came from local citizens' and business groups and was executed through municipal authorities. In 1929 Gov Franklin D. Roosevelt vetoed a bill that would have authorized municipal and county governments to pass ordinances regulating or licensing "gypsies." Direct attacks on Gypsy camps were rare, but an attack on a Rom camp in Rochester in 1902 spurred press criticism of the police for providing inadequate protection to the Gypsies. In 1926 a group dressed in Ku Klux Klan garb attacked Rom near Baldwin Place (Putnam Co).

Historically sedentary, unlike the other groups, Gypsies from eastern Slovakia immigrating in the late 19th and early 20th centuries settled primarily in New York City, making their living as professional musicians in saloons, hotels, and theaters. Since the 1970s Gypsies from Yugoslavia, Hungary, and Macedonia—groups not previously represented in the United States—have immigrated to New York.

Travelers, Romnichels, and Ludar

Irish and Scottish Travelers do not identify themselves as Gypsies but are sometimes referred to as such by observers. Irish Travelers immigrated to the United States in the last half of the 19th century and specialized in tinsmithing, horse trading, and floor-covering sales. Scottish Travelers immigrated from the mid–19th century well into the 20th, specializing in horse trading, textile and fur selling, and home repairing.

The Romnichels, for the most part, emigrated from the British Isles from 1850 to 1900, often in groups of several related families. Association with England is a source of ethnic pride. Horse trading while traveling became the backbone of the Romnichel economy through the first quarter of the 20th century. New England Romnichels traveled to the state to buy horses for their urban sales stables. Secondary occupations were selling rustic furniture and basketry, and fortune-telling, especially in summer resort areas. Romnichels established seasonal fortune-telling camps on rented land near Brooklyn's Prospect Park and the Bronx Zoo. Driveway paving and septic tank cleaning become important Romnichel livelihoods in the 1950s.

The Romnichel ethnic language, known as Rom'nes, contributes to group cohesion and privacy. Eloping is traditional, although some marriages are arranged by parents. An ideological system distinguishing the ritually clean from the unclean *(mokadi)* regulates private behavior and separates Romnichels from non-Gypsies. Land ownership often facilitated nomadism, providing an assured camping place and loan collateral or income. Following patrilineal ideology, postmarital residence favors patrilocality. Romnichels are Protestant, and in the late 20th century fundamentalist Christian congregations led by Romnichel pastors came to define Romnichel ethnic identity and social organization.

Ludar, who speak a dialect of Romanian and are Orthodox Christians, emigrated from Bosnia from the 1880s. Their marriages are traditionally arranged, with a bride-price paid. Some specialized in the exhibition of trained animals and arrived with their bears and monkeys. In the late 1930s, Stanley George's Russian brown bears, adept at roller-skating, riding tricycles and scooters, and performing a tightwire act, participated in the WPA Circus in New York City. Horse trading was important through the first third of the 20th century. Carnival concessions, the manufacture and sale of outdoor furniture, and driveway paving have more recently become Ludar livelihoods.

Ludar established permanent large camps in New York City and made seasonal journeys or commuted to tell fortunes house to house. The Ludar camp just outside the Bronx Zoo, in use from about 1905, drew objections from zoo director William C. Hornaday, and by 1916 the Ludar had left the Bronx for campsites in Jamaica (to about 1925) and Maspeth (*ca* 1925–39) in Queens, the last of which, after frequent Health Department scrutiny, was razed in 1939.

Rom

Rom from Serbia and the Russian empire arrived in the United States from the late 19th century to the first quarter of the 20th. Conflict within the group is resolved by a formal gathering of male elders (the *kris*), with enforcement through fines or the threat of banishment. A purity code pervades many aspects of Rom life. Arranged marriages are sealed by payment of a bride-price, but eloping is also common. Rom consider themselves Roman Catholic or Eastern Orthodox, and much of Rom traditional ritual echoes that common in Serbian Orthodox practice. Rom participation was highlighted in Aimee Semple McPherson's revival movement, as in Rochester in 1921, but had no long-term effect on beliefs and practices. However, the growing Pentecostal Christian movement among the Rom since the late 1970s preaches against earlier practices. Pentecostal churches led by Rom pastors have been established in New York City.

Rom specialized in horse trading and the repair of copper industrial equipment and camped in or near cities where such equipment was used. They developed fortune-telling businesses in rented New York City storefronts by 1914, and fortune-telling became more important after the use of copper and horses declined. Steve Kaslov (Lolya), a New York City Russian Rom leader in the 1930s, corresponded with Pres Franklin D. Roosevelt and Eleanor Roosevelt from 1937 to 1941. Through the latter, Kaslov was introduced to the Welfare Council of New York, which established the Romany Coppersmiths workshop (1939–40) to bolster the flagging coppersmith business. Eleanor Roosevelt supported the workshop through her "My Day" column and commissioned work.

Gropper, Rena C. *Gypsies in the City: Culture Patterns and Survival* (Princeton, NJ: Darwin Press, 1975)

Lockwood, William G., and Sheila Salo. *Gypsies and Travelers in North America: An Annotated Bibliography* (Cheverly, Md: Gypsy Lore Society, 1994)

Salo, Matt T., and Sheila Salo. "Gypsy Immigration to the United States." In *Papers from the Sixth and Seventh Annual Meetings,* ed. Joanne Grumet (New York: Gypsy Lore Society, 1986)

Salo, Sheila. "Lolya's Story: Steve Kaslov and His Memoirs," *Journal of the Gypsy Lore Society* 5 (1995): 38–50

Matt T. Salo and Sheila Salo

gypsum. A soft mineral containing calcium sulfate and water, described chemically as $CaSO_4$-$2H_2O$. New York State gypsum is quarried from Salina Group rocks, which formed about 420 million years ago in a shallow, salty sea extending across the future central and western parts of the state. Gypsum occurs beneath the surface in a narrow band running through Niagara, Erie, Genesee, Monroe, Ontario, Wayne, Seneca, Cayuga, Onondaga, and Madison Cos. From colonial times into the early 19th century, New York State imported gypsum from the Maritime Provinces. Disruption of this trade during the War of 1812 initiated quarrying in Madison and Onondaga Cos. Gypsum was added to soil as a fertilizer in the early 19th century. Starting in 1893 a plant in Oakfield (Genesee Co) used gypsum in making building plaster. In 1905 manufacturers of Portland cement began using small amounts of gypsum to retard setting time. A sandwich of gypsum plaster between sheets of heavy paper has been marketed as wallboard since around 1906. By 1917 New York State was producing over 600,000 tons (544,300 MT) of gypsum from western New York State mines at Akron, Garbutt, Wheatland, Victor, Union Springs, Fayetteville, Jamesville, and Lyndon. In 1948 the yield was 1.4 million tons (1.3 million MT) of crude gypsum, worth $3.3 million. In 2000 four active gypsum plants in the state produced a total of 1.5 million tons (1.3 million MT) of calcined gypsum, worth $27.5 million. The US Gypsum Co and Oakfield Mine, a processing plant and commercial mine in Oakfield (Genesee Co), maintain operations at the beginning of the 21st century. Gypsum mined out of the state is processed at plants in Rensselaer, Rockland, and Westchester Cos.

Van Diver, Bradford B. *Roadside Geology of New York* (Missoula, Mont: Mountain Press Publishing, 1985)

John J. Chiment and Victoria J. Chiment

H

Habitat for Humanity. An international Christian organization dedicated to increasing the supply of affordable housing for low-income families through new construction and the renovation of existing structures. Founded in 1976 in Georgia by Millard Fuller, a millionaire entrepreneur, Habitat for Humanity (HFH) has grown to over 2,000 independent chapters, called affiliates. The first affiliate in New York State was the Lower East Side HFH, established in 1982. Former president Jimmy Carter began his involvement with Habitat in 1984 with the renovation of an apartment building on Manhattan's Lower East Side, energizing the organization statewide. The Lower East Side affiliate later consolidated with other area affiliates to form the New York City HFH in 1986. New York State had 18 affiliates in 1990, including those in Albany, Buffalo, Rochester, and Syracuse. In the mid-1990s, HFH undertook an "urban initiative" to increase its activities and funding in big cities. New York City was designated as a site in the Jimmy Carter Work Project 2000, during which 20 new projects were completed in one week, including HFH's 100,000th home at West 134th St in Harlem. By the end of 2001 the 56 New York State affiliates had built or renovated 700 homes and donated $1.6 million to Habitat homes in foreign countries.

Baggett, Jerome P. *Habitat for Humanity: Building Private Homes, Building Public Religion* (Philadelphia: Temple Univ Press, 2001)

Katherine B. Killoran

Hackensack Indians. A group of Munsee-speaking communities whose homeland stretched along the river valley bearing their name from present-day Rockland Co south to Staten Island. Their name may derive from Munsee words for hook-shaped river mouth. The Hackensack population probably ranged from 200 to 400 at the beginning of European settlement. Colonial records document major communities on uplands bordering the Hackensack Meadowlands in New Jersey. Oratam, Tantaqua (known to settlers as Hans), and other Hackensack leaders became important intermediaries between their Munsee neighbors and Dutch and English settlements clustering around nearby New Amsterdam. Living near the center of colonial expansion, devastated by epidemic disease, and depopulated by war and outmigration, the Hackensack could only delay colonists intent on acquiring their lands. As early as 1630 Hackensack sachems signed deeds conveying lands bordering New York Harbor on Staten Island and the Bayonne peninsula. Driving settlers away during the Peach War in 1655, the Indians sold land rights on the recaptured island back to the Dutch in 1657. English settlers finally extinguished remaining Hackensack claims to Staten Island in 1670. Other Hackensacks put their marks on the great Orange Co Kakiat, Chesecock, Wawayanda, Minisink, and Minisink Angle Patents made between 1696 and 1704. Most Hackensacks joined communities led by Taphow and other Indians moving from western Connecticut to the Ramapo Valley and the great drowned land meadows around the upper reaches of the Wallkill River along contested borderlands between New York and New Jersey. These communities in turn became part of a widespread network of dispossessed Indian people moving along remote Appalachian upland hollows. Ranging from New England to West Virginia, most were forced to abandon the region by 1800. Today, many of their descendants belong to Delaware, Munsee, and Mohican (Mahican) communities in Ontario, Wisconsin, Kansas, and Oklahoma. Others claiming descent from the Hackensack continue to live in remote upland communities along the New York–New Jersey border.

Esposito, Frank J. "Indian-White Relations in New Jersey" (PhD diss, Rutgers Univ, 1976)
Grumet, Robert S. "The Minisink Settlements: Native American Identity and Society in the Munsee Heartland, 1650–1778." In *The People of Minisink: Papers from the 1989 Delaware Water Gap Symposium,* ed. David G. Orr and Douglas V. Campana (Philadelphia: Mid-Atlantic Region, National Park Service, 1991)
Kraft, Herbert C. *The Lenape-Delaware Indian Heritage: 10,000 BC to AD 2000* (Elizabeth, NJ: Lenape Books, 2001)

Robert S. Grumet

Hadley. Town (pop 1,971) in NW Saratoga Co. It is bounded on the east by the Hudson River, and the land is rough and hilly. The town was settled by Europeans in ?1788 and formed in 1801 from Greenfield. Its economy was dependent upon logging, small woodenware factories, tanneries, and a paper mill. The Adirondack Railroad (built 1863–65) provided improved access but, by about 1900, the woods-dependent industries declined because of overharvesting. The Conklingville Dam, on the west border, was constructed from 1927 to 1930 to regulate the Sacandaga River; it created a market for summer cottages on the shore of Great Sacandaga Lake, which partly bisects the town.

Field Horne

Hagaman [HAY-GA-MIN]. Village (pop 1,357) in Amsterdam (Montgomery Co). In 1777 Joseph Hagaman settled on the North Chuctanunda Creek and built grist- and sawmills. After the Civil War, the Anchor and Star knitting mills were established, making woolen knit underwear and hosiery. The village was incorporated in 1892. In the early 21st century, it is primarily a bedroom community for nearby municipalities.

James Crawford

Hagen, Walter (Charles) (*b* Rochester, 21 Dec 1892; *d* Traverse City, Mich, 5 Oct 1969). Professional golfer. Raised by his mother and blacksmith father a mile from the Country Club of Rochester, Hagen began regularly skipping school to caddy in 1905. By age 15 he had become the club's assistant golf pro, brought about in part at the urging of George Eastman. Walter Hagen continually worked to hone his golf skills, and he finished fourth at the 1913 US Open golf championship. A talented athlete, Hagen also pitched the Rochester Ramblers to three city semi-pro baseball championships and played in spring training with the Philadelphia Phillies. But he opted for golf when Ernest Willard, a former Rochester newspaper editor, offered to pay Hagen's way to the 1914 US Open in Chicago. Hagen won that tournament by one stroke, the first of 75 career tournament victories, which included 40 events on the Professional Golfers' Association (PGA) tour that he helped found in 1916. His five PGA tournament titles (1921, 1924–27) remain a record. He also won four British Opens (1922, 1924, 1928–29) and two US Opens (1914, 1919). Hagen's 11 major tournament wins rank third best all-time behind Jack Nicklaus and Bobby Jones. One of the first Americans to play professional golf full-time, in 1940 "the Haig" became an inaugural member of the PGA Hall of Fame. Hagen raised the social status of professional golfers, and his flamboyance on and off the golf course helped to popularize the game worldwide. He captained the US Ryder Cup team in matches against Great Britain six times (1927, 1929, 1931, 1933, 1935, 1937) and was named captain for 1939 and 1941, though no matches were played. Hagen ended his professional career in 1940. He continued to play in exhibitions, touring more than 100 countries over the course of his career. Living in Michigan, Hagen worked with the Wilson Sporting Goods Co and developed a popular line of golf equipment. He died of throat cancer at age 76.

Hagen, Walter, and Margaret Seaton Heck. *The Walter Hagen Story* (New York: Simon & Schuster, 1956)
Pitoniak, Scott. "Walter Hagen: The First Giant of American Golf," *Rochester Democrat and Chronicle,* 17 Sept 1995

Scott Pitoniak

Hague. Town (pop 854) in NE Warren Co. Settled *ca* 1765, the town was formed from Bolton in 1807 as Rochester and renamed Hague in 1808. Rogers' Rock State Campground, on the shores of Lake George, is near the site where Robert Rogers escaped from pursuing Indians in 1758. British forces encamped at Sabbath Day Point (1757–59). Samuel Adams acquired the Sabbath Day Point Tract by a 1766 grant and built an inn. In the 19th century lumbermen floated logs down the lake to Ticonderoga (Essex Co). Graphite for pencils was mined from 1887 until 1924–25. The YMCA's Silver Bay Association (1904) serves as an educational and religious center. The Hoax Fest in July commemorates "George the Monster," a supposed sea serpent fabricated in a 1906 prank. Tourism drives the town's economy.

Marilyn J. Van Dyke

Haitians. The first wave of Haitian immigration to New York State was during the Haitian Revolution (1791–1803), when Whites, free Blacks, and black slaves fled or were brought from what was then the French colony of St. Domingue. For New York State African Americans in the 19th century, the very existence of Haiti, a state in which former slaves ruled themselves, became a beacon of hope and pride. There were several largely abortive schemes for African Americans to settle in Haiti, although contact continued throughout the century. The US occupation of Haiti (1915–34) prompted another wave of Haitian émigrés, including Elie Garcia and Jean-Joseph Adam, who became members of Marcus

Garvey's separatist Universal Negro Improvement Association. Starting in the 1960s a new wave of Haitians fled poverty, the Duvalier dictatorship (1957–86), and the troubled times that followed. Although many Haitians immigrated legally after the end of the quota system in 1965, many also came as undocumented immigrants. Until the mid-1970s most immigrants were members of the Haitian elite and the middle class, but then came increasingly from working-class and peasant backgrounds.

In 2002 they lived mainly in New York City, especially Crown Heights, Flatbush, Canarsie, and Flatlands in Brooklyn; the Upper West Side in Manhattan; Laurelton, Rosedale, Queens Village, and Springfield Gardens in Queens; Hempstead, Valley Stream, and Mineola in Nassau Co, as well as in Suffolk and Rockland Cos. A larger group of Haitian migrant farmworkers lived in the area around Rochester and Ithaca. The 2000 US Census reported 160,319 people of Haitian birth or descent in New York State, but community activists have claimed much higher numbers, up to 375,000 or more.

Social Networks and Politics

In many cases the immigration of a Haitian family is started by a woman, whether spouse, daughter, or sibling, who then brings in her family over the years. Remittances from immigrant Haitians sustain many families in Haiti. Haitians have formed a great number of professional, political, and cultural organizations, including soccer clubs and Masonic temples. Hometown associations such as *Les Amis des enfants de Lascahobasto* support relief activities in Haiti. Haitians also find support in Haitian neighborhood centers such as the large Haitian-Americans United for Progress (HAUP) center that opened in 1975 in Queens. The community supports the local weekly newspapers, such as *Haiti-Observateur* (1971), *Haiti-Progrés* (1983), and *Haitian Times* (2000), the latter targeting the English-speaking second generation. The New York City affiliate of Radio Soleil and local radio stations such as Radio Tropicale, Radio Perspectives, Radio Samba, and Moments Créoles are also popular.

Until the 1980s politically active Haitian immigrants tended to focus more on reforming Haiti than on American politics. This changed when the Food and Drug Administration advised the rejection of blood donations from Haitians, citing a high incidence of AIDS among donors. On 20 April 1990 over 80,000 Haitians and their supporters demonstrated in Manhattan and Brooklyn, and continued protests until the measure was rescinded a few weeks later. In August 1997 the Haitian immigrant Abner Louima was tortured by four policemen in the 70th precinct in Brooklyn, leading to prolonged demonstrations for justice.

Education and Culture

Haitians speak Kreyol (Creole), which developed from French and African languages. A minority has mastery of the French language. Haitians mainly enter the workforce as low-paid wage workers in the service and manufacturing sectors. In the New York City area they work in healthcare, hotels, office cleaning, and transportation services. There is an emerging class of managers and public employees. Most Haitians are Catholics, among them Pierre Toussaint (?1766–1853), who was brought to New York City in the 1780s as a slave. Known for his philanthropies and dignity, he was declared venerable in 1997 by the Catholic Church and is a candidate for sainthood. In New York City the largest Haitian parish is St. Jerome at 2900 Newkirk Ave in Flatbush (Kings Co). Haitians celebrate Mass with drums and in Kreyol. A growing number of immigrants belong to Protestant congregations. At the same time, most Haitians believe in serving the spirits *(lwa)* of Vodoun, an African-derived religion. Vodoun is also an ancestor cult and a system of folk medicine. Rituals integrate singing and the use of drums, and provide guidance, comfort, and healing, in particular when immigrants face difficulties in adjusting to their new life. Haitian art, in particular Haitian painting, has achieved international reputation and is shown in museums. Modern Haitian music has also gained attention. Compas, the most important form of Haitian dance music, is played in many New York City nightclubs. So is root music, which blends Vodoun rhythms and rock. Young immigrants in Rockland Co founded one of the most influential bands of this genre, Bookman Experians, in 1978. The father of Brooklyn-born artist Jean-Michel Basquiat was born in Haiti. Wyclef Jean of the group Fugees moved to New Jersey after a long period of residence in Brooklyn, and writer Edwidge Danticat still lives in Brooklyn.

Laguerre, Michel. *Diasporic Citizenship: Haitian Americans in Transnational America* (New York: St. Martin's Press 1998)

Stepick, Alex. *Pride against Prejudice: Haitians in the United States* (Boston: Allyn & Bacon 1998)

Carolle Charles

Halcott. Town (pop 193) in W Greene Co. The area was settled in 1809 and the town was formed from Lexington in 1851. Halcott encompasses four valleys, which are drained by streams flowing to the Delaware River. Vly Mountain, at an elevation of 1,000 feet (300 m), is not crossed by roads and separates Halcott from the rest of the county. Much of Halcott is forested, and the valleys are occupied by farms and by seasonal and year-round residences.

Field Horne

Hale, Nathan (*b* Coventry, Conn, 6 June 1755; *d* New York City, 22 Sept 1776). Schoolteacher, army officer, and spy. One of 12 children, Hale taught school after graduating from Yale in 1773. In 1775 he enlisted in the Connecticut Militia, which joined Gen George Washington's forces near Boston and followed them to New York City. Defeated by the British on Long Island in August 1776, Washington sought a spy to infiltrate their lines. The 21-year-old Hale, now a captain, was the only volunteer. According to a manuscript acquired by the Library of Congress at the beginning of the 21st century, Hale confided the nature of his mission to a tory, Robert Rogers, who informed British authorities. Hale set out in mid-September; the British, under Gen William Howe, invaded Manhattan a few days later. Hale was captured in Manhattan on the night of 21 Sept 1776, interrogated by Howe, and hanged the next morning, probably where 3d Ave intersects East 66th St. A plaque at this site commemorates Hale. Subject of much fable and few facts, Hale is renowned for 14 words, which he paraphrased from the play *Cato* by Joseph Addison: "I only regret that I have but one life to lose for my country." A fellow officer, William Hull, reported Hale's alleged declaration years later, saying he heard it from a British officer present at the hanging.

Kelby, William. "Site of the Execution of Captain Nathan Hale" *New-York Historical Society Quarterly* (April 1918)

Schecter, Barnet. *The Battle for New York: The City at the Heart of the American Revolution* (New York: Walker, 2002)

Seymour, George Dudley. *Documentary Life of Nathan Hale* (New Haven, Conn, 1941)

Richard E. Mooney

Half Moon. Dutch exploration ship captained by Henry Hudson in 1609. The *Half Moon (Halve Maen)* was built by the Dutch East India Co in Amsterdam in 1608. It was about 65–70 feet (20–21 m) in length and had a carrying capacity of nearly 80 English (long) tons (81 MT). It was square-rigged with a probable sail area of 2,757 feet^2 (256 m^2). On 4 Apr 1609 Henry Hudson set sail from Amsterdam with the *Half Moon* on the voyage that eventually brought the ship to North America. It was with this ship that he explored New York Bay and navigated the Hudson River near the later site of Albany. After Hudson's voyage the ship was captained by Laurens Reale, who departed for the East Indies in 1611. The ship's fate is not absolutely known, but it likely was destroyed in the East Indies sometime by the early 1620s. Full-size replicas of the *Half Moon* were constructed in 1909 and 1989. Although the 1909 replica no longer exists, the 1989 replica is used in annual re-creations of Hudson's trip up the river and in educational programs while under sail and in ports on the Hudson River and elsewhere.

Hendricks, Andrew A. "Construction of the 1988 Half Moon," *de Halve Maen* 66 (Fall 1993): 42–47

Johnson, Donald S. *Charting the Sea of Darkness: The Four Voyages of Henry Hudson* (Camden, Maine: International Marine, 1993)

New Netherland Museum, http://www.newnetherland.org

Paul Otto

Halfmoon. Town (pop 18,474) in SE Saratoga Co. Named for the bend in the Mohawk River, its southern boundary, it was initially settled by Dutch traders in the 17th century. Formed as a district in 1772, it was recognized as a town in 1788, and its name was Orange from 1816 to 1820. The town was crossed by the Champlain (1823) and Erie (1823) Canals. At Crescent an aqueduct 1,150 feet (350 m) in length crossed the Mohawk River and stimulated business, including a bank (1842). There was little manufacturing in town, and farming predominated until suburbanization was made possible by the Northway (1960). Halfmoon's population had a fourfold increase between 1960 and 2000.

Field Horne

Hall, James (*b* Hingham, Mass, 12 Sept 1811; *d* Bethlehem, NH, 6 Aug 1898). Geologist and paleontologist. In 1832 Hall received a bachelor of natural science from Rensselaer School (later Rensselaer Polytechnic Institute), and an MA degree the next year. He was professor of chemistry at Rensselaer School from 1835 to 1841. In 1836

Hall started work on the Adirondack counties for the New York State Geological Survey, becoming principal geologist of the western district in 1837. In identifying geological strata from their fossils, Hall gained experience that led to his 1843 appointment as state paleontologist. This position resulted in *The Paleontology of New York,* 13 volumes published from 1847 to 1894. Hall was professor of geology at Rensselaer Polytechnic Institute from 1854 to 1876. In 1863 Congress named Hall a charter member of the National Academy of Sciences. Hall was appointed curator of the New York State Cabinet of Natural History (later the New York State Museum) in 1865. He served as the museum's director until 1894, making Albany a center for the study of paleontology. One of Hall's contributions was the identification of stromatolites (Precambrian limestone- or dolomite-layered sedimentary structures) as having biogenic origin.

See also ANCIENT LIFE.

Clarke, John M. *James Hall of Albany: Geologist and Paleontologist, 1811–1898* (1923; repr New York: Arno, 1978)

Pamela Cooper

Hall of Fame for Great Americans. The first institution of its kind in the United States and the model for many others, the hall is located at West 181st St and University Ave on the campus of Bronx Community College. Its outdoor colonnade contains portrait busts, designed by some of the country's greatest sculptors, honoring illustrious American statesmen, inventors, writers, artists, composers, educators, jurists, and scientists. The Hall of Fame was the idea of Henry Mitchell MacCracken, chancellor of New York University (NYU), who purchased property in 1894 to build a new NYU campus. Architect Stanford White designed three buildings on a ridge overlooking the Harlem River valley: the rectangular halls of philosophy and languages flanking the circular, domed Gould Memorial Library. Construction was financed by gifts from Jay Gould and his daughter Helen Gould Shepard. Because the ridge left unsightly basement windows overlooking the valley, White built a 630 ft (192 m) serpentine terrace around the buildings, topped by a colonnade. MacCracken decided to use the terrace as an educational tool recognizing the accomplishments of prominent Americans.

The Hall of Fame opened in 1900 with 29 honorees. Until 1976 a national panel of electors chosen by the hall's Board of Trustees periodically considered nominations of native-born or naturalized Americans dead at least 25 years. Over one-quarter of those inducted have New York State connections, including Franklin D. Roosevelt, Theodore Roosevelt, Grover Cleveland, James Fenimore Cooper, William Cullen Bryant, Washington Irving, Susan B. Anthony, James Kent, Samuel F. B. Morse, Alexander Graham Bell, and Edwin Booth. In 1973 NYU sold the property to the Dormitory Authority of the State of New York, and it became the campus of Bronx Community College. With the 1976 election the number of honorees reached 102, matching the number of available bust spaces. NYU then suspended its contributions to the hall's operating expenses, leading to the resignation of the hall's Board of Directors on 1 July 1979. Although renovations were undertaken by Bronx Community College in the 1980s, no new additions are contemplated. The hall attracts about 10,000 visitors per year.

Morello, Theodore, ed. *Great Americans: A Guide to the Hall of Fame for Great Americans,* rev ed. (New York: New York Univ, 1977)

Lloyd Ultan

Hambletonian. See HARNESS RACING.

Hamburg. Town (pop 56,529) and village (pop 10,116) in W Erie Co. On Lake Erie and settled in 1804, the town was formed in 1812 from Willink [now Aurora]. In 1806 the first gristmill in Erie Co outside of Buffalo was established on Eighteenmile Creek. Many Germans settled in town beginning in the early 1830s. The first railroad was the Buffalo and State Line (1852); later, trolley service (1901–32) helped make Hamburg a commuter suburb. In the mid–19th century Water Valley was the site of the Haviland and Cadwell woolen factory and of a foundry. The Village of Hamburg incorporated in 1874. Late 19th-century industries were Hamburg Canning Co (1881) and Pierce Glass Co (1910–16). Resorts on Lake Erie were developed, including Idlewood (1882) and Woodlawn Beach (1891). Industries in the 20th century included Bethlehem Steel Co, a Ford stamping plant, Eaton Bros, Chemtrol, and Electro-Refractories Corp. In the early 21st century rubber goods and optical products were manufactured. The New York State Thruway crossed the town in 1957. Hilbert College (1969) and the Erie County Fair (1868), the largest county fair in the United States, are located in Hamburg. It is one of several locations claiming to be the birthplace of the hamburger.

Andrew C. Maines

Hamden. Town (pop 1,280) in central Delaware Co. Settled about 1779, the town was formed from Delhi and Walton in 1825. Settlers worked at lumbering. The Ontario and Western Railroad (1872–1957), providing an outlet for dairy products, encouraged the establishment of creameries. Late in the 19th century, a large tannery operated at De Lancey. Once a thriving business center, the hamlet of Hamden declined as the railroad was abandoned and farming waned. Landmarks include the Hamden Inn (1844) and a covered bridge (1859), restored in 2001, which is one of three in the county still in public use.

Dorothy Kubik

Hamilton. Town (pop 5,733) and village (pop 3,509) in SE Madison Co. Settled in 1792, the town was formed from Paris (Oneida Co) in 1795. First called Payne's Settlement, the Hamilton post office opened in 1806. A Baptist seminary incorporated in 1817 grew into Madison University (1846), which changed its name to Colgate University in 1890. The town was served by the Chenango Canal (1837–78) and three railroads. From 1955 to 1992 the American Management Association operated White Eagle Conference Center and created Americana Village (1967), a museum village now abandoned. Village boundaries were expanded in the late 20th century into Madison and Eaton in order to annex Hamilton Municipal Airport. The university employs many area residents and provides cultural activities, including exhibitions at the Picker Art Center. Hamilton Village Historic District, organized around a New England–style village green, is listed on the National Register.

See also BAPTISTS.

William F. Helmer

Hamilton, Alexander (*b* Nevis, West Indies, ?1757; *d* Weehawken, NJ, 12 July 1804). Revolutionary War officer and statesman. Born out of wedlock, Alexander Hamilton became a New Yorker in 1773, when he enrolled at King's College (now Columbia University) at the age of 16. He entered as the crisis for independence from Great Britain was breaking, wrote his earliest pamphlets on behalf of the American cause, helped rescue the loyalist college president from a hostile crowd, and began to study the art of artillery. Having joined the Continental army as a captain, Hamilton spent most of the war as aide-de-camp to George Washington, with the rank of lieutenant colonel. Despite his youth he was in a position to speak with Washington's authority to the highest-ranking generals and never lost the perspective he gained. At the end of the conflict he returned to field service and took an active part in the Battle of Yorktown.

Hamilton married Elizabeth Schuyler in 1780, daughter of Philip Schuyler. Hamilton's origins aside, the New York elite was open to talent, and the marriage guaranteed him a place in its top rank. When the war ended he studied law for 10 intense months and entered the bar in October 1782. He already had been chosen as a New York State delegate to the Continental Congress. Returning to writing, he began his habit of composing long, insightful letters about the condition of the state and of the United States, invariably stressing the theme of fostering economic development. His analysis of "the rulers" of his adopted state was scathing. His highest compliment was for a man who "meant to do well whenever he can hit upon what is right." The fundamental division, he believed, was between people whose view was continental and those whose view was limited to the good of the state.

Hamilton's *Continentalist* essay series (1782–83) developed the theme that national power was an absolute necessity. Postwar persecution of loyalists seemed ludicrous to him,

Alexander Hamilton, John Trumbull, 1806.

because it flouted the peace treaty and harmed American credibility and because it drove out talented businessmen. His *Letters from Phocion* (1784–85) developed these themes, and he represented a number of former loyalists in court, most notably in *Rutgers v Waddington* (1784). In this case the mayor's court of New York City interpreted the state's antiloyalist Citation Act in a way that it did not conflict with the treaty. He played the predominant role in organizing the Bank of New York, the city's first formal banking institution, in 1784. He also began rallying Hudson Valley landlords, city merchants, and professionals, whom he called the "principal people," to make common cause for their "own defence" so that men "whose principles are not of the levelling kind" would replace the "truly alarming . . . present legislature" and the "the power of government" would be "entrusted to proper hands."

Hamilton took part in the meeting at Annapolis, Md, in 1786 that proposed the federal Constitutional Convention, entered the state legislature in the session of 1787 precisely so that he could be elected to the convention, and became one of the state's three delegates. As a legislator he demonstrated his passion for regularity and predictability rather than ad hoc decision making. His performance at the Philadelphia convention was limited, perhaps because he was frustrated by his two Antifederalist New York colleagues, Robert Yates and John Lansing Jr. But the part he took in the ratification struggle was enormous. He wrote 56 of the 85 *Federalist* essays whose intended readership was "the considerate citizens of New York." He spoke strongly at the ratifying convention at Poughkeepsie in 1788 and helped broker the agreement that split the Antifederalist majority and led to New York becoming the 11th state. Although Hamilton lacked the common touch, his position and arguments enjoyed strong support among New York City artisans, who honored him with the fully rigged "Federal Ship *Hamilton*" in the parade that celebrated ratification.

As early as 1786 Hamilton was casting himself in the role of national minister of finance, inspired both by Jacques Necker in France and by the British cabinet post of chancellor of the exchequer. He leaped on the chance to become secretary of the treasury (1789) when George Washington offered it to him and held that office until 1795. It allowed him to pull all his themes together in a general plan for fostering a vibrant, capitalist, national economy. That plan took the form of the four *Reports* prepared between 1789 and 1791, three for Congress and one, on the constitutionality of establishing a Bank of the United States, for Washington. During most of his cabinet service he was based in Philadelphia, which replaced New York City as national capital in 1790. As inspector general he accompanied the army that put down the Whiskey Rebellion (1794) in western Pennsylvania, a role he was to reprise in 1798 against Fries' Rebellion in the same state. He returned to New York State to practice law when he left formal public service. The cases he argued helped to establish the commercial law of the early United States.

By that time Hamilton was a deeply partisan High Federalist, and he enjoyed informal domination over the cabinet of Pres John Adams. His roles in giving the deadlocked presidential election of 1800 to his old enemy Thomas Jefferson rather than to Aaron Burr and in denying Burr the governorship in 1804 led to a duel between Hamilton and Burr at Weehawken, NJ, and to Hamilton's death.

The Law Practice of Alexander Hamilton, ed. Julius Goebel Jr et al, 5 vols (New York: Columbia Univ Press, 1964–81)

The Papers of Alexander Hamilton, ed. Harold C. Syrett et al, 27 vols (New York: Columbia Univ Press, 1961–87)

McDonald, Forrest. *Alexander Hamilton: A Biography* (New York: Norton, 1979)

Mitchell, Broadus. *Alexander Hamilton,* 2 vols (New York: Macmillan, 1957–1962)

Edward Countryman

Hamilton, William (*b* New York City, 1773; *d* ?New York City, 9 Dec 1836). Abolitionist writer and preacher. Perhaps the most prominent and important African American leader in New York City during the early republic, Hamilton was born free to a black mother and white father (reputedly Alexander Hamilton). As a young man he worked as a carpenter, and during the early 1800s he rose steadily into the ranks of New York City's black elite. In 1808 he cofounded the New York African Society for Mutual Relief, which was initially formed as a burial society. It was officially incorporated in 1810, and Hamilton served as president. He helped establish education clubs, such as the Phoenix and Philomathean Societies, and he served as a ward chairman for abolitionist-run schools.

During the late 1820s Hamilton became part of a group that criticized the paternalistic attitudes of white educators. As a result, many African schools came under the more direct control of the black community in 1832. A renowned orator and writer, Hamilton continually agitated for black justice by giving orations from the African Methodist Episcopal Zion Church in New York City, by addressing the African Society, by meeting with white allies in and around New York City, and by publishing pamphlets critical of racism, the overseas slave trade, and the growth of slavery in America. His pamphlets brought praise from New York City's black community and were passed down to succeeding generations of reformers. In 1834 Hamilton was honored as president of the National Convention of the Free Persons of Color, where he gave one of his last major addresses, criticizing the rising popularity of the American Colonization Society. Hamilton was part of an inaugural generation of black activists, both in New York State and nationally, who set the stage for subsequent generations of African American reformers.

Hodges, Graham. *Roots and Branch: African Americans in New York and East Jersey, 1613–1863* (Chapel Hill: Univ of North Carolina Press, 1999)

Newman, Richard, Patrick Rael, and Philip Lapsansky, eds. *Pamphlets of Protest: An Anthology of Early African-American Protest Literature, 1790–1860* (New York: Routledge, 2000)

Richard Newman

Hamilton College. Private college in Clinton (Oneida Co). Founded in 1793 by Samuel Kirkland, a Congregationalist minister who served as a missionary to the Oneida Nation. Originally named Hamilton-Oneida (after Alexander Hamilton, a trustee of the school), the school's initial mission was to educate children of the Oneida Nation and European settlers of Central New York. Chartered in 1812 as Hamilton College, it is the third oldest college in New York State. The college suffered fiscal difficulties early on but flourished after the Civil War, offering a traditional curriculum in the classics. Hamilton was established as an all-male institution, but in 1968 the board of trustees established Kirkland College, an undergraduate institution for women on adjacent land. Ten years later the two colleges merged. Noteworthy features of the 1,300-acre (526 ha) campus include Kirkland Cottage (1792), home of the founder and the oldest building on campus; Buttrick Hall (1812); the chapel (1827), designed by Philip Hooker and thought to be the earliest remaining three-story church in the United States; and Root Glen, a 7.5 acre (3 ha) wooded garden and ravine. Hamilton's enrollment in 2002 was 1,707. Famous graduates include Elihu Root, US secretary of war and secretary of state, who was born on the campus, and poet Ezra Pound.

Pilkington, Walter. *Hamilton College, 1812–1962* (Clinton, NY: Hamilton College, 1962)

Kenneth J. Blume

Hamilton County (1,720 mi^2/4,455 km^2; pop 5,379). Created in 1816 from Montgomery Co and named in honor of Alexander Hamilton, it began functioning fully in 1838. Subsequent boundary changes took place with Fulton Co in 1860 and with Essex Co in 1915. The county is presently subdivided into nine towns containing one incorporated village, Speculator. The unincorporated hamlet of Lake Pleasant serves as county seat. Throughout the 20th century it was the least densely populated of all of the counties in the United States east of the Mississippi River and north of Florida. Within New York State, it has one-fourth the population and, at 3.1 persons per square mile, about one-seventh the density of the next ranked counties, Schuyler and Lewis, respectively.

Elevations range from 771 ft (235 m) on the shore of Sacandaga Lake in the county's extreme southeast corner to 3,899 ft (1,188 m) at the summit of Snowy Mountain in the Town of Indian Lake. Hamilton Co lies entirely within the Adirondack Upland physiographic province. The east and central portions are part of the Adirondack Mountain Peaks subregion, including the northeast- to southwest-oriented valleys that contain Long, Indian, and Piseco Lakes. The remaining area lies within the Adirondack Low Mountains subregion. Bedrock throughout is primarily composed of granitic gneiss and charnockites with seams of metamorphosed sedimentary rocks. Outcroppings of Adirondack anorthosite form the summit of Snowy Mountain and are also present around Speculator. All these rock types were metamorphosed during the Grenville orogeny in the middle Proterozoic age (1,300–1,000 million years ago) and have recently been uplifted. The predominant northeast to southwest orientation of the ridges and valleys resulted from faulting of the Precambrian bedrock during the Taconian orogeny (430–500 million years ago). Coincidentally, the most recent glacial advance followed the southwest-oriented fault lines and enlarged and shaped the broad valleys present today.

Hamilton Co is part of four major watersheds. Waters in the east drain into the Hudson River,

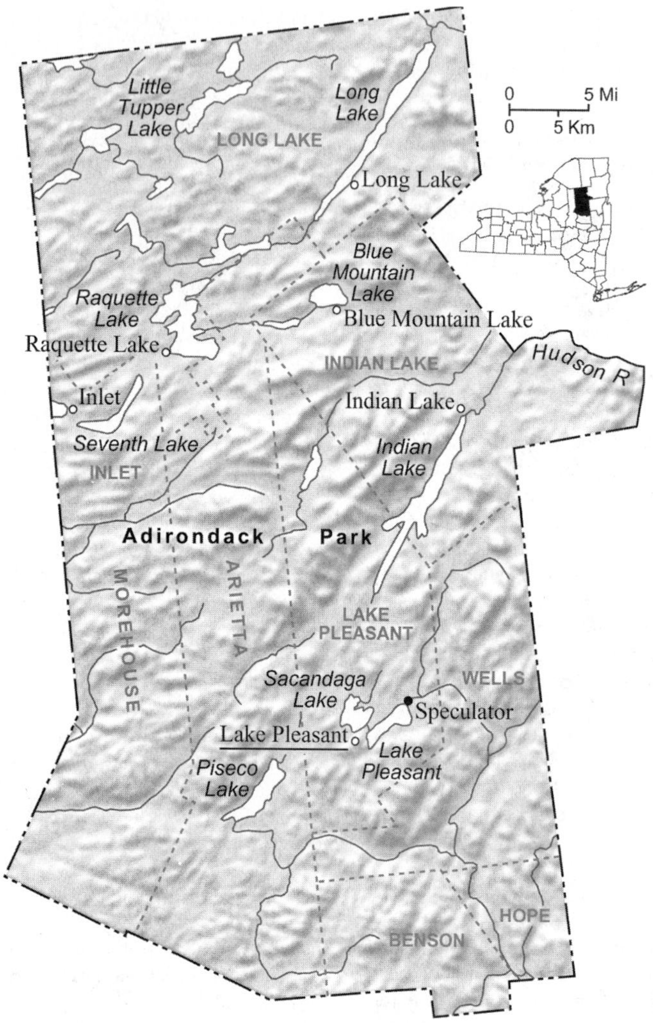

either via north-flowing Indian River or southward via the Sacandaga River. West and East Canada Creeks rise in the southwest quarter and flow south to the Mohawk. Waters along the western boundary flow into Lake Ontario via the Black River system. From its headwaters near Raquette and Blue Mountain Lakes, the Raquette River carries water from the north and central parts of the county northward to the St. Lawrence River. Soils are sandy, thin, and nonarable by modern agricultural standards.

The climate of Hamilton Co is humid-continental. As measured in Indian Lake, average January and July temperatures are 14°F (-10°C) and 64°F (18°C), respectively. Temperatures in the higher elevations are consistently lower. Below 0°F (-18°C) readings are a significant part of winter. Summertime highs of 90°F (32°C) or above occur occasionally in the valleys but not at the higher elevations. Average annual precipitation varies from 41 inches (104 cm) at Indian Lake to 58 inches (147 cm) at Piseco. Seasonal snowfall averages vary greatly from over 200 inches (508 cm) in the high eastern elevations to less than 80 inches (203 cm) in the Sacandaga River valley. The county's primeval forest cover consisted of an Adirondack hardwood community, dominated by beech, sugar maple, yellow birch, hemlock, and white pine intermixed with a spruce-fir community dominated by red spruce, balsam fir, and paper birch. The Adirondack hardwood association dominated the southern quarter of the county, and spruce-fir association dominated the rest. Because New York State has withheld some parcels of land from logging since the 1890s, Hamilton Co contains some of the last remaining primeval forestland in the eastern United States. In the early 21st century, approximately 98% is forested. Hamilton Co lies entirely within the Adirondack Park Blue Line.

American Indians and Early Settlement

The central Adirondacks were used lightly by the Indians. The territory that is now Hamilton Co was hunting territory north of the homeland of the Mohawk Nation. Archaeological evidence of their camps has been found on the shores of various lakes. Colonial and early national land patents conveyed title to the land long before settlement was practicable even in the limited areas that were later populated. The first was Vrooman's Patent (1768), which included part of Morehouse. The Totten and Crossfield Purchase (1771) included a large part of the county's north but was not divided and sold until after the Revolution. A total of 10 grants by the colony or state were made.

Two Indians were Hamilton Co's first permanent residents. Sabael Benedict, a Penobscot/Abenaki, and Peter Sabattis, an Abenaki, both located in Indian Lake about the time of the Revolution. Their descendants were long part of the communities and served as guides. White settlement commenced by 1792 at Wells with the arrival of Joshua and Mary Wells from Long Island, the first to attempt farming in the relatively low and flat land of the Sacandaga Valley. Settlers came to most areas of the county between 1790 and 1810, although Morehouse was not settled until 1832, while the northern communities of Indian Lake and Long Lake, home of the Benedict and Sabattis families, first attracted white settlement *ca* 1840. Most were from New York and New England, but French, German, and Dutch settlers were among the arrivals in Morehouse. The county was 4.2% Irish born in 1855, and the foreign-born population crested in 1900 at 9%. The 1820 census listed one slave and one free Black, and the minority population has always been minuscule. As recently as 1940 the census listed only one nonwhite resident. The 2000 census reported that 2% of the population was nonwhite, by far the highest total in the county's history.

Transportation

The first trail through the county ran north through the Sacandaga Valley and was used by Sir John Johnson and his Indian allies in the Revolution. During the War of 1812 it was improved as a military road to Sackets Harbor, but by 1820 it become overgrown with brush from a point near Cedar Lake, 14 miles (23 km) north of Lake Pleasant; the southern part continued to be the main access to the farming towns of the county's southeast. Other state-designated roads ran from Newkirk's Mills (Fulton Co) to Piseco, legislated in 1841 at Andrew K. Morehouse's request, and from Crown Point (Essex Co) to Carthage (Jefferson Co) by way of Indian Lake and Blue Mountain Lake by 1860.

Railroads came late. The Manheim and Salisbury Railroad was proposed in 1834 to connect at Raquette Lake with the water route to the St. Lawrence Valley, and the Sackets Harbor and Saratoga Railroad was proposed in 1848 to cross the wilderness from southeast to northwest. A successor of the latter company was the Adirondack Railroad, which reached North Creek in 1871, providing much improved access to the north by stage connections from its terminus. Hamilton Co finally acquired rail service via the Mohawk and Malone in 1892, although it ran through the unpopulated west. It took the construction of two short lines—the Raquette Lake Railroad (1900–1933) and the Marion River Carry Railroad (1900–1929)—to provide service to the Raquette Lake and Blue Mountain Lake region, some miles east of the trunk line. The modest tourism of the county's southeast benefited from the Gloversville and Northville Railroad, completed in 1875.

Poor roads were the norm, but because of the absence of navigable waterways or railroads, residents and tourists depended upon them. The highway along the Sacandaga, successor to the ancient trail, was improved beginning in 1912 and completed to Speculator in 1926 and paved in concrete in 1938. A 20 mi (32 km) gap remained unpaved from Speculator to Indian Lake until 1955, when Rte 30 was completed as a continuous north-south highway.

Economic Development

Even though there were vast forest resources, transporting forest products was difficult. Consequently, Hamilton Co's first settlers were subsistence farmers. In 1855, 500 men were farmers,

HAMILTON CO POPULATION CENSUS FIGURES

	White	Nonwhite	Total Population	Foreign-Born
1820	1,249	2	1,251	6
1830	1,324	1	1,325	23
1840	1,904	3	1,907	—
1850	2,186	2	2,188	184
1860	3,021	3	3,024	284
1870	2,958	2	2,960	306
1880	3,906	17	3,923	346
1890	4,744	18	4,762	422
1900	4,920	27	4,947	462
1910	4,352	21	4,373	358
1920	3,966	4	3,970	344
1930	3,923	6	3,929	265
1940	4,187	1	4,188	161
1950	4,103	2	4,105	145
1960	4,263	4	4,267	144
1970	4,703	11	4,714	93
1980	5,011	23	5,034	134
1990	5,248	31	5,279	111
2000	5,257	122	5,379	82

Notes: "Nonwhite" includes African Americans, Asians, American Indians, and Pacific Islanders and, for 2000, also the mixed race and other race categories. Through the 1960 census these figures primarily reflect the African American population. Foreign-born figures for 1820 and 1830 include only those not naturalized, and for 1930 and 1950, the foreign-born totals include Whites only. Other years include all foreign-born in the population.

and the Town of Hope, with 6,729 acres (2,723 ha), had the most farmland, followed by Wells and Lake Pleasant. The first sawmill was at Lake Pleasant in 1795, and the provisional county had 22 sawmills by 1825. Lumbering developed relatively late and used the Schroon and Hudson; the Sacandaga was improved following state legislation of 1854 so that it could float its lumber to market. In 1855 the number of sawmills remained high, but lumbering was still limited as a full-time occupation, with only 10 lumbermen listed in the census. When pulp paper production was begun regionally in the late 1860s, the market for lumber increased. The heyday of Hamilton Co lumbering was in the 1880s and 1890s, after which the heavily cut forests took decades to recover. Shingles were a significant product of southern communities from 1850 to 1880, and 14 men appeared in the 1855 census as shingle makers. Other woods products, made by individuals or in small shops or mills, included bakers' peels, shoe lasts, clothespins, hoe handles, washboards, butter tubs, and fiddle butts. Spruce gum, gathered in the forest, was another source of income in the late 19th century.

The tanning of leather, using hemlock bark from the forest, spread northward from Johnstown and Gloversville (Fulton Co). The first known tannery was operating in 1820 at the mouth of Mill Creek in Wells. In 1855, 43 men worked in the leather industries of Hope, Wells, and Morehouse, and Hope Falls was a busy tannery hamlet in the Civil War era but, by the 1890s, hemlock had grown scarce. Few other industries were ever pursued in Hamilton Co. According to oral tradition, gold was mined in Arietta in the 1840s, and the Fulton County Marble Co (1874) quarried limestone briefly. Fish for the Saratoga Springs hotel market was taken from Blue Mountain Lake and Indian Lake. In Hope and Wells, women stitched gloves for the Northville factories, as many as 46 of women working in their homes in 1925, and from 1941 to 1965 the Serfis Glove Corp had a plant in Wells.

Even though demand for capital was limited, Hamilton Co banking began early, with a private bank operated by Andrew K. Morehouse at Piseco during its brief boom period in the 1840s. The Bank of Hope Falls had a brief existence in the 1850s. The Bank of Hamilton Co (1929) consolidated in 1955 with the Manufacturers' National Bank of Troy, a Marine Midland (now HSBC) affiliate, and moved its office from Wells to Speculator in 1961.

Lumbering recovered in the mid–20th century and is once again economically significant, but tourism became Hamilton Co's bread and butter in the late 19th century. A May 1836 article in *American Monthly* reported on a fishing trip to Lake Pleasant a decade earlier, and John Todd of Boston published his short book *Long Lake* in 1845. Boardinghouses such as the Lake Pleasant Hotel (1845–1904) appeared to serve hunters and fishers. But it was William H. H. "Adirondack" Murray's 1869 classic, *Adventures in the Wilderness,* that led to the rush to explore the mountains that very summer. More boardinghouses were built, as were some grand hotels, such as the 300-room Prospect House (1880) at Blue Mountain Lake.

In 1876 William West Durant began building and selling what came to be called Great Camps, especially around Raquette Lake. Within 25 years much of northern Hamilton Co was assembled into large tracts such as Whitney Park and Nehasane Park, where captains of industry spent summer vacations. Smaller camps followed on the shores of lakes. Nevertheless, the southern communities of Benson, Hope, and Wells did not become significant destinations. Even though roads were poor in the county, the advent of auto touring affected its tourism. The first major campground was built 3 miles (5 km) south of Wells in 1920. Winter sports, developed at Speculator in the 1920s, added a season to the traditional short summer. After World War II the remaining hotels and boardinghouses lost business to campgrounds, motels, and rental cottages. Snowmobile trails developed after 1960 further strengthened the winter trade.

Religion, Education, and Culture

Rev Elisha Yale of Kingsboro Presbyterian Church [now in Gloversville] made preaching visits to the present county as early as 1804 and established small religious libraries. When the Montgomery County Bible Society was formed in 1816, it had three representatives in each of Hamilton's three towns. Methodist circuit riders were the first religious workers to create a network in the county, but the usual number attending church was relatively low: in 1855, 5% of residents, compared to 25% in Montgomery Co. In 1875 there were eight churches in Hamilton Co, five of them Methodist; there was one Roman Catholic church in Morehouse.

Common schools were created in Hamilton Co following the state legislation of 1812 and 1814, as population required. A union free school district was created in Long Lake hamlet in 1893 and merged with three other common school districts in 1907. Indian Lake established a high school, which graduated its first class in 1908, and Long Lake's union district began a high school program in 1924. Perhaps because of the small populations in the districts, centralization proceeded quickly in the 1920s. Benson formed a central school district in that decade, later merging with Northville; Lake Pleasant and Wells both consolidated in 1926. Long Lake, with its Union Free School District and high school program, became a central school in 1947. Inlet continued to operate its two-room common school in 2003, one of the few remaining in New York State. Many high school students are bused long distances. Lake Pleasant and Piseco send students 50 miles (80 km) to Johnstown; Morehouse students travel 30 miles (48 km) to Poland (Herkimer Co).

The county's first newspaper was the *Hamilton County Sentinel* (1845) at Lake Pleasant. The *Hamilton County News* (1946) is a weekly published at Speculator. There is no radio or television station. The hamlets of Long Lake, Indian Lake, Piseco, and Wells and the Village of Speculator have public libraries, which are served by the Southern Adirondack Library System. The Adirondack Museum (1957) and the Adirondack Lakes Center for the Arts (1967), both at Blue Mountain Lake, are the chief cultural attractions.

Politics

Hamilton Co's political history is unique in the state. The legislature, responding to the excessive size of Montgomery Co, formed it provisionally in 1816. Until it contained 1,288 taxable inhabitants qualified to vote for members of the assembly, the new county was to act in conjunction with Montgomery. Population growth was slow, and it was not until 1837, with the contiguous portion of Montgomery about to become Fulton Co, that the legislature authorized Hamilton Co to organize. Officers were elected in 1838, and

POPULATIONS OF TOWNS, HAMILTON CO

Town, Year Founded	1840	1880	1920	1960	2000
Arietta, 1836	209	294	176	235	293
Benson, 1860	—	402	119	87	201
Gilman, 1839–60[a]	98	—	—	—	—
Hope, 1818	711	651	203	234	392
Indian Lake, 1858	—	615	1,031	1,186	1,471
Inlet, 1901	—	—	171	307	406
Lake Pleasant, 1812	296	343	393	718	876
Long Lake, 1837	59	324	1,116	896	852
Morehouse, 1835	169	181	109	65	151
Wells, 1805	365	1,113	652	539	737

[a]Gilman was dissolved 6 Apr 1860. In 1855 it was the least populated town in the state, with only 90 people.

Lake Pleasant was chosen as the county seat. Nevertheless, there were some seven serious attempts to dissolve the county, the final one in 1930.

Since its population never has achieved the threshold required, Hamilton is the only county in New York State never to have a separate member of the assembly; it shares its representative with Fulton Co. Until the system of paved roads was completed, transportation was a serious problem for the Board of Supervisors. Although Lake Pleasant was the county seat, meetings of the board were held in Hope to accommodate its members' needs. Supervisors from Inlet, Indian Lake, and Long Lake had to travel great distances. The Long Lake supervisor usually went to North Creek by wagon, then by rail via Albany and Fonda to Northville, completing the journey to Hope by wagon, while the Inlet supervisor made a similar journey via Utica and Fonda. In 2003 the county was still governed by a Board of Supervisors, which adopted weighted voting according to population in 1969. Voters have historically been conservative; in the early 21st century the ratio is four Republicans to one Democrat.

RECENT HISTORY

The state's Forest Preserve (1885) was incorporated into the Adirondack Park (1892), affecting changes in Hamilton Co in the 20th century. The 1971 creation of the Adirondack Park Agency (APA) placed the entire park under regional planning and put absolute limits on growth. Since Hamilton Co lies entirely within the Adirondack Park, two regulating bodies have power over property rights: the Department of Environmental Conservation (DEC) and the APA. Land swapping, the burning of long-held hunting and fishing camps, and the razing of lean-tos and fire towers in the backcountry stirred up strong feelings at the end of the 20th century. Bush pilots and their seaplanes were restricted in access to lakes traditionally theirs to use, and many quit or went out of business. Wetlands legislation made large tracts of land unusable for development. The environmental program of the APA and DEC limited the amount of land available for homes and tourist facilities. These restrictions, seen by many as intrusions, on the daily lives of residents created a great deal of animosity toward the state. To ameliorate the situation, the government agencies were forced to moderate their stands in the 1990s.

Among the requirements in the Adirondack environment has been that all solid waste generated within the park be trucked outside it for disposal. Local governments initially resisted this mandate, but the state provided ample funding to close landfills, pay for trucking costs, and subsidize disposal fees. Tourism, however, has continued to grow and represents the region's economic future. Aside from the Adirondack Museum, the SS *Durant* cruise line and Camp Sagamore give visitors a culturally based experience. Lumbering continues on private lands, with scientific approaches preventing a repeat of the overcutting and clear-cutting that destroyed the industry around the turn of the 20th century.

There is no centennial era book, but Hamilton Co has one of the best of the state's 20th-century county histories: Ted Aber and Stella King, *History of Hamilton County* (1965). It is based almost entirely on primary sources and is comprehensive. Harold K. Hochschild, *Township 34* (1952) is a scholarly history of Blue Mountain Lake and Raquette Lake. Also useful are Howard I. Becker, *A History of South Pond and Origin of Long Lake Township* (1963) and *Historical Book of the Town of Arietta* (1986).

Field Horne

Hamlin. Town (pop 9,355) in NW Monroe Co. Located on Lake Ontario, the town was settled in ?1809, formed from Clarkson as Union in 1852, and renamed Hamlin in 1861. German farmers came to town in the mid–19th century. The Rome, Watertown and Ogdensburg Railroad (1875; later New York Central) connected it with Rochester. Agriculture, particularly fruit, has been its mainstay; Duffy Mott operated a fruit-processing plant (1929–77), employing up to 200 workers seasonally. A Civilian Conservation Corps camp (1935) helped develop Hamlin Beach State Park; during World War II the camp housed prisoners of war. Since 1960 Hamlin's population has more than tripled and suburbanized, but the town retains a rural character.

Nancy Martin

Hammon, Jupiter (*b* Lloyd Neck, Suffolk Co, 17 Oct 1711; *d* Lloyd Neck *ca* 1790–95). Poet and preacher. Born into slavery on the Lloyd Manor, he was provided an education there alongside the family's children by Nehemiah Bull, a Harvard graduate, and Daniel Denton, an English missionary. He was apparently given access to the family's library and allowed time to read. His duties for the Lloyds included managing accounts and handling money, although he was also described as being good with tools. What brought him recognition during his lifetime, however, were his religious convictions and powers of expression; he had a reputation as an excellent preacher. His Christian faith is reflected in seven publications, four of them poems, which he published between 1760 and 1787. His first poem, "An Evening Thought: Salvation by Christ" (1760), is the earliest published poem by an African American author. During the American Revolution, Hammon lived with the Lloyds in Hartford, Conn, returning to Long Island after the war. Two published sermons, "A Winter Piece" and "An Evening's Improvement" (1782), exhorted readers to conversion. In a more celebratory mode, he published a 20-stanza poem (1778) dedicated to Phillis Wheatley, who, like Hammon, was an enslaved African American poet. In "An Address to the Negroes in the State of New York" (1787), he stated that he was prepared to bear his own servitude patiently but called for the freedom of young Blacks. Sidney Kaplan and Emma Nogrady Kaplan have written that Hammon's ambivalence on slavery reflects his "titanic struggle for a position as a Black and a slave in a white world that called itself Christian." He was essentially forgotten until 1915, when literary critic Oscar Wegelin published the first biography.

Day, Lynda R. *Making a Way to Freedom: A History of African Americans on Long Island* (Interlaken, NY: Empire State Books, 1997)

Kaplan, Sidney, and Emma Nogrady Kaplan. *The Black Presence in the Era of the American Revolution* (Amherst: Univ of Massachusetts Press, 1989)

Ransom, Stanley A., Jr, ed. *America's First Negro Poet: The Complete Works of Jupiter Hammon of Long Island* (1970; repr Port Washington, NY: Kennikat Press, 1990)

Lynda R. Day

Hammond. Town (pop 1,207) and village (pop 302) in SW St. Lawrence Co. Settled in 1812 with an influx of Scots in 1818–21, the town was formed from Morristown and Rossie in 1827. Scottish settlers built stone houses that are still a prominent feature in the landscape. Lumber was shipped on the St. Lawrence from Hammond, and a customhouse, served by the Black River and Morristown Railroad (1876), operated in the 19th century. The village incorporated in 1901. Hammond, which includes a number of the Thousand Islands, is the site of Singer Castle (1896–1904) on Dark Island, which opened to the public in 2003, of Chippewa Bay, where Frederic Remington summered, and of Cedar Island State Park. Away from a riverside strip of second homes the town is agricultural.

Richard E. Mooers

Hammond, Jabez D(elano) (*b* New Bedford, Mass, 2 Aug 1778; *d* Cherry Valley, Otsego Co, 18 Aug 1855). Politician and historian. Educated in common schools in Woodstock, Vt, Hammond practiced medicine in that state before moving to Orange Co in 1803, where he studied law while supporting himself as a schoolteacher. In 1805 he began a prosperous legal practice in

Cherry Valley; De Witt Clinton was among his clients. A Clintonian Republican, he served in the House of Representatives (1815–17) and for two terms as a state senator (1818–21), where his service for a year on the Council of Appointment provided him with an excellent vantage point to view the political scene. After practicing law in Albany in the early 1820s, Hammond spent the rest of his life in Cherry Valley and was an Otsego Co judge (1838–43) and a regent of the University of the State of New York (1845–55). He is best known for *The History of Political Parties in the State of New-York,* to which he added a third volume in 1848, *Life and Times of Silas Wright.* Well received in Hammond's time, these volumes remain essential reading for students of the era. Hammond also wrote an antislavery novel, *The Life and Opinions of Julius Melbourn,* published anonymously in 1847 but acknowledged as Hammond's in the 1851 second edition.

Hammond, Jabez D. *The History of Political Parties in the State of New-York from the Ratification of the Federal Constitution to December, 1840,* 2 vols (Albany: C. Van Benthuysen, 1842)

———. *Life and Times of Silas Wright, Late Governor of the State of New York* (Syracuse: Hall & Dickson, 1848)

Donald M. Roper

Hammondsport. Village (pop 731) in Urbana (Steuben Co). Settled in 1796, the village at the head of Keuka Lake was surveyed in 1808 by Judge Lazarus Hammond. Improvements were slow until the Crooked Lake Canal (1833–77) joined Keuka Lake with the Erie Canal, and Hammondsport became a commercial port. The village was incorporated in 1856. The Bath and Hammondsport Railroad (1874–1967) transported wine and champagne, products of the vineyards surrounding the village. Aircraft manufacturing began by 1908 under Glenn H. Curtiss and grew into Mercury Aircraft. The population dropped by 21% in the 10 years after Taylor Wine Co closed in the early 1990s. A Mercury Aircraft spin-off, Clark Specialty Co, was still a local industry in 2003. A major summer tourist destination, Hammondsport is the site of the Glenn H. Curtiss Museum.

Virginia L. Wright and Jerry Wright

Hampton. Town (pop 871) in E central Washington Co. Probably settled before the American Revolution, the town was formed in 1786. Hampton was the home of William Miller (1782–1849), whose preaching gave birth to the Adventist churches. At Low Hampton, bar iron for blacksmith use was made from Champlain Valley ore. Other industries included a woolen factory, a wrapping-paper mill, a blasting powder factory (*ca* 1850–?1874), and many slate quarries, some of which remained in production in 2003. The Carver Falls power plant on the Poultney River dates from 1894 and still generates power for Central Vermont Public Service Corp. Farming remains the predominant land use; many residents commute to Granville or Rutland. The William Miller House (1815) and Chapel (1848) are on the National Register.

R. Paul McCarty

Hampton Bays. Locality (pop 12,236) in Southampton (Suffolk Co). Known as Good Ground, it acquired a post office by that name in 1829 and became a Long Island Rail Road station in 1869. In 1922 the post office changed its name to Hampton Bays. The Shinnecock Canal (built 1884–92) is the hamlet's eastern boundary. The area attracted Manhattan merchants selling dresses, pianos, and crystal to storefronts along the Montauk Highway. The Canoe Place Inn, a favorite summertime haunt of Gov Alfred E. Smith in the 1920s, also attracted eloping Southampton society youth. In 1970 the permanent population was 1,862 but since then has increased more than sixfold. Much of the growth is attributable to teachers, service workers, and others employed in the Hamptons and attracted by affordable housing near limited-access highways.

Sherrill Foster

Hamptonburgh. Town (pop 4,686) in central Orange Co. In 1712 proprietor Christopher Denne induced 18-year-old Sarah Wells (1694–1796) to precede his family accompanied only by Indians and carpenters; her courage has been made subject of legend. The hamlet of Campbell Hall is named for Capt Lachlan Campbell from Islay in the Hebrides; he purchased the land *ca* 1740 but returned to Scotland to fight under the duke of Cumberland. The town was formed in 1830 from Goshen, Blooming Grove, Montgomery, New Windsor, and Wallkill. Hamptonburgh was crossed by the Wallkill Valley (1867) and Ontario and Western (1873) Railroads. By the mid–19th century dairy farming took precedence, and in the early 21st century the town still has some farming but is becoming residential, with many New York City commuters. Landmarks include the stone Bull House (1722–27), listed on the National Register, and Hill Hold (1769), with its working farm.

Hamptons, the. Regional designation (Suffolk Co). The Hamptons is a loosely defined term that can denote the entire area from Westhampton to Montauk, but in terms of cultural and celebrity dynamics it usually refers to the South Fork of Long Island. The two towns of Southampton and East Hampton gave rise to the term, which was well established by the 1960s. Until the latter part of the 19th century the area was rural and isolated. In the 1870s a number of prominent artists stumbled upon the South Fork and were taken by its rustic charm, quaint villages, and the stunning "Hampton Light," so named because of the fork's encirclement by water. Visitors like Winslow Homer were followed by longer-term residents such as Thomas Moran, William Merritt Chase, Mary Nimmo, and Childe Hassam. The artistic presence and the paintings they created attracted summer vacationers to modest boardinghouses and wealthier families to cottages built for them.

The reputation of the Hamptons as a playground of the rich was cemented in the 1920s. A number of extremely wealthy families set up summer compounds in Southampton. The South Fork became dotted with the large houses, often hidden behind 10–12 ft (3–4 m) high privet hedges. The depression slowed the colonization of the Hamptons by wealthy families from New York City and elsewhere, but the foundations of the South Fork's reputation as a resort for the upper classes was firmly established. The Hamptons went through fundamental changes after World War II. It enjoyed a renewal of its artistic community. Jackson Pollock and his wife Lee Krasner settled in the Springs district of East Hampton. A little further south, Alfonso Ossorio turned his Georgica Pond estate, the Creeks, into a center of the new art. Somewhat later, Willem de Kooning, another important figure in late 20th-century art, took up residence in East Hampton. The cultural ferment also lured writers seeking a respite from Manhattan without losing the companionship and support of their fellow authors. James Jones, Truman Capote, John Steinbeck, Peter Mathiessen, Joseph Heller, and Willie Morris were among those who made their homes in different parts of the South Fork in the 1950s and 1960s. As home to artists and literati the Hamptons probably peaked in the 1960s and 1970s. The famous names today are more likely to come from popular media rather than art and literature. Billy Joel, Jerry Seinfeld, Martha Stewart, Matt Lauer, Peter Jennings, and Steven Spielberg are typical of the personalities who have dominated upscale Hamptons social life in the new century.

The luminaries who adopted the South Fork as their home established a number of cultural institutions that continue to thrive. The activities of both the Parrish Art Museum in Southampton and the Guild Hall in East Hampton are supported by the patronage of the active arts and culture community. The prestige of their sponsors, coupled with the generous level of funding, allows the Parrish and the Guild Hall to host exhibits and performances far above the level of most regional institutions. In recent years the East Hampton Film Festival has joined the older organizations as a dynamic component in the Hamptons art scene.

While best known for its affluent and celebrity communities, the Hamptons has also experienced more conventional middle-class suburbanization, and the number of year-round residents has increased noticeably. Like much of the island, it has seen steady growth in the Latino population drawn to the service sector jobs that have opened up as the population expanded. Adding to the mix are the descendants of pre–Civil War families, known as Bonackers, a term derived from Accabonac Creek. Many still ply the traditional agricultural and sea-oriented trades, though both these fields are in decline. The continual loss of open or undeveloped land in the Hamptons, combined with the overall increase in the size of homes being built, has led to calls for greater preservation and stricter zoning; Suffolk Co pioneered in the Purchase of Development Rights (PDR) strategy for farmland preservation, some of which took place in the Hamptons. Conflicts between developers and environmentalists/preservationists increased in number and intensity during the 1990s. In 2000 the towns of both Southampton and East Hampton instituted temporary moratoriums on construction permits. While the Hamptons remains one of the most attractive and unique parts of Long Island, continued uncontrolled development threatens to destroy the very qualities that have made it so alluring.

Gaines, Stephen. *Philistines at the Hedgerows* (Boston: Little, Brown, 1998)

Mathiessen, Peter. *Men's Lives* (New York: Random House, 1986)

Richard F. Welch

Hancock. Town (pop 3,449) and village (pop 1,189) in SW Delaware Co. Settled before the American Revolution, the town was formed from Colchester in 1806. The East Branch of the Delaware River crosses the town and meets the West Branch in the Village of Hancock, which became a major lumbering and rafting center. In the mid–19th century French Settlement was created by selling small lots of land to French and German settlers. The Erie (1848) and Ontario and Western (1872–1957) Railroads aided the growth of the village, which was incorporated in 1888. After Delaware Co's first wood acid factory was built at Kerryville in 1878, the wood chemical industry flourished, with more than 10 plants in the town. This, along with tanneries and bluestone quarries, drove the economy in the late 1800s. Railroad service declined in the 1950s, and the reconstruction of Rte 17 (I-86) as a four-lane highway in the 1960s reduced the tourist business. In 2003 lumbering and quarrying supported the economy.

Dorothy Kubik

Hand, (Billings) Learned (*b* Albany, 27 Jan 1872; *d* New York City, 18 Aug 1961). Federal judge. The son, nephew, and grandson of attorneys, Hand was raised in Albany and attended Albany Academy. Learned was his mother's maiden name. He graduated from Harvard, where he had been primarily interested in philosophy. Rather than continuing his studies in that subject, however, he consented to taking up the family trade and graduated from Harvard Law School in 1896. Returning to Albany, he practiced law and taught briefly at Albany Law School. Between 1902 and 1909 Hand worked for two New York City law firms but experienced professional dissatisfaction, as he had in Albany. He was appointed a district court judge to the Southern District of New York in 1909. While espousing a legal philosophy of judicial restraint, Hand was politically active at times, especially in supporting Progressive causes following World War I. In 1924 he was elevated to the Court of Appeals for the Second Circuit located in New York City. Joined on that court by Thomas Swan and his cousin, Augustus Hand, the three men served together for more than 25 years. In 1939 Learned Hand became the court's chief judge. His numerous letters, speeches, and legal writings, and his eloquent, thoughtful judicial opinions profoundly affected the development of American jurisprudence. One of Hand's most important achievements was in *Masses Publishing Co v Patten* (1917), in which he set forth a "direct incitement" test for evaluating potentially seditious speech, a more libertarian standard than Justice Oliver Wendell Holmes's "clear and present danger" test. Eventually Hand's broader standard was accepted. Oft mentioned but never nominated to the US Supreme Court, he would nonetheless become perhaps the best-known jurist of his era. His 1944 I Am an American Day address to new citizens in Central Park in Manhattan included his characteristic defense of tolerance and dissent: "the spirit of liberty is the spirit which is not too sure that it is right." The speech brought fame beyond legal circles. After his retirement in 1951, Hand continued to serve the Second Circuit in a semiretired capacity until his death. His Holmes Lectures at Harvard University in 1958 revealed the aged Hand's continuing commitment to judicial restraint and doubts about the judicial direction of the Warren Court.

For illustration see COURTS, FEDERAL.

Gunther, Gerald. *Learned Hand: The Man and the Judge* (New York: Knopf, 1994)

Timothy P. Gordinier

Handsome Lake [Ganiodaio; Skanyadariyoh] (*b* Canawaugus [now Avon, Livingston Co], *ca* 1735; *d* Onondaga Indian Reservation [loc in Onondaga Co], 10 Aug 1815). Seneca prophet, chief, and warrior. Relatively little is known of his early life, and his birth name is not known. A half-brother of the Seneca war chief Cornplanter, at some point he gained the hereditary title Handsome Lake, by which he is commonly known. He supported the alliance with the British during the Revolutionary War but was not particularly active in Seneca political affairs, although he signed the 1797 Treaty of Big Tree, and had a reputation as a drunkard.

The Seneca after the Revolutionary War faced a daunting series of problems. The entire Iroquois culture experienced major destructive changes, including ongoing loss of land, a new reservation system, instability in the traditional family unit, alcohol abuse, and accusations of witchcraft. Cultural, religious, and political factionalism grew increasingly prevalent. Compounding these changes, ancient rituals used to treat diseases continued ineffective against illnesses introduced by Europeans.

Living a dissolute life on Cornplanter Grant in Pennsylvania on the Allegheny River, Handsome Lake emerged from a trance on 15 June 1799 and began preaching a new message of salvation to his people. He reported that he had died and been transported to heaven by three celestial beings. This was the first of a series of trances in which he saw the destructive effects of white culture. The traditional importance of dreams and their interpretation among the Iroquois partially explains his visions being so easily accepted among his people. Recovering in health, Handsome Lake began to advocate a series of prohibitions aimed at moral salvation for the Iroquois.

The new message, often called the Code of Handsome Lake, or Gaiwiio (Good News or Good Word), prohibited alcohol, sexual promiscuity, abortion, witchcraft, and gambling. It is the basis in the 20th and 21st centuries of some Iroquois opposition to casinos on reservations. Handsome Lake believed that much of the Seneca problem came from the evil workings of witches, who were urged to confess and repent, and predicted that evil would eventually result in the fiery destruction of the world. He advocated for family stability and the care of children and the elderly. The influence of various missionary efforts among the Seneca was evident in his code, and Handsome Lake incorporated elements from both traditional and Christian systems into a new Iroquois religion. He especially advocated keeping four Seneca traditions performed at the annual midwinter ceremonies: the Drum Dance, the Great Feather Dance, the Personal Chant, and the Great Bowl Game.

Handsome Lake would spend the remainder of his life proselytizing his vision. He moved to Cold Spring on the Allegany Indian Reservation in 1803. Although his message was initially accepted among the Seneca, his overzealous focus on witchcraft led to both his and his dogma's rejection. Several Seneca accounts during this period tell of witches being executed. Eventually, Handsome Lake moderated his views, especially following his accusation of a member of a prominent Lenape family resident among the Seneca. In 1809 he moved to the Tonawanda Indian Reservation. He died during a missionary trip to the Onondaga, who had invited him. Handsome Lake had a foreboding of his death and reported a visitation of the corn spirit but chose to continue to travel regardless. Following his death several adherents, including Gov Blacksnake, took up his message and contributed to its spread, which continued into the 21st century.

Deardorff, Merle H. "The Religion of Handsome Lake: Its Origin and Development." In *Symposium on Local Diversity in Iroquois Culture,* ed. William N. Fenton. Bureau of American Ethnology Bulletin 149 (Washington, DC: Smithsonian Institution, 1951)
Parker, Arthur C., "The Code of Handsome Lake, the Seneca Prophet." In *Parker on the Iroquois,* ed. William N. Fenton (Syracuse: Syracuse Univ Press, 1968)
Wallace, Anthony F. C. *The Death and Rebirth of the Seneca* (New York: Knopf, 1970)

George H. J. Abrams

Handy, W(illiam) C(hristopher) (*b* Florence, Ala, 16 Nov 1873; *d* New York City, 28 Mar 1958). Songwriter and music publisher. Son of an African Methodist Episcopal minister and musically trained, Handy was the most successful, though not the first, arranger and popularizer of the African American rural southern folk music that emerged around 1900. While traveling in the Mississippi Delta, he first heard authentic rural blues and soon was adding blues and other folk arrangements to his band's repertoire. In 1905 he moved to Memphis, Tenn, where he became the leading bandleader, with compositions including "The Memphis Blues" (1912) and "St. Louis Blues" (1914). In 1913 he formed a music publishing company with Harry H. Pace, and they moved their company to New York City in 1918, setting up offices in Times Square. This was the peak of his success as a publisher. After Pace left the partnership in 1921 to found Black Swan Records, Handy suffered devastating reverses. He re-formed his business as a small family-run enterprise while living in Harlem and gradually regained his financial footing, with successful new arrangements of his songs recorded by leading artists of the swing era. From 1943 on, Handy lived in Tuckahoe (Westchester Co).

Hurwitt, Elliott S. "William Christopher Handy." In *International Dictionary of Black Composers,* vol 1, ed. Samuel Floyd (Chicago: Fitzroy Dearborn, 1999)

Elliott S. Hurwitt

Hannibal. Town (pop 4,957) and village (pop 542) in W Oswego Co. Settled in 1802 the town was formed from Lysander (Onondaga Co) in 1806. The Western Emigration Co formed in Hannibal in 1834 and sent a colony to settle in Kenosha, Wisc. In the 19th century the town produced lumber, barrels and barrel staves, cheese and cheeseboxes, and tobacco; the latter crop persisted until the mid-1950s. The village incorporated in 1860. The Rome, Watertown and Ogdensburg Railroad (1873) connected farmers to markets. In addition to farming, residents commute to Oswego, Fulton, and Syracuse.

Barbara J. Dix

Hanover. Town (pop 7,638) in NE Chautauqua Co. The site of many Indian villages, the area became the home of Chautauqua Co's first European American settler, Amos Sottle, in 1796. A harbor was built at the mouth of Cattaraugus Creek in the 1830s; its breakwater was rebuilt in 1983. In the 19th century shipbuilding, lumbering, grain-cleaning machinery, grape farming, and furniture manufacturing were paramount. The town acquired rail service in 1851–52, and the Thruway opened through town in 1957. The Cattaraugus Indian Reservation abuts the town. A famous historical curiosity is Sottle's fiddle, made of a horse skull.

Vincent Martonis

Hanson, Howard (*b* Wahoo, Nebr, 28 Oct 1896; *d* Rochester, 26 Feb 1981). Composer and educator. Hanson attended Luther College in Wahoo and the University of Nebraska at Lincoln, continuing his studies at the Institute of Musical Art in New York City and at Northwestern University. In 1916 he started teaching composition and music theory at the College of the Pacific in San Jose and became dean of its Conservatory of Fine Arts in 1919. In 1921 he was awarded the Prix de Rome and studied in Rome for three years. Hanson became the director of Rochester's Eastman School of Music (1924–64), and during his tenure the school developed into one of the world's major centers for the training of professional musicians. As a teacher of composition, he influenced a generation of American composers and encouraged American music through the American Composers' Concerts (1925), which became the annual American Music Festival (1931–71).

Hanson made his conducting debut in 1924, directing the New York Symphony Orchestra in the premiere of his tone poem, *North and West.* He conducted many other orchestras, including the Boston Symphony, which premiered his *Symphony No. 2* (Romantic) in 1930, acknowledging its affinities to Respighi, with whom he had studied in Rome, and such late-Romantic composers as Sibelius and Grieg. At the same time Hanson tried to cultivate a distinctively American style both in the sound and themes of his music. He made numerous recordings as a conductor, largely of American compositions and often with the Eastman-Rochester Orchestra. His compositions include an opera, *Merry Mount,* premiered by the Metropolitan Opera in 1934, many choral works, a piano concerto, several symphonic poems, seven symphonies, other works for orchestra, a string quartet, and works for wind ensemble. In 1944 Hanson was awarded the initial Pulitzer Prize for music for *Symphony No. 4* (Requiem) and was the recipient of numerous other honors throughout his life.

Perone, James E. *Howard Hanson: A Bio-Bibliography* (Westport, Conn: Greenwood, 1993)

Vincent Lenti

harbormasters. A 1911 state law empowered the governor to appoint harbormasters to regulate the anchorage of vessels in any municipality on the Hudson River north of New York City. The law was prompted by a 1911 accident in which a steamer damaged a motorboat. It was determined that the motorboat owner could not collect damages because it was not anchored in a designated anchorage. The case led legislators to argue for having local officials in charge of cooperating with federal authorities about the designation of proper anchorage areas. Aside from the harbormasters named for Hudson (Columbia Co) and Rondout (Ulster Co) in 1911 and for Tarrytown (Westchester Co) in 1912, no other appointments were ever made for the unpaid position. In 1925 Gov Alfred E. Smith recommended that the office be abolished. The New York State Reorganization Commission agreed, and a bill eliminating harbormasters moved their function into the Department of Public Works in 1926.

Robert Allan Carter

Hardenbergh Patent. Land tract. In 1707 Johannis Hardenbergh and his seven partners parlayed a deed to a few thousand acres of Ulster Co backlands into the largest of the great patents granted by Gov Edward Hyde, Viscount Cornbury during his administration (1702–8). The vaguely worded document was signed by an otherwise unknown Esopus Indian named Nanesinos. The final tract totaled 1.5 million acres (607,000 ha) entirely within the Catskill Mountain region and encompassing large parts of what are now Delaware, Greene, Sullivan, and Ulster Cos. Encountering difficulty in finding tenants willing to lease the remote and rocky lands and unable to stop Indians from ejecting his surveyors, the cash-poor Hardenbergh was forced to enter into a consortium with several major Hudson Valley land barons. This syndicate, whose members included the rich and influential Robert Livingston, negotiated final Indian sales of all patent lands in 1746. Settlers began moving onto the lands only after the Indians abandoned, under duress, their ancestral territories at the end of Revolutionary War. By the summer of 1844 the Hardenbergh tenants had joined the antirent movement. Although authorities put down each outbreak, continuing resistance forced the landowners to grant fee-simple ownership to farmers on patent lands by the end of the 1860s.

Ellis, David Maldwyn. *Landlords and Farmers in the Hudson-Mohawk Region, 1790–1850* (Ithaca: Cornell Univ Press, 1946)
Kim, Sung Bok. *Landlord and Tenant in Colonial New York: Manorial Society, 1664–1775* (Chapel Hill: Univ of North Carolina Press, 1978)
Mark, Irving. *Agrarian Conflicts in Colonial New York, 1711–1775* (New York: Columbia Univ Press, 1940)

Robert S. Grumet

Hardenburgh. Town (pop 208) in W Ulster Co. Settled in the 1790s, the town was formed in 1859 from Shandaken and Denning. In the 19th century its forest produced lumber, shingles, butter trays, handles, and scoops. Tourism developed by the end of the century, and Hardenburgh became the site of several large private parks, including the vast George J. Gould estate at Furlough Lake, still owned by a descendant in 2003. The town's mountainous upland is noted for four-season recreation; 43% of the town is state owned. The Forge and Tappan covered bridges (1906, kingpost truss) and the Grants Mills covered bridge (1902, town truss) are landmarks.

Ruth Piwonka

Hare Krishna. Religious movement. Common nickname for the International Society for Krishna Consciousness (ISKCON). In 1965 A. C. Bhaktivedanta Swami came to Brooklyn from India to fulfill the instructions of his spiritual master to teach the Caitanya cult in the West. While aligned with Hinduism, the Krishna consciousness taught by Bhaktivedanta traced its roots to the 16th-century Krishna bhakti movement founded by Sri Caitanya Mahaprabhu, who preached that all people, regardless of caste, could reach spiritual realization through service to Krishna (God).

Initiates vowed to chant 16 rounds of the Hare Krishna mantra daily on a string of prayer beads and to abstain from meat, illicit sex, intoxicants, and gambling. They also committed themselves to distributing their guru's translations of and commentaries on various sacred Vedic texts in airports and other public locations. Initially Bhaktivedanta focused on the young people living in the Bowery on New York City's Lower East Side. After he was observed chanting in Tompkins Square Park, word spread among the musicians and bohemian crowd of the area, and several of those interested in the Swami and his teachings helped establish a small temple. During his first year in New York, Bhaktivedanta, now called Prabhupada by his followers, initiated 19 disciples. In 1966 he formally incorporated ISKCON, which underwent major changes in the beginning of 1967 when he traveled to the emerging hippie community in San Francisco, where ISKCON developed a communal living structure and recruited 150–200 converts within two years. By 1975 there were 36 ISKCON communities and preaching centers in North America with 40 more worldwide. By 1983 the total worldwide had grown to nearly 200, and by 2,000 to over 300. Before his death in 1977, Bhaktivedanta initiated approximately 5,000 disciples into his movement, and by 2001 there were an estimated 50,000 members in the United States. After his death ISKCON faced ongoing succession problems and structural change. Its communal structure largely disintegrated in North America as married people were forced to find employment and establish independent households. The increasing involvement of East Indian immigrants within ISKCON's North American communities since the late 1970s has furthered a shift toward congregationalism. In 2001 there were four temples in metropolitan New York serving about 1,000 members, with fewer than 50 resident members. Once a controversial religious sect, ISKCON has increasingly accommodated to mainstream US culture.

Rochford, E. Burke, Jr. "Hare Krishna in America: Growth, Decline, and Accommodation." In *America's Alternative Religions,* ed. Timothy Miller (Albany: SUNY Press, 1995)

E. Burke Rochford Jr

Harford. Town (pop 920) in SW Cortland Co. Settled in 1803, the town was formed from Virgil in 1845. It consists of broken and rugged uplands. The railroad came through in 1869, providing an outlet for both lumber and produce, and the first cheese factory was built in ?1874. In the 1960s Suburban Propane constructed a reservoir in town for the saltwater it pumped from underground caverns needed to store gas; the caverns, under most of the town, remain in use in the early 21st century. Many residents commute to Cortland, Ithaca, or Binghamton.

There are several dairy farms in town, including the Cornell University's Animal Science Teaching and Research Center.

Cathy A. Barber

Harkness, Georgia Elma (*b* Harkness, Clinton Co, 21 Apr 1891; *d* Claremont, Calif, 21 Aug 1974). Theologian and church leader. Born in a town named after her paternal grandfather, Nehemiah Harkness, she was raised a Methodist. After receiving a bachelor's degree from Cornell University in 1912, Harkness taught high school in Schuylerville (Saratoga Co) and Scotia (Schenectady Co) from 1912 to 1918. She later earned two master's degrees and a PhD from Boston University. She taught philosophy and religion as a faculty member at Elmira College (1922–37) and received a teaching fellowship at the Union Theological Seminary (1935–37) before moving on to Mount Holyoke College (1937–39). Harkness became the first woman to hold an academic chair in theology at an American theological seminary, serving as professor of applied theology at Garrett Biblical Institute in Evanston, Ill (1939–50), and Pacific School of Religion in Berkeley, Calif (1950–61). She received an honorary doctorate from Elmira College in 1962. A prolific author, Harkness published over 30 books and numerous articles on theology, including *The Dark Night of the Soul* (1945) and the popular hymn "Hope of the World" (1954). A prominent leader in the international ecumenical movement and American Methodism, she played an important role in the decision of the Methodist Church to grant full ordination to women in 1956. Following her retirement in 1961, she remained active as a church leader.

Keller, Rosemary Skinner. *Georgia Harkness: For Such a Time as This* (Nashville: Abingdon Press, 1992)

Christopher H. Evans

Harlan, John Marshall, II (*b* Chicago, 20 May 1899; *d* Washington, DC, 29 Dec 1971). Associate justice of the US Supreme Court. Grandson of his namesake who also served on the US Supreme Court, he attended Princeton, graduated in 1920, went to Oxford as a Rhodes Scholar, and earned his law degree from the New York School of Law in 1925. He practiced with the prominent New York City firm of Root-Clark throughout his career, with stints off for public service, which included prosecuting Prohibition cases from 1925 to 1927 and heading a 1928 corruption probe that led to a conspiracy conviction of a former Queens borough president. From 1951 to 1952 Harlan served as chief counsel to the New York State Crime Commission that investigated organized crime's hold on the New York City waterfront. In 1954 he was nominated to the US Court of Appeals, Second Circuit, and later that year Pres Dwight D. Eisenhower appointed him to the US Supreme Court. A conservative on the activist Warren Court, Harlan espoused a respect for precedent and a limited role for the Court.

Yarbrough, Tinsley E. *John Marshall Harlan: Great Dissenter of the Warren Court* (New York: Oxford Univ Press, 1992)

Daniel J. Linke

Harlem. Neighborhood in Upper Manhattan in New York City. Named after the Dutch city, the initial settlement was at what is now about 125th St on the Harlem River in the 1650s. Upon Manhattan's capture by the English in 1664, Nieuw Amsterdam became New York, but the name Harlem perpetuated the island's Dutch colonial past. Although Harlem has always been legally a part of New York City, without independent political status, for its first two centuries its distance from the downtown city gave it a degree of autonomy. Harlem has never had fixed limits, and the common view of the boundaries has fluctuated over time; through the end of the 18th century much of the upper half of Manhattan was considered Harlem. During the Revolutionary War Gen George Washington, as part of his retreat, made a successful stand against the British on 16 Sept 1776 in the Battle of Harlem Heights, in what is now the neighborhood of Washington Heights. Harlem remained a British outpost until the war's end. In 1806 Manhattanville was formed in the same valley as the earlier battle site, situated northwest of Harlem around what is now Broadway and 125th St near the Hudson River. The city immediately began to improve the river-to-river road linking the two shoreline villages. Although an outlying sector of Harlem, Manhattanville soon flourished into a distinct transportation, manufacturing, and residential hub, and was the homestead of Daniel F. Tiemann, mayor of New York (1858–60) and state senator (1872–73).

Students in sculpture class at the Harlem Community Art Center. Photograph by Berenice Abbott, 1939.

Transportation and Expansion

The opening of the New York and Harlem Railroad in 1837 spurred Harlem's transformation from a place of exhausted farmlands and declining country estates into one of potential suburban appeal. After the Civil War, transportation improved, culminating around 1879 with the extension of elevated rail lines into Harlem, which increased land speculation. By the mid-1880s the "els" and surface rail networks had promoted building activity north of Central Park as far as 125th St, between 5th and 8th Aves, and that growth was poised to continue further uptown. The resulting genteel suburban residential development was marked by freestanding villas and cottages and the architecturally significant row-house blocks concentrated in such enclaves as Hamilton Heights and Sugar Hill, Mount Morris Park, and St. Nicholas and Jumel Terrace Historic Districts. The later opening of the Interborough Rapid Transit (IRT) subway lines on Lenox Ave and Broadway in 1904 touched off an apartment building boom in Harlem and Manhattanville.

Jewish and Italian Harlem

After the Civil War German Jewish merchants from the Lower East Side became the first distinguishable Jewish population in Harlem, and by 1917, with around 80,000 Jewish residents, only the Lower East Side had a larger Jewish immigrant community. But overcrowding and the opening of new housing led to a Jewish migration to Manhattan's Upper West Side, the Bronx, and other neighborhoods. By 1930 only about 5,000 Jews remained in the neighborhood, leaving behind many synagogues and other architectural reminders. The Italian presence also started in the 1870s. Managers of the 1st Ave trolley lines brought Italians to East Harlem from Italy and Lower Manhattan as strikebreaking laborers. The continued availability of jobs on transportation and construction projects fueled Harlem's emergence as the country's largest Italian enclave by the 1890s. The depression aggravated poverty, poor health conditions, and inadequate housing, which prompted increased numbers of residents to leave Harlem's Little Italy in the 1930s and 1940s. Our Lady of Mount Carmel Church, built on East 115th St in 1884, reflects the once thriving Italian enclave.

The Growth of Black Harlem

In Manhattan, social conventions and property covenants traditionally restricted housing for African Americans, who at the turn of the 20th century were densely concentrated in the blocks of the West 50s and 60s. By 1903 anticipation of the IRT subway lines produced new tenements in Harlem in a spate of overdevelopment around 135th St that failed to attract tenants. The crisis enabled African American realtor Philip A. Payton to persuade white Harlem property owners to rent or sell to black tenants. Payton obtained the management of a building around West 135th St east of Lenox Ave and founded the Afro-American Realty Co (1904). Better housing opportunities motivated legions of Blacks to pay above market rate for uptown rentals. Harlem became the scene of some of the most important real estate transactions in New York City's history for housing African Americans. Several influential black churches, including St. Philip's Church (Protestant Episcopal), Mother AME Zion, and Abyssinian Baptist, also relocated uptown and remain institutional pillars in the community. As Blacks moved west of Lenox Ave, white landlords organized to oppose the "invasion" but without success. While economic necessity caused Harlem's mostly working-class and poor residents to subdivide many houses into smaller rental lodgings, the allure of its private houses and modern apartments gave rise to the world's most affluent African American community. By 1930 Negro Harlem was thriving roughly from 110th St in the south to 155th St in the north, and from Madison Ave in the east to St. Nicholas Ave in the west; Harlem had become the de facto African American capital in the United States, and despite its heterogeneity, the name became chiefly identified with its black population.

Cultural Energy and Civil Unrest

During the 1920s the emergence of an elite black Harlem captivated the American mainstream as a fashionable phenomenon, highlighted by interracial social mixing at such chic nightclubs as Happy Rhone's, Small's Paradise, and Nest Club, and at "rent parties." The legendary Cotton Club featured Blacks as entertainers but barred them as clientele. The decade saw a flowering of literary and artistic activity known as the Harlem Renaissance, whose leading figures included writers Alain Locke, James Weldon Johnson, Countee Cullen, Zora Neale Hurston, Claude McKay, Jean Toomer, and Langston Hughes; artist Aaron Douglas; and performers Paul Robeson, Florence Mills, Fats (Thomas Wright) Waller, Bessie Smith, and Ethel Waters. Artistic production was championed by white literary and social arbiters like critic Carl Van Vechten and financial patron Charlotte Mason.

Major African American periodicals circulating in Harlem included the newspapers *New York Age* and the *Amsterdam News* and the magazines *Crisis*, and *Opportunity*, published, respectively, by the NAACP and the National Urban League. By the 1930s Blacks were occupying many of the exclusive houses on Harlem's Hamilton Heights and Sugar Hill. The era's political climate was diverse, with influential leaders ranging from the moderate Rev Adam Clayton Powell Sr, pastor of the Abyssinian Baptist Church, militant antisegregationist W. E. B. DuBois, a leader of the NAACP, and black separatist Marcus Garvey, founder of the Universal Negro Improvement Association.

The Great Depression sparked a downward turn in the housing market and precipitated Harlem's decline. On 19 Mar 1935 unfounded rumors that employees of a five-and-ten store killed a teenage shoplifter incited rioting. Mayor Fiorello La Guardia appointed a biracial commission to investigate underlying social and economic conditions but suppressed the report for a more than a year. The commission recommended measures and reforms surrounding racial discrimination in employment, education, and recreation; integration of hospital staffs; and processing of citizens' complaints against police. The riot led to the construction of the Harlem River Houses in 1937, the country's first federally funded housing projects. During World War II the government initially rejected African American labor in the war effort, heightening deep-seated racial tensions in urban centers around the country and in Harlem, where riots erupted on 1 Aug 1943. But a decade of increased racial polarization also galvanized local leadership, exemplified in November 1944 when Rev Adam Clayton Powell Jr of the Abyssinian Baptist Church won an election that would make him Harlem's (and New York State's) first black congressman.

A continuing decline of economic and social conditions contributed to black skepticism toward national policies after World War II. The frustrated progress of the civil rights and voting rights movements of the 1950s and 1960s made Harlem activists receptive to both the nonviolent advocacy of Dr Martin Luther King Jr and the militant separatism encouraged by Malcolm X, pastor of the Harlem mosque of the Nation of Islam. The polemic atmosphere of the 1960s spawned Harlem's Black Arts Movement, whose vanguard included Amiri Baraka (LeRoi Jones), Sonia Sanchez, Nikki Giovanni, Ed Bullins, Addison Gayle Jr, Larry Neal, Maulana Karenga, and Toni Cade Bambara, considerably less integrationist and more politically militant than its artistic predecessors in the 1920s.

Changing Neighborhoods

Puerto Rico came into the possession of the United States as a result of the Spanish-American War in 1898. Emigrants from the island established an East Harlem enclave by the 1930s. In the late 1940s Spanish Harlem, later known as El Barrio, was the country's foremost Puerto Rican neighborhood and home to Pedro Albizu Campos, a leader of the Puerto Rican independence movement. But by 2000 Harlem's largest Latino population was Dominican, whose influx since the 1960s constituted the city's fastest growing immigrant group as a result of relaxed immigration laws and the US occupation of the Dominican Republic.

Harlem's extraordinary cultural and architectural legacies are today generating a resurgence of tourism, home purchases, and business investments. Commercial revitalization is being spearheaded by prominent corporations including the Upper Manhattan Empowerment Zone (UMEZ), the Abyssinian Development Corp, and the 125th Street Business Improvement District (BID). In 2001 former president Bill Clinton's decision to lease office space in Harlem had symbolic impact. Homeowners' associations reflect an influx of middle-class Blacks and Whites in Harlem's officially landmarked residential districts. Gentrification is apparent in the high-market sales of fine row houses and in improved neighborhood services.

See also Finns; Harlem renaissance; Jazz; Lesbians, gays, bisexuals, and transgendered people.

Gurock, Jeffrey S. *When Harlem Was Jewish, 1870–1930,* (New York: Columbia Univ Press, 1979)
Lewis, David Levering. *When Harlem Was in Vogue,* (1981; repr New York: Penguin, 1997)
Orsi, Robert Anthony. *The Madonna of 115th Street: Faith and Community in Italian Harlem, 1880–1950,* 2d ed. (New Haven, Conn: Yale Univ Press, 2002)
Osofsky, Gilbert. *Harlem: The Making of a Ghetto: Negro New York, 1890–1930,* 2d ed. (1971; repr Chicago: Ivan R. Dee, 1996)
Riker, James. *Revised History of Harlem (City of New York): Its Origins and Early Annals,* rev Henry Pennington Toler, ed. Sterling Potter (1904; repr Bowie, Md: Heritage Books, 2001)

Eric K. Washington

Harlem Heights, Battle of. Revolutionary War engagement. On 15 Sept 1776 Gen George Washington evacuated his forces from the southern part of New York City and retreated to Harlem Heights on the northern end of Manhattan after Gen William Howe's British and German regulars landed at Kip's Bay on the east side of the island, now roughly from 27th to 34th Sts. Early the next morning an American reconnaissance party of 120 skirmished with 400 British troops near present-day 106th St and fell back to Harlem Heights. Deciding to trap Howe's men, Washington sent in more troops to lure the British forward while a second detachment moved behind them. The second force fired prematurely, and Howe's soldiers hurriedly retreated. Washington pursued with 2,000 soldiers and steadily drove the British back to the area of that morning's skirmish. Not wanting to bring on a general engagement with 5,000 British reinforcements arriving on the field, Washington recalled his men by midafternoon on 16 September. Howe suffered 14 killed and 154 wounded; Washington had 30 dead and 100 wounded or missing. The engagement lifted American morale following their defeats at Long Island and Kip's Bay and the loss of New York City to the British. The area of the skirmish is now known as Washington Heights.

Bliven, Bruce, Jr. *Battle for Manhattan* (New York: Henry Holt, 1956)

Michael P. Gabriel

Harlem Renaissance. A movement that occurred between World War I and World War II and celebrated African American culture. Although not limited geographically to Harlem in Upper Manhattan (Washington, DC, with Howard University, Los Angeles, Chicago, and Buffalo also were major hubs), Harlem was its epicenter. The relocation following World War I of large numbers of African Americans to New York City in general and to the Upper Manhattan neighborhood of Harlem in particular made Harlem the center of African American life and the nation's largest and most culturally influential city.

Although there were many aspects to the flourishing community in Harlem, its cultural production was perhaps the most dramatic. The Harlem branch of the YMCA, the 135th St branch of the New York Public Library (now Schomburg Center for Research in Black Culture), and other cultural institutions, such as the Dark Tower (home of A'Lelia Walker, daughter of the beauty product millionaire Madam C. J. Walker), helped to create a collective identity among the black intelligentsia. They provided a forum for political debates and activism, outlets for cultural expressions for artists, writers, and musicians, and community educational programs.

Literature

Although there had been a flowering of black culture in the 19th century, including the publi-

Builders, by James Lesesne Wells, 1929.

cation of Paul Lawrence Dunbar's poetry, Anna Julia Cooper's *A Voice from the South* (1892), and historian George Washington Williams's important works, it was not until the 1920s that there was a true blooming of black literary culture. The literary movement that centered in Harlem had its genesis in the intellectual movement that occurred worldwide at the turn of the 20th century. The notion that a renaissance in African American literature was taking place in the 1920s was vigorously promoted by Howard University philosopher Alain Locke, who edited a collection of essays, *The New Negro* (1925), which discussed different aspects of contemporary black culture. Locke argued that the "New Negro" was characterized by a renewed commitment to struggle for equal rights and a willingness to celebrate black culture. An essay included in Locke's collection was "The Negro Digs Up His Past," by bibliographer Arthur A. Schomburg, who argued that Blacks in the United States had to discover the African roots of their culture.

Harlem Renaissance writers' themes included their living conditions in the North and their quest for political and social equality, racial consciousness, politics, and integration. Although there was much social critique, the dominant mood of the era was one of celebration, a joyful embrace of black urban life and African American existence in its complexity and richness. Literature took many forms and included poetry, drama, fiction, and essay. Prominent among the poets were Langston Hughes and Claude McKay. Hughes published "The Negro Speaks of Rivers," which first appeared in the NAACP's journal *Crisis* in 1921 and celebrated African and diaspora experiences and the spirit of African Americans. "I've known Rivers / I've known rivers ancient as the world and older than the flow of human blood in human veins / I've known rivers / Ancient, dusky rivers / My soul has grown deep like the rivers." McKay, an immigrant from the West Indies, captured the spirit of many newcomers when he authored "If We Must Die" in 1919, a poem about the increasing number of lynchings that occurred throughout the United States. If we must die, the poem argued, "let it not be like hogs / Hunted and penned in an inglorious spot." But, "If we must die, O let us nobly die / So that our precious blood may not be shed / In vain; then even the monsters we defy / Shall be constrained to honor us though dead."

McKay's poetry suggests a new militancy arose among New York's African American population. In no uncertain terms, he argued for black self-protection. Other literary figures such as poet Countee Cullen, novelist and short story writer Dr Rudolph Fisher, and Howard University professor Sterling A. Brown also focused upon contemporary and historical accounts of black life, and the migrant community of Harlem continued to provide the subject matter. Zora Neale Hurston, a novelist, anthropologist and playwright, was perhaps the best-known female writer of the Harlem Renaissance. She studied at Howard University and Barnard College. Her most famous book, *Their Eyes Are Watching God* (1937), is a love story in which the protagonist Janie is on a quest for self-identity. In the process, she defies the traditional role of wife and mother that women were compelled to play. Poet Georgia Douglas also pursued themes that had escaped respectable women artists when she published her anthology *An Autumn Love Cycle* (1928), which spoke of the various states of love.

Music and Art

Music and art also were important components of the cultural movement. Ragtime, jazz, spirituals, and blues reigned in clubs such as Smalls Paradise, where middle-class Blacks and Whites gathered, and at rent parties, where working-class migrants entertained. Music styles, particularly blues and jazz, exhibited the elegance and sophistication of black culture. The big bands of Fletcher Henderson and Duke Ellington, the Harlem stride piano of Fats Waller and Willie "the Lion" Smith, and the sounds of Coleman Hawkins on tenor sax and Louis Armstrong on trumpet celebrated the culture of Harlem.

Some Americans and Europeans adapted Harlem Renaissance literary dialogue into their creative works. Poet e. e. cummings, photographer Carl Van Vechten, and others found models in black America. African American artists were able to reap the benefits of this movement and gathered patrons and supporters from among white artists and writers, who were centered largely in Greenwich Village in Manhattan. Sculptor Augusta Savage created busts of Marcus Garvey, W. E. B. DuBois and other black leaders. In 1924 Savage won the Julius Rosenwald Fellowship for her sculpture of a young African American boy, titled *Gamin* (1929). The prize money enabled her to spend a year studying in Paris. Many artists of the period portrayed Blacks as sensual and primitive; this was a theme often explored in art and was an expression against civilization and one that black artists, like Savage and Aaron Douglas, felt compelled to repudiate through their work.

Politics and Activism

The political power of African Americans increased during the Harlem Renaissance. Blacks succeeded in electing officials and in securing political appointments in government. W. E. B. DuBois established the NAACP headquarters in Harlem (1909) and announced with banners each new lynching that occurred. Marcus Garvey's Universal Negro Improvement Association was also located in Harlem and called for black self-sufficiency, which challenged DuBois's integrationist philosophy. The noncommunist socialist A. Philip Randolph organized the most influential black labor union in 1925, the International Brotherhood of Sleeping Car Porters and published the *Messenger* at its headquarters in Harlem.

The Harlem Renaissance was primarily a movement for artists and intellectuals. For most Harlem residents the celebration of black culture was less important than dealing with increased segregation, inadequate housing, and rising levels of violence perpetrated against Blacks. But African American culture flourished at an unprecedented level, and there was a greater recognition of that culture from the larger white society during the years of the Harlem Renaissance. In the 1930s, with the grimmer realities of the depression and the new importance of left-wing, class-based politics, the buoyant aesthetic of the Harlem Renaissance gradually faded.

See also Literature, new york city area.

Huggins, Nathan Irvin. *Harlem Renaissance* (New York: Oxford Univ Press, 1971)

Lewis, David L. *When Harlem Was in Vogue* (New York: Knopf, 1981)

———. *Harlem Renaissance: Art of Black America* (New York: Studio Museum in Harlem, 1987)

Lillian S. Williams

Harmony. Town (pop 2,339) in S Chautauqua Co. Settled in 1809 the town formed from Chautauqua in 1816. North Harmony was taken off in 1919. Lumbering was important in early years, and dairy and other farming continue to be significant industries in the early 21st century.

Michelle Henry

Harmony Mills. Incorporated around 1837 as Harmony Manufacturing Co, Harmony Mills operated in Cohoes (Albany Co) for a century, becoming one of the largest cotton textile enterprises in North America. The mills primarily produced print cloth from cotton shipped in from southern states. The first building began production in 1838 with 3,000 spindles, and 2,000 more were added the following year. Spindle capacity increased steadily, reaching 7,000 by 1841 and 36,000 by 1854, when new construction expanded the facility. An entirely separate building with 20,000 spindles was added in 1857. Preparations for a third mill, opposite the first, were begun in 1866. Workers excavating the site unearthed the remains of a mastodon, now on display at the New York State Museum in Albany. By the early 1900s Harmony Mills had a capacity of 285,000 spindles and 6,500 looms. The management acquired rights to more than 1.5 miles (2.4 km) along the bank of the Mohawk River to provide water for the 13 boilers and 17 turbines that ran the spindles, looms, and other machinery.

The mills were managed successfully by three generations of the Johnston family (Robert, his son David, and grandson D. S.) between 1850 and 1910, when the operation was sold to the Draper Corp of Hopedale, Mass, which dominated the worldwide cotton-weaving machinery market. Harmony Mills was known for its contribution to the growth of the city of Cohoes as well as for the unusual benefits afforded its thousands of resident workers, such as street maintenance and provisions for religious observances. Like other cotton textile manufacturers in the state, Harmony Mills fell victim to the southward migration of the industry as advances in electric power allowed mills to operate closer to the source of their raw material. The company was finally liquidated in 1937. In the early 21st century the Harmony Mills complex has deteriorated, though some buildings remain in use as warehouses or rental space for retail outlets.

Bagnall, William R. *The Textile Industries of the United States, Including Sketches and Notices of Cotton, Woolen, Silk, and Linen Manufactures in the Colonial Period* (1893; repr New York: A. M. Kelley, 1971)

Walkowitz, Daniel J. *Worker City, Company Town: Iron and Cotton Worker Protest in Troy and Cohoes, New York, 1855–1884* (Urbana: Univ of Illinois Press, 1978)

Allen Fannin

harness racing. The modern form of the sport evolved during the early 1800s in and around Boston, New York City, and Philadelphia, with New York City as its center. It emerged out of spontaneous races known as brushing matches between drivers on the smooth and firm roads of the expanding cities. The roads were particularly suited to speed at the trotting gait and allowed the wheels of the vehicles the horses pulled to roll freely without jarring the driver out of the seat or causing the vehicle to slow the horse. Bloomingdale Rd and Harlem Lane were popular courses for racing in New York City, with Jamaica Turnpike their counterpart on Long Island; after *ca* 1835 Manhattan's Third Ave came into favor.

Illegal in New York State between 1802 and 1821, harness racing remained on public roads until 1823. On 27 May, the day of the famed North versus South race between thoroughbreds Eclipse and Henry at the Union Course in Jamaica (Queens Co), a trotting race also debuted on the racecourse. Although horses had been driven in informal races, they were ridden when trotting first came to the tracks. The first trotting race was won by Topgallant, trained by George Woodruff, uncle of Hiram Woodruff, who became the preeminent trainer of trotters in the 19th century. In 1825 the New York Trotting Club was formed and it, along with men like Hiram Woodruff, Cornelius Vanderbilt, and Robert Bonner, shaped and promoted the sport in its early years. With northern thoroughbred racing as their model, these harness-racing pioneers organized races in which the horses had to win two out of three heats of 2–3 miles each to win a race. The New York State model was used as harness racing spread west.

The horses that dominated and popularized the sport of trotting during the 19th century were both native New Yorkers. Lady Suffolk, born in Smithtown (Suffolk Co), raced from 1838 to 1853 and won 90 of the 162 races that she entered. Her first 50 races were under saddle, but she raced her remaining matches in harness, pulling both four-wheeled race wagons and two-wheeled sulkies, as racing in harness became the dominant style. Flora Temple, foaled in Oneida Co and bought from a Dutchess Co farmer, raced from 1850 to 1861, winning 86 of her 103 career starts. No harness racer would reach the popularity and dominance of these two New Yorkers until the 20th century, and none would ever claim their durability and longevity. Known as the Old Gray Mare and the Bob-Tailed Nag, respectively, they were celebrated in popular songs of the era.

American trotting horses were not yet a breed in the modern sense when these mares were racing, but they tended to descend from only a few families of horses. Born in Sugar Loaf (Orange Co), William Rysdyk's horse Rysdyk's Hambletonian (1849–76) is considered the foundation of the American standardbred. A blending of the Messenger and Bellfounder trotting families, he and his 1,331 offspring were so successful that by 1871, when a stud book was compiled, his family alone had begun to dominate harness racing. With the founding of the National Association of Trotting Horse Breeders in New York State in 1876 and the requirement, initiated in 1879, that a harness horse be able to trot or pace 1 mile in under the 2 min 30 s standard, the American standardbred became a recognized breed of horse.

In the mid–19th century, harness racing became a mainstay of county fairs and of the New York State Fair in Syracuse, which was the first home to the Hambletonian Stake, harness racing's richest race. The State Fair was its official host from 1926 through 1929, with rain-outs in 1927 and 1929 forcing postponements of the races, which were eventually held in Lexington, Ky. The race took place at Good Time Park in Goshen (Orange Co) from 1930 to 1956 before moving out of state. Although harness racing gained national popularity, New York State continued to be a major force; its governing body, the US Trotting Association (1939), was headquartered in Goshen in the 1940s. Trainer Billy Haughton (1923–86), one of the sport's best-known 20th-century figures, was a Gloversville (Fulton Co) native and won 4,910 races and over $40 million. He won the Hambletonian Stake four times and the Little Brown Jug, the premier race for pacers, a record five times.

In 1939 a constitutional amendment to permit pari-mutuel betting at authorized horse tracks was approved, and in 1940 the legislature provided for the creation and regulation of a pari-mutuel system. Although harness racing declined at the county fairs in the late 20th century, New York State supported seven major pari-mutuel harness tracks in 2004—Batavia Downs, Buffalo Raceway (Hamburg), Monticello Raceway, Saratoga Equine Sports Center, Syracuse Mile, Vernon Downs, and Yonkers Raceway—as well as the non-pari-mutuel Goshen Historic Track.

Overall attendance at New York State facilities declined during the last 20 years of the 20th century, in part because of patrons' lack of discretionary time and funds, the initiation of off-track betting, the simulcasting of programs from tracks outside the state, competition from other sports and from television, the loss of Roosevelt Raceway (Nassau Co), and the opening of New Jersey's Meadowlands Racetrack. Attending New York State's tracks in 2002 were 570,843 people, betting $59,238,000. The Harness Racing Museum and Hall of Fame (1951) at Goshen preserves and interprets the sport's history.

Adelman, Melvin L. *A Sporting Time: New York City and the Rise of Modern Athletics, 1820–1870* (Urbana: Univ of Illinois Press, 1986)
Hervey, John. *The American Trotter* (New York: Coward, McCann, 1947)
Longrigg, Roger. *History of Horse Racing* (New York: Stein & Day, 1972)

Elizabeth Redkey

Harper, Martha Matilda (*b* Oakville [now in Ont], 10 Sept 1857; *d* Rochester, 3 Aug 1950). Entrepreneur and women's advocate. Harper was bound out at age 7 and remained a servant until age 31. In 1882 she moved to Rochester, bringing with her a hair tonic formula. She continued working as a domestic until 21 Aug 1888 when she opened a manufacturing center and Rochester's first beauty salon. Her logo, a cornucopia, was trademarked that year. A symbol of plenty, its implicit message was "feed yourself, free yourself," and her enterprise attracted servant girls by representing the benefits of becoming salon owners, called Harperites. Harper's mentor and customer, Susan B. Anthony, and other suffragists supported Harper. Social connections through people like Rochester lawyer John Van Voorhis and his family also provided a conduit for Harper's Hairdressing Parlor to attract an affluent clientele—which would eventually include Pres Calvin and Grace Coolidge—who enjoyed Harper's healthful methods and products. Harper's own floor-length hair was an important marketing tool in the early years. Customers brought out-of-town visitors who demanded that similar shops be opened in their communities. In 1891 Harper, influenced by the organizational structure and values of Christian Science, created a new form of retailing, franchising, to economically empower her working-class sisters, tap their loyalty and service commitment, raise needed capital, and ensure quality and brand identification. That year, Harper's first franchise opened in Buffalo. Only authorized products, processes, and trained Harper personnel were employed in Harper shops. In 1920 she married Robert A. MacBain, her junior by 24 years.

By the late 1920s Harper had over 500 franchises in the United States and internationally, two manufacturing centers, and five training schools, with headquarters in Rochester. Unlike the mainstream beauty industry, Harper considered hair dyes and permanents dangerous and prohibited them from her operation. After Harper retired, these products were introduced under new management into Harper shops in the 1940s and promoted as safe and stylish. As a beauty industry pioneer, she ignored the industry's mass marketing of beauty aids and believed that salons ought to work on releasing people's inner beauty; Harper's salon operators promoted healthy skin and hair, and customers received neck, shoulder, and head massages to relieve stress. Harper's customers included Britain's Sir Anthony Eden, Woodrow Wilson, George Bernard Shaw, and Jacqueline Kennedy. Harper retired in 1932, and her husband then managed the business until the mid-1940s. The company's name was changed to the Harper Method Inc in 1935, and after Harper's husband died in 1965 the business continued to operate under a series of owners until 1972, when its assets were purchased. The manufacturing and training operations were closed by competitor Wilfred Academy. The last active Harper salon is her original shop. It is the oldest, continuously operating salon in the country and is in the Temple Building in Rochester.

Plitt, Jane R. *Martha Matilda Harper and the American Dream: How One Woman Changed the Face of Modern Business* (Syracuse: Syracuse Univ Press, 2000)

Jane R. Plitt

Harpersfield. Town (pop 1,603) in NE Delaware Co. Settled in 1771 by Col John Harper and others, the town was abandoned in 1777, but settlers returned after the Revolution and the town was formed in 1788. In the first half of the 19th century, Penfield axes, made at a Harpersfield axe factory, were widely used, and in 1875 Harpersfield produced the second-largest quantity of maple sugar (153,700 lb/69,717 kg) of any town in the state. Failure of the Susquehanna Turnpike in the mid–19th century, the lack of a railroad, and the decline of farming prevented significant growth. Dairy products, cauliflower cultivation, and poultry provided a living for most residents until the mid–20th century. In 2003 Harpersfield was a rural residential community.

Dorothy Kubik

Harpur, Robert R. (*b* Ballybay, Ireland, 25 Jan 1731; *d* Harpursville, Broome Co, 25 Apr 1825). Educator, statesman, and land developer. Born to Scottish parents, he studied at Glasgow University before immigrating to America in 1761 and joining the faculty of King's College (now Columbia University) in New York City. He became the college's first librarian and was politically active as a member of the New York Provincial Congress (1776–77) and the New York State Assembly (1777–84). Harpur was secretary of the Regents of the University of the State of New York (1784–87) and deputy secretary of state for New York State (1778–95). In the latter position he is credited with giving many towns of the New Military Tract their classical names, including Cicero, Homer, Pompey, and Brutus. Harpur left public life in 1795 and purchased 30,000 acres (12,000 ha) from the state along the Susquehanna River, where he founded the village of Harpursville. In 1950 the Triple Cities College of Syracuse University was renamed in his honor. Today Harpur College is a unit of SUNY Binghamton.

Dictionary of American Biography, sv "Harpur, Robert"

Dick Case

Harrietstown. Town (pop 5,575) in SE Franklin Co. Settled *ca* 1812, the town was formed from Duane in 1841. Its economy was based on lumbering, and logs were floated down the Saranac River, but mills were few because local demand was limited and shipping costly. From 1857 to 1861 the Philosophers' Camp at Ampersand Lake attracted Ralph Waldo Emerson, James Russell Lowell, and their circle. Most of Harrietstown's population and employment are centered in the Village of Saranac Lake. The Adirondack Regional Airport is located in town.

Thomas W. Perrin

Harriman. Village (pop 2,252) in Woodbury and Monroe (Orange Co). The locality, first known as Centerville, grew up along the Ramapo River in the early 19th century. It became a station on the Erie Railroad (1841) and acquired a post office named Turner in 1843. The first train order transmitted by telegraph originated there in 1851. Railroad magnate E. H. Harriman (1848–1909) created a 20,000-acre (8,000 ha) estate and a mansion, Arden House (1905), adjacent to the village. The post office was renamed in Harriman's honor in 1910, and the village was incorporated in 1914. The original MIA flag was created in Harriman and first flown in the village on 10 Nov 1974.

Alan Hunter

Harriman, E(dward) H(enry) (*b* Hempstead [now in Nassau Co], 20 Feb 1848; *d* Arden, Orange Co, 9 Sept 1909). Railroad executive. In 1861 he left school to work as an office boy on Wall St, where he advanced to messenger clerk. At the age of 22, he bought a seat on the New York Stock Exchange with a loan from an uncle. After his marriage to Mary Williamson Averell in 1879, he became a director on her father's New York State railroad, the Ogdensburg and Lake Champlain. Harriman's major railroad career began in 1883 when he was elected director of the Illinois Central Railroad. In 1885 he bought the Parrott estate, named Arden, in the Ramapo Highlands of Orange Co, which became the Harrimans' permanent summer home. His greatest achievement was the reorganization and rebuilding of the Union Pacific Railroad starting in December 1897. Under Harriman's leadership as president, the railroad acquired the Southern Pacific Railroad in 1901 after a bidding war with J. P. Morgan and Co; it later reconstructed the Central Pacific Railroad. His ideas on competition and organization significantly improved the capacity and productivity of railroad systems. By 1905 additional tracts of land increased the Harrimans' estate to almost 19,200 acres (7,770 ha). At his death, Harriman also owned a 20,000-acre (8,000 ha) forest preserve in Orange Co; a substantial part of this land was donated to New York State and became Harriman State Park. Harriman's son Averell was a noted diplomat and governor of New York State.

Kennan, George. *Edward Henry Harriman: A Biography* (Boston: Houghton Mifflin, 1922)
Klein, Maury. *The Life and Legend of E. H. Harriman* (Chapel Hill: Univ of North Carolina Press, 2000)
Mercer, Lloyd J. *E. H. Harriman: Master Railroader* (Boston: G. K. Hall, 1985)

Lloyd J. Mercer

Harriman, W(illiam) Averell (*b* New York City, 15 Nov 1891; *d* Yorktown Heights, Westchester Co, 26 July 1986). Financier, diplomat, and governor. The fifth of six children born to railroad magnate E. H. Harriman and Mary Averell, W. Averell Harriman was reared in New York City and at Arden, the family's estate in Orange Co. He was educated at private schools in New York City, at Groton School in Massachusetts, and at Yale University. Although frail in his youth, Harriman was an avid sportsman who played polo in international competition during the 1920s. His marriage to Kitty Lanier Lawrance, mother of his two daughters, ended in divorce in 1929. Soon thereafter, he married Marie Norton Whitney, who died in 1970. As a financier in the 1920s and 1930s, Harriman engaged in high-profile business ventures ranging from shipbuilding, shipping, and aviation to manganese mining in the former Soviet republic of Georgia. After 1931 he was a partner in the private investment bank Brown Bros Harriman and Co, and from 1932 until 1946 he was chairman of the board of Union Pacific Railroad. In 1933 Harriman joined the New Deal's National Recovery Administration (NRA), beginning a government career that eventually included service in five Democratic administrations over half a century. In March 1941 he was posted in London as expediter of US arms and war supply shipments to Great Britain, and from 1943 until the conclusion of World War II, he was ambassador to the Soviet Union. With the return to peacetime, Harriman opted not to resume his business career. In the ensuing years of the Cold War, he served as ambassador to Great Britain, secretary of commerce, European coordinator of the Marshall Plan, and chief of the Mutual Security Administration.

Although he lacked the natural skills for elective politics, Harriman yearned to hold office in his own right. In 1952 he campaigned unsuccessfully for the Democratic presidential nomination but in 1954 was elected governor of New York State, defeating US senator Irving M. Ives. Staffed with veterans of the Roosevelt and Truman administrations plus young aides such as future senator Daniel P. Moynihan, the Harriman administration was socially progressive and fiscally cautious. It was marked by important initiatives in consumer protection, mental health, and services for the elderly, but the efforts were overshadowed by tax and budget battles between the administration and the Republican-led legislature. With the backing of former president Harry S. Truman, Harriman made a second bid for the Democratic presidential nomination in 1956 but won little support outside his home state. Running for reelection as governor two years later, he was branded as a captive of Tammany Hall and lost to Nelson A. Rockefeller by more than half a million votes. Harriman had naively provided the vehicle for Rockefeller to launch his political career by appointing him chairman of the Temporary State Commission on the Constitutional Convention. Following his term as governor, Harriman served as assistant secretary of state, undersecretary of state, and special envoy for Presidents John F. Kennedy, Lyndon Johnson, and Jimmy Carter. His third wife, Pamela Digby Churchill Hayward, with whom he had a wartime liaison while she was the daughter-in-law of Prime Minister Winston Churchill, was with him when he died, four months shy of his 95th birthday.

Abramson, Rudy. *Spanning the Century: The Life of W. Averell Harriman, 1891–1986* (New York: William Morrow, 1992)

Rudy Abramson

Harriman State Park. See BEAR MOUNTAIN AND HARRIMAN STATE PARKS.

Harrington, (Edward) Michael (*b* St. Louis, 24 Feb 1928; *d* Larchmont, Westchester Co, 31 July 1989). Writer and political activist. Raised in St. Louis, he was educated in the city's Catholic schools before attending Holy Cross, Yale Law School, and the University of Chicago. He was a member of the radical pacifist Catholic Worker movement from 1951 to 1952, when he lived among the poor in the Bowery of New York City. In 1952 he joined the socialist movement, and would remain a tireless advocate of democratic socialism for the remainder of his life. Although his radicalism made him a marginal figure in the national politics of the McCarthy era, in the 1960s Harrington was well known in left-wing circles for advocating a liberal-labor coalition within the Democratic Party. After writing the influential book *The Other America: Poverty in the United States* (1962), which helped inspire Pres Lyndon Johnson's War on Poverty in 1964, Harrington became known as "the man who discovered poverty." Widely regarded as Norman Thomas's heir apparent, he was elected chairman of the Socialist Party in 1968. He joined the Political Science Department at Queens College in 1972. In 1973 he founded a new organization at a New York City convention, the Democratic Socialist Organizing Committee (DSOC), which later became the Democratic Socialists of America (DSA). In his last decade he campaigned to defend the legacy of the New Deal and the Great Society against its conservative detractors.

Isserman, Maurice. *The Other American: The Life of Michael Harrington* (New York: PublicAffairs, 2000)

Maurice Isserman

Harris, Elisha (*b* Westminster, Vt, 5 Mar 1824; *d* Albany, 31 Jan 1884). Physician, medical statistician, and public health reformer. After receiving his MD from the College of Physicians and Surgeons (now part of Columbia University) in 1849, Harris established private practice in

New York City. In 1855 he was appointed superintendent of the Staten Island Quarantine Hospital. Harris also held offices at the US Sanitary Commission, New York City Metropolitan Board of Health, New York State Board of Health, Prison Association of New York, and Citizens' Association Special Council of Hygiene and Public Health from the 1850s to the 1880s. He gained an international reputation by improving the accuracy of methods to gather and compile vital statistics and by showing how to use statistics on epidemics, sanitation, public utilities, crime, vaccination, and social welfare to the best advantage of public health. Harris was one of the founders of the American Public Health Association in 1872 and its president in 1877.

Duffy, John. *A History of Public Health in New York City, 1625–1866* (New York: Russell Sage Foundation, 1968)

Fox, Daniel M. "Harris, Elisha." In *Dictionary of American Medical Biography* (Westport, Conn: Greenwood, 1984)

Eric v. d. Luft

Harris, Ira (*b* Charleston, Montgomery Co, 31 May 1802; *d* Albany, 2 Dec 1875). US senator. Graduating from Union College in 1824, Harris studied law in Albany and was admitted to the bar in 1827. His political career began in 1844 with his support for the antirent movement that had arisen when quasi-aristocratic Hudson Valley landlords had tried to collect unpaid rents from their tenants. Harris served in the state assembly (1845–46) and senate (1847–50). In 1847 he became a justice of the New York State Supreme Court, serving until 1859. An early member of the Republican Party, Harris was elected easily by the legislature to the US Senate in 1860, outmaneuvering Horace Greeley and William M. Evarts. He was a close friend and confidante of Pres Abraham Lincoln, and Harris's daughter and her husband (Harris's stepson) were with Lincoln when he was assassinated. Harris was defeated for reelection in 1866 and retired from politics; he then became a professor at Albany Law School (1867–75), which he had helped found in 1851. He also held positions with Vassar College, Union College, Albany Medical College, and University of Rochester.

Memorial of Ira Harris (Albany: J. Munsell, 1876)

Jon Sterngass

Harrisburg. Town (pop 423) in NW Lewis Co. Settled in 1802, the town was formed in 1803 from Lowville, Champion (Jefferson Co), and Mexico (Oswego Co). German Americans from the Mohawk Valley followed the first settlers in 1806. Peppermint oil production was an early source of income. The John Rice Glass Factory (1841) operated only a short time. Harrisburg became a dairy town, and cheese making was the principal industry until the last cheese factory closed in 1949. In the 1930s natural gas was discovered, and a company formed to supply gas to Lowville, but the wells were soon depleted.

Arthur Einhorn

Harris Hill. Locality (pop 4,881) in Clarence (Erie Co). In 1807 Asa Harris built a tavern on a slight knoll on the Buffalo Rd (now Rte 5), which became the center of a hamlet. County offices moved there briefly after the burning of Buffalo in 1813. A post office named Harris Hill operated from 1842 to 1902. In the early 21st century Harris Hill has a small commercial district, but it is primarily suburban, with developments off Harris Hill Rd and Main St (Rte 5).

Nancy B. Mingus

Harrison. Coextensive town and village (pop 24,154) in SE Westchester Co. In 1696 John Harrison purchased the tract from the Indians. In the 1720s it was settled by Quakers, who built a meetinghouse in 1727. During the Revolutionary War era, many of them manumitted African Americans, who created a community nearby in "The Hills." By 1774 Harrison was electing town officers, and in 1788 the state confirmed its status as a town. In 1870 a station on the New Haven Railroad was established, and the community that grew up around it became predominantly Italian. West Harrison was developed in the 1890s with Italians, Germans, and Lithuanians. The northeast part of the town, Purchase, developed into an estate district in the 19th century and became the site of Westchester County Airport (1945), Manhattanville College (1952), and SUNY Purchase (1971). I-287 was completed through town in 1960 and attracted several corporate headquarters, including PepsiCo (1970) and Texaco (1977). The village incorporated in 1975 to be coextensive with the town. Postwar suburbanization resulted in a fourfold increase in the town's population between 1920 and 1960. In 2000 about 5.5% of the town's population was Asian. Keio Academy (1990) is operated by Keio University in Japan.

Harrisville. Village (pop 653) in Diana (Lewis Co). Foskit Harris purchased property along the Oswegatchie River from Joseph Bonaparte and built a sawmill (1833) and a gristmill (1835); his enterprises were followed in 1858–59 by those of Joseph Pakud, a Swiss capitalist. The village incorporated in 1892. A paper mill operated by the St. Regis Paper Co closed in the mid-1950s. Many residents work in St. Lawrence or Jefferson Cos; others operate tourist-oriented businesses. The village is the home of a large central school district.

Arthur Einhorn

Hart, Kitty Carlisle [Conn, Katherine] (*b* New Orleans, 3 Sept 1910). Actress, singer, and arts advocate. Educated in Switzerland, at the Sorbonne in Paris, and at the London School of Economics, she studied acting at the London Royal Academy of Dramatic Art. She moved to New York City in the early 1930s when she took her stage name. Carlisle's first appearance on Broadway was in *Champagne Sec* in 1934. That same year, she starred in the film *Murder at the Vanities* and the following year in the Marx Brothers' classic *A Night at the Opera*. She was married to playwright and director Moss Hart from 1946 until his death in 1961; they had two children. She portrayed the title character in the first New York City production of Benjamin Britten's opera *The Rape of Lucretia* (1948) and made her Metropolitan Opera debut in 1967 as Prince Orlofsky in Johann Strauss Jr's *Die Fledermaus*. She was a regular panelist on the television show *To Tell the Truth* from 1956 to 1977.

Her advocacy on behalf of women led to her appointment as chair of the New York State Conference of Women (1966) and as special consultant to Gov Nelson A. Rockefeller on women's opportunities (1968). In 1971 Gov Rockefeller appointed her vice chair of the New York State Council on the Arts, and she served as chair from 1976 to 1996. She has also served as a member of the board of SUNY Empire State College and is an honorary trustee of the Metropolitan Museum of Art and the Museum of Modern Art. She appeared in the 1984 revival of the musical *On Your Toes*, and later film appearances include Woody Allen's *Radio Days* (1987) and *Six Degrees of Separation* (1993). In 1996 she resumed her singing career and began performing her one-woman show, *My Life upon the Wicked Stage*, nationwide.

Hart, Kitty Carlisle. *Kitty: An Autobiography* (New York: St. Martin's Press, 1988)

Al Berr

Hartford. Town (pop 2,279) in central Washington Co. Settled permanently about 1782, the town was formed from Westfield [now Fort Ann] in 1793. Still predominantly agricultural in 2003, it was the top potato-growing town in the state in 1860, and the crop was shipped via the nearby Champlain Canal. After the Civil War dairy grew more important, and fluid milk was shipped generally after *ca* 1900. Nineteenth-century manufactures included leather, hats, wool cloth, and shoes. The town is the site of the Howard Hanna Civil War Museum, located in a shop used as an enlistment center, and of the privately operated Log Village Grist Mill Museum, which includes a 17 ft (5.2 m) breast-type waterwheel.

R. Paul McCarty

Hartford Treaty. Throughout its history, New Netherland was involved in boundary disputes with English colonies. No dispute caused more problems than the conflict over ownership of the Connecticut River valley, which was explored in 1614 by the Dutch captain Adriaen Block. In June 1633, to secure the valuable fur trade afforded by the river for the Dutch West India Co, Director Wouter van Twiller authorized the purchase from the local Indians of a parcel of land on the Connecticut River. The Dutch promptly erected a small trading fort called Fort Good Hope, located near what would become Hartford, Conn, only to face an unwelcome English intrusion as men from Plymouth Colony established their own trading house above the Dutch fort. For seven years the conflict over ownership continued off and on between the English and Dutch. By 1640 the Dutch, who had been unable to match the population growth of the English, finally lost control of the Connecticut River valley. The main area in dispute then became Long Island, but negotiations were prevented by the English Civil War. Therefore, before his departure for New Netherland as the new director general, Petrus Stuyvesant was instructed by the Dutch West India Co to negotiate a provisional settlement with the English colonies in America. Soon after his arrival in 1647 Stuyvesant wrote to Gov John Winthrop of Massachusetts asking for a meeting to discuss the boundary dispute. After several delays, a meeting was held at Hartford in September 1650. This was attended by Stuyvesant and commissioners from the United Colonies of New England (Massachusetts Bay, Plymouth, New Haven, and Connecticut Colonies). The resulting provisional treaty mandated that Long Island east of Oyster Bay would belong to the English and that the western part would remain in Dutch hands. On the mainland the boundary would start on the west side of Greenwich, Conn, and run north. Although this meant that the Dutch relinquished their claim to the Connecticut River valley and the eastern part of Long Island, it also meant that they gained recognition of their rights to the rest of New Netherland. However, the First Anglo-Dutch War (1652–54) prevented the necessary ratification of the treaty in Europe for a time, but in 1656 the States General of the Netherlands finally ratified the agreement. Such approval was not forthcoming from England because the English colonies apparently never sent the treaty to London. Nevertheless, the English colonies generally did adhere to the treaty. Although the Hartford Treaty could not prevent the English conquest of New Netherland in 1664, it did postpone it for a number of years.

Cohen, Ronald D. "The Hartford Treaty of 1650: Anglo-Dutch Cooperation in the 17th Century," *New-York Historical Society Quarterly* 53 (1969): 311–32

"Extract of the Articles of Agreement, Made and Concluded at Hartford, situate in Conitticot, the 19th September, 1650 . . ." In *Documents Relative to the Colonial History of the State of New York,* 15 vols, trans and ed. E. B. O'Callaghan and B. Fernow (Albany: Weed, Parsons, 1856), 1:611–12

Jacobs, Jaap. "The Hartford Treaty: A European Perspective on a New World Conflict," *de Halve Maen* 68 (Winter 1995): 74–79

Jaap Jacobs

Hartland. Town (pop. 4,165) in E central Niagara Co. Settled in 1803 on the site of a large windfall, the town was formed from Cambria in 1812. A circular earthwork, thought to be a prehistoric Indian site, was plowed down in 1828. Southwest of Johnson Creek, salt springs created a barren area where nothing grew; salt was manufactured in this area before the Erie Canal made it cheaper to ship from Syracuse. There was also a brick manufacturer north of Middleport in the 1870s and a broom factory at Johnson Creek in the 1900s. Throughout its history Hartland has been primarily a fruit growing town.

Nancy B. Mingus

Hartsdale. Locality (pop 9,830) in Greenburgh (Westchester Co). The Odell House (1732), now a museum, was the headquarters of the Comte de Rochambeau in 1781. The area was served by the Harlem Railroad (1844) and by Central Park Ave (Rte 100, 1871), now a major retail corridor. It was known as Hart's Corners and acquired a post office by that name in 1872; the name was changed in 1886. The Bronx River Parkway (1925) further stimulated suburban development. Hartsdale, a residential suburb, is the site of a working farm, Westchester Greenhouses; Hartsdale Pet Cemetery (1896), the nation's first; and a branch of Empire State College. The Asian population, present since the 1970s, reached 10.2% in 2000, the majority either Japanese or Asian Indian.

Scott C. Monje

Hartsville. Town (pop 585) in W Steuben Co. Settled in 1809, the town was formed from Hornellsville in 1844. Characterized by steep and rocky hills, the area yielded lumber until *ca* 1855. After the timber thinned out, dairying predominated, which helped to support a number of local cheese manufacturers. In the early 21st century Christmas tree farming is an important local industry, and about 55% of the houses are vacation homes for Buffalo and Rochester residents. Call Hill (2,401 ft/731.8 m) is the highest point in the county.

Virginia L. Wright and Jerry Wright

Hartwick. Town (pop 2,203) in central Otsego Co. Lutheran minister John Christopher Hartwick (1714–96) obtained an Indian deed (1752) and a patent (1761) for 21,500 acres (8,700 ha), which he intended for a spiritual community he referred to as a "New Jerusalem." Settlement began in 1784 and accelerated after 1791 when William Cooper began acting as Hartwick's agent. After Hartwick's death, money from the sale of lands to New Englanders was used to establish Hartwick Seminary (1815–1934), a Lutheran seminary. The town was formed from Otsego in 1802. Population peaked at 2,772 in 1830. Manufacturing included the Union Cotton Factory (1809) in Toddsville and the Clinton Cotton Mills (1815) in Clintonville, as well as several foundries in the Civil War era. Hops was an important crop until the 1910s. Hartwick hamlet, an interurban trolley center in the early 20th century, declined rapidly later in the century and became primarily a bedroom community to Oneonta and Cooperstown. The three contiguous hamlets of Hartwick Seminary, Hyde Park, and Index became a tourist-oriented commercial strip in the 1990s, with a shopping center, motel, and the Cooperstown Dreams Park, a youth baseball camp (1996).

Hugh C. MacDougall

Hartwick College. Private coeducational liberal arts college in Oneonta (Otsego Co). Hartwick Seminary was founded 25 miles (40 km) north of Oneonta in 1797 to train Lutheran theologians. Incorporated in 1816 by the state legislature as both a seminary and a classical academy, Hartwick began accepting women in 1851. In 1928 the trustees decided to expand the curriculum to include collegiate courses. Citizens of Oneonta donated land and raised money to locate the new college there, which opened as Hartwick College in 1929. A nursing program was started in 1943, and in 1968 the college separated from the Lutheran Church to become an independent institution. Eight miles (13 km) from the main campus, Hartwick operates a 914-acre (370 ha) environmental campus at Pine Lake. In 2003 the college enrolled 1,400 students in 30 programs of study.

Ronald H. Bailey. *Hartwick College: A Bicentennial History, 1797–1997* (Oneonta, NY: Hartwick College Press, 1997)

Sarah E. DeSanctis

Hasidism. Beginning in the latter half of the 18th century, the Hasidic movement sought to revitalize Jewish life in central and eastern Europe. Hasidim (from the Hebrew word meaning pious ones) share many commonalities with other Orthodox Jews but generally are distinguished by their common history, distinctive customs and dress, joyful approach to the performance of religious ritual, and their unique organization into "courts" or communities. Varying in size from a few hundred to several thousand families, courts are organized around familial allegiance to a particular rebbe (Hasidic religious leader) and that rebbe's special teachings and philosophy.

The first surge of Hasidic immigration to New York City coincided with the overall wave of Jewish immigration to New York State between the 1880s and 1920s, especially to the Lower East Side of New York City. Yet, among these immigrants were few devout Hasidim, as most rebbes, fearing the openness and freedom of America, had discouraged their followers from leaving Europe. Those who did emigrate found themselves, and certainly their children, quickly overwhelmed by the social pressures to assimilate and shed distinctive practices.

After World War II, the second wave of immigration took place as Hasidic Jews who survived the Holocaust followed their rebbes to Brooklyn, where they successfully re-created the language, clothing, and customs of their communities in Europe. The largest group in New York and the United States, the Satmarers, originated in Hungary and settled in the Williamsburg section of Brooklyn. The Satmar rebbe Joel Teitelbaum was particularly notable for his strident anti-Zionism and renunciation of modernity. He established a satellite enclave near Monroe (Orange Co), incorporated as the Village of Kiryas Joel in 1977. His nephew Rabbi Moshe Teitelbaum was made his successor following his death in 1979. The village has been the subject of controversy since 1989 when it created a special public school district in order to receive state services for its children with disabilities. The US Supreme Court voided the district in 1994. In 1999 the governor signed into law a bill with broader criteria that has so far withstood court challenges.

The best-known Hasidic group, the Lubavitchers, also known as Chabad, established themselves in the Crown Heights area of Brooklyn at 770 Eastern Parkway when the sixth Lubavitcher rebbe, Rabbi Joseph Schneerson, settled there in 1940 and began a campaign to revitalize Jewish communities around the world. Upon his death in 1950, his son-in-law, Menachem Mendel Schneerson, became the seventh Lubavitcher rebbe, expanding the Lubavitch mission of imparting the Chabad philosophy and Orthodox Jewish practice to the wider Jewish community by developing a vast network of outreach programs and strategies. In contrast to the Satmars, the Lubavitchers have involved themselves in Israeli politics, sometimes creating great dissension in the Jewish world, such as when the rebbe supported legislation that would have delegitimized non-Orthodox religious conversions in Israel. In the decades before and even after the rebbe's death in 1994, many Jews were alienated by the cult of personality that some Lubavitchers created around Schneerson and their claim that he was the Messiah. No successor to Schneerson was appointed. In August 1991 the accidental death of a black child by a Lubavitch motorist and the subsequent murder of a Hasidic student touched off weeks of rioting in Crown Heights, which was finally diffused by local community activists from both sides.

Along with some Satmar families, several other Hasidic groups—including the Bobovers, the Belzers, Stoliners, and Vizhnitzers—helped to transform Borough Park into perhaps the largest group of Hasidim in the United States by the

1980s. It was estimated in 2000 that approximately 200,000 Hasidim reside in Brooklyn. In addition to Kiryas Joel, other important Hasidic enclaves in the state include Monroe and Harriman (Orange Co) and Monsey, Spring Valley, and New Square (Rockland Co).

Heilman, Samuel. *Defenders of the Faith: Inside Ultra-Orthodox Jewry* (New York: Schocken Books, 1992)
Hundert, Gershon David, ed. *Essential Papers on Hasidism: Origins to the Present* (New York: New York Univ Press, 1991)
Mintz, Jerome R. *Hasidic People: A Place in the New World* (Cambridge, Mass: Harvard Univ Press, 1992)

Zion Zohar

Hastings. Town (pop 8,803) in S Oswego Co. Settled in 1789 the town was formed from Constantia in 1825. Archaeological excavations have uncovered many Indian burials. The Fort Brewerton Blockhouse Museum is located near the original site of Fort Brewerton (1759). In the 19th century lumbering and barrel making (for Syracuse salt and Oswego flour) were major industries. At Caughdenoy 1,000 eels were taken from the Oneida River daily for four months each year, continuing the Indian practice of harvesting eels, and shipped to cities for market. Central Square is the town's only incorporated village. Little France is a hamlet settled by immigrants from Alsace-Lorraine prior to 1880. There are still some farms in the town but no industry. I-81 (1959–60) has promoted land development and facilitated commuting.

Barbara J. Dix

Hastings-on-Hudson. Village (pop 7,648) in Greenburgh (Westchester Co). A Revolutionary War skirmish, the Battle of Edgar's Lane, took place 30 Sept 1778. Marble was quarried from 1834 until the early 1870s. The Hudson River Railroad came through in 1849, making the area accessible for country homes. The village was at that time the site of three large factories that attracted workers of many national origins: the Hudson River Steam Sugar Refinery (1853–77, under various names), Zinsser Chemical Co (1897–1955) and National Conduit (later Anaconda Wire and Cable; 1880–1975). Incorporated in 1879, Hastings-on-Hudson is a commuter village with a small business district.

Henry Steiner

Haudenosaunee. See IROQUOIS CONFEDERACY.

Hauppauge [HOP-POG]. Locality (pop 20,100) in Smithtown and Islip (Suffolk Co). An area of scrub forest and swamp, its name means "overflowed land." Irish immigrants built St. Patrick's Church in 1845, and a post office opened in 1856. The Brooklyn Industrial School Association operated from 1907 to 1954. Hauppauge remained agricultural until after World War II, when the area became more accessible because of the Northern State Parkway and the Long Island Expressway (1964). The population, only 804 in 1940, grew to 13,957 by 1970. It is the site of the Vanderbilt Industrial Park, the second largest development of this kind in the United States (with more than 1,350 companies), and of county and state office buildings.

Noel J. Gish

Hauptman, Herbert A. (*b* Bronx Co, 14 Feb 1917). Mathematician. The son of Israel and Leah Rosenfeld Hauptman, his interest in mathematics began at an early age. He went to public schools in the Bronx and then to Townsend Harris High School (1930–33). Hauptman earned a BS from City College of New York (1937), an MA in mathematics from Columbia University (1939), and a PhD from the University of Maryland (1954). During the war years 1943–46 he was a weather officer in the US Army Air Corps. He joined the US Naval Research Laboratory (NRL) in Washington, DC, in 1947. While at NRL, starting about 1950, he studied the diffraction pattern of X rays through a crystal and, with physicist Jerome Karle, developed the "direct methods" mathematical approach to determine the three-dimensional position of atoms in the crystal based on the pattern. In 1970 Hauptman left NRL to direct the Mathematical Biophysics Lab at the Medical Foundation of Buffalo (MFB), since 1994 the Hauptman-Woodward Medical Research Institute. Since 1970 he has also served as research professor in the Department of Biophysical Sciences at SUNY Buffalo. In 1985 Hauptman shared the Nobel Prize in chemistry with Karle for their work. Their research with the mineral colemanite has since been used to establish the structures of 50,000 molecules, leading to 5,000 new chemicals and drugs for treating cancer, heart disease, high blood pressure, and AIDS. In 1986 Hauptman was named president of MFB. His recent research interest is identifying additional molecular structures.

Herbert A. Hauptman. "Autobiography," http://www.nobel.se/chemistry/laureates/1985/hauptman autobio.html

John Tepper Marlin

Haverstraw. Town (pop 33,811) and village (pop 10,117) in E central Rockland Co. Formed as a precinct in 1719 and recognized as a town in 1788, Haverstraw was named for the Dutch word meaning oat straw. Beginning in 1815 its clay deposits were used for brick making on a large scale, and the work drew many Irish families. In 1852 Richard Ver Valen of Haverstraw invented an improved brick machine, which was manufactured locally and sold widely. The village, an important river landing, was surveyed in 1837 and incorporated in 1854 as Warren; its name was changed in 1874. In the late 19th century as many as 42 brickyards operated at a time, but the business declined after 1900, and the last company closed in 1942. Letchworth Village (1907–96) near Thiells was the state's largest institution to serve people with developmental disabilities. The Palisades Interstate Parkway opened through town in 1953. Puerto Ricans began settling in Haverstraw in 1945 and were joined by Dominicans in the 1960s. People of Latino ethnicity constituted 59% of the village's population in 2000 and African Americans constituted 12%. Much of the western part of town is preserved in Harriman State Park. High Tor Mountain was protected from being quarried in the 1930s, in part through *High Tor,* a verse drama by noted playwright Maxwell Anderson that lamented the despoiling of the Hudson Valley. The land was acquired by the Hudson River Conservation Society and became a state park in 1943.

Haverstraw Indians. A Munsee-speaking community on the west bank of Haverstraw Bay centering around the present-day Hudson Valley community of Haverstraw (Rockland Co). The name, used by colonists between 1657 and 1686 to identify Indian people living at the location, derives from the Dutch words for oat straw. References in documents dating between 1649 and 1664 explicitly identify the terms Rumachenanck, Remahenonck, and Rewechnongh as Munsee cognomens for Haverstraw. These are probably related to the term Rechgawawank, still widely used to identify Indians living on northern Manhattan Island and the adjacent mainland. Whatever their identity or affiliation, most Haverstraw people probably either moved north to Esopus communities or west to join Hackensack or Minisink friends and relatives following final sale of their last land rights in the area in 1686.

Grumet, Robert S. "On the Identity of the Rechgawawanck." *Bulletin and Journal of Archaeology for New York State* 83 (1982): 1–7
Kraft, Herbert C. *The Lenape-Delaware Indian Heritage: 10,000 BC to AD 2000* (Elizabeth, NJ: Lenape Books, 2001)

Robert S. Grumet

Hawkins, Micah (*b* Head of the Harbor, Suffolk Co, 1 Jan 1777; *d* New York City, 29 July 1825). Merchant, poet, humorist, and composer. Trained as a coach maker, from 1802 until his death he was an innkeeper and the "musical grocer" of Catherine Slip on the New York City waterfront. Largely self-taught, he played piano, flute, violin, and viola, and was a singer, comedian, and mimic. He improvised verses for the entertainment of his patrons, accompanying himself on a keyboard concealed beneath his grocery counter. He compiled several tune books; the earliest, *Book of Notes for the German Flute,* was begun in 1794 and contains over 200 melodies, mostly popular airs, dances, marches, and patriotic songs. Hawkins is most important for his humorous and satirical works, including the first opera by an American composer on an American subject, *The Saw-Mill, or a Yankee Trick* (1824), which played at Chatham Garden Theatre in Lower Manhattan and was set in northwestern New York State.

His work is populist in spirit, championing underdogs and the lower classes over the old Dutch elite, who are portrayed as pompous and ridiculous. Keenly interested in African Americans and their music, he wrote two popular songs in African American dialect: "Backside Albany" (*ca* 1815) and "Massa Georgee Washington and General La Fayette" (1824). Hawkins was closely associated with his nephew, the artist William Sidney Mount.

Lawrence, Vera Brodsky. "Micah Hawkins, the Pied Piper of Catherine Slip," *New York Historical Society Quarterly* 62 (1978): 138–65

Elliott S. Hurwitt

Hawley, Gideon (*b* Huntington, Conn, 26 Sept 1785; *d* Albany, 17 July 1870). Superintendent of common schools. Hawley graduated from Union College in 1809, where he taught the succeeding year. In 1812 he was admitted to the bar and became the New York State's first superintendent of common schools, a position he held until the Clintonian party lost control of the legislature in 1821. Considered the founder of state's common school system, Hawley organized the state into school districts and managed the first continuous disbursement of state funds for education. He served as secretary to the Regents of the University of New York (1814–41) and as a regent from 1842 until his death. Hawley was also a founding trustee of Albany Female Academy in 1821, a founding regent of the Smithsonian Institution (1846–61), and a board member of the state's first normal school, located in Albany (1844–61). Hawley was a director of the Mohawk and Hudson Railroad and financial officer of the Utica and Schenectady Railroad. He also wrote the philosophical treatise *Essays on Truth and Knowledge, Relating Chiefly to the Definition of Truth and to the Definition and Division of Knowledge* (1856).

Pruyn, John V. L. *Remarks on the Life and Character of the Late Gideon Hawley, LLD* (?1870; repr Glen Rock, NJ: Microfilming Corp of America, 1978)
Who Was Who In America 1607–1896 (Chicago: Marquis Who's Who, 1967)

Thomas J. Mauhs-Pugh

Hawthorne. Locality (pop 5,083) in Mount Pleasant (Westchester Co). Originally Unionville it grew in significance with the founding of Unionville Reformed Church (1818) and a station stop on the Harlem Railroad (1846). It was an important transfer station for cattle drovers until the early 20th century. The post office (1851) was named Neperan. In 1901 Sr Mary Alphonsa [Rose Hawthorne Lathrop] founded Rosary Hill Home for incurable cancer patients, and the station and post office were renamed for her father, the famous novelist Nathaniel Hawthorne. Suburbanization began with the Sherman Park development from 1891 to 1894 and accelerated after World War II. The Hawthorne Traffic Circle at the junction of the Bronx, Taconic, and Saw Mill Parkways was a landmark from 1931 to 1968, when it was replaced by a three-level interchange.

Field Horne

hay. Perennial grasses such as clover and timothy, often called English hay, were imported by the first European settlers in the early 1600s and were cultivated, cut, and dried for use as winter feed for cattle, sheep, and horses. Salt hay was cut from native grasses in the salt marshes near Long Island Sound. Hay barracks were common; a staddle, or square log foundation, supported a simple roof with corner posts. English and Dutch barn-building traditions predominated, and barns were primarily storage buildings for hay and grain rather than housing for livestock. Hay was pitchforked loose into the mow until the mid-1800s, when the invention of dump rakes, which could turn large amounts of hay quickly, and of mowing machines allowed farmers to make enough hay to winter over large herds. This played a key role in the development of large-scale dairying in Central and Northern New York because farmers were able to keep parts of their herds producing throughout the year. At the same time, hay's value as a cash crop rose as cities grew and the number of urban horses without pasturage increased. The state's 1855 agricultural census recorded a hay harvest of 3,256,949 tons (2,954,652 MT), with St. Lawrence and Oneida Cos the leaders in production. Hay storage evolved as well. By the mid-1800s the English barn, with its gable-roofed, three-bay frame and doors in the long walls, superseded the Dutch barn and soon developed into the bank barn, the foundation of which cut into a hill to allow ground-level entry at both the mow and basement "floors." Increasing production in the late 1800s encouraged a shift to gambrel-roofed barns with larger mow capacities. Loading hay into the barn changed as well. By this time hay harpoons, which used horses and pulleys to move loose hay in large quantities, were used widely. In the 20th century the protein-rich legume alfalfa was commonly grown for hay as well, and with tractor power in the 1920s and 1930s, square-baling became common. Hay production peaked early in the 20th century, with greatest production, 6,914,000 tons (6,272,270 MT), in 1916 and greatest number of acres, 5,067,000 (2,050,542 ha), in 1924. In 2000 New York State farmers cut 1,520,000 acres (615,122 ha) to produce 3,098,000 tons (2,810,456 MT). At the beginning of the 21st century, much of the crop is round-baled, wrapped in plastic, and left in the meadow until used, leaving the mows of many New York State barns empty.

Harper, Douglas A. *Changing Works: Visions of a Lost Agriculture* (Chicago: Univ of Chicago Press, 2001)
Hedrick, U. P. *A History of Agriculture in the State of New York* (New York: Hill & Wang, 1966)

Jessie Ravage

Hay, Mary Garrett (*b* Charlestown, Ind, 29 Aug 1857; *d* New Rochelle, Westchester Co, 29 Aug 1928). Suffragist. Hay was educated and began her career in politics in Indiana, where she worked for the Woman's Christian Temperance Union, eventually meeting Carrie Chapman Catt and moving to New York City in 1895 to assist in the formulation of the organization committee of the National American Woman Suffrage Association (NAWSA). She organized suffrage movements throughout the country with Catt. Hay resigned from NAWSA in 1900. She held various positions in New York suffrage organizations, including president of the Federation of Women's Clubs (1910–12), director of the General Federation of Women's Clubs (1914–18), president of the New York Equal Suffrage League (1910–18), and president of the Woman Suffrage Party of Greater New York (1912–18). Through these organizations, she lobbied for a state constitutional amendment giving women the right to vote. A staunch Republican, Hay in 1918 was elected as a delegate to the New York Republican Convention and made part of the state party's executive committee, and she became chair of the Republican Women's National Executive Committee in 1919. Her efforts in 1919 to block the Republican Party's renomination of New York's incumbent US senator James W. Wadsworth Jr—an opponent of woman suffrage—undercut her position in the party; she was dropped from the state party's executive committee in 1920. Hay remained active as chair of the New York City League of Women Voters from 1918 to 1923, and she later worked as a prohibition advocate in the Republican Party.

Louis, James P. "Hay, Mary Garrett." In *Notable American Women, 1607–1950: A Biographical Dictionary*, ed. Edward T. James (Cambridge, Mass: Belknap Press, 1950)
Perry, Elisabeth Israels. "Defying the Party Whip: Mary Garrett Hay and the Republican Party, 1917–1920." In *We Have Come to Stay: American Women and Political Parties, 1880–1960*, ed. Melanie Gustafson, Kristie Miller, and Elisabeth Israels Perry (Albuquerque: Univ of New Mexico Press, 1999)

Kerry Delaney

Head of the Harbor. Village (pop 1,447) in Smithtown (Suffolk Co). Settled in 1677, the area remained rural until the Long Island Rail Road came through in 1872, initiating tourism and other development. Stanford White was a resident beginning in 1884. The village incorporated in 1928. One of the Three Villages, along with Stony Brook and Nissequogue, Head of the Harbor is residential with considerable historic character. Mills Pond House (1838) and Deepwells Manor (1845) are open to the public and listed on the National Register.

Bronwyn Hannon

Health, Department of. Through education, research, and improved access to medical care, the department seeks to promote good health practices and protect the public from disease and injury. Organized to implement public health statutes passed in 1880–81, the New York State Board of Health employed a staff of 13 and spent $10,306 in its first full year. Its initial goal was to standardize, simplify, and monitor the public health ordinances, terminologies, and practices that had proliferated among the state's 20 municipalities, excluding New York City and Buffalo, which had effective local health bureaus in place. Within a few years the board was assembling data on births, deaths, marriages, and incidences of contagious diseases; regulating the preparation and burial of dead bodies; providing assistance to communities afflicted by epidemics; and working to discover and prevent adulteration of food and drugs. In 1901 the agency became the Department of Health, under a commissioner appointed by the governor, with expanded powers including inspection of public works.

The largest expansion of the department's responsibilities came with passage of the Hill-Burton Act (1946), which combined federal and state governmental efforts in creating and upgrading health care facilities neglected during the Great Depression and World War II. In ensuing decades a burgeoning elderly population and Medicaid legislation (1965) led to the department's involvement in the oversight and regulation of hospitals, HMOs, nursing and private home care, medical personnel, and other health-related agencies. The department was reorganized in 1977 to comprise the Office of Health Systems Management, which regulates healthcare institutions and providers, and the Office of Public Health, which administers other functions such as disease control and prevention. Crises like the discovery of toxic waste contamination in the Love Canal area of Niagara Falls in the late 1970s expanded the department's role in environmental oversight. The appearance of AIDS (1981) and West Nile virus (1999) and the reemergence of tuberculosis in the 1980s and 1990s, especially in the New York City area, have again centered attention on contagious diseases. The threat of bioterrorism is another recent concern.

As of 2004 the Department of Health operates the Roswell Park Cancer Institute in Buffalo, the Helen Hayes Hospital for physical rehabilitation in West Haverstraw (Rockland Co), the Wadsworth Center research facilities in the Capital District, and Veterans Nursing Homes in Batavia (Genesee Co), Montrose (Westchester Co), Oxford (Chenango Co), and the St. Albans area of Queens Co. The department's School of Public Health is a joint venture with SUNY Albany. While the Health Department continues to be involved in scientific research and regulation of healthcare institutions and personnel, it increasingly focuses on the health needs of specific groups of New Yorkers—children, women, families, and the elderly—through initiatives like the ambitious Child Health Plus insurance program (1991) and the EPIC drug coverage plan for seniors (1987).

See also INSURANCE, HEALTH.

New York State. Department of Health. *Annual Report* (1880–)

Sexton, Anna M. *A Chronicle of the Division of Laboratories and Research, New York State Department of Health: The First 50 Years, 1914–1964* (Lunenburg, Vt: Stinehour Press, 1967)

Teresa K. Lehr

Health and Human Service Union 1199 SEIU. Founded in 1932 during the militant left-wing industrial union campaigns of that era by a small group of drugstore clerks in New York City as the Pharmacists' Union of Greater New York. In 1936 the union hired Leon J. Davis to be its first full-time salaried organizer, and union members decided to affiliate with the American Federation of Labor as Local 1199. The next year Local 1199 joined with other industrial unions in the movement that led to the formation of the Congress of Industrial Organizations. Also in 1937, Local 1199 launched a successful effort to secure jobs for African Americans as pharmacists in Harlem drugstores. By 1940 more than 700 workers belonged to Local 1199; that year Davis was elected president, a position he held until his retirement in 1981.

In 1957 Davis, looking to expand Local 1199's organizational base, recruited Elliot Godoff, who for more than two decades had sought to unionize New York City hospital workers. Recognition for the union and a negotiated contract came in December 1958 after a prolonged campaign at Montefiore Hospital in the Bronx. Encouraged by this victory, Local 1199 began recruiting workers in other hospitals across the five boroughs. On 8 May 1959, some 3,500 workers in seven New York City hospitals took part in an unprecedented 46-day strike. The negotiations that ended the strike produced a Memorandum of Understanding that gave the workers limited grievance machinery and established a 12-member board, the Permanent Administrative Committee (PAC). The PAC was to hold annual reviews of wage demands and worker grievances at which union representatives might appear. The hospitals also agreed to rehire strikers. In 1962 Local 1199 struck at Beth El Hospital (now Brookdale Medical Center) and at Manhattan Eye and Ear Hospital, demanding formal union recognition. The union agreed to end this strike in return for a pledge from Gov Nelson A. Rockefeller to introduce and push for legislation that would grant hospital workers collective bargaining rights under the state's labor relations act. The law that passed in 1963 was limited to workers in nonprofit hospitals in New York City, but two years later it was extended to cover workers in hospitals throughout New York State.

Firmly entrenched in New York City, Local 1199 in 1968 secured a breakthrough contract with the League of Voluntary Hospitals of New York that gave workers a $100-per-week minimum salary. The following year, attempting to build on its success in the metropolitan area, the union launched a Union Power, Soul Power national campaign and four years later established itself as the National Union of Hospital and Health Care Employees. Through the 1960s, Local 1199 tried to organize workers in hospitals across New York State. By 1974, 1199NY, which included New Jersey and Connecticut, represented more than 60,000 workers. By the late 1970s, seeking to organize healthcare workers into a single union nationally, 1199 officials initiated merger discussions with leaders of the Service Employees International Union (SEIU). Issues of succession and merger preoccupied the union during the 1980s. On 1 June 1989 the merger of Local 1199 with the SEIU was accomplished. In 2002 the union for Local 1199/SEIU had 215,000 members throughout New York State.

Fink, Leon, and Brian Greenberg. *Upheaval in the Quiet Zone: A History of Hospital Workers' Union, Local 1199* (Urbana: Univ of Illinois Press, 1989)

Brian Greenberg

healthcare and hospitals. The quality of healthcare for New Yorkers in the 18th century was determined by their environment and social class. Malaria and typhoid fever, generated in the wetlands of the frontier, were perennial maladies. Much of the population lived in remote areas where medical help was distant or nonexistent, and medicines were derived from roots and leaves of plants. Infants and the elderly were especially at risk, women often died in childbirth, and men in the prime of life were highly vulnerable to injuries. Well-to-do patients could enjoy visits from physicians and had domestic servants to nurse them back to health. The less affluent could consult apothecaries for advice. In closely knit settlements and communities, female relatives and neighbors often nursed the sick.

As newcomers swelled the population of New York City, it became clear that a facility to house a growing indigent population was necessary. In 1736 an almshouse, with infirmary, opened at what is now the site of City Hall. The infirmary eventually moved to former farmland on the East Side, where it became the forerunner of Bellevue Hospital. New York Hospital, an early private and voluntary facility (chartered 1771), primarily saw charity cases as well. After 1824 the state legislature required all counties to establish almshouses. Treatment in an almshouse infirmary was less than ideal; a physician was present only when needed and healthy inmates served as nurses. Funding was minimal and periodic inspections reported poor maintenance and neglected patients.

HOSPITALS IN THE 19TH CENTURY

For the first three-quarters of the 19th century, training for physicians varied from apprenticeships to attending lectures at small medical schools organized as business enterprises by private physicians. To enroll as many students as possible, these proprietary schools kept entry requirements minimal. Some students pursued medical degrees in the few American colleges granting them, like the College of Physicians and Surgeons (affiliated with Columbia from 1860), or in Europe. Because the Medical Society of the State of New York, established in 1806 by the legislature, could not force citizens to patronize licensed practitioners, it ceded licensing powers to county medical societies in 1844.

Competing medical theories—homeopathy, Thomsonianism, magnetism, osteopathy, mesmerism, hydropathy, eclecticism, and allopathy—appeared to be equally effective against diseases. In midcentury a series of medical advances took place that gave physicians of the allopathic, or "regular," school an advantage. The discovery of the anesthetic properties of ether; the formulation of the germ theory, which led to sterile operating environments; and the promotion of immunization during smallpox epidemics revolutionized the way medical professionals understood and treated illness. Nevertheless, some of the alternative medical therapeutics, notably homeopathy, achieved durable success. In 1845 the nation's first homeopathic dispensary was created in New York City, and homeopathic facilities spread statewide in the following decades, including the Homeopathic Hospital of Albany (1872), Rochester Homeopathic Hospital (1887), and Hahnemann Hospital (1889) in Rochester, Gowanda State Homeopathic Hospital (1894) in Collins (Erie Co), and Syracuse Homeopathic Hospital (1895). In the early 20th century, however, the homeopathic and eclectic hospitals closed or gradually transformed themselves into respectable allopathic institutions.

By the late 19th century three kinds of hospitals treated the sick in the large cities: public, religious, and nondenominational voluntary hospitals. At public institutions such as Buffalo General Hospital (1858), Rochester City Hospital (1864), and the system of New York City municipal hospitals including Bellevue, Kings County Hospital (1831), and Harlem Hospital (1887), patients were separated by gender into wards where 20 or more could be tended efficiently by a few nurses and their progress observed by a resident physician. As long as a public hospital was governed by local political officials, few advances were made. Toward the end of the century, however, inspections revealed the often deplorable conditions in these institutions, and medical schools increasingly viewed them as valuable teaching laboratories where new treatments could be demonstrated. Bellevue, with ties to three university medical schools (New York University, Columbia, and Cornell), was the first hospital to use hypodermic needles (1856) and to provide an ambulance service (1869), innovations thereafter introduced to the western part of the state by Buffalo General, affiliated with University of Buffalo Medical College. Patients benefited, and the reputation of public institutions for the sick improved.

As Catholic immigration, particularly from Ireland and Germany, mushroomed in midcentury, religious orders established institutions where the newcomers would feel welcome, where their languages were spoken, and where their religious traditions might be continued. In addition to the Buffalo hospital bearing their

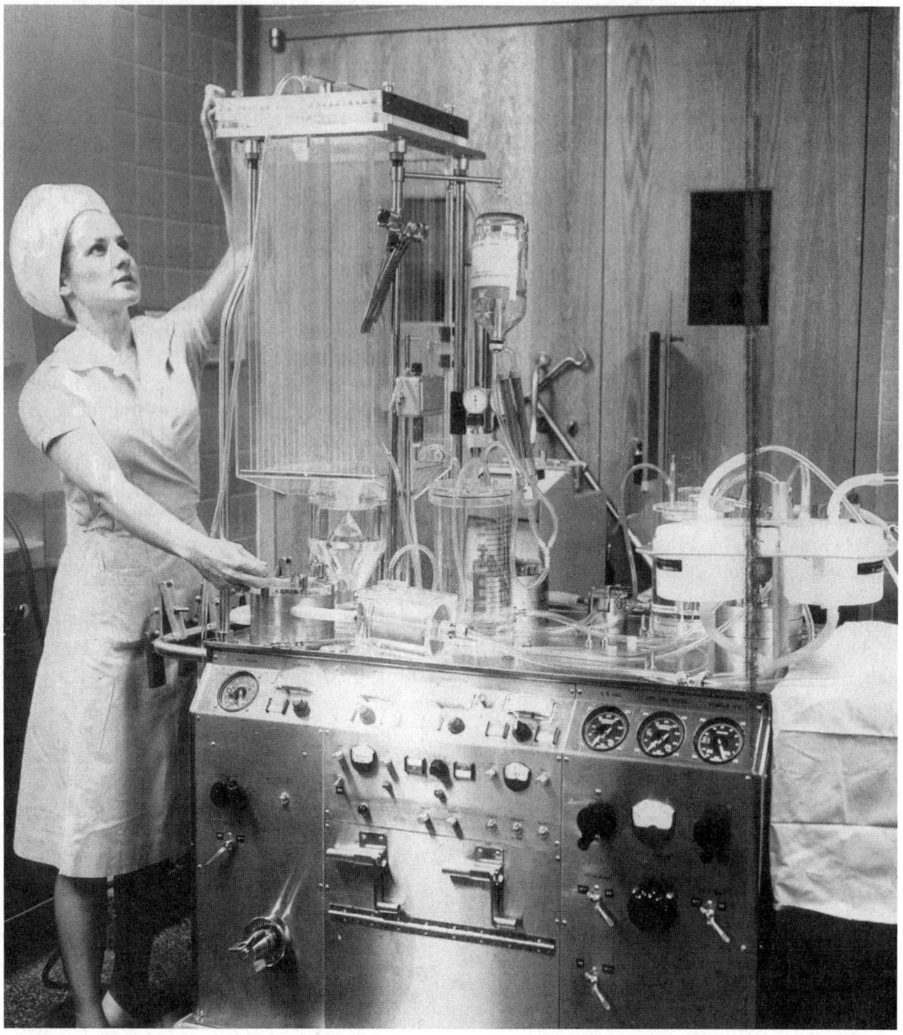

Heart-lung machine used in open-heart surgery at the SUNY Upstate Medical University in Syracuse, 1967.

name (1848), the Sisters of Charity opened St. Mary's Hospital in Rochester (1857) and operated Troy Hospital in Rensselaer Co (1850); Franciscans established St. Elizabeth's Hospital in Utica (1866) and St. Joseph's Hospital in Syracuse (1869); and nurses from the Sisters of Mercy created St. Peter's Hospital in Albany (1869). Some of these were operating years before public institutions began serving the same areas. Other religious denominations also started hospitals, such as Syracuse's House of the Good Shepherd (Episcopal, 1872); Albany's Child's Hospital (Episcopal, 1874); Brooklyn's Lutheran Medical Center (1883) and Methodist Hospital (1887); and Manhattan's St. Luke's (Episcopal, 1846), Presbyterian (1872), and Mt. Sinai (founded as Jews' Hospital, 1855).

From midcentury groups of citizens established private, nondenominational hospitals in areas where existing services were overburdened or inferior. By 1847 Brooklyn Hospital had joined New York Hospital in serving the metropolitan area on a voluntary basis, and Albany Hospital in 1849 became the state's first private institution outside the New York City region. The trend accelerated in the decades after the Civil War, the massive casualties of which exposed the inadequacies of existing healthcare resources. German Hospital (1868) and Roosevelt Hospital (1871) were founded in Manhattan, followed by the Syracuse Women's Hospital and Training School for Nurses (1887) and Rochester's Genesee Hospital (1887) and Highland Hospital (1889). By this time, city leaders had designated a segment of their citizenry as the "worthy" poor, who deserved better care than was available in spartan public institutions. Clerks, crafters, abandoned women and children, widows, marooned travelers, and the aged were major concerns.

Voluntary hospitals were directed by boards of private citizens, supported by subscriptions from the public, and run on a tight budget, sometimes depending on individuals for donations of food, linens, and equipment. Physicians treated ward patients free of charge, gaining prestige in return by being associated with the institutions. Although these hospitals were committed to helping the poor, they could also refuse patients who carried a particular disease or exhibited objectionable behavior. Public healthcare institutions, on the other hand, had to accept everyone who entered their doors. As knowledge about diseases and their prevention grew and as treating the sick became more successful, voluntary hospitals increasingly attracted affluent patients by furnishing comfortable private rooms.

Citizens had come to depend on and respect "professional" medicine. Responsibility for promoting and maintaining good health had shifted from the individual to the community. Better-educated physicians and more skillful surgeons, assisted by improving technologies, allowed hospitals to shed their reputation as places of despair. Furthermore, the rising profession of nursing promised women rewarding work in one of the few fields in which formal training gave them respect.

Hospitals in the 20th Century

At the turn of the 20th century patients outside the main urban centers often had to travel considerable distances to find hospital care. But as populations grew, areas that had been rural built their own hospitals, such as Shattuck Memorial (1908) in Ticonderoga (Essex Co), Bassett (1922) in Cooperstown (Otsego Co), and Oneida City (1936) in Madison Co. New suburban hospitals were also created, like Huntington Hospital (1916) in Suffolk Co, and existing ones were expanded. From its original total of nine beds in 1900, Nyack Hospital (Rockland Co) enlarged to 80 in 1926 and to 125 in 1952 (its capacity has since tripled).

More and bigger facilities, however, did not always mean higher standards of care or medical instruction. In 1910 the Flexner Report, a scathing exposé of America's proprietary medical schools and hospitals, resulted in the closing of underfunded and poorly run diploma mills. In 1918 national accreditation of hospitals began, with disastrous results: only 13% of the 692 hospitals reviewed passed. Unsurprisingly, economic factors contributed to the poor performance. Local communities were hard pressed to support the new institutions and services, and access to improved medical techniques threatened to become a prerogative of the wealthy. The 1946 Hill-Burton Act reduced economic and geographic disparities in quality of care by awarding federal funds to rural areas for the construction or upgrade of community hospitals, with the proviso that recipient facilities provide subsidized services to the poor. Low-interest federal loans and other incentives helped urban hospitals to modernize after years of austerity during the depression and World War II.

With regular evaluations, hospitals strove to keep their physical plants and their staffs up to date. Affiliation with university medical schools brought well-trained and research-oriented students to hospital floors, and increasingly full-time professors took over teaching responsibilities from physicians in private practice. The length of hospital stays has declined drastically, partly because of antibiotics and partly because of the lessons of World War II, which demonstrated that surgical patients recovered faster when encouraged early to become physically active. Laparoscopy, a minimally invasive surgical technique using lasers, has shortened recovery times as well. The proliferation of nursing homes and home-care programs have made it possible for many elderly patients and those with chronic conditions to avoid extended hospital stays.

The flow of federal and state funds to healthcare institutions, however, has had mixed results. The character of these institutions, which were formerly supported by religious contributions and community donations, has changed dramatically. The involvement of governmental agencies has led to an emphasis on institutional accountability and frequent reporting, forcing an upsurge in nonmedical staffing. In 1960 the

LARGEST HOSPITALS IN NEW YORK STATE

Name	Certified Beds	County
Mount Sinai Hospital	1,171	New York
Bellevue Hospital Center	912	New York
Beth Israel Medical Center/Petrie Campus	894	New York
Kings County Hospital Center	888	Kings
New York–Presbyterian Hospital at Columbia Presbyterian Center	888	New York
New York–Presbyterian Hospital at New York Weill Cornell Center	880	New York
New York University Hospitals Center	879	New York
Long Island Jewish Medical Center	827	Nassau
St. Vincent's Hospital Manhattan	758	New York
Strong Memorial Hospital	750	Monroe
Buffalo General Hospital	742	Erie
North Shore University Hospital	731	Nassau
Maimonides Medical Center	705	Kings
Montefiore Medical Center at Henry and Lucy Moses Division	679	Bronx
Lenox Hill Hospital	652	New York
Westchester Medical Center	635	Westchester
Albany Medical Center Hospital	631	Albany
Nassau University Medical Center	631	Nassau
Winthrop-University Hospital	591	Nassau
New York Methodist Hospital	570	Kings
Crouse Hospital	566	Onondaga
Memorial Hospital for Cancer and Allied Diseases	565	New York
Erie County Medical Center	550	Erie
St. Luke's–Roosevelt Hospital at St. Luke's Hospital Division	541	New York
Rochester General Hospital	528	Monroe

Source: New York State Department of Health, http://www.health.state.ny.us/nysdoh/hospital/main.htm.

Hospital Review and Planning Council began to work with regional hospital councils to monitor services statewide, and for 10 years beginning in 1975 a Health Planning Committee assisted the governor in formulating health policy. In the late 20th century, in an effort to increase efficiency but maintain autonomy, hospitals and related healthcare facilities in some localities began merging into large systems, promising patients "seamless" care from the cradle to the grave. Examples include Continuum Health Partners in New York City; North Shore–Long Island Jewish Health System; Health Quest Systems in Dutchess and Putnam Cos; Northeast Health in the Capital District; United Health Services, comprising hospitals in Broome, Chenango, and Delaware Cos; Bassett Healthcare in and around the Mohawk Valley; and Kaleida Health in the Buffalo vicinity.

Early in the 21st century healthcare consortia battle strenuously for personnel, patients, and resources. Competition among health insurance providers has likewise intensified, creating a volatile healthcare environment in which institutions with century-long traditions are regularly forced to close or downgrade. In 2001 Genesee Hospital closed its doors and Crouse Hospital in Syracuse (descendant of the Women's Hospital) filed for bankruptcy.

See also LABOR; NURSES.

Atwater, Edward C. "Women, Surgeons, and a Worthy Enterprise: The General Hospital Comes to Upper New York State." In *The American General Hospital: Communities and Social Contexts,* ed. Diana E. Long and Janet Lynne Golden (Ithaca: Cornell Univ Press, 1989)

Dowling, Harry F. *City Hospitals: The Undercare of the Underprivileged* (Cambridge, Mass: Harvard Univ Press, 1982)

Ludmerer, Kenneth. *Learning to Heal: The Development of American Medical Education* (1985; repr Baltimore: Johns Hopkins Univ Press, 1996)

New York State. Department of Health. *Annual Reports* (Albany: Author, 1880–)

Opdycke, Sandra. *No One Was Turned Away: The Role of Public Hospitals in New York City since 1900* (New York: Oxford Univ Press, 1999)

Richardson, Jean. "Catholic Religious Women as Institutional Innovators: The Sisters of Charity and the Rise of the Modern Urban Hospital in Buffalo, NY, 1848–1900" (PhD diss, SUNY Buffalo, 1996)

Rosner, David. *A Once Charitable Enterprise: Hospitals and Health Care in Brooklyn and New York, 1885–1915* (1982; repr Cambridge: Cambridge Univ Press, 2004)

Starr, Paul. *The Social Transformation of American Medicine* (New York: Basic Books, 1982)

Teresa K. Lehr

health maintenance organizations. See HEALTHCARE AND HOSPITALS; INSURANCE, HEALTH.

Hearst, William Randolph (*b* San Francisco, 29 Apr 1863; *d* Beverly Hills, Calif, 14 Aug 1951). Publisher and politician. The son of Phoebe Apperson Hearst, a future philanthropist, and George Hearst, a millionaire miner, William Randolph Hearst's publishing career began in March 1887 when he was named editor and publisher of his father's newspaper, the *San Francisco Examiner.* Having boosted the circulation and reputation of the *Examiner,* in 1895 he bought the *New York Morning Journal,* which he redesigned and published as, in turn, the *New York Journal,* the *New York Journal and Advertiser,* the *New York American and Journal,* and then, beginning in 1902, the *New York American.* In 1896 he began publication of a second English language New York City paper, the *New York Evening Journal.* The two papers were consolidated in 1937 into the *New York Journal-American,* which ceased publication in 1966. The Hearst publishing empire was extended into magazines with the purchase of *Cosmopolitan* in 1905, *Good Housekeeping,* and *World Today,* later renamed *Hearst's International,* in 1911, and *Harper's Bazaar* in 1912. During the first three decades of the 20th century Hearst also continued to acquire newspapers, including several in New York State: the *Syracuse Telegram* and the *Rochester Journal* in 1922, the *Albany Times-Union* in 1924, and the *Syracuse Journal* in 1925. He began publication of his only tabloid, the *New York Daily Mirror,* in 1924.

Hearst effectively used his publications to make a name for himself in the 1890s and 1900s as a leading urban progressive, a "trust-buster," and an advocate of municipal control of public utilities. Nominated for Congress from a Manhattan district by the Tammany Hall–controlled Democratic Party, Hearst served two terms from 1903 to 1907. In 1904 he campaigned for the Democratic presidential nomination. Even without the support of Tammany, he mounted an effective national campaign but came in second for the nomination, losing to another New Yorker, Alton B. Parker. In 1905 he ran for mayor of New York City as the candidate of his own third party, the Municipal Ownership League but, through blatant electoral fraud, lost to Mayor George B. McClellan Jr, the Tammany candidate. In 1906, this time with the support of Tammany Hall, Hearst ran for governor of New York State and was narrowly defeated by Charles Evans Hughes, the Republican candidate backed by Pres Theodore Roosevelt.

In 1914 Hearst entered the moving picture industry as producer of newsreels, serial films, and features. His first serial film, *The Perils of Pauline,* was shot and edited in Ithaca. In 1919 he formed Cosmopolitan Productions, entered into a partnership with Adolph Zukor to distribute his feature films, and built one of the largest moving-picture studios on the East Coast in Upper Manhattan. Although Hearst would, by the middle 1920s, spend most of his time in California at his San Simeon estate, he kept his Manhattan residence on Riverside Drive and continued to invest heavily in New York City real estate. In 1935 *Fortune* magazine assessed the value of these holdings at $41 million. Much of Hearst's property in the city had to be sold in 1937 when the Hearst Corp came close to bankruptcy as a result of declining publishing revenues, accumulated debt, and Hearst's own extravagant spending on art and real estate. Hearst was never divorced from his wife Millicent, who remained in New York City with their five sons, but he lived with actress Marion Davies for more than a quarter century before his death.

Nasaw, David. *The Chief: The Life of William Randolph Hearst* (Boston: Houghton Mifflin, 2000)

Procter, Ben. *William Randolph Hearst: The Early Years, 1863–1910* (New York: Oxford Univ Press, 1998)

David Nasaw

Hebrew Union College–Jewish Institute of Religion. The Jewish Institute of Religion (JIR) was founded by Stephen S. Wise in 1921 and opened in 1922 on West 68th St in Midtown

Manhattan. Wise objected to the anti-Zionism of the Hebrew Union College (HUC) in Cincinnati and wanted a school where he could train rabbis to serve *Klal Israel*, all of the Jewish people. The faculty included scholars such as Harry A. Wolfson, Salo W. Baron, Julian Obermann, and Shalom Spiegel, and prominent European scholars such as Ismar Elbogen and Felix Perles, who came on a visiting or part-time basis. Following a diminishing of ideological differences, the two institutions merged in 1950 to form HUC-JIR. In 1954 the school added a third center in Los Angeles and in 1963 a fourth in Jerusalem. A new campus, the Brookdale Center, opened in 1979 and is located next to New York University (NYU) on West 4th St in Greenwich Village in Lower Manhattan. It includes the Minnie Petrie Synagogue, which displays Israeli artist Yaacov Agam's stained-glass windows of the 12 tribes. The Klau Library has over 130,000 volumes of Hebrew literature, Jewish history and thought, and Jewish music. Because of its proximity to NYU, HUC-JIR has been able to offer joint courses and cosponsor conferences with the Skirball Department of Hebrew and Judaic Studies. The New York City campus houses the School of Sacred Music, which is the main professional program for the training of Reform cantors. In 2003 the school had 155 students studying at the New York City campus.

Karff, Samuel E. *Hebrew Union College–Jewish Institute of Religion at 100 Years* (Cincinnati: Hebrew Union College Press, 1976)

Dana Evan Kaplan

Hebron [HE-BRON]. Town (pop 1,773) in E central Washington Co. A patent encompassing this town was granted to Highland Scots who fought in the French and Indian War. Settled in 1769–70, the firstcomers were joined by some of the Scots patentees in 1774–75. Meetings were held by 1774 as the district of Black Creek, but the settlement formed as a town in 1786. Red slate was quarried at Slateville from 1853 to the 1940s. West Hebron had a starch factory after the Civil War and, in the late 19th and early 20th centuries, produced seeds and seed potatoes. Some vacation-home development began in the 1970s, but the predominant land use in the early 21st century remains farming.

R. Paul McCarty

Heck [née Ruckle], Barbara (*b* Ballingrane, Ireland, 1734; *d* Prescott [now in Ont], 17 Aug 1804). Lay Methodist leader. Barbara Ruckle became a Methodist about 1752 and married Paul Heck in 1760. The Hecks, with other Irish Palatines, immigrated to North America, arriving in New York City on 10 Aug 1760. Though loyal Methodists, they attended the Trinity Lutheran Church because there was no Methodist society in New York City. This changed when, according to tradition, sometime in 1766 Heck discovered her brother and some friends playing cards and, believing this contrary to Methodist principles, angrily swept the cards into the fireplace. She thereafter went to her cousin Philip Embury, who had been a Methodist preacher in Ireland, and urged him to resume Methodist preaching. In October 1766 Embury began preaching in his home to a small group that included the Hecks and a slave woman named Betty. This meeting marks the origin of Methodism in New York. Embury's home was too small to accommodate the growing Methodist congregation. After meeting for a while in a rigging loft at 120 William St, with Heck's encouragement and design they built a permanent stone chapel on John St in Manhattan (now John Street United Methodist Church), which officially opened on 30 Oct 1768. Around 1770 the Hecks moved to Camden Valley [now in Washington Co] and were active in Methodist work in nearby Cambridge. After the Revolutionary War began, the Hecks, who were loyalists, moved to Canada, where they continued to support Methodism and founded at least one Methodist society. For her remarkable piety and role in the denomination, Heck is known as the "Mother of American Methodism."

Baker, Frank. *From Wesley to Asbury* (Durham, NC: Duke Univ Press, 1976)
Crook, William. *Ireland and the Centenary of American Methodism* (London: Hamilton, Adams, 1866)

Charles Yrigoyen Jr

Heck, Oswald D. (*b* Schenectady, 13 Feb 1902; *d* Schenectady, 21 May 1959). Speaker of the assembly. Raised by German immigrant parents, Heck attended Union College, graduating in 1924. Enrolling in Albany Law School, he dropped out after one year and completed his legal education by reading the law, and was admitted to the state bar in 1928. Elected as a Republican to the state assembly from Schenectady in 1931, with exceptional debating skills, Heck was chosen as Speaker in 1936. He occupied the post for 22 consecutive years (1937–59), making him the assembly's longest-serving Speaker (twice as long as any predecessor). From 1937 to 1941 Heck led a successful battle against Democratic governor Herbert H. Lehman to achieve greater legislative control over the state budget. After Republican Thomas E. Dewey's 1942 election as governor, Heck and Dewey (who held similar views on the state government's need to expand social policy) formed a close political partnership. Between 1943 and 1954, Heck guided Dewey's agenda through the assembly, leading to tremendous growth in state government: the state budget rose 304% in this period. During World War II Heck also headed the state's childcare program that provided childcare for mothers employed in defense plants (at its height in July 1945 more than 10,800 children were enrolled statewide). As Speaker, Heck's remarkable ability to muster support for controversial measures was demonstrated in the passage, over intense opposition from his own party, of Dewey's Ives-Quinn bill in 1945 (America's first nondiscrimination employment law). In the early 1950s Heck became the champion for a state compulsory automobile insurance law. After overcoming significant legislative resistance, he successfully directed the legislation through the assembly in 1956, signed later that year by Gov W. Averell Harriman. In 1958 Heck made a drive for his party's gubernatorial nomination but abandoned the bid when polling showed he could not defeat Nelson A. Rockefeller. A liberal Republican, Heck served as Speaker under four governors and was perhaps the state's most influential legislator of the 20th century. As of 2002 he remains the last assembly Speaker not from New York City or Long Island.

Smith, Richard N. *Thomas E. Dewey and His Times* (New York: Simon & Schuster, 1982)

Tod M. Ottman

Hector. Town (pop 4,854) in NE Schuyler Co. The town is bounded on the west by Seneca Lake where high bluffs, upward of 300 ft (90 m), rise almost perpendicular; many streams and waterfalls, notably Hector Falls, drop into the lake. Settled in 1791, the town was formed in 1802 from Ovid (Seneca Co) and was, in sequence, part of five different counties before Schuyler Co was formed. The town was served by the main line of the Lehigh Valley Railroad (1892). In the late 19th century, fruit baskets, barrels, and crates were manufactured in at least seven shops in town; other products included mittens and grain cradles. In 2002 Hector was noted for its fruit-growing industry, primarily grapes. The Hazlitt 1852 Vineyards and Chateau LaFayette Reneau wineries are located in town. Tourism is also important to the economy. Most of the 16,302-acre (6,597 ha) Finger Lakes National Forest (1985), the only national forest in New York State, is located in the town and encompasses the Hector Backbone, a high ridge with dramatic vistas.

Glenda Gephart

Hedrick, U(lysses) P(rentiss) (*b* Independence, Iowa, 15 Jan 1870; *d* Clifton Springs, Ontario Co, 14 Nov 1951). Horticultural scientist and administrator, historian, and author. Hedrick grew up on a farm on the northern Michigan frontier, graduated from Michigan Agricultural College in Lansing in 1893, and served as an assistant horticulturalist there for two years while earning an MS degree. After teaching at Oregon Agricultural College (now Oregon State University, Corvallis), Utah Agricultural College (now Utah State University, Logan), and his alma mater, in 1905 he was appointed a horticulturalist at the New York State Agricultural Experiment Station at Geneva (Ontario Co). He was promoted to vice director in 1921 and became director in 1928.

For the next decade he presided over a professional staff that grew from 56 to 91 people and was integrated into the State College of Agriculture at Cornell. Hedrick collaborated with station colleagues to publish popular illustrated books on different fruit of New York State, beginning with *The Apples of New York* (1905). His best-known independent publication was *A History of Agriculture in the State of New York* (1933), noted for its focus on the social and cultural aspects of rural life. During Hedrick's years at the station, many new strains of fruit trees, grapes, and berries were developed. He served as president of the New York State Agricultural Society (1936) and various horticultural associations. Hedrick continued such voluntary service after his retirement in 1938 and published *Fruits for the Home Garden* (1944), *Grapes and Wines from Home Vineyards* (1945), memoirs of his youth, *The Land of the Crooked Tree* (1948), and *A History of Horticulture in America to 1860* (1950). He also pursued his hobby of collecting rare books and etchings.

Gates, Paul. "Ulysses Prentiss Hedrick: Horticulturist and Historian," *New York History* 47 (July 1966): 219–47

Kathryn A. Boardman

Hell Gate Bridge. A 1,017 ft (310 m) span, this two-hinged steel arch is the chief bridge in a 17,000 ft (5,182 m) viaduct between the Bronx and western Long Island carrying New York Connecting Railroad over Hell Gate, a tidal strait between Ward's Island, an island in the East River, and Queens. Hell Gate Bridge was built jointly by Pennsylvania Railroad and New York, New Haven and Hartford Railroad. Gustav Lindenthal served as chief engineer, assisted by Othmar H. Ammann and David B. Steinman. When completed in 1917 it was the longest steel arch in the world, at a cost of $20 million, and formed the final link in the Northeast Corridor, the busiest intercity passenger rail route in the United States connecting eastern seaboard cities between Boston and Washington, DC. Hell Gate Bridge carried heavy freight traffic until the Penn Central merger of 1968, when much traffic was diverted to a Hudson River crossing at Castleton (Rensselaer Co). At the beginning of the 21st century, about 24 passenger trains traveled the bridge per average weekday. The structure's grace belies its massive scale, which dwarfs the railroad trains crossing it. Capable of carrying trains on all four of its tracks at once, Hell Gate is one of the strongest long-span bridges ever built.

Reier, Sharon. *Bridges of New York* (New York: Quadrant Press, 1977)

Thomas R. Flagg

Hempstead. Town (pop 733,432) in Nassau Co. English proprietors received a patent from New Netherland director Willem Kieft in 1644, a year after purchasing land from the Indians. The "town spot" (now Village of Hempstead) was in the center of the island, at the southern edge of the Hempstead Plains and between two streams (now underground). Most of the settlers left the town spot to live on their farms. Others moved east and west to establish other towns. Early Hempstead residents farmed, raised sheep and cattle, fished in streams and bays, and hunted deer and wildfowl. The Hempstead Plains were common pastureland, and Rockaway and other peninsulas were also used for grazing. Salt hay from South Shore marshes was harvested in the fall for fodder. Streams powered paper mills, sawmills, and gristmills.

In 1775 Hempstead pledged its support to the king and refused to elect representatives to a provincial convention that was to select delegates to the Second Continental Congress. The patriot sentiment was strongest in the northern part of town, and it seceded on 23 Sept 1775, creating de facto the town of North Hempstead. To protect cattle and sheep from the British, the patriot authorities ordered stock to be taken inland, and 1,400 cattle were driven to the Hempstead Plains. After the British victory at the Battle of Long Island on 27 Aug 1776, however, the occupation of Long Island began. The 16th and 17th Light Horse Dragoons wintered in Hempstead, using the Presbyterian Church as a barracks and riding school; other British and Hessian troops were stationed elsewhere in the town. Long Island supplied food and firewood for the British forces in New York City. In 1783 hundreds of Hempstead loyalists left for Nova Scotia and New Brunswick. The state legislature divided Hempstead in 1784, officially confirming North Hempstead's 1775 secession.

In the 19th century Hempstead was primarily agricultural and provided food for Brooklyn and New York City, particularly fish, shellfish, dairy products, and vegetables. The Queens County Agricultural Society held its first fair in Hempstead in 1842, and the town gave the society 40 acres (16 ha) for its fairgrounds in 1866, where the Mineola Fair was held until 1952. Rockaway, with large hotels, was a popular seaside resort in the 19th century. Among the larger businesses in the early 20th century were John Lewis Childs's seed business in Floral Park (to 1923) and, in Garden City, the Curtiss aircraft factory (1918–31), and Doubleday's publishing plant (1910–88).

When New York City expanded in 1898 and incorporated western Long Island towns, Hempstead lost much of the Rockaway Peninsula to Queens. After Nassau Co was formed in 1899, Mineola became the county seat, with the courthouse and other county buildings located on land donated by the Garden City Co and later on the Agricultural Society's former fairgrounds. The flat Hempstead Plains had been used for horse racing beginning in 1668. Colonial militia trained on the plains, and military camps included Camp Winfield Scott (1861), Camp Black (1898), and Camp Mills (1917–18) in East Garden City. The plains became the site of many pioneering aviation flights in the early decades of the 20th century with airfields, including Roosevelt Field (1918–51) and Mitchel Field (an army air base, 1918–61).

Brooklyn bought a number of ponds in Hempstead in the mid–19th century to supply its water and constructed a storage reservoir, pumping station, and conduit. Sunrise Highway (Rte 27) was built over the pipeline route in the 1920s after New York City had shifted to upstate water. Robert Moses secured much of the water supply land for parks and parkways, creating Valley Stream and Hempstead Lake State Parks (1925) and the Southern State, Meadowbrook, and Wantagh State Parkways. A referendum in 1926 ceded the town's barrier beach to the state, enabling the creation of Jones Beach State Park (1927).

Commuting to New York City became more practical after the Long Island Rail Road's tunnel under the East River provided a direct connection to Manhattan in 1910. Population increased dramatically in the next two decades in railroad suburbs in the western part of the town. It more than doubled in the 1920s and then nearly tripled from 1940 to 1960 with Levittown and other housing developments. Large shopping centers opened in 1956 on two former airfields, Roosevelt Field (East Garden City) and Green Acres (Valley Stream). The town's population peaked in 1970 and thereafter has been relatively stable because little land is available for development and the population is aging. Diversity has increased in recent decades, particularly the Latino population with an influx of Salvadoran, Columbian, and Dominican immigrants.

Hempstead has the largest population of any town in the state and is the most populous municipality in the state besides New York City. It encompasses 142.6 miles^2 (369.33 km^2) and has 32 school districts, 22 incorporated villages, and 34 unincorporated communities. It has been the home base of the powerful Nassau Co Republican Party; J. Russel Sprague, county executive from 1938 to 1952, was the Republican boss in his era. In a revolt against the county's fiscal crisis, two Democrats were elected to the Hempstead town board in 1999, the first since 1905. From 1932 to 2000 Hempstead was governed by four councilmen and two supervisors, each elected at large. The presiding supervisor was the town executive and the two supervisors also sat on the county's Board of Supervisors until replaced by a legislature in 1995. Since then one supervisor is elected in a townwide vote, and the six council members are elected from districts.

Hempstead first adopted a preservation ordinance in 1983. By 2001 it designated 24 buildings as landmarks, including Rock Hall, the town's 1767 house museum in Lawrence. There are numerous other museums, including the Cradle of Aviation Museum and the Long Island Children's Museum in East Garden City. The town owns 1,400 acres (570 ha) of park land including 22 pool complexes, two golf courses, ocean and bay beaches, a marine nature study area, and sport and recreation fields in 46 staffed parks. Annual festivals include Hofstra University's Dutch Festival (May), the Belmont Stakes (June), and Family Festival by the Sea (September), as well as many local community and ethnic festivals.

Natalie A. Naylor

Hempstead. Village (pop 54,554) in Hempstead (Nassau Co). The first English settlers came from Connecticut in 1644. The Duke's Laws convention met at this "town spot" in 1665. The oldest and largest settlement in the area, as well as the marketing and trading center, Hempstead led what would become Nassau Co in many services: newspaper (1831), fire department (1832), village incorporation (1862), and gas streetlights (1866). Population increased significantly beginning in the 1920s. The Franklin Shops (1927–60) were located in a six-story commercial building, the largest business building east of Brooklyn when built, and Hempstead had multistory apartments and department stores by the 1930s. Abraham and Straus (1952–?1992) was the largest department store. Hempstead's business district declined beginning in the 1960s despite urban renewal efforts because of nearby shopping malls. The black population increased beginning in the 1960s and the Latino population in the 1970s. In 2000 African Americans were 52% of the population, and those of Latino ethnicity made up 32% of the population. On the National Register of Historic Places are St. George's Rectory (1793) and Church (1822), and the post office (1933). Museums include the African American Museum of Nassau County and the Hofstra University Museum.

Natalie A. Naylor

Hempstead Plains. Prairie grasslands in Nassau Co. In 1670 Daniel Denton described the plains as "sixteen miles long and four broad" with "very good pasture for sheep or other cattle." As early as 1668 horse racing took place on the plains, and in the same era they were first used for military training. The Town of Hempstead retained most of the plains as common grazing land until 1869, when Alexander T. Stewart purchased 7,170 acres (2,902 ha) to develop Garden City. Originally thought unsuitable for cropland, parts were farmed in the 19th century; others were covered with a profusion of birdfoot violets, which bloomed in May. In the 20th century the treeless plains were used for pioneering flights and for airfields, while military encampments continued at Camp Mills and at Mitchel Field Army Air Corps Base. After World War II the plains were developed to create Levittown and other suburban communities. Nassau Co and the Nature Conservancy are preserving a remnant of 79 acres (32 ha) of the plains on Mitchel Field.

Furman, Gabriel. "The Hempstead Plains" [1845]. In *The Roots and Heritage of Hempstead Town,* ed. Natalie A. Naylor (Interlaken, NY: Heart of the Lakes Publishing, 1994)

Neidich, Carol. "The Hempstead Plains and the Bird-foot Violet," *Long Island Forum* 43 (June 1980): 108–15

Watson, Winslow C. "The Plains of Long Island" [1859], *Nassau County Historical Journal* 17 (Spring 1956): 1–36

Natalie A. Naylor

Henderson. Town (pop 1,377) in SW Jefferson Co. New Englanders settled the town in 1802 and were joined by a colony from Perthshire, Scotland, in 1803. The town was formed from Ellisburg in 1806 and named for William Henderson, the proprietor, who platted Naples [now Henderson Harbor]. It was an important lake port, shipping grain and stock to Kingston, Ont, until *ca* 1870. By the 1840s Henderson was a sports-fishing destination, and tourism has been the town's main industry since the late 19th century. A smallmouth bass tournament and a yacht club regatta are among the town's annual events. Henderson, the childhood home of Charles Grandison Finney, is the site of Westcott Beach State Park and of Henderson Shores State Unique Area. Association Island, now a recreational vehicle resort, was a retreat for General Electric employees from 1912 to 1956.

Laura Lynne Scharer

Henrietta. Town (pop 39,028) in S Monroe Co. Settled in 1806 after an abortive attempt between 1790 and 1792, the town was formed from Pittsford in 1818. The town was primarily agricultural, with German farmers arriving after 1850 and Italians in the 20th century. Ellwanger and Barry operated 134 acres (54 ha) of nursery land from 1850 to 1920. F. B. Pease Co, makers of food-processing machinery, moved to Henrietta in 1927. From 1939 to 1973 the town was the site of the Ray Hylan School of Aeronautics. Aside from cottages at River Meadows in the 1920s, there was little suburban development until 1954, when the West Henrietta Thruway exit opened. The 120-acre (49 ha) Genesee Valley Regional Market (1956) is a centrally located food distribution center that leases space to 200 tenants. Industrial operations include General Electric Supply Co (1956, sales), McKesson-Robbins (1958, warehouse), Strasenburgh Labs (1958), and Riverwood, the Kodak Marketing Education Center. Rochester Institute of Technology moved to Henrietta in 1968. Although known for Marketplace Mall and the Jefferson Rd commercial corridor, only 6% of its land is zoned for commercial use, while 80% is zoned residential, of which about half is undeveloped. Antoinette Brown Blackwell (1825–1921), the first American woman to be ordained a minister, was a native of Henrietta.

Carolyn Vacca

Henry, Edward Lamson (*b* Charleston, SC, 12 Jan 1841; *d* Ellenville, Ulster Co, 11 May 1919). Genre artist. Henry lived in New York City from the age of 7, studied at the Pennsylvania Academy of Fine Arts in Philadelphia, and in 1860 went to Paris, where he studied with Charles Gleyre and Gustave Courbet. Returning from Europe, Henry made New York City his home and from 1862 to 1885 kept a studio at the Tenth Street Studio Building along with many of the city's foremost artists. In 1869 Henry was elected to full membership in the National Academy of Design. His scenes of 18th- and early 19th-century life appealed to audiences nostalgic for colonial and antebellum America. Antiquarian by nature, Henry used his collection of antiques, architectural elements, and vehicles as props in numerous genre scenes. After 1883 Henry and his wife, Frances Livingston Wells of Johnstown (Fulton Co), spent summers at the house they built at the Cragsmoor art colony near Ellenville (Ulster Co), and in 1887 this became their home. Henry was involved in several historic preservation efforts, including an unsuccessful letter-writing campaign (1913–18) to New York City officials and the *New York Times* against the destruction of St. John's Church on Varick St. One of the most popular artists of his time, Henry depicted numerous historic New York State buildings and landmarks in his compositions.

McCausland, Elizabeth. *The Life and Work of Edward Lamson Henry, NA, 1841–1919.* New York State Museum Bulletin, no. 339 (Albany: Univ of the State of New York, 1945)

Ronald J. Burch

Henry, Joseph (*b* Albany, 17 Dec 1797; *d* Washington, DC, 13 May 1878). Scientist. Born to poverty, Henry attended elementary school first in Albany and then after age 7 in nearby Galway (Saratoga Co). Henry's father, William, was a teamster who died by the time Henry was 13. As a teenager Henry took an apprenticeship with an Albany watchmaker. Intrigued by science, Henry returned to school at the Albany Academy in 1819, where he graduated three years later; he stayed on at the academy as an assistant lecturer in chemistry through 1824, and he also took a series of teaching jobs in and around the city. While in Albany, Henry experimented with electromagnets, which led him in 1831 to invent the world's first electric (reciprocating) motor. Henry was also interested in meteorology, a passion he cultivated by collecting weather data for the New York State Board of Regents. This foreshadowed a nationwide meteorological program Henry would establish, the first of its kind in the United States and a precursor to the National Weather Service. Henry's work on the electric motor brought him significant national attention, and in 1832 he accepted a chair at the College of New Jersey (now Princeton University).

While at Princeton, Henry continued research into fundamental ideas about electricity and magnetism. He was invited by Michael Faraday to lecture on the mathematical theory of electromagnetism at the Royal Institution in London in 1837. In addition to important theoretical discoveries, including the phenomena of induction, his work on electromagnetic relays contributed to the development of the telegraph. Henry was appointed chief executive officer of the newly created Smithsonian Institution in 1846. He shaped the early history of the Smithsonian with his particular understanding of conditions for the practice of science in the United States. Henry believed that the top priority at the Smithsonian was the support of research. He fought off efforts to use the Smithsonian's endowment to establish a library, a popular museum, or a lecture series or to support applied research. Instead Henry chose to support research and scholarly publications in those fields of science he considered to be most rigorous, such as physics and chemistry, as well as those he thought showed promise, such as natural history, meteorology, and anthropology. Henry's articulation and staunch defense of the research ideal created a context for the first major institutional support of scientific investigation in America. By the Gilded Age Henry was perhaps America's most prominent scientist, and in 1868

Silhouette of Joseph Henry; detail by Augustin Edouart, 1843.

he was awarded the presidency of the National Academy of Sciences. Three years later he was appointed chairman of the United States Light-House Board. He held both of these positions, plus his position as head of the Smithsonian, until his death. In 1893 the standard electrical unit of inductive resistance was named the "henry."

Moyer, Albert. *Joseph Henry: The Rise of an American Scientist* (Washington, DC: Smithsonian Institution Press, 1997)

Loren Butler Feffer

Hepburn, A(lonzo) Barton (*b* Colton, St. Lawrence Co, 24 July 1846; *d* New York City, 25 Jan 1922). Banker. Raised on a farm, Hepburn received his early education at St. Lawrence Academy (1861–67) in Potsdam. He moved on to Middlebury College in Vermont in 1868 but left the following year due to economic circumstances. He read the law at an Ogdensburg (St. Lawrence Co) law firm and was admitted to the state bar in 1871. Three years later he won a seat in the state assembly as a Republican. In July 1879 Hepburn led an assembly investigation into rate collusion between state railroads and the Standard Oil Co (the probe was one of the earliest investigations of the petroleum giant). Hepburn left the assembly in 1880 when Gov Alonzo B. Cornell appointed him to head the Banking Department, a state post he held for three years. In 1883 Hepburn returned to St. Lawrence Co, where he was successful in the timber trade. In 1893 he was appointed as president of the Third National Bank, a major New York City financial institution. Hepburn moved to Chase National, another New York City bank, six years later. Remaining the rest of his life at Chase, Hepburn served in numerous capacities, becoming board chairman in 1911. Under his guidance Chase's deposits mushroomed from $41 million in 1899 to $315 million by 1922. Viewed as a man of tremendous integrity, Hepburn was integral to Chase's rise as a premier financial institutions in America. Hepburn closely advised US Sen Carter Glass in his drafting of the 1913 Federal Reserve Act that established the Federal Reserve Bank system. A notable philanthropist, he gave away more than $5 million of his personal fortune, much of which went to the North Country. Hepburn gave $1.1 million to the hospital at Ogdensburg, $535,000 to build seven public libraries in St. Lawrence Co, and $276,500 to St. Lawrence University.

Bishop, Joseph Bucklin. *A. Barton Hepburn: His Life and Service to His Time* (New York: C. Scribner's Sons, 1923)

Tod M. Ottman

Herkimer. Town (pop 9,962) and village (pop 7,498) in central Herkimer Co. Settled in 1725–26 by Palatine Germans and known as German Flatts, it was attacked and mostly destroyed in 1757 during the French and Indian War. Fort Dayton (1776) was a major defensive fortification on the western frontier during the Revolutionary War. A district was formed in 1772 as German Flatts, but when the town was formed in 1788 it was named instead for Gen Nicholas Herkimer. Becoming the county seat in 1791, the future village was platted in 1793 and incorporated in 1807. The Herkimer Manufacturing and Hydraulic Co (1833–59) dammed West Canada Creek and created a canal to supply waterpower, attracting factories producing cotton and woolen cloth, and, later, hats, paper, broom handles, plaster, shoes, and wooden products. The Utica and Schenectady Railroad (1836; later New York Central) supported the industries with shipping. Major firms included Herkimer Paper (1866–early 1970s; became International Paper in 1898), H. M. Quackenbush (1871; air pistols, nutcrackers, and other products), Standard Furniture (1886–1976; office desks; employed 675 workers in 1912), Marks Knitting, and Union Mills Knitting. A small Jewish community formed in the 1850s; Polish and Italian workers came for factory jobs later in the 19th century. Between 1880 and 1920 Herkimer's population nearly quadrupled, peaking at 12,327 in 1930 and then slowly declining. In the mid–20th century, the Library Bureau opened a plant (1947–1990s) and Mohawk Data Services (1964; data recorders) operated plants both in the village and at East Herkimer. The New York State Thruway opened its Herkimer exit in 1964. The 2002 closing of the East Herkimer plant of Guilford Mills was a significant loss of employment; H. M. Quackenbush, an innovative metal finishing firm headquartered in the village, remains family owned. Herkimer is the site of Herkimer County Community College (1967). Born and raised in Herkimer, boxer Lou Ambers (Luigi Giuseppe D'Ambrosio), the "Herkimer Hurricane," was a lightweight world champion (1936–38, 1939–40).

James Crawford

Herkimer, Nicholas [Herchheimer, Johan Nicholas] (*b* German Flatts [now in Herkimer Co], ?1728; *d* Herkimer Home [now Danube, Herkimer Co], ?17 Aug 1777). Militia officer. Herkimer was from a prosperous and influential Palatine family in the Mohawk Valley. As a second lieutenant in the militia during the French and Indian War, he commanded a successful defense of Fort Herkimer in what is now German Flatts on 30 Apr 1758. Herkimer attended the first meeting of the Tryon County Committee of Safety on 24 May 1775 and served as its chair from June to December of that year. On 26 Aug 1775 the committee elected Herkimer commander of the Tryon County Militia. The New York Provincial Convention commissioned him a brigadier general of militia on 5 Sept 1776. Herkimer's troops were ambushed at the Battle of Oriskany on 6 Aug 1777 while attempting to relieve the siege of Fort Stanwix [now Rome, Oneida Co]. Wounded in one leg, which was then amputated, Herkimer died shortly after the battle. His home, built in 1764, is maintained as a state historic site.

Herkimer Home State Historic Site in Little Falls, built in the 1750s.

Penrose, Maryly B. *Mohawk Valley in the Revolution: Committee of Safety Papers and Genealogical Compendium* (Franklin Park, NJ: Liberty Bell Associates, 1978)

Christine Sternberg Patrick

Herkimer County (1,411 mi²/3,654 km²; pop 64,427). Created in 1791 from Montgomery Co and named after Revolutionary War general Nicholas Herkimer. Subsequent boundary changes occurred with the creation of Onondaga (1794), Chenango (1798), and Oneida (1798) Cos. Territory was also lost to Montgomery (1797) and Clinton (1801) but gained from Otsego (1816) and Montgomery (1817). Herkimer Co is presently subdivided into the City of Little Falls and 19 towns that contain 9 incorporated villages. The Village of Herkimer serves as the county seat. Elevation ranges from approximately 300 feet (90 m) where the Mohawk River leaves the county to over 2,756 feet (840 m) on an unnamed summit in the Town of Ohio. Herkimer Co straddles three landform provinces. The far south lies within the Susquehanna Hills subregion of the Appalachian Upland where ice-rounded hills typically rise several hundred feet above a base elevation that is from 1,000 to 1,500 feet (300–460 m) above mean sea level. The region is underlain by Devonian and Silurian sandstones and shales. The Mohawk Valley subregion of the Hudson-Mohawk Lowland lies immediately to the north. Here the Mohawk River flows through an entrenched inner valley that narrows and becomes more sharply defined to the east. The surrounding country lies 200–700 feet (60–210 m) above the river's floodplain.

Bedrock consists of Ordovician shales, siltstones, limestones, dolomites, and some Cambrian dolomites. The northern two-thirds of the county fall within the Adirondack Upland, specifically the Western Adirondack Hills and the Adirondack Low Mountains, where Precambrian crystalline silicates, interspersed with some Middle Proterozoic marble, form the bedrock. The Adirondack Hills stretch along the western margins in the north and turn southeast across the county. The low mountain country in the northeast is higher (by nearly 1,000 ft/300 m) and significantly more rugged. Herkimer Co was glaciated, as evidenced by extensive deposits of glacial till in the south, outwash and lake deposits in the lowlands, and numerous Adirondack water bodies whose existence stems from moraine deposits that serve as natural dams. Herkimer Co's most famous geological characteristic is the presence of Herkimer diamonds, quartz crystals of some beauty but little value; they are mined for and by tourists and rock and mineral collectors.

The county lies within four major watersheds. Ocquionis Creek and the Unadilla River in the far south are part of the Susquehanna River system. The remainder of the county's southern third, including East and West Canada Creeks and Mill Creek, empty into the east-flowing Mohawk River. Most of the north is part of the Black River watershed. Besides the headwaters of the Black, important tributaries include the Beaver, Independence, and Moose Rivers. The extreme north is drained by the West and Middle Branches of the Oswegatchie River, which empties into the St. Lawrence. Arable soils are limited to the county's southern third. The most extensive areas of superior farmland are in the

eastern half north of the Mohawk River and in the high, hilly country of the far south. Lands north of the Poland-Dolgeville line hold no agricultural potential.

Herkimer Co's climate is humid-continental. Mean January temperatures range from 13°F (-11°C) at Stillwater Reservoir in the western Adirondacks to 26°F (-3°C) at Little Falls in the Mohawk Valley. Below 0°F (-18°C) temperatures are a significant part of every winter, especially in the north, where the nation's coldest temperature for the day is occasionally reported. Mean July temperatures range from 65°F (18°C) at Stillwater Reservoir to 73°F (23°C) at Little Falls. Daytime highs reach or exceed 90°F (32°C) every summer, most frequently in the south. Average annual precipitation ranges from 42 inches (107 cm) at Little Falls to 52 inches (132 cm) in Russia. Seasonal snowfall amounts vary from 71 inches (180 cm) near West Winfield in the southwest to over 200 inches (508 cm) near Old Forge. The primeval forest cover consisted of three communities. Alleghenian hardwoods dominated by beech, sugar maple, hemlock, white pine, and basswood covered the county south of the Mohawk River. Arable lands to the north supported an Adirondack hardwood community principally of beech, sugar maple, yellow birch, hemlock, and white pine. The rest of the county was cloaked in a mix of Adirondack hardwoods, along with red spruce, balsam fir, and paper birch. The proportion of spruce and fir increased with elevation. In 2000 over three-quarters of the county was covered with second- and third-growth forest. The northern two-thirds of Herkimer is within the Adirondack Park.

American Indians and Early Settlement

Herkimer Co has been inhabited for about 10,000 years. An Owasco period (*ca* 1300–1700) site has been excavated at Weaver Lake in the south. The forerunners of the Iroquois established themselves in the area *ca* AD 1000. The Mohawk were the primary inhabitants. Small numbers of French, Dutch, and British explorers, traders, and missionaries began to penetrate the area by the late 1500s. The Mohawk allied themselves with the Dutch and later with the English. The only important Mohawk settlement in the county during the Contact period was the Upper Mohawk Castle in Canajoharie [now in Montgomery Co]. All other traces of Mohawk occupancy are of seasonal hunting camps.

The first European settlers were German Palatines. In 1723 land between the present towns of Frankfort and Little Falls on both banks of the Mohawk was surveyed, and on 25 Apr 1725 it was patented to Gov William Burnet. Named in the patent were 92 Palatines, to whom the land was given, subject to the usual quitrent. They settled on it in 1725–26. Johan Jost Herkimer built a stone house around 1740 on the south side of the Mohawk that was later fortified as a military post during the French and Indian War and known as Fort Herkimer. Soon afterward a French and Indian raid destroyed the unfortified settlement on the north side of the river, killing 40 and carrying 100 captive into Canada.

In 1769 the king of England gave British Indian agent Sir William Johnson the Royal Grant, or "Kingsland," covering 80,000 acres (32,375 ha), 66,000 acres (26,710 ha) of which lay in the future Herkimer Co between East and West Canada Creeks. Johnson's 1774 death contributed to the weakening of British power in the region. The Palatines generally supported the patriot cause, but many neighbors and families were divided politically during the Revolutionary War. The percentage of the African American population likely reached its high point during the colonial period, when wealthy landowners were large slaveholders (Gen Nicholas Herkimer held 33 slaves).

In 1776 Col Elias Dayton of the Third New Jersey Regiment took charge of building Fort Dayton in Herkimer. In 1777 Gen Herkimer led a force of 800 Palatines from this fort to aid Fort Stanwix [now Rome, Oneida Co], then threatened with capture by an army of British and Indians led by Col Barry St. Leger. Although caught in an enemy ambush near Fort Stanwix, Herkimer's army fought attackers to a draw in the 6 Aug 1777 Battle of Oriskany, an action that prevented St. Leger from advancing down the Mohawk Valley. Herkimer died 11 days later at his home near Little Falls. Loyalists and British-allied Iroquois raided the Mohawk Valley later in the war, notably at Andrustown on 18 July 1778. Many Loyalist settlers fled to Canada during and after the war, while the Mohawks were resettled near what is now Brantford, Ont.

HERKIMER CO POPULATION CENSUS FIGURES

	White	Nonwhite	Total Population	Foreign-Born
1800	14,410	69	14,479	—
1810	21,905	141	22,046	—
1820	30,685	332	31,017	253
1830	35,518	352	35,870	346
1840	37,190	287	37,477	—
1850	38,041	203	38,244	3,614
1860	40,310	251	40,561	5,537
1870	39,696	233	39,929	5,785
1880	42,491	178	42,669	5,260
1890	45,465	143	45,608	5,933
1900	50,828	221	51,049	6,652
1910	56,147	209	56,356	10,313
1920	64,813	149	64,962	11,123
1930	63,931	75	64,006	9,430
1940	59,471	56	59,527	7,067
1950	61,350	57	61,407	5,911
1960	66,222	148	66,370	4,950
1970	67,461	172	67,633	3,280
1980	66,327	387	66,714	2,383
1990	65,341	456	65,797	1,415
2000	63,031	1,396	64,427	1,297

Notes: "Nonwhite" includes African Americans, Asians, American Indians, and Pacific Islanders and, for 2000, also the mixed race and other race categories. Through the 1960 census these figures primarily reflect the African American population. Foreign-born figures for 1820 and 1830 include only those not naturalized, and for 1930 and 1950, the foreign-born totals include Whites only. Other years include all foreign-born in the population.

Economic Development

With peace, former soldiers from the New England states came to live on the fertile land, with English and Irish immigrants soon following. The African American percentage of the population probably fell at this time; it would remain small over the next two centuries, (generally less than 1% of the total). Construction of the Mohawk Turnpike (now Rte 5) in 1803 and of the Military Road (from present Dolgeville to Prospect through Manheim, Salisbury, Norway, and Russia) a few years later aided migration. Most settled on hill farms north or south of the Mohawk Valley and, like the valley farmers, cultivated wheat as their chief cash crop. The county's population bounded from near 3,000 in 1790 to near 31,000 in 1820, with many of the Yankee settlers exploiting upland streams such as Steele Creek and Cold Brook for mills and small metalworking and textile manufactories. Completion of the Erie Canal in 1825 improved and extended the Mohawk River waterway, which carried Herkimer Co wheat east easily and cheaply. The Utica and Schenectady Railroad, the county's first, was in operation by 1836. In 1853 it became part of the newly formed New York Central and was double-tracked by 1874 to serve as part of the Central's famed Water Level Route between New York City and Chicago.

From the 1830s into the 1910s, many towns had local, independent banks. One of these, Herkimer County Bank (1833; after 1917, Herkimer County Trust Co) in Little Falls, survives in the 21st century as part of the Savings Bank of Utica. By the 1850s the influx of western wheat into eastern markets caused many Herkimer Co farmers to move into dairying and the production of cheese, and by 1875 Little Falls was a major cheese distribution center.

Also by the 1850s most hill-region industries had disappeared or moved closer to the canal. Ilion's Remington Armory (1816; from 1888, Remington Arms Co) moved to land near the canal in 1828, then boomed during the Mexican-American and Civil wars. During the 1870s the Remington firm diversified into farm machinery, sewing machines, and typewriters, and by the 1890s into bicycles. From the mid-1800s a range of industries also flourished in the southern part of the county. Little Falls produced steel and brass tools, textiles, paper, plaster, and starch; Dolgeville, piano parts; Herkimer, guns, steel tools, paper, flour, finished lumber, furniture, and textiles; and Frankfort, farm machinery, locks, powdered milk, textiles, and tanneries. Industries drew waves of new immigrants: in the 1840s, many potato-famine Irish; from the 1850s, Germans and German and central European Jews; from the 1870s, Francophone Canadians; and from the 1880s, Italians, Poles, Slovenians, Russians, and Ukrainians. The foreign-born percentage peaked in Herkimer Co in 1910 at 18%.

Following the Civil War, the county's northern section—then almost untouched wilderness despite such projects as Charles Herreshoff's 1800–1810 iron foundry at Old Forge—began to open up to logging and associated harvesting of hemlock bark for use in tanneries. Many Francophone Canadians worked in the logging camps, and most members of the other new groups worked in Mohawk Valley factories. The Erie Canal, reconstructed as the New York State Barge Canal, remained a vital commercial waterway through the 1950s. In 1912 Little Falls was an industrial city, with 50 factories employing 3,876, and Mohawk Valley industries flourished during World War I, especially Remington Arms (11,000 employees). In 1928 a spin-off company of Remington Arms, Remington Typewriter Co, merged with other business machine companies to form Remington Rand, with manufacturing facilities in Ilion.

Religion, Education, and Culture

Palatine settlers established two Reformed churches at the settlement of Burnetsfield in 1723, and German language services continued through the mid-1800s. Other early German immigrants formed Lutheran congregations in Schuyler (1764) and Stark (1792). New Englanders organized Presbyterian congregations at Burrell's Corners (1795) and in Norway and Litchfield. Baptist congregations, formed largely by settlers from Rhode Island, arose in Litchfield (1795), at Burrell's Corners (1800), and in Jordanville. In 1806 the county's first Episcopal church, Trinity, was founded in Fairfield; the church building was completed in 1809. Methodism made strong gains in the county; in 1855 there were 29 Methodist churches, 12 Baptist congregations, 7 Dutch Reformed, 7 Presbyterian, and 7 Universalist. The first Roman Catholic parish was formed at Little Falls in 1833, acquiring a building in 1847. Polish, Italian, and Ukrainian Roman Catholic parishes followed in the first years of the 20th century. A Russian Orthodox church was founded in Herkimer in 1916; descendants of this congregation dedicated a new church at East Herkimer in 1965. The Jewish community, which had established a Hebrew Aid Society in 1915 and a cemetery in 1927, built Temple Beth Joseph in Herkimer in 1949. Later, Seventh-day Adventist (1938) and Jehovah's Witness (by 1976) congregations also formed.

One-room schools served Herkimer Co from the 1730s until after passage of the state's Central School Act (1913). In 1803 the first secondary

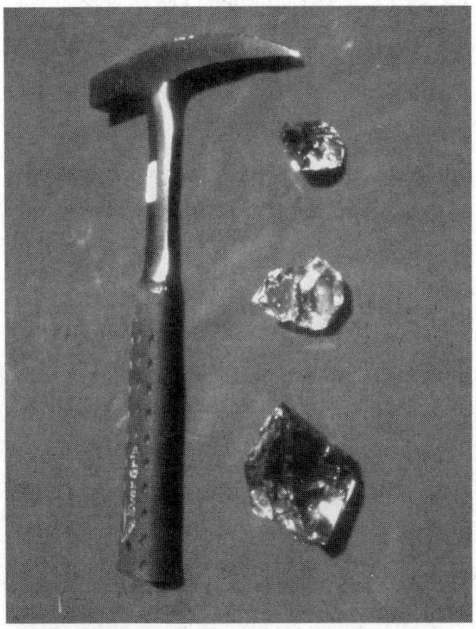

Herkimer diamonds, found in the southern Adirondacks, are a form of quartz crystal that closely resembles real diamonds in appearance.

POPULATIONS OF TOWNS AND CITIES, HERKIMER CO

Town or City, Year Founded	1800	1840	1880	1920	1960	2000
Columbia, 1812	—	2,129	1,616	911	1,327	1,630
Danube, 1817	—	1,960	1,235	746	911	1,098
Fairfield, 1796	2,065	1,836	1,656	1,337	1,282	1,607
Frankfort, 1796	946	3,096	3,025	6,483	7,550	7,478
German Flatts, 1772[a]	1,637	3,245	6,746	14,089	15,742	13,629
Herkimer, 1772[b]	2,534	2,369	3,593	11,982	11,568	9,962
Litchfield, 1796	1,976	1,672	1,218	747	963	1,453
Little Falls, 1829	—	3,881	6,913	684	1,188	1,544
Little Falls (city), 1895	—	—	—	13,029	8,935	5,188
Manheim, 1797	1,037	2,095	2,421	3,886	3,872	3,171
Newport, 1806	—	2,020	1,953	1,700	1,907	2,192
Norway, 1792	1,913	1,046	1,045	488	427	711
Ohio, 1823[c]	—	692	961	583	480	922
Russia, 1806[d]	—	2,298	2,177	1,433	1,761	2,487
Salisbury, 1797	716	1,859	1,884	1,418	1,551	1,953
Schuyler, 1792	963	1,798	1,452	1,007	1,893	3,385
Stark, 1828	—	1,766	1,476	811	783	767
Warren, 1796	2,445	2,003	1,430	959	918	1,136
Webb, 1896	—	—	—	1,357	1,562	1,912
Wilmurt, 1836–1918[e]	—	60	271	—	—	—
Winfield, 1816	—	1,652	1,597	1,312	1,750	2,202

Note: In 1800 the Towns of Manheim and Salisbury were in Montgomery Co.

[a]Formed as Kingsland District; recognized as Town of German Flatts 1788.

[b]Formed as German Flatts District; recognized as Town of Herkimer 1788.

[c]Named West Brunswick until 1836.

[d]Union until 1808.

[e]Dissolved in 1918; divided between Towns of Ohio and Webb.

school, Fairfield Academy, was chartered. In 1812 the state-chartered College of Physicians and Surgeons of the Western District of New York (1812–41; known as Fairfield Medical College) located on the academy's campus. It was the second medical college in New York State and the first outside New York City. In 1893 piano manufacturer Alfred Dolge established the first kindergarten in the state at Dolgeville. The county's first centralized school was at Van Hornesville (1931). In 2003 there were 10 central school districts, and the Town of Webb Union Free School District operated a K–12 program in one building. The county's Board of Cooperative Education Services (BOCES) was founded in 1954, and Herkimer County Community College was founded in 1962.

The county's first newspaper was the *Telescope*, published at Herkimer in 1802. In the 19th century many communities had their own newspapers. Two of these, *Herkimer Evening Telegram* (1898) and the *Little Falls Evening Times* (1886), continue to function as important cultural institutions. Of the theaters that existed in the larger communities, only one, Little Falls's Valley Cinema, survived in 2003. Realtor Frank Basloe established a Herkimer Co–based professional basketball team, the Basloe Globe Trotters (1903–26), and Ilion's Best Garage sponsored a semi-pro football team (1931–35). Another semi-pro team, the Frankfort Falcons, played from 1959 into the early 1960s. Herkimer Co sports figures include Dolgeville's Harold "Prince Hal" Schumacher, pitcher for the New York Giants; the "Herkimer Hurricane," boxer Lou Ambers; Herkimer-born golfer Wayne Levi; Little Falls basketball coach Wilbur Crisp; and Herkimer football coach Elmer Morgan. The Dolgeville Central School players were the New York State Class D football champions in 2000–2001.

Politics

Herkimer Co was active in the abolitionist movement. Stalwarts included Abby Kelley Foster of Litchfield, John Curtiss Underwood, a Litchfield native, and Zenas Brockett of Brockett's Bridge [now Dolgeville]. After the Civil War the county generally voted Republican, with a decreasing number of Democratic holdouts. Among the leading political figures were the Democrat Gen Francis Elias Spinner (1802–90), a Herkimer Co sheriff (1834–37) who later served in the House of Representatives (1855–61) and as treasurer of the United States (1861–75), and Republican Warner Miller (1838–1918), a US senator (1881–87). The Board of Supervisors, as formed in 1791, was composed of each town's supervisor. The US Supreme Court's one person–one vote decision in 1964 resulted in a new, more representative body, the Herkimer County Legislature (1968).

Herkimer Co has had an active labor movement. The strike against Little Falls knitting mills in 1912 and 1913 was the largest strike in New York State led by the anarcho-syndicalist Industrial Workers of the World. Following a 1936 strike by Remington Rand employees in Ilion, the company simply removed its typewriter works but left other production facilities. Many farmers were active in the Grange movement from the 1870s through the 1930s, and the Dairy Farmers Union repeatedly struck for better milk prices, especially in the 1930s.

Recent History

Herkimer Co's population has been stable since 1920, fluctuating between 59,000 and 67,000. From the 1960s, as much traditional manufacturing left the northeast, Remington Rand's (from 1928, Rand Corp) high-technology business prospered, partly offsetting closures of area textile and metalworking plants. Rand also helped generate other like businesses, such as the Herkimer-based Mohawk Data Systems (1964–90). Agriculture in the county has declined. Between 1950 and 1997, the number of farms decreased from 1,869 on 387,277 acres (156,725 ha) to 583 on 141,847 acres (57,403 ha). At the beginning of the 21st century, Ilion's Remington Arms, with almost 1,000 on its payroll, and county government are large employers. Manufacturers in 2003 included Feldmeier (formerly Cherry Burrell), Burrows Paper Corp, Salada Foods, and LaSalle Laboratories in Little Falls; Rawlings' Adirondack Bat Co, Gehring Tricot, and North Hudson Woodcraft Corp in Dolgeville; F. E. Hale Manufacturing Co (office furniture), Granny's Kitchen (bakery), and Union Tool in Frankfort.

See also Architects and architecture, Mohawk Valley.

Four histories of the county have been published: Nathaniel S. Benton, *History of Herkimer County* (1856); F. W. Beers and Co, *History of Herkimer County* (1879); George A. Hardin, ed., *History of Herkimer County* (1892); and Josephine E. Case, ed., *Herkimer County at 200* (1992), an exemplary modern project. A Norway newspaper in the late 19th century published historical material on that town and its neighbors, reprinted by the Kuyahoora Valley Historical Society: Fred Smith, ed., *Norway Tidings, 1887–1890,* 2d ed. (2003). The books of Jane Dieffenbacher are of a high standard: *Middleville, New York, the Story of a Village* (1990) and *This Green and Pleasant Land: Fairfield, NY,* 2d ed. (2003). Other well-researched local histories include Clara V. O'Brien, *God's Country* (1982), covering Eagle Bay and Fourth Lake, and Margery Foss et al, eds., *A Glimpse in Passing: Newport, NY* (1991). Eleanor Franz's *Dolge* (1980) is a careful biography that provides a history of the early years of Dolgeville.

Susan R. Perkins

Hermon. Town (pop 1,069) and village (pop 402) in central St. Lawrence Co. Settled before 1812, largely from Vermont, the town was formed as DePau in 1830 from Edwards and De Kalb; the name was changed to Hermon in 1834. The village was incorporated in 1877. Hematite was mined in the Civil War era. Agriculture remains the most important element in the town's economy, but soil and slope conditions are not as favorable for farming as elsewhere in the county, and much of the town has reverted to forest. The village, largely a bedroom community for Canton, has instituted several progressive initiatives, such as sewer system and water system improvements, to stem population loss.

Richard E. Mooers

Herrings. Village (pop 129) in Wilna (Jefferson Co). Watertown businessman William P. Herring founded the village in 1894 with the establishment of the Jefferson Paper Co. A post office named Herring opened in 1899 and changed to Herrings in 1950. In 1911 the community and the paper mill were both sold to the St. Regis Paper Co. Herrings was incorporated in 1921 at the same time as Deferiet, another St. Regis–

owned village. The Herrings St. Regis mill closed in 1965. In 2004 Herrings residents worked and shopped in Carthage and Watertown.

Laura Lynne Scharer

Herrman, Augustine (*b* Prague, Bohemia [now in Czech Republic], 1621; *d* Bohemia Manor [now in Cecil Co, Md], ?1685). Merchant, surveyor, draftsman, and diplomat. During the turmoil of the Thirty Years War Herrman emigrated from Prague to Amsterdam, where he continued his education, later exhibiting exceptional skills in languages and mapmaking. Before settling in New Netherland he worked as both a public surveyor and a tobacco planter in Virginia. Sometime before 1644, as an agent for a private trading firm, he moved to New Amsterdam. In 1647 he was elected to the body of Nine Men, an advisory council serving the director general and council. Because of his linguistic and diplomatic skills he was called on to represent New Netherland at several intercolonial gatherings; the most famous was his 1659 embassy to Maryland, where he successfully defended Dutch interests in the Delaware. Herrman is best known for his depiction of New Amsterdam on the 1656 Adriaen van der Donck map of New Netherland and his map of Chesapeake Bay, which was commissioned by Lord Baltimore. As payment for his services Herrman was granted a large tract of land in Cecil Co, Md. Before his death he was persuaded by the Labadists Jasper Danckaerts and Peter Sluyter to bequeath his estate to their group for the purpose of establishing a religious colony.

Capek, Thomas. *Augustine Herrman of Bohemia Manor* (Prague: State Printing Office, 1930)

Gehring, Charles T., trans and ed. *Delaware Papers, 1648–1664.* New York Historical Manuscripts, Dutch series (Baltimore: Genealogical Publishing, 1981)

Charles T. Gehring

Heuvelton [HEW-VEL-TON]. Village (pop 804) in Oswegatchie (St. Lawrence Co). Platted *ca* 1805, the village incorporated in 1912. It acquired rail service from the Rome, Watertown and Ogdensburg Railroad (1862). Heuvelton has long been a major center of dairy processing; in 2003 it was the site of three large cheese plants, including McCadam Cheese Co (1876; sold to Agri-Mark in 2003) and Heritage Cheese House, which serves Amish dairy farmers in the surrounding towns. In addition, from 1893 to 1928 the village was the world's largest dressed-turkey market. Heuvelton was one of the centers of the Dairy Farmers Union strike that roiled much of the North Country in 1939. The US-Canada joint defense agreement was signed 17 Aug 1940 by Pres Franklin D. Roosevelt and Prime Minister Mackenzie King in a private railcar on a Heuvelton siding.

Richard E. Mooers

Hewitt, J(ohn) N(apoleon) B(rinton) (*b* Tuscarora Indian Reservation [loc in Niagara Co], 16 Dec 1857; *d* Washington, DC, 14 Oct 1937). Ethnologist and linguist. He was educated first at home, then at the local reservation school, and subsequently at high schools in Wilson and Lockport (Niagara Co), where he was enrolled in the academic department. He was recruited in 1880 and trained as an assistant by Erminnie A. Smith, then collecting the Tuscarora and other Iroquois languages for the Bureau of American Ethnology. After Smith's death in 1886, he applied to the bureau for the opportunity to upgrade the manuscript of the Tuscarora dictionary and grammar that she had already submitted, a task he never completed in his 51 years at the bureau. Hewitt spent the rest of his life collecting the traditional history, culture, folklore, and languages of the Iroquois. In addition to his native Tuscarora, he taught himself to speak Mohawk and Onondaga, and he transcribed texts in various of the Six Nations languages. Some of his most valuable published works appeared in the *Annual Report of the Bureau of American Ethnology: Iroquois Cosmology* (1903, 1928) and *Seneca Fiction, Legends, and Myths* (1918), which was edited by Hewitt and contained materials both he and Jeremiah Curtin collected. He contributed many articles to the two-volume *Handbook of American Indians North of Mexico* (1907, 1910). His article "Orenda and a Definition of Religion," published in *American Anthropologist* in 1902, has become a classic. His papers are in the National Anthropological Archives at the Smithsonian Institution in Washington, DC.

American National Biography, sv "Hewitt, John Napoleon Brinton"

Swanton, John R. "John Napoleon Brinton Hewitt," *American Anthropologist* 40 (1938): 286–90

Barbara Graymont

Hewlett {Hewlett, locality (pop 7,060) in Hempstead, Nassau Co; Hewlett Bay Park, village (pop 484) in Hempstead; Hewlett Harbor, village (pop 1,271) in Hempstead; Hewlett Neck, village (pop 504) in Hempstead}. George Hewlett, an English immigrant, was granted land in the area in 1654. The Rockaway Branch Railroad established a station in 1869 named Hewletts after the landowners. The line's successor, the Long Island Rail Road (LIRR), designated the station Fenhurst from 1892 to 1897, but local opposition, led by Augustus J. Hewlett, convinced the LIRR to rescind the change, and the station reverted to its original name. The Hewlett-Woodmere school district was established in 1898. Hewlett Bay Park was the name of a racetrack developed in 1913 by the Hewlett Bay Co. Land around the racetrack had been surveyed into building lots, and by 1914 gracious homes had been built on lots of 1–10 acres (.4–4.1 ha); the village incorporated in 1928. Hewlett Harbor originated with the purchase of land by Samuel Auerbach in 1900; he built his home on 450 acres (182 ha). In 1925 the Seawane Corp purchased his land to create the Seawane Golf and Country Club and a golf-centered community. Hewlett Neck was originally part of Brower's Point, which was purchased for development in 1869 by Samuel Wood. During the 1920s some residents sought to maintain their exclusive neighborhoods and one-acre zoning by incorporating as villages; Hewlett Harbor incorporated in 1925, Hewlett Neck in 1927, and Hewlett Bay Park in 1928. Hewlett's population more than doubled between 1940 and 1960; Hewlett Harbor's nearly quadrupled in the same period. The three Hewlett villages are among the most exclusive residential communities on Long Island and border on Macy Channel, which leads to Hewlett Bay. The Keystone Yacht Club is in Hewlett Neck.

John A. Hewlett

Hiawatha. See IROQUOIS CONFEDERACY; IROQUOIS GOVERNMENT AND RELIGION.

Hicks, Granville (*b* Exeter, NH, 9 Sept 1901; *d* Franklin Park, NJ, 18 June 1982). Author. After graduating from Harvard University (1923), Hicks married Dorothy Dyer in 1925 and taught briefly at Smith College in Northampton, Mass, before accepting a position in 1929 as an English professor at Rensselaer Polytechnic Institute (RPI). The remainder of his life was devoted to literary pursuits, and he was a frequent visitor to Yaddo, an artists' and writers' haven in Saratoga Springs and in 1970–71 was its executive director. Hicks had joined the Communist Party by the winter of 1935 and was subsequently dismissed from the RPI faculty. During his Marxist years he was an editor of the Communist Party weekly *New Masses* and wrote *The Great Tradition* (1933) and *Figures of Transition* (1939), which presented a Marxist approach to American and British literature, respectively. In *I Like America* (1938), Hicks tried to demonstrate the compatibility of Marxism and American patriotism. He renounced Communism in 1939 following the signing of the Nazi-Soviet Pact. Hicks purchased an old farmhouse in Grafton (Rensselaer Co) in 1932 and remained there until his health failed in 1978. He was instrumental in founding the town's first library in 1943 and wrote a popular nonfiction work about Grafton (*Small Town,* 1946) as well as four novels based on his relationships with its residents. His other works include *Where We Came Out* (1954), a retrospective look at his former interest in communism, and his honest yet unapologetic autobiography, *Part of the Truth* (1965).

Levenson, Leah, and Jerry Natterstad. *Granville Hicks: The Intellectual in Mass Society* (Philadelphia: Temple Univ Press, 1993)

Long, Terry L. *Granville Hicks.* Twayne's United States Authors Series 387 (Boston: Twayne Publishers, 1981)

Warren F. Broderick

Hicks family {Hicks, Elias (*b* Hempstead [now in Nassau Co], 19 Mar 1748; *d* Jericho [now in Nassau Co], 27 Feb 1830); Hicks, Isaac (*b* Westbury [now in Nassau Co], 19 Apr 1767; *d* Westbury, 10 Jan 1820); Hicks [née Seaman], Rachel (*b* Westbury, 10 Apr 1789; *d* Westbury, 13 Aug 1878)}. During the 18th and 19th centuries, this Long Island family produced leaders in New York and American Quakerism (Society of Friends). Elias Hicks grew up on the farms of his father and, after his mother's death, of an older brother. At 17 he was apprenticed to a carpenter and also studied surveying. He married Jemima Seaman, a fellow Quaker from Jericho, in 1771 and settled on her parents' farm. Recorded a Quaker minister in 1778, over the next half century he traveled extensively among most of the Friends meetings in North America. An outspoken opponent of slavery, he refused to use any of its products, such as cotton clothing or sugar. He advocated traditional Quakerism and scorned Friends who joined with non-Quakers in reform and humanitarian work because he saw such ties as a threat to Quaker distinctiveness. During the American Revolution he was involved in negotiations with both British and American authorities to defend Quaker interests. While forward-looking in his opposition to slavery, he was steadfastly conservative in other ways, such as his criticism of the

Erie Canal as an irreligious attempt to improve God's creation. He was at the center of the separation of 1827–28, during which American Quakers split into factions of Hicksites and Orthodox Friends over doctrinal disputes.

Isaac Hicks, a cousin of Elias, received a good education from his father, a tailor. He settled in New York City in 1789 and the following year married Sarah Doughty, a fellow Quaker. Between 1790 and 1804, first as part of the firm of Hicks and Loines and then in Alsop and Hicks, he developed one of the city's largest import-export and commission businesses, specializing in whale oil, cotton, and dry goods. In 1805 he retired to a farm in Westbury. He became more active in Quaker affairs, working with the New York Manumission Society and traveling with Elias as a companion.

Rachel Hicks was a leading figure among Hicksite Friends after the separation. In 1815 she married Abraham Hicks, a nephew of Elias, who died in 1827. From 1836 to 1860 she traveled widely as a Quaker minister. In the 1840s and 1850s New York Hicksite Friends with radical reform sympathies saw her as one of their chief opponents and deplored her influence. After 1860 she traveled less extensively but was still active on a variety of New York Yearly Meeting committees. A controversial figure and a conservative force, she was critical of anything that tended to weaken Quaker distinctiveness, such as participation in the abolitionist or women's rights movements.

Davison, Robert A. *Isaac Hicks: New York Merchant and Quaker, 1767–1820* (Cambridge, Mass: Harvard Univ Press, 1964)

Forbush, Bliss. *Elias Hicks: Quaker Liberal* (New York: Columbia Univ Press, 1956)

Hicks, Rachel. *Memoir of Rachel Hicks* (New York: Putnam's, 1880)

Ingle, H. Larry. *Quakers in Conflict: The Hicksite Reformation* (Knoxville: Univ of Tennessee Press, 1986)

Thomas D. Hamm

Hicksville. Locality (pop 41,260) in Oyster Bay (Nassau Co). Valentine Hicks first planned the community in 1834; as a trustee of the Long Island Rail Road, he was able to ensure a station stop when the railroad began operations in Hicksville in 1837. By the mid–19th century the vicinity was home to Irish and German farmers; Hicksville's first newspaper was the German language *Long Island Central Zeitung* (1873). Hicksville farmers raised cucumbers to supply pickle works but shifted to potato growing after a blight. After World War II farms were sold for development; Hicksville's population peaked in 1960 at 50,405. It is a busy transportation and shopping hub, with Broadway Mall (opened in 1956 as Mid-Island Plaza) and the most heavily used railroad station east of Jamaica (Queens Co). The Hicksville Gregory Museum interprets earth science. Rock musician Billy Joel spent his childhood in the area.

Lynda R. Day

Higgins, Frank W(ayland) (*b* Rushford, Allegany Co, 18 Aug 1856; *d* Olean, Cattaraugus Co, 12 Feb 1907). Governor. Higgins grew up in Poughkeepsie and graduated from the Riverview Military Academy in 1873. He moved to Michigan in 1875 and started a successful mercantile business, but returned home in 1879 and joined his father's company in Olean, which ran small grocery stores in central New York State. By 1884 Higgins was running the entire business and speculating in western iron and timberlands. Elected as a Republican member of the state senate from Cattaraugus and Chautauqua Cos in 1893, he held the position until 1902, when he was elected lieutenant governor under Benjamin B. Odell Jr. In 1904 Higgins received the nomination for governor, and with the support of Pres Theodore Roosevelt he defeated his Democratic opponent. Higgins supported small government and lower taxes, and there was a state treasury surplus of $11 million when he left office. His administration was marred, however, by massive gas and insurance scandals that revealed the corrupt relationship between corporate business interests and the Republican Party. Higgins supported a progressive revision of the state insurance laws but was unable to successfully maneuver among Republican power brokers Odell, Roosevelt, and Thomas C. Platt in the complicated world of New York State politics. He declined to run for a second term and suffered a fatal heart attack six weeks after leaving office.

McCormick, Richard. *From Realignment to Reform: Political Change in New York State, 1893–1910* (Ithaca: Cornell Univ Press, 1981)

Public Papers of Frank W. Higgins, Governor (Albany: J. B. Lyon, 1906–7)

Jon Sterngass

higher education

Early Colleges and Universities

New York City's Kings College (1754), the first college in New York, typified the pre–Revolutionary War "one college per colony" pattern. Anglicans dominated its governing board, but the college charter prohibited discriminating against students from other denominations. A 1784 act gave a religiously heterogeneous Board of Regents control over the renamed Columbia College, which closed during the American Revolution. The act also gave the Regents nonexclusive authority to charter other colleges, schools, museums, and libraries; the legislature retained concurrent authority to charter colleges until 1892. It also granted the Regents exclusive authority to prescribe rules for admission to professional schools and the professions. In 1787 the legislature created a separate board for Columbia, reserving supervision of education in the state to the Regents. In 1795 the Regents chartered nonsectarian Union College (Schenectady), the state's second college and the first with a campus planned by an architect (Joseph Jacques Ramée). During the 19th century the Regents and the legislature chartered nonsectarian and denominational colleges; founders failing to meet more stringent Regents criteria often requested legislative charters. Hamilton College (1812) in Clinton (Oneida Co) justified its charter by noting the absence of a college in the state's western district. Colleges founded in the 19th century, often by Protestant denominations and often located near the Hudson River and the Erie Canal, included Hobart College (1825), an Episcopal college in Geneva (Ontario and Seneca Cos); Madison University (1846; now Colgate University), a Baptist institution in Hamilton; the University of Buffalo (1846); the University of Rochester (1850), a Baptist university; St. Lawrence University (1856), a Universalist university in Canton; St. Stephens College

Nott Memorial at Union College, Schenectady.

(1860; now Bard College), an Episcopal college in Annandale-on-Hudson (Dutchess Co); and Syracuse University (1870), a Methodist school that was the product of a merger between Genesee College (1851) in Lima (Livingston Co) and Geneva Medical College (1834).

Older colleges often helped spawn newer schools. Madison University trustees helped to found the breakaway University of Rochester; six Rochester trustees later helped to establish nonsectarian Vassar College (chartered 1861, opened 1865) in Poughkeepsie (Dutchess Co). Vassar trustees helped form Sarah Lawrence College (1926) in Bronxville (Westchester Co). Union graduate John Raymond became president of Vassar in 1864, one of 90 former students of Union who became college presidents during the 19th century. Union graduate Henry Tappan became president of the University of the City of New York (now New York University) when it opened in 1832 as a nondenominational response to Columbia's Episcopalian ties. Many Catholic colleges for men opened in cities or suburbs with substantial immigrant populations: St. Johns College (opened 1841, chartered 1846; now Fordham University) in Fordham Manor [now in Bronx Co]; the Academy of the Holy Infancy (1853; now Manhattan College) in Bronx Co; St. John's College (1870; now St. John's University, in Queens and Staten Island) in Brooklyn; St. Francis College (1884) in Brooklyn; Canisius College (1870) in Buffalo; Niagara University (1883) in Niagara Falls and Buffalo; LeMoyne College (1946) in Syracuse; Siena College (1937) in Loudonville (Albany Co); and St. John Fisher College (1948) in Rochester. St. Bonaventure University (1858) in Olean (Cattaraugus Co) was exceptional for its rural location.

Public higher education in New York State included the upstate normal colleges—New York was the second state with normal schools, institutions for teaching training—the contract or statutory colleges, City College and Normal College in New York City, and the military colleges. Outside of New York City, antebellum public higher education was restricted to a normal school in Albany (1844). In Oswego a normal school for elementary schoolteachers opened in 1863. In 1866 the legislature authorized establishment of not more than four additional normal schools: Brockport (1867) in Monroe Co, Fredonia (1868) in Chautauqua Co, Cortland (1869), and Potsdam (1871) in St. Lawrence Co were selected. Demand for teachers removed the restriction, and New York State had six more normal schools by the end of the 19th century: Buffalo (1871), Geneseo (1871) in Livingston Co, New Paltz (1886) in Ulster Co, Oneonta (1889) in Otsego Co, Plattsburgh (1890), and Jamaica (1893–1906) in Queens Co. Albany Normal, devoted to preparing secondary-level teachers, was the first of the state's normal colleges to offer college-level instruction and later became the first to move from a three- to four-year program, with degree-granting authority conferred in 1942. Albany would be the only normal school to move to university level after the opening of the multicampus State University of New York (SUNY) in 1948. The need to house a predominantly female normal school population led to creation of the New York State Dormitory Authority (1944).

Specialized Education and Women's Colleges

Curricula changed with the level of instruction: the balance of liberal and professional studies changed as normal schools moved from serving as local secondary schools to according primacy to teacher preparation. As local governing boards were transformed into weak boards of visitors, increased New York State Education Department (NYSED) control over teachers colleges during the 20th century helps to explain the contentious jurisdictional battle over their governance after the 1948 founding of SUNY, which was resolved in SUNY's favor in 1949. Several groups competed for the federal support provided by the 1862 Morrill Land Grant, which gave each state land or scrip equal to 30,000 acres (12,141 ha) for each US representative and senator to open at least one college. The objective of the college, according to the act, should be "without excluding other classical or scientific studies, and including military tactics, to teach such branches of learning that are related to agriculture and the mechanic arts." Ezra Cornell, a member of the group receiving final legislative approval, added a $500,000 contribution to the funds derived from the land scrip sale to create a substantial endowment for a university in Ithaca and donated the land used for the campus. Cornell University (1870), a chartered private corporation, included several ex officio public representatives. Its sponsorship of contract colleges exemplified the New York State pattern of private stewardship of specialized education. The contract colleges included the Veterinary College (1894; now New York State College of Veterinary Medicine); the New York State College of Agriculture (1904; now New York State School of Agriculture and Life Sciences); and the College of Home Economics (1925; now New York State College of Human Ecology). Two other private colleges successfully challenged Cornell's primacy: the New York State School of Clay-Working and Ceramics at Alfred University (1900; now New York State College of Ceramics) and the New York State College of Forestry at Syracuse University (1911; now SUNY College of Environmental Science and Forestry).

New York City sponsored a liberal arts competitor to the city's private colleges. The Free Academy of New York (1847) evolved into City College of New York (1866), the first of several municipal colleges offering free tuition and a short degree program. Young women enrolled in the Female Normal and High School (1870), renamed the Normal College of the City of New York shortly after opening and then Hunter College in 1914. Brooklyn College (1930) and Queens College (1937) opened under the auspices of the Board of Higher Education, which was established in 1926. In 1961 the municipal colleges were brought together as the City University of New York (CUNY). The municipal colleges engaged in little graduate-level work. Private universities began to add postbaccalaureate instruction in the 1880s, retaining dominance until CUNY Graduate School and University Center (1961) opened and SUNY established four university centers at Buffalo, Stony Brook, Binghamton, and Albany in the 1960s.

By 1895 New York State chartered and hosted 14 medical schools, 7 law schools, and 13 schools of theology; many freestanding schools affiliated or merged with the state's universities. Technical schools included Polytechnic University (1854) in Brooklyn and Farmingdale [now in Nassau Co]; Rochester Institute of Technology (1944); Rensselaer School (1824; now Rensselaer Polytechnic Institute) in Troy (Rensselaer Co); and Clarkson University (1896) in Potsdam. New York State's military colleges included the US Military Academy (1802) at West Point (Orange Co), the State Nautical School (1875; now SUNY Maritime College) in Fort Schuyler [now in Bronx Co] and the United States Merchant Marine Academy (1943) in Kings Point (Nassau Co). The first junior colleges, including Packer Collegiate Institute (1919; originally Brooklyn Female Academy, 1845), Seth Low in Brooklyn (1928–38), and Sarah Lawrence (provisional charter 1926, permanent charter 1931), were private. Columbia closed Seth Low as New York City's municipal colleges grew; Sarah Lawrence became a four-year college in 1932. By 1954 New York State had 29 junior and community colleges; another 17 colleges offered two- and four-year curricula, though only 37 of these 46 public and private colleges granted the associate of arts or associate of science degrees.

Most 19th-century colleges were single-sex institutions. St. Lawrence University claims to be the oldest continuously coeducational institution of higher learning in the state. The legislature chartered coeducational Alfred University, previously a coeducational academy founded by Seventh-Day Baptists, in 1857. Colleges for women—many opened as seminaries or academies—included Elmira (1855), whose first president, Augustus W. Cowles, was another Union College graduate; Ingham University (1857–92; founded 1841 as Le Roy Female Seminary) in Le Roy (Genesee Co); Rutgers Female College (1867–95) in New York City; Barnard College (1889) in New York City; and Skidmore College (1903) in Saratoga Springs. In 1943 Hobart joined with William Smith (1908), a women's college in Geneva, to form the coordinate Colleges of the Seneca. The College of New Rochelle (1904) in Westchester Co was the state's first Catholic college for women; other Catholic women's colleges, often located in or removed to suburbs, included the College of Saint Rose (1920) in Albany and Nazareth College (1924) in Rochester. Most nondenominational and Catholic single-sex colleges joined the national movement for coeducation in the 20th century; four women's colleges were exceptions: Barnard, Marymount (1907) in Tarrytown (Westchester Co), Russell Sage (1916) in Troy, and Wells (1868) in Aurora (Cayuga Co).

Development of the SUNY System

Private colleges and universities, claiming to act in the public interest and to perform a public function under the Regents general supervision, dominated higher education in New York State during the first half of the 20th century. Public activity and financial support played a supplementary role. "Emergency collegiate centers," for example, established between 1933 and 1938 by NYSED under the jurisdiction of private colleges, replicated the contract college pattern. The 21 centers offered adults subjects in the freshman and sophomore curricula of the five sponsoring colleges. Similarly private colleges absorbed some of the postwar GI influx by contracting to run three two-year colleges, collectively known as the Associated Colleges of Upper New York, on former military facilities. Contracting for public services, critics charged, was not a remedy for inadequate public higher education opportunity in New York State. In 1910 Commissioner of Education Andrew S. Draper called for the conversion of several upstate private colleges into tuition-free public municipal colleges and for a scholarship program enabling selected students to attend any college in the state. Private college opposition led Draper to drop the conversion plan, but in 1913 the legislature passed a bill calling for $100 Regents Scholarships for 3,000 students; in 1865 the state had established the Cornell University Scholarships, also distributed geographically. Critics considered these awards, distributed by assembly district, inadequate to meet the demand for higher education.

Religious and racial discrimination accompanied the economic barriers that the Cornell and Regents Scholarships were designed to ameliorate. By World War I Jewish students dominated City College and the New York University downtown campus. In response, some private colleges sifted out applications from minority students. The Regents' Inquiry into the Character and Cost of Public Education in New York State (1938) threatened neither discriminatory admissions practices nor private college dominance. It reported that "New York is adequately supplied with private colleges, though it does not have a free state university. No additional state funds should be spent during this generation to set up new colleges." But the post–World War II GI influx and protests from minority groups placed the private colleges on the defensive. The Temporary Commission on the Need for a State University (1946) found significant geographic, economic, and racial-religious barriers to higher education. Three years of legislative debate, plus issuance of the report of the President's Commission on Higher Education (1947) just as New York's Republican governor Thomas E. Dewey began his run for president against incumbent Harry S. Truman, provided the context for enactment of the State University Law (1948). SUNY absorbed most public higher education institutions, including the state's teachers colleges, fostered the opening of two-year colleges, and took over several private institutions, including the Syracuse University College of Medicine and Long Island College of Medicine (1950), the Syracuse University satellite campus in Binghamton (1950; Harpur College, the core of SUNY Binghamton), and the University of Buffalo (1962; the core of SUNY Buffalo). Private college discrimination against Jewish, Catholic, and African American students abated after the opening of SUNY and passage of the Fair Education Practices Act (1948). Expansion of CUNY and SUNY helped to meet the increased demand for higher education in the 1960s brought about by the postwar Baby Boom. SUNY converted the teachers colleges into comprehensive colleges with liberal arts divisions and built up its research universities, specialized units, and community colleges.

CUNY's commitment to expansion included the opening of new campuses: Eugenio Maria de Hostos Community College (1968) in the Bronx was aimed at Latino students; York (1966) in Queens and Medgar Evers (1968) in Brooklyn, both four-year CUNY colleges, attracted many African American students. CUNY also targeted minority populations through special admissions programs. The New York State legislature, for example, funded Search for Education, Elevation, and Knowledge (SEEK, 1966), aimed at placing high school graduates from designated poverty areas into special programs at CUNY's senior colleges. In 1970 CUNY implemented open admissions, which guaranteed admission of all New York City high school graduates to a CUNY unit; the 1975 New York City budget crisis initiated a retreat from this commitment and an end to the free tuition policy in place since the founding of City College. Growing expenditures for public higher education during the 1960s and 1970s prompted Gov Nelson A. Rockefeller and the legislature to increase aid to private colleges. Aid vehicles included the Tuition Assistance Plan, which would replace examination-based Regents Scholarships and need-based Scholar Incentive Awards, and "Bundy funds," which provided funds for each degree recipient. During the 1960s and 1970s, Catholic colleges, desiring a share of increased public funding, attempted to meet the church-state strictures imposed by the Blaine Amendment to the New York State Constitution by opting for lay boards of trustees.

Current Trends

At the end of the 20th century, state allocations to public higher education declined proportionately, and sometimes absolutely, as competing budgetary demands increased. Scholarship aid increased—the state awarded $637 million in need-based undergraduate grants in 1997–98—but so did SUNY and CUNY tuition levels. SUNY's 68 units are located in most upstate counties; community college branches are located in many cities and towns lacking larger units. CUNY includes 21 units: 10 senior colleges, 6 community colleges, a 4-year technical college, a doctoral-granting graduate school, a law school, an accelerated medical program, and a medical school, enrolling over 200,000 degree candidates plus 150,000 students in adult and continuing education. In New York State, as in the United States, there were more private than public colleges (230 versus 89), but more students enrolled in the public institutions (567,893 versus 456,605 in fall 1997). New York State exports college students; in fall 1996 the difference between the number of New Yorkers attending college out of state and the number of students from other states attending college in New York State was 3,244. A 2000 New York State Lottery–funded program, designed to right the balance, awarded a scholarship to one graduate of each New York State high school attending college in the state.

See also Libraries; Medical education; Nurses; Theological education.

Abbott, Frank C. *Government Policy and Higher Education: A Study of the Regents of the University of the State of New York, 1784–1949* (Ithaca: Cornell Univ Press, 1958)
Barba, William C., ed. *Higher Education in Crisis: New York in National Perspective* (New York and London: Garland Publishing, 1995)
Carmichael, Oliver C., Jr. *New York Establishes a State University* (Nashville: Vanderbilt Univ Press, 1955)
Folts, James D. *History of the University of the State of New York and the State Education Department, 1784–1996* (Albany: NYS Education Department, 1996); see http://www.nysl.nysed.gov/edocs/education/sedhist.htm
Glazer, Judith S. "Nelson Rockefeller and the Politics of Higher Education in New York State," *History of Higher Education Annual* 9 (1989): 87–114
Gordon, Sheila C. "The Transformation of the City University of New York" (PhD diss, Columbia Univ, 1975)
Martens, Freda R. H. *Growth of Higher Education in New York State from Colonial Days to the Present* (N Manchester, Ind: Hechman Bindery, 1961)
New York State. Temporary Commission on the Need for a State University. *The Report of the Temporary Commission on the Need for a State University* (Albany: Williams Press, 1948)
Sherwood, Sidney. *The University of the State of New York: Higher Education in the State of New York.* Contributions to American Educational History, no. 28, ser ed. Herbert B. Adams (Washington, DC: Government Printing Office, 1900)

Harold S. Wechsler

Higher Education Services Corporation (HESC). The agency is the successor to Higher Education Assistance Corp formed in 1959. Created as a State Education Department agency in 1974, HESC manages financial aid and savings programs for students and grants for schools, colleges, and universities. The agency coordinates administration of loan programs with financial institutions and state and federal agencies. The HESC reports to the governor and is managed by a 15-member board of trustees. Its major initiatives include implementation of the 1968 Bundy Report, which provided state aid for private institutions; the Higher Education Opportunity Program (1969), which assists financially and educationally disadvantaged students; and the Keppel Report (1973), which expanded state aid for students. The Tuition Assistance Program (TAP) (1974), HESC's most recognized program, is the largest tuition program in the United States and offers grants to students based on financial need. In the 1980s the federal grant program GEAR UP was implemented to prepare at-risk middle school students for college. It manages the Science and Technology Entry Program, which offers assistance to qualifying minority students in high school who pursue education in the science or healthcare fields. The College Savings Program, one of the most successful savings programs in the country, is co-managed by the Office of the New York State Comptroller and allows parents to reduce taxes while saving for their children's college education. In 2001–2 HESC managed 10 grant programs and distributed nearly $709 million to students. TAP grants were distributed to 350,000 students and totaled $675 million. The agency also managed 10 loan programs and 1 savings program, which had nearly 250,000 accounts and $1.1 billion in assets.

Folts, James D. *History of the University of the State of New York and the State Education Department, 1784–1996* (Albany: University of the State of New York, 1996)

Christine A. Ohl

High Falls Brewing Company. Founded as the Genesee Brewing Co in Rochester in 1878, it was bought by the Bartholomay Brewing Co, another Rochester brewery, in 1889. A few years later Louis Wehle acquired the Genesee name and plant. After the repeal of Prohibition in 1933, Wehle opened a new Genesee Brewing Co that quickly became the dominant brewery in Rochester. By 1939 it was producing 275,000 barrels of beer annually, far more than any other Rochester brewery. After several decades of growth, by 1988 it had become the industry's seventh largest brewery with annual sales of 2.65 million barrels. During this period of rapid growth, Genesee marketed its beers in Pennsylvania, New Jersey, and New England but continued with its long-standing strategy of focusing mainly on western New York and surrounding New York State regions. The company brewed eight beers under the Genesee name and also made beers under the Shea's Brewery, Dundee's Brewery, and Fred Koch Brewery labels. By 1999 beer sales had dropped to 1.6 million barrels annually. The next year it was purchased by its management and renamed High Falls Brewing Co.

Van Wieren, Dale. *American Breweries II* (West Point, Pa: Eastern Coast Brewiana Association, 1995)

Martin Stack

Highland. Locality (pop 5,060) in Lloyd (Ulster Co). It developed as a hamlet around the landing for the Poughkeepsie ferry and acquired a post office named New Paltz Landing in 1821, with a name change to Highland in 1865. Its economy, centered on shipping and transport, benefited as the terminus of the New Paltz Turnpike (1832). The Highland Foundry and Machine Shop was an employer in the era after the Civil War; later, summer boarding and ice cutting were dominant. The community acquired rail service from the West Shore in 1883 and a river crossing with the Mid-Hudson Bridge in 1930. Major employers in 2003 were the Rocking Horse Ranch, Zumtobel Staff Lighting, and Phoenix Electronics.

Ruth Piwonka

Highland. Town (pop 2,404) in SW Sullivan Co. Settled in 1784, the town was formed from Lumberland in 1853. The Revolutionary War Battle of Minisink, at which a group of Indians and tories under the command of Col Joseph Brant routed a small contingent of Goshen (Orange Co) militia, took place within the present town in 1779. Lumbering and poor farming sustained the settlers. The Delaware and Hudson Canal (1828–98) entered New York State in Highland, and the canal's Delaware Aqueduct, designed and built by John Roebling in 1848, has been restored by the National Park Service. It is the oldest wire-rope suspension bridge in the world. When the Erie Railroad arrived in neighboring Shohola, Pa, in 1848, it boosted Highland's small industries such as timber and bluestone and, beginning in the 1870s, promoted the upper Delaware for vacationers. The river and Highland's lakes still constitute a "sportsman's paradise." Highland is the year-round home to a growing population of bald eagles.

John Conway

Highland Falls. Village (pop 3,678) in Highlands (Orange Co). The locality, just south of the US Military Academy at West Point, acquired a post office in 1849 named Buttermilk Falls; the name was changed in 1866. It became a summer resort for such notables as financier J. P. Morgan (1837–1913). Its resident population, which worked in hotels, at West Point, and in nearby iron mines, was Irish American and, later, Italian American. The large Cozzen's Hotel became Ladycliff Academy (1900–1980) and is now the West Point Visitor's Center and Museum. The village was incorporated in 1906. Completion of the Bear Mountain Bridge (1924), US 9W (1930s), and Palisades Interstate Parkway (1958) contributed to tourism. Highland Falls was the birthplace of naturalist Edgar Alexander Mearns (1856–1916). The Carpenter Gothic Cragston Dependencies and the Highland Falls Railroad Depot (1882) are listed on the National Register of Historic Places.

Stella Bailey

Highlands. Town (pop 12,484) in E Orange Co. Settled *ca* 1723, the town was formed in 1872 from Cornwall. There was little arable land. West Point became a military post during the Revolutionary War and, in 1802, the US Military Academy. It still occupies a large part of the town's area. Fort Montgomery, which fell in 1777, is a National Historic Landmark and became a state park in 2002. The Storm King Highway (1916–22; now Rte 218), an engineering marvel, is listed on the National Register.

High-Minded Federalists. Political group. Believing the Federalist Party to be moribund, 55 of its members announced the end of their party in New York State by endorsing "To the Independent Federal Electors of the State of New-York," dated 14 Apr 1820 and published three days later in New York City's *American;* it also appeared as a broadside and in pamphlet form. Less organized than their opponents, less prone to cultivate voters, and less committed to the recent conflict with Great Britain, Federalists had also seen their policies taken over by a national administration that had launched a new national bank and used an expanded navy to defend American commerce. Out of power and out of office, these dissident Federalists of New York State, whom Clintonian Federalists quickly and sarcastically labeled as "high-minded," proclaimed their support for the Bucktail Republicans, whom they praised as guardians of democratic institutions and promoters of federal policies like the Missouri Compromise. The High-Minded Federalists followed a path similar to that followed in the mid-1810s by the Coodies, a group of American Federalist Party members named for their founder, New Yorker Gulian Crommelin Verplanck, who used the pseudonym Abimelech Coody. Like the Coodies, the High-Minded condemned what they viewed as Gov De Witt Clinton's political and personal ambition, and warned that he could disrupt New York State's Republican Party and, conceivably, endanger the Union by exploiting Federalist resentment of southern domination of the federal government to build an all-northern political following.

A highly articulate and rather youthful elite (largely in their 30s), the High-Minded were predominantly lawyers, Episcopalians, closely interrelated among themselves, and extensively related to other state-level political participants active from 1815 through 1828. Some of the ex-Federalists, such as John Sudam and Thomas G. Waterman, provided valuable Bucktail leadership in the New York State legislature during the early 1820s. Others, like Charles King, who had taken over as managing editor of the *American* in May 1823, parted company with the Albany Regency. Though James A. Hamilton long stood by Martin Van Buren, like most of the High-Minded who remained politically active, he eventually became a Whig. Two of the men, Charles King and William Duer, later served as presidents of Columbia College. John Duer helped produce the state's Revised Statutes of 1829 and advanced to chief judge of the New York City Superior Court in 1857. In 1856 John A. King, running as a Republican, won the office of governor.

Hanyan, Craig, and Mary Hanyan. *De Witt Clinton and the Rise of the People's Men* (Montreal: McGill-Queen's Univ Press, 1996)

Livermore, Shaw. *The Twilight of Federalism: The Disintegration of the Federalist Party, 1815–1830* (Princeton, NJ: Princeton Univ Press, 1962)

Craig and Mary L. Hanyan

high society. New York State and especially New York City have historically been home to the nation's largest and most influential social elite. This elite, however, changed radically in the early decades of American independence. After the British army left New York City in 1783, the old landed loyalist families, strong supporters of the British Crown during the Revolutionary War, were supplanted by a "patriot" elite. Until the turn of the century, Federalists like John Jay, Rufus King, and Gouverneur Morris retained control of the affairs of New York City. Aristocratic in their attitude toward social issues, they favored an established social hierarchy. Their wealth, dress, and elegant homes on Broadway and around Bowling Green in Manhattan, remote from log cabin life on the frontier, defined an upper-class ethos for the period. Jay's wife Sarah was the undisputed leader of postrevolutionary New York society. Long after the Federalist Party itself had waned in the 1820s, elite values persisted in the drawing rooms of Lafayette Place and 5th Ave. Later New Yorkers would look back with nostalgia at the "good families" of the era and their supposed ideals of republican simplicity.

The most populous state in the Union by the 1830s, New York had the largest manufacturing base and the greatest commerce, and led the nation in banking and transportation. The fruits of that economic preeminence were revealed in the increasing wealth of New Yorkers. Their magnificent homes on 5th Ave and their great country estates, like the Greek Revival Livingston home in Staatsburg (Dutchess Co) built in 1832, reached new levels of ostentation. With the exception of civic-minded families, such as the Roosevelts at Oyster Bay (Nassau Co), by the 1860s the traditional elite like the Brevoorts and Schermerhorns, of Knickerbocker origin, had ceased to play a dominant role in public life. Rather, they were insular, anxious to restrict contact with the "vulgar" masses. They deplored and feared the "new money" represented by the Vanderbilts, Jay Gould, and Jim Fisk, whose fortunes were founded on the railroads, telegraphy, stock market speculation, and other emerging enterprises. Over time accommodation was inevitable. The problem facing the traditional elite was how the process could be managed and controlled to their own advantage.

The institutions they created reveal something of the tone of social life in the Empire State. Beginning in the 1830s among the social clubs formed in New York City were the Union Club (1836) and the Century Association (1846). Modeled after exclusive London clubs, they formed a defensive phalanx of "old money." No Jews, Catholics, or African Americans were considered. Decisions on membership were taken by a secret ballot of black and white balls, with the black ball readily used to settle scores and to exclude undesirables. At successful clubs prospective members routinely had to wait five years or more to advance to election. A study in the 1870s revealed that one-half of club memberships in the city went to as few as 20 families, with many men holding multiple memberships. A network of exclusive private associations, as well as country clubs and similar bodies for yachtsmen, golfers, coaching enthusiasts, and aviators further contributed to the aristocratic ambience of New York high society.

Upper-class social life in New York City was organized into a "season" coinciding with opera performances at the Academy of Music (1853–85) and the Metropolitan Opera (1883). The opera and museums like the Metropolitan Museum of Art (1870), with their great opportunities for display, were the social elite's greatest contribution to the city's culture. The most exclusive events on the social calendar—limited to 25 august citizens of impeccable social position and wealth, and their invited guests—were the Patriarch Balls held at Delmonico's Restaurant under the control of Ward McAllister. With the leading hostess, Mrs William Astor, McAllister played an important role in preserving an elite social world. He was the originator of the "Four Hundred," an imprecise but influential tally of the New York City aristocracy, reflecting McAllister's sense of its ideal size. Attempts to define the boundaries of "society," beginning with the publication of the *Social Register* in 1887, became something of a parlor entertainment.

Club members formed a natural clientele for upscale consumption. A market for hand-manufactured luxury carriages arose to satisfy their tastes, and New York City was the center of trade in fine arts, silver work, jewelry, dresses, and furs. Merchants like A. T. Stewart imported the fine carpets and consumer goods needed to fill the mansions of the elite. The American fine arts market was centered on New York City, and the leading architectural practices of Richard Morris Hunt and of McKim, Mead and White, among others, executed commissions for mansions in Newport, RI, northern New Jersey, and Long Island as well as on 5th Ave, largely replacing the Greek Revival style with Gothic confections like Renwick Castle (later Yates Castle) in Syracuse and Lyndhurst in Tarrytown (Westchester Co). The banks of the Hudson River had long been the preferred location for country estates, such as Kykuit, built by the Rockefellers at Pocantico Hills (Westchester Co). Wealthy New Yorkers differed from the landed gentry of England in that they did not expect to make money from the land or believed that their children would choose to live in their mansions. Few estates remained in the ownership of a single family for long.

The building of a railroad line to Saratoga Springs in the 1830s led to the creation of the first national summer resort devoted to nothing but pleasure and relaxation. Saratoga was a matrimonial marketplace, a venue for political intrigue, and a place where new dances were introduced. Women enjoyed a prominence and an access to social resources there unprecedented in American life. "Saratoga is famous," wrote Henry James, "as the place where women adorn themselves most, or as the place, at least, where the greatest amount of dressing may be seen by the greatest number of people." New York's metropolitan social elite established residential colonies on the North Shore of Long Island, which became known as the Gold Coast; in exclusive communities like Bedford, Harrison, and Bronxville in Westchester Co; and at unique communities such as Tuxedo Park (Orange Co), developed by Pierre Lorillard in 1886. Unlike the celebrities and Wall St barons who in recent times have flooded enclaves like the Hamptons, the 19th-century upper crust preferred exclusivity to fame or notoriety.

Although the role of money as a basis for social prominence was obvious, elites in the age of Mrs Astor were proud of their family lineage, and there were some figures of modest means among McAllister's Four Hundred. In the 20th century, however, wealth became a more reliable measure of social status. By the 1920s it was evident that money was defining new forms of social celebrity. F. Scott Fitzgerald's novel *The Great Gatsby* (1925) is set among the great mansions of Long Island, where Nick Carraway, Tom and Daisy Buchanan, and the new-money aspirant Jay Gatsby settled. Their parties were crowded by showgirls, boxers, bootleggers, and speakeasy types. The socialites of the 20th century embodied a restless self-confidence that no family pedigree or social exclusivity could dampen, opening the doors to a new elite culture of money, celebrity, and boldness.

The role of old families had largely faded, but New York City social clubs were rejuvenated in the 1980s and 1990s, and remain bastions of social conservatism and exclusivity. With the great bull market of the 1990s, Wall St millionaires were once again hiring butlers and English nannies, and debutante balls were chronicled in the *New York Times*. The city was richer than it had ever been before and happy to flaunt its wealth. Works of modern art and Park Ave penthouse apartments fetched record sums. Although the market downturn of the late 1990s curbed the extravagance, the history of New York high society suggests a bright future for conspicuous consumption.

Aslet, Clive. *The American Country House* (New Haven, Conn: Yale Univ Press, 1990)
Homberger, Eric. *Mrs. Astor's New York: Money and Social Power in a Gilded Age* (New Haven, Conn: Yale Univ Press, 2002)
Jaher, Frederic Cople. *The Urban Establishment: Upper Strata in Boston, New York, Charleston, Chicago, and Los Angeles* (Urbana: Univ of Illinois Press, 1982)
Wilson, Derek. *The Astors, 1763–1992: Landscape with Millionaires* (New York: St. Martin's Press, 1993)

Eric Homberger

highways. See INTERSTATE HIGHWAYS; ROADS.

hiking and camping. The popularity of these two related activities in the state has grown continuously since the Civil War. Resident and tourist interest in being outdoors to enjoy nature was evident in the 1880s and 1890s in the Adirondacks with the protection of the public forest lands, the formation of more than 60 associations and hunting and fishing clubs, construction of numerous camps from compact summer places to the rustic "great camps," and the formation of hiking organizations like the Adirondack Trail Improvement Society (1897). By the 1920s the automobile had made the population more mobile, and the new activity of "car camping" began along roads and in campgrounds. As people began to travel a series of hiking organizations also emerged in the 1920s, such as the Adirondack 46ers (those who climbed all of the 46 mountains in the Adirondacks at 4,000 feet [1,219 m] or higher), Adirondack Mountain Club, Appalachian Trail Conference, and the New York–New Jersey Trail Conference. Public demand and the efforts of such organizations as the Civilian Conservation Corps spurred the construction of trails, forest roads, and campgrounds through the 1930s and 1940s.

Hiking in the state ranges from easy walks in the woods to long-distance treks like the Northville–Lake Placid Trail (1922), a 133 mi (214 km) footpath created by the Adirondack Mountain Club; the 2,167 mi (3,487 km) Appalachian Trail (1923) with 88 miles (142 km) through southeastern New York State; and the Finger Lakes Trail (1962), 552 miles (888 km) connecting the Catskill and Allegheny Mountains. In 1998, 3.1 million state residents (21% of the population) were joined by many tourists in hiking on the thousands of miles of trails on state and private lands, and 1.9 million residents (13% of the population) camped at facilities on state and private lands. In 2002 public camping facilities included 66 campgrounds operated in state parks by the Office of Parks, Recreation, and Historic Preservation and 52 campgrounds on Adirondack and Catskill Forest Preserve lands managed by the Department of Environmental Conservation. Backcountry camping is generally allowed on many state forest and Forest Preserve lands within the Adirondack and Catskill Parks. Commercial camping facilities are available at 1,145 locations, with more than 82,900 campsites, offering services, and state parks and commercial campgrounds offer more than 6,600 cabins.

New York State Office of Parks, Recreation, and Historic Preservation. *Statewide Comprehensive Outdoor Recreation Plan 2003* (Albany: Author, 2002)

Chad P. Dawson

Hilbert College. Private four-year college on a 47-acre (19 ha) campus 15 miles (24 km) south of Buffalo in Hamburg (Erie Co). It was founded as Immaculata College in 1957 by the Franciscan Sisters of St. Joseph to train its members for the teaching profession. The school began admitting laywomen in 1964. By 1969 it built a new campus adjacent to its original convent location, became coeducational, and its mission broadened to include academic disciplines outside of education. At that time it was renamed Hilbert College, after Mother M. Colette Hilbert, who founded the order in 1897. Four-year degree programs became available in 1992. The school is home to the Institute of Law and Justice and maintains the McGrath Library Law Collection, one of the largest academic law collections open to the public in western New York State. In 2003 it was one of only two schools in the country that offered a BA degree in economic crime investigation. Hilbert had a student body of 964 in 2003.

Marianne Rahn-Erickson

Hill, David B(ennett) (*b* Havana [now Montour Falls, Schuyler Co], 29 Aug 1843; *d* Albany, 20 Oct 1910). Governor and US senator. Hill moved to Elmira in 1863, was admitted to the bar in 1864, served in the state assembly in 1871 and 1872, but did not run for office again until 1882, when he became mayor of Elmira. Hill served as lieutenant governor of New York State under Grover Cleveland from 1883 to 1885, then ascended to the governorship in January 1885 when Cleveland became president. Reelected governor in 1885 and 1888, Hill won the second time even though Pres Cleveland failed to carry New York State and lost his reelection bid. As a Democratic governor facing a Republican-controlled legislature, Hill opposed civil service reform and Prohibition, vetoed the 1885 Census Bill as an unnecessary extravagance, and generally supported the rights of labor unions. His partisanship was exemplified in his claim "I am a Democrat!" in a speech during his bid for reelection in 1885. The motto, which would be linked to Hill for the rest of his career, implied that he would not support civil service or any of Cleveland's reforms and made it clear that he did not want the votes of Mugwumps, Republicans who deserted their party in 1884 to vote for Cleveland.

Hill's career reached its zenith when New York State's first Democratic legislature in a decade chose him as US senator in early 1891. Hill did not take up those duties immediately but instead continued to act as governor, a decision that stirred great controversy as he simultaneously held claim to both offices. During that year Hill successfully overturned the election of three Republican state senators and replaced them with Democrats, giving his party control of the state legislature, but fallout from this action damaged his future political prospects. Hill assumed his duties as senator in January 1892 after completing his gubernatorial term. His interest in the Democratic nomination for president that year failed to materialize, though, and he never challenged Cleveland at the party convention. In 1894 Hill reluctantly accepted the nomination for the governorship but was easily defeated by

Gov David B. Hill appearing in W. Duke and Sons Co tobacco advertisement, 1888.

Levi P. Morton in the aftermath of the panic of 1893. Hill served the remainder of his term in the senate but never ran for public office again, even refusing the Democratic Party nomination for vice president in 1900. In 1904 he managed Alton B. Parker's failed presidential campaign and then enjoyed a successful law practice in Albany.

Alexander, De Alva Stanwood. *Four Famous New Yorkers: The Political Careers of Cleveland, Platt, Hill, and Roosevelt* (1923; repr New York: I. J. Friedman, 1969)

Bass, Herbert. *"I Am a Democrat": The Political Career of David Bennett Hill* (Syracuse: Syracuse Univ Press, 1961)

Hill, David. *Public Papers of David Bennett Hill: Governor/Senator of New York* (Albany: Albany Argus, 1885–92)

Jon Sterngass

Hillburn. Village (pop 881) in Ramapo (Rockland Co). Originally called Woodburn, it is located in a small valley hemmed in by the Ramapo Mountains. A charcoal forge (1848) manufactured merchant iron; a rolling mill (1852–72) and, later, the Ramapo Iron Works (1881) also provided employment. The Ramapo Wheel and Foundry Co of nearby Ramapo platted the present Hillburn in 1872 to provide homes for its workers. The Hillburn post office opened in 1882, and the village incorporated in 1893. Long the home of the triracial Ramapo Mountain People, the village developed a substantial minority population. Hillburn had the last legally segregated public school in New York State. It finally was closed in 1943, after a 12-year campaign by a local NAACP branch and the efforts of national civil rights figures, including Thurgood Marshall. Its 2000 population was 40% minority, including 13.6% black, 17.6% American Indian, and 22% of mixed heritage. The village is the location of the Thruway interchange with I-287 and Rte 17, but it does not benefit from the limited-access traffic.

Hillcrest. Locality (pop 7,106) in Ramapo (Rockland Co). Developed by William Moles beginning in 1910, it was first known as Moleston. It is residential with a commercial strip on Rte 45. In 2000 the population was 51% African American and 15% Asian American.

Hill Cumorah Pageant. Religious drama produced by the Church of Latter-day Saints (LDS) and performed annually in Manchester (Ontario Co). The pageant is staged on the Hill Cumorah, revered by Mormons as the place where Joseph Smith Jr discovered golden plates that had been buried by the angel Moroni. In 1830 Smith translated this record and published it in Palmyra (Wayne Co), four miles to the north of Hill Cumorah, as the Book of Mormon, which Latter-day Saints regard as scripture written by ancient American Christians.

In 1907 LDS Church president Joseph F. Smith bought several sacred sites in Western New York. Hill Cumorah was purchased in 1928, but Mormon celebrations there actually began with the 1917 Pioneer Day commemoration of Brigham Young's arrival in Utah, and Mormon missionaries started the Palmyra Celebration in 1922. LDS theatrical productions at Hill Cumorah began in 1935 with the dedication of a 40 ft (12.2 m) statue of Moroni. In 1937 Harold I. Hansen began his 40-year directorship of the program. Over the years he streamlined the script, limiting scenes solely to events depicted in the Book of Mormon. In 1957 Crawford Gates composed a musical score recorded by the Mormon Tabernacle Choir and the Utah Symphony. A new version of the pageant, written by best-selling science fiction author Orson Scott Card, debuted in 1988.

Rooted in the early 20th-century fondness for grandiose outdoor theater, the pageant has become increasingly sophisticated. Guided by Mormons in the entertainment industry, it was presented, by the 1980s, on a recontoured hill and a seven-level stage with pyrotechnics, a booming musical score, ornate costumes, and dramatic depictions of good versus evil climaxing with the visit of Jesus Christ to the Americas after his resurrection. It is run entirely by LDS volunteers, including the 600-member cast of young performers.

The Hill Cumorah Pageant is the most dramatic aspect of a complex of LDS pilgrimage sites in Western New York, including the Smith Family Farm, a visitors center, and a temple that was dedicated in 2000. It is also one of the most successful public relations events of the LDS Church, drawing the faithful, the curious, and the hostile, often in the form of conservative Protestants who distribute literature disputing the pageant's theological claims. With more than 100,000 visitors each July, the pageant proves to be a very popular tourist attraction in the area.

Armstrong, Richard N., and Gerald S. Argetsinger. "The Hill Cumorah Pageant: Religious Pageantry as Suasive Form," *Text and Performance Quarterly* 2 (1989): 153–64

Hill Cumorah Pageant Web Guide, http //pageant.ensignct.com/pageant/history.html

Whitman, Charles W. "A History of the Hill Cumorah Pageant, 1937–1964" (PhD diss, Univ of Minnesota, 1967)

Eric A. Eliason

Hillman, Sidney (*b* Zagare [now in Lithuania], 23 Mar 1887; *d* Point Lookout, Nassau Co, 10 July 1946). Labor leader. Hillman was active with the socialist General League of Jewish Workers (the Bund), then emigrated to New York City in 1907. In 1909 unemployment led him to Chicago, where he worked as a fabric cutter. He became immersed in the labor movement, leading a garment workers strike in Chicago in 1910. Opposed to the elitism and craft orientation of the United Garment Workers union, Hillman and others founded the Amalgamated Clothing Workers of America (ACW) in New York City on 26 Dec 1914. As president (1914–46), Hillman was committed to industrial unionism, collective bargaining, and social welfare reform. He was a founding member of the Committee of Industrial Organization in 1935 and served as a vice president until his death. Hillman also served on Franklin D. Roosevelt's labor advisory board (1933–36) and was the only representative of labor on the National Defense Advisory Commission in 1940. This body was replaced by the Office of Production Management in the same year, and as associate director, Hillman was charged with ensuring labor peace during World War II and was a crucial advisor for New Deal labor policy.

Fraser, Steven. *Labor Will Rule: Sidney Hillman and the Rise of American Labor* (New York: Free Press, 1991)

Christopher Martin

Hillsdale. Town (pop 1,744) in SE Columbia Co. Settled ?1719 and known as Nobletown, it was settled primarily by New Englanders with some Dutch in its western part, formed as a district from Claverack in 1782, and recognized as a town in 1788. Iron was mined from 1833 to *ca* 1890 and plows produced, woolen cloth was woven beginning 1816, and French immigrants burned charcoal for the Copake Iron Works. Farm products included wool, hay, buckwheat, and, after the Harlem Railroad (1852), dairy. Summer boarders began to arrive after the Civil War, and in the last quarter of the 20th century weekend homes became common. Hillsdale had an unusually heavy concentration of "investor farms" in the 1980s and is known for beef cattle. It is the site of Catamount ski area and the annual Falcon Ridge Folk Festival.

Hilton. Village (pop 5,856) in Parma (Monroe Co). The Rome, Watertown and Ogdensburg Railroad came to the hamlet of North Parma in 1875. The village was incorporated in 1885 under that name but was changed to Hilton in 1896. In the 20th century the village grew as a result of businesses processing fruit and vegetables, including an evaporator, a cannery, a vinegar plant, and a sauerkraut factory; Italian immigrants worked in the plants. Buttons were manufactured from 1915 to 1933. Suburbanization from 1960 to 2000 resulted in a more than fourfold population growth. Every fall the Hilton Apple Fest attracts thousands of visitors.

Nancy Martin

Hindus. The roots of Hinduism in New York State date from the late 19th century. The Vedanta Society of New York, first in the United States, was established in New York City in 1894 by Swami Vivekananda (1863–1902), a disciple of Sri Ramakrishna. Aided by a growing interest in Eastern philosophy, Vivekananda drew wide acclaim for his historic 1893 addresses to the Parliament of World Religions in Chicago and gave subsequent lectures in Brooklyn, Manhattan, and elsewhere, attracting a group of American disciples in New York City. After Vivekananda's departure, four other swamis from India, Abhedananda, Bodhananda, Pavitrananda, and Tathagatananda, led the society until the end of the 20th century.

In 1921 the Vedanta Society bought its headquarters on West 71st St near Central Park. Since 1962 it has held annual 4 July Vivekananda Festivals at Moss Hill Farms, a country home in Carmel (Dutchess Co). Other Hindu gurus (teachers) with their own philosophies, meditation and yoga practices, and styles of leadership came to the state beginning in the 1930s. The teachings of Swami A. C. Bhaktivedanta, who arrived in 1965, stressed an ascetic lifestyle and an ecstatic form of Hindu worship known as bhakti (devotional singing). He incorporated the International Society for Krishna Consciousness (ISKCON), popularly known as the Hare Krishna movement, in a Manhattan storefront in 1966. The mainly European American congregations of both the Vedanta Society of New York and ISKCON were eventually joined and revitalized by new Indian immigrants.

Following the Immigration Act of 1965, Indian professionals and their families began settling in Flushing (Queens Co). The growing immigrant community improvised ways to continue their religious traditions in America. Humble beginnings in homes, apartments, basements, rented halls, storefronts, and converted buildings led to the first traditional Hindu temples in the West. In 1970 the Hindu Temple Society of North America was incorporated by Alagappa Alagappan, a former UN civil servant from Chettinad in South India. After raising funds, the group purchased a defunct Russian Orthodox church on Bowne St in a residential Flushing neighborhood. In 1975 the society demolished the church and began building an immense, elaborate edifice in the traditional architectural style of a South Indian Hindu temple. Consecrated on 4 July 1977, it was devoted to Ganesha, the elephant-headed god of wisdom and remover of obstacles. The temple's official name later changed to Sri Maha Vallabha Ganapati Devasthanam, but it is more commonly known as the Ganesha temple. It became a model for temples across the United States and a vital center for the Hindu community.

As the community grew into a microcosm of the Indian subcontinent, various groups specialized in regional traditions. By 2000, seven more temples had been built in Flushing, forming the country's largest and most diverse concentration of Hindu temples. Flushing remains a major residential area for South Asians and the cradle of the Hindu community in the United States. Although South Asian immigrants initially met with some hostility from neighbors, in later years the annual street parade to celebrate Ganesh Chaturthi (the birthday of Ganesha) in late summer became a colorful tradition attracting over 10,000 people. Diwali, the autumn "Festival of Lights" that marks the beginning of the Hindu new year, draws even bigger crowds each year to South Street Seaport in Lower Manhattan. When the enterprising pioneers of the early community moved on, larger South Asian commercial areas developed in Jackson Heights and Richmond Hill in Queens, in Manhattan, and in Edison, NJ. Later generations, including an increasingly diverse mix of Hindu immigrants from the Caribbean and other areas of the global Indian diaspora, face different challenges of adaptation as they try to translate Hinduism for a new age.

Figures for the Hindu population are difficult to determine. The census of India estimates that 80% of the population of India is of Hindu background. In the 2000 US census, 251,724 persons in New York State claimed Asian Indian ancestry, 170,899 of them in New York City, and a substantial majority are Hindus. In the early 21st century, there are at least 84 Hindu temples and centers in New York State. Most are in New York City; others are in Albany, Monroe (Orange Co), Buffalo, Syracuse, Getzville (Erie Co), Rochester, Richville (St. Lawrence Co), Rush (Monroe Co), Thousand Island Park (Jefferson Co), and Stone Ridge (Ulster Co).

See also INDIANS AND SOUTH ASIANS.

Hanson, R. Scott. "City of Gods: Religious Freedom, Immigration, and Pluralism in Flushing, Queens–New York City, 1945–2000" (PhD diss, Univ of Chicago, 2002)

Hawley, John Stratton. "Global Hinduism in Gotham" In *Asian American Religions: Borders and Boundaries*, ed. Tony Carnes and Fenggang Yang (New York: New York Univ Press, 2003)

Khandelwal, Madhulika S. *Becoming American, Being Indian: An Immigrant Community in New York City* (Ithaca: Cornell Univ Press, 2002)

R. Scott Hanson

Hinsdale. Town (pop 2,270) in SE Cattaraugus Co. Settled in 1806, the town was formed from Olean in 1820. The first sawmill in the county was built in Hinsdale in 1807. Farmers in town protested in the bloodless Dutch Hill War" (1844–45) against the lease and eviction policy of the Holland Land Co. After exhausting the lumber supply, settlers turned to farming and dairying; cheese making became the main industry. The Erie Railroad (1851), Genesee Valley Canal (1856–78), and Buffalo, New York and Philadelphia Railroad (1872; later Pennsylvania Railroad) all served the town. Rte 17 (I-86) was built in the 1970s. In the early 21st century many residents commute to Olean. Lock 102 of the Genesee Valley Canal is a landmark. Heritage Days are held in August, and Sprint Speedway, a flat oval racetrack for cars and go-carts, is a Hinsdale attraction.

Bruce D. Fredrickson and Madelynn P. Fredrickson

hip hop. Musical style with funk, rhythm and blues, and ethnic roots, characterized by a strong beat, intricate mixing of recorded music, DJing, and rhythmic song-speech known as MCing or "rapping." Rap evolved in the Bronx in the mid-1970s as part of a wider subcultural movement that also included break dancing, graffiti, and other cultural practices.

Origins

Pressing poverty, political grievances, and a wide mixture of persons of African descent, including Haitians, US-born blacks, Jamaicans, Puerto Ricans, Dominicans, and Cubans, contributed to the distinctive nature of hip hop culture, which allowed inner-city youth to establish individual and neighborhood identities in a competitive, largely nonviolent forum. Hip hop competition also brought disparate ethnic groups into a forum where musical ideas were shared and improvisational musical conventions evolved.

Prominent local ethnic groups contributed crucial ingredients to the hip hop formula. Cuban and Puerto Rican musical culture can be found in the percussive style of early hip hop. Early hip hop DJs made intensive use of timbales, salsa beats, and Tito Puente records; Barbadian bongo style is also prominent. Jamaican traditions brought to hip hop competitive DJing and a communal sense of song ownership. Rapping, the vocal component of hip hop, may have antecedents in Jamaican music genres of talkover and dub, both of which feature song-speech called toasting. Other antecedents may be found in domestic black oral culture. The lyrical content of many early raps is reminiscent of schoolyard verbal abuse games, like the dozens ("Your mama is so ugly that . . ."). Several early rappers cite the album *Hustler's Convention* (1973), a collection of prison recitations put to music by the Last Poets, as their primary inspiration. Others suggest that rapping began simply as a means to make announcements during dances or as a means of promoting favorite DJs.

Jamaican-born DJ Kool Herc (Clive Campbell) was one of the first well-known DJs in the Bronx. His powerful sound system, innovative techniques, and funky and obscure playlist produced numerous imitators. Herc also pioneered "cutting and mixing," playing the most danceable drum breaks in succession on two turntables, a practice favored by competitive dancers. Former gang member Afrika Bambaataa (Kevin Donovan) publicly promoted hip hop as an alternative to gangs, and his single "Planet Rock" (1982) was one of the earliest and most influential hip hop songs. Bronx DJ Grandmaster Flash (Joseph Sadler) composed the critically acclaimed hip hop classic "The Message" (1982) and revolutionized DJing by introducing numerous turntable techniques, including the playing of increasingly small snippets of songs ("cutting"), using the sounds of records played backward ("backspinning"), and creatively manipulating the speed of play ("phasing"). Flash's companion Grand Wizard Theodore (Theodore Livingstone) pioneered "scratching," in which a record is rapidly moved back and forth with the turntable's stylus in the groove, making the turntable a rhythmic instrument and allowing the DJ to evolve from passive medium to active musician.

THE 1980S

The first hip hop record was probably the New Jersey–based Sugar Hill Gang's "Rapper's Delight" (1979), which found a national audience, opening the door for other hip hop artists. With the exception of Mercury Records, which signed Kurtis Blow in 1980, major record companies failed to mine the hip hop talent in New York City, leaving it to minor labels. Blow's album sales were modest but captured the spirit of Bronx-style rapping. The first group to have significant critical and commercial appeal was Run DMC from Hollis (Queens Co), which released a nationally successful album in 1984. Middle class and well versed in hard rock, members Run (Joseph Simmons), DMC (Darryl McDaniels), and Jam Master Jay (Jason Mizell; killed in 2002) worked closely with New York University art student Rick Rubin to produce a hard-edged, guitar-heavy brand of hip hop. Following closely behind were the Beastie Boys, an all-white rap group that, using a formula similar to Run DMC's, sold millions of records and established the commercial viability of hip hop.

In the late 1980s hip hop acts and styles, several of which evolved in New York City and many of which reached a national audience through MTV, steadily proliferated. "Old School" hip hop, which included mostly Bronx- and Harlem-based artists such as L. L. Cool J., Big Daddy Kane, Kool Moe Dee, and Rakim, emerged from the core group of early hip hop performers, retaining a funk and rhythm and blues (R&B) rhythmic framework and a lyrical focus on boasting and disparaging others. Many suburban-based acts, such as Public Enemy and De La Soul (both from Long Island), A Tribe Called Quest, and Digable Planets, known as the "New School," expanded the musical parameters of hip hop, all promoting, albeit in differing tones, positive self-awareness and political consciousness for Blacks. Bronx native Teddy Riley popularized the so-called New Jack Swing sound via his production work with artists like Keith Sweat, Heavy D and the Boyz (from Mount Vernon, Westchester Co), and even Michael Jackson. This musical innovation borrowed more heavily from contemporary R&B to create a highly danceable musical style with broad commercial appeal. Other well-known New York hip hop acts from this period also expanding the boundaries of hip hop include all-female groups Salt-N-Pepa and Stetsasonic and dance-oriented artists like Rob Base and DJ EZ Rock.

SINCE 1990

In the 1990s the hegemony of New York City in the hip hop world eroded, especially with the rise of scenes in Los Angeles and Oakland, Calif. Verbal feuding between rap stars based in New York and Los Angeles may have led to the much-publicized murders of Tupac Shakur (originally from New York City) in 1996 and the Notorious B.I.G., a New York City–based artist on Sean "Puff Daddy" Combs's Bad Boy record label, in 1997. Combs, also later known as P. Diddy, from Mount Vernon, became by the mid-1990s a prominent pop music impresario, producing a string of hits that appealed to a wide mainstream audience and that were met with derision by many in the hip hop community. Jay-Z (Shawn Carter) from Brooklyn also emerged as a major star in the 1990s, launching his career on his own record label.

The marriage of hard rock and hip hop became something of a subgenre all its own, with New York City–based heavy metal band Anthrax jointly recording with Public Enemy, and with groups including Korn, Limp Bizkit, Rage Against the Machine, Slayer, the Red Hot Chili Peppers, and Kid Rock spreading the popularity of rap rock into new white suburban market niches. By the early 21st century hip hop was an influential cultural force worldwide, influencing the direction not only of popular music but areas as disparate as fashion, language, and politics.

George, Nelson. *Hip Hop America* (New York: Viking Press, 1998)

Hager, Steven. *Hip Hop: The Illustrated History of Break Dancing, Rap Music and Graffiti* (New York: St. Martin's Press, 1984)

Rose, Tricia. *Black Noise: Rap Music and Black Culture in Contemporary America* (Middletown, Conn: Wesleyan Univ Press, 1994)

Steve Graves

Hiscock, Frank (*b* Pompey, Onondaga Co, 6 Sept 1834; *d* Syracuse, 18 June 1914). Lawyer and politician. The son of a farmer, Hiscock attended Pompey Academy, studied law, and was admitted to the New York Bar in 1855. District attorney of Onondaga Co from 1860 to 1863, Hiscock served in both the US House of Representatives (1877–87) and the US Senate (1887–93). As a senator, he was a member of the Ways and Means Committee and chaired the Appropriations Committee. He later practiced law in Syracuse. His nephew Frank H. Hiscock, chief judge of the New York Court of Appeals (1916–26), founded the Hiscock Legal Aid Society in Syracuse.

National Cyclopedia of American Biography, sv "Hiscock, Frank"

Dick Case

historical archaeology. This discipline is distinguished from prehistoric archaeology in New York State as being subsequent to the date of first contact between Indian and European cultures. Prehistoric and historic archaeology use essentially the same techniques for data retrieval in the field and for artifact analysis, but historical archaeology uses additional documentary resources for interpretation.

Deliberate collection of artifacts from historic sites occurred in New York City as early as the late 18th century. Sites in New York State previously occupied by Indians aroused the greatest interest, however. Scholars attempting to interpret these finds included De Witt Clinton and Henry Rowe Schoolcraft. Attention to artifacts from French and Indian War and Revolutionary War sites also increased after about 1830 as surviving veterans died. Discoveries of Revolutionary War burials became especially frequent in Brooklyn, Manhattan, the Saratoga battlefields, and elsewhere. Eighteen-year-old Harvard student Francis Parkman found French and Indian War artifacts at Lake George; Jeptha Simms, Benson J. Lossing, Jared Sparks, and others wrote of colonial sites and artifacts.

The work of Joshua V. H. Clark, Lewis Henry Morgan, Ephraim G. Squier, and others furthered the study of historic Iroquois sites through major works published between 1848 and 1852. Combining documentary research and interviews with Iroquois chief John Blacksmith on the Tonawanda Indian Reservation [loc in Erie, Genesee, and Lewis Cos] in 1847, Orsamus Marshall identified Boughton Hill (now Ganondagan State Historic Site in Victor, Ontario Co) as the Seneca village site destroyed during the 1687 expedition led by Marquis de Denonville. This first step enabled archaeologists a century later to determine the historical sequence of Seneca village sites back to 1550. Squier recorded visible remains of a palisaded fort on a hilltop adjacent to Boughton Hill in 1848. After the Civil War, Dr David Kellogg of Plattsburgh collected historical artifacts at sites around Lake Champlain. In 1886 he attempted to protect the wreck of the *Royal Savage,* sunk in 1776 near Valcour Island [now in Clinton Co] and had divers who were looting the wreck arrested. In 1888 Stephen Pell discovered artifacts in the ruins of Fort Ticonderoga (Essex Co), inspiring its eventual reconstruction. After 1890 historical archaeology developed rapidly. New York State Museum bulletins on Indian trade artifacts appeared by 1898; excavations of contact sites occurred in the Buffalo/Niagara region and on Long Island. Historical sequences of Onondaga and Seneca village sites were first proposed, as it became recognized that entire cultures should be studied through archaeology.

Before the 1960s, work at military sites in New York predominated. Annie Witherbee, one of the first women active in historical archaeology, excavated at Crown Point (Essex Co) in 1912 and received favorable recognition for her work. William L. Calver and Reginald P. Bolton studied Revolutionary War sites in the New York City and lower Hudson Valley areas. In the early 20th century, often just ahead of the steam shovels as the city rapidly expanded, they rescued historical information and artifacts that would have been lost forever. With extraordinary skill, diver Lorenzo F. Hagglund raised the 1776 gunboat *Philadelphia* in Lake Champlain in 1935. Late 1950s excavations at Johnson Hall [now Johnstown, Fulton Co], Fort Montgomery (Orange Co), Crown Point, Ticonderoga, Fort William Henry [now in Lake George, Warren Co], Lewiston (Niagara Co), and the Saratoga battlefields initiated the momentum in historical archaeology toward professionalism and research, going beyond collection.

Important advances also began in the 1950s in the study of post-Contact Indian sites. The 1550–1687 Seneca village site sequence, after many years of research, was published in 1953. A synthesis of Oneida Iroquois research appeared in 1976, followed by studies of the Onondaga in 1987 and of the Mohawk in 1995. Excavations revealed Mohican (Mahican) sites of the 16th and 17th centuries in the Albany and mid-Hudson regions. This work was greatly encouraged and advanced in this period by the New York State Archaeological Association with its annual statewide and frequent regional chapter meetings. At these meetings, both professionals and amateurs discuss research, exchange ideas, and report findings on both historic and prehistoric archaeological sites. Fifteen chapters are established across New York State.

In the 1960s historic preservation and the protection and management of archaeological re-

Five Points. New York City's most notorious 19th-century slum, named for the intersection of what used to be Orange, Cross, and Anthony Sts in Lower Manhattan. The open intersection was portrayed in period lithographs as throbbing with illicit activities. Contemporary writing characterized the inhabitants as prostitutes, drunkards, and criminals. The construction of a federal courthouse at Foley Square in the 1990s required archaeological excavation of a block that abutted the Five Points intersection. The investigation of 14 historic lots bound by what are now Pearl, Park Row, and Baxter Sts exposed former tenement foundations, cellar floors, courtyards, and 50 backyard features. Artifacts were recovered from 22 of the features, most of which were either wood- or brick-lined privies. Several cisterns, a large cesspool, and an icehouse were also discovered.

The earliest artifact assemblages that were recovered dated to the early 19th century when artisans worked and lived along Pearl St. As the neighborhood filled up with immigrant workers, the early houses were subdivided into apartments; by midcentury, several multistory tenements had been built. Artifacts associated with tenements on Pearl St provided insights into the lives of Irish families who had fled the potato famine of the 1840s. Individual households appear to have owned Staffordshire dinnerware and tea sets in fashionable styles. Residents decorated their apartment with plants and figurines and provided their children with inscribed dishes meant to teach manners and pride in personal property. Although fish would have been less expensive, they continued to prefer pork following Irish custom. Artifact assemblages and food remains associated with the Jewish secondhand clothing dealers on Baxter St were distinctive. Findings suggest that they too used material possessions and traditional foodways to maintain their ethnic identity in their new homes.

While the finds do not confirm the stereotypical picture of Five Points residents, the excavation did reveal overcrowded and unsanitary living conditions. Front and back tenements on single lots left only tiny courtyards in between, filled with privies and cesspools.

Anbinder, Tyler. *Five Points: The 19th-Century New York City Neighborhood That Invented Tap Dance, Stole Elections, and Became the World's Most Notorious Slum* (New York: Free Press, 2001)

Stott, Richard B. *Workers in the Metropolis: Class, Ethnicity, and Youth in Antebellum New York City* (Ithaca: Cornell Univ Press, 1990)

Yamin, Rebecca, ed. *Tales of Five Points: Working-Class Life in 19th-Century New York*, 6 vols (West Chester, Pa: John Milner Associates, 2000)

Rebecca Yamin

sources became a national priority. With new federal legislation and procedures for cultural resources management (CRM), surveys to locate sites and excavations to mitigate adverse impacts of new construction, especially in urban areas, generated extensive new data. In 1970–71 excavations by the New York State Historic Trust and by the National Park Service, respectively, uncovered parts of Dutch Fort Orange (1624–76) in Albany and of Fort Stanwix [now Rome, Oneida Co]. New York City projects in the 1980s produced a wealth of information from the 17th through 19th centuries. Major projects of the 1990s included the African Burial Ground and Five Points excavations, both in Manhattan. A significant 1986 project in Albany at the Key-Corp site revealed 17th-century Dutch remains. In advance of Albany construction projects in the 1990s, colonial archaeological sites were discovered at the new locations of the New York State Dormitory Authority, the Department of Environmental Conservation, and the Dean Street Parking Garage. In 2001 remains of a mid-17th-century brickyard and a complete 18th-century distillery were uncovered. Noteworthy projects since 2001 have included the exhumation and study of 1,200 skeletons from the late 19th-century Albany Almshouse cemetery and excavations at the site of the Daniel Pieter Winne house near Albany, firmly dated to 1751 through dendrochronology.

Calver, William L., and Reginald P. Bolton. *History Written With Pick and Shovel* (New York: New-York Historical Society, 1950)

Cantwell, Anne-Marie, and Diana diZerega Wall. *Unearthing Gotham: The Archeology of New York City* (New Haven, Conn: Yale Univ Press, 2001)

Hart, John P., and Charles L. Fisher, eds. *19th and Early 20th Century Domestic Site Archaeology in New York State* (Albany: NYS Museum, 2000)

Huey, Paul R. "The Origins and Development of Historical Archaeology in New York State," *Bulletin: Journal of the New York State Archaeological Association* 113 (1997): 60–96

Starbuck, David R. *The Great Warpath: British Military Sites from Albany to Crown Point* (Hanover, NH: Univ Press of New England, 1999)

Yamin, Rebecca. "New York's Mythic Slum: Digging Lower Manhattan's Infamous Five Points," *Archaeology* 50 (Mar/Apr 1997): 44–53

Paul R. Huey

historical markers. As part of the national celebration of the 150th anniversary of the American Revolution in 1926, New York State approved funding to support commemorative markers "to designate sites that are of historic significance in the colonial, revolutionary or state formative period." Small cast-iron markers could be acquired for as little as $2 from the Education Department, after approval of the proposed text, location, and supporting historic documentation. Approximately 2,800 small blue-and-gold roadside markers dealing with subjects ranging from American Indian archaeology to modern industrial history were put up between 1926 and 1936. It is estimated that more than 60% of them remain.

Funding ran out in 1939, but active coordination of markers by the Education Department's Office of State History continued into the 1960s. At that time a program was initiated with the Thruway Authority and the Department of Public Works (now Department of Transportation) to install oversized historic area markers on state lands such as highway rest areas and campsites. This was seen as the start of an ongoing program to identify historic sites for educational purposes, but emphasis shifted from individual sites to summary regional histories. The unintended result was to supplant the smaller roadside markers, which were considered inappropriate for highways. Markers of the traditional size, style, and colors continue to be erected using private funds.

Lord, Philip, Jr. "The State Historic Marker Program: A Summary History," http://www.nysm.nysed.gov/research_collections/research/history/hismarkers.html

Philip L. Lord Jr

historic preservation and restoration. Since the early 19th century, New York State's citizens and government agencies have been national leaders in the effort to save and restore historic buildings and have worked to promote the significance of historic buildings for educational purposes, as well their relationship to quality of life. While the earliest preservation efforts were concerned with buildings and sites relating to colonial and revolutionary New York, the focus of preservationists expanded in the mid–20th century to include buildings of architectural and cultural significance.

An early effort to preserve a historic site occurred at Ticonderoga (Essex Co) when William Ferris Pell acquired Fort Ticonderoga in 1820 to prevent its destruction, which facilitated its eventual restoration in 1907–9. The first action in the country by a governmental body to preserve a historic building was New York State's acquisition in 1850 of George Washington's Headquarters (Hasbrouck House) in Newburgh (Orange Co). The building had been occupied by Washington during the final two years of the Revolutionary War and was typical of the sorts of buildings that were the focus of preservation efforts in the state for the next century. The 1876 centennial kindled interest in buildings affiliated with America's colonial past. In 1887 the state acquired the Senate House in Kingston (Ulster Co), built in 1676, where the state senate met during the Revolution. Other early state acquisitions included Johnson Hall in Johnstown (Fulton Co) in 1906, Philipse Manor Hall in Yonkers in 1908, and Schuyler Mansion in Albany in 1911. Although the properties were owned by the state, maintenance was provided by the Trustees of Scenic and Historic Places and Objects in the State of New York (later American Scenic and Historic Preservation Society).

Nongovernmental preservation efforts varied throughout the state during the early 20th century. In 1925 a private group's survey of pre-1776 Dutch buildings around New York State resulted in the book *Dutch Houses in the Hudson Valley before 1776* by Helen Wilkinson Reynolds in 1929. George Chapman purchased the Seabury-Tredwell House (1832) in Manhattan in 1934,

Aerial view of Fort Ticonderoga, by Clyde Smith.

along with all of its original furnishings, with the goal of turning it into a museum. Under the auspices of the Historic Landmark Society, it was opened to the public in 1936 as the Old Merchant's House. In 1940 John D. Rockefeller Jr set up a $50,000 fund to save a portion of Philipsburg Manor in Sleepy Hollow (Westchester Co) from a developer who wanted to build 14 houses on the property. The house was renovated in the 1940s for use as the headquarters for the Tarrytown Historical Society; since 1951 Sleepy Hollow Restorations (renamed Historic Hudson Valley in 1988) has operated the property.

The formation of the National Trust for Historic Preservation in 1949 signified a greatly increased awareness in historic buildings nationally, and a major change in attitude occurred in the 1950s, when interest developed in using historic buildings as part of everyday life instead of only as museums. Several organizations dedicated to local and regional preservation issues were founded in response to this change. For example, in 1957 residents of the Stockade in Schenectady established an association to advocate the preservation of their distinctive neighborhood, which had its origins in the 17th century. The Schenectady City Council in 1962 established the Stockade as the first municipal historic district in New York State. In another case, in reaction to the demolition of Pennsylvania Station in Manhattan in 1963, Mayor Robert F. Wagner Jr established the New York City Landmarks Preservation Commission in 1965 to identify and designate city landmarks, which were protected through a review process. That same year Brooklyn Heights became the first historic district in New York City. Such developments were implemented in several communities throughout the state to establish locally based legislative efforts to maintain historically designated properties through restrictions on alterations and standards for exterior appearance.

After the National Historic Preservation Act was passed in 1966, the preservation of historic buildings became a national policy with a unique federal-state partnership, and the New York State Historic Trust (now New York State Office of Parks, Recreation, and Historic Preservation) was designated the State Historic Preservation Office (SHPO). Charged with conducting a statewide survey of historic properties and administering a grant program for preservation, the trust also nominated properties to the National Register of Historic Places. New York State passed its own Historic Preservation Act in 1980, modeled after the federal act. Properties listed on the state and national registers are provided protection from state and federal actions that may affect the listed, or eligible, properties. Having a property listed, however, does not limit private actions as long as local laws are followed.

In response to these legislative developments, several more private, not-for-profit preservation groups were established. Such organizations include the Landmark Society of Western New York (1937), the Society for the Preservation of Long Island Antiquities (1948), Historic Ithaca (1966), the Hudson-Mohawk Industrial Gateway (1972), the Saratoga Springs Preservation Foundation (1977), and the statewide Preservation League of New York State (1974). As a measure of New York State's successes in preservation, by 2003 over 4,300 properties made up of nearly 80,000 individual resources around the state were listed on the National Register of Historic Places, ranging from ships and industrial buildings to vernacular residences, museums, and monuments of local, state, or national significance. Approximately 175 municipalities also enacted local historic preservation legislation.

See also ARCHITECTS AND ARCHITECTURE, NEW YORK CITY; COURTHOUSES; NATIONAL PARK SERVICE AREAS; STATE HISTORIC PARKS, SITES, AND HERITAGE AREAS.

Hosmer, Charles B., Jr. *Presence of the Past: A History of the Preservation Movement in the United States before Williamsburg* (New York: G. P. Putnam's Sons, 1965)

———. *Preservation Comes of Age: From Williamsburg to the National Trust, 1926–1949*, vol 1 (Charlottesville: Univ Press of Virginia, 1981)

Shaver, Peter D., and Preservation League of New York State. *The National Register of Historic Places in New York State* (New York: Rizzoli, 1993)

John G. Waite and Jennifer R. Breslin

historic sites. See NATIONAL PARK SERVICE AREAS; STATE HISTORIC PARKS, SITES, AND HERITAGE AREAS.

HIV. See AIDS (ACQUIRED IMMUNE DEFICIENCY SYNDROME).

Hmong. See SOUTHEAST ASIANS.

HMOs. See HEALTHCARE AND HOSPITALS; INSURANCE, HEALTH.

Hoag, William C(lark) (*b* Allegany Indian Reservation [loc in Cattaraugus Co], 17 Aug 1860; *d* Allegany Indian Reservation, 31 July 1927). Seneca politician. Hoag attended the local Quaker school and, at age 8 after the death of his father, ran the family farm. He began his political career in the Seneca Nation of Indians as treasurer at age 22 and held office for more than 40 consecutive years, from 1883 to 1891 alternately as clerk and treasurer and from 1892 to 1927 as treasurer and president. Early in his career, in 1892, he played a significant part in negotiating the 99-year lease with the City of Salamanca (Cattaraugus Co). During his reign as president and treasurer of the Seneca Nation, Hoag helped defeat every effort by the United States to allot Seneca lands via the Dawes Act. Passed in 1887, the act imposed private ownership of property on American Indians and ultimately led to the loss of two-thirds of their landholdings by 1934. Hoag was a successful businessman and political opportunist who would go on to become the most powerful politician of the elective era of Seneca politics.

Cutter, A. M. *Genealogical and Family History of Western New York* (New York: Lewis Historical Publishing, 1912)

Randy A. John

Hobart. Village (pop 390) in Stamford (Delaware Co). Located on the West Branch of the Delaware River and settled before the American Revolution, it was called Waterville until 1828, when the Hobart post office was named. Dairy farmers found an outlet for their products when the railroad reached Hobart in 1884. The village was incorporated in 1888. In 2003 Tyco Health Care/Mallinckrodt employed 500 workers and manufacturing pharmaceuticals in a 250,000 ft^2 (23,226 m^2) facility. Hobart is also the home of the A. Lindsay and Olive B. O'Connor Foundation, which supports preservation activities and historical interpretation in Delaware Co. The Catskill Scenic Trail passes through Hobart along the old railroad bed.

Dorothy Kubik

Hobart, John Henry (*b* Philadelphia, 14 Sept 1775; *d* Auburn, Cayuga Co, 12 Sept 1830). Episcopal bishop and author. After graduating from the College of New Jersey (now Princeton University) in 1793, Hobart studied for the ministry under William White. He was ordained a deacon in the Episcopal Church in 1798 and priest in 1801. He served briefly in congregations in Pennsylvania, New Jersey, and Long Island and in 1801 was appointed assistant minister of Trinity Church in New York City. He quickly became an important figure in the Episcopal Diocese of New York. He was elected assistant bishop in 1811 to aid the ailing Benjamin Moore and became bishop of the diocese and rector of Trinity Church in 1816. Known as an energetic bishop and an advocate of the High Church position within Anglicanism, he renewed the practice of episcopal visitations and sometimes traveled over 4,000 miles a year to visit his huge diocese. Through his labors the state's Episcopal Church increased in size eightfold. As a High Church apologist he emphasized distinctive Episcopal doctrines, particularly the belief that sincere Christian ministry needed to be connected to the apostles through a succession of bishops. His motto was Evangelical Truth and Apostolic Order. This involved him in a number of public controversies with other Protestant clergy and Episcopalians who preferred a more conciliatory approach to other religious groups. He was responsible for the founding of both the General Theological Seminary (1817) in Manhattan and Geneva College (1822; now Hobart and William Smith Colleges) in Seneca Co. He died of fever while touring his diocese and is buried in Trinity Church.

Mullin, Robert Bruce. *Episcopal Vision/American Reality: High Church Theology and Social Thought in Evangelical America* (New Haven, Conn: Yale Univ Press, 1986)

Robert Bruce Mullin

Hobart, John Sloss (*b* Fairfield, Conn, 6 May 1738; *d* New York City, 4 Feb 1805). Patriot and jurist. Hobart spent his childhood in Fairfield and graduated from Yale College in 1757. He apparently read law for a time in New York City, although there exists no evidence that he practiced law. He married Mary Grinnell in 1764, and they moved to Eatons Neck in Huntington (Suffolk Co) in 1765. Before the American Revolution, Hobart was a strong advocate of the patriot cause, serving in the New York Committee of Correspondence (1774), the provincial convention (1775), and provincial congresses (1775–77). In 1777 he was appointed an associate justice of the New York State Supreme Court. The Hobarts moved to Throgs Neck [now in Bronx Co] in 1794. He retired from the state supreme court in 1797 and was appointed as a Federalist by the state legislature to the US Senate in January 1798. On 16 April of that year he resigned to accept an appointment as US judge for the District of New York, a position he held until his death.

Voyse, Mary. *John Sloss Hobart: Forgotten Patriot.* Pamphlet (Huntington, NY: Huntington Historical Society, 1976)

James R. Belpedio

Hobart and William Smith Colleges. Private coeducational liberal arts college in the City of Geneva (Ontario Co). Founded in 1796 as Geneva Academy and chartered by the legislature in 1813, it closed temporarily in 1818. Through the support of Episcopal bishop John Henry Hobart and the community, it reopened in 1822 as Geneva College and was chartered in 1825. Its Episcopal Church affiliation continues in the early 21st century. Elizabeth Blackwell completed her medical studies at the head of her otherwise all-male class in 1849. The college was renamed Hobart Free College in 1852. In 1908 a gift of Geneva nurseryman and philanthropist, William Smith, established William Smith College nearby as a coordinate school for women. The relationship between the institutions evolved gradually through a common commencement ceremony (1922), corporate identity, and name (1943). In 2001 the colleges had an enrollment of 1,843 students.

See also Lacrosse.

Smith, Warren H. *Hobart and William Smith: The History of Two Colleges* (Geneva, NY: Hobart and William Smith Colleges, 1972)

Marla A. Bennett

hockey. See Ice hockey.

Hoffman, John T(hompson) (*b* Sing Sing [now Ossining, Westchester Co], 10 Jan 1828; *d* Wiesbaden, Germany, 24 Mar 1888). Governor and New York City mayor. A Union College graduate, Hoffman was admitted to the bar in 1849 and established a practice in New York City. A Tammany Hall Democrat, he was elected city recorder in 1860 and presided over the draft riot trials before becoming mayor of New York City (1865–68). He was picked by Tammany boss William M. Tweed to be the 1866 Democratic gubernatorial candidate as part of Tweed's unsuccessful attempt to gain statewide political control. He won the governorship in 1868, again running with Tweed's endorsement, through an election widely viewed as corrupt. As governor he ordered protection for marchers during New York City's Orange Riots and signed legislation creating the American Museum of Natural History. Reelected in 1870 and mentioned as a possible presidential candidate for the 1872 election, his political career was curtailed by Tweed's downfall. Retired from politics in 1872, he resumed practicing law and traveled abroad. Hoffman Island, located east of Staten Island, is named after him.

Stebbins, Homer Adolph. *A Political History of the State of New York, 1865–1869* (1913; repr New York: AMS Press, 1967)

John Marino

Hoffman, Michael (*b* Halfmoon [now in Saratoga Co], 11 Oct 1787; *d* Brooklyn, 27 Sept 1848). Lawyer and politician. A lawyer in Herkimer and a member of Martin Van Buren's Bucktail Republicans, he served in US Congress (1825–33), as judge of Herkimer Co (1830–33), and as the state canal commissioner (1833–35) before becoming federal land registrar (1836–37) in Saginaw, Mich. Upon returning to New York State, Hoffman served in the state assembly (1841, 1842, 1844). A leading state Democrat and supporter of Andrew Jackson, he opposed the construction of unprofitable feeder canals that increased New York State's debt and led the Stop and Tax movement (1841–42) that restored the state's credit. At the 1846 Constitutional Convention, Hoffman secured provisions that would pay off the canal debt, prohibit the state from extending its financial credit to private individuals and corporations, and limit state debts to $1 million, restrictions that inspired similar curbs in other states. From 1845 to 1848 he served in the civilian post of naval officer of New York City, appointed by Pres James K. Polk.

Gunn, L. Ray. *The Decline of Authority: Public Economic Policy and Political Development in New York State, 1800–1860* (Ithaca: Cornell Univ Press, 1989)
Henretta, James A. "The Strange Birth of Liberal America: Michael Hoffman and the New York Constitution of 1846," *New York History* 77 (Apr 1996): 151–76

James A. Henretta

Hofstra University. Private university in Hempstead (Nassau Co). By the terms of the will of Kate Mason Hofstra, her estate was designated for use as a memorial to her husband William. Nassau College–Hofstra Memorial, a two-year, coeducational commuter college, opened in 1935 under the auspices of New York University. In 1937 it became an independent, four-year institution and was renamed Hofstra College. Granted a full charter in 1940, it became a university in 1963. After the North Campus was acquired in 1966, high-rise dormitories were built, attracting out-of-state students and fostering a stronger campus community. Hofstra has grown to 111 buildings on a 240-acre (97.1 ha) campus, offering 130 undergraduate majors and employing more than 500 full-time faculty. The university is known for its law school, drama department, radio station, art museum, scholarly conferences, and football team, and is the summer home of the New York Jets. Its library houses an important collection of manuscripts and other materials for the study of Long Island history. The campus is a registered arboretum because of the great variety of trees, ornamental shrubs, and other plantings on its beautifully landscaped grounds. The student body numbers about 13,400, which includes 8,300 full-time undergraduates.

Lord, Clifford Lee. *The Hofstra Story, 1935–1971* (Hempstead, NY: Hofstra University Press, 1972)

Lynda R. Day

Holbrook. Locality (pop 27,512) in Islip and Brookhaven (Suffolk Co). The Long Island Rail Road came through the territory in 1844 and a 5,000-acre (2,000 ha) tract was platted in lots ranging from 5 to 20 acres (2 to 8 ha) by Alexander McCotter in 1848. A post office was established in 1862. The one significant industry was the 1875 Nevins and Griswold cigar factory, located in the railroad depot. As late as 1931 the population stood at only 321. In 1966 the Long Island Expressway reached the area, and between 1965 and 1975 it mushroomed from 2,500 to 15,000, with many of its new residents New York City and Nassau Co policemen and firemen. Holbrook is the site of Sachem Central School District, New York's largest suburban district in 1998, with 14,500 students.

Holiness-Wesleyan Movement. The theology and practice of most associated groups is built on the Christian perfectionism of Phoebe Palmer, a Methodist autodidact who with her sister Sarah Lankford established in the 1830s a series of "Tuesday meetings for the promotion of holiness" in the parlor of her New York City home. Originally a women-only group, it soon accepted men and non-Methodists. Attended and supported by many of northern Methodism's leaders, including New Yorkers Nathan Bangs, George Peck, Bishop Jesse T. Peck, and Bishop Randolph S. Foster, these meetings promoted Palmer's brand of "entire sanctification," the postconversion experience first articulated by John Wesley, in which one's heart was cleansed from sin and directed entirely toward love of God and humankind. Palmer added that this new level of living could be attained immediately and required only that one "lay one's all on the altar," that is, turn oneself totally and exclusively over to Christ. By 1886 over 200 similar meetings were operating in the United States and several other countries.

In 1867, intent on spreading this message to all of America, a group of pro-Holiness northeastern Methodist ministers started the National Camp Meeting Association for the Promotion of Holiness (NCMAPH). The association, whose founders included several prominent New Yorkers, grew rapidly through the 1870s and 1880s, with multiple annual camp meetings along the east coast. New York City minister John Inskip served as NCMAPH president from 1867 to 1884, presiding over 48 of the 52 national camp meetings held during his tenure and editing the association's organ, the *Christian Standard,* from 1876 to his death in 1884. During his tenure the camp at Round Lake (Saratoga Co) became the most used national camp meeting venue. The first national camp meeting held there, in 1869, hosted some 20,000 people. During the 1880s regional Holiness associations, some more radical than NCMAPH, spread south and west. By the 1890s the heyday of the NCMAPH and the formative influence of New York State leaders in the movement had ended, and many regional adherents began "coming out" of Methodism and forming separate Holiness denominations. The NCMAPH persists today much transformed, under the name of the Christian Holiness Partnership (CHP), in which most of the state's Holiness denominations and groups hold membership. Several denominations arose from the Methodist camp meeting movement, including the Church of God and the Church of the Nazarene.

The Wesleyan Methodists and the Free Methodists are the earliest Wesleyan Holiness denominations. The Wesleyan Methodist Connection (now Wesleyan Church) originated in Utica in 1843 under the leadership of abolitionists who left the Methodist Episcopal Church (MEC). One such leader was Orange Scott, a semiliterate laborer from Vermont who as a young man had risen rapidly in the ministry. In 1842 Scott and two fellow ministers began publishing the *True Wesleyan* in Utica. By 1844 the Wesleyan Methodist Connection held its first General Conference; at that point Scott was made publisher of the *True Wesleyan,* then headquartered in New York City. The new church forbade slaveholding and membership in secret societies, and laid down a number of regulations concerning personal holiness, including the forbidding of alcohol. It drew significant support from western and central New York State's evangelical Burned-over District and made its earliest headquarters in New York City. In 1883 the Wesleyan Church founded Houghton College (Allegany Co).

The Free Methodist Church was founded by members of the MEC's Genesee Conference in Western New York out of disputes in the 1850s over the reputed worldliness of the day's Methodist Church and its leaders. These Nazarites, as their opponents called them, espoused antislavery and Holiness teachings, and rejected pew rental and "worldly" church fund-raising practices. Under Benjamin Titus Roberts, the group formed their new denomination in 1860 at Pekin (Niagara Co). In 1866 the Free Methodists founded Chili Seminary (now Roberts Wesleyan College) in Rochester. The Salvation Army arose in 1878 out of the London mission work of William and Catherine Booth, erstwhile members of the Methodist New Connexion, and established its American headquarters in New York City in 1880. Although sharing the wider movement's emphasis on sanctification, it differed from the other two groups in its hierarchical structure and British origins. The Holiness denominations continued to grow in the 20th century into one of the major branches of Protestantism. Despite the movement's New York State roots, the greatest strength of Holiness denominations is generally in the south and west.

Dieter, Melvin E. *The Holiness Revival of the 19th Century* (Metuchen, NJ: Scarecrow Press, 1980)

Jones, Charles Edwin. *Perfectionist Persuasion: The Holiness Movement and American Methodism, 1867–1936* (Metuchen, NJ: Scarecrow Press, 1974)

Christopher R. Armstrong

Holland. Town (pop 3,603) in SE Erie Co. Settled in 1807, the town was formed from Willink [now Aurora] in 1818. Germans settled beginning in the 1830s, and by the middle of the century the town was the site of a huge tannery. The Buffalo, New York and Philadelphia Railroad (later Pennsylvania Railroad) came through in 1872. After World War II Polish farm families arrived. Late 20th-century industry included Trimold (a division of Fisher-Price), Ramblewood Manufacturing, and Vimco (1919; industrial lighting). In the early 21st century, agriculture, including dairying, remained the predominant land use. The town is the site of Holland International Speedway (1960).

Andrew C. Maines

Holland Land Company. Largest private land developer in early New York State. After some initial investments in US public securities in the 1780s, the company (consisting of the Dutch financial houses of Pieter Stadnitski and Son, Nicholas and Jacob van Staphorst, P. and C. Van Eeghen, and Ten Cate and Vollenhoven) began to acquire extensive tracts of undeveloped land in North America starting in 1792. It organized formally in 1796. Buying at cut rates, the investors hoped that ensuing settlement would greatly increase land value over time. By the early 1800s the company had purchased three separate tracts of land in the State of New York and a fourth in northwestern Pennsylvania.

One of the firm's initial purchases was a central New York State tract of over 100,000 acres (40,500 ha), which extended southward from what became Cazenovia [now in Madison Co]. Two other parcels near the upper Black River, known as the Oldenbarneveld settlement, were also acquired about this time. The Dutch owners

Surveyor's compass used by Augustus Porter to survey the Holland Land Patent, *ca* 1790.

struggled to develop the Cazenovia lands from 1793 to 1841, building grist- and sawmills, opening roads and market outlets, and trying to strike the right balance of sternness and forbearance with the poor settlers. Beyond developing land at their Oldenbarneveld settlement, they attempted to build a maple sugar business. Making profits in the Black River region, however, was challenging, because the Dutch investors faced the same knotty problems of the central New York tract, where collecting debt payments from cash-poor settlers proved difficult.

The Dutch proprietors put most of their resources, however, into developing lands in western New York State, portions of these lands including the fertile Genesee Valley. The area became known as the Holland Land Purchase, and widespread settlement began in 1800 after some surveys had been completed. In that year the Dutch investors selected Joseph Ellicott to serve as their resident land agent. He formulated and implemented a pragmatic strategy for developing the area. The first wave of settlers Ellicott hoped to attract would be transients; although they could not properly pay for the land, they would do the initial hard work of clearing the properties. Any significant payments for the firm's lands would have to wait until a second wave of wealthier and more established farmers moved in to buy partially improved land. Ellicott and the Dutch investors were counting on this second wave to make the sort of permanent agricultural improvements that would raise land values throughout the Holland Land Purchase and, ultimately, help them realize their profits.

Yet the settlers of the purchase had their own objectives. Drawn to the region in the hope of a better life, they grew food, raised livestock, and made potash, in ways more suitable to themselves than to the company's economic gain. Moreover, the large amount of open land and the small number of settlers hindered the Dutch investors, forcing them, for a time, to give wide latitude to the settlers. Soaring land debt coupled with falling land values after the national economic panic of 1819 prompted the Dutch investors to dismiss Ellicott in 1821 and get tough with the thousands of delinquent settlers. As the company moved aggressively to assert direct control, primarily by getting rid of the most notorious debtors and trying to force the remaining settlers to integrate fully into the local cash economy, conflicts erupted. In 1836 settlers from the more isolated "back towns" destroyed the Mayville (Chautauqua Co) land office, threatened the one in Batavia (Genesee Co), and forcibly resisted efforts by local officials and the militia to dispossess any of the debtors. Another conflict, known as the Dutch Hill War, inflamed Hinsdale (Cattaraugus Co) in 1844–45. As public opinion turned against the Dutch investors, reflecting the strong egalitarian sentiments of the era, the company decided to cut its losses, and by 1846 it had sold all of its lands in western New York State to various US investors.

See also LAND COMPANIES AND PATENTS; TUSCARORA NATION.

Brooks, Charles E. *Frontier Settlement and Market Revolution: The Holland Land Purchase* (Ithaca: Cornell Univ Press, 1996)

Charles E. Brooks

Holland Patent. Village (pop 461) in Trenton (Oneida Co). A grant of about 20,000 acres (8,100 ha) made in 1769 to Henry Fox, Lord Holland, was sold to others before 1797, when the locality was surveyed and settled. Among the first settlers was Pascal de Angelis, a West Indies–born Italian, but many of the early settlers were Welsh. The Black River and Utica Railroad came through in 1855, and the first cheese factory opened in 1861. The Clarendon Hotel (1876) attracted summer visitors. The village incorporated in 1885. The Steffens Publishing Co and Oneida County Rural Telephone were employers in 2002.

Holland Tunnel. The New York metropolitan region's first interstate vehicular crossing of the Hudson River, completed in 1927 and connecting Lower Manhattan with Jersey City, NJ, through two two-lane tubes passing under the river, each measuring about 8,400 ft (2,560 m) long. Designed by Clifford M. Holland, the tunnel is one of the few public works named after its engineer. The New York–New Jersey Tunnel Commission built the structure using shield-driven, compressed-air technology, and the Port of New York Authority (now Port Authority of New York and New Jersey) has operated it since 1930. Holland was the first long, mechanically ventilated, underwater, vehicular tunnel in the world. With 20 ft (6.1 m) wide roadways, the cast-iron tubes were nearly twice the diameter of earlier subway tunnels. The innovative ventilation system became the model for later tunnels. Huge fans and longitudinal ducts force fresh air in, below the roadway, and stale air out, above the roadway. Canal St and Rte 9A (West St) are the main New York approaches, with the New Jersey Turnpike and the Pulaski Skyway the key connectors in New Jersey. From 1970 tolls have been collected eastbound only, as part of the Hudson River/Staten Island one-way tolls system, later incorporating an electronic (E-Z Pass) system. Named a National Historic Civil and Mechanical Engineering Landmark in 1984, the tunnel carried approximately 29.2 million vehicles in 2001.

Leon Goodman

Holley. Village (pop 1,802) in Murray (Orleans Co). Located on the Erie Canal, Holley's post office opened in 1823, and the village was incorporated in 1850. The Niagara Falls Branch of the New York Central Railroad (1852) provided rail service. Aside from some small industries, such as a plow factory and machine shop and barrel factory, Holley was a center for fruit buying and processing. Duffy-Mott operated in the village in the mid–20th century, and Diaz Chemical Corp produced dyes and chemicals in the last quarter of the century. Holley is a bedroom village but has a new industrial park housing Precision Packaging Products (plastics) and Clarendon Cheesecakes. The Holley Central School District is believed to have lost more men per capita during the Vietnam War than any other district in the nation.

Marsha DeFilipps

Holley, Marietta (*b* Giddingsville, Jefferson Co, 16 July 1836; *d* Giddingsville, 1 Mar 1926). Writer. The youngest of seven children, she grew up in modest circumstances, worked on her family farm, and gave piano lessons. Beginning in 1857 her poetry was published under pseudonyms in the *Jefferson County Journal;* 12 years later she sold a story to *Peterson's Magazine.* By the time she entered the literary world, the tradition of Yorker comic writing was abating, but a rural audience for it persisted. Her work was a unique combination of three idioms: domestic fiction, literature by women for women, and local-color writing. But, more significantly, it was both feminist and prohibitionist. While others had created comic figures of women, especially women's rights advocates, Holley's most significant creation, Samantha Allen, was an admirable foil to figures exemplifying intemperance and antisuffrage. Sometimes called the female Mark Twain, she identified with the character she created and used the pseudonym "Josiah Allen's wife" in her early books. She entered the mainstream of American popular literature when, in 1872, Elisha Bliss of the American Publishing Co commissioned her first book, later published under the title *My Opinion and Betsey Bobbit's,* in which women's rights were debated. Her 1877 title, *Samantha at the Centennial,* essayed temperance. In 1887 *Samantha at Saratoga* was the year's best-seller. In all she published 21 books and many short stories; those after 1879 were under her own name. She avoided public appearances, left Jefferson Co for the first time at the age of 45, and in later years spent winter months in a New York City hotel. Her outspoken positions on the day's issues gained her the friendship of Susan B. Anthony and Clara Barton, an invitation to address Congress on women's rights (which she declined), and an audience in the Grover Cleveland White House. Her writing earned her a comfortable living, and after her retirement in 1915 she devoted herself to the creation of a remarkable garden on the family farm, where she had built a large house. She also founded the Holley Library at Adams (Jefferson Co).

Winter, Kate H. *Marietta Holley: Life With "Josiah Allen's Wife"* (Syracuse: Syracuse Univ Press, 1984)

Field Horne

Holley, Myron (*b* Salisbury, Conn, 29 Apr 1779; *d* Rochester, 4 Mar 1841). Canal proponent and political activist. The son of Sarah Dakin and Luther Holley, he graduated from Williams College in Williamstown, Mass, in 1799. He studied law under James Kent in Cooperstown (Otsego Co) but soon abandoned that career. In 1803 he settled in Canandaigua (Ontario Co) and opened a bookshop. After a stint as county clerk (1810–14), he was elected to the assembly (1816, 1820–21), where he was an active proponent of the Erie Canal. He also served as an acting commissioner and treasurer of the Canal Board (1816–24), a full-time position that regularly brought him to construction sites. Accused of embezzling canal funds in 1824, Holley retired to a farm in Lyons (Wayne Co). He became a leader of the Antimasonic Party in Wayne Co, authored the main address of the Antimasonic National Convention in Philadelphia (1830), and edited party newspapers in Lyons (1831–34) and Hartford, Conn (1834–35). Disappointed with the Antimasons' absorption into the Whig Party, he turned to farming in Rochester. There he was drawn into the fight against slavery and became a leading advocate for an abolitionist political party. After launching the *Rochester Freeman* (1839–41) to spread his views, he was a principal founder of the Liberty Party (1840). Holley never attended church, yet he offered his own sermons to family, neighbors, and the poor, and viewed political action on behalf of equality as a religious obligation. He opposed what he saw as the elitism of Freemasonry as well as the degradation of slavery. The Village of Holley (Orleans Co) was named in his honor.

Goodman, Paul. *Towards a Christian Republic: Antimasonry and the Great Transition in New England, 1826–1836* (New York: Oxford Univ Press, 1988)
Wright, Elizur. *Myron Holley; and What He Did for Liberty and True Religion* (Boston, 1882)

Scott C. Monje

Holly, Birdsill (*b* Auburn, Cayuga Co, 8 Nov 1820; *d* Lockport, Niagara Co, 27 Apr 1894). Inventor. He grew up in Seneca Falls, where he was trained as a machinist. His 1855 patent for an elliptical rotary pump revolutionized firefighting engines. In 1859 he moved to Lockport as engineer with the Lockport Hydraulic Race Co, beginning work in 1864 on an underground raceway tunnel that was completed in 1866. At the same time, a large industrial complex of stone buildings, called Holly Manufacturing, was built over the raceway. Surplus water from the nearby Erie Canal was released into the tunnel at the top of the locks. The 54 ft (16.5 m) drop created the power needed to run the complex, which made sewing machines, pumps, and hydraulic machinery. After a series of devastating fires in Lockport, Holly designed and installed a fire hydrant system throughout the city, centrally connected by underground pipes and in operation by December 1864. Lockport was the first city in the world to have this system of water supply and fire protection, which was widely adopted elsewhere. He later invented a district steam heating system, which created steam from a central boiler and forced it through underground pipes to heat buildings. By 1878 Lockport was the first city in the world to be heated by central district steam heat. Despite his various inventions, Holly died a poor man, never having achieved any financial success from his work.

Fredrickson, Madelynn. *The Life and Times of Birdsill Holly* (Blue Spruce Press, 1996)
Pierce, Morris. "The Introduction of Direct Pressure Water Supply, Cogeneration, and District Heating in Urban and Institutional Communities, 1863–1882" (PhD diss, Univ of Rochester, 1993)

Madelynn P. Fredrickson

Holmes, John Haynes (*b* Philadelphia, 29 Nov 1879; *d* New York City, 3 Apr 1964). Minister and social activist. Educated at Harvard, he served

Unitarian churches in Massachusetts before moving to the Church of the Messiah in New York City in 1907. Holmes advocated the social application of liberal religion, embracing socialism as "political Christianity" and focusing on the church's role in progressive political causes. An outspoken pacifist unhappy with the Unitarian commitment to World War I, Holmes distanced himself from his denomination and in 1919 led his church to change its name to the Community Church of New York. A fire destroyed Holmes's church later that year, and the congregation met in rented space until 1940. He was a founder of the NAACP in 1909 and served as national vice president for 50 years. In 1914 he helped organize the American Union Against Militarism, which became the American Civil Liberties Union (ACLU), and in 1915 was a founder of the American chapter of the International Fellowship of Reconciliation, headquartered in Nyack (Rockland Co). Holmes supported Margaret Sanger's birth control movement and developed strong ecumenical and interreligious ties, especially with the Jewish community through his longtime friend Rabbi Stephen S. Wise. He chaired the City Affairs Committee (1929–38), which exposed corruption in New York City in the administration of Mayor Jimmy Walker and assisted in the reform efforts of Mayor Fiorello La Guardia. Holmes's play *If This Be Treason,* produced on Broadway in 1935, anticipated the 1941 attack on Pearl Harbor and examined how a pacifist president might have responded. Holmes retired in 1949 but kept busy writing a biography of Indian leader Mohandas Gandhi and preaching on occasion at the Community Church until 1959.

Holmes, John Haynes. *I Speak for Myself: The Autobiography of John Haynes Holmes* (New York: Harper & Bros, 1959)

David E. Bumbaugh

Holt [née Hunter], **Elizabeth** (*b* Hampton, Va, ?1727; *d* Philadelphia, Pa, 6 Mar 1788) and **Holt, John** (*b* Williamsburg, Va, ?1721; *d* New York City, 30 Jan 1784). Newspaper publishers. The Holts married in Virginia in 1749, and in 1755 John Holt became junior partner to James Parker of New York City. In 1760 Parker placed Holt in charge of his *New-York Gazette; or, The Weekly Post-Boy.* In May 1762 Holt began running the newspaper on his own under a four-year lease. In 1765 the Sons of Liberty paid £440 to keep a debt-ridden Holt out of prison. The *Gazette* criticized the British Stamp Act, often using incendiary language. When Holt's lease expired in 1766, the pro-British Parker took back the newspaper.

Subsidized by the Sons of Liberty, Holt launched *The New-York Journal, or General Advertiser* in May 1766. He continued to criticize Britain's "tyrannical Designs," while he educated Americans about their rights and encouraged their resistance. In August 1776 British occupation forced him to leave New York City. He revived publication in Kingston (Ulster Co) in July 1777. In August he was appointed state printer, a position he held until his death. When the British burned Kingston in October, Holt escaped to Poughkeepsie (Dutchess Co) and resumed printing in May 1778. He suspended newspaper publication in January 1782. After the war, a destitute Holt returned to New York City and in November 1783 established the *Independent New-York Gazette,* which soon became the *Independent Gazette; or The New-York Journal Revived.* On 18 Mar 1784, seven weeks after Holt's death, Elizabeth Holt—already appointed state printer—renamed the newspaper the *New-York Journal, and State Gazette.* In June 1785 she turned over the *Journal*'s proprietorship to son-in-law Eleazer Oswald, a Philadelphia newspaper publisher, because other printers were undermining the *Journal*'s operation and seeking the state printership. She retired to Philadelphia to live with her daughter and son-in-law.

Featherston, James S. "John Holt." In *American Newspaper Journalists, 1690–1872,* ed. Perry J. Ashley (Detroit: Gale Research, 1985)
Hudak, Leona M. *Early American Women Printers and Publishers, 1639–1820* (Metuchen, NJ: Scarecrow Press, 1978)

Gaspare J. Saladino

Holtsville. Locality (pop 17,006) in Brookhaven (Suffolk Co). The Long Island Rail Road established a station called Waverly in 1843. When the post office opened in 1860, the name was changed to Holtsville. A large IRS Service Center opened in 1972. A landfill, closed in 1973, became the 144-acre (58 ha) town-operated Holtsville Ecology Site and Park (1979). The Empire State Carousel Museum (2003) is an attraction.

Holy Trinity Russian Orthodox Monastery. This institution in Jordanville (Herkimer Co) began its existence in 1928 when priest-monk Panteleimon (Nizhnik) and monk Jacob (Masheruk) made a $25 down payment on a 300-acre (121 ha) farm. Since that time Jordanville's monastery has become the chief cultural and ideological center of the Russian Orthodox Church outside of Russia, serving simultaneously as a pilgrimage site, seminary, publishing house, icon studio, apiary, dairy farm, and cemetery. The community celebrates its largest feasts annually on the days of Pentecost and St. Job of Pochaev (Labor Day weekend), attracting pilgrims and tourists. Their solemn liturgical services disperse clouds of imported incense and use as many as 10 deacons and 40 priests. In 1948 Archbishop Vitaly (Maximenko) and Archimandrite Iosif (Kolos) established theological classes for novices that grew into the Holy Trinity Seminary, an accredited New York State institution attracting students from around the world and graduating priests, deacons, monks, and choir directors. The main monastery building was built from 1952 to 1957, housing the monks' cells, refectory, and printing press. The work of noted iconographer Archimandrite Kiprian (Pizhew) covers the interior of the monastery cathedral. Jordanville's print shop of St. Job of Pochaev traces its origins to Ukraine and Czechoslovakia. Jordanville has been a central international source for Russian language sources concerning Orthodoxy. Besides serving the émigré community, Jordanville's publications made their way to the Soviet Union, where they were clandestinely distributed and reprinted, contributing to the maintenance of Orthodox Christianity. Of all the Orthodox monastic communities in New York State, Jordanville most closely and consciously evokes the traditions and atmosphere of prerevolutionary Russia. In the early 21st century approximately 40 monks live at the monastery, while 45 students attend the Holy Trinity Seminary.

The Holy Trinity Monastery (Jordanville, NY: St. Job of Pochaev Press, 1996)

Nadieszda Kizenko

home economics. A course of instruction, both in public schools and on the collegiate level, that taught young women the scientific study of domesticity. Home economics was distinguished from earlier education in housewifery, domestic arts, and domestic science by efforts to create a profession with an association, scholarly journal, and graduate programs and degrees.

Origins

Both the name and the movement grew out of a series of conferences held at the Lake Placid Club (Essex Co) between 1899 and 1909. In the first year only 11 people attended, including Melvil Dewey, the New York State librarian, and his wife, Annie Dewey, who supported home economics education because they believed that enlightened homemakers improved civic life and health. Since a number of land grant colleges in the West and Midwest were already supporting domestic arts programs, the Deweys and other New Yorkers discussed the possibility of seeking state funds to support home economics at Cornell University, the land grant institution in Ithaca. The Lake Placid group first developed a resolution for state funds in 1899. In March 1900 a bill cosponsored by local branches of the Association of Collegiate Alumnae was introduced into the legislature authorizing funds for a department of home economics at Cornell. The bill failed, but that year Melvil Dewey established a home economics department at the New York State Library to answer inquiries, and by 1909, 700 people attended the Lake Placid conference. That year the American Home Economics Association (AHEA) was organized and began publication of the *Journal of Home Economics.*

The spread of home economics in New York State was eventually linked to efforts to revitalize agriculture and rural communities by Liberty Hyde Bailey, a professor of horticulture at the College of Agriculture at Cornell. Bailey made frequent trips to Albany where he met Dewey and discussed the future of home economics education in the state. In 1900 Bailey asked Martha Van Rensselaer, a former school commissioner from Randolph (Cattaraugus Co), to organize at Cornell a reading course for farm women that would be comparable to a course already available for farm men. In 1901 the College of Agriculture published Van Rensselaer's *Saving Steps,* a pathbreaking bulletin that introduced the idea that household work could be easier and more efficient if homemakers followed scientific principles. In addition to the Farmers' Wives Reading Courses and associated Cornell Study Clubs, in 1903 the College of Agriculture offered the first resident course for credit in home economics and in 1905 added a noncredit winter course open to any woman in the state.

Establishing the College of Home Economics

Home economics was institutionalized as a field of study under the leadership of Van Rensselaer and Flora Rose, a nutritionist with an MA from Columbia University who in 1907 joined the new Department of Home Economics within the College of Agriculture. In 1910 the legislature approved a request for funds to erect a home economics building, and a year later the first three students graduated with a BS in home economics. In 1911 Van Rensselaer and Rose were granted the first full professorships for women at Cornell and the next year were named co-directors of the Home Economics Department. The following year the new building opened. By 1919 the department became the School of Home Economics within the College of Agriculture, but an attempt in 1920 to create a separate state college of home economics was defeated in the legislature. The first MS degree in home economics was granted in 1922, and autonomy finally was achieved in 1925 when the legislature established the New York State College of Home Economics. In 1930 the first PhD in home economics was awarded, and in 1933, with the help of Eleanor Roosevelt, who lobbied for money to erect a building, the Martha Van Rensselaer Hall opened.

Growth of the Field and New Careers

Both federal and state legislation spurred the growth of collegiate home economics. The 1914 Smith-Lever Act supported home economics education through the extension program of the US Department of Agriculture. The 1917 Smith-Hughes Act provided federal funds for home economics training and made the education of home economics teachers a priority. When the Purnell Act was passed by the state legislature on 1 July 1925, Albert R. Mann, dean of the College of Agriculture, allocated a liberal share of the funds to home economics for research on vitamins and rural home management. In 1929 the state also earmarked funds for research in the economics of the household, and the 1935 Bankhead-Jones Act supplied federal money for the study of human nutritional needs. Throughout the 20th century faculty in the state college were associated with innovations in food conservation and preparation, product and housing design, textiles, home management and budgeting, and new scientific ideas about child development. Beginning in 1925 the faculty's empirical research in child health, behavior, and guidance was supported by the Laura Spelman Rockefeller Memorial based in New York City. Until Farm and Home Week ended in the 1960s, thousands of New Yorkers attended this annual event on the Cornell campus that demonstrated the latest developments in the application of science to family and home life.

In the period from 1911 to post–World War II, the College of Home Economics was a major pathway into higher education for young women in the state because tuition was affordable and the training useful. In addition to preparing for marriage and motherhood, home economics graduates taught in the public schools, worked as demonstration agents for the cooperative extension system, and filled management roles in hospitals, hotels, and power companies. In the Progressive era home economists were associated with improving public health and hygiene in both rural and urban areas statewide; during World War I they assisted in maximizing food resources; in the depression they helped families cope with limited incomes; after World War II they worked in product design and marketing for industry, such as Corning Glass Works (Steuben Co), and in media, such as NBC in New York City.

Educational Changes

Although home economics was taught at Vassar College and the College of New Rochelle, it did not gain acceptance at most of the elite liberal arts colleges for women, and it had to struggle for status and recognition at research universities such as Cornell. At Teachers College of Columbia University it was offered as "household arts" and reflected that institution's commitment to vocational education geared to the needs of modern society. By World War I both Cornell and Teachers College developed well-regarded scientific nutrition and nutrition education programs; many of the early home economics faculty at Cornell received graduate training at Teachers College. Home economics programs were also part of the undergraduate curriculum at many state normal and technical schools, and at units of the City University of New York.

By the 1960s broad changes in American universities and in American women's economic and social roles made education in home economics seem old-fashioned. Many college programs were transformed and given new names that dropped the connection to domesticity and that reflected a broader perspective. In 1969 the New York State College of Home Economics became the New York State College of Human Ecology. In 1972, as a result of Title IX, a federal antidiscrimination mandate, public schools had to offer similar instruction to both boys and girls. Home economics (for girls) and industrial arts (for boys) were replaced by "home and career skills" for both genders, and Future Homemakers of America was recast as the Family, Career and Community Leaders program. Home economists also began to shape a new professional identity. In 1992 the AHEA became the American Association of Family and Consumer Sciences, and public schoolteachers in the newly named field began to organize their curriculum around specialized courses in parenting, infant psychology, entrepreneurship, and career decision making.

Eagles, Juanita, Orrea Pye, and Clara Taylor. *Mary Swartz Rose, 1874–1941, Pioneer in Nutrition* (New York: Teachers College Press, 1979)

From Domesticity to Modernity: What Was Home Economics? http://rmc.library.cornell.edu/homeEc

Rose, Flora. *A Growing College: Home Economics at Cornell University/New York State College of Human Ecology* (Ithaca: NYS College of Human Ecology, 1969)

Stage, Sarah, and Virginia Vincenti, eds. *Rethinking Home Economics: Women and the History of a Profession* (Ithaca: Cornell Univ Press, 1997)

Joan Jacobs Brumberg

homelessness. While the term is contemporary, the problem in New York State dates back to the beginning of European settlement. In early records it is not always easy to distinguish homelessness from other forms of poverty, such as widows unable to support themselves or their children, the aged poor, or people needing a loan to carry them over a bad stretch. All classes of poverty often found themselves in the care of the poorhouse. In New Netherland the poorhouse, which was initially administered by the Dutch Reformed Church, provided food and lodging in exchange for work. One in New Amsterdam [now New York City] probably opened in 1653, and another in Beverwijck [now Albany] opened in 1655. In the Dutch period, however, the percentage of the population that was truly homeless was tiny, and the government gradually assumed responsibility for the indigent. In 1736 the New York City Common Council erected the first public almshouse in Manhattan. Care for the poor, however, remained an important religious obligation, and every denomination, Dutch Reformed, Lutheran, Anglican, and Jewish, cared for its own indigent members.

Police stations were the primary place where the homeless were sheltered in New York City in the late 19th century; detail from *Harper's Weekly*, 13 Dec 1873.

The close connection between religion and homelessness reinforced the widespread perception of a distinction between the "deserving" and the "unworthy" poor: the former being poor through no fault of their own, and the latter poor through their own moral failings. This dichotomy has shaped all attempts to deal with homelessness in New York State. The purpose of poor relief was to get people back, if possible, to being productive members of the community.

During the early years of the Republic the number of homeless in New York State rapidly increased because of economic recession or depression, immigration, and changed public policy. When the problem failed to abate on its own, the state initiated a more systematic approach. In 1824 the legislature passed the County Poorhouse Act, which directed counties to levy special taxes of up to $7,000 to construct poorhouses to provide for the homeless and other indigents. All costs of operating these institutions were to be borne by the respective counties, but major cities, which by now operated their own facilities, were exempt. Like almshouses, county facilities provided shelter in exchange for work. The 1824 statute brought about significant change, particularly in rural areas; by 1832, 48 counties had opened poorhouses. Nevertheless, actual operations across the state were in many places troubling. An 1838 report on conditions at the poorhouse in Genesee Co revealed decrepit buildings and dangerous overcrowding, and similar conditions were reported the following year in Montgomery Co. Such reports, however, had little effect. By 1856 New York State had 55 county poorhouses providing shelter for 4,936 people, 25% of whom were children.

During the second half of the 19th century, many of the homeless in urban areas were routinely provided nighttime shelter by the police at station houses. Beginning in 1857 the New York City Police Department was required by law to provide such lodging. Other private institutions, such as the Salvation Army, also extended aid. Established in New York City in 1880, that organization quickly opened missions offering food and lodging in other cities in the state, including Albany and Syracuse. It was one of the few organizations that made no distinctions among the poor.

The state and local governments gained an increasing role in dealing with the indigent in the early 20th century, and the Great Depression brought with it the country's and New York State's greatest crisis yet in homelessness. Those numbers were stark. The total number of homeless who slept in Buffalo's shelter system per year climbed from 24,633 in 1929 to 461,646 for 1933. In response the state government created, in 1931, the Temporary Emergency Relief Administration (TERA) to aid the jobless; TERA set up work programs and provided medical care, clothing, and food to the unemployed. Initially it had no specific program to aid the homeless, but in 1933 such funds became available. Between 1933 and 1935 TERA's Transient Division operated a statewide homeless care network, again providing shelter in exchange for labor. Under it, homeless workers in Elmsford (Westchester Co) made furniture, and others at Camp Greenhaven (Dutchess Co), Camp Saratoga in Saratoga Springs, and Camp Stony Brook in Dansville (Steuben Co) worked in state parks. Overall the state operated 15 such camps, giving shelter on average to more than 10,000 homeless per month. TERA was closed in late 1935 for lack of additional funding. The gravity of the homeless problem in New York State during the depression is captured in William Kennedy's Pulitzer Prize–winning novel *Ironweed* (1984), which revolves around the life of a homeless man eking out a meager existence in late 1930s Albany.

With the onset of World War II the problem declined and New York State entered a near 30-year period of stable figures on homelessness. The problem was limited primarily to downtown urban areas with concentrations of people with alcoholism, such as the Gut and Arbor Hill neighborhoods of Albany. Starting in the late 1970s, however, on the heels of a stagflation and high levels of unemployment, New York State once again experienced a great surge in homelessness. It was most visible in New York City, and the most comprehensive judicial decision on the right to shelter for the homeless, *Callahan v Carey* (1979) was rendered there. A number of factors contributed to the sudden increase. Changed federal policy led to cutbacks such as the conversion of low-income housing (eg, of single-room occupancy units) to commercial property or rental units for more affluent groups, meaning the loss of thousands of low-income units throughout New York State. Between 1970 and 1980 the gap between the number of households requiring low-cost rental units and the number of such units in New York City's housing stock increased by over 400,000. In addition, beginning in the 1980s, New York State deinstitutionalized thousands of limited-income mental patients into this shrinking low-income housing market. Between 1982 and 1989, the average number of single, homeless adults in New York City's shelter system at any one time increased from 3,700 to 9,700 and the number of families from 2,137 to 5,091. In 1999 more than 25% of New York City residents who rented an apartment spent more than 50% of their income on rent.

Bahr, Howard. *Disaffiliated Man: Essays and Bibliography on Skid Row, Vagrancy, and Outsiders* (Toronto: Univ of Toronto Press, 1970)

Burt, Martha. *Over the Edge: The Growth of Homelessness in the 1980s* (New York: Russell Sage Foundation, 1980)

Katz, Michael. *Poverty and Policy in American History* (New York: Academic Press, 1983)

Mike Fabricant

homeopathy. See ALTERNATIVE MEDICINE.

Homer. Town (pop 6,363) and village (pop 3,368) in NW Cortland Co. Settled in 1791 the town was formed in 1794. Two branches of the Tioughnioga River flow through town. Homer became industrialized at an early date; a cotton factory was established soon after 1800, and an edge tool factory, a nail factory, and a foundry followed. Despite the prosperity, it lost its bid to be the county seat in 1810. The village incorporated in 1835 and acquired a railroad link to Syracuse and Binghamton in 1854. After mid-century dairying increased in importance, and the first cheese factory was built in 1864. Sleighs, butter tubs, wagons, and fishing line were later factory products. Homer was home to David Hannum, the model for Edward Noyes Westcott's *David Harum*. I-81 (1966) improved road access and has made the commute to Syracuse more feasible for Homer residents.

Cathy A. Barber

Homer, Winslow (*b* Boston, 24 Feb 1836; *d* Prout's Neck, Maine, 29 Sept 1910). Artist. Homer began his career in 1857 in Boston, working as a freelance illustrator for publishers of books and magazines. In 1859 he moved to New York City where he maintained a studio for more than 20 years. In the 1860s his studio was in the University Building on Washington Square and for much of the 1870s in the Studio Building on West 10th St. During his time in Boston and New York he drew more than 200 illustrations on original subjects for popular pictorial magazines, notably *Harper's Weekly*. His many New York City subjects ranged from views of fashionable society in Central Park to depictions of the poor in hovels.

He exhibited his first paintings in 1863 at the National Academy of Design in New York City. His election in 1865 to full membership in the National Academy was a notable honor for a largely self-taught artist. In 1875 his slowly growing income as a painter allowed him to end his career as an illustrator. Always a realist, his paintings throughout his career depicted many aspects of contemporary life but nothing of urban culture in New York City or elsewhere. His oils and watercolors up to 1881 reflect his visits to several locales in New York State, including East Hampton, Mountainville, Leeds, and other rural communities in the Hudson River valley, and Keene Valley and Minerva in the Adirondacks. Homer typically depicted figures in bright natural light in outdoor settings but with little suggestion of narrative.

In 1881 he sailed to England and spent 18 months in Cullercoats, a fishing village on the North Sea, where he became keenly interested in marine subjects. A year following his return to New York City he moved to Prout's Neck, where he painted timeless struggles in nature, including the contest of sea against shore. From his small studio-home overlooking the Atlantic he traveled extensively. Commencing in 1889 Homer visited the Adirondacks most years to the end of his life, always to fish and sometimes to paint, making his last visit to Minerva in June 1910. He never married. Among his best-known oils are *Prisoners from the Front* (1866), a Civil War subject; *Snap the Whip* (1872), a scene of boys at play; and *Northeaster* (1895), in which a storm-driven wave breaks on weather-beaten rocks. Watercolors set in New York State include his *Fresh Air* (1878), painted in Mountainville, and *Casting—A Rise* (1889), an Adirondack subject. By 1890 the originality of his subjects, the sharpness of his vision, and the vigor and freshness of his style had established Homer as one of America's greatest painters.

For illustration see ADIRONDACK GUIDES.

Cikovsky, Nicolai, Jr, and Franklin Kelly. *Winslow Homer* (Washington, DC: National Gallery of Art, 1995)

Tatham, David. *Winslow Homer in the Adirondacks* (Syracuse: Syracuse Univ Press, 1996)

David Tatham

home rule. General-purpose local governments (counties, cities, towns, and villages) obtained full power to elect or appoint their officeholders during the 19th century and the power to adopt local laws during the 20th.

CONTROL OF LOCAL GOVERNMENTS AND OFFICERS

Under British colonial rule, qualified adult white males elected town officers such as supervisors, tax assessors, and overseers of highways. The governor and council appointed county clerks, sheriffs, and justices of the peace. Freemen of the cities of New York and Albany, both chartered in 1686, elected aldermen and constables, but the mayors and certain other officers were appointed by the governor and council. Under the 1777 Constitution all the appointive county, city, and town offices were filled by the Council of Appointment. Shifts in political control of the council led to the appointment of hundreds of new local government officers. Responsive to the popular demand for more direct, democratic control of local government offices, the Constitution of 1821 made county clerks, sheriffs, and coroners elective; mayors appointive by the city council; and justices of the peace appointive by the county board of supervisors and the county judges. After 1826 justices of the peace were elected in each town. The mayor of New York City was made elective by a constitutional amendment of 1833, and all other city mayors were made elective by an amendment of 1839. The 1846 Constitution made judges elective, ending state appointment of locally based officers.

By their colonial charters the cities of New York and Albany had received extensive lands and special privileges, resources that allowed them to function as quasi-private, autonomous corporations. Disposition of city-owned property and assertion of state legislative power eliminated that autonomy. In legislative practice and emerging legal theory, the state legislature created and controlled all local governments. A 1788 statute formally divided the entire state into counties and towns, although many of them were continued from the colonial period. The compiled statutes of 1802 stated the "powers, duties and privileges of towns," and in 1828 the legislature declared that "no town shall possess or exercise any corporate powers" except those granted by the Revised Statutes. Tight legislative control resulted in numerous special laws erecting towns or altering their boundaries, granting or amending city and village charters, and otherwise attempting to manage local affairs. An 1838 statute empowered counties to construct public buildings and roads, and the 1846 Constitution empowered the legislature to delegate more functions to the counties. A general law of 1847 provided for the administration of villages and their incorporation by local referendum, under county supervision. Whenever this law did not suit local needs, the legislature still incorporated villages; an 1874 constitutional amendment barred it from doing so. An 1849 statute authorized county boards of supervisors to erect new towns.

Cities

A commission appointed by Gov Samuel J. Tilden recommended in 1877 that cities be given considerable administrative autonomy. This and many similar proposals over several decades failed because of upstate Republicans' deep distrust of the New York City Democratic machine. The 1894 Constitutional Convention long debated and finally rejected plans to give cities a measure of "home rule," as local government control of local affairs became known by the late 19th century. The new constitution did require that mayors be notified of the passage of special bills affecting their cities and that they accept or reject such legislation; however, the bill could be repassed at the next legislative session with no mayoral veto. (This system ended in 1924.)

The General City Law of 1909 standardized city administration in a few areas not covered by legislative charters. A 1913 amendment to that law gave all cities a vague general authority to manage their local affairs. Statutes of 1906 and 1914 provided optional models for government of smaller cities. The reformist 1915 Constitutional Convention proposed that all cities be granted full control over strictly local affairs and the right to amend their charters and also that special laws affecting individual cities and counties be strictly limited; these proposals were lost, though, when voters rejected the revised constitution. Substantive home rule for cities was finally granted by a 1923 constitutional amendment and a 1924 statute. Cities received the power to enact local laws relating to their "property, affairs, or government" and to adopt and amend their own charters by local law. The local laws could not be inconsistent with the constitution or the general laws affecting all cities but could supersede special laws. The state legislature could pass no special law concerning the "property, affairs, or government" of a particular city, except by request of the city government or (until 1938, and again after 1963 except for New York City) in an emergency as certified by the governor.

Counties, Villages, and Towns

While each city government functioned under a unique charter, counties outside New York City operated under general laws codified in 1892, 1909, and 1950. A 1938 constitutional amendment gave counties and villages of over 5,000 population home-rule powers similar to those enjoyed by cities. The state legislature also enacted special forms of government for Nassau and Westchester Cos in the mid-1930s. Under the Optional County Government Law of 1937 and the Alternative County Government Law of 1952, counties could choose from several organizational models, but only one county (Monroe) did so. A 1958 constitutional amendment gave all counties outside New York City the authority to devise and adopt alternative forms of government. Sixteen larger counties did so between 1959 and 1983, despite the stringent requirement that these county "charters" be approved in a double or even triple referendum by voters in the cities, in the towns outside cities, and in the villages if their services were affected. A new local government article in the constitution, adopted in 1963, clarified and broadened home-rule provisions and contained a bill of rights for local governments. The Statute of Local Governments confirming their basic powers could be amended only by two successive legislatures, with the governor's approval. The Municipal Home Rule Law of 1964 governed the adoption of local laws and city and county charters. All towns and smaller villages now were granted home rule powers. In 1962 certain "suburban" towns, mostly near large cities, had already received local law powers and administrative flexibility. In 1976 nonsuburban towns were empowered to supersede some provisions of the Town Law in restructuring their governments.

Employing their home-rule powers, many local governments have altered their organizational and administrative structures. However, the state legislature retains full power to pass general laws controlling local governments, limited only by the basic constitutional guarantee of home rule in the matters of "property, affairs, or government." The appellate courts have broadly interpreted the legislature's authority in matters of "state concern," which include taxation and debt, education, transportation, health, water supply, social services, aspects of civil service, and local courts. Therefore, a local government generally cannot legislate in those areas. Home-rule provisions tend to protect the powers of existing local governments, and consolidating local government entities or sharing services is difficult to accomplish. Local government autonomy is diminished by the increasing costs of services mandated by state law and by constitutional real property tax and debt limits and other restrictions on revenue generation.

See also City government.

Galie, Peter J. *Ordered Liberty: A Constitutional History of New York* (New York: Fordham Univ Press, 1996)

Hartog, Hendrik. *Public Property and Private Power: The Corporation of the City of New York in American Law, 1730–1870* (Chapel Hill: Univ of North Carolina Press, 1983)

New York State. Department of State. *Local Government Handbook*, 5th ed. (Albany: Author, 2000)

James D. Folts

Hondurans. Honduran Garifunas, of mixed Indian, European, and African descent, from the Caribbean coast first arrived during the late 1940s and early 1950s as sailors with the United Fruit Co. Soon after they were settling in New York, mainly in Brooklyn and the Bronx and often in communities with Garifunas from other Central American countries, notably Belize, Nicaragua, and Guatemala. A second wave of Hondurans emigrated when armed conflicts and political turmoil erupted in the 1980s in Central America. After political stability was restored, however, economic hardships persisted and large-scale, internal labor migration to urban centers continued in the early 1990s. Many immigrated to the United States on temporary protected status following the devastation caused by Hurricane Mitch in 1998. An estimated 300 Hondurans were leaving for the United States each day in January 1999.

According to the 2000 US census and an independent report, the Honduran growth rate in the United States during the 1990s was the largest of any single Latino group. The 1990 census tallied 26,169 Hondurans in New York State. The 2000 figure was 43,314 foreign-born Hondurans. New York State's Honduran population ranks third in the country in the early 21st century. It is concentrated in the Bronx (12,774), mainly in the Melrose area, with small populations also in East Harlem, Brooklyn (9,117), and Queens (6,019), primarily in Jackson Heights.

Hondurans in New York State host the annual Honduran Day Parade in the Bronx in celebration of their 15 September Independence Day. They have also formed numerous business and civic associations in New York City, including a community-based umbrella organization created in 1990, the Federation of Honduran Organizations of New York (FEDHONY). In 2000 the FEDHONY-sponsored New York–Honduras Telethon raised $10,000 in aid sent back to Honduras. Another notable group, founded in 1992, is Hondurans Against AIDS. The Garifuna creole language, unrelated to Spanish, has been approved as a second language in New York City's public school system.

International Organization for Migration. *World Migration Report: 2000* (Geneva, Switzerland: UN Publications, 2000)

Ana Margarita Cervantes-Rodríguez and Michael C. English

Honeoye [HONEY-oi] **Falls.** Village (pop 2,595) in Mendon (Monroe Co). Settled in 1791 close to the falls on Honeoye Creek, it was known first as Norton's Mills. It acquired a post office in 1826 as West Mendon and was incorporated as a village under its present name in 1838. Flour milling along Honeoye Creek shaped the economy of the village for over a century. Several old mill buildings, adapted to new uses, are extant. Honeoye Falls was on the New York Central Railroad's Peanut Line (1853–1939) and the Lehigh Valley Railroad from 1892 into the early 1960s. Products manufactured in the village have included axes, woolen cloth, foundry work, paper, woodworking machinery, bean separators, pianos, and agricultural implements. Honeoye

Falls also processed fruits and vegetables and was the home of the Dibble Seed Co (1891–1967). In the late 20th century a transition was made to services and light industry. A cherished local icon is the iron figure of a firefighter, trumpet in hand atop the village hall. Allegedly pilfered from St. Catharines, Ont, it has been the object of numerous capture plots since its installation in 1891.

Carolyn Vacca

Honeywell International. See ALLIED-SIGNAL.

Hooker, Philip (*b* Rutland, Mass, 28 Oct 1766; *d* Albany, 31 Jan 1836). Architect, builder, surveyor, and politician. Son of Samuel Hooker, a carpenter, and Rachel Hinds Hooker, Philip moved with his family to Albany ?1773. While nothing is known of his education, he surely gained carpentry skills from his father before moving to New York City around 1793. There, he may have received formal tutoring in drafting, and his training in surveying probably occurred after his return to Albany in 1795. In 1797–99 Hooker designed and constructed Albany's First Church in association with Elisha Putnam, a builder from Lansingburgh (Rensselaer Co) and relative of the Revolutionary War general Israel Putnam, and Gideon Putnam, founder of Saratoga Springs. Hooker built numerous Albany buildings with Putnam during their 1797–1803 partnership. New England buildings and English pattern books influenced his early work. His New York State Bank (1803) in Albany drew on the work of English architects Robert and James Adams, for instance. Within a few years, a French influence, best seen in Albany's Mechanics' and Farmers' Bank (?1811–12) and Albany Academy (1815–16), began to shape his designs.

With the rise of the Democratic Party dynasty known as the Albany Regency (*ca* 1820–1842), Democrat Hooker became politically active, holding positions on the Albany Common Council (1818–21), as city surveyor (1819–32), and as city superintendent (1821–27). By the late 1820s he responded to Revival styles then becoming nationally popular. The consistory house for Albany's First Dutch Reformed Church (*ca* 1828–30) and City Hall (1829–32) are his most notable Greek Revival efforts. His only documented assay in Gothic Revival is Albany's St. John's Church (1827–28). The Albany region's most famed architect of the early 19th century, Hooker received commissions as far west as Lewis Co (Lowville Academy, 1825–26) and as far north as Essex Co (Port Kent's Elkanah Watson House, 1826–28), as well as Hyde Hall (1818, 1827–35) in Springfield (Otsego Co). Late in his career Hooker worked with junior partners Robert Higham (1810–51) and James Kelly (*fl* 1835). His work strongly influenced early 20th-century architects, including Charles A. Platt (1861–1933) and Marcus T. Reynolds (1869–1937).

Bucher, Douglas G., and W. Richard Wheeler. *A Neat Plain Modern Stile: Philip Hooker and His Contemporaries, 1796–1836* (Amherst: Univ of Massachusetts Press, 1993)

Root, Edward Wales. *Philip Hooker: A Contribution to the Study of the Renaissance in America* (New York: Charles Scribner's Sons, 1929)

Walter Richard Wheeler

Hooker Chemical Company. Elon Hooker founded Hooker Electrochemical Co in 1909 at Niagara Falls as a subsidiary of the Development and Funding Co, established in 1903 to explore investment projects. Hooker Chemical, as the company was commonly known, grew around application of the Townsend cell, which facilitated the passage of electricity through brine to produce valuable chlorine and caustic soda, with the hydrogen gas produced vented as waste. Starting in 1918 Hooker hydrogen was used by the nearby Hydrofats Co (partly owned by Hooker) to hydrogenate vegetable oils to produce solid shortenings. Hooker also produced intermediate coal-tar products for medicines and dyes, greatly expanding its petrochemical product list after World War I. Among its developments was the insecticide Lindane. By the 1950s Hooker Chemical employed more than 3,000 people and produced over 100 chemicals at eight US plants. From 1942 to 1953 it buried chemical wastes at Love Canal, a neighborhood in Niagara Falls. In 1968 the company was acquired by Occidental Chemical, a multinational firm headquartered in Dallas, which at the beginning of the 21st century maintained a production facility with 260 full-time employees in Niagara Falls.

Thomas, Robert E. *Salt and Water, Power and People: A Short History of Hooker Electrochemical Company* (Niagara Falls: Hooker Electrochemical, 1955)

Thomas Fletcher

Hoosick. Town (pop 6,759) in NE Rensselaer Co. Settled by Dutch farmers in ?1724, it was formed as a district in 1772 and recognized as a town in 1788. Hoosick was the site of the Battle of Bennington (1777). Mills on the Hoosic River and other streams made scythes, woolen and flannel cloth, shawls, paper, and rope. A circus company organized in 1835 and practiced for a year before touring. Hoosick was made famous by Grandma Moses (1860–1961), who lived after 1905 just over the Washington Co line near Eagle Bridge. Many of her distinctive, primitive paintings depicted scenes of Hoosick's farm and village life. In the early 21st century, the town's land remains predominantly agricultural.

Kathryn T. Sheehan

Hoosick Falls. Village (pop 3,436) in Hoosick (Rensselaer Co). The Hoosic River powered two early cotton factories, the Caledonian (1823–68) and the Tremont (1831–60). The village was incorporated in 1827. Its best-known industry, the Walter A. Wood Mowing and Reaping Machine Co (1854–1924), employed 775 in 1870 but was forced to close because it failed to adapt to gasoline power. Hoosick Falls was home to several other agricultural machinery manufacturers and foundries, as well as to a factory producing machinery for cotton and woolen mills. In the late 20th century Oak Industries (now Oak-Mitsui) was a large employer; it continued in 2003 to produce copper foil for circuit boards on a smaller scale, while Saint-Gobain Corp manufactured films, foams, and fabrics.

Kathryn T. Sheehan

Hoosic River (69 mi/111 km). Rising in Cheshire, Mass, the Hoosic flows northwest through Vermont before entering New York State, running 40 miles (64 km), and emptying into the Hudson River in Schaghticoke (Rensselaer Co) at Lock 4 State Canal Park. It is broad and shallow until it reaches the waterfalls and a deep, winding, rocky gorge in Schaghticoke. The 720 mi² (1,865 km²) watershed drains the Taconic and Green Mountains, Berkshire Hills, and Rensselaer Plateau, passing through scenic farmland. An Indian trail followed the Hoosic River valley from a very early date, followed in the mid–18th century by roads connecting the Hudson River valley with northwestern Massachusetts. During the French and Indian War the river corridor was the route followed by both British forces and French and Indian raiding parties to and from Fort Massachusetts [now North Adams, Mass] and eastward to the Connecticut River valley. Historic iron and covered wooden bridges survive at Johnsonville and Buskirk (Rensselaer Co). In recent years polluting industries, primarily in Massachusetts, have either closed down or installed wastewater treatment facilities, substantially improving water quality and renewing interest in the river's fishery resources. Power plants operate at Hoosick Falls (Rensselaer Co), Johnsonville, and Schaghticoke. Relicensing agreements for them have increased boat access to the river. With significant navigable stretches between dams, the Hoosic has become popular for canoeing between North Adams, Mass, and the river's mouth.

Niles, Grace G. *The Hoosac Valley: Its Legends and Its History* (1912; repr Bowie, Md: Heritage Books, 1997)

Schmitt, Claire. *Natural Areas of Rensselaer County, New York,* 2d ed. (Troy, NY: Rensselaer-Taconic Land Conservancy, 2002)

Warren F. Broderick

Hope. Town (pop 392) in SE Hamilton Co. Settled *ca* 1790, the town was formed in 1818 from Wells. By 1825 it had 1,343 sheep, nearly double the number of people. Until *ca* 1900, lumbering and tanning were its chief industries, and some women sewed for Northville glove shops; small farming continued into the 20th century. Modern access was provided by an improved Rte 30 (1912, concrete 1938). Farming had disappeared by 1960, however, and Hope has no industry and no tourism except for seasonal camps.

Hopewell. Town (pop 3,346) in central Ontario Co. Settled in 1789, the town was formed in 1822 from Gorham. Many of the early settlers were from Maryland. Hopewell is the site of the Seneca village of Ohnaghee, depopulated by smallpox in the second quarter of the 18th century. In 1789 Oliver Phelps built a gristmill at Chapin on the Canandaigua Lake outlet that helped establish the market for Genesee wheat. Crossed by the state road from Utica to Avon authorized in 1794, it is a grain farming district and has some light manufacturing. It is the site of the Ontario Co offices.

Marla A. Bennett

Hopkinton [HAWP-KIN-N]. Town (pop 1,020) in SE St. Lawrence Co. Settled in 1802, the town was formed in 1805 from Massena. In 1814 the British seized a large amount of flour stored in a Hopkinton barn during a raid. In the 1850s three potato starch factories were in operation. In the early 21st century most of the town is forested and within Adirondack Park. Much of it is industrial forest land, but there are some very large farms along the northern park boundary and a large dairy calf rearing operation near Nicholville.

Richard E. Mooers

Hopper, Isaac T(atem) (*b* Deptford Township, NJ, 3 Dec 1771; *d* New York City, 7 May 1852). Quaker abolitionist. Hopper was active in antislavery and Society of Friends circles in Philadelphia before moving in 1829 to New York City, where he ran a bookstore supporting the Hicksite branch of the Quakers, published Quaker literature, and worked on behalf of fugitive slaves. From 1840 to 1845 Hopper was treasurer and book agent of the American Anti-Slavery Society. His connection with the *National Anti-Slavery Standard*, a publication that criticized the behavior of some Quakers toward abolitionists, led to a controversy among New York Quakers, and in 1842 the New York Yearly Meeting (Hicksite) disowned Hopper. He remained a Quaker although in his last years without formal membership. From 1845 until his final illness, he worked as an agent for the Prison Association of New York, finding jobs for released convicts and assisting the association's Female Department. The Home for Discharged Female Convicts begun by the New York Prison Association was later renamed the Isaac T. Hopper Home in his honor.

Bacon, Margaret. *The Lamb's Warrior: The Life of Isaac T. Hopper* (New York: Crowell, 1970)

Christopher Densmore

hops. The cultivation of a perennial vine that produces cones, called hops, was the first specialized agricultural industry in New Netherland, introduced by the Dutch in 1629. Hop is a primary ingredient in beer, a dietary staple for the early settlers. The vines, however, were not grown in large amounts in New York State until 1808, when they were planted in Bouckville (Madison Co) by James Coolidge, who in 1816 was the first to sell his crop in New York City. Cultivation spread to Oneida Co in 1821 and by 1828 to Chenango, Franklin, Otsego, Herkimer, Montgomery, and Schoharie Cos, where the naturally rich soil retained the proper acidity for hop cultivation and where reasonably level fields were protected by low hills. By 1835 Otsego Co was the leading producer in the state. By 1839 New York State led the country in hop production. Throughout much of the second half of the 19th century Central New York was the largest hop-producing region in the nation. In 1879 the state produced just over 10,500 tons (9,530 MT) of hops, over 80% of the national total. Over the next two decades, however, competition from the Pacific Northwest dramatically cut the New York State share of national production. In 1890 the figure was 10,000 tons (9,070 MT), about 50% of the national total. In 1900 production was down to 8,500 tons (7,710 MT), or 35%.

Most farmers cultivated hops as one of many crops, planting from 4 to 6 acres (1.6–2.4 ha). However, some planted exclusively hops in amounts exceeding 100–200 acres (40–81 ha). James F. Clark, who cultivated 150 acres (60.7 ha) just south of Cooperstown (Otsego Co) was the largest hop producer in the state from 1876 to 1900, employing nearly 1,000 people at harvest time and operating his seven hop houses day and night during the picking season. Hop growing, though profitable for many, was risky. The initial investment was costly; cultivation, harvesting, and drying were demanding; and the market varied dramatically. Extra workers had to be hired to help with the harvest, which usually began in late August and lasted from two to four weeks, and most were housed and fed at the grower's expense. Men working as tenders carried vine-entwined poles to hop boxes stationed throughout the field, where pickers, usually women and children, plucked the conelike flowers from the vines. In hop houses the cones were dried in a process that took 10–12 hours. After cooling the dried cones were pressed into bales. Dealers bought hops from growers and sold them to brewers or other buyers throughout the United States and Europe. Prices were set even before the crop had matured, a gamble for both the dealer and the grower. An especially bad epidemic of hop mildew, or "blue mold," struck New York State in 1909, crippling the industry. Prohibition dramatically decreased the demand for hops, and by the 1920s hop growers were out of business in the state. In the 21st century, with the popularity of home brewing and microbrewing, interest in producing hops as a specialty crop has increased. The desire to preserve historic crops and ways has also encouraged hop cultivation at home, and can be found at the Pederson Farm in Seneca (Ontario Co) and at historic sites such as the Farmers' Museum in Cooperstown.

Tomlan, Michael. *Tinged with Gold: Hop Culture in the United States* (Athens: Univ of Georgia Press, 1992)

Suzan D. Friedlander

Cultivating hops with a grubber in Otsego Co, 1894.

Horicon. Town (pop 1,479) in N central Warren Co. Settled *ca* 1810, the town was formed from Hague and Bolton in 1838, and its settlers worked at farming and lumbering. Beginning *ca* 1840, tanneries attracted Irish immigrant workers, who produced 20,000 hides annually. Limestone and marble were quarried, and a cedar oil distillery was among many 19th-century mills. Beginning with the Wells House (1872) at Adirondack, hotels, boardinghouses, and cottages made Horicon a resort area, especially around Brant and Schroon Lakes. At what residents called the Rat Farm, Victor Schwentker raised rodents from the 1930s until 1963, supplying laboratory animals to the military during World War II and helping popularize the gerbil as a pet.

Marilyn J. Van Dyke

Hornby. Town (pop 1,742) in SE Steuben Co. Settled in 1814, it was formed in 1826 from the town of Painted Post. Hornby's timber-covered hills provided its main economic activity through most of the 19th century; when the timber was gone, many residents turned to dairy farming. In the late 19th century a rake factory operated in Hornby. The Syracuse, Geneva and Corning Railroad (1877; later New York Central) served the town. The Hornby picnic, started in 1911 and still ongoing in 2002, remains a popular annual event. In 2003 agriculture, especially dairying, dominated the Hornby economy, with much of the rest of the town consisting of state forest land. Many residents work in Corning and Painted Post.

Thomas Dimitroff

Hornell. City (pop 9,019) in W Steuben Co. The locality was settled in 1790 and named for Judge George Hornell, who arrived in 1793. In 1850, when the Erie Railroad reached the town, extensive rail shops and yards were built and the population grew rapidly. Other industries before and after the Civil War included sash and blind works, a foundry, a tannery, shoemaking, and furniture making. Incorporated as a village in 1852, it became the City of Hornellsville in 1888 and was renamed Hornell in 1906. In the 20th century it produced silk goods, tile, brick, fence wire, gloves, shoes, and electrical machinery. Dr Roswell Park began his medical practice at a cancer sanatorium here, eventually founding the Roswell Park Cancer Institute in Buffalo. In the 1970s the downtown area was split with the construction of the Rte 36 arterial. The old Erie shops closed after Conrail absorbed the bankrupt Erie Lackawanna Railroad in 1976. Hornell's economy revived in the 1990s when first Morris-Knudsen and later Alstom Transportation opened railcar facilities in the city. In 2002 Alstom employed 850 locally and received a $961 million contract from the state's Metropolitan Transportation Authority to build 660 subway cars (the largest subway car purchase by MTA) for the New York City system at the Hornell facility.

Virginia L. Wright and Jerry Wright

Hornellsville. Town (pop 4,042) in W Steuben Co. Settled in 1793, the town was formed from the town of Canisteo in 1820. Muck farming began in the 1830s, and there was a boom in celery cultivation in the late 19th and early 20th centuries. After the disastrous flood of July 1935, Arkport and Almond Dams were built to protect downstream land from flooding.

Virginia L. Wright and Jerry Wright

Horseheads. Town (pop 19,561) and village (pop 6,452) in central Chemung Co. Settled in 1789, the town was formed in 1854. The name derives from the slaughter, in 1779, of 30 to 40 war-worn horses by Maj Gen John Sullivan's troops at this location. The village was incorporated in 1837 as Fairport and changed its name to Horseheads in

1845; the post office name was changed in 1853. Beginning in 1840 it was known for the manufacture of brick; other products included agricultural implements, architectural ironwork, woolen cloth, hardware, screen doors and windows, bridges, and structural iron. A canal feeder for the Chemung Canal (1833–78) put Horseheads on a major transportation route; it was the site of the canal's toll collector. The town was crossed by the Erie Railroad in 1849 and was later served by four other lines and an electric railroad. The Horseheads Celery Co (1887) shipped the produce of its muckland; tobacco was another cash crop. Because of its rail systems, Horseheads was selected by the US Army for the Elmira Holding and Reconsignment Point, a supply depot, in 1942. The vast (35-acre/14 ha) Ann Page plant (1965) produced grocery items for the A&P Co until the 1980s. Rte 17 (I-86) was completed in town in 1971. In the early 21st century, large employers in Horseheads include Cutler-Hammer Eaton Corp, Imaging and Sensing Technology Corp, and Toshiba Display Devices. The Hanover Square Historic District is the commercial center of the village, which is for the most part Romanesque Revival. Teal Park and the 1855 Extension District are also listed on the National Register, as is the Zimmerman House (1890), home of Eugene Zimmerman (1862–1935), cartoonist and illustrator for *Judge.*

Heather A. Wade

horse racing. See HARNESS RACING; THOROUGHBRED RACING.

horses. Dutch settlers are credited with bringing the first horses—of a stocky, continental European breed, well suited to farmwork—to New Netherland in the 1600s. Dutch farmers preferred horses to oxen, unlike New England farmers, who preferred oxen to their own horses of English breeds. Once fields were cleared, horses were able to work at a faster rate than oxen. In the early 1800s universal replacement of oxen by horses for farmwork increased productivity and spurred expansion of cultivated lands. Over the same period, horse-powered stagecoach lines proliferated, with the first New York City to Boston stage in operation by 1784; stages would continue to serve smaller localities throughout the state into the 20th century. Horses also served as the first draft animals on the Erie Canal, which opened in 1825.

The 1855 census recorded 579,715 horses in the state, or about 1 horse for every 6 persons. They were the main power for hauling goods and transporting people within cities, with as many as 200,000 horses in New York City around 1900. The New York City police had 800 horses in 1904, primarily used to control traffic jams. Although the horse population increased in the late 19th century—in 1910 the state had 591,008 horses on farms and 303,256 horses in nonfarm areas—the ratio of horses to human beings fell during that era; in 1910 the state counted 1 horse for every 10 humans. By 1930, with 339,000 equines recorded, the ratio was 1:37; by 2000, 1:113.

During their 19th-century heyday, urban horses presented a number of problems. They needed housing in stables and stores of grain for feed. There was also equine pollution. The average horse produces approximately 2–3 gal (8–11 l) of urine and 30–50 lb (14–23 kg) of manure a day. In New York City much of the manure was gathered from the streets and then stored in areas sometimes known as manure blocks. Many thought the droppings were a grave public health hazard. However, much of the manure was sold to farmers on Long Island, and the fertilizer helped that region become one of the nation's leading areas for truck farming in the late 19th century. The bodies of the horses themselves also created a pollution problem. The life of a city horse was frequently brutal and short (on average 2–4 years), and an estimated 15,000 horses died on the streets of New York City each year. The carcasses were taken to offal docks and then transported to rendering plants, by law kept some distance from developed urban areas.

The era of the urban horse started to wane with electrification of streetcar lines between 1888 and 1892. In 1906 motorbuses replaced horse-driven omnibuses on Manhattan's 5th Ave, and by 1912 cars outnumbered horses in New York City. But workhorses remained, in dwindling numbers, on the city's streets through World War II. On many farms, tractors did not replace workhorses until the late 1940s or 1950s.

Horses as race animals have always been important in New York State. In the mid-1660s the first English governor of New York Colony laid out North America's first official racehorse track—a 4 mi (6.4 km) wide, 16 mi (25.8 km) long stretch—on Salisbury Plain [now Hempstead, Nassau Co]. The National Museum of Racing and Hall of Fame (for thoroughbreds) is located in Saratoga Springs, and the Harness Racing Museum and Hall of Fame is located in Goshen (Orange Co). The Saratoga Race Course, dating to 1864, is one of the oldest and most storied North American thoroughbred race courses. Each June Belmont Park in Elmont (Nassau Co) hosts the Belmont Stakes, the final race in the Triple Crown, the most prestigious of thoroughbred racing series. Famous trotters bred in the state include Lady Suffolk, inspiration for the folksong "The Old Gray Mare," who was foaled at Smithtown (Suffolk Co) in 1833, and Hambletonian, foaled at Sugar Loaf (Orange Co) in 1849. Hambletonian was the first standardbred, a fast but steady horse capable of trotting or pacing a distance of 1 mi (1.6 km) in 2.5 minutes, and Orange Co became an important breeding center for the type.

A 2000 survey found 168,000 horses, valued at $1.7 billion, and total equine-related assets of $6.2 billion. The state's equine owners and operators spent over $700 million for operating and capital expenses. Quarterhorses and thoroughbreds were the most common breeds, with 30,000 animals each. Standardbreds ranked third at 11,500; Appaloosas, Morgans, and Arabians each boasted populations of about 9,000; paints followed at 6,800. There were 15,300 racehorses and 11,500 draft horses, indicating new interest in the use of horses on small farms. In addition, the state's breeders claimed more than 25,000 broodmares and almost 5,000 stallions. Most horses in the state are used for recreation, and many are used in horse shows, rodeos, and pulling contests. The Saratoga-bred gelding, Funny Cide, won the Kentucky Derby and Preakness Stakes in 2003.

See also HARNESS RACING; SARATOGA SPRINGS; STREET RAILWAYS; THOROUGHBRED RACING.

Gates, P. W. *The Farmer's Age: Agriculture, 1815–1860 (New York: Holt, Rinehart & Winston, 1960)*

H. F. Hintz

horticulture. Interest in domestic commercial horticulture emerged in the late colonial period, a time when seeds and seedlings for most fruits, flowers, vegetables, and ornamentals were imported from Europe. William Prince established the first commercial nursery in America in 1737, the Linnaean Botanic Garden at Flushing (Queens Co). Prince wanted to reduce reliance on food imports by supplying quality fruit tree seedlings.

The first vegetable seeds produced for sale in the United States were grown by the New Lebanon (Columbia Co) Shaker community in 1789 or 1790. Grant Thorburn established the first seed house in the state in New York City in 1805, and he became a major importer and supplier to communities statewide. Patrick Barry, who became a leading American horticulturist in the second half of the 19th century, and George Ellwanger established the Mount Hope Nurseries in Rochester in 1840. Mount Hope introduced many varieties from Europe, such as fruit trees on dwarfing stock and the cut-leaf weeping birch. Following the Civil War other growers and suppliers, including Joseph Harris and Hiram Sibley, established firms that flourished in Rochester. By the late 1870s Rochester and Western New York had become the horticultural center of the nation.

Nursery catalogs of the mid–19th century included not only fruit trees but a wide variety of perennial flowers and flowering shrubs. Multifarious roses were offered in the early catalogs of the Mount Hope Nurseries and Geneva Nursery (Ontario Co). Ellwanger's son, Henry B. Ellwanger, gained national recognition with the publication of *The Rose* (1882). James Vick of Rochester and John Lewis Childs of Floral Park (Nassau Co) were other 19th-century horticulturalists who gained national reputations. To respond to changes in the horticultural industry following the Civil War, Patrick Barry advocated the establishment of the New York State Agricultural Experiment Station in Geneva, which opened in 1882. Barry recognized that research by university-trained scientists was necessary to improve fruit culture and farming practices if New York State were to succeed in competing with western nurseries and fruit growers.

In *Cyclopedia of American Horticulture* (1900), horticulturist and botanist Liberty Hyde Bailey, who retired as dean of the College of Agriculture at Cornell University in 1913, divided the field into four branches: "pomology, or fruit-growing; olericulture, or vegetable-growing; floriculture, or raising ornamental plants . . . ; [and] landscape horticulture, or growing plants for their use in the landscape (or in landscape gardening)." By the turn of the 20th century, nurseries had been established throughout the United States, and the states of California and Washington were becoming centers of fruit and vegetable production. At the same time the growth of suburbs stimulated demand for landscaped homes. Ornamental trees and shrubs gradually replaced fruit trees as the most important source of annual revenue for commercial nurseries in New York State. Andrew Jackson Downing of Newburgh (Orange Co) had been an early and influential voice for residential landscaping and open landscaped urban spaces. Downing's *A Treatise on the Theory and Practice of Landscape Gardening* (1841) is a foundation work of American landscape design. Downing is credited with the concept for New York City's Central Park, which he advocated in the August 1851 *Horticulturist.*

The great nurseries and seed houses of the 19th century did not endure. The Linnaean Botanic Garden continued as a family-run business through midcentury. In 1887 George Ellwanger and Patrick Barry donated 22 acres (9 ha) to the City of Rochester, which became the nucleus of Highland Park. In 1918, suffering from competition and labor strife, Mount Hope Nurseries became a realty company to convert nursery lands into subdivisions. W. Atlee Burpee Co of Philadelphia absorbed James Vick's Sons in the late 1920s. The home grounds of W. T. and E. Smith Geneva Nurseries were last used in the 1990s by Garden Galleries, a wholesale business now in Phelps (Ontario Co). Joseph Harris Co was consolidated as Harris Moran Seed Co in the 1990s with corporate offices in California.

Since Earth Day 1970, there has been a shift in the industry from beautifying to conservation. In 2002 smaller regional and local growers (2,227 statewide) and landscapers produce ornamental trees, shrubs, and perennial plants. The New York State Nursery and Landscape Association, with headquarters in Baldwinsville (Onondaga Co), represents the interests of these businesses. In New York State in 2002 there were 27,500 acres (11,129 ha) in nursery stock and 25 million ft^2 (2.3 million m^2) in enclosed greenhouse space. Landscape sales in the state were $2.7 billion, with nursery revenues ranked second among farm commodities in the state and among the top 10 nationally.

See also BOTANICAL GARDENS.

Chapman, P. J., and E. H. Glass. *The First 100 Years of the New York State Agricultural Experiment Station at Geneva, NY,* ed. R. E. Krauss (Geneva, NY: NYS Agricultural Experiment Station, 1999)

Grebinger, Paul, and Ellen M. Grebinger. *To Dress and Keep the Earth: The Nurseries and Nurserymen of Geneva, New York* (Geneva, NY: Geneva Historical Society, 1993)

McKelvey, Blake. "The Flower City: Center of Nurseries and Fruit Orchards," *Rochester Historical Society Publications* 18 (1940): 121–29

Paul Grebinger and Monette Goodridge

Hosack, David (*b* New York City, 31 Aug 1769; *d* New York City, 22 Dec 1835). Physician, surgeon, botanist, and medical educator. After attending Columbia College from 1786 to 1788 and studying medicine privately under Richard Bayley in 1788, Hosack received a BA from the College of New Jersey (now Princeton University) in 1789. Following further private medical study under Nicholas Romayne (1789–90), he received an MD from the University of Pennsylvania in 1791 and then practiced in Alexandria, Va. From 1792 to 1794 he studied medicine and botany in Edinburgh and London. Back in medical practice in New York City in 1794, he became professor of botany in 1795 and of materia medica in 1796 at Columbia College. For the next 35 years, Hosack was a leading figure in New York science, medicine, and education. In 1801 his interest in botany led him to purchase 20 acres (8.1 ha) for the Elgin Botanic Garden, located where Rockefeller Center now stands. Hosack was surgeon-in-attendance at the 1804 duel between Alexander Hamilton and Aaron Burr. The founder and president of Rutgers Medical College in 1826, Hosack retired when the New York State Supreme Court dissolved the school in 1830.

See also BOTANICAL GARDENS; MEDICAL EDUCATION; SCIENTIFIC CULTURE (19TH–21ST CENTURIES).

Robbins, Christine Chapman. *David Hosack: Citizen of New York* (Philadelphia: American Philosophical Society, 1964)

Eric v. d. Luft

hospitals. See HEALTHCARE AND HOSPITALS.

hotels. See RESORT HOTELS; URBAN HOTELS.

Hough, Franklin B(enjamin) (*b* Martinsburg, Lewis Co, 22 July 1822; *d* Lowville, Lewis Co, 11 June 1885). Physician, historian, and forester. Educated at Lowville Academy and Black River Institute in Watertown, Hough demonstrated an early interest in mineralogy. He graduated Union College in Schenectady in 1843 and went on to receive an MD from Cleveland Medical College in 1848, just before the death of his wife, Maria Eggleston. He practiced medicine in Somerville (St. Lawrence Co), where in 1849 he married Mariah Kilham, with whom he would have eight children. In 1852 he moved to Albany to write New York State history, publishing histories of St. Lawrence, Franklin, Jefferson, and Lewis Cos while working for the state government. In 1855 he was appointed superintendent of the New York State Census, in which he compiled the first state agricultural and industrial records. In 1861 Hough moved his family back to Lowville. During the Civil War he joined the US Sanitary Commission, then became surgeon for the 97th New York Regiment, and later worked for the Bureau of Military Statistics. In 1865 he returned to the state census and participated in the 1870 federal census. Hough's analysis of agricultural and trade statistics demonstrated a decline in forests and lumber production in the eastern states. In 1874 Hough and Verplanck Colvin produced the *First Annual Report of the Commissioners of State Parks,* recommending the creation of a timber preserve in northern New York State. Hough served as the US Department of Agriculture's forestry agent from 1876 through 1883, founded the *Journal of American Forestry,* and achieved international recognition for his publications on the influence of forests on climate. His work led to the Forest Preserve Act of 1885 and the New York State Forest Preserve. A mineral he discovered was named houghite in his honor. His son Romeyn also worked in forestry.

Einhorn, Arthur. "Franklin B. Hough: An Incipient Anthropologist of the Early 19th Century." In *American Anthropology, The Early Years,* ed. John V. Murra (Princeton, NJ: West Publishing, 1976)

Pilcher, Edith. "Biography of Franklin B. Hough." In *With Hand and Heart: The Courtship Letters of Franklin B. Hough and Mariah Kilham, January through May 1849,* ed. Vivian G. Smith (Utica: North Country Books, 1993)

Houghton, Alanson B(igelow) (*b* Cambridge, Mass, 10 Oct 1863; *d* South Dartmouth, Mass, 16 Sept 1941). Industrialist, politician, and diplomat. Raised in Corning (Steuben Co) and educated at Harvard College, Houghton labored at Corning Glass Works (now Corning Inc), which was founded by his grandfather, Amory Houghton, for 30 years. While serving as president (1910–18) and chairman of the board (1919–28), he transformed Corning Glass Works into a multimillion-dollar corporation with international sales and institutionalized the company's commitment to industrial science and engineering. A Republican, he became an important political figure after his 1918 election to Congress. Pres Warren G. Harding appointed him ambassador to Germany in 1922, and Pres Calvin Coolidge named him ambassador to Great Britain in 1925. Houghton championed three diplomatic achievements while abroad: the Dawes Plan, the Locarno Treaties, and the Kellogg-Briand Pact. After fending off pleas to run for the New York State governorship in 1926, he emerged as a leading vice presidential candidate two years later. When this boom failed, he became New York State's 1928 Republican nominee for US senator but lost narrowly to Royal S. Copeland. He then returned to London until retiring from public service in 1929; he lived primarily in Washington, DC. Though retired, he remained the controlling shareholder of Corning Glass Works and served on several boards, including the Brookings Institution and the Carnegie Endowment for International Peace. Despite political defeats, contemporaries hailed Houghton as the greatest American diplomat in recent memory, expressing regret that he was never appointed secretary of state.

Matthews, Jeffrey J. "The Businessman Diplomat: A. B. Houghton, A Case Study," *Business and Economic History* 28 (Winter 1999): 137–44

———. "The Pursuit of Progress: Corning Glass Works, Alanson B. Houghton, and America as World Power" (PhD diss, Univ of Kentucky, 2000)

Jeffrey J. Matthews

Houghton College. Located in Houghton (Allegany Co), this private, Christian, liberal arts college began in 1883 as a high school seminary under the Wesleyan Methodist Connection. Coeducational from its founding, Houghton operated as a secondary school for its first 15 years. In 1899 a few college classes were offered. The college department's first diploma was awarded in 1901. While early principals were Wesleyan Methodist pastors willing to accept the job, in 1908 Houghton acquired its first academically trained president, James S. Luckey, who served until his death in 1937. Houghton College received its provisional charter from New York State in 1923 and awarded its first 19 baccalaureate degrees two years later. A permanent charter was granted in 1927, and accreditation by the Middle States Association of Colleges and Secondary Schools came in 1935. Stephen W. Paine succeeded Luckey and served as president until 1972. Under Paine's leadership the college expanded from about 300 students to 1,200, necessitating the addition of new buildings, and the percentage of faculty holding earned doctorates tripled. Daniel R. Chamberlain, president since 1976, has overseen the construction of several other major campus buildings and an extensive adult degree-completion program. Houghton College continues its historical connection with the Wesleyan Church. As of 2001 it offers baccalaureate degrees in 48 fields, and a recent gift of

$15 million will allow the faculty to develop a master's degree course in music, the first master's program at Houghton. Enrollment for the fall 2000 semester was 1,246, plus 111 in an adult degree-completion program at a site near Buffalo.

Gillette, Frieda, and Katherine Lindley. . . . *And You Shall Remember: A Pictorial History of Houghton College* (Houghton, NY: Houghton College, 1982)
Smith, Willard G. "The History of Church-Controlled Colleges in the Wesleyan Methodist Church" (PhD diss, New York Univ, 1950)

Richard L. Wing

Hounsfield. Town (pop 3,323) in W Jefferson Co. Settled in 1800, its most important locality, Sackets Harbor, was founded the following year. The town was formed in 1806 from Watertown. A hydraulic canal from Huntington's Mills to Sackets Harbor provided power to mills from 1832 to *ca* 1842. Hops growing was a major agricultural pursuit in the first half of the 19th century but was replaced around 1850 by dairy farming and market gardening. Few farms remain in 2003. Summer residents have been important to Hounsfield since the 1870s; cottage associations, like Knobby Knoll and Campbell's Point, line the lakeshore. The Watertown International Airport (1929) and Dexter Marsh State Wildlife Management Area are located in the town, which includes a number of islands in Lake Ontario, the largest of which are Galloo and Stony Islands.

Laura Lynne Scharer

Housing Finance Agency (HFA). Public benefit corporation. Created in 1960 to finance low-income housing through the sale of municipal bonds, with proceeds used to make mortgages to eligible borrowers, the agency also administers several loan programs, as well as a tax credit program, designed for the creation and rehabilitation of affordable multifamily rental housing units. Its borrowers include limited-profit, nonprofit, and urban rental housing companies, owners of multifamily housing units, nonprofit nursing home and medical corporations, and community development corporations. The original mandate has expanded to include financing the construction of educational and healthcare facilities. However, creating and preserving affordable housing, especially in high-cost areas, remains its primary concern. A president/chief executive officer (CEO) manages the agency under the guidance of a seven-member board. Four members are appointed by the governor, three of whom (commissioner of the Division of Housing and Community Renewal, commissioner of taxation and finance, and director of the budget) are ex officio. The president/CEO also serves as the CEO of the State of New York Mortgage Agency (SONYMA), which is co-located with the HFA. As of 2001 the agency had sold over $4.8 billion in bonds to finance approximately 89,000 units of housing. In 2003 a staff of 210 administered HFA activities, the New York State Affordable Housing Corp, the New York State Project Finance Agency, and the State of New York Municipal Bond Bank Agency.

New York State. Housing Finance Agency. *Annual Report* (New York: Author, 1960–)

Jeffrey Kraus

Howard. Town (pop 1,430) in NW Steuben Co. Settled 1806, the town was formed in 1812 from Bath and Dansville. In the early 19th century the Bath and Lake Erie Turnpike was built east to west across the town. Artist Otis Bullard (1815–53), a native of Howard, gained fame by showing his 1,000 ft (305 m) canvas panorama of New York City in a series of national tours. Rte 17 (I-86) was built through the town just north of the hamlet in 1968–69. Dairying has been the principal industry for more than a century. Annual events include the Ice Festival in February and Old Home Day in July.

Virginia L. Wright and Jerry Wright

Howe, Louis McHenry (*b* Indianapolis, Ind, 14 Jan 1871; *d* Bethesda, Md, 18 April 1936). Political adviser. In 1873 Howe's family moved to Saratoga Springs. Howe eventually became coeditor of his father's weekly newspaper, the *Sun*, but then turned to freelance writing. He met Franklin D. Roosevelt while covering state politics for the *New York Herald*, which hired Howe in 1906. In 1912 Roosevelt asked Howe to run his New York State Senate reelection campaign and later his gubernatorial campaign. Howe served as his secretary during his term as governor of New York from 1929 to 1933, working in New York City to secure Roosevelt the Democratic Party's presidential nomination in 1932. On taking office, Roosevelt appointed Howe his personal secretary, a position Howe held until his death. Howe played a key role in developing many New Deal programs, including the Civilian Conservation Corps, Subsistence Homestead Program, and various anticrime initiatives.

Rollins, Alfred B. *Roosevelt and Howe* (New York: Knopf, 1962)
Stiles, Lela. *The Man behind Roosevelt: The Story of Louis McHenry Howe* (New York: World Publishing, 1954)

Barry Mowell

Howe Caverns. Cavern network near Cobleskill (Schoharie Co). Howe Caverns has hosted over 13 million visitors since it opened to the public as a tourist attraction in 1929. Formed over 6 million years by running water eroding prehistoric limestone deposits, the cavern network stretches more than 1 mile (1.6 km) and is composed of a series of passageways, stalagmite- and stalactite-filled chambers, an underground stream, and a subterranean lake that hosts a fleet of flat-bottom tour boats. The Mohawk originally called the cavern Ostgargee, meaning cave of the great galleries. The caves take their present name from farmer Lester Howe, the first white settler known to have explored them when he stumbled upon them in 1842. Howe developed the site as a tourist attraction and built the Cave House Hotel over the cavern entrance in 1847. The cool air from the cave's mouth provided an early form of air conditioning inside the build-

Underground boating through Howe Caverns on the *Alcestis*, 1930.

ing. In 1888, with public interest waning, Howe sold the caverns to private investors who began mining limestone from the cave. In 1926 John Mosner and Walter Sagendorf hatched a plan to install elevators and electric lighting in the cavern, making it again a tourist destination. The restored site opened for public tours in 1929.

Cudmore, Dana. *The Remarkable Howe Caverns Story* (Woodstock, NY: Overlook Press, 1990)

Barry Mowell

HSBC Bank USA. The Marine Bank of Buffalo was founded in 1850 and, by merging with the Buffalo Trust Co in 1925, became one of the largest trust companies in the United States, the Commercial Trust Co of Buffalo, which merged with Marine Midland Trust Co of NY in 1951. Marine Midland acquired Grace National Bank of New York in 1965 to become Marine Midland Grace Trust Co New York City. The Marine Midland headquarters, Buffalo's tallest building, was finished in 1974. In 1980 the Hongkong and Shanghai Bank (HSBC), headquartered in London, acquired 51% of Marine Midland Bank; in 1987 it acquired the remaining 49%. In 1999 the US bank name was changed to HSBC Bank USA, with headquarters in Buffalo, and the Republic National Bank of New York was acquired. At the beginning of the 21st century, HSBC Bank USA had over 400 branches in New York State.

Hubbard, J. T. W. *For Each, the Strength of All: A History of Banking in the State of New York* (New York: New York Univ Press, 1995)

Pamela Cooper

Hubbard, Elbert (Green) (*b* Bloomington, Ill, 19 June 1856; *d* at sea, Irish Sea, 7 May 1915). Writer and decorative artist. Hubbard made his original fortune selling soap for the Larkin Co in Buffalo after 1875, run by his brother-in-law John Larkin. In 1894 he quit his job and went to Europe, visiting the Kelmscott Press of British arts and crafts movement leader William Morris. He briefly attended Harvard College then in 1895 established the Roycroft Press in East Aurora (Erie Co), primarily to publish his own writings. Modeled after Morris's enterprise, Roycroft periodicals included the *Philistine: A Periodical of Protest, Little Journeys,* which described visits to homes of famous people, and the *Fra.* First published in the *Philistine* in 1899, Hubbard's "A Message to Garcia," a tale of heroic endurance and obedience, sold a purported 9 million copies by the time of Hubbard's death. The Roycroft community became a self-contained and self-supporting arts and crafts business producing mission-style furniture, fine bookbinding, and metalwork. While maintaining Morris and John Ruskin's ideal of satisfaction in labor, Hubbard also exploited Roycroft's commercial potential, overseeing one of the few profit-showing communities of this type. Hubbard also raised funds in extensive lecture tours, bringing Roycroft and its ideas and ideals to a wider audience until his untimely death on the *Lusitania.*

Champney, Freeman. *Art and Glory: The Story of Elbert Hubbard* (New York: Crown Publishers, 1968)

Nancy E. Green

Hudson. City (pop 7,524) in W Columbia Co. A largely Quaker group of seafarers and merchants from Nantucket and Edgartown, Mass, and Newport and Providence, RI, purchased the site of Hudson, then called Claverack Landing. Their business had been affected by the Revolution, leading them to seek a more protected seaport. Forming a stock corporation and as proprietors, they platted Hudson in 1785 with a main street running back from the river along a ridge. The same year the city withdrew from Claverack and became the third incorporated city in the state. It grew rapidly to 1,500 in 1786 and to 2,584 in 1790, when it was the 24th-largest city in the United States.

The proprietors' original intention was to follow their accustomed maritime pursuits. Shipbuilding, begun in 1784, was the leading industry, along with associated trades, including cordage (1785) and sail-duck (1787), a type of canvas, as well as tanneries using Spanish hides and sealskins. Hudson's coastal shippers and exporters loaded beef and pork, lumber, hoops, staves, and heading from the back country. This large agricultural hinterland encompassed all of Columbia Co, most of Berkshire Co in Massachusetts, and a part of northwest Connecticut. They also sent out whaling vessels and produced whale oil and candles. Hudson was a port of entry from 1790 to 1815. Due to its high-volume shipping, it became the terminus of five turnpikes, built between 1799 and 1806 and radiating like the spokes of a wheel. Hudson's growth was evident: a newspaper began in 1785, three libraries opened between 1786 and 1797 and a post office in 1792, water came to its streets by aqueduct in 1790, and Hudson Academy opened in 1805, the same year the city was made the county seat.

Following the Embargo of 1807 and subsequent war, Hudson, which depended heavily on trade, went into decline. It responded by developing the manufacture of goods no longer readily available; a woolen satinet factory and an iron foundry were operating by 1815. The increase of travel and trade on the Hudson River helped the young city, and until 1932 Hudson was the head of navigation on the river. Its leaders sought advantages from newer transportation technology as well, operating several steamboat lines and initiating the Hudson and Berkshire Railroad (1838); later it was served by the Hudson River Railroad (1851). Its whaling industry revived from 1830 to 1845, bringing significant prosperity. Hudson's seaport also fostered illegal activities, including prostitution, which thrived until the mid–20th century, and gambling.

In the mid–19th century Hudson developed an iron industry. Hudson Iron Co (1851) and Columbia County Iron Co (1858) were followed by more specialized factories, such as the Clapp and Jones Manufacturing Co (1870; steam fire engines), Philips Spiral Corn-Husker Co (1871), and Hudson Paper Car-Wheel Co (1873; railroad-car wheels with paper cores). Clothing, cigars, and knit goods also entered the picture in the third quarter of the century, as did the Hudson Portland Cement Co (1850s–1908). James Clark's ready-made clothing factory employed 400 workers in 1858.

Many Irish came to Hudson around 1850 during the potato famine emigrations; by 1855 nearly 20% of the population was Irish-born. At the end of the 19th century new ethnic groups began arriving, among them Italians, Poles, Hungarians, Jews, and Ukrainians. In the 20th century Hudson produced machinery, knit woolens, ginger ale, matches, clothing, flypaper, and cement, but it was chiefly a county seat and market town. Its superb Federal townscape and architecture remained largely unaltered and were discovered in the 1980s by artists and art and antique dealers, who began the process of restoration. In the early 21st century Hudson is increasingly a tourist destination, although still a manufacturing city, with Kaz (electrical equipment; 400 workers), L. B. Furniture Industries (wood and metal restaurant furniture), and W. B. McGuire Co (millwork). The 2000 census reported that 24% of the population was African American. Those of Latino ethnicity numbered 8%.

Hudson is home of the American Museum of Firefighting and of Hudson Correctional Facility (1887). Landmarks include the Hudson Opera

Armory in Hudson, early 20th century.

House (1855) and Promenade Hill (1785; also known as Parade Hill), a park integral to the original townscape. Hudson was the childhood home of artist Sanford Robinson Gifford (1823–80) and home of William Woodworth (1780–1839), inventor of the first practical planing machinery.

Hudson, Henry (*fl* late 16th century–early 17th century). English mariner and explorer. Little of Henry Hudson's life is known before about 1607. Hudson sailed for both the English and the Dutch and is chiefly known for his explorations and discoveries in North America. The Hudson River, Hudson Strait, and Hudson Bay are all named after him. His final four voyages are documented; all of these focused upon exploration for a northern passage to Asia. In his first two (11 May–25 Sept 1607 and 2 May–5 Sept 1608), he sailed for the Muscovy Co, first exploring the Arctic Ocean between Greenland and Spitzbergen [now in Norway], and then between Spitzbergen and Novaya Zemlya [now in Russia]. In his third (4 Apr–17 Nov 1609), under the employ of the Dutch East India Co, he journeyed first north into the Arctic. Upon finding his way blocked by ice, he turned westward to North America, where, he was led to believe through his correspondence with Capt John Smith, a passage to the East might lie. In his fourth (departed 2 May 1610), undertaken for a group of English merchants, he explored the waterways later named after him in Canada—Hudson Strait and Hudson Bay.

It was on his third voyage that Hudson and his crew explored and mapped New York Bay and the Hudson River to a point 25 miles (40 km) beyond the later site of Albany. He undertook this voyage in a Dutch-built ship, the *Half Moon (Halve Maen),* that he sailed as far north as Albany. Beyond that point five of his crew explored the river in a small boat. During exploration of the Hudson River, Hudson and his crew had numerous encounters with Native Americans, including Mohicans (Mahicans) and various bands of Munsee speakers. Some of these encounters were peaceful; others ended in bloodshed on both sides. On his return to Europe, Hudson was detained by English authorities, but his reports reached his Dutch employers. Information concerning his interaction with native people who offered valuable furs in exchange for inexpensive items of European manufacture immediately led to Dutch exploitation of the fur trade and eventually to Dutch colonization of the area. His third voyage also helped complete the mapping of the Atlantic coast of North America.

On his fourth voyage, while bound by ice in Hudson Bay, most of his crew mutinied, casting him adrift on 3 July 1611 with his son John and seven other men, most of them ill. Although later voyages to the same region searched for him, no sign of him or his men was found.

Asher, G. M. *Henry Hudson the Navigator: The Original Documents in Which His Career Is Recorded.* Hakluyt Society, First Series, no. 27 (London: Printed for the Hakluyt Society, 1860; repr New York: Burt Franklin, 1963)
Johnson, Donald S. *Charting the Sea of Darkness: The Four Voyages of Henry Hudson* (Camden, Maine: International Marine, 1993)
Otto, Paul. "Common Practices and Mutual Misunderstandings: Henry Hudson, Native Americans, and the Birth of New Netherland," *de Halve Maen* 72 (Winter 1999): 75–83

Paul Otto

Hudson Falls. Village (pop 6,927) in Kingsbury (Washington Co). Serving as the county's half-shire town from 1795 until 1993, the village incorporated in 1810 as Sandy Hill. Its industry, based on the waterpower of the Hudson River, produced significant quantities of paper (starting 1844) and lumber. The Glens Falls Feeder Canal was made navigable in 1832, and the Glens Falls Railroad (1869; later Delaware and Hudson Railroad) also provided transport. Many Francophone Canadians and Irish came for employment, and beginning in 1888 a group of aristocratic Lithuanians settled along River St. In 1910 the village changed its name to Hudson Falls. Twentieth-century industries included Standard Wallpaper (1895–1928), and Union Bag and Paper Co, which employed 1,100 of the village's 1,700 workers in 1940; in 1951 the paper mill became a General Electric manufacturing facility. The Sandy Hill Corp (1857–1990), manufacturer of papermaking machinery, was the dominant industry in the 20th century; in 2003 its facility was owned by Metso Paper USA, which services papermaking equipment.

R. Paul McCarty

Hudson-Fulton Celebration of 1909. A historic festival commemorating the 300th anniversary of Henry Hudson's exploration for the Dutch East India Co of what is now the Hudson River and the 100th anniversary of the demonstration by Robert Fulton of the first practical steamboat on this same body of water (though the actual anniversary of the latter was 1907). The celebration began on 25 September in New York Harbor, continued with events in Newburgh, Poughkeepsie, Kingston, Catskill, Hudson, Albany, and Troy, and ended 11 October in Cohoes (Albany Co). Planning began with the formation of the Hudson-Fulton Celebration Commission, which Gov Frank W. Higgins signed into law on 27 Apr 1906; the commission included private individuals, mayors of cities, presidents of villages in the Hudson Valley, and members of the state legislature. Presiding over it was Stewart L. Woodford of New York City, former lieutenant governor of New York (1867–69) and former minister of Spain (1897–98).

Citizens' committees worked in the communities where celebrations were planned along the Hudson River and in all the boroughs of New York City. The objectives were fourfold: to create an educational celebration, to generate an increased awareness of New York State history, to engage New York State residents of all nationalities, and to promote international friendship. Two replica vessels served as focal points for the celebration. The Netherlands Hudson-Fulton Commission donated the *Halve Maen,* a replica of the Dutch East India Co ship that Henry Hudson commanded. The Royal Shipyard at Amsterdam built this replica between October 1908 and April 1909, and the Holland-America Steamship Line transported it to New York Harbor. The commission contracted the Staten Island Shipbuilding Co to build the replica of Robert Fulton's *Clermont* at Mariners Harbor (Richmond Co).

The centerpiece of the celebration was a naval rendezvous and parade in New York Harbor on 25 September followed by the transit of the *Halve Maen* and the *Clermont* replicas in company with an escort fleet to upriver celebrations. Community events in the Hudson Valley included the dedication of parks and monuments, concerts, lectures, exhibitions, museum shows, dedications, and parades. There were also aeronautical displays by Glenn Curtiss and Wilbur Wright, fireworks, and the illumination of buildings and skylines with electric searchlights (a novelty at the time). Newspaper accounts estimated that 1 million people watched the naval parade and that some 2 million participated in related events in New York City. Several hundred thousand took part in the events throughout the Hudson Valley. The gathering of warships from many nations in New York Harbor was the largest to that date, and the related naval parade involved more than 1,500 vessels. Wright's demonstration flight on 29 September circling the Statue of

THE HUMAN FLAG COMPOSED OF 2500 ALBANY N.Y. SCHOOL CHILDREN. H.&F. CELEBT'N.1909.

2,500 schoolchildren form a human flag on the steps of the State Capitol for the Hudson-Fulton Celebration, Albany, 1909.

Liberty was the first air travel over water in the United States and provided a public relations boost to the nascent aviation industry. The celebration served as a catalyst for the further development of the Palisades Interstate Park with New Jersey and the creation of parkland in the Hudson Highlands and elsewhere in the Hudson Valley.

Hudson-Fulton Celebration Commission. *The Hudson-Fulton Celebration, 1909, the Fourth Annual Report of the Hudson-Fulton Celebration Commission to the Legislature of the State of New York* (Albany: J. B. Lyon, 1910)

New York Times, 26 Sept–10 Oct 1909

William T. Reynolds

Hudson Highlands fortifications. From the beginning of the American Revolution, British and American military leaders recognized the strategic importance of the Hudson River. If the British were to gain control of the river, New England would be cut off from the rest of the colonies. Such an accomplishment would be a serious and perhaps fatal blow to American independence. Immediately after the Battles of Lexington and Concord in 1775, New York and the Continental Congress began investigating the problem of defending the Hudson River. It was in the Hudson Highlands between Tarrytown (Westchester Co) and Newburgh (Orange Co) that Americans focused their efforts. The terrain and course of the river combined to create a number of spots where passage by British warships could be impeded.

The first effort to construct fortifications was in 1775 on Martelaer's Rock (now Constitution Island), across the river from West Point (Orange Co) where the river narrowed and made a sharp S curve. In September 1775 construction of a "grand bastion," also known as Fort Constitution, began on the island under the direction of engineer Bernard Romans. It did not take long, however, for the poorly conceived plans of Romans and the slow pace of construction to attract considerable criticism. In February 1776 Romans was replaced, and the focus of efforts to fortify the Highlands shifted south to the vicinity of Popolopen Creek on the west side of the river. To the north and south of where the creek flows into the Hudson, engineers constructed Fort Montgomery in Orange Co and Fort Clinton in what is now Rockland Co. On the opposite bank, below a point on the river known as Anthonys Nose [now in Cortlandt, Westchester Co], Fort Independence was built. Under the direction of engineer Thomas Machin, an 1,800 ft (550 m) chain was laid between Fort Montgomery and Anthonys Nose in the spring of 1777 to prevent the passage of British ships into the Highlands.

In October 1777 Sir Henry Clinton led a British force up the Hudson with the intention of reaching Albany to link up with Gen John Burgoyne's campaign marching south from Canada. On 6 October Clinton captured Forts Clinton and Montgomery and subsequently cut the chain. He continued north and took Constitution Island on 8 October after it was deserted by its militia garrison. Two weeks after he arrived in the Highlands, Clinton decided to return to New York City, having heard no word from Burgoyne. As they withdrew back down the river, Clinton's men demolished Forts Constitution, Clinton, Montgomery, and Independence.

After the British departed, American forces reoccupied the Highlands and began building new fortifications, this time focusing their efforts at West Point. Under the direction of Polish engineer Thaddeus Kosciuszko, a comprehensive system of fortifications was designed and constructed, including another chain across the river between West Point and Constitution Island. Also under the supervision of engineer Thomas Machin, the 65-ton, 500 ft (59 MT, 150 m) chain was forged at the Sterling Ironworks in Warwick (Orange Co) and emplaced on 30 Apr 1778. In place to protect the chain were Constitution Island, batteries along the river, and Fort Clinton on the West Point plain above the river. A second ring of forts, the most important of which was Fort Putnam above the West Point plain, protected Fort Clinton and the river batteries. A third ring of redoubts was constructed and armed to provide mutual support.

The second chain was never directly challenged by the British. After 1777 Sir Henry Clinton tested American control of the Hudson Highlands only twice. In May 1779 he advanced upriver and seized Stony Point [now in Rockland Co], on the west bank of the Hudson 11 miles (18 km) south of West Point, as well as Fort Lafayette, just across the river in Westchester Co. The Americans responded by reinforcing West Point and then sent a force south to counterattack the British at Stony Point. A bayonet attack led by Gen Anthony Wayne recaptured Stony Point on 16 July 1779, which induced Clinton to return to New York City. The following year Clinton tried to secure West Point through negotiations with garrison commander Gen Benedict Arnold, but his efforts were frustrated when the Americans uncovered the plot and captured Maj John André, Clinton's aide-de-camp.

After the war, the US government decided to maintain a garrison at West Point but abandoned the other posts along the Hudson. In 1802 the United States Military Academy was established at West Point, making it the nation's longest continuously occupied military post.

Links of the Hudson River chain on display at West Point, 1911.

Diamant, Lincoln. *Chaining the Hudson: The Fight for the River in the American Revolution* (New York: Carol Publishing Group, 1989)

Palmer, Dave Richard. *The River and the Rock: The History of Fortress West Point, 1775–1783* (New York: Hippocrene Books, 1969)

Ethan S. Rafuse

Hudson locomotives. Most celebrated type of fast passenger locomotive developed by New York Central Railroad (NYC) for its Water Level Route from New York City to Chicago. On 14 Feb 1927 American Locomotive Co (ALCO) at Schenectady completed the first Hudson: No 5200, Class J-1. The Hudson featured a 4–6–4 type (four leading wheels, six driving wheels, and four trailing wheels), the last able to support a very large firebox. The locomotive combined high steaming capacity with large 79 in (201 cm) driving wheels to produce over 53,000 lbs (24,000 kg) of starting tractive effort, enough to handle 25 steel passenger cars at speeds of 90 mph (145 kph). NYC was soon operating Hudsons of three different classes and in 1937 ordered 40 ALCO-built J-3 Super Hudsons with even higher boiler pressure. A year later NYC ordered 10 Henry Dreyfuss–designed streamlined Hudsons, bringing their inventory to 275 Hudsons. The locomotive type pulled NYC's famed Twentieth Century Limited, Empire State Express, and Commodore Vanderbilt; these trains often ran in multiple sections of 15 or more cars. The 4–6–4 type was adopted by other railroads, but none of their engines ever gained the same renown. From 1937 Lionel Corp and others produced popular toy models of the Hudson, increasing the engine's fame. In the mid-1940s NYC's more powerful freight- and passenger-service Mohawk (4–8–2) and Niagara (4–8–4) challenged the Hudson's primacy; the last NYC Hudson was built in 1938. All were retired by May 1956 and scrapped shortly afterward.

Stagner, Lloyd E. *North American Hudsons,* 3d ed. (David City, Nebr: South Platte Press, 1992)

David R. Gould

Hudson River (315 mi/507 km). It ranks among the most important rivers in North America. Its headstream begins in the Adirondacks on the southwestern slope of Mt Marcy, 4,322 feet (1,317 m) above sea level at Lake Tear of the Clouds. For 52 miles (84 km), as it flows due south from the lake, it appears as little more than a faint squiggle on maps. On the ground hikers see the Opalescent River, a swift mountain stream that drops an average of 64 feet (20 m) per mile. Just south of the abandoned titanium mines at Tahawus (Essex Co), it joins the outlet of Sanford Lake and becomes the Hudson. From there it flows south southeast while gathering the waters of assorted creeks and those of the Indian, Schroon, and Sacandaga Rivers. After turning decidedly east near the Village of Corinth (Saratoga Co), the river leaves its old, preglacial channel and follows a newly carved route to Glens Falls (Warren Co). There it turns almost due south and becomes the principal stream in the 1,200 mi (1,930 km) long Appalachian or Great Valley that stretches from south of Montreal to northern Alabama. Still more tributaries, the Batten Kill, Fish Creek, and Hoosic River, join the Hudson on its way to Troy (Rensselaer Co). There the Hudson meets its greatest tributary, the Mohawk River, which more than doubles the master stream's volume and helps make the last 150 miles (241 km) the Hudson River that so many know. South of West Point (Orange Co) the river leaves the Great Valley and follows a fjord that cuts through a section of the Appalachian Mountains, more frequently referred to as the Highlands. Forty-five miles (72 km) further south the river reaches the southern tip of Manhattan and empties into New York Bay. Altogether the Hudson's water comes from three mountain ranges (Adirondacks, Catskills, and Berkshires), the sea, and other areas, making up nearly 14,000 mi^2 (36,300 km^2) of watershed.

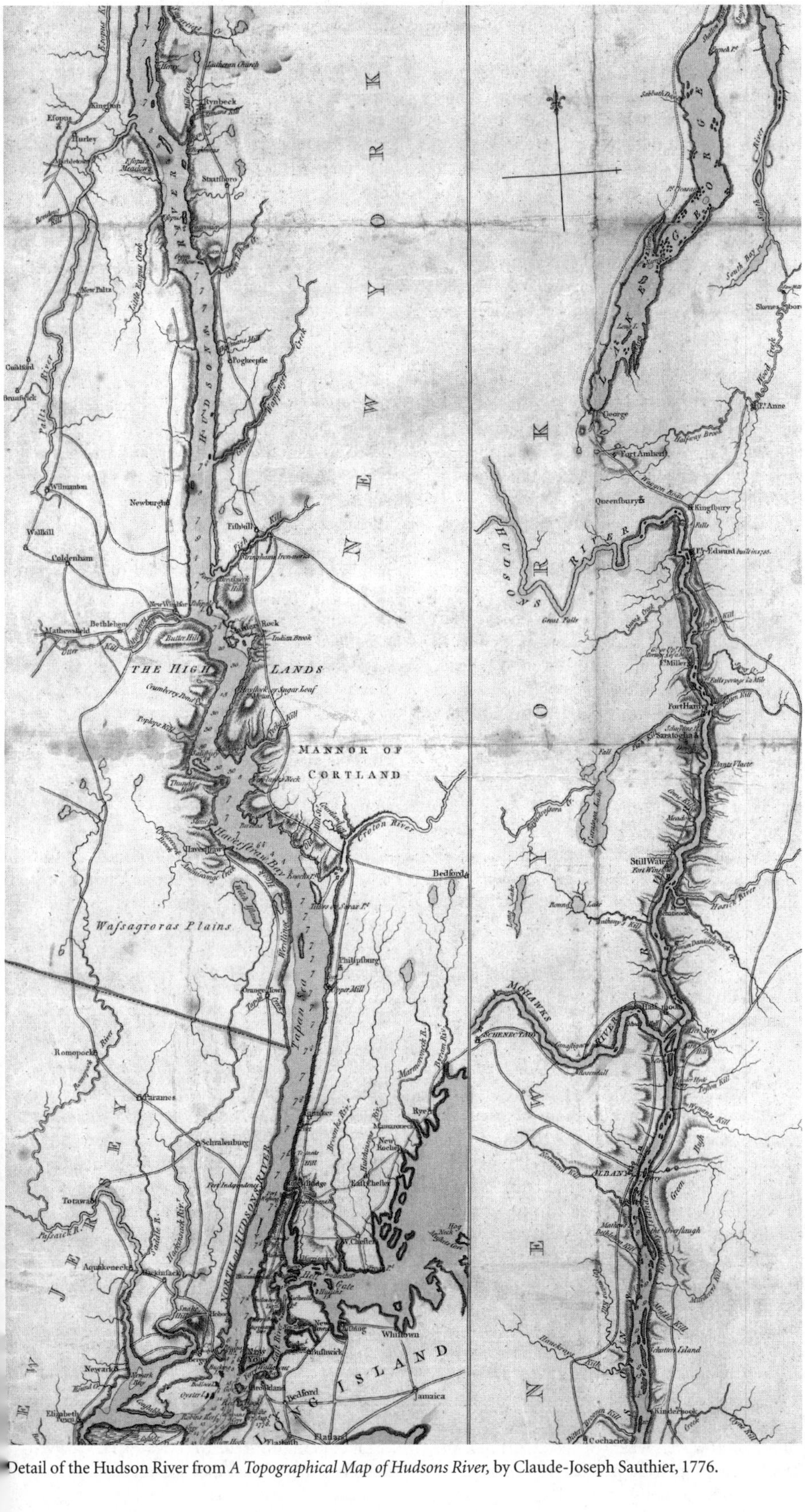

Detail of the Hudson River from *A Topographical Map of Hudsons River,* by Claude-Joseph Sauthier, 1776.

The Hudson is a tidal river below Troy. Other tributaries, including the Esopus, Catskill, Wallkill, Kinderhook, and Croton, feed the river along the way. For much of the river's passage from Albany to New York City, the Catskill Mountains, although five or more miles away, dominate its western shore, while to the east and further removed lie the gentler slopes of the Taconic Range. In the Highlands below West Point, the valley narrows to a mere 150 feet (46 m). A dozen or so miles further downstream at Haverstraw Bay, the river expands to its widest breadth of over 3 miles (5 km), which is part of the broad expanse known as the Tappan Zee. From here south the river's width averages nearly a mile, despite narrowing to 0.6 mi (1 km) near West 14th St in Manhattan. On the western shore opposite Yonkers and the northern end of Manhattan Island, the land rises to form a sheer cliff of igneous rock, known as the Palisades, formed during the Jurassic period. The Hudson's landscape is among the most dramatic of any river in North America.

Natural History

The age of the Hudson River remains uncertain, but it may date back 75 million years to the Cretaceous period when the surrounding country was generally flat and featureless. During the succeeding Tertiary period the earth's bedrock was thrust upward at various times to create the uplands now known as the Catskill, Adirondack, and Taconic Mountains, thereby increasing the downward-cutting capacity of the river and its tributaries. Much more recently the Laurentide ice sheet advanced southward down the valley, plucking and grinding the bedrock of the riverbed and the adjacent valley and substantially deepening and widening both. Even though the river channel is filled with huge quantities of gravel, the river bottom is below sea level as far north as Troy. The deepest point is World's End, midchannel between Gee's Point and Constitution Island directly in front of West Point, where the river's gravel bottom lies 202 feet (62 m) below the water surface, but its bedrock bottom lies nearly 790 feet (240 m) below the surface. The location is not coincidental. The movement of the south-flowing ice sheet was impeded by the Hudson Highlands and further constricted by the narrow channel that the river had previously used to pass through the mountain barrier. The resulting pressures substantially increased the down-cutting action of the ice, no doubt widening the narrow breach in the mountain barrier as well as deepening it. Just how that breach was originally formed remains unclear. However it was formed, the ice carved the narrow, preglacial valley into a fjord.

Beginning about 20,000 years ago the ice sheet began to retreat from its point of furthest advance south of Manhattan at the Narrows. A meltwater lake known as Glacial Lake Albany later formed behind the terminal moraine across New York Bay, extending north to Glens Falls, or approximately 200 miles (320 km). At its maximum extent—over 400 feet (120 m) deep at present-day Albany—the lake existed for 4,000–5,000 years and in a number of ways helped shape much more recent human activity along the river's margins. Fine sediments settled to the lake's bottom, for instance, forming extensive beds of clay that were mined to make untold millions of bricks at Kingston (Ulster Co) and other towns during the 19th and 20th centuries. Also at this time the clays were utilized to create thousands of molds used to cast iron storefronts, stoves, machine parts, and more at Troy, Albany, New York City, and elsewhere. Streams that emptied into the lake formed deltas later selected as settlement sites for river towns such as Albany, Newburgh, Red Hook, Kingston, Hudson, Kinderhook, and Glens Falls.

The hills south of the highlands act as a funnel directing sea breezes upriver as far as Iona Island, about 40 miles (64 km) upstream from Manhattan. The saltwater also moves upriver, as far north as Poughkeepsie in times of very low flow and drought. The Hudson estuary, where fresh- and saltwater merge, supports a rich diversity of aquatic life. Scientists have counted 186 species of fish, including 73 saltwater varieties. Saltwater shad and striped bass swim near small- and largemouthed bass and eels, lobsters walk the river's floor off the southern tip of Manhattan Island, barnacles attach to pilings off 40th St, and oysters lie under the George Washington Bridge. Seals sometimes swim up the river, a school of dolphins once made the trip to Albany, and whales can at times be spotted off 42d St. Divers off the coast of Manhattan occasionally report seeing great sea turtles floating in the murk. Conversely, native brook trout inhabit the cold, crystal-clear headwaters of the river. At Troy the tide crests at 5 feet (2 m). Depending on direction of flow, tides can accelerate or impede a boat's travel by about 3 miles (5 km) an hour. Indeed, a log dropped in the river at Troy will float 8 miles (13 km) downstream and 7 miles (11 km) upstream in a single day. It will take about 10 months for it to reach outer New York Harbor. With such tidal activity, it is no wonder some American Indians called the Hudson "the stream that flows both ways."

After the waters of the Hudson flow through the Narrows between Brooklyn and Staten Island, into the Atlantic and southeast toward the Ambrose Light, the river seems to end. About 10,000–15,000 years ago, however, the continent extended approximately 130 miles (210 km) further to the rim of the continental shelf. The river flowed through a channel before dropping into a deep gorge carved at a much earlier time. In the 21st century the floor of this great submerged gorge, known as the Hudson Canyon, lies between 9,000 and 15,000 feet (2,740–4,570 m) beneath the North Atlantic's surface. The gorge is home to still more varieties of fish.

Early History through the American Revolution

Algonquian-speaking Indians occupied the territory along the Hudson River, north and east of Albany and to the west and east of the middle and lower Hudson Valley. They were likely the groups that European explorers encountered when they sailed into the river. Giovanni da Verrazano was the first to record his visit in 1524; Henry Hudson arrived in his 90 ton (81 MT) ship, the *Half Moon,* about 12 Sept 1609. An Englishman sailing for the Dutch East India Co, Hudson explored the river as far north as the head of navigation at Cohoes [now in Albany Co], where they "found it to be at an end for shipping to go in" and turned back. Although frustrated in their efforts to discover a passage to the east, the Dutch recognized the economic importance of Hudson's discovery. The chief river of the colony had many names, but for the most part the Dutch called it the Noordt, or North, River. Although the name North River was used into the 20th century, cartographers initially identified the river as Hudson's River, and a simplified version of this name became the standard name.

The first Dutch settlement along the Hudson River was established in 1624 at Fort Orange [now Albany]. In 1626 Dutch West India Co Director Peter Minuit purchased the island of Manhattan from local Indians, and early Dutch colonial efforts focused on that area. As the colony grew, Dutch settlers exploited the riverway as they would have in the Netherlands, using it to move goods and people. Dutch settlers used the waterway as the main avenue of communication and trade. Sloops brought traders and people to the northern frontier of Fort Orange and Rensselaerswijck [now in Albany, Columbia, and Rensselaer Cos] and returned with beaver pelts and lumber. The river served as a broad entranceway to the north via Lakes George and Champlain and to the west via the Mohawk River. Like the Dutch, the English continued to exploit the Hudson as a means of moving settlers and commercial goods, and trade on the river flourished.

The Hudson River, with its close connection to the Lake George–Champlain corridor, was of great strategic significance in the British and French colonial wars of the late 17th and 18th centuries. From the fort at Albany, New York Colony's northernmost fortification, Pieter Schuyler, a colonel in the Albany Militia, joined with forces from New England in two abortive marches on French Canada, first in 1690 during King William's War and then in 1709 during Queen Anne's War. During the French and Indian War (1755–63) that followed, Albany became one of the principal garrisons for British troops, who used it for a series of attacks on French forts at Ticonderoga and Crown Point (Essex Co).

Control of the Hudson River and Valley held the key to victory in the American Revolution. If the British gained control they would be able to separate the rebel hotbed of New England from the rest of the new nation. The British general William Howe realized this fact in 1776 when he captured Manhattan Island. Retreating northward, George Washington ordered a chain placed across the river at Anthony's Nose a few miles south of West Point to prevent a British advance. But in October 1777 Gen Henry Clinton sailed upriver, captured the chain, and destroyed the forts protecting it. British control of the Hudson Highlands lasted just 13 days, though, before Clinton and his troops retreated to New York City after British defeats at Saratoga. On Washington's orders Col Thaddeus Kosciuszko strengthened the fort at West Point and placed another chain across the river. A sharp S bend at the point and the swift and treacherous water currents helped make the Hudson impregnable. West Point was nearly captured, however, when Benedict Arnold, the Revolutionary patriot turned traitor, hatched a treasonous plot to turn the fort over to the British.

The river was the site for nearly a third of all battles of the Revolution. After the British captured New York City in 1776, the legislature of New York State moved up the Hudson to White Plains (Westchester Co), Fishkill (Dutchess Co), and, ultimately, to Kingston in February 1777. That April delegates meeting in Kingston's Ulster County Courthouse approved New York's first constitution, and in July George Clinton took the oath there as the state's first governor. Kingston remained New York State's capital until October, when, as part of Gen Henry Clinton's brief offensive, the British burned the city. In April 1782 Washington made Newburgh (Orange Co) the headquarters for the American army. At Dobbs Ferry (Westchester Co) in 1783, Washington negotiated the evacuation of the British forces with Gen Guy Carleton, and on 25 Nov 1783, as the last of the British troops embarked from New York City, Washington and Gov George Clinton raised the American flag over the Battery.

Transportation and Commerce since Independence

In the 19th century the Hudson was the stage for revolutionary developments in technology and engineering, commerce and industry, and the first flowering of American art and letters. Each had a profound effect upon the river and its landscape. The developments in technology and engineering were numerous. By 1750 a distinctive watercraft, the Hudson River sloop, had been devised that combined stability, large cargo capacity, and shallow water navigability. Beginning around 1800 as commercial trade expanded, sloop construction mushroomed all along the river at places like Troy, Albany, Haverstraw (Rockland Co), and, above all, Nyack (Rockland Co). Approximately 1,000 were launched between 1796 and 1835, making these craft the mainstay of the Hudson River fleet until steam replaced wind as the primary energy source. In 1804 John Stevens demonstrated the first practical steamboat in New York Harbor. Three years later Robert Fulton piloted a steamboat up the Hudson River from Manhattan to Albany in 36 hours. Fulton and his financial underwriter Robert R. Livingston enjoyed a monopoly on steam travel on the river until 1824, when the US Supreme Court decided in *Gibbons v Ogden* that Congress had the right to regulate interstate commerce and nullified New York State's grant of a monopoly. Steamboats, used largely for passenger traffic after 1860, would remain a feature of Hudson River travel until 1971, with the retirement of the *Alexander Hamilton.*

The development of canals connecting the Hudson with the north and west helped transform the valley. The Erie Canal (1825) followed the natural corridor up the river and west through the canal's 83 locks to Lake Erie. Each year thousands of people, many of whom were immigrants recently arrived through the Port of New York, made the journey to the west. The canal changed the economy of the Hudson: the rising volume of traffic brought prosperity to river cities, especially Albany and Troy, which became nationally significant industrial centers. At the same time, however, the importation of cheaper grain from the west destroyed the livelihood of some of the valley's farmers.

HUDSON RIVER BRIDGES AND TUNNELS

Name	Location	Length in Feet (Meters)	Year Opened
Waterford Bridge	Waterford (Saratoga)–Troy (Rensselaer)	743 (226.5)	1909
One Hundred and Twelfth Street Bridge	Cohoes (Albany)–Troy	809 (246.6)	1996
Collar City Bridge	Colonie (Albany)–Troy	2,238 (682.1)	1981
Green Island–Troy Bridge	Green Island (Albany)–Troy	630 (192.0)	1982
Congress Street Bridge	Watervliet (Albany)–Troy	1,024 (312.1)	1969
Troy-Menands Bridge	Menands (Albany)–Troy	1,512 (460.9)	1932
Patroon Island Bridge	Albany-Rensselaer	1,795 (547.1)	1968
Albany Railroad Bridge	Albany-Rensselaer	1,272 (387.7)	1866
Private Parker F. Dunn Memorial Bridge	Albany-Rensselaer	981 (299.0)	1969
Castleton-on-Hudson Bridge	Coeymans (Albany)–Schodack (Rensselaer)	5,330 (1,624.6)	1959
Alfred H. Smith Memorial Railroad Bridge	Coeymans-Schodack	5,249 (1,599.9)	1924
Rip Van Winkle Bridge	Catskill (Greene)–Hudson (Columbia)	5,041 (1,536.5)	1935
George Clinton Kingston–Rhinecliff Bridge	Ulster (Ulster)–Rhinebeck (Dutchess)	7,793 (2,375.3)	1957
Poughkeepsie Railroad Bridge	Highland (Ulster)–Poughkeepsie	6,767 (2,062.6)	1889[a]
Franklin D. Roosevelt Mid-Hudson Bridge	Lloyd (Ulster)–Poughkeepsie	3,000 (914.4)	1930
Newburgh-Beacon Bridge	Newburgh (Orange)–Beacon (Dutchess)	7,855 (2,394.2)	1963[b]
Bear Mountain Bridge	Highlands (Orange)–Cortlandt (Westchester)	2,255 (687.3)	1924
Governor Malcolm Wilson Tappan Zee Bridge	Nyack (Rockland)–Tarrytown (Westchester)	15,840 (4,828.0)	1955
George Washington Bridge	Fort Lee, NJ–Manhattan	4,760 (1,450.9)	1931
Lincoln Tunnel (North Tube)	Weehawken, NJ–Manhattan	7,482 (2,280.5)	1945
Lincoln Tunnel (Center Tube	Weehawken, NJ–Manhattan	8,216 (2,504.2)	1937
Lincoln Tunnel (South Tube)	Weehawken, NJ–Manhattan	8,600 (2,621.3)	1957
Amtrak (Pennsylvania Railroad) Tunnel	Weehawken, NJ–Manhattan	7,218 (2,200.1)	1910
Holland Tunnel (North Tube)	Jersey City, NJ–Manhattan	8,558 (2,608.5)	1927
Holland Tunnel (South Tube)	Jersey City, NJ–Manhattan	8,371 (2,551.5)	1927
PATH Tube (northern)	Jersey City, NJ–Manhattan	5,571 (1,698.0)	1908
PATH Tube (southern)	Jersey City, NJ–Manhattan	5,571 (1,698.0)	1909

Sources: B. J. Cudahy, *Rails under the Mighty Hudson: The Story of the Hudson Tubes, the Pennsy Tunnels, and Manhattan Transfer,* 2d ed. (2002); New York State Department of Transportation, http://www.dot.state.ny.us/.

Note: Bridges and tunnels arranged from northernmost to southernmost crossings of the Hudson from Troy to Manhattan.

[a]Closed to traffic in 1974.

[b]Second span opened in 1980.

The canals, railroads, and emerging industrialization changed the commerce and life of the port towns on the river. Poughkeepsie became famous for its Vassar brewery, the Eastman National Business College (later Eastman School of Business), and Vassar Female College (now Vassar College). Heavier industry also flourished, including iron foundries in Troy and textiles in Cohoes, whose population between 1840 and 1850 jumped from 150 to more than 4,000. Troy and Albany competed for canal and railroad traffic from the south, north, and west. In 1840 New York City, Albany, and Troy were, respectively, ranked 1st, 9th, and 21st among the most populated cities in the United States. Other port towns, including Hudson (Columbia Co), Newburgh, Kingston, and Catskill (Greene Co), grew less dramatically in part because they were connected by primitive roads to the interior of the state.

Tow winding throug. Highlands, West Point.

Northbound caravan of canalboats, lashed together, pass West Point on the Hudson River. Illustration by Augusta Brown, 1896.

Two other canals linked the port of New York via the river to commerce in the north and west. The Champlain Canal (1823) provided water access to Lake Champlain and ultimately to the St. Lawrence River in Canada. The Delaware and Hudson Canal (1828) connected the port of Kingston with Pennsylvania's anthracite fields, enabling low-cost coal shipment to Kingston, and ultimately to the furnaces and stoves of New York City. Both waterways contributed substantially to the industrial expansion of the towns along the river, especially with regard to the iron and steel industry. The Croton Aqueduct (1842) followed the east bank of the Hudson from the Croton River in Westchester Co to New York City.

Railroads also transformed the river and the valley, beginning with the first railroad built in the state, the Mohawk and Hudson. It opened in 1831 for the primary purpose of carrying passengers from Albany to Schenectady, thus bypassing the most inefficient section of the Erie Canal. Exactly 20 years later the Hudson River Railroad began running up the east shore of the river, cutting travel time between New York City and Albany to five hours and giving steamboat and other water traffic its first taste of competition. That same year the Erie Railroad began operations between Dunkirk (Chautauqua Co) and Piermont (Rockland Co), creating a hinterland that stretched the length of the state. Two years later the Erie extended its line along the river's west shore to Jersey City, NJ, thereby helping to create a major freight and passenger terminus and manufacturing district opposite Manhattan. In 1853 Cornelius Vanderbilt consolidated a string of rail lines into the New York Central and Hudson River Railroad, thereby providing full service from New York City, through the Hudson Valley, and on to Buffalo. Its main route between New York City and Albany is still used by Amtrak in the early 21st century. Its trackage, which in places is located mere feet from the river's east bank, provides a spectacular view of the Hudson.

By comparison many of the river's west-bank communities remained disconnected from the nation's growing rail network and increasingly dependent upon river transport. In 1872 the New York, Kingston and Syracuse (after 1875, the Ulster and Delaware) was built from Rondout [now Kingston] to Phoenicia (Ulster Co) to Stamford (Delaware Co), but it remained without links to any other rail lines for a decade. In 1883 the New York, Ontario, and Western reoriented its main line to end at Cornwall (Orange Co), where it joined the just completed New York, West Shore, and Buffalo Railroad that provided rail service to west river towns. Construction was delayed for several reasons, among which were high construction costs through difficult terrain, an economically weak service hinterland, and adequate, if not ideal, river transport. The line was later acquired by New York Central Railroad. In the early 21st century, it continues to function as a freight-only line in the CSX Transportation system.

If the Hudson was an extraordinarily useful north-south conduit, its width made east-west passage difficult. Ferries date back to New Netherland, and through the 20th century there were dozens of ferry crossings. The ferrying of freight across the Hudson by lighterage, particularly between New Jersey and Manhattan, made the lower Hudson River one of the busiest commercial rivers in the world. In 1885 the Poughkeepsie Railroad Bridge opened, the first permanent structure across the river below Albany. It was not until 1908, with a tunnel connecting Manhattan and Hoboken, NJ, that the river was crossed at New York City. In 1910 the Pennsylvania Railroad Co's tunnel under the river permitted the opening of the imposing Pennsylvania Station. Although railroads were first, vehicular crossing proved to be more important. The Bear Mountain Bridge (1924) was a bellwether of future crossings, including the Holland Tunnel (1927), the Lincoln Tunnel (1937), the Mid-Hudson Bridge at Poughkeepsie (1930), the George Washington Bridge (1931), the Rip Van Winkle Bridge at Catskill (1935), and the Tappan Zee Bridge (1955). The Hudson crossings and the valley roads that led to them enabled unprecedented numbers of people and industries to settle on the river. In the two decades after the Tappan Zee Bridge opened, the population density of the formerly isolated Rockland Co on the west shore increased from 500 to 1,300 people per square mile. Just below the Hudson River, at the Narrows in New York Bay, a similar population surge took place on Staten Island after the Verrazano-Narrows Bridge opened in 1964.

The Hudson as a Cultural Resource

Beginning in 1825 the Hudson River valley drew the interest of numerous artists, writers, and distinguished visitors. Artists like Thomas Cole, Asher B. Durand, Jasper Francis Cropsey, and Frederic Edwin Church were among those comprising the Hudson River school, a significant movement in American art. Some of the more famous Hudson River school paintings had the river as its subject. These include Cole's *Sunny Morning on the Hudson* (*ca* 1827), Cropsey's *Autumn on the Hudson River* (1860), and Church's many paintings of the river from Olana, his hilltop house on the east shore near the City of Hudson. For the most part these painters chose to gaze on the wilder aspects of the landscape, ignoring the increasing commercial traffic on the great river itself. As Cole put it, "The Hudson for natural magnificence is unsurpassed."

Washington Irving's tales often cloaked the Hudson River with a supernatural aura. In his *Knickerbocker's History of New York* (1809), which captured Dutch culture on the river, Irving virtually created literary culture in America; his portraits of Rip Van Winkle and Ichabod Crane in the *Sketch-Book* (1819–20) showed "the witching effect" of the Hudson Valley's landscape upon the imagination. In a similar vein is Joseph Rodman Drake's once popular long narrative poem, "The Culprit Fey" (1819). Set near West Point, it relates the tale of a fairy who falls in love with a mortal maid. The early 20th-century American composer Henry Hadley wrote a successful symphonic poem of the same name in 1908. James Fenimore Cooper also made extensive use of Hudson River settings. From a peak in the Catskills, Cooper's Leather-Stocking proclaims that he can see the Hudson and "all creation," and the author's novel *Satanstoe* (1845) considers 18th-century culture in the valley.

As opportunities for travel increased in the 19th century, the river drew visitors from across the nation as well as Europe. They came to experience personally the landscape and culture made famous by the Hudson's artists and writers. In his 1899 guidebook to the United States the encyclopedic German travel writer Karl Baedeker compared the river to Europe's Rhine—and declared the Hudson to be superior.

In the 20th century the Hudson River continued to have a prominent place in literature. Novelist Edith Wharton set her *Hudson River Bracketed* (1929) at her aunt's house near Rhinebeck (Dutchess Co) and remembered her visits there in her autobiography, *A Backward Glance* (1934). In *World's End* (1987), named after the channel passage near West Point, T. Coraghessan Boyle considers the burdens of the myths and history associated with the Hudson Valley. The novel's 20th-century characters have to contend with the mythic power of the Hudson and its mountains as well as the actions of their 17th-century forebears.

The Hudson was also the subject of music and poetry in the 20th century. The New York City–born composer Ferde Grofé created the *Hudson River Suite* (1955), which includes a musical evocation of the lower Hudson and the Palisades and a portrait of Rip Van Winkle. Paul Goodman's poem "The Lordly Hudson" was set to music by Ned Rorem in 1948. It includes the lines, "This is our lordly Hudson / and has no peer in Europe or the East / This is our lordly Hudson hardly flowing / under the green-grown cliffs." Songwriter Alec Wilder's "Did You Ever

Sheet music cover depicting Hudson River view from Hyde Park.

Cross Over to Sneden's?" (1947), about the ferry crossing at Sneden's Landing (Rockland Co), has become a well-known standard.

Since the Livingstons and Van Rensselaers of the 18th century, wealthy families built estates on the Hudson. Those constructed in the 19th century eclipsed those built by their predecessors. Alexander Jackson Davis's majestic Gothic Revival mansion Lyndhurst (1838) at Tarrytown (Westchester Co) helped create a vogue for vast estates. Lyndhurst was purchased in 1880 by the railroad financier Jay Gould. Many of Gould's peers at the pinnacle of the American economic system, among them the Vanderbilts, Astors, and Rockefellers, also purchased or built estates on the Hudson. In the 19th century John D. Rockefeller acquired about 3,400 acres (1,380 ha) of land at Pocantico (in Tarrytown), where he built an opulent family mansion, Kykuit. Springwood, at Hyde Park (Dutchess Co), was purchased by James Roosevelt, father of Pres Franklin D. Roosevelt, after the Civil War and is now the center of the Franklin D. Roosevelt National Historical Site. Life at these estates was captured in Edith Wharton's novel *The Age of Innocence* (1920). However, during the 20th century many families on great estates found themselves desperately clinging to their houses with few resources to maintain them. The imposition of the federal income tax and estate tax early in the century made their hold only more tenuous. Many prominent families, Vanderbilts and Livingstons among them, gave their houses to historic trusts. At the same time, the state government created great public parks along the Hudson, including the Palisades Interstate Park (1900) and Bear Mountain State Park (1916).

Environmental Issues

Transportation advances and increased population along the river opened the way for both commercial development and environmental degradation. During the 19th century tannery operators in the Catskills clear-cut stands of hemlock and drained wastes into tributary streams, severely polluting them. Stockyards and slaughterhouses along the Hudson's shore dumped manure and discarded animal parts directly into the river, while towns and cities put their untreated sewage into the waterway. Rock quarriers mined much of the Palisades for fashionable brownstone houses in New York City. At Sing Sing [now Ossining, Westchester Co] in 1825 convicts began quarrying the stone used to construct the prison that was to house them. The facility was intentionally located at the base of the marble rich Mt Pleasant, where later inmates cut and dressed stone and loaded it on ships for buildings along the Hudson. Above Glens Falls the river was used for log drives to feed that town's sawmills well into the 20th century. Fishing, especially of shad, grew into an industry. As there were no regulations or concepts of fish management, harvests averaged roughly 3 million pounds (1.4 million kg) a year between 1880 and 1901.

Increasing knowledge of the complex ecology of the Hudson River and its vast watershed led to a greater understanding of the environment. In 1872 Verplanck Colvin discovered the Hudson's rising at Lake Tear of the Clouds. As superintendent of the state's topographical survey, which mapped the Adirondacks and many of the tributaries that contribute to the Hudson, Colvin told the legislature of the effects of deforestation upon the Hudson watershed, warning that clear-cutting had dried up many of the river's feeder streams and brooks. In 1892 the state created the 2.8 million-acre (1.1 million ha) Adirondack Park. Over time the forests grew back and thus replenished the streams that feed the Hudson.

Colvin's emphasis upon the environment was echoed by others. Robert Barnwell Roosevelt was one of the first to study the declining shad population and to begin educating fishers about overharvesting in the late 19th century. Others concerned with the Hudson and its valley in the 19th century included architects Frederick Law Olmsted, Calvert Vaux, and Andrew Jackson Downing. Naturalists John Burroughs, Theodore Roosevelt, and E. H. Harriman were disturbed by the deforestation and quarrying.

Profound environmental changes affected the Hudson River and valley during the 20th century. As more automobiles, factories, and people entered the valley, they brought more pollution. By the 1960s industrialists and most people regarded the Hudson as an open trough of toxic water that they could use as they saw fit. At Fort Edward (Washington Co), the General Electric Co (GE) discharged more than 1 million pounds (450,000 kg) of polychlorinated biphenyls (PCBs) into the river. Raw sewage dumped by Troy, Albany, Watervliet (Albany Co), and Rensselaer often rendered the river incapable of sustaining any aquatic life. Manhattan added 165 million gallons (625 million l) of raw sewage a day to the water. From Albany to New York City the Hudson was off limits to swimmers. One by one, species of birds (eg, osprey and bald eagles), plants (eg, wild celery and wild rice), aquatic creatures (eg, mussels and crabs), and fish (eg, shad and bass) died back or moved away from the polluted waters and compromised land.

Citizen action eventually stopped the degradation of the river, and the Hudson became central to a new chapter in US history, one that emphasized the importance of the environment. In 1963 the Scenic Hudson Preservation Conference was formed to oppose Consolidated Edison's proposal for an electrical-generating plant at Storm King Mountain in Cornwall (Orange Co) just north of West Point. In a landmark decision of 1965, later sustained by the US Supreme Court, the federal Circuit Court of Appeals held that the "preservation of natural beauty and of national historic shrines" had to be considered before the project could be approved. The denouement of the case played out over the next 15 years until December 1980, when Con Edison signed the Hudson River Compact. In exchange for Scenic Hudson's agreement to drop all lawsuits, Con Edison abandoned the Storm King project, donated the mountain property to a park, and gave $12 million for a foundation devoted to the study of the river's fish. The company also installed new devices to reduce fish kills at its Indian Point nuclear-generating facilities, established fish hatcheries, and agreed to study the impact of the power plants on the Hudson's aquatic life.

As a result of the Storm King controversy, other environmental groups were founded on the Hudson. Among the most important were Clearwater (1969), the Hudson River Fishermen's Association (1966), and the Hudson Riverkeeper (1983). Clearwater, begun in part by folksinger Pete Seeger, has its own Hudson sloop, the *Clearwater*, a floating laboratory classroom educating people about the value of the river. The Hudson River Fishermen's Association, begun by the environmental activist and writer Robert Boyle, encourages "the responsible use of aquatic resources and protection of habitat." Boyle also began the Hudson Riverkeeper, which inspects the river daily for evidence of polluters. At the end of the 20th century these groups, along with other citizen organizations, joined together to press for GE to clean up the PCBs that it had dumped in the river decades earlier and that had contaminated fish and other wildlife. Because of the efforts of determined and vigilant environmentalists, the Hudson River and Valley are cleaner in the early 21st century than at any time in the last century.

See also Bridges and tunnels; Pollution; Waterfronts.

Adams, Arthur G. *The Hudson River Guidebook* (New York, Fordham Univ Press, 1996)

———. *The Hudson through the Years*, 3d ed. (New York: Fordham Univ Press, 1996)

Boyle, Robert H. *The Hudson River: A Natural and Unnatural History*, rev ed. (New York: W. W. Norton, 1969)

Carmer, Carl. *The Hudson* (New York: Rinehart, 1939)

Cronin, John, and Robert F. Kennedy Jr. *The Riverkeepers* (New York: Scribner's, 1997)

Howat, John K. *The Hudson River and Its Painters* (New York: Viking Press, 1972)

Lossing, Benson J. *The Hudson: From the Wilderness to the Sea* (1866; repr Hensonville, NY: Black Dome Press, 2001)

O'Brien, Raymond J. *American Sublime: Landscape and Scenery of the Lower Hudson Valley* (New York: Columbia Univ Press, 1981)

Smith, Elizabeth McKelden, ed. *The Great Estates Region of the Hudson River Valley* (?Tarrytown, NY: Historic Hudson Valley Press, 1998)

Stanne, Stephen P., Roger G. Panetta, and Brian E. Forist. *The Hudson: An Illustrated Guide to the Living River* (New Brunswick, NJ: Rutgers Univ Press, 1996)

Van Zandt, Roland. *Chronicles of the Hudson: Three Centuries of Travel and Adventure* (1971; repr Hensonville, NY: Black Dome Press, 1992)

Wilstach, Paul. *Hudson River Landings* (1933; repr Port Washington, NY: Ira J. Friedman, 1969)

Tom Lewis

Hudson River ferries. The 200 miles (322 km) from the Narrows between Long Island and Staten Island to Fort Edward (Washington Co) on the Hudson River are a continuous north-south navigable waterway. Before the era of large bridges and tunnels, this unbroken stretch of water was a formidable obstacle to east-west travel. From an early date, therefore, ferries were necessities at major settlements and at intersections of major travel routes, as at Kings Ferry (between Rockland and Westchester), Kingston (Ulster Co), the Narrows, and Manhattan Island.

At first, the ferries were primarily used for trading and bringing produce to the market and were usually operated by American Indians in canoes and dugouts. Early settlers soon began to ferry market-goers in their own rowboats or sailboats as well. With the growth of traffic, however, organization and regulation were clearly needed. Consequently, charters or franchises were sold for specific locations and periods of time. The earliest recorded, issued by the Dutch West India Co, dates from 1637 at Beverwijck [now Albany]. In later years municipalities, royal gover-

PRINCIPAL ROUTES OF HUDSON RIVER FERRIES

Towns Served	Dates in Service	Details
Upper Hudson		
Schuylerville (Saratoga)–Clarks Mill (Washington)[a]	1800–*ca* 1930	Known as Sarles Rope Ferry
Stillwater (Saratoga)–Crandall Corners (Washington)[a]	1800–*ca* 1930	Known as Powers-Briggs Rope Ferry
Bemis Heights (Saratoga)–Schaghticoke (Rensselaer)[a]	*ca* 1750–*ca* 1865	Known as Bemis Heights Rope Ferry
Watervliet (Albany)–Troy (Rensselaer)	*ca* 1700–*ca* 1860	Known as Ashley's Ferry
Albany-Rensselaer	1831–1904	Known as Albany-Bath North Ferry
Albany-Rensselaer	1684–*ca* 1880	Known as Albany-Greenbush South Ferry
Albany-Rensselaer	*ca* 1635–84	Known as Albany-Crawlier Ferry
Albany-Rensselaer	1836–*ca* 1880	Known as Albany-Greenbush Railroad Ferry; owned by New York Central and Hudson River RR after 1869
Middle Hudson		
Coxsackie (Greene)–Newton (Nutten) Hook (Columbia)	1800–1938	
Athens (Greene)–Hudson (Columbia)	1778–1947	
Catskill (Greene)–Hudson	*ca* 1800–1935	
Catskill–Greendale (Columbia)	1851–1935	
Saugerties (Ulster)–Tivoli (Dutchess)	1800–1938	
Kingston (Ulster)–Rhinecliff (Dutchess)	*ca* 1700–1957	
Highland (Ulster)–Poughkeepsie	1793–1941	
Milton (Ulster)–Camelot [now Poughkeepsie]	*ca* 1760–*ca* 1865	
Newburgh (Orange)–Beacon (Dutchess)	1743–1963	
Cornwall (Orange)–Storm King (Putnam)	1850–92	
West Point (Orange)–Cold Spring (Putnam)	*ca* 1700–	Operated by US Army; now serves only military personnel
West Point–Garrison (Putnam)	*ca* 1680–	Operated by US Army; now serves only military personnel; until 1924 carried vehicles and general public and was privately owned
Lower Hudson		
Jones Point (Rockland)–Peekskill (Westchester)	1800–*ca* 1900	Known as Caldwell's Ferry
Stony Point (Rockland)–Verplanck (Westchester)	*ca* 1700–*ca* 1800, 1922–24	Known as King's Ferry
Haverstraw (Rockland)–Peekskill	1835–*ca* 1900	
Haverstraw (Rockland)–Verplanck	1837–*ca* 1900	
Haverstraw (Rockland)–Crugers (Westchester)	*ca* 1850–*ca* 1900	
Haverstraw–Ossining (Westchester)	2001–	Operated by New York Waterway
Nyack (Rockland)–Tarrytown (Westchester)	1834–1941; 1956	
Piermont (Rockland)–Irvington (Westchester)	1841–61; 1932–41	
Piermont–Duane St, Manhattan	*ca* 1850–68	Operated by Erie RR
Sneden's Landing (Rockland)–Dobbs Ferry (Westchester)	1698–1944	
Alpine, NJ–Yonkers	*ca* 1700–*ca* 1750; 1876–82; 1885–95; 1923–56	

nors, and finally New York State would issue ferry charters.

Other early chartered routes crossed the Narrows from Long Island to Staten Island (1647) and linked Manhattan both to Brooklyn (1642) and to Communipaw (1661), which later became Jersey City, NJ. Fares, freight rates, hours, and conditions of operation were formalized, as were type and quality of vessel and crew requirements. Flat-bottomed scows, rafts, and capacious, stable, flat-decked sailing vessels called periaugers were most commonly used, supplemented from the 1690s by faster sloop-rigged sailing vessels. Periaugers were about 50 feet (15 m) long with unencumbered decks to accommodate carriages, cattle, and horses, as well as merchandise and passengers. Sail-ferry arrival and departure times were not dependable, and sail crossings were often rough, dangerous, and uncomfortable. Team boats powered by horses, mules, oxen on a treadmill turning paddle wheels, or current-propelled rope ferries were used wherever feasible. Above the falls at Troy, barges, flatboats, and scows predominated, and a rope ferry stayed in use into the 1920s.

In 1811 Col John Stevens (1749–1838) established the first steam ferry, *Juliana,* from Hoboken, NJ, to Barclay St in Manhattan. In 1814 Robert Fulton put his steamboats *Jersey* and *York* on a route from Manhattan's Cortlandt St to Jersey City's Paulus Hook [now Exchange Place], with these "primitive" steamboats making the crossing in 15 minutes, close to the 11 minutes of "high-speed" 21st-century ferries on the same route. Steam became the new standard along the Hudson and in New York Harbor. Early steam ferry operators included Cornelius Vanderbilt (1794–1877), Daniel D. Tompkins (1774–1825), and Robert L. Stevens (1787–1856). From the 1830s into the 1960s, railroads terminating on the New Jersey and Long Island shores across from Manhattan became major operators of ferries.

The typical steam ferry was a double-ended, bidirectional craft, the design of which eliminated any need to turn the boat for loading and unloading. Team gangways for the vehicles ran down the middle of the ship, with passenger cabins along either side, outboard and on the upper deck. Most boats were 150–200 feet (46–61 m) long, averaged 40–70 feet (12–21 m) wide, and operated between 12 and 18 mph (19–29 kph), accommodating up to 2,000 passengers without overcrowding. In 1888 Hoboken Ferry Co introduced the new *Bergen* with screw propellers at each end, replacing sidewheels. This technology gradually became the standard for both steam ferries and the diesel ferries introduced in the 1930s. The last steam sidewheeler built was the *Charles W. Galloway* (1922) for a Staten Island–New Jersey line that operated until 1948. The first diesel ferries, *Piermont* and *Irvington,* named for the Rockland and Westchester Co communities they ferried between, went into operation in 1932.

During the later 19th and early 20th centuries, the Hudson River ferry business reached its zenith. Many lines came under the control of connecting railroad and streetcar lines, operating from West Shore terminals to numbers of Manhattan slips with up to 20-boat fleets of sleek and speedy steam vessels. From 1900 into the 1940s the development of the automobile briefly stimulated the ferry business, reviving many defunct upriver crossings, but a series of large bridges built between 1924 (Bear Mountain) and

PRINCIPAL ROUTES OF HUDSON RIVER FERRIES (*continued*)

Towns Served	Dates in Service	Details
Englewood Cliffs, NJ–Manhattan	1860–?84	Sporadic service; likely ended in 1884 when Palisades Mountain House was burned down
Englewood Cliffs, NJ–Dyckman St, Manhattan	1915–42; 1948–51	
Fort Lee, NJ–Carmansville [now Washington Heights], Manhattan	*ca* 1660–*ca* 1800	Burdette's Ferry
Fort Lee, NJ–Manhattanville [now Morningside Heights], Manhattan	1880–96	
Fort Lee, NJ–Canal St, Manhattan	1832–*ca* 1910	Operated by Manhattan and Fort Lee Steamboat Co
Edgewater, NJ–125th St, Manhattan	1888–1950	Main operators: Public Service Ferry; Electric Ferry Co
Bulls Ferry, NJ–Spring St, Manhattan	1788–1909	
Guttenberg, NJ–42d St, Manhattan	1902–22	Operated by New York Central RR
Guttenberg, NJ–Spring St, Manhattan	1832–1909	Operated by Manhattan and Fort Lee Steamboat Co
Weehawken, NJ–Manhattan	1700–1834; 1859–1959; 1986–	West Shore RR, New York Central RR Co (1883–1959); currently operated by New York Waterway
Weehawken, NJ–Manhattan	1926–43; 1989–	Currently operated by New York Waterway
Hoboken, NJ–14th St, Manhattan	1886–1942	Operated by Delaware, Lackawanna and Western RR
Hoboken, NJ–Barclay St [now North Cove], Manhattan Ferry	1774–1967; 1989–	Main operators: John Stevens; Barnet DeKlyn; Hoboken Co; Delaware, Lackawanna and Western RR; Erie Lackawanna RR; NJ Transit RR; in 2003, New York Waterway
Pavonia (Jersey City, NJ)–Manhattan (various points)	1733–1959; 1989–	Main operators: Archibald Kennedy; Homer Ramsdall; Long Dock Co; Erie RR; in 2003, New York Waterway
Paulus Hook [now Exchange Place, Jersey City, NJ]–Cortlandt St, Manhattan	1764–1949; 1988–	Main operators: Cornelius Van Voorst; John Stevens; Robert Fulton; Pennsylvania RR; Direct Line; in 2003, New York Waterway
Communipaw (Jersey City, NJ)–Manhattan; Brooklyn (various points)	1661–1967; 1975	Main operators: William Jansen; Pieter Hetfelsen; Central RR of NJ; Circle Line; in 2003, New York Waterway
Staten Island–Manhattan	1624–	Known as Staten Island Ferry; operated by New York City
Staten Island–Brooklyn	*ca* 1645–1964	Operated by New York City

Note: Ferry lines arranged from northernmost to southernmost routes. Table accurate through the end of 2003.

[a]Exact locations shifted over time.

Compiled by Arthur G. Adams

1964 (Verrazano-Narrows) eliminated the need for it. In 1967 no ferries operated on the Hudson River proper, and only the Manhattan–Staten Island route remained on the Upper Bay.

In 1980 ongoing redevelopment of the Lower Manhattan and New Jersey waterfronts plus advocacy by the Hudson River Navigation Co, a holding company with coal-mining interests, spurred the Port Authority of New York and New Jersey, those states' governors, and developer Arthur Imperatore Sr to conceive a new solution. It entailed an 8 mi (13 km) rapid-transit railway connecting the waterfront cities of Bayonne, Jersey City, Hoboken, and Weehawken, and restored passenger ferry services from Weehawken and Hoboken to Manhattan. Two new giant ferries connecting Staten Island and Manhattan were built in the following two years. The *Andrew J. Barberi* (1981) and the *Samuel I. Newhouse* (1982) were both diesel-powered ships measuring 300 feet (91 m) long and 70 feet (21 m) wide, operating at 20 mph (32 kph), and carrying up to 6,000 passengers. In 1986 Imperatore restored ferry operations from Weehawken to Manhattan's West 38th St with small, passenger-only, single-ended diesel vessels. In 1989 Imperatore's Port Imperial Ferry Co, later reorganized as New York Waterway, began operations from Hoboken Terminal to Lower Manhattan on behalf of the Port Authority and New Jersey Transit Railroad. Imperatore soon opened other routes on the East River, in Upper New York Bay, and on the Hudson. In 2002 the Hudson-Bergen Light Rail line, planned since 1980, opened for operation from Bayonne to Hoboken, and will ultimately continue north to Nyack (Rockland Co).

At the beginning of the 21st century, New York Waterway operates over 50 vessels and has commenced construction of a large new rail-ferry terminal at Weehawken. Other operators have also entered the field with experimental and emergency lines. Following the 11 Sept 2001 destruction of the World Trade Center and downtown Port Authority Trans-Hudson (PATH) rapid-transit line station, ferries provided immediate emergency and evacuation services. In subsequent months, they also provided the main access to Lower Manhattan for thousands of passengers from the south and west. Continued waterfront redevelopment promises regrowth of ferry services with larger and faster vessels. There is also pressure to reopen upriver ferry lines to connect with Metro-North and Amtrak trains operating along the eastern bank of the Hudson.

Adams, Arthur G. *The Hudson through the Years,* 5th ed. (New York: Fordham Univ Press, 2003)

Baxter, Raymond J., and Arthur G. Adams. *Railroad Ferries of the Hudson,* 2d ed. (New York: Fordham Univ Press, 1999)

Cudahy, Brian J. *Over and Back: The History of Ferryboats in New York Harbor* (New York: Fordham Univ Press, 1990)

Smith, H. J. *The Romance of the Hoboken Ferry* (Hoboken, NJ: Hoboken Ferry, 1931)

Arthur G. Adams

Hudson River fortifications and chains. See HUDSON HIGHLANDS FORTIFICATIONS.

Hudson River Railroad. Chartered in 1846, the Hudson River Railroad company (HRRR) operated a rail line between New York City and East Greenbush (Rensselaer Co), across the Hudson River from Albany, from 1851 to 1869. It faced serious problems both before and during construction. Initially investors hesitated to buy company stock for fear that locomotives could not compete with the Hudson River steamboats. But chief engineer John B. Jervis argued successfully that, regardless of season, trains could make the 140 mi (225 km) trip in half the steamboats' 10–11 hours. Plans called for the road to run along the river's east bank. Convincing property owners, among whom were many prominent landowners, to grant easements was difficult. The company, as well as citing economic advantages, pushed the idea that the railroad would enhance the natural beauty of the environs and within a few months obtained most easements. Actual construction of the railroad was routine, involving the laying of 7 in (17.8 cm) square chestnut ties to support T-shaped iron rails. The challenge was building the roadbed. The rock of the Hudson Highlands was difficult to cut through, particularly at Breakneck Mountain, near Cold Spring (Putnam Co). The company hired several contractors before finding one who could complete Breakneck Mountain's 842 ft (257 m) tunnel, which is still in use. Completed to East Greenbush in 1851, HRRR concentrated on passenger business. Its flat, water-level route allowed trains to reach speeds of nearly 50 mph (80 kph) when pulled by specially designed locomotives. In 1853 HRRR connected with newly organized New York Central Railroad, which ran between Buffalo and Albany. This benefited New York City because the two roads reinforced its hold on the western hinterland. During the 1850s, because of price wars with steamboats, the company often operated at a loss. This situation changed in the early 1860s, when steamboat line-owner Cornelius Vanderbilt and his son William H. Vanderbilt acquired influence in HRRR. Cornelius Vanderbilt, who became president of the company in 1867, merged HRRR with New York Central in 1869 to create one of the largest trunk lines in the country.

Hungerford, Edward. *Men and Iron: A History of the New York Central* (New York: Thomas Y. Crowell, 1938)

F. Daniel Larkin

Hudson River school. Artistic movement. The term Hudson River school refers to a school of American landscape painting that began in the 1820s, reached its apogee in the middle of the 19th century, and continued to the end of the century. The term itself is misleading. It was first used in the 1870s by critics who looked askance at the virtuosic canvases of American landscape artists whose technical brilliance they regarded as empty display. To denigrate these artists, critics coined the term Hudson River school, by which they meant narrow and insular, in contrast to the Barbizon school of landscape painting in France, which they admired. In fact, artists of the Hudson River school were well traveled, and some had received academic training in Europe. Moreover, the Hudson River valley did not provide the setting for most of the work done by artists of this school in the second half of the 19th century. The term is accurate in one important sense: the school of landscape painting that dominated US art for a half century did have its origins in New York City and the Hudson Valley.

Thomas Cole and the First Phase

A likely starting point for the Hudson River school was a day in 1825 when prominent US artist John Trumbull (1756–1843) saw several landscape paintings in a framing shop in New York City. They made such an impression that he purchased one and showed them to two friends, engraver Asher B. Durand and critic William Dunlap, who also purchased paintings. The artist was Thomas Cole (1801–48), the founder of the Hudson River school. He was born in Lancashire, England. As a youth he took nature walks with his sister, read Wordsworth, and in the words of his friend and biographer Louis Legrand Noble, dreamed of "the natural beauties of the North American states." Cole came to the United States with his family in 1818 and then went to Philadelphia in 1823, hoping to become an artist. He received little formal training, was essentially self-taught, and was never comfortable with the human figure. Upon arriving in New York City in 1825, he devoted himself completely to landscape painting. To this genre he brought a romantic vision that was shared by contemporaries such as James Fenimore Cooper and William Cullen Bryant. For Cole, landscape was Edenic and an expression of primal innocence; as an artist he looked to an idealized past rather than to an America that was being tamed and subjected to human mastery.

Kaaterskill Falls (Greene Co) had become a tourist attraction by the early 19th century, and a mountain house and viewing tower had been built, along with a handrail along the ledge for the convenience of tourists. None of these modern appurtenances are seen in Cole's *Falls of Kaaterskill* (1826), which anachronistically includes an Indian gazing at a world from which his people had been displaced. Like Cooper, whom he admired, Cole was uneasy about the democratic forces welling up in America and about the westward movement that would transform the United States in the name of progress. Cole never traveled to the American West, but he did travel to Europe twice, in 1829–32 and 1841–42. Italian ruins helped inspire allegorical paintings, such as *The Course of Empire* (1834–36), a set of five large works that expressed Cole's apprehensions over civilizations that invested heavily in material progress. Cole's allegorical paintings stand apart from works that portray scenes of the Hudson Valley and settings along the eastern seaboard. Of these, his *View from Mount Holyoke* (1836) is particularly noteworthy.

Cole's success was instantaneous when Trumbull discovered him in 1825. Well-connected in the art world and socially prominent, Trumbull brought Cole to the attention of important patrons, and by the late 1820s Cole had become one of America's leading artists, enjoying the support of wealthy collectors such as Luman Reed, Philip Hone, Samuel Ward, and William Paterson Van Rensselaer. Cole's writings on art added to his stature, as did the praise of William Cul-len Bryant. Cole cofounded the National Academy of Design in Manhattan in 1826, which, along with the Arts-Union, became an important base of training and institutional support for Hudson River school artists. To measure Cole's importance one need only consider his influence on other artists: Asher Durand (1796–1886), Jasper Francis Cropsey (1823–1900), Sanford Robinson Gifford (1823–80), Worthington Whittredge (1820–1910), and most importantly Frederic Edwin Church (1826–1900), all of whom turned to landscape in the 1840s and became prominent in the second phase of the Hudson River school after Cole's unexpected death in 1848.

The Second Phase

After Cole, the most important artist of the school was Frederic Edwin Church, who lived in Cole's house in Catskill (Greene Co) from 1844 to 1846. Church's *To the Memory of Cole* (1848) includes a tree stump from which new growth appears, expressing the idea that the Hudson River school would continue. In the years after Cole's death, Church worked in the manner of his mentor—ruminative, nostalgic, and reverent before the mystery and beauty of nature. His style changed when he traveled to South America to see the landscapes that German naturalist Alexander von Humboldt had praised so highly. Out of this and other trips to South America, the Arctic, Europe, and the Middle East came the spectacular, very large works for which Church is best known. It was in works such as *The Heart of the Andes* (1859), *Cotopaxi* (1862), and *Rainy Season in the Tropics* (1866) that Church's fame reached its apex. Large audiences in the United States and Europe purchased tickets to see Church's sensational paintings, which were sometimes placed on a stage behind drapes and then unveiled for viewers to see through opera glasses or metal tubes.

It was in a gallery of the Tenth Street Studio Building, designed by Richard Morris Hunt in 1858, that Church first displayed his paintings. Church and many other Hudson River school artists had studios in this building. Artists of the school fell loosely into clusters according to their different interests and styles. Some, including Durand, Whittredge, Gifford, Cropsey, and the lesser-known John Casilear (1811–93), Thomas Rossiter (1818–71), William Hart (1823–94), James M. Hart (1828–1901), and Homer Dodge Martin (1836–97), chose settings in the Hudson Valley. Among the artists who traveled to the West was Albert Bierstadt (1832–1902), who received training in Germany and traveled widely in Europe from 1853 to 1857. In a series of trips to the American West, Bierstadt made sketches for the sensational canvases that he painted after returning to New York. He celebrated the natural beauty of the Rockies, Yellowstone, and Yosemite in virtuosic canvases of immense size that rivaled Church's in popularity. At the peak of his career in the 1860s, canvases sold for high prices and brought him fame and fortune in America and Europe. *The Rocky Mountains* (1865) was purchased by an English railroad financier for $25,000, an enormous price for the time.

The splendor of Bierstadt is in sharp contrast to the landscape paintings of another group of Hudson River artists, the Luminists, which included Fitz Hugh Lane (1804–65), Martin Johnson Heade (1819–1904), John Frederick Kensett (1816–72), and Sanford Gifford. An interest in atmospheric effects connects these artists to Cole, but they also drew inspiration from provincial English marine paintings and from the 17th-century French artist Claude Lorrain. The Luminist style is polished, brush strokes are suppressed, and compositions have a strong horizontal emphasis. There is a sense of calm that is far removed from the theatrical effects of some Hudson River artists.

The Final Phase

In the 1860s and 1870s, attacks from critics of the Hudson River school's leading figures helped undercut the movement. Church began to suffer from arthritis of the hand in the 1860, his output diminished, and by the time of his death in 1900 he was all but forgotten. It was Bierstadt who took the brunt of the critics' attacks. His reputation began to suffer in the 1870s, and when his *Last of the Buffalo* (1888) was rejected for display by the Corcoran Art Gallery in Washington, DC, in 1889 it was in serious eclipse, as was the Hudson River school. Taste was changing from landscape to scenes of domestic and urban life in a finished academic style or in the Impressionist style, to which some American artists converted in the 1880s and 1890s. By 1900, the year of Church's death, the Hudson River school was definitively over. However, interest in the school began to revive by 1910, and exhibitions in the 1930s and since have assigned it a prominent place in US art history. Outstanding collections can be found in Manhattan's Metropolitan Museum of Art and New-York Historical Society and in the Albany Institute of

The Falls of Kaaterskill, by Thomas Cole, 1826.

History and Art. Thomas Cole's restored house can be seen in Catskill, and Frederic Church's house, Olana, near Hudson (Columbia Co) is a museum.

For other illustrations see CATSKILL MOUNTAIN HOUSE; DURAND, ASHER B(ROWN); LAKE GEORGE.

Flexner, James Thomas. *The Wilder Image: The Native School from Thomas Cole to Winslow Homer* (New York: Dover, 1970)

Howat, John K. *The Hudson River and Its Painters* (1972; repr New York: American Legacy Press, 1983)

Novak, Barbara. *Nature and Culture: American Landscape and Painting, 1825–1875* (New York: Oxford Univ Press, 1995)

Wilmerding, John, and Lisa Fellows Andrus, eds. *American Light: The Luminist Movement, 1850–1875* (Washington, DC: National Gallery of Art, 1980)

Warren Roberts

Hudson River sloops. For two centuries sloops dominated river traffic on the Hudson. Dutch settlers brought their indigenous watercraft designs to the New World, and over time local builders adapted those forms to suit regional needs. By 1750 a distinctive new type had emerged. Hudson River sloops used a tall, powerful rig of gaff mainsail (four-sided sail fixed to a sliding spar attached to the after-side of the mast), jib (triangular sail lashed to the mast's forward stays), and square topsail (run high on the mast) for speed within the valley. Their broad shallow hulls, up to 70 feet (21.3 m) long and 28 feet (8.5 m) wide, conferred stability, cargo capacity, and shoal-water capability. Large luxurious cabins under a raised quarterdeck accommodated a dozen or more passengers. In the early 1800s commercial pressures, scheduled packet service, and competition from steamboats placed a premium on speed. Centerboards, invented around 1815, permitted larger rigs on fast shallow hulls. Sloop construction boomed, with builders from all along the Hudson, in New York Bay, and on Long Island Sound launching more than 1,300 sloops between 1796 and 1835. Nyack was by far the largest producer, followed by Marlborough, Albany, Haverstraw, and Troy. But steamboats attracted the lucrative passenger trade, and cargo traffic economics made schooners, which required smaller crews, more attractive. By the mid-1830s many owners were abandoning sloops for steamboats or adapting schooners, either by conversion or through new construction. Fewer than 25 new sloops were built between 1855 and 1867. The main means of transportation, on land or water, in the Hudson Valley for 200 years, the sloops had supported the region's growth, which in turn aided the Port of New York's commercial and financial development. The sloops also came to symbolize the river. In the 1960s, when a campaign began to reclaim the river's environmental heritage, a replica, *Clearwater,* was built to serve as both an educational platform and a symbol of the valley's history and promise. At the beginning of the 21st century, *Clearwater* remained home-ported at Poughkeepsie.

Fontenoy, Paul E. *The Sloops of the Hudson River: A Historical and Design Survey* (Mystic, Conn: Mystic Seaport Museum, 1994)

Paul E. Fontenoy

Hudson River steamboat lines. The world's first successful commercial steamboat, Robert Fulton and Robert R. Livingston Jr's *North River Steamboat,* often called *Clermont,* made its first regularly scheduled trip from Manhattan to Albany on 4 Sept 1807, a journey lasting over 36 hours. Fulton and Livingston, who enjoyed a statewide steamboat monopoly, soon built other Hudson River steamers. By the early 1820s, improved design of the craft reduced most trips to 20 hours, with the ships operating day and night. They carried passengers and express freight, both at premium prices, but with a high level of dependability.

In 1824 the US Supreme Court decision in *Gibbons v Ogden* ended the monopoly, and by 1840, there were more than 100 steamboats on the Hudson. Almost all were side-paddle wheelers featuring walking-beam engines with vertical cylinders. The ships averaged between 15 and 18 mph (24–29 kph). Manhattan-Albany trips averaged between 9 and 10 hours. Because speed was at a premium on day boats, racing and attendant collisions, fires, and boiler explosions were common. Beginning in the mid-1820s some steamboats towed safety barges, engineless replicas of the steam vessels, for riders who feared boiler mishaps. Night boats, which also carried freight, emphasized comfort and luxury rather than speed.

During the 1830s and 1840s, competition drove fares sharply down and led to price-fixing by the North River Association and other owner groups. But competition continued to create faster, more elegant ships, lower fares, and higher traffic volumes. By 1835 Daniel Drew founded People's Line to compete with North River Association ships, undercutting their prices so that People's Line lost $10,000 in its first year. Rivalry between Albany and nearby Troy generated new lines as well, because many Troy citizens refused to ride on ships that terminated at Albany.

By October 1851 Hudson River Railroad offered a four-hour trip from Manhattan to Greenbush [now Rensselaer] across the Hudson from Albany; the trains ran throughout the year, even when ice closed the river and cut off steamboat travel. Much freight and passenger traffic was lost to trains, but tourists and those seeking comfort and low fares preferred steamboats. Hudson River Day Line, formed in 1856, acquired fast boats, averaging 200 feet (61 m) in length, such as *Daniel Drew,* originally built for People's Line, *Alida, Armenia,* and the streamlined twins *Albany* and *New York*. Hailed as "Speed Queens," boats of this type were popular through the 1880s. In the 1890s larger ships began serving day-trippers and the Adirondack, Catskill Mountain, and Saratoga Springs resorts. People's Line in 1896 added giant *Adirondack* and, renamed Hudson Navigation Co, acquired *C. W. Morse* in 1903. Day Line launched the 379 ft (115.5 m) *Hendrick Hudson* in 1906, added luxury liner *Robert Fulton* in 1909, and added the 400 ft (121.9 m) *Washington Irving* in 1913. Licensed to carry 5,000 passengers, the *Washington Irving* featured private parlors, gourmet dining, a symphony orchestra, and fine commissioned artworks. Also in 1913 Hudson Navigation Co enrolled *Berkshire*, at 422 feet (128.6 m) the largest steamboat ever to operate on the Hudson.

Steamboat travel on the Hudson reached its height in the 1920s, with Day Line adding screw propeller–driven *DeWitt Clinton* in 1920, sidewheeler *Alexander Hamilton* in 1924, and the single-screw *Peter Stuyvesant* in 1927. The lines served 2.5 million passengers during the peak year of 1925. Overnight boats remained cheaper and more comfortable than railroad sleeping cars. Passenger traffic continued fairly steady on Hudson River Night Line, a successor to Hudson Navigation Co, but high stevedoring costs in Manhattan forced the company to close in 1939. As late as 1948 Day Line's four ships often carried 15,000 passengers daily to Indian Point, Bear Mountain, West Point, Poughkeepsie, Kingston Point, and Catskill. High costs of vessel and pier replacement and a short operating season led to a decline in the daily excursion business. The 1971 motor ship *Dayliner* ceased regularly scheduled trips in 1987. Corporate successor Hudson River Day Line, an affiliate of Manhattan's Circle Line, discontinued regular upriver trips, but in 2002 the company restored limited service to Bear Mountain and West Point with chartered high-speed ferries.

Adams, Arthur G. *The Hudson through the Years* (New York: Fordham Univ Press, 1996)
Dayton, Fred Erving. *Steamboat Days* (New York: Frederick A. Stokes, 1925)
Ringwald, Donald C. *Hudson River Day Line: The Story of a Great American Steamboat Company* (1965; repr New York: Fordham Univ Press, 1990)

Arthur G. Adams

Hughes, Charles Evans (*b* Glens Falls, Warren Co, 11 Apr 1862; *d* Osterville, Mass, 27 Aug 1948). Governor and US Supreme Court justice. Educated at Madison College (now Colgate University), Brown University, and Columbia Law School (1884), he practiced law in New York City for 20 years, interrupted by a two-year hiatus teaching at the Cornell University Law School (1891–93). In 1905 he was appointed counsel to New York State legislative committees investigating abusive business practices by utilities and life insurance companies. He became the Republican candidate for governor in 1906 and defeated Democrat William Randolph Hearst.

Hughes labored during his first year in office to assert his primacy over the party Republicans who dominated the state legislature. He removed officials he believed unfit for office or lacking in administrative ability and secured the adoption of legislation giving him power to initiate investigations of executive agencies and departments. The centerpiece of his legislative program was his successful proposal to establish public service commissions with strong investigative and rate-fixing authority over utilities and transportation companies. Hughes supported labor reform legislation, including the nation's first workers' compensation law. He also secured support for his proposals to ameliorate the conditions of aliens, improve the probation system, control the spread of tuberculosis, and regulate the sale and labeling of drugs. He helped strengthen the existing policy of environmental conservation, and his crusade to end racetrack gambling ultimately overcame the hostility of the political establishment and the power of racing interests.

Reelected in 1908, Hughes resigned in October 1910 after accepting Pres William H. Taft's offer of a seat on the US Supreme Court, where he served as associate justice for six years, writing a number of decisions broadly construing congressional power to regulate interstate commerce. In June 1916 he resigned to stand as the Republican candidate to oppose incumbent president Woodrow Wilson. While garnering about 52% of New York State ballots, Hughes was hurt by the perception that his victory might take the country into World War I, trailed Wilson in the popular vote nationwide, and suffered a narrow electoral college defeat, receiving 254 to Wilson's 277 electoral votes. Resuming the practice of law in 1917 in New York City, Hughes was appointed secretary of state by Pres Warren G. Harding in 1921. During his four-year tenure, Hughes negotiated a separate US peace treaty with Germany, supported the Dawes Plan as a way to ease Germany's World War I reparations burden, and oversaw efforts to improve US relations with Latin America. He also negotiated a significant naval disarmament agreement among the world's leading military powers during a 1921–22 international conference in Washington, DC. Hughes again returned to private law practice in New York City in 1925.

Named chief justice of the United States by Pres Herbert Hoover in 1930, Hughes guided the Supreme Court through the turbulent years of the Great Depression. His fidelity to the Bill of Rights was reflected in opinions broadly interpreting First Amendment freedoms. After initially voting to strike down major components of New Deal regulatory legislation, Hughes later led the Court in a more moderate direction, writing the key decision in 1937 that upheld the constitutionality of the National Labor Relations Act (Wagner Act). He helped defeat Pres Franklin D. Roosevelt's proposal to increase the size of the Supreme Court with a letter to the US Senate Judiciary Committee stating the Court was abreast of its docket and would function less efficiently with more members. Remembered most for his work with the Supreme Court, from which he retired in 1941, Hughes also served on the Permanent Court of International Justice and wrote several books on foreign relations and the Supreme Court itself.

See also LIBERALISM. For illustration see LAWYERS AND LAW FIRMS.

The Autobiographical Notes of Charles Evans Hughes, ed. David J. Danelski and Joseph S. Tulchin (Cambridge, Mass: Harvard Univ Press, 1973)
Pusey, Merlo J. *Charles Evans Hughes*, 2 vols (1951; repr New York: Garland Publishing, 1979)
Wesser, Robert F. *Charles Evans Hughes: Politics and Reform in New York, 1905–1910* (Ithaca: Cornell Univ Press, 1967)

Robert A. Klump

Hughes, John J(oseph) (*b* 24 June 1797, Annaloghan, Ireland; *d* 3 Jan 1864, New York City). Catholic bishop. Raised in County Tyrone in Ireland, Hughes moved to Chambersburg, Pa, in 1817, where his father was living. He entered Mount St. Mary's Seminary in Emmitsburg, Md, and was ordained in 1826. He gained a reputation as a staunch defender of Catholic rights. He became coadjutor bishop of New York in 1838 and found New York's churches deep in debt when he arrived, with lay trustees resisting the bishop's hiring decisions. Having opened St. Joseph's Seminary (1840–60) and St. Johns College (1841; now Fordham University) in the Bronx, he became bishop in 1842 and held the first diocesan synod to establish uniform discipline. In 1850, with new dioceses established in the state, he became the state's first archbishop. In 1842 he won the support of Gov William H. Seward to end the monopoly over distribution of state educational funds by the Public School Society, a private organization with a Protestant character. Although the state legislated that public funds would henceforth be distributed through locally elected school supervisors, Hughes, like other American bishops, developed his own parochial school system, securing diocesan control of the Sisters of Charity and establishing other orders of women teachers. When anti-Catholic violence threatened to spread to New York from Philadelphia in 1844, he surrounded his churches with armed men. In 1858 he laid the cornerstone for the new St. Patrick's Cathedral. An American patriot, he rallied his diocese, much of it Irish or German, to support the Mexican War and later the Civil War, though he rejected emancipation as its purpose. In 1861–62, at Pres Abraham Lincoln's request, he journeyed to Paris and Rome to dissuade Emperor Louis Napoleon and Pope Pius IX from recognizing the Confederacy. He helped quell the draft riots in July 1863 and opened a new St. Joseph's Seminary in Troy (Rensselaer Co) in 1864.

See also CATHOLIC EDUCATION.

Shaw, Richard. *Dagger John: The Unquiet Life and Times of Archbishop John Hughes of New York* (New York: Paulist Press, 1977)

Gerald P. Fogarty, SJ

Huguenots. Reformed Protestants of ancien régime France. French Protestant mercantile houses played a role in the European expansion into the Atlantic world, and Huguenot merchants, as well as migrating Huguenot peasant families, were early European settlers in New Netherland. Among them were merchants Jacques Cousseau from La Rochelle and Gabriel Minvielle from Bordeaux, who served as New York City mayor in 1684. Most early Huguenot settlers came from the French provinces of Picardy, Normandy, and Saintonge, and from the cities of La Rochelle and Calais. By the 1650s a small Huguenot community emerged on Staten Island, and Huguenot pastor Michel Cipierre ministered at Harlem on Manhattan Island from 1658 to 1663. In 1678 a group of 12 men, living in the Esopus area, mostly from the province of Artois by way of the German Palatinate, established the Village of New Paltz [now in Ulster Co].

New York's Huguenot population remained, however, largely amorphous until the 1680s, when King Louis XIV's policy in France of eradicating Calvinism, culminating in the 1685 revocation of the act of religious toleration known as the Edict of Nantes, resulted in widespread persecutions. In the late 1680s several hundred Huguenot refugees arrived in New York fleeing France by way of England and from the French West Indian colonies of St. Christopher, Guadeloupe, Marie Galante, and Martinique. By 1689 seven French Reformed congregations existed in and about New York City. In 1682 Pierre Daillé, a former professor at the Protestant Academy of Saumur, organized New York City's first French congregation, which conducted services in Fort James. Daillé also ministered to congregations on Staten Island, at New Paltz, Bushwick [now in Kings Co], and Schraalenburg [now in NJ]. Another New York City congregation formed under Pierre Peiret, who arrived in 1686 from Foix and erected a church on Petticoat Lane, now Marketfield St, in 1688. This structure was replaced in 1704 by a stone edifice, Eglise du St. Esprit, at Church and Pine Sts. In 1686 a group of investors began to purchase land in Westchester Co for a refugee colony, finalized with Jacob Leisler's purchase of 6,100 acres (2,470 ha) at New Rochelle in 1689. David Bonrepos, a former pastor on St. Christopher, ministered to that community from 1688 to 1695.

By the early 18th century, Huguenots accounted for about 9% of New York City's population. Huguenot merchants Stephen DeLancey, Auguste Jay, and Gabriel Laboyteau were among the city's leaders, and Huguenot craftsmen, especially silversmiths Bartholomew Le Roux, Simeon Soumaine, and Peter Quintard, were distinguished. But without continued immigration, the Huguenot population rapidly assimilated. Daillé's New York City congregation became defunct in the 1690s, and in the early 18th century the other congregations affiliated with either Anglican or Dutch Reformed or Presbyterian Churches. Elias Neau, a convert to Anglicanism, operated from 1704 to 1722 a catechizing school for the Society for the Propagation of the Gospel (SPG) to educate enslaved African New Yorkers. By the 1750s most former French Reformed congregations had abandoned the French language. Only New York City's Eglise du St. Esprit remained independent until merging with the Episcopal Church in 1804; it continues to serve French-speaking Protestants in the 21st century. The Huguenot Society of America, formed in New York City in 1883, and the Huguenot Historical Society, formed in New Paltz in 1894, are dedicated to preserving Huguenot history.

Butler, Jon. *The Huguenots in America: A Refugee People in New World Society* (Cambridge, Mass: Harvard Univ Press, 1983)

Carlo, Paula Wheeler. "Anglican Conformity and Nonconformity among the Huguenots of Colonial New York." In *From Strangers to Citizens: The Integration of Immigrant Communities in Britain, Ireland, and Colonial America, 1550–1750,* ed. Randolph Bigne and Charles Littleton (London: The Huguenot Society of Great Britain and Ireland; Brighton and Portland, England: Sussex Academic Press, 2001)

———. "The Huguenots of Colonial New Paltz and New Rochelle: A Social and Religious History" (PhD diss, CUNY, 2001)

David William Voorhees

Human Rights, Division of. This state agency enforces New York State's antidiscrimination laws, providing an alternative to the court system for victims of bias based on race, age, sex, creed, national origin, or disability. A commissioner, appointed by the governor with senate approval, heads the agency at the governor's pleasure. The division began as the State Commission against Discrimination (SCAD), created by the Ives-Quinn Act of 1945 and charged with the elimination of discrimination in employment. Before World War II, discrimination in the private sector job market in New York State and elsewhere was widely considered to be a matter of private preference. Thus northern states that had laws prohibiting segregation or discrimination in public accommodations or public sector employment generally did not police the private labor market. The US government, through Executive Order 8802 issued in June 1941, prohibited racial and religious discrimination by employers who held defense contracts during World War II, and New York was the first state to enact a peacetime "fair employment" law in 1945.

Ives-Quinn tried to show that employers and unions could open jobs to minorities without legal compulsion. Like the 1935 National Labor Relations Act, or Wagner Act, Ives-Quinn established an administrative, nonjudicial forum to resolve disputes. It gained a widely favorable consensus among state employers, the media, politicians, and the public in its first years of operation. Advocates of federal civil rights legislation often pointed to the success of New York State's law in support of a national statute. Groups like the NAACP, American Jewish Congress, and National Urban League had been among the most ardent supporters of the New York State law but were disappointed that the commission did not act more aggressively against racial discrimination. In part the commission was reluctant to impose race-conscious or quota policies on employers. The commission's critics formed a watchdog group, the Committee to Support the Ives-Quinn Law, in the late 1940s to monitor the agency. It issued critical reports that the commission ignored or rebutted, and by the 1950s civil rights activism turned to new directions.

In the wake of the US Supreme Court's *Brown v Board of Education* (1954) and the acceleration of civil rights demands later in that decade, the commission came under increasing pressure to do more to attain racial equality. The state legislature extended the commission's authority to public accommodations in 1952, public housing in 1955, age discrimination in employment in 1958, and sex discrimination in 1965. The commission became a political issue in the 1954 gubernatorial campaign, when Democratic nominee W. Averell Harriman pushed for a more aggressive state civil rights campaign against Republican US senator Irving Ives, a cosponsor of the original Ives-Quinn Act. Gov Harriman appointed Charles Abrams, a real estate attorney and founder of the New York City Housing Authority, as chairman of the commission in 1955. Abrams had already established a controversial reputation as an advocate of "benevolent quotas" in public housing. Although some academics saw the need for race-conscious approaches to the problem of discrimination in the mid-1950s, Abrams clashed with state legislative leaders, principally New York State Assembly Speaker Oswald Heck, and was too controversial to be an effective commission chairman. Republican governor Nelson A. Rockefeller replaced Abrams with the more conservative Elmer Carter, National Urban League activist, in 1959.

Carter responded to calls for a more active enforcement of civil rights laws and was chairman when the state legislature renamed the agency the New York State Commission on Human Rights in 1962 (becoming the New York State Division of Human Rights in 1968). The commission became more forceful in its campaign against labor union discrimination, especially in the urban building trades. In 1964 it won its first major court contest in *Local 28, Sheet Metal Workers International Association v EEOC* (1986), although it would be another 20 years before the union fully complied with nondiscrimination orders. When the federal Civil Rights Act of 1964 was being debated, some civil rights groups held up the New York State Commission on Human Rights as a model, and others pointed to its inadequacies. In particular Herbert Hill, labor secretary of the NAACP, published a scathing attack in 1965 on state fair employment commissions, and it remains the most widely cited evaluation of their work. But Title VII of the Civil Rights Act of 1964 did adopt most of the features of New York State's law. Federal civil rights laws allow state agencies like the New York State Division of Human Rights to make the initial attempt to settle discrimination complaints. The division remains the more effective forum for the settlement of small-scale grievances. Complainants who have more time and money avail themselves of the US Equal Employment Opportunity Commission (EEOC) and federal judicial remedies. Moreover the New York State division has enforcement over smaller employers and covers a wider range of groups that have no grounds to complain or sue under federal law. The division had 185 employees in 2000, and 5,727 complaints were filed from 1999 to 2000.

Moreno, Paul. *From Direct Action to Affirmative Action: Fair Employment Law and Policy in America, 1933–72* (Baton Rouge: Louisiana State Univ Press, 1997)

Paul Moreno

Hume. Town (pop 1,987) in NW Allegany Co. A part of the town was in the Caneadea Reservation (1798–1826). Settled in 1806, the town was formed from Pike (Wyoming Co) in 1822. A furnace, foundry, and machine shop at Wiscoy established in 1842 produced plows, mill gearings, steam engines, sawmills, cheese factory furniture, and farm implements. In the same period a furniture factory operated at Mills Mills, a place named for Roger Mills. The Mixville Association at Wiscoy was a brief Fourierist experiment in 1844–45. The Genesee Valley Canal (1851–76) and the Erie and Pennsylvania Railroads provided transport. Ethnic farmers included the Irish, who first came during canal construction in 1838–40, and the Germans, who settled Dutch Hill *ca* 1850. Dairying became the town's focus, with potatoes a commercial crop in the mid–20th century. The locality of Fillmore, created by the canal and quiescent ever since, observed its centennial in 1951 under the distinctive slogan of A Century of Rigor Mortis.

Humphrey. Town (pop 721) in central Cattaraugus Co. Settled in 1815, the town was formed from Burton [now Allegany] in 1836. About 1856 John Meachum built a pearling oven to convert potash to pearl ash and a gassing room to convert pearl ash to saleratus. Lumbering was succeeded by dairying. Sugartown was a center of maple sugar production. In 1880 National Transit Co built an oil pipeline across town. In the early 21st century much of Humphrey is forestland. Pumpkinville, at Sugartown, is an annual event in autumn.

Bruce D. Fredrickson and Madelynn P. Fredrickson

Hungarians. From the mid–19th century, New York City has served as the primary gateway to the United States for most Hungarians as well as a primary focus of Hungarian American life. Hungarians first arrived in New York State after their nation's revolution of 1848–49. The mostly male immigrants primarily stayed in or near New York City. The new arrivals founded a short-lived Hungarian glee club, New York-i Magyar Dalárda, in 1851, and the first Hungarian religious congregation, Magyar Egyház, an ecumenical group that met in Lower Manhattan in 1852. New York City–based immigrants also founded the first Hungarian American newspaper, *Számüzöttek Lapja* (Exiles' News) in 1853 and the first Hungarian association of long duration, New York-i Magyar Egylet, in 1865.

From 1890 to 1914 close to 700,000 new immigrants reshaped the social composition and image of Hungarians in America. In contrast to the gentry-class refugees of 1848, they were primarily peasants. Some found employment in the factories of New York City, Albany, and Buffalo, but most moved on to the coal mines, steel mills, and industrial plants of other eastern and midwestern states. From 1948 to 1953, 27,000 displaced persons (DPs) from Hungary entered the United States. About a third of these entrants settled in or near the New York City metropolitan region. After the failed rebellion of 1956, 40,000 refugees entered the United States, with perhaps less than a third of these remaining in New York State. Both groups included large numbers of professionals, and in time members of the two migrations filled many high positions in US society. Strongly anticommunist, they agitated for the liberation of Hungary and founded scores of cultural, political, and professional organizations. By the 1970s they entered US politics, and they tended to be conservative. In 1994 George E. Pataki, a third-generation Hungarian American, was elected New York State governor.

The US Census of 2000 found 96,593 persons of Hungarian ancestry living in the state, with nearly a third of the total residing in Brooklyn and Queens and two smaller concentrations in and around Buffalo and Albany. The locations of Hungarian organizations mirrored this settlement pattern. Of 45 organizations active in the 1990s, New York City was home to 36 of the groups; 4 were in Buffalo, 3 in Albany, 1 in Kerhonkson (Ulster Co), and 1 in Fillmore (Allegany Co). Reflecting religious affiliation in Hungary, about 66% of Hungarian Americans are Roman Catholic, 20% Reformed, and the remaining 15% either Lutheran, Greek or Byzantine Catholic, Eastern Orthodox, or Jewish. There is also a substantial Hungarian Gypsy population in New York State.

Puskás, Julianna. *Ties That Bind, Ties That Divide: 100 Years of Hungarian Experience in the United States.* Trans Zora Ludwig (New York: Holmes & Meier Publishers, 2000)

Tezla, Albert. *The Hazardous Quest: Hungarian Immigrants in the United States, 1895–1920* (Budapest: Corvina Press, 1993)

Várdy, Steven Béla. *The Hungarian-Americans* (Boston: Twayne Publishers, 1985)

Steven Béla Várdy

Hunkers. Opponents applied this name to conservative New York State Democrats between 1835 and the early 1850s. Equal Rights Party members, or Locofocos, first used the label when accusing their Democratic opponents of "hankering" or "hunkering" after office. Locofocos battled over banking policy with Hunkers, who tended to favor continued chartering of banks by individual legislative acts, a process Locofocos considered corrupt. Led by *Albany Argus* editor Edwin Croswell, Lt Gov and US Sen Daniel S. Dickinson, and legislator and later governor Horatio Seymour, the Hunkers opposed attempts to derail government spending and speculation in the 1830s, including Pres Andrew Jackson's efforts to reduce the circulation of small denomination banknotes as currency and to reign in the use of federal funds deposited in state banks as speculative capital. They supported an aggressive canal-building policy for New York State, one at odds with the more cautious approach favored by Barnburners, a Democratic faction that worked to limit government spending.

Although they faced defeat with passage of the Stop and Tax Law of 1842, Hunker William C. Bouck was elected governor that year, and Hunkers benefited from patronage when Pres James K. Polk selected Hunker and former governor William L. Marcy as secretary of war in 1845. Fearing that the Whigs would defeat Bouck in the 1844 gubernatorial election, Democratic leaders persuaded US Sen Silas Wright, a leading Barnburner, to run. Wright was successful, but the Hunkers regained party dominance after he lost his reelection bid in 1846 and died in 1847. The slavery issue reinforced party divisions in 1848, when the Barnburner faction walked out of the state convention after Hunkers backed the national Democratic platform by refusing to support the antislavery Wilmot Proviso. The state party split, leaving the Hunkers in control until the factions reunited in 1850. The Hunkers then divided into two segments: the Hardshells, who disdained cooperation with the Barnburners, and the Softshells, who wished to heal party wounds. The split lasted through the 1850s.

Donovan, Herbert D. A. *The Barnburners* (1925; repr Philadelphia: Porcupine Press, 1974)

Niven, John. *Martin Van Buren and the Romantic Age of American Politics* (New York: Oxford Univ Press, 1983)

Robert D. Sampson

Hunt, Richard Morris (*b* Brattleboro, Vt, 31 Oct 1827; *d* Newport, RI, 31 July 1895). Architect. Hunt was the first American to study at France's Ecole des Beaux-Arts. Under the patronage of Hector Lefuel, he was appointed inspector of works for the Tuileries/Louvre project and helped design the Louvre's Pavillon de la Bibliothèque. In 1855 Hunt settled in New York City. His first major building there was the Tenth Street Studio, completed in 1857. The Stuyvesant, built in 1869, introduced the French flat to Manhattan. During the 1870s and 1880s Hunt's commissions in the New York City area included the Lenox Library, the Tribune Building, mansions for the Astors and Vanderbilts, and the Vanderbilt mausoleum—the only structure that survives—in the New Dorp Moravian Cemetery on Staten Island. Among his public buildings were the pedestal for the Statue of Liberty, the US Naval Observatory, and the Administration Building of the 1893 Chicago World's Fair. Known as the "dean of American architecture," Hunt was a founder of the American Institute of Architects (1857) and later served as its president (1888–91). The generation of students he trained moved away from classic English forms and obtained broad artistic and professional education. Hunt helped found New York City's Municipal Arts Society (1893), which in 1898 erected a memorial to him on 70th St opposite of where his Lenox Library once stood.

Baker, Paul R. *Richard Morris Hunt* (Cambridge, Mass: MIT Press, 1980)

Stein, Susan R., ed. *The Architecture of Richard Morris Hunt* (Chicago: Univ of Chicago Press, 1986)

George J. Lankevich

Hunt, Ward (*b* Utica, 14 June 1810; *d* Washington, DC, 24 Mar 1886). State judge and US Supreme Court justice. Educated at Oxford and Geneva Academies, Hunt attended Hamilton College for a year, then attended Union College, graduating in 1828. He began preparation for the bar the following year in Litchfield, Conn, and then clerked in Judge Hiram Denio's Utica office. Hunt was admitted to the bar in 1831 and, after a year in New Orleans to improve his health, became Denio's partner. By 1837 he was a solo practitioner. Hunt was elected to one term in the assembly in 1838 and served as mayor of Utica in 1844. An antislavery Democrat, Hunt supported Martin Van Buren's 1848 presidential candidacy and made two unsuccessful runs for judgeships on the State Court of Appeals as a Democrat. He later gravitated to the Republican Party, where he made the important connection with his fellow Utican, Roscoe Conkling, and was finally elected to the Court of Appeals as a Republican in 1865 and was designated commissioner of appeals after the 1867 court reorganization. When the "New York seat" became vacant on the US Supreme Court in 1872, Hunt was appointed largely because of Conkling's (now a US senator) backing. Hunt's most enduring marks are his 1873 jury charge, while riding circuit, that guaranteed Susan B. Anthony's conviction for violating New York State's election law and his dissent to the Court's *United States v Reese* (1876) decision that severely limited the effectiveness of the 15th Amendment. Hunt's ill health prevented him from hearing cases most of his last five years on the Court, but he refused to resign until Congress provided him with an adequate pension, which it did in 1882.

Kutler, Stanley I. "Ward Hunt." In *The Justices of the United States Supreme Court, 1789–1969: Their Lives and Major Opinions,* ed. Leon Friedman and Fred L. Israel, 5 vols (New York: Chelsea House, in association with Bowker, 1969–78)

Donald M. Roper

Hunt, Washington (*b* Windham, Greene Co, 5 Aug 1811; *d* New York City, 2 Feb 1867). Governor and US representative. Educated in common schools, Hunt later studied law, was admitted to the bar (1834), and established a practice at Lockport (Niagara Co). After an unsuccessful bid for US Congress (1836), he was appointed judge (1836–41) in Niagara Co. A Whig, he served three terms in US Congress (1843–49) but refused a fourth term. He subsequently served as state comptroller (1849–50) and governor (1851–52). While governor, he sought Erie Canal expansion funded by the sale of canal revenue certificates, a plan that was later deemed unconstitutional. After losing his reelection bid in 1852, Hunt retired to his Lockport farm. He served as temporary chairman of the Whig Party's last national convention (1856) and joined the Democrats when the Whig Party disintegrated. In 1860 he declined the Democratic nomination for US vice president and later served as a Democratic National Convention delegate (1864).

Holt, Michael F. *The Rise and Fall of the American Whig Party: Jacksonian Politics and the Onset of the Civil War* (New York: Oxford Univ Press, 1999)

John Marino

Hunter. Town (pop 2,721) and village (pop 490) in S Greene Co. Part of the Hardenbergh patent, the town was first settled in the 1780s. It was formed from Windham in 1813 as Greenland, and the name changed in 1814. The main street of the village was surveyed in 1817 by Col William Edwards of the New York Tannery Co, and tanning was initially its main industry, drawing Irish Catholic workers by 1836. It was succeeded by chair making when the tanbark was depleted. An expanded small boardinghouse in 1823 became the Catskill Mountain House, one of the Hudson Valley's chief landmarks and accessible after 1902 by the Catskill Mountain Railroad and the funicular known as the Otis Elevating Railroad. Christmas tree cutting was important by the end of the 19th century, and modern lumbering began in 1903. Residential parks were developed in the eastern part of town from 1887 to 1889, notably Onteora Park. Starting with Simon Epstein's Grandview House in 1893, the number of Jewish summer boardinghouses increased rapidly. After World War II the hotel and boarding business declined, and the state burned the derelict ruins of the Catskill Mountain House in 1963. Hunter Mountain Ski Bowl opened in 1960.

Field Horne

Hunter, Robert (*b* Edinburgh, October 1666; *d* Jamaica, 31 Mar 1734). Royal governor of New York and New Jersey (1710–19). Robert Hunter rose rapidly in the British military to the rank of lieutenant colonel, serving as aide-de-camp to John Churchill, Duke of Marlborough, in the War of the Spanish Succession. As a reward for his participation in the Battles of Blenheim (1704) and Ramillies (1706), Hunter was appointed lieutenant governor of Virginia under Gov George Hamilton, Earl of Orkney. Hunter sailed for Virginia in 1707 but was captured by French pirates en route. Exchanged in 1709 he was awarded the highly lucrative post of governor of New York and New Jersey. Hunter arrived in New York on 13 June 1710, bringing with him 2,814 Palatine refugees who were to establish a naval stores project on the Hudson River at the expense of the Whig government of England. When that government fell, Hunter extended his own credit to incur a personal debt of over £21,000, which was never repaid; the project was ultimately abandoned. Hunter had greater success in Indian relations, securing the allegiance of the Iroquois Confederacy in the ongoing war between the French and the English.

Convening his first assembly in 1710, Hunter immediately encountered resistance when the merchant-dominated assembly insisted that its treasurer, rather than the Crown's representative, pay the colony's bills, contrary to Hunter's instructions. Consequently the assembly refused to raise any money for either Hunter's salary or government expenses. The impasse between assembly and governor continued until 1715, when Hunter agreed that the assembly would control the disbursement of funds, receiving in return a revenue bill to support government for five years. Although he was aware he had sacrificed the royal prerogative by his actions, he felt he had little choice. With assurance of support for all ordinary government expenses, Hunter ensured the remainder of his years in New York would be serene by achieving a pro-administration landowner majority in the assembly. He also discredited his enemies, previous New York governor Edward Hyde, Viscount Cornbury, and Francis Nicholson, with the 1714 publication in New York City of a satirical play, *Androboros,* the first play printed in America.

Using similar successful tactics to calm dissent in New Jersey, Hunter returned to England in 1719 to oversee his personal affairs. In 1720 he exchanged posts with Controller of Customs William Burnet. He remained at that post until 1728, when he was appointed governor of Jamaica. One of the most effective of New York governors, Robert Hunter managed to bring relative tranquility to New York, a province noted throughout colonial history as one ridden by factionalism and disorder. Hunter achieved success primarily because of his ability to compromise, realizing that the resistance he encountered in New York was aimed not so much at him as at the royal government he represented. Given extensive powers by the home government, neither he nor any other governor was given the means to enforce those powers. The lack of money for defense was itself sufficient to cause governors to make concessions to assemblies, thereby weakening the royal prerogative. Hunter, who unsuccessfully urged Parliament to directly supervise New York, accurately predicted that the colonies would separate from the mother country if they were permitted to continue challenging royal authority.

Lustig, Mary Lou. *Robert Hunter (1666–1734): New York's Augustan Statesman* (Syracuse: Syracuse Univ Press, 1983)
Smith, William, Jr. *The History of the Province of New York.* Ed. Michael Kammen, 2 vols (Cambridge, Mass: Belknap Press, 1972)

Mary Lou Lustig

Hunter College. New York City public college that became part of the City University of New York (CUNY). Under Pres Thomas Hunter, the Female Normal and High School first held classes on 14 Feb 1870 at 691 Broadway, moving to Park Ave at 68th and 69th Sts in 1873. The nation's first tuition-free college for women, the Normal School offered teacher training to both black and white women. The school became a degree-granting institution on 19 June 1888, offering teaching and academic curricula, and awarded its first baccalaureate degree on 23 June 1892. The name was changed to Hunter College of the City of New York on 4 Apr 1914. Hunter developed strong programs outside teaching; Gertrude Elion, class of 1937, and Rosalyn Yalow, class of 1941, won the Nobel Prize in medicine. The School of Social Work was established in 1956. In 1964 Hunter College officially became coeducational. In fall 2002 it enrolled 10,126 full-time and 5,368 part-time undergraduate students, and 918 full-time and 4,195 part-time graduate students.

Patterson, Samuel W. *Hunter College: 85 Years of Service* (New York: Lantern, 1955)

Pamela Cooper

hunting. A popular sport, recreational hunting has affected wild game populations throughout the state's history. Hunting of heath hen, grouse, quail, and turkey were restricted in some counties in 1708, and colonial authorities regulated white-tailed deer hunting in 1741 to protect a dwindling population. Turkey, elk, and black bear populations were gone by about 1850, the last native moose was shot in 1861, and cougars, wolves, and passenger pigeons vanished over the next few decades. In many cases changes in land use affected wild fauna as much as or more than hunting. About 75% of the land in New York State was cleared for farming and settlement by 1890, and this dramatically reduced animal habitat. Cottontail rabbits and squirrels remained plentiful, and foxes, ruffed grouse, and various waterfowl were hunted throughout the state.

DEER HUNTING

Deer are New York State's foremost game animal. The Adirondacks have always been a favorite location for deer hunting, and wealthy sportsmen established vast private clubs there in the 1880s and 1890s. Logging of the interior mountains in the 1880s created more of the "edge" habitat, between forests and fields, which deer favored, and as the herd grew, hunters called for regulations to maintain it. In 1887 Theodore Roosevelt organized the Boone and Crockett Club in New York City, whose members included Sen Henry Cabot Lodge, painter Albert Bierstadt, and William Temple Hornaday, the first director of the New York Zoological Society. The club was influential in pushing for regulation of hunting and conservation of game habitat nationwide.

The state established a per person limit of three deer per year in 1886, which was reduced to two in 1892. The use of hounds and the jacklighting of deer with lanterns at night were banned in 1897. Despite these efforts few deer remained outside of the Adirondack and Catskill Mountains by 1900. Licenses were required for nonresidents in 1905 and for residents in 1908, with revenues supporting fish and game programs. In 1909, 12,100 deer were taken, and in 1912 the state restricted the hunt to deer with antlers at least 3 inches (7.6 cm) long. There are separate seasons for various game animals, usually set to avoid breeding periods.

As farms reverted to forest and wild land in the 20th century, deer populations increased statewide, and deer hunting became widely popular outside of the Adirondacks. Seasons were

The Turkey Shoot, by Tompkins Harrison Matteson, 1857.

determined by individual counties beginning in 1930, and all of the state's nonurban counties had legalized deer hunting by 1948. Deer hunting was increasingly regulated with separate rules for northern and southern zones. Bow hunting was allowed beginning in 1929 with a separate season established in 1948. Seasons for hunting with muzzle-loading firearms were established in 1977. With increasing deer populations becoming problematic in some regions, the state began a controlled return to the hunting of deer without antlers starting in Steuben Co in 1941. The state issues Deer Management Permits that allow limited hunting of antlerless deer for several specific ecological areas. In 2001 new hunters are required to take a 10-hour training course, and a separate course is required for bow hunters.

Deer hunting increased in popularity until the 1980s, with license sales peaking at about 800,000. The number dropped to about 650,000 resident and 44,000 nonresident licenses in the 1999–2001 season, with over 200,000 deer taken each year from a population of over 1 million. Hunting laws have been administered by a series of evolving agencies, beginning with the Fisheries, Game, and Forest Commission in 1895 and since 1970 by the Department of Environmental Conservation.

Other Game Populations

Black bears also returned as woodland habitat increased during the 20th century. There are as many as 5,000 bears in separate populations in the Adirondacks, Catskills, and western Southern Tier, and hunters annually take between 500 and 750, most incidentally while deer hunting. Through much of the century, hunters also avidly pursued Chinese ring-necked pheasants, first released on Gardiners Island in 1892 and then near Geneseo (Livingston Co) in 1903. The Geneseo birds were the progenitors of millions that lived in the counties bordering the Great Lakes. In 1968 more than 500,000 birds were taken, but changing farming practices were already reducing suitable habitat, and fewer than 170,000 were taken annually by the 1990s, probably the majority of those raised by the state-operated game farms.

The decline of pheasant hunting was balanced by the surge in popularity of turkey hunting in the 1980s. Some wild turkeys filtered into the state from Pennsylvania and were augmented by an aggressive trap-and-transfer program that resulted in large flocks in most of the state by 2000. Moose returned in the 1990s, migrating from Canada and New England. There was a breeding population of several dozen by 2000, but whether there will ever be a huntable population is open to question.

Despite the loss of land to urban sprawl and the posting of private property, hunting continued to be a popular activity and a boon to the state's tourist economy at the end of the 20th century. Hunters remained active through the purchase of their own lands, agreements with private landowners, state-sponsored cooperative programs, and the use of extensive public lands, including about 180,000 acres (73,000 ha) of Wildlife Management Areas and nearly 3.6 million acres (1.5 million ha) of state forests and forest preserves.

Hammond, S. H. *Wild Northern Scenes* (1857; repr Harrison, NY: Harbor Hill Books, 1979)
Jamieson, Paul. *The Adirondack Reader* (Lake George, NY: Adirondack Mountain Club, 1982)
Severinghaus, C. W., and C. P. Brown. "History of the White-Tailed Deer in New York," *New York Fish and Game Journal*, July 1956

John C. Pitarresi

Huntington. Town (pop 195,289) and locality (pop 18,403) in NW Suffolk Co. Settlers from New England bought land from the Matinecock Indians in 1653; the earliest town minutes date from 1658. Originally functioning apart from both New England and New Netherland, Huntington came under New York Colony control in 1664. Settlement clustered near the Town Spot, the present village green. The colonial economy was a mix of farming and maritime pursuits, including coastal trading, whaling, and shipbuilding, although there was also a brickyard and a tannery. In June 1774 Huntington adopted the Declaration of Rights affirming that taxation without representation was a violation of the rights of British subjects. Residents suffered for having done so after the defeat of American forces at the Battle of Long Island in August 1776, when the island was occupied by British forces that established a garrison at Huntington.

After the Revolution Huntington was rebuilt and established a post office in 1799. The commercial center shifted westward to the present downtown. Northport became a shipbuilding center, and Cold Spring Harbor a whaling port. With the arrival of the Long Island Rail Road (1867) growth accelerated. Wealthy New York City residents created so-called Gold Coast estates, especially along the shore, while the middle class enjoyed several resorts, including Cold Spring Harbor. Brickmaking was an important industry at Lloyd Harbor and Fort Salonga in the late 19th century, and pottery was made at Huntington Harbor. There was abundant civic endeavor in the 20 years around the turn of the 20th century, including waterworks, an electric company, a library (1892), the Town Hall (1910), and a new firehouse (1911) housing Long Island's first motorized fire engines. The Great Depression halted growth, but after World War II the prewar population of 32,000 exploded, reaching 126,000 by 1960. The Northern State Parkway was built across town in 1949–52, and the Long Island Expressway reached Rte 110 in 1962, rendering the town even more accessible for commuters. Population growth continued at a reduced but steady rate to 2000. The town is governed by a town board of the supervisor and four part-time members, elected at large to four-year terms. Landmarks include Jaynes Hill, at 401 feet (122.2 m) the highest point on Long Island, the Heckscher Museum of Art, and Eatons Neck Lighthouse (1799). Famous residents include Walt Whitman, whose birthplace is a state historic site, and Fred Waller, who is credited with the 1925 invention of water skiing.

Robert C. Hughes

Huntington, William Reed (*b* Lowell, Mass, 20 Sept 1838; *d* Nahunt, Mass, 26 July 1909). Episcopal priest and church leader. Educated at Harvard College and Norwich University, a military preparatory school in Vermont, he studied for the ministry under Frederick D. Huntington (later first Episcopal bishop of Central New York). He was ordained in 1862 and served for 21 years at All Saints Church in Worcester, Mass. In 1883 he was called to be rector of Grace Church in New York City. Despite many other offers, including a number of bishoprics, he served the rest of his ministry at Grace Church.

Because of his active role in national church affairs he was often considered the leading Episcopal priest of his era. Throughout his ministry Huntington emphasized four key concerns. In *The Church-Idea* (1870) he advocated the uniting of American Christians on the four principles of Scripture, the ancient creeds, the sacraments of Baptism and the Lord's Supper, and the historic episcopate. These principles became the basis of the Chicago-Lambeth Quadrilateral, which has been the fundamental ecumenical document for Episcopalians since 1886 and for other Anglicans since 1888. Also concerned with women's ministry, he championed the deaconess movement within the Episcopal Church. Huntington was the principal architect behind the 1892 revision of the *American Book of Common Prayer,* and many of his more far-reaching reforms were later incorporated into the 1928 *Prayer Book.* A strong advocate for the cathedral movement, he served as a trustee for the Episcopal Cathedral of St. John the Divine in New York City from 1887 to 1909, taking an active role in its design.

Woolverton, John F. "William Reed Huntington and Church Unity: The Historical and Theological Background of the Chicago-Lambeth Quadrilateral" (PhD diss, Columbia Univ, 1963)

Robert Bruce Mullin

Huntington Bay. Village (pop 1,496) in Huntington (Suffolk Co). Huntington Bay was the site of Nathan Hale's landing in 1776 en route to New York City to spy on British forces. It remained agricultural until large estates were built in the late 19th century. The most prominent resident was coal, steel, and real estate magnate August Heckscher (1848–1941), who was a generous local benefactor and gave the village, which incorporated in 1924, a park and the Heckscher Museum of Art in 1917. From 1906 to 1957 the famed Chateau des Beaux Arts operated as a hotel and dining casino. Musician Harry Chapin (1942–81) was a resident.

Robert C. Hughes

Huntington Station. Locality (pop 29,910) in Huntington (Suffolk Co). Formerly a privately owned racetrack known as Fairground, it became the location of the railroad station serving Huntington in 1867. Its post office was called Fairground from 1890 to 1912, after which it was changed to Huntington Station. Often a gateway for immigrants, Huntington Station was made an urban renewal area in the 1960s, its downtown business district demolished but never rebuilt. Home to a thriving if poor immigrant community, Huntington Station remained the focus of revitalization efforts in 2003.

Robert C. Hughes

Hurley. Town (pop 6,564) in central Ulster Co. Settled by the Dutch in 1662 as Nieuwe Dorp, the area was renamed Hurley in 1669 and officially formed by a town patent in 1708. In 1777 it served briefly as the state capital. Sojourner Truth (?1797–1883) was born into slavery in Hurley, where she spent her early years. The Ulster and Delaware (1870) and Ontario and Western (1902) Railroads provided service. As many as 50 bluestone quarries, worked in large part by Irish miners, operated in the 1880s. The construction of Ashokan Reservoir (1907–17) drew a large number of Italian laborers, as well as other immigrants and African Americans. The opening of the reservoir resulted in the loss of several hamlets and a considerable amount of good farmland but there are still rich farms, some raising large quantities of sweet corn. The nearby IBM plant (1955) helped increase population. Hurley Historic District is famous for its street of colonial stone houses, open to the public on the second Saturday of July. The town is the site of the New York Conservatory for the Arts (1986), a musical theater arts education program, and the Hurley School, which was the inspiration for Winslow Homer's paintings *Snap the Whip* and *The Country School.*

Ruth Piwonka

Huron. Town (pop 2,117) in NE Wayne Co. The first non-Indian settlers were about 70 slaves who cleared land for William and Thomas Helm of Virginia *ca* 1796. Bounded on the north by Lake Ontario and on the west by Sodus Bay, the town was formed from Wolcott in 1826 as Port Bay; its name was changed to Huron in 1834. The hamlet of Resort, on the bay, began about 1808 as a shipping port for salt and produce at the terminus of the Old Galen Rd. North Huron formed around a saw- and gristmill (1809), and Huron developed around the town hall (1849). Apples, grapes, and other fruits are grown, and wine is produced. Marshall Farms is a large breeder of pet ferrets. There are numerous summer cottages near the bay and lake. Chimney Bluffs State Park and part of the Lake Shore Marshes State Wildlife Management Area are located in town.

Scott C. Monje

Hurricane Agnes/Flood of 1972. The storm, with maximum winds of 75–95 mph (121–153 kph), was responsible for the most destructive and widespread flooding on record in New York State. Active 15–25 June 1972, the tropical disturbance moved north from the Yucatán Peninsula and was declared a hurricane on 18 June. Hitting the Florida panhandle 19 June and moving over Georgia and the Carolinas, it traveled out to the Atlantic before returning to land in New York State. By 19–20 June rain from the storm caused numerous homes in the greater New York City area to flood, necessitating rescues by boat. Roads including the Bronx River, Hutchinson River, Saw Mill River, and Taconic Parkways became impassable. The storm made landfall in New York State on 22 June, moving north toward Poughkeepsie, and then turned westerly and hovered for several days over the New York–Pennsylvania border. Heavy rains caused extensive flooding of the Allegheny, Susquehanna, and Chemung Rivers; a dam broke at Big Flats near Elmira, spurring the evacuation of 20,000 people; tens of thousands more were evacuated from communities like Corning, Hornell, Olean, Salamanca, and Wellsville. More limited flooding occurred on the Genesee River south of Rochester. National Guard troops were activated to assist with rescue and cleanup. Agnes was the costliest mainland US hurricane up to that time; New York State suffered approximately $703 million in damages, and at least 24 deaths in the state were attributed to the storm. Because of the severity and extent of the damages, 14 counties were declared federal disaster areas, making federal funds available to them for recovery. The storm spurred extensive work on flood-control measures for the state's waterways to prevent a recurrence of catastrophic flooding.

Report of Flood Tropical Storm Agnes, June 1972: Summary Report (Buffalo: US Department of the Army, Buffalo District, Corps of Engineers, 1973)

Brian W. Rossmann

hurricane of 1938. On 21 Sept 1938 a devastating hurricane struck New York State without warning, affecting the Lower Hudson region, New York City, and Long Island. The storm first hit land in New York State at 3 PM and caused local flooding and power outages. Although a dozen lives were lost, New York City itself was only lightly scathed. In the Lower Hudson region the hurricane came after four days of rain, flooding much of Westchester Co. Several homes in the northern suburbs were damaged, and hundreds of trees were downed, making roads impassable, but there was no loss of life. Long Island bore the brunt of the hurricane, whose center ran through Babylon (Suffolk Co). Coastal communities along the barrier dunes from south central Suffolk Co to the East End suffered the most damage. Waves as high as 50 feet (15 m) crashed upon the shore, submerging low-lying areas and rendering evacuation by sea impossible. Heavy wind and water erosion created the Shinnecock Inlet and widened Moriches Inlet. Impassable roads, flooding, and uncertainty over which summer homes were occupied or vacant hampered rescue efforts. At least 50 people lost their lives on Long Island. Thousands of homes were damaged and hundreds destroyed, and communities lost outside contact when telephone poles fell. Millions of trees were uprooted, including some of the oldest on Long Island. Long Island's fishing industry barely survived the storm because of the extensive loss of boats, and farmers struggled with the devastation of crops and livestock. After striking Long Island, the hurricane continued northward and caused more deaths and destruction in New England. In total the hurricane of 1938 claimed nearly 700 lives, 100 of them in New York State.

Allen, Everett S. *A Wind to Shake the World: The Story of the 1938 Hurricane* (Boston: Little, Brown, 1976)

Gregory Dehler

hurricanes. Violent cyclones that originate in equatorial waters between June and November, with wind speeds from 74 to over 200 mph (119–322 kph). In addition to the damage potential from high wind velocities, the associated very low air pressures lead to a buildup of water between the storm and the coastline, immersing large areas of shoreline. Coastal and lowland flooding are behind 90% of fatalities related to hurricanes. The most vulnerable areas in the state are eastern Long Island, New York City, and the lower Hudson Valley, but some storms, notably Hurricane Agnes (23 June 1972), track inland, crossing New York State farther west and causing severe flooding.

Some of the most notable hurricanes in the state's history include the Great Gale of 1815 (21–23 September), which caused tides to rise 12 feet (4 m) above normal, inundating coastal towns and requiring numerous rescues by boat from rooftops and second-story windows in Manhattan. Making landfall near what is now Center Moriches (Suffolk Co), the storm of 3 Sept 1821 flooded New York City's Battery and washed ships ashore on Rockaway Beach in Queens Co. Another memorable storm was the September Gale of '69 (8 Sept 1869). The hurricane of 21 Sept 1938 caused enormous damage on Long Island, creating waves 50 feet (15 m) high, destroying homes and boats, and decimating the fishing industry. Wind and water erosion created the Shinnecock Inlet and widened Moriches Inlet, and 700 people died, 100 of them in New York State. Hurricane Agnes (15–25 June 1972) centered on the same area before moving on through southern and western New York State, where it caused the most destructive flooding in the state's history.

Some recent non-hurricanes, such as the Ash Wednesday storm of 6 Mar 1960, the Halloween storm of 31 Oct 1991, and the "storm of the century" on 12–14 Mar 1993 are examples of recent coastal storms that have caused as much damage as or more damage than hurricanes Brenda (1960), Donna (1960), David (1979), Gloria (1985), Bob (1991), and Alberto (1994). The National Oceanic and Atmospheric Administration (NOAA) reports 9 hurricanes making landfall in New York State in the 20th century; 3 category I (winds 74–95 mph/119–153 kph); 1 category II (winds 96–110 mph/155–177 kph); and 5 category III storms (winds 111–139 mph/179–224 kph), with no category IV or V storms.

Elsner, James B., and A. Birol Kara. *Hurricanes of the North Atlantic: Climate and Society* (New York: Oxford Univ Press, 1999)

Ludlum, David M. *Early American Hurricanes, 1492–1870* (Boston: American Meteorological Society, 1963)

C. G. Rose

Hyde, Edward [Viscount Cornbury] (*b* ?London, 28 Nov 1661; *d* London, 31 Mar 1723). Colonial governor and military officer. Born to a prominent family, Viscount Cornbury was the first cousin of Queen Mary II and Queen Anne owing to the marriage of his aunt, Anne Hyde (1637–71), to the Duke of York, later James II.

Cornbury was educated primarily at L'Academie de Calvin in Geneva, from 1680 to 1682, and was appointed lieutenant colonel of the Royal Regiment of Dragoons in 1683. In the Glorious Revolution of 1688, Viscount Cornbury was the first English officer to defect to the invading Prince William of Orange. His devotion to the Church of England and his connection to the Protestant court of Princess Anne were leading motives in his break from the Catholic James II. Yet, because of Cornbury's defense of Princess Anne's right of succession, William and Mary dismissed him from his regiment. His family entered a time of financial distress from which it never fully recovered.

William eventually appointed Cornbury governor of the royal colony of New York in 1702; Queen Anne added the governorship of New Jersey soon after. Cornbury strengthened New York's defenses during Queen Anne's War (1702–13) and reduced political tensions that had plagued the colony since Leisler's Rebellion in 1689. Long divided by land disputes, New Jersey was less easily tamed. An opposition party in New Jersey, led by landowner and politician Lewis Morris, employed rumor and salacious print to attack Cornbury's reputation and force his recall to England. Among the charges were accusations of financial corruption and transvestism. The New Jersey Assembly subsequently withheld Cornbury's salary, driving him into debt in New York. When he was succeeded as governor by John Lord Lovelace, Baron of Hurley in December 1708, the New York court placed him under house arrest at the suit of his creditors, who feared his departure for England.

On the death of his father in 1709, Cornbury succeeded to the title of third Earl of Clarendon. He returned to England in 1710, where he successfully defended his administration as royal governor. He was appointed to the Privy Council, served as Queen Anne's envoy to the court at Hanover [now in Germany] in 1714, and took a leading role in the House of Lords from 1710 until his death.

Bonomi, Patricia U. *The Lord Cornbury Scandal: The Politics of Reputation in British America* (Chapel Hill: Univ of North Carolina Press, 1998)

Singer, Samuel Weller, *The Correspondence of Henry Hyde, Earl of Clarendon, and of His Brother Laurence Hyde, Earl of Rochester; with the Diary of Lord Clarendon from 1687 to 1690,* 2 vols (London: H. Colburn, 1828)

Patricia U. Bonomi

Hyde Park. Town (pop 20,851) in W central Dutchess Co. Part of the Great Nine Partners (1697), Pawling (1696), and Fauconnier (1703) Patents, it was settled between 1730 and 1740 and named for the royal governor, Edward Hyde, Viscount Cornbury, around 1765. The town was formed from Clinton in 1821. Its river frontage became the site of large estates owned by wealthy families, such as the Roosevelts, Vanderbilts, and Millses, that have became historic sites. Nineteenth-century industries, such as a nail factory and an ice tool factory (1858), shipped goods from river landings. Early in the 20th century violet growing was an important industry. After World War II lower Hyde Park became a Poughkeepsie suburb and its main artery (US 9) the site of shopping malls. In 1972 the Culinary Institute of America opened in one of the former estates.

William P. McDermott

hydrology. See WATER AND HYDROLOGY.

hydropathy. See ALTERNATIVE MEDICINE.

hymnody and gospel hymnody. The singing of hymns goes back three centuries in New York State, accompanied by the composition and publication of music for worship. Songs ranged from metrical psalms to works influenced by religious awakenings, the Sunday school movement, urban revivalism, and developments within denominations. Numerous hymns survived and remain current.

Dutch and French Protestant settlers sang in their languages to identical psalm melodies in early New Amsterdam [now New York City] churches. For the colony's first Psalter in English, *The Psalms of David* (1767), published for the city's Reformed Dutch Church (founded 1628), Philadelphian Francis Hopkinson translated lyrics and adapted tunes from the earlier Dutch Psalter and added hymns of his own. From New England came the singing school movement, which brought forth a number of tune books in New York State, including Thomas Atwill's *New York Collection,* his *New York and Vermont Collection,* and Louis Edson Jr's *Social Harmonist,* all published around 1795 to 1800. Louis Edson Sr composed "Lenox" (to "Blow ye the trumpet, blow"), found in altered form in present-day hymnals. Publication of the first shape-note tune book, *The Easy Instructor,* moved to New York City from Philadelphia in 1802, then Albany in 1805 to serve growing interest in the music outside those cities. Shape-note composers Nehemiah Shumway (1761–1843) and others authored tunes named for New York State locales such as Newburgh (Orange Co), North Salem (Westchester), Whitestown (Oneida Co), and New Lebanon (Columbia Co). Shumway's "Schenectady" and "Ballstown" (for Ballston, Saratoga Co) remain in shape-note repertoires today.

Revivalism and the Patriotic Hymn

The Great Awakening had an impact on New York and other colonies, resulting in widespread use of the psalms and hymns of English reverend Isaac Watts. During the Second Great Awakening, *The Christian Lyre* (1831) was compiled by *The Evangelist's* editor Joshua Leavitt in Brooklyn to aid in the popular revival meetings of Charles Grandison Finney of Jefferson Co and included the folk tune "Pleading Savior" ("Jesus, thou divine companion") and "O sacred head now wounded," both still found in contemporary hymnals. In response to *The Christian Lyre,* composers Thomas Hastings of Utica and Lowell Mason of Boston published *Spiritual Songs for Social Worship* (1833), aiming to provide a more dignified church music. This collection introduced "My faith looks up to thee" by Ray Palmer, later a Congregational pastor in Albany. Hastings, a prolific composer of both hymn texts and tunes, is chiefly remembered for setting "Rock of Ages, cleft for me" to music in 1830. Both text and tune to the popular "We three kings of Orient are" (1857) were written by John Henry Hopkins Jr, an Episcopal clergyman who served churches in New York State. The famous preacher Henry Ward Beecher, pastor of Brooklyn's Plymouth Congregational Church from 1847 to 1887, published the influential *Plymouth Collection* (1855) with musicians Darius E. Jones and John Zundel, remembered as the composer of the tune "Beecher" (1870, "Love divine, all loves excelling").

Rise of the Sunday School

Children's hymns played an important role in the rapidly growing institution of Sunday school, where appropriate verses and music of interest to children were needed. New York State composers influenced by this movement of the 1820s onward include Horace Waters, Philip Phillips, Isaac B. Woodbury, William B. Bradbury, and Robert Lowry. Bradbury, active from 1840, composed several tunes in use today. In 1862 he added music to the poem "Jesus loves me! This I know" by Anna and Susan Warner of Constitution Island (Putnam Co) and to "He leadeth me, O blessed thought" by Joseph H. Gilmore, a pastor and University of Rochester professor. Bradbury, also a music publisher, encouraged blind New York City poet and teacher Fanny Crosby to write hymns. From the 1860s on, using more than 90 pseudonyms, she wrote perhaps 8,000 for Sunday school collections, including "Awake! Awake! O heart of mine!" and "Tell me the story of Jesus." Lowry is best known for "Shall we gather at the river" (1864), written while minister at Brooklyn's Hanson Place Baptist Church, but wrote many others and edited 16 songbooks. Mary Artemesia Lathbury, the "Poet Laureate of Chautauqua," wrote several hymns, including "Day is dying in the west" in 1877 for use at the Chautauqua Assembly.

The Gospel Hymn

The term "gospel hymn" arose in the 1870s from the popular book of that name originally published in New York City by Biglow and Main (1875), successors to William Bradbury. George C. Stebbins, a composer with formal training at Buffalo and Rochester, assisted in editing *Gospel Hymns* and made several contributions such as "Jesus is tenderly calling thee home." The gospel movement reflected work of independent preachers and singers who traveled throughout New York and elsewhere holding revival meetings, often carrying *Gospel Hymns* with them, keeping it in publication for two decades.

THE 20TH CENTURY

Among hymns considered standard, several are of the 20th century and written by New York City ministers and theologians. Henry Van Dyke, author of "Joyful, joyful, we adore thee" (1907, to Beethoven's "Ode to Joy"), Maltbie D. Babcock, author of "This is my Father's world" (1901), and William P. Merrill, who wrote "Rise up, O men of God" (1911) for men's meetings, all served as pastors of Brick Presbyterian Church. Methodist minister Frank Mason North wrote a missionary hymn on the city, "Where cross the crowded ways of life" (1903). Walter Russell Bowie, Episcopal rector and professor, wrote a hymn of the Social Gospel, "O holy city, seen of John," published in *Hymns of the Kingdom* (1910), coedited by Henry Sloan Coffin, hymn translator and later president of Union Theological Seminary. One of the century's most widely sung hymns, "God of grace and God of glory," was written in 1930 for the dedication of Manhattan's Riverside Church by its pastor, Harry Emerson Fosdick. An unusual ascension hymn, "And have the bright immensities received our risen Lord" by Episcopal clergyman and seminary professor Howard Chandler Robbins, was published the following year.

New York City contributed to hymnody in other ways. Musical editor of Episcopal hymnals Charles Winfred Douglas supported the restoration of medieval plainsong melodies to the hymnals of 1916 and 1940. His own works include "St. Dunstan's" (1917, "He who would valiant be"). T. Tertius Noble, composer of "Ora Labora," also contributed to the volumes. Later contributors to Episcopal hymnals included Calvin Hampton, Gerre E. Hancock, David Hurd, David McKinley Williams, and Alec Wyton. The Hymn Society in the United States and Canada was established in New York City in 1922, and Union Theological Seminary produced several influential figures. Clarence Dickinson, founder of Union's School of Sacred Music (1928–74), edited the Presbyterian hymnal of 1933. Dickinson's successor, Hugh Porter, with wife Ethel Porter, edited the *Pilgrim Hymnal* (1958) for the United Church of Christ. Hymnists educated at Union include Austin C. Lovelace, Carlton R. Young, V. Earle Copes, and Russell Schulz-Widmar.

In the late 20th century shape-note or sacred-harp singing gained new audiences, and a gathering of shape-note singers met for the first New York State Sacred Harp Convention at Ithaca in 1989. By 2001 more than 10 local groups were formed statewide.

Cross, Virginia Ann. "The Development of Sunday School Hymnody in the United States of America, 1816–1869." (DMA diss, New Orleans Baptist Theological Seminary, 1985)

Foote, Henry Wilder. *Three Centuries of American Hymnody* (Cambridge, Mass: Harvard Univ Press, 1940)

Wilhoit, Melvin Ross. "A Guide to the Principal Authors and Composers of Gospel Song of the 19th Century." (DMA diss, Southern Baptist Theological Seminary, 1982)

The Cyber Hymnal, http://www.cyberhymnal.org

Harry Eskew

I

IBM. Computer and technology manufacturer. The predecessor firm, Computing-Tabulating-Recording Co (C-T-R) of Endicott (Broome Co), was formed in 1911 under the leadership of Charles R. Flint. It was a merger of International Time Recording Co (ITR) of Endicott, formed in 1900, with the Computing Scale Co of Dayton, Ohio, and Tabulating Machine Co of Washington, DC. ITR had in turn been formed in Endicott in 1900 from the merger of three New York State companies that made time-clock machines: Bundy Manufacturing Co (1889, Binghamton), Dey Time Register Co (1893, Syracuse), and Willard and Frick Manufacturing Co (1894, Rochester). The Tabulating Machine Co had been formed by Buffalo-born and -raised and New York City–educated Herman Hollerith in 1896, whose development of punch-card technology was instrumental in tabulating the 1890 US census in a timely fashion.

In 1914 CTR hired Thomas J. Watson, an aggressive 18-year veteran of the National Cash Register Co, who soon became the company's president. Watson made the leasing of Hollerith sorters a cornerstone of the business and in 1924 renamed the company the International Business Machines Corp. The name change reflected international clientele and operations that burgeoned following World War I. That year the firm had plants in Endicott, Washington, Dayton, France, and Germany and employed about 3,500 people worldwide. Watson's support of IBM in Germany received the personal approbation of Adolf Hitler, a later embarrassment. Its primary business was in automated methods of recording and assembling data using printed, punched paper cards. Maintenance of a sales division as important as manufacturing was key to IBM operations when sales personnel became leaders and advisers in product development. Watson introduced the terse motto "Think" to employees, which became a symbol of the company, as was the unofficial dress code of dark suits and white shirts worn by IBM men. An exponent of "welfare capitalism" in the 1930s, IBM was one of the country's first companies to offer retirement benefits and paid vacations.

Production of typewriters, achieved with the acquisition of Electromatic Typewriters of Rochester in 1933, joined production of machines for accounting and banking needs at Endicott. This was followed by wartime manufacture of some three dozen gun, aircraft device, and ordnance parts. Engineers also worked with different universities to build the automatic sequence controlled calculator (ASCC) in 1944, followed by the electronic numerical integrator and computer (ENIAC) for use at the army's proving grounds in Aberdeen, Md, in 1946, and the selective sequence electronic calculator (SSEC) in 1948, based on a Harvard graduate student's concept of digital computing. All three were gymnasium-size machines designed to do mathematical calculations for ballistics and other sciences. After World War II, manufacturing and circuit-board technologies were the focus of Endicott research.

IBM's second major manufacturing center was built at Poughkeepsie in 1942 and became the site of electric printing systems engineering and manufacture in 1944. An experimental version of the "typeball" was introduced at Poughkeepsie in 1946 and was offered commercially to consumers in the 1961 IBM Selectric typewriter. IBM's first electronic computer was the 701 or "Defense Calculator" developed at Poughkeepsie's South Road Lab in 1952, the company's answer to Remington Rand's Univac. Nineteen of the enormous 701 machines, operating with vacuum tubes, were built between 1952 and 1954. The early computing language FORTRAN (FORmula TRANslation) was developed at Poughkeepsie in 1954, the year a new research lab was built. In 1958 Poughkeepsie produced the 7000-series mainframes, IBM's first solid-state, transistorized machines.

Federal work was expanded in the 1950s with the new Airborne Computer Laboratory at Vestal (Broome Co) in 1954, followed by a large facility at Kingston (Ulster Co) in 1956, and IBM Owego (Tioga Co) in 1957. Kingston and Vestal were two of four sites in the 1950s working on magnetic "sliders" to read and write computer data. Kingston also worked on project SAGE (Semi-Automatic Ground Environment) to build air defense computers; an air force BOMARC interceptor missile at Cape Canaveral, Fla, was launched from Kingston in 1958. It also produced the Russian translation machine shown at the 1964 World's Fair. IBM System/360 of 1964, the first computer with separate components configured to suit customers' needs, had magnetic media storage drums developed at Kingston. This was a major success, boosting IBM's share of the computer market, and IBM became 1 of the 10 largest US companies. Cathode-ray-tube displays and air traffic control and cryptographic systems were other Kingston products of the 1960s and 1970s.

Additional New York State facilities built in the 1960s included the Thomas J. Watson Research Center, Yorktown Heights (Westchester Co), opened in 1961; two manufacturing plants at East Fishkill (Dutchess Co), 1963 and 1964; and new corporate headquarters at Armonk (Westchester Co), 1964. In 1961 IBM was estimated to have 81% of the computer market. Its industry dominance was reflected in company expansion but brought a federal antitrust suit in 1969 (dropped in 1982).

In the 1970s and 1980s IBM facilities in New York State continued to work on products and computer networking under myriad corporate divisions. Research labs and plants produced the floppy disk for information storage, the scanning grocery check-out system, and a consumer transaction facility for automated banking. IBM introduced its personal computer in 1981. IBM Kingston made a major investment in plasma flat-screen display development in the 1980s.

By the late 1980s the computer industry was moving away from corporate consumers, the source of IBM's strength, to individual consumers, and numerous companies began to succeed in the personal computer marketplace. The 1980s also brought attempts to unionize IBM workers, efforts that had little or no support at New York State sites even into the 1990s, when IBM moved some manufacturing and support services jobs to independent contractors and foreign countries, and benefits began to be eroded. Downturns in business and efforts to restructure the company under CEO Louis V. Gerstner Jr, hired in 1993, had wide impact but were felt especially hard in the mid–Hudson Valley when the IBM Kingston plant, which once employed 6,200 people, closed in 1995. IBM Owego, which once had 5,000 employees, was sold to Loral Aerospace in 1994. IBM Poughkeepsie saw its lowest employment number that year at 5,000 workers, and IBM East Fishkill went to 4,100 in 1996 (down from about 9,200 in 1993) even though a new research facility was built in 1990.

In 1982 the two IBM facilities in Dutchess Co employed nearly 25,000 people, more than 23% of all workers in the county. By the end of 2001 fewer than 12,000 of those jobs (10% of the county total) remained. In 2002 local entrepreneurs formed Endicott Interconnect Technologies (EIT) to purchase the IBM site at Endicott. IBM then leased back office space for approximately 2,000 administrative personnel and became an EIT customer for its circuit board products. IBM Poughkeepsie employees continued to develop and build the company's largest computers and numbered 5,800 at the end of 2002, although the IBM Poughkeepsie golf course designed by Robert Trent Jones in 1944 was sold in 2003. IBM East Fishkill employed 5,400 at the end of 2002 and expanded with a new microchip manufacturing plant in 2003, but the trend continued away from computer manufacture to computer-related consulting. IBM headquarters remained at Armonk in 2003, and the company still operated at several other Westchester Co locales, as well as in Dutchess, Broome, Orange, and Rockland Cos; New York City; eight other sites in the United States; one in Canada; one in Mexico; one in Israel; seven in Europe; two in India; and nine in Asia. It employed 316,000 people worldwide.

Bashe, Charles J., et al. *IBM's Early Computers* (Cambridge, Mass: MIT Press, 1985)

Carroll, Paul. *Big Blues: The Unmaking of IBM* (New York: Crown Publishers, 1993)

Garr, Doug. *IBM Redux: Lou Gerstner and the Business Turnaround of the Decade* (New York: Harper Business, 1999)

John Tepper Marlin

ice ages. An informal term for the global climate changes of the last 2 million years. Deep-sea climate records show that there have been at least six major and many more minor glacials, or cold stages, during this time. These are separated by interglacials, or warm stages, such as Earth is experiencing at present. Glacial-interglacial cycles are driven by small and gradual changes in Earth's orbit. These changes vary the seasonal distribution of solar radiation over many thousands of years, and, in general, glacials occur when summers are colder in the Northern Hemisphere. This allows continental ice sheets to develop at midlatitudes of North America and Eurasia and triggers a complex series of feedbacks within Earth's climate system to cause worldwide cooling. Peak glacial conditions during the past few glacial-interglacial cycles of the Pleistocene epoch (1.81 million–10,000 years ago) have been spaced about 100,000 years apart.

Retreat of the Laurentide Ice Sheet

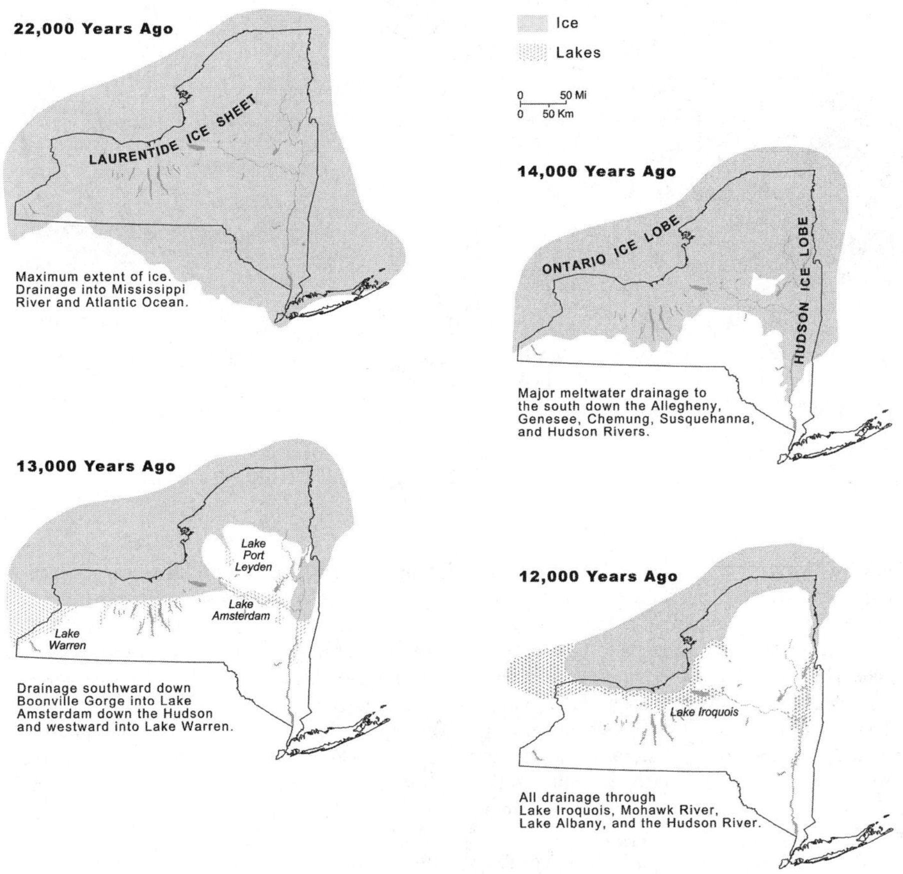
22,000 Years Ago
LAURENTIDE ICE SHEET
Maximum extent of ice. Drainage into Mississippi River and Atlantic Ocean.
Ice
Lakes
0 50 Mi
0 50 Km
14,000 Years Ago
ONTARIO ICE LOBE
HUDSON ICE LOBE
Major meltwater drainage to the south down the Allegheny, Genesee, Chemung, Susquehanna, and Hudson Rivers.
13,000 Years Ago
Lake Port Leyden
Lake Amsterdam
Lake Warren
Drainage southward down Boonville Gorge into Lake Amsterdam down the Hudson and westward into Lake Warren.
12,000 Years Ago
Lake Iroquois
All drainage through Lake Iroquois, Mohawk River, Lake Albany, and the Hudson River.

NOTE: All dates are approximate and are in uncalibrated radiocarbon years before present.

SOURCE: Adapted from Y. W. Isachsen, et al, *Geology of New York: A Simplified Account* (1991).

In North America, the Laurentide ice sheet developed during each glacial and then melted away during each interglacial. This ice sheet was centered in the Hudson Bay area, and at its maximum extent covered about 5 million mi^2 (13 million km^2) of Canada and the northern United States. There is evidence for its southern margin reaching into New York State during two glacials, in the Wisconsinan stage between 40,000 and 12,000 ^{14}C years ago and during an earlier glacial that is presumed to have been the Illinoian stage. (^{14}C years are uncalibrated radiocarbon-derived ages that have not been corrected for changes in atmospheric abundance of ^{14}C through time.) Ice flow was focused into distinct ice sheet lobes that occupied the Champlain and Hudson Valleys in the east and the Lake Ontario and Lake Erie basins in the west. Thinner and slower flowing ice overspread intervening areas. Rapid ice flow southwestward down the Lake Erie basin drew ice away from adjacent areas of the Appalachian Upland and left a small area near Salamanca (Cattaraugus Co) as the only part of New York State that has never been glaciated. The area of Long Island south of the Harbor Hill Moraine in the west and the Ronkonkoma Moraine in the east consists of materials deposited by the meltwaters of the ice sheet.

Glacial Erosion

The main effect of erosion by glacial ice is to make valleys wider, deeper, and straighter. Ice will be thicker and flow faster over preexisting river valleys, and so these will be preferentially enlarged if they are parallel to ice flow. For example, the major lake valleys of the Finger Lakes region were aligned with ice flowing southward from the Lake Ontario area and so were eroded into the broad valleys that we see today. In contrast, the glens of this region were at right angles to ice flow and beneath thinner and slower-flowing ice covering the hilltops and so were not glacially enlarged. Broad glacial valleys from which modern streams drain in opposite directions are called through valleys and are found in many areas of the Appalachian Upland. These show that significant glacial erosion also occurred to the south, east, and west of the Finger Lakes region.

The Laurentide ice sheet at its maximum extent was thicker than the highest peaks of the Adirondacks. Many of these summits appear smoothed and rounded on their north sides because of glacial abrasion, where rocks and sediment embedded in the bottom of the ice sheet wore down the underlying bedrock in a sandpaper-like effect. The south faces of these peaks are often rough and craggy because glacial plucking ripped out chunks of bedrock from the downflow mountainside. Parallel scratches and grooves called striations are caused by abrasion and record the direction of ice flow. Striations can be found in many areas of New York State and are best developed in relatively soft rocks such as limestone and dolostone.

Glacial Deposition

Distinctly different glacial deposits formed beneath, at the margin, and beyond the Laurentide Ice Sheet. These three depositional zones migrated northward across New York State as the ice sheet retreated back toward Canada.

Till is an unsorted mixture of clay, silt, sand, gravel and boulders deposited directly from glacial ice. The exact composition of till reflects the type of rock from which the sediment was derived. For example, till in the Adirondack Upland tends to be sandy, whereas till in the Erie-Ontario Lowland is much finer grained and clay rich. Drumlins are small hills that are often composed of till and that formed beneath the Laurentide ice sheet. Glacial erratics are boulders of a rock type that is not local to an area and, like striations, give clues as to ice flow directions. Common erratics in New York State include igneous and metamorphic rocks that were transported from Canada and deposited on the sedimentary strata of the Appalachian Upland.

End moraines are accumulations of sediment that formed at the outer edges of Laurentide ice sheet. As such, they mark places where the ice margin was stationary for a few years following an advance or during retreat. They are usually composed of till and appear as ridges, mounds, and hummocks that parallel the former ice lobe edge. In some areas meltwater formed poorly sorted deposits of sand and gravel against the ice margin. These are called kame moraines if deposited at the end of a lobe or kame terraces if they accumulated between the side of the lobe and a hillside. Eskers are sinuous sand and gravel ridges that formed in meltwater tunnels in the ice sheet and are typically oriented at right angles to nearby end moraines.

Glacial meltwater carried sediment beyond the Laurentide ice sheet margin. Glacial river deposits of horizontally bedded sand and gravel are called outwash, and they form deposits hundreds of feet thick in some valleys of the Appalachian Upland. Kettles are depressions, often filled with water, that formed when ice buried beneath outwash melted away. Clay and silt settled out in proglacial lakes that formed wherever water was trapped between the ice margin and adjacent elevated areas. Beaches and deltas developed around the margins of these lakes and mark their changing water levels during retreat of the Laurentide ice sheet. Some of these proglacial lakes drained catastrophically, and dry channels such as at Clark Reservation near Jamesville (Onondaga Co) and Altona Flat Rocks (Clinton Co) record scouring by these outburst floods.

Wisconsinan Glacial Events

Almost all of the glacial deposits at the land surface of New York State today were formed during the Wisconsinan stage. During this time the Laurentide ice sheet eroded older glacial deposits, with the exception of a few sheltered sites or places beyond the limit of Wisconsinan glaciation.

The Laurentide ice sheet advanced into western and central New York State around 40,000–35,000 ^{14}C years ago during the middle Wisconsinan. The ice margin retreated in western New York State and maybe elsewhere before readvancing after 24,000 ^{14}C years ago during the late Wisconsinan. The maximum stand occurred about 22,000 ^{14}C years ago when the southern limit of ice extended southeast from Salamanca, through northern Pennsylvania and New Jersey, to reach the Atlantic Ocean at Long Island.

Retreat from the late Wisconsinan maximum was underway by 19,000 ^{14}C years ago. Ice may have withdrawn into the Erie-Ontario Lowland before readvancing to the Valley Heads moraine about 14,000 ^{14}C years ago. This major moraine marks the southern end of the Finger Lakes valleys and forms the drainage divide between the Chesapeake and the St. Lawrence watersheds. Meltwater drainage was focused into the Allegheny, Susquehanna, and Hudson Rivers.

As retreat continued after 14,000 ^{14}C years ago, proglacial lakes developed in north-draining valleys where water was trapped by the ice margin. These lakes in western, central, and northern New York State expanded and merged as the ice margin withdrew northward, and water levels sequentially dropped as successively lower outlet channels emerged from under the retreating ice. Proglacial lakes also developed in the Mohawk Valley between the Ontario ice lobe and the Hudson ice lobe, and in the Hudson and Champlain Valleys. The last of these proglacial lakes drained as the Laurentide ice sheet withdrew north of the Adirondack Upland about 12,000 ^{14}C years ago.

LONG-TERM EFFECTS OF GLACIATION

The great weight of the Laurentide ice sheet pushed the land surface beneath it downward, and this glacio-isostatic depression was greatest in northern New York State, where the ice was thickest. Marine water flooded the St. Lawrence–Champlain Lowland to elevations as much as 525 feet (160 m) above modern sea level immediately following deglaciation. This Champlain Sea lasted for about 1,700 years and gradually drained as postglacial rebound raised the area back above sea level.

Rivers and soils of New York State were also greatly affected by glaciation. The Allegheny River formerly drained northward into Lake Erie but was permanently diverted southward into Pennsylvania during the Pleistocene by deposition of end moraines at Steamburg (Cattaraugus Co). The enlargement of many valleys during glaciation produced misfit rivers that today are disproportionately small relative to their valleys. The poor infiltration into clay-rich soils on former proglacial-lake beds resulted in the formation of wetlands such as the Montezuma National Wildlife Refuge. In contrast, the productive Palmyra soils developed on well-drained outwash deposits.

See also GEOLOGY AND PLATE TECTONICS.

Cronin, Thomas M. *Principles of Paleoclimatology* (New York: Columbia Univ Press, 1999)
Isachsen, Yngvar W., et al, eds. *Geology of New York: A Simplified Account,* 2d ed. (Albany: NYS Museum, 2000)
Muller, E. H., and Calkin, P. E. "Timing of Pleistocene Glacial Events in New York State," *Canadian Journal of Earth Sciences* 30 (1993): 1829–45
Pair, Donald L., and Rodrigues, Cyril G. "Late Quaternary Deglaciation of the Southwestern St. Lawrence Lowland, New York and Ontario," *Geological Society of America Bulletin* 105 (1993): 1151–64

David Barclay

Ice boating on Keuka Lake.

ice boating. Ice boats probably originated in northern Europe and were introduced to New York by Dutch settlers in the 18th century. Ice boating expanded during the second half of the 19th century, with regional variations in hull and rig form suited to environmental conditions and needs. The South Bay scooter, native to the Great South Bay off the southern shore of eastern Long Island, is a small flat-bottomed boat with a pointed bow and rounded stern. Capt Wilbur Corwin of Bellport (Suffolk Co) is credited with inventing the first scooter by attaching brass runners to a waterfowl gunning punt in the early 1870s. Lifesaving crews and others favored scooters, which traverse both ice and water, important in winters when the Great South Bay frequently freezes only partially. Ice boats also have a lengthy history as pleasure and racing craft, and the Hudson Valley was a center of ice boat competition and design. The Poughkeepsie Ice Yacht Club started in 1861. John E. Roosevelt organized the Hudson River Ice Yacht Club in 1869; his nephew, Franklin D. Roosevelt, was at one time an officer of the club. The largest ice boat of the Hudson fleet was John E. Roosevelt's *Icicle:* 67 feet (20 m) long with a sail area of over 1,000 ft^2 (90 m^2). Long straightaways made the Hudson ideal for ice boating, and racing steam trains where the track ran parallel to the river was a favorite activity. On 20 Jan 1871 the *Icicle* made history when it beat the Chicago Express train on a run between Poughkeepsie and Ossining (Westchester Co). The Hudson River continued to be the focal point of New York State ice boating in the early 20th century, with other venues at Orange and Chautauqua Lakes. Ice boats served as winter rumrunners on lakes bordering Canada during Prohibition. In the 20th century ice boats evolved from traditional wood hull forms steered from the stern to very light hulls, essentially no more than a fiberglass cockpit with steel runners, steered from the bow. The Hudson River Ice Yacht Club continues to promote the sport, while the Saratoga Lake Ice Report encourages ice boating on Saratoga Lake. Other ice boating locales include Rensselaer Co's Long Pond, Wayne Co's Sodus Bay, and Albany Co's Watervliet Reservoir.

Liebers, Arthur. "Iceboating." In *The Complete Book of Winter Sports* (New York: Coward, McCann, 1963)
Schoettle, Edwin J. "Ice Boating." In *Sailing Craft,* ed. Edwin J. Schoettle (New York: Macmillan, 1928)

Daria E. Merwin

ice fishing. Early settlers probably learned techniques of ice fishing from American Indians, who had been using decoys and spearing fish on frozen lakes in what would become New York State since at least AD 1000. Ice fishers have used a variety of devices, collectively known as tip-ups, to tell them when a fish is on their line. On Oneida Lake in the early 1870s, members of the Oneida Community used primitive wooden tip-ups secured to the ice with spikes and fitted with wire loops and reels of linen or cord line that ran through the loops. Walleyes, perch, bass, and ling were among the fish they caught. Sticks about 18 inches (46 cm) long were also used to jig perch eyes and other bait. The ice was cut with long, heavy chisels known as spuds, or with axes. They learned these techniques from James D. Spencer, who had arrived in the area in the 1840s and who probably adopted methods practiced there for many years. On Chautauqua Lake, a center by the 1890s, anglers used wooden decoys in the American Indian fashion to lure fish for spearing and angling. Lake Champlain, the bays and coves on Lake Erie and Lake Ontario, and portions of some Finger Lakes are also popular locations. In the 20th century hand and power augers, electronic fish finders, portable shelters, and special rods, reels, and lines made ice fishing easier. Walleyes, northern pike, perch, bluegills, sunfish, crappies, pickerel, and tiger muskellunge are favorite targets. On some waters trout can also be kept. Ice fishers may use two rods or hand lines and up to five tip-ups in New York State. Creel limits for game fish vary by species, and limits for more plentiful, easier-to-catch panfish species were imposed in the 1990s in response to what had been an unregulated, informal commercial fishery on many lakes.

Capossela, Jim. *Ice Fishing: A Complete Guide, Basic to Advanced* (Woodstock, Vt: Countryman Press, 1992)

John C. Pitarresi

ice hockey. King's College School, founded in Windsor, NS, in 1788 by New York loyalists who named their institution after King's College (now Columbia University), holds a unique place in the history of ice hockey. The forerunner of modern ice hockey, derived from field hockey games such as Irish hurley, Scottish shinny, and French hocquet, emerged around

Syracuse Stars home game, 1930s.

1800 on the playing fields and frozen ponds of King's College School. Another prerequisite for the modern game of hockey, artificial ice, was apparently first introduced to North America in New York City by William Newton in 1870, although a more celebrated rink was constructed in the original Madison Square Garden in 1879.

Canadian hockey developed over the course of the 19th century, entering the United States in the century's later decades. The American Amateur Hockey League, formed in 1889, included the St. Nicholas Club, the New York Athletic Club, the Skating Club of Brooklyn, and the Crescent Athletic Club, also of Brooklyn. In 1894 American and Canadian university students who met at Niagara Falls discussed their different versions of the new game and set up a series of matches; the Canadian game prevailed. An ice rink opened at Lexington Ave and 101st St in Manhattan on 14 Dec 1894, and less than a year later the St. Nicholas Arena opened one block from Central Park at Columbus Ave and 66th St. A New Jersey man, Ken Gordon, is credited with assembling the hockey team at St. Nicholas in 1896.

Hobart Amory Hare ("Hobey") Baker, who at Princeton University was considered the best American collegiate player of his day, turned down lucrative offers to turn professional, preferring to remain in New York, starring for the amateur St. Nicholas Club from 1914 to 1916, when he began training as a fighter pilot. Baker was killed at the age of 26, only a month after completing services in World War I, when his plane crashed in December 1918. In his honor, the Hobey Baker Memorial Trophy is awarded each year to the most valuable player in National Collegiate Athletic Association (NCAA) hockey. St. Nicholas continues as a prestigious amateur club whose roster is largely filled by former professional and collegiate players living in the New York City area.

In 2003 there were 107 minor hockey associations statewide, divided by four geographical regions: central, east, north, and west, each with tier I, II, and III skill levels. There are 7 adult men's recreational organizations. Women have 13 established programs, and there is 1 Senior A women's team, the New York Stars. There are 53 programs for girls, 18 high school league programs, and 5 junior programs. Special programs include All-Island Sports Sled Hockey, 3 programs dedicated to the developmentally challenged, and 7 summer league programs.

The 1932 and 1980 Winter Olympics, both held in Lake Placid (Essex Co) at a time when only amateurs were eligible, boosted the fortunes of American hockey. In 1932 the United States team won the silver medal, losing to Canada. In the 22 Feb 1980 "Miracle on Ice," undoubtedly the most famous hockey game ever played in the state, the US team of collegiate players defeated and eliminated the favored Soviet team, which had regularly defeated professional National Hockey League (NHL) all-star teams, and then went on to win the gold medal.

Collegiate Hockey

The Intercollegiate Hockey League began in 1900 with Columbia University, Dartmouth College, Harvard University, Princeton University, and Yale University. Cornell University joined in 1910. There was a noticeable rise in participation after the sport was showcased at the 1932 Lake Placid Winter Olympics. By the 1950s college hockey was the cornerstone of most national teams and US Olympic teams. Rensselaer Polytechnic Institute (RPI) was the first New York school to win the NCAA Division I title, in 1954. Clarkson University, St. Lawrence University, Colgate University, Union College, RPI, and Cornell University play in the Eastern College Athletic Conference (ECAC). Hamilton College and Skidmore College play in the ECAC East Division, and Hobart College, Elmira College, and the Rochester Institute of Technology participate in the ECAC West Division. Several Cornell alumni went on to play in the NHL, including Hall of Fame goaltender Ken Dryden and forwards Joe Nieuwendyk and Kent Manderville. Dryden backstopped Cornell to the 1967 NCAA championship; the school repeated the feat in 1970. The RPI Engineers picked up a second national championship in 1985, led by future NHL star Adam Oates. Thirteen other colleges play hockey in the state, including an eight-team State University of New York Conference. Seven junior colleges also field teams.

Women's ice hockey began as a club event, often to meet Title IX requirements, before it became an established sport. Hamilton College began its women's ice hockey club in 1975; it became a varsity team in 1996. NCAA Division I women's teams include Clarkson University, Colgate University, Cornell University, Niagara University, St. Lawrence University, and Union College. Division III teams include SUNY Buffalo, SUNY Cortland, Elmira College, Hamilton College, Manhattanville College, SUNY Plattsburgh, RPI, Rochester Institute of Technology, and Utica College. In 1994 Erin Whitten of Glens Falls (Warren Co), goaltender for Team USA, became the first winner of the USA Hockey Women's Hockey Player of the Year Award, the equivalent of the Hobey Baker Award.

Professional Hockey

While there are various reports of certain teams paying some players small stipends to suit up for their clubs earlier in the 20th century, it is generally recognized that professional hockey started in the United States in 1925 when the NHL's Hamilton (Ont) Tigers were sold to a group of New York investors for $75,000, and the franchise was moved to Manhattan. The team was renamed the Star Spangled Skaters, although that was changed to the Americans before the team opened the 1925–26 NHL season at Madison Square Garden before about 17,000 fans. Starting in 1926 the Americans had to share home ice at Madison Square Garden with the better-funded New York Rangers, and fan support and publicity were lost to the newer team. The Americans continued through the 1941–42 season, playing as the Brooklyn Americans in their last season (though continuing to play home games in Manhattan) before folding. The Rangers were league champions in their early years, winning the Stanley Cup in 1928, 1933, and 1940 but not again until 1994. The Buffalo Sabres joined the NHL as an expansion franchise for the 1970–71 season. In fall 1972 the New York Islanders, whose home ice is Nassau Veterans Memorial Coliseum in Uniondale (Nassau Co), joined the NHL, and the New York Raiders, whose home ice was Madison Square Garden, joined the World Hockey Association. Although the Raiders folded after one season, the Islanders would become a dominant team, winning four straight Stanley Cups from 1980 through 1983.

Minor league professional hockey arrived in New York State as early as 1928 with the creation of the Buffalo Bisons. The Bisons would remain a fixture in Buffalo (with a brief hiatus in the late 1930s) until 1971, when the city acquired an NHL franchise. Although Rochester and Syracuse both had minor league franchises in the 1930s, it was not until the postwar period that they acquired enduring teams, the Rochester Americans, or Amerks, since 1956, and the Syracuse team under a variety of names, most prominently the Syracuse Blazers, and since 1994, the Syracuse Crunch. There have been teams in localities around the state from Long Island

PROFESSIONAL ICE HOCKEY TEAMS IN NEW YORK STATE

Years in League	Team	League
Albany		
1990–91	Albany Choppers	International Hockey League
1993–	Albany River Rats	American Hockey League
Binghamton		
1973–77	Binghamton Dusters	North American Hockey League
1977–80	Binghamton Broome Dusters	American Hockey League
1977–90	Binghamton Whalers	American Hockey League
1990–97	Binghamton Rangers	American Hockey League
1997–2002	Binghamton BC Icemen	United Hockey League
2002–	Binghamton Senators	American Hockey League
Buffalo		
1928–29	Buffalo Bisons	Canadian Professional Hockey League
1929–36	Buffalo Bisons	International-American Hockey League
1930–31	Buffalo Americans/Majors	American Hockey Association
1931–32	Buffalo Majors	American Hockey Association
1936	Buffalo Bisons	American Hockey League
1940–70	Buffalo Bisons	American Hockey League
1970–	**Buffalo Sabres**	National Hockey League
1975–76	Buffalo Norsemen	North American Hockey League
Clinton (Oneida Co)		
1954–73	Clinton Comets	Eastern Hockey League
Commack (Nassau Co)		
1961–73	Long Island Ducks	Eastern Hockey League
1973–75	Long Island Cougars	North American Hockey League
Elmira		
2000–	Elmira Jackals	United Hockey League
Glens Falls (Warren Co)		
1979–99	Adirondack Red Wings	American Hockey League
1999–2004	Adirondack IceHawks	United Hockey League
2004–	Adirondack Frostbite	United Hockey League
New York City		
1925–41	**New York Americans**	National Hockey League
1926–	**New York Rangers**	National Hockey League
1931–32	Bronx Tigers	Canadian-American Hockey League
1933–34	Bronx Tigers	Eastern Amateur Hockey League
1933–34	New York Athletic Club	Eastern Amateur Hockey League
1933–34	New York–Hamilton Crescents	Eastern Amateur Hockey League
1933–34	Saint Nicholas Hockey Club	Eastern Hockey League
1934–35	New York–Hamilton Crescents	Eastern Hockey League
1935–48	New York Rovers	Eastern Amateur Hockey League
1937–38	Bronx Tigers	Eastern Amateur Hockey League
1941–42	**Brooklyn Americans**	National Hockey League
1942–43	Brooklyn Arma Torpedoes	Eastern Amateur Hockey League
1942–43	Jamaica Hawks (Queens Co)	Eastern Amateur Hockey League
1942–43	Manhattan Arrows	Eastern Amateur Hockey League
1943–44	Brooklyn Crescents	Eastern Amateur Hockey League
1947–49	New York Rovers	Quebec Senior Hockey League
1949–52	New York Rovers	Eastern Amateur Hockey League
1959–61	New York Rovers	Eastern Hockey League
1964–65	New York Rovers	Eastern Hockey League
1972–73	**New York Raiders**	World Hockey Association
1973–74	**New York Golden Blades/New Jersey Knights**	World Hockey Association
1985–86	New York Slapshots	Atlantic Coast Hockey League
Niagara Falls		
1926–30	Niagara Falls Cataracts	Canadian Professional Hockey League
1929–30	Niagara Falls Cataracts	International Hockey League

PROFESSIONAL ICE HOCKEY TEAMS IN NEW YORK STATE (continued)

Years in League	Team	League
Rochester		
1935–36	Rochester Cardinals	International Hockey League
1956–	Rochester Americans	American Hockey League
Sands Point (Nassau Co)		
1942–43	Sands Point Tigers	Eastern Amateur Hockey League
Schenectady		
1981	Schenectady Chiefs	Atlantic Coast Hockey League
Syracuse		
1930–36	Syracuse Stars	International-American Hockey League
1936–40	Syracuse Stars	American Hockey League
1951–54	Syracuse Warriors	American Hockey League
1962–63	Syracuse Braves	Eastern Professional Hockey League
1967–73	Syracuse Blazers	Eastern Hockey League
1973–77	Syracuse Blazers	North American Hockey League
1974–75	Syracuse Eagles	American Hockey League
1979–80	Syracuse Firebirds	American Hockey League
1980	Syracuse Hornets	Eastern Hockey League
1994–	Syracuse Crunch	American Hockey League
Troy (Rensselaer Co)		
1951–59	Troy Bruins	International Hockey League
1952–53	Troy Uncle Sam's Trojans	Eastern Amateur Hockey League
1986–87	Troy Slapshots	Atlantic Coast Hockey League
1990–93	Capital District Islanders	American Hockey League
Uniondale (Nassau Co)		
1972–	**New York Islanders**	National Hockey League
Utica		
1973–77	Mohawk Valley Comets	North American Hockey League
1978–79	Utica Mohawks	Northeastern Hockey League
1979–80	Utica Mohawks	Eastern Hockey League
1981–85	Mohawk Valley Stars	Atlantic Coast Hockey League
1985–87	Mohawk Valley Comets	Atlantic Coast Hockey League
1987–93	Utica Devils	American Hockey League
1993–94	Utica Bulldogs	Colonial Hockey League
1994–97	Utica Blizzard	Colonial Hockey League
1998–2001	Mohawk Valley Prowlers	United Hockey League

Source: Dan Diamond et al, *Total Hockey: The Official Encyclopedia of the National Hockey League* (1998).

Note: Major league franchises appear in bold.

Compiled by Andrew Podnieks

to Niagara Falls, including Binghamton, Glens Falls, and Utica. New York City has had a number of minor league teams, with franchises in the Bronx, Brooklyn, and Queens as well as Manhattan. The comedy *Slap Shot* (1977), which starred Paul Newman and was filmed in part in Syracuse, Utica, and Hamilton (Madison Co), depicted the tough, gritty, and often profane world of minor league hockey in New York State.

Through the 2002–3 season, 67 natives of New York State have played in the NHL. Two have been inducted into the Hall of Fame. Billy Burch, born in Yonkers in 1900, played most of his career (1922–33) with the New York Americans. Joe Mullen, who learned to play hockey on roller skates on the streets of Hell's Kitchen in Manhattan, became during the course of his career (1979–97) the first American-born player to have more than 500 goals and 1,000 assists.

Diamond, Dan, ed. *Total Hockey: The Official Encyclopedia of the National Hockey League* (Kansas City, Mo: Andrews McMeel Publishing, 1998)

Farrington, S. Kip, Jr, *Skates, Sticks, and Men: The Story of Amateur Hockey in the United States* (New York: David McKay, 1972)

Fischler, Stan, and Shirley Fischler. *Everybody's Hockey Book* (New York: Charles Scribner's Sons, 1983)

Andrew Podnieks and Angus Gillespie

ice industry. From the early 19th century to well into the 20th century, ice boxes, supplied by the ice-harvesting and -shipping industry, were a fundamental part of most households. Before they appeared, meat was salted or dried, and perishable items were stored in a cellar or at nearby cold springs. As more of the population moved to towns and cities, however, ice boxes became the only available method of refrigeration, with a typical family using a 25–100 lb (11–45 kg) block of ice every two or three days. Each community had its own source from nearby lakes and ponds.

Although ice was commercially harvested in many regions of the state, the industry centered on the Hudson River, which provided the main supply for New York City, Philadelphia, and points as distant as Cuba. Ice harvesting and shipping were major industries from 1840 to 1925. Harvesting took place from Newburgh (Orange Co), at the "salt line" of ocean water brought in by the tides, north to Albany. Initially, when naturally frozen Hudson River ice was shipped from Coxsackie (Greene Co) to New York City in 1828 and introduced in hotels, many feared that it was "too cold" for good health. Demand grew quickly, however, and by the Civil War the ice industry was fully underway. The leading companies changed names and

Ice harvesting on the Hudson River at Stuyvesant Landing, 1912.

investors, but the Knickerbocker Ice Co had the most icehouses and enjoyed the greatest longevity among the major Hudson River companies. These firms had vertically integrated systems and owned the icehouses, barges, and city delivery routes. Even their horses rotated from the ice to the city streets. Smaller, family-owned operations such as Seaman, Howland, and Bedell, sold ice to local delivery routes or, when the price was right, in wholesale lots to the city suppliers.

Harvest was mainly in January and February. When core samples showed that the ice was thick enough, a "pond" was staked out and the ice marked into squares. A "pond gang" cut the ice with horse-drawn saws, broke it into chunks and floated the ice to shore through harvesting channels opened with a metal-prowed scow. The ice was broken into blocks and sent on a continuously running conveyor to be stored in wooden icehouses, windowless structures some 40 feet (12 m) high and 100–200 feet (30–61m) long, insulated with sawdust. Inside, the blocks slid down a chute to the level being filled. The "house gang" included skilled men called switchers, who would heave each block to the correct location, where it would be carefully positioned and the space between blocks filled with sawdust. Between 1890 and 1910, the average pay for this perilous and hard labor in excruciating cold was usually $1.75 a day; the workday started at around 7 AM and ended about 5 PM. Those who came in at 3 AM to work overtime, feeding the horses and breaking open the channels, could earn an extra dollar. The lowest paid was the muggin boy, who cleaned up the ice after the horses, and the highest paid were the engineers and crew bosses. Some rural schools near the river closed so boys could work on the crews and girls could help with the meals. By about 1870 continuous-flow ice elevators and other special harvesting equipment on land, run by steam power, greatly increased the annual harvest. By the turn of the 20th century, one icehouse loaded 43 blocks per minute, each measuring 22 x 15 in^2 (142 x 97 cm^2) and weighing about 230 pounds (104 kg). The icehouses were emptied beginning in March when tows of 10–12 barges made the first trips to city markets. Auxiliary craft called bumboats supplied beer, peanuts, tobacco, and other items to men unloading icehouses in isolated locations or on islands.

At its height (1900–1910), there were at least 8,000 men, 1,000 horses, and almost 100 barges involved in harvesting, packing, shipping, and delivering ice on the Hudson. There were more than 170 commercial icehouses along the Hudson, ranging in capacity from 10,000 to 100,000 tons (9,070–90,720 MT). In all, about 5 million tons (4.5 million MT) were usually in storage by the end of the harvest.

The size of the industry led to allegations and investigations of corruption and monopolistic practices by some of the larger companies. There were questions as well about the purity of the ice from various sources. Ice companies would urge consumers to "Buy Only PURE Lake Ice." In Central New York, harvesting ice from the Erie Canal was discouraged. The availability of artificially produced ice and alternative means of refrigeration led to a decline of ice harvests. By 1940 most homes had electric refrigerators, but a few small one- or two-person ice-harvesting operations continued in more rural areas. Ice delivery routes were found in cities up until 1950, but most of what they delivered was artificially made. Spectacular fires destroyed some icehouses along the Hudson River; others were converted in the 1930s for mushroom farming. In the early 21st century, few remnants remain, and ice harvesting only exists as a wintertime activity for a few museums. Weather permitting, the Tully Area Historical Society (Onondaga Co), holds an ice-harvesting event on a nearby lake, and the Greene County Historical Society has an ice-harvesting exhibit at the Bronck House.

Cumming, Richard O. *The American Ice Harvests: A Historical Study in Technology, 1800–1918* (Berkeley: Univ of California Press, 1949)

Barbara S. Rivette

ice storms. Prolonged spells during which ice accumulates instead of snow, often to the point of regional, statewide, or national emergency. While less frequent than snowstorms, ice storms are particularly hazardous to life and property. The critical difference between them is the vertical temperature profile. During snowstorms the lower atmosphere remains below the freezing point, 32°F (0°C), keeping precipitation in the form of snow. With ice storms a significant portion of the lower atmosphere remains above freezing, allowing the precipitation to melt on its way to the ground. A shallow layer of subfreezing air near the surface causes the rain to freeze on contact with the ground, forming freezing rain. When these conditions persist, ice can accumulate significantly. If the subfreezing layer near the surface is deeper, the rain will refreeze before striking the ground, forming sleet, a hazardous condition in its own right. Local terrain features can play a significant role in the development of ice storms. Valleys can trap cold air near the ground while warmer air is transported aloft, leading to a potential localized icing event.

The effects of an ice storm can linger after the storm passes. Travel may be impossible for days because of the accumulation of ice on roads and walkways. Widespread power outages may result from the weight of ice building up on power lines and may not be repaired for extended periods because of the simultaneous difficulty of reaching the downed lines. Extensive tree damage can result from significant ice accumulation. New York State has experienced several major ice storms in recent times. On 4–5 Dec 1964 a particularly devastating event struck the Mohawk and upper Hudson Valleys, leaving ice over 1 inch (2.5 cm) thick and resulting in a loss of power for at least 30,000 homes in the Capital District and hazardous travel throughout the region. Thousands were forced to live in shelters for several days, and damages were estimated at $5 million. An ice storm on 15 Feb 1990 toppled thousands of trees and caused 80,000 residents in western New York State to lose electricity. Freezing rain fell for a record 22.6 hours on 3–4 Mar 1991, leaving much of the western half of the state encased in up to 2 inches (5.1 cm) of ice and depriving almost 325,000 people of electricity. Particularly hard hit was Rochester, where 120,000 trees were destroyed and schools closed for a week. With $300 million in damage to the city alone, the storm is believed to be the most expensive natural disaster in New York State history. Ice accumulated to 1–3 inches (2.5–7.6 cm) across the North Country on 6–9 Jan 1998, leaving more than 100,000 without power for days, causing over $11 million in damages, and resulting in six deaths. On 4–5 Apr 2003 an eight-county area of Western and Central New York saw ice accumulation of up to an inch; 65,000 Rochester residents lost electricity, some for a week or more.

Ahrens, C. Donald. *Meteorology Today: An Introduction to Weather, Climate, and the Environment,* 6th ed (Pacific Grove, Calif: Brooks/Cole, 2000)
National Climatic Data Center. *Storm Data* (1959–)

Scott Rochette

ILGWU. See INTERNATIONAL LADIES' GARMENT WORKERS' UNION.

Ilion. Village (pop 8,610) in German Flatts (Herkimer Co). The village incorporated in 1852. After the Erie Canal began operations (1821), Eliphalet Remington bought land at the present village site and, in 1828, moved his gun barrel manufacturing there, later producing rifles. Becoming E. Remington and Sons, the firm expanded into agricultural machinery (1856), sewing machines (1870), and typewriters (1873). The production of bicycles and textiles, including those of Ilion Knitting Mill (1886), was overshadowed by the Remington plant, which employed 6,000 workers by 1940. Ilion was also the center of strawberry shipment from around 1862 into the 20th century. The West Shore Railroad (1883) provided direct service. In the 20th century Remington Rand (1928–71), successor to the Remington typewriter business, became an important employer, producing punch-card data systems. The Thruway came through in 1954. Remington Arms remains Ilion's main employer in the early 21st century; Herkimer Foods (1949) markets the region's distinctive cheddar cheese and other products. The village is the site of the Remington Arms Museum.

See also GUNS AND ORDNANCE INDUSTRY.

James Crawford

illegal immigration. See UNDOCUMENTED IMMIGRATION.

I♥NY. In 1977 New York State's commissioner and assistant commissioner of commerce, John Dyson and William Doyle, unveiled an advertising campaign to promote tourism. Inspired by the successful Virginia Is for Lovers campaign, they persuaded Gov Hugh Carey and the state legislature to allocate $4 million for the project. They engaged the firm of Wells, Rich, and Greene to develop the campaign. Rejected slogans included New York, New York, It's a Heck of a State and I Live in New Hampshire but I Love New York, which would become simply I Love New York. Graphic artist Milton Glaser of Push Pin Studios, whose work included logos for *New York Magazine* and Brooklyn Brewery, was enlisted to design the logo and graphics. Steve Karmen composed the signature song, also entitled "I Love New York." The chorus consists of repeating the phrase "I love New York" three times. The song debuted during the May 1977 ad campaign and has become the unofficial state song. The initial television ads featured images of New York State and performers from *A Chorus Line.* Both Glaser and Karmen donated their services. Glaser's logo, which he had initially sketched on a paper napkin, was almost immediately bootlegged and adapted for other locales and special interests, from cheese to Zimbabwe. The image soon graced products such as T-shirts, tote bags, and coffee mugs. The campaign has been ongoing since 1977 but was renewed after the attack on the World Trade Center on 11 Sept 2001. Glaser revamped his logo, adding the words "More Than Ever." He abandoned his pursuit of copyright infringement by manufacturers using the logo without permission, thus allowing for the further proliferation of the logo. The new campaign, designed as the original was to boost the state's economic and moral spirits, featured former New York City mayor Rudolph Giuliani and Gov George E. Pataki.

Glaser, Milton. *Art Is Work* (New York: Overlook Press, 2000)

ilton Glaser's logo for New York's tourism promotion mpaign.

Lawrence, Mary Wells. *A Big Life in Advertising* (New York: Knopf, 2002)

Jennifer Steenshorne

immigration. The populating of New York State has depended upon the movement of people from other parts of the globe. Even the Iroquoian and Algonquian nations that occupied the territory prior to European discovery had originally come from the north or the west, as had earlier native peoples.

New Netherland

European immigration began in 1624 with the arrival of 30 Walloon families from the Spanish-controlled southern Netherlands [now Belgium]. A policy to encourage agricultural settlements to be known as patroonships took shape in 1629 and resulted in a decade of gradual immigration. To accelerate the process, the Dutch government and the Dutch West India Co (WIC) agreed in 1640 that the WIC would give up its fur-trade monopoly. Population continued to increase, although economic troubles and religious persecution, both of which impelled emigration from the British Isles, were largely absent in the Netherlands. David Cohen's study of the origins of New Netherland residents, based on a little over 900 heads of families, found that those of Dutch ethnicity were a bare majority of immigrants to the colony, constituting only 51% of those who emigrated from the Netherlands, with an additional 7% from present-day Belgium. Many of New Netherland's immigrants were, in fact, non-Dutch resident in the Netherlands. The colony included French (7%), Scandinavians (16%), and Germans (18%) fleeing the Thirty Years War and turbulence at home.

A small but significant number of English settlers also came to the present New York. Some assimilated into the dominant Dutch culture in Dutch communities, but most lived in English villages, either those on eastern Long Island sent out by New Haven Colony starting in 1640 or those on western Long Island created under the authority of New Netherland starting in 1644. One of the smallest groups was Africans.

New York Colony

Dutch immigration dried up overnight with the English takeover in 1664. English immigrants, with modest numbers of Lowland Scots, took up much of the slack. Huguenots had arrived in small numbers during the Dutch administration, settling on Staten Island and near Kingston [now in Ulster Co]; in 1678 a colony acquired and settled New Paltz [now in Ulster Co] and with the revocation of the Edict of Nantes (1685), hundreds more fled France and its West India colonies. A group of resident Huguenots acquired New Rochelle (Westchester Co) in 1689, by which year there were seven Huguenot congregations in the colony. The French were about 9% of the New York City population in the early 18th century but were quickly assimilated into English and Dutch subcultures.

Lowland Scots, who had been resettled in Ulster in Ireland in the 17th century following an English decree of 1609, were impelled to emigrate in the early 18th century by several economic forces: a mercantile system that favored London over the provinces; the Wool Act (1699), which forbade export of finished product; and high rents. In addition, these Presbyterian Scots sought greater religious freedom than was possible under an Anglican Church establishment. Poverty caused many immigrants from Ireland to come under indenture, and they remained after their terms expired. Scots-Irish immigration was greatest during five short pulses, the first in 1717–18 and the last beginning in 1771, triggered by a collapse in the linen industry and terminated by the outbreak of war. Many settled together, as they did before 1720 in Wallkill (Ulster Co) and Goshen, Bethlehem, and Monroe (Orange Co); at Cherry Valley (1741) and Middlefield (*ca* 1755) [now in Otsego Co]; in the present Fulton Co (*ca* 1760–72); and in New Perth (1764) [now Salem, Washington Co].

German immigration began as a component of Dutch colonization but was thereafter mostly in abeyance until a number of forces came together just after the turn of the 18th century. During the War of the Spanish Succession (1702–13), France attacked Germany, wreaking havoc on its populace. Taxation by their own government and overpopulation, along with a particularly severe winter in 1708–9, inspired many Palatine Germans to emigrate. The first arrived in New York in 1708 and formed a colony at the present Newburgh (Ulster Co). A second very large group came in the year following and under government sponsorship formed seven *dorfs* (villages) in and near the present Germantown (Columbia Co) and West Camp (Ulster Co) to produce naval stores. They quickly dispersed: to the Schoharie Valley in 1712 and thence to Pennsylvania (1717–23) and the central and western Mohawk Valley (1723–25).

Immigration from Scotland was sporadic during the 18th century. But rule from London, the development of the sheep industry, and the resulting enclosures created strong incentives for leaving. A colony of 472 Argyllshire Presbyterians arrived in 1738–40 expecting to receive land from the governor but were rebuffed; they settled in various locations and finally, in 1764, received a town patent for Argyle [now in Washington Co]. Although the overwhelming majority of immigrants were Presbyterian, Sir William Johnson invited a group of Roman Catholic Highlanders to settle in the Johnstown area [now in Fulton Co] in 1773; his death shortly afterward and the outbreak of war resulted in the colony's departure for Canada.

The nonvoluntary immigration of Africans to New York Colony continued throughout the colonial period. Africans as a percentage of the colony's population probably peaked around 1720 at 16%, declining to a little less than 12% in the year of the final colonial census in 1771. This was so despite the continuing slave imports, with over 6,000 Africans entering the colony between 1712 and 1760. At midcentury the largest populations of Africans were in New York and Albany Cos, but slavery was prevalent throughout the colony. Most slaves from New York Colony came from homelands in Congo (in the area of what is now Angola), the Gold Coast (in the area of what is now Ghana), and other locations in West and West Central Africa. They retained and expressed their African heritage in numerous ways. Until after the Revolution the free black population remained very small, and manumission was more common in New York City than in rural areas. By 1820, when 95% of the Blacks in New York City were free, on rural Staten Island almost 90% of the black population remained enslaved. In that year African Americans constituted less than 3% of the state's population. The percentage would not return to double digits until 1970.

Immigration in the New Republic

The start of the Revolutionary War in 1775 ended immigration to New York, although some British and Hessian soldiers who came with the invading army ultimately remained. But almost immediately upon the 1783 peace, immigration resumed. The largest component of new residents in the state for the years up to 1820 was an interregional migration from New England, which was experiencing population pressures. The complementary enticement was the vast amount of New York land placed on the market by investors enabled by state policy and by the extinguishing of Indian claims. Some New England towns transplanted themselves, in part, to towns in central and western New York State. A smaller migration came from New Jersey and from Pennsylvania; very small numbers of southerners, mostly from Maryland or Virginia, arrived via the Susquehanna River corridor.

Political upheaval in France pushed small numbers of Royalists and, later, Bonapartists to plant colonies in Lewis, Jefferson, Chenango, and Allegany Cos; most of the settlers, ill suited for frontier life, returned home upon changes in the French government. Meanwhile, Dutch investors sought out financial opportunities, including land in Oneida and Madison Cos and the vast Holland Land Purchase; most of their settlers were Yankee migrants, but they did establish a Dutch community called Olden Barneveld [now Barneveld, Oneida Co] in 1793.

More significant numerically was the stream of immigrants from the British Isles. Among them were a Welsh group that settled Steuben and Remsen (Oneida Co) in 1795, later sending out settlements into surrounding towns and counties. Irish immigrants came in increasing numbers, and a group of political émigrés from the failed rebellion of 1798 would play important roles in the political and legal life of New York State.

Other source of immigration were the Caribbean and Latin America. This phenomenon dated to New Netherland. Many of the slaves brought to New York Colony did not come directly from Africa but were either born or had spent extended time in the Caribbean. Slaveholders often favored slaves who had spent at least a decade in the West Indies; they were thought to make better workers. Slaves from Latin America, often called Spanish slaves, were common in New York Colony. A group of 50 Spanish slaves, captured during the War of Jenkins' Ear (1739–41), successfully sued for freedom after the end of the war. The Haitian Revolution at the turn of the 19th century brought as many as 4,000 slaveholders, slaves, and free Blacks to New York State, most of whom later relocated elsewhere.

Voluntary immigration from Central and South America started as early as 1654 in New Amsterdam with the arrival of 23 Jews from Recife, Brazil, marking the beginning of the Jewish presence in North America. The extensive trading networks between New York Colony and the Caribbean led to population exchanges. Richard Morris, the patriarch of the prominent Morris family, came to New York from Barbados in the 1660s. Other well-known West Indian immigrants included Samuel Fraunces, whose tavern became a favored meeting place in post-Revolutionary New York City, and Alexander Hamilton, born and raised on the island of Nevis. Immigration from Latin America was as yet limited, though some sailors did make extended stays in New York City, which became a haven for political exiles. Francisco de Miranda sailed from New York City with a crew of 200 in 1806 to raise a rebellion in his native Venezuela. Father Felix Varela, exiled from Cuba for political opposition to Spanish rule, arrived in New York City in 1824. He became an influential writer and administrator for local Catholics and, among other duties, ministered to the city's small Spanish-speaking population. —*FH*

Passengers on the steerage deck of the SS *Pennland* on the way to Ellis Island, 1893.

Northern European Influx

In the decades following the cessation of the Napoleonic Wars in 1815, immigration to New York State began an upsurge that would continue, despite periodic downturns, until the outbreak of war in Europe in 1914. Throughout the 19th and early 20th centuries, immigration to the state swelled as a result of population pressure in Europe, which increased the number of landless and impoverished peasants, and economic change (principally the rise of industrial production), which threatened the livelihood of European artisans. The migratory process accelerated at times of natural disasters such as the Great Famine in Ireland in 1845–49, caused by failure of the potato crop, and the phylloxera plague, which ravaged wine-producing regions in parts of western Europe in the 1870s. The inflow of immigrants also increased in particular eras as a result of political upheaval, such as the European revolutions of 1848–49 and the pogroms waged against Jews in Russia in the 1880s.

European immigrants were drawn to New York State in greater numbers than they were to anywhere else in the United States because it was the most prosperous state in the Union and home to the largest city and port in the New World. Between 1855 and 1892 newcomers entered New York through a landing site at Castle Garden, located at the southern tip of Manhattan. In 1892 a new immigration center was opened on Ellis Island, and during its years of operation (1892–1932), approximately 12 million immigrants entered the country by way of this facility.

The growth and maintenance of the statewide transportation network did much to disperse immigrants. Many millions of northern European immigrants traveled through the state by way of the Hudson River and the newly completed Erie Canal in the first half of the 19th century. Although travelers often intended to go farther west, many decided instead to settle in manufacturing towns along the route of the canal. Once members of particular ethnic groups had settled in a locality in New York State, they frequently wrote to friends and relatives, encouraging them to follow, thus contributing to the process known as chain migra-

NEW YORK STATE'S FOREIGN-BORN POPULATION BY SELECTED PLACE OF BIRTH

Origin	1860	1870	1880	1890	1900	1910	1920
Africa	69	92	156	299	473	900	1,528
Asia[a]	206	105	81	358	1,744	420	744
Austria	—	3,928	6,530	33,135	78,491	245,004	151,172
Belgium	860	984	1,288	1,342	1,787	3,484	5,300
Canada[b]	55,273	79,042	84,182	93,193	117,535	124,580	114,614
Central America[c]	55	49	65	237	1,048	2,803	8,645
China	77	177	1,015	3,135	6,880	4,482	4,559
Cuba[d]	—	1,824	2,227	4,065	2,195	17,483	—
Denmark	1196	1,701	3,145	6,238	8,746	12,544	14,222
France	21,826	22,302	20,321	20,443	20,008	23,472	32,252
Germany	256,252	316,902	355,913	498,602	480,026	436,911	295,651
England	106,011	110,071	116,362	144,060	135,685	146,870	135,541
Ireland	498,072	528,806	499,445	483,375	425,553	367,889	284,747
Scotland	27,641	27,282	28,066	35,332	33,862	39,437	37,656
Wales	7,908	7,857	7,223	8,108	7,304	7,464	6,763
Greece	35	60	94	413	1,573	10,097	26,117
Holland	5,354	6,426	8,399	8,366	9,414	—	—
Hungary	—	709	4,440	15,598	37,168	96,843	78,374
India	—	102	310	349	403	361	624
Italy	1,862	3,592	15,113	64,141	182,248	472,201	545,173
Japan	—	9	32	209	392	1,163	2,393
Mexico	116	127	237	330	353	555	2,999
Norway	539	975	2,185	8,602	12,601	25,013	27,573
Pacific Islands[e]	11	6	96	112	113	220	320
Poland[f]	2,296	4,061	11,999	22,718	70,255	—	247,519
Portugal	353	237	295	284	362	660	1,481
Russia	1,013	1,473	5,438	58,466	165,610	558,256	529,243
South America[c]	312	442	754	921	1,130	—	—
Spain	809	818	1,216	1,603	1,614	3,766	12,722
Sweden	1,678	5,522	11,164	28,430	42,708	53,705	53,025
Switzerland	6,166	7,916	10,721	11,557	13,678	16,315	15,053
Turkey[g]	39	71	180	427	1,915	14,482	5,250
West Indies[d]	1,957	1,303	1,734	—	4,241	—	38,288

Source: US Census.

[a]Does not include China, Japan, and India, which are listed separately.

[b]Includes French and English Canada and Newfoundland.

[c]The data for Central American in 1910 and 1920 include South America.

[d]The data for Cuba in 1890 and 1910 include other West Indies, except Puerto Rico after 1890; since 1900 persons born in Puerto Rico have been counted as native-born.

[e]Does not include the Philippine Islands and other US possessions.

[f]For the census of 1910 the Polish population is reported under Austria, Germany, and Russia.

[g]From 1910 Turkey is divided into Turkey in Asia and Turkey in Europe. The data for Turkey in Asia and Turkey in Europe for 1910 are, respec-tively: 5,004 and 9,478; for 1920: 3,200 and 2,050.

Compiled by Jacqueline Villarrubia-Mendoza

tion. Some, particularly Welsh, German, and Scandinavian immigrants, opted to settle in the rural areas and take up farming. The Irish, however, remained overwhelmingly concentrated in urban areas.

Lower Manhattan became a patchwork of ethnic enclaves in this period, as did neighborhoods in many of the smaller cities in the rest of the state. Overall, the Irish and Germans were the two most prominent immigrant groups before the Civil War, except in Oneida Co, where the Welsh outnumbered the Germans, and Chautauqua Co, where Swedes and Norwegians were especially prominent. Jews, coming largely at this point from German-speaking lands, also arrived in significant numbers. By 1860 there were 40,000 Jews, mostly from Germany and central Europe. There were 27 synagogues in New York City, and congregations were formed in urban areas in the rest of the state.

Some of the Jews outside of New York City worked initially as itinerant peddlers, and many others pursued trades, as in Rochester, where German Jews played a prominent role in the creation of the local garment industry. Many skilled German workers came to America with experience in trade unionism and political radicalism, and thus provided part of the leadership for the nascent labor and socialist movements. Limited by their lack of education and training, most Irish immigrant men worked as common laborers and factory workers, and many Irish women secured work as seamstresses and domestic servants. In New York City the Irish found in Tammany Hall an avenue to political power by the 1860s. In the second half of the 19th century and into the 20th, many Irish and other immigrants became involved in machine politics in the state's urban areas.

With approximately a half-million foreign-born residents, 39% of its overall population, New York City was America's preeminent center of immigrant life in 1880. The New York cities with the next largest foreign-born populations were Brooklyn, 177,694 immigrants (31% of the overall local population); Buffalo, 51,268 (33%); Rochester, 26,622 (29%); and Albany, 23,765 (26%). Schoharie Co, with only 1.8% of its population foreign-born in 1880, was the area least affected by immigration. Some ethnic groups had their greatest population concentrations outside of New York City, such as the English and Welsh, who made up 28% of the overall population of Oneida Co (compared to 6% in New York City). Germans accounted for 16% of Erie Co, compared to 13% in New York City.

The growing prominence of immigrants in the life of the state had an unsettling effect on many New York State residents for a variety of reasons during the first half of the 19th century. Work-

NEW YORK STATE'S FOREIGN-BORN POPULATION BY COUNTY

County	1860	1870	1880	1890	1900	1910
Albany	34,288	39,314	37,977	37,267	31,531	32,764
Allegany	3,216	3,546	3,187	3,628	2,374	2,200
Broome	2,770	4,045	3,956	5,869	5,154	8,776
Cattaraugus	5,716	5,665	7,071	7,986	7,819	8,371
Cayuga	7,503	9,238	9,353	9,617	8,519	10,009
Chautauqua	8,172	9,282	10,818	14,944	17,549	23,389
Chemung	2,853	4,553	5,118	6,224	6,411	6,173
Chenango	1,795	2,779	1,879	1,876	1,664	1,815
Clinton	12,627	12,677	10,605	7,746	6,117	5,370
Columbia	5,443	5,859	4,962	5,331	4,641	6,075
Cortland	1,666	1,888	1,735	1,986	1,523	2,001
Delaware	3,247	3,469	2,521	2,689	2,227	2,077
Dutchess	9,822	12,103	11,671	12,053	12,093	13,460
Erie	54,904	60,907	65,378	103,453	119,470	144,231
Essex	4,391	4,633	5,047	3,820	2,384	3,848
Franklin	7,793	6,950	6,161	6,324	6,033	7,163
Fulton	2,239	2,515	2,931	3,984	4,945	6,568
Genesee	6,223	2,486	1,994	5,797	5,379	6,910
Greene	2,190	5,833	5,694	1,862	2,067	2,579
Hamilton	284	306	346	422	462	358
Herkimer	5,537	5,785	5,260	5,933	6,652	10,313
Jefferson	9,270	10,036	8,788	10,013	11,739	12,828
Kings	109,077	153,811	188,312	272,895	355,697	572,512
Lewis	5,477	5,232	5,036	4,088	2,949	2,104
Livingston	6,232	5,837	5,614	5,397	4,861	5,416
Madison	4,077	4,816	4,127	3,901	3,216	3,319
Monroe	31,172	33,764	38,342	51,997	51,059	71,276
Montgomery	3,052	4,280	4,847	7,475	8,229	13,690
Nassau	—	—	—	—	11,063	19,396
New York	386,345	419,094	478,670	639,943	850,884	1,257,597
Niagara	14,312	13,227	12,840	15,031	17,691	24,373
Oneida	26,368	25,707	23,435	25,255	24,477	33,804
Onondaga	20,048	24,073	23,384	31,056	32,227	40,234
Ontario	7,134	7,350	7,681	7,539	6,910	6,864
Orange	9,753	14,259	12,422	15,231	14,723	19,222
Orleans	4,601	4,243	4,799	6,225	5,520	5,804
Oswego	11,886	13,255	11,195	9,215	7,318	8,101
Otsego	2,456	2,733	2,650	2,523	2,294	2,332
Putnam	1,432	2,451	2,233	2,631	2,119	3,265
Queens	14,090	19,075	22,001	35,146	44,812	79,237
Rensselaer	21,324	25,621	26,573	27,706	22,982	2,172
Richmond	8,375	10,113	10,961	14,779	18,687	24,339
Rockland	5,073	5,350	4,593	7,442	7,249	9,719
Saratoga	6,682	7,709	7,586	8,105	7,881	9,007
Schenectady	3,792	3,686	3,744	5,569	9,689	21,055
Schoharie	951	901	742	618	659	651
Schuyler	979	1,048	898	751	706	614
Seneca	3,876	3,845	3,964	3,700	3,355	3,528
Steuben	6,170	5,884	6,477	7,081	6,041	5,703
St. Lawrence	17,588	18,219	15,412	13,903	13,829	13,239
Suffolk	4,001	4,877	5,601	9,990	14,757	22,289
Sullivan	5,990	5,822	4,262	3,326	3,041	4,488
Tioga	1,697	1,902	1,637	1,434	1,049	925
Tompkins	1,503	2,127	2,173	2,137	2,076	2,487
Ulster	12,746	12,740	10,319	10,385	9,276	14,233
Warren	2,648	2,578	2,497	2,592	2,628	2,978
Washington	6,656	8,294	6,354	5,864	5,220	6,106
Wayne	7,304	7,411	7,891	7,654	6,899	7,425
Westchester	27,823	37,344	23,710	38,392	46,682	81,285
Wyoming	4,929	4,051	3,946	3,912	3,287	3,397
Yates	1,512	1,755	1,799	1,878	1,630	1,411

Source: US Census (1920).

Compiled by Jacqueline Villarrubia-Mendoza

ing-class, native-born Americans felt threatened by competition from foreign-born workers. The temperance movement had inspired considerable enthusiasm among many Americans in the aftermath of the religious revivals of the 1820s and 1830s, and a significant portion of the public was therefore horrified by the centrality of alcohol to the social life of many immigrants. Some Protestants were also alarmed by the rising prominence of Catholic immigrants; they considered them to be members of a fundamentally un-American, antidemocratic religion. In addition, the growing power of Tammany Hall, which depended largely on the support of poor immigrants, seemed to many Americans to be a danger to democracy in America. In response to these anxieties, the anti-immigrant American or Know-Nothing Party rose briefly to prominence in statewide politics in the period immediately preceding the outbreak of the Civil War.

Southern and Eastern European Newcomers

After 1880 the number of northern European immigrants living in New York State began to decline. Statewide, the Irish population went from 483,375 in 1890 to 367,889 in 1910. Similarly, New York's German population, at 498,602 the largest single group of foreign-born in the state, had dropped to 436,911 in 1910. In the meantime, the number of southern and eastern Europeans coming to New York State increased dramatically. Like the Irish before them, a significant minority of the first southern and eastern Europeans worked on transportation projects, most notably the expansion of the state railroad system in the decades following the Civil War. In 1880 there were 13,421 Italians living in New York City and Kings Co, 186 in Buffalo, and 51 in Rochester. Within 10 years, there were 39,951 Italians in New York City, 1,832 in Buffalo, and 516 in Rochester, and by 1920 their numbers had jumped to 390,832, 16,411, and 19,468 respectively. There were over a half-million Italians living statewide by 1920, more than the number living in three adjoining states (Pennsylvania, New Jersey, and Massachusetts) combined.

The number of immigrants from eastern Europe also expanded. In 1890 New York State was home to 105,911 eastern European immigrants, but by 1920 there were more than 400,000 (principally from Czechoslovakia, Hungary, Yugoslavia, Poland, and Romania). Many ethnic Poles settled in manufacturing cities and towns. Some 30,000 Poles were living in Buffalo in 1920; smaller Polish and Ukrainian communities were found in Rochester, Utica, and other localities.

The Chinese Exclusion Act (1882) and the so-called Gentlemen's Agreement (1907) severely restricted Asian immigration to America in this period, and by 1910, the entire state was home to only 12,578 Asians, including immigrants from the Indian subcontinent, and most of them lived in New York City. Buffalo, with 133 Asians, had the largest number of any city outside the New York City, and Utica had only 3 in 1910. However, a small but significant number of other non-European immigrants (notably Turks, Syrians, Lebanese, and Armenians) made their way into communities throughout the state between the late 19th century and the outbreak of World War I.

A large proportion of eastern European immigrants were Jews, and most of these newcomers stayed in New York City. Indeed, Jews remained the most highly urbanized of the principal immigrant groups in this period. The overwhelming majority of Italian immigrants resided in urban areas (70% in New York City, 16% in the state's other cities in 1920). However, the Italians were not nearly so centered in New York City as were eastern European Jews because a significant minority of Italians lived in small cities and rural areas, where some engaged in farming. Poles and other non-Jewish eastern Europeans seem to have been more inclined than Italians to pursue farming, although they, too, remained largely urbanized.

The Watershed of World War I

World War I marked the end of the era of unlimited immigration and ended the heyday of European immigration to the United States. The Atlantic became dangerous to traverse, and young men, who constituted a disproportionately large percentage of immigrants, were subject to conscription in their homelands and therefore barred from emigrating during the war. In the meantime, tension over the war fueled belief in racist doctrines, which had first started to circulate in the late 19th century, holding that immigrants from southern and eastern Europe were inherently inferior and therefore undesirable additions to American life. This perspective was most effectively embodied in New Yorker Madison Grant's *Passing of the Great Race in America*, published in 1916.

Anxieties concerning the impact that immigration was having on New York State and on democracy in America intensified between 1910 and 1920 as a result of the rising prominence of southern and eastern Europeans, particularly Jews, in the socialist and labor movements. A series of disruptive strikes, especially in the textile and garment industries, had an unsettling effect on Americans who had complacently held that such unrest was inherently a European problem. From the strike in 1909 involving 30,000 workers, mainly immigrant women, against shirtwaist manufacturers in New York City, to the labor unrest that affected the state in 1919, immigrant factory workers progressively became more vocal and organized in support of their interests at the workplace. At the same time, the Socialist Party, which drew its power predominantly from immigrant eastern European Jews and Germans, experienced a rise in power that hit a crescendo in the national elections of 1916 and in several municipal elections (eg, in Schenectady and Buffalo) in 1917. The rise of socialism, which was indelibly linked to foreigners in the minds of many Americans, became unsettling to a patriotic general public during World War I. It did not help that the Socialist Party advocated pacifism in that conflict.

Manifestations of ethnic nationalist sentiment also proved to be unsettling for many New York State residents. In New York City and other state urban centers, immigrants and ethnic groups representing the spectrum of powers involved in the war participated in demonstrations in favor of their homelands. German Americans and many Irish Americans supported Germany, Britain's (and later America's) enemy, before 1917. Italian Americans rose to the defense of their homeland, which came into the war on the side of the Allies in 1915. Thousands of Poles volunteered for the American and Polish armies to fight for the liberation of their homeland, and British immigrants volunteered to defend the Empire. Other immigrant and ethnic groups, such as Turks, Lebanese, and Jews, also found that their loyalties were affected by the war. Urban New York State therefore came to reflect, in miniature, the conflicts raging across the ocean, and many established Americans saw in this spectacle a threat to the future health and stability of the United States. —*PAB*

An Era of Restrictionist Legislation: 1924–1964

The surge in immigration in the early years of the 20th century, particularly from Italy, Russia, and other eastern European countries, resulted in increased anti-immigrant fervor in the country. There were fears that the nation would be inundated with Bolshevik insurgents and a widespread belief, stoked by "scientific" theories, in the racial inferiority of these newest immigrants. The culmination of these anxieties was the Johnson-Reed Immigration Act of 1924, which slashed immigration quotas for southern and eastern Europeans first imposed in 1921, from 156,000 annually to just 20,000. There was a more modest reduction in the quota for northern and western Europeans, from 198,000 to 141,000. The effect of the law was immediate, with the overall flow of immigrants to New York State falling 60% (to 68,000) in 1925; the flow of Italians, Russians, and Poles plunged over 80%. The quota system was made permanent and fully operational with the passage of the 1929 National Origins Act, which largely preserved the favorable quotas for northern and western Europe. Immigration from Canada and Mexico continued to be free of any numerical limits.

Despite these restrictions, large flows in the early 1920s, coupled with the entry of many dependents later in the decade, increased the overall foreign-born population of New York State to 3.26 million in 1930. The largest group was Italians, who made up nearly one-fifth of the foreign-born population, followed by Russians (15%), and Poles (11%). Many of the Russians and Poles who came to New York State were ethnic Jews. Those born in northern and western Europe were less than one-third of the foreign-born, reflecting the larger flows from southern and eastern Europe since the closing years of the preceding century. Although over 70% of New York State's foreign-born residents in 1930 lived in New York City, approximately 90% of those born in Russia, Romania, and Austria lived there. These groups, primarily Jewish, were concentrated on the Lower East Side of Manhattan, Brownsville in Brooklyn, and a few other neighborhoods. Those born in the West Indies were also heavily represented in New York City, with more than 9 in 10 settling there, primarily in Harlem. New York City was also home to 70% of the 629,000 Italian immigrants in New York State, but there were substantial concentrations in other cities. The 24,000 Italians in Rochester constituted nearly one-third of that city's foreign-born population; 19,000 settled in Buffalo, and 9,000 in Syracuse. Buffalo was also home to the largest Polish immigrant concentration (27,000) after New York City (238,000). Constituting over one-fifth of Buffalo's immigration population and largely Catholic and Jewish, many Poles settled on Buffalo's East Side. Among the other major foreign-born groups, Canadians

NEW YORK STATE'S FOREIGN-BORN POPULATION BY PLACE OF BIRTH

	1930	1940[a]	1950	1960	1970	1980	1990	2000
Total Population	12,588,066	13,479,142	14,830,192	16,783,604	18,236,882	17,558,072	17,990,455	18,976,457
Foreign-Born Population	3,262,278	2,916,645	2,578,973	2,289,314	2,109,776	2,388,938	2,851,861	3,868,133
Foreign-Born (%)	25.9	21.6	17.4	13.6	11.6	13.6	15.9	20.4
Birthplace								
Europe	2,961,265	2,644,647	2,277,832	1,933,562	1,438,531	1,108,392	842,395	879,307
Austria	142,298	172,347	149,955	107,101	65,606	38,779	19,275	11,299
Czechoslovakia	56,176	41,798	44,111	42,021	32,363	24,041	17,660	13,246
Denmark	17,407	14,304	11,627	9,462	6,366	3,681	2,778	—
England[b]	146,772	117,370	100,280	86,343	67,860	52,105	68,434	62,237
Finland	17,444	15,101	12,897	9,765	6,605	3,541	2,141	—
France	32,273	26,373	28,185	27,639	23,681	20,852	18,411	20,310
Germany	349,196	316,844	270,661	250,173	183,754	134,991	92,322	69,327
Greece	33,387	34,800	36,757	36,579	44,478	54,738	44,316	42,335
Hungary	70,631	75,254	65,276	60,382	43,506	31,732	22,337	17,401
Ireland	251,704	205,323	182,581	131,764	93,818	66,639	53,949	41,934
Northern Ireland	41,521	30,432	4,171	18,749	10,651	3,418	—	—
Italy	629,322	584,075	503,175	440,063	352,711	283,990	190,305	147,729
Netherlands	14,909	13,842	13,393	13,132	11,421	8,462	7,379	6,545
Norway	44,882	37,169	33,073	27,125	17,371	10,540	5,924	—
Poland	350,383	281,080	254,065	234,742	168,370	113,262	88,230	93,187
Romania	51,014	43,950	32,270	29,040	25,485	21,827	22,369	25,059
Russia[c]	481,307	436,028	354,197	245,068	147,993	112,725	98,576	94,595
Scotland	67,623	57,639	48,304	41,396	29,184	19,861	—	—
Sweden	61,233	48,317	36,747	23,516	13,534	7,741	4,646	4,305
Wales	7,037	4,752	4,725	3,383	2,200	1,495	—	—
Caribbean	64,466	14,986	73,305	100,997	246,099	463,759	682,991	1,004,344
Cuba	—	6,632	14,531	30,632	72,224	56,895	52,064	36,642
Dominican Republic	—	—	3,265	9,643	52,700	131,313	241,941	408,086
Haiti	—	—	445	3,180	21,466	55,363	87,215	125,475
Jamaica	—	—	6,081	12,441	44,916	107,130	146,829	226,470
Central and South America	20,145	14,322	24,252	41,540	110,892	250,474	448,353	726,079
Guatemala	—	—	415	692	1,793	7,049	17,883	33,208
Honduras	—	—	410	1,748	4,934	—	20,955	43,314
Panama	—	—	970	6,070	10,810	—	28,257	26,202
Colombia	—	—	1,775	5,477	25,502	48,486	82,767	111,727
Ecuador	—	—	980	3,019	17,105	42,426	68,954	139,226
Guyana	—	—	—	—	—	33,398	81,386	142,154
Peru	—	—	890	1,565	4,572	12,966	26,647	43,753
Asia	47,610	39,840	59,179	77,022	133,114	290,456	556,662	916,597
China[d]	7,512	—	14,752	22,251	42,425	68,839	155,352	301,735
India	920	—	1,475	2,013	8,537	33,434	66,851	117,238
Korea	—	—	346	822	3,965	27,104	71,975	97,933
Philippines	—	—	4,132	5,037	10,264	27,493	50,245	72,408
Turkey[e]	16,673	20,507	19,520	15,105	13,397	12,332	11,569	16,228
Canada	155,526	129,810	120,011	111,280	85,176	73,142	56,795	54,876
Mexico	5,218	3,567	4,290	4,496	4,806	10,676	43,505	161,189
All others	8,048	6,358	20,104	20,417	91,158	192,039	221,160	125,741

Source: US Census.

[a]In 1940 the foreign-born populations for specified countries includes only Whites; this was also true for most regions and countries in 1950.

[b]Includes Scotland, Wales, and Northern Ireland in 1990 and 2000.

[c]For the years 1940–90 includes the non-Baltic Republics of the USSR.

[d]Includes Hong Kong in 2000.

[e]1930 and 1940 include Asian population only; from 1950 includes European population as well.

Compiled by Timothy Calabrese

were the most widely dispersed: nearly 50% concentrated in counties bordering Canada, and just 29% lived in New York City.

In the 1930s immigration dropped dramatically, more a result of the Great Depression than of restrictionist legislation. Fewer than 700,000 immigrants arrived in the United States over the decade; 272,000 made their home in New York State, many of them Jews fleeing Nazi persecution. Emigration from the United States actually exceeded immigration in the 1930s. By 1940 New York State's foreign-born population dropped to 2.9 million (22% of the total population). During World War II the immigration law was amended, as it conflicted with US foreign policy goals. Chinese exclusion, in effect since 1882, was repealed in 1943, in large part because it was inconsistent with China's status as a wartime ally. While the war kept flows at low levels in the early 1940s, immigration increased later in the decade as the law was changed again to account for postwar realities. The War Brides Act, which went into effect in December 1945, brought in approximately 120,000 spouses and children of those serving in the US armed forces, and the Displaced Persons Act of 1948 brought in over 400,000 refugees, primarily from Poland

NEW YORK STATE'S TOTAL AND FOREIGN-BORN POPULATION FOR SELECTED COUNTIES AND CITIES

	1920	1930	1940	1950	1960	1970	1980	1990	2000
Total Population									
New York State	10,385,227	12,588,066	13,479,142	14,830,192	16,783,604	18,236,882	17,558,072	17,990,455	18,976,457
New York City and Nassau and Westchester Cos	6,090,604	7,754,446	8,435,301	9,190,538	9,892,376	10,216,975	9,259,820	9,484,778	10,266,281
New York City	5,620,048	6,930,446	7,454,995	7,891,957	7,783,314	7,894,798	7,071,639	7,322,564	8,008,278
Yonkers	100,176	134,646	142,598	152,798	190,634	204,367	195,351	188,082	196,086
Albany Co	186,106	211,953	221,315	239,386	272,926	286,742	285,909	292,594	294,565
Albany (city)	113,344	127,412	130,577	134,995	129,726	115,875	101,727	101,082	95,658
Erie Co	634,688	762,408	798,377	899,238	1,064,687	1,113,491	1,015,472	968,532	950,265
Buffalo	506,775	573,076	575,901	580,132	532,759	462,781	357,870	328,123	292,648
Monroe Co	352,034	423,881	438,230	487,632	586,387	711,917	702,238	713,968	735,343
Rochester	295,750	328,132	324,975	332,488	318,611	296,233	241,741	231,636	219,773
Onondaga Co	241,465	291,606	295,108	341,719	423,028	472,746	463,920	468,973	458,336
Syracuse	171,717	209,326	205,967	220,583	216,038	197,332	170,105	163,860	147,306
All others	2,880,330	3,143,772	3,290,811	3,671,679	4,544,200	5,435,011	5,830,713	6,061,610	6,271,667
Foreign-Born Population									
New York State	2,825,375	3,262,278	2,916,645	2,578,973	2,289,314	2,109,776	2,388,938	2,851,861	3,868,133
New York City and Nassau and Westchester Cos	2,134,163	2,542,835	2,309,072	1,961,952	1,784,088	1,661,697	1,932,947	2,410,839	3,314,875
New York City	2,028,160	2,358,686	2,138,657	1,784,206	1,558,690	1,437,058	1,670,199	2,082,931	2,871,032
Yonkers	25,796	34,314	28,816	25,695	27,229	27,513	32,582	38,067	51,687
Albany Co	29,322	29,760	25,050	20,924	18,256	15,902	15,849	16,127	19,228
Albany (city)	17,695	18,024	15,243	12,475	10,178	7,808	7,102	7,785	8,222
Erie Co	147,309	148,692	119,598	97,900	90,144	69,640	56,357	42,950	42,886
Buffalo	121,824	118,941	92,401	70,150	55,020	35,252	22,025	14,741	12,856
Monroe Co	79,491	87,377	72,130	62,041	58,490	56,395	50,722	45,573	53,743
Rochester	71,411	74,839	60,238	49,127	42,044	31,230	20,275	14,423	16,077
Onondaga Co	41,517	44,539	36,055	31,624	30,818	26,576	25,187	21,597	25,929
Syracuse	32,383	35,150	27,632	23,495	21,196	15,707	13,026	10,576	11,214
All others	393,573	409,075	354,740	404,532	307,518	279,566	307,876	314,775	411,472
Foreign-Born (%)									
New York State	27.2	25.9	21.6	17.4	13.6	11.6	13.6	15.9	20.4
New York City and Nassau and Westchester Cos	35.0	32.8	27.4	21.3	18.0	16.3	20.9	25.4	32.3
New York City	36.1	34.0	28.7	22.6	20.0	18.2	23.6	28.4	35.9
Yonkers	25.8	25.5	20.2	16.8	14.3	13.5	16.7	20.2	26.4
Albany Co	15.8	14.0	11.3	8.7	6.7	5.5	5.5	5.5	6.5
Albany (city)	15.6	14.1	11.7	9.2	7.8	6.7	7.0	7.7	8.6
Erie Co	23.2	19.5	15.0	10.9	8.5	6.3	5.5	4.4	4.5
Buffalo	24.0	20.8	16.0	12.1	10.3	7.6	6.2	4.5	4.4
Monroe Co	22.6	20.6	16.5	12.7	10.0	7.9	7.2	6.4	7.3
Rochester	24.1	22.8	18.5	14.8	13.2	10.5	8.4	6.2	7.3
Onondaga Co	17.2	15.3	12.2	9.3	7.3	5.6	5.4	4.6	5.7
Syracuse	18.9	16.8	13.4	10.7	9.8	8.0	7.7	6.5	7.6
All others	13.7	13.0	10.8	11.0	6.8	5.1	5.3	5.2	6.6

Source: US Census.

Note: The foreign-born populations for the above counties in 1920 and 1930 and for counties and cities in 1950 include only Whites.

Compiled by Timothy Calabrese

and the Baltic states, as well as Jews and Germans. The flow of newly arrived immigrants to New York State, however, was not large enough to counteract mortality among older immigrant cohorts and the outflow of immigrants to other states, and the total foreign-born population dipped to 2.6 million in 1950.

The relaxation of immigration restrictions in the prior decade distinguished the 1952 McCarran-Walter Act (also known as Immigration and Nationality Act), especially with regard to Asians. While the law maintained national-origin quotas, it provided the Asian-Pacific region with a quota of 2,000 and permitted Asians and other non-Whites to naturalize. Significant for New York State, the law imposed an annual quota of 100 on colonies, severely restricting immigration from the West Indies, which had previously been covered under the large British quota. Overall immigration increased to nearly 2.5 million in the 1950s, of which 627,000 settled in New York State, but the total foreign-born population continued to fall, dropping to 2.29 million in 1960.

Economic opportunities expanded in the postwar years, as did government loans for aspiring homeowners and other GI benefits, all of which propelled many southern and eastern Europeans into the middle class. Many left cities, such as Buffalo, Rochester, Syracuse, and Albany, to take up residence and the opportunities offered in the developing suburbs. At the same time, these cities were starting to lose manufacturing jobs at an alarming rate and were unable to attract large flows of new immigrants. The inflow of southern African Americans into the state's largest

Percentage Foreign-Born

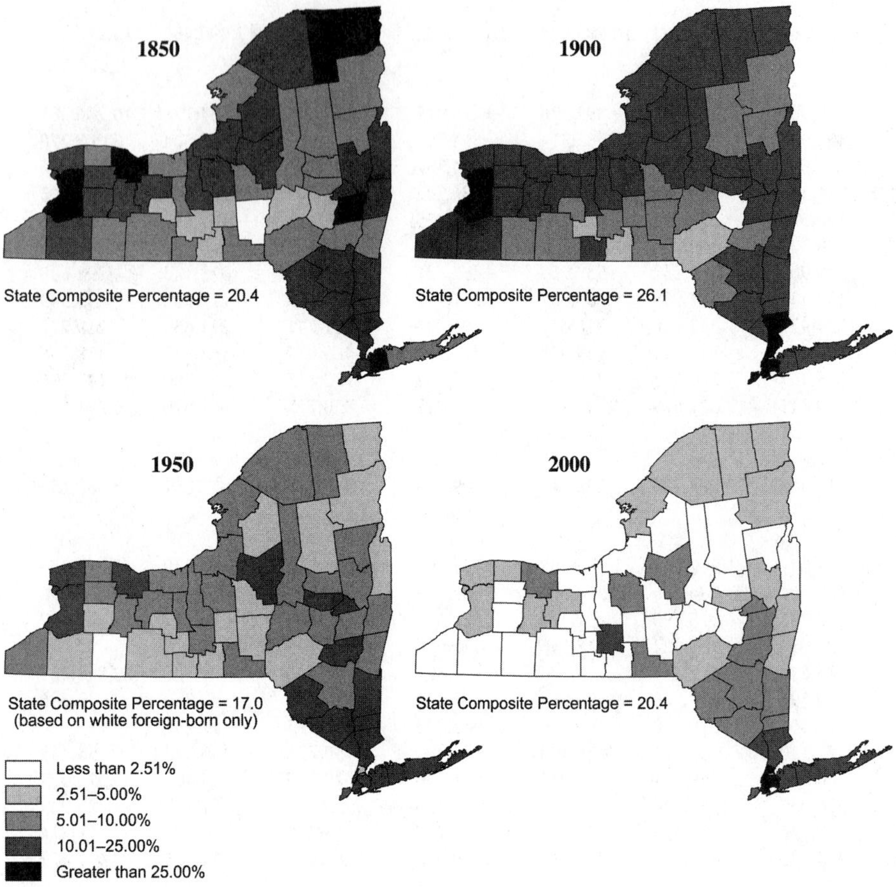

SOURCE: US Census.

cities could not compensate for the large outflow of European ethnics; many cities in New York State began to decline in population, even as the population of the counties in which they were located continued to grow, at least initially.

Although New York City also experienced large-scale white exodus from many of its neighborhoods, the city's population was stabilized by substantial domestic inflows of Blacks and Latinos from the southern United States and from Puerto Rico, respectively, as well as continued immigration. With the overhaul of immigration law in 1965, new immigrants would soon play a vital role in shoring up these neighborhoods and reshaping New York's City's population.

New Immigration

In the 1960s antirestrictionist forces finally prevailed and forced passage of amendments to the Immigration and Nationality Act in 1965. The law as amended abolished immigration quotas based on national origins and made family reunification the main path of entry to the United States. It also allowed the entry of those with employment skills required in the United States and the admission of refugees, defined as those fleeing communist or communist-dominated countries. Though there was an annual ceiling on immigration from the Eastern Hemisphere, "immediate relatives" of US citizens were not subject to any numerical limitation. While the law created opportunities for immigration from all countries, the framers of the law expected immigrants to be overwhelmingly European because they were thought to be the prime beneficiaries of family visas. What was not anticipated, however, was the decline in demand for visas from Europe, or the high demand from non-European sources for the pool of employment visas, whose numbers were being augmented by unused family visas. The law resulted in increased flows, totaling 3.2 million in the 1960s, of whom 747,000 settled in New York State.

The full impact of the 1965 law was felt in the 1970s, with New York State receiving 942,000 immigrants in that decade. This upward trajectory continued for two decades, with immigration flows topping 1 million in the 1980s and reaching nearly 1.3 million in the 1990s. Since 1965, 8 in 10 immigrants to New York State have settled in New York City and have helped counterbalance large domestic outflows from the city. Because of immigration, New York City's population reached an all-time high of 8 million in 2000. Newly arrived immigrants were also settling in the suburbs of New York City. In the 1990s Nassau and Westchester Cos received more immigrants than any other county outside of New York City; close to 5% of all immigrants to New York State settled in Nassau and 4% in Westchester. The rest of New York State received under 11% of immigrants to the state, many of them refugees. Buffalo, Rochester, Syracuse, and Albany have been unable to attract the large numbers of immigrants they did in prior decades. These cities have suffered substantial domestic outflows, resulting in continued drops in their populations.

The effect of large-scale immigration to New York State in the post-1965 years can be seen in the increasing size and share of its foreign-born population. The total foreign-born population, which had bottomed out at 2.1 million in 1970, increased to 2.4 million in 1980 and to 2.9 million in 1990. By 2000 the foreign-born hit the 3.9 million mark, accounting for over 20% of New York State's population, up from 12% in 1970. The foreign-born population in 2000 reached a new peak both in New York City (2.9 million) and in Nassau and Westchester Cos. Approximately 36% of New York City's population in 2000 was foreign-born, close to the same percentage it was at the height of the 1920 wave of immigration. On the other hand, in 2000 the foreign-born population reached its lowest point since before 1900, although there were increases in the number and share of the foreign-born in Rochester, Syracuse, and Albany.

The 1965 law not only boosted immigration levels but also changed the state's immigrant composition. Between 1972 (when computerized records were first available) and 1998, the top 10 source countries of immigrants to New York State were the Dominican Republic, China, Jamaica, the former Soviet Union (mainly the Ukraine and Russia), Guyana, Haiti, India, Colombia, Ecuador, and Trinidad and Tobago. Only one European entity is in the list. Overall flows from Europe represented under one-fifth of the numbers during this period. The unprecedented mix of immigrants has resulted in major changes in the racial and ethnic makeup of New York State, which was 87% white as recently as 1960. By 2000, 35 years after the passage of the 1965 law, the white population was 62%. Given New York City's status as the primary destination for immigrants, racial and ethnic changes were even more dramatic, with the white share of the city's population declining from 85.3% in 1960 to 44.7% in 2000. African Americans accounted for 26.6%; Asians were 9.8%. Those of Latino ethnicity (which can include persons of any race) were 27% of the city's population.

The racial diversity in New York City was complemented by enormous ethnic diversity within the major racial groups. Among Latinos, for example, Puerto Ricans, though still the largest group, were succeeded in neighborhoods such as East Harlem in Manhattan and in the West Bronx by Dominicans and Mexicans. The largest concentration of Dominicans, however, is in Washington Heights in Manhattan, once a bastion for Irish and later German Jewish immigrants. Other Latino groups such as Ecuadorians and Colombians are a major presence in Jackson Heights and Elmhurst in Queens. Among African Americans across southeastern Queens and central Brooklyn, native-born residents with origins in the southern states were being succeeded by immigrants from Caribbean nations such as Jamaica, Haiti, and Guyana. In the 1990s African immigrants from Ghana and Nigeria started settling in the Bronx and in the northern Manhattan neighborhood of Harlem. The fastest growth is among Asians, and three Chinatowns have emerged: the original Chinatown in Lower Manhattan, Sunset Park in western Brooklyn, and Flushing in northern Queens.

Immigrants from the Ukraine and Russia, who are primarily Jewish, settled in the vicinity of Brighton Beach in southern Brooklyn, succeeding native-born eastern European Jews whose roots in the neighborhood go back to the 1920s.

Racial transitions were not as marked outside of New York City, with Whites accounting for 85% of the population in 2000. However, shifts in racial composition were more noticeable in the counties adjacent to New York City, because of their large immigrant populations. In Westchester and Nassau, the immigrant presence was concentrated in urban areas, fed by both a direct flow of new immigrants and immigrant outflows from New York City. Among foreign-born Latinos, there were concentrations of Dominicans in Yonkers; Mexicans in New Rochelle, Yonkers, and White Plains; and Salvadorans in Hempstead and Freeport. Indians and Filipinos were the major foreign-born Asian group in Yonkers, while Jamaicans and Haitians were the largest Caribbean-born groups in Mount Vernon and Yonkers. Whites accounted for just 71.3% of Westchester's population in 2000 and 79.3% of Nassau's.

Refugee flows from the former Soviet Union and Vietnam (including Amerasian children) have left their mark on smaller cites such as Binghamton and Utica, as well as on Rochester, Buffalo, Syracuse, and Albany. Refugees from the former Yugoslavian republic of Bosnia and Herzegovina had a notable presence in Utica. The largest Caribbean presence in New York State outside of New York City, Jamaicans, had concentrations in Rochester and Poughkeepsie. Among foreign-born Latinos, Mexicans had a large presence in Newburgh (Orange Co) and Poughkeepsie, while there were significant clusters of Cubans in Rochester and of Dominicans in Albany. The largest Asian groups, Chinese and Indians, had a small presence across New York State outside of the New York City metropolitan area. Despite low immigration, many of these cities experienced dramatic changes in their racial composition. In 2000 Whites made up 48% of Rochester's population, 54% of Buffalo's, 63% of Albany's, and 64% of Syracuse's. Whites constituted roughly 90% of the population for all of these cities in 1960. However, these changes were more a result of the vacuum created by white losses than an influx of new immigrant groups; most of the nonwhite population consists of native-born African Americans.

New York State's ethnic mix continues to change because of high levels of intermarriage. A majority of Whites have a spouse of a different ethnic background. For the children of such unions, ethnicity is mainly symbolic, and ethnic identity is a matter of choosing among multiple backgrounds. This phenomenon is also increasingly evident among Latinos, where intermarriage between Latino ethnic groups is common. The growth in racial marital unions has substantially added to the racial/ethnic mix of New York State, with 3% of residents listing themselves as multiracial in the 2000 census.

Continuing immigration is likely to diversify further New York State's population because of the "diversity visa" legislation first passed in 1986 and made permanent in the 1990 Immigration Act. This program makes visas available to people from nations that are underrepresented in the flow of immigrants to the United States. The diversity flow in the 1990s helped Bangladeshis, Ghanaians, and Nigerians, among others, establish a presence in New York State. *—JJS and APL*

See also UNDOCUMENTED IMMIGRATION.

Alba, Richard. "The Melting Pot: Myth or Reality?" In *Race and Ethnicity in the United States,* ed. S. Steinberg (Malden, Mass: Blackwell, 2000)

———, et al. "Neighborhood Change under Conditions of Mass Immigration: The New York City Region, 1970–1990," *International Migration Review* 29 (1995): 625–56

Berrol, Selma. *The Empire City: New York and Its People, 1624–1996* (Westport, Conn: Praeger, 1997)

Binder, Frederick, and David Reimers. *All the Nations under Heaven: An Ethnic and Racial History of New York City* (New York: Columbia Univ Press, 1995)

Burrows, Edwin G., and Mike Wallace. *Gotham: A History of New York City to 1898* (New York: Oxford Univ Press, 1999)

Cohen, David S. *The Dutch-American Farm* (New York: New York Univ Press, 1992)

Daniels, Roger. *Coming to America: A History of Immigration and Ethnicity in American Life,* 2d ed. (New York: Harper Collins, 2002)

Foner, Nancy. *From Ellis Island to JFK: New York's Two Great Waves of Immigration* (New Haven, Conn: Yale Univ Press, 2000)

———, ed. *New Immigrants in New York,* 2d ed. (New York: Columbia Univ Press, 2001)

Jackson, Kenneth T., ed. *The Encyclopedia of New York City* (New Haven, Conn: Yale Univ Press, 1995)

Klein, Milton M., ed. *The Empire State: A History of New York* (Ithaca: Cornell Univ Press, 2001)

Knoblauch, Edward H. "Mobilizing Provincials for War: The Social Composition of New York Forces in 1760," *New York History* 78 (Apr 1997): 147–72

LeMay, Michael C. *From Open Door to Dutch Door: An Analysis of US Immigration Policy since 1820* (New York: Praeger, 1987)

Lobo, Arun Peter, and Joseph J. Salvo. "The Role of Nativity and Ethnicity in the Residential Settlement of Blacks in New York, 1970–1990." In *Immigration Today: Pastoral and Research Challenges,* ed. Lydio Tomasi and Mary Powers (New York: Center for Migration Studies, 1999)

Lobo, Arun Peter, Ronald J. O. Flores, and Joseph J. Salvo. "The Impact of Hispanic Growth on the Racial/Ethnic Composition of New York City Neighborhoods," *Urban Affairs Review* 37 (2002): 703–27

Lobo, Arun Peter, Joseph J. Salvo, and Vicky Virgin. *The Newest New Yorkers: 1990–1994: An Analysis of Immigration to New York City in the Early 1990s* (New York: New York City Department of City Planning, 1996)

Waters, Mary. *Ethnic Options: Choosing Identities in America* (Berkeley: Univ of California, 1990)

Philip A. Bean, Field Horne, Arun Peter Lobo, Joseph J. Salvo

impossibility defense. The New York State Court of Appeals decision in *People v Jaffe* (1906) offered a significant precedent for the legal impossibility defense. Lawyers for Samuel Jaffe, charged with attempting to receive stolen property, argued that he had not committed a crime because while the defendant thought he was buying stolen goods, they were not in fact stolen. The court sided with the defense, ruling that an individual could not be convicted of attempting to commit a crime when facts unknown to the defendant would have made the completion of the perpetration of the crime impossible. New York State upheld this ruling until the revision of the Penal Code in 1967, when it sought to eliminate the defense of impossibility. In 1977 the New York State Court of Appeals reiterated this idea in *People v Dlugash* by emphasizing the defendant's mental "frame of reference": that what was in the actor's mind should be the standard for determining his/her criminal liability. Thus the state could prosecute someone for attempted murder, even though the victim may have already been dead. It is no defense that the crime was factually or legally impossible if the crime could have been committed had the circumstances been as the defendant believed them to be.

Hasnas, John. "Once More unto the Breach: The Inherent Liberalism of the Criminal Law and Liability for Attempting the Impossible," *Hastings Law Journal* 54 (Nov 2002)

Gary Gershman

Independence. Town (pop 1,074) in SE Allegany Co. Although a squatter was present as early as 1798, the area was settled in 1818; it was formed as a town in 1821 from Alfred. In the mid–19th century Whitesville was a small manufacturing center that had a tannery, a woolen factory, a foundry, and an agricultural implement factory, and in 1896 it had a beehive manufactory. In 1875 Independence led Allegany Co in potato and maple sugar production and ranked second in butter. Whitesville celebrates Memorial Day with an annual parade and barbecue.

Independence Party. Political party. Formed before the 1994 gubernatorial election as the Independence Fusion Party, it achieved official status after that year's statewide elections and changed its name to the Independence Party shortly thereafter. Socially liberal and inclusive, it lacks articulated stances on social issues but emphasizes representation of the independent voter, fiscal responsibility, and government accountability and efficiency. Many of its original activists either supported Ross Perot's bid for president in 1992 or were dissatisfied with the Democratic and Republican candidates. Some sought to create a third party as a way to cross-endorse other party candidates in the governor's race. The Independents backed Rochester-area billionaire B. Thomas Golisano for governor in 1994, 1998, and 2002, with Golisano backing each campaign with millions of dollars of his own money and placing third in each race with 217,490, 364,056, and 633,000 votes, respectively. The party supported Perot in the 1996 presidential race but distanced itself from the national Reform Party in the late 1990s and backed its own candidate, physicist John Hagelin, in the 2000 presidential elections. Some of the Independent Party's greatest influence has been in municipal and town elections, where its cross-endorsement of major party candidates has often provided the margin of victory. In 2003 the party was the state's third largest, with 273,056 enrolled members—including 83,462 New York City residents—and was not affiliated with any national party.

Independence Party of New York State, http://ipny.org/

Sifry, Micah L. *Spoiling for a Fight: Third-Party Politics in America* (New York: Routledge, 2002)

John Evers

Independent Reflector. Journal published from 30 Nov 1752 to 22 Nov 1753. Initiated, written, and edited by William Livingston, a New York lawyer and pamphleteer, with the collaboration of fellow Yale graduates, William Smith Jr, John Morin Scott, and others. The group's object was to promote the cultural development of the province by essays on manners and morals, along the lines of the English journals the *Tattler* and the *Spectator*, but the publication soon became a lively, crusading paper, criticizing many of the colony's shortcomings. Its most controversial numbers were six essays protesting plans to establish a college in the colony under Anglican auspices and chartered by the Crown. Livingston proposed a less sectarian institution chartered by the assembly. Under pressure from the DeLancey-controlled provincial government, printer James Parker terminated publication abruptly. The paper and Livingston became widely known throughout the colonies. The journal's challenge to royal prerogative was an important precursor to the ideology of the American Revolution.

Klein, Milton M., ed. *The Independent Reflector, or, Weekly Essays on Sundry Important Subjects, More Particularly Adapted to the Province of New-York,* by William Livingston (Cambridge: Harvard Univ Press, 1963)

Milton M. Klein

Indian Defense League of America (IDLA). The oldest American Indian rights group still in existence. It was organized originally to protest the restrictions of the Immigration Act of 1924, which had been interpreted to prohibit Indians from Canada from crossing into the United States. On 1 Dec 1926 Clinton Rickard from the Tuscarora Indian Reservation [loc in Niagara Co] and Indians from Canada living in Niagara Falls formed the Six Nations Defense League as a means of working to restore Indian rights to cross the border, keeping with the provisions of the Jay Treaty of 1794. The group shortly thereafter changed its title to the Indian Defense League of America to represent all Indian peoples on both sides of the border. In 1927 Rickard met with members of Congress and other government officials in Washington, DC, to secure their support of legislation permitting Indians to cross the Canadian border into the United States.

A separate lawsuit brought by a Philadelphia law firm on behalf of Paul Diabo, a Caughnawaga Mohawk ironworker from Quebec, was a major breakthrough on the border-crossing issue. *McCandless, Commissioner of Immigration v US ex rel Diabo* was decided in favor of the Indians in the US district court in 1927 and upheld in the US Court of Appeals in 1928. A bill supporting Indian border-crossing rights presented in 1927 at Rickard's urging worked its way through Congress and was signed into law by Pres Calvin Coolidge in 1928. In recognition of its victory in Congress, on 14 July 1928 the IDLA held a border-crossing celebration combined with a recognition of traditional Indian culture. This celebration continues to be held on the third Saturday in July between Niagara Falls and Niagara Falls, Ont, in alternating directions every other year. After winning the border-crossing struggle, the IDLA continued to speak to the many concerns of the Indian people. In the 1970s it conducted labor negotiations between Algonquin fur workers from Quebec and the owner of a mink ranch in Ontario Co, succeeded in having the substandard housing of the workers satisfactorily upgraded, and won a workers' compensation case for one worker. At the height of its influence in the 1930s and 1940s, the IDLA had branches in Niagara Falls and Buffalo but was active on reservations in New York State, Ontario, and Quebec. The organization continues into the 21st century.

Graymont, Barbara, ed. *Fighting Tuscarora: The Autobiography of Chief Clinton Rickard* (Syracuse: Syracuse Univ Press, 1973)
Hauptman, Laurence M. *The Iroquois Struggle for Survival: World War II to Red Power* (Syracuse: Syracuse Univ Press, 1986)

Barbara Graymont

Indian Lake. Town (pop 1,471) in E Hamilton Co. Sabael Benedict (*d* 1855), a Penobscot/Abenaki, was the first permanent resident, about the time of the Revolutionary War. The first white settler arrived *ca* 1840, and a colony of Irish from Ticonderoga (Essex Co) settled at Tirrell Pond in 1851. The town was formed from Long Lake, Wells, and the extinct town of Gilman in 1858. Lumbering got underway in the mid–19th century. Novelist Ned Buntline (Edward Zane Carroll Judson) lived at Eagle Lake from 1856 to 1862. Sportsmen came as early as 1853, and after the Civil War, hotels were built to accommodate them, the most notable being the Prospect House (1881–1903). They were facilitated by the railroad terminus (1871) at nearby North Creek (Warren Co). The town remains a tourist destination, especially because of the Adirondack Museum (1957). Indian Lake, enlarged in 1845 by a loggers' dam and again in 1898, has been joined by two other lakes, Adirondack (1909), with a floating island, and Abanakee (1951). Blue Mountain Lake is the town's natural large body of water.

Indians. See AMERICAN INDIANS.

Indians and South Asians. Indians (also known as Asian Indians, East Indians, or South Asians) are an ethnic group from the Indian subcontinent, which comprises the countries of India, Pakistan, Bangladesh, Sri Lanka, and Nepal. South Asian immigrants also come from Great Britain; countries in East, Central, and South Africa; the Malayan Peninsula, Hong Kong, and Fiji; and the Caribbean countries of Trinidad and Tobago and Guyana. The 2000 US census tallied approximately 350,000 people of South Asian descent in New York State, about one-fifth of the total Indian population in the United States. Although dispersed across the state, they live primarily in urban areas, about 60% in New York City. Within the city, Queens has the largest concentration of Indians, Brooklyn the most extensive Pakistani and Bangladeshi neighborhoods, and the Bronx a concentration of Guyanese and Trinidadian Indians. An additional 23% live in suburban counties around New York City. There are also significant concentrations in the Buffalo, Rochester, Syracuse, and Albany metropolitan areas.

History and Demography

The earliest Indian immigrants came to New York State in the mid–19th century, most of them either businessmen or students in Protestant seminaries. Hindu emissaries, including Swami Vivekananda (1863–1902), began arriving in the United States by the 1890s, establishing the first Vedanta Center in New York City in 1894 for the pursuit of universal aspects of the spiritual wisdom of the Hindu traditions. By the early 20th century graduate students from India began coming for advanced studies in New York City, among them B. R. Ambedkar, who received a doctorate from Columbia University in 1916, a leader of so-called low castes and a co-framer of India's constitution (1949). India's independence from Great Britain in 1947 cut some of those traditional educational ties, and increasing numbers of students came to New York State universities. In addition, the Immigration and Nationality Act of 1965 further relaxed quotas, and many professionally qualified scientists, engineers, and physicians came to stay. The number of Indian immigrants jumped from 2,459 in 1966 to about 10,000 in 1970 and totaled upward of 20,000 annually by 1977. A significant number of South Asians from the Caribbean countries, South Africa, Malaysia, and Fiji are descendants of indentured plantation workers hired by British colonialists in the 19th century.

The education level of Indians is unusually high for a new immigrant group; many who entered in the 1980s and 1990s under family or relative visa preference have had some college background. And while those who came in 1960s and 1970s were scientists, engineers, physicians, and educators, more recent immigrants work in a variety of professions, including nursing and management. Many are small entrepreneurs and flourish in the construction, garment, computer, motel and hotel, convenience store, newsstand, and taxi businesses. Research has shown that many Indians are overqualified for the jobs they hold, evidence that participation in the American marketplace has not been without problems. The group is unique, however, in that first-generation immigrants have often managed middle- or upper-middle-class status.

Culture and Religion

The Indian community in New York State is a microcosm of the complex and variegated culture of the Indian subcontinent, which contains 23 different languages and a variety of food habits, religious observances, and social customs. Interactions between Indians in America and relatives and friends at home help maintain a sense of cultural identity. Although English serves as a common language for South Asian immigrants in the United States, the different languages commonly set off the different groups and establish the limits of marriages, foods, music, literature, and often religion. The more widely spoken languages are Gujarati, Punjabi, Bengali, Malayalam, and Hindi-Urdu, although the latter is underrepresented in United States in comparison with its prevalence in India. Other common languages among South Asians are Assamese, Baluchi, Dogri, Kannada, Kashmiri, Konkani, Marathi, Nepali, Odiya, Pushto, Rajasthani, Sindhi, Sinhala, Tarnil, and Telugu. There are cultural-literary associations of these languages, and most have magazines, newspapers, and radio and television programs. Many of these languages are taught at religious meeting places or schools. The more numerous language groups have more than one newspaper and radio and television programs.

Approximately 200 ethnic grocery stores sell ingredients for Indian foods and religious ceremonies, and there are at least that many restaurants in New York State. Indian cuisine is known for its distinctly spiced tandoori dishes of chicken or meat on skewers cooked in the intense heat of a clay oven. But in the Indian community the variety of regional cuisines is wide, including Bengali, Gujarati, South Indian, and Kashmiri. Ethnic shopping areas in Queens and Manhattan offer a variety of Indian restaurants and fashion and jewelry shops.

Almost 60% of the Indian and South Asian population are considered Hindu. This ancient tradition is followed by worship at home (where small shrines are maintained) or at one of the 90 temples in urban areas of New York State. Many temples have full-time priests who also visit homes for special services and marriages, funerary rites, and other significant occasions. New York State has a variety of Indian spiritual masters and their ashrams for earnest seekers, visited by Hindus and non-Hindus alike for yoga, meditation, and other spiritual practices.

Among South Asians Islam has the most adherents after Hinduism, primarily Pakistani and Bangladeshi immigrants, but many from India as well. Distinct Indian Islamic groups present in New York State include the Ismaili Shiites under the Aga Khan, the Dawoodi Bohras of Gujarat, and the Ahmadiyyas, who have had a presence in New York City since the early 1920s.

Other religious traditions include Sikhism, which originated in the Punjab region and uses that language in its temples. Sikhism combines the teachings of Hindu Bhakti (devotion) and the Muslim Sufis. There are 22 Sikh places of worship in New York State, with the majority in New York City. Estimates of Sikh population in the state range between 30,000 and 50,000. Jainism is another tradition; it views life as a gift of togetherness, accommodation, and assistance in a universe teeming with interdependent constituents. There are over a dozen Jainist places of worship in New York State and approximately 3,500 adherents. Approximately 4,000 Zoroastrians, who stress the importance of good words, good thoughts, and good deeds, live in New York State and have three associations in New York City. There is a small group of Marathi-speaking Bene Israeli Orthodox Jews from the Konkan coast of India. Indian Christians in the state belong to many different denominations, and some attend churches in their communities, but a significant number are Malayalam speakers from Kerala who worship in the native Orthodox church called Mar Thoma. Roman Catholic and Protestant Christians speaking Tamil, Telugu, Gujarati, Punjabi, and Hindi have their own congregations, and some have their own radio programs.

Most marriages are arranged by families, friends, caste members, and professional marriage bureaus; very few, mainly the highly educated, marry outside of the Indian community. Additionally, prospective spouses are found through magazines like *India Abroad,* which feature classified marriage advertisements. Family ties are important, and the elderly live mostly with their children.

New York City and State have a large number of active business and professional organizations of South Asians—physicians, hoteliers, builders, jewelers, diamond merchants, financiers, accountants, pharmacists, social workers, newsstand owners, taxi drivers—cutting across religious, linguistic, and country of origin lines to work for economic and professional betterment. Political fund-raising at various levels of local and state government is one way South Asians work to influence public policy related to their profession. All the important community functions, notably India's Independence Day of 15 August and the Diwali (Festival of Light) of late October, draw huge crowds and many political leaders. New York City offers a vibrant theater, a movie industry, Indian dance events, and Hindi film music with visiting Mumbai artists. Indian food, music, dance, movies, literary works, spiritual practices, and intellectual and professional achievement help define the Indian community. Local print media, radio, and television also help create community consciousness and recognition by mainstream New Yorkers of the existence of a unique ethnic group that adds to the rich diversity of the state.

Eck, Diana L. *A New Religious America: How a "Christian Country" Has Become the World's Most Religiously Diverse Nation* (New York: Harper San Francisco, 2001)

Khandelwal, Madhulika S. *Becoming American, Being Indian: An Immigrant Community in New York City* (Ithaca: Cornell Univ Press, 2002)

Williams, Raymond Brady. *Religions of Immigrants from India and Pakistan: New Threads in the American Tapestry* (Cambridge and New York: Cambridge Univ Press, 1988)

Bharat L. Bhatt

Industrial Workers of the World. A radical labor union formed in Chicago in June 1905, the Industrial Workers of the World (IWW) advocated boycotts and strikes to promote working-class interests. Known also as the Wobblies, this union attempted to organize all workers, regardless of trade or ethnic, racial, or gender background. Active primarily in the mining and lumber industries of the West, the IWW also was involved in notable strikes in New York State. In 1906 the IWW organized one of America's first recorded sit-down strikes, involving 3,000 workers at the General Electric plant in Schenectady. In New York City, the IWW, led by Elizabeth Gurley Flynn, Joseph Ettor, and Arturo Giovannitti, assisted 18,000 hotel and restaurant workers in a strike starting on 7 May 1912. After a seven-week walkout, the workers were ultimately defeated. New York City IWW organizers achieved one of the union's most notable victories in 1912 when Ettor and Giovannitti led a Lawrence, Mass, textile strike that ended with management agreeing to worker demands. That year the IWW was involved in a textile strike in Little Falls (Herkimer Co). IWW's rank and file has greatly diminished since the late 1920s. In 2001 total membership was approximately 1,100, with the IWW–New York City branch numbering 12 persons.

Dubofsky, Melvyn. *We Shall Be All: A History of the IWW* (New York: Quadrangle Books, 1969)

John Cashman

Influenza Pandemic, 1918–19. Influenza epidemics were common during fall and winter months, but the strain that caused the 1918–19 epidemic was remarkable in its virulence. Although the flu is usually deadly in the very young and the elderly, this strain, erroneously named "Spanish Influenza," was fatal more often in persons aged 15–45. The rapid spread of disease was linked to army and navy personnel crowded into training camps during the final months of World War I. Soldiers taking leave in nearby cities and traveling in public conveyances increased civilian exposure. Being near a military installation or acting as a transportation hub predisposed a community to greater danger, but cooperation among public and private authorities resulted in more effective control even in densely populated communities. New York City, for example, had a lower fatality rate than many other cities and towns in the state.

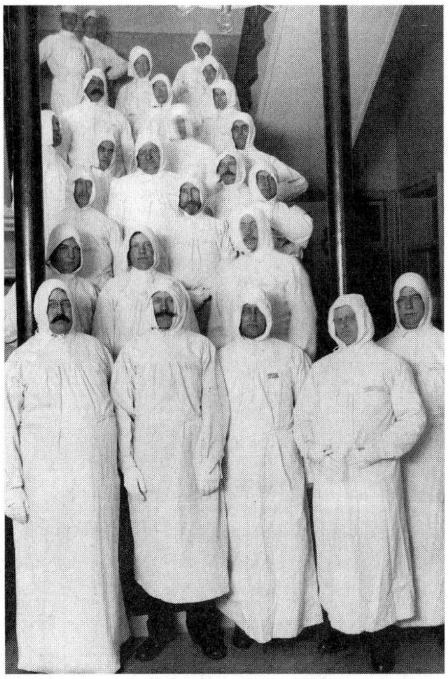

Medical personnel during the Influenza Pandemic, Buffalo, 1918.

The *New York Times* reported that the first cases in the state were merchant mariners who shipped into New York Harbor on 13 Sept 1918. They were promptly quarantined. When civilian cases appeared in Manhattan, Health Commissioner Royal S. Copeland declared influenza a reportable disease; all physicians were required to inform the Board of Health of new cases. By late September incoming travelers who appeared to have the "grippe" were detained and examined at railroad stations. They were not allowed to ride public transit to their destinations in the city. Shortly afterward the Board of Health ordered the opening and closing times of businesses, factories, and theaters to be staggered, thereby thinning crowds during rush hours. Copeland ordered tight monitoring of the availability of hospital beds and divided the city into districts for more efficient medical and nursing care. Despite opposition, he refused to close schools, declaring them more healthful places for students than their own homes.

Other communities came under the jurisdiction of the State Department of Health, which quickly declared influenza a reportable disease, made "unguarded" coughing and sneezing in public a misdemeanor, and flooded localities with literature about avoiding contagion and caring for victims. Less than two weeks after it appeared in New York City, the epidemic skipped northward to Victory Mills and Schuylerville (Saratoga Co) and then westward to Oswego. As a Great Lakes port and with the Fort Ontario Army Hospital on the city's outskirts, Oswego was more vulnerable than other municipalities of comparable size. The disease struck approximately 3,500 of Oswego's 23,000 inhabi-

INFLUENZA AND PNEUMONIA DEATHS IN NEW YORK STATE CITIES, 1918–19

City	Sept–Dec 1918	Jan–June 1919	Total	Excess[a]
Albany	623	225	848	646
Buffalo	2,474	857	3,331	2,548
Rochester	1,125	333	1,458	1,125
Syracuse	943	203	1,146	951
Boroughs of New York City				
Bronx	2,899	1,483	4,382	3,181
Brooklyn	8,497	4,535	13,032	9,165
Manhattan	9,418	5,260	14,678	9,857
Queens	1,778	877	2,665	1,976
Richmond	673	282	955	764
New York City total	23,265	12,437	35,702	24,943

Source: Bureau of the Census, *Mortality Statistics, 1919* (1921).

Note: Only cities of 100,000 or more in population are included.

[a]Excess numbers are based on the corresponding death totals for 1915, which are assumed to represent normal rates.

Compiled by Jacqueline Villarrubia-Mendoza

tants by the first week of October. With half its normal complement of physicians and nurses in military service, the community faced a crisis it could not handle. The Health Department quickly sent aid: physicians in the Communicable Diseases Division and supervising nurses of the Public Health Nursing Division. They established central information bureaus, organized nurses, and created temporary hospitals. When the situation came under control, the state medical personnel were reassigned to Dunkirk (Chautauqua Co), Binghamton, Syracuse, Schenectady, and other communities paralyzed by the epidemic. Meanwhile, scientists in the State Division of Laboratories and Research worked to develop an effective vaccine, volunteering themselves for inoculation. A $50,000 federal grant to the state funded additional help from US Health Service physicians and nurses.

Most major communities in the state adopted measures similar to New York City's. Indiscriminate spitters, coughers, and sneezers were arrested and fined. Public conveyances were fumigated, and their windows were kept open despite cold weather. At the epidemic's height theaters, taverns, and schools were closed by municipal ordinances. Churches voluntarily suspended services. Although the occurrence of disease waned in November, new cases of influenza and its attendant complication, pneumonia, continued into the new year. More than a half million New Yorkers were afflicted, and the death toll reached into the tens of thousands.

Crosby, Alfred W. *America's Forgotten Pandemic: The Influenza of 1918* (1976; repr New York: Cambridge Univ Press, 1989)

Teresa K. Lehr

Ingham University. The first women's university in the United States began as the Le Roy Female Seminary (Genesee Co), founded by sisters Marietta Ingham and Emily Ingham in 1837. Ingham University was chartered by New York State in 1857 with authority to grant college degrees at the baccalaureate and master's levels. Several noted educators served on its faculty, including portraitist Phineas Staunton, head of the art department, chosen as chief artist for an 1867 Smithsonian Institution South American expedition. Ingham University was organized into three major divisions: a literary college, an art college, and a conservatory of music. Only women were admitted to the literary college, though men could study in the other two. During its 35 years Ingham graduated 346 women and 5 men, the latter in art.

The university was originally the property of the Ingham sisters. However, the 1867 deaths of Marietta and of Emily's husband, Phineas Staunton, who succumbed to yellow fever while on his South American expedition, the opening of state normal schools in nearby Geneseo (Livingston Co) and Brockport (Monroe Co), and the depression in 1873 led the trustees to transfer the university to Presbyterian Synod of Genesee. In 1883 it was passed to a Le Roy business group. When the university closed in 1892 in bankruptcy, the property was purchased by a Le Roy banker and later conveyed by bequest to Yale University. Eventually the buildings were demolished, the founders' remains were moved from their campus burial plot, and in 1908 the land was sold to the Le Roy school district. In 1999 a marker was erected at the university site by the women of Le Roy in memory of the Ingham alumnae.

Wing, Richard L. "Ingham University, 1857–1892: An Exploration of the Life and Death of an Early Institution of Higher Education for Women" (PhD diss, SUNY Buffalo, 1990)

Richard L. Wing

Inlet. Town (pop 406) in W Hamilton Co. Camps were built on Fourth Lake in the 1870s, and the Mohawk and Malone (1892) and Raquette Lake (1900) Railroads made the town easily accessible. Inlet was formed in 1901 from Morehouse. By the 1920s it was a major vacation spot and remains an important summer destination. Inlet Common School, one of the last in the state, continues to educate the town's children; older students travel to Webb (Herkimer Co) for the upper grades.

Inness, George (*b* Newburgh, Orange Co, 1 May 1825; *d* Bridge-of-Allan, Scotland, 3 Aug 1894). Artist. Inness's family moved to New York City soon after his birth but relocated to Newark, NJ in 1829. Inness attended the Newark Academy for a short time and had only minimal formal education afterward. His first art teacher, John Jesse Barker of Newark, was an itinerant painter. About this time (1841) Inness moved back to New York City and began an apprenticeship with the mapmaking firm of Sherman and Smith. He studied with his most significant teacher, French landscape painter Régis-François Gignoux, in New York City in 1843. The next year Inness had his first exhibition at the National Academy of Design and by the late 1840s was exhibiting regularly in New York City. Elected as an associate of the academy in 1853, he was also an early member of the Society of American Artists. The Hudson River school influenced his early work, but Inness later began to engage and express the ideals of the Barbizon landscape style. In 1860 he moved to Massachusetts. Although known for his landscapes, Inness is also recognized for the allusive religious serenity of his work, showing the influence of the Swedish mystic Emanuel Swedenborg. Some of his major paintings are *Spring Blossoms, Montclair, New Jersey* (?1891) at the Metropolitan Museum of Art, *Coming Storm* (1878) at the Albright-Knox Art Gallery in Buffalo, and *June, 1882* at the Brooklyn Museum of Art.

Cikovsky, Nicolai, Jr. *George Inness* (New York: Harry N. Abrams, 1993)

David B. Malone

insanity defense. According to New York State law in 2004, a defendant may be found not criminally responsible for an offense because of "mental disease or defect." The current insanity defense is the result of a long evolution through the New York State court system. Traditionally, American law in most of the 50 states relied on the English precedent known as the McNaughtan Rule, established in 1843. Under that rule, defendants had to show they suffered from a mental disease causing a defect in their reasoning powers and that as a result they either did not understand the "nature and quality" of their act or did not know that the act was wrong. One of New York State's most famous 19th-century cases involving an insanity defense was the trial of William Freeman, accused of murdering four people in Fleming (Cayuga Co) and found guilty in 1846.

The McNaughtan Rule was affirmed by the Court of Appeals, New York State's highest court, in *Flanagan v People* (1873). The reasoning in Flanagan was embodied in late 19th-century statutes passed by the New York State legislature. These standards were clarified throughout the first half of the 20th century in a variety of cases. No significant changes were made until 1965, when the legislature instituted language that modified the law and raised the bar for pleading a defense of insanity by redefining key phrases such as "knowledge" and what constituted knowing the difference between right and wrong. These changes reflected growing disenchantment with the McNaughtan Rule that permeated not only New York State but also the country as a whole. Five years later, in *People v Adams* (1970), the state's high court interpreted and tested the new standard. In discussing the differences with McNaughtan, the court noted the new rule was a more realistic assessment of the mental state of the defendant than the total impairment demanded under the old rule. The Court of Appeals also emphasized that defendants could now be held criminally responsible only if they had some concrete understanding of the offense rather than just a surface understanding.

In the wake of the Torsney case (Robert Torsney, a police officer, was arrested for a cold-blooded killing, found not guilty by reason of insanity, and later released) and the ensuing public outcry, the New York legislature passed the Insanity Defense Reform Act of 1980, which created more stringent guidelines regarding the insanity defense, especially in the continuing evaluation and eventual release phase. This did not put the issue to rest, and four years later the legislature again amended the statutory provisions of the insanity defense. In that law, standards were set forth that are in effect at the start of the 21st century. In *People v Kohl* (1988) the Court of Appeals upheld this subsequent adjustment and declared it was acceptable to make the insanity defense an affirmative one, placing the burden of proof on the defendant. *Kohl* also upheld the new statutory construction as not violating the due process clause of either the New York State or US Constitutions. These changes mirrored revisions on the national level in the federal Insanity Defense Reform Act of 1984. Such attempts in the 1980s to restrict the use of the insanity defense reflected the outcry over cases such as that of John Hinckley, who had attempted to assassinate Pres Ronald Reagan in 1981. Thus, in 2003, the New York Code (§40.15) demands the defendant show at the time of the commission of the crime a lack of "substantial capacity" to know or appreciate either the nature and consequences of such conduct or that such conduct was wrong.

Simon, Rita J., and David E. Aaronson. *The Insanity Defense* (New York: Praeger, 1988)

Gary Gershman

insurance, automobile. As soon as cars and trucks appeared on New York State roadways in the early 20th century, insurance companies offered policies to cover costs resulting from accidents. Insurers who offered auto coverage included fire and life companies such as Liberty Mutual and Prudential. Yet few policies were sold because there were only a small number of cars. With the affluence of the 1920s, however, car ownership skyrocketed. In 1928 alone New York State recorded 2,582 deaths caused by motor vehicle collisions. In response, pressure arose for legislation encouraging drivers to be both more responsible and insured. Gov Franklin D. Roosevelt signed the Safety-Responsibility bill, effective 1 Sept 1929 and sponsored by the American Automobile Association, requiring drivers to compensate injured parties in an accident within a specified time and depriving those who did not comply of their right to drive. The law proved reasonably effective, although by the end of the 1930s rising accident rates, caused in part by high speeds on newly constructed parkways, led to a push for more comprehensive coverage.

Although there were already calls for compulsory insurance, the Page-Anderson bill, effective 1 Jan 1942, merely required all drivers involved in an accident to post either $15,000 in cash, a surety bond, or present proof of insurance. The bill's sponsors hoped that the provisions of the law were onerous enough to raise the coverage rate, and approximately 60% of motor vehicles registered in the state during World War II had liability insurance. In 1946 the Assigned Risk Plan made insurance mandatory for high-risk owners of vehicles, and these policies were spread among many insurers to mitigate risk. The creation of the Motor Vehicle Liability Security Fund in 1947 provided protection to drivers insured by companies that became insolvent, but New York State still lacked a compulsory auto insurance law. Such a law was championed by Assembly Speaker Oswald D. Heck, who sponsored and passed through the lower house a compulsory auto insurance bill in both 1954 and 1955. Yet Heck's bill was defeated each time in the state senate by that Majority Leader Walter J. Mahoney; closely tied to insurance interests, Mahoney saw the legislation as unnecessary. Rapid increases in both car ownership and in uninsured accidents, however, forced Mahoney to relent.

The compulsory legislation, effective 1 Jan 1957, required all motor vehicle owners registered in the state to carry $10,000 in liability insurance. However, the law, following the tort-liability system, led to frequent lawsuits, which inhibited quick restitution to drivers, increased the state court's caseload dramatically, lowered insurance company profits, and raised the cost of auto insurance. In 1973 the state legislature responded by passing legislation, which Gov Nelson A. Rockefeller signed that February, creating a no-fault auto insurance system. State residents could now opt for a no-fault insurance policy, enabling quick settlements between parties (damage had to be less than $500) without assigning fault to any driver. Trial lawyers and some consumer groups opposed the law, arguing the legislation limited drivers' legal rights. The state legislature amended the no-fault system law over time with an eye toward limiting litigation even more, but no-fault insurance remains. In 1989 New York State government began to arbitrate some claims, but in 1999 the disputes began to be taken by the American Arbitration Association. Historically, New York State's motor vehicle owners have consistently paid higher premiums than most other states.

Mehr, Robert I., and Emerson Cammach. *Principles of Insurance* (Homewood, Ill: R. D. Irwin, 1985)

Thomas E. Mertes

insurance, fire, marine, and casualty. Marine insurance covers property and casualty losses incurred on the high seas. During most of the colonial period, after an act of Parliament in 1719 banned the founding of stock insurance firms in British America, mariners in New York relied on European insurers. After the American Revolution, however, marine underwriters began to appear in New York State. In 1796 New York Insurance Co became the state's first insurance firm to write marine coverage. Less than 15 years later New York City had more than 10 companies. The Board of Underwriters, which set industry-wide guidelines, was founded in New York City in 1820. Because significant amounts of capital were needed to establish an insurance concern, New York City became home to many of the nation's marine underwriters. The powerful Atlantic Mutual Co was created in New York City in 1842. Yet with the dominance of the British Merchant Marine and British underwriters for the remainder of the century, the American and New York State market declined. This situation reversed after World War II, and the Chubb Group of Insurance Cos (founded in 1882 in New York City), became a postwar world leader in marine insurance. Increases in the international oil trade, the globalization of the airline industry, and general increases in world markets stimulated by free trade agreements have all solidified the dominance of New York State marine underwriters.

The Knickerbocker Fire Insurance Co, based in New York City, was the first concern to write fire policies in the state. Founded in 1787, it was built upon the techniques and practices of marine insurers as well as upon the pioneering work of Benjamin Franklin and his Union Fire Co. Other fire insurers were formed as Manhattan expanded, but the state's fire insurance industry was devastated by New York City's Great Fire of 1835; the conflagration consumed the city's downtown of nearly 600 buildings, bankrupting 23 of the 26 fire insurers in the state and opening the state's fire insurance market to competitors. One lesson from the disaster was the need for insurance firms to diversify their policies geographically to spread risk. In the 1850s many New York City underwriters began to organize themselves as mutual rather than stock companies in an attempt to meet the growing capitalization demands of the burgeoning insurance market. One of these new mutual fire insurers was the Utica Fire Insurance Co of Oneida Co, formed in 1903. Again a disastrous fire, this time in Chicago in 1871, led to numerous bankruptcies of New York State firms and undermined support for underwriters organized by the mutual company arrangement, which tended to have fewer reserve funds than a stock company. In response to this and other nefarious industry practices, the state legislature, in 1886, passed and Gov David B. Hill signed into law the Standard Fire Policy. This policy, enforced by the State Insurance Department, mandated a plain and straightforward fire contract, thereby standardizing fire contracts statewide; over time New York State's fire policy became the standard for the entire fire insurance industry.

In the early 20th century New York State companies formed the American Foreign Insurance Association, a consortium of fire and marine companies that sought foreign business. However, New York State's fire insurance companies faced serious challenges in the modern era. In 1949 the state legislature passed and Gov Thomas E. Dewey signed legislation that allowed underwriters who offered group or homeowner policies to offer fire coverage. Opening the market to multiple-line insurers, this legislation essentially eliminated the need for single-line insurers like fire underwriters. In 1968 the New York Property Insurance Underwriting Association was created to offer fire coverage in inner cities where many individual companies refused to write insurance after the civil unrest and riots of the mid-1960s. In 2002 no single-line fire insurers in stock or mutual forms existed in New York State. There are assessment cooperatives still offering single-line fire policies, but they represent only a small part of the fire insurance policy market.

Mitchell, C. Bradford. *A Premium on Progress: An Outline History of the American Marine Insurance Market, 1820–1970* (New York: Newcomen Society in North America, 1970)

Thomas E. Mertes

insurance, health. By the end of the 19th century, European industrialized nations had implemented programs of social insurance to provide medical care to their citizens.

The Early 20th Century: Thwarted Efforts

The European programs were thoroughly reviewed in Washington, DC, and by individual states, and in 1916 a resolution was introduced in the US House of Representatives authorizing a federal commission to prepare a plan for a national insurance fund against sickness, invalidity, and unemployment. A similar proposal introduced the same year in the New York State Senate was referred to the Judiciary Committee and reintroduced in 1917. A year later the New York State Federation of Labor succeeded in obtaining a modification to meet the demands of labor unions, which sought solutions to such problems in a spirit of voluntarism rather than government intervention, and a revised bill was then produced. In 1919 the State Reconstruction Commission urged passage of compulsory health insurance legislation, resulting in yet another bill. It was passed by the senate but defeated in the assembly. Subsequent senate bills contained modified provisions, all aimed at reducing the number of those to be covered, in an attempt to reach a consensus.

Despite these repeated efforts, opposition to the development or expansion of new welfare programs proved too great for legislation of this kind to pass. Nevertheless, the proper role of government in healthcare continued to be actively debated. Advocates of health insurance drew a parallel with public education, insisting that health insurance should be considered a public good and should be publicly funded and universally available. Opponents were led by associations of medical practitioners. These groups warned that forcing physicians to answer to "political superiors" would injure their self-respect. A 1920 article in the *New York Medical Journal* described national or compulsory health insurance plans as "health insurance propaganda."

The issue of national health insurance coverage was largely deflected by World War I and the period of prosperity that followed it, but arose again during the Great Depression. Some New Deal programs included health insurance measures for large segments of the population, and their success caught the attention of policy makers. But in 1934 the American Medical Association (AMA) responded by formulating 10 principles, the first of which stated that all medical services and all medical practice should be under the control of the medical profession. Other principles held that no third party should come between the doctor and patient and that the profession should assume leadership of any new methods of providing medical services to the community. The political power of the medical associations was enough to prevent the implementation of any universal health insurance program.

Midcentury: New Ideas, Major Programs

Notwithstanding the opposition, changes were occurring that increased the number of workers and their dependents covered by health insurance. During World War II, when wage and price controls eliminated the option of increasing workers' wages, employers were allowed to provide increased benefits, including health insurance. Even earlier, commercial insurance carriers and new types of group medical plans had begun to appear, initially on the West Coast. In 1937 Group Health Insurance (GHI) was established as the first tax-exempt, nonprofit health insurance program in New York State, followed by Blue Cross Blue Shield (1939), which eventually served the state through seven regional programs, and Health Insurance Plan (HIP), which began as a prepaid group health insurance provider in 1947 and operated principally within the New York City area. These plans were licensed by the state to fill a public need by supplying health insurance to a wide segment of the population at a cost close to that of the benefits provided, with the risk spread over the entire community of beneficiaries.

GHI subsequently became a model for the developing cooperative health insurance movement and provides an excellent example of the type of coverage made widely available throughout the United States in the mid–20th century. By the late 1970s GHI, originally organized as a "health cooperative," had become a "health service corporation" with prepaid medical groups and health maintenance organizations (HMOs). GHI was the first medical insurance carrier to offer paid-in-full service benefits without regard to the patient's income. Participating physicians and other providers of health services accepted GHI's scheduled allowances as full payment for services provided. Emphasis was placed on preventative medicine and healthcare, including annual physical examinations, well-baby care, and immunizations.

By the 1950s health insurance was generally available to workers and their dependents through employer-sponsored plans, but the retired and the unemployed too often lacked the personal resources needed to buy health insurance. The introduction in 1965 of Medicare and Medicaid was a major step toward covering those not working. Medicare, a federally funded and administered program, is available to all elderly citizens. However, state-administered Medicaid programs, funded only in part by federal resources, are means-tested. Under Gov Nelson A. Rockefeller, New York State established a very comprehensive Medicaid program (1965). Originally administered by the Department of Social Welfare, in cooperation with the Health Department (which was responsible for establishing standards of medical care), the program has been attacked from the beginning as excessively costly. Movements over the past few decades to reduce welfare rolls have resulted in a decline in the number of those eligible for Medicaid benefits.

The 1970s to the Present: Slow Gains

Several universal health insurance plans have been proposed in recent decades. In 1971 Assemblyman Albert Blumenthal of Manhattan introduced legislation for a comprehensive insurance program aimed at reducing medical costs and distributing them more equitably. The plan called for a group medical and hospital program to provide coverage for unlimited inpatient and outpatient care, along with prescription drugs. An individual's contributions to the plan would be deductible from federal income taxes. All funds would be channeled to a single public agency, the New York State Health Insurance Corp. Although Blumenthal's bill failed, assembly reports in 1984 and 1988 reiterated the need for a comprehensive program that would require reallocating and reorganizing the current system, and the Health Department introduced another proposal in 1989. Called UNY*Care, for Universal New York Health Care, it promised affordable healthcare for all New Yorkers using a combination of tax-based programs and expanded private insurance. Residents would be issued a card enrolling them in the system, and all providers would be served by a central, state-administered payer. Primary care would be provided for all residents from birth to age 17, and primary care benefits in employers' insurance packages would be strengthened. Catastrophic benefits would be extended to the underinsured and full benefits to the uninsured. Like similarly ambitious measures before it, UNY*Care never became a reality, but aspects of it have been preserved in more modest programs.

The state government has since issued several reports on issues related to health insurance. In 1991 the Senate Democratic Task Force on Health Insurance produced a document citing problems with the existing healthcare system—gaps in coverage, insurers avoiding high-risk or very sick clients, and the challenges posed by new threats like AIDS—and examining four approaches to universal insurance: a public-based system such as Canada's; a modified public system relying on strong centralized health insurance with some private-sector involvement; a combined public-private system that would require employers to provide coverage to their workers or pay a tax ("play or pay"); and an expanded private-sector approach with the government providing tax credits or subsidies. The following year a study by the Health Department found that 2.1 million New Yorkers were uninsured and that the majority of uninsured adults were employed. Innumerable legislative commissions have been appointed and public hearings held to determine the causes of the growth in the state's uninsured and underinsured populations and to recommend corrective actions.

Although the problem of the uninsured remained a constant, those with insurance experienced major changes in coverage options in the 1990s. The managed care and HMO movement proved very successful in New York State, with enrollment in HMOs growing from about 2.4 million in 1990 to 6 million by 1996. The number of Medicaid recipients served by HMOs likewise increased dramatically over these years. By the end of the decade membership in HMOs had stabilized, in part because of the competition from new and hybridized managed-care products such as preferred provider organizations (PPOs).

Although no program has yet been implemented to include all New York residents, there have been significant attempts to expand coverage. Since 1987 the Elderly Pharmaceutical Insurance Coverage (EPIC) program has helped pay for medications for older citizens with modest incomes above Medicaid levels. The Child Health Plus program, administered by the Health Department, provides fully or partly subsidized health insurance to children from low-income families who are not eligible for Medicaid, and unsubsidized coverage is available to children from higher-income families. Between 1991, when coverage began, and 1997, the program was state funded from surcharges levied on hospital bills. In 1998 a federal program designed to improve children's health insurance coverage began providing funds; in 2000 New York State received $257 million for the program, and 536,000 children were served. The success of Child Health Plus led to the establishment in 1999 of a new program, Family Health Plus, which provides comprehensive healthcare to parents and single and childless individuals aged 19–64 who cannot afford private insurance but are not eligible for Medicaid.

The New York State Health Insurance Partnership Program was established in 1996 to assist small-business employers and sole proprietors without employees in purchasing small-group health insurance policies. Now called Healthy New York, the program was initially funded with an annual allocation of $6 million from the Health Care Initiatives Pool established as part of the 1996 Health Care Reform Act, which deregulated New York State's hospital system. The Health Care Reform Act of 2000 created a health insurance and tobacco control program funding pool using tobacco settlement money allocated to New York State. A significant portion of the tobacco funding went toward Family Health Plus. Although these programs have made modest, incremental progress toward the goal of providing health insurance for all residents, in 2000 the US Census Bureau estimated the number of uninsured in New York State at 2.8 million, or 15.2% of the population.

New York State. Assembly Committee on Health. *Report of the Subcommittee on National Health Insurance* (1976)

New York State. Council on Health Care Financing. *Health Insurance: Public Policy in New York* (1984)

———. *Policy Options for the Uninsured in New York State* (1988)

New York State. Department of Health. *Proposal for Universal New York Health Care* (1989)

New York State. Office of the State Comptroller. *Department of Health: Management of the Child Health Plus Program.* Report 97-S-10 (1997)

New York State. Senate Democratic Task Force on Health Insurance. *Report on Universal Health Care Initiatives* (1991)

Carol Whittaker

insurance, life. A contract that offers a payment at the end of a specified time, usually the insured's death, in return for a premium paid in advance. In 1818 the state legislature chartered the Manhattan Co of New York City with the right to sell life insurance. New York Life and Trust Co, chartered in 1830 and headquartered in New York City, followed and was the first US company to employ agents to sell life policies. During this period the life insurance market was small. By the 1840s, however, with the emergence of aggressive sales techniques on part of underwriters, a vibrant market began. The majority of life insurers, such as Mutual of New York (1842; now MONY), adopted a mutual form, owned by policyholders rather than by stockholders, and this type of structure gave policyholders part of company surpluses, allowed for lower capitalization, and offered the potential for policyholders to direct the company. Other New York City life companies emerged, including New York Life Insurance Co in 1849 and Equitable Life Assurance Society, founded by Henry Hyde, 10 years later. Equitable became a dominant insurance company by developing the tontine; known also as the semi-tontine or deferred dividend, these plans invested annual payments made for the first years of the policy, usually 5, 10, or 20 years. After the years fixed, annuities began to be paid back to the policyholder. Some insurers appealed to specific ethnic communities; the most successful was probably the Germania Life Insurance Co (1860), renamed the Guaranty Life Insurance Co in 1918.

By the end of the century Mutual, Equitable, and New York Life, known as the Big Three, were America's largest life insurers. Two other New York City–area firms, Prudential and Metropolitan Life (Met Life), challenged their dominance. Prudential, founded in 1875 in Newark, NJ, pioneered the concept of industrial life insurance. Geared to the needs of lower-income families, industrial life insurance had no investment aspect (as most policies did at the time) but instead term insurance that paid a death benefit. Premiums, collected by company agents on a regular basis, were inexpensive. Met Life, founded in 1863 in New York City, began selling its own industrial life policies. Together, these four instate insurers, plus Prudential, became second only to banks as the largest institutional investors in New York City financial markets. They were large purchasers of railroad and corporate bonds, urban and rural mortgages, and real estate, and played a crucial role in the call money market for broker's loans.

With the growth of the life insurers, however, came complaints of large-scale abuses, including nepotism, creative bookkeeping, lavish salaries, and questionable investments. Tontines were a particular area of corruption, where for decades in almost all cases the accounting for these funds by life insurers was underestimated and incomplete, resulting in complaints and lawsuits. The state legislature's Armstrong Committee's investigations of 1905 highlighted these problems, especially at Equitable, and led New York State to craft a series of laws that set the national standard for insurance regulation. They discontinued tontines, made more stringent requirements for reserve investments, disentangled banks and life insurance companies, and increased regulatory powers. In the subsequent decades the industry moved toward marketing group life insurance as well as annuities. Group insurance sales increased in the 1910s under the leadership of companies such as Equitable. In part, the buyers of group life insurance and group annuities included large industrial firms. Helping to defuse union-organizing activities, these insurance and annuity plans once offered to workers usually led management to succeed in their demands for an open shop. Group insurance would grow faster than life insurance through much of the remainder of the century. The not-for-profit financial institution Teachers Insurance and Annuity Association, founded in New York City in 1918, would eventually, in a partnership with College Retirement Equities Fund (TIAA-CREF), become one of the largest managers of pension and insurance funds. The financial success of the insurance business as a whole was perhaps best demonstrated by Met Life, which by 1929 had $2.25 billion in policies insuring more than 1.3 million customers.

The innovative years of the 1920s were followed by the lean years of the 1930s. New Deal attempts to address the problems of the Great Depression led to antitrust actions and new investigations of the insurance industry, this time at the federal level, by the Temporary National Economic Committee. The 1935 Social Security Act was seen as both capturing part of the market in annuities and threatening to industrial insurance. The depression and World War II drove companies out of the stock market and toward corporate and government bonds, which would impair higher returns in the postwar era. After 1945, then, to revitalize business, state life insurers turned to a variety of new products that offered higher returns, such as individual and group annuities, which provided both annual payments after retirement and a death benefit. Annuities would overtake term-life policies as the most popular insurance product. As the state progressively lifted restrictions on life insurer investments, firms were able to compete more effectively with banks in pensions and money management. One important new venue was underwriting real estate developments. Met Life built two housing projects in New York City, which addressed the city's housing needs and offered the company a stable real estate investment. The first was Parkchester in Bronx Co, an apartment complex built between 1939 and 1942 that housed 12,000 families, and the second was Stuyvesant Town, built between 1943 and 1947 in Manhattan and offering 8,756 apartments.

Wall Street's economic performance in the 1970s, characterized by high inflation and a sharply declining equity market, hurt life insurers. Bonds, a mainstay of the life insurers' investment portfolio, were savaged by rising inflation. With traditional life insurance products offering less financial opportunity, life insurers moved aggressively into offering new investment services. In 1969 Gov Nelson A. Rockefeller promoted and signed into law a bill that allowed life insurers to create or buy financial service subsidiaries. State life insurers began to sell money market funds, mutual funds, and certificates of deposit in direct competition with banks and other financial institutions. There were also new products. Equitable, for instance, began to write home and auto policies in 1974. The number of mergers between insurance companies and other financial concerns increased rapidly. In 1988, after the necessary legislation became New York State law under Gov Mario M. Cuomo's signature, many mutual insurance companies turned themselves into stock companies. Demutualization provided insurers much greater access to capital markets, easing their transformation into full-service financial companies. The first of New York's Big Four to take that step was Equitable in 1992, followed by MONY in 1998, and Met Life in 2000. New York Life remains a mutual company. In 1999 Congress ended most remaining federal barriers to the consolidation of the financial sector with the repeal of the Glass-Steagall Act.

Keller, Morton. *The Life Insurance Enterprise, 1885–1910: A Study in the Limits of Corporate Power* (Cambridge, Mass: Belknap Press, 1963)

Rousmaniere, John. *The Life and Times of the Equitable* (New York: The Equitable Cos, 1995)
Stalson, J. Owen. *Marketing Life Insurance* (Cambridge, Mass: Harvard Univ Press, 1942)

Thomas E. Mertes

Insurance Department. Created in 1859 by the New York State legislature in response to revelations of insolvency and fraud among several fire insurance companies, its mission is to guarantee the fiscal soundness of insurance companies, ensure the prompt payment of claims, eradicate fraud and unethical conduct from the industry, and promote the insurance industry's growth within the state. The department is headed by a superintendent appointed by the governor and confirmed by the New York State Senate.

During the 19th century major insurance companies made financial contributions to the Democratic and Republican Parties to influence the appointment of friendly superintendents. Though early appointees often were accused of working for the companies and not the policyholders, the department quickly made significant contributions to insurance regulation. Believing that insurance companies would be financially sounder, more responsive to consumers, and easier to regulate if they were to specialize, in 1865 Superintendent William Barnes banned the provision of more than one line of insurance by the same company. After the Chicago fire of 1871, most other states similarly prohibited multiple-line insurance companies until the 1940s; the New York laws were not changed until 1949. In 1871 Superintendent George W. Miller organized and presided over the first convention of state insurance officials, creating the National Insurance Convention (now National Association of Insurance Commissioners), which sought to adopt uniform national standards for insurance company reporting and regulation. The department's Standard Fire Policy of 1886 served as a model for most other states. Although the intent of the department was to create a plain and unambiguous contract that would be just to both insured and insurer, this policy provided many loopholes for insurance companies to avoid paying claims. Finally, an administrative rule devised in 1901 by Deputy Superintendent Henry D. Appleton required insurance companies nationwide to comply with New York legislation as a condition of doing business in the state. Although the Appleton Rule clearly affected interstate business, the Supreme Court upheld its legality in *Fireman's Insurance v Beha* (1929); the rule was incorporated into New York's insurance laws in 1939.

The regulation of the life insurance industry, largely based in New York City, also fell under the jurisdiction of the Insurance Department. In 1905 Superintendent Francis Hendricks reluctantly investigated accusations of unethical practices at the Equitable Life Assurance Society. His report substantiated the allegations and prompted the New York legislature to create a special committee to examine the conduct of all life insurance companies operating within the state. Known as the Armstrong Committee, with Charles Evans Hughes appointed as lead counsel, it severely chastised the department for permitting malpractice throughout the industry and recommended a wide array of reform measures. Most of these measures were adopted as part of the New York State Insurance Code, and 19 other states followed New York's legislative lead. The department's enforcement of the Appleton Rule spread the stringent New York laws nationwide.

As new lines of insurance, such as auto, workers' compensation, and health, came into the market during the first half of the 20th century, New York expanded its regulations to cover them. It became the first state to create insurance guaranty funds to pay claims against insolvent insurers, establishing the Workmen's Compensation Security Fund in 1935, the Life Insurance Guaranty Corp in 1941, and the Motor Vehicle Liability Security Fund in 1947. Department consumer guides, published since the mid-1960s, help consumers compare companies and policies. The Insurance Frauds Bureau, established in 1981, is charged with the investigation and prosecution of all insurance fraud cases. Since the mid-1990s it has been particularly concerned with the rise in fraudulent medical claims that have been submitted under its no-fault auto insurance plan. In 1998 New York State passed the landmark External Appeal Law, granting health insurance consumers who have been denied coverage the right to request an independent review of their insurers' decision. Oversight of insurance web sites and quotes from on-line companies came under the department's jurisdiction in 1999. Department personnel and representatives from the insurance industry began to staff the Insurance Emergency Operation Center immediately after 11 Sept 2001 to gather information and to coordinate responses to insurance concerns. As of March 2001 the department had approximately 900 employees, employed at the main office in New York City and in other staff offices in Albany, Buffalo, Mineola, Oneonta, Rochester, and Syracuse.

Meier, Kenneth J. *The Political Economy of Regulation: The Case of Insurance* (Albany: SUNY Press, 1988)
New York State Insurance Department, http://www.ins.state.ny.us/

Sharon Ann Murphy

intellectual émigrés. The most characteristic representatives of the immigrants coming from Nazi Germany and Nazi-occupied Europe during the 1930s were less the "huddled masses" of Emma Lazarus's famous poem than the cultivated urban middle classes, often from the cultural and intellectual elite of their home countries. The numbers were relatively small—only about 130,000 of the 500,000 people who left Nazi Germany after 1933 and Austria after 1938 came to the United States, of whom more than half settled in New York City. Their cultural importance for New York City and New York State was immense. They had left Germany because either they were representatives of the Weimar Republic (mainly democrats and social democrats), or they were, by National Socialist definitions, Jews. Many were supporters of the modern social sciences and the culture of the avant-garde. Under the Nazis the German and Austrian universities lost more than a quarter of their teaching staff, and in the social sciences and in some of the subdisciplines of the natural sciences more than 60%. The situation at theaters, concert halls, and publishing houses was similar.

Within American Academia

Though the 1930s was a time of xenophobia and high immigration barriers in the United States, some farsighted Americans created places for refugee scholars in American universities. The Rockefeller Foundation started a special aid program in 1933 that enabled more than 300 German-speaking scholars to continue their academic career in the United States. An additional 335 people were supported by the Emergency Committee in Aid of Displaced German/Foreign Scholars, which was created in New York City at the same time by Stephen Duggan. He was the director of the Institute of International Education and had already founded the Russian Student Fund after the Russian Civil War of 1918–20 to allow more than 500 young Russians to finish their academic education in the United States. The Rockefeller Foundation and the Emergency Committee agreed to pay the salary of the refugee scholars for several years if the sponsoring university would later include them in their budget. Although they were placed nationwide, the largest group was in New York State, in part because of an abundance of contacts and the state's renowned institutions of higher learning. The Emergency Committee, for example, placed 111 scholars in New York State. No other state had more than 27. Of the 111, 21 went to the New School for Social Research and 13 apiece to Columbia and New York Universities. The municipal colleges of New York City also received an infusion of émigré intellectual talents, especially Brooklyn College, where economists Gerhard Bry and Stephanie Browne and historian Hans Rosenberg joined the faculty. There was no other place in which refugee intellectuals influenced American culture in as many areas as they did in New York City.

The best-known home for émigré scholars was the University in Exile at the New School for Social Research. Among its contributions, the University in Exile provided intellectual grounding for the New Deal and the Keynesian revolution; scholars like Gerhard Colm, Emil Lederer, and Adolph Lowe, for example, influenced the fields of public finance and cyclical and growth theory. Political scientists Arnold Brecht, Hans Simons, and Hans Speier opened the horizons for isolationist America for international questions and became instrumental during the war for the Roosevelt administration in planning reeducation in and democratization of Germany after Nazi rule. A second University in Exile at the New School was founded with Ecole Libre des Hautes Etudes in 1942, which among others included figures like ethnologist Claude Lévi-Strauss and philosophers Alexandre Koyré and Boris Mirkine-Guetzévitch. In contrast to the Germans, the teaching staff of the Ecole Libre, an intellectual outpost of the Free French movement of Gen Charles de Gaulle, immediately after the war returned to France, where most of them became high-ranking officials.

The other main center for German intellectuals in New York City academic life was at Columbia University, where the Institute of Social Research (ISR), the so-called Frankfurt school, found a home after 1934. The ISR's influential achievements included the combination of a Marxist perspective skeptical of the possibility of achieving a socialist society with other currents in contemporary thought, notably Freudian psychoanalysis. These scholars' analyses of modern mass society were influenced by the work of Max Weber and his thesis of the process of a rationalization of the modern world as well as by their experience of Nazism, which they saw in part as an unfortunate consequence of modernity.

Among the members of the ISR who would find a place at Columbia were philosophers Max Horkheimer, Theodor W. Adorno, and Herbert Marcuse, psychoanalyst Erich Fromm, and political scientist Franz Neumann. Neumann's *Behemoth* (1942) played an important role in the developing theory of totalitarianism in postwar America. ISR scholars often tempered their former reliance on the Germanic post-Hegelian tradition with the pragmatically and empirically oriented American understanding of science. Their empirical research on the authoritarian personality and the dynamics of prejudice had a major impact on the development of American sociology. Adorno cooperated in the comprehensive interdisciplinary Radio Research Project at Columbia University, which was directed by the Austrian emigrant Paul Lazarsfeld, a former "Austro-Marxist" who, on the basis of this project, later became one of the founders of US market research. Other influential members of the ISR in New York City were Karl August Wittfogel, a student of "oriental despotism," and Siegfried Kracauer, who studied films and war propaganda on behalf of the Museum of Modern Art.

New York University (NYU) also benefited from the presence of émigré intellectuals. The prestige of its Institute of Fine Arts was to a large extent grounded on the German emigrants' impact. Even before 1933, Erwin Panofsky, a leader of the school of iconographic analysis of art, taught at the institute as a visiting professor. After 1933 refugee scholars made up over half of the teaching staff at certain times. In 1945 NYU hired Ludwig von Mises, a leader of the so-called Austrian school, an orthodox branch of neoclassical economic theory. Fritz Machlup and Oscar Morgenstern, former students of Mises in Vienna, also taught at New York State universities. At NYU, management theorist Peter Drucker had a great impact after 1950. Mathematician Richard Courant from Göttingen established a center for applied mathematics at NYU, which was initially funded by the Rockefeller Foundation and named after Courant in 1958. Nuclear physicists Leo Szilard and Enrico Fermi, from Hungary and Italy respectively, taught at Columbia, while Hans Bethe taught at NYU and Cornell, and Victor Hess at Fordham. In the life sciences, biochemist Erwin Chargaff at Columbia University helped lay the foundation for the analysis of DNA. A number of the leaders of the psychoanalytic movement came to New York City, including Otto Rank and the humanistic psychologist Alfred Adler, who became professor at the Long Island College of Medicine in Brooklyn, while art psychologist Rudolf Arnheim of the New School and Erich Fromm represented at the time its expanding subdisciplines. The German Protestant philosopher of religion Paul Tillich from Frankfurt taught at Union Theological Seminary after 1933, and many leading figures of Jewish learning also came to New York City, including Ismar Elbogen and Abraham Joshua Heschel at the Jewish Theological Seminary, and Salo W. Baron at the Jewish Institute of Religion and Columbia University.

Emigrés in the Arts

European émigrés made a major contribution to New York State's artistic culture. The presence of surrealist and other modernist artists such as André Breton, André Masson, Max Ernst, George Grosz, Marc Chagall, and Salvador Dalí in New York City, as well as previous émigrés such as Marcel Duchamp, acted as a catalyst for the incipient New York school of abstract expressionism. As a result, New York City supplanted Paris as the central city in the international art scene. In music, Kurt Weill, the composer of *Die Dreigroschenoper* (*The Three Penny Opera;* 1930), had a successful career as creator of Broadway musicals such as *Lady in the Dark, One Touch of Venus,* and pageants such as *The Eternal Way,* a history of Jews from the vantage of the tribulations of the 1930s. Composers such as the Hungarian born Béla Bartók and conductors including Bruno Walter, George Szell, and Fritz Reiner enlivened New York City's musical life. German émigrés Alfred Lion and Francis Wolff started the influential Blue Note jazz record label in 1939. Journalists Stefan Lorant and Max Frankel, publishers Kurt Wolff and Gershom Schocken, and photographers Alfred Eisenstaedt and André Kertész also made major contributions to American culture. German stage directors and composers had an enriching impact on the political theater of the New Deal era. Dramatists and directors Bertolt Brecht and Erwin Piscator, who created the Dramatic Workshop at the New School in 1940, tried to undermine the audience's identification and illusions with characters by creating "epic theater." Their influence on the next generation of actors was immense.

As a group, the refugees—the product of the permanently crisis-ridden new republics in Germany and Austria after World War I—belonged to a segment of intellectuals and artists deeply sensitive to the complex process of technologically induced modernity. This philosophy and sensibility came to New York State at a time when the New Deal was seeking economic and political answers to the problems of the depression.

Coser, Lewis A. *Refugee Scholars in America: Their Impact and Their Experiences* (New Haven: Yale Univ Press, 1984)

Fermi, Laura. *Illustrious Immigrants: The Intellectual Migration from Europe* (Chicago: Univ of Chicago Press, 1968)

Fleming, Donald, and Bernard Bailyn, eds. *The Intellectual Migration: Europe and America, 1930–1960* (Cambridge, Mass: Harvard Univ Press, 1969)

Jackman, Jarrell, and Carla M. Borden, eds. *The Muses Flee Hitler: Cultural Transfer and Adaption, 1930–1945* (Washington, DC: Smithsonian Institution Press, 1983)

Claus-Dieter Krohn

intercity bus lines. Connections between urban centers rather than within them or to suburbs. Traditionally such lines are privately owned, for-profit organizations, not publicly sponsored or subsidized by government funds.

The Colonial Coach Corp was incorporated in Watertown in January 1925. Its purpose was to connect the area between the Canadian border and Binghamton, an area inadequately served by the railroads. A dozen individual operators, one running since 1913, were combined into a system of routes connecting Oswego, Syracuse, and Utica with Plattsburgh on Lake Champlain. Two interstate routes between New York City and Syracuse were instituted in 1928; both ran through northern New Jersey, one via Scranton, Pa, and Binghamton, the other along the west shore of the Hudson River and via Albany and Utica. Cross-state service from Buffalo through Albany and Pittsfield, Mass, to Boston began in spring 1929, and Colonial advertised that it was then running a system covering 1,500 miles (2,414 km) with 100 buses. Colonial was bought out and reorganized as Eastern Greyhound Lines of New York in 1930, the first holding of the expanding Greyhound system, marking its entry into the Northeast. The New York Central Railroad purchased 50% of the stock, and the company was renamed Central Greyhound Lines of New York (CGLNY) in 1935.

International bus service between New York City and Montreal via the Hudson Valley and both banks of Lake Champlain was begun in August 1929 by a partnership of Fifth Avenue Coach Co and Provincial Transport, the Gray Line sightseeing association affiliates in those cities. Champlain Coach Lines, as it was called, passed to CGLNY in 1942. Greyhound bought out the railroad's interest in 1947 and, after a series of corporate simplifications, merged its New York State operations into Eastern Greyhound Lines in 1955.

Several early operators that connected with New York Central West Shore Division trains and Hudson River Day Line boats were instrumental in the development of the resort areas north of Albany and west of the Hudson. The most important were Hudson Transit Lines, based in Newburgh (Orange Co) and organized in 1922 to consolidate service to the Catskills and extended to New York City in 1933; and Adirondack Transit Lines (so named in 1934), which started in Kingston (Ulster Co) as Rip Van Winkle Lines in 1926 and ran between New York City and Albany. Both joined the Short Line association in the 1930s when it was recruiting members with the goal of becoming a nationwide bus system.

When the Short Line association broke up in 1937, both Adirondack and Hudson Transit continued as independent line operators; Adirondack joined the new Trailways association, and Hudson Transit continued to use the Short Line trade name. Both companies flourished as resort carriers until rising automobile ownership after World War II significantly affected that segment of their business. They continued as line operators with Short Line running to Binghamton via Monticello, Liberty, and Roscoe (Sullivan Co), and to Carbondale, Pa, via Port Jervis (Orange Co). Short Line later acquired airport, tour, and sightseeing services in New York City; Adirondack continued service to Malone (Franklin Co) and Massena (St. Lawrence Co) via Saranac Lake (Franklin and Essex Cos) or Plattsburgh.

Western New York Motor Lines (trade name, Blue Bus Lines) was organized in 1924 to combine the rights of operators that had started service in 1916 between Batavia (Genesee Co) and Rochester. These were joined in 1925 with a Batavia-Buffalo line started in 1921 to provide through service from Rochester to Buffalo. Rochester-Penfield Bus Co (later Valley Trailways) was organized in 1934, and it acquired Blue Bus Lines in 1958, continuing operations under that name. The system then comprised lines from Buffalo via Rochester and Oswego to Watertown and to Syracuse, in addition to service between Rochester, Corning (Steuben Co), and Elmira. The name Empire State Trailways was adopted in 1962 and shortened to Empire Trailways in 1975. Adirondack acquired the Empire routes in 1994, operating them separately as New York Trailways. Hudson Transit Lines and its affiliates were sold to conglomerate Coach

USA in July 1998, continuing in the line-haul and tourist markets. Greyhound, while shedding its unprofitable branchlines, continues to serve its mainline routes between the principal cities of the state.

Bail, Eli, and Albert E. Meier. "Central Greyhound Lines," *Motor Coach Age*, Oct 1999

Goldmann, Stephen M. "Hudson Transit Lines," *Motor Coach Age*, Sept 1969

Sullivan, Charles. "Empire Trailways," *Motor Coach Today*, Oct 1996

"Turnpikes Turn to Bus Routes in Empire State," *Bus Transportation Magazine*, July 1922

Eli Bail

Interlaken. Village (pop 674) in Covert (Seneca Co). Known as Farmer from its post office name of 1819, it was renamed Interlaken when the village incorporated in 1904. A contest was held, and a teacher proposed the name after the Swiss resort town. Enoch Covert's saddlery (1863–1951) supplied a silver-plated harness set for the Russian imperial coach and also outfitted US cavalry mounts in World War I. Other manufactured products included fruit baskets, metal goods, cleaning products, hardware, axe handles, and baseball bats; the Seneca Creamery Co employed 119 workers in 1895. Rail service was provided by the Geneva and Ithaca Railroad (later Lehigh Valley Railroad) between 1873 and the 1960s. In the early 21st century, Interlaken had two wineries.

Lisa Compton

international bridge authorities. Three separate state public authorities each operate an international highway bridge between New York State and Ontario. The Thousand Islands Bridge Authority, created by the state legislature in 1933, operates an 8.5 mi (13.68 km) bridge complex spanning the St. Lawrence River between Collins Landing (Jefferson Co) and Ivy Lea, Ont. The complex, which opened in 1938, traverses four islands and includes two suspension bridges, two arch bridges, and a truss bridge. A board of four Americans and three Canadians manages the authority. The Buffalo and Fort Erie Public Bridge Authority was created by the New York State legislature (with US congressional consent) in 1933 and Canada in 1934 to take over operation of the Buffalo Peace Bridge; the bridge is a 5,800 ft (1,767.8 m) long span that crosses the Black Rock ship canal, connecting Buffalo to Fort Erie, Ont. Opened in 1927, the bridge is composed of five steel-arch spans. A 10-member board of directors, half American, half Canadian, oversees the authority. The Ogdensburg Bridge and Port Authority, created in 1958 by the state legislature, operates and manages a variety of infrastructure assets that facilitate trade between New York State and Canada. The Ogdensburg-Prescott International Bridge, which opened in 1961, is the authority's main property. Crossing the St. Lawrence River between Ogdensburg (St. Lawrence Co) and Prescott, Ont, this suspension bridge is 1,150 feet (350.5 m) long. A seven-member board, appointed by the governor with the senate's consent, governs the authority; each member serves a five-year term, and no Canadians sit on the board.

Thomas A. Birkland

International Brotherhood of Sleeping Car Porters (BSCP). The first successful African America labor union, founded on 25 Aug 1925 at 160 West 129th St in New York City with the goal of representing Pullman Palace Car Co porters in labor negotiations. The BSCP's chief organizer and first president was civil rights activist A. Philip Randolph.

From its start in 1867, the Pullman Co hired only Blacks as porters. At a time when few opportunities for nonagricultural employment were available to Blacks, the job offered prestige and a steady salary. Yet despite the company's proclaimed paternalism, the pay was poor and hours were long and unpredictable. Porters had to buy their own uniforms and supplies, and their dependence on tips enforced subservience. Pullman had crushed previous attempts at unionizing.

Persuaded to become involved by Ashley L. Totten, a porter later fired for his organizing work, Randolph began his campaign in the pages of his radical magazine, the *Messenger*. Even in New York City, where he was enthusiastically received, he had to proceed in secret to avoid company reprisals against union members. To evade company spies, porters sometimes enlisted their wives to hold meetings and do union business. Membership fluctuated, but Randolph attracted a core of remarkably devoted organizers. He had to persuade the porters that Pullman could be effectively opposed, that collective bargaining could prevail in labor disputes, and that a black union could negotiate with a white company on equal terms. Randolph's most formidable aide was Milton P. Webster, who organized the Chicago local and later became first vice president of the national organization. Beginning with a $10,000 grant from the liberal Garland Fund, BSCP launched a nationwide effort despite inadequate, uncertain funding and numerous setbacks. Over time Pullman tried to undermine Randolph in various ways, from attempting to have him arrested to sending him a substantial bribe.

Four months after the passage of the Railway Labor Act in May 1926, Randolph began trying to use it to force Pullman to accept the BSCP as the porters' representative. A strike effort in 1928 aimed at compelling the company to accept arbitration by a mediation board under the act nearly destroyed the union. Randolph "postponed" the strike on the advice of William Green, president of the American Federation of Labor (AFL), who in 1928 secured federal charters for individual BSCP locals. Randolph also had to combat racism within the AFL, the threat of communist takeover of the union, and the opposition of much of the black establishment, especially the black press (New York City's *Amsterdam News* being one notable exception). But New Deal labor legislation in 1934 and 1935, specifically the Amended Railway Labor Act and the Wagner-Connery Act, improved the BSCP's position, and on 1 June 1935 the union was certified as the porters' official representative. Further, in 1935 the AFL granted the BSCP an international charter. Pullman finally signed a contract with the BSCP on 25 Aug 1937. The union negotiated a succession of agreements for the porters, greatly improving their pay and working conditions. Other Pullman railway service workers were brought into the union, and in 1952 BSCP representation was extended to all railway porters. As it grew stronger, the union made important contributions to Randolph's other civil rights initiatives. But the post–World War II decline in rail transportation progressively weakened the union, and in 1978 it was merged into the Brotherhood of Railway and Airline Clerks.

Brazeal, Brailsford R. *The Brotherhood of Sleeping Car Porters: Its Origin and Development* (New York and London: Harper & Bros, 1946)

Harris, William H. *Keeping the Faith: A. Philip Randolph, Milton P. Webster, and the Brotherhood of Sleeping Car Porters, 1925–1937* (1977; repr Urbana: Univ of Illinois Press, 1991)

Veronica F. Towers

International Brotherhood of Teamsters. In 1899 the American Federation of Labor (AFL) chartered the Team Drivers International Union (TDIU), the first national trade union of drivers of carts drawn by teams of horses. Among the seven locals making up the new organization was a group of team drivers—teamsters—from New York City. The TDIU subsequently split into two groups but was reunified in 1903 at Niagara Falls as the International Brotherhood of Teamsters (IBT). Although the IBT grew from 32,000 members to more than 46,000 in its first two years, it was riven by factionalism, much of it centered in New York City. In 1906 locals in New York City led a secession movement that resulted in the formation of the United Teamsters of America (UTA). Several of the New York City locals were subsequently persuaded to reaffiliate with the IBT, which led to vicious interunion fights in the city. By 1911 almost all the New York City locals had returned to the IBT. In the following year, 9,000 of the IBT's 42,000 members were in New York City.

Through the 1910s and 1920s, the New York City locals attracted new members by winning substantial wage raises and reductions in working hours. Average wages per hour for drivers of two-horse teams in New York City was increased from 26¢ per hour in 1913 to 75¢ per hour in 1928, and the average workweek declined from 60 hours to 54 hours in the same period. In the 1930s the union began organizing drivers of motor trucks, which were rapidly replacing horse-drawn carts as the principal vehicles for transporting goods.

Several New York City Teamster leaders were convicted of embezzling funds from their unions and of taking payoffs from employers in exchange for lower wage demands. The efforts of Local 807 in New York City to use violence and intimidation to force employers to pay union rates provided the basis for passage by Congress of the Hobbs Anti-Racketeering Act in 1946, which made illegal such coercive measures by unions. Investigations conducted by the New York State Crime Commission in the early 1950s revealed that Joseph Papa, president of Local 202 in New York City, had embezzled $37,000 from the local and received at least $46,000 in cash from a firm in exchange for forcing its competitor out of business. During this period officers in locals in other parts of New York State were also accused of corruption. Binghamton Local 693 and Yonkers Local 445 were placed under trusteeship by Dave Beck, who succeeded Dan Tobin as IBT president in 1952, following allegations of improper conduct by local leaders. Perhaps the most notorious New York City Teamster was John Dioguardi, "Johnny Dio," who served three years in a state prison during the 1930s for extortion against trucking companies. He later became well known as a major racketeer in the garment industry as both an employer and a union officer. In the mid-1950s Dioguardi and Detroit Teamster leader Jimmy Hoffa were alleged to be partners in setting up various phony Teamster "paper locals" in order to swing the New York Joint Council 16, a coalition of Teamster locals in New York City, behind Hoffa's bid for the IBT presidency. Their partner in the scheme was New York City gangster Tony "Ducks" Corallo. In 1957 the AFL-CIO expelled the IBT for corrupt practices, and the union was not readmitted until 1988.

Despite the many accusations of corruption, by 1955 the membership of New York Joint Council 16 had reached 122,938, the largest metropolitan organization in the national union. Through the next three decades, Joint Council 16 remained both a major force within the national union and a frequent source of corruption. In 1989 the US Justice Department used a racketeering suit to force the IBT to sign a consent decree mandating federal oversight of the union's financial activities and elections and established an independent review board (IRB) to investigate corruption and influence of organized crime in the union. The IRB remained in operation in 2003. Ron Carey, who as president of Local 804 in Queens gained a reputation as a reformer, was elected in 1991 as general president of the IBT. However, Carey was subsequently deposed from office and expelled from the union in 1998 by the federal overseer when it was revealed that he had used substantial portions of the union's treasury to finance his campaign for reelection in 1996. In a second election in 1998, James P. Hoffa, son of Jimmy Hoffa, was elected IBT president. In 2002 the IBT membership in New York State was approximately 200,000.

Russell, Thaddeus. *Out of the Jungle: Jimmy Hoffa and the Remaking of the American Working Class* (New York: Knopf, 2001)

Thaddeus Russell

International Ladies' Garment Workers' Union (ILGWU). Established in New York City on 3 June 1900, primarily by eastern European Jews, the ILGWU proved to be the most stable and enduring of a series of unions that since the 1880s sought to organize immigrant workers in the city's garment industry. For almost a decade the union foundered, with few members and little funds. A turning point for the ILGWU came in 1909, when its female shirtwaist (a popular kind of blouse) makers—a group the union's male leadership had at first been hesitant to organize—went on strike in the "Uprising of the 20,000," inspired by leaders like Clara Lemlich (later Shavelson) and Pauline Newman. Their action focused sympathetic public attention on the plight of immigrant garment workers and emboldened others in the industry. The following year nearly 60,000 male ILGWU cloak makers walked out in a general strike. Its success led to the kind of industry-wide bargaining the ILGWU would rely on for more than a half-century. The strike was settled in part through the arbitration of the progressive jurist Louis Brandeis, who proposed a model of labor-management cooperation called the Protocol of Peace. In this agreement the union ceded to management the right to hire and fire but won significant wage increases and preferential treatment for union members in hiring. Although the protocol lasted only six years before being replaced by industry-wide collective bargaining, it brought stability to the union. Membership soared to 90,000 by 1913, allowing the union to introduce a range of services, including a health center, a Pennsylvania resort for members, and educational and recreational programs.

The union was divided by political factionalism in the 1920s. On taking the presidency in 1923, Morris Sigman tried to expel communists from the union's leadership. With their significant support among the rank and file, however, communists won election to key positions in the ILGWU's New York City locals in 1925; the Joint Board of Cloak, Skirt, Dress and Reefer Makers' Unions, which set policy for most of these locals, was likewise under the control of communists like Charles Zimmerman and Louis Hyman. They called a cloak makers' strike in 1926, which ended in a costly defeat. Following this debacle the communists left to form the Needle Trades Workers' Industrial Union (NTWIU). Sigman reestablished control of the ILGWU, but stepped down in 1928 so that others, such as Vice Pres David Dubinsky, could repair the debilitated union. Dubinsky became president in 1932, and the ILGWU reabsorbed the NTWIU two years later. The New Deal also helped revitalize the union, which under Dubinsky's leadership played a key role in the formation of the Committee for Industrial Organization (CIO) in 1935. When the American Federation of Labor (AFL) responded by ejecting CIO-affiliated unions, the ILGWU withdrew from both the AFL and CIO, remaining independent until rejoining the AFL in 1940. The war and postwar boom further strengthened the union, with membership climbing to an all-time high of 457,517 in 1969, three years after Dubinsky's retirement. Beginning in the 1970s competition from garment imports and the rapidly changing demographic profile of garment workers led to the union's decline. Over several decades the workforce in New York City had become largely African American and Latina, yet union leaders remained largely male and Jewish. This contributed to a growing tension between leadership and the rank and file at a time when the industry was contracting. Membership had fallen to 108,000 by 1995, when the ILGWU merged with the Amalgamated Clothing and Textile Workers Union to form the Union of Needletrades, Industrial and Textile Employees (UNITE).

Levine, Louis. *The Women's Garment Workers: A History of the International Ladies' Garment Workers' Union* (New York: B. W. Huebsch, 1924)

Tyler, Gus. *Look for the Union Label: A History of the International Ladies' Garment Workers' Union* (Armonk, NY: M. E. Sharpe, 1995)

Daniel E. Bender

International Longshoremen's Association. Labor union founded in Chicago as the Longshoremen of the Lakes in 1877. Joined by Canadian workers, the organization became the International Longshoremen's Association (ILA) in 1895, and shortly thereafter became an American Federation of Labor (AFL) affiliate. By 1905 ILA membership had reached 100,000. The first New York State branch, Local 791 in the Port of New York, was formed in May 1908. Joseph Patrick Ryan became president of ILA's Atlantic District in 1918 and was elected the national union's president-for-life in 1943. In October 1945, 35,000 ILA members struck at the Port of New York to protest a contract proposed by Ryan. In addition to wage increases and modifications to the hiring system, workers wanted more control over their union; many ILA locals rarely met, and corruption, including racketeering and kickbacks, was increasing. Although an arbitrator ultimately granted most worker demands, in 1951 Gov Thomas E. Dewey created the New York State Crime Commission to investigate criminal behavior on the waterfront. As a result of this investigation in 1953 the AFL expelled the ILA on corruption charges, the New York–New Jersey Waterfront Commission was formed to help thwart illegal practices, and Ryan was ousted as ILA president. Those efforts to combat malfeasance on the waterfront had only limited effect.

Corruption and interunion competition contributed to a major strike, beginning in the Port of New York and extending along the entire East Coast, on 16 Nov 1956. The strike lasted intermittently until February 1957, and the Longshoremen won benefits such as paid holidays and vacations. The ILA was readmitted into the AFL-CIO in 1959. The number of ILA rank and file declined in the 1960s as a result of mechanization and containerization and the growth of airlines. During Teddy Gleason's presidency (1963–87) Longshoremen in 1966 secured from the New York Shipping Association (an organization that represented Port of New York employers) a guaranteed annual wage. Although the union is greatly reduced in size since its peak years following World War II, it remains an active institution. Union headquarters are in New York City, and in 2002 national membership was approximately 65,000.

Freeman, Joshua Benjamin. *Working-Class New York: Life and Labor since World War II* (New York: New Press, 2000)

John Cashman

International Railroad Bridge. First railroad bridge across the Niagara River above the falls, connecting Fort Erie, Ont, and the Black Rock section of Buffalo. This crossing replaced a railroad ferry that had operated since 1857. Construction of the iron structure began in 1870 under the supervision of Sir Casimir S. Gzowski, a founder and partner in Gzowski-MacPherson Co, with E. P. Hannaford as chief engineer and Joseph Hobson as resident engineer. The $1.5 million bridge opened 3 Nov 1873. The main bridge, from the Canadian shore to Squaw Island, consisted of seven fixed spans varying in length from 193.5 feet (58.98 m) to 248 feet (75.6 m) and a draw span of 362 feet (110.3 m); the smaller bridge across the Erie Canal at Black Rock had a fixed span of 219 feet (66.8 m) and a draw span of 218 feet (66.5 m). The iron-truss superstructure was replaced by steel in 1901, and the canal span underwent a major reconstruction with conversion of the Erie Canal to the New York State Barge Canal. This bridge continues to be one of the most important international railroad crossings in North America, permitting direct rail service between Buffalo, Detroit, and Chicago, around the north side of Lake Erie. It is owned and maintained by the

Canadian National Railway Co, the successor to the Grand Trunk Railroad, which originally contracted to build the bridge.

Greenhill, Ralph. *Spanning Niagara: The International Bridges, 1848–1962.* Catalog of Exhibition at Buscaglia-Castellani Art Gallery of Niagara Univ (Lewiston, NY: Niagara Univ, 1984; distributed by Univ of Washington Press)

Bogacki, Charles J., Stanley T. Maitland, and Victoria B. Katorski. *The International Railroad Bridge, Fort Erie to Buffalo, 1873–1973, and Colonel Sir Casimir S. Gzowski* (Buffalo: Buffalo and Erie County Historical Society, 1973)

Paul J. Bartczak

International Sematech. Semiconductor industry consortium composed of 10 members, including microchip industry leaders Intel, IBM, and Advanced Micro Devices (AMD), that put a research center at SUNY Albany. Although a 1987 effort to attract the Austin, Tex–based nonprofit research group to New York State failed, the state's second attempt proved successful. In July 2002 Gov George E. Pataki announced the creation of International Sematech North at SUNY Albany, raising hopes that the Capital District would join the ranks of technology-saturated areas such as Austin and California's Silicon Valley. The state's pledge of a $210 million financial package to help defray spiraling cost increases in microchip development and its commitment to making SUNY Albany a premier nanoscience research destination proved appealing to Sematech, which pledged $193 million to the project over its five-year life. The consortium established its presence at SUNY Albany's Center for Excellence in Nanoelectronics, a project that built the world's only university-based semiconductor production line employing 300 mm silicon wafers, the latest industry standard. Sematech researchers will use the tools at the Center for Excellence to develop extreme ultraviolet (EUV) lithography techniques at SUNY Albany; EUV is an important step in reducing the size of microchip transistors. Sematech's first workers arrived at the university's Albany NanoTech complex in 2003, and though it will employ about 25 people in Albany, hundreds of jobs are expected to be attached to the consortium's research. The state's investment appeared to pay dividends just months after the initial Sematech announcement, when another major semiconductor player, Tokyo Electron, announced its own plans to put a research and development center at Albany NanoTech.

"Chip Facility Bound for Albany," *Albany Times-Union,* 18 July 2002

Kenneth Aaron

International Union of Electrical, Radio, and Machine Workers (IUE). A product of the Cold War that emerged after nine years of bitter struggle between left- and right-wing unionists in the United Electrical, Radio, and Machine Workers of America (UE). In November 1949 the UE was expelled from the Congress of Industrial Organizations (CIO) by CIO president Philip Murray, and the IUE immediately formed at the 11th constitutional convention of the CIO in Cleveland. The same month, the IUE held its inaugural convention in Philadelphia and elected James B. Carey, former UE leader and CIO secretary-treasurer, as the head of the new union.

The competition between left- and right-wing electrical workers continued well into the next decade as the two unions competed for members throughout the nation. In New York State that battle took shape in New York City, Buffalo, Syracuse, Seneca Falls, Fort Edward, and most dramatically in Schenectady. There, approximately 25,000 unionized blue-collar workers at the General Electric (GE) works remained loyal to the UE but were continually lobbied by local IUE activists to abandon their left-wing union and rejoin the mainstream of the American labor movement through the IUE-CIO.

State and federal government efforts to isolate and marginalize the UE and to offer tacit support to the IUE through the Taft-Hartley Act of 1947, with its requirement that union leaders sign noncommunist affidavits, and through the intervention of local politicians, the Catholic Church, the FBI, and congressional investigation committees, placed additional pressures on UE leaders. By 1953 the IUE had drawn over 300,000 members away from the UE and grew even larger when the largest of the UE locals, Local 301 at Schenectady, broke away and joined the IUE in 1954.

In subsequent years, the UE and the IUE did manage to forge some cooperative links, particularly in their battles with GE's take-it-or-leave-it-bargaining strategy, inaugurated by GE vice president and director of employee relations Lemuel R. Boulware. They waged major national strikes in 1955–56 against Westinghouse and in 1960 and 1969 against GE. They engaged in coordinated bargaining with GE and on several occasions discussed the prospect of reuniting, but never did. Declining union membership in the 1970s and through the end of the century seriously eroded the IUE's strength. In October 2000, following the trend established by other weakened AFL-CIO unions, the 160,000 members of a much diminished IUE merged with the Communications Workers of America (CWA) to form a union of 740,000 members. In 2003 membership in the IUE-CWA stood at about 150,000, with New York State membership between 10,000 and 14,000. The UE's national membership in 2003 totaled 35,000, and its New York State membership was between 1,000 and 1,200.

Filippelli, Ronald L., and Mark D. McColloch. *Cold War in the Working Class: The Rise and Decline of the United Electrical Workers* (New York: SUNY Press, 1995)

Schatz, Ronald W. *The Electrical Workers: A History of Labor at General Electric and Westinghouse, 1923–1960* (Urbana: Univ of Illinois Press, 1983)

Gerald Zahavi

International Workingmen's Association (IWA). Known also as the First International, the IWA was founded in London on 28 Sept 1864. Its members included a broad cross section of socialists, anarchists, and nationalists. Its mission ranged from encouraging labor organization to making overt challenges to the capitalist system. Karl Marx was not involved in the initial founding of the IWA, but he and his followers took an intense interest in its activities and came to dominate the organization, seeing it as a possible vehicle for radicalizing the working class. New York City provided the first US affiliate in 1867, and it grew rapidly. In 1870 the IWA in London issued credentials to Robert Hume of Long Island and Cyrenus Osbourne Ward, a Brooklyn machinist and a later official at the federal Bureau of Labor Statistics, to organize additional American sections of the organization. At its peak in early 1872 it claimed 5,000 members nationwide, with New York City as its center. Most IWA members in New York City were German immigrants. However, sections (branch locals) also represented immigrants from France and Ireland, and Czechs from Austria-Hungary, as well as the American-born and a sprinkling of labor union locals. The IWA hosted controversial events in New York City honoring the Paris Commune in July 1871, and approximately 10,000 marched in December 1871 to protest executions of Communards in France. In January 1874 another demonstration led to a notorious riot with police at Manhattan's Tompkins Square. As a way of distancing the IWA from some of its European critics, the headquarters of the IWA was moved to New York City in 1872, and New Yorker and German immigrant Friedrich A. Sorge was chosen as general secretary. However, the IWA remained badly faction ridden in the United States, and Sorge, in frequent correspondence with Marx, soon initiated a purge of elements he considered reformist. This resulted in separate organizations trying to claim the IWA mantle. Membership declined rapidly thereafter, and by 1876 the IWA had dissolved. Successor organizations of the IWA included the Working Men's Party of the United States, precursor of the Socialist Labor Party, and the International Labor Union, a forerunner of the Knights of Labor. Famous New York City IWA members included Adolf Strasser and Samuel Gompers, who were later instrumental in establishing the American Federation of Labor.

Bernstein, Samuel. *The First International in America* (New York: Augustus Kelley, 1962)

Stephen Burwood

interstate highways. New York State played an important role in the creation of the nation's Interstate Highway System. Pres Dwight D. Eisenhower first proposed the project, the largest ever built, to a July 1954 meeting of governors in Bolton Landing (Warren Co), and Bertram Tallamy, designer of the New York Thruway (1946–56), became the first head of the Federal Highway Administration (FHWA), charged with building the new national road system. Passage of the Federal Aid Highway Act of 1956 enabled New York State to create 1,499 miles (2,412.4 km) of high-speed, divided, limited-access roadway. The FHWA, which oversaw construction, also incorporated most of the New York Thruway into the Interstate Highway System by 1958. As federal funds paid for 90% of construction costs, with state and local funds sharing the balance, the FHWA set roadway standards, which included travel lanes 12 feet (3.7 m) wide, breakdown lanes 10 ft (3.1 m) wide, road signs of uniform colors and sizes (green for entrances and exits, blue for services), 16 ft (4.9 m) minimum heights for underpasses, and curves angled to allow speeds of 70 mph (113 kph).

Among the most important routes in New York State are I-90 from Buffalo to Massachusetts, incorporating much of the east-west section of the New York Thruway; I-81 (1954–71), reaching from the Pennsylvania state line through Binghamton and continuing north through Watertown to the Canadian border; I-84 (1963–71), from the Pennsylvania state line at Port Jervis (Orange Co) via Newburgh (Orange Co) to the Connecticut state line; I-86 (formerly Rte 17, begun in 1950 and incorporated into the interstate system in stages starting in 1999); I-87 (1960–67 for sections north of Albany to the Canadian border and not part of the New York Thruway), from the Major Deegan Expressway in the Bronx to the Canadian border via the New York State Thruway to Albany and then through Glens Falls (Warren Co) and the Adirondack Park to Plattsburgh and Champlain (Clinton Co); I-88 (1974–82), from Binghamton to Schenectady; and I-95 (1958), from the New Jersey state line to the Connecticut state line through Manhattan, the Bronx, and Westchester Co. I-87, however, is really an intrastate rather than interstate as it begins and ends within the state's borders.

Completion of the interstate highways in 1972 brought profound changes as important as those over a century earlier from the opening of the Erie Canal and the coming of the railroads to the social and economic fabric of New York State. Since completion of the interstates, New Yorkers have come to rely upon the trucking industry for delivery of goods and upon the automobile, over passenger trains and buses, for personal transportation. All of the major interstates, especially after the North American Free Trade Agreement (NAFTA) in 1994, have become important links in the trucking routes between Canada and the rest of North America. I-495 (1955–72), the Long Island Expressway, helped to change Long Island into an automobile suburb of New York City, while I-490 (1963–74) and I-590 around Rochester and I-287 around the north and west of metropolitan New York City had a similar effect. In the two decades after the 1955 opening of the Tappan Zee Bridge (I-87/287) across the Hudson River, the population density of west bank Rockland Co increased from 500 to 1,300 people per square mile (2.6 km^2).

Many of the hundreds of interstate entrances and exits attracted lively economic development, with farms and fallow lands at such interchanges sold to motel and fast-food chains, shopping malls, and big-box retailers. From the early 1980s properties near developed interchanges have seen the growth of "edge cities," new centers of living and commerce that include housing developments, shopping centers, and corporate parks; edge cities flourish near White Plains and Tarrytown (Westchester Co) and near Great Neck and Lake Success (Nassau Co).

Some changes brought by the interstates have had their costs. The highways sometimes bisected farms, rendering them economically inefficient, and before passage of the National Environmental Policy Act (1970), engineers often built the roads through wetlands, damaging fragile ecosystems. In particular, interstates have drawn people and economic vitality from older cities to newer suburban communities and hastened the demise of trolleys and passenger trains. Planners often further degraded urban environments by building the highways through public parks and along riverbanks. In addition, strict federal standards for width and speed required engineers to destroy thousands of acres of land and thousands of houses in constructing the roads and their approaches, and, after completion, the interstates poured thousands of cars and trucks onto streets ill equipped to handle the increased traffic flow. For better or worse, from the 1970s interstates have supplanted railroads as the economic spine of the state. At the beginning of the 21st century, New Yorkers rely on the highways as an integral part of the delivery of their goods and services, as well as a key element in their own transportation.

Lewis, Tom. *Divided Highways: Building the Interstate Highways, Transforming American Life* (New York: Viking, 1997)

Seely, Bruce E. *Building the American Highway System: Engineers and Policy Makers* (Philadelphia: Temple Univ Press, 1987)

Tom Lewis

interurban railways

Origins

The interurbans usually carried passengers short distances. Freight was incidental, with express and less-than-carload shipments transported in attached trailers or box motors. Major lines in New York State sold tickets and checked baggage in the same fashion as steam railways. They also used steel cars resembling new steam railway passenger coaches. Some smaller lines used zone fares and the high-windowed coaches typical of city streetcars or trolleys. Almost all interurbans were powered throughout their routes by trolley poles attached to overhead electrified wires. A few ran on third rail systems for a portion of their routes. The economical interurbans, which used publicly maintained roads and needed only small crews, provided more frequent service than the longer-haul steam railways.

Nationally, most construction of electric railway lines occurred between 1899 and 1908. The lines served areas with cities surrounded by prosperous agricultural land. In New York State electric routes sprang up mainly in the northern, central, and western sections of the state. Major cities in close proximity were an ideal market; one of the first interurbans, built in 1895, connected Buffalo and Niagara Falls. Shortly before World War I the state interurban network peaked at 1,129 miles (1,817 km).

Development

The most prominent interurban lines in New York State, like rail and canal traffic, followed the Mohawk corridor. International Railway, which built the Buffalo–Niagara Falls line and also operated streetcars in both cities, soon extended another line from Buffalo to Lockport and Olcott (Niagara Co). This linked Buffalo, through Lockport, with a series of interurbans running parallel to the New York Central Railroad main line and reaching nearly across the state. Two syndicates, New York State Railways, controlled by New York Central, and Empire United Railways, controlled by Clifford D. Beebe of Syracuse, operated most of these lines. New York State Railways operated Rochester and Sodus Bay Railway, Rochester and Eastern Rapid Railway, running from Rochester to Geneva (Ontario Co), and Oneida Railway, linking Syracuse and Utica along an electrified section of New York Central's West Shore line from Rochester to Utica. Empire United's principal property was Rochester, Syracuse, and Eastern Railroad, a heavily built, high-speed line constructed parallel to New York Central's main line between Rochester and Syracuse. Beebe's syndicate also owned Empire State Railroad connecting Syracuse and Oswego, the Auburn and Syracuse, and Syracuse Northern Railroad running from Syracuse to South Bay (Madison Co) and Brewerton (Onondaga Co) on Oneida Lake. The linked system of the two syndicates reached its easternmost point on New York State Railway line at Little Falls (Herkimer Co). The gap of 30 miles (48 km) to the Fonda, Johnstown and Gloversville Railroad, which joined the electric railway complex at Schenectady, Albany, and Troy (Rensselaer Co), was never filled. Long interline trips were used to publicize the industry in its early years, but the typical interurban passenger traveled a short distance on a single carrier.

Interurbans also served other areas of New York State. The Buffalo and Lake Erie ran west to Erie, Pa, providing through weak connections an interchange with the Ohio-Indiana system. The Southern New York Railway, which began as a street railway in Oneonta (Otsego Co), ran north to Cooperstown (Otsego Co) and met New York State Railways in Herkimer. The Broadhead family, owners of the street railway in Jamestown (Chautauqua Co) adjacent to the Erie Railroad, also maintained interurbans that traveled each side of Chautauqua Lake to Westfield (Chautauqua Co) on the New York Central main line. Small networks of electric railways started from Bradford, Pa, and Elmira and fed into the Erie Railroad main line. The Capital District network included Schenectady Railways, which operated lines to Albany and Troy; the Hudson Valley Railway, a subsidiary of Delaware and Hudson Railroad, which ran north to Glens Falls and Warrensburg (Warren Co); and the Albany and Hudson, a third rail line extending 28 miles (45 km) south from Albany. Several small isolated lines, such as the Penn Yan, Keuka Lake and Branchport, resembled New England rural lines, featuring wooden cars open to the weather in summertime.

Decline

The World War I years were difficult for electric interurbans, which were caught between the rigid fare structures of the lines' municipal charters, or "franchises," and rising wage rates. In 1915 the Buffalo and Lake Erie went bankrupt, and Beebe's network began to fragment. Several companies—a reorganized Buffalo and Lake Erie, now Buffalo and Erie; Albany and Hudson; and Fonda, Johnstown and Gloversville—reequipped with lightweight cars, but most New York lines continued to operate heavy steel equipment through the 1920s. The overall prosperity of the decade failed to help the industry, which crumbled as automotive transport spread. In 1928 Rochester tried to remove interurbans from downtown streets by creating a subway route for them built in an old canal bed. The depression forced the abandonment of much New York State interurban mileage: Albany and Hudson ceased operations in 1929; most of New York Central's network and Beebe's lines were abandoned between 1929 and 1931; Buffalo and Erie closed in segments during 1932 and 1933; and Utica and Mohawk Valley, serving Rome (Oneida Co), Utica, and Little Falls, closed in 1933. The state's interurbans had negligible freight revenues, and most could not handle railroad freight cars. They were unable to integrate

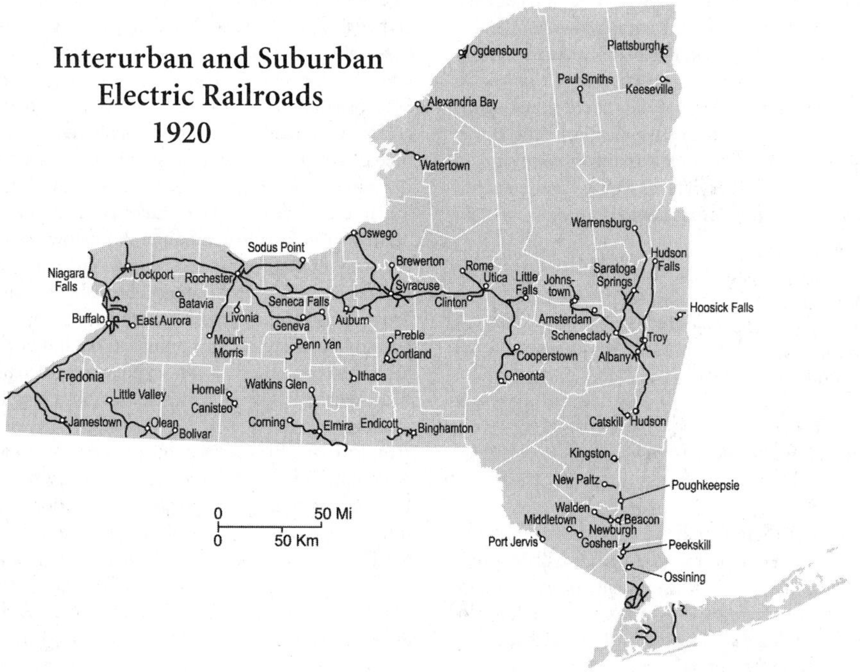

SOURCE: Adapted from Doubleday, Page and Co, *Geographic Manual and New Atlas* (1918).

into the freight railroad system that preserved some midwestern and western interurbans for several more years. Two New York lines, Southern New York Railway and Jamestown, Westfield and Northwestern, were exceptions. They did not parallel steam railroads and developed enough interchange freight traffic to survive as freight-only short lines until 1941 and 1950, respectively. Overall, New York State interurbans were short-lived, and physical evidence of their existence is already rare.

Hilton, George W., and John F. Due. *The Electric Interurban Railways in America* (Stanford, Calif: Stanford Univ Press, 1960)

Middleton, William D. *The Interurban Era* (Milwaukee: Kalmbach Publishing, 1961)

George W. Hilton

invasive species. See EXOTIC SPECIES; TREE DISEASES AND PESTS.

investment banks. See SECURITIES INDUSTRY.

Inwood. Locality (pop 9,325) in Hempstead (Nassau Co). As Northwest Point, Inwood was granted in 1663 by the Town of Hempstead to six freeholders who settled on the shore of Jamaica Bay. Baymen shipped the famous Rockaway clams to New York City. Development followed the Rockaway Branch Railroad (1869). In 1871 the locality became Westville but was renamed Inwood in 1889 when a post office opened. The home of turn-of-the-century Nassau Co Republican leaders, Inwood was made part of New York City in 1898, but the leaders sponsored legislation resulting in its transfer to Nassau Co the following year. Blacks came to Inwood before 1900, and Italians and Albanians followed in the new century. Inwood's population reached 8,022 in 1940. African Americans made up 26% of the population in 2000. The 300-acre (121 ha) Inwood Country Club (1901), founded by wealthy German Jews, was the site of the 1923 US Open championship.

John A. Hewlett

Iona College. Private college. Founded in 1940 in New Rochelle (Westchester Co) by the Congregation of Christian Brothers. Iona and its Rockland Graduate Center in Orangeburg (Rockland Co) offer bachelor's and master's degrees. The college is noted for its programs in social work, business, and peace and justice studies. Until 1969 only men were enrolled. By 2001, 53% of undergraduates were women. That year Iona had 2,506 full-time undergraduate and 1,571 graduate students, and 1,734 evening school students.

Iona College, http://www.iona.edu

Carl A. Westerdahl and Susan S. Clarke

Ira. Town (pop 2,426) in NE Cayuga Co. Settled in 1800, the town was formed from Cato 1821. It contains drumlins, streams, and wetlands with gentle, rolling land that is very productive. The Southern Central Railroad (1869) provided service to Ira. In 2003 farmers produced dairy products along with soybeans, field corn, hay, wheat, and kidney beans. In the early 21st century, Ira experienced growth as a result of Onondaga Co commuters moving to town.

Dorothy Southard

Iranians. After California, New York State is home to the second largest Iranian community in the United States. Immigration from Iran has occurred in two distinct phases. The first, from 1953 to 1977, came with the expansion of education in Iran. More than 20,000, mostly intellectuals and professionals, came as visitors, students, and interns, eventually changing their status to permanent residents. The second phase began in 1978 and became significant in the early 1980s, the period immediately before and after the Islamic Revolution in Iran in 1979. (The most significant "refugee" from the revolution to arrive in New York State was the shah of Iran. The decision of the Carter administration to admit him to the United States for medical treatment in a New York City hospital on 22 Oct 1979 evoked protests by the Iranian government and precipitated the takeover of the US Embassy in Tehran on 4 Nov 1979.) That second wave, which continues in the early 21st century, is highly diversified in terms of social class, education, occupation, and age. The mostly involuntary immigration of middle- and upper-class families was crucial to the making of New York State's Iranian community. With a median income around 20% higher than the national average in 2000, Iranians are among the most affluent immigrant groups in the United States. They are also among the most educated and are widely successful in professions and corporations. They are a dominant force in the rug industry and own scores of businesses, from automobile dealerships to jewelry enterprises.

The heterogeneous Iranian American population includes Jews (concentrated on Long Island), Armenians, Assyrians, Zoroastrians, and Bahá'ís. The majority are Shi'ite Muslims, though with a predominantly secular orientation. However, a growing religious cohesiveness among Iranian Shi'ites is indicated by such establishments as the Imam Ali Mosque and Islamic school (also known as the Islamic Institute of New York), founded in Woodside (Queens Co) in the early 1990s, and the Ferdowsi School, founded in 1990 in Greenvale (Nassau Co). *Anjomans* (cultural associations) and *dowreh* (informal networks of relatives and friends) are the cornerstones of the Iranian American communities. The *Iranian Yellow Pages* has been published annually since 1986, and numerous television and radio programs are broadcast. The Iranian-American Society of New York, founded in 1990 in Greenvale, celebrates Nowruz (the Iranian new year festival) on the first day of spring and Mehregan (the Iranian fall festival).

Prominent individuals include the scholar Ehsan Yarshater, founder and editor of the *Encyclopaedia Iranica* (begun in 1979) at Columbia University; Masood Khatamee, professor at New York University School of Medicine and executive director of the Fertility Research Foundation in New York City; Sorosh Roshan, an obstetrician/gynecologist, internationally recognized humanitarian, and president of the International Health Awareness Network and the National Council of Women of the United States; and Farhad Talebian, a surgeon and president of the Iranian American Society of New York. The 2000 US census counted 17,323 Iranian-born individuals in New York State; a total of 22,856 persons statewide claimed Iranian ancestry, up from 18,183 in 1990, and numbers continue to rise. Over 80% of New York State's Iranian population lives in the greater New York City area, including over 40% of the state's total in Nassau Co.

Ansari, Maboud. *The Making of the Iranian Community in America* (New York: Pardis Press, 1992)

Maboud Ansari

Iraq War. War between the United States and Iraq that began on 19 Mar 2003 with the US invasion of Iraq. The US government accused the Iraqi government of Saddam Hussein of widespread human rights abuses, harboring weapons of mass destruction, and having links to Islamic terrorist groups. When the Iraqi government did not satisfy US concerns on these matters, the invasion commenced. Some of the most memorable debates leading up to war took place in the United Nations headquarters in Manhattan. On

5 Feb 2003 Secretary of State Colin Powell addressed the Security Council, laying out in detail the case that the Iraqi government possessed weapons of mass destruction. After intense discussions over several weeks, the Security Council did not authorize a resolution backing the American position. Opinion in New York State before the war was divided. An antiwar demonstration on 15 Feb 2003 brought at least 100,000 participants to rallying points around 1st Ave in Manhattan and resulted in 295 arrests.

In anticipation of retaliation for US attacks on Iraq, New York City mayor Michael Bloomberg and Police Commissioner Raymond W. Kelly presented Operation Atlas, a plan to protect New York City and its inhabitants. On 25 Mar 2003, six days into combat, the US government resumed the 24-hour patrol of New York City airspace that had followed the 11 Sept 2001 attack on the World Trade Center.

A number of New York State units were activated for the war. The 105th Military Police Co, Army National Guard, based in Buffalo and Rochester, had been ordered to state active duty on 11 Sept 2001 to provide security support in New York City; it was federally mobilized in February 2003. New York State army reserves were also activated, including the 479th Engineer Battalion, based at Fort Drum, near Watertown, and the 301st Area Support Group, based at Fort Totten (Queens Co). By the end of 2003, 21 military personnel from New York State had been killed in the war.

Pamela Cooper

Irish

Colonial New York

The Irish presence in the area of North America that became New York State extends through its development from Dutch outpost to British colony, and from 19th-century agricultural and industrial powerhouse to political and cultural arbiter in the 20th century. Irish emigration to North America during the 17th century was typically via continental Europe where Catholic elites, in flight from political, economic, and religious oppression, often took up service in the armies of France or Spain. However, the liberal immigration policies of the Dutch did attract some enterprising Irish immigrants to New Netherland, such as the surgeon William Hays who was in New Amsterdam in 1647 and the baker Thomas Powell who resided in Beverwijck [now Albany] from 1656 to 1671. In general the Irish presence in the colony was discrete, and archival evidence is complicated by phonetic spellings in the Dutch church registers and other civil records; as late as 1701, the Albany cooper and licensed innkeeper John Finn from County Waterford appears as "Jan Fyne" or "Johannes Fine."

After 1664 the British transatlantic empire inevitably brought career administrators to New York, including the colony's Gov Thomas Dongan. A native of County Kildare and Stuart loyalist, Dongan's term (1682–88) was a brief expression of tolerance marked as much by his 1686 Charter of Liberties and Privileges as by the appearance of Irish Catholics in his entourage such as the Jesuit priest Henry Harrison. Maj Thomas Jones (?1665–1713), a native of Strabane, County Tyrone, exiled after the Stuart defeat at the Battle of the Boyne (1690), acquired 6,000 acres (2,430 ha) on the south shore of Long Island as part of his wife's dowry in 1696. Among several Queens Co appointments he subsequently held was ranger general, which permitted him to monopolize the local whaling industry from what is now the East Bath House in Jones Beach State Park.

From the 1730s New York City had an important trade relationship with Ireland, particularly in the export of flaxseed that soared from 950 hogsheads (226,532 l) around 1736 to 18,850 (4.5 million l) in 1766–67. A small but significant portion of this seed was directly exchanged for finished linen goods with Dublin and the manufacturing towns of Belfast, Londonderry, and Newry; as late as 1770–72 Ireland accounted for 75% of all linen sold in New York City. Much of this flaxseed-linen commerce was in the hands of local Irish merchants who ranged from general goods retailers to specialists in the trade, such as Greg, Cunningham & Co.

A labor shortage in the early 18th century attracted Irish workers to the colony, particularly Protestants from the northern parts of Ireland who traveled on cargo vessels returning from flaxseed delivery. A modest proportion of these emigrants were indentured servants channeled through Irish agents like William Neilson. More were freemen, but in general the Irish preferred not to trade their landlord system at home for the one operating in the Hudson Valley. Nevertheless, there were Irish Presbyterian congregations established in Goshen (Orange Co), Bethlehem (Orange Co), and Wallkill (Ulster Co) in the 1720 and 1730s, and Irish names begin to appear with regularity in the civil, religious, and military records of Orange, Ulster, and Albany Cos from that time. Among them was Charles Clinton (1690–1773) from Corbay, County Longford, father of Gov George Clinton (1739–1812), who settled Little Britain (Orange Co) with about 90 other Irish immigrants in 1729–30. Thereafter, New York City–based men such as Sir Peter Warren from County Meath and Anthony Duane from County Galway became involved in land speculation in the Mohawk Valley, settling Irish immigrants in what is now Montgomery and Schenectady Cos. The stability of the Canadian border after the Peace of Paris (1763) opened up areas of the colony even farther north, and Irish immigrants were directed to settle, for example, in Essex and Washington Cos by landowning compatriots in New York City.

As early as 1700 Irish soldiers were stationed in New York Colony as part of British garrison forces, and in 1741 several of those from Fort George in Lower Manhattan were arrested as part of the "Negro Plot." But it was the French and Indian War that accelerated the numbers of Irish enlisted men in the colony. Many petitioned for service-bonus land grants, particularly in Ulster Co. One of the major beneficiaries was Sir William Johnson, originally from County Meath, who received 100,000 acres (40,470 ha) north of the Mohawk River, eventually acquiring a significant portion of what became Herkimer, Oneida, Fulton, and Otsego Cos. This land base allowed Johnson to dispense patronage to scores of kin and emigrants from Ireland, especially in connection with his estate at Johnstown [now in Fulton Co]. Although in 1766 Johnson became the first master of St. Patrick's Lodge, the earliest Masonic lodge in western New York, he also permitted Fr Peter McKenna to hold Catholic services for his Irish tenants even though penal laws still in effect in the colony on the eve of the Revolution barred Catholic services.

The ethnoreligious makeup of the 18th-century Irish in the colony was far more diverse than it would be a century later. There were congregations to support Anglo-Irish, Scots-Irish, German (Palatine)-Irish, as well as Huguenots and Quakers from Ireland. The Irish mercantile elite in New York City worshiped at Trinity Church on Broadway, although Robert and John Murray, whose parents were from County Armagh, were Quakers, as was Thomas Eddy, whose parents were from Dublin and Belfast. There was a significant degree of assimilation despite such religious distinctiveness, particularly among Irish Anglicans who frequently intermarried with old Dutch and English families. Dissenters from Ireland were more likely to emigrate in family or community groups, thus preserving Irish identity somewhat longer. Irish Presbyterians from Ulster were particularly associated with the First Presbyterian Church (Wall St) and the Rutgers Church (Henry St). Many Palatine immigrants from Ireland (especially those whose families had lived in Ireland for two generations) were early Methodists. Philip Embury, a carpenter from County Limerick, established a Methodist society in 1766 and its first American church on John St two years later. He died in 1772 at Ash Grove (Washington Co), where he and other Irish Methodists had taken up a land grant.

Likewise, the political diversity of the 18th-century Irish was clearly defined by the American Revolution. Many, like the heirs of William Johnson, who had profited by their relationship to the British Crown and its North American administrators, remained loyal to England and either fled to Canada or had their lands confiscated. On the other hand, patriot Irish like Capt Thomas Randall and James Duane fled New York City for the duration of the British occupation. The loyalist flaxseed merchants Hugh and Alexander Wallace spent four months in late 1776 in prison even though Belfast native Hugh Gaine, a tory who had been public printer to the colony since 1768, was little inconvenienced. The British general Lord Francis Rawdon was able to recruit 250 local men for his Volunteers of Ireland unit in 1779 by having Maj John Lynch play up ethnicity. Other Irish were among the rebels, ranging from Timothy "Sure Shot Tim" Murphy, the son of County Donegal immigrants who as a rifleman defended the New York State frontier and helped turned the tide at the second Battle of Saratoga (1777), to the New York City brothers Hercules and Hugh Mulligan, the former a Son of Liberty and a merchant tailor who outfitted British officers, the latter a supplier to the British army, and both were undercover agents for George Washington. Gen Richard Montgomery, a member of New York's First Provincial Congress who had emigrated in 1772 from County Donegal and died in the assault upon Quebec in 1775, was long remembered as a hero among the New York Irish.

Independence to the 1840s

Following the evacuation of the British, a new chapter in the history of the Irish in New York State began with the establishment in 1784 of the Friendly Sons of St. Patrick. This fraternal society, based in New York City, was purposely nonpolitical and helped restore social and cultural relations between men who had been on opposite sides during the American War of Independence. Many of the original members of the Friendly Sons became involved in rural New York State land deals at the end of the 18th century, partly the fortuitous circumstances of having ethnic connections in the governor's mansion. Under George Clinton, the legislature passed a land act whose first beneficiary was Alexander Macomb. Macomb, who had emigrated with his parents from County Antrim in 1755 and made his wealth in the fur trade, purchased 640,000 acres (259,000 ha) along the Canadian border (the St. Lawrence Ten Towns, including what became Ogdensburg) in 1787. His partners in this deal were Daniel McCormick, an auctioneer from County Antrim, and William Constable, a native of Dublin in the India and China trade, (together the first three presidents of the Friendly Sons), with whom he also concluded the Macomb Purchase in 1791, acquiring an additional 3.6 million acres (1.5 million ha) across northern New York State.

Such ethnic and business networks often solidified connections between the Irish in rural and urban parts of the state in the early national period, while marriage reinforced it; for example, three of the nine children of merchant John McVickar, a founding member of the Friendly Sons from County Antrim who was a protégé of McCormick, married Constables. Dynastic evidence survives in places like Constableville (Lewis Co) and Russell (formerly Ballybean) and Louisville (St. Lawrence Co). The Macomb Purchase was sold off in smaller pieces to a host of developers, among whom were other Irish men such as Michael Hogan, who settled Bombay and Hogansburg (Franklin Co).

The results of this activity were not yet evident in the 1790 census of New York State, which counted approximately 25,500 persons of Irish nationality, about 7.5% of the total population. Their distribution is significant, with nearly one-third in the Mohawk Valley (Albany and Montgomery Cos), just over one-third in the counties on the eastern side of the Hudson Valley (Westchester, Dutchess, Columbia, and Washington Cos), and about one-eighth in Orange and Ulster Cos. Almost another quarter was in the area encompassing New York City and Long Island. The number of Irish in New York State increased with the new century; working-class Catholics in particular were lured by employment opportunities on major turnpike- and canal-building projects. By 1820 there were large numbers of non-naturalized persons in Jefferson, St. Lawrence, Clinton, Oneida, and Herkimer Cos, partly the result of efforts by the Irish Emigrant Association (1817), which urged immigrants from Ireland to leave New York City for the northern frontier. Similarly the Shamrock Friendly Association between 1815 and 1818 found employment for 1,200 new migrants throughout the country. The leaders of these organizations were middle-class professional Irish men, many of them political exiles from the United Irish rebellion (1798) who had emigrated after the repeal of the Alien and Sedition Acts (1804). They formed the nucleus of a nascent ethnic community, at whose center was Thomas Emmet (1764–1827). Again through the influence of Gov George Clinton, Emmet was admitted to the New York Bar and began a spectacular legal career that led to his appointment as state attorney general (1812–13).

From 1790 to 1808 the Diocese of Baltimore had jurisdiction over the Roman Catholic Church in New York State; during that period, St. Peter's in New York City (1784) and St. Mary's in Albany (1787) were the state's two principal parishes. The County Galway–born merchant Dominick Lynch, founder of Lynchville [now Rome, Oneida Co] in 1796, and Cornelius Heeney, from King's County [now County Offaly] in Ireland and a merchant in the fur trade with considerable property in Brooklyn, were among the many Irish trustees of St. Peter's. The parish itself was administered by Irish-born Dominican priests (William and Matthew O'Brien, John Connell, and Anthony McMahon) and by Bishop John Connolly (1750–1825), who oversaw the new Diocese of New York (1808), which encompassed the entire state. In 1815 there were 17,000 Catholics in New York City, mostly Irish, when St. Patrick's Cathedral was dedicated on Mott St (near Houston). Across the East River in Brooklyn, Irish immigrants from Counties Derry and Donegal (including the parents of John McCloskey, the first American-born cardinal) had been settling in the neighborhood of the Brooklyn Navy Yard since 1801. St. James was opened for them in 1823.

The establishment dates of parishes in the upper regions of New York State track the settlement of immigrants along the path of the Erie Canal, the construction of which already involved more than 3,000 Irish workers by 1818. The first public masses for Catholics were said at Utica in 1819 and in Rochester in 1820. The following year Fr Patrick Kelly was sent as a missionary priest to the canal workers, and Bishop Connolly visited Irish work camps in 1823. By the end of the decade, there were 50,000 natives of Ireland along the canal route between Buffalo and New York City. These were often migrants who had disembarked at Quebec or Montreal and whose settlement in New York State was facilitated by the northern ports of Ogdensburg and Oswego; generally, transatlantic fares were cheaper to Canada than to New York City before 1838. The growth of Albany, Utica, Syracuse, and Rochester at this time is directly related to the influx of Irish, not only as canal laborers but also as subcontractors who bid for up to 3 mi (5 km) sections and as teamsters for its mule barges. Likewise, the creation in 1847 of separate dioceses for Albany and Buffalo can be attributed to the increased number of Irish Catholics settled in these districts, including prominent laymen such as Nicholas Devereux, a Utica merchant-banker, James Maher and John Cassidy, both local politicians in Albany, and the merchant-salt manufacturers Thomas McCarthy and James Lynch of Syracuse.

Mid-19th to Early 21st Centuries

The completion of the Erie Canal anticipated a need for Irish labor on extension projects, feeder canals, and railroads throughout the state for the next 30 years. The 1850 census counted 39 male Irish laborers and 34 female Irish domestic servants in the Putnam Co town of Southeast, a brand new stop on the Harlem Railroad, illustrating how closely such employment opportunities and intrastate migration operated for 19th-century Irish. Once infrastructure contracts were completed, local industries such as salt, grain, lumber, stone quarrying, and leather tanning absorbed the Irish (eg, Split Rock in Onondaga Co). One of the most ambitious undertakings to employ the Irish and direct their settlement within the southern part of the state was the Croton (Westchester Co) water system begun in 1837. Thousands of Irish laborers worked on the aqueduct, tunnels, and bridges that brought mountain water to New York City and in the process created ethnic enclaves in places like High Bridge [now in Bronx Co] and Croton-on-Hudson (Westchester Co). Nevertheless, the state's rural-agricultural economy continued to attract some Irish, including Catholics at Plattsburgh and Protestants at Tyrone (Schuyler Co). County Clare immigrants began to farm at New Ireland near Limestone (Cattaraugus Co) at midcentury.

From the middle of the 19th century, the Irish became political capital in the struggle for power between New York City and Albany. A significant yet often overlooked example is the creation in 1847 of the New York State Commissioners of Emigration to reform immigration at the Port of New York. This commission was brought into being through the combined efforts of Bishop John Hughes (1797–1864) and Andrew Carrigan (1804–72), who were both of Irish birth, along with John E. Develin (son of Irish immigrants) and Thurlow Weed. It wrested control of bond monies from the City of New York and by 1855 had instituted state-backed procedures for processing immigrants at Castle Garden (now Castle Clinton) and caring for sick arrivals at hospital facilities on Ward's Island. The timing could not have been more propitious, as during this period (1847–55) 43% of all foreign-born arrivals at the Port of New York were from Ireland.

Nearly 900,000 refugees fled from a devastating famine, begun in 1845, the social and economic consequences of which were felt in transatlantic migration patterns for the remainder of the century. The existence of established communities like Dublin in Rochester, the Old First Ward in Buffalo, Gander Bay in Albany, and Vinegar Hill in Brooklyn fed chain migration, and in many cases the famine exodus substantially increased their Irish-born populations. The number of Albany Irish was 10 times larger in 1855 than it had been in 1830, while approximately half the population of the Rochester almshouse was Irish during the 1850s. New York City was the most affected; its Sixth Ward (including the Five Points slum) was 42% Irish-born in 1855 and comprised hundreds of emigrants from Counties Kerry and Sligo whose passage was paid for by their landlords. At the same time, there were substantial numbers of Irish people living in all of Manhattan's 22 wards, including the more rural districts north of 50th St where the Irish had been homesteading. In 1857, on the basis of eminent domain for Central Park, the state legislature appropriated Seneca Village, where Irish and African Americans had been farming for more than 20 years.

Catholic parishes, charities, social services, and educational institutions throughout the state were created in direct response to the needs of famine and postfamine immigrants. Examples include St. Vincent's Hospital (Manhattan), the New York Catholic Protectory (Westchester Co), St. Dominic's Home (Blauvelt, Rockland Co, the Mission of the Immaculate Virgin (Richmond Co), the College of Mount Saint Vincent (Bronx

Co), and the College of New Rochelle (Westchester Co). Often staff was recruited in Ireland for specific service in the New York City area, thereby establishing religious communities such as the Sisters of Mercy (1846), the Franciscan Brothers of Brooklyn (1858), the Religious of the Sacred Heart of Mary (1877), and the Carmelities (Province of St. Elias, 1889). The state's Catholic hierarchy remained Irish American even as its flock became more ethnically heterogeneous during the century following the famine: Bishops McCloskey, Conroy, McNeirny, Burke, Cusack, and Gibbons in Albany; Bishops Timon, Ryan, Quigley, Colton, Dougherty, Turner, Duffy, and O'Hara in Buffalo; Bishops McQuaid, Hickey, O'Hern, Mooney, and Kearney in Rochester; Bishops Ludden, Grimes, Curley, and Duffy in Syracuse; Bishops Loughlin, McDonnell, and Molloy in Brooklyn; and Archbishops Hughes, and Corrigan, and Cardinals McCloskey, Farley, Hayes, and Spellman in New York City.

Likewise, the arrival of the Irish coincided with the development of representational politics in New York State. After the extension of suffrage to all white males in the 1820s, the increasing number of Irish immigrants who were naturalized became significant in state elections, particularly as Democratic voters. Essential to the development of the urban machine, the Irish vote was most often exchanged for jobs, housing, food, even bail, in an era devoid of social welfare legislation. They participated at all levels in the political system although not as party "boss" until the ascendancy of Hugh McLaughlin (Brooklyn, 1861), "Honest" John Kelly (New York City, 1871), and Patrick "Packy" McCabe (Albany, 1900).

While famine migration irrevocably associated the Irish in New York State with Catholicism and the Democratic Party, the Irish presence was equally as important in urban-industrial areas and wage labor for the next 100 years. By 1870 the most populated Irish counties in New York State were New York, Kings, Albany, Rensselaer, and Erie; indeed, the Irish presence in the cities of these counties gave New York State the largest foreign-born urban concentration in the nation. Despite a popular impression that an Irish underclass in these cities was the cause of myriad social problems, the proverbial "paddy wagon" was as likely to be driven by an Irish policeman as to have an Irish criminal on board. In fact, for every legally executed Irishman in New York State, there was a Thomas Murray, Michael Moran, Clarence Mackay, or Anthony N. Brady making his fortune in capitalist ventures. The majority of Irish were neither destitute nor rich; rather they were solid middle- and working-class people who prized family and job security over individual advancement. Factory-based employment drew the Irish to specific concentrations in both trade and place; for example, garment workers in New York City, carpet workers in Yonkers, iron molders and collar workers in Troy (Rensselaer Co), and brickmakers in the Haverstraw Bay area of Rockland Co. A unique example is the Dunbartons Mill, which transplanted skilled workers from Gilford in northern Ireland to Greenwich (Washington Co) to manufacture linen thread from 1880 to World War I.

The expansion of New York City required an insatiable supply of day laborers for infrastructure projects including another phase of the Croton water system and the Brooklyn Bridge. Firms such as the Crimmins Contracting Co and Kingsley and Keeney became conduits for regular work for unskilled Irish men. As a result, the Irish emerged in the front ranks of the labor movement in the second half of the 19th century. Kate Mullaney and Esther Keegan, for example, organized collar laundresses in Troy in 1864, and Robert Blissert, Matthew Maguire, and P. J. McGuire were instrumental in the first Labor Day observances in 1882. Irish union officials were influential throughout the next century, from Kate Hogan (Interborough Association of Women Teachers, 1906) and Michael J. Quill (Transport Workers Union, 1934) to George Meany (New York State Federation of Labor, 1934; AFL, 1952; AFL-CIO, 1955), and John J. Sweeney (Service Employees International, 1980; AFL-CIO, 1995). Even though all New York cities had their corps of domestic servants drawn from the ranks of Irish immigrant women, this employment sector, more than any other, was rife with discrimination; newspapers like the *Brooklyn Eagle* and the *New York Times* ran "Help Wanted" advertisements that specified "No Irish need apply," while jokes and cartoons about inept "Bridget" were widely circulated.

Such prejudices had a long-standing history, rooted in Anglo-Saxon attitudes toward Catholicism that periodically surfaced in racist actions such as the burning of St. Mary's in New York City in 1831. The Irish response was to organize the Ancient Order of Hibernians (AOH) to protect Catholic citizens and church property; the first division was established at St. James's parish in New York City in 1838. By the 1880s this Catholic fraternal organization had an estimated 22–24,000 members in 18 New York State counties, although the majority of Hibernians were attached to Manhattan or Brooklyn divisions. In most places by the late 19th century, the AOH marched in St. Patrick's Day parades alongside veterans of the Civil War. (St. Patrick's Day was celebrated in Amsterdam [now in Montgomery Co] as early as 1747.)

There had been at least 20 specifically Irish units in the New York State Volunteers (NYSV). Corcoran's Irish Legion and the Irish Brigade included many companies recruited upstate, such as the 63d Regiment's Company K (Faugh-a-Ballagh) from Albany and Companies G, H, and I of the 105th (Western Irish Regiment) from Rochester. The 69th, known as the Fighting Irish, Kerrigan's Rangers, and Irish Rifles, were recruited in New York City and Brooklyn. The Red Hand logo of the Ulster Guard, mustered at Kingston, was a direct reference to the legacy of the county's original Irish settlers although there was no known ethnic presence in the rank-and-file of the 20th/80th NYSV. In July 1863 the Irish rioted against conscription with devastating consequences for New York City. There was also civil unrest in Troy, to a lesser extent along the Harlem and New Haven Railroads in Westchester Co. In other parts of the state, the Irish did not violently protest the draft, and Rochester actually exceeded its quotas. About 7,000 Civil War veterans, members of the Fenian Brotherhood (a secret militant Irish nationalist organization), assembled in Buffalo and invaded Canada in June 1866 in an attempt to wrest independence for Ireland from Great Britain. A second unsuccessful attempt was made at Malone that same year and at Hogansburg (Franklin Co) in 1870.

Civil War recruitment poster for Corcoran's Irish Legion, 1862.

Thereafter New York State remained the base for expatriate nationalist activities on behalf of Irish independence. The Fenians commissioned County Clare native John P. Holland (1840–1914) to build a submarine prototype, which as the *Fenian Ram* was tested successfully in the Hudson River in 1881. The Fenian splinter group, Clan na Gael (1867), under the leadership of John Devoy (1842–1928, emigrated to New York in 1871), directed Irish American militant republicanism and offered support for the Easter Rising of 1916. Two of the executed leaders of this rebellion had New York State connections: the socialist James Connolly had spent several years organizing workers in Troy, and Tom Clarke had been managing editor of Devoy's newspaper, the *Gaelic American* (1903).

The life of the man who would become the most prominent leader of postindependence Ireland was spared in the aftermath of the Easter Rebellion partly because of his American citizenship: Eamon de Valera (1882–1975), born in New York City to an Irish servant girl and a Spanish music teacher, spend 18 months touring the United States in 1919–20 to garner attention for Ireland's claim to self-determination. From his headquarters in New York City, de Valera made brief stops in Albany, Syracuse, and Rochester. In Rochester he also visited with his mother, who had settled there in 1895. Irish activists in New York City, such as Paul O'Dwyer (1907–98), continued to draw public attention to nationalist issues throughout the 20th century, including the partition of Ireland; civil rights violations in Northern Ireland during the 1960s and 1970s, followed by the deaths of 10 political prisoners there while on hunger strike in 1981; and Immigration and Naturalization Service (INS) deportation proceedings against republicans living in New York State, such as Joe Doherty (1983–92).

The elections of Edward Murphy (1875), Michael Nolan (1878), and William R. Grace (1880) to the mayoralties of Troy, Albany, and New York began a period of Irish ascendancy in local and state politics. Its pinnacle was reached in 1918 when Alfred E. Smith, with maternal Irish roots, was elected Governor of New York State. The influence of key Democratic bosses such as Daniel P. O'Connell, Charles F. Murphy, and Edward J. Flynn helped mobilize the Irish voting bloc, a tradition broken only when suburbanization after World War II diluted the machine's old neighborhood base. Nevertheless, the state's representatives in Washington, DC, continued to be Irish Americans, such as Robert F. Kennedy and Daniel Patrick Moynihan.

The creation of greater New York City in 1898 combined the state's two major Irish centers of population, Manhattan and Brooklyn, instantly making the metropolitan area the most Irish place on the planet. Other cities in the state declined in relevance from that time; there were 275,000 persons of Irish birth living in New York City in 1900 (with as many or more claiming Irish ancestry) compared with about 10,000 in Albany. In 1960 New York City claimed 311,000 persons of Irish ancestry, plus another 66,350 in neighboring Nassau and Westchester Cos, not to mention those New Jersey counties included in the standard metropolitan statistical area. New immigrants from Ireland in the 1920s, 1950s, and 1980s clustered in New York City, especially in ethnic neighborhoods in northern Manhattan, the Bronx, and Queens. The Irish Immigration Reform Movement, which operated out of offices in Woodside (Queens Co) during the late 1980s, successfully lobbied Congress to redress legislation enacted in 1965 that had made thousands of young Irish migrants illegal aliens. The result was a multiyear lottery scheme with implications for all undocumented workers in the United States.

After the Second World War, East Durham (Greene Co) became a summer resort for the Irish. Two institutions preserve community there: the Irish American Heritage Museum (1986) and the Michael J. Quill Irish Cultural and Sports Center (1987). A state education amendment in 1998 led to the creation in 2001 of the Great Irish Famine Curriculum, to teach grades 4–12 about mass starvation in 19th-century Ireland and its consequences for New York State. In 2002 the president of Ireland, Mary McAleese, and Gov George E. Pataki unveiled a striking landscape memorial in Battery Park City (New York Co) to commemorate the sesquicentennial of the Irish famine.

The Irish contribution to New York State's literary history has been considerable. Edmund Bailey O' Callaghan and James Sullivan have written notable histories of the state; Michael J. O'Brien and Richard Purcell have chronicled the early Irish presence in it; and novelists such as William Kennedy (Albany), Jimmy Breslin (Queens), and Alice McDermott (Long Island) as well as poets like Terence Winch (the Bronx) have documented the contemporary period. Two weekly newspapers, the *Irish Echo* (1928) and the *Irish Voice* (1987), as well as a monthly magazine, *Irish America* (1993), are published in New York City for national circulation. Likewise, American popular culture and musical theater have benefited from New York Irish influences. Irish Americans were active as minstrel performers, such as the Troy-born Bryant Brothers, who introduced "Dixie" to the nation in 1859. A later generation of Irish-American composers wrote quintessentially "Irish" Tin Pan Alley tunes like "Mother Machree" (1910) and "When Irish Eyes Are Smiling" (1912). Irish American playwrights and actors included Dion Boucicault, the team of Edward Harrigan and Tony Hart, George M. Cohan, and Eugene O'Neill. New York City in the 1920s and 1930s also became a center of Irish traditional music and recordings, such as those by the Sligo-style fiddler Michael Coleman. In the early 21st century New York City remains the gateway for the dissemination of Irish trends in American popular culture, ranging from the world's largest annual St. Patrick's Day Parade (150,000 marchers with millions on the sidelines) to more than 600 performances of the stage show *Riverdance on Broadway* (2000–2001).

As the 21st century opened, 2.5 million people in New York State (13% of its total population), claimed single or multiple Irish ancestry. The longevity and intricacy of ties between the state and Ireland were crystallized on 11 Sept 2001: New York City not only lost hundreds of second- and third-generation Irish accountants, financial services professionals, and fire, police, and rescue personnel, but also the unique archaeological remains from a 1991 excavation of the Irish Five Points (New York Co) that were warehoused in the basement of the World Trade Center.

See also CATHOLICS; ETHNIC PRESS; LABOR; ROCHESTER (CITY); TROY; URBAN GANGS.

Almeida, Linda Dowling. *Irish Immigrants in New York City, 1945–1995* (Bloomington: Indiana Univ Press, 2001)

Bayor Ronald H., and Timothy J. Meagher, eds. *The New York Irish* (Baltimore: Johns Hopkins Univ Press, 1995)

Casey, Marion R. "Irish." In *Encyclopedia of New York City*, ed. Kenneth T. Jackson (New Haven, Conn: Yale Univ Press, 1996)

Dolan, Jay P. *The American Catholic Experience: A History from Colonial Times to the Present* (Notre Dame, Ind: Univ of Notre Dame Press, 1992)

Erie, Steven P. *Rainbow's End: Irish Americans and the Dilemmas of Urban Machine Politics, 1849–1985* (Berkeley: Univ of California Press, 1988)

From Shore to Shore: Irish Traditional Music in New York City. Dir Patrick J. Mullins (VHS) (Truckee, Calif: Cherry Lane Productions, 1993)

The Great Irish Famine Curriculum, http://www.emsc.nysed.gov/nysssa/gif/curriculum.html

McKelvey, Blake. "The Irish in Rochester: An Historical Retrospect," *Rochester History* 19 (Oct 1957): 1–16

McNickle, Chris. *To Be Mayor of New York: Ethnic Politics in the City* (New York: Columbia Univ Press, 1993)

Miller, Kerby A. *Emigrants and Exiles: Ireland and the Irish Exodus to North America* (New York: Oxford Univ Press, 1985)

Murphy, Richard C., and Lawrence J. Mannion, *The History of the Friendly Sons of St. Patrick in the City of New York, 1784–1955* (New York: J. C. Dillon, 1962)

Purcell, Richard J. "Irish Contribution to Colonial New York," *Studies: An Irish Quarterly Review of Letters, Philosophy and Science* 29 (1940): 591–604; 30 (1941): 107–20

Rowley, William E. "The Irish Aristocracy of Albany, 1798–1878," *New York History* 52 (July 1971): 275–304

Truxes, Thomas M. *Irish-American Trade, 1660–1783* (New York: Cambridge Univ Press, 1988)

Marion R. Casey

iron and steel industry. Cornelius Board in 1736 discovered iron ore along the Orange Co–New Jersey border, and local iron manufacturing began there almost immediately. The first pig iron was produced *ca* 1750 on Philip Livingston's estate [now in Columbia Co]. By the Revolutionary War, charcoal blast furnaces, bloomery furnaces, and forges were operating east of the Hudson River in Dutchess Co in Amenia, Beekman, Dover, and Fishkill, where they exploited rich local hematite ore deposits. A second set of iron-manufacturing facilities developed west of the Hudson in the Highlands of Orange Co and what is now Rockland Co at the same time. The oldest, largest, and most productive of these facilities was Sterling Iron Works near present-day Warwick (Orange Co). Board, the original prospector, and Timothy Ward established this works. Originally built to produce anchors, the Sterling Works later manufactured the chain that stretched across the Hudson at West Point (Orange Co) in 1778. At this time, Abel Noble and Peter Townsend owned the property and made it a productive iron producer for the Continental army. Much of the ore smelted here came from the nearby Forest of Dean mine, which operated until 1942 and is now part of the United States Military Academy's reservation at West Point.

At the start of the 19th century, large iron ore deposits in the Lake Champlain watershed began to be mined, and the first of many furnaces, forges, bloomeries, and later rolling mills appeared in Essex and Clinton Cos. Blessed with abundant supplies of high-grade ore, waterpower, and wood, the region's iron industry grew impressively when the Champlain Canal was completed in 1823. By 1840 the two-county region produced over 10,000 tons (9,070 MT) of iron annually. Beginning in the 1830s a less significant fourth cluster of ironworks began to appear in eastern Jefferson and nearby St. Lawrence Cos and in Oneida and Wayne Cos. Between 1800 and 1830, New York State was second only to Pennsylvania as an iron producer.

These early iron-manufacturing complexes had much in common. Until at least the 1830s all facilities used the same technology. Most iron was produced by smelting iron ore with charcoal fuel and limestone flux in stone furnaces while subjecting the mixture to blasts of air produced by large waterpowered bellows. The resulting molten metal was poured into sand molds whose form determined the product's name. Metal cast in long, cylindrical ingots destined to be reworked was pig iron; metal cast into the shape of a finished product was cast iron. Blast furnaces were the center of an involved operation that included numerous buildings, extensive land, and a sizable work force that operated the furnace 24 hours a day, 7 days a week and cut timber, manufactured charcoal, and hauled iron ore, limestone, and charcoal to the furnace site. Fuel requirements substantially exceeded those of iron ore in volume, thus the location of these iron plantations was based more on a ready and reliable wood supply than on a nearby iron ore source. These same fuel requirements meant that the furnaces were well spaced and modest in size. The insatiable requirements of these iron plantations wrought a significant environmental legacy. Entire forests, such as the Forest of Dean in Orange Co, were cut to provide charcoal fuel; waterways were dammed to supply waterpower and diverted to create canals; abandoned mines collapsed and filled with water; and slag piles dotted the landscape. Finally, iron making often spurred initial settlement such as the Orange Co villages of Monroe and Southfield [now Tuxedo Park], and the locality of Sloatsburg in Rockland Co, settlements that long outlasted the industry itself.

Most pig iron was further refined into wrought or bar iron. This refining was done at a forge, where the metal was heated until hot and then beaten with a hammer, a very labor-intensive process that removed the carbon from the metal and produced an iron that could be bent and shaped, welded, and tempered. Forges were often not closely associated with furnaces but instead were established close to markets for the finished product. A small percentage of wrought iron was produced directly from ore at bloomery furnaces. Sometimes referred to as Catalan forges, bloomeries were usually small, much less efficient operations requiring far fewer workers and considerably less investment than blast furnaces.

Production technologies began to shift during the 1830s as anthracite and bituminous coal, converted first to coke, were introduced as alternative fuel sources. Coke is a high-grade, high-temperature fuel made of nearly pure carbon. It is produced by burning coal in the absence of oxygen; coal is to coke as wood is to charcoal. Dwindling wood supplies combined with cheap and convenient transport via the Delaware and Hudson Canal led to the building of at least 10 anthracite-fueled furnaces in the Hudson-Champlain Valley corridor by 1860. Anthracite furnaces had a substantially larger capacity, approximately 70 tons (64 MT) of iron per week as opposed to 25 tons (23 MT) at a charcoal facility; charcoal fuel furnaces were limited in size as charcoal tended to be crushed if ore was piled too high. The larger anthracite furnaces required workforces proportionately larger, and location was determined by access to navigable waterways. Rolling mills, an alternative and much more efficient method of producing wrought iron, also developed in the 1830s. A typical rolling mill processed nearly as much iron as a charcoal furnace produced. During this same period the Champlain region rose to national prominence as local magnetite ore deposits were tapped and larger, more efficient regional transport and manufacturing facilities were built. Most notable was the Town of Moriah (Essex Co), whose ores and locally produced pig iron were in demand throughout the Northeast. In 1880 Essex Co was the second-leading iron ore–producing county in the country. Beyond the Champlain Valley, the three urban centers of New York City, Troy (Rensselaer Co), and Buffalo also emerged as important New York State centers of iron and steel fabrication.

New York City

New York City's involvement in the industry dates from the 1760s, when cast and wrought iron were produced. Expansion of the city's shipbuilding industry, however, promoted iron founding to a major industry and led to the establishment of a number of huge foundries capable of producing boilers weighing several tons. Allaire Ironworks was the first of these. By 1840 the list included Columbian Foundry, Novelty Ironworks, Delameter Works, and Morgan Ironworks. By the early 1850s the Novelty works covered two city blocks and employed over 1,000 workers. During the 1840s another group of foundries emerged and specialized in the production of cast-iron architecture. Capitalizing on James Bogardus's idea of cast-iron building facades, Daniel Badger and his Architectural Iron Works pioneered producing cornices, columns, and complete storefronts. A third facet of New York City's founding industry focused on the manufacture of stoves. One of the largest of these firms was the J. L. Mott Iron Works established by Jordan Mott in 1846 on 400 acres (162 ha) of land that later became known as Mott Haven [now in Bronx Co]. The city's iron-founding industry as a whole reached its height around 1860, after which rising real estate values and operating costs began to take their toll. By 1928 there were only five foundries still operating in Manhattan; by 1982 there were none.

Troy

Troy's association with iron and steel began in 1807 when the Albany Rolling and Slitting Mill opened on Wynants Kill (Rensselaer Co). Two years later the Troy Iron and Nail Co was built a short distance upstream. Henry Burden, a Scottish immigrant, arrived at this company in 1819 and soon rose to superintendent. Over the next quarter century, he patented a number of machines including a wrought-iron nail-and-spike machine that mass-produced railroad spikes, a rotary concentric squeezer that converted puddled iron into blooms, and a horseshoe machine capable of producing 60 horseshoes per minute. Burden's engineering genius extended to the mill itself, where he constructed a massive 60 ft (18 m) diameter overshot waterwheel that generated 1,200 horsepower. The Civil War spurred tremendous expansion that included development of a 45-acre (18 ha) plant site along the Hudson River at South Troy (Rensselaer Co) and a near quadrupling of the workforce from 370 to more than 1,400 employees. By the end of the 1860s, the company's annual production included 600,000 kegs of horseshoes, comparable numbers of kegs of bolts, rivets, and spikes, plus thousands of tons of wrought-iron bars (Burden's Best).

Erastus Corning bought the Albany Rolling mill in 1826 and, assisted by ironmaster John F. Winslow, guided the facility's expansion into one of the nation's foremost producers of iron railroad rail and sheet iron by the Civil War. A fourth important member of Troy's iron and steel fraternity was John A. Griswold, agent for the Rensselaer Iron Works. In 1861 Griswold, in collaboration with Winslow, contracted for and produced the iron plate for the Union navy's ironclad USS *Monitor,* which was assembled at the Continental Iron Works in Greenpoint, Brooklyn, a year later. During these years, Irish workers dominated the Troy iron industry. In 1860, 66% of the unskilled laborers and 50% of the skilled laborers were Irish. By 1875 the Rensselaer Works was putting out 270 tons (245 MT) of steel ingots a day. A decade later the company's successor, Albany and Rensselaer Iron and Steel, built three modern blast furnaces in South Troy and the processing facilities needed to keep pace with the daily production of 450 tons (408 MT) of steel. In 1888, 4.5% of the nation's steel rail production was allotted to the Troy facility. But the numbers are deceiving; overextended and poorly located to compete, the company was sold to receivers in 1893 and never reopened. This firm's fate is emblematic of the situation steel producers throughout the Hudson-Champlain corridor faced; the facilities were poorly positioned to compete successfully in the national market and were thus abandoned. All regional works had shuttered by 1906.

Troy also became an important iron-founding center. Ideally situated at the confluence of the Erie Canal and the Hudson River and with large local deposits of molding sand to draw upon, Trojan foundries most famously produced stoves and ranges beginning in 1815. By 1860 Albany and Troy were each producing upwards of $1 million worth of stoves yearly. The Rathbone Stove Works of Albany was producing more than 35,000 stoves annually by the mid-1860s. In 1875 the 32 stove foundries in the Troy-Albany area produced 450,000 stoves. Clinton Stove Works, the largest, turned out 200 different models. By the end of the 1890s, these same companies became less competitive in the face of growing competition from midwestern firms that capitalized on iron and steel industry innovations and proximity to an expanding market. The result was amalgamation, bankruptcy, and migration to new locations and increased labor unrest, especially among the molders and puddlers.

Troy had a long tradition of organized labor with the molders striking in 1859 over wages and working conditions. The 1870s were particularly strike prone and violent. The puddlers organized a 6-month strike in 1873–74, which resulted in Troy's ironmasters importing nonunion labor, a tactic that led to a so-called reign of terror. Burden and other ironmasters were forced to house these scab workers in guarded warehouses converted to dormitories to ensure their safety. On 18 May 1875, after having been unemployed for nearly 50 weeks, the puddlers agreed to end their strike. These strikes combined with the 1873–77 depression caused widespread poverty and hardship among those working in the iron industry.

Buffalo

Buffalo's association with the iron and steel industry dates from 1846 and the establishment of the Buffalo Iron and Nail Works rolling mill. But the region's rise to industrial prominence began in the 1890s largely in response to the expansion of the Lake Superior iron ranges and the emergence of Lake Erie ports as transshipment points in the ore trade. In 1892 iron ore receipts at Buffalo and Tonawanda (Erie Co) were slightly less than 200,000 tons (181,500 MT); in 1903 ore tonnage exceeded 2 million (1.8 million MT). In 1890 western New York State's steel industry consisted of one blast furnace and one rolling mill. By 1904 the area contained an additional blast furnace and a second rolling mill, three new steelworks, plus the integrated blast furnace, rolling mill, and steelworks complex of Lackawanna Steel (Erie Co). In 1905, 11 of the 22 furnaces operating in the state were clustered in or around Buffalo. By 1926 the ratio was 21 of 25. During the early 1930s the Lackawanna plant, purchased by Bethlehem Steel in 1922, built a large capacity, continuous sheet and wide strip mill to supply the expanding automobile industry based in Detroit and the domestic appliance industry centered at General Electric's facilities in Schenectady.

World War II brought change on a number of fronts. In 1942 Republic and Jones and Laughlin opened new iron-ore mines in the area of Clifton (St. Lawrence Co), and a resurgence of activity at the large mines at Lyon Mountain (Clinton Co) and Moriah occurred. War demands also resulted in a more than 10% increase in the Buffalo area's steelmaking capacity. By the end of the war the Buffalo area was the third-largest steel-manufacturing center in the country. During the 1950s depletion of the richest Lake Superior ores, combined with the competitive advantage Central and Western New York enjoyed regarding shipping costs associated with Labrador ores via the newly opened St. Lawrence Seaway, prompted speculation of further expansion of the state's steel industry at Buffalo. Buffalo's steelmaking capacity rose from 6 million tons (5.4 million MT) to 9 million tons (8.2 million MT) of steel between 1957 and 1970. At the same time, however, the number of primary plants dropped from five to three. The largest closing was Republic Steel's Tonawanda plant, which opened in 1907 and closed in 2001.

Throughout this period Bethlehem Steel's Lackawanna plant remained the preeminent production facility within the state and that company's principal supplier to the Midwest. In the late 1950s the company decided to build a new out-of-state integrated facility at the south end of Lake Michigan. This left the Lackawanna plant poorly positioned to supply the biggest steel markets. In late 1970 Bethlehem reduced its Buffalo facility's production capacity from 6.7 million tons (6.1 million MT) to 4.8 million tons (4.4 million MT) of steel per annum, thereby launching a downward spiral that by 1985 included closure or drastic cutbacks in the plant's rail, bar, structural, and sheet steel facilities. But the problem extended far beyond a single firm.

The American steel industry generally and large integrated steel producers in particular faced a set of problems not easily solved. In the 1970s and early 1980s a steep decline in internal markets occurred, especially in the Northeast, as the national and regional economies moved away from durable goods production. Shrinking foreign markets, heightened environmental concerns and controls, and dramatic growth in highly competitive, domestic minimill steel facilities compounded this situation. Together these developments spelled closure for integrated steel plants across the country's traditional manufacturing belt.

At the end of the 20th century, New York State was no longer a major center of steel production. The three largest mills in operation all confined production to high-priced specialty steels. The Crucible Materials Corp plant at Camillus (Onondaga Co) dates from 1876 and was the largest steel plant in New York State in 2002, employing more than 2,000 workers. The plants at Purchase (Westchester Co) and Dunkirk (Chautauqua Co), which are minimill operations, date from the mid-1960s and mid-1970s respectively. All three plants were foreign owned and the second two employed approximately 1,000 workers each.

See also Great lakes shipping lines and watercraft; Labor; Technology.

Gordon, Robert B. *American Iron, 1607–1900* (Baltimore: Johns Hopkins Univ Press, 1996)
Moravek, John R. "The Iron Industry: A Geographic Force in the Adirondack-Champlain Region of New York State, 1800–1971" (PhD diss, Univ of Tennessee, 1976)
Ransom, James M. *Vanishing Ironworks of the Ramapos* (New Brunswick, NJ: Rutgers Univ Press, 1966)
Seely, Bruce. "Blast Furnace Technology in the Mid-19th Century: A Case Study of the Adirondack Iron and Steel Company," *Journal of the Society for Industrial Archeology* 7 (1981): 27–54
Temin, Peter. *Iron and Steel in 19th-Century America, an Economic Inquiry* (Cambridge, Mass: MIT Press, 1964)
Walkowitz, Daniel J. "Statistics and the Writing of Working Class Culture: A Statistical Portrait of the Iron Workers in Troy, New York, 1868–1888," *Labor History* 15 (1974): 416–68

Marie Johnson

Irondequoit. Town (pop 52,354) in NE Monroe Co. Settled permanently in 1800, the town was formed from Brighton in 1839. Located between Irondequoit Bay, Lake Ontario, and the Genesee River, plentiful water and fertile soil promoted agricultural growth, giving rise to the nickname Market Garden Town by the 1870s. The town still had many market gardens as late as 1950, but the nurseries that had supplied almost 3 million apple trees annually across the nation succumbed to western competition by 1890. Crossed by the Rome, Watertown and Ogdensburg Railroad (1875), it was affected more by the Rochester and Lake Ontario Railroad (1879–1936), which helped develop a string of beach resorts and hotels. Part of Rochester's urban ring, Irondequoit farmlands were among the first in Monroe Co to be developed, beginning as early as 1919. Irondequoit's population tripled during the 1920s and experienced another decade of extraordinary population growth during the 1950s, increasing 62%. Since 1960, like many inner suburbs, its population has stabilized and slightly declined. Sea Breeze, an amusement park created in 1879 by the Rochester and Lake Ontario Railroad Co, continues in operation in the 21st century. The chaotically organized House of Guitars has a national reputation for its selection of instruments and recorded music. It is the home of Durand-Eastman Park. In 2002 the Irondequoit Land Use Coalition was created to protect the town's remaining environmentally sensitive land.

Carolyn Vacca

Irondequoit melon. A muskmelon variety created by William Sutton of Irondequoit (Monroe Co) that made its debut in the seed catalog of James Vick of Rochester in 1889. The melon was prized by muskmelon connoisseurs for its aroma and sweetness, and was featured prominently on Rochester tables for several decades. Although they were cultivated at first by garden farmers in Irondequoit, the melons subsequently were grown by farmers throughout Central and Western New York. Irondequoit melons rotted easily and their soft rinds made them difficult to ship long distances, and by 1930 farmers began switching to the hardier Bender and Bender Surprise melons, often marketed as Irondequoit melons. A fungus blight in the late 1930s largely ended cultivation of the original Irondequoit and Bender melons, though blight-resistant hybrids, such as the Iroquois, are still sold as Irondequoit-type melons.

"The Irreplaceable Irondequoit Melon," *Rochester Democrat and Chronicle,* 8 Aug 2002

Peter Eisenstadt

Iroquois art. The artistic traditions of the Iroquois people are deeply rooted. From an early bone comb delicately carved with the image of a beaver to a contemporary artist's airbrushed painting of the Tree of Peace, Iroquois art reflects and reinforces both creative expression and cultural continuity.

Archaeological evidence has shown that long-standing artistic traditions used local and traded materials such as shell, bone, antler, and wood. After Europeans arrived and trade increased, the materials in Iroquois art changed. Rather than porcupine quills and shell beads for embroidering clothing, multicolored glass beads took center stage. Geometric designs were complemented by floral patterns. But the cultural identity of Iroquois art remained. Finely woven black-ash splint baskets reflect the significance of the natural world to the Iroquois. Carved wooden spoons and bowls were enhanced with images of clan animals. A baby's wooden cradleboard was carved with floral designs or the animal image of the child's clan. Silver was a medium for making brooches, using these cultural symbols as well as symbols adopted from European cultures such as the Irish heart and hands often seen in Iroquois silver brooches.

Painting and sketching developed in Iroquois art in the 19th and early 20th centuries. Images reflected the Iroquois way of life during the period or illustrated stories and historical accounts. One of the earliest-known Iroquois painters was Dennis Cusick, a Tuscarora who in the 1820s depicted scenes showing the combining of cultures. In one, Iroquois children at the Seneca Mission School on the Buffalo Creek Reservation [now in Erie Co] are painted wearing traditional Iroquois clothing while engaged in lessons taught by the white missionaries. By the early 20th century Seneca artist Jesse J. Cornplanter worked with Arthur C. Parker, a Seneca Indian and director of the Rochester Museum of Arts and Sciences (now Rochester Museum and Science Center), making sketches of contemporary Iroquois life. His work is important because he drew accurate portraits of the way people dressed at the time. Jesse Cornplanter has influenced many Iroquois painters and artists because of his faithful documentation of the critical moments in Iroquois legend and ritual.

Gustoweh (hard hat), by Rick Hill (Tuscarora), 1989.

A number of Iroquois painters participated in the Temporary Emergency Relief Administration (TERA) arts and crafts project, which began in the 1930s. Seneca watercolorist Sanford Plummer portrayed in a realistic style the legends, ceremonial dances, and important historical scenes of Iroquois culture. Ernest Smith, a Seneca from the Tonawanda Indian Reservation [loc in Erie, Genesee, and Lewis Cos], painted to preserve as accurately as possible the memory of Iroquois customs he felt were being lost. His work also produced more nostalgic portraits of the past. Painting was not the only art form encouraged during the TERA project, however. Several Iroquois artists began to carve in wood, creating human figures doing traditional activities, often reflecting the pre-Contact era. The TERA project lasted until World War II, when all of the Work Projects Administration art programs were eliminated.

During the late 1960s and 1970s, carving in stone became a popular new form of artistic expression. Sculptors used steatite, alabaster, and other stone to express religious symbols, clan animals, and figures from Iroquois legends, giving narrative traditions a visual form. Seneca-Cayuga artist Tom Huff is a renowned stone carver of Iroquois themes. He has also produced satirical found-object sculptures that comment on social inequity, as in *Tonto's Revenge Dance Party,* related to the Cayuga land claim dispute in New York State. The art of carving bone and antler was rediscovered when Stanley Hill, a Mohawk high-steel worker, began sculpting eagles, turtles, bears, and Iroquois symbols out of moose and deer antlers. Over the past 30 years, Hill has become the foremost Iroquois antler carver, and his success has inspired other Iroquois to pursue the art of carving.

Traditional Iroquois pottery was abandoned after metal pots and European ceramics were introduced in the 17th century. In the late 1960s, however, a few Iroquois artists revived the traditional art of pottery making, notably at the potteries run by the late Oliver and Elda Smith on the Six Nations Reserve near Brantford, Ont, and by Onondaga artist Peter B. Jones in Versailles (Cattaraugus Co). As in stone and bone sculptures, clay pots are infused with symbolic images. Some artists have expanded the medium into clay sculptures, often using the human form to speak to concerns about contemporary issues such as gambling, alcoholism, racial bias, and sovereignty.

Seneca beaded cloth bag, mid–19th century.

Seneca cradle board or baby frame, mid–19th century.

Contemporary Seneca artist G. Peter Jemison references the past in his paintings. He has intermixed family images with the portrayal of traditional Haudenosaunee symbols, such as the bald eagle, Five Nations wampum belt, and the Three Sisters (corn, beans, and squash). An eighth-generation descendant of Mary Jemison (?1743–1833), the white woman who was captured in childhood and later formally adopted by the Seneca, Jemison displays his vast knowledge of Iroquois history in his artwork.

The artistic media has continued to expand with incorporation of photography among Iroquois artists. Onondaga Jeffrey M. Thomas photographs contemporary American Indian people. His work has been shown throughout Canada and the United States and was the subject of a documentary film, *Shooting Indians: A Journey with Jeffrey Thomas,* which appeared at the Toronto International Film Festival in 1997. Photographer and art historian Jolene Rickard references her Tuscarora heritage in her work, which combines traditional and modern elements.

Iroquois artists of the 21st century continue to work in a variety of media, creating baskets, wooden utensils, and traditional objects in addition to paintings, photographs, and sculpture. They create not only for aesthetics or to retain traditional skills but to speak to all people about their concerns for our world. In coping with the challenges of a modern society, today's Iroquois artists often become the "visual voices" of their people. Through art they address the issues of vital importance to a modern people while continuing to help ensure the existence of an enduring culture.

Hanks, Christina J. *Visual Voices of the Iroquois* (Howes Cave, NY: Iroquois Indian Museum, 1992)

Jemison, G. Peter. *Haudenosaunee Artists: A Common Heritage* (Brockport, NY: Tower Fine Arts Gallery, SUNY College at Brockport, 1992)

Jemison, G. Peter, et al. *The Pan-American Exposition Centennial: Images of the American Indian* (Buffalo: Burchfield-Penney Art Center, 2001)

McMaster, Gerald, and Arthur Renwick. *Reservation X: The Power of Place in Aboriginal Contemporary Art* (Hull, Que: Canadian Museum of Civilization, 1998)

New York State. Office of Parks, Recreation, and Historic Preservation. *Art from Ganondagan: The Village of Peace* (Waterford, NY: Author, 1986)

Rogers, Bertha. *Iroquois Voices, Iroquois Visions: A Celebration of Contemporary Six Nations Arts* (Treadwell, NY: Bright Hill Press, 1996)

Van Horn, Elizabeth H. *Iroquois Silver Brooches (as-ne-as-ga) in the Rochester Museum* (Rochester: Rochester Museum and Science Center, 1971)

Stephanie Shultes, Nancy Weekly

Iroquois Confederacy. Native American league, originally of the Mohawk, Oneida, Onondaga, Cayuga, and Seneca, joined in the 1720s by the Tuscaroras; also known as the Iroquois League, the Great League of Peace, the Five Nations, the Six Nations, and the Haudenosaunee, a Seneca term meaning "the lodge extended" or "the longhouse." The name Iroquois probably originated in a Basque epithet used by late 16th-century European and Indian traders. In the 17th and 18th centuries, Haudenosaunee country stretched from the Mohawk to the Genesee River valleys. In 1995, 16,754 people were reportedly affiliated with eight reservations within New York State's borders: Oneida, Onondaga, Tuscarora, the Mohawk reservation of Akwesasne (St. Regis), and the Seneca reservations of Allegany, Cattaraugus, Tonawanda, and Oil Spring.

Origins and Characteristics

The founding date of the Iroquois League is uncertain, but it was probably between 1450 and 1525. Tradition, confirmed by archaeological evidence, describes an era when Iroquois made ceaseless war against outsiders and each other. These conflicts reflected a cultural pattern of "mourning wars" common among eastern American Indians. A person's death, from whatever cause, was believed to decrease the spiritual power of the deceased's extended family. Grieving kinswomen often urged young men to raise a war party to take prisoners who would make up the loss, either literally through adoption into the family or symbolically through ritual execution. Such raids, of course, provoked counter-raids and endless feuding. Tradition says that such conflicts particularly affected a man called Hiawatha (He Who Combs). Enraged by the deaths of his daughters, he wandered into the forest, where he met a man of supernatural origins named Deganawida (the Peacemaker). Offering Hiawatha strings of the sacred shell beads called wampum, Deganawida spoke three "Rare Words of Condolence." The first dried Hiawatha's tearful eyes and let him see clearly again. The second opened his unhearing ears and helped him listen to reason. The third unstopped his throat and allowed him to speak plainly. These condolence rituals were the core of the Peacemaker's message, the Great Law. Cere-

The Council with Tadodaho at the Time the League Was Started, by Ernest Smith (Tonawanda Reservation), 1936.

mony, rather than warfare, would restore the spiritual power depleted by death and bring strength and harmony to people.

The Peacemaker and Hiawatha spread the Great Law to other nations but encountered many obstacles along the way. The most formidable resistance came from an Onondaga chief named Thadodaho, whose mind was so filled with murderous rage that his hair had become a writhing mass of snakes. The Peacemaker and Hiawatha straightened Thadodaho's hair, rubbed his body with wampum beads to soothe him, and spoke the Rare Words of Condolence to calm his mind. Thus rehabilitated, Thadodaho joined Hiawatha and the Peacemaker in uniting the Five Nations around the Great Law. In recognition of the Onondaga's prominent role, his people became the "firekeepers" for a council of approximately 50 chiefs from each of the nations, and the main Onondaga village became the league's capital.

The league chiefs were divided into two sides, or moieties—one composed of the Mohawk, Onondaga, and Seneca and the other of the Oneida and Cayuga—that performed the rituals that Deganawida prescribed. When one of the chiefs died, members of the "clear-minded" side recited the story of the Peacemaker and the Great Law, offered the Rare Words of Condolence, and restored the loss by conferring the deceased's name upon his chosen successor. Thus the league renewed itself and its people. The office of chief was semihereditary in particular lineages of *rotiyanehr* (nobles). From kinsmen of the appropriate age, the elder women of the lineage made the choice. They could also replace a leader who failed to meet expectations.

The main duty of a chief, as well as the principal purpose of the league, was to keep the peace through ceremony and through the preaching of the Great Law. In societies that did not rely on the coercive power of a state-organized government, such public acts were vitally important. Only if everyone shared in the climate of goodwill could order be preserved. Therefore the league council was apparently not designed to make policy decisions in the sense familiar to western European governments; such decisions were likely to provoke division rather than consensus. Leaving contentious matters to local village councils, the league operated on a plane perhaps better described as religious than political.

17th-Century Transformations

When the European colonization of North America began, the Five Nations, with a probable population of 21,000 people, had powerful mechanisms for maintaining cultural unity and for dealing with outsiders who shared basic assumptions about the meaning of peace. Yet their political mechanisms were almost entirely local. In practical terms individual villages, not the league as a whole, faced the challenges unleashed by the European invasion. Among the most important of those challenges resulted from competition over imported European goods such as glass beads, woolen cloth, and metal tools and weapons. With their inland location, the Five Nations were severely disadvantaged in acquiring the new commodities until 1614, when Dutch traders opened for business at what would later be known as Albany, only about a day's journey from the easternmost Mohawk village. Thenceforth the Iroquois enjoyed ample access to Dutch suppliers of cloth, metal tools, and countless other items, including, by the mid-1630s, firearms. These and other imported weapons they turned against rivals who had better access to the beaver and various furs that European suppliers demanded.

But conflicts over fur supplies and trade routes were quickly overshadowed by more desperate struggles provoked by another great force unleashed by European colonization, epidemic disease. Initially the same interior location that had isolated the Five Nations from trade protected them from viral invaders to which Indians had no immunity. In the 1630s, however, a smallpox pandemic spread from New England to the Great Lakes, and by 1640 at least half of the Haudenosaunee people had perished. By 1700, repeated outbreaks of smallpox, measles, influenza, and other maladies reduced the northeastern North American population as a whole by roughly 90%. Amidst so much death, the mourning war tradition metastasized into ever spiraling conflicts as native peoples fought desperately for captives to replace the victims. In these 17th-century conflicts, there were no real winners, only survivors. But the Five Nations' economic connections to the Dutch gave them a weapons advantage that allowed them to fare better than most. Iroquois forces—recruited by war chiefs from one or more nations but apparently not under any central league direction—conquered the Huron, the Petun, the Erie, the Neutral, and other nations, incorporating vast numbers of captives into their villages. By the 1660s the total population of Iroquoia remained at about its 1640 level of 10,000, yet over half of those people were war captives, and their homelands stood almost empty of human inhabitants. The strains that these wars placed on the league and its message of peace were profound. Respected chiefs, and perhaps even entire lineages entitled to choose their successors, succumbed to disease. Massive numbers of newcomers had somehow to be assimilated. And the decentralized way in which kin groups and villages waged wars inevitably led to intra-Iroquois conflicts over strategy and in some cases over possession of prisoners. Beginning in the 1660s the strains became increasingly intense. In making war on Indian enemies, the Iroquois fell into conflict with the European trading partner of many of those foes, New France, of which the French Crown assumed direct control in 1663 and reinforced its royal troops. This show of force encouraged Seneca, Cayuga, Onondaga, and Oneida headmen to make peace with the French and their allied Indians in 1665. Just as important, however, was the conquest of New Netherland by British forces in 1664 and the consequent disarray of trading relationships. Some Iroquois were more eager to gain access to French markets than they were intimidated by French military might.

Most Mohawks, close enough to Albany to be assured at least some trade goods and embittered by more intense conflict with New France than others had experienced, rejected the peace until after the French invaded their country and burned their villages in 1666. For the better part of the next decade, the Five Nations rested uneasily in the French economic and diplomatic orbit. Jesuit missionaries worked in Iroquois villages and convinced hundreds of people to move to missions on the St. Lawrence River, most notably the community near Montreal today known as Kahnawake (Akwesasne was a mid-18th-century offshoot of Kahnawake). Those who remained in Iroquoia were deeply divided over questions of religion and relations with the French. Meanwhile, devastating wars with Mohicans (Mahicans), Southern New England Algonquians, and Susquehannocks continued, and trade ties to the Hudson River were further disrupted by a short-lived Dutch reconquest of New York in 1673.

When English government returned in 1674, Gov Edmund Andros reinvigorated New York's Indian trade and cultivated ties with anti-French factions in the Five Nations. Emboldened by their new political and economic connections, these factions expelled French Jesuit missionaries from their villages and waged aggressive new wars against French-allied Indians in the Great Lakes region. As in previous decades, Iroquois forces sought both captives and furs, and their actions pulled New France into the fray. New York openly joined the conflict in 1689, when England entered Europe's War of the League of Augsburg, but supplied little material and almost no military support for the Iroquois. Meanwhile, French invasions of Iroquoia in 1687, 1693, and 1696 struck devastating blows, and well-armed, French-allied Indians turned the tide against the Five Nations. After the English and French made peace in the Treaty of Ryswick of 1697, each power claimed the Five Nations as subjects, each insisted that the Iroquois could neither be covered by the European pact nor negotiate as independent agents, and each supported influential headmen who nearly paralyzed the councils of the Five Nations. By 1700 seemingly intractable political conflict combined with continued attacks by French-allied Indians to jeopardize Iroquois survival.

During this difficult period, controversies spread beyond individual villages to mobilize like-minded interests across all of the Five Nations. Beginning in at least the early 1680s, headmen from each nation had met regularly at the village at Onondaga to thrash out bitter differences among advocates of the alliance with the English, supporters of peace with New France, and those who struggled to find some neutral path. Although these meetings followed many of the ceremonial forms of the league council, the participants for the most part were not league chiefs, who apparently remained aloof from divisive politics. It is useful to distinguish, therefore, between a centuries-old Iroquois League that maintained the Great Peace and a newer Iroquois Confederacy that coordinated diplomatic and military policy for the Five Nations.

The 18th-Century Confederacy

After bitter struggles during the war of the 1690s, neutralists came to dominate confederacy councils. The turning point was marked by simultaneous treaties with the French at Montreal and the English at Albany in 1701. In this "Grand Settlement," the confederacy ended its war with the French and the French-allied Indians, and established a future agenda of aggressive neutrality. At Montreal, Iroquois spokesmen pledged neutrality in exchange for French promises to mediate disputes between the Five Nations and their former Indian enemies in the Great Lakes region. At Albany, diplomats reaffirmed their Covenant Chain relationship with the English while offering the Crown a "deed" to the same Great Lakes territories. By thus seeming to acknowledge the sovereignty of both European crowns at once, the confederacy's headmen hoped to preserve the Five Nations' autonomy. The balance-of-power strategy also had the advantage of drawing on all Iroquois factions. Headmen with ties to New France were instrumental in negotiating an end to hostilities with the French and their allies. Those with ties to Albany were just as important in redefining the relationship with the English. Without their willing support, the neutralists could not have achieved their objectives.

To one degree or another, neutrality guided Iroquois interactions with their European and native neighbors throughout the first half of the 18th century. Nevertheless the confederacy's diplomacy continued to be based in factional politics, and neutrality was often imperfectly applied. Friends of the British (particularly among the Mohawk) and of the French (particularly among the Seneca) maintained close ties to New York and New France, respectively, and on occasion groups of Iroquois would join one or another imperial power as military allies. This was particularly the case during the French and Indian War from 1754 to 1763, when many Mohawks fought beside the British against the French while some Onondagas and Senecas took up arms in support of the French.

The massive British victory in that war, which expelled French government from North America, made balance-of-power neutrality policy no longer possible. Drawing on long-standing personal political connections—particularly those between Mohawks and Superintendent of Indian Affairs Sir William Johnson—the Six Nations moved into an ever closer cooperation with the British. Johnson regarded the Iroquois as imperial overlords of other Indian peoples and thus attempted to systematize relations with numerous, formerly hostile, nations of the continental interior and to mediate conflicts more effectively between Indians and aggressively expansionist British colonists. By manipulating its diplomatic role, the confederacy was able to protect its own interests and lands but often at the expense of other Indian peoples for whom it purported to make decisions, in particular the Delaware and Shawnee.

At the outbreak of the US War of Independence, the recent history of cooperation between the Iroquois and the Crown led many rebels to see the former as a major threat. Revolutionaries forced the Mohawk to flee their homes in the Mohawk Valley. Most relocated to Niagara, from which their warriors launched stinging raids against New York's frontiers. In retaliation, in 1779 the United States mounted a three-pronged invasion of Iroquoia commanded by James Clinton, John Sullivan, and Daniel Brodhead. Nearly all Onondaga, Cayuga, and Seneca villages were destroyed, and their residents were forced into exile at Niagara. Despite all this, the War of Independence was deeply divisive for the Six Nations. Many Oneidas and Tuscaroras threw in their lot with the United States, and many other Iroquois struggled to revive the neutrality strategy by playing the revolutionaries off the Crown. Amid such bitter disputes, the political Iroquois Confederacy ceased to operate. Its council fire was extinguished in January 1777, and henceforth each nation, or fragment of a nation, went its own diplomatic and military way. In light of the destruction that US forces wreaked on Iroquois communities, it would have been a supreme irony if the revolutionaries had, as has sometimes been asserted, taken the Iroquois League as the inspiration for the federal Union. While some of the framers of the US Constitution genuinely admired the league, there is no evidence that they understood its workings in sufficient detail to use it as a model.

Destruction and Rebirth in the 19th and 20th Centuries

At the end of the War of Independence, however powerful the unifying cultural ideal of the league may have remained, Iroquois people were scattered. The majority of Mohawks moved to present-day Ontario, taking up lands that the British Crown allotted them at Grand River and on the Bay of Quinte; the small Akwesasne community remained on the St. Lawrence, straddling the new international border between Canada and New York. Some Senecas joined the Mohawk at Grand River, but most returned to their traditional country and settled at Tonawanda, Buffalo Creek, Cattaraugus, and Allegany, and on the Genesee River. Most Oneidas and some Onondagas and Cayugas returned to their homes. Others went to Grand River, and still others to Buffalo Creek. The Tuscarora also dispersed, some to Grand River, and others eventually on the Niagara River. Two separate league council fires were kindled, at Buffalo Creek and Grand River. By the early 19th century, each council maintained its own roster of league chiefs. In this period the "New Religion" of the prophet Handsome Lake gained many adherents among the New York Iroquois.

Relentless pressure from unscrupulous white land speculators chipped away at the Six Nations' remaining New York lands. The nadir came at the Treaty of Buffalo Creek of 1838, in which the Ogden Land Co purported to purchase every remaining square inch of Seneca country, on the assumption that the nation's people would remove to what is now Kansas. The signatures of 41 Seneca chiefs appeared on the treaty, only about half of those entitled to participate. Many of the signatures were purchased with bribes, and others were forged. With the aid of Quakers and other Whites disgusted by the fraud, the Seneca were able to negotiate a compromise in 1842 whereby they regained the Allegany and Cattaraugus Reservations. Buffalo Creek, however, was lost, and the status of Tonawanda remained in dispute. At Allegany and Cattaraugus, outrage over the Buffalo Creek Treaty led in 1848 to the establishment of a new government called the Seneca Nation of Indians, which replaced semihereditary chiefs with an elected council. The Tonawanda Seneca did not join the nation, largely because their argument against the treaty depended on the fact that their chiefs had not signed it. Onondaga Nation also retained its system of chiefs, and the league council fire was moved from Buffalo Creek to their reservation. But with the Seneca Nation no longer participating and with few Mohawks, Oneidas, and Cayugas still resident in New York State, the Onondaga league council's claim to speak for all Six Nations became largely symbolic. The extent to which that claim was accepted by other Iroquois remained contested throughout into the 21st century.

From its beginning, however, symbolism, ritual, and an ideology of cultural unity rather than more literal forms of political representation had been the core of the league's significance. In keeping with that tradition, during the late 20th-century renaissance of Native American culture, the Onondaga league council found itself at the forefront of cultural and political activism, with its chiefs acting as powerful spokesmen for Indian sovereignty on an international stage. In the early 21st century, the league remained a potent, and controversial, force in New York State history.

See also LACROSSE; PREHISTORIC ARCHAEOLOGY; WAR OF 1812.

Brandão, José António. *"Your Fyre Shall Burn No More": Iroquois Policy toward New France and Its Native Allies to 1701* (Lincoln: Univ of Nebraska Press, 1997)

Fenton, William N. *The Great Law and the Longhouse: A Political History of the Iroquois Confederacy* (Norman: Univ of Oklahoma Press, 1998)

Graymont, Barbara. *The Iroquois in the American Revolution* (Syracuse: Syracuse Univ Press, 1972)

Hauptman, Laurence. *Conspiracy of Interests: Iroquois Dispossession and the Rise of New York State* (Syracuse: Syracuse Univ Press, 1999)

———. *The Iroquois Struggle for Survival: World War II to Red Power* (Syracuse: Syracuse Univ Press, 1986)

Jennings, Francis, et al, eds. *The History and Culture of Iroquois Diplomacy: An Interdisciplinary Guide to the Treaties of the Six Nations and Their League* (Syracuse: Syracuse Univ Press, 1985)

Richter, Daniel K. *The Ordeal of the Longhouse: The Peoples of the Iroquois League in the Era of European Colonization* (Chapel Hill: Univ of North Carolina Press, 1992)

Trelease, Allen W. *Indian Affairs in Colonial New York: The 17th Century* (1960; repr Lincoln: Univ of Nebraska Press, 1997)

Vecsey, Christopher, and William A. Starna, eds. *Iroquois Land Claims* (Syracuse: Syracuse Univ Press, 1988)

Wallace, Anthony F. C. *The Death and Rebirth of the Seneca* (New York: Vintage Books, 1969)

Daniel K. Richter

Iroquois government and religion. The Haudenosaunee, or as they are commonly called, the Iroquois, historically were centered in what is now Central and Western New York. The original Iroquois Confederacy consisted of five nations, the Mohawk, Oneida, Onondaga, Cayuga, and Seneca. In the early 18th century it was joined by the Tuscarora, a nation that had been forced out of North Carolina. In the pre-Contact period the Iroquois League's domain extended into Pennsylvania, and its political influence stretched as far west as the Mississippi River and as far south as Georgia. Much of the strength and organization of the confederacy can be attributed to its government and religion, or more properly to Ongwehonweheka ("the way of life of the original people"). The chiefs and clan-mothers serve as both the political and the religious leaders. The two pillars of Haudenosaunee religion and government are the creation story and the Peacemaker's message.

CREATION

Although there is some difference in various accounts of the creation narrative, the basic Haudenosaunee story describes how the Skywoman fell through a hole in the sky where all spiritual beings lived. She landed on the back of a turtle, which grew supernaturally to make a land base large enough for all to live on. The Skywoman gave birth shortly thereafter to a daughter, who grew quickly and delivered twin boys through a virgin birth. The evil twin, Flint, tore his way out of his mother's body through her armpit, which killed her. The good twin, Sapling, buried her with great ceremony, after which she became Mother Earth. The good twin became the Creator, and the evil twin did all that he could to undermine the Creator's work. A contest was held to determine who would have supremacy on Turtle Island. Although Skywoman sided with Flint, the Creator won. After the Creator made many life-forms, including woman, man, animals, and plants, he gave each one special duties. All of creation was to fulfill these duties, which dictated how each being should act toward each other and toward the Creator. For example, the Creator taught the animals that they were to give their lives to woman and man for food, clothing, and bone tools; woman and man should treat all life with respect; plants should provide medicines and food to animals and people. Giving

Sky Woman, by Ernest Smith (Tonawanda Reservation), 1936.

thanks in all things was part of this duty. After Skywoman died, Flint came back to fight for her body. In the struggle, he pulled off her head and threw it high in the air. She became the moon, or Grandmother Moon. The Elder Brother was the sun and the Grandfathers continued to live in the Spirit World in the sky.

The Haudenosaunee believe that although animals and humans eventually lost their ability to communicate verbally with each other, they should still give thanks to both the animal and the Creator in taking the life of a plant or an animal for its gift of life. Thankfulness for all things and respect for all life continues to be a critical element of Haudenosaunee spiritual philosophy.

The Peacemaker and the Great Law

Although the formation of the Iroquois League is considered to have been anywhere from the first century AD to as late as 1743, most scholars generally believe it to have been at or around the middle of the 15th century. Oral tradition holds that the Haudenosaunee were scattered and engaged in warfare with each other without restraint. A divine being from the Huron Nation, called the Peacemaker, or Deganawida, came to the Mohawk, Oneida, Onondaga, Cayuga, and Seneca people and converted them to the way of peace (health and order), power (unity and civil authority), and righteousness (a good mind and justice). Hiawatha and a powerful Iroquoian woman named Jikonsaseh assisted him in this difficult effort. Thadodaho, a very evil and powerful wizard of the Onondaga Nation, was so resistant to this message of peace that he used his magic to have Hiawatha's three daughters killed. Through the process of grieving, combined with divine events, Hiawatha discovered the funeral and mourning rituals that became the foundation of Haudenosaunee condolence ceremonies. It was supernaturally revealed to him that wampum is sacred and should be used at councils and funerals. Hiawatha forgave Thadodaho and personally combed the snakes out of his hair when he finally became converted. Thadodaho was then appointed by the Peacemaker to be the most noble and central of all chiefs.

The Peacemaker chose 50 leaders as chiefs, or sachems, to make up the Grand Council. He selected 9 Mohawks, 9 Oneidas, 14 Onondagas, 10 Cayugas, and 8 Senecas and endowed them with chieftain duties and names. The chiefs that would succeed them would be chosen from the same clan and inherit the same original chieftain titles as given by the Peacemaker. The Peacemaker also set apart 50 women, each of whom were to be one specific chief's clanmother. The Peacemaker restructured the clan system so that there were at least three different clans in each nation. Various clans were in each nation; the collective nations constituted the league or confederacy.

The chiefs all buried their weapons of war beneath the Tree of Peace and tied their arrows together to symbolize their united strength. The Peacemaker placed an eagle on top of the tree for protection, signifying that if any Haudenosaunee person saw danger to the league, they should inform everyone. The branches reached far, indicating that anyone from anywhere who was in need and willing to live under the tenets of the Great Peace could take refuge under the branches of the league. A fire was established, representing the life of the confederacy. The Peacemaker instructed that one string of wampum from each nation be bound together at one end as a symbol of their unity. The Peacemaker outlined through the Great Law how the confederacy should operate its government and religion, which included a moral code of conduct. This is considered to be the constitution of the Haudenosaunee, and it is still recited at designated times. The Peacemaker set up a metaphorical longhouse, with the Mohawk Nation guarding the eastern door, the Seneca Nation guarding the western door, and the Onondaga Nation at the center to hold and guard the fire and keep the wampum of the confederacy. Thus, Haudenosaunee means "People of the Longhouse."

Gaiwiio—The Code of Handsome Lake

After the American Revolution, the Haudenosaunee people were so torn apart and in such social and political disarray that many of them readily accepted Gaiwiio, the Good Message of the Seneca prophet Handsome Lake. Handsome Lake had fought in the American Revolution and afterward abused alcohol and medicines. Nearing what he thought was certain death in 1799, living on the Cornplanter Grant in northern Pennsylvania near the New York State border, he had the first in a series of visions from the Creator, who restored his health once Handsome Lake repented and determined to change his ways. Four messengers from the Sky World also appeared to him from time to time to give him instruction.

Handsome Lake taught that the original instructions of the Peacemaker must be maintained, but he altered some of the practices and meanings to adjust to the new Haudenosaunee society. He taught the people how to practice the Great Law in the "modern" world where the European American culture was threatening to overcome them. The evils of the Whites, such as cardplaying, alcohol consumption, fiddle dances, and syphilis, were condemned. Handsome Lake also zealously pursued the eradication of witchcraft. However, he endorsed some aspects of white culture, such as improved housing and agriculture.

Handsome Lake suppressed some of the old ceremonies and medicine societies and affirmed and encouraged greater participation in others, but in the end he restored most of the old ceremonies. He promoted self-sufficiency, sobriety, and good moral conduct. Leaders had a greater responsibility to do good. Some of the tenets of Gaiwiio are that a man should never strike a woman, one should never make fun of the way a person looks, a person should still burn tobacco as thanks before picking medicines, and that a 10-day feast should be held to honor the dead. Many aspects of Gaiwiio are similar to Christian teachings such as imperatives to feed the poor, not to steal, to have respect for one's parents, that pride is wrong, that abortion is wrong, and that a person should repent for one's wrongdoing. Handsome Lake also preached a new concept that involved cruel punishments after death inflicted by the Punisher in the house of torment for specific offenses committed in this life.

Some of the Haudenosaunee accepted his message, while others rejected it or accepted only parts of it. Because his writings were recorded by Quaker friends, some Haudenosaunee were convinced that Quakers had influenced his message. Even today, some of the Mohawk people reject Gaiwiio as too much of a compromise with Christianity. However, most of the traditional Haudenosaunee now accept Gaiwiio and follow its tenets; they consider it to be an extension and clarification of the Creator's and the Peacemaker's messages.

Government Structure and Function

Although the Great Law was and continues to be recited through the reading of wampum strings at special gatherings, a number of Haudenosaunee speakers have written several versions of it over time. The most widely accepted version is the 1912 Gibson-Goldenweiser Manuscript as narrated by the Seneca chief John Arthur Gibson. Although the Haudenosaunee have had to adapt many customs and practices over the years because of non-Indian policies, practical considerations, and geopolitical factors, the Great Law continues to be the basis and authority upon which the confederacy operates.

The Haudenosaunee government provides that every person's ideas and concerns can be addressed in council through their chiefs. Clan meetings are held where any individual may bring up his or her concerns to the entire clan. If the clan believes that the issue affects their entire nation, a national meeting is held during which the clan's chief presents his clan's concerns. Again, if the issue affects the whole confederacy, a Grand Council is held and the issue is brought forward by the nation's chief and all the chiefs of the confederacy discuss the item and make a consensual decision.

The Grand Councils, which are meetings of all six nations, are called by the Onondaga and held at the Onondaga Council House. Runners, who carry special wampum as an invitation to attend, are sent to each of the other five nations. The chiefs of each nation bring their national wampum to the Grand Council as a symbol that they represent their people and have a right to participate actively. Either the Younger Brothers (the Oneida, Cayuga, and Tuscarora) or the Elder Brothers (the Mohawk and Seneca) can bring an issue to council and have equal authority. If the decision of both the Elder and the Younger Brothers is unanimous, the Onondaga review and confirm the decision. If they cannot reach a consensus on any issue, the Onondaga may choose to table the discussion for a later time or to "cover it in ashes," which means it will not be discussed again. By following these procedures, all chiefs leave with "one heart, one mind, and one law." A clanmother, who also attends the Grand Councils, can veto any decision of the Grand Council through her chief. Individual members may be asked to speak on an issue they are familiar with or may request to speak if they have important information to share with the council.

The unity of the confederacy does not prevent each nation from having the autonomy to pursue its own interests. In national meetings, the seating and procedural structure is analogous to that of the Grand Council meetings. The nation is divided into different moieties, or sides, based on their clans. The chiefs of the various clans pass issues over the fire to each other to reach a consensus. The clan composition of each moiety varies from nation to nation, as each nation is composed of different clans. The Wolf, Bear, Turtle, and Deer are among the most common.

Funerals are an important part of the government and religion of the Haudenosaunee. To simplify a complex ritual, the opposite moiety of the deceased conducts the mourning and burial rites, thus comforting the mourners of the deceased's moiety. For example, among the Oneida and Mohawk, if a Wolf Clan member dies, it is the responsibility of the "clear-minded"—in this case the Bear and Turtle Clans—to cook and serve the feast foods and to conduct the ceremony designed to lift the grief of the Wolf Clan.

If a chief dies, the funeral is a much larger matter. Runners are sent to all the nations, informing them to come to a Big Condolence. These ceremonies are designed not only to console the family and friends of the chief but also to "raise" a new chief. If a Cayuga, Oneida, or Tuscarora chief dies, the Seneca, Mohawk, and Onondaga conduct the ceremonies; if a Seneca, Mohawk, or Onondaga chief dies, the Cayuga, Oneida, and Tuscarora conduct the ceremonies. Ideally, a chief is raised three days after the funeral of his predecessor. The authority of the chief is vested in the horns or deer antlers, which are attached to a *gustoweh* (Haudenosaunee man's headdress) and were traditionally placed on his head by his clanmother during the Condolence Ceremony. In more recent times, this procedure is replaced by a formal presentation of the chieftain wampum string that represents his title. Large condolences are also held for clanmothers.

Women's Roles and the Raising of Chiefs

Haudenosaunee women have been critical to the operations of the Haudenosaunee government since the formation of the Iroquois Confederacy. When the Peacemaker arrived and attempted to spread his great message of peace, the first person to accept and promote his message was Jikonsaseh. Recognizing the strength and wisdom of women, the Peacemaker made Jikonsaseh the first of 50 clanmothers, and he incorporated the role of women throughout the functions of the Haudenosaunee government. Children were to follow the matrilineal system and marry only outside of their clan.

The most noble of the women is the clanmother, whose title is passed down to her through her family. She is entrusted by the Great Law with a number of responsibilities, such as to bestow names, participate in councils, hold clan meetings, and promote harmony and happiness within her clan. The clanmother's main responsibilities, though, are to raise a chief from her own clan, watch over the behavior of her chosen chief to ensure that he follows the principles of the Great Law, and if necessary, reprimand him or remove him from his position. The clanmother also has a wampum string that symbolizes her right to choose a chief. Her decision for the chief nomination is taken to each level for approval: the clan, the nation, and then the confederacy. She looks for a chief who is honest, humble, kind, wise, dedicated, and generous. The chiefs are to listen to and truly care for the people and never to lord over them in any way. These chosen chiefs are responsible for selecting Thadodaho. They are also responsible for selecting the Pine Tree chiefs, who are men demonstrating exceptional wisdom and caring. Pine Tree chiefs help the other chiefs in any matter needing their assistance, and they may attend and participate in councils if they so choose.

Faithkeepers and Religious Ceremonies

The Peacemaker established the role of religious caretakers, called faithkeepers, in Haudenosaunee life. These are men and women from the community who are responsible for organizing and running the religious ceremonies. They are chosen for their spirituality and their commitment to attending and participating in ceremonies, and they usually keep their positions for life. Safeguarding and maintaining the religion and spirituality of the people is such an important job that faithkeepers are not allowed to hold any other titles. They also have their own set of names that are passed down from faithkeeper to faithkeeper. One woman and one man are chosen from each side of the moiety to be in charge of each ceremony.

These festivals, or ceremonies, and the approximate times of the year they are held are Midwinter, early February; Maple, early March; Strawberry, mid- to late June; Bean, mid-August; Corn, early September; Harvest, mid-October; and Thunder and End of Season Ceremonies, mid-December. The Midwinter Festival is held when the Pleiades are directly overhead. Up until the middle of the 19th century, two white dogs were sacrificed during this time. This ceremony was performed to maintain balance by getting at the root of a person's deepest problems and desires through the interpretation of their dreams and by atoning for their sins. Today, the practice is replaced with the Ribbon Ceremony during which a basket with ribbons is burned. During the Harvest and Midwinter Festivals, the children are given their names by their respective clanmothers. The children are only allowed to take the name of someone in their clan who has passed away, since the belief is that the spiritual beings become confused if two living people have the same name. The peach stone bowl game is played at these two special festivals, which reminds the people of the great battle fought between the forces of good and evil at creation.

A special feast is also held periodically in honor of the dead who had not received the 10-day feast at the time of their death. Special foods that the deceased had liked are prepared, and the people dance throughout the night. Secret medicine societies, although not incorporated by the Peacemaker, became superfluous over time and appeared to peak during the 17th and 18th centuries, though they still have followings. The societies were responsible for war and peace, good hunting, and healing. Once Handsome Lake suppressed but then later allowed them, they changed focus to curing illnesses and maintaining well-being among the people. Individuals can become members of a medicine society only if they have been healed through it or if they or someone else dreams that they should join. Some medicine societies are considered so sacred that they cannot be discussed in everyday conversation.

Seneca headdress, mid–19th century.

Survival of the Longhouse

Although there had been significant conversions to Christianity during the colonial period, the divisions of the Revolutionary War and the catastrophic loss of land that followed in the postcolonial settlements provided a real challenge to the survival of the Longhouse religion. The American Revolution tore apart the confederacy and individual nations. The British offered land to their Iroquois allies in what is now Ontario, to which nearly 2,000 Haudenosaunee moved. The Six Nations Reserve on the Grand River near Brantford [now in Ont] accommodated individuals from each of the six nations. Joseph Brant, a Mohawk captain who led the Iroquois in the British effort, took half of the confederacy belts to Canada to establish the Longhouse there. The other half of the belts remained with the Haudenosaunee who stayed in New York. There were now two Iroquois Confederacies. Both Longhouses were short of chiefs, and in many cases new chiefs were raised in both countries, with duplicate titles and names. Despite an 1876 act that forbade Indian ceremonies and raids in the 1920s by the Royal Canadian Mounted Police, who arrested Longhouse chiefs, confiscated ceremonial materials, and padlocked the longhouses, traditional religion survives, and in the early 21st century there are four longhouses at Grand River, all of which follow Gaiwiio.

The Longhouse in New York State remained surprisingly viable throughout the 19th and 20th centuries in the face of tremendous change. There were many converts to Christianity, yet many Christian chiefs and clanmothers continued in their traditional roles. The followers of the Longhouse religion persist among the Haudenosaunee residing in New York State. Akwesasne (St. Regis Indian Reservation), a Mohawk reservation that lies on the border of the United States and Canada, currently follows the traditional religion and government through the Mohawk Nation Council of Chiefs, which operates on both sides of the border. However, the same community also has an elected council on each side of the border: the St. Regis Mohawk Tribal Council in New York State and the Mohawk Council of Akwesasne in Ontario. The Mohawk have maintained their language the most effectively among the Haudenosaunee and are often called upon to conduct various parts of ceremonies at the Haudenosaunee headquarters at Onondaga.

Most of the Oneidas who moved to Wisconsin during the 1830s and 1840s had abandoned the traditional religion for Christianity. At the start of the 21st century, most of them continue to follow Christianity and operate an elective system, although there is a small contingency of Longhouse people who returned to the ancient religion and who meet in a longhouse. From 1839 to 1845, about 650 more Oneidas moved to the Thames River near London, Ont, where they maintained the Longhouse religion and government as much as possible under Canada's forced elective system. They continue to practice their Longhouse religion but hold elections for political leaders. The small group of Oneidas who were left in New York State, following the moves of most Oneidas to Canada and Wisconsin, gave their fire (wampum) to the Onondaga to hold for them until they could raise chiefs again. In 1975 they switched from an elective to a traditional form of government and religion, but as of 2003 did not have any chiefs in place and did not recognize nor attend Grand Council meetings as a nation.

Most of the Onondagas in New York State returned to their original homeland following the American Revolution. The Onondagas who had been living in Buffalo Creek [now in Erie Co] among the Seneca returned with their sacred wampum to the Onondaga territory near Syracuse in 1847 and rekindled the confederacy fire there. Although a number of Protestant churches have operated in Onondaga territory, the traditional governmental system remains viable, and no elections have ever been held. As the firekeepers and the keepers of the wampum, the Onondagas have faithfully condoled the position of Thadodaho. In the early 21st century, they hold daily national meetings, except during ceremonies and funeral rites, and continue to call and hold Grand Council meetings, which chiefs and other Haudenosaunee leaders travel far to attend.

The Senecas who stayed in New York State were divided about how best to survive as a people. The Seneca Nation of Indians was created in 1848 on the Cattaraugus Indian Reservation [loc in Cattaraugus, Chautauqua, and Erie Cos] and the Allegany Indian Reservation [loc in Cattaraugus Co]. It has a written constitution and an elective system. Although these Senecas do not participate at Grand Councils, there are still some traditional people in both the Cattaraugus and Allegany communities. The Tonawanda Seneca continue to hold fast to the ancient Longhouse practices and have condoled chiefs and clanmothers that attend Grand Councils.

The Cayuga lost the bulk of their lands shortly after the American Revolution, and for the most part those who remained in New York State moved to the Cattaraugus Reservation to live with the Seneca and were no longer traditional. The Seneca-Cayuga Nation of Oklahoma, consisting of Senecas and Cayugas that once lived on the Little Sandusky River in Ohio, also no longer follows the Longhouse ways. In recent years, many of the Cayugas in the United States have returned to the ancient religion and government and participate in Grand Councils. The Tuscarora Indians live on the Tuscarora Indian Reservation [loc in Niagara Co]. Many of them are Christians, and they do not have a longhouse. However, they continue to maintain a traditional form of government in which clanmothers raise traditional hereditary chiefs who attend the Grand Councils.

In spite of the tremendous pressures and obstacles the Iroquois Confederacy has faced over the past 225 years or so, it remains surprisingly strong and viable. With few exceptions, every Haudenosaunee community at the start of the 21st century has a traditional spiritual longhouse where civic and religious activities may be carried out. The confederacy on both sides of the US-Canadian border work together, attending and participating in each other's condolences and ceremonies. There have been recent efforts by both Longhouses to reunite the two into one.

Fenton, William N. *The Great Law and the Longhouse: A Political History of the Iroquois Confederacy* (Norman: Univ of Oklahoma Press, 1998)

———, ed. *Parker on the Iroquois* (Syracuse: Syracuse Univ Press, 1968)

Hewitt, J. N. B. *Iroquoian Cosmology.* Annual Report of Bureau of American Ethnology, 1899–1900. (Washington, DC, 1903)

Hill, Rick. "The Lessons of the Great Law," *Niagara Gazette,* 20 Jan 1997

North American Indian Travelling College. *Traditional Teachings* (Cornwall Island, Ont: Author, 1984)

Richter, Daniel K. *The Ordeal of the Longhouse: The Peoples of the Iroquois League in the Era of European Colonization* (Chapel Hill: Univ of North Carolina Press, 1992)

Thomas, Jacob. "The Legend of the Peacemaker, Part 1." MS, 1968

———. "The Great Laws of Peace, Part 2." MS, 1968

Woodbury, Hanni, et al, ed. *Concerning the League: The Iroquois League Tradition as Dictated in Onondaga by John Arthur Gibson* (Winnipeg, Man: Algonquian and Iroquoian Linguistics, 1992)

Elizabeth A. Obomsawin

Iroquois wars. The Iroquois Indians, French colonists living in the St. Lawrence River valley (New France), and native peoples in the Great Lakes region fought a series of wars primarily between 1640 and 1698. Written records left by European friends and foes of the Iroquois provide statistics. Up to 1701 the Iroquois were involved in 465 recorded hostilities, of which they initiated 354 (76%) and were on the receiving end of 111. The heaviest fighting took place from 1640 to 1669 and from 1680 to 1698. During the middle decades of the 17th century, the Iroquois were involved in 297 hostilities (an average of 99 hostilities per decade), 247 (83%) of which they initiated. In the latter 20 years of the 17th century they were involved in 120 hostilities (60 per decade), of which they initiated 81 (67%). The French were attacked 123 times, the Huron 73 times, and the Ottawa Valley Algonquin 23 times.

Furs were an important economic resource for New York and New France, and trade alliances forged with native peoples provided allies for wars to assert political control over large, contested regions of northeastern North America. The Iroquois were the main fur suppliers to the Dutch and English and were also, conveniently, foes of the French, with whom the Dutch and the English competed for furs and land. Early historians explained the Iroquois wars by focusing on the influence of the fur trade. The "beaver wars" theory, which has dominated thinking about these wars, contends that Iroquois culture was changed as a result of contact with Europeans. The Iroquois quickly became dependent on European goods and began to hunt more aggressively for the furs needed to trade for such goods. As a result they depleted their fur resources and

Seneca war club.

began to raid against other native groups to steal furs and to drive these groups from prime fur-bearing areas. The wars against the French were to diminish competition in the fur trade.

Recent scholarship suggests that possible causes of the Iroquois wars include revenge, honor, prestige, and the capture of people for torturing or for replacing the dead. These pre-contact motives for warfare remained important after contact with Europeans. Replacing people who had died actually became more important because new diseases brought by Europeans caused widespread death. By 1701 the Iroquois had captured 3,810–4,176 people. Adding on the number of people thought "lost" to the Iroquois (2,277–2,795), but whom were almost all captured rather than killed, puts the number of people captured by the Iroquois at 6,087–6,971. The number of captives was actually higher in the latter decades: 1,434–1,568 by 1669 and 2,384–2,608 from 1680 to 1700 (a 60% increase). This suggests that the goal of taking captives increased in importance over time.

The Iroquois ranged over a large portion of northeastern North America in pursuit of military conquest—from Virginia to Lac St. Jean [now in Que] and from Green Bay [now in Wisc] to Tadoussac [now in Que]—but most of their hostilities were centered in the St. Lawrence Valley and the upper Great Lakes. By 1701 the Iroquois had captured or killed 8,103–9,329 people in northeastern North America. They had managed to keep French settlement confined to the St. Lawrence River and to the fortified towns of Quebec, Montreal, Three Rivers, and their surrounding areas; destroy several nations of native peoples, including the Huron, Erie, and Neutral; and reshape the human geography of the region. As early French writers noted, this concentration of raiding suggests that Iroquois warfare aimed at creating a buffer zone between the Iroquois and their neighbors. This tactic, added to the capturing of people to bolster their population, helped ensure the survival of the Iroquois as a nation. Because of their political and economic alliances with the Dutch and, after 1664, the English authorities of what came to be New York State, Iroquois warfare played an important role in New York's development. The Iroquois helped limit French power in North America, and their warfare, waged for their own reasons, served to support New York's power and expansion in the early colonial period.

Brandão, José António. *"Your Fyre Shall Burn No More": Iroquois Policy toward New France and Its Native Allies to 1701* (Lincoln: Univ of Nebraska Press, 1997)

Hunt, G. T. *The Wars of the Iroquois: A Study in Intertribal Trade Relations* (Madison: Univ of Wisconsin Press, 1940)

Richter, Daniel K. *The Ordeal of the Longhouse: The Peoples of the Iroquois League in the Era of European Colonization* (Chapel Hill: Univ of North Carolina Press, 1992)

José António Brandão

Irving, Washington (*b* New York City, 3 Apr 1783; *d* Tarrytown, Westchester Co, 28 Nov 1859). Author. The youngest of eight surviving children of Scottish English parentage, Irving became the first internationally known writer from the United States. He attended private schools and was admitted to the bar in 1806 but ended his law career in 1809.

Surrounded by Dutch American in-laws, neighbors, friends, and acquaintances, he acquired considerable familiarity with Dutch as it was spoken in the Hudson Valley of his day. His use of 17th-century Dutch sources reveals he was able to read the language in printed form. Most of his early reading was 18th-century neoclassical English literature. Gothic romances, notably Ann Radcliffe's, and later Sir Walter Scott's poetry appealed to his antiquarian bent and romantic spirit, which had been nourished by his youthful explorations of rural Manhattan, the Hudson Valley, and points north, and by travel in Europe undertaken for his health (1804–6). These interests are reflected in the prominence of history and popular culture in his major works.

Irving contributed to newspapers edited by his brother Peter and became known for his satirical commentary on New York society in "Letters of Jonathan Oldstyle, Gent.," which appeared in Peter's *Morning Chronicle* (1802–3). Social and political satire interspersed with essays or sketches by brothers William and Washington Irving and James Kirke Paulding, William's brother-in-law, appeared in *Salmagundi* (1807–8). Profound sadness touched Washington Irving during the composition of his instantly popular and profitable burlesque *History of New York* (1809) with the death of his fiancée Matilda Hoffman in April 1809. Although he later contemplated marriage, his financially uncertain condition contributed to his remaining a bachelor.

The success of his first major work notwithstanding, literature remained a secondary pursuit. While engaged in his merchant family's business and serving as colonel of the New York State Militia during the War of 1812, he compiled some of Thomas Campbell's poetry (1810), revised *History* (1812), and edited the *Analectic Magazine* (1813–14). In 1815 he left for Liverpool to assist his brother Peter in the family business, which failed in 1818. Emboldened by *History*'s success in England and the advice of Sir Walter Scott, whose encouragement led him to study German, he now endeavored to earn a living by his pen.

Several prose collections narrated by Geoffrey Crayon followed, whose diffidence, nostalgia, and occasional self-mockery are Irving's, as is his role as spectator. Their tales, placed between sketches and essays that are mostly set in England, mark a beginning in the writing of short fiction. While retaining aspects of the familiar essay, they exhibit several characteristics of the modern short story in English. Best known among them are the Knickerbocker folktales named for the historian of *History*, who functions here as a posthumous narrator. Set mainly in New York, their supernatural content is faithful to Dutch oral folk traditions as Irving had absorbed them in the Hudson Valley of his youth. Only in "Rip Van Winkle" and "The Legend of Sleepy Hollow," located in *The Sketch-Book* (1819–20), do the supernatural events follow the simple plots of tales Irving found in German folklore collections. These Knickerbocker tales were chiefly intended, however, as realistic portrayals of Hudson Valley country manners, as were "Dolph Heyliger" in *Bracebridge Hall* (1819–20) and "Wolfert Webber, or Golden Dreams" in *Tales of a Traveller* (1824), a collection of short fiction in four parts. While the first two volumes were highly acclaimed, the third received a poor critical reception, causing Irving to all but cease writing for several years.

In 1826, having acquired fluency in Spanish, Irving accepted the post of diplomatic attaché in Spain, where he produced a scholarly *History of the Life and Voyages of Christopher Columbus* (1828) and a humorous *Chronicle of the Conquest of Granada* (1829), and began work on *The Alhambra* (1832), the so-called Spanish *Sketch-Book*. After 3 years as secretary of the legation in London (1829–32) and a total absence of 17 years, he returned to the United States to great acclaim. In 1835 he purchased and enlarged a Dutch farmhouse overlooking the Hudson River near Tarrytown. Sunnyside, as he named it, would be his home for his remaining years.

A voyage to the West in 1832 produced *A Tour on the Prairies* (1835), one of his three-part *Crayon Miscellany; Astoria* (1836), an account of fur trader John Jacob Astor, written with his nephew Pierre Irving; and *The Adventures of Captain Bonneville, U.S.A.* (1837). Diplomatic appointments took him to Europe in 1842. He served as US minister to Spain until 1845 and returned home in 1846, assisting with negotiations in London. Two collections of American sketches followed: *A Book of the Hudson* (1849) and *Wolfert's Roost* (1855). Irving wrote several biographies, notably his five-volume *Life of George Washington* (1855–59), which remained definitive until the 20th century. Ailing through much of its composition, Irving succumbed less than a year after its completion.

Irving's talent was not for invention; rather, his imagination drew upon a superior ability to absorb what he read, heard, and observed with the eye of the painter he once contemplated of becoming, and to re-create his subject in a graceful, gently satirical manner. His Knickerbocker works made that name a household word. His poetic rendering of the essentially Dutch life on the Hudson ensured its survival and made him America's first folklorist.

See also KNICKERBOCKER'S HISTORY OF NEW YORK; ST. NICHOLAS.

Funk, Elisabeth Paling. "Washington Irving and His Dutch-American Heritage as Seen in *A History of New York, The Sketch Book, Bracebridge Hall,* and *Tales of a Traveller*" (PhD diss, Fordham Univ, 1986)

———. "Washington Irving and the Dutch Heritage." MS, 2002

Hedges, William L. *Washington Irving: An American Study, 1802–1832* (Baltimore: Johns Hopkins Univ Press, 1965)

Irving, Washington. *The Complete Works of Washington Irving.* Ed. Richard Dillworth Rust et al, 30 vols (Madison: Univ of Wisconsin Press; Boston: Twayne Publishers, 1976–89)

Pochmann, Henry A. Introduction. *Washington Irving: Representative Selections* (New York: American Book, 1934)

Reichart, Walter A. *Washington Irving and Germany* (Ann Arbor: Univ of Michigan Press, 1957)

Roth, Martin. *Comedy and America: The Lost World of Washington Irving* (Port Washington, NY: Kennikat Press, 1976)

Rubin-Dorsky, Jeffrey. *Adrift in the Old World: The Psychological Pilgrimage of Washington Irving* (Chicago: Univ of Chicago Press, 1988)

Wagenknecht, Edward. *Washington Irving: Moderation Displayed* (New York: Oxford Univ Press, 1962)

Williams, Stanley T. *The Life of Washington Irving,* 2 vols (New York: Oxford Univ Press, 1935)

Elisabeth Paling Funk

Irvington. Village (pop 6,631) in Greenburgh (Westchester Co). The Justus Dearman farm was surveyed into lots in 1850, with a main street ending at the just completed railroad and a ferry to Piermont. A post office established in 1851 was named Dearman's, but the community was renamed Irvington in 1854 for author Washington Irving, whose home lay just north. The village was incorporated in 1872 and became the center of an estate district. Earlier houses included those of Louis C. Tiffany, Cyrus W. Field, and John Jacob Astor III. Phrenologist Orson S. Fowler built his in an octagon shape. Later on, Vertner Tandy, the first prominent black architect, built Villa Lewaro for Madam C. J. Walker, an African American entrepreneur. The one large industry of the village was the Lord and Burnham Co (1870–1988), manufacturer of greenhouses and heating systems; in 2003 its building housed apartments and the village's library. By the early 21st century Irvington had become a commuter village with a historic business district. Its population, 3,657 in 1950, nearly doubled in the second half of the 20th century.

Henry Steiner

Ischua [ISH-U-AH]. Town (pop 895) in E central Cattaraugus Co. Settled in 1814, the town was formed from Hinsdale in 1846 as Rice; the name was changed in 1855. In the second quarter of the 19th century, industries included a brickyard, foundry, tannery, and hat factory. With the growth of dairying after the Civil War, four cheese factories were built. The Buffalo, New York and Philadelphia Railroad (later Pennsylvania Railroad) came through in 1872. The Oil Spring Indian Reservation, which is leased by the Seneca Nation to non-Indians, abuts the town. The Olean Municipal Airport is located in Ischua.

Bruce D. Fredrickson and Madelynn P. Fredrickson

Islam. New York State has the second largest concentration of Muslims in the United States. In 1995 there were at least 662,000 Muslims in the state (including 138,000 Shi'ites); current estimates range from 800,000 to 2 million. These include American-born Muslims, immigrants, and the children of immigrants who are raised and educated in the United States. Islam may now be the fastest-growing religion in the state and the country. Three demographic factors are responsible: immigration, birth rates, and conversions.

Early History

Although there were probably adherents of Islam among African slaves and a small presence throughout the 19th century, the first documented Muslim institution in the state was the short-lived American Moslem Brotherhood (1893), founded by the American convert Alexander Russell Webb, a native of Hudson (Columbia Co) and former US consul to the Philippines. The American Mohammedan Society was founded in 1907 by immigrants from Poland, Russia, and Lithuania; in 1931 they opened a mosque in Williamsburg, Brooklyn. In 1939 Moroccan-born Sheikh Daoud Ahmed Faisal organized the Islamic Mission of America in Brooklyn Heights, which, while originally serving a largely Arab and Middle Eastern population, began to attract native converts. Many Arab Muslims arrived in the city after 1948, clustering in particular around Atlantic Ave in Brooklyn. Although the modern interest of New York City Blacks in Islam can be traced to the 1920s, the founding of the Nation of Islam Mosque no. 7 in Harlem in 1946 and the powerful influence, beginning in 1954, of Malcolm X (1925–65) sparked the rise of an Islamic movement among Blacks. The presence of the United Nations in New York City after 1945 brought Muslims to the city from Asia and Africa. The Islamic Cultural Center of New York was founded in Manhattan in 1955.

Post-1965

Since changes in immigration laws in 1965, immigrants have been coming from an increasing number of countries, representing much greater diversity. The New York City metropolitan area is home to the most heterogeneous group of Muslims in the United States, most of them immigrants who have come since 1980. The immigrant Muslim community of New York State is now made up of representatives of a wide variety of ethnic and national backgrounds. They include immigrants from Pakistan, Bangladesh, Egypt, Iran, Turkey, Lebanon, Palestine, Afghanistan, Syria, Iraq, Yemen, Africa, Eastern Europe, Guyana, Malaysia, and Indonesia. New York City is the port of entry for most Muslim immigrants to the United States. In recent years political troubles at home have often brought Muslims to settle in New York State, including Afghanis fleeing civil war and the Taliban, Bosnians escaping from a disintegrating Yugoslavia, and Iranians leaving their troubled homeland before and after the downfall of the shah in 1979. With this latter group, Shi'ite Muslims arrived in New York State for the first time in large numbers.

With the new immigration, the Muslim presence in the state spread beyond the New York City area, predominantly with Pakistanis, Yemenis, and Turks. The Rochester Muslim population is primarily Turkish families who moved to the city in the late 1960s to work in the men's clothing industry, Bangladeshi and Pakistani immigrants, and a substantial African American Muslim community. After Muslim inmates protected guards during the 1971 uprising at Attica, officials tolerated proselytizing and preaching by Muslim organizations inside the prison system, and many Blacks serving time in prison gained a new lease on life through conversion to various branches of Islam. African American Muslims have undergone considerable changes in recent decades. Although the Nation of Islam continues to practice its unique heterodox version of Islam, many African American Muslims have adopted orthodox Sunni Islam. Controversial new sects incorporating some aspects of Islam with other elements, such as the Nuwaubians and the Five Percent Nation, a New York–centered offshoot of the Nation of Islam founded in 1964 by Clarence 13X, have made a significant impact on urban street culture and hip hop slang. There are large concentrations of African American Muslims in New York City, Albany, Rochester, Syracuse, Jamestown, Buffalo, and the Poughkeepsie area. Latin American Muslim conversions and organizations have been growing steadily since the late 1980s.

About two-thirds of the state's total Muslim population are first- or second-generation immigrants. The heterogeneity of the Muslim population in New York State has led to the founding of numerous mosques along ethnic and religious lines. A substantial demographic shift in the Muslim population occurred in the late 1970s, with an influx of students from abroad who have had a significant and ongoing impact on the Islamization of Muslim communities. With the new educated and professionally oriented immigrant Muslims, a new wave of mosques has flourished since the 1970s. They range from simple storefronts to the large modern mosque at 3d Ave and 96th St in Manhattan (built by the Islamic Cultural Center with financial support from Kuwait), which opened in 1991 after years of delays. By 2003 there were at least 280 mosques and centers in the state. New York City had the heaviest concentration, around 100, twice as many as a decade earlier and almost five times as many as 20 years earlier. Neighborhoods with a relatively high number of mosques and Islamic centers include Jamaica, Brownsville, Harlem, and East New York. In 2002 there were at least 80 mosques in Brooklyn and Queens alone; Albany had 8; Buffalo, 7; Rochester, 6; and Syracuse, 3. Most are Sunni, but at least 18 are Shia, including a mosque belonging to the Ithna Asharriyya (Twelver) Shi'ite sect in Woodside, Queens. There are a few sectarian centers such as Ahmadiyya, a 19th-century movement of Indian origin with a center in Holliswood, Queens; the African American separatist Assaru Allah in Brooklyn; and several Sufi centers in New York City.

Many mosques have ethnic identities, reinforced by serving as community centers for new immigrants and converts. Mosques and Islamic centers in New York State and across the country have become the focal point for Muslim life in nontraditional ways, taking on functions including weddings, funeral services, counseling, fund-raising, social and cultural events, language instruction, and computer training courses. Some 50 Islamic schools are scattered throughout the state, with more than 30 in New York City (Queens and Brooklyn each have a dozen or more). Nassau Co has eight schools, Syracuse, two, and Schenectady, two. Others include the Medina School in Albany and Sister Clara Muhammad Schools in Poughkeepsie and Rochester.

New York City is home to numerous nongovernmental Muslim organizations advocating freedom of religion, including the Islamic Circle of North America and the Muslim Alliance in North America. In the late 1970s, fundamentalist fringe leaders including Sheikh Omar Abd al-Rahman began setting up small associations in Brooklyn and New Jersey to support the anti-Soviet resistance in Afghanistan and other political causes. After the 1993 World Trade Center bombing, the Muslim community in New York City entered a period of introspection. Meanwhile, the city and state experienced tremendous growth in the immigrant Muslim population and the opening of new mosques and Islamic schools throughout the 1990s. The destruction of the World Trade Center on 11 Sept 2001 by radical Muslim terrorists from Saudi Arabia, Egypt, United Arab Emirates, and Lebanon created a crisis for ordinary Muslims in New York City. More than 100 bias assaults against innocent Muslims were reported in the city in the days immediately following the attacks, and undisclosed numbers of Muslim immigrants were detained by the federal government and held without charges.

In September 2002 in the First Ward of Lackawanna (Erie Co), a Yemeni American neighborhood of about 3,000 outside Buffalo, federal agents arrested several US citizens of Yemeni descent who had traveled to Al Qaeda training camps in Afghanistan. The men, who became known as the Lackawanna Six, pled guilty to providing material support to the enemy under the Patriot Act. Whether they constituted a sleeper cell plotting terrorist crimes or merely a motley group of ideological zealots and religious seekers led astray is unresolved. National security entry and exit registration requirements for nonimmigrant foreigners from predominantly Muslim countries, put in place after 11 Sept 2001, were suspended in December 2003. Reactions to 11 September and the ensuing wars in Afghanistan and Iraq have led to new organizations to oppose terrorism and promote cultural awareness, civil rights, tolerance of diversity, and a positive public image of the Muslim community.

See also INDIANS AND SOUTH ASIANS; SEPTEMBER 11TH, 2001; UTICA: BOSNIANS IN UTICA.

Ansari, Maboud. *The Making of the Iranian Community in America* (New York: Pardis Press, 1992)
Dodds, Jerrilynn D., and Edward Grazda. *New York Masjid: The Mosques of New York City* (New York: Powerhouse Books, 2002)
Haddad, Yvonne, and Adair Lummis. *Islamic Values in the United States* (New York: Oxford Univ Press, 1987)
Haddad, Yvonne, and J. Smith, eds. *Muslim Communities in North America* (Albany: SUNY Press, 1994)
Koszegi, M., and G. Melton. *Islam in North America* (New York: Garland Publishing, 1992)

Maboud Ansari

Islandia. Village (pop 3,057) in Islip (Suffolk Co). The Long Island Expressway reached the present village in 1964, encouraging residential developments, one of which was called Islandia. Until the village incorporated in 1985, its territory was considered part of Central Islip and Hauppauge. Proponents of the village were accused of attempting to gain zoning control to attract industry and to create a tax haven for businesses. In 1998 there were 162 businesses in the village, including the world headquarters of Computer Associates. It is the site of the Islandia Center mall.

Daria E. Merwin

Island Park. Village (pop 4,732) in Hempstead (Nassau Co). The village is located on what was known as Hog Island in the 17th century. The island was sold in 1874 to Sarah Barnum, who resold it for use as the Queens Co poor farm; the Board of Supervisors renamed the island Barnum Island after her. Located in Middle Bay, the island was served after 1880 by the railroad line from Lynbrook to Long Beach. Between 1901 and 1914 the island was sold repeatedly to syndicates of speculators who planned its development as a resort with a racetrack. Finally in 1922 the Island Park–Long Beach Corp gave the area a new name and developed it rapidly on reclaimed land. Island Park became a summer colony, acquiring a post office in 1925 and incorporating on the western part of the island in 1926. By the 1950s Island Park was a year-round community with a large Italian and Greek population. It grew most rapidly from 1950 to 1970, and in the 1990s the Latino population increased significantly, to 18% of the total. It is the longtime home and political base of Sen Alfonse D'Amato.

Georgina Martorella

Islip. Town (pop 322,612) and locality (pop 20,575) in SW Suffolk Co. William Nicoll acquired land in the eastern half of the present town from the Secatogue Indians between 1683 and 1697, while a number of patentees acquired the western half between 1692 and 1708. Islip was formed as a precinct, and its earliest surviving minutes date from 1720. Because the proprietors' families retained most of their landholdings, settlement lagged behind other Suffolk Co towns. The main line of the Long Island Rail Road came through in 1842, but it was the South Side Rail Road (1868) that heralded the summer resort industry. Oystering in Great South Bay expanded beginning in 1840, and clamming was also important; the Doxsee Cannery (1866–1905) in Islip hamlet shipped clams and chowder worldwide. Islip hamlet also became a yachting center, and Capt Hank Haff served aboard several America's Cup winners. Sunrise Highway (1929) and Heckscher State Parkway (1959) improved Islip's accessibility. The town's population, only 20,709 in 1920, began to expand rapidly after World War II, more than doubling between 1950 (71,465) and 1960 (172,959), and nearly doubling again by 2000. Historically, town politics have been dominated by conservatives, from Loyalists in the 18th century to Republicans in the 21st century. Islip MacArthur Airport (1942) at Ronkonkoma is now the center of industry in the town. Heckscher State Park and Bayard Cutting Arboretum are attractions, and St. Mark's Episcopal Church (1880) at Islip hamlet, built in the style of a Norwegian stave church with funding by William K. Vanderbilt, is a landmark. In 2000 the town's population was 9% Black and 2% Asian. In addition, 20% of the total population were of Latino ethnicity.

Daria E. Merwin

Islip Terrace. Locality (pop 5,641) in Islip (Suffolk Co). The area was wooded until 1914, when Andrew Wolpert and sons began building houses on speculation. They marketed them to German immigrants, and the development was known as Germantown. Lingering resentment from World War I resulted in a name change to Islip Terrace when the post office opened in 1922. Many residents worked in the Central Islip State Hospital or the Great River branch of Northrop Grumman, both of which closed in 1997.

Daria E. Merwin

Israelis. There were few immigrants to the United States from Israel in the two decades following the latter's establishment in 1948. During the 1950s an estimated 18,000 Israelis lived in New York State, almost all settled in New York City. Beginning in the 1970s Israelis immigrated in large numbers, with New York City remaining a prime destination. Like other immigrants to the United States following passage of the 1965 Immigration Act, the allure of broadened economic opportunities, a high living standard, and the variety of educational programs available were among the factors motivating Israeli immigrants. Also important for many were conditions in Israel: tension from the continuing conflict between Arabs and Jews; a sense of limited opportunity in a small, isolated nation; and among Israelis of Middle Eastern origin (Sephardim), resentment over their low status in a society dominated by those of European background (Ashkenazim).

In many ways Israelis differ from most other recent immigrant populations as well as from eastern European Jewish immigrants who arrived in great numbers during the late 19th and early 20th centuries. They come from a nation with a democratic political system, an industrial economy, and universal schooling. According to the 1990 census, more than 85% of the Israelis in New York State had graduated from high school, and 54% had attained at least some college education. The employment pattern of Israeli New Yorkers is also unusual. Rather than being concentrated in a few occupations, as is common with recently arrived ethnic groups, their education and training enable them to work in a wide variety of jobs; almost half hold managerial, professional, or technical positions. Their high rate of self-employment is second only to Korean Americans.

In contrast to traditional immigrant patterns, New York State's Israelis have neither established their own ethnic benevolent societies or cultural organizations, nor to any significant degree associated themselves with those of the American Jewish community. Though heavily concentrated in Queens and Brooklyn, there are no specifically Israeli neighborhoods. Israelis have not sunk ethnic roots because most, even after many years in residence, consider their stay in the United States temporary. Their attachment to their homeland is extremely strong, frequent trips back to Israel are common, and they have a much higher rate of return than other recent immigrant groups. Their children often spend summer vacations with relatives in Israel. While resistant to committing themselves to ethnic organizations, Israelis do frequent Israeli restaurants and coffee bars. They subscribe to Israeli publications, read the New York City–published Hebrew newspaper *Israel Shelanu* (Our Israel), and listen to Israeli radio programs. Israelis also increasingly use the Internet to stay connected to events in Israel. However, despite hopes and expressed intentions to return home, the majority of Israelis have remained. A growing number have married American Jews, and Israeli children, in contrast to their parents, show an attraction to American culture and identity. By the mid-1990s Israeli consulate officials estimated the presence of 250,000–350,000 Israelis in the United States with 100,000–150,000 resident in New York City and its suburbs. The 2000 census reported that 29,300 people who had been born in Israel were living in the state.

"Just Don't Call Us 'Yordim,' " *Jerusalem Post International Edition,* week ending 19 Mar 1994
Shokeid, Moshe. *Children of Circumstances: Israeli Emigrants in New York* (Ithaca: Cornell Univ Press, 1988)

Frederick M. Binder

Italians. Although Giovanni da Verazzano led the first European expedition into New York Bay in 1524, there were few Italians in New York State before 1860. Those present generally hailed from northern Italy. Wolfgang Amadeus Mozart's best-known librettist, Lorenzo Da Ponte, a native of the Veneto region, came to New York City in 1805 and was appointed the first professor of Italian literature at Columbia College in 1825. Adelina Patti, probably the most famous opera singer in the world in the second half of the 19th century, arrived in New York in 1847 and made her debut at the New York Academy of Music in 1859. Exiled revolutionaries from northern Italy, including Giuseppe Garibaldi, lived on Staten Island in the decade preceding the American Civil War. By the late 1850s and early 1860s, handfuls of northern and southern Italians had begun to appear in some communities beyond New York City, including Rochester and Utica. Many worked as organ-grinders, itinerant musicians, peddlers, and image makers (artisans who made decorative figurines and small busts from plaster). Only 1,862 of the 998,640 foreign-born residents of New York State in 1860 were Italian, and the vast majority of these lived in New York City.

During the American Civil War, approximately 100 New York Italians served as officers in the Union army, including Francis B. Spinola, who rose to the rank of brigadier general and led a unit known as Spinola's Empire Brigade. Italians from New York State also served in the Garibaldi Guard.

Mass Immigration

In the half century following the Civil War, increasingly more Italian immigrants came to New York State. Most were male and came predominantly from the central and southern Italian regions of Molise, Abruzzo, Lazio, Campania, Apulia, Basilicata, Calabria, and Sicily. By the 1870s a still small but growing number of southern Italian laborers began to use New York City as a base from which they are known to have migrated for seasonal work in the Hudson Valley, Buffalo, Rochester, Utica, Albany, and surrounding areas. Much of this work was in laying track for railroads and streetcar lines, road paving, canal repair, and other construction projects. When winter set in and construction became difficult, they typically migrated either to New York City, where some had families, or to Italy. Over time greater gender balance developed in many communities, but in some cities, notably Albany and Syracuse, the percentage of female Italian immigrants remained below 40% as late as 1920.

"Little Italy," Lower East Side, New York City. Drawing by Arthur W. Grumbine, 1950.

The seasonal migrations of the 1870s and 1880s established an array of smaller urban areas statewide as potential places of settlement and extended the reach of migratory chains leading from particular communities in Italy to cities and towns throughout New York State. In addition, the expansion of manufacturing in the closing decades of the 19th century increased significantly the regional demand for semiskilled and unskilled labor. The growing availability of such work statewide gave more Italian immigrants, who were largely unskilled peasants, an incentive to settle year-round in cities and manufacturing towns to the north and west of New York City. By 1890 there were embryonic Italian colonies in the principal manufacturing towns along the route of the Erie Canal. Buffalo's colony, numbering 1,832 immigrants in 1890, was the largest outside of New York City's greater metropolitan area. However, with 39,951 Italians, New York City was the principal center of Italians in the entire country. Additionally, Brooklyn, which had not yet consolidated with the City of New York, was in 1890 home to another 5,685. In the decade that followed, the Italian immigrant population of New York City, which by then included Brooklyn, expanded dramatically to 145,433, a threefold increase. Italian colonies outside of New York City grew at a comparable or greater rate in that 10 years. The Italian communities in Buffalo, Rochester, Syracuse, and Utica were among the 25 largest in the country by the turn of the century.

By 1920 almost 400,000 Italian immigrants lived in New York City. The smaller Italian colonies stretching across the center of the state had also grown significantly. Rochester (19,468) had the largest population, but Buffalo (16,411), Utica (8,435), Syracuse (6,756), and Schenectady (5,378) were also important centers. Smaller but still significant Italian populations thrived in Niagara Falls, Rome, Auburn, Amsterdam, Troy, Binghamton, Elmira, Jamestown, Poughkeepsie, Newburgh, Mount Vernon, and New Rochelle. A relative handful of New York State's Italians also settled in agricultural communities like Canastota (Madison Co), transforming local mucklands into onion farms.

Religious Practices and Social Institutions

Once established in a community, immigrants tried to re-create some semblance of the life they had known in Italy. For many, this included the development of religious institutions that literally and figuratively spoke their language. Almost all Italian immigrants were Catholics.

The small sprinkling of Protestants included a Waldensian congregation in Manhattan and small Baptist congregations in the state's principal urban areas. In 1866 the Catholic Archdiocese of New York created St. Anthony's in Greenwich Village in Manhattan as the first Italian "national" parish in the state. In 1884 another Manhattan parish in East Harlem built the first church in the state specifically for Italian Catholics. During the 1890s the first Italian parishes were established in other communities.

The annual observance of patron saint feast days, typically culminating in processions in which statues of the patron saints of particular southern Italian villages were carried through the streets, occupied a central place in the religious life of Italian immigrants. New York's first known *festa* occurred in 1882 in East Harlem, and in the decades that followed, *feste* honoring an array of southern Italian patron saints enlivened streets annually throughout the state. Mother Francesca Xavier Cabrini joined the ranks of the saints in 1946, when she became the first Italian immigrant canonized. However, Italian Americans were not admitted into the hierarchy of the American church until 1954, when Joseph Pernicone was named among 13 auxiliary bishops of New York City.

Apart from parish churches, Italian immigrants established an array of other institutions in communities. Mutual aid societies open to immigrants from particular villages, provinces, and regions of southern Italy were often among the earliest organizations in each Italian colony. Such institutions provided focal points for the state's often isolated, nascent immigrant communities as well as sources of assistance in times of need. Immigrants also set up religious confraternities to organize *feste* and maintain chapels dedicated to their patron saints. Every Italian colony had one or more marching bands that played a prominent role in *feste* and in other community events. The Order of the Sons of Italy was prominent in every colony throughout the state by 1920, and in some communities there were multiple lodges of the Sons of Italy in the first half of the 20th century.

Work

A reasonably large number of Italian immigrants were engaged in skilled trades and business throughout the state, particularly prominent in barbering, stone masonry, stonecutting, shoemaking, and tailoring. However, most in the early 20th century were construction workers, common laborers, and factory workers. In Buffalo and New York City significant numbers worked on the docks, and many others were employed by the railroads statewide. Many immigrants also worked as bootblacks and itinerant musicians, particularly in the early days of Italian migration.

New York City was home to several Italian American luminaries of the early 20th century labor and radical movements. These included Arturo Giovannitti, the poet and socialist editor of the newspaper *Il Proletario;* Joseph Ettor, the American-born son of Italian immigrants who became an organizer for the Industrial Workers of the World (IWW); and the widely respected anarchist Carlo Tresca. The immigrant response to the labor movement before World War I was uneven, as Italians sometimes acted as strikebreakers in the late 19th and early 20th centuries. Nevertheless, many Italians played an important role in disruptive and frequently successful labor disputes, particularly after 1910. The Italian presence was especially evident in the International Ladies' Garment Workers' Union, the Amalgamated Clothing and Textile Workers Union, and the Hod Carriers' Union.

New York State Italians also made their mark in business. Some immigrants opened their own garment shops in the tailoring centers of the state, and in every immigrant community there was a prominent class of retail grocers and fruit and nut peddlers. By the end of the 1930s, Italians owned some 10,000 grocery stores in New York City alone, and large numbers also joined the ranks of small retailers throughout the rest of the state. The heyday of the Italian American "mom and pop" stores, which represented an avenue of social mobility open to immigrants and their children, began to wane after World War II as supermarkets began to dominate the retail grocery trade. Many Italians continued in food importing and the wholesale business. Progresso Foods, later best known for its canned soups, was founded as a food importer and distributor in New York City in 1927. In many communities, particularly before the onset of the depression, there was a proliferation of *pastafici,* or fresh pasta shops. Particularly after World War II, Italian restaurants, bakeries, and pizzerias grew in popularity among non-Italians in urban areas, introducing more New Yorkers to pasta, cannoli, and pizza.

Newspapers

The first Italian language newspaper in the state, the *Progresso Italo-Americano* (1879), and two of its competitors, *L'Eco d'Italia* (1883) and the *Araldo Italiano* (1889), were founded in New York City. In 1897 Buffalo's *Corriere Italiano* became the first Italian newspaper outside the metropolitan area and was followed by Utica's *L'Avvenire* (1900), Albany's *La Lotta* (1901), Schenectady's *Corriere* (1903), the *Corriere di Rochester* (1905), and the *Gazzetta* of Syracuse (1906). Mount Vernon was the last community to get its own Italian newspaper, the *Cronaca Illustrata,* in 1915. By the mid-1920s, the *Progresso Italo-Americano* had become the leading Italian immigrant paper, with a nationwide circulation of 120,000. By the 1940s Italian language publications began to close down because of declining readerships. *Il Progresso* continued to be published until 1988 and was succeeded by the New Jersey–based *America Oggi.*

Loyalty and Conflict

Immigrant identification with Italian nationalism was manifest in their response to Italy's entrance in World War I in June 1915. Thousands of Italian immigrants fought in the American armed forces in 1917–18, but thousands more had already returned to fight for Italy in 1915–17. Among them were approximately 1,700 from Rochester and nearly 300 who left Utica on a single day in June 1915. The *New York Times* reported in September 1915 that between 3,000 and 5,000 Italians were leaving every week through the Port of New York to serve in the Italian armed forces. Not all Italian immigrants in New York State were nationalist or supported the rise of the fascist government of Benito Mussolini after World War I. Immigrant opposition to Italian nationalism was led by the radical left, many immigrant labor leaders, assimilationists of Italian descent, and fervently antifascist newspapers like Frank Bellanca's *Il Nuovo Mondo* and Carlo Tresca's *Il Martello.* Violent clashes between the dictator's supporters and detractors occurred, particularly in the aftermath of the murder of Giacomo Matteotti, the popular socialist parliamentarian, by fascist thugs in Italy in 1924.

Nevertheless, Mussolini's war of conquest against Ethiopia in 1935–36 united much of the immigrant community in an outpouring of nationalist fervor. Italian Americans collected large amounts of cash, copper, and gold for the Italian war and war relief efforts. In 1936, 100,000 women in New York, New England, and northern New Jersey reportedly donated their gold wedding rings to these campaigns. Additional drives throughout the state collected thousands of other gold objects to support the Italian war effort. Mussolini's proclamation of the end of the war in June 1936 sparked jubilation in many Italian communities in New York State but also heightened tensions between Italian Americans and African Americans living in Harlem.

With the outbreak of World War II, however, Italian Americans actively supported the American war effort. Many who fought in the war had grown up in an America where they were members of a still somewhat marginalized, generally poor ethnic group, but they returned with a new sense of identity born of the indisputable patriotic credentials they had earned in a widely supported American war. The GI Bill, in turn, gave an unprecedented number of Italian Americans access to higher education and social mobility throughout the state in the 1940s and 1950s.

New York City's Francis B. Spinola was the first Italian American to serve in Congress (1887–91). Born in Stony Brook (Suffolk Co) in 1821 and educated in Dutchess Co, Spinola served in the New York State Assembly and Senate in the 1850s before becoming a general in the Union army in 1862. For the most part, however, Italians did not become a significant force in New York State politics until around World War I. Many initially joined the Republicans and remained in that party even after the onset of the Great Depression. In New York City, the percentage of the Italian American vote that went to the Republicans significantly increased between 1936 and 1944. Yet, the Republican Party seems to have failed to get the support of the bulk of Italians in many communities for two reasons. First, Prohibition and immigration restriction, both championed by the Republicans, were unpopular among Italian immigrants. Second, the growing popularity of Alfred E. Smith and Franklin D. Roosevelt and the help provided by the New Deal inspired many Italian immigrants to ally with the Democrats in this period. However, Fiorello La Guardia, the most significant Italian American politician in New York State in the first half of the 20th century, was a Republican and a liberal congressman from New York City. La Guardia decried the influence of Tammany Hall and was elected mayor of New York City in 1933, a position he would retain for a dozen years.

By the 1920s Italians began to displace Irish Americans in urban political machines. In Utica the Democratic machine led by Rufus Elefante was the dominant force in local politics between 1930 and 1960. In Rochester Italians also began to gravitate more decisively toward the Democratic camp during this time. By the late 1940s Italians had begun to emerge as the leaders of the Democratic city and county organizations in Manhattan. Carmine DeSapio, who began his rise by defying the Irish American Democratic leadership in Greenwich Village in 1939, took control of the county Democratic organization in 1949. He dominated city politics from 1953 until he was successfully challenged by reform Democrats in 1961.

In his efforts to supplant the old Tammany Hall establishment, DeSapio also enjoyed the strong support of New York City organized-crime boss Frank Costello. Prohibition brought new prominence to organized crime and criminal leaders, and many, such as Brooklyn-born Al Capone and New York City gangster Charles "Lucky" Luciano, were of Italian descent. In the 1950s public scrutiny increasingly focused on Italian American criminals in New York State, and widely publicized investigations transformed figures like Costello into household names. Many Italian Americans were resentful of what they considered an unfair emphasis on criminality in their community, and the public backlash had a damaging effect on the political careers of several rising Italian American political leaders in New York, most notably that of DeSapio.

As Italian Americans began to move into the suburbs after World War II, a new generation of Republican politicians emerged. Particularly notable were Joseph Margiotta and Sen Alfonse M. D'Amato, both of the powerful Nassau Co Republican machine. Rudolph Giuliani served as mayor of New York City from 1994 to 2001 and Mario M. Cuomo as governor from 1979 to 1994. In 1984 Congresswoman Geraldine A. Ferraro became the first woman to be nominated to the vice presidency. Rensselaer Co Republican Joseph L. Bruno has served in the state senate since 1976 and has held the position of majority leader since 1995.

Suburbanization

The statewide population of Italian immigrants peaked around 1930; the 1940 census registered the first decrease in the Italian immigrant population of the state since the onset of mass Italian immigration in the late 19th century. A discriminatory new immigration law introduced in 1924, which drastically reduced the flow of newcomers, set the stage for this decline. Although there was a small influx of skilled Italians into the state in the 1950s and 1960s, their numbers could not compare with the great wave that had crested just before the World War I. In addition, in the closing decades of the 20th century, a significant portion of a generally more prosperous population left the urban neighborhoods they had inhabited for several generations. In New York City the movement to Staten Island was greatly facilitated by the opening of the Verrazano-Narrows Bridge in 1964. New Jersey also absorbed many Italian Americans seeking life in the suburbs. In 2000, 2,737,146 New York State residents, just over 14% of the state's population, reported in the census that their descent was Italian. In New York City, only 8.7% claimed Italian descent. The suburban counties around New York City were home to a greater concentration: Putnam (32%), Suffolk (29%), Nassau (24%), and Westchester (21%). Other large concentrations included Schenectady (22%), Dutchess (22%), and Oneida (20%) Cos.

See also Ethnic press; Harlem; Organized crime; Rochester (city).

Accardi, Leonard. *Italian Contributions to Albany in the 19th Century* (Albany: La Capitale Publishing, 1941)

Bean, Philip A. "The Irish, the Italians, and Machine Politics, a Case Study: Utica, New York (1870–1960)," *Journal of Urban History* (Feb 1994)

———. *La Colonia: Italian Life and Politics, 1860–1960* (Utica: Ethnic Heritage Studies Center, Utica College, 2004)

Briggs, John W. *An Italian Passage: Immigrants to Three American Cities, 1890–1930* (New Haven, Conn: Yale Univ Press, 1978)

Diggins, John P. *Mussolini and Fascism: The View from America* (Princeton, NJ: Princeton Univ Press, 1972)

Mangione, Jerre, and Ben Morreale. *La Storia: Five Centuries of the Italian American Experience* (New York City: Harper Collins, 1992)

Salamone, Frank A. *Italians in Rochester, New York, 1900–1940* (Lewiston, NY: Edwin Mellen Press, 2000)

Philip A. Bean

Italy. Town (pop 1,087) in SW Yates Co. Settled in ?1790, the town was formed from Naples (Ontario Co) in 1815. Italy includes three ridges divided by two valleys in which the streams drain into the St. Lawrence and Susquehanna watersheds. Until 1933 the Big Elm at Italy Hollow was a landmark, having a trunk circumference of 29 ft (8.8 m). The Middlesex Valley Railroad (1892; later Lehigh Valley Railroad) crossed the town's northwest corner. Italy reached its maximum population of 1,698 in 1845, but between 1960 and 1990 the population increased 262%, largely because of the conversion of second homes into permanent residences. Reforestation of marginal farmland in the 1930s created the 5,000-acre (2,023 ha) High Tor State Wildlife Management Area.

Gwen Chamberlain

Ithaca. Town (pop 18,198) and city (pop 29,287) in central Tompkins Co. Located at the headwaters of Cayuga Lake, Ithaca was visited from 1786 to 1788 and settled in 1789. Abraham Bloodgood acquired 1,400 acres (567 ha) from the state on land called the Flats, which he conveyed in 1794 to his widowed son-in-law Simeon DeWitt. DeWitt had a subdivision survey made and offered lots for sale. He named his land Ithaca, first mentioned on a map of 1807; in 1808 the first hotel took the name Ithaca Hotel. The settlement flourished with DeWitt's encouragement and served as a transshipment point for salt and gypsum mined at Salina (Onondaga Co). In 1810 Ithaca was linked to Owego (Tioga Co) by a turnpike. Ithaca was named county seat in 1817 and the town was formed in 1821 from Ulysses; the village incorporated in that year, governed by a president and trustees.

Steamboats operated from Ithaca on Cayuga Lake beginning in 1821, carrying plaster, salt, pork, whiskey, and flour, and service continued until early in the 20th century. The Ithaca and Owego Railroad was built in 1834; by the 1850s there were rail lines north and south. The final links, connecting Ithaca to all the major rail lines, were built between 1871 and 1874. A small industrial center had developed along Fall Creek, including plaster mills, gristmills, sawmills, paper mills (1818) and carding mills (1819); in 1827 a cotton factory was established. Economic decline followed the 1837 depression. Ithaca exhibited the major social enthusiasms of the Burned-over District, including revivalism, abolitionism, and temperance. In the 1830s Irish Roman Catholics joined the primarily Protestant population of mostly white settlers. More African Americans, fleeing the South or moving further into the North from Pennsylvania and New Jersey, arrived in the period before the Civil War. The population increased following the 1868 opening of Cornell University, which provided the community with economic stability and became one of the county's two largest employers by 1900, soon ascending to first rank. The Village of Ithaca became a city in 1888, governed by a mayor and aldermen. A public library, endowed by Ezra Cornell, opened in 1866. The Ithaca Street Railway Co provided trolley service (1884–1935). Ithaca College began as the Ithaca Conservatory of Music in 1892, moving to a location on South Hill in 1965.

Post–Civil War industry included the Ithaca Agricultural Works (1867–83), the Ithaca Calendar Clock Co (1868), Phoenix Iron Works (1869–1939), the Ithaca Gun Co (1888; moved to Genoa, Cayuga Co, 1990s), and Land and Reynolds machine shop (1865–1921). In the 1890s Italian and Hungarian workers appeared in Ithaca, and in the 1910s immigrants came from Greece. These groups grew and by 1990 in the city and town there were communities of American Indians, Chinese, Indians, Vietnamese, Koreans, Japanese, South Americans, Russians, and Western Europeans. In 1992 Tibetans established the Namgyal Monastery. The size of the population grew steadily throughout the 20th century with a significant jump following World War II when the university expanded and Ithaca Gun Co flourished. From 1912 to 1920 Ithaca hosted a silent movie industry. Products made in 20th-century Ithaca include cigars, pianos, organs, and airplanes; manufacturing companies include Morse Chain (Ithaca operations, 1906–80s) and National Cash Register Co (1943; later Axiom, 1995).

Local press includes the daily *Ithaca Journal* (1815), the *Cornell Daily Sun* (1880), the weekly *Ithaca Times* (1977), and the literary journal *Bookpress* (1990). Ithaca's cultural life is rich, with an opera company, the Center for the Arts in Ithaca (1965) offering summer theater and

Tobogganing in Ithaca, early 20th century.

arts education, and numerous smaller drama, choral, instrumental, and dance groups. Major museums include the Sciencenter (1983), Museum of the Earth (2002), Cornell's Johnson Art Museum, and Tompkins County Museum. The city and region are served by the Cayuga Medical Center, and Ithaca hosts a giant Friends of the Library Book Sale every fall. In 1997 the *Utne Reader* voted the city "The Most Enlightened Community in the United States" based on the amount of citizen participation in local affairs, concern for the environment, and cultural activities. Since 1950 the population of the Town of Ithaca has more than doubled, while the population of the city has remained relatively unchanged. The city faces increasing financial strain as it attempts to continue to provide expected and mandated services.

See also ARCHITECTS AND ARCHITECTURE, SOUTHERN TIER (EASTERN).

Abt, Henry. *Ithaca* (Ithaca: Ross Kellogg, 1929)

Dieckmann, Jane M. *A Short History of Tompkins County* (Ithaca: DeWitt Historical Society, 1986)

Kammen, Carol. *Peopling of Tompkins County: A Social History* (Interlaken, NY: Heart of the Lakes Publishing, 1985)

Carol Kammen

Ithaca College. Private four-year college. Founded as the Ithaca Conservatory of Music in September 1892, the school rented rooms above Rothschild's Department Store until November 1910, when it mortgaged a house at 120 East Buffalo St. The conservatory expanded through the 1920s, adding affiliated programs that included drama, physical education, and speech correction. In 1931 the school received a college charter. In 1960 ground was broken for Egbert Union, the first building on the new South Hill Campus. Friends Hall, the first classroom building, was built in 1961 and named to honor the Friends of Ithaca College, a community group whose financial contributions facilitated the move from downtown Ithaca to the South Hill campus. In 2003 the campus comprised nearly 70 buildings. Still renowned for its School of Music, the college also has nationally recognized programs in its School of Health Sciences and Human Performance and the Roy H. Park School of Communications. In 2003 the school enrolled 6,200 undergraduates in 92 academic programs and 200 graduates in 17 graduate programs.

Ithaca College, http://www.ithaca.edu

Sarah E. DeSanctis

Ives, Irving M(cNeil) (*b* Bainbridge, Chenango Co, 24 Jan 1896; *d* Norwich, Chenango Co, 24 Feb 1962). Politician. Ives served in the army in World War I. He graduated in 1920 from Hamilton College and entered the banking and insurance business in New York City with Guaranty Trust Co of New York and then with Manufacturers Trust Co in Norwich. He won election as a Republican to the New York State Assembly in 1930 and held several leadership roles over the next 15 years. During the 1940s Ives sponsored legislation to create the New York State Department of Commerce (now Empire State Development Corp) and the New York State School of Industrial and Labor Relations at Cornell University. He also led the effort to pass the Ives-Quinn bill, which became the first state law in the nation to outlaw employment discrimination based on race, creed, or national origin. In 1945 Ives became the first dean of the School of Industrial and Labor Relations. He was elected to the US Senate a year later and won reelection in 1952. A moderate Republican who usually enjoyed solid support from unions, Ives regularly sponsored labor-related legislation, such as antidiscrimination in employment bills. His 1954 bid to become governor of New York State failed, and his political career ended in 1958 when he chose not to seek reelection to the Senate for health reasons.

Ives, Irving McNeil. Papers. Cornell Univ Library, Ithaca

Timothy N. Thurber

Ives-Quinn Law. Enacted in New York State in 1945, it was the first law in the nation to ban employment discrimination and to create a permanent fair employment agency, unlike the federal Fair Employment Practices Committee, created in 1941 and allowed to expire in 1946. In 1943 Gov Thomas E. Dewey appointed Alvin S. Johnson head of New York's Committee on Discrimination in Employment, a temporary wartime agency dedicated to eradicating employment discrimination in defense industries. Seeing the current war rooted in Nazi racial hatred, Johnson believed that racism must be eradicated for peace to exist in the postwar era. He committed himself to enacting a law banning employment discrimination and to creating a permanent fair employment agency. In March 1944 Johnson persuaded Dewey to form a planning commission to make policy recommendations. Submitted to the state legislature on 28 Jan 1945, the commission's bill was coauthored by Johnson and the assembly majority leader Irving M. Ives (R-Chenango Co). Known as Ives-Quinn, for legislative cosponsors Ives and Sen Elmer Quinn (D-Manhattan), the bill banned employment discrimination on the basis of race, national origin, and religion; made employment without discrimination a civil right; and created the State Commission Against Discrimination (SCAD). The state business lobby forcefully opposed Ives-Quinn, but with Dewey's vigorous support, the bill passed the legislature in late February and was signed into law on 12 March. By 1955, 10 states had followed New York State's lead and enacted similar laws.

See also HUMAN RIGHTS, DIVISION OF.

Ottman, Tod M. " 'Government That Has Both a Heart and a Head': The Growth of New York State Government During the World War II Era, 1930–1950" (PhD diss, SUNY Albany, 2001)

Tod M. Ottman

J

Jackson. Town (pop 1,718) in S Washington Co. Settled between 1761 and 1765 by New Englanders, Scots, and northern Irish, the town was formed from Cambridge in 1815. It was crossed by the Delaware and Hudson Railroad (1852). In the 19th century its farms produced potatoes and flax for sale. In 2003 the predominant land use remained agriculture. Hedges Lake and Lake Lauderdale, two small lakes, are surrounded by summer cottages. Tourist attractions include the freight and excursion short-line Batten Kill Railroad (1994) and three covered bridges that cross the Batten Kill at the hamlets of Rexleigh, Shushan, and Eagleville.

R. Paul McCarty

Jackson, Robert H(oughwout) (*b* Spring Creek, Pa, 13 Feb 1892; *d* Washington, DC, 9 Oct 1954). Lawyer and US Supreme Court justice. Jackson grew up in Frewsburg (Chautauqua Co) and was admitted to the bar in 1913 after attending Albany Law School for one year and reading law in Frank Mott's Jamestown (Chautauqua Co) office. Already involved in Democratic Party politics, Jackson's highly successful law practice, bar association involvement, and the minority status of the party provided a fast track for his advancement. He became acquainted with Franklin D. Roosevelt in the World War I era and campaigned for and advised him during his governorship. From 1934 to 1937 Jackson skillfully served the New Deal in a number of capacities, as well as advising Pres Roosevelt. The president designated him solicitor general in March 1938 and attorney general in early 1940, and named him to the US Supreme Court in June 1941—the last justice not to be a law school graduate—and Roosevelt may have implied Jackson's eventual appointment as chief justice.

Jackson's constitutional jurisprudence generally allowed the elected branches of government free rein, with notable exceptions, including his poignant statement on religious liberty in the flag-salute case of *West Virginia State Board of Education v Barnette* (1943), his articulate defense of individual liberty in his dissent in *Korematsu v United States* (1944) against the Japanese internment policy, and his concurrence in *Youngstown Sheet and Tube Co v Sawyer* (1952). Generally aligned with Felix Frankfurter in the often acrimonious division on the Court over the judiciary's role, Jackson's conflict with Hugo Black was central to the feud. In April 1945 Jackson accepted the controversial position of chief US prosecutor at the Nuremberg trials. After Chief Justice Harlan Fiske Stone's death in April 1946, both Black and Jackson were rumored as his successor and both asserted resignation if the other was made chief justice. Pres Harry S. Truman appointed Fred M. Vinson to the position, and Black and Jackson remained on the Court. Jackson wrote two significant works on the Court: *The Struggle for Judicial Supremacy* (1941) and *The Supreme Court in the American System of Government* (1955).

Gerhart, Eugene C. *America's Advocate: Robert H. Jackson* (Indianapolis: Bobbs-Merrill, 1958)
Jackson, Robert H. *That Man: An Insider's Portrait of Franklin D. Roosevelt,* ed. John Q. Barrett (New York: Oxford Univ Press, 2003)
Schubert, Glendon A., ed. *Dispassionate Justice: A Synthesis of the Judicial Opinions of Robert H. Jackson* (Indianapolis: Bobbs-Merrill, 1969)

Donald M. Roper

Jacobs, Harriet Ann (*b* Edenton, NC, ?1813; *d* Washington, DC, 7 Mar 1897). Fugitive slave and author. Born into slavery, Jacobs grew up in the household of her master, Dr James Norcom. By 1829 Jacobs found herself threatened sexually by Norcom. In an effort to protect herself, she took a white lover, Samuel Tredwell Sawyer, from whom she bore two children. In 1835 Sawyer arranged to purchase the children from Norcom, giving Jacobs the strength to flee herself. She spent seven years in hiding in the South before making her way North in 1842. She spent the next seven years moving frequently around the Northeast, evading slave catchers. In 1849 she was in Rochester, where she worked in the Anti-Slavery Office and Reading Room, located in the rooms above the offices of Frederick Douglass's *North Star.* While in Rochester, Jacobs lived with Amy and Isaac Post, Quaker reformers and abolitionists. Amy Post urged Jacobs to write her memoir, and although hesitant and doubtful of her abilities, Jacobs finally began writing in 1853. Her manuscript was completed in 1858. Difficulties in finding a publisher delayed its appearance until 1861, when *Incidents in the Life of a Slave Girl, Written by Herself* was published. The book appeared under a pseudonym, Linda Brent, since Jacobs was still a fugitive slave. Although Jacobs was well known as the author in abolitionist circles, by the 20th century both she and her narrative had been largely forgotten, and many thought the book was a novel. The discovery of Jacobs's letters in the Post Archive at the University of Rochester made it possible to authenticate her authorship in 1981. In the late 20th and early 21st centuries, *Incidents in the Life of a Slave Girl* has been widely regarded as a major slave narrative and has earned a place in the canon of writings by African American women. During the Civil War and Reconstruction, she moved to Virginia and Georgia to help freed slaves and later lived in Boston.

Yellin, Jean Fagan. Introduction. *Incidents in the Life of a Slave Girl, Written by Herself,* by Harriet A. Jacobs (1861; repr, ed. Lydia Maria Child, Cambridge, Mass: Harvard Univ Press, 1987)

R. A. R. Edwards

Jacobs [née Butzner], Jane (*b* Scranton, Pa, 4 May 1916). Urban activist and writer. Daughter of a prominent physician and a nurse, she grew up outside Scranton. At age 20 she moved to New York City, working various secretarial jobs while freelance writing for such magazines as *Vogue* and *Harper's Bazaar.* Following two years at Columbia University's School of General Studies (1938–40), she served as an editor of the *Iron Age,* a metallurgical industry trade magazine, from 1940 to 1943. She worked for the US government from 1943 to 1952, in the Office of Wartime Information and later the Overseas Information Agency. During that time she married architect Robert Hyde Jacobs Jr, purchased a home in Manhattan's Greenwich Village, and bore three children.

Following a series of inquiries by her employer, the US Department of State, that focused primarily on her membership in the American Labor Party (early 1940s–1949) and the United Public Workers of America (1943–51), Jacobs left the government and became an editor at *Architectural Forum* in 1952. Inspired by William Kirk, director of the Union Settlement in East Harlem, she began to question the assumptions of architecture and city planning that underlay postwar urban renewal projects. After her criticisms of such projects appeared in *Fortune* magazine in April 1958, the Rockefeller Foundation offered Jacobs a grant to develop her ideas further in a book. *The Death and Life of Great American Cities* (1961) characterized desirable city life in terms of four "generators," or conditions, for urban diversity: mixed uses (commerce, industry, residence), small blocks, buildings of various kinds and ages, and concentrated population. According to Jacobs, modernist planners and architects failed to recognize the gap between their idealized visions and the complexity of urban life, and she blamed them for destroying cities. Her text became a touchstone in the debate between modernist planners and their critics.

After leaving *Architectural Forum* in 1962, Jacobs organized and led community-based protests, drawing on the principles in her book. Her allies ranged from Tammany Hall Democrat Carmine DeSapio to Republican US Congressman (and later mayor of New York City) John Lindsay. Her most significant victories included the defeat of urban renewal plans for the West Village neighborhood (1961–62), the development of an alternative middle-income housing project designed by West Village residents themselves (1962–74), and the halt on implementing a proposed Lower Manhattan expressway (1962 and 1968). Amidst the tumultuous political climate of the late 1960s, Jacobs was arrested twice, once for demonstrating against US policy in Vietnam and once for disrupting a state expressway hearing. In 1968 Jacobs moved her family to Toronto, where she continued defending neighborhoods from highway projects and other threats, and authored seven additional books, including *The Nature of Economies* (2000).

Fulford, Robert. "When Jane Jacobs Took on the World," *New York Times Book Review,* 16 Feb 1992

Christopher Klemek

Jacobstein, Meyer (*b* New York City, 25 Jan 1880; *d* Rochester, 18 Apr 1963). US congressman, banker, and publisher. Jacobstein's father was an immigrant Jewish tailor, and his family moved to Rochester in 1882. He attended the Rochester Free Academy and the University of Rochester (1900–1902) and completed his education at Columbia University, where he received a BA (1904), an MA (1905), and a PhD (1907). Jacobstein taught economics at the University of Rochester from 1913 to 1918. He was elected to the US Congress in 1922, winning an upset victory as a Democrat in Rochester's 38th District, a Republican stronghold, and served until 1929. Jacobstein was founding president (1929–33) of the First National Bank and Trust Co of Rochester, which merged into Rochester's Lincoln-Alliance Bank and Trust Co in 1936. He became publisher of the *Rochester Evening Journal* and the *Sunday American,* the Hearst newspapers in Rochester, in 1933 and continued so until they ceased in 1937. Jacobstein moved to Washington, DC, where he worked as a researcher at the Brookings Institution (1939–46) and the Library of Congress (1947–52). He retired in 1952 and returned to Rochester in 1956. He led a study on employment opportunities in the Rochester area at the request of Gov W. Averell Harriman in 1957.

Barnes, Joseph W. "Rochester's Congressmen Part II, 1869–1979," *Rochester History* 41 (Oct 1979): 12–13

Karl S. Kabelac

Jamaicans. Individuals from the island of Jamaica have lived in New York State since the colonial era. The first large immigration occurred during the first three decades of the 20th century, when about 140,000 West Indians, mainly Jamaicans, moved to the United States. Most settled in New York City, which because of its large black population (especially in Harlem) proved particularly attractive to first-wave West Indian immigrants. Jamaican immigrants, such as the charismatic leader of the Universal Negro Improvement League Marcus Garvey and poet Claude McKay, greatly influenced the development of black nationalism and left-wing politics in the United States. In the 1940s and 1950s, there was a second wave of Jamaican migrants, many becoming farm and factory laborers in areas such as Genesee Co, and some reuniting with relatives already living in the United States. A third wave came after 1965.

In 2000 about 200,000 Jamaican-born immigrants, including several thousand illegal immigrants, lived in New York State, mostly in the New York City area. They have tended to settle in central Brooklyn (Crown Heights, Flatbush, East Flatbush), southeastern Queens (Laurelton, Cambria Heights), and north Bronx (Williamsbridge, Wakefield). Other sizable concentrations can be found in Mount Vernon (Westchester Co), Rockland Co, and Nassau Co along the border with Queens. Smaller numbers also live in the Buffalo and Rochester areas. Jamaican immigrants have a high labor force participation rate and tend to hold multiple jobs. Many of the women are employed in the personal service and healthcare industries, and men often work in construction and various service industries, such as the private transportation industry (as jitney drivers) in New York City. However, upward mobility through higher education is a cultural ideal in Jamaica, and many immigrants are entering such professions as law, medicine, engineering, and teaching.

Jamaicans have created a variety of fraternal and political associations; private schools; and ethnic, mainly Protestant, churches. Rastafarians, originally from the most downtrodden segment of Jamaican society, have been a major cultural force in Jamaica and among immigrants in the United States because of their emphasis on the dignity of black people, their values and lifestyle, and the popularity of reggae music, although the number of Rastafarians in New York City is small. Important immigrant Jamaican organizations include the Jamaican Progressive League in the Bronx, the Jamaica Foundation in Hempstead (Nassau Co), and the Jamaican Ex-Constabulary Association of New York for former police officers. The Friends of Needy Children in Jamaica supports relief activities. Jamaican immigrants share a strong feeling of common culture with other English-speaking West Indians and tend to join West Indian institutions. West Indian–oriented publications such as the weekly *New York Carib News* and the magazine *Everybody's* include extensive treatment of Jamaican issues. In Buffalo there is the Jamaican-American Association, and in Rochester there is the Club Caribbean for Jamaicans and other West Indians. Jamaican foodways, such as jerked chicken, have become part of the American cultural landscape. Reggae, dance hall, and ska, all music of Jamaican origin, have influenced American rap, hip hop, and rock music. A number of popular hip hop artists, notably Busta Rhymes, Heavy D, and Shinehead, are of Jamaican ancestry. Persons of Jamaican background in New York State politics include Ronald Blackwood, mayor of Mount Vernon from 1985 to 1995, and Allan Thompson, mayor of Spring Valley (Rockland Co) from 1993 to 2001. Una Clarke was a Democratic member of the New York City Council (40th District, Brooklyn) from 1991 to 2001 and was succeeded by her daughter Yvette Clarke in 2001. Nick Perry completed 10 years as a Democratic member of the New York State Assembly (58th District, Brooklyn) in 2002. Colin Powell, America's first African American secretary of state, is the son of Jamaican immigrants and grew up in the Bronx.

Kasinitz, Philip. *Caribbean New York: Black Immigrants and the Politics of Race* (New York: Cornell Univ Press, 1992)
Vickerman, Milton. *Crosscurrents: West Indian Immigrants and Race* (New York: Oxford Univ Press, 1999)
Waters, Mary C. *Black Identities: West Indian Immigrant Dreams and American Realities* (New York: Russell Sage Foundation; Cambridge, Mass: Harvard Univ Press, 1999)

Milton Vickerman

James, Duke of York and Albany (*b* Stirling Castle, Scotland, 4 Oct 1633; *d* Saint-Germain-en-Laye, France, 5 Sept 1701). Second surviving son of Charles I, he was named Duke of York (1644–85), and after the execution of his father in 1649, spent many years in exile on the continent. After the English took possession of New Netherland in 1664, he was named proprietor. The former Dutch colony included New York Colony east of the Mohawk Valley, portions of what is now New Jersey, and portions of Delaware, Massachusetts, and Maine. The Duke's Laws, promulgated in 1665, were the colony's first legal code. On the death of his brother, Charles II, in 1685 he succeeded to the throne as James II, and New York became a royal colony. James's policy of centralization and elimination of colonial charters led to its incorporation into the Dominion of New England in 1685. Extremely unpopular in many circles because of his Catholicism, James was deposed in the Glorious Revolution of 1688 and exiled to France. Across the Atlantic in New York Colony, his fall sparked Leisler's Rebellion (1689–91).

The bestowal of place-names is likely the most enduring legacy of James, Duke of York to his colony. He named the colony New York in 1664, and the colony's largest settlements were named after his ducal titles, New York City and Albany. In 1683, when the county system was established in the colony, all colonies then created were named after him and his relatives. Albany, New York, and Ulster Cos (he was Earl of Ulster) were named for him. Dutchess Co was named after his wife, Mary Beatrice d'Este. Kings, Suffolk, and Westchester Cos were named after his brother, Charles II, Duke of Suffolk and Earl of Chester. Queens Co was named for Charles II's wife, Catharine of Braganza, and Richmond Co was named in honor of his nephew, Charles Lennox, Duke of Richmond. Ironically, Orange Co was named in honor of his daughter, Mary Stuart of England, and son-in-law, William of Orange, who would supplant him in 1688.

Miller, John. *James II* (New Haven, Conn: Yale Univ Press, 2000)

Jennifer Steenshorne

James family. Celebrated for the psychologist and philosopher William James (1842–1910) and his brother, the novelist and essayist Henry James Jr (1843–1916), the family traces its New York State roots to the late 18th century. William James (1771–1832) was a Presbyterian who emigrated from Ireland in 1789. By 1793 he settled in Albany, where he operated a successful produce business. By the 1820s he owned real estate in Buffalo, Rochester, Syracuse, Troy, and Utica, and was an investor in the Erie Canal, a partner in land development companies, and the officer of two local banks. In 1824 James bought 250 acres (101 ha) of swampy marshland that became the City of Syracuse and became president of the Syracuse Salt Co. James St, a major Syracuse thoroughfare, is named for William James and his role in the development of the city and its salt industry. He was also a major benefactor of Union College, from which his son Henry James Sr (1811–82) graduated in 1830. At William James's death in 1832 his estate was one of the largest in the United States, and Henry, 1 of 11 children, became financially independent.

After his marriage to Mary Walsh of New York City, Henry settled in the neighborhood on Washington Square in Greenwich Village in Manhattan. Their children, in addition to William and Henry Jr, included younger brothers Garth Wilkinson (1845–83) and Robertson (1846–1910). The youngest child, Alice James (1850–92), was a writer of considerable ability whose posthumously published diary received much literary attention. After an extended trip to France and England in 1844–45, the family lived on West 14th St in New York City from 1845 to 1855. During his New York City years Henry Sr was active as a lecturer and writer. In *Letters to a Swedenborgian* (1847) and *Lectures and Miscellanies* (1852) he presented his philosophy, one that evolved from the works of Swedish mystic Emanuel Swedenborg. The elder James rejected emphasis on the self as an egoism that damages the human personality and prevents it from achieving human fellowship.

The family spent several years in Europe and then resided in Newport, RI, during the Civil War before settling in Cambridge, Mass, where William attended Harvard College from 1861 to 1863 and graduated from Harvard Medical School in 1869. He taught at Harvard from 1874 to 1907. He was significantly attached to the Adirondacks in New York State, particularly Keene Valley in Essex Co, and spent portions of many summers there, enjoying the valley of the Ausable River and the steep side of Round Mountain. During a visit to Keene Valley in 1898, he spent a night outdoors and experienced overwhelming emotions, which he later wrote about in *The Varieties of Religious Experience* (1902). William James's other best-known works deal with theories of knowledge and belief: *The Will to Believe* (1897), *Principles of Psychology* (1890), and *The Meaning of Truth* (1909). As a leading exponent of pragmatism he evaluated ideas in terms of their outcomes, emphasizing that true ideas are those that emerge over time because they have led human beings to successful outcomes.

Henry James Jr spent the first six months of 1875 in two furnished rooms on East 25th St in New York City, where he wrote book and theater reviews for the *Nation.* Although his fiction stressed international themes, particularly that of the American in Europe, it also included vivid impressions of New York State. The opening chapters of *An International Episode* (1878) describe a stifling August 1874 in the hotels, offices, and streets of New York City. *Daisy Miller* (1878) is largely set in Rome, but the heroine and her family have Schenectady origins; the main action of *Washington Square* (1880) takes place in 1840s New York City. The vividly realized Albany home of Isabel Archer in *Portrait of a Lady* (1881) draws on James's memory of childhood visits to his extended family. He later used the impressions he gathered of the working-class areas around 2d Ave in 1875 for the early section of *The Bostonians* (1886). After each of three visits James made to New York over the next 35 years he wrote short stories set in the city. James's observations of America during his visit of 1904–5 resulted in *The American Scene* (1907), which includes four lengthy chapters on New York City and an account of his trip to the Hudson Valley. Early 20th-century New York City appears in "The Jolly Corner" (1908), "Julia Bride" (1908), and "Crapy Cornelia" (1909).

During his final stay in New York City, occasioned by the death of William James in 1910, Henry James Jr set his last short story, "A Round of Visits" (1910), in a luxurious New York City apartment house. His memoir, *A Small Boy and Others* (1913), covering the time up to when he was 15, describes his reactions to the midcentury Manhattan and the vivid life of his family's household. The *New York Edition* (1907–9) of his novels and tales, perhaps James's most lasting tribute to his birthplace, contains illuminating prefaces to his works.

Edel, Leon. *Henry James: A Life* (New York: Harper & Row, 1985)
Habegger, Alfred. *The Father: A Life of Henry James Sr* (New York: Farrar, Straus & Giroux, 1994)
Lewis, R. W. B. *The Jameses: A Family Narrative* (New York: Farrar, Straus, & Giroux, 1991)

Barbara J. Dunlap

Jamestown. City (pop 31,730) in SE Chautauqua Co. Located at the southeastern end of Chautauqua Lake, 7 miles (11 km) north of the Pennsylvania border, Jamestown's hilly terrain is part of the Allegheny Plateau. Its region was Seneca Indian hunting territory when first known to Europeans. The French discovered they could reach their Mississippi River territories by carrying vessels from Barcelona to Mayville, navigating Chautauqua Lake and its outlet and, ultimately, reaching the Allegheny River. A 1739 journey by Baron de Longueuil was the first documented use of this route. In 1806 a search for lost horses brought James Prendergast to the Chadakoin River where the powerful rapids and surrounding pine forest impressed him. Two years later he purchased 1,000 acres (405 ha) and, by 1814, built a sawmill, gristmill, and dam to generate waterpower. The community he founded was first known as the Rapids, but by 1816, when a post office opened, it was called Jamestown after its founder. It incorporated as a village in 1827.

As early as 1816 the area's lumber resources led to furniture production, which ultimately expanded to be its largest industry. Manufacturing was fostered by rail service, with the Atlantic and Great Western (1860) providing a direct route to New York City. Lines to Buffalo and Westfield followed. By 1900 three-quarters of the industrial goods produced in Jamestown were either furniture, fabric, metal products, or photographic paper. Among the important plants was N. W. Gokey and Son (1881–1920), one of the largest shoe factories in the state, and the Automatic Voting Machine Co (1896–1982), which introduced the first practical mechanical voting machine. Though Jamestown was a pioneer in the manufacture of metal furniture beginning in 1888, wooden furniture manufacturing eventually dominated the economy; in sheer numbers of firms and employees, it was the city's lifeblood and gave it a national reputation second only to Grand Rapids, Mich. Jamestown's Furniture Exposition Building (1917–82) hosted semiannual furniture shows attended by manufacturers from across the country.

Before the 1860s most of the settlers of Jamestown were Yankees emigrating from New England and eastern New York State, along with some Pennsylvanians. A small African American population settled in an area called Africa and included Catherine Harris, who achieved some renown for her aid to escaped slaves. Swedes first arrived in Jamestown in 1849 to work in the furniture factories. More settled after the Civil War, and they soon became the dominant ethnic group. By 1920 almost 40% of Jamestown residents were of Swedish descent. A substantial Italian population beginning in 1887 and smaller numbers of Greeks (1886–), Albanians (1903–), and others were also attracted by industrial employment.

Jamestown was chartered as a city in 1886. Nonpartisan mayor Samuel A. Carlson (1908–27, 1929–33, 1935–37) became nationally known for creating the city's Board of Public Utilities, which continues to generate and provide its own electrical power to residents of the city and adjacent areas at reduced rates, a reflection of Swedish ideas of social democracy and municipal ownership. The city has a strong mayoral form of government with a nine-member city council, whose members are elected to two-year terms, with six of them elected from wards and three serving at large. The mayor serves a four-year term.

In the second half of the 20th century most of Jamestown's factories closed, leaving tool and die makers and Crawford Furniture. Other important employers of Jamestown residents are located outside the city limits, including Clark Laboratories (medical test kits) in Ellicott, Fancher Chair Co in Falconer, and Cummins Engine Co (known as Jamestown Engine Plant) in Busti. Like many cities Jamestown has undergone a substantial population decline from a peak of 45,155 in 1930. A multicounty railroad authority was created in 2000 to guarantee continued freight traffic along the Norfolk Southern branch rail line through Jamestown between Hornell (Steuben Co) and Pennsylvania. The 1998 designation of the western portion Rte 17 as I-86 is expected to help attract business and industry. Though unemployment was relatively low in 2000, almost 20% of Jamestown residents lived at or near the federal poverty level.

Among prominent Jamestown residents and natives were Reuben E. Fenton (1819–85), a founder of the Republican Party, New York State governor (1865–69), and US senator (1869–75); Robert H. Jackson (1892–1954), associate justice of the US Supreme Court and chief US prosecutor at the Nuremberg war crimes trial; and Walter E. Washington (*b* 1915), the first black mayor of a major American city (Washington, DC, 1966–78). The most celebrated Jamestown native is undoubtedly Lucille Ball (1911–89), who left the area as a teenager to pursue a modeling and acting career.

The daily newspaper, the *Jamestown Post-Journal,* is the successor to a newspaper begun in 1826. Jamestown's educational institutions include Jamestown Business College (1886) and Jamestown Community College (1950). It is the site of the Fenton History Center (1963), the Roger Tory Peterson Institute of Natural History (1984), and the Lucy Desi Museum (1996); the Reg Lenna Civic Center is a venue for cultural programming. A recent addition to the city's educational life is the Robert H. Jackson Center for Justice (2001). The Jamestown Savings Bank Ice Arena (2002) is the keystone of plans for revitalization of the downtown west side.

Gregory P. Rabb

Jamestown Business College. Private two-year college. Founded in 1886 to provide an inexpensive education in practical subjects, its early programs were six to nine months long. The Jamestown Business College (JBC) moved several times, locating at its present Fairmount Ave site in Jamestown (Chautauqua Co) in 1955. The classroom building was built in 1969, and the administrative building in 1992. In recent years more general studies have been added to the curriculum. JBC offers a one-year certificate in office administration and in medical technology, and associate degrees in business administration and administrative assistant. The college enrollment was approximately 300 in 2002.

Jamestown Business College, http://www.jbcny.org

Pam Kirst

Jandreau, Leo E(ugene) (*b* Schenectady, 4 Nov 1904; *d* Schenectady, 30 Mar 1978). Labor leader. Jandreau left high school to work at General Electric Co's main facility in Schenectady. In 1922 he transferred from office work to the machine shop, where he helped organize the Electrical Industry Employees Union (EIEU) in 1933. Jandreau was elected recording secretary in 1934 and president in 1935. In 1936 the Schenectady EIEU became Local 301 of the new United Electrical and Radio Workers Union (renamed United Electrical, Radio, and Machine Workers of America in 1937), a charter member of the Congress of Industrial Organizations

(CIO). Jandreau was elected business agent in 1937, a position he held until 1965. A popular and controversial leader, Jandreau denied persistent allegations of Communist Party membership, charges that ended only when he led Local 301 into the anticommunist International Union of Electrical, Radio, and Machine Workers in 1954.

Kannenberg, Lisa. "The Product of GE's Progress: Labor, Management, and Community Relations in Schenectady, New York, 1930–1960" (PhD diss, Rutgers Univ, 1999)

Lisa Kannenberg

Japanese. The history of Japanese communities in New York State begins with the six Japanese businessmen who arrived in New York City on the liner *Oceanic* in 1876 and established trading firms to import silk and other Japanese goods. Small numbers of business owners, students, and clergymen followed. By 1900 between 500 and 1,000 Issei (Japanese immigrants) had settled in New York State, almost exclusively in New York City. They began to forge a distinctive community in the decades that followed. The Japanese population of New York State was tiny, never exceeding 5,000 until the 1960s. In comparison, over 200,000 Issei settled in Hawaii and Pacific Coast states before the Gentlemen's Agreements of 1907–8, which restricted immigration of Japanese laborers. Furthermore, while the Issei of the Pacific Rim communities were primarily agricultural workers, New York State's Issei included business people, students, artists, writers, and domestic servants in New York City, plus a handful of residents scattered throughout the broader state, mostly students at Cornell University in Ithaca. Although economic discrimination restricted Issei laborers (apart from a contingent of ship workers at the Brooklyn Navy Yard) to domestic service or employment in Japanese-owned businesses, the community's strong intellectual and commercial character gave it a uniquely cosmopolitan flavor. A number of outstanding Japanese, notably chemist Jokichi Takamine, medical researcher Hideyo Noguchi, playwright-critic Sadakichi Hartmann, and poet-novelist Yone Noguchi, resided in New York City in the first quarter of the 20th century.

Japanese American Harry Yasuda working in Rochester for the Ledger Printing and Publishing Co, 1944.

The dominant institutions of the New York City community were the Japanese Methodist Church, founded in 1901; the Nippon Club, a social organization founded in 1905; and the Japan Society, an interracial cultural and artistic foundation formed in 1907. In addition, the Japanese Association, a mutual assistance fraternity, founded a New York City chapter in 1914. The chief newspaper for the community was the *Japanese American Commercial Weekly (Nichi-Bei Shuho)*, published from 1901 to 1925. After the passage of the federal National Origins Act of 1924, which barred Japanese immigration and limited other visas, the New York City community gradually changed shape. The *Japanese American Commercial Weekly* newspaper was succeeded by the *Japanese American (Nichi-Bei Jiho)*, published from 1924 to 1941. Affluent Issei spread to suburbs such as Scarsdale and New Rochelle (Westchester Co) and to Long Island. As New York City became a dominant global cultural center, students and intellectuals, such as Ministers Toru Matsumoto and Alfred Akamatsu, writer Bunji Omura, and activist Haru Matsui, migrated to the metropolis. In addition some 100 Japanese artists, including Yasuo Kuniyoshi, Eitaro Ishigaki, and Taro Yashima, worked in New York City during the interwar years. Meanwhile New York State became home to an outstanding Nisei (American-born) population, including sculptor Isamu Noguchi, entertainer Sono Osato, journalists Tooru Kanazawa and Larry Tajiri, lawyer George Yamaoka, sociologist T. Scott Miyakawa, memoirist Kathleen Tamagawa, and poet Kikuko Miyakawa. Community institutions evolved to serve the Nisei. In 1930 Japanese Association leaders sponsored the all-Nisei Tozei Club. The following year the *Japanese American* began an English language section, which split off in 1939 to become the *Japanese American Review.*

The coming of World War II transformed New York State's Japanese community. In the months before Pearl Harbor, the Japanese consulate in New York City and Japanese businesses throughout the state began to shut down; in mid-1941 the Japanese American Committee for Democracy (JACD), an antifascist group, was formed in New York City. Once war broke out, all Japanese-owned businesses were shut down statewide and the Nippon Club was seized and sold off. Issei community leaders were interned at Ellis Island. Although there was no mass incarceration of Japanese Americans in New York State during the war, as occurred in the states of the Pacific Coast, there were incidents of discrimination. Mayor Fiorello La Guardia refused to allow Japanese Americans to participate in a New York City–wide victory parade in 1942, and many businesses refused to hire Japanese Americans. Nevertheless, New York State's ethnic Japanese found ways to prove their loyalty. Japanese writers and translators joined the federal Office of War Information. JACD activists organized bond rallies and blood drives. Dozens of Nisei volunteered for the US armed forces. New York State's Japanese Americans also volunteered to assist a wave of Japanese Americans resettling from the camps to find housing or jobs. The new arrivals included such standouts as artist-writer Miné Okubo, activist Yuri Kochiyama, and dancer Yuriko Amemiya. In 1944 when the federal War Relocation Authority announced plans to open a hostel in Brooklyn to house resettled Japanese Americans and La Guardia publicly expressed his opposition, dozens of liberal groups responded by forming a citizens' committee that successfully championed resettlement. Outside New York City charitable and church groups sponsored internees, and the War Relocation Authority opened offices in Rochester and Buffalo to assist resettlers, who took jobs ranging from nursing to dairy farming.

New York State's ethnic Japanese population slowly increased during and after World War II. While many community members, mainly wartime resettlers, migrated west, others remained in New York City or took up residence in diverse areas of the state; for example, activist Toshi Ohta Seeger moved to Beacon (Dutchess Co), architect Minoru Yamasaki, the future designer of the World Trade Center, settled in Larchmont (Westchester Co), and writer Lydia Minatoya grew up in Albany. After Japanese immigration was relegalized in 1952 a small number of Japanese, including artist-singer Yoko Ono, settled in New York City. More followed after federal Asian immigration quotas were abolished in 1965, and the state's Japanese communities again became dominated by immigrants. Many Japanese settled in suburbs as well as in Riverdale (Bronx Co) and the East Village in Manhattan. By 2000 the US Census listed 37,279 people of Japanese ancestry in New York State, about 5% of the state's ethnic Asian population, of whom somewhat over half lived in New York City.

Hosler, Akiko S. *Japanese Immigrant Entrepreneurs in New York City: A New Wave of Ethnic Business* (New York: Garland Publishing, 1998)

Sawada, Mitziko. *Tokyo Dreams, New York Nights: Urban Japanese Visions of America, 1890–1924* (Berkeley: Univ of California Press, 1996)

Greg Robinson

Jasper. Town (pop 1,270) in SW Steuben Co. Settled in 1807, the town was formed in 1827 from Canisteo and Troupsburg. Lumbering was succeeded by dairying when the timber stands were exhausted. In the mid–20th century Jasper was the second-largest milk-producing town in Steuben Co, and dairy farming remains the predominant land use in the early 21st century. In the 1990s an Amish farming community noted for woodworking and quilting settled in Jasper. The Wigwams Museum, an idiosyncratic building constructed by George Countryman in the 1930s to house his Indian artifact collection, is maintained by the Jasper Historical Society.

Virginia L. Wright and Jerry Wright

Java [JAY-VAH]. Town (pop 2,222) in SW Wyoming Co. Settled in 1809, the town was formed from China [now Arcade] in 1832. The first Irish came in 1829, and by 1880 more than half the town was of Irish birth or parentage. The Tonawanda Valley and Cuba Railroad (1880; later the Buffalo, Attica and Arcade) provided a rail link. Duoform Medicine Co manufactured patent medicines in town from 1912 to 1918. Java Lake was developed as a resort in 1928. In the 1940s Java was home to Ed Don George, the world heavyweight wrestling champion. In the early 21st century, the town's primary enterprise remains dairy farming. Small shops produce screwdrivers (Farrant Screw Machine Products, 1968), wooden doors, and foundry work. The Beaver Meadow Audubon Center (324 acres/131 ha) is in Java. A mastodon was unearthed in 2001 while a pond was being dug.

Javits, Jacob K(oppel) (*b* New York City, 18 May 1904; *d* Palm Beach, Fla, 7 Mar 1986). Politician. The son of Jewish immigrants, Javits worked as a traveling salesman before enrolling in law school at New York University. He graduated in 1926 and joined his brother's law practice until service in World War II. Javits's military experiences inspired him to deal more directly with social problems, and he turned to politics. He was elected to the first of four consecutive terms in the House of Representatives in 1946, representing Manhattan's Upper West Side. Javits, with a socialist upbringing and an overwhelmingly Democratic district, was more liberal than most of his Republican colleagues, especially on domestic issues. He enjoyed unusually strong support from unions for voting against the Taft-Hartley bill in 1947 and favoring increases in the minimum wage. Javits also expressed concern that anticommunist investigations by the House Committee on Un-American Activities constituted grave threats to civil liberties. Javits won election as New York State attorney general in 1954 and to the US Senate in 1956. There, too, he acquired a reputation as a liberal Republican for his support of civil rights, labor, federal aid to the arts, healthcare, and antipoverty programs. In 1964 he joined several other liberal Republicans in refusing to endorse Barry Goldwater, the party's archconservative presidential nominee. Though he was an early supporter of US involvement in Vietnam, Javits grew critical of the war and played a leading role in drafting the War Powers Act of 1973. A staunch friend of Israel, he was also involved in Middle East peace negotiations in the late 1970s. Javits's political career ended in 1980 when, already in declining health, he lost in the Republican primary to conservative Alfonse D'Amato and then lost in the fall election while running on the Liberal Party ticket. Javits subsequently taught at Columbia University's School of International Affairs.

Javits, Jacob K., with Rafael Steinberg. *Javits: The Autobiography of a Public Man* (Boston: Houghton Mifflin, 1981)
MacKown, Craig, and Arnold Bortz. *Jacob K. Javits: Republican Senator from New York* (Washington, DC: Grossman Publishers, 1972)

Timothy N. Thurber

Jaws. A 1974 novel by Peter Benchley adapted into a 1975 film by Steven Spielberg. Benchley's popular book finds Sheriff Martin Brody, a former New York City police officer, in a struggle of human versus monster as residents of Amity, a fictional summer beach community located on Long Island's South Shore, are preyed upon by a 25 ft (8 m) shark. Universal Studios optioned the screenplay and entrusted it to the young director Steven Spielberg. Universal's gamble paid off: the film earned $100 million within six months of its release on 30 June 1975. With the aid of an ichthyologist (Richard Dreyfuss) and a professional fisher (Robert Shaw), Brody (Roy Scheider) is pressed to hunt down the shark, after the ineffective mayor has disregarded public safety, leading to a handful of deaths. Though Universal planned on filming in Sag Harbor (Suffolk Co), the studio worried that the location would be overrun with tourists during the summer months and settled instead with Edgartown in Martha's Vineyard, Mass, though the film convincingly re-created Benchley's conceived geographic locale.

Gottlieb, Carl. *The Jaws Log* (New York: Dell Publishing, 1975)

Matt Kirsch

Jay. Town (pop 2,306) in N Essex Co. Settled in 1796 the town was formed in 1798 from Willsboro. In the same year the first forge was established at Lower Jay, one of the first interior Adirondack settlements; later the hamlets of Au Sable Forks and Jay were centers of ironworks and mills. Lumbering operations and boardinghouses were scattered through the town. The J. and J. Rogers Co operated ironworks, including a rolling mill and nail factory, at Au Sable Forks (Essex and Clinton Cos) beginning in 1870. The firm converted the mill to pulp and paper manufacturing; 250 jobs were lost when it closed in 1966. Jay was the site of the Land of Make Believe (1952–70) amusement park and of Asgaard Farm, home of artist Rockwell Kent. In the 1960s, prior to the enactment of subdivision restrictions, a large recreational development, Ausable Acres (now known as Timberland), was created in the northeast part of town. Tourism in the early 21st century dominates the economy, with some lumbering and quarrying of granite.

Thomas A. Rumney

Jay, John (*b* New York City, 12 Dec 1745; *d* Bedford, Westchester Co, 17 May 1829). First chief justice of US Supreme Court, diplomat, and governor. Educated at King's College (now Columbia University), Jay graduated in 1764, trained in the law office of loyalist Benjamin Kissam, and was admitted to the bar in 1768. There was little sign that the strife that began with the Stamp Act (1765) would catapult him to the forefront of American leadership. His personal background seemed to point him toward the British, and he appeared content to practice law. Nevertheless, he joined such figures as Robert R. Livingston, whose cousin Sarah he married, in what might be described either as the radical wing of the old elite or the conservative wing of the revolutionary leadership. Their stance toward Britain was militant; their concern, in the face of rising popular radicalism, was to thwart what they saw as a serious challenge to the power and the property of their own sort.

Jay accepted independence reluctantly but led the committee given the vital task of drafting a new state constitution, which was adopted in 1777. The document he produced provided a strong governorship, an independent state senate elected by substantial property holders, and property requirements for voting for the new state assembly. Perhaps reflecting Jay's Huguenot and Dutch Calvinist heritage, the new constitution also contained a veiled attack on Catholicism, though not an outright exclusion of Catholics from voting or holding office.

Jay became chief justice of the supreme court of New York State in 1777 but left after two years for service in Congress, including its presidency. Congress sent him to Spain as informal American minister, where he endured great frustration from the Spanish government's refusal to recognize him or the United States. He joined Benjamin Franklin and John Adams in Paris to negotiate the treaty of 1783 making peace with Britain. Returning home, he became secretary for foreign affairs, holding the office until Thomas Jefferson became secretary of state in 1790. He also joined the New York Manumission Society, founded in 1784.

A supporter of the movement that led to the federal constitution, Jay wrote five of the eighty-five essays of "The Federalist" series. George Washington appointed him as the first chief justice of the US Supreme Court, a post he held concurrently with the foreign secretaryship until Jefferson arrived from France. Jay returned to diplomacy once more, when Washington sent him to London to negotiate a new treaty with Britain. Jay's Treaty of 1795 was the result.

Jay was the Federalist candidate for governor in 1792, and he apparently did win the vote, only to lose after the totals in some counties were challenged. He was elected governor in 1795, however, and reelected in 1798. In 1800, when Jeffersonians won the state legislature and the right to choose New York's presidential electors, Jay scornfully rejected a suggestion from Alexander Hamilton that he convene the outgoing Federalist legislature so that it could choose the electors and keep Jefferson from the presidency. When Jay left the governorship in 1801 his public career ended. His wife died the same year, and he lived as a quiet widower in Westchester Co until his own death in 1829.

Johnson, Herbert A. *John Jay, Colonial Lawyer* (New York: Garland Publishing, 1989)
Morris, Richard B. *John Jay, the Nation, and the Court* (Boston: Boston Univ Press, 1967)
Morris, Richard B., et al, eds. *John Jay: The Making of a Revolutionary* (New York: Harper & Row, 1975)

Edward Countryman

Jay's Treaty. First American pact to arouse domestic dissent. In 1795 Pres George Washington sent Chief Justice John Jay to London to resolve issues left over from the settlement of the American Revolution. These included the presence of British troops on American soil along the Canadian boundary and issues that had emerged from Britain's war against revolutionary France, such as Franco-American trade and the impressment into the Royal Navy of "British" seafarers from American vessels. Jay secured withdrawal of the troops. He did not, however, win recognition of American neutral rights, and he gave up the American right to retaliate against British commerce for 10 years. Democratic-Republican opponents of the treaty and Federalist supporters of it launched campaigns of public meetings and mass petitions. Despite the opposition the treaty took effect.

Combs, Jerald A. *The Jay Treaty: Political Battleground of the Founding Fathers* (Berkeley: Univ of California Press, 1970)

Edward Countryman

jazz. A distinctively American musical genre created through the amalgamation of African American musical traditions, various forms of popular music, and the diverse personal styles of individual performers. Rooted in the blues and other folk music forms but expressed primarily through band and orchestral instruments of European origin, jazz represents a dynamic mixture of musical tradition and innovation. It places particular emphasis on improvisation and personal expression, and therefore on live performance. During the early development of jazz, this emphasis on live performance brought the most talented jazz musicians to the entertainment districts of a number of major cities, most importantly New Orleans, Chicago, Kansas City, and New York City, and they became focal points in the evolution and dissemination of jazz as an American art form. New York City became especially significant in this context, and since the 1920s it has been widely recognized as the jazz capital of the world. It serves as a key center of innovation in the genre, as the most important locale for jazz performance and recording, and as a proving ground for new musicians. Although New York City has a number of important native jazz musicians, the most important New Yorkers in jazz came to the city as adults, including Louis Armstrong (1901–71), Duke Ellington (1899–1974), Charlie Parker (1920–55), Miles Davis (1926–91), and Ornette Coleman (1930–).

Early Jazz and Swing

Although much of the early development of jazz took place primarily among musicians in New Orleans and Chicago, some elements of the new genre began to gain popularity in New York City prior to World War I. Syncopated dance music, which in its rhythmic accents shared much in common with jazz, became highly fashionable during the 1910s and appeared in dance halls, cabarets, and restaurants. The African American composer and bandleader James Reese Europe (1881–1919) played a major role in the popularization of this music through the Harlem performances of his Club Clef Orchestra and later with the 369th Infantry "Hellfighters" Band, a group composed of members of an African American regiment. During World War I the band introduced jazz to France. Around the same time the growing popularity of jazz in New York City made it an increasingly important destination for touring jazz bands from New Orleans, Chicago, and elsewhere. The Original Dixieland Jazz Band, a group of white musicians from New Orleans, opened a sensational engagement at Reisenweber's Restaurant, just south of Manhattan's Columbus Circle, in January 1917. Shortly thereafter they made the first jazz recording for Columbia Records. An instant success, the recording sold over 1 million copies and marked the beginning of New York City's dominance of the jazz recording industry. The rambunctious piano style known as Harlem Stride, which was the first important New York jazz style, emerged from ragtime around the same time. Its major figures—James P. Johnson (1894–1955), Willie "the Lion" Smith (1897–1971), and Fats Waller (1904–43)—were all from the New York City metropolitan area.

By the 1920s New York City was becoming the primary center of jazz performance. The vast migration of African Americans to New York City during the early 20th century created a substantial following for African American music, particularly in Harlem, where African American arts were flourishing. Blues singers such as Mamie Smith (1883–1946), Ethel Waters (1896–1977), and Bessie Smith (1894–1937) attracted large followings and sold many records. African American musical revues generally had a jazz flavor, and in the 1920s, from Eubie Blake's (1883–1983) *Shuffle Along* (1921) to Fats Waller's *Hot Chocolates* (1929), they became a staple of New York City's popular theater scene. New York City also served as the primary center for music publishing, recording, and radio broadcasting, all elements of the music industry's expanding infrastructure. The city's cosmopolitan audience, which was particularly open to new forms of artistic expression, provided significant support for music and the arts.

These developments, along with the continued popularity of jazz as dance music, created a vibrant musical scene in New York City, where jazz musicians found large audiences, abundant performance opportunities, and high salaries. As a result, top players such as Louis Armstrong and Bix Beiderbecke (1903–31) moved to New York from Chicago, the leading northern jazz city before 1920. Fueled by this infusion of talent, the rising popularity of jazz was accompanied by the establishment of new clubs and ballrooms. Harlem became the focus of these developments with the founding of the Cotton Club (1922), the Savoy Ballroom (1926), and countless other performance venues. As young jazz musicians moved into Harlem, after-hours jam sessions in the smaller clubs became a proving ground where they could test their skills against better-known players.

During the 1920s and early 1930s, a number of key figures in jazz achieved prominence within the dynamic atmosphere of Harlem's clubs and of venues like Roseland Ballroom in Midtown Manhattan. The first significant jazz big band was that of Fletcher Henderson (1897–1952), whose orchestra performed regularly at the Roseland Ballroom starting in 1924. Henderson and his arranger, Don Redman (1900–1964), established many of the musical conventions of big-band jazz. Henderson's band featured a series of important musicians, including Coleman Hawkins (1904–69) and Louis Armstrong, who first came to New York City to play with Henderson. Armstrong's dynamic sense of swing transformed the Henderson band, and New York City jazz, during his stint with the band (1924–25). In 1929 Armstrong left Chicago and returned to New York City, which thereafter remained his home. His influential recordings in the late 1920s and early 1930s largely created what would be the swing era synthesis of jazz treatments of pop standards. In the early 1940s he moved to Corona in Queens (where the Louis Armstrong House and Archives opened as a museum in 2003).

Other significant figures in big-band jazz in New York City included Rochester-born Cab Calloway (1907–94), whose orchestra had a long tenure at the Cotton Club in the early 1930s. Jimmie Lunceford (1902–47) and Chick Webb (1909–39) also led influential bands that helped introduce the swing style to New Yorkers. Webb, whose band held a long residency at the Savoy Ballroom, first brought Ella Fitzgerald (1918–96) to the public's attention by employing her as his featured singer. Count Basie (1904–84), a key figure in the development of swing in Kansas City, Mo, significantly expanded his popularity after moving to New York City in 1937, where he introduced a more propulsive vocabulary of swing. A member of the Basie band, Lester Young (1909–59) introduced a highly influential smoother style of playing the tenor saxophone. His playing was featured, along with other soloists, on the recordings of Billie Holiday (1915–59), the most important swing era jazz singer. Holiday moved to New York City from her native Baltimore in 1928 and made her first recordings at age 18 in 1933. Native New Yorker Benny Carter (1907–2003) was another important swing era bandleader. He made his first recordings in the 1920s and remained active into the early 21st century.

White musicians also played an influential role in making New York a center of jazz. Paul Whiteman (1890–1967), although considered by many to be more of a jazz-influenced performer than a bona fide jazz artist, led the most popular jazz orchestra of the time. In 1924 he commissioned and debuted George Gershwin's (1898–1937) *Rhapsody in Blue* at the Aeolian Hall at 29 West 42d St. The same year, the midwestern band the Wolverines introduced trumpeter Bix Beiderbecke to New York City audiences at the Cinderella Ballroom. Beiderbecke later played with Whiteman.

The most significant swing era bandleader was Duke Ellington, a native of Washington, DC, who came to New York City in the early 1920s. In the late 1920s and early 1930s, his orchestra performed regularly at the Cotton Club and made a number of seminal recordings. Ellington and his sidemen, such as Johnny Hodges (1907–70), Cootie Williams (1911–85), and Barney Bigard (1906–80), established new standards of musicianship, composition, and arrangement for jazz big bands. The early 1940s are often cited as the pinnacle of Ellington's career. His orchestra was unmatched in its sheer virtuosity. Ellington and his close collaborator Billy Strayhorn (1915–67) penned their most important compositions during this period. These included "Ko-Ko," "Harlem Air Shaft," and Ellington theme song and New York City anthem, "Take the A Train." In 1943 Ellington debuted his first, and probably his most important, extended piece, "Black, Brown, and Beige," in the first of a series of annual concerts at Carnegie Hall. He continued to compose and tour until his death. The influential swing bandleader Benny Goodman (1909–86) played a central role in making jazz more acceptable to a wider audience, especially with his landmark 1938 concert at Carnegie Hall, which featured his own group as well as guest soloists from the Ellington and Basie bands. Other significant swing era musicians associated with New York City included trumpeters Bunny Berigan (1908–42) and Roy Eldridge (1911–89), vibraphonist Lionel Hampton (1908–2002), and tenor saxophonist Coleman Hawkins, who made his famous recording of "Body and Soul" upon his return to New York City in 1939 after an extended stay in Europe.

Bebop and Hard Bop

The rise of swing also coincided with the growth of Manhattan's 52d St as a key entertainment district. By the late 1930s numerous small clubs (most in the block between 5th and 6th Aves), began to replace Harlem's clubs and ballrooms as the city's center for jazz performance. Venues such as the Onyx Club, the Famous Door, the Three Deuces, and the Hickory House served as primary outlets for bringing leading swing musicians before a large, cosmopolitan audience. Because these clubs could not easily accommodate big bands, they most often presented smaller ensembles of swing musicians. Still, they became strongly associated with the swing style of jazz, and 52d St came to be known by the nickname of Swing Street. The rise of small-group jazz coincided with the growing commercialization of the swing style of jazz. One response to this was Dixieland revival, in which musicians, many of them based in New York City including Pee Wee Russell (1906–69) and Eddie Condon (1905–75), played in a manner that harkened back to jazz styles of the 1920s.

Younger musicians who felt that swing did not provide them with an adequate creative outlet by the early 1940s embarked on a reinterpretation of jazz tradition, working out new approaches to rhythm, harmony, melody, and improvisation in the form of bebop. One of bebop's original appeals to young musicians derived in part from its difficulty, which challenged players and listeners alike. After-hours clubs in Harlem, particularly Minton's Playhouse and Clarke Monroe's Uptown House, provided the context in which bebop emerged during the early 1940s. The central figure in its creation was the Kansas City alto saxophonist Charlie Parker, who moved to New York City around 1942. His style of playing, daring in its harmonies and performed with improvisational bravura, soon found its admirers. Parker's life was cut short by his heroin habit, but he was among the most influential of all modern jazz players. Close to Parker in his influence was trumpeter Dizzy Gillespie (1917–93), who played with him in small groups of the mid-1940s and thereafter led his own groups and big band.

Many other important bebop figures either were native to New York City, such as pianist Bud Powell (1924–66), alto saxophonist Jackie McLean (1932–), and tenor saxophonist Sonny Rollins (1930–), or moved to the city at a very early age, such as pianist Thelonious Monk (1917–82) and drummer Max Roach (1924–). By the mid-1940s, bebop began to appear in the jazz clubs on 52d St in Manhattan, where it captured an even larger audience. Recordings of the new style of jazz were popular, and bebop became the founding movement in modern jazz. In response to its popularity, a number of new clubs specifically associated with bebop were established along Broadway near 52d St, including Bop City, the Royal Roost (which displayed the nickname "the Metropolitan Bopera House" on its awning), and Birdland (which was named in honor of Charlie "Bird" Parker).

The diversity of musical influences in New York City contributed significantly to modern jazz's ongoing process of innovation and continued as its premier center of performance and recording. The growing Latino and Cuban presence in New York City contributed to the Afro-Cuban style of jazz, which brought together elements of bebop and Latin American music. Best-known examples are the collaborations of Dizzy Gillespie and Cuban drummer Chano Pozo (1915–48), who performed together in a landmark concert at Carnegie Hall in 1947. By the late 1940s and early 1950s, some jazz musicians also began to turn away from some of the more ebullient sides of bebop and toward more subdued textures. This new "cool" style of jazz was most strongly associated with the West Coast, but New York City musicians contributed to its development as well. While the 1949 "Birth of the Cool" session with trumpeter Miles Davis and other New York City jazz musicians helped introduce the style, as did the recordings of pianist Lennie Tristano (1919–78), the longest lasting and most influential exemplar of this style was the Modern Jazz Quartet. Led by vibraphonist Milt Jackson (1923–99) and pianist John Lewis (1920–2001), the quartet emerged in the early 1950s as a major proponent of the cool style and a leader in efforts to incorporate elements of classical music into jazz.

New York City remained the focus of developments within the mainstream of modern jazz, exemplified by the hard bop style of the 1950s and 1960s, which transformed bebop through its use of darker and earthier styles of playing and its greater reliance on African American folk music rather than on the popular song. Prominent exponents of hard bop included pianist Horace Silver (1928–), and drummer Art Blakey (1919–90); Blakey led the Jazz Messengers through a variety of changing ensembles. Miles Davis, who moved to New York City in 1944, also extended the lessons of bop. He led his ensembles through a variety of different styles from the 1950s through the early 1990s. Bassist Charles Mingus (1922–79) was another protean composer and post-bebop experimenter who made a number of significant midsize ensemble recordings in the 1950s and 1960s.

As the 1960s progressed the nationwide audience for jazz began to decline as rock and roll and rhythm and blues emerged as dominant forms of American popular music. This trend actually reinforced the importance of New York City as the capital of jazz, however, because it continued to accommodate the greatest opportunities for jazz musicians. The declining popularity of jazz was reflected in the relocation of the center of jazz performance by the late 1950s to Lower Manhattan around Greenwich Village, where a diverse, bohemian culture thrived. This was music for listening, not for dancing. There, clubs like the Five Spot, the Half Note, the Jazz Gallery, the Village Gate, and the venerable Village Vanguard featured the leading jazz musicians. Technological improvements had significantly increased the quality of live recordings by this time, and these clubs also served as venues for a large number of historic jazz recordings.

Free Jazz and Beyond

In 1959 the free jazz scene was inaugurated in New York City at the Five Spot by a performance of tenor saxophonist Ornette Coleman, whose controversial style aroused opposition but also spawned many followers. Among the most prominent figures on the New York City free jazz scene in the early 1960s were saxophonists Eric Dolphy (1928–64) and saxophonist Albert Ayler (1936–70); pianist Cecil Taylor (1929–), a native of New York City; and saxophonist John Coltrane (1926–67), undoubtedly the most influential musician in this idiom. During the late 1960s and 1970s, an important jazz community also emerged in the so-called loft scene in Lower Manhattan, which provided an outlet for a new generation of musicians experimenting in free jazz. Studio Rivbea, established by saxophonist Sam Rivers (1930–) in Manhattan's SoHo district, was an especially important venue for avant-garde jazz.

Since the early 1980s jazz has undergone a renaissance of sorts during which both traditional and experimental forms of the music have found new audiences, and New York City has again played a key role in this process. Jazz festivals and older jazz clubs like the Village Vanguard have become major tourist destinations, and various new clubs have sprung up, including the Blue Note, a revitalized Birdland, Iridium, Smalls, and the Knitting Factory. New York City also remains an important center of innovation in the early 21st century. The M-BASE movement, centered in Brooklyn and led by saxophonist Steve Coleman (1956–), has brought together a collective of jazz musicians concerned with new conceptual approaches based on a variety of African and African American musical structures. Similarly, the eclectic "downtown" music scene in Lower Manhattan has continued to attract musicians interested in the avant-garde and the fusion of jazz with other musical forms. At the same time, the jazz tradition has taken on an institutional presence in New York City through Jazz at Lincoln Center, the world's largest not-for-profit jazz organization. Under music director Wynton Marsalis (1961–), the Lincoln Center Jazz Orchestra has promoted jazz as an American art form through its repertory of the classic works of jazz's greatest composers and musicians.

Jazz Elsewhere in New York State

While the rest of the state cannot rival New York City as a jazz center, its contributions have not been negligible. The Glen Island Casino in New Rochelle (Westchester Co) in the 1930s and 1940s hosted important engagements by mainstream swing big bands, including Benny Goodman and Glenn Miller (1904–44). Soprano saxophonist Sidney Bechet (1897–1959) had several extended stays at the Log Cabin in Fonda (Montgomery Co) in the late 1930s, where he made recordings that heralded the Dixieland revival. The Van Dyck of Schenectady showcased top musicians beginning in 1947. Rochester's Pythodd club in the 1950s and 1960s was a center for touring hard bop performers. Buffalo's notable jazz clubs included the Colored Musicians Club and the Anchor Bar. Saratoga Springs (since 1978), Syracuse (since 1983), and Rochester (since 2002) continue to have popular annual jazz festivals in the early 21st century. Jazz musicians raised in New York State outside of New York City include bassist Scott LaFaro (1936–61) of Geneva (Ontario Co), drummer Mel Lewis (1929–90) and saxophonist Grover Washington Jr (1943–99) of Buffalo, clarinetist Michael "Peanuts" Hucko (1918–2003) and singer Mark Murphy (1932–) of Syracuse, saxophonist Nick Brignola (1936–2002) of Troy, arranger Johnny Richards (1911–68) of Schenectady, and brothers and bandleaders Chuck (1940–) and Gap (1938–) Mangione of Rochester.

Balliett, Whitney. *Collected Works: A Journal of Jazz, 1954–2000* (St. Martin's Press, 2000)

Charters, Samuel Barclay, and Leonard Kunstadt. *Jazz: A History of the New York Scene* (1962; repr Cambridge, Mass: Da Capo Press, 2000)

DeVeaux, Scott Knowles. *The Birth of Bebop: A Social and Musical History* (Berkeley: Univ of California Press, 1997)

Giddins, Gary. *Visions of Jazz: The First Century* (New York: Oxford Univ Press, 2000)

Gitler, Ira. *Swing to Bop: An Oral History of the Transition in Jazz in the 1940s* (New York: Oxford Univ Press, 1985)

Haskins, James. *The Cotton Club* (New York: Hippocrene Books, 1994)

Kernfeld, Barry, ed. *New Grove Dictionary of Jazz* (New York: St. Martin's Press, 1994)

Litweiler, John. *The Freedom Principle: Jazz after 1958* (New York: Morrow, 1984)
Ostransky, Leroy. *Jazz City: The Impact of Our Cities on the Development of Jazz* (Englewood Cliffs, NJ: Prentice-Hall, 1978)
Shaw, Arnold. *The Street That Never Slept: New York's Fabled 52nd Street* (New York: Coward, McCann and Geoghegan, 1971)

Roger W. Stump

Jefferson. Town (pop 1,285) in SW Schoharie Co. Settled in 1794 by New Englanders who left their mark with a village green in the hamlet of Jefferson, the town was formed from Blenheim and Harpersfield [now in Delaware Co] in 1803. Most of Jefferson is hilly upland; a high ridge passing through the center of the town forms the watershed between the Delaware and Mohawk Rivers. Scotch Valley (1962–98) was a ski area on Bald Mountain. In the early 21st century, agriculture, primarily dairying, is the principal economic activity. Vacation homes owned by urban dwellers dot the landscape.

Peter Johnson and Dawn Johnson

Jefferson County (1,272 mi²/3,294 km²; pop 111,738). Created in 1805 from Oneida Co and named after Thomas Jefferson. In 1808 territory was surrendered to and in 1810 and 1813 annexed from Lewis Co. Jefferson Co is subdivided into 1 city, Watertown (the county seat), and 22 towns that contain 20 incorporated villages. Elevation ranges from approximately 250 feet (76 m) along the St. Lawrence River to 1,723 feet (525 m) on an unnamed Tug Hill summit in the southeast corner of the Town of Worth. The county's shoreline with Lake Ontario and the St. Lawrence River, including various offshore islands, extends for over 150 miles (240 km).

Jefferson Co straddles three major physiographic provinces. The western Adirondack Hills subregion of the Adirondack Upland stretches across the northeastern portion of the county and the nearby St. Lawrence River islands. Bedrock here consists of highly resistant Precambrian gneiss, granite, and marble, and is part of the Frontenac Arch that links the Adirondack Upland with the Canadian Shield across the river and forms the Thousand Islands. It is exposed in places to form roche moutonnées (sheepback rocks). The Eastern Ontario Hills and the Black River Valley lie immediately to the southwest. Together these areas occupy the bulk of the county's territory and are subregions of the Erie-Ontario Lowland physiographic province. Elevations lie between 250 feet (76 m) in the north and west to over 700 feet (210 m) near Carthage. Local relief is modest. Bedrock, often covered by just a thin layer of soil, consists of Devonian limestone and dolostone. The Tug Hill Plateau, composed largely of Devonian shale and sandstone, rises sharply and occupies the county's southeast corner. Streams have cut 100–250 ft (30–76 m) deep narrow channels (locally referred to as gulfs) that run for a mile or more down the slope of the escarpment. Jefferson Co was covered by the Laurentide ice sheet as evidenced by a layer of glacial till, by groves (striations) cut into the bedrock by the advancing ice, and by drumlins south of Watertown. The ice retreated only about 10,000 years ago.

Jefferson Co lies entirely within the Lake Ontario and St. Lawrence River watersheds. Aside from the St. Lawrence, which serves as the county's northern boundary, the Black River is by far the most important stream. Flowing from east to west across the county's middle, the waters of the Black powered dozens of mills that served as nuclei for a string of villages and the City of Watertown. Other important streams include the Indian River, which drains most of the northeast quarter of the county, and Sandy and South Sandy Creeks, which drain most of the south. Soil quality ranges from scattered areas of highly arable land capable of supporting modern agriculture, especially dairy farming, to lands that offer no agricultural potential, such as those of Fort Drum and much of the Tug Hill.

Jefferson Co's climate is humid-continental. Mean January temperatures range from approximately 20°F (-7°C) in the southwest to around 16°F (-9°C) in the northeast. Below 0°F (-18°C) temperatures are an important part of every winter. Mean July temperatures hover between 68° and 70°F (20–21°C) depending on elevation. Daytime highs reach or exceed 90°F (32°C) a few times each summer in the lower elevations, less often on the Tug Hill. Annual precipitation varies sharply from less than 35 inches (90 cm) at Watertown to nearly 60 inches (150 cm) on the upper sections of the Tug Hill Plateau. Seasonal snowfall ranges from less than 70 inches (178 cm) along parts of the St. Lawrence to 200 or more inches (508 cm) in the Towns of Rutland, Rodman, and Worth. Single storms can drop over 100 inches (254 cm) of snow on Watertown and areas to the south over the course of three or four days. With the exception of scattered areas of wetland forest and some limited areas of oak-hickory forest along the shore of Lake Ontario, the county's primeval forest cover was composed of northern hardwoods. An Adirondack hardwood community dominated by beech, sugar maple, yellow birch, hemlock, and white pine, mixed with red spruce and balsam fir, covered the Tug Hill country and most of the northeast. The remaining area was blanketed by an Alleghenian hardwood community dominated by beech, sugar maple, hemlock, white pine, and basswood. At the present time approximately half the county is covered by second- or third-growth forest.

AMERICAN INDIANS AND EARLY SETTLEMENT

Archaeological evidence indicates that there has been human habitation in what is now Jefferson Co for 12,000 years. Diverse sites, perhaps hundreds of them, represent a wide variety of cultures including the Point Peninsula (AD 350–500) and Pillar Point (AD 1000–1200). By AD 1200 the area was inhabited by the St. Lawrence Iroquois, a group related to the Neutral and Huron in Ontario and to the Five Nations Iroquois. It is estimated that there were as many as 55 St. Lawrence Iroquois village sites in the county's land area, although only a few were occupied at any one time. European diseases, warfare, and dislocation are named as causes of the disappearance of these people by 1580. The area then became hunting grounds for the Oneida and was part of the territory ceded to the United States at Fort Schuyler in 1788.

Except for the small, disputed Penet's Square tract, the county was part of Macomb Purchase (1791), which was divided into large tracts for sale to speculators. They included James Le Ray de Chaumont, a member of the family that housed Benjamin Franklin in Paris during the American Revolution; Peter Chassanis, Le Ray's brother-in-law, as agent for the Castorland colony planned as a refuge for French émigrés; and Thomas Boylston, who bought 817,155

JEFFERSON CO POPULATION CENSUS FIGURES

	White	Nonwhite	Total Population	Foreign-Born
1810	15,100	40	15,140	—
1820	32,812	140	32,952	787
1830	48,354	139	48,493	1,306
1840	60,843	141	60,984	—
1850	67,962	191	68,153	4,556
1860	69,616	209	69,825	9,270
1870	65,178	237	65,415	10,036
1880	65,888	215	66,103	8,788
1890	68,562	244	68,806	10,013
1900	76,521	227	76,748	11,739
1910	80,099	283	80,382	12,828
1920	82,097	153	82,250	11,410
1930	83,373	201	83,574	10,246
1940	83,858	145	84,003	8,027
1950	85,351	170	85,521	6,528
1960	87,483	352	87,835	5,057
1970	88,074	434	88,508	3,277
1980	87,318	833	88,151	2,910
1990	101,154	9,789	110,943	3,146
2000	99,118	12,620	111,738	4,116

Notes: "Nonwhite" includes African Americans, Asians, American Indians, and Pacific Islanders and, for 2000, also the mixed race and other race categories. Through the 1960 census these figures primarily reflect the African American population. Foreign-born figures for 1820 and 1830 include only those not naturalized, and for 1930 and 1950, the foreign-born totals include Whites only. Other years include all foreign-born in the population.

acres (330,691 ha) in Jefferson and Lewis Cos that became known as the Black River tract.

European settlement, begun in 1794 by the Castorland Co at Long Falls [now Carthage], was centered in the Black River valley. By 1810 there were 15,143 people in Jefferson Co. The number more than doubled in the following decade, and by 1850 the population reached 68,153. The earliest settlers were New Englanders from Vermont and Connecticut. Quakers from Pennsylvania settled in Philadelphia and Orleans. Le Ray's European marketing efforts brought French and Swiss settlers, especially to Cape Vincent. Palatine Germans migrated from the Mohawk Valley. Francophone Canadians arrived after the Canadian Rebellion (1837–42). There were 40 African Americans (22 enslaved, 18 free) in the county in 1810. Their numbers grew to 247 during the War of 1812, then leveled off at about 150.

Economic Development

Subsistence farming and manufacturing for local consumption were the basis of the economy in the early years. Potash, the first cash export, was shipped down the St. Lawrence River to Montreal. Dependence upon the river for transport created a strong economic bond between Jefferson Co and Canada. With the Embargo Act (1807), smuggling became endemic. When the War of 1812 cut off Canadian markets, textile manufacturing took up much of the slack. In the north and east, the iron industry flourished for several years with mines in Antwerp and Philadelphia, and production in Philadelphia and Carthage. Shipbuilding was important along Lake Ontario and the St. Lawrence River for most of the century. In 1825 there were 55 gristmills, 98 sawmills, 33 distilleries, 139 asheries, 27 carding machines, 27 fulling mills, 4 cotton and woolen manufactories, 3 forges, 1 furnace, and 10 trip-hammers.

The dairy industry began in 1834 when John A. Sherman acquired a dairy herd from Canada to make cheese. Cheese making soon became a major industry; Limburger was first made in the United States in Rodman in 1853. In 1861 the county's first cooperative cheese factory was opened, and by 1870 there were 70 such factories. The Watertown Cheese Board was opened in 1874 and for many years sold nearly 9 million pounds (4.1 million kg) of cheese annually, with daily sales up to $200,000. Buyers came from across the country. The market disbanded around 1920, when fluid-milk production became dominant over cheese making. Raising hay for city markets was also a major agricultural activity.

The Erie Canal (1825) had a negative effect on the use of the St. Lawrence River for shipping, but the 1851 arrival in Watertown of the Rome, Watertown and Ogdensburg Railroad provided easier and cheaper transportation to downstate markets. This, along with cheap power supplied by the rivers and streams, created a manufacturing boom, with Watertown at its center. The city became one of the most prosperous of its size in the country. By 1880 the Black River was lined with tanneries, machine shops, foundries, engine works, gristmills, cotton and woolen mills, paper mills, lumber mills, woodworking establishments, a large wagon factory, furniture factories, and the Davis Sewing Machine Co, among others.

The most important industry in the late 19th century was papermaking. The new technology using wood pulp to make paper was well suited to the region. Between 1870 and 1910 the Black River valley was one of the greatest papermaking regions in the world. In 1900 there were 26 paper and pulp mills along the river between Carthage and Dexter, including Taggart Bros (1864) and the Dexter Sulphite Pulp and Paper Co (1887). As the supply of wood for pulp was depleted, the paper industry declined, but it was still the predominant industry in 1950. Two of Jefferson Co's largest businesses were New York Air Brake Co (1890), a maker of railway brakes and hydraulic pumps, and Bagley and Sewall (1882), a manufacturer of papermaking machines.

The county's favored position on the St. Lawrence River and on Lake Ontario gave it potential for another industry, tourism. As early as 1840 some people were coming to fish. Cottage colonies developed early, such as Westminster Park (1853) and Thousand Island Park (1875). Pres Ulysses S. Grant's visit to the Thousand Islands in 1872 attracted national attention. In the early 21st century, Alexandria Bay, Chaumont, Clayton, Henderson Harbor, and Theresa are especially dependent on the dollars of tourists who come for sailing, sportfishing, duck hunting, or simply touring; major attractions include Boldt Castle, the Antique Boat Museum, and Sackets Harbor State Historic Site.

The Military Presence

The military has always been an important part of Jefferson Co life. Federal troops were first stationed in 1808 to try to control smuggling and have been almost continuously there since that time. During the War of 1812 Sackets Harbor was army headquarters for the Northern Frontier and the most important naval and shipbuilding port on Lake Ontario; it was the site of a battle on 29 May 1813 when British vessels attempted to take its shipyard. The village was crowded with thousands of soldiers and sailors. Gen Jacob Brown (1775–1828), for whom Brownville is named, was commander of the militia on the Northern Frontier during the war. Following its end, a military post, Madison Barracks (1816–1945), was built at Sackets Harbor.

In 1909 the government acquired 10,000 acres (4,050 ha) of the pine barrens in the northeast corner of the county as a summer training area. As World War II approached, 75,000 acres (30,400 ha) were added. Five entire villages and 525 homes were taken over. Three divisions were trained at Pine Camp during the war. The large number of young soldiers in the area led to many marriages between them and local women. Many liked the area so well that they settled there. Pine Camp became Camp Drum in 1951 and Fort Drum in 1974. In the 1980s it became the base of the 10th Mountain Division. A huge expansion took place between 1984 and 1989, and hundreds of federal jobs became available. Thousands of new people moved into the area, and the county's economy flourished. There was a 10-fold increase in the minority population of Jefferson Co during the 1980s.

Religion, Education, and Culture

The earliest New England settlers were primarily Baptists and Congregationalists, and the latter formed the first religious society in the county in 1801 at Burrville. Baptists, Congregationalists, and Methodists benefited greatly from the religious revivalism of the 1820s. Jefferson Co was a center of the Second Great Awakening. Charles Grandison Finney, one of its main exponents,

POPULATIONS OF TOWNS AND CITIES, JEFFERSON CO

Town or City, Year Founded	1800	1840	1880	1920	1960	2000
Adams, 1802	—	2,966	3,302	3,194	3,964	4,782
Alexandria, 1821	—	3,475	3,135	3,567	3,574	4,097
Antwerp, 1810	—	3,109	3,414	2,569	1,905	1,793
Brownville, 1802	—	3,968	2,624	3,856	3,985	5,843
Cape Vincent, 1849	—	—	3,143	2,111	1,756	3,345
Champion, 1800	143	2,206	2,259	2,854	3,878	4,361
Clayton, 1833	—	3,990	4,214	3,618	3,753	4,817
Ellisburg, 1803	—	5,349	4,810	3,192	3,285	3,541
Henderson, 1806	—	2,480	1,842	1,229	1,207	1,377
Hounsfield, 1806	—	4,146	2,770	2,297	2,722	3,323
Le Ray, 1806	—	3,721	2,660	2,366	3,627	19,836
Lorraine, 1804[a]	—	1,699	1,435	790	609	930
Lyme, 1818	—	5,472	2,277	1,642	1,448	2,015
Orleans, 1821	—	3,001	2,318	1,869	1,982	2,465
Pamelia, 1819	—	2,104	1,143	988	1,414	2,897
Philadelphia, 1821	—	1,888	1,750	1,549	1,297	2,140
Rodman, 1804[b]	—	1,702	1,517	1,027	765	1,147
Rutland, 1802	—	2,090	1,796	1,810	2,229	2,959
Theresa, 1841	—	—	2,389	1,762	1,635	2,414
Watertown, 1800	119	5,027	1,264	1,116	2,492	4,482
Watertown (city), 1869	—	—	10,697	31,285	33,306	26,705
Wilna, 1813	—	2,591	4,393	7,014	6,809	6,235
Worth, 1848	—	—	951	545	193	234

Note: In 1800 the Towns of Champion and Watertown were in Oneida Co.

[a]Malta until 1808.

[b]Harrison until 1808.

grew up in Henderson and had his religious conversion in Adams in 1821. He began preaching at Evans Mills and returned throughout much of his career as a Presbyterian preacher. Another Presbyterian minister from Jefferson Co, Jedidiah Burchard, was sometimes criticized for his "vulgar" and "wild" preaching style, but he conducted successful revivals in Jefferson Co and elsewhere in New York State.

Other denominations in the county reflected the variety of ethnic groups that settled prior to 1850. Friends meetings were formed at Indian River [now Philadelphia], Chaumont, and Pleasant Creek [now Le Ray] around 1810–15. The first Roman Catholic parish, which served both French and Irish Catholics, was formed at Carthage in 1819. Germans formed the first Evangelical Lutheran congregation at Stone Mills in 1840. There were five Universalist churches in 1855. Interest was also found in the Church of the New Jerusalem (Swedenborgian), the Mormons, and spiritualism.

While the Methodists and Baptists remained prominent throughout the 19th and early 20th centuries, Roman Catholicism was gaining rapidly. By 1875 there were 12 Catholic churches, and Catholics outnumbered every group except the Methodists. The concentrated population of the City of Watertown allowed for Irish, French, and Italian Catholic parishes. It also supported the formation of an African Methodist Episcopal Zion church (1892), a synagogue (1903), and a Greek Orthodox parish (*ca* 1920). The expansion of Fort Drum (1984–89) resulted in many new churches, including three Korean churches of different denominations, an Islamic center, and a variety of pentecostal, interdenominational, and nondenominational churches.

By 1802 there were small schools in Watertown and Adams, and schools became widespread following 1812 and 1814 state legislation establishing common districts. The Watertown Board of Education was incorporated in 1865 and opened a high school. Private academies were also established, including Watertown Female Academy (1824); Black River Literary and Religious Institute (1836); Adams Seminary (1832) for girls; and Union Academy (1828) at Belleville. Later, the Hungerford Collegiate Institute (1855) was established at Adams and the Ives Seminary (1856) at Antwerp.

Small rural and village schools centralized between 1926 and 1955 in order to build more modern facilities and to offer more services. A number of common schools in Watertown, Lorraine, and Worth, along with a few scattered others, were still operating in 1958, when a second wave of consolidation into larger school districts occurred. In 2001 there were 11 public school districts and 35 public schools in Jefferson Co. There were also 10 private schools, all with religious affiliations. St. Vincent de Paul Seminary in Orleans had a brief existence beginning in 1838, but after its move to Fordham [now in Bronx Co] became St. John's College (now Fordham University). Jefferson Community College (1961) at Watertown is the only college within a 50 mi (80 km) radius of the city.

Watertown founder Henry Coffeen published the county's first newspaper, probably in 1809. The *Hemisphere* became the *American Eagle* in 1810. Dozens of papers followed, both in Watertown and in at least 10 other communities. *Le Phare des Lacs* (1859–65) of Watertown was a French language paper serving some of the county's 6% Canadian-born residents (as of 1865) and the 5% born in France. In 2003 the *Watertown Daily Times* (1870) was the county's daily newspaper, and three weeklies were published: the *Jefferson County Journal* at Adams, the *Thousand Islands Sun* at Alexandria Bay, and the *Carthage Republican Tribune* at Carthage. The first radio station, WANT, began broadcasting at Watertown in 1941 and remained in operation with nine others in 2003. The first television station, WCNY, broadcast from Champion in 1954; in 2003 there were five television stations.

The county's best-loved literary figure remains Giddingsville's Marietta Holley (1836–1926), who wrote under the pseudonym of Josiah Allen's Wife. Most of her 21 books were a remarkable synthesis of three idioms: domestic fiction, literature by women for women, and local-color writing. Her chief creation, Samantha Allen, made her point by serving as a foil to other characters who personified intemperance or antisuffrage.

Politics

Since the Civil War Jefferson Co has been overwhelmingly Republican. Few non-Republicans have been elected to local offices, but Watertown's Roswell P. Flower (1835–99), a pro-Tammany Democrat, served as the area's congressman (1881–83) and as governor (1892–94). Other government leaders from Jefferson Co included Lt Govs Allen C. Beach (1868) and George H. Cobb (1910). Watertown has been home to two prominent US secretaries of state, Robert A. Lansing (1915–20) and his nephew, John Foster Dulles (1953–59), who also served briefly as a US senator. Dulles's brother, Allen Welsh Dulles, headed the CIA from 1953 to 1961.

A Board of Supervisors consisting of one representative from each town and varying numbers from the City of Watertown originally governed Jefferson Co. In response to the US Supreme Court's one person–one vote decision, differences in population were adjusted by a weighted voting system. In an effort to equalize representation the county changed to a 15-person Board of Legislators in 1996. The first county administrator was hired in 1987 to run day-to-day government affairs.

Recent History

World War II brought prosperity to Jefferson Co, but by the 1960s it was fading. Construction of the St. Lawrence Seaway (1955–59) and of I-81 (1959–66), both expected to benefit the area, proved detrimental. Instead of bringing goods and people to Jefferson Co, they made it easier to bypass it. The county has suffered from a sluggish economy with high unemployment and low wages, but the population remained constant. The 1984–89 Fort Drum expansion created a population explosion, especially in Le Ray, and between 1980 and 1990 the population grew by almost 25%. Population distribution has changed as city and village residents have moved into rural areas. In 2001 Fort Drum was the county's largest employer with more than 10,000 soldiers and nearly 2,500 civilian jobs. Prisons at Watertown and Cape Vincent, built in the 1980s, provided another 2,000 jobs. Other major employers included hospitals, school systems, and federal, state, and local governments. Tourism has become a year-round business as visitors come for water sports, hunting, river rafting, fishing, snowmobiling, and a host of outdoor activities. The county contains 13 state parks.

In the early 21st century, only 11% of jobs come from manufacturing. There are about 100 manufacturing plants, including New York Air Brake Co, still the largest but with a fraction of its former employees, and Car-Freshner Corp (1952), maker of the "little trees." Agriculture remains important. In the second half of the 20th century the number of farms in the county declined steeply (4,440 in 1950 and only 916 in 1997), but because of the increasing size of the surviving farms, the number of acres was cut only in half during that period, and Jefferson Co remains 16th in the state in percentage of land in farms. It is third in the state in dairy production and first in honey production. Hay and forage growth continues to be strong. Animals raised include sheep, goats, bison, and deer. Crowley Foods at La Fargeville and Great Lakes Cheese of New York at Adams are the largest food processors. Some significant county residents include Frank W. Woolworth (1852–1919), founder of the Woolworth chain; highwayman Charles E. Boles (1829–?1917, also known as Black Bart; and Melvil Dewey (1851–1931), creator of the Dewey Decimal System.

See also THOUSAND ISLANDS RESORTS.

The first county history was written when many of the first settlers were living; Franklin B. Hough's *History of Jefferson County* (1854) was expanded by S. W. Durant and H. B. Peirce in *History of Jefferson County* (1878). Four others followed, each with some material of value: William H. Horton, *Geographical Gazetteer of Jefferson County* (1890), John A. Haddock, *The Growth of a Century: History of Jefferson County* (1894), Edgar C. Emerson, *Our County and Its People: Jefferson County* (1898), and Jere Coughlin, *Jefferson County Centennial* (1905). Three histories of Watertown have been published: *Watertown, NY: A History* (1876), Joel H. Monroe, *Through 11 Decades of History: Watertown* (1912), and Harry F. Landon, *150 Years of Watertown* (1950). Cape Vincent is also the focus of several books, including Elizur H. Pratt, *Historical Sketch of the Town of Cape Vincent* (1876) and Nelie H. Casler, *Cape Vincent and Its History* (1906). The Thousand Islands region is documented in a recent study by Susan W. Smith, *The First Summer People: The Thousand Islands, 1650–1910* (1993). Marianne Perciacante, *Calling Down Fire: Charles Grandison Finney and Revivalism in Jefferson County, New York, 1800–1840* (2003) contains a thorough sociological and geographic analysis of the county's early development. Once a quarterly publication, the *Bulletin of Jefferson County Historical Society* (1959–) published irregularly at the end of the 20th century.

Laura Lynne Scharer

Jefferson Valley. Locality (pop 14,891) in Yorktown (Westchester Co). A post office was established for the farming district of Jefferson Valley in 1850. Nearby Lake Osceola became a small resort with a hotel during the Civil War era, a function continued in 2003 by the Osceola Beach and Picnic Grounds. The Taconic Parkway provided highway access in 1932, but the area remained agricultural until 1958 when the 680-acre (275 ha) "New Town" was begun by developer David Bogdanoff; it grew to include houses and apartments as well as retirement housing and the Jefferson Valley Mall (1983).

Amy Surak

Jeffersonville. Village (pop 420) in Callicoon (Sullivan Co). Beginning in 1840, it became home to German and Swiss immigrants who called their community Winkelried. When Charles Langhorn was told by his doctor to settle in an area abundant with hemlock trees, he chose Winkelried and in 1846 built a hotel he called the Jefferson House. The post office adopted the name Jeffersonville in 1849. It was home to a German language newspaper, the *Sullivan Volksblatt* (1870). The village incorporated in 1924. In the early 21st century, Jeffersonville's Main St was revitalized by new arrivals from the New York City metropolitan area.

John Conway

Jehovah's Witnesses. Religious organization. Founded in 1879 by Charles Taze Russell (1852–1916) as the Watch Tower and Tract Society, the organization moved its headquarters from Allegheny, Pa, to Brooklyn in 1909, where it has remained, adopting its current name in 1931. After Russell's death, Joseph F. Rutherford (1869–1942) became president, and when he died one-man rule began to come to an end. Their Adventist theology propounds the imminent return of Christ and the culminating battle of Armageddon that will destroy all nonbelievers. The faithful will live forever on earth in paradise where no pain, sorrow, or sin will exist, while only the 144,000 who are the elect will spend eternity in heaven to rule the earth. Witnesses reject military service, saluting the flag, and blood transfusions, all issues that have led to protracted court battles. Until 1999 they were not permitted to vote in civic elections. Followers spread their message through persistent door-to-door proselytizing and the distribution of tracts. Members meet five times a week for Bible study in buildings called Kingdom Halls. The Witnesses have extensive real estate holdings in Brooklyn Heights—"Brooklyn ruled" is a familiar catchphrase within the denomination referring to an edict of the governing body—and in Wallkill (Ulster Co), where they own 28 buildings, a large printing factory, and a 670-acre (271 ha) dairy farm. The Wallkill complex is used for administration and education, and can accommodate 1,200 people. In 2001 there were approximately 6.1 million members worldwide and about 66,000 in New York State.

Bergman, Jerry. *Jehovah's Witnesses: A Comprehensive and Selectively Annotated Bibliography* (Westport, Conn: Greenwood, 1999)
Penton, M. James. *Apocalypse Delayed: The Story of Jehovah's Witnesses* (Toronto: Univ of Toronto Press, 1997)
Rogerson, Alan. *Millions Now Living Will Never Die: A Study of Jehovah's Witnesses* (London: Constable, 1969)

Jerry Bergman

Jell-O. In 1897 Pearle B. Wait of Le Roy (Genesee Co) introduced a new flavored gelatin dessert, which his wife, May Wait, named Jell-O. Although not the first prepared gelatin dessert, it became the most famous. The first four flavors were strawberry, raspberry, lemon, and orange. For two years, Wait prepared and packaged Jell-O but was unable to create a market for it. In 1899 he sold the rights for $450 to Orator Woodward, a successful Le Roy businessman and owner of the Genesee Pure Food Co. The first nationwide advertisement for the product appeared in magazines such as the *Ladies' Home Journal* during the spring of 1902. In 1904, 4-year-old Elizabeth King was introduced as the Jell-O girl. Her image

Jell-O advertisement, 1916.

appeared in advertising and on packaging for over 40 years. There was also Jell-O Ice Cream Powder and Jello-O Pudding, and as of 2003 the brand name was carried on 158 products. In 1923 the Genesee Pure Food Co became the Jell-O Co, which was acquired in 1925 by the Postum Co of Battle Creek, Mich. The latter became a subsidiary of General Foods in 1929. Jell-O advertising and recipe books were illustrated by such noted artists as Rose O'Neill, Maxfield Parrish, and Norman Rockwell, and after 1934, the product was promoted by Jack Benny in his weekly radio show. General Foods (now Kraft Foods) closed the factory in Le Roy in 1964 and moved production to Dover, Del. The Le Roy Historical Society opened the Jell-O Gallery in 1997, during the gelatin product's 100th anniversary.

Wyman, Carolyn. *Jell-O: A Biography: The History and Mystery of America's Most Famous Dessert* (New York: Harcourt, 2001)

Lynne Belluscio

Jemison [née Lee], **Alice Mae** (*b* Cattaraugus Indian Reservation [loc in Cattaraugus, Chautauqua, and Erie Cos], 9 Oct 1901; *d* Washington, DC, March 1964). Activist and politician. Eldest of three children of a prominent Seneca Nation political family, Alice Mae Lee lived on the Cattaraugus Reservation in Western New York during her childhood, graduated from Silver Creek High School, just off the reservation, in 1919, and soon after married LeVerne Leonard Jemison, also from Cattaraugus. The couple had two children, but they separated in December 1928.

Jemison entered the world of politics in 1929 and soon became a Seneca lobbyist in Washington, DC. Best known for her firm beliefs in Indian sovereignty and that the Bureau of Indian Affairs should be abolished, she worked actively in Washington against the Indian Reorganization Act (1934) as well as the Selective Service Act (1917), seeing them incompatible with tribal sovereignty, and was an active member of the American Indian Federation (1934), a group formed to resist federal interference in tribal affairs.

Hauptman, Laurence M. "Alice Mae Lee Jemison." In *Notable American Women: The Modern Period: A Biographical Dictionary,* ed. Barbara Sicherman and Carol Hurd Green (Cambridge, Mass: Belknap Press, 1980)

Martha Symes

Jemison, Mary [Dehgewanus] (*b* at sea, Atlantic Ocean, ?1743; *d* Buffalo Creek Reservation [now in Erie Co], 1833). Adopted Seneca woman. Born to a Scots-Irish family that emigrated from Ireland to central Pennsylvania, she was taken captive during the French and Indian War by Shawnee warriors and their French allies on 5 Apr 1758. The only member of her family to survive the raid, Jemison was marched to Fort Duquesne [now Pittsburgh]. She was adopted by a pair of Seneca sisters to replace a brother they had lost in the war, reflected in the name she was given, translated as "Two Voices Falling."

Instructed in the language and ways of the Seneca, she took her place in the community of Seneca women, married a Delaware warrior named Sheninjee, and had two children, only one of whom survived. Sheninjee died of illness in 1763. Jemison rejoined her adopted sisters near what is now Geneseo (Livingston Co). She soon married a Seneca named Hiokatoo, with whom she had six more children, and remained married until his death in 1811.

After the war Jemison was given numerous opportunities to rejoin white society but declined, saying that white prejudice would preclude her and her children from living normal lives. During the Revolutionary War, Jemison was part of the massive flight of Iroquois from Gen John Sullivan's invading army in 1779. Unlike most Seneca, however, she resettled afterward along the Genesee River. She held on to Genesee lands her entire life but not without difficulty. She was formally granted a parcel of land in the 1797 Treaty of Big Tree. Her 18,000-acre (7,284 ha) tract, known as the Gardeau Reservation [now in Wyoming Co], was reduced through a number of questionable transactions, one notably with a man who purported to be a long-lost cousin from Ireland. On 19 Apr 1817 the New York legislature granted her citizenship and officially recognized her title to the remaining land, all of which was ceded before her death.

Jemison achieved wide renown through the publication of her life story, which she related in 1823 at the age of 80 to James E. Seaver, a western New York State doctor. Seaver published the heavily edited memoir to great acclaim. *A Narrative of the Life of Mrs. Mary Jemison* sold over 100,000 copies in its first year and has since been reprinted and republished more than two dozen times. In the book, which capitalized on the popularity of the captivity narrative genre, she provided a sympathetic view of Indian life, especially of women's lives. She also chronicled the social disintegration that attended the Seneca in the post-Revolutionary period, with particular emphasis on the disruptive effects of alcohol. One of her sons murdered his two brothers in separate drunken rages and was himself later killed in an alcohol-related incident. Despite these tragedies, in 1823 Jemison had 39 grandchildren and 14 great-grandchildren; her descendants today number in the thousands. A statue in her honor was erected in Letchworth State Park in 1910.

Namias, June. *White Captives: Gender and Ethnicity on the American Frontier* (Chapel Hill: Univ of North Carolina Press, 1993)
Seaver, James E., ed. *A Narrative of the Life of Mrs. Mary Jemison* (1824; repr Syracuse: Syracuse Univ Press, 1990)

Karim M. Tiro

Jericho. Locality (pop 13,045) in Oyster Bay (Nassau Co). Its colonial population was predominantly Society of Friends (Quaker), and its meetinghouse (1787) is still in use. Jericho was home to Elias Hicks (1748–1830), the influential Quaker preacher, starting in 1770. Jericho Quakers manumitted their slaves in the 1770s as an act of conscience. The farming community changed little from the Revolutionary War era until World War II. Jericho had only 551 residents in 1940, but a Hicks descendant subdivided her farm in 1952, beginning rapid growth; the population reached 10,795 by 1960. In 1958 the construction of the Long Island Expressway destroyed many of the old buildings. Jericho is a commuter community, with office parks near the expressway along Jericho Turnpike, which divides the locality. In 2000 its population was 10.7% Asian, predominantly Korean.

Richard A. Winsche

Jerry Rescue. Fugitive slave incident. On the morning of 1 Oct 1851, William "Jerry" Henry (*b* ?1812), an escaped slave from Missouri, was arrested in a Syracuse cooperage shop by federal marshals and local police in a test of the 1850 Fugitive Slave Act. Syracuse was a center of abolitionism, and the Liberty Party was holding a convention that morning in the city's Congregational Church. The pealing of church bells was a signal to the members of the Syracuse Vigilance Committee that a slave had been captured. Prominent abolitionist Gerrit Smith quickly agreed to serve as defense counsel in a hastily convened court proceeding that day at the office of the US commissioner at Water and Clinton Sts. While the hearing was ongoing, at about 2:30 PM an interracial crowd entered the commissioner's office trying to free Jerry. This effort temporarily succeeded, though he was recaptured on the nearby Lock Street Bridge. Jerry was put in leg irons and taken to the police office in the Journal Building on Clinton Square. The abolitionists debated their next move. Jermain Wesley Loguen, a prominent African Methodist Episcopal Zion minister, and Gerrit Smith felt that a forcible rescue would make the most dramatic possible statement against the Fugitive Slave Act, while Unitarian minister Samuel J. May, a Garrisonian pacifist, was confident that Jerry would be peacefully released due to popular pressure. Active confrontation carried the day. These actions were aided by the refusal of most local national guard and militia units to assemble and defend the federal marshals, despite being ordered to do so by the Onondaga County sheriff.

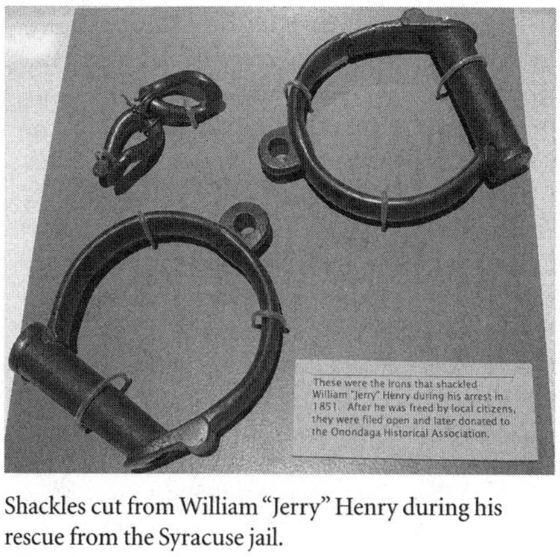

Shackles cut from William "Jerry" Henry during his rescue from the Syracuse jail.

That evening a crowd of around 2,000 people gathered outside the police office and around 8:00 PM broke into the building, using a battering ram to open the door to the room holding Jerry. After he was released and freed from his chains, he was eventually brought, by way of Oswego, to Kingston [now in Ont], where he died of tuberculosis in 1853. Subsequent attempts to try 25 of the leaders of the Jerry Rescue for violation of the Fugitive Slave Act resulted in only one conviction. A countereffort to try a US deputy marshal for violation of New York State's personal liberty law ended in acquittal. Syracuse hosted annual celebrations of the Jerry Rescue, usually featuring Gerrit Smith as keynote speaker, throughout the 1850s. It remains a source of civic pride; Jerry's shackles are a prized possession of the Onondaga Historical Association in Syracuse, and in 1990 the Jerry Rescue Memorial, a sculpture by Sharon BuMann, was dedicated close to the site of the original rescue.

Sernett, Milton C. *North Star Country: Upstate New York and the Crusade for African American Freedom* (Syracuse: Syracuse Univ Press, 2002)
Yacovone, Donald. *Samuel Joseph May and the Dilemmas of the Liberal Persuasion, 1797–1871* (Philadelphia: Temple Univ Press, 1991)

Peter Eisenstadt

Jerusalem. Town (pop 4,525) in S central Yates Co. Evidence of prehistoric human occupation is found at the "Old Fort" at Sherman's Hollow and at stone structures on Bluff Point. The town was formed in 1790, and the first settlement in its present territory followed in 1794 when Jemima Wilkinson (1752–1819) and her followers moved west from Torrey. At Branchport industrial production beginning in the 1830s included iron, shoes, steel springs, fruit baskets, and spokes. Summer cottages, built as early as 1875, were facilitated by the electric Penn Yan, Keuka Park and Branchport Railroad (1897–1927). Grape cultivation began in the late 19th century; by 1894, 129 grape growers harvested 438 acres (177 ha) in town. Landmarks include Garrett Memorial Chapel on Bluff Point, the 7 mi (11 km) long peninsula between the arms of Keuka Lake, and the Jemima Wilkinson House (1814). The town is the site of Keuka College (1888) and Keuka Lake State Park. A Groffdale Conference Mennonite community located in Jerusalem around 1980. In the early 21st century, agriculture (especially grape culture), recreation, and tourism drove the economy.

Gwen Chamberlain

Jervis, John B(loomfield) (*b* Huntington, Suffolk Co, 14 Dec 1795; *d* Rome, Oneida Co, 12 Jan 1885). Civil engineer. Jervis moved with his parents in 1798 to Fort Stanwix [now Rome, Oneida Co], where he completed elementary school and worked on his family's farm. When construction began on the Erie Canal in 1817, chief engineer Benjamin Wright gave him a job as axeman with a survey party. By 1819 Jervis rose to resident engineer, through reading and observing other engineers. In 1825 Wright hired Jervis as his assistant on the Delaware and Hudson Canal (D&HC) project. After Wright's departure in 1827, Jervis became chief engineer and Port Jervis (Orange Co), on the canal route, bears his name. He also built the "gravity" Carbondale Railroad, which linked Carbondale, Pa, with D&HC and was the first US line to experiment with steam locomotives. Between 1830 and 1833 Jervis constructed New York State's first two railroads: the Mohawk and Hudson, which ran between Albany and Schenectady, and the Saratoga and Schenectady. Both used steam power. While working with Mohawk and Hudson, Jervis designed the first locomotive to use a forward movable truck to guide it around curves, an innovation that evolved into a standard for locomotives. In 1833 Jervis left the railroads to construct the Chenango Canal between Binghamton and the Erie Canal at Utica. In 1834 he married Cynthia Brayton, who died together with a newborn daughter in 1839. Thirteen months later he married Eliza Coates. Between 1836 and 1849 Jervis worked on what he considered his greatest project, Croton Aqueduct, which supplied abundant water to New York City. Jervis built the aqueduct's massive stone High Bridge over the Harlem River and pioneered the reverse-curve spillway for dams. After completing Croton, he served as consulting engineer on Cochituate Aqueduct in Boston. In 1847 Jervis became chief engineer of Hudson River Railroad between New York City and Albany and in 1850 took a similar position on Michigan Southern and Northern Indiana Railroad (MS&NIRR), becoming company president in 1852. From this date until 1858, he served intermittently as president of MS&NIRR and of Rock Island Railroad. During the early 1860s he acted as general superintendent and chief engineer of the financially shaky Pittsburgh, Fort Wayne and Chicago Railroad. After reviving this line, Jervis returned to Rome, where in 1868 he helped found Merchant Iron Mill, working there until his death.

Larkin, F. Daniel. *John B. Jervis: An American Engineering Pioneer* (Ames: Iowa State Univ Press, 1990)

F. Daniel Larkin

Jesuits. Members of the Society of Jesus, a Catholic religious order founded in the 16th century. Although specifically proscribed in New York Colony for most of its history, Jesuit missionaries among the Indian tribes of what is now Central New York included Isaac Jogues, who, with two other Jesuits, was tortured and martyred by Mohawks in Ossernenon [now Auriesville, Montgomery Co] in 1646. Fr Simon Le Moyne worked with the Onondaga from the 1654 to 1661. Kateri Tekakwitha (1656–80), born at Ossernenon, was baptized by Jesuits and was beatified in 1980. The first public mass in the state was said by two Jesuits on 14 Nov 1655 at Indian Hill, near what is now Manlius (Onondaga Co). The colony's only Catholic governor, Thomas Dongan, arrived in New York in 1683 with Rev Thomas Harvey, an English Jesuit, as chaplain. Harvey and two Jesuit colleagues formed a Jesuit school near or on the site of the present Trinity Church in Manhattan. Leisler's Rebellion in New York and the 1688 Glorious Revolution in England ended Dongan's regime, the school, and an effective Jesuit presence in New York.

In 1808 the Jesuit Anthony Kohlmann became the administrator of the Diocese of New York. In this capacity he helped found St. Patrick's Old Cathedral in 1809. In 1846 Bishop John J. Hughes sold the college he started in 1841 (now Fordham University) to the Society of Jesus, which has maintained it since. In 1847 a small contingent from Fordham founded St. Francis Xavier College in New York City for day students, which within a few years enrolled more students than other Catholic colleges on the East Coast. In 1912 it phased out its collegiate levels, becoming Xavier High School. The Buffalo Mission (1869–1907), established by the Jesuit German province, cared for numerous new German-speaking immigrant parishes in Western New York and established several colleges, including Canisius College (1870) in Buffalo. The mission merged with the local Jesuit province when the need for separate language services diminished. Jesuits started Le Moyne College (1946) in Syracuse and founded McQuaid Jesuit High School (1952) in Rochester.

Jesuits served Italian immigrants with their Loretto Mission at the Church of the Nativity in Manhattan (1891) and helped Latino Catholics with programs, including the Nativity School. Jesuit-style retreats, modeled on the Spiritual Exercises of their founder, St. Ignatius Loyola, are in Manhasset (Nassau Co), Staten Island, and Cornwall (Orange Co). The province has administered numerous parishes throughout the state, including seven in 2002, and other high schools, including Fordham Prep, Loyola School, and Regis High School in New York City. Membership in the New York province of the Society of Jesus (which includes northern New Jersey and several foreign missions) in 2002 totaled 580, including 467 priests, 85 seminarians, and 27 brothers.

See also EXPLORATION; NEW FRANCE.

Bangert, William V., SJ. *A History of the Society of Jesus*, rev ed. (St. Louis: Institute of Jesuit Sources, 1986)
Curran, Francis X., SJ. *The Return of the Jesuits* (Chicago: Loyola Univ Press, 1966)

Thomas C. Hennessy, SJ

Jewett. Town (pop 970) in central Greene Co. A part of the Hardenbergh Patent located in rough, high terrain, the area was settled in 1783. Zadock Pratt, who later founded Prattsville, operated a tannery in Jewett from 1802 to 1815. The town was formed from Lexington and Hunter in 1849. Beginning in 1951 Ukrainian immigrants living in New York City purchased many of the town's poorer farms for summer homes. They also built the landmark St. John the Baptist Church (1961). Jewett, known for its copious snowfalls, has many vacation houses, used both in summer and during the ski season at Hunter and Windham ski areas.

Field Horne

Jewish Agricultural Society. An aid organization that promoted the resettlement of Jewish immigrants as farmers outside the urban areas of the Northeast. In 1900 the Baron de Hirsch Fund reorganized its Committee on Agricultural and Industrial Settlements as the Jewish Agricultural and Industrial Aid Society (JAIAS), renamed the Jewish Agricultural Society (JAS) in 1922. German American Jews served in leadership positions and encouraged the movement of Russian and Romanian Jews away from New York City. From 1908 to 1959 the society published the *Jewish Farmer* in Yiddish and English. The JAIAS originally promoted agricultural colonies as the most expedient way to turn Jewish immigrants into farmers and to encourage the emergence of Jewish institutions like synagogues and benevolent societies in the newly settled areas. Within a decade, however, the JAIAS had largely abandoned this approach in favor of providing loans to individuals and families for the purchase of land, granting 2,000 loans totaling $1 million between 1900 and 1910. From 1904 to 1910 it ran a test farm on Long Island to train farmers and in 1908 began extension activities to advise farmers on agricultural practices and marketing. Also in 1908 the JAIAS created a Farm Labor Bureau to provide Jewish immigrants with agricultural experience by placing them as workers on Jewish-owned farms. By 1913 the JAIAS established settlement and rural sanitation departments, many Jewish farms in the Catskills having begun to take in boarders to supplement their income.

Sullivan and southern Ulster Cos emerged as the center of Jewish farming in New York, with pockets extending into Greene, Rockland, Orange, and Putnam Cos. The society played a role in establishing Catskill synagogues and other Jewish institutions, such as a Workmen's Circle chapter in Ellenville (Ulster Co) in 1911 and a Hebrew school in Leurenkill (Ulster Co). From 1919 to 1945 the group operated a regional office in Ellenville, helping Jewish farmers organize credit unions, farm loan associations, cooperative health and personal insurance associations, fire insurance associations, and, in response to the depression, the Inter-County Farmers Cooperative Association (1934). Outside the Catskills, Jewish farmers established a significant presence in southern Rensselaer Co. With JAIAS assistance the Hebrew Benevolent Farmers' Association was created there in 1909, a rural credit union in 1911, and a mutual fire insurance company in 1928. During the 1930s the JAS settled Jewish refugees from Germany in 10 New York locations, again mainly in the Catskills, and from 1947 to 1953 placed 75 families of Holocaust survivors on New York farms, primarily as poultry farmers. Jewish farming declined rapidly between 1955 and 1965 because of mechanization, competition from agribusiness, and elimination of price supports for eggs. At the same time, Jewish immigration to the United States waned, and an increasingly professionalized urban Jewry found the JAS's services less attractive. The organization disbanded in 1972.

Gold, David. "Jewish Agriculture in the Catskills, 1900–1920," *Agricultural History* 5 (Jan 1981): 31–49
Goodwin, Edward A., and Herman Levine. "A Historical Review of Farming by Jews in New York." In *Report of the General Manager, 1956* (New York: Jewish Agricultural Society, 1957)
Lavender, Abraham, and Clarence Steinberg. *Jewish Farmers of the Catskills: A Century of Survival* (Gainesville: Univ Press of Florida, 1995)

Harvey Strum

Jewish education. The first Jewish arrivals in New Amsterdam in 1654 were permitted to practice their religion privately and to educate their children at home. The colony's first Jewish school was organized in 1731 by the congregation Shearith Israel and reorganized in 1755 to teach religious and secular subjects. As the Jewish population grew in the early 19th century, to about 1,150 in 1830, Jews moved beyond New York City and settled across the state, especially after the opening of the Erie Canal in 1825. Jewish merchants, artisans, and peddlers established congregations in Albany (1838), Syracuse (1842), Rochester (1848), Buffalo (1848), and Utica (1848). The need to provide a Jewish education to the young was recognized, but struggling congregations found it difficult to find teachers; there were no ordained rabbis in the United States until the 1840s. If they found a rabbi or hazan, he usually served as teacher as well. A Jewish school was virtually synonymous with its teacher and usually closed when the teacher left. In this period many primary schools in the state were private, church related, and Christian in outlook. There were efforts to found Jewish day schools so that Jewish children could receive their secular studies along with Jewish rather than Christian religious instruction. In the early 1850s New York City was home to seven synagogue-affiliated day schools, enrolling about 850 children. These schools often employed gentile teachers for secular subjects and Jewish teachers for religious studies. Some affluent Jews sent their children to a few private, single-sex Jewish day and boarding schools, the latter attracting statewide and even national student bodies. Rochester had two Jewish day schools in the late 1850s.

By the middle of the 19th century Jewish students in New York State were increasingly enrolling in tuition-free public schools. Changes in state education law in the 1850s led to a reduction in overt Christian influences in public education, and Jewish immigrants, wanting to assimilate, were attracted to recent improvements in buildings, instruction, and curricula. In Buffalo Jewish students were enrolled in the public schools by the late 1840s. All the congregational day schools in New York City had closed by the late 1850s and those in Rochester and Syracuse by the late 1860s. Religious instruction shifted to supplementary after-school or weekend programs, attended by about one-third the school-age Jewish population. In 1917 there were 277,000 Jewish children enrolled in New York City public schools and fewer than 1,000 in Jewish day schools. Jewish Sunday or Sabbath schools, modeled on Philadelphia's Hebrew Sunday School (1838), were created in New York City in the 1840s. Following the Civil War they spread across the state, especially among Reform congregations such as Rochester's B'rith Kodesh, which organized a Sunday school in 1869.

The growing number of poor German Jewish immigrants in New York State after the Civil War prompted the established Jewish community to found special schools, often called Hebrew Free Schools, to counter Christian proselytizing activities, provide free religious training to immigrant children, and "Americanize" and modernize newcomers. Attendance at such schools often had as a precondition enrollment in the city's public schools. At Hebrew Free Schools in New York City (1865), Syracuse (1885), Buffalo (*ca* 1900), and Utica (1903), cultural and political assimilation of new immigrants assumed an importance equal to religious instruction. The arrival of large numbers of eastern European Orthodox Jews from the 1880s to the 1920s led to the founding of traditional, religiously Orthodox schools, the first of which were Machzike Talmud Torah (1883) and Etz Chaim (1886) in New York City. In the 1880s individual teacher-entrepreneurs established cheders, fee-based supplementary schools that met after school hours and taught mechanical reading of Hebrew. These schools, usually only for boys, were created in Buffalo, New York City, Rochester, and other communities with recent immigrant Orthodox populations.

Early in the 20th century there were attempts in New York City, Buffalo, Rochester, and Utica to establish community-wide supplementary schools, usually called Talmud Torahs, to provide comprehensive religious studies for all Jewish youth and to bridge the growing differences in theology and religious practices. The New York City Bureau of Jewish Education (1910), led by Samson Benderly and Rabbi Mordecai Kaplan, developed the New Jewish Education system, built on Talmud Torahs, to prepare American Jewish youth for life in two worlds, secular America and religious Judaism. New curricula, teacher training methods, and teaching materials were developed that merged religious, historical, and artistic studies within a cultural Zionist context. In the 1920s and 1930s New Jewish Education was carried across the state and nation by educators prepared at the bureau.

Whereas the American public school system was thoroughly coeducational, the education of Jewish girls tended to lag behind that of boys. Hebrew Free Schools, though generally open to both sexes, were more popular with girls than boys. Education of Orthodox girls tended to be neglected until the 1920s, when Orthodox day schools with enhanced learning opportunities for girls and young women were established; these included the coeducational Yeshiva of Flatbush (1928), the all-girls Shulamith School (1929) in Brooklyn, and Manhattan's Ramaz School (1937). The ultra-Orthodox, who began arriving in the 1930s, maintained separate schools for the sexes, creating yeshivot for boys and the first ultra-Orthodox girls school in America, Bais Yaakov in Brooklyn (1937). Since World War II the number of ultra-Orthodox schools has grown along with the community itself in New York City and Rockland Co. Among Reform, Conservative, and Reconstructionist Jews, the importance of religious education for girls is reflected in the acceptance of the Bat Mitzvah—a ceremony to initiate girls into the adult Jewish community, analogous to the Bar Mitzvah for boys—first celebrated at the Society for the Advancement of Judaism in New York City in 1922. In modern Orthodox synagogues different but parallel ceremonies are also becoming common.

The movement of Jews to new urban and suburban neighborhoods had a profound impact on Jewish education. As old synagogues moved with their congregants to new neighborhoods and new congregations were established, the older Talmud Torahs and other community-wide educational programs were marooned in their old neighborhoods. The communal schools in New York City, Utica, Rochester, and Buffalo ultimately closed. Further undermining community-based Jewish education were the growing divisions among Orthodox, Conservative, Reform, Reconstructionist, and ultra-Orthodox Jews, and the presence of committed Yiddishists and cultural secularists. Reflecting demographic trends among the state's Jews, suburban synagogues were built as "Jewish centers," where all social, welfare, and religious services, including religious instruction, were to be provided under one roof. The vigorous growth of suburban congregational schools in the 20th century had significant gender implications. Women often founded, directed, and staffed the Hebrew schools, and girls received religious instruction along with boys. Nearly all supplementary Jewish education now takes place in congregational schools, with women continuing to provide much of the energy and direction.

The most dramatic change in the past 40 years has been the rapid increase in day school enrollments. In 2000 over 100,000 children attended Jewish day schools in the state. The majority are sponsored by Orthodox and ultra-Orthodox communities, but some are affiliated with the Conservative and Reform branches of Judaism and with community-wide groups. In the 1999–2000 school year about one-third of New York State's school-age Jewish children attended day schools. Enrollment is highest at the elementary level, but secondary enrollment has been growing rapidly. Day schools are concentrated in New York City and surrounding counties, especially Rockland Co. Many of the Jewish children enrolled in public schools receive some Jewish religious education at afternoon or weekend schools.

In addition to religious education, secular Jewish organizations such as the Workmen's Circle have provided instruction in Yiddish language and culture since the late 1910s. Schools were founded throughout the state, and a few continue into the 21st century. Many of the state's colleges and universities have Jewish studies programs. Manhattan's Yeshiva University and the Jewish Theological Seminary of America were both founded in 1886. The Jewish Institute of Religion, established in New York City in 1922, merged with the Cincinnati-based Hebrew Union College (1875) in 1950, becoming Hebrew Union College–Jewish Institute of Religion (HUC-JIR). There are also several ultra-Orthodox yeshivot in New York City. Jewish adult education programs sponsored by schools, congregations, and community agencies can be found in many locations. The quality and breadth of Jewish instruction, as well as the degree of participation, is greater at the beginning of the 21st century than at any previous time in the state's history.

Adler, Selig, and Thomas E. Connolly. *From Ararat to Suburbia: The History of the Jewish Community of Buffalo* (Philadelphia: Jewish Publication Society of America, 1960)

Brumberg, Stephan F. *Going to America, Going to School: The Jewish Immigrant Public School Encounter in Turn-of-the-Century New York City* (New York: Praeger, 1986)

Eisenstadt, Peter. *Affirming the Covenant: A History of Temple B'rith Kodesh, Rochester, New York, 1848–1999* (Rochester: The Temple, 1999; distributed by Syracuse Univ Press)

Stephan F. Brumberg

Jewish Institute of Religion. See HEBREW UNION COLLEGE–JEWISH INSTITUTE OF RELIGION.

Jewish liturgical music. Music, composed or improvised, that appears in the context of a Jewish worship ritual. Jewish liturgical music in New Amsterdam began with the arrival of the colony's first Jews in 1654. While the exact music used in the largely Dutch Sephardic congregation is unknown, it likely involved men singing solo and choral-led metrical melodies, and excluded women and musical instruments by religious mandate. A large influx of Jews from central Europe starting in the middle of the 19th century changed the face of Jewish worship music. Many of these Jews had been involved in the European Jewish Reform movements and searched for ways to bring the service up-to-date to comply with the musical standards of US society. By 1846 the congregation of Beth El in Albany, through the influence of Rabbi Isaac Mayer Wise, began to utilize a mixed gender choir and to sing hymns in English and German rather than in Hebrew. New York City's Temple Emanu-El installed an organ in its new sanctuary about 1850. By 1875 the choir-and-organ format had become standard in several of New York State's most prominent synagogues, providing a sense of decorum and grandeur during worship.

The face of Jewish liturgical music changed once again with the immigration of over 2 million eastern European Jews to New York State between 1880 and 1924. Many of the newcomers were Orthodox in their religious observance and their musical worship tradition focused around a vocalist known as a cantor, or *hazzan.* The greatest *hazzanim* gained legendary status, packing synagogues first in eastern Europe and then in New York. Numerous European-born cantors such as Yossele Rosenblatt (1880–1933), David Roitman (1884–1943), and Zavel Kwartin (1874–1953) took cantorial positions at major synagogues in New York City. Their highly ornate and emotional compositions were treasured by congregants and immortalized in recordings and sheet music.

After World War II the near annihilation of European Jewish culture forced American Jewry to create and perpetuate Jewish liturgical music on its own. The three major streams of American Judaism—Reform, Conservative, and Orthodox—established schools for cantorial study at their religious seminaries in Manhattan between 1947 and 1964. Joining the cantorial instructors were a bevy of composers interested in creating an American sound for Jewish worship, including Abraham Wolf Binder (1895–1966), Isadore Freed (1900–1960), and Lazar Weiner (1897–1982). Each attempted to write works that fused contemporary art music idioms with what they saw as traditional Jewish modes and feelings. Temple Emanu-El and the Park Avenue Synagogue in Manhattan, Temple B'rith Kodesh in Rochester, and other New York State synagogues supported composers by commissioning new liturgical works.

A new creativity in Jewish liturgical music emerged in the 1960s, strongly influenced by folk styles in the United States and Israel. Kutz Camp Institute, established in Warwick (Orange Co) in 1965, served as an incubator for new Reform Jewish music talent and helped develop the careers of such liturgical music artists as Debbie Friedman, Jeffrey Klepper, and Michael Isaacson. In the Conservative movement, Ramah camps in Wingdale (Dutchess Co) and Nyack (Rockland Co) reinforced the movement's own set of young people's prayer melodies. At the end of the 20th century, New York City remained a center of Jewish liturgical music. People packed the Carlebach Shul on the Upper West Side of Manhattan every Sabbath to sing and dance to Rabbi Shlomo Carlebach's (1925–94) songs; Congregation B'nai Jeshurun, a few blocks north, held standing-room-only "new age" musical services. A host of traditional, innovative, and hybrid forms of liturgical music continue to bring relevancy and meaning to the prayer experiences of congregants.

Katz, Israel J. "The Sacred and Secular Musical Traditions of the Sephardic Jews in the United States," *American Jewish Archives* 44 (Spring–Summer 1992): 331–56

Slobin, Mark. *Chosen Voices: The Story of the American Cantorate* (Urbana: Univ of Illinois Press, 1989)

Judah Cohen

Jewish Theological Seminary of America (JTS). Rabbinical school of the Conservative movement. Founded by Sabato Morais in 1886, the seminary began offering courses in January 1887 in the vestry of Shearith Israel, New York City's oldest Jewish congregation. The institution was intended as a traditional rabbinical program, designed to offer an alternative to the students at Hebrew Union College in Cincinnati, and promised to remain "faithful to Mosaic Law and ancestral traditions." When it faced financial difficulties at the turn of the century, a group of wealthy Jewish philanthropists from Reform congregations in New York City, led by Louis Marshall and Jacob Schiff, stepped forward to offer funding. They believed it was important to create an institution to train Americanized rabbis who could serve the huge numbers of eastern European immigrants who had settled into Jewish ghettos. The reconstituted seminary recruited prominent scholar Solomon Schechter from Cambridge University in 1902. Schechter built an impressive academic and religious institution on Lexington Ave between 58th and 59th Sts. As president, Cyrus Adler (1915–40) moved the seminary to Broadway, between 122d and 123d Sts on Morningside Heights, opposite Columbia University. After a long and acrimonious debate, in 1985 JTS ordained its first female rabbis. In addition to a rabbinical school, the seminary has a cantorial school, undergraduate and graduate schools, and several research centers and special programs. In 2002 JTS had 197 undergraduate students, 301 master's and doctoral and students, 38 cantorial students, and 126 rabbinical students.

Wertheimer, Jack, ed. *Tradition Renewed: A History of the Jewish Theological Seminary*, 2 vols (New York: Jewish Theological Seminary of America, 1997)

Dana Evan Kaplan

Jews and Judaism

Colonial Era and Early Republic

The Jewish community of New York City is the oldest Jewish settlement in what is now the United States. The original group of 23 Sephardic settlers (tracing their ancestry to Spain) arrived in New Amsterdam in 1654. Director General Petrus Stuyvesant was reluctant to admit the presence of the Jews, and he objected to their opening a public place of worship, but he relented under pressure from the Dutch West India Co. Immigrants from Holland later joined this group. After 1664 Ashkenazim (Jews of German and northern European origin) began to arrive and soon reached parity with the Sephardim. Over the next century Jews of both groups continued to arrive from countries such as England, Holland, Spain, Portugal, and Germany, often via other colonial ports in the Caribbean. By 1695 the Jewish community of 100 persons constituted 2.5% of the population of New York City. By the mid–18th century, that city's Jewish population reached 300, with an overwhelming Ashkenazi majority. New York Colony permitted the naturalization of Jews in 1720 and full citizenship in 1727.

Despite their small numbers, Jewish merchants played a significant economic role locally and internationally in the extensive Atlantic trade system that linked the American colonies, Africa, and the colonial powers of Europe. Prominent Jewish merchants made up New York City's Jewish elite who, along with their families, played high-profile roles in the community's religious and social life. Jacob Franks emigrated from England around 1708 and later married Abigail Levy, a merchant's daughter. Luis Moses Gomez arrived from Spain via France at about the same time. Gomez became the patriarch of a large clan encompassing three generations based in New York City and forming kin networks throughout Europe, colonial port cities, and the hinterlands of the North American frontier. Although the colony's Jewish population was concentrated in New York City, there were Jewish families in Newburgh [now in Orange Co] and on Long Island by the 1760s.

In the first half of the 18th century, the Franks and Gomez families, the former Ashkenazi and the latter Sephardi, together led New York City's preeminent Jewish religious institution, Shearith Israel, the first congregation in North America. Formed in 1654 shortly after the arrival of New York's first Jewish immigrants, the congregation adopted the Sephardic style of worship. By the 1720s Shearith Israel had purchased land for a cemetery and a new synagogue building, completed in 1730 on Mill St [now South William St]. Gomez played an integral role in the building of New York's first permanent synagogue. After his death in 1740, his son Mordecai took up the mantle of leadership alongside Franks. Also that year, Isaac Mendes Seixas defied the Spanish-Portuguese Jewish elite of New York City by marrying Rachel Levy in a wedding across the Sephardi-Ashkenazi divide, solidifying the familial and social bonds between the two groups. Shearith Israel represented a wealthy elite who not only worshiped together but provided for the Jewish poor and transients in the city. All aspects of Jewish life took place within the purview of the synagogue. Nevertheless, to some, the Jewish community suffered from religious laxity and a failure to enforce religious discipline. The Jews of New York City overwhelmingly sympathized with the patriot cause during the American Revolution. All but seven fled the city when the British seized the area in late 1776, returning after the British left.

Gershom Mendes Seixas, born in 1745 to Rachel and Isaac Mendes Seixas, became the first Jewish cleric born in the New World. Serving as *hazzan* (cantor or service leader) at Shearith Israel from before the Revolution to the time of his death in 1816, he defined the role of Jewish religious leadership in the late colonial and early national eras. He was the Jewish counterpart to the Protestant minister who guided his congregants morally and represented his community in the broader American public, while the lay leadership continued to look to the European rabbinate for guidance on questions of Jewish law. Although the Jewish community had long taken care to tend to the ill and indigent, and to properly bury the dead, these functions were formalized with the creation of the Kalfe Sedaka Mattan Besether (1798) and Hebra Hased Va Amet (1802).

German Jewish Immigration

In 1820 German-speaking Jews seeking to escape anti-Semitism and to improve their economic prospects began to arrive in New York State, primarily from Bohemia, Alsace-Lorraine, and German states including Bavaria, Baden, and Württemberg. The overwhelming majority of immigrants came with very few resources and intended to earn their livelihoods as peddlers and storekeepers. New philanthropic, religious, and mutual-aid institutions emerged to meet their needs, further undermining the unity of Jewish communal life with synagogue life. In 1822 Ashkenazi members of Shearith Israel formed the Hebrew Benevolent Society, which become the preeminent Jewish philanthropy organization in New York City by the 1840s.

In 1825 these Ashkenazim, likely bolstered by the presence of new arrivals, seceded from Shearith Israel to form B'nai Jeshurun, not only to establish the Ashkenazi rite of worship and stricter ritual observance but to lower the cost of ritual privileges such as blessing the Torah. The secession had a splintering effect on Jewish religious institutions in the city and precipitated the formation of a number of synagogues, mostly along national lines, among them Ansche Chesed, She'arey Tzedek, and Rodeph Sholem. German Jews associated with leaders of Ansche Chesed and Temple Emanu-El founded the German Hebrew Benevolent Society, which distributed funds exclusively to German Jews. From the 1820s through the 1850s, large and small charities proliferated, including a significant number of women's benevolent societies. In 1855 members of Shearith Israel opened the Jews' Hospital in the City of New York, renamed Mount Sinai Hospital in 1866. Benevolent societies merged to found the Hebrew Benevolent and Orphan Asylum Society in 1860.

Jewish charities played an important social as well as a philanthropic function. Annual balls provided both the base of funds and the opportunity for regular social events. German Jewish immigrants also joined together in mutual-aid organizations and fraternal orders to provide each other with sick benefits, burial services, and the society of their peers. One of the earliest and most important of these groups was B'nai B'rith, which was founded on New York City's East Side in 1843 as a secular Jewish organization with a structure of local lodges along the model of American fraternal orders like the Freemasons. B'nai B'rith quickly expanded throughout New York State and beyond.

With the advent of German immigration, Jewish communities formed beyond New York City. In 1825 the charismatic Jewish leader (and influential Jacksonian politician) Mordecai M. Noah enthusiastically promoted a scheme to settle Jews on Grand Island, near Buffalo, but nothing came of the plan. New York City utopians founded Sholom, a short-lived (1837–42) Jewish agricultural colony in Wawarsing (Ulster Co). Permanent Jewish communities took root in the booming cities of central and western New York State in the 1840s. The opening of the Erie Canal in 1825 and the development of railroads had made the hinterlands accessible for settlement and provided an outlet for intensifying German Jewish immigration. The establishment of Jewish communities in cities like Albany, Buffalo, Rochester, Syracuse, and Utica followed a similar pattern: a wave of German Jewish immigrants joined the few pioneers in what had been frontier villages and quickly created a range of institutions such as synagogues and mutual-aid societies. These early immigrants engaged in a variety of economic pursuits, including work as peddlers, dry goods sellers, carpenters, tailors, and watchmakers. In 1838 Joseph Sporborg and others founded a synagogue, Beth El, in Albany. In Rochester and Buffalo, the first Jews arrived in the late 1830s and soon established their first congregations, B'rith Kodesh (1848) and Beth El (1847), respectively. Jews in each city formed a B'nai B'rith lodge within two years of each other in the mid-1860s, and Rochester, Buffalo, and Albany each had a Hebrew Benevolent Society by the mid-1850s.

The Civil War divided the Jews in New York State over the question of group participation in the Union cause. Most chose not to highlight their Jewish identity but to contribute to the war effort as citizens, not as part of a specifically Jewish undertaking. Only Syracuse Jews opted to recruit a Jewish unit, in 1862, as a manifestation of a discretely Jewish patriotism. The war brought prosperity to the large and small cities of New York State, and consolidated the economic position of German Jews as major manufacturers, particularly in the fledgling ready-made clothing industry. German Jews also emerged as influential retailers responsible for the creation of the modern department store, of which R. H. Macy (1858), purchased in 1888 by Isidor and Nathan Straus, and Bloomingdale's (1872) in New York City were early pioneers.

The Emergence of Denominational Judaism

Reform Judaism in New York State emerged out of a confluence of factors including a precipitous decline in Jewish worship and the breakdown of traditional authority to enforce dietary laws or to certify marriages and other life-cycle rites. Reformers implemented changes in religious practice to gain the respect of their fellow citizens and to attract a younger generation to a form of Judaism more modern in its trappings, with the heavy use of the vernacular, choirs, and mixed seating. A more prominent role for women in religious life was one significant aspect of American mainstream religion adopted by Jewish reformers. Immigrant German Jews brought the seeds of Reform Judaism to the United States, and New York State was an important testing ground for major trends.

Rabbi Isaac Mayer Wise, the preeminent advocate of Reform in the United States in the 19th century, emigrated in 1846 from Bohemia [now in Czech Republic] to Albany, where he took up the pulpit at Congregation Beth El. There he instituted the radical reform of "family pews" where men and women worshiped together. (This was likely the first congregation in the history of Judaism that did not separate men from women.) By 1850 Wise faced such fierce opposition within Beth El that violence erupted at Rosh Hashanah holiday services. Over 70 of Wise's supporters then formed Anshe Emeth, where Wise served as rabbi until moving to Cincinnati in 1854.

Temple Emanu-El, founded in 1845 in New York City by lay leaders newly arrived from Germany, introduced major changes in worship, including the abolition of payment for ritual privileges, regular sermons, a new emphasis on decorum during worship, and the use of a German hymnal for those who did not understand Hebrew. Guided by the radical Reform rabbi Leo Merzbacher, Emanu-El did away with many aspects of traditional Judaism over the next 15 years, including the wearing of prayer shawls and head coverings during prayer, much of the standard Hebrew liturgy in favor of German and English, and separation of the sexes during the service. A minister and choir now recited prayers for the congregation. Merzbacher's Reform prayer book *Seder Tefilah* and Isaac Mayer Wise's more moderate *Minhag Amerika* both strongly affected the development of Reform Judaism after 1860 when it gained popularity throughout the state in established German Jewish communities. Rochester's Congregation B'rith Kodesh made a decisive move toward Reform when it adopted *Minhag Amerika* in 1862, on its way to becoming a preeminent institution of radical Reform in the United States. Its own prayer book, published in 1884, later influenced the standard liturgy of the Reform movement. By 1880 there was a confluence of religious, business, and philanthropic German Jewish elites within flagship Reform institutions in cities throughout the state.

As a result of the consolidation of denominational Reform, traditional congregations like Shearith Israel and B'nai Jeshurun increasingly identified as specifically Orthodox, or disaffected minorities within transforming synagogues split off to found Orthodox congregations. Rochester's Congregation Aitz Raanon broke from B'rith Kodesh in 1870. In 1886 leaders of established congregations like Shearith Israel and Ahawath Chesed joined with national leaders to found the Jewish Theological Seminary of America in New York City as a defense against Reform. The seminary later evolved into the rabbinical institution of Conservative Judaism. On the eve of mass migration from eastern Europe, how-

Rehearsing for the parents and children service held at Temple Adath Yeshurun in Syracuse, *ca* 1960.

ever, Orthodox Jewish practice in New York State and throughout the United States was negligible.

Immigration from Eastern Europe

From 1880 to 1924 over 2 million Jews from eastern Europe came to the United States, with Russia, Poland, Ukraine, Belarus, Lithuania, and Romania as the most common source areas. In 1875 there were 3,000 Jews living in Rochester, and by 1910 there were 11,000. About 80,000 Jews lived in New York City in 1880, constituting 9% of its population and by 1910 between 800,000 and 1,500,000 lived there. Some 37,000 Sephardic Jews from Turkey, the Balkan countries, Greece, and Syria also emigrated during this era. Traditional Judaism flourished among eastern European Jews in the myriad small synagogues called *khevres* or shuls formed by *landslayt* (immigrants from the same town or region in eastern Europe) that combined worship with mutual-aid functions. In 1887 the Orthodox Union was created to bring together large and small Orthodox congregations, most of them in New York City, to prevent attenuation of traditional Judaism under the forces of assimilation and to manage the accommodation of Orthodoxy to American life. Shuls such as Manhattan's Kehilath Jeshurun, founded in 1872, led the way to Modern Orthodoxy and away from *khevre*-style worship by emphasizing decorum and introducing English language for the benefit of the younger generation.

The small workshops of the city's garment industry were concentrated in the immigrant neighborhood of the Lower East Side. Eastern Europeans—men, unmarried women, and children alike—overwhelmingly earned their livelihoods in the needle trades before 1910. Alongside other new arrivals from southern and eastern Europe, Jewish immigrant workers of this era made their mark on the labor movement in the United States. In the political arena, the Socialist Labor Party and later the Socialist Party both had influential Yiddish sections. The unions of the clothing trades such as the United Hebrew Trades (1888), International Ladies' Garment Workers' Union (1900), and the Amalgamated Clothing Workers of America (1914) consisted primarily of Jewish members. Especially after 1900, unions dominated by eastern European immigrant Jews played a prominent role in labor. They were decisive in the widespread strikes of 1909 and 1910 that earned labor major concessions. Jews helped to elect the first Socialist congressman from New York State in 1914, Meyer London of the Lower East Side.

Radical Yiddish periodicals published in New York City enjoyed an avid readership among immigrants nationwide, including the anarchist *Freie Arbeiter Stimme (Free Voice of Labor)* and the radical journal *Tsukunft (Future)*. The largest of them all, *Forverts (Forward)*, edited by Abraham Cahan, claimed to be the voice of the Jewish worker movement. The mainly socialist Workmen's Circle, founded in New York City in 1892 as a mutual-aid society and becoming a national order in 1900, combined aspects of a mutual-aid society and a fraternal order. In the first decades of the 20th century, leftists founded two more fraternal orders along sectarian lines. Immigrants also formed hometown organizations known as *landsmanshaftn* based on political or religious affinities to provide members with health and life insurance, burial benefits, and, in some cases, places of worship.

Beginning in the World War I era, an increasing number of women's clubs and *landsmanshaftn* auxiliaries in New York City exerted a strong influence on immigrant communal life in their philanthropy on behalf of Jews in Europe and in managing secular Jewish schools for children based on the Yiddish language. A lively Yiddish theater developed in New York City at the end of the 19th century, first around the Bowery and later on 2d Ave. The first Yiddish production, Avrom Goldfadn's *Koldunya; or, The Witch,* took place in the Bowery in 1892. By 1914 there were 14 resident Yiddish theater companies in New York City offering comedies, operettas, melodramas, and translations of the classics.

Despite some German Jewish resistance to the mass immigration of Jews from eastern Europe, philanthropy was the central connection between Germans and eastern Europeans in New York State. As part of a broad-based reform impulse on the part of the middle and upper classes in the United States to improve the lot of southern and eastern European immigrants and to assimilate them into American society, a number of German Jewish social welfare institutions acted, led by notable philanthropists such as the investment banker Jacob Schiff. Early efforts in New York City include B'nai B'rith, the Baron de Hirsch Fund, and the Reform body the Union of American Hebrew Congregations. In the 1880s the United Hebrew Charities provided food, shelter, and medical care, among other goods and services. Vocational schools for boys and girls, the Young Men's and Young Women's Hebrew Associations, and the Hebrew Free School provided education in the 1880s and 1890s. Some of these institutions joined forces in 1889 to form the Educational Alliance, a community center that offered classes, meeting rooms, a library, a gymnasium, and a wide range of cultural events. In 1909 the Hebrew Sheltering Society (1889) merged with the Hebrew Immigrant Aid Society (1902) to form the Hebrew Immigrant Aid Society (HIAS) in New York City. The HIAS provided crucial aid for immigrants immediately upon their arrival, one exception to German dominance in immigrant social welfare in the city.

Developments in the cities of the central and western parts of the state mirror those in New York City. Eastern European immigrant workers concentrated in the garment industry and initially settled in immigrant neighborhoods in Buffalo and Rochester. Not all Jews supported labor activity. In late 1890, for example, Rochester's men's clothing manufacturers, dominated by German Jews, established the Rochester Clothiers Exchange to quell labor protest. Other Jews, though, formed *landsmanshaftn* and branches of nationwide organizations such as the Workmen's Circle and the Labor-Zionist Poalei Zion. Union organizing had some early victories in Rochester, an important regional garment center. Garment workers, some of whom were affiliated with the Knights of Labor, agitated in 1888 for a nine-hour day. Although the United Garment Workers founded two union locals in Rochester in the 1890s, and a substantial group of Jewish tailors took part in the Socialist Labor Party at that time, Jewish unions in Rochester did not enjoy success until 1913, when thousands of members of the United Garment Workers marched in the streets to secure a 52-hour workweek and overtime pay. The Jews of Rochester also helped to elect three socialists to city government in 1917. Despite class tensions between Jewish workers and bosses, the German Jewish philanthropies of Rochester joined in 1882 to form the United Jewish Charities to coordinate aid to eastern European immigrants.

In Buffalo beginning in 1903, the German Jewish Federation performed philanthropic work on behalf of eastern European immigrants. The Jewish Orphan Asylum of Western New York opened its doors in Rochester in 1877. As in the social reform movement nationwide, Jewish women played central roles in settlement house activity. The sisterhood societies of the Reform congregations in Buffalo and Rochester respectively took charge of Zion House and the Baden Street Settlement House and remained active in these endeavors for many decades.

From the beginning of the eastern European immigrant era, new immigrants, often facing anti-Semitism at the more established resorts in Saratoga Springs and the northern Catskills, made a home in rural areas of Ulster and Sullivan Cos north of New York City, establishing the southern Catskills as an important Jewish farming and summer resort community. Jews were drawn to the region by the prospect of farming, although few had an agricultural background. By 1900 the typical Jewish farming family combined dairy farming with summer boarding of Jewish guests from the city to make ends meet. Thriving Jewish ethnic economies consisting of merchants, artisans, and kosher butchers in communities like Ellenville (Ulster Co) developed to support a network of surrounding farms. With the help of the Jewish Colonization Association (renamed Jewish Agricultural and Industrial Society in 1922) and the bustling summer season, Jewish farmers provided dairy products, eggs, and, later, kosher poultry to New York City well into the 1960s. The Jewish agricultural collective, the Inter-County Farmers' Cooperative Association, was a pioneer in large-scale egg production during the 1940s.

World War I to World War II

By World War I eastern European Jews had begun to penetrate the elite religious and charitable institutions of German Jewry. Reform congregations such as Rochester's B'rith Kodesh and Emanu-El in New York City admitted eastern European Jews to their ranks who had, like German Jews, assimilated into middle-class society. New organizations were established in New York City to defend Jewish interests, such as the American Jewish Committee, founded in 1906. Louis Marshall, a Syracuse native and a leading lawyer in New York City, was the organization's president from 1912 to 1929. Its effort to expand beyond its base among German Jews by forming in 1908 the New York Kehillah, a community-wide organization, was only partially successful. Among its activities, the American Jewish Committee defended American Jews against acts of anti-Semitism, such as the blood libel accusations in Massena (St. Lawrence Co) in 1927.

Starting in 1914, however, Jewish organizations turned much of their attention to the crisis in European Jewry, which served to unify the Jews of New York State across the lines of nationality and class. Germans, eastern Europeans, radicals, workers, storekeepers, and business owners joined together in a large-scale campaign to raise funds and other forms of assistance for the Jews of Europe who now faced the upheaval of war, poverty, and pogroms. The American Jewish Joint Distribution Committee, founded in 1914 by many of those active in the American Jewish Committee, helped coordinate relief efforts. In 1917 wealthy philanthropists like Felix M. Warburg created the Federation for the Support of Jewish Philanthropic Societies of New York City (later known as Federation of Jewish Philanthropies) to coordinate the considerable fund-raising energies of the city's vast network of Jewish organizations across the ideological spectrum in the Jewish War Relief Campaign. In collective and individual campaigns, Jews throughout New York State played a decisive role in the survival of many Jewish communities abroad during World War I and after.

The restrictive federal immigration law of 1924 brought an end to the era of mass migration. By the 1920s workers buoyed by union victories earned higher wages, which allowed them to leave the garment shop to open small businesses as Jewish communities expanded to the outer boroughs of New York City. In 1910 over 500,000 Jews resided in the Lower East Side, but extensive Jewish settlement in other parts of the city had already begun. Between 1899 and 1904, for example, the Jewish population of Brownsville in Brooklyn rose from 10,000 to 50,000. Encouraged by the expansion of mass transit and a building boom in the 1920s, 160,000 Jews by 1930 left the Lower East Side for new neighborhoods in Upper Manhattan, Brooklyn, and the Bronx. Synagogue centers built in this era, such as the Brooklyn Jewish Center, combined worship, recreational, and social functions to cater to the needs of this new Jewish middle class. The Jacob H. Schiff Center in the Bronx boasted a complex with a swimming pool, gymnasium, auditorium, and sanctuary. Most of the new centers affiliated with the Conservative movement, the denominational choice of acculturated eastern European Jews and their American-born children. Conservative Judaism hit its stride as a middle ground between Orthodoxy and Reform under the leadership of Solomon Schechter, who headed the Jewish Theological Seminary from 1902 until his death in 1915. Other denominational institutions established in New York City during the 1920s—a period of growth and experimentation in Jewish life—include Modern Orthodoxy's Yeshiva University, the Jewish Institute of Religion, and Mordecai M. Kaplan's Society for the Advancement of Judaism, which later became the center of Reconstructionism, Judaism's fourth movement within the United States.

Zionism, the movement to establish a Jewish homeland, was a contentious issue that divided Jewish leadership in the early decades of the 20th century. There was much opposition to Zionism, particularly from within the Reform movement, but the foundation in New York City in 1912 of the women's Zionist organization Hadassah signaled that Zionism was on its way to becoming a popular movement among American Jews. Reform rabbi Stephen S. Wise, founder of the Free Synagogue in New York City in 1907, became an outspoken leader of American Zionism. In 1917, upset by the non-Zionist American Jewish Committee, he helped found the rival American Jewish Congress (which he led until his death in 1949), and in 1922 he helped establish the Jewish Institute of Religion in New York City as an alternative to Hebrew Union College, the Reform seminary in Cincinnati. By the 1930s most sectors of the American Jewish community were increasingly hospitable toward Zionism.

The crisis in Germany after 1933 led the American Joint Distribution Committee, B'nai B'rith, the American Jewish Committee, and the American Jewish Congress to organize to rescue European Jewry and resolve the refugee crisis. Although they succeeded in drawing attention to the horrible situation for Jews in Germany, their efforts were hobbled by many factors, including inaction at the highest levels of government and internal dissension. During World War II Jews of all ideological convictions united against Hitlerism. Of the 150,000 German Jewish refugees who found their way to the United States in the 1930s and 1940s, nearly 40,000 settled in the Washington Heights neighborhood of northern Manhattan, among them Henry Kissinger. Less well known is the group of German Jews, used to living in rural areas, who with the help of some resettlement agencies became cattle dealers in Central New York. In large areas of Cortland, Chenango, and Broome Cos, German Jewish refugees dominated the cattle-trading industry for several decades. They also established summer guest houses and camps in the area.

Political Activism

Jews have an established tradition of political activism and were among leaders of the Socialist Party in the first decades of the 20th century and leaders of the Communist Party in the interwar years. Jews played a major role in the American Labor Party during the 1930s and 1940s, and in its anti-Communist rival, the Liberal Party, from the 1940s through the 1980s. The first Jewish candidate for governor, Oscar S. Straus, was the Progressive Party candidate in 1912. But most Jewish political activity has been directed toward the major political parties. Samuel Koenig was elected secretary of state in 1906 on the Republican ticket, the first Jewish candidate elected to statewide office. In 1932 Democrat Herbert H. Lehman was elected the state's first (and through the early 21st century, the state's only) Jewish governor. In 1949 Lehman became the first Jewish US senator from New York State. From the 1950s through the 1970s prominent Jewish politicians in the state included US senator Jacob K. Javits (1957–81), state comptroller Arthur Levitt (1954–78), and state attorney general Louis J. Lefkowitz (1957–78).

Emanuel Bernard Hart, a New York City merchant, was the first Jew elected to the House of Representatives from the state, in 1850. Many have followed, among them Gloversville (Fulton Co) industrialist Lucius N. Littauer (1897–1907), Brooklyn Democrat Emanuel Celler (1923–73), Rochester economist Meyer Jacobstein (1923–29), and New York City activist Bella Abzug (1971–79). There have also been three Jewish members of the US Supreme Court from New York State: Benjamin N. Cardozo (1932–38), who had been a judge on the New York State Court of Appeals since 1917; Arthur Goldberg (1962–65), who was the unsuccessful Democratic candidate for governor in 1970; and Ruth Bader Ginsburg (1993–).

After World War II

The Holocaust was felt by New York State's Jewish population in ways direct and indirect. Many knew of relatives who had not survived the war. Most felt that the creation of a Jewish state was a necessity in a world in which Jewish persecution on such a scale was possible. It was in Lake Success (Nassau Co) in 1947 that the United Nations approved the partition plan that led to the creation of Israel, and most New York Jews were fervent supporters of the new country. After the war, another kind of Jewish refugee came to New York State; Hasidim (ultra-Orthodox Jews), refugees from Hungary and to a lesser extent Poland, settled in the Brooklyn neighborhoods of Williamsburg, Crown Heights, and Borough Park. In their dress and customs they consciously stayed apart from the assimilating tendencies of most American Jews. They were divided into numerous sects, each centered around the charismatic figure of their rebbe. For the most part they did not join the postwar exodus to the suburbs but remained in Brooklyn. Hasidic sects also formed rural-suburban communities within easy commuting distance to New York City, including New Square, Monsey (Rockland Co), and Kiryas Joel (Orange Co), the largest Hasidic settlement outside of Brooklyn with a population of 13,138 in 2000. Kiryas Joel, an incorporated village, created unique church-state relationships that were litigated before the US Supreme Court.

In the late 1940s and 1950s, the Jewish population burgeoned in the areas surrounding New York City, including Westchester Co to the north, Nassau and Suffolk Cos on Long Island, and Bergen Co in New Jersey. By 1960 Brownsville in Brooklyn and the Lower East Side of Manhattan, once at the heart of the city's Jewish working class, had lost almost all of their Jewish population. The Bronx, too, which in 1930 had the highest Jewish percentage of any of the boroughs of New York City, was losing many of its Jewish residents. In 1960 Westchester Co had approximately 135,000 Jews and Nassau Co had over 330,000. Congregations throughout the state followed their members to the suburbs, where they built new sanctuaries, as did Rochester's B'rith Kodesh and Albany's long-standing Reform congregation, Beth Emeth.

Feminism has had an important impact on all

New York City rabbi A. M. Eisenbach studying a Torah scroll. Photograph by Seymour Edelstein, 1988.

aspects of Judaism. The Reconstructionist and then Reform seminaries were the first to ordain female rabbis, and women immediately took up pulpits in New York State in the early 1970s. After a fierce debate at the Jewish Theological Seminary, the Conservative institution in New York City began admitting women to its rabbinical program during Chancellor Gerson Cohen's tenure (1972–86); 32 women had received rabbinic ordination at the seminary by 1992. All Jewish denominations with the exception of Orthodoxy have granted full ritual privileges to women. In the early 1990s Elat Chayyim Spiritual Retreat Center, New York State's first post-denominational institution, was founded in Accord (Ulster Co).

In the postwar era, the Catskill summer resort industry, ranging from large hotel complexes to bungalow colonies to efficiency cabins, continued as it had since the 1920s to offer Jews from New York City a place to meet potential spouses and to sample the talents of emerging entertainers. Among the performers were Eddie Fisher and Woody Allen, who honed their skills on Catskill audiences before moving on to Broadway, film, and television careers. Others who had early success in the borscht belt were Sid Caesar, Milton Berle, and Barbra Streisand. In August 1969 Jewish farmer Max Yasgur allowed his farm in Bethel (Sullivan Co) to be used for the Woodstock Festival. Changes in vacation patterns, rises in land values, and consolidation in the egg and poultry markets brought a decline to both Jewish resorts and Jewish agriculture in the region. During the summer months in the 21st century, Hasidim from Brooklyn occupy many of the camps and bungalows that had been used by earlier generations of Jews.

A new Jewish population arrived in New York State in the 1960s and 1970s, with a growing number of Sephardic Jews from Syria, Iraq, Egypt, Iran, Morocco, and other Arab and Middle Eastern countries. Many of these migrants settled in Brooklyn and Queens. Beginning in the 1970s there was a massive immigration of Jews from the Soviet Union who settled especially in the Brooklyn neighborhoods of Brighton Beach and Manhattan Beach. A 2002 study estimated that there were 202,000 Russian-speaking Jews in the New York City metropolitan area (New York City, Long Island, and Westchester Co), with 62% living in Brooklyn. Although most came from eastern Europe, there was also a substantial population of Bukharan Jews from Central Asia.

Since the late 19th century, New York State and especially New York City have been the center of the cultural, intellectual, and institutional life of the American Jewish community. This remains true in the early 21st century, even though the percentage of the nation's Jews living in the state has been declining. In 1960, 46% of Jews in the United States lived in New York State; by 1990 that number had decreased to 31%. A 2002 study of the New York City metropolitan area suggests that the region's Jewish population, at about 1.4 million, remains largely unchanged from recent years. In 2000, though, the Jewish population of New York City, at about 972,000, fell below the million mark for the first time in a century. Still, almost 70% of the Jewish population of the metropolitan area live in New York City, with almost half (456,000) living in Brooklyn. Manhattan had 243,000; Queens, 186,000; Nassau Co, 221,000; Westchester Co, 129,000; and Suffolk Co, 90,000. About one-fifth of the Jews in the metropolitan region consider themselves to be Orthodox, making the area the largest concentration of Orthodox Jews in the United States.

See also ANTI-SEMITISM; BORSCHT BELT; CATSKILLS; CENTRAL ASIANS; FORT ONTARIO EMERGENCY REFUGEE SHELTER; GERMANS; HARLEM; LITERATURE, NEW YORK CITY AREA; LOWER EAST SIDE; MODERN DANCE; MUSICAL THEATER; ORGANIZED CRIME; RUSSIANS.

Adler, Selig, and Thomas E. Connolly. *From Ararat to Suburbia: The History of the Jewish Community of Buffalo* (Philadelphia: Jewish Publication Society of America, 1960)
Diner, Hasia R. *Lower East Side Memories: A Jewish Place in America* (Princeton, NJ: Princeton Univ Press, 2000)
Eisenstadt, Peter. *Affirming the Covenant: A History of Temple B'rith Kodesh, Rochester, New York, 1848–1998* (Syracuse: Syracuse Univ Press, 1998)
Feingold, Henry L. *A Time for Searching: Entering the Mainstream, 1920–1945* (Baltimore: Johns Hopkins Univ Press, 1992)
Gerber, Morris O. A. *Pictorial History of Albany's Jewish Community* (Albany: Author, 1986)
Grinstein, Hyman B. *The Rise of the Jewish Community of New York, 1654–1860* (Philadelphia: Jewish Publication Society, 1945)
Karp, Abraham J. *Haven and Home: A History of the Jews in America* (New York: Schocken Books, 1985)
Levine, Rhonda F. *Class, Networks, and Identity: Replanting Jewish Lives from Nazi Germany to Rural New York* (Lanham, Md: Rowman & Littlefield, 2001)
Marcus, Jacob Rader. *The Colonial American Jew, 1942–1776* (Detroit: Wayne State Univ Press, 1970)
Moore, Deborah Dash. *At Home in America: Second Generation New York Jews* (New York: Columbia Univ Press, 1981)
Rischin, Moses. *The Promised City: New York's Jews, 1870–1914* (Cambridge, Mass: Harvard Univ Press, 1962)
Rosenberg, Stuart E. *The Jewish Community in Rochester, 1843–1925* (New York: Columbia Univ Press, 1954)
Rudolph, Bernard G. *From a Minyan to a Community: A History of the Jews of Syracuse* (Syracuse: Syracuse Univ Press, 1970)
Shaigel, Baila, and Harold L. Drimmer. *The Jews of Westchester: A Social History* (Fleischmanns, NY: Purple Mountain Press, 1994)
Wenger, Beth S. *New York Jews and the Great Depression: Uncertain Promise* (New Haven, Conn: Yale Univ Press, 1996)

Jocelyn Cohen

jitney service. See TAXI AND CAR SERVICES.

Joel, Billy [William Martin] (*b* Bronx, 9 May 1949). Singer and songwriter. Joel's father was a German-born engineer, and his family moved to the Hicksville/Levittown area (Nassau Co) when he was a child. He was interested in music from a young age and at 14 joined his first band. Joel attended Hicksville High School, dropping out shortly before graduation. In 1972 he released his first solo album, *Cold Spring Harbor.* He moved to Los Angeles in 1973, and that year his first hit single, "Piano Man," came out on an album of the same name. A year after returning to New York State in 1975 he released the jazz-inflected ballad "New York State of Mind," popular among many residents and others. His first number-one album was *52d Street* (1979). Joel won five Grammy Awards between 1978 and 1980 and the Grammy Legend Award in 1990. He was inducted into the Rock and Roll Hall of Fame in 1999. In 2001 he released *Fantasies and Delusions,* an album of solo classical piano compositions. *Movin' Out,* a Broadway musical based on his songs, with choreography and direction by Twyla Tharp, opened in 2002 and won two Tony Awards in 2003.

Geller, Debbie. *Billy Joel: An Illustrated Biography* (New York: McGraw-Hill, 1985)

J. Justin Gustainis

Jogues, Isaac. See NORTH AMERICAN MARTYRS.

John Jay College of Criminal Justice. New York City public college, part of the City University of New York (CUNY). Cooperative education under the auspices of the College of the City of New York and the New York City Police Department began on 23 Apr 1925, when the Police Academy opened in City College's Commerce Building at Lexington Ave and 23d St. In 1940 City College initiated a program for training policemen. An associate degree curriculum in police science began in 1955 at the Baruch School of Business and Public Administration. Created in 1964, with the main building at 899 10th Ave near 59th St in Manhattan, John Jay College of Criminal Justice took over the program. To enhance academic coursework, the college offers students internships in such fields as corrections administration and fire science as well as in criminal justice. John Jay College confers both baccalaureate and master's degrees, including a master's program in forensic psychology, and administers the CUNY PhD in criminal justice. In fall 2000 the college enrolled 6,617 full-time and 2,942 part-time undergraduate students, and 240 full-time and 813 part-time graduate students.

Roff, Sandra Shoiock, Anthony M. Cucchiara, and Barbara J. Dunlap. *From the Free Academy to CUNY: Illustrating Public Higher Education in New York City, 1847–1997* (New York: Fordham Univ Press, 2000)

Pamela Cooper

Johnsburg. Town (pop 2,450) in NW Warren Co. Crane Mountain (3,289 ft/1,002.5 m) is a landmark. John Thurman (1730–1809) patented the land and built his home in 1790; the town was formed from Thurman in 1805. John Thurman built a cotton factory and calico print works (1797), the latter believed to be the first in the United States. A large tannery (1833–85) at Wevertown was the first of several. The Wesleyan Methodist Church was a center of Underground Railroad activity. The Adirondack Railroad (1871) opened Johnsburg to tourism. In 1878 Henry H. Barton successfully processed garnet for industrial abrasives, and it has been mined at various locations ever since. The town helped popularize winter sports following the 1932 Winter Olympics at Lake Placid; the first commercial ski area in the East (1933), ski trains (1934–41), the first electric ski lift (1947), and the state-owned Gore Mountain ski facility (1964) are some of the attractions. The Hudson River White Water Derby (1957) attracts canoeists and kayakers annually, and in the late 20th century, recreational rafting became popular. The Upper Hudson River Railroad runs scheduled tourist trains on the old line. Johnsburg was the birthplace and childhood home of Eben E. Rexford (1847–1916), author of the popular song "Silver Threads among the Gold."

Marilyn J. Van Dyke

Johnson, Alexander Bryan (*b* Gosport, England, 29 May 1786; *d* Utica, 9 Sept 1867). Banker and philosopher. He was of Jewish descent, a fact he kept closely hidden his entire life. Johnson received a limited education until 1801, when, at the age of 14, he and the rest of his family emigrated and joined his father in Utica, where he had settled in 1787. He worked in his father's store until he was 21, then left to operate a glass factory near Albany. This was not satisfying, so Johnson moved in 1811 to New York City, where he studied finance. In 1812 he returned to Utica, where he became interested in banking and in 1819 was appointed president of the Utica branch of the Ontario Bank of Canandaigua (Ontario Co). Simultaneously, Johnson studied law and was admitted in 1822 to the New York State Bar, though he did not engage in legal practice. Instead, he continued as president of the Ontario bank until 1855. Johnson is best remembered for his writings, especially on language. Although neglected at the time, *The Philosophy of Human Knowledge* (1828), *A Treatise on Language* (1836), and *The Meaning of Words* (1854) argue for the limitations of language as a means of understanding external reality and anticipate some of the insights of logical positivism and 20th-century linguistic philosophy. Other of his books include *Religion in Its Relation to the Present Life* (1841), a moral treatise; *An Encyclopedia of Instruction* (1856); *An Inquiry into the Nature of Value and of Capital* (1813), an innovative work of economic theory.

Todd, Charles L., and Robert Sonkin. *Alexander Bryan Johnson: Philosophical Banker* (Syracuse: Syracuse Univ Press, 1977)

John R. Deitrick

Johnson, Alvin S(aunders) (*b* Homer, Neb, 18 Dec 1874; *d* Upper Nyack, Rockland Co, 7 June 1971). Educator and political activist. The son of Danish immigrants, Johnson attended the University of Nebraska, receiving a BA in 1897 and an MA the following year. In 1898 he moved to New York City to attend Columbia University, earning a PhD in economics in 1902. After graduating he taught economics at Columbia (1902–6) and Cornell Universities (1912–16). Johnson then worked as an editor for the *New Republic* (1917–23) and for the *Encyclopedia of the Social Sciences* (1928–34). But Johnson's greatest accomplishments came in educational administration. In 1919 he was one of the founders of the New School for Social Research in New York City, a pioneering institution in the area of adult higher education. He served as the New School's director from 1923 to 1945. A champion of academic freedom, in 1933 Johnson founded the University in Exile at the New School. By 1941 this program had provided refuge for more than 170 European scholars fleeing from the Nazi and other fascist regimes. Johnson was also a state-level political activist on matters of race. He headed the Committee on Discrimination in Employment (1943–45), coauthored New York's antidiscrimination Ives-Quinn bill (1945), and led a successful drive to ban admissions discrimination in New York State's private colleges (1946–48). After 1948 Johnson retired from public life, keeping busy with writing projects and developing adult education programs at the New School. A prolific scholar Johnson was learned in a wide range of disciplines, authoring 10 books and more than 100 articles.

Johnson, Alvin S. *Pioneer's Progress: An Autobiography* (New York: Viking Press, 1952)

Tod M. Ottman

Johnson, Guy (*b* County Meath, Ireland, ?1740; *d* London, 5 Mar 1788). Loyalist officer and British superintendent of Indian affairs. Johnson, a nephew of Sir William Johnson who arrived in America in 1756, served as a provincial officer in the French and Indian War and participated in both the 1759 expedition against Fort Niagara [now in Porter, Niagara Co] and Maj Gen Jeffery Amherst's campaign of 1759–60. In 1763 he married Sir William's youngest daughter, Mary, and settled in the Mohawk Valley. With his uncle's patronage, Johnson rose steadily in the ranks of the Indian Department, becoming a deputy agent in 1762 and a secretary in 1765. He was also a Tryon Co militia officer, chief justice of the Court of Common Pleas in 1772, and Colonial Assembly representative from 1773 to 1775. After Sir William's death in 1774, Gen Thomas Gage appointed Johnson to replace his uncle as interim superintendent of Indian affairs. Unable to contain growing revolutionary activity in the Mohawk Valley, in May 1775 Johnson and his family left their estate, Guy Park [now in Amsterdam, Montgomery Co]. The Americans later confiscated the property. At a stopover at Oswego during their flight to Canada, Mary died in childbirth.

After hearing of Maj John Campbell's appointment as superintendent of Indian affairs in Quebec, Johnson journeyed to England, accompanied by Joseph Brant, Daniel Claus, and other loyalists, in December 1775 seeking clarification of his powers. He returned in 1776 as superintendent of the Six Nations with orders to assist the British army in its operations around New York City, but his role was peripheral. Only when he returned to Fort Niagara in 1779 did he effectively encourage Iroquois loyalty and military expeditions against the New York frontiers. In 1781 Johnson's reputation was tarnished in a scandal involving the Indian Department's accounts with the Niagara trading firm Taylor and Forsyth. Sir John Johnson, his cousin and brother-in-law, replaced him as superintendent in 1782. Johnson returned to England after the war to defend his conduct in court and present loyalist claims. He died during the trial and was posthumously exonerated. Guy Park is now a New York State historic site.

Gibb, Harley L. "Colonel Guy Johnson, Superintendent General of Indian Affairs, 1774–82," *Papers of the Michigan Academy of Science, Arts, and Letters* 27 (1941): 595–613

Sullivan, James, Alexander C. Flick, and Milton W. Hamilton, eds. *The Papers of Sir William Johnson*, 14 vols (Albany: Univ of the State of New York, 1921–65)

David L. Preston

Johnson, Henry L(incoln) (*b* Winston-Salem, NC, 1897; *d* Washington, DC, 2 July 1929). World War I hero. In 1917 Johnson left his job as a baggage handler at Albany's Union Station to enlist in the US Army. He was assigned to the 369th Infantry, the Harlem Hellfighters or Black Rattlers, which was sent to Europe to serve under the French army. On 14 May 1918 a German raid party attacked a post he guarded in France's Argonne Forest. Johnson killed three Germans and rescued a comrade. He was awarded France's highest military honor, the Croix de Guerre, making him not only the first American to receive that honor but also a celebrated hero among the African Americans. He was promoted to sergeant before being discharged in 1919. When the Hellfighters arrived back in the United States, Johnson was featured in a parade up 5th Ave in Manhattan. He returned to Albany, where people also celebrated his bravery. He remained there but, debilitated from war injuries, was unable to work steadily. He died in a military hospital in Washington, DC, and was buried with full military honors at Arlington National Cemetery in Virginia. In 1991 a portion of Northern Blvd in Albany was renamed Henry Johnson Blvd. The city later erected a monument and bronze bust of Johnson in Washington Park. In 1996 he was awarded a Purple Heart and at the Pentagon on 13 Feb 2003 received the army's second highest honor, the Distinguished Service Cross. As of 2003 long-standing efforts to award Johnson a Medal of Honor had not been successful.

DiSanto, Victor J. "Henry Johnson's Paradox: A Soldier's Story," *Afro-Americans in New York Life and History* 21 (July 1997): 7–18

Victor DiSanto

Johnson, Sir John (*b* Mount Johnson [now Fort Johnson, Montgomery Co], 5 Nov 1741; *d* Montreal, 4 Jan 1830). Loyalist officer and Indian agent. Son of Sir William Johnson and Catherine Weissenburg, John Johnson was knighted in 1765. On his father's death in 1774 he inherited a baronetcy and an extensive estate in the Mohawk Valley but fled to Canada in 1776 after Gen Philip Schuyler issued a warrant for his arrest on the basis of his loyalist sympathies. Commissioned a lieutenant colonel by Canadian governor Guy Carleton in June 1776, Johnson recruited New York loyalists for the King's Royal Regiment of New York. In the summer of 1777 he commanded this regiment during the siege of Fort Stanwix [now Rome, Oneida Co] and at the Battle of Oriskany on 6 August. In 1780 Johnson led combined forces of loyalists, British regulars, and Indians on two raids that destroyed homes and farms in the Schoharie and Mohawk Valleys. In 1782 he was promoted to brigadier general and commissioned superintendent general and inspector general of the Six Nations Indians and those in the Province of Quebec. After the war he supervised the settlement of loyalist refugees in Canada, continued to advocate for the welfare of Indians, and served on the Legislative Council of Quebec from 1786 to 1791. When Upper Canada was established in 1791, he failed to secure the governorship. Following this disappointment he moved to London for several years before returning to Canada in 1796. Soon after, he accepted a position on the Legislative Council of Upper Canada and continued to acquire substantial real estate holdings in both Upper and Lower Canada.

Thomas, Earle. *Sir John Johnson: Loyalist Baronet* (Toronto: Dundurn Press, 1986)

Christine Sternberg Patrick

Johnson, Sir William (*b* Smithstown, Ireland, ?1715; *d* Johnstown [now in Fulton Co], 11 July

1774). Influential landowner, soldier, diplomat, and British superintendent of Indian Affairs.

EARLY CAREER

Born into a prominent Anglo-Irish family, Johnson emigrated to New York in 1738 as a client of his uncle Peter Warren, a Royal Navy captain. Warren's marriage to Susannah DeLancey and ties to Gov George Clinton shaped Johnson's early political connections. Johnson developed his uncle's estate, Warrensburgh, near the Mohawk community of Tiononderoge [now Florida, Montgomery Co], and entered the fur trade around 1739, securing a lucrative contract to supply the British post at Oswego. By that time he was living with a runaway indentured servant named Catherine Weissenburg; they had three children but were never legally married. Johnson acquired large tracts of land and took great pride in his efforts to bring colonists into the Mohawk Valley. Accompanying his economic success was even greater political activity, especially as an ally of Gov Clinton. He became justice of the peace (1745), a colonel of the militia (1748), and a member of the governor's council (1751).

His relations with his Mohawk neighbors made Johnson an important negotiator in Anglo Iroquois diplomacy. During King George's War (1744–48) he organized Mohawk scouting parties against the French in the St. Lawrence and Champlain Valleys. He gained a reputation for fair trading with the Mohawks, who named him Warrighiyagey ("Doer of Great Things" or "In the Midst of Affairs"). He learned to speak Mohawk and became familiar with Iroquois diplomatic rituals. Throughout his life, Johnson's influence among the Iroquois was based upon his Mohawk connections, particularly the sachem Theyanoguin [Hendrick Peters; King Hendrick] and later Joseph and Molly Brant. He consistently exploited opportunities for self-promotion and advancement, resigning from a New York provincial post in Indian affairs in 1751 when the assembly would not reimburse his wartime expenditures, and seeking instead the royal position of superintendent of Indian Affairs of the Northern Department, which he got in 1756.

THE FRENCH AND INDIAN WAR

In 1755 Gen Edward Braddock commissioned Johnson to command an expedition against the French at Fort St. Frédéric [now Crown Point, Essex Co]. Although they failed to capture the fort, Johnson's provincials gained a victory over the French at Lake George that raised British morale sunk after the defeat of Braddock's army in the Ohio Valley that summer. Johnson suffered a leg wound that continuously affected his health. His Mohawk ally Theyanoguin was killed. The victory heightened Johnson's transatlantic prestige, and in 1755 the Crown awarded him a baronetcy. He was nonetheless unable to budge the Iroquois Confederacy from their neutrality in a war that by 1757 the French seemed to be winning. In July 1759 after Gen John Prideaux's death at the British siege of Fort Niagara [now in Porter, Niagara Co], Johnson temporarily assumed command of the British forces, although he was not a commissioned British officer. He won some Seneca and Mohawk support during the siege, which was successfully concluded and hailed as a major victory.

Sir William Johnson, *ca* 1760.

Johnson was a prominent figure in reshaping the British Empire in North America after the conquest of New France. His influence upon British policy was evident in the Board of Trade's 1764 plan for Indian affairs. Though never fully implemented, the plan reflected Johnson's ideas on centralizing the functions of Indian diplomacy and regulating trade and land sales with the Indians. He worked to conclude a peace with western Indian nations during Pontiac's War (1763–65), extending to them the Covenant Chain alliance in 1766. Fearing the resurgence of pan-Indian confederacies, Johnson fomented diplomatic divisions between the Iroquois Confederacy and the western Indian nations.

LANDLORD AND SUPERINTENDENT

By the 1760s Johnson had become one of the wealthiest landholders in colonial New York, amassing thousands of acres of land. Largely responsible for the European settlement of the Mohawk Valley, he attracted hundreds of Irish, Scottish, and Palatine German tenants to his estates. His extant Georgian-style homes, Fort Johnson [now in Montgomery Co], built around 1749, and Johnson Hall, begun in 1763, were symbols of his prestige and the scenes of frequent interactions among Indians, Europeans, and Africans. Johnson owned at least 40 slaves in his lifetime. Indians were a ubiquitous presence at Johnson's homes and his estates reflected a blending of Indian material culture and expensive British consumer goods. Molly Brant, an influential Mohawk matron and sister of Chief Joseph Brant, became Sir William's common-law wife after Catherine Weissenburg's death in 1759. Molly was one of Johnson's crucial links to the Iroquois; their union lasted for roughly 15 years, until his death, and produced eight children.

After the French and Indian War, unrestrained settlement, racial violence, and land disputes frustrated Johnson's plans to regulate the colonial frontiers. His health also continued to decline. Indian nations in the trans-Appalachian west increasingly espoused united resistance to British expansion. Johnson's plans for an independent Indian Department were compromised by Britain's postwar deficits, ministerial changes, and disputes with its colonies. His last major achievement was negotiating a boundary line between Indian nations and the northern colonies, resulting in the 1768 Treaty of Fort Stanwix, in which the Iroquois gave up their claim to lands in the Ohio Valley. Six years later, as Johnson listened to Indian grievances over violations of the treaty at Johnson Hall, he collapsed and a few hours later died. His nephew Guy Johnson and eventually his son by Catherine Weissenburg, John Johnson, succeeded him as superintendent of Indian Affairs. John Johnson also inherited his father's baronetcy. Many of Johnson's tenants and most of his family, including Molly Brant and their eight children, fled to Canada during the Revolutionary War. An opponent of the colonial resistance movement, he did not live to see the war destroy the patriarchal society he had helped to create.

Johnson was the foremost Indian diplomat in the northern British colonies during the 18th century. His diplomacy enabled white settlers and Indians to coexist, although uneasily, on the New York frontiers until the American Revolution. But his promotion of settlement, trade, Christian missions, imperial authority, and divisions between Indian confederacies eroded the autonomy of Indian nations in eastern North America. Fort Johnson and Johnson Hall are maintained as New York State historic sites.

See also IRISH; MUNSEE.

Anderson, Fred. *Crucible of War: The Seven Years' War and the Fate of Empire in British North America, 1754–1766* (New York: Knopf, 2000)

Hamilton, Milton W. *Sir William Johnson, Colonial American, 1715–1763* (Port Washington, NY: Kennikat, 1976)

Sullivan, James, Alexander C. Flick, and Milton W. Hamilton, eds. *The Papers of Sir William Johnson*, 14 vols (Albany: Univ of the State of New York, 1921–65)

David L. Preston

Johnson City. Village (pop 15,535) in Union (Broome Co). In 1890 Lester Bros of Binghamton built a factory; felt, furniture, washing machine, and box factories followed. Lestershire, which acquired a post office the year before the shoe factory was completed, incorporated as a village in 1892. Lester Manufacturing Co, under the leadership of George F. Johnson, was renamed Endicott Johnson Co in 1902; Lestershire was renamed Johnson City in 1916. The company built parks, carousels, a library, and low-cost homes for workers. Due to its excellent labor relations, commemorated by the "Square Deal" arch (1920) at the village border, the company attracted immigrants, including Slovaks, Poles, and Italians, from port cities and Pennsylvania coalfields. Other 20th-century products of village factories included paper, irons, cameras, and shoe lasts and heels. After World War II Endicott Johnson gradually declined. Shopping malls now anchor the economy, and employment opportunities are dispersed. Recent immigrants have arrived from Southeast Asia, Korea, Eastern Europe, and elsewhere. Practical Bible College (1900) is located in Johnson City but has its own post office, Bible School Park (1911).

Charles J. Browne

Johnson Hall. Historic house in Johnstown (Fulton Co). With the removal of the French threat from the Mohawk Valley, Sir William Johnson drew plans for a house on 700 acres (283 ha) of his 50,000-acre (20,200 ha) Kingsborough Patent to reflect his new position as superintendent of Indian Affairs for the Six Nations. In 1763 he contracted with Samuel Fuller, a Boston-trained carpenter, to build a Georgian house of wood made to look like stone. Johnson Hall became the nucleus of Johnson's working estate. A mill, formal gardens, blacksmith shop, Indian store, barns, servant and slave housing, and other buildings were developed over 11 years. Stone dependencies flanked the mansion.

In 1774, during a tense conference with 600 Indians at Johnson Hall, Sir William collapsed and died. His son John inherited the estate but, as he was a loyalist, it was confiscated at the close of the American Revolution and sold at auction. The estate remained a private residence under a succession of owners until 1906, when New York State acquired the house, one remaining flanking stone house, and 20 acres (8 ha) of the original 700-acre farm. As trustees, the Johnstown Historical Society operated Johnson Hall as a museum until 1950, when New York State assumed full control of the site. It is operated by the New York State Office of Parks, Recreation, and Historic Preservation.

Feister, Lois M. *Johnson Hall Outbuildings, Landscape History, and Forgotten Features: Documentary and Archeological Research Conducted between 1945 and 1991, Johnstown, Fulton County, New York* (Waterford, NY: Bureau of Historic Sites, 1995)

Wanda Burch

Johnstown. Town (pop 7,166) and city (pop 8,511) in central Fulton Co. Settled in 1760, Johnstown developed around Johnson Hall (1763), the home of Sir William Johnson, patentee of much of the surrounding territory. He developed the community with a gristmill (1766), a church, and modest tradesmen's houses. When Tryon Co was formed in 1772, a courthouse and jail, both of which remain standing, were added. Johnson's tenant settlers came from Germany, Scotland, England, and Ireland, reinforced by migration from Massachusetts and Connecticut. Johnson encouraged craft industries (including silk experimentation), iron and potash works, and the introduction of sheep and new breeds of cattle. The town was formed from the old town of Caughnawaga in 1793. The village incorporated in 1808 and became a city in 1838. Johnstown is credited with the first glove and mitten factory in the United States (1808), and it soon developed a large industry: 60 firms produced 1,272,000 pairs in the 1890s, and leather, paper boxes for gloves, and glove-cutting machines were also manufactured. Other industrial products included saws and files, straw board for the glove boxes, and cheese from factories serving the town's farmers. The Fonda, Johnstown and Gloversville Railroad provided service starting in 1870, connecting with the main line of the New York Central at Fonda (Montgomery Co). The Knox Gelatine Co (1890–1975) was the first to produce granulated gelatine. Starting in the 1950s glove making declined, and only one firm was active in 2002, although a number of leather finishers continued in business. In addition to Johnson Hall, the late 18th-century Drumm House and the Jimmie Burke Tavern (?1781), both small vernacular structures, are historic house museums.

Wanda Burch

Johnson Hall; detail from panoramic map of Johnstown, 1888.

Johnstown, Battle of. Last significant battle of the American Revolution. In the fall of 1781, six days after Lord Charles Cornwallis surrendered at Yorktown, a British detachment under the command of Maj John Ross was sent from Fort Haldimand on Carleton Island [now in Jefferson Co] to Johnstown [now in Fulton Co]. By early October the British assembled over 600 troops at Oswego, consisting of army units, loyalist militia, and Indian allies. One-quarter of the force were Butler's Rangers, veterans of Mohawk Valley warfare. Capt Walter Butler, despised in the region for his participation in the Cherry Valley raid, accompanied the troops and served as second in command. On 11 Oct 1781 they proceeded up the Oswego River to Oneida Lake. The raiders traveled south of the Mohawk River and successfully bypassed Continental troops at Fort Dayton [now Herkimer] and Fort Rensselaer, later known as Fort Plain [now in Montgomery Co].

On the morning of 24 October, Ross's force initiated a raid in the vicinity of Fort Hunter [now in Montgomery Co]. Their arrival was soon reported to Col Marinus Willett at Fort Rensselaer, who marched with almost 500 men to intercept. Now aware of the pursuit, Ross crossed the Mohawk River on 25 October and moved through what was the village of Johnstown. His troops took up a position in the fields north of Johnson Hall, the former home of Sir William and Sir John Johnson. Willett divided his forces late in the morning on 25 October, planning to fight a direct action until a column under the command of Maj Aaron Rowley could attack Ross's flank. A delay in Rowley's attack divided the Battle of Johnstown into two stages. In the midafternoon, Ross and Butler drove Willett from the field.

Less than an hour after the first encounter, the flanking attack surprised the British at their most disorganized moment. The sounds of renewed battle reached Willett in the village, and he managed to rally a portion of his force to return to the battle. The fighting claimed approximately 40 lives on each side; Willett's men captured about 50 prisoners of war. As darkness fell Ross and Butler pulled their men out of the fight and headed for high ground to the north. The next day Ross abandoned all plans for further operations and retreated north and west, pursued by Willett's scouts. On 30 October Ross was able to put his beleaguered force across West Canada Creek. While attempting to rally Ross's rear guard, Butler was shot by an Oneida Indian and scalped. With the British in complete disarray, Willett's men returned to the valley, where the news of Yorktown added to the excitement of their own victory.

Lowenthal, Larry. *Marinus Willett: Defender of the Northern Frontier* (Fleischmanns, NY: Purple Mountain Press, 2000)

William S. Helmer

Jones, J(ohn) Raymond (*b* St. Thomas [now in US Virgin Islands], 19 Nov 1899; *d* New York City, 9 June 1991). Democratic Party leader. Jones immigrated to the United States as a teenager and came to New York City in 1918. For several years he worked on behalf of the Democratic Party in Manhattan's North Harlem as the protégé of the 22d Democratic district leader John Kelly. In 1921 he founded in Harlem the Five Cent Fare Club and in 1943 the famous Carver Democratic Club, which quickly became Harlem's most important political organization. In 1944 Jones won election as Democratic Party district leader, a post he held until 1953; five years later he returned to help his sometime friend and sometime foe Rep Adam Clayton Powell Jr stave off a primary challenge. Jones held a series of patronage appointments, culminating with his service as a deputy housing commissioner (1947–50) under mayor of New York City William O'Dwyer. In 1963, after supporting Mayor Robert F. Wagner Jr against Democratic leader Carmine DeSapio, Jones replaced DeSapio as the head of Tammany Hall. As leader of the Manhattan Democratic Party (1963–67), he was Tammany Hall's first black and last effective leader. Jones's skillful politicking and mastery of arcane electoral rules earned him the sobriquet "The Harlem Fox." Jones helped launch the careers of numerous black politicians in the state, including first black secretary of state Basil Paterson (1979–83) and first African American mayor of New York City David Dinkins (1989–93). Jones left politics in 1967 after feuding with US senator Robert F. Kennedy and other reform state Democrats over the slating of candidates for judgeships. He retired in St. Thomas.

Walter, John C. *The Harlem Fox: J. Raymond Jones and Tammany, 1920–1970* (Albany: SUNY Press, 1989)

Richard M. Flanagan

Jones, John W(alter) (*b* Leesburg, Va, 22 June 1817; *d* Elmira, 26 Dec 1900). Underground Railroad conductor. Jones was born a slave on the Sally Elzy plantation. He escaped and settled in Elmira in July 1844. Three years later he was appointed sexton of the First Baptist Church. Jones utilized his small home next to the church as a depot for escapees, concealing as many as 30 slaves at one time. Over the next nine years, Jones engineered the freedom of approximately 800 slaves who traveled the Underground Railroad destined for St. Catharines [now in Ont]. A majority of fugitives were stowed away on Jones's 4 AM Freedom Baggage Car via Watkins Glen (Schuyler Co) or Niagara Falls. Named sexton of Elmira's Woodlawn Cemetery in 1859, Jones oversaw burials of nearly 3,000 Confederate soldiers from the Elmira Prison Camp. In the early 21st century, a museum in his honor was under development in Chemung Co.

Ramsdell, William S. "John W. Jones, 1817–1900: Woodlawn's Sexton," *Chemung Historical Journal* (Sept 1997): 4668–71

Glenn Reynolds

Jones, Louis C(lark) (*b* Albany, 28 June 1908; *d* Haverford, Pa, 25 Nov 1990). Historian and folklorist. Reared in Albany, Jones graduated from Hamilton College (1930), then earned an MA (1931) and PhD (1941) from Columbia University. He began his career teaching English but was influenced by his colleague Harold W. Thompson to turn his attention to folklore. He achieved recognition as an authority on American folk culture through his writings, including *Cooperstown* (1949) and a classic compendium of ghost lore, *Things That Go Bump in the Night* (1959). Jones served as executive director of the New York State Historical Association at Cooperstown (Otsego Co) for a quarter century (1946–72), energizing its programs and publications. While there he gained a national reputation as director of the innovative Farmers' Museum, one of the first living-history museums to feature actors in period re-creations. It opened to the public in 1944 with a collection of 5,000 artifacts on the site of a 19th-century farm once owned by James Fenimore Cooper. Jones developed the American folk art collection at Fenimore House, making it one of the largest of its kind in the United States. He also created adult education programs and in 1964 inaugurated the Cooperstown Graduate Program (CGP), a joint undertaking of the New York State Historical Association and SUNY Oneonta. With Jones as director (1964–82), CGP provided specialized training in the field of historic preservation, contributing to the professionalization of museology and the advancement of museum studies in America. Jones's last book on the folk culture of New York State, *Three Eyes on the Past,* appeared in 1982.

Somewhere West of Albany . . . : A Festschrift in Honor of Louis C. Jones. New York Folklore 1 (Summer 1975)

Frank K. Lorenz

Jones, Rosalie (Gardiner) (*b* New York City, 24 Feb 1883; *d* Brooklyn, 12 Jan 1978). Suffragist. Jones grew up in New York City. Her wealthy family had extensive landholdings on the North Shore of Long Island, including a country home. She toured Long Island and Ohio with English suffragist Elisabeth Freeman in a yellow "Votes for Women" wagon in 1912, holding open-air meetings. She was president of the Nassau Co chapter of the National American Woman Suffrage Association (1912–13). Jones gained national fame when she organized a 140 mi (225 km) pilgrimage from New York City to Albany to present a woman suffrage petition to William Sulzer on the eve of his becoming governor in December 1912. They were joined by local suffragists all along the Hudson Valley and garnered much publicity during the 13-day hike. "General Jones," as she was known to her "troops," became a celebrity and followed up with a similar trek in February 1913 from Newark, NJ, to Washington, DC, to participate in the famous suffrage parade on the eve of Woodrow Wilson's presidential inauguration. Jones continued to work for suffrage in New York State and campaigned in western states.

Jones pursued her education at Adelphi College (AB, 1919), Washington College of Law (LLB, 1919), George Washington University (MA, 1919), and American University, where she received a doctorate in civil law (1922). She married a Democratic senator from Washington State, Clarence Dill, in 1927, but the couple divorced nine years later, and Jones resumed her birth name. She managed her family's landholdings and did pro bono legal work. She lived in Laurel Hollow (Nassau Co) and spent the last decades of her life in Brooklyn. Jones helped pioneer radical tactics and greatly publicized suffrage, but because she conducted most of her suffrage activities independent of suffrage organizations, her reputation has faded.

Mathews, Jane. " 'General' Rosalie Jones, Long Island Suffragist," *Nassau County Historical Society Journal* 47 (1992): 23–34

Natalie A. Naylor

Jones Beach State Park (2,413 acres/977 ha). Located on a sandy barrier island off Long Island's south shore, this oceanfront state park is 5 miles (8 km) long. The name comes from the family of Thomas and Freelove Jones, the first white settlers to arrive in the Massapequa region in 1696. A cottage colony, High Hill Beach (*ca* 1900), and a small hotel (*ca* 1920) were accessible by ferry from Bellmore [now in Nassau Co]. The state park, conceived of by Robert Moses as early as 1922 and planned by him, opened 4 Aug 1929. Moses proposed "a simply developed beach" that would provide recreation for New Yorkers. It was difficult for businessmen and politicians to see Moses's grand vision in the mosquito-infested tidal pools and windswept dunes of the isolated and inaccessible sandbar. In its first full year of operation, it encompassed,

Beach and boardwalk at the central mall of Jones Beach State Park, *ca* 1957.

in addition to a splendid beach, a roller rink, an archery range, umbrella, chair, and rowboat rentals, and deck tennis. The park features a boardwalk, a swimming pool, facilities for games and sports, a nature center, a gift shop, restaurant, and snack bars. Undeveloped areas of the park are especially appealing to nature lovers, including birdwatchers, fishers, and boaters. The Jones Beach Marine Theater has provided concerts by the sea since it opened in 1952. For more than 20 years, the theater's musicals and concerts were often headlined by Freeport [now in Nassau Co] resident Guy Lombardo. Since the 1980s the theater has produced a popular rock concert series during the summer season and recently expanded its seating capacity from 8,200 to 14,354. Open every day of the year, the park attracts between 7 and 8 million visitors annually.

Caro, Robert. *The Power Broker: Robert Moses and the Fall of New York* (New York: Vintage Books, 1974)

Kramer, Peter. "An Inside View of Jones Beach." In *Robert Moses: Single-Minded Genius,* ed. Joann P. Krieg (Interlaken, NY: Heart of the Lakes Publishing, 1989)

Moses, Robert. "The Building of Jones Beach." In *Robert Moses: Single-Minded Genius,* ed. Joann P. Krieg (Interlaken, NY: Heart of the Lakes Publishing, 1989)

Lynda R. Day

Joplin, Scott. See RAGTIME.

Jordan. Village (pop 1,314) in Elbridge (Onondaga Co). Trade on the Erie Canal gave birth to the village and several mills and factories on Skaneateles Creek. The village was incorporated in 1835, and the Rochester and Syracuse Railroad came through in 1851. Nineteenth-century industries included Sperry and Rockwell (*ca* 1850; wheelbarrows), A. D. Peck (1872; wheelbarrows), Peck and Tracy (1876; horse powers [horse treadmills for operation of machinery] and steam engines), Garrison and Taylor (1871; bedsteads), and Hardy and Putnam (1865; straw board). The Erie Canal bed was converted to a landscaped park in the 1930s. In the early 21st century, manufacturing includes Omega Wire Co and Bennett Bolt Works.

Barbara S. Rivette

Jorgensen, Christine [George William Jr] (*b* New York City, 30 May 1926; *d* San Clemente, Calif, 3 May 1989). Transsexual. Born the son of Danish immigrant parents, George William Jorgensen Jr always felt different, preferring girls' activities to boys' while growing up in the Bronx. After graduating from Christopher Columbus High School, he tried desperately to act in ways society considered masculine, trying twice to enlist in the US Army, being rejected, but finally being drafted in 1945. He served and was honorably discharged in 1946. Five years later he went to Denmark, ostensibly to pursue a career as a photographer; there he underwent a series of sex-change operations. When news of these broke in December 1952, Christine Jorgensen found that her procedure, the first highly publicized operation of its kind, had stirred a media frenzy. She returned to the United States in February 1953 and moved to Massapequa (Nassau Co) the same year. The public was fascinated, and television shows, magazines, and newspapers lavished Jorgensen with attention. Attractive and poised, Jorgensen parlayed this fame into a highly successful nightclub act and spoke candidly about her sex-change procedure, which she explained as having corrected a mistake nature had made. After her parents' death, Jorgensen moved to California and wrote *Christine Jorgensen: A Personal Autobiography* (1967), which then became a movie, *The Christine Jorgensen Story* (1970).

Jorgenson, Christine. *Christine Jorgensen: A Personal Autobiography,* 2d ed. (San Francisco: Cleis Press, 2000)

Meyrowitz, Joanne. *How Sex Changed: A History of Transsexuality in the United States* (Cambridge, Mass: Harvard Univ Press, 2002)

Donna L. Halper

Joseph Crater disappearance. Joseph Force Crater (*b* 1889) was a prominent New York City lawyer, active in Tammany Hall politics, who was appointed by Gov Franklin D. Roosevelt on 8 Apr 1930 to fill the place of Joseph Proskauer, who had resigned from the New York State Supreme Court. Those in New York's Democratic circles expected that Crater would be nominated as their candidate for that seat in November's election. However, sometime after 9:15 PM on 6 Aug 1930, Crater left a steakhouse on 45th St between 8th and 9th Aves, hailed a cab, waved goodbye to his friends, and was never seen again. Crater's Tammany Hall associates assured his wife that everything was fine and that her husband would soon resurface. News of Crater's absence was closely guarded, so as not to impede his chances at the polls, and the vanishing was kept from the press until 3 September. By that time, police and private investigators had learned that Crater was juggling extramarital affairs. Crater had also, along with other Tammany officials, come under scrutiny of the state's Seabury Investigations for alleged corruption and financial misdealings. There was speculation on whether the judge had fled the country to avoid prosecution or had perhaps been murdered to keep from testifying. A $5,000 reward offered by the New York City Police Department for information produced reported sightings of Crater nationwide, but none were accurate. Crater was declared dead in June 1939, and his whereabouts and the reason for his vanishing remain unknown.

Crater, Stella, and Oscar Fraley. *The Empty Robe* (Garden City, NY: Doubleday, 1961)

Judge Crater Disappears: A Collection of Newspaper Clippings, 1930–1980 (New York: New York Public Library Microfilm, 1985)

William M. Sternberg

Judicial Conduct, Commission on. State agency responsible for reviewing complaints of misconduct against any of the more than 3,500 judges or justices of New York State's unified court system. Before the legislature created the Temporary State Commission on Judicial Conduct in 1974, judges essentially policed each other by convening disciplinary bodies. The new commission endowed a full-time professional staff with the authority to investigate allegations of misconduct against judges, to "admonish" or make confidential suggestions to judges, and in serious cases to recommend formal disciplinary proceedings in the appropriate court. This commission ran from January 1975 through August 1976, when the permanent Commission on Judicial Conduct was established by a state constitutional amendment. The commission's authority derives from Article 6, Section 22 of the state constitution. A second constitutional amendment, effective in April 1978, created the present commission, with expanded jurisdiction and increased membership.

A judge or justice may be publicly admonished, censured, or removed for misconduct in office, persistent failure to perform duties, habitual intemperance, and conduct on or off the bench that is deemed to be prejudicial to the administration of justice. The chief administrator of the courts, with the approval of the New York State Court of Appeals, issues Rules Governing Judicial Conduct, and the New York State Bar Association adopts the Code of Judicial Conduct to which judges and justices must adhere.

The commission deals with formal charges and allegations regarding improper demeanor, conflicts of interest, violations of defendants' or litigants' rights, favoritism, bias, prejudice, gross neglect, corruption, and some prohibited political activity. By law all complaints must be signed and in writing. The decision to investigate lies with the commission, which may dismiss a complaint at any stage during its investigation or adjudication. When circumstances warrant, the commission may also issue a confidential letter of dismissal and caution to a judge, despite a dismissal of the complaint. A judge or justice also may be retired if mental or physical disability prevents the proper performance of duties. The Court of Appeals reviews all determinations by the commission. The chief judge gives written notice to the involved judge or justice, who may either accept the decision or make a written request to the chief judge for a review.

The 11 members of the commission serve four-year terms. Appointments are apportioned among the governor, the chief judge of the Court of Appeals, and each of the four majority and minority leaders of the legislature. Four members must be judges, at least one must be an attorney, and at least two must be from outside the legal profession. Commission members serve part-time, without compensation, and elect one of their number to serve as chairperson. A lawyer is the clerk of the commission, and a full-time administrator and counsel hires and directs the staff. There are commission offices in New York City, Albany, and Rochester. Complaints increased substantially during the 1990s.

New York State Archives. "New York State Commission on Judicial Conduct." Unpublished agency history (1981)

Christine Karpiak

judicial review. Power of a court to annul a law it deems unconstitutional. The concept was introduced in New York State before the US Supreme Court, with the *Marbury v Madison* decision in 1803, made it a permanent national legal principle. The New York State Constitution of 1777 established a Council of Revision to decide on the constitutionality of all bills that passed both legislative houses, thus implementing a form of judicial review. The council was composed of the governor, the chancellor of the chancery court, and at least two of the three judges of the state supreme court. If the council ruled that a bill was unconstitutional, a two-thirds vote of both houses could override the decision. Otherwise, the legislature was required to incorporate the council's objections before the bill became law. If the council took no action for 10 days, the bill automatically became law. This mechanism stayed in place until 1821, when the state's constitutional convention abolished the council.

During the same period, state and local courts had been sporadically applying the principle of judicial review. A prominent and controversial decision was rendered in *Rutgers v Waddington* (1784). At issue was the 1783 Trespass Act, a state law that made it easier for citizens to sue loyalists for property damages or occupation of such properties during the Revolutionary War. Alexander Hamilton, the attorney for the defendant, persuaded the New York City mayor's court to declare unconstitutional a portion of the law because it violated the federal Treaty of Paris. Other early New York State cases affirming judicial review were *Dash v Van Kleeck* (1811), *Livingston v Van Ingen* (1812), and *Gardner v Village of Newburgh* (1816).

Although the principle of judicial review is firmly set in New York State, several decisions have limited its scope. *Matter of Fuller* (1901) established that if a part of a statute is unconstitutional, the remainder may still be valid, and *People ex rel Simpson v Wells* (1904) established that courts will not determine the constitutionality of a statute until a concrete case arises in which a decision is unavoidable. *Matter of Herlands v Surpless* (1939) declared that courts cannot interfere with a legislative act unless there is an infringement on citizen rights or unless a legal wrong is being committed. In *Trio Distributor Corp v City of Albany* (1956) it was ruled that courts do not have general veto power over legislation and cannot void a law because judges do not favor it.

In certain instances judicial review is guaranteed by the law. Article 6, Sections 3(b)(1) and (2) of the state constitution and Section 5601(b) of the Civil Practice Law and Rules expressly state when a question of a lower court concerning the constitutionality of a particular law may of right be taken directly to the state's court of appeals. Although there have been periodic attempts to abolish or severely limit judicial review in New York State through legislation or constitutional amendment, none has been successful.

Corwin, Edward S. "The Extension of Judicial Review in New York: 1783–1905," *Michigan Law Review* 15 (Feb 1917): 281–313

Langer, Laura. *Judicial Review in State Supreme Courts: A Comparative Study* (New York: SUNY Press, 2002)

Robert Allan Carter

Juilliard School. Private music, dance, and drama conservatory. Founded in New York City by Frank Damrosch in 1905 as the Institute of Musical Art, it received a generous endowment with James Loeb's $500,000 gift. Loeb specified that the institute would not discriminate against race, color, sex, or religious creed. The institute moved in 1910 from its first home, Manhattan's Lenox Library at 5th Ave and 12th St, to 122d St and Claremont Ave. In 1926 the institute, still headed by Damrosch, merged with a new school, the Juilliard Graduate School, set up with a $12.5 million bequest by textile merchant Augustus D. Juilliard. The resulting entity was known as the Juilliard School of Music. The graduate school initially occupied 49 East 52d St, then a second structure was built at 122d St. Those buildings were sold to the Manhattan School of Music when Juilliard moved to Lincoln Center in 1969 to a building designed by Pietro Belluschi. To reflect the addition of dance in 1951 and drama in 1968, it changed its name to the Juilliard School. After Damrosch the school has been headed by John Erskine, Ernest Hutcheson, William Schuman, Peter Mennin, and Joseph Polisi. Those who have attended Juilliard include Richard Rodgers, Van Cliburn, Philip Glass, Leontyne Price, Miles Davis, Robin Williams, Patti LuPone, Kelsey Grammar, Meredith Willson, James Levine, Wynton Marsalis, Yo-Yo Ma, Kevin Kline, and Christopher Reeve. In 2001 the student body numbered about 730, of whom about 100 were dance or drama students.

Olmstead, Andrea. *Juilliard: A History* (Urbana: Univ of Illinois Press, 1999)

Andrea Olmstead

Junction Canal. Waterway that linked the North Branch Extension Canal, at the juncture of the Susquehanna and Chemung Rivers at Athens, Pa, with the Chemung Canal at Elmira. The private Junction Canal Co was originally chartered by the New York State legislature in 1846, but construction never began and the canal was rechartered on 16 Apr 1852. Built primarily to ship anthracite from the Wyoming Valley in Pennsylvania to Central New York and the Great Lakes region, the canal also benefited regional farmers and the semianthracite coal interests in Bradford County, Pa. Work began in March 1853 and the main portion of the channel was completed in 1854. Construction problems along the North Branch Extension Canal caused delays until November 1856, when the first coal barges from Pittston, Pa, arrived in Elmira; the North Branch Extension was not fully functional until 1858. The Junction's construction cost was $530,637. The 18 mi (29 km) canal extended 15.75 miles (25.4 km) into New York State. There were eight lift locks and three guard locks of white pine construction supported by three canal dams to feed the canal line. The high mark of the canal was 1864, with 256,044 tons (232,279 MT) of freight, including 156,104 tons (141,615 MT) of coal. A March 1865 flood along the Chemung and Susquehanna Rivers caused severe damage to the North Branch Extension Canal. The canal systems were rebuilt, but the North Branch Extension and Junction Canals had their last season in 1871. The Extension was closed in April 1872, and the Junction Canal did not reopen for business.

Petrillo, F. Charles. *Anthracite and Slackwater: The North Branch Canal, 1828–1901* (Easton, Pa: Center for Canal History and Technology, 1986)

Whitford, Noble E. *History of the Canal System of the State of New York, Together with Brief Histories of the Canal of the United States and Canada*, vol 1 (Albany: Bandow Printing, 1906)

F. Charles Petrillo

Junius. Town (pop 1,362) in NW Seneca Co. Settled in 1795, the town was formed from Washington [now Fayette] in 1803. An active Quaker community (1815–63) contributed to social reform movements. Orchards, dairy farms, gravel quarries, and peat beds formed Junius's agrarian economy. Crossed by the New York State Thruway (1954), Junius is the site of the Waterloo Premium Outlet Mall (1995), a popular destination for national and international tourists. In the early 21st century farmers, raise dairy products, soybeans, and corn.

Lisa Compton

jury system. The right to trial by jury is guaranteed by the New York State Constitution of 1894, as that right existed under previous constitutions, statutes enacted before 1894, and the common law in force in 1777. The right was established in colonial New York. The Duke's Laws of 1665–66 provided for trial juries of 6–7 men in local courts and 12 men in the provincial Court of Assizes. After 1683 the common-law courts used trial juries of 12 men and grand juries of 24, as in England. Justices of the peace and city magistrates tried small suits, and litigants could obtain a six-man jury. A 1732 statute authorized those officials to try misdemeanors without a jury if the person accused did not give bail to be tried in a higher court. Since 1824 a person charged with a misdemeanor outside New York City has had the right to a six-person jury trial. Within New York City, a circumscribed right to a jury trial of a misdemeanor charge was abolished in 1897. It was restored in 1970, after the exemption was declared unconstitutional.

Jury trials have been made optional in most cases for reasons of efficiency and economy. Submission of complex commercial cases to referees, without jury trial, was regularized by a 1768 statute. The common-law right to waive jury trial in civil cases was incorporated in the Constitutions of 1846 and 1894. A 1935 amendment permitted less than unanimous (five-sixths) verdicts in civil cases. Waiver of jury trial in felony cases (except for crimes punishable by death) was authorized by a constitutional amendment in 1937. Six-person juries for civil trials in supreme and county courts were permitted in 1962 and made standard in 1972. In 2003 fewer than 5% of civil and criminal court cases go to jury trial.

Juror Selection

Qualifications for jury selection have been revised frequently. Property qualifications for jurors were first established by an act in 1699 and fixed at £60 in 1741, $150 in 1801, and $250 in 1829. Qualified jurors were identified using tax assessment rolls. The list, or panel, of persons summoned by the sheriff for jury duty was attached to the writ returned to the court. A jury summons was not always welcome, and the courts frequently fined those who failed to appear. After 1798 town and city officials prepared lists of those eligible for jury service, again using tax assessment rolls. The county clerks recorded names on slips of paper to be drawn at random from a box, and the sheriff or deputy summoned the jurors for a court term. In rural counties this system operated with little change well into the 20th century. Commissioners of jurors handled the administrative functions in New York City starting in 1847 and in Kings Co starting in 1858. Statutes passed from 1894 to 1897 required commissioners of jurors in other larger counties.

The juror selection law was complex, and reformers worked for a simpler system. Juror pools for several different courts were used experimentally in New York City in 1937 and routinely beginning in 1959. The county clerks within New York City again became responsible for administering juror selection in 1940. They were required to use written questionnaires in identifying qualified jurors. In 1954 the legislature required every county outside of New York City to have a commissioner of jurors, but several small counties were soon exempted. A uniform, statewide juror selection law was finally enacted in 1977. In most counties the commissioner of jurors is appointed by a county jury board composed of two Supreme Court justices, the senior county judge, and a county legislator. Within New York City and in at least six small counties, the county clerk serves as commissioner. Although the nominal $250 property requirement lasted until 1967, sources of potential juror names had broadened beyond the tax rolls. Commissioners of jurors in New York City had long used voter lists and city directories, and in 1954 the use of any "general source of names" and of questionnaires was mandated statewide. In New York City "special" trial juries, handpicked for difficult or notorious cases, were authorized in 1896 and abolished in 1965. During the 1930s Thomas E. Dewey, as special prosecutor and New York Co district attorney, employed these "blue ribbon" juries to expose racketeering.

Exemptions from Service

Legal exemptions from jury service were first enacted in 1801 for groups such as militia, fire company members, and prison officials. The number of exemptions multiplied over the years. The courts came to rely on small pools of permanently qualified jurors, who tended to be retired white males who wanted to occupy their time and earn a little money. Women did not gain the right to serve on juries until 1937, and until 1975 they could claim exemption on the basis of gender. The 1977 juror selection law declared that juries must be "selected at random from a fair cross-section of the community . . . and that all eligible citizens shall have the opportunity to serve." The law's intent was thwarted by automatic disqualifications (elected and major appointed government officials and military personnel) and numerous exemptions (eg, medical professionals, attorneys, clergy, police and corrections officers, firefighters, persons caring for children, and persons over age 70). All these disqualifications and exemptions were abolished effective in 1996, increasing the size of the statewide juror pool by about 1 million. As of 2003 a juror must be a citizen aged 18 or older, a resident of the county in which he or she is called for service, not a convicted felon, and able to communicate in English. A juror is excused if he or she is mentally or physically unable to serve or if service would pose "undue hardship or extreme inconvenience." After the mid-1990s, shorter and less frequent terms of service, higher pay, and better accommodations have made jury service less burdensome. About 600,000 New Yorkers were summoned for jury service in 2002. Some 25,000 were called for grand jury services.

Grand and Special Juries

Grand juries usually have 23 persons; 16 form a quorum and 12 are needed to indict a person for criminal prosecution. The proceedings are secret. Witnesses are subpoenaed by the district attorney or, rarely, by the grand jury itself. They appear without counsel present, unless a witness waives immunity from prosecution. Grand juries routinely approve the draft indictments prepared by the district attorney; some observers have therefore considered the indictment process superfluous. A 1973 constitutional amendment permitted defendants to waive indictment by the grand jury in certain cases. A grand jury also has the power to investigate and report on misconduct, nonfeasance, or neglect by public officials. That power was declared illegal by the Court of Appeals in 1961 but restored with procedural safeguards by the legislature in 1964.

Mayers, Lewis. "The Constitutional Guarantee of Jury Trial in New York," *Brooklyn Law Review* 7 (1937): 180–204

New York State. Unified Court System. *Continuing Jury Reform in New York State: January 2001 Report* (2001)

James D. Folts

Women and Jury Service. The New York State woman suffrage victory in 1917 did not award women access to jury service. For the next 20 years the Women's City Club of New York, the League of Women Voters, and the state's women's bar associations made such access a priority. They were not alone in this quest. Before national woman suffrage was ratified in 1920, 16 states allowed women to vote but only 6 (Utah, Washington, Kansas, New Jersey, California, and Michigan) permitted women to serve on juries. By 1923, 12 more states and the Territory of Alaska allowed but did not necessarily oblige women's jury service.

The first victory in New York State came through the actions of Doris I. Byrne, a Democrat representing the Bronx, and Jane H. Todd, a Republican representing Westchester Co, in the New York State Assembly. From 1935 on they introduced repeated bills for mandatory women's jury service. Passed by the assembly, the state senate defeated them on the basis that rural women opposed being forced to travel to county seats to serve, but nonetheless the bills prepared the way for women performing some kind of service. In 1937 Sen Philip M. Kleinfeld introduced a bill that permitted women to serve on juries but that also gave them an automatic exemption. This bill passed both houses, and Gov Herbert H. Lehman, long a supporter of women's jury service, signed it into law.

To prove that large numbers of women wanted jury service, the state's League of Women Voters ran "jury schools" to help demystify the courtroom and to encourage women to forgo their exemptions. On 1 Sept 1937, the day the law went into effect, 1,345 women filed for service in New York Co alone; thousands of women served in the ensuing years. Still, women civic activists were not satisfied. Arguing that women's citizenship status should be equal to men's, they continued to campaign for mandatory service. Until the early 1950s, the Women's City Club of New York and the Federation of Business and Professional Women's Clubs spearheaded this campaign. During World War II they even tried to get a mandatory bill passed as a "war measure" on the basis of the difficulty of finding qualified male jurors. A mandatory service bill passed the assembly in 1944 but went no further. Early in 1952 the clubs announced that the opposition of rural women was still so strong that they would drop active work toward a mandatory bill and endorsed their last bill on the issue in 1953. Little action was taken after that to achieve mandatory women's jury service in New York State, but the issue worked its way through other state courts and finally reached the US Supreme Court. When the Court ruled in *Taylor v Louisiana* (1975) that all juries had to be drawn from a pool that excluded no element of the community, the issue of New York State women's voluntary versus mandatory service became moot.

Kerber, Linda K. *No Constitutional Right to Be Ladies: Women and the Obligations of Citizenship* (New York: Hill & Wang, 1998)

Lemons, J. Stanley. *The Woman Citizen: Social Feminism in the 1920s* (Urbana: Univ of Illinois Press, 1973)

Perry, Elisabeth Israels. "Rhetoric, Strategy, and Politics in the New York Campaign for Women's Jury Service, 1917–1975," *New York History* 82 (Winter 2001): 53–78

Elisabeth Israels Perry

juvenile justice system. A House of Refuge in New York City opened in 1824 as the nation's first shelter for juvenile delinquents. It also accepted vagrants. Reform or industrial schools were established as early as the 1840s with the goal of socializing troubled youth through discipline derived from hard work and serious study. The Children's Aid Society (1853) developed a placing-out system in which orphaned children were removed from New York City to be adopted by farm families in the country. Following the lead set by Chicago's Cook Co juvenile court system in 1899, reformers set up a special court to handle only cases involving juveniles arrested in Buffalo (1901), Manhattan and the Bronx (1902), and Brooklyn (1903). A 1909 court act coined the term "juvenile delinquency" and stipulated that children could no longer be tried as adults. The 1922 Children's Court Act created a separate juvenile justice system intended to shield delinquent children from the harsh punishments meted out by the adult criminal courts. Adolescent misbehavior was attributed to dysfunctional families, gang-infested slums, ineffective schooling, and the adjustment difficulties of recent immigrants.

To safeguard the best interests of children,

judges often placed them under the supervision of probation officers to provide counseling and guidance. A number of landmark US Supreme Court cases starting in the mid-1960s, however, granted youthful offenders constitutional safeguards similar to those enjoyed by adults because the courts often failed to deliver meaningful rehabilitative services. Since 1962 juvenile offenses are often handled through each county's family court, in which the county attorney, or the corporation counsel in New York City, handles delinquency charges and young Persons in Need of Supervision (PINS), who are truants, runaways, or incorrigible in disobeying their parents. The family courts do not demand bail, seek grand jury indictments, or conduct jury trials. In some cases in which a juvenile is accused of committing a serious violent crime the prosecution may seek to waive the case to the state supreme court, and if found guilty the youth will be deemed a juvenile offender and subject to more severe punishment than a juvenile delinquent. While New York State considers children from the age of 7 to age 16 to be juveniles, in most states the upper limit extends past age 16. In 1978 the New York State legislature enacted the nation's toughest juvenile offender law, enabling prosecutors to bring murder charges against children as young as 13. Both public and private detention facilities hold juvenile delinquents and offenders for anywhere from two weeks up to a year or more and include secure, limited secure, and nonsecure centers, community group and foster homes, and mental health care facilities. Approximately 16,500 youths enter these facilities each year.

See also CRIMINAL JUSTICE.

Jones-Brown, Delores, Elsie Chandler, and Susan Decker. *Criminal Justice in New York* (Boston: Allyn & Bacon, 2000)

Charles Lindner and Andrew Karmen

K

Kalm, Pehr [Peter] (*b* Angermanland, Sweden, 6 Mar 1716; *d* Abo, Sweden, 15 Nov 1779). Naturalist. Pehr Kalm became a student of Carl von Linné (Linnaeus) at Sweden's Uppsala University at a time when interest in scientific agriculture was awakening in that nation. When the Swedish Academy of Science decided to send a scholar to North America to investigate useful plants and trees, Kalm was chosen. He sailed in August 1748 on a two-and-a-half-year journey. From a base at the old Swedish colony of Raccoon [now Swedesboro, NJ], he explored Pennsylvania, New Jersey, New York, and Quebec. He reached New York City in June 1749, proceeding up the Hudson to Albany, visiting the Cohoes Falls and Crown Point [now in Essex Co] on his way to Quebec; in October he returned by the same route, adding to his observations of both Albany and New York City. His journals, published as *En Resa til Norra America* (3 vols, 1753–61), provide some of the earliest scientific observations of the New York environment and its native and European peoples.

Adolph B. Benson, ed. *Peter Kalm's Travels in North America* (1937; repr New York: Dover, 1987)

Field Horne

Kanatsiohareke Mohawk Community. Contemporary Mohawk settlement on the north side of the Mohawk River 4 miles (6 km) east of Canajoharie (Montgomery Co). Seeking to reoccupy their traditional homeland, Mohawks from Akwesasne (St. Regis Indian Reservation) [partly loc in Franklin Co], led by Tom Porter, established the current settlement in 1993 on 322 acres (130 ha) of land purchased at auction. The Mohawk name refers to "the place of the clean pot," a series of large, circular limestone formations found near Canajoharie. The community is located on the site of an old Mohawk village but more recently was the site of a Montgomery Co nursing home. The buildings on the property include a large multifamily residence, barn, and several auxiliary buildings. Residents adhere to the traditional Iroquois Longhouse religion and its seasonal calendar of ceremonies and maintain the property from revenue earned from a bed and breakfast and from the sale of books, apparel, and traditional crafts.

Kanatsiohareke Mohawk Community, http://www.mohawkcommunity.com

Snow, Dean R. *The Iroquois* (Cambridge, Mass: Blackwell, 1994)

Christina Rieth

Kaplan, Mordecai M(enahem) (*b* Swenziany, Lithuania, 11 June 1881; *d* New York City, 8 Nov 1983). Founder of Reconstructionism. Kaplan immigrated with his family to New York City in 1889 and studied at a local yeshiva, the Jewish Theological Seminary (JTS), City College of New York, and Columbia University. Ordained in 1902, he became associate rabbi at Kehilath Jeshurun, an Orthodox shul, and in 1909 began teaching at JTS. Kaplan conceived of Judaism as a dynamic cultural phenomenon and reconsidered attitudes regarding miracles, faith, the messiah, and chosenness, re-envisioning the synagogue as a cultural center, with God to be found through cultural expressions of the Jewish people. He revised traditional liturgies and prayers and introduced the bat mitzvah, a coming-of-age ceremony for girls, beginning with his daughter in 1922. Many of these changes occurred at institutions that Kaplan founded and led in the city, including the Jewish Center (1918), the Society for the Advancement of Judaism (1922), and the Young Men's Hebrew Association (1929). In the mid-1930s Kaplan formalized this movement, known as Reconstructionism, often considered the fourth major Jewish denomination, and published *Judaism as a Civilization* (1934). Although often considered one of the 20th century's greatest Jewish thinkers, he was excommunicated by the Union of Orthodox Rabbis in 1945. He retired in 1963 but continued to write and speak prolifically for some time.

Gurock, Jeffrey S., and Jacob J. Schacter. *A Modern Heretic and a Traditional Community: Mordecai M. Kaplan, Orthodoxy, and American Judaism* (New York: Columbia Univ Press, 1997)

Jonathan Gill

Kaser. Village (pop 3,316) in Ramapo (Rockland Co). Kaser, incorporated in 1990, is the home of the Visnitz group of Hasidic Jews that fled from the Soviet Ukraine to Brooklyn. The group moved to what was then part of Monsey. In the mid-1980s its leaders began investigating incorporation to counter Ramapo's zoning code, which restricted high-density residential construction favored by the community's large families. Kaser's population nearly doubled during its first decade as a village. It is now the international headquarters of the Visnitz Hasidim.

Kayaderosseras Patent. This large land grant, containing 406,404 acres (164,466 ha) north and west of the Mohawk and Hudson Rivers, originated in a 1703 petition to the assembly by Attorney General Sampson Shelton Broughton for himself and 12 other New York City investors. They asked for authorization to purchase the tract from the Mohawks. In 1704, without having received such permission, Broughton obtained a deed from certain Mohawk leaders for a very small portion of the land and petitioned for a patent, justifying it by the Indian deed. A new petition of 1708 by Nanning Harmense, one of the proprietors, was confirmed by a patent of Edward Hyde (Lord Cornbury), acting for Queen Anne. It specified a quitrent of £4. No division or survey was done, and the matter remained unsettled. In 1754 the Mohawks were shocked to discover New York Colony believed that the Mohawks had, by the 1704 deed, sold their best hunting grounds. The patent was called a "notorious fraud" by Sir William Johnson, superintendent of Indian affairs in the northern colonies. Nevertheless the assembly took no action to cancel it. After the 1763 peace, settlement was at last safe and practical, land values increased, and in 1768 the proprietors' heirs permitted a few "poor, industrious" people to settle near Saratoga Lake. The Mohawks drove them off and appealed to Johnson, who championed the Mohawks' cause. To settle the dispute Gov Henry Moore met with the Indians, ordered a survey, and negotiated a compromise. The heirs paid the Mohawks 5,000 Spanish dollars and relinquished the western part of the claim. Each of the 25 allotments were divided into 13 shares and surveyed in 1771; they provide the basis for modern land title in most of Saratoga Co.

Higgins, Ruth L. *Expansion in New York* (Columbus: Ohio State Univ, 1931)

Field Horne

Kaye [née Smith], **Judith** (*b* Monticello, Sullivan Co, 4 Aug 1938). Chief judge, Court of Appeals. Kaye's parents were eastern European immigrants who farmed and ran a clothing store in Monticello. Kaye graduated from Barnard College in 1958 and from New York University (NYU) School of Law in 1962. She worked for the New York City firms of Sullivan and Cromwell, IBM, NYU School of Law, and beginning in 1969 for the commercial law firm of Olwine, Connelly, Chase, O Donnell, and Weyher, where she eventually made partner. In 1983 she became the first woman to serve as associate judge on the New York State Court of Appeals, the state's highest court. Ten years later Gov Mario M. Cuomo appointed Kaye to the state's highest judicial position, chief judge of the Court of Appeals and chief judge of New York State. Kaye's writings and rulings have emphasized the importance of state constitutional law, common-law principles, and the role of the law in social change. She has been commended for bringing intellectual rigor to family law. Her reforms of state court administration have included the introduction of drug treatment, community, and domestic violence courts.

Kaye, Judith. "A Life in the Law," *Seton Hall Law Review* 30 (2000): 752

"Tribute to Chief Judge Kaye." In *1994 Annual Survey of American Law*, bk 1 (New York: New York Univ School of Law, 1995): ix–lxiii

Ellen Sexton

Kazakhstanis. See CENTRAL ASIANS.

Keating, Kenneth B(arnard) (*b* Lima, Livingston Co, 18 May 1900; *d* New York City, 5 May 1975). Politician. After serving in the army during World War I, Keating attended the University of Rochester and graduated in 1919. He graduated from Harvard Law School in 1923 and practiced law in Rochester until World War II, when he served in the army in the Far East. He was elected to the House of Representatives in 1946, where he served six terms, and to the US Senate in 1958. Keating had a conservative record in the House, but by the early 1960s he had joined liberal Northeast Republicans in support of many domestic social programs favored by Presidents John F. Kennedy and Lyndon Johnson. He was a strong supporter of civil rights legislation. Keating cosponsored the House bill that became the 1957 Civil Rights Act, voted for the 1964 Civil Rights Act, and advocated granting the District of Columbia electoral college votes in presidential elections. Many African Americans in New York State considered him a political ally. Keating burst into the national spotlight in August 1962 when he warned that the Soviet Union was building missile bases in Cuba. For several weeks

Keating led the Republicans who charged Pres Kennedy with hiding this information from the public and underestimating a serious threat to national security. In 1964 Keating was defeated in his reelection bid by Robert F. Kennedy. He failed not only because Kennedy was a tough opponent but because of sharp divisions within the Republican Party: Keating had refused to endorse archconservative Barry Goldwater, the 1964 Republican presidential nominee. Keating was elected to the New York State Court of Appeals in 1965 and served there until Pres Richard M. Nixon named him ambassador to India in 1969. A long-time supporter of Israel, Keating became ambassador to that nation in 1973, a position he held until his death.

White, Mark J. *The Cuban Missile Crisis* (Basingstoke, Hampshire, England: Macmillan, 1996)
Keating, Kenneth. Papers. Univ of Rochester

Timothy N. Thurber

Keene. Town (pop 1,063) in N Essex Co. Keene encompasses 8 of New York's 46 highest peaks, including Mt Marcy, as well as the source of the Hudson River. Settled in 1795 the town formed in 1808 from Elizabethtown and Jay. Asher B. Durand and other painters began visiting Keene Valley in the 1840s, forming the nucleus of a remarkable artistic and intellectual community. Town residents earned a livelihood through small farms and lumbering until after the Civil War, when tourism grew rapidly; by 1878 there were almost 1,000 rooms available in town. Putnam Camp (1875–1920s), the favorite retreat of philosopher William James, and the Glenmore School for the Social Sciences (1890–1910), founded by Thomas Davison, attracted numerous intellectual leaders. Summer tourism endured after the passing of Keene Valley's intellectual eminence in the 1920s. The proximity of the Northway (1967) has made the area more accessible; a mix of lumbering, outdoor recreation, and tourism continues.

Plunz, Richard, ed. *Two Adirondack Hamlets in History: Keene and Keene Valley* (Fleischmanns, NY: Purple Mountain Press, 1999)

Thomas A. Rumney

Keeney, Calvin N(oyes) (*b* Le Roy, Genesee Co, 1849; *d* Le Roy, 31 Oct 1930). Creator of the stringless green bean. Keeney joined his father in the agricultural produce business after the Civil War. N. B. Keeney and Son Co dealt in dry beans, apples, potatoes, and wool, and sold feed, farm supplies, coal, and lumber. In 1878 Keeney began working with Thorburn's Refugee Wax bean and eventually developed the first stringless bean and 25 varieties of it, as well as other bean varieties, by isolating small plots of beans in the middle of cornfields. He then moved beehives into the small plots to cross-pollinate the flowers, introducing Keeney's Stringless Refugee Wax in 1884 and Improved Black Wax in 1885. It is generally believed that most, if not all, of the modern snap beans can be traced to Keeney's bean breeding. His most significant variety was Burpee's Stringless Green Pod (1894), which became a favorite of home gardeners, commercial growers, and canners. In 1927 he helped form the Associated Seed Growers, a merger of N. B. Keeney and Son, Everett B. Clark Seed Co of Connecticut, a specialist in sweet-corn breeding, and the John H. Allen Seed Co of Wisconsin, known for pea-seed breeding. In 2003 the company continued as Asgrow Seed Co.

Lynne Belluscio

Keeseville. Village (pop 1,850) in AuSable (Clinton Co) and Chesterfield (Essex Co). The first permanent settlement was in ?1806–7; an iron rolling mill was in operation by 1815. Irish immigrants arrived by 1822. The village, which straddles the Ausable River, became a manufacturing center, producing iron and wood products until well into the 20th century. Keeseville incorporated in 1878. The last of its industries, R. Prescott and Sons (wood products) closed in the late 1960s. In the early 21st century only a Pepsi-Cola bottling franchise remained in what had become a residential and commercial center. Keeseville's stone arch bridge (1842–43), with its 110 ft (33.5 m) span, is a landmark.

Thomas A. Rumney

Kellogg [née Cornelius], Minnie (Laura Meriam) (*b* Oneida Indian Reservation [loc in Wisc], 10 Sept 1880; *d* ?1947). Indian rights activist. One of four children born to Adam Poe Cornelius and Celisha Bread, she grew up on a farm near the reservation boundary and attended a public elementary school. After graduating from a private girls school in Wisconsin in 1898, she attended, without receiving a degree, Stanford University, Barnard College, the New York School of Philanthropy (now Columbia University School of Social Work), Cornell University, and the University of Wisconsin. In 1911 she helped found and became secretary of the American Indian Association (later Society of American Indians), where she focused on educational and economic issues, arguing for Indian self-sufficiency and against government intervention. In 1912 she married non-Indian Minneapolis attorney Orrin Kellogg, and they lived together on her family farm. She was opposed to the Bureau of Indian Affairs and in 1920 published *Our Democracy and the American Indian,* which criticized US policies toward American Indians. Her ability to speak articulately in English, Oneida, and Mohawk helped her gain national attention. Her promises of legal action to regain Oneida and Iroquoian Indian land in New York State inspired the hopes of many Indians. To raise funds for their work, the Kellogg Party (as she and her supporters became known) sold certificates to those who expected a return on any land claims settlement in New York State. Kellogg and her husband lived on the money raised primarily from the Iroquois reservations, and this system eventually led to accusations of fraud. The land claims settlement never materialized during her lifetime, but she left behind a trail of paperwork that became the basis of the modern Oneida Indian land claims case. The US district court dismissed her suit in 1927, and her politics of self-reliance were increasingly unfashionable in the 1930s. Kellogg was largely forgotten and died in obscurity.

Hauptman, Laurence M. "Designing Woman: Minnie Kellogg, Iroquois Leader." In *Indian Lives,* ed. I. G. Moses and Raymond Wilson (Albuquerque: Univ of New Mexico Press, 1985)
McLester, Thelma C. "Oneida Women Leaders." In *The Oneida Indian Experience: Two Perspectives,* ed. Jack Campisi and Laurence M. Hauptman (Syracuse: Syracuse Univ Press, 1988)

Thelma C. McLester

Kempton, (James) Murray (*b* Baltimore, 6 Dec 1917; *d* New York City, 5 May 1997). Reporter, columnist, and author. Born and educated in Baltimore he joined the *New York Post* in 1942, left the newspaper to serve in the armed forces during World War II, and returned after the war. In the 1950s he advanced a liberal version of anticommunism that criticized the communist movement but defended individual communists against McCarthyism. Except for periods when he worked for the *New Republic* and the *New York World-Telegram,* Kempton stayed at the *Post* until 1981. He left to become a columnist for *Newsday.*

An eclectic reporter, Kempton ranged over subjects as varied as race, jazz, politics, and the Mafia. He was always suspicious of the corrupting tendencies of power. His dogged reporting, sharp but complex prose, historical perspective, and egalitarian conscience made him an admired presence in New York City newspapers. Winner of a National Book Award in 1973 for *The Briar Patch: The People of the State of New York vs Lumumba Shakur, et al* and a Pulitzer Prize for commentary in 1985, Kempton wrote regularly until his death.

Kempton, Murray. *Rebellions, Perversities, and Main Events* (New York: Times Books, 1994)

Robert W. Snyder

Kendall. Town (pop 2,838) in NE Orleans Co. Settled in 1812, the town was formed in 1837 from Murray. Until the Erie Canal made Syracuse salt readily available, brine was boiled for salt at Kendall. A library opened in 1822 and operated until common school libraries came into use. In 1825 a colony of 53 Norwegians settled in the town's northeast, the first organized emigration from Norway to the United States; all but two moved on to LaSalle Co, Ill in 1834. Fruit growing (apples, pears, peaches, and quinces) became important early in the town's history. Kendall was served by the Rome, Watertown and Ogdensburg Railroad (1876; called Ho-Jack). In the 20th century its agricultural products included wheat, corn, fruit, and vegetables; fruit was processed in dry houses and in a vinegar plant. The Lake Ontario State Parkway (1970) runs along the shore and aids some Rochester-bound commuters. Other residents continue to work the town's large farms.

Joette Knapp

Kenmore. Village (pop 16,426) in Tonawanda (Erie Co). In 1888 real estate agent Louis Phillip Adolph Eberhardt (1860–1939) purchased land and began development the following year of a suburban village. A trolley from Buffalo began operating in 1893, facilitating its growth, and the village was incorporated in 1899. During World War I Kenmore was a testing ground for the Curtiss Aeroplane Co. From 1920 to 1930 the village experienced fivefold population growth, and by the early 21st century it was a mature suburb of Buffalo. The sandstone Eberhardt Mansion (1893) is listed on the National Register of Historic Places.

Nancy B. Mingus

Kennedy, Robert F(rancis) (*b* Brookline, Mass, 20 Nov 1925; *d* Los Angeles, 6 June 1968). Politician. The seventh of the nine Kennedy children, Robert served briefly in the navy during the

1940s and graduated from Harvard and the University of Virginia Law School. He began his political career during the 1950s by managing his brother John F. Kennedy's successful 1952 US Senate campaign and then by working as counsel for Senate committees investigating communist influence in the federal government and corruption in labor unions. Like many other Democrats of that era, Robert was a strong anticommunist. Upon John's election as president in 1960, Robert became US attorney general and was his brother's closest advisor on several important matters, including civil rights and the Cuban Missile Crisis. After John's assassination, Robert resigned as attorney general and became a senator from New York State in 1964 by defeating Republican Kenneth B. Keating despite accusations that Kennedy was a "carpetbagger" without a record of extended prior residence in the state. As senator, Kennedy focused mostly on national issues, such as race relations, poverty, and Vietnam, rather than on narrower New York affairs, but he did lead an effort to develop the Bedford-Stuyvesant neighborhood of Brooklyn. His attempts to revive the sagging fortunes of the Democratic Party in New York State proved less successful. An outspoken critic of Pres Lyndon Johnson's foreign and domestic policies, Kennedy sought the Democratic presidential nomination in 1968. That campaign ended when he was assassinated after winning the California primary.

Dooley, Brian. *Robert Kennedy: The Final Years* (New York: St. Martin's Press, 1996)

Timothy N. Thurber

Kennedy, William (*b* Albany, 16 Jan 1928). Writer. Kennedy grew up in Albany in a close-knit Irish American community that has played an important role in the themes and style of his writing. After college and a stint in the army, he lived for seven years in Puerto Rico. Kennedy returned to Albany in 1963 and wrote a series of articles on communities within the city. The work was eventually expanded into the successful book *O Albany!* (1983) and formed a source of the rich local imagery that would typify his "Albany cycle" of novels. Kennedy's first published novel, *The Ink Truck* (1969), draws upon his experience as a journalist to depict the closing months of a bitter newspaper strike. *Legs* (1975) traces the life of Albany gangster Jack "Legs" Diamond, and *Billy Phelan's Greatest Game* (1978) follows a gambler's struggle to live an ethical life in an amoral world. Kennedy's breakthrough novel was *Ironweed* (1983), a Pulitzer Prize–winning account of the life of a homeless man. Kennedy also penned the script for the 1987 movie version of *Ironweed* and for the 1984 film the *Cotton Club* (co-written with Francis Ford Coppola). The novel *Quinn's Book* (1988) looks back to the ancestors of characters who populate the Albany cycle, while *Very Old Bones* (1992) brings the chronicle up to the middle of the 20th century. *The Flaming Corsage* (1996) fills in details of the interconnected lives of the Phelan, Taylor, and Daugherty families, and *Roscoe* (2002) outlines the political world in which the Albany cycle takes place. Other works include the nonfiction *Riding the Yellow Trolley Car* (1993); two children's books coauthored with his son Brendan; and a play, *Grand View* (1996). With money from a MacArthur Fellowship (1983) he helped found the Albany-based New York State Writers Institute and has served as its executive director.

Gillespie, Michael Patrick. *Reading William Kennedy* (Syracuse: Syracuse Univ Press, 2001)
Michener, Christian. *From Then into Now: William Kennedy's Albany Novels* (Scranton, Pa: Univ of Scranton Press, 1998)

Michael Patrick Gillespie

Kensett, John Frederick (*b* Cheshire, Conn, 22 Mar 1816; *d* New York City, 14 Dec 1872). Painter. Trained by his father and uncle, Kensett began his career as an engraver and apprenticed with printers in New Haven, Conn, New York City, and Albany. In 1838 he worked in New York City engraving banknotes but also began painting and exhibiting his work. He left for Europe in 1840 to study painting. After returning to New York City in 1847 Kensett became affiliated with the Hudson River school. He was elected associate member of the National Academy of Design in 1848. Kensett painted scenes of Europe and the eastern United States, but his New York landscapes earned him respect and fame. He captured the grandeur of the New York wilderness using light and imagery. His works *Along the Hudson* (1852) and *Lake George* (1856) were highly acclaimed. Kensett was admired for his paintings of the Catskill and Adirondack Mountains, Niagara Falls, Long Island, and the Hudson River valley. He was the president of the Artists' Fund Society and a founder of the Metropolitan Museum of Art.

Driscoll, John Paul, and John K. Howat. *John Frederick Kensett, an American Master* (New York: Norton, 1985)

Nancy Knechtel

Kensington. Village (pop 1,209) in North Hempstead (Nassau Co). This part of the Great Neck peninsula was purchased in 1909 by the Rickett-Finlay Realty Co, which planned a model community on an English pattern; they duplicated the gates of England's Kensington Gardens for its entrance. The 135-acre (55 ha) village was incorporated in 1917. It remains an exclusive residential area in the early 21st century.

Richard A. Winsche

Kent. Town (pop 14,009) in N central Putnam Co. Formed from a part of the old town of Frederickstown in 1795 as Frederick, its name was changed to Kent in 1817. It was home to "teenage Paul Revere" Sybil Ludington (1761–1839). In the 19th century Farmers Mills enjoyed abundant waterpower and turnpike transportation to the Hudson, but railroads bypassed the town, and the mills lost their waterpower to New York City's expanding reservoir system. Beginning in the 1930s Kent attracted sportsmen's clubs and summer colonies, and its population began to increase rapidly. Transportation improved with the Taconic Parkway (1935) and I-84 (1968–70); resulting suburbanization produced a 257% population increase between 1960 and 2000. The Great Buddha Hall of Chuang Yen Buddhist Monastery (1997) is a landmark.

Sallie S. Sypher

Kent, James (*b* South Precinct, Dutchess Co [now Kent, Putnam Co], 31 July 1763; *d* New York City, 12 Dec 1847). Jurist. After completing his war-interrupted studies at Yale College in 1781, he took a legal apprenticeship with New York State attorney general Egbert Benson and was admitted to the state bar in 1785. That same year he entered a law practice with Gilbert Livingston in Poughkeepsie. Debates over the US Constitution during these years introduced Kent to state and national political figures, including Alexander Hamilton, who became a close friend. Kent was a vigorous Federalist and was elected to the state assembly from Dutchess Co in 1790 and 1792. In the assembly he was a staunch opponent of the Antifederalist New York State governor George Clinton. In 1793 Kent ran for US Congress but was defeated by his Antifederalist brother-in-law. Disillusioned, he quit his practice with Livingston that same year and moved to New York City, where his Federalist friends secured for him Columbia College's first professorship of law. Though Kent held the Columbia post for five years, there was little interest in his courses, which he only offered his first two years. Kent's emergence as a figure of prominence came through the judiciary, first as a master of chancery (1796) and New York City recorder (1797), then as a State Supreme Court justice (1798–1814), and finally as chancellor of the Court of Chancery (1814–23). Kent gained influence as a jurist by insisting that his decisions be recorded and published. His chancery decisions were recognized by US Supreme Court justice Joseph Story as recording important American legal precedents. Following his 1823 retirement from the bench, Kent resumed teaching at Columbia. His lectures, now more successful, provided him with the material for his massive four-volume *Commentaries on American Law,* published between 1826 and 1830. The books passed through six editions in his lifetime. Kent's most lasting contributions to American law, through the *Commentaries* and his decisions, lay in preserving legitimacy for the British common-law tradition and in the institution of written decisions, to which state and federal judges turned for precedent. His decisions incorporated not only common law but also an expansive reading that provided him the reputation of being able to dominate judicial fellows in argument. Kent's conservatism led him to oppose abandoning property qualifications for suffrage at the New York State Constitutional Convention in 1821. Kent spent his final years continuing his life-long arduous study and preparing new editions of his *Commentaries.*

Langbein, John H. "Chancellor Kent and the History of Legal Literature," *Columbia Law Review* 93 (Apr 1993): 547–94

Bryan Waterman

Kent, Rockwell (*b* Tarrytown, Westchester Co, 21 June 1882; *d* Plattsburgh, 13 Mar 1971). Artist. Kent attended private school in Tarrytown and the Horace Mann School in New York City, and spent two summers at William Merritt Chase's art colony Shinnecock (Suffolk Co). In 1902 he left architecture studies at Columbia University to enroll in the New York School of Art, directed by Paul Henri, who was a significant influence on Kent. A lifelong advocate for world peace, organized labor, and pro-Russian and antifascist causes, Kent joined the Socialist Party in 1904. In 1927 he bought a farm near Au Sable Forks (Essex Co) and named it Asgaard

(Norse for "farm of the gods"). He produced oils, murals, mystical woodcuts, lithographs, advertisements, and illustrations for books, such as for Herman Melville's *Moby Dick.* His love of harsh climates, rugged terrain, and manual labor motivated extended trips to remote places, including two to Greenland that he recounted in *Salamina* (1935). In 1948 Kent's insertion of "Vote for Wallace" in bottle caps sparked a boycott against his dairy's "Russian milk." His run for US Congress on the American Labor Party ticket that year garnered him less than 3% of the vote. After taking the Fifth Amendment before Sen Joseph McCarthy's investigative committee in 1953, Kent's passport was rescinded, and the sale of his work ceased. His passport was restored after the landmark US Supreme Court case *Kent v Dulles* (1958), and gradually commissions returned. Known more widely for radical politics than for creativity during his lifetime, Kent is only now considered a major 20th-century artist and illustrator.

Traxel, David. *An American Saga: The Life and Times of Rockwell Kent* (New York: Harper & Row, 1980)

Miriam Steinhardt Soffer

Kernan, Francis (*b* Wayne, Steuben Co, 14 Jan 1816; *d* Utica, 7 Sept 1892). US senator. Son of Irish Roman Catholic immigrants, he was a 1836 graduate of Georgetown College before he built a thriving law practice in Utica and joined the Democratic Party. After holding minor political posts, he gained statewide prominence campaigning for the Free-Soil Party (1848) and as official reporter for the Court of Appeals (1854–57) and as assemblyman (1861). As a US congressman (1863–65), he supported the Union but opposed emancipation. From 1871 to 1874 Kernan backed Samuel J. Tilden's crusade against the Tweed Ring, and he earned the Democratic nomination for governor in 1872. Unable to carry the largely Protestant regions of the state, he lost the election, but Democrats, when they gained control of the legislature in 1874, elected him as US senator (1875–81). While in the US Senate, Kernan served as chairman of the Committee on Patents. An unsuccessful candidate for reelection, he spent the remainder of his life practicing law and furthering education, chiefly as a school commissioner in Utica and as a member of the state's Board of Regents (1870–92).

Alexander, DeAlva Stanwood. *A Political History of the State of New York,* 4 vols (1906; repr Port Washington, NY: I. J. Friedman, 1969)

Jerome Mushkat

Keuka College. Private college in Keuka Park (Yates Co). The college was founded in 1890 by Rev George Harvey Ball (1819–1907) as part of a trio of educational and religious institutions that included Keuka Institute and Lake Keuka Assembly. Its primary benefactors were the Central Association of Freewill Baptists (also founded by George Ball) and the Ball brothers (nephews of George and owners of the Ball Mason Jar Co of Muncie, Ind). Offering religious and secular education to local and regional students of all ages and denominations at a minimal cost, the college opened in 1892 as a coeducational institution. The first class enrolled in 1896 and consisted of three women. The assembly closed in 1905, and the institute in 1915. Keuka College also closed in 1915 because of financial problems but reopened in 1920 as Keuka College for Women, a liberal arts school associated with the American Baptist Church. By 1942 the college had instituted its field period program, in which students transformed their studies into practical experience. Keuka College became coeducational in 1985, but women still enroll at higher rates than men. In 2002 the school offered 33 undergraduate majors and 3 master's programs and enrolled 1,057 students.

Africa, Philip A. *Keuka College: A History* (Valley Forge, Pa: Judson Press, 1974)

Laura J. McClusky

Keuka Lake (18 mi²/47 km²). Keuka, called Crooked Lake until *ca* 1860, is identified by its Y shape, formed by Bluff Point jutting into the lake from the north. One million years BP Keuka was a south-flowing river. As a glacier moved southward, it scraped the valley bare and piled a huge dam of debris at the southern end, preventing drainage and leaving behind a lake 19.6 miles (31.54 km) long, 183 feet (55.8 m) at its deepest, and 1.9 miles (3.06 km) at its widest point. Penn Yan (Yates Co) is at the top of the east branch and Branchport (Yates Co) atop the west, with Hammondsport (Steuben Co) near its south end. Municipal water systems for Hammondsport and Penn Yan draw water from the lake. The Crooked Lake Canal (1833–77) through the Keuka Lake Outlet between Keuka and Seneca Lakes facilitated the shipment of local grain, fruit, and manufactured goods via the Erie Canal. The Penn Yan and Dresden Branch of the Fall Brook Railroad (1884) replaced the abandoned canal. The natural waterway is now the centerpiece of the Keuka Lake Outlet Trail.

Navigation on Keuka by settlers began in 1798 when a New York City–built flatboat was used to move a family to the lake's west branch. The first steamboat, the *Keuka,* was launched in 1837. Over the next 60 years, steamboats carried passengers and goods up and down the lake. In March 1908 Hammondsport's aviation pioneer Glenn H. Curtiss used Keuka's ice as the runway to launch his plane *Red Wing.* That November he launched the *Loon,* the first amphibious aircraft, from Keuka's waters.

Keuka's steep hillsides provide ideal grape-growing conditions. Rev William Bostwick planted Catawba and Isabella vine cuttings near Hammondsport in the 1830s. One hundred twenty years later, Dr Konstantin Frank started a New York State wine industry expansion when he planted on Keuka's western shore the first European *Vitis vinifera* to be grown in the eastern United States. In the early 21st century, Keuka Lake is a popular year-round recreational destination.

Dyson, Katharine Delavan. *The Finger Lakes Book: A Complete Guide* (Lee, Mass: Berkshire House Publishers, 2001)

Gwen Chamberlain

KeySpan Corporation. Gas and power distributor for New York State. The company dates to 1825, when Brooklyn Gas Light Co was chartered by the state legislature. It did not secure a contract to supply gas until 1847; it began supplying in 1849 from a plant located next to the Brooklyn Navy Yard at Hudson Ave at the East River. Over the next 40 years, 15 more gas companies would open in Brooklyn and Queens. In 1895 the merger of seven firms—Brooklyn Gas Light, Fulton Municipal Gas, Citizens' Gas Light, Metropolitan Gas Light, Williamsburg Gas Light, People's Gas Light, and Nassau Gas Light—created Brooklyn Union Gas (BUG). Between 1896 and 1910 BUG acquired six more companies, increasing its customer accounts to 387,000. As the demand for street lighting grew, the company expanded its cooking gas business and began supplying gas for water heating and industrial purposes. During the 1930s it entered the home heating business and began selling refrigerators and stoves as another avenue for selling gas.

Originally both a manufacturer and supplier of distilled coal gas, BUG became a supplier of natural gas in 1950–52. In 1957 it expanded service to Staten Island by acquiring New York and Richmond Gas Co and two years later absorbed Kings Co Lighting Co and Brooklyn Borough Gas Co. In 1998 it created a holding company, KeySpan Energy Corp (after 1999, KeySpan Corp), which acquired some of the assets of Long Island Lighting Co (LILCO), and agreed to deliver power to the 1.1 million customers of Long Island Power Authority, the nonprofit successor to LILCO. KeySpan is also under contract to manage Long Island Power Authority's electric transmission and distribution systems. In 2000 KeySpan expanded into New England by acquiring Eastern Enterprises, a natural gas utility with more than 800,000 customers in Massachusetts and New Hampshire. In 2003 KeySpan had more than 13,000 employees. The subsidiary KeySpan Energy Delivery, formerly BUG, manages regulated natural gas utilities, distributing natural gas to 2.5 million customers in New York City, Nassau and Suffolk Cos, and New England. The company has headquarters in Brooklyn and Hicksville (Nassau Co) as well as in Boston.

Larson, Edwin S. *Brooklyn Union Gas: Fueling Growth and Change in New York City* (New York: Newcomen Society, 1987)
Murphy, Robert E. *Brooklyn Union: A Centennial History* (Brooklyn: Brooklyn Union Gas, 1995)

Jeffrey Kraus

Kiantone. Town (pop 1,385) in SE Chautauqua Co. Settled in 1807 the town was formed from Carroll in 1853. The residents of Harmonia or "the Domain," a Spiritualist commune, built round and octagon houses (1853–58); the commune was gone by 1870, and the houses have also disappeared. Because of its close proximity to Jamestown, Kiantone is partly suburban with some dairy farming.

Michelle Henry

Kiantone Community. In 1853 John Murray Spear, an abolitionist and Universalist preacher turned spiritualist, founded a utopian society on 123 acres (50 ha) near Kiantone (Chautauqua Co), where local springs were believed to have curative powers. Variously known as Harmonia, the Association of Beneficents, or the Domain, the community endorsed free love and female liberation, and hosted Spiritualist gatherings. Up to 40 summer residents lived in 10 octagonal or oval structures, following Spear's spiritually inspired designs. Spear brought a machine called the New Motor to nearby Randolph. He developed an elaborate ritual for the machine, which he considered both alive and divine, and which he hoped would provide humanity with a limitless source of power. However, in Spear's account it was soon destroyed by scandalized citizens. In 1859 the society was reconstituted as the Sacred Order of Unionists, some of whom traveled west and set up a colony in Patriot, Ind. The order foundered, and both communities were given up in 1863.

Duino, Russell. "Utopian Themes with Variation: John Murray Spear and His Kiantone Domain," *Pennsylvania History* 29 (Apr 1962): 140–50

Glenn Wright

Kichtawank Indians. Munsee-speaking community whose settlements centered around the Croton River valley in northern Westchester and Putnam Cos. The Jansson-Visscher map of 1635 noted Indian communities identified as Noch Peem, Pasquasheck, and Keskistkonck along the southern and eastern slopes of the Hudson Highlands and an Indian village identified as Kestaubniuck at what is now Peekskill (Westchester Co). Kichtawanks first appeared in written records when two of their sachems, Mamarranack and Wapgaurin, were noted among envoys from several Hudson Valley Indian nations seeking peace with colonists at Stamford, Conn, on 6 Apr 1644 at the height of Kieft's War. Although Kichtawank warriors may have joined other Highlands Indians in attacks on colonists during the Peach and Esopus Wars between 1655 and 1664, their sachems managed to maintain neutrality during both conflicts. Many Wiechquaeskecks moved to Kichtawank territory, where Wessecanow, Oscawanna, and other sachems signed a series of deeds that conveyed the last Indian lands there by 1699. No longer mentioned by name after moving north and east away from the area, they are commemorated as the namesakes of the unincorporated locality of Kitchawan (Westchester Co). The name of the Croton River is traditionally believed to be based on the alleged chief, Croton, though an alternative derivation is from the Greek city-state, Crotone.

Brawer, Catherine, ed. *Many Trails: Indians of the Lower Hudson Valley* (Katonah, NY: Katonah Gallery, 1983)
Trelease, Allen W. *Indian Affairs in Colonial New York: The 17th Century* (Ithaca: Cornell Univ Press, 1960)

Robert S. Grumet

Kidd, William (*b* Scotland, ?1645; *d* London, 23 May 1701). Pirate. A minister's son, William Kidd left Greenock, Scotland, for a life on the sea. In 1689 he captained a ship commissioned as a privateer by the governor of Nevis, but in the following year he settled in New York. As royal authorities arrived to suppress Leisler's Rebellion, Kidd aided the military commander, Maj Richard Ingoldsby, positioning himself for favor with the winning side. He then married a rich widow and bought a pew in Trinity Church, both signs of substance and respectability, but in 1695 he went to London on a trading voyage with the plan to seek letters as a privateer. He arrived as concern was rising about the pirates who were threatening the trade of the Dutch East and West India Cos. William III awarded a syndicate a royal patent to outfit a ship for attacking both pirates and vessels of Britain's enemy, France. The company gave Kidd command of the *Adventure Galley,* a 287-ton (260 MT), 30-gun ship. He sailed it to New York, seizing a French vessel on the way before heading for the waters between Madagascar and India in 1697. Although Kidd captured two Muslim vessels sailing under French passes, rumors circulated that he had become friendly with the "Red Sea Men," the pirates of that region. Growing apprehensive, he set course for America in 1698. After a stop in the West Indies he sailed north for Boston, where Richard Coote, Earl of Bellomont, a principal in the company that had engaged Kidd, was governor of New York and New England. On 25 June 1699 Kidd stopped at Gardiners Island, where he left several chests and bales of goods along with an inventory. When he reached Boston, Bellomont denounced him as a pirate and imprisoned him. He was sent to England in chains in 1700 and was hanged. Whether Kidd had actually engaged in piracy or was simply a privateer caught on the wrong end of the London policy shift remains unsettled. Several centuries of treasure seekers have sought Capt Kidd's buried chests on Gardiners Island and elsewhere on Long Island but to no avail.

Ritchie, Robert C. *Captain Kidd and the War against the Pirates* (Cambridge, Mass: Harvard Univ Press, 1986)

Richard F. Welch

Kieft, Willem (*b* ?Amsterdam, 1602; *d* Swansea, Wales, 29 Sept 1647). Director of New Netherland. Son of an elite Amsterdam family with important connections to the Dutch West India Co (WIC), Kieft directed, between 1638 and 1647, New Netherland's transition from fur-trading post to colonial settlement and was responsible for the purchase of much of the land around the Manhattan rim from the local Indians. Because there were not enough Dutch settlers for the land on western Long Island, Kieft granted charters for three English villages (Hempstead, Gravesend, and Flushing) between 1644 and 1645 and for the Dutch village of Brooklyn in 1646. Although unable to hold back the English incursions in the Connecticut Valley, Kieft, with the help of the Swedes in the area, managed to expel English settlers from the Delaware River. He was criticized, however, for his role in instigating the series of increasingly violent confrontations between New Netherland and the native Munsee-speaking peoples, known as Kieft's War (1640–45), that caused great destruction to both sides. Angered by the economic and population loss caused by the war and by Kieft's autocratic style of governing, leading Dutch colonists successfully petitioned the WIC in 1644 to have him replaced. Kieft died when the *Princess Amalia,* the ship carrying him and several of his opponents back to the Netherlands, wrecked off the southern coast of Wales.

Frijhoff, Willem. *Wegen van Evert Willemsz.: Een Hollands weeskind op zoek naar zichzelf, 1607–1647* (Nijmegen, Netherlands: SUN, 1995)
Haefeli, Evan. "Kieft's War and the Cultures of Violence in Colonial America." In *Lethal Imagination: Violence and Brutality in American History,* ed. Michael A. Bellesisle (New York: New York Univ Press, 1999)

Evan Haefeli

Kieft's War. Occurring from 1640 through 1645, it was the first armed struggle between American Indians and Europeans in and around New Amsterdam. Shortly after Willem Kieft took over as director of New Netherland in 1638, the Dutch West India Co abandoned its monopoly on the fur trade and offered to give land on generous terms to colonists. As more Europeans entered the colony, tensions developed between the Indians and the colonists. The Indians' crops were destroyed by the Europeans' hogs and cattle, and the colonists resented the continued presence of Indians within their settlements. To add to the mounting tension, Kieft in 1639 taxed the Indians' corn and furs to help with colony expenses. In spring 1640 the Raritan Indians tried, unsuccessfully, to capture the Dutch sloop sent to trade with them. In May they refused to make reparations for the hogs they were accused of killing on Staten Island. Kieft sent troops to demand payment, in the course of which "several" Indians were killed and the sachem's brother tortured.

Relations remained quiet until June 1641, when the Raritans killed four farmers on Staten Island. Kieft offered a reward to induce other Indians to fight the Raritans, who, after pressure from the Long Island Indians and the Tankitekes from the lower Hudson Valley, made peace. Meanwhile, a Wiechquaeskeck killed a colonist on Manhattan, and a Hackensack killed another at Newark Bay in 1642. Kieft was determined to subdue the Indians to his authority rather than negotiate. Over the course of 1643–44 he launched a series of expeditions with West India Co soldiers and colonial militiamen (many of them recent immigrants from New England), massacring scores of often unsuspecting Indians and destroying their crops in villages north, east, and west of Manhattan. The Indians retaliated, driving colonists from their destroyed farms around New Amsterdam to take refuge in Fort Amsterdam.

One group of leading colonists protested the brutal conduct of the war and demanded that Kieft be replaced, but others—with Kieft's encouragement—continued to attack villages on Long Island and the mainland across the Sound. Finally, in August 1645, in the presence of Mohawks, the Indians signed a peace settlement with the Dutch. After five years of war the Indians had lost 900–1,000 lives, and the colonists some 50. Many colonial farms had been burned, and uncounted numbers of colonists fled the colony.

Haefeli, Evan. "Kieft's War and the Cultures of Violence in Colonial America." In *Lethal Imagination: Violence and Brutality in American History,* ed. Michael A. Bellesisles (New York: New York Univ Press, 1999)
Trelease, Allen W. *Indian Affairs in Colonial New York: The 17th Century* (1960; repr, intro William A. Starna, Lincoln: Univ of Nebraska Press, 1997)

Evan Haefeli

Kinderhook. Town (pop 8,296) and village (pop 1,275) in N Columbia Co. Settled in the 17th century by the Dutch and others, Kinderhook formed as a district in 1772 and was recognized as a town in 1788. Niverville was served by the Albany and West Stockbridge Railroad (1841) and later by the Kinderhook and Hudson (1890), but the Village of Kinderhook, incorporated in 1838, had no rail connection. At Niverville industries included cotton wadding, silk thread, and mowing machines; at Kinderhook they included a steam cotton mill (1846–*ca* 1870), several hat factories, a hoopskirt factory (1860s), and the Kinderhook Knitting Co (1882). Peat beds northwest of Niverville were worked until the 1870s. Kinderhook Lake was stocked with pickerel as early as 1818 and became a modest resort, with recreational facilities from *ca* 1870, which became Electric Park (1901–?1920), an amusement park. In the village, the Vanderpoel House (*ca* 1820) is a historic house museum, as are Lindenwald (1797), known as Martin Van Buren National Historic Site, and the Luycas Van Alen House (1737) in the town. The village is also the home of the Columbia County Historical Society and the North Pointe Cultural Arts Center. American Bio Medica, which produces medical diagnostic testing kits, employs 70.

King, John A(lsop) (*b* New York City, 3 Jan 1788; *d* Jamaica, Queens Co, 7 July 1867). Governor and US representative. He was educated in Europe while his father, Rufus King, served as US minister to Great Britain. He served as a lieutenant of cavalry during the War of 1812. He relocated to Jamaica after the war and farmed before undertaking decades of political service, including six terms as assemblyman (1819–21, 1832, 1838, 1840) and one as state senator (1823); he also held diplomatic positions (1825) with his father in Great Britain. King was elected as a Whig to Congress (1849–50), where he opposed the Fugitive Slave Act. After the dissolution of the Whigs, he served as New York State's first Republican governor (1857–58). While in office, he advocated for revision of the existing excise law, popular education initiatives, increased voting rights for Blacks, and the completion of public works projects. Declining renomination to a second term, he retired to his Jamaica farm.

Alexander, DeAlva Stanwood. *A Political History of the State of New York*, 4 vols (1906; repr Port Washington, NY: I. J. Friedman, 1969)

John Marino

King, Preston (*b* Ogdensburg, St. Lawrence Co, 14 Oct 1806; *d* New York City, 13 Nov 1865). US senator and congressman. King graduated from Union College in 1827 and studied law in the office of Silas Wright. In 1830 he became editor of the *St. Lawrence Republican.* As a staunch Jacksonian, he served in the state assembly from 1835 to 1838, becoming the minority leader. King encouraged armed New Yorkers to cross the border and support the Canadians against the British in the uprisings of 1837, and attempted to rescue Americans captured during the revolt. An antislavery Democrat during his first years in the US House of Representatives (1843–47), he was a founder of the Free Soil Party and served two terms as a Free Soil congressman from the Ogdensburg area (1849–53). After a brief return to the Democratic Party, he became one of the organizers of the Republican Party in New York State in the mid-1850s. He was elected US senator in 1856 and served one unremarkable term. Appointed collector of customs in New York City in 1864, King committed suicide by jumping from a ferryboat into New York Harbor.

Muller, Ernest. "Preston King: A Political Biography" (PhD diss, Columbia Univ, 1957)

Jon Sterngass

King, Rufus (*b* Scarborough [now in Maine], 24 Mar 1755; *d* Jamaica, Queens Co, 29 Apr 1827). US senator. Born into a wealthy family, King served briefly in the American Revolution and then practiced law in Massachusetts. As a Massachusetts delegate to the Continental Congress (1784–87), he advocated a strong central government, played a major role in the inclusion of the antislavery legislation in the Northwest Ordinance of 1787, and served that year as a member of the US Constitutional Convention. King married Mary Alsop, the daughter of a successful New York City merchant, in 1786 and moved to the city in 1788, from which he was promptly elected to the state assembly. In 1789 he was elected to the US Senate, where he vigorously supported Alexander Hamilton's economic policies and served on the board of directors of the first Bank of the United States. His defense of the Jay Treaty helped lead to his appointment as minister to Great Britain (1796–1803). In 1804 he moved to Jamaica. A Federalist Party leader, King was its unsuccessful vice presidential candidate in 1804 and 1808 and its last presidential candidate in 1816. After the War of 1812 began, the New York State legislature returned King to the US Senate (1813–25), where he expressed only lukewarm support for the war. As a senator he opposed any expansion of slavery and voted against the Missouri Compromise of 1820. In 1824 he declined reelection but was again appointed minister to Great Britain (1825–26).

Ernst, Robert. *Rufus King: American Federalist* (Chapel Hill: Univ of North Carolina Press, 1968)
King, Charles, ed. *The Life and Correspondence of Rufus King*, 6 vols (1894–1900; repr New York: Da Capo Press, 1971)

Jon Sterngass

King George's War. The third of four great imperial wars between Great Britain and France. King George's War (1744–48) was the American component of the European War of the Austrian Succession. Driven by commercial interests, the primary issue in North America was over control of the Newfoundland fisheries. Britain took Newfoundland from France at the close of Queen Anne's War (1702–13) and sought to defend it against the threat posed by the French fortress at Louisbourg on Ile Royale [now Cape Breton Island, NS]. New York Colony was distracted by internal politics, much as it had been during King William's (1689–97) and Queen Anne's Wars. New York's politically unwise governor, George Clinton, was harried by a provincial assembly determined to expand its own power at the expense of the royal prerogative. The legislature had wrested control of New York Colony's affairs from the executive by manipulating its powers of appropriation. The war provided ample opportunity to continue that effort. By denying Clinton money to prosecute the war, the assembly forced neutrality on him and exposed the poorly defended frontier to incursions from Canada.

The main action of the war was a Massachusetts-led expedition against Louisbourg during May and June of 1745, for which New York Colony was asked to contribute troops and money. Restricted by the assembly, Clinton was only able to send ten cannon. Louisbourg fell to the superior English forces, and New York's debility was revealed by its absence from the campaign. In response, the cleric Abbé François Picquet led a French and Indian war party against Saratoga [now Schuylerville, Saratoga Co] in November 1745, killing 30 residents and capturing nearly 100. The following spring and summer, skirmishes in the forests around Schenectady killed 12 more New Yorkers. As a result, settlements north and west of Albany were largely abandoned for the duration of the war.

Without funds from the assembly, Clinton conducted the war by borrowing money from London. He opened a council with the Iroquois on 19 Aug 1746 and attempted to recruit them into the war effort, but they held fast to the neutrality they declared in 1701. Sir William Johnson convinced the Mohawk to participate, but this was largely a symbolic gesture. The Iroquois Confederacy understood New York's political disorder and were skeptical about the depth of Great Britain's commitment to the war. In 1747 their suspicions were confirmed when an attack on the French at Fort St. Frédéric [now Crown Point, Essex Co] was called off at the last moment. The war ended with the Treaty of Aix-la-Chapelle on 18 Oct 1748. All territorial conquests were canceled, including Louisbourg, and Britain's North American provinces were compensated for expenses incurred in prosecuting the war. Neither the war nor the peace settled any of the major controversies between Great Britain and France.

Kammen, Michael. *Colonial New York: A History* (New York: Scribner's, 1975)
Katz, Stanley N. *Newcastle's New York: Anglo-American Politics, 1732–1753* (Cambridge, Mass: Belknap Press, 1968)
Peckham, Howard H. *The Colonial Wars, 1689–1762* (Chicago: Univ of Chicago Press, 1964)

Daniel A. Piazza

King Hendrick [Theyanoguin] (*b* Westfield, Mass, 28 Mar 1692; *d* Lake George, Warren Co, 8 Sept 1755). Mohawk chief, diplomat, and orator. Born to a Mohegan father and a Mohawk mother, Theyanoguin played a prominent role in New York colonial affairs during the first half of the 18th century. He also was known to the British as Hendrick Peters (later King Hendrick), an alias that has caused many historians to confuse Theyanoguin with Tejonihokarawa, another Mohawk chief who was also often referred to as Hendrick Peters. Hendrick Peters Tejonihokarawa was a member of the Wolf Clan and was born *ca* 1660, and Hendrick Peters Theyanoguin was a member of the Bear Clan born in 1692. It was Tejonihokarawa, not Theyanoguin, who was one of the so-called Four Indian Kings who visited Queen Anne in England in 1710. A portrait painted on that trip clearly shows his Wolf Clan affiliation. Tejonihokarawa was deposed by clan matrons in 1712–13 and restored with the name Soiengarahta in 1720, a famous episode that is often incorrectly attributed to Theyanoguin. Tejonihokarawa died sometime after April 1735, about the time when Theyanoguin began to rise to political importance.

Theyanoguin also made a trip to England but in 1740. He visited Boston in 1744 and received Conrad Weiser at his home at Canajoharie [now in Montgomery Co] in 1745, the same year he attended a conference in Albany. He went to Montreal with a Mohawk delegation in 1746 and around that time moved his home to Yosts [now in Montgomery Co] to be closer to Sir William Johnson, with whom he had many dealings in the years following. He participated in the

Albany Plan of Union in 1754 and traveled to Philadelphia the following winter, making speeches for which he later became famous. He was killed alongside British forces under the command of Johnson fighting the French at Lake George.

Fenton, William N. *The Great Law and the Longhouse* (Norman: Univ of Oklahoma Press, 1998)
Hamilton, Milton W. "Theyanoguin." In *Dictionary of Canadian Biography*, vol 3 (Toronto: Univ of Toronto Press, 1974)
Silverstsen, Barbara J. *Turtles, Wolves, and Bears: A Mohawk Family History* (Bowie, Md: Heritage Books, 1996)

Dean R. Snow

Kingsbury. Town (pop 11,171) in W central Washington Co. Patented in 1762 with township privileges, it was settled in 1765. Kingsbury was recognized as a town in 1786. It was traversed by the Champlain Canal (1819) and a railroad (1848; later Delaware and Hudson Railroad). Limestone was quarried at Smiths Basin. By 1878 the town had the largest proportion of cleared land in the county. In 2003 bluestone was still being quarried near the Warren Co border, and Kingsbury was one of two leading dairy farm towns in Washington Co.

R. Paul McCarty

Kings County. See BROOKLYN [KINGS COUNTY].

Kings Park. Locality (pop 16,146) in Smithtown (Suffolk Co). The area was lightly settled until the Society of St. Johnland (1869), the first of many social service institutions, established an affiliated orphanage and home for the disabled and mentally ill affiliated with the Episcopal Church. A railroad station was built in 1872. The post office, named St. Johnland when it opened in 1876, was renamed Kings Park in 1890. In 1885 the Kings County Farm opened, becoming the Kings Park State Hospital for the mentally ill in 1895 and closing in 1996. Other institutions included Indian Head Farm (1905), which taught farming skills to immigrant Jews, and the Howard Colored Orphan Asylum (1910–18). Hospital work attracted Irish Catholic, Jewish, and Italian workers. Kings Park is the site of the 1,266-acre (512 ha) Gov Alfred E. Smith/Sunken Meadow State Park and the 153-acre (62 ha) Nissequogue River State Park.

Joshua Ruff

Kings Point. Village (pop 5,076) in North Hempstead (Nassau Co). Located on the northern part of Great Neck peninsula, Kings Point is named for Gov John A. King, who built a mansion on its rocky shoreline in 1854. Kings Point became home to numerous celebrities, including store owner Henri Bendel, car manufacturers Alfred P. Sloan and Walter P. Chrysler, and showman George M. Cohan. The village was incorporated in 1924. The Chrysler estate was purchased by the US government in 1942 to be the home of the US Merchant Marine Academy.

Lynda R. Day

Kingston. Town (pop 908) and city (pop 23,456) in NE Ulster Co. Kingston's territory was a stronghold of the Esopus Indians, from whom the Dutch settlement (1652) took its name. Tension between settlers and Indians led to the concentration of the settlement within a palisaded area in 1658 and culminated in the First Esopus War (1659–60). The Second Esopus War began in 1663 and was ended by treaty in 1664. Esopus received its village charter in 1661 and was called Wiltwijck. It was renamed Kingston by the English in 1668, although during the 1673–74 Dutch administration it was called Swaenenburgh.

Kingston was an important and long-term supply source for the Continental army during the American Revolution, and colonial legislators met there in 1777 to ratify a constitution for the State of New York. On 16 Oct 1777 British Gen John Vaughan and 3,000 men landed at Rondout, marched to Kingston, and burned the village. Although rebuilt, Kingston lost its position as state capital to Poughkeepsie. The village, incorporated in 1805, merged with the Village of Rondout and the hamlet of Wilbur to form the City of Kingston in 1872. The city's incorporation and the 1879 creation of the Town of Ulster left the Town of Kingston small in area and population, as it was in 2003, and not contiguous to the city. The town's 19th-century industry was quarrying, and an Irish community supported a Roman Catholic church and an Ancient Order of Hibernians lodge.

The completion of the Delaware and Hudson Canal (from Rondout Landing to Honesdale, Pa) in 1828 magnified Kingston's commercial status by making it an important transshipment entrepôt for Pennsylvania coal bound for New York City and other points in the state. Boatbuilding, limestone quarrying, brickmaking, lime production, and hydraulic cement manufacturing, chiefly by the Newark Lime and Cement Manufacturing Co (1851), built an industrial economy. Goods were shipped largely by sloop and steamboat to New York City. Irish and Germans settled in Rondout; Jews founded synagogues at Kingston (1853) and Rondout (1854); and three black churches were formed (1848, 1852, 1853). Railroads brought increased prosperity beginning with the Ulster and Delaware Railroad (1870) to the west and the Wallkill Valley Railroad (1872) to the southwest; the riverside West Shore line opened in 1883.

Kingston's economy fluctuated in the 20th century. Cement production peaked around 1900 and then declined. By the 1940s brickmaking had also waned, and only the Hutton and Staples brickyards remained in operation. The Dwyer and Feeney boatyards and the Fessenden, Fuller, and Jacobson shirt factories were major producers in that period. Electrol produced airplane hydraulics during World War II. In 1955 IBM opened a plant in Ulster (Ulster Co), creating jobs for Kingston residents. For 40 years it produced advanced computer systems such as SAGE (Semi-Automatic Ground Environment), an air defense network. In 1994, when the IBM plant closed, Kingston leaders formed the Kingston/Ulster Empire Zone. In 2003 the zone provided tax benefits to more than 150 businesses, including restaurants, craft retailers, clothing retailers, and financial and real estate firms. These businesses and Kingston's rich history attracted young professionals and tourists. Kingston was the birthplace and home of 19th-century painters John Vanderlyn (1775–1852) and Jervis McEntee (1828–91). A landmark is the Senate House Museum, the 1676 structure in which the state legislature held its first session and in which legislators convened in 1777 to draft and ratify the first constitution for New York State.

Karen Nichols

Senate House, Kingston, built in 1676 by Abraham van Gaasbeek and a state historic site since 1887.

King William's War. The first of the wars in North America between England and France, it was also known in Europe as the War of the League of Augsburg (1689–97). In 1688 the Glorious Revolution ousted Catholic James II and brought Protestant William of Orange, an enemy of France's Louis XIV, to the English throne. As a result England and France declared war in 1689, and the two nations' North American colonies and their Indian allies became embroiled in the conflict. That same year political uncertainty in New York Colony led to Leisler's Rebellion and divided the province into pro- and anti-Leislerian factions.

The first action of the war in North America was a French and Indian attack on Schenectady in February 1690 that laid waste to the settlement. Following the attack, Jacob Leisler called for an intercolonial conference in April 1690. The participants included New York, Massachusetts Bay, Plymouth, and Connecticut. A two-pronged attack of New France was planned, and Leisler levied taxes to pay for New York's share of the expenses. A fleet led by Sir William Phips left Massachusetts in August 1690 to attack Quebec via the St. Lawrence River but was unsuccessful. A land assault on Montreal through New York Colony under the command of Fitz-John Winthrop of Connecticut got underway in July–August 1690, but it was forced to turn back. The campaign was a failure: supplies that were supposed to arrive en route never materialized, and Iroquois allies never arrived because they were suffering from a smallpox epidemic. There were no other intercolonial offensives for the duration of the war.

Arriving in New York Colony in March 1691, newly appointed governor Henry Sloughter was a political enemy of Leisler. Upon his arrival Gov Sloughter arrested Leisler and 36 others; Leisler was tried and executed in May 1691. The governor was informed that the Iroquois were growing restless under New York Colony's half-hearted war effort. To placate them, Albany mayor Peter Schuyler led New York Militia and Iroquois allies on an attack of La Prairie, across the St. Lawrence River from Montreal, on 10 Aug 1691. For nearly two years afterward, the New York frontier remained quiet. A French attack in 1693 destroyed several Mohawk villages in what is now Montgomery Co. Schuyler and New York governor Benjamin Fletcher led more than 800 troops and Iroquois allies against the French in response. This prompt action pleased some Iroquois, but for many it was both too little and too late; they opened peace talks with Canadian governor Comte de Frontenac.

Another lull, lasting nearly three years, settled on the New York frontier. By 1696 Frontenac was under pressure from Versailles and civil officials in New France to defeat the Iroquois once and for all. The aging governor mustered more than 2,000 French troops and Indian allies for an attack on the Onondaga and Oneida. Arriving at Onondaga Lake in August 1696, Frontenac's army advanced on the two villages to find them burned by the fleeing Iroquois. This was one of the last actions of the war in New York Colony, as the conflict between England and France ended the following year with the Peace of Rijswijk. The Iroquois Confederacy eventually made its own peace with New France in 1701.

Peckham, Howard H. *The Colonial Wars, 1689–1762* (Chicago: Univ of Chicago Press, 1964)
Trelease, Allen W. *Indian Affairs in Colonial New York: The 17th Century* (Ithaca: Cornell Univ Press, 1960)

Daniel A. Piazza

Kinzua Dam controversy. In the 1920s the US Army Corps of Engineers proposed construction of dams on the Allegheny River in Pennsylvania for power production. Potential reservoir areas included the Allegany Indian Reservation [loc in Cattaraugus Co] of the Seneca Nation of Indians in New York State, confirmed to the Seneca in Article 3 of the 1794 Treaty of Canandaigua, and the Cornplanter Grant, the last Indian-owned land in the Commonwealth of Pennsylvania. Indian protests began in 1935. In 1936 a record-setting flood in Pittsburgh shifted the focus to flood control, and the future Kinzua Dam was included in flood control acts passed by Congress in 1936 and 1938. Opposition from the Departments of Justice and Interior based on the Treaty of Canandaigua halted further development until the administration of Pres Dwight D. Eisenhower in 1953, when the departments reversed their position. In 1957 the Seneca Nation, with the strong support of the Philadelphia Yearly Meeting of Friends (Quakers), launched a national public relations campaign to rally support for alternate dam locations, identified by Dr Arthur E. Morgan, that would not violate the 1794 treaty. In the sociopolitical context of the Cold War, protests against the dam focused on the moral issue of a nation keeping its word. By 1958 efforts centered on an unsuccessful attempt to defeat the House public works appropriations bill, and New York governor W. Averell Harriman urged the state's representatives to oppose the dam and vote to delete the Kinzua appropriation. Seneca Nation attorney Edward O'Neill argued in federal court that a special act of Congress was required to break the 1794 Treaty of Canandaigua, but US District Judge Joseph McGarraghy in Washington, DC, denied his request, citing the appropriation as evidence of congressional intent, and the US Supreme Court refused review in June 1959.

The Seneca Nation shifted its campaign from opposing the dam to obtaining the best possible settlement. The 1958 Seneca Nation election resulted in the transfer of power to a new party whose core consisted of educated veterans of World War II and Korea. For the next six years George Heron and Basil Williams led the Seneca Nation as president and treasurer, respectively. With the continuing support of the Philadelphia Quakers, the people of the Allegany Reservation organized themselves into numerous committees to determine their future course. The 179 ft (54.6 m) Kinzua Dam in Warren, Pa, 11 miles (18 km) from the New York State border, flooded a third of the Allegany Reservation, leaving only wooded hillsides and towns occupied by Whites under leases executed by Congress in the late 19th century. Of the total resident population of the area, 1,103 in 1962, 550 people lost their homes and land, and an additional 98 lost much of their land. The final settlement in 1964 (Public Law 88-533, 78 Stat 738) provided individual Senecas and the Seneca Nation with $14,613,550, the bulk of which was devoted to addressing the cultural impact on the Seneca Nation. The Seneca used these funds to create a scholarship program and to build two office complexes, two libraries, a bowling alley, and a museum. As a result, Seneca educational levels increased significantly, and the Seneca Nation's government has become an institutionalized bureaucracy. Women, who played a major role in fighting dam construction and planning relocation, received the right to vote (1964) and hold office (1966), and have rapidly moved into formal political roles.

Bilharz, Joy A. *The Allegany Senecas and Kinzua Dam: Forced Relocation through Two Generations* (Lincoln: Univ of Nebraska Press, 1998)
Hauptman, Laurence. *The Iroquois Struggle for Survival: World War II to the Emergence of Red Power* (Syracuse: Syracuse Univ Press, 1986)

Joy A. Bilharz

Kirkham, Charles B. (*b* Thurston, Steuben Co, 2 Nov 1881; *d* Middletown, Orange Co, 31 Dec 1969). Aviation and automotive engineer. From 1901 to 1905 his family's foundry in Urbana (Steuben Co) made motorcycle engines for Glenn H. Curtiss, who worked with Kirkham on several projects. The Kirkham brothers developed automobile and airplane engines, which helped achieve new speed and distance records. In 1910, while the family firm continued to produce engines, Kirkham and mechanic Fred Eells began building Curtiss-type airplanes. A year later Kirkham founded Charles B. Kirkham Motors in Savona (Steuben Co), by 1912 developing one of the nation's first tractor-type airplanes. A successor company failed in 1914, and Kirkham joined Curtiss Motor Co in Hammondsport (Steuben Co) in 1915, quickly becoming chief engineer and improving engine power from 80 horsepower to 375 horsepower in two years. Second in command to Curtiss at the Curtiss engineering plant in Garden City (Nassau Co) in 1917–19, Kirkham developed an early supercharger and a high-altitude triplane. He later became a consulting engineer for many firms and by 1926 also ran his own company in Garden City, Kirkham Products, which undertook specialized contract work. About 1930 he moved this business to Farmingdale (Nassau Co), where it became Liberty Aircraft Production Co in 1938. Kirkham retired in 1940.

Roseberry, C. R. *Glenn Curtiss: Pioneer of Flight* (Garden City, NY: Doubleday, 1972)

Kirk W. House

Kirkland. Town (pop 10,138) in S central Oneida Co. Beginning in 1784 Kirkland was home to the Brothertown community, a settlement of Christian Indians who received 24,000 acres (9,712 ha) from the Oneida tribe and moved to Wisconsin around the 1840s. White settlement commenced in 1787, and the town was formed from Paris in 1827. It was the site of the Hamilton-Oneida Academy (1793), which was created to educate both Indians and Whites; the school was chartered in 1812 as Hamilton College. Iron ore (Clinton hematite) was discovered in 1797, and Kirkland firms such as Manchester Manufacturing Co (1815–54) and Clinton Iron Co (1874), as well as Franklin Iron Works (1852–1905) at Franklin Springs, used the ore for production. Mining of Clinton hematite continued until 1963. The Chenango Canal (1837–78) and three rail lines that opened between 1866 and 1884 served the industries. Other industrial products included nails, hats, bricks, paint, pottery, scythes, and leather. Hind and Harrison Plush Co (1890s–1940s) operated at Clark Mills. Lithia water was bottled at Franklin Springs (1888–*ca* 1970). Dairy and truck farming continued in Kirkland in 2002. The town's largest employers are Lutheran Care Ministries Network (1919), Hamilton College, and the public school system. James H. Rhodes Co of Franklin Springs produces electronic components. Many residents commute to the Utica area for employment.

Kirkland, Samuel (*b* Norwich, Conn, 1 Dec 1741; *d* Clinton, Oneida Co, 28 Feb 1808). Missionary and educator. Son of a Congregationalist minister and influenced by experiences during the Great Awakening, young Kirkland expressed an interest in evangelism. In 1760 he became the first white student in Moor's Charity School, a boarding academy in Lebanon, Conn, founded by Eleazar Wheelock for training American Indians as missionaries to their kin. Two years later he entered the College of New Jersey (now Princeton University) as a sophomore and received an AB degree in 1765. It was awarded *in absentia,* however, because Kirkland had left school in the autumn of 1764 and began living as a missionary among the Seneca Nation of the Iroquois League in Kanadasegea [now Geneva, Ontario Co]. There he learned the local language and was honored by adoption into the nation. But exhaustion and illness set in by the spring of 1766, forcing Kirkland to leave the Seneca and recuperate in Connecticut, where he was ordained and married to Jerusha Bingham, a niece of Wheelock. He returned as a missionary to other Iroquois nations, the Oneida, and neighboring Tuscaroras.

In August 1766 Kirkland established residence at Kanonwarohale/Canowaroghare [now Canajoharie, Montgomery Co], or Oneida Castle, a traditional American Indian stronghold 16 miles (26 km) west of Fort Stanwix [now Rome, Oneida Co], the nearest white settlement. Except for interruptions during the American Revolution, his mission there lasted 40 years. Funded through an arrangement with the Society in Scotland for the Propagation of Christian Knowledge, the struggling missionary spent most of his money to improve Native American welfare. Kirkland was convinced that Indians faced two choices: survive by adapting to white culture or face oblivion by retaining traditionalist patterns, and he erected a church for worship services, a school for elementary education, sawmills, blacksmith shops, and gristmills for acculturation. He used missionary funds to buy seeds, oxen, and iron tools, encouraging Indians to be industrious and sober. His influence helped convince the Oneida in 1775 to remain neutral when Shawnees tried to recruit them in Lord Dunmore's War in Virginia, but that same year opposition from Anglican missionaries caused him to suspend his mission. Thereafter he was assigned as director of Indian scouts and chaplain at Fort Stanwix, serving also for a time as brigade chaplain under Maj Gen John Sullivan and accompanying the troops on the Sullivan-Clinton campaign. In 1780 Kirkland returned to missionary work among the Seneca, Oneida, Cayuga, and Onondaga. Four years later he served the American cause again by persuading the Seneca to accept the Treaty of Fort Stanwix.

Facing old age, illness, and diminishing prospects, Kirkland accepted in 1789 a grant of land that amounted to some 4,000 acres (1,619 ha) near Utica. To this gift from Oneidas and New York State he received a contiguous 2,000 acres (809 ha) as payment for his role in the Phelps and Gorham Purchase. He harbored on the land grant longtime Indian friends who were being threatened by white encroachment. He still thought that agriculture and literacy were keys to Indian survival, and so in 1793 he endowed a new school through which he intended to provide for the spiritual and temporal welfare of American Indians. Alexander Hamilton endorsed the plan, and the institution was called the Hamilton-Oneida Academy. From 1788 to 1795 Kirkland's concern for the Oneida was compromised to some degree by his fundraising and favor-trading deals with donors to the academy. Few Indian students ever attended the school, which in 1812 received a new charter and the name Hamilton College. Kirkland was the victim of financial reverses and painful illness during his final years, and he died at his home near the campus.

Lothrop, Samuel K. *The Life of Samuel Kirkland, Missionary to the Indians* (Boston: Little, Brown, 1847)
Pilkington, Walter. *Hamilton College, 1812–1962* (Clinton, NY: Hamilton College, 1962)
Pilkington, Walter, ed. *The Journals of Samuel Kirkland: 18th-Century Missionary to the Iroquois, Government Agent, Father of Hamilton College* (Clinton, NY: Hamilton College, 1980)

Henry Warner Bowden

Kirkwood. Town (pop 5,651) in S Broome Co. Settled in 1789, the town was formed from Conklin in 1859. Lumbering was the first industry. The Erie Railroad was completed through town in 1848. Three book manufacturers, a very large Frito-Lay Co plant, and the Kirkwood Industrial Park (1965) on a former state hospital farm are all adjacent to I-81 (1961). Residents work in town or commute to the greater Binghamton area.

Charles J. Browne

Kiryas Joel [KEER-YAS YO-EL]. Village (pop 13,138) in Monroe (Orange Co). The village was created as a community for Satmar Hasidim. The Satmar moved to the United States and New York City after World War II, where, under the leadership of Grand Rabbi Joel Teitelbaum (?1887–1979), they primarily settled in the Williamsburg area of Brooklyn. Following unique codes for dress, kosher food, and personal conduct, they are among the most uncompromising of the Hasidic communities of New York City in their rejection of secularism, and they contemplated a move out of the city to avoid the corrupting influences of urbanism and modernity. The Satmar began settling in the Town of Monroe in 1974, and in 1977 the community incorporated as a village, separating Kiryas Joel ("the village of Joel") from Monroe. Physical separation from New York City has not meant isolation, however, and a connection, although at times contentious, has been maintained between Kiryas Joel's leaders and those of the Satmar and other Hasidic communities in the city. In addition, because of a lack of local industries, most of the men from Kiryas Joel commute to jobs in New York City.

From its outset the village has been deeply involved in a variety of separation of "synagogue and state" questions, most prominently dealing with education. Although the Satmar were able to educate most of their children without government interference by sending them to private religious schools, they were unable to secure adequate resources to provide special education for their children with disabilities. A special public school district created by the New York State legislature in 1989 was voided by the US Supreme Court in *Board of Education of Kiryas Joel Village School District v Grumet* (1994). In a splintered 6–3 decision, the district was deemed an improper "fusion of governmental and religious functions" whose primary purpose was to advance religion in violation of the Establishment Clause. The New York State legislature immediately revised the law to address the Supreme Court's objections, providing for the establishment of special school districts in any community that met specific criteria regarding such things as community size, growth potential, and the income of residents. That 1994 law, as well as a 1997 successor with broader criteria, were both found unconstitutional by New York State courts, which felt the criteria were primarily defined so the laws would be applicable to Kiryas Joel. A third version of the law, with even broader criteria, was signed by the governor in August 1999 and has withstood court challenges so far.

Kiryas Joel has also experienced internal conflict. Resident Joseph Waldman has been a prominent dissenter against the village's Satmar hierarchy, claiming in lawsuits filed against the village in 1995 and 1997 that its government is excessively entangled with the ruling religious body, the Congregation Yetev Lev, and that the rights of dissenters in the village are suppressed. And in June 2001 the village's first contested mayoral race was held.

Mintz, Jerome R. *Hasidic People: A Place in the New World* (Cambridge, Mass: Harvard Univ Press, 1992)
Wiese, Philip R. "*Board of Education of Kiryas Joel Village School District v. Grumet:* Crossing the Line of Establishment Clause Jurisprudence," *Ohio Northern Univ Law Review* 21 (1994): 629–53

Timothy P. Gordinier

Kissinger, Henry (Alfred) [Heinz] (*b* Fürth, Germany, 27 May 1923). US government official, consultant, and historian. In August 1938 Kissinger and his family settled in the German Jewish community in Washington Heights, Manhattan. After high school, he studied evenings at City College of New York until 1943, when he was conscripted and then naturalized by the US Army. Kissinger earned his PhD in history at Harvard in 1954. While a member of the Harvard faculty (1954–69), he wrote *Nuclear Weapons and Foreign Policy* (1957), which was published by the Council on Foreign Relations in New York City and made him known in foreign policy circles. He served as a project director for the Rockefeller Brothers Fund (1956–58) and was at various times a consultant to Gov Nelson A. Rockefeller and several federal agencies, including the US Department of State. He remained a registered Democrat until his involvement in Gov Rockefeller's unsuccessful bids in 1964 and 1968 for the Republican presidential nomination. Kissinger served Presidents Richard M. Nixon and Gerald R. Ford as national security adviser (1969–75) and secretary of state (1973–77), winning the Nobel Peace Prize in 1973 for negotiating a peace accord that was ultimately unsuccessful but did allow the withdrawal of US troops from Vietnam. In July 1982 he founded Kissinger Associates, an international consulting firm on Park Ave in New York City. He has also served on numerous corporate boards. In 1980 he briefly considered running for US senator from New York State, and in 1986 he contemplated a run for governor of the state.

Isaacson, Walter. *Kissinger: A Biography* (New York: Simon & Schuster, 1992)

Scott C. Monje

klezmer music. The term originally used to describe the music played by Jewish musicians in eastern Europe (klezmer, sg; klezmorim, pl). Forming small itinerant ensembles *(kapelyes)* these musicians provided music at Jewish weddings and other important (sometimes non-Jewish) community functions. A *kapelye* typically consisted of one or two melodic instruments, usually violins or clarinets but occasionally a trumpet, and a rhythm section with some combination of bass, hammer dulcimer *(tsimbl)*, and drums. During the large-scale immigration of Jews from eastern Europe in the late 19th and early 20th centuries, a number of younger klezmorim came to live and work in the United States, specifically to New York City. Among the more prominent were Abe Schwartz (1881–1963), a violinist who produced some of the first American klezmer recordings, and Harry Kandel (1885–1943), a clarinetist. Slightly later arrivals included the clarinetists Naftule Brandwein (?1884–1963) and Dave Tarras (1897–1989). Descended from families of Russian klezmorim, these two men with contrasting personalities and playing styles eventually came to rank among the music's most celebrated players in the United States.

Interest in klezmer music began to wane after open immigration to the United States ended in 1924. By the 1950s to listen to klezmer music, one had to travel to the Catskills, where musicians such as Tarras and Brandwein still played regularly at Jewish resort hotels and campgrounds. Starting in the early 1970s, young, conservatory-trained Jewish musicians searching for "roots" music began to rediscover klezmer. Taking mostly from old 78 rpm recordings and interviews with aging klezmer musicians, they reconstituted the techniques and instrumentations of their spiritual forebears and began performing publicly. Ensembles based in New York State such as Kapelye and the Andy Statman Klezmer Orchestra gained recognition as local founders of an international klezmer revival. KlezKamp, a gathering for klezmer musicians and Yiddish culture enthusiasts, began at the Concord Hotel in Kiamesha Lake (Sullivan Co) in late December 1985 and continued to be held in the region through 1999. Subsequent groups in the state formed soon after, including the Klezmatics, Metropolitan Klezmer, and Isle of Klezbos. They built on the work of their predecessors by fusing klezmer music with jazz, funk, and other styles, and by giving the music a progressive ideological bent. At the turn of the 21st century, New York State was home to over a dozen klezmer groups performing out of Ithaca, Oneonta, Mamaroneck, Rochester, and New York City. Two New York City–based labels, Jewish Alternative Movement (JAM) and Tzadik: Radical Jewish Culture, distributed many of the new klezmer revival recordings; and an entire "scene" of self-styled progressive musicians, including John Zorn, Frank London, and Alicia Svigals, played klezmer-infused music regularly at downtown New York City clubs such as the Knitting Factory and Tonic.

Rogovoy, Seth. *The Essential Klezmer* (Chapel Hill, NC: Algonquin Books of Chapel Hill, 2000)
Sapoznik, Henry. *Klezmer! Jewish Music from Old World to Our World* (New York: Schirmer Books, 1999)
Slobin, Mark, ed. *American Klezmer: Its Roots and Offshoots* (Berkeley: Univ of California Press, 2002)

Judah Cohen

knickerbocker. Netherlands immigrant Hermen Jansen van Wyekycbacke adopted the Anglicized surname Knickerbacker when he settled in Albany Co in the 1680s. This surname became part of New York State lore when Washington Irving, a relative of the Knickerbackers, published *A History of New York* (1809). He used a pen name, Diedrich Knickerbocker, distorting the spelling of the name. Illustrations by C. R. Leslie and Washington Allston, George Cruikshank, and Felix O. C. Darley brought the querulous narrator to life. They also inspired the ubiquitous knee breeches of Irving's characters to be christened knickerbockers. Irving's epigones, such as James Kirke Paulding, formed what was known as the Knickerbocker school of literature. By the 1820s the term knickerbocker stood for an invented Dutch past caricatured with sentimental affection, whimsical exaggeration, and a satirical bite that targeted local politics, Dutch culture, and people living in the Hudson River valley and New York City. Irving's parody initially met with a cool reception from established Dutch families, but by the mid–19th century knickerbocker was synonymous with regional identity and compared to the term Yankee used to identify New Englanders.

The use of the appellation in New York City included *Knickerbocker* magazine (1833–65), the first significant American literary periodical, and the Knickerbocker Base Ball Club (1845), which formulated the rules for the first modern baseball game. The name was also attached to a life insurance company (1846), a popular brand of beer (1867), an elite men's club (1871), and a theater (1896). The term somewhat declined in popularity in the 20th century but was used by Kurt Weill and Maxwell Anderson in the Broadway musical *Knickerbocker Holiday* (1938), which was loosely based on Irving's history. The term is kept alive by the New York Knickerbockers (1946), the professional basketball team commonly known as the Knicks. Elsewhere the term was used by Knickerbocker Yacht Club (1874) in Port Washington (Nassau Co). Knickerbocker was part of the title of a series of daily newspapers in Albany from 1879 to 1988. There is a Knickerbocker Golf Course in Cortland Co, a Knickerbocker Pond in Sullivan Co, and a Knickerbocker Lake in Columbia Co, as well as Knickerbocker, Tex, founded by two relatives of Washington Irving.

Dayton, Abram Child. *Last Days of Knickerbocker Life in New York* (New York: G. P. Putnam's Sons, 1887)
Sokol, David, et al. *Visions of Washington Irving: Selected Works from the Collections of Historic Hudson Valley* (Irvington, NY: Historic Hudson Valley, 1991)

Kathryn Clippinger Kosto

Knickerbocker's History of New York. *A History of New York, from the Beginning of the World to the End of the Dutch Dynasty, by Diedrich Knickerbocker,* by Washington Irving was first published on 6 Dec 1809. This burlesque history in seven books saw several more editions, the most important being the third (1819) for its illustrations by Washington Allston and C. R. Leslie, and the second (1812) and final (1848) for significant changes in the text. With his brother Peter, Irving began a parody of Samuel Latham Mitchill's historical and descriptive *The Picture of New York* (1807). Upon Peter's departure for Europe, Irving abandoned this model and limited himself to the little-known Dutch colony of New Netherland. The fictional Knickerbocker was given flesh and blood reality through kinship with an Albany-area family of Dutch descent, his landlord's claim within the *History,* and newspaper announcements around the time of publication that established him as an elderly missing person. The crotchety, nostalgic, and comically inconsistent historian's commentary on his subject, comparisons with situations of his own time, and reflections on humankind's foibles make Knickerbocker a major character in the *History.* His inflated claims of the historian's role cast doubt on the value of historiography.

Comic distortion extends to his presentation, which makes a mockery of structure. Book 1 ridicules unbridled scholarship in its cosmogony and recital of theories regarding America's discovery and population. Book 2 describes the early Dutch colony, beginning with Hudson's voyage. Considering in detail only three of New Netherland's directors, Book 3 concerns Wouter van Twiller, a portrait that differs most from the historical figure. Book 4 deals with Willem Kieft, his tenure a Federalist critique of Jeffersonian politics and his portrait a satire of that president, although the characterization rings true for its subject. Books 5–7 are Petrus Stuyvesant's, ending with the English takeover in 1664. The final edition, without some of the earlier, youthful zest, adds a partially developed subplot involving the patroonship of Rensselaerswijck that surfaces within each director's narrative. Throughout, Knickerbocker depicts government and its functionaries, along with the struggle for popular participation, and dwells on the administration of civil and criminal justice. The colony's relations with its neighbors are mostly presented as conflict: the Indians at Swanendael and the Peach War, the Swedes at Forts Casimir and Christina, and the English at "Fort Goed Hoop" and Oyster Bay. The historical influx of Connecticut squatters mirrors the friction caused when increasing numbers of New Englanders moved into New York's rural areas during the 18th century.

The burlesque rendered Irving's work unsuitable as history even in his day. Nevertheless his genuine penchant for history and access to hitherto unexplored sources made it more informative regarding New Netherland than the meager or biased accounts from earlier historians such as William Smith or Benjamin Trumbull. Innumerable literary allusions parody or imitate an array of major literary works, among them *Mirror of the Old and New Time[s]* (*Spiegel van den Ouden en Nieuwen Tyt,* 1632) by Dutch author Jacob Cats (1577–1660), who retained his immense popularity at home and among the descendants of New Netherland's pioneer families well into the 19th century. A collection of popular sayings interspersed with Cats's poetry, this emblem book also provided Irving with realistic portraits of 17th-century Netherlandic daily life.

The *History* is a treasure trove of early Dutch American folklife. Details of structures, interiors, and dress are given; food, drink, and tobacco habits are depicted while they accentuate the differences between population groups and serve the burlesque. Genuine New Netherland names serve Irving's remarkable skill at bilingual punning, reflecting the zest for wordplay among Dutch Americans of his day and beyond. Institutions, administrators, and populace are represented in explanatory or descriptive tall tales that draw upon existing Dutch and English stereotypes. Customs of social and family life are accurately rendered, as are legends and folk beliefs, even when incorporated into fictive situations or employed to emphasize the struggle between the Dutch and the English. Noteworthy are a few lines concerning the *Flying Dutchman,* a legendary ghost ship that was later popularized in stories, opera, and film, which constitute the first mention of this figure in American literature. Many of these traditions survived to become part of the regional or national popular culture. None is more remarkable than Irving's adoption of the Dutch St. Nicholas, both as secular folk hero and as legendary patron saint, whose feast day he celebrated with the *History*'s first publication. His transformation of the traditional, stern bishop into a jolly, 17th-century Dutch settler became the origin of the most widespread character in national folklore: the American Santa Claus.

Irving's *History* presented New York with the first record entirely devoted to its European beginnings. The pursuit of his sources, known and obscure, was scholarly and serious, but he chose to present his material in a comic vein, blurring hardship and bloodshed. Occasionally he simplified, altered a date, selected only those names that would affirm a homogeneously Dutch New Netherland, and expanded particles of historic truth to fit a character or event that would carry his point. Yet the *History*'s incidents of pure fiction are few and are meant to be instantly recognizable. A solid foundation of knowledge and truth underlies Irving's creation, which includes the elements of Dutch popular culture as they had survived in the New York of his youth. The *History*'s success made the appellation Knickerbocker nearly synonymous with New Yorker in Irving's lifetime. It remains current for New York businesses, sports clubs, and other endeavors.

Black, Michael L. "Political Satire in Knickerbocker's *History*." In *The Knickerbocker Tradition,* ed. Andrew B. Myers (Tarrytown, NY: Sleepy Hollow, 1974)

Cats, Jacob. "Spiegel van den Ouden en Nieuwen Tyt." In *Alle de Wercken van den Heere Jacob Cats,* vol 1 (1962; repr Utrecht, Netherlands: De Banier, 1712)

Funk, Elisabeth Paling. "Washington Irving and His Dutch-American Heritage as Seen in *A History of New York, The Sketch Book, Bracebridge Hall,* and *Tales of a Traveller*" (PhD diss, Fordham Univ, 1986)

———. "Washington Irving and the Dutch Heritage." MS, 2002

Irving, Washington. *A History of New York* [1812]. Ed. Edwin T. Bowden (New Haven: New College and University Press, 1964)

———. "A History of New York" [1809]. In *History, Tales, and Sketches,* ed. James W. Tuttleton (New York: The Library of America, 1983)

———. *A History of New York* [1848], vol 7 of *The Complete Works of Washington Irving,* ed. Michael L. Black and Nancy B. Black (Boston: Twayne Publishers, 1984)

Williams, Stanley T., and Tremaine McDowell. Introduction. *Diedrich Knickerbocker's A History of New York,* by Washington Irving (New York: Harcourt, Brace, 1927)

Elisabeth Paling Funk

Knights of Columbus. Roman Catholic fraternal order. Established in New Haven, Conn, in March 1882 by Fr Michael J. McGivney, the Knights provided opportunities for socialization among an emerging Irish Catholic middle class. They also sponsored programs to promote Catholic education, provide assistance to the indigent, and support the families of deceased members through their insurance program. The Knights organized themselves into local councils in cities with large concentrations of Catholics. In June 1891, 29 men gathered in Brooklyn to establish Council 60, the first in New York State. Four years later the Knights expanded with Council 124, which represented New York City. The order established a second council in Brooklyn that same year and extended into Rochester with Council 178 in June 1896. Archbishop Michael A. Corrigan of the Archdiocese of New York and Bishop Bernard J. McQuaid of the Diocese of Rochester viewed the order with skepticism, anxious about the ceremonies used to install new members. The bishops' concerns were serious enough for Knights New York State deputy John J. Delaney to meet with them to explain the purpose of the order. Neither Corrigan nor McQuaid took action against the Knights, and by 1900, 54 councils had been established in the state.

The Knights spread throughout New York State in the 20th century. They followed the national leadership in encouraging American patriotism among Catholics and defended the church against those who questioned the patriotism of a denomination led by a pope in Rome. The New York State Council has been active in promoting annual Columbus Day parades throughout the state. The first parade was held in New York City in 1909. The Knights also devoted themselves to assisting men in service during times of war. Beginning with the Spanish-American War, the New York State Knights raised funds to provide for the needs of veterans, cooperating with the YMCA and other social service organizations. The Knights established recreation centers, arranged for weekly religious services, and provided personal sundries for Catholic soldiers in the United States and overseas. New York State councils are grouped into 106 districts that are further consolidated into 12 chapters.

Finucane, Eugene, and James A. Foy. *History of the Knights of Columbus in New York State, 1891–1987* (New York: NYS Council, Knights of Columbus, 1987)

Foley, James E., and Nicholas Virgadamo, eds. *The Knights of Columbus in the State of New York, 1891–1968* (New York: NYS Council, Knights of Columbus, 1968)

Kauffman, Christopher J. *Faith and Fraternalism: The History of the Knights of Columbus, 1882–1982* (New York: Harper & Row, 1982)

Timothy Walch

Knights of Labor. Founded in Philadelphia in 1869, the Noble Order of the Knights of Labor became the major national labor organization of 19th-century America. The Local Assembly (LA) was the basic unit of the Knights of Labor, and in 1896 there were over 12,000 Local Assemblies in 5,000 communities nationwide. With innovative "mixed" assemblies composed of people from different industries complementing trade assemblies, the Knights recruited 3 million workers, including women, ethnic minorities, and African Americans, in many occupations. The Knights' legislative agenda included legalization of unions, elimination of child and convict labor, and nationalization of transportation and communications. They supported their demands for an eight-hour day and equal pay for equal work with strikes and boycotts. They also advocated replacing the wage system with a cooperative commonwealth.

Knights of Labor Assemblies, 1878–96

SOURCE: J. Garlock, *Guide to the Local Assemblies of the Knights of Labor* (1982).

In 1873 in New York City the Knights formed their first assembly in the state. Following initial upstate activity in 1876–78, the Knights began to organize heavily: 450 LAs in 1880–85, 554 LAs in their banner year of 1886, and 290 LAs in 1887–96. LAs were formed in every locality with over 2,000 residents and in many smaller communities as well. Much of the organizing was concentrated in towns and cities, with a District Assembly (DA) coordinating clusters of LAs in Albany, Amsterdam, Brooklyn, Buffalo, Cohoes, Elmira, Gloversville, Kingston, Middletown (Orange Co), New York City, Norwich, Olean, Oneida, Oswego, Rochester, Syracuse, Troy, Utica, and Watertown.

While some Knights in small rural communities belonged to trade LAs, often of railroad employees, most belonged to mixed assemblies and worked as iron miners, iron bloomers, farmers (Clintonville), watchcase makers (Sag Harbor), salt workers (Warsaw), starch workers (Glen Cove), cotton workers (New Hartford), and textile mill operatives (Chadwicks Mills [now Chadwicks]). These LAs were generally solitary and small.

In larger towns and small cities, where there was more employment and often more than one LA, most Knights belonged to trade assemblies and worked in specifically local industries as tapestry weavers (Yonkers), longshoremen and seamen (Oswego), saw makers (Middletown), axe and edge-tool makers (Ballston Spa), and mitten and glove makers (Gloversville). Other Knights belonged to LAs of telegraphers, carpenters, plumbers, and painters. Assemblies in communities such as Binghamton, Auburn, Jamestown, Elmira, Poughkeepsie, Watertown, Ogdensburg, Lockport, Hornell, and Schenectady were usually larger than rural LAs. But some small towns had sizable assemblies: a Nyack (Rockland Co) local of buttonhole operators on shoes had 348 members, while a mixed LA in Brockport (Monroe Co) had 707 members.

In larger cities, membership in the Knights was almost entirely within trade LAs. The building trades were well represented by LAs, as were occupations involving services (barbers, tailors, printers), food preparation (bakers, brewers), transportation (teamsters, street railroad employees), and miscellaneous manufacture (coopers, shoemakers, glassblowers, cigar makers). These communities had clusters of LAs in major industries: clothing and textiles (Utica, Troy, Cohoes), port work (Buffalo), and clothing and shoes (Rochester). With so many workers in single trades, Knights in these cities often formed assemblies of members in specific occupations within these trades. In Rochester, for example, 2,000 Knights belonged to five shoe industry LAs: shoe operatives, stock cutters, shoe cutters, shoemakers, and custom shoemakers.

The New York City–Brooklyn Knights had 441 locals, presenting extraordinary organizing opportunities and organizational challenges. LAs had German, Italian, black, and women workers, and most were trade LAs of specialized workers. Entire DAs consisted of LAs whose members worked at the same trade, including telegraphers, printers, streetcar drivers and conductors, plumbers and steamfitters, shoemakers, carpet weavers, hatmakers, glassblowers, lithographers, and machinists. Several of these DAs became National Trade Assemblies with LAs beyond New York City. In contrast, District Assembly 49, the "Home Club," included LAs in varied occupations. Claiming 366 LAs and over 60,000 members in 1886, DA 49 was not only the largest district in New York State but the largest component of the entire organization. Jurisdictional disputes inevitably arose both within the Knights (among DA 49 and its own LAs, other DAs, and the General Executive Board), and between DA 49 and unions affiliated with the emerging American Federation of Labor.

Such problems, compounded by personal rivalries and ideological differences, and replicated in other parts of the country, contributed to the demise of the Knights of Labor during the 1890s. Although workers in many trades and communities in New York State have since been represented by trade unions, the Knights' vision of uniting all producers in "One Big Union" has vanished.

See also CARPET INDUSTRY; LABOR.

Close, Beatrice. "District Assembly 49 of the Knights of Labor: A Radical Approach to Labor Problems" (MA thesis, New York Univ, 1968)
Garlock, Jonathan. *Guide to the Local Assemblies of the Knights of Labor* (Westport, Conn: Greenwood, 1982)
———. "A Structural Analysis of the Knights of Labor: A Prolegomenon to the History of the Producing Classes" (PhD diss, Univ of Rochester, 1974)
Grob, Gerald N. *Workers and Utopia: A Study of Ideological Conflict in the American Labor Movement, 1865–1900* (Evanston, Ill: Northwestern Univ Press, 1961)

Jonathan Garlock

Knolls Atomic Power Laboratory (KAPL). Based in Niskayuna (Schenectady Co), with the 3,511-acre (1,421 ha) Kenneth A. Kesselring Site (begun 1952) in Milton and Galway (Saratoga Co), the laboratory is operated by Lockheed-Martin for the US Department of Energy and the US Navy. Research and development are carried out for the design and operation of naval nuclear propulsion plants. The Niskayuna site was begun in 1946 as a civilian nuclear power plant project and shifted to naval uses in 1950; it was operated by General Electric until 1993. It transmitted the first power for civilian use generated by atomic energy in July 1955. KAPL employed 2,600 people and had a budget of $450 million in 2003.

Knolls Atomic Power Laboratory, http://www.kapl.gov

Field Horne

Know-Nothings. The American Party, commonly known as the Know-Nothing Party, emerged in 1854 as a national third political party coalescing around antebellum nativist, anti-Catholic agitation. It evolved from the Order of the Star Spangled Banner, a secret fraternity founded in New York City in 1849 and dedicated to eliminating Catholic and immigrant participation in politics and public office. Members swore to support only American-born Protestant candidates. Outside queries about the organization's agenda or structure were to be dismissed with the statement "I know nothing," hence furnishing the order's popular name. In 1853 the order spread across New York State under the leadership of New York City merchant James W. Barker, a former Whig. Know-Nothing organizers set up local lodges throughout the state.

As the country sank into an ever deepening sectional crisis, some Americans, including former president Millard Fillmore from Buffalo, sympathized with nativists who believed national unity could be restored by a campaign against foreign influence and immigration and that nativism could transcend the slavery issue. In June 1854 Know-Nothings formed a National Grand Council and launched a nationwide organizing effort. The following year Know-Nothings founded the American Party. Know-Nothingism initially proved popular throughout the country, enrolling about a million members, mostly young Protestant men in white-collar and skilled occupations.

In the 1854 election the new party attempted to unite northern and southern voters behind a party platform favoring temperance, opposing tax support for parochial schools, and endorsing a 21-year waiting period for naturalization. It aimed to reduce immigrant and Catholic political power and discourage further immigration to the United States. The party's national electoral peak came in 1854 when it won a number of seats in the House of Representatives election, including Francis Edwards of Chautauqua and Cattaraugus Cos, William Valk of Flushing (Queens Co), and Thomas Whitney of New York City.

Running former Whig Fillmore for US president in 1856, the party hoped to prevent a majority winner in the electoral college, throwing the decision to the House of Representatives. Fillmore drew about 21% of the votes in New York State and 22% of the votes nationally, and the party made no gains in Congress. Ironically, in the face of defeat the party split over the very same sectional issues it had sought to transcend with a nativist campaign. Many of the former American Party members became affiliated with the new Republican Party.

Anbinder, Tyler. *Nativism and Slavery: The Northern Know Nothings and the Politics of the 1850s* (New York: Oxford Univ Press, 1992)
Scisco, Louis Dow. *Political Nativism in New York State* (New York: Columbia Univ Press, 1901)

M. Stephen Pendleton and Jean Richardson

Knox. Town (pop 2,647) in NW Albany Co. Settled by the Dutch before 1750 and further populated by migrants from Stonington, Conn *ca* 1790, the town was formed from Berne in 1822. As many as six factories along with home workshops made pillboxes from local basswood from 1806 until *ca* 1900. Both marble and Helderberg bluestone were quarried in Knox; hops were raised in the late 19th century. Knox Cave was operated commercially (1933–58), and spelunkers continue to explore the town's caverns. In the early 21st century, some land remains agricultural, but most residents commute to Capital District jobs.

Knox [née Markward], Rose (*b* Mansfield, Ohio, 18 Nov 1857; *d* Johnstown, Fulton Co, 27 Sept 1950). Businesswoman. Markward was educated in Mansfield and moved with her family to Gloversville (Fulton Co) in the late 1870s. She worked sewing gloves until she met Charles Briggs Knox and married 15 Feb 1883. After selling knit goods in New York City and Newark, NJ, the couple settled in Johnstown, where they opened the Knox Gelatin Co in 1890. In 1896 Knox published a booklet, *Dainty Desserts,* in an attempt to popularize gelatin as a common kitchen ingredient. When her husband died in 1908, Knox assumed control of the business. She became a pioneer in the labor movement by instituting a five-day workweek and providing vacation and sick time to her employees in 1913. Knox authored another booklet, *Food Economy* (1917), wrote newspaper columns, spent over $500,000 on research for uses of gelatin, and in 1929 was the first woman elected to the board of directors of the American Grocery Manufacturers' Association. She retired as president of the company at age 90 but remained as chair of the board until her death. In 1973 the Lipton Tea Co purchased Knox, and in 1994 Nabisco acquired Knox Gelatine, a unit of Nabisco/Kraft in 2002.

Lovett, Robert W. "Knox, Rose Markward." In *Notable American Women, 1607–1950; A Biographical Dictionary,* ed. Edward T. James (Cambridge, Mass: Belknap Press of Harvard Univ Press, 1950)

Kerry Delaney

Knox, Seymour H(orace), Jr (*b* Russell, St. Lawrence Co, 11 Apr 1861; *d* Buffalo, 16 May 1915). Businessman. Knox joined his cousins Frank W. and Charles Woolworth in a venture designed to open numerous five-and-ten stores starting in 1886. Knox purchased Frank Woolworth's interest in the Erie, Pa, Buffalo, and Lockport (Niagara Co) stores in 1889 and established the independent S. H. Knox chain. In 1911 F. W. Woolworth and Co absorbed Knox's firm and its 112 stores. At his death Knox was chairman of the Marine Trust Co and a vice president at F. W. Woolworth. The Knox family graced Buffalo and New York State with philanthropy throughout the 20th century. Knox donations built a high school and a town hall in Russell, and Seymour II was a major financial supporter of the Albright-Knox Art Gallery in Buffalo. Grandsons Northrup and Seymour III brought the professional hockey team Buffalo Sabres to Western New York in 1969.

Brough, James. *The Woolworths* (New York: McGraw-Hill, 1982)

R. Jake Sudderth

Knox Trail. At the 150th anniversary of the American Revolution in 1926, New York State created a commission "to investigate and report on marking the trail over which Gen Henry Knox conducted the artillery train and supplies from Fort Ticonderoga to Boston in the winter of 1775–76." Knox's efforts helped Gen George Washington force the British out of Boston early in 1776, providing an important American victory. In consultation with the Massachusetts Historical Commission, a route was selected based on historic documents and research into the roadways of the late 18th century. The New York State portion of the trail begins in Essex Co at Fort Ticonderoga, extends south parallel to the Hudson River to Columbia Co, and then turns east to the Massachusetts border. By 1927, 56 granite and bronze monuments had been established at intervals along the route, 30 in New York State and 26 of a different design in Massachusetts. These markers, indicating one of the first heritage trails in the United States, still stand in the early 21st century.

Philip L. Lord Jr

Koch, Ed(ward Irving) (*b* Bronx Co, 12 Dec 1924). Mayor of New York City. Raised in New York City and Newark, NJ, Koch enrolled in the City College of New York but left in 1943 to join the US Army. Completing his service in 1946 Koch returned to college, earning a law degree from New York University in 1948; he started practicing law the following year. Koch began his political career as a street corner speaker for 1952 Democratic presidential candidate Adlai Stevenson. In 1956 he moved to Manhattan's Greenwich Village, and he cofounded the Village Independent Democrats (VID), a grassroots organization that challenged Tammany Hall, espousing a good government program. An important VID victory was Koch's 1963 defeat of party boss Carmine DeSapio for Democratic district leader. In 1966 Koch was elected to the City Council, and in 1969 he was elected to the US Congress, serving four consecutive terms.

In 1977 Koch was elected mayor in a campaign in which he challenged public unions, supported the death penalty, and promised to untangle the city's severe fiscal problems. Once elected Koch helped restore the city's fiscal integrity. He was reelected in 1981, with Republican support and an endorsement from Pres Ronald Reagan, and again in 1985, with nominal Republican and liberal opposition. Positioning himself as a moderate to conservative Democrat and as a tough and effective administrator, his core supporters were white Catholics and Jews in the "outer boroughs." He did less well among traditional liberals, Blacks, and Latinos, who saw him as too close to real estate interests and as racially polarizing. Koch rode a public bus to his first mayoral inauguration, and he frequently walked the streets, asking passersby his trademark question, "How'm I doin?"

In 1982 Koch made a bid for his party's gubernatorial nomination. Facing a relatively unknown lieutenant governor, Mario M. Cuomo, Koch was heavily favored to win. But shortly before the primary Koch, in a *Playboy* interview, spoke critically of the state outside of New York City, calling Albany "small town life at its worst" and the suburbs "sterile," and he characterized rural life as having to drive "20 miles to buy a gingham dress or a Sears Roebuck suit." The interview likely resulted in his loss to Cuomo in the primary by 53% to 47%. In Koch's final mayoral term fiscal improprieties emerged in the city's Parking Violations Bureau, entangling Donald Manes, one of the mayor's closest associates. Although Koch was never implicated, the furor surrounding the scandal, combined with Koch's perceived insensitivity toward racial minorities, led to Koch's failure to capture his fourth Democratic primary bid for mayor in 1989, and he lost to Manhattan Borough president David Dinkins. Since leaving office he has continued to write and offer opinions for a variety of New York City print, radio, and television companies.

Mollenkopf, John. *A Phoenix in the Ashes: The Rise and Fall of the Koch Coalition in New York City Politics* (Princeton, NJ: Princeton Univ Press, 1992)

Thomas A. Birkland

Kodak. See Eastman Kodak Company.

Kohlmann, Anthony (Kaisersberg, France, ?13 July 1771; Rome, Italy, 11 Apr 1836). Roman Catholic priest. He attended college in Fribourg, Switzerland, and was ordained in 1796. In 1800 he entered the Jesuit order in Russia and was sent in 1806 to teach at Georgetown College in Washington, DC, then under Jesuit direction. He was then sent to New York City to become the administrator of the Diocese of New York (1808–15) and to quell the lay trustee movement, which held that laypeople should choose their own pastors. As pastor of St. Peter's Church in New York City, he founded the old St. Patrick's Cathedral in Lower Manhattan in 1815 and established the short-lived New York Literary Institute for boys (1808–15) on the site of the present St. Patrick's Cathedral. He was sued in 1812 when he refused to divulge the identity of a thief who confessed to him during confession (though Kohlmann arranged to have the stolen property returned). In the Court of General Sessions, De Witt Clinton upheld the privacy of the confessional, a ruling that attracted national attention and set a crucial precedent in civil law. In 1815 he returned to Georgetown, became superior of the American Jesuits, and from 1824 taught at the Gregorian University in Rome and was a consultor to several papal congregations (administrative departments within the Roman curia).

Shelley, Thomas J. *The History of the Archdiocese of New York* (Strasbourg, France: Editions du Signe 1999)

Gerald P. Fogarty, SJ

Mayor Ed Koch *(left)* at Syracuse Hancock International Airport with Mayor Lee Alexander *(center)* of Syracuse, 1982.

Koreans. From the early 1900s onward, a few hundred Koreans, mainly students, lived in New York City. They founded the still existing New York Korean Methodist Church on 633 West 115th St in Manhattan in 1921 and supported the Korean struggle for independence from Japan. Among these immigrants was the novelist and memorist Younghill Kang, who in the 1930s wrote about the lives of Korean immigrants in works such as *East Goes West* (1957).

After the passage of the 1965 Immigration Act, Korean immigration rose sharply, with perhaps 100,000 immigrating to New York State. Many were Christians originating from North Korea. Most settled in the Greater New York City area. Approximately 70% of the Koreans in New York City settled in Queens, especially in Flushing, Woodside, Elmhurst, Bayside, and Little Neck. Some 25% live in Flushing, and Koreatown there is the residential, commercial, and social-cultural center for the city's Koreans. Several hundred Korean stores bearing signs in Korean line Union St's Hanin Sanga (the Korean business district) between Roosevelt Ave and Northern Blvd. These businesses serve Korean food, groceries, and other culturally distinctive items. Another area in the city where Koreans and Korean stores are highly visible is the so-called Broadway Korean Business District in Manhattan, a 10-block area from 24th to 34th Sts between 6th and 5th Aves.

Post-1965 immigrants include a large number of college students and employees working for branches of Korean companies located in the area. Korean immigrants to New York are usually well educated, but many often are unable to find jobs commensurate with their education largely because of English language skills. The language handicap, combined with strong family ties and access to ethnic credit associations for business capital, has led many to open small businesses. These are heavily concentrated in produce and grocery retailing, dry cleaning, manicure shops, garment subcontracting, and wholesale and retail trading of imported Asian goods. The cultural gap between Korean shopkeepers and their customers has occasionally created tensions, especially in black and Latino neighborhoods. Between 1981 and 1991 there were five long-term boycotts of Korean stores in black neighborhoods in Manhattan, Queens, and Brooklyn. The longest and most publicized began in the Church Ave–Fulton St area in Brooklyn in January 1990 and lasted more than a year.

Korean organizations in the New York City area include approximately 600 Protestant churches, 20 Catholic churches, 20 Buddhist temples, about 100 alumni associations, 60 Korean merchant associations, 50 cultural organizations, 40 social service agencies, 40 professional associations, and the Korean Association of New York, an umbrella organization. Although Christians are only 25% of the population in South Korea, 75% of the Korean immigrants in New York are affiliated with Protestant and, to a lesser degree, Catholic churches. Korean churches serve a number of functions for immigrants, including social services, fellowship, and maintenance of Korean culture. The controversial Unification Church of Korea evangelist Sun Myung Moon has had a substantial presence in New York City since the mid-1970s. In addition, three Korean dailies published in New York City, including *Hankook Ilbo*, five Korean TV stations, and two Korean radio stations provide Korean language programs and news about Korea, the Korean community, and the larger US society. In 2000 about 130,000 Koreans and their descendants live in New York State. Most are in New York City and its suburbs. About 65% of this population was foreign-born. Outside of the New York City area, the largest Korean community is in the Albany area.

Prominent Korean Americans include Hae-Jong Kim, United Methodist bishop for Western New York from 1992 to 2000, Sung Bok Kim, an influential historian of the American colonial era who teaches at SUNY Albany, and novelist Chang-Rae Lee, who was raised in Westchester (Westchester Co).

Kim, Illsoo. *New Urban Immigrants: The Korean Community in New York* (Princeton, NJ: Princeton Univ Press, 1981)

Min, Pyong Gap. *Changes and Conflicts: Korean Immigrant Families in New York* (Boston: Allyn & Bacon, 1998)

Pyong Gap Min

Korean War. On 25 June 1950 the communist North Korean People's Army (NKPA) crossed the 38th parallel on the Korean peninsula and invaded the Republic of Korea (ROK) in the south. Continued action by the NKPA pushed the ROK and US troops into the southeast corner around Pusan by 4 Aug 1950. The first winner of the congressional Medal of Honor of the Korean War was Pfc William Thompson of the Bronx, who was mortally wounded on 6 Aug 1950 when his machine gun fire provided cover that allowed his platoon to retreat to higher ground. After a massive amphibious landing of US forces on the coast west of Seoul on 15 Sept 1950, the Eighth Army fought out of the Pusan Perimeter and began driving north. Seoul fell to US troops on 26 September, and the Eighth Army crossed the 38th parallel on 7 Oct 1950. Chinese People's Volunteer (CPV) forces joined the NKPA and halted the advance in late November.

National Guard units had been federalized to augment the regular army since August 1950. Three New York State Army National Guard commands went to Korea. The 955th Field Artillery Battalion arrived in February 1951 and went into action at Suim-Ni in April. The 101st Signal Battalion served from 7 Apr 1951. The 773d Antiaircraft Artillery Gun Battalion landed at Pusan on 18 Oct 1952 and provided defense for new military construction. Three New York Air National Guard commands, the 102d and 114th Bomber Squadrons and the 136th Fighter Interceptor Squadron, served in the United States to enhance national security. The 137th Fighter Bomber Wing served in France.

Many of the leaders of the war effort were from New York State. Gen Matthew Bunker Ridgway (West Point, 1917), son of a distinguished New York family, on 11 Apr 1951 replaced Gen Douglas MacArthur as supreme commander of UN forces in Korea. When Ridgway was named supreme allied commander of the North Atlantic Treaty Organization (NATO) in Europe on 12 May 1952, he was replaced by Gen Mark W. Clark, a native of Madison Barracks (Jefferson Co).

Another New Yorker was Charles E. Wilson, who rose from poverty in the Hell's Kitchen district of Manhattan to become president of General Motors and director of the Office of Defense Mobilization from 1950 to 1952. Wilson's revitalization of the American defense industry provided for the continued vigilance of the Cold War as well as the demands of the Korean War. At the Watervliet Arsenal in Albany Co, the workforce increased from 1,505 in July 1950 to 4,850 at the beginning of 1952, with a six-day week for some units during the height of production in 1951. Many of the Watervliet workers were women returning to positions they had held during World War II. Overall, postwar American industry supplied war materiel without major disruption to the consumer market. As the increased output had the potential to initiate inflation, Wilson instituted wage and price controls in January 1951. After a conflict with Pres Harry S. Truman over wages and prices in steel manufacturing, Wilson resigned his position in March 1952 and returned to private industry.

A cease-fire was signed on 27 July 1953, ending the Korean War in a stalemate. New York lost 2,379. For many decades there was little in the way of formal commemoration of the war's veterans. The New York State Korean War Veterans Memorial in Albany was dedicated on 25 June 1990. The national Korean War Veterans Memorial, with murals by Louis Nelson of New York City, was dedicated in Washington, DC, on 27 July 1995.

Berebitsky, William. *A Very Long Weekend: The Army National Guard in Korea, 1950–1953* (Shippenburg, Pa: White Mane Publishing, 1996)

Soffer, Jonathan M. *General Matthew B. Ridgway: From Progressivism to Reaganism, 1895–1993* (Westport, Conn: Praeger, 1998)

Pamela Cooper

Kornberg, Arthur (*b* Brooklyn, 3 Mar 1918). Biochemist. A son of Austrian immigrants, he grew up in impoverished circumstances in Brooklyn. He earned a BS from City College of New York and an MD from University of Rochester in 1941. Kornberg began his career as a physician, serving as a ship's doctor in the US Coast Guard. After conducting nutrition research at the National Institutes of Health, Kornberg in 1946 began to focus on enzymology, initially working in the laboratory of Severo Ochoa at New York University School of Medicine. In 1956 he demonstrated the enzymatic synthesis of DNA, for which he was awarded the Nobel Prize in medicine with Ochoa in 1959. Kornberg investigated DNA replication for many years at Stanford University, creating a viable virus in 1967. Kornberg married Sylvy R. Levy from Rochester; they had three sons. Kornberg was honored by the University of Rochester in 1997, when the Arthur Kornberg Awards for achievement in biomedical research were established at the School of Medicine and Dentistry, and in 1999, when a major facility was named the Arthur Kornberg Medical Research Building.

Kornberg, Arthur. *For the Love of Enzymes: The Odyssey of a Biochemist* (Cambridge, Mass: Harvard Univ Press, 1989)

Adam Bostanci

Kortright. Town (pop 1,633) in NE Delaware Co. Settled in 1774, the town was formed from Harpersfield in 1793. In the 19th century Bloomville was a thriving business community, served by the Ulster and Delaware Railroad (1891–1976). Sheffield Farms creamery (1893–1960) was the first business in the United States to pasteurize milk on a commercial scale. In 2003 there were 23 dairy farms still operating. The old railroad bed from Bloomville to Roxbury has been designated the Catskill Scenic Trail and set aside for hikers, cross country skiers, bicyclists, and snowmobilers.

Dorothy Kubik

Kosciuszko, Thaddeus [Kociuszko, Tadeusz] (*b* ?Mereczowszczyzna, near Kosow [now Kossovo, Belarus], 12 Feb 1746; *d* Solothurn, Switzerland, 15 Oct 1817). Military officer, engineer, and Polish nationalist. Son of a minor nobleman, Kosciuszko was educated at military academies in Poland and France. Faced with limited prospects in Poland, he traveled to Philadelphia to obtain a position in the Continental army in August 1776. He was commissioned a colonel of engineers in October 1776 and appointed Gen Horatio Gates's chief engineer in March 1777. His recommendation for defenses at Mt Defiance to protect Fort Ticonderoga [now in Essex Co] went unheeded, and the fort was captured by the British, under Maj Gen John Burgoyne, on 5 July 1777. Two months later Kosciuszko chose Bemis Heights [now in Saratoga Co] as the location for the Continental defenses under Gates's command, in preparation for a decisive battle with Burgoyne. The American victory at the Battle of Bemis Heights (the second Battle of Saratoga) led to Burgoyne's surrender in October 1777. In March 1778 Kosciuszko was assigned to West Point (Orange

Co), where he developed a defensive system that included an enormous iron chain across the Hudson River. In June 1780 he accompanied Gates to South Carolina as chief of engineers and he served there for the remainder of the war. Kosciuszko then returned to Poland and led several campaigns against Russian troops in defense of Poland. He was captured in 1794, imprisoned for two years, and lived the remainder of his life in exile.

Pula, James S. *Thaddeus Kosciuszko: The Purest Son of Liberty* (New York: Hippocrene Books, 1999)

Jennifer Steenshorne

kosher foods. Kosher means "fit to eat" in Hebrew and refers to the foods permissible to eat under the Jewish laws of Kashrut, dietary restrictions that have been part of Judaism since biblical times and are codified in the Talmud and other tracts of Jewish law. Orthodox Jews observe the kosher laws faithfully, but Reform and Conservative Jews vary. A specially trained rabbi, known as a mashgiach, almost always an Orthodox rabbi, inspects, supervises, and provides a heksher (certification that the food is kosher).

The first Jewish congregation in North America, Congregation Shearith Israel, founded in 1654, provided for supervised kosher slaughter of animals. By the mid-1700s, kosher butchers in New York City exported beef to congregations in British Jamaica and Dutch Curaçao, but the market for kosher foods remained relatively small. In the 1880s, as massive waves of Jewish immigrants came to New York State from eastern Europe, the demand for more kosher butchers, kosher bakeries, and kosher dairies increased dramatically. Some immigrants became well known for providing products needed by Jewish homes. Polish-born Israel Rokeach, for example, opened his first factory in 1890 on Manhattan's Lower East Side. Rokeach and Sons Manufacturing still markets gefilte fish, borscht, and many other kosher foods and products. Others, like Isadore Pinckowitz, made American food available to the kosher consumer; his company, Hebrew National Foods in New York City, began producing kosher frankfurters in 1905; bought out by ConAgra, Hebrew National kosher frankfurters are produced in the early 21st century in Jericho (Nassau Co). Throughout the early to mid-1900s, new kosher companies proliferated, such as Streit's Matzoh, founded in Manhattan in 1916, and Empire Kosher Poultry, founded in Liberty (Sullivan Co) in 1938, operating in 2003 in Mifflintown, Pa. By the 1920s, numerous cities outside of the five New York City boroughs had established kosher delicatessens.

By the 1960s kosher food was being advertised to the non-Jewish audience, as "kosher" had become synonymous with "clean" or "higher quality." Hebrew National hot dogs and Levy's rye bread were among the first to take this approach. And while New York City remained the home of most of the agencies that oversaw kosher products, Orthodox rabbis in Albany and Buffalo established their own local vaad to supervise the sale of kosher food and to ensure consumer protection. Although the number of kosher butchers declined (from 3,800 in New York City in 1940 to 400 in 1984), they remain crucial to the Jewish community. Kosher restaurants also thrive. In 2003 the Manhattan telephone directory lists 122 kosher restaurants in the borough. The Union of Orthodox Jewish Congregations of America, which began in the late 1890s as an educational organization, is today the largest of the many organizations that supervise kosher food production and employs more than 50 rabbis at its New York City headquarters.

The preparation of kosher food has often been accompanied by controversies. Having a captive market of observant Jews, kosher meat sellers have at times been accused of making unfair profits. A dispute between meat wholesaler and retailers in May 1902 caused a steep jump in prices, leading hundreds of Jewish women, mostly impoverished immigrants in the Lower East Side of Manhattan and the Bronx, to riot in protest. Similar issues were raised in 1910, 1929, and 1937.

Not all determinations of kosher status are alike, and some observant Jews prefer the stricter glatt kosher status to ordinary kosher food, and glatt kosher establishments have in recent decades become increasingly common in New York City. The legal status of kosher designations remains controversial. In 1915 New York State enacted legislation creating the nation's first kosher food law, forbidding the labeling of nonkosher food as kosher; it became a model for all subsequent kosher food legislation. But in August 2000, in a decision upheld by the US Supreme Court in 2003, a federal judge ruled kosher laws unconstitutional because they entangled the government in a religious matter, violating constitutional guarantees separating the two. While efforts continue to find a legal basis for kosher determination, the practical consequences of voiding a legal kosher status have been relatively limited because those who are observant have long made their purchases based on the heksher of a mashgiach rather than on its legal confirmation.

See also MEATPACKING INDUSTRY.

Freedman, Seymour E. *The Book of Kashruth: A Treasury of Kosher Facts and Frauds* (New York: Bloch, 1970)

Donna L. Halper

Kossuth, Lajos [Louis] (*b* Monok [now in Hungary], 19 Sept 1802; *d* Turin, Italy, 20 Mar 1894). Hungarian statesman. After failing to gain his country's independence from Austria in the Hungarian Revolution of 1848–49, Kossuth fled his homeland in August 1849. When he arrived in New York City on 6 Dec 1851 seeking American support for his continued struggle against the Austrian empire, close to 200,000 people greeted him as a hero. During his seven-month sojourn in the United States, Kossuth spent over five weeks in New York City and nearly five weeks touring the state, visiting Albany, Buffalo, Niagara Falls, Auburn, Syracuse, Utica, and Schenectady. Kossuth attracted widespread admiration as an exponent of human freedom and national independence. As the Protestant adversary of a Roman Catholic autocrat, he also drew support from US nativists then fearful of Roman Catholic immigrants. Although unsuccessful in his mission—Pres Millard Fillmore received him coolly in January and February 1852 and held to the US policy of nonintervention in European affairs—Kossuth's rousing speeches generated a "Kossuth craze" throughout New York State, with the community of Kossuth (Allegany Co) taking his name in 1852. Kossuth returned to Europe the same year, settling in Turin in 1861. Abraham Lincoln's Gettysburg Address of 1863 was probably influenced by a Kossuth speech delivered 7 Feb 1852 in Columbus, Ohio.

Komlós, John H. *Kossuth in America, 1851–1852* (Buffalo: East European Institute, 1973)
Várdy, Steven Béla. "Louis Kossuth's Words in Abraham Lincoln's Gettysburg Address," *Eurasian Studies Yearbook* 71 (1999): 27–32

Steven Béla Várdy

Krasner, Lee [Krassner, Lena; Krasner, Lenore] (*b* Brooklyn, 27 Oct 1908; *d* New York City, 19 June 1984). Artist. Krasner, who adopted the first name Lenore while in her teens, knew from an early age that she wanted to be an artist. From 1926 to 1932 she studied at Cooper Union in Greenwich Village and the National Academy of Design, where she learned traditional figure drawing and painting. In 1937, while employed by the Works Progress Administration's Federal Art Project, she began taking classes at Hans Hofmann's Cubist-oriented art school on West 8th St, where she developed a semiabstract aesthetic. Such radical revisions, or "breaks," as she called them, would come to characterize her artistic evolution. Krasner was a first-generation member of the New York school of abstract expressionism, which flourished in the 1940s and 1950s. After her 1945 marriage to painter Jackson Pollock, she kept her surname professionally but changed the spelling. The couple moved to East Hampton (Suffolk Co), and Krasner began to make fully abstract paintings with impacted, mosaic-like surfaces. A series of collage paintings, including *City Verticals* (1953) and *Burning Candles* (1955), incorporate fragments of rejected works that she cannibalized and reconfigured. By the time of Pollock's death in 1956, she was moving toward paintings in which references to plant life and human forms appear, such as *The Seasons* (1957) and *Cool White* (1959). In the last 20 years of her career, Krasner created lacy, impressionistic canvases, hard-edge abstractions, and another collage series. Never satisfied with a so-called signature style, she was consistent in her devotion to experimentation and self-expression, which she also encouraged in others. The Pollock-Krasner Foundation, created under the terms of her will, perpetuates that legacy by providing financial support to needy and worthy artists.

Hobbs, Robert. *Lee Krasner* (New York: Abbeville Press, 1993)
Landau, Ellen G. *Lee Krasner: A Catalogue Raisonné* (New York: Abrams, 1995)
Rose, Barbara. *Lee Krasner: A Retrospective* (New York: Museum of Modern Art, 1983)

Helen A. Harrison

Krol, Bastiaen Jansz (*b* Harlingen, Netherlands, 1595; *bur* Amsterdam, 14 Mar 1674). Colonial official. Krol was in New Netherland for seven months in 1624 as the first comforter of the sick, a lay office to which he had been appointed by the Amsterdam Consistory of the Reformed Church. After a winter in the Netherlands, he returned in 1625 to New Netherland with additional authority to baptize and marry. In 1626 he began a new career, having been appointed by the Dutch West India Co to the directorship at Fort Orange [now Albany], where a predecessor had been killed in battle against the Mohawk.

Krol, who had some fluency in the language, established long-lasting peaceful relations.

He visited the Netherlands briefly in late 1629 and early 1630, returning to his post at Fort Orange, with instructions from Kiliaen van Rensselaer to purchase land for his colony (often referred to as a patroonship) of Rensselaerswijck, which Krol accomplished. In March 1632 he replaced Peter Minuit as New Netherland's director, serving until the arrival of Wouter van Twiller 13 months later. Krol returned briefly to Fort Orange but sailed for the Netherlands in July 1633. He was back at Fort Orange in 1638 and continued to serve until 1643, sometimes being called commis (in charge of trade goods and West India Co stores) and sometimes commandant. In July 1644 he was a member of the Council of New Netherland at New Amsterdam and later that year returned permanently to Amsterdam.

American National Biography, sv "Krol, Bastiaen Janszen"
Dictionary of American Biography, sv "Krol, Bastiaen Jansen"
Eekhof, Albert. *Bastiaen Jansz. Krol, Krankenbezoeker, Kommies en Kommandeur van Nieuw-Nederland, 1595–1645* (The Hague, Netherlands: Martinus Nijhoff, 1910)

Peter R. Christoph

Krupsak, Mary Anne (*b* Schenectady, 26 Mar 1932). Legislator and lieutenant governor. Krupsak was raised in Amsterdam (Montgomery Co). She earned a BA from the University of Rochester (1953) and a law degree from the University of Chicago (1962). A lifelong Democrat, Krupsak held a variety of staff positions for both houses of the New York State legislature and was on the staff of Gov W. Averell Harriman (1954–58). In 1969 she became the assemblywoman for Montgomery and parts of Albany and Schenectady Cos. She served two terms before being elected in 1972 as state senator. Krupsak established herself as an advocate for economic development, governmental reform, and women's rights. In 1974 she became the first woman in New York to win a statewide election, becoming the state's first female lieutenant governor (1975–78). While serving in that position, Krupsak made the I Love New York campaign a primary focus of her office and initiated a successful campaign to save Radio City Music Hall. Frustrated with the pace of dealing with the state's problems, Krupsak challenged Gov Hugh Carey in the 1978 gubernatorial primary and was defeated. After leaving office she worked from 1978 to 1989 as a lawyer. In 1993 she moved to Geneva (Ontario Co), serving as president of the Finger Lakes Association in Penn Yan (Yates Co) from 1997 to 2001. In 1998 Krupsak coordinated the 150th anniversary celebration of the first women's rights convention at Seneca Falls (Seneca Co).

The New York Red Book (1969–70, 1973, 1975)
Weinstein, Helene E. *Lawmakers: Biographical Sketches of the Women of the N.Y.S. Legislature (1918–1988)* (Albany: Legislative Women's Caucus, ?1988)

Jane R. Plitt

Ku Klux Klan. A secret society espousing white Protestant superiority. Revived in 1915, the Klan's popularity after World War I was a national phenomenon that capitalized on xenophobia and racism. It decried anyone who was not "100% American": Catholics, Jews, rumrunners, immigrants, Bolsheviks, Blacks, and other minority groups. By enlisting the help of respected citizens—often the local Protestant minister—and by tailoring its message to the concerns of a specific region, the Klan was able to attract millions of recruits nationwide. In 1923 the *New York Times* estimated that there were 200,000 Klan members in New York State. While the Ku Klux Klan distributed its literature throughout the state, burned crosses at numerous locations, and intimidated many people who did not adhere to its concept of morality or of "Americanism," it also actively promoted itself as a philanthropic, community-centered organization.

Nassau and Suffolk Cos were major strongholds. The group arrived in the area at the end of 1922, emphasizing the dangers of Catholicism, immigration, and lax Prohibition enforcement. A 1923 rally in Central Islip (Suffolk Co) included the initiation of 1,500 recruits and oratory denouncing Jews and Catholics. The following year, a Klan march in Freeport (Nassau Co) attracted a crowd of 30,000 admiring spectators who watched some 2,000 parading Klansmen and Klanswomen, led by the village's chief of police. Scholars have estimated that in 1924 one of seven people in Suffolk Co belonged to the Klan. In 1924 Klan-backed candidates were elected to Suffolk's Republican Party County Committee, including the chairman, who was widely reported to be a Klan organizer. The Klan also engaged in vigilante law enforcement, especially regarding Prohibition, formed "vigilance committees," and routinely assisted federal Prohibition agents patrolling Long Island roads.

Binghamton was another center for Klan activity. Klan members arrived in the city in 1923, acquiring a building the next year for the Klan's state headquarters. Binghamton Common Council president Hubert D. Ballard presided at a Klan rally and later became Binghamton's "kleagle." Their dominance of local Binghamton Republican politics sharply declined after 1925. Chapters were also organized in Albany, Troy, Utica, Syracuse, Elmira, and Rochester and were active in almost every part of the state in the early 1920s. In 1922 the Klan initiated a recruiting drive in Buffalo and attracted 6,000 members. In response to Klan agitation, Mayor Frank Schwab ordered an investigation of its activities, and a police officer infiltrated the organization. Secret files were stolen from Klan headquarters on 3 July 1924 and eventually reached the mayor, who permitted two alleged membership lists to be viewed by the public. This and consequent reactions and crises, such as the marking of Klan houses during the night, boycotts, the suicide of a person whose name appeared on the list, and charges of embezzlement, precipitated the organization's demise in Buffalo.

The Klan never made serious inroads in New York City, with its large Catholic, Jewish, and African American population. Almost as soon as it arrived, it was denounced by political officials and religious leaders. New York City mayor John F. Hylan called the Klan "a menace to the city, state, and nation." The Klan's biggest legal obstacle came from the state's 1923 Walker Law. Making exceptions for labor, benevolent orders, and student fraternities and sororities, the law required organizations to report annually to the state their membership lists, bylaws, and oaths. To circumvent the law the Klan attempted to incorporate itself as fraternity Alpha Pi Sigma, but this ruse failed. The US Supreme Court upheld the law in 1928. The Walker Law, in conjunction with internal problems and scandals, diminished the Klan's power and influence in New York State. Although there were brief revivals in the years following World War II, the Klan never again achieved the success it had achieved in the 1920s.

Gombieski, Jane S. "Klokards, Kleagles, Kludds, and Kluxers: The Ku Klux Klan in Suffolk County, 1915–1928, Part 1," *Long Island Historical Journal* 6 (1993): 41–62
Jackson, Kenneth T. *The Ku Klux Klan in the City, 1915–1930* (New York: Oxford Univ Press, 1967)
Lay, Shawn. *Hooded Knights on the Niagara: The Ku Klux Klan in Buffalo, New York* (New York: New York Univ Press, 1995)

Lenora M. Henson

Kunstler, William M(oses) (*b* New York City, 7 July 1919; *d* New York City, 4 Sept 1995). Defense attorney. A 1941 graduate of Yale University, Kunstler served in the Pacific with the Signal Corps during World War II and was awarded the Bronze Star. He graduated from Columbia Law School in 1948 and spent the first years of his legal career engaged chiefly in divorce and estate law in New York City. During the 1960s he represented the Freedom Riders and other civil rights activists, including Martin Luther King Jr. Kunstler was committed to several radical causes, successfully defending the Chicago Seven in fall 1969 and playing a controversial role during the rebellion at the Attica Correctional Facility. Primarily an informal mediator between prison inmates and state officials, Kunstler was an advocate for prisoners' rights as well. Also involved with Native American causes, Kunstler represented Indian activist Leonard Peltier. Kunstler's eclectic list of clients included poet Dylan Thomas, radical Abbie Hoffman, philosopher Bertrand Russell, mobster John Gotti Sr, and Lee Harvey Oswald's killer, Jack Ruby. In his later years Kunstler defended El Sayyid Nossir, who was acquitted of the 1990 assassination of hard-line Zionist rabbi Meir Kahane; Yusef Salaam, one of the defendants in a widely publicized 1990 case of a jogger raped in Central Park; Sheik Omar Abdel-Rahman, one of the alleged leaders behind the 1993 bombing of the World Trade Center; and in 1994 he briefly represented Colin Ferguson, the Long Island Rail Road killer. Kunstler had a reputation not only for disruptive courtroom antics, such as jumping on tables and haranguing judges, but also for being an effective, brilliant advocate. To his supporters, Kunstler was a selfless crusader for the downtrodden and despised. To his critics, who made many unsuccessful attempts to have him disbarred, Kunstler was an egotistical, unprincipled attorney who made media circuses out of judicial proceedings and exploited legal technicalities to free guilty clients.

Kunstler, William M., with Sheila Isenberg. *My Life as a Radical Lawyer* (Secaucus, NJ: Carol Publishing, 1994)
Langum, David J. *William M. Kunstler: The Most Hated Lawyer in America* (New York: New York Univ Press, 1999)

Timothy P. Gordinier

Kyrgyzstanis. See CENTRAL ASIANS.

L

labor. Labor existed in many forms in New Netherland and colonial New York, including compensated and uncompensated, agricultural, commercial, and industrial, and free and unfree. The dominant form of labor in New York during this period was agricultural work. Commercial agriculture (primarily on the large Hudson River estates) was common by the late 17th century, and wheat was shipped in large quantities to the Caribbean. Most of those who farmed in colonial New York, though, were semisubsistence farmers who primarily worked to provide for themselves and their family, selling any surplus for ready cash. There were a variety of types of nonagricultural work as well, including fur trade and soldiering on the frontier and artisanal crafts in the cities (shipwrights, cartmen, coopers, blacksmiths, and many others).

New Yorkers worked in a variety of circumstances. The goal for many was financial independence, to own one's farm if one toiled in the fields, or to be a master craftsman if one worked in the artisanal trades. Some achieved these goals, but many more did not. Many farmed on one of the four huge Hudson River manors, where land was leased, not purchased. For every master craftsman there were more who worked as journeymen or apprentices. Many apprentices were bound to a master for a number of years, some, but not all, formal indentures. Women in New York Colony worked as house servants, farmhands, and child rearers. Often they were not directly compensated for their labor.

On the lowest rung of the ladder of labor were enslaved Africans, both male and female. In the colonial census of 1723, 15% of the people counted in New York Colony were Africans, almost all of them enslaved. Slaves performed the same work as free laborers, such as working on farms, as servants, and in various artisanal capacities. Slaves took part in both direct and indirect forms of rebellion against their enslavement, including revolts in New York City in 1712 and the murky Negro Plot of 1741 (which may or may not have been a slave revolt), escaping to freedom, and volunteering to serve in the military. Slave labor remained legal until 1827, when New York State's gradual manumission provisions reached culmination.

Well into the 19th century, farmwork was the dominant form of labor in New York State. The 1855 census listed 321,930 farmers, almost as many as in all the other job categories combined. (By 2000, in contrast, there were only 24,609 workers recorded in the category of "farming, fishing, and forestry," a mere 0.3% of the state's labor force.) The image of the yeoman farmer, owner, and cultivator of his own acres is persistent but in many ways misleading. The situation of lease tenure on the manors was a constant political issue, one that was not resolved until the antirent movement of the 1840s. Even after the end of manorial tenure, many people in New York State continued to lease farmland. In 1900 sharecroppers and lessees constituted almost a quarter of all farms in New York State, and the percentage remained high until the number of farms began to radically contract after World War II. Traditionally, few on farms worked for a salary. This practice also changed during the 20th century, and many now engaged in agricultural work (35% of them at the beginning of the 21st century) earn regular wages just like workers in urban settings.

Antislavery advocates, pleased that New York State had abolished slavery in 1827, regularly touted the state as a home of free labor in contrast to the South's dominant use of slave labor. The condition of labor in the North, even its most squalid forms, was indeed profoundly different from the systematic degradation of slavery. There were still many New Yorkers, however, who claimed that, in significant ways, labor in the state was not free of coercion and control from the owners of businesses and from laws biased against the rights of labor. It is from this urban, artisanal labor force that the labor movement arose.

Artisans and Mechanics

In the late 18th and early 19th centuries, most manufacturing in New York State was done by hand in small shops. Much of it was concentrated in New York City but was also present in other urban areas, including Albany and Hudson (Columbia Co). Blacksmiths, bread makers, cabinetmakers, tailors, and shoemakers were crucial to New York State's economy, supplying essential commodities to shop owners and merchants. The hierarchical structure of the trades placed the most experienced craftsmen at the top and the less skilled journeymen at the bottom. Most learned their trade through the apprentice system, which gave men (there were no female apprentices) a hands-on education in the trades.

New York State's mechanics demonstrated an early awareness of their social and legal status, and many formed their own journeymen societies, organized along craft lines. One of the most prominent was New York City's General Society of Mechanics and Tradesmen, founded in 1785. Smaller mechanic societies sprung up in Albany, Catskill, Lansingburgh, Hudson, and Poughkeepsie in the early 1790s. The journeymen had finely calibrated political consciousnesses, supporting, as did merchants, the Federalists (who favored tariff protections) during and after the ratification of the US Constitution in 1788. This support lasted through the mid-1790s, when journeymen abandoned the Federalists and backed the Democratic-Republicans. Many workers continued to support the Jeffersonian Republicans and later the nascent Democratic Party in the 1820s. The Democrats returned their support with policies that favored workingmen, such as the provision in the Constitution of 1821 that removed all property qualifications for suffrage for white men. They also formed their own political organizations, notably the Working Men's Party, which was established in 1829. Led by the fiery Thomas Skidmore, the Working Men's Party advocated an egalitarian distribution of property among the populace and sought to abolish commercial banks. Members also desired equal amounts of clothing and food for all.

Divisions between masters and journeymen occasionally resulted in conflict, which began because of wage disputes and because masters occasionally hired men outside of the exclusive craftsmen's societies. Although most journeymen resolved workplace disagreements through meetings with the master craftsmen, on some occasions the journeymen responded with aggressive tactics such as organizing boycotts and strikes and advertising their protests in daily newspapers. In the face of exploitation by masters, many workers joined trade unions. Boilermakers, carpenters, painters, masons, tailors, and bakers all formed organizations to defend their traditional work practices. Organized workers planned strikes, which were initially illegal. Early labor law privileged masters over journeymen; courts frequently ruled against strikers, charging them with conspiracy. The militia occasionally broke strikes and arrested labor leaders. In 1809 New York City authorities disciplined cordwainers (shoemakers) for striking against their master in *People v Melvin,* and in 1836 a New York judge fined and scolded 21 tailors for organizing in the *Twenty-one Journeyman Tailors* case. In response to this punishment, 30,000 people protested for labor rights. Elsewhere in the state the Mechanics Society was formed in Buffalo in 1812. In 1829, in Utica, the *Mechanics Press* started publishing, and the following year workers on the Erie Canal in Rochester formed the Boatmen's Mutual Relief Society.

Despite an unfriendly legal environment, workers in New York State engaged in a number of strikes and were politically active in the 1820s and 1830s. There were massive, militant work stoppages by New York City weavers and dockworkers. After the Working Men's Party dissolved in 1831, the General Trades' Union was formed, and it supported over 40 strikes between 1833 and 1836. The expansion of infrastructure facilitated industrial development, introducing to factory work greater numbers of New Yorkers, including increasing numbers of immigrants from Ireland and Germany. By midcentury, in fact, over half of New York City workers were foreign-born, offering employers a sizable supply of labor. The workforce was ethnoculturally divided with the native-born workmen getting the best occupations and the immigrants often working the less desirable jobs.

Increasingly, workers in different trades tried to form joint organizations. In 1850 radical thinker Wilhelm Weitling, a onetime colleague of Karl Marx, sought to unite New York City's German American workers into the German Central Committee of United Trades in New York. Many of the same German immigrants founded the Communist Club in New York City during the depression of 1857. The Workingman's Assembly, formed in Rochester in 1863 out of a failed Typographical Union strike, was probably the first central trades council in the United States. The Trades Assembly of New York State, an organization that lobbied politicians in Albany for pro-worker legislation, was formed in that city in 1865.

Although white workmen fought for a more equitable society, they often prohibited women and Blacks from joining their organizations, and racial violence occurred occasionally. In 1862 a group of mostly Irish workers attacked black workers at a Brooklyn tobacco factory, forcing the employer to fire all black employees and hire more Irish. Irish workers also kept Blacks from working on the New York City waterfront. The climax of the Irish–African American tension came in the draft riots of July 1863, in which a primarily Irish mob attacked and killed upward of 100 people; labor tensions were a major contributing factor to the rioting. There were also smaller antidraft riots in Yonkers, Albany, Buffalo, and Troy. Because of their exclusion from most trade unions, African Americans and women formed their own work-based organizations. One such example is the American League of Colored Laborers, which was established in 1850 and promoted industrial education for black artisans. In 1853 African American waiters in New York City went on strike, and they successfully obtained a 25% wage increase. Almost 300 women formed the United Tailoresses Society in 1831 in New York City, and the Female Industrial Organization of New York City followed in 1845, uniting women from a variety of trades. Elsewhere in the state, Rochester seamstresses formed a union in 1853, and Syracuse women established the Sewing Women of Syracuse Protective Union in 1865. Women in Troy formed the Collar Laundry Union in 1864. They had an unsuccessful strike in 1869 over pay increases and the recognition of their union.

Post–Civil War Organizing

Industrialization increased rapidly in New York State after the Civil War. Large numbers of New Yorkers who had been artisans, farmers, or European peasants became industrial laborers. New York City was important for its needle trades, Albany and Troy emerged as iron manufacturing centers, Schenectady was home to an important locomotive works, Utica housed textile and garment manufacturing plants, Rome was a leading center of copper products, Rochester produced garments and became the world's biggest center of photographic equipment manufacturing in the 1890s. Industrialized workers struggled against the low pay, unpleasant and dangerous working conditions, mechanization, and long hours instituted by owners.

In 1870 New York State was home to over 300 trade unions, making it the most organized state in the nation. The Noble and Holy Order of the Knights of Labor (KOL), established in Philadelphia in 1869, admitted both skilled and unskilled workers and was especially active in fighting for higher wages and decent working conditions. The well-organized KOL ran candidates in local elections, organized boycotts, and spoke for all producers, advocating a cooperative republic of workers. It was a fraternal order that stressed the importance of brotherhood, pride, morality, and secrecy (the secrecy requirement was dropped in 1882). The KOL had a strong presence in New York City, forming its first assembly there in 1873 and forming District Assembly 49 in 1882 with 60,000 members. The KOL was active in Rochester, Buffalo, Albany, Syracuse, Utica, Watertown, and Troy, along with more sparsely populated areas throughout the state where it helped organize protests and supported demonstrators. In a particularly dramatic case, the KOL in 1885 helped organize a successful strike against pay cuts that involved 3,000 carpet weavers, mostly women, employed by the Alexander Smith mill in Yonkers. The five-month strike won a 10% pay increase.

In 1877 New York State railroad workers took part in one of the nation's most disruptive work stoppages after the Baltimore and Ohio Railroad announced a 30% wage cut. This nationwide strike affected Albany, Syracuse, and Buffalo, halting a vital transportation system throughout much of the state. In Buffalo, police and 300 deputy sheriffs and Civil War veterans broke the strike. Very active in the national strike, the KOL became a national organization at its annual meeting in 1878. Several years after the strike, in 1883, the Brotherhood of Railway Trainmen was organized in Oneonta (Otsego Co). In 1890 KOL railway workers organized a strike against New York Central Railroad after the company fired 20 men, each of whom had over 10 years of experience. Unable to win support from the American Federation of Labor (AFL) or match the resources of New York Central, this strike ended in failure, resulting in a sharp drop in the KOL's New York State membership. By 1893 there were hardly any KOL members in Albany, Syracuse, or Buffalo.

Broad associations of workers emerged in cities around the state. Central labor unions sprang up in New York City, Albany, Troy, Syracuse, and Buffalo. Serving as umbrella organizations, central labor unions helped unite the state's diverse employees and assisted them politically by endorsing candidates and campaigning for pro-labor legislation. German workers organized a German Trades Union in New York City in the early 1880s that merged with the Central Labor Union in 1882 and sponsored the radical United Hebrew Trades in 1888. The Workingmen's Federation of the State of New York appeared in 1898, and its first president was James Lavery of the Typographical Union.

The struggle for shorter hours united the state's varied unionists. Workers staged strikes from Buffalo to New York City, seeking to convince politicians to pass legislation for fewer hours. As early as 1864 the Iron Molders' International Union held its convention in Buffalo to discuss the importance of the eight-hour day, and New York City was the site of several large strikes for the eight-hour day during the 1860s and 1870s. Widespread agitation for shorter hours convinced state politicians to pass an eight-hour law for some employees in 1867. In 1872 over 100,000 workers in the building trades went on strike for three months to demand an eight-hour day, and New York City brewery employees in 1881 organized a strike and boycott of nonunion beer, which won them a decreased workweek.

New York's wage earners took tremendous pride in their work and sought to achieve broad respectability. In 1882 New York City's Central Labor Union began a yearly tradition when it sponsored a massive Labor Day parade. Wage earners also staged Labor Day marches in Albany and Brooklyn. Similar marches continued each year, and in 1894 Labor Day became a national holiday. The Socialist Labor Party (SLP), a Marxist organization that saw itself as an alternative to the Democratic and Republican Parties, was founded in 1877. The SLP was only marginally successful in winning the support of New York City's workers, who were generally loyal to the immigrant-friendly Democrats. Henry George, a pro-labor politician who was morally appalled by industrial capitalism and upset by the city's hostility toward strikes and other forms of working-class protest, believed private ownership of land was the root of poverty; he advocated a plan for a single tax, just on land. Backed by the Central Labor Union, the SLP, and the KOL, George challenged Democrat Abram S. Hewitt for the position of mayor of New York City in 1886. George garnered an impressive 68,110 votes (31% of votes cast), but he lost in a three-way contest.

In 1881 the Federation of Organized Trades and Labor Union was founded, evolving into the American Federation of Labor in 1886. It was headed by Samuel Gompers, an English-born former cigar maker who lived in New York City and was active in the Cigar Makers International Union (CMIU) during the 1860s and 1870s. The AFL's strategy included staging boycotts, strikes, and demonstrations of craft workers. The AFL was composed of an amalgamation of trade unions of carpenters, cigar makers, iron molders, and printers. Unlike earlier labor organizations, the AFL was not a political association, although it occasionally lobbied politicians for reforms. It restricted membership to skilled crafters, barring most unskilled workers and African Americans from their unions.

The Early 20th Century

In the beginning of the 20th century, both organized and unorganized workers continued to struggle for better conditions, exerting pressure on employers and politicians. Transit workers, bartenders, and teamsters all staged protests around this time. The Knights of Labor helped organize a five-week strike of Brooklyn trolley workers in 1895; they succeeded in mobilizing hundreds of protesters in blocking strikebreakers from operating cars. In 1900 New York City cigar makers, mostly women, left water faucets turned on before beginning a strike, causing property damage. A strike organized by the rank and file in 1907 involving black and white members of the Longshoremen's Union Protective Association in New York City halted maritime traffic for over a month.

One of the most significant labor conflicts involved mostly Jewish and Italian female garment workers in New York City's Lower East Side in 1909–10. In the "Uprising of the 20,000," the strikers wanted their employers to recognize their union, Local 25 of the International Ladies' Garment Workers' Union (ILGWU). They were supported by Mary Dreier, president of the New York Women's Trade Union League (NYWTUL), along with working-class activists Rose Schneiderman and Leonora O'Reilly. This work stoppage eventually resulted in the Protocol of Peace, an industry-wide labor-management agreement. Though its terms only lasted for six years, the Protocol of Peace, which set wage rates and limited hours in return for a no-strike pledge from workers, legitimized labor unions and encouraged workplace cooperation.

In 1912 New York City–based journeymen tailors helped organize a major strike by garment workers in Rochester, calling for union recognition and a 10% wage increase. Organizers from the newly formed Amalgamated Clothing Workers of America (ACW) appealed to the ethnically diverse workforce by giving speeches in Italian, Polish, and Yiddish. Internal conflicts and strong employers resulted in the strike's defeat. ACW organizing, however, continued, and ACW leaders, such as Sidney Hillman, advocated a grassroots unionism predicated on the idea that the locals were controlled by the needs of their members rather than by national leadership. Other major strikes of the early 20th century included the textile workers at New York Mills in Whitestown and New Hartford (Oneida Co) in 1912, uniting workers from Poland, Italy, and many other countries. In 1915 members of the Papermakers and the Pulp, Sulphite, and Paper Mill Unions in Deferiet (Jefferson Co) went on strike against the St. Regis and Remington paper plants. Workers were evicted from company housing, and the National Guard arrested large numbers of workers. After two years, the unions won recognition from management.

Industrial accidents and fires have long been the bane of workers. In 1854, 15 children were killed in an explosion of a gunpowder factory on 10th Ave in Manhattan. In 1913 a fire at the Binghamton Clothing Factory claimed the lives of 35 workers. But the largest loss of life in an industrial fire occurred in 1911 at the Triangle Shirtwaist Factory; 146 employees died. This disaster raised the nation's consciousness about the dangers of industrial workplaces, triggering widespread activism and several important statewide reforms. Organizations such as the New York State Consumer League and the NYWTUL lobbied politicians for workplace improvements, spread information about the horrors of industrial conditions, and supported strikes and other forms of working-class protests. State Senator Robert F. Wagner Sr and Assemblyman Alfred E. Smith sponsored reforms to improve workplace conditions in the wake of the fire. In 1911 the Factory Investigating Commission (FIC), headed by Wagner and Smith, began inspecting industrial sites across the state. Through their efforts, the Democratic Party attracted increasing support from progressive, pro-labor voters.

Many labor voters, however, looked elsewhere than the two major parties. In 1901 the Socialist Party of America established a chapter in New York City, with Morris Hillquit as one of its leaders. The membership consisted of workers in addition to professionals such as journalists and lawyers. No Progressive era labor organization was more militant than the Industrial Workers of the World (IWW), a syndicalist group founded in Chicago in 1905 that organized unskilled workers and advocated mass strikes. The IWW helped organize workers throughout New York State, making crucial inroads in Mohawk Valley mill towns like Little Falls (Herkimer Co) and heavy manufacturing centers like Schenectady, where they organized a sit-down strike of 3,000 workers in the General Electric (GE) plant. Mainstream labor organizations such as the AFL distanced themselves from radical groups like the IWW. More moderate socialists and pro-labor residents of Schenectady elected socialist George R. Lunn to head the city in 1911. As mayor, Lunn funded free health and dental care for workers and oversaw the construction of new schools and playgrounds in the city's working-class neighborhoods.

Racial divisions continued during the Progressive era. Employers fostered racial factionalism by importing African American strikebreakers during strikes in the Buffalo steel industry and New York City hotel business. The pervasiveness of racism convinced African Americans to form their own unions, including the Colored Musicians Union in Buffalo (established in 1917) and trade unions for those working in New York City's hotels. Additionally, many established unions had segregated locals. In 1925 African Americans formed the International Brotherhood of Sleeping Car Porters (BSCP) in New York City. Led by the charismatic A. Philip Randolph, the BSCP represented more black workers (over 12,000 nationwide) than any other union. Women unionists gained important victories during the 1910s. Syracuse garment worker Nellie Kelly became the first female member of the New York State Federation of Labor Executive Council in 1915; she served until 1921, paving the way for other women.

New York State's labor movement received valuable concessions from the federal government during World War I. With the AFL firmly backing the war effort, Pres Woodrow Wilson supported the right of wartime workers to form unions. In return for Wilson's liberal stance, the AFL agreed to refrain from calling strikes during the war. Labor unions sprang up throughout the state, and many workers joined unions for the first time. Leaders of labor (including Samuel Gompers), business, and the federal government talked confidently about America's new period of industrial democracy. Yet, industrial relations became conflict-ridden following the war. New York City longshoremen and garment workers, Schenectady electrical workers, and steelworkers throughout the state organized postwar strikes. Employees of the Lackawanna Steel Co (Erie Co) participated in an AFL-backed national steel strike involving 350,000 steelworkers throughout the county. Lackawanna's workers struck from September 1919 until June 1920 and elected a socialist mayor, John Gibbons, in the midst of the conflict. The strike, however, was unsuccessful. The organizing of copper workers in Rome led to a general strike in May 1919. The attempt to break the strike led to a riot and martial law, but the strike was won in August.

While steelworkers engaged in a nationwide battle, dissidents throughout the state came under increased scrutiny, and hundreds of militants were jailed as a result of the Palmer Raids of 1918–21. Initiated by US Atty Gen A. Mitchell Palmer, these raids were aimed at socialists, anarchists, and IWW members. In the New York State legislature in 1919, the Lusk Committee performed a similar role in trying to root out alleged subversives. This antiradical crusade culminated when five duly elected members of the state assembly were expelled in April 1920 for belonging to the Socialist Party. All of this contributed to an antilabor atmosphere that was readily used by employers.

The 1920s

Employers used lockouts, firings, blacklists, and government raids in the 1920s to try to keep factories union-free and to undermine radicalism. One effective strategy used by employers was to provide benefits as a means of warding off unionization drives—a practice known as welfare capitalism—by trying to create a climate of mutual understanding and respect between wage earners and managers. Endicott Johnson, a major shoe manufacturer outside of Binghamton, Buffalo's Larkin Co, and Eastman Kodak in Rochester offered health insurance, profit sharing, housing, retirement benefits, and vacations. Some employers created "company unions," management-led associations meant to deter the formation of worker-run unions. Employer-sponsored company unions functioned in ways similar to traditional trade unions, but workers had little say over important issues, such as pay rates or control of the workplace.

Although the 1920s were generally a low point for the union movement, the Communist Party rose as a militantly left-wing force. After an abortive effort in the late 1920s and early 1930s to form their own unions under the auspices of the Trade Union Unity League, Communist Party members tried to influence existing unions, with varying degrees of success. Their influence in the ILGWU in the 1920s was blocked by union president David Dubinsky, and they were largely forced out of the union. Communists did retain considerable following in the Fur and Leather Workers Union and the Transit Workers Union, among others. Even in a conservative era, labor had considerable influence in New York State. Gov Al Smith and his successor, Franklin D. Roosevelt, counted on labor as a critical element of their support. Maverick New York City Republican Congressman Fiorello La Guardia was friendly to the Socialist Party, and he championed labor's cause by sponsoring pro-labor legislation, speaking out against social inequality, and walking picket lines.

Rise of the CIO

Labor activism took center stage during the 1930s. The Great Depression caused employers to cut welfare programs, reduce wages, and lay off thousands of workers, demonstrating the limits of corporate paternalism. Workers responded by participating in one of the most spectacular organizing drives in American history, resulting in the rise of the Committee for Industrial Organization within the AFL in 1935. The CIO was expelled from the AFL in 1937 and changed its name to the Congress of Industrial Organizations (CIO) in 1938. The CIO became a national union representing thousands of unskilled and semiskilled workers, in contrast to the more exclusive AFL. Bitter strikes in Buffalo's steel mills, New York City's garment factories, and Schenectady's immense GE plants forced employers to recognize new, progressive unions. Sidney Hillman of the ACW and David Dubinsky of the ILGWU were founding members of the CIO. (The ILGWU returned to the AFL in 1940.) Hillman and Dubinsky joined Alex Rose in founding the American Labor Party (ALP) in 1936 to give voters an alternative to the Tammany-controlled Democratic ticket to support Roosevelt in the presidential election.

The United Electrical, Radio, and Machine Workers of America (UE), one of the CIO's most progressive unions, held its founding convention in Buffalo in 1936 and joined the CIO in 1938. In that latter year dairy farmers, talc miners, aluminum workers, and pulp and paper workers formed the CIO-backed Northern Federation of Farmers and Trade Unions. A 1936 strike against Remington Rand, at the time the world's largest maker of office equipment, lasted a year, and brought out workers in Syracuse, Ilion (Herkimer Co), Tonawanda (Erie Co), and North Tonawanda (Niagara Co). The labor movement also had an important impact on public policy in the 1930s. Frances Perkins, the secretary of labor for Pres Roosevelt, had held similar positions for Roosevelt when he had been governor. Many initiatives that had started in New York State became national policy, among them pro-labor legislation dealing with wages, hours, and workplace conditions. Sen Robert F. Wagner Sr sponsored the National Labor Relations Act in 1935. Also known as the Wagner Act, the law protected the right to organize, protest, and use free speech, and it outlawed the company union.

The labor-liberal coalition was severely tested during World War II. Pres Roosevelt showed a willingness to support organized labor as long as it demonstrated support for the war effort. In the face of labor shortages and demands for increases in manufacturing, leaders of organized labor signed a no-strike pledge, ensuring uninterrupted production for the duration of the war. Several union leaders from the state served the president in high-level positions. Sidney Hillman, the most prominent, worked as associate director of the Office of Production Management. Wartime labor shortages also helped transform the gender and racial characters of factory floors. Women began working in the state's traditionally male-only factories, and African American trade unions, led by A. Philip Randolph, pressured Roosevelt to sign an executive order prohibiting racial discrimination in wartime production facilities. This order resulted in the creation of the Fair Employment Practices Committee in 1941.

Postwar Problems

The wartime unity of workers and employers did not last into the postwar period. Peacetime meant lower production demands that resulted in shorter hours and layoffs. The end of price controls led to higher prices and demands for higher wages. The end of the war especially affected women because many were laid off to free up jobs for returning soldiers. Salary disputes caused a nationwide strike in 1946 at GE and Westinghouse, in which thousands of workers represented by Local 301 of the UE in Schenectady participated. A general strike in Rochester started on 25 May 1946 among municipal employees of the American Federation of State, County, and Municipal Employees (AFSCME) union. The unprecedented show of solidarity when 50,000 people walked off the job forced Rochester's administrators to recognize the union.

Alarmed by these strikes and the community support they received, employers went on the offensive, lobbying politicians to pass antilabor laws and creating savvy public relations campaigns designed to create a wedge between union activists and the general public. Organized collectively in groups such as the National Association of Manufacturers (NAM), business leaders sought to demonstrate that the labor movement wounded the country's economy and threatened the nation's democratic values. In 1947 Congress passed the Taft-Hartley Act, which forced unionists to sign pledge cards to ensure that they were not communists and prevented third party boycott of goods and services, secondary boycotts, and sympathy strikes (as happened in Rochester in 1946). New York State established its own draconian antiunion laws. Following a 1947 strike involving Buffalo schoolteachers, state politicians passed the Condon-Wadlin Act that banned strikes by public-sector unions and mandated the firing of all strikers. Businesses also placed antiunion advertisements in the press and on the radio, singling out unions for their supposed irresponsibility.

The Cold War had an exceptionally disconcerting impact on the labor movement, provoking internal fighting between Communist and liberal anti-Communist unionists. Leaders of the latter played an active role in defining appropriate political ideas. In 1944 David Dubinsky left the American Labor Party to form the Liberal Party. Dominated by Dubinsky and Alex Rose, president of the Millinery Workers Union, the Liberal Party would be an important influence on politics in the state for decades and a stronghold of anticommunist liberalism. In 1949 the CIO expelled 11 left-wing unions, including the UE and the International Fur and Leather Workers Union, which had a strong presence in New York State. In 1955, after establishing itself as an uncompromising anticommunist outfit, the CIO merged with the AFL under the leadership of George Meany, a former plumber from New York City who was a leader of the New York State Federation of Labor between 1934 and 1940. By the 1950s left-wing activists had little influence on the state's trade unions. The percentage of workers in unions was significant: 34.4% of the workforce was unionized in 1953, and the national average in that same year was 32.6%. Additionally, wages in the manufacturing sector were high, allowing many members of the working classes to buy suburban homes, send their children to college, and retire in relative comfort. Around the same time, a number of heavy manufacturing jobs left the urban centers for the suburbs. For example, Long Island, home to some of the state's largest suburbs, experienced the emergence of many new heavy manufacturing jobs, especially in the aviation industry, during the 1940s and 1950s.

Yet militant union efforts did not come to an end in the postwar era. In 1959 New York City teachers won a massive pay raise after striking for three weeks. That same year hospital and nursing home employees unionized across the state, especially in New York City, where the militant AFL Local 1199 of the Health and Human Services Union, representing largely African American and Puerto Rican workers, organized large-scale protests. Gov Nelson A. Rockefeller signed a bill in 1963 guaranteeing hospital workers in New York City the right to unionize, which was expanded to all state hospital employees in 1965. Organized labor rewarded Rockefeller for his pro-labor support by endorsing him in several elections.

In 1966 New York City was shaken by a 12-day transit strike by the Transport Workers Union, which cost the city $100 million a day. The strike's disruptions forced politicians to review labor laws. Gov Rockefeller appointed a commission, headed by the University of Pennsylvania's George W. Taylor, to recommend changes to the Condon-Wadlin Act. In 1967 the commission created the Public Employees' Fair Employment Act, popularly known as the Taylor Law. Like the Condon-Wadlin Act, the Taylor Law prohibited strikes, but it also strengthened public-sector unions by guaranteeing employees the right to form unions without employer interference. A three-member Public Employment Relations Board (PERB) was created to implement the law.

The 1968 strikes by the United Federation of Teachers (UFT) in New York City about community control in Brooklyn's Ocean Hill–Brownsville School District only peripherally concerned traditional union concerns such as wages or hours. Rather, the episode centered on questions of community involvement in personnel decisions and soon became a nasty battle in which questions of race and anti-Semitism dominated all other questions. After three bitterly divisive strikes, which closed the city's schools for almost two months, the UFT won a grudging victory; still, bitter divisions remained in the labor movement and the city as a whole.

If the school strike marked something of a turn from postwar liberalism, this was accentuated when traditional labor organizations occasionally clashed with the New Left in the late 1960s and 1970s as civil rights activism and the Vietnam conflict split the nation. Many union leaders, notably George Meany, and rank-and-file members supported the Vietnam conflict. College and high school student activists, on the other hand, were virulently against the war. In 1970 the two sides clashed in New York City as construction workers, then involved in building the World Trade Center, violently attacked antiwar protesters in Lower Manhattan. The Hardhat Rebellion, as it became known, was emblematic of the right-wing shift of much of organized labor. Disagreements over the nature of US foreign policy continued to divide traditional labor and left-wing activists during the 1970s and 1980s. Under the leadership of George Meany and his successor, Lane Kirkland, the AFL-CIO continued to support the federal government's interventions throughout eastern Europe, Latin America, Africa, and the Middle East.

The country's long postwar boom came to a dramatic halt in the early 1970s as workers confronted both high levels of inflation and unemployment and plant closings. New York State was hit especially hard. Major steel, metal, and textile firms shut down and relocated to the south or overseas where labor costs were low. The elimination of jobs and capital flight transformed previously strong economic centers like Troy, Schenectady, Binghamton, Amsterdam, Utica, Syracuse, Rochester, and Buffalo into "rust belt" cities. The percentage of the state's unionized workers declined considerably during this period, from 40.2% in 1970 to 24.2% in 1994. Plant shutdowns and the threat of shutdowns had a disciplinary effect on organized labor: employers used the unpromising economic climate to their advantage and forced concessions. Public-sector unions were not immune from the economic downturn. Urban fiscal emergencies during the 1970s forced municipal unions, like the AFSCME, to make wage and benefit concessions. In 1974 New York City had a debt of $11 billion, and Democratic mayor Abe Beame temporarily stopped city hiring. The city's municipal unions agreed to a variety of deferrals of wage increases, benefit reductions, and the purchase of $2.5 billion in state and municipal bonds to help the city through the fiscal crisis of 1974 and 1975.

The decline in heavy manufacturing, the New York City fiscal crisis, and the attacks on unions did not prevent employees from organizing for better conditions. Graduate student employees and professors in the New York City and New York State university systems began unionizing in the 1970s. During the 1990s telephone opera-

Construction worker in Syracuse, 1983. A combination of protest and government action opened the building trades to women and minorities in the 1960s and 1970s.

tors, janitors, and truck drivers demonstrated solidarity in a number of strike actions, and the Communications Workers of America (CWA), the Service Employees International Union (SEIU), and the International Brotherhood of Teamsters all won important strikes in the state. Despite radical changes in the economy, New York remained one of the most unionized states in the country.

The labor movement has entered a new phase in the post–Cold War period. Under the headship of Bronx-born John J. Sweeney, the AFL-CIO invested heavily in organizing, hoping to reverse the decline in unionization rates. Organized labor has become more welcoming to traditionally underrepresented groups. Greater numbers of women, African Americans, and new immigrants from Asia and Latin America have benefited from recent organizing drives. In some cases, women and minorities lead powerful, multiracial unions. In 1986 AFSCME's D.C. 37, New York City's largest union, elected African American Stanley Hill as president. In 1989 Puerto Rican–born Dennis Rivera was elected president of the powerful Local 1199, and in the 1990s Sandra Feldman became president of the UFT. Intellectuals and college student activists have teamed up with organized labor to fight corporate globalization and sweatshop abuses, indicating a revival of the labor-left alliance. One of the sharpest expressions of this renewed partnership occurred in October 1996, when college professors, graduate students, union organizers, and labor leaders organized a well-attended conference at Columbia University entitled "The Fight for America's Future: A Teach-In with the Labor Movement."

Labor in New York City was profoundly affected by the attacks on the World Trade Center on 11 Sept 2001. Among the approximately 2,750 deaths were hundreds of unionized firefighters, police officers, clerks, and other workers. In the aftermath of this tragedy, organized labor throughout New York State offered a helping hand. New York State unionists organized memorial services, participated in candlelight vigils, and launched fund-raising campaigns for the victims and their families.

See also Binghamton; Buffalo; Child labor; Dairy industry; Irish; Italians; *Lochner v New York;* Poles; Riots and civil disturbances; Troy; Workers' education; World war I.

University Libraries, University at Albany. "Documenting Labor Inside and Out," http://library.albany.edu/speccoll/documentinglabor/table_of_contents.htm

Dubofsky, Melvyn. *When Workers Organize: New York City in the Progressive Era* (Amherst: Univ of Massachusetts Press, 1968)

Freeman, Joshua B. *Working-Class New York: Life and Labor since World War II* (New York: New Press, 2000)

Fuller, David L. *The History of Labor in New York State: A Poster Map of the Most Important Events in Labor History from 1600 to Present Day* (New York: New York Labor History Association, 1998)

Huston, Reeve. *Land and Freedom: Rural Society, Popular Protest, and Party Politics in Antebellum New York* (New York: Oxford Univ Press, 2000)

Montgomery, David. *The Fall of the House of Labor: The Workplace, the State, and American Labor Activism, 1865–1925* (Cambridge: Cambridge Univ Press, 1987)

Rock, Howard B. *Artisans of the New Republic: The Tradesmen of New York City in the Age of Jefferson* (New York: New York Univ Press, 1979)

Roediger, David R. *The Wages of Whiteness: Race and the Making of the American Working Class* (New York: Verso, 1991)

Wilentz, Sean. *Chants Democratic: New York City and the Rise of the American Working Class, 1788–1850* (New York: Oxford Univ Press, 1984)

Yellowitz, Irwin. *Labor and the Progressive Movement in New York State, 1897–1916* (Ithaca: Cornell Univ Press, 1965)

Zahavi, Gerald. *Workers, Managers, and Welfare Capitalism: The Shoeworkers and Tanners of Endicott Johnson, 1890–1950* (Urbana: Univ of Illinois Press, 1988)

Zieger, Robert. *The CIO, 1935–1955* (Chapel Hill: Univ of North Carolina Press, 1995)

Chad Pearson

Labor, Department of. Formed in 1901 by consolidating the Bureau of Labor Statistics (1883), the Department of Factory Inspection (1886), and the Board of Mediation and Arbitration (1886), the new agency arose during an era of expanded regulation involving workplace safety, apprenticeships, wages, hours, and children's and women's labor. The first department of labor established in the country, the agency administers and enforces various programs to serve and protect the state's workforce, including federally mandated unemployment insurance and job training and placement, state-funded administration of labor legislation, and federal- and state-funded collection of labor market data and research.

Public demand for reform after the 1911 Triangle Shirtwaist Factory fire in New York City and other abuses led to a reorganization of the department in 1913. The Division of Industrial Hygiene was added to conduct research on occupational health and safety, and in 1915 the first state employment bureau was established. Throughout the 1920s, 1930s, and 1940s, the department was at the forefront of research and social legislation. The department's Division of Women in Industry, established in 1922, was influential in women's issues, minimum wage, and youth employment. Frances Perkins was the state's first female industrial commissioner (1929–33), as the head of the department was then known, and the first female US cabinet member, serving as labor secretary (1933–45) under Pres Franklin D. Roosevelt.

In 1933 the Wagner-Peyser Act created the US Employment Service, and two years later the Social Security Act created the unemployment insurance program. In 1937 the state's arbitration and collective bargaining regulation processes were established with their separate boards, the Labor Relations Board and the State Mediation Board. Although the industrial commissioner headed both, they were not part of the Department of Labor proper. During World War II the State Employment Service came under federal control but returned to state hands in 1946. The Workers' Compensation Board became a separate entity (1944–45), and the Division of Research and Statistics emerged chiefly from the Bureau of Labor Statistics and the research sections of the Division of Women in Industry, its enforcement component becoming the Division of Labor Standards.

The department headquarters in Albany and is headed by the commissioner of labor, who is appointed by the governor. The department's response to the Workforce Investment Act of 1998 has led to partnerships with allied government and nonprofit agencies, often in One-Stop Centers, where social service agencies work together to help welfare recipients and those with varied needs. Employment at the department peaked at 13,000 in the 1970s but has since declined, in part because some services became available by telephone and Internet. As of 2002 the Labor Department employed about 5,000 people, with approximately 88% of those positions financed by federal grants. The agency had an operating budget of $5.4 billion, which includes money collected from employers for unemployment insurance claims.

New York State Department of Labor, http://www.labor.state.ny.us

Padula, Ferdinand. *Stand Fast! A Chronicle of the Workers' Movement in New York State* (Albany: NYS Department of Labor, 1993)

R. Ashley Hibbard

Laboratory Institute of Merchandising. Private fashion college located in Manhattan. The school was founded in 1939 by Maxwell F. Marcuse. Originally located on West 34th St, a thriving center for department stores and specialty shops, the school created a professional curriculum in merchandising and the fashion industry. Its first class of 79 women graduated in 1941. In 1959 it moved Midtown to 5th Ave and since 1965 has been in a town house at 12 East 53d St. Although still attended primarily by women, the school officially became co-ed in 1971. It received accreditation in 1977 and issued its first bachelor's degree in 1985. The school combines a core program in the liberal arts with four professional areas: fashion, visual, business, and the arts and communications. It grants an associate in applied sciences degree, a bachelor's of business administration, and a bachelor's of professional studies. In 2003 the student body numbered 405.

Marianne Rahn-Erickson

Labor Day. The New York City labor movement, dominated by the Knights of Labor, initiated this holiday devoted to the American worker.

Matthew Maguire, a machinist from Paterson, NJ, and secretary of the New York City Central Labor Union, suggested the holiday. That year the first Labor Day parade took place on Tuesday, 5 September 1882 when thousands of workers marched around Union Square in New York City. In 1884 the Knights of Labor chose the first Monday in September as the permanent holiday, and subsequently Labor Day has been celebrated in many localities nationwide. Oregon passed the first state law to recognize Labor Day in February 1887. Later the same year New York and three other states designated Labor Day a holiday. Amid growing labor unrest during a presidential election year, Rep Amos J. Cummings, a Democrat from New York State (11th District), sponsored a bill that Pres Grover Cleveland signed into law, making Labor Day a national holiday in 1894. To disassociate American labor from any connection with socialism, the first Monday of September was chosen to honor American workers rather than 1 May, which in 1889 the Second Socialist International in Paris had designated as International Workers Day.

Observance of Labor Day has changed since its early years. Labor Day in New York City was originally celebrated by a street parade followed by political speeches and a picnic for the workers and their families. In recent years, with the labor movement membership declining to less than 15% of the regular workforce, Labor Day is seen by many as the last long weekend of summer rather than as a day to celebrate organized labor. Labor parades no longer take place every year in New York City or elsewhere, nor do they always take place on the actual day. In 1998 labor officials led a ceremony making Union Square, site of the first Labor Day parade, a National Historic Landmark.

US Department of Labor. "The History of Labor Day," http://www.dol.gov/opa/aboutdol/laborday.htm
Grossman, Jonathan. "Who Is the Father of Labor Day?" *Monthly Labor Review* 95 (Sept 1972): 3–6

John F. Lyons

Lackawanna. City (pop 19,064) in W Erie Co. The Lackawanna Iron and Steel Co purchased land in 1899 for a steel mill that was in production in 1903. The city was incorporated in 1909. It grew rapidly with Polish, Hungarian, Italian, Serbian, Croatian, and Greek workers, and the population reached 23,948 in 1930. Other firms, quantity users of steel, also built plants in the city. Due to the excellent infrastructure and power sources, Lackawanna Iron and Steel's corporate headquarters relocated from Scranton, Pa. In 1922 it merged with Bethlehem Steel Co to become the second largest such company in the United States. At its peak the Bethlehem plant in Lackawanna produced about 5% of the nation's annual steel output. In the 1970s the steel industry declined steadily, and the plant closed in 1983, leaving the city without industry and in a desperate economic situation. The Our Lady of Victory Basilica and National Shrine (1925), built by Fr Nelson Henry Baker (1841–1936), who also founded the Home of Charity for needy boys, was restored at the end of the 20th century and is a tourist and religious destination. In 2002 six Lackawanna men were arrested because of links to the Al Qaeda terror network; all of the men pleaded guilty to charges of supporting terrorism.

See also BOTANICAL GARDENS; IRON AND STEEL INDUSTRY.

Andrew C. Maines

Lackawanna Steel Strike of 1919. When a national walkout of steel workers began on 22 Sept 1919, workers at the Lackawanna Iron and Steel Co (Erie Co) were receptive to the American Federation of Labor's (AFL's) national effort to organize the steel industry. Always a dangerous occupation with long hours, making steel in the massive Lackawanna mill became even more oppressive after World War I. Disarmament cut back on demand for steel, leading to layoffs and salary cuts averaging about 36% at the Lackawanna plant. In addition the cost of living had jumped by 84.2% in Lackawanna between December 1914 and June 1919, exacerbating the steelworkers' economic plight. The company's initial response to the possibility of a job action in support of unionization was to fire hundreds of workers who attended union rallies, using Red Scare tactics to discredit union activists and armed plant guards with billy clubs and machine guns. The steelworkers were not intimidated. On the first day of the national steel strike, 98% of Lackawanna Steel's 6,000 workers stayed home. On the second day, while throngs of strikers threw stones at steel company police as they left the Lackawanna plant, company guards fired into the crowd, killing two, including a twice-decorated World War I veteran, and wounding two others. This began what strikers called a "reign of terror," in which city leaders, headed by the Democratic mayor of Lackawanna John Toomey, called in state police reinforcements to help squelch the strike. In November, as the strike was waning nationally, Lackawanna's voters rebelled against the violence associated with the Toomey administration and elected Socialist John Gibbons as mayor. With the support of a friendly city administration, the strikers managed to hold out until June 1920, six months after the strike collapsed nationally.

Brody, David. *Labor in Crisis: The Steel Strike of 1919* (Philadelphia: Lippincott, 1965)
Scheuerman, William. "The Politics of Protest: The Great Steel Strike of 1919–20 in Lackawanna, New York," *International Review of Social History* 31, prt 2 (1986): 121–46

William Scheuerman

Lacona. Village (pop 590) in Sandy Creek (Oswego Co). The Rome, Watertown and Ogdensburg Railroad (1851) stimulated growth of the hamlet of East Sandy Creek, which incorporated as Lacona in 1880. With waterpower supplied by the Sandy Creek, it had gristmills, cheese factories, and a tannery. In 1925 the First National Bank of Lacona gave permission to the Coterie Club to erect an ornamental clock, which still stands. I-81 (1961) facilitates commuting to Watertown and Syracuse.

Barbara J. Dix

lacrosse. Known as the "fastest game on two feet" and Canada's national game, it is the oldest team sport in North America. Indians throughout the Mississippi River drainage system and the Great Lakes region played various stick and ball games prior to the arrival of French and English colonists in the 17th century. Although many Indian tribes have ancient ball game traditions, the Mohawk game became modern lacrosse. The sport developed into three different versions in the 20th century: field lacrosse, played outdoors by collegiate men and high school boys with 10 players on each side; box or indoor lacrosse, a rougher game played by teams of 6 men on dry hockey rink floors; and women's lacrosse, an outdoor game with minimal body contact and 12 players on each side.

THE COLLEGIATE GAME

Mohawks from Canada introduced lacrosse to Brooklyn in 1863 and to New York City in 1869, and throughout the 1870s and 1880s clubs from Montreal, the Caughnawaga Indian Reservation, and Akwesasne (St. Regis Indian Reservation) [partly loc in Franklin Co] played private clubs in lacrosse contests, inspiring the creation of clubs in Manhattan, Brooklyn, and Staten Island and in New Jersey. Delegates from these clubs and from Boston met at the Astor House in New York City in June 1879 and formed the US National Amateur Lacrosse Association. Among the clubs was a men's team from New York University (NYU), the country's first collegiate squad. Members of the Crescent Athletic Club of Brooklyn, which dominated competition in the United States during the early 20th century, cultivated the game at other nearby colleges and high school campuses. In Central New York lacrosse at the college level spread slowly after a Canadian professor introduced lacrosse to Hobart College in Geneva (Ontario Co) in 1897. The Syracuse University program was born in 1916, founded by landscape engineering pro-

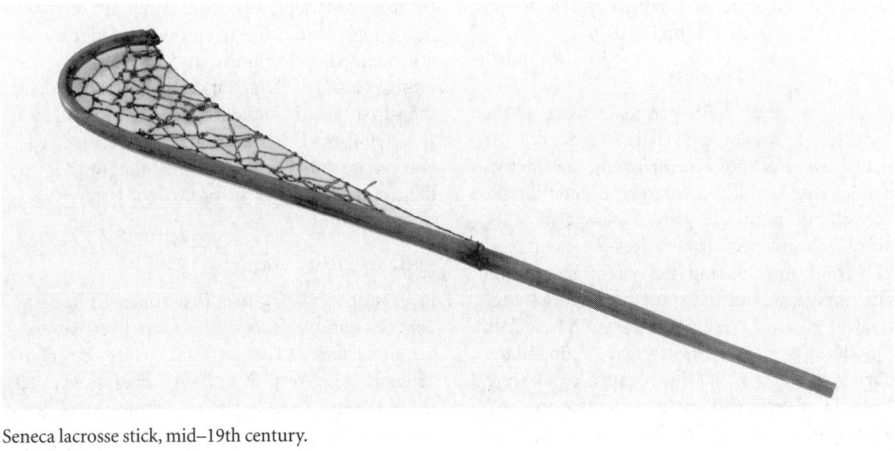

Seneca lacrosse stick, mid–19th century.

fessor Laurie Cox, who served as head coach through the 1930 season.

By 1922 NYU, Syracuse University, Cornell University, Colgate University, Hobart College, and West Point had teams. The number of college teams in the state grew to 35 by 1970. After the replacement of Indian-made wood lacrosse sticks with those made from synthetic materials, the sport's popularity grew during the late 20th century, and by 2003 New York State had 51 collegiate men's lacrosse teams—the most in the country. The teams hailed from 14 Division I, 8 Division II, and 29 Division III schools; 17 junior colleges also fielded teams.

From 1881 to 1970 the US Intercollegiate Lacrosse Association awarded championship honors to one or more schools annually. Five schools from New York won or shared (indicated by an asterisk) the national title, including NYU (1895), Cornell (1907*), Syracuse (1922*, 1924), West Point (1923, 1944, 1945*, 1951*, 1958, 1959*, 1961*, 1969*), and Rensselaer Polytechnic Institute (1952). The National Collegiate Athletic Association (NCAA) began sponsoring a national championship tournament in 1971. Only two schools from New York State have won the Division I men's title: Cornell (1971, 1976, 1977) and Syracuse (1983, 1988, 1989, 1990, 1993, 1995, 2000, 2002, 2004). The Cornell championship teams from 1976 and 1977 featured three-time All-American Eamon McEneaney, who later died in the 11 Sept 2001 terrorist attack on the World Trade Center. Throughout the 20th century and into the 21st century, Syracuse had the most dominant collegiate program in the state. Led by coaches Roy Simmons Sr (1931–70) and Roy Simmons Jr (1971–98), the team featured players such as National Football League Hall of Famer Jim Brown, Oren Lyons Jr, Tim O'Hara, Tim Nelson, twin brothers Gary and Paul Gait, Tom Marachek, and brothers Casey, Ryan, and Michael Powell. From 1972 to 1993 Hobart won 16 titles in other NCAA tournaments, and Adelphi University won 7 NCAA titles from 1979 to 2001.

Women's lacrosse became popular in the 1930s, after the US Women's Lacrosse Association was formed in 1931, and clubs in Baltimore, Boston, New York City, and Philadelphia were organized the following year. By 1958, 16 colleges in New York State included women's lacrosse in their physical education programs. In the 1970s the NCAA began sponsoring tournaments for Division I (1982), Division III (1985), and Division II (2001) schools. There were 45 colleges in New York State with women's lacrosse in 2003, but only 1 has won a national crown. C. W. Post Campus of Long Island University captured the 2001 Division II title.

High School Lacrosse

As early as 1905 boys played lacrosse at the Brooklyn Polytechnic Preparatory School. By 1917 several schools competed in the Metropolitan Interscholastic Lacrosse League for the championship of the greater New York City, Brooklyn, and eastern New Jersey region. Austere conditions during the Great Depression hurt the game, but the sport experienced a revival after World War II in and around New York City. The game spread swiftly across Long Island during the 1960s, mainly because of Howard "Howdy" Myers, who started a lacrosse program at Hofstra University in 1949. Statewide, there were 199 high schools with boys' programs in 1982 and 321 by 2003. Boys' teams began competing in a state championship tournament in 1977. Organizers divided schools into Class A and Class B in 1986 and added Class C in 2000. From 1981 to 2003 West Genesee High School of Camillus (Onondaga Co) won 12 state titles. However, high schools in the New York City metropolitan area have dominated the tournaments. Ward Melville High School (East Setauket, Suffolk Co), Yorktown High School (Yorktown Heights, Westchester Co), and Garden City High School (Nassau Co) each won multiple championships.

Some high schools added lacrosse to their physical education programs for girls after 1945. In 1958 there were 37 secondary schools with girls' lacrosse, mainly in downstate New York. Girls' teams have contested for a state championship since 1995 in two divisions. There were 242 high schools competing in girls' lacrosse in 2003.

Inside the Iroquois Confederacy

Play by American Indians in New York State predates the founding of the United States. Teams representing the Mohawk, Oneida, Onondaga, Cayuga, Seneca, and Tuscarora Nations reinforced alliance ties through lacrosse contests. However, with the creation of the modern reservation system and the displacement of Indians out of New York State, these relationships became difficult to maintain. During the late 19th century, teams from reservations regularly played against elite clubs in New York City, Boston, Toronto, and Montreal and overseas in Britain. In 1901 Seneca Indians staged exhibition matches at the Pan-American Exposition in Buffalo. In the 20th century Iroquois Indians played field lacrosse, box lacrosse, and a ceremonial medicine game. Indian clubs played contests against colleges, barnstormed across the northeastern United States, and played in an elimination tournament to decide what team would represent the United States at the 1932 Olympics. The Iroquois team was defeated by the Crescent Athletic Club, which suffered a loss against the eventual tournament winner, Johns Hopkins University. Individual Indian athletes have played for collegiate field lacrosse programs and Canadian box lacrosse clubs. During the 1990s clubs such as the Akwesasne Thunder, Newtown Golden Eagles, and Onondaga Athletic Club competed for various league championships.

In 1983 Onondaga faithkeeper Oren Lyons Jr and Tuscarora stickmaker Wes Patterson created the Iroquois Nationals field lacrosse team. The team recruited players from different reservations, represented the Iroquois Confederacy in international exhibitions, and traveled on Iroquois passports. The Nationals participated in their first World Games of field lacrosse in 1990 as a member of the International Lacrosse Federation. In 2003 Canada defeated the Iroquois in the championship game of the inaugural World Indoor Games.

Professional Lacrosse

Professional box lacrosse first appeared in New York State in the form of the short-lived American Box Lacrosse League (1932). Harry Smith, a Mohawk who lived in Buffalo during the Great Depression, earned notice as a professional box lacrosse player in the 1930s before moving to California, changing his name to Jay Silverheels, and playing Tonto on *The Lone Ranger.* The National Lacrosse League (1974–75) briefly resurrected the sport in New York State before the Major Indoor Lacrosse League (MILL) was born in 1987. The MILL has included five franchises in the state: the New York Saints, Buffalo Bandits, Rochester Knighthawks, Syracuse Smash, and Albany Attack. The Bandits won championships in 1992, 1993, and 1996, and the Knighthawks won the league crown in 1997. After the completion of the 1997 season, the MILL combined with a rival group of owners to form the National Lacrosse League. Since 1991 Gary and Paul Gait have dominated the league in scoring and all-league honors. Founded by former SUNY Cortland lacrosse player Jake Steinfeld (chairman of Body by Jake Enterprises), an outdoor field lacrosse league called Major League Lacrosse began play in 2001 with two franchises in New York State: the Long Island Lizards and the Rochester Rattlers. Led by the Gait brothers, the Lizards won the league's inaugural championship.

Fisher, Donald M. *Lacrosse: A History of the Game* (Baltimore: Johns Hopkins Univ Press, 2002)

Vennum, Thomas, Jr. *American Indian Lacrosse: Little Brother of War* (Washington, DC: Smithsonian Institution Press, 1994)

Donald M. Fisher

LaFayette. Town (pop 4,833) in central Onondaga Co. The Onondaga Nation had a mound village (?1681) in what is now LaFayette, and the town was the site of Indian Orchard (Tueyahdasso), examined by botanist John Bartram in 1743. The modern Onondaga Indian Reservation adjoins the town. Settled in 1791, the town was formed from Pompey and Onondaga in 1825. The Syracuse, Binghamton and New York Railroad was built in 1854 and began running milk trains in 1888. I-81 (1957) improved access to Syracuse. It remains a farming town with large apple orchards dominating the landscape. The LaFayette Apple Festival has attracted visitors for crafts and for apple desserts on Columbus Day weekend since 1972.

Marla A. Bennett

La Grange. Town (pop 14,928) in central Dutchess Co. Part of the Beekman (1697) and Rombout (1685) Patents, it was formed as Freedom in 1821 and renamed in 1828 after the Marquis de Lafayette's home. The Taconic Parkway was built through town in 1947, providing access to James Baird State Park (1949). Following World War II, IBM facilities in Poughkeepsie and East Fishkill drew residents, increasing La Grange's population sixfold by the century's end. George Huntington (1850–1916), the physician who identified Huntington's disease in 1872, was a resident (1874–1901, 1903–15).

William P. McDermott

La Guardia, Fiorello H(enry) (*b* New York City, 11 Dec 1882; *d* Bronx Co, 20 Sept 1947). Mayor and congressman. The son of a US Army bandleader of Italian ancestry and an Austrian-born Jewish mother, La Guardia spent his childhood throughout the American West. He entered public service at age 17, when he began working for the US Consulate Service in Europe. While abroad he mastered Italian, Yiddish, German,

French, and Croatian—language skills that would later prove invaluable as mayor. Returning to New York City after his father's death, La Guardia completed high school, earned a law degree at New York University (1910), and landed a translator's position at the US Immigration Service on Ellis Island. There he became convinced of the need to rid government of corruption and minimize its bureaucracy. Running on a platform that reflected these goals, he was elected to Congress in 1916 from Lower Manhattan as a Republican; he was the first member of Italian descent to serve in that body. La Guardia's congressional term was interrupted by World War I, in which he was a US Army pilot-bombardier in Europe.

In 1919 La Guardia was elected president of the New York City Board of Aldermen, where he introduced some of the progressive reforms that would later characterize his mayorship. Three years later La Guardia was reelected to Congress, this time from East Harlem, where he became a fiery pro-labor advocate. In 1932 he cosponsored the Norris–La Guardia Act, which barred the use of antilabor injunctions. As a progressive Republican from New York City, La Guardia was in the unenviable position of being denounced by members of his own party, where laissez-faire attitudes dominated, and by Tammany Hall Democrats. Three years prior to the passage of the Norris–La Guardia Act, he lost decisively in a bid for New York City mayor to Tammany regular Jimmy Walker. However, in a second attempt for the post in 1933, La Guardia captured City Hall by cobbling together a City Fusion ticket consisting of Republicans, Socialists, and other reformers after political scandal weakened the Tammany machine.

Holding the mayor's office for three consecutive terms (1934–45), La Guardia was arguably New York City's most influential chief executive of the 20th century. Taking office in January 1934 La Guardia instituted a set of emergency fiscal measures and claimed unprecedented executive powers to mitigate the devastation of the depression. Some politicians, such as Democratic governor Herbert H. Lehman, charged that these actions were dictatorial. Despite gubernatorial censure, La Guardia supported Lehman's successful bid for reelection in 1938, a stance that angered Republican gubernatorial nominee Thomas E. Dewey. Although a lifelong Republican, La Guardia again exhibited his political ambidexterity by securing millions of dollars in federal aid for the city from the Democratic president Franklin D. Roosevelt, funds that the mayor used to build a wide array of new infrastructure, including bridges, parks, subways, and public housing on a scale never seen before or since in New York City.

While in office La Guardia promoted a progressive social agenda. Setting out to rid the city's government of the corruption of Tammany Hall, La Guardia expanded the ranks of the civil service to make government officials more responsive while ensuring that such positions were acquired by merit rather than by patronage. Other aspects of his agenda included in 1943 the founding of the City Center as the people's theater and the establishment of the Health Insurance Plan (HIP), originally open to municipal employees and moderate- to middle-income New Yorkers for a fee. These two initiatives were criticized for their expense, especially as Americans faced the economic hardships of war. As his time in office progressed, the mayor was often denounced for his refusal to listen to criticism, which detractors claimed made him increasingly arrogant. By his last mayoral term La Guardia began to seek other venues for his energy. In late 1945, after completing his third term, La Guardia left city politics to head the United Nations Relief and Rehabilitation Administration based in Washington, DC.

Kessner, Thomas. *Fiorello H. La Guardia and the Making of Modern New York* (New York: McGraw-Hill, 1989)

Dominique Padurano

Lake Carmel. Locality (pop 8,663) in Kent (Putnam Co). Lake Carmel was founded in 1930 as a vacation-home community. Arthur and Warren Smadbeck surveyed small lots surrounding an artificial lake and advertised them through the *New York Daily Mirror*'s subscription department. Beginning in the 1950s summer cottages were enlarged and winterized, creating year-round homes at reasonable prices. In 2001 only 12% of structures were still seasonal. High-density and inadequate septic systems have threatened lake and drinking water quality, but residents have resisted sewer construction because of the cost.

Sallie S. Sypher

Lake Champlain (435 mi²/1,127 km²). Popularly referred to as the West Coast of New England and, by some, as the sixth Great Lake, much of its length marks the border between New York State and Vermont. The lake has a shoreline of 587 miles (945 km) and is 120 miles (193 km) long. Although 400 feet (122 m) at its deepest, the lake's average depth is 64 feet (20 m). From its southern end at Whitehall (Washington Co), it drains northward via the Richelieu River into the St. Lawrence River. The Lake Champlain watershed area is 8,234 mi² (21,326 km²) and lies in the states of New York and Vermont and in the Canadian province of Quebec. It is one of the largest freshwater lakes in the United States.

To Indian, colonial, and postcolonial residents of the lake basin, Lake Champlain has served as a conduit for human migration, trade, ideas, and information. It and its basin have also provided natural resources for direct consumption through fishing and hunting, agriculture, mining, and forestry, and for indirect consumption through recreation and tourism. It played a strategic role in political and economic struggles over territory between colonists and indigenous peoples, the British and the French, the British and American revolutionaries. It also had an effect on the conduct and outcome of the War of 1812.

Physical Characteristics

The physiography of the basin was shaped by mountain-building processes over millions of years. The geological record reveals ancient sedimentary and metamorphic rocks. Glacial erosion and deposition have more recently influenced the lake's environment. The last ice age, the Pleistocene (ending about 10,000 years ago), scoured the lake bed and blocked its outflow with glacial debris, resulting in Lake Vermont, which was later transformed into the Champlain Sea before returning to its freshwater state as Lake Champlain. In hydrological terms, the lake has five distinct segments. The South Lake, which extends from the Poultney River to Crown Point (Essex Co), is narrow and shallow and acts much like a river. The Main Lake, from Crown Point north to Rouses Point (Clinton Co) and west of the Champlain Islands, is much deeper and colder; it contains more than 80% of the lake's volume. The three other segments, Mallett's Bay, the Inland Sea, and Missisquoi Bay, are constrained in their circulation through the construction of causeways and bridges and in general are shallower than the Main Lake.

Historic and Strategic Importance

Human activities in the Lake Champlain region began with indigenous societies such as the Abenaki, Iroquois, and Huron Nations. In 1609 French explorer and cartographer Samuel de Champlain initiated European contact, and colonial and postcolonial domination of the area followed. The basin has been the scene of conflict between indigenous groups and then between French and British colonial influences, especially on its western shore. The 1776 Battle of Valcour Island, while a defeat for Brig Gen Benedict Arnold's American fleet, delayed the British invasion from Canada until the following year, when the Americans would be victorious at the Battle of Saratoga. The American victory over the British in the Battle of Plattsburgh (1814) under Commodore Thomas Macdonough was a pivotal event in the War of 1812.

The commercial dimension of the lake was strengthened in the 19th century with communities in the basin developing a variety of specialized functions. On the New York side, the iron industry developed in the region surrounding Port Henry (Essex Co). Water-based transportation was a key facet of the economic development of the basin with connections via canal to both the St. Lawrence and Hudson Rivers. Many see the 19th century as the golden age of waterborne commerce for the lake with myriad vessel types powered by sail and later by steam. Examples include sailing canalboats (which were towed on the canals and then sailed on the lake), horse ferries, and an array of steam-powered passenger and freight vessels. Sunken examples of many of these, such as the *Champlain II* (a side-wheel steamer that ran aground off Westport in Essex Co in 1875), are part of underwater historic preserves. In 1929 the Lake Champlain Bridge at Crown Point was opened, putting many ferries out of business. In 2003 ferry crossings remained in operation at Ticonderoga, Essex, Port Kent (Essex Co), and Cumberland Head at Plattsburgh.

The introduction and consolidation of passenger and freight railroad operations during the 19th century influenced the growth and viability of lake communities and water-based transportation in complex ways. Some communities thrived, while others declined. By the end of the century the primacy and viability of water-based transportation and the commercial focus on the lake had waned. In recent decades, however, the lake has become a focus for recreation and tourism, especially sailing and motorboating but also canoeing, fishing, and swimming. In the 21st century the economy of the basin relies less on natural resource and manufacturing sectors and more on employment in the service sector, with Burlington, Vt, and Plattsburgh as its largest cities.

ENVIRONMENTAL PLANNING

Past planning efforts for the Lake Champlain watershed have been undermined by a lack of funding or political consensus among jurisdictions or a combination of both. In political terms, the basin includes territory in two states and a Canadian province, and comprises more than 200 municipalities and local governments. In New York State, 74% of the basin falls within the boundary of the Adirondack Park. Efforts by New York and Vermont to engage in joint planning for Lake Champlain and to confront the challenges of water pollution began at the turn of the 20th century and have waxed and waned. The most recent water resources planning process in the United States portion of the basin was initiated when the US Congress signed into law the Lake Champlain Special Designation Act in 1990. The federal legislation and subsequent funding were the impetus and provided the primary funding for a comprehensive watershed-based planning effort that ties the environmental welfare of the lake to coordinated actions of New York and Vermont and wherever possible the Province of Quebec under the auspices of the Lake Champlain Basin Program. The planning effort also sought to couple environmental issues with a broader array of policy issues including recreation, cultural heritage, and economic development. Resulting agreements have addressed environmental concerns about the lake, including toxic substances in lake sediments, eutrophication and nonpoint source pollution, phosphorus and other nutrients, threats to the human consumption of fish, and nonnative species (such as zebra mussels first confirmed in the lake in 1993).

CHAMP

In common with many other deep lakes, especially the famous Loch Ness in Scotland, Lake Champlain's history is replete with reported sightings of a large elusive sea creature. Newspaper accounts of the creature, which began in 1819 with a report in the *Plattsburgh Republican*, continue into the 21st century. The mysterious creature, nicknamed Champ, has become a tourist attraction and part of the lore of the lake. It is featured in the logos and names of businesses, serves as a mascot for the Vermont Expos minor league baseball team, and is the focus of a children's book.

See also NEW FRANCE.

America's Historic Lakes, http://www.historiclakes.org

Lake Champlain Basin Program. *The Lake Champlain Atlas* (Grand Isle, Vt: Author, 1999)

———, http://www.lcbp.org

Lake Champlain Committee. *Essays on Lake Champlain* (Burlington, Vt: Author, 1988)

Versteeg, Jennie G., ed. *Lake Champlain: Reflections on Our Past* (Burlington, Vt: Center for Research on Vermont, 1987)

Richard S. Kujawa

Lake Champlain ferries. The long, narrow character of Lake Champlain gave rise to cross-lake transport from the earliest days of settlement. The first ferries were little more than crude rowboats or canoes, used primarily by owners for their own purposes. Those who entered the business of transporting people and goods early on did so simply because they happened to live at strategic sites along the lakeshore. With the rapid increase in settlement after the Revolution, however, ferries became more formalized and required charters from the New York State or Vermont legislatures.

In the 1820s horsepowered ferries were introduced at a number of crossings, augmenting the small sail- and rowboats already in use. Sail and steam-powered ferries evolved toward the end of that century. The first steamboat used as a Lake Champlain ferry was the *General Greene*, put in service between Burlington, Vt, and Port Kent (Essex Co) in 1825. The earliest documented horsepowered ferry was *Experiment*, which traveled between Chimney Point, Vt, and Port Henry (Essex Co) beginning in 1826. Until about 1860, 10 such horseboats operated on the lake. Sail ferries, which stepped their masts on the gunwale, operated on the lake until the early 20th century and featured flat bottoms, a design that allowed them to sail in either direction, and steering was provided by an oar placed at either end of the boat. With their masts on the side of the boat, the sail ferries provided an open deck space for wagons. In the early 20th century the ferries that survived the building of the Crown Point Bridge (1929) and Rouses Point Bridge (1936) adapted to the less costly internal combustion engine.

As of 2003 four ferry crossings operated across Lake Champlain, traveling on long-established routes. The crossing between Larrabee's Point, Vt, and Ticonderoga (Essex Co) operated from May through October and used a cable to guide a tugboat-powered barge across the passage. Further north, the Lake Champlain Transportation Co crossing between Charlotte, Vt, and Essex (Essex Co) was recently transformed from seasonal to year-round, and the Burlington–Port Kent ferry operated as a seasonal crossing from May through October. The Cumberland Head (Essex Co)–Grand Isle, Vt, ferry route evolved since 1976 into a dynamic year-round link in the regional transportation system, moving almost a million vehicles across Lake Champlain each year.

Crisman, Kevin, and Arthur B. Cohn. *When Horses Walked on Water: Horse-powered Ferries in 19th-Century America* (Washington, DC: Smithsonian Institution, 1999)

Ross, Ogden J. *The Steamboats of Lake Champlain, 1809–1930* (Quechee, Vt: Vermont Heritage Press, 1997)

Arthur B. Cohn

lake effect snow. A major feature of winter in areas east or downwind of Lakes Erie and Ontario is lake effect snow (LES). Cold air masses from the north and west pass over the relatively warm waters of the lakes, which impart heat and moisture to the air. Heating from below destabilizes the air mass, leading to rising air, clouds, and precipitation. Ascent is also enhanced by friction as the air moves from water to land. The intensity of LES depends heavily on three major factors. First is the temperature difference between the relatively warm surface of the lake and the colder low-level air traveling across it; greater temperature differences lead to greater instability in the air mass and more intense snowfall. Second is low-level wind direction; precipitation is greatest when the wind is aligned with the east-west axes of the lakes, carrying air over longer stretches of water. Third is the height of the stable layer of overlaying warm air, or capping inversion, beneath which clouds form; the higher the capping inversion, the thicker the clouds and the more intense the resultant snowfall. LES is often deposited in narrow geographic bands, leaving neighboring areas unaffected. Lightning and thunder are not uncommon.

LES is most common during the late fall and early winter months, when the water-air temperature contrast is greatest. Areas downwind of Lake Ontario, which almost never freezes, have a longer LES season, contributing to average seasonal snowfall topping 200 inches (508 cm) in eastern Oswego and western Lewis Cos. Lake Erie is much shallower and often freezes over, inhibiting production of LES during the late winter; nonetheless, portions of Erie and Chautauqua Cos experience snowfall averaging 150 inches (381 cm) or more. In records compiled between 1971 and 1999, the four largest cities in the LES belt recorded the following average seasonal snowfalls: Syracuse, 121 inches (307 cm); Watertown, 113 inches (287 cm); Rochester, 100 inches (254 cm); and Buffalo, 97 inches (246 cm). In 1976–77 the hamlet of Hooker (Lewis Co) set the state record for seasonal snowfall at 467 inches (1,186 cm), and the mark for a single month, 192 inches (488 cm), was established at Bennett Bridges (Oswego Co) in January 1978. In recent years there have been several significant episodes of LES. On 11–12 Jan 1997, Montague (Lewis Co) experienced 77 inches (196 cm) of snowfall in a 24-hour period, an unofficial record. Between 24 Dec 2001 and 1 Jan 2002, 81 inches (206 cm) or more fell in Buffalo and 127 inches (323 cm) in Montague. An LES event on 28–31 Jan 2004 dropped 86 inches (218 cm) of snow on Parish (Oswego Co) and 22 inches (56 cm) on Syracuse, with precipitation of 1 foot (.3 m) or more stretching in a band from the Rochester area to eastern Oneida Co.

National Climatic Data Center. *Storm Data* (1959–)

National Weather Service Forecast Office, Buffalo. "Lake Effect Weather Page," http://www.erh.noaa.gov/buf/lakeeffect/indexlk.html

Scott Rochette

Lake Erie (9,910 mi²/25,667 km²). The fourth largest of the Great Lakes, Lake Erie is 241 miles (388 km) long and 30–57 miles (48–92 km) wide. Its surface area makes it the 11th largest lake in the world. Approximately 6% (554 mi²/1,435 km²) of its surface area lies within New York State. With a maximum depth of 210 feet (64 m), an average depth of 62 feet (19 m), and an elevation of 569 feet (173 m), it is the shallowest of the Great Lakes and the only one with no point below sea level. Slightly larger in area than Lake Ontario, it contains only one-fourth as much water. It is fed from Lake Huron via the Detroit River, Lake St. Clair, and the St. Clair River, and it drains into Lake Ontario via the Niagara River. Lake Erie is the warmest and the most biologically fertile of the Great Lakes. It freezes in winter and accounts for high snowfall along its leeward shore, especially in the Appalachian Upland, south of Buffalo. The lake's shores are soft and unstable, and because it has no natural deepwater harbors, artificial harbors have been built at Buffalo and Dunkirk (Chautauqua Co).

In prehistoric times, the site contained an east-

Whitecaps along Lake Erie shoreline, early 20th century.

ward-flowing river. Ice Age glaciers scoured the valley into a lake basin and then filled it in as they melted. The original lake, blocked to the north by remaining glaciers, was 200 feet (61 m) deeper than it is today and drained southward through the Maumee River. Drainage shifted to the Niagara River as the glaciers continued to recede.

Exploration and War

In the 17th century the Erie, the tribe for whom the lake was named, and the Huron were displaced by the Iroquois from the northern and southern shores of Lake Erie. Subsequently, the Wyandot (a Huron group) settled along the western shore of the lake in the early 1700s. Erie was the last of the Great Lakes to be explored by the French, who—to avoid the Iroquois and to get to Lake Huron—long favored the northern route via the Ottawa River and Lake Nipissing. The first recorded European visitor was Louis Jolliet, who in 1669 entered Lake Erie from the Detroit River and followed the north shore eastward. An early French name was Lac du Chat (Lake of the Cat), actually a reference to the abundant raccoons.

The first ship on Lake Erie, and on the Great Lakes, was the *Griffon,* which René-Robert Cavelier de la Salle had built on the Niagara River in 1679 and then used in his search of the upper lakes for furs and the Northwest Passage. As the French neglected it, English traders came to Lake Erie and began to divert the fur trade south from the French outpost on the Straits of Mackinac. Frequent disputes between the French and English eventually led to the French and Indian War (1754–63), with a young George Washington's skirmish with French scouts outside Fort Le Boeuf [now Waterford, Pa] being one of several incidents that sparked the conflict. After the war, Detroit became the principal English stronghold in the west. Beginning in the 1760s local American Indians launched a series of wars to hinder European settlement of the area. Shipwrights from what is now Oswego Co came to the Niagara River to build two 80-ton (73 MT) schooners, the first ships to sail Erie since the *Griffon,* to supply the besieged Fort Detroit during Pontiac's War in 1763. The English, who kept Forts Detroit and Niagara until 1796, encouraged Indian raids both during and after the American Revolution. After the War of 1812 the United States and Great Britain entered into the Rush-Bagot agreement of 1817 to demilitarize the Great Lakes. This symbolized the final abandonment of British efforts to hinder US expansion toward the west, and settlement along the lakeshore accelerated.

Shipping and Commerce

In the postwar period, Lake Erie was destined to become a focal point of shipping and commerce in the Great Lakes region once the obstacle of Niagara Falls could be overcome. The solution came with the opening of numerous canals. The completion of the Erie Canal in 1825 connected the lake at Buffalo to the Hudson River; the opening of the Welland Canal in Upper Canada [now Ont] in 1829 connected it to Lake Ontario; and canals linking the Ohio River to the lake at Cleveland in 1832 and at Toledo in 1845 opened the interior of Ohio to New York State markets.

The first steamer on Lake Erie, the 330-ton (299 MT) *Walk-in-the-Water,* was built in 1818 at Black Rock [now in Erie Co]. The lake, shallow and turbulent, was less favorable to wind-powered craft than was nearby Lake Ontario, and steamships quickly came to dominate the passenger trade. The flow of passengers to the Midwest swelled with the opening of the Erie Canal and even more with the arrival of rail service between Albany and Buffalo in 1842. In the 1850s many steamships exceeded 1,000 tons (907 MT); the *City of Buffalo,* built in 1857 at 2,200 tons (1,996 MT), was said to rival ocean-going vessels in size and elegance. Although the prevalence of railroads after the mid–19th century had gradually diminished the importance of the Port of Buffalo, it was not until the opening of the expanded Welland Canal in 1932 and the St. Lawrence Seaway in 1959 that Buffalo's role as a transshipment center came to an end. Ships could now sail directly between the upper lakes and the ocean. Iron ore, coal, and grain remained the principal cargoes.

Fisheries and Environment

Lake Erie's shallow waters warm quickly in the spring and summer, contributing to its biological productivity. Commercial fishing was well established by the mid-1800s, but by the 1880s signs of distress became apparent. The commercially desirable whitefish and sturgeon were nearly depleted by the 1920s. The herring catch, 32.2 million pounds (14.6 million kg) in 1924, collapsed to 5.7 million pounds (2.6 million kg) in 1925 and never recovered. Studies at the time attributed the decline primarily to overfishing and secondarily to pollution. Fishers also discovered Lake Erie's first lamprey, an invasive species that would have a devastating impact on the major commercial species. The Lake Erie herring collapse stimulated biological research and the first multistate/binational conservation efforts on the Great Lakes, although effective collaboration was not achieved at that time. As the most desirable catches declined, fishers turned to rough fish that could be sold for fish meal, oil, or fertilizer. After 1935 rainbow smelt, an invasive species, became the most abundant forage fish for local predators, fulfilling the former ecological role of the herring.

As early as the 1920s researchers issued warnings about pollution in Lake Erie, where, because of its shallow waters, human, agricultural, and industrial waste had a concentrated impact. By the 1950s phosphorus from laundry detergents and other nutrients from industrial and agricultural runoff were producing enormous algae blooms, which, when they died and decayed, created offensive odors and depleted the water's oxygen supply (eutrophication). With some exaggeration, environmentalists declared Lake Erie "dead" in the early 1970s.

In response, the United States and Canada signed the Great Lakes Water Quality Agreement (GLWQA) in 1972 to control the flow of nutrients into the lakes. Because of growing concern with industrial contaminants, comprising those that accumulate in fish, the GLWQA was amended in 1978 to include eliminating toxic substances in the water, such as dioxins, furans, PCBs, mercury, and DDT. By the late 1980s the lake was healthier than it had been in decades, and recreational fishing for walleye and smallmouth bass was becoming more popular. Lake trout, a coldwater fish, was never abundant in Lake Erie but found a niche in the lake's eastern basin near New York State, which now actively stocks trout. While whitefish managed to recover their numbers through diet adaptation, reductions in the numbers of forage fish, because of reduced phosphorus levels, may threaten the continued recovery of the more commercially desirable predators.

In the late 1990s Lake Erie suffered from renewed algae blooms and eutrophication. This time the problem was not industry but zebra mussels, which consume enormous amounts of phytoplankton (depriving many other species of food) and then produce wastes high in phosphorus. Other recent problems are the fishhook water flea, an invasive species that consumes zooplankton, and an outbreak in 2000 of avian botulism, which killed hundreds of waterfowl. To combat these problems and to search for remedies, the New York State Department of Environmental Conservation monitors fish populations from a station at Dunkirk (Chautauqua Co).

Ashworth, William. *The Late, Great Lakes: An Environmental History* (New York: Knopf, 1988)
Bogue, Margaret Beattie. *Fishing the Great Lakes: An Environmental History, 1783–1933* (Madison: Univ of Wisconsin Press, 2000)
Hatcher, Harlan. *Lake Erie* (Indianapolis: Bobbs-Merrill, 1945)

Scott C. Monje

Lake Erie Beach. Locality (pop 4,499) in Evans (Erie Co). Developed in the 1920s, Lake Erie Beach was originally a summer resort. The Home Guardian Co of New York City divided farms near the lake into small lots, advertised them in Buffalo newspapers, and sold hundreds. Primarily constructed for summer occupancy, most homes were later winterized, and Lake Erie Beach is now a year-round residential community.

Andrew C. Maines

Lake George (44.4 mi^2/115 km^2). A glacial lake within the Adirondack Park along the northeast border of New York State. The lake is spring and brook fed, 32 miles (51.5 km) long, with a depth up to 195 feet (59.4 m), a maximum width of 3 miles (4.8 km), and over 107 miles (172.2 km) of shoreline. Without navigable inlets or outlets, it is 316 feet (96.3 m) above sea level.

In May 1646, on the eve of the Feast of Corpus Christi, the first European, Jesuit missionary Isaac Jogues, arrived here and named the lake Lac du Saint Sacrement (Lake of the Blessed Sacrament). A strategic component of the corridor between New York City and Montreal, the lake was the scene of many battles during the French and Indian War and the American Revolution. Sir William Johnson defeated the French in the Battle of Lake George (1755). Following the battle, Johnson built Fort William Henry (Warren Co) at the southern end of the lake, which he renamed Lake George to honor King George II of England. The British were besieged and defeated in 1757 by Marquis de Montcalm's troops, depicted in James Fenimore Cooper's novel *The Last of the Mohicans* (1826). In the Battle of Ticonderoga (1758), British Maj Gen James Abercromby gathered 16,000 troops at the southern end of the lake and launched an unsuccessful attack on French forces at Fort Carillon (Essex Co), renamed Fort Ticonderoga when the British captured it in 1759. During the American Revolution, the fort was captured by the Americans in 1775 and retaken by the British in 1777.

Small towns and hotels began to appear along the Lake George shoreline by 1800. Early settlers came here for the hunting and fishing, and soon they began developing the region's lumber and tourist resources. Steamboat travel started in 1817 when the Lake George Steamboat Co's *James Caldwell* began ferrying passengers from Caldwell [now Lake George, Warren Co] to Ticonderoga (Essex Co) as part of the important transportation link between New York City and Montreal. The Lake George Steamboat Co is the oldest continually operating transportation company in the United States. Beginning in 1882 the Delaware and Hudson Railroad provided service to Lake George. By 1900 wealthy visitors built luxurious summer estates along a 10 mi (16 km) stretch on the lake's western shoreline between Caldwell and Bolton Landing (Warren Co), giving this shoreline the name Millionaires' Row. Many of these mansions still stand, although their acreage has been subdivided many times to make room for motels, summer homes, and marinas. The Sagamore Hotel on Green Island near Bolton Landing, first opened in 1883 and rebuilt since because of fires, is the last of the grand old hotels on the lake. Construction began on the third Sagamore Hotel on the site during the 1920s.

The Lake George region became easily accessible during the 1960s with the completion of the Northway and is a popular resort area offering many forms of recreation year-round. The lake contains nearly 200 islands, 17 private and the remainder owned by New York State, which manages approximately 387 campsites on 44 islands. Issues of concern include Eurasian milfoil, an invasive species of aquatic plant first discovered in the lake in 1985, and zebra mussels, which were discovered in the lake in 1999.

Lake George, depicting a view of Tongue Mountain Range on Northwest Bay, by John Frederick Kensett, 1869.

See also RESORT HOTELS.

Smith, H. P. *History of Warren County* (Syracuse: D. Mason, 1885)

William Preston Gates

Lake George. Town (pop 3,578) and village (pop 985) in E Warren Co. Settled before the Revolutionary War, the town was formed from Queensbury, Bolton, and Thurman in 1810 as Caldwell. The name did not change to Lake George until 1962. The town was the site of Fort William Henry (1755–57) and other fortifications, and of the Battle of Lake George (September 1755). In 1780 James Caldwell of Albany began to promote settlement on his Lake George lands, and the locality grew as a shipping depot for lumber and other goods being sent to Ticonderoga. Tourists began visiting for the scenery and the sportfishing, leaving early residents saying that they lived "on fish and strangers." A steamboat was placed on the lake in 1817, but freight service fell into disuse with the opening of the Glens Falls Feeder Canal in 1832. The Village of Lake George served as the county seat from 1815 to 1963. The Fort William Henry Hotel (1855), the Prospect Mountain House (1877), and the inclined railway on Prospect (1895–1903) encouraged tourism, as did the extension of the railroad from Glens Falls (1882). In addition to hotels and cottages, a group of lakefront estates were built during the Gilded Age. The post office was renamed from Caldwell to Lake George in 1871, and the village incorporated under its present name in 1903. Despite changes in style, Lake George's tourist business thrived through the 20th century and into the 21st, becoming year-round with the development of a winter sports program in 1934. Attractions include Fort William Henry (reconstruction, 1954), Veterans Memorial Highway (1969), excursions of the Lake George Steamboat Co, the Million Dollar Beach, and the Lake George Submerged Heritage Preserve, underwater remains of historic vessels designated by the state for visits by divers.

Marilyn J. Van Dyke

Lake George, Battle of. In 1755 Great Britain planned to seize the French-held Fort St. Frédéric at Crown Point on Lake Champlain in present-day Essex Co. In September 1755 Maj Gen William Johnson assembled 2,300 New York and New England militia and their Mohawk allies on Lac St. Sacrement, which Johnson renamed Lake George. He assembled another 500 troops on the Hudson River at Fort Lyman, later renamed Fort Edward [now in Washington Co]. Meanwhile, Baron Jean-Armand Dieskau, the French commander in Canada, massed over 3,000 French regulars, Canadian militia, and Indians at Ticonderoga [now in Essex Co], south of Crown Point. Deciding to strike Fort Lyman to disrupt Johnson's supply lines, Dieskau advanced south along Lake Champlain with over 1,500 troops and approached his objective by 7 September. Dieskau's Indian allies proved reluctant to assault the recently reinforced fort, so he decided to attack Johnson's army encamped at Lake George.

Johnson detected the French advance and sent 1,200 men to support Fort Lyman on the morning of 8 September. Dieskau ambushed them, inflicting heavy losses, and the survivors fled back to Johnson's camp. The French general tried to pursue, but the victory had disorganized his troops. When he regained control and advanced to Lake George, Johnson had organized a defense. Dieskau's regulars attacked, but after several hours of fighting Johnson's artillery and musket fire shattered the French forces. Around dusk the French retreated, leaving behind their wounded commander. Johnson, also wounded, did not pursue. As the French force regrouped at the site of the morning's ambush, 200 troops from Fort Lyman, marching to Johnson's aid, struck them. The French suffered heavy casualties, scattered, and retreated to Ticonderoga. Throughout the three engagements, Johnson lost 331 men, with 223 dead. The French had 149 killed, 163 wounded, and 27 captured, including Dieskau. Following the battle Johnson built Fort William Henry on Lake George, and the French built Fort Carillon at Ticonderoga. Although Johnson failed to drive the French out of Crown Point, he secured an important victory for British morale.

Anderson, Fred. *Crucible of War: The Seven Years' War and the Fate of Empire in British North America, 1754–1766* (New York: Knopf, 2000)
Steele, Ian K. *Betrayals: Fort William Henry and the "Massacre"* (New York: Oxford Univ Press, 1990)

Michael P. Gabriel

Lake George Steamboat Company. The first steamboat company on Lake George was chartered by the New York State legislature on 15 Apr 1817, with James Caldwell and John Winans among the directors. The first steamer, the 80 ft (24.4 m) *James Caldwell,* was completed at Ticonderoga (Essex Co) in 1817 and operated until 1819, when the vessel burned at its dock at the southern end of the lake. There were several discontinuous periods of service during the first 37 years, but four steamboats, the *Mountaineer, William Caldwell, John Jay,* and *Minne-Ha-Ha,* plied the lake before the company was fully acquired by the Champlain Transportation Co in 1868. That same year the Champlain company was itself taken over by the Rensselaer and Saratoga Railroad, and in 1871 all the company's assets were leased to the Delaware and Hudson Canal Co (later Delaware and Hudson Railroad Co). Four wooden steamboats were placed in service from 1869 to 1895: the *Ganouskie, Horicon I, Ticonderoga I,* and *Mohican I.* Three steel-hulled steamboats—the *Sagamore, Mohican II,* and *Horicon II*—were launched from 1902 to 1911 and were operated successfully by the company until the Great Depression. In 1939, with only the *Mohican II* in service, Delaware and Hudson sold the remaining assets to Capt George Stafford. In 1945 the downsized steamboat company was purchased by Wilbur E. Dow Jr, who revived the company as a tourist attraction (still in operation in 2003), by modernizing the *Mohican II* and by adding the 168 ft (51.2 m) *Ticonderoga II,* a former naval vessel. In 1969 the company built the 103 ft (31.4 m) *Minne Ha-Ha II* and added the 190 ft (57.9 m) *Lac du Saint Sacrement* in 1989.

Bellico, Russell P. *Sails and Steam in the Mountains: A Maritime and Military History of Lake George and Lake Champlain,* 2d ed. (Fleischmanns, NY: Purple Mountain Press, 2001)

Russell P. Bellico

Lake Grove. Village (pop 10,250) in Brookhaven (Suffolk Co). The landmark New Village Congregational Church (1817) was the nucleus of this village on Middle Country Rd, which acquired a post office named New Village in 1831. Called Ronkonkoma from 1866 to 1870, it was renamed Lake Grove. The population more than tripled in the 1960s, from 2,253 to 8,133. The Smithaven Mall, built in 1968, lies partly in the village and helped stimulate its incorporation the same year. The former Gould Feed Co (1873), which served duck farmers, became the village hall.

Luise Weiss

Lake Luzerne. Town (pop 3,219) in S central Warren Co. Settled *ca* 1765, the town was formed from Queensbury in 1792 as Fairfield; the name was changed to Luzerne in 1808 and to Lake Luzerne in 1963. By 1820 lumbering and hemlock-bark harvesting were conducted on a large scale. Thomas Garner and Co (1867–1905) produced sheepskin for binderies. The first pulp mill in America using American-made machinery was built by Albrecht Pagenstacher in 1869. The resort industry began with Rockwell's Hotel (1832), and the Wayside Inn (1869) was among the most prominent. The town was the site of the East's first dude ranch; six were operating in the mid-1960s. The Ketchum Manufacturing Co (1922) produces ear tags for animals. The Luzerne Music Festival is an annual summer event, and the Pulp Mill Museum and Frances G. Kinnear Museum interpret the community's history.

Marilyn J. Van Dyke

Lake Ontario (7,600 mi²/19,684 km²). Easternmost and smallest of the Great Lakes. Of Lake Ontario's surface area, 3,446 miles² (8,925 km²) are in New York and the rest in Canada. It ranks 12th in area among the natural freshwater lakes of the world. Lake Ontario is 193 miles (311 km) long and 53 miles (85 km) at its greatest width, with a maximum depth of 802 feet (244 m) and an average depth of 283 feet (86 m). Its surface elevation is 246 feet (75 m), and its lowest point lies 556 feet (169 m) below sea level. It is fed primarily by the waters of Lake Erie via the Niagara River and drained by the St. Lawrence River. Other tributaries in New York are the Genesee, Oswego, and Black Rivers, with the communities of Rochester and Oswego, historically, its principal ports. The lake, which never freezes, has a moderating effect on climate that sustains a substantial fruit belt, but it also generates significant snow squalls in winter.

Origins

The lake basin most likely began as the western extension of the St. Lawrence Valley. Ice Age glaciers ground it into a lake basin, carrying away shale and sandstone and depositing it as till. The initial lake (Lake Iroquois) covered large portions of New York State; it shrank to its present size as the receding glacier allowed the water to drain northeastward, reforming the St. Lawrence River.

Exploration and War

When the first Europeans arrived, Lake Ontario was dominated by the Iroquois Confederacy to the south and by the Huron League to the north. Etienne Brulé and Samuel de Champlain explored the lake in 1615. The French built Fort Frontenac [now Kingston, Ont] in 1673 and Fort Niagara [now in Porter, Niagara Co] in 1678 to control access to the fur region, although fur traders preferred the northern route, via the Ottawa River, through the 17th century. In 1722 the English built a trading post and in 1727 a fort at Oswego, which established their only foothold on Lake Ontario for nearly 40 years, which in turn created a commercial and military rival out of Frontenac.

The lake's importance to the 18th-century fur trade ensured it a role in the French and Indian Wars. In 1756 and 1758, Oswego and Frontenac were destroyed. British troops reoccupied Oswego and seized Niagara in 1759. Oswego became a rallying point for loyalists during the American Revolution and, in 1777, the starting point for British Gen Barry St. Leger's advance toward Albany. The British refused to abandon Oswego, Niagara, or other frontier outposts until 1796, 13 years after the war had ended. Following the War of 1812, Lake Ontario was never again a strategic factor in military operations. The Rush-Bagot agreement of 1817 effectively demilitarized the Great Lakes, although the United States briefly threatened to revoke it in 1865 because of cross-border raids by Confederate guerrillas based in Canada.

Shipping and Commerce

Early travel was by canoe and bateau. In 1755 the *Oswego,* a war sloop, was the first sailing ship on Ontario and the second on the Great Lakes. The first steamboats on the Great Lakes were the *Frontenac* in 1816, from Kingston, and the *Ontario* in 1817, from Sackets Harbor. The latter served Lewiston (Niagara Co), Oswego, and Ogdensburg (St. Lawrence Co). Sailing by wind, however, was not especially problematic, and the full transition to steam progressed very slowly. The progression was hastened by the opening of the Welland Canal in 1829 through Canada, which allowed freight and passengers from the upper lakes to bypass Niagara Falls. Nevertheless, it was 40 years from the first launchings before steam dominated Lake Ontario.

The lake enabled early settlers in western New York State to ship their potash, wheat, pork, and whiskey to Montreal, but some resented the loss of trade to American markets, and memories of the War of 1812 made others reluctant to rely on the British-controlled route. In addition, two events in the 1820s hindered the development of US shipping on the lake. With the Canada Trade Act of 1822, the British Parliament placed restrictions on US shipping on the St. Lawrence River, cutting off the lake's outlet to Montreal and the sea. In 1825 the Erie Canal captured the trade of Western New York (and the Midwest via the Port of Buffalo) and funneled it away from the lake to the Hudson River, although a branch came to Lake Ontario via Oswego.

Most US shipping was limited to carrying grain, salt, timber, and passengers between one Lake Ontario port and another. Canadians and Americans were granted equal access to all the lakes and the St. Lawrence in 1871, but by then railroads had captured most of the traffic in both countries, and the New York port trade began to decline. One exception was coal; Pennsylvania coal was carried to Canada from Rochester, Oswego, Sodus Point (Wayne Co), and Fair Haven (Cayuga Co) into the 1960s. The opening of the Welland Canal in 1931–32 and of the St.

Lawrence Seaway in 1959 increased shipping on the lake, but most of it carried steel, iron ore, grain, and other bulk cargoes between the upper lakes and the Atlantic without stopping at any Lake Ontario port. New York manufacturers never relied heavily on the lake for transportation, and cross-lake passenger service ended in 1950.

By the 1990s the Port of Oswego was the only active deepwater port on the New York shore, handling aluminum ingots, fertilizer, cement, road salt, materials for recycling, and heavy machinery. The Port of Rochester has been rebuilt for the launching of a Rochester-Toronto fast ferry.

Fisheries and Environment

In the 1800s Lake Ontario offered commercial fishers whitefish, trout, herring, sturgeon, and one of the world's largest reservoirs of freshwater Atlantic salmon. Many of these varieties were seriously depleted during the 19th century because of overfishing, the construction of mill dams on spawning streams, pollution, deforestation, and habitat destruction. Invasive species—introduced through canals, fish-stocking operations, and later the ballast water of ships—competed with native species for food. Most notable among invasive species, the alewife proved poisonous to Atlantic salmon when eaten, and the sea lamprey became a predator of many food fish. By 1898 the Atlantic salmon population had completely died out, and as the preferred fishing species were depleted, fishers turned to herring, but they too were in decline by the early 1900s. In addition, the lake trout population collapsed between 1930 and 1960.

Since the late 20th century, whitefish taken mainly in eastern Canadian waters has been the principal commercial catch. After several fluctuations, only a remnant whitefish population survived in the 1960s and 1970s, but by the 1980s they had recovered. The population peaked in 1993 (at twice the level of 1900) and then declined again apparently because of competition from new invasive species, particularly zebra and quagga mussels. The alewife became the most prominent species in the lake. The sea lamprey eventually suffered from pollution, the collapse of the populations they preyed on, and control efforts with chemical poisons.

By the 1960s phosphorus from laundry detergents and from municipal, industrial, and agricultural runoff sustained huge algal blooms on the lake. These masses proliferated along two-thirds of the shoreline to the west of Rochester and 79% of the shoreline to the east. When they died, they decayed and depleted the water of oxygen (eutrophication). Normal aquatic life, except carp and white perch, almost disappeared near highly populated and industrial areas. This phenomenon prompted the United States and Canada in 1972 to sign the Great Lakes Water Quality Agreement (GLWQA) to control the flow of nutrients into the lakes. Because of growing concern with industrial contaminants, including those that accumulate in fish, the GLWQA was amended in 1978 to include a focus on eliminating toxic substances in the water, such as dioxins, furans, PCBs, mercury, and DDT. Subsequently, there were substantial improvements in the quality of offshore and nearshore waters, but eutrophication continues as a problem in tributaries, bays, and marshes—the most visible and often recreational areas—because of nonpoint sources of pollution. New York State and Ontario monitor toxic substances in fish and advise against consuming certain varieties.

Early efforts to restore Atlantic salmon populations to sustain commercial fishing commenced in the 1870s but were largely ineffective. Carp were introduced, but they proved unpopular and their foraging disturbed the habitats of other species. In the 1960s New York State and Ontario began stocking Pacific salmon (primarily chinook and coho) as well as brown, steelhead, and lake trout to support sportfishing and succeeded in creating an important recreational fishery. Most of these fish come from the Salmon River Hatchery in Oswego Co. Sportfishing on Lake Ontario peaked in the early 1990s and then declined. Stocking had to be reduced because of smaller numbers of forage fish, especially alewives. Ironically, reduced phosphorus levels since the 1970s have led to a decline in zooplankton and, consequently, in fish production in the lake. After 25 years of stocking, salmon and especially trout began to show some signs of sustaining a natural population.

Ashworth, William. *The Late, Great Lakes: An Environmental History* (New York: Knopf, 1986)

Bogue, Margaret Beattie. *Fishing the Great Lakes: An Environmental History, 1783–1933* (Madison: Univ of Wisconsin Press, 2000)

Great Lakes Information Network, http://www.greatlakes.net

Makarewicz, Joseph C. *New York's North Coast: A Troubled Coastline: Lake Ontario Embayments Initiative* (Penn Yan, NY: Finger Lakes–Lake Ontario Watershed Protection Alliance, 2000)

Scott C. Monje

Lake Placid. Village (pop 2,638) in North Elba (Essex Co). Lake Placid remained undeveloped until the 1840s. In 1852 the Nash House opened to cater to tourists, and by the 1870s a number of hotels were established. The grandest was the Lake Placid Club (1895–1980), which initiated a winter season based on skiing and skating in 1904. The village was chosen to host the 1932 and 1980 Winter Olympics; the Olympic Training Center, operated year-round to develop Olympic-class athletes, continues the village's involvement in Olympic competition. In the early 21st century Lake Placid remains a renowned resort and center for winter sports.

Thomas A. Rumney

Lake Placid Winter Olympics 1932. The first Olympic Winter Games held in the United States took place in Lake Placid (Essex Co), a village famed for its winter resort facilities, from 4 Feb to 15 Feb 1932. Godfrey Dewey, son of Lake Placid Club founder Melvil Dewey, first lobbied to bring the Olympics to Lake Placid. While attending the 1928 Winter Games in St. Moritz, Switzerland, Dewey managed the US ski team, carried the American flag at the opening ceremony, and researched how the event was administered. He returned convinced that his community could organize the Winter Games, and in July 1928 a local chamber of commerce guaranteed a bond of $50,000 to support the bid. Despite bids by others, including Yosemite Valley, Calif, and Montreal, Lake Placid's skiing and skating facilities, as well as its building plans, impressed International Olympic Committee members, who awarded Lake Placid the Third Olympic Winter Games in 1929. Dewey had gained the support of Gov Franklin D. Roosevelt, who signed a bill authorizing the state to build a bobsled run on private lands if Lake Placid were awarded the Winter Olympics. Roosevelt also helped acquire additional state funds; most of the $1.05 million cost of the games came from the state legislature. At Mt Van Hoevenberg, on land owned by the Dewey family, Lake Placid built the first US bobsled run. A 60 m ski jump and an indoor skating arena, a Winter Olympic first, were also constructed.

In a speech calling for world peace, Gov Roosevelt officially opened the Games, which featured 252 athletes from 17 nations. Controversy brewed among Europeans when the International Skating Union decided to run the speed skating events in the North American pack racing style. Lake Placid native Jack Shea won the 500 m and 1,500 m races, and the Bronx's Irving Jaffee won the 5,000 m and 10,000 m races. Both American bobsledding teams also won golds. The two-man team consisted of Lake Placid's Curtis and Hubert Stevens, and the four-man team included Eddie Eagan, who had won a gold medal in boxing at the 1920 Olympics and remains the only person to win gold medals in both the Winter and Summer Olympics. The United States won 6 gold medals out of 14 events; Norway followed in second with 3, including Sonja Henie's gold in women's figure skating. Final paid attendance for the Games was slightly over 58,000. Although they were small in scope, and depression and political instability in Europe and Asia affected attendance, the 1932 Winter Olympics were successful in establishing Lake Placid as one of the world's leading centers for winter sports competition and furthered its reputation as a winter resort. After the Games were completed, world championships in skating, skiing, and bobsledding, and collegiate hockey championships were held at its facilities. The Winter Olympics returned to Lake Placid in 1980.

Flags and the Olympic torch for the 1980 Winter Olympics at Lake Placid.

Buchanan, Ian, and Bill Mallon. *Historical Dictionary of the Olympic Movement,* 2d ed. (Lanham, Md: Scarecrow Press, 2001)

Ortloff, George Christian, and Stephen C. Ortloff. *Lake Placid: The Olympic Years, 1932–1980* (Lake Placid, NY: Macromedia, 1976)

Bill Mallon

Lake Placid Winter Olympics 1980. The Village of Lake Placid (Essex Co) hosted its second Olympics in February 1980. More than 500,000 people visited, spending an average of $125 a day. Over 1,000 athletes from 37 countries participated. This included the Soviet Union, despite international tensions over the Soviet invasion of Afghanistan the previous year. Several athletes excelled, including American speed skater Eric Heiden, who won five gold medals, setting a world record in the 10,000 m race and Olympic records in the 500 m, 1,000 m, 1,500 m, and 5,000 m races. Both ski jumping events set Olympic records: Austria's Anton Innauer jumped 266.3 meters from the 70 m hill, and Finland's Jouko Törmänen jumped 271 meters from the 90 m hill. Alpine skier Ingemar Stenmark won two gold medals for Sweden, and skier Hanni Wenzel won two golds for Liechtenstein. Overall the Soviet Union won 10 gold medals, including 3 from cross-country skier Nikolai Zimatov, and East Germany won 9. The United States won six gold medals: five by Heiden and one by the Miracle on Ice hockey team.

Lake Placid's athletic and tourist facilities were expanded and upgraded for the Olympics, including the construction of two new arenas and renovation of the ski jump venues and the luge run. Estimates of the cost of the preparations run as high as $170 million. In 1981 the legislature created the New York State Olympic Regional Development Authority to improve and manage the Olympic facilities, and a US Olympic training center was established in Lake Placid in 1982. Hundreds of athletes, both American and foreign, train at the Olympic venues. The Olympic rink has been used by the Buffalo Sabres, Ottawa Senators, and New York Islanders of the National Hockey League as a preseason training base, and ice shows and other recreational attractions are held there. In February 2000 the Goodwill Winter Games were held in Lake Placid. In many ways, though, Lake Placid retains the character of a small village: during the snow season, the Olympic venues often are available to weekend athletes. Other Olympic facilities have been converted for alternate use, such as the Olympic Village in nearby Ray Brook, which was transformed into a medium-security prison.

The 1980 Olympics and subsequent events using the Lake Placid facilities, which are continually improved, made the area into a more popular tourist destination. The effects are felt throughout the region, in places such as Wilmington, Saranac Lake, Keene, Tupper Lake, and Paul Smiths, especially with limited accommodations in Lake Placid. Twenty years after the Olympic Games, with tourism expanded from a seasonal to a year-round enterprise, the Lake Placid area was drawing 700,000 visitors annually.

Lake Placid 80 (Salt Lake City, Utah: Sport and Culture USA, 1980)

Larry Felser

Lake Pleasant. Town (pop 876) in central Hamilton Co. Settled *ca* 1795, the town was formed in 1812 from Johnstown [now in Fulton Co]. It began as a community of small farmers, but the growing season was very short and in the late 19th century residents turned to shingle making and lumbering. Lake Pleasant hamlet (post office, 1820) has been the county seat since 1838 but was known as Sageville from 1844 to 1893. A state fish hatchery was created on Mill Creek in 1887. Tourism began with the Lake Pleasant Hotel (1845–1904) and, beginning in 1889, private cottages. In the early 21st century Lake Pleasant is a resort town.

Lake Ronkonkoma. See RONKONKOMA.

Lake Success. Village (pop 2,797) in North Hempstead (Nassau Co). Lake Success, a glacial kettle hole, is named from the Matinecock Indian word *Sacut,* meaning "at the outlet." Dutch settlers built an octagonal church in 1732. By the 1830s the village was known as Lakeville and was the site of the resort hotel Lake Ville House. The village was incorporated in 1926, although it had a mere 203 residents as late as 1940. The next year the Sperry Gyroscope plant was built, attracting new development. The plant became headquarters for the United Nations (UN) Secretariat and Security Council (1946–51), and was the site of such epochal events as the decision to create a Jewish state in Palestine and to commit UN forces to the Korean conflict. The village is now an upscale community bisected by the Northern State Parkway and the Long Island Expressway, permitting easy commuting, and has extensive corporate and medical offices. Asian Americans make up 15% of its population.

Georgina Martorella

Lakeview. Locality (pop 5,607) in Hempstead (Nassau Co). The area, known as Hempstead Swamp, was lightly settled through much of the 19th century, and by 1870 it was the site of the Woodfield railroad station. When made, Hempstead Lake was projected in 1873 to be a reservoir for the City of Brooklyn, but the project was a failure. The station's name was changed to Lake View about 1903. The area became home to commuters and to employees of the publishing firm Doubleday in nearby Garden City. Since the 1960s Lakeview has attracted many African American homeowners, who made up 85% of the population in 2000. Most of Hempstead Lake State Park is in Lakeview.

Georgina Martorella

Lakewood. Village (pop 3,258) in Busti (Chautauqua Co). Lakewood developed as a summer resort with the building of two large hotels along the lakeshore, the Cowing House (1870) and the Kent House (1875), and the establishment of a passenger station on the main line of the Erie Railroad; the village incorporated in 1893. With the rail link, the ice business became important but declined with the growth of refrigeration. Later, summer residents winterized their homes and others built new houses, giving the village a reputation for comfortable affluence as a suburb of Jamestown. A busy commercial corridor has developed along Rte 394 in the southern half of the village.

Helen Ebersole

Lamb, John (*b* New York City, 1 Jan 1735; *d* 31 May 1800). Militia leader, merchant, and politician. In the fall of 1765, Lamb helped organize the Sons of Liberty in New York City to oppose British revenue acts of the 1760s. In 1775, after learning of the skirmishes at Lexington and Concord in Massachusetts, Lamb and the Sons of Liberty seized New York City's customhouse and the British military stores at Turtle Bay in Manhattan. Lamb was commissioned a captain by the New York Provincial Congress in July and raised an artillery company for continental service under Brig Gen Richard Montgomery during the unsuccessful 1775 Quebec campaign. Wounded and captured during the battle, he was freed in a 1776 prisoner exchange and, on resuming military service, promoted to colonel. In October 1777, now in command of Forts Montgomery and Clinton (Orange Co), Lamb evacuated both as British forces advanced. He was

Ski jumps constructed for the 1980 Winter Olympics at Lake Placid.

commander of artillery under Benedict Arnold at West Point in 1779–80, unaware of Arnold's treason pertaining to the fortification plans. In 1781 Lamb served with Gen George Washington at the Battle of Yorktown and ended his service in New York. Lamb was later elected to the New York State Assembly and then served as collector of customs for the Port of New York. On behalf of his ally Gov George Clinton, Lamb led the opposition to New York's ratification of the US Constitution. Lamb was an officer of the Society of the Cincinnati and the Humane Society of the City of New York. After a clerk absconded with substantial customhouse assets, Lamb covered the losses and died impoverished.

Shannon, Dennis Michael. " 'Restless Genius': John Lamb and Revolutionary New York" (PhD diss, Univ of California, Berkeley, 1994)

Martin Bannan

Lancaster. Town (pop 39,019) and village (pop 11,188) in central Erie Co. Settled in 1803, the town was formed in 1833 from Clarence. Germans arrived *ca* 1830 and Irish *ca* 1850. The village was incorporated in 1849. Beginning in the early 1840s five east-west railroads were built across town. In the last half of the 19th century bedsteads, leather, and plows were produced. Glassblowers in Lancaster were active until 1904, and the Lane Industrial Glass Co produced glass mechanically from 1907 to 1965. Two electric railroads between 1893 and 1931 contributed to suburban growth. Scott Aviation was a major employer in the late 20th century. Landmarks include the Warren Hull House (*ca* 1810), thought to be the oldest "substantial masonry residence" in Erie Co, and the Town Hall/Opera House (1896).

Nancy B. Mingus

land companies and patents. The process by which most land in New York State was transferred from government to private hands involves an interesting contradiction. With the notable exception of the New Military Tract, most of New York State was deeded in large patents to individuals, partnerships, or land companies. This process was nearly complete by 1800. Yet by the mid–19th century, except for the nonarable tracts in the Adirondacks and the Tug Hill and Appalachian Plateaus, most land in the state was held by small-scale farming families, and few people had made fortunes from large-scale landholdings. The colonial manor lords are a partial exception to this generalization. Thus a process designed to channel public assets to an elite few with influence or capital served less to create a landed aristocracy than to allow small freeholders to take possession of affordable farms. This contradiction between the intent and results of policy began with the Dutch and continued through the English colonial and early American periods.

The Dutch Period

The Dutch East India Co's 1629 Charter of Freedoms and Exemptions allowed the company to give large feudal estates called patroonships to its major stockholders and to deed small lots to freehold farmers. Although at least eight attempts were made to establish patroonships within New Netherland, which included the present New Jersey and Delaware as well as New York State, only the one started by Amsterdam diamond merchant Kiliaen van Rensselaer satisfied the requirement that 50 adult settlers populate the patroonship within four years. Van Rensselaer acquired secure title to most of present-day Albany and Rensselaer Cos, nearly 1 million acres (405,000 ha), and his descendants acquired wealth and power from this asset.

More significant in the long run, however, were the approximately 600 small freehold farms established during the Dutch period on Manhattan, Long and Staten Islands, and in the lower Hudson Valley. These small independent holdings were evidence that colonial authorities needed a secure agricultural base more than they needed to support the aristocratic pretensions of the few. They also created a natural restraint on all subsequent attempts to establish a landed gentry. The ready availability of cheap land within and beyond the colony inhibited efforts by landowners to attract a stable class of tenant farmers but did not entirely prevent it.

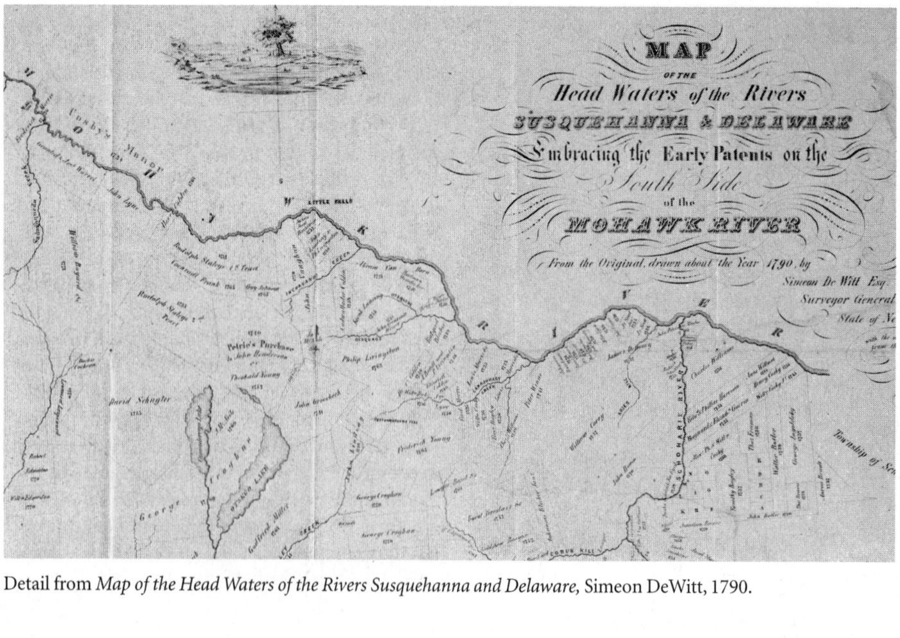

Detail from *Map of the Head Waters of the Rivers Susquehanna and Delaware,* Simeon DeWitt, 1790.

The English Period

The period of English rule (1664–1776) was marked by governors aggressively deeding large patents to influential persons, so that colonial New York developed the most aristocratic character of any northern colony. By the end of the Revolutionary War most of New York's colonial territory had passed into or through the hands of elites. This process began when James, Duke of York, became sole proprietor of the colony in 1664. James confirmed the earlier Dutch patents and permitted his governors to grant patents and, when politically expedient, manorial status to loyal subjects. Besides ownership of a designated tract of land, a manor grant included the honorary title of lord and, in some cases, a permanent seat in the Colonial Assembly. By law, lordships could only be bestowed upon individual families. Thus lands granted to nonfamilial partnerships could not be made manors, regardless of size, while at times eligible families opted for a patent rather than a manor. Notable early grants included an extensive but vaguely defined increase to the Van Rensselaer holdings known as the Lower Manor, or Claverack [now in Columbia Co]; Robert Livingston's 3,000-acre (1,200 ha) patent that expanded into the 160,000 acre (65,000 ha) Livingston Manor; and the 90,000-acre (36,000 ha) Philipsburg Manor awarded to Frederick Philipse I. Other early grants included the Saratoga Patent to four partners: 75,000 acres (30,000 ha) to Francis Rumbout; 7,000 acres (2,800 ha) to Pieter Schuyler; 2,000 acres (800 ha) to Peter Fauconnier; and 35,000 acres (14,000 ha) in the Hoosic Valley to Maria van Rensselaer (1645–89), Hendrick van Ness, Jacobus van Cortlandt, and Gerrit Finnise.

The awarding of large patents escalated after the colony reverted to the English Crown when its proprietor became King James II in 1685. Govs Benjamin Fletcher (1692–98); Richard Coote, Earl of Bellomont (1698–1701); and Edward Hyde, Viscount Cornbury (1702–8) gave away most of the colony east of the Hudson River and south of the Van Rensselaer domain. This largesse included Philipse's Highland Patent of 205,000 acres (83,000 ha) [now most of Putnam Co] to Adolph Philipse and 86,000 acres (34,800 ha) to Stephanus van Cortlandt, forming Cortlandt Manor. Others parcels were the 18,000-acre (7,300 ha) Little Nine Partners tract to Samuel Boughton and associates and the 160,000-acre (65,000 ha) Great Nine Partners Patent to Caleb Heathcote and friends. Heathcote was also awarded the Manor of Scarsdale. The Rhinebeck Patent of nearly 22,000 acres (8,900 ha) and another 100,000 acres (40,000 ha) in southern Dutchess Co went to Henry Beekman Sr. On Long Island 32,000 acres (12,900 ha) in present Suffolk Co went to Col William Smith.

Lands farther from settled areas were often granted in even larger parcels. During just six years in office, Gov Hyde bestowed the 120,000-acre (49,000 ha) Wawayanda Patent on John Bridges and 11 partners; the approximately 130,000-acre (53,000 ha) Minisink Patent on Stephen DeLancey, Matthew Ling, and 22 others; the 400,000-acre (162,000 ha) Kayaderosseras Patent on 13 associates; and the nearly 1.5 million-acre (610,000 ha) Hardenbergh Patent on Johannis Hardenbergh and five partners. At the same time, many small farmers acquired land

Selected Land Patents and Tracts

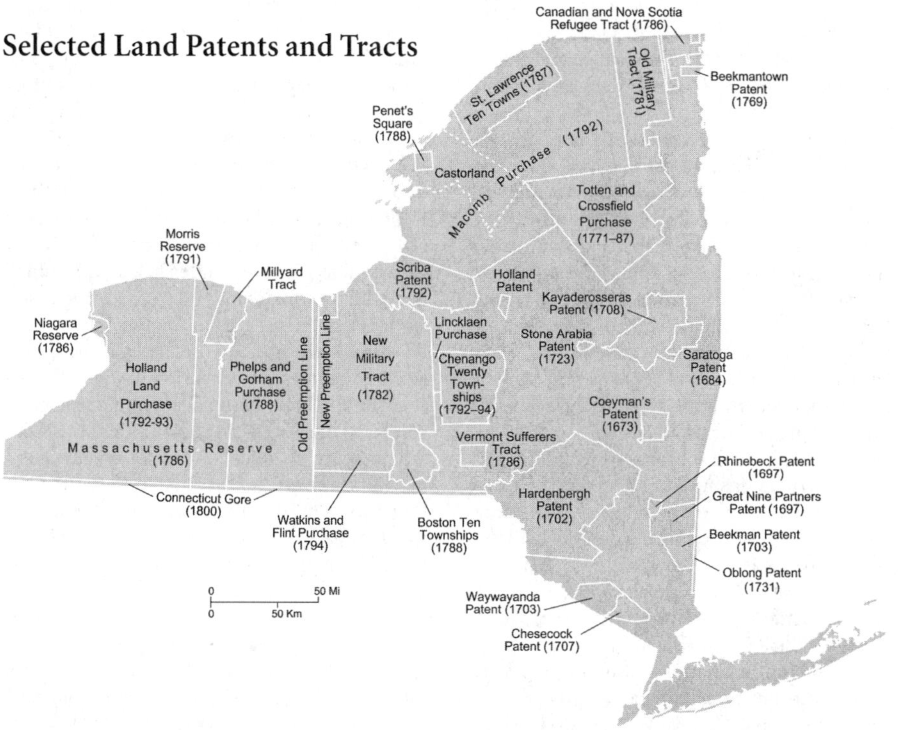

either through special pleas to the government or by banding together to acquire patents that could later be subdivided. Much of Ulster Co, including the patents of New Paltz, Hurley, Marbletown, and Rochester, passed into farmers' hands in this manner. Because of these small freehold farms, the west side of the Hudson River was less fashionable among the upper classes than were older estates east of the river. Nevertheless, the proliferation of freeholders reinforced the notion that farming families should own their own land. A relative lull in land alienation occurred between 1708 and 1728, but from 1729 until 1776 the governors patented nearly 4 million acres (1.6 million ha) to the colony's social elite. All of the land involved lay east of the Unadilla River, much of it north of previously patented tracts.

Some of the most successful land investors acquired tracts by negotiating with the Indians before approaching the governor. In this manner Sir William Johnson obtained more than 500,000 acres (200,000 ha) near his estate at Johnstown [now in Fulton Co]. Although not finalized until after the Revolutionary War, front men Joseph Totten and Stephen Crossfield sought ownership of a 1,150,000-acre (465,000 ha) tract by first negotiating with the Mohawk Indians in 1771, only afterward seeking the colonial government's approval. To acquire patents during the later colonial period, land seekers developed a number of strategies to circumvent the limit on the size of grants imposed by the Crown on colonial governments. The limit was set at 2,000 acres (809 ha) in 1708 and reduced to 1,000 acres (405 ha) in 1753. A common strategy was to have a number of legal-sized patents pass through the hands of dummy partners before they were acquired by the actual investors. Governors in turn charged exorbitant fees or required kickbacks for their connivance with such schemes, benefiting from the many transactions required for this purpose.

This system of conveyance allowed for a great deal of fraud throughout the colonial period. Bribery of officials, control of courts by a small number of elite families, manipulation of contracts with Native Americans, and the use of vague descriptions of the extent of lands being purchased all served to concentrate large portions of the colony in the hands of elites. For example, Livingston Manor, which began with two tracts totaling 2,000 acres (809 ha), was stretched to 160,000 acres (65,000 ha) because of vague wording in Livingston's contract with the Mohican (Mahican). Similarly, Philipse's Highland Patent began with a deal for only 15,000 acres (6,070 ha) from the Wappinger Indians but was extended nearly to the Connecticut border because of wording in Gov Fletcher's grant to Philipse and included 190,000 additional acres (77,000 ha) that still legally belonged to the Indians. Its later proprietors successfully manipulated the courts to defend this fraudulently acquired title.

As a result, in the late colonial period, acquiring large patents became a costly, involved, and business-like process. For example, George Clinton, governor from 1743 to 1753, charged fees of £12 6s for each 1,000-acre (405 ha) grant, and Cadwallader Colden charged $31.25. Legal expenses could add considerably to costs. Small farmers, deprived of the opportunity to gain freehold estates from the large proprietors, resisted the terms of tenancy by both legal and violent means. A number of quasi-feudal practices had persisted throughout the colonial period. Tenants were often required to pay quitrents and taxes, to provide labor, and to give the landlord one-quarter or one-half of the sales price if the improvements and lease were sold to another. Failure to do so could result in eviction. This occasionally led to violent tenant revolts on the Philipse, Van Rensselaer, Livingston, and Van Cortlandt holdings between 1711 and 1766.

Furthermore, land companies and individual investors often went into debt and required a quick return on their investment through resale rather than a slow return through tenant leases. As a result, the acquisition of a large patent no longer ensured recipients immediate access to upper-class status. Instead it typically came with the risks and prospective rewards associated with most businesses. The solvency of the final buyer, the small-scale farming family, became the critical factor in determining success or failure.

The Postrevolutionary Period

The transition of land dealing from a process by which a select few established or reinforced their status, wealth, and power to a tough and risky business where few were successful reached its pinnacle during the first decade after independence. Over a period of just 10 years, 15 million acres (6.1 million ha) of New York State passed as large patents into the hands of investors. Many lost great fortunes in the process. The rapid pace of the postrevolutionary land grab occurred partly because the former colonies were in desperate need of revenue. This included New York State and Massachusetts, the latter having acquired the right to negotiate with the American Indian inhabitants for ownership of extensive tracts of New York territory, including most of the land west of Seneca Lake.

In 1786 the state legislature established the Board of Land Commissioners to help facilitate the distribution of state lands. Methods included laying out townships of 15,000–92,000 acres (6,000–37,000 ha) for sale at public auction. Two of the larger such tracts were the St. Lawrence Ten Towns and the Chenango Twenty Townships. Smaller, individual parcels included Sidney, Randolph, Warren, and Fayette townships in the lower Susquehanna Valley. Five percent of the land in each town was set aside for highways, and two lots were set aside to endow education and religion. Invariably, speculators won the bidding at prices of 16–90¢ an acre, despite intentions to encourage settlers to buy the land. Alexander Macomb, for example, acquired nearly all of the land contained in the St. Lawrence Ten Towns (almost 640,000 acres/260,000 ha). Macomb, a fur trader with considerable frontier experience, also acquired nearly 3,670,000 acres (1,485,000 ha) in six great tracts constituting much of the northern and western Adirondacks that were subsequently distributed among silent partners or subdivided and sold. George Scriba was another investor who acquired a substantial tract for the modest price of just 16¢ an acre, yet he lost his entire fortune promoting its settlement. Elsewhere, John W. Watkins and Royal W. Flint purchased 336,380 acres (136,128 ha) in the Chemung region for 80¢ an acre in 1794, and William Bingham, a Philadelphia merchant, acquired a large narrow tract bordering Pennsylvania where he founded the City of Binghamton.

The Commonwealth of Massachusetts patented its New York State lands to investors for very low prices. In 1787 the 230,400-acre (93,240 ha) Boston Ten Townships tract was sold to Samuel Brown and 10 partners for 12.5¢ an acre. In 1788 Massachusetts patented 6 million acres (2.4 million ha) west of Seneca Lake to Nathaniel Gorham and Oliver Phelps. The price was first estimated to be 3¢ an acre, payable in Massachusetts securities; however, those securities quickly appreciated, leaving Phelps and Gorham unable to complete the purchase. As a result, they relinquished any claim to the westernmost 4 million acres (1.6 million ha), returning it to Massachusetts in 1790 in exchange for clear title to the eastern 2 million acres (809,000 ha). They then sold 1.2 million acres (490,000 ha) to Robert Morris for approximately $75,000. In turn, Morris sold the land for £75,000 to an English partnership that included Sir William Pulteney, John Hornby, and Patrick Colquhoun and was fronted by Charles Williamson. Phelps and Gorham sold about 50 townships directly to individuals and small land companies, including 20,000 prime acres (8,100 ha) along the Genesee River acquired by Jeremiah Wadsworth for $1 an acre. Wadsworth's nephews, James and William, held most of this land, acquired more, and became the largest individual owners of cultivated land in the state. In 1791 Robert Morris, with silent partners probably including Samuel Ogden, Gouverneur Morris, R. Loderston, and William Constable, bought from Massachusetts the western 4 million acres (1.6 million ha) returned by Phelps and Gorham. Morris acquired secure title from the Seneca Nation for $100,000, then sold more than 3 million acres (1.2 million ha) to the Holland Land Co, a syndicate of Dutch bankers, for a substantial profit in 1792. He retained 750,000 acres (304,000 ha) known as the Morris Reserve, selling it in large parcels (15,000–150,000 acres/6,100–61,000 ha) until financial problems elsewhere forced him to surrender what remained.

Farmers Take Final Possession of the Land

The problem that land companies and individual investors faced in profiting from large land patents remained the same across time. More often than not farmers, the ultimate purchasers of frontier land, had insufficient capital and inadequate access to profitable markets to make their scheduled payments. The experience of the Holland Land Co illustrates this point: for 36 years beginning in 1800 it retailed much of western New York State to farmers but made only modest profits for its shareholders. The company faced so many problems in extracting land payments from farmers that by 1820 farmers owed it more than $4 million. In 1835 the company had to sell its holdings to American investors because of political resentment fostered by its debtors.

The companies' ability to extract profits from their holdings depended on the ability of farmers to profit from their labors. Quality of land was key to farmer success: investments in northern Adirondack lands, for example, tended to be unsuccessful at any but very low prices. Providing access to markets and to vital services like sawmills and gristmills became a vital function for land companies. The Dutch investors in Cazenovia [now in Madison Co] spent more on improvements to attract settlers and help them succeed ($128,000 by 1797) than they did in purchasing the tract ($87,000) in the first place. Charles Williamson, manager of the Pulteney Purchase, invested nearly $1.4 million in improvements by 1799, including roads and a central village.

In the end, however, few land companies profited from their investments. The most successful land traders in New York State were the less ambitious but more methodical investors who moved to the frontier and lived among their holdings and customers. They tended to be the merchants and lawyers who participated in the development of growing communities, and for whom land trading was merely an adjunct to other activities. They provided important functions in making sure that the farmers—their neighbors, clients, and customers—could afford and make payments on appropriately sized parcels of land.

New York State ended up mostly in the hands of small-scale farming families because the processes changed little across time. During the first century of Dutch and English settlement, governors awarded large patents to influential figures for little or no cost. These landowners attempted to establish large estates but were unable to attract a contented tenant class. Instead they sold lots to farmers for modest sums, often profiting by little more than small annual quitrent payments, until most of their patents passed from their hands.

During the last half century of English possession, governors patented equally large tracts to investors. However, they extracted such large bribes or commissions that investing in land became a risky business requiring quick subdivision and resale. This process accelerated during the early national period, when land companies and individual investors acquired much of the rest of the state, sometimes in immense tracts. Because most of these purchases came at competitive auctions and involved terms of credit, purchasers quickly sold smaller tracts to speculators, who in turn sold even smaller tracts to smaller-scale investors, until the land eventually came into the possession of those with the means of paying for it in manageable lots through the hard work of farming.

Brooks, Charles E. *Frontier Settlement and Market Revolution: The Holland Land Purchase* (Ithaca: Cornell Univ Press, 1996)

Friedenberg, Daniel M. *Life, Liberty, and the Pursuit of Land: The Plunder of Early America* (Buffalo: Prometheus Books, 1992)

Hugill, Peter J. *Upstate Arcadia: Landscape, Aesthetics, and the Triumph of Social Differentiation in America* (Boston: Rowman & Littlefield, 1995)

Mark, Irving. *Agrarian Conflicts in Colonial New York, 1711–1775* (New York: Columbia Univ Press, 1940)

Price, Edward T. *Dividing the Land: Early American Beginnings of Our Private Property Mosaic* (Chicago: Univ of Chicago Press, 1995)

Rayback, Robert. "New York: Land Policy in Three Eras." In *Richards Atlas of New York State,* ed. Robert Rayback (Phoenix, NY: Frank E. Richards, 1957–59)

Sakolski, A. M. *The Great American Land Bubble: The Amazing Story of Land-Grabbing, Speculations, and Booms from Colonial Days to the Present Time* (New York: Harper & Brothers, 1932)

Wyckoff, William. *The Developer's Frontier: The Making of the Western New York Landscape* (New Haven, Conn: Yale Univ Press, 1988)

Scott W. Anderson

landfills. Early refuse disposal was performed primarily in surface enclosures and waste piles maintained privately by the affiliated homeowner or industry. Between 1844 and 1994 as much as 20% of the landmass of New York City, 45,650 acres (18,474 ha), was at one time or another used for waste disposal. Although some refuse, such as manure, was recycled, unusable wastes were put on scows and dumped at sea. It was not until the late 19th century that New York City started a systematic process of treating waste and reusing it in low-lying areas. This system was soon adopted by other cities in the state. In the 1960s refuse disposal facilities in New York State peaked at roughly 1,600. Prior to 1962 there was no form of state regulation for waste disposal. In that year the New York State Public Health Council mandated that refuse disposal was to be managed as a "sanitary landfill," and all incinerators were to operate within federal air pollution standards. New York State mandated in 1966 that all solid waste planning on a county or regional level be fully reimbursed. In 1970 the Department of Environmental Conservation (DEC) complemented this mandate with the legalization of a 50% state aid match for all municipal solid waste planning and construction costs. As of 1988 DEC regulations require that a landfill, hazardous or otherwise, be lined with two layers of geomembrane fabric in order to be issued an operation permit. Annually the agency conducts more than 700 inspections of hazardous waste treatment and containment facilities. Typically, 60% of the facilities inspected are found to be in compliance with state hazardous waste management regulations, 35% of inspections find medium-priority violations, and 5% of inspections reveal high-priority violations.

The state's solid waste totaled 18 million tons (16 MT) in 2001; 9.4 million tons (8.5 MT) were placed in landfills within the state, 3.7 million tons (3.4 MT) were used to process energy, and 4.9 million tons (4.4 MT) were exported to other states or to Canada. The state generated approximately 73.6 million tons (66.8 MT) of hazardous waste in 1998, compared to approximately 66.6 million tons (60.4 MT) in 1997.

Legal waste disposal methods in 2002 included burning nonhazardous municipal solids in an incinerator and disposing of the ash in a municipal solid waste landfill or collecting the waste and immediately encapsulating it in a municipal landfill. It is estimated that more than 80% of all municipal solid waste is deposited in a landfill. As of 31 Dec 1999, New York State had 28 operating municipal solid waste landfills. Landfill gas, created by the anaerobic decomposition of organic materials, is burned on site or used in projects that harness the energy of the methane in the gas. New York State supported 15 landfill gas-to-energy facilities, which generated 256 million kWh of electricity in 1998. Fresh Kills landfill in Staten Island produced 2% of the world's methane in 1995. At approximately 2,200 acres (890 ha), it was the largest operating landfill in the state and at its peak in the late 1980s took in more than 27,000 tons (24,500 MT) per day of solid waste. The landfill officially stopped accepting municipal solid waste on 22 Mar 2001, and full completion of the landfill closure is expected in 2010.

See also Love Canal; Pollution; Sanitation and Sewage.

Hammond, Stephen. *Generation and Management of Hazardous Waste in New York.* Hazardous Waste Report, 1998 (Albany: Department of Environmental Conservation, June 2000)

Samuel H. Sage

landforms. For its areal extent New York State's physical base displays more diversity than any other state in the Union. Geomorphologists divide the state into nine major landform regions; most can be further divided into subregions that contrast sometimes subtly, sometimes dramatically. The land is shaped by a number of diverse conditions and forces that start with the nature of the bedrock, how that bedrock is arranged and fractured, and how resistant it is to the forces

Landform Regions

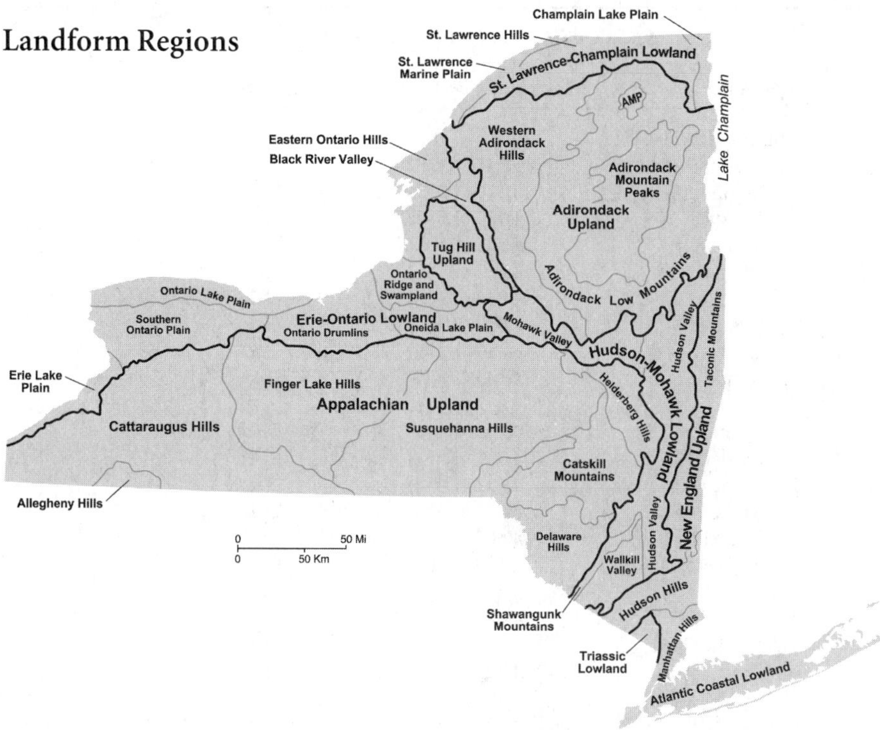

of erosion. The tectonic forces that cause the bedrock to rise or shift en masse are countered by erosional forces that include flowing water, waves, and sheets of moving ice, wind, chemical action, and the downward shifting movement of unconsolidated materials. Together these forces would have worn down the lands of the state to a near uniform, level plain in the course of 30–40 million years were it not for the opposing forces of uplift and volcanism that resulted in the creation of mountains and broad regional plateaus. Overall the flatter, lower regions of the state, like the Hudson, Champlain, and St. Lawrence Valleys and the areas bordering Lakes Erie and Ontario, are composed of softer, more easily eroded bedrock than are the high areas like the Adirondacks, the Taconics, and the Appalachian Plateau. This differential resistance to erosion is often the basis for New York State's most famous landscape features, such as Niagara Falls, the Thousand Islands, the Palisades, the Helderberg Escarpment, and Taughannock Falls.

While continental glaciation is probably the best-known land shaping force associated with New York State's landforms, it is not the most significant. The glaciers altered the appearance of the landforms without changing their basic form or structure. The ice and meltwaters widened, deepened, and modified the profile of valleys, rounded and smoothed hilltops, and buried most of the bedrock under a layer of loose rock and related debris (drift) previously embedded in the ice, but glaciers neither created nor eliminated the uplands or lowlands. By comparison the tectonic forces that forged the uplands and the erosional forces that have removed thousands of feet of bedrock from the Adirondack and Taconic regions over millions of years, for example, far exceed the influence of the ice sheets on landform development. Some of the more conspicuous present-day land-altering processes include wave-induced changes to the southern Long Island shoreline and those brought about by human activity. The latter include the creation of artificial lakes (reservoirs), the leveling of sand dunes on Long Island and the Pine Bush near Albany for tract housing, the creation of new land around the shore of Manhattan, the filling in or draining of wetlands, especially around major cities, the creation of spoil banks and artificial hills associated with industry or waste disposal, massive excavations and fills along major highways, and the oversteepening of hillsides that result in instability and landslides.

Adirondack Upland

This heavily eroded upland is composed largely of ancient Precambrian, crystalline rock consisting primarily of quartzites, gneisses, marles, and anorthosites. The Adirondack Upland is tied to the Canadian Shield by the Frontenac Arch, which extends across the St. Lawrence Lowland to the north and forms the Thousand Islands in the St. Lawrence River. Vast quantities of younger rock that once overlaid the region have been almost entirely eroded away, facilitated by the much more recent and ongoing uplifting of the area creating the near circular dome that presently exists. The central parts of the region are characterized by a series of straight and long valleys that formed along faults and fracture zones. The most pronounced valleys run northeast-southwest, and many contain streams or lakes. A secondary series of fracture zones runs perpendicular to the first, giving many of the lakes and streams a distinct angular pattern as exemplified by Upper Saranac Lake, Lake Placid, and Long Lake. The region was heavily glaciated, which resulted in a smoothing of the exposed elevations, especially north-facing slopes, and a widening of many valleys. The region contains a variety of depositional features related to glacial retreat. While the region's drainage pattern is radial, individual drainage courses are often confused and circuitous because of randomly laid glacial deposits.

The Adirondack Upland physiographic province is divided into three major subregions. The Adirondack Mountain Peaks area is located in the eastern half of the upland and is its most rugged and highest section. Summits rise to a minimum of 3,000 feet (910 m) and in two cases exceed 5,000 feet (1,520 m), Mt Marcy and Algonquin Peak. Local relief can vary by 2,000 feet (610 m). The Adirondack Low Mountains subregion surrounds the High Peaks area. Summits can exceed 2,000 feet (610 m) and local relief 1,000 feet (305 m). This region contains a large number of lakes. The Western Adirondack Hills subregion lies to the west, particularly the northwest, of the higher Adirondack country. Elevations range from 500 to 2,000 feet (150–610 m). Local relief is typically 200–300 feet (60–90 m) but reaches 500 ft (150 m) in select locations. Roche moutonnée (rounded mounds of exposed bedrock), a consequence of glaciation, abound in parts. Water bodies are noticeably less abundant than in the low mountain area to the east.

Appalachian Upland

Extending from the west margin of the Hudson Valley to the Pennsylvania border in the west, the Appalachian Upland is the largest physiographic region in the state. With limited exception, surficial bedrock consists of nearly flat-lying Devonian sedimentary rocks that dip gently to the south and west. From Central New York east the region's northern boundary is sharply defined by the Helderberg scarp face that allows stunning views of the low country to the north. Although this region contains the only area in New York State that was never glaciated, most of it has been altered by continental glaciation.

The Helderberg Hills subregion occupies the extreme northeastern section of the upland and rises sharply almost 2,000 feet (610 m) from the bordering Hudson and Mohawk Valleys. The plateau is capped by a massive layer of resistant Coeymans limestone, which overlays a layer of Manlius limestone. The latter contains the largest collection of caverns in the northeastern United States. These caves predate the glaciation that did much to alter the classic karst surface features by filling sinkhole depressions with glacial drift and by studding the land surface with drumlins.

The Catskill Mountains form the subregion immediately south of the Helderbergs. Elevations commonly exceed 3,000 feet (910 m), and Slide and Hunter Mountains rise above 4,000 feet (1,220 m). Like the rest of the Appalachian Upland, the Catskills are a heavily eroded plateau rather than an area that has undergone more typical mountain-building processes. Local relief is upward of 1,000 feet (305 m), in places substantially more. The region is marked by a series of cuestas, the most pronounced being a 2,000 ft (610 m) escarpment known locally as the Wall of Manitou along the region's eastern margin. The Catskills are also characterized as an area of relatively few valleys and correspondingly large intervening highlands. The landscape displays the effects not only of continental glaciation but of valley and mountain glacial activity.

The Delaware Hills is a heavily eroded and glaciated area with high elevations ranging from 2,000 feet (610 m) in the north to 1,200 feet (365 m) in the south. Local relief ranges from 1,000 feet (305 m) in the west to less than 500 feet (150 m) in the southeast. Glacial drift is nearly ubiquitous but ranges in depth from a foot or less on hilltops to over 100 feet (30 m) in many valleys.

The Susquehanna Hills subregion is characterized by blocks of elongated upland that reach 1,700–2,100 feet (520–640 m) in height separated by substantial, north-south-trending valleys widened and deepened by advancing ice and subsequently by large meltwater rivers. These valleys presently contain small "underfit" streams. Near level land is limited and confined to portions of the larger valleys and to some of the tops of the more extensive interfluves. Hillsides are steep and in places composed of sheer rock ledges.

The Finger Lake Hills are generally lower and more gently rolling than the other subregions of the Appalachian Upland. The area is dissected by a complex network of north-south-trending through valleys, which deepen and take a more pronounced U shape in the higher elevated south. Some of these valleys are occupied by water, such as the Finger Lakes. As typical of glacially scoured valleys, the main valley walls are interrupted by deeply incised valleys such as Watkins Glen; most are hanging valleys with dramatic waterfalls, the most spectacular being 215 ft (66 m) Taughannock Falls.

Comparatively flat-topped uplands interrupted by valleys characterize the Cattaraugus Hills subregion, which extends over most of southwestern New York. Hilltop elevations increase modestly toward the southeast, where they can exceed 2,000 ft (610 m). Valley sides become steeper and the landform region as a whole more rugged. The northern boundary of the Allegheny Hills subregion, known also as the Salamanca Re-entrant, runs roughly parallel but a few miles north of the Allegheny River in southwestern New York. Largely contained within the Allegany State Park, the area is the only unglaciated region in the state. The valleys are more V shaped, the landforms more angular, and the bedrock more exposed.

Atlantic Coastal Lowland

The Atlantic Coastal Lowland includes all of Long Island and most of Staten Island. The bedrock consists of Cretaceous-age sedimentary rock that dips gently southward and lies buried beneath huge quantities of glacial deposits that range from 400 to over 2,000 feet (120–610 m) deep. Deposits are the consequence of two continental glaciers. The more recent Wisconsinan ice sheet overrode the meltwater deposits of a previous ice sheet and reached its maximum southern extent along the Ronkonkoma terminal moraine, which reaches almost 400 ft (120 m) above sea level and extends from Montauk Point to the west. The ice sheet retreated then readvanced, creating the Harbor Hill Moraine, which forms the island's north flake and runs west from Orient Point to Lake Success (Nassau Co) before dipping southwest, burying the original ice front, and continuing to the west end of Long Island, across Staten Island to Perth Amboy, NJ. Verrazano Narrows marks the gap in the Harbor Hill Moraine created by the erosive powers of the Hudson River. The sequence of peninsulas on the north shore of Long Island, commonly referred to as the Necks, were formed when north-flowing tributaries of the river that drained Long Island Sound cut deep valleys into the moraine deposits that were subsequently drowned when the ice melted and sea levels rose. The gently sloping land south of the moraine complex is the result of meltwater deposition.

SELECTED SUMMIT ELEVATIONS

Summit	Elevation in Feet (Meters)	County
Adirondacks[a]		
Mount Marcy	5,344 (1,629)	Essex
Algonquin	5,114 (1,559)	Essex
Haystack	4,960 (1,512)	Essex
Skylight	4,926 (1,501)	Essex
Whiteface	4,867 (1,483)	Essex
Dix	4,857 (1,480)	Essex
Boundary	4,840 (1,475)	Essex
Gray	4,840 (1,475)	Essex
Iroquois	4,840 (1,475)	Essex
Basin	4,827 (1,471)	Essex
Gothics	4,736 (1,444)	Essex
Colden	4,714 (1,437)	Essex
Giant	4,627 (1,410)	Essex
Santanoni	4,607 (1,404)	Essex
Redfield	4,606 (1,404)	Essex
Nippletop	4,600 (1,402)	Essex
Wright	4,580 (1,396)	Essex
Saddleback	4,515 (1,376)	Essex
Panther Peak	4,442 (1,354)	Essex
Table Top	4,427 (1,349)	Essex
Rocky Peak	4,420 (1,347)	Essex
McComb	4,405 (1,343)	Essex
Armstrong	4,400 (1,341)	Essex
Hough	4,400 (1,341)	Essex
Seward	4,361 (1,329)	Franklin
Marshall[b]	4,360 (1,329)	Essex
Allen	4,340 (1,323)	Essex
Esther	4,220 (1,286)	Essex
Big Slide	4,220 (1,286)	Essex
Upper Wolfjaw	4,185 (1,276)	Essex
Lower Wolfjaw	4,175 (1,273)	Essex
Street	4,166 (1,270)	Essex
Phelps	4,161 (1,268)	Essex
Donaldson	4,140 (1,262)	Franklin
Seymour	4,120 (1,256)	Franklin
Sawtooth	4,100 (1,250)	Franklin
Lookout	4,100 (1,250)	Essex
Cascade	4,098 (1,249)	Essex
South Dix	4,060 (1,237)	Essex
Porter	4,059 (1,237)	Essex
Colvin	4,057 (1,237)	Essex
Emmons	4,040 (1,231)	Franklin
Dial	4,020 (1,225)	Essex
Yard	4,018 (1,225)	Essex
East Dix	4,012 (1,223)	Essex
MacNaughton	4,000 (1,219)	Essex
Green	3,980 (1,213)	Essex
Blake	3,980 (1,213)	Essex
McDonnel	3,960 (1,207)	Essex
Cliff	3,960 (1,207)	Essex
Moose	3,899 (1,188)	Essex
Snowy	3,899 (1,188)	Hamilton
Nye	3,895 (1,187)	Essex
Kilburn	3,893 (1,187)	Essex
North River	3,880 (1,183)	Essex
Blue Ridge (Cloud Cap)	3,868 (1,179)	Hamilton
Panther	3,865 (1,178)	Hamilton
McKenzie	3,861 (1,177)	Essex
Witchopple	3,842 (1,171)	Essex
Bartlett Ridge	3,840 (1,170)	Essex
Gooseberry	3,840 (1,170)	Essex
Sentinel	3,838 (1,170)	Essex
Lyon	3,830 (1,167)	Clinton
Couchsachraga	3,820 (1,164)	Essex
Averill Peak	3,810 (1,161)	Clinton
Avalanche	3,800 (1,158)	Essex
Buell	3,786 (1,154)	Hamilton
Boreas	3,776 (1,151)	Essex

SELECTED SUMMIT ELEVATIONS (continued)

Summit	Elevation in Feet (Meters)	County
Little Nippletop	3,760 (1,146)	Essex
Wakely	3,760 (1,146)	Hamilton
Blue	3,759 (1,146)	Hamilton
Henderson	3,752 (1,144)	Essex
Lewey	3,742 (1,141)	Hamilton
The Brothers (Twin Mtns)	3,721 (1,134)	Essex
Wallface	3,700 (1,128)	Essex
Hurricane	3,694 (1,126)	Essex
Hoffman (Blue Ridge)	3,693 (1,126)	Essex
Cheney Cobble	3,683 (1,123)	Essex
Little Moose	3,630 (1,106)	Hamilton
Calamity	3,620 (1,103)	Essex
Sunrise	3,614 (1,102)	Essex
Stewart	3,602 (1,098)	Essex
Slide	3,584 (1,092)	Essex
Gore	3,583 (1,092)	Warren
Dun Brook	3,580 (1,091)	Hamilton
Noonmark	3,556 (1,084)	Essex
Fishing Brook	3,550 (1,082)	Essex
Adams	3,535 (1,077)	Essex
Little Santanoni	3,500 (1,067)	Essex
Jay	3,340 (1,018)	Essex
Catskills		
Slide	4,204 (1,281)	Ulster
Hunter	4,025 (1,227)	Greene
Black Dome	3,990 (1,216)	Greene
Blackhead Peak	3,937 (1,200)	Greene
Thomas Cole	3,935 (1,199)	Greene
Cornell	3,906 (1,191)	Ulster
Graham	3,890 (1,186)	Ulster
Peekamoose	3,863 (1,177)	Ulster
Table	3,856 (1,175)	Ulster
Plateau	3,855 (1,175)	Greene
Wittenberg	3,802 (1,159)	Ulster
Sugarloaf	3,782 (1,153)	Greene
West Kill	3,777 (1,151)	Greene
Panther	3,760 (1,146)	Ulster
Lone	3,740 (1,140)	Ulster
Big Round Top	3,723 (1,135)	Ulster
Big Indian	3,721 (1,134)	Ulster
Balsam Cap	3,700 (1,128)	Ulster
Rusk	3,680 (1,122)	Greene
High Peak	3,660 (1,116)	Greene
Twin	3,647 (1,112)	Greene
Rocky	3,620 (1,103)	Ulster
Fir	3,619 (1,103)	Ulster
North Dome	3,593 (1,095)	Greene
Balsam	3,590 (1,094)	Ulster
Indian Head	3,585 (1,093)	Greene
Balsam	3,565 (1,087)	Greene
Halcott	3,537 (1,078)	Greene
Evergreen	3,531 (1,076)	Greene
Vly	3,529 (1,076)	Greene
Spruce Top	3,520 (1,073)	Greene
Dry Brook Ridge	3,510 (1,070)	Delaware-Ulster
Windham High Peak	3,505 (1,068)	Greene
Bearpen	3,500 (1,067)	Delaware-Ulster
Round Top	3,470 (1,058)	Greene
Huntersfield	3,450 (1,052)	Greene
Bloomberg	3,448 (1,051)	Delaware
Stoppel Point	3,425 (1,044)	Greene
Belle Ayr	3,406 (1,038)	Ulster
Spruce	3,380 (1,030)	Ulster
Mill Brook Ridge	3,380 (1,030)	Delaware-Ulster
Pisgah	3,365 (1,026)	Delaware
Wildcat	3,268 (996)	Ulster
Hemlock	3,264 (995)	Ulster
Van Wyck	3,260 (994)	Ulster

continued on page 868

The shallow estuaries on Long Island's south shore are former meltwater channels that now open onto tidal flats, salt marshes, and lagoons containing hundreds of low islands, all of which are protected from the Atlantic Ocean by a series of barrier islands.

Erie-Ontario Lowland

Divided into nine major subregions, this area of low relief lies immediately south and east of Lakes Erie and Ontario. The bedrock consists of southward-dipping deposits of Silurian and Ordovician limestones, sandstones, shales, and dolostones. With the exception of the Niagara Escarpment, which rises to ground level in Monroe Co and becomes more pronounced as it extends westward to the Niagara River and Canada, the region's most conspicuous landform features are sculpted by continental glaciation or postglacial activity. Capped by resistant Lockport dolostone, the escarpment is the basis for the state's most famous landform feature, Niagara Falls, and the 7 mi (11 km) Niagara Gorge carved by the river during the past 12,000 years. Drainage throughout much of the lowland is poor, resulting in extensive areas of wetland, some of which have been artificially drained to expose highly productive muckland soils.

The Lake Erie Plain is a narrow strip of land that runs along the south shore of Lake Erie and rises up to 200 feet (60 m) above the lake surface near the base of the Cattaraugus Hills. Aside from steep-walled ravines cut by streams flowing into the lake, the topography is subdued and consists of various lacustrine features formed when postglacial water levels were higher. The Ontario Lake Plain stretches from the Niagara River to Sodus Bay and south to the base of the Niagara Escarpment. It is similar to the Lake Erie Plain except for the presence of a prominent beach ridge formed by postglacial Lake Iroquois, which is followed by Rte 104. The Southern Ontario Plain is a zone of rolling topography and low relief formed by substantial amounts of glacial drift that lies between the Niagara Escarpment and the Appalachian Upland to the south.

The Ontario Drumlins subregion extends from Rochester to Syracuse and is arguably the most distinct physiographic region within the greater lowland. Although present in other subregions, the thousands of inverted teaspoon-shaped hills, drumlins, that formed under the ice and that range from tens to several hundreds of feet in elevation constitute one of the largest drumlin swarms in the world. The Ontario Ridge and Swampland extends east from the City of Oswego and north of Oneida Lake. It is dominated by numerous wetlands whose drainage is impeded by a series of low ridges composed of glacial till that trend east-west. The Oneida Lake Plain is a nearly featureless area that extends south and east of the lake and contains several extensive swamps and muckland areas. The Eastern Ontario Hills subregion is composed of flat-lying beds of Ordovician limestone and sandstone that is overlain by a mantle of glacial till that is very thin on the headlands that project into Lake Ontario in the north. Further south the lakeshore features an extensive area of sand dunes, sand spit, bay bars, and wide beaches. Elsewhere relief varies from level to gently rolling, interrupted by steep rock ledges. Wedged between the Tug Hill and Adirondack Uplands the Black River Valley consists of a sequence of flat-lying, till-covered, limestone-

SELECTED SUMMIT ELEVATIONS (continued)

Summit	Elevation in Feet (Meters)	County
McGregor	3,253 (992)	Delaware
Morrisville Range	3,253 (992)	Delaware
Plattekill	3,250 (991)	Delaware
Giant Ledge	3,218 (981)	Ulster
Richmond	3,213 (979)	Greene
Utsayanthe	3,213 (979)	Delaware
Mongaup	3,150 (960)	Ulster
Overlook	3,150 (960)	Ulster
Rose	3,123 (952)	Ulster
Denman	3,051 (930)	Sullivan
Mombaccus	3,000 (914)	Ulster
Taconic Hills		
Bald	2,693 (821)	Rensselaer
Harvey	2,065 (629)	Columbia
Perry Peak	2,060 (628)	Columbia
Hudson Hills		
North Beacon	1,602 (488)	Dutchess
Spy Rock	1,463 (446)	Orange
Bear	1,210 (369)	Orange
Shawangunk Mountains		
Near Sam's Point	2,289 (698)	Ulster
Susquehanna Hills		
Hooker Hill	2,325 (709)	Otsego
Finger Lakes Hills		
Connecticut Hill	2,095 (639)	Tompkins
Cattaraugus Hills		
Alma Hill	2,548 (777)	Allegany
Call Hill	2,401 (732)	Steuben
Allegheny Hills		
Flatiron Rock	2,387 (728)	Cattaraugus
Tug Hill Upland		
Gomer Hill	2,080 (634)	Lewis

Source: J. H. Thompson, *Geography of New York State* (1966).

[a]The Adirondack peaks considered part of the traditional 46 peaks over 4,000 feet do not include Boundary, Lookout, Yard, or McNaughton. Included in the traditional 46 are Blake, Cliff, Nye, and Couchsachraga.

[b]Formerly known as Clinton.

floored terraces that rise to the base of the Tug Hill escarpment. The subregion's northernmost area is covered by a sand delta associated with a postglacial lake.

Hudson-Mohawk Lowland

Part of the notably larger ridge and valley province, most of the region is underlain by folded sedimentary and metamorphic rock, much of it soft and easily eroded. By providing a comparatively easy route from seaboard to the Great Lakes Lowland and the continental interior, this region has played a significant role in the settlement and economic development of New York State and the lands farther west.

The Hudson Valley is a 10–20 mi (16–32 km) wide lowland bounded on the east by the Taconics and on the west by the Catskills, Helderbergs, and Adirondacks. The geology of the east and west sides of this lowland are markedly different. The bedrock in the western half is composed of shales, sandstones, and limestones that have been folded into north-south-trending ranges of hills and ridges of low-to-modest elevation. Three of the more conspicuous of these are the Kalkberg and Hoogeberg in Greene Co and Marlboro Mountain in Ulster Co. Slate underlies most of the lowland's eastern half, and relief is more subdued. As the Wisconsinan ice retreated, the Hudson Lowland was drowned under glacial Lake Albany, and many side streams built substantial deltas along the lakeshore, forming landforms that are now the sites of several of the region's larger settlements, including Albany, Schenectady, Newburgh, Kingston, Hudson, Glens Falls, and Saratoga Springs.

Lying between the Adirondack and Appalachian Uplands, the Mohawk Valley is an east-west-trending lowland floored by soft shales. Drained by the eastward-flowing Mohawk River, which is confined within a narrow inner valley, the broader lowland extends 10–30 miles (16–48 km) north-south and rises to as much as 1,000 feet (305 m) at the margins. This was at one time the primary drainage route for the entire Great Lakes watershed; the Iro-Mohawk River was thus much larger and more powerful than the present Mohawk. The valley's bedrock is disrupted by a series of block faults that have raised or lowered various parts of the valley's floor. Water gaps were cut in raised blocks (horsts) at Little Falls (Herkimer Co), the Noses (east of Canajoharie, Montgomery Co), and less conspicuously at Hoffmans (Schenectady Co). The massive size of the potholes on Moss Island at Little Falls provides further evidence of the amounts of water that flowed through the channel. The extensive sand plain between the Cities of Schenectady and Albany marks the location of a delta formed where the Iro-Mohawk emptied into glacial Lake Albany.

Guarded by the Shawangunk ridge on the northwest and the Hudson Highlands on the southeast, the Wallkill Valley is a 20 mi (32 km) wide by 65 mi (105 km) long lowland floored by folded Ordovician shales and graywackes. Having served as a channel for lobes of continental ice and as a basin for postglacial lakes, the valley's topography varies from gently rolling to flat plain at the southern end. The valley drains to the northeast via the Wallkill River. While clearly not a lowland, the Shawangunk Mountains are structurally part of the Hudson-Mohawk Lowland. Separating the Wallkill Valley from the Port Jervis trough on the west, the "Gunks" are an extension of Kittatinny Mountain that begins in eastern Pennsylvania over 100 miles (160 km) to the southwest. The narrow ridge is a flat-topped, anticlinal formation composed of severely folded Ordovician shales, siltstones, and graywackes capped by an erosion-resistant Silurian conglomerate that rises 1,000 feet (305 m) in the north. An extensive section of vertical cliff on the east face offers some of the best technical climbing in the eastern United States.

Drumlin known as Mormon Hill, south of Palmyra.

New England Upland

An extension of the Appalachian Mountains, this area of low mountains and hills is the most geologically complex area of New York State. It has undergone multiple episodes of mountain building (orogenies) when the North American tectonic plate collided with other tectonic plates followed by periods of erosion. The bedrock is old and consists largely of intensely fractured, folded, and, in places, refolded metamorphic rock. The higher elevations are composed of resistant gneisses, quartzites, and schists, and many of the valleys are marble floored. The region is divided into three major subregions.

The Taconic Mountains rarely exceed 2,000 feet (610 m) in elevation in their 100 mi (160 km) extent along the state's eastern border. The precise origin of these steep-sided and forest-covered highlands remains a subject of long-standing debate. One theory holds that the present Taconics were once the steep western front of a Himalayan-scale mountain range now represented by the Berkshires. The front broke free from the primary mountain mass and skidded westward as a massive landslip known as a klippe. The sliding mountain mass also pushed up a 20 mi (32 km) wide belt of bedrock immediately to its west, transforming it into a contorted and chaotic collection of rock structures that form the basis for the apron of hills west of the higher Taconics. The Hudson Hills, or Highlands, subregion extends in a northeast direction as a narrow band, called the Reading Prong, across the southeastern part of the state. Elevations range from 787 feet (240 m) below sea level at the bedrock bottom of the Hudson River to 1,329 feet (405 m) atop North Mount Beacon. The area is exceptionally rugged and scenic, especially where the Hudson River cuts through the highlands. How the Hudson carved a breach in this hard rock barrier to form one of the most dramatic landform features in the state remains the subject of another long-standing debate. The Manhattan Hills, also known as the Manhattan Prong, is a landscape of rolling hills and valleys that extend south from the Hudson Highlands near the Dutchess-Westchester county line to the tip of Manhattan Island. The unencumbered character of this subregion's topography can be observed in some of New York City's green spaces, notably Inwood Hill, Fort Tryon, and Bronx Park.

St. Lawrence–Champlain Lowland

The flat-lying bedrock consists primarily of Cambrian-age sandstone and Ordovician-age limestone. Depressed by the weight of an ice sheet to an estimated depth of as much as 550 feet (168 m), the region was subsequently flooded by seawater for a time after the ice sheet melted, leaving extensive portions of the region covered by a layer of marine clay. The bedrock has since "bounced back," a process known as isostatic rebound, which remains ongoing.

The St. Lawrence Marine Plain is a narrow band immediately south of the St. Lawrence River. Relief is smooth and, at most, gently rolling and includes a number of east-west-trending moraines. Bedrock underlying the adjacent St. Lawrence Hills tilts upward toward the Adirondack Upland to the south. Elevations rise from below 200 feet (60 m) at the shore of the St. Lawrence to over 1,200 feet (365 m) along the subregion's southern margin. Local topography is largely the result of glacial deposition and typically less than 100 feet (30 m). The Champlain Lake Plain bedrock is broken into numerous fault blocks. Gently rolling country, elevations range from 100 ft (30 m) at the lakeshore to 400 ft (120 m) at the western margins. The Ausable, Saranac, and Salmon Rivers have cut substantial gorges into the bedrock, which is covered with glacial till.

Triassic Lowland

Bounded on the northwest by the Ramapo Highlands (Reading Prong) and on the east by the Manhattan Hills (Manhattan Prong), this small triangular-shaped area in the southeastern corner of the state includes western Staten Island and the eastern two-thirds of Rockland Co. The lowland is characterized by several wide, gentle valleys floored by soft, reddish-brown mudstone and sandstone and separated by northeast-southwest-trending ridges of the erosion-resistant igneous rock diabase. The ridges range from 200 to 500 feet (60–150 m) above sea level. The most conspicuous is the Palisades, a 400 ft (120 m) high cliff that borders the west shore of the lower Hudson River. The region is exceptional within New York State because it experienced post-Paleozoic sedimentation and is the only part of the state where dinosaur fossils are found. Completely glaciated, the lowland is covered with a mantle of glacial till and outwash deposits that are more than 500 ft (150 m) thick in places.

Tug Hill Upland

Composed of flat-lying Paleozoic sandstones, limestones, and shales that dip decidedly to the west and south, this is an outlier of the Appalachian Plateau region. The region's northern and eastern margins are marked by an imposing cuesta that rises as much as 800 feet (240 m) above the adjoining Black River Valley subregion of the Erie-Ontario Lowland. Streams have cut a number of deep, narrow ravines, locally referred to as gulfs, into the cuesta's bedrock. The region's southern slope is substantial but more gradual, while the region's western margin merges imperceptibly with the Ontario Lowland. Much of the plateau is poorly drained because of ground moraine deposits.

Isachsen, Yngvar W., et al, eds. *Geology of New York: A Simplified Account,* 2d ed (Albany: NYS Museum, 2000)

Roseberry, C. R. *From Niagara to Montauk: The Scenic Pleasures of New York State* (Albany: SUNY Press, 1982)

Tesmer, Irving H., ed. *Colossal Cataract: The Geologic History of Niagara Falls* (Albany: SUNY Press, 1981)

Thornbury, William D. *Regional Geomorphology of the United States* (New York: John Wiley & Sons 1965)

Van Diver, Bradford B. *Roadside Geology of New York* (Missoula, Mont: Mountain Press Publishing, 1985)

James W. Darlington

Lansing. Town (pop 10,521) and village (pop 3,417) in N central Tompkins Co. Settled in 1791, the town was formed from Genoa (Cayuga Co) in 1817. At Bower Settlement, German immigrants established a church in 1803. Two railroads entered Lansing in 1871–73. The town's first salt company, eventually named International Salt, operated from 1892 to 1962. Portland Point Cement Co (1899–1947; later Penn Dixie) produced cement. Many immigrant workers found jobs in those industries, especially Syrians in the salt plant. In the early 21st century, New York State Electric and Gas operates Milliken Station (1955), a steam electric-generating station; Cargill (1970) mines salt in a 2,400 ft (731.5 m) deep mine, the deepest in the United States and one of the largest. Borg-Warner Automotive (1975; formerly Morse Chain) makes industrial machine and automotive products. The village was incorporated in 1974 to administer the rapidly growing number of apartments, motels, and malls near the Ithaca border that developed beginning in 1963. The Ithaca post office and YMCA and the county airport (1956) are located in Lansing. Some town residents farm, while many work in Ithaca. Two Youth Division centers at South Lansing help girls (1968) and boys (1993) in need of supervision. The Rogues Harbor Inn (1830) at South Lansing continues to serve meals in the early 21st century.

Jane Dieckmann

Lansing, John, Jr (*b* Albany, 30 Jan 1754; *d* ?New York City, ?12 Dec 1829). Moderate Antifederalist politician and jurist. Son of an Albany trader and minor officeholder, Lansing studied law under Robert Yates and was admitted to the bar in 1775. He served as Gen Philip Schuyler's military secretary for two years before returning to his legal practice in 1778. In 1781 Lansing married Cornelia Ray, and over time they had 10 children. In the 1780s he represented Albany Co in the state assembly, in which he served two terms as Speaker. Lansing served in the Confederation Congress in 1784 and 1787 and on the 1786 commission that settled the disputed western New York State land claims of Massachusetts. As members of the New York delegation at the Constitutional Convention of 1787, Lansing and Robert Yates left in July to protest the majority's efforts to create a strong centralized federal government. As a delegate to the New York State convention at Poughkeepsie in 1788, Lansing voted against the ratification of the US Constitution. He was mayor of Albany from 1786 to September 1790, when he was appointed as judge of the state supreme court; he became chief justice in 1798 and chancellor in 1801. He served on the commissions that settled the New York State–Vermont land and boundary controversies in 1790 and 1791. He was also named a regent of the University of the State of New York. After his retirement from public service in 1814, he resumed his law practice in Albany and managed his landholdings. Lansing vanished on 12 Dec 1829 after leaving his hotel room in New York City to deliver a letter. The case was never solved and his body never found.

The Delegate from New York; or Proceedings of the Federal Convention of 1787: From the Notes of John Lansing, Jr. Ed. Joseph Reese Strayer (Princeton, NJ: Princeton Univ Press, 1939)

Brad L. Utter

Laotians. See Southeast Asians.

Lapeer. Town (pop 686) in SW Cortland Co. Settled in 1799 by Primus Grant, a native of Guinea, settlers of European ancestry followed three years later. The town formed from Virgil in 1845. The land is hilly with steep ravines. The first cheese factory was built in 1875, and agriculture remains the basis for the town, while many residents commute to Cortland or Binghamton. Hunts Falls is a 71 ft (21.6 m) cascade.

Cathy A. Barber

Lapham, Elbridge G(erry) (*b* Farmington, Ontario Co, 18 Oct 1814; *d* near Canandaigua, Ontario Co, 8 Jan 1890). US representative and senator. The son of Quaker farmers, Lapham was educated in public schools and at Canandaigua Academy. After further study in civil engineering, he worked for Michigan Southern Railroad and then turned to the study of law, gaining admission to the bar in 1844. The same year he married Jane McBride (the couple would have eight children) and opened a law practice in Canandaigua, soon winning fame as a trial lawyer. From 1848 an antislavery Democrat, Lapham joined the new Republican Party in 1856. He was a delegate to the New York State Constitutional Convention of 1867–68 and then served as US representative (1875–81) from the 27th District in Ontario Co. In 1876 he helped conduct impeachment proceedings against Secretary of War William W. Belknap. In 1881 the New York State legislature chose him to complete the 1881–85 term of resigned US senator Roscoe Conkling, and he served as chairman of the Senate's Committee on Fish and Fisheries (1881–83). He retired from politics and resumed his Canandaigua law practice in 1885.

"Elbridge Gerry Lapham." In *Biographical Directory of the US Congress* (Alexandria, Va: CQ Staff Directories, 1997)

Jeffrey Kraus

La Présentation. The French established a mission in 1749 where the Oswegatchie River meets the St. Lawrence River [now Ogdensburg, St. Lawrence Co]. Led by Sulpician priest François Picquet, the palisaded settlement was attacked and burned that same year, possibly by Mohawk Indians. In 1750 the French rebuilt it as a larger earthwork fortification and mission. By the mid-1750s, among the numerous Algonquin and Iroquois pro-French Indians who moved to La Présentation, the greatest number were Onondagas. Not all of the Indian residents converted to Christianity, but many did support the French during the French and Indian War (1754–63). Regardless of origin, Indians who relocated at the post were often referred to as Oswegatchies.

With an impending British attack in 1760, the French abandoned the fort to consolidate their forces at Fort Lévis on Isle Royale [now Chimney Island, St. Lawrence Co]. The British occupied La Présentation after 1760 and renamed it Oswegatchie, retaining possession of it until 1796 when it was relinquished to the United States in compliance with the Jay Treaty. By this time what would become the City of Ogdensburg was growing around the fort. The remaining Indians living in the vicinity left by 1807, following local complaints and a New York State order. American troops used the fort during the War of 1812 and from there launched several raids on Canada. It was captured and briefly held by the British in 1813 and no longer used following the war. A reconstruction of the fort is planned by the Fort La Presentation Co.

Blau, Harold, Jack Campisi, and Elizabeth Tooker. "Onondaga." In *Northeast,* vol 15 of *The Handbook of North American Indians,* 20 vols, ed. Bruce G. Trigger (Washington, DC: Smithsonian Institution, 1978)

Douglas J. Pippin

Larchmont. Village (pop 6,485) in Mamaroneck (Westchester Co). After the New Haven Railroad (1848) was built, an unsuccessful attempt was made in 1854 to sell lots in the area. The 1872 survey by the Larchmont Manor Co was more successful. The Larchmont Yacht Club (1880) on Long Island Sound was joined by several resort hotels in the 1890s, notably the Royal Victoria (1895). The village was incorporated in 1891. By 1930, when the population reached 5,284, the village was almost fully developed. The hotels closed soon after. The New England Thruway (1958) provided rapid road access for commuters to New York City. Poet Phyllis McGinley (1905–78) was a resident from the late 1930s onward; humorist Jean Kerr (1922–2003) moved to Larchmont in 1955; and comedian Joan Rivers (1933–) was raised in the village. In their work, all three women gently satirized suburban life, as in Kerr's *Please Don't Eat the Daisies* (1957). In the early 21st century Larchmont is a mature commuter suburb.

Larkin Company. Manufacturer and mail order house. John D. Larkin (1845–1926) founded J. D. Larkin Co, a soap manufacturer, in 1875 in Buffalo. In 1885 the company began selling directly to customers through the mail, called the Larkin Idea. Larkin's motto was From Factory-to-Family: Save All Cost Which Adds No Value. Elbert Hubbard, Larkin's brother-in-law and founder of the Roycroft community in East Aurora (Erie Co), developed the premium inducements and other sales promotions. During the 1890s the company created Larkin Clubs of Ten, or cooperative buying clubs, in which "secretaries" recruited club members who bought Larkin products in bulk in exchange for premiums and coupons. The company incorporated in 1892 and by the turn of the century had become the largest soap manufacturer in Buffalo in terms of employees and one of the nation's largest mail order businesses, with sales rising from $220,000 in 1892 to $15 million by 1906. After 1900 it expanded to include food and household products, and established branch offices in urban centers including Brooklyn and Manhattan. The company shortened its name from J. D. Larkin to Larkin Co in 1904, when it employed over 2,250 workers in Buffalo. Frank Lloyd Wright designed the Larkin Administration Building (1906–50), Wright's first commercial commission and one of his most important early buildings, as well as homes for several Larkin executives in Buffalo. Responding to new forms of retail competition in the late 1910s, the company opened a department store, numerous food markets, gasoline stations, and homecraft stores in Buffalo, Western and Central New York, and in Peoria, Ill, where Larkin had a large operation. The death of John D. Larkin in 1926, the departure of other key executives, the failed attempt to operate retail stores, the onset of the depression, and other external changes led to financial reverses. By 1939 Larkin Co, under new ownership and having undergone a major restructuring, had been reduced to a shadow of its former self.

Larkin, Daniel I. *John D. Larkin: A Business Pioneer* (Amherst, NY: Author, 1998)
Stanger, Howard R. "From Factory to Family: The Creation of a Corporate Culture in the Larkin Company of Buffalo, New York" *Business History Review* 74 (Autumn 2000): 407–34

Howard R. Stanger

La Salle, René-Robert Cavelier de (*b* Rouen, France, 21 Nov 1643; *d* ?, 19 Mar 1687). French explorer. Shortly after abandoning his studies for the Jesuit priesthood in 1667, La Salle immigrated to Montreal. Two years later in an effort to explore the Ohio Territory, La Salle left Montreal with a Sulpician missionary party. After crossing Lake Ontario they met with the Seneca nation at Ganondagan [now Victor, Ontario Co] to try and obtain a guide. Breaking off from the Sulpician group, La Salle went further into the interior and explored until returning to Montreal in 1673. He received permission in 1674–75 to build a fort on Lake Ontario, which he named Fort Frontenac [now Kingston, Ont]. In the winter of 1678–79, he built a stockade and shipyard on the Niagara River. The stockade was named Fort Conti and was located at the site that would later become Fort Niagara [now in Porter, Niagara Co]. It burned within months of its construction. The shipyard was placed above the falls near the confluence of the Niagara River and Cayuga Creek [now Niagara Falls]. It produced only the 42 ton (38 MT) ship *Griffon,* which La Salle used to explore the Great Lakes. After he sent it back from what is now Green Bay, Wisc, in 1679 loaded with furs, the *Griffon* disappeared. On 9 Apr 1682 La Salle reached the Mississippi River's delta and claimed the entire river basin for Louis XIV. He attempted to colonize the mouth of the Mississippi River in 1685 but through navigational error landed instead at Matagorda Bay [now in Texas]. His party tried for two years to find the Mississippi River until his desperate men mutinied and killed him, probably in what is now Texas.

Galloway, Patricia Kay, ed. *La Salle and His Legacy: Frenchmen and Indians in the Lower Mississippi Valley* (Jackson: Univ Press of Mississippi, 1982)
Parkman, Francis. *La Salle and the Discovery of the Great West* (1869; repr New York: Modern Library, 1999)

Daniel A. Piazza

Last of the Mohicans: A Narrative of 1757. Novel. Published in 1826, *The Last of the Mohicans* is the most famous of James Fenimore Cooper's Leatherstocking Tales. Set during the French and Indian War, the novel follows the journey of Cora and Alice Munro, daughters of an English colonel, from Fort Edward [now in Washington Co] to Fort William Henry [now in Lake George, Warren Co], which their father commands. The sisters, along with Maj Duncan Heyward, a Virginian serving in the British army, are led astray by the treacherous Magua, a former scout for the British now secretly serving the French. Having been previously ill treated by Col Munro, Magua decides to gain revenge by kidnapping his daughters, but the plan is thwarted by the appearance of Hawkeye (Natty Bumppo, or Leatherstocking), an American scout, and of the Mohicans Chingachgook and his son Uncas. Later, during a dramatic battle at Glens Falls [now in Warren Co], the Munro sisters are captured by Magua and must be freed by Hawkeye and his Mohican allies. The reunited party avoids detection and finally arrives at Fort William Henry. During these initial events Cooper highlights an unspoken attraction between Cora and Uncas. Col Munro, under attack by the French, decides to surrender when reports confirming that reinforcements had not been sent fall into enemy hands. The French commander, Marquis de Montcalm, promises the British army safe conduct, but the retreating British are ambushed and massacred by the French-aligned Iroquois. During the battle Cora and Alice are again taken by Magua. Hawkeye, Heyward, and the Mohicans give chase, pursuing Magua to the Canadian border. In the lengthy struggle to free the Munros, Uncas and Cora are killed, and Magua is shot by Hawkeye. Alice and Heyward plan to wed and return to civilization, while Hawkeye and Chingachgook, now the last of the Mohicans, choose to remain in the wilderness.

From its initial publication the novel has been one of the most influential works of American literature. Its success turned the attention of many American artists to the wellspring of US history and the wonders of the untamed wilderness. Cooper's reliance on an actual historical episode, the massacre at Fort William Henry, to center his narrative proved that America had a complex history that could serve as the basis for a national literary tradition. His treatment of American Indians, albeit somewhat wooden, also opened up settlement history as a subject for artistic production. Almost immediately on the novel's publication, Cooper's use of New York State geography and landmarks increased tourism to the region, as visitors, national and international, flocked to see the picturesque landscapes he described.

The novel's themes of mythic frontier heroes battling on an epic landscape have inspired numerous imitations and adaptations. Just after the book appeared in 1826, Thomas Cole painted two canvases depicting scenes from its conclusion. In 1831 *The Last of the Mohicans* was adapted for the stage and enjoyed several runs in various US cities. A Parisian ballet company turned Cooper's narrative into a ballet, *Les Mohicans,* a decade after its publication, illustrating the early transatlantic popularity of the text. As technology advanced, new kinds of representations proliferated. Magic lantern shows of the mid–19th century depicted key events from the novel, largely through images of New York State's landscapes. At least a dozen film adaptations have been undertaken, from D. W. Griffith's silent film of 1909 to Michael Mann's 1992 Hollywood epic. Productions by other studios and the BBC, as well as animated versions, have also appeared. Quite often they have simplified Cooper's treatment of European American colonial and American Indian histories and shied away from the issue of miscegenation implicit in the attraction between Uncas and Cora. Adaptations have instead typically focused on the grandeur of New York State scenery. The novel's vision of frontier history has remained a central part of American culture.

Kelly, William P. *Plotting America's Past: Fenimore Cooper and the Leatherstocking Tales* (Carbondale: Southern Illinois Univ Press, 1983)

McWilliams, John. *"The Last of the Mohicans": Civil Savagery and Savage Civility* (New York: Twayne Publishers, 1993)

Duncan Faherty

Latham. Locality in Colonie (Albany Co). Lying at the intersection of the Troy-Schenectady Turnpike (Rte 7) and the Albany-Saratoga Rd (US 9) at Latham Corners, Latham acquired a post office, named for the owner of its hotel, in 1899. The intersection was made a traffic circle in 1929. After World War II the population grew rapidly, reaching 9,661 in 1960, the year the Northway opened parallel to US 9. Latham Circle Mall, the region's first indoor shopping center, opened in 1956. In the early 21st century, Latham is an inner suburb of Albany, with significant industrial and wholesale facilities, and the site of Albany International Airport.

Amy Braig-Lindstrom

Latin music. Several streams converged to form Latin popular music, the most prominent of which are Cuban *son,* the music style most fundamental to the development of the caliente (hot) salsa styles of the 1960s and 1970s, and a thriving Puerto Rican community in New York City, whose population by the mid-1950s equaled that of the San Juan metropolitan area.

Puerto Rico to New York

Puerto Rican migration to New York City began in earnest immediately after US citizenship was granted to Puerto Ricans in 1917. One of the early presences of Puerto Rican musicians in the city, and one of the earliest collaborations between African American and Puerto Rican musicians, can be traced to the celebrated World War I military band of James Reese Europe and his 369th Infantry Hellfighters, the group credited with introducing European audiences to jazz. Europe had gone to Puerto Rico to find men of African descent trained in municipal military bands and recruited 18. After the war the band toured the United States, was greeted in Manhattan with a parade up 5th Ave, and briefly recorded and played in a club Europe opened in Harlem. Other Puerto Ricans in Harlem's jazz scene of the 1920s and 1930s included valve trombonist Juan Tizol, a longtime member of the Duke Ellington Orchestra, whose compositions include the Latin-influenced "Caravan" (1937). Working-class Puerto Rican communities emerged in East Harlem, later known as El Barrio, in the 1920s and in the Hunt's Point, Longwood, and Mott Haven neighborhoods of the South Bronx in the 1940s. Both were sites of tremendous Latin music creativity and by the 1950s boasted numerous theaters, dance halls, clubs, and music stores.

The other dominant group in the New York City Latin music scene was Cuban, whose traditions of *son, danzón, guajira, guaracha,* and bolero had been popular in Puerto Rico since the 1920s. They took hold in New York City, and, though less popular, Puerto Rican *plena* and *jíbaro* music was also part of the mix. Groups ranged from trios to large ensembles, and many included both Puerto Ricans and Cubans, such as Cuarteto Caney and Cuarteto Machín. Notable groups in the 1920s and 1930s included Cuarteto Mayarí and groups led by influential Puerto Rican patriot, poet, and composer Rafael Hernández; Manuel "Canario" Jiménez, best known for popularizing the Puerto Rican *plena;* Piquito Marcano; and patriotic nationalist Pedro Flores.

The Mambo and Cha-cha-cha Era

In the 1950s people throughout the Americas and Europe were swept up in the mambo craze, a dance and music rooted in the Cuban *son* that had become internationally popular in the late 1920s and 1930s. In the 1930s Arsenio Rodríguez introduced into *son* the *montuno,* or mambo, a rhythmic section that allowed for solo improvisation; this caught on with *son* groups in Cuba, Puerto Rico, and New York. At the same time Israel "Cachao" López added a mambo section to the *danzón orquesta* (later called *charanga*), an ensemble modeled after European salon orchestras with violins and flute, which played elite society dances for predominantly white Cubans and Europeans. In the late 1930s Rodríguez introduced mambo as a form in its own right in his *son conjuntos.*

In New York City in the late 1940s, three bandleaders came to be known as the Mambo Kings—Francisco "Machito" Grillo (1909–84), a Cuban, and Tito Rodrígue (1923–73) and Tito Puente (1923–2000), both Puerto Rican. All three adapted mambo and other Cuban-based styles to a Latin music version of the big swing bands. The relationship of African American, Cuban, and Puerto Rican music can also be seen in Mario Bauzá's and Cuban percussionist Chano Pozo's work with jazz bandleader and trumpet player Dizzy Gillespie in the 1940s. In the 1950s the cha-cha-chá from Cuba became a major dance fad in New York City and internationally. Played by *charanga orquestas,* it evolved from the mambo section of *danzón* and was adapted to New York City's mambo big bands. After the Cuban Revolution (1959) *charanga orquestas* became established here, playing *danzón* and other Cuban-based music styles as well as the New York–born *pachanga* dance fad. Eddy Zervigón's *charanga,* Orquestra Broadway, began a successful career that continued into 2004. The careers of Charlie Palmieri and his Charanga Duboney, Johnny Pacheco y Su Charanga, and a host of other New York Latino musicians were launched on Al Santiago's Alegre label, founded in 1956. Key dance venues included the Palladium Ballroom in Manhattan, East Harlem's Park Palace, and the Bronx's Hunts Point Palace. Mambo and cha-cha-chá were appropriated by the mainstream music industry in pop versions by Rosemary Clooney, Tommy Dorsey, Little Anthony and the Imperials, and others.

The New York Sound

Until the rupture of diplomatic relations with Cuba in the early 1960s, the interaction between the New York and Havana music scenes enabled a somewhat parallel Latin music development, but even by the 1940s, New York bands had begun to take on a distinct, often jazz-influenced sound and style. New York Puerto Ricans, who had grown up amidst both African American and Latin music, briefly explored Latin *bugalú,* a bilingual Latinized version of the boogaloo, a black music-and-dance fad of the late 1960s and early 1970s. The civil rights and black identity movements of the 1960s inspired the Latino identity movements of the 1970s. There was a new sense of pride in *puertorriqueñidad* (Puerto Rican-ness) and Latino identity, and music was a primary vehicle for expressing this new consciousness. With an increasingly diverse Latino population, rhythms such as the Colombian *cumbia* and Dominican merengue were either musically alluded to or incorporated.

By the early 1970s, New York's Latin popular music became known as salsa after Fania Records (co-owned by New York Dominican flutist and bandleader Johnny Pacheco, and founded in 1964), the most influential record label in Latin music history, adopted the new name. Most musicians and bands such as Manny Oquendo y Libre continued to honor the older Cuban forms even as they explored new directions. The most popular music—especially as performed by such *salseros* as "bad boys" Willie Colón and Héctor Lavoe; Larry Harlow, known as *El Judio Maravilloso* (The Marvelous Jew); Celia Cruz (the Queen of Salsa); Ray Barretto; Rúben Blades; Victoria "La Lupe" Loli; and Pete "El Conde" Rodríguez—was aggressive and brassy and reflected the reality and diversity of urban Latino life. Other groups, such as Jerry González's Fort Apache band and Mario Rivera's Salsa Refugees, joined Cuban rhythms with jazz harmonies and instrumentation.

As Latinos spread out from New York City the music moved with them. Latin bands, many with non-Latino players, can be found throughout the state in cities such as Rochester and Buffalo, which have strong Puerto Rican communities. In the Capital District Alex Torres y Orquesta Los Reyes Latinos became a prominent group. An industry-led movement of sentimental *salsa romántica,* characterized by crooners, occurred in the 1980s. In reaction to the perceived superficiality of this music, a *salsa dura* movement began to take hold in the mid-1990s; bands of earlier years, such as Eddie Palmieri's reconstituted La Perfecta, are regaining popularity among another generation of fans, and another generation of musicians, such as Jimmy Bosch, are making their voices heard.

Caliente = Hot: Cuban and Puerto Rican Musical Expression in New York (New World Records NW 80244, 1977)

Glasser, Ruth. *My Music Is My Flag: Puerto Rican Musicians and Their New York Communities, 1917–1940* (Berkeley: Univ of California Press, 1995)

Lamento Borincano—Early Puerto Rican Music: 1916–1939 (Arhoolie 7037–38, 2001)

Singer, Roberta. " 'My Music Is Who I Am and What I Do': Latin Popular Music and Identity in New York City" (PhD diss, Indiana Univ, 1982)

Washburne, Christopher John. *New York Salsa* (Philadelphia, Pa: Temple Univ Press, 2004)

Roberta L. Singer

Lattingtown. Village (pop 1,860) in Oyster Bay (Nassau Co). Richard Latting purchased land in the area in 1660, and Josiah Latting later harvested reeds for thatching. By 1740 the community had been named for the family. In 1915 two attorneys purchased 400 acres (162 ha) and demolished some 60 houses to make room for their estates. Concern over the possible loss of ability to control development led the inhabitants to incorporate as a village in 1931. Population doubled in the 1950s. It has remained an exclusive residential community and is the site of St. Josephat's Ukrainian Orthodox Monastery (1944), located on a 118-acre (48 ha) estate. Another landmark is the 42-acre (17 ha) Bailey Arboretum, a county park.

Tom Kuehhas

Latvians. Since the Middle Ages Germanic knights, Poland, and Sweden ruled portions of Latvian territory before Russia absorbed Latvia in 1795 and ruled it until 1918. While the first Latvian immigrants settled in New York in the 1600s, often coming in company with other northern European ethnic groups such as Swedes, the first major wave occurred between 1890 and 1905. It resulted largely from the czarist policy of Russification among the empire's non-Russian minorities. By 1900, 4,309 Latvians officially arrived in the United States, though this statistic underrepresents the number of Latvian immigrants because US officials frequently misclassified them as Russian or Scandinavian. These early Latvian arrivals were mainly individual males who later sent for other family members. Overwhelmingly of peasant origin, they chose to settle in urban areas, especially New York City, where they took unskilled factory and foundry work, later turning to construction work. The Latvian-Estonian Lutheran missionary Hans Rebane was instrumental in organizing a number of Latvian parishes throughout New York State for the Lutherans' Missouri Synod. The first Latvian Lutheran congregation formed on New York City's Upper East Side in 1902.

The second influx of Latvian immigrants to the United States, comprising about 5,000 persons, resulted from the failed Russian Revolution of 1905. Many of these immigrants represented a radical political orientation and returned to Russia during the revolutions of 1917; while in New York State—primarily in New York City—most worked in skilled trades, in publishing, or as union organizers. The existence of an independent Latvia from 1918 to 1940 greatly reduced emigration from the country, but that changed after World War II. Following Soviet reoccupation of Latvia in 1944, over 40,000 Latvians fled to North America, bringing with them strong nationalist sentiment as well as professional and organizational skills. It was from this end-of-war period that significant Latvian communities grew in Buffalo, Poughkeepsie, and other urban regions outside New York City. Since 1951 the American Latvian Association, based in Washington, DC, functioned as the dominant secular organization in an increasingly middle-class and professional Latvian American community.

Latvian settlement in New York State has been overwhelmingly urban and largely organized around the Lutheran Church, to which about 85% of Latvian New Yorkers belong at the beginning of the 21st century. People of Latvian descent remain scattered among urban centers of the state, such as Buffalo, Poughkeepsie, Albany-Schenectady, Syracuse, and Long Island City; Melville (Suffolk Co) also boasts many Latvians. In eastern Schoharie Co and Warren Co rarer agricultural communities existed from the 1900s. But these farming communities were greatly diminished by the beginning of the 21st century because of assimilation and intermarriage. On the 2000 US Census, 9,937 New Yorkers claimed Latvian ancestry. New York City remains the center of New York State's Latvian community, with about 3,000 active members, many associated with the Latvian Evangelical Lutheran Church in Brooklyn.

Anderson, Edgar. "Latvians." In *Harvard Encyclopedia of American Ethnic Groups,* ed. Stephan Thernstrom (Cambridge: Belknap Press of Harvard Univ Press, 1980)

Karklis, Maruta, Liga Streips, and Laimonis Streips, eds. *The Latvians in America, 1640–1973: A Chronology and Fact Book.* Ethnic Chronology Series, no 13 (Dobbs Ferry, NY: Oceana Publishing, 1974)

Martin Fedor Ziac

Laurel Hollow. Village (pop 1,930) in Oyster Bay (Nassau Co). The area, called Wauwepex by the American Indians, was purchased by settlers in 1653 and was known as Laurel Hollow by 1700. In 1872 Oliver L. Jones built the popular Laurelton Hotel, and the locality took Laurelton as its name. Louis C. Tiffany built the massive Laurelton Hall (1905–57) in the village. Incorporated as Laurelton in 1926, the village assumed its present name in 1935. The Cold Spring Harbor Laboratory (1890), renowned for its work on biology and genetics, is located on 107 acres (43 ha) in Laurel Hollow; three of its scientists have received the Nobel Prize. The village is also the site of the Cold Spring Harbor Fish Hatchery (1883).

Tom Kuehhas

Laurens. Town (pop 2,402) and village (pop 277) in S central Otsego Co. Its 1773 settlement of migrants from New Jersey was uprooted by the Revolutionary War; permanent settlement followed in 1784. The town was formed in 1810 from Otsego. Its population reached 2,235 in 1835, then declined, not exceeding that number until 2000. Laurens was the site of a number of industries powered by Otego Creek, including the Otsego Cotton Mill (1846–73), a tannery, a foundry, a hammer factory (1840) that employed 20 a decade later, and a mill that made bags for wool. Prosperous farmers and business people built handsome houses in the village, which incorporated in 1834, and in the hamlets of West Laurens and Mount Vision. Farming, which once included hop raising, declined in the 20th century. Now largely a residential community, most workers in Laurens commute to Oneonta.

Hugh C. MacDougall

Lavender, Ellen Elizabeth [Mother Lavender] (*b* Macon, Ga, ?1841; *d* Utica, 8 Sept 1928). Evangelist and humanitarian. Born into slavery and separated from her family at age 7, she became the slave of a harsh plantation owner in South Carolina. After emancipation Ellen moved north with her son Amos, the result of a forced mating with another slave. She settled in Albany, where she was introduced to Christianity. She later married Nicholas Lavender, and after his death she became Sister Lavender, an evangelist. Around 1893 she and sons Amos and Nicholas Jr moved to Utica, where she began a ministry of providing meals and a place to sleep in her home to anyone in need. Poor and illiterate herself, she also assisted the sick and dying. In 1901 Mother Lavender, as she had become known, introduced an annual New Year's Day dinner, open to anyone in need; some years as many as 900 attended. For 40 years after her death, the annual meals were held without interruption. In Utica the name Mother Lavender continues to be equated with sacrifice and sharing. She is buried in Utica at the New Forest Cemetery.

Cardarelli, Malio J. *Utica's Mother Lavender: I'll See You in Heaven* (New Hartford, NY: Author, 1999)

Malio J. Cardarelli

Law, Department of. See ATTORNEY GENERAL.

Lawrence. Town (pop 1,545) in E St. Lawrence Co. Settled in 1806, the town was formed in 1828 from Hopkinton and Brasher. At Lawrence hamlet, a potato-starch factory began operating in 1847 and was the first of many in town. In 1849 a large, 30-saw gang sawmill began operating; others followed. The Northern Railroad (later Rutland Railroad) initiated service in 1850. The town is predominantly agricultural on good soils. In the early 21st century a Kraft General Foods milk plant operates in North Lawrence.

Richard E. Mooers

Lawrence. Village (pop 6,522) in Hempstead (Nassau Co). Antigua-born merchant Josiah Martin acquired land in this part of Rockaway and built Rock Hall, a Georgian-style mansion, in 1767; it is now a town museum. The Rockaway post office opened in Lawrence in 1840. Development by the Lawrence brothers began when the Rockaway Branch Railroad established a Lawrence station in 1869. There were fox hunts, steeplechases and, later, polo matches at the Rockaway Hunting Club (1884), and the Osborne House hotel (1884) and Isle of Wight Hotel (1885) further helped define the area's exclusive image. The village incorporated in 1897, and its population reached 3,649 in 1940. It has a church, four synagogues, and four Jewish day schools, in addition to a large and growing Jewish population.

John A. Hewlett

lawyers and law firms. After the Revolutionary War the practice of law in New York State lacked uniformity, but a developing, Americanized common law increased the importance of judges and allowed a flexible interpretation of the law. Aspiring young lawyers generally apprenticed with established ones, learning the mechanisms of the profession through experience rather than academic preparation. Admission to the bar occurred after an examination by a state supreme court justice or court-appointed attorney. This system of reading law enabled talented men of humble origins to join the profession and potentially to rise through the ranks of society and become officeholders; a disproportionate number of lawyers were active in local, state, and federal politics. Martin Van Buren of Kinderhook (Columbia Co), for example, entered the legal profession in 1796 at the age of 14 and apprenticed with different lawyers for the required seven years. He passed the bar in 1803 and practiced law for 25 years, while holding the posts of attorney general and US senator before becoming governor of New York State and president of the United States.

More formal training in schools was introduced in the late 18th century, and the apprenticeship system gradually declined. James Kent offered law lectures at Columbia College from 1793 to 1798, when he was appointed to the state supreme court. Columbia did not offer a course in law again until 1858, when Theodore Dwight assumed the professorship and the School of Law was established. New York University opened a short-lived School of Law in 1835; it was reestablished in 1858 and combined with the Metropolitan Law School in 1895 to offer night classes. Albany Law School began as Union University's Department of Law in 1851.

In the 1800s the rapid increase in the volume and complexity of commerce contributed to the need for more formally trained lawyers, as did a newly industrializing and consolidating state.

Charles Evans Hughes.

Advances in transportation and manufacturing called for new laws, which required a more uniform court structure, regular selection procedures for judges, and systematic qualification of attorneys. The practice of law also changed. Before the mid-1800s New York State lawyers were generally sole practitioners. The first private law firms developed as industrialization necessitated representation of corporations in increasingly complicated business transactions. In Buffalo, for example, Hodgson Russ, founded in 1817, assisted in bringing the Erie Canal there and in developing the city's first charter. The firm later provided counsel to railroads.

Regulating the Profession, 1860s–1940s

Several developments damaged the reputation of the legal profession in New York State in the second half of the 19th century. Among these were the questionable involvement of lawyers in new business opportunities, collusion with railroad companies battling for supremacy through consolidation, and involvement in corrupt New York City politics. Few formal constraints on the actions of lawyers existed because no bodies policed the profession. Bar admission requirements, furthermore, were minimal. Only in 1870 was the Bar Association of the City of New York incorporated to correct judicial abuses and raise professional standards. In 1871 the state legislature shifted power over admission to the profession to the New York State Court of Appeals and adopted new regulations, requiring bar applicants to be men at least 21 years old who had completed a three-year clerkship with a practicing attorney.

The creation of the New York City Bar prompted the establishment in 1877 of the New York State Bar Association, which attempted to strengthen requirements for admission to the profession. In 1882 the Court of Appeals mandated a college education as a prerequisite for clerkships. In 1895 the state legislature established the State Board of Law Examiners, empowered to administer a bar admission exam. Additional rules established in 1911 required bar applicants to complete three years of study at an accredited law school (four years for noncollege graduates). Attorneys from other states could be admitted to the bar in New York State after five years of practice in any jurisdiction and upon application to the Court of Appeals. Bar associations also agitated for a code of conduct, with the first national code released by the American Bar Association in 1908. Several new law schools opened, including Cornell School of Law (1887), University at Buffalo Law School (1887), New York Law School (1891), Syracuse University College of Law (1895), Brooklyn Law School (1901), Fordham University School of Law (1905), and St. John's University School of Law (1925).

New York City became the center of American finance, spawning the creation of corporate law firms that were copied throughout the country. Between 1872 and 1924 the number of private practice law firms in the city with four or more attorneys increased from 17 to over 1,000. Cravath, Swaine, and Moore, which arose from the 1853 merger of Blatchford, a Manhattan firm, and Seward, an Auburn firm, was the archetype of the large law firm. Cravath began the practice of hiring first-rank graduates of leading law schools to do research for clients in exchange for salary, training, and increased responsibility leading toward partnership. Associates were required to work exclusively on firm business and allowed to develop their own practice only after they made partner. Partners in other firms generally shared profits equally until 1940, when Root Clark (later Dewey Ballentine) tied profits to the amount of business a partner brought into the firm.

Since World War II

Attorneys supported the war effort during World War II by volunteering for the armed forces, donating their services to the Red Cross, and initiating projects that provided legal services to servicemen's wives and widows and others. The National Lawyers Guild, founded in 1937, represented on a pro bono basis consumers accused of violating Office of Price Administration mandates and families of servicemen evicted by landlords. After the war attorneys again organized through local bar associations to help veterans. Although minorities and women were increasingly successful in opening their own firms throughout the state, the majority of law firms remained homogeneously white and male.

During the 1950s the rift between New Deal progressive lawyers and more conservative corporate attorneys widened as the American Bar Association condemned attorneys who represented members of the Communist Party. The National Lawyers Guild in New York City saw a decline in its membership in the state and elsewhere as lawyers were called to testify before the House Committee on Un-American Activities. In the early 1960s, as southern civil rights activists called for more legal support, volunteer New York State lawyers responded, such as Faith Seidenberg of Syracuse, who went south to assist the movement. New York City–based organizations, such as the National Lawyers Guild, the American Civil Liberties Union, and the Lawyers Constitutional Defense Committee, organized these efforts.

The focus on business aspects of law during the 1960s and 1970s influenced significant changes. Firms that developed new departments to address the increasing need for legal specialists became "mega firms," with the attorney staff numbering in the hundreds. In some cases specialty, or boutique, law firms developed. In 1964 the erosion of the rule against soliciting new business opened up the profession to market forces. The US Supreme Court struck down minimum-fee schedules in 1975 and decided in 1977 that lawyers could advertise. The growing complexities of economic transactions, corporate structures, and the law itself increased the demand for lawyers, especially at large law firms.

Many of the large firms in New York City developed new specialties related to corporate takeovers, which became more numerous and fueled tensions between notions of professionalism and commercialism. Skadden, Arps, Slate, Meagher and Flom, founded in 1948, both influenced and reflected the changing needs of corporate clients. As corporate takeovers increased Skadden, Arps developed a specialization in that work. It is also recognized for its hiring of minorities, women, and gay and lesbian attorneys from a wide range of law schools.

In the early 1970s few firms were inclined to branch out beyond their locations and fields of practice. They would establish satellite offices only if loyal clients had interests elsewhere. National corporations generally used a different firm in each city. Finely Kumble was the first to merge with smaller firms in cities where it desired to open branch offices. In 1979 New York State law firms began to expand internationally, signifying greater globalization and need for representation for American clients doing business abroad and for foreign clients wanting to do business in the United States. Market forces and the changing economy fostered new signs of competition among law firms in the 1980s, manifested in lateral mobility and the rush to establish branches in other American and foreign cities. Large firms were financially successful because of a wave of mergers and acquisitions. Older firms, still operating under the rules of etiquette of the early 1900s, responded to intense pressure to become more competitive by borrowing management techniques from investment banking and corporate clients.

The tensions between the dictates of the market and the duties of the profession became even more of an issue when the increase in corporate transactions opened the possibility of making much money. Pressure to bill long hours created greater stress for associates in large firms and distracted them from the commitment to pro bono work. The increasing firm salaries in the 1970s aggravated the imbalance between private-practice and public-interest attorneys. New York State has developed models for public-interest law firms, for-profit and not-for-profit entities that provide legal representation to traditionally underserved populations or focus on specific issues. For-profit public-interest law firms such as Rabinowitz Boudin, founded in 1944 in New York City, and Walter, Thayer and Mishler, founded in Albany in 1981, represent unions, criminal defendants, plaintiffs in civil rights cases, tenants, and consumers.

Not-for-profit public-interest legal organizations such as the American Civil Liberties Union (1920) and the Center for Constitutional Rights (1966), both founded in New York City, litigate class-action lawsuits. Law communes or collectives, such as Lefcourt Garfinkle, founded in New York City in 1969 (the nation's first), were committed to representing progressive political causes and people. These public-interest law firms were particularly influential in securing rights for traditionally underserved or unpopular clients.

The first organized effort in New York State to provide representation to the poor was the Legal Aid Society, created in 1876 as a service organization for German immigrants. In 1963 federal grants provided impetus for creating experimental civil legal services offices, most notably Mobilization for Youth (MFY) Legal Services in New York City. In 1965, through the Office of Economic Opportunity (OEO), Legal Services (replaced by the Legal Services Corp in 1975) provided federal money for a network of civil legal services offices throughout New York State. A network of public-defender offices developed concurrently and continues to represent indigent criminal defendants free of charge. The total number of public-interest attorneys in New York State is hard to tally because the category covers lawyers working in district attorneys' offices, criminal legal aid and civil legal services offices, government agencies, and public-interest law firms.

Although solo practitioners and small law offices still abound statewide, the mega firms also remain a fixture, with several firms having numerous New York State and international branches. In 2002 six firms based in New York City employed more than 500 lawyers in their main office: Skadden, Arps, Slate, Meagher and Flom (857); Simpson, Thatcher and Bartlett (635); Weil, Gotshal and Manges (565); Shearman and Sterling (559); Davis, Polk and Wardwell (527); and Sullivan and Cromwell (520). Sizable Buffalo firms include Hodgson Russ, with 142 lawyers, and Phillips, Lytle, Hitchcock, Blaine and Huber, with 120 lawyers in its main office. In Rochester, Nixon Peabody had 119 lawyers in its main office; Harter, Secrest and Emery employed 92 lawyers, and Harris Beach, 87. In Syracuse, Bond, Schoeneck and King retained 102 lawyers, while Hancock and Estabrook employed 74 lawyers in its main office. In East Meadow (Nassau Co), Certilman, Balin, Adler, and Hyman retained 73 lawyers. According to the 1999 Attorney Census, New York Co had the largest number of working lawyers, with 60,211, an average of 1 lawyer for every 26 residents. The lowest ratio was in Orleans Co, with 25 lawyers, 1 for every 1,801 residents. Hamilton Co had the fewest number of lawyers at 5.

The law continues to be a burgeoning profession. In 2003, 15 law schools operated in New York State, including several established after World War II: Hofstra Law School (1970), Cardozo Law School of Yeshiva University (1976), Pace University School of Law (1976), Touro College Law Center (1980), and CUNY School of Law at Queens College (1983). In February 2003, 3,293 people took the state bar exam, and 1,531 passed.

Abel, Richard L. *American Lawyers* (New York: Oxford Univ Press, 1989)

Auerbach, Jerold S. *Unequal Justice: Lawyers and Social Change in Modern America* (New York: Oxford Univ Press, 1976)

Chester, Alden. *Courts and Lawyers of New York: A History, 1609–1925* (New York: American Historical Society, 1925)

Henke, Jack. *Lawyers and Law in New York: A Short History and Guide* (Albany: Charles Evans Hughes Press, 1979)

Greater Upstate Law Project. "An Overview of Programs: Civil Legal Service Offices in New York State," http://www.gulpny.org/legal%20services/State_Funding/snapshots.pdf

Houseman, Alan W., and Linda E. Pearle. *Securing Equal Justice for All: A Brief History of Civil Legal Assistance in the United States* (Washington, DC: Center for Law and Social Policy, 2003)

New York State Defenders Association. "New York State Chief Defenders List," http://www.nysda.org/AboutNYSDA/Chief_Defenders/chief_defenders.html

Amy Ruth Tobol

League of American Wheelmen. National bicyclist advocacy and promotional organization. As bicycling gained popularity in the late 19th century, riders faced adverse behavior by drivers of horse-drawn vehicles and governmental restrictions on cyclists, such as regulations forbidding the use of park roads. After local bicycle clubs proved ineffective in addressing cyclists' concerns, the New York City Bicycle Club called for the formation of a national organization, and in 1880 the League of American Wheelmen (LAW) was formed in Rhode Island. Separated into divisions by states, the LAW had a particularly active and effective staff in New York. The state's 27,000 members in 1897 comprised 26% of the country's total. In addition to seeking to protect cyclists' rights, the LAW was instrumental in the Good Roads Movement. It also produced a series of innovative route books complete with road maps, put up road condition signs, compiled lists of hotels providing lodging and meals to cyclists at fixed prices, administered amateur bicycle racing, and sponsored bicycle tours. As bicycling enthusiasm waned in the early 20th century, LAW membership declined precipitously. The organization was revived in the 1940s without strong state divisions and since 1994 has been known as the League of American Bicyclists.

Mason, Philip P. "The League of American Wheelmen and the Good-Roads Movement, 1880–1905" (PhD diss, Univ of Michigan, 1957)

Geoffrey N. Stein

League of Women Voters. Successor organization to the National American Woman Suffrage Association (NAWSA) after women gained the vote. A local chapter was founded in New York City as early as 2 June 1919, although the national league was not officially founded until February 1920, during the convention of NAWSA in Chicago. New York State was active from the beginning in increasing women's participation in elections. Buffalo started a chapter in 1920, as did smaller cities like Ogdensburg (St. Lawrence Co). In some cities, such as Rochester, chapters were not formed until the end of the 1920s because the organization was seen as competing with established women's clubs. Although the league was nonpartisan, some Republicans and Democrats found their advocacy of such issues as ending child labor, gaining equal pay for working women, guaranteeing maternal and infancy benefits for the poor, and supporting the League of Nations as potential political threats. But the league's priority was to provide women with objective information about all candidates and to encourage women to become politically active locally and regionally. Like the national league, the New York State league sponsored candidates' forums and political debates, first on radio and later on television. As society's attitude about careers for women changed, however, fewer women were available to do volunteer work, and membership had declined substantially by the 1970s. By 1995 the pioneering Buffalo chapter had to merge six Erie Co chapters into one. Meager funds nearly caused the New York City chapter to close in late 2000, but corporate donations came through at the last minute. Despite these declines, the New York State league remained active, with 59 local chapters and a membership of about 7,000 in 2003. While continuing to sponsor candidates' nights, to help immigrants understand the voting process, and to teach students about citizenship, the New York State League of Women Voters participates in the study and investigation of public issues such as the protection of natural resources, welfare reform, solid waste reduction, and strengthening the United Nations.

League of Women Voters of New York State, http://www.lwvny.org
McKelvey, Blake. "Woman's Rights in Rochester: A Century of Progress," *Rochester History* 10 (July 1948): 1–24

Donna L. Halper

Leather Man. In the third quarter of the 19th century, a tramp clothed entirely in leather laced together with thongs was seen along roads in Westchester and Putnam Cos and adjacent Connecticut on an apparently regular circuit of about five weeks. He accepted food at farmhouse doors, returning to the same kitchens year after year, but spoke little. It was believed he spoke an uneducated French as well as some English. He slept in caves and in simple huts he assembled. By 1887 it was apparent he was suffering from a cancer in his lip and jaw; on 24 Mar 1889 he was found dead near Briarcliff Manor (Westchester Co). His marked grave is in Sparta Cemetery; his leather bag is in the collection of the Connecticut Historical Society. In the year of his death his story was taken up by New York City newspapers, and stories of his origins appeared, none of which has ever been documented. All research has focused on the supposed Jules Bourglay of Lyon, France, said to have left there after an ill-fated romance about 1857. There is no indication in the sources that a more likely Quebecois origin was ever investigated. The mystery was of great popular interest in the region through the middle of the 20th century, when those who remembered seeing him in childhood were still living.

Albee, Allison. "The Leather Man," *Quarterly Bulletin of the Westchester County Historical Society* 13 (1937): 29–38, 68–77, 90–110

Field Horne

Lebanon. Town (pop 1,329) in S central Madison Co. Settled in 1792, the town was formed from Hamilton in 1807. Once served by three railroads, its treasured landmark is the Lebanon Depot of the abandoned Syracuse and Chenango Valley Railroad (1872–1937), now a community center. Limestone quarried in the early 19th century furnished material for many houses, especially along River Rd near Randallsville. Dairy farms supplied milk stations along two railroad lines in the late 19th century. Dairy farming remains productive in the early 21st century.

William F. Helmer

Ledyard. Town (pop 1,832) in SW Cayuga Co. On the east shore of Cayuga Lake, this town contains a pre-Iroquoian village archaeological site near Levanna, dating from *ca* AD 1000. During the Revolutionary War the town also contained a Cayuga settlement, Chonodote, which was partly destroyed by a Continental army raiding party in 1779. European settlement began 10 years later, and the town was formed from Scipio in 1823. From 1873 to 1974 the Cayuga Lake Railroad served the town, with passenger service ending in 1948. In 2002 much of the land remained in dairy farms, corn, or soybeans, because the soil is highly productive and fertile. Ledyard is the site of Long Point State Park.

Laurel Auchampaugh

Lee. Town (pop 6,875) in N central Oneida Co. The town was formed from Western in 1811 after the area's settlement in 1790. In its early years lumbering and tanning were major occupations, succeeded by dairying and cheese making after the Civil War. In 1912 the Mohawk River was dammed in Lee's southeastern corner to provide water for the Barge Canal, creating Lake Delta and flooding the hamlet of Delta. At that time Olney and Floyd Canning Co moved from Delta to Lee Center, closing in the late 1960s. Near the dam a sizable suburban-type community of workers from Griffiss Air Force Base more than doubled the town's population in the 1950s. The population continued to increase until the closing of the base in the 1990s.

Lee, Ann (*b* Manchester, England, 29 Feb 1736; *d* Niskayuna [now Watervliet, Albany Co], 8 Sept 1784). Shaker leader. Daughter of John Lees, a blacksmith, she joined a small group of religious enthusiasts known as Shaking Quakers in 1758. Members of the society, including Lee, were arrested repeatedly for confrontational tactics and disturbing public worship. She married Abraham Standerin (Standley) in 1762. None of their four children survived infancy. A charismatic visionary, Lee led a handful of followers to America in 1774, arriving in New York City. For some years her activities are unknown. Later in the decade, separated from her husband, she and her followers relocated to Niskayuna in 1776 and lived in isolation, which ended in 1780 when members of the sect, including Lee, were imprisoned in Albany for failure to support the American Revolution. Between May 1781 and September 1783 Lee and some disciples traveled throughout eastern New York State and New England, gathering converts. During this missionary journey she experienced physical abuse and persecution, but the young sect won several hundred followers. Although opponents depicted Lee as a violent, promiscuous woman, the Shakers revered "Mother Ann" as a miracle worker and inspired prophet, the embodiment of the Christ Spirit. Her teachings shaped the religious ideals and structures of the community after her death.

Stein, Stephen J. *The Shaker Experience in America: A History of the United Society of Believers* (New Haven, Conn: Yale Univ Press, 1992)
Testimonies of the Life, Character, Revelations and Doctrines of Our Ever Blessed Mother Ann Lee . . . (Hancock, Mass: J. Tallcott & J. Deming, 1816)

Stephen J. Stein

Lee, Luther (*b* Schoharie, Schoharie Co, 30 Nov 1800; *d* Flint, Mich, 13 Dec 1889). Religious reformer. A Methodist preacher in Chenango and Cayuga Cos, he entered the Methodist Episcopal Church's itinerant ministry in 1827 and was assigned to the Malone (Franklin Co) preaching circuit. Convinced of the evils of slavery, Lee served as a New York State Anti-Slavery Society traveling agent in 1838 and 1839. At an 1839 abolitionist meeting in Albany, Lee argued strenuously for the formation of an independent antislavery party, which was later established as the Liberty Party. In 1843 Lee joined a group who seceded from the Methodist Episcopal Church to form a thoroughgoing antislavery denomination, the Wesleyan Methodist Connection, in Utica. From 1847 to 1867 Lee was the most visible leader of the Connection, particularly while editor of the *True Wesleyan*, the denominational paper published in Syracuse. In South Butler (Wayne Co) he preached the sermon for the 1853 ordination of Antoinette Brown (later Antoinette Brown Blackwell), often considered to be the first ordained clergywoman. Lee later moved to Michigan to teach at Adrian College.

Kaufman, Paul Leslie. *"Logical" Luther Lee and the Methodist War against Slavery* (Lanham, Md: Scarecrow Press, 2000)

Douglas M. Strong

Lee, Spike [**Shelton Jackson**] (*b* Atlanta, 20 Mar 1957). Film director, writer, and actor. Lee's mother was a teacher, and his father a jazz musician. The family moved to Brooklyn before Lee's third birthday. A graduate of John Dewey High School in Brooklyn (1975), he received his BA in communications at Morehouse College in Atlanta (1979) and earned his MA in film studies at New York University (1982). During the 1980s he established his own production company, Forty Acres and a Mule Filmworks, in Brooklyn. Many of Lee's films are set in Brooklyn, including the comedy *She's Gotta Have It* (1986), his first theatrical feature. The commercial success of the film not only brought Lee to the forefront of the 1980s independent cinema movement but also opened doors for an emerging generation of black directors and screenwriters. In his films Lee often confronts racial issues, exploring the place of African Americans in a white-dominated society as well as interracial conflict. In one of his most significant Brooklyn films, *Do the Right Thing* (1989), set in Bedford-Stuyvesant, he examines racial tensions between Blacks and Italian Americans. Other films with a New York City setting include *Jungle Fever* (1991), *Malcolm X* (1992), *Crooklyn* (1994), *Summer of Sam* (1999), and *25th Hour* (2002).

Fuchs, Cynthia, ed. *Spike Lee: Interviews* (Jackson: Univ Press of Mississippi, 2002)

Lefkowitz, Louis J(acob) (*b* New York City, 3 July 1904; *d* New York City, 20 June 1996). Attorney general. The son of a garment center vest maker, Lefkowitz grew up in a cold-water flat on Manhattan's Lower East Side, attended public schools in New York City, and received his law degree from Fordham University in 1925. In 1928 he was elected to one term as a New York State assemblyman as a Republican in the heavily Democratic New York Co Sixth District, where he became well known for his personal style of campaigning. His law practice was interrupted with several jobs in appointed positions, including a year as deputy state tax commissioner (1943). He served as general counsel to the Republican Party in the state, and in 1957 the New York State legislature appointed him attorney general to replace Jacob K. Javits, who had been elected to the US Senate. The next year Lefkowitz won the first of his five consecutive four-year terms in the position, serving until 1978, making him the state's longest-serving attorney general. The Republican candidate for mayor of New York City in 1961, he lost to Robert F. Wagner Jr by 400,000 votes. Lefkowitz took an aggressive approach to the attorney general's job, moving the office from the narrow task of defending the state in lawsuits to the broader and more proactive role of protecting the consumer by filing lawsuits on residents' behalf. After retiring from his post he worked as a lawyer and after 1979 served on the Board of Trustees of the Boys Club of New York, a group he had joined as a child on the Lower East Side.

Ravo, Nick. "Louis Lefkowitz, 22-Year Attorney General, Dies at 91," *New York Times,* 22 June 1996

John R. Deitrick

left-wing summer camps. By the end of the 19th century, secular socialist colonies had been created and children's summer camps organized by reformers concerned with the negative impact of urban life on young people. Jewish summer camps were organized for children of each section of the organized Jewish community, from Orthodox religious to secular socialist and Zionist. Later, as members of the working class gained summer vacations and the pay to support them, workers' organizations, especially those on the left, acquired land for vacations and socializing.

By the early 20th century New York City was a center for radical activity, especially in the large eastern European Jewish immigrant communities. Contentious radical groups organized three types of vacation retreat within a 100 mi (161 km) radius of New York City: summer bungalow colonies, resorts, and children's camps. Bungalow colonies were communities of cottages shared by like-minded radicals, who bought land together but built or owned houses individually, or in some cases rented cottages from a single owner. They featured organized social and political activities such as weekend lectures. Left-wing resorts were similar to the nonradical resorts that spread through the Catskills during the first part of the 20th century but with many more organized activities for adults and children. Radical culture was given full sway, with concerts by Pete Seeger and Paul Robeson and regular lectures by left-wing notables. Some resorts were linked to children's camps, where these cultural figures also presented programs. The network of children's camps reflected the full variety of the New York–based movement. They were organized to provide alternative education and socialization for the children of radicals and to create oases that might be a model for the kind of racially integrated and socially progressive society they wanted to create.

Among the bungalow colonies were the communist-oriented Followers of the Trail in Peekskill (Westchester Co), the socialist Three Arrows Colony in Putnam Co, and the Mohegan Colony in Peekskill, founded by anarchists and later including various types of radicals. Goldens Bridge (Westchester Co) was a communist-associated bungalow colony, evidently linked to the first interracial camp in the United States, Wo-Chi-Ca (Workers' Children's Camp, 1933–51) in Port Murray, NJ. Arrow Park in Sterling Forest (Orange Co) was founded in 1949 by young pro-Soviet Russian Americans and later sold to Ukrainians. Camp Nitgedaiget splintered off from Camp Unity; both resorts were organized by people from the Allerton Ave "Coops," a communist-sponsored housing cooperative in the Bronx.

Camp Kinderland of the International Workers' Order, founded on Sylvan Lake in Hopewell Junction (Dutchess Co) in 1923 and still existing in Massachusetts, is the oldest radical children's camp. Like its neighboring adult resort, Lakeland, it was oriented toward Yiddish culture and heavily influenced by the Communist Party. Kinderland had a heated political rivalry with the anticommunist Kinder Ring, founded by the Socialist-oriented Workmen's Circle between 1927 and 1930 and located on the other side of Sylvan Lake. Both Kinder Ring and the affiliated Circle Lodge adult resort continue in the early 21st century but with an emphasis more Jewish than socialist. Camp Woodland in Phoenicia (Ulster Co), created by radicals associated with the Progressive education movement, specialized in folk music and the culture of the Hudson Valley. The Pioneer Youth of America was an independent organization in the 1930s and 1940s, associated for a time with the Workers Education Association. Another left-wing children's camp was Camp Ma-Ho-Ge in the Adirondacks. Camp Hemshekh (1956–77) in the Catskills served the Yiddish-speaking children of the socialist Jewish Labor Bund, whose parents were often Holocaust survivors; future World Trade Center architect Daniel Libeskind was a counselor there. Camp Hurley was operated by the interracial United Community Service Centers of East New York in Brooklyn, which also ran Twin-Link Camp in Accord (Ulster Co; 1959–68). Located near the Ashokan Reservoir from the late 1950s to the 1970s, Camp Hurley was reestablished in Huntington (Suffolk Co) in 1993.

Left-wing camps were controversial institutions in the context of Cold War politics and the social upheavals of the Civil Rights Movement. The Non-Criminal Investigations Unit of the New York State Police spied on communist children's camps, and in a famous incident Robeson's 1949 concert at the Mohegan Colony was attacked by an anticommunist mob. All the camps, resorts, and bungalow colonies created spaces for fellowship, political debate, and recreation. In these summer places New York radical movements became more than political organizations, developing their own cultures that nurtured activists and their families through historical and socioeconomic change.

Joselit, Jenna Weissman, and Karen S. Mittelman, eds. *A Worthy Use of Summer: Jewish Summer Camping in America* (Philadelphia: National Museum of American Jewish History, 1993)
Mishler, Paul C. *Raising Reds: Young Pioneers, Radical Summer Camps, and Communist Political Culture in the United States* (New York: Columbia Univ Press, 1999)
New York State. "Communist Indoctrination and Training of Children in Summer Camps." In *Report of the Joint Legislative Committee on Charitable and Philanthropic Agencies and Organizations* (Albany: Williams Press, 1956)

Paul C. Mishler

"Legend of Sleepy Hollow." Short story by Washington Irving (1783–1859), published in 1819, set in "Tarry Town," or Tarrytown (Westchester Co), on the eastern shore of the Hudson River during the post-Revolutionary period. The story tells of the arrival of the gangling Ichabod Crane, an acquisitive and gullible Yankee. Taking up schoolteaching in the somnolent Dutch community, he woos Katrina Van Tassel, the daughter of a prosperous local farmer. Pursuing his suit with vigor and a thinly disguised sexual rapacity, Ichabod attracts the antagonism of Brom "Bones" Van Brunt, a daredevil horseman and rival for Katrina's hand. After an evening at the Van Tassels' farm, where the company is entertained by stories of witchcraft and the legend of a headless horseman reputed to haunt the locality, the superstitious Ichabod returns home on a borrowed plow horse. Suddenly he finds himself pursued and overtaken by the apparition of a demonic horseman without a head. As the ghostly figure sweeps past it flings a round object, apparently its detached head, at the terrified schoolteacher, and then disappears into the darkness. Ichabod is never again seen in Sleepy Hollow, although the following morning a shattered pumpkin is discovered at the bridge where the incident took place. The old wives of the village insist he was spirited away supernaturally, but rumor has it he has resurfaced at a safe distance, in the new guise of lawyer and local politician. Brom, suspected by some of being the prankster behind the whole affair, marries Katrina, and the community returns to its peaceful and timeless existence.

First published in *The Sketch-Book of Geoffrey Crayon, Gent.,* the story is presented as a manuscript discovered among the papers of "Diedrich Knickerbocker," the fictitious Dutch historian of Irving's earlier *History of New York* (1809). Important literary sources are the demonic horseback chase through Kirk Alloway in Robert Burns's comic epic poem *Tam O'Shanter* (1787) and Gottfried August Bürger's 1785 ballad "The Wild Huntsman." The throwing of a false head occurs in the Rübezahl legends of Germany. Like its companion piece "Rip Van Winkle," Irving's legend naturalizes European folktale in a rural American setting and is a conscious exercise in national mythmaking. Ichabod Crane, an original creation, supplied the characteristic qualities for the prototypical Yankee of satire and caricature.

Irving settled in 1836 on his Sunnyside estate in Tarrytown close to the location of his legend. The tale of the headless horseman has been adapted for the stage, screen, and opera. Sleepy Hollow has imprinted itself on the local landscape. Tourist brochures refer to the area as Sleepy Hollow Country, and it has been used in the names of cemeteries, country clubs, and other local institutions. In 1996 the Village of North Tarrytown adopted the name Sleepy Hollow.

Hedges, William L. *Washington Irving: An American Study, 1802–1832* (Westport, Conn: Greenwood, 1980)
Rubin-Dorsky, Jeffrey. "The Value of Storytelling: 'Rip Van Winkle' and 'The Legend of Sleepy Hollow' in the Context of *The Sketch Book,*" *Modern Philology* 82 (1985)

Susan Manning

legislature. Achieving representative government was a persistent objective of colonial New Netherlanders and New Yorkers. New York was first a Dutch corporate and then a British proprietary colony, ruled after 1685 by an appointed governor and council. In New Netherland, following Dutch custom, delegates from each village could attend a Colonial Assembly called by the director general and council to address problems of colony-wide concern. Such assemblies were infrequent and were called only three times (1653, 1663, 1664).

Richard Nicolls, the first governor appointed by the patentee James, Duke of York, after the British conquest in 1664, imposed the Duke's Laws, which did not provide for a representative assembly. Following a 14-month restoration of Dutch rule, British authority was reestablished in 1674. Soon thereafter Gov Edmund Andros proposed the creation of a representative assembly in New York, but the duke continued to resist. Under Gov Thomas Dongan, appointed in 1682, an election for a General Assembly of Freeholders was authorized by James. It met in 1683 and proposed a Charter of Liberties and Privileges that called for an elected assembly that would meet at least once every three years. However when his brother, King Charles II, died in February 1685, James became king and New York became a royal colony. As monarch, James II vetoed the charter but not before the colony could hold its first and only real election before the Glorious Revolution. New York's assembly meet three times between 1683 and 1687.

William III, successor to James II, appointed Henry Sloughter as governor. Faced with the unrest caused by Leisler's Rebellion (1689–91), Sloughter called an assembly into session. It first met in New York City in 1691 and annually thereafter, with short intervals when an assembly was dissolved or arrangements were being made for a new session. Because calling the assembly to meet and dissolving it at will remained an important executive power, a fixed term of office was seen as providing a potential source of independence for elected representatives. Although the assembly met annually, the time of elections to that body and the length of its sessions were not fixed: between 1691 and 1775 there were 31 assembly elections, 4 necessitated by deaths of monarchs and 25 conducted after governors dissolved the assembly. Thus colonists' desire for regularly scheduled elections and meetings of their representative body persisted unsatisfied until the eve of the American Revolution. The Colonial Assembly last met on 3 Apr 1775, and the legislature created by the first state constitution convened on 10 Sept 1777 in Kingston (Ulster Co).

State Legislature: Size, Terms, and Term Limits

The state constitution adopted in 1777 made the legislature the principal repository of governmental power in New York's constitutional system of separate institutions sharing powers. The assembly created by the constitution had 70 members apportioned among 14 counties in accord with their number of qualified voters and elected annually. The senate had 24 members, a quarter of whom were elected annually to four-year terms from within four multimember districts: eastern (3 members), southern (9 members), middle (6 members), and western (6 members). The assembly was much larger and the senate somewhat smaller than the Colonial Assembly, which had also used counties as the primary basis of representation.

The 1777 Constitution allowed for the growth in the size of the legislature up to a limit of 300 assembly members and 100 senators, levels never reached. The state's constitutional convention in 1801 fixed the number of senators at 32 (fewer than the 43 then serving) and assembly members at 100, with both houses apportioned according to population. Two assembly members per year could be added as counties were created, up to a limit of 150. In 1821 a guarantee for one assembly member per county was added, and the number of senate districts increased from four to eight. Further revisions made by the 1846 Constitutional Convention provided for election of 32 senators and 128 assembly members from single-member districts, the former for two-year terms, the latter still for one year.

Theodore Roosevelt began his political career by serving 3 terms in the New York State Assembly, 1882–84. Photograph by William Notman, 1883.

A proposal in 1867 to return to county-based elections (with multimember rather than single member districts), adopt four-year staggered terms for the senate, and increase the assembly's size to 139 members failed to be adopted. A similar fate befell an 1873 proposal made by New York State's first Constitutional Commission to return the state to electing its 32 senators at large from eight multimember districts.

The 1894 Constitutional Convention increased the size of the senate to 50 and allowed it to grow under specified conditions. In 2004 it had 62 members. The assembly's size was fixed and remained at 150 members (except in 1966 when it reached 165 because of a brief-lived reapportionment later found to be in violation of the state constitution). The two-year term for the assembly was adopted by constitutional amendment in 1937; several attempts before this date and since to adopt a four-year senate term have failed. Perhaps because New York State never adopted initiative and referendum procedures, there has been no serious effort to institute term limitations for its legislators.

Powers of the Legislature

Most governmental authority was located in the state legislature by the 1777 Constitution, and relatively few constraints were placed upon it. Periodically in the eras that followed, particularly in the 19th century, discontent with legislative performance—corruption, favoritism, spending excesses, imprudent borrowing—led to the adoption of constitutional provisions limiting what the legislature could do, prescribing its procedures, and empowering others in areas formerly regarded as legislative.

Of all developments restricting the legislature's power, the creation over time of a very strong governorship was most important. The executive veto was adopted in 1821, and the item veto followed in 1874. After a long struggle in the early 20th century, Progressive era thinking came to fruition with adoption of the four-year term for governor (effective 1938); gubernatorial appointment of most executive agency heads, albeit with senate advice and consent; and, of transcendent importance, the creation of a constitutionally based executive budget

ASSEMBLY SPEAKERS, FROM 1899

Name	Dates of Service	Residence
S. Frederick Nixon (R)	1899–1905	Westfield (Chautauqua Co)
James W. Wadsworth Jr (R)	1906–10	Mount Morris (Livingston Co)
Daniel D. Frisbie (D)	1911	Middleburg (Schoharie Co)
Edwin A. Merritt Jr (R)	1912	Potsdam (St. Lawrence Co)
Alfred E. Smith (D)	1913	Manhattan
Thaddeus Sweet (R)	1914–20	Phoenix (Oswego Co)
H. Edmund Machold (R)	1921–24	Ellisburg (Jefferson Co)
Joseph A. McGinnies (R)	1925–34	Ripley (Chautauqua Co)
Irwin Steingut (D)	1935	Brooklyn
Irving M. Ives (R)	1936	Norwich (Chenango Co)
Oswald D. Heck (R)	1937–59 (part)	Schenectady
Joseph F. Carlino (R)	1959 (part)–64	Long Beach (Nassau Co)
Anthony J. Travia (D)	1965–68 (part)	Brooklyn
Moses M. Weinstein (D)	1968 (part)	Queens
Perry B. Duryea, Jr (R)	1969–74	Montauk (Suffolk Co)
Stanley Steingut (D)	1975–78	Brooklyn
Stanley Fink (D)	1979–86	Brooklyn
Mel Miller (D)	1987–91	Brooklyn
Saul Weprin (D)	1991–94	Queens
Sheldon Silver (D)	1994–	Manhattan

Source: New York Red Book.

TEMPORARY PRESIDENTS AND MAJORITY LEADERS OF THE NEW YORK STATE SENATE, FROM 1874

Name	Dates of Service	Residence
William H. Robertson (R)	1874–81	Katonah (Westchester Co)
Dennis McCarthy (R)	1881,[a] 1884–85	Syracuse
John C. Jacobs (D)	1883	Brooklyn
Edmund L. Pitts (R)	1886–87	Medina (Orleans Co)
Henry R. Low (R)	1888	Monticello (Sullivan Co)
J. Sloat Fassett (R)	1889–91	Elmira
Jacob A. Cantor (D)	1892–93	New York City
Charles T. Saxton (R)	1894	Clyde (Wayne Co)
Edmund O'Connor (R)	1895	Binghamton
Timothy E. Ellsworth (R)	1896–1902	Lockport (Niagara Co)
John Raines (R)	1903–9	Canandaigua (Ontario Co)
Jotham P. Allds (R)	5 Jan–23 Feb 1910	Norwich (Chenango Co)
George H. Cobb Sr (R)	Elected 11 Mar 1910	Watertown
Robert F. Wagner (D)	1911–17 Oct 1913	New York City
John F. Murtaugh (D)	1914	Elmira
Elon R. Brown (R)	1915–18	Watertown
J. Henry Walters (R)	1919–20	Syracuse
Clayton R. Lusk (R)	1921–22	Cortland
James J. Walker (D)	1923–24	New York City
John Knight (R)	1925–9 Apr 1931	Arcade (Wyoming Co)
George R. Fearon (R)	9 Apr 1931–32	Syracuse
John J. Dunnigan (D)	1933–38	New York City
Perley A. Pitcher (R)	4 Jan–20 Feb 1939	Watertown
Joe R. Hanley (R)	27 Feb 1939–1943	Perry (Wyoming Co)
Benjamin F. Feinberg (R)	1944–49	Plattsburgh
Arthur H. Wicks (R)	30 Mar 1949–18 Nov 1953	Kingston (Ulster Co)
Walter J. Mahoney (R)	1954–64	Buffalo
Joseph Zaretzki (D)	1965	New York City
Earl W. Brydges (R)	1966–72	Niagara Falls
Warren M. Anderson (R)	1973–88	Binghamton
Ralph J. Marino (R)	1989–94	Syosset (Nassau Co)
Joseph L. Bruno (R)	1995–	Troy (Rensselaer Co)

Source: New York Red Book.

[a]No choice was made in 1882.

process (1927). The legislature retained crucial taxing and appropriation authority, but the governor came to define spending priorities and to control actual spending.

Until the mid-1960s the legislature commanded relatively little professional staff to balance the expertise available to the executive. Abbot Low Moffat, Republican chair of the Assembly Ways and Means Committee, reportedly did much of the detail work himself in the 1930s. Legislators' concerns focused largely on their districts. Moreover, they were in session and could exercise collective power for only a few months of the year. Although members were likely to win when they sought reelection, their tenures were short and their political prospects dependent on the resources and good will of strong county party organizations. County leaders were, in turn, responsive to their respective state organizations and its head. Concentration of governmental power (and control of patronage) in the executive eventually allowed governors to gain control over formerly independently powerful state party leaders. For the Democrats, this change began with Franklin D. Roosevelt and accelerated under Herbert H. Lehman. For the Republicans, it was achieved by Thomas E. Dewey. Through them chief executives made the party an additional tool for dominance of the legislature, at least during those long periods in which majorities in both houses were their co-partisans.

The resurgence of legislative power began in the 1960s, fueled by changes in the nature of membership, the geographic distribution of power, shifts in partisan control resulting from reapportionment, and a national movement for the professionalization of state legislatures. Elected legislators served longer, and more of them came to regard legislative service as their careers and legislative work as a full-time occupation. Offices and staff were provided for members both in Albany (eventually in a legislative office building completed in 1973) and in each district. Legislative sessions lengthened, as did the leaders' time served in leadership positions. First with Republican and then with Democratic governors, assembly speakers and senate majority leaders beginning in the mid-1960s built fiscal, legal, and policy staffs to generate an independent capacity to assess gubernatorial priorities. Soon such leaders as Assembly Speaker Stanley Fink (1979–86) and Senate Majority Leader Warren M. Anderson (1973–88) were devoting staff resources to proactive development of legislative initiatives in key areas of policy. Legislative independence became more obvious in 1976 when Gov Hugh Carey's veto of a bill to ensure New York City's proportion of education aid was overridden in the legislature, the first veto override since 1870. More frequent assertion of legislative power followed. Techniques and structures were enacted by the legislature to ensure that executive agencies acted in accord with legislative intent and to check regulatory incursions on legislative prerogatives. During the governorship of George E. Pataki (1995–), the state budget again became a focus of conflict over the distribution of power between the executive and legislative branches.

With regard to procedure, the New York State Constitution at the beginning of the 21st century prohibits bills in the legislature to be amended following their final reading or made applicable by reference. Private bills must be limited to one subject, identified in the title. Tax laws must clearly identify the nature and object of taxation. Bills must be printed and on members' desks in final form for three calendar days before passage, unless a Message of Special Necessity is received from the governor (such messages have become routine). Two-thirds majorities are needed in each house to support spending public funds for private or local purposes.

Substantively, the constitution names 14 areas where the legislature is barred from passing private or local bills and prohibits gifts or loans of state credit for private purposes. Preemptive and constraining constitutional provisions restrict the legislature in its borrowing authority, policies toward state workers, use of state lands, and actions with regard to local governments. And it is affirmatively directed to act by other constitutional provisions in such areas as education and in relief of the poor.

Hierarchy and Partisanship

The majority party dominates the business of each house of the legislature, with minority party members marginalized. Although the state constitution designates the lieutenant governor as the senate's presiding officer, real power in the senate resides in the elected majority leader, designated its temporary president. Each majority elects a leader (the speaker in the assembly, the majority leader in the senate) and invests extraordinary power in this person. For their respective houses, these leaders control the flow of business, assign committee members, appoint key staffers and direct their work, determine the allocation of political opportunities and fiscal resources to members, and designate colleagues for committee chairs and other leadership positions. The basic level of compensation of legislators is established by law, but leadership positions and ranking minority status bring additional compensation (payments in lieu of expenses, or "lulus").

The leaders' strength is enhanced, too, by their control of political resources. One effect of the reapportionment revolution in New York State brought about by the US Supreme Court and the federal Voting Rights Act (1965) was to shift the responsibility for determining legislative districts within counties from county boards and the New York City council to the state legislature. This change gave the speaker and majority leader a crucial role in shaping members' districts and therefore in determining their prospects for political survival. As political party strength diminished in the late 1960s and early 1970s, majority and minority party legislative leaders began to raise funds to finance legislative campaigns in efforts either to gain or to retain the majority in each house. In the later decades of the 20th century, incumbents for legislative office in both the senate and assembly were rarely defeated: average success rates for assembly and senate incumbents in the 1980s and 1990s exceeded 95%, and in 2002 only one incumbent in each house who sought reelection was defeated. Even raising a serious challenge to a sitting member, whether in a primary or general election, became a formidable task. Most funds gathered by the majority and minority party campaign committees in each house came to be used, therefore, to influence candidate selection, to fund campaigns in a few selected districts with vulnerable incumbents, and to wage strong contests in targeted districts with no incumbents. As a result, aspirants to office often incurred political obligations to legislative leaders even before they were legislators.

Assembly speakers and senate majority leaders have sometimes been criticized as too empowering of staff and insufficiently responsive to views of rank-and-file members. However, their great power and the relationships they develop with individual members over time bolsters sitting leaders' security. Moreover, organizing within each house to achieve a leadership change is very difficult and, as the failure of Majority Leader Michael Bragman's challenge to Speaker Sheldon Silver in 2000 illustrated, the consequences of trying and failing are dire. When Bragman's attempted coup became public, the Speaker stripped two key supporters of committee chairmanships and most support in the Democratic Conference melted away. The power of the two leaders and that of the governor has led to the description of high policy making in New York State as "three men in a room" government.

Democratic Party strength in the legislature has long been centered in New York City, and Republican strength has been outside that city. Since the late 20th century, there have been a significant number of Democratic representatives from suburban and rural areas and Republican senators from New York City, forcing both the speaker and the majority leader to manage important regional differences in their conferences. The greater size and demographic diversity of the assembly, however, made the leadership task in this house more of a challenge than in the senate. (In 2001 the total number of women and minorities in the Assembly Democratic Conference was greater than the total membership of the Senate Republican Conference.) For example, the majority leader can distribute the benefits of being the majority party to all the members of the conference, but the speaker must often require junior members to wait their turn.

A strong relationship with the speaker or majority leader is most important for majority party legislators who seek to build legislative careers in Albany. It is somewhat less important for those with ambitions in public sector opportunities elsewhere, such as the US Congress, the judiciary, or executive branch positions in local or state government. Frustrated by their lack of real power, many minority party legislators return home to seek elected leadership positions in local government or, if the occasion arises, to enter the administration of governors of their party. Some members of both parties use the contacts and skills they develop to build careers as lobbyists after they leave the legislature.

The Legislative Process

The legislature convenes annually on the first Monday after the first Wednesday in January to receive the governor's constitutionally required, agenda-setting State of the State message. In the final decades of the 20th century, the legislature remained in session through June or later. Members are generally in Albany two days a week in January and February and three days per week thereafter. To deal with the logjam that arises as deals negotiated through the session are consummated, around-the-clock meetings at the close are common. The constitution provides procedures for calling additional special legislative sessions for specified purposes, but the modern practice of recessing rather than adjourning allows leaders to call the body back easily to Albany at their discretion.

The formal powers of the senate and assembly are almost identical. One difference is that the senate must confirm many gubernatorial appointees to cabinet-level executive positions. Because members of the Board of Regents, at the head of the State Education Department, are elected by the legislature sitting jointly with each member having one vote, the more numerous assembly dominates this process. Senators are likely, to the annoyance of assembly members, to think of their body as the upper house. Long-running divided partisan control of the legislature notwithstanding, even relatively powerless minority party senators are not likely to switch houses to gain majority status. Majority party assembly members rarely seek seats in the senate, where they would be in the minority. Minority party assembly members do regularly seek election to the senate, where they would gain majority status.

Bills may be introduced in either house. "Unibills" are introduced simultaneously in both houses. Members may introduce unlimited numbers of bills until a published deadline and 10 bills each for a limited period after the deadline. Assistance with bill drafting is provided by a Bill Drafting Commission. In accord with the state constitution, budget bills are introduced by the governor. Bills are live for an entire two-year session and may gather many cosponsors in addition to the prime sponsor, who controls the legislation. Referral to committee is by staff responsive to the speaker in the assembly and majority leader in the senate. Where committee jurisdiction is unclear, the power to refer is significant. Committees may amend, defeat, or hold bills, or report them for consideration on the floor. Hearings may be used to build support for a measure or give visibility to its sponsors. In each session far more bills are introduced than are enacted. Bills with little chance of passage are often introduced to begin policy discussions or to satisfy constituents that action is being taken on a matter. At a specified date in the session, all business is referenced to the leadership-controlled Rules Committee in each house. Throughout the session, the leaders control access to the floor. At any phase, bills can be given priority or stopped by the speaker or the majority leader. On the floor, partisan discipline prevails, with outcomes known before matters are debated; debate is perfunctory, and the unexpected rarely occurs. Bills must be passed in identical form in both the senate and the assembly before submission to the governor. If the governor fails to approve or veto a bill within 10 days, it becomes a law. If the legislature adjourns, preventing a bill's return, the bill must be approved by the governor within 30 days to be a law. With the consent of sponsors and leaders, bills may be sent back for changes to meet gubernatorial objections and avoid veto. Since the legislature no longer adjourns (which would leave the executive 30 days to deal with the crush of business at the close of the session), bills are sent to the governor's counsel office for consideration by the governor in a phased manner.

Districting and Apportionment

The New York State Constitution of 1777 was the first to provide for occasional redistricting to deal with population movements. The 1821 Constitution stipulated that districting of the assembly be based on inhabitants except for "aliens, paupers and persons of colour not taxed," an exclusion that disadvantaged urban areas. Senate districts of unequal population developed at midcentury because of an 1846 constitutional limitation barring division of any county for the purpose of apportionment unless it was entitled to more than one seat. The growth in southern New York's proportion of the state population resulted in 1892 in Republican legislation on districting to limit the representation of New York City, Brooklyn, and the surrounding counties to 15 of 32 senate seats. In 1894 provisions were embedded in the state constitution that ensured overrepresentation of rural areas and underrepresentation of New York City in both the assembly and the senate for the next 70 years. Because rural New York State was a Republican Party bastion, both houses of the legislature were mostly controlled by the Republicans for this entire period, described by Democratic governor Alfred E. Smith as "constitutionally Republican."

The application by the US Supreme Court of the one person–one vote principle to New York State in *WMCA v Lomenzo* (1964) enhanced the representation in the legislature of suburban areas and diminished that of rural areas, shifting the locus of Republican legislative strength. Still largely Democratic, New York City achieved legislative representation proportional to its population, but by this time its share of the state population had diminished. The Democratic Party's 1964 national landslide put Democrats in control of both legislative houses in New York State for the first time since 1935, but outgoing Republicans reapportioned before the Democratic legislature was seated. Democrats retained control of the senate for only one year and the assembly for four years. Republicans regained the assembly majority in 1969 and held it through 1974.

Over the course of the 20th century the state legislature became more diverse in its representation. The first African American member, Edward A. Johnson, a Republican from New York City, was elected to the assembly in 1917. The first female legislator, Republican Ida B. Sammis of Suffolk Co, won election to the assembly in 1918. The first Latino to serve was Puerto Rican native Oscar Garcia Rivera, who won an assembly seat representing East Harlem in 1937. No Asian American had yet served by the beginning of the 21st century. Because of very low minority voting rates, amendments in 1970 to the federal Voting Rights Act (1965) resulted in Kings,

Bronx, and New York Cos being subject to US Justice Department scrutiny to ensure fair representation of minorities. This legislation accelerated the increase in numbers of minority party members and women in the legislature. In 2001 there were 34 members of the Black, Puerto Rican, and Hispanic Legislative Caucus, 25 in the assembly and 9 in the senate. In the same year, there were 35 female members of the assembly and 8 female senators.

Two effects of the Voting Rights Act—the application of the one person–one vote standard and the public reaction to Republican scandals in Washington, DC—led in 1974 to Democrats winning control of the assembly. Bipartisan gerrymanders in 1980, 1990, and 2000 ensured continued Democratic control of the assembly and Republican control of the senate. A permanent staff reporting to a joint task force designs the districts. With gubernatorial acquiescence, decisions are controlled by the senate Republicans for their house and by assembly Democrats for theirs. As of 2004, this has resulted in the longest continuously divided partisan control of a contemporary bicameral legislative body in the United States; the senate has been Republican since the 1966 session, and the assembly has been Democratic since the 1975 session.

REFORM

The concentration of budgetary power in leaders' hands, the regular failure of the legislature to produce timely budgets, growing debt, concerns about noncompetitive elections, publicity given to conflicts of interest, increased burdens on local governments, and the national movement for campaign finance reform all led to calls for reforms of the legislative process in the late 20th century. In response, some steps were taken to diminish conflict of interest in the legislature (1987); a statute was passed suspending legislative pay if a budget was not adopted by the beginning of the state fiscal year (1995); and the beginnings of a conference committee system were established to consider more openly and inclusively budgetary issues (1995). A series of other budget process reforms were also under consideration, and, with decennial redistricting on the agenda, there was the revival of the idea (included in the failed constitution of 1967) that this process be taken from the legislature and be given to a less self-interested redistricting commission, as was done for the New York City Council in the 1989 charter.

See also APPORTIONMENT AND DISTRICTING; COLONIAL NEW YORK; PARTY SYSTEM; TAXATION.

Benjamin, Gerald, ed. *The New York State Constitution: A Briefing Book* (New York: Temporary State Commission on Constitutional Revision, 1994)

Benjamin, Gerald, and Robert Nakamura, eds. *The Modern New York Legislature: Redressing the Balance* (Albany: Nelson A. Rockefeller Institute of Government, 1991)

Bonomi, Patricia U. *A Factious People: Politics and Society in Colonial New York* (New York: Columbia Univ Press, 1971)

Galie, Peter J. *Ordered Liberty: A Constitutional History of New York* (New York: Fordham Univ Press, 1996)

Schneier, Edward, and John Brian Murtaugh. *New York Politics: A Tale of Two States* (Armonk, NY: M. E. Sharpe, 2001)

Stonecash, Jeffrey. "The Rise of the Legislature." In *New York Politics and Government,* ed. Sarah F. Liebschutz (Lincoln: Univ of Nebraska Press, 1998)

Ward, Robert. *New York State Government: What It Does, How It Works* (Albany: Rockefeller Institute Press, 2002)

Gerald Benjamin

Lehigh and Hudson River Railroad. The first trackage, completed in Orange Co by predecessor Warwick Valley Railroad Co in 1862, extended from Warwick to a connection with the New York and Erie Railroad at Greycourt [now Chester] and with the Erie Branch to Newburgh. Grinnell Burt, president of the Lehigh and Hudson River Railroad (L&HR) and its predecessors, was the driving force behind this enterprise. L&HR was formed by merger and completed its line to Belvidere, NJ, in 1882. Opening of the Poughkeepsie Railroad Bridge in 1889 enabled the railroad to connect with New England lines after extending to Maybrook (Orange Co). This gave the L&HR a through line of 85.8 miles (138.08 km) from Maybrook to Easton, Pa, including trackage rights. By then coal had replaced agricultural products as the main traffic. In 1905, to block a takeover by the New Haven Railroad, several other connecting lines took a controlling interest in the L&HR. Passenger service, never of much consequence because of the rural character of the territory, ended in 1939. The changeover from steam to diesel power was accomplished in 1950–51. Although well managed and profitable for many years, L&HR could not survive the general collapse of the northeastern railroads. It fell into bankruptcy in 1972 and was merged into Conrail in 1976.

Boyd, Jim, and Tracy Antz. *Lehigh and Hudson River: History and Operations of the L&HR, 1860–1976* (Scotch Plains, NJ: Morning Sun Books, 2001)

Pennisi, Bob. *The Northeast Railroad Scene, Vol 2: The Lehigh and Hudson River* (Flanders, NJ: Railroad Avenue Enterprises, 1977)

Larry Lowenthal

Lehigh and New England Railroad. Small, mainly freight railroad centered in the Pennsylvania anthracite, or hard coal, region and Lehigh River Valley that connected with New York, New Haven and Hartford Railroad at Campbell Hall (Orange Co). Originally chartered as South Mountain and Boston Railroad Co in 1872, Lehigh and New England was purchased by Lehigh Coal and Navigation Co in 1904. The railroad served as a conduit for anthracite and other freight heading northeast to New England via the Poughkeepsie Bridge across the Hudson River. Anthracite traffic declined after World War II, and trucks carried most of the Lehigh Valley region's other major commodity, cement. The railroad tried to capture general freight moving from the Allentown, Pa, area to the rail interchange at Campbell Hall, but this venture failed. Lehigh and New England filed for abandonment or government permission to cease operations in 1960; it was one of the first railroads in the nation to do so. All operations terminated on 31 Oct 1961.

Crist, Ed. *The Lehigh and New England Railroad* (Newton, NJ: Carstens Publications, 1980)

Jeff Schramm

Lehigh Valley Railroad. Primarily a carrier of anthracite, or hard coal, from the mountains of northeast Pennsylvania, the line maintained facilities in and around New York City and in central and western New York State. Lehigh Valley Railroad originated in northeast Pennsylvania in 1846 with the incorporation of the Delaware, Lehigh, Schuylkill and Susquehanna Railroad. In time the company, renamed LVRR in 1853, expanded north to Sayre, Pa, on the New York State border, and east to Perth Amboy and Jersey City, NJ. In 1876 it moved into New York with the acquisition of the Geneva, Ithaca and Sayre Railroad and by 1892 reached Buffalo. The main line in Central and Western New York stretched from Sayre through Geneva (Ontario Co) and Batavia (Genesee Co) to Buffalo, and branchlines linked to Rochester, North Fair Haven, Camden, Elmira, and Cortland. From the 1890s to 1917, LVRR operated lake steamers that transported coal from railroad docks at North Fair Haven (Cayuga Co) to many points on the Great Lakes. The company also owned waterfront terminals in Brooklyn, Manhattan, and the Bronx. As anthracite revenues fell from the 1930s through the 1960s, LVRR trimmed its branchlines and, by 1961, eliminated passenger service. Pennsylvania Railroad took control of the company in 1962 but operated it separately. By the early 1970s LVRR was bankrupt like many other northeastern carriers. Absorbed by Conrail on 1 Apr 1976, most of the company's New York State properties were abandoned.

Archer, Robert F. *Lehigh Valley Railroad* (Berkeley, Calif: Howell-North Books, 1977)

Hamilton-Dann, Mary. *Upstate Odyssey: The Lehigh Valley Railroad in Western New York* (Rochester: Railroad Research Publications, 1997)

Jeff Schramm

Lehman, Herbert H(enry) (*b* New York City, 28 Mar 1878; *d* New York City, 5 Dec 1963). Governor and US senator. After graduating from Williams College in Williamstown, Mass, in 1899, he worked for a New York City textile company, becoming vice president and treasurer after six years. In 1908 he was made a full partner at Lehman Bros, a major investment banking firm. Early in his career he also began to support the Henry Street Settlement on Manhattan's Lower East Side, developing a lasting passion for social reform. During World War I, Lehman held several key federal administrative positions, including those that supervised relief efforts. He managed Alfred E. Smith's winning gubernatorial campaign in 1926, and two years later Lehman left private business to lead the national Democratic Party's finance committee in Smith's presidential drive. At the same time he won the lieutenant governor's position in the election in which Franklin D. Roosevelt was chosen for his first term as governor; both were reelected in 1930. Lehman proved invaluable as an active lieutenant governor who resourcefully handled banking crises, state hospital improvements, and prison disturbances.

Upon Roosevelt's ascension to the presidency, Lehman was elected as the state's first Jewish governor in 1932 and reelected in 1934, 1936, and 1938, the latter for a four-year term. Through his leadership New York State enacted what later became known as the "Little New Deal," a series of relief programs modeled after Roosevelt's national New Deal. With a calm but persuasive resolve born of his business career and his dedicated liberalism, Lehman led successful fights to set a minimum wage, guarantee job insurance, provide public housing, expand the legal rights of organized labor, and increase unemployment relief. Skilled at working with special interest groups, powerful politicians, and bureaucrats, he also enhanced state government operations, brought new regulation to utilities, secured changes in the criminal justice system, and managed to turn a $106 million deficit in 1932 into an $80 million surplus 10 years later.

In December 1942 Lehman resigned as governor to become director of the Office of Foreign Relief and Rehabilitation Operations, a post he held for three years. Although he ran an unsuccessful campaign for the US Senate in 1946, Lehman won a special election in 1949 after the retirement of Robert F. Wagner Sr and then won a full six-year term in 1950. He supported most of Pres Harry S. Truman's programs and consistently promoted liberal causes. He cosponsored a bill to strip Sen Joseph McCarthy of committee chairmanships and advocated his censure in the Senate. In 1956 Lehman retired from politics. From 1959 to 1961, he worked with Eleanor Roosevelt and others in a reform Democratic movement that led to the defeat of Tammany Hall boss Carmine DeSapio. Lehman was a noted philanthropist for numerous causes, and in 1960 he and his wife Edith donated $500,000 to establish the Children's Zoo in New York City's Central Park. Lehman died of a heart attack shortly before he was to receive the Presidential Medal of Freedom.

See also LIBERALISM; WORLD WAR II.

Ingalls, Robert P. *Herbert H. Lehman and New York's Little New Deal* (New York: New York Univ Press, 1975)

Nevins, Allan. *Herbert H. Lehman and His Era* (New York: Charles Scribner's Sons, 1963)

William Rainbolt

Lehman, Irving (*b* New York City, 28 Jan 1876; *d* Port Chester, Westchester Co, 22 Sept 1945). Jurist. Lehman, a child of immigrant parents who had flourished in commodity trading, was raised in the privileged world of New York City German Jews. He was educated at Columbia University, where he received his BA (1896), MA (1897), and LLB (1898). He practiced law in New York City until he was elected to the New York State Supreme Court in 1908. He served on that court in New York City until 1923, when he was elected to the New York State Court of Appeals, the state's highest appellate court. Reelected in 1936, he became its chief judge in 1940 and sat in that capacity until his death. Lehman best expressed his judicial outlook when he wrote that the judge must use law "as an instrument with which to do justice between man and man; but he also has the responsibility of preserving and even molding the law so that human relations can be fitly ordered by it in the future." From 1921 to 1940 he served as president of the Jewish Welfare Board in New York City. Brother and sometime advisor of Gov Herbert H. Lehman, he was one of the nation's most eminent state jurists.

"The Influence of the Universities on Judicial Decision," *Cornell Law Quarterly* 10 (1924): 1–16

Wiecek, William M. "The Place of Chief Judge Irving Lehman in American Constitutional Development," *American Jewish Historical Quarterly* 60 (Mar 1971): 280–303

William M. Wiecek

Lehman College. New York City public college, part of the City University of New York (CUNY) at 250 Bedford Park Blvd West in the Bronx. The Bronx campus of Hunter College opened in 1931 in one building near Jerome Park Reservoir; campus construction finished in 1936. The extension suspended classes during World War II to accommodate a Navy training center. From March to August 1946, the campus housed the sessions of the UN Council and General Assembly. The regular college program resumed in 1946, when male students were accepted but attended separate classes. In September 1951 the Board of Higher Education allowed men to matriculate at the Bronx campus. Renamed for former governor Herbert H. Lehman, the extension became an independent college on 1 July 1968. The Lehman Center for the Performing Arts opened in 1980. Lehman College offers professional programs in health and education in cooperation with Bronx institutions and houses the CUNY PhD program in plant sciences. In fall 2003 Lehman enrolled 4,584 full-time and 3,010 part-time undergraduate students, and 110 full-time and 2,008 part-time graduate students.

Roff, Sandra Shoiock, Anthony M. Cucchiara, and Barbara J. Dunlap. *From the Free Academy to CUNY: Illustrating Public Higher Education in New York City, 1847–1997* (New York: Fordham Univ Press, 2000)

Pamela Cooper

Leicester [LES-TER]. Town (pop 2,287) and village (pop 469) in W Livingston Co. Long a center of Seneca settlement, from 1797 to 1826 the hamlet of Cuylerville, on the Genesee River, was the location of the Big Tree, Squakie Hill, and Little Beard's Town Reservations of the Seneca and allied Indian nations. Leicester is also the site of the Boyd-Parker Memorial, erected in honor of two men killed by Indians during the 1779 Sullivan-Clinton campaign, which destroyed much of Indian life in the Genesee Valley. Initial white settlement began in 1789. The town was formed in 1802 as Lester; the spelling changed in 1805. The Genesee Valley Canal operated through town from the early 1840s to 1878. The village was incorporated in 1907 as Moscow but changed its name in 1917. Salt extraction began in the 1890s, and part of the Akzo salt mine near Cuylerville collapsed in 1994, causing polluted wells and weakened foundations. Salt mining ended the following year. The principal industries are CPAC, manufacturer of pollution control systems, and the Seneca food-processing plant, a division of Curtice-Burns. Agriculture remains an important land use.

Joyce Rapp

Leisler, Jacob (*bap* Frankfurt am Main, Germany, 31 Mar 1640; *d* New York City, 16 May *os*/26 May *ns* 1691). Merchant and governor of New York Colony. A son of Frankfurt's French Reformed minister, Leisler arrived in New Amsterdam as a soldier in the employ of the Dutch West India Co in 1660. Shortly thereafter he abandoned a military career for mercantile pursuits. By the 1670s he was the predominant New Yorker engaged in the Chesapeake tobacco trade. Through marriage he also became heir to one of New York's largest fortunes when his mother-in law, Marritje Jans Loockermans, died in 1677. Subsequent attempts by his in-laws, the Bayard and Kierstede families, to break Marritje Jans's will resulted in a bitter feud that colored New York politics for decades.

Leisler was appointed as a tax assessor in 1674, an Admiralty Court justice in 1683, and a New York City justice of the peace and a captain of the militia in 1685. He also served as New York agent for the Colony of Maryland and as Suffolk Co's agent to the provincial government, and represented Huguenot interests in the province, purchasing 6,100 acres (2,470 ha) in Westchester Co for their settlement of New Rochelle in 1689. A Dutch Reformed Church deacon, Leisler espoused a precisionist brand of Calvinism and in 1676 was a litigant in a suit arising from Orthodox efforts to have Albany Dominie Nicholas van Rensselaer, who had been ordained in the Anglican rather than the Dutch Reformed doctrine, removed from the pulpit.

With the collapse of royal government in the wake of England's 1688 Glorious Revolution, the Committee of Safety in June 1689 elected Leisler as interim provincial chief executive. His populist and theologically rigid administration eventually antagonized many New Yorkers who did not share his points of view. Upon the arrival of royal English governor Henry Sloughter in March 1691, Leisler was arrested, tried for treason, and, at the insistence of his in-laws, hastily executed by hanging "til halfe dead" then beheaded. In 1695 England's Parliament reversed the New York court sentence and restored his estate to his heirs.

Special Issue on Jacob Leisler, *de Halve Maen* 67 (Spring 1994)

Voorhees, David William. "The 'fervent Zeale' of Jacob Leisler," *William and Mary Quarterly*, 3d ser, 51 (July 1994): 447–72

David William Voorhees

Leisler's Rebellion

BACKGROUND

In the 1680s New York Colony experienced explosive population growth from natural increase as well as an influx of Huguenot refugees. A pietist movement known as the Nadere Reformatie (Further Reformation) swept Reformed congregations, challenging the clergy's authority. Rising land prices, widening class differences, a deepening recession, and increasingly bitter intrafamilial estate feuds within New York's elite added tensions. King James II's disallowance of the 1683 Charter of Liberties and a provincial assembly, which he had granted when the duke of York, as well as conflicting Dutch and English judicial systems, caused legal confusion. Dissatisfaction with the crown intensified when in 1688 New York was subsumed into the Dominion of New England, and steep economic depression quickly followed the removal of governmental offices to Boston. Fears that King James II, a Roman Catholic, was forcing Catholicism upon the population were exacerbated by his creation of a manorial system and placement of his coreligionists in provincial offices.

News that the Protestant William, Prince of Orange, stadtholder of Holland, and son-in-law of King James II had in November 1688 invaded England to "save it from popery" and that James had subsequently fled the throne threw England's colonial governments into disarray. In April 1689 Boston overthrew the Dominion of New England government, imprisoned Gov Sir

Edmund Andros, and 22 prominent citizens formed the Committee of Safety to oversee local affairs. Following Boston's example, at the beginning of May the towns of Suffolk Co on eastern Long Island ousted James's officials and sent their militias to seize the government in New York City. Rebellion rapidly spread to Queens and Westchester Cos. On 31 May *os*/9 June *ns* 1689 the New York City militia rebelled and took Fort James on behalf of the Prince of Orange. A week later James's New York lieutenant governor, Francis Nicholson, fled to England.

Leisler in Power

With Nicholson's flight the New York militia captains, as the Council of War, called for a provincial convention to oversee affairs while awaiting instructions from England. Beginning on 27 June *os*/7 July *ns* 1689 representatives from two East New Jersey counties, eventually all New York counties except Albany, and two observers from Connecticut convened in New York City. The convention, known as the Committee of Safety and dominated by Samuel Edsall and Peter Delanoy, oversaw civil affairs, while the Council of War, dominated by senior militia captain Jacob Leisler, oversaw military affairs. A militant Calvinist faction, strongly supporting William's claim to the English throne, now controlled the government. On 28 June *os* /8 July *ns* 1689 the convention appointed Leisler "captain of the fort" and on 16 Aug *os*/26 Aug *ns* 1689 named him provincial commander in chief. With the appointment of Leisler, who for over a decade had been battling his in-laws, the Bayard, Kierstede, and Van Cortlandt families, over his wife's inheritance, the rebellion now acquired a bitter personal tone.

As anti-Catholic hysteria swept New York, popular hostility turned against King James II's Dominion officials. New York councilors Nicholas Bayard and Stephanus van Cortlandt, although members of the Dutch Reformed Church, were attacked by a mob and forced to flee to Albany, which had formed its own convention under Van Cortlandt's brother-in-law, Albany mayor Pieter Schuyler. Here they organized the opposition. In September 1689 the Committee of Safety called for elections to obtain those offices still held by James II's appointees. To force elections in Albany Co, the committee sent Jacob Milborne with a contingent of militia in October. Milborne retreated when a party of Mohawk Indians favorable to Schuyler's faction threatened to attack his men.

In December 1689 arrived the long awaited royal letters, addressed to Francis Nicholson, or "in his absence to such as for the time being take care" of the government. Notified by Massachusetts president Simon Bradstreet that the letters were intended for Leisler, Leisler assumed the title lieutenant governor, dissolved the Committee of Safety on 16 Dec *os*/26 Dec *ns* 1689, and appointed a council. He then began arresting the opposition leadership, including Nicholas Bayard, who had returned to the city believing that the royal letters were intended for the old council members. In February 1690 a bloody French and Indian raid of Schenectady added further fears of a Roman Catholic plot. Sweeping arrests of Roman Catholics, Quakers, and other alleged Jacobites followed. Schuyler's Albany faction capitulated to Leisler, who then called a provincial assembly to raise governmental revenues but dissolved it when the delegates insisted on discussing the condition of those imprisoned. The towns of eastern Suffolk Co, meanwhile, voted after much debate to join Connecticut, the government under which they had been prior to 1664.

In May 1690 delegates from New York, Massachusetts, Plymouth, and Connecticut met in New York City to plan at Leisler's request a military expedition against French Canada. This was North America's first intercolonial conference independent of English authority. The expedition, overseen by Leisler, was undertaken in summer 1690 with Fitz-John Winthrop of Connecticut commanding the land forces and William Phips of Massachusetts commanding the naval forces. The land expedition ended in complete failure when the Indian allies, racked by smallpox, failed to produce the promised forces and supplies. Leisler's subsequent imprisonment of Winthrop for insubordination antagonized his New England supporters. Leisler, meanwhile, faced increasing resistance at home. His confiscation of matériel for the expedition outraged many merchants. In June 1690 an assassination attempt was made against him in New York City. The passage of a tax and the breaking up of monopolies by his second assembly in fall 1690 further eroded support. An uprising in Queens Co in October was quickly suppressed by Jacob Milborne and Samuel Edsall.

English politics, however, determined Leisler's fate. The French had captured his initial packets to England, allowing Francis Nicholson's version of events to reach Whitehall first. The Committee of Safety's agent to England, Joost Stol, was politically inept. And, Leisler tied himself too closely to radical English Whigs, who in 1689 fell out of royal favor. In Jaunary 1690 the Crown commissioned Henry Sloughter, whose political views were hostile to Leisler's, as New York governor, with James II's old New York councilors, now in prison or exile, as his council. Not until fall 1690, when Whigs were again in favor, did Leisler's agent Benjamin Blagge receive a favorable hearing and instructions for Sloughter. By then it was too late; Sloughter had left England.

In late January 1691 a contingent of English regulars, commanded by Maj Richard Ingoldsby, that had separated from Sloughter's convoy arrived in New York Harbor. Leisler refused to surrender the government to Ingoldsby, who was unable to produce his commission. A violent confrontation between pro- and anti-Leislerian factions for control of the city ensued, and several people were killed. The province now hovered on the brink of civil war. Gov Sloughter finally arrived on 19 Mar *os*/29 Mar *ns* 1691 and proclaimed his commission. Although Leisler surrendered the fort the following day, Sloughter nonetheless arrested him and 36 of his faction. The resulting treason trials of Leisler and his associates, presided over by their most bitter enemies, were a travesty of English justice. Leisler and Jacob Milborne, who had become Leisler's son-in-law a mere two months earlier, were condemned to death, and, after riots broke out, hastily executed.

Aftermath

Leisler had remained popular with the majority of New Yorkers, who saw in his execution an act of martyrdom. To allay further violence, Gov Sloughter instituted a policy of moderation, which was short-lived because he died suddenly two months later. The anti-Leislerian council appointed Richard Ingoldsby as interim governor and exacted revenge. Scores were sued, fined, and jailed, and had their properties confiscated. Gov Benjamin Fletcher, who arrived in 1692, continued this partisan favoritism and rewarded anti-Leislerian leaders with enormous land grants, often parceled from confiscated Leislerian lands. With a Whig ascendancy at King William III's court, however, a lobby led by Jacob Leisler Jr gained increasingly favorable hearings. In 1692 the Crown ordered all prosecutions of Leislerians to end, and in May 1695 Parliament reversed the New York court sentences and upheld the legality of Leisler's seizure of the fort on behalf of William III.

Parliament's decision did not end the dispute. The arrival in 1698 of a Whig governor, Richard Coote, Earl of Bellomont, placed the Leislerians in power, who in turn sought vengeance. They instituted a new round of suits against the anti-Leislerians, culminating with the 1702 treason trial of Nicholas Bayard, who narrowly avoided execution. When in May 1702 Edward Hyde, Viscount Cornbury, a Tory, arrived as governor, power again shifted to the anti-Leislerians. This rise and fall of the factions, dependent on the royal governor's political outlook, continued for several more decades, although issues and personal alignments increasingly took on new configurations. While partisan feelings relating to Leisler were still so strong in 1764 that the Colonial Assembly appended to its published minutes, for the "Satisfaction of the Public," Parliament's 1695 act exonerating Leisler, the 1729 marriage of Leisler's granddaughter, Elizabeth Rynders, to Nicholas Bayard's grandson and heir, Nicholas Bayard the Younger, truly marks the dispute's end.

Leisler's Rebellion was New York's most divisive conflict until the American Revolution. Ethnic, religious, economic, and social tensions all contributed to the turmoil that rent every community throughout the province. Although a provincial extension of England's Glorious Revolution, at the core of its peculiar bitterness was an intrafamilial feud that had increasingly divided New York's elite for over a decade prior to 1689 and that had brought forward the leaders of both factions. From their manipulation of public opinion and royal favor during a period of intense crisis emerged colonial New York's strong two-party system.

Archdeacon, Thomas J. *New York City, 1664–1710: Conquest and Change* (Ithaca: Cornell Univ Press, 1976)

Balmer, Randall. *A Perfect Babel of Confusion: Dutch Religion and English Culture in the Middle Colonies* (New York: Oxford Univ Press, 1989)

Christoph, Peter R., ed. *The Leisler Papers, 1689–1691* (Syracuse: Syracuse Univ Press, 2002)

Leder, Lawrence H. "Records of the Trials of Jacob Leisler and His Associates," *New-York Historical Society Quarterly* 36 (Oct 1952): 431–57

McCormick, Charles Howard. *Leisler's Rebellion* (New York: Garland Publishing, 1989)

Merwick, Donna, *Possessing Albany, 1630–1710: The Dutch and English Experiences* (New York: Cambridge Univ Press, 1990)

Ritchie, Robert C. *The Duke's Province: A Study of New York Politics and Society, 1664–1691* (Chapel Hill: Univ of North Carolina Press, 1977)

Voorhees, David William. "The 'Fervent Zeale' of Jacob

Leisler," *William and Mary Quarterly,* 3d ser, 51 (July 1994): 447–72

David William Voorhees

Lemmon v The People. See SLAVE TRANSIT.

Le Moyne College. Private coeducational liberal arts college. In April 1945, anticipating the large number of veterans eligible for the GI Bill, the bishop of the Diocese of Syracuse, Walter A. Foery, purchased the 103-acre (42 ha) Gifford Farm on Salt Springs Rd for the future site of a Jesuit college. Classes began in downtown Syracuse in spring 1946, while construction began on the Gifford Farm, which became known as Le Moyne Heights. Classes moved to there in June 1948. Organized social action on campus began in 1962 with the founding of International House under the leadership of Rev Daniel J. Berrigan. The college, which originally emphasized its industrial relations program, is now known for its liberal arts curriculum. Enrollment in 2002 numbered 2,228 full-time and 257 part-time undergraduates and 803 graduate students.

Langdon, John W. *Against the Sky: The First 50 Years of Le Moyne College* (Syracuse: Le Moyne College, 1996)

Sarah E. DeSanctis

Lenape. See MUNSEE.

Lenox. Town (pop 8,665) in N Madison Co. Originally encompassed by the Oneida Indian Nation Reservation, the town was formed in 1809 from Sullivan. It benefited from its location on the Erie Canal (1819) and the Syracuse and Utica Railroad (1839; later New York Central); it is crossed by the New York State Thruway (1954). A large expanse of muckland near Canastota was drained by ditching and put into intensive agricultural use, ultimately controlled by Italian farming families; onions remain the town's main product. Quality Hill hamlet acquired its name, in local tradition, from the many "persons of quality" living there in the early 1800s.

William F. Helmer

Leon. Town (pop 1,380) in W Cattaraugus Co. Settled in 1818, the town was formed from Conewango in 1832. Early settlers arrived in 1818 and briefly engaged in the lumber industry and erected several sawmills. Dairying became the leading occupation, and cheese factories and creameries were built. An Amish colony from Ohio settled in the Conewango Valley beginning in 1949, and in the early 21st century, the Amish carry on such traditional farming practices as piling hay in cocks and stacking grain in sheaves. Their goods and services are in demand by the public. In 2003 dairying was the predominant land use.

Bruce D. Fredrickson and Madelynn P. Fredrickson

Le Ray. Town (pop 19,836) in central Jefferson Co. Settled in 1802, the town was formed from Brownville in 1806 and named for Frenchman James Le Ray de Chaumont (1760–1840), whose elaborate, high-style mansion (1827) still stands. Settlers were a mixture of French, New Englanders, and Pennsylvania Quakers. The town was served by the Rome, Watertown and Ogdensburg Railroad (1855). In 1941 the federal government took half the town for Pine Camp [now Fort Drum]. Its expansion between 1984 and 1989 created a population explosion, and Le Ray became the most populated town in the county, more than tripling in a decade from 5,039 (1980) to 17,973 (1990). Fast food restaurants, shopping plazas, and service businesses developed along the US 11 corridor; the number of farms, already declining, dropped even further. Twenty years later growth continued but more slowly. The presence of Fort Drum has made Le Ray the most ethnically diverse town in Jefferson Co; in 2000 its racial composition was 16% African American and 2% Asian; people of Latino ethnicity constituted 11%.

Laura Lynne Scharer

Le Roy. Town (pop 7,790) and village (pop 4,462) in E Genesee Co. Settlement occurred in 1797, and the town formed from Caledonia (Livingston Co) in 1812 as Bellona; the name was changed the following year. The village incorporated in 1834 and has had many industrial enterprises, including patent medicine, brooms, crushed stone, salt (1883–1928), Lapp Insulator (1919–), and Union Steel Chest (1932–73). Le Roy Female Seminary, which moved to the village in 1837, was chartered as Ingham University (1857–91), the first university for women in the United States. A documented route of the Underground Railroad can be explored by a 17 mi (27 km) tour. In 1897 Pearle B. Wait developed Jell-O. Lacking funds, he sold his formula to Orator Woodward, who successfully marketed it to make it "America's Most Famous Dessert." Though the Jell-O plant left town in 1964, a Jell-O Museum is open year-round. The annual Oatka Festival is held in July. The Thruway and I-490 (1964) facilitate commuting to Rochester and Batavia.

Susan L. Conklin

lesbians, gays, bisexuals, and transgendered people

CONSENSUAL SODOMY LAWS

American Indian culture provided an honored place for the berdache, or transgendered person, although evidence for the practice among the nations of the Iroquois Confederacy or the Algonquian-speaking Indians in the southern reaches of the state is thin. A toleration for homosexual behavior was not shared by the European colonizers. In the early 17th century, the Dutch colony of New Netherland controlled the lands of the future New York State and punished homosexual acts with death. Harmen Meyndertsz van den Bogaert, a Dutch West India Co (WIC) official whose travel journal is an early and important ethnographic account of the Iroquois, was accused of sodomy with a black slave and died in 1647, escaping imprisonment. In 1660 Jan Quisthout van der Linde, a WIC soldier, was convicted of sodomy, tied in a sack, and cast into one of Manhattan's rivers.

In 1664 when England gained authority over the colony, a death penalty for sodomy remained in force. After the Revolution, New York State adopted a 1787 law also mandating the death penalty for such activity. In 1796 the penalty became a maximum of 14 years of either solitude or hard labor; subsequent revisions increased or lessened prison time. In 1886 a new law was passed that included penalties for oral sex; previously the law had covered anal sex only. Neither the 1886 or earlier laws included women in their purviews. The consensual sodomy law (1886) underwent further changes before it was almost eliminated in the Penal Code revision of 1967 but was maintained, although the offense was reduced to a misdemeanor. The Catholic Church was the most influential group supporting the retention of the sodomy statute. In 1980 the New York Court of Appeals struck down the consensual sodomy statute on privacy and equal protection grounds in their ruling in *People v Onofre et al.*

PASSING WOMEN

Although for much of New York State's history sodomy laws did not apply to women, lesbians had to contend with economic and social systems requiring dependence on a male supporter and protector. Some women, such as Lucy Ann Joseph Lobdell, circumvented these restrictions by "passing." Born in Albany Co in 1829, Lobdell lived as a man in Delaware Co from the mid-1850s. A well-known hunter, she also served as a Methodist minister and married. In 1880 she was admitted to a Seneca Co almshouse and when her gender became known was transferred to that county's Willard Asylum for the Insane.

Ingham University; detail from panoramic map of Le Roy, 1892.

In New York City the 1901 death of Tammany Hall political organizer Murray Hall attracted wide attention when it was revealed that he was actually a woman. Edward Stevenson's *The Intersexes* (1908) reports on a 1903 case of a Buffalo railway worker, Harry Gorman, who was one of a number of passing women working for New York Central Railroad.

Meeting Places in the 19th Century

During the 1880s and 1890s politicians, doctors, and other authorities complained of organized meeting places for homosexuals in communities across the state and not only in the largest cities. According to testimony before an 1899 state committee investigating New York City public officials, these places included Manhattan's Manilla Hall, Paresis Hall, and Artistic Club, among others. One habitué of the Paresis dance hall, pseudonymous writer Earl Lind, wrote of a late-19th-century group called Cercle Hermaphroditos, which met there to "unite for defense against the world's bitter persecution."

Harlem Renaissance

As New York State entered the 20th century, its rapidly growing cities provided more meeting places for homosexual men and women. Women gathered in bars and restaurants and at resorts such as Fire Island's Cherry Grove (Suffolk Co). In addition to these places, men met at public parks, restrooms, bus or train stations, cheap hotels, and bathhouses, and in certain streets and alleys. As the Jazz Age dawned in 1920, and for a decade and a half afterward, Harlem became a center for African American artists, performers, writers, and intellectuals, many of them lesbian, gay, bisexual, or transgendered (LGBT). Historian Eric Garber has documented many of the speakeasies, cabarets, costume balls, and "buffet flats" (apartments where sexual performances took place and prohibition liquor was served). Some clubs were established specifically for the "pansy trade" (homosexual men), and lesbian and bisexual entertainers were common among Harlem club acts. Gladys Bentley, a large, masculine-looking lesbian, performed nightly in a white top hat and tails at 133d St's Clam House. Also, entertainers like Ma Rainey, Bessie Smith, Alberta Hunter, Josephine Baker, and Moms Mabley may have gravitated to some clubs to limit their own social contact with men and to live in a largely female world. The Harlem Renaissance attracted black artists and intellectuals from all over the country, and white tourists came to experience the free life of its clubs and speakeasies.

Police Activity

With the increase in gay meeting places came an increase in police activity. In 1916, at the instigation of the Manhattan-based New York Society for the Prevention of Vice, the police raided a downtown bathhouse, with 35 customers and employees going to prison. The club manager committed suicide. In 1929 an anonymous German tourist described another Manhattan raid: "Various people were struck down, kicked, in short, the brutality of these officials was simply indescribable." The police also began to notice women's activities. In the 1950s and 1960s, lesbians arrested at Manhattan's Sea Colony bar were taken to the nearby Women's House of Detention, and it was not uncommon after such raids to hear women calling out to friends and lovers through the jail's narrow street-side windows. Wisconsin senator Joseph McCarthy (1908–57) had equated homosexuality with the communist menace, and the ensuing antihomosexual panic commonly targeted bars and baths in the nation's cities. During this era New York's State Liquor Authority (SLA) could revoke a liquor license for serving homosexuals, with police throughout the state using entrapment—policemen posing as homosexuals—to provoke illegal solicitations. Social historians Madeline Davis and Elizabeth Kennedy note that many Buffalo bars serving working-class lesbians were closed by the late 1960s.

Censorship Law

In 1926 a newly translated French play, *The Captive*, dealing with the story of an innocent young woman seduced by an older, predatory lesbian, opened in New York City. Despite its negative portrayal of homosexuality, a public outcry condemned the play's discussion of the topic. Following warnings to Broadway producers to "clean up the stage," in raids of 9 Feb 1927 Mayor Jimmy Walker shuttered *The Captive* and two other plays, *Sex*, starring Mae West, and *The Virgin Man* and authorized the arrests of their casts and producers. After the courts overturned Walker's actions, the plays reopened to larger audiences, but later in 1927 the New York State legislature outlawed any depiction of "sex degeneracy or sex perversion" on the state's stages via the "Wales Padlock Bill." Though not always enforced, this legislation remained on the books until the general revision of the Penal Code in 1967. By the late 20th century and into the 21st, depictions of homosexuality on New York stages and in film and on television were common. Many continued to show LGBT persons in a negative light, notably William Friedkin's film *Cruising* (1980), protested by gay leaders in the year of its release. While other characterizations were more positive, few challenged the greater society's beliefs about the LGBT community or portrayed its complex relationships.

Early Organizations

After World War II gay veterans returning to New York City or settling there for the first time formed the social organization Veteran's Benevolent Association, soon known as the League. It provided something of a haven during the antihomosexual panic of the early 1950s when the dangers of exposure, job loss, blackmail, or arrest were very real. At the same time, men also began to organize on the West Coast to end discrimination against homosexuals with the Mattachine Society, founded in Los Angeles in late 1950 and claiming a handful of local chapters around the country by the mid-1950s. In 1955 after rumors of a police investigation cut attendance at League meetings, two League members, Sam Morford and Tony Segura, decided to establish a New York State chapter of the Mattachine Society (MSNY). Using names and addresses supplied by the parent organization, Segura and Morford called a 10 Jan 1956 first meeting of MSNY at Manhattan's Diplomat Hotel. By April the new group had just over a dozen members, most of whom accepted the psychiatric profession's view of homosexuality as an illness. MSNY meetings were usually lectures or discussions led by medical or legal professionals. MSNY also provided legal referrals and assistance to arrestees. But MSNY also began the process of quietly educating lawmakers and others to end harassment and persecution.

While women were welcome in MSNY, and a few were members, it was predominantly a male organization. At the 1958 Mattachine Society national convention, Del Martin and Phyllis Lyons, who founded the lesbian organization Daughters of Bilitis (DOB) in San Francisco in 1956, invited New York State women to meet with them in MSNY's Upper West Side Manhattan headquarters. One attendee, librarian Barbara Gittings, then organized a first meeting of DOB-NY on 20 Sep 1958 in the MSNY offices. The women of DOB-NY wanted a place to meet and to be together, but were afraid that overtly social functions might lead to accusations of pandering, so they adopted an educational format of discussions and lectures.

By the mid-1960s the lecture-centered activities of the MSNY and DOB-NY were no longer sufficient for some members. On 19 Sept 1964 activist Randy Wicker led members of two small, recently founded groups, the Homosexual League and the League for Sexual Freedom, in organizing a 10-person picket line at the US Army's induction center on Manhattan's Whitehall St. The pickets, dressed respectably in suits and ties or in dresses, protested the lack of confidentiality of army draft records and the dishonorable discharges given gay men and women. A year later, Wicker, joined by MSNY president Dick Leitsch and other Mattachine members, picketed at the United Nations to protest Cuban treatment of gays. Leitsch increased MSNY's quiet lobbying of city officials to end police harassment and entrapment and in 1965 directly challenged the SLA's indirect ban on serving homosexuals. While there were no specific regulations about serving homosexuals, the SLA deemed gay bars disorderly or unsavory per se and thus subject to closure. After some difficulty in finding a bar to refuse them service, Leitsch and a handful of Mattachine members were turned away from Julius's, a bar already having problems with the SLA for catering to gays, in Greenwich Village. MSNY filed a complaint with the SLA against Julius's, hoping to establish grounds for a court case challenging the SLA itself. But the authority simply denied that it had any regulation prohibiting the serving of gay people. MSNY faced similar problems fighting entrapment. During efforts to bring the subject before public scrutiny, police officials denied the practice or blamed misguided local precincts.

In the 1960s there was a slow and increasingly more public growth in New York State and the nation of what were then called homophile organizations. In 1966 the first gay college group boasting official school recognition was formed, Columbia University's Student Homophile League, and in 1967 the Oscar Wilde Memorial Bookstore opened on Manhattan's Mercer St. At the end of the decade, Buffalo's first gay organization, the Mattachine Society of the Niagara Frontier, was established. The stage was set for an event of gay anger and pride that would resound nationally and internationally.

The Stonewall Riots

In the early morning of 28 Jun 1969, the New York City Police, headed by Deputy Inspector Seymour Pine, raided the Stonewall Inn, a gay bar on Greenwich Village's Christopher St. Customers reacted in anger and were soon joined by LGBT people from the street, with rioting occurring that night and on successive nights. Although not the first homosexual riot (a 1967 raid on a Los Angeles bar had also caused a brawl between police and patrons), it was the most extensive and serious confrontation to date, and "Stonewall" soon became the founding myth of the modern gay liberation movement.

MSNY leaders called for calm, but younger members demanded some kind of organized response. Led by Michael Brown, they formed the Mattachine Action Committee, which began by calling the gay community to a forum at Greenwich House, the usual venue for Mattachine events. On 31 July, Brown and other members of the new committee, including Martha Shelley and Marty Robinson, formed a new organization, the Gay Liberation Front (GLF), at a public meeting held at Alternate University in New York City. The GLF soon divided into a number of caucuses or cells, many of which later became separate organizations. Members formed consciousness-raising groups, were opposed to any concept of leadership, and sought to align themselves with larger radical causes and to convince the American left that homosexuals were an oppressed people; GLF activists were outspoken supporters of the Black Panthers, for instance. During its short lifetime (July 1969–December 1972), the GLF mounted a handful of demonstrations, produced a 9-issue newspaper, *Come Out* (1969–72), briefly attempted a community center, and organized the first gay dances. GLF-Women organized the first all-women dances. In the year after Stonewall, gay groups sprang up in most cities and on most college campuses in the state. On account of the divisions existing within American society and because of GLF's tendency to create separate cells, groups based on age, class, race, and gender were established.

Some members, including Columbia University graduate student in philosophy Arthur Evans, carpenter Marty Robinson, and US Air Force veteran and peace activist Jim Owles, soon found the GLF's lack of structure and its courting and support of the left detrimental to the cause of gay liberation. In December 1969 this group founded the more formally structured Gay Activists Alliance (GAA), which sought a wide constituency for the gay movement and focused on the single issue of homosexual liberation. The GAA, with Owles serving as its first president, experienced the same tensions that plagued GLF, but its structured democracy enabled it to function despite divisions. At its height in 1970–71, GAA drew several hundred, mostly white, men to weekly membership meetings. Saturday dances, held at its Wooster St headquarters, "the Firehouse," in Manhattan's Soho section, regularly drew 1,000 partyers. GAA viewed itself primarily as a political organization and demanded that politicians "speak to the homosexual," confronting candidates and elected officials in highly public, loud, nonviolent confrontations, or "zaps."

In 1971 GAA introduced a gay civil rights bill in the New York City Council through Liberal Eldon Clingan and Democrat Carter Burden. Though it would be 15 years (long after GAA ceased to exist) before passage of a similar bill, GAA made use of the proposed measure as a rallying point and as a hook for press coverage of the discrimination faced by homosexuals. GAA members joined others in calling on the state legislature for repeal of the sodomy laws, and in 1970 the GAA joined with other organizations to form the New York State Coalition of Gay Organizations (NYSCGO). NYSCGO maintained no formal headquarters but claimed members across the state (New York City, Buffalo, Syracuse, Utica, Watertown, and Albany) and on State University of New York campuses and at other colleges throughout the state. On 14 Mar 1971 NYSCGO brought 3,000 demonstrators—including some dozen GAA members who had walked 150 mi (241 km) from Manhattan's Times Square through the communities along the Hudson River—to the State Capitol in Albany.

While small groups of women participated in both GLF and GAA, both organizations were largely male. Many lesbians were active members of the National Organization for Women (NOW) but found themselves unwelcome if open about their sexuality. In late 1969 author Rita Mae Brown and others left NOW for GLF and attempted to draw lesbians in the women's movement and in the gay movement together in consciousness-raising groups. In May 1970 Brown and others presented a paper, "The Woman Identified Woman," describing how the concerns of lesbians were central to the concerns of the women's movement, at the Second Congress to Unite Women, held in New York City. Their point was reiterated through wall posters urging congress participants to "Take a Lesbian to Lunch" or proclaimed "The Women's Movement is a Lesbian Plot," and by lesbians wearing T-shirts reading "Lavender Menace" in large, red letters. At the end of the conference, a new group, Radicalesbians, was formed.

Also from early 1970, DOB president Ruth Simpson favored joining with other lesbian and gay groups in a more active stance, but most of the DOB membership preferred their quiet meetings and discussions. On 8 Oct 1970 at their regular business meeting, as the DOB women passed a motion stating their unwillingness to use picketing as a tool, two policemen abruptly entered the meeting and demanded a certificate of occupancy. Simpson initially refused to show papers demanded by the officers, who threatened to take her to the precinct house. When the policemen finally departed, leaving Simpson with a summons, the DOB meeting immediately approved a public demonstration to coincide with Simpson's court appearance. Yet after relocating to a purchased building in another precinct, the DOB was again harassed by the police, and by the end of 1971, DOB members' fear of ongoing harassment and lack of activity almost ended the organization.

For the next two years, GAA's women's committee was arguably the most active place for a New York City lesbian to be. Yet American men did not suddenly lose their sexist attitudes when they walked through the door of the Firehouse, and GAA's interpretation of its one-issue rule left little room for many issues important to lesbians. Just as gay women had been unable to convince NOW that lesbian issues were women's issues, they were unable to convince gay men that women's issues were lesbian issues. Almost from the beginning, the women of GAA discussed the feasibility of a separate lesbian activist organization, with Jean O'Leary an early voice for separation. GAA vice president Nath Rockhill and other women resisted this move until May 1973, when GAA itself was clearly past its peak. Rockhill, O'Leary, Ginny Vida, and others then founded Lesbian Feminist Liberation as a separate organization.

The day of activist organizations was nearly over, at least for the next decade. In 1973 two other organizations, the first of several with a national scope, formed in New York City. Bruce Voeller left the GAA presidency to joined with Rockhill and others in creating the National Gay Task Force (NGTF), headquartered on Manhattan's 5th Ave until its 1986 move to Washington, DC. New York City lawyer and former GAA member William J. Thom established the Lambda Legal Defense and Education Fund, first headquartered in Manhattan; this followed a New York State Supreme Court decision overturning a lower court ruling that had denied the group recognition as a legal defense and education fund. The 1980s were primarily a decade of quiet growth on the local and state levels. By 1985 a California-published directory of homosexual organizations listed 89 New York State LGBT associations outside New York City and an additional 230 within the New York City's five boroughs.

The AIDS Epidemic

On 5 June 1981 the *New York Times* reported cases of gay men with a rare and fatal form of cancer, and close to this date the federal Centers for Disease Control reported unusual, fatal pneumonia cases among gay men. First called Gay-Related Immunodeficiency Disorder, the new threat to the gay community would soon be termed Acquired Immune Deficiency Syndrome (AIDS). The community responded with the establishment of social and health services agencies, such as the Gay Men's Health Crisis, founded in 1981 in New York City, and similar organizations soon launched in cities around the state. Education became a major weapon in the AIDS fight as it became clear that transmission occurred through the transfer of body fluids via sexual contact or via shared needles. The prejudice of the wider society, which preferred to ignore or blame gays and addicts, made this education difficult, and American sex phobia worked to hamper—and at times prevent—any but abstinence education, particularly for the young. As the epidemic continued and gay men faced the death of many in their social circles, the community gathered to provide care, assist in mourning, and combat a growing public outcry against gays. Conservative commentator William F. Buckley went so far as to call for the tattooing of all gay men.

In 1985 Gay and Lesbian Alliance Against Defamation (GLAAD) was founded in New York City to combat negative media images of gays. Two years later, a call for activism during a meeting at Manhattan's West Village Gay and Lesbian Community Services Center sparked formation of the AIDS Coalition to Unleash Power (ACT UP). ACT UP sought to force federal, state, and municipal governments to take the epidemic seriously, develop needed drugs, and care for the already infected. Independent chapters, such as ACT UP of Western New York, soon arose in other parts of the state and nation. By 2000 the availability of better drugs to manage AIDS and the resulting lower death rate quieted some of the urgency. While a strong rise in AIDS cases continued, especially among gay youth, minority groups, and women, New York State communities continued to resist, or even forbid, meaningful sex education.

Community Centers

The idea of providing space for the LGBT community to gather, receive services, and create new organizations arose soon after the Stonewall riots. GLF in New York City made such an attempt as early as 1969. Early community centers were generally little more than organizational headquarters with space for dances and other organization events. By the mid-1970s this type of center existed in New York City, Buffalo, Rochester, Albany, and other cities throughout the state. Beginning in the 1980s a new type of center began to appear, based in part on the settlement house model of the early 20th century. These centers are, themselves, organizations providing a variety of social services plus space for new organizations to form and grow. In 2002 the National Association of LGBT Community Centers counted 10 such centers in New York State.

Transgender Rights Law

Transgendered persons were a part of organized gay life in the pre-Stonewall era, playing a visible part during the Stonewall riots as well. From their inceptions, New York City's Street Transvestite Action Revolutionaries (1969) and the more middle-class charitable organization Imperial Court of New York (1986) were prominent at gay pride parades and events throughout the state. At the same time they were often marginalized, both by society as a whole and by many within the lesbian and gay community. Most gay men recognized the fun of a night's drag and perhaps appreciated the satirical element in such events, but few felt akin to those for whom a cross-gender lifestyle was an ongoing expression of their true identity. In the early to mid-1970s, women especially often saw male-to-female drag as a parody of women, which degraded them in the way "black-face" impersonations degraded African Americans. Female-to-male cross-dressing was looked upon, at best, as aping heterosexual society and its male power games. These perceptions began to change in the 1990s as the transgendered community asserted itself within the wider LBGT community. Organizations like New York City's short-lived Transgender Menace of the mid-1990s plus the coming together of transgendered persons in gender identity programs at community centers around the state fostered a new consciousness, both among the transgendered themselves and in the lesbian and gay community as a whole. In 1998 Ithaca was the first New York State community to cite gender identity in its human rights law. Rochester and Suffolk Co followed suit in 2001, and a year later both Buffalo and New York City extended their civil rights ordinances to protect the transgendered. These laws were quietly passed through the efforts of Empire State Pride Agenda (ESPA), founded in 1990 from the merger of two earlier lobbying groups (New York City's Friends and Advocates for Individual Rights PAC [FAIRPAC] and Albany's New York State Lesbian and Gay Rights Lobby), and other groups.

ESPA was also the most visible lobby for a state equal rights law, an early version of which was first introduced in the 1970s at the instigation of NYSCGO. From the early 1990s such legislation passed the Democratic-led assembly every session but failed in the Republican-controlled senate. But in December 2002 both bodies approved the Sexual Orientation Non-Discrimination Act, which was then signed into law by Gov George E. Pataki; this law, however, does not cover transgendered persons. ESPA continues as the main lobby for LGBT rights in the state, advocating transgender inclusion in civil rights law as well as marriage rights for LGBT individuals and public focus on the continuing AIDS epidemic.

The issue of marriage rights drew national attention to New York State in late February 2004: two weeks after San Francisco became the first municipality in the United States to perform same-sex marriages, New Paltz (Ulster Co) became the second. The village's mayor officiated at 25 same-sex marriages before an injunction from the Ulster Co district attorney halted the proceedings. The district attorney later charged the mayor with multiple counts of solemnizing a marriage without a license. Leading politicians in the state were split on the advisability of same-sex marriages. Gov Pataki felt there was no legal authority for such marriages to be performed. Atty Gen Eliot Spitzer refused to stop the same-sex marriages in New Paltz, though he issued an advisory opinion that such marriages appeared to be illegal under terms of the state's Domestic Relations Law.

Chauncey, George. *Gay New York: Gender, Urban Culture, and the Making of the Gay Male World, 1890–1940* (New York: Basic Books, 1994)

Clendinen, Dudley, and Adam Nagourney. *Out for Good: The Struggle to Build a Gay Rights Movement in America* (New York: Simon & Schuster, 1999)

Garber, Eric. "A Spectacle in Color: The Lesbian and Gay Subculture of Jazz Age Harlem." In *Hidden from History: Reclaiming the Gay and Lesbian Past*, ed. Martin Duberman, Martha Vicinus, and George Chauncey Jr (New York: New American Library, 1989)

Ingram, Gordon Brent, Anne-Marie Bouthillette, and Yolanda Retter, eds. *Queers in Space: Communities, Public Places, Sites of Resistance* (Seattle: Bay Press, 1997)

Katz, Jonathan. *Gay American History: Lesbians and Gay Men in the USA* (New York: Thomas Y. Crowell, 1976)

Kennedy, Elizabeth Lapovsky, and Madelind D. Davis. *Boots of Leather, Slippers of Gold: The History of a Lesbian Community* (New York: Penguin, 1994)

Loughery, John. *The Other Side of Silence, Men's Lives and Gay Identities: 20th-Century History* (New York: Henry Holt, 1998)

Marotta, Toby. *The Politics of Homosexuality* (Boston: Houghton Mifflin, 1981)

Newton, Esther. *Cherry Grove, Fire Island* (Boston: Beacon Press, 1993)

Roscoe, Will, ed. *Living the Spirit: A Gay American Indian Anthology* (New York: St. Martin's Press, 1988)

Teal, Donn. *The Gay Militants*, 2d ed.(New York: St. Martin's Press, 1995)

Williams, Walter L. *The Spirit and the Flesh: Sexual Diversity in American Indian Culture* (Boston: Beacon Press, 1986)

Richard C. Wandel

Letchworth State Park (14,350 acres/5,807 ha). A scenic area extending from Mount Morris (Livingston Co) to Portageville (Wyoming Co). Letchworth's Genesee Gorge was carved some 12,000 years ago when glaciers moved through the region, where the Genesee River cuts through cliffs that rise in places to 600 ft (183 m). The park contains three canyons and three waterfalls. At its core is the former Gardeau Reservation of the Seneca Indians, famed as the home of Indian captive Mary Jemison, the "White Woman of the Genesee." The 1826 Treaty of Buffalo Creek extinguished the remaining Seneca rights to land in the Genesee Valley. Subsequently William Pryor Letchworth, a merchant from Buffalo, acquired 1,000 acres (405 ha) of land in 1859 at the heart of the old reservation. His home, Glen Iris, still stands as an inn and restaurant. In 1872 Letchworth purchased and reassembled a Seneca council house on his property, where it still stands, next to Mary Jemison's old cabin. In 1907 he deeded his property to New York State, and through the years additional land was added; the state park was established in 1911. Camping, cross-country skiing, and other seasonal recreation is available year-round. The William Pryor Letchworth Museum contains geological specimens and American Indian antiquities. The park attracts 1 million people annually.

See also Genesee river.

Wooster, Margaret. *Somewhere to Go on Sunday: A Guide to Natural Treasures in Western New York and Southern Ontario* (Buffalo: Prometheus Books, 1991)

Loretta J. Gabriel

Levitt, Arthur (*b* Brooklyn, 28 June 1900; *d* New York City, 6 May 1980). Lawyer and comptroller. Levitt spent his childhood in Brooklyn and enlisted in the US Army in 1917. He graduated from Columbia University with a BA in 1921 and a law degree in 1924. He practiced law in New York City until 1941, when he reentered the US Army as a captain in the Judge Advocate General's Corps. After promotion to colonel, he served until the end of World War II as commander of the corps' training center in Queens. After involvement in Democratic politics and a term as president of the New York City school board, he was elected state comptroller in 1954. He would be elected for six consecutive terms, serving until 1978, the longest serving comptroller in the state's history. He was recognized for pursuing aggressive general statewide audits on a nonpartisan basis. At the behest of Democratic Party regulars, he ran against incumbent Robert F. Wagner Jr in the 1961 Democratic primary for mayor of New York City, Levitt's only electoral defeat. He became chairman of the New York Democratic Party State Convention in 1965 and served as a delegate to the 1968 and 1976 Democratic National Conventions. He declined the nomination for a seventh term as state comptroller in 1978 and returned to private life as a bank investment officer in New York City.

Levitt, Arthur. Papers. New York State Archives, Albany

James R. Belpedio

Levittown. Locality (pop 53,067) in Hempstead (Nassau Co). It began as a development of 17,500 houses built between 1947 and 1951 on the Hempstead Plains. The region was known as the "island of trees," or Island Trees, in the 19th century. After the Civil War, Germans, Irish, and, later, Italians came from New York City and Brooklyn and took up small farms in the area. By 1900 Island Trees had been subdivided into truck farms, speculative parcels awaiting development. Abraham Levitt and Sons, under the leadership of William J. Levitt, began construction in 1947 at the peak of the postwar housing boom, using cost-effective, mass-production techniques developed for defense-worker housing during World War II. The subdivision, one of the largest by a single developer, pioneered the use of "assembly line" techniques in housebuilding. Levitt's use of press releases during the construction phase established both builder and development as icons of postwar suburbia.

Initially, the houses were four-room, shingled cottages on a concrete slab. A hot-water coil system was embedded within the slab, providing radiant heating and eliminating the need for a basement. The first 2,000 houses were rental units. As soon as feasible, Levitt made the houses available for purchase under the terms of the Servicemen's Readjustment Act of 1944 (GI Bill), which provided mortgage insurance for veterans and eliminated the need for a down payment. To enhance the houses' marketability, Levitt created "village greens," with swimming pools, playgrounds, and shopping areas, providing gathering places. On completion of the first phase in 1948, Levitt changed the development's name from Island Trees to Levittown so that the planned post office would carry the family name, a change met with opposition from some residents, particularly those few whose homes predated Levitt. However, as most houses were Levitt rental units, Levitt had the power to name the community as he saw fit.

In the 1950s Levittown was criticized for the bland sameness of its houses and the homogeneity of its residents. Much criticism came because, for the first time in the United States, the working class was being offered new suburban housing. Prior to World War II the suburban homeowner was assumed to be a member of the middle class. The GI Bill made the single-family house accessible to veterans of all backgrounds. The community and its residents were severely scrutinized, and many critics attributed to Levittown problems that were characteristic of larger social changes. Despite, or perhaps because of, the criticism, the residents of Levittown spent considerable time and money on their homes.

By 1957 many of the four-room Cape Cods had become seven- and eight-room, two-story houses in a wide range of styles, and by 1987 it had become almost impossible to find an unaltered house within the development. Nevertheless, the negative stereotypes persist in the popular press, where the name Levittown is often synonymous with suburban sprawl. As the houses became more expansive, their purchase prices rose accordingly. As a result, second- and third-generation homeowners are drawn from a more affluent segment of the population than that of the first. Because of racial restrictions, the original population of Levittown was almost entirely white. The Federal Housing Administration, under whose auspices the mortgage insurance was issued, favored projects that were termed "harmonious" or segregated projects. Levitt incorporated this restriction into the covenant that governed the purchase terms for Levittown, and the development remained segregated until the covenant expired in the 1970s. Since that time a number of families of Middle Eastern and Asian descent have moved into Levittown, but very few African Americans. In 2000 about 45% of Levittown is Roman Catholic and about 25% is Jewish. Near the end of the 20th century a number of Hindus and Muslims arrived. In 2000 about 3% of Levittowners were Asian.

The weekly *Levittown Tribune* provides news coverage of the area. In 2002 the pools and playgrounds continued to serve the residents, but the shopping areas were less successful. These were part of Levitt's attempts to re-create the prewar small town using the technology and funding mechanisms of the postwar era. However, his vision of stay-at-home mothers shopping while their children played nearby was short-lived. By 1960 the village green as a shopping center had succumbed to the rise of the two-car family, the supermarket, and the shopping mall, as in most US communities. The village greens now house services such as delicatessens and card shops. Levittown was emblematic of the transition of America's working population from urban tenants to suburban homeowners. Although initially greeted with a degree of skepticism by the original inhabitants, Levittown's residents quickly took their place within the suburban milieu of Nassau Co.

Kelly, Barbara M. *Expanding the American Dream: Building and Rebuilding Levittown* (Albany: SUNY Press, 1993)

"Levittown at 50." In *Long Island: Our Story* (Melville, NY: Newsday, 1998)

Liell, John Thomas. "Levittown: A Study in Community Planning and Development" (PhD diss, Yale Univ, 1952)

Barbara M. Kelly

New homes in Levittown, 1951.

Lewis. Town (pop 1,200) in NE Essex Co. Settled in 1796 the town was formed from Willsboro in 1805. Through much of the 19th century its most important industry was a forge (?1837). In the 20th and early 21st centuries, outdoor recreation was a source of income, made possible by Northway (1967) access, while some residents worked at farming or lumbering. Lewis was the home of millwright and lumberman Joseph Call, a champion wrestler who competed in international matches as the Lewis Giant (*fl* 1820–30).

Thomas A. Rumney

Lewis. Town (pop 857) in SW Lewis Co. Settled in 1798, the town had a large influx of German, French, and Swiss immigrants beginning around 1831. It was formed in 1852 from Leyden and West Turin. Forest products provided livelihoods and included bird's-eye maple planks for European cabinetmakers, white ash oars for Boston whalers, and black ash hoops for Connecticut and Massachusetts oyster-keg makers. Lumbering, along with dairy farming and outdoor recreation, remain important in the early 21st century. The town encompasses the headwaters of the Mohawk and Salmon Rivers.

Arthur Einhorn

Lewis, (Mary) Edmonia (*b* Greenbush [now Rensselaer], *ca* 1840; *d ca* 1910). Neoclassical sculptor. The first African American sculptor to achieve international recognition, Lewis was born to parents of African American and American Indian heritage. Little is known about her early life, and she herself often told conflicting stories, except that she was orphaned by about age 9. Some accounts have her living with two Mississauga Indian aunts near the Canadian side of Niagara Falls, but others place her in Newark, NJ. During the 1850s Lewis attended New York Central College, a Baptist abolitionist school in McGrawville [now McGraw, Cortland Co]. From 1859 to 1863 she attended Oberlin College in Ohio, then went to Boston and studied with neoclassic portrait sculptor Edward Brackett. Sales of plaster-cast copies of her bust of Union army colonel Robert Gould Shaw (1864) financed her travels in 1865 to Florence and in early 1866 to Rome, where she became part of the White Marmorean Flock, as Henry James called a group of women sculptors working there. Lewis frequently used American Indians and African Americans as her subjects and was particularly intrigued by the themes of abolitionism and women who were able to overcome struggles. Her works include *Forever Free* (1867–68), the first celebration of the Emancipation Proclamation by an African American sculptor, and *The Death of Cleopatra* (1874–76), which attracted much attention when it was exhibited at the 1876 Philadelphia Centennial Exposition and the 1878 Chicago Exposition. About the time neoclassical sculpture began to fall out of favor, Lewis slipped into obscurity. The last known reference to her being alive is from 1909. The details of her death are unknown.

Bearden, Romare, and Harry Henderson. *A History of African-American Artists: From 1792 to the Present* (New York: Pantheon, 1993)

Alexandra Schein

Lewis, Francis (*b* Llandaff, Wales, 1 Apr 1713; *d* New York City, 31 Dec 1802). Merchant and signer of the Declaration of Independence. The only child of Anglican minister Francis Lewis and Amy Pettingal, he was orphaned as a youth and raised by his mother's Welsh and Scottish relatives, who purportedly imbued him with an antipathy for English oppression. Educated at Westminster School in London and trained at a London mercantile house, Lewis reached Philadelphia in 1738 and was living in New York City by 1740. He married Elizabeth Annesley, sister of his deceased business partner, in 1743. Three of their seven children survived infancy. As a civilian commissary at Oswego in 1756 in the French and Indian War, Lewis was captured, sent to France, and later exchanged. Supported by Isaac Sears and the radical Whigs in New York City, Lewis was elected to the Committee of Fifty-One (1774), the Committee of Sixty (1774), and the Provincial Convention (1775). A member of the Continental Congress (1775–79), he served diligently on the Marine, Secret, Commercial, and Claims Committees and signed the Declaration of Independence. Congress appointed him in 1779 to the Board of Admiralty. In 1781, he retired from all public and private business. He was the father of Morgan Lewis, governor of New York from 1804 to 1807.

Burlingham, Charles C. *Francis Lewis: One of the New York Signers of the Declaration of Independence: Historical Sketch* (1926)
Delafield, Julia. *Biographies of Francis Lewis and Morgan Lewis,* 2 vols (New York: A. D. F. Randolph, 1877)

Joseph S. Tiedemann

Lewis, Morgan (*b* New York City, 16 Oct 1754; *d* New York City, 7 Apr 1844). Governor. The son of prominent merchant and revolutionary leader Francis Lewis and Elizabeth Annesley, Morgan Lewis graduated from the College of New Jersey (now Princeton University) in 1773 and then read law with John Jay. During the Revolutionary War, he served in various capacities. As Gen Horatio Gates's chief of staff, Lewis received the British surrender at Saratoga. After the war, he resumed practicing law. In 1779 Lewis married Robert R. Livingston's daughter Gertrude; they had one child. The marriage helped make Lewis one of the largest landowners in the state.

Elected to the assembly in 1789 and 1792, Lewis used the Livingston family's break with Federalism in favor of Gov George Clinton's faction to gain the attorney generalship in 1791 and appointment to the state supreme court the following year. In 1801 he was promoted to chief justice. Largely by default, Lewis was the Livingston-Clinton faction's successful gubernatorial candidate against Aaron Burr in 1804, only to be largely responsible for splitting the Republican Party with his inadequate combination of Lewisites (labeled Quids by the Clintonians) and Federalists. As a result Lewis lost his bid for reelection in 1807 to Daniel D. Tompkins. His four terms in the state senate, 1811–14, marked the end of his political career and coincided with his military service in the War of 1812. The latter role included quartermaster general of the Northern Department at the rank of brigadier general, appointment as major general in 1813, brief assumption of the northern army's command during its commander's illness, accompanying a mistaken campaign against Montreal that began late in 1813, and command of the defense of New York City in 1814. Lewis's retirement included presidency of the New-York Historical Society, 1832–36, and two positions he held until his death: grandmaster Mason of the state from 1830 and president general of the Society of the Cincinnati from 1839. Lewis Co is named after him.

Alexander, DeAlva Stanwood. *A Political History of the State of New York,* 4 vols (1909; repr Port Washington, NY: I. J. Friedman, 1969)
Delafield, Julia Livingston. *Biographies of Francis Lewis and Morgan Lewis* (New York: Anson D. F. Randolph, 1877)

Donald M. Roper

Lewisboro. Town (pop 12,324) in NE Westchester Co. Part of Cortlandt Manor and of the Oblong (1731), the town was settled from Connecticut, probably in the 1730s, and government was in operation by 1747. It was confirmed as a town in 1788 as Salem and became South Salem in 1806 and Lewisboro in 1840. The Harlem Railroad (1847) served the town at Goldens Bridge. Boot and shoe manufacturing supplemented the farming industry in the 1870s. Cross River Reservoir (1905) inundated valley farmland. Lake Kitchawan (1925) and the Goldens Bridge Cooperative Colony (1927) were resort developments, the latter created by Jewish working-class owners. I-684 (1967) carries heavy traffic through the town's western end. Four Winds Hospital (1925), a psychiatric facility, employs about 500 staff. After 1960 Lewisboro developed into a commuter community. Part of Ward Pound Ridge Reservation is in Lewisboro, and a landmark in Cross River is the Fifth Division Market, a 19th-century general store still in service. Vice President and Secretary of Agriculture Henry A. Wallace (1888–1965) ran his experimental Farvue Farm here from 1946 until his death.

Lewis County (1,275 mi²/3,302 km²; pop 26,944). Created in 1805 from Oneida Co and named for Gov Morgan Lewis. Subsequent boundary changes were made with Jefferson Co in 1808, 1809, and 1813. Lewis Co is subdivided into 17 towns that contain 9 incorporated villages. Lowville serves as the county seat. Elevations range from under 740 feet (226 m) where the Black River exits the county to over 2,110 feet (643 m) at Gomer Hill's summit in the Town of Turin.

Lewis Co straddles three major physiographic provinces. The Black River Valley subregion of the Erie-Ontario Lowland province runs the county's full length and separates the Tug Hill Upland province in the southwest from the Western Adirondack Hills subregion of the Adirondack Upland province in the east-northeast. Till and meltwater deposits indicate that all of the county was glaciated. The Black River courses northwest while descending 130 feet (40 m) across the county and flows along the valley region's eastern margin south of Lowville. Its route approximates the boundary between the Precambrian igneous and metamorphic rocks of the Adirondacks from the Ordovician-age sedimentary rocks in the west. Much of the valley is underlain with limestone, which forms a series of pronounced, nearly level terraces that rise to over 1,200 feet (365 m) and extend west 4–6 miles (6–10 km) to the base of a 500 ft (150 m) high cuesta that marks the edge of the Tug Hill Upland. The valley's eastern slopes rise less regularly into the Western Adirondack Hills, which range from about 1,000 to 1,700 feet (305 to 520 m) in elevation and consist of low east-west-trending ridges of middle Proterozoic granitic gneiss and metamorphic sedimentary rock, intermixed with Pleistocene alluvial sediments. The Tug Hill is a westward-dipping, glacially smoothed mesa composed of late Ordovician sandstone and shale deposits overlain with uneven layers of glacial till.

The Black River and its tributaries, most notably the Deer, Beaver, Sugar, Moose, and Independence Rivers, drain more than two-thirds of the county and empty into Lake Ontario. Waters in the southwest corner also drain into Lake Ontario via the Salmon River and the East Branch Fish Creek. The headwaters of the Mohawk River lie in the Towns of Lewis and West Turin and flow to the Hudson. The Indian and Oswegatchie Rivers drain the northeastern part of Lewis Co into the St. Lawrence River. Extensive portions of Black River Valley soils are well suited to modern commercial agriculture. Moderately fertile soils are found on the Tug Hill south and west of Constableville. Elsewhere the soils hold little or no agricultural promise.

Lewis Co's climate is humid-continental. Mean January temperatures range from 14°F (-10°C) near Beaver Lake to 18°F (-8°C) in the southwest. Winters are long, and below 0°F (-18°C) temperatures are common. Mean July temperatures range from 65°F (18°C) near the eastern border to 69°F (21°C) in the Town of Pinckney. Daytime highs of 90°F (32°C) or more occur a few times nearly every summer, most frequently in the Black River Valley. Average annual precipitation amounts range from 39 inches (99 cm) near Beaver Falls to 60 inches (152 cm) in Montague. Seasonal snowfall amounts vary from 98 inches (249 cm) at Beaver Falls to 280 inches (711 cm) in Montague, which is the highest average seasonal snowfall for any place east of the Rocky Mountains on the continent.

Primeval forest cover consisted largely of northern hardwoods. By far the most extensive was an Adirondack hardwood community dominated by beech, sugar maple, yellow birch, hemlock, white pine, spruce, and fir that covered both the Tug Hill and Adirondack Uplands. A similar community without the spruce and fir covered the southern half of the Black River Val-

ley, while the northern half supported an Alleghenian complex dominated by beech, sugar maple, hemlock, white pine, and basswood along with some areas of wetland forest with hemlock and black ash. Over 75% of Lewis Co is presently covered with second- or third-growth forest. The county's eastern margins lie within the Adirondack Park.

American Indians and Early Settlement

Human occupation in the Black River Valley is shown by archaeological investigation to extend back at least 10,000 years. In the Contact period, Lewis Co was part of the territory of the Oneida Nation and used for seasonal hunting. The Oneida ceded it to the State of New York by the Treaty of Fort Schuyler (1788). In 1792 the state sold the land of the present county to Alexander Macomb as part of the Macomb Purchase. He, in turn, sold land to speculators who marketed tracts to potential settlers. Settlement began in Leyden in 1794 and progressed in the valley towns through 1803, although New Bremen and Diana remained unsettled until 1818–19. The highlands in the west were settled even later: the present Osceola by squatters in 1822 and Montague by removals from St. Lawrence and Jefferson Cos in 1846.

The Castorland enterprise in Lyonsdale (Lewis Co) and Carthage (Jefferson Co) commenced in 1794. The people involved were French aristocrats fleeing the French Revolution, but with an unforgiving climate, relatively poor soils, and a lack of farming skills among the settlers, their colonies in Lyonsdale, Carthage, Croghan, New Bremen, and Greig were soon given up, and by 1814 all traces were gone. The French remained a significant minority in the county, however, following a renewed immigration beginning about 1830. In 1855 there were 1,267 French-born residents concentrated in New Bremen, Croghan, and Lewis, some 5% of the county's population. Vincent Le Ray de Chaumont, son of one of the original proprietors, employed an agent at Dunkirk, France, in the mid–19th century, resulting in continuing immigration. Joseph Bonaparte, the former king of Spain, bought land in Diana in 1828 and was for a short time a resident.

Yankees were probably the largest single group, coming from Connecticut, Massachusetts, and Washington Co. Palatine Germans from the Mohawk Valley were among the early settlers of Harrisburg. German speakers from German states, Alsace, and Switzerland came to Lewis, Croghan, New Bremen, and West Turin beginning about 1830; Welsh settled in Turin; and, after the canal-building era, Irish immigrants put down roots in West Turin. In 1865, 19% of the county's residents were foreign-born, and the percentages ranged as high as 38%, registered by Croghan. In that same year the Irish, at 5.6%, were the county's largest foreign-born group, followed by Germans (4.4%), French (3.3%), and Welsh (1.2%).

Transportation

Although Lewis Co is bisected by the Black River, which flows north and west to Lake Ontario, the direction of settlement was mostly from the south and required overland travel from the Mohawk Valley to reach the upper reaches of the Black. This retarded settlement and development, and was the impetus for residents' demands for a canal beginning in 1825. It was not in service until 1851. Steamboats offered service on the Black River below the canal.

Soon, however, railroads began to compete. The Utica and Black River (1867) connected Utica and Watertown by way of the Black River Valley. In 1885 it provided 10 passenger trains daily through Lowville; the following year it was leased to the Rome, Watertown and Ogdensburg, which, in turn, leased it to the New York Central in 1891. Other lines were built from this road across Diana (1886) and to Croghan (1906). Passenger service through Lowville ended in 1961, and the track between Lyons Falls and Lowville was taken up in 1964, although freight service continues northward and southward from those points, operated by the Mohawk, Adirondack and Northern. The Lowville and Beaver River Railroad continues operation of the short line to Croghan.

Roads, too, were few and late. The first macadam was laid in 1910 from Lowville to the top of the hill in Martinsburg. Most initial paving was accomplished between 1912 and 1917 and between 1931 and 1935. Rte 12 was relocated and rebuilt, beginning with the stretch from Glenfield to Lyons Falls in 1965, but most roads are primarily for local use. There is no interstate or other four-lane highway in the county.

Economic Development

In the 19th century Lewis Co developed an economy based upon forest products and agriculture. With the opening of the Black River Canal, its vast resources of lumber could be shipped economically. This led to the development of large industrial mills, such as T. B. Basselin (1883–1909) at Castorland and the Beaver River Lumber Co (1890), which employed 400 men. Pulp and paper were also produced on an industrial scale once technology had created the capability. Paper mills operated in Croghan, Diana, Lyons Falls, Port Leyden, and even in remote Greig. Many other products made in small- to medium-sized factories scattered around the county drew upon forest trees for their materials: bird's-eye maple for cabinets, white oak for oars, and black oak for hoops, furniture, caskets, boxes, excelsior, matchsticks, chicken incubators, piano sounding boards, bowling pins, pumps, toys, and sash and blinds. A hemlock extract plant, successor to small tanneries that used the hemlock bark itself, was producing 12 barrels of extract daily in 1884. Spruce gum was gathered seasonally in the late 19th century. Even those products not based on wood were mostly extracted: talc in Diana, bog iron in Watson, and peppermint oil in Harrisburg. There was some ironwork produced in Denmark, Diana, and Port Leyden, and a modest amount of textile manufacturing was carried out in Copenhagen and Port Leyden (the latter through the 1990s).

With thin soils and a cold climate, Lewis Co was quickly determined to be best for grazing. In 1833 Levi Bowen of West Rd shipped and sold the first load of butter and cheese to Deerfield (Oneida Co). Dairying became an important endeavor, and farmers embraced the cheese factory idea, building 49 by 1875, which made the county ninth in the state. Refrigerated cars for

LEWIS CO POPULATION CENSUS FIGURES

	White	Nonwhite	Total Population	Foreign-Born
1810	6,404	29	6,433	—
1820	9,184	43	9,227	124
1830	15,156	83	15,239	396
1840	17,777	53	17,830	—
1850	24,522	42	24,564	4,358
1860	28,541	39	28,580	5,477
1870	28,642	57	28,699	5,232
1880	31,324	92	31,416	5,036
1890	29,729	77	29,806	4,088
1900	27,397	30	27,427	2,949
1910	24,836	13	24,849	2,104
1920	23,690	14	23,704	1,283
1930	23,416	31	23,447	1,816
1940	22,798	17	22,815	1,348
1950	22,501	20	22,521	1,055
1960	23,230	19	23,249	739
1970	23,614	30	23,644	411
1980	24,918	117	25,035	376
1990	26,454	342	26,796	337
2000	26,451	493	26,944	305

Notes: "Nonwhite" includes African Americans, Asians, American Indians, and Pacific Islanders and, for 2000, also the mixed race and other race categories. Through the 1960 census these figures primarily reflect the African American population. Foreign-born figures for 1820 and 1830 include only those not naturalized, and for 1930 and 1950, the foreign-born totals include Whites only. Other years include all foreign-born in the population.

dairy products were introduced on the railroad in 1899. Meanwhile other products proved advantageous. Potatoes were grown, especially in Watson, and in 1874, 3,295 acres (1,333 ha) were planted in the county. Lewis Co ranked third in the state in maple sugar production in 1875. Lewis Co business operators were forced to bank in Utica or Watertown until the 1830s, when two banks were established: the Lewis County Bank (1834) in Martinsburg and the Bank of Lowville (1838).

Religion, Education, and Culture

Religious life was a priority to settlers. In West Turin, settled in 1796, prayer meetings were held in the first summer. In 1803 Baptist churches were organized in Leyden and West Turin, and a Congregational church was formed in Lowville. The first church building was erected in Martinsburg in 1806. French and German settlers brought the Roman Catholic faith and the first church was St. Vincent de Paul Church at Belfort, organized ?1832. While 15 Methodist churches were in the majority in 1855, as they were in most New York counties, there were 9 Baptist churches, and 7 Roman Catholic churches. In addition, Mennonites in New Bremen and Croghan had immigrated directly from Europe and did not have church buildings.

The first school was probably taught in 1798 between Constableville and Lyons Falls, but others soon followed, such as those in Turin (1801), Leyden Hill (1802), and Martinsburg (1804), supported by assessments based on attendance. After 1812 schools benefited from state authorization and, after 1814, state funding; a comprehensive network of schools developed. The only successful private school was Lowville Academy (1808). It became a Union Free School in 1905, although its property remained privately managed until 1924. Centralization began in 1923 at Port Leyden. Harrisville and Copenhagen centralized in 1936, Beaver River in 1945, and Lowville in 1952. The process was completed in 1961 with the creation of the South Lewis Central School District that resulted from the consolidation of three central districts: General Martin (1925), Lyons Falls (1927), and Constableville (1929). The last common school, Indian River, ceased operating in 1962. Vocational education was advanced by BOCES starting in 1965, now part of St. Lawrence–Lewis BOCES based in Canton. Two parochial schools have operated: Father Leo Memorial School (1916–78) in Croghan, a successor to earlier schools, and St. Peter's School (1959) in Lowville. There is no institution of higher education in the county.

The first newspaper was the *Black River Gazette* (1807) at Martinsburg, the earliest paper north of Utica. In 2004 the *Journal and Republican* and *Adirondack Mountain Sun* are published weekly at Lowville. WBRV-AM radio began broadcasting from Leyden in 1955 and added FM in 1989. It was joined by WLLG-FM in 1986. All three have a country music format.

Franklin B. Hough (1822–85), who served as the first forestry director in the US Department of Agriculture, was author of the first county history, an early environmentalist, and a theorist of forest management. The critic Edmund Wilson (1895–1972) had a summer house at Talcottville, and he wrote extensively on Lewis Co and its people in *Upstate* (1971). The county has several important museums, especially Constable Hall (1949) housed in a Georgian mansion at Constableville and built in 1810–19, the American Maple Museum at Croghan, and the Mennonite Heritage Farm at Kirschnerville. Lewis Co has a rich tradition of folk fiddle playing, which is commemorated at the American Fiddlers' Hall of Fame and Museum at Osceola (1976). The museum's founder, the late Alice Colvin Clemens, is the best known of its tradition bearers.

Politics

The county was formed from Oneida in 1805, simultaneous with its northwestern neighbor, Jefferson. The county seat was established at Martinsburg; the courthouse, built in 1812, still stands. Government remained there until 1864, when it moved to Lowville, Lewis Co's largest village. Several towns have small populations, making governance costly. Highmarket, formed in 1852, declined in population in the 20th century to a point that residents voted for it to be annexed by West Leyden in 1976. Until 1970 the county was governed by a board of town supervisors, when it established a 10-district county legislature. The legislature first appointed a county manager in 1988, although the position was vacant between 1997 and 2002.

Recent History

Despite Lewis Co's large expanse of forested, even rugged, terrain, about 60% of its area was occupied by 4,124 farms in 1875; half of this acreage was unimproved. The area in farms increased slightly in the following quarter century, but the number of farms had already started to decline. After World War I, some of the farms given up by their longtime operators were taken up by new immigrants; Hungarians settled in Greig and Hungarians and Poles in West Turin, but ultimately only the best of the county's land could support modern agriculture. The number of farms declined dramatically in the 20th century, to 623, occupying 22% of the county, but an increase in farms' acres took place concurrently, from an average of 128 acres (52 ha) to 288 acres (117 ha) in 1997. Concentrated in the Black River Valley, farming emphasizes dairying; a part of its production serves the kosher market in New York City. In recent years some Amish farmers have moved in, separate from the long-established Mennonites elsewhere in the county. In the 20th century Lewis Co continued to have a significant industrial sector. Furniture was made in Lowville from 1905 to 1931, knit goods in Port Leyden from 1907 until the 1990s, and bowling pins in Croghan from 1918 to 1961. Pulp paper was an important product, made by St. Regis in Diana until the mid-1950s and by Gould in Lyons Falls until 2001. Lowville products included cardboard boxes, imitation leather, bowling pins, and cream cheese. The Hale Ski Lift Co operated in Turin from 1949 to 1962.

In 2003 fewer industries remained. Wood and other forest products were harvested. Manufacturers included Burrows Paper Corp, Kraft (cream cheese), Climax (boxes), AMF (bowling pins, flooring), Fibermark (paperboard), Beaverite (binders, gaskets), Otis Technology (gun-cleaning products), Harrisville Dry Kiln, Viking Cives (snowplows), and Interface Solutions (gaskets). Suzorite Mineral Products continues to mine talc in Diana, a town that lost a large part of its usable land area to state reforestation efforts in the 1930s and to the expansion of Pine Camp [now Fort Drum] beginning in 1941. Fort Drum's growth in the 1980s spilled over into neighboring towns and

POPULATIONS OF TOWNS, LEWIS CO

Town, Year Founded	1800	1840	1880	1920	1960	2000
Croghan, 18410	—	—	3,374	2,551	2,697	3,161
Denmark, 1807	—	2,388	2,204	1,905	2,214	2,747
Diana, 1830	—	883	2,026	2,181	1,641	1,661
Greig, 1828[a]	—	592	1,570	635	693	1,365
Harrisburg, 1803	—	850	1,089	619	423	423
Highmarket, 1852–1973[b]	—	—	941	316	95	—
Lewis, 1852	—	—	1,161	753	587	857
Leyden, 1797	622	2,438	1,933	1,515	1,715	1,792
Lowville, 1800	300	2,047	3,188	3,915	4,635	4,548
Lyonsdale, 1873	—	—	1,475	918	942	1,273
Martinsburg, 1803	—	2,272	2,386	1,566	1,469	1,249
Montague, 1850	—	—	975	450	73	108
New Bremen, 1848	—	—	2,414	1,609	1,963	2,722
Osceola, 1844	—	—	666	431	181	265
Pinckney, 1808	—	907	1,152	688	357	319
Turin, 1800	440	1,704	1,386	1,016	878	793
Watson, 1821	—	1,707	1,470	707	781	1,987
West Turin, 1830	—	2,042	2,006	1,929	1,905	1,674

Note: In 1800 the Towns of Leyden, Lowville, and Turin were in Oneida Co.

[a]Brantingham until 1832.

[b]Annexed to Town of West Turin 1973.

resulted in a modest increase in racial and ethnic diversity.

Tourism is Lewis Co's growth industry. Several of its lakes began attracting vacationers in the 19th century. Joseph Bonaparte's retreat in Diana was located on what is now called Lake Bonaparte, the site of many private camps. Brantingham Lake in Greig had a famous resort hotel, the Brantingham Inn (1876–1966). Others scattered around the county included the Fenton House (1826) at Number Four, the Lowville Mineral Springs House (1872), and Forest Home and the Hermitage at Lake Bonaparte. Winter sports became significant soon after World War II. Since the Tug Hill Plateau has the most snow in the East, Turin was selected for the site of Snow Ridge Ski Area (1945) and its Swiss Ski School. Winter recreation dispersed in the 1960s with the rise of snowmobiling; the western upland towns, especially Osceola and Pinckney, have become major snowmobile destinations.

The pioneer county histories are those by Franklin B. Hough, *History of Lewis County* (1860) and the much expanded second edition (1883). They were competently updated to 1965 by G. Byron Bowen, *History of Lewis County, NY, 1880–1965* (1970). A scholarly book on the French settlement is Edith Pilcher's *Castorland: French Refugees in the Western Adirondacks* (1985). There is little literature of good quality on the towns and villages; while not scholarly, two books by Matt J. Conway are comprehensive: *Highmarket "As You Were"* (1977) and *Port Leyden, "the Iron City"* (1989).

Field Horne

Lewiston. Town (pop 16,257) and village (pop 2,781) in W central Niagara Co. Louis-Thomas Chabert de Joncaire (*d* 1739) established a trading post in 1720. The area was resettled in 1792 and again *ca* 1800 and was burned by the British in 1813. The site was reserved by the state and patented in single lots. The town was formed from Cambria in 1818, and the village incorporated in 1822. The Rome, Watertown and Ogdensburg Railroad (1876) provided transportation, as did the electric Niagara Falls and Lewiston Railroad (1895). Model City (1893) was a planned development that never took off but became the site of Erie Preserving Co (processed fruits and vegetables). The town surrounds the territory of the Tuscarora Indian Reservation. Efforts by the New York Power Authority to condemn a part of the reservation led to a landmark, although ultimately unsuccessful, court challenge in 1958 by the Tuscarora Nation. The Power Authority operates the Power Reservoir, the Robert Moses Niagara Power Plant (1961), and the Lewiston Pump Generating Plant. Suburbanization and industrial development led to a doubling of the town's 1950 population of 6,921 within a decade. Lewiston landmarks include Frontier House (1824–26), an early hotel that now houses a McDonald's restaurant, and the Basilica of the National Shrine of Our Lady of Fatima (1954). Lewiston is the site of Niagara University (1856) and its Castellani Art Museum (1978), of Earl W. Brydges Artpark State Park (1974; performing arts center), and of Joseph Davis and Reservoir State Parks.

Nancy B. Mingus

Lexington. Town (pop 830) in SW Greene Co. It was formed from Windham in 1813 as New Goshen, becoming Lexington almost immediately. Much of the town is high, forested Catskill Mountain land, but the Schoharie Kill passes through the northeast corner and its tributary, West Kill, drains a 9 mi (14 km) valley. The Shandaken Tunnel was constructed from 1917 to 1924 to carry Schoharie Reservoir water to Esopus Creek, where it joins the south-flowing New York City water supply. Boardinghouse business developed in the late 19th century. After World War II Norwegians and Ukrainians from New York City established enclaves of summer homes.

Field Horne

Leyden. Town (pop 1,792) in SE Lewis Co. Settled in 1794, with many of the initial wave coming from Haddam, Middlefield, and Middletown, Conn, the town was formed in 1797 from Steuben [now in Oneida Co]. Its rich land supported dairy farms, and in the late 19th and early 20th centuries, most of its milk was sent to nearby cheese factories. The county's first radio station, WBRV, was established in Leyden in 1955. C. Hart Merriam (1855–1942), a founder of the National Geographic Society and member of the 1899 Harriman Alaska Expedition, was a resident of the hamlet of Locust Grove, and critic and essayist Edmund Wilson (1895–1972) resided summers in the hamlet of Talcottville. The Natural Bridge, where the Sugar River disappears into an underground channel, is a natural wonder.

Arthur Einhorn

L'Hommedieu, Ezra (*b* Southold, Suffolk Co, 30 Aug 1734; *d* Southold, 27 Sept 1811). Politician. L'Hommedieu graduated from Yale College in 1754 and practiced in Southold and New York City. In 1775 he signed the patriot Agreement of Association and was elected delegate to the First Provincial Congress. He served on subsequent congresses, and as a member of the fourth congress, he assisted in drafting the 1777 state constitution. He served on the Committee of Safety and supplied the Suffolk Co militia. He was a delegate to the Continental Congress (1779–83) and after independence served as Suffolk Co clerk (1784–1811), state senator (1784–92, 1794–1809), chairman on the Council of Appointment (1784–98), and member of the Board of Regents from its founding until his death (1784–1811). As a lawyer and politician he was a cosigner of the 1798 treaty with the Mohawks that ceded tribal lands to the state. In 1801 he was a delegate to the state constitutional convention.

Wood, Clarence Ashton. *Ezra L'Hommedieu: Island Statesman* (Amityville, NY: Long Island Forum, 1949)

Jennifer E. Steenshorne

libel. Four categories of the English common law of libel applied in 17th- and 18th-century New York Colony. Blasphemous libel and obscene libel aimed at protecting religion and public morality. Private libel protected individual reputations through civil suits for monetary damages, though criminal prosecution could be initiated where the libel was especially irresponsible and dangerous. Seditious libel, the most significant for the American colonies, was defined as malicious criticism of the government that tended to lower its reputation, inclining people to faction and sedition. It posed the greatest danger to public debate in the colonies. In cases involving seditious libel, juries were limited to determining whether the material was directed at the king or his ministers and whether the defendant had published the material. Truth was not a defense according to the common-law maxim, "the greater the truth, the greater the libel," and judges determined if the words in question were libelous.

The acquittal of John Peter Zenger in 1735 at his famous trial for seditious libel did not establish a legal precedent in New York Colony, but it did stimulate debate. Thereafter responsibility for prosecutions shifted from the courts to the Colonial Assembly, but prosecutions were rare in either forum. For the remainder of the 18th century publishers were uninhibited and largely ignored seditious libel laws. The 1777 Constitution did not contain a free speech clause, and Article 35 actually continued English common law unless modified by the legislature.

The national Sedition Act of 1798, though viewed as repressive from a contemporary perspective, embodied reforms advocated by Zenger's counsel: that truth should be a defense and that juries should be permitted to decide both law and facts. In 1804 New York State governor George Clinton obtained a common law indictment for seditious libel against Harry Croswell, editor of the *Wasp*, a Federalist newspaper published in Hudson (Columbia Co). Croswell was convicted under common-law standards. On appeal to the state's highest court, his lawyer, Alexander Hamilton, argued that the truth, published with good motives and justifiable ends, should be a complete defense. Judge James Kent accepted most of Hamilton's arguments in *People v Croswell.* Kent's restatement provided the basis for an 1805 statute allowing truth, published "with good motives and for justifiable ends" as a defense. This statute was constitutionalized in Article 6, Section 8 of the 1821 New York State Constitution. The state's standard gradually became the position adopted by most states, and it governed press freedom in the state and most of the nation throughout the 19th and nearly two-thirds of the 20th centuries. Criminal libel was dropped from the New York State Penal Law in 1965.

The laws involving civil libel were revolutionized based on the Supreme Court decision in *New York Times Co v Sullivan* (1964). Henceforth civil libel suits brought by public officials would require proof that the statements were known to be false or made with reckless disregard of the truth. Reflecting the result of America's distasteful experience with seditious libel, the Court announced that seditious libel prosecutions were inconsistent with the requirements of the First Amendment. The New York State Court of Appeals, relying on the state constitution in *Chapadeau v Utica Observer-Dispatch, Inc* (1975) and *Immuno A. G. v J. Moor-Jankowski* (1991), among others, has granted even greater protection to the press from libel suits than is required by the US Supreme Court.

See also Rights.

Levy, Leonard W. *Emergence of a Free Press* (New York: Oxford Univ Press, 1985)

Roper, Donald M. "James Kent and the Emergence of New York's Libel Law," *American Journal of Legal History* 17 (1973): 223–31

Peter J. Galie

liberalism. New York State has experienced three phases of liberalism, each emphasizing a different aspect of its three fundamental principles of self-government, legal equality, and individual rights. Between 1830 and 1890 classical liberalism stressed limited government and the primacy of property rights. From 1890 to 1940 regulatory liberalism bolstered the powers of state government and placed limits on property rights. After 1940 social welfare liberalism used state authority and resources to enhance legal equality and to provide material benefits to various social and economic groups.

Classical Liberalism

The American Revolution and the New York State Constitution of 1777 introduced liberal ideas into the quasi-aristocratic government and society of colonial New York. The constitution mandated a representative government based on the sovereignty of the people and a republican system reflecting the liberal principle of self-rule. Although the constitution did not contain a bill of rights protecting individual liberty, it guaranteed religious freedom, trial by jury, and the protection of private property. Despite such liberal features, the political system of 1777 primarily reflected classical republican principles. The constitution largely limited self-rule to male property owners, disenfranchising all women and excluding 40% of the adult men from voting in assembly elections and 70% from contests for the governor and state senate. The constitution also protected the quasi-feudal property rights of the Van Rensselaers, Livingstons, and other Hudson River valley manorial lords. Moreover, the state's political leaders ignored the liberal political economy advanced by Adam Smith, whose *Wealth of Nations* (1776) celebrated free markets and condemned government economic intervention. Instead, they pursued a policy of neomercantilism, providing state assistance to merchants, land speculators, and entrepreneurs for projects that would enhance the "commonwealth" of the society.

A liberal system of government, economic policy, and cultural ideals emerged in New York State after 1830 as newly professional party politicians, rural smallholders, and an entrepreneurial urban bourgeoisie seized political power. In the 1810s Martin Van Buren, a Jeffersonian Republican and future Jacksonian Democrat, repudiated classical republicanism because it disparaged political parties. Van Buren argued that parties mobilized the popular will and believed that the "majority should govern" was a fundamental maxim in free governments. Recruiting self-made lawyers and journalists, Van Buren created the first modern political party. At the Constitutional Convention of 1821 Van Buren's followers extended the suffrage to nearly all adult men, replacing a "republican" definition of citizenship based on property with a "liberal" conception based on the autonomy of individuals. Influenced by patriarchal values and the legal rules of coverture (which excluded married women from legal equality), the delegates did not extend voting rights to women and excluded most African Americans from the polls. The delegates did however, insert a bill of rights into the 1821 Constitution, thereby protecting many liberal political and legal rights.

During the 1820s the Van Burenites challenged the state's neomercantilist policies, which had chartered 30 commercial banks and invested state funds in the banks' stock. Invoking the classical liberal principles of Smith, they limited the number of new banks and regulated existing ones. Under the terms of Van Buren's Safety Fund System of 1829 (a precursor of the Federal Deposit Insurance Corp of 1933), state-appointed commissioners oversaw the affairs of member institutions and settled claims against failed banks.

During the 1830s the state's Jacksonian Democrats intensified the campaign for a laissez-faire political economy, condemning "the whole vile progeny of class legislation . . . the chartered monopolies, artificial credit system, fraudulent paper currencies, the perpetual taxation of public debt." William Leggett, a radical Democrat, demanded "Equal Rights" and the end of government subsidies to corporations. Logrolling local legislators created a substantial state debt by adding unprofitable feeder canals to the Erie Canal and by loaning $3 million to the New York and Erie Railroad. When Whig governor William H. Seward doubled the state debt to $27 million by expanding the canal system in the early 1840s, Van Burenite Michael Hoffman led successful movements to stop canal construction and to revise the state's constitution.

The 1846 Constitution gave the force of fundamental law to liberal principles. First, it greatly expanded self-rule for men (while explicitly rejecting it for women) by making nearly all state and local offices elective positions and allowing voters to call a new constitutional convention every 20 years. Second, the constitution limited the power of the state government and enhanced the rights of private property. A delegate representing New York City's merchants and bankers declared that the "sole object" of government was "to afford political protection to mankind in their lawful pursuits" and won provisions that diminished the state's traditional police powers by abolishing all offices for inspecting goods. Defending the interests of rural taxpayers, Hoffman and his allies limited the state's role in the economy. The constitution prohibited the state from extending loans or financial credit to private individuals or corporations and limited future state debts to $1 million, except as funded by specific taxes approved in a popular referendum. In the words of Hoffman, "We will not trust the legislature with the power of creating indefinite mortgages on the people's property."

Third, the new constitution strengthened the judiciary. It made judges elected officials who served limited terms, thus giving the judiciary a mandate from the sovereign people, like the legislature and the governor. Empowered by popular election, New York judges struck down legislation that violated the constitution's debt limits and other provisions. Classical liberal judges also redefined legal doctrines to give greater protection to private property. Historically, due process of law had meant procedural rights, such as a jury trial. However, in *Westervelt v Gregg* (1854), the New York State Court of Appeals gave due process a substantive interpretation, ruling that the Married Women's Property Act of 1848 had unlawfully transferred the property of husbands to their wives. In *Wynehamer v People* (1856), the court invalidated a statute seizing alcoholic beverages: "Where rights are acquired by the citizen under the existing law, there is no power in any branch of government to take them away." And finally, the new constitution struck a significant blow against the quasi-feudal land system of the Hudson Valley. It limited future agricultural leases to 12 years and prohibited restraints on land transfers, transforming manorial land into a marketable commodity.

Classical liberal ideas soon altered economic policy and social institutions. In 1850 the General Railroad Act allowed any group of entrepreneurs with the requisite capital stock of $10,000 per mile to incorporate a railroad and, using the state's power of eminent domain, to run its lines anywhere. In 1853, under the leadership of Charles Loring Brace, who had been inspired by the English political philosopher Herbert Spencer, the Children's Aid Society was formed with its base in New York City. It applied a classical liberal approach to the welfare of orphan children by repudiating the discipline of traditional orphan asylums and set up voluntary dormitories and industrial schools. Brace believed this would help create self-reliant and autonomous individuals.

New York State's political system now embodied a laissez-faire ethos celebrating individual economic opportunity, religious tolerance, fiscal conservatism, and limited state government. Fearing statewide laws that would restrict their religious and cultural practices, immigrant Irish and German Democrats championed "home rule" for cities. Rural and small-town Republicans opposed state levies for roads, prisons, and the Erie Canal. In 1873 they won constitutional guarantees against using local taxes to subsidize railroads and other corporations, and in 1880 rural legislators imposed taxes on business corporations. Wealthy New Yorkers likewise invoked classical liberal principles to demand frugal government. Citing the excessive patronage and corrupt deals of party politicians, they unsuccessfully proposed to redefine the liberal principle of self-rule by limiting voting on financial issues to taxpayers. Influenced by aissez-faire principles, in the 1880s Gov Grover Cleveland vetoed legislation that would have reduced the hours worked by trolley conductors and limited subway fares to 5¢. Additionally, the Court of Appeals in the landmark case of *In re Jacobs* (1885) invalidated a law regulating the working conditions of cigar makers in tenement dwellings as violating their freedom of contract.

Classical liberalism, once a radical antiaristocratic ideology that proclaimed the virtues of self-rule, legal equality, and individual freedom for all citizens, had become an instrument for protecting the property rights of small landholding farmers and the urban bourgeoisie. When Samuel Gompers of the American Federation of Labor proposed a public works project to assist workers during the depression of 1893, Gov Roswell P. Flower replied that "in America, the people support the government; it is not the province of the government to support the people."

Regulatory Liberalism

In the 1870s the upper-class New Yorkers who demanded "good government" began a reform movement that eventually altered the meaning of liberalism. Reformers ousted the corrupt Tammany Hall administration of Mayor William M. Tweed and endorsed the railroad regulation proposals advocated by the legislature's Hepburn Commission and the National Anti-Monopoly League. In 1886 middle-class voters in New York City won legislation setting natural gas prices. In rural areas women's temperance advocates campaigned successfully for local ordinances regulating the sale of alcoholic beverages and, with the passage of the Raines Law in 1896, secured state control of the liquor industry. Government regulation gradually replaced property rights at the center of the political agenda.

Regulatory liberalism exploded into public consciousness in 1905 when a legislative committee probed overcharging by the Consolidated Gas Co. The committee's chief lawyer, Charles Evans Hughes, established a pattern of overcapitalization, fraudulent bookkeeping, and tax evasion that gave huge profits to Consolidated Gas. To eliminate these abuses, Hughes won laws reducing the cost of gas and creating a publicly financed Commission of Gas and Electricity. To deter intervention by classical liberal judges, the law specified that the commission's regulations were to be reviewed by the courts only if there was a clear deprivation of property rights. Hughes then investigated the nation's life insurance industry, which was centered in New York City. His probing revealed corrupt insurance policies, including bias against the purchasers, speculative investments, and political payoffs. These revelations resulted in 10 laws forbidding political contributions, regulating lobbying, and setting rules for investment and underwriting—legislation that moved New York State decisively toward a new system of political economy based on regulation, administration, and planning.

As Republican governor from 1906 to 1910, Hughes expanded the scope of regulatory liberalism to include administrative efficiency, political reform, and workers' rights. His main goal was to restore power to citizens of middling means by curbing corporate abuses and machine politicians and by creating an efficient state government. To address political corruption, the governor secured laws limiting political contributions by corporations and replacing patronage jobs with competitive civil service positions. To increase government efficiency Hughes won passage of the Moreland Act (1907), which allowed the governor to oversee city and county officials and semiautonomous state government departments. More important, in 1910 Hughes partially implemented an executive budget, beginning the process that would transfer prime responsibility for fiscal policy from legislative committees to the governor's office and result in the Executive Budget Amendment of 1927. These legislative and political initiatives defined the character of modern state government.

The expansion of state power assisted New York's working classes. Initially Hughes espoused classical liberal principles by rejecting special legislation for the "working classes or any other classes." Motivated by similar concerns, the Court of Appeals had recently struck down legislation regulating the working conditions of bakers in the case of *Lochner v New York*, a decision upheld by the US Supreme Court in 1905. Once in office, Hughes came to realize that society was "so interdependent that . . . the opportunities for labor" should be enlarged by government action. Urged on by assembly representatives and state senators representing urban immigrants of European ancestry, Hughes used his legal skills to craft regulatory legislation that would not be voided by classically liberal judges. As a result, both the Page-Prentice Act of 1907, setting an 8-hour day and 48-hour week for factory workers under 16, and the Dangerous Trades Act, barring young workers from 30 occupations, survived legal challenge because they applied only to young workers or those in dangerous occupations. To enforce these regulations, the governor reorganized the Department of Labor and created a new bureau for immigrant issues. In 1910 the Worker Compensation Act established a compulsory plan of compensation for workers injured in hazardous industries and a voluntary system for other workers. Alleging that the act infringed on liberty of contract, New York State judges struck it down the following year, prompting workers and middle-class reform liberals to amend the state's constitution and enact a more inclusive insurance plan.

Just as farmers and the urban bourgeoisie defined the political program of classical liberalism, so an alliance of middle-class "social progressives" and urban workers set the legislative agenda of regulatory liberalism. Following the Triangle Shirtwaist Factory fire in 1911, Assemblyman Alfred E. Smith and Senator Robert F. Wagner Sr won the support of middle-class organizations, including the Citizens Union of the City of New York, Consumers' League of the City of New York, American Association for Labor Legislation, and Child Labor Committee. With their support they enacted legislation regulating fire safety and sanitation in factories, limiting working hours for women and children, setting minimum wages for state canal workers, and creating a State Industrial Board. This cross-class alliance continued during Smith's eight years as governor between 1919 and 1928. Advised by reformers Belle Moskowitz and Robert Moses, Smith won legislation that would increase the state's bureaucracy and give the governor extensive budgetary powers.

Smith's major accomplishment was ending the classical liberal era of limited state government. During his tenure as governor, the state's revenue rose (in constant dollars) from $50 million per year to nearly $190 million, while the state and local taxes paid by individuals increased from $20 to $52 per capita. Smith, and later Democratic governor Franklin D. Roosevelt (1929–33), achieved this fiscal revolution by making deals with rural representatives. In return for legislation increasing state revenue, Smith returned most of the proceeds to local communities for schools, roads, and libraries. By 1930 state subsidies accounted for 25% of the revenue of New York State's towns and villages and 50% of the expenditures of many farming communities. To win the support of urban voters for this fiscal program, Smith kept property taxes low and raised the levies paid by corporations and wealthy individuals. By 1930 property taxes accounted for only 12% of the state's revenue, while levies on corporations, stock transfers, and estates brought in 67%. The classical liberal era of small government and private property rights had given way to a regulatory liberal regime that used wealth for public purposes.

The depression temporarily halted the expansion of the state budget but cemented the triumph of regulatory liberalism. Democratic governor Herbert H. Lehman (1932–42) during the first years of his tenure focused on the pressing financial issues facing the state. These included balancing the state's budget while paying down its depression-induced debt of $100 million, providing homeowners with mortgage relief, saving the commercial mortgage industry, and winning a $40 million bond issue to provide relief for 500,000 unemployed New Yorkers. The social cost of restoring finances while providing relief was high. Sharp cuts in state spending would affect aid to the elderly, increased state income taxes hit the middle class, and the poor were burdened by regressive sales and gasoline taxes.

Lehman commanded the support of trade unions and urban workers by backing labor legislation, which since Hughes has been a key element in the program of regulatory liberalism. In 1933 Lehman advocated the passage of 25 bills dealing with labor issues, and in 1935, with Democratic majorities in the assembly and the senate, he extended this ambitious agenda. Bills setting a 40-hour week on public works contracts, banning yellow-dog contracts, and declaring that labor is not a commodity won legislative approval. The legislature also cut the power of antiunion judges by requiring jury trials for individuals accused of violating court injunctions in labor disputes. Private insurers and bureaucrat-wary legislators opposed Lehman's proposal for a state agency to manage the workers' compensation system, and he settled for a special fund that would pay workers' claims against bankrupt firms and insurers. Finally, Lehman won approval for a system of unemployment insurance that placed contributions from employers, employees, and the state in a single pooled fund from which laid-off workers could draw benefits for 16 weeks. Rejecting arguments by corporate lawyers that pooled coverage arbitrarily transferred private property and violated due process, the New York State Supreme Court narrowly upheld the new law. As regulatory liberal ideals became dominant, judges increasingly ignored or repudiated the classical liberal doctrine of substantive due process.

By 1940 New Yorkers had redefined liberalism as positive government. In 1893 Gov Flower had reflected classical liberal sentiment when he condemned aid to the unemployed as "official paternalism." A half century later, Gov Lehman celebrated the efforts of reform liberals to provide people with economic security, praising governmental "social welfare services" precisely because they were paternalistic, believing it to be at the heart of democracy and the promotion of the general welfare.

Social Welfare Liberalism

Over the next half century a massive infusion of money from the federal government, higher state taxes, and increased borrowing by government agencies and authorities brought the social welfare state to New York. The government bureaucracy increased dramatically in size and provided citizens with more and more services. Legislators and public officials implemented neomercantilist governmental policies that encouraged economic development and enhanced the prosperity of various interest groups. A political alliance of middle-class progressives and new arrivals to the state, primarily southern-born African Americans and Puerto Ricans, campaigned for laws prohibiting racial discrimination and for taxpayer-funded social assistance to needy and disadvantaged residents.

Housing policy reflected one of the aspects of social welfare liberalism. In the late 19th century, state and municipal governments had enacted building codes regulating tenements and other dwellings, but they had not directly subsidized construction. During the 1920s New York City promoted construction of 500,000 market-priced units by exempting them from local taxation while Gov Smith secured the State Board of Housing, which granted tax exemptions to private companies that built low-cost housing. Publicly owned and managed housing came to New York State only in 1936 with the completion of the First Houses project on New York City's Lower East Side, financed by the Federal Relief Administration. Many additional units were built after Congress enacted the Wagner-Steagall Housing Act of 1937 in which federal loans would cover 90% of the cost of public units and the 1938 state ratification of a constitutional amendment that allowed the state government to loan the remaining 10% to local housing authorities. By 1942 Democratic social welfare liberals were calling for a bond issue of $200 million to finance public housing for low-income families.

These liberal dreams became a reality, and eventually a fiscal nightmare, during the succeeding decades. In 1955 the legislature enacted the Mitchell-Lama Act, which subsidized middle-income housing by allowing the issue of voter approved tax-exempt bonds and reducing local real estate taxes. Five years later it created the State Housing Finance Agency to provide additional funding. However, in 1964 and again in 1965 the state's voters rejected bond issues (of $165 and $200 million) to clear slums and construct low-income public housing. In response, Republican Gov Nelson A. Rockefeller (1959–73) won legislation in 1968 to create the Urban Development Corp (UDC). The UDC had the power to condemn existing buildings, acquire land by eminent domain, override local building codes, and finance new construction by borrowing up to $2 billion. By 1972 it had 30,000 low-rent housing units under construction.

The initial success of the UDC obscured two problems, one racial and the other financial. Beginning in the 1930s the Lehman administration had courted the growing African American community in Harlem, working through trade union leader A. Philip Randolph and Lester Granger of the National Urban League. Lehman and Charles Poletti, who served briefly as governor in 1942, had pressured businesses to hire black workers, insisted on racial integration in publicly subsidized housing, and in 1938 won a constitutional provision prohibiting discrimination against an individual's civil rights on the basis of race, color, or religion. In 1945 the Ives-Quinn Law echoed these sentiments by prohibiting discrimination on the basis of race and religion in employment, housing, and other areas of life. By the 1950s social welfare liberals in New York City had affirmed their commitment to equal treatment of African Americans by prohibiting exclusionary labor practices in the city's construction contracts. However, many labor unions refused to admit Blacks and used their political influence to prevent enforcement of this regulation. The city's Fair Housing Law of 1958, the first in the nation, likewise failed to achieve racial integration in public housing. Thousands of white tenants left the public housing system in the 1960s and 1970s, complaining that the racial quotas devised by the Housing Authority broke up established ethnic communities and increased the amount of crime. The liberal promise of legal equality and an integrated, color-blind society floundered on the rocks of racial suspicion and conflict.

Race complicated housing initiatives, and dubious financing during the Rockefeller administration threatened the housing program and many other governmental initiatives with disaster. As a program of government initiatives in the provision of services, social welfare liberalism in New York reached its apogee during the Rockefeller era. During that 15-year period, the number of state employees nearly doubled, rising from 109,000 to 215,000, the annual budget rose from $1.7 billion to $7.8 billion (roughly doubling in constant dollars), and the government provided massive funding for higher education, health, highways, and environmental concerns. To finance the increased size and scope of the state, the governor and the legislature doubled the level of taxes; state and local levies took 3.5% of citizens' income in the 1950s and 7.5% in the 1970s. Moreover, Rockefeller won voter approval for $4 billion in bonds to improve water quality, highway and mass transit systems, and the environment, thereby raising the per capita state debt by nearly 350%.

Finally, the Rockefeller administration resorted to dubious financing schemes that contravened the spirit of the state's constitutional tradition and the liberal tenet of self-rule. To finance and direct his ambitious building and social welfare programs, the governor expanded existing agencies, such as the Dormitory Authority, and won legislative approval of dozens of semiautonomous public authorities, such as the UDC and the Housing Finance Agency. In addition, he entered into controversial leaseback agreements with local governments, using their bonding authority to raise funds for state initiatives, including the massive Albany office project now known as the Governor Nelson A. Rockefeller Empire State Plaza. Most of these bonds were issued without voter approval and were backed not by the "full faith and credit" of the government but only by a "moral obligation." The boom in government activity yielded impressive results. In 1959 the SUNY System enrolled 38,000 students on 28 campuses; 15 years later it boasted 264,000 students on 64 campuses. Hundreds of government-financed nursing homes, hospitals, and mental health clinics served communities across the state, and thousands of poor families lived in low-cost public housing. State funding improved highways and public transit systems, and state agencies provided health services to the aged and the poor.

In 1975 this spending boom ended in a spectacular fiscal bust. A decrease in federal rent subsidies for low-income families undermined the fragile financing of the UDC, raising the prospect it would default on hundreds of millions of dollars of moral obligation bonds. To preserve the state's capacity to borrow money, the legislature and ultimately the state's taxpayers had to assume responsibility for the bonds issued by the UDC and other public authorities. This fiscal crisis of the mid-1970s, like that of the 1840s, brought a reassessment of the ideology of liberalism and the role of government. By the early 1970s some New Yorkers, of both African and European ancestry, were questioning whether the creation of a homogeneous culture through integrated schooling was the best way to realize the liberal values of equality and self-rule. As an alternative, they increasingly advanced the notion of multiculturalism and community-based schools and institutions. Other citizens noted the existence of contradictory interests within the liberal movement. They pointed out that the success of reform liberals in fostering public-sector labor unions and in providing their members with substantial salaries and benefits made it difficult for state and local governments to find sufficient resources to expand social welfare programs for minorities and the poor.

Inspired by Pres Ronald Reagan (1981–89), New York City mayor Rudolph Giuliani (1994–2002) and Gov George E. Pataki (1994–) initially invoked classical liberal principles to challenge the legitimacy of the social welfare state. They cut taxes and the number of government workers, implemented strong anticrime policies, and reduced the number of people on welfare. However, to retain political support, both officials soon increased government spending, improving the infrastructure (roads, bridges, subway cars, and hospitals), and enhancing social entitlement programs. Between 1997–98 and 2002–3, the state budget jumped from $67 billion to $91 billion, funded in part by the boom economy of the late 1990s and in part by substantial borrowing. By 2002 the debt of New York State had risen to $38 billion, while that of New York City had increased to $42 billion. (By way of comparison, the debt of California was only $25 billion.)

To maintain or create political alliances among the state's diverse social and economic groups, including African Americans, Jews, Hispanics, middle-class progressives, and white urban workers, the leaders of both political parties continued the ambitious public agendas of reform and social welfare liberals. Thus in 2000, despite a looming budget deficit, Republican governor Pataki and the Democratic assembly enacted a new entitlement program, Family Health Plus. This offered fully subsidized healthcare to 600,000 low-income adults and helped to ensure employment for the 220,000 members of 1199 SEIU, a minority-dominated healthcare union. It remains to be seen if New York State and city governments can sustain massive entitlement programs in addition to a large regulatory bureaucracy and very substantial public debts. In the early years of the 21st century, yet another redefinition of liberalism seemed a distinct possibility.

Baker, Paula. *The Moral Frameworks of Public Life: Gender, Politics, and the State in Rural New York, 1870–1930* (New York: Oxford Univ Press, 1991)

Buenker, John D. *Urban Liberalism and Progressive Reform* (New York: Scribner's, 1973)

Corwin, Edward S. "The Extension of Judicial Review in New York: 1783–1905," *Michigan Law Review* 15 (Feb 1917): 281–313

Galie, Peter J. *Ordered Liberty: A Constitutional History of New York* (New York: Fordham Univ Press, 1996)

Gunn, L. Ray. *The Decline of Authority: Public Economic Policy and Political Development in New York State, 1800–1860* (Ithaca: Cornell Univ Press, 1989)

Ingalls, Robert P. *Herbert H. Lehman and New York's Little New Deal* (New York: New York Univ Press, 1975)

McCormick, Richard L. *From Realignment to Reform: Political Change in New York State, 1893–1910* (Ithaca: Cornell Univ Press, 1981)

Niven, John. *Martin Van Buren: The Romantic Age of American Politics* (New York: Oxford Univ Press, 1983)

Underwood, James E. *Governor Rockefeller in New York: The Apex of Pragmatic Liberalism in the United States* (Westport, Conn: Greenwood Press, 1982)

Wesser, Robert F. *Charles Evans Hughes: Politics and Reform in New York, 1905–1910* (Ithaca: Cornell Univ Press, 1967)

Yearley, Clifton K. *The Money Machines: The Breakdown and Reform of Governmental and Party Finance in the North, 1860–1920* (Albany: SUNY Press, 1970)

Yellowitz, Irwin. *Labor and the Progressive Movement in New York State, 1897–1916* (Ithaca: Cornell Univ Press, 1965)

James A. Henretta

Liberal Party. Perhaps the most enduring and influential minor party in American political history, the Liberal Party often played a significant role in deciding the outcomes of New York City and statewide elections. In 1944 trade union leaders David Dubinsky and Alex Rose, both pro–New Deal and anticommunist, founded the Liberal Party by withdrawing from the communist-dominated American Labor Party. Sharing a Jewish-Polish ancestry, Rose (president of the United Hatters, Cap and Millinery Workers International Union) and Dubinsky (head of the International Ladies' Garment Workers' Union) dominated the Liberal Party until the 1970s.

The new party hoped to maintain a balance between the Democratic and Republican Parties, which it saw as dominated, respectively, by the bossism of Tammany Hall and by powerful and wealthy special interests. For many decades the party could count on 5% to 8% of the statewide electorate, its support concentrated in New York City, with a strong following among Jews and former socialists. The party also had many intellectual supporters, among them Adolph Berle and Reinhold Niebuhr. In its political philosophy the party supported positions such as rent control, affordable housing, consumer and environmental protection, civil rights, and equal rights for women, and called for the adoption of a direct primary and referendum.

The Liberal Party often played a decisive role in important elections, as when it provided the margin of victory to elect W. Averell Harriman as governor in 1954. The party offered Democrats or Republicans the opportunity to run as an independent if they had been denied their own nomination. Many times the Liberal Party exercised influence over major party nominations by promising to provide a major candidate a multiparty endorsement or by threatening to run its own candidate and deprive the two major parties of votes. For example, in the 1966 gubernatorial election the Liberal Party ran Franklin D. Roosevelt Jr as its own candidate. The Roosevelt name produced a record 507,234 votes for the party (well above its quarter of a million vote average in statewide elections), thereby ensuring the defeat of the Democratic nominee Frank D. O'Connor and securing the victory for Republican governor Nelson A. Rockefeller. The Liberal Party provided critical support to the campaigns of New York City mayors Robert F. Wagner Jr and John Lindsay. In what was perhaps the Liberal Party's finest hour, Lindsay, after losing the Republican primary, was reelected in 1969 on the Liberal line, garnering over a million votes. The party also gave a boost to the political aspirations of Mario M. Cuomo, backing him once for the mayoralty and four times for governor.

After the mid-1970s the Liberal Party steadily lost enrollment, declining from about 120,000 votes in 1970 to near 60,000 some 20 years later. In the 1980s the Liberal Party's aged leadership, its ties to the decaying garment industry, and the emergence in New York State of more vigorous third parties, such as the Conservative Party and the Right-to-Life Party on the Right and the Green Party and Working Families Party on the Left, led to its steady decline. Although its strong support of Rudolph Guiliani led to positions of influence for party leaders in his administration, it did nothing to staunch the erosion of its political base and the perception among many that patronage had become more important to the party than crusading liberalism. In November 2002 the Liberal Party failed to meet the 50,000 vote minimum as mandated by law to keep itself on the statewide ballot as an organized party, and in February 2003 the party disbanded.

Flournoy, Houston I. "The Liberal Party in New York State" (PhD diss, Princeton Univ, 1956)

McNickle, Chris. *To Be Mayor of New York* (New York: Columbia Univ Press, 1992)

Erik van den Berg

Libertarian Party. Political party committed to maximizing individual liberty and limiting government. Favoring voluntary cooperation as the means to achieve progress, the party opposes the proliferation of government and subsidy programs such as Social Security, foreign aid, the funding of political campaigns, price controls, and other measures that interfere with the free-market economy.

The Libertarian Party was established in New York State in 1972 and ran Francine Youngstein for mayor of New York City in 1973. Adherents referred to themselves as Free Libertarians in the early 1970s to avoid confusion with the state's Liberal Party. During the mid-1970s the party found support outside New York City among those who advocated gun rights and tax reform and championed social issues such as women's rights, abortion rights, and, in the 1980s, gay rights. Lawyer Gary Greenberg traveled statewide campaigning for his candidacy for the 1978 gubernatorial race, stressing traditional libertarian principles and legalization of certain drugs. The 1978 campaign resulted in a stronger party with a statewide network of chapters.

After the 1983 Libertarian Party National Convention in New York City, political infighting resulted in inactivity within the New York State party, which, in 1986, failed to nominate any candidates for statewide office. Except for that year, the party has fielded candidates for the governorship in every election since 1974, although its gubernatorial candidates have never drawn more than 1% of the total vote. Its lowest draw was 4,722 votes in 1998, and its highest was 24,611 in 1990. In 1994 the party received national notoriety when radio personality Howard Stern was nominated for governor; Stern withdrew from the race after four months. As well as fielding candidates for state and local offices, the party has endorsed candidates for president, US senator, and US representative. Norma Segal, Libertarian candidate for the US Senate in 1992, drew more than 108,000 votes and finished with close to 2% of the votes cast.

Never an officially recognized political party under state law because of its inability to garner more than 50,000 votes in any gubernatorial race, it uses the nominating petition process to put forth candidates for political office. The state party closely follows the national party's platform. It maintains a political structure with a chair and executive board, publishes the newsletter *FreeNY,* and maintains operations through dues and volunteer efforts. During the late 1980s membership rebounded from around 150 to the estimated original level of 1,200–1,400, where it remained at the start of the 21st century. Members belong to county or local chapters, which numbered around 12 in 2002, or to one of several college chapters. A 2003 federal court decision (and subsequent revised state voter registration form) allowed voters to register with the Libertarian Party even though it does not legally qualify as a party.

Libertarian Party. "The Libertarian Party: Our History," http://www.lp.org/organization/history

John Evers

Liberty. Town (pop 9,623) and village (pop 3,975) in central Sullivan Co. Settled 1793–94, the town formed from Lumberland in 1807. Early residents worked at lumbering, tanning, and farming. Liberty was the site of the Liberty Normal Institute (1847), and the village incorporated in 1870. With the arrival of the Ontario and Western Railroad (1872–1953), the village became the center of a prosperous resort industry and the home of dozens of prominent hotels beginning in the 1880s, including the Wawonda (1891–1914), the largest structure in the county at the time. Beginning in 1889, the railroad touted the health benefits of the region's air, leading to the creation of the Loomis Sanitorium for tuberculosis patients (1896–1938). Many of the institution's architecturally noteworthy buildings still stand; when antibiotics caused the decline of tuberculosis, Loomis Sanitorium was sold to strongman Bernarr Macfadden, became a health resort, but closed in 1942. Tubercular patients tended to discourage the resort trade, but an influx of Jewish vacationers after 1900 gave birth to Jewish bungalow colonies, summer camps, and resorts, including the world-renowned Grossinger's Hotel (1919–85). Access to Liberty improved with the completion of the limited-access Rte 17 (I-86) between 1958 and 1960, but changing social customs caused the resorts to decline and close beginning about 1965, although the famed Stevensville at Swan Lake reopened as the Swan Lake Resort.

John Conway

Liberty Party. Abolitionist political party. Frustrated by the antislavery movement's relative lack of success, many abolitionists in the late 1830s favored abandoning moral suasion, the voluntary persuasion of individuals, as the principal tactic used to end slavery. William Lloyd Garrison, the American Anti-Slavery Society founder, refused to consider political action as a valid antislavery tactic, but leading abolitionists, such as New Yorkers Joshua Leavitt, Gerrit Smith, Myron Holley, and William Goodell, believed that effective change could occur only through the elective process. The Whig and Democratic Parties, however, both seemed hopelessly tied to Southern slave interests; so in March 1838 Goodell, Alvan Stewart, and other political abolitionists met in Utica and proposed a distinctly Christian, antislavery "liberty-party." The idea garnered limited support at an Albany abolitionist convention in May 1839, and a few antislavery candidates in New York State ran that year on independent tickets for local offices. At an antislavery convention held in November 1839 at the Presbyterian Church in Warsaw (Wyoming Co), supporters made the first independent abolitionist nominations for US president. The Liberty Party was formally constituted in Albany in April 1840, and James G. Birney, a Kentucky native then living in New York City, was nominated for the presidency.

Though never large the number of Liberty votes grew in the early 1840s, especially in New York State's religiously radical Burned-over District of Central and Western New York. Out of about 62,300 Liberty votes cast nationwide in the 1844 election, 15,812 were cast in New York State, and almost all of those were from the Burned-over District. Because most New York State Liberty voters had previously voted as Whigs, many historians contend that the Liberty vote in 1844 was sufficient to deny the Whig presidential candidate, Henry Clay, the electoral votes of New York State, thus handing the election to Democrat James K. Polk. In the late 1840s many Liberty politicians favored a broad-based coalition with other northern "free soil" politicians. Some Liberty leaders, especially those from Central and Western New York like Goodell and Smith, decried the coalition, considering it a dilution of abolitionist principles. While the Free Soil Party was officially established in Buffalo, remaining Liberty members held various conventions in 1847, one in Macedon Lock (Wayne Co) and one in Buffalo. In the 1848 election New York State's political abolitionists split their votes between the Liberty and the Free Soil candidates. The Liberty Party continued through the 1850s as a tiny remnant of its former self, consisting almost solely of a few die-hard New York State abolitionists. The party managed to field candidates for national and statewide office through 1860, and its platform became increasingly radical, calling for the extension of suffrage to all persons, white and black, men and women.

Kraut, Alan M. "The Forgotten Reformers: A Profile of Third Party Abolitionists in Antebellum New York." In *Antislavery Reconsidered: New Perspectives on the Abolitionists,* ed. Lewis Perry and Michael Fellman (Baton Rouge: Louisiana State Univ Press, 1979)
Strong, Douglas M. *Perfectionist Politics: Abolitionism and the Religious Tensions of American Democracy* (Syracuse: Syracuse Univ Press, 1999)

Douglas M. Strong

libraries. There are approximately 7,000 libraries in New York State. They range from those considered among the greatest research libraries in the world to small community and school libraries that bring books and other information resources to all corners of the state and the state's diverse citizenry.

EARLY LIBRARY TYPES

The origins of libraries in New York can be traced to the early 18th century, but development was understandably spotty and limited to the few centers of population. Perhaps the first formal library was established in New York City when a small collection of books was deposited in Trinity Church in 1698 for the use of Anglican clergy and probably made accessible to others.

When early libraries were referred to as "public libraries," it was to distinguish them from the private libraries of individuals. These were usually established with some variation of a subscription method and were known as association or society libraries. The model for these libraries was the Library Company of Philadelphia established by Benjamin Franklin and others in 1731. Such a library was established in East Hampton (Suffolk Co) in 1753. The New York Society Library was established in 1754 and the Albany Society Library in 1758. Other early libraries to which the public had access were attached to academies, which were established by legislation in 1787. With funding available from state grants, representative small academy libraries included the Kingston Academy (Ulster Co), the Washington Academy in Salem (Washington Co), the Lansingburgh Academy (Rensselaer Co), and Erasmus Hall in Flatbush (Kings Co). In 1796 the legislature made provisions for li-

New York Public Library in 1932.

brary societies, which developed rapidly in small towns and older communities across the state. The earliest examples of these so-called farmers' libraries in Western New York were the Batavia Library (Genesee Co) in 1804 and the Wheatland Library (Monroe Co) in 1805.

Lending libraries operated for a profit, usually by a bookseller, were another type that began to appear in the late 18th century. Such collections, typically called circulating libraries, often had a larger proportion of fiction in their holdings than other libraries of the time. The first of these libraries was opened in New York City by Garret Noel in 1763, and the most renowned commercial circulating library in the early period was operated by Hocquet Caritat, a French immigrant, in New York City from 1797 to 1804.

In the early 19th century a new type of library developed in the growing cities of the state. They targeted young workingmen in the mechanical and commercial trades. The Mercantile Library Association in New York City and the Apprentice Library in Albany were organized in 1820. Other similar young men's association libraries were founded in Troy (Rensselaer Co), Rochester, and Buffalo, and these collections often became absorbed by, or formed the basis of, free public libraries later in the century.

The New York State Library was established in Albany in 1818 "for the use of the government and the people of this state." It developed important research collections and served as a resource for the legislature and others in state government. With 95,000 volumes in its collections in 1876, it was the largest state library in the country. Other early specialized libraries included those of historical societies. The library of the New-York Historical Society had 60,000 volumes by 1876, and other large historical collections were held by the Long Island Historical Society in Brooklyn (now Brooklyn Historical Society), the Albany Institute (now Albany Institute of History and Art), and the Buffalo Historical Society (now Buffalo-Erie Historical Society). In addition, the Astor Library (1854) opened in New York City as a research library that by the end of the century was combined with the Lenox Library (1870), formed by James Lenox and the Tilden Trust (a bequest from Gov Samuel J. Tilden to establish a free library in the city), to form the New York Public Library (1895).

Libraries and Education

New York was an early pioneer in the development of school libraries, recognizing the intimate connection between libraries and education. In 1835 the legislature approved a revolutionary plan to establish school district libraries across the state. Districts were empowered to levy a tax to purchase a library but initially the number of districts to do this was relatively small. Development of such libraries accelerated after 1838, when the state authorized an annual payment of $55,000 from the US government to school districts for the purpose of acquiring libraries. Although the districts were required to match the funds, the growth in school district libraries, which were designed also to serve the needs of the community, was dramatic. By 1848 there were libraries in nearly all of the state's 11,000 districts, with the number of volumes totaling nearly 1.3 million. The school district libraries were not sustained, however, because provisions in the law in later years enabled districts to divert funds to other purposes, such as improving teacher salaries. Still, the program established the practice of providing state funding for public libraries and the view that support for libraries was inextricably connected to support for education.

Institutions of higher learning possess some of the richest library resources in New York. The oldest academic library is Columbia University's, established by 1757, just three years after the univeristy's founding as King's College in 1754. In the 19th century smaller colleges often had libraries associated with literary societies in addition to those owned by the college. The expansion of higher education and of graduate programs, which required research collections, stimulated the growth of academic libraries in the 20th century. The creation of the State University of New York system in 1948, and particularly of four university centers at Albany, Binghamton, Buffalo, and Stony Brook (Suffolk Co), greatly strengthened research libraries in the state. Many special collections in these libraries, such as the Fiske Icelandic collection at Cornell, are unsurpassed.

Melvil Dewey, whose decimal classification system influenced libraries worldwide, had a significant impact on libraries in New York State. As the librarian at Columbia College (now Columbia University), Dewey established the first school to train librarians in 1887. Two years later, he accepted the position of state librarian and moved his fledgling school to Albany, where it flourished until 1926, when it returned to New York City to join with the New York Public Library's Library School to form Columbia University's School of Library Service. Although this closed in 1992, New York State still has seven graduate school programs in library and information science for the education of librarians, more than any other state in the country.

State Librarian Dewey pioneered a number of statewide library ventures. He was a driving force behind new legislation in 1892 that brought the public libraries in the state under the Regents of the University of the State of New York. The law provided for state aid for libraries and provided for the creation of "traveling libraries" to be loaned out to small towns by the State Library, which took on a central role in promoting library services across the state. Dewey was also instrumental in establishing the New York Library Association (NYLA) in 1890, which has always proved a force for improving library services statewide and for lobbying the legislature for increased state aid.

Modern Improvements

The growth in free public libraries in the early 20th century was furthered by gifts from Andrew Carnegie, who provided funds for the construction of about 40 library buildings in upstate New York and 66 branch libraries in New York City. The growth in book collections in free public libraries was also dramatic, increasing nearly 20 times in the 40 years after the new library legislation of 1892.

The major development in the organization of libraries in the second half of the 20th century was the creation of regional library systems to allow for more efficient services to the public and for services for smaller libraries without sufficient resources of their own. There are 23 public library systems, offering services such as on-line catalogs and circulation systems, cooperative cataloging and acquisition programs, and training for staff members. Over 1,000 public libraries and neighborhood branches receive state support through the public library systems. School library systems were established in 1984; 42 serve over 4,500 school library media centers in both public and nonpublic schools. In 1966 the legislature established a series of reference and research library resources systems or councils, commonly called the 3Rs. The purpose of the 3Rs is to enhance the capabilities of the state's academic, medical, law, business, and special libraries by enabling them to acquire services and share resources cooperatively. There are nine reference and research library resources councils that work with the public and school library systems and more than 900 academic, law, medical, business, and other special libraries. The 3Rs play an important role in supporting library access to electronic resources, including the New York On-line Virtual Electronic Library (NOVEL). They also provide interlibrary loan services and help coordinate state funding programs.

Like libraries everywhere, New York's libraries have seen tremendous changes in recent years as information resources are increasingly available electronically. The Regents Commission on Library Services conducted an extensive study and issued a report in 2000 that lays out a plan for further development of library services that would capitalize on the ability to deliver information resources electronically to ensure that all New Yorkers have equitable access to information necessary for education and economic development.

See also Blindness.

Cole, George Watson. "Early Library Development in New York State (1800–1900)," *Bulletin of the New York Public Library* 30 (Nov–Dec 1926): 849–57, 917–25

Ditzion, Sidney H. "The District School Library, 1835–55," *Library Quarterly* 10 (Oct 1940): 545–77

Lopez, Manuel D. *Bibliography of the History of Libraries in New York State* (Tallahassee: Journal of Library History, School of Library Science, Florida State Univ, 1971)

Meeting the Needs of All New Yorkers: Library Service in the New Century. Final Report of the Regents Commission on Library Services (Albany: University of the State of New York, 2000)

New York State Library, http://www.nysl.nysed.gov

Tolman, Frank L. "Libraries and Lyceums." In *History of the State of New York,* vol 9, ed. Alexander C. Flick (Cooperstown: NYS Historical Association, 1962)

US Department of the Interior, Bureau of Education. *Public Libraries in the United States of America: Their History, Condition, and Management, Part I* (Washington, DC: Government Printing Office, 1876)

Philip B. Eppard

Liederkranz cheese. In 1873 Bavarian-born Julius Wettstein founded the Monroe Cheese Co (Orange Co) to manufacture fancy, European-style cheeses. In 1891 Jacob Weisl, a native of Bohemia [now in Czech Republic], purchased Monroe Cheese, and the Weisl family would guide the firm for the next 38 years. Sometime between 1891 and 1898, the company's Swiss-born cheesemaker, Emil Frey, created a new cheese to rival German Bismarck cheese. By 1902 Frey's strongly flavored and strongly scented cheese was sold under the name Liederkranz—in honor of the famed German American singing society founded in New York City in

1847—although this name was not registered with the US Patent and Trademark Office until 1909. On 15 May 1915 a Monroe newspaper reported that the company shipped an average of 1 ton (.9 MT) of cheese a day. The Monroe plant closed in July 1926, with operations moving to Van Wert, Ohio. Sold to the Borden in 1929, the Ohio facility continued to make Liederkranz until 1981. Fisher Cheese Co of Wapakoneta, Ohio, produced Liederkranz from 1982 until 1985. Cheese connoisseur John Steele Gordon has described Liederkranz as one of America's three great native cheeses, the other two being monterey jack and brick. At the beginning of the 21st century ConAgra Foods, headquartered in Downers Grove, Ill, owns the rights to the famed variety but does not currently produce it.

James Nelson

lieutenant governor. Dating to the state constitution of 1777, the position was appointed during the colonial era. Under the current constitution, the formal qualifications for governor and lieutenant governor are identical: US citizenship, a minimum age of 30 years, and five years' residence in New York State. Singular among statewide offices but like the vice presidency in the federal government, the lieutenant governorship bridges the separation of powers divide. The governor's and lieutenant governor's offices are created in the constitution's executive article. An amendment adopted in 1953 requiring the governor and lieutenant governor to be elected on a single ballot links the two offices even more closely. Yet the lieutenant governor's sole constitutional duty is legislative: to preside over the state senate.

The most important function of the lieutenant governor is to ensure continuity in state governance: becoming governor if the governor should die, resign, decline to serve, or be removed from office, and acting as governor if the governor is impeached, is absent from the state, or is unable to discharge the duties of office. The first lieutenant governors to succeed to the governorship served as acting governors. They were John Tayler (1817), Nathaniel Pitcher (1828), and Enos T. Throop (1829). David B. Hill, who came to the office after Grover Cleveland resigned to take the presidency in 1885, was the first to be sworn in as governor. Throop and Hill later won the office in their own right. Others who reached the governorship by succession were Horace White (1910), Martin H. Glynn (1913), and Charles Poletti (1942). Malcolm Wilson—the last lieutenant governor (1959–73) to become governor this way in the 20th century—gained the office when Nelson A. Rockefeller resigned in 1973. Even if a vacancy does not arise, the lieutenant governorship is a formidable political base from which to seek the governor's seat, as the careers of De Witt Clinton, Hamilton Fish, Frank W. Higgins, Herbert H. Lehman, and Mario M. Cuomo attest. It is the practice of New York State's major political parties to nominate geographically and demographically balanced tickets for statewide office as an electoral tactic. This resulted in the lieutenant governorship serving as a point of access to high elective office for Italian Americans (Charles Poletti, 1939–42) and women (Mary Anne Krupsak, 1975–78).

With one foot in each of the political branches, the lieutenant governor may stand firmly in neither. The constitution grants a casting vote, but the rules of the state senate, combined with partisanship and long practice, render the lieutenant governor almost entirely powerless in that body. Effectiveness on the executive side depends entirely on the lieutenant governor's relationship with the governor. Malcolm Wilson was part of the inner circle in the Rockefeller administration, as was Stan Lundine when he served as Gov Cuomo's lieutenant governor (1987–94). But Govs Hugh Carey, Mario M. Cuomo, and George E. Pataki each marginalized their first lieutenant governors, respectively Mary Anne Krupsak, Alfred B. DelBello (1983–85), and Betsy McCaughey Ross (1995–98).

Differences arise because politicians aspiring to be lieutenant governor may have independent political bases. Although elected on a single ballot with the governor, nominees for lieutenant governor are chosen by statewide primary, sometimes without the support of their party's gubernatorial candidate. Moreover, once elected the lieutenant governor serves the same fixed term as the governor, cannot be removed by the gover-

LIEUTENANT GOVERNORS

Name	Elected or Succeeded to Office	Residence
Pierre Van Cortlandt (RW, DR)	1777	Croton Landing (Westchester Co)
Stephen Van Rensselaer (F)	1795	Albany
Jeremiah Van Rensselaer (DR)	1801	Albany
John Broome (JR)	1804	New York City
John Tayler[a] (JR)	29 Jan 1811	Albany
De Witt Clinton[b] (JR)	30 Apr 1811	New York City
John Tayler (JR)	1813	Albany
Erastus Root (VBR)	1822	Delhi (Delaware Co)
James Tallmadge (D)	1824	New York City
Nathaniel Pitcher[c] (JD)	1826	Sandy Hill (Washington Co)
Peter R. Livingston (AJ)	16 Feb 1828	Rhinebeck (Dutchess Co)
Charles Dayan (JD)	7 Oct 1828	Lowville (Lewis Co)
Enos T. Throop[d] (JD)	1828	Auburn (Cayuga Co)
Charles Stebbins (JD)	12 Mar 1829	Cazenovia (Madison Co)
William M. Oliver (D)	5 Jan 1830	Penn Yan (Yates Co)
Edward P. Livingston (VBR)	1830	Clermont (Columbia Co)
John Tracy (JD)	1832	Oxford (Chenango Co)
Luther Bradish (W)	1838	Malone (Franklin Co)
Daniel S. Dickinson (D)	1842	Binghamton
Addison Gardiner (D)	1844	Rochester
Hamilton Fish[e] (W)	1847	New York City
George W. Patterson (W)	1848	Westfield (Chautauqua Co)
Sanford E. Church (D)	1850	Albion (Orleans Co)
Henry J. Raymond (W)	1854	New York City
Henry R. Selden (R)	1856	Rochester
Robert Campbell (R)	1858	Bath (Steuben Co)
David R. Floyd Jones (D)	1862	Oyster Bay (Nassau Co)
Thomas G. Alvord (R)	1864	Syracuse
Stewart L. Woodford (R)	1866	Brooklyn
Allen C. Beach (D)	1868	Watertown
John C. Robinson (R)	1872	Binghamton
William Dorsheimer (R)	1874	Buffalo
George G. Hoskins (R)	1879	Bennington (Wyoming Co)
David B. Hill (D)	1882	Elmira
Dennis McCarthy[f] (R)	6 Jan 1885	Syracuse
Edward F. Jones (D)	1885	Binghamton
William F. Sheehan (D)	1891	Buffalo
Charles T. Saxton (R)	1894	Clyde (Wayne Co)
Timothy L. Woodruff (R)	1896	Brooklyn
Frank W. Higgins (R)	1902	Olean (Cattaraugus Co)
Matthew Linn Bruce (R)	1904	New York City
Lewis Stuyvesant Chanler (D)	1906	Barrytown (Dutchess Co)
Horace White[g] (R)	1908	Syracuse
George H. Cobb (R)	21 Oct 1910	Watertown
Thomas F. Conway (D)	1910	Plattsburgh
Martin H. Glynn[h] (D)	1912	Albany
Robert F. Wagner Sr[i] (D)	17 Oct 1913	New York City
Edward Schoeneck (R)	1914	Syracuse
Harry C. Walker (D)	1918	Binghamton
Jeremiah Wood (R)	1920	Lynbrook (Nassau Co)
George R. Lunn (D)	1922	Schenectady
Seymour Lowman (R)	1924	Elmira
Edwin Corning (D)	1926	Albany

LIEUTENANT GOVERNORS (continued)

Name	Elected or Succeeded to Office	Residence
Herbert H. Lehman (D)	1928	New York City
M. William Bray (D)	1932	Utica
Charles Poletti (D)	1938	New York City
Joe R. Hanley[j] (R)	3 Dec 1942	Perry (Wyoming Co)
Thomas W. Wallace (R)	1942	Schenectady
Joe R. Hanley[k] (R)	17 July 1943	Perry (Wyoming Co)
Joe R. Hanley (R)	2 Nov 1943	Perry
Frank C. Moore (R)	1950	Buffalo
Arthur H. Wicks[l] (R)	29 Sept 1953	Kingston (Ulster Co)
Walter J. Mahoney[m] (R)	6 Jan 1954	Buffalo
George B. DeLuca (D)	1954	New York City
Malcolm Wilson (R)	1958	Yonkers
Warren M. Anderson[n] (R)	18 Dec 1973	Binghamton
Mary Anne Krupsak (D)	1974	Amsterdam (Montgomery Co)
Mario M. Cuomo (D)	1978	Queens
Alfred B. DelBello (D)	1982	Lewisboro (Westchester Co)
Warren M. Anderson[o] (D)	1 Feb 1985	Binghamton
Stan Lundine (D)	1986	Jamestown (Chautauqua Co)
Betsy McCaughey Ross[p] (R)	1994	New York City
Mary O. Donohue (R)	1998	Troy (Rensselaer Co)

Source: New York Red Book.

Note: Unless otherwise noted, before 1821 lieutenant governors assumed office on 1 July of the election year. From 1821 to the present, they assume office 1 Jan of the year following election.

Abbreviations: AJ: Anti-Jacksonian; D: Democrat; DR: Democratic-Republican; F: Federalist; JD: Jacksonian Democrat; JR: Jeffersonian Republican; R: Republican; RW: Revolutionary Whig; VBR: Van Buren Republican; W: Whig.

[a]Tayler was elected president of the senate after Broome died.

[b]Elected under a special act.

[c]When Clinton died, 11 Feb 1828, Pitcher became governor; Livingston and Dayan were successively presidents of the senate.

[d]Throop succeeded Martin Van Buren as governor; Stebbins and Oliver were successively elected presidents of the senate.

[e]When Gardiner was elected judge of the Court of Appeals, Fish filled the vacancy under an act passed in Sept 1847.

[f]Hill succeeded Grover Cleveland as governor; McCarthy was elected president of the senate.

[g]White succeeded Charles Evans Hughes as governor, 6 Oct 1910; Cobb succeeded White as president of the senate.

[h]Glynn succeeded Gov William Sulzer, who was removed from office 17 Oct 1913.

[i]Wagner succeeded Glynn as lieutenant governor.

[j]Hanley succeeded Poletti, who became governor on 3 Dec 1942, when Gov Lehman resigned.

[k]Hanley succeeded Wallace, who died 17 July 1943.

[l]Wicks succeeded Moore, who resigned 29 Sept 1953.

[m]Mahoney succeeded Wicks, who resigned 19 Nov 1953.

[n]Anderson succeeded Wilson, who became governor.

[o]Anderson succeeded DelBello, who resigned 1 Feb 1985.

[p]Residence presumed to be in the metropolitan New York City area.

nor, and is automatically considered by observers to be a candidate in waiting for the governorship.

Cuomo, Mario M. *The Role of the Lieutenant Governor: A Proposal* (Albany: Office of the Lieutenant Governor, 1982)

Zimmerman, Joseph F. *Roles of the Lieutenant Governor, Attorney General, and Comptroller in New York State* (Albany: SUNY Albany, Graduate School of Public Affairs, 1984)

Gerald Benjamin

lighthouses. In the 1760s New York City merchants, distressed by shipwrecks on Sandy Hook, NJ, a spit of land stretching into the navigational channel for New York Harbor, raised money for a lighthouse through two lotteries sponsored by the New York colonial government. The Sandy Hook Lighthouse opened in 1764 and is the oldest operating lighthouse in the United States. It continued under New York State ownership until 1789, when the US Congress created the US Lighthouse Establishment to have federal jurisdiction over lighthouses. The oldest lighthouse in New York State and the first in the country to be built with money appropriated by the US government stood at Montauk Point (Suffolk Co) on Long Island. Pres George Washington proposed the lighthouse to Congress in 1792; it was built in 1796, put in service in 1797, and continues to operate. By the middle of the 19th century, concern over the effectiveness and quality of these aids to navigation led Congress to pass legislation in 1852 establishing a US Lighthouse Board (1852–1910) to manage the country's lighthouses, which included updating many of them with new Fresnel lenses and eventually with electrical lights. By 1910 Congress abolished the Lighthouse Board, creating instead the Bureau of Lighthouses, better known as the Lighthouse Service. In 1939, administration of the lighthouses was transferred to the US Coast Guard.

Of the more than 70 lighthouses built in New York State between 1796 and 1991, 46 were constructed before 1860. They represent a variety of architectural styles that depend on their locations. Originally, the light keepers were employees of the Lighthouse Establishment, with appointments requiring presidential approval and often patronage positions, but by 1896 they were civil servants. Both men and women were hired to keep the light, and many of them lived in housing adjacent to the lighthouses with their families. One of the best known was Kate Walker, who was her husband's assistant keeper at the Robbin's Reef Lighthouse in New York Harbor off Staten Island from 1883 until his death in 1886. She kept the light going while raising her two children, rowing them to Staten Island to attend school, and was finally named lighthouse keeper in 1894, serving until 1919.

With its 1,850 miles (2,977 km) of shoreline and 127 miles (204 km) of coastline, New York State had 74 lighthouses in 2002 located on New York Harbor, the Hudson River, the Atlantic Ocean, Long Island Sound, Lake Champlain, parts of the St. Lawrence Seaway, and the Great Lakes (see table page 901). Thirty-three of the lights were active as aids to navigation maintained by the US Coast Guard and were fully automated. The remaining 41 have been phased out by the Coast Guard as aids but are maintained by museums, historic and preservation societies, state parks, and as private residences. In 1987 the US Coast Guard turned over historic Montauk Point light to the Montauk Historical Society, which maintains the structure and opens it to the public. Many of those in New York State are protected by landmark status, including the still active Staten Island Lighthouse and the deactivated Barcelona Lighthouse on Lake Erie, which are National Landmarks. Others, such as the Blackwell Island Lighthouse and the New Dorp Lighthouse (Swash Channel Rear Range Lighthouse) are listed on the National Register of Historic Places. One of the most famous is the Statue of Liberty on Ellis Island, which served as a lighthouse from 1886 to 1902 and is now a National Monument. Lighthouses in private hands include the Stony Point (Henderson) and the Selkirk (Salmon River) Lighthouses, both on Lake Ontario, and the Sands Point Lighthouse on Long Island Sound, among whose various owners was William Randolph Hearst in the 1930s. The Coast Guard put the newest light in the state into service in 1991 atop the Marine and Academic Center on the campus of Kingsborough Community College on Manhattan Beach in Brooklyn. Its white light flashing every 4 seconds is a modern aid to navigation as were the early kerosene and gas lamps lit by hardy light keepers in the previous three centuries.

Montauk Lighthouse, the oldest lighthouse in New York State, built in 1792.

Crowley, Jim. *Lighthouses of New York* (Saugerties, NY: Hope Farm Press, 1999)

Francis J. Duffy

lighting. See POWER AND LIGHTING.

Lilac Festival. Annual festival in Rochester celebrating the extensive lilacs and other plantings in the city's Highland Park. Landscaped by Frederick Law Olmsted, Highland Park, on the south side of Rochester, was created in 1888, and four years later horticulturist John Dunbar planted the first 20 varieties of lilacs. By 1898 the lilacs in full bloom were sufficiently spectacular to attract a crowd of 3,000 on one Sunday. This led to the city establishing an annual Lilac Sunday. In May 1908 Lilac Sunday had an attendance of 25,000; by the 1940s attendance had risen to 100,000. In 2003 the Lilac Festival attracted over 500,000 people to the 10-day free event, which showcases over 1,200 flowering lilacs of more than 500 varieties. It is the Rochester area's largest annual festival, including multiple stages for music and a wide variety of foods and activities.

Lilac Festival, http://www.lilacfestival.com

Eric L. Kline

LILCO. See LONG ISLAND POWER AUTHORITY (LIPA).

Lily Dale. Spiritualist community. Beginning in 1844 a group of early Spiritualists congregated in Laona (Chautauqua Co), forming the First Spiritualist Community of Laona in 1855. Meetings were held at Willard Alden's farmstead on Middle Cassadaga Lake from 1873, and in 1879 the group purchased 20 acres (8 ha) of adjacent property, establishing the Cassadaga Lake Free Association. The community expanded steadily in the 1880s and 1890s, adding a hotel, school, lecture hall, library, post office, stores, and cottages. A newspaper, the *Sunflower,* appeared in 1898. The spiritualist enclave emerged as a hotbed of radical politics and was visited by suffragist Susan B. Anthony, feminist Rev Anna Howard Shaw, and opponent of religion Robert Green Ingersoll. Sir Arthur Conan Doyle, Franklin D. and Eleanor Roosevelt, and Mohandas Gandhi also visited. In 1906 the community took the name Lily Dale Assembly. The Hydesville (Wayne Co) home of sisters Kate and Margaret Fox, who as teenage mediums gave sensational impetus to the American Spiritualist movement, was acquired by and transported to Lily Dale in 1916; it burned down in 1955.

Although spiritualism as a popular phenomenon declined in the first half of the 20th century, Lily Dale survived as a pilgrimage destination for spiritualists and occult enthusiasts worldwide, and as a regional attraction for summer tourists. The Lily Dale Museum and Historical Society opened in 1986. In the early 21st century Lily Dale Assembly is both the largest and oldest continuously functioning Spiritualist community in the United States, with over 250 year-round residents, including more than a dozen professional mediums. Approximately 25,000 visitors arrive each summer to communicate with deceased friends and family members, participate in "psychic development" training, observe clairvoyance demonstrations, conduct research, and attend talks, workshops, and retreats by visiting psychics and Spiritualist leaders. The general offices of the National Spiritualist Association of Churches (1893) are located at Lily Dale.

Wicker, Christine. *Lily Dale: The True Story of the Town That Talks to the Dead* (San Francisco: Harper San Francisco, 2003)

Glenn Wright

Lima [LYE-MA]. Town (pop 4,541) and village (pop 2,459) in NE Livingston Co. Settled in 1788, the town was formed in 1796 as Charleston and in 1808 changed its name to Lima. The village was incorporated in 1867. Genesee Wesleyan Seminary (1832–1941) was an early coeducational school; among its graduates were Belva Ann Lockwood (1830–1917), first woman to run for president, and Sen Kenneth B. Keating (1900–1975). It shared its campus with Genesee College (1850–72). The seminary campus was later used for Genesee Junior College (1947–51) and, since 1951, by the pentecostal Elim Bible Institute (1924). Porcelain insulators were manufactured from 1904 to ?1986. Lima is home to Lakeland Concrete Products (concrete forms) and Shawndra Products (industrial filters) but remains primarily agricultural. The muckland at South Lima has been used since the 1870s to grow potatoes, onions, celery, cabbage, and lettuce. Much of the Village of Lima is a National Historic District.

Joyce Rapp

lime-burning industry. Limestone was quarried in New York State since the earliest European settlement. While much of it was unsuitable for building purposes, it could be calcined, or burned without fusing, to produce quicklime. When treated with water, quicklime forms calcium hydroxide, or hydrated lime. In a number of locations, mostly in Central New York, lime was mined from marl beds associated with wetlands. Burned or hydrated lime was used in tanning, bleaching, and the manufacture of paper, whitewash, paint, glass, and beet sugar. Lime has long been used as a fertilizer and since the early 19th century in the manufacture of cement and concrete. Until the mid–19th century lime was burned in stone- or brick-lined kilns surrounded by earth. The most famous description of such a kiln in use is found in Nathaniel Hawthorne's story "Ethan Brand" (1850). Later lime kilns were freestanding stone structures, superficially resembling iron furnaces of the same era. Even larger brick, stone, and masonry kilns were in use well into the 20th century. A few major lime-burning operations are noteworthy. In Glens Falls (Warren Co) a series of kilns, which later became a large consolidated operation, dates from 1824. Near Middle Falls (Washington Co) large lime kilns from the mid–19th century remain standing. A great deal of limestone was quarried and burned in Onondaga Co, where it was used in the manufacture of soda ash by Solvay Process Co. One set of kilns stood at Chazy (Clinton Co) into the 1980s (having ceased operation in the 1930s). Remains of a few of the larger kilns and scattered hillside kilns can still be found across the state. Lime continues to be manufactured by a modern burning process in a few places in Central and Western New York, including Medina, Lockport, Munnsville, Holley, Albion, and Sodus.

Ries, Heinrich. *Lime and Cement Industries of New York.* Bulletin of the New York State Museum, vol 8, no. 44 (Albany: Univ of the State of New York, 1901)
Rolando, Victor. *200 Years of Soot and Sweat: The History and Archaeology of Vermont's Iron, Charcoal, and Lime Industries* (Manchester, Vt: Vermont Archaeological Society, 1992)

Warren F. Broderick

Limestone. Village (pop 411) in Carrollton (Cattaraugus Co). Mills built in 1828 gave the name Tunungwant Mills to the first post office in 1838, which was renamed Carrollton in 1848 and Limestone in 1850 for the appearance of disintegrating bones found nearby in ancient mounds. A huge tannery (1858) and the Bradford Branch of the Erie Railroad (1866) contributed to growth, but oil interests were the greatest stimulant. Limestone was platted in 1876 and incorporated in 1877, at which time its population was about 1,200, its numbers greatly boosted by an oil boom in the late 1870s. Adjacent to Allegany

LIGHTHOUSES OF NEW YORK STATE

Name	Station Established	Body of Water	Town (County)
Atlantic Region			
Blackwell Island[a]	1872	East River	Roosevelt Island (New York)
Cedar Island[a]	1839	Long Island Sound	East Hampton (Suffolk)
Cold Spring Harbor[a]	1890	Long Island Sound	Huntington (Suffolk)
Coney Island (Nortons Point)	1890	Lower New York Bay	Brooklyn (Kings)
Eatons Neck	1799	Long Island Sound	Huntington (Suffolk)
Execution Rock	1850	Long Island Sound	New Rochelle (Westchester)
Fire Island	1827	Atlantic Ocean	Islip (Suffolk)
Fort Wadsworth[a]	1903	Upper New York Bay	Staten Island (Richmond)
Great Beds	1880	Lower New York Bay	Staten Island (Richmond)
Horton Point	1857	Long Island Sound	Southold (Suffolk)
Huntington Harbor (Lloyd Harbor)	1857	Long Island Sound	Huntington (Suffolk)
Kingsborough Community College	1991	Lower New York Bay	Brooklyn (Kings)
Latimer Reef	1804	Long Island Sound	Southold (Suffolk)
Little Gull Island	1806	Long Island Sound	Southold (Suffolk)
Long Beach Bar (Bug Light)[b]	1990	Long Island Sound	Southold (Suffolk)
Montauk Point	1796	Atlantic Ocean	East Hampton (Suffolk)
New Dorp (Swash Channel Rear Range)[a]	1856	Lower New York Bay	Staten Island (Richmond)
North Brother Island[a]	1869	East River	Bronx (Bronx)
North Dumpling	1849	Long Island Sound	Southold (Suffolk)
Old Field Point	1823	Long Island Sound	Brookhaven (Suffolk)
Old Orchard Shoal	1893	Lower New York Bay	Staten Island (Richmond)
Orient Point	1899	Long Island Sound	Southold (Suffolk)
Plum Island (Plum Gut)[a]	1827	Long Island Sound	Southold (Suffolk)
Prince's Bay[a]	1828	Lower New York Bay	Staten Island (Richmond)
Race Rock	1879	Long Island Sound	Southold (Suffolk)
Robbin's Reef (Kate's Light)	1839	Upper New York Bay	Staten Island (Richmond)
Romer Shoal	1898	Lower New York Bay	Staten Island (Richmond)
Sands Point[a]	1809	Long Island Sound	North Hempstead (Nassau)
Staten Island (Rear Range)	1909	Lower New York Bay	Staten Island (Richmond)
Statue of Liberty[a]	1886	Upper New York Bay	Liberty Island (New York)
Stepping Stones	1877	Long Island Sound	North Hempstead (Nassau)
Throgs Neck	1827	Long Island Sound	Bronx (Bronx)
West Bank (Front Range)	1901	Lower New York Bay	Staten Island (Richmond)
Great Lakes Region			
Barcelona (Portland Harbor)[a]	1829	Lake Erie	Westfield (Chautauqua)
Braddock Point	1896	Lake Ontario	Parma (Monroe)
Buffalo Breakwater	1872	Lake Erie	Buffalo (Erie)
Buffalo Main	1818	Buffalo River	Buffalo (Erie)
Buffalo Harbor South Entrance (Bottle Light)[a]	1903	Lake Erie	Buffalo (Erie)
Cape Vincent Breakwater[a]	1900	St. Lawrence River	Cape Vincent (Jefferson)
Charlotte-Genesee (Port of Genesee)[a]	1822	Lake Ontario	Rochester (Monroe)

continued on page 902

State Park, Limestone benefits from outdoor recreational opportunities. Casey's Limestone Hotel (1864–65) is a landmark and was long a center of community life.

Bruce D. Fredrickson and Madelynn P. Fredrickson

limestone quarrying. Nonfuel mineral production industry. Although substantial limestone formations were discovered near Chittenango (Madison Co) in 1818, quarries did not proliferate in the state until after 1880, facilitated by the invention of steam drills and channel technology and by a rising demand for road-building material. By 1900, 190 quarries were clustered in four regions within the state: Jefferson and St. Lawrence Cos, a corridor from Buffalo to Albany, a corridor from Albany to Ellenville (Ulster Co), and the lower Hudson Valley. Throughout the 20th century, Erie, Genesee, Onondaga, Dutchess, and Ulster Cos delivered the highest volumes of crushed and block limestone, and the industry remained in volume and value the state's top nonfuel mineral producer. In the 1990s limestone production declined, reflecting decreased construction demand associated with a weak economy. By 2001 limestone was processed only as crushed stone used for construction and road building. In that year 33,069,400 tons (30 million MT) of limestone and limestone-dolomite were produced by 63 quarries, at a value of $168 million. In 2002 the largest producer was London-based Hanson PLC, with five quarries and five processing plants in New York State; an estimated 5,000 workers were still employed across the industry.

Tepordei, Valentin, and Susan M. Copland. "Stone, Crushed." In *Metals and Minerals*, vol 1 of *Minerals Yearbook* (Washington, DC: US Department of the Interior, US Geological Survey, 2001)

Karen Nichols

limners. Artists and painting style. The term limner defines a group of colonial artists who specialized in portraits. Often referred to as the first American art school, limner paintings have a simple style featuring flat, two-dimensional fig-

Abraham Wendell, by John Heaten, *ca* 1737. Wendell was an Albany miller.

LIGHTHOUSES OF NEW YORK STATE (continued)

Name	Station Established	Body of Water	Town (County)
Crossover Island[a]	1848	St. Lawrence River	Hammond (St. Lawrence)
Dunkirk (Point Gratiot)	1826	Lake Erie	Dunkirk (Chautauqua)
East Charity Shoals	1877	Lake Ontario	Brownville (Jefferson)
Fort Niagara[a]	1872	Lake Ontario	Porter (Niagara)
Galloo Island[a]	1820	Lake Ontario	Hounsfield (Jefferson)
Grand Island (Old Front Range)[a]	1917	Niagara River	Grand Island (Erie)
Horse Island (Sacketts Harbor)[a]	1831	Lake Ontario	Hounsfield (Jefferson)
Horseshoe Reef[a]	1856	Niagara River	Buffalo (Erie)
Ogdensburg Harbor[a]	1834	St. Lawrence River	Ogdensburg (St. Lawrence)
Oswego Harbor West Pierhead	1822	Lake Ontario	Oswego (Oswego)
Rochester Harbor	1822	Lake Ontario	Rochester (Monroe)
Rock Island[a]	1848	St. Lawrence River	Orleans (Jefferson)
Selkirk (Salmon River)	1838	Lake Ontario	Richland (Oswego)
Sodus Outer	1871	Lake Ontario	Sodus (Wayne)
Sodus Point[a]	1825	Lake Ontario	Sodus (Wayne)
South Buffalo North Side[a]	1903	Lake Erie	Buffalo (Erie)
Stony Point (Henderson)[a]	1830	Lake Ontario	Henderson (Jefferson)
Sunken Rock	1847	St. Lawrence River	Alexandria (Jefferson)
Thirty Mile Point	1875	Lake Ontario	Somerset (Niagara)
Three Sisters Island[a]	1870	St. Lawrence River	Hammond (St. Lawrence)
Tibbetts Point	1827	St. Lawrence River	Cape Vincent (Jefferson)
Hudson/Champlain Region			
Barbers Point[a]	1873	Lake Champlain	Westport (Essex)
Bluff Point (Valcour Island)[a]	1874	Lake Champlain	Plattsburgh (Clinton)
Crown Point[a]	1858	Lake Champlain	Crown Point (Essex)
Cumberland Head	1838	Lake Champlain	Plattsburgh (Clinton)
Esopus Meadows (Middle Hudson River)	1839	Hudson River	Esopus (Ulster)
Hudson-Athens (Hudson City)	1874	Hudson River	Hudson (Columbia)
Jeffrey's Hook (Little Red Lighthouse)	1889	Hudson River	Manhattan (New York)
Point Aux Roches[a]	1858	Lake Champlain	Beekmantown (Clinton)
Rondout Creek (Kingston)	1838	Hudson River	Kingston (Ulster)
Saugerties	1836	Hudson River	Saugerties (Ulster)
Split Rock Point	1838	Lake Champlain	Essex (Essex)
Stony Point	1826	Hudson River	Stony Point (Rockland)
Tarrytown (Kingsland Point)[a]	1883	Hudson River	Mount Pleasant (Westchester)

Source: National Park Service, Inventory of Historic Light Stations, New York Lighthouses, http://www.cr.nps.gov/maritime/light/ny.htm.

[a]Inactive as of 2003.

[b]An earlier lighthouse was operational at this site from 1871 into the 1940s; that building burned down in 1963.

Compiled by Francis J. Duffy

ures and stylized backgrounds. Broad expanses of color and unique perspective gave these portraits a folk-art appeal. Between 1695 and 1750 limners from the Hudson River valley and from New Jersey's Raritan Valley painted portraits and scriptural themes. Limners were self-taught and based their technique on English portrait mezzotints and woodcut illustrations from Dutch bibles. Most limners worked in New York City or Albany, but many traveled to rural outposts searching for patrons.

New York City's best-known limners were the Duyckincks. Gerrit Duyckinck (1660–?1712) was a limner-glazier in New York City. He painted mostly city residents, and 10 portraits are attributed to him including a self-portrait. Evert Duyckinck III (?1677–1727), Gerrit's nephew, painted at least 20 portraits of New York City and Albany residents, including members of the Beekman family. Gerardus Duyckinck (1695–1746), Gerrit's son, formerly identified as the DePeyster limner, taught drawing and sold looking glasses and art supplies near Old Market Slip in New York City. He painted nearly 50 known subjects including Hudson Valley merchants, clergymen, and politicians, such as New York City mayor Abraham DePeyster (*ca* 1730). Besides the Duyckincks, Scotsman John Watson (1685–1768) worked in New York City and is credited with 20 portraits. He settled in Perth Amboy, NJ, in 1714 and worked in the Raritan Valley. He painted New York City and Albany residents and members of the Van Rensselaer family, including a 1735 portrait of Maria van Cortlandt van Rensselaer (1680–*ca* 1750).

The upper Hudson Valley limners included Nehemiah Partridge (1683–?1737), Pieter Vanderlyn (1687–1778), and John Heaten (?1698–?1758). Partridge was formerly identified as the *Aetatis Suae* limner since he inscribed the Latin phrase on his paintings. He was from New Hampshire and by 1717 moved to New York City. From 1718 to 1725 he painted in Albany, New England, and Virginia. More than 60 portraits have been attributed to Partridge, including one of Ariantje Coeymans (?1717–23) in Albany Co, the first life-size portrait of a woman in the colonies. Peter Vanderlyn settled in Albany in 1726 and painted Gansevoort family portraits before moving to Poughkeepsie in the late 1730s. Many of the 25 portraits assigned to Vanderlyn were of people from the Mohawk and mid-Hudson Valleys. He worked in Kinderhook (Columbia Co), Kingston (Ulster Co), and Hurley (Ulster Co). John Heaten, a native of England, lived in Albany during the 1730s and was formerly identified as the Wendell limner. Heaten's 20 known subjects, painted between 1730 and 1745, include the Van Bergen family and the Van Bergen overmantel (?1733), a farm scene in Catskill (Greene Co). Trained European artists settled the colonies in the 1760s and replaced limners, who were considered amateurs.

Belknap, Waldron Phoenix, Jr. *American Colonial Painting: Materials for a History* (Cambridge, Mass: The Belknap Press of Harvard Univ Press, 1959)

Black, Mary C. "Early Colonial Painting of the New York Province." In *Remembrance of Patria: Dutch Arts and Culture in Colonial America,* ed. Roderic H. Blackburn and Ruth Piwonka (Albany: Albany Institute of History & Art, 1988)

Mary Alice Mackay

Lincklaen [LINK-LA-EN]. Town (pop 416) in NW Chenango Co. Settled in 1796, Lincklaen was formed in 1823 from German. Historically a dairying town, its marginal lands were acquired by the state in the 1930s to form Lincklaen State Forest. From 1967 to 1974 Solvent Savers, a chemical waste recovery facility, operated in the town, creating a toxic waste problem still present in the early 21st century. In 2003 Lincklaen had four large dairy farms as well as field corn and alfalfa; many residents commuted to Cortland and Syracuse.

Lincoln. Town (pop 1,818) in NE Madison Co. Conrad Klock and a group of Palatine Germans from the Mohawk Valley settled at Clockville in 1792. Lenox Iron Works (1815–47) was a manufacturer of stoves and plows. Other 19th-century products of the town were scythes, hay forks and rakes, and wool cloth. Lincoln was formed from Lenox in 1896. The last hop yard and kiln in the county, at the Durwood Eisaman farm, ceased operations in 1952.

William F. Helmer

Lincoln Center for the Performing Arts. Performing arts center. Located on Manhattan's West Side and bordered by 62d and 66th Sts, and Columbus and Amsterdam Aves, it covers 15.5 acres (6.3 ha) and includes seven buildings, one park, and three plazas. Lincoln Center was conceived in the mid-1950s by Charles Spofford (1902–91), a Metropolitan Opera and Juilliard School of Music board member, as a response to the perceived overcrowded and outmoded facilities of New York City's major arts organizations, including the Metropolitan Opera, New York Philharmonic, and Juilliard School. It was largely funded with private money, particularly from John D. Rockefeller III (1906–78). Robert Moses, the head of the Mayor's Committee on Slum Clearance, used his authority to clear the necessary land, which resulted in the eviction of substantial numbers of moderate- to low-income families and businesses from the former Lincoln Square neighborhood.

Six well-known architects were chosen, each to design a building that the Lincoln Center fund-raisers would pay for outright rather than burden the member arts constituents with a mortgage. The architects were Wallace K. Harrison (Metropolitan Opera), Eero Saarinen (Vivian Beaumont Theater), Philip Johnson (New York State Theater), Gordon Bunshaft (Library of the Performing Arts), Max Abramovitz (New York Philharmonic), and Pietro Belluschi (Juilliard). The buildings all were to share a common exterior material, travertine marble from Italy. Construction began in 1959, and Philharmonic Hall (renamed Avery Fisher Hall in 1973) was the first completed (September 1963), followed by the New York State Theater, home of the New York City Ballet (1964) and New York City Opera (1966); the Library and Museum of the Performing Arts (1965) (later renamed the New York Public Library of the Performing Arts); the Metropolitan Opera House, which opened 16 Sept 1966; and the Lincoln Center Theater (home of the Vivian Beaumont and Mitzi E. Newhouse Theaters). In 1969 the Juilliard School, including Alice Tully Hall, was completed, and the Film Society of Lincoln Center and the Chamber Music Society of Lincoln Center were formed. In 1987 the New York City Ballet and the School of American Ballet joined Lincoln Center, and in 1991 the Samuel B. and David Rose Building was completed, containing offices, rehearsal rooms, and dormitories for the School of American Ballet and the Juilliard School. Jazz at Lincoln Center was added in 1996, with a new 100,000 ft^2 (9,300 m^2) facility scheduled to open at Columbus Circle in 2004. A nonprofit corporation manages the center's buildings and administers the Lincoln Center Institute for the Arts in Education, which sends performers to public schools. Regular features include the PBS *Live from Lincoln Center* series and the summer Lincoln Center Festival. In 1991–92 the constituent members of Lincoln Center collaborated in programming all the works of Mozart in more than 500 concerts. In the season ending in 2000, Lincoln Center had 4.7 million visitors. It has fulfilled its founders' visions of revitalizing the Upper West Side of Manhattan and of providing a model for performing arts centers worldwide.

Stern, Robert A. M., Thomas Mellins, and David Fishman. *New York 1960: Architecture and Urbanism between the Second World War and the Bicentennial* (New York: Monacelli Press, 1995)

Young, Edgar B. *Lincoln Center: The Building of an Institution* (New York: New York Univ Press, 1980)

Andrea Olmstead

Lincoln Tunnel. Perhaps the busiest underwater vehicular tunnel in the world, its three two-lane tubes connect Midtown Manhattan to Weehawken, NJ. The tubes under the Hudson River are each about 8,000 feet (2,440 m) long, with roadways 21.5 feet (6.55 m) wide. Built by the Port of New York Authority (now Port Authority of New York and New Jersey), the first tube opened in 1937, the second in 1945, and the third in 1957. Direct ramps lead from the New York City end of the tunnel to Manhattan's Port Authority Bus Terminal. Both ramps and bus terminal—one of the world's largest—were completed in 1950. By 1970 a 2.5 mi (4.02 km) contra-flow expressway bus lane provided quick access to the New Jersey entrance. An extensive system of approaches facilitated optimum use of the tubes. Since 1957 an intelligent transportation system (ITS) featuring variable message signs, traffic signals, and television cameras has managed these approaches. Since 1970 tolls have been collected from eastbound traffic only, as part of the Hudson River/Staten Island one-way tolls system that later incorporated an electronic (E-Z Pass) system. For the year 2001 almost 42 million vehicles passed through the tunnel.

Leon Goodman

Lindenhurst {Lindenhurst, village (pop 27,819) in Babylon, Suffolk Co; North Lindenhurst, locality (pop 11,767) in Babylon}. Located on the South Side Rail Road (1867), Lindenhurst began as Breslau, a planned community for German immigrants, and in 1870 it acquired a post office. About 1872 a factory building was erected to attract industry, initially producing papier-mâché and, later, buttons; another produced dress trimmings. The post office was renamed Lindenhurst in 1891. Factories in the late 19th and early 20th centuries produced safety pins, artificial flowers, Swiss embroidery, and cigars. Until World War I, the German holiday Pfingst Sunday *(Whitsunday)* was observed. When incorporated as a village in 1923, Lindenhurst had 2,775 residents. In the mid-1920s large developments were platted, and in the scrub oak north of the village, a development was begun in 1925 based on a rumor that the Long Island Rail Road would move its repair shops to the area; when the rumor proved false, half-finished homes were abandoned for more than a decade. The village's 1940 population of 4,756 increased to 20,905 in 1960, and similar growth occurred in North Lindenhurst. In the early 21st century Lindenhurst is both residential and industrial, producing electrical goods, aircraft parts, and metal products, among others. In North Lindenhurst, Zahn's Airport (1945) became an industrial park in 1980.

Evelyn Ellis

Lindenthal, Gustav (*b* Brünn [now Brno, Czech Republic], 21 May 1850; *d* Metuchen, NJ, 31 July 1935). Civil engineer and bridge builder. Lindenthal trained as a mason and carpenter during his youth but left Brünn at age 20 to pursue engineering. In 1874 he moved to the United States, where formal training was not needed to work in the field. His successful work in Pennsylvania led to his appointment as commissioner of bridges for New York City in 1902. Lindenthal pursued an ambitious plan to build a bridge over the Hudson River that would allow direct entry to Manhattan from New Jersey but lost his politically appointed position after the 1903 elections, and the project failed to materialize. Instead he designed several other bridges in the New York City area, including the Blackwell's Island Bridge (now the Queensboro Bridge) spanning the East River (1909). The following year he pursued the daunting task of linking the Bronx and Queens over the dangerous Hell Gate channel, providing Manhattan with direct rail service to New England. Completed in 1917, the Hell Gate Bridge is considered Lindenthal's crowning achievement. His dream of building a bridge across the Hudson River never died, however, and he developed proposals until one of his former apprentices, Othmar H. Ammann, built the George Washington Bridge (1931).

Petroski, Henry. *Engineers of Dreams: Great Bridge Builders and the Spanning of America* (New York: Knopf, 1995)

Frank E. Griggs Jr

Lindley. Town (pop 1,913) in SE Steuben Co. Col Eleazer Lindsley purchased the land that was to become Lindley in 1789 and, the following year, brought a colony of 40 people from Morristown, NJ, to settle it. The town was formed in 1837 from Erwin. In 1839 the Corning and Blossburg Railroad was completed across town, carrying coal and lumber from Pennsylvania to the state's canal system at Corning. Lumbering was the chief economic activity until its decline in the 1870s, when it was replaced by tanning, which lasted until *ca* 1900. Farming was also central to the town, especially tobacco after the 1850s. Dairying succeeded it and remained important in 2003. Residents not involved in farming are employed in Corning and Painted Post.

Thomas Dimitroff

Lindsay, John (Vliet) (*b* New York City, 24 Nov 1921; *d* Hilton Head, SC, 19 Dec 2000). Congressman and mayor. Raised in Manhattan, John Lindsay graduated from Yale University, served in the navy during World War II, and received a law degree from Yale in 1948. In 1955 he became executive assistant to US Attorney General

Herbert Brownell, serving as the Justice Department's liaison to Congress and the White House. Three years later Lindsay won election to Congress from Manhattan's affluent East Side on the Republican ticket. Reelected three times, he compiled a liberal voting record, often supporting legislation of Democratic presidents. Even as a junior congressman, his reputation as a party maverick and his personal appeal attracted national attention. In 1965, running on the Republican and Liberal lines, Lindsay won election as the mayor of New York City. He faced a challenging first term marked by municipal union strikes amid a city brimming with social unrest. Defeated in the Republican primary, Lindsay won reelection on the Liberal Party line in 1969. In his second term, Lindsay oversaw an expansion of social services that forced the city to impose new taxes and increase borrowing.

In 1971 he became a Democrat, citing the Republicans' abandonment of progressive causes and its continuation of the Vietnam War, and launched an abortive run for his new party's 1972 presidential nomination. Rejecting a run for a third term as mayor, Lindsay in 1974 returned to the practice of law. He made an unsuccessful bid for the Democratic nomination to the US Senate in 1980 and then chaired the Lincoln Center Theater in New York City from 1984 to 1991. In 1995 Lindsay's failing health and mounting medical bills led Mayor Rudolph Giuliani and City Council Speaker Peter Vallone to appoint him city commissioner for the United Nations, which provided him with health insurance and a city pension.

Cannato, Vincent. *The Ungovernable City: John Lindsay and His Struggle to Save New York* (New York: Basic Books, 2001)

Lindsay, John V. *Journey into Politics: Some Informal Observations* (New York: Dodd, Mead, 1967)

Timothy Sullivan

Link, Edwin (Albert) (*b* Huntington, Ind, 26 July 1904; *d* Binghamton, 7 Sept 1981). Inventor. Link had a peripatetic childhood, living and attending public schools in Indiana, Illinois, California, Pennsylvania, West Virginia, and New York. In 1922, while living in Binghamton, he dropped out of high school and went to work for Western Electric and then for his father's music company, where he became skilled in organ building and repair. After learning to fly in 1927, Link began work on a mechanical device with a fuselage and controls that simulated flying and could be used to teach rudimentary piloting skills. Two years later he filed a patent application for his Pilot-Maker and formed the Link Aeronautical Corp in Binghamton to market the invention. The Link Trainer, which had been modified to teach instrument flying, secured its first major customer in 1934: the US Army Air Corps. Sales to Japan, the Soviet Union, and other countries soon followed.

The Link Trainer, popularly known as the Blue Box, came into widespread use during World War II. With factories in Binghamton and Gananoque, Ont, Link employed some 1,500 people and manufactured 80 trainers a week during peak wartime production, when more than 500,000 pilots used some 10,000 ANT-18 trainers. After the war the Link company developed more sophisticated electronic training devices, later called simulators, for advanced jet aircraft. In 1953, Link gave up active management of his aeronautics enterprises and turned to underwater archaeological work. To facilitate this work, he developed several innovative devices, including a submersible decompression chamber and a deep-diving submersible. Although his contributions to the exploration of the sea brought him well-deserved recognition, Link's name continues to be associated with his pilot training device, designated a Historical Mechanical Engineering Landmark by the American Society of Mechanical Engineers in June 2000.

Kelly, Lloyd L., and Robert B. Parke. *The Pilot Maker* (New York: Grosset & Dunlap, 1970)

William M. Leary

Linowitz, Sol M(yron) (*b* Trenton, NJ, 7 Dec 1913). Businessman, diplomat, and attorney. Linowitz graduated from Hamilton College in 1935 and Cornell Law School in 1938. He was a practicing attorney in Rochester from 1938 to 1942. During World War II Linowitz held legal positions in Washington, DC, with the Office of Price Administration and the US Navy, then returned to Rochester in 1946 to resume his law practice. Several years later he joined the Haloid Co and soon became vice president in charge of the patent and licensing division, where he played a vital role in protecting Haloid's xerography patents from numerous challenges. As chairman of the executive committee, general counsel, and, from 1960 to 1966, chairman of the board at Haloid's successor, Xerox Corp, Linowitz was a key figure in the company's overseas expansion and helped make public service an important element of its corporate culture. With David Rockefeller, he formed the International Executive Service Corps in 1964 to promote modern market economies in developing countries. In 1966 he began a diplomatic career, serving for three years in a dual appointment as ambassador to the Organization of American States and US representative on the Inter-American Committee of the Alliance for Progress. Linowitz was heavily involved in negotiating the Panama Canal Treaties in 1977–78 and facilitated Middle East peace talks from 1979 to 1981. He received the Presidential Medal of Freedom in 1998 and was the honorary chairman of the board at the Academy for Educational Development in 2003.

Linowitz, Sol M. *The Making of a Public Man: A Memoir* (Boston: Little, Brown, 1985)

Martin Stahl

Lisbon. Town (pop 4,047) in NW St. Lawrence Co. Fort Levi, site of the last large battle of the French and Indian War, was located on Chimney Island on the town's northern border. An Oswegatchie Indian village was located on Indian Point in Lisbon's northwest corner from after the Revolution until *ca* 1806, when they resettled at Akwesasne (St. Regis Indian Reservation). Settled by Whites largely from Washington Co in 1799, the town was formed in 1801. The Northern Railroad (later Rutland Railroad) initiated service in 1850. The town's population in 1855 included 1,045 Irish-born residents, 30% of the total. Extensive areas were flooded as a result of St. Lawrence Seaway construction (1959), and the New York Power Authority has since retained ownership of a strip of shoreline. The town remains agricultural and has large areas of wetland. It is the site of the undeveloped Galop Island State Park. Lisbon Town Hall (1889), with an elaborate Stick-style auditorium/gymnasium, is listed on the National Register. Lisbon's population increased by 25% between 1960 and 2000 as the City of Ogdensburg extended its suburbs and as seasonal homes along the St. Lawrence were converted to year-round use.

Richard E. Mooers

Lisle [LIE-UL]. Town (pop 2,707) and village (pop 302) in NW Broome Co. Settled around 1792, the town was formed in 1801 from Union. Lumber, leather, and potash were produced by early industries. A distillery and factories producing scales, combs, hats, and wagons were among later enterprises. The Union Free Library (1814–39) was the first in the county and was supported by taxes. A railroad came through in 1854, and a village around the depot was incorporated in 1867. A rifle factory operated in Lisle in the decades after the Civil War. Dairy farming is now the dominant use of land.

Charles J. Browne

Litchfield. Town (pop 1,453) in SW Herkimer Co. Settled around 1786 by New Englanders, the town was formed from German Flatts in 1796. Early industries were Litchfield Furnace (*ca* 1816), maker of hollowware, and a tannery at Cedarville (1824); lime was processed at North Litchfield. Eliphalet Remington, the founder of Remington Arms, made his first gun barrel at a forge in the Ilion Gorge in 1816. Columbia Spring was a minor resort with a hotel in the mid– to late 19th century. In the early 21st century, the predominant land use is agriculture.

Susan R. Perkins

literacy. Ability to read, write, and speak a language, and to compute and solve problems at levels of proficiency necessary to function in society. New York State provides English literacy instruction in reading, writing, math, communication, problem solving, and language skills. Literacy education in New York State originally focused primarily on new voters. An amendment to the state constitution in 1921 required that all newly registered voters after 1 Jan 1922 "be able, except for physical disability, to read and write English." A 1923 law required new voters to provide proof of literacy subject to review by election inspectors. Conclusive proof was a literacy certificate issued by the Board of Regents; 28,402 such certificates were issued in 1923. The literacy requirement for voting was suspended in 1965 after the federal government passed the Voting Rights Act and was terminated 10 years later.

In 1928–29 the Bureau of Adult Education was established within the State Education Department and became responsible for literacy education. With this change, the focus of literacy instruction moved from immigration and voting requirements to the broader goal of providing evening classes to the general adult population. Vocational subjects, such as home-

High school boys reading on the subway, *ca* 1920.

making and industrial and commercial courses, were added as part of the literacy program.

In 1966 the bureau was renamed the Office of General and Continuing Education. That same year Title III of the federal Elementary and Secondary Education Act Amendments provided the first major federal legislation funding adult education. It established a state-administered program focused on enabling adults to acquire the basic education skills necessary for literate functioning within the family, community, and workplace. Federal funding expanded services and provided administrative funds to the State Education Department. Statistics indicate that the number of adults served grew from 78,195 in 1984 to 191,349 in 1993. As of 2000 programs were offered by public schools, libraries, colleges, community-based organizations, correctional facilities, and proprietary schools. Union and workplace facilities and public television provide other venues for literacy instruction. Programs in family literacy are designed to provide integrated literacy activities between children and parents, training for parents as the primary teachers for their children, parent literacy training leading to economic self-sufficiency, and age-appropriate education to prepare children for success in school. The state also receives federal funding for literacy programs through the Workforce Investment Act (1998) and Even Start legislation. The New York State legislature provides approximately $100 million each year to support and upgrade services and curriculum to meet education standards.

Brustein, Michael, and Marty Mahler. *The Administrator's Guide to the Adult Education and Family Literacy Act of 1998* (Washington, DC: National Adult Education Professional Development Consortium, 1998)

Barbara Shay

literature, beyond New York City. In the colonial period most of the province's literature was produced in New York City. During and after the Revolutionary War, this began to change. As European Americans headed north and west, newspapers, a good gauge of the spread of printing, began to appear outside of New York City. The *Albany Gazette* was published as early as 1771. Often containing fiction, verse, and sermons, newspapers appearing over the next few decades included the *Whitestone Gazette* (1793), published in the Utica area, and the *Otsego Herald* (1795) in Cooperstown (Otsego Co). In 1804 the *Ontario Repository* started in Canandaigua (Ontario Co), followed by the *Buffalo Gazette* (1811). By 1816, when the *Rochester Gazette* first appeared, newspapers, as well as books and other kinds of publications, were being produced across the state.

Antebellum Literature

New York State's frontier was the initial theme of upstate literature. It was the first American frontier to receive extended literary treatment and profoundly shaped the genre's development. Eleven years of farming in Orange Co inspired a utopian view of the American spirit in French immigrant J. Hector St. John de Crèvecoeur's (1735–1813) influential collection of essays, *Letters from an American Farmer* (1782). Washington Irving's stories, especially "Rip Van Winkle" and "The Legend of Sleepy Hollow" (from *The Sketch-Book*) 1819–20, helped popularize the Catskill and lower Hudson regions, and perpetuate comic stereotypes of the Dutch, which were central to Irving's satirical *A History of New York* (1809). In *From the Beginning of the World to the End of the Dutch Dynasty,* Diedrich Knickerbocker (1809) helped form popular notions of the Catskill's mystique.

Irving's close friend James Kirke Paulding (1778–1860) collaborated with him on works, including *History of New York* (1809). Paulding set *The Dutchman's Fireside* (1831) in the pre-Revolutionary mid–Hudson Valley. His *Old Continental* (1846) portrays the war itself in rural New York. Another Irving friend, Joseph Rodman Drake (1795–1820) wrote the romantic poem "The Culprit Fey" (1819) in the *Croaker Papers.* Set in the lower Hudson Valley near West Point (Orange Co), it tells of a fairy in love with a mortal. *Our Travels* is an account of the author's flight from the 1822 New York City yellow fever epidemic, which describes in detail a trip by boat and stagecoach across the state to Niagara and back. James Fenimore Cooper (1789–1851) was the greatest exponent of New York State's frontier theme. Thinly disguising Cooper's father as the fictional Judge Marmaduke Temple, *The Pioneers* (1823) depicts the settlement of Otsego Co. Other Leatherstocking Tales include *The Last of the Mohicans* (1826) and *The Deerslayer* (1841). The canny backwoodsmen and -women, the loyal Indian, and the fearsome savage who populate these stories of the settlement of colonial New York became popular American images.

When the opening of New York's frontier dispossessed the Iroquois and other Indian nations, American Indians became an important theme in upstate literature. In the posthumously published *The History of Maria Kittle* (1790–91), Ann Eliza Bleecker (1752–83), one of America's first female authors, tells of an Indian attack and a woman's captivity near present-day Melrose (Rensselaer Co). James E. Seaver's *Narrative of the Life of Mrs. Mary Jemison* (1824) published in Canandaigua (Ontario Co), relates Mary Jemison's capture and life with the Seneca, one of the most enduring of the captivity narratives. One of the earliest Indian authors in the state was David Cusick, a Tuscarora who published *Sketches of Ancient History of the Six Nations* (1828). Amid the proliferation of Indian tales and stories drawing on New York State Indians in the first half of the 19th century, Rochester lawyer Lewis Henry Morgan's classic *The League of the Ho-dé-no-sau-nee, or Iroquois* (1851), brought a new anthropological sophistication to the interest in the state's first inhabitants.

The 19th-century outpouring of revivalism and religious heterodoxy in Central New York left its mark on literature. In *Lectures on Revivals of Religion* (1835), the preacher Charles Grandison Finney reflects upon his upstate experiences. John Humphrey Noyes, founder of the Oneida Community, reviews the history of 19th-century utopias in *History of American Socialisms* (1870). His son, Pierrepont Burt Noyes, and granddaughter, Constance Noyes Robertson, a well-known popular novelist, also wrote memoirs and histories of the Oneida Community. In 1830 E. B. Grandin of Palmyra (Wayne Co) published the first edition of the *Book of Mormon,* which Joseph Smith Jr translated from the "reformed Egyptian."

Religious ferment was a powerful force in generating themes of abolitionism and African American freedom in upstate literature. In 1845 Frederick Douglass published his autobiography and in 1848 moved to Rochester, where he produced a more comprehensive version, *My Bondage and Freedom* (1855). In *Twelve Years a Slave* (1858) Solomon Northup, a free Black born in Minerva (Essex Co), told of his kidnapping and sale to slaveholders in Louisiana and of his eventual return to New York State. Harriet Ann Jacobs (?1813–97) worked in an abolitionist reading room above the office of Frederick Douglass's newspaper, the *North Star,* to publish a memoir of her early life, *Incidents in the Life of*

Washington Irving and His Literary Friends, by Christian Schussle, 1863.

a Slave Girl (1861), which began as a series of anonymous letters to the *New York Times.* Sojourner Truth's narrative of her life in slavery in Ulster Co first appeared in 1850.

Popular literature by women proliferated in the first half of the 19th century. Frances Miriam Berry Whitcher's (?1811–52) sketches and poems appeared in *Godey's Lady's Book,* and her stories satirizing the people of Whitesboro (Oneida Co) were published posthumously as *The Widow Bedott Papers* (1855) and as a play. In the 1840s Emily Chubbuck Judson (1817–54), a teacher at Utica Female Seminary, wrote sketches and religious poetry for the *New York Mirror* in the 1840s and seven novels, sometimes as Fanny Forrester. Writing as Grace Greenwood and married in 1853 to the owner of *Lippincott Magazine,* Leander K. Lippincott, Sara Clarke (1823–1904) wrote *Greenwood Leaves* (1850) and *Queen Victoria* (1883).

Susan Warner's (1819–85) *The Wide, Wide World* (1850), told the story of how religion helped an orphan adapt to an oppressive life on a Columbia Co farm. One of the century's best-selling novels, its theme, detailed setting, and attention to native speech set a trend for domestic fiction. In this melodramatic genre, characterized by increasingly suspenseful cliff-hangers, females in a hostile world relied on religion to make the difficult transition from childhood to adulthood. Warner wrote over 25 novels, in addition to 15 novels and children's books in collaboration with her sister Anna Bartlett Warner (1824–1915). Anna's 41 books include novels, children's stories, and gardening manuals. The sisters lived on Constitution Island and in Highland Falls (Orange Co).

Susan Fenimore Cooper's evocation of Cooperstown's landscape, weather, and wildlife in *Rural Hours* (1850) was a successful work of nature writing. Her other works include an anthology of poetry, *The Rhyme and Reason of Country Life* (1854), three books on nature, and several children's stories. Others in this vein include William H. H. Murray's (1840–1904) *Adventures in the Wilderness; or, Camp Life in the Adirondacks* (1864) and Joel T. Headly's (1813–97) *The Adirondacks; or, Life in the Woods* (1869). Charles Fenno Hoffman (1806–84) was author of *Greyslaer: A Romance of the Mohawk* (1840), which was based on a celebrated murder case, and also wrote poetry, including *Love's Calendar* and *Lays of the Hudson.*

The Late 19th and Early 20th Centuries

After the Civil War, the dominant themes in the state's literature focused on regional themes. In 1872 the *Atlantic Monthly* published the first of Philander Deming's (1829–1915) short stories. Local color genre stories, they detail hard-scrabble life in the Adirondacks and Champlain Valley. Deming's keen observations reflect his careers as a newspaper reporter and as a court stenographer for the Third Judicial District of the State Supreme Court in Albany. Orange Co resident E(dward) P(ayson) Roe (1838–88) left the ministry after his literary success. He wrote *Barriers Burned Away* (1872) and *Opening a Chesnut Burr* (1874), the first of his many pious, sentimental novels. Utican Charles Austin Fosdick (1842–1915), writing under the name of Harry Castlemon, mined the success of the Horatio Alger juvenile genre in works such as *Frank the Young Naturalist* (1864) and *Boy Trapper* (1878). Marietta Holley (1836–1926) lived in the village of Adams (Jefferson Co) and in July 1871 *Peterson's Magazine* published her first story. Holley's first book, *My Opinions and Betsy Bobbet's,* appeared in 1873. The popular Samantha series followed. Often visiting upstate towns in novels such as *Samantha in Saratoga* (1887), Samantha, the 200 lb (91 kg) garrulous wife of a farmer, expresses opinions about religion, ethics, and a woman's role in life.

Set in "Syrchester," modeled after Syracuse, Edward N. Westcott's (1846–98) best-seller *David Harum* (1898) depicts lingering mistrust between Dutch and German settlers and more recent arrivals from New England as among the changes brought on by the Erie Canal. Harum, who stays barely within the law in his rise from shrewd peddler to successful banker, became a stereotype of a western New Yorker. Using a folksy tone, a touch of nostalgia, and a naturalist's eye, Irving Bacheller (1859–1950) wrote 29 novels about rugged North Country life. They include *Eben Holden* (1900) and *Silas Strong, Emperor of the Woods* (1906). Brooklyn-born Robert W. Chambers (1865–1933) was an illustrator for *Vogue* before settling in Broadalbin (Fulton Co). His 72 nostalgic, sentimental, historical romances, most of them best-sellers set in the Mohawk Valley during the colonial period and the Revolutionary War, include accounts of Iroquois legends and ceremonies. His *Tracer of Lost Persons* (1906), with an international setting, was the basis for a 1930s radio series.

A writer whose work has proved more lasting was Harold Frederic (1856–98), born and raised in Utica, an editor for the *Utica Observer* and the *Albany Evening Observer,* and author of novels and short stories set in the Mohawk Valley. Frederic draws on his legislative reporting in Albany for the political theme in *Seth's Brother's Wife* (1887) and *In the Valley* (1890) depicts the 1777 Battle of Oriskany. In his masterpiece, *The Damnation of Theron Ware* (1896), a minister gains knowledge and loses faith when new ideas about religion, art, and science come to a small conservative town. In *The Copperhead* (1893) and other Civil War stories, Frederic describes communities affected by distant battles and arguments over slavery. The war and its aftermath was an important theme for other authors in the state, among them Albion W. Tourgée (1838–1905). A long-time resident of Chautauqua Co who had attended the University of Rochester, Tourgée wrote *A Fool's Errand* (1879), perhaps the best novel of Reconstruction. The best-known Civil War novel, Stephen Crane's *Red Badge of Courage* (1895), is based on the experiences of the 124th New York State Volunteers from Orange Co. Crane also wrote a series of stories based on experiences in Sullivan Co.

Nature writing, an important New York State tradition, arguably peaked with John Burroughs (1837–1921). Born in Roxbury (Delaware Co), he lived in West Park (Ulster Co), on the Hudson, and nearby he built Slabsides, a rustic cabin. Burroughs's publications celebrate the Catskills and articulate his philosophical and political views. His 23 books of essays begin with *Wake Robin* (1871). John Jay Chapman, another prominent political and cultural critic, lived in Barrytown (Dutchess Co); his essays championed the individual against the forces of modernity.

Often considered New York State's greatest 19th-century poet, Walt Whitman (1819–92) is primarily associated with New York City and Long Island. However, some of his best known poems, such as "By Blue Ontario's Shore," have upstate locales. His love of the outdoors made a profound impression on other authors, including John Burroughs, whose first book, *Notes on Walt Whitman as Poet and Person* (1867), was the first biography of Whitman. The state's rich Indian and colonial history inspired poetry, such as Alfred Billings Street's (1811–81) *The Burning of Schenectady* (1842) and *Frontenac* (1849), and William H. C. Hosmer's (1814–77) *Yonnondio, or Warriors of the Genesee* (1844). Other poems were collected in the volumes edited by Ina Russelle Warren, *Poets and Poetry of Syracuse* (1884) and *Poets and Poetry of Rochester* (1885). The region's most distinguished poet of the era was Adelaide Crapsey (1878–1914), who lived most of her life in Rochester. Her posthumously published *Verse* (1922) introduced the cinquain, a short verse form influenced by haiku.

From 1920 to the 21st Century

Regionalism dominated upstate fiction for most of the 20th century. Walter D. Edmond's (1903–98) Erie Canal novel *Rome Haul* (1929) and his Revolutionary War novel *Drums Along the Mohawk* (1936) are probably the best-known New York State regional novels of midcentury. Samuel Hopkins Adams's (1871–1958) *Canal Town* (1944) and *Sunrise to Sunset* (1950) use upstate communities and the Erie Canal to explore the interaction of people and nature and how they change one another. Carl Carmer (1893–1976) incorporated folklore and oral history in his *Listen to the Sound of the Lonesome Drum* (1936) and other collections. His novels include *Genesee Fever* (1941) and *The Farm Boy and the Angel* (1970), an account of early Mormonism. *The Taven Lamps Are Burning* (1964) is a noteworthy anthology of upstate literature. Carmer was one of a number of writers who researched rural folklore in "York State" (basically New York State north of the Bronx). Harold W. Thompson wrote *Body, Boots, and Britches: Folktales, Ballads and Speech from Country New York* (1939), and Louis C. Jones, director of the New York State Historical Association, published collections of ghost stories including *Things That Go Bump in the Night* (1959). Urban writers include Jerre Mangione (1909–98), the coordinating editor of the Work Projects Administration's Federal Writers' Project who set *Mount Allegro* (1943) in an Italian Rochester neighborhood. Set in "Cato" (Utica), Helen Barolini's (1925–) *Umbertina* (1979) describes the female immigrant experience and how a fourth-generation Italian American family resolves lingering conflicts.

One of New York State's most distinguished writers, critic Edmund Wilson (1895–1972) set his sexually frank *Memoirs of Hecate County* (1946) in a suburb north of New York City. His *Upstate* (1971) is part memoir and part review of the state's literature. In *Apologies to the Iroquois* (1959), Wilson tells of his discovery of the state's Indian culture. His onetime friend and subsequent antagonist Vladimir Nabokov taught from 1948 to 1959 at Cornell University and had New York State settings in several novels, including *Pnin* (1957) and *Lolita* (1958). Mary McCarthy (1912–89), once married to Wilson, provided a compelling account of nine Vassar women and foreshadowed the reemergence of the feminist movement in the best-seller *The Group* (1963).

Prominent 20th-century poets include Hayden Carruth (1921–), who taught at Syracuse University after 1979. The title poem from his collection *The Oldest Killed Lake in America* (1985), was a tribute of sorts to Onondaga Lake. A. R. Ammons (1926–2001) taught after 1964 at Cornell University and was known for his experiments in prosody, such as *Tape for the End of the Year* (1965), a poem drafted on a narrow ribbon of calculator tape on a manual typewriter. John Logan (1923–87), who taught at SUNY Buffalo (1966–85), was a leading "confessional" poet, and in collections such as *The Bridge of Change* (1979) was concerned with the problems and emotions of everyday life. BOA Editions in Rochester (1976), one of the few presses in the United States that publishes only poetry, has a distinguished roster of authors, including Li-Young Lee, William Heyen, Lucille Clifton, and W. D. Snodgrass.

Successful novelists who set works in New York State include Kurt Vonnegut (1922–), who worked at General Electric in Schenectady and fictionalized the city as "Illium" in satiric novels such as *Player Piano* (1952), *Cat's Cradle* (1963), and *Hocus Pocus* (1990). Recurring character Kilgore Trout in Vonnegut's fiction is a Cohoes (Albany Co) resident. In *World's End* (1987), T. Coraghessan Boyle explores the Dutch colonial period, the 1949 riots, and the tumult of 1968 in Peekskill (Westchester Co), his hometown. John Crowley's (1942–) *Little Big* (1981) is partly set in a mythified rural New York State. *Aegypt* (1987), *Love and Sleep* (1993), and *Daemonomania* (1999) speculate on the mystical history of the world and the philosophy of 16th-century English magus John Dee in the fictional town of Blackbury Jambs, near Bethel (Sullivan Co).

Gail Godwin (1937–), author of best-selling novels including *A Mother and Two Daughters,* has lived in Woodstock (Ulster Co) since 1976. John Gardner (1933–82), raised in Batavia (Genesee Co) had New York State settings in *The Sunlight Dialogues* (1972), *Nickel Mountain* (1973), and *October Light* (1976). Ishmael Reed (1937–), born in Buffalo, has published numerous collections of poetry, as well as novels and essays, and is one of the leading African American authors of his generation. Born in Lockport (Niagara Co), prolific author Joyce Carol Oates (1938–) writes novels that often explore violence. In *We Were the Mulvaneys* (1996), the date rape of 16-year-old Marianne Mulvaney tears apart a happy family. *Middle Age* (2002) tells the story of dissolute residents in upscale "Salthill-on-Hudson." Her short story "Au Sable" (2001) examines an aging man's decision to commit suicide with his wife in their Adirondack summer cottage. *Mohawk* (1986) and *Risk Pool* (1988), by Richard Russo (1949–) are set in "Mohawk," a once prosperous town that resembles Gloversville (Fulton Co), where Russo grew up. *Nobody's Fool* (1993) is set in fictional settings that resemble Saratoga Springs and Ballston Spa (Saratoga Co).

Widely acclaimed novelist William Kennedy (1928–), former reporter for *Albany Times-Union,* set *The Ink Truck* (1969) amidst a newspaper strike. *Legs* (1975), *Billy Phelan's Greatest Game* (1978), the Pulitzer Prize–winning *Ironweed* (1983) and *Roscoe* (2002) are among the novels in his Albany Cycle. They explore 19th- and 20th-century history through characters that include gangsters, former baseball players, derelicts, and politicians. Often focusing on Irish Americans, Kennedy writes about ethnicity, leadership and corruption, and the nature of city life in New York State.

See also Yankee migration.

Bergmann, Frank, ed. *Upstate Literature: Essays in Memory of T. O'Donnell* (Syracuse: Syracuse Univ Press, 1985)

Carmer, Carl. *The Tavern Lights Are Burning: Literary Journals through Six Regions and Four Centuries of New York State* (1964; repr New York: Fordham Univ Press, 1996)

O'Donnell, Thomas F. "The Regional Fiction of Upstate New York" (PhD diss, Syracuse Univ, 1957)

———. "Mr. Keen Where Are You? Robert W. Chambers Is Lost," *NAHO* 11 (Winter 1978–79): 2–9

———. "The Secret Passion of Philander Deming," *NAHO* 12 (Winter 1979–80): 13–15

Wood, Ann D. "The 'Scribbling Women' and Fanny Fern: Why Women Wrote," *American Quarterly* 23 (Spring 1971): 3–24

Miriam Steinhardt Soffer

literature, New York City area. The New York City area's literary roots lie in political pamphlets and journalism associated with the Revolution. Important precursors include the city's first newspaper, the *New-York Gazette* (1725), and the first journal, the *Independent Reflector* (1752–53), by William Livingston, William Smith Jr, and John Morin Scott. Prominent works from the Revolutionary era are the pamphlets of Thomas Paine, including *Common Sense* (1776), and the newspaper essays of Alexander Hamilton, James Madison, and John Jay, compiled as *The Federalist Papers* (1787–88).

Independence to the Civil War

The main characteristics of New York City's literature—urbanity, irony, and skepticism—emerged early and can be said to have begun with Philip Freneau and Washington Irving. Freneau (1752–1832) is referred to as the poet of the American Revolution for his satirical verse (1775). His poems such as "The Indian Burying Ground" (1787) and "The Wild Honey Suckle" (1786) are seen as harbingers of the romanticism that dominated literature until the Civil War. Washington Irving (1783–1859) came to prominence with the satirical *History of New York* (1809), narrated by the fictional Diedrich Knickerbocker. Irving had previously worked with James Kirke Paulding (1778–1860) in the creation of *Salmagundi* (1807–8), a series of pamphlets satirizing New York society. Irving and Paulding were the core of the club that came to be known as the Knickerbockers and included Fitz-Greene Halleck (1790–1867) and other literati. Knickerbocker Joseph Rodman Drake (1795–1820) and Halleck published the *Croaker Papers* (1819), which included Drake's romantic legend of the lower Hudson, "The Culpret Fey." Charles Brockden Brown (1771–1810), who spent several crucial years in New York City, was the nation's first professional novelist. His factually realistic "gothic" novels include *Arthur Mervyn* (2 vols, 1799–1800), which depicts the city's 1798 outbreak of yellow fever. Susanna Rowson (1762–1824) was an actress-turned-writer of plays, poems, and novels, including *Charlotte Temple: A Tale of Truth* (1791), a cautionary tale set mostly in New York City and read widely for several decades. Early African American authors include the slave Jupiter Hammon (1711–*ca* 1790) from Lloyd Neck (Suffolk Co), who in 1760 became the first published African American poet. Venture Smith's (1729–1805) narrative (1798) told of his life as a slave on Long Island.

James Fenimore Cooper (1789–1851), a sometime resident in Westchester Co, had recently published *The Spy* (1821) when he moved to New York City in 1822 for several years before settling in Cooperstown (Otsego Co), and it was there he founded the literary Bread and Cheese Club. Fellow member William Cullen Bryant (1794–1878) moved to New York City in 1825 and soon became a center of the city's literary scene. A distinguished poet, he was the promoter of a distinctive American literature. Other literati included James Gates Percival, a poet, William Dunlap, a playwright and historian, and James A. Hillhouse, who wrote verse dramas. Gulian Crommelin Verplanck (1786–1870), a lawyer, politician, and journalist, published *Discourses and Addresses on Subjects of American History, Arts, and Literature* (1833).

New York City vied for cultural prominence at

first with Philadelphia, then Boston, but by the mid–19th century it had become the nation's main publishing center. Evert Augustus Duyckinck (1816–78), editor of *Literary World* (1847–53), was in a sense "dean of letters" and was the author of the authoritative *Cyclopaedia of American Literature* (1855), a catalyst for literary activity. Cornelius Mathews (1817–1889), a Duyckinck protégé, wrote prolifically in a variety of forms. In *Big Abel and the Little Manhattan* (1845), a Manhattan Irishman gives a returned native "Manhatto" a tour of the city. Among those in the Duyckinck circle were Herman Melville (1819–91) and Edgar Allan Poe (1809–49). Melville grew up in New York City and the Albany area and wrote his early novels and much of *Moby Dick* (1851) in New York City. Most of *Pierre* (1852) is set in the city, as are several stories, including "Bartleby the Scrivener" (1853). Poe edited the *Broadway Journal* from 1837 to 1838 and from 1844 to 1849 and published many of his own tales, poems, and essays in it, including "The Literati of New York City" (1846). The passing scene in Manhattan was described with a genteel sensibility by Nathaniel P. Willis (1806–67) and with more directness by George G. Foster's (1814–56) works such as *New York Naked* (1854). Mid-19th-century New York City was described with considerable passion and power by Walt Whitman (1819–92), who worked for the *Brooklyn Eagle* (1846–47) and other newspapers. His *Leaves of Grass* (1855 and many revised editions to 1892) asserted an exuberant and urban poetic voice in a new open verse form.

The Civil War to World War II

In the decades after the Civil War, romanticism was largely left behind in favor of various forms of realism and naturalism. The many volumes of Horatio Alger Jr (1832–99), with their rags-to-riches stories of boys on the streets, prefigured the adventurous, moralizing "dime novels" that became popular in the third quarter of the 19th century. These would be the precursors of the "pulp" magazines that flourished in the early years of the 20th century. Stephen Crane's (1871–1900) more aesthetically sophisticated and less optimistic *Maggie, A Girl of the Streets* (1893) examined the violence and miseries of tenement life. Besides *The Red Badge of Courage* (1895), Crane wrote innovative free verse and for papers including the *New York Tribune.* O. Henry (William Sydney Porter) (1862–1910) found subject matter for his remarkable surprise endings in the bars, dance halls, and brothels of the Gramercy Park and Tenderloin neighborhoods (14th–24th Sts along 6th Ave).

Literary realism extended to other social levels of city life, most notably in works by William Dean Howells (1837–1920), Henry James Jr (1843–1916), and Edith Wharton (1862–1937). Howells, who went to New York City in 1891, wrote novels that explored class issues, incorporating ethnic and labor problems with concerns of a troubled middle class. James, a native New Yorker, set some of his best-known works in New York City, including *Washington Square* (1881) and *The Bostonians* (1886), which takes place almost as much in New York City as in Boston. Wharton examined the moral plight of New York City's new aristocracy in *Ethan Frome* (1911), *The House of Mirth* (1905), the first of several "naughty" portraits of high society in New York and the lower Hudson Valley, and *The Age of Innocence* (1920). *Old New York* (1924) is a fictional social history of New York City society from the 1840s to the 1870s.

In the early 20th century, a new "bohemianism" came to prominence in the literature of New York City, challenging the supposedly stale genteel conventions of the Victorian era. The center of this new sensibility was in Greenwich Village, espoused by poets like Edna St. Vincent Millay, e. e. cummings, and Sara Teasdale. This was the preeminent era of "little magazines," erudite publications committed to the politics and aesthetics of international modernism, with an influence far beyond their circulation figures. For most of the 20th century, it was a dominant forum for the city's litterateurs. The *Little Review* arrived from Chicago in 1913 and published Hart Crane's "The Bridge" in 1922. The more staid *Dial*, edited for a time by Marianne Moore (1887–1972), came to New York in 1917 and provided space for Conrad Aiken and Van Wyck Brooks. Writers for the leftist *Masses* (1911–17) included Max Eastman, Carl Sandburg, Louis Untermeyer, John Reed, and Theodore Dreiser. Some of this new approach appeared in magazines with a national circulation. *McClure's Magazine* (1893–1929), perhaps best known for its muckraking exposés, featured much contemporary literature, including the works of Frank Norris, Edwin Arlington Robinson, Sinclair Lewis, Lincoln Steffens, Sherwood Anderson, and Willa Cather. The *Smart Set* (1890), a witty literary journal, was prominent from about 1914 to 1930 under the joint editorship of George Jean Nathan (1882–1958) and H. L. Mencken (1880–1956). In the 1920s *Vanity Fair* (1868–1939) featured many of the members of the so-called Algonquin Round Table, including Dorothy Parker, Alexander Woollcott, and Robert Benchley. The *New Yorker* (1925), one of the few surviving mass-circulation magazines with literary pretension, published E. B. White, A. J. Liebling, Joseph Mitchell, James Thurber, and other chroniclers of New York City life.

In the 1920s, Prohibition and World War I heightened the sense of rebellion against propriety. Jazz-age New York City was epitomized by F. Scott Fitzgerald (1896–1940) in such novels as *This Side of Paradise* (1920), *The Beautiful and the Damned* (1922), and *The Great Gatsby* (1925), the latter largely set in Nassau Co's Gold Coast. Other novels of the 1920s include *I Thought of Daisy* (1929) by Edmund Wilson (1895–1972) and *Manhattan Transfer* (1925) by John Dos Passos (1896–1970), which portrayed a fragmented, socially diverse city in conflagration. Thomas Wolfe (1900–1938) viewed the city as opposed to the sensibilities of the individual and the artist in novels such as the semi-autobiographical *The Web and the Rock* (1939) and *Look Homeward, Angel* (1929). Fanny Hurst (1889–1968) became one of the most popular female writers of the day with novels like *Back Street* (1930) and *Imitation of Life* (1933), as well as with stories of working-class and immigrant women for *Cosmopolitan* and *Saturday Evening Post.* Dawn Powell (1896–1965) is best known for her satirical novels of New York City, including *Angels on Toast* (1940) and *The Locusts Have No King* (1948).

Jewish and black literature also became prominent in the interwar decades. Originating mainly in immigrant communities in the Lower East Side, Brooklyn, and the Bronx, Jewish literature affirmed a new Jewish American identity. Abraham Cahan (1860–1951) was editor of the Yiddish *Forverts* (1897) and wrote the English novels *Yekl: A Tale of the New York Ghetto* (1896) and *The Rise of David Levinsky* (1917), both influential depictions of immigrant life. Sholem Asch (1880–1957) came to New York in 1914, and his works in Yiddish, including *The Mother* (1930), set in the Lower East Side, were widely translated. Isaac Bashevis Singer's (1904–91) Yiddish stories became immensely popular in translation, especially after "Gimpel the Fool" appeared in *Partisan Review* in 1953. Other powerful treatments of Jewish life in New York City are *Call It Sleep* (1934) by Henry Roth, *In Dreams Begin Responsibilities* (1938) and *The World Is a Wedding* (1948) by Delmore Schwartz. Saul Bellow's *Humboldt's Gift* (1975) is based on Schwartz's life.

The Harlem Renaissance, an eruption of African American intellectual and artistic talent, can be dated from 1910 when W. E. B DuBois took over the *Crisis,* the organ of the National Association for the Advancement of Colored People (NAACP). *The New Negro* (1925) was a groundbreaking anthology. In *The Weary Blues* (1926), Langston Hughes (1902–67) incorporated jazz rhythms into poetry. *The Big Sea* (1940) and *I Wonder as I Wander* (1956) recount his life in the 1920s and 1930s. Claude McKay's (1889–1948) *Home to Harlem* (1928) was a best-seller, a signal of a gradual acceptance of African American literature.

The impact of the depression turned many writers away from flouting convention to trying to understand and correct society's manifest ills. The literature of social protest included Michael Gold's *Jews without Money* (1930) and James Agee's *Let Us Now Praise Famous Men* (1941). A group of young leftist writers, including Herman Spector, Joseph Kalar, Edwin Rolfe, and Sol Funaroff, published poems in *We Gather Strength* (1933). The Federal Writers' Project of the Works Progress Administration produced the *New York City Guide* (1939) with staff that included Richard Wright and John Cheever.

World War II to the Millennium

The moral seriousness of the 1930s continued into the 1940s and 1950s, though domestic and international communism became the major political and ethical issue of the day. For a time it seemed that postwar possibilities in literature were circumscribed by the emotionally unencumbered plain style with which John Hersey (1914–93) described atomic devastation in *Hiroshima,* first published in the *New Yorker* in 1946. In response, Mary McCarthy (1912–89) predicted that fiction after the atomic bomb would no longer be possible. The Holocaust also called into question complacent assumptions about literature's independence of political events. The questions of war and peace became a preoccupation of the "New York intellectuals," and no journal was more identified with their efforts than the *Partisan Review* (1934). Its editors included Delmore Schwartz, William Phillips, Dwight Macdonald, Philip Rahv, F. W. Dupee, Mary McCarthy, Elizabeth Hardwick, Harold Rosenberg, and Lionel Abel. Boundaries between fiction and nonfiction was challenged by authors like Norman Mailer (1923–), who wrote the bitter war novel *The Naked and the Dead* (1948). With *Advertisement for Myself* (1959) he inaugurated a series of assertive nonfiction works that vehemently engaged in political and cultural events. Truman Capote's (1924–84) *In Cold Blood* (1966) led to the definition of a new form, the "nonfiction novel." Another model was provided by Mary McCarthy in her novels *Memories of a Catholic Girlhood* (1957), *The Company She Keeps* (1942), and *The Group* (1963). In the 1950s and 1960s the *New Yorker* continued to be a medium for its special brand of sophisticated short stories examining urban and suburban life, and frequently featured John Updike and John Cheever.

The 1950s and early 1960s were a time of rebellion, exemplified in the work of such "migrants" to New York City as Carson McCullers, Paul Bowles, Murray Kempton, Elizabeth Hardwick, and Joseph Heller. In their hands literature often took on the ironies of black humor and the mock heroic. Anxiety streamed beneath the rebelliously intellectual sentimentality of *Catcher in the Rye* (1951) and other stories by J. D. Salinger (1919–). A seminal work for the Beat generation, Allen Ginsberg's (1926–97) *Howl* (1956) was in effect a manifesto of a new order and extended poetry to include the personal experiments of rough street life (including sexual experience) and affirmed a new openness of form. Jack Kerouac's (1922–69) *On the Road* (1957) is a central Beat novel, while *The Subterraneans* (1958) is written in a "bop" style, influenced by jazz improvisation. William Burroughs's (1914–97) *Junkie* (1953) and *Naked Lunch* (1959) portray the addict's experience, and the latter uses an innovative and disorienting "cut-up" technique of composition. The *Evergreen Review,* founded in New York in 1957 by Barney Rossett at Grove Press, published Beat writers including Kerouac, Ginsberg, Burroughs, and poet Gary Snyder (1930–). Long Island novelist Thomas Pynchon's (1937–) tragicomic allegories included *V* (1963), in which the city's sewers were populated with albino alligators.

One landmark anthology for poetry, *New American Poetry: 1945–1960,* edited by Donald M. Allen, inaugurated what was to become a dominant alternative tradition in poetry that rejected most attributes of academic verse. Leading figures included Frank O'Hara (1926–66), Kenneth Koch (1925–2002), and John Ashbery (1927–), who were influenced by French surrealism and abstract expressionist; their work eschewed conventional logic in favor of images and musicality. O'Hara's *Meditations in an Emergency* (1957) captures the intimacies of daily life in Manhattan, while Koch's work ranges from a dense obscurity to lyrical humor. Ashbery, who authored plays, a novel, and art and literary criticism, wrote *Self Portrait in a Convex Mirror* (1975) and is known as a difficult, deliberately nonlogical poet. More formalist poets include James Merrill (1926–95), whose "An Urban Convalescence" (1962) and *Lost in Translation* (1976) recount his youth in the city, and Anthony Hecht (1923–2004), also a critic, whose works include *The Laws of the Poetic Art* (1995). Galway Kinnell (1927–), a darker and more symbolic author, is known for his *Avenue Bearing the Initial of Christ into the New World* (Ave C on the Lower East Side) (1974) and the novel *Black Light* (1966). Other important poets include Richard Howard (1929–), also a translator of French literature, poet and critic John Hollander (1929–), and W. S. Merwin (1927–), whose formal style became gradually more image oriented and experimental. Other New Yorkers in this generation are Muriel Rukeyser (1913–80), poet and author of the novel *The Orgy* (1965), Louis Auchincloss (1917–), Frederick Morgan (1922–2004), and Howard Moss (1922–), for many years poetry editor of the *New Yorker.*

Leading critical voices included Edmund Wilson (1895–1972), whose broad humanistic erudition was central to the city's intellectual life by midcentury. Wilson arrived in 1916 and was associated with *Vanity Fair,* the *New Republic,* and then the *New Yorker* until 1948. Other key voices were Columbia professors Lionel Trilling (1905–75), notably in *The Liberal Imagination* (1950), and Mark Van Doren (1894–1972), who taught Allen Ginsberg, John Berryman, Thomas Merton, Herb Gold, and Jack Kerouac. Susan Sontag's (1933–2004) works, including "Against Interpretation" (1966), were influenced by European intellectual tradition but also aspects of popular life such as film, photography, and disease. *Commentary* (1945), under the conservative editorship of Norman Podhoretz, edged out *Partisan Review* as the focus of discussion and controversy. The more vehement *New Criterion* (1982), edited by Hilton Kramer and Samuel Lipman, set out to protect US culture from the 1960s counterculture, which they perceived to be anti-intellectual and anti-authority threats. The *New York Review of Books* (1963) displaced the *New York Times Book Review* (1896) as the city's premier source for critical response to new publications. In 1997 Bard College began the publication *Conjunctions,* which emerged as the place to look for "advanced" writing.

African American writer James Baldwin (1924–87) wrote of growing up in Harlem in *Go Tell It on the Mountain* (1953), *Notes of a Native Son* (1955), and the angrier *The Fire Next Time* (1963). Ralph Ellison's (1914–94) *Invisible Man* (1952) found immediate acceptance in the literary establishment. Umbra (1963), a Lower East Side black writers' group that included Ishmael Reed (1937–), was formative in the Black Arts Movement that emerged in the mid-1960s, which included writers like Larry Neal, Nikki Giovanni, and Amiri Baraka (Leroi Jones).

As Jewish writers entered the literary mainstream, their anxieties over estrangement and loss of community came to epitomize the universal anxieties of the 20th century. Critic Alfred Kazin (1915–98) wrote most notably *On Native Grounds: An Interpretation of Modern American Prose Literature* (1942) and a series of autobiographical works about growing up in Brooklyn. Critic Irving Howe (1920–93) was the founding editor of *Dissent* (1954). Bernard Malamud (1914–86) in *The Magic Barrel* (1958), *The Assistant* (1957) and *The Tenants* (1971) wrote of tensions within the Jewish community, often with other ethnic groups. Persistently controversial, Philip Roth (1933–) enraged parts of the Jewish community with a ribald comic treatment of middle-class Jewish anxieties in *Portnoy's Complaint* (1969) and in a series of novels having main character Nathan Zuckerman explore the role of the Jewish American novelist. The secular Jewish upper middle class got a comic treatment in Julie Hecht's *Do the Windows Open?* (1997) while Cynthia Ozick (1928–) critiques secular Jews in *The Puttermesser Papers* (1997) and *Quarrel and Quandry* (2000). Allegra Goodman (1967–) wrote more gently in *The Family Markowitz* (1996), *Kaaterskill Falls* (1998), and *Paradise Park* (2001).

The century came to a close with a kaleidoscope of new writing, often dominated by themes of multiculturalism, sexual orientation, and feminism. Gay and lesbian themes in fiction became an important component of the city's literature, starting with such works as Hubert Selby Jr's *Last Exit to Brooklyn* (1964) and continuing later with such authors as Christopher Bram (1952–) in *Almost History* (1992) and *Father of Frankenstein* (1996), and Edmund White (1940–) in *The Beautiful Room Is Empty* (1998). The AIDS crisis dominated gay fiction in the 1980s and 1990s in works such as Ethan Morden's *I've a Feeling We're Not in Kansas Anymore: Tales of Gay Manhattan* (1985), Andrew Holleran's (1943–) *The Beauty of Men* (1996), and Michael Cunningham's (1952–) *The Hours* (1999). Rita Mae Brown in *Rubyfruit Jungle* (1973) described lesbian life in New York City in the 1970s. Audre Lorde (1934–92), born and raised in Harlem and a self-described "black lesbian, mother, warrior, and poet," was the author of *Zami* (1982) and *Sister Outsider* (1984).

Ethnic literature remained a staple of writing about New York City. Brooklyn-born Frank McCourt (1931–) wrote of the years he spent in Ireland between the ages of 4 and 19 in his novel *Angela's Ashes* (1996), and the sequel, *'Tis* (1999), continues his story as an immigrant in New York City. Other chroniclers of Irish American life include Mary Gordon (1951–), whose works include *Final Payments* (1978) and *The Shadow Man* (1998), a memoir of her father, an anti-Semite who hid his Jewish background. Alice McDermott writes of suburban Irish in Brooklyn and eastern Long Island in *These Nights* (1987) and *Charming Billy* (1998). Latino culture is treated by the Cuban American Oscar Hijuelos (1951–), best known for *Our House in the Last World* (1983) and *The Mambo Kings Play Songs of Love* (1989), and Julie Alvarez in *How the Garcia Girls Lost Their Accents* (1991) and *Something to Declare* (1998). Chang-Rae Lee (1965), born and raised in Westchester Co, writes of Korean immigrants and their assimilation into American culture in *Native Speaker* (1995) and *A Gesture of Life* (1999).

There was a remarkable outpouring of writing on New York City itself in the last part of the 20th century. E. L. Doctorow's (1931–) novel *Ragtime* (1975) was a self-reflexive picture of the city in the early 20th century. Doctorow also used New York City, often historical, in *World's Fair* (1986), *Billy Bathgate* (1989), and *City of God* (2000). In *The Bonfire of the Vanities* (1987), Thomas Wolfe writes of the greedy, materialistic culture of New York City during the 1980s and the city's contrasts between great wealth and poverty. Don DeLillo (1936–) has often used New York City settings in his work, as in *Great Jones Street* (1973), a street in Greenwich Village. In *Underworld* (1998), DeLillo uses the 1951 play-off game between the Brooklyn Dodgers and New York Giants as a backdrop to explore recent American history. New York City becomes a character in *Motherless Brooklyn* (1999), by Jonathan Lethem (1964–), while his *Fortress of Solitude* (2003) follows the life of a boy growing up in Brooklyn from the 1970s to 2003. The impact of the terrorist attack on the World Trade Center on 11 Sept 2001 on the city's literature will no doubt be profound. It has just begun to be felt, as in Pete Hamill's (1935–) *Forever* (2002) and in *110 Stories: New York Writes after September 11* (2002), edited by Ulrich Baer.

See also HARLEM RENAISSANCE, NEW YORK INTELLECTUALS; ST. NICHOLAS.

Ashton, Dore. *The New York School: A Cultural Reckoning* (New York: Viking, 1973)

Atlas, James. "The Changing World of New York Intellectuals," *New York Times Magazine* (23 Aug 1985)

Bender, Thomas. *New York Intellect: A History of Intellectual Life in New York City, from 1750 to the Beginning of Our Time* (New York: Knopf, 1987)

Cole, William, ed. *New York: A Literary Companion* (Wainscott, NY: Pushcart Press, 1992)

Lewis, David Levering. *When Harlem Was in Vogue* (New York: Knopf, 1981)

Maurice, Arthur Bartlett. *The New York of the Novelists* (New York: Dodd, Mead, 1917)

Wallock, Leonard. *New York: Cultural Capital of the World, 1940–1965* (New York: Rizzoli, 1988)

Wilson, Edmund. *Classics and Commercials: A Literary Chronicle of the Forties* (New York: Farrar, Straus, 1950)

———. *The Shores of Light: A Literary Chronicle of the Twenties and Thirties* (New York: Farrar, Straus & Young, 1952)

William Wilson

Lithuanians. Lithuanians did not become a presence in New York State until the middle of the 19th century, although an immigrant from Lithuania, Alexander Carolus Curtius (Kursius), became headmaster of New Amsterdam's [now New York City] Latin school and its first physician in 1659. Determining the number of immigrants is difficult because of Lithuania's shifting political boundaries and its ethnic complexity, which included Poles, Germans, and Jews, as well as ethnic Lithuanians. Indeed, the largest group of immigrants to New York State from the area of Lithuania from 1880 to 1920 were Jewish Lithuanians, often known as Litvaks, who settled in large numbers in New York City and elsewhere. The number of immigrants from Lithuania declined following the imposition of immigration quotas in the 1920s. Lithuanian refugees after World War II were primarily from the intellectual and professional classes.

Ethnic Lithuanians were largely Roman Catholics. Their early churches were Polish Lithuanian until the first permanent Lithuanian parish, St. Mary of the Angels, was established in Brooklyn in 1894. Parishes sponsored cultural programs and language classes for children and adults. Mutual benefit societies were created, such as St. Casimir's, founded with Polish immigrants in 1875 in New York, and the Alliance of All Lithuanians (now Lithuanian Alliance of America [LAA]), founded in Pennsylvania in 1889, with its executive offices in New York City since 1910. The LAA began publishing a Lithuanian newspaper, *Vienybe,* in 1889. At the turn of the 20th century, Lithuanians in the United States were split ideologically between freethinkers and Roman Catholic activists. In Brooklyn Dr Jonas Sliupas organized the Alliance of Lithuanian Freethinkers in 1900, active through 1915. A year later, the LAA met in Pennsylvania; members were unable to heal the rifts, which led to the formation of an alternative group by the Catholic faction called the Lithuanian Roman Catholic Alliance of America. Eventually, the latter alliance began publishing its own official newspaper, *Garsas,* in Brooklyn in 1917; it was later based in Pennsylvania. In 1903 the Lithuanian Gymnastics Club was established in Brooklyn and continues today as the New York Lithuanian Athletic Club.

Throughout the 20th century, associations acted to preserve Lithuanian cultural identity and campaigned for Lithuania's independence during its occupations by czarist Russia, Germany, and the Soviet Union. Relief efforts on behalf of Lithuanian refugees of both world wars was widespread, and the passage of the Displaced Persons Act in 1948 opened America's doors to 30,000–37,000 Lithuanian refugees. With their arrival, many institutions in New York State sprang up to meet their needs: in 1949, the Representative Committee of Lithuanian Women (which became the Federation of Lithuanian Women's Clubs in 1963); in 1951, the American Lithuanian Engineers and Architects Association and the Lithuanian Community of the United States (to promote ethnic culture); in 1953, the Assembly of Captive European Nations, represented by nine separate national committees, including the Committee for a Free Lithuania. Renewed efforts to protest the Soviet occupation of Lithuania occurred in 1965 with the establishment in New York of the Committee to Restore Lithuania's Independence. Institutions and associations, such as the Lithuanian Cultural Center in Brooklyn, founded in 1974, and the Lithuanian-American Community, continue to uphold Lithuanian culture and unity. Rochester has a Lithuanian language radio program, *Dainos Aidas.*

Although primarily farmers in the old country, most early Lithuanian immigrants settled in urban areas and worked in factory settings. Concentrations included workers in the General Electric factories in Schenectady, where they worked in the electrical machine factories, in the Endicott Johnson shoe factories in the Binghamton area, in Amsterdam (Montgomery Co), in the Brooklyn shipyards, and in Manhattan's garment district. Lithuanian garment workers united to form the Lithuanian Tailoring Cooperative in Brooklyn in 1913, which existed until 1960. Substantial Lithuanian communities in New York State are established in New York City (after Chicago, the largest Lithuanian community in the United States), Amsterdam, Rochester, Utica, Schenectady, Albany, Binghamton, Niagara Falls, Great Neck, and Herkimer. Famous Lithuanians in the state include tennis player Vitas Gerulaitis, writer Jonas Valaitis, and composer Elisabeth Swados. In 2000 there were approximately 49,000 Lithuanians in New York State.

Budreckis, Algirdas M., comp and ed. *The Lithuanians in America, 1651–1975: A Chronology and Fact Book* (Dobbs Ferry, NY: Oceana Publications, 1976)

Kalinauskaite, D. "Lithuanians Abroad." In *Lithuania: Past, Culture, Present,* ed. Saulius Zukas (Vilnius, Lithuania: Baltos Lankos, 1999)

Kucas, Antanas. *Lithuanians in America.* Trans Joseph Boley (Boston: Encyclopedia Lituanica, 1975)

Victor A. Varis

Littauer, Lucius N(athan) (*b* Gloversville, Fulton Co, 20 Jan 1859; *d* New Rochelle, Westchester Co, 2 Mar 1944). Industrialist, politician, and philanthropist. The son of glove manufacturer Nathan Littauer, he was educated at Wells Seminary in Gloversville and the Charlier Institute in New York City before earning a bachelor's degree from Harvard in 1878. Littauer entered the family business but returned to Harvard in 1881 to coach one season of football, becoming the first full-time coach in American collegiate athletics. Under his guidance Littauer Bros Glove Co became one of the industry's largest enterprises. Littauer won a seat in the US House of Representatives as a Republican in 1897 and was an ardent protectionist on trade issues until stepping down in 1907. He formed the Glove Manufacturers Association in 1902 and the following year faced accusations of conflict of interest related to the federal government's purchase of Littauer gloves. A member of the New York State Board of Regents from 1912 to 1914, Littauer resigned following his conviction for evading import duties on a diamond tiara bought in Europe.

In 1928 Littauer sold his glove industry holdings for approximately $7 million and thereafter distributed nearly an equal sum in philanthropic activities. He created the Graduate School of Public Administration at Harvard (1936) and made major bequests to the New School for Social Research and the Jewish Theological Seminary in Manhattan. Littauer funded medical research at New York University and other institutions, and honored his father by establishing the Nathan Littauer Hospital in Gloversville (1894). The Lucius N. Littauer Foundation (1929) continues to support library collections and humanistic research on Jewish topics.

Engel, Herbert M. *Shtetl in the Adirondacks: The Story of Gloversville and Its Jews* (Fleischmanns, NY: Purple Mountain Press, 1991)

Glenn Wright

Little Beard's Town. Indian reservation. In 1797, at the federal treaty with the Seneca at Big Tree, north of present-day Cuylerville (Livingston Co), the US government recognized Little Beard's Town, a 2 mi^2 (5 km^2) parcel of land on the west side of the Genesee River, upon the site of today's Cuylerville. Little Beard, also known as Hanging Spear (Segwidow'gai), was one of the more prominent chiefs of the Seneca in the last quarter of the 18th century. Little Beard's Town was called De-o-nun'-dä-gä-a ("Where the Hill Is Near"). In 1779 the Sullivan-Clinton campaign destroyed the apple orchards, extensive cornfields, and the 128 houses in Little Beard's Town, seen by George Washington as the principal place of Seneca military forays in the Genesee Valley during the American Revolution. In 1802 the Seneca, in a properly ratified treaty with the federal government, sold this reservation to Oliver Phelps. In 1806 Little Beard was killed in a drunken brawl at Leicester (Livingston Co). Many of Little Beard's Town residents eventually made their way to the Tonawanda Indian Reservation to live in the early 19th century.

Doty, Lockwood L. *History of Livingston County, New York,* 2d ed. (Jackson, Mich: W. J. Van Deusen, 1905)

Turner, Orsamus. *History of the Pioneer Settlement of Phelps and Gorham's Purchase* (Rochester: William Alling, 1851)

Laurence M. Hauptman

Little Falls. Town (pop 1,544) and city (pop 5,188) in SE Herkimer Co. First settled under the Burnetsfield Patent of 1723 mostly by Palatine Germans, the present city was the site of a canal (1795) built by the Western Inland Lock Navigation Co around the falls. The village incorporated in 1811, and the town was formed from

Gulf Curve train wreck in Little Falls, 1940.

Fairfield, Herkimer, and German Flatts in 1829. More than a dozen large saw- and gristmills had been built on the Mohawk River by the time the Erie Canal opened in 1821 to the west and 1822 to the east. Rapid industrial development followed, beginning with a paper mill (?1828) and including the production of yarn, woolen cloth, knit goods, hammers, starch, mowing machines, leather, and paper boxes. It also became the site of a nationally significant outdoor wholesale cheese market in the mid–19th century. The city was incorporated in 1895. Drawn by factory work and joining earlier Irish and German immigrants were Russians, Poles, Slovenians, Ukrainians, and Italians. In October 1912 many of these immigrant workers struck the Phoenix and Gilbert knitting mills, protesting a wage cut, and were organized by the Industrial Workers of the World. Twentieth-century industry centered on the knitting mills but also included sectional bookcases, felt shoes, dresses, food packaging, gift wrap, bicycles, knitting machines, milking machines, and mattresses. The New York State Thruway crossed the town in 1954; a later exit in Danube was linked by an arterial to the city. Most of the mills closed after World War II, but the Burrows Paper Corp (1903) remained in operation in 2003, joined by LaSalle Labs (cosmetics manufacture). Attempts to develop the area's tourism potential have been successful, including Canal Place, a textile mill renovated for art and craft shops and restaurants.

James Crawford

Little Gull and Great Gull Islands. Two oversized rock piles left by the retreating glacier at the eastern end of Long Island Sound, these islands have long served as aids to navigation. Great Gull Island, 17 acres (6.9 ha) in size, is 7 miles (11.3 km) east of Orient Point; Little Gull, 1.5 acres (.6 ha), is 1 mile (1.6 km) further east. On Little Gull Island, an 81 ft (24.7 m) high lighthouse (1806) was automated in 1976. On Great Gull Island, Fort Michie, a US Army installation (1896–1948), has become a world-famous tern colony. The War Assets Administration presented the island to the American Museum of Natural History as a research station. More than 10,000 roseate terns *(Sterna dougallii)* thrive on the isolated island. Twenty ornithologists and assistants live there from April to October. Because terns are extremely sensitive to human beings, the scientists use the tunnels and ruins of Fort Michie to move about the area. After the terns leave, 500 or more harbor seals *(Phoca vitulina)* gather for the winter season. Special permits must be obtained before visiting these islands.

Sherrill Foster

Little Theatre. Rochester movie house. The Little Theatre was a part of the little cinema movement that began in 1925. Little theaters were built in Chicago, Philadelphia, Cleveland, and Buffalo and were dedicated to experimental, silent, and foreign films. Rochester architect Edgar Phillips designed the Art Deco theater, which opened on 17 Oct 1929 with the screening of *Cyrano de Bergerac.* Although it had financial trouble during the depression, the theater achieved a national reputation for its devotion to the art of cinema, and in 1949 the Little Theatre was chosen as the site for the national premier of Laurence Olivier's *Hamlet.* Despite the decline of downtown Rochester and the competition of multiplexes, the Little Theatre, now the Little Theatre Film Society, a nonprofit corporation, is still dedicated to experimental, foreign, and independent cinema.

Bogue, Gary. "A Little Story," *Cornerstone* 37 (Jan–Feb 1999): 3
"History of the Reel World," http://www.littletheatre.com/history.php

R. A. R. Edwards

Little Valley. Town (pop 1,788) and village (pop 1,130) in central Cattaraugus Co. A settlement of 1807 was given up; the town was settled permanently in 1815–16 and was formed from Perry [now Perrysburg] in 1818. The village was platted in 1851, when the the Erie Railroad came. By an act of 1865 the county seat was moved to Little Valley to have railroad access, and the courthouse was erected in 1867–68. The village incorporated in 1876. In the late 19th century Cattaraugus Cutlery Co employed 125 workers; other employers were the Kellogg Washing Machine Co and a Borden milk plant. In the early 21st century, the town's land use is chiefly agricultural; Little Valley was the only Cattaraugus Co town in which assessed agricultural acreage was greater in 1995 than it had been a quarter century earlier. In 2003 Bush Industries was a manufacturer of wooden furniture. The 6,015-acre (2,434 ha) Rock City State Forest encompasses Rock City, a tract covered with huge conglomerate boulders. The Cattaraugus County Fair is held in Little Valley in midsummer.

Bruce D. Fredrickson and Madelynn P. Fredrickson

Liverpool. Village (pop 2,505) in Salina (Onondaga Co). Haudenosaunee (Iroquois) tradition holds that the Great League was founded at a site in the present Liverpool. French Jesuits operated a mission to the Onondaga, Sainte Marie de Gannentaha, from 1656 to 1658. Liverpool was carved from the Salt Springs Reservation in 1797 and incorporated in 1830. Salt was shipped to market on the Erie and Oswego Canals, and Liverpool crafters produced baskets and furniture from willow, a skill introduced by German immigrants in 1852 that declined in the 1920s. Salt production also declined, ending in 1926. The Moyer touring car was produced in the village from 1908 to 1914. Automobiles and the Onondaga Lake Parkway (1933) transformed the village into a Syracuse suburb, and the New York State Thruway opened a Liverpool interchange in 1954. The village is the site of Onondaga Lake Park (1932), Sainte Marie among the Iroquois Living History Museum (1933), the Salt Museum (1934), and the Willow Museum (1994). Heid's of Liverpool, a hotdog stand that originated in 1886, is a landmark.

Daniel A. Piazza

livery service. See TAXI AND CAR SERVICES.

Livingston. Town (pop 3,424) in SW Columbia Co. Bought from the Indians in 1683–86, the area was settled when a Livingston house was built at the mouth of the Roeliff Jansen Kill in 1699 and a sawmill with 12 saws was constructed a year later. Palatine Germans and a few Scots arrived after 1710. Livingston was formed as a district in 1772 and as a town in 1788. Manufacturing in the 19th century included woolen and cotton cloth, blocks, straw paper, hosiery, and fishing nets; the Hudson River Ore and Iron Co (1883–1901) mined at Burden. Served by the Hudson River Railroad (1851), the town in the mid–19th century was a large producer of rye, and in the 20th century apples and small fruits dominated. In 2003 Iron Mountain at Burden holds underground vaults for business records storage.

Livingston [née Schuyler], **Alida** (*b* Beverwijck [now Albany], 28 Feb 1656; *d* Livingston Manor [now in Columbia Co], May 1727). Businesswoman and matriarch of the Livingston family in America. The third of 10 children of Philip Pietersz Schuyler and Margareta van Slichtenhorst, she was raised in Albany and at age 19 married Rev Nicholas van Rensselaer, director of the colony of Rensselaerswijck [now in Albany, Columbia, and Rensselaer Cos]. In July 1679, eight months after Nicholas's death, she married Robert Livingston (1654–1728), a Scottish immigrant who as an adolescent had lived in the Dutch Republic and in early 1675 had settled in Albany. She bore him nine children and was his partner and adviser throughout his career as a merchant and politician. Aside from a brief stay in Connecticut in 1690–91, at the time of the Leisler troubles, she never left the Hudson Valley. During Robert's increasingly frequent trips to New York City and, on two occasions, England, Alida looked after the family's interests, first in Albany and after about 1700 at Livingston Manor, which she ran with acumen and in spite of numerous challenges turned into a profitable enterprise. Some 175 extant letters to her husband from 1680 to 1726 (in Dutch) attest to her entrepreneurial skills and political insights.

Biemer, Linda Briggs. "Business Letters of Alida Schuyler Livingston, 1680–1726," *New York History* 63 (1982): 183–207

———. *Women and Property in Colonial New York: The Transition from Dutch to English Law, 1643–1727* (Ann Arbor, Mich: UMI Research Press, 1983)

Leder, Lawrence H. *Robert Livingston, 1654–1728, and the Politics of Colonial New York* (Chapel Hill: Univ of North Carolina Press, 1961)

Jos van der Linde

Livingston, (Henry) Brockholst (*b* New York City, 25 Nov 1757; *d* Washington, DC, 18 Mar 1823). State judge and US Supreme Court justice. In his teens Livingston moved with his family to New Jersey, where his father, William, would become governor in 1776, and was educated at the College of New Jersey (now Princeton University). He was an officer on Philip Schuyler's staff during the Saratoga campaign and an aide to brother-in-law John Jay's Spanish mission (1780–82). Captured at sea in March 1782 while returning from Europe, Livingston was paroled two months later and, after reading law with Peter W. Yates, was admitted to the bar at Albany in 1783. He ranked with Alexander Hamilton at the head of New York City's bar and was an active land and securities speculator. Like his cousin Robert R. Livingston, Brockholst changed his politics from Federalist to Republican and opposed Jay's gubernatorial campaigns (1792, 1795) and Jay's Treaty (1794). Livingston served in the assembly (1788–89, 1800–1801), was part of the successful campaign to win New York State for Thomas Jefferson in 1800, and was appointed to the state supreme court in 1802. His ready wit and willingness to break from crusted precedent is seen in his *Pierson v Post* (1805) dissent, in which he ridiculed the notion that law courts should settle sportsmen's disputes over wild animal carcasses. Perhaps because he so differed from his colleagues in interpreting the law, Livingston sought a change that was achieved with his appointment to the US Supreme Court, where he served from 1807 to 1823. Livingston regularly found agreement on the Marshall Court but prevented institution of a federal criminal common law and maintained New York State's doctrine that contracts were subject to existing insolvency laws. Livingston married three times, and his first two wives bore 11 children.

Dunne, Gerald T. "Brockholst Livingston." In *The Justices of the United States Supreme Court, 1789–1969: Their Lives and Major Opinions*, ed. Leon Friedman and Fred L. Israel, 5 vols (New York: Chelsea House, in association with Bowker, 1969–78)

Donald M. Roper

Livingston, Edward (*b* Clermont [now in Columbia Co], 28 May 1764; *d* Annandale-on-Hudson, Dutchess Co, 23 May 1836). Lawyer and statesman. He was born the youngest of 11 children to Robert R. Livingston, a New York State landowner and judge, and Margaret Beekman. Livingston attended the College of New Jersey (now Princeton University), was admitted to the New York State Bar in 1785, and married Mary McEvers in 1788. As a New York City congressman in the US House of Representatives (1795–1801), he opposed the Jay Treaty, the Quasi-War with France, and the Alien and Sedition Acts. He also supported Thomas Jefferson's presidential nomination during the turbulent election of 1800. After the death of his wife, Livingston became the federal district attorney for New York State and mayor of New York City (1801–3). When more than $40,000 was discovered embezzled from the district attorney's office, Livingston assumed responsibility for the loss. He resigned his public offices and moved to New Orleans. He weathered false accusations of taking part in the Aaron Burr conspiracy, an abortive attempt by the former vice president in 1807 to recruit mercenaries and presumably seize parts of Louisiana Territory and Mexico to form a personal empire. Livingston remarried in 1805 and eventually returned to Washington, DC, as a Louisiana congressman in 1822 and a senator in 1828. He then served in Pres Andrew Jackson's administration, first as secretary of state in 1831 and then as US minister to France in 1833. In May 1835 Livingston moved back to his Hudson River estate, Montgomery Place, where he died the following year.

Hatcher, William B. *Edward Livingston: Jeffersonian Republican and Jacksonian Democrat* (Baton Rouge: Louisiana State Univ Press, 1940)

Thomas H. Cox

Livingston, Philip (*b* Albany, 15 Jan 1716; *d* York, Pa, 12 June 1778). Merchant and politician. Born into a prominent Scottish family, Livingston graduated from Yale College in 1737. He returned to Albany, became a merchant, and prospered supplying the army during King George's War and the French and Indian War. Moving to New York City and becoming active in politics, Livingston served on the Common Council (1754–62) and in the Colonial Assembly (1758), becoming Speaker in 1768, and was a delegate to the Stamp Act Congress (1765) and register in chancery (1768–69). Livingston helped found the New York Society Library (1754), the Chamber of Commerce (1768), and New York Hospital (1771). Despite writing a pamphlet against independence, *The Other Side of the Question* (1774), he was a conservative revolutionary and did sign the Declaration of Independence in 1776 as a member of the Continental Congress (1775–78). He was a member of the state assembly (1776) and senate (1777). Livingston died during a congressional session meeting.

Kierner, Cynthia A. *Traders and Gentlefolk: The Livingstons of New York, 1675–1790* (Ithaca: Cornell Univ Press, 1992)

Mark G. Spencer

Livingston, Robert (*b* Ancrum, Scotland, 13 Dec 1654; *d* Livingston Manor [now in Columbia Co], 1 Oct 1728). Colonial merchant and politician. A member of a Reformed family fleeing persecution in Scotland, Livingston spent much of his childhood in the Netherlands. He immigrated to Albany in 1674, where he used his fluency in Dutch and English as Albany town clerk and secretary to Nicholas van Rensselaer of Rensselaerswijck [now in Albany, Columbia, and Rensselaer Cos]. By 1675 he was also the clerk of the Board of Indian Commissioners. His marriage in 1679 to Alida Schuyler van Rensselaer, the widow of his deceased former employer, provided him with social status and political connections. He amassed 160,000 acres (64,700 ha) of land on the Hudson River, which he named Livingston Manor, and traded in numerous commodities, including furs, rum, and sugar. He led Albany's resistance to Jacob Leisler's 1689 rebellion, largely out of fear that a fanatic and inept administration might strangle commerce. After Leisler's execution in 1691, Livingston entered provincial politics in earnest. He was appointed provincial secretary of Indian affairs (1695), named to the governor's council (1698), elected to the provincial assembly (1709–11, 1715–25), and served as the assembly's speaker (1718–25). Livingston personally traveled to Onondaga after King William's War to reconfirm the Covenant Chain alliance. In 1710 he cooperated with Gov Robert Hunter's plan to resettle Palatine German refugees on Livingston Manor. In 1722 he hosted an intercolonial conference on Indian affairs that attempted to control Iroquois expansion into the Pennsylvania and Virginia frontiers. Livingston retired from public life in 1725. His son Philip assumed much of his role as landowner and politician.

Leder, Lawrence H. *Robert Livingston, 1654–1728, and the Politics of Colonial New York* (Chapel Hill: Univ of North Carolina Press, 1961)

Daniel A. Piazza

Livingston, Robert R(obert), Jr (*b* New York City, 27 Nov 1746; *d* Clermont, Columbia Co, 25 Feb 1813). Lawyer and diplomat. He was the oldest of 11 children of Robert R. Livingston, a colonial lawyer and landowner, and Margaret Beekman. After attending King's College (now Columbia University), Livingston became a lawyer and in 1768 began a partnership with college friend John Jay. In 1770 he married Mary Stevens, the daughter of New Jersey landowner John Stevens. Livingston served as recorder for the City of New York (1773–75), attended the First Continental Congress in 1774, and signed the Articles of Association. He then served in New York's provincial congress and the Second Continental Congress in 1775. While in Philadelphia, Livingston urged caution and abstained from voting for outright independence. Although Congress appointed him to a committee to draft the Declaration of Independence,

Robert R. Livingston. Print by Charles B. J. Févret de Saint-Mémin.

Livingston contributed little to the document's creation. He instead returned to New York and helped create the state's 1777 Constitution, under which he became the state's first chancellor, serving on the Council of Revision and as chief justice of the New York State Court of Equity. Throughout the war, Livingston was a New York State senator, delegate to the Continental Congress, and secretary of foreign affairs for the Confederation government (1781–83). In 1784 Livingston returned to the state legislature, and he was appointed by Congress to settle a boundary dispute between New York and Massachusetts, which was resolved in 1786.

Alarmed at the democratic forces unleashed by the American Revolution, he joined other local elites to support the ratification of the US Constitution in 1788. The following year Livingston administered the presidential oath of office to George Washington in the gallery of Federal Hall in New York City. Dismay at being rejected for a cabinet position and distrust of Federalist economic policies soon led Livingston to identify with the Jeffersonian Republicans. He actively campaigned for George Clinton as governor in 1792, opposed the ratification of the Jay Treaty in 1795, and ran against Jay in an unsuccessful bid for governor in 1798.

Turning briefly away from politics, Livingston and his partners, brother-in-law John Stevens and Nicholas Roosevelt, attempted to build a commercially successful steamboat. In 1798 Livingston secured from the state legislature an exclusive monopoly to operate steamboats on New York State waters. His attempts at steam navigation failed until service as US minister to France (1801–4) took him to Paris, where he met scientist and inventor Robert Fulton. After a scandalous effort to take sole credit for the Louisiana Purchase, Livingston returned to his Hudson River estates, where he published essays on animal husbandry and continued to experiment with steamboats. On 17 Aug 1807 Fulton and Livingston successfully sailed their ship, the *North River Steamboat* (often called *Clermont*), from New York City to Albany. Livingston renewed his New York State monopoly in 1808 and, with the help of his younger brother Edward, secured similar rights in the Territory of New Orleans. The US Supreme Court ruled the New York monopoly unconstitutional in *Gibbons v Ogden* (1824), a decade after Livingston had died of apoplexy.

Brandt, Clare. *An American Aristocracy: The Livingstons* (New York: Doubleday, 1986)
Dangerfield, George. *Chancellor Robert R. Livingston of New York, 1746–1813* (New York: Harcourt, Brace, 1960)

Thomas H. Cox

Livingston, William (*b* Albany, 30 Nov 1723; *d* Elizabethtown, NJ, 25 July 1790.) Lawyer and statesman. A son of Philip Livingston, who was the second lord of Livingston Manor, William graduated from Yale in 1741 and then studied law as an apprentice under James Alexander and William Smith Sr. His practice was moderately successful, and he became a leader of the New York Bar, seeking to elevate standards and improve the quality of the profession. In this he was joined by two fellow Yale graduates and lawyers, William Smith Jr and John Morin Scott. The trio was known as the "Presbyterian triumvirate" and became anathema to Church of England leaders by opposing the plan to create King's College (now Columbia University) as an Anglican institution in 1753–55 and to establish an Anglican bishop in the colonies (1768–69). Livingston fought these battles with his pen, founding New York's first journal, the *Independent Reflector* (1752–53) and writing a series of newspaper essays under the pseudonym "The American Whig" (1768–69). He married Susanna French of New Jersey in 1745. His poem *Philosophic Solitude* (1747) made him colonial New York's principal poet. He moved to New Jersey in 1772, where in 1776 he was elected the first governor of the state and was reelected every year thereafter until his death, serving a total of 14 years.

Dillon, Dorothy R. *The New York Triumvirate: A Study of the Legal and Political Careers of William Livingston, William Smith, Jr., John Morin Scott* (New York: Columbia Univ Press, 1949)
Klein, Milton M. *The American Whig: William Livingston of New York* (New York: Garland Publishing, 1993)
Sedgwick, Theodore, Jr. *A Memoir of the Life of William Livingston* (New York: J & J Harper, 1833)

Milton M. Klein

Livingston County (632 mi²/1,637 km²; pop 64,328). Created in 1821 from Genesee and Ontario Cos and named after Chancellor Robert R. Livingston. Boundary adjustments were made with Steuben (1822), Monroe (1825), Allegany (1846, 1857), and most recently Ontario (1922) Cos. Livingston Co is divided into 17 towns that contain 9 incorporated villages; Geneseo serves as the county seat. Elevations range from 520 feet (159 m) where the Genesee River exits the county to 2,244 feet (684 m) at the Tabor benchmark in the Town of Springwater. Most of Livingston Co is located in the Appalachian Upland landform province. The area east of Canaseraga Creek valley is part of the Finger Lakes Hills subregion; the area to the west lies within the Cattaraugus Hills subregion. The uplands consist of rolling hills, dissected by narrow, steep-sided valleys that trend north-south. Relative relief in the southeast is as much as 900–1,000 feet (274–305 m). The Southern Ontario Plain subregion of the Erie-Ontario Lowland extends across the county's north. It is an undulating surface that varies from 600 to 900 feet (183–274

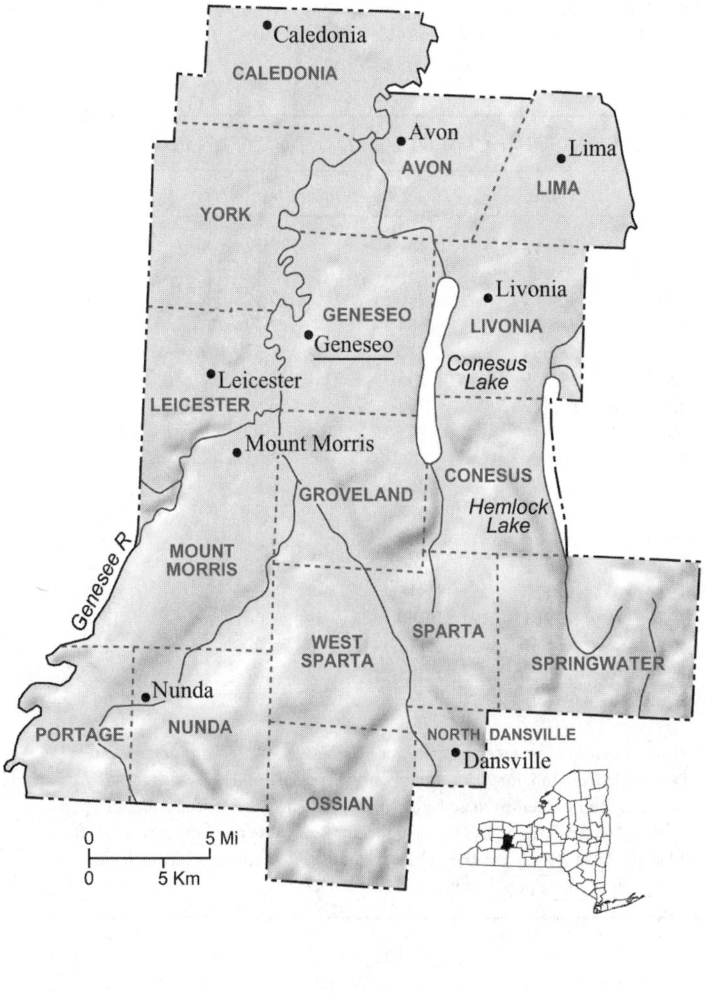

m) in elevation where 50–120 ft (15–37 m) high drumlins provide relief. The Portage Escarpment separates the lowlands from the uplands but is not readily distinguished. Except for a band of limestone and dolostone that transects the county's northern reaches, bedrock consists of sandstone and shale. Aside from some Silurian-aged material in the Town of Caledonia, the bedrock is Devonian. The landscape was smoothed and rounded by continental glaciation, which also filled valleys with unconsolidated materials, diverted water channels including the ancestral Genesee River, and scoured out the valleys containing the westernmost Finger Lakes and Hemlock and Conesus Lakes. Most of the county lies within the Genesee River watershed. The exception is a small area in the southeast, which drains into the Susquehanna River via the Cohocton River. Most of the county's prime agricultural land is concentrated in the north half and in Canaseraga and Keshequa Creek valleys. Moderately fertile soil is found scattered throughout the area south and southeast of Conesus Lake.

Livingston Co's climate is humid-continental. Seasonal temperatures are remarkably consistent at Avon, Mount Morris, and Dansville. All three report mean January temperatures of 24°F (-4°C) and mean July temperatures of 70°F (21°C). Readings are slightly lower in the higher elevations. Occasional below 0°F (-18°C) temperatures are anticipated every winter, while daytime summer highs reach 90°F (32°C) or above at least once every summer. Average annual precipitation amounts range from 30 inches (76 cm) at Mount Morris to about 35 inches (89 cm) in the far northwest. Mean seasonal snowfall amounts vary from 51 inches (130 cm) at Dansville to over 80 inches (203 cm) in the northwest and higher elevations elsewhere. The primeval forest cover was a mosaic of four different communities. Swamp forest of black ash, red maple, sycamore, and hemlock covered the flatland bordering the lower Genesee River and Canaseraga Creek. Substantial stands of Alleghenian hardwoods consisting of mixed stands of beech, sugar maple, hemlock, white pine, basswood, oak, and chestnut covered portions of the south and west, while Central hardwood forests of beech, sugar maple, basswood, and in places oak and chestnut dominated the southeast and northwest. Oak-chestnut forests occupied the margins of the lower Genesee and the Canaseraga Valleys. Letchworth State Park, with its deep gorge dubbed "the Grand Canyon of the East," was carved by the Genesee River in the southwest.

American Indians and Early Settlement

The area that is now Livingston Co was the home of American Indians for many centuries before the arrival of Europeans. Owasco period (*ca* 900–1350) sites have been found in West Sparta. By the 18th century, the Seneca, the Keepers of the Western Door (the westernmost nation of the Iroquois Confederacy) dominated the region. In 1779 the Sullivan-Clinton expedition reached the area. Gen George Washington had sent this military party to break the power of the Iroquois, most of whom supported the British. Monuments in the towns of Leicester and Groveland commemorate Americans killed when the expedition reached the Genesee River region. The Treaty of Big Tree, signed in Geneseo in 1797, removed most of the American Indians to the south and west and hastened the development of the region by European settlers. Nevertheless, no area of the state had more reservations than Livingston Co. Under that treaty, five reservations were established: Canawaugus [now in Caledonia], Squakie Hill, Little Beard's Town, and Big Tree [now in Leicester], and Gardeau [now partly in Mount Morris]. All were relinquished by treaty in 1826.

After the American Revolution, Seneca territory was sold to the Phelps and Gorham Co and its successor, the Pulteney Associates. They, in turn, sold the land in townships to speculators and in farms to settlers, some of whom had first seen the country as soldiers in the Sullivan expedition. Among its largest landowners were brothers James and William Wadsworth, the founders of Geneseo, who purchased thousands of acres of rich Genesee Valley land; they farmed it and leased farms to tenants. Most land, however, was sold in freehold. In consequence, settlement proceeded rapidly, beginning with the territories of the present Towns of Geneseo and Lima in 1788 and most other towns between 1789 and 1795. A projected city, Williamsburg, was begun in what is now Groveland in 1792 but was soon given up. Three towns in the south and southeast, Nunda, Ossian, and Springwater, were the last to be settled, between 1804 and 1807.

The earliest settlers were generally Protestants of English, Scots-Irish, and German ancestry; several groups of Scots immigrated to Caledonia beginning in 1798. Irish Catholics began to settle in the 1830s and 1840s and amounted to just under 10% of the county's population in 1855. Some of the settlers brought enslaved Blacks with them, for slavery was legal in the state until 1827. After the Civil War a community of former slaves from Virginia settled in the Town of Caledonia. Around the turn of the century, there was a large influx of Italian immigrants, especially to Mount Morris, as well as smaller numbers of Slavic people.

LIVINGSTON CO POPULATION CENSUS FIGURES

	White	Nonwhite	Total Population	Foreign-Born
1830	27,595	134	27,729	53
1840	35,000	140	35,140	—
1850	40,666	209	40,875	5,128
1860	39,362	184	39,546	6,232
1870	38,094	215	38,309	5,837
1880	39,269	293	39,562	5,614
1890	37,549	252	37,801	5,397
1900	36,816	243	37,059	4,861
1910	37,674	363	38,037	5,416
1920	36,468	362	36,830	4,264
1930	37,082	478	37,560	3,423
1940	27,970	540	28,510	2,681
1950	39,597	660	40,257	2,136
1960	43,135	918	44,053	1,548
1970	52,791	1,250	54,041	1,296
1980	55,887	1,119	57,006	1,261
1990	60,091	2,281	62,372	1,309
2000	60,494	3,834	64,328	1,668

Notes: "Nonwhite" includes African Americans, Asians, American Indians, and Pacific Islanders and, for 2000, also the mixed race and other race categories. Through the 1960 census these figures primarily reflect the African American population. Foreign-born figures for 1830 include only those not naturalized, and for 1930 and 1950, the foreign-born totals include Whites only. Other years include all foreign-born in the population.

Transportation

The completion of the Erie Canal in 1825 just a few miles north of the county line created economic opportunity for Livingston Co farmers. The Genesee Valley Canal, which joined the Erie Canal at Rochester, reached the southern part of Livingston Co in the early 1840s, allowing goods and commodities to be shipped by water to almost anywhere in the world. The Genesee Valley Canal was never extended to the Allegheny River as originally planned, and it was abandoned in 1878.

The railroads replaced the canal as the principal means of shipping products to market. The first was the Buffalo, Corning, and New York (later Buffalo Division of the Erie), built through the county's eastern towns in 1852–53. The Rochester and Genesee Valley reached Geneseo in 1856. The Erie and Genesee Valley came to Dansville in 1872, as did the Delaware, Lackawanna and Western in 1882, completing the county's four north-south trunk lines.

Livingston Co has always had a road system, some of the earliest following American Indian trails. Rte 5 in the north has been a main east-west thoroughfare since the early 19th century; Alexis de Tocqueville traveled that road during his celebrated visit to America in 1831. Today, most of the county's agricultural and manufactured goods are transported by truck; I-390 opened on a north-south route from Avon to Dansville in 1981.

Economic Development

The importance of wheat farming grew after the opening of the Erie Canal facilitated the ship-

POPULATIONS OF TOWNS, LIVINGSTON CO

Town, Year Founded	1800	1840	1880	1920	1960	2000
Avon, 1797[a]	535	2,999	3,459	3,350	4,404	6,443
Caledonia, 1802[b]	—	1,987	1,927	1,988	3,067	4,567
Conesus, 1821[c]	—	1,654	1,397	814	1,221	2,353
Geneseo, 1791	348	2,892	3,340	3,007	4,337	9,654
Groveland, 1812	—	2,000	1,342	2,920	3,373	3,853
Leicester, 1802[d]	—	2,415	1,679	1,686	1,392	2,287
Lima, 1796[e]	1,060	2,176	2,782	1,890	2,716	4,541
Livonia, 1808	—	2,719	3,119	2,600	3,526	7,286
Mount Morris, 1818	—	4,576	3,931	4,470	4,567	4,567
North Dansville, 1846	—	—	4,178	4,793	6,095	5,738
Nunda, 1808	—	2,637	2,790	2,272	2,309	3,017
Ossian, 1808	—	938	1,204	596	489	751
Portage, 1827	—	4,721	1,295	860	733	859
Sparta, 1796	505	5,841	1,201	833	1,019	1,627
Springwater, 1816	—	2,832	2,279	1,416	1,293	2,322
West Sparta, 1846	—	—	1,157	695	817	1,244
York, 1819	—	3,049	2,482	2,640	2,695	3,219

Notes: In 1800 the Towns of Avon, Geneseo, Lima, and Sparta were in Ontario Co. In 1840 the Towns of Nunda, Ossian, and Portage were in Allegany Co.

[a]Hartford until 1808.

[b]Southampton until 1806.

[c]Freeport until 1825, then Bowersville until later that same year.

[d]Lester until 1805.

[e]Charleston until 1808.

ment of products to the Port of New York and then as far as England. Specialized agriculture included nurseries in North Dansville (1851) and vegetable farming on muckland around South Lima (1870s) and between Mount Morris and Dansville. Dansville was Livingston Co's chief manufacturing village; it had the first paper mill in Western New York (1810) and also produced flour, iron, cloth, leather, and lumber. But smaller communities also produced goods and commodities for sale during the 19th century: brooms in Mount Morris; agricultural tools and machinery in Avon, Caledonia, Livonia, Mount Morris, Springwater, and York; gypsum and woolen cloth in Caledonia; and wooden items in Springwater.

Salt, extracted from deep mines, became an important product of York in 1884 and of Leicester a few years later. In Nunda, caskets (1879–1979) and paving machines (until 1955) were the economy's mainstay. The Mount Morris Knitting Mill (1920s) was important to that village. The Livonia Cement Block Factory operated from 1903 until the 1930s, and porcelain insulators were a Lima product from 1904 until about 1986. At the start of the 20th century, Dansville produced for a short time an automobile with the unfortunate name of Klink. Throughout the 20th century, the Foster Wheeler Energy Corp (1900–2003) manufactured steam-power equipment.

Mineral springs created minor resorts at Avon (1821) and Nunda (1867). The Genesee River Gorge attracted tourists by midcentury when the Cascade House (?1852) was built in Portage, and hotels were built on both Conesus and Hemlock Lakes in 1856. The Genesee Gorge, the county's greatest natural attraction, became a part of Letchworth State Park in 1907. Down the valley from Letchworth, the flood-control Mount Morris Dam (1948–51) removed land from private ownership and public use, but it is normally not inundated.

Religion, Education, and Culture

Several distinctive religious communities have made Livingston Co their home. Mennonites settled in Livonia by 1827, one of three such colonies in New York State prior to World War II. A Shaker community was in Groveland from 1837 to 1894. The Roman Catholic Society of the Divine Word built a seminary (1924–68) on the shores of Conesus Lake. The Abbey of the Genesee (1951), a monastery of the Order of Cistercians of the Strict Observance (Trappist), has become well known for both its spirituality and its production of bread.

The first school was probably opened in Lima in 1792–93, and between 1800 and 1810 schools were in operation in Avon, Caledonia, and Conesus. Genesee Wesleyan Seminary (1830–1941) in Lima was an important educational institution in the 19th century and claimed as former students Belva Ann Lockwood, the first woman to argue before the Supreme Court, and Henry J. Raymond, first editor of the *New York Times*. It was affiliated with Lima's Genesee College (1850–71), which became Syracuse University. SUNY Geneseo is generally recognized as one of the outstanding undergraduate colleges of the system. Opened in 1871 as a teacher training school, it has become a nationally recognized liberal arts college with an enrollment of about 5,000. Other institutions of higher education have used the former Genesee Wesleyan Seminary campus: Genesee Junior College (1947–51) and Elim Bible Institute (1951–). A branch of Genesee Community College operates at Lakeville.

Centralization of schools under state incentives began with Dansville Central School in 1926; Mount Morris was the last to consolidate, in 1952, although a number of common school districts remained independent entities as late as 1958. There are eight public high schools and one parochial high school in the county, but nine school districts outside the county draw students from Livingston Co. Its first newspaper was the *Genesee Farmer* (1817), published at Moscow [now Leicester]. In 2003 the weekly *Genesee Country Express* (1924) is published at Dansville, and the *Livingston County News* and *Lake and Valley Courier* are published at Geneseo. Radio stations broadcast from Genesee, Avon, and Dansville.

The county has been known for several important medical and health establishments. Our Home Hygienic Institute (1858) in Dansville offered a mineral spring "cure" and pioneered innovative exercise and diet regimens. It became the Jackson Sanatorium in 1883 and was taken over by Bernarr Macfadden as the Physical Culture Hotel, finally closing in 1971. Near the close of the 19th century, the state purchased the abandoned Shaker property at Sonyea in Groveland and established Craig Colony (1896–1968), a residential facility for people with epilepsy. Later, the facility was converted to a developmental disability facility, and it is now home to two state correctional facilities. A state tuberculosis hospital was established by Gov Franklin D. Roosevelt at Mount Morris. The impressive buildings of all of these health-related facilities still exist. Dansville was the birthplace of the American Red Cross, founded by Clara Barton in 1881; Chapter No. 1 is still active in the village.

The most famous annual event in Livingston Co is the Genesee Valley Hunt, among the nation's oldest. Fox hunting has been popular in the region since the 19th century, and Theodore Roosevelt enjoyed riding to hounds there. Because of its size and agricultural richness and diversity, Livingston Co has two county fairs, the Hemlock Fair in the southeast and the Caledonia Fair in the northwest. Other annual festivals take place in other towns and villages.

Politics

During and after the Civil War, Mount Morris, Groveland, and Sparta stood against the typical pattern of Republican voting, generally supporting Democratic candidates. Mount Morris has continued to do intermittently and has the greatest percentage of registered Democrats, a legacy of Italian immigration and loyalty. But, overall, Livingston Co is Republican territory.

The county is governed by a Board of Legislators, elected by town and serving also as supervisors. Weighted voting was instituted in 1968; exclusion of student and prisoner populations ended in 2002, resulting in recalculation. In 1984 a Republican-Democratic coalition proposed streamlining government by placing efficient county-level departments in charge of most of the functions of towns and villages. Although this plan was not realized, the coalition initiated the computerizing of county government records and created Economic Development and Solid Waste Departments. In 1989 day-to-day operations were placed in the hands of a county administrator, Dominic Mazza; he remained in office in 2003.

Recent History

The biggest business of Livingston Co is agriculture. It ranks fifth in New York in acres under cultivation and produces wheat, potatoes, and vegetables such as beets and dry beans. However, the principal crops are hay and corn for animal feed, because Livingston is also one of the largest milk-producing counties in New York. Although most agricultural produce is shipped elsewhere for processing in the early 21st century, Seneca Foods operates a plant in the Town of Leicester, and there is a winery in Conesus. Other specialized agriculture includes a beef cattle operation in Ossian, potato growing in Springwater, and horses in and around Avon.

In 1994 part of the Akzo salt mine near Cuylerville collapsed, and salt extraction ended a year later, but American Rock Salt Co (1997) began shipping from a new mine at Hampton Corners in Groveland in 2001; the Genesee and Wyoming Railroad built a new spur to serve it, completed in 2000. Kraft's Cool Whip is manufactured exclusively in Avon. Other industrial employers in 2003 included Allen-Bailey Tag and Label Co, Jones Chemical, and CEN Electronics in Caledonia; CPAC (pollution control equipment) in Leicester; Lakeland Concrete Products and Shawndra Products (industrial filters) in Lima; ADM and Sweeteners Plus in Livonia; and Atofina Chemicals in York. In Nunda small industries such as Nunda Mustard Co and Once Again Nut Butter Co are recent additions. Much of the recent job growth has been in service professions, especially education, healthcare, and law enforcement. Livingston Co's biggest employer at the beginning of the 21st century is SUNY Geneseo. Noyes Memorial Hospital in Dansville and healthcare generally are important to the economy, as are Groveland (1982) and Livingston (1991) Correctional Facilities in Groveland. Many residents commute to Rochester or elsewhere.

The population of Livingston Co has grown slowly. In the 1860 census (the first after the boundaries of the county assumed their present form), Livingston Co had a population of 39,546. Between 1960 and 2000, it increased 46%, to 64,328, but this figure includes students at SUNY Geneseo and inmates at the two large correctional facilities. At the end of the 20th century persons of Latino heritage, primarily Puerto Ricans and Mexicans, began to arrive in the county and were 2.3% of the population in 2000; they are concentrated in Geneseo, Groveland, Mount Morris, and North Dansville. East and South Asians, still under 1% of the population, are living primarily in Geneseo.

Livingston Co has been home to two US presidents, Millard Fillmore, who worked at a mill in what is now West Sparta, and Chester A. Arthur, who lived for several years in York and attended Temple Hill Academy in Geneseo. James W. Wadsworth Jr of Geneseo and Kenneth B. Keating of Lima both represented New York in the US Senate in the 20th century. Sen Wadsworth's son, James Jeremiah Wadsworth, served as ambassador to the United Nations at the end of the second Eisenhower administration. Other prominent natives and residents include Francis Bellamy (1855–1931), author of the Pledge of Allegiance and a native of Mount Morris, as was John Wesley Powell (1834–1902), explorer of the Grand Canyon. Astronaut Col James Adamson of Groveland has made two space flights. Perhaps the most famous athlete to reside in Livingston Co was Vic Raschi, a pitcher for the New York Yankees, the St. Louis Cardinals, and Kansas City Athletics (1946–55).

The standard county histories are James H. Smith, *History of Livingston County* (1881); Lockwood Doty, *History of Livingston County* (1905) and *History of the Genesee Country,* 4 vols (1925); and the contemporary and well-illustrated William R. Cook, *Celebrating Our Past: Livingston County in the 20th Century* (2000). Early town histories include Orson Walbridge, *Early History of the Town of Springwater* (1887); William P. Boyd, *History of the Town of Conesus* (1887); Levi Parson, *Centennial Celebration, Mount Morris* (1894); H. O. Bunnell, *Dansville* (1902); and H. Wells Hand, *Centennial History of the Town of Nunda* (1908; repr 1993). More recently, towns have been documented in Mary R. Root, *History of the Town of York* (1940); Mary Preston, *Avon: Heart of the Genesee Country* (1976); and J. Marilyn Yasso, *History of Retsof* (1987). Daniel Fink's *Barns of the Genesee Country, 1790–1915* (1987), broader in content than its title, is a regional history.

William R. Cook

Livingston family. Influential New York State family in politics and civic affairs during the colonial and Revolutionary War periods. In 1675 Robert Livingston (1654–1728), a Scots Presbyterian whose family had fled to the Netherlands to escape religious persecution, settled in Albany and succeeded in the fur trade. His success was facilitated by his marriage to Alida Schuyler van Rensselaer and by his ties to the town's Dutch elite. Livingston also became a valued adviser to the colony governors. In 1686 Gov Thomas Dongan rewarded his service with a 160,000-acre (64,750 ha) land grant, which became known as Livingston Manor [now in Columbia Co] and included Clermont [now in Columbia Co], the manor seat.

The Livingstons were among the most successful entrepreneurial families in the colony, and the manor was the centerpiece of their family business. The manor lords built saw- and gristmills to process produce for local sale or export. Robert's eldest son, Philip (1686–1749) inherited the manor and erected the colony's first ironworks in Ancram [now in Columbia Co] in 1743. Philip's son Robert (1708–90) became the manor's third proprietor in 1749 and expanded the ironworks significantly. Others in the family were prominent members of New York City's merchant community. Just as the first Robert Livingston exported goods from his store in New York City while Alida oversaw the manor's enterprises, their sons and grandsons acted as commercial agents for later proprietors of the family's landholdings, which were populated mainly by tenant farmers.

During the colonial era the Livingstons were active in politics and civic life. Nine men bearing the Livingston surname sat in the Colonial Assembly, and three served on the governor's council. Those living in New York City were among the founders of the New York Society Library (1754), the New York Chamber of Commerce (1768), and New York Hospital (1771), and they participated in the movement to establish a college in the colony. By the 1760s the Livingstons were emerging as leaders of a coalition of lawyers, landowners, and non-Anglican Protestants, a faction that came to lead New Yorkers' resistance to British imperial authority. The Livingstons were reluctant revolutionaries who accepted both independence and war with Britain as necessary to defend American liberty. Two Livingstons represented New York in the Continental Congress and another was New Jersey's revolutionary governor. New York's first chancellor, Robert R. Livingston of Clermont, also played a leading role in drafting the first state constitution.

After the Revolutionary War, the family's public stature lessened because of their aristocratic antipathy toward competitive popular politics. Only Edward (1764–1836), the chancellor's youngest brother, held important elective offices. The Livingston wealth diminished as grain production moved westward and tenants continually challenged title to the manor. The enfranchisement of all white men made politicians more responsive to the grievances of tenant farmers. In 1846 the state abolished long-term leases, which were gradually converted to fee-simple ownership, thereby effecting the dissolution of Livingston Manor.

Brandt, Claire. *An American Aristocracy: The Livingstons* (Garden City, NY: Doubleday, 1986)
Kierner, Cynthia A. *Traders and Gentlefolk: The Livingstons of New York, 1675–1790* (Ithaca: Cornell Univ Press, 1992)

Cynthia A. Kierner

Livingston Manor. On 22 July 1686 Gov Thomas Dongan created Livingston Manor for merchant Robert Livingston (1654–1728). The tract contained 160,000 acres (64,750 ha) in what is now Columbia Co. By 1707, 10 families settled along Roeliff Jansen Kill in the vicinity of the manor house [now in Clermont, Columbia Co]. Because of imprecise geographical calculations, portions of Livingston's tract fell within the Van Rensselaer domain, thwarting serious settlement plans. Livingston sold 6,000 acres (2,428 ha) at East Camp [now Germantown, Columbia Co] in 1710 to Gov Robert Hunter for a Palatine settlement. In 1715 Hunter reconfirmed the manor boundaries and allowed Livingston an assembly seat and courts. Livingston offered new settlers a variety of rent terms instead of perpetual leases. He granted an average of 84 acres (34 ha), and rents were about 28s annually. Livingston bequeathed more than 140,000 acres (56,700 ha), the manor proper, to his son Philip (1686–1749). Philip remained in Albany but scrupulously managed affairs with assistance of an overseer. He developed Ancram (Columbia Co) in 1741, where he constructed two mills and an iron factory. By 1766 he had 266 tenants and preferred German, Dutch, and Highlander Scot farmers to New England farmers. Another son, Robert (1688–1775), inherited 13,000 acres (5,300 ha), which included the manor house. He hired a clerk to manage affairs and was assemblyman for the manor (1726–27). Around 1730 he built Clermont, a Georgian-style mansion in Clermont, which became his permanent residence in 1743, and his son, Robert R. (1718–75), acquired the property.

Philip bequeathed land to his son Robert (1708–90), who spent years trying to still agitated tenants. Protests began on the east manor in 1751. Rioters were spurred by David Ingersoll of Massachusetts Bay Colony, who claimed Massachusetts owned 26,000 acres (10,500 ha), including part of Claverack [now in Columbia Co]. For years both colonies wrangled over ownership. Fearing an uprising, Livingston arrested and evicted tenants. Protesters, called Taconic Insurgents, attacked Livingston's ironworks, arrested workers, and raided farms, while Livingston loyalists destroyed property and crops.

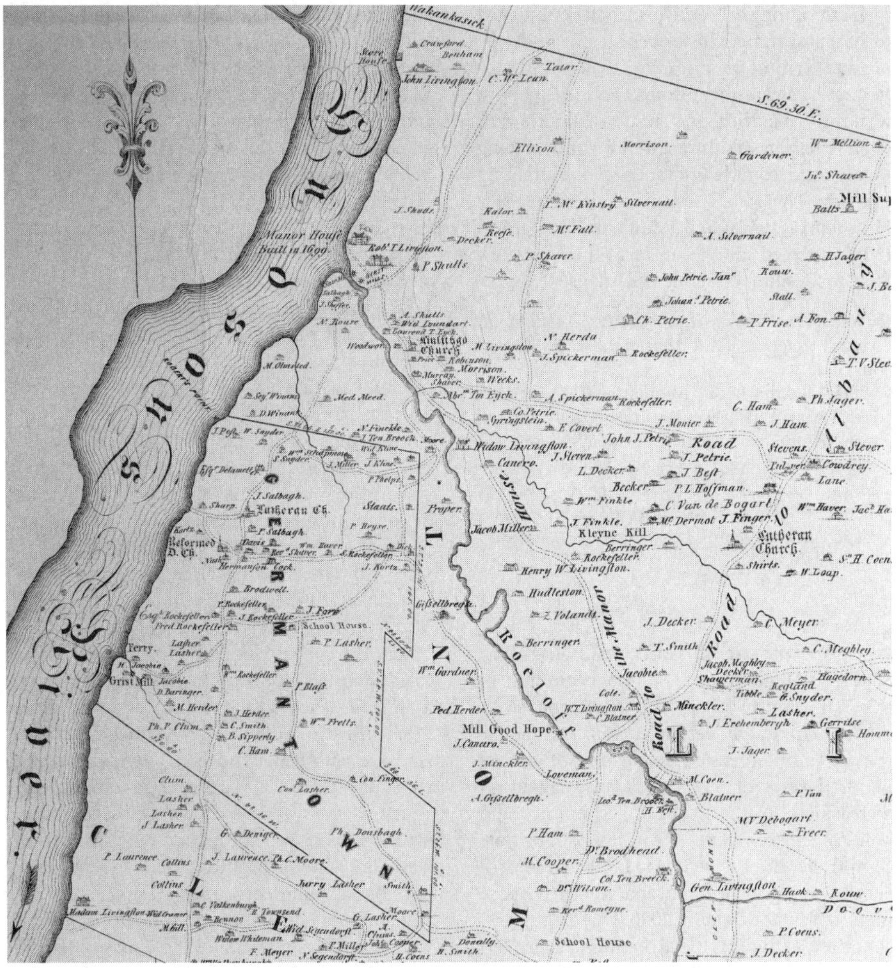

Detail of Livingston Manor in 1798, by John Wigram, 1850.

Raids ended after the Board of Trade interceded in 1757. In June 1766 the same Massachusetts rebels enticed 200 tenants to march to Livingston's house, but the mob met with armed guards and disbanded. Rancor remained intense, and when the Revolutionary War commenced many eastern tenants sided with the British. The British burned the manor house in 1777, but Margaret Beekman Livingston rebuilt it by 1782. Her son, Chancellor Robert R. (1746–1813), inherited the property. Livingston financed Robert Fulton's *North River Steamboat,* often called *Clermont,* the first steam-powered vessel, which sailed in 1807. In 1786 the manor became part of newly formed Columbia Co. To protest the manor system, tenants organized uprisings in 1790, 1811–12, and 1844. In 1846 the manor proper was politically dissolved, but the family retained the manor house. In 1962 heir Alice Livingston willed Clermont to the state. The mansion and grounds were designated a National Historic Landmark in 1972. Clermont was a state historic park and museum in 2003 on 500 acres (202 ha) of land.

See also MANOR SYSTEM.

Kim, Sung Bok. *Landlord and Tenant in Colonial New York: Manorial Society, 1664–1775* (Chapel Hill: Univ of North Carolina Press, 1978)

Tricia A. Barbagallo

Livonia. Town (pop 7,286) and village (pop 1,373) in E Livingston Co. A European American settlement primarily settled by New Englanders, it began in 1789, and the town was formed from Pittstown [now Richmond, Ontario Co] in 1808. A Mennonite society was organized in 1827, and by 1848 Irish immigrants had formed a community as well. Early manufacturing included grain cradles, made from 1843 to 1855 until reapers rendered them archaic. The Erie, the first of several railroads, came through in 1852–53. Lakeville, a resort, is located at the north end of Conesus Lake, and a hotel (1856) and cottages on Hemlock Lake's west shore made it an early popular resort. But the lake came into use as a water supply for Rochester starting in 1872, and by the early 20th century its cottages had been bought out. The Village of Livonia was incorporated in 1882. Livonia Cement Block Factory was an important employer from 1903 to the 1930s. In the late 20th century, employers included Western New York Syrup Corp (1971; now Archer Daniels Midland) and Sweeteners Plus (1983). Increasingly suburban, Livonia's population doubled between 1960 and 2000, and many residents commute to the Rochester area. A center of Genesee Community College is located at Lakeville.

Joyce Rapp

Lloyd. Town (pop 9,941) in SE Ulster Co. Formed in 1845 from New Paltz, the town was served by the West Shore Railroad (1883) and by the Central New England (1889–1983), which crossed the Poughkeepsie Railroad Bridge. Important products included hay, ice, bluestone, bentwood goods, and fruit packages. A bluff along the Hudson River is noted for fruit farming, especially apples and grapes, and in the 1920s currants were a significant crop. Italians came to work the area's farms and orchards in the 1920s. The Mid-Hudson Bridge (1930) crosses the Hudson from the southeast part of town. In the early 21st century the town is mixed residential and agricultural, with concentrated population and business at Highland. It is the site of the Hudson Valley Laboratory of the Cornell University College of Agriculture (1923).

Ruth Piwonka

Lloyd Harbor. Village (pop 3,675) in Huntington (Suffolk Co). The Lloyd family acquired Lloyd Neck in 1676 but did not live there until 1711. Poet Jupiter Hammon was born as a slave in the latter year and died *ca* 1790. In the late 19th century wealthy families established estates on both West and Lloyd Necks. The village was incorporated in 1926. The 1922 estate of Marshall Field III became 1,413-acre (571 ha) Caumsett State Park in 1961. A Nike missile base (1955–63) became the campus of Friends World College (1966–91). Lloyd Neck is also the site of the 80-ac (32 ha) Target Rock National Wildlife Refuge. Other estates have been subdivided for residences, but Lloyd Harbor remains one of the wealthiest communities in the nation. The Henry Lloyd House (1711) and Joseph Lloyd House (1763) are open to the public.

Robert C. Hughes

lobbyists. In the early 1800s the term lobbyist originated as the description of a legislative advocate or person who frequented the state capitol's lobby and hallways in hopes of getting the ear of a senator or member of the assembly. It was nearly a century, however, before the practice was formally regulated. The Armstrong Committee of 1905 required lobbyists to register with the secretary of state, but beyond this registration, there was no regulatory oversight or power to control lobbying.

In 1977, through a combined effort of Gov Hugh Carey and the legislature, the Regulation of Lobbying Act was adopted. This law recognizes that in a functional democracy people and groups have the right to voice their opinions and to seek change from governmental officials and institutions. The first new regulation on state lobbying in 70 years, the act called for full disclosure from special hired interests trying to influence both the legislature and the governor's office. It defines the term lobbyist as every person or organization retained, employed, or designated by any client to engage in lobbying but does not include the lobbying activities of any officer, employee, counsel, or agent of the state or any municipality or subdivision of the state. Although the advocacy efforts of public employees often mirror those of privately paid lobby firms, they are not subject to the same level of public scrutiny under the law.

The 1977 act also required that a temporary state commission monitor and publicly document the identities, activities, and expenditures of those seeking to influence legislation, rules, regulations, and rate-making actions of the government. Commonly known as the New York Temporary State Commission on Lobbying, it consists of six members chosen by the governor and legislative leaders to ensure a bipartisan balance. The executive director, who serves a two-year term, heads the commission and is appointed jointly by the commission's chair and vice chair. The Lobbying Act applies to lobbyists, public corporations, and clients of lobbyists who spend more than $2,000 annually on lobbying activities. Lobbyists working on behalf of not-for-profit organizations, such as the Sierra Club, are subject to the same regulations.

The Lobbying Act was amended in 1999 to expand the definition of lobbying activities to include those at the local level. This section took effect on 1 Apr 2002 and applies to any attempt to influence legislation through a municipality or its subdivisions with more than 50,000 people, including counties, towns, cities, and villages, but excluding school districts. The law also applies to lobbying of public corporations. It prohibits employing a lobbyist with compensation contingent on the outcome of the lobbying effort and bans lobbyists from offering gifts that exceed $75 in value to public officials. State courts have been actively interpreting what constitutes a gift and how the amounts are calculated. Government watchdog groups, such as the New York Public Interest Research Group, assert that lawmakers are routinely offered trips, tickets, transportation, and other perks in excess of $75 by special interests such as trade associations, ideological groups, and unions. However, most of these expenses are not filed as official lobbying expenses and therefore are not included in the lobbyists' reports to the commission.

According to the commission's data for 2002, 1,835 clients represented by 3,332 lobbyists and 48 public corporations spent $92 million on lobbying activities. The continual increase in lobbying expenditures reflects the perception that money spent pursuing public money is worth the rewards. The top three interest groups in 2002 were healthcare ($18 million), trade associations ($10.1 million), and education unions ($8.6 million). While New York State seeks to increase the transparency of lobby activities, critics contend that decision makers and candidates for elected office are still heavily driven by their concern to increase their campaign treasuries.

Matthew J. Lindstrom

local government historians. New York State's 1919 Historian's Law mandated the creation of official historians for each city, town, and village in the state. New York was the first state to create such a network of public historians, but the unsalaried positions attracted relatively little interest, and by the beginning of 1921, only 735 of the possible 1,550 positions had been filled. Their first large task was compiling the local records of World War I. Though most municipal historians have had relatively little renown, their ranks have included Franklin D. Roosevelt, who served as Hyde Park (Dutchess Co) town historian from 1926 to 1932. Borough historians were added for New York City in 1921, and in 1933 the position of county historian was formally recognized. In 1998 the borough president of Manhattan appointed a community historian to serve each of the borough's 12 community districts, the first step toward a more comprehensive inclusion of New York City within the local government historians program. Supervised by the state historian, local government historians are appointed by their jurisdiction's chief executive, such as the city mayor. Their terms run concurrently with their appointing officer. The main tasks assigned to local government historians include researching and writing the history of their communities; acting as a history resource for local schools; working in historical preservation activities such as designation of historical sites; and helping to organize commemorations and promoting tourism. The state's organizations of County Historians (1967) and Municipal Historians (1971) merged in 1999 to form the New York State Association of Public Historians.

Kammen, Carol. *Plain as a Pipestem: Essays about Local History* (Interlaken, NY: Heart of the Lakes Publishing, 1989)

Wellman, Judith. "Local Historians and Their Activities," New York State Museum, Local Government Historians, http://www.nysm.nysed.gov/srvlocal.html

Winslow, Edward J. "Local Historians in New York State," New York State Museum, Local Government Historians, http://www.nysm.nysed.gov/srvlocal.html

Peter Eisenstadt

local government jurisdictions. New York State's local governance at the beginning of the 21st century is not the systematic result of planned, orderly design. It is instead the intricate, multidimensional outcome of several hundred years of institutions adapting to an increasingly complex social, economic, and political environment. According to the state comptroller there were 10,643 local government entities, component units, and special-purpose units in New York State in 2000. This included 57 counties (excluding the five counties in New York City), 62 cities, 932 towns, 554 villages, 705 school districts, 866 fire districts, 810 independent and discrete special-purpose units, 132 county districts, and 6,525 town special districts that employed 1,055,800 (more than half in education). Using different assumptions for counting, thus arriving at different totals, the US Bureau of the Census ranked New York State ninth in number of local governments in 1997. Bureau statistics show the number of local governments in New York State as having declined between 1952 and 1982, reflecting a dramatic reduction in the number of school districts, and rising after 1982 as school consolidation slowed and the number of special districts grew.

New York State has a highly layered local government structure. It is one of only 11 states in which a citizen might live within the jurisdiction of three general-purpose governments (county, town, and village) simultaneously. Most New Yorkers living outside New York City support and are served by two general-purpose local governments (county and town or city) and, except in cities, a separate school district. School district boundaries are often not coterminous with municipalities or other local governments. New York City is the only place in the state with a single general-purpose local government; consolidation in 1898 resulted in the elimination of county, city, town, and village governments within its new boundaries. The four types of general-purpose local governments rely heavily on the property tax for their source revenue and perform multiple functions. Public safety is a priority for most jurisdictions. Highways are important to all and constitute the major expense in rural jurisdictions. Unlike their counterparts in most other states, counties in New York State spend most heavily on social services and healthcare. Counties and towns are top-down entities, originally established by the state at its own initiative over its entire territory to provide the minimal governmental services essential for the functioning of a rural society. Cities and villages are bottom-up entities, chartered by the state in response to local requests to provide the more extensive services required by more densely settled places. Over time, in response to growth and suburbanization, all types of general-purpose local government in New York State came to have similar powers, but few were dissolved or abolished.

School districts and fire districts are supported by property tax. Tolls, fees, or other charges provide most of the support for other special-purpose governments. Created to achieve efficiencies of scale, insulate decision making in key or controversial policy areas from popular or political pressure, and/or provide needed services without increasing the general property tax levy, these entities perform a single function, often within boundaries different than those of general-purpose localities. Examples include toll-supported regional bridge and highway authorities such as the Buffalo and Fort Erie Public Bridge Authority, providing a service across established municipal boundaries, and fee-supported town water and sewer districts, which often serve parts of towns whose users pay for the services provided. Local governments in New York State spent $109.2 billion in 2001 and raised $27.5 billion in property taxes. Other revenue sources were nonproperty taxes (including sales and consumer utility), licenses and fees, and federal and state aid. Although the layering and complexity of local government in New York increases costs and reduces the accountability of elected officials to the citizenry, efforts to reduce the number of local governments have met with little success. Such reform threatens the jobs of local employees and elected officials and creates uncertainty about property values and the quality of local services after the proposed change. Furthermore, citizens identify existing local government structures with their idea of community and resist linkage to places that might be less affluent or more racially and ethnically diverse. Thus reformers have come to advocate consolidating local services as an alternative to restructuring.

Benjamin, Gerald, and Richard Nathan. *Regionalism and Realism: A Study of Governments in the New York Metropolitan Area* (Washington, DC: Brookings Institution Press, 2001)

New York State. Secretary of State. Division of Local Government Services. *Local Government Handbook* (Albany: Office of the Secretary of State, 2001)

Gerald Benjamin

***Lochner v New York,* 198 US 45 (1905).** Landmark US Supreme Court decision overruling an 1895 New York State law limiting the hours of labor in bakeries to 10 hours per day or 60 hours per week.

The Bakeshop Law

The statute was aimed at the state's urban bread-baking industry, which was dominated by small shops committed to laborious hand methods. To cut costs, employers typically located their shops in tenement basements, where conditions were abysmal: ceilings were as low as 5.5 feet (1.7 m);

floors were typically wood or dirt, with sewers running throughout; the inadequately ventilated shops with few windows alternated between stiflingly hot and bitterly cold and provided no outlet to dissipate dust and fumes. Bakers faced arduous work and poor pay, but their major complaint was long hours. Workers were hired and paid by the week or day. Since there was no standard workday, employers usually demanded long hours. By 1895 it was typical for bakers to work 74 hours per week. Some worked as much as 126 hours per week without extra pay.

When the bakeshop law was proposed in 1895, the political atmosphere was not conducive to such legislation. Thomas C. Platt's Republican machine, which dominated both houses of the state legislature, tended to be sympathetic to business interests and opposed to economic regulation. Moreover organized labor, split into three factions, was uncoordinated and weak. The paths of two men coincided to bring about passage of the bakeshop bill. Henry Weismann, an energetic, ambitious, and articulate leader of the Journeymen Bakers' and Confectioners' International Union of America, had made the shorter hours law his organizing principle. Edward Marshall was the Sunday editor of the *New York Press* and a member of the Tenement House Committee of 1894. Commonly called the Gilder Committee, this group of about eight members was organized to study the living and working conditions of the state's urban slums. As a result of his work on the committee, Marshall became a crusader for bakeshop reform. In a series of articles in the *Press,* he exposed the unhealthy conditions and dreadful hours of labor in the industry. More important he linked the bakeshop bill to the tenement reform movement. With prominent and influential mainstream reformers behind it, the measure passed the state assembly by a vote of 120–0. The state senate followed with a vote of 20–0, and on 2 May 1895 Gov Levi P. Morton signed the bill into law.

New York State Court of Appeals

In 1902 bakeshop owner Joseph Lochner of Utica was convicted in Oneida County Court of violating the bakeshop law by "requiring or permitting" one of his employees to work more than 60 hours in one week. The trial court sentenced him to pay a $50 fine or spend 50 days in jail. Lochner appealed to the Appellate Division of the Supreme Court, which upheld his conviction by a vote of 3–2. Arguing that the limitation on the hours of work was an unconstitutional infringement on his liberty, Lochner then took his case to the state's highest court, the New York State Court of Appeals, which voted 4–3 to uphold once again his conviction. Writing the opinion, Chief Judge Alton B. Parker maintained that regulations such as the bakeshop act were legitimate efforts by the state to deal with modern problems. He explained that individual liberty is not absolute and must yield to the general welfare.

In New York State 140 legislators, the governor, and 7 state judges had approved the bakeshop law, with only 5 state judges dissenting. The law's demise would come from the US Supreme Court and, ironically, its former champion, Henry Weismann. In 1897 following a dispute over finances, Weismann was expelled from the bakers' union. He then opened several bakeshops of his own and studied law on the side. Although he was never admitted to the New York State Bar, Weismann took over Lochner's case in 1904. Affiliating with Brooklyn attorney Frank Harvey Field, he successfully appealed the state court's opinion to the US Supreme Court.

US Supreme Court

The Supreme Court's decision to overrule the lower court in *Lochner v New York* came by a vote of 5–4. Justice Rufus Peckham, formerly a judge on the New York Court of Appeals, wrote the majority opinion. Peckham reasoned that the law's limit on working hours violated the liberty of both the employer and employee to enter into contracts of their choosing. The state did not have the authority to interfere with this "liberty of contract," he reasoned, unless in doing so it was exercising its "legitimate police power." The state in this case would need to demonstrate that the law was enacted to protect the health and safety of the public. In Peckham's view the state had failed to do so, and thus the statute was unconstitutional.

In his dissent Justice Oliver Wendell Holmes disagreed with the majority's underlying premise. He argued that the doctrine of liberty of contract is not expressly stated in the Constitution. It was a creation of judicial interpretation of the 14th Amendment guarantee that no state shall deny any person life, liberty, or property without due process of law. For those who agreed with Justice Peckham, the protection of liberty in this amendment included liberty of contract. But Holmes maintained that Peckham was simply using the vagueness of the amendment to attach his own economic views to the Constitution. The majority opinion was based not on the Constitution, he argued, but "upon an economic theory [laissez-faire] which a large part of the country does not entertain."

Scholars have debated whether the Lochner case had any real impact on business regulation by the states, and some believe that the decision reflected long-standing American traditions. Nevertheless the case has come to symbolize the antidemocratic nature of Supreme Court opinions and the abuse of judicial power. Because of the Court's continued use of the theory developed in *Lochner* to overrule state attempts to regulate economics matters, the next several decades of constitutional history became known as the laissez-faire era or the Lochner era. Although *Lochner* was overruled by *West Coast Hotel v Parrish* (1937), it endures as a touchstone in the debate over the power of the Court relative to popular will.

Kens, Paul. *Lochner v New York: Economic Regulation on Trial* (Lawrence: Univ Press of Kansas, 1998)

Paul Kens

Locke. Town (pop 1,900) in SE Cayuga Co. Settled in 1790, the town was formed from Milton [now Genoa] in 1802. Traces of an Iroquois settlement were found just west of Locke hamlet. During the Civil War era, two woolen factories operated. A cider mill and jelly factory was built in 1872 and shipped its products to New York City and Philadelphia markets. The Southern Central Railroad (1870; later Lehigh Valley Railroad) connected Locke to Auburn. In 1975 an oil tanker truck with brake failure careened downhill and started a fire that destroyed 11 buildings in the hamlet. The 857-acre (347 ha) Fillmore Glen State Park is partly in Locke.

Esther Thornton

Lockport. Town (pop 19,653) and city (pop 22,280) in central Niagara Co. Settled in 1805, the town was formed in 1824 from Cambria and Royalton. An 1816 act of the New York State legislature convinced speculators that the Erie Canal would pass through the area that was to become Lockport, and the Holland Land Co began to sell land to both speculators and Quakers. The village site was surveyed and occupied in 1821 and chosen the following year as the county seat. An advertisement appeared in New York City papers in 1821 seeking canal workers for the Lockport section (1821–25) of the Erie Canal, one of the hilliest stretches of the canal. A wave of Irish immigrants looking for work swelled Lockport's population to 2,500 in 1825. On 25 Oct 1825 the Erie Canal officially opened, and

Lockport, by George Catlin, 1825.

the twin flights of locks, from which the village and town were named, were put in service. Lockport was incorporated as a village in 1829.

Excess water from the top of the locks was passed to the bottom through raceways, creating power to run grist- and sawmills, a cotton factory (1833), boot and shoe shops, a tannery, a sash and blind factory, and a furnace and plow factory, all of which were in operation by 1835. The town was served by the Lockport and Niagara Falls Railroad (1836–51), the Rochester, Lockport and Niagara Falls (1852; later New York Central Railroad), and the Buffalo and Lockport (1853). Birdsill Holly, who invented the Holly system for supplying water from a central pumping station, built an industrial complex on the banks of the canal. The state enlarged the canal between 1838 and 1859. Lockport incorporated as a city in 1865. It was the site of the first commercial telegraph company (1845) and the first commercial producer of aluminum (1882). Late 19th-century firms included Merchant's Gargling Oil (1854–95) and Pound Manufacturing Co (1869; steam engines); products included glass (1840), barrel-making machinery (1858), hoisting blocks (1864), saws (1869), mill machinery (1869), pulp paper (1886), limestone, and hydraulic cement, as well as pear trees from Niagara Nurseries (1839).

The final enlargement of the canal at Lockport began in 1908 and ended in 1918. New industries appeared in the 20th century, such as Simonds Saw and Steel and Harrison Radiator (now Delphi-Harrison Thermal Systems). These industries infused new prosperity into the local economy after Holly Manufacturing moved to Buffalo in 1904 following a bitter strike.

In the early 21st century, Delphi-Harrison Thermal Systems (1910; now a General Motors subsidiary) employs 6,500 workers. Lockport's workforce is a relatively high 21% in manufacturing. Other large employers are Sherwood (500 workers; valves), Cadillac Rubber and Plastic (200; plastic injection moldings), Pivot Punch (150), Metal Cladding (100), Great Lakes Container (100; corrugated cartons), and Diversified Manufacturing (100; precise machining). Tourism and service industries are expanding. The Erie Canal locks and Holly's raceway tunnel (accessible through Lockport Cave Raceway Tour) are attractions, as are Captain Murphy's excursions on the canal and through the locks. NASA astronaut Lt Col William Gregory (1957–) is a Lockport native, as was businessman and politician John J. Raskob (1879–1950). The Niagara County Fairgrounds are in Lockport; the Kenan Center (1967) is a regional arts facility; and an apple festival is held in October. The population of the city remained relatively stable in the second half of the 20th century, but the town has undergone considerable suburbanization, changing the ratio between the respective populations from 6:1 in 1950 to 1.2:1 in 2000.

Bruce D. Fredrickson

Lockwood [née Bennett], **Belva Ann** (*b* Royalton, Niagara Co, 24 Oct 1830; *d* Washington, DC, 19 May 1917). Educator, attorney, and social activist. Her early years were spent on her parents' farm in Royalton. She became a teacher at age 15. In 1884 she married Uriah H. McNall, a local farmer. At his death six years later she returned to teaching, but, discovering her pay was half that of male teachers, she quit to attend Genesee College in Lima (Livingston Co). After graduating in 1857 she became principal of the McNall Seminary in Oswego. She became increasingly involved in women's issues, especially suffrage, and following the Civil War she moved to Washington, DC, where she studied at National University Law School. In 1868 she married the dentist Ezekiel Lockwood. Their home became a national hub for feminist activity. Lockwood received her law degree in 1873, becoming one of the first women admitted to the bar in the United States. In 1879 she became the first woman to plead a case before the US Supreme Court. Lockwood headed the National Equal Rights Party's presidential ticket in 1884 and 1888, and was involved in the peace movement, serving as US delegate to the 1889 Universal Peace Congress in Paris. She helped author the legislation that secured woman suffrage in Oklahoma, Arizona, and New Mexico in 1903, and represented the Cherokee Nation in a successful lawsuit against the United States in 1906.

Norgren, Jill. "Before It Was Merely Difficult: Belva Lockwood's Life in Law and Politics," *Journal of Supreme Court History* 23 (1999): 16–42

Winner, Julia Hull. "Belva A. Lockwood—That Extraordinary Woman," *New York History* 39 (1958): 321–40

Matthew Taylor Raffety

Locofocos. Also known as the Equal Rights Party, this segment of New York City's Democratic Party coalesced in 1835 as Pres Andrew Jackson's battle against the Second Bank of the United States spilled into state legislatures. At issue was the continued restriction of banking to those who obtained individual legislative charters, a process opponents believed was rife with corruption. After Democratic legislators reneged on an 1834 campaign promise to oppose such charters, a faction with roots in the Working Men's Party (1829–31) and inspired by *New York Evening Post* editor William Leggett and former "Workie" Alexander Ming Jr sought to commit the city's Tammany Hall–controlled Democratic Party to support antimonopoly measures, including a general incorporation law for banking. On 29 Oct 1835 Democrats gathered at Tammany Hall to make legislative nominations. After the regular organization pushed through its slate, the Equal Rights faction seized the platform to nominate its own. At that moment, the gas supplying the hall's lighting was cut off and the room went dark. Anticipating the familiar Tammany tactic, several members produced the new friction matches, called locofocos, to light candles, thereby illuminating the hall and allowing them to proceed.

Although the Equal Rights Party ticket failed in November, it polled strongly, establishing the Locofocos, as they were subsequently called by Democratic and Whig opponents, as a significant political threat. Two of its members were elected to the state assembly in 1836. Unable to gain support for their own legislation in the state legislature, Locofocos gave the Whig-sponsored Free Banking Act of 1838 mixed reviews; while the act put an end to individual legislative bank charters, it also created requirements enabling only the very wealthy to operate banks. By the end of the 1830s, the Equal Rights Party had faded away as a number of its members saw Pres Martin Van Buren's embrace of the Independent Treasury plan as acceptance of their antimonopoly banking principles. Many Locofocos later supported Van Buren's unsuccessful bid for the Democratic presidential nomination in 1844. Though the group had disbanded, Whig publicists continued into the 1840s to use "Locofocos" to describe Democrats as dangerous radicals.

Byrdsall, Fitzwilliam. *The History of the Loco-Foco or Equal Rights Party* (1842; repr New York: Burt Franklin, 1967)

Spann, Edward K. *Ideals and Politics: New York Intellectuals and Liberal Democracy, 1820–1880* (Albany: SUNY Press, 1972)

Robert D. Sampson

Locomotive 999. Probably America's best-known steam engine. In 1892 George H. Daniels, passenger agent for New York Central and Hudson River Railroad (NYC&HRRR), proposed construction of a high-speed locomotive to pull the company's premier train, Empire State Express, at the Columbian Exposition of 1893 in Chicago. NYC&HRRR's William Buchanan designed the new engine with the wheel configuration of a standard American locomotive—four leading wheels, four driving wheels, and no trailing wheels—but employed enormous driving wheels (86 in/218 cm) . Completed at the West Albany shops in April 1893, the locomotive was capable of high speeds with limited tractive effort. On 9 May 1893 Locomotive 999, whose number was chosen for dramatic impact, drew Empire State Express at 102 mph (164.2 kph) west of Batavia (Genesee Co). The next day engineer Charles Hogan drove the locomotive to a still debated world record speed of 112.5 mph (181.05 kph). Star attraction of the Columbian Exposition, the speeding engine captured the public imagination as an embodiment of American power and mechanical genius. Unsuited for reliable starting and acceleration, 999's tall driving wheels were replaced by 70 in (178 cm) ones after assignment out of Syracuse in 1899, and the engine then took over branchline, local, and milk runs. In 1906 the Oswego shops removed 999's wagon-top boiler, and in 1913 it was renumbered 1086. The locomotive barely escaped scrapping following the end of regular service in 1921. Beginning in 1923 it appeared, often under its own steam, at celebrations including the 1939 World's Fair in New York City and the 1948 Chicago Railroad Fair. Donated to the Chicago Museum of Science and Industry in 1962, the engine was recently restored to its mid-1920s appearance.

Stauffer, Alvin F. *New York Central's Early Power* (Carrollton, Ohio: Author, 1967)

David R. Gould

Lodi. Town (pop 1,476) and village (pop 338) in SW Seneca Co. Settled in 1789, the town was formed from Covert in 1826. Fossenvue (1875–1900) was a lakeside summer cultural colony. Queen's Castle (1899) was built as a birthday gift to its founder, suffragist Elizabeth Smith Miller, and is now owned by the Finger Lakes National Forest, which is in part in Lodi. The town was served by the Seneca Lake line of the Lehigh Valley Railroad (1892). In the late 19th century its orchards were extensive, and fruit baskets were manufactured for shipment. The Lodi Historical Society houses the state's oldest E. and G. G. Hook pipe organ (1852).

Summer cottages dot the shore of Seneca Lake. In 2003 there were six wineries, and grain was raised for dairy cattle feed.

Lisa Compton

Loening, Grover Cleveland (*b* Bremen, Germany, 12 Sept 1888; *d* Miami, Fla, 29 Feb 1976). Aeronautic engineer. Born during his father's service abroad as US consul, Loening attended schools in and around New York City. He attended Columbia University, where he founded Columbia's Aero Club and received in 1910 the nation's first master's in aeronautics. The same year Loening joined Queen Aeroplane Co in New York City, and engineered water flyers, in which he made his first flight in 1912. He continued work on flying boats with the Wright Co in 1913. As Signal Corps aeronautical engineer for the US Army's Aviation Section at San Diego (1914), Loening condemned the army's unsafe Wright and Curtiss "pushers," biplanes with stern propellers, forcing American makers to adopt European designs. Loening's engineering division became permanent, and his published lectures became official texts for the US and British military. Leaving the army to organize Sturtevant Aeroplane Co in Boston in 1915, he developed the nation's first all-steel airplane. Two years later he founded Loening Aeronautical Engineering Corp in Long Island City (Queens Co), soon transferring operations to East 31st St in Manhattan; the company produced seaplanes for northeastern airlines, Arctic exploration, military use, and sport. Loening sold his firm to Keystone in 1928, and a year later, it became Keystone-Loening Division of Curtiss-Wright. His Grover Loening Aircraft Co, established in Garden City (Nassau Co) in 1929, built research aircraft and provided consulting to other manufacturers, including Grumman and Curtiss-Wright, as well as to securities companies with aviation interests. During the 1930s Loening also served as a director of Pan American World Airways, headquartered in Manhattan. Loening closed his company in 1936 on becoming aviation advisor to the US Maritime Commission. During World War II he held similar positions with the War Production Board and National Advisory Council on Aeronautics. Following the war, he helped design the heliport atop the Pan Am Building (now MetLife Building) in Manhattan. An important figure in establishing engineering rigor, Loening was the recipient of numerous awards.

Loening, Grover Cleveland. *Takeoff into Greatness: How American Aviation Grew So Big So Fast* (New York: Putnam's, 1968)

Kirk W. House

log drives. Transporting single softwood logs to market by water, or log driving, was begun in the Adirondacks by Alanson and Norman Fox on the Schroon River branch of the upper Hudson River in 1813. Before this, logs had been banded together in rafts for transport on larger lakes and rivers. In 1806 New York State legislation was passed to regulate rafting of logs on state rivers, which had begun in the 1780s outside the Adirondacks. Logs were usually cut in fall and winter, then skidded to frozen ponds or stream banks to await the spring thaw. Dams made of logs and rock-filled cribs captured heads of water for holding ponds, which would create pressure to push logs downstream once released. Head and tail booms, a series of logs chained or roped together, held the timber. Logs were branded and sorted according to their destination mills. Depending on weather and volume, logs traveled approximately 2 mph (3 kph), and most of the wood went through in a matter of days, but marooned logs could take years to reach their destinations.

Cutting and transporting timber was big business in the Adirondacks, Catskills, and headwaters of the Susquehanna and Allegheny Rivers between 1850 and 1950. Driving costs varied according to seasonal conditions, volume of logs, and wage rates. The season would last approximately two months, and on average 50–60 men would work a drive. As more operators moved into the Adirondack woods, first cooperative and then partnership drives, begun in 1862 and governed by contract, managed the drives. The Hudson River Boom Association, which managed the major partnership, built the Big Boom at Glens Falls (Warren Co) between 1849 and 1851, corralling millions of logs.

Log driving was dangerous, demanding workers who were agile, reckless, and fearless. Drivers kept logs moving downstream, prevented logjams, and broke up any by hand or with dynamite. Risks included injury, death, illness, exhaustion, and premature crippling by muscular rheumatism. French Canadians predominated among log drivers. Like western cattlemen, log drivers were a special breed who inspired legend and lore chronicled in ballads, songs, and obituaries. Three-man crews operated large, sturdy riverboats called bateaux or jamboats. They worked seven days a week in icy water or along the shore, from before dawn until after dark, sleeping at campsites on the way. Their tools were a 5 ft (1.5 m) ironwood peavey (cant hook) for gripping and turning logs and a 12 ft (3.7 m) black spruce or ash pike pole capped with an iron screw spike or hook. They wore felt hats, calked (studded) boots to prevent slipping, red and black Mackinaw shirts, and pants stagged (cut off) at the calf. Log drivers were fueled by four meals a day totaling 7,000 calories. Great rivalries developed as crews vied to complete the drives, and rivermen were notorious for holding drunken celebrations after the drives. By 1940, 11 companies operating on the Hudson River had driven more than 1 billion board feet of timber. By 1950 log driving was becoming obsolete as railroads and trucks became more cost effective.

Fox, William Freeman. *History of the Lumber Industry in the State of New York* (1901; repr Harrison, NY: Harbor Hill Books, 1976)

Hochschild, Harold K. *Lumberjacks and Rivermen in the Central Adirondacks, 1850–1950* (Blue Mountain Lake, NY: Adirondack Museum, 1962)

Welsh, Peter C. *Jacks, Jobbers, and Kings: Logging the Adirondacks, 1850–1950* (Utica: North Country Books, 1996)

Caroline M. Welsh

logging and lumbering. The forested lands of New York State attracted the attention of colonists during the 17th century. White pines growing along the Hudson River valley and the shores of Lake Champlain provided good stock for ship masts, becoming an important economic commodity. For over 200 years they were harvested and floated to shipyards and mills. Whole and sawn logs were tied together to form large rafts, some measuring 48 ft x 160 ft (15 m x 49 m) and containing close to 180,000 board feet of lumber. When this supply was depleted in the mid–19th century, lumberjacks logged in the forests north of Albany, where rapids and falls on the Hudson River and its tributaries made transportation more difficult. Sawmills were established in the North Country at many settlements as part of the initial land-clearing process. The first sawmill at Wing's Falls [now Glens Falls, Warren Co] began operating in 1765. Significant logging operations in the Adirondacks began in 1813, when Norman and Alanson Fox of Brant Lake (Warren Co) floated individual logs down

Logjam on the Hudson River above Fort Edward, 1913.

Logging sleds of the Streever Lumber Co, Ballston Spa, *ca* 1915.

the Schroon River to the Hudson and then to mills at Glens Falls; others quickly followed their lead. In 1820 Saratoga Co reported 27,700 pine logs sawed, and Clinton Co recorded 38,100. Much of the lumber cut at these early mills was used locally, but the abundant forests promised lucrative rewards for those who could get logs to larger markets in industrial towns and cities.

Among lumber towns that developed in the state during the 19th century were Wanakena (St. Lawrence Co), Boonville (Oneida Co), and Jamestown, Carroll, Forestville, and Poland (Chautauqua Co). After 1900 many logging camps developed into lumber towns. The Emporium Lumber Co purchased a sawmill and camp at Conifer (St. Lawrence Co) in 1910 that grew into a settled community.

By 1850 logging had penetrated to the center of the Adirondacks, and New York State ranked first in the nation in lumber cut. Around the same time entrepreneurial lumbermen began purchasing large tracts of timberland in the northern counties and hiring men to cut and transport logs to mills. Logging in Township 34, the Blue Mountain Lake region in the central Adirondacks, began around 1849 and continued until 1906. Jones Ordway, the owner of the land, established large-scale lumbering operations in the area in 1854; 20 years later, his Morgan Lumber Co owned 5 mills and employed around 200 men. The company continued to grow after Ordway's death in 1890 and was incorporated as International Paper Co in 1898, owning over 60,000 acres (24,000 ha) of timberland. Other lumber companies, such as Finch Pruyn and Co of Glens Falls, were harvesting well over 100,000 logs per year and hiring hundreds of men. However, production in the upper Hudson region had already peaked in 1872 at 213.8 million board feet and declined thereafter because of overharvesting. The destruction of forests concerned many in the state, including sports enthusiasts and the affluent owners of private camps and resorts. Through their lobbying and the geographic surveys of Verplanck Colvin and others, the state legislature established the Adirondack Forest Preserve in 1885 to repurchase and protect lands in the Adirondacks. Thereafter the lumber industry was sharply curtailed in New York State, declining from over 1.3 billion board feet sawed in 1869 to under 200 million (including timber harvested out of state) in 1928. By 1930 the state ranked 23d in the nation in lumber manufacturing. In the mid-1930s, new demand for hardwoods stimulated the development of logging around the headwaters of the Hudson River.

Lumberjacks were generally single men who developed reputations for rowdiness and heavy drinking. Their lives were filled with hard work and danger. Before the automobile, they lived in camps consisting of a few rough log structures near timber stands. Up to 40 men slept and dined together in one poorly ventilated and usually insect-infested building. Lumberjacks became legendary for folk music, tall tales, and the vast amounts of food they consumed. Logging activities were regulated by the seasons. Hemlock bark for tanneries was harvested in summer, but most activity began in autumn, when lumber and pulpwood trees were cut. The New York State Lumberjacks Association, organized in the early 1970s, preserves and promotes traditional lumber harvesting skills at state and national athletic competitions.

Mechanization eliminated many logging jobs throughout the 20th century, and concerns over environmental protection have led to close regulation, but in the 21st century logging is thriving. Lumber and wood products businesses can be found in Chautauqua, Erie, and numerous other counties. In 1999 the state had 250 fixed-location sawmills and at least 1,300 seasonal or limited portable sawmills producing a total of about 189 million ft^3 (5.4 million m^3) of roundwoods including sawlogs and hardwoods, the highest reported levels since the early 1900s. At the turn of the 21st century the lumber industry employs 52,000 workers in New York State and contributes approximately $4 billion annually to the economy.

See also ADIRONDACKS; BINGHAMTON; CATSKILLS; ENVIRONMENTAL LAW; ENVIRONMENTALISM; FORESTRY; SUSQUEHANNA RIVER.

Hochschild, Harold K. *Lumberjacks and Rivermen in the Central Adirondacks, 1850–1950* (Blue Mountain Lake, NY: Adirondack Museum, 1962)
McMartin, Barbara. *The Great Forests of the Adirondacks* (Utica: North Country Books, 1994)
Welsh, Peter C. *Jacks, Jobbers, and Kings: Logging the Adirondacks, 1850–1950* (Utica: North Country Books, 1995)

Douglas McCombs

logging railroads. Lines operated solely to haul forest products to mills and to return supplies into the woods. While some conifer logs were rafted down major rivers into the 20th century, floating hardwood logs was problematic. Logging railroads enabled easy transport of both hardwood and conifer logs. Some of the first lines of the late 1860s used wooden rails and horse power. In the Adirondacks, some 30 steam-powered, iron-railed lines developed in the 1880s and 1890s following the establishment of the New York Central and Delaware and Hudson trunk lines. Not all 30 operated simultaneously. By the 1930s many lumber and paper companies had closed. The last Adirondack logging railroad, Grasse River, shut down in 1957. Although there were few logging railroads in other parts of the state, notable ones were the Fenwick Lumber Co in the Catskills and Glenfield and Western and Williamstown and Redfield, two Tug Hill companies. In 2000 the Adirondacks continued to ship pulp to paper mills but via highways.

Allen, Richard S., et al. *Rails in the North Woods: Histories of 10 Adirondack Short Lines,* 2d ed. (Utica: North Country Books, 1999)

Michael Kudish

Loguen, Jermain Wesley [Logue, Jarm] (*b* ?1813, Davidson Co, Tenn; *d* Saratoga Springs, 30 Sept 1872). Abolitionist and minister. Born Jarm Logue, likely the child of an involuntary liaison between his slave mother and her master, he escaped slavery sometime around 1834. He made his way to St. Catharines [now in Ont], moving in 1837 to Rochester, where he worked as a waiter. After learning to read at age 23, from 1839 to 1841 he studied at the interracial, abolitionist-inspired Oneida Institute in Whitesboro, starting a school for black children in nearby Utica in 1841. He became a licensed deacon in 1843 at the African Methodist Episcopal Zion (AMEZ) Church, adopting the better-known form of his name around this time. He would serve AME Zion churches in Bath (1844–46), Ithaca (1846), Syracuse (1846–48, 1851–55, 1858–62; 1864–66), Troy (1848–50), and Binghamton; he also served in Montrose, Pa (1862–64). He was in Troy when the Fugitive Slave Act of 1850 was enacted but returned to Syracuse, feeling that the city would be safer for a prominent fugitive, and became a visible leader in the fight against the act. He helped as many as 1,500 fugitive slaves to freedom and took a leading role in the Jerry Rescue in Syracuse in 1851. Indicted for his participation in November, he escaped to Canada, returning to the United States the following year, and was never tried. Loguen was a strong advocate for woman suffrage and supported John Brown's secret plans for fomenting a slave rebellion. In 1859 he published his autobiography, *The Rev. J. W. Loguen as a Slave and as a Freeman.* In 1868 he was elected both as AMEZ bishop and as president of the State Convention of Colored People meeting in Utica. He was reelected bishop in 1872 but resigned because of ill health and died shortly thereafter.

Hunter, Carol M. *To Set the Captives Free: Reverend Jermain Wesley Loguen and the Struggle for Freedom in Central New York, 1835–1872* (New York: Garland, 1993)

Sernett, Milton C. " 'A Citizen of No Mean City': Jermain W. Loguen and the Antislavery Reputation of Syracuse," *Syracuse University Library Associates Courier* 22 (Fall 1987): 33–53

Peter Eisenstadt

Long Beach. City (pop 35,462) in SW Nassau Co. The first residents of this barrier beach came in 1849 to staff a lifesaving station. Austin Corbin built his New York and Long Beach Railroad in 1880 to provide access; he also constructed the huge Long Beach Hotel, but this soon failed. In 1907 the Town of Hempstead sold the area to the flamboyant former state senator William H. Reynolds, the builder of Dreamland in Coney Island, and development began in earnest. Millions of cubic yards of sand were pumped in to add land area. Reynolds built a boardwalk and sold lots restricted to white Protestant ownership and modest Mediterranean-style houses; he called it the "Riviera of the East." Reynolds also went bankrupt in 1918. Nevertheless Long Beach incorporated as a village in 1918 and as a city in 1922, with Reynolds its first mayor. Its large hotels made it a major summer resort, and the city developed a reputation for free living, rumrunning, and corruption during Prohibition. By the 1960s its appeal as a resort was fading, and decisions to house deinstitutionalized mental health patients and the homeless in some of the former hotels continued the city's deterioration. In the early 1980s pressure was brought by local residents to restore the oceanfront, and the turnaround has been significant. In 2000, 13% of residents were of Latino ethnicity; racially, 6% of residents were black. Actor Billy Crystal (1947–) grew up in Long Beach and lived there until 1976. The Granada Towers (1929) condominiums are on the National Register of Historic Places.

Richard A. Winsche

Longhouse religion. See IROQUOIS GOVERNMENT AND RELIGION.

Long Island. At 1,374 mi^2 (3,558 km^2) it is the largest island adjoining the continental United States and is 118 miles (190 km) long and 24 miles (39 km) at its widest. It is home to Kings, Queens, Nassau, and Suffolk Cos, with a combined population at the 2000 census of 7,439,618 (39% of the state's population). But in speaking of Long Island one must separate the physical from the cultural and political geography. Since 1898 Kings and Queens Cos, as the Boroughs of Brooklyn and Queens respectively, have been part of New York City. The eastern portion of Queens Co, which did not join the consolidated city, formed Nassau Co in 1899. Since then the two eastern and two western counties have developed different identities. Queens and Brooklyn have increasingly been pulled into the orbit of New York City and in 2000 accounted for 59% of the city's population. The two eastern counties have developed their own distinctiveness. When people speak of "the island" today, they are invariably referring to Nassau and Suffolk. Yet the separation between "the city" and "the island" on Long Island has been gradual and never complete. Many Brooklyn and Queens institutions still bear the name of Long Island. Five daily newspapers published in the two boroughs in the 20th century carried the name Long Island in their mastheads. Long Island University was founded in Brooklyn in 1926, and the Long Island Rail Road (LIRR) and Long Island Expressway run the length of the island. Long Island is a place of great contrasts, containing much of the largest city in the United States, one of the nation's largest suburban areas, and an agricultural East End.

EARLY HISTORY

The present Nassau and Suffolk Cos remained rural for the first 270 years of European settlement. Self-governing Puritan pioneers passed on a propensity for independence, along with their skill in farming, fishing, and navigation, to future generations. The Hempstead Plains and Montauk Downs, America's first prairies, served as range for livestock well into the mid–19th century. Antebellum industries were limited to shipbuilding and whaling, which during their brief but spectacular heyday fostered ancillary activity in sail making, nautical stores, and repairs. Before the time of improved roads, transportation was mainly by boat, a method that came naturally to residents of an island endowed with accessible harbors along its 1,180 miles (1,899 km) of shoreline. The LIRR, completed in 1844, ran inland because its original purpose was to link New York City and Boston, not to serve the island's populated north and south shores. Competing railroads were built along the shores and, by the 1880s, consolidated into the LIRR. The extension to Montauk (1895) added impetus to the already significant reputation of the Hamptons as a summer resort. Increasing numbers found the island an ideal venue for all sorts of recreation, including boating, fishing, swimming, golf, tennis, and hiking. Some German, Irish, and Dutch migration occurred in the 19th century, but the population remained primarily English and Scottish, with some African Americans and a declining number of Indians. Beginning in the 1880s, Long Island became the site of hundreds of mansions on its Gold Coast estates on Long Island Sound and around Islip.

In western Long Island, Brooklyn, settled about 1635, grew from a rural town to a small city and suburb of New York City in the early 19th century and by midcentury was one of the largest cities in the United States. In 1890, with a

Long Island Farmhouses, by William Sidney Mount, 1862–63.

population of 806,343, it was the third largest city in the United States and had in the process incorporated most of Kings Co. There was also a more gradual but distinct urbanization of the western towns and cities of Queens Co. As late as 1850, a majority of the county's population lived in the three eastern towns (Hempstead, North Hempstead, and Oyster Bay) that would later be part of Nassau Co. By 1890 two-thirds of the residents lived in the western portion of the county that became part of New York City in 1898.

Consolidation and Suburbanization

The consolidation of Greater New York City in 1898 was the political confirmation of the growing connections between western Long Island and New York City that had been ongoing for years. In many ways the most dramatic sign of these links was the completion of the Brooklyn Bridge in 1883, the first permanent connection between Long Island and Manhattan Island. By 1920 four additional bridges across the East River had been built. The first trolley tunnel under the river was completed in 1892. In 1908 the first of many subway tunnels under the East River was opened. Especially significant for the suburbanization of Long Island was the opening of the Queensboro Bridge in 1909 and the completion of an East River tunnel of the LIRR in 1910. One could now live in the country and work in Manhattan with no need for a ferry crossing.

The coming of the automobile age, combined with the many parkways, bridges, and tunnels built by Robert Moses, increased the flow of traffic in and out of the city, just as his parks and beaches enhanced the well-established quality of Long Island as a resort. For all their wealth and power, the Gold Coast estate owners failed to prevent the surge of suburban growth. The great influx of middle-class commuters turned into a post–World War II population explosion, sparked by the guaranteed, low-rate mortgages that the GI Bill extended to veterans and their growing families. Farms turned into mass-market housing tracts, typified by Levittown's more than 17,400 low-cost homes in the late 1940s and 1950s. This dramatic expansion created a corresponding demand for schools, churches and temples, libraries, hospitals, malls, and places of employment.

The aviation industry flourished in Nassau and Suffolk Cos, from experimental flights to the manufacture of planes by Glenn Curtiss and others to Charles Lindbergh's solo nonstop trip from Roosevelt Field to Paris in 1927. Queens Co became the home of the area's two major airports, La Guardia and John F. Kennedy International. Heavy industry, hitherto concentrated in Kings and Queens Cos, finally came to Nassau and Suffolk Cos as war clouds gathered in Europe: Grumman, Republic, Sperry Gyroscope, and many other firms ensured American preeminence in waging war and exploring space.

Recent Trends

In the second half of the 20th century Nassau and Suffolk Cos increased in population from 948,894 to 2,753,913, becoming the two most populated counties in the state outside of New York City. In the process they evolved from a suburban backdoor to the city to a postsuburban society, distinct from New York City and with their own economy and culture. By 1970 the two counties (with the exception of the East End) were densely packed and crisscrossed by parkways and limited-access highways. Housing developments interspersed with light-industrial parks, campuslike office complexes, medical centers, educational institutions, shopping malls, outlet stores, and corporations such as Computer Associates International, Symbol Technologies, and Cablevision System Corp. From 1970 onward at least four of every five employed residents of Nassau and Suffolk Cos have worked in these counties. In 2000, 278,000 workers commuted into New York City, while 992,000 worked in Nassau and Suffolk Cos.

With the dramatic population increase in these counties, there were also changes in its racial and ethnic composition. In 1957 the Diocese of Rockville Centre (Nassau Co) was established, a sign of the region's growing Catholic population. In the early 21st century, slightly more than half of the population of the two counties profess Roman Catholicism, and 1 in 10 is Jewish. The largest single ethnic group is Italian (27%), followed by Irish (22%) and German (20%). Of the minority population in 2000 (18%, up from 3% in 1950), 8.5% were black and 2.4% Asian. Latinos were 10% of the population. In 2000 Queens was 44% white, 20% black, and 17% Asian, with those of Latino ethnicity at 25%; Brooklyn was 41% white, 36% black, 8% Asian, and 20% of Latino ethnicity. For the four counties of Long Island, Whites make up 58% of its population.

Politics

There is no political entity called Long Island. The Boroughs of Queens and Brooklyn firmly operate as part of New York City. Nassau and Suffolk Cos share problems of overdevelopment, road congestion, pollution, high rates of AIDS and breast cancer, and many others, but each county executive speaks separately. There have been proposals of statehood or regional union for Nassau and Suffolk Cos, but they have failed to gain public approval, perhaps because of each county's devotion to autonomy and concern with the loss of individual freedom associated with larger political bodies. Because there is no overarching unity, there is the problem of segmentation, of layers of bureaucracies from the village to town to county levels. Brooklyn is strongly Democratic in its voting patterns, Queens less reliably so, and Nassau and Suffolk have been strongly Republican, though the party's strength is waning. Throughout the 20th century, only three Democratic candidates for president carried both Nassau and Suffolk Cos.

In the early 21st century one can see both similarities and differences between the eastern and western portion of Long Island. As more minorities move to Nassau and Suffolk Cos, they have become, like Brooklyn and Queens, multiracial, multiethnic, and filled with recent immigrants. They share the problems of disparities between wealth and poverty, of adjusting to postindustrial economies and aging infrastructures, of managing environmental concerns, and of providing services to a huge and sprawling population.

See also Airports; Aviation; Climate and weather; Long island rail road; Policing; Suburbanization; Water supply and use (non–new york city watershed); Whaling.

Bailey, Paul. *Long Island: A History of Two Great Counties,* 3 vols (New York: Lewis Publishing, 1949)
Bookbinder, Bernie. *Long Island: People and Places, Past and Present,* 2d ed. (New York: Harry N. Abrams, 1998)
Long Island: Our Story (Melville, NY: Newsday, 1998)
MacKay, Robert B., and Richard F. Welch, eds. *Long Island: An Illustrated History* (Sun Valley, Calif: American Historical Press, 2000)

Roger Wunderlich

Long Island, Battle of. Revolutionary War engagement in which the British defeated but failed to destroy the American army. Having forced the British to evacuate Boston in March 1776, Gen George Washington moved his army to the New York City area anticipating an attack, deployed most of his soldiers on Manhattan, but placed 4,000 in Brooklyn under Gen Nathanael Greene. On 25 June, as the Americans entrenched, Gen William Howe's British army arrived and landed unopposed on Staten Island and received reinforcements. By August his forces numbered 32,000 British and Hessian troops, supported by 30 warships mounting 1,200 guns, and 400 transports. This represented the largest force that Britain deployed in the 18th century. Washington's force numbered some 20,000 by this time, but many were untrained. Rather than sailing up the Hudson River and cutting Washington's line of retreat, Howe opted to seize Brooklyn, hoping to force the Americans to abandon New York City.

On 22 August Howe began landing troops on Long Island and had 20,000 ashore within three days, most encamped near Flatbush (Kings Co). Separating the British and American positions was a heavily wooded ridge called the Heights of Guana, stretching approximately east-west beginning at what are today Green-Wood Cemetery and Prospect Park. Four roads crossed the ridge and led toward Brooklyn: the Gowanus Rd along the coast, Flatbush Pass, Bedford Pass, and Jamaica Pass in what is now East New York (Kings Co). Rather than let them approach his lines at Brooklyn Heights unopposed, Washington contested the British advance. He sent 3,000 reinforcements to Gen Israel Putnam, who replaced the ailing Greene as commander. An additional 800 men were stationed in each of the first three passes, and another 500 were assigned to Jamaica Pass. This last detachment did not reach the pass in time, however, and it was guarded by only five militia officers.

Howe reconnoitered the American defenses and decided to outflank them using Jamaica Pass. On the night of 26 August, he led 10,000 troops eastward, captured the five officers at the pass, and enveloped the American position undetected. The next morning, as other British detachments launched diversionary attacks from the front, Howe's column descended on them from behind. Struck from two directions, the Americans were quickly routed from Bedford and Flatbush Passes. Ill-trained units disintegrated, and soldiers fled singly and in small groups to the main American line near Brooklyn. The Americans stood firm only at the Gowanus Rd pass. There Gen William Alexander, Lord Stirling, held the British at bay for several hours until he was overwhelmed by superior numbers. His brave stand allowed hundreds of American troops to escape across the swampy Gowanus Creek. By 2:00 PM on 27 August the fighting had ceased, and Howe had won a resounding victory, killing 200 and taking nearly 900 prisoners, including Gen Alexander and Gen John Sullivan. British losses totaled 392 killed, wounded, and captured. Although victorious, Howe failed to attack the main American entrenchments at Brooklyn Heights immediately after the battle. This allowed Washington time to evacuate his battered army to Manhattan on the night of 29–30 August and to continue the fight for American independence.

Manders, Eric J. *The Battle of Long Island* (Monmouth Beach, NJ: Philip Freneau Press, 1978)

Schecter, Barnet. *The Battle for New York: The City at the Heart of the American Revolution* (New York: Walker, 2002)

Michael P. Gabriel

Long Island Baymen. The numerous bays and lagoons of Long Island have engaged generations of shellfishers. American Indians harvested clams and scallops and valued the shells for tribute, barter, and decoration before the arrival of Europeans. The fortunes and livelihoods of Long Island baymen (both women and men) have grown and declined since the bonanza years of the 19th century. In Jamaica Bay, the Great South Bay, the Great and Little Peconic Bays, and Gardiners Bay, oysters, scallops, and clams once yielded bountiful harvests to individual baymen and shellfish companies. Early baymen using open boats and long-handled tong rakes to dig for clams or oysters fit the image of New England baymen of the early 1800s. For many that method gave way at midcentury to the steel dredge that scraped the bay bottom. By the 1870s huge quantities of the famous Great South Bay oyster went by sailing sloop to New York City and other markets. At some fish shanties on the South Shore, oysters were shucked before being packed on ice for shipment to inland markets. In 1901 Nassau Co baymen in operations large and small harvested 3.5 million pounds (1.6 million kg) of oysters in boats using dredges. On the North Shore, Manhasset Bay and Hempstead Harbor provided work for hundreds of baymen and their families. From the 1830s to the early 1900s, Port Washington [now in Nassau Co] supported an extensive oyster and clam industry. In Nassau Co's Oyster Bay, Roslyn, Glen Cove, and Glen Head, baymen became a force in local politics via their local processing places, the fish shanties.

Since the early 1900s, however, full-time baymen have been "going ashore," giving up a way of life with diminishing returns. By 1905 many of the bays and harbors close to New York City were polluted and determined to be off-limits for shellfishing by the New York State Department of Health. The state closed large areas of Manhasset Bay and Hempstead Harbor in 1925 following a typhoid outbreak linked to contaminated oysters. In the last half of the 20th century, shellfishing declined sharply as a major Long Island industry because of overfishing and water quality degradation. East End baymen blamed the collapse of the bay scallop and oyster industry in the 1980s and 1990s on the brown tide, loss of wetlands, and overdevelopment of surrounding shorelines. Nitrate-nitrogen concentrations in groundwater streams adjacent to Great South Bay increased fivefold between 1963 and 1976, affecting both water quality and the ecosystem. In 1987 historian Jeffrey Kassner linked the closure of large shellfishing areas in Great South Bay to suburbanization. The associated population growth and land use increased runoff into surface waters, contributing to coliform bacteria growth and other contamination. According to one estimate, just 150 full-time baymen remained on the North and South Forks in 1999. But the voice of the baymen has not gone unheard. The ambitious, well-funded Peconic Estuary Program, a federal, state, and local management plan released in 2001, has seemed the best hope for restoring and protecting some of Long Island's East End bays and the livelihoods of the baymen.

Kassner, Jeffrey. "Suburbanization and the Decline of the Shellfish Industry in New York." In *Long Island: The Suburban Experience,* ed. Barbara M. Kelly (Interlaken, NY: Heart of the Lakes Publishing, 1990)

"Long Island: Our Story," http://www.newsday.com/community/guide/lihistory/

Matthiessen, Peter. *Men's Lives: The Surfmen and Baymen of the South Fork* (New York: Random House, 1986)

Shodell, Elly. *Cross Currents: Baymen, Yachtsmen and Long Island Waters, 1830s–1990s* (Port Washington, NY: Port Washington Library, 1993)

Catherine A. McKeen

Long Island ducks. Fowl descended from 20 Pekin ducks that arrived in Stonington, Conn, from near Peking [now Beijing, China] in three shipments in 1873 and 1875. These ducks were larger than any in the United States and had a mild, succulent taste. According to some sources, descendants of these ducks had arrived in the Eastport-Speonk area (Suffolk Co) by 1883 and marked the start of a thriving full-time industry. Henry Raynor of Speonk may have been the first duck farmer on Long Island to obtain Pekins; Brewster Tuttle and D. Parshall Tuttle of Eastport were early duck raisers who obtained their breeders from Raynor. Eugene O. Wilcox of Speonk listed Pekin breeders in his January 1884 inventory. The region is well suited to duck farming because it is humid and has an abundance of both fresh water essential for raising breeding ducks and sandy soil to aid in the ducks' digestion.

In the first half of the 20th century, the largest duck farms in the world were located on Long Island, including those owned by W. H. Pye of Eastport, A. J. Hallock of Speonk, and A. B. Soyers and Hollis V. Warner of Riverhead (Suffolk Co). In 1949 Warner's was the largest duck farm in the world and raised about 500,000 ducks per year. By 1959 too many producers led to a saturated market on Long Island, and profits began to wane. Additionally, many small duck farms, unable meet the restrictions set up to reduce the water pollution caused by duck excrement and fermenting feed, were forced to close. In 2002 there were four duck farms on Long Island that generated $18 million in sales. Duck feathers, once picked by women and girls and now machine plucked, are an additional source of income.

Wilcox, LeRoy. "Duck Industry." In *Long Island: A History of Two Great Counties, Nassau and Suffolk,* vol 2, ed. Paul Bailey (New York: Lewis Historical Publishing, 1949)

Suzan D. Friedlander

Long Island Expressway (LIE). Long Island's only east-west, limited-access highway for passenger and commercial vehicles. It runs 71 miles (114 km) from Queens-Midtown Tunnel, at the island's western edge, to an eastern terminus at Riverhead (Suffolk Co), at the head of Peconic Bay. Along with the Long Island Rail Road, it is one of the major transportation lifelines, both economic and social, for New York City and the two counties to the east, Nassau and Suffolk.

The LIE was constructed in several sections, which were initially called by various local names. The first section, Borden Avenue Expressway, was completed in 1940 and linked the Queens-Midtown Tunnel to the Brooklyn-Queens Expressway (BQE). Work continued after World War II, with completion in 1958 of the Horace Harding Expressway section, extending eastward from Queens Blvd to the Queens-Nassau border. Built through Nassau Co by 1963, the full length of the expressway was open to Riverhead by 1972. The original LIE construction provided at least six lanes in all sections, with additional lanes at key points, such as at the interchanges with Van Wyck Expressway, Grand Central Parkway, Queens Blvd, and the BQE. The two-level LIE section at the BQE has the added lanes on the lower level.

Following World War II, LIE usage patterns developed from an interplay of social, economic, and transportation factors. The GI Bill housing loan program facilitated residential development in Nassau and Suffolk Cos, and during the same period, construction of the LIE and expansion of existing parkways greatly improved mobility throughout Long Island. Commercial growth included construction of aircraft factories and other manufactures, service businesses for the growing population, and offices for high-technology, financial, and other firms. Continuing growth of weekday work travel and weekend recreational travel resulted in recurring congestion on the Long Island highway system. Delays on the LIE became severe and long lasting because of the road's strategic, central location and its role as the only limited-access route for trucks through Queens, Nassau, and Suffolk Cos.

In 1971 a 2.2 mi (3.5 km) long, contra-flow bus/taxi lane began operating on the Queens-Midtown Tunnel approach during the morning peak period, allowing for improved travel time and reliability for the numerous express bus commuters from Queens into Manhattan. By 1983 the whole of the LIE formed part of the Interstate Highway System as I-495. While used for interstate trips, the LIE was most heavily used on weekdays for commuting and on weekends for recreational and shopping trips. One of the most intensively utilized highways in the world, in 1999 its average daily traffic at peak points reached more than 181,000 vehicles in Nassau Co and over 204,000 in Queens Co. Because 80% of all trips that Nassau and Suffolk residents made to work were within these same counties, most expressway trips were relatively short, averaging 12 miles (19 km) during weekday peaks. The expressway was not, as was commonly believed, a major conduit for working commuters between Nassau and Suffolk Cos and Manhattan; Manhattan was the destination for only 7% of all morning peak westbound trips on the LIE.

Improvement programs in the 1970s and 1980s related primarily to vehicular flow and included some interchange reconstruction as well as introduction of INFORM, a system of vehicle detectors, television, and changeable message signs providing drivers with routing advice. The LIE

High Occupancy Vehicle (HOV) Program, begun in the early 1990s, planned to add HOV lanes to a 40 mi (64 km) section from Medford (Suffolk Co) to the Queens-Nassau line by 2004. Other projects to reduce congestion included a $130 million road widening and bridge replacement program where the LIE meets the Cross Island Parkway, which was completed in 2003, and a $200 million road upgrade from the Queens-Midtown Tunnel to the Grand Central Parkway.

Long Island Transportation Plan 2000, http://www.LITP2000.com

Leon Goodman

Long Island ferries. Before bridges and tunnels spanned the East River, ferryboats were the principal transport for travelers bound east to and west from Long Island. In the colonial period, commercial ferries powered by sail operated on the river and the Long Island Sound. In the late 18th century, these were replaced by paddle-wheel ferryboats, powered by draft animals lashed to on-board treadmills. In 1814 Robert Fulton inaugurated a mechanically powered Long Island ferry service when he placed the steam-powered *Nassau* on a regular run between Brooklyn and Lower Manhattan.

By the mid–19th century, dozens of ferryboat routes served the lower East River, with two firms emerging as the dominant operators. Union Ferry Co ran seven separate crossings, including the original Fulton Ferry, and Williamsburg Ferries claimed a series of routes, with a principal Long Island terminal at the foot of Broadway (Kings Co). The Long Island Rail Road (LIRR) was also an important East River ferryboat operator, with a direct route between its passenger terminal in Long Island City (Queens Co) and the foot of Manhattan's East 34th St, plus another route linking Long Island City with Lower Manhattan's James Slip. Other 19th-century East River ferryboat companies included Greenpoint Ferry Co, Nassau Ferry Co, and the trustees of St. Patrick's Cathedral, who operated a route between the foot of Manhattan's East 23d St and Long Island City's Penny Bridge, near the cathedral's Calvary Cemetery.

Important ferry routes also served Long Island across the relatively open waters of Long Island Sound. LIRR inaugurated service in 1836 and by 1844 was one of the first links in an intercity rail-water service between New York and Boston. Union Ferry Co provided the initial connection between Lower Manhattan and the foot of Atlantic Ave in Brooklyn, and a steamboat ferry linked LIRR's easternmost terminal in Greenport (Suffolk Co) with the Norwich and Worcester Railroad at a point near New London on the Connecticut side of the Sound.

Bridges and tunnels began to supplement the East River ferries and eventually replaced them as commerce across the lower East River thrived and the width of the river made such construction possible. In 1883 the Brooklyn Bridge opened for traffic, and over the next decades additional bridges and tunnels allowed swifter passage across the river. In the early decades of the 20th century, private operators abandoned ferry businesses, and New York City officials tried to retain key East River ferry crossings as municipal services. But famed Fulton Ferry was discontinued in 1924 after a mere two years of municipal operation, and the last ferry service across the lower East River, between the foot of Manhattan's East 23d St and Brooklyn's Greenpoint Ave, ran its final boats in 1933. Municipal operation lasted a few years longer on several crossings connecting points further east. Service between Clason Point (Bronx Co) and College Point (Queens Co), for instance, remained in operation until the opening of the Bronx-Whitestone Bridge in 1939.

At the beginning of the 21st century, despite heavy use of bridges and tunnels across the lower East River, important ferry services continue to serve eastern Long Island. Car ferries link Bridgeport, Conn, with Port Jefferson (Suffolk Co) and New London, Conn, with Orient Point (Suffolk Co). Shelter Island (Suffolk Co) can only be reached by one of two ferry services, while Fire Island's (Suffolk Co) resort areas are served by several fleets of modern ferryboats that cross Great South Bay from points such as Sayville (Suffolk Co).

Cudahy, Brian J. *Over and Back: The History of Ferryboats in New York Harbor* (New York: Fordham Univ Press, 1990)

Pierrepont, Henry E. *Historical Sketch of the Fulton Ferry and Its Associated Ferries* (Brooklyn: Union Ferry, 1879)

Brian J. Cudahy

Long Island Motor Parkway. One of the country's first reinforced concrete, limited-access highways, extending 48 miles (77 km) from near Flushing in northern Queens to Lake Ronkonkoma (Suffolk Co). The roadway was designed by William K. Vanderbilt Jr and friends to foster American auto racing. Vanderbilt donated a trophy for races held on Long Island public roads from 1904 to 1910. When two spectators were killed during a race in 1906, however, Vanderbilt decided to construct both a private roadway for car racing and a public use highway. Construction between Garden City and Bethpage (Nassau Co) began 6 June 1907. The first 10 miles (16 km) of the 16 ft (4.9 m) wide Long Island Motor Parkway opened in 1908. To help cover the $2 million construction cost, a $2 toll was charged for public access. Races were run and autos tested in 1908, 1909, and 1910. Four spectators were killed and 20 injured in 1910, after which the New York State legislature banned auto racing anywhere but on racetracks. By 1911 the road had been extended eastward to its full length and widened to 22 feet (6.7 m). Tolls dropped to $1 in 1917 and, after Robert Moses's adjacent, toll-free Northern State Parkway opened in 1933, to 40¢ in 1935. The loss of racing, the move of automakers to Detroit, and the competition from the Northern Parkway forced the roadway to close on Easter 1938. The right-of-way in Queens became a bicycle and hiking path; in Nassau and in western Suffolk Cos it became a high-tension line right-of-way for the Long Island Power Authority. The last remaining portion still open in 2003 was 13 miles (21 km), from Dix Hills to Ronkonkoma (Suffolk Co), designated County Rd 67.

Miller, Robert. "The Long Island Motor Parkway: Prelude to Robert Moses." In *Robert Moses: Single-Minded Genius,* ed. Joann P. Krieg (Interlaken, NY: Heart of the Lakes Publishing, 1989)

Long Island Motor Parkway, http://www.osi3.net/limp/

S. Berliner III

Long Island Power Authority (LIPA). Nonprofit, publicly owned electric utility created in 1986. In April 1965 investor-owned Long Island Lighting Co (LILCO) announced plans to build a nuclear power plant in Shoreham (Suffolk Co). Construction began in 1973. Cost overruns were massive. The project was originally budgeted at $65–75 million but cost about $5.5 billion when it was ready for low-power testing in August 1985. Opponents contended that these costs had led LILCO to charge the nation's highest utility rates. In 1986 the New York State legislature created LIPA, authorizing it to acquire LILCO assets and securities, to decommission—reduce radioactive materials below a certain level—and close the Shoreham plant. LIPA commenced operations in January 1987 but failed in efforts to acquire LILCO.

In 1988 Gov Mario M. Cuomo reached an agreement with LILCO whereby it agreed to transfer Shoreham Nuclear Power Plant to LIPA for decommissioning and to assume the cost of doing so. LILCO was allowed to raise its rates. In 1992 it transferred Shoreham's title to LIPA for $1. LIPA decommissioned the plant in the course of what was the nation's first decontamination of a Nuclear Regulatory Commission (NRC)-licensed commercial nuclear facility. In 1996 LIPA entered additional negotiations with LILCO for the company's assets. By 1998 it had acquired LILCO's electric transmission and distribution system and its interest in the Nine Mile Point Two nuclear plant in Scriba (Oswego Co). At the same time, LILCO's natural gas system and Long Island–based power plants were transferred to a new holding company formed by a merger of LILCO and KeySpan Energy Corp (the former Brooklyn Union Gas and now KeySpan Corp). KeySpan Corp provides electricity from these generating facilities to LIPA via a management service agreement. In 1998 LIPA began to sell electricity to former LILCO customers, with significant rate reductions of approximately 20%. In addition, LIPA issued an aggregate refund of approximately $200 million to more than 1 million customers. LIPA is governed by a board of trustees, with its 15 members serving four-year terms. The governor appoints nine trustees and the board's chair. In 2003 LIPA was headquartered in Uniondale (Nassau Co) and had 80 employees and a customer base of 1.1 million in Nassau and Suffolk Cos and the Rockaways area of Queens.

Grossman, Karl. *Power Crazy* (New York: Grove Press, 1986)

New York State. Law Department. *Report on the Investigation of Executive Severance Compensation Payments by the Long Island Lighting Company* (Albany: Bureau of Investor Protection and Securities, 1999)

New York State. Office of Comptroller. *Long Island Power Authority: Staff Study: Disposition of the Shoreham Nuclear Power Plant* (Albany: Division of Management Audit, 1996)

Jeffrey Kraus

Long Island Rail Road (LIRR). With 82.2 million passengers in 1999, 60% of whom were commuters, the LIRR has the distinction of being the busiest commuter railroad in the country. Of the roughly 144,000 daily riders, 25,000 travel to Flatbush Ave (Kings Co), 5,000 to Hunters Point (Queens Co), and the rest to Pennsylvania Station in New York City.

The 19th Century

Chartered in 1834, the LIRR is the third oldest railroad in the country and the only one still bearing its original name. (The original spelling, Long Island Railroad, was changed in 1944.) The first train operated on 18 Apr 1836. Financial problems and the 1837 depression delayed the completion of the road from Jamaica (Queens Co) to the terminus at Greenport (Suffolk Co) until 1844. The LIRR was built to cut the travel time from New York City to Boston from 16 hours to 8 hours; at Greenport passengers took a ferry to Stonington, Conn. The completion of the New Haven Railroad along the Connecticut shore in 1850 destroyed the LIRR's monopoly of a fast route to Boston. Because the route through the sparsely settled interior of Long Island provided neither passenger nor freight traffic, in 1850 the railroad plunged into bankruptcy and a 15-year depression. After the Civil War, the South Side Rail Road and the Flushing, North Shore and Central Railroad competed with the LIRR for business at Jamaica, Flushing (Queens Co), Hempstead (Nassau Co), and Babylon (Suffolk Co). In 1877 this competition drove the LIRR and its rivals into bankruptcy. In 1881 the courts restructured the roads into one system under LIRR management. Prior to 1889 the LIRR leased competing lines but merged them into itself to simplify its corporate structure. The railroad prospered in the 1880s and 1890s as passenger traffic greatly increased, especially during summer, and freight business soared. New York City residents discovered Long Island's beaches, picturesque villages, and recreational possibilities of the north and south shores.

The 20th Century

The Pennsylvania Railroad bought out the LIRR in 1900, constructed the four East River tunnels between 1903 and 1908, and built the imposing Pennsylvania Station, which opened in 1910. Beginning in 1905 the electrification of the Pennsylvania Railroad and the LIRR stimulated an explosive increase in the population of the villages on the western end of Long Island, especially in Queens Co, and transformed the LIRR from a largely seasonal to a commuter railroad. The years after World War I increased the ridership, but soon trucks cut into the freight revenue, and with the completion of the subways into Queens in 1917 and elevated lines in 1937, the LIRR lost the bulk of its Queens passengers. In 1954 the Long Island Transit Authority took over the railroad, which ceased to be a private corporation, and extensively regenerated it. In 1965 the New York City Transit Authority (NYCTA) acquired the LIRR. In 1968 the NYCTA, which was a reorganization of the earlier Board of Transportation, became part of the Metropolitan Transit Authority. Politics and labor turmoil were the forces behind these various incarnations.

In the last 30 years of the 20th century, extensive improvements were made, including purchases of new cars—760 M1s, 172 M3s, and 192 M7s—and the opening of a new car yard on New York City's West Side in 1988. All stations were rebuilt with raised platforms, a modern shop facility was built during 1984–91 at Hillside (Queens Co) to service the whole electric fleet, and electrification was extended to Huntington and Ronkonkoma (Suffolk Co). Because the freight haulage fell from 17,131 carloads and 1.1 million tons (997,902 MT) in 1987 to 11,683 carloads and 865,857 tons (785,492 MT) in 1996, the LIRR sold the freight business to the New York and Atlantic Railroad in May 1997 for a 20-year period; the New York and Atlantic runs seven trains a day, five days a week, and operates out of the Fresh Pond (Queens Co) yard. In 1997–98 the LIRR introduced modern bilevel cars and dual-mode locomotives able to operate in both diesel and electric territory. To accommodate these new features, two new yards were added: in 1999 a nine-track maintenance yard at Port Jefferson (Suffolk Co) and in 2000 an air-conditioning repair shop and yard at Huntington. The LIRR plans to pursue entry into Grand Central Terminal via the East Side Access (63d St tunnel).

Stations and Branches

Jamaica Station is the heart of the LIRR system of approximately 124 stations, a number that varies from time to time owing to additions and abandonments. Except for the North Shore branch that runs directly to Pennsylvania Station, passenger routes pass through Jamaica Station, which has eight passenger tracks serving its five passenger platforms, a pair of express tracks by which rush-hour trains can bypass the platforms, six lay-up tracks for storing trains, and a network of switches and crossings. The appearance of Jamaica Station will be drastically changed when the light-rail AirTrain to John F. Kennedy International Airport is connected to the present passenger platforms. This new transfer facility was designed to provide easy access to the airport and to speed up traveling time. The LIRR covers approximately 701 miles (1,128 km) of track. The main line of the LIRR is 94 miles (151 km) long, extending from New York City to Greenport. The Montauk Division extends 114 miles (183 km) from Long Island City (Queens Co) to Montauk (Suffolk Co). Nine shorter branches include the Port Jefferson branch from Hicksville (Nassau Co) to Port Jefferson, the Oyster Bay branch from Mineola to Oyster Bay (Nassau Co), the North Shore branch from Woodside (Queens Co) to Port Washington (Nassau Co), the Hempstead branch from Floral Park to Hempstead (Nassau Co), the West Hempstead branch from Valley Stream (Nassau Co), the Long Beach branch to Long Beach (Nassau Co), the Atlantic branch to Laurelton (Queens Co), the Far Rockaway branch to Far Rockaway (Queens Co), and the freight-only Bay Ridge line running from Fresh Pond Junction (Queens Co) to Bay Ridge (Kings Co).

Condit, Carl W. *The Port of New York: A History of the Rail Terminal System* (Chicago: Univ of Chicago Press, 1981)

Seyfried, Vincent F. *The Long Island Rail Road: A Comprehensive History*, 7 vols (1961–84)

Vincent F. Seyfried

Commuters boarding the Long Island Rail Road, *ca* 1955.

Long Island Sound. Lying between the eastern shore of Bronx Co, the southern shores of Westchester Co and Connecticut, and the northern shore of Long Island, the Sound is a tidal estuary opening into the East River on the west. Seawater pushes strong currents through the Race, an inlet between Plum and Fishers Islands, on the east. A mix of freshwater from tributaries and saltwater from the ocean, the Sound stretches 110 miles (177 km) from New York City eastward along Long Island's North Shore. It is 21 miles (34 km) at the widest point and varies in depth from 65 to 350 feet (20 to 107 m), with a mid-Sound average of 65 feet. From the island's moraines, sediments, layered cliffs, and boulders, geologists theorize the Sound is about 15,000 years old and was formed when a retreating glacier widened and rising sea levels filled in a river canyon carved out millions of years earlier. Because it is a partially enclosed estuary, the coastlines in the Sound do not have the pounding Atlantic surf, making the ecosystem unique.

Native inhabitants used the Sound for travel and trade between the Long Island and Connecticut shores, as did Europeans when they arrived in the 17th century. Decades before the Revolution the Sound teemed with sailing vessels carrying cargo, passengers, and mail between Long Island communities, Connecticut, and Manhattan. From protected harbors such as Oyster Bay, sloops and brigs set off for trade along the Atlantic coast and in the Caribbean Sea. The Sound became less of a transportation

Long Island Sound. Photograph by Robert L. Harrison.

link with the development of railroads, improved roadways, and widespread use of the automobile. From about 1880 to 1920, the era of luxurious yachts plying the Sound coincided with the heyday of North Shore Gold Coast estates. At the beginning of the 21st century a few ferries regularly connect Long Island and Connecticut, a small number of tankers and barges transport oil to power plants, and recreational boating and fishing contribute about $5 billion to the region's economy.

The Long Island Sound lobster fishery had grown during the 1970s and 1980s to the third largest in the country. In 1997 the combined catch in western and eastern Long Island Sound peaked at 7.7 million pounds (3.5 million kg). The catch declined by 2 million pounds (910,000 kg) in 1999 when harvesters reported traps filled with dead or dying lobsters, mostly in the western Sound. In January 2000 the US government declared the Long Island Sound lobster fishery a disaster. In that year the catch in the western Sound fell to 542,000 pounds (245,800 kg) and in the eastern Sound to 1.3 million pounds (590,000 kg). The US Congress, US Environmental Protection Agency, and New York and Connecticut governments responded with funds for alleviation and research, some earmarked to examine the possible link between lobster deaths and a pesticide used to fight the mosquito-borne West Nile virus.

In 1985 New York, Connecticut, and the federal government initiated the Long Island Sound Study to address water quality degradation. The two states invested heavily in sewage plant upgrades to reduce the nitrogen-related hypoxia that was killing marine life. More federal funds in 2000 for Sound restoration prompted the Department of Environmental Conservation, other state agencies, and a variety of citizen groups to expand the goals for restoring the Sound's ecosystem, including the creation of shoreline open space reserves and parklands. Beginning in the mid-1970s, observers noted a slow, steady increase in the number of harbor seals wintering in the Sound. That number rose sharply in the early 1990s. Harp, hooded, and gray seals have also been sighted regularly, increasingly in the western Sound. The seal population increase results partly from a federal law passed in 1972 strictly regulating seal killing and possibly from cleaner water.

Fagin, Dan. "The Evolution of LI Sound." In *Long Island: Our Story,* ed. Newsday (Melville, NY: Newsday, 1998)

"Long Island: Our Story," http://www.newsday.com/community/guide/lihistory/

Villani, Robert. *Long Island: A Natural History* (New York: Abrams, 1997)

Weigold, Marilyn. *The American Mediterranean: An Environmental, Economic, and Social History of Long Island Sound* (Port Washington, NY: Kennikat, 1974)

Catherine A. McKeen

Long Island Sound Bridge. Proposed bridge connecting Long Island's Nassau or Suffolk Co with the north shore of Long Island Sound to avoid the circuitous and congested route through New York City. Proposals for cross-Sound bridges emerged in the 1950s. Among them were Oyster Bay–Rye, Port Jefferson–Bridgeport, Shoreham–New Haven, and Orient Point–Watch Hill. In 1967 the state legislature authorized the Triborough Bridge and Tunnel Authority to build the Oyster Bay (Nassau Co) to Rye (Westchester Co) span. The proposed 6.1 mi (9.8 km) bridge with a 1,200 ft (366 m) cable-stayed suspension main span would have linked Cross Westchester Expressway (I-287) with Nassau Co's Seaford–Oyster Bay Expressway (Rte 135). The plan aroused opposition over environmental issues, and in 1973 Gov Nelson A. Rockefeller scrapped it. In the early 21st century, cross-Sound traffic detours through Queens to the Throgs Neck Bridge over the East River or uses improved Port Jefferson–Bridgeport or Orient Point–New London ferries. Although largely dormant, the bridge proposal has resurfaced from time to time.

Caro, Robert A. *The Power Broker: Robert Moses and the Fall of New York* (New York: Vintage Books, 1974)

Robert A. Olmsted

Long Island Sound steamboat lines. The first shipping lines on Long Island Sound were maintained by sailing ships, usually owned by their individual captains. Faster boats operated as packets or regularly scheduled boats and usually made one run per week. Schooners, two- (or more) masted sailing ships with triangular fore and aft sails, and barks, three-masted vessels with square sails on the fore and main masts, carried freight upon demand and remained active in this trade through the steam era. Robert Fulton and Robert R. Livingston's North River Steamboat Co, which operated on the Hudson River from 1807, did not immediately run lines on Long Island Sound. The owners feared British warships during the War of 1812 and worried that steamboats could not cross the rough water of Hell Gate, the point where the East River rushes past Ward's Island into the Sound. But in 1816 North River's *Fulton* made its first passage through Hell Gate, continuing through the Sound to New Haven, Conn.

Within a brief time *Fulton,* joined by *Connecticut,* was serving New London and Norwich, Conn, and Newport and Providence, RI. In 1817 the company's *Firefly,* built in 1812, began short runs from Providence. North River's New York State monopoly kept rival companies out of New York State ports. After the breakup of the monopoly in 1824 the Connecticut River Steamboat Co established service between New York City and Hartford with the *Oliver Ellsworth.* In 1826 North River's *Chancellor Livingston* began a run from New York City to Providence.

Development was rapid for North River and its new rivals. Early operators included Chester W. Chapin and John Brooks as well as New York City residents Capts Elijah Peck, Jacob Vanderbilt, and Cornelius Vanderbilt, and Cadwallader Colden, George Law, Daniel Drew, and Richard Peck. Corporations, lines, and routes formed and re-formed continually over the next decades. Most of the lines originated at the Hudson. Principal companies were New Haven Line (1815–1937), Providence Line (1822–1937), Hartford Line (1824–1937), Bridgeport Line (1833–1937), New London and Norwich Line (1836–1935), Stonington Line (1837–1900), Fall River Line (1847–1937), Boston Lines (1907–41), and Colonial Providence Line (1910–42). Many famous boats such as *Fulton, Connecticut, Richard Peck, Chester W. Chapin, Comet,* and *Arrow* served different routes and different companies on the Sound.

From the 1830s, Long Island steamboats connected with railroads such as Boston and Providence (1835), Housatonic (1840), Norwich and Worcester (1840), and New York, Providence, and Boston (1893). Between 1844 and 1847 the Long Island Rail Road also ran boats from Greenport (Suffolk Co) to Norwich and Stonington, Conn, in a bid for the New York City to Boston through traffic. It failed, despite maximum rail and minimum water distances. By the late 19th century, most of the steamboat lines were under the control of the New Haven Railroad's marine subsidiary, New England Navigation Co, later renamed New England Steamship Co.

Around 1900, with completion of the New Haven and Shoreline Railroad and the bridging of the mouth of the Connecticut River, land travel became faster and more economical. In 1917 rail-only Hell Gate Bridge provided another nonwater option for passengers and freight bound east from Manhattan. In 1937 New England Steamship Co terminated all Long Island Sound service after labor trouble. Eastern Steamship Co and Colonial Providence Line continued in operation a few years longer. Eastern Steamship closed on 29 Nov 1941, as did Colonial Line on 29 Mar 1942, after military requisition of vessels and threat of German submarine attacks. Long Island Sound steamboats never returned after World War II. Tankers and barges with bulk cargoes and ferries from Long Island to Bridgeport and to New London continue to travel the Sound, but this usage is only a fraction of its former water traffic.

Dayton, Fred Erving. *Steamboat Days* (New York: Frederick A. Stokes, 1925)

Foster, George H., and Peter C. Weiglin. *Splendor Sailed the Sound: The New Haven Railroad and the Fall River Line* (San Mateo, Calif: Potentials Group, 1973)

Hilton, George W. *The Night Boat* (Berkeley, Calif: Howell-North Books, 1968)

Arthur G. Adams

Long Island State Park Commission. Administrator and planner Robert Moses (1888–1981) originated the idea of regional park commissions for New York State in his *State Park Plan for New York State* (1922), published by the New York State Association, a private reform organization founded two years earlier in New York City. In April 1924 Gov Alfred E. Smith signed the bill that created 10 park regions, each administered by a separate commission within the New York State Conservation Department. The governor appointed the commissioners, and the presidents of each commission together formed the New York State Council of Parks. Robert Moses served as president of the Long Island State Park Commission (LISPC) as well as president of the State Council of Parks from 1924 until his resignation in 1962.

LISPC was charged with acquiring lands for conservation and public recreation and with developing and maintaining park facilities and parkways in the Long Island region. The original legislation, as drafted by Moses, included provisions granting significant powers to LISPC and the other regional commissions. Specifically, the law allowed LISPC to appropriate property simply by occupying a site and stating that it desired ownership, leaving owners to apply for compensation. The 1924 bill's broad definitions of terms also assisted LISPC. For example, "parks" encompassed parkways, boulevards, docks, piers, and bridges, and "real estate" included underwater lands as well as uplands.

Even with these powers, LISPC's early years were beset with conflicts: legal challenges to the methods of acquisition; hostility from individual Long Islanders and from organized groups fearing the loss of private property and local control; and the state legislature's resistance to Smith's and Moses's ever increasing budget requests. But under Moses's adamant leadership, LISPC pressed forward with acquisition of properties—farmland, woodland, watershed supply areas, former estates, and predeveloped recreational facilities such as golf courses—from farmers, other private landowners, public entities, and municipalities. Metropolitan New York's burgeoning population and the newly affordable automobile were creating an urgent desire for open space suitable for recreational purposes. Parks were a popular issue in the 1920s, often winning bipartisan support that also cut across regional and other divisions. Moses and the LISPC carefully crafted political alliances, combined the powers and resources of different agencies, and, pushed by Moses's indomitable will, often initiated projects that lacked adequate funding by banking on the idea that it was more difficult to stop a project already in motion than one still on paper.

In 1926 LISPC established its headquarters at the former August Belmont estate in Babylon (Suffolk Co). This was soon home to a vast workforce of architects, engineers, surveyors, masons, carpenters, mechanics, landscape workers, and others charged with implementing an array of design projects. These included the transformation of Long Island's remote barrier beach into Jones Beach State Park (1926–52) and the creation of a 200 mi (322 km) network of "linear parks," or landscaped roadways, connecting New York City's parks with access roads (1926–66). By the end of the 1928 summer season, LISPC had established 14 state parks on Long Island, on a total of 9,700 acres (3,930 ha) that had already been visited by over 500,000 persons. Over the next three decades, LISPC acquired, improved, and developed Long Island's extensive parks and parkways, ultimately incorporating thousands of acres of protected lands, waterways, and shorelines and providing recreational and transportation facilities for millions of visitors. This development, especially on the island's south shore, helped usher in the era of massive suburbanization.

In 1972 a new agency, the New York State Office of Parks, Recreation, and Historic Preservation, was granted direct authority for park development and maintenance under a single commissioner. Although the regional commissions were retained, their function was redefined as largely advisory to this new commissioner. In 1977 LISPC's ceded its authority over Long Island's parkways to the New York State Department of Transportation (DOT). In 2003 there were 32 state parks in the Long Island Park Region occupying 25,520 acres (10,328 ha); the DOT manages 12 parkways in the region.

Blakelock, Chester R. *History of Long Island State Parks* (New York: Lewis Historical Publishing, 1959)

Caro, Robert A. *The Power Broker: Robert Moses and the Fall of New York* (New York: Vintage Books, 1975)

Alison M. Cornish

Long Island University. Private university. The oldest of Long Island University's (LIU's) three residential campuses, Brooklyn Campus, was founded in 1926 and merged with the Brooklyn College of Pharmacy (1886) in 1929. Its founders and early trustees, mostly from Booklyn's Protestant business class, intended to open higher education to the growing numbers of Jews and Catholics in Brooklyn and greater New York City. In fall 2001 Brooklyn Campus, in downtown Brooklyn, had 10,631 students. LIU expanded to Nassau Co when the C. W. Post Campus opened in Brookville (1954) on the former Gold Coast estates of Marjorie Merriweather Post and W. E. and E. F. Hutton. The Tilles Center for the Performing Arts (1980), part of LIU on the Post Campus, is home to the Long Island Philharmonic and is a presenting venue for other arts organizations. Post had 12,931 students in 2001. Suffolk Co hosts Southampton College, opened in 1963 on the former estate of textile baron Arthur B. Claflin. The Friends World Program based at the college has seven overseas centers. Southampton's student body totaled 3,981 in 2001. LIU's three branch satellite locations—Brentwood Campus (1959) in Suffolk Co, Westchester Graduate Campus (1975) in Purchase, and Rockland Graduate Campus (1976) in Orangeburg—had a combined enrollment in 2001 of 1,642. LIU was the nation's eighth largest private university, with 29,774 students, as of fall 2001.

Cory, Christopher T., ed. *Access and Excellence: 75 Years of Long Island University* (Brooklyn: LIU Press, 2001)

Long Island University, http://www.liu.edu/liu_start.html

Catherine A. McKeen

Long Lake. Town (pop 852) in N Hamilton Co. The first resident, Capt Peter Sabattis, an Abenaki, arrived about the time of the Revolutionary War and speculator Theophilus Anthony of New York City built a summer home before the area was permanently settled in the early 1830s. Named for the 15 mi (24 km) Long Lake (more accurately a widening of the Raquette River), the town was formed in 1837 from Arietta, Lake Pleasant, Morehouse, and Wells. Other significant bodies of water are Raquette and Blue Mountain Lakes. The town was accessible by the state road from Crown Point (Essex Co) to Carthage (Jefferson Co), authorized in 1841. Two books popularized the area for 19th-century sports enthusiasts: Rev John Todd's *Long Lake* (1845) and William H. H. Murray's *Adventures in the Wilderness* (1869). William West Durant began developing "Great Camps" in 1877 and helped to attract many wealthy men to invest in retreats such as Nehasane Park (1894) and the private Whitney Park, facilitated by the Mohawk and Malone Railroad (1892). Long Lake remains a resort town, with extensive lumbering interests. The Hotel Adirondack (*ca* 1900) is an operating landmark.

Loomis Gang. In the decades before the American Civil War, the Loomis Gang of Sangerfield (Oneida Co) ran an extended interstate syndicate that trafficked in stolen horses, livestock, and counterfeit currency. At the center of the syndicate was the Loomis family itself, which operated from its headquarters, overlooking Nine-mile Swamp (Madison Co) just south of the Great Western Turnpike [now US 20]. Having purchased the land sometime earlier, George Loomis brought his bride, Rhoda Mallet, to Sangerfield in 1814. Both came from New England families with pretensions to gentility and a predilection for petty crime.

By the mid-1840s, their son George Washington Loomis, known as "Wash," had become the leader of the gang, which had grown to include scores of operatives in several states. By 1848 outraged local citizens had determined to take matters into their own hands, and a search of the Loomis homestead revealed overwhelming evidence of robbery and theft. Wash escaped prosecution by heading for the gold fields of California, but a brother was sentenced in 1850 to two months in jail and a fine after a vigorous prosecution by young Oneida Co district attorney Roscoe Conkling. Wash returned in the winter of 1850 and, after the death of his father in 1851, reorganized and expanded the family business. The gang's depredations increased in frequency and scope after that, and a number of mysterious disappearances and violent and sometimes fatal attacks were attributed to the outlaw clan. The final act of hubris came on the night of 10 Oct 1864, when the Madison Co courthouse in Morrisville was burned to the ground, taking with it the indictments prepared for a new round of prosecutions.

Just more than a year later, early Halloween morning, four men sought out Wash at the homestead and crushed his skull, leaving him to die later that night. On 17 June 1866 a much larger party of local vigilantes burned the homestead and terrorized the evicted inhabitants. On 3 June 1867 Conkling, now a rising US senator, successfully quashed the murder indictment pending against Waterville constable Jim Elkins, the leader of the Halloween raid. Thereafter, the younger members of the clan dispersed, living out the remainder of their lives peaceably. The remnant in and around Sangerfield contented itself with nuisance-level misdemeanors and internecine strife. Rhoda died in 1887, and the last of Wash's generation died in Canada in 1911. *The Loomis Gang,* a movie produced by Waterville (Oneida Co) native Brian Peter Falk, had its world premier April 2002 in Waterville.

Torrey, E. Fuller. *Frontier Justice: The Rise and Fall of the Loomis Gang* (Utica: North County Books, 1992)

William S. Helmer

Lorraine. Town (pop 980) in S Jefferson Co. Settlement, begun in 1802, was aided by the Rome-Brownville Turnpike (1804). The town was formed as Malta in 1804 from Mexico [now in Oswego Co] and was renamed in 1808. It was a lumbering district until the mid–19th century and became a dairy farming town after 1863, when the first cheese factory opened; after *ca* 1900 fluid milk was shipped. It was also the site of an egg-pickling factory (1872–after 1886). In the early 21st century few farms remain, and the town is a bedroom community for Watertown and Syracuse. Much of the land is used for hunting, fishing, and snowmobiling.

Laura Lynne Scharer

lotteries. For many state and local governments in the 17th through 19th centuries, lotteries were an important source of revenue. New York, like all other colonies and original states, saw a profusion of public and private lotteries, which peaked in the early 1800s. Although public lotteries often existed for some public purpose—both Columbia and Union Colleges received funding from lotteries as early as 1795—many private lotteries were run dishonestly for the benefit of their owners. Indeed, the corruption inherent in largely unregulated lotteries in New York State was revealed in a spectacular 1818 libel trial in New York City, in which newspaper editor Charles Baldwin, defending against a libel action, provided extensive details about private lotteries. His revelations, combined with general concerns over the morality of lotteries and gambling, resulted in an 1820 state constitutional prohibition on lotteries (ratified in 1821). The constitutional ban was ignored, however, when the City of Albany authorized an 1821 lottery to dispose of public lands and two years later when New York City ran a lottery to raise funds for a hospital. In response the state legislature passed laws in 1833 and 1834 to enforce the constitutional prohibition, thereby effectively ending lotteries in New York State. Eight other states had also banned lotteries by 1834. No longer an accepted method of finance, lotteries throughout the United States were largely reduced to a quasi-legal status for over a century. By the 1960s, however, state-run lotteries began to return; New Hampshire instituted the first in 1964. On 8 Nov 1966 New York State followed when voters approved a constitutional amendment to establish a state-run lottery; the first drawing took place on 1 June 1967. The Division of the Lottery, a separate and independent unit of the Department of Taxation and Finance, manages the Lottery. The commissioner of Taxation and Finance appoints the Lottery director. Opposition to the reinstitution of the State Lottery was centered in the New York Council of Churches, a coalition of Protestant denominations that attacked the Lottery on moral grounds. Most of these objections were overcome, however, by the state constitutional requirement (in Art 1, § 9) that Lottery revenues support public schools; this commitment was more stringent than other states' revenue dedication provisions.

In fiscal year 2000–2001, the State Lottery offered six regular games and numerous instant games that raised $4.19 billion in ticket sales; 54% ($2.27 billion) of that money was paid out in prizes, 35% ($1.45 billion) went to education, and the remaining 11% ($464 million) went to satisfy retailer commissions, administrative costs, and contractor fees. Although the money dedicated to education was a substantial sum, it constituted only 5% of total state educational spending for 2000–2001. The Lottery has occasionally funded noneducational projects, including the 1980 Winter Olympics in Lake Placid and a 1991 scratch-off game established by the state legislature for New York City to finance youth anticrime programs. Through an aggressive advertising campaign, the Lottery has made itself among the best-known and ubiquitous of state institutions. Those on the "draw team" who select nightly the winning numbers on television have become minor celebrities. Despite its popularity, the Lottery remains controversial. In 1989 the legislature required it to post signs providing information on help for compulsive gamblers, and, like most state lotteries, it continues to face criticism for its marketing practices and its effect on the poor and on minorities.

Nibert, David. *Hitting the Lottery Jackpot: Government and the Taxing of Dreams* (New York: Monthly Review Press, 2000)

Thomas A. Birkland

Loudonville. Locality in Colonie (Albany Co). Elias H. Ireland leased land in the area from Stephen Van Rensselaer in 1832, and a post office called Ireland Corners opened in 1850. One-half mile to the south lay Loudonville hamlet, named for John Campbell, Lord Loudoun (1705–82), British commander-in-chief in North America who built the military road (now US 9) in 1756. The Ireland Corners post office was renamed Loudonville in 1871 and since the late 19th century has been Albany's preeminent suburb. A mix of small estates and housing developments, it is the site of Siena College (1937).

Wesley G. Balla

Louisville [LEW-IS-VIL]. Town (pop 3,195) in NW St. Lawrence Co. Settled in 1800, the town was formed in 1810 from Massena. In the late 19th century, pumps and other wooden goods were made at Chase Mills. During construction of the St. Lawrence Seaway (1955–59), Louisville Landing hamlet, a former port of entry, and several working farms were flooded, while islands (Barnhart and Long Sault, among others) were created in Lake St. Lawrence. Apart from a few remaining farms, the town is a rural bedroom community for Massena. The New York Power Authority owns a continuous strip of river shoreline. Croil Island State Park (undeveloped) and the Wilson Hill State Wildlife Management Area are located in town.

Richard E. Mooers

Love Canal. In 1892 William T. Love proposed a waterway to link Lake Ontario with the Niagara River about 4 miles (6 km) above Niagara Falls and expected to generate hydroelectric power and provide shipping with a way around the falls. Excavation began in 1894, but the plan was abandoned, leaving a water-filled trench about 3,000 feet (914 m) long and less than 100 feet (30 m) wide. In the early 20th century, the land was sold at public auction and became a dumping site in what is now the City of Niagara Falls. From 1942 to 1953, Hooker Chemical Co buried 22,000 tons (20,000 MT) of hazardous wastes in the site.

In 1953 Hooker sold the property to the Niagara Falls School District for $1; the property deed, which included a clause explaining that chemicals were buried there, attempted to absolve the company of future liability. An elementary school was built directly above the site, and a neighborhood grew on both sides. Residents reported small explosions and fumes emanating from Love Canal in the 1960s, and the state government investigated chemical contamination of basements and sewers in nearby homes in 1976. Heavy winter snow and spring rain in 1978 percolated into the canal and flushed the chemicals to the ground surface and into buildings, including the 99th Street School and neighborhood homes. Natural deposits of clay underneath the canal prevented the chemicals from seeping downward, so they had nowhere to go but upward and outward, a process that has been described as the bathtub effect. The chemicals may also have been transported through underground swales, old streambeds that were filled in by housing developers when the neighborhood was built.

In June 1978 the New York State Department of Health issued the first of three health orders to the people living nearby. The first was a health warning for pregnant women and for children under the age of 2. The other two were evacuation orders for all residents within given perimeters. Concerned residents organized themselves into four protest groups, the largest of which was the Love Canal Homeowners Association led by Lois Gibbs. In August 1978 a federal state of emergency was declared for part of the area, the largest ever for a technological hazard. In May 1980 the emergency declaration area was expanded, leading to the permanent evacuation of approximately 950 families and to an agreement between the federal and state governments to compensate residents at fair market value for their homes. A number of health studies were also conducted on the people who lived there, some of which continued into the 21st century.

The Love Canal crisis inspired the federal Comprehensive Environmental Response, Compensation, and Liability Act of 1980 (CERCLA), the Superfund program, which is aimed at cleaning contaminated sites throughout the United States. CERCLA prevents companies responsible for chemical contamination from absolving their own liability when selling contaminated properties, as Hooker had done, and requires the companies found to be responsible for chemical contamination to pay for the full cost of cleanup and containment of the pollution. At Love Canal this was achieved by removing chemicals from the topsoil, flushing them from sewers, and dredging nearby creeks. A barrier drain system was installed on both sides of the canal to collect the chemicals that seep out of it. The effluent is treated at a wastewater treatment facility located on the site. Since 1990 homes have been resold in one section of the area, now called Black Creek Village. Most of the other homes and buildings in the neighborhood had to be demolished because of the extent of contamination. In 2004 the Environmental Protection Agency proposed removing Love Canal from the Superfund list, a move signaling that cleanup of the site had been completed.

Fletcher, Thomas. "Neighborhood Change at Love Canal: Contamination, Evacuation, and Resettlement," *Land Use Policy* 19 (4) 2002: 311–23

———. *From Love Canal to Environmental Justice: The Politics of Hazardous Waste on the Canada-US Border* (Peterborough, Ont: Broadview Press, 2003)

New York State. Department of Health. *Love Canal: A Special Report to the Governor and Legislature* (Albany: Author, 1981)

Thomas Fletcher

Lovelace, Francis (*b* Berkshire, England, ?1618; *d* Oxfordshire, England, ?1683). Second governor of the province of New York. James, Duke of York appointed Lovelace governor of the province in April 1667, and he arrived in Manhattan in March 1668. Lovelace was responsible for laying out the settlements of Marbletown and Hurley [now in Ulster Co], and he established monthly mail service to Boston. Lovelace was in Connecticut in July 1673 when a Dutch force stormed Fort James and recaptured New York. He returned to England humiliated and out of favor with James, who confiscated his assets as compensation for the lost province. Although the Treaty of Westminster restored New York to the English in February 1674, Lovelace spent the rest of his life fending off lawsuits from creditors and was briefly imprisoned in the Tower of London before his death.

New York State. *Minutes of the Executive Council of the Province of New York: Administration of Francis Lovelace, 1668–1673.* Ed. Victor H. Paltsits (Albany: State of New York, 1910)

Ritchie, Robert C. *The Duke's Province: A Study of New York Politics and Society, 1664–1691* (Chapel Hill: Univ of North Carolina Press, 1977)

Daniel A. Piazza

Lowenstein, Allard (*b* Newark, NJ, 16 Jan 1929; *d* New York City, 14 Mar 1980). Social activist and congressman. The son of a New York City restaurateur, Lowenstein graduated from Horace Mann School in New York City in 1945 and University of North Carolina in 1949. That year he entered politics as a legislative assistant to the liberal senator Frank Porter Graham of North Carolina. Lowenstein received a law degree from Yale University in 1954. He worked with Eleanor Roosevelt in 1956–57 as educational consultant to the American Association for the United Nations. He began a New York City law practice in 1960 and explored the possibility of running for Congress. He taught law and politics at several universities, including City College of New York during 1967–68. In 1967 he garnered national attention for his leadership of the New York Coalition for a Democratic Alternative, the "Dump Johnson" movement that helped keep Pres Lyndon Johnson from seeking renomination in 1968. Lowenstein was elected to Congress as a Democrat from the Fifth District, which extended from Queens to Oyster Bay (Nassau Co) in 1968. In 1970 Lowenstein's district was redrawn by the Republican-controlled legislature, and he lost in the November general election to Republican state senator Norman Lent. He lost in four subsequent congressional campaigns between 1972 and 1978. He was active in a number of liberal social and political causes, managing to reach number seven on Pres Richard M. Nixon's political enemies list. Dennis Sweeney, a former protégé, shot Lowenstein at his law office at 50 Rockefeller Plaza, and he died at St. Clare's Hospital in Midtown Manhattan.

Chafe, William H. *Never Stop Running: Allard Lowenstein and the Struggle to Save American Liberalism* (New York: Basic Books, 1993)

John David Rausch Jr

Lower East Side. The neighborhood known as the Lower East Side, a swathe of Manhattan east of the Bowery and north of Fulton St, did not get this name until the end of the 1930s, and it was not until the 1960s that the name became fixed. Where commentators used the phrase "lower east side" or some variant of it before the 1960s, they did not use capital letters and were just as likely to refer to this urban space as "downtown," "east side," "the ghetto," or the "Hebrew quarter." Since the end of World War II and particularly after the 1960s, the Lower East Side became thoroughly associated with the eastern European Jews who immigrated to the area from the 1880s onward. The name became firmly attached to the neighborhood, and historians, other writers, and the public at large believed that the Lower East Side was an exclusively eastern European Jewish neighborhood and that it was known by that name. The descendants of those immigrants, few of whom lived in the neighborhood, have marked it off as having deep meaning to the American Jewish experience. They have memorialized it in fiction, film, pageantry, tours, and a variety of commercial ventures. The sacralization of the Lower East Side, however, has erased its long and complex history.

Historians, writers, and others who have commented upon the Lower East Side and its significance to American Jews have not necessarily agreed on where the neighborhood's boundaries should be fixed. While most have agreed that the neighborhood lies east of the Bowery, its northern boundary remains the subject of dispute. Some commentators have cited 14th St as its uppermost border whereas others have drawn the line at Houston St. The latter is probably more accurate, but many of the sites associated with eastern European Jewish life in New York City—the Yiddish theater district, the Hebrew Technical Institute, Union Square, Cooper Union, the Asch Building where the Triangle Shirtwaist Factory operated—all lie beyond Houston. These places have played an important part in the romance of the Lower East Side.

Early History and Settlement

The neighborhood was home to free black settlers in the 17th century. Many of the small holdings operated by these marginal farmers were consolidated into larger ones, the most important being that owned by James DeLancey, whose name is remembered by Delancey St, a major thoroughfare of the neighborhood. DeLancey, a British loyalist, lost his land with the successful completion of the American Revolution. The area became a magnet for petty artisans and shopkeepers and their families, and by the 1830s it was a major area of Irish settlement. Within its borders was the notorious Five Points neighborhood, and in the 1830s the first tenement buildings went up to accommodate the influx of Irish immigrants.

German immigrants also settled in the neighborhood. Of them, many were Jews. These Jewish residents of what was then called Kleindeutschland, or Little Germany, built synagogues in the neighborhood, established a variety of stores, including some that served the Jewish community in particular, and created a vibrant Jewish culture. On Essex St, for example, a number of Jewish men who had been rejected for membership in the Masons met in 1843 at Sinshimer's Tavern and founded a secret benevolent society; it was the forerunner of the B'nai B'rith, the world's oldest Jewish fraternal organization. In the middle decades of the 19th century, Jews from Hungary, Bohemia [now in Czech Republic], Posen [now in Poland], Moravia [now in Czech Republic], and elsewhere in central Europe flocked to this neighborhood as soon as they arrived in the United States. As early as the 1850s, they were joined by handfuls of eastern European Jews. The first Russian Jewish congregation, Beth Hamedrash Hagadol, was established in 1852 on Bayard St. In 1857 Reb Pesach Rosenthal opened the Downtown Talmud Torah, which offered instruction in Yiddish.

The greatest influx of newcomers, including Russian, Lithuanian, Polish, Romanian, Hungarian, and Galician Jews, as well as Italians, Greeks, Chinese, and other non-Jews from eastern Europe, took place in the 1880s. The growth of the population of the Lower East Side coincided with the great migration from eastern and southern Europe, which did not subside until the 1920s. The immigrant Jews, including a contingent of Jews from Greece and Syria, made up about half the neighborhood's residents, the percentage varying depending on where the lines of the neighborhood were drawn. In 1892 about 75% of all New York City Jews lived in the 7th, 10th, and 13th Wards that made up the Lower East Side. In 1910 the number of Jews residing in the neighborhood peaked at 500,000. After 1910 newly arriving eastern European Jews avoided the Lower East Side, instead choosing to make their homes in Harlem, Washington Heights, and the Brooklyn neighborhoods of Brownsville and Williamsburg. By 1920 the Jewish population of the neighborhood dipped to 400,000, and it declined precipitously with each passing decade. Even as Jews moved to other neighborhoods, however, they tended to return to the Lower East Side. It was the place to go to see Yiddish plays and films through the 1930s and 1940s. New York City Jews from other neighborhoods went there to purchase iconic Jewish foods, such as bread, pickles, and fish, Jewish books and ritual objects, and matzo and other goods for Passover.

At its height as an immigrant neighborhood, the Lower East Side was considered one of America's worst slums. Jacob Riis used photographs of the neighborhood to depict the lives of the impoverished in *How the Other Half Lives* (1890), and Jewish and Christian reformers arrived to improve the lives of residents through settlement work and other kinds of uplift. The horrendous housing conditions of the Lower East Side inspired a major movement for housing reform, which led to citywide legislation in 1878 and 1901. The neighborhood was also a zone of intense cultural productivity. The settlements themselves, like the Educational Alliance and the Henry Street Settlement, encouraged the flourishing of painting, theater, and dance. The Jewish immigrant community sponsored an array of artistic, journalistic, and political endeavors.

SINCE THE 1930S

The Jewish population of the Lower East Side declined as new areas of the city opened up and as they were able to afford better housing. Some Jews remained, particularly in the housing cooperatives established by the Amalgamated Clothing Workers of America. Some Jewish institutions, like the Eldridge Street Synagogue, have remained in continuous use since the end of the 19th century. By the 1930s the Jewish population of the Lower East Side tended to be older, poorer, and more observant than New York City's Jewish population as a whole. The makeup of the neighborhood changed drastically. By the end of World War II, migrants from Puerto Rico occupied the apartments that Jews were leaving. They were followed by successive waves of newcomers from the Dominican Republic, Korea, the Philippines, India, Bangladesh, and especially China. Like the earlier immigrants these new immigrants also moved on to other neighborhoods when their resources permitted. By the beginning of the 21st century, the Lower East Side has been rediscovered not only as a site for historical walking tours and Jewish pilgrimages. Young people, Jews heavily represented among them, have begun moving to the Lower East Side to take advantage of lower rents. A number of them have been musicians, painters, and performance artists, and the neighborhood has emerged as one of Manhattan's "hottest" areas for culture and the arts.

Diner, Hasia R. *Lower East Side Memories: A Jewish Place in America* (Princeton, NJ: Princeton Univ Press, 2000)
Howe, Irving. *The World of Our Fathers* (New York: Harcourt Brace Jovanovich, 1976)
Rischin, Moses. *The Promised City: New York Jews, 1870–1914* (Cambridge, Mass: Harvard Univ Press, 1962)

Hasia R. Diner

Lower Manhattan Development Corporation. Joint city-state body created in 2001 by New York City Mayor Rudolph Giuliani and Gov George E. Pataki to aid in rebuilding Lower Manhattan, the entire area south of Houston St, following the terrorist attack of 11 Sept 2001. It was also charged with creating a permanent memorial to honor those lost in the destruction of the World Trade Center (WTC). The Lower Manhattan Development Corp (LMDC), a subsidiary of the Empire State Development Corp and a public benefit corporation, is governed by a 16-member board of directors (half appointed by the mayor and half by the governor) and funded through congressional appropriations administered by the US Department of Housing and Urban Development (HUD). Gov Pataki appointed former US Deputy Secretary of State John C. Whitehead first chairman of LMDC's board. In March 2002 LMDC helped plan and finance an interim WTC memorial in Manhattan's Battery Park, incorporating Fritz Koenig's sculpture *Sphere*, the only WTC artwork to survive the terrorist attack. LMDC also worked with WTC site owner Port Authority of New York and New Jersey to establish viewing platforms around the site perimeter and a wall bearing the name of each victim lost there. In February 2003, after a design competition in which LMDC received over 400 submissions, the corporation selected German architectural firm Studio Daniel Libeskind to plan a new building complex. LMDC has also proposed construction of a Lower Manhattan transportation hub, located at Fulton St and Broadway. In April 2003 LMDC opened a competition for the design of the permanent WTC memorial, and in November 2003 eight finalists were chosen from among the 5,201 submissions. The winning design, *Reflecting Absence* by Michael Arad and Peter Walker, was selected in January 2004. In 2003 LMDC employed a staff of 40.

Draft Mission Statement and Program for World Trade Center Memorial (New York: Lower Manhattan Development Corp, 2003)

Jeffrey Kraus

Lowville [LAU-VIL]. Town (pop 4,548) and village (pop 3,476) in central Lewis Co. Settled in 1798 by a company from Westfield, Mass, the town was formed in 1800 from Mexico (Oswego Co). Dairy farming flourished because of the rich soil on the Black River flats, and most of the town is still in agricultural use. The village incorporated in 1854 and was designated the county seat in 1864. With the Black River Canal (1851), the Rome, Watertown and Ogdensburg Railroad (1867), and the Lowville and Beaver River Railroad (1906), industries flourished, including the Asbestos Burial Casket Co (1885–1955), J. E. Habener Furniture Co (1905–31), Payne-Jones/Pajco (1935; imitation leather for books and US passports), AMF (1957; bowling pins), Kraft (1965), the largest cream cheese plant in the country, and Climax (1980; cardboard boxes). In 2002 Marks Farm was a major supplier to the kosher milk market in New York City, with hundreds of cows and a resident rabbi. Lowville is the site of the county offices, fairgrounds, a general hospital, and a shopping mall serving the county.

Arthur Einhorn

loyalists and loyalism. Also known as tories, royalists, and King's men by their contemporaries, loyalists supported Great Britain during the American Revolution. They represented a cross section of colonial society: rich and poor, rural and urban, male and female, white, black, and Indian. Religion also played a role, dividing Anglicans and Presbyterians, as many prominent loyalist families were Anglican. The strength of loyalist support in the Colony of New York has been the subject of historical debate because of variations in the meaning and definition of loyalism. Writers who use military rolls as their primary source for determining loyalist strength estimate that 23,500 male residents of New York served in the British forces. Those who rely on loyalist claims to Great Britain find that 1,107 New Yorkers filed petitions to the Loyalist Claims Commission. Both figures are problematic; the latter represents only those heads of households or their heirs who lost property in the war and survived to make a claim, and both sources overlook the women and children identified as loyalists in historical records and the thousands of Indians who served alongside the British army. These approaches also ignore changes of allegiances throughout the war.

ORIGINS OF LOYALISM

Following the end of the French and Indian War in 1763, many future loyalists disagreed with Britain's attempts to impose taxes on the colonies. Provincial assemblymen such as James DeLancey and William Smith Jr supported sanctions against Britain. What separated these men and other future loyalists from the patriots was their belief that independence was a threat to their economic security. Loyalism in New York involved more than an unquestioned allegiance to the Crown. Self-interest was also an important factor. Merchants such as William Bayard, Oliver DeLancey, and Isaac Low built their fortunes on Britain's transatlantic trade networks. Until his death in 1774, Sir William Johnson profited through his land speculation in the Mohawk Valley while in the post of superintendent of Indian Affairs of the Northern Department. Despite Johnson's considerable holdings, his family, including his son Sir John Johnson and his nephew Guy Johnson, was forced to flee the valley during the American Revolution. Indian leaders such as Joseph Brant and John Deseronto, both Mohawks, and Seneca war chief Sayenqueraghta sought support from King George III in protecting their lands from white settlement.

Although loyalism garnered support, a strong loyalist leadership failed to develop in New York in the years prior to the American Revolution for several reasons. Among their difficulties, prominent loyalists had different priorities and could not agree on a platform. In one case, William Smith Jr proposed in the provincial assembly that Britain reorganize its relationship with the colonies by appointing a lord lieutenant and creating an American parliament, but the idea lacked widespread support from other loyalists. In addition, political factions in the assembly derailed debate on the colony's future, pitting the loyalist DeLancey family against the patriot Livingstons. Although the DeLanceys had opposed Britain's actions during the 1760s when the Livingstons held power, they became associated with loyalism at the start of the Revolution because they held power in the assembly and needed the Crown's support to maintain control. Finally, the outbreak of armed conflict at Lexington and Concord in April 1775 coincided with rumors of an Indian war against white settlement on New York's western frontier. This divided the loyalists in New York about which conflict was the greater threat: a war on the frontier or colonists taking up arms against the British.

LOYALISTS DURING THE REVOLUTION

New York communities became polarized during the war as local committees of public safety asked men to demonstrate their citizenship by providing financial assistance to New England patriots, taking an oath in support of the Continental Congress, and joining their neighborhood night watch. Individuals who resisted fell under suspicion. Through the summer of 1776, the New York Provincial Congress expanded its efforts to find and punish loyalists by creating committees for detecting conspiracies, conferring power upon them to take custody of suspects and to confine them to house arrest or exile. By the year's end, hundreds of loyalists and suspected loyalists were imprisoned.

Several loyalist corps were raised to fight for the British, including Sir John Johnson's King's Royal Regiment of New York in 1776 and Butler's Rangers in 1777, both operating out of Western New York and Canada, and DeLancey's Brigade in 1776 for the defense of New York City and Long Island. Several nations of the Iroquois Confederacy, especially the Seneca and Mohawk, pledged support to the British, although the Oneida and Tuscarora supported the Continental army. The Burgoyne campaign of 1777 was an effort to take control of Albany and the rich farmlands of the Mohawk Valley to cut off New England from the rest of the colonies. Hoping to enlist loyalist support along the way, British troops moved south from Canada and west from Lake Ontario through the Mohawk Valley. In spite of early victories but hampered by poor communication and an overestimation of the loyalist support, British general John Burgoyne surrendered at Saratoga on 17 Oct 1777.

The British surrender had dire consequences for loyalists in New York State. Men who had joined the loyalist corps were sent into exile either in Canada or New York City, and thousands appeared before their local committees to explain why they had supported the British or deserted patriot forces and returned home. The legislature also enacted 30 new laws punishing loyalists. The 1779 New York Act of Attainder allowed local committees to exile loyalists, confiscate their property, and sell it to finance the patriots' war effort. By 1780 committees were permitted to exile the families of loyalists, sending them behind British lines.

The defeat at Saratoga also devastated the Iroquois Confederacy, but with the persuasion of Joseph Brant and his sister Molly, the British maintained the support of their mostly Mohawk and Seneca allies. From August to September 1779 Maj Gen John Sullivan and more than 5,000 Continental army soldiers tried to end Iroquois participation in the war by destroying their villages, fields, and orchards in the Finger Lakes. This campaign was in part because of loyalist and Indian attacks at Cherry Valley (Otsego Co) and Pennsylvania's Wyoming Valley the previous year. Thousands of Iroquois were forced to take refuge at Fort Niagara [now in Porter, Niagara Co]. From 1780 to the end of the war, Iroquois warriors and loyalist forces took revenge by raiding white settlements along the New York and Pennsylvania frontiers.

After the Revolution

In areas of strong loyalist support, including Kings, Queens, Richmond, and Suffolk Cos, it was possible for loyalists to retain their land and possessions after the war. The repercussions were hardest on those who were evicted for their loyalist support. Although affluent New Yorkers went to England, the majority of refugees established new colonies in North America where the British government promised free land grants. Over 30,000 loyalists chose Nova Scotia and created a separate loyalist province called New Brunswick. A smaller group comprising about 8,000 refugees migrated north to settle Canada's upper St. Lawrence Valley, which became Upper Canada in 1791. When Indian leaders discovered that King George III had given away their lands to the Americans as part of the peace settlement in 1783, Canada's governor Sir Frederick Haldimand offered them land on the Niagara peninsula, extending 6 miles (9.7 km) from either side of the Grand River, from its source to its mouth at Lake Erie. Joseph Brant and over 2,000 Iroquois settled there, and a smaller group of Mohawks led by John Deseronto relocated at Tyendinaga on the Bay of Quinte, in what is now Ontario.

Whether New York loyalists left by force or by choice, their initial years of resettlement were hard. Many families remained away from New York State, and some loyalists who returned to their former homes faced prosecution for treason. The Commission for Claims and Losses, or the Loyalists Claim Commission, was created in Great Britain in 1783. Loyalists making claims for loss of property had to demonstrate proof of loyalty and an inventory of lost or confiscated possessions, with an evaluation from reliable witnesses. Compensation received was usually less than the declared value. The number of migrants was considerably higher than the total number of claims filed by loyalists because most refugees were poor farmers, with little or no property to claim.

See also CANADA.

Allen, Robert S. *His Majesty's Indian Allies: British Indian Policy in the Defense of Canada, 1774–1815* (Toronto: Dundurn Press, 1993)

Ranlet, Philip. *The New York Loyalists* (Knoxville: Univ of Tennessee Press, 1986)

Tiedemann, Joseph S. *Reluctant Revolutionaries: New York City and the Road to Independence* (Ithaca: Cornell Univ Press, 1997)

Michelle Leung-Elder

Lucia, Carmen (*b* Calabria, Italy, 1902; *d* Rochester, 19 Feb 1985). Labor organizer. One of 14 children, Lucia settled with her family in Rochester in 1904 and was educated at the Sacred Heart School. She witnessed the clothing workers' uprising in Rochester in 1913 and was a frequent visitor to Rochester's Labor Lyceum. In 1916 Lucia began working in Rochester's clothing factories and soon became shop steward for the Amalgamated Clothing Workers of America (ACW). She was secretary to Rochester ACW head Abraham Chatman from 1924 to 1930 and attended the Summer School for Women Workers in Industry at Bryn Mawr College in Pennsylvania. Lucia married Leo Kowski in 1931, moved to New York City, and found employment with the Necktie Workers Union. In 1935 she began a 40-year stint with the United Hatters, Cap and Millinery Workers International Union, organizing workers throughout the United States and abroad, rising to vice president in 1946. She was also instrumental in organizing retail clerks in California, where she lived to retirement in 1974. Lucia returned to Rochester in 1979 and resided at St. Anne's Heritage Home.

"The Hatters' Fighting Lady," *Rochester Democrat and Chronicle,* 3 Feb 1980

Lucia, Carmen. Oral history, 1978–79. Twentieth Century Trade Union Woman collection. Bentley Library, Wayne State Univ, Detroit

Christopher Martin

Ludington (Ogden), Sybil (*b* ?Branford, Conn, 5 Apr 1761; *d* Unadilla, Otsego Co, 26 Feb 1839). Patriot. When an infant she was taken to Fredericksburgh [now Kent, Putnam Co], where her father Henry operated mills. He was named colonel of the Dutchess Co militia, and on 26 Apr 1777 a rider arrived at their house with news of Maj Gen William Tryon's attack on Danbury, Conn. Sixteen-year-old Sybil was sent to alert the militiamen, a task that required a night ride of 40 miles (64 km) through the present towns of Kent and Carmel (Putnam Co) and East Fishkill (Dutchess Co). In 1784 she married Edmond Ogden, bore one son, and in 1792 removed to Catskill (Greene Co), where her husband died. She was licensed as an innkeeper (1803) but apparently went to live with her son at Unadilla *ca* 1810. She made no mention of her ride in her 1837 pension application based on her husband's war service, and the tale first appeared in print in a family memoir and in a magazine article, both 1907. Sculptor Anna Hyatt Huntington helped commemorate Ludington with her equestrian bronze, placed in Carmel (Putnam Co) in 1961, and a US postage stamp was issued in 1975.

Dacquino, V. T. *Sybil Ludington: The Call to Arms* (Fleischmanns, NY: Purple Mountain Press, 2000)

Field Horne

Luhan [née Ganson], **Mabel Dodge** (*b* Buffalo, 26 Feb 1879; *d* Taos, N Mex, 13 Aug 1962). Arts patron and writer. Born into a wealthy Buffalo family and widowed as a young woman, she lived in Italy with her second husband, Edwin Dodge, from 1904 until 1912. Returning to the United States, she hosted a famous salon at 23 5th Ave in New York City. Her circle included Gertrude Stein, Emma Goldman, Margaret Sanger, Alfred Stieglitz, Max Eastman, John Reed, and other avant-garde intellectuals. She joined the feminist Heterodoxy Club, supported birth control, and advocated free love. An early proponent of psychoanalysis, she became a patient of A. A. Brill and wrote about Freudian theories in a regular column for Hearst newspapers. An influential hostess, she helped fund modern dance pioneer Isadora Duncan, promoted the postimpressionist Armory Show (1913) held in the 69th Regimental Armory at 25th St and Lexington Ave, and was an organizer of the Madison Square Garden pageant (1913) in support of striking Paterson, NJ, silk workers. Divorced from Dodge in 1916, Mabel moved with her new husband, artist Maurice Sterne, to Taos, N Mex, where, as she later wrote, her "life broke in two." She divorced Sterne, married Pueblo Indian Antonio Luhan, and embraced the climate, terrain, and Native American cultures of the Southwest as healing forces for mind and body. She was instrumental in transforming Taos into an artist colony during the 1920s and 1930s, attracting such luminaries as D. H. Lawrence and Georgia O'Keeffe. While in Taos, Luhan wrote the multivolume *Intimate Memories* (1933), a chronicle of intellectual and artistic life in the early 20th century.

Frazer, Winifred L. *Mabel Dodge Luhan* (Boston: Twayne Publishers, 1984)

Christine Kleinegger

lulus. Slang term for extra compensation above regular salary for New York State legislators. Beginning in 1948 it was used as a popular nickname for payment in lieu of expenses, when the legislature used a lump-sum system to reimburse work-related expenses. As the term evolved it came to represent special bonuses over and above per diem expenses that legislative leaders paid out to reward and control members. The system was cloaked in secrecy, with leaders revealing who got a lulu and how much money only at the end of each session, giving rank-and-file members a strong incentive to cooperate with the leaders by voting for controversial legislation. The leaders' ability to hand out lulus, coupled with their absolute power to appoint the chairs of committees and their control of campaign funds, created one of the most leadership-dominated legislatures in the nation. Controversy erupted over lulus during the government reform movement of the 1970s. The *Albany Times-Union* mounted a campaign against lulus, portrayed by a cartoonist as a buxom dance hall girl. Reform groups filed a well-publicized legal challenge but lost with the courts upholding the legislature's authority to set its own salary and expense payments. Emboldened by its success in fighting off criticism, the legislature expanded the number of committee chair positions and minor leadership slots that were deemed worthy of a lulu. By the early 1990s, almost every member of the legislature got a lulu, ranging from $48,000 for the assembly speaker and senate majority leader, to $9,000 for ranking minority members on less important committees, but legislative leaders did regularize the payments and spell them out in advance in state law.

Rosen, Hy, and Peter Slocum. *From Rocky to Pataki: Character and Caricatures in New York Politics* (Syracuse: Syracuse Univ Press, 1998)

Peter Slocum

lumber and timber products. For centuries before the arrival of European settlers, the Native American inhabitants of present-day New York State depended on the region's forests for firewood, bark, pole-building materials, bowls for food storage, and many other products. They developed the unique birchbark canoe and the basket of black ash splints. European settlers brought their own heritage of using trees and wood, along with iron-cutting tools, and found a rich mix of tree species suitable for making everything from buildings to furniture to musical instruments to kitchen utensils to burial caskets. Bernhard Fernow, a forester active in the Adirondack region of the state from the 1890s to 1910s, is alleged to have proclaimed, "From cradle to grave, you are surrounded with wood." At the beginning of the 21st century, New York State firms that use wood continue to show a tremendous diversity of products.

Colonial Times

In 18th-century New York, most wood was cut for cooking and heating. Labor was relatively plentiful but machines were lacking, in contrast to 21st-century conditions, in which labor is expensive and machines are used to reduce costs. Trees were felled by axes, and logs were moved short distances usually by animal power. Logs were employed as structural timbers in buildings, sometimes as round pieces and sometimes squared on two sides with hand tools. Workmen used wedges and other hand tools to split smaller pieces out of larger logs. Most wooden items produced in colonial New York were utilitarian. During this period both precision-finishing woodworking tools and much fine furniture was imported from Europe.

Building styles usually depended on the backgrounds of the settlers. Buildings constructed from entire logs—the log cabins of early American history—were mainly built by immigrants from Scandinavia in areas where softwood timber was plentiful. Dutch, English, and German settlers, who predominated in early New York, built half-timbered buildings using a mix of brick and wood, while southern European settlers used more stone and very limited amounts of wood. The advent of water-powered sawmills greatly increased the use of wood, but these mills were small, the logs still transported only short distances to the mills, and the lumber used locally. Better homes were often constructed entirely of stone.

Settlers also exploited many tree species for roofing and siding material, producing shakes (thin, boardlike pieces of wood split from a larger piece) and shingles (similar pieces sawn, rather than split, from a log). In colonial times the heartwood of old-growth white pine was widely used for shakes and shingles. Ash and oak were also employed for this purpose.

The 19th Century

Widespread development occurred in New York State in the 19th century, with almost every area settled and urban centers growing. From the 1820s the Erie Canal facilitated long-distance transport, and beginning in the 1830s and 1840s, railroads increased such transport. Lumber and wood products were shipped great distances, and with the development of water and steam power, manufacturing facilities sprang up across much of the state. While timber harvesting was still labor intensive by later standards, the introduction of steam engines facilitated movement of logs out of the forest. In the Adirondacks and the Tug Hill area of northern New York, logs—principally buoyant softwoods such as spruce, fir, and pine—were floated down streams and rivers to sawmills. Glens Falls (Warren Co) and the surrounding area on the upper Hudson River became a major lumber-producing region, shipping through the port of Albany to the growing cities of North America; it is said that in 1865 more lumber passed through the port of Albany than any other US port. Elsewhere in the state, hardwoods and softwoods were mainly harvested for local use. In 1869, New York State's peak lumber production year, its sawmills employed about 7,500 people and milled 1.3 million board feet of lumber, of which 80% was softwood and 20% hardwood. New York State led the nation in lumber production during the 1860s and 1870s.

Many small shake and shingle mills operated, with northern white cedar replacing white pine as their chief raw material by the 1870s. By the end of the 19th century virtually all wooden shakes and shingles used in New York were imported from the cedar forests of Maine.

Into the 20th Century

By the beginning of the 20th century, New York State's major urban centers and their growing populations consumed huge quantities of wood products. Softwood lumber was a major home-building material, though brick, concrete, and iron were employed in large urban structures. Hardwoods were used for many products, especially furniture. Furniture manufacturers developed, with western New York State's Jamestown (Chautauqua Co) already one of the nation's furniture centers by 1850. Firms such as Jamestown Stirling, Harden of McConnellsville, Ethan Allen of Falconer and Boonville, and Stickley of Manlius and Fayetteville employed cherry and maple lumber, for example, from New York's forests to manufacture fine furniture, and these companies became widely known by 1900. Smaller firms producing specialty products—from shoe forms and brush handles to cabinets, boxes, and caskets—located across New York during the same period.

By the mid-1800s many observers had expressed concern over the management of Adirondack forests, which were threatened by major forest fires and overharvesting of timber during the latter 19th century. New York City's water supply came from the Hudson River, whose headwaters originated in the Adirondack Mountains, and in 1883 the influential *New York Tribune* called for protection of "the fountainheads of the noble streams that conserve our physical and commercial prosperity." Sentiments against timber harvesting in the Adirondacks hardened further, and an 1885 constitutional amendment ruled all tree cutting forbidden on state lands within the newly designated Adirondack Forest Preserve. This decision, along with the spread of softwood lumber harvesting across North America, led to a drastic reduction in total lumber

Lumberyard, Streever Lumber Co, Ballston Spa, *ca* 1915.

production in New York State as well as to a rise in the importance of the state's hardwood lumbering.

RECENT EVENTS

At the beginning of the 21st century, the state's annual lumber production is approximately 560 million board feet, of which 80% is hardwood and 20% softwood. Virtually all lumber used in the state for home construction comes from other states. New York is a major importer of all kinds of wood products.

Over half the New York State firms manufacturing wood products are located within the New York City metropolitan area. Some employ only a few people to create very special products; others employ hundreds and produce items such as pianos, kitchen cabinets, and lawn furniture. The huge consumer market in the metropolitan region and ready access to transportation allow the production of made-to-order specialty items, thus making the area attractive to small manufacturing plants. Elsewhere in the state, small plants have developed from part-time, single-person operations; the Catskill region has recently fostered the growth of many such firms. Furniture continues to be an important component of New York's wood-processing industries. The state ranks among the ten chief furniture-producing areas in the country, and its furniture industry employs 17,000 people and has annual sales of over $1.6 billion.

Wooden pallets, widely used in the transportation industry and manufactured across the state, are fabricated from millions of board feet of low-grade lumber annually and are important to the economic health of the state's sawmills. An estimated 57 New York State firms produce wooden pallets, with combined annual sales of $60.6 million; the state ranks 12th nationally in pallet production.

Wood-based manufacturing in New York State faces a number of challenges: energy costs higher than in many areas of the country, high wage rates, changing furniture styles requiring industry flexibility, and concerns over reuse or disposal of residues and wastes, especially for firms in urban locations. Some residues, excluding sawdust and other fine wastes, serve as fuel for industrial and home heating, and state regulations governing discharge of substances into water bodies or the atmosphere are strict. Foreign competition has increased dramatically in recent years, with furniture components shipped in from Asia.

Wood products manufacturing remains an important segment of the state's economy, employing over 30,000 people and shipping over $30 billion worth of goods annually. The industry ranks among the ten largest manufacturing activities in New York State. It provides a market for timber from the state's forests, enabling owners of private forests to achieve better long-term management of the trees, water, and wildlife on their lands.

Canham, Hugh O. *Forest Wood Products.* New York State Forest Resources Assessment, no. 7 (Albany: NYS Department of Environmental Conservation, 1981)

Canham, Hugh O., and George R. Armstrong. *Long Term Trends in New York's Timber Industries and Their Implications* (Albany: NYS Office of Planning Coordination, 1969)

Canham, Hugh O., and Kevin S. King. *Just the Facts: An Overview of New York's Wood-Based Economy and Forest Resource* (Albany: Empire State Forest Products Association, 1998)

Hugh O. Canham

Lumberland. Town (pop 1,939) in S Sullivan Co. Settlement along the Delaware River preceded the Revolutionary War, and the town formed from Mamakating in 1798. While lumbering was its chief industry, bluestone quarries near Pond Eddy shipped their product by canal or railroad to New York City. Glen Spey was named *ca* 1870 by George Ross MacKenzie, vice president of Singer Sewing Machine Co, who built mansions for himself and for each of his seven children along with a schoolhouse, a church, and other buildings, many of which still stand. After World War II Glen Spey became a resort for over 200 Ukrainian families who continue to hold an annual festival. Lumberland is the site of several of the reservoirs built along the Mongaup River to provide hydroelectric power; they lie in the Mongaup Valley State Wildlife Management Area, home to a growing population of bald eagles.

John Conway

lunar modules. Spacecraft used by US astronauts to land on the Moon during the late 1960s and early 1970s. On 7 Nov 1962 the Grumman Aircraft Engineering Corp of Bethpage (Nassau Co) won a $345 million contract (renegotiated to $387.9 million the following January) to design and build the lunar modules (LMs) for the Apollo program. The LMs were the first spacecraft—vehicles that operate totally outside Earth's atmosphere—to be operated by crew onboard, and they carried the first people to the lunar surface. By 1966 Grumman, Long Island's largest manufacturing employer, had 6,500–7,000 people working on the LMs, had become a multimillion-dollar corporation, and had gained distinction as NASA's second largest contractor.

The LM was a two-stage spacecraft. Many contemporaries called it the "bug" because of its four insect-like landing legs. The legs attached to the gold Mylar-covered, cube-shaped descent stage that held the engine that allowed the LM to descend to the lunar surface. On top of the descent unit rested the ascent stage with the ship's control room and the engine that lifted it off the Moon. Perhaps the most important LM was not the first one that landed on the Moon on 20 July 1969 during the Apollo 11 mission but the one used during the Apollo 13 mission from 11 to 17 Apr 1970. After an explosion in the Apollo service module, the three Apollo 13 astronauts had to abandon their lunar landing attempt and live for more than three days in their LM, a ship designed to sustain two people for 48 hours. With instructions from Grumman and NASA engineers, the astronauts converted their LM into a "lifeboat" that safely returned them to Earth. By the end of the Apollo program in 1972, Grumman had built 12 operational LMs, 6 of which landed on the Moon.

Kelly, Thomas J. *Moon Lander: How We Developed the Apollo Lunar Module* (Washington, DC: Smithsonian Institution Press, 2001)

Pellegrino, Charles R., and Joshua Stoff. *Chariots for Apollo: The Untold Story behind the Race to the Moon* (1985; repr New York: Avon Books, 1999)

David H. Onkst

Lunn, George R(ichard) (*b* Lenox, Iowa, 23 June 1873; *d* Rancho Santa Fe, Calif, 27 Nov 1948). Minister and politician. Lunn served in the Spanish-American War and graduated in 1901 from Union Theological Seminary in New York City. Ordained a Presbyterian minister, Lunn served at the Lafayette Presbyterian Church in Brooklyn from 1901 to 1904. From 1904 to 1909 he was pastor of the First Reformed Church in Schenectady, where his preaching for social reform and against corruption angered many in the congregation and led to his resignation. In 1911, deciding on a career in politics, Lunn joined the Socialist Party and was elected mayor of Schenectady—the first Socialist mayor in New York State—by a rapidly growing working-class electorate. The rise of Schenectady's working-class population was due to the founding of General Electric Co in 1892. Between 1900 and 1910 the city's Socialist Party grew considerably, from 32 votes for Socialist candidates in the 1900 presidential election to 2,628 votes in the 1910 election.

Upgrading the city's infrastructure was a primary concern of the Lunn administration, as was instituting municipal reform, expanding the park system, ensuring the rights of strikers, and improving areas of public health. In the 1913 mayoral election Lunn lost to a Fusion ticket of Republicans, Democrats, and Progressives. In 1915 he ran for mayor again and won; the next year he was elected to Congress as a Democrat. For a short time he served as both congressman and mayor. In 1917 he lost the mayoral election and was defeated for a second congressional term in 1918. He was reelected as a Democrat to his third and fourth terms as Schenectady mayor in 1919 and 1921, resigning on 1 Jan 1923 to run successfully for lieutenant governor of New York State under Gov Alfred E. Smith that year. Lunn was appointed public service commissioner of New York State in 1925, a position he held until 1942, when he resigned because of ill health.

Gardner, George R. Lunn. *The Schenectadians: The Story of Schenectady's 20th Century and Two Men Who Helped Shape It* (Lincoln, Nebr: iUniverse, Writer's Club Press, 2001)

Hendrickson, Kenneth. "George R. Lunn and the Socialist Era in Schenectady, New York, 1909–1916," *New York History* 47 (Jan 1966): 22–38

Brian Keough

Lusk Committee [Joint Legislative Committee to Investigate Seditious Activities]. Established on 26 Mar 1919 at the height of the Red Scare, the committee questioned individuals and organizations suspected of advocating the overthrow of the American government in violation of state criminal anarchy statutes. Between June 1919 and March 1920, the committee, named for its chairman, Clayton Lusk, a freshman state senator from Cortland, capitalized on public fear of radicalism to raid offices, infiltrate meetings, examine documents, and subpoena witnesses. The committee investigated 77 organizations, most in New York City, including the Russian Soviet Bureau, the Rand School of Social Science, and the Industrial Workers of the World; local Communist Party and Socialist Party chapters in cities across the state; and publishers of radical newspapers. In addition to obtaining membership lists to assist district attorneys in prosecuting alleged radicals, the committee held hearings that resulted in over 3,000 pages of testimony, primarily from law enforcement officials, detectives, and educators, concerning the proliferation of seditious organizations. The committee's final report, submitted on 24 Apr 1920, had over 4,000 pages of text and evidence. In an effort to protect the state's youth from radical teachings, the committee recommended several educational reforms. Removing candidates of the Socialist and Communist Parties from all state ballots and creating a secret service to investigate further those individuals suspected of anarchy and sedition were also recommended. Eventually laws regarding teacher loyalty oaths and state licensing of private schools were enacted in 1921; however, Gov Alfred E. Smith successfully fought for their repeal upon returning to office in 1923. As public fear of radicalism waned, so did the committee's influence. Lusk suffered a similar fate. Once touted as a potential Republican gubernatorial candidate, he was linked by the press to bribery scandals and decided not to seek reelection in 1924.

Jaffe, Julian F. *Crusade against Radicalism: New York during the Red Scare, 1914–1924* (Port Washington, NY: Kennikat Press, 1972)

New York State Legislature. Joint Committee Investigating Seditious Activities. *Revolutionary Radicalism: Its History, Purpose, and Tactics* (Albany: J. B. Lyon, 1920)

Todd Pfannestiel

Lutherans. Protestant denomination. Founded by the German reformer Martin Luther (1486–1546), it sought to rectify perceived abuses within Roman Catholicism, emphasizing worship in the vernacular, upholding the office of ministry as a divine institution, and establishing a congregational structure with lay responsibility for calling ordained pastors.

The first congregations formed at Fort Orange [now Albany] and New Amsterdam [now New York City] in 1649 barely survived the 17th century with only intermittent pastoral leadership. They were revived when Justus Falckner, the first Lutheran ordained in America, accepted a call to the original two congregations in 1703, rebuilding both and ministering to Lutherans throughout the area of the Hudson Valley, including eastern New Jersey. By 1750 the number of congregations grew to 23 with increased immigration. In 1786 the New York Ministerium—a synodical organization composed of pastors and lay representatives—was organized to supervise further growth and development. Massive 19th-century immigration from Germany and Scandinavia established the modern Lutheran Church of New York State, composed of multiple synods and urban concentrations in Buffalo, the Schoharie Valley, Albany, metropolitan New York City, and the Middle Hudson and Long Island regions.

New York Lutheranism developed a distinctive pattern, with many groups embracing either orthodoxy or pietism, but with a developing group of moderate church bodies as well. The New York Ministerium developed a pronounced Lutheran orthodoxy emphasizing confessional theology, dogma, and liturgical renewal. This was reinforced as 19th-century German immi-

Rev Alfred J. Schroeder, pastor of the Lutheran Church of the Resurrection, Syracuse, 1979.

gration brought new waves of orthodox Lutherans, who formed hundreds of new congregations. The Buffalo Synod, under the leadership of Buffalo minister Johannes Andreas Augustus Grabau, emphasized the ordained ministry as a divinely instituted office and demanded orthodoxy and congregational obedience to pastors. Another faction joined an eastern district of the Missouri Synod of Lutherans, which emphasized the centrality of the congregation in their polity, and a debate ensued among German Lutheran immigrants. The debate created schisms in the Buffalo Synod and the New York Ministerium, and dissidents in both eventually moved into the Missouri Synod. The Buffalo Synod survived, though much smaller in size and more amenable to a democratic spirit. All the Lutheran groups in New York State emphasized religious education and established numerous parish schools, preseminaries, seminaries, and two institutions of higher education—Concordia College and Bronxville and Wagner College. Lutheran pietism, which had roots in colonial New York, appealed to acculturated, English-speaking Lutherans. Two Albany-area synodical bodies—the Hartwick and Franckean Synods—introduced revivalistic practices as well as a strong emphasis on moral reform, including the abolition of slavery.

By the early 20th century New York State Lutherans had become among the most diverse group of Lutherans in any state, with 14 of the 24 Lutheran groups found in the United States located in the state. A significant cluster of Norwegian Lutheran congregations in Brooklyn and Staten Island developed in the late 19th century and supported an influential deaconess community and hospital. Swedish and Finnish immigrants also established congregations in the metropolitan New York area. Immigrant groups from the West Indies established African American congregations in Harlem and Queens. In these and other congregations a strong identity, both ethnic and religious, has sustained ethnic and cultural diversity. The close proximity of different Lutheran church bodies in urban areas and lay impatience with secondary theological differences, which different synods represented, stimulated a pan-Lutheranism and numerous mergers throughout the 20th century. The earliest, the United Lutheran Synod of New York (1928), provided leadership for the United Lutheran Church of America (1918) and later the Lutheran Church in America (1962). Both organizations established their national headquarters in New York City. Lutheranism in New York State has strongly influenced national Lutheran church bodies, including the Lutheran Church–Missouri Synod and the recently formed Evangelical Lutheran Church in America (1988), with its emphases on inter-Lutheran cooperation, liturgical renewal, social ministry, and advocacy of public issues. In the early 21st century, Lutherans in New York State worship in 20 different languages from German and English to Swahili and Arabic. There are approximately 1 million New York State residents with Lutheran roots, including 300,000 baptized members of approximately 500 Lutheran congregations.

Kreider, Harry J. *The Beginnings of Lutheranism in New York* (New York: United Lutheran Synod, 1949)

Nelson, E. Clifford. *The Lutherans in North America* (Philadelphia: Fortress Press, 1980)

Scholz, Robert. *Press toward the Mark: History of the United Lutheran Synod of New York and New England, 1830–1930.* American Theological Library Association Monograph Series, no. 37 (Metuchen, NJ: Scarecrow Press, 1995)

Robert F. Scholz

Lyme. Town (pop 2,015) in W Jefferson Co. Settled in 1802, Lyme grew little until after the War of 1812. It was formed from Brownville in 1817 and a colony of Quakers from Philadelphia settled in 1818. The first of many limestone quarries opened in 1825; quarrying reached its peak around World War I. Shipbuilding began in 1832 and continued for 50 years. Completion of the Rome, Watertown and Ogdensburg Railroad connection in 1852 created new industries and allowed others to expand, including commercial fishing for whitefish and lake herring, and hay growing for downstate markets. Since the 1920s tourism has been the major industry. Point Peninsula is part of the town and is the site of Long Point State Park.

Laura Lynne Scharer

Lynbrook. Village (pop 19,911) in Hempstead (Nassau Co). The locality at the intersection of Merrick Rd, Hempstead Ave, Broadway, and Atlantic Ave was known as Bloomfield and then as Pearsalls Corners. It acquired a railroad station in 1867 and then, as Pearsalls, a post office in 1873. Its population grew rapidly, and many of its new residents were Brooklyn transplants. In 1894 it chose its current name by inverting the syllables of Brooklyn, and incorporated in 1911. Population growth was 274% in the 1920s and continued at a more gradual pace until a 1970 peak. The village was home to the nationally known Henri's (1915–1930s), operated by Henri Charpentier, inventor of the crêpe suzette, and to Whittaker Chambers in his childhood and retirement.

Lynda R. Day

lynching. The history of New York State, in common with that of other northern states, reveals no consistent pattern in the use of this summary, extralegal punishment, which did not always imply hanging and was not directed solely at African Americans. In New York Colony, at least 18 black slaves were publicly hanged, burned, and broken on the wheel after the slave revolt of 1712, and after the suspected slave conspiracy of 1741 from 13 to 31 were executed. But these brutal punishments, which followed quickly on apprehension, do not qualify as lynchings because they were inflicted after trials.

Although lynching originally had a wider meaning, embracing other and occasionally nonlethal extralegal actions, such as tarring and feathering, by the 1830s the term was largely limited to signify extralegal death at the hands of a mob. In New York City during the draft riots of 13–15 July 1863, there were a number of lynchings, that is, hangings, burnings, and drownings, of African Americans. In the aftermath, many Blacks left the city, leading to a 20% drop in their numbers as recorded by the census of 1865.

There are four, possibly five, known records of individual lynchings in New York State. A black man accused of raping a white girl was reputedly lynched in Saratoga Co during the 1860s. Robert Jackson, "alias Robert Lewis," a 22-year-old African American accused of raping a white woman, was hanged at Port Jervis (Orange Co) on 2 June 1892, despite the efforts of town notables to save him; an inquest followed but brought no indictment. Another Black, John Johnston, accused of murder, was lynched at Auburn (Cayuga Co) on 14 Nov 1893. A white vagrant, George H. Smith, accused of murdering his father-in-law, was shot by a posse at Ransomville (Niagara Co) on 10 Jan 1896, and Paulo Boleta, probably an Italian immigrant, was accused of murderous assault and lynched at Greenwich (Washington Co) on 14 Dec 1916. There are also occasional records of narrowly averted lynchings, as in Harlem in 1909, when an African American youth, Edward Ashford, shot white Joseph Hughes in the leg. Ashford, who said he had been menaced by Hughes and other whites, was saved from a mob through the intervention of socially prominent Charles Collis, who reportedly told the crowd, "We don't lynch here. This is not the South." There were likely unrecorded lynchings as well. But the persistent threat of lynching was never used as a means to enforce a social caste system in New York State. It was not employed systematically, as in the post–Civil War South, to intimidate African Americans.

Dray, Philip. *At the Hands of Persons Unknown: The Lynching of Black America* (New York: Random House, 2002)

Waldrep, Christopher. *The Many Faces of Judge Lynch: Extralegal Violence and Punishment in America* (New York: Palgrave Macmillan, 2002)

Janice K. Dunham

Depiction of a lynching during the New York City draft riot, week of 13 July 1863; detail from the *Illustrated London News*, 15 Aug 1863.

Lyndon. Town (pop 661) located in E Cattaraugus Co. Settled in 1808, the town was formed in 1829 from Franklinville. A post office named Elgin operated in Lyndon from 1828 to 1903. The town was briefly renamed Elgin in 1857–58. General farming shifted to dairying in the mid–19th century. After more than a century of gradual population loss, the number of inhabitants started to increase in the 1970s. Agriculture remains the predominant land use.

Bruce D. Fredrickson and Madelynn P. Fredrickson

Lyndonville. Village (pop 862) in Yates (Orleans Co). In early years it was the site of a brickyard and a foundry; a gristmill (1836) continued to use waterpower until 1937, three years before it closed. A post office opened in 1846 and became a station on the Rome, Watertown and Ogdensburg Railroad (1876; called Hojack). The village was incorporated in 1903. Employers in the 20th century included the Lyndonville Canning Co (1916), Speas Manufacturing Co vinegar plant, P. D. Patten Manufacturing Co (gas engines), Monroe Electronics, and a DuPont insecticide plant. In 2004 Lyndonville employers included fruit processors Nakano Foods, Bowman Apple Products, and H. H. Dobbins.

Elena Ames

Lynds, Elam (*b* Litchfield, Conn, 1784; *d* Brooklyn, 8 Jan 1855). Prison warden and reformer. Initially apprenticed to a hatter, Lynds became involved in the New York State Militia as a young man, rising to the rank of major and serving in the US Army during the War of 1812. Lynds became principal keeper of the Auburn Prison (Cayuga Co) in 1817 and head warden in 1821. There he applied the discipline of his military background in creating the Auburn system, which became the leading method for prison construction and management worldwide. Lynds reorganized the prison architecture, dividing living quarters into cell blocks for easier surveillance and control, instituting single-occupant cells, and creating general workhouse space for the prisoners during the day. He mandated uniforms, a rule of silence, and lockstep movement from place to place, and supported liberal use of the lash. Lynds believed the Auburn system changed the focus of the prison from containment to reform of the convict. Though his reforms were studied and emulated, Lynds was a controversial figure, eventually being ousted as warden in 1825 due to persistent complaints of prisoner abuse. Lynds was almost immediately given the job of constructing a new prison in Ossining (Westchester Co). Over four years he built Sing Sing Prison, entirely with convict labor, and became its first head warden. Like Auburn, Sing Sing became a model prison. Nevertheless accusations continued to follow Lynds and his methods. Though a lengthy investigation exonerated him of charges of abuse and financial mismanagement, he resigned in disgust in 1830. Eight years later he returned to head Auburn but was forced to step down under the cloud of a grand jury indictment the next year. In 1843 Lynds was back heading Sing Sing, only to be removed a year later under charges of cruelty and misappropriation, finally leaving public service for good. Despite his checkered career, his reforms influenced the construction and management of penal institutions for more than a century.

History of New York State Prisons, "'Sent Up the River': Sing Sing Correction Facility," http://www.geocities.com/MotorCity/Downs/3548/facility/singsing.html

Lewis, W. David. *From Newgate to Dannemora: The Rise of the Penitentiary in New York, 1796–1848* (Ithaca: Cornell Univ Press, 1965)

Matthew Taylor Raffety

The Rochester, Syracuse, and Eastern interurban railroad passing above the Erie Canal in Lyons, *ca* 1909.

Lyons. Town (pop 5,831) and village (pop 3,695) in S central Wayne Co. The town was settled in 1789; in 1794 Pulteney estate agent Charles Williamson initiated settlement of the village. Lyons was formed from Sodus in 1811; the village, the county seat, was incorporated in 1831. The Erie Canal (1822) and New York Central Railroad (1853) crossed the town. Lyons was once home to several peppermint oil companies, including H. G. Hotchkiss Essential Oils (1841–1990), and in the 19th century produced half the nation's output of peppermint oil. Pottery was also an important industry. In 2003 Silgan Containers manufactured cans, and Parker Hannifin produced refrigeration and air-conditioning parts; the town's farms produced a variety of field crops. The county courthouse (1854) is a landmark. The motion picture *Lady in White* (1988) was filmed in Lyons. The Peppermint Days Festival is held each July.

Scott C. Monje

Lyonsdale. Town (pop 1,273) in SE Lewis Co. The area was settled briefly in 1792 by the French refugee Castorland colony and permanently in 1819. Tanneries using hemlock bark from the forest were the first industries. The town was formed in 1873 from Greig. In the 19th and 20th centuries the Moose River's waterfalls powered a rag paper mill, sawmills, and, beginning in 1888, pulp mills. Gould Paper Co (1896) in Lyons Falls bought the pulp mills and continued annual spring log drives until 1947. The lower Moose River, classified a IV to V+ stream on the International Rating Scale, attracts kayakers from across the nation.

Emily Williams

Lyons Falls. Village (pop 591) in West Turin and Leyden (Lewis Co). Mills took advantage of the waterpower from falls (70 ft/21.3 m) on the Black River. The Black River Canal (1851–1924) and the Rome, Watertown and Ogdensburg Railroad (1867) provided transportation. In 1896 Gordias H. P. Gould established a large pulp and paper mill. It stimulated the growth of the village, which incorporated in 1900. After 1951 the mill passed through a series of owners, including Georgia-Pacific; it closed in 2001, idling 180 workers and creating a serious economic downturn. Its hydroelectric plant continued operating under new ownership. The picturesque Three Way Bridge (1853–1964; two successive structures) was a landmark at the junction of the Moose and Black Rivers just above the falls.

Arthur Einhorn

Lysander. Town (pop 19,285) in NW Onondaga Co. The first settler arrived in 1793, and the town was formed in 1794. In the 19th century its level land was farmed, with tobacco, small fruits, and grain as principal crops. Onondaga Co's first planned community, Radisson, was created in 1969 by the state's Urban Development Corp on land used by the federal government for explosives manufacture during World War II. In 2003 Radisson had an Anheuser-Busch brewery, technology plants, and 2,100 residential units. A part of the explosives test range is now the 3,611-acre (1,461 ha) Three Rivers State Wildlife Management Area, a classic lake plain habitat. Lysander has 30 miles (48 km) of waterfront on Cross Lake and the Seneca River. In the western part of town, dairying and crop and small fruit farming continue, and Plainville Turkey Farms raises and processes more turkeys than any other farm in the northeastern United States.

Barbara S. Rivette

M

MacCracken, Henry Noble (*b* Toledo, Ohio, 19 Nov 1880; *d* Poughkeepsie, 7 May 1970). Educator. He graduated from New York University (NYU) in 1900, and after gaining further degrees at NYU and Harvard, he studied at Oxford University and taught literature at Yale University and Smith College. In 1915 he became the fifth president of Vassar College in Poughkeepsie. MacCracken, a suffragist, guided the pioneer women's college to international prominence, encouraging its recently enfranchised graduates to be active citizens. A man of boundless energy, he fostered change both in college governance and curriculum and in creating institutions such as the first county health organization in the United States for Dutchess Co (1916), the American Junior Red Cross (1917), the Kosciuszko Foundation (1925), the Seven Sisters organization (1925), Sarah Lawrence College in Bronxville (1926), and the National Conference of Christians and Jews (1939). During the depression he was secretary of the Dutchess Co Works Administration and head of the Temporary Emergency Relief Administration. From his retirement as president of Vassar in 1946 until his death, he undertook projects to preserve and popularize Dutchess Co history.

Chronology of Vassar History, 1861–1975, http://faculty.vassar.edu/daniels

Daniels, Elizabeth A. *Bridges to the World: Henry Noble MacCracken and Vassar College* (Clinton Corners, NY: College Avenue Press, 1994)

Elizabeth A. Daniels

Macdonough, Thomas (*b* The Trap [now MacDonough, Del], 31 Dec 1783; *d* at sea, Atlantic Ocean, 10 Nov 1825). Naval officer. The sixth of nine children, Macdonough was orphaned by age 12 and worked as a clerk until an elder brother used political connections to get him a midshipman's warrant in the US Navy in February 1800. While serving in the Mediterranean during the Barbary War, Macdonough supervised construction of gunboats in Italy. In 1810 he obtained a furlough from the navy and made a voyage from New York City to England and India as captain of the merchant brig *Gulliver*. Upon hearing of war with Britain two years later, Macdonough returned to the navy on 17 July 1812 and that September took command of US naval forces on Lake Champlain. For the next two years he built vessels at Burlington and Vergennes, Vt. When the British invaded from Canada in September 1814, he positioned his squadron off Plattsburgh to await attack by a slightly superior British squadron. In the ensuing battle on 11 Sept 1814, Macdonough's flagship *Saratoga* was under heavy fire by HMS *Confiance* until he used skillfully deployed spring lines to turn his ship around, bringing a fresh broadside to bear, thereby forcing British Capt George Downie to surrender. The Battle of Plattsburgh, one of the most decisive engagements in naval history, compelled the British to withdraw to Canada and led London to seek peace with the United States. Macdonough commanded the US Navy's yard at Portsmouth, NH (1815–18), sailed to Russia as commander of the *Guerriere* (1818–20), then oversaw completion of the *Ohio* at the New York Navy Yard in Brooklyn (1820–24). While commander of the *Constitution* (1824–25) during a Mediterranean tour, as the ship was returning to New York City, Macdonough died.

Eckert, Edward. "Thomas Macdonough: Architect of a Wilderness Navy." In *Command under Sail*, ed. James C. Bradford (Annapolis, Md: Naval Institute Press, 1985)

James C. Bradford

MacDowell, Edward Alexander (*b* New York City, 18 Dec 1861; *d* New York City, 23 Jan 1908). Composer, pianist, and teacher. Originally trained as a pianist, MacDowell studied composition and piano in Germany. In 1888 he and his wife Marion returned to Boston, where MacDowell became a popular and highly regarded composer, introducing such works as his *Piano Concerto No. 2* (1885) and *"Indian" Suite* for orchestra (1896). In 1896 MacDowell was invited to be Columbia University's first professor of music. He built up the department but left in 1904 after quarreling with the school's new president. After a car accident, his health declined. MacDowell was the most popular 19th-century American composer, particularly for his piano music, which included four sonatas and many suites such as *Woodland Sketches* (1896), in the romantic style of Schumann and Grieg. Individual pieces such as "To a Wild Rose" remain popular with pianists.

Levy, Alan. *Edward MacDowell: An American Master* (Lanham, Md: Scarecrow Press, 1998)

David Raymond

Macedon [MASS-E-DIN]. Town (pop 8,688) and village (pop 1,496) in SW Wayne Co. Settled in 1789, the town was formed from Palmyra in 1823. The village, a creation of the Erie Canal (1822) and New York Central Railroad (1853), incorporated in 1856. Nearby Wayneport was a major coaling station for the New York Central. In 1847 the Liberty League, the "uncompromising" faction of the abolitionist Liberty Party, selected Gerrit Smith as its presidential candidate at a convention in Macedon. The firm of Bickford and Huffman developed a grain drill in 1849, which was especially popular with farmers in the south until trade was disrupted by the Civil War. In 1946 Howard and Richard Samuels founded the Kordite Co, which revolutionized the packaging business with its plastic bags. In 2003 the Exxon Mobil Chemical film division maintained headquarters, Baldwin Richardson made condiments and dessert toppings, and Fleischer's Bagels was a leading bagel producer. Also in 2003 the Finger Lakes Aerosport Park at Long Acre Farms, the state's first aerotow hang gliding park, opened. Owing to its proximity to Rochester, Macedon experienced significant suburban development; its population increased by 239% between 1950 and 2000. To guard against sprawl, the town purchased the development rights of some farms.

Scott C. Monje

Machias [MATCH-EYE-AS]. Town (pop 2,482) in NE Cattaraugus Co. Settled in 1807, the town was formed from Yorkshire in 1827. The Cattaraugus County Poor-House (1868) was located in Machias; an addition is now the Machias Nursing Home, and the original stone building has been proposed for a county museum. Farming, cheese making, and sugaring were the residents' chief livelihoods. The Buffalo, New York and Philadelphia Railroad (1872; later Pennsylvania Railroad) and the Rochester and State Line Railroad (1878; later Buffalo, Rochester and Pittsburgh Railway) served Machias. Spring-fed Lime Lake is a summer resort. Agriculture is the predominant land use in the early 21st century. The town's population increased 45% between 1960 and 2000.

Bruce D. Fredrickson and Madelynn P. Fredrickson

Mackenzie, William Lyon. See *CAROLINE* AFFAIR AND THE CANADIAN REBELLION OF 1837.

Macomb. Town (pop 846) in SW St. Lawrence Co. Settled ?1805–6, Macomb was formed in 1841 from Gouverneur and Morristown. The Mineral Point Lead Manufacturing Co (1839) mined a number of sites on Black Lake through the mid–19th century; in the late 1870s, pumps were manufactured at Pope Mills. Farm fields, though on fertile alluvial soil, are small, irregular, and dispersed in much of the town. An established pattern of farm abandonment has been broken by a growing Swartzentruber Amish population, which has made some land productive again. That, the varied landscape, and the views of Black Lake give Macomb great charm. It is the site of the Fish Creek Marsh State Wildlife Management Area.

Richard E. Mooers

Macomb Purchase. State land purchase agreement. The largest parcel ever granted by New York State, the sale was made possible by a 1791 law authorizing the land office commissioners to sell public lands "in such parcels, on such terms, and in such manner as they shall judge most conducive to the interest of the state." The acknowledged purpose was to promote settlement, but opportunities for collusion were transparent. In June an application was filed by state assemblyman Alexander Macomb; although he alone was named, he was in partnership with William Constable and Daniel McCormick.

A Protestant Irish-born fur trader, Macomb (1748–1831) had relocated from Detroit to New York City at the end of the American Revolution and, in 1786, had begun to invest in land to support an increasingly lavish lifestyle and a large family. On 10 Jan 1792 the agreement was formalized, promising the ultimate transfer of 3,670,000 acres (1,485,200 ha)—12% of the state's surface area—covering all of Lewis Co, most of St. Lawrence, Franklin, and Jefferson Cos, and a small piece of Oswego Co. The terms of the agreement required one-sixth payment within one year, with the remainder in five annual installments. A family was to be settled on every square mile within seven years and, as was customary, any gold or silver mines were reserved to the state. Islands in the St. Lawrence were omitted due to the continuing uncertainty over the international border, and Akwesasne (St. Regis Indian Reservation) was excluded.

With the January 1792 annual report of the land commission to the legislature, public reaction to the deal erupted, and it intensified through the winter and spring. Although accusations were never substantiated, the purchase price of 8d an acre (contrasted with 1s 8d to 3s 1d an acre for similar sales) strongly suggested collusion. But Macomb—who had also speculated in bank stocks, the China trade, and land in Ohio and Maine—was severely overextended. By June his finances were collapsing, and he assigned his interest to his partners. Only Constable, despite financial reverses of his own, was able to hold on to a share.

Ultimately the land was sold in smaller tracts to other speculators and was settled under their direction. Samuel Ward acquired the 817,000-acre (331,000 ha) Boylston Tract. William Inman acquired the 74,000-acre (30,000 ha) Brantingham and 25,000-acre (10,000 ha) Inman's Triangle tracts. William and James Constable acquired most of Great Tracts 4, 5, and 6, and Daniel McCormick acquired most of Great Tracts 1, 2, and 3. McCormick failed and lost his investment to nine other speculators. The Constables sold the 600,000-acre (243,000 ha) Great Tract 4 to the Antwerp Co of Holland which, in turn, sold most of it to James Le Ray de Chaumont. They also sold 210,000 acres (85,000 ha) to another French aristocrat, Peter Chassanis; the 290,000-acre (117,000 ha) Eleven Towns Tract to Nicholas Low and three partners; 61,000 acres (25,000 ha) from Great Tract 5 to James Watson; and 210,000 acres (85,000 ha) to John Brown of Providence, RI.

Dill, David B., Jr. "Alexander Macomb and His Career Shift: Taking the Main Chance," *St. Lawrence County Historical Association Quarterly* 40 (1995): 1–14

Macy, W(illiam) Kingsland (*b* New York City, 21 Nov 1889; *d* Islip, Suffolk Co, 15 July 1961). Politician. Born to wealth, Macy received a BA from Harvard University in 1912. He joined the Union Pacific Tea Co in 1913 and rose rapidly to president. In 1926 he left business to enter politics, becoming the Suffolk Co Republican chairman (1926–51). As county boss Macy constructed a tightly knit political machine built on patronage and personal loyalties. He also served as New York State Republican chairman (1930–34). From that position Macy spurred an ideological shift within the party, moving away from its traditional conservatism toward a more electorally viable progressive republicanism. He played a critical role in promoting more liberal and dynamic Republican candidates like Fiorello La Guardia for mayor of New York City and Thomas E. Dewey for both New York Co district attorney and later for governor. From 1941 to 1953 Macy served on the state Board of Regents. In 1946 he won election to the New York State Senate from Suffolk Co, and later that year he went on to represent his district in the US Congress (1946–50). Macy's fall from power was spectacular. In 1950 he released a confidential letter to the public indicating that Gov Dewey had allegedly offered to pay off Lt Gov Joseph Hanley to keep Hanley out of the upcoming gubernatorial race. Although Macy released the letter to discredit Dewey, public outrage following the incident actually brought about the demise of Macy. In November 1950 Macy lost his reelection bid for Congress, forcing his resignation as Suffolk Co boss. In 1953, after he was not reappointed for another term on the Board of Regents, Macy's political career was over. A longtime power in the New York State Republican organization, Macy remains most noted for his effort to realign his party.

Smith, Richard Norton. *Thomas E. Dewey and His Times* (New York: Simon & Schuster, 1982)

Tod M. Ottman

Macy's. See R. H. MACY.

Madison. Town (pop 2,801) and village (pop 315) in E Madison Co. Settled in 1792, the town was formed from Hamilton in 1807, the year James Coolidge grew the county's first hops crop. The village incorporated in 1816. Both were served by the Third Great Western Turnpike (1803–11), the Chenango Canal (1837–78), and the Ontario and Western Railroad (1870). Two large cider manufactories operated in Bouckville in the 1860s. Many buildings were built with cobblestones dug out by canal workers, including Coolidge's five-sided Landmark Tavern (1847–51). The state's first windmill farm for electrical power generation occupies a ridge just east of the Village of Madison. The town's land remains predominantly agricultural, and many residents commute to Utica, Rome, or Syracuse. The Madison Central School District is a large employer. The Madison-Bouckville Antiques Show, one of the largest in the Northeast, draws large crowds every summer along US 20.

William F. Helmer

Madison Barracks. Located west of Watertown, Fort Volunteer was hastily built in 1812. Fort Pike, an adjacent construction named for Zebulon M. Pike, was established in 1815 on the northeastern end of Sackets Harbor. A 40-acre (16 ha) site was acquired in 1816, gray limestone barracks encompassing a small parade ground were built between 1816 and 1819, and the installation was named for Pres James Madison. The post was intermittently garrisoned through the Civil War and nearly abandoned after an 1877 fire destroyed half the structures. Ulysses S. Grant used his influence to have the post rebuilt. Additional construction from 1893 to 1899 added a new parade ground, brick officer housing, and a hospital of gray limestone. Madison Barracks was used primarily as a hospital post in World War I and training post in World War II; it closed in 1945. An early example of a designed military complex and renowned for its diverse architecture, the restored Madison Barracks site with its parade ground is a National Register Historic District.

Roberts, Robert B. *Encyclopedia of Historic Forts: The Military, Pioneer, and Trading Posts of the United States* (New York: Macmillan, 1988)

Michael J. Stenzel

Madison County (656 mi²/1,699 km²; pop 69,441). Created in 1806 from Chenango Co and named for James Madison, fourth president of the United States. Madison Co is subdivided into 1 city, Oneida, and 15 towns containing 10 incorporated villages. Wampsville serves as the county seat. Elevation ranges from 368 feet (112 m) at Oneida Lake's shore to 2,142 feet (653 m) on Morrow Mountain in the Town of Georgetown. The county's northern quarter lies within the Oneida Lake Plain subregion of the Erie-Ontario Lowland and includes near level glacial lakebed, outwash terrace, and low hill landforms. The rest of the county is part of the Susquehanna Hills subregion of the Appalachian Plateau. Here relief increases toward the south, where hilltops are often 500–600 feet (150–180 m) above adjoining valley bottoms. The north-facing Helderberg Escarpment, in places a near vertical outcrop of Onondaga limestone up to 250 feet (76 m) high, marks the boundary between the two landform regions and is the basis for 167 ft (51 m) high Chittenango Falls. Devonian limestone, shale, sandstone, and siltstone underlie the Susquehanna Hills. Lake plain bedrock consists of Silurian-

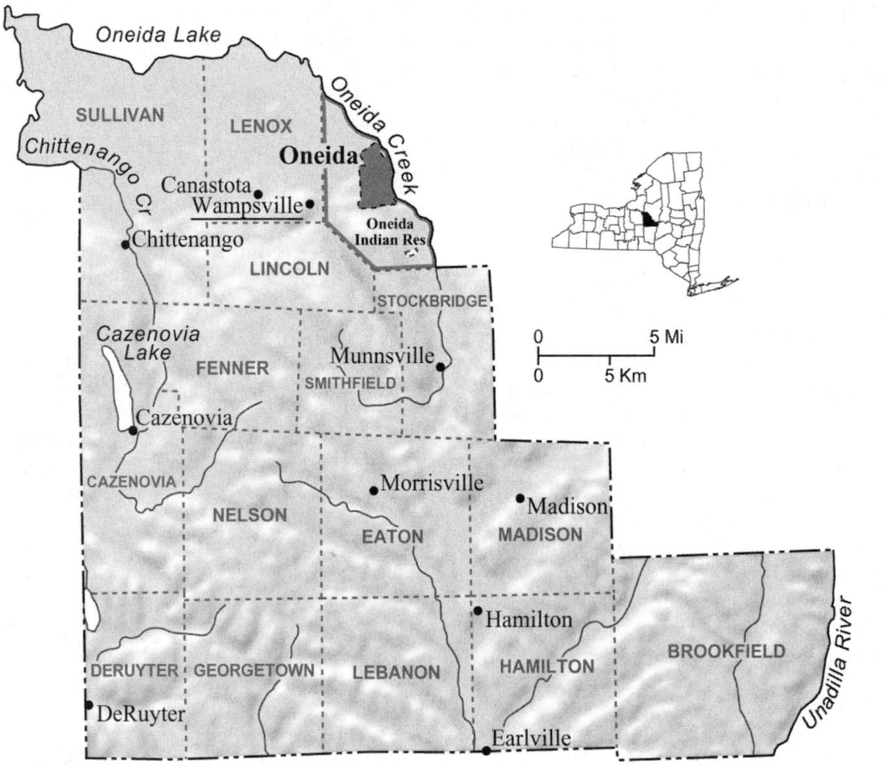

age dolomite, limestone, sandstone, and shale. Madison Co was glaciated throughout, as evidenced by the glacial lake plain in the north, rounded hills and deeply scoured valleys in the south, and a mantel of glacial till nearly everywhere. The Oneida Lake watershed extends across the northern half of the county. The Susquehanna River watershed, via the Unadilla, Chenango, Otselic, and Tioughnioga Rivers, drains the southern half except for part of the Town of Madison, which lies in the Mohawk River watershed. Soil quality is highly variable in terms of agricultural potential, but most of the land supports modern farming.

Madison Co's climate is humid-continental. Mean January temperatures range from 18°F (-8°C) near Morrisville to 22°F (-6°C) in the northwest at the border with Onondaga Co. Winter lows can be expected to fall below 0°F (-18°C) every year. Mean July temperatures range from 67°F (19°C) at Morrisville to 70°F (21°C) near Oneida Lake; and daytime highs reach the 90s°F (32–37°C) at least once or twice every summer. Average annual precipitation amounts range from 39 inches (99 cm) near Canastota to 43 inches (109 cm) in the Tioughnioga River valley. Seasonal snowfall amounts vary from 84 inches (213 cm) in the southeast to 119 inches (302 cm) in the northwest near the eastern end of Oneida Lake. The primeval forest consisted of three distinct communities. Alleghenian hardwoods made up primarily of beech, sugar maple, hemlock, white pine, and basswood covered all but the wettest parts of the uplands and limited areas of the lake plain. Some of the lake plain supported less diverse central hardwood communities of beech, sugar maple, and basswood. Swamp forest occupied the poorly drained lands south of Oneida Lake and in the Chenango and Sangerfield River valleys.

American Indians and Early Settlement

Iroquoian peoples, including the Oneida, formed the League of the Iroquois in the years before European contact. The Oneida were early occupants of what is now Madison Co. At least 24 Oneida villages occupied sites at various times in Stockbridge, Cazenovia, Fenner, and elsewhere, as well as in neighboring Oneida Co and southward to the present Pennsylvania. Archaeological investigations at Nichols Pond in Fenner, once thought to be the site of Samuel de Champlain's 1615 attack on an Onondaga village, have shown it to be a much earlier Oneida stockaded settlement with artifacts pointing to a date of *ca* 1480 and no evidence of any battle in the vicinity. The southern shore of Onondaga Lake is now accepted as the probable site of Champlain's attack.

By the 1820s the Oneidas began to leave New York State for the vicinity of what is now Green Bay, Wisc; another migration began in 1839–40 to the Thames River District in Upper Canada [now Ont]. By the time of the 1855 census, only 151 Oneidas remained in New York State, most occupying reservation land in Madison Co. By 1926 Oneida territory consisted of 32 acres (13 ha) on the West Rd in the outside district of the City of Oneida.

In the New York State and Oneida Nation treaty of 22 Sept 1788 at Fort Schuyler, the state acquired a large tract in what is now southern Madison and northern Chenango Cos from the Iroquois. Designated as the Chenango Twenty Townships, it was surveyed by Horace P. Schuyler in 1789. North of the tract, the 200,000-acre (81,000 ha) Oneida Indian Nation Reservation was set aside for the Oneida in the 1784 Fort Stanwix treaty, but it was soon abrogated. In 1794, however, fur trader Peter Smith negotiated with some Oneidas for a 50,000-acre (20,200 ha) tract, which eventually became known as New Petersburgh. This tract and the larger Lincklaen Purchase (1792) in the county's southwest were then sold to potential settlers.

Madison Co was settled very rapidly, beginning with a community of squatters on Oneida land in the present Sullivan (1790). By 1795 there were settlers in each of the county's towns except Georgetown, where others arrived in 1804. The county's population, 8,036 in 1800, tripled in one decade to 25,144, after which it grew more gradually. Most of the settlers were from New England or eastern New York State, but Nelson attracted a distinctive Welsh colony. Some Irish immigrants came in the mid–19th century (they were 5% of the population in 1855), and at the end of the century, Italians arrived, eventually forming a significant part of the population of Lenox, Sullivan, and Canastota. A small group of freed African Americans settled around Peterboro, the home of abolitionist Gerrit Smith. Many more enjoyed his hospitality while passing through as fugitives.

MADISON CO POPULATION CENSUS FIGURES

	White	Nonwhite	Total Population	Foreign-Born
1810	24,932	212	25,144	—
1820	32,016	192	32,208	67
1830	38,811	227	39,038	192
1840	39,785	223	40,008	—
1850	42,774	298	43,072	2,801
1860	43,245	300	43,545	4,077
1870	43,124	398	43,522	4,816
1880	43,646	466	44,112	4,127
1890	42,501	391	42,892	3,901
1900	40,185	360	40,545	3,216
1910	38,940	349	39,289	3,319
1920	39,276	259	39,535	3,295
1930	39,574	216	39,790	2,951
1940	39,425	173	39,598	2,490
1950	45,933	281	46,214	2,189
1960	54,246	389	54,635	1,848
1970	62,299	565	62,864	1,467
1980	64,236	914	65,150	1,555
1990	67,453	1,667	69,120	1,448
2000	67,006	2,435	69,441	1,558

Notes: "Nonwhite" includes African Americans, Asians, American Indians, and Pacific Islanders and, for 2000, also the mixed race and other race categories. Through the 1960 census these figures primarily reflect the African American population. Foreign-born figures for 1820 and 1830 include only those not naturalized, and for 1930 and 1950, the foreign-born totals include Whites only. Other years include all foreign-born in the population.

Transportation

Madison Co's central location in the state on the Oneida Lake Plain ensured that major transportation routes would cross its territory as the new nation expanded westward. To the north the main Indian pathway was developed as the Genesee Rd (1794) and then as the Seneca Turnpike (1800), the major migration route to the western New York State frontier. In the south, the Third Great Western Turnpike (1803; later Cherry Valley Turnpike) followed a similar westward course. These and other primitive roads were muddy, dusty, or snowdrifted, depending on the weather and the season. The opening of the first section of the Erie Canal (1819) across the northern part of the county through Canastota and Chittenango eased travel and contributed to the growth of those villages. The portion through Madison Co was part of the "long level" that required no locks.

One of the branch canals constructed to feed the Erie, the Chenango Canal (1837–78) from Utica and Binghamton, passed through the Towns of Madison and Hamilton. It required 116 locks along its 97-mile (156 km) route and never paid its operating expenses. By the time of its abandonment, the canal had been paralleled and replaced by a faster, all-weather mode of transport, the railway. Within a few more years, the county claimed a network of six separate railroad companies. The first in Madison Co was the Syracuse and Utica Railroad, which was to become an integral part of the New York Central System. This line and its parallel, leased subsidiary, the West Shore, followed the Hudson and Mohawk Rivers on opposite banks and across the Oneida Lake Plain westward.

Five lines running north and south—Lehigh Valley; Delaware, Lackawanna and Western; Unadilla Valley; New York, Ontario and Western; and Chenango Branch of the West Shore—carried farm products, especially fluid milk, south to the New York City metropolitan area and brought Pennsylvania coal northward. When this north-south traffic vanished or took to the highways, the lines were abandoned, except the Lackawanna branch, now operated by the New York, Susquehanna and Western. The east-west

POPULATIONS OF TOWNS AND CITIES, MADISON CO

Town or City, Year Founded	1800	1840	1880	1920	1960	2000
Brookfield, 1795	1,973	3,695	3,685	2,092	1,990	2,403
Cazenovia, 1795	3,080	4,153	4,363	3,343	4,968	6,481
DeRuyter, 1798	310	1,799	1,584	1,141	1,290	1,532
Eaton, 1807	—	3,409	3,799	2,223	3,196	4,826
Fenner, 1823	—	1,997	1,272	780	900	1,680
Georgetown, 1815	—	1,130	1,490	854	633	946
Hamilton, 1795	2,673	3,738	3,912	3,354	5,438	5,733
Lebanon, 1807	—	1,794	1,586	940	880	1,329
Lenox, 1809	—	5,440	10,246	5,536	7,729	8,665
Lincoln, 1896	—	—	—	821	1,102	1,818
Madison, 1807	—	2,344	2,474	1,629	1,915	2,801
Nelson, 1807	—	2,100	1,649	1,099	1,170	1,964
Oneida (city), 1901	—	—	—	10,541	11,677	10,987
Smithfield, 1807	—	1,699	1,226	767	804	1,205
Stockbridge, 1836	—	2,320	2,023	1,413	1,574	2,080
Sullivan, 1803	—	4,390	4,803	3,002	9,369	14,991

Note: In 1800 the Towns of Brookfield, Cazenovia, DeRuyter, and Hamilton were in Chenango Co.

main track, formerly the New York Central, is operated by CSX for freight and by Amtrak for passengers. No railroad station remained open in the county in 2004.

Economic Development

The lowland soil of the county's northern section supports grain and vegetable crops, and is especially productive in the mucklands around Canastota. The more hilly land of the south, with elevations exceeding 2,100 feet (640 m) above sea level, is better suited to dairying, sand and gravel quarrying, and general farming. Here in the rolling countryside sheep raising became widespread in the early 1800s, and mills for processing their wool prospered. Hops were first planted in New York State at McClure's Settlement [now Bouckville] in 1808. For more than a century, hop farms flourished throughout this southern portion, but "blue mold" disease and Prohibition led to a precipitous decline in hop culture by 1930. Butter and cheese manufacture gave way to fluid-milk production as improved transport systems provided better access to urban areas, especially New York City.

Madison Co's hamlets utilized waterpower and, later, steam to produce a variety of manufactured goods. Most were the usual products of Upstate New York in the 19th century: woolen cloth, leather, paper, plows and stoves, farm tools and agricultural machinery, edge tools, and augers. Glass was made in Smithfield and Canastota. Distinctive goods included town clocks made in Cazenovia, telescopes made in Canastota, and silos, manufactured in Brookfield as late as 1966. The economy also benefited from a limited resort industry. White Sulphur Springs in Sullivan had a brief heyday in the 19th century, but Cazenovia became a fashionable resort after the Civil War.

Religion, Education, and Culture

The first organized worship in Madison Co by Europeans took place at French Jesuit missions directed to the Indians in the late 17th century. The first church organization was the First Baptist Church (1797) at Hamilton. By 1855 the county was dominated by Baptists, with 21 congregations, and Methodists, with 29. There were also 11 Congregational, 10 Presbyterian, and 7 Universalist churches, but only 3 Roman Catholic parishes: St. Patrick Oneida (1843), St. James Cazenovia (1847), and St. Patrick Chittenango (1853). In the early 21st century there are 8 Roman Catholic parishes and 2 missions.

The common school system developed following 1812 state legislation. Theological, classical, or literary academies and institutes or seminaries flourished alongside, but at a loftier level than, the public one-room schoolhouses during the 19th century. Two present-day Madison Co collegiate communities had religious beginnings and often served as training grounds for the Protestant ministry and for overseas missions. The Hamilton Literary and Theological Institute (later Madison University) was founded by Baptists in 1819 and the Seminary of the Genesee Conference by Methodists in 1824. Colgate University (1846) evolved from the former and Cazenovia College from the latter. Both are now nondenominational and coeducational. A much later addition came in 1910, when the New York State School of Agriculture took over the former county courthouse, clerk's office, and adjacent buildings in the Village of Morrisville. This new arrival stressed vocational learning rather than the classical or liberal arts instruction of Cazenovia and Colgate.

Madison Co's villages and larger hamlets all established Union Free School districts in the late 19th and early 20th centuries, some with high school programs. Centralization, which began at Stockbridge Valley in 1927, swallowed up these union districts and rural common schools. By 1958 there were 12 central districts and the Oneida City School District; three smaller central districts (Earlville, Georgetown, and Leonardsville) were subsequently consolidated into adjacent districts. In 2004 Madison Co was served by 10 school districts.

The first newspaper in the county, the *Freeholder,* was published in 1807 at Peterboro. The long-lived *Madison Observer* (1822–96) was the newspaper of record for the county. In 2003 the *Oneida Daily Dispatch* (1851; originally a weekly) circulated, along with metropolitan papers; the *Hamilton Mid-York Weekly* provided local coverage. There were two radio stations but no television broadcasting. At the beginning of the 21st century, it has the respected Picker Art Gallery (1966) at Colgate University, the Stone Quarry Hill Art Park, an outdoor sculpture gallery in Cazenovia, and a number of history museums.

Reform and Politics

During the years before the outbreak of the Civil War, considerable abolitionist sentiment was expressed in public meetings and church assemblies whose participants came at the behest of reformer and philanthropist Gerrit Smith (1797–1874), son of pioneer landowner Peter Smith. Gerrit Smith held strong positions not only on slavery but on woman suffrage and temperance. Although the family mansion in Peterboro burned down in 1936, the estate is on the National Register and the Peter Smith Land Office is a National Historic Landmark. Another

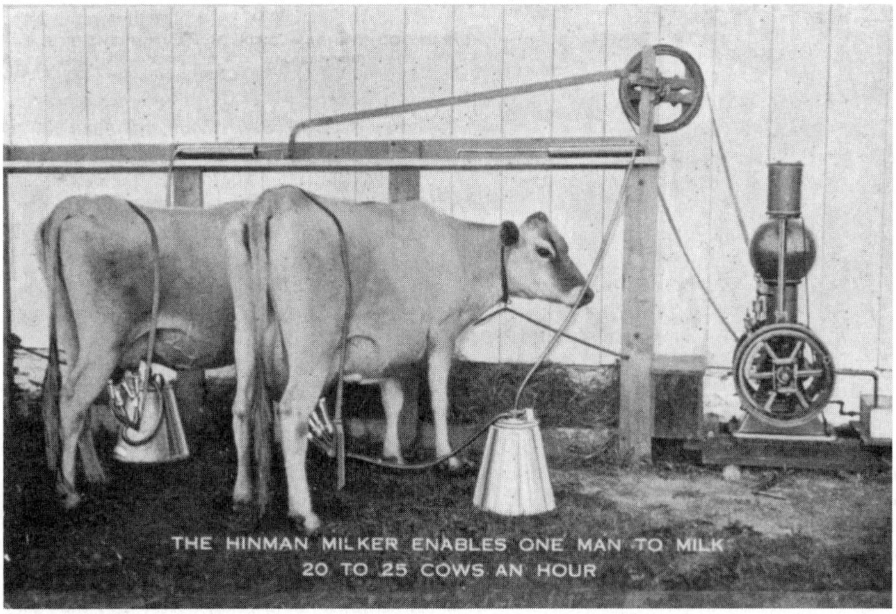

Hinman milking machine, invented by Arthur V. and Ralph L. Hinman in Stockbridge.

controversial reformer with unusual ideas on the role of women in society, temperance, and relations between the sexes was John Humphrey Noyes (1811–86), who led a band of religious Perfectionists from Vermont to settle Oneida. Noyes believed in the benefits of communal living, rejected monogamous marriage, and founded the Oneida Community in 1848. It dissolved in 1881, becoming a joint-stock company that continues to manufacture tableware early in the 21st century. The community's Mansion House is listed on the National Register. Notoriety of a different kind was achieved by a band of thieves, arsonists, and all-around outlaws known as the Loomis Gang, headquartered near the Ninemile Swamp. The group kept central New York State residents in a state of apprehension and, often, terror for years until outraged citizens raided their family farm and ended their reign in 1867.

The first county seat, Cazenovia, was not selected until 1810. That village's position on the extreme southwest border of the county was considered inconvenient, and in 1817 the county seat was moved to Morrisville, a more central and more accessible location. As the Erie Canal and the railroads opened in the north, the Villages of Oneida and Canastota grew in population, industry, and political power, soon demanding the county seat be relocated again. Morrisville had but one rail connection, and detractors noted that it was about 2 miles (3 km) from the village. Consequently, almost every other community in the county touted its own superior advantages and amenities. At one point, county officers considered a half-shire arrangement that would have established duplicate government offices in the northern section, in the vicinity of Oneida. Finally, in a 1907 referendum, voters approved Wampsville, between the rival communities of Oneida and Canastota, as the new county seat. Its claim to ample rail service found emphasis in the orientation of the courthouse, built to face the New York Central and West Shore Railroads' main lines rather than the public highway. Until 1930 frequent interurban passenger service was furnished by the Utica-to-Syracuse "third rail," the electrified section of the West Shore line. The county buildings in Morrisville were vacated at the end of 1909 and immediately put to use for the new state school of agriculture.

RECENT HISTORY

Completion of the New York State Thruway (1954) resulted in the diversion of motor traffic from roads such as Rte 5 and US 20 and gave superhighway access to a single Madison Co community, Canastota, despite efforts by Oneida officials to secure an exit of their own. The near exit to the city is a few miles away at Verona (Oneida Co). A 1985 US Supreme Court decision found merit in the claim of the Oneida Indians to land in the county on the basis that state treaties had been executed without the required federal approval. Subsequently, the Oneida acquired tracts of land in Madison and Oneida Cos and began enterprises, including a gaming casino. As a sovereign nation, the Oneida have claimed exemption from all local, state, and federal taxation, which has led to controversy with local governments, landowners, and business owners in the region. Negotiations continued in 2003. Manufacturing in Madison Co is much reduced but, in 2003, still included Diemolding Corp and Owl Wire and Cable in Canastota and the Ferris Co in Munnsville, makers of commercial mowers. Electricity is generated by the state's first wind farm, in the Town of Madison, and another in Fenner, which began operations in 2000.

Mrs. L. M. Hammond, *History of Madison County* (1872), taps into memories of pioneers; it includes anecdotes, sometimes romanticized, but is generally reliable. Gurdon Evans, "A General View . . . of the County of Madison," in *Transactions of the New York State Agricultural Society,* 11 (1851), is a brief but excellent account. Two volumes, James H. Smith, *History of Chenango and Madison Counties* (1890) and John E. Smith, *Madison County* (1899), are detailed and trustworthy. *Country Roads* (1976) and Barbara Giambastiani's *Country Roads Revisited* (1984) are collaborative works including short town histories and emphasizing historic preservation. Of the many local histories, David Alvord's *Oneida, NY: A Bit of America at Its Best* (2001) is concise and essentially complete. Other noteworthy community histories are those on Cazenovia: Russell A. Grills, *Cazenovia: The Story of an Upland Community* (1977), Henry Severance, *Owahgena, Being a History of the Town and Village of Cazenovia* (1984), and Peter J. Hugill, *Upstate Arcadia: Landscape, Aesthetics, and the Triumph of Social Differentiation in America* (1995). Anzolette D. Ellsworth and Mary E. Redmond's *New Woodstock and Vicinity* (1901), about a hamlet in the Town of Cazenovia, and the Brookfield Township Historical Society's *Remembered Years* (1976) are both useful, as is Dorris Lawson's *Italians in Canastota* (1976). The semiannual *Madison County Heritage* (1977–) publishes articles on county and local topics.

William F. Helmer

Madison Square Garden. Entertainment and sporting venue. Originally located at the intersection of 26th St and Madison Ave and converted from the abandoned depot of the New York and Harlem Railroad, the site housed the P. T. Barnum Hippodrome and bandmaster Patrick Gilmore's Concert Garden after 1874. It opened as Madison Square Garden on 31 May 1879. The first Garden is remembered for its horse and flower shows, boxing matches, and P. T. Barnum's famous import, Jumbo, the African elephant.

Difficulties with heating the cavernous space, however, led to starting over with architect Stanford White's $3 million Neo-Moorish Madison Square Garden, which opened on 16 June 1890 and had an 8,000-seat auditorium, a 32-story tower topped with a nude copper statue of Diana, sidewalk arcades, and a roof garden cabaret. The roof garden was the site of the sensational murder of White on 25 June 1906 by the jealous husband of White's mistress. One of the last major events at the second Garden was the 1924 Democratic National Convention, which after 103 roll calls nominated John W. Davis as its candidate. The New York Life Insurance Co, which owned the land, decided about this time to demolish the building and build its headquarters on the site.

The third Garden, which opened in December 1925 on the site of the former trolley car barns at the northwest corner of 8th Ave and 49th St, was an undistinguished boxlike structure designed by theater architect Thomas Lamb and developed by boxing promoter George Lewis "Tex" Rickard and circus owner John Ringling. At the same time, Rickard and Ringling created the Madison Square Garden Corp, allowing investors to put their money into a corporation dedicated solely to profitable sporting events. From 1925 to 1945 the arena hosted 32 world championship fights. It was here that the New York Rangers hockey team debuted in 1926 and that the New York Knickerbockers basketball team appeared in 1946.

In the early 1960s a decision was made to move downtown using the new Pennsylvania Station's air rights. A circular building 13 stories high and 425 feet (129.5 m) in diameter was built at 7th Ave between 31st and 33d Sts on the site of the original Pennsylvania Station, which had been razed in 1963. This fourth Garden was inaugurated in February 1968. In addition to the 20,000-seat arena, the $116 million complex included a 5,600-seat multiuse theater, an exposition rotunda, and a 48-lane bowling alley. It was the site of the historic 1971 boxing match between undefeated heavyweights Muhammad Ali and Joe Frazier, the mass 1982 wedding of 2,075 couples by Sun Myung Moon (founder of the Unification Church), the 1992 Democratic National Convention, and the 2004 Republican National Convention.

Durso, Joseph. *Madison Square Garden, 100 Years of History* (New York: Simon & Schuster, 1979)

Leonard Benardo

Madrid [MAD-RID]. Town (pop 1,828) in central St. Lawrence Co. Settled in 1801, the town was formed from Lisbon in 1802. Scottish immigrants settled the south and west parts of town. Columbia Village [now Madrid hamlet] was attacked by Canadian militia in 1814 to recapture goods seized from a ship on the St. Lawrence. Bog ore was mined in the late 1830s, and a small woolen factory operated in the mid–19th century. Because of fertile soils, some of St. Lawrence Co's largest farms are located in Madrid. The town is known for its annual Bluegrass Festival in July.

Richard E. Mooers

magic, folk. Beliefs and practices that cross the boundaries of popular healing, ritual, religion, shamanism, and the occult. With ethnically diverse sources, New York State's folk magic extends from prehistory to the early 21st century. Within the state's white population, it experienced dramatic outbursts in the first decades of the 19th century and the last decades of the 20th.

From colonial times until the widespread impact of cultural anthropology and multiculturalism in the 20th century, many white Americans dismissed American Indian religious beliefs and practices as both superstition and magic. Christian polemics against differing cosmologies notwithstanding, Indians had concepts paralleling European distinctions between "white" and "black" magic. The Algonquian-speaking Indians and the Iroquois had special practitioners whose rituals of healing, metaphysical intercession, amulets, and oral charms against evil parallel worldwide traditions of folk magic and shamanism.

COLONIAL PERIOD TO THE EARLY 1800S

European settlement brought Judeo-Christian varieties of folk magic to the area. Accusations of witchcraft were made among Whites sporadically from the late 1600s to the late 1800s. Manuscripts containing incantations and magic formulas for healing or protection have survived in Dutch, English, German, ancient Hebrew, and Yiddish from the colonial era. One such manuscript is "Divine Magia" by the English colonist Caleb Gilman, who described Jesus as "the Greatest Magus that ever was, or will be." Another is an alchemical treatise by an anonymous German sectarian minister living in Manhattan in the 1780s. Although all ethnic and immigrant groups have oral traditions of folk magic, New York State's writings on the occult have come primarily from those of British and continental European extraction.

Astrology was of special interest to early New Yorkers. By knowing the moon's daily position in the zodiac, common people could determine what to do or to avoid each day. This involved comparing astrological almanacs with occult folklore or handbooks. English colonists stopped buying John Holt's popular New York almanac in 1767 because it omitted astrological information. His next almanacs reintroduced it. German-speaking residents printed their own astrological almanacs and obtained occult handbooks published by Pennsylvania Germans. Thomas Longworth's New York City directory provided astrological almanacs from 1797 until 1840. Folk magic appealed to literate New Yorkers, both urban and rural.

Since the colonial period Manhattan's publishers have been a principal source of America's occult handbooks, varying from penny chapbooks to weighty volumes. Throughout the 1700s there were multiple printings of *The Complete Fortune Teller* and Erra Pater's *Book of Knowledge.* Anonymous treatises such as *Aristotle's Masterpiece* and the *Book of Fate,* covering palmistry, astrology, divination by physiognomy, and related arts, were printed in New York City in the late 1700s and through much of the 19th century. Even village bookstores advertised occult works to early residents of the state, while in rural areas hundreds of peddlers hawked "forbidden books" door-to-door, including rare books and recent occult publications from abroad. After the Revolution folk magic became so prevalent that Lutheran clergyman Frederick Quitman wrote a pamphlet in 1810 against the "many thousands" who participated in it. At the same time, the state legislature outlawed "pretending to have skill in physiognomy, palmistry, or like crafty science, or pretending to tell fortunes, or to discover lost goods." Nevertheless, thousands of New York State residents continued to participate in occult practices in the early 1800s.

Treasure Digging

The most dramatic and controversial manifestations of folk magic involved treasure digging. By the 1820s this was a cottage industry in various sections of the state. For example, hundreds of Onondaga Co residents descended on the Town of Manlius, where they used incantations and divining rods in an attempt to unearth treasure. From Lake Champlain to Rochester to Broome Co, village mystics also used "peep stones" or "seer stones" to search for buried gold and silver. Statewide, those who sought treasure by supernatural means included landowners and vagrants, church members and the unchurched, moneygrubbing charlatans and devout believers who accepted no money for their metaphysical services. However, Wayne and Ontario Cos received the lion's share of publicity for these activities because of treasure seer Joseph Smith Jr. After a decade of treasure seeking in Palmyra and Manchester, Smith published the Book of Mormon in 1830 and began leading a successful religion, the Church of Latter-day Saints. Because of his movement's emphasis on historical preservation, artifacts of this early New York State folk culture are recorded in published photographs of the Smith family's magic parchments ("lamens") for treasure digging, of various seer stones, and of a Jupiter talisman inscribed according to instructions in Francis Barrett's 1801 occult handbook, *The Magus.*

Decline and Resurgence

New York State's crescendo of folk magic in the first two decades of the 19th century would remain unequaled until the 1960s. Between 1820 and 1850 revivalism doubled the membership in Protestant churches, whose clergy overwhelmingly attacked folk magic. From the late 1840s onward the Spiritualism of the Fox sisters can be interpreted as a new version of the occult, with the whisperings of a medium replacing the incantations of a magus and expensively crafted crystal balls replacing such objects as inscribed daggers and seer stones. However, the Empire State's other occult traditions got little publicity for nearly a century. The most visible evidence of occult practice was in the classified listings for astrology, fortune-telling, numerology, and palmistry in city directories and telephone books, though these listings did not include the more numerous practitioners of noncommercial folk magic. Two murders allegedly connected to witchcraft garnered widespread publicity: those of a man in Sullivan Co in the 1880s and of Clothilde Marchand in Buffalo in 1930.

Folk magic among minorities remained peripheral to mainstream society until the "occult explosion" of the late 1960s, which led to the "discovery" by Whites of traditions of folk magic long known to other New Yorkers—shamanism, wicca, Santeria, and voodoo. As a result, publishers in the state have continued to print how-to books for every conceivable manifestation of the occult. As New York State entered the 21st century, folk magic and the occult continued to attract practitioners as well as the attention of academics, legitimate journalists, tabloid reporters, and the public.

Blanchard, David. "Who or What's a Witch?: Iroquois Persons of Power," *American Indian Quarterly* 6 (Fall/Winter 1982): 218–37

Freedland, Nat. *The Occult Explosion* (New York: Putnam's, 1972)

Gonzales-Wippler, Migene. *Santeria, the Religion: A Legacy of Faith, Rites, and Magic* (New York: Harmony, 1989)

Harring, Sidney L. "Red Lilac of the Cayugas: Traditional Indian Law and Culture Conflict in a Witchcraft Trial in Buffalo, New York, 1930," *New York History* 73 (Jan 1992): 65–94

Lewis, James R., ed. *Magical Religion and Modern Witchcraft* (Albany: SUNY Press, 1996)

Porterfield, Amanda. "Witchcraft and the Colonization of Algonquian and Iroquois Cultures," *Religion and American Culture* 2 (1992): 103–24

Quinn, D. Michael. *Early Mormonism and the Magic World View,* 2d ed. (Salt Lake City, Utah: Signature Books, 1998)

D. Michael Quinn

Mahicans. See Mohicans [mahicans].

Mahopac. Locality (pop 8,478) in Carmel (Putnam Co). The locality consists of Mahopac and Mahopac Falls; the latter was originally Red Mills, an important mill site from the 1740s. It lost its waterpower in the 1870s when New York City claimed water rights to Lake Mahopac, Putnam Co's largest natural lake, and lowered its water level. The Mahopac Hotel (1834) was the first of many lakefront resorts. The Mahopac Railroad reached Lake Mahopac hamlet in 1871 and contributed to the hotel's success. A huge development plan went bankrupt after the 1873 panic, and in the 1890s the old hamlet was relocated to protect the New York City watershed. Both hamlets now consist mostly of single-family suburban homes.

Sallie S. Sypher

Mailer, Norman (Kingsley) (*b* Long Branch, NJ, 31 Jan 1923). Author and journalist. Mailer grew up in Brooklyn, where his family moved in 1927, and graduated from Boys' High School in 1939. He began writing as a student at Harvard University (1939–43) and in 1941 his essay won *Story* magazine's contest for collegiate writers. He graduated with a BS degree in aeronautical engineering. Mailer served in the US Army (1944–46) as a sergeant in the South Pacific, afterward writing the critically acclaimed, best-selling World War II novel *The Naked and the Dead* (1948), drawing heavily from his combat experiences. Subsequent novels, *Barbary Shore* (1951) and *The Deer Park* (1955), were not well received critically or commercially. In the 1950s Mailer lived in Manhattan's Greenwich Village and was a founder of the *Village Voice* in 1955. His collection *Advertisements for Myself* (1959) includes the influential essay "The White Negro: Superficial Reflections on the Hipster" (1956). In his journalism in the 1960s he was among the first to take a subjective and novelistic approach to reporting. This was exemplified in an account of a 1967 anti–Vietnam War protest at the Pentagon, *The Armies of the Night* (1968), for which he won a Pulitzer Prize. In 1969 he made an unsuccessful run for mayor of New York City, calling for the city to secede and become the 51st state, garnering over 41,000 votes in the Democratic primary. In 1979 Mailer wrote the "true-life novel" *The Executioner's Song,* which won the Pulitzer Prize. He was president of the American chapter of PEN, an international literary organization, from 1984 to 1986 and served as New York State Author from 1991 to 1993. Author of 39 books, he lives in Provincetown, Mass.

Mills, Hilary. *Mailer: A Biography* (New York: McGraw-Hill, 1984)

Brett Forman

Maine. Town (pop 5,459) in W Broome Co. Settled in ?1794 by New Englanders, residents were joined by Scottish immigrants at Mt Ettrick beginning in 1836 and by Irish immigrants at New Ireland beginning in 1844. A tannery operated at the hamlet from 1832 until after 1885. The town was formed from Union in 1848. Maine's population declined after the Civil War but later stabilized. The town's rake factory closed in 1928. Dairy farming remains the dominant land use; the town is also a bedroom community for the Triple Cities (Binghamton, Endicott, and Johnson City). Binghamton Regional Airport (1951) is in town, and the Cyrus Gates House (1851) has a strong claim as a stop on the Underground Railroad.

Charles J. Browne

malls. See SHOPPING CENTERS AND MALLS.

Malone. Town (pop 14,981) and village (pop 6,075) in N Franklin Co. The town was settled in 1802 by Vermonters, and the village was settled one year later. The town was formed from Chateaugay in 1805 as Harison; the name was changed to Ezraville in 1808 and to Malone in 1812. The first county courthouse was built here in 1811–12. Malone was briefly occupied by the British army and ransacked by militiamen and Indians in 1814. With good waterpower on the Salmon River, Malone had varied industrial enterprises, including sawmills, brickyards, tanneries, distilleries, woolen mills (1825–80), and paper mills (starting 1872). Sandstone was quarried in the town, and around 1880 there was a boom in hop growing, with 253 growers planting 918 acres (371.5 ha). Malone acquired rail service in 1850, and the Northern Railroad (later Rome, Watertown and Ogdensburg Railroad) built its shops in 1857; after 1892 it was a rail junction and shop location for the New York Central. Malone was a staging point for the Fenian raids into Canada in 1866 and 1870. It drew Irish immigrants in addition to a large number of Francophone Canadian migrants; in 1940 the population was 60% bilingual. People in another immigrant group, the Chinese, were intercepted trying to cross the international border on trains, and up to 600 at a time were detained in or near the jail from 1902 to 1911. Franklin (1986), Bare Hill (1988), and Upstate (1999) correctional facilities provide significant employment opportunities and increase the population without adding to school taxes, but a division of Wolverine footwear closed in 2000, eliminating 400 jobs. Other employers include Cleyn and Tinker (woolen fabrics), Valco (furniture), Alice Hyde Medical Center, and the Tulloch Campus of North Country Community College. Malone was the home of William A. Wheeler, US vice president during Rutherford B. Hayes's presidency (1877–81).

Thomas W. Perrin

Malta. Town (pop 13,005) in central Saratoga Co. Connecticut settlers arrived between 1762 and 1764 from a riverfront settlement to the east. The town was formed in 1802 from Stillwater. Having few mill sites, it never supported manufacturing. The sandy plain covering large parts of town was not good farmland. The town borders Saratoga Lake and Round Lake, where a camp meeting in 1868 grew into a village. The Luther Forest, an experimental plantation (1898), consisted of 7,000 acres (2,800 ha) in Malta and Stillwater; its Malta portion was converted to housing and light manufacturing starting in 1975, benefiting from excellent Northway (I-87) access. The landmark Parade Ground where the militia trained is the only true village green in Saratoga Co. A retail center was developed near the Parade Ground in the 1990s to serve a suburban population nearly six times that of 1960.

Field Horne

Malverne. Village (pop 8,934) in Hempstead (Nassau Co). The farms of this area, originally known as Norwood, were subdivided by the Amsterdam Development and Land Co beginning in 1911. As Malverne, a post office was acquired in 1916, and the village was incorporated in 1921. Development accelerated after World War II. In the 1960s the Malverne School District, which included the predominantly black locality of Lakeview, attempted to integrate the schools in the district and an emotional struggle ensued. Malverne is a suburb with a predominantly white population in the early 21st century. One of Nassau Co's two surviving farms is in the village: the 7-acre (2.8 ha) Grossmann's Farm, which has been in the same family since 1895.

Lynda R. Day

Mamakating. Town (pop 11,002) in SE Sullivan Co. Settled soon after 1728 by Manuel Gonsalus, a Spanish Protestant, its settlers were chiefly Dutch from eastern towns until about 1790, when a Yankee influx began. Mamakating was formed as a precinct in 1743 and as a town in 1788. The Shawangunk Mountains run through the town, and it is the site of Bashakill State Wildlife Management Area. The Delaware and Hudson Canal (1828–98) served Mamakating. By 1855 it was a dairy town; the Ontario and Western Railroad (1871–1953) carried milk to market and brought vacationers. Most resorts were concentrated on the Shawangunk Mountains to take advantage of the views. At Mastens Lake, the Sullivan County Club (now Mamakating Park) was created by wealthy New Yorkers in 1892. Wurtsboro Hills, a large resort community, became year-round in the 1950s. The railroad was superseded by Rte 17 (I-86), a limited-access highway completed in town between 1956 and 1958. The town had the greatest population increase, 1,214 (11%), in the county in the 1990s, largely due to an influx of people who work in Orange Co and in the New York City metropolitan area.

John Conway

Mamaroneck [MAM-AR-O-NECK]. Town (pop 28,967) and village (pop 18,752) in SE Westchester Co. Purchased by John Richbell from the Siwanoy Indians in 1661, it was sold by his widow to Caleb Heathcote in 1697 and became part of his Manor of Scarsdale. Mamaroneck first elected town officers in 1697, and the town was confirmed in 1788. The Westchester Co Manufacturing Society built a dam and factory in 1811, but a series of businesses housed in the latter were unsuccessful. The New Haven Railroad was built through town in 1848. The village, which is partly in Rye, incorporated in 1895. D. W. Griffith (1875–1948) made films at a studio on Orienta Point from 1919 to 1924. In 1940 factories produced motor oil, perfume, and woolen cloth. Mamaroneck's population more than doubled between 1920 and 1930 (7,801 to 19,040), reaching 29,107 in 1960. In the early 21st century Mamaroneck is a commuter suburb of New York City.

mammals. Class of warm-blooded higher vertebrates whose offspring are born live and nursed on milk. Eighty-one species regularly appear in New York State. The land-based mammals are represented by the taxonomic orders Didelphidae (1), Insectivora (10), Chiroptera (9), Lagomorpha (5), Rodentia (22), Carnivora (21), and Artiodactyla (2). The marine mammals belong to the order Cetacea (27).

Least weasel *(Mustela nivalus).*

The majority of the terrestrial mammals can be found across most of the state, although many species, such as the white-tailed deer *(Odocoileus virginianus)* and eastern chipmunk *(Tamias striatus)*, do better in some regions than others. For some species New York State marks, or is very near, the northern, southern, western, or eastern limits of their range. Of the major terrestrial habitat types or ecological zones, the Northern Appalachian–Boreal type dominates the Adirondack region and the Tug Hill Plateau. It is primarily a mixture of beech, maple, birch, and various conifers including white pine, balsam fir, and spruce. Among the associated mammals are the moose *(Alces alces)*, American marten *(Martes americana)*, rock vole *(Microtus chrotorrhinus)*, and snowshoe hare *(Lepus americanus)*. The state's other ecoregions are decidedly more temperate and have a mixture of oak, hickory, maple, hemlock, and pine. Mammals inhabiting primarily these areas include the gray squirrel *(Sciurus carolinensis)*, eastern cottontail *(Sylvilagus floridanus)*, and opossum *(Didelphis virginiana)*. Records of the fox squirrel *(Sciurus niger)* and least weasel *(Mustela nivalis)* are largely confined to the extreme west of the state and the New England cottontail *(Sylvilagus transitionalis)* to the extreme eastern portion.

The impact of human beings on mammalian species in New York State has been profound. Although the role of Paleolithic immigrants from Asia in the disappearance of the Pleistocene mammals is uncertain, that of later European arrivals is clear. Farmers first occupied the more fertile and warmer regions appropriate for growing crops; mammals in those regions were thus the first to disappear. Species that suffered most were either valued for food or for commerce, such as white-tailed deer, elk *(Cervus elaphus)*, and beaver *(Castor canadensis)*, or were considered a personal or economic threat, such as wolves *(Canis lupus)* and cougars *(Felis concolor)*. The first mammal to disappear in historic times was probably the elk, the last of which was shot near Bolivar (Allegany Co) in 1842. The wolverine *(Gulo gulo)*, if ever a full-time resident, was extirpated from its Adirondack habitat around the same time. Moose were temporarily eliminated from the state in 1861.

Although the state's lands were almost entirely forested when Europeans arrived, by the 1880s roughly 75% was devoted to agriculture, causing the decline of many of the larger mammals. The cougar, wolf, and lynx *(Lynx canadensis)* were certainly gone by the turn of the century, and the beaver probably was as well. Many other species were at historic lows but not eliminated entirely. White-tailed deer disappeared everywhere but in the Adirondacks and a small portion of the southwest Catskills. The fisher *(Martes pennanti)*, otter *(Lontra canadensis)*, black bear *(Ursus americanus)*, and marten suffered similar reductions in numbers and distribution. At the same time, species such as the meadow vole *(Microtus pennsylvanicus)* were probably at their peak population because they largely escaped the direct attention of humans yet benefited from the clearing of land.

Also during the late 1800s the public began to realize that the natural resources of the state were not inexhaustible and would be lost if action was not taken. The State Forest Commission was established in 1885, and laws and regulations to control the harvest of wildlife were passed. Restoration of the beaver in the early 1900s was a success, but similar efforts with elk and moose failed. The abandonment of marginal farmlands and increased migration to the cities allowed for the return of many species. White-tailed deer reoccupied essentially the entire state by the end of the 1930s, and the fisher, otter, and black bear are slowly expanding into much of their historical range at varying rates. Moose returned to the Adirondacks in the 1980s, and the eastern coyote *(Canis latrans)* now occupies most of the state. Many of the marine mammals that had suffered from excessive harvest and hunting are recovering as well, most notably the fin *(Balaenoptera physalus)* and humpback whales *(Megaptera novaeangliae)*, which are occasionally sighted off the beaches of Long Island and sometimes become stranded or wash up dead on the beaches.

Today the greatest threat to mammals is not direct harvest but the ever expanding and more mobile human population. Country homes dot the forests, displacing species where sheep pastures displaced them over 100 years before. The right whale is now threatened not by the harpoon but by accidental ramming by ships, entanglement in fishing gear, and reduction of fish stocks on which they depend for food. The introduction of exotic species, including parasites, has caused the severe decline of a number of native trees, shrubs, and aquatic invertebrates, and is a growing concern for mammal populations. The long-term implications of global climate change remain obscure but are potentially staggering.

MAMMALS OF NEW YORK STATE

Family	Species	Common Name
Order Didelphimorphia		
Didelphidae	*Didelphis virginiana*	Virginia opossum
Order Insectivora		
Soricidae	*Blarina brevicauda*	northern short-tailed shrew
	Cryptotis parva	least shrew
	Sorex cinereus	masked shrew
	Sorex dispar	long-tailed shrew
	Sorex fumeus	smoky shrew
	Sorex hoyi	pygmy shrew
	Sorex palustris	water shrew
Talpidae	*Condylura cristata*	star-nosed mole
	Parascalops breweri	hairy-tailed mole
	Scalopus aquaticus	eastern mole
Order Chiroptera		
Vespertilionidae	*Eptesicus fuscus*	big brown bat
	Lasionycteris noctivagans	silver-haired bat
	Lasiurus borealis	eastern red bat
	Lasiurus cinereus	hoary bat
	Myotis leibii	eastern small-footed bat
	Myotis lucifugus	little brown bat
	Myotis septentrionalis	northern long-eared bat
	Myotis sodalis	Indiana bat
	Pipistrellus subflavus	eastern pipistrelle
Order Lagomorpha		
Leporidae	*Lepus americanus*	snowshoe hare
	Lepus californicus	black-tailed jackrabbit
	Lepus europaeus	European hare
	Sylvilagus floridanus	eastern cottontail
	Sylvilagus transitionalis	New England cottontail
Order Rodentia		
Sciuridae	*Glaucomys sabrinus*	northern flying squirrel
	Glaucomys volans	southern flying squirrel
	Marmota monax	woodchuck
	Sciurus carolinensis	eastern gray squirrel
	Sciurus niger	eastern fox squirrel
	Tamias striatus	eastern chipmunk
	Tamiasciurus hudsonicus	red squirrel
Castoridae	*Castor canadensis*	American beaver
Dipodidae (Zapodinae)	*Napaeozapus insignis*	woodland jumping mouse
	Zapus hudsonius	meadow jumping mouse
Muridae (Sigmodontinae)	*Peromyscus leucopus*	white-footed mouse
	Peromyscus maniculatus	deer mouse
Muridae (Arvicolinae)	*Clethrionomys gapperi*	southern red-backed vole
	Microtus chrotorrhinus	rock vole
	Microtus pennsylvanicus	meadow vole
	Microtus pinetorum	woodland vole
	Ondatra zibethicus	muskrat
	Synaptomys cooperi	southern bog lemming
Muridae (Murinae)	*Mus musculus*	house mouse
	Rattus norvegicus	Norway rat
	Rattus rattus	black rat
Erethizontidae	*Erethizon dorsatum*	porcupine

Chapman, William K., and Dennis Aprill. *Mammals of the Adirondacks* (Utica: North Country Books, 1991)

Connor, Paul F. *The Mammals of Long Island, New York* (Albany: Univ of the State of New York, 1971)

New York State, Department of Environmental Conservation, http://www.dec.state.ny.us

Alan Hicks

Manchester. Town (pop 9,258) and village (pop 1,475) in N Ontario Co. Settled in 1793, the town was formed from Farmington as Burt in 1821; the name was changed to Manchester in 1822. The Ontario Manufacturing Co built a woolen mill in 1812; other textile and flour mills followed. Joseph Smith Jr, founder of the Church of Latter-day Saints (Mormon), was a resident from 1818 to 1830. At Hill Cumorah he purportedly found the tablets that became the Book of Mormon, whose history is recounted in an annual pageant at the site. The Erie Canal (1825) passed through the town at Port Gibson. Manchester first acquired rail service with the Auburn and Rochester Railroad (1841), but it was the Lehigh Valley Railroad (1892) that made Manchester a railroad town with its division end, transfer yards, and shops, drawing Syrian, Italian, Ukrainian, and Polish workers. The railroad attracted the Swift and Co icehouse and the Manchester Produce Co. Rte 96 bypassed the village in 1951, and in 1954 the Thruway was opened across the town. The Lehigh Valley Railroad went bankrupt in 1976, and the line was taken over by the Ontario Central Railroad.

MAMMALS OF NEW YORK STATE (continued)

Family	Species	Common Name
Order Cetacea		
Balaenidae	*Eubalaena glacialis*	right whale
Balaenopteridae	*Balaenoptera borealis*	sei whale
	Balaenoptera musculus	blue whale
	Balaenoptera physalus	fin whale
	Balaenoptera acutorostrata	minke whale
	Megaptera novaeangliae	humpback whale
Delphinidae	*Delphinus delphis*	short-beaked saddleback dolphin
	Globicephala melas	long-finned pilot whale
	Grampus griseus	Risso's dolphin
	Lagenorhynchus acutus	Atlantic white-sided dolphin
	Lagenorhynchus albirostris	white-beaked dolphin
	Orcinus orca	killer whale
	Pseudorca crassidens	false killer whale
	Stenella attenuata	pantropical spotted dolphin
	Stenella coeruleoalba	striped dolphin
	Stenella frontalis	Atlantic spotted dolphin
	Stenella longirostris	spinner dolphin
	Tursiops truncatus	bottlenose dolphin
Monodontidae	*Delphinapterus leucas*	beluga whale
Phocoenidae	*Phocoena phocoena*	harbor porpoise
Physeteridae	*Kogia breviceps*	pygmy sperm whale
	Kogia simus	dwarf sperm whale
	Physeter macrocephalus	sperm whale
Ziphiidae	*Mesoplodon densirostris*	Blainville's beaked whale
	Mesoplodon europaeus	Gervais's beaked whale
	Mesoplodon mirus	True's beaked whale
	Ziphius cavirostris	Cuvier's beaked whale
Order Carnivora		
Phocidae	*Cystophora cristata*	hooded seal
	Halichoerus grypus	gray seal
	Phoca groenlandica	harp seal
	Phoca vitulina	harbor seal
	Phoca hispida	ringed seal
Canidae	*Canis familiaris*	domestic/feral dog
	Canis latrans	coyote
	Urocyon cinereoargenteus	gray fox
	Vulpes vulpes	red fox
Ursidae	*Ursus americanus*	black bear
Procyonidae	*Procyon lotor*	raccoon
Mustelidae	*Lontra canadensis*	river otter
	Martes americana	American marten
	Martes pennanti	fisher
	Mustela erminea	ermine
	Mustela frenata	long-tailed weasel
	Mustela nivalis	least weasel
	Mustela vison	mink
Mephitidae	*Mephitis mephitis*	striped skunk
Felidae	*Felis catus*	domestic/feral cat
	Lynx rufus	bobcat
Order Artiodactyla		
Cervidae	*Alces alces*	moose
	Odocoileus virginianus	white-tailed deer

Compiled by Joe Bopp and Roland W. Kays

Moderate suburbanization resulted in a 33% population increase between 1960 and 1990.

Marla A. Bennett

Mangione, Jerre [Gerlando] (*b* Rochester, 20 Mar 1909; *d* Haverford, Pa, 16 Aug 1998). Writer. Of Sicilian parentage, Mangione grew up in an Italian American enclave of Rochester. He received his BA from Syracuse University in 1931 and served as national coordinating editor for the Federal Writers' Project from 1937 to 1940. In 1943 he published his first book, *Mount Allegro,* a memoir of his early years in Rochester. *Mount Allegro* gave literary visibility and identity to a poorly understood ethnic group, and did so with great artistry. In this work Mangione's amiable and appealing ethnic Rochester becomes an icon for American ethnic experience as a whole. Mangione hoped the memoir would "dispel some of the more spurious cliches pinned to the image of Italian Americans by an uninformed American public." Between 1948 and 1992 he published nine other books, including two novels, an autobiography, studies of Sicilians and Italian Americans, and a history of the Federal Writers' Project (1935–43), and served as professor of English and creative writing at the University of Pennsylvania from 1961 to 1977. He was the recipient of numerous awards, including Italy's Premio Nazionale Empedocle.

Gardaphe, Fred. *Italian Signs, American Streets* (Durham, NC: Duke Univ Press, 1996)
Mangione, Jerre. *An Ethnic at Large: A Memoir of America in the Thirties and Forties* (Philadelphia: Univ of Pennsylvania Press, 1983)

Eugene Paul Nassar

Manhasset. Locality (pop 8,362) in North Hempstead (Nassau Co). An attempt by colonists from Lynn, Mass, to settle here in 1640 was disrupted by the Dutch. Part of a purchase by English settlers in 1643 from the native inhabitants, it was used as common pastureland until 1677, when it was occupied for farming. A small commercial center called Head of Cow Neck acquired a post office in 1812, which was renamed Manhasset in 1837. A railroad trestle (1898) across Manhasset Bay made commuting practical; businesses gathered around the station while houses were built to its north and east. Since 1907 it has been the seat of North Hempstead town government. Manhasset is noted for the fashionable shopping strip called the Miracle Mile; actually about three miles (5 km) long, it dates to the 1940s and draws shoppers from many affluent communities. Jim Brown, the football great, starred at Manhasset High School in the early 1950s. Manhasset landmarks include Greentree, the estate of the late Mr and Mrs John Hay Whitney, the Lakeville African Methodist Episcopal Zion Church (1833), and the Horatio Gates Onderdonk House (1836). The Manhasset Peninsula, extending into Long Island Sound, is the site of a number of other exclusive villages and localities.

Joan Gay Kent

Manhattan [New York County] (23 mi^2/60 km^2; pop 1,537,195). The county, the smallest in the state in area, was created in 1683 as coextensive with the City of New York. It is the only county in the state without a history of division into towns and subsidiary municipal governments. It is bounded by the Hudson, Harlem, and East Rivers, all three of which are tidal estuaries of the Atlantic Ocean. Although Manhattan Island dominates the county, it also includes adjacent islands, among them Governors, Liberty, Roosevelt, Ward's, and Randall's Islands, as well as part of Ellis Island, whose sovereignty is shared with New Jersey. New York Co and City expanded north onto the mainland with two territorial annexations from lower Westchester Co in 1874 and 1895. The consolidation of New York City in 1898 created the Borough of Manhattan, while the Annexed District north of the Harlem River became the Borough of the Bronx. Though located physically in the Bronx, the neighborhood of Marble Hill continued to be administered by Manhattan after 1895, when the dredging of the Harlem River Ship Canal separated the neighborhood from Manhattan Island.

The Borough of the Bronx remained a part of New York Co until 1914, when Bronx Co was formed.

Early History

Before European contact, the Algonquian-speaking Indians inhabited the area and cultivated maize, beans, squash, and other crops. The word *Manna-hata* is Algonquian, but its meaning is uncertain. Educated guesses abound, but the most popular is "hilly island," since the topography of Manhattan Island was quite rugged prior to the early 19th century, when it was leveled to make way for a gridded street plan. The northern portion of the island was the highest in elevation, although what became East Harlem was not much above mean sea level, and wetlands were prevalent. The East Side was considerably flatter than the West Side, and there was also relatively rocky terrain in what is now Central Park. The name of the island was spelled as "Manhattan" as early as 1614. In 1624 the Dutch established New Amsterdam as their principal settlement on Manhattan Island. A year later plans were drawn for constructing a military fort on the southern tip of the island, strategically located at the confluence of the Hudson and East Rivers. Although the fur trade with the Indians remained their primary interest, the Dutch also established farms, pastures, and orchards. There was little differentiation between commercial and residential neighborhoods during this period, with servants' quarters located within their household of employment and citizens living alongside or above their businesses. The English took control of New Amsterdam in 1664, and both the city and colony were named for the new proprietor—James, Duke of York—while retaining the older name of Manhattan for the island itself.

From the 1620s through the end of the 19th century, the city expanded northward, the most significant growth occurring during the second half of the 19th century. In 1664 settlement did not extend much past the present Wall St, at one time a fortified barrier, although there were several small villages in what is now Harlem. The Boston Post Rd, Bloomingdale Rd [now part of Broadway], and Kingsbridge Rd were main thoroughfares into the villages and farmlands of northern Manhattan and beyond. British New York experienced the expansion of public culture: ornamental gardens, theaters, taverns, and coffee shops. Because transatlantic trade was vital to the regional economy, the municipal government leased lots along the island's waterfront, initially concentrated on the East River, to entrepreneurs to facilitate commercial growth. Water lot grantees were required to build streets and wharves, and in return they could collect fees from ship owners and merchants who utilized the waterfront property.

During the American Revolution, the British captured Manhattan (1776–83), and the city was largely in ruins by the end of the war. When the patriots returned they began reconstructing it. Wall St became the new governmental and commercial core of the city. The old City Hall building on Wall and Nassau Sts was renamed Federal Hall and served as the national capital from 1789 to 1790. On 8 Mar 1817 the New York Stock and Exchange Board (renamed New York Stock Exchange in 1863) was organized, ushering in a new era in which Manhattan became the nation's leading financial center.

The 19th Century

Manhattan in the 19th century was a place of rapid growth and transformation, as the modestly sized "walking city" became the sprawling industrial and financial center of America. As the population grew to more than half a million by midcentury, municipal authorities faced increasing demands for clean drinking water, sewers, and other public services. Yellow fever and cholera epidemics were frequent, largely affecting poorer residents who, unlike wealthy citizens, did not have country homes in which to take refuge. In response the city built the Croton

Depiction of New Amsterdam, Nicolaes Visscher, *ca* 1655.

Aqueduct (1842) and constructed a public sewer system. In 1798 New York City instituted a numbered ward system, which extended up the island until the creation of the 21st and 22d Wards in 1853. However, nothing was to transform Manhattan more than the implementation of the gridded streets of the Commissioners' Plan of 1811. The pregrid landscape was a mosaic of farmland and dispersed settlements amid hills, wetlands, and streams. The development of the grid plan required that both topography and private property boundaries conform to the new standardized blocks of the grid. As the city expanded, real estate speculators such as John Jacob Astor bought undeveloped land on the outskirts, then subdivided and sold it, making large profits.

By 1830 New York City had overtaken Philadelphia and Boston as the leading port city in America. The rapid influx of immigrants from Europe provided cheap labor for industrial production throughout the 19th century. To accommodate the demographic and commercial growth of the city, landfill was dumped into the surrounding waterways, extending the shoreline and increasing the total land area south of the present City Hall by 33%. Residential development expanded northward as streets and avenues were constructed in accordance with the grid plan. By the 1850s the frontier of urban development extended to 42d St, and northward expansion continued throughout the remainder of the century.

In 1853 the state legislature passed a law authorizing the city to acquire land for a public park in Manhattan. The Central Park Commission, established in 1857, held a design contest for the proposed park. Frederick Law Olmsted and Calvert Vaux submitted the winning entry, which replicated an idealized version of an English pastoral landscape. While Olmsted hoped that Central Park would provide an oasis of civility amid the turmoil and chaos of an expanding metropolis, it was so far uptown that many working-class families who lived in Lower Manhattan could not afford to visit the park regularly. Instead it boosted adjacent property values and encouraged northward expansion in Manhattan. By 1870 an estimated 48% of the New York City population lived above 14th St, a street that did not exist at the turn of the century.

Exclusive neighborhoods developed along 5th Ave and Washington Square in the 19th century. A fire in 1835 destroyed much of the remaining residential parts of downtown Manhattan and sparked a major uptown movement. Anchored at Washington Square to the south and extending north along 5th Ave to Central Park, Millionaires' Row was lined with political clubs, brownstones, mansions, and opulent department stores. During the Gilded Age (end of the 19th century), the architect Richard Morris Hunt built colossal homes for the Vanderbilts, Tiffanys, and Villards along 5th Ave.

It was also during the 19th century that poor neighborhoods expanded. Tenement districts like the Lower East Side, Five Points, and Hell's Kitchen experienced a rapid influx of new immigrants. Five Points, built on an in-filled marsh, had been bypassed by the first waves of affluent development. Irish, German, and Italian families settled into cramped five- and six-story walk-ups that often housed several families per apartment. Tenement apartments had little ventilation or plumbing and few amenities. Five Points and other neighborhoods were depicted in the photographs of Jacob Riis's *How the Other Half Lives* (1890), and the public outcry over the squalid living conditions of the urban poor inspired a process of municipal intervention and urban planning. Between 1887 and 1894 the city bought and leveled most of the Five Points neighborhood (often anathematized as the

MANHATTAN (NEW YORK CO)
POPULATION CENSUS FIGURES

	White	Nonwhite	Total Population	Foreign-Born
1790	29,661	3,470	33,131	—
1800	54,122	6,367	60,489	—
1810	86,550	9,823	96,373	—
1820	112,820	10,886	123,706	5,390
1830	183,136	13,976	197,112	17,773
1840	296,352	16,358	312,710	—
1850	501,732	13,815	515,547	240,989
1860	801,095	12,574	813,669	386,345
1870	929,199	13,093	942,292	419,094
1880	1,185,843	20,456	1,206,299[a]	478,670
1890	1,489,627	25,674	1,515,301[b]	639,943
1900	2,006,891	43,709	2,050,600[c]	850,884
1910	2,693,228	69,294	2,762,522[d]	1,257,597
1920	2,168,906	115,197	2,284,103	928,144
1930	1,631,756	235,556	1,867,312	641,618
1940	1,577,625	312,299	1,889,924	582,895
1950	1,556,599	403,502	1,960,101	461,102
1960	1,271,822	426,459	1,698,281	374,698
1970	1,089,302	449,931	1,539,233	307,630
1980	841,204	587,081	1,428,285	348,581
1990	868,120	619,416	1,487,536	383,866
2000	835,610	701,585	1,537,195	452,440

Notes: "Nonwhite" includes African Americans, Asians, American Indians, and Pacific Islanders and, for 2000, also the mixed race and other race categories. Through the 1960 census these figures primarily reflect the African American population. Foreign-born figures for 1820 and 1830 include only those not naturalized; other years include all foreign-born in the population.

[a]Includes 41,626 in Annexed District, now in the Bronx.
[b]Includes 74,085 in Annexed District, now in the Bronx.
[c]Includes 200,507 in Bronx Borough.
[d]Includes 430,980 in Bronx Borough.

worst slum in the United States); the area is now the site of judicial buildings and Columbus Park. Reformers attempted to deal with the overcrowding in many areas. By the end of the 19th century, neighborhoods in the Lower East Side had densities as high as 1,560 people per acre. In 1910 Manhattan's population peaked at 113,363 per square mile. (In 2000 the borough had 68,017 persons per square mile.)

THE 20TH CENTURY

With the consolidation of New York City in 1898, Manhattan became just one of five boroughs in the city. It now had a borough president and for the first time a governmental structure separate from that of New York City. But far from diminishing its status, the change made Manhattan dominant in a larger city. Economically, politically, and culturally, it remained the center of New York City. While not determining the city's growth, the development of new transportation systems facilitated urban expansion. With the opening of the 9th Avenue Elevated (or the El), an elevated rail line that snaked through Lower Manhattan beginning in 1868, the era of mass transportation in New York City began. Its construction overshadowed the once vibrant street life of the Bowery. The elevated network expanded later in the 19th century, but the opening of the first subway in 1904 marked the beginning of the dispersion of Manhattan's population. Bridges to cross the Harlem River had been built as early as 1693, but the East River was first spanned by the Brooklyn Bridge in 1883 and the Hudson River by the Hudson Tubes (now part of the Port Authority Trans-Hudson [PATH] system) in 1908 and 1909. The first vehicular crossings were the Holland Tunnel (1927), followed by the George Washington Bridge (1931).

Manhattan also grew vertically as major corporations built tall office buildings in the 20th century. Located in Midtown, where a second business district had emerged, the 1,250 ft (381 m) Empire State Building (1931) was the tallest building in the world until the twin towers of the World Trade Center surpassed it in the early 1970s. In 1931 work began on Rockefeller Center. John D. Rockefeller Jr originally intended to build a new Metropolitan Opera House and three office buildings, but the stock market crash of 1929 led him to devote the entire complex to commercial development. The emergence of skyscrapers in the Downtown and Midtown business districts defined the Manhattan skyline, which became a universal symbol of the modern city.

By the first quarter of the 20th century, Manhattan neighborhoods were highly segregated by ethnicity and class. Harlem had been the focus of African American migration during the early 20th century. Italian enclaves were in Greenwich Village and along Canal St in Lower Manhattan, where there was also a sizable Chinese community. Jewish immigrants were clustered along 2d Ave in the Lower East Side, and most of the German population was in Yorkville in the Upper East Side. By the early 20th century, the main theater district in the city had moved from 14th St to Times Square and the adjacent streets of Broadway. Jazz was featured in Harlem from the late 1920s to the early 1950s, along 52d St from the 1930s into the 1950s, and after the 1950s in Greenwich Village after the 1950s. The latter was home to a group of young writers, artists, and political radicals who scorned a middle-class lifestyle.

After midcentury the Lower East Side slowly lost its Jewish character as Jews moved elsewhere in the city and to suburbs. Greenwich Village bohemia expanded into neighborhoods east and south that then became known as the East Village and SoHo (South of Houston St). Post–World War II Manhattan suffered from a loss of manufacturing jobs and middle-class flight to the suburbs. Stable working-class neighborhoods were decimated by unemployment, poverty, and crumbling infrastructure. The elimination of discriminatory immigration quotas in 1965 resulted in a large influx of Asians and Latinos into already marginalized neighborhoods, including East Harlem, where Puerto Ricans had already settled in large numbers. These neighborhoods suffered extensive landlord abandonment and arson in the 1960s and 1970s, leaving behind an inhospitable landscape of vacant lots and run-down buildings. In 1980, after a steady decline since 1910, Manhattan's population fell to 1,428,285, its lowest population in the 20th century. This soon began to turn around. In the 1980s a new form of neighborhood change, gentrification, emerged. Areas of the Lower East Side, Harlem, and the Upper West Side that had always been popular with artists, were bought up and renovated by returning middle-class residents.

In 2001 New York City remained a symbol of the economic power of the United States and became a target of international terrorism, resulting in the destruction of the World Trade Center on 11 September. The rebuilding of the site is one of the great challenges Manhattan faces in the early 21st century.

See also DEPARTMENT STORES; JAZZ; NEW YORK CITY SUBWAY; STREET RAILWAYS; TAXI AND CAR SERVICES; THEATER, NEW YORK CITY.

The literature on Manhattan, unlike that for New York City or specific Manhattan neighborhoods and topics, is relatively sparse. For the period before the consolidation of 1898, when New York City was largely limited to the Island of Manhattan, the standard work is Edwin G. Burrows and Mike Wallace, *Gotham: A History of New York City to 1898* (1999). A general work of great utility is Kenneth T. Jackson, ed., *The Encyclopedia of New York City* (1995). A classic work of great comprehensiveness is I. N. Phelps Stokes, *The Iconography of Manhattan Island, 1498–1909,* 6 vols (1915–28). Valuable studies of the growth of Manhattan Island include Ann L. Buttenwieser, *Manhattan Water-Bound: Manhattan's Waterfront from the 17th Century to the Present* (1999); Eric Homberger, *The Historical Atlas of New York City: A Visual Celebration of Nearly 400 Years of New York City's History* (1994); David Scobey, *Empire City: The Making and Meaning of the New York City Landscape* (2002); David Ward and Olivier Zunz, *The Landscape of Modernity: New York City, 1900–1940* (1992); Paul E. Cohen and Robert T. Augustyn, *Manhattan in Maps, 1527–1995* (1997); Max Page, *The Creative Destruction of Manhattan, 1990–1940* (1999); and Henry Moscow, *The Street Book: An Encyclopedia of Manhattan Street Names and Their Origins* (1978).

Reuben Skye Rose-Redwood and Kristina Gibson

Lower Manhattan; detail from panoramic map of New York City, 1910.

Manhattan, purchase of. See PURCHASE OF MANHATTAN.

Manhattan College. Independent Catholic liberal arts college. In 1848 the Brothers of Christian Schools founded the Academy of the Holy Infancy on Canal St in Manhattan to teach French-speaking immigrant children. The school moved to 131st St in 1853, added college-level studies in 1859, and adopted the name Manhattan College in 1861. In 1892 a school of engineering was added. The college moved to its Riverdale campus in the Bronx in 1924 and became coeducational in 1973. In 2002 there were about 3,400 students from 60 nations studying in its five undergraduate schools, arts, business, engineering, education, and science.

Butler, W., and W. Strode, eds. *Manhattan College: Then and Now* (Prospect, KY: Harmony House Publishers, 1991)

Carl A. Westerdahl and Susan S. Clarke

Manhattan Project. Name given to the secret work by the US government that led to the development of a working atomic bomb in July 1945. In 1942 the task of producing such a weapon was placed in the hands of the Manhattan Engineering District (MED) of the US Army Corps of Engineers. Named to avoid attention, the unit was only briefly headquartered in New York City; the MED stretched nationwide. Critical to the project was the fissionable uranium-235 (U-235) isotope. Early work on developing methods for separating the isotope from its constituents took place at Columbia University in Morningside Heights. The unit assigned the task of devising both gaseous diffusion and centrifuge separation was code-named the Substitute Alloy Materials (SAM) laboratory.

Linde Air Products Co of Tonawanda (Erie Co) was one of the few American companies experienced in working with uranium ores. Prior to World War II, Linde refined uranium to produce agents needed to color ceramic glazes. Because U-235 existed only in minute amounts, vast quantities of uranium had to be processed to acquire the volume needed, and no potential source was overlooked. Late in 1942, the US Army awarded the company a contract to build a pilot refinery in Tonawanda to extract uranium oxide from a concentrated sludge of vanadium tailings. Because it was not known which of several methods of isotope separation would be most productive, research took place simultaneously on a variety of approaches. Linde's long experience in commercial gas production put it in good stead for a contract to develop a gaseous diffusion process. Experiments were conducted at the company's original 1907 factory site on Chandler St in Buffalo. In 1943 the Electro Metallurgical Co constructed a plant at Niagara Falls for converting uranium-bearing compounds into metal and for extracting uranium from scrap metal. Other New York State companies contributed in varying degrees to the success of the Manhattan Project, including Hooker Electrochemical Co, a Niagara Falls–based electrochemical producer, and the American Chicle Co, the maker of Chiclets chewing gum. Headquartered in Long Island City (Queens Co), American Chicle did experimental work on the company's printing presses for making barriers for the gaseous diffusion process.

Groueff, Stephane. *Manhattan Project: The Untold Story of the Making of the Atomic Bomb* (Boston: Little, Brown, 1967)

William E. Worthington Jr

Manhattan topography. There is little evidence today that more than 2,200 acres (890 ha) of the Manhattan shoreline is filled land, that high hills and rocky prominences once formed a backbone down its center, and that networks of rivers, streams, and ponds flowed from it into the Hudson and East Rivers. Leveling hills enabled city officials and private landowners to build streets for a transportation system, to fill inland watercourses for development plots, and to expand the island into surrounding rivers to create a premier maritime economy. The pattern of altering Manhattan's natural topography was applied elsewhere in the state. Portions of New York City's outer boroughs were also flattened and grew outward, as were, for example, portions of Albany, Buffalo, and Syracuse.

Manhattan's Original Landform

The 1639 Manatus map shows a much thinner island. Using contemporary streets as reference points, its southern boundaries were at the original high-water mark, Pearl St (all street names in the entry refer to the current configuration of Manhattan) on the east and Greenwich St on the west. The Hudson River shoreline generally followed Washington St from Reade to West 13th St. The island's western borders were 10th, 11th, and 12th Aves as far as West 42d St, after which 12th Ave defined the outer limits to the northern terminus at Spuyten Duyvil Creek. On the East Side Cherry St formed the rim from Dover to Jefferson St. The East River touched 1st Ave at Stuyvesant's Meadow (between East 12th and 25th Sts) and at 89th St; in between, most of the original limits of the land remain. The banks of Manhattan's third and narrowest body of water, the Harlem River, which once separated Marble Hill from the Bronx, have been minimally expanded. A small group of islands were in the river at 155th St, and an inlet at Sherman Creek pierced the rocky edge of the river between Dyckman and West 202d Sts.

Originally substantial creeks flowed from several blocks inland into the Hudson and East Rivers. These disappeared as the street grid laid out in the 1811 Plan was implemented. They also became land after adjacent, low-lying meadows and swamps were drained for other, more salubrious or economically lucrative uses and as a health measure. Stuyvesant Creek ran from a meadow into the East River at 18th St and 1st Ave, a crowded, 19th-century tenement district. A large stream ran into Turtle Bay between East 45th and 48th Sts, the site of 19th- and 20th-century stockyards considered to be a public nuisance. The Saw Kill crossed what would become Central Park from 10th Ave and entered the East River at 74th St. Another kill ran from the salt meadows in Harlem to the East River at 124th St. Only two large creeks were on the West Side. Strykers Bay entered the Hudson from West 96 through 99th Sts but was most likely filled in by 19th-century railroad construction and Robert Moses's West Side Highway. The mouth of the Great Kill, the confluence of three smaller streams, was at 11th Ave and 40th St. The move of 12th Ave northward to make room for shipping and associated uses in the late 19th and early 20th centuries probably caused the demise of this kill. Early maps also show large ponds, swamps, and meandering streams throughout Manhattan's interior. The 1811 Plan called for a strict grid that obliterated these water bodies as well as the original shoreline. The Collect Pond between Broadway and Baxter, from Duane to Canal Sts, was the largest and most famous of the depressions. It was a source of drinking water until after the Revolution, and it took 10 years, beginning in 1803, to fill in this pond. Beekman's and Lispenard's Swamps downtown, Sunfish Pond in the East 30s, Minetta Stream in SoHo, Bestaver's Killitje around 14th St and 5th Ave, and several streams running through what would become Central Park also dotted the original landscape.

New Land

Manhattan's topography in the 17th century also included hills, which in their natural and leveled states have aided the needs of the city. A rocky ridge ran from the island's northern rim at Spuyten Duyvil into Lower Manhattan. Fort Washington at 175th St and Mount Pitt (or Jones Hill) near Grand St were two of many high points that were used as early fortifications. Many of the downtown hills were leveled prior to and just after the Revolutionary War. The crest of Potbaker's Hill, between Reade and Duane Sts, was used to create land for the first Hall of Records. Other prominences at this time became streets and filled swamps. A 30 ft (9 m) hill between Worth, Canal, and Broadway became Franklin St, Verlettenberg Hill became Exchange Place, and another hill between Broadway and Leonard Sts helped fill Lispenard's Swamp.

On the edges of the island the debris from leveling the hills, along with ballast, sunken ships, building and roadway excavations, wastes, ashes, and street sweepings, were collected and deposited in the East and Hudson Rivers to make new land. In 1623 Dutch settlers began to fill in the East River between the low- and high-water marks along Pearl St to create the city's first wharves. Over time, various charters and laws increased the city's ownership up to 400 ft (122 m) into the rivers and beyond. Subsequent fills from the 1890s to the 1930s altered the island to its present state. Highways such as the East River Drive, regularized the East River shoreline from Montgomery to East 93d St, and West St/12th Ave/Henry Hudson Parkway straightened the Hudson's edge from Battery Park to the Bronx. Waterside, built on an ingenious platform between East 25th and 30th Sts (1961–73), extended the shore for housing, as did Battery Park City on 90 acres (36 ha) of fill (1961–76). By 1978 the North River Wastewater Treatment Plant deck extended into the Hudson River and in 1993 Riverbank State Park was built on top of the plant.

Manhattan's original topography continues to influence its physical shape. Developers have blasted out the gneiss forming the island's early backbone to build skyscrapers, constantly elevating the skyline. Surface swamps, ponds, and streams no longer exist on the surface, but construction companies must be mindful of their presence. In 2002 a stream that fed the original Great Kill flooded excavations for a new theater on West 42d St. In the early 21st century the island south of City Hall is 33% larger than when Peter Minuit bargained with the Indians for its control. Environmental laws have temporarily halted expansion into the rivers, but the need for additional space for housing downtown has prompted the city to reconsider, recommending massive decking over the lower East River.

Buttenwieser, Ann L. *Manhattan Water-Bound: Manhattan's Waterfront from the 17th Century to the Present* (Syracuse: Syracuse Univ Press, 1999)

Stokes, I. N. Phelps. *The Iconography of Manhattan Island, 1498–1909* (1915–28; repr New York: Arno Press, 1967)

Ann L. Buttenwieser

Manhattanville College. Independent liberal arts college. In 1841 the Religious Order of the Sacred Heart, a French teaching order, founded the Academy of the Sacred Heart in Manhattan's Lower East Side as a boarding school for Catholic girls. The school moved in 1847 to Convent Ave in Manhattanville on the Upper West Side and was chartered as a women's college with the name Manhattanville College in

1917. It moved to the former estate of Whitelaw Reid in Purchase (Westchester Co) in 1952 and became coeducational in 1969 and nondenominational in 1971. Ophir Hall, renamed Reid Hall in 1969, was listed in 1974 in the National Register of Historic Places. In 2002 the college offered programs in the liberal arts, sciences, management, and education to about 1,400 undergraduates and 750 graduate students, most of the latter in its education program.

Manhattanville College, http://www.manhattanville.edu

Carl Westerdahl and Susan S. Clarke

Manheim. Town (pop 3,171) in E Herkimer Co. Settled around 1755, the town was formed from Palatine (Montgomery Co) in 1797 and was annexed to Herkimer Co in 1817. A nail factory was in operation by 1800 on East Canada Creek. In the 19th century Manheim was a cheese-making town, producing over 1 million pounds (454,000 kg) a year in 1855 and 1865 and ranking second in the state. Manheim's industrial employment was concentrated in Dolgeville, with its piano and felt-slipper factories. The Daniel Green Co (1894), a shoe manufacturer, closed in 2001, eliminating 500 jobs. The major industries in 2003 were Rawlings' Adirondack Bat factory, North Hudson Woodcrafters, and Tricot (curtains and lace), along with dairy farming. Its Violet Festival is held the second weekend in June.

Susan R. Perkins

Manlius. Town (pop 31,872) and village (pop 4,819) in E Onondaga Co. Settled in 1790, the town was formed in 1794. Manufacturing included paper mills, carpentry tools, harvesters, yarn, and cement, much of it within the Village of Fayetteville. The Village of Manlius was settled in 1792 and incorporated in 1813. The Erie Canal (1819) passed through the northern part of the town. Manlius Military Academy, founded in 1869 as St. John's School for Boys, merged with DeWitt's Pebble Hill School in 1970. Two ice holes, depressions where ice forms in winter and remains frozen well into the summer, were used to harvest ice. Green Lakes State Park (1936) encompasses two lakes and several ponds. As Syracuse suburbanized, the population of Manlius increased rapidly, from 10,221 in 1950 to 19,351 in 1960.

Marla A. Bennett

Mannsville. Village (pop 400) in Ellisburg (Jefferson Co). Settled *ca* 1800, the village was named for Maj H. B. Mann in 1823, when the post office was established. One of several trading centers in the town, it was particularly important because it was on the Rome, Watertown and Ogdensburg Railroad (1851). During the 1840s and 1850s Mannsville was the center of the Jefferson Co antislavery movement. The village was incorporated in 1879. Mannsville became a bedroom community after World War II, and in 2003 residents commuted to Watertown, Fort Drum, and Syracuse (since I-81 opened in 1961).

Laura Lynne Scharer

Manorhaven. Village (pop 6,138) in North Hempstead (Nassau Co). On Manhasset Peninsula, this locality is largely surrounded by water, and one part of it was known as O'Gorman's Island. Farming and boat building were principal occupations; from 1871 until 1925 much of the land was mined for building sand. In 1926 O'Gorman's Island was sold to a syndicate that renamed it Manhasset Isle, and landfill broadened the causeway connecting it to the rest of the peninsula. The summer cottages that were built were later converted to year-round use. The village was incorporated in 1929. From 1937 to 1940 Manhasset Bay was the base of overseas seaplane operations; the hangars were taken over for aircraft parts manufacture during World War II. Manorhaven's population includes many families with Italian, Asian, and Latino backgrounds. Expensive condominiums, small boatyards, marinas, a municipal beach and pool, and some light industry are near the waterfront.

Joan Gay Kent

manor system. European nations that created colonial possessions developed systems of estate holdings. The Dutch created the patroon system, the French had seigniories, and the English established the manor. New York Colony's manor system was an offshoot of the failed patroon system of the New Netherland period. When the English gained political control of the colony in 1664, several manors were established, both for economic and political reasons and to promote settlement and agriculture. The manor system was a vital part of the colony during the late 17th and early 18th centuries, and allowed affluent men to acquire vast landholdings and to rent farms to tenants. Manors declined after the Revolutionary War and were defunct after 1846.

FROM PATROONSHIP TO ENGLISH PATENT

To alleviate the economic burdens associated with colonization, the Dutch West India Co offered extensive land grants to Europeans as a strategy to populate the colony. In 1630 company shareholder and merchant Kiliaen van Rensselaer acquired a grant and established the first privately owned patent, called a patroonship, in New Netherland. Rensselaerswijck [now in Albany, Columbia, and Rensselaer Cos], consisted of 850,000 acres (344,000 ha). Five patroonships subsequently were created in New Netherland, under which each patroon had jurisdiction over tenants, served as the governmental authority, and had the right to establish local courts. Although patroons managed some tenants on their estates, they were not successful in promoting settlements because of the financial burdens associated with defense, the subsidizing early settlers, and the costs of transportation. Besides Rensselaerswijck the majority of patroonships failed because of a lack of administrative abilities, the extensive costs involved, and the need to wait years to see a return on initial investments.

After 1664, when the English took control of the colony, royal governors recognized Dutch land rights but introduced their own system of land distribution. They offered land to colonists, not European investors, and made grants in British territories located in the colonies of New York, Massachusetts, and Rhode Island. English

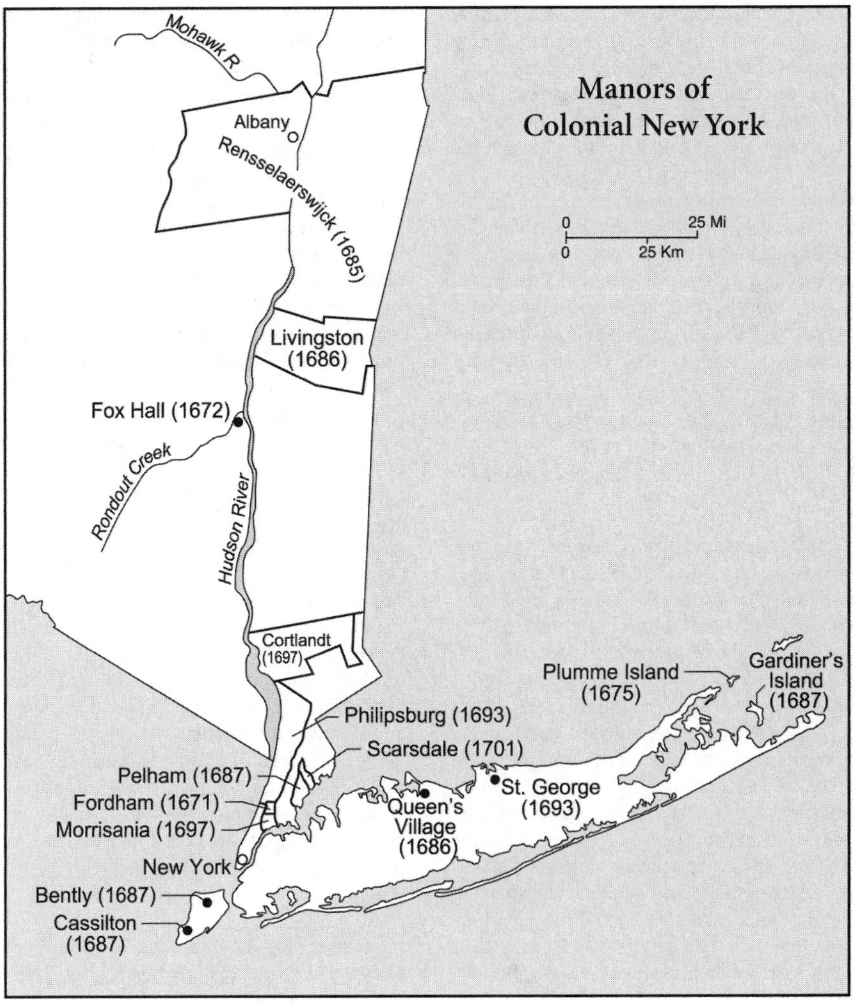

governors established manors primarily to gain political control and for economic reasons, but they also showed a degree of favoritism and bestowed land grants to politicians. As governors sought to organize the colony, they tried to curb authority of the remaining Dutch patroonships. Rensselaerswijck and Colendonck (Westchester Co), however, protested the new policy and aimed to gain territory so they could maintain the political autonomy they enjoyed under the Dutch. In 1664 Gov Richard Nicolls confirmed the Van Rensselaer title to Rensselaerswijck Manor but stripped the family's claim to Albany. Nicolls established three manors in eastern Long Island: Gardiner's Island (1665), 3,300 acres (1,340 ha); Shelter Island (1666), 8,000 acres (3,200 ha); and Fisher's Island (1668), 4,000 acres (1,600 ha). He also granted a 9,166-acre (3,709 ha) tract in Westchester Co to physician Thomas Pell in 1666, which Gov Thomas Dongan established as Pelham Manor in 1687.

Gov Francis Lovelace succeeded Nicolls and granted over 24,000 acres (9,700 ha) of undeveloped land to wealthy men politically connected to government. To promote settlement, in 1671 he granted a 3,900-acre (1,580 ha) tract to merchant John Archer called Fordham [now in Bronx Co]. Lovelace granted 230 acres (93 ha) at Esopus [now Kingston, Ulster Co] in 1672 to Thomas Chambers, called Fox Hall Manor, which served as a military base. Gov Lovelace granted two patents in New England. He established Tisbury Manor on Martha's Vineyard [now in Massachusetts] in 1671 for Thomas and Matthew Mayhew. He also granted 4,160 acres (1,683 ha), called Sophy Manor, or Prudence Island, on Narragansett Bay, RI, to Boston merchant John Pine in 1672. Gov Edmund Andros made only one grant during his term. He approved an 820-acre (332 ha) tract on Plum Island in eastern Long Island in 1675 to Samuel Wyllys of Hartford, Conn. Because the first manors were small and landowners were mainly New Englanders and absentee landlords, manors or patents were mostly investments and not entirely successful in terms of colonization or agriculture.

Rise of the Manor System

During the 1680s colonial governors approved major land grants, making a success of the manor system. All manors were located east of the Hudson River, from Long Island north to Albany Co, and most existed in Westchester Co. Of all the governors Thomas Dongan granted the most land. He ceded over 500,000 acres (202,000 ha) between 1685 and 1687 and bestowed vast grants to those who served in a political or military capacity. In 1685 Dongan reconfirmed the Van Rensselaer title to lands and granted the family a seat in the provincial assembly and an additional 250,000 acres (101,000 ha), which formed Claverack Manor, or the Lower Manor (Columbia Co). With Dongan's grant the Van Rensselaers held the largest land claim in the colony: 1 million acres (405,000 ha) of undeveloped land.

In 1685 Dongan granted an additional 64,000 acres (25,900 ha) to the Mayhews on Martha's Vineyard (1685) and approved 2,900 acres (1,170 ha) for Boston merchant Henry Lloyd to form the Queen's Village Manor [now Lloyds Neck, Suffolk Co]. In 1686 Dongan created a manor for politician Robert Livingston: Livingston Manor [now in Columbia Co] on 160,000 acres (65,000 ha). Dongan also created some smaller manors in the colony. In 1686 he formed Eaton Manor for Milford, Conn, merchants Richard and Alexander Bryan. Eaton was located in Huntington (Suffolk Co) and contained 1,500 acres (610 ha). In 1687 Dongan granted two manors on Staten Island: Cassiltown, a 25,000-acre (10,100 ha) tract for New York and New England politician John Palmer, and Bentley Manor, a 3,165-acre (1,281 ha) tract for Christopher Billopp, a captain in the Royal Navy.

Gov Benjamin Fletcher designated six new manors and bestowed that status on extant land patents. In 1693 he formed Philipsburg Manor (Westchester Co) for merchant Frederick Philipse, granting him 92,000 acres (37,200 ha). He ceded the 64,000-acre (25,900 ha) St. George Manor in Brookhaven (Suffolk Co) to Chief Justice and British Army Col William Smith. Fletcher created a 300,000-acre (120,000 ha) manor in his own name, Fletcherdon (Orange and Ulster Cos), in 1694 for Navy Capt John Evans. Fletcher upgraded patents purchased by Stephanus van Cortlandt to establish Cortlandt Manor in 1697. Manor status connected noncontiguous parcels or approximately 86,000 acres (34,800 ha) of Van Cortlandt property. Fletcher gave Van Cortlandt a seat in the assembly, which secured the latter's political career. For the mayor of New York City, Nicholas Bayard, Fletcher founded Kingsfield Manor in 1695, a small tract in Albany Co. In 1697 he established Morrisania [now in Bronx Co], a 1,920-acre (777 ha) tract for the governor of New Jersey and the New York province chief justice Lewis Morris. In 1701–2 Lt Gov John Nanfan established the last manor, an 11,500-acre (4,650 ha) tract called Scarsdale (Westchester Co) for New York City mayor Caleb Heathcote.

Manor Lords' Rights and Privileges

By 1700 four manors—Rensselaerswijck, Livingston, Cortlandt, and Philipsburg—comprised over 50% of the undeveloped land in the province. All landowners had some form of legal jurisdiction over tenants that depended on the terms of their manor grant. Most royal land grants contained an advowson provision where proprietors had the right to appoint a clergyman and the power to tithe the tenants to pay the clergyman's salary; there is little evidence, however, that tithing was introduced. Royal governors granted landowners court leet, or rights to settle disputes and resolve social misconduct issues not punishable under English law. Three manors—Cortlandt, Livingston, and Rensselaerswijck—were entitled to send representatives to the assembly. Before 1750 they rarely exercised this privilege because the major landholders had family members either seated on the colonial council or closely associated with the governors. After 1750 a subtle repositioning in the colony's politics left the assembly holding more influence. At that point manors with rights to send a representative to the assembly began exercising that privilege.

Of all the manors, Rensselaerswijck, Livingston, Philipsburg, Morrisania, and Cortlandt were the most successful because of significant land grants but also because manor lords developed property for agriculture and commerce, making them attractive to farmers, craftsmen, families, and shippers. Large landowners such as the Van Rensselaers, Van Cortlandts, and Philipses populated the land, developed self-contained economic entities, and thereby enhanced their standing in society as members of the colonial aristocracy. These families were major agents in commerce and agriculture and became a major force in politics. Most manor lords were politically involved in colonial affairs prior to receiving substantial land grants. The combination of wealth gained from commercial activities and their place in local government provided the opportunity to acquire vast land grants. To declare their continued subservience to the feudal system, wealthy individuals were obligated to demonstrate their fealty with a token annual payment to the governor, who was the Crown's representative. Using their wealth and connections, manor lords often cunningly added to their vast estates. From the 1680s to the 1770s, Cortlandt, Livingston, and Rensselaerswijck had significant mills, landing sites, and farms, which influenced the formation of port towns that later became important communities, such as Albany, Kingston, and Tarrytown (Westchester Co).

Proprietors were entitled to claim escheat (the reversion of a farm after the death of a tenant or after the eviction of a tenant), and nonpayment of rent also produced a land reversion to the landowner. Proprietors drew income when a tenant sold improvements to the property to the next owner. The manor lord could claim a percentage of the profits from the sale, known as a quarter sale. Landowners earned additional income by lending money with interest to farmers and by operating the local supply store.

Tenants and Leases

Before the Revolutionary War manor lords oversaw more than 5,000 tenant farms. Although farmers were not required to fealty or to commit allegiance as in Europe, they owed annual stipends or perpetual fees for the rented farms. Leases stipulated that tenants were required to pay rent in either cash, produce, wood, or grain, and in some cases they were required to work a certain number of days per year in lieu of cash or to produce payments. Some leases stipulated that the landowner was automatically entitled to a portion of the crop at harvest time. Other leases required tenants to clear land in a certain number of years. By the mid-1700s a set fee replaced labor requirements on some manors. At Philipsburg and Cortlandt Manors, once rent fees were established they never increased. Leases stipulated that proprietors had rights over minerals, hunting and fishing, milling, and lumber, which economically limited the prosperity of tenants. Proprietors owned mills, which the tenants were expected to use for a fee. At Livingston, Rensselaerswijck, and Cortlandt, manor lords and their agents supervised industrial activities. Tenants were offered farms on differing terms that were at the discretion of landlords. Some tenants rented farms for specific terms, such as 1 to 99 years, while other leases were for one, two, or three lives, or terms.

Decline

On the eve of the Revolutionary War, major manors continued to operate except for Cortlandt, which remained a manor in name only. By the mid-1750s Cortlandt had been divided into smaller parcels and distributed to heirs. The remaining manors faced their own difficulties. Although annual rents were not overly burdensome on tenants, conflicts arose because tenants toiled on land for a lifetime but had no chance to purchase the property they developed. During the last half of the 18th century, New England settlers rented land on New York's manors. Some newcomers were satisfied to rent, but others were agitated by the lack of opportunity to buy land. These properties in contention lay on the border between colonies, on lands whose ownership was disputed by Indian groups or by New England colonies. Tenants organized to discuss rights and rallied for better lease terms. In 1763 and 1766 military forces were needed to quell tenant uprisings, primarily at Livingston Manor and in the northeastern sector of Cortlandt Manor.

Despite the economic and political power of the proprietors, politicians had difficulty controlling the activities of tenants and manor lords during the Revolutionary War. In 1779 the state accused Philipsburg Manor's Frederick Philipse III of treason and confiscated his land, farms, and mills. His land was sold to speculators or to his tenants who could prove their patriotism. Cortlandt, Rensselaerswijck, and Livingston Manors remained in family hands; most other manors were politically dissolved before the war ended.

Over time the manor lords modified lease terms and began to entertain the possibility of outright land sales. Cortlandt Manor lands were available for sale to tenants from the late 1760s. Rensselaerswijck tenants, however, were compelled to pay a perpetual rent well into the 19th century. Rent and the obligation to present the landlord a portion of profits fueled resentment. After the so-called last patroon, Stephen Van Rensselaer, died in 1839, his sons tried to evict tenants whose rents were in arrears. Armed conflicts ensued and were halted by the militia. By 1840 there was widespread agitation throughout the state for modifications of lease terms. Thousands of tenants petitioned the legislature seeking redress. Under political and social pressure, the Van Rensselaers reached amicable terms with their tenants. With lingering tenant unrest in other regions of the state, revisions were made in 1846 to the state constitution, which abolished nearly all manorial rights and limited lease terms to 12 years. Over the next 10 years the remaining land tenure claims were resolved.

See also ANTIRENT MOVEMENT.

Irving, Mark. *Agrarian Conflicts in Colonial New York, 1711–1775* (1940; repr Port Washington, NY: I. J. Friedman, 1965)

Judd, Jacob, ed. "A Loyalist Claim: The Philipse Estate." In *The Loyalist Americans: A Focus on Greater New York,* ed. Robert A. East and Jacob Judd (Tarrytown, NY: Sleepy Hollow Restorations, 1975)

Kim, Sung Bok. *Landlord and Tenant in Colonial New York: Manorial Society, 1664–1775* (Chapel Hill: Univ of North Carolina Press, 1978)

Jacob Judd

Manorville. Locality (pop 11,131) in Brookhaven (Suffolk Co). Originally known as Punk's Hole, its railroad station (1844) was named St. George Manor after the colonial land grant, but when a post office was established in 1845 it was called Manorville. Cordwood, some of it for railroad use, was cut nearby. It was a center of cranberry production from *ca* 1880 until the 1960s, producing 25,000 bu (900 m³) in a good year. Production ceased in 1976 after bog maintenance had become uneconomical. Population growth was marked in the 1970s and 1990s. In the early 21st century, suburban tracts are intruding into this area, which is otherwise characterized by golf courses, game preserves, and county parkland.

Richard F. Welch

Man o' War. Considered by many the greatest racehorse of the 20th century. Sired by Fair Play out of Mahuba by Rock Sand, Man o' War was foaled at August Belmont II's Nursery Stud in Lexington, Ky, on 29 Mar 1917. Samuel D. Riddle of Saratoga Springs purchased him in 1918. The bright chestnut won 20 of 21 races, never by less than a length, and he ran all but 3 of those races in New York State. His single defeat occurred in the Sanford Stakes at Saratoga on 13 Aug 1919. Man o' War was pointed the wrong way as the race began and got off next to last. He ironically finished second by half a length to a horse named Upset.

Man o' War did not run in the Kentucky Derby. In a decision that was not unusual then, Riddle skipped the derby, but "Big Red" won all the other major stakes for 3-year-olds in 1920, including the Preakness, Belmont, Withers, Travers, and Jockey Club Stakes. His career earnings of just under $250,000 broke a 27-year record. Man o' War was retired to Walter Jeffords Sr's Faraway Farm in Lexington, where he died on 1 Nov 1947.

Bowen, Edward L. *Man o' War* (Lexington, Ky: Eclipse Press, 2000)

Hotaling, Edward. *They're Off! Horse Racing at Saratoga* (Syracuse: Syracuse Univ Press, 1995)

Edward Hotaling

Mansfield. Town (pop 800) in central Cattaraugus Co. Settled in 1818, the town was formed from Little Valley in 1830 as Cecilius; the name was changed to Mansfield in 1831. In 1829 settler Daniel Smith discovered evidence of iron tools having been used in a sugar maple with 125 growth rings; speculation attributed this to Francophone Canadian explorers. In the early 21st century, farming continues, but the nearness to Holiday Valley ski resort has resulted in construction of camps and homes, and US 219 permits some residents to commute to the Buffalo area. Mansfield Coach and Cutter, a four-season horse park, offers hay, sleigh, and carriage rides.

Bruce D. Fredrickson and Madelynn P. Fredrickson

Mantle, Mickey (Charles) (*b* Spavinaw, Okla, 20 Oct 1931; *d* Dallas, 13 Aug 1995). Baseball player. Raised in Commerce, Okla, Mantle debuted with the New York Yankees at age 19 and played his entire career with the club (1951–68). Joe DiMaggio's successor in center field, Mantle encouraged a growing celebrity with his remarkable speed, strength, and ability to hit prodigiously long home runs, like his 565 ft (172 m) "tape measure shot" against the Washington Senators in 1953. In 1956 Mantle led the American League in home runs, batting average, and runs batted in, garnering Most Valuable Player (MVP) honors. He repeated as MVP in 1957 and 1962. Injuries and alcoholism slowed him by the mid-1960s, but by the end of his career he had amassed 536 home runs and an additional 18 in World Series play, a record. Mantle coached for the Yankees during the early 1970s, and he was inducted into the Baseball Hall of Fame in 1974. Banned from professional baseball in 1983 for taking a public relations job with an Atlantic City, NJ, casino, Mantle was reinstated in 1985. Three years later he opened a restaurant and sports bar in New York City. In 1995 an ailing Mantle received a liver transplant but died of liver cancer two months later. Mantle's reputation endures as a symbol of the 1950s Yankees dynasty. Among the most popular athletes in America during his playing days, Mantle was a focal point for the 1980s sports memorabilia boom, and he was named to Major League Baseball's All-Century Team in 1999.

Herskowitz, Mickey. *Mickey Mantle: An Appreciation* (New York: William Morrow, 1995)

Scott Pitoniak

Manton, Martin T(homas) (*b* New York City, 2 Aug 1880; *d* Fayetteville, Onondaga Co, 17 Nov 1946). Federal judge. Manton attended public schools in Bayside (Queens Co). In 1901 he graduated from Columbia Law School and was admitted to the New York State Bar. Manton had been practicing in New York City for 15 years when in August 1916 Pres Woodrow Wilson nominated him to serve on the US District Court for the Southern District of New York. In March 1918 he was elevated to the US Court of Appeals for the Second Circuit. Manton was the senior judge on that court until 1939, when he resigned following the release of a letter to the Judiciary Committee of the US House of Representatives, in which New York Co district attorney Thomas E. Dewey accused Manton of corruption. Later that year Manton was indicted and convicted of accepting loans or gifts amounting to $186,000 from litigants in eight cases. Most involved patent infringement, though one was a criminal case. Following 19 months in federal prison in Lewisburg, Pa, Manton moved to Fayetteville where he died at his son's home.

Borkin, Joseph. "Martin T. Manton." In *The Corrupt Judge: An Inquiry into Bribery and Other High Crimes and Misdemeanors in the Federal Courts* (New York: Clarkson N. Potter, 1962)

Ellen Sexton

manumission. As early as 1669 slaves were manumitted in New York Colony; 14 were freed in New York City before 1701. Because slaves were personal property, masters granted freedom on private terms, but after New York City slaves organized an insurrection in 1712, emancipation became a legal issue. In response, the assembly passed the colony's first restrictive manumission law on 12 Dec 1712. The law required masters to pay an expensive £200 fee for each freed slave. Manumission was rare before 1760.

In 1777 delegates at New York's constitutional convention passed a resolution urging the end of slavery, but the state's first act of manumission did not come until 1781, when the legislature freed slaves who served in the militia. Urged by groups like the New York Manumission Society, the legislature in 1785 considered a gradual emancipation bill, but it included restrictions on voting, holding public office, marrying Whites, and testifying against Whites. The

Council of Revision vetoed the bill because of these restrictions. Smaller steps met with more success: a 1785 law prohibited importing slaves, and a 1788 act outlawed auctioning slaves for export. After this, however, long-term lease arrangements disguised what were in effect sales. In some instances slaves negotiated their freedom by asking masters to establish manumission terms in a will in return for exemplary service.

After years of petitions from manumission societies the assembly passed the gradual emancipation act of 1799, which freed slaves born after 4 July 1799, but women were not freed until age 25, men until age 28. Even with this very gradual manumission, which enabled New York State slaveholders to keep the next generation of slaves in bondage through their most productive years, the law had further loopholes for masters. Slaveholders could abandon children born after 1799 to the state, receive maintenance stipends, and reclaim children as slaves (this was repealed in 1804). Encouraged by Gov Daniel D. Tompkins, the legislature enacted an emancipation law in 1817, when there were about 10,000 slaves in the state, that became effective 4 July 1827 and manumitted slaves born before 1799. New York became the first state to pass a retroactive, uncompensated abolition law, although it required slaves to wait 10 years before becoming free. At the 1821 Constitutional Convention, James Tallmadge Jr demanded an amendment for immediate abolition without success. In July 1827, 2,800 slaves were freed, but nonresidents, mostly southerners, were allowed to bring slaves into the state for periods up to 9 months. In 1841 this provision was repealed, effectively ending slavery in New York State.

Hodges, Graham Russell. *Root and Branch: African Americans in New York and East Jersey, 1613–1863* (Chapel Hill: Univ of North Carolina Press, 1999)
McManus, Edgar J. *Black Bondage in the North* (Syracuse: Syracuse Univ Press, 1973)
Zilversmit, Arthur. *The First Emancipation: The Abolition of Slavery in the North* (Chicago: Univ of Chicago Press, 1967)

Kathryn Clippinger Kosto

maple syrup. Sap of the sugar maple tree *(Acer saccharum),* harvested almost exclusively in North America and Russia, and concentrated by boiling. Maple trees are tapped in February, March, and April when the sap flows from the trunk into the branches during the warm days and back into the trunk in freezing nights. "Sugar weather" may last up to six weeks, ending when buds appear.

Maple sugar, cultivated by the earliest European settlers, was the main sweetener in Canada and the northern American colonies. Cane sugar was available but too expensive for most households. After the Civil War, the development of railroads significantly lowered transportation costs, making cane sugar more affordable. Maple syrup continued to flourish, however, as producers now sold their syrup to the broader national market that the railroad provided. Production techniques—sap flowed out of spiles (taps) and was collected in pails or storage tanks—remained basically the same from the colonial period into the 1990s, when some producers began to use vacuum systems to enhance production volumes. Sap ranges from 1% to 6% sugar, and water is boiled off in evaporators until the sap is concentrated to 66–67% sugar. Further evaporation produces maple sugar. Forty to fifty gallons (150–190 l) of sap are needed to produce one gallon (3.8 l) of syrup. In 2003 three rating systems to grade the syrup on color and flavor existed; US Department of Agriculture (USDA), Canada, and Vermont each had similar criteria for four main grades. New York State producers use the USDA system.

There were 1,525 producers of maple products in the state in 2000, up from 1,450 in 1995. New York State has been one of the top three national producers of maple syrup, along with Maine and Vermont. The state produced in 1999 and 2000 about 200,000 gal (760,000 l) for each year. Fluctuations in syrup volume result from the length of the sugar season and the sap sugar concentration. A severe ice storm in January 1998 shut most production down for that year in the northern Adirondacks. Maple syrup is produced in more than 50 of the state's counties; the leading counties in 2000 were Lewis, Wyoming, St. Lawrence, Clinton, and Montgomery, collectively accounting for 46% of the state's production.

Ike Smith boiling maple sap, Tompkins Co, 1907.

At the start of the 21st century the state's maple producers are represented by the New York State Maple Producers Association, which advocates for the interests of the industry at the state capital. The American Maple Museum in Croghan (Lewis Co) holds a wide range of exhibits and photographs illustrating the history of maple syrup production. The state's maple producers are also supported by the Cornell Sugar Maple Research and Extension Program. Administered by Cornell University, the program researches sugar maple forests and sap production, with staff located throughout the state and at the Uhilein Field Station near Lake Placid (Essex Co).

Lasky, Kathryn. *Sugaring Time* (New York: Macmillan, 1983)
Maple/New York Crop Reporting Service (1987–)

Eric L. Kline

mapping. See CARTOGRAPHY AND MAPPING.

Marathon. Town (pop 2,189) and village (pop 1,063) in SE Cortland Co. Settled in 1794, the town formed from Cincinnatus in 1818 as Harrison, gaining the present name in 1827. The land is hilly, and the Tioughnioga River flows through town, forming a narrow valley. The Syracuse and Binghamton Railroad was completed here in 1854, aiding a shift to dairying, but leather making and lumbering were also important. The village incorporated in 1861. Small industries developed, including wagon making (1882) and the Climax Road Machine Co (1887–1932), which produced a stone crusher. I-81 (1966) provided highway access with an exit at the village. The town's population grew 29% between 1960 and 2000. Dairying and maple sugaring remain important, while some residents commute to Cortland, Syracuse, or Binghamton. The Marathon Maple Festival is held each spring.

Cathy A. Barber

marathons and running. On 19 Sept 1896 the first US marathon was run from Stamford, Conn, to Columbia Oval in the Bronx. New York City lithographer John J. McDermott won this race and also won the first Boston Marathon in 1897. John J. Hayes, a clerk at Bloomingdale Bros department store, became America's first gold medalist in the marathon at the 1908 Olympics. A marathon boom in New York City from 1908 to 1910 established the official distance of 26 miles 385 yards (42.195 km). The first continuing marathon in New York State was the Yonkers Marathon from 1907 through 1917. In 1925 a marathon was started at Port Chester (Westchester Co) and held annually through 1939. Reinstated in 1935 the Yonkers Marathon continues as a source of civic pride. The New York Road Runners Club (NYRRC) was organized in 1958, with former Olympic marathoner Theodore Corbitt as president, and held its first marathon in 1959 at Macombs Dam Park in the Bronx. The Syracuse Chargers Track Club (SCTC) was founded in 1969 to encourage long-distance running as well as track and field in Central New York. The NYRRC started the New York City Marathon in 1970 and the 10 km Mini-Marathon for women in 1972.

On 10 Sept 1972 Frank Shorter, who grew up in Middletown (Orange Co), became the second US gold medalist in the Olympic Marathon. Shorter's victory increased both participation in long-distance running and the number of races. Earle C. Reed established the Boilermaker 15 km Road Race in Utica in 1976; with over 9,000 runners in 2002, it was the largest US road race of that distance. A women's race that began in Albany in 1979 has become Freihofer's Run for Women, the USA Women's 5 km Championship, attracting top competitors from all over the world. Both the SCTC and the NYRRC have expanded their programs to include track events. In 1998 the SCTC established the Ed Stabler Syracuse Chargers National Distance Running Collection at the Syracuse University Library, probably the world's most extensive resource for research on running.

Cooper, Pamela. *The American Marathon* (Syracuse: Syracuse Univ Press, 1998)

Pamela Cooper

Marbletown. Town (pop 5,854) in central Ulster Co. Settled in 1669, the area was patented in 1703, briefly the state capital in 1777, and recognized as a town in 1788. Crossed by the 17th-century Old Mine Rd, the Delaware and Hudson Canal (1828–98), and the Ontario and Western Railroad (1902), it produced hoop poles, bluestone, and, at High Falls, cement. The Mohonk Mountain House (1869) lies in the town's extreme south. Boardinghouses and hotels were built in the late 19th and early 20th centuries. Marbletown is noted for its more than 130 surviving stone dwellings dating from the 17th through 19th centuries in the hamlets of Marbletown, Stone Ridge, and High Falls. Stone Ridge is the site of Ulster County Community College (1962, campus 1969) and the D and H Canal Museum is located at High Falls. Kinetics Thermal Systems (refrigeration and test equipment) employed 130 in 2003.

Ruth Piwonka

Marcantonio, Vito (*b* New York City, 12 Dec 1902; *d* New York City, 8 Aug 1954). Congressman. Born in the Italian immigrant neighborhood of Manhattan's East Harlem, he became an aide in the early 1920s to Fiorello La Guardia, then a congressman from New York City. Like his boss, Marcantonio was a liberal Republican who opposed the corruption of New York City's Democratic Tammany machine. After La Guardia lost his 1932 bid for reelection, Marcantonio won the seat himself in 1934 on the Republican and City Fusion Parties' tickets. He was defeated in 1936, but he won the seat back in 1938 with the help of the state Republican landslide of that year and the endorsement of the newly formed American Labor Party (ALP). Popular among his constituents, he strongly supported the New Deal, opposed discriminatory policies like the quota system—which commonly victimized Italians and Jews at that time—and endorsed independence for Puerto Rico. Marcantonio's support of some Communist Party positions, particularly on civil rights, made him increasingly a political pariah. He often ran in both the Democratic and Republican primaries, winning the nomination of one and sometimes both parties. In 1947 the state legislature, seeking a means to curtail Marcantonio's electoral career, passed the Wilson-Pakula Act, which ended the open primary system, making it difficult for a candidate registered in one party to run in another party's primary. Despite having only the ALP endorsement in 1948, he was narrowly reelected, but in 1950, a candidate having joint Republican, Democratic, and Liberal support defeated him. In 1949 he ran as the ALP candidate for mayor of New York City, which he lost. His biographer, Gerald Meyer, called Marcantonio "the most electorally successful radical American politician in the twentieth century."

Meyer, Gerald. *Vito Marcantonio, Radical Politician, 1902–1954* (Albany: SUNY Press, 1989)

Peter Eisenstadt

Marcellus. Town (pop 6,319) and village (pop 1,826) in W central Onondaga Co. Settled in 1794, the town was formed the same year. Beginning around 1812, products made included gunpowder by Marcellus Powder Co, until it was sold to DuPont in 1881, and wool cloth, until the Crown Mill Co closed in 1961. The Syracuse and Auburn Railroad (1838; later New York Central) served the area. The village was incorporated in 1853. In 1869 resident Emory Wilson Mills (*d* 1882) developed the first self-propelled steam engine, predecessor of modern farm machinery. Important 19th-century crops included teasels and tobacco, and the F. B. Mills Seed Co flourished at Rose Hill from 1887 to 1953. Paper manufacturing began by 1832, and the Martisco Paper Co (1874) was still in operation in 2003. Dairy farming remained the predominant land use. At Marietta water has been drawn from the north end of Otisco Lake for public water systems since 1907. Marcellus is the site of county-run Marcellus Park (1936) and of Baltimore Woods Nature Center (1970).

Barbara S. Rivette

Marchand murder. When 12-year-old Henri Marchand Jr arrived home from school on 6 Mar 1930 he found his mother Clothilde beaten to death. His father, a French sculptor who constructed lifelike dioramas at the Buffalo Museum of Science, identified Lila Jimerson, a Cayuga who lived on the Cattaraugus Indian Reservation [loc in Cattaraugus, Chautauqua, and Erie Cos], as the murderer. Jimerson was arrested a few hours later. She implicated Nancy Bowen, an elderly Cayuga traditional healer, as her accomplice, and Bowen was also arrested. What began as an ordinary murder case quickly assumed a sensational quality that engulfed Buffalo in controversy when it was revealed that Lila posed nude above the waist for Marchand in many of the "Iroquois village scenes" that he created for the museum. More confounding evidence was revealed when the *Buffalo Times* published love letters sent from the sculptor to his model. Henri and Lila had been in a two-year affair. Lila, promised marriage by Henri, engaged in traditional Cayuga witchcraft to expedite Clothilde's death and her own marriage to Marchand. Marchand was suspected as having been behind the killing, which mimicked a traditional Cayuga witch killing.

The case gave rise to an Indian rights movement defending Nancy and Lila and unsuccessfully challenging the jurisdiction of the Buffalo court. The social and legal position of American Indians in Western New York became an issue, with the continued existence of witchcraft symbolizing a great cultural gulf in the early 20th century. In the context of the assimilationist policy followed by the Cayuga during the period, the continuation of witchcraft proved that supporters of traditional Cayuga culture were not assimilating. Marchand, who remarried an 18-year-old during the year-long controversy, claimed that having sex with his models meant nothing and was part of his culture. Henri's attitude may have influenced the verdict. Lila, after a second trial, was acquitted of murder charges in March 1931. Nancy Bowen pleaded "guilty" to second-degree manslaughter, was sentenced to time served, released from jail, and sent home to the Cattaraugus Reservation.

Harring, Sidney L. "Red Lilac of the Cayugas: Traditional Indian Law and Culture Conflict in a Witchcraft Trial in Buffalo, New York, 1930," *New York History* 73 (Jan 1992): 65–94

Sidney L. Harring

Marchi, John J(oseph) (*b* Staten Island, 20 May 1921). State senator. Raised by Italian immigrant parents, he attended Manhattan College, graduating in 1942. During World War II Marchi served in both the US Coast Guard and the US Navy. In 1953 he received a doctor of juridical science from Brooklyn Law School. Elected to the New York State Senate in 1956, he became an influential lawmaker for New York City. As chair of the senate's Committee on the City of New York, Marchi was a major architect of the city's School Decentralization Law in 1969. That same year he captured the Republican nomination for mayor of New York City, defeating Mayor John Lindsay, but lost to the latter running as a Liberal and Independent in the general election. In 1973 Marchi ran as the Republican mayoral nominee again but lost to Democrat Abe Beame. Marchi was chair of the state senate's Finance Committee from 1973 to 1988. In this capacity he was instrumental in crafting legislation that rescued New York City from fiscal insolvency in the mid-1970s. Considered one of the founders of Staten Island's secession movement (a drive by residents to leave New York City), Marchi had legislation passed in the senate in 1989 permitting the borough to do so, but the measure died in the assembly. Still a member of the senate in 2002, Marchi is now the state's longest-serving legislator and the longest-serving incumbent state lawmaker in the United States. From 1980 to 2000 he received the Democratic as well as the Republican state senatorial nomination.

Marchi, John J. Papers. College of Staten Island, City Univ of New York.

Daniel C. Kramer

Marcy. Town (pop 9,469) in E Oneida Co. The town is the site of "the Neck," New York State's first short canal, constructed in 1730. Settled in 1793 the town was formed from Deerfield in 1832. Industry began with the development of Glassville (1809), where two window-glass factories employed 300. Limestone was quarried at Stittville beginning around 1833. Marcy State Hospital (1919–91) provided psychiatric care; Mid-State Correctional Facility (1983) and Marcy Correctional Facility (1988) were constructed adjacent to the hospital. The town has also been the site of the Utica Municipal Airport (1928–59) and Chaminade Prep, a Marianist novitiate (1947–69). The Thruway opened through Marcy in 1954, and suburbanization of parts of the town followed. Major employers in 2002 were the SUNY Institute of Technology at Utica/Rome (1969), a Wal-Mart regional distribution center (1994), and a New York Power Authority transmission station.

Marcy, William L(earned) (*b* Southbridge, Mass, 12 Dec 1786; *d* Ballston Spa, Saratoga Co, 4 July 1857). Governor and US senator. Raised in Massachusetts, Marcy graduated from Brown University in 1808, moved to Troy (Rensselaer Co), and was admitted to the bar in 1811. After becoming active in local politics and serving as city recorder (1816–18, 1821–23), he became a leader of the political faction known as the Albany Regency, which made key Bucktail Republican patronage decisions. He served as state comptroller (1823–29), associate justice of the New York State Supreme Court (1829–31), and US senator (1831–33). Marcy defended Martin Van Buren's appointment as minister to England by claiming that to "the victor belong the spoils of the enemy"; the speech contributed to the rise of the term "spoils system." Marcy resigned his senate seat on 1 Jan 1833 after his election as governor of New York State and served three terms as a loyal Jacksonian Democrat before he was defeated by William H. Seward in 1838. During his administration, the New York State Geological Survey (1836) was created, and Mt Marcy in the Adirondacks was named in his honor. He served as an efficient secretary of war under Pres James K. Polk (1845–49) and successfully prosecuted the Mexican War. Marcy, who always tried to avoid committing himself to a definite position on the slavery question, was briefly the leading presidential candidate of the deadlocked Democratic National Convention of 1852 before the nomination went to dark horse Franklin Pierce. Marcy served Pierce as secretary of state (1853–57). Only four months after leaving office, Marcy died suddenly while vacationing.

Silhouette of William L. Marcy, by Augustin Edouart, 1839.

Mattina, Benjamin. "The Early Life of William Learned Marcy, 1789–1832" (PhD diss, Georgetown Univ, 1949)

Spencer, Ivor. *The Victor and the Spoils: A Life of William L. Marcy* (Providence, RI: Brown Univ Press, 1959)

Jon Sterngass

Margaretville. Village (pop 643) in Middletown (Delaware Co). A woolen mill (1844) helped to create the hamlet and was followed by a tannery (1863), cooperage (1865), and foundry (1867). After the Ulster and Delaware Railroad reached nearby Arkville in 1872, tourism became an important business. Margaretville was later served directly by a branch of the Delaware and Northern (1905–42). It incorporated in 1875 and was the trading hub for the surrounding area. In the 1930s and 1940s it served as the center for exporting the cauliflower harvest to outside markets; in 1950 there were 581 growers in the vicinity. Tourism remains an important business. The Galli-Curci movie theater, named for Metropolitan opera soprano Amelita Galli-Curci (1889–1963), who had a home nearby, is now an antique center.

Dorothy Kubik

Margiotta, Joseph M(ichael) (*b* Brooklyn, 6 June 1927). County political leader. Margiotta's family moved to Uniondale (Nassau Co) in 1938, and he attended local schools and graduated from Hempstead High School. After serving in the navy (1945–46), he graduated from Hofstra College (1950) and Brooklyn Law School (1953), joined his father in legal practice in Uniondale, and became active in the local Republican Party. Margiotta held appointed positions in Albany for four years before he was elected to the state assembly, where he served from 1965 to 1977. Within a few years he headed the Nassau and then the Long Island delegation in the legislature, where he fought for increased funding for suburban school districts.

In 1968 Margiotta became head of the Nassau Co Republican Committee, a position he retained until 1983. He perfected the party organization through computer analysis of election results, political polls, extensive campaign literature produced in the party's own print shop, political patronage, and successful fund-raising. Three-fourths of the party's nearly 2,000 committee members held government jobs, and they were expected to contribute 1% of their salaries to the party. By 1980 Nassau Republicans were raising more than $2 million annually. Margiotta was the party boss who selected candidates and influenced awarding public contracts, patronage appointments, and promotions of municipal employees. In the late 1970s, Margiotta came under attack for fee splitting and insurance kickbacks, and in a case brought by the US attorney for the Eastern District of New York, a federal jury convicted him on charges of extortion and mail fraud in 1981; he served 14 months in federal prison. After release, unable to regain his former power, Margiotta started a new career as a political consultant and lobbyist. He regained his law license in 1999 and resumed his legal practice in Uniondale.

"At Last, a Last Hurrah for Margiotta?" *New York Times*, 8 May 1983

Natalie A. Naylor

Maria College. Independent, two-year Roman Catholic college. Established in 1958 in Albany, the college served as a liberal arts college by and for the Religious Sisters of Mercy. It opened its enrollment to all women in 1964 and seven years later became coeducational. At the start of the 21st century it offers associate degrees and certificates in numerous fields including early childhood education, nursing, and physical and occupational therapy. In 1986 a convent (now Marian Hall) located on the college grounds was designated by the Historic Albany Foundation as a historic building. With a predominantly lay faculty in 2003 the college had an adult education focus offering courses in day, evening, and weekend divisions to nearly 1,000 students annually.

Maria College, http://www.mariacollege.org

Christine Karpiak

Marilla. Town (pop 5,709) in E Erie Co. Part of the Buffalo Creek Reservation until 1826, it was probably settled in that year. Marilla was formed from Alden and Wales in 1853. Apples for shipment and sale were dried in the early 20th century in an evaporator. The population, 2,252 in 1960, more than doubled in the next 40 years as Buffalonians moved outward. In the early 21st century the land is primarily agricultural.

Andrew C. Maines

Marine Midland Bank. See HSBC BANK USA.

Marion. Town (pop 4,974) in central Wayne Co. Settled in 1795, chiefly from New England and New Jersey, the town was formed from Williamson as Winchester in 1825; it was renamed in 1826. The private Marion Collegiate Institute (1855–1904) became a public high school. The town has a sizable expanse of muckland, growing celery, carrots, onions, and lettuce; fruit is cultivated elsewhere in town. Food processing is the principal industry. Marion Canning Co was founded in 1918 and became part of Seneca Foods in 1970. It is engaged both in the canning of vegetables and in the manufacture of cans for its own use and for sale to other companies. Seneca Foods, the nation's largest private-label vegetable canner, moved its headquarters to Marion in 2001.

Scott C. Monje

Marist College. Independent liberal arts and sciences institution on the eastern shore of the Hudson River in Poughkeepsie. Founded as a seminary on property purchased in 1905 by the Marist Brothers, a Roman Catholic religious order, the site was named Saint Ann's Hermitage. Beginning in 1929 it allied with Fordham University and Catholic University of America, and offered college-level courses. The New York State Board of Regents granted Marian College, as it was known then, a temporary charter in 1946. The charter became permanent in 1950 and in 1960 the name was changed to Marist College. The school began enrolling lay male students in 1957, while women were allowed into the evening division in 1966 and into the day division, making the school fully coeducational in 1968. The following year ownership of the college transferred to the Marist College Educational Corp with an independent board of trustees. In 2001 the school offered 28 baccalaureate and 7 master's degree programs, and enrolled approximately

3,900 full-time undergraduates, 55% female and 45% male. Adult and continuing education students numbered 1,120, with an additional 881 full- and part-time graduate students.

Marist College, http://www.marist.edu
Murray, Dennis J. "A Lasting Ideal in a Changing World: A History of Marist College," *Dutchess County Historical Society Yearbook* 74 (1989): 42–65

Thomas W. Casey

Marlborough. Town (pop 8,263) in SE Ulster Co. Settled in the first quarter of the 18th century mostly from Long Island and Westchester Co, the town was formed from Newburgh precinct as New Marlborough precinct in 1772 and recognized as a town in 1788. Marlboro hamlet was platted in 1764. At both Marlboro and Milton, a great variety of products were made in the 19th century: woolen cloth, blankets, shoddy, rag carpets, knit goods, pins, buttons, liquid dyes, glue, paper, brick, agricultural implements, wheelbarrows, iron mortars and pestles for druggists, baskets, and crates. The town, which by 1880 was a summer resort, had rail service with the West Shore line beginning in 1883. In the 20th century fruit growing, including both apples and grapes, became important; in the 1930s Italians, Irish, and southern Blacks came to work on the fruit farms, and there were several notable wineries in 2003. Shell Oil built a tank farm on Milton dock *ca* 1934. In the early 21st century, Chelsea Modular Homes employs 120. Type designer Frederic W. Goudy (1865–1947) was a resident from 1923 until his death.

Ruth Piwonka

Married Women's Property Act. Until 1848, New York State law, based on common law, dictated that any property belonging to a woman was signed over to her husband's control upon marriage. In 1837 Thomas Herttell, a Democratic assemblyman, introduced a bill giving married women more property rights. Herttell, an advocate for legal equality of the sexes, appealed to men's economic interests when arguing for women's property rights. He noted that the system as it stood was confusing, and he appealed to legislators' concerns about the instability of the economy, contending that the law could protect family assets that might otherwise be lost by unscrupulous husbands. The bill never emerged from judiciary committee; legislators feared women would gain too much independence and that the provisions would undermine marriage itself. Herttell continued to petition the legislature between 1837 and 1848, and the issue was debated in national periodicals.

Paulina Wright Davis, Ernestine Rose, and Elizabeth Cady Stanton led the drive for legislation, and in 1848 a largely Whig legislature passed a comprehensive statute giving married women rights to control property. With this act, New York was one of the first states to grant property rights to married women, and it served as a model for other states. The statute granted women full legal control of all property of inheritance or earning that they owned at or acquired after marriage. An amendment granting contractual powers that allowed married women to pass on and set up real and personal property was added in 1849. Additional amendments through 1860 include a wife's right to guardianship in the case of divorce, equal laws of intestacy, and the right to sue and be sued. With the decline of pressure from women's groups in 1862 (by which time Stanton and Susan B. Anthony were focused on abolition), sections of the statute were repealed, affecting not only property but also women's rights to their children and the right to convey property through court permission. Throughout the remainder of the 19th century the act continued to be adjusted to extend property rights for women; revisions in 1866 resulted in a recovery of rights, and in 1884 women gained full contractual capacity.

Basch, Norma. *In the Eyes of the Law: Women, Marriage, and Property in 19th-Century New York* (Ithaca: Cornell Univ Press, 1982)
Salmon, Marylynn. *Women and the Law of Property in Early America* (Chapel Hill: Univ of North Carolina Press, 1986)

Amy Surak

Marshall. Town (pop 2,127) in S Oneida Co. Beginning in 1784, the area of Marshall was home of the Brothertown community. The town was formed from Kirkland in 1829. It was crossed by the Chenango Canal (1837–78) and the Utica, Clinton and Binghamton Railroad (1870). Hop growing was significant in the 19th century, and a milk plant (1902–83) began with condensed milk and later processed fluid and dry milk. In 2003 Schwartz Forge and other small businesses employed some residents. Others worked in surrounding towns or nearby cities including Utica and Syracuse.

Marshall, Louis (*b* Syracuse, 14 Sept 1856; *d* Zurich, Switzerland, 11 Sept 1929). Lawyer and conservationist. Born into a German Jewish family and educated at Dwight Law School (now Columbia Law School) in New York City, Marshall was admitted to the New York State Bar in 1878 and began practice in Syracuse. He quickly earned a reputation as a successful trial lawyer, arguing many cases before the New York State Court of Appeals. In 1894 he became a founding member of the New York City firm Guggenheimer, Untermeyer, and Marshall. Marshall also served as a delegate to the New York State Constitutional Convention of 1894, where he championed the cause of conservation in the Adirondacks. He married Florence Lowenstein in 1895. Marshall grew into a nationally acclaimed specialist in constitutional law. In addition he fought for the rights of Jews and other minority groups. He was president of the American Jewish Committee from 1912 to 1929 and attended the Paris Peace Conference after World War I, where he worked to ensure minority rights. A summer resident on Lower Saranac Lake, in 1911 he helped to found a forestry college (now SUNY College of Environmental Science and Forestry) in Syracuse and in 1915 advocated for Adirondack conservation at another state constitutional convention.

Rosenstock, Morton. *Louis Marshall, Defender of Jewish Rights* (Detroit: Wayne State Univ Press, 1965)

Philip G. Terrie

Marshall, Robert (*b* New York City, 2 Jan 1901; *d* Washington, DC, 11 Nov 1939). Conservationist. Marshall was the third child of noted constitutional lawyer, influential Jewish leader, and minority-rights advocate Louis Marshall and Florence Lowenstein. His parents, who were active conservationists, maintained a summer residence on Lower Saranac Lake in Franklin Co. An energetic explorer, the young Marshall, together with his brother George and guide Herbert Clark, climbed all 46 of the Adirondack summits above 4,000 ft (1,219 m) between 1916 and 1925, inspiring many later recreational hikers. In 1924 Marshall earned a degree from Syracuse's New York State College of Forestry and began a career in the US Forest Service. In 1934 he suggested formation of a federal wilderness planning board to identify sites that might then be preserved by acts of the US Congress. A year later he cofounded, in Washington, DC, the Wilderness Society to lobby for this idea. After Marshall's sudden death from a heart attack, 25 years elapsed before Congress passed the Wilderness Act (1964), which included many of Marshall's recommendations. In 2000 the Wilderness Society had 200,000 members worldwide.

Glover, James. *Wilderness Original: The Life of Bob Marshall* (Seattle: Mountaineers Books, 1985)

Brad Edmondson

Marshall, Thurgood [Thoroughgood] (*b* Baltimore, 2 July 1908; *d* Bethesda, Md, 24 Jan 1993). Civil rights lawyer and US Supreme Court justice. The grandson of a slave, Marshall spent most of his childhood in Baltimore. In 1930 he received a bachelor's degree from Lincoln University in Chester, Pa, and three years later a law degree from Howard University in Washington, DC. In 1938 he accepted the chief counsel position at the National Association for the Advancement of Colored People (NAACP) in New York City and led their Legal Defense and Education Fund (LDF) from its beginnings in 1940 until 1961. Independent from the NAACP since 1957, the LDF today handles over 100 cases. At the NAACP Marshall led numerous challenges against state-sponsored discrimination, most notably the Hillburn case (Rockland Co) that in 1943 closed the last legally segregated public school in New York State, and he also spoke out in support of the Ives-Quinn bill. Enacted into state law in 1945, this made New York the first state in the nation to establish a permanent commission dedicated to combating racial and ethnic discrimination in employment. He was transformed into a prominent public figure after his victory in the 1954 landmark US Supreme Court decision *Brown v Board of Education,* which found unconstitutional the "separate but equal" doctrine that had been followed in many of the nation's public schools. Appointed to the US Court of Appeals for the Second Circuit in 1961, four years later Marshall became US solicitor general, and in 1967 he was named the first black associate justice of the Supreme Court.

Tushnet, Mark V., ed. *Thurgood Marshall: His Speeches, Writings, Arguments, Opinions, and Reminiscences* (Chicago: Lawrence Hill Books, 2001)

Robert B. Ward

Martinsburg. Town (pop 1,249) in central Lewis Co. Settlers from Salem (Washington Co) and Westfield, Mass, came in 1801, and the town was formed from Turin in 1803 and served as the county seat from 1805 to 1864. Its eastern and central parts are dairy country; in 1895 the town had 14 cheese factories, the most of any Lewis Co town. The West Martinsburg Cheese Factory sent a 5-ton (4.5 MT) "Big Cheese" to the San Francisco exposition in 1916; Goudy's (1872–1959), the state's longest-operating cheese factory, supplied soft cheese for the New York City Jewish market. The Keystone Chemical Co (1927–29) briefly operated a large wood-chemical plant in town. Whetstone Gulf State Park (1928) has a 3-mile-long gorge. Martinsburg built a one-room school as late as 1950 (closed 1952).

Emily Williams

Marx Brothers {Marx, Chico [Leonard] (*b* New York City, 22 Mar 1887; *d* Beverly Hills, Calif, 11 Oct 1961); Marx, Harpo [Adolph] (*b* New York City, 23 Nov 1888; *d* Hollywood, Calif, 28 Sept 1964); Marx, Groucho [Julius] (*b* New York City, 2 Oct 1890; *d* Los Angeles, 19 Aug 1977); Marx, Gummo [Milton] (*b* New York City, 23 Oct 1893; *d* Palm Springs, Calif, 21 Apr 1977); Marx, Zeppo [Herbert] (*b* New York City, 25 Feb 1901; *d* Palm Springs, 30 Nov 1979)}. Motion picture and stage comedy team. The sons of German Jewish immigrants, the brothers grew up in poverty in Yorkville, a neighborhood on the Upper East Side of Manhattan. None graduated from high school, although some attended Public School 86 on 96th St. The driving force behind the brothers was their mother, Minnie, who molded them into a vaudeville singing act that found success when it switched to comedy. Their humor was rooted in the New York stage and vaudeville. Their clowning embodied the essence of New York City street savvy; its major component involved lampooning the social order while carrying out frantic comical anarchy.

The brothers moved to Chicago in 1910 and toured the vaudeville circuit with their mother as stage manager. Gummo was drafted during World War I and later managed the group. They arrived on Broadway in 1924 in the hit musical comedy *I'll Say She Is.* Two of their follow-up productions, *The Cocoanuts* (1925) and *Animal Crackers* (1928), were adapted for the screen in 1929 and 1930; both were filmed in Paramount Pictures' Astoria studio in Queens. In 1931 the brothers left New York City for Hollywood, where they starred in such masterpieces as *Duck Soup* (1933) and *A Night at the Opera* (1935). Their final screen appearance as a team came in *Love Happy* (1950). Groucho continued in show business with the popular quiz show *You Bet Your Life* (radio 1947–56; television 1950–61) and returned to New York City for a celebrated one-man show at Carnegie Hall in 1972.

At their zany best, the Marx Brothers played fast-talking—or, in the case of the ever-silent Harpo, fast-acting—hustlers who outwitted foils and bystanders alike and were always ready with sharp rejoinders and mocking puns. Groucho was famed for his stoop-postured walk and painted moustache, his leer and ever-present cigar. Chico spoke with an exaggerated Italian accent and was the co-conspirator of the child-like, curly-wigged Harpo. Zeppo rarely participated in his brothers' comic madness, playing straight man on stage and in their initial films.

Louvish, Simon. *Monkey Business: The Lives and Legends of the Marx Brothers* (New York: St. Martin's Press, 2000)

Maryknoll. The Catholic Foreign Mission Society of America was founded as the first official society dedicated to overseas missions and evangelization on behalf of the Catholic Church in the United States. Formally authorized by the Vatican in 1911, its permanent home base of operations was established in 1912 at Ossining (Westchester Co) on a hilltop, Maryknoll, dedicated to the Blessed Virgin Mary. In 1912 Mary Josephine Rogers (Mother Mary Joseph), who had helped found the society, formed a women's group that became, in 1920, the Foreign Mission Sisters of St. Dominic; known as the Maryknoll Sisters, this group established a cloister in 1932. The society's first four missionaries were sent to Yeungkong, China, in 1918, and by World War II, Maryknoll had opened missions in southern China, Manchuria [now in China], Korea, Japan, and the Philippines. New mission territories were extended into Latin America and Africa, and an outreach to Asian immigrants throughout the United States was launched. The Lay Mission Program joined the society in 1974, and the Mission Association of the Faithful joined in 1994. The society's educational activity continues through the magazine *Maryknoll,* the successor to *A Field Afar* (1907), and through Orbis Books (1971). In 2001 there were over 550 Maryknoll priests and brothers and over 700 sisters working throughout the world.

Dries, Angelyn, OSF. *The Missionary Movement in American Catholic History* (Maryknoll, NY: Orbis Books, 1998)

Kathleen L. Riley

Maryland. Town (pop 1,920) in SE Otsego Co. Settled about 1793, the town was formed from Worcester in 1808. Its principal hamlet, Schenevus, developed around a station on the Albany and Susquehanna Railroad (1865) and became an incorporated village in 1870, at which time it had a large tannery, a plaster mill, and a sash and blind factory; the hamlet of Maryland had a bobbin factory and a wood acid factory. Its land was best for grazing, although hops were grown, but agriculture declined in the late 20th century. I-88 opened through the town in 1979, making it easier for residents to work in Oneonta or Cobleskill (Schoharie Co). In 1996 Schenevus dissolved its village corporation to eliminate the cost of separate village services.

Hugh C. MacDougall

Marymount College of Fordham University. Private women's college. Established as Marymount Academy in Tarrytown (Westchester Co) by Mother Joseph Butler of the Religious of the Sacred Heart of Mary as a secondary school for girls in 1907, it became a liberal arts college in 1919. Its study abroad program began in 1924, and Mother Butler served as president until 1926. By 1972 Marymount ended its affiliation with the Religious of the Sacred Heart of Mary and in 1969 named its first lay president and became more heterogeneous and secular. The coeducational Weekend College was established in 1975. By the mid-1970s, a combination of overexpansion, declining enrollments, and an inadequate endowment created financial difficulties and unionization of the faculty. Financial and academic motivations led Marymount to consolidate with Fordham University in July 2002. Marymount's enrollment in spring 2002 was 947.

Burton, Katherine. *Mother Butler of Marymount* (New York: Longmans, Green, 1944)

Doran, Micheileen. "A History of Marymount College, Tarrytown" (EdD diss, Teachers College, Columbia Univ, 1979)

Elisa Carrillo

Marymount Manhattan College. Private liberal arts college. The school was founded in 1936 at 5th Ave and 84th St by the Religious of the Sacred Heart of Mary, an order with roots in France, as a junior college for women affiliated with Marymount College in Tarrytown (Westchester Co). It became a four-year college in 1947, moved to its present location at 221 East 71st St in 1948, became independent in 1961, and began admitting men in 1989. It offers programs in liberal arts, business, fine arts, and education, and is noted for preparing teachers of people with hearing and speech impairments. In 2002 enrollment stood at about 1,600 full-time and 670 part-time students.

Egan, Jogues. *Marymount Manhattan College: The First 50 Years, 1936–1986* (New York: Marymount Manhattan College, 1986)

Yayin Chu-Reimer

Masons. See FREEMASONS.

Masonville. Town (pop 1,405) in SW Delaware Co. Settled in 1792, the town was formed from Sidney in 1811. Settlers worked at lumbering, floating pine planks down the river to Philadelphia. In the mid–19th century, dairy farming became important. Later, neighboring railroads shipped dairy products to wider markets, but the town lost nearly half its population between 1880 and 1920. In 2003 lumbering and stonecutting were still important industries. Many small businesses have opened, and the population has grown with new residents from metropolitan areas. A substantial minority of the town's area is owned by the state, including Camp Brace, a facility of the New York State Office of Children and Family Services.

Dorothy Kubik

Massachusetts Reserve. Territorial claim comprising all of western New York State from the present Ontario-Seneca county line westward. The claim was made by Massachusetts on the basis of its 1629 and 1691 charters, which defined its western boundary as the Pacific Ocean. At a 1786 conference in Hartford, Conn, between representatives of Massachusetts and New York State, Massachusetts gained the rights to buy the land from the Indians, except for the Mile Reserve along the Niagara River, while New York State retained political jurisdiction. This agreement also gave Massachusetts the rights to the Boston Ten Townships in what is now Broome, Tioga, Tompkins, and Cortland Cos. Speculators Oliver Phelps and Nathaniel Gorham intended to buy the entire Massachusetts Reserve, but their finances permitted them to close only on the eastern third in 1788. Philadelphia merchant Robert Morris bought the western two-thirds in 1789, then acquired most of Phelps and Gorham's holdings the following year. Morris managed to sell some of the land profitably to British and Dutch investors before going bankrupt in 1798.

Livermore, Shaw. *Early American Land Companies: Their Influence on Corporate Development* (New York: Commonwealth Fund, 1939)

Turner, Orsamus. *History of the Pioneer Settlement of Phelps and Gorham's Purchase, and Morris' Reserve* (1851; repr Geneseo, NY: James Brunner, 1976)

Francis P. Boscoe

Massapequa {East Massapequa, locality (pop 19,565) in Oyster Bay, Nassau Co; Massapequa, locality (pop 22,652) in Oyster Bay; North Massapequa, locality (pop 19,152) in Oyster Bay}. Settled in 1796 as South Oyster Bay with its own post office from 1814 to 1861, it was a popular summer resort, especially after the opening of the South Side Rail Road in 1867. The post office reopened under the name Massapequa in 1902. Suburbanization started after the electrification of the railroad (1926). The site of Frank Buck's Jungle Camp, a privately run zoo (1934–1950s) in East Massapequa, is now an enclosed shopping mall. The Massapequas developed quickly after World War II; populations and school enrollments peaked in 1970 and then decreased. East Massapequa's residents adopted the name in 1970 to deemphasize its historic association with Amityville (Suffolk Co). A famous graduate of Massapequa High School is comedian Jerry Seinfeld.

William J. Johnston

Massapequa Indians. Indian community centered in what is now southern Nassau Co. It is not clear whether Massapequas spoke Munsee or Unami dialects of Delaware or a variant of Quirpi, a closely related southern New England Indian language. The name may derive from Delaware words for "large river." Massapequa first appears in an Indian deed dated 15 Jan 1639 in which the sachem Mechoswodt ceded his "patrimonial lands" to the Dutch West India Co. The deed allowed the Indians the right to make a living on the land and placed them under Dutch protection. While some Massapequas remained friendly with the colonists, others did not. Determined to avenge the murders of friends and kinsfolk and angered after Mechoswodt's son Tackapousha conveyed the western half of their lands to Hempstead settlers on 13 Nov 1643, many Massapequas joined the war against the Dutch. Retaliatory Dutch attacks finally compelled them to join in a general peace ending the fighting on Long Island on 24 May 1645. Never again openly going to war against the Dutch, Massapequa warriors remained at peace during the Peach War (1655) and fought alongside Dutch soldiers during the Esopus Wars between 1659 and 1664. Tackapousha became the key intermediary between all western Long Island Indians and colonists following the English conquest in 1664. Periodic treaties adjudicated disputes and allayed fears of rumored attacks and conspiracies.

A particularly thorny dispute with Hempstead settlers using the 1639 and 1643 agreements to claim all Massapequa lands dragged on until Tackapousha agreed to accept a 200-acre (80 ha) reservation at Cow Neck at Oyster Bay on 24 Mar 1685. Other communities were maintained at Rockaway and Fort Neck at the south end of Oyster Bay Township at Fort Neck. Most Massapequas spent increasing amounts of time among friends and relatives elsewhere as English settlers bought most of their last remaining lands in Nassau Co by 1710. Some gradually moved to Delaware communities west of the Hudson River. Others settled at Poospatuck in Mastic (Suffolk Co). Wherever they moved, most chose to spend part of each year traveling through Long Island towns, where they camped on lands of sympathetic settlers or squatted on unwanted swampy backlands along the fringes of colonial settlement. Dispossessed and impoverished, they made meager livings as laborers, farmhands, servants, and peddlers of homemade brooms, bowls, baskets, and herbal remedies. Most people tracing descent from Massapequa Indian ancestors belong to the present-day Matinecock and Poospatuck Indian communities.

Grumet, Robert S. "The Indians of Fort Massapeag," *Long Island Historical Quarterly* 8: 26–38
Strong, John A. *The Algonquian Peoples of Long Island from Earliest Times to 1700* (Interlaken, NY: Empire State Books, 1997)

Robert S. Grumet

Massapequa Park. Village (pop 17,499) in Oyster Bay (Nassau Co). Real estate promoters developed it as Stadt Wurtemberg *ca* 1870 to attract German settlers, but the venture failed. In 1927 Michael J. Brady, the head of a group of developers hoping that road construction for nearby Jones Beach would make the area more accessible, purchased 1,400 acres (567 ha). Changing the ethnic appeal, they described it as "a bit of old Erin" and offered lots for sale under the name Massapequa Park. The village incorporated in 1931 and acquired a post office in 1934. Fitzmaurice Field airport was located here from 1929 to 1951. With a population of 488 in 1940, rapid growth followed the end of World War II; in the 1950s the village grew 753%.

Richard A. Winsche

Massena. Town (pop 13,121) and village (pop 11,209) in N St. Lawrence Co. Settled in 1792 and largely occupied under Revolutionary War land warrants starting in 1798, the town was formed in 1802 from Lisbon. US barracks built in 1812 were burned by British forces in 1813. Massena Springs, now within village limits, was a 19th-century resort, and its first hotel was built in 1822. The village, which is partly in Louisville and Norfolk, was platted in 1831 and incorporated in 1886. Industrial products included woolens, starch, leather, and furniture. The population expanded dramatically after 1902, when Pittsburgh Reduction Co (now Alcoa) began producing hydroelectricity from the St. Lawrence River for reduction of aluminum; Armenians, Francophone Canadians, and Italians, as well as laborers of other nationalities, came to dig the power canal and stayed to work for Alcoa. A 1928 incident in which local Jews were unjustly accused of the ritual slaughter of a young girl gave Massena much unwanted national publicity. The St. Lawrence Seaway project (opened in 1959) included the Moses-Saunders Power Dam, which generated sufficient electricity to enable Alcoa to expand and for Reynolds Metals (now part of Alcoa) and General Motors to construct aluminum reduction and manufacturing facilities. Massena's population has declined 25% since 1960 because of manufacturing job losses and suburban housing expansion in surrounding towns. Newer industries are located in a successful industrial park (1979) and elsewhere in town. Robert Moses State Park and Eisenhower and Snell Locks are located near the power dam. Massena is connected to Canada via the Seaway International Bridge. The St. Lawrence Centre (1990) is a midsized retail and entertainment facility.

Richard E. Mooers

Mastic {Mastic, locality (pop 15,436) in Brookhaven, Suffolk Co; Mastic Beach, locality (pop 11,543) in Brookhaven}. A Pochaug Indian settlement survived in the area as late as 1882. The Manor of St. George was granted to William "Tangier" Smith in 1693 and 1697. During the Revolution the British turned the manor house into Fort St. George, which was raided by the Americans in 1780. The Tangier Development Co began the development of Mastic in 1910 but failed; a Mastic post office opened in 1925. Mastic Beach was platted in 1926 by Warren and Arthur Smadbeck's Home Guardian Co, which created 19,730 lots measuring 20 x 100 feet (6.1 x 30.5 m) that were sold for $55 through advertisements in the *Brooklyn Citizen.* A Mastic Beach post office opened in 1930. Development resumed in the late 1950s and offered low-cost housing, but there were few jobs in the area, and the commute was hard. The result was many abandoned houses: in 1980, 1 of 11 was vacant. Revitalization began in 1982. The Mastics are the site of the Poospatuck Indian Reservation, the William Floyd House (1724), home of the signer of the Declaration of Independence on a 613-acre (248.1 ha) National Park Service tract, and the Manor of St. George on Smiths Point, with an 18th-century house on 127 acres (51.4 ha).

Matinecock. Village (pop 836) in Oyster Bay (Nassau Co). The Matinecock Friends Meeting built its meeting house just across the village border in Glen Cove in 1725; it burned in 1986 but was immediately rebuilt. A number of Gold Coast estates were built in the village beginning in the 1890s, and the Piping Rock Club was organized in 1912. In 1928 the residents incorporated under the historic name of Matinecock, an Indian tribal name. An exclusive residential village with a 1995–96 median home price of $1,472,000, it is consistently listed among communities with the highest per capita incomes in the nation.

Tom Kuehhas

Matinecock Indians. Use of the word Matinecock, variously translated as island edge and hilly land, expanded from a local place-name for a neck of land in the Town of Oyster Bay (Nassau Co) to a general term identifying related Delaware- and Quirpi-speaking Indian communities stretching across the north shore of western Long Island from Flushing (Queens Co) to Huntington (Suffolk Co). Indians identified in colonial records as people or proprietors of Matinecock were closely linked by blood and affection with nearby Massapequa, Setauket, Rockaway, Merrick, and Canarsee communities, and more distantly, with eastern Long Island Indians from Nissaquogue, Unquachog (Unkechaug), Shinnecock, and Montaukett.

Matinecocks were first mentioned in written records during Gov Willem Kieft's administration when "Gawarowe, sachem of Matinneconck" signed a peace treaty with the Dutch on behalf of Indians living at Matinecock, Massapequa, and Setauket on 15 Apr 1644. One year later, Montaukett sachem Wyandanch included

Matinecocks taking refuge at Nissaquogue among Indians he had taken under his protection at a meeting with Dutch authorities. Wyandanch and Massapequa sachem Tackapousha each claimed authority over Matinecocks and their lands in the years that followed. Linked by blood and marriage to the families of both men, Matinecock sachem Asharoken, his successor Suscaneman, and their relatives signed nearly 150 deeds conveying tracts ranging in size from 1 to 200 acres (.4–81 ha) to contending Hempstead, Oyster Bay, and Huntington townspeople between 1653 and 1710. Rival settlers used these deeds to bolster land claims in title and boundary disputes that dragged on throughout the colonial era. Suscaneman and his people employed uncertainties generated by this situation as part of a delaying strategy that helped Matinecocks remain on ancestral lands as their population dwindled from several hundred to fewer than two or three families during this time. Most Matinecocks gradually moved to Bayside (Queens Co) and Great Neck (Nassau Co) by the 1800s. Marrying Indians from other nations and non-Indians, most continued to fish and tend family garden plots as they found wage work as field hands, servants, and laborers in local shops, farms, and households. Today, several hundred Long Islanders chiefly residing in Queens and Nassau Cos trace descent from the Matinecock.

Grumet, Robert S. "Suscaneman and the Matinecock Lands, 1653–1703." In *Northeastern Indian Lives, 1632–1816*, ed. Robert S. Grumet (Amherst: Univ of Massachusetts Press, 1996)

Strong, John A. *The Algonquian Peoples of Long Island from Earliest Times to 1700* (Interlaken, NY: Empire State Books, 1997)

Robert S. Grumet

Matthias [Matthews, Robert] (*b* Cambridge, Washington Co, 1788; *d* ?1841). Raised by rigidly Calvinist Scots Covenanters, Matthews was orphaned at the age of 7 and sent to live first with a farmer and later with a carpenter, who taught him their trades. About 1808 he was working as a journeyman carpenter in New York City. From the beginning Matthews combined his religious devotion with anger, particularly against women, resulting in a conviction for assault in 1811. He returned to Cambridge, opened a store, and in 1813 married Margaret Wright. His business failed, and in 1816 he returned with his family to Manhattan, where two of his young sons died, and he also became very ill. During this time, he underwent a religious conversion, which led him to denounce his Christian background and claim that he was a prophesying Hebrew, like Jesus himself. When his health returned, Matthews moved back to Washington Co, then to Albany in 1825–26. There he tried to join the Presbyterian Church of Rev Edward N. Kirk, one of the state's rising middle-class evangelicals. The church rejected Matthews, partly because of his reputation as a wife beater and poor provider, but began proselytizing his abused wife and children. At this point Matthews turned to Bible study, began growing his beard, and claimed a vision that Albany was in the path of destruction. He tried to persuade his wife to leave, but when she refused, Matthews fled with three of their children to Argyle (Washington Co), where he was apprehended and briefly confined to an insane asylum.

In June 1831 Matthews traveled to Western New York, Washington, DC, and Manhattan, having discovered himself as the Prophet Matthias, scourge of disobedient women and effeminate or weak men. Preaching in the streets, his somewhat incoherent message was that he was the Spirit of Truth, or God, and would usher in a post-Christian era and save the world from devils, meek Christian men, and their disobedient, prophesying wives. The world would end in 1851, he claimed. Afterward he and his patriarchs would inhabit a purified world in which men would share resources and govern their wives and children without interference. Matthias began conscripting converts, including Elijah Pierson, a Manhattan merchant and evangelical reformer whose household Matthias joined, some of Pierson's friends, and Isabella Van Wagenen (born Isabella Baumfree, a slave), a servant and companion who would change her name to Sojourner Truth after the collapse of the "Kingdom of Matthias." With money from wealthy followers, Matthias created a costly wardrobe and a royal household and moved from Pierson's house to that of Sylvester Mills. By July 1833 he had moved to the estate of his new disciples Benjamin and Ann Folger in Sing Sing [now Ossining, Westchester Co].

In time he had a vision in which he and Ann Folger were "match spirits." In late 1833 Matthias used his spiritual position to convince Benjamin Folger to give up his wife to him. He then arranged to have his 20-year-old daughter, Isabella Laisdell, herself a bride of only one month, join them in Sing Sing and be offered as a substitute wife to Benjamin Folger. While rumors about the cult grew and Isabella's first husband raised a public outcry about the fate of his wife, finally reclaiming her, Elijah Pierson was mysteriously poisoned. Matthias was prosecuted for the murder and acquitted, but was convicted on assault charges for beating his daughter Isabella and sentenced to three months in the county jail. His kingdom then disbanded. On his release from jail in autumn of 1835 Matthias visited the Mormons at Kirtland, Ohio, but Joseph Smith Jr ran him out of town. Matthias headed west, where reports had him in Arkansas and Iowa and then dead in the early 1840s. A minor though sensational figure, Matthias, like his fellow (and far more successful) New York State prophet, Smith, permits a glimpse at the roles of gender and authority within new religious movements.

Johnson, Paul E., and Sean Wilentz. *The Kingdom of Matthias: A Story of Sex and Salvation in 19th-Century America* (New York: Oxford Univ Press, 1994)

Paul E. Johnson

Mattydale. Locality (pop 6,367) in Salina (Onondaga Co). Its nearness to Syracuse resulted in development of an early suburb (*ca* 1910) named after the farm of Frank Matty (1850–1939), Syracuse mayor and political power. In 1943 the Army Air Force built an airport, radar installation, and housing nearby, and part of the facility became Hancock International Airport (1949). Northern Lights shopping plaza (1951) drew much of the trade from older businesses. Population increased rapidly after World War II and was estimated at 8,292 in 1970.

Barbara S. Rivette

May, Samuel J(oseph) (*b* Boston, 12 Sept 1797; *d* Syracuse, 1 July 1871). Unitarian minister and radical reformer. After graduating from Harvard College (1817) and Harvard Divinity School (1820), May occupied pulpits in Connecticut, Massachusetts, and New York, and in 1825 married Lucretia Flagge Coffin, with whom he had four children. In the 1820s May embraced education reform and temperance, supported movements against capital punishment, and espoused free press. In 1830 William Lloyd Garrison brought May into the radical immediatist antislavery movement, a choice that cost May his family and local church support. He helped organize the New England Anti-Slavery Movement (1832), the American Anti-Slavery Movement (1833), and the Non-Resistance Society (1838). He moved to Syracuse in 1845, in large part because his stance on abolition was not appreciated in Boston. In Syracuse May was a minister at the Church of the Messiah (1845–68), which was renamed the May Memorial Church Universalist Society in 1885. He was a major supporter and advocate of Garrison's nonviolent principles to resist slavery, although in 1851 in Syracuse May participated in the somewhat violent rescue of escaped slave William "Jerry" Henry. He led the fight for economic rights for working women and spent his last years promoting freedmen's aid societies, women's rights, and education reform. He is buried in Syracuse's Oakwood Cemetery.

Yacavone, Donald. *Samuel Joseph May and the Dilemmas of the Liberal Persuasion, 1797–1871* (Philadelphia: Temple Univ Press, 1991)

Graham Russell Hodges

Maybrook. Village (pop 3,084) in Hamptonburgh and Montgomery (Orange Co). Originally called Orange Junction, it grew up around the 1889 junction of the Central New England and the Lehigh and Hudson River Railroads. A Maybrook post office opened in 1890. In 1906 the New York, New Haven and Hartford Railroad acquired a half interest in the Central New England and built an important switching terminal at Maybrook. Many rooming houses were built to accommodate the workers. The village was incorporated in 1925. During World War II 1,500 people were employed in the yards, but all rail activity ceased in 1974 because of the Poughkeepsie Railroad Bridge fire. Employers since the railroad have been Osram Sylvania (1984–2003) and Yellow Freight System (1980), which employed as many as 1,000 in the mid-1990s. It is the site of the Maybrook Railroad Museum (1988).

Marcus H. Millspaugh

Mayfield. Town (pop 6,432) and village (pop 800) in NE Fulton Co. Settled *ca* 1760 by Scots, German, and Irish tenants of Sir William Johnson, the town was formed from the old town of Caughnawaga in 1793. The townspeople raised hay, buckwheat, and potatoes, but, as early as 1795, Mayfield had tanneries and had grown into a manufacturer of grained leather and Saranac gloves. In 1892 it supported eight glove shops. Other 19th-century products included woodenware, paper, steel traps, saws, and limestone. The Fonda, Johnstown and Gloversville Railroad reached Mayfield in 1875. The village incorporated in 1896. In 1916 resident

William C. Brower invented and patented the first sap gravity-flow tubing system to run from maple tree to sugarhouse. Much of the town's best farmland was inundated by the Great Sacandaga Lake (1930). The Alvord Glove Co (1917), with its trademark 24 ft (7.3 m) lumberjack figure on Rte 30, was the last survivor of the local leather industry, changing ownership *ca* 2000. Cynthia Nickloy (1902–61) of Mayfield was a Munchkin in *The Wizard of Oz* (1939).

mayors. See NEW YORK CONFERENCE OF MAYORS AND MUNICIPAL OFFICIALS (NYCOM).

Mayville. Village (pop 1,756) in Chautauqua. Settled in 1804 it was a transshipment point for the salt trade between Onondaga (Onondaga Co) and Pittsburgh (?1805–?1819). It became the county seat in 1811 and was incorporated in 1830. The last public hanging in New York State was held in Mayville in 1836. The village was served by steamboats on Chautauqua Lake; the Chautauqua House (1868–93) was a large hotel at the landing. Railroads (1867–1978) provided shipping for the ice industry (1871–1935), the dairy industry (1914–76), and the Ethan Allen furniture factory. Mayville is the home port of the steamboat *Chautauqua Belle* and site of the annual Ice Castle Extravaganza, begun in 1987. It was the home of author and statesman Albion W. Tourgée (1838–1905) after 1881.

Devon Taylor

McAuley, Jeremiah (*b* County Kerry, Ireland, 1839; *d* New York City, 18 Sept 1884). Founder of rescue missions. Raised in Ireland as a nonpracticing Roman Catholic, he was sent to New York City at the age of 13 to live with a married sister. A self-proclaimed "rogue," he took up a career as a river thief and moved to Water St in the notorious Fourth Ward. In 1857 he was convicted of highway robbery and sentenced to 15 years in Sing Sing Prison. After five years he experienced a religious conversion that transformed his life, and he was released on 8 Mar 1864. Assisted by Alfredic Smith Hatch, a wealthy Wall St banker, McAuley was able to find stable work. Despite his newfound personal success, he felt a divine call to help the destitute men of the Fourth Ward. With Hatch's financial assistance, McAuley opened the Helping Hand for Men Mission in 1872, reincorporated four years later as the Water Street Mission. A nondenominational Protestant mission, it provided lodging for 5,144 men and served over 26,000 meals during its first year. Religious services marked by preaching and singing were punctuated by testimonies of renewed lives. McAuley's rescue mission model spread quickly to other regions of the city and nation. He was directly involved in the discussions that led to the formation of the Bowery Mission in 1879. In 1882 he founded the Cremore Mission, located at 104 West 32d Street in the city's notorious Tenderloin region. He also helped Michael Dunn, an ex-convict, establish a halfway house for men recently released from prison, and Dunn went on to establish similar houses in Detroit, San Francisco, Philadelphia, and Brooklyn.

Bonner, Arthur. *Jerry McAuley and His Mission,* rev ed. (Neptune, NJ: Loizeaux Bros, 1990)
McAuley, Jerry. *Transformed; or, The History of a River Thief, Briefly Told* (Author, 1876)
Offord, R. M., ed. *Jerry McAuley: An Apostle to the Lost,* 7th ed. (Freeport, NY: Books for Libraries Press, 1970)

David P. Setran

McCall, H(erman) Carl (*b* Boston, 17 Oct 1935). Senator, comptroller, and gubernatorial candidate. One of six children raised by his mother, a single parent, McCall received his BA from Dartmouth College (1958), studied at the University of Edinburgh (1961–62) and took his MA (1963) from the Andover-Newton Theological School. He moved to New York City in 1964 and became involved in local government and politics, serving as a deputy administrator of the New York City Human Resources Administration (1966–69) and co-owner and editor (1971–73) of the *Amsterdam News* weekly newspaper. A Democrat, he was elected to the state senate from the 28th District and served three terms (1975–79). McCall subsequently served as deputy US ambassador to the United Nations (1979–81), state commissioner for human rights (1983–84), board member for the Port Authority of New York and New Jersey (1985–89), vice president of Citicorp/Citibank (1985–93), and president of the New York City Board of Education (1991–93). In 1993 the state legislature appointed McCall as state comptroller, filling the vacancy created by Edward Regan's resignation. McCall was elected comptroller in 1994 and 1998, becoming the first African American elected to statewide office in New York. As comptroller McCall oversaw the growth of the state pension fund from $5.6 billion in 1994 to $112 billion in 2002. He was the Democratic candidate for governor in 2002, losing to Gov George E. Pataki. After leaving office, he returned to the private sector and served on several boards of directors.

Jeffrey Kraus

McCarthyism. See COLD WAR AND MCCARTHYISM.

McClintock, Barbara (*b* Hartford, Conn, 16 June 1902; *d* Huntington, Suffolk Co, 2 Sept 1992). Geneticist. McClintock and her family moved to Brooklyn when she was 6; she graduated from that borough's Erasmus Hall High School in 1919. She attended the New York State College of Agriculture at Cornell, where she received a BS (1923) and MS (1925) in botany; in 1927 she earned a PhD in the same subject at Cornell. She was hired as Cornell's first female science teacher, a position she held from 1927 to 1931. McClintock taught at a variety of other colleges until 1941, when she took a research position at the Cold Spring Harbor Laboratory (Suffolk Co). Dedicating the rest of her life to research at Cold Spring, McClintock's work focused on the genetics of maize and the relationship between plant reproduction and mutation. In 1944 she became the first woman to be president of the Genetics Society of America. In 1951 she published research arguing how genetic information was suppressed or expressed from one generation of maize plants to another, theories that were far in advance of molecular biology at that time. The scientific community did not fully comprehend her revolutionary work in genetics until the late 1970s. McClintock's 1951 discovery of transposable genetic elements, which she further expanded in later years with research trips to study maize cultivation in South America and Mexico, earned her the 1983 Nobel Prize in physiology or medicine. She was the first woman to receive an unshared Nobel Prize in that category.

Keller, Evelyn Fox. *A Feeling for the Organism: The Life and Work of Barbara McClintock* (San Francisco: W. H. Freeman, 1983)

Mary Anne Hansen

McCrea, Jane (*b* Bedminster [now Lamington, NJ], ?1752; *d* near Fort Edward, Washington

Detail from *The Murder of Jane McCrea,* drawing made for an uncompleted painting by John Trumbull, *ca* 1790.

Co, 27 July 1777). Revolutionary War martyr. Orphaned in 1769 by the death of her father, Scots-Irish immigrant and Presbyterian minister James McCrea, Jane moved in 1770 to Argyle (Washington Co) to live with her eldest brother, John, a lawyer. By 1776 most accounts have her affianced to David Jones, a loyalist, whose sentiments she shared, from the upper Hudson Valley serving in the British army under John Burgoyne. Early on 27 July 1777, McCrea went from Argyle to the home of her loyalist friend, Sarah Fraser Campbell McNeil, cousin of Burgoyne's brigadier Simon Fraser, near Fort Edward. What happened next has been obscured by the weight of legend, romance, propaganda, and conflicting contemporary reports, but the most enduring versions hold that either Mohawk or Ottawa allies of Burgoyne captured the two women, stripped them naked, and dragged them to the British camp. McNeil survived, but McCrea was killed, either by the sword or gunshot. An alternative version holds she was killed by American pickets in pursuit of the Indian forces. Patriots exploited the McCrea incident, arguing that if Burgoyne could not protect even his own supporters from his Indian allies, how much less safe were the families of rebels. John Vanderlyn's painting, *The Murder of Jane McCrea* (1804), in which a terrified woman is about to be tomahawked by two towering loinclothed Indians, is a classic depiction of American attitudes toward Indian savagery.

American National Biography, sv "McCrea, Jane"
Holden, James A. "Influence of the Death of Jane McCrea on the Burgoyne Campaign." In *Proceedings of the New York State Historical Association* ([New York?]: The Association, 1913)
Namias, June. "Jane McCrea and the American Revolution." In *White Captives: Gender and Ethnicity on the American Frontier* (Chapel Hill: Univ of North Carolina Press, 1993)

Eric v. d. Luft

McDonough. [MICK-DOUGH-NAH]. Town (pop 870) in SW Chenango Co. Settled in 1795 as one of the Chenango Twenty Townships, the town was formed from Preston in 1816. Genegantslet Lake is in the western part of McDonough and covers about 150 acres (61 ha). In the 19th century the town had tanneries, a woolen factory, a foundry and machine shop, and a cheese factory, but by the 1940s most residents worked in nearby towns. McDonough is the site of Bowman Lake State Park and, since 1998, of a Buddhist retreat.

Michele A. McFee

McDougall, Alexander (*b* Islay, Scotland, ?July 1732; *d* New York City, 9 June 1786). Continental army general and merchant. After moving with his family to New York City at age 6, McDougall later went to sea and eventually became a merchant. During the French and Indian War (1754–63), he captained two ships as a privateer. In 1769 McDougall published a broadside critical of the New York provincial assembly, claiming partisan misuse of public funds. His arrest and brief imprisonment for the accusations made him a celebrity; he was subsequently active in the patriot cause. McDougall served as colonel of the First New York Regiment of militia in 1775. He was promoted to brigadier general in the Continental army in 1776 and to major general a year later. McDougall took part in the Battles of Long Island (Kings Co) and White Plains (Westchester Co) in 1776. After Maj Gen Benedict Arnold's treason was discovered in September 1780, McDougall was put in command of West Point (Orange Co). He served briefly in the Continental Congress in 1781. After the war he became the first president of the Bank of New York and served in the New York State Senate from 1783 until his death.

Champagne, Roger J. *Alexander McDougall and the American Revolution in New York* (Schenectady: NYS American Revolution Bicentennial Commission, in conjunction with Union College Press, 1975)

Jennifer Steenshorne

McEnroe, John (Patrick) (*b* Wiesbaden, Germany, 16 Feb 1959). Tennis player. McEnroe grew up in Douglaston in Queens, began playing tennis at age 8, and honed his talent at the Trinity School in Manhattan and Port Washington Tennis Academy. Enrolled at Stanford University in 1977, he helped the team win the NCAA Championship as a first-year student when he took the singles title. He returned to Queens to win the 1979 US Open, his first of 17 Grand Slam event victories. In 1981, 1983, and 1984 he won Wimbleton and was on five winning US Davis Cup teams. His explosive temper brought him numerous fines and forced him to default from the 1990 Australian Open after he yelled at an umpire and broke his racket. McEnroe left the tour in 1992, served as captain of the US Davis Cup team for 14 months in 1999 and 2000, and later became a television sports analyst and game show host.

Evans, Richard. *McEnroe: Taming the Talent* (New York: Viking Penguin, 1990)

Joshua Ruff

McGlynn, Edward (*b* New York City, 27 Sept 1837; *d* Newburgh, Orange Co, 7 Jan 1900). Roman Catholic priest and social activist. He was ordained a priest in 1860 and from 1866 to 1887 served as pastor of St. Stephen's Church on East 28th St, then the largest parish in Manhattan. An active member of the Academia, an intellectual discussion group composed of liberal-minded New York City clerics, he quickly drew the suspicion and ire of church officials because of his radical opinions. McGlynn supported the social theorist Henry George, and when George ran for mayor of New York City in 1886, McGlynn publicly endorsed his candidacy despite having been warned not to do so by Archbishop Michael Corrigan. Like George, McGlynn called for the institution of a single tax on all income not derived from one's own labors. He was made president of the Anti-Poverty Society, a group dedicated to advancing the theories of George. This inaugurated a series of events that eventually led to McGlynn's formal excommunication by Pope Leo XIII on 3 July 1887. He remained immensely popular and in 1892 was reinstated. In 1894 Corrigan named him pastor of St. Mary's Church in Newburgh.

Isacsson, Alfred. *The Determined Doctor: The Story of Edward McGlynn* (Tarrytown, NY: Vestigium Press, 1996)
———. *Edward McGlynn: Studies Marking the Centenary of His Death* (Tarrytown, NY: Vestigium Press, 1999)

Anthony D. Andreassi

McGraw. Village (pop 1,000) in Cortlandville (Cortland Co). Settled in 1809, it was known as McGrawsville by 1829. From 1849 to 1861 it was the site of New York Central College, the first US college to have a racially integrated faculty. The village incorporated in 1869 as McGrawville; the post office was changed to McGraw in 1898 and that became the village's name in 1932. Dr. L. C. Warner invented the "health corset" here in 1873. By 1876 he employed 115 but moved his factory to Bridgeport, Conn; other corset factories continued the business locally, and in 1895 half a million corsets a year were made by 450 workers. In the early 21st century, the Vesta Corset Co (1913) continues the tradition.

Cathy A. Barber

McGraw, John (Joseph) (*b* Truxton, Cortland Co, 7 Apr 1873; *d* New Rochelle, Westchester Co, 25 Feb 1934). Baseball player and manager. The eldest son of Irish immigrant John McGraw, a railroad worker, and Ellen Comerfort McGraw, he left his abusive father after his mother's death. He then left public school, held menial jobs, and discovered a love for baseball. After apprenticeship as a minor league player for Olean (Cattaraugus Co) in the New York–Pennsylvania League (1890), Wellsville (Allegany Co) in the New York State League (1890), and Cedar Rapids, Iowa, in the Illinois-Iowa League (1891), McGraw joined the major leagues and played third base with the Baltimore Orioles (1891–99, 1901–2), St. Louis Cardinals (1900), and New York Giants (1902–6). In 1,099 major league games, McGraw had a .334 batting average, scored 1,024 runs, and stole 436 bases. A player-manager for Baltimore (1899, 1901–2), "Little Napoleon" managed the New York Giants (1902–32), which he led to a record 10 National League pennants, with World Series championships in 1905, 1921, and 1922. A master of strategy and motivation, he garnered 2,763 managerial victories, second highest in the game's history, and a .586 winning percentage. McGraw was elected to the Baseball Hall of Fame in 1937.

Alexander, Charles C. *John McGraw* (New York: Viking Press, 1988)

William M. Simons

McKelvey, Blake F(aus) (*b* Centralia, Pa, 10 June 1903; *d* Rochester, 13 Sept 2000). Historian. After graduating from Williamsport High School, McKelvey entered Syracuse University intending to be a medical missionary but became interested in history. After graduating he received an MA from Clark University (1929) and a PhD from Harvard (1933), with a dissertation on American prisons. Named assistant city historian for Rochester in 1936, he helped establish Rochester's first (of nine) Sister City relationship with Rennes, France. He was a founding member of the Montgomery Settlement House (now Montgomery Neighborhood Center). He edited the Rochester Historical Society's Publication Fund Series through 1947 and established *Rochester History*, the quarterly journal of the Office of the City Historian, in 1939. As writer and editor and as city historian (1948–73) he helped define the role of the nonpolitical public historian, studying the intricacies of urban development and often taking an active role in preservation, planning, and social justice work.

A founding member of the Urban History Group, he taught urban studies at the University of Michigan, Sir George Williams University, Rochester Institute of Technology, and the University of Rochester. His four-volume scholarly history of Rochester, published between 1945 and 1961, and its subsequent one-volume abridgment and update, makes the city one of the best documented in the nation. His studies helped city planners make informed decisions and understand the cultural transitions brought on by successive waves of immigrants. In 1959 he warned that if issues of housing, education, and unemployment among the growing black community were not soon addressed there would be serious problems; in July 1964 Rochester experienced one of the first racial riots of the 1960s. He continued to work after he retired in 1973, and he completed a biography of Xerox founder Joseph C. Wilson shortly before his death.

Ruth Rosenberg-Naparsteck

McKim, Mead and White. Established in 1879, the New York City architectural firm achieved an unprecedented level of critical praise because it contributed mightily to the form of both grand public buildings and elite private residences. The three men transformed American urbanism using classical forms and principles not only as an esthetic choice but also as a way of expressing a concept of the national character as rooted in the ideals of the ancient world, particularly the democracy of Greece and the republic of Rome. The firm received nearly 1,000 commissions from 1879 to 1919 and was said to be the largest architectural firm in the world before 1910. During its peak years, from 1900 to 1910, it employed more than 100.

The three principal architects had strong and distinctive personalities; indeed, the differences among them seemed to be a key factor in their collective success. Charles Follen McKim (1847–1909) was the son of a well-known abolitionist. He studied at the Ecole des Beaux-Arts in Paris and worked in New York City for the architect H. H. Richardson. In 1871 he began to accept independent commissions and the following year shared an office with William Rutherford Mead (1846–1928). Born to artistic parents Mead graduated from Amherst College (1867) in Massachusetts, then studied in Florence. Stanford White (1853–1906), born in New York City, was the son of a noted critic and Shakespearean scholar through whom he met many leading artists and architects. He lacked formal training but excelled at opulent compositions and was legendary as a bon vivant.

During the 1880s the firm became well known for its highly inventive houses and social clubs, designed in the so-called Shingle Style, which brought together myriad design influences, including early American houses and buildings in France and Japan. One such work was the Newport Casino (1880) in Rhode Island. Among the firm's outstanding works in New York City were White's Madison Square Garden (1891) and the Henry Villard houses (1885) at 451 and 457 Madison Ave. They did master plans and several buildings for both New York University (1892–1901) and Columbia University (1893–1902), as well as designs for the University Club (1900), the J. P. Morgan Library (1907), and, perhaps most important, Pennsylvania Station (1911). The station, based in part on the ancient Roman baths of Caracalla, was a paradigmatic synthesis of efficient planning, state-of-art technology, and imposing architecture. The memorable gateway to a great city, Pennsylvania Station succumbed to the wrecking ball in 1963. The firm also designed buildings throughout New York State, including Buffalo's Metcalf residence (1882) and houses at Delaware and North Aves (1899). In Albany they designed the Arnold house (1905) at 465 State St. In Rochester they completed the Eastman School of Music (1921) and the Eastman Theatre. On 25 June 1906 actress Evelyn Nesbit's husband killed White after Nesbit and White had been publicly identified while attending a musical performance on the rooftop of Madison Square Garden. The event was widely covered in the media and became a scandal. McKim died three years later in 1909. Mead officially retired in 1919 and lived until 1928. The three architects left an indelible mark on New York City and the state, forging a uniquely American architecture grounded in the grandeur of the past.

Baker, Paul R. *Stanny: The Gilded Life of Stanford White* (New York: Free Press, 1989)

Moore, Charles. *The Life and Times of Charles Follen McKim* (Boston: Houghton Mifflin, 1929)

Roth, Leland M. *McKim, Mead and White: Architects* (New York: Harper & Row, 1983)

Thomas Mellins

McKinley assassination. On 6 Sept 1901 at the Pan-American Exposition in Buffalo, Leon F. Czolgosz shot Pres William McKinley at close range. McKinley died in Buffalo on 14 September. The president had given a speech at the exposition on 5 September, and after visiting Niagara Falls the next morning, he returned to attend a public reception at the Temple of Music. Guarding him were 3 Secret Service officers, 4 Buffalo detectives, 15 exposition police, and 10 army soldiers. Czolgosz, carrying a gun covered by a handkerchief, joined the line to shake the president's hand and shot him twice. He was wrestled to the ground and turned over to the Secret Service. The president was taken by motor ambulance to the exposition's first aid station. One bullet, deflected by a button, did not penetrate, but the other went through his stomach. Ironically, doctors did not find it because they failed to use a new technology displayed at the exposition, the X-ray machine. Cabinet members and Vice Pres Theodore Roosevelt, who was vacationing on Isle La Motte on Lake Champlain, rushed to Buffalo, as did New York governor Benjamin B. Odell Jr. That evening thousands of angry citizens gathered outside the police station that held Czolgosz. Buffalo police had to use force to keep the crowd back from the station.

Medical bulletins and newspaper headlines in the following days raised optimism about McKinley's recovery. Meanwhile, after Czolgosz identified himself as an anarchist, police looked for evidence of a conspiracy, attempting to link anarchist Emma Goldman, who had lived in Rochester and New York City, to the shooting. No connection to any anarchist group was proved, but in the wake of the shooting widespread hostility toward anarchists developed in New York State and across the nation. McKinley's condition worsened: by 13 September gangrene had set in and at 2:15 the next morning McKinley died. Roosevelt, who had resumed his vacation, hurried back to Buffalo, where he took the oath of office the same day. Federal, state, and city governments declared 19 September a day of mourning. In Brooklyn thousands congregated at Borough Hall to express their grief, and 10,000 people gathered in Manhattan's Herald Square to listen to the tolling of bells as McKinley was buried in Canton, Ohio.

Born in Detroit in 1873 of Polish immigrant parents, Leon Czolgosz had worked in factories in Ohio and Pennsylvania. Three years before the assassination he suffered a mental breakdown. His decision to shoot McKinley was apparently inspired by the Italian American anarchist Gaetano Bresci's assassination of King Humbert I of Italy in 1900. Tried in state supreme court on 23–24 September in Buffalo, Czolgosz was found sane and guilty of first-degree murder. Sentenced to death by Justice Truman C. White on 26 September, Czolgosz went to the electric chair at Auburn Prison (Cayuga Co) on 29 Oct 1901.

Johns, A. Wesley. *The Man Who Shot McKinley* (New York: A. S. Barnes, 1970)

Harvey Strum

McKinney-Steward [née Smith], **Susan (Maria)** (*b* Brooklyn, ?1846; *d* Wilberforce, Ohio, 7 Mar 1918). Physician. Of American Indian, African American, and French descent, she received her MD in 1870 from the predominantly homeopathic New York Medical College and Hospital for Women. She finished postgraduate studies at the Long Island Medical College and became the first African American woman physician in New York State and the third in the nation. From 1870 to 1895 she practiced homeopathic medicine in Brooklyn, in 1881 cofounded the Brooklyn Woman's Homeopathic Hospital and Dispensary, and after 1892 served on the board of the Brooklyn Home for Aged Colored People (now Brooklyn Home for the Aged). In 1874 she married Rev William Guillard McKinney. Widowed in 1895 she married Rev Theophilus Gould Steward one year later. They settled in 1898 at Wilberforce University in Ohio, where he taught history and she served as resident physician until her death.

Seraile, William. "Susan McKinney Steward: New York State's First African-American Woman Physician," *Afro-Americans in New York Life and History* 9 (July 1985): 27–44

Eric v. d. Luft

McMaster, James Alphonsus (*b* Duanesburg, Schenectady Co, 1 Apr 1820; *d* Brooklyn, 29 Dec 1886). Journalist and writer. The son of Jane Brown McMaster and Gilbert McMaster, a Scots-Irish Presbyterian minister, James McMaster was educated at Union College in Schenectady and, as a convert to Episcopalianism by 1840, at the General Theological Seminary in New York City. His disillusionment with Episcopalianism led to a conversion to Catholicism in 1845 and a brief period of study for the Roman Catholic priesthood in Belgium. McMaster settled in New York City in 1846 and began a career in journalism. In 1848 he bought the *New York Freeman's Journal and Catholic Register* and made it one of the most important Catholic newspapers in the United States. In 1850 he married Gertrude Fetterman. They had seven children, four of whom survived to adulthood.

McMaster was outspoken in his political and theological views, and filled his newspaper with fierce attacks on his opponents. A Copperhead Democrat with southern sympathies, he was imprisoned briefly at the outset of the Civil War for criticism of the Lincoln administration. In religion he championed the authority of the pope, interpreting papal infallibility in the broadest terms, and staunchly defended parochial schools. McMaster continued to edit his newspaper until his death.

Kwitchen, Mary Augustine. *James Alphonsus McMaster: A Study in American Thought* (Washington, DC: Catholic Univ of America Press, 1949)

Thomas J. Shelley

McQuaid, Bernard J(ohn Joseph) (*b* New York City, 15 Dec 1823; *d* Rochester, 18 Jan 1909). Bishop and educator. The son of Bernard McQuaid and Mary Maguire McQuaid, he was orphaned at age 9 and raised by the Sisters of Charity in the Roman Catholic Orphan Asylum in New York City. He was educated at Chambly College in Chambly [now in Quebec] and St. Joseph's Seminary in Fordham [now in Bronx Co]. Following ordination as a priest of the Diocese of New York on 16 Jan 1848, he was assigned to Madison, NJ, where he established the state's first parochial school. He served as rector of St. Patrick's Cathedral in Newark, NJ (1853–56, 1857–68), founded Seton Hall College and Seminary (1856), and assisted Mother Mary Xavier Mehegan in establishing the Sisters of Charity of St. Elizabeth (1859). On 3 Mar 1868 McQuaid was named the first bishop of the newly established Diocese of Rochester, a see that he administered until his death. He built a network of parishes, Catholic schools, charitable institutions, and two model seminaries, St. Andrew's Preparatory Seminary (1870) and St. Bernard's Seminary (1893; now St. Bernard's Institute). McQuaid was one of the youngest bishops at Vatican Council I (1869–70) and played a national role in the American Catholic Church as a respected leader of its conservative wing.

McNamara, Robert F. *The Diocese of Rochester in America, 1868–1993*, 2d ed. (Rochester: Diocese of Rochester, 1998)

Zwierlein, Frederick J. *The Life and Letters of Bishop McQuaid*, 3 vols (Rochester: Art Print Shop, 1925–27)

Thomas J. Shelley

Mead, James M. (*b* Mount Morris, Livingston Co, 27 Dec 1885; *d* Lakeland, Fla, 15 Mar 1964). Congressman and senator. Mead's family moved to Buffalo in 1890. The son of a Lackawanna Railroad employee, he began working on the railroad at age 12 as a water boy and eventually as a switchman. He attended night classes at the Caton School of Engineering in 1904 and the Buffalo Institute of Technology in 1905. In 1911 he moved to Washington, DC, to work on the Capitol police force. Mead became active in Democratic politics upon his return to Buffalo in 1912, and he was elected to the Erie Co Board of Supervisors in 1913 in a strongly Republican area. He was elected to the state assembly the following year and to Congress in 1918. Mead continued to represent his constituents in the Buffalo-area district until being elected to the Senate in 1938 to fill the vacancy caused by the death of Royal S. Copeland; in 1940, he was elected to a full term and served until 1947. A staunch supporter of Pres Franklin D. Roosevelt's New Deal, Mead was Roosevelt's candidate for New York State governor in the 1942 primary election. He was defeated by Atty Gen John J. Bennett Jr, the candidate of James A. Farley, state Democratic Party chair. Mead ran for governor again in 1946 but lost to the incumbent Republican governor Thomas E. Dewey by one of the largest margins ever in a state gubernatorial election. Mead served on the Federal Trade Commission from 1949 to 1955 and was appointed by Gov W. Averell Harriman as director of the New York State Commerce Department in 1955, retiring in September 1956.

Mead, James M. *Tell the Folks Back Home* (New York: Appleton-Century, 1944)

John David Rausch Jr

Meagher, Thomas Francis (*b* Waterford, Ireland, 3 Aug 1823; *d* Fort Benton, Montana Terr, 1 July 1867). Irish nationalist and general. As an Irish independence activist advocating violence to free his homeland from British rule, he was convicted by the British in 1848 of high treason and banished to Van Diemen's Land [now Tasmania]. In 1852 Meagher escaped to New York City, where his support of Irish nationalism made him an important lecturer, lawyer, and political leader for Irish immigrants. In 1861 he recruited a company for both the 69th New York Volunteer Militia Regiment and the Irish Brigade, which drew many of its soldiers from New York City. As a Union brigadier general, he commanded the Irish Brigade in the Peninsular, Second Bull Run, Antietam, and Fredericksburg campaigns. In 1865–66 he served as the acting territorial governor of Montana, where he drowned in the Missouri River.

Athearn, Robert G. *Thomas Francis Meagher: An Irish Revolutionary in America* (New York: Arno Press, 1976)

Bernadette Zbicki Heiney

Meany, (William) George (*b* New York City, 16 Aug 1894; *d* Bethesda, Md, 10 Jan 1980). Labor union leader. Meany grew up in the Bronx and attended school until age 14. His father was president of a plumbers' union in the Bronx, and Meany became a plumber's helper at age 16, attending trade school at night. In 1917 he joined his father's union, Bronx Local 463, one of the largest in the nation, as a journeyman plumber. He was elected to the local's executive board in 1920 and as business agent in 1922. In 1932 he was elected to the executive board of the New York State Federation of Labor, and two years later he was chosen to head the 800,000-member state federation. Meany had close alliances with leading state Democrats such as Gov Herbert H. Lehman and Sen Robert F. Wagner Sr and worked to gain passage of several important labor laws. In 1940 he became secretary-treasurer of the American Federation of Labor (AFL). He served on the War Labor Board during World War II, and afterward he was one of the most outspoken anticommunist labor leaders. In 1952 Meany was elected AFL president and in 1955 helped end the rivalry between the AFL and the industrial unions that made up the Congress of Industrial Organizations (CIO). He became the first president of the unified AFL-CIO, the largest union organization in the United States. Gruff and autocratic, Meany held the federation together in years of massive decline for labor. He was a supporter of the Civil Rights Movement, particularly against job discrimination. Meany retired as president in 1979.

Robinson, Archie. *George Meany and His Times* (New York: Simon & Schuster, 1981)

Richard A. Greenwald

meatpacking industry. Meatpacking is the industrialized purchasing of livestock, its conversion into salable products, and its distribution to consumers. The meatpacking industry emerged during the mid–19th century as railroads replaced turnpikes as the dominant mode of transporting livestock from rural farms to urban population centers. Although butchers and slaughterhouses have been present in New York State since the 17th century, they tended to serve local populations. During the 19th century, the advent of improved transportation networks and increased demands for cattle, hogs, and sheep spurred the growth of meatpacking as an integrated industry embracing the shipping, slaughter, and sale of meat and meat by-products.

Early Practice

New York State farmers sold livestock to drovers who transported the animals to market. The earliest drovers were stock owners who drove their own animals. Prior to the first quarter of the 19th century, all of the livestock driven to market in the state was bred and slaughtered in-state. One of the earliest livestock markets in New York State was founded in 1676 in Manhattan between Pine and Wall Sts. Livestock was driven down drove roads paralleling major rivers, such as the Hudson and Mohawk, into New York City markets. Turnpikes, such as the Cherry Valley Turnpike and the Hamilton and Skaneateles Turnpike, became major livestock routes. During the late 18th and early 19th centuries, drovers established central collection points outside of New York City where droves were consolidated before moving on to the city. Many of these collection points were tavern stands where drovers and their animals rested and were fed along the drive. As the droves increased in size and frequency in the early 19th century, specialized drovers' taverns or drove yards developed throughout the state, many of which were founded by livestock entrepreneurs and drovers.

New York State's roads often became clogged corridors with cattle, sheep, hogs, and birds jockeying for space as they were driven to markets. Flocks of turkeys and geese were driven along the same turnpikes as their four-footed counterparts. While hog and cattle drovers were mainly concerned with shrinkage (weight loss) during the drives, fowl drovers had to protect the birds' feet by "shoeing" them in the traditional British manner of covering the feet with pitch and adding a layer of sand to help the birds endure the drive. Onondaga Co's Gooseville Corners is one enduring legacy of the early fowl drives.

Drove yards during the 18th and 19th centuries provided regular, full-service resting places along the livestock routes for drovers and their stock. The stock were watered, fed, and housed in pens and roosts while their human overseers took advantage of the amenities provided by innkeepers. In the New York City hinterlands, drove yards such as the Wayside Inn—purchased in 1775 by James and Michael Varian, whose brothers Isaac and Richard were butchers in New York City markets—sprouted along roads leading into the city. Dutchess Co drovers Ebenezer and Hebron Hurd likewise divided their time between driving cattle and slaughtering in New York City. By 1825 farmers elsewhere in the state had integrated the breeding, shipping, and sale of livestock into kin-based entrepreneurial ventures.

Entrepreneurs

The introduction of cattle driven from Ohio, Kentucky, Virginia, and Pennsylvania to New York City markets contributed to the emergence of New York State's livestock entrepreneurs. In 1817 the first drove of 200 corn-fattened Ohio cattle arrived at Bull's Head Tavern in the Bowery in New York City. Established by Richard Varian during the American Revolution, the Bull's Head rapidly became the center of New York City's nascent meatpacking industry. Its drove yards and adjacent slaughterhouses attracted drovers from throughout the eastern United States, forcing the Bull's Head in 1825 to seek more space at 24th St and 3d Ave. In 1830 drover Daniel Drew bought the Bull's Head and was its proprietor for eight years before he moved on to fame as a Wall St operator. Persistent legend holds that the phrase "watered stock" entered the world of finance from Drew's years as a drover.

While New York City was attracting livestock and butchers from the rest of the state and beyond, other meat entrepreneurs were taking advantage of increased livestock traffic and availability. Troy (Rensselaer Co) butcher Samuel Wilson was dubbed "Uncle Sam," and the name stuck after he began provisioning troops during the War of 1812. Barrels of his meat were stamped "U.S.," and his meat became known as Uncle Sam's beef or Uncle Sam's pork. Wilson's moniker became synonymous with the American government, and Uncle Sam became a popular American icon.

Expanding the Industry

During the 1840s railroads began to absorb most of the livestock traffic through New York State. By the Civil War there were direct lines between New York City and Chicago, the nation's emerging meatpacking and livestock brokering center. Cattle became the dominant animal shipped on the hoof to urban markets. As livestock became a leading commodity transported on the nation's expanding railroads, drove yards grew at railheads and along trunk lines to facilitate the transfer of stock to railcars. Some of New York State's livestock entrepreneurs were drawn to Chicago on the eve of the Civil War, including Dutchess Co drovers John B. Sherman and Samuel W. Allerton, whose family had been driving livestock into New York City since the turn of the 19th century. Allerton in 1865 was the leading force behind the founding of the Chicago Union Stock Yards.

By the mid-1870s the American meatpacking industry had fully crystallized. New York State's livestock entrepreneurs, such as Allerton, Sherman, and Timothy C. Eastman (New York City), John B. Dutcher (New York City), and Jacob Dold (Buffalo), profited from every animal shipped by rail from Chicago to New York City. Continuing the integration strategies forged by

Dold Packing Plant, Buffalo, 1917.

earlier farmers-drovers-butchers, these livestock entrepreneurs formed close ties to the trunk-line railroads and opened stockyards in New York City, Buffalo, and Albany, as well as in Pennsylvania, Illinois, Missouri, and other western states. They also opened slaughterhouses in New York City (Allerton, Eastman) and Buffalo (Dold) with satellite slaughterhouses in midwestern cities closest to the livestock supplies.

Reform and Decline

Public nuisances wrought by slaughterhouses prompted changes in health codes, resulting in the consolidation of slaughterhouses in more concentrated areas surrounding the railroads' terminal stockyard facilities. In New York City this was the "Butchertown" area around Turtle Bay along the East River. Rather than deal with increasingly restrictive health codes prohibiting livestock drives through city streets, the railroads and their stockyard operators and meatpackers chose to relocate their facilities across the Hudson River in Jersey City, NJ. New York City's Butchertown disappeared in the late 1940s with the construction of the United Nations complex, and Buffalo's stockyards, which opened in 1861, were closed in 1983.

New York State's meatpacking industry grew and contracted with changing demands for meat, new transportation and distribution networks, and increased regulations governing the location of noisome nuisance industries. Many of the state's meatpackers and traditional butchers have disappeared, replaced by midwestern agribusinesses with large integrated breeding farms and slaughterhouses. Rochester sausage maker Zweigle's, founded in 1880 by German butcher C. Wilhelm Zweigle, is now known for its hot dogs (Red Hots and White Hots) and other deli meats. Zweigle's remains a family-owned enterprise. Buffalo's F. Wardynski and Sons, founded in 1920 by immigrant Polish butcher Frank Wardynski and now selling its products via the Internet, has successfully adapted to changing markets, livestock supply, and product demands. Schaller and Weber, another family meatpacking enterprise, still does business in New York City's historically German Astoria neighborhood in Queens.

When the meatpacking industry abandoned urban areas such as New York City after the 1960s, specialty butchers catering to changing ethnic populations and old-line religious foodways, emerged to fill the void. In the years following World War II, meat industry analysts noted more than 2,400 kosher butchers stores in New York City alone; by the late 1990s there were just more than 50 remaining. One of the firms that serves New York City's, and much of the East Coast's, kosher meat needs is International Glatt, headquartered in Brooklyn. Its butchers—shohets clad in USDA-approved coats and hard hats hiding their yarmulkes—travel to slaughterhouses and kill lambs and beeves on kosher days, alternating with Muslim halal butchers and regular butchers.

Palmer, Richard F. "The Era of the Drover," *New York Folklore Quarterly* 30 (Dec 1974): 226–31

Skaggs, Jimmy M. *Prime Cut: Livestock Raising and Meatpacking in the United States, 1607–1983* (College Station: Texas A&M Univ Press, 1986)

Yeager, Mary. *Competition and Regulation: The Development of Oligopoly in the Meat Packing Industry* (Greenwich, Conn: JAI Press, 1981)

David S. Rotenstein

Mechanicville. City (pop 5,019) in E Saratoga Co. It originated as a mill hamlet at the mouth of Tenendaho Creek; the Champlain Canal (1823) gave it improved access, as did the Rensselaer and Saratoga Railroad (1835). American Linen Thread Co (1850) was the first major industry. Mechanicville incorporated as a village in 1859

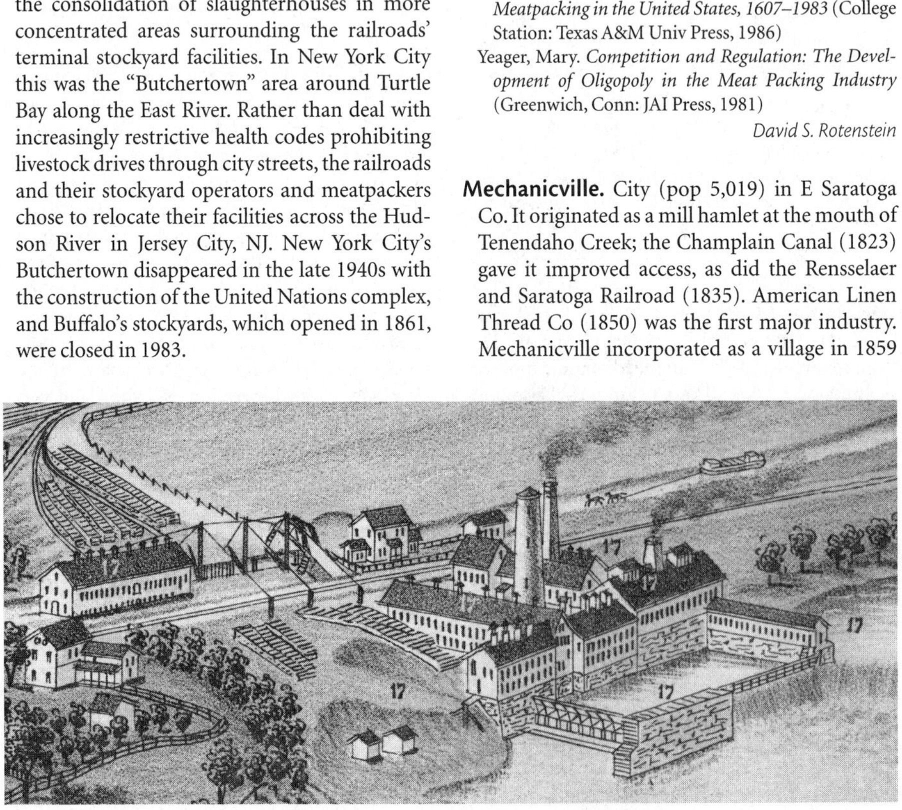

Hudson River Water Power and Paper Co; detail from panoramic map of Mechanicville, mid-1880s.

and as a city in 1915. Industrial growth followed the Civil War, with the Hudson River Water Power and Paper Co (now West Virginia Pulp and Paper Co) (1885) and the Boston and Maine Railroad yards (1912), which had a peak capacity of 1,475 cars. Significant Italian and Lithuanian communities developed after 1895. Population peaked at over 10,000 in 1925 and declined sharply with the closure of the mill in 1971 and the decline of rail yards in the 1980s. Col Elmer E. Ellsworth (1837–61), the first Union officer killed on the Virginia front, was a Mechanicville resident.

Field Horne

Medaille College. Private college. Founded by the Sisters of St. Joseph in Buffalo in 1875 as a preparatory institute for teachers in religious orders. In 1937 the school was chartered by the state as Mount St. Joseph Teachers College to grant baccalaureate degrees in education to women in religious orders. The state granted a new charter in 1968 creating Medaille College, a coeducational, nonsectarian, liberal arts–based, four-year institution. The college offers bachelor and associate degree programs, certificates of study, and master's degrees in education and business administration. An accelerated degree program for working adults attracts students from Western and Central New York and southern Ontario. Total enrollment in 2001 was 1,752 with a student-faculty ratio of 16:1 and a women-men ratio of 70:30. Dormitory housing is provided for approximately 110 students. A branch campus for business programs opened in Amherst (Erie Co) in 1997, and enrollment in 2001 was 350. In 2002 the college opened a Rochester branch campus in Brighton (Monroe Co), also for the accelerated business program.

Medaille College, http://www.medaille.edu

Nancy E. Frazier

Medford. Locality (pop 21,985) in Brookhaven (Suffolk Co). The Long Island Rail Road (1843) created a station, from which stages ran to Patchogue and Port Jefferson. Some lots were platted, and a post office opened in 1886, but little development took place until 1897, when the O. L. Schwenke Land and Development Co began selling lots. From 1907 to 1927 Medford was the site of Hal B. Fullerton's 80-acre (32 ha) Long Island Rail Road Experimental Farm, which demonstrated methods of making Long Island's less productive soils into successful operations. Medford's population, only 902 in 1950, exploded in the second half of the 20th century. Its largest industry is Gershow Recycling Corp (1973).

Medgar Evers College. Public college. Located in Brooklyn, the school was named for the civil rights leader murdered in 1963. Founded in 1968 as part of the University of the City of New York (CUNY), the college opened as a four-year college in 1971 with a mission to serve the educational, cultural, and social needs of its central Brooklyn community, which was predominantly African American. Evers reflected the tension over the financing of CUNY after the New York City fiscal crisis of 1976 when the state legislature denied the school support for all but a few four-year programs between 1978 and 1993. During this period New York City funded two-year programs at the school, which regained its official, full four-year college status in 1994. Through its Schools of Liberal Arts and Education, Science, Health and Technology, and Business, Evers offers 17 baccalaureate and 9 associate degree programs. It realizes its community role through extensive external and continuing education programs and cultural events. The college sponsors a Middle College High School in cooperation with the New York City Board of Education. Dr Betty Shabazz, civil rights leader and widow of Malcolm X, was appointed to the Evers faculty as associate professor of health sciences in 1976, and in 1985 she assumed administrative duties until her death in 1997. In 2002 the college enrolled 2,677 full-time and 2,196 part-time students.

Roff, Sandra Shoiok, Anthony M. Cucchiara, and Barbara J. Dunlap. *From the Free Academy to CUNY: Illustrating Public Higher Education in New York City, 1847–1997* (New York: Fordham Univ Press, 2000)

Barbara J. Dunlap

medical education. A colonial American who wanted to become a physician or surgeon could either serve as a doctor's apprentice, take private lessons from a doctor, or obtain formal medical education in Europe. The second medical school in the Western Hemisphere, the Medical Faculty of King's College, was founded in New York City in 1767, suspended in 1776, reopened in 1784 as the Medical School of Columbia College, reorganized in 1807 as the College of Physicians and Surgeons in the City of New York, and is now the College of Physicians and Surgeons of Columbia University.

Medical Education in Early New York State

In late 18th-century America nothing prevented doctors from running private medical schools and graduating new doctors. This enterprise was common in all major American cities. In New York City in 1787 Nicholas Romayne established a private school, which he affiliated in 1792 with Queen's College (now Rutgers University). This school closed in 1793, but Romayne remained active in medical education, mainly at the College of Physicians and Surgeons, where he was president of the medical school (1807–11). Following a quarrel with Columbia, Romayne in 1812 revived the Faculty of Physic of Queen's College at 204 Duane St, Manhattan, but it lasted only until 1816. Other rivals to Columbia emerged. David Hosack, after several failed attempts to place himself in the vanguard of medical teaching in New York City, spent $20,000 of his own money in 1826 to establish a regular medical school at 68 Duane St, loosely under the auspices of Rutgers College of New Jersey, which would grant the degree. But his political enemies at Columbia secured passage of a law in 1827 denying his graduates the right to practice medicine in New York State because their degrees were granted in New York by an out-of-state institution. Hosack then asked his friend, Bishop John Henry Hobart, founder of Geneva College (now Hobart and William Smith Colleges), to reaffiliate the school within New York State. Hobart quickly created the Rutgers Medical Faculty of Geneva College, which trained physicians at Duane St until the New York State Supreme Court closed it in 1830 on the grounds that Geneva College had no right to maintain a medical school off-site. Hosack thus paved the way for the permanent, on-site medical school that Edward Cutbush created at Geneva College in 1834. The New York County Medical Society, dominated by Hosack's enemies, founded the New York School of Medicine in 1831, but dissolved it in 1833. The University of New York Medical Department, founded in 1841, merged in 1898 with Bellevue Hospital Medical College, founded in 1861, to form the University and Bellevue Hospital Medical College, which became the New York University College of Medicine in 1935 and the New York University School of Medicine in 1960.

The first formal medical education outside of New York City was offered by Fairfield Academy (Herkimer Co) in 1809. The College of Physicians and Surgeons of the Western District of the State of New York, replacing the medical school of Fairfield Academy, was incorporated on 12 June 1812. Before it dissolved in 1841, it graduated a disproportionate number of eminent physicians for its size and location, including Charles Brodhead Coventry, Nathan Smith Davis, Asa Gray, Frank Hastings Hamilton, and Frederick Hyde. In the early 19th century, small, unregulated proprietary medical schools flourished nationwide, teaching all varieties of medicine. With the Erie Canal creating one of the most transient, prosperous, and rapidly growing populations in the world at that time, Central and Western New York was a hotbed of such activity. Usually these schools were short-lived, but one that enjoyed moderate success was Auburn Medical School (Cayuga Co), which existed from 1824 to 1839. One proximate cause of the demise of medical education in Fairfield and Auburn was the founding of Geneva Medical College. Regular, or allopathic, medical education was further enhanced when Alden March and James Armsby founded Albany Medical College (1839), and Millard Fillmore and Austin Flint Sr founded the Department of Medicine at the University of Buffalo (1846). In 1849 Geneva graduated Elizabeth Blackwell, the world's first woman to earn a regular medical degree.

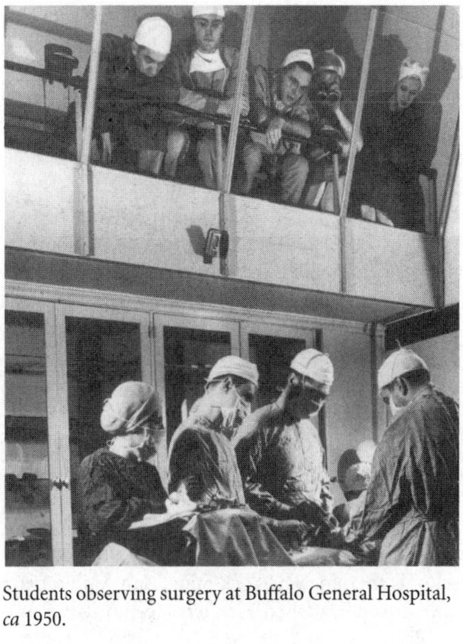

Students observing surgery at Buffalo General Hospital, *ca* 1950.

Late 19th-Century Developments

In 1850 a high-minded group of Manhattan physicians founded the New York Medical College to actualize the ideals of medical education promoted by the American Medical Association (AMA), which had been founded three years earlier. Although it attracted students and created several innovations in accordance with AMA principles, the school never won the respect of physicians; the hostility of the medical community forced it to close in 1864. In 19th-century America, women were admitted more often to homeopathic, eclectic, botanic, or other "irregular" medical schools than to those approved by the state medical societies and the AMA. An 1853 MD graduate of the eclectic Syracuse Medical College, Clemence Sophia Lozier, founded the predominantly homeopathic New York Medical College and Hospital for Women (NYMCHW) in 1863. It graduated many prominent women physicians, including the first African American woman physician in New York State, Susan McKinney-Steward, in 1870. A group including William Cullen Bryant founded the New York Homeopathic Medical College (NYHMC) in 1860 in Manhattan. It absorbed NYMCHW in 1918 and evolved into the New York Medical College in Valhalla (Westchester Co). In 1865 Elizabeth and Emily Blackwell obtained a charter for the Woman's Medical College of the New York Infirmary for Women and Children. Under Emily Blackwell's administration, it ran a medical school for women from 1868 to 1899. She closed the school only after she was convinced that Cornell University Medical College would give equal training to both sexes and after she had arranged for all her students to transfer to Cornell.

Medical Curriculum: The Flexner and Weiskotten Reports

Typical American requirements for the MD degree in the first half of the 19th century were three years of study with a "reputable practitioner" in a tutor-to-preceptor or apprentice-to-master relationship, two semesters of lectures, successful examinations, and a written thesis. To matriculate, a candidate only had to demonstrate proficiency in Latin, English, and natural science, and to be of good character. A bachelor's degree was not necessary. In the 1870s the idea gained acceptance that medical colleges should admit students according to common academic criteria, usually a bachelor's degree, and that all students should pass the same fundamental medical curriculum. The three-year graded curriculum became standard, and the thesis requirement was abolished. Early in the 20th century the ideal American medical school had a four-year graded curriculum, intensive laboratory instruction in the first two years, broad clinical training in the last two years, and affiliation with a large urban hospital or medical center. To ensure that medical schools met these new standards, the Carnegie Foundation, with the cooperation of the AMA and the Association of American Medical Colleges, hired Abraham Flexner in 1908 to visit all medical schools in the United States and Canada. The Flexner Report (1910) resulted in the demise of about half the medical schools surveyed. Of the 11 medical schools then in New York State, only Columbia and Cornell satisfied Flexner. He thought that Syracuse Medical College and New York University could survive. He wanted to abolish Albany, Buffalo, Long Island College Hospital Medical School, NYHMC, NYMCHW, the Eclectic Medical College of the City of New York (1866–1913), and the Fordham University School of Medicine (1905–21), but only the last two succumbed. In 1934 the AMA Council on Medical Education and Hospitals appointed Herman Gates Weiskotten, dean of the Syracuse University School of Medicine (1922–51), to design and direct a new national medical school survey, a second Flexner Report. The Weiskotten team approved all 9 schools in New York State but found about 20 of the 89 American and Canadian schools below accepted standards, placed some on probation, and required others to make specific adjustments.

The Turn of the Millennium

In early 21st century there were 12 medical schools in New York State: Albany Medical College of Union University (1839); Albert Einstein College of Medicine of Yeshiva University (1955); Columbia University College of Physicians and Surgeons (1767); Mount Sinai School of Medicine of the City University of New York (1968); New York Medical College, Valhalla (1860); New York University School of Medicine (1841); SUNY Buffalo School of Medicine and Biomedical Sciences (1846); SUNY Stony Brook School of Medicine (1971); SUNY Downstate College of Medicine (1858); SUNY Upstate Medical University College of Medicine (1834); University of Rochester School of Medicine and Dentistry (1920); and Weill Medical College of Cornell University, New York City (1898).

See also Alternative medicine.

Beebe, Richard T. *Albany Medical College and Albany Hospital: A History, 1839–1982* (Albany: Miss Marion Van Benthuysen Fund of Albany Medical Center, 1983)

Ludmerer, Kenneth M. *Time to Heal: American Medical Education from the Turn of the Century to the Era of Managed Care* (New York: Oxford Univ Press, 1999)

Spiegel, Allen D. "New York Medical College: An Early Center of Excellence in American Medical Education," *Journal of Community Health* 18 (Oct 1993): 293–315

Stookey, Byron Polk. *A History of Colonial Medical Education in the Province of New York, with Its Subsequent Development, 1767–1830* (Springfield, Ill: Charles C. Thomas, 1962)

Wershub, Leonard Paul. *One Hundred Years of Medical Progress: A History of the New York Medical College, Flower and Fifth Avenue Hospitals* (Springfield, Ill: Charles C. Thomas, 1967)

Eric v. d. Luft

Medical Society of the State of New York. Not-for-profit, principal professional organization for physicians. The Weekly Society of Gentlemen, an informal group meeting in New York City to discuss medicine, formed the short-lived Medical Society of the State of New York (MSSNY) in 1794. County-level societies formed in the following years. On 4 Apr 1806 MSSNY was reorganized, joining county societies under one name, and first met in Albany in 1807. In 1823 MSSNY adopted the first code of medical ethics in the country. Members John McCall and Nathan Smith Davis drew on their experiences with the state society to advocate for a national medical organization during the 1830s and 1840s; the American Medical Association first convened at New York University in May 1846. A splinter group, the New York State Medical Association, organized in 1884 to protest a new code of ethics adopted by MSSNY, but the two groups reunited in 1905.

MSSNY has 44 committees and panels within 8 major departments and divisions addressing such issues as communications, governmental affairs, information technology, public health and education, and sociomedical economics. In 1999 MSSNY approved a collective bargaining unit for negotiations between physicians and managed care organizations. In the early 21st century, MSSNY lobbied on healthcare issues, regulated medical education, offered physician education programs, and provided public health research and education.

Ische, John P. "Chronology of the History of Medicine in New York State," *New York State Journal of Medicine* 57 (1 Feb 1957): 620–36

Walsh, James Joseph. *History of Medicine in New York State* (New York: National Americana Society, 1919)

Kathy Ray

Medina [MUH-DYE-NA]. Village (pop 6,415) in Ridgeway and Shelby (Orleans Co). Platted in 1824, the village was incorporated in 1832. The Erie Canal came through in 1824, and in 1836 the wood-railed Medina and Darien Railroad was built to Akron (Erie Co) but was given up after about four years. The village was later served by the Niagara Falls Branch of the New York Central (1852). The waterpower of Oak Orchard Creek powered gristmills, barrel manufactories, and foundries. Other industries included Bignall Manufacturing Co (1862; iron and brass pumps), Medina Manufacturing Co (1873; wood pumps), and Ives and Hubbard Pail Co (1875; paper pails). In addition to the goods from the numerous food-processing plants such as H. J. Heinz Co, 20th-century village products included chemicals, furniture, firefighting equipment, and shirts. Fisher-Price manufactured toys in the village from 1970 to 1995. Early 21st-century employers include BMP American (textiles for electronics), American Sigma (electronics), Acme Manufacturing (metal goods), Bernz-O-Matic (torches), and Medina Cold Storage.

Melville. Locality (pop 14,533) in Huntington (Suffolk Co). Although it had a post office in 1852–53 and from 1876 to 1906, Melville remained rural until after the Long Island Expressway reached Rte 110 in 1962. It was the site of several institutions, including St. Rose's Industrial School for Girls (1907) and the Suffolk State School (1965–93). A 1950 attempt at incorporation was unsuccessful. The town's 1961 master plan projected offices along Rte 110, and in 2003 it was an important business address, the site of *Newsday* and Estée Lauder, among many others.

Robert C. Hughes

Melville, Herman (*b* New York City, 1 Aug 1819; *d* New York City, 28 Sept 1891). Author. The grandson of two heroes of the American Revolution, Melville spent his childhood in New York City and then in the Albany area, where his family fled to escape creditors. He studied at the Albany Academy and the Albany Classical School. But when his once prosperous father died in

1832, leaving a large family in poverty, Melville was obliged to find whatever temporary employment he could, clerking in his brother Gansevoort's Albany store, working the fields on his uncle Thomas's farm near Pittsfield, Mass, and teaching school nearby. In May 1838 poverty forced the family to move up the Hudson River to Lansingburgh (Rensselaer Co), where Herman studied surveying and engineering at Lansingburgh Academy in an unsuccessful effort to find work on the Erie Canal. Following a period of sporadic and transient employment, he signed on the whaling ship *Acushnet,* bound for the Pacific, in the last days of 1840. The cruise was unprofitable and unpleasant, leading Melville and a shipmate, Richard Tobias Greene, to desert at Nuku Hiva in the Marquesas Islands on 9 July 1842. They took refuge with the Taipi people, who, despite their reputation as cannibals, welcomed the two. Shortly, Greene left to seek medical aid for an infection Melville had developed and failed to return. On 9 August, Melville shipped aboard an Australian whaler, the dilapidated and poorly officered *Lucy Ann.* In Tahiti the crew refused duty, and after an easygoing confinement ashore, Melville signed aboard a passing whaler. He arrived in the Sandwich Islands [now Hawaiian Islands] in May 1843, and three months later enlisted aboard a US Navy frigate headed for Boston.

At home in Lansingburgh he wrote a novel about his experiences with the Taipi. The exotic and successful *Typee* (1846) established his reputation as a novelist of the sea. Newly arrived in the nation's literary forefront, Melville wrote of his *Lucy Ann* experiences in *Omoo* (1847), which was also well received. On 4 Aug 1847 he married Elizabeth Shaw, daughter of the chief justice of the Massachusetts supreme court. Melville's more ambitious third novel, *Mardi* (1849), which looks forward to his mature work, disappointed readers with its obscure metaphysics. *Redburn* (1849) and *White-Jacket* (1850) mollified his readers without challenging them. In 1850 he moved to Pittsfield, where he met Nathaniel Hawthorne and bought a farm. After two years of work, Melville completed his masterpiece, *Moby-Dick* (1851), which opens with its narrator, Ishmael, in the "insular city of the Manhattoes." Despite the novel's consummate achievement, the reception of the great whaling story fell far short of what it deserved. Melville then wrote short stories, some set in New York State. "Bartleby, the Scrivener," a meditation on the dehumanizing nature of the 19th-century corporate workplace, ranks among the most enduring stories in American literature. Melville also produced three more poorly received novels: *Pierre* (1852), largely set in New York City, a domestic tragedy with hints of incest; *Israel Potter* (1855), a bleak story of the American Revolution; and *The Confidence-Man* (1857), an opaque narrative in which the victim of the confidence game may be the reader.

Herman Melville. Photograph by Rodney H. Dewey, 1861.

In 1863, at the height of the Civil War, Melville moved from Pittsfield to New York City, and from there made a visit to the front, riding out into guerrilla country with a cavalry patrol. In late April 1864 he traveled on to the camps of the army of the Potomac in Culpepper, Va, where he visited Gen Ulysses S. Grant on the eve of Grant's crucial spring offensive. Based partially on these experiences he wrote a book of war poems, *Battle-Pieces and Aspects of the War* (1866), which probably helped him obtain an appointment that year in the New York Customs House. With that Melville all but disappeared as a literary figure. He published *Clarel* (1876) at his own cost, a long religious poem inspired by his visit to Palestine in 1857, but it was little noticed. In 1867 he lost a son, probably by suicide. Then his mother died, followed by his closest uncle, both of his remaining brothers, and two of his four sisters, so that when he retired late in 1885, most of his family was gone. But with his new leisure, he returned to serious writing, publishing (in small numbers and at his own expense) two books of poetry, *John Marr* (1888) and *Timoleon* (1891). At his death he left two more books in manuscript, *Weeds and Wildings,* a poetic tribute to his wife, and *Billy Budd,* a masterpiece of a short novel. But his passing was little noticed, and it was not until the 1920s that he was rediscovered and, over time, recognized by many readers as a great author.

Garner, Stanton. *The Civil War World of Herman Melville* (Lawrence: Univ Press of Kansas, 1993)
Howard, Leon. *Herman Melville: A Biography* (Berkeley: Univ of California Press, 1951)
Parker, Hershel. *Herman Melville: A Biography,* 2 vols (Baltimore: Johns Hopkins Univ Press, 1996–2002)

Stanton Garner

member items. Legislative appropriations for local projects. Member items emerged in the last quarter of the 20th century as a state-funded pork barrel system for financing popular local projects or organizations. Each house of the state legislature allotted a certain portion of the state budget to individual legislators for use in their local districts. Funded projects ranged from well-managed senior citizen centers and health clinics to less essential items such as Little League uniforms and, infamously in the 1980s, a cheese museum in Rome (Oneida Co). The governor and legislative leaders doled out these projects to win rank-and-file support for the overall budget. Almost all funds were allocated to each house's majority party members to ensure continued control. Although the amounts were less than 1% of the overall state budget, or $550 million out of $90,000 million in 2002–3, the direct personal connection between legislators and local constituents was politically valuable to incumbents.

Rosen, Hy, and Peter Slocum. *From Rocky to Pataki: Character and Caricatures in New York Politics* (Syracuse: Syracuse Univ Press, 1998)

Peter Slocum

Memorial Art Gallery of the University of Rochester. Located at 500 University Ave in Rochester, the gallery represents an unusual combination of university art museum and community art center. In 1904 the university's president, Rush Rhees, developed an expansion plan that included an art gallery. Eight years later he persuaded local art collector Emily Sibley Watson to memorialize her son, architect James G. Averell, by funding construction. Rhees and Watson picked George Herdle, president of the Rochester Art Club and a painter known for assembling remarkable modern exhibitions, as the gallery's first director. At his untimely death in 1922, Herdle was succeeded by his daughter Gertrude Herdle Moore, who would occupy the post for the next 40 years. Built in classical Renaissance style in 1913, the gallery grew from 14,000 feet^2 (1,300 m^2) to 125,500 feet^2 (11,660 m^2) through a series of expansions in 1926, 1968, and 1985–87. The collection comprises some 11,000 objects. The holdings cover a historical and geographical range from ancient Egypt to contemporary America and are especially strong in American art; contemporary crafts, particularly by Western New York artists; medieval European sculpture; 17th-century Dutch and 19th-century French painting; and 18th-century British portraiture. Works of note include John Sloan's *Election Night at Herald Square* and Everett Shinn's *Sullivan Street.* About half the objects are works on paper. The Creative Workshop, the gallery's community art school, offers classes in various artistic media, art history, and computer graphics to over 4,000 children and adults annually. The research collections and archives of the gallery's Charlotte Whitney Allen Library are open to the public. In the early years of the 21st century, the gallery has an annual attendance of 300,000 and over 10,000 members. Over 1,200 volunteers, including 120 docents, assist a staff of some 40 full-time employees.

Brayer, Elizabeth. *Magnum Opus: The Story of the Memorial Art Gallery* (Rochester: Memorial Art Gallery of the Univ of Rochester, 1988)
Peters, Susan Dodge, ed. *Memorial Art Gallery: An Introduction to the Collection* (Rochester: Univ of Rochester in association with Hudson Hills Press, 1988)

Elizabeth Brayer

Memorial Day. An official US holiday honoring military personnel who have died protecting the nation. Henry C. Welles, a Waterloo (Seneca Co) druggist, is attributed with first suggesting the idea in 1865, and Gen John B. Murray, the Seneca Co clerk, is accredited with organizing the first formal ceremony in Waterloo on 5 May 1866. Two years later on the day, Maj Gen John A. Logan, commander of the Grand Army of the Republic, an organization of Union veterans, proclaimed 30 May as a day of remembrance, which became known as Decoration Day. The first national observance was held on 30 May 1868 at Arlington National Cemetery, where flowers were placed on soldiers' graves. Initially established to honor Northern troops killed during the Civil War, the holiday was not recognized by Southern states until after World War I, when it was expanded to honor US casualties of all wars. A 1966 presidential proclamation recognized Waterloo as the official birthplace of Memorial Day. In 1968 Congress passed a bill (enacted in 1971) declaring Memorial Day a federal holiday to be commemorated on the last Monday of every May.

Memorial Day, http://usmemorialday.org

Bernadette Zbicki Heiney

Menands. Village (pop 4,646) in Colonie (Albany Co). The Erie Canal (1823) passed through alluvial flats where French immigrant Louis Menand (1807–1900) established a commercial horticultural business in 1842. The village became a stop on the Albany Northern Railroad (1853; later Delaware and Hudson) and later on an interurban trolley system, making it convenient for estates of wealthy Albany businessmen. Albany interests also established businesses such as the Albany Felt Co (1905), International Harvester, and Montgomery Ward Co (1929). Menands was incorporated in 1924 to prevent Albany from possibly annexing it. The Menands Regional Market, with 300 farmers' stalls and 100 buyers' stalls, opened in 1934. Menands Heights (now Dutch Village Apartments), opened in 1940, are thought to have been the first garden apartments in upstate New York. In the early 21st century Menands remains a popular Albany suburb and is home to a number of industrial facilities, including Albany Steel, Morgan Linen Co, and Simmons Machine Tool Corp.

Wesley G. Balla

Mendon. Town (pop 8,370) in SE Monroe Co. Settled in 1791, the town was formed in 1812 from Bloomfield (Ontario Co). Mendon's glacial landscape, consisting of drumlins, kames, eskers, and kettles, is distinctive, with some preserved in Mendon Ponds Park (1928). In the early 19th century it was a region of wheat growing and small industry, including chair factories. Mendon's best-known furniture maker was Brigham Young, who lived in Mendon from 1829 to 1833, during which time he joined the Mormon Church. Other industries included carding machines and agricultural implements, Rudolph Tischner's ocarina factory (1880–1921), and Searjeant Metal Products (1949–68). Though Mendon had little or no industry in 2002, it has become a thriving and comfortable Rochester suburb. Large-scale development started in 1969. One-third of its land area was classified agricultural in the 2000 census, and the town intends to maintain this distribution through a variety of strategies.

Carolyn Vacca

Mennonites. See ANABAPTISTS.

mental health care. In 1665 James, Duke of York, proprietor of the Colony of New York, decreed that the cost of caring for "distracted persons" should not be borne by the individual towns where these people lived but by all the towns in that "rideing," or district. One hundred years before the American Revolution, New Yorkers were already dealing with two issues that have concerned them ever since: the need to care for people with severe mental problems and the question of who should take responsibility for that care. The history of mental health treatment in New York State can be divided into three phases. From the colonial period to the Civil War, if families could not care for their mentally ill members, local governments took responsibility for them. From the mid–19th century to the mid-20th, the state played the leading role. In the current phase, which began in the 1950s, responsibility has shifted back to the local level, although with extensive support from the state and some from the federal government.

Care Close to Home: Colonial Times to the Civil War

Because colonial New Yorkers generally thought of mental disability as an affliction from God rather than as a disease, they placed little emphasis on trying to cure it or identify its different forms. Dependent "lunatics" who had no relatives to care for them were generally boarded out at public expense with local families or placed in the poorhouse. But most mentally ill people had some kind of family support, and they were generally able to make a place for themselves in the community, even if they were quite disabled. Newcomers with mental problems might well be driven out of town, and dangerous individuals might be kept locked up, but colonial New Yorkers tolerated a fair level of mental dysfunction from their own neighbors. This social pattern began to change during the early 19th century. As rising immigration increased New York State's population, particularly in the cities, and as the expansion of roads, railroads, and canals fostered greater mobility, families dispersed and many more Americans found themselves living among strangers. Under these conditions the old informal acceptance of mental disability among longtime neighbors declined, and increasing numbers of mentally ill people were placed in county almshouses—spartan and overcrowded facilities whose one special provision was generally a caged area in the cellar for the most disturbed inmates. The only major institution in the state designed specifically for the mentally ill, New York Hospital's Bloomingdale facility in New York City (1821), was well regarded, but its services were generally limited to those who could pay for their care. Three localities in the state established public facilities specifically for the mentally ill: New York City in 1839, Kings Co in 1852, and Monroe Co in 1863.

Creating separate facilities did little to improve their quality. In New York, as in many other states, the wretched care provided to the mentally ill caused growing comment from the 1820s on; Charles Dickens, who visited the New York City asylum on Blackwell's Island [now Roosevelt Island] in 1842, was just one of many to express shock and outrage. A compelling alternative began to emerge in the 1790s, when French physician Philippe Pinel developed a new therapeutic approach to mental illness, called "moral treatment." At the same time, the English Quaker William Tuke created a retreat for the mentally ill that blended education, physical exercise, rehabilitative work, religious training, and kind personal relations. Offering for the first time the hope of actually curing mental illness, the ideas of Pinel and Tuke energized US reformers. In 1833 Massachusetts opened the first public asylum in the country based on moral treatment, and three years later the state legislature in New York approved the construction of the New York State Lunatic Asylum (now Mohawk Valley Psychiatric Center), to be built in Utica. When the facility opened in 1843, counties were instructed to send their most curable patients there. The facility was soon deluged, however, and in 1850 it was announced that patients who had been hospitalized for more than a year would not be accepted. This left the local almshouses nearly as crowded as before, particularly when Utica began sending back to them anyone who required more than a year of treatment. By 1854 Utica was serving fewer than 300 of New York State's more than 2,400 "pauper lunatics," and county superintendents were begging the state to open a facility for chronic patients. Their pleas acquired more force when Sylvester Willard, secretary of the state's Medical Society, was commissioned by the legislature to review conditions in the county facilities. His devastating report, released in 1865, convinced many readers that the task of caring for the mentally ill had to be taken out of local hands.

The State Takes Charge: The 1860s to the 1950s

The 1869 opening of Willard Asylum for the Insane in the Town of Ovid (Seneca Co) represented the formal beginning of state leadership, as every county in the state was instructed to send its long-term mental patients to Willard. However, the facility filled up so rapidly that in less than two years counties were again allowed the option of caring for their own mentally ill. The state's growing role in mental health services was also reflected in the appointment of a state commissioner in lunacy in 1873, to be replaced by a three-member commission in 1889, and in the opening of four more state asylums, in Poughkeepsie, Middletown (Orange Co), Buffalo, and Binghamton. But since most of their admissions were new patients, taken straight from the community, the county facilities remained as crowded as ever. By 1890 there were still roughly 1,500 mental patients in local almshouses, about the same number as in 1865—and living under similarly squalid conditions.

This situation led to the passage of the State Care Act of 1890. Under the new law, counties were again ordered to transfer all their mentally ill patients to state institutions. The only facilities excepted, the county asylums in Manhattan, Brooklyn, and Rochester, were taken over by the state within a few years. To make space for the county patients, all state facilities for the mentally ill were required to accept chronic as well as acute cases, and a seventh facility was opened in St. Lawrence Co. In addition the state established the Board of Alienists, which over the next 30 years arranged the deportation of about 15,000 state mental patients who were not US citizens. The state takeover of mental health services in New York—the first in the nation—coincided with a change in clinical thinking about mental illness. Most mental hospitals were far too large and too crowded to provide the intensive programs and personalized attention called for in moral treatment. In any case, the rise of scientific medicine between 1890 and 1920 inclined researchers to look for medical rather than environmental explanations for mental illness.

Psychiatrists too were eager to identify their field with the ongoing successes of medical science: state "asylums" became "hospitals" in 1890, and the Commission in Lunacy became the State Hospital Commission in 1912.

Meanwhile other perspectives on mental illness were also gaining ground. The writings of Sigmund Freud crossed the Atlantic soon after 1900, and although relatively few New Yorkers actually underwent psychoanalysis, Freud's insights about sexuality, the role of the unconscious, and the significance of early childhood experience affected the practice of many therapists. The popularization of these ideas during the 1920s significantly influenced American beliefs about the sources of mental illness. Another powerful set of ideas emerged when a former mental patient, Clifford Beers, introduced the concept of mental hygiene, which, like the later term mental health, emphasized patients' strengths rather than their disabilities. The National Committee for Mental Hygiene, founded by Beers and others in 1909 and based in New York City from 1912, made a systematic, widely publicized case for community-based prevention and early intervention as an alternative to long-term hospitalization. These efforts led to the creation of New York State's first local mental health clinics, whose services included pioneering work in the treatment of children. The movement founded by Beers also represents an early example of activism by consumers of mental health care, a trend that would play an increasingly important role in the years ahead.

However, neither the mental hygiene movement nor Freud's ideas had much influence on actual practice in the state's mental hospitals. The patient population continued to climb, rising from about 30,000 in 1909 to more than 93,000 in 1954. Staffing and funding were generally very tight, and most care was custodial at best. Although other states were experiencing similar problems, New York's situation was particularly dramatic because it had America's largest state hospital system, accounting for one-fifth of all institutionalized patients in the country. Starting in the 1920s state facilities did make more use of occupational therapy, which utilizes purposeful activity to reduce emotional stress, build patients' self-esteem, and enhance their capacity to care for themselves. Most of the treatments introduced during this period, however, were medical interventions: fever therapy, insulin and Metrazol shock, electroshock, and prefrontal lobotomies. Despite the serious side effects and inconclusive evidence of the effectiveness of these treatments, many thousands of New Yorkers in both public and private facilities were subjected to them.

Two developments helped produce a change in mental hospital practice. First, a wave of exposés shortly after World War II publicized the wretched condition of state hospitals; these included a widely read photo-essay in *Life* magazine (1946), Mary Jane Ward's novel *The Snake Pit* (1946) and the movie based on it (1948), and *The Shame of the States* (1948) by the journalist Albert Deutsch, who devoted four chapters to facilities in New York State. The mounting publicity given the grim, overcrowded facilities and the inadequate or even abusive care encouraged reformers and public officials to seek an alternative to large-scale institutional treatment. Second, a new family of drugs, the phenothiazines, appeared on the scene in the mid-1950s. These, along with many other psychotropic medications developed in the years that followed, proved strikingly effective in reducing the most crippling symptoms of mental illness. For the first time it appeared possible that most mental patients could be treated in the community. The landmark New York State Community Mental Health Services Act, passed in 1954, offered state funds to help local governments bring the revolution about.

Back to Care in the Community: the 1950s to the Present

Perhaps the best way to understand the challenges faced by mental health care in New York State from the 1950s on is to compare the momentum of deinstitutionalization, or the discharge of patients from the state's mental hospitals, with progress in community treatment, the pattern of care expected to replace hospitalization. In the early 21st century, it is clear that the former has been implemented in New York State much more thoroughly than the latter. Deinstitutionalization itself consisted of two processes. Annual discharges from New York's state facilities for treating mental illness and alcoholism rose from an average of about 10,000 per year in the early 1950s to a peak of 42,000 in 1968, and then leveled off at more than 30,000 per year for the next two decades. Meanwhile, as admission criteria were tightened, annual admissions fell from about 38,000 in 1970 to 15,500 in 1997. The combined effect of these trends was a drop in the patient population from an all-time high of 93,000 in 1955 to just over 8,000 in 1997, a level last seen in the 1890s.

Community treatment received an important boost when the federal Community Mental Health Centers Construction Act of 1963 made extensive federal funding available for the first time for local mental health services. Two years later legislation creating Medicare and Medicaid committed the federal government to subsidizing approximately half the cost of most medical care, including mental health services, for the poor, elderly, and disabled. These huge programs, along with a variety of state funding arrangements and the growing willingness of health insurers to cover mental health care, produced an array of community-based services in New York State, including clinics, support groups, day hospitals, child guidance programs, and psychiatric units in general hospitals. Although Medicaid paid for extended institutional care, most community services were primarily designed to treat moderately troubled people who were already living in the community; they did relatively little for the thousands of severely disabled patients being discharged from state hospitals.

Living arrangements for discharged patients presented additional problems. Periodic exposés revealed that many former state hospital patients, particularly in the New York City area, were living in squalid, for-profit adult homes and nursing homes that offered poor physical care and no mental health support. While the state Office of Mental Health (est 1977) did not operate or supervise these facilities, it attracted bitter criticism for continuing to place patients in them. Meanwhile other discharged patients, especially in larger cities, cycled among homeless shelters, jails, and the streets, sharing their bleak circumstances with troubled people who had never been hospitalized but who in an earlier era probably would have been. The Office of Mental Health responded to these problems by encouraging more local services for severely disabled patients, initiating its own programs for the underserved groups and seeking better coordination of state and local efforts. Solutions were made more difficult, though, by a retrenchment in social spending by the federal government that included significant cuts in mental health funding, the courts' insistence on the right of the mentally ill to refuse treatment, and the reluctance of many communities to accept as neighbors people with severe mental disabilities. At the same time, the promised financial savings from deinstitutionalization were diminished by the need to improve the quality of care in state hospitals. In addition, labor unions and community leaders exerted political pressure that kept state psychiatric centers in rural areas open for many years despite their sharply declining patient populations.

At the start of the 21st century, New Yorkers are once again receiving most of their mental health

TRENDS IN INPATIENT POPULATION (1869–1997)

Year	Census	Admissions	Discharges
1869	745	605	366
1889	5,201	1,739	1,141
1909	29,363	6,625	3,246
1929	45,319	10,750	4,605
1950	82,906	20,902	10,575
1955	93,314	21,459	9,554
1960	88,768	26,773	16,819
1965	84,859	33,254	23,674
1970	64,384	37,986	38,190
1975	35,222	33,879	35,147
1980	25,531	31,592	31,897
1985	22,929	32,563	31,871
1990	17,183	30,822	31,957
1995	10,574	21,179	22,162
1997	8,308	15,522	16,483

Source: NYS Office of Mental Health.

Note: Numbers include mental health and alcoholism services.

care in their own communities, just as they did 200 years earlier. A host of new treatments and medications have replaced moral therapy, the state government has a recognized, if sometimes contested, role in local services, and there is a vastly expanded array of programs for the moderately disabled. But two key issues continue to concern New Yorkers, as they did in 1665: the need to care for people with severe mental problems, and the question of who should take responsibility for that care.

Deutsch, Albert. *The Shame of the States* (New York: Harcourt, Brace, 1948)
Dowdall, George W. *The Eclipse of the State Mental Hospital: Policy, Stigma, and Organization* (Albany: SUNY Press, 1996)
Dwyer, Ellen. *Homes for the Mad: Life Inside Two Nineteenth-Century Asylums* (New Brunswick, NJ: Rutgers Univ Press, 1987)
Gamwell, Lynn, and Nancy Tomes. *Madness in America: Cultural and Medical Perceptions of Mental Illness before 1914* (Ithaca: Cornell Univ Press, 1995)
Grob, Gerald. *The Mad among Us: A History of the Care of America's Mentally Ill* (New York: Free Press, 1994)
Hurd, Henry M. *The Institutional Care of the Insane in the United States and Canada,* vol 3 (1916; repr New York: Arno Press, 1973)
Malzberg, Benjamin. *Mental Disease in New York State, 1910–1960: A Study of Incidence* (Albany: Research Foundation for Mental Hygiene, 1967)

Sandra Opdycke

Mental Hygiene, Department of. State agency serving people with mental illness, developmental disabilities, and substance abuse problems. New York State assumed responsibility for the care of people deemed insane or feeble minded during the antebellum period. Although the vast majority either remained at home or were placed in local almshouses or jails, a select few thought likely to benefit from intensive intervention gained admission to the State Lunatic Asylum (now Mohawk Valley Psychiatric Center) in Utica, which opened in 1843, and the State Asylum for Idiots in Syracuse, which opened in 1855.

After the Civil War, mounting public concern led the state to build new custodial facilities for the insane and to regulate almshouses and other institutions for dependent people. These trends gave rise to the State Commission in Lunacy (1873), a powerful policy-making body, and the State Care Act (1890), which made the state exclusively responsible for the care of the insane. These changes, intended to promote active treatment, spawned an ever growing system of custodial care. In 1896 the State Commission in Lunacy (renamed the State Hospital Commission in 1912) presided over 12 state hospitals that housed 19,500 patients. By 1921 the number of patients had increased to 41,000 and the number of hospitals to 14.

The state's care of the feeble minded (a group that included people with developmental disabilities, cerebral palsy, and severe epilepsy, and, in some instances, unruly children and adolescents) became increasingly custodial. Four additional state schools were established between 1886 and 1908, and in 1918 the State Commission on the Feeble Minded (renamed State Commission for Mental Defectives in 1919) was created to administer these institutions. The schools initially emphasized preparation for independent or semi-independent living; social and economic pressures, however, gradually made them into custodial facilities where students spent their entire lives.

In 1926 the newly created Department of Mental Hygiene replaced the State Hospital Commission and the State Commission for Mental Defectives, but the situation did not fundamentally change. The number of state hospitals gradually grew to 20, the state schools to 7, and the patient population swelled. In 1955, when the number of people housed in department-run institutions peaked at almost 113,000, the number of psychiatric inpatients per capita was far higher in New York than in any other state, and the department's operations accounted for approximately one-third of the state's annual budget.

These circumstances helped to propel passage of the landmark Community Mental Health Services Act (1954), which encouraged the establishment of local outpatient psychiatric programs. However, the decline of state custodial institutions, which began in earnest in the 1960s, was less the result of conscious planning than of changing social attitudes, new federal benefits for the elderly and the disabled, and legal challenges concerning the rights of people with disabilities and the state's obligation to provide adequate care. Even though the number of inpatients in state hospitals declined by more than 60% between 1955 and 1975, the department continued to focus on providing long-term psychiatric care.

In 1977 concern that it was not devoting enough attention to people with developmental disabilities or substance abuse problems (a pop-

NEW YORK STATE PSYCHIATRIC FACILITIES

Facility	County	Type	Opened
Binghamton	Broome	Adult	1881
Bronx	Bronx	Adult	1963
Bronx Children's	Bronx	Pediatric	1969
Brooklyn Children's	Kings	Pediatric	1996
Buffalo	Erie	Adult	1880
Capital District	Albany	Adult	1975
Central Islip[a]	Suffolk	Adult	1896
Central New York	Oneida	Forensic	1977
Creedmoor	Queens	Adult	1912
Elmira	Chemung	Adult	1973
Gowanda[b]	Erie	Adult	1898
Harlem Valley[b]	Dutchess	Adult	1924
Hudson River	Dutchess	Adult	1871
Hutchings	Onondaga	Adult	1973
Kings Park[c]	Suffolk	Adult	1896
Kingsboro[d]	Kings	Adult	1895
Kirby Forensic	New York	Forensic	1985
Manhattan Children's[e]	New York	Pediatric	1970
Manhattan[d]	New York	Adult	1902
Marcy[f]	Oneida	Adult	1935
Mid-Hudson Forensic	Orange	Forensic	1973
Middletown	Orange	Adult	1874
Nathan S. Kline Institute	Rockland	Research	1952
New York State Psychiatric Institute[g]	New York	Research	1895
Pilgrim	Suffolk	Adult	1931
Queens Children's	Queens	Pediatric	1970
Rochester[d]	Monroe	Adult/Forensic[h]	1891
Rockland	Rockland	Adult	1931
Rockland Children's	Rockland	Pediatric	1970
Sagamore Children's	Suffolk	Pediatric	1969
South Beach	Richmond	Adult	1972
St. Lawrence	St. Lawrence	Adult	1890
Utica/Mohawk Valley[i]	Oneida	Adult	1843
Western NY Children's	Erie	Pediatric	1970
Willard[e]	Seneca	Adult	1869

Source: NYS Office of Mental Health.

[a]Closed in 1997.

[b]Closed in 1994.

[c]Closed in 1996.

[d]Previously operated as a county asylum.

[e]Closed in 1995.

[f]Became part of Mohawk Valley Psychiatric Center in 1985.

[g]Originally the Pathological Institute of the New York State Hospitals.

[h]Forensic facilities treat incarcerated patients or those admitted by court order, pursuant to a judicial finding of "incompetent to stand trial" or "not responsible by reason of mental disease or defect."

[i]New York State Lunatic Asylum, 1843–90; Utica State Hospital, 1890–1974; Utica Psychiatric Center, 1974–85; Mohawk Valley Psychiatric Center, 1985– .

ulation for which it assumed responsibility in 1966) propelled lawmakers to split the department into three autonomous divisions: the Office of Mental Health (OMH), the Office of Mental Retardation and Developmental Disabilities (OMRDD), and the Office of Alcoholism and Substance Abuse Services (OASAS). Each office helps shape and regulate a complex, decentralized array of in- and outpatient services offered by state, federal, and local governments and nonprofit organizations. In 2000 OMH and its local government and nonprofit partners provided in- and outpatient treatment, housing, and support services to 400,000 adults and 100,000 children. They also operated 17 psychiatric centers for adults and 6 for children. OMRDD and its partners provided housing, employment, educational programs, and family services to more than 120,000. OASAS employs 1,200 professional treatment specialists and 400 prevention specialists and operates 13 treatment centers throughout the state, providing assistance to 123,000 people, most on an outpatient basis.

See also DRUG ADDICTION AND TREATMENT.

Grob, Gerald N. *Mental Illness and American Society, 1875–1940* (Princeton, NJ: Princeton Univ Press, 1983)

New York State. Department of Mental Hygiene. *History of the Department of Mental Hygiene* (Albany: 1955)

Trent, James W., Jr. *Inventing the Feeble Mind: A History of Mental Retardation in the United States* (Berkeley: Univ of California Press, 1994)

Bonita L. Weddle

mental retardation and developmental disabilities. Before the mid–19th century, medical authorities in New York State, as in most of the United States, paid little attention to disabilities that originated in developmental years. Most authorities and citizens considered such childhood disabilities as idiocy and imbecility (in current usage, mental retardation), fits (epilepsy), slurred speech and a crippled gait (cerebral palsy), and some forms of lunacy (eg, autism) as sources of humor or as opportunities for Christian benevolence. They were often regarded primarily as legal problems, especially in the management of estates. Yet in the 1840s, reports from Europe began to suggest the previously unthinkable: that idiots could be educated.

New York State Asylum for Idiots

Encouraged by these reports, Frederick Backus, a physician and state senator from Rochester, chaired a legislative committee whose January 1846 report recommended that a state asylum for idiots be created. With backing from Amariah Brigham, superintendent of the New York State Lunatic Asylum, Backus in 1851 persuaded the state legislature to fund the New York State Asylum for Idiots, which was directed by Hervey B. Wilbur. Located first in Albany, the asylum moved to Syracuse in 1855. French immigrant Edward Seguin, whose writings on the education of idiots at the Parisian insane asylum Bicêtre had influenced Backus and Wilbur, visited the asylum frequently. Convinced that idiots could learn and become productive citizens, Wilbur and Seguin shifted the public discussion of intellectual disabilities from charitable and legal concerns to education. Wilbur championed the instruction of so-called simple idiots, who had neither physical disabilities nor epilepsy, and did not exhibit the destructive behavior that characterized (in the language of the day) the imbecile. All asylum residents were children of school age. They participated in a nine-month school year, usually returning home for the summers. Wilbur expected his students to complete their education, return to their communities, and secure employment.

Long before his death in 1883, however, Wilbur found that communities were hardly eager to receive asylum graduates. Educated feeble minds could not find employment, especially during economic downturns when local officials did not want idiots, however trained, to take jobs from able-minded citizens. At the same time, Wilbur was pressured to admit imbeciles who were suited neither for the prison nor the poorhouse, as well as more severely disabled inmates. Medical superintendents also found greater professional legitimacy if they stressed the pathology of their inmates over the capacity of their pupils to learn. Under these conditions, the educational focus of care for the feeble-minded began to give way to a custodial orientation.

Custodial Institutions

When Josephine Shaw Lowell founded the New York State Custodial Asylum for Feeble-Minded Women at Newark (Wayne Co) in 1878, she was beginning a process of institutional custodialism that Wilbur could not postpone. The Newark asylum and other institutions, such as Rome State Custodial Asylum (Oneida Co) and Letchworth Village in Thiells (Rockland Co), that would open in New York State over the next century were primarily custodial. The population of the state's institutions was 2,239 in 1905, a figure that grew significantly during the 20th century.

Staff at State Custodial Asylum, Rome, *ca* 1920.

The eugenics movement, at its height in the 1910s with effects lingering through the 1960s, contributed to that growth. For proponents of eugenics, controlling the breeding of inferior human beings would lead to a more efficient population and, in turn, fewer social problems; people with developmental disabilities were increasingly seen as a social menace. From 1910 to 1920, many political and charitable organizations, including the New York arm of the Committee on Provision for the Feeble-Minded, advocated building more and larger custodial institutions, restricting marriage laws, and sterilizing breeding-age "defectives." A law allowing involuntary sterilization was passed by the state legislature in 1912 but determined unconstitutional in 1918 and repealed.

A parallel development was the rise of public special education programs, first introduced in New York City in 1900. Rochester followed suit in 1906, and by the start of World War I most public school systems in the state had at least one such class. These programs multiplied after 1930 as state officials sought an alternative to residential institutions for children. The graduates of these programs were usually institutionalized as adults. Special education was intended to prepare children for this life; in these classes, pupils learned to read and do basic arithmetic and acquired skills in housework, agriculture, and handicrafts.

Changes in the family after World War II also contributed to the sustained growth of custodial institutions. The war encouraged small, mobile families, leaving postwar Americans seemingly unable to care for their disabled children. Physicians counseled families against keeping developmentally disabled children at home. Under pressure from physicians, social workers, and parents, state officials in the early 1950s began to admit toddlers and occasionally infants. By 1965 New York State's institutions had a collective population of more than 20,000.

Deinstitutionalization

With this increase in the institutional population, national voices began to question the conditions and the costs of large residential facilities. Geraldo Rivera's 1972 exposé of Willowbrook State School (Staten Island) and Letchworth Village, two of the state's largest institutions, generated support among state officials and ordinary citizens for deinstitutionalization. Federal legislation such as the Rehabilitation Act of 1973 and federal court decisions such as *Wyatt v Stickney* (1971) provided the legitimacy for change, and changes to the Medicaid program provided a financial incentive to depopulate the institutions and transfer the cost of running the facilities from the state to the federal government. Beginning in the mid-1970s, New York State shifted its policies and programs away from special education and segregated institutions to "mainstreaming" in regular schools and independent living in regular communities. In the process, education for children became more inclusive, and employment and housing for adults became more typical. By 1998 the average daily population of the residential institutions in New York State was down to 2,910. At the beginning the 21st century, most New York State citizens with developmental disabilities, adults and children, live in communities, either independently or with various levels of social and economic assistance.

See also PRISONS AND JAILS.

Ferguson, Philip M. *Abandoned to Their Fate: Social Policy and Practice toward Severely Retarded People in America, 1820–1920* (Philadelphia: Temple University Press, 1994)

Rothman, David J., and Sheila M. Rothman. *The Willowbrook Wars* (New York: Harper & Row, 1984)

Trent, James W., Jr. *Inventing the Feeble Mind: A History of Mental Retardation in the United States* (Berkeley: Univ of California Press, 1994)

James W. Trent Jr

Mentz. Town (pop 2,446) in central Cayuga Co. Settled in 1797, the town was formed from Aurelius in 1802 as Jefferson; the name was changed in 1808. The building of the Erie Canal in 1819 began a period of growth lasting until about 1850, especially at Port Byron. A woolen cloth mill opened in 1820, and a grain cradle factory opened around 1845. After the construction of the Auburn and Syracuse Railroad nearby (1838) and of the New York Central through Mentz (1853), the canal became less of an economic factor and was abandoned in 1918. The Thruway was built through town in 1954. In 2003 the principal industry was farming, and many residents commuted to nearby cities.

Michael Riley

merchants (17th century). Commercial entrepreneurs responsible for the international and regional movement of capital and goods and a driving force in the development of New Netherland and New York. Private merchant activity in New Netherland began within two years after Henry Hudson's voyage in 1609. As Amsterdam investors funded voyages to collect furs, a lively competition developed among Dutch merchants who sent their employees to the Hudson River valley to trade with the Indians. The chartering of the state-sponsored Dutch West India Co (WIC) in 1621 officially banned private trading, but Dutch merchants continued to influence the growth of New Netherland by both legally investing in the WIC and illegally circumventing WIC regulations. When the WIC abolished its fur-trading monopoly in 1640, these same private merchants eagerly pursued the colony's commercial opportunities.

In the 1640s and 1650s, New Netherland's resident merchants were a combination of representatives of Amsterdam investors (factors like Govert Loockermans and Cornelis Steenwyck, or family members like Johannes Pietersen Verbrugge and Timotheus Gabry), private traders from other American colonies (Englishmen like Isaac Allerton and Thomas Willet) or WIC employees (Oloff Stevenson van Cortlandt and Frederick Philipse I, for example). Merchants congregated in two main areas: New Amsterdam, the staple port for the entire colony, and Beverwijck [now Albany]. They sent furs from the Hudson and Delaware River valleys, along with tobacco from the Chesapeake, to markets in Holland. Fish, flour, and other "country produce" were exported to WIC colonies in Brazil and Curaçao, and a wide variety of goods were imported from the Netherlands. By the 1660s resident merchants were experiencing a commercial boom and had secured local governments in New Amsterdam and Beverwijck that protected their trade and status.

English control of the colony in 1664 did not immediately alter the flow of capital and goods. As English denizens under the surrender agreement, New York merchants continued to rely on Dutch capital and markets. English investors who entered the New York trade did so in partnership with Dutch and New York merchants. After 1674 the blending of English and Dutch capital increased and sought new opportunities in the Caribbean, exporting foodstuffs and barrel staves and importing rum, molasses, slaves, sugar, and logwood, while maintaining the tobacco and fur trade. Newly arrived merchants reflected merchant capital's ethnic and geographic combination. In 1674 Englishman Lewis Morris arrived in New York City from Barbados; Robert Livingston (1654–1728), a Presbyterian Scot, left Rotterdam for Albany in 1674; and Stephen DeLancey, a French Huguenot refugee, arrived in New York from London in 1686.

After the upheavals of Leisler's Rebellion (1689–91), New York merchants remained heavily committed to exporting foodstuffs to the Caribbean. They continued to diversify their trade by sending foodstuffs to southern Europe, purchasing furs from Canada, importing wine from Madeira off of Portugal, buying slaves in West African and Madagascan ports, and risking commerce with pirates. As the 17th century ended, New York's merchant entrepreneurs began to adjust to new conditions caused by a decline in Dutch investment, war between England and France, and a tightening English imperial system.

Maika, Dennis J. "Commerce and Community: Manhattan Merchants in the 17th Century" (PhD diss, New York Univ, 1995)

Matson, Cathy. *Merchants and Empire: Trading in Colonial New York* (Baltimore: Johns Hopkins Univ Press, 1998)

Rink, Oliver A. *Holland on the Hudson: An Economic and Social History of Dutch New York* (Ithaca: Cornell Univ Press, 1986)

Dennis J. Maika

merchants (18th century). By the close of the 17th century, New York City surpassed Boston in the number of vessel clearances, tonnage, and the value of numerous exported commodities. The city was steadily gaining preeminence over its satellite region of small producers and growing settlements. Only well into the next century would Philadelphia overtake New York in the value and volume of coastal and West Indian commodities passing through the cities. The number of both eminently successful and rising middling wholesale merchants grew from roughly 135 during the 1690s, to over 200 in the 1720s, to nearly 400 in the 1750s. Although ethnic quarrels and cultural distinctions between Dutch and English commercial families did not fade entirely as the century progressed, their most visible public and political signs often blended in mutual pursuit of new markets and goods. England's imperial domination over the Low Countries during the 18th century did not entirely quash advantageous ties of trade, credit, and banking between the colony and Amsterdam. Even as merchants shifted their attention more toward the English firms that could supply colonial needs and desires, the Dutch trade did not vanish. Indeed, merchants from all parts of European empires in the Western Hemisphere remarked about the nature of a trading community in New York City that grasped at business opportunities and risks in all known parts of the commercial world at that time. New York City merchants were instrumental in the local urban and wider regional rise as well. They welcomed the material prosperity that their ships and long-distance liaisons brought to the growing province, especially by opposing restrictions on commerce that limited importation, and they channeled their captains to widening sources of consumer goods.

In the midst of this expansion, consequential differences arose within the merchant community that reflected economic maturation as well as imperial and urban social tensions. Merchants of outstanding fortune rose to the top of the city's social scale by diversifying into new ports of call, continuing to cultivate their strong connections to England, risking new manufactures, extending loans to their needy provincial government, and introducing the luxuries that consumers desired in ever greater amounts. These extremely successful merchants, always a minority of the city's wholesalers, also began to specialize in the types of voyages they undertook individually. Further, the great wholesalers often were secure enough to trade "on their own accounts" as sole venturers or to form small partnerships of wealthy traders who ventured to southern Europe and western Africa regularly. The wealthiest city traders developed diverse routes of trade, elaborate kinship networks and credit liaisons, and specialized knowledge about particular markets, such as those for flour, rum, sugar, or flaxseed.

Over the century new city traders were getting a start from exporting agricultural staples and country manufactures that were now produced in large quantities in the economic region surrounding New York City and kept their business interests focused on trade with North American coastal ports and the West Indies. Often men of modest means or humble family background, middling traders were adversely affected by the gyrations of the colonial economy to a greater degree than their more successful peers. Wars, for example, were a mixed blessing. King William's War (1689–97) and Queen Anne's War (1702–13) produced acute shortages of goods and ships, which made entry into commerce difficult. Warfare from the 1730s to the 1750s brought huge sums of money into some colonial merchants' hands, lucrative government supply contracts, and increased opportunities for privateering and smuggling with French and Spanish Caribbean ports, but it also uprooted the regular channels of coastal trade and competitive markets of numerous middling traders. Recessions brought on by severe currency contractions, as well as a series of poor harvests, also brought hard times in the early 1720s and early 1730s. In addition middling traders attained less success as a group, and they tended to rise and fall more dramatically than the great traders did when struck by the vicissitudes of war, recession, or harvests. They rarely achieved economies of scale, and they protected coastwise and West Indies trade with large partnerships and dispersed ownership of vessels. Middling merchants—always the majority of traders in New York during this century—often grew dependent on exportable agricultural surpluses from their own economic region and rarely could afford to become specialized in their services.

By the mid-1730s great and middling merchants carried sugar, salt, logwood, wine, whale oil, fish, molasses, and numerous other commodities from coastal and West Indies trade into New York and reexported large quantities of goods to southern Europe, southern France, and the Low Countries. Nearly 25% of New York imports were textiles from England, and an increasing flow of dry goods from numerous English and European towns filled the holds of the city's greatest traders. From New York producers, ships continued to carry furs but increasingly devoted their cargoes to flour, wheat, and timber products such as shingles and potash. By the mid-1730s New York merchants owned 67% of the vessels going to the West Indies, 60% of those plying coastal ports, and about 25% of those going to southern Europe. While New Yorkers owned just 30% of the city's vessels bound for London in the 1730s, they owned nearly 50% by 1764. By the later year New York built vessels carried 89% of the city's coastal trade from Newfoundland to Charles Town [now Charleston, SC].

By the mid-1740s eminent New York traders were adorning their persons and homes in ways comparable to their successful London peers. Luxuries such as coaches, silks, snuff, and perfume; homes of three stories; ships registered at 280 tons (254 MT); and other signs of the elite's accomplishments became accepted signs of commercial success. In these continuing years of periodic currency shortages, infrequent opportunities for manufacturing or institutional development, and fears about unstable paper money, the most successful merchants offered fellow merchants personal bonds at slightly more than the legislated interest rate of 6%; became personal bankers who lent sums of money and credit against goods for particular voyages of trusted relatives and friends; and loaned money to both Crown officials and local retailers. Speculating in bills of exchange became widespread. A few city merchants opened auction houses after the 1740s, and a handful of eminent traders began to underwrite marine insurance premiums that covered commercial risks. A far larger number of merchants began investing in landed estates and urban real estate, but few retained the value of this property through the American Revolution era.

Harrington, Virginia. *The New York Merchant on the Eve of the Revolution* (New York: Columbia Univ Press, 1935)
Matson, Cathy. *Merchants and Empire: Trading in Colonial New York* (Baltimore: Johns Hopkins Univ Press, 1998)
White, Philip L. *The Beekmans of New York in Politics and Commerce, 1647–1877* (New York: New-York Historical Society, 1956)

Cathy Matson

Mercy College. Private liberal arts college. The college was founded in 1950 in Tarrytown (Westchester Co) by the Sisters of Mercy as a junior college for Catholic women. In 1958 the Sisters bought Dobbs Ferry Midgrove, the former Westchester Co estate of Edwin Gould, for the college and Our Lady of Victory Academy. Mercy College began to award bachelor's degrees in 1961 and became coeducational in 1967 and independent and nonsectarian in 1969. Mercy offers undergraduate degrees, and since 1982 master's degrees as well, in the liberal arts, health sciences, education, and business. The college has branches in White Plains and Yorktown (Westchester Co), the Bronx and Manhattan, and eight extension centers. Since the 1970s the college has focused on teaching adult and immigrant students and has had bilingual degree programs partially taught in Spanish and Korean. In 2002 the college enrolled about 7,000 undergraduate and 3,000 graduate students.

Mercy College. *Annual Report to the Community* (Dobbs Ferry, NY: Author, Fall 2001)

Carl A. Westerdahl and Susan S. Clarke

Meredith. Town (pop 1,588) in N central Delaware Co. Settled in 1797, largely by Scots and Scots-Irish, the town was formed from Franklin and Kortright in 1800. Dairy farming reached its peak with Meridale Farms (1888), known for first-class Jersey cattle. The Ulster and Delaware Railroad reached East Meredith in 1900, providing access to city markets for Hanford Mills (1820–1968), an industrial complex operated by the Hanford family for 130 years. In 1973 the 70-acre (28 ha), 16-building Hanford Mills property became a working museum. The John T. McDonald Farm, where hydro power was applied for farm purposes in the 1880s, was reputedly the first such operation in the state; it is listed on the National Register.

Dorothy Kubik

Meridian. Village (pop 358) in Cato (Cayuga Co). Settled in 1804, it acquired a post office in 1824 named Cato Four Corners, which was changed to Meridian in 1850. It was incorporated as a village in 1854. In the 19th century the village had small industries, including an agricultural implement factory (1833), a carriage factory (1876), and a tannery (1877). In 2002 there was no manufacturing, and it was a bedroom community. Many residents lived in 19th- and 20th-century houses and worked in Syracuse.

David A. Dudley

Merrick {Merrick, locality (pop 22,764) in Hempstead, Nassau Co; North Merrick, locality (pop 11,844) in Hempstead}. The name is derived from the Mericoke Indians, who inhabited the region before English settlers arrived in 1644. In the 19th century it was an agricultural trading center with access to the ocean for boats. There were also four paper mills on the Merrick River. The South Side Rail Road arrived in 1867, beginning the growth of Merrick. The Long Island Camp Meeting Association began a Methodist campground in 1869 on 60 acres (24 ha) that are now part of North Merrick. Cottages were built and used for the meetings until the 1920s; the circular plan and many of the houses remain. Growth accelerated after World War I; electrification of the railroad (1925) and construction of the Southern State Parkway (1927) made suburban Merrick more accessible. In 1940 in Merrick had 2,935 residents and North Merrick, 2,072; growth leveled off in both after 1970.

Georgina Martorella

message of necessity. The 1894 Constitutional Convention, with almost no explanation or debate, added a clause to the constitution stating that the governor may tell the legislature to take an immediate vote on a bill rather than wait the mandated three days after its introduction. At the 1915 Constitutional Convention, criticism of the alleged abuses of this device, especially the frequency of its usage and its employment on complex legislation such as budget bills, persuaded the delegates to approve a proposal that would remove the message of necessity clause from the proposed constitution. Voters defeated the proposed constitution at the polls, however, and the message of necessity has survived two subsequent constitutional conventions, court challenges, and criticism from both the left and right wings of the private sector. It is considered by some to be an essential tool for expediting necessary legislation.

Lincoln, Charles Z. "Consideration and Passage of Bills." In *The Constitutional History of New York,* vol 3 (Rochester: Lawyers Cooperative Publishing, 1906)

Robert Allan Carter

meteorites. Between 30,000 and 40,000 meteoroids—pieces of rock from space or cometary dust burning in the atmosphere—fall toward Earth every year, mostly in tiny fragments. Meteoroids that reach the ground, of which perhaps 500 a year are fist-sized or larger, are called meteorites. Most, about 93%, are "stony," looking and feeling like ordinary rock, but metallic meteorites, "irons," are much heavier than typical rock. In November 1883 a meteor shower is said to have started multiple fires in the woods in Guilford (Chenango Co), in what was then the hamlet of Colesville. Period accounts tell of streaks of light and of a meteorite impact behind a local tavern. It was reported that the meteorite remained intensely hot for days, preventing anyone's approach. Although a bright meteor shower might well have occurred as part of the Leonid meteor event (a meteor shower that appears to emanate from the constellation Leo) reports of fire and brimstone and predictions of the end of the world were exaggerated. No meteorite has been reported found in the vicinity of Guilford. Since 1818, 11 meteorites, both stones and irons, have been recovered in New York State, mainly from the Hudson and Mohawk Valleys, where population density or farming activities are high. Meteorites have surely fallen in the Adirondacks, the Southern Tier, and elsewhere with the same frequency but have remained undiscovered.

Two recent meteorites hit human-made objects: a house in Schenectady in 1968 and a car in Peekskill (Westchester Co) in 1992. The Peekskill meteorite provided a wealth of data because it fell on a warm October night and was seen by many, including 16 persons who videotaped the event. Visible as a fireball for more than 40 seconds as it traveled 440–500 miles (700–800 km) to the ground, it was observed to break into at least 12 fragments at an altitude of 25 miles (40 km), but only one piece was found during a search. When

Recorded Meteor Finds

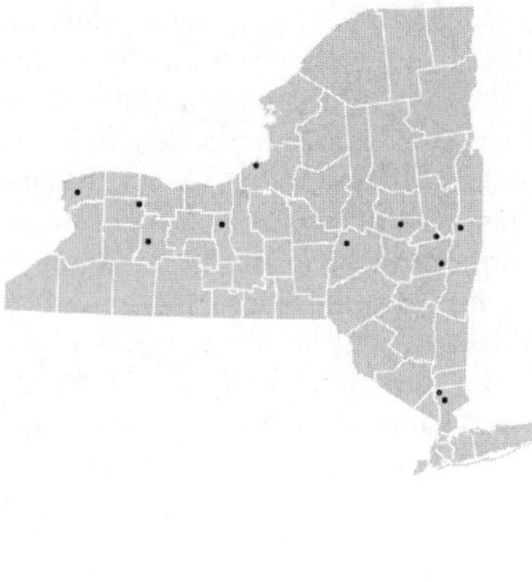

first photographed it was at an altitude of 29 miles (47 km) and traveling at about 9 miles (15 km) per second. The fireball had a greenish glow as bright as a full moon and crackled like a sparkler. The prefragmentation object probably had a diameter of 3–7 feet (1–2 m) and weighed from 2 to 16 tons (1.8–14.5 MT). The Peekskill meteorite is only the fourth in the world for which the orbit is known; it originated at the inner edge of the solar system's asteroid belt.

Recently fallen meteorites have a thin, black, glassy crust, which then weathers to a smooth dark brown. Interior color varies, ranging from light tan to black. A polished piece will usually reveal small grains of metal. New York State has a history of mining and smelting, and the products of these industries, in the form of magnetite ore or furnace slag, are often mistaken for meteorites.

Dodd, H. T. *Thunderstones and Shooting Stars* (Cambridge, Mass: Harvard Univ Press, 1986)

William M. Kelly

Methodism. Methodism traces its origins to the 18th-century evangelical revival within the Church of England led in England by John Wesley (1703–91). Wesley taught that all are free to respond to God's offer of salvation and must utilize those disciplines that cultivate a holy life. With its rejection of predestination joined to an emphasis on the possibility of achieving divinely inspired personal and social holiness, Methodism became one of the most dynamic religious movements in the United States. Methodists started to arrive in North America by the early 1760s. Among the first were Irish immigrants Barbara Ruckle Heck and Philip Embury, who, with Capt Thomas Webb, a British army officer, were instrumental in establishing the Wesley Chapel on John St in Lower Manhattan in 1768, which was the first Methodist chapel built in America. The present United Methodist congregation at 44 John St occupies the site of the original structure. Methodist societies grew in number and size over the next 15 years, and in 1784 in Baltimore, Md, the Methodist societies in America formally organized into the Methodist Episcopal Church. The Methodist message of divine grace available to all appealed to a broad range of people. Methodism grew rapidly in the succeeding years. By 1800 in New York State there were 6,363 church members, including both Whites and African Americans. By 1813 membership in New York State had increased more than threefold to 17,928 Whites and 1,131 African Americans.

Growth and Divisions

The spread of Methodism in the early 19th century was furthered by itinerating ministers who "rode the circuit," covering up to 500 miles (805 km) per month on horseback while keeping as many as 60 preaching engagements. Methodism rapidly became a central feature of religious life and social activity in the state, nowhere more so than in Central and Western New York, the so-called Burned-over District, where the evangelical fires of the Second Great Awakening were at their most incandescent. But the rapid growth of Methodism was statewide. The influential Methodist leader Nathan Bangs (1778–1862), who lived in New York City from 1810 to his death, saw the number of Methodist congregations increase from 2 or 3 to over 60 churches. His ministerial career was typical of a transitional generation that moved from circuit riding toward more rooted, socially prominent Methodist clergy and church members. By the time of his death, there were approximately 150,000 Methodists in the state.

Among the earliest and most enthusiastic followers of Methodism were African Americans. There were, however, both subtle and overt forms of discrimination, especially a heavy-handed paternalism that thwarted efforts by black Methodists to chart their own religious course. This resulted in the formation of two new Methodist denominations. The African Methodist Episcopal Church (AME) was created in Philadelphia in 1816, with Richard Allen as the first bishop. Black Methodists in New York City did not follow Allen's lead, and in 1821 James Varick, Peter Williams, Christopher Rush, and others created the African Methodist Episcopal Zion Church. Race and slavery profoundly shaped American Methodism in the first half of the 19th century. Divisions over slavery led to a rupture of American Methodism into separate northern and southern denominations in 1844. The year before the split, when some antislavery clergy from New York and the New England states felt that the northern church was wavering over slavery, they formed the Wesleyan Methodist Church (now Wesleyan Church) in Utica. The church has a small membership in New York (approximately 12,000) and maintains Houghton College (Allegany Co). The Free Methodist Church was formed at Pekin (Niagara Co) in 1860 as a result of another schism. It too was an antislavery denomination that opposed renting pews and emphasized a strict standard of holy living for its members. Major support for the new church came from New York Methodists who left the Methodist Episcopal Genesee Annual Conference to join the new denomination. The Free Methodists have a small membership in New York State (approximately 8,000) and operate Roberts Wesleyan College in Rochester.

Holiness and Reform

The first mission statement of the Methodist Episcopal Church stated its purpose: "To reform the Continent, and to spread scriptural Holiness over these Lands." This involved both personal and collective efforts at achieving holiness. One important aspect of holiness involved efforts at education and reforming society. American Methodism has been actively involved in educational ministries since its origins. More than 40 schools and academies with direct connections to Methodism were begun in the state, though most of these are no longer extant. The first was Wesleyan Seminary, opened in 1819 in Lower Manhattan. Syracuse University was founded by the Methodist Episcopal Church in 1870 with help from the City of Syracuse; it remains the only United Methodist institution of higher education in the state.

Abolitionism was another way to spread holiness. Almost all Methodist clergy in New York State were abolitionists and also active in other reform movements. Concern for the poor and immigrant population was a high priority, especially in New York City. With denominational support they opened Five Points Mission in Lower Manhattan in 1850 and distributed food and clothing to the needy, housed social services for women and children, and included evangelistic outreach. In 1888 the Methodist Episcopal Woman's Home Missionary Society began the Alma Mathews House in Greenwich Village to provide shelter for immigrant women. Other ministries for immigrants and sailors were supplied by Methodism, including the famous Bethel Ship, which served Scandinavian sailors from its anchorage in New York Harbor from 1845 until 1879. The New York Methodist Hospital in Brooklyn, chartered in 1881, was the first of several Methodist hospitals across the nation. United Methodists are actively engaged in other social welfare ministries, such as the Children's Home of the Wyoming Conference in Binghamton, the Bethel Homes (nursing and rehabilitation) in Croton-on-Hudson (Westchester Co), and Gateway-Longview, Inc. (care and treatment services for children, youth, and families) in Buffalo. The 19th-century Holiness movement left its mark on New York Methodism in the number of personal and social reforms it promoted. Methodists were especially prominent in reforms that advanced what they considered to be a proper Christian lifestyle. As early as 1866, Methodists were vocal in prohibiting business openings on Sunday and in forbidding gambling of any kind. Temperance was a major crusade for the Methodist Church, and it rejoiced when national prohibition became law in 1919. The 1919 *Central New York Annual Conference Journal* exulted, "King Alcohol is now an outlaw in the United States, and there will be no truce until his treacherous subjects are fully beaten and he himself is driven back to Hell."

Organization

In 1939 the Methodist Episcopal Church reunited with the Methodist Protestant Church and the Methodist Episcopal Church, South to form the Methodist Church. In 1968 the Methodist Church and the Evangelical United Brethren Church joined to become the United Methodist Church, which remains the second largest denomination of American Protestantism. It has six geographical annual conferences that minister in the state; they are Western New York, North Central New York, Wyoming, Troy, New York, and Greater New Jersey. According to the 1998 *General Minutes of the Annual Conferences of the United Methodist Church,* the conferences in New York State had approximately 322,000 members, 1,500 churches, and 1,900 clergy. Although most of these churches are predominantly white, there are many congregations that are African American, Latino, or Asian. In recent years Methodist membership has been declining in New York State, where United Methodist membership declined 15–20 percent from 1968 to 1998. Each annual conference is supervised by a bishop, who appoints the clergy to the churches and acts as the spiritual and administrative head of the conference. Clergy and lay delegates from the local churches meet annually at the conference to conduct business and to plan strategies for their ministry. Both men and women may be ordained in United Methodism. Two general agencies of the United Methodist Church are located in New York City: the General Commission on Christian Unity and Interreligious Concerns, the denomination's ecumenical agency, and the General Board of Global Ministries, the church's official missions agency and its largest administrative unit.

See also CHAUTAUQUA INSTITUTION; HOLINESS-WESLEYAN MOVEMENT.

Bradley, David H. *A History of the A.M.E. Zion Church* (Nashville: Parthenon Press, 1956)
Harmon, Nolan B., ed. *The Encyclopedia of World Methodism,* 2 vols (Nashville: United Methodist Publishing House, 1974)
Marston, Leslie R. *From Age to Age a Living Witness: A Historical Interpretation of Free Methodism's First Century* (Winona Lake, Ind: Light & Life Press, 1960)
McLeister, Ira Ford. *History of the Wesleyan Church of America* (Marion, Ind: Wesley Press, 1959)
Ransom, Reverdy C. *Preface to the History of the A.M.E. Church* (Nashville: A.M.E. Sunday School Union, 1950)
Seaman, Samuel A. *Annals of New York Methodism from A.D. 1766–A.D. 1890* (New York: Hunt & Eaton, 1892)
Ward, William Ralph, Jr. *Faith in Action: A History of Methodism in the Empire State* (Rutland, Vt: Academy Books, 1986)

Charles Yrigoyen Jr

Metro-North Railroad. Commuter rail system serving Manhattan, the Bronx, and the northern New York City suburbs of Westchester, Putnam, Dutchess, Rockland, and Orange Cos, as well as Connecticut's Fairfield and New Haven Cos. A part of the Metropolitan Transportation Authority (MTA), the system has been officially known as MTA Metro-North Railroad since 1993. It operates the Grand Central Terminal–based Harlem, Hudson, and New Haven commuter lines, the last in partnership with the Connecticut Department of Transportation. The Harlem line, running 82 miles (132 km) to Wassaic (Dutchess Co), began as the New York and Harlem Railroad in 1832, and the Hudson line, running 74 miles (119 km) to Poughkeepsie, originated as the Hudson River Railroad in 1846. Both railroads later formed part of the New York Central Railroad System. From 1848, the New Haven line, extending 72 miles (116 km) to New Haven, Conn, shared Harlem line tracks into New York City. In 1871 these railroads began using Grand Central Depot at 42d St in Manhattan. After railroads began to be powered by electricity and the Grand Central Terminal was built in 1913, suburban passenger traffic grew significantly, but following World War II commuter services were curtailed because of increasing competition from automobiles.

In 1965 the state created Metropolitan Commuter Transportation Authority (after 1968 the MTA) to preserve commuter rail service. In 1968 New York Central and Pennsylvania Railroads merged as Penn Central, absorbing New Haven Railroad in 1969. MTA contracted with Penn Central to run New Haven trains in 1971 and Hudson and Harlem trains in 1972. Conrail took over the operation in 1976, but after federal law required Conrail to discontinue passenger trains, the New York State legislature created the Metro-North Commuter Railroad Co on 1 Jan 1983. The MTA subsidiary initiated a series of improvements, including purchasing new cars and locomotives, rehabilitating yards and shops, extending electrification, rebuilding stations with raised platforms and added parking spaces, improving track and signals, repairing viaducts and tunnels, and renovating Grand Central Terminal. Ridership rose from 48 million passengers in 1984 to 73 million in 2001. By the beginning of the 21st century, the system comprised 384 miles (618 km) of route, 775 miles (1,247 km) of track, 119 stations, and about 950 cars and engines. Metro-North also contracts with New Jersey Transit to provide service, using pooled equipment of both companies, on a 95 mi (153 km) route from Hoboken, NJ, to Port Jervis (Orange Co) and on a 31 mi (50 km) route from Hoboken to Spring Valley (Rockland Co). The two commuter services have operated since 1974 and 1983, respectively.

Olmsted, Robert A. "A History of Transportation in the Bronx," *Bronx County Historical Society Journal* 26 (Fall 1989): 68–91

Robert A. Olmsted

Metropolitan College of New York. Private four-year college. Educator Audrey Cohen founded the Women's Talent Corps in 1964 as an outgrowth of her work with CORE (Congress of Racial Equality) and the American Friends Service Committee. The name changed to Talent Corps once men were admitted. In 1970 the school became known as the College for Human Services, the name it held until 1992, when it became Audrey Cohen College. In 2002 the school, headquartered in Manhattan, became known as Metropolitan College of New York. Initially the school's goal was to provide experientially based educational opportunities for low-income and working people whose needs were not being addressed by traditional academics. Today the school still focuses on the needs of students who are part of the full-time workforce. It operates on a three-semester per calendar year schedule so students can complete their degrees more quickly than in a two-semester system. There are two bachelor degrees, five master's, and two associate degree programs offered. Classes are held at four locations around New York City. In 2003, the student body numbered nearly 1,600.

Marianne Rahn-Erickson

Metropolitan Museum of Art. Members of the Union League Club, including Frederick Law Olmsted, Henry Bellows, and William Cullen Bryant, wished to create something uplifting to the nation after the Civil War, and this goal spurred the founding of the Metropolitan Museum of Art (the Met). Incorporated on 15 Apr 1870, the museum and its collections were to instruct the public at large, from workers and artisans to scholars, about art. Since 1880 the Met has been located at 5th Ave and 82d St in New York City. The original building was a red brick Neo-Gothic structure designed by Calvert Vaux and Jacob Wrey Mould. Additions bear the architectural signatures of designers such as Richard Morris Hunt, Theodore Weston, and the Beaux Arts firm McKim, Mead and White. A number of additions were made from 1971 through 1991. The Robert Lehman Wing (1975) houses his collection of the works of Old Masters, Impressionists, and Postimpressionists. The Sackler Wing (1978) houses the Temple of Dendur. The American Wing (1980) includes 24 rooms depicting domestic life as well as art of different periods; the Michael C. Rockefeller Wing (1982) presents art from the Americas, Africa, and Oceania; and the Lila Acheson Wallace Wing (1987) shows modern art. Other permanent collections include the Egyptian, Greek and Roman (including the Cesnola Collection of Cypriot antiquities), Far Eastern, Ancient Near Eastern, European Arms and Armor, European Sculpture and Decorative Arts, European Paintings, American Paintings and Sculpture, and Prints and Photographs.

The building is leased from the City of New York, which contributes to yearly expenses; private patrons, however, have always been responsible for amassing its collections. The Cloisters, Romanesque, and Gothic ruins brought from Europe and reassembled in Fort Tryon Park in Upper Manhattan, is a museum branch that houses medieval art. The Met's public and educational programs attract approximately 350,000 participants annually, and researchers study the museum's collections at the on-site Watson Library. At the beginning of the 21st century the Met has gross assets at $2.3 billion and draws about 6 million visitors annually.

Metropolitan Museum of Art, http://www.metmuseum.org
Tomkins, Calvin. *Merchants and Masterpieces: The Story of the Metropolitan Museum of Art* (New York: Henry Holt, 1989)

Dorothy M. Browne

Metropolitan Opera. In 1880, 70 wealthy subscribers formed the Metropolitan Opera Co (the Met) to build a new opera house at 39th St and Broadway. Designed by Josiah Cleaveland Cady and built at a cost of $1.7 million, it seated 3,045. The initial performance, Charles Gounod's *Faust,* was held on 22 Oct 1883. In the first season all operas were sung in Italian. In the following seven, under new management, all were sung in German, many conducted by Anton Seidl. A fire on 27 Aug 1892 badly damaged the opera house. To fund the rebuilding, 35 stockholders, 19 original and 16 new, formed the Metropolitan Opera and Real Estate Co and raised $2.1 million. By the next season, the redesigned Met was again the scene of operas performed in German, French, and Italian by international artists on lavish sets. Over the next several decades the Met became firmly established as one of the leading opera companies in the world. Outstanding performers were many, including brothers Jean and Edouard de Reszke, Nellie Melba, and the American singers Geraldine Farrar, Lawrence Tibbett, and Rosa Ponselle, but none were more associated with the Met than tenor Enrico Caruso, who sang in every opening night performance except one between 1903 and 1920. Longtime managers of the first Met were Maurice Grau (1898–1903), Heinrich Conried (1903–08), Giulio Gatti-Casazza (1908–35), and Edward Johnson (1935–50). Conductors included Arturo Toscanini (1907–15) and Arthur Bodansky (1915–39). Under Gatti-Casazza two Giacomo Puccini operas premiered at the Met, *La Fanciulla del West* (1910) and *Il Trittico* (1918).

Revenues dropped precipitously during the depression, and plans to build a new opera house in Rockefeller Center in the 1930s proved abortive. The formation of the Metropolitan Opera Association in 1932, and the Metropolitan Opera Guild in 1935 helped stabilize the finances. After the transfer of the assets of the opera house from the Metropolitan Opera and Real Estate Co to the Metropolitan Opera Association after a successful fund-raising campaign, the Met entered a new phase of financial support by public subscription. Among the singers featured during the 1930s and 1940s were Bidù Sayão and Jussi Björling, the incomparable

Wagnerians Kirsten Flagstad and Lauritz Melchior, and numerous conductors and singers displaced by World War II, including Bruno Walter, George Szell, and Lotte Lehmann. The Met first broadcast on the radio on Christmas Day in 1931 with a performance of Engelbert Humperdinck's *Hänsel und Gretel.* From 1940 through the 2003–4 season, the broadcast sponsor was Texaco (now Chevron Texaco).

From 1950 to 1972 Rudolph Bing served as the somewhat autocratic general manager. During his tenure in 1955 the great contralto Marian Anderson became, belatedly, the first black singer there in January 1955. Bing oversaw the move to the Met's new home at Lincoln Center for the Performing Arts in 1966. Designed by Wallace K. Harrison, costing about $50 million and seating 4,019, it opened on 16 Sept 1966 with the world premiere of Samuel Barber's *Antony and Cleopatra.* Schuyler Chapin (1972–75) and Anthony Bliss (1975–85) were the next managers, followed by Bruce Crawford (1985–1989) and Joseph Volpe (1990–). In 1975 James Levine was named music director and principal conductor, and subsequently artistic director. Through 2003 he has conducted at the Met in 2,000 performances of 75 different operas. Mainstays of the Met in recent decades include Leontyne Price, Marilyn Horne, Luciano Pavarotti, and Placido Domingo. World premieres have included John Corigliano's *The Ghosts of Versailles* (1991) and John Harbison's *The Great Gatsby* (1999).

Mayer, Martin. *The Met: 100 Years of Grand Opera* (New York: Simon & Schuster, 1983)

Janet Daley

Metropolitan Transportation Authority (MTA). Public authority that operates the transportation agencies of New York City and seven suburban counties. The forerunner to the MTA, the Metropolitan Commuter Transportation Authority, started operations on 1 June 1965. Chaired by William J. Ronan, it acquired the nearly bankrupt Long Island Rail Road (LIRR) in 1966. Plans were soon made to expand the scope of the new agency, and the renamed MTA came into being on 1 Mar 1968. Its creation was prompted by the insolvencies of the region's commuter rail lines and the growing financial needs of New York City's mass transit system, and its establishment was part of a long-term trend toward the increasing authority of state government over the affairs of New York City. The MTA permitted a more coordinated approach to planning and funding regional transportation, with the authority setting fares and tolls. A key to the expansion of the MTA was the incorporation of the Triborough Bridge and Tunnel Authority (TBTA) and the use of its toll revenue surpluses to defray mass transit deficits. The powerful head of the TBTA, Robert Moses, agreed to the MTA's takeover of the TBTA only after Gov Nelson A. Rockefeller assured him a seat on the board of the new authority and, according to some accounts, Rockefeller's support for Moses's plan for a Long Island Sound bridge. Neither came to pass, and the creation of the MTA marked the end of the 35-year reign of Moses as a great power in New York City and State affairs.

In 2002 the MTA consisted of the New York City Transit Authority, operating bus and subway services in New York City; the LIRR, serving the Hudson Valley; and the Metro-North Railroad, serving Connecticut. The latter two are the largest and second-largest commuter rail lines in the United States. The MTA's other agencies include Long Island Bus (1973), which links 96 communities in Nassau and Suffolk Cos, and the Bridges and Tunnels agency, consisting of seven bridges and tunnels in New York City (the former TBTA). Ronan served as the authority's first chairman during its first and most difficult years. As a result of the New York City fiscal crisis, budgetary shortfalls in Albany, recurring labor disputes, and the high rate of inflation that characterized most of the 1970s, the authority's annual operating deficit mushroomed from $100 million in 1971 to $500 million four years later. From 1970 to 1976 the MTA's labor costs jumped 60%, its energy costs increased by 162%, and ridership fell by 22%; by 1979 average subway ridership had fallen by 1.2 million passengers per day from 10 years earlier. As a result the MTA was forced to slash routine maintenance and suspend equipment purchases. In response, in 1981 the state legislature declared a "transportation emergency" and set out to reenergize the authority.

Under the leadership of Chairman Richard Ravitch the authority implemented in 1982 its first in a series of five-year capital improvement plans that over time substantially improved system conditions. The key to this turnaround was the state legislature's and Gov Mario M. Cuomo's approval for the MTA to have the ability to issue debt with state backing. With this new power, between 1982 and 2000 the MTA spent $34 billion to replace and upgrade facilities and equipment. In 1983 the MTA took over Conrail's passenger service, which became Metro-North. The MTA has made its systems significantly cleaner and more reliable than they were when the authority was first formed. From 1991 to 2000 ridership increased 15% on the LIRR, 23% on Metro-North, and 25% on the subways. A 17-member board governs the MTA; the governor, the New York City mayor, and the county executives of the seven suburban counties in which the MTA operates appoint the board members, who are confirmed by the state senate. The Power Authority of the State of New York provides, at the cost of production, the electricity that powers much of the MTA's trains and subways. In 2001 the MTA had 62,800 employees, long-term bonded debt of $15.3 billion, and total operating expenses of $6.7 billion.

Caro, Robert A. *The Power Broker: Robert Moses and the Fall of New York* (New York: Vintage Books, 1974)
Connery, Robert H., and Gerald Benjamin. *Rockefeller of New York: Executive Power in the Statehouse* (Ithaca: Cornell Univ Press, 1979)

Thomas A. Birkland

Mexicans. In the 1920s a small group of Mexicans from the Yucatán Peninsula settled in New York City, but Mexican immigration to New York State began in earnest only in the 1940s and 1950s, when families from the Mixteca area in central Mexico arrived. A massive chain migration followed. In 1980 there were approximately 40,000 Mexicans in the New York City area and in 1990, 100,000, the majority still from the Mixteca area. Most immigrants, especially the large number of those undocumented, worked as laborers in industry and agriculture, and some in the Mexican restaurants that became popular in the 1980s. The 1986 Immigration Reform and Control Act legalized the status of many immigrants, who were then able to bring their families. As economic conditions in Mexico worsened, the number of Mexican Americans jumped. Including the undocumented, an estimated 400,000–450,000 people with Mexican heritage, of whom about 147,000 were Mexican-born, lived in New York State in 2000 and were the third-largest Hispanic group in New York City after Dominicans and Puerto Ricans.

About 275,000 lived in New York City, with other concentrations in Hudson Valley towns, such as Newburgh (Orange Co) and Mount Kisco (Westchester Co). In New York City, Little Mexicos have sprung up in several places: Jackson Heights in Queens; El Barrio, or Spanish Harlem, in Manhattan; Sunset Park and Williamsburg in Brooklyn; the South Bronx; and recently in Staten Island. Because of their geographic dispersion, the number of Mexican American associations is not yet proportional to their population. Civic leagues can be found in most boroughs of New York City, such as the Comité Cívico Mexicano de Nueva York, which organizes Cinco de Mayo parades on Mexico's national holiday in all five boroughs, Yonkers, and Newburgh. Yonkers also has an organization, Comunidad Mexicana de Yonkers. The nonprofit organization Mexican Cultural Institute of New York is a branch of the Mexican consulate that focuses on artistic and cultural events. New Rochelle (Westchester Co) has the Club Mexicano Bellas Artes. Mexican amateur soccer teams are members of the Federation of Mexican Sports Clubs. Several Mexican American associations help Mexican immigrants who are exploited in the labor market. For example, Joel Magallan Reyes SJ founded a Catholic labor organization, the Asociación Tepeyac, in 1997; another is the Asociación Mexico-Americana de Trabajadores (Mexican American Workers Association), founded by Gerry Dominguez. Most Mexican Americans in New York State are Catholic, but because of their dispersed residence patterns, most do not worship in Mexican American congregations. A few churches are Mexican, though, such as Our Lady of Guadeloupe on West 14th St in Manhattan.

An important issue for the Mexican American community is the high rate of school dropouts among their children. In New York City about 47% of Mexican Americans between 16 and 19 years of age have left school. There are also perceptions of racial discrimination in employment, especially against US-born Mexican Americans. Another issue is their lack of political representation in New York City. One reason is that many Mexicans are recent immigrants, sometimes undocumented, and thus cannot vote, and another is that they are widely dispersed and have not formed strong political organizations.

Smith, Robert C. "Mexicans in New York City: Membership and Incorporation of New Immigrant Group." In *Latinos in New York: Communities in Transition,* ed. Sherrie Baver and G. Haslip Viera (Notre Dame, Ind: Univ of Notre Dame Press, 1996)
———. "Mexicans: Social, Educational, Economic, and Political Problems and Prospects in New York."

In *New Immigrants in New York,* ed. Nancy Foner (New York: Columbia Univ Press, 2001)

Robert C. Smith

Mexican War. Conflict between the Republic of Mexico and the United States from 13 May 1846 to 17 Mar 1848. New York State played an active role in supporting American military efforts, sending two volunteer infantry regiments, one to California and the other to Mexico, to serve during the hostilities. Hundreds of individual citizens from the state also enlisted in the regular army regiments formed during the early stages of the war. Although the public enthusiastically supported the war, the state's Whig delegation in Congress opposed it, seeing it as an attempt to spread slavery. In opposing it, they saw an opportunity to gain control of the White House. Congressman Hugh White argued for an amendment to Pres James K. Polk's wartime appropriations bill, precluding the possibility of extending slavery into newly acquired territory. New York's Whigs were sustained by Horace Greeley's *New York Tribune,* which argued vehemently against the war. Whig resistance was clearly defined in that the party supported American troops in the field but protested Polk's conduct of the war.

In June 1846 Polk chose Col Jonathan D. Stevenson of New York City to form a volunteer "California" regiment. The government's instructions declared the regiment's recruits were to be single men of high physical and moral standing with a desire to remain in California when the conflict was over. On 30 June Stevenson, an experienced militia officer and state legislator, received permission from Gov Silas Wright to raise his regiment. It comprised 10 companies, 7 recruited in New York City, 1 in Albany-Troy, 1 in Norwich (Chenango Co), and 1 in Bath (Steuben Co). On 1 Aug 1846 the regiment was sworn into federal service as the Seventh Regiment at Governors Island in New York Harbor; during 1847, the designation was changed to the First Regiment. They arrived in California during March and April of 1847, took part in numerous expeditions, and served garrison duty. In March 1848 the regiment engaged Mexican forces at Todas Santos, Baja, Calif, forcing the Mexicans from the peninsula. The First Regiment was not returned to its place of origin; many of the men stayed in California, some becoming prominent citizens.

The Second New York Volunteers was formed in December 1846 and originally designated the First, but while serving in Mexico became the Second Regiment. Commanded by Col Ward B. Burnett, a West Point graduate, it fought in Mexico as part of the Volunteer Division under Maj Gen John A. Quitman. The regiment joined Gen Winfield Scott's army in February 1847, was among the first volunteer regiments from east of the Appalachians to arrive in Mexico, and fought in all major engagements thereafter. Of the 38 officers in the regiment, 4 were killed in action or mortally wounded, including Lt Col Charles Baxter, who led the regiment at Chapultepec after Col Burnett was seriously wounded at Churubusco. Seven other officers also suffered wounds in various engagements. The Second Regiment returned home in August 1848.

Few New Yorkers received greater distinction during the Mexican War than William Jenkins Worth (1794–1849), a native of Hudson (Columbia Co). After service in the War of 1812 and as commandant of cadets at West Point (Orange Co), Brig Gen Worth commanded the forces at Chapultepec, was briefly commander of the Department of Texas, and gave his name to the City of Fort Worth. His body was returned to his native state in 1857 and interred at the intersection of Broadway and 5th Ave at Madison Square in Manhattan, where it remains, along with a 51 ft (15.5 m) obelisk erected over his tomb.

Bauer, K. Jack. *The Mexican War, 1846–1848* (New York: Macmillan, 1974)

Biggs, Donald C. *Conquer and Colonize: Stevenson's Regiment and California* (San Rafael, Calif: Presidio Press, 1977)

Brett Michael Mills

Mexico. Town (pop 5,181) and village (pop 1,572) in N Oswego Co. The town was formed in 1792 from Whitestown [now in Oneida Co] and is called "Mother of Towns" because it initially included all of the present area of Onondaga and Cortland Cos and all of eastern Oswego Co. In the 19th century the town produced lumber, barrels, leather, and woolen cloth, and raised stock and made dairy products. French Street is a locality settled before 1850 by Alsatian immigrants, including stone carvers; Alsatian glassblowers followed by the late 1860s. The village incorporated in 1851. The town was a site of Underground Railroad activism, including providing brief refuge for William "Jerry" Henry after his rescue from Syracuse in 1851. The high school (1937) entrance hall is the only place in the world where the high-quality pictorial mural wallpaper *La Guerre d'Independence* (1930), by Zuber et Cie, can be seen intact. At Mexico Point Park, open to the public, Casey's Cottage is a reproduction medieval cottage created in the 1930s by Dr William C. Casey and German artist Severin Bischof. Most residents commute to work in other places.

Barbara J. Dix

Mid-Atlantic region. Although New York State is generally considered as one of the Mid-Atlantic states, there is no agreement on that region's boundaries. Three states—New York, Pennsylvania, and New Jersey—are invariably included in the Mid-Atlantic region, but many scholars have alternative maps of the region. Delaware and Maryland are often included, and historian Robert J. Gough, in an 1983 article, "The Myth of the Middle Colonies," suggested that there are really two regions: one encompassing eastern New York State and northern New Jersey and the other eastern Pennsylvania and southern New Jersey. There are also questions about whether parts of New York State should be grouped with New England and if parts of Delaware and Maryland should be grouped with the South.

Delaware and Maryland

While there are good reasons to include Maryland and Delaware in the Mid-Atlantic region, they fall on the other side of the most famous regional divide in American history, the Mason-Dixon Line, demarcating of the border between colonial Pennsylvania and Maryland. It is an oversimplification to say that the Mason-Dixon Line became the dividing line between the slaveholding South and the free North. In fact it is not a single line. The Mason-Dixon Line begins with a semicircle 12 miles (19 km) in radius around New Castle, Del. From a point on the circumference of this semicircle, Charles Mason and Jeremiah Dixon in the 1760s surveyed a tangent line running south down the middle of the Delmarva Peninsula to form the western boundary of Delaware and the eastern boundary of Maryland. From another point on the semicircle, they ran a line west to form the southern boundary of Pennsylvania and the northern boundary of Maryland. Thus the Mason Dixon Line not only divides Maryland from Pennsylvania but also is the boundary between Delaware and Maryland.

It is true that what distinguished Maryland and Delaware from Pennsylvania, New Jersey, and New York by 1860 was that Maryland and Delaware both were slave states. Delaware, however, was originally the so-called Lower Counties of Pennsylvania under a grant in 1682 from James, Duke of York to William Penn. Although the Lower Counties had their own legislature, it was not until 1703 that Delaware became a colony separate from Pennsylvania. Delaware continued to share the same governor with Pennsylvania until the American Revolution. In cultural terms the northern counties of Delaware are similar in folk architecture and agriculture to southeastern Pennsylvania and southern New Jersey. Thus there are both political and cultural reasons for including Delaware as one the Mid-Atlantic states. The southern counties of Delaware are similar to the eastern shore of Maryland, which is linked economically and culturally to the Chesapeake Bay and to Virginia. The southernmost part of the Delmarva Peninsula is actually within Virginia. The Appalachian Mountains region of western Maryland is culturally and politically similar to central Pennsylvania, as Gen Robert E. Lee discovered after the Battle of Antietam in 1862. While the tobacco-growing, slave-owning eastern shore of Maryland was pro-South, there was little sympathy for secession in the Maryland uplands. Therefore if we include Delaware in the Mid-Atlantic states region, we should also include Maryland.

Pre-Contact History

New York, New Jersey, Pennsylvania, and Delaware share an overlapping history from pre-Contact through the colonial period. The Indians of New York State were part of a greater Eastern Woodland culture area that extended from the Midwest to New England. In linguistic terms, however, there were two different Native American language families represented in New York State. Eastern Pennsylvania, New Jersey, and the lower Hudson Valley were inhabited by the Delaware Indians, so named by Europeans because they lived on either side of the Delaware River. The Lenape, as they called themselves, spoke a language that was part of the Algonquian linguistic family. By the beginning of the 19th century most, if not all, of them had left the region and begun their long migration westward, eventually ending up in Oklahoma, Wisconsin, and Canada. The central and western sections of New York State were and still are inhabited by the Iroquois-speaking Five Nations (the Seneca, Oneida, Onondaga, Cayuga, and Mohawk). Later, in the mid–18th century, they were joined by the Tuscarora, another Iroquois-speaking tribe that migrated from North Carolina after a disastrous war with the English colonists.

Interrelationships

The establishment of the competing European colonies in the early 17th century continued the political and ethnic interrelationships between New York, New Jersey, Pennsylvania, and Delaware. New Netherland (1624–64) and New Sweden (1638–55) in the Hudson and Delaware Valleys had an influence that outlasted their brief existence as colonies. Historical geographer Terry Jordan has demonstrated that the material culture of New Sweden, especially the log cabin, introduced by the Finns who had prior experience as fur traders on the Russian frontier, diffused from the Delaware Valley into the Appalachian Mountains and eventually into the American West. The Dutch influence survived the conquest of New Netherland by the English in 1664. Many cultural traits of the Dutch culture area, such as the regionally distinct Dutch American farmhouse and the New World Dutch barn, did not take shape until the first half of the 18th century. Aspects of Dutch American material culture, religion, and language—"Jersey Dutch" in the lower Hudson Valley, and *de tawl,* or *de taal,* in the Mohawk Valley—survived in the New York and New Jersey countryside until the first half of the 20th century.

The English conquest of New Netherland created a new web of interrelationships. King Charles II granted the land between the Connecticut and Delaware Rivers as a proprietary colony to his brother James, Duke of York, later King James II. James retained for himself the so-called Duke's Province (New York) and regranted the rest to his friends Sir George Carteret and John, Lord Berkeley. This became the Colony of New Jersey, so named after Carteret's estate on the Isle of Jersey. In 1674 Berkeley sold his shares to two Quakers, Edward Byllynge and John Fenwick. But Fenwick and Byllynge quarreled, and William Penn was called in to arbitrate their differences. Byllynge's creditors asked Penn and two other Quakers to become trustees for Byllynge. Fenwick established his own colony in Salem, NJ, in 1675.

In 1676 the Colony of New Jersey was divided into East and West New Jersey. Carteret died in 1680, and his shares were purchased by another group of English Quakers, which also included William Penn. Thus Penn was a proprietor of both East and West New Jersey well before he became involved in Pennsylvania. Quaker influence continues in present day in New Jersey. Eventually East New Jersey passed to a group of Scottish proprietors and West Jersey to a group of Anglicans. Finally the proprietors of both East and West New Jersey in 1702 petitioned the Crown to reunite them as the royal Colony of New Jersey. However, New Jersey continued to share a governor with New York until 1738.

In 1681, in repayment of a loan made by Penn's father, who was an admiral in the royal navy, Charles II granted the younger Penn a colony on the west side of the Delaware River, which became Pennsylvania. Penn himself came to his colony in 1682 to supervise the layout of Philadelphia. He recruited Palatinate Germans and Ulster Irish (or Scots-Irish, as they became known in America) to settle in his Quaker commonwealth. Both the Germans and the Scots-Irish migrated from central Pennsylvania south through the Great Valley of the Appalachian Mountains into the upland regions of Maryland. They were responsible for the diffusion into the American frontier of two significant material cultural traits, the Lancaster, or long, rifle and the Conestoga, or covered, wagon.

Cultural Connections

If one considers the Mid-Atlantic region as a grouping of states (New York, New Jersey, Pennsylvania, Delaware, and Maryland), the region might be seen as being crosscut by several culture areas, defined in terms of clusters of culture traits, such as language, folk architecture, and material culture. Linguist Hans Kurath divided the eastern United States into three major speech areas, each of which he divided into subregions. Kurath included all of New York State and northern New Jersey within the Northern area, which he subdivided into Upstate New York, the Hudson Valley, and Metropolitan New York. He included southern New Jersey, the southern two-thirds of Pennsylvania, northern Delaware, and the upland part of Maryland in the Midland area. Kurath subdivided the Midland area into the Delaware Valley (the Philadelphia area), the Susquehanna Valley, the Upper Ohio Valley (the Pittsburgh area), and the Upper Potomac and Shenandoah Valleys. The eastern shore of Maryland, southern Delaware, and the part of Virginia on the lower Delmarva Peninsula he classified as the Delmarva subdivision within the Southern dialect area.

Folk architecture confirms Kurath's dialect areas. Folklorist Henry Glassie mapped what he calls the Mid-Atlantic culture area defined in terms of a farmhouse type named by historical geographer Fred Kniffen as the I-house and the forebay, or Pennsylvania Dutch, bank barn. Glassie's Mid-Atlantic folk culture area coincides with Kurath's Midland dialect area. According to Glassie, the three-bay English barn, exemplified by barns he studied in Otsego Co can be found in western New York State, northern Pennsylvania, eastern Long Island, and throughout New England. The New World Dutch barn has been mapped by John Fitchen and others throughout the Schoharie, Mohawk, and Hudson Valleys, northeastern New Jersey, and western Long Island. Glassie also documented that the pounded-ash basketmaking tradition of the Adirondack Mountains links this part of New York State to New England, in contrast to the split-oak baskets of the southern Appalachian Mountains.

Material folk culture studies have also established a Maritime Coastal region that links the Chesapeake Bay, Delaware Bay, Barnegat Bay in New Jersey, and the Great South Bay of Long Island in terms of decoy carving and traditional wooden boatbuilding. While there are variations of styles between these areas, there is an overall similarity in the traditional activities of hunting, trapping, and gathering (especially clamming and oystering). There also is evidence of cultural exchange between these maritime subregions, such as the influence of Barnegat Bay decoy carvers on Chesepeake Bay carvers and the migration of eastern shore oyster-house workers from Crisfield, Md, to Shell Pile, NJ.

Local historian Lloyd Graham has identified another culture area in western New York State: Niagara Country, or Niagara Frontier. This area from Buffalo to Rochester was historically oriented to the Great Lakes and Canada. In the colonial period it was the battleground between the French and the British for the control of Canada, especially at Fort Niagara, strategically located at the mouth of the Niagara River. In the early 19th century, after the completion of the Erie Canal, this area, as well as a larger area of New York State west of the Hudson Valley became what historian Whitney Cross has termed the Burned-over District, the birthplace of spiritualism, Mormonism, communitarian movements such as the Oneida Community, and various other reform movements such as abolitionism and women's rights.

Conclusion

The trait that characterizes the Mid-Atlantic region first and foremost is its religious and ethnic diversity. It may be said that the region is the birthplace of American pluralism. Among the religious and ethnic groups that settled the region were Roman Catholics, Quakers, German Reformed, Moravians, Mennonites, Amish, Dutch Reformed, Scots-Irish and Scottish Presbyterians, Puritans, and Anglicans. The region also played a vital role as the incubator of new religious and communal experiments. Finally, the Mid-Atlantic region was the main theater of the American Revolution and the hearth of American democracy where both the Declaration of Independence and the US Constitution were drafted.

Bodle, Wayne. "The 'Myth of the Middle Colonies' Reconsidered: The Process of Regionalization in Early America," *Pennsylvania Magazine of History and Biography* 113 (1989): 527–48

Cohen, David Steven. *The Dutch-American Farm.* American Social Experience Series, no. 24 (New York and London: New York Univ Press, 1992)

Cross, Whitney R. *The Burned-over District: The Social and Intellectual History of Enthusiastic Religion in Western New York, 1800–1850* (Ithaca: Cornell Univ Press, 1950)

Fitchen, John. *The New World Dutch Barn: A Study of Its Characteristics, Its Structural System, and Its Probable Erectional Procedures* (Syracuse: Syracuse Univ Press, 1968)

Glassie, Henry. "William Houck: Maker of Pounded Ash Adirondack Pack Baskets," *Keystone Folklore Quarterly* 12 (1967): 23–54

———. "Eighteenth-Century Cultural Process in Delaware Valley Folk Building," *Winterthur Portfolio* 7 (1972): 29–57

———. "The Variation of Concepts within Tradition: Barn Building in Otsego County, New York." In *Man and Cultural Heritage: Papers in Honor of Fred B. Kniffen,* ed. H. J. Walker and W. G. Haag (Baton Rouge: School of Geoscience, Louisiana State Univ, 1974)

Gough, Robert J. "The Myth of the 'Middle Colonies': An Analysis of Regionalization in Early America," *Pennsylvania Magazine of History and Biography* 107 (1983): 393–419

Greenberg, Douglas. "The Middle Colonies in Recent American Historiography," *William and Mary Quarterly* 36 (1979): 396–427

Kurath, Hans. *A Word Geography of the Eastern United States* (Ann Arbor: Univ of Michigan Press, 1949)

Thompson, John H., ed. *Geography of New York State* (Syracuse: Syracuse Univ Press, 1966)

David Steven Cohen

Middleburgh. Town (pop 3,515) and village (pop 1,398) in E central Schoharie Co. The land is primarily hilly upland divided by the Schoharie Creek. Settled by Palatines in 1712 as

Weiser's Dorf, it was the site of the Middle Fort, which successfully withstood an attack by Mohawk-led Indians and tories in 1780. The town was formed from Schoharie as Middletown in 1797 and renamed Middleburgh in 1801. According to local lore Middleburgh's first settlers jointly purchased the valley's first horse, which immediately foaled, providing two horses for the price of one; the horse appears on the county's official seal. Nineteenth-century manufacturing produced wrapping paper, gloves, cigars, and fruit baskets; farming centered on broom corn and hops as cash crops. The Middleburgh and Schoharie Railroad connected to main lines from 1868 to 1936. The village, incorporated in 1881, had become residential by the early 21st century. It is also the site of the Dr. Best House medical exhibition. The Middleburgh Telephone Co (1897) was in 2003 one of the few independent telephone companies left in the state.

Peter Johnson and Dawn Johnson

Middlebury. Town (pop 1,508) in N Wyoming Co. Settled largely by former Vermont residents in 1802, the town was formed from Warsaw in 1812. The Buffalo Division of the Erie Railroad established a station in town in 1852. Salt brine was struck in 1878, and in the early 21st century there are two salt brine facilities at Dale. Hillside, a 52-room summer residence built in 1851 for a Kentucky family, was made an artists' colony before World War I by its owner; in 2003 it was a bed-and-breakfast. The town remains primarily agricultural. The New Farm, a large weekly farm market, is located on the Warsaw town line. The Carlton Hill State Multiple Use Area is in Middlebury.

middle colleges. Located on community college campuses, these high schools target at-risk students, aiming to increase their likelihood of college attendance. In 1972 Janet Lieberman, a Fiorello H. LaGuardia Community College (Queens Co) administrator with experience in educating at-risk students, and LaGuardia president Joseph Shenker proposed a school that used LaGuardia's facilities to address the academic, vocational, and affective development of at-risk adolescents. An interdisciplinary curriculum met New York State graduation requirements. The college location permitted high school students to interact with older, successful students from similar backgrounds and to earn college credits. Middle College High School (MCHS) opened in 1974 after obtaining city and state approval. MCHS modeled credit-earning, unpaid internships after LaGuardia's cooperative education program. A "house" system, "teacher-counselors," and individual, group, and peer counseling addressed affective development. About 40% of a typical entering class required reading remediation, over 50% were two or more years behind in mathematics, and all students showed multiple absences and ninth grade course failures. But by 1985, MCHS graduated 83% of its students and sent almost 75% of these graduates to college. In 1985 the New York State legislature funded International High School at LaGuardia (1986)—for immigrant students whose limited English proficiency placed them at risk of dropping out—and middle college replications at other CUNY units. The Ford Foundation awarded funds for a nationwide replication (1987–88); other schools opened independently. Middle colleges enroll more than 15,000 at-risk students at about 30 sites, including 6 in New York City; several schools have achieved charter school status.

Cullen, Cecelia L. "Middle College High School: Its Organization and Effectiveness" (EdD diss, Columbia Univ, 1991)

Lieberman, Janet E., ed. *Collaborating with High Schools,* special issue of *New Directions for Community Colleges,* no. 63 (Fall 1988)

Wechsler, Harold S. *Access to Success in the Urban High School: The Middle College Movement* (New York: Teachers College Press, 2001)

Harold S. Wechsler

Middlefield. Town (pop 2,249) in N central Otsego Co. Settled as Newtown-Martin *ca* 1755 by Scots-Irish settlers, its population was scattered during the American Revolution, and it was resettled *ca* 1790. The town was formed from Cherry Valley in 1797. Phoenix Mills (1815–1912) manufactured cotton cloth until 1866, then woolen cloth, and finally knit goods; around 1900, it employed 400 workers. Other 19th-century shops produced shoe lasts, cheeseboxes, and pumps. Summer camp facilities were established along the east shore of Otsego Lake between 1914 and 1946. In 2003 many residents commuted to Cooperstown, making Middlefield the second-wealthiest town per capita in Otsego Co. The Otsego County Correctional Facility and the Meadows, the county nursing home, are located in town, as is the Cooperstown-Westville Airport (1955). The four-county 4-H Junior Livestock Show (1948) is held annually at Iroquois Farm. Landmarks include Kingfisher Tower (1876) and the Asher Benjamin–designed Middlefield Baptist Church (1826). The Middlefield Village Print Shop (1829) is now at the Farmers' Museum in nearby Otsego.

Hugh C. MacDougall

Middle Island. Locality (pop 9,702) in Brookhaven (Suffolk Co). A settlement on the important Middle Country Rd, it acquired a post office called Middletown in 1795, was renamed Brookhaven in 1796, and became Middle Island in 1821. Many residents made their living cutting cordwood. In 1910 pilot Ralph Johnstone was forced down in this area after setting an altitude record of 8,471 feet (2,582 m). Middle Island is the site of the 320 ac (130 ha) Cathedral Pines County Park, a white pine forest planted in 1812. Suburban development followed the 1970 extension of the Long Island Expressway.

Suzanne Johnson

Middleport. Village (pop 1,917) in Royalton and Hartland (Niagara Co). Middleport grew up on the Erie Canal (1824) and later on the Niagara Falls Branch of the New York Central Railroad (1852). It developed a livestock and produce trade, had a dry dock on the canal, and was the site of a blast furnace (1840) and a paper mill (1870s). The village was incorporated in 1859. The Niagara Sprayer and Chemical Corp (1904) was sold in 1943 but continued operating; in 2003 it was a formulation plant for FMC Agricultural Products Group. Landmarks include the Freeman House (1820s) and the cobblestone Universalist Church (1841).

Nancy B. Mingus

Middlesex. Town (pop 1,345) in NW Yates Co. Settled in 1789, the town was formed in 1796 as Augusta, and the name was changed in 1808. The town is bounded on the west by Canandaigua Lake. After the Civil War, grape culture became important, especially in Vine Valley. In 1894, 97 vineyards cultivated grapes, and in the early 21st century, vineyards are still present. A resort hotel built on the lake at Vine Valley in the 1860s was short-lived. Its site is now occupied by a recreational vehicle park and other tourist businesses. The Middlesex Valley Railroad (1892; later Lehigh) crossed the town. The Bare Hill State Unique Area, an area nearly destitute of forest growth with plentiful boulders, is in Middlesex.

Gwen Chamberlain

Middletown. City (pop 25,388) in central Orange Co. Settled 1760–70, residents built the First Congregational Church in 1786. A tannery (1805) was the first industry. A post office was acquired in 1816 and renamed South Middletown in 1829; the original name was resumed in 1849. Middletown incorporated as a village in 1848. Its industrial development followed the Erie Railroad, for which it was the western terminus from 1843 to 1846. Products included ironwork (1843), wool hats (1853), saws (1853), carpet bags (1853), and files (1856). Later rail lines (Middletown, Unionville and Water Gap, 1868; Middletown and Crawford, 1871; and Ontario and Western, 1873) helped expand its industrial base, which was broad and extensive in the early 20th century, including a large Borden Condensed Milk Co plant, Ontario and Western repair shops, and Howell-Hinchman and Co tannery. The State Homeopathic Asylum for the Insane (now Middletown Psychiatric Center) opened in 1874. Middletown incorporated as a city in 1888. Rte 17/I-86 and I-84, which intersect just east of the city, place it within an easy drive of the New York City metropolitan region. The Webb Horton House (*ca* 1906) on the campus of Orange County Community College (1950) is a landmark. In 2000 the racial composition of Middletown was 69% White and 15% African American. Those of Latino ethnicity made up 25% of the population.

Middletown. Town (pop 4,051) in SE Delaware Co. Settled in 1763 by Dutch Americans from Hurley (Ulster Co), New Kingston was settled by those burned out of Kingston by the British. The town was formed in 1789 from the Towns of Woodstock and Rochester (Ulster Co). Lumbering was the major occupation, followed by dairying. The Ulster and Delaware Railroad (1872–1976) brought summer boarders and provided an outlet for dairy products and cauliflower, a profitable crop in the first half of the 20th century. The Pepacton Reservoir (1955) inundated the hamlet of Arena and flooded valley farmland. By 2003 most farms had been subdivided for second-home use, and tourism sustained the economy. Landmarks include Halcottsville's Kelly Round Barn (1893) with a round silo at its center, and Dunraven's stone schoolhouse (1820). The Delaware and Ulster Rail Ride at Arkville is an attraction.

Dorothy Kubik

Middleville. Village (pop 550) in Fairfield and Newport (Herkimer Co). Site of an early (1810) bridge over the West Canada Creek, Middleville developed as an industrial hamlet. The large factory of the Herkimer Manufacturing Co (1814) originally produced cotton cloth and iron tools; it shifted to knit goods in 1886 and to felt in 1902. It was taken down in 1932. A tannery operated from 1814 until 1973, when it closed, a casualty of the declining leather industry and of its pollution. Other products included the Raithel Covered Carriage (a convertible baby carriage with both wheels and runners) made by the Raithel brothers (1885–1935). Middleville was served by the Herkimer, Newport and Poland Narrow Gauge Railway (1881; after 1892, Mohawk and Malone Railroad). The village was incorporated in 1890. In the early 1940s the E. J. Willis Marine Equipment Co became Middleville's largest employer, producing marine hardware, ships' bells, and parts for industry. Tourists are drawn by the famed Herkimer Diamond Mines, just outside the village, as well as by trout fishing, canoeing, and kayaking.

Susan R. Perkins

Midtown Plaza. Nation's first urban enclosed shopping mall. It was designed in the International style by Austrian-born architect and city planner Victor Gruen (1903–80), who in the 1950s had designed the first suburban enclosed mall, Southdale, outside of Minneapolis. Midtown Plaza opened in downtown Rochester in 1962. In addition to retail space, the complex included a bus terminal, auditoriums, offices, and, until 1980, a hotel. Gruen's intent was to recreate the traditional European town square to serve as a civic and cultural gathering space as well as a commercial center. The idea had been initiated in 1956 by two downtown department store owners, Gilbert J. C. McCurdy and Maurice R. Forman, who were concerned about competition from suburban shopping centers. Praised as a model of downtown revitalization, the mall was the catalyst for the construction of office towers and other buildings, which were then connected to it by a network of skyways. It was expanded in the 1970s and 1980s. In the 1990s the two original lead stores closed, and most of their space was converted to offices. The structure was 40% vacant in the early years of the 21st century and various proposals were being considered for its revitalization. A distinguishing feature is the 28 ft (8.5 m) Clock of Nations, in which animated puppets represent various cultures of the world.

Gruen, Victor. *The Heart of Our Cities* (New York: Simon & Schuster, 1964)

McKelvey, Blake. *Rochester on the Genesee: The Growth of a City*, 2d ed. (Syracuse: Syracuse Univ Press, 1993)

Scott C. Monje

Midwinter Ceremony. See Iroquois government and religion.

migrant farmworkers. Agricultural laborers who travel in search of temporary employment, such as picking fruit and vegetables or working in nurseries and greenhouses. Migrant workers are sometimes distinguished from seasonal workers who are recruited locally. Migrant workers in New York State have almost always been members of minority ethnic groups. Their composition shifted during the 1980s and 1990s from predominantly African American to predominantly Mexican. No reliable statistics regarding migrant workers exist, but an estimate of the total number of hired farmworkers in the state at the beginning of the 21st century was about 62,000, with 20,000 year-round workers and 42,000 migrant and seasonal workers. Most migrant workers labor in the fruit- and vegetable-growing areas of the state, including the Great Lakes fruit belt, the Hudson Valley, and Suffolk Co on Long Island. Living and working conditions are frequently substandard, but the migrants' temporary residence and social and physical isolation hamper their organizing for improvement, and the New York State Labor Relations Act (Art 20, §§ 701, 703), originally passed in 1937 and known as the New York State Labor Law, denies agricultural workers the right of collective bargaining.

History

In the 1800s sufficient harvest help was found locally, even if schools closed for two weeks to allow students and teachers to participate. But the need for outside labor grew in the 1900s as specialized commercial farming expanded and population shifted from rural to urban areas. During World War I farmers recruited male workers, usually inexperienced in agriculture, from nearby cities. In the 1920s and 1930s, there was increased seasonal use of hoboes, drifters, and other unemployed persons who required boarding. Hired in small numbers by individual farmers, they sometimes lived with their employers. Canadians and unemployed coal miners from Pennsylvania were also recruited. During the severe labor shortages of World War II, the state's farmers leased Italian and German prisoners of war from the US Army and contracted workers from the British West Indies, principally Jamaica. With the advent of the H-2 (now H-2A) visa program in 1952, which permits the hiring of foreign agricultural workers if US workers are unavailable, farmers again looked beyond the United States for workers. The New York State Farm and Food Processing Labor Program, created during World War II, led to the creation of the State War Council's Farm Manpower Service, which recruited 375,000 workers between 1943 and 1945. The Extension Service (now Cornell Cooperative Extension) assumed primary responsibility for coordination but assigned recruitment of labor to the Employment Service.

African American migrant workers, mostly from the south (particularly Florida), became prominent after World War II. Growers' associations advertised for workers, and Florida, with the US Department of Labor, brought officials from East Coast states who needed migrant workers together with migrant crew leaders at annual meetings. Some H-2A workers came from Caribbean islands, such as Jamaica and the Bahamas. Laborers also came from Puerto Rico under a special federal program and later from Haiti. Together, these individuals formed the East Coast stream of migrant workers. Texas- and California-based streams, primarily Mexican and Mexican American, occasionally fed workers into this stream.

Many of the East Coast migrants picked citrus in Florida in the winter and spring months. Some worked in Virginia, Maryland, the Carolinas, and Georgia in the spring before moving on to New York State. In the early years workers remained in the state from May until November, shifting from one type of crop to another as the harvest season progressed. Work opportunities decreased as farms became more specialized and crops less varied. Harvesting also became increasingly mechanized; mechanical bean pickers, onion toppers, and potato harvesters, for example, eliminated thousands of jobs in the 1960s. Hand harvesting was generally retained for easily bruised fruits and vegetables that had

Migrant farmworkers harvesting potatoes in Livingston Co, *ca* 1970.

to be kept presentable, such as fresh-market apples. These factors reduced the migrant labor season to the apple-picking season of September through October, except for some vegetable planting and greenhouse and nursery work, prominent on Long Island, in the early spring.

The demographics began shifting in the mid-1980s. Some African Americans settled out of the migrant stream, finding jobs in northern factories or in Florida's growing tourist and service industries. Employers also considered the rising demands of Blacks for better pay and living conditions to be unreasonable. New York State farmers shifted to a predominantly Mexican workforce of documented and undocumented aliens, and the state received closer attention from the Immigration and Naturalization Service and the Border Patrol. The Immigration Reform and Control Act of 1986 greatly increased the number of documented Mexicans by legalizing those already in the country; New York State ranks among the top five destinations of H-2A visa holders. In addition to harvesting and seasonal work in processing plants, Mexicans replaced locally recruited Whites on dairy farms, where the work tended to be year round.

Conditions

Migrants are generally men traveling alone or in crews recruited by contractors or crew chiefs. Some travel with their families, which is often more difficult for transnational migrants. Crew chiefs mediate between workers and farmers, often exercising extensive control over migrants' lives—in June 2002 six people were indicted in Buffalo on charges of forced labor. As workers come to know the jobs and the farmers, they may decide to deal directly with their chosen employer. Thus, the use of crew chiefs declined in the 1970s and 1980s, but rose again with the increased reliance on foreign, non-English-speaking workers. Annual incomes for migrant farmworkers are normally well below poverty level. Work is seasonal, irregular, and interrupted by adverse weather. Wages in the fruit industry are frequently paid in the form of piecework. No minimum wage for farmworkers existed in New York State until 1967, when legislators instituted one lower than the regular minimum wage. In 2000 the state adopted the standard federal minimum wage for its farm laborers.

For most of the postwar period, farmers provided housing—as barracks or smaller detached units—free or for a minimal charge deducted from wages. Migrant housing in New York State is inspected by the Department of Health, but only for farms with a past payroll of more than $3,000 that intend to hire five or more people and usually only if the farmer reports that intention to the state. Regulations govern the number and proximity of showers and toilets. In the 1990s more farmers stopped providing housing and required workers to find their own, which did not lead to improved conditions. All agricultural workers are explicitly excluded from many federal and state labor, health, and safety regulations, and many of those laws that do apply are weakly enforced. Typical occupational hazards include exposure to pesticides, falls from ladders in orchards, and infectious diseases, especially in barracks-style camps.

The CBS broadcast of *Harvest of Shame* (1960) introduced many to East Coast migrants' living and working conditions, which became a political issue in the 1960s. In September 1967 Wayne Co civic organizations invited US senators Robert F. Kennedy and Jacob K. Javits to survey its farms. Kennedy, who was confronted by a farmer with a shotgun at one camp, decried the conditions as appalling and disgraceful and insisted that Gov Nelson A. Rockefeller take remedial action. Some improvements did occur, such as passage of the agricultural minimum wage law and voluntary installation of indoor plumbing. Cornell University also was touched by controversy when workers protested its attempts to close a migrant camp belonging to a demonstration farm it had received in a bequest. The incident led to the establishment in 1971 of the Agricultural Manpower Project (renamed Cornell Migrant Program in 1979), which collects data and offers workers services and classes in healthcare, nutrition, housing, education, and immigration issues. Other state agencies and private secular and religious organizations, such as the Independent Farmworkers Center, Florida (Orange Co); Rural and Migrant Ministry, Poughkeepsie and Brockport (Monroe Co); Farmworker Legal Services of New York, Rochester, and New Paltz (Ulster Co); and Rural Opportunities, Rochester, have also been formed to address problems associated with migrant life. In 1996 advocacy groups initiated marches on Albany and annual Farm Workers' Advocacy Days. New state laws in the late 1990s required the provision of drinking water, toilets, and hand-washing facilities in the fields. Repeated attempts to amend the labor law to allow collective bargaining for farmworkers have failed to pass the New York State Senate.

Friedland, William H., and Dorothy Nelkin. *Migrant: Agricultural Workers in America's Northeast* (New York: Holt, Rinehart & Winston, 1971)

Hahamovitch, Cindy. *The Fruits of Their Labor: Atlantic Coast Farmworkers and the Making of Migrant Poverty, 1870–1945* (Chapel Hill: Univ of North Carolina Press, 1997)

Heppel, Monica L., and Sandra L. Amendola. *Immigration Reform and Perishable Crop Agriculture* (Washington, DC: Univ Press of America, 1992)

Lehmann, Joyce Woelfle, ed. *Migrant Farmworkers of Wayne County, New York: A Collection of Oral Histories from the Back Roads* (Lyons, NY: Wayne County Historical Society, 1990)

Scott C. Monje

Milan [MY-LIN]. Town (pop 2,356) in N central Dutchess Co. Part of the Little Nine Partners Patent (1706) and settled by tenant farmers in the late 1740s, the town was formed from North East in 1818. Rugged terrain limited agricultural productivity; in the late 19th century it still had a number of leasehold farms and clouded land titles. Lafayetteville, once an active hamlet, and its hotel were named to honor Marquis de Lafayette. Once known for exporting violets to New York City, Milan has developed a mix of weekend homes and commuters. It is the site of Lafayetteville Mountain Multiple Use Area and Wilcox County Park.

William P. McDermott

Milborne, Jacob (*b* Putney, England, 1648; *d* New York City 16 May *os*/26 May *ns* 1691). Merchant and political agitator. Milborne arrived in New York City in 1668 as clerk and bookkeeper for merchant Thomas Delavall. He subsequently acquired Delavall's estate and, as factor for a group of London merchants, became a successful merchant. A member of a radical English nonconformist family, Milborne appears in various accounts of London and New York political intrigues. In 1688–89 he was in Rotterdam, Netherlands, where he associated with the English Whigs in exile who later formed King William III's government. He returned to New York in late summer 1689 to find the provincial government headed by Jacob Leisler. He immediately gained Leisler's favor and became his chief aide. Once in a position of power, Milborne promoted the leveling views of London's Protestant fringe. He served Leisler in Albany during the winter of 1689–90, was active in putting down riots on Long Island in fall 1690, and served as Leisler's provincial secretary. In March 1691 he was arrested by newly arrived English governor Henry Sloughter, tried for treason, and executed by beheading three months after marrying Leisler's daughter Mary.

Leisler, Jacob. Papers. Fales Library, New York Univ, New York City

Voorhees, David William. "'Fanatiks' and 'Fifth Monarchists': The Milborne Family in the Seventeenth-Century Atlantic World," *New York Genealogical and Biographical Record* 129 (Apr 1998): 67–75; (July 1998): 174–82

David William Voorhees

Milford. Town (pop 2,938) and village (pop 511) in central Otsego Co. Settled *ca* 1770, its residents were dispersed during the American Revolution, and it was resettled from New England in 1783. The town was formed from Unadilla in 1796 as Suffrage; the name was changed in 1800. The Village of Milford, incorporated in 1890, was served by a Delaware and Hudson Railroad branchline from 1869 to 1931. Goodyear Lake (1907) was formed by a hydroelectric dam on the Susquehanna and was quickly surrounded by summer cottages. A notorious 1934 murder of a client by former speakeasy owner Eva Coo, one of the few women sent to the electric chair in New York State, took place on Crumhorn Mountain in Milford. An unusually shaped, nationally distributed pineapple cheese was produced in Milford from 1903 to 1955; a microbrewery (1995) occupied the same premises in 2003. Astrocom Electronics (1961) manufactures communications equipment in Colliersville. Since 1996 the Leatherstocking Railway Historical Society has operated rail excursions from Milford to Cooperstown.

Hugh C. MacDougall

Military and Naval Affairs, Division of. Supervisory body for the New York Army National Guard, New York Air National Guard, New York Guard, New York Naval Militia, and State Emergency Management Office. When established in 1926 within the New York State Executive Department, the Division of Military and Naval Affairs (DMNA) was also responsible for the State Soldiers' and Sailors' Home at Bath (now Bath VA Medical Center), the State Monuments Commission, the Bureau for the Relief of Sick and Disabled Veterans, and the State Bonus Commission. Responsible for memorializing the participation of New York soldiers in the Civil War, the Monuments Commission was organized in 1913 and was composed of three veterans appointed by the adjutant general. The adjutant general, comptroller, and attorney general sat on the New York Veterans Relief Commission, which was founded in 1922 to assist disabled World War I veterans financially; the Bureau for the Relief of Sick and Disabled Veterans under the adjutant general replaced the commission in 1923. A year after a constitutional amendment passed in 1923 permitting the state to distribute direct bonus payments to World War I veterans who were honorably discharged, the Bonus Commission was established; it included the adjutant general, comptroller, attorney general, and treasurer. The Division of Veterans Affairs, created in 1945 to assist returning World War II veterans, assumed responsibilities for veterans' support. Most of the other commissions were annulled in 1952.

Created as an independent organization within the Executive Department, the State Civil Defense Commission (SCDC) prepared the state's defense against potential attacks. It was transferred to the DMNA in 1973 and became responsible for coordinating the state's disaster planning. Renamed the State Emergency Management Office (SEMO), it provides training, coordinates response, and distributes information and resources in the event of natural disasters, toxic hazards, and other emergencies in the early 21st century. SEMO maintains headquarters in Albany and five regional offices.

Michael J. Stenzel

militia. Compulsory military service was required under Dutch and British colonial rule, continued under New York State, and abolished in 1846. The volunteer Army National Guard, Naval Militia, and Air National Guard are now the state's organized militia. The New York Guard is an in-state reserve force.

Colonial Militia

The Dutch West India Co (WIC) employed professional soldiers of several nationalities; they were augmented by the burgherguard, as the Dutch called its citizen militia. A burgherguard for New Amsterdam was formed by Director Willem Kieft and the council in May 1640. They were required to have a gun always kept in good condition; assigned to a position under a corporal, they were to go to their places at the sound of three canon shots. During the 1650s and 1660s, rising tensions with the English and several conflicts with the Indians led Director General Petrus Stuyvesant to increase reliance on the militia. Guards were organized by the Dutch at Esopus [now Kingston, Ulster Co] and Beverwijck [now Albany].

The Duke's Laws of 1665 and Colonial Assembly acts first passed in 1691 established the colony's militia. The governor issued military commissions and acted as commander in chief. White and free black men aged 16–60 enrolled in a militia company in the city, town, precinct, or manor where they lived. Exemptions from militia training were granted to provincial and county officials, ministers, physicians, schoolmasters, Quakers, and slaves. Local companies of foot soldiers and troops of horsemen trained four days a year. County regiments assembled at least once a year. Men absent from training without an excuse were fined. A foot soldier was required to furnish a musket and ammunition; a trooper was to supply his own horse, saddle, and weapon. Gov George Clarke reported in 1738 that "the people are generally expert in the use of firearms." Commissioned officers usually belonged to the local gentry, but an observer remarked in 1755 that private soldiers were "raw country men."

During war, militia musters were recruiting grounds for the provincial troops, who were paid by assembly appropriations, often with large British subsidies. If not enough men volunteered, the assembly authorized the governor to "detach" (draft) militiamen to meet the quotas. During King William's War (1689–97), Queen Anne's War (1702–13), and King George's War (1744–48), troops were assembled from New York and other colonies to invade Canada via Lake Champlain. Each time the plan collapsed from logistical, financial, and political strains. During the French and Indian War (1754–63), monetary bounties for volunteers and occasional drafts of militiamen, drifters, and even convicts helped fill the ranks of New York provincial troops. They took part in the 1758 capture of Fort Frontenac [now Kingston, Ont] and the siege of Fort Niagara [now in Porter, Niagara Co] in 1759. Militia rangers patrolled the frontiers of Albany, Ulster, and Orange Cos against Indian raiders.

Revolutionary War and the Early New York State Militia

New York City revolutionaries formed a militia in April 1775, and the Provincial Congress soon assumed control of military affairs. A new militia law enacted that August continued the basic requirements of the colonial militia service, but privates now had to have an edged weapon (bayonet or tomahawk) as well as a firearm. Company members selected their officers. Regiment and brigade officers were appointed by the Provincial Congress, which issued all commissions. Local militia companies trained monthly, and regiments assembled twice a year. Under the 1777 Constitution, militia officers were appointed by the Council of Appointment and commissioned by the governor. Men over age 50 were exempted from regular militia training, but those up to age 55 (age 60 after 1780) were placed in companies that could be called out in case of invasion or other emergency. The greatest mobilization of the militia during the Revolution occurred during the Burgoyne–St. Leger campaign to invade New York in 1777, when Mohawk Valley Militia units suffered over 400 casualties at the Battle of Oriskany.

Militiamen who volunteered or were drafted for short terms of service were called the levies. Men were occasionally drafted into New York's Continental regiments to meet the state's quotas. Special regiments of levies were organized to guard and patrol New York's western and northern frontiers against loyalist and Indian attacks. The state troops were supposed to receive the pay of Continental soldiers, but payments often fell years behind. Desertions were common, and recruitment was difficult. In 1778 the legislature authorized future land grants to officers and soldiers who served in the state levies and the Continental line. After the war state lands in the New Military Tract and elsewhere were allotted to the individuals holding these land bounty rights, but the rights were often sold to speculators for cash.

Militia in the 19th Century

The US Constitution gave Congress the responsibility of organizing and equipping the militia, and states appointed officers and trained the men. The federal Uniform Militia Act of 1792 required all free white males aged 18–45 to be enrolled in the state militia. Exempted were county, state, and federal officials, clergymen, teachers, mariners, firemen, some factory workers, Quakers, and, after 1820, other conscientious objectors. (Blacks were not allowed to serve until 1872.) Commissioned officers were appointed by the Council of Appointment until the 1821 Constitution made most military offices elective. Soldiers elected their company officers, and commissioned officers elected the regimental and battalion field officers, who elected the brigadier generals. The governor appointed the adjutant general and most staff officers and, with senate approval, major generals and brigade inspectors. Neither the militia elections nor political appointments tended to select officers on the basis of military ability. Militia offices became important vehicles for political advancement.

A major test of the state militia occurred in the War of 1812, when thousands of New York militiamen were drafted into federal service for short periods. Indifferently armed and trained, the militia occasionally refused to cross the state line into Canada and frequently deserted, especially when their pay was late. Four thousand militiamen were fined for avoiding wartime drafts. At the Battle of Queenston Heights [now Queenston, Ont] on 13 Oct 1812, New York Militia refused to advance across the Niagara River in support of the American attack. This forced Winfield Scott to surrender to the British and their Iroquois allies, with more than 1,000 troops captured, killed, or wounded.

In 1830 the New York Militia had 37 divisions, 81 brigades, 338 regiments, and 188,526 men "present at inspections." These numbers included infantry, artillery, cavalry, and rifle units: an imposing army, but only on paper. The annual "general training day" had become mostly a holiday. The adjutant general reported in 1843 that "insubordination and lack of discipline" had infected not only the rank and file but also many officers. The one bright spot was the increasing number of volunteer "uniform" companies in cities and larger villages. Although part of the militia, these companies purchased uniforms and standard weapons, rented armories, and trained more frequently. The elite uniform companies included the Buffalo City Guard, the Rochester Union Grays (an artillery unit), the Syracuse Citizens Corps, the Utica Citizens Corps, the Albany Burgesses Corps, and many units in New York City, where a majority of the militia were now foreign-born.

Compulsory militia duty ended in 1846. Each eligible man could now commute his militia obligation by paying a 50–75¢ annual fee, a process discontinued in 1870. An 1846 statute provided that the existing uniform companies form the basis of a reorganized, volunteer militia. For the first time the state paid for arms and equipment but not for uniforms, which were now required. The state also paid militiamen who were on active duty ($1.25 a day for a private). Despite these incentives, many of the authorized companies were slow to organize, even with a required minimum of 32 men. In 1857 the legislature appropriated monies for building or renovating arsenals in New York, Brooklyn, Albany, Rome, Corning, and Buffalo, and armories in several other cities. Summer militia parades, held in public, attracted many spectators. In 1860 the organized state militia numbered about 18,000 men, with 8 divisions, 26 brigades, and 62 regiments. In 1862 the state militia was renamed the National Guard, and the 1916 National Defense Act required that all organized state militias use that name.

EARLY 21ST-CENTURY MILITIA

All resident males aged 17–45 are legally members of the "unorganized militia," which the governor may call to duty in time of imminent danger. New York State's military establishment includes the Army National Guard, the New York Guard, the Air National Guard, and the Naval Militia. The New York Guard was formed in 1917 after the National Defense Act allowed the president to federalize the National Guard in times of war or national emergency. The mission of the New York Guard is primarily to support the deployment of the National Guard units within New York State. New York Guard units have responded to natural and civil disasters in the state, including the 1997 ice storm in northern New York and the terrorist attacks of 11 Sept 2001.

Aimone, Alan C., and Eric I. Manders. "A Note on New York City's Independent Companies, 1775–1776," *New York History* 63 (Jan 1982): 59–73
Kutolowski, John F., and Kathleen Smith Kutolowski. "Commissions and Canvasses: The Militia and Politics in Western New York, 1800–1845," *New York History* 63 (Jan 1982): 5–38
Mahon, John K. *History of the Militia and the National Guard* (New York: Macmillan, 1983)

James D. Folts

milk. See AGRICULTURE; DAIRY INDUSTRY.

Millay Colony for the Arts. A retreat for creative artists in Austerlitz (Columbia Co). Opened in 1973 the Millay Colony is named for poet Edna St. Vincent Millay (1892–1950), winner of the 1923 Pulitzer Prize for poetry. Born in Rockland, Maine, Millay lived most of her life in New York State, first as a student at Vassar College, then as a young poet in New York City, and finally with her husband at their farm, Steepletop, in Austerlitz. Millay's sister Norma Millay Ellis became the executrix of her estate, and to honor her sister's contribution to American letters, Ellis established a retreat for writers, composers, and visual artists on Millay's property, using outbuildings for studios and living quarters. Each artist is selected by a panel of evaluators based on the artist's work to date, recommendations, and project proposal, and spends one month at the colony with five other artists. Some meals and a studio are provided free of charge. While residents may socialize, the emphasis is on work and quiet. Over the past three decades, more than 1,000 artists from all over the United States and abroad have worked at the Millay Colony. Chosen artists range from those well established in their field to newcomers, and they may return for additional stays, going through the application process each time. Former guests include Pulitzer Prize–winning playwright James Lapine and American composer Seymour Shifrin.

The Millay Colony, http://www.millaycolony.org

Paul Lamar

Millbrook. A 4,000-acre (1,600 ha) estate in Dutchess Co near the village of the same name, which became the home to a commune called the Castalia Foundation. Castalia was established in August 1963 by two former professors at Harvard: Timothy Leary (1920–96), known for his experimentation with lysergic acid diethylamide (LSD), and Richard Alpert (1931–), later known as Baba Ram Dass. The Millbrook estate, built in the 1890s with a turreted 64-room mansion, a gatehouse, cottages, barns, and a bowling alley, belonged to millionaire William Mellon Hitchcock and his twin brother Tom. They were not only supporters of Leary's research but also were related to great wealth as grandsons of Gulf Oil founder William Larimer Hitchcock and as nephews of Pittsburgh financiers Andrew and Richard Mellon. They were introduced to Leary by their sister Peggy, who was a member of the New York branch of Leary's group, the International Federation for Internal Freedom, founded to promote the right to expand one's consciousness. Leary and Alpert had been expelled from the Harvard faculty earlier in 1963 for using student volunteers in LSD experiments and, after a brief stay in Mexico, took up residence at the Millbrook estate.

The commune at Millbrook served as a space for psychedelic experimentation and as a haven for Leary's numerous and ever changing followers. Writers such as Ken Kesey, Allen Ginsberg, Thomas Pynchon, R. D. Laing, and William Burroughs, artists such as jazz trumpeter Maynard Ferguson and his wife and children, and some of New York's intelligentsia were willing to pay to attend the Castalia Center. At any given time, the commune could be inhabited by as many as 45 adults and 15 children.

The commune attracted national attention but also aroused local concerns, as residents of the village became increasingly alarmed that it might attract hard-core drug addicts. Their complaints prompted authorities to make a series of midnight raids. In April 1966 local police, led by Assistant District Attorney G. Gordon Liddy, arrested four of the residents on drug possession charges, Leary among them. Charges against Leary were dropped because of Liddy's failure to read him his newly instituted Miranda rights. Although Leary left Millbrook soon afterward, the city police department continued to monitor the activities at the estate and conducted further raids but only found members of a Hindu ashram who lived there with William Hitchcock's permission. Finally, in 1968, the remaining residents of Millbrook were evicted by the Mellon Hitchcock family.

Liddy achieved his own notoriety as the chief architect of the 1972 Watergate burglary that led to the resignation of Pres Richard M. Nixon. Leary spent some 15 years in and out of prison in the years following Liddy's raid on Millbrook, but by 1976 he was a free man; always an advocate for the legalization of drugs, Leary earned his living through lectures and book publications, including a 1982 lecture tour on the pros and cons of drug use with his onetime nemesis, Liddy. The Millbrook estate remains one of the earliest and most influential of the 1960s East Coast communes.

Kleps, Art. *Millbrook: The True Story of the Early Years of the Psychedelic Revolution* (Oakland, Calif: Bench Press, 1977)
Miller, Timothy. *The 60s Communes: Hippies and Beyond* (Syracuse: Syracuse Univ Press, 1999)

John R. Deitrick

Millbrook. Village (pop 1,429) in Washington (Dutchess Co). Originally a station on the Dutchess and Columbia Railroad (1869), the area quickly grew into a small commercial village incorporated in 1895. A milk condensing plant of the US Condensing Co encouraged the production of fluid milk on nearby farms. Halcyon Hall, an ornate six-story country home (1893) became Bennett College (1924–77). In the late 1960s the village was briefly the home of Dr Timothy Leary's psychedelic group. Still an important hub of the weekend house region, the village is becoming a tourist attraction.

William P. McDermott

Miller, Frieda Segelke (*b* La Crosse, Wisc, 16 Apr ?1889; *d* New York City, 21 July 1973). Labor reformer and administrator. A graduate of Milwaukee-Downer College (1911), Miller did graduate work at the University of Chicago (1911–15) and taught briefly at Bryn Mawr College in Pennsylvania (1916–17) before becoming executive secretary of the Women's Trade Union League in Philadelphia. She relocated to New York City in 1924, working as a factory inspector for the International Ladies' Garment Workers' Union (ILGWU) and later as a research investigator for the State Charities Aid Association and the New York Welfare Council. In 1929 she became director of the State Labor Department's Division of Women in Industry and Minimum Wage and was a key figure in the passage and enactment of the state's Minimum Wage Law for Women and Minors (1933). From 1938 to 1942 Miller served as New York State's industrial commissioner, overseeing implementation of an ambitious unemployment insurance program and promoting industrial job growth. She joined the US Department of Labor in 1944 as director of its Women's Bureau. Her efforts on behalf of women did not extend to support for the Equal Rights Amendment, which she saw as a threat to essential protections for women in the workforce. Miller left the Labor Department in 1953 but continued to work on labor and women's issues with various international organizations until 1967.

Wallace, Teresa Ann. "Frieda Segelke Miller: Reformer and Labor Law Administrator, 1889–1973" (PhD diss, Boston University, 1983)

Glenn Wright

Miller, Nathan L(ewis) (*b* Solon, Cortland Co, 10 Oct 1868; *d* New York City, 26 June 1953). Governor. Miller's first public office was as a school commissioner in Cortland Co (1894–1900). He served as county Republican chairman until he was appointed state comptroller from 1901 until 1903, when he was appointed to a vacancy in the state supreme court, where he served until 1913. He later served in the Court of Appeals for New York State (1913–15). After resigning from the court he practiced law in Syracuse, becoming general counsel to Solvay Process Co. He ran for governor in 1920 and gave Alfred E. Smith his first political defeat. Miller was a staunch conservative, leading some, including Eleanor Roosevelt, to refer to him as a reactionary. While in office he strengthened the laws against suspected radicals, was suspicious of the political power of newly enfranchised women, and was skeptical of the progressive reforms of Al Smith. In 1922 Smith defeated Miller in the governor's race, and Miller retired from active politics. At the time of his death, Miller was general counsel for US Steel Corp. Colleagues regarded him as a fiscal conservative in politics and a "lawyer's lawyer" in the courtroom.

Branche, Lewis. *Governors of New York* (Watertown: Watertown Daily Times, 1958)

Dick Case

Miller, Warner (*b* Hannibal, Oswego Co, 12 Aug 1838; *d* New York City, 21 Mar 1918). Congressman and senator. Miller attended common schools near Northville (Fulton Co), the Charlotteville Seminary (Schoharie Co), and Union College in Schenectady, where he graduated in 1860. In 1861–62 he served as a private and later as a sergeant major in the Fifth New York Cavalry, and he was captured by the Confederates at Winchester, Va. After the war he worked in a Fort Edward (Washington Co) paper mill, becoming its superintendent, and went to Belgium to study the process. He purchased a Herkimer mill around 1865, forming the Herkimer Paper Co to manufacture pulp paper; he perfected paper-making machinery and is credited with substantially lowering the cost of production. A Republican, he served in the state assembly (1874–75) and the House of Representatives (1879–81), and he was appointed to succeed Roscoe Conkling in the Senate (1881–87), where he supported passage of the oleomargarine bill, eight-hour days for letter carriers, and increased pensions for disabled veterans. In 1888 Miller ran unsuccessfully for governor and returned to his business career. In the early 1890s he served as president of the Nicaragua Canal Co, formed to build a rail and water route between the Atlantic and Pacific oceans.

Green, Nelson, ed. *History of the Mohawk Valley: Gateway to the West* (Chicago: S. J. Clarke Publishing, 1925)

James Crawford

Miller, William (*b* Pittsfield, Mass, 15 Feb 1782; *d* Hampton, Washington Co, 20 Dec 1849). Adventist leader. Raised a Baptist in Hampton, Miller moved from skeptical deism at the turn of the 19th century to religious conversion during the War of 1812. Bible study revealed to him that the prophecies of Christ's Second Coming would be fulfilled in 1843, and in 1831 he began preaching these ideas in nearby communities in New York and Vermont and then throughout the Champlain Valley. Within two years his lecturing carried him to the Hudson and Mohawk Valleys, and in Poughkeepsie, New York Mills (Oneida Co), and Utica, several preachers began promulgating Millerism on their own. In 1839 a group of Boston and New York City professional reformers took charge of the campaign, which spread through the northern states and to England. The Great Disappointment of 1844, which saw his prophecies unfulfilled, led to the rapid dwindling of Millerism, and Miller retired to his farm.

Rowe, David L. *Thunder and Trumpets: The Millerites and Apocalyptic Thought in Upstate New York* (Chico, Calif: Scholars Press, 1985)

David L. Rowe

Miller, William E(dward) (*b* Lockport, Niagara Co, 22 Mar 1914; *d* Buffalo, 24 June 1983). Congressman and vice presidential candidate. Raised in Lockport, Miller returned there to practice law after graduating from Notre Dame University and Albany Law School. He joined the army in 1942 and served as an assistant prosecutor at the Nuremberg trials of Nazi war criminals. Returning to Lockport, Miller's war record propelled him to become Niagara Co district attorney in 1948 and congressman in 1950. He compiled a conservative voting record, although he supported civil rights legislation. Miller's fondness for the political rough-and-tumble and his biting partisan humor helped him become chairman of the Republican National Committee in 1961. In 1964 Miller chose not to run for reelection to Congress when Republican Barry Goldwater picked him as presidential running mate. Defeated in the election, Miller returned to his private law practice in Buffalo. Although he never ran for elective office again, Miller chaired the Niagara Frontier Transportation Authority from 1971 to 1974, overseeing the modernization of the Buffalo airport. A decade after the 1964 election, Miller made light of his obscurity by proclaiming in an American Express television commercial that he traveled with his card in order to be recognized.

Miller, William E. Papers. Kroch Library, Cornell Univ, Ithaca
Southwick, Leslie H. *Presidential Also-Rans and Running Mates, 1789–1980* (Jefferson, NC: McFarland, 1984)

Timothy Sullivan

Miller Place. Locality (pop 10,570) in Brookhaven (Suffolk Co). Andrew Miller settled here in 1671. A post office, established 1825, was called Miller's Place until 1894 when the current form was adopted. Miller Place had been a farming district, but in the 19th century its Long Island Sound landing became a stop for schooners supplying cordwood to New York City. It was also served by the Long Island Rail Road from 1894 until 1938, when service east of Port Jefferson was discontinued. Dominated by suburban tracts in the early 21st century, the hamlet retains an impressive array of 18th- and 19th-century buildings listed on the National Register of Historic Places.

Richard F. Welch

Millerton. Village (pop 925) in North East (Dutchess Co). North East Station on the Harlem Railroad was established in 1850 and led to the growth of a trading center, renamed Millerton in 1860. New railroads linking it to southern Dutchess Co, Poughkeepsie, and Connecticut in the 1870s strengthened its position, and it incorporated in 1875. Eddie Collins Memorial Park (1964) was dedicated to the Baseball Hall of Famer (1887–1951). All rail service was discontinued in 1980. It remains a market village serving nearby localities and farms.

William P. McDermott

Mill Neck. Village (pop 825) in Oyster Bay (Nassau Co). The village is bounded on the east by Oyster Bay Harbor. Shortly after Oyster Bay's 1653 founding, the town's leaders granted Henry Townsend land along the Mill River, and he built a gristmill (1661). The land west of this stream was known as Mill River Neck, shortened to Mill Neck in the late 18th century. The village was incorporated in 1925 and remains an exclusive residential community. The former Lillian Dodge estate is now the Mill Neck Manor School for the Deaf (1951).

Tom Kuehhas

Millport. Village (pop 297) in Veteran (Chemung Co). Lumbering was the first industry; later there was a woolen factory (1823), tannery (1825), boat shop (1834), and furniture factory (by 1853). The Mill Port post office opened in 1832 in advance of the opening of the Chemung Canal (1833–78). The village was served by the Northern Central Railway (1849; later Pennsylvania Railroad). Population declined after the closing of the canal, but the Millport Bridge Works produced iron highway bridges in the 1880s. From 1869 to 1930, the village school was a two-story octagon building. Millport began to invest in restoration by 1990. Early 21st-century industry includes manufacture of industrial swabs and tire brushes.

Heather A. Wade

Milo. Town (pop 7,026) in E central Yates Co. Settled in ?1788, many of Milo's settlers were followers of Jemima Wilkinson, the Public Universal Friend. The town was formed from Benton in 1818. Industrial development occurred along the Crooked Lake Outlet, where waterpowered mills processed corn, wheat, timber, flaxseed, and wool. After the Civil War grape culture became important, and the Seneca Lake Grape and Wine Co (1867) began harvesting the state's largest (100-acre/40 ha) vineyard a few years later. Milo was served by the Northern Central Railway (1851) and Fall Brook Railroad (1877). In the 1890s many Danes settled on its farms. A Morton Salt plant (1970–79) near Himrod had a brief existence. In the early 21st century Milo is a farming town with summer recreation, tourism, and four wineries. A Groffdale Conference Mennonite community located in town around 1980.

Gwen Chamberlain

Milton. Town (pop 17,103) in central Saratoga Co. It was settled from 1772 to 1773 and formed from Ballston in 1792. While chiefly agricultural, the abundant waterpower of the Kayaderosseras Creek powered 55 saw- and gristmills in 1824. Later it powered paper mills in a string of villages along its length, as well as a tannery and an ax and scythe works; only Cottrell Paper Co survives into the 21st century. Ballston Terminal Railroad (1896), later Eastern New York Railroad, although electric, handled the mill freight until it closed in 1928. Starting in 1952 the Kenneth A. Kesselring Site of Knolls Atomic Power Laboratory became the largest employer in town and stimulated suburban growth. Most of Ballston Spa, the county seat, is in the town.

Field Horne

Mina. Town (pop 1,176) in SW Chautauqua Co. It was settled in 1816 by Alexander Findley on the shore of the lake named for him. The town formed in 1824 from Clymer. Lakeside Assembly (1895–1915), established by the United Brethren on Findley Lake, was modeled on the Chautauqua Institution. The lake provides year-round recreation, and the hamlet of that name has flourished with tourism and improved access via Rte 17 (I-86), completed through Mina in 1983.

Michelle Henry

Minden. Town (pop 4,202) in SW Montgomery Co. Minden was the site of an important

Mohawk Indian fort along the Otsquago Creek 4 miles (6 km) southwest of Fort Plain. Settled by Palatine Germans in the early 18th century, it was raided often during the Revolutionary War, and in 1780 the women of the community armed themselves and defended it. The town was formed in 1798 from Canajoharie. Minden's 19th-century agriculture emphasized dairy and hops. The Thruway was built across the town in 1954. Most of Minden remains farmland, enhanced by a growing Amish community.

James Crawford

Mineola. Village (pop 19,234) in Hempstead and North Hempstead (Nassau Co). The village of Hempstead Branch developed after the Long Island Rail Road built a branch (1839) from the main line to Hempstead. Its post office (1844) was renamed Mineola in 1858. Mineola became the county seat of Nassau Co when it was formed in 1899. The village incorporated in 1906. In the early 1900s Jericho Turnpike was part of the Vanderbilt Cup racecourse. During World War I soldiers from Camp Mills in Garden City patronized Mineola businesses, bringing prosperity that continued until the depression. In 1937 the county took over the old Mineola fairgrounds for a government center and expanded it in 1952. Population growth was greatest in the 1920s and again in the 1940s and 1950s. A residential community with light industry and many law offices, Mineola is the political and legislative center of Nassau Co. It has a significant Portuguese American population and is the site of Winthrop-University Hospital.

Georgina Martorella

Minerva. Town (pop 796) in SW Essex Co. Settled in 1804 the town was formed from Schroon in 1817. Its hemlock and spruce forest was developed for commercial lumbering beginning around 1840, and there was a tannery (*ca* 1840–67) and an ironworks (*ca* 1870). The North Woods Club (1886) is a private enclave with clubhouse and cottages. In the early 21st century lumbering and outdoor recreation businesses dominate. It was the home of the folksinger "Yankee" John Galusha (1859–1950) and seasonal residence of Winslow Homer.

Thomas A. Rumney

Minetto. Town (pop 1,663) in W Oswego Co. The town was formed in 1915 from the Town of Oswego. The Minetto Shade Cloth Factory (1879) was taken over in 1914 by Columbia Mills, which manufactured venetian blinds, cotton bagging, surgical gauze, label cloth, and book cloth. The company built homes and recreation buildings for its employees. The name was changed to Minetto-Meriden Co before closing in 1977. At Minetto is a complex bridge (1915–17) consisting of a multispan, reinforced concrete arch over the Oswego River and a steel truss over the canal.

Barbara J. Dix

minimum wage. The legally established minimum pay rate for workers, according to New York State law, must be "sufficient to provide adequate maintenance and to protect health." The Factory Investigating Commission, led by state senator Robert Wagner and state assemblyman Alfred E. Smith, recommended a minimum wage for women and minors in 1915. Smith went on to press for minimum wage legislation when he was elected governor in 1919, but pressure did not reach a critical level until the Great Depression resulted in drastic wage cuts. The National Consumers League, based in New York City, led the drive for minimum wage legislation and Gov Herbert H. Lehman signed the state's first minimum wage law in 1933. Under this legislation state-appointed wage boards would set minimum wage levels on an industry-by-industry basis. Although unions would be the chief advocates for later minimum wage increases, at the time labor opposed state involvement in setting wages and instead focused on collective bargaining to determine pay rates. Under deteriorating economic conditions, the law met with little opposition from businesses and their Republican allies in the legislature. The US Supreme Court declared the law and others in the nation unconstitutional in *Morehead v New York ex rel Tipaldo* (1936) based on an earlier ruling, *Adkins v Children's Hospital* (1923), that minimum wage legislation infringed on the freedom of employees and employers to make their own employment contracts. However, the Court reversed itself the following year when a single justice changed his position. New York State passed new minimum wage legislation immediately thereafter. These early minimum wage provisions applied only to women and minors. In 1944 the legislation was amended to include men.

Under Gov Nelson A. Rockefeller the first statewide minimum wage of $1 per hour was instituted in 1960. The statewide standard eventually replaced the industry-specific wage boards, although separate standards were maintained for agricultural workers, hotel and restaurant employees, domestic workers, and a few other exceptional categories. The statewide minimum wage has been increased several times, sometimes as a direct result of state statute and sometimes as a result of federal minimum wage increases that were made automatic in state legislation. The rate was increased from $4.25/hr to $5.15/hr in 2000, bringing the state minimum wage in line with the federal rate. Unions and other advocates for the poor and working class continue to press for a higher minimum wage, insisting that the minimum rate should provide a "living wage" sufficient to allow workers and their families to avoid poverty. Organizations representing small businesses, such as the Business Council of New York State and the Retail Council of New York State, have opposed increases, arguing that higher wages hurt their businesses and harm competitiveness.

Ingalls, Robert P. "New York and the Minimum Wage Movement, 1933–1937," *Labor History* 15 (Spring 1974): 179–98

Waltman, Jerold. *The Politics of the Minimum Wage* (Urbana: Univ of Illinois Press, 2000)

Brian Obach

mining and mineral industry. The abundant mineral wealth of New York State was known to Native American peoples, who established specific, widely known sites for the extraction of chert or rough flint for projectile points, of clay for pottery, and of iron and manganese minerals for red, yellow, and black pigments. As soon as Europeans arrived in New Netherland, they began to search for mineral wealth, particularly precious metals. Initially they traded for such metals with Native Americans. The settlers never found gold and silver in economic quantities, but they encountered other metals of greater importance for daily life. Iron was first extracted from bog deposits, small pockets of limonite [FeO(OH)] located in swamps on eastern Long Island in the 1640s. By the 1750s settlers of the eastern Hudson Highlands were taking limonite from weathered pockets of rock. Although these deposits were scanty, further exploration revealed more plentiful deposits of magnetite (Fe_3O_4). This became the iron ore of choice in mines in Orange Co. Local refineries reduced the ore to metal, which was used for cookware, tools, weapons, and construction materials. The lead ore galena (PbS) and copper-bearing chalcopyrite ($CuFeS_2$) were mined in the Hudson Valley and mid-Hudson region, in particular at Ellenville (Ulster Co) and in northeastern Dutchess Co. Because galena contains traces of silver, attempts were made to establish mines for silver but were unsuccessful. In addition to mineral ores, the colonists quarried stone—marble, limestone, and sandstone—for building purposes. Clay, common in the Hudson Valley, was used for manufacturing brick and rough pottery.

The 19th Century to World War I

New York State's mining industry enjoyed its heyday during the 19th century. The center of iron mining shifted from the lower Hudson Valley to the Adirondacks, with operations at Mineville, Port Henry, and Crown Point (Essex Co) by 1825, although the mid-Hudson limonite mines and siderite ($FeCO_3$) mines continued to produce iron ore. At the time of the Civil War, iron from the Adirondacks constituted 25% of the nation's production and was critical to the Union war effort. Iron from North Country blast furnaces was used for many essential items, from stoves to cannons to horseshoes. Between 1880 and 1918, 23 million tons (20.9 million MT) of iron ore worth $70 million were mined statewide, mostly in the Adirondacks. During the same period, entrepreneurs established a range of other works in the region: galena mines, for lead; pyrite (FeS_2) mines, for sulfur; graphite (C) mines, supplying raw material for pencils, crucibles, and electrical components; garnet mines, producing garnet for abrasives; and talc mines, primarily supplying paint and soap factories. From 1892 a single mine at Wilmurt

Garnet is crushed for use in making abrasives. Photograph by Shannon P. Quinn.

(Herkimer Co) in the southern Adirondacks yielded diatomaceous earth, a soil bearing microscopic fossilized shells, which was marketed as infusorial earth and used for polishing.

Beginning in 1895, emery—a natural mixture of magnetite, corundum (Al_2O_3), and other minerals—was mined at Peekskill (Westchester Co); the emery was used as an abrasive. From 1890 quartz sand was extracted from deposits in Durhamville and Dumbarton (Oneida Co), supplying factories in Lancaster, Ithaca, Syracuse, Lockport, and Clyde that used the sand in glass manufacturing. From 1894 quarry workers cut quartz in Wawarsing and Rochester (Ulster Co) for locally manufactured grindstones. Some of this rock, crushed to sand, also supplied the glassworks at Corning (Steuben Co). Several companies recovered molding sand from shallow deposits, primarily a few inches below the surface of Albany Co, to supply the iron-casting industry of nearby Troy (Rensselaer Co) and other markets.

Quarries across the state continued to cut granite, sandstone, slate, marble, and limestone for construction purposes and for millstones. Statewide, more than 400 concerns mined clay for brick, terra cotta, roofing tile, and coarse grades of pottery. From about 1825 iron mines worked hematite (Fe_2O_3) deposits in Madison Co and elsewhere in Central New York; these mines also yielded pigment for mineral paints, providing the raw material for "barn red" paint. During the same period, Welsh quarry workers in Granville and other Washington Co towns cut red and green slate for roofing shingles, and waste slate was finely ground for paint pigment. Mining attracted Irish and Italian workers and others from various immigrant groups.

Throughout the 19th century, halite (salt, NaCl) and gypsum ($CaSO_4 \cdot 2H_2O$) were mined in Central and Western New York. Miners dug salt, used as a preservative and in chemical processes, from underground mines and also extracted it from the brines of specially prepared wells; through 1908 New York State controlled a large portion of the nation's salt-brine industry. The Syracuse area, Ithaca, Watkins Glen (Schuyler Co), and Retsof (Livingston Co) had notable salt mines and wells. Gypsum, used in fertilizer and plaster, was mined in open cuts; construction of the Erie Canal spurred development of gypsum mines in Union Springs (Cayuga Co), Seneca Falls (Seneca Co), Phelps (Ontario Co), Le Roy (Genesee Co), and Wheatland (Monroe Co). Limestone of a special composition—high calcium, low magnesium, a modest amount of aluminum, and a little iron—was mined for the raw material for Portland cement across the state where it was available.

Modern Period

From the end of World War I to the beginning of World War II, there was a decline in mining activity, though mines for sphalerite (ZnS), a primary zinc ore, were established in Balmat (St. Lawrence Co) in 1920 and prospered into the early 21st century. Graphite mining in the state ceased in 1921, and building-stone quarries closed or slowed production beginning in the early 20th century. Only the largest iron mines such as those at Mineville and Port Henry survived through the 1940s, and just two garnet mines remained in operation into the same era. Of two small emery mines in Westchester Co, one failed by the 1950s, but the other continued to produce emery until the 1980s.

World War II revived some quarters of the mining industry. The need for domestic sources for certain raw materials rejuvenated large iron mines in Essex, Clinton, and St. Lawrence Cos. From 1938 to 1945, the mines at Mineville alone produced more than 8 million tons (7.2 million MT) of ore. A 19th-century iron mine at Tahawus (Essex Co) reopened as an ilmenite ($FeTiO_3$) mine, providing titanium dioxide, an essential component of paint pigment and chemical smoke screens. These mines continued to operate for as long as 40 years, though all had closed by 1982. In the 1950s a new commodity—the mineral wollastonite ($CaSiO_3$)—entered the market as a filler material and found particular utility in the manufacture of molded resin automobile body panels. At the beginning of the 21st century, two Adirondack mines at Willsboro (Essex Co) and at Harrisville (Lewis Co) produce a third of the world's wollastonite supply. The last of New York State's gypsum mines closed in 1999 at Oakfield (Genesee Co); all the state's iron and titanium mines had closed by this date as well.

In the late 20th century, industrial talc mines in St. Lawrence Co remained viable, with the discovery of new uses for talc as filler in paper, ceramics, and synthetic rubber. Halite, extracted as both rock salt and brine, remains an important commodity at the beginning of the 21st century, as does clay for bricks and Portland cement. Small mines located throughout the state continue to produce peat for agricultural purposes. Garnet is still produced for abrasives and water filtration, and granite, slate, and bluestone or sandstone quarries show continued strength from the strong construction economy of the 1990s. By far the most important mines in the state during the modern period are those producing construction aggregates: crushed stone, sand, gravel, and Portland cement. At the beginning of the 21st century, 2,500 mines operate, providing direct employment for about 5,000 people and indirect employment for between five and nine times that number. Mines for construction aggregates—used to build roads, houses, schools, and airports, and for many other projects requiring fill, concrete, or asphalt—represent 90% of all these mines. Among comparative state rankings in the early 21st century, New York State is first in wollastonite and garnet, third in salt, fourth in talc, sixth in dimension stone, and eighth in Portland cement. The value of raw minerals produced in 2000 was conservatively estimated at $1 billion, and the state ranks 16th in the United States in terms of value of mineral production, excluding oil and gas.

Isachsen, Y. W., et al. *Geology of New York: A Simplified Account* (Albany: NYS Museum, 1991)
Newland, David H. *The Mineral Resources of the State of New York* (Albany: NYS Museum, 1921)

William M. Kelly

Minisink. Town (pop 3,585) in SW Orange Co. Settled around 1725–30, the community was raided by Joseph Brant and allied Indians in 1779. Formed in 1788 from Goshen, the town was the county's largest producer of Goshen butter in the 1840s; after the New Jersey Midland Railroad came through in 1868, it was a milk-shipping town. In the early 21st century, intensive agriculture continues on the muck soils in the southeast along the Wallkill River.

Minoa. Village (pop 3,348) in Manlius (Onondaga Co). It was settled *ca* 1810 by Palatine Germans from the Mohawk Valley and German speakers from Alsace-Lorraine *ca* 1825 who later formed St. Mary's Roman Catholic Church (1837), a parochial school (1841), and a Lutheran church (1855). Served by the Syracuse and Utica (1839) and West Shore (1883) Railroads, both incorporated into the New York Central, the post office was called Manlius Station from 1855 to 1895. In 1913, 14 female property owners exercised their right to vote by supporting an incorporation petition; the village incorporated that year. The East Syracuse Railroad yards expanded eastward in 1940, providing additional employment and operating 24 hours a day. The growth of residential subdivisions has more than doubled the village population since 1970.

Barbara S. Rivette

minority-owned businesses. Although racial minorities in New York State, especially African Americans, had owned businesses since the 18th century, opportunities were severely circumscribed by hardened attitudes toward race. Notable exceptions in the 19th century included the Albany-based real estate developer Dinnah Jackson and a meat supply business in Rochester owned by Austin Steward. As Manhattan's Harlem emerged as the state's center of black life at the turn of the 20th century, numerous black-owned enterprises surfaced there. They included the newspapers *New York Age* (1887) and *Amsterdam News* (1909), the United Mutual Life Insurance Co founded in 1930, and numerous law and medical offices such as the dentistry practice of Bessie Delany, which operated from the 1920s into the 1940s.

A significant expansion in New York State's black businesses had to wait for the emergence of the modern Civil Rights Movement. In 1969 Pres Richard M. Nixon created the Office of Minority Business Enterprise (MBE; from 1979, Minority Business Development Agency) within the US Commerce Department, and in 1971 the US Congress funded the office, authorizing it to provide monies to both national and local minority business development organizations. While opponents contended that the programs benefited only a few politically connected firms, proponents argued that these programs evened a playing field historically warped by racism and discrimination. From 1970 on, federal law expanded to include other minorities besides African Americans, such as Latinos, Asians and Pacific Islanders, American Indians, and Alaska natives.

The federal Public Works Employment Act of 1977 required that 10% of all federal public works contracts be awarded to minority businesses, and in 1980 the US Supreme Court ruled in *Fullilove v Klutznick* that such set-asides were constitutional. After the US Congress passed the 1982 Surface Transportation Act, which allocated large sums for federal, state, and local transportation projects, New York State established the Disadvantaged Small Business Program in the same year to assist minority-owned firms in gaining some of the resulting contracts. But the New York City Transit Authority was slow to comply with the federal act. Partly in response to this situation, in 1985 the New York State Unified Minority/Women Business Enterprise Certification Program was established to improve qualification procedures in all MBE programs, in particular, to prevent fraud and abuse by firms that were not at least 51% minority owned. The certification program provided a pool of verified firms for use in procurement programs for all state agencies and public authorities.

In a 1989 ruling, *City of Richmond v Croson,* the US Supreme Court required states to prove a pattern of discrimination against any potential beneficiaries of MBE programs before such programs could be instituted. Proofs would involve expensive disparity studies that states and municipalities were unwilling to undertake. After the *Croson* decision, the Port Authority of New York and New Jersey eliminated its mandatory goals but kept other initiatives. In 1992, in response to a survey in New York City revealing inequality in city contract awards, Mayor David Dinkins formed the New York City Minority and Women-Owned Business Enterprise Program, and in the following year this program allocated $272 million in 18 contracts through set-asides; it was phased out in 1998.

A 1997 report of the Survey of Minority-Owned Businesses indicated that New York led all states with the largest number of black-owned businesses (86,469). It ranked second in Asian and Pacific Islander–owned businesses (123,258). Of these, 51,023 were owned by ethnic Chinese, 29,288 by Asian Indians, and 20,244 by Koreans. The state ranked fourth in Latino-owned businesses; of 104,189 firms, 60,603 were owned by Latin Americans and 17,124 by Puerto Ricans. Black business ownership had more than quadrupled since 1977, when only 17,530 enterprises in the state were owned by Blacks, but had not kept pace with the growth in numbers of Latino-owned firms (5,151 in 1977) and of Asian and Pacific Islander–owned firms (6,093 in 1977). New York State's businesses owned by American Indians and Alaska natives numbered 2,911 in 1977 and 6,443 in 1997. Of all US minority-owned firms, 40–45% operated in the service sector.

According to the 2002 list published by New York City–based *Black Enterprise* of the top 100 black businesses, the city was home to the 4 top black-owned investment firms and 5 of the top 10 black-owned private equity firms in the nation. Additionally, Carver Federal Savings Bank, founded in 1949 at 53 West 125th St, was the largest black-owned bank in the country. Hip hop has been a boon to New York City's black-owned businesses. Phat Farm (Russell Simmons), Sean John (Sean "P. Diddy" Combs), and Roc-A-Wear (Jay-Z) apparel companies—all headquartered in New York City and capitalized at more than $100 million each—have become important in the international urban fashion scene.

Wainwright, Jon S. *Racial Discrimination and Minority Business Enterprise: Evidence from the 1990 Census* (New York: Garland Publishing, 2000)

Walker, Juliet E. K. *History of Black Business in America: Capitalism, Race, Entrepreneurship* (New York: Macmillan, 1998)

Quincy T. Mills

minstrelsy. Performance involving singing, dancing, and comedy done in blackface makeup. With roots in both African and European traditions but originating in New York City and other northern cities in the early 1830s, the form spread quickly throughout the country. American theatrical works in blackface go back to at least the 1751 performance of *Othello.* Comic characters in blackface appeared later in the 18th century. The first American comic song performed in blackface and African American dialect was "Backside Albany" (*ca* 1815) by New York City composer Micah Hawkins. Athletic dancing was a critical element in early minstrel performance. The African American dancer Henry Lane, known as Juba, from the Five Points area of Manhattan, was a key figure in the development of minstrel dance.

One of the first minstrel stars in New York State was George Washington Dixon, a white Virginian who came north around 1825. Dixon worked with Blanchard's Family Circus in Buffalo, then with the Albany Circus Co in 1827–28. He sang the sentimental blackface song "Coal Black Rose" at New York City's Bowery Theatre, Chatham Garden Theatre, and Park Theatre in 1829. In 1834 Dixon introduced the song "Zip Coon" about a stereotypical flashy and pretentious African American, its melody surviving as "Turkey in the Straw." Minstrel star Thomas Dartmouth "Daddy" Rice (1808–60) made his career dancing as a character named Jim Crow, a shambling, ill-kempt black man. He first performed it in Cincinnati around 1829–30 and brought it to the Bowery in 1833, where it became a sensation. The Bowery theaters were leading venues for minstrel performances. The early audience consisted primarily of young, lower-class white males such as newsboys and street toughs known as Bowery boys. In the early decades especially, imitation and mockery of African Americans was leavened with lampoons of lawyers, politicians, and other members of the upper class. Rice's burlesque skit *Rochester Knockings* (*ca* 1850) spoofed the supposed spiritual powers of the Fox Sisters.

Around 1840 the minstrel show repertoire and format were more or less standardized and gentrified, as bawdy material was banished by the most popular troupes. The lineup typically consisted of four to eight men who sang and played instruments, mostly banjo, fiddle, tambourine, and bones. The percussion was played by two comics or "end men," known as Tambo and Bones, flanking the others. The music included quasi-sentimental love ballads, songs of frontier river life, and parodies of opera, along with comic routines. The most enduring repertoire to emerge from minstrel culture were the plantation songs of Stephen Foster (1826–64), such as "Oh! Susanna" (1847), "Old Folks at Home" (1851), and "My Old Kentucky Home, Good Night" (1853). Foster spent the last years of his life in New York City.

Christy's Original Virginia Minstrels, among the most popular troupes of the 1840s and 1850s, originated in Buffalo in 1842 and toured western and northern New York State between 1843 and 1845. The troupe's leader, Edwin P. Christy (1815–62), was from Philadelphia; cofounder George Harrington (1827–68), who adopted Christy as his name, hailed from Palmyra (Wayne Co). Daniel Emmett (1815–1904), who came to New York City in November 1842, achieved renown as the composer of "Old Dan Tucker" (1843). On 4 Apr 1859 in New York City, while performing with Bryant's Minstrels, he gave the first performance of his composition "Dixie Land," which would soon become the unofficial anthem of the Confederacy.

After the war, African Americans established their own minstrel troupes, reclaiming material that had been based on their culture. The leading black composer was James Bland (1854–1911), born in Flushing (Queens Co) and the composer of "Carry Me Back to Old Virginny" (1878) and "Oh Dem Golden Slippers" (1879). Among the many great stars of black minstrelsy were the Bohee Brothers and the comedians Billy Kersands and Sam Lucas. Performers starting out in black minstrelsy included songwriter W. C. Handy and comedian Tom Fletcher.

Aspects of minstrelsy lasted well into the 20th century. Leading white singers and comedians, including Eddie Cantor and Al Jolson, gained fame in blackface around 1915. Black vaudeville retained many characteristics of minstrelsy during the years when it was a training ground for the likes of Ma Rainey, Bessie Smith, and Jelly Roll Morton. The great black shows of the 1920s, such as *Shuffle Along* (1921) by Eubie Blake and Noble Sissle, featured black comedians in blackface. The myriad difficulties that minstrel shows present for contemporary sensibilities should not obscure their role as the first significant genre of the American musical theater.

Cockrell, Dale. *Demons of Disorder: Early Blackface Minstrels and Their World* (New York: Cambridge Univ Press, 1997)

Lott, Eric. *Love and Theft: Blackface Minstrelsy and the American Working Class* (New York: Oxford Univ Press, 1993)

Mahar, William J. *Behind the Burnt Cork Mask: Early Blackface Minstrelsy and Antebellum American Culture* (Urbana: Univ of Illinois Press, 1999)

Elliott S. Hurwitt

Minuit, Peter (*b* Wesel [now in Germany], ?1589; *d* West Indies, 1638). Director of New Netherland. In 1624–25 Minuit served as a "volunteer" under the provisional director, Willem Verhulst. His commission to inspect the resources of New Netherland provided him with valuable information about the river systems and access to the fur trade. When he became director in 1626 he already was well acquainted with the colony's strengths and weaknesses. Among his immediate accomplishments were recognizing the strategic importance of Manhattan Island and reestablishing peaceful relations with the Mohawks near Fort Orange [now Albany] after the fort's commander interfered in local Indian affairs. Minuit consolidated settlers on the island for protection after purchasing it from American Indians. He became embroiled in a struggle between two factions of the West India Co over whether to promote colonization to make the colony self-sufficient or to maintain dependence on the company to prevent competition and smuggling. Minuit's interest in colonization was one of the reasons for his recall in 1631. Although deposed as director of New Netherland, Minuit was soon employed in a Swedish venture to establish a colony in the New World. In 1638 Minuit sailed aboard the *Kalmar Nyckel* with men and equipment to begin a Swedish trading colony in the Delaware Valley. Minuit's earlier knowledge of the region led him to an area where the Dutch were weak and the prospects of trade with the Indians were the best. Soon after land was purchased from the local Lenape Indians at the mouth of the Christina River, Minuit set sail for Sweden with a cargo of riches from New Sweden. A visit aboard the Dutch ship *Het Vliegende Hert* at St. Christopher [now Saint Kitts] in the Caribbean led to his death when a hurricane forced ships to leave port. He was never seen again.

Jameson, J. Franklin, ed. *Narratives of New Netherland, 1609–1664* (1909; repr New York: Barnes & Noble, 1967)

Van Laer, A. J. F., ed. and trans. *Documents Relating to New Netherland, 1624–1626* (San Marino, Calif: Henry E. Huntington Library and Art Gallery Press, 1924)

Weslager, C. A. *A Man and His Ship: Peter Minuit and the "Kalmar Nyckel"* (Wilmington, Del: Kalmar Nyckel Foundation of Wilmington, 1989)

Charles T. Gehring

Miracle on Ice. Olympic hockey game between the United States and the Soviet Union on 22 Feb 1980. Played at the Lake Placid Olympic Arena, a US team of current and former college players went against the heavily favored Soviet team, which had defeated National Hockey League all-star teams in pre-Olympic games. The Soviets led 3-2 at the start of the third and final period. A goal by Mark Johnson tied the game, and midway through the period, team captain Mike Eruzione scored to put the United States ahead 4-3. Goalie Jim Craig frustrated the Soviet players for the last 10 minutes. As the game ended with an American victory, the jubilant crowd left the rink chanting "U-S-A!" The remarkable victory by the underdog American team was set against an increase in cold war tensions, highlighted a month earlier by Pres Jimmy Carter's threat to boycott the 1980 Summer Olympics in Moscow over the Soviet invasion of Afghanistan. The game, played during the ongoing hostage crisis in Tehran, seemed to many to restore American pride after a series of international and domestic reverses, and the sporting event was soon widely hailed as a miracle on ice. Almost an afterthought, the American team beat Finland to win the gold medal two days later.

Eskenazi, Gerald, and Dave Anderson. *Miracle on Ice* (New York: Bantam, 1980)

Larry Felser

missions. In 1796 Presbyterians, Dutch Reformed, and Baptists established the New York Missionary Society, one of the new nation's first missionary organizations. This interdenominational association originally concentrated on Indians but quickly turned its attention to establishing new Protestant churches and evangelizing settlers in western territories. Interest in domestic missions accelerated in the 19th century in response to growing religious diversity. In New York it also arose from significant local factors including the rapid settlement of Western New York and the influence of revivals, particularly the preaching of Charles Grandison Finney (1792–1875) in Central and Western New York, which became known as the Burned-over District. This became a breeding ground for a generation of missionaries and social reformers. Local voluntary societies grew out of these revival settings and supported numerous missionaries in the state. The Female Missionary Society of the Western District (1817), for example, raised sufficient funds in its first year to send six missionaries for one- to six-month tours of Western New York. Missionary fervor led to the establishment of colleges throughout the country between 1812 and 1860. In Hamilton (Madison Co), Baptist settler Samuel Payne helped organize the Hamilton Missionary Society (1807) and the Baptist Education Society (1817) (now Colgate University). Samuel Kirkland, Presbyterian missionary to the Oneida Indians, founded Hamilton Oneida Academy (1793) in nearby Clinton (Oneida Co). The school was renamed Hamilton College in 1812.

The Catholic Church in the United States was officially a mission church until 1908. Early New York Catholic missionaries endeavored to convert American Indians but by the 1830s turned their attention to immigrant Catholics through "city missions." Catholics and Protestants created urban missionary organizations to alleviate moral and social problems they found in New York City. In 1812 the interdenominational Society for Supporting the Gospel Among the Poor of the City of New York formed to send missionaries into prisons, almshouses, and hospitals. In the same year the New York Religious Tract Society organized to distribute evangelical literature throughout the state. This was one of the precursors to the American Tract Society (1825), still active in 2002. The New York City Tract Society formed in 1827. Prominent New York philanthropists, such as Arthur Tappan, dedicated themselves to this cause. By 1816 the Young Men's Missionary Society of New York, the Female Missionary Society for the Poor of New York, and the New York Evangelical Society all focused on the moral and economic plight of New York City's poor. By 1851 the Young Men's Christian Association (YMCA), founded in London, began providing food, shelter, and the gospel to New York's poor. Perhaps the most significant New York City mission, the Five Points House of Industry founded by Methodists in 1854, sought to save souls through evangelization, temperance, job training, and education. Other mission charities included the Howard Mission and Home for Little Wanderers (1861) and the New York Colored Mission (1865).

After the Civil War prominent urban mission movements, including the Women's Christian Temperance Union, a national organization that evolved out of activism in Chautauqua Co in the early 1870s, and the Salvation Army, founded in England and established in Manhattan in 1880, continued to see New York City as a particularly acute moral problem requiring a suitable evangelical solution. From the 1880s until about 1910, many Protestant evangelicals turned their attention to Jewish communities in New York City, and converts such as Hermann Warzawiak and Leopold Cohn preached, published tracts, and established congregations. Jehovah's Witnesses, a Christian millennialist sect founded in the 1870s, brought their headquarters to Brooklyn in 1909, seeking converts through door-to-door missionizing throughout the state.

In 1894 Swami Vivekananda brought the Hindu Vedanta Society to New York City. His successful mission to the West began primarily among New York City's most prominent citizens. Father Divine's Peace Mission, established in Brooklyn in 1914 and headed by George Baker (1879–1965), opened interracial homeless shelters and employment bureaus in New York City and the Hudson Valley. One of the most influential of 20th-century New York City missions was the Catholic Worker movement, started by Roman Catholic convert Dorothy Day (1897–1980), who devoted her life to promoting peace through "voluntary poverty," working and living with the city's poor. At the same time Protestant missions continued to proliferate, often resulting in surprising results that reflected the state's changing religious and demographic landscape. For example, convert Joseph S. DeRogatis (1888–1976) founded Calvary Chapel (now Olivet Presbyterian Church) on Staten Island in the 1950s as a Protestant mission church to Italians. Other missionary groups that recruit members on New York City streets include the International Society for Krishna Consciousness, known as the Hare Krishnas, active since the 1960s; the Nation of Islam, centered in Harlem, which has focused efforts within the African American community since the 1960s; and Sun Myung Moon's Unification Church, active since the 1970s. Because New York attracts people from all over the world, its religious diversity continues to present distinct challenges and opportunities for missionaries of every tradition.

See also AMERICAN INDIAN MISSIONS.

Ariel, Yaakov *Evangelizing the Chosen People: Missions to the Jews in America, 1880–2000* (Chapel Hill: Univ of North Carolina Press, 2000)

Smith-Rosenberg, Carroll. *Religion and the Rise of the American City: The New York City Mission Movement, 1812–1870* (Ithaca: Cornell Univ Press, 1971)

Winston, Diane. *Red-Hot and Righteous: The Urban Religion of the Salvation Army* (Cambridge, Mass: Harvard Univ Press, 1999)

Amy DeRogatis

Mitchill, Samuel Latham (*b* North Hempstead [now in Nassau Co], 20 Aug 1764; *d* New York City, 7 Sept 1831). Scientist, editor, and politician. After studying medicine with Dr Samuel Bard in New York City, Mitchill traveled to Edinburgh and received a medical degree with honors at Edinburgh University in 1786. Returning to New York City, he practiced at New York Hospital and studied law. In 1792 he was hired as chair of natural history, chemistry, and agriculture at Columbia College, and in the following year he became a professor of botany. Intrigued by taxonomy, he collected and classified many minerals, flora and fauna, and aquatic organisms throughout New York State. As a chemist he debated with Joseph Priestley over the nature of oxygen, and he gained international recognition for his doctrine of explaining epidemic disease through atmospheric effluvia. In 1797 he founded, with Elihu Hubbard Smith and Edward Miller, the *Medical Repository,* the first American scientific journal, which Mitchill edited until 1821. A Jeffersonian Republican, Mitchill was elected from Manhattan to the state assembly in 1791 and 1798, to the US House (1801–4, 1810–13), and to the US Senate (1804–9). He used these offices to promote the development and use of the steam engine and to advocate for the purchase and exploration of the lands of the Louisiana Purchase. In 1807 he helped found the College of Physicians and Surgeons (now part of Columbia University), where he was professor of chemistry, natural history, botany, and materia medica. In 1826 he resigned to help form Rutgers Medical College (originally based in New York City but sponsored by Rutgers College of New Jersey), where he was vice president for four years. He participated in numerous New York City intellectual societies, including the Philological Society and the Friendly Club, and helped found many others, such as the New-York Historical Society in 1804 and the Lyceum of Natural History (now New York Academy of Sciences) in 1817. Mitchill was a leading shaper of intellectual life in New York City in the first quarter of the 19th century.

Aberbach, Alan David. *In Search of an American Identity: Samuel Latham Mitchill, Jeffersonian Nationalist* (New York: Peter Lang Publishing, 1988)

Bryan Waterman

modern dance. An experimental concert dance form that arose in the early 20th century. New York City was the natural or adopted home of almost all the significant pioneers of American modern dance. Beginning with the introduction of expressive dance routines into the bills of fare at burlesque houses in the late 19th century, modern dance integrated itself into New York City's theatrical world. Its leading exponents, predominantly female, saw it as a radical act, rejecting the stilted idioms of the ballet. Often expressing the ideals of the women's rights movement, the dancers addressed many relevant social issues of the day, including labor organizing, antifascist politics, and racism.

Early Pioneers

Isadora Duncan (1877–1927) arrived in New York City from California in 1895. She was soon performing her own dances, which theatricalized the American aesthetic gymnastic dance tradition, in the salons of wealthy New Yorkers. Duncan's style was characterized by natural posture and locomotion and motions derived from nature, such as water and waves. She deepened this physically expressive tradition through the use of personal, emotional, and at times left-wing political themes danced to symphonic and operatic music. Her concerts at the Metropolitan Opera House, Carnegie Hall, and the Brooklyn Academy of Music between 1898 and 1923 were markers in her development.

Martha Graham. Photograph by Nickolas Muray, 1926.

Two other early modern dance pioneers, Ruth St. Denis (1879–1968) and Ted Shawn (1891–1972), met and married in New York and settled in Los Angeles in 1915 to launch Denishawn, their company and school. In the early 1920s, several former Denishawn company dancers, Martha Graham (1894–1991), Doris Humphrey (1895–1958), and Charles Weidman (1901–75), settled in studios in and around Greenwich Village in New York City to launch careers as choreographers. Graham came to New York City in 1923 and presented her first concert in 1926 at the 48th Street Theatre; the vast majority of her more than 200 dances premiered in theaters in New York State. Of all the early moderns, Graham most radically upended traditional notions of what dance should look like by eschewing fluidity and romanticism in motion and by drawing from a vocabulary that favored stark, angular, taut, and asymmetrical design. Heroic themes, including Greek mythology filtered through a psychological lens, and the celebration of Americana folklore dominated the themes of her dances. By collaborating with contemporary artists, Graham enhanced her dances by using modernist sculptures and mobiles as set pieces and dissonant music as scores.

Doris Humphrey and Charles Weidman premiered their company in 1928 in concerts in Brooklyn and New York City. Unlike Graham, Humphrey's dances presented a more harmonious, often utopian, view of humankind. Humphrey's movement vocabulary favored fluid, musically phrased, curvilinear motion. Hanya Holm (1893–1992) brought influences to America from the European strand of modern dance when she moved to New York City in 1931. She opened a studio based on the work of her German mentor, Mary Wigman (1886–1973), and her dances reflected a strong social conscience and a populist spirit tinged with humor. Holm was a master at designing group movements full of surprising changes of direction and level that ebbed and flowed through the stage space. She was one of the first modern dancers to choreograph for the Broadway stage, and she won awards for *Kiss Me, Kate* (1948) and *My Fair Lady* (1956), among others. Holm ran her own dance studio in New York City from 1936 to 1967. José Limón (1908–72) launched a company in New York City in 1946, showcasing his own and Humphrey's dances. *The Moor's Pavane* (1949), an intricately constructed and passionately danced treatment of the story of Othello, survives as one of his signature works.

Midcentury Dance

A different strand of modern dance reflected the urban experience of working-class Jewish American and African American artists. The flavor of life in the streets of New York City permeated the dances of the next generation of modern dancers. Helen Tamiris (1905–66), whose early training began at the Henry Street Settlement in New York City, created vibrant works tinged with jazz rhythms that both celebrated and questioned the American commitment to democracy, as seen in the work *Walt Whitman Suite* (1934). The solos of Tamiris's husband, Daniel Nagrin (1917–), include *Strange Hero* (1949) and his anti-Vietnam work *The Peloponnesian War* (1968). The latter was developed during a guest residency at SUNY Brockport; it did not use heroic archetypes but instead featured conflicted, ambiguous characters plucked from the contemporary life. Anna Sokolow (1910–2000), who grew up in the New York City tenements, later taught at the Juilliard School for many years. In works examining topics such as the Spanish civil war and the Holocaust, Sokolow employed the amplification of gesture as a communicative tool.

Notable African American modern dancers include Pearl Primus (1919–94), a student of African, Caribbean, and southern black culture who earned a doctorate from New York University. Katherine Dunham (1912–) was a Chicago anthropologist and dancer who staged nightclub revues that theatricalized Afro-Caribbean legends and restaged authentic social dances from ethnographic research. She also set a new version of *Aida* for the Metropolitan Opera in 1963, performed in musicals including *Cabin in the Sky* (1940), and later worked in Hollywood films.

Postwar Avant-Gardists

Erick Hawkins (1909–94), Paul Taylor (1930–), and Merce Cunningham (1919–) were all former members of Graham's company who formed their own companies. Hawkins devised dances that used undistorted, unforced movements to explore spiritual states. Taylor discovered dance while studying visual art at Syracuse University on a swimming scholarship. He moved to New York City in 1952 and founded his first company in 1954 while still a member of Graham's company. His dances are built on basic locomotor actions that are pushed to extremes through distortion, augmentation, or fragmentation. Cunningham employs the raw materials of dance—the body through space over time—with energy and no conscious overlay of emotional intent. He incorporated the chance procedures of his long-time collaborator, composer John Cage (1912–92), into many of his works and launched his full company in 1954.

Other significant modern dancers include Alwin Nikolais (1910–93), an assistant of Hanya Holm, who started his company in 1954. Nikolais disguised the human figure and face through the psychedelic use of lights, slide projections, props, and fabric, with accompaniment by electronic scores. In 1989 Nikolais merged his company with that of former company member Murray Louis (1926–), a crafter of witty kinesthetic portraits. Alvin Ailey (1931–89) founded the Alvin Ailey American Dance Theatre in New York City in 1958. Ailey's work revealed both the pain and the survival spirit of the African American experience. His signature works included *Revelations* (1960) and *Cry* (1971). Since Ailey's death, the company has been under the artistic directorship of Judith Jamison.

The Judson Dance Theatre, founded in 1962 by young choreographers performing at the Judson Church on West 4th St in Greenwich Village, drew on the innovations of Merce Cunningham. Using performers with little or no training, they developed programs emphasizing minimalist movement, gender role reversals, and rituals created around everyday events. They performed at a variety of locations around New York City, including rooftops, Central Park, museums, and Grand Central Terminal. Judson veteran alumna Twyla Tharp (1941–) used an eclectic mixture of ballet, jazz, social dance, tap, and modern dance to reinvigorate postmodern dance at a time when it was concerned with cerebral, formalistic investigations. Tharp enjoys crossover fame as a choreographer who works with both ballet and modern dancers and has created works such as *Push Comes to Shove* (1976), commissioned by the American Ballet Theatre and featuring Mikhail Baryshnikov. Tharp's collaboration with composer Billy Joel, *Movin' Out*, opened on Broadway in 2002. Another Judson alumna, Trisha Brown (1936–), cofounded Judson and Grand Union (1970), an improvisational company. In addition to performing dances on rooftops, Brown's 1971 piece *Walking on the Wall* found dancers supported by mountain climbing gear as they dangled from walls and ceilings in Manhattan lofts and museums.

Significant recent choreographers include Garth Fagan (1940–), who founded The Bottom of the Bucket, But . . . Dance Theatre (now Garth Fagan Dance) in Rochester while teaching at SUNY Brockport. The dancers he developed in community classes in Rochester became the basis for his original company. Fagan's cross-cultural mix of modern dance, Afro-Caribbean dance, and ballet features undulating torsos, quick transitions from earth to air, and freely flung limbs, all performed at breathtaking speeds. Fagan choreographed the Broadway version of *The Lion King* (1997).

The dances of Bill T. Jones (1952–) marked a return to frank emotional expression and direct political statement in modern choreography. While an athlete at SUNY Binghamton, Jones met his future collaborator, Arnie Zane (1947–88). Together they launched the American Dance Asylum (1974) in Binghamton, which became Bill T. Jones/Arnie Zane and Dancers in 1982. Headquartered in New York City, the choreographers created dances filled with striking juxtapositions of politically charged or personally confessional texts, among them *Last Supper at Uncle Tom's Cabin/The Promised Land* (1990), and explored terminal illness in *Still/Here* (1994). Ballet, modern, theater, and opera companies commission new works from Jones, and his company tours internationally. After a significant career as a performer with a number of New York City modern companies, Mark Morris (1956–) formed the Mark Morris Dance Group in 1980. A highly musical choreographer with a background in folk dance forms, he creates dances that are filled with quirky movement choices that purposely contrast the elegance of the classical and operatic music he favors. He opened a school and company headquarters in Brooklyn in 2001.

Professional presenting venues for modern dance performances have flourished in New York City. Some of the sites that have contributed greatly to building enthusiastic audiences for modern dance include Dance Theatre Workshop, Brooklyn Academy of Music, the Joyce Theatre, La Mama, City Center, the Danspace Project at St. Mark's Church, P.S. 122, the 92nd Street Young Men's Hebrew Association, Symphony Space, Alice Tully Hall, Aaron Davis Hall, the Nikolais-Louis Dance Lab, and the Cunningham Studio.

Banes, Sally. *Terpsichore in Sneakers: Post-Modern Dance* (Middletown, Conn: Wesleyan Univ Press, 1977)
Bremser, Martha, ed. *50 Contemporary Choreographers* (New York: Routledge, 1999)
Foulkes, Julia L. *Modern Bodies: Dance and American Modernism from Martha Graham to Alvin Ailey* (Chapel Hill: Univ of North Carolina Press, 2002)
Graff, Ellen. *Stepping Left: Dance and Politics in New York City, 1928–1942* (Durham, NC: Duke Univ Press, 1997)
Lowenthal, Lillian. *The Search for Isadora: The Legend and Legacy of Isadora Duncan* (Pennington, NJ: Princeton Book Co, 1993)
Magriel, Paul, ed. *Nijinsky, Pavlova, Duncan: Three Lives in Dance* (New York: Da Capo Press, 1977)
Maynard, Olga. *American Modern Dancers: The Pioneers* (Boston: Little, Brown, 1965)
Perpener, John O., III. *African-American Concert Dance: The Harlem Renaissance and Beyond* (Urbana: Univ of Illinois Press, 2001)

Robin Lakes

Modern Times. A 90-acre clearing in the pinewoods of northern Islip (Suffolk Co), Modern Times was founded in 1851 by Josiah Warren (1798–1874), one of America's early propounders of philosophical anarchism, and his writing partner, Stephen Pearl Andrews (1812–86), a lawyer, linguist, and self-styled "universologist." Modern Times was created to prove the merit of "equitable commerce," a design for living based on Warren's two major tenets: "sovereignty of the individual" entitled people to live as they pleased, providing this did not impede the right of others to do the same; "cost the limit of price" committed them to swap labor, exchange goods at cost, and coin currency known as labor notes that promised payment in hours of work at the issuer's occupation. Contrasted with the religious, property-sharing majority of experimental communities, property was private, households were nuclear, and freethinkers far outnumbered believers.

Private but profitless enterprise could not prevail against a burgeoning market economy. Cash-poor pioneers, never more than 150 strong, could acquire land and build houses but otherwise settled for a lifestyle rich in discussion of social problems but poor in standard of living. Indifference to whether couples lived in or out of wedlock evoked a lurid reputation in the eyes of the outside world, compounded in 1853 when a cluster of sexual radicals made an unsuccessful effort to enlist Modern Times in the cause of "free love" (women's rights to its advocates but random sex to critics). When wealthy buyers started bidding for property, the cost principle broke against the power of the dollar. In 1864 the residents ended their experiment and changed the name of Modern Times to Brentwood.

As a factor in Long Island history, Modern Times was an early settlement on the empty tracks of the Long Island Rail Road, then bankrupt after completion of a line on the mainland shattered its hope to link New York and Boston. The gardens and orchards of Modern Times/Brentwood showed skeptics that the disparaged soil of the pine barrens could be cultivated. Although the practice of equitable commerce failed to endure, Modern Times's toleration of unwed couples forecast future flexibility in legally sanctioned living arrangements.

Codman, Charles A. "A Brief History of 'The City of Modern Times,' Long Island, New York—and a Glorification of Some of Its Saints," *ca* 1905, Brentwood Public Library, Brentwood, NY
Martin, James J. *Men against the State: The Exposition of Individualist Anarchism in America, 1827–1908* (1953; repr Colorado Springs: Ralph Myles Publisher, 1970)
Wunderlich, Roger. *Low Living and High Thinking at Modern Times, New York (1851–1864)* (Syracuse: Syracuse Univ Press, 1992)

Roger Wunderlich

Moffat, Abbot Low (*b* New York City, 12 May 1901; *d* Hightstown, NJ, 19 Apr 1996). Assemblyman. Raised in Manhattan, Moffat earned a BA from Harvard (1923) and an LLB from Columbia University (1926). He entered the state assembly in 1929 with his election from Manhattan's Upper East Side. During the 1930s Moffat, in coordination with other Republican politicians, successfully redirected the state Republican Party toward a new, more politically viable progressive conservatism. As chairman of the assembly's Ways and Means Committee (1936–43), he reached the pinnacle of his power, playing a seminal role in the development of new and expansive state policies in public housing, labor, and highways. He is most publicly noted for his prolonged fight with Democratic governor Herbert H. Lehman. In response to spiraling public expenditures, from 1937 to 1942 Moffat and the Republican leadership in the legislature continually reduced the governor's budget. Though fiscally conservative, Moffat strongly believed in an active state government. He left the assembly in 1943 to begin a second career at the US Department of State. Among his duties Moffat met with Vietnamese nationalist leader Ho Chi Minh in 1946 and urged unsuccessfully for US cooperation with nationalist movements in Southeast Asia. Moffat retired from public life in 1962.

See also NEW YORK STATE THRUWAY.

"Abbot Low Moffat." In *The Modern New York State Legislature: Redressing the Balance,* ed. Gerald Benjamin and Robert T. Nakamura (Albany: Nelson A. Rockefeller Institute of Government, 1991)

Tod M. Ottman

Mohawk. Town (pop 3,902) in N central Montgomery Co. Settled in 1713, the town was formed in 1837 from Johnstown [now in Fulton Co]. It was crossed by the Utica and Schenectady Railroad (1836; later New York Central). A mill at Berrysville produced paper (1860s) and cotton cloth (1890s). The Log Cabin on Rte 5 near Yosts was a well-known jazz venue in the 1930s and 1940s, frequented by saxophonist Sidney Bechet and others. In the early 21st century much of the town's land remains agricultural. Mohawk is the site of Fulton-Montgomery Community College (1964), the National Kateri Tekakwitha Shrine, and the Mohawk-Caughnawaga Indian Museum (1949).

James Crawford

Mohawk. Village (pop 2,260) in German Flatts (Herkimer Co). Mohawk began developing in the 18th century and was the site of mills and a plow factory before the Erie Canal (1821) was put in use, but it grew more rapidly afterward and was incorporated in 1844. Until the Midland and Susquehanna Railroads were built to the south, Mohawk was the farm trading point for a considerable region because of an early road to Richfield Springs. Ironwork, knit goods, and fishing reels were manufactured. The West Shore Railroad (1883) provided direct transportation. In the 20th century most residents worked in the Duofold mill (1906; knit underwear) or for the Remington factories in nearby Ilion. In the early 21st century, residents work for Remington, in service industries, or at jobs to which they commute. Gregory B. Jarvis (1944–86), a graduate of Mohawk High School, was killed in the *Challenger* disaster.

James Crawford

Mohawk Airlines. The nation's premier regional air carrier during the 1960s. Mohawk Airlines began in 1945 as Robinson Aviation, an air taxi service between Ithaca and New York City, founded by C. S. Robinson. In February 1948 the renamed Robinson Airlines obtained a temporary certificate from the Civil Aeronautics Board (CAB) as a local service carrier with authority to fly scheduled routes from Ithaca throughout New York State. Operating a fleet of DC-3s, Robinson in 1950 expanded service to include a major north-south line between Watertown and New York City, and an east-west route between Buffalo and Albany. The company was renamed Mohawk Airlines on 1 Jan 1953, and the next year Robert E. Peach, who started work as a pilot with Robinson, became president. By 1955, when it received a permanent certificate from the CAB, Mohawk Airlines served 28 cities in the Northeast and carried nearly 250,000 passengers, with operating revenue in excess of $3 million.

Mohawk continued to expand over the next 15 years, gaining a reputation as an aggressive, innovative air carrier. Based at Oneida County Airport near Utica after 1957, Mohawk was the first local service carrier to fly pressurized aircraft (1955) and gained widespread publicity in 1957 when it hired the first African American stewardess to fly for a scheduled airline in the United States. In 1962 Mohawk became the first scheduled airline to adopt a computerized reservation system and took the lead in bringing pure jet transports to local service carriers when it ordered four 79-passenger, British-built BAC One-Elevens. By 1969 Mohawk flew to 87 cities in an area bounded by Minneapolis, Toronto, and Washington, DC. Operating a fleet of 23 BAC One-Elevens and 17 turboprop Fairchild Hiller FH-227s, it carried 26 million passengers. Mohawk, however, fell on hard economic times in 1969–70 as it struggled to pay for its new equipment. In 1971 it approached economic collapse as a result of a 154-day pilot strike. The weakened company was acquired and absorbed by Allegheny Airlines on 12 Apr 1972.

Davies, R. E. G. *Airlines of the United States since 1914*, rev ed. (Washington, DC: Smithsonian Institution Press, 1982)

William M. Leary

Mohawk and Hudson Railroad. New York State's first railroad, Mohawk and Hudson (M&HRR), was chartered on 17 Apr 1826 to build a line between Albany and Schenectady. The prime mover behind the project was George W. Featherstonhaugh of Schenectady. He enlisted the support of Albany's Stephen Van Rensselaer, who became company president. The railroad was intended to complement the Erie Canal by providing canalboat passengers with a direct 16 mi (26 km) land route between the cities as an alternate to the circuitous 28 mi (45 km) canal route. Initially capitalized at $300,000, M&HRR had 33 original stockholders, most of whom, including John Jacob Astor, lived in New York City. In 1830 John B. Jervis became the railroad's chief engineer, replacing Peter Fleming, who had made little progress in constructing the line. Jervis used white pine rails capped by wrought-iron strips. Stone blocks supported the tracks, and a macadamized horse path ran between the rails, because horses were needed to pull cars along the slippery rails in winter. Steep grades descended to both river-level terminuses, and 12-horsepower stationary steam engines were required to draw the cars up these inclines; M&HRR was the third US railroad to use steam locomotives. The first track of the projected double-track line opened on 9 Aug 1831, with the locomotive DeWitt Clinton pulling a wood car and six passenger cars from Albany to Schenectady. Regular service started the next month with one-way trips averaging 40 minutes. The Saratoga and Schenectady Railroad, which began operation in 1832, aided M&HRR's passenger business by extending rail travel beyond Schenectady. The M&HRR's freight trade, begun in 1831, was helped by other railroads expanding west of Schenectady. By 1843 six railroads operated between Schenectady and Buffalo, ensuring another decade of prosperity for M&HRR, renamed Albany and Schenectady Railroad in 1847. The company acquired modern, powerful locomotives and completed its conversion to all-iron rails by 1849. Four years later, New York's first railroad merged with seven others to become New York Central and Hudson River Railroad.

Larkin, F. Daniel. *Pioneer American Railroads: The Mohawk and Hudson and the Saratoga and Schenectady* (Fleischmanns, NY: Purple Mountain Press, 1995)

F. Daniel Larkin

Mohawk corridor. A lowland that separates the Adirondack Upland to the north from the Appalachian Plateau to the south and extends west from the Hudson Valley at Albany approximately 100 miles (160 km) to the Ontario Lake Plain at Utica and the edge of the extensive Great Lakes basin. The Mohawk corridor is, when combined with the Hudson Valley, the only low-level breach in the 1,200 mi (1,930 km) long Appalachian Mountains, which extend from Quebec to northern Alabama. The breach permitted comparatively uninterrupted travel between the Atlantic seaboard and the continent's interior lowlands. Although broadened and deepened by ice and torrents of water during the Pleistocene, the corridor is flattest and lowest along the floodplain of the eastward-flowing Mohawk River. Benches rise on both sides of the river to 500 feet (150 m) amid rolling country that is occasionally interrupted by the incised valleys of tributary streams, thus hindering east-west travel beyond the river's floodplain.

Early History

Archaeological evidence in the form of chert (flint) indicates that Paleo-Indian groups were traveling back and forth along this route 10,000–12,000 years ago. Much more recent archaeological evidence shows habitation during the Owasco period, between AD 1000 and 1300. By the 16th century the Mohawk were established in the lowland that bears their name; by the late 1500s European trade goods were finding their way west along the corridor. Aware of the direct connection with the Great Lakes basin and the vast fur resources of the continental interior, the Dutch established Fort Orange in 1624 at the strategic east end of the Mohawk Valley on the west shore of the Hudson River, near what is now Albany. What had been the back door of the previously westward-facing Iroquois Confederacy became the front portal through which European goods such as iron tools, guns, wampum beads, and other trade items flowed west in exchange for furs. In 1634 smallpox spread west along the same route. Later that year Harmen Meyndertsz van den Bogaert became the first resident of New Netherland to venture west along the Mohawk. As a consequence of disease, Mohawk numbers plummeted from an estimated 7,000 to about 2,000 by 1640. Nevertheless the Mohawk held firm control of the gateway. Fur traffic peaked in 1657, when 38,000 pelts were traded at Beverwijck [now Albany]. In 1661 a group of Dutch farmers established the settlement of Schenectady, an advanced post on what was known as Mohawk Flatt, in part to participate in the fur trade.

The valley's strategic importance made it a focus of attention during the colonial wars between Britain and France, beginning with King William's War, when a combined French and Indian force laid waste to Schenectady in 1690. Dutch, Palatine German, Scots-Irish, and English took up lands farther west along the broader lowland in the decades following. Fort Hunter [now in Montgomery Co] was built in 1711 during Queen Anne's War to protect the valley's eastern half while simultaneously extending the trading frontier. During the early 1700s, as European numbers and influence mounted, a majority of the Mohawks abandoned the valley and moved north of the Adirondacks. The French and Indian War led to renewed military activity when the British built Fort Bull [now in Oneida Co] beyond the valley's western mouth in 1756 to guard the Oneida Carrying Place. Within a year French forces overran the fort and went on to destroy the settlement at Herkimer. The British responded by erecting forts at the present-day sites of Utica and Rome (Oneida Co). The fur trade had declined dramatically by 1770, when white settlement extended throughout the length of the corridor. The Revolutionary War brought renewed fighting to the valley and adjacent uplands. No theater was witness to more protracted or intense military activity. More than two centuries later the Mohawk corridor continues to exhibit its past military importance in the form of place-names, military roads, fortified farmhouses, and military markers.

Independence and the opening of Iroquois lands to white settlement led to a stream and soon a flood of settlers from the Hudson Valley and New England traveling up the Mohawk bound for Central and Western New York. Travel was generally undertaken in winter, when roads were more easily traversed. In the span of three days in February 1795, approximately 1,200 sleighs carrying pioneer families were reported to have passed through Albany heading west through the corridor. During the rest of the year, freight often went by river and bateau. Recognizing this fact, the state legislature authorized the incorporation of the semiprivate Western Inland Lock Navigation Co in 1792. Its goal was to clear debris from existing stream channels, to build wing dams to create straighter and deeper channels, and to construct short canals around rapids and other obstacles in the Mohawk and waterways farther west. Although never a financial success, the company did facilitate travel through the corridor by making it possible for much larger Durham boats to make the passage from Schenectady to Oneida Lake. A settlement destined to become Utica began to take form at the west end of the corridor in 1788 at the site of the original Fort Schuyler and a fording point on the Mohawk. Ideally situated to serve as a gateway town, the thriving village soon became the principal supply center and transportation hub for all of Central and Western New York. Stagecoach lines operated along the full length of the corridor by 1794, the same year the state authorized the construction of the Genesee Road from Utica west to Canandaigua (Ontario Co). By 1802 no less than nine stage lines spread from the town to destinations as far apart as Ogdensburg (St. Lawrence Co), Buffalo, and Binghamton. Land travel was further improved with the Albany and Schenectady Turnpike (built 1802–5) and then with the Mohawk Turnpike between Schenectady and Utica and the Seneca Turnpike following the route of the Genesee Road.

The War of 1812 once again illustrated the strategic importance of the Mohawk corridor, as troops and supplies moved west from Albany to places like Sackets Harbor (Jefferson Co) and the Niagara Frontier. Moreover, problems associated with transporting war materials in a timely manner underscored the need for an artificial waterway that would take advantage of the Mohawk lowland and link the Hudson River with the Great Lakes. Completed in 1825, the Erie Canal carried an unprecedented volume of traffic through the corridor. In the canal's first year, over 1,000 boat passengers passed through Utica daily. Freight figures were more remarkable. Two years after the canal's completion over 625,000 barrels of Genesee flour were moved along the corridor to the Port of New York. The canal was such an economic and financial success that in 1835 the state legislature approved a major enlargement program that would triple its capacity. Initially nearly all of the goods moving east originated in Central and Western New York, but by midcentury a majority of the east-bound traffic originated in the upper Midwest. The canal and, by extension, the Mohawk corridor formed the neck of an hourglass through which the bulk of the foodstuffs and other products of the nation's expanding heartland flowed to the Atlantic seaboard, with finished goods and people moving west in return.

The Railroad Era

In 1831 an alternative form of transportation appeared in the corridor when the Mohawk and Hudson, the first railroad in the state, made its inaugural run between Albany and Schenectady. Another railroad, the Utica and Schenectady, began operations along the north shore of the Mohawk River in 1836. Starting in 1843 it was possible to travel from Albany to Buffalo entirely by train, but only by riding on seven different railroads. Initially perceived as primarily passenger carriers, these and other lines merged to form the New York Central Railroad in 1853. Traffic rose steadily, and in 1869 the New York Central and Hudson River Railroad (NYC&HRRR) linked New York with Chicago via Albany, Buffalo, and the Mohawk Valley. By 1875 the route was quadruple-tracked, with freight traffic far exceeding passenger traffic. Although the route from New York City to the Ohio state line was 31 miles (50 km) longer than that of its keenest competitor, the Pennsylvania Railroad, the NYC&HRRR was able to compete effectively because of its nearly level, comparatively straight trackage. In the 1880s a second railroad, the West Shore, was built along the south bank of the Mohawk River and was soon acquired by the NYC&HRRR. Hundreds of passenger trains passed through the corridor every week, carrying many thousands of passengers between the Hudson River and the Great Lakes basin and points west. A large proportion traveled first class; but many were immigrants traveling second class to urban centers in New York State, including communities in the corridor itself, and to the cities or agricultural lands of the upper Midwest and the eastern Great Plains.

Freight traffic volume was equally impressive, as the nation's industrial heartland and its associated economy grew at a rapid rate and the import and export trade out of the Port of New York continued to expand. Nearly all of the higher-value freight moved by rail, leaving the Erie Canal with low-value bulk goods like grain and lumber. Although traffic through the corridor continued to rise in absolute terms, the proportion that passed through the Mohawk Valley en route from the Atlantic Coast to the trans-Appalachian west declined as rail networks grew in size and importance.

The 20th Century

The 20th century brought further change to the transportation facilities along the corridor, beginning in 1903 when work began on a new and much larger canal, one that would dredge and straighten the Mohawk River and make it an integral part of a canal that could accommodate 30,000-ton (27,200 MT) self-propelled barges. Completed in 1918, the Barge Canal was an engineering marvel that never came close to achieving traffic expectations. Freight tonnage peaked in the mid-1950s but by the mid-1990s had disappeared entirely. The canal, renamed the Erie Canal, has attracted thousands of recreational boaters annually in recent years. Rail traffic has also changed dramatically over the century. Passenger service, including trains like the Twentieth Century Limited, remained strong until after World War II. The four-tracked main line of the New York Central was still heavily trafficked at midcentury, although truck transport had a negative impact. As highway traffic made further gains during the 1960s, the four tracks were reduced to two. In the early 21st century the route remains one of the most important freight lines in the eastern United States and is owned by CSX Corp, while Amtrak runs passenger trains through the valley.

The former Albany and Schenectady Turnpike and Mohawk Turnpike, along with the old Genesee Road, were taken over by the state early in the century, and by 1910 much of what came to be designated Rte 5 was paved and attracted early automobile enthusiasts. The road quickly became the most heavily trafficked long-distance, east-west highway in the state. Other parallel highways followed, including Rte 5S on the opposite shore of the Mohawk and US 20 on the southern margin of the corridor. The scenic quality of the latter's route, combined with limited urban development, made it especially popular among seasonal tourists. In response to rapidly expanding highway traffic after World War II, the state built the limited-access New York State Thruway. Opened in 1954, it followed the Mohawk corridor from Utica to Albany. It was later incorporated into the federal interstate system as part of I-90, one of the state's major arteries for passenger and truck traffic.

Ayres, Steven E. "Measuring the Difficulty of Terrain for Railroad Operation: Northeastern United States" (MA thesis, Syracuse Univ, 1969)
Bradley, James W. *Evolution of the Onondaga Iroquois: Accommodating Change, 1500–1655* (Syracuse: Syracuse Univ Press, 1987)
Thompson, John H., ed. *Geography of New York State* (Syracuse: Syracuse Univ Press, 1966)
Ullman, Edward L. "The Railroad Pattern of the United States," *Geographical Review* 39 (1949): 242–56

James W. Darlington

Mohawk Nation. Nation of the Iroquois League. The traditional territory of the Mohawk people is the river valley that bears their name, centered in what is now Montgomery Co. According to tradition, the Mohawk were the first of the Iroquois nations to accept the message brought to them by the Peacemaker at the founding of the league, more than a century before the arrival of Europeans in what is now New York State. The name Mohawk comes from Algonquian-speaking Indians in the Hudson River valley. The Mohawk call themselves Kanien'kehaka ("People of the Flint/Splint"). The easternmost of the Iroquois nations, the "keepers of the eastern door," they conducted external diplomatic relations with eastern Indians and later with Europeans.

A 1609 French expedition under Samuel de Champlain, along with Algonquin and Montagnais allies, defeated the Mohawk in a battle near Ticonderoga [now in Essex Co]. This attack was the first of what would become almost a century of hostilities between the Mohawk and the French. Difficulties in French-Mohawk relations also extended to French missionary politics. The Jesuit missionary Isaac Jogues, with two other priests, sought and found martyrdom among the Mohawks at Ossernenon [now Auriesville, Montgomery Co] in 1646. When wars with France were opposed by Iroquois Christian converts, they moved to villages on the St. Lawrence River with French Jesuit missionaries.

The center of Mohawk-European trade and diplomacy was Albany, begun on Mohican (Mahican) land in 1614 as Fort Nassau, enlarged for trade as Fort Orange in 1624. The Mohawks then fought the Mohicans, and by 1628 the Mohawks had won both the area and the Dutch trade monopoly. The palisaded Mohawk villages in the valley northwest of Fort Orange were called castles by the Dutch. Seven of the villages were visited in 1634 by surgeon Harmen Meyndertsz van den Bogaert, soon after a devastating smallpox epidemic. Located in present-day Montgomery Co, the three largest villages—Ohnekak'ONKE, Skanatis'ON, and TionONTOKEN (known to Van den Bogaert as Onekagoncka, Schanidisse, and Tenotoge)—had 32–55 longhouses each and the four smaller villages had 6–16.

In 1664 the English replaced the Dutch, and New Netherland was renamed New York. To the north, the French remained a distinct hostile force to the Mohawk. They maintained an alliance with the English because of their proximity and their strategic position along the Mohawk River. The Covenant Chain alliance between the British colonies, with New York as the mediator, and numerous Indian nations began in the 1670s. The Iroquois League took the leading role among the Indian nations in reaffirming the Covenant Chain with the British, almost on a yearly basis for the next century. As a sign of their favor with the British, three Mohawks were among the four chiefs, known as the Four Indian Kings, who traveled to London in 1710 to meet with Queen Anne.

Nevertheless, following a treaty of peace with the French in 1701, the Mohawk and the other Iroquois nations tried to remain neutral in the British-French wars of the 18th century. Neutrality became more difficult for these Indians, however, as these conflicts progressed. Sir William Johnson was the dominant figure in Mohawk-British diplomacy from the 1740s until his death in 1774. He developed a relationship with the Mohawk chief Theyanoguin, also known as King Hendrick or Hendrick Peters. In 1755 Theyanoguin accompanied Johnson in a campaign against the French at Fort St. Frédéric [now in Crown Point, Essex Co], but he was killed at the Battle of Lake George.

The Revolutionary War left the pro-American Oneidas and Tuscaroras in conflict with the pro-British Mohawks and Senecas and the neutral Onondagas. Chief Joseph Brant and his sister Molly, the common-law wife of Sir William Johnson, were influential Mohawks who greatly contributed to Mohawk support of the British during the war. Gen George Washington used his Iroquois allies to fight the Mohawk and to invade the territory of the Seneca and Cayuga in the 1779 Sullivan-Clinton campaign. Almost all of the Mohawk people left the Mohawk Valley during the war. Those from the upper Mohawk River village of Canajoharie [now in Montgomery Co] followed Joseph Brant to the Niagara region. Those from the lower settlement of Fort Hunter [now in Montgomery Co] followed Mohawk chief John Deserontyon to Lachine in Quebec.

After the Revolutionary War, when the 1783 Treaty of Paris failed to provide for Great Britain's Indian allies, the Americans were in possession of the traditional Mohawk territory. Canadian governor Sir Frederick Haldimand obtained land along the Grand River on the Niagara peninsula and at the Bay of Quinte on the north shore of Lake Ontario for those Iroquois who fled to Canada. These reserves were settled, respectively, by Brant and Deserontyon and their followers. The Treaty of Canandaigua of 1794 between the Iroquois and the United States established the Iroquois reservations in New York State but did not make any provision for Mohawk reservations. Only one Mohawk representative arrived from Canada for the negotiations. In 1819 a new survey of the international boundary between Canada and northern New York created a Mohawk reservation in New York State. The Canadian Mohawk village of Akwesasne, formerly the Jesuit mission of St. Regis, was split in two after the border was moved.

The Akwesasne community today is partly in New York State, the St. Regis Indian Reservation [loc in Franklin Co], and partly in Quebec and Ontario. The administration of Akwesasne involves several different parties among the Mohawk and numerous non-native governments. The Canadian provincial and national governments recognize the Mohawk Council of Akwesasne, New York State recognizes a separate St. Regis Mohawk Tribal Council. Longhouse religion adherents on both sides recognize only the traditional chiefs of the Mohawk Nation Council. Independent Mohawk communities have more recently been established in New York: Ganienkeh in 1974 on Moss Lake (Herkimer Co), which was relocated in 1977 to Miner Lake (Clinton Co) because of local, non-Indian opposition, and Kanatsiohareke near Canajoharie in 1993.

From the mid- to late 20th century, both revitalization and conflict were a part of life for the Mohawk. In the 1940s Mohawk teacher Ray Fadden organized the Akwesasne Mohawk Counselor Organization to teach crafts, history, and traditional ways to children. A decade later he went on to found the Six Nations Indian Museum in Onchiota (Franklin Co). At approximately the same time, however, Mohawk people at Kahnawake (near Montreal) and Akwesasne fought the construction of the St. Lawrence Seaway. The subsequent industrial buildup along the river near these reservations led to numerous ongoing environmental problems. In December 1968 Mohawks from Akwesasne blockaded the international bridge from Cornwall, Ont, to Massena (St. Lawrence Co) to protest Canadian violations of the 1794 Jay Treaty, in which Indians were guaranteed free access across the border without the payment of customs duties. Early in 1969, shortly after the Canadian government removed their restrictions and duties, the influential activist newspaper *Akwesasne Notes* was founded. The controversial Mohawk Warrior Society was founded in 1973 as a traditionalist organization during the peak of the Red Power movement.

Starting in the late 19th century, men from Akwesasne and Kahnawake started to work as steelworkers in building skyscrapers and other structures, developing a reputation for their fearlessness in working at great heights. By the late 1940s there was a community of about 400 Mohawks living in the Gowanus neighborhood of Brooklyn. Many Mohawks continue to work in construction in New York City. On 11 Sept 2001, Mohawks working around the World Trade Center were among the first responders to the site where many had worked 30 years earlier.

See also AMERICAN INDIANS IN LITERATURE: INDIGENOUS AUTHORS.

Calloway, Colin G. *The American Revolution in Indian Country* (New York: Cambridge Univ Press, 1995)
Campisi, Jack, and William A. Starna. "When Two Are One: The Mohawk Indian Community at St. Regis (Akwesasne)," *European Review of Native American Studies* 14 (2000): 39–45
Hauptman, Laurence M. *The Iroquois Struggle for Survival: World War II to Red Power* (Syracuse: Syracuse Univ Press, 1986)
Snow, Dean. *The Iroquois* (Cambridge, Mass: Blackwell, 1994)

Roy A. Wright-Tekastiaks

Mohawk or Mohican hairstyle. Although many variant forms of the haircut exist, the commonly accepted image is of the head shaved close on both sides and upright hair like a coxcomb, or crest, from the forehead to the nape of the neck. The names refer to Indian nations of New York Colony and New England whose hairstyle was recorded by 17th- and 18th-century explorers. Historians and novelists have long presumed the style was used by Indians when engaged in warfare, which indeed it often was. Recent research suggests it may also have had symbolic significance associated with clan affiliation and sexual abstinence—many Indians practiced sexual abstinence before going into battle. During early years of the United States, many paintings and lithographs depicted famous Indians with the distinctive hairstyle, among them the Mohawk chief Joseph Brant. Although the Mohawk and Mohican names have been popularized in association with the hairstyle, many other Native American groups also were identified with it historically, including the Shawnee, Cherokee, Pawnee, Caddo, and Sauk.

At some point before the mid–20th century, an Indian-style haircut was in vogue with teenage boys attending summer camps, and it was sometimes used as an initiation ceremony by college fraternities. The sudden emergence of the unconventional style may have had its impetus from World War II newsreels showing army and marine recruits receiving mandatory crew cuts, with occasional bizarre variations that imitated the classic Indian style. Whatever the inspiration was, the style came to be called a "Mohawk," with "Mohican" also used at times. In the 1980s the style appeared in punk culture with some people sporting the shaved head with the coxcomb dyed in blaring colors, lending an almost carnival flair to the style.

Leach, Edmund R. "Magical Hair," *Journal of the Royal Anthropological Institute* 88 (1958): 147–64
Wallace, Paul A. W., ed. *30,000 Miles with John Heckewelder* (Pittsburgh: Univ of Pittsburgh Press, 1958)

Arthur Einhorn

Mohawk River (148 mi/238 km). It raises as a series of small, parallel, fast-flowing brooks that drain a large portion of the south slope of the Tug Hill Plateau. Beginning near the rural crossroads of Mohawk Hill (Lewis Co), the East Branch drops rapidly from nearly 1,800 feet (550 m) at its source to 700 feet (210 m) where it joins its first major tributary, Lansing Kill. The stream flows south to Rome (Oneida Co), site of the strategic portage known in colonial times as the Oneida Carrying Place, which links the river and westward-flowing Wood Creek. The Mohawk then makes a decisive turn to the east and follows the lowland that bears the river's name. Gathering waters from the Adirondack Mountains to the north (most notably East and West Canada Creeks) and from the Appalachian Plateau to the south (mainly Schoharie Creek), the river's natural flow increases substantially before emptying into and doubling the size of the Hudson River at Cohoes (Albany Co). The river drops from 450 ft (137 m) at Rome to less than 20 ft (6 m) at its mouth in the process. Even though the river was interrupted by waterfalls at Cohoes and Little Falls (Herkimer Co) and by an assortment of rapids that included rifts known as Wolf, Keator's, and Knock'em Stiff, east of Rome it was generally navigable. Its route was confined to an inner valley carved by the meltwaters of former glacial Lake Iroquois, including dramatic water gaps at Little Falls and east of Canajoharie (Montgomery Co) at the Noses.

The Iroquois called the river Tenonanatche ("river flowing through mountains"). It played a major role in the society of the Mohawk, whose primary villages were located close by the river, approximately midway between the Hudson and the Oneida Carrying Place, and in the society of the Oneida, who occupied the site between the Hudson and Lake Ontario watersheds. For the Dutch and, more significantly, the British colonial powers, the Mohawk River played an important role in their quests to gain political and economic control over an expanse of the continental interior. The Mohawk River region was a major battleground during the American Revolution.

After the war, astute business and political leaders of New York State and the United States as a whole perceived and then utilized the Mohawk River as a critical avenue of trade. The waterway provided a key link between the Port of New York, the greater Atlantic seaboard, and Europe with the underdeveloped but promising regions of central and western New York State and the Great Lakes country beyond. The Mohawk River east of Rome fostered substantial industrial development and consequent community growth in the age of waterpower. In the 1790s the quasi-public Western Inland Lock Navigation Co improved the river's navigability by focusing its flow with a series of wing dams and short canals at German Flatts (Herkimer Co) and Little Falls. Another canal joined Wood Creek, and indirectly Lake Ontario, with the Mohawk at Rome. The economic development of the Mohawk River region required the dispossession of the Mohawk and Oneida Indians. The state largely completed this task by the end of the 18th century.

By 1820 facilities were being designed and built to divert Mohawk River water to fill the eastern third of the original Erie Canal and years later the Enlarged Erie. When plans for the third generation of the Erie, the Barge Canal, were developed early in the 20th century, the Mohawk River was made an integral part of the new canal between Cohoes and Frankfort (Herkimer Co). The river was channelized by dredging and straightening its course and by installing a series of movable dams and a sequence of locks. The once infamous rifts were dug out, drowned, and in some instances replaced by a lock. The falls at Cohoes and Little Falls were bypassed by the canal and thus remain, but the water flowing over them is significantly diminished. The channelized portion of the Mohawk River, renamed the Erie Canal in 1992, no longer carries any freight traffic but caters exclusively to recreational boaters.

The story of the Mohawk River north of Rome is decidedly different. This section was never navigable. The river did power a few small- to modest-sized grist- and sawmills, a few of which became nuclei for small communities. Beginning in the 1850s, water from the river and its tributaries was diverted to fill the Black River Canal. When the much larger Barge Canal was built, a large concrete dam was constructed approximately 5 miles (8 km) north of Rome, impounding the waters of the upper Mohawk to supply water for the Rome summit level of the new canal. Named for a small community covered by its waters, part of reservoir and surrounding shore is now Delta Lake State Park.

Hislop, Codman. *The Mohawk* (New York: Rinehart, 1948)

Lord, Philip, Jr. *The Navigators: A Journal of Passage on the Inland Waterways of New York (1793)* (Albany: NYS Museum Bulletin 498, 2003)

Whitford, Noble E. *History of the Barge Canal of New York State* (Albany: Brandow Printing, 1906)

James W. Darlington

Mohawk Valley Psychiatric Center. The first mental institution funded by New York State, it opened in 1843 as the New York State Lunatic Asylum in Utica. Dominated by the colonnaded Main Building, the institution was built to house 250 patients but within 10 years tended an average of 400. The institution admitted only those thought curable. Patients followed a strict routine of rest, recreation, and light work in the institution's fields and workshops. The asylum was noted for its avoidance of physical restraint but helped popularize the Utica Crib, a restraining device consisting of a mattress in a wooden cage, which was sometimes suspended by ropes and gently rocked. After 1890, when state lawmakers mandated the transfer of mentally ill paupers to state institutions, the asylum lost its distinctive therapeutic orientation. Renamed Utica State Hospital, in 1890 it became a custodial facility for long-term patients. By the early 20th century, its patient population averaged approximately 1,000. Increasing demand for beds led to the 1919 opening of a satellite campus in nearby Marcy (Oneida Co); in 1935 this facility became Marcy State Hospital. The patient census at Utica State Hospital peaked at approximately 2,500 in 1957–58. Thereafter, sweeping changes in mental health policy fostered a steady decline in the patient population. Renamed the Utica Psychiatric Center in 1974, it was merged with the Marcy facility in 1985. The resulting institution, the Utica-based Mohawk Valley Psychiatric Center, had an inpatient population of approximately 150 adults and 25 children in 2000. The Main Building, a National Historic Landmark, has been vacant since the early 1990s. In 2002 the state announced plans to use it as a storage facility for the records of the New York State Office of Mental Health.

Dwyer, Ellen. *Homes for the Mad: Life Inside Two 19th-Century Asylums* (New Brunswick, NJ: Rutgers Univ Press, 1987)

Bonita L. Weddle

Mohegan Lake. Locality (pop 5,979) in Yorktown and Cortlandt (Westchester Co). The construction of a hotel by 1851 attracted visitors, and avenues built in 1857 on the lake's east side opened up land for summer residences and the Mount Pleasant House (?1859) and the St. Nicholas Hotel (?1872). In 1880 the military Mohegan Lake School opened, operating until the early 1930s. By 1900 Mohegan Lake was a quiet resort for wealthy New Yorkers. The Mohegan Colony (1923), a community of anarchists, ran its own school from 1925 to 1937; bungalow colonies catering to urban laborers followed. Suburbanization of the area after World War II changed its character, as tract developments proliferated. In 2002 Mohegan Lake is a commuter suburb.

Field Horne

Mohicans [Mahicans]. Eastern Algonquian-speaking Indians. Their territory, at the time of first European contact in the 17th century, extended from the southern shores of Lake Champlain to what is now Dutchess Co, and from west of Schenectady to the Housatonic Valley of Massachusetts and Connecticut in the east. Their population was then an estimated 5,000–8,000. The clan structure was matrilineal, and the three major clans of the 17th century were the Turtle, Wolf, and Turkey. Villages were led by sachems. The chief sachem, usually a nephew of a previous leader, was assisted by counselors, a messenger, and a war leader when needed.

With the erection of Fort Nassau in 1614 and of Fort Orange in 1624 [both now in Albany], and the growth of the fur trade, part of the Mohican population shifted north from mid-Hudson sites to locations on the east side of the river near the forts. The early Mohican role in the fur trade and relations with the Dutch was challenged by the Mohawk, a longstanding enemy. The Dutch permitted the Mohawk to trade at Fort Orange, and the Mohican lost their monopoly in trade. In 1626 they asked the commissary of Fort Orange, Daniel van Crieckenbeeck, to help them against a Mohawk war party, which he agreed to do even though this was against the Dutch policy of neutrality. The Mohawk defeated the Mohican and killed Van Crieckenbeeck and four of his men. After the Mohican sued for peace with the Mohawk in 1629, the latter assumed rights to the land on the west shore of the Hudson and near Saratoga Lake. After 1630 farms at Rensselaerswijck [now in Albany, Columbia, and Rensselaer Cos] and adjacent areas further reduced Mohican land. In 1664 Mohicans joined with New England Indian nations in a war against the Mohawk that lasted until November 1671.

With the death in 1674 of Jeremias van Rensselaer, the director of Rensselaerswijck, whom they considered their friend, the Mohican feared Mohawk attacks and announced a defensive alliance with two friendly Algonquian-speaking nations, the Wappinger and Wekquaesgeck, to the south. During the 1676 King Philip's War, the Mohican remained neutral but welcomed New England Indian fugitives. Some Mohicans from the Housatonic Valley moved back into New York Colony for safety. The Mohican did subsequent service for the British. In 1696 Mohicans, asked by the English to help protect Albany, moved into locations above the city to intercept raids from Canada. In 1709 and 1711 Mohicans served on expeditions against Canada and also fought for the English as paid soldiers in King George's War and the French and Indian War at midcentury.

By the early 18th century, the Hudson Valley Mohicans had little arable land left. Their numbers were greatly reduced by war and disease. Ampamit, a sachem, complained at a 1722 Indian conference at Albany that Europeans were taking more land than was intended to be sold and depriving the Indians of their land. By the 1730s, Christian missions were begun among them. The most extensive was at Stockbridge, Mass, where the Mohicans were granted a town so they could have a school and a missionary. A small mission was established in Brainard [now in Rensselaer Co] at the Mohican village of Kaunaumeek on Kinderhook Creek in 1743. Within a year, the converts moved to Stockbridge. From 1742 to 1746 and again for six months in 1749, there was a Moravian mission at Shekomeko, a Mohican village [now Pine Plains, Dutchess Co.] In the first half of the 18th century the Mohican continued to leave their ancestral home. Many went to Oquaga and Otsiningo [both now in Broome Co], intertribal villages on the Susquehanna River. Others went to Pennsylvania, Ohio, Canada, and other places west. In the Revolutionary War, at least 15 Mohicans fighting for the Americans died in battle at Kingsbridge [now in Bronx Co], and others served elsewhere. Despite their services, Mohicans were unable to obtain land as veterans.

In 1784, having lost most of their land, the Christianized Indians of Stockbridge, Mass, removed to New Stockbridge [now Stockbridge, Madison Co], where they established a new town in Oneida territory. They built houses, a mill, and a church and established a farming community. The residents, however, divided into two church factions: one following Rev Samson Occom, a Mohegan, who believed in keeping their Indian language and customs, the other following the missionary John Sergeant Jr from Stockbridge, who advocated more thorough-going assimilation. Although the two churches joined after the death of Occom in 1792, the communities did not. In the early 19th century influential Stockbridge Indians, among them Hendrick Aupaumut, were advocating their removal to the west. In 1818, led by John Metoxen, a quarter of the residents of Stockbridge left for land on the White River of Indiana but found on their arrival that the land had been ceded to the government. In 1822 a treaty was negotiated giving the Stockbridge Indians land on the Fox River in Wisconsin. Over the next several years the remaining Stockbridge in New York moved to Wisconsin. Aupaumut and his wife were among the last to leave New Stockbridge in 1829, a year before his death. In 1834 the US government moved the Stockbridge and Brotherton groups to a reservation on the shore of Lake Winnebago. In 1887 Congress passed the Dawes Act, which allowed individuals to sell their reservation allotments. This policy resulted in the sale of segments of valuable reservation pinelands. In 1938 the Mohican ratified a new constitution and were federally recognized as the Stockbridge-Munsee Band of Mohican Indians. In 2001 almost half of the more than 1,500 enrolled Mohicans resided on the Mohican Nation Reservation in Red Springs and Bartelme townships in Shawano Co in northeastern Wisconsin.

Brasser, Ted. "Mahican." In *Northeast,* ed. Bruce G. Trigger, vol 15 of *Handbook of North American Indians,* ed. William C. Sturtevant (Washington, DC: Smithsonian Institution, 1978)

Dunn, Shirley W. *The Mohicans and Their Land, 1609–1730* (Fleischmanns, NY: Purple Mountain Press, 1994)

———. *The Mohican World, 1680–1750* (Fleischmanns, NY: Purple Mountain Press, 2000)

Frazier, Patrick. *The Mohicans of Stockbridge* (Lincoln: Univ of Nebraska Press, 1992)

Shirley W. Dunn

Mohonk Mountain House. Victorian era hotel perched at the foot of a small lake in the Town of Marbletown (Ulster Co) in the Shawangunk Mountains above New Paltz (Ulster Co), 90 miles (145 km) north of New York City. In 1858 John Stokes purchased Mohonk Lake and approximately 300 acres (121 ha) surrounding it and opened a small tavern at its northern end in 1859. Ten years later, he sold the property to Albert Smiley. Albert's twin brother Alfred was resident manager until 1879, when he opened the Lake Minnewaska Mountain House nearby. In the same year, Albert took up residence and two years later was joined by his half-brother, Daniel, and Daniel's wife Effie. A devout Quaker, Albert associated his resort with the altruistic impulses of the late Victorian era and thus made Mohonk a pioneer in the holding of conferences. The Conference on International Arbitration (1895) and the Conference of Friends of the Indian and Other Dependent Peoples (1883) assembled at Mohonk annually until both groups suspended meetings during World War I.

The various components of the Mountain House have been built of stone since 1879, reducing the risk of fire. The last major addition to the structure was the expansion of the dining-room wing, completed in 1910. Unaltered in its basic appearance since that time, the hotel is one of the best-preserved examples of high Victorian resort architecture in the United States. The design features many noteworthy details, such as the towering central staircase and the parlor wing built over the edge of the lake. Extensive gardens adjoin the structure, and trails wind away from the lake in all directions, including several that lead to the Memorial Tower that crowns "Sky Top," the rocky knob that rises above the lake. Carriageways and trails have been designed to present guests with sudden and spectacular views of the mountain scenery. The unique look of the resort was captured in the film *The Road to Wellville* (1994) starring Anthony Hopkins and Matthew Broderick. In 1986 Mohonk was named a National Historic Landmark. Adjacent to the resort, which was still in the hands of the Smiley family in 2003, is Mohonk Preserve, 6,400 acres (2,590 ha) of land with 40 miles (64 km) of foot trails and an entry point at Gardiner (Ulster Co). Activities include golf, tennis, swimming, boating, riding, concerts, and theme programs. The 251-room hotel is open all year.

Burgess, Larry. *Mohonk: Its People and Spirit,* rev ed. (Fleischmanns, NY: Purple Mountain Press, 1996)

William S. Helmer

Moira. Town (pop 2,857) in W Franklin Co. Settled in 1803, the town was formed from Dickinson in 1828. The Northern Railroad came through in 1850 and encouraged the development of the dairy industry. In 1883 the Northern Adirondack Railroad, serving the lumbering industry in southern Franklin Co, formed a junction with the earlier railroad at the hamlet of Moira. Starch was processed from local potatoes (the first starch factory opened in 1851) until cornstarch drove the potato product from the market in the early 20th century. In the early 21st century, Moira remains a dairy town.

Thomas W. Perrin

Molloy College. Private college. The school was established in Rockville Centre (Nassau Co) in 1955 by the Dominican Sisters of the Congregation of the Holy Cross, Amityville. It was chartered as the Molloy Catholic College for Women and named for Archbishop Thomas E. Molloy of Brooklyn, who was instrumental in helping found it. In 1971 its name was changed to Molloy College. In 1972 it began accepting men into the nursing program and in 1982 became fully coeducational. Molloy's academic strengths are in the service fields, particularly nursing, education, social work, and speech therapy. The college offers 5 associate, 30 bachelor's, and 2 graduate degree programs. Enrollment for 2002–3 was approximately 2,500 students, 2,010 of whom were undergraduates, 72% full-time (1,449), and 77% women (1,548).

Comer, Colleen. "Molloy College . . . The Dimensions of Our Roots." In *Molloy College Chrysalis* (1996)

Patrick Ziegler

Mongolians. See CENTRAL ASIANS.

Monroe. Town (pop 31,407) and village (pop 7,780) in SE Orange Co. It was the home of the legendary "cowboy" Claudius Smith, who terrorized Ramapo Valley patriots until he was hung at Goshen in 1779. The town was formed from Cornwall in 1799 as Cheesecocks; it was renamed Southfield in 1801 and Munroe in 1808, assuming its modern spelling during Pres James Monroe's presidency. The Erie Railroad (1841–1983) encouraged dairy farming, especially milk shipment, and several iron mines operated between 1797 and 1880. In 1863 the town was divided into Monroe, Highlands, and Southfield but was reunited in 1865. In the late 19th century, boardinghouses supported a summer tourist business; they were later supplanted by bungalow colonies. The village was incorporated in 1894. The Monroe Cheese Co (1873–1926) was the originator of Liederkranz (1902) and Velveeta (*ca* 1920) cheeses. The New York State Thruway (1954) and the four-lane

Mohonk Mountain House, early 20th century.

Rte 17/I-86 (1955) made commuting by automobile practical, and Monroe's population grew rapidly in the late 20th century.

Alan Hunter

Monroe County (659 mi²/1,707 km²; pop 735,343). The county was created in 1821 from parts of Ontario and Genesee Cos, and a small portion of Livingston Co was added in 1825. Named for James Monroe, fifth president of the United States, Monroe Co is divided into 1 city and 19 towns that contain 10 incorporated villages. Rochester serves as the county seat. Elevations range between 245 feet (75 m) along the shores of Lake Ontario to over 1,031 feet (314 m) in the Hopper Hills at the extreme southeast corner. The county falls within two major landform provinces. The Erie-Ontario Lowland occupies the northern two-thirds and is further divided into the Ontario Lake Plain, the Southern Ontario Plain, and a small portion of the Ontario Drumlin Field in the east. The Finger Lakes Hills, a subregion of the Appalachian Upland, extend across Monroe Co's southern third. Ordovician shales make up the bedrock in the north, while most of the county is underlain by Silurian sandstones. There is a band of Devonian limestone in the far south. Strata throughout dip gently southward, and evidence of continental glaciation is present. Notable features include hundreds of drumlins, a generally thick layer of glacial till, and a clearly defined beach ridge formed by glacial Lake Iroquois that extends east-west across the entire county and that essentially is the path of Rte 104. Glaciers helped deflect the path of the Genesee River, whose original mouth was Irondequoit Bay, itself a drowned valley. All surface waters drain into Lake Ontario, some directly from modest local streams, and some via tributaries of the Genesee River, which flows north through the county's center. Fine arable soil is present throughout most of the county.

Monroe Co has a humid-continental climate. Mean January temperatures vary only slightly, from 24°F (-5°C) in the southern hills to 25°F (-4°C) near Brockport. Mean July temperatures are 70°F (21°C) and 72°F (22°C), for the same locations. Below 0°F (-18°C) lows are expected every winter, as are occasional midday summer highs above 90°F (32°C). Annual average precipitation amounts range from 30 inches (76 cm) in the northwest to 34 inches (86 cm) near Rochester. Seasonal snowfall ranges from 60 inches (152 cm) in the south to as much as 100 inches (254 cm) closer to the lakeshore, the higher amounts reflecting local lake effect. Lake Ontario also affects temperature patterns by moderating springtime temperatures near the lakeshore downward and by delaying the onset of frosts in the fall. The primeval forest cover, none of which remains, consisted of three forest communities. Central hardwoods, primarily beech, sugar maple, and basswood along with some oak, chestnut, and hickory predominated. Swamp forest covered significant portions in the south along the Genesee River and Black and Honeoye Creeks. Oak-hickory forest covered a narrow band from the hills in the southeast to Irondequoit Bay.

Settlement

Paleo-age artifacts discovered in the Town of Wheatland indicate that human occupation in the area dates back 11,000 to 12,000 years; there is evidence of Algonquin sites that predate the arrival of the Seneca *ca* AD 1300. The Seneca exerted control over the region and consequently were later known as "keepers of the western door." Seneca villages within the present county were probably limited to Totiakton, in the southeast, and Casconchiagon, at the falls on the Genesee. Early white visitors included scout Etienne Brûlé in 1610 and René-Robert Cavelier de la Salle in 1669. Marquis de Denonville came to Irondequoit Bay in 1687 to forge an alliance with the Seneca but failed. As the most powerful of Britain's Indian allies during the Revolutionary War, the Seneca were a primary target of the Sullivan-Clinton campaign of 1779. That campaign effectively destroyed Iroquois control over central and western New York State. It simultaneously provided American troops the opportunity to consider firsthand the region's agricultural promise. The British wanted control of Irondequoit Bay, hoping to build a fort; the Indians saw no particular benefit in this, but Col John Butler was permitted to camp there, in present-day Charlotte and at the oxbow in Ellison Park. There were no military engagements within the present county.

In accordance with the Hartford Convention of 1786, Massachusetts acquired preemption rights to all the land in Monroe Co and much more. Two years later Massachusetts sold its right to negotiate with the Iroquois for land ownership to a consortium of investors led by Oliver Phelps and Nathaniel Gorham, who in 1788 purchased from the Seneca Nation 2.6 million acres (1.05 million hectares) of land located primarily east of the Genesee River. To acquire the land west of the river, later known as the Mill Tract, Phelps promised to build a mill to grind Seneca corn. Financier Robert Morris purchased Phelps and Gorham's land, including much of present-day Monroe Co, in 1790, selling it two years later to the Pulteney Associates. In 1791 Morris acquired from Massachusetts and the Seneca most of the lands west of the Genesee River, including the western portion of the county known as the Triangle Tract.

By 1800 the region that later became Monroe Co had attracted nearly 1,200 settlers, including 42 free Blacks in the Town of Rush. The first record of slaveholding dates from 1812. The first evidence of village growth began about 1800, at Charlotte, a port of entry, and at millsites such as Scottsville, Norton's Mills [now Honeoye Falls], and Rochester. However, Pittsford—as site of the first school (1794), library (1803), church building (1804), post office (1811), and newspaper (1815), as well as an early mill—was developed relatively early. With about 700 residents, Rochester became an incorporated village in 1817. By 1825 the county's population exceeded 39,000, including 263 Blacks. The Erie Canal spurred further dramatic growth in existing communities like Rochester and in new ones like Brockport, Fairport, and Spencerport. Irish immigrants began arriving in substantial numbers in the 1830s and 1840s as canal laborers, and Germans came in the early 1850s to work in Rochester industries. Most immigrants lived in the city, but those who could afford land became farmers, as the Irish did in Greece, the Scots in Wheatland, and the Germans in Webster. At midcentury Monroe Co's population approached 90,000; over one-third lived in Rochester.

Economic Development

Monroe Co's early market economy focused on the growing and processing of wheat. In 1789 Ebenezer Allan built and operated the first gristmill, which Phelps had promised would be done, at the falls just west of the present-day Court Street Bridge, but Allan sold it in 1792. Nathaniel Rochester's party found the structure abandoned when they arrived at the site in 1803 to take possession of their Hundred-Acre Tract. By

MONROE CO POPULATION CENSUS FIGURES

	White	Nonwhite	Total Population	Foreign-Born
1830	49,390	465	49,855	1,338
1840	64,247	655	64,902	—
1850	86,951	699	87,650	26,077
1860	100,081	567	100,648	31,172
1870	117,263	605	117,868	33,764
1880	144,149	754	144,903	38,342
1890	188,750	836	189,586	51,997
1900	217,005	849	217,854	51,059
1910	281,918	1,294	283,212	71,276
1920	350,064	1,970	352,034	79,575
1930	420,739	3,142	423,881	87,377
1940	434,452	3,778	438,230	72,130
1950	479,385	8,247	487,632	62,041
1960	561,320	25,067	586,387	58,490
1970	655,821	56,096	711,917	56,395
1980	613,525	88,713	702,238	50,722
1990	602,177	111,791	713,968	45,573
2000	581,961	153,382	735,343	53,743

Notes: "Nonwhite" includes African Americans, Asians, American Indians, and Pacific Islanders and, for 2000, also the mixed race and other race categories. Through the 1960 census these figures primarily reflect the African American population. Foreign-born figures for 1830 include only those not naturalized, and for 1930 and 1950, the foreign-born totals include Whites only. Other years include all foreign-born in the population.

then grist- and sawmills were in place elsewhere in the area. However, limited and restricted Canadian markets, prohibitively expensive transport costs to the east and south, and the disruption of the War of 1812 effectively stifled wheat and flour shipments until 1815. The crest of the prominent, well-drained, beach ridge soon evolved into the region's premier east-west route: the Ridge Rd. In 1823 the Erie Canal was completed between Monroe Co and Albany, by which time Rochester had seven modest gristmills. But the canal's low fares and shipping rates quickly transformed the village into America's first boomtown. By 1835 Rochester's population had grown to 14,000, and 18 mills crowded around the falls with a combined capacity to convert 20,000 bu (705,000 l) of wheat into 5,000 barrels of flour daily. The opening of markets energized local farmers to transform larger amounts of local forestland into wheat fields. The canal stimulated other manufacturing. In 1827 nine sawmills at Rochester produced approximately 100,000 board feet of lumber, most supplied from nearby forests. In following years those same mills depended upon rafts of sawlogs coming from further up the Genesee Valley. Rochester also rose to become perhaps the Erie's biggest boat-building center. The area's first bank, the Bank of Rochester, opened in 1824.

Wheat production in the county began to falter in the late 1830s because of the unrelenting planting of the crop and consequent mining of the region's soil nutrients, weevil infestation, and effects of the panic of 1837. Rochester millers covered the widening shortfall by purchasing greater quantities of Midwestern wheat, which further encouraged local decline. Although Rochester's flour production continued to expand, reaching 1.7 million barrels in 1847, change was in the air. In 1837 the Tonawanda Railroad opened between Rochester and Batavia (Genesee Co), followed soon after by the Auburn and Rochester Railroad. By the early 1850s two more rail lines served Monroe Co: the Rochester, Lockport and Niagara Falls and the Rochester and Syracuse. All became part of the New York Central Railroad in 1853. A wide-gauge line from the Southern Tier was soon added. North of the Ridge Rd, farmers long interested in apple and other fruit production continued to expand their orchards. The first large commercial plant nursery was established in 1834, but it was not until the 1840s that local horticultural operations blossomed into an industry of national significance. By the 1870s more than 4,000 acres (1,600 ha) in the Towns of Brighton, Gates, Greece, Irondequoit, and Penfield were planted in ornamental trees and scrubs, in addition to flowers and vegetables grown for seed. Within Rochester, by 1850 the shoe and clothing industries had evolved and were poised for dynamic growth, based on new production procedures that included ready-made, standard-size formats. Of Monroe Co's population at midcentury (87,650), 36,403 lived in Rochester.

The city's population increased by about one-third in the 1850s, while the rest of the county stayed essentially the same. By 1860 there were 60 trains departing Rochester daily. Shipments from Rochester on the Erie dropped from $8,400,000 in 1854 to $2,830,000 in 1860, while the total freight carried by the New York Central increased 60% in its first year (1854). Flour milling entered a period of decline and survived only to supply regionally. Sawmilling and shipbuilding were no longer viable local industries. Shoemaking, men's clothing production, and metalworking were of national significance and the city's largest industrial employers. The garment trades proved particularly attractive to German and eastern European Jewish immigrants and, by 1890s, Italians and Poles. Cigarette manufacturing became a major local employer for about 30 years beginning in the 1870s, employing over 800 workers (mostly women and girls).

Local firms also rose to become the nation's foremost supplier of nursery stock. In 1860 the county led the state in orchard products and was second in garden produce. Various industries appeared in the towns and villages. Some, such as mills producing blasting powder, were based on natural resources; others, like McCormick's reapers (made in Brockport), were linked to agriculture, which remained the core of the local economy. Hilton and Webster each attracted apple-processing plants, which in turn spurred further apple production. By 1890 Monroe Co was second in the nation in the value of its agricultural produce. Railroad tracks crossed all parts of the county by then, and Rochester became an impressive trolley hub.

There was a manufacturing shift in the late 1800s toward more technical and exacting products, the most famous being those of Eastman Kodak; it began production of photographic supplies in 1880 and grew rapidly. Kodak's first buildings were near the falls, but in 1891 it began building on land in the Town of Greece, thereby becoming the first industry to expand away from the center city (land that was later annexed by the city). Bausch and Lomb, a local optical firm since the 1840s, grew impressively, partially in response to orders from Kodak. Gleason Tool Co, a machine-tool manufacturer, developed precision gear cutting machines that attracted acclaim and much business. Other important instrument manufacturers included Ritter (dental equipment) and Taylor Instrument (precision measuring devices).

Religion, Education, and Culture

The first church building, Northfield Baptist, was built in what is now Pittsford in 1804. The local revivals of the 1830s, most led by Charles Grandison Finney, attracted large, diverse crowds and placed Rochester and the surrounding area at the forefront of the Burned-over District. The first rural Roman Catholic parish in New York State, known then as St. Ambrose, was formed in Greece in 1832. The first Jewish congregation, B'rith Kodesh, was organized in 1848. By 1855 there were 151 houses of worship in the county, with 46 located in Rochester. Baptist, Methodist, and Presbyterian were the best represented among the Protestant denominations. There were also 12 Catholic churches and one Jewish congregation.

The county's first school was built at Pittsford in 1795, and many others quickly followed. The first secondary schools were Rochester High School and Monroe Academy in Henrietta; both were established in 1827. By 1850 there were 12 academies operating. The Rochester School for the Deaf, founded in 1876 as the Western New York Institute for Deaf Mutes and known for the Rochester Method of signing, remained vital in 2003. School centralization began at Brockport in 1927 and continued at an uneven pace through the interwar years. In 2003 there were 16 central school districts, 1 union free district, 1 city school district, and 2 BOCES districts. County residents were also served by 6 school districts headquartered in adjoining counties.

The Rochester Athenaeum (1829) became

POPULATIONS OF TOWNS AND CITIES, MONROE CO

Town or City, Year Founded	1840	1880	1920	1960	2000
Brighton, 1814	2,336	3,736	2,911	27,849	35,588
Chili, 1822	2,174	2,274	1,780	11,237	27,638
Clarkson, 1819	3,486	2,100	1,403	2,339	6,072
East Rochester, 1981[a]	—	—	3,901	8,152	6,650
Gates, 1813[b]	1,728	1,988	1,419	13,755	29,275
Greece, 1822	3,669	4,848	3,350	48,670	94,141
Hamlin, 1852[c]	—	2,556	1,999	2,755	9,355
Henrietta, 1818	2,085	2,243	1,910	11,598	39,028
Irondequoit, 1839	1,252	1,986	5,123	55,337	52,354
Mendon, 1812	3,435	3,193	2,509	3,902	8,370
Ogden, 1817	2,404	2,967	2,681	7,262	18,492
Parma, 1808	2,652	3,180	2,923	6,277	14,822
Penfield, 1810	2,842	2,955	2,087	12,601	34,645
Perinton, 1812	2,513	4,030	7,799	16,314	46,090
Pittsford, 1814	1,983	2,236	4,614	15,156	27,219
Riga, 1808	1,984	2,221	1,649	2,800	5,437
Rochester (city), 1834	20,191	89,366	295,750	318,611	219,773
Rush, 1818	1,929	1,741	2,091	2,555	3,603
Sweden, 1813	1,884	5,734	3,984	7,224	13,716
Webster, 1840	2,235	2,950	3,976	16,434	37,926
Wheatland, 1821[d]	2,871	2,599	2,076	3,711	5,149

[a]Incorporated as a village within the Towns of Perinton and Pittsford 1906; recognized as a town 1981. Populations for 1920 and 1960 are for the village.

[b]Northampton until 1812.

[c]Union until 1860.

[d]Inverness when formed; renamed same year.

Mechanics Institute in 1885 and is now the Rochester Institute of Technology, which includes the National Technical Institute for the Deaf. SUNY Brockport began as a Baptist college in 1834, became the Collegiate Institute in 1842, and was a state normal school until the late 1940s. The University of Rochester and Colgate Rochester Divinity School were both founded as Baptist institutions in 1850, while Roberts Wesleyan College began as Chili Seminary in 1866. Nazareth College (1942) and St. John Fisher College (1951) are both in Pittsford, and Monroe Community College (1962) has an expanding campus in Brighton.

Rochester's first newspaper was the *Weekly Gazette* (1816), and its first daily was the *Daily Telegraph* (1827). Although in 1900 there were six daily newspapers in Monroe Co, in 2003 only one remained, the *Rochester Democrat and Chronicle* (1833). Some of the largest cultural institutions are the Rochester Museum and Science Center (1912), Memorial Art Gallery (1913), Rochester Philharmonic Orchestra (1922), George Eastman House, International Museum of Photography and Film (1949), Genesee Country Village and Museum (1966), GEVA Theater (1972), and the Strong Museum (1980). Rochester's first radio station, WHAM (1922), was identified by the federal government in 1928 as 1 of just 24 class 1-A clear channel stations nationwide.

The Rochester city parks system dates from 1888 and includes the work of Frederick Law Olmsted, a Robert Trent Jones golf course, Seneca Park Zoo (1894); it also hosts the annual Lilac Festival. The Monroe County Park Commission (1926) began operating five large city parks in 1961, and the county also bought Springdale Farm, a working farm in Northampton Park. Sports fans have made Rochester a "baseball city," supporting its Red Wings club and local hockey, lacrosse, and soccer franchises. The Rochester Royals basketball team (1945–57) won the NBA championship in 1951. The Oak Hill Country Club (1901), located in Pittsford since 1926, has hosted many important tournaments, including the 2003 PGA Championship. Famed golfer Walter Hagen began on local courses, and Olympic speed skater Cathy Turner is a native of Hilton.

Politics

The area has a long history of activism and reform. Both Frederick Douglass and Susan B. Anthony lived here as they struggled to achieve equal rights and civil justice, often moving in the same circles. Douglass generated local support for the Underground Railroad and abolition, while Anthony, a temperance and abolitionist lecturer, recruited support for woman suffrage. A board of supervisors governed the county from 1821 until 1967, when the county charter created the legislature, with 29 members casting equal votes. In 1980 the appointed county manager position was replaced by an elected county executive. An elected mayor and City Council administer Rochester; elected supervisors and boards manage the 19 towns; and elected mayors and trustees govern the 10 villages. The Republican Party dominates town-, village-, and county-level politics (with the exception of Brighton), and this has been the case historically with few exceptions. Rochester tends to elect Democratic candidates. These affiliations have produced tensions that hinder cooperation and have framed the recurring debates over metropolitan government.

The 20th Century

In 1900 Monroe Co had 5,889 operating farms covering 381,941 acres (154,566 ha). Most were dairy, fruit, or vegetable farms, and there were about 40 nurseries. The manufacturing sector led by Eastman Kodak, dominated the economy. More photography-related firms sprang up, as did other companies like General Railway Signal (1904) and North East Electric (1908; later Delco, a subsidiary of General Motors). Population in the towns and villages remained stable until the early 1920s, when inner-ring towns around Rochester began experiencing significant population growth and simultaneous loss of farmland. This scenario was prompted by the proliferation of the automobile and of trolley service, which also fueled the expansion of Kodak Park and other industrial facilities on the city's margins. Beginning early in the century, George Eastman set an enviable standard of philanthropic support within the region that permeated local business and culture.

By midcentury Monroe Co's population approached 500,000, nearly 70% of which lived in Rochester. Orchard, vegetable, and dairy farming remained important, but the number of active farms had declined to 3,147. Major employers like Eastman Kodak, Bausch and Lomb, and others benefited from government war contracts and made successful transitions to peacetime production, largely because of their technological orientation. One local firm that met spectacular success after 1950 was Haloid (now Xerox). The expanding workplace became evident in various ways. The African American population doubled in the 1950s as many arrived from the South. Shortly after, Puerto Ricans began making the area their home, followed by a variety of other groups, including refugees from around the globe. Despite the influx, in 2000, one in four county residents claimed German heritage. Suburban development expanded at increasing rates, due in part to new high-speed, limited-access highways, such as the expressway (I-490) connecting Rochester's Inner Loop with the New York State Thruway in 1961, that dramatically transformed the urban and rural landscapes. Concurrently, the city's population declined, and by 2000 the proportion of county residents living in Rochester (30%) was the lowest it had been since 1830. The Rochester population, however, included three-quarters of the county's poor.

For a variety of reasons the prosperity and expansion that marked much of the century turned to narrow profit margins and reduced workforces during the 1980s and 1990s for many local companies, including Kodak and Xerox. The strategy has been to diversify the economy through the creation of many smaller businesses and industries, especially in the area of high technology, education, and medicine; fast-growing companies like Pac Tec Communications and Harris Interactive led the way. By concerted private and public efforts, Monroe Co experienced an 8% growth in jobs during the 1990s. In that same decade, however, nearly a quarter of the population aged 25–34 left. Still, the county remains one of the highest per capita exporters in the nation, and 22% of the workforce remains involved in manufacturing. It is very active in the global marketplace and is designated an Empire Zone and a Foreign Trade Zone, exporting more products to foreign markets than 40 US states.

As a new century begins, local governments and residents are looking to major projects, including a fast ferry to Toronto, a downtown bus terminal, and a performing arts center, to revitalize the city, and innovations in technology, such as University of Rochester's Center for Optics Manufacturing and local biomedical research, to expand business and employment opportunities.

See also SUBURBANIZATION.

An early account of Monroe Co is in Orsamus Turner, *History of the Pioneer Settlement of Phelps and Gorham's Purchase, and Morris' Reserve* (1851). The standard histories of the county are W. H. McIntosh, *History of Monroe County* (1877) and William F. Peck, *Landmarks of Monroe County* (1895). The Federal Writers' Project's *Rochester and Monroe County: A History and Guide* (1937) gives a rare interwar perspective. A brief modern history is provided by Howard C. Hosmer, *Monroe County* (1971); while unannotated, it is a detailed narrative. With the domination of the county by the City of Rochester, Blake F. McKelvey's four-volume scholarly history, *Rochester* (1945–61) is foundational. The journal of the Rochester Historical Society, *Rochester History*, contains many fine articles on aspects of the city and surrounding area. Most of the towns have histories and other publications. Carl F. Schmidt, *History of the Town of Wheatland* (1953), offers a detailed chronological history. Other quality publications are Helen R. Williams, *Sesquicentennial History of the Town of Brighton* (1964), Mary Conners, *East Rochester, NY: 100 Years of History, 1897–1997*, Eleanor Kalsbeck, *Henrietta Heritage* (1977), Leith L. Wright, *Hilton U.S.A.* (1984), Katherine Wilcox Thompson, *Penfield's Past 1810–1960* (1960), and *Perinton Papers* (1971), a collection of strong essays. The early history of seven towns is traced in Margaret Schmitt MacNab, *Northfield on the Genesee* (1981).

Carolyn Vacca

Monsey. Locality (pop 14,504) in Ramapo (Rockland Co). Originally called Kakiak, it acquired the name Monsey when the Erie Railroad (1841) established a station; a post office followed in 1848. It was the site of a number of social welfare institutions in the early 20th century, including St. Zita's Home for Friendless Women (1890) and the Herriman Farm School. From the 1920s until around 1960, Monsey was a summer resort with hotels and bungalow colonies catering primarily to a Jewish clientele. After World War II suburban developments increased in density and ended Monsey's appeal as a resort, but it became home to a thriving Orthodox Jewish population.

Montague. Town (pop 108) in W Lewis Co. Settled in 1846, mostly by migrants from St. Lawrence and Jefferson Cos, the town was formed in 1850 from West Turin. Lumbering was the main industry, and the first sawmill was built in 1847–48. Farming supported cheese factories (1882–*ca* 1945). A forestry-oriented prison camp operated from 1936 to 1940. A peak population of 975 in 1880 dropped to 32 by 1980; in the last two decades of the 20th century the number of residents tripled with an influx of second-home owners and small service businesses. The forests are harvested for local paper mills. Because of Montague's heavy annual snowfall, recent growth in winter sports has stimulated service businesses. The Tug Hill State Wildlife Management Area is in Montague.

Arthur Einhorn

Montauk. Locality (pop 3,851) in East Hampton (Suffolk Co). Bounded by Block Island Sound to the north and the Atlantic Ocean to the east and south, the end of Montauk Point is the easternmost point of New York State. Montauk is an Algonquian word meaning a place of observation or a fortified place. The Montaukett Indians were its original inhabitants, but English settlers negotiated treaties (1648–1703) with them, leading to incremental loss of Montaukett autonomy. Strategically important to early American shipping routes, Montauk became the site of New York State's first lighthouse in 1796; it remains a landmark. In 1839 the *Amistad*, a Cuban slave ship under the control of its cargo, was intercepted by the US Coast Guard and landed at Montauk. The area remained ruggedly exotic until the late 19th century and was visited by few. Its beauty was elegized in poetry by Walt Whitman.

In 1879 the land was purchased by New York financier Arthur Benson for a private hunting and fishing resort. One of his visitors, Austin Corbin, president of the Long Island Rail Road (LIRR), planned a transoceanic steamboat terminal at Fort Pond Bay, but it was never realized. Both Benson and Corbin ignored Indian land claims and enforced relocation to suit their purposes. The Montaukett engaged in a lengthy legal battle ending in a New York State Supreme Court defeat in 1910, in which a judge falsely deemed them extinct.

After the LIRR reached Montauk in 1895, it received increased public attention. It was the quarantine for US Army soldiers returning from the Spanish-American War, including the Rough Riders. It also became a tourist destination because of its beautiful shoreline and recreation such as deep-sea fishing. Carl Fisher, the developer of Miami Beach, attempted to build a grand resort in 1926, but the plan was aborted by the Great Depression and the 1938 hurricane. Despite cottage construction beginning in the late 1940s and motel construction in the 1960s, more than half of Montauk's land is protected in Hither Hills and Montauk State Parks. In the early 21st century it remains one of the state's most popular tourist destinations.

Joshua Ruff

Montaukett (Montauk) Nation. American Indian inhabitants of the eastern end of the South Fork of Long Island. Paleoperiod fluted points found in the area indicate a native inhabitancy of more than 10,000 years. They were maritime-oriented fishers, gatherers, and hunters who spoke a variant of the Algonquian language similar to Mohegan-Pequot. In a series of 16 deeds and documents from 1648 to 1794 they incrementally alienated their land to the settlers. Grave goods from the Pantigo burial ground, east of the Village of East Hampton, reveal that the Montaukett became highly integrated into the European economic sphere between 1675 and 1725. From the earliest days of colonial settlement, Montaukett men tended the animals pastured at the tip of Montauk (Suffolk Co) and carried out shore whaling for the settlers and extensive ocean whaling voyages later. The women worked for colonist families as nurses, midwives, household help, laundrywomen, dairymaids, and basket and scrub makers, and in other service occupations. Montaukett and other Long Island native men served in the colonial militia and later fought in the Revolution and subsequent American wars. They also served as guiding hunters in the Indian Field reserve at the tip of Montauk, providing rides to the beaches, woodworking, ice delivery, and livery service.

In 1785 a group of Montaukett and other Long Island natives left for a new Christian Indian home at Brothertown in Oneida territory, at the site of what is now Marshall (Oneida Co). They were led by the Mohegan reverend Samson Occom, who spent most of his professional life at Montauk and married a Montaukett, Mary Fowler. Her brothers Jacob and David, who were among the 27 colonial era American Indians educated in the English manner, were important teachers and missionaries to the Iroquois, as well as translators at the October 1776 Treaty of Fort Pitt and other parleys before and during the Revolution. With much of their land at Brothertown taken by trespassers from New England, the Brotherton and other New York Indians used money from the sale of their New York land to purchase Menominee land in 1821–22 and to establish a new Brothertown in Wisconsin.

In the 1880s, as developer Arthur Benson purchased land from individuals and not from the tribe as a whole, the Pharaoh family, often leaders of the Montaukett, and the Fowler family remaining at Montauk were cajoled off Indian Field and into Freetown, an African American area north of the Village of East Hampton, and Eastville, east of Sag Harbor (Suffolk Co). A court case to regain their land lasted until they were declared extinct as a tribe by state supreme court justice Abel Blackmar in 1910, questionably upheld upon appeal in 1913 and 1917. At the end of the 20th century, the scores of Montaukett descendants in the Town of East Hampton and the hundreds more in enclaves throughout Suffolk Co petitioned the Bureau of Indian Affairs for federal recognition, the first step in gaining recompense for the land taken from them.

Stone, Gaynell, ed. *The History and Archaeology of the Montauk* (Stony Brook, NY: Suffolk County Archaeological Association, 1993)

Strong, John. *The Algonquian Peoples of Long Island From Earliest Times to 1700* (Interlaken, NY: Heart of the Lakes Publishing, 1997)

———. *"We Are Still Here!" The Algonquian Peoples of Long Island Today* (Interlaken, NY: Heart of the Lakes Publishing, 1996, 1998)

Gaynell Stone

Montcalm, Marquis de [Montcalm-Gozon, Louis-Joseph de; Marquis de Saint-Véran] (*b* Château de Candiac, France, 28 Feb 1712; *d* Quebec, 14 Sept 1759). French field commander. Montcalm was a frequently wounded and much decorated cavalry veteran of several European wars when King Louis XV appointed him major general in command of all French North American forces in January 1756. Despite friction with civilian colonial authorities in Quebec, especially the Marquis de Vaudreuil, Montcalm was successful in the field. For the next three years, mostly in the Champlain Valley, he consistently outfoxed the British under Sir William Johnson, Sir William Shirley, and Sir James Abercromby. He captured Oswego on 14 Aug 1756 and Fort William Henry on 9 Aug 1757. Following the victory of his 3,800 men over Abercromby's 15,000 at Ticonderoga on 8 July 1758, he was promoted to lieutenant general and given the powers of a field marshal. On 13 Sept 1759, he was surprised and defeated by Maj Gen James Wolfe on the Plains of Abraham, just west of the citadel of Quebec. Both commanders were mortally wounded in this battle, which ended French colonial influence in northeastern North America.

Anderson, Fred. *Crucible of War: The Seven Year's War and the Fate of Empire in British North America, 1754–1766* (New York: Knopf, 2000; distributed by Random House)

Lewis, Meriwether Liston. *Montcalm: The Marvelous Marquis* (New York: Vantage Press, 1961)

Eric v. d. Luft

Montebello. Village (pop 3,688) in Ramapo (Rockland Co). In 1900 financier Thomas Fortune Ryan (1851–1928) built a mansion named Montebello on his 822-acre (332.7 ha) estate. His wife, Ida Barry Ryan (*d* 1917), built a church, a seminary, a girls school, and the original Good Samaritan Hospital (1902). The mansion later served as an office for Phelps Dodge Corp (1951–82). The School for Living (1934–45) and the Bayard Lane Community (1936–45) were well-known back-to-the-land experiments founded by Ralph Borsodi. Montebello incorporated as a village in 1986 to control zoning and to limit development.

Montezuma. Town (pop 1,431) in W Cayuga Co. Settled in 1798, the town was formed from Mentz in 1859. Settlers were drawn by its salt springs, and a number of attempts were made to develop them, including one with state funds around 1860. The Richmond Aqueduct, the second longest on the Erie Canal, was built in 1856 to carry the canal over the Seneca River; it consisted of 31 stone arches, spanning 894 ft (272.5 m). It was designed by Van Rensselaer Richmond, who also developed an innovative system for the New York Central Railroad (1853) crossing of Montezuma Marsh that involved a crib of wood and stone that "floated" on the soft ground. Seven aqueduct arches remain standing in Montezuma. The New York State Thruway (1954) crosses the town without an exit. Dairy and crop farming were the main sources of employment in 2003.

Cheryl Longyear

Montezuma Marsh. See CAYUGA MARSHES.

Montezuma National Wildlife Refuge. New York State's first national wildlife refuge, covering 7,068 acres (2,860 ha) in Seneca, Wayne, and Cayuga Cos in the Montezuma Marsh (Cayuga Marsh) at the north end of Cayuga Lake. Dr Peter Clark first used the name Montezuma for his nearby farmhouse in 1806. Internal improvements significantly drained the marshlands in the 19th and early 20th centuries. In 1937 the Bureau of Biological Survey (now US Fish and Wildlife Service) acquired 6,432 acres (2,603 ha), and the Civilian Conservation Corps built dikes to reclaim wetlands, which became the Montezuma Migratory Bird Refuge in 1938 before becoming the Montezuma National Wildlife Refuge (MNWR). Despite birder protests in the 1950s, the state constructed the New York State Thruway through the refuge with the approval of the US Department of the Interior.

Beginning in 1976 North America's first successful bald eagle hacking experiment, in which federal and state biologists unobtrusively fed immature eagles in artificial nests on caged platforms atop high towers, reestablished the species at Montezuma. Significant as a major staging area for waterfowl migration in the Northeast because it lies in the Atlantic flyway (approximately 1 million migratory birds of all types annually pass through the Montezuma Wetlands Complex), the area is also home to endangered and threatened species (black terns, pie-billed grebes, and least bitterns, among others). Although the National Audubon Society designated it the first Important Bird Area in New York State in 1997, the complex continues to be threatened by possible expansion of a local landfill, runoff from cropland, and the introduction of invasive flora and fauna. The refuge has expanded somewhat from its original size, and in 2002 the MNWR acquired 150 acres (61 ha) of former farmland to attract migratory grassland species, such as meadowlarks, plovers, and bobolinks, which are among the continent's fastest declining populations. The state-run Northern Montezuma Wildlife Management Area is adjacent to the refuge.

Montezuma National Wildlife Refuge, http://www.fws.gov/r5mnwr

Scott C. Monje

Montgomerie, John (*b* Scotland; *d* New York City, 1 July 1731). Royal governor of New York and New Jersey (1728–31). Montgomerie served in the War of the Spanish Succession and was then elected to Parliament. George II rewarded Montgomerie for his past loyalty by offering him a choice of offices. The ambitious Montgomerie chose the government of New York and New Jersey as offering the best chance for monetary gain. He was named to replace William Burnet in 1727. On his arrival in New York in April 1728, Montgomerie allied with the merchant faction, which had been Burnet's opposition. The assembly passed a revenue bill to cover all ordinary government expenses for five years and voted to reduce the salary of opposition leader Chief Justice Lewis Morris (1671–1746). Montgomerie's refusal to erect chancery courts or to serve as chancellor was regarded by the opposition as weakening the royal prerogative. Montgomerie, indifferent to imperial concerns, at the urging of merchants repealed the act passed during Burnet's administration that outlawed the Albany-Montreal trade. He died in New York City of a stroke and is considered by some to be among New York's worst provincial governors.

Smith, William, Jr. *The History of the Province of New York.* Ed. Michael Kammen, 2 vols (Cambridge, Mass: Belknap Press, 1972)

Mary Lou Lustig

Montgomery. Town (pop 20,891) and village (pop 3,636) in N Orange Co. Settled around 1720 by Palatine German, Dutch, and Scots-Irish immigrants, its most prominent early resident was Lt Gov Cadwallader Colden (1689–1776), a physician and natural scientist who moved to his estate, Coldengham, in 1727. Organized as Hanover Precinct in 1772 and changed to Montgomery Precinct in 1782, it was recognized as a town in 1788. Montgomery Academy organized in 1787, and its 1820 building is a landmark. The village grew around a mill on the Wallkill River and acquired a post office named Wardsbridge in 1792. The village was incorporated in 1810. The Montgomery Cotton Factory was built about 1813. In 1880 the village was the home of Crabtree and Patchett, worsted yarn makers, and of Walker's Paper Mill, but most of the town's industry was in Walden. The Town of Montgomery was served by two north-south rail lines, the Wallkill Valley (1867–72) and Central New England (1889). It remained agricultural until the late 20th century, when urbanization resulted in housing development and population increase. The town grew 13% in the 1990s, and the village increased 35%. The Union Street/Academy Hill and Bridge Street Historic Districts in the village as well as many other sites in town are listed on the National Register of Historic Places.

Robert Williams

Montgomery, Helen Barrett (*b* Kingsville, Ohio, 31 July 1861; *d* Summit, NJ, 19 Oct 1934). Author and stateswoman. Montgomery's family moved to Rochester when she was a child. Her father attended Rochester Theological Seminary and became pastor of Lake Avenue Baptist Church (1876). She graduated from Wellesley College in Massachusetts in 1884 and taught at Rochester Free Academy (1884–85) and then at Wellesley Preparatory School in Philadelphia (1885). In 1887 she married William A. Montgomery, an industrialist and later philanthropist in Rochester. She became active in civic organizations, advocating progressive educational methods and greater opportunities for women. With Susan B. Anthony, she formed the Women's Educational and Industrial Union in 1893 and served as its first president. The union assisted poor working women, providing legal aid, vocational training, playgrounds, and health education. Much in demand as a platform speaker, Montgomery was elected president of the New York State Federation of Women's Clubs in 1896. From 1898 to 1900, she worked with Anthony to raise $50,000 for the University of Rochester, which helped persuade its trustees to admit women as regular students.

In 1899 she was elected to the Rochester City School Board and served for 10 years; she was the first woman ever elected to public office in the city. Innovations during her tenure included kindergartens, manual and domestic training, school lunches, night schools, and mothers' clubs. During this time, she continued her involvement with Anthony and the suffrage movement as a member of the Women's Political Equality Club of Rochester. She made a North American tour in 1910–11 in support of missionary work and wrote several study books on that topic for church use. Her reputation as a platform speaker rose to national prominence as a result. From 1914 to 1924, she served as president of the Woman's American Baptist Foreign Mission Society. During one of her overseas trips, she devised the idea of a World Day of Prayer, which became a Protestant institution in 1922. In 1921 Montgomery was elected president of the Northern Baptist Convention, becoming the first woman in the United States to be elected to a major denominational post. During her tenure she presided over an historic debate between fundamentalists and liberals at the annual meeting of the convention. In 1924 she completed the *Centenary Translation of the New Testament* from Greek, the first woman to translate that work. A thorough ecumenist, in later years she wrote in favor of cooperative women's work and missions. She was awarded an honorary master's of arts degree from Brown University in 1917, a doctor of humane letters degree from Franklin College, and doctor of letters degrees from Denison University in 1922 and Wellesley College in 1925.

McKelvey, Blake. *Rochester: The Quest for Quality, 1890–1925* (Cambridge, Mass: Harvard Univ Press, 1956)

Montgomery, Helen B. *From Campus to World Citizenship* (New York: Revell, 1940)

William H. Brackney

Montgomery, Richard (*b* Swords, Ireland, 2 Dec 1738; *d* Quebec City, Canada, 31 Dec 1775). Military commander. After attending Trinity College in Dublin, Montgomery joined the British army in 1756 and fought in the French and Indian War. He saw action in several major campaigns, including Louisbourg on Cape Breton Island, NS (1758), Fort Ticonderoga and Crown Point [now in Essex Co] (1759), and the capture of Montreal (1760). Montgomery settled in England after the war but by 1773 returned to New York Colony, bought a farm at Kings Bridge [now in Bronx Co], married Margaret Livingston, and settled near Rhinebeck (Dutchess Co). In 1775 he was elected to the New York provincial congress and appointed by Congress as brigadier general of the Continental army. Montgomery led an invasion of Canada, gained notoriety for conquering Montreal in November 1775, and was promoted to major general in December although he never learned of the promotion. He and Benedict Arnold headed attacks on Quebec City and on Cape Diamond, and Montgomery was shot and killed. His body, abandoned by his flustered troops, was recovered by the British and buried in Quebec. Congress established a memorial for Montgomery at St. Paul's Chapel in Lower Manhattan, where his remains were interred in 1818 after they had been exhumed in Quebec. His death, seen as a heroic tragedy, was memorialized by John Trumbull in his famous painting, *The Death of General Montgomery in the Attack on Quebec* (1786). Montgomery Co was named in his honor in 1784.

Shelton, Hal T. *General Richard Montgomery and the American Revolution: From Redcoat to Rebel* (New York: New York Univ Press, 1994)

Mark G. Spencer

Montgomery County (405 mi²/1,049 km²; pop 49,708). Created in 1772 from Albany Co and originally named Tryon Co after colonial governor William Tryon, its name was changed in 1784 to honor Revolutionary War general Richard Montgomery. The county initially covered a huge territory that included much of northern and western New York State. Major territorial changes occurred with the formation of Ontario (1789), Herkimer (1791), Otsego (1791), Tioga (1791), Hamilton (1816), and Fulton (1838) Cos. Lesser adjustments took place with Herkimer Co in 1797 and with Clinton, Essex, Saratoga, and Washington Cos in 1817. Montgomery Co is divided into 1 city, Amsterdam, and 10 towns that contain 10 incorporated villages. Fonda is the county seat.

Elevations range from just under 240 feet (73 m) along the banks of the Mohawk River where it exits the county to over 1,600 feet (490 m) in the southwest. Montgomery Co is part of the Mohawk Valley subregion of the Hudson-Mohawk Lowland landform province. The Mohawk River flows eastward across the county's breadth within a well-entrenched former glacial spillway. Those steep-sided walls rise abruptly 200–500 feet (60–150 m) above the valley floor, most dramatically at the narrow gap known as the Noses east of Canajoharie, to a broad surrounding lowland whose rolling surface increases in elevation as it extends to the Helderberg Escarpment in the south and the Adirondack Upland to the north. Ordovician shales and sandstones underlie most of the county. Some limestone and dolostone lie in the northeast. Cambrian-age limestone and dolostone are found in scattered areas of north central and northwest Montgomery Co. The county was glaciated, as evidenced by rounded hills, extensive deposits of glacial till, and lake-bed and outwash deposits. It lies entirely within the Mohawk River watershed. Numerous tributaries, most notably Canajoharie, East Canada, and Schoharie Creeks, approach the master stream at right angles, some in deeply incised ravines. Soil quality varies greatly, but high- to medium-quality agricultural land is found throughout the county's western third and in a substantial area west of Amsterdam.

The climate is humid-continental. Mean January temperatures vary only slightly, ranging from 19°F (-7°C) in the north to a couple of degrees warmer in the southeast. Early morning lows drop below 0°F (-18°C) a few times nearly every winter. Mean July temperatures range from the upper 60s°F (18–20°C) in the southwest to approximately 70°F (21°C) in the northwest and east. Summertime temperatures reach or exceed 90°F (32°C) at least once most years. Average annual precipitation amounts range from slightly less than 39 inches (99 cm) at Tribes Hill to about 45 inches (114 cm) in the southwest. Seasonal snowfall amounts vary from over 100 inches (254 cm) in the southwest to less than 60 inches (152 cm) close to the Mohawk River in the east. The primeval forest cover consisted of two communities. The inner valleys of the Mohawk River and Schoharie Creek were covered by a central hardwood forest dominated by beech, sugar maple, and basswood. An Alleghenian hardwood forest, dominated by beech, sugar maple, hemlock, white pine, and basswood, blanketed the remainder.

American Indians and Early Settlement

The excavated Snell site is evidence of Owasco occupation (1000–1300). The present area of Montgomery Co was at the center of Mohawk territory in early Contact times. In the 17th century they lived in palisaded villages dominated by longhouses. Some of the largest were Onekagoncka, Canawarode, Schanidisse, and Tenotoge. The Dutch established trade relations with the Mohawk shortly after their establishment of Beverwijck [now Albany] in the 1620s. As early as 1634–35, Harmen Meyndertsz van den Bogaert journeyed through the Mohawk Valley to determine why the fur trade had decreased. The French also established connections with the Mohawk and made strenuous efforts to convert them to Catholicism, with mixed results. Several Jesuit missionaries were martyred at the hands of the Mohawk, the most noted being Fr Isaac Jogues in 1646 at Ossernenon [now Auriesville]. Ossernenon was later the birthplace of Kateri Tekakwitha (1656–80), one of the first generation of Mohawk converts to Catholicism; she was beatified by the Roman Catholic Church in 1980.

The county's major land patents included the Kayaderosseras, Harrison, Corry's, and Williams Patents; each contained more than 12,000 acres (4,900 ha). The first settlers were the Dutch and Palatine Germans. The Dutch pushed west from Schenectady beginning in 1713 as far as the present town of Palatine. In the spring of 1723 a group of Palatine German families settled near the Mohawk River on the 12,700-acre (5,140 ha) Stone Arabia Patent in Palatine. Population increased with these settlements, but it was the 1711 construction of Fort Hunter that opened the area up to trade. The fort (150 ft²/14 m²) contained a two-story blockhouse with double loopholes and a 24 ft² (2 m²) chapel.

The dominant figure in the county in the late colonial period was Sir William Johnson, who came from Ireland in 1738 to administer the 15,000-acre (6,100 ha) estate of his uncle, Sir Peter Warren, at the mouth of Schoharie Creek in what is now the Town of Florida. Active in the fur trade, Johnson became friendly with the

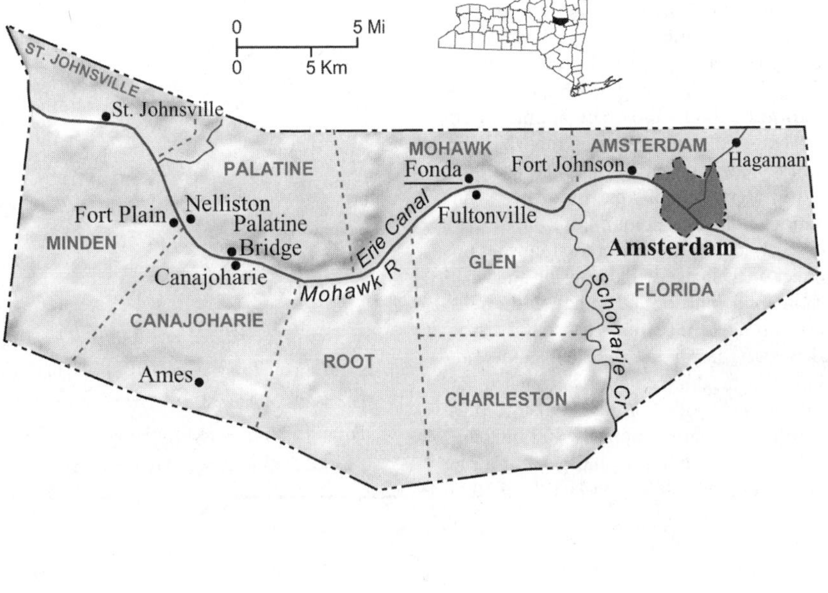

MONTGOMERY CO POPULATION CENSUS FIGURES

	White	Nonwhite	Total Population	Foreign-Born
1790	28,219	629	28,848	—
1800	21,226	474	21,700	—
1810	40,137	1,077	41,214	—
1820	36,641	928	37,569	93
1830	43,004	711	43,715	261
1840	35,230	588	35,818	—
1850	31,518	474	31,992	3,116
1860	30,509	357	30,866	3,052
1870	34,102	355	34,457	4,280
1880	37,997	318	38,315	4,847
1890	45,425	274	45,699	7,475
1900	47,273	215	47,488	8,229
1910	57,344	223	57,567	13,690
1920	57,706	222	57,928	12,363
1930	59,859	217	60,076	11,108
1940	58,940	202	59,142	9,212
1950	59,315	279	59,594	7,911
1960	56,989	251	57,240	5,819
1970	55,607	276	55,883	3,891
1980	52,424	1,015	53,439	2,684
1990	50,189	1,792	51,981	1,848
2000	47,160	2,548	49,708	1,574

Notes: "Nonwhite" includes African Americans, Asians, American Indians, and Pacific Islanders and, for 2000, also the mixed race and other race categories. Through the 1960 census these figures primarily reflect the African American population. Foreign-born figures for 1820 and 1830 include only those not naturalized, and for 1930 and 1950, the foreign-born totals include Whites only. Other years include all foreign-born in the population.

Mohawk, learned their language and customs, and eventually became superintendent of Indian Affairs of the Northern Department. He used his influence with the Mohawk and the Iroquois to defend British interests against the French during the French and Indian War. Johnson's prominence in the Mohawk Valley gave him much control, including in politics. He provided land and money for the construction of the Tryon Co courthouse in Johnstown [now in Fulton Co] in 1772. Due to his great influence, Johnson's family members and friends were appointed to official positions by Gov Tryon.

Revolutionary War

Anti-Crown sentiment was developing in coastal cities, but it did not immediately reach the Mohawk Valley. By 1774, upon the death of Sir William Johnson, however, dissension between those loyal to the Crown and those in opposition to it was becoming apparent. In that year, Tryon Co officials signed a document affirming their loyalty while disapproving of some of the Crown's actions and maintaining certain personal and political liberties. On 5 May 1775 a liberty pole was raised at Caughnawaga [now Fonda] by a group of 300 patriots. After a confrontation with Guy and John Johnson, the rally dispersed, but the authority of the Johnsons was no longer unchallenged. In the spring and fall of 1780, Sir John Johnson led Indian and loyalist raiders through the county, wreaking havoc. Residents were terrorized and their homes ravaged by their neighbors. Reports estimated that 197 people were killed and 121 taken captive during the raids; approximately 700 buildings were destroyed. The largest engagement in the county during the war was the Battle of Stone Arabia on 19 Oct 1780. In an open field about 2 miles (3 km) northeast of the present village of Palatine Bridge, Col John Brown and a force of about 200 militia fought Johnson's combined army of British troops, loyalists, and Indians. Greatly outnumbered, Americans lost about 30 men, including their commander. With fewer casualties, Johnson's force continued westward, burning buildings as they marched.

There were relatively few Mohawks left in the present county at the war's end. Those who sided with the British moved to Canada and settled on lands granted them by the British government. Unoccupied land in what is now Montgomery Co, particularly in the south, were taken up by farmers from New England and eastern New York State. Attracted by the fertile land, the postwar immigrants settled on properties confiscated from loyalists or became tenants on tracts such as Corry's Patent, whose landlord, George Clarke, leased farms for three lives (ie, the lifetimes of three individuals party to the lease).

Transportation

Initial travel occurred along Indian trails and by canoe along the Mohawk River and tributary streams. By 1730 flatboats and bateaux transported grain, potash, and pearl ash on the Mohawk. In 1800 the Mohawk Turnpike was built by a corporation from Scotia to Utica along the north bank of the river, with tollgates at various points. In 1822 the Erie Canal opened across the county. Workers had particular difficulty with its construction adjacent to the steep, rocky slopes of the Noses east of Sprakers. At Fort Hunter, where the Schoharie Creek created hazardous flood conditions, an aqueduct was built in 1841 to carry the canal over the creek, replacing earlier guard locks and a rope tow across the crosscurrent.

The Utica and Schenectady Railroad began operating in 1836; in 1853 it became part of the New York Central Railroad. Fonda became its junction with a small feeder, the Fonda, Johnstown and Gloversville, in 1870. The West Shore Railroad (1883) on the south shore unsuccessfully challenged the New York Central and was acquired by it in 1886. The speed and lower costs of railroads attracted business, and the Erie Canal suffered and its tolls were eventually abolished. It was replaced by the New York State Barge Canal in 1918. Local public transportation began with horsecar lines in Amsterdam (1873) and in Fonda and Fultonville (1875). These were later electrified and joined by interurbans running to Gloversville and Schenectady in 1902–3 but were driven out of business by bus lines in 1936–38.

Economic Development

Montgomery Co was part of the region called the "Breadbasket of the Revolution." Farming centered on grain and hay, as evidenced by the

POPULATIONS OF TOWNS AND CITIES, MONTGOMERY CO

Town or City, Year Founded	1800	1840	1880	1920	1960	2000
Amsterdam, 1772[a]	1,064	5,333	11,710	3,130	5,400	5,820
Amsterdam (city), 1885	—	—	—	33,524	28,772	18,355
Canajoharie, 1772[b]	2,266	5,146	4,294	3,784	4,233	3,797
Charleston, 1793	2,001	2,103	1,334	785	546	1,292
Florida, 1793	1,238	5,214	3,249	1,651	2,168	2,731
Glen, 1823	—	3,678	2,622	1,782	1,734	2,222
Minden, 1798	2,929	3,507	5,100	4,366	4,560	4,202
Mohawk, 1837	—	3,112	2,943	2,353	3,070	3,902
Palatine, 1772[c]	3,517	2,823	2,786	2,232	2,556	3,070
Root, 1823	—	2,979	2,275	1,198	1,243	1,752
St. Johnsville, 1838	—	1,923	2,002	3,123	2,958	2,565

Note: In 1800 Montgomery Co included the Towns of Broadalbin, Johnstown, Mayfield, and Northampton [now in Fulton Co], and the Towns of Manheim and Salisbury [now in Herkimer Co].

[a]Formed as Mohawk District; recognized as Town of Caughnawaga 1788; name changed 1793.

[b]Formed as district; recognized as town 1788.

[c]Formed as Stone Arabia District; name changed to Palatine 1773; recognized as town 1788.

many Dutch barns still extant. The Erie Canal made possible cheap shipment of western grain, causing a shift to dairy; in the early years of railroad service, no refrigeration was available for fresh milk so farmers made and shipped cheese. In 1855 Montgomery Co produced 1,538,000 pounds (697,600 kg) of cheese and 1,211,000 pounds (549,300 kg) of butter. In the second half of the 19th century, hops were a significant cash crop in the towns south of the Mohawk, where 1,111 acres (450 ha) planted in 1875 placed Montgomery seventh among New York counties. Hop producers in the western United States caused fluctuations in pricing, which in addition to a blight and Prohibition ended hop growing locally.

While the canal encouraged industry by providing cheap, efficient transportation, both Amsterdam and Fonda developed waterpowered industries on tributary streams early in the 19th century. Carpet manufacturing began in Amsterdam in 1842 and became the county's largest industry; employing 9,300 workers in 1920. Knit goods were Amsterdam's second industry, and they were also produced in Fonda, Fultonville, Fort Johnson, Fort Plain, Hagaman, and St. Johnsville. Other significant 19th-century products were brushes and brooms (Amsterdam, Fonda, Fultonville), paper bags (Canajoharie), furniture (Fort Plain), and agricultural implements (St. Johnsville). The Imperial Packing Co (1891), which grew into Beech-Nut, dominated in Canajoharie throughout the 20th century. Fultonville relied on the White Mop Wringer Co (1904–2003). Fort Plain Furniture ceased production in 1932; Arkell and Smith, paper bag producers, left Canajoharie in 1952, and Amsterdam lost its two huge carpet firms in 1955 and 1968.

In the early 21st century fewer, smaller industries are scattered through the county's communities. Amsterdam has Cranesville Block Co, Ward Products, and Noteworthy Corp, all post–World War II arrivals, which together employ over 1,000 workers. Keymark Corp/Kasson and Keller in Fonda is the county's largest single manufacturer, while Beech-Nut in Canajoharie and Sentinel Products in St. Johnsville are the larger firms upcounty. Heralding a newer form of employment, the Target Distribution Center in Florida is expected to begin operations in 2005.

Religion, Education, and Culture

The first house of worship erected in the county was the chapel financed by Queen Anne and built at Fort Hunter in 1711. It was Anglican, but the vast majority of the settlers were Reformed or Lutheran. Palatine Germans organized the Reformed Dutch Church of Stone Arabia in 1739. A congregational split about 20 years later gave birth to Trinity Lutheran Church. Methodist circuit riders appeared at the end of the 18th century, and by 1855 there were 12 Methodist congregations, but the county's Dutch and Palatine roots were evident in its 16 Reformed and 8 Lutheran churches. The first Catholic worship took place at Amsterdam in 1837, and a church organized in Florida in 1844. Jewish immigrants began settling in Amsterdam in the 1860s, forming a Reform synagogue in 1874 and an Orthodox synagogue in 1887.

The *Canajoharie Telegraph* (1825) was the first newspaper published in the county. The *Canajoharie Radii* (1837), published by Levi S. Backus, who was deaf, received state appropriations to

Cassidy Building, Amsterdam, 1905.

circulate the paper to deaf-mute residents of the state. The *Amsterdam Democrat* (1878) was the first daily paper. In 2003 the *Amsterdam Recorder* is the daily, and the *Courier-Standard-Enterprise* (1876) is a weekly published at Fort Plain and serving the upcounty towns. Radio broadcasting is provided by WCSS-AM (1948), and WBUG-FM.

Education began under subscription support before the 1812 state legislation authorizing common schools; the Union Academy of Palatine (1795) was among the first, located at Stone Arabia. The Central Asylum for the Deaf and Dumb (1823) at Buel in the Town of Canajoharie was established to educate deaf-mutes for productive lives; one of four such schools in the country and the first to teach the sign language alphabet in printed form, it closed in 1836 because of decreased state funding. During the late 1840s Susan B. Anthony taught at Canajoharie Academy (1824). One of the county's largest schools was the coeducational Fort Plain Seminary and Collegiate Institute (1853), whose first class numbered 513.

In 1869 there were 117 one-room schools in Montgomery Co. The first parochial school was St. Mary's Institute (1881) in Amsterdam, which began with a high school program; three additional schools for elementary education were founded between 1902 and 1931. In the latter year almost 18% of Amsterdam's 8,000 registered students attended parochial schools. Centralization was a state initiative beginning in the 1920s and was resisted in Montgomery Co. St. Johnsville centralized in 1942, Canajoharie in 1944, Fort Plain in 1951, and Fonda-Fultonville in 1953. The Amsterdam city district was enlarged after 1958 by annexing rural schools, but many held out, and as late as 1969 one district was still in court. County officials joined with Fulton Co officials to established Fulton-Montgomery Community College in 1963. Classes began in 1964 and its campus, in the Town of Mohawk on the Fulton Co line, was begun in 1967. Its 2003 enrollment included 150 students from other countries.

Cultural institutions include the Canajoharie Library and Art Gallery, with its collection of American representational art, and Old Fort Johnson (1749). The National Shrine of North American Martyrs at Auriesville and the National Kateri Tekakwitha Shrine west of Fonda commemorate and interpret the story of 17th-century Mohawk converts to Roman Catholicism. Actor Kirk Douglas, born Issur Danielovitch in Amsterdam in 1916, is perhaps the county's most famous native son.

Politics

Supervisors elected every four years in each of the 10 towns and the 5 Amsterdam wards administer Montgomery Co government. One member is elected by peers to preside over the Board of Supervisors for the coming year. The practice was to alternate between supervisors from upcounty and those from the city but in recent years the vote has not followed this tradition. Each supervisor had an equal vote until 1972 when proportional voting was instituted, using a weighted vote based upon the population represented. The position of county administrator was created by resolution in 1978 to oversee the day-to-day activities of county offices, but it was eliminated in the spring of 2003. At various times throughout the 20th century, constituents proposed relocating the county seat to Amsterdam, but Fonda remains the official location of all county business. Voters have favored Republican candidates in national elections except when there are very strong Democratic candidates. A leading political figure from Montgomery Co was Mary Anne Krupsak, lieutenant governor under Gov Hugh Carey.

Recent History

Transportation improvements, urban renewal, and the loss of manufacturing were the most significant changes in the county after World War II. Rail service was reduced, although the track through the Mohawk Valley remains the main New York-to-Chicago trunk line; Amsterdam alone retains a station. But the New York State Thruway, completed in 1954, placed Montgomery Co on the state's modern transportation artery and made its city and villages, except tiny Ames, easily accessible to commercial traffic via three exits. The City of Amsterdam's landscape was drastically altered as a result of urban renewal from 1965 to 1979, including construction of arterial highways, public housing, and the Amsterdam Mall (1977). Meanwhile, village shopping districts once thriving with "mom and pop" stores have been unable to compete with larger, more diverse shopping centers.

Montgomery Co had 542 farms in 1997, a slight increase from five years earlier, encompassing 134,940 acres (54,608 ha); both numbers were the largest in eastern New York. Its 52.1% of land in farms is fifth highest in New York State. Some of the relative viability of farming can be traced to a significant Amish immigration, which began in 1986 in Palatine and subsequently spread to Minden. While fewer in number, the arrival of a community of Akwesasne Mohawk in 1993, also in Palatine, has similar implications for both land stewardship and tourism potential. Still more cultural diversity is provided by Amsterdam's Latino population, amounting to 16% in 2000.

The county lost many important manufacturers over the second half of the 20th century, including the carpet industry in Amsterdam. Life Savers in Canajoharie moved its operations south in 1988, attracted by cheaper labor and better access to raw materials. Moreover, the Montgomery Co population in 2000 was down more than 10% from its 1969 total of 55,970 because of job losses. While manufacturing has declined, it remains one of the principal employment sectors and includes baby food, candy, printing and publishing, rubber and plastics, and metal fabrication. The Target Distribution Center in Florida will offer a large number of warehouse jobs. Having increased the sales tax by 1% in 2003, county officials look toward stimulation of the economy through establishing industrial parks and capitalizing on cultural tourism.

F. W. Beers, *History of Montgomery and Fulton Counties* (1878) is the standard county history. Jeptha R. Simms, *Frontiersmen of New York* (1882) is widely used for the early period, since the author gathered firsthand accounts. Also useful for the western part of the county is Nelson Greene, *The Story of Old Fort Plain and the Middle Mohawk Valley* (1913). Washington Frothingham, *History of Montgomery County* (1892), although almost a duplicate of the Beers's work, provides useful material. Hugh P. Donlan, *Outlines of History, Montgomery County, New York, 1772–1972* (1973) is a strong example of a county history from the bicentennial period. Although not every community has a published history, there are a few that stand out, including Hugh P. Donlon, *Annals of a Milltown in the Mohawk Valley* (1980), which provides a comprehensive treatment of Amsterdam with helpful treatment of the 20th century; Katherine M. Strobeck, *Port Jackson: An Erie Canal Village* (1989); Nelson Greene, *Fort Plain–Nelliston History, 1580–1947* (1947); Ruth Lupo, *Waymarks of Nelliston, 1878–1978* (1978); and Annie Coddington, *Randall Gleanings* (2001).

Kelly A. Yacobucci Farquhar

Monticello [MON-TI-SEL-OH]. Village (pop 6,512) in Thompson (Sullivan Co). Settled in 1804, it won designation as county seat in 1809 and was incorporated as a village in 1830. Situated on a ridge 1,387 feet (423 m) above sea level, Monticello was primarily a government and trading center in the 19th century, although in 1860 it had an iron foundry, and during the Civil War Zack Taylor made banjo and drum heads in the village. It missed being on the main line of the Ontario and Western Railroad but had rail service via Port Jervis (Orange Co) (1871–1953). Cigar making employed residents in the 1890s, and a long-lived tannery burned in 1924. In the 20th century, industrial products included gloves, Christmas tree lights, toy trucks, and flavorings produced by Synfleur Scientific Laboratories (1904–1980s). Monticello Raceway (1958) is a harness-racing track. Once an important commercial center, Monticello lost much of its downtown business to malls outside the village; many residents commute to work in surrounding areas.

John Conway

Montour. Town (pop 2,446) in S Schuyler Co. Settled in 1788, the town was formed in 1860 from Catharine. In 2002 employment was centered in the Village of Montour Falls. The town-owned Havana Glen Park (1937) features a hiking trail through a gorge carved by glaciers. The Lee School Museum was a 1960 gift of the local school district when it ceased operating. Catharine Creek, a renowned trout stream, flows into Seneca Lake.

Glenda Gephart

Montour Falls. Village (pop 1,797) in Montour and Dix (Schuyler Co). The village was the site of a Seneca community, Catharine's Town, which was destroyed in 1779 by Continental army general John Sullivan and his troops. European settlement began nine years later. The Catharinestown post office was established in 1802, and its name was changed to Havana in 1828. It became a prosperous manufacturing village producing, at various times, linseed oil, woolens, stoneware, agricultural implements, bench vises, plaster, and yeast. A major manufacturer was Shepard Niles (1878), a crane and hoist producer, which continued as a service firm in 2003. Incorporated as a village in 1836, Havana served as the county seat from 1860 to 1868. The village's name was changed to Montour Falls in 1895. Chequagua Falls, 156 feet (47.6 m) high, dramatically overlooks Main St, which also features a group of 19th-century buildings in the "Glorious T" National Register Historic District. Bethesda Sanitarium (1881) was a private chronic hospital; Schuyler Hospital now serves the county. Montour Falls was the site of the People's College of the State of New York (incorporated 1854; operated 1864–65; Cook Academy (1873–1943). St. John's Seminary (1950–68) subsequently occupied the academy's site, which by 1974 was occupied by the Senator Frederick L. Warder Academy of Fire Science.

Glenda Gephart

Montour family {Montour, Louis Couc (*b* Trois-Rivières, Canada, 1659; *d* Seneca Nation territory, 1709); Montour, Isabelle Couc (*b* ?Trois Rivières, Canada, 1667; *d* ?Ohio Valley, ?1753); Montour, Andrew (*b* ?Oneida Nation territory, ?1710; *d* ?Ohio Valley, ?1775)}. Interpreters and traders. Few in early America were truly multilingual in both European and American Indian languages, and those who were became invaluable to both trade and diplomacy. Among them were several generations of the Montour family, which were involved in the fur trade in New York Colony, Canada, and throughout the Great Lakes.

The Montour family name originated when Louis Couc adopted it as his fur trade name in the early 1680s. His parents were Pierre Couc, a French immigrant to Canada, and Marie Miteouamegoukoué, an Algonquin woman. In 1708 Louis Montour guided members of the Miami, Wyandot, and other western Indian nations to Albany to open trade with the English, circumventing French law decreeing that all fur trade go through Montreal. A year later, he was leading a group of Ojibways across New York Colony when he was reputedly murdered by rival French trader and interpreter Louis-Thomas Chabert de Joncaire.

Isabelle Couc Montour, or Madame Montour, as she was usually known in the English records, was Louis Couc Montour's sister. After his death she took over his role in the fur trade and later served as interpreter for New York governor Robert Hunter. She had one recorded marriage in New France in 1684, to Joachim Germano. By the early 18th century, she was married to the Oneida leader Carandowana; it is uncertain if she was married a third time. In 1711 she served as an official interpreter and produced hundreds of wampum belts for New York Colony's abortive invasion of Canada, the so-called Glorious Enterprise.

After 1720 and for most of the next three decades, Madame Montour and her family lived in the Susquehanna Valley near the present locations of Williamsport and Sunbury, Pa. Her family continued participation in the fur trade with Albany. Her son Andrew Montour acted as a go-between for both Sir William Johnson and George Croghan with Iroquois and other Indian nations. He interpreted several languages at treaty conferences in New York up until the American Revolution.

Hirsch, Alison Duncan. "The Celebrated Madame Montour: 'Interpretress' across Early American Frontiers." In *Explorations in Early American Culture*, vol 4 (University Park: Pennsylvania Historical Association, 2000)

Merrell, James H. *Into the American Woods: Negotiators on the Pennsylvania Frontier* (New York: Norton, 1999)

Alison Duncan Hirsch

Mooers. Town (pop 3,404) in Clinton Co. Settled in 1796 the town, which is bounded on the north by Canada, was formed from Champlain in 1802. Its Yankee settlers were later joined by Quebecois; their descendants are predominant, with some Irish and Scots mixed in. The Northern Railroad (later Rutland Railroad) opened up eastern markets beginning in 1848; it was joined by the Mooers branch of the New York and Canada Railroad (1852). The town's economy was based on farming, forest products, and ironwork. Mooers hamlet was an incorporated village between 1899 and 1995. In the early 21st century, some residents work at the border crossing, while others farm or work outside of town; maple sugar is a distinctive product.

Thomas A. Rumney

moose *[Alces alces]*. The largest member of the deer family. A full-grown male may be 6 feet (1.8 m) tall at the shoulder and weigh 1,400 pounds (635 kg). Cows typically breed at 28 months, with the calf remaining with the mother until she calves again. Moose are generally solitary, but individuals—other than adult males—may join together during the winter. They prefer mixed forests of quaking aspen, balsam fir, and paper birch; they also favor wetlands with sodium-rich water plants. Moose were once common in the northern areas of New York State, especially in the Adirondacks. Intensive hunting resulted in their extinction, with one of the last moose, a cow, killed in August 1861 near Raquette Lake (Hamilton Co). Between 1894 and 1895, 11 moose were imported from Canada and released near Nehasane (Hamilton Co). Between 1902 and 1903, another 12 were released near Raquette Lake. Both efforts failed to reestablish a viable population. Occasional migrants were noted from 1935 to 1980, but all left the state or were killed. In 1980 six moose migrated from the New England area to Raquette Lake and remained. Their recovery may be related to a decrease in logging and subsequent regrowth of prime moose habitat. As of 2000 the state boasted an estimated 80–110 moose, with sightings reported in 39 counties.

Franzmann, Albert W., and Charles C. Schwartz, eds. *Ecology and Management of the North American Moose* (Washington, DC: Smithsonian Institution Press, 1997)

Brad Coon

moral obligation debt. Nonguaranteed debt. Bonds issued by states or other public entities not backed by the state's "full faith and credit" have a long history in the United States. Such debt normally commands higher interest rates to compensate lenders for assuming greater risk. Although not backed by the guarantees set forth in Article 7, Section 16 of the New York State Constitution, it has been contended that the state nonetheless has a liability, an implicit moral obligation, to fulfill the commitments of entities or agencies that the state itself has created.

The issue surfaced from time to time beginning in 1852, when it was referred to in a court case on the constitutionality of a canal debt issue. The debt had been authorized by the legislature but not approved by the voters as required by the recently adopted Constitution of 1846. Cited with greater frequency following the emergence of the public authority, or public benefit corporation in the 1920s, it achieved its greatest prominence in New York State during the 1960s. In 1960 a new authority, the New York State Housing Finance Agency (HFA), was authorized to sell bonds and lend the proceeds to companies engaged in the construction of middle-income housing. To increase the marketability of HFA bonds, at interest rates low enough to enable companies to rent apartments to middle-income tenants, the law creating HFA provided that its debt service would be backed not only by a dedicated income stream, such as rent, but by an explicit provision, known as a make-up clause, requiring that if the HFA had to draw down its capital reserve to service its debt it would notify the governor and the state budget director of the amount required to restore the reserve. The bond prospectuses issued by the agency included similar assurances but stipulated that they were not legally binding on the state. It did, however, guarantee that the matter would come to the state's attention. A similar guarantee was later included in the laws governing the operation of a wide variety of other public authorities.

So-called moral obligation borrowing, which bypassed public referendums and other constitutional restrictions, played a major role in financing the enormous New York State construction programs of the 1960s and indeed supported the bonds issued by public authorities in many other states. Unavoidably, the explosion of such debt significantly contributed to the fiscal crisis in New York State and New York City in the 1970s. The state has continued to use nonguaranteed debt to finance construction. However, it has largely removed the make-up clauses from state law and has taken a number of other steps to regulate both the volume and pace of state borrowing. Among the most important have been the creation of the Public Authorities Control Board in 1976 and the enactment of a comprehensive debt reform act in 2000.

Quirk, William J., and Leon E. Wein. "A Short Constitutional History of the Entities Commonly Known as Authorities," *Cornell Law Review* 56 (Apr 1971): 521–97

Utevsky, Michael D. "The Future of Nonguaranteed Bond Financing in New York," *Fordham Law Review* 45 (Mar 1977): 860–84

Robert P. Kerker

Moran, Mary Nimmo (*b* Strathaven, Scotland, 16 May 1842; *d* East Hampton, Suffolk Co, 25 Sept 1899). Etcher. A leading artist of the painter-etcher movement, Mary Nimmo emigrated with her family in 1852, settling near Philadelphia. Their neighbor, landscape painter Thomas Moran (1837–1926), became Nimmo's teacher in 1860, and in 1862 the two were married. They spent 1866–68 abroad, where she developed an appreciation for the Barbizon school's plein air method of directly capturing nature. In 1878 the Morans first visited East Hampton (Suffolk Co). In the following year she produced her first etchings, and together the Morans helped ignite a resurgence of interest in printmaking in America. The immediacy and intimacy of her landscapes, etched out-of-doors, earned her honors at the 1893 World's Columbian Exposition, as well as membership in the New York Etching Club and England's Royal Society of Painter-Etchers.

Siegel, Nancy. *The Morans: The Artistry of a 19th-Century Family of Painter-Etchers* (Huntingdon, Pa: Juniata College Press, 2001)

Brian Edward Hack

Moran Towing Company. In 1850 Thomas Moran, an unemployed stonemason, left Kill Lara, in the County of West Meath, Ireland, bound for New York with his wife, who died on the ship, and seven children, including 17-year-old Michael. The family settled in Frankfort (Herkimer Co), on the Erie Canal, where Michael Moran went to work driving mules along the canal. By 1855 he bought his first canal barge and continued to expand his barge business. Seeing the future in steam tugs, in 1860 he moved to New York City, where his older brother Dick owned a sailing sloop, but he decided to purchase interest in a steam towboat instead, the *Ida Miller*. He started a towboat agency on South St in Manhattan and by the mid-1880s had an interest in 10 tugboats working New York Harbor. The Moran boats, visible by the large white M on the black stacks and named for family members or close friends, towed freighters and tankers around the harbor, docked ocean liners and windships, performed rescue operations for ships in distress, and had an exclusive contract to haul the garbage from New York City out to sea. Two of Michael Moran's five sons, Eugene and Joseph, joined the family business, and in 1905 the Moran Co incorporated. By Moran's death on 28 June 1906, Moran Towing Corp was a leader in the Port of New York and by 1956 was the largest fleet in New York Harbor. In the 20th century, under nearly 70 years of leadership of Michael's grandson, Edmond J. Moran, the company opened or bought out other tugboat companies to operate from Maine to Texas. The business remained family owned and managed until 1994 when it was sold to Mormac Marine Group in Stamford, Conn. In 2002 Moran Towing Corp, headquartered in Greenwich, Conn, was a $150 million company with 16 tugboats in New York Harbor alone, as well as boats in the ports of Albany and 13 more in other states.

Moran, Eugene F., and Louis Reid. *Tugboat: The Moran Story* (New York: Charles Scribner's Sons, 1956)

Francis J. Duffy

Moravia. Town (pop 4,040) and village (pop 1,363) in SE Cayuga Co. Settled in 1790, the town was formed from Sempronius in 1833. Mill Brook provided waterpower for industry, including a cotton mill (1831–56), woolen mills, a spoke factory, a brickyard, carriage works, and a fluting- and polishing-iron factory. Rogers and Skinner manufactured Jethro Wood's cast-iron moldboard plow beginning in 1823, a ground-breaking agricultural invention. The village was incorporated in 1837, and the Southern Central Railroad (1870) contributed to its prosperity. After the Civil War the town was a destination for Spiritualists because several notable mediums were residents. Fillmore Glen State Park, 857 acres (346 ha), is partly in town. In the village's historic district, St. Matthew's Episcopal Church is noted for its seven oaken carvings by Hans Meyer of Oberammergau, Germany. Jennings Department Store (1860) is one of New York State's oldest in continuous operation. At Moravia Downs, pony-cart racing takes place every summer. Moravia was the childhood home (1843–50) of John D. Rockefeller Sr (1839–1937). In 2002 manufacturers included Crosible (filters) and UPSCO (meters for natural gas). Moravia, whose population increased 60% between 1960 and 2000, is a bedroom community for Auburn, Ithaca, and Cortland. Fertile land continues to produce in hay and corn.

Arlene Murphy

Moravian Church (Unity of the Brethren). Protestant Episcopal denomination with roots reaching back to the 15th-century Hussite movement in Bohemia and Moravia [both now in Czech Republic]. Reformer Jan Hus was martyred in 1415. His followers eventually organized as the Unity of the Brethren in 1457, which grew as a religious force in the region and predated the Reformation ministries of Martin Luther and John Calvin. In 1736 Bishop August Gottlieb Spangenburg of the Unity of the Brethren, who had immigrated to the United States with Swiss colonists a year earlier, visited New York City, and in 1739 the Brethren commissioned Christian Heinrich Rauch to preach to American Indians in New York Colony. He arrived at Shekomeko Village [now Pine Plains, Dutchess Co] in 1740, and 10 converts were organized into the Shekomeko Congregation in 1742. On the basis of a 1744 act requiring that all preachers be licensed, provincial authorities ordered the mission closed by 1745. Partly as a result of suspicions arising from their pacifism, the Moravians were denied a license, and the congregation moved to Pennsylvania in 1746. In what is now Onondaga Co, missionary David Zeisberger lived among the Iroquois for months at a time between 1745 and 1766.

Efforts with European settlers were more successful. In 1741 Peter Boehler preached the first Moravian sermon in New York City, and the first congregation there was organized in 1748. Staten Island was a center of Moravian activity in the 18th century, and the New Dorp Moravian Church was established in 1763, followed by three more between 1873 and 1889. Churches were also established in Brooklyn and Queens, and a mission in Utica was formed in the mid–19th century. The church today continues to emphasize a Christ-centered piety and social outreach. There were 11 Moravian congregations in New York State in 2002, 10 in New York City and 1 in Utica, organized under the Eastern District of the Northern Province of the Moravian Church in North America.

Stocker, Harry Emilius. *A History of the Moravian Church in New York City* (New York: First Moravian Church, 1922)

Westmeier, Karl Wilhelm. *The Evacuation of Shekomeko and the Early Moravian Missions to Native North Americans* (Lewiston, NY: Edwin Mellen Press, 1994)

Elisabeth Sommer

Moreau. Town (pop 13,826) in NE Saratoga Co. Settled in 1766 and formed in 1805 from Northumberland, the central and southeastern parts are fertile, and the rest has sandy soil; the western part lies in the Palmertown Mountains. The Champlain Canal (1823) passed along its eastern side. The Feeder Dam on the Hudson River near the western border was the point at which logs were taken out of the river to avoid the waterfalls at Glens Falls. The adjacent community of South Glens Falls developed as a manufacturing village. The first American temperance society was formed at Clark's Corners in 1808. Moreau Lake State Park covers 4,110 acres (1,663 ha) and is located primarily within the town.

Field Horne

Morehouse. Town (pop 151) in SW Hamilton Co. Settled in 1832, the town was formed in 1835 from Lake Pleasant. In 1834 speculator Andrew K. Morehouse began development, attracting French, German, and Dutch people to settle in the wilderness. A tannery (1854) and lumbering (1890s) provided a livelihood, but the town never met Morehouse's expectations. In 1953 it became the last of New York's 932 towns to acquire electrical power. Its population was only 65 in 1960. It remains a lumbering and resort town.

Moreland Act investigations. Clean government provision. Section 6 of the New York State Executive Law, commonly referred to as the Moreland Act, provides for the creation of special investigations or commissions appointed and empowered by the governor to examine the affairs of any New York State government department, bureau, board, or commission with a goal of documenting and exposing any mismanagement, fraud, or wrongdoing.

Background and Provisions

Forms of similar executive oversight date to the 19th century. The governor's authority to remove or recommend removal of certain state and local government officials was granted by the Constitutions of 1821, 1846, and 1894, and by various statutes. Investigations of public officers by the governor, by commissioners appointed by him, or by local district attorneys were explicitly authorized by several laws enacted between 1866 and 1892. Commissioners were empowered to issue subpoenas, take testimony, and make reports to the governor. Numerous gubernatorial investigations were conducted during the latter 19th century, a period of frequent mismanagement and corruption in state and local government.

The Moreland Act was adopted in 1907. Authored by Assemblyman Sherman P. Moreland (1868–1951), a Republican lawyer from Chemung Co, the act was drafted in response to two ad hoc legislative investigatory panels in 1905. Both the Stevens (public utilities) and Armstrong (insurance) investigations precluded a role for the governor even though the findings of the investigations directly affected the executive and the administration. The narrowness of each investigation, the exclusion of the executive branch, and the need to seat new investigators and commissioners for each investigation led Assemblyman Moreland, with advice from Gov Charles Evans Hughes (who had served as counsel to both the Armstrong and Stevens investigations prior to his election as governor in 1906), to draft the law.

Under terms of the Moreland Act, the independent, governor-appointed commissions enjoy the power to subpoena and examine witnesses under oath, and the governor is solely responsible for choosing the number of commissioners or acting as the investigator. The governor defines the nature of the investigation, which can be very broad and may overlap with the work of government departments. Final reports of the investigations are often issued to the governor, after which the commission ceases to exist and is disbanded. The governor utilizes the findings as he deems appropriate, often using the reports to recommend changes to state law and regulations.

The act does not preclude the legislature from calling for special investigations, and other government agencies, such as the Attorney General's Office, remain empowered to investigate alleged abuses of wrongdoing within New York State as needed. Further, the governor's power to investigate is not limited to the appointment of Moreland commissions. New York State's chief executives also have used special commissions, specific departmental inquiries, and other investigatory bodies to investigate government activities.

Investigations

There have been at least 58 Moreland Act investigations through the early 21st century, although many individual investigations have issued more than one report. Between 1907 and 1928 New York State governors commenced 36 Moreland investigations. Gov William Sulzer alone seated four such investigations in 1913. Moreland investigations have generally concentrated on large state agencies and other significant state institutions. The reorganization and consolidation of state government during the 1920s gave the governor more control over the executive branch, and the need to seat Moreland Act commissions to investigate minor mismanagement or corruption decreased.

Between 1929 and 1963 governors established only 15 Moreland Act investigations. Several focused on agency administration and efficiency, such as an investigation of quasi-judicial functions by state boards and commissions (1939). Other investigations centered on the state's role in supervising and administering state programs; in particular, during this period they concentrated on the administration of state-regulated industries and state-supported benefit programs. These included bingo, harness racing, alcoholic beverages, and the administration of public welfare programs and benefits. The management of workers' compensation was the subject of three separate Moreland Act investigations (1942, 1953, 1955). Some investigations, such as those pertaining to the administration of public welfare programs and the operation of bingo, involved several levels of government. Gov Nelson A. Rockefeller named Moreland Act commissions to investigate the enforcement of law by local governments (1962) and the administration of the Alcoholic Beverage Control Law (1963).

After 1963 the act was not invoked again until Gov Hugh Carey named Moreland commissions to investigate the New York State Urban Development Corp and the operations of nursing homes and residential facilities, both in 1975. Gov Mario M. Cuomo appointed commissions to investigate the criminal justice system and the use of force (1985), government corruption and abuse of public office (1987), the effectiveness of the returnable beverage container act (1989), and educational structures and policies (1993). Gov George E. Pataki impaneled a Moreland commission to investigate the management and control of the New York City School System (1999). The commission had issued five separate reports by summer 2002 on topics including attendance and enrollment; school construction, maintenance, and related problems; and Capital Plan budget gaps.

Breuer, Ernest H. *Moreland Act Investigations in New York: 1907–65* (Albany: Univ of the State of New York, 1965)

Missal, John E. *The Moreland Act* (New York: King's Crown Press, 1946)

John Evers

Morgan, Edwin B(arber) (*b* Aurora, Cayuga Co, 2 May 1806; *d* Aurora, 13 Oct 1881). Politician and entrepreneur. He was the eldest son of successful businessman Christopher Morgan and Nancy Barber Morgan, and the son-in-law of Judge Walter Wood, one of Central New York's wealthiest land dealers and manufacturers. After Wood's death in 1827, Morgan bought the family store in Aurora, which traded in locally produced wool, grain, and pork. There he met Henry Wells, a grain shipper for a mill in Port Byron (Cayuga Co). Morgan was a founding investor with Wells in the American Express Co (1850) and the express service Wells, Fargo and Co (1852), serving as president of the latter until 1856.

Morgan was elected to Congress from New York's 25th district as a Whig and Republican for three terms (1853–59), but his greatest impact on Central New York was as an investor and philanthropist. He invested in Adams Express Co and the United States Express Co, as well as in banks, railroad companies, and the Oswego Starch Co. A founder of the *New York Times* in 1851 and its largest stockholder, Morgan was also a major benefactor of Wells College in Aurora and of Auburn Theological Seminary. His relatives included New York governor Edwin D. Morgan and financier J. P. Morgan.

Biographical Review: The Leading Citizens of Cayuga County, New York (Boston: Biographical Review Publishing, 1894)

History of Cayuga County, New York (Auburn, NY: Cayuga County Historical Society, 1908)

Scott W. Anderson

Morgan, Edwin D(enison) (*b* Washington, Mass, 8 Feb 1811; *d* New York City, 14 Feb 1883). Governor and US senator. In 1822 Morgan's family moved from Massachusetts to Connecticut, where he received a minimal formal education before beginning work as a clerk at his uncle's general store in 1828. A year later Morgan entered Hartford politics. In 1837 he moved to New York City, where he founded a successful mercantile firm before moving gradually into banking and brokerage services. He refused to flee New York City during the 1849 cholera epidemic, instead remaining to help those stricken with the disease. The popularity Morgan accrued from this helped him win election as a Whig to the state senate, where he served from 1850 to 1855. As senator he introduced and shepherded through the legislation that created Central Park in New York City. In 1855 he played a crucial role in the formation of the Republican Party; Morgan was the New York Republican state chair (1856–58) and the first chair of the Republican National Committee (1856–64). He also served as a commissioner on the New York State Board of Emigration (1855–58) and as president of the Hudson River Railroad.

In 1858 Morgan was elected governor, winning a four-way race by a plurality of 17,000 votes. In his first term he helped reduce the state debt, increased the revenue from the Erie Canal tolls, successfully advocated for a voter registry law, and vetoed a group of corrupt railroad bills. He supported William H. Seward's failed bid for the presidential nomination in 1860, though he campaigned for Abraham Lincoln's election. Morgan himself was reelected in 1860 by a wide margin. He took a moderate position in the secession crisis, but after the assault of Fort Sumter he rallied New York State to support the Union and focused his energies on recruiting soldiers. When the state was made a military department in 1861, Lincoln commissioned Morgan as a major general of volunteers (1861–63).

Morgan declined to run for reelection in 1862, instead pursuing election to the US Senate, where he served from March 1863 until March 1869. In 1865 he declined Lincoln's offer of a cabinet position as secretary of the treasury. Morgan voted for the Wade-Davis bill, an act that attempted to install control of Reconstruction in the hands of Congress, and initially tried to work with Pres Andrew Johnson. But Morgan supported black citizenship and voted to override Johnson's veto of the 1866 civil rights bill. Morgan usually voted with the more progressive Republicans, passing the Military Reconstruction Acts and supporting New York State's attempt to enfranchise Blacks through constitutional revision in 1867–69. He also voted against Johnson during the president's impeachment trial in 1868. After he was defeated for reelection to a second term in the Senate, Morgan returned to his home on 5th Ave and to his private business and philanthropic concerns in New York City. He ran for governor in 1876 but was defeated by Lucius Robinson. In 1881 Morgan turned down the secretary of the treasury position offered by Pres Chester A. Arthur, one of his old New York friends and protégés. In an age famous for political scandals, Morgan was noted for his personal integrity and charity, giving especially large sums to the Union Theological Seminary and Williams College in Williamstown, Mass, and serving on the boards of several New York City hospitals.

See also CIVIL WAR: CIVIL WAR REGIMENTS.

Booraem, Hendrik. *The Formation of the Republican Party in New York* (New York: New York Univ Press, 1983)

Rawley, James. *Edwin D. Morgan, 1811–1883: Merchant in Politics* (1955; repr New York: AMS Press, 1968)

Jon Sterngass

Morgan, J(ohn) P(ierpont) (*b* Hartford, Conn, 17 Apr 1837; *d* Rome, 31 Mar 1913). Investment banker. The son of an American businessman operating a merchant banking firm in London, John Pierpont Morgan was educated in Boston, Switzerland, and Germany, and graduated from Harvard. He started in his father's London business, taking a junior position on Wall St in 1857. Four years later he opened J. P. Morgan and Co to sell and distribute European securities; the firm's £10 million loan to France during the Franco-Prussian War established Morgan as an international financier and advisor to governments. In 1871 J. P. Morgan and Anthony J. Drexel formed the investment banking firm of Drexel, Morgan and Co. With the failure of Jay Cooke and Co during the Panic of 1873, Morgan became the leading distributor of US bonds issued both domestically and abroad. He secured his position as America's foremost banker through marketing railroad securities; he had a close association with the New York Central Railroad and undertook numerous railroad reorganizations. The dominant financial figure of his time, Morgan specialized in industrial mergers, the best known being his fashioning, in 1901, of United States Steel, America's first billion dollar corporation. During the Panic of 1907 he acted on behalf of the Roosevelt administration, using government funds to stabilize major New York City banks. Morgan left an art collection worth about $60 million at the time of his death to the Metropolitan Museum of Art. His collection of books, manuscripts, prints, and old master drawings became the Morgan Library, now a complex of buildings housing a research center and museum on Madison Ave in New York City.

Chernow, Ron. *The House of Morgan: An American Banking Dynasty and the Rise of Modern Finance* (New York: Atlantic Monthly Press, 1990)

Pamela Cooper

Morgan, Lewis Henry (*b* Aurora, Cayuga Co, 21 Nov 1818; *d* Rochester, 17 Dec 1881). Anthropologist. Morgan grew up along the shores of Cayuga Lake. During his childhood the burial mounds and arrowheads left by the Cayuga served as a reminder of the Indian past while the Erie Canal represented the ascendant market civilization. As an adult Morgan became a pioneer of anthropology, a social science that emerged from the rupture between "traditional" society and the industrial world. He experienced this rupture firsthand, and in his scholarship he offered a comprehensive theory to explain it.

Lawyer and Ethnographer

After graduating from Union College in Schenectady, Morgan returned home to study law in 1840 and soon passed the bar. Beginning in 1843 under the name Skenandoah, he also became the leading force behind a ritualistic fraternity known as the Grand Order of the Iroquois. The organization was part of a larger attempt to break away from Europe by inserting Indians as the heroic cultural ancestors of the American republic; as New Yorkers, the white "warriors" tried to learn what they could about the real Iroquois. This quest took a lucky turn in 1844, when Morgan had a chance encounter in an Albany bookstore with Ely S. Parker, a 16-year-old Tonawanda Seneca. Through Parker, Morgan gained access to the Tonawanda Reservation [loc in Erie, Genesee, and Niagara Cos], eventually becoming an adopted member of the Hawk Clan, and was able to pursue ethnographic research of an unprecedented depth. That same year he opened a law practice in Rochester, where he lived until his death. As a lawyer and sometime politician, Morgan was part of the Rochester establishment and on the vanguard of the type of progress exemplified by the history of the Empire State in the 19th century.

Morgan's first book, *The League of the Ho-dé-no-sau-nee, or Iroquois* (1851), a detailed examination of all aspects of Iroquois society, is an ethnographic classic. Elaborating on John Locke's argument that before the institution of civil society humans are governed by family relationships, he showed how an extensive kinship organization permeated all aspects of Iroquois life. In the book he celebrated the "equality," "boundless freedom," and "hospitality" of traditional Iroquois society, and explained why this society was doomed and why civilization was ultimately worth the cost. The same year *The League* was published, Morgan married his first cousin Mary Elizabeth Steele. In the following years, he made a substantial fortune from the railroad business and from an iron mine that bore his name. A staunch Republican, he served in the New York State Assembly (1861) and Senate (1868–69). Throughout his life he was an advocate for American Indians and an active citizen of Rochester, but he made his great impact as a scholar.

After 1854 Morgan was able to discuss and refine his scientific work at the monthly meetings of the Pundit Club, an organization that he cofounded with the other leading scientists, scholars, and educators of Rochester, and that became his intellectual home. Morgan's second book, *The American Beaver and His Works* (1868), remains a classic study of the mammal whose pelt once inspired the avarice of European colonists. His enthusiasm for ethnography was rekindled during the late 1850s when he discovered that what he had previously considered the unusual family organization of the Iroquois was in fact common among American Indians. This encouraged him to attempt to prove the connection between all American Indians, their common Asiatic origin, and, ultimately, the unity of humankind. Between 1859 and 1862 he made four trips across the West collecting ethnographic information. After two of his three children died in 1862, he retreated from business to devote himself to his expanding kinship project. His *Systems of Consanguinity and Affinity of the Human Family* (1870) was a pioneering work in kinship studies, a new branch of anthropological research devoted to family structure.

Social Theorist

Morgan's most famous work is *Ancient Society* (1877). Dividing the human experience into three "ethnical periods," which he labeled "savagery," "barbarism," and "civilization," he argued that the changing definition, distribution, and accumulation of property was the motor behind progress. His theory fit human existence into a universal pattern, from small kinship-based tribes with rudimentary technology and common property, to large "civilized" states based on clearly marked external borders, private property, and the exchange of commodities in an increasingly impersonal market. For evidence of this theory, he pointed to his own civilization spreading across the North American continent, while Native American societies could do nothing to stem the tide.

Yet Morgan believed that what he regarded as an excessive emphasis on the accumulation of property would be replaced in the future by an enlightened democratic community that would be a revival in new form of the "liberty," "equality," and "fraternity" of primitive peoples. He maintained a particularly American faith in the future and never embraced anything resembling the European left. Embodying nostalgic primitivism and a belief in progress, his misgivings about the encroaching market civilization influenced many writers, most famously Karl Marx and Friedrich Engels.

Final Years

In his final years Morgan achieved a scholarly preeminence signified by his 1879 election as president of the American Association for the Advancement of Science. Exhibiting the constancy of his scholarly interests, in his last book, *Houses and House-Life of the American Aborigines* (1881), he extolled the "communism in living" practiced by the same peoples his theory of social evolution branded as "barbaric." When Morgan died he left his estate to the University of Rochester for the advancement of women's education. His legacy as a scholar is complex. His work provided the foundation for a generation of anthropologists. In the 20th century his influence declined as grand theories of social evolution lost favor, but he remains one of the most significant American social theorists of the 19th century, almost certainly the only one to be cited by Marx, Charles Darwin, and Sigmund Freud. Morgan's innovative and influential explanation for the schism between the primitive and the civilized stands as perhaps his most significant accomplishment.

See also AMERICAN INDIANS IN LITERATURE: NONINDIGENOUS AUTHORS.

Resek, Carl. *Lewis Henry Morgan, American Scholar* (Chicago: Univ of Chicago Press, 1960)

Trautmann, Thomas. *Lewis Henry Morgan and the Invention of Kinship* (Berkeley: Univ of California Press, 1987)

Daniel N. Moses

Morgan, William (*b* Culpeper Co, Va, 7 Aug 1774; *d* ?Fort Niagara [now in Porter, Niagara Co, Sept ?1826). Stonemason and activist. It is possible that Morgan was a veteran of the War of 1812 with the rank of captain, but no firm record survives. He settled eventually in Western New York about 1820 and worked at his trade. Hoping to enhance his social status, he was elected a Royal Arch Mason at Le Roy (Genesee Co) in 1825. When he applied for membership in the more prestigious lodge at nearby Batavia, however, he was denied admission, some accounts suggest because of a drinking problem. In retribution, he wrote or contributed to an exposé of the Freemasons, *Illustrations of Masonry,* in 1826. On 11 September of that year, Morgan was arrested on trumped-up petty theft charges and taken to Canandaigua (Ontario Co) for trial. He was never with certainty seen again. Some reports indicate he was incarcerated at Fort Niagara, after which he may have been drowned in Lake Ontario or escaped to parts unknown. Human remains washed ashore at Oak Orchard (Monroe Co) in October 1827, and newspaper reporter Thurlow Weed argued the body was Morgan's, but this was later disproven. Because of his revelation of Masonic secrets, it was supposed that Morgan was murdered by Masons, though a state investigation failed to produce any substantial evidence. A monument was erected in Morgan's memory in the Batavia Cemetery by a local group of antisecret society enthusiasts. Outrage over Morgan's death provided the impetus for the Antimasonic movement.

See also ANTIMASONRY.

Mock, Stanley Upton. *The Morgan Episode in American Free Masonry* (East Aurora, NY: Roycrofters, 1930)

William H. Brackney

Morgenthau, Henry, Jr (*b* New York City, 11 May 1891; *d* Poughkeepsie, 6 Feb 1967). Farmer, publisher, and public official. Morgenthau was the only child of Josephine Sykes and Henry Morgenthau Sr, an entrepreneur, Democratic Party activist, and diplomat of German Jewish descent. Henry Jr attended Cornell University, leaving before completing his degree and in 1913 purchased a farm in East Fishkill (Dutchess Co). There he befriended his neighbor, Franklin D. Roosevelt, and became involved in Democratic politics, promoting the party in rural areas of New York State. In 1922 Morgenthau purchased the weekly *American Agriculturist,* which he published in New York City, and advocated conservation, scientific farming, and pro-farmer public policies. Gov Roosevelt named Morgenthau chairman of the state's Agricultural Advisory Commission (1928) and then commissioner of conservation (1930). As commissioner, Morgenthau implemented a reforestation program that was a precursor to the Civilian Conservation Corps. In 1933 Roosevelt, then US president, made Morgenthau head of the Federal Farm Board and its successor, the Farm Credit Administration. In 1934 he was made secretary of the treasury, a position he held until 1945, and Morgenthau helped create the World Bank and the International Monetary Fund. In July 1945 he retired from government and returned to his farm, where he devoted time to philanthropic activities.

Blum, John Morton. *Roosevelt and Morgenthau* (Boston: Houghton Mifflin, 1970)

Scott C. Monje

Moriah. Town (pop 4,879) in E Essex Co. Benjamin Porter settled Moriah in 1766 but left during the Revolution when his mill was destroyed, returning and rebuilding after the war. The town was formed from Crown Point and Elizabethtown in 1808. Moriah contains the largest iron district in the Adirondacks, worked extensively beginning in the 1840s, ultimately controlled by Witherbee-Sherman Corp (1862), a consolidation of smaller interests. From the late 19th century into the mid–20th century, Moriah was the most populous town in Essex Co. Housing for miners was provided in Witherbee (*ca* 1905), a planned hamlet, and Grover Hills (1942–43). Republic Steel leased mines here from 1937 to 1971 and was the last operation to close; the town has since worked to create new economic opportunities. In the early 21st century the Moriah Shock Incarceration Facility (1989) in Mineville and a developmental disabilities service organization are employers.

Thomas A. Rumney

Moriches [MO-RICH-ES] {Center Moriches, locality (pop 6,655) in Brookhaven, Suffolk Co; East Moriches, locality (pop 4,550) in Brookhaven; Moriches, locality (pop 2,319) in Brookhaven}. Early bayfront hamlets of shellfishers and farmers, each acquired a post office at an early date: Moriches in 1802, East Moriches in 1849, and Center Moriches in 1854. A paper mill operated in the 1870s. The Pekin duck was introduced to farms in 1873, making it a duck-farming region. The Long Island Rail Road was built through Center Moriches in 1881, creating an important resort industry. Competition from the Hamptons and destruction wrought by the 1938 hurricane ended the business. Center Moriches successfully revitalized its business district in the 1980s. In 1996 TWA Flight 800 broke up in flight off East Moriches, placing the locality in the international spotlight.

Luise Weiss

Mormons (Latter-day Saints). The Church of of Latter-day Saints (LDS) was organized on 6 Apr 1830 in Fayette (Seneca Co) at the house of Peter Whitmer. The town's German Reformed pastor wrote that new believers called themselves "Die wahre Nachfolger Christi" (the True Disciples of Christ). Formally adopting the name Latter-day Saints, the church's adherents were popularly known as Mormons, in reference to their scriptural Book of Mormon, published at Palmyra (Wayne Co) in March 1830. Mormonism evolved from the metaphysical experiences of Joseph Smith Jr in Western New York. Most early converts lived in Wayne, Ontario, Livingston, Seneca, and Broome Cos, places where Smith had traveled since his initial revelation in 1820. Martin Harris of Palmyra was one of Smith's initial converts, his first scribe, and a participant in Mormonism's early revelatory history. William W. Phelps, a newspaper editor in Canandaigua (Ontario Co), was the most socially prominent of the early believers. Church leaders remained in the state until 1831, when they led about 200 followers to Ohio. Brigham Young and Heber Kimball, who would become Smith's "apostles," joined them there in 1833 after converting in Mendon (Monroe Co) in 1832.

Doctrines and Beliefs

While Mormonism has experienced dramatic changes during its history, it retains doctrines first announced in Western New York. First, God chose farmboy Joseph Smith Jr as a modern prophet who conversed with deity and angels. As later described, Smith's "First Vision" occurred near his family's farm at Manchester (Ontario Co) in the spring of 1820, when he saw God and Jesus as separate "personages" in human form.

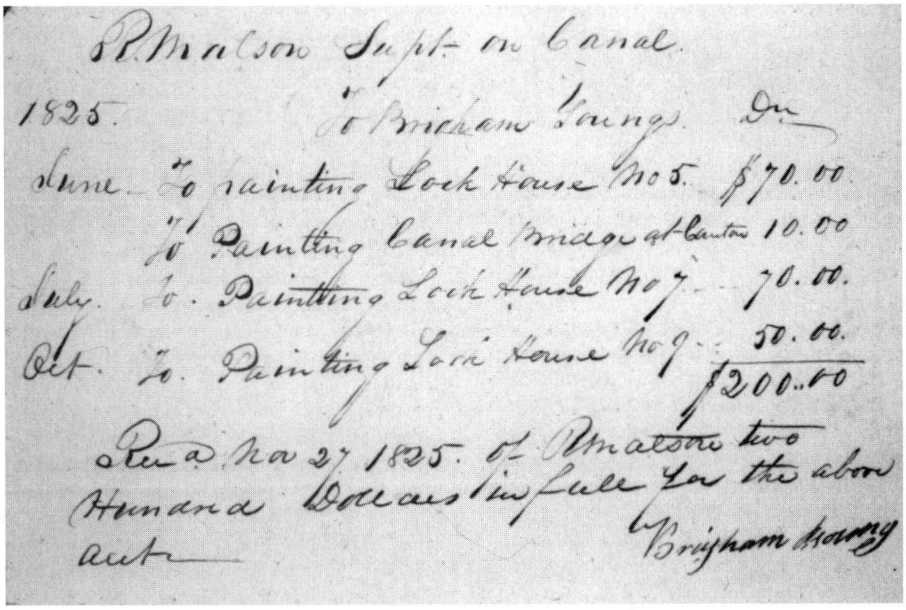
P. Watson Supt. on Canal
1825. To Brigham Young Dr
June To painting Lock House No 5. $70.00
To Painting Canal bridge at Canton 10.00
July. To. Painting Lock House No 7 70.00
Oct. To. Painting Lock House No 9 50.00
$200.00
Recd Nov 27 1825. of P Watson two Hundred Dollars in full for the above acct
Brigham Young

Brigham Young's receipt for working on the Erie Canal, 1825.

Second, his first religious duty was to translate by revelatory methods the text of the Book of Mormon, chronicling God's dealings with Israelite peoples of pre-Columbian America: the Nephites and Lamanites, who flourished from *ca* 600 BC to AD 421, and the Jaredites, from the fall of the Tower of Babel to sometime after 279 BC. Third, Jesus and his atonement are central to this scripture and to the church organized in 1830. Fourth, continued revelations to a living prophet are necessary for the governance of God's church, which required restoration in "the latter days" because of an absence of divine authority since the death of Christ's ancient apostles. Twenty-five revelations Smith announced in New York State between 1823 and 1831 are published as scripture in *Doctrine and Covenants.* Fifth, because of Christianity's loss of authority, baptism is valid only when performed by LDS priesthood. Sixth, Christ's second coming will soon usher in a millennium of peace, for which Latter-day Saints must prepare.

After leaving the state, Smith further separated the LDS Church from other Christian denominations. Ecclesiastically, he claimed that, in addition to a living prophet, God's church must have 12 living apostles who trace authority to Peter, James, and John. Doctrinally, he affirmed that all people have individual existence before birth, that these pre-mortal spirits are literal children of their Heavenly Father, and that relatively few mortals—only those who hate God eternally—will suffer damnation, while nearly all will have an afterlife in one of three heavenly "degrees." In the highest degree, the "celestial kingdom," nuclear families that began on earth will continue eternally. To secure those blessings for all who have lived without knowledge of Mormon teachings and authority, specially constructed temples perform proxy ordinances of baptism, "endowment" (a ritualized set of instructions lasting several hours), and "sealing" of marriage "for time and eternity." Thus, Mormons promote genealogical research and preservation of vital records through microfilming in such disparate places as New York State's county courthouses, Poland's Catholic parishes, and Japan's Buddhist shrines. Although Mormons originally considered New York State the ancient home of Nephites, Lamanites, and Jaredites, Smith later shifted attention to archaeological sites from Mexico southward. By the mid–20th century Mormons generally regarded Mesoamerica as the location of this ancient history, though interest continues in Western New York as the site of nearly all events in the Book of Mormon.

Mormon Presence, 1832–1900

Because most Mormons migrated to Utah in the 19th century, national attention focused on their commonwealths in the Midwest and later in a vast western region centering on Salt Lake City. Nevertheless, church emissaries and converts remained active throughout New York State. At Chenango Point (Broome Co) missionaries baptized 100 people in 1832. In 1837 Apostle Parley P. Pratt introduced Mormonism to Manhattan and Brooklyn, where he organized fledgling branches and published the church's first proselytizing tract, *A Voice of Warning.* Forty-one British Mormons arrived at New York Harbor in 1840 but continued westward to LDS headquarters, which for economic reasons diverted its transatlantic immigrants to New Orleans for the next 15 years. The most prominent convert in the state during this period was Long Island newspaperman James Arlington Bennet, who accepted baptism in 1843 but lost interest in the church after Smith's murder by an Illinois mob in June 1844. Also in 1844 the *Prophet* became New York City's first LDS newspaper, followed by the *New York Messenger* a year later.

At least 20 native New Yorkers were among the 230 Mormons who sailed from New York Harbor in 1846 on the *Brooklyn* around Cape Horn to California, answering Brigham Young's call for westward migration after Smith's martyrdom. Some remained in northern California and became millionaires during the Gold Rush. Others joined Young's colonists, who traveled overland from Illinois to Utah, where Young in 1852 publicly promoted the legalization of slavery in the state, prohibited the ordination of anyone of black ancestry to LDS priesthood, and declared that God wanted Mormon men to marry polygamously—three policies that would embroil Mormonism in ongoing controversy. The *Mormon* became the church's third Manhattan newspaper in 1855, the year LDS immigrant ships resumed docking in New York Harbor. Sixty-five thousand European Mormons passed through New York City's Castle Garden immigration depot from 1855 to 1890.

The 20th Century

With most of New York's converts having migrated west, only a few hundred Mormons lived in the state in 1900, when Brigham H. Roberts was formally barred from assuming the seat in the US House of Representatives he had won in 1898. Congress regarded Utah's election of this polygamist "general authority" as an insulting violation of his church's 1890 abandonment of polygamy. Manhattan's newspapers likewise gave sensational coverage of the three-year struggle (1904–7) by Utah senator and apostle Reed Smoot, a monogamist, to avoid expulsion from Congress because some prominent Mormons continued to marry polygamously. In 1919 Sen Smoot dedicated Brooklyn's chapel, the first built with LDS funds east of the Mississippi since 1846. In 1922 Roberts, still a polygamist, became president of the Eastern States Mission in New York City.

By this time LDS headquarters had already taken steps to make Western New York a site for pilgrimages. In 1907 it bought the Manchester farm where Smith experienced his theophany, and in 1917 missionaries of the Eastern States Mission spontaneously commemorated events there in a celebration that became an official annual event in 1922. The Hill Cumorah, where Smith claimed to have recovered the text of the Book of Mormon, was acquired in 1928. A spectacular pageant, recreating events from Mormon scripture, has been staged annually since 1937, when 13,000 people attended opening night. There were other signs of Mormons' growing prominence in the state as well, partly as a result of Mormon outmigration from Utah after the 1920s and partly because LDS headquarters encouraged Mormons outside Utah to remain where they converted. In 1932 teenagers in the church's New York District sang for a *Church of the Air* broadcast on the CBS Radio Network. In 1934 membership was sufficient to organize the New York Stake, similar to a diocese. Thirty-five thousand attended the Hill Cumorah Pageant in 1940. The pageant was suspended during World War II, but on resuming in 1948 drew 100,000 attendees. Mormons, often Utah-born, became executives of major corporations in Manhattan. In 1962 Utah headquarters purchased shortwave radio station WRUL in New York City to broadcast LDS programming worldwide.

The 1964–65 World's Fair in Flushing Meadows (Queens Co) featured the $3 million Mormon Pavilion, which hosted a million visitors and transformed local proselytizing. Whereas there had been 6 convert baptisms in the surrounding area in 1963, 1,000 baptisms took place in each of the two years the fair was open. After disassembly its concrete panels were used to construct the stake center in Plainview (Nassau Co). In 1975 LDS president Spencer W. Kimball dedicated the New York Stake Center within the church's 36-story complex near Lincoln Center in Manhattan.

The church ended its policy of excluding those

with black ancestry from priesthood and temple marriage in 1978, but there were continued vigorous efforts by the Utah leadership to marshal political activism in support of socially conservative positions. Mormons took over the 1977 International Women's Year conference in Salt Lake City and voted down profeminist resolutions. This began a five-year, Utah-directed campaign of LDS minorities in 20 states to defeat the Equal Rights Amendment (ERA). New York, the 16th state to ratify the ERA, was spared this conflict. Since 1994 similar tactics have been used to oppose protections for homosexuals in New York and other states.

In 1995 LDS headquarters announced that New York State would have its own temple. After five years of legal wrangling with the owners of neighboring property, the church gave up plans to build the temple in Harrison (Westchester Co). For historical reasons Palmyra was ultimately selected as the location of the 100th temple worldwide, and church president Gordon B. Hinckley dedicated it on 6 Apr 2000. The entry records of 22 million European immigrants who passed through the Port of New York between 1892 and 1924 were transcribed by 12,000 Mormon volunteers, constructing an electronic database for the American Family Immigration History Center, which opened on Ellis Island in April 2001. The LDS Church also provided funding, genealogical software, computers, and expertise for the project. In July 2002 Hinckley dedicated a new visitors' center on the Hill Cumorah and a month later announced that a special temple would be established on the Lincoln Center property in Manhattan. In September 2003 ground was broken for the first LDS meeting house in Harlem, where a branch was formed in 1997. Despite this activity, LDS membership in New York State has never recovered from the departure of church headquarters in 1831. While New York's approximately 75,000 Mormons represent only .375% of the state's population, the church's 12 million adherents across the globe—more than half are outside the United States—regard New York State as part of their spiritual heritage. Millions have visited sacred sites in the Finger Lakes region.

See also BURNED-OVER DISTRICT.

Acosta, R. Vivian, and Alejandro Soffiantini. *Zion in the Brooklyn District: One Heart, Many Voices: A History of the Church of Jesus Christ of Latter-day Saints in Brooklyn and Staten Island, New York, 1837–1997* (Brooklyn: New York District of the Church of Jesus Christ of Latter-day Saints, 1997)

Baugh, Alexander L., and Andrew H. Hedges, eds. *Regional Studies in Latter-day Saint Church History: New York–Pennsylvania* (Provo, Utah: Brigham Young Univ, 2002)

Berrett, LaMar C., and Larry C. Porter, eds. *New York and Pennsylvania,* vol 2 of *Sacred Places: A Comprehensive Guide to Early LDS Historical Sites* (Salt Lake City, Utah: Bookcraft, 2000)

Deseret Morning News 2004 Church Almanac (Salt Lake City: Deseret News, 2003)

Olive, Phyllis C. *The Book of Mormon Lands of Western New York* (Salt Lake City, Utah: DMT Publishers, 1998)

Porter, Larry C., Milton V. Backman Jr, and Susan Easton Black, eds. *Regional Studies in Latter-day Saint Church History: New York* (Provo, Utah: Brigham Young Univ, 1992)

Quinn, D. Michael. *The Mormon Hierarchy: Origins of Power* (Salt Lake City, Utah: Signature Books, 1994)

———. *The Mormon Hierarchy: Extensions of Power* (Salt Lake City: Signature Books, 1997)

Quinn, D. Michael, trans and ed. "The First Months of Mormonism: A Contemporary View by Rev Diedrich Willers," *New York History* 54 (July 1973): 317–33

The Ship Brooklyn Association Newsletter (1996–)

D. Michael Quinn

Morris. Town (pop 1,867) and village (pop 591) in SW Otsego Co. Settled around 1770, the town was formed in 1849 from Butternuts. Originally patented in 1769 to a British army officer, it was transferred after the American Revolution to his nephew Gen Jacob Morris (1755–1844), son of Lewis Morris, signer of the Declaration of Independence. Jacob settled in 1787 and built Morris Manor (1805). What is now the Village of Morris was settled as Louisville by a group of French royalist refugees in 1790; a Quaker colony followed, building a meeting house in 1811. Cotton (1812) and woolen (1815) factories and a tannery were early industries. Later 19th-century products included chairs, butter paddles, inkstands, and tobacco boxes. The village incorporated in 1870. In the early 21st century, some farming continues, but most residents commute to employment outside the town. Morris is the site of the Otsego County Fair. Landmarks include a monument marking the fatal fall from a horse of William Cooper's daughter Hannah (1801) and All Saints Chapel (1870) at Morris Manor.

Hugh C. MacDougall

Morris, Gouverneur (*b* Morrisania [now in Bronx Co], 31 Jan 1752; *d* Morrisania, 6 Nov 1816). Diplomat and politician. Son of one of colonial New York's great families, Gouverneur Morris described to Thomas Penn a mass meeting of New York City citizens in May 1774. "The mob begin to think and to reason," he wrote, calling them "poor reptiles" who basked in the "vernal morning" and would "bite" before noon. The imagery was strong, and it rested on Morris's perception that "men of property" were sorting themselves out from "tradesmen and mechanics." Yet despite personal attitude and social background, including a loyalist mother and a half-brother who was a member of parliament and a British lieutenant general, Morris chose the American side in the Revolution.

Morris was schooled at the Academy of Philadelphia (1761–64), graduated from King's College (now Columbia University) (1764–68), and studied law in the office of William Smith Jr. He was licensed to practice law at the age of 19 in 1771. Elected to the New York Provincial Congress in May 1775, Morris helped draft the first state constitution and was a delegate to the Second Continental Congress in October 1777, serving until 1779. He took a nationalist position there, including favoring recognition for Vermont's claim to independence from New York, and he lost his seat in 1779. Invited to assist continental financier Robert Morris (1735–1806; no relation), he stayed in Philadelphia and represented Pennsylvania rather than New York at the federal constitutional convention (1787). He was in Europe between 1788 and 1798, part of the time as a private businessman and part as American minister to France. He deeply opposed the French Revolution, using his diplomatic status to assist some of its aristocratic victims, and suggested military intervention to the British prime minister. He observed the French events carefully, and the journal that he kept is a primary source for the period. When he came home he returned to New York, settling at the family manor, Morrisania, and in 1800 the state legislature chose him to complete the three remaining years of an unexpired term in the US Senate. His retirement from public life afterward was only nominal. He supported the Hartford Convention of 1814 and joined in advocating the Erie Canal.

Despite his fears of social upheaval Morris may have chosen the American side because his temperament was fundamentally radical. At independence he proposed amalgamating the former colonies into one nation, replacing them with districts with new boundaries for political representation. That suggestion foreshadowed the change in France from the provinces of the old order to *departements* as well as the phrase "We the People of the United States of America" in the federal constitution, which he proposed, as opposed to "We the People" of the separate states. Drafting New York's state constitution, he helped to overcome proposals to exclude Catholics from political life. He accepted Vermont's independence early. He argued an antislavery position so strongly in the federal convention that South Carolina and Georgia nearly withdrew. Never completely predictable, he summed up the contradictions of his time.

Adams, William Howard. *Gouverneur Morris: An Independent Life* (New Haven, Conn: Yale Univ Press, 2003)

Mintz, Max M. *Gouverneur Morris and the American Revolution* (Norman: Univ of Oklahoma Press, 1970)

Swiggett, Howard. *The Extraordinary Mr. Morris* (New York: Doubleday, 1952)

Edward Countryman

Morris, Lewis (*b* Morrisania [now in Bronx Co], 15 Oct 1671; *d* Trenton, NJ, 21 May 1746). Politician. Morris' political career began in New Jersey, where he opposed the proprietary government and was instrumental in removing Edward Hyde, Viscount Cornbury, as governor of New Jersey and New York Colonies in 1708. A rival of the DeLancey faction, he was elected to the New York Assembly in 1710. He was appointed chief justice in 1715 but was removed in 1733 by Gov William Cosby because he supported Cosby's nemesis, Rip van Dam. Morris and his supporters in the Morris party, which represented landed interests in politics, used John Peter Zenger's *New York Weekly Journal* to conduct a press war against Cosby, which resulted in a libel suit against Zenger in 1735. Because of his connections in London, Morris was appointed the first royal governor of New Jersey after its 1738 separation from New York Colony. His regime was marked by much factious infighting and Morris died in office. His manor, Morrisania (1697) gave name to that section of the Bronx.

Sheridan, Eugene R., ed. *Lewis Morris, 1671–1746: A Study in Early American Politics* (Syracuse: Syracuse Univ Press, 1981)

Jennifer Steenshorne

Morris, Lewis (*b* Morrisania [now in Bronx Co], 8 Apr 1726; *d* Morrisania, 22 Jan 1798). Congressman. Son of Lewis Morris (1698–1762), he graduated from Yale in 1746 and was the final lord of Morrisania, the family manor. He received a royal appointment as judge of the Court of Admiralty in 1760 and served until 1774. He was elected to the Colonial Assembly in 1769, but his political rivals, the DeLanceys, had him expelled from office since he lived outside his Westchester jurisdiction. Unlike most manor lords, Morris sided with the American cause during the Revolutionary War and in 1775 became a delegate to both the colony's provincial congress and the Continental Congress. During the summer of 1776, Morris served as brigadier general of the Westchester Co militia, fought to block the British invasion of New York City, and found time to sign the Declaration of Independence in Philadelphia. After leaving Congress in 1777, Morris served as Westchester Co judge (1777–78), as state senator (1777–81, 1784–88), and on the Board of Regents (1784–98). He favored ratification of the US Constitution at the state's 1788 Constitutional Convention. During the Revolution the British burned Morrisania, causing him great financial loss, and he spent considerable time restoring his estate.

Bakeless, John. *Signers of the Declaration* (Boston: Houghton Mifflin, 1969)

Chris Brooks

Morris, Robert (*b* Liverpool, England, Jan 1734; *d* Philadelphia, 8 May 1806). Merchant and politician. In 1747 Morris immigrated to Oxford, Md, and was apprenticed with merchant Charles Willing in Philadelphia. In 1757 he and Willing's son, Thomas, formed Willing and Morris, which traded in England, Spain, Portugal, and the West Indies. Morris served in the Continental Congress (1775–78) and worked on several committees, including the Secret Committee of Trade, and used Willing and Morris to procure military supplies for Congress. In 1781 during a national fiscal crisis, Congress elected him superintendent of finance and agent of marine. Morris struggled to increase Congress's revenues, established the Bank of North America, and contracted with merchants to supply the Continental army. He established military contracts with New Yorkers Comfort Sands, Walter Livingston, and William Duer, who supplied all troops based in New York. Lack of resources to pay these contracts and army personnel contributed to the 1783 Newburgh Affair, where army officers threatened mutiny.

Morris resigned from the Office of Finance in 1783 and became involved in international trade; he was half-owner of the *Empress of China*, the first American vessel in the China trade. The *Empress* sailed from New York Harbor on 22 Feb 1784. Morris formed a partnership in 1784 with Gouverneur Morris, William Constable, and John Rucker. Their firm, located on Great Dock St [now Pearl St], managed voyages to China and handled Morris's tobacco trade with the French Farmers General. A US senator (1789–95) from Pennsylvania, Morris played a major role in relocating the national capital from New York City to Philadelphia and then to Washington, DC.

He was a leading New York State land speculator. In 1790–91 he purchased 5 million acres (2 million ha) of the Phelps and Gorham tract in the Genesee region and sold more than 3 million (1.2 million ha) in 1793 to European investors of the Holland Land Co. He retained a tract, called the Morris Reserve, which included more than 600,000 acres (240,000 ha) west of the Genesee River. He divided the reserve and sold portions of it to investors. When his land investments later failed, he lost the remaining land to creditors, went bankrupt, and was imprisoned for debt (1798–1801) in Philadelphia. After his release he lived off his wife's pension from the Holland Land Co.

Ferguson, E. James, ed., et al. *The Papers of Robert Morris, 1781–1784* (Pittsburgh: Univ of Pittsburgh Press, 1988)

Mary A. Y. Gallagher

Morris family. Large, politically prominent family from which the Morrisania section of the Bronx, Morristown, and Morris Co, NJ, derive their names. Established in America by Richard Morris, a Welsh veteran of Oliver Cromwell's army who along with his brother Lewis became a merchant in Barbados, the family entered the history of New York Colony in the 1660s when Richard, his wealthy wife, Sarah Pole, and his brother Lewis purchased 500 acres (202 ha) north of the Harlem River in what is now the Bronx. After both Richard and his wife died in 1672, Lewis Morris, a strict Quaker, adopted their infant son, also named Lewis, expanded the Morrisania estate to over 1,900 acres (770 ha), and acquired large holdings in New Jersey, all of which were inherited by the younger Lewis Morris (1671–1746). In May 1697 the New York estate officially became the Morrisania Manor, and the younger Lewis obtained the title of first lord of the manor. His children included Lewis Morris (1698–1746), second lord of the manor, and Robert Hunter Morris (*ca* 1700–1764), chief justice of New Jersey and royal governor of Pennsylvania, who inherited the New Jersey estates.

The second lord of the manor Lewis, speaker of the New York Assembly and judge of the Admiralty Court, fathered nine children during his two marriages, the first to Tryntje Staats of a landed Dutch New York family and the second to Sarah Gouverneur of a New York City mercantile family of Huguenot descent. The nine, though divided by sibling rivalries and political loyalties, played prominent roles in law, politics, and business in revolutionary New York and the early republic.

Gouverneur Morris (1752–1816) and his half-brothers Lewis (1726–98) and Richard (1730–1810) were on the patriot side of the revolutionary struggle. His mother, Sarah Gouverneur Morris, however, whose Morrisania estate lay within British lines, was a loyalist, and Staats Long Morris (1728–1800) was a general in the British army who became a member of the British Parliament and governor of Lower Canada [now Quebec] (1797–1800). Of the five Morris daughters, two were married to loyalists, Martin Wilkins and Vincent Pearse Ashfield, and left New York with their families during the British evacuation in 1783.

Of the three patriot sons, Lewis (third and last lord of the manor, a member of the Continental Congress [1775–77], and signer of the Declaration of Independence) and Richard (lawyer, state senator, and chief justice of the state supreme court) were eclipsed by their brilliant and adventurous young stepbrother Gouverneur. He entered the Provincial Congress in 1775–77, worked with John Jay and Robert R. Livingston to draft the first state constitution, served as a member of the Continental Congress (1777–79), acted as assistant to Superintendent of Finance Robert Morris (no relation) from 1781 to 1784, and was the most vocal member of the Constitutional Convention of 1787. He was a minister to France during the French Revolution and became one of the chief backers of the Erie Canal.

A few members of the next generation achieved some prominence during the same eras. Two of the sons of Lewis Morris, signer of the Declaration of Independence—Lewis (1754–1824) and Jacob Morris (1755–1844)—served as aides to Gen Nathanael Greene, while a third, Richard Valentine Morris (1768–1815), was commissioned captain in the US Navy in 1798 and commanded a squadron sent to combat the North African corsairs. Their cousin, Lewis R. Morris (1760–1825), son of Richard, served as assistant secretary of foreign affairs under Robert R. Livingston during the Revolutionary War and later became a Vermont landowner and congressman (1798–1803). The Morrisania estate, badly damaged during the war, was acquired in 1789 by Gouverneur Morris, who bought out his brothers' shares of the property. It was inherited by his son, Gouverneur Morris Jr (1813–88), a railroad developer whose fortune was valued at over $1 million in the mid–19th century.

Adams, William Howard. *Gouverneur Morris: An Independent Life* (New Haven, Conn: Yale Univ Press, 2003)
Kline, Mary-Jo. *Gouverneur Morris and the New Nation, 1775–1788* (New York: Arno Press, 1978)
Lefferts, Elizabeth Morris. *Descendants of Lewis Morris of Morrisania, b. 1671, d. 1746, First Governor of New Jersey as a Separate Province* (New York: T. A. Wright, 1907)
Sheridan, Eugene R. *Lewis Morris, 1671–1746: A Study in Early American Politics* (Syracuse: Syracuse Univ Press, 1981)
Smith, Samuel S. *Lewis Morris: Anglo American Statesman, 1613–1691* (Atlantic Highlands, NJ: Humanities Press, 1983)

Elizabeth M. Nuxoll

Morris Reserve. Tract of land in Western New York that Philadelphia merchant and financier Robert Morris (1734–1806) bought from Massachusetts in 1791. Part of the original Phelps and Gorham Purchase (1788), the land was within the portion that Oliver Phelps and Nathaniel Gorham reconveyed to Massachusetts after failing to complete installment payments. After Morris profitably sold 1.2 million acres (486,000 ha) purchased from Phelps and Gorham in 1790 to the Pulteney Associates in 1791–92, he bought the 4 million-acre (1.6 million ha) reconveyed tract with plans to market it to other European investors. He sold more than 3 million acres (1.2 million ha) to the Holland Land Co but retained Morris Reserve as security for a loan and to sell through his Canandaigua-based son, Thomas Morris (1771–1849). The reserve included much of what are now Allegany, Wyoming, Genesee, Orleans, Livingston, and Monroe Cos. To fulfill the responsibility to extinguish Indian land claims, Thomas Morris negotiated the Treaty of Big Tree (1797) with the Seneca Nation. When Robert Morris's fortune collapsed in 1798, he assigned large tracts in the reserve to his preferred creditors. Thomas Morris, for whom Mount Morris was named, remained until 1803, representing Ontario Co in the state legislature from 1794 to 1800 and, for one term, in Congress, from 1801 to 1803.

Chernow, Barbara Ann. *Robert Morris: Land Speculator, 1790–1801* (New York: Arno Press, 1974)
Oberholtzer, Ellis P. *Robert Morris: Patriot and Financier* (1903; repr New York: Burt Franklin, 1968)
Turner, Orsamus. *History of the Pioneer Settlement of Phelps and Gorham's Purchase, and Morris' Reserve* (1851; repr Geneseo, NY: James Brunner, 1976)

Elizabeth M. Nuxoll

Morrissey, John (*b* Templemore, Ireland, 12 Feb 1831; *d* Saratoga Springs, 1 May 1878). Boxer, businessman, and politician. Morrissey and his family left Ireland for Troy (Rensselaer Co) in 1834. His early involvement with Troy's street gangs honed his fighting skills, and he eventually started to fight for money. In 1849 Morrissey moved to New York City, and his skill soon earned the attention of Tammany Hall supporter Isaiah Rynders, who enlisted him to help turn out the Tammany vote at election time. Morrissey soon gained a reputation as a tough and tenacious fighter. In 1851 he moved to California. The following year he defeated George Thompson in his first professional fight. Returning to New York City, Morrissey continued to work for Tammany and fight professionally, wearing an American flag around his waist. He became the country's heavyweight champion after a 37-round fight with Yankee Sullivan in 1853. Morrissey retired after defeating John C. Heenan in 1858. During the 1860s he became one of the most successful owners of saloons and gambling establishments in New York City and Saratoga Springs. Morrissey was instrumental in getting the funding to build the Saratoga Race Course in 1864. After success in Saratoga, Morrissey entered politics and won election to Congress from Manhattan. Frustrated with Tammany Hall's hierarchical power structure, Morrissey founded the Young Democracy in 1870 in an attempt to reform New York politics and to end Tammany's domination. He served in Congress from 1867 to 1871 and in the New York State Senate from 1875 to 1877.

See also SARATOGA SPRINGS.

Gorn, Elliott J. *The Manly Art: Bare-Knuckle Prize Fighting in America* (Ithaca: Cornell Univ Press, 1986)
Hotaling, Edward. *They're Off! Horse Racing at Saratoga* (Syracuse: Syracuse Univ Press, 1995)

Jennifer Steenshorne

Morristown. Town (pop 2,050) and village (pop 456) in W St. Lawrence Co. The town, at the downstream end of the Thousand Islands, was settled in 1799, and the village and Edwardsville hamlet were platted at that time. An influx of English immigrants took place in 1817–18, and the town was formed in 1821 from Oswegatchie. Served by the Black River and Morristown Railroad (1876), the village incorporated in 1884. Industrial enterprises have included W. H. Comstock Co, maker of Dr. Morse's Indian Root Pills (1867–1960; until after World War I the single largest employer), Nestle's Condensed Milk (?1917–*ca* 1930; 150 workers), and Long Valley Ore Co (1937–42; graphite). Until 1953 Morristown had ferry service to Brockville, Ont. The town's St. Lawrence River and Black Lake shorelines are lined with cottage colonies, second homes, and year-round homes, but some of the farmland in between has become overgrown with brush. In 2003 the town and village were bedroom communities for Ogdensburg, and Amish from neighboring towns had settled near Brier Hill and Edwardsville. The Morristown Village Multiple Resource Area has secured National Register listing for a number of important buildings, many of them stone, including a land office (1821), store (*ca* 1821), school (*ca* 1824), and grist windmill (1825). Jacques Cartier State Park is located on the St. Lawrence River.

Richard E. Mooers

Morrisville. Village (pop 2,148) in Eaton (Madison Co). Settled in 1797 as Morris's Flatts, it took its present name when it incorporated in 1819. Located on the Third Great Western Turnpike (1803–11), Morrisville served as county seat from 1817 to 1910. The Gurley comb factory was in operation from 1808 to *ca* 1840. Tillinghast and Son (1839) made leather from South American hides, and Cross Brothers foundry (1830) manufactured cast-iron plows and stoves. It also had several woolen factories and, in the 1850s, a sewing-silk factory. A state school of agriculture opened in 1910 in former county government buildings, becoming the State University College of Technology at Morrisville, the largest employer in the area. Madison Hall (1865), a college building that was once the courthouse, is listed on the National Register.

William F. Helmer

Morse, Samuel F(inley) B(reese) (*b* Charlestown [now Boston], 27 Apr 1791; *d* New York City, 2 Apr 1872). Artist and telegraph inventor. He was the son of Jedidiah Morse, a Congregational clergyman and geographer. Attending Yale College, Samuel Morse heard lectures on electricity, but he was more enthusiastic about painting portraits. In 1811 his parents sent him to England to study painting. After returning home in 1815, he struggled to earn a living from painting. When he was painting in New Hampshire, he met Lucretia Pickering Walker, who became his first wife in 1818. Morse settled in New York City in 1823. To improve the status of artists, he helped found the National Academy of Design in 1826 and served as its president (1826–45). From 1828 to 1829 he painted in Central New York locales such as Utica and Cooperstown (Otsego Co). Believing that easy immigration into the United States threatened its stability, in 1836 and 1841 he ran unsuccessfully for New York City mayor on nativist tickets. In 1832 he conceived of an electromagnetic telegraph. In the next few years, while professor of art at what later was called New York University, he worked to develop a telegraph. By 1837 Morse abandoned painting for telegraphy. By 1838 he developed the dots and dashes that became known as Morse code and in 1840 patented his telegraph. After securing congressional funds in 1843 to construct an experimental telegraph line between Washington and Baltimore, on 24 May 1844 he sent the first message: "What hath God wrought!" In 1847 Morse bought Locust Grove, a farm overlooking the Hudson River near Poughkeepsie. His first wife having died, he married Sarah Ann Griswold of Utica in 1848. Although rivals challenged his telegraph rights, in 1854 the US Supreme Court affirmed Morse's rights to the patent. In his later years he became a trustee of Vassar College and divided his time between his West 22d St brownstone in New York City and his farmhouse in Poughkeepsie. In 1864 he ran unsuccessfully for US Congress as a Democrat opposing President Abraham Lincoln. Since 1980 his farmhouse (now the Samuel F. B. Morse Historic Site) has been open to the public.

Kloss, William. *Samuel F. B. Morse* (New York: Abrams, 1988)
Mabee, Carleton. *The American Leonardo: A Life of Samuel F. B. Morse* (1943; repr Fleischmanns, NY: Purple Mountain Press, 2000)
Morse, Edward Lind, ed. *Samuel F. B. Morse: His Letters and Journals*, 2 vols (Boston: Houghton Mifflin, 1914)

Carleton Mabee

Morton, Levi P(arsons) (*b* Shoreham, Vt, 16 May 1824; *d* Rhinebeck, Dutchess Co, 16 May 1920). Governor, vice president, and businessman. Following a basic education at Shoreham Academy, he became a store clerk in Enfield, Mass, at age 15. The 20-year mercantile career that followed included ownership of a store in Hanover, NH, a partnership in a Boston mercantile firm, and the establishment of a dry goods business in New York City. In 1863 he established L. P. Morton and Co, an international banking firm. Sir John Rose, the finance minister of Canada, later joined him, and the new firm, appointed as the financial agent of the US government in 1873, played a significant role in funding the national debt and settled the *Alabama* claims against Great Britain over shipping violations during the Civil War.

Morton's political career began with his defeat as Republican candidate for the House of Representatives in 1876. He was elected to the House in 1878 and reelected in 1880, resigning when appointed minister to France in 1881. During his tenure he successfully negotiated recognition of American corporations in France and, on 4 July 1884, formally accepted the Statue of Liberty from the French people. In 1887 he purchased an estate, Ellerslie, in Rhinebeck, which remained his home until his death.

Morton was elected vice president with Pres Benjamin Harrison in 1888 but was not renominated in 1892. Elected governor of New York State in 1894, he worked for civil service reform and signed legislation allowing the consolidation of New York City and empowering the governor to remove New York City mayors from office. Morton left public life in 1896 following his unsuccessful candidacy as New York State's "favorite son" for president. He created the Morton Trust Co and spent the remaining years of his life in investment and philanthropic activities.

McElroy, Robert. *Levi Parsons Morton: Banker, Diplomat, and Statesman* (New York: G. P. Putnam's Sons, 1930)

William P. McDermott

Moses [née Robertson], **Grandma** [Anna Mary] (*b* Greenwich, Washington Co, 7 Sept 1860; *d* Hoosick Falls, Rensselaer Co, 13 Dec 1961). Painter. Born on a farm, Anna Mary Robertson attended school occasionally before going to work at a neighbor's farm at age 12. In 1887 she married Thomas Moses and the couple moved to the Shenandoah Valley in Virginia, where they had 10 children. In 1905 the family moved to a farm in Eagle Bridge (Rensselaer Co). When Thomas Moses died in 1927, Anna Mary Moses continued to run the farm with her children's help.

Moses had always decorated objects around her home but did not deliberately paint pictures until the late 1930s when she became too old to do her usual routine of farmwork. She painted simple and happy scenes of farm life and the countryside, focusing mainly on rural New York State. She illustrated romanticized images drawn from her own experiences, including *The Old Oaken Bucket* (1943), *Out for Christmas Trees* (1944), *Apple Pickers* (1954), and her signature piece, *Sugaring Off* (1940), a scene that she painted more than 20 times. Moses also painted occasional Revolutionary War historical scenes, such as *The Battle of Bennington* (1953). Her clumsy human figures, often with just a slash for the mouth and two dots for the eyes, blended wonderfully with her beautifully represented nature scenes of rolling hills, valleys, farms, and villages. Her attractive images depicted the necessities of farm life and how the seasons dictate the work to be done, though conveying little of the grim realities that can intrude on rural life.

In 1938 Louis Caldor, an art collector from New York City, noticed Moses's work in a drugstore in Hoosick Falls and bought 19 of her paintings in one day. In October 1939 he loaned three to the Museum of Modern Art in New York City for the *Contemporary Unknown Painters* exhibition. Her pastoral paintings touched a national nerve, portraying a world in harmony far removed from the Great Depression and World War II. In October 1940 Otto Kallir's Galérie St. Etienne in New York City held a one-woman show of 35 Moses paintings, titled *What a Farm Wife Painted.* She quickly became the most renowned primitive style painter in the United States. The inspired sobriquet "Grandma Moses" appeared for the first time in an article in the *New York Herald Tribune* on 8 Oct 1940.

The popularity of her joyful preindustrial scenes (she never painted an urban setting) increased during the Cold War when her public persona matched key components of the American self-image: she was a self-taught woman who had dutifully served as wife and mother before proving the democratic individualist creed that everyone had talents and could accomplish something. Her personality also charmed America. She was unconcerned with money and said she painted simply to occupy her time. Nevertheless, her paintings hang in the major American museums, including the Metropolitan Museum of Art and the Museum of Modern Art in New York City. At the age of 100, she beautifully illustrated the famous poem " 'Twas the Night before Christmas" (also named "A Visit from St. Nicholas") and continued to paint until her death at 101. In the previous two decades, she had painted more than 1,500 paintings.

Moses, Grandma. *My Life's History* (New York: Harper & Row, 1952)
Kallir, Jane, et al. *Grandma Moses in the 21st Century* (New Haven, Conn: Yale Univ Press, 2001)
Kallir, Otto. *Grandma Moses* (New York: Harry Abrams, 1973)

Moses, Robert (*b* New Haven, Conn, 18 Dec 1888; *d* West Islip, Suffolk Co, 29 July 1981). Park and public works administrator. The son of a New Haven department store owner and his wife, both of German Jewish descent, who moved to New York City in 1897, Moses attended boarding school and Yale College, graduating in 1909. He continued his studies at Oxford University, where he wrote a thesis on the British civil service, which he presented for a PhD at Columbia University in 1914.

Early Career and Smith Years

Moses began his career with the New York Bureau of Municipal Research (now Institute of Public Administration), a private organization, developing efficiency ratings for New York City's Civil Service Commission, chaired by Madison House headworker Henry Moskowitz. In 1919 Henry's wife, Belle Moskowitz, tapped Moses to serve as chief of staff and director of research on Gov Alfred E. Smith's Reconstruction Commission, which was created to propose solutions to the social turmoil brought by World War I. Smith's electoral defeat in 1920 ended the commission's work, but Smith was impressed by Moses's contributions, particularly his proposals for a strong gubernatorial office. When Smith returned as governor in 1923, he increasingly relied on the ambitious young reformer. After Moses drafted enabling legislation for a system of state parks and connecting landscaped motor routes called parkways, Smith appointed him chairman of the State Council of Parks and one of its regional bodies, the Long Island State Park Commission. As State Council of Parks head, Moses became the driving force behind 11 regional commissions, with de facto control over plans and budgets for the largest state park system in the United States and a potentially huge network of parkways. With Smith's ardent support, Moses pressed land acquisition on Long Island, which helped create by 1929 some 9,700 acres (3,930 ha) of parkland, including Sunken Meadow, Montauk Point, Gilgo Beach, Fire Island, the remarkable recreation grounds at Jones Beach, and the Southern State Parkway, which stretched 21 mi (34 km) from Queens to Babylon (Suffolk Co). Moses got projects done on time, under budget, and without graft.

Public Works in Depression and War

With the onset of the Great Depression, Moses's public works experience was relied upon by Democratic governors Franklin D. Roosevelt and Herbert H. Lehman to garner federal funds to employ the jobless. Roosevelt appointed Moses to co-chair the State Emergency Public Works Commission, which planned New Deal–funded parkways, including the Taconic and housing projects such as Knickerbocker Village on Manhattan's Lower East Side. In 1934 Mayor Fiorello La Guardia made him New York City's park commissioner, though Moses was careful not to draw a salary on these multiple positions. As park commissioner, he utilized New Deal funds, particularly from the Works Progress Administration (WPA), to put thousands to work building and refurbishing hundreds of baseball diamonds, sandboxes, and swimming pools, making New York City's parks the state's largest WPA effort. After La Guardia appointed Moses head of the Triborough Bridge Authority in 1934, he oversaw the New Deal's largest public works authority project: the bridge and its connecting highways. At the same time he managed the sprawling Henry Hudson Parkway project, which covered the West Side Railroad tracks to complete Riverside Park and joined with the Saw Mill River Parkway in Westchester Co. City planners marveled how Moses realized New York's urban future.

Moses extended his domain further during World War II. Triborough Bridge Authority tolls funded planning and construction of the Brooklyn-Battery Tunnel, Bronx-Whitestone Bridge, and Gowanus Expressway arterials to meet national defense needs. In 1941 he pressed Mayor La Guardia to appoint him to the City Planning Commission, which Moses immediately dominated. Wearing both park and planning hats, Moses claimed that decent housing required nearby recreation space, a formula that convinced La Guardia to allow Moses to influence project decisions at the New York City Housing Authority. When La Guardia wanted a plan for postwar public works in 1943, Moses headed the commission that drew up the list of highways, slum clearance sites, public schools, and other projects.

The Coordinator

In 1946 New York City mayor William O'Dwyer formalized Moses's accumulated power and named him the city's construction coordinator. Moses set his Triborough staff to work on new expressways to connect with Long Island and Westchester Co parkways, including the Cross Bronx, which tore through a neighborhood, Van Wyck (Queens Co), and Cross Westchester. While on the Long Island State Park Commission, he encouraged the Long Island Expressway and Sunrise Highway Extension. He drove the Housing Authority to pursue slum clearance in Harlem, Brownsville (Kings Co), and the South Bronx, which provided low-rent units, but concentrated African Americans and Latinos within existing ghettos. In 1949 Moses arranged with federal and city officials to redevelop slum sites under the federal Title I program, including Manhattan's Washington Square Southeast, the New York University–Bellevue Medical Center, Manhattantown on West 97th St, and Lincoln Center for the Performing Arts, a festival place grafted onto a middle-class housing project. While critics called Moses's Title I projects, notably Manhattantown, ruthless exercises in "Negro removal," they had to admire Moses's virtuoso use of power at Lincoln Center. Elsewhere in New York State, Moses's expertise and drive proved indispensable. In 1954 Gov Thomas E. Dewey appointed him chairman of the Power Authority of the State of New York. Moses undertook the $720 million Niagara River project, which condemned one-fifth of the Tuscarora Indian Reservation [loc in Niagara Co] for the Robert Moses Power Dam, Lewiston State Park, and the Robert Moses State Parkway. At Massena (St. Lawrence Co), along the St. Lawrence Seaway, he built another dam, completed in 1958 and also named after himself.

Declining Influence

By the late 1950s the mood in New York City turned against Moses's highways, such as a proposed route across Washington Square, and his Title I projects that seemed aimed at keeping African Americans and Latinos in poor neighborhoods. Mayor Robert F. Wagner Jr stripped away his city planning post and rejected his housing proposals. But Moses's real nemesis was Gov Nelson A. Rockefeller, perhaps the only New Yorker whose power matched his own. In 1962 Rockefeller obtained Moses's resignation from the State Council of Parks and in the following year from the Power Authority. Moses remained chairman of the Triborough Bridge and Tunnel Authority until Rockefeller forced him aside in 1968. In retirement Moses sneered at his critics, labeling them timorous liberals with small ideas, and withstood the torment of Robert Caro's scathing biography *The Power Broker.* Moses died on Long Island, near his beloved Gilgo Beach, convinced that he had been democracy's builder who gave the people what they wanted.

See also POWER AUTHORITY OF THE STATE OF NEW YORK; STATE PARKS; WORLD'S FAIRS.

Caro, Robert A. *The Power Broker: Robert Moses and the Fall of New York* (New York: Alfred A. Knopf, 1974)
Moses, Robert. *Public Works: A Dangerous Trade* (New York: McGraw-Hill, 1970)
Rodgers, Cleveland. *Robert Moses: Builder for Democracy* (New York: Henry Holt, 1952)
Schwartz, Joel. *The New York Approach: Robert Moses, Urban Liberals, and Redevelopment of the Inner City* (Columbus: Ohio State Univ Press, 1993)

Joel Schwartz

Moskowitz [née Lindner], **Belle Israels** (*b* New York City, 5 Oct 1877; *d* New York City, 2 Jan 1933). Social reformer and political strategist. The daughter of East Prussian immigrants who ran a jewelry and watch repair shop in Harlem, Lindner was educated at city schools, at Horace Mann High School for Girls, and briefly at Columbia University's Teachers College. In 1900 she took up settlement work at the Educational Alliance on Manhattan's Lower East Side and in 1903 married architect Charles Henry Israels, with whom she had three children. From about 1905 to 1910 she wrote for the *Survey,* the premier journal for social work, and volunteered with the Council of Jewish Women–New York Section, pursuing dance hall reform. This campaign resulted in a 1910 state law for the licensing and regulation of dance halls. Her husband died in 1911. Belle Israels participated in the New York State Progressive Party campaign of 1912 and from 1913 to 1916 worked for the Dress and Waist Manufacturers' Association on labor issues. She married Henry Moskowitz, fellow Progressive Party activist and industrial reformer, in 1914, and from 1916 to 1918 ran an industrial consultant firm. Although she opposed Tammany Hall, in 1918 Moskowitz supported Alfred E. Smith for governor and organized the state's women's vote for him. When his victory coincided with the conclusion of World War I, Moskowitz suggested he appoint a reconstruction commission to assess the state's economic and political needs and to outline necessary reforms. Smith agreed, making her the commission's executive secretary. The commission's reports later formed the core of his legislative program. When Smith lost reelection in 1920 and was put in charge of the commission that created the Port of New York Authority, Moskowitz was responsible for the port's public relations program. After Smith's reelection in 1922, he named her publicity director for the State Democratic Committee, a job she created. In this capacity she managed Smith's reelection campaigns and presidential nomination in 1928. After his defeat she stayed on as publicity agent for the Empire State Building and continued to support Smith's presidential ambitions. She died following a fall.

Perry, Elisabeth Israels. *Belle Moskowitz: Feminine Politics and the Exercise of Power in the Age of Alfred E. Smith* (New York: Oxford Univ Press, 1987)

Elisabeth Israels Perry

MOST (Museum of Science and Technology). Hands-on museum founded in 1981 in Syracuse as the Discovery Center of Science and Technology. It was designed as a gathering place and learning center that would directly involve the public in state-of-the-art science and technology–based projects and displays. Early attractions included the Silverman Planetarium and the Hands on Science Arcade, where visitors could experience the feeling of being inside a bubble or speak into a microphone and observe their voiceprints created on an oscilloscope screen. In 1992 the institution was renamed the Milton J. Rubenstein Museum of Science and Technology. Films are screened in the Bristol Omnitheatre, which opened in 1996. Many MOST programs are designed to initiate interest in science in schoolchildren and are linked to school curricula. The museum sponsors science fairs, camp-ins, birthday parties, discovery fairs, and workshops. The MOST, located at 500 South Franklin St, hosts about 220,000 visitors annually.

Milton J. Rubenstein Museum of Science and Technology, http://www.most.org/

Motion Picture Division. State film censorship office. In 1921 New York State entered an era of film censorship that would last 44 years and result in the review of 73,000 films. Responding to public calls for censorship of objectionable films, the New York State legislature on 14 May 1921 created the Motion Picture Commission, whose job was to examine films before commercial exhibition to determine if they were "obscene, indecent, immoral, inhuman, sacrilegious, or . . . would tend to corrupt morals or to incite to crime." Offending scenes or dialogue were ordered removed, and in some cases, censors completely rejected films. Inspectors checked theaters to ensure that exhibitors showed only licensed films. Only six other states conducted similar film censorship, though many other states followed the findings of New York's censors. Under a general state reorganization in 1927, the Motion Picture Commission became part of the Education Department, where it came under the supervision of the Board of Regents. Films denied licenses could appeal first to the director of the renamed Motion Picture Division and then to the Board of Regents, but appeals were rarely successful. Film distributors could also appeal to the courts, but until 1952 none was successful in convincing judges to overrule the censors' determination. While few license denials led to appeal, several famous New York censorship cases went to the US Supreme Court, including one involving the Italian film *The Miracle.* The resulting 1952 decision in *Burstyn v Wilson* extended free speech protection to films for the first time and declared censorship based on sacrilege to be unconstitutional. Succeeding cases also struck down censorship for "immoral" content, and by the 1960s New York State censored only for obscenity. When the US Supreme Court decision *Freedman v Maryland* (1965) required substantial changes in state censorship statutes, the legislature failed to pass new laws to meet the guidelines laid down by the Supreme Court, and the Board of Regents voted to stop operations of the division as of 30 Sept 1965. The records of the Motion Picture Division, including all 73,000 original scripts, are housed at the New York State Archives, whose web site includes a searchable database.

Carmen, Ira H. *Movies, Censorship and the Law* (Ann Arbor: Univ of Michigan Press, 1966)
Motion Picture Division Files. New York State Archives, Albany; see http://iarchives.nysed.gov/MPD/rr_other_film_search.jsp
Randall, Richard S. *Censorship of the Movies* (Madison: Univ of Wisconsin Press, 1968)

Laura Wittern-Keller

motorcycling. The maturation of bicycle design and production, combined with the development of internal combustion engines in the 1890s, produced early experimental motorcycles. One such motor bicycle, now in the collections of the Buffalo and Erie County Historical Society, was built by Nelson Hopkins of Williamsville (Erie Co) in 1894–95. Most early motorcycle manufacturers were surviving or former bicycle builders, such as the E. R. Thomas Motor Co of Buffalo, which was among the pioneering US firms to market on a broad scale, with perhaps 1,000 motorcycles sold for the 1901 season. The first motorcycles revealed their bicycle antecedents with diamond frames, wire suspension wheels, and supplementary pedal propulsion systems. During the first two decades of the 20th century, motorcycle equipment evolved toward greater weight, more robustness, and more power. Two-, three-, and four-cylinder engines arrived, as did clutches and multigear transmissions.

Competitive riding began almost simultaneously with motorcycle development. Early contests included endurance runs and hill climbs. Sheepshead Bay in Brooklyn was a significant early venue for wheel-to-wheel races, while the mile course at the State Fairgrounds in Geddes (Onondaga Co) long served as the premier venue for national caliber races. Early racing was dangerous and involved many fatalities. Modern competitive events include scrambles, motocross, enduros, and observed trials. Noncompetitive, early, organized recreational riding took the form of motorcycle club rides and gypsy tours, informal runs with destinations such as picnics. Meets and rallies have remained popular, from the annual state Federation of American Motorcyclists conventions during the 1910s to the annual Americade rally held at Lake George (Warren Co), begun in 1983 under the name Aspencade East.

Despite attempts to market motorcycles for commercial purposes, such as light delivery, and as an alternative to walking or using streetcars, automobiles became the universal, economical, and motorized transportation once envisioned for motorcycles, since they appeared safer and more socially acceptable. Some manufacturers tried to produce motorcycles more closely related to automobiles than bicycles, such as the Neracar, which had a sheet metal body and drag link steering produced by Ner-A-Car Corp of Syracuse (1920–28). Others built inexpensive, lightweight motor bicycles, such as the Evans Power Cycle by Cyclemotor Corp of Rochester and later G. R. S. Products of Menands (Albany Co) (1915–26). By the end of the 1920s, though, most motorcyclists were recreational riders, and New York State's motorcycle manufacturing ceased. Many years later the Yankee Motor Co in Schenectady (1966–75) claimed it was introducing the first new American motorcycle in 30 years, but its line of on- and off-road motorcycles was short-lived. Though the major suppliers of motorcycles to New York State's seasonal riding

Nelson Hopkins with prototype motorcycle, *ca* 1895.

public are outside the state, there remains a cottage industry turning out custom motorcycles.

Motorcycle registration began in New York State in 1916, more than a decade after the licensing of automobiles. By the end of that year, 25,106 motorcycles had been registered, compared to 265,753 pleasure cars. Other regulations were imposed in the 1960s, in part because of the proliferation of inexpensive Japanese motorcycles among new riders. In 1965 a special motorcycle operator's license became mandatory, and other regulations required daytime headlight use on state roads and annual safety inspection of registered motorcycles. The state's safety helmet law, effective since 1 Jan 1967, remains the subject of protests and lobbying by motorcyclists claiming it infringes on their freedom to ride. Organizations such as the American Motorcyclists Association, American Bikers Aimed Toward Education (ABATE of New York), and the New York State Off-Highway Recreational Vehicle Association provide sophisticated defenses of motorcyclists' privileges. In 2001 New York State had 217,546 registered motorcycles, compared to 8,803,170 registered automobiles.

Stein, Geoffrey N. *The Motorcycle Industry in New York State: A Concise Encyclopedia of Inventors, Builders, and Manufacturers* (Albany: Univ of the State of New York, State Education Department, and NYS Museum, 2001)

Geoffrey N. Stein

motor vehicle industry. As experiments with internal combustion engines during the 1890s foretold an era of motorization, New York State, with a precision metal products manufacturing history, was ripe to become a center for automobile production. Especially during the first three decades of the 20th century, small-scale builders produced cars statewide, often in locations previously important for bicycle or carriage manufacture.

Early Automobile Manufacture

One of the earliest concerns that attempted to manufacture cars in the state was would-be pioneer Hitchcock Manufacturing Co of Cortland, a carriage and sleigh manufactory. In 1894 it announced that it would be building two- and four-wheel machines to the design of Edward J. Pennington of Cleveland, but it was bankrupt the following year. Electric and steam power were briefly used—the Lane Motor Vehicle Co in Poughkeepsie produced steam cars—but the gasoline engine dominated after the first decade of the 20th century. The Selden Motor Vehicle Co in Rochester was associated with George B. Selden, whose 1877 internal combustion–powered automobile patent was the subject of extended litigation in the early 20th century; the Selden Co built about 7,500 autos between 1907 and 1914 before turning attention to motor trucks.

Early designs also experimented with the number of wheels. The E. R. Thomas Motor Co of Buffalo offered a line of two-, three-, and four-wheeled vehicles in 1900. Thomas soon dropped the three-wheelers and split its operation into separate motorcycle and automobile companies, the latter specializing in expensive automobiles. Other luxury-car builders included the Lozier Motor Co of Plattsburgh, the Abendroth and Root Manufacturing Co of Newburgh (Orange Co), coach builder James Cunningham and Son of Rochester, and Brewster and Co of Long Island City (Queens Co), another respected carriage maker, turned to automobiles. Additionally, New York City–based importers traded in expensive European cars, which in the first decade of the 20th century were often considered more sophisticated and advanced than domestic autos. Subsequently, the products of several foreign enterprises, notably Mercedes and Fiat, were assembled in New York State.

Perhaps the most significant New York State–based automobile manufacturers were the Pierce-Arrow Motor Car Co, which specialized in luxury automobiles, and the Franklin Automobile Co, known for its use of an air-cooled engine. William C. Durant, who resided on 5th Ave in Manhattan, is credited with the creation of General Motors (GM). After twice being forced from control of the company, he organized Durant Motors in January 1921. With corporate offices in Manhattan, Durant built 130,000 Star automobiles and 23,000 Durants at a factory in Long Island City and its other US plants for only the 1923 model year. But Durant Motors began to decline, and in 1927 the Long Island City plant was sold to the Ford Motor Co. A few attempts to build cars in New York State were made by independent companies between the 1940s and 1960s, including the Motorette Corp, which specialized in three-wheel cars and trucks, and the Playboy Motor Corp and Griffith Motors, both of which produced sports cars, the latter using a tubular chassis, Ford engine, and imported body.

Trucks and Other Vehicles

Trucks have also been an important product of the state's motor vehicle industry. Produced more economically in smaller numbers than were contemporary automobiles, trucks were assembled by a number of builders, especially from the 1910s through the 1930s. The Selden Motor Vehicle Co focused on motor trucks from 1914 through 1932. The Walter Automobile Co also shifted from car to truck production after

Franklin Series 10 cars awaiting hood installation, Syracuse, 1923.

SELECTED NEW YORK STATE AUTOMOBILE MANUFACTURERS

Company	Location(s)	Years Operated in New York State	Approximate No. of Cars Produced
Abendroth and Root Manufacturing Co[a]	Newburgh (Orange Co)	1906–13	200
American Mercedes	Long Island City (Queens Co)	1905–7	—
Brewster and Co	Long Island City	1915–25	—
Cortland Cart and Carriage Co[b]	Sidney (Delaware Co)	1916–24	1,500
Durant Motors[c]	Long Island City	1921–25	—
E. R. Thomas Motor Co	Buffalo	1900–1913	8,000
Fiat Automobile Works	Poughkeepsie	1910–17	—
Franklin Automobile Co	Syracuse	1902–34	150,000
Griffith Motors	Syosset (Nassau Co) (1964), White Plains (Westchester Co) (1965), Plainview (Nassau Co) (1966)	1964–66	300
Harvey Allen Moyer	Syracuse	1911–15	400
James Cunningham and Son	Rochester	*ca* 1900–1931	—
Lane Motor Vehicle Co[d]	Poughkeepsie	1900–11	800
Lozier Motor Co	Plattsburgh	1905–10	1,000
Maxwell-Briscoe Motor Co[e]	North Tarrytown [now Sleepy Hollow, Westchester Co]	1904–13	40,000
Mobile Co of America[e]	North Tarrytown	1900–1904	600
Mora Motor Car Co	Newark (Wayne Co)	1906–11	500
Motorette Corp	Buffalo	1946–48	4,000
Noma Motors Corp	New York City	1919–23	600
Pierce-Arrow Motor Car Co	Buffalo	1901–38	85,485
Playboy Motor Corp	Buffalo	1947–51	—
Selden Motor Vehicle Co	Rochester	1907–14	7,500
Singer Motor Co	New York City and Mount Vernon (Westchester Co)	1914–20	1,400
Spaulding Automobile and Motor Co	Buffalo	1902–3	100
Stearns Steam Carriage Co	Syracuse	1901–3	100
Walter Automobile Co	Manhattan	1902–6	250

[a]Produced Frontenac cars.

[b]Produced Hatfield cars.

[c]Produced Durant and Flint cars.

[d]Produced steam cars.

[e]Produced Maxwell cars.

Compiled by Geoffrey N. Stein

1906. Other truck brands produced in the state have included Stewart, Chase, Sullivan, Ward LaFrance, Atterbury, Larrabee-Deyo, and Mack. The final New York State–built heavy truck was the Brockway, last assembled in 1977 in Cortland by a subsidiary of Mack Trucks. Additionally, the state's builders of fire apparatuses contributed to that specialized area of truck manufacture. Leading names include Sanford, Childs, Buffalo, Mack, and Ward LaFrance vehicles. In Elmira, for three-quarters of a century, American-LaFrance fire apparatuses figured among the most important custom trucks in the United States; in 1985 manufacturing moved to Virginia. The cab-forward design, introduced in volume by the Series 700 of 1947, is an American-LaFrance contribution to apparatus design. Bus manufacture, including contemporary fabrication of transit buses by Orion Bus Industries in Oriskany (Oneida Co), complements historical efforts such as production by the Fifth Avenue Coach Co in New York City in the first third of the 20th century.

A Changing Industry

Following the concentration of the automobile industry in Michigan, several assembly plants survived in New York State as branches of Detroit-based companies. The Ford Motor Co began building Model Ts in Buffalo in the 1910s in the former John R. Keim Co factory. New assembly plants were added on Main St and on Fuhrmann Blvd, the latter closing in 1958 to end automobile assembly for Ford in New York State. GM ran an assembly plant on East Delavan Ave in Buffalo, producing Chevrolet automobiles before shifting to axle manufacture. GM maintained the longest-operating motor vehicle factory in the state, building Chevrolet automobiles from 1914 to 1996 in a Stanford White–designed factory at North Tarrytown [now Sleepy Hollow, Westchester Co]. Between 1900 and 1910 the factory's first two occupants, the Mobile Co of America and the Maxwell-Briscoe Motor Co, also constructed automobiles.

In 1930 a reported 13,000 people were employed in 12 Western New York auto factories. At the turn of the 21st century, the automotive industry in the broadest sense remains significant to the state's economy, with, as in other states, facilities providing for the sale, servicing, and repair of motor vehicles as well as for the infrastructure of their operation. In addition, a manufacturing presence remains in the form of component fabrication by the major automakers and by independent manufacturers, which have over the past century numbered in the tens if not hundreds. In 1949 Ford added a stamping plant for doors, hoods, and other panels in Hamburg (Erie Co), and a Ford radiator plant operated from 1923 to 1988 in Green Island (Albany Co). A GM engine factory in Tonawanda (Erie Co), built in 1927, was by 1985 the corporation's largest such facility, and with 16,000 employees that year, made GM Western New York's largest industrial employer. GM's other facilities included a forge plant in Tonawanda, completed in 1953, and the Harrison radiator operation (now part of Delphi Automotive Systems) in Lockport (Niagara Co) and Buffalo.

Independent component manufacturers have included the Mott Wheel Works (later Williams Steel Wheel and Rim Co) at Utica and Trico Products Corp, a maker of windshield wipers, at Buffalo. Custom-body builders included Willoughby in Utica, Brunn in Buffalo, and Rollston in New York City. The Willys-Morrow Co, a subsidiary of the Willys Corp, manufactured metal parts at Elmira until its demise in 1934; in 1920, 3,000 men had been employed. The Herschell-Spillman Motor Co of North Tonawanda (Niagara Co) and the Rochester Motors Corp, among other manufacturers, supplied engines to car builders. Syracuse has been a center of gear manufacture, with major producers Brown-Lipe (1895), Dunston Gear Corp, and Syracuse Gear Co. In 1922 the Brown-Lipe operation was acquired by GM and later operated as part of its Fisher Guide Division, manufacturing plastic parts. New Venture Gear traces its roots to 1888; as New Process Gear Corp (formerly New Process Rawhide Co) it became part of Chrysler Corp in 1934, and New Venture Gear was created in 1990 as a joint venture of GM and Chrysler. In 2000 the company employed some 4,000 people in the Town of DeWitt (Onondaga Co).

Automobile Trade Journal (1912–28)
Bellamy, James F. *Cars Made in Upstate New York* (Red Creek, NY: Squire Hill Pub, 1989)
Facts and Figures of the Automobile Industry (1920–33)
Kimes, Beverly Rae, and Henry Austin Clark Jr. *Standard Catalog of American Cars, 1805–1942,* 3d ed. (Iola, Wisc: Krause Publications, 1996)

Geoffrey N. Stein

Motor Vehicles, Department of (DMV). New York was the first state to license motor vehicles (954 in 1901) and motor vehicle operators (2,382 in 1903). Its first Motor Vehicle Act was passed in 1904. The issuance of license plates began in 1910, and their manufacture at Auburn Prison (Cayuga Co) in 1923. The statewide requirement that all drivers be licensed dates to 1924, but liability insurance for all motor vehicles was not compulsory until 1957. Administrative responsibility for motor vehicle regulation was initially in the office of the secretary of state. Between 1910 and 1916, licensing revenues grew from $398,000 to $4,000,000. The development of these fees as a major revenue source led in 1921 to a shift of responsibility at the state level for motor vehicle and operator licensing to the State Tax Commission, and at the local level county clerks were authorized to open local motor vehicle offices. Motor vehicle laws were administered through the department's Automobile Bureau through 1924, when the bureau became the Bureau of Motor Vehicles and the Office of Commissioner of Motor Vehicles was created. In 1926 the bureau became part of the newly instituted Department of Taxation and Finance, and the State Police took over enforcement of the Highway Law. By 1929 revenue from licenses had grown to $40,000,000.

The Department of Motor Vehicles was established by constitutional amendment as one of 20 named state departments in 1959. The following year the Bureau of Motor Vehicles was eliminated, and the DMV took over its responsibilities. Organized in its present form in 1961, the DMV "registers and titles motor vehicles, examines and licenses drivers, dealers, repair shops, inspection stations and driving schools, and collects fees for these activities," according to the *New York Red Book.* The department ensures that all vehicles are insured, receives and investigates repair shop complaints, and administers the vehicle emission inspection process. The DMV also adjudicates noncriminal traffic violations in the Cities of Buffalo and Rochester, in New York City, and in western Suffolk Co.

The Commissioner of Motor Vehicles heads the 14-member Governor's Traffic Safety Committee, established by law and executive order in accord with federal requirements in 1967 to protect the state's eligibility for highway construction and traffic safety funding. In connection with this responsibility, efforts against drunk driving are spearheaded in the department, and accident statistics are maintained. Efforts to improve highway safety resulted in a steady decline in the rate of vehicular accidents involving death in the last decade of the 20th century. Persons killed per 100 million vehicle miles of travel dropped from 2.1 in 1990 to 1.1 in 2000.

In 1984 New York State was last in the nation to include a photograph on drivers' licenses. Nine years later a *New York Times* article described the DMV, an agency unusual in the palpable impact of its work on most New Yorkers, as "the most hated bureaucracy" in state government. Unlike the offices run by elected county clerks, the agency's branch offices in New York City and populous urban/suburban counties were infamous for gross inefficiency and indifference to citizen service. Declaring that the DMV needed a "culture change," Commissioner Patricia B. Adduci, former clerk of Monroe Co, launched an 18-month effort to increase efficiency, effectiveness, and responsiveness. Symbolic of change was the reduction of the state's 19-digit driver's license number to 9 digits. New offices were opened. Mail- and machine-based transactions were introduced. Average waiting time was measured and reduced, and efforts were made to be more accommodating to those waiting. Improvements, later built upon with the use of Internet, have been acknowledged statewide and nationally.

In 2001 DMV's work was done through 28 regional offices in Albany, Onondaga, Rockland, Westchester, Nassau, and Suffolk Cos and in New York City, and through the agency of elected county clerks in the state's other counties. There were 10,706,563 vehicles registered in New York State and 11,014,805 licensed drivers in 2001.

"Motor Vehicle and Driver Regulation in New York State: A Brief History," http://www.newyorkplates.com/history.html
"Motor Vehicles Moves to Shed Its Poor Image," *New York Times*, 22 Mar 1993
New York Red Book (2000–2002)

Gerald Benjamin

Mount, William Sidney (*b* Setauket, Suffolk Co, 26 Nov 1807; *d* Setauket, 18 Nov 1868). Artist. Descendant of Long Island farmers and storekeepers, Mount apprenticed in 1824 in New York City as a sign painter with his brother Henry, who encouraged Mount to enroll in the National Academy of Design (1826). He settled in Stony Brook (Suffolk Co), although he and his brothers opened a studio in New York City in 1829. Mount's religious works and portraits met with praise, but he turned to rural genre scenes that depicted everyday life and contained complex symbolism, for which he also received acclaim and patronage. Mount observed his Long Island neighbors and transformed them into vivid characters on his canvases: threshers, horse dealers, courting couples, and musicians. He was among the first American artists to depict African Americans in a dignified manner, in paintings as *Farmers Nooning* (1836), *Eel Spearing at Setauket* (1845), and *The Bones Player* (1856). Although a Democrat, Mount parodied both Whigs and his own party, and his works are filled with scathing allusions to political imbroglios. Mount's *Painter's Triumph* (1838) shows a professional artist exhibiting his painting to a farmer and celebrates art for common people. After his mother and brother died in 1841, Mount retired for almost a year, then studied with Thomas Cole in Catskill (Greene Co). Mount's images from the Civil War and postbellum years reflect his increasing political cynicism. Mount patented the Cradle of Harmony, a new type of violin, in 1853 and left a legacy of numerous fiddle tunes, many of which have been recorded. His house in Stony Brook was designated a National Historic Landmark in 1965.

For illustrations see LONG ISLAND; SETAUKET.

Johnson, Deborah J., and Elizabeth Johns. *William Sidney Mount: Painter of American Life* (New York: American Federation of Arts, 1998)

Kathryn Clippinger Kosto

mountains. See LANDFORMS.

Mount Hope. Town (pop 6,639) in W Orange Co. The town was formed in 1825 from Wallkill, Minisink, and Deerpark as Calhoun; the name was changed in 1833. After the Erie Railroad crossed the town in 1848, fluid milk became its chief agricultural product. Lumber and shingles were produced at Mount Hope hamlet, the Erie Lead Mine Co began operations at Guymard about 1863, and Otis and Co ran the

Cider Making, by William Sidney Mount, 1840–41.

Shoddy Hollow Mill on the Shawangunk Kill in the 1870s. The City of New York operated a municipal tuberculosis sanatorium near Otisville from 1903 to 1955. Its site became Otisville Correctional Facility (1977), a medium security state facility. This facility and the Federal Correctional Institute at Otisville (1980) are the town's largest employers. In the early 21st century, some dairy farms remain in operation. The Eleazer Harding House (*ca* 1790) is a museum.

Mount Ivy. Locality (pop 6,536) in Haverstraw (Rockland Co). Originally called Gurnee's Corner, it acquired a station of the New Jersey and New York Railroad (1874) and a post office (1882–1928), both named Mount Ivy. Sand and gravel were quarried in the 1920s. In the early 21st century the locality is residential.

Mount Kisco. Coextensive town and village (pop 9,983) in N central Westchester Co. A station on the Harlem Railroad (1847) gave birth to the community; by the 1860s it was a small manufacturing center producing cotton and woolen cloth, shoes, and shirts. The village was incorporated in 1874. Spencer Optical Co (1874–88) employed 200 workers. Dairy farms in the surrounding country were gradually supplanted by estates in the late 19th century. Italian laborers formed a strong community in the village. The Canadian Radium and Uranium Corp (1943–66) processed uranium, including some for the Manhattan Project. Automobile commuting was encouraged by the construction of the Saw Mill River Parkway (1949). As the retail center for northeast Westchester Co, its concentration of business increased in the 1970s with facilities such as the Shoppers Bazaar mall (1977). The village was taken from Bedford and New Castle and made a town in 1978. In the early 21st century Mount Kisco remains a center of trade and the site of the regionally important Northern Westchester Hospital (1916), and has a growing Latino community, 24.5% of the population in 2000, which finds work primarily on the nearby estates.

Mount Marcy (5,344 ft/1,629 m). Highest point in New York State and center of the High Peaks region of the Adirondack Mountains. Located near Lake Placid in Essex Co, it is sometimes called Tahawus, an Iroquois word meaning "cloudsplitter." Mt Marcy is a part of the Canadian Shield geological formation lying at the heart of what is now Adirondack Park. With its bare rock crown, severe weather can threaten hikers even in midsummer. Ebenezer Emmons, leader of New York State Geological Survey, made the first recorded ascent of Mt Marcy on 5 Aug 1837 and named the peak for Gov William L. Marcy, who supported the survey. The first trail was blazed up the mountain in 1861 by Orson "Old Mountain" Phelps, a colorful Keene Valley guide. In September 1901 Vice Pres Theodore Roosevelt was hiking down the mountain when he learned that an assassin had shot and fatally wounded Pres William McKinley and that he would become president.

Mt Marcy is protected by the state constitution's 1894 forever wild clause, which prohibits development or timber cutting on state-owned wilderness and forestland. Improved highway access and the development of lightweight hiking and camping gear in the late 20th century opened the mountain, once the province of hardy hikers only, to thousands of novices. By 2002 the Adirondack Mountain Club estimated that at least 10,000 hikers, skiers, and snowshoers reached the summit annually via the peak's five trails. This increased use led to trail erosion, which in turn led to mandatory camping and hiking restrictions in 2001.

Weber, Sandra. *Mount Marcy: The High Peak of New York* (Fleischmanns, NY: Purple Mountain Press, 2001)

Peter Slocum

Mount Morris. Town (pop 4,567) and village (pop 3,266) in SW Livingston Co. Permanent European American settlement began in 1793 in this longtime home to the Seneca Indians. The town was formed from Leicester in 1818, and the village incorporated in 1835. The Genesee Valley Canal (1840–78) and several railroads starting in 1859 contributed to Mount Morris's economic growth. Broom manufacturing began in 1830; in 1881 the town had 10 broom factories. Other industrial products included glass, turbines, and spoke-making machines. Fruits and vegetables were canned and dried; the first cannery opened in 1878. Italian immigrants came for work on the railroads, in canneries, and in the Mount Morris Knitting Mill (1920s), and constituted a large proportion of the population. In the late 20th century, Puerto Ricans came to work in the Seneca Foods plant, which remains in operation in the early 21st century. In 2000 about 5% of the town was of Latino ethnicity.

Letchworth State Park (1907) surrounding the Genesee River ravine runs the length of the town; the 282 ft (86 m) high Mount Morris Dam (constructed 1948–51 for flood control) spans the valley. The campus of Murray Hill State Tuberculosis Hospital (1936–71) is now the site of Livingston Co offices and a skilled nursing facility. Mount Morris is the birthplace of John Wesley Powell (1834–1902), the explorer of the Grand Canyon, and Francis Bellamy (1855–1931), author of the "Pledge of Allegiance." The town is the site of the 160 x 200 ft (49 x 61 m) Black and White Farm Barn listed on the National Register of Historic Places.

Mary Jo Marks

Mount Pleasant. Town (pop 43,221) in central Westchester Co. The Dutch first settled the area with the development of Philipsburg Manor Upper Mills (1682; restoration 1968) by Frederick Philipse I. In the northeast corner of the present town a number of English Quaker families settled after 1725. All land tenure was by leasehold from the Philipse family until 1785, at which time it was sold by the state as freehold farms. The town was formed in 1788; Ossining was taken off in 1845. Harlem (1846) and Hudson River Railroads traversed it, improving access to New York City. After 1891 suburban development accelerated. Industrial pursuits were limited to marble quarrying and, in the 20th century, the General Motors plant on the Hudson. Important landmarks are the Philipsburg Manor Upper Mills, Old Dutch Church of Sleepy Hollow (1697), and Kykuit (1913), the John D. Rockefeller estate.

Field Horne

Mount Saint Mary College. Private college. The Sisters of St. Dominic of Newburgh (Orange Co) established Mount Saint Mary College in 1930 as a teacher training school for members of the order. In 1960 the college opened its doors to lay students and began accepting men *ca* 1968. The 72-acre (29 ha) campus overlooks the Hudson River. A liberal arts college, the school offers degrees in 47 undergraduate majors, as well as graduate degrees in business, education, and nursing. Undergraduate enrollment for the 2002–3 academic year included 1,915 students, 75% full-time and 70% women.

Patrick Ziegler

Mount Sinai. Locality (pop 8,734) in Brookhaven (Suffolk Co). On land purchased from the Setauket Indians in 1664, the protected Mount Sinai Harbor was the landing site for Col Benjamin Tallmadge's surprise attack on British-held Fort St. George in Mastic in 1780. The locality, known as The Old Mans after retired British Maj Daniel Gotherson, acquired a post office named Mount Sinai in 1840 and was a shipbuilding center throughout the 19th century. In 1891 a 76-acre (31 ha) residential park named Crystal Brook was begun, encompassing simple summer cottages, a chapel (1902), and a community house, all of which remain largely intact in 2003. Mount Sinai, whose population tripled in the 1970s with suburban development pressure, is the site of the town-operated Cedar Beach on Long Island Sound.

Luise Weiss

Mount Vernon. City (pop 68,381) in S Westchester Co. In 1851 under the leadership of merchant tailor John Stevens, the socialist Industrial Home Association No. 1 of the City of New York was formed by 1,000 mechanics, tradesmen, and laborers. The association purchased five farms along the New Haven Railroad in Eastchester to create a commuter suburb of affordable, owner-occupied houses. By the following summer 300 homes had been started. It incorporated as a village in 1853. Other associations created adjacent communities: South Mount Vernon (1851); East Mount Vernon (1851) and West Mount Vernon (1852), both created by German immigrants; and Central Mount Vernon (1853). A steam-powered factory was built in 1857 by a corporation that leased it to a series of industries, beginning with a cartridge producer during the Civil War. West and Central Mount Vernon incorporated as West Mount Vernon in 1869, consolidating with Mount Vernon in 1878. It became a city in 1892.

Oil, coal, produce, and building supplies were brought up Eastchester Creek and shipped through the city to the rest of Westchester Co and New York City. Manufacturing grew during the 20th century, and important employers included Lillian Vernon Corp (1951; catalog sales) and Consumers Union (publisher of *Consumer Reports*), both of which left the city in the early 1990s. Its African American population, 7% in 1945, grew steadily and reached 60% in 2000; among its well-known black residents have been Dr Betty Shabazz, widow of Malcolm X, and Sadie and Bessie Delany, who wrote the autobiography *Having Our Say* (1993). In the 1980s Mount Vernon emerged as a center of rap music and was home to musicians Sean "Puff Daddy"

South 4th Ave, Mount Vernon, early 20th century

Combs and Heavy D. In the early 21st century, with the city's white population concentrated north of the New Haven tracks, it continues to struggle to create a racially balanced community and school system. Major employers in 2003 included Michael Anthony Jewelers (jewelry manufacturer), Reliable (industrial machinery), and Semi-Alloys (semiconductors). St. Paul's Church Eastchester (present building 1763–87) is a National Historic Site. The election that resulted in the Zenger trial took place on the church's green in 1733.

Amy Surak

Moynihan, Daniel Patrick (*b* Tulsa, Okla, 16 Mar 1927; *d* New York City, 26 Mar 2003). Professor and US senator. Raised in New York City and honored as valedictorian of Benjamin Franklin High School, Moynihan entered City College in 1943, enlisted in the navy the following year, and studied primarily at Tufts University (BA 1948, MA 1949, PhD 1961). He served as an aide to Gov W. Averell Harriman (1955–58) and then taught at Syracuse University. As assistant secretary of labor under Pres John F. Kennedy and Lyndon Johnson, he helped draft the War on Poverty legislation and wrote a controversial report, *The Negro Family: The Case for National Action,* which argued that dysfunctional families, often characterized by weak or absent fathers, were one of the causes for multigenerational black poverty.

After running unsuccessfully for president of the New York City Council in 1965, Moynihan joined the Harvard faculty and was recognized as a leading expert on urban problems. As an adviser to Pres Richard M. Nixon from 1969 to 1970, he helped draft the Family Assistance Plan, a welfare reform program that would have guaranteed a minimum income to the nation's poor. He also stirred controversy with a memo recommending "benign neglect" of racial issues. From 1973 to 1975 he was US ambassador to India and from 1975 to 1976 was US ambassador to the United Nations. During this period he was a leading neoconservative critic of liberal excesses but became an equally stern opponent of conservative shibboleths during the Reagan era. After narrowly winning the Democratic primary in 1976, he served four terms in the US Senate from New York until retiring in 2001.

Moynihan's major support base in all four elections came from New York City, while nonurban upstate voters most often favored his Republican challengers. His principal legislative concerns included Social Security reform, transportation policy, and the environment, and he was an architect of the Tax Reform Act of 1986, as well as chair of the Senate Finance Committee in 1993–95. Author of nearly two dozen books on ethnicity, family issues, international affairs, and politics, Moynihan was a unique figure who moved regularly between academia and government under both Democrats and Republicans. He died of complications from an emergency appendectomy in early 2003.

Hodgson, Geoffrey. *The Gentleman from New York: Daniel Patrick Moynihan—A Biography* (New York: Houghton Mifflin, 2000)

Katzman, Robert A., ed. *Daniel Patrick Moynihan: The Intellectual in Public Life* (Baltimore: Johns Hopkins Univ Press, 1998)

Jonathan Entin

MTA. See METROPOLITAN TRANSPORTATION AUTHORITY (MTA).

muck farming. Agricultural technique based on soil composition. Muck is a lightweight, dark, silty soil found in wetlands. It contains high concentrations of decomposed organic matter and minerals making it extremely fertile. Beginning in the 1820s farmers drained wetlands, cleared vegetation, and farmed what they called black dirt or black beach. Large muck farms, 60–100 acres (24–40 ha), existed by the 1850s in Madison, Oneida, and Orange Cos, and by the 1860s in Orleans, Genesee, Oswego, Yates, Ontario, and Steuben Cos. Farmers installed pipe drains since they routinely contended with flooding. Muck contained high levels of phosphorus and produced larger vegetables, making soil ideal for truck crops.

In the 1840s in Florida (Orange Co) and Canastota (Madison Co) English and Irish farmers planted potatoes, hemp, and small crops of onions in muck. Since onion crops were more profitable and required intensive hand labor, in the 1880s immigrants were hired as sharecroppers. They established their own farms, became the dominant farmers, and made a million-dollar business out of muck crops in New York State. In the 1880s Polish émigrés farmed 10,000 acres (4,000 ha) of muck in Orange Co. By 1920 Italians in Canastota had more than 200 muck farms, which averaged 10–40 acres (4–16 ha); there were over 8,000 acres (3,200 ha) of muck farms in Madison Co. Farmers built shacks, onion sheds, and barns, and lived seasonally on farms. In the 1930s farmers invented the muck truck to transport vegetables. The roof, rear seats, and trunk were removed from old cars, creating an odd flatbed truck that was unique to the state.

Muck farms fueled the cash crop industry and perfected a specialized agricultural technique. Farmers mainly produced onions, giving Canastota the name Onion Town, and Florida was called the Onion Capital of the World. Onion farms were the primary agricultural product of Orange, Madison, and Oswego Cos. Most farmers planted Ebenezer set or Yellow Globe onions for local stores and for markets in New York City, Albany, New Jersey, and Canada. Celery, lettuce, carrots, cabbage, and asparagus also were major crops. Because farms were profitable, the US and New York State Departments of Agriculture constructed networks of ditches to control flooding. In 1939, 14,900 acres (6,030 ha) of muck onions were farmed in the state.

By the late 1940s muck farming declined in some counties. In Central New York major floods eroded soil, and Thruway construction destroyed muck since road salt saturated soil. Younger generation farmers abandoned agriculture for professional careers, but muck farming flourished in the Finger Lakes region and in Orange Co. In 1965, 16,400 acres (6,637 ha) of seed and set onions were farmed in the state, mainly in Orange Co (8,050 acres/3,258 ha). By 1970 many farms were abandoned and in the 1980s were residential property. In the 1990s there was a resurgence in muck farming. In 2000, 26,957 acres (10,909 ha) were farmed, of which 10,983 acres (4,445 ha) were onions. Current muck crops include turf grass or sod (Madison, Monroe, and Westchester Cos), potatoes (Madison and Oneida Cos), and corn (Ontario, Steuben, Orange, and Yates Cos). Farmers in Oswego Co market muck onions as New York Bolds. They are major competitors with the Vidalia, onions from Georgia. In 2001 New York State ranked fifth nationally in onion production, and nearly 11,000 acres (4,452 ha) of onions were farmed in the mucklands of Orange, Orleans, Oswego, Madison, and Wayne Cos.

Canastota Oral History Project. Interviews. Everett Needham Case Library, Colgate Univ, Hamilton, NY

Wilkinson, Albert E. *Muck Crops: A Book on Vegetable Crops Raised on Reclaimed Land* (New York: Orange Judd, 1916)

Tricia A. Barbagallo

Mugwumps. Late 19th-century reformers who, in response to the widespread scandals of the age, advocated civil service examinations, laissez-faire economics, and limited government as a way to restore political morality and achieve the common good. *Mugwump* is an Algonquian word for leader. The first Mugwumps were those Republicans who coalesced around the issue of corruption in Ulysses S. Grant's administration and backed the editor of the *New York Tribune,* Horace Greeley, for president in 1872. The term came into wider use in the election of 1884 when some Republicans backed the New York State reform governor, Grover Cleveland, over the scandal-ridden Republican candidate, James G. Blaine. Well-known New Yorkers played an especially prominent role in the movement, including Edwin L. Godkin (editor of the *Nation*), George William Curtis (editor of *Harper's Monthly*), Brooklyn mayor Seth Low, and Utica journalist Harold Frederic. Mugwumps backed reforms such as the Pendleton Act (1883) for civil service reform as a way to eliminate the spoils system and depoliticize government employment.

In New York State an alliance of mostly Republican Mugwumps joined with the Cleveland wing of the Democratic Party to do battle with politicians from both sides of the aisle; the enemies list included Republicans like Roscoe Conkling and Thomas C. Platt as well as Democrats like David B. Hill and, above all, the operatives of Tammany Hall. The reputation of the Mugwumps has varied greatly; they are often characterized as wealthy upper-class men who cherished order and good manners over the interests of immigrants, African Americans, farmers, and the poor. Supporters, however, admire their honesty and commitment to public virtue and see them as precursors to the Progressives. Cleveland's narrow victories in 1884 and 1892 were directly because of the influence of the Mugwumps, and the electoral successes of Low in Brooklyn and New York City imply a wider range of support for the Mugwump platform than a few elitists.

McFarland, Gerald. *Mugwumps, Morals, and Politics, 1884–1920* (Amherst: Univ of Massachusetts Press, 1975)

Tucker, David. *Mugwumps: Public Moralists of the Gilded Age* (Columbia: Univ of Missouri Press, 1998)

Jon Sterngass

Muhlenberg, William Augustus (*b* Philadelphia, 16 Sept 1796; *d* New York City, 8 Apr 1877). Episcopal priest and ecumenical pioneer. Muhlenberg's distinguished German Lutheran family worshiped in the Episcopal Church for language reasons. He graduated from the University of Pennsylvania in 1815, was ordained a deacon in 1817, and until his ordination to the priesthood in 1820 was assistant to Bishop William White. He served as rector (1820–26) of St. James Church in Lancaster, Pa, then became rector of St. George's Church in Flushing (Queens Co). In 1828 he began the Flushing Institute, a private boys school that expanded into St. Paul's College (1838–?1845) at Strattonport [now College Point, Queens Co]. After a European journey he founded the Church of the Holy Communion (1845) in New York City, an early "free church" with no sold or rented pews. Embellishments such as new musical settings, flowers, and altar candles were borrowed from Lutheranism and Roman Catholicism. Holy Communion was also noted for community service, which led to the founding of St. Luke's Hospital (1858). To assist with these varied ministries Muhlenberg helped found the Sisterhood of the Holy Communion in 1845 (formalized in 1852), the oldest Episcopalian women's religious community. Muhlenberg, interested in ecumenism, described his position as "Evangelical Catholic," combining Protestant and Catholic elements. His *Muhlenberg Memorial* (1853), a petition to the church's general convention, advocated a united church with the Episcopal Church at its center. In 1869 he founded the Society of St. Johnland, a self-sufficient ecumenical community for the poor, disabled, and elderly in Smithtown (Suffolk Co).

Skardon, Alvin. *Church Leader in the Cities: William Augustus Muhlenberg* (Philadelphia: Univ of Pennsylvania Press, 1971)

Robert Bruce Mullin

Muldowney [née Roque], **Shirley** (*b* Burlington, Vt, 19 June 1940). Drag racer. Muldowney grew up in Schenectady, where she became a street racer, and raced on her first dragstrip, the Fonda Speedway (Montgomery Co), in 1958. In 1965 she became the first woman licensed by the National Hot Rod Association (NHRA) to drive a gasoline-powered dragster. After competing in the top gas class, she began racing a funny car, a nitromethane-powered drag racer, and won her first funny-car event at Lebanon Valley Dragway in West Lebanon (Columbia Co) and her first national event on the International Hot Rod Association (IHRA) circuit in 1971. After four fires she switched to the safer and faster top fuel class and reached the finals of the 1974 and 1975 US Nationals. At the 1975 finals she became the first woman to break the 5-second barrier, finishing in 5.98 seconds. In 1976 she became the first woman to win a NHRA top fuel drag race event. In 1977, the same year she received an Outstanding Achievement Award from the US Congress, Muldowney became the second driver to top 250 mph for the quarter-mile, posting the sport's fastest time (5.77 seconds) and top speed (253 mph) to date. She remains the only driver to have won three NHRA season points championships (1977, 1980, 1982). Profiled in the 1983 film *Heart Like a Wheel,* Muldowney, who competed in a signature pink race car and was popularly known for a time as "Cha-Cha," was almost killed in a 1984 crash. After returning to racing in 1987, she won her 18th NHRA national event in 1989, made the finals in five consecutive IHRA circuit events in 1996, and drove the quarter-mile in record-breaking time (4.69 seconds) and speed (312.5 mph) at IHRA's 1998 Northern Nationals. In 1990 Muldowney became the first female and second drag racer inducted into the Motor Sports Hall of Fame. In 1998 the state senate honored her as one of New York State's Women of Distinction. She retired from racing in 2003.

Shirley Muldowney, http://www.muldowney.com/shirley_home.htm

Post, Robert C. *High Performance: The Culture and Technology of Drag Racing, 1950–1990* (Baltimore: Johns Hopkins Univ Press, 1994)

Doug Sherman

mules. Hybrid offspring of a male donkey (jack or jackass) and a female horse (mare), sterile except under rare circumstances. They have given significant service to New York State as draft animals on farms and in cities, as pack animals, and more recently as mounts for recreational trail riding. Farmers in the state have always kept fewer mules than horses; mules were much more popular in the southern states, where they were often preferred to horses as work animals because of their longer working lives and tolerance for hot weather. New York State's 1855 census, which recorded almost 580,000 horses, found only 2,254 mules. But following the Civil War, mules gained fame for their useful labor on the towpaths of the state's canals, soon largely displacing horse teams. Thomas Allen's Erie Canal song "Low Bridge, Everybody Down" (1913), composed when the towpath-less New York State Barge Canal (1911) was putting mules out to pasture permanently, nostalgically lauds Sal the mule as "a good old worker and a good old pal." In 1900 the mule population was 3,313, doubling to approximately 6,000 mules by 1930. In 2000 there were about 2,500 mules and donkeys in the state, making up about 1.5% of the equine population.

H. F. Hintz

Mullaney, Kate (*b* Ireland, 1845; *d* Troy, 17 Aug 1906). Labor organizer. Kate emigrated with her parents from Ireland to Troy and became the family breadwinner after her father died. With her mother in ill health, Kate experienced the poor working conditions of Troy's collar-and-cuff industry. In 1864 she organized and became the first and only president of the Collar Laundry Union of Troy, following the example of larger cities in forming a union to protest wage scales, hours, and working conditions imposed on the women in the collar factories. Women made up 25% of Troy's labor force, and laundresses were the lowest paid in the collar industry, despite how essential the laundering and starching of collars and cuffs were to the quality of the product. Mullaney achieved national recognition in 1868 when she was appointed assistant secretary of the National Labor Union, the first female appointment to a national labor union office. With about 200 fellow workers, she organized a strike in 1869, asking for a 25% wage increase; although this move failed, it prompted the women to organize a laundry cooperative and a cooperative to manufacture collars and cuffs. The Collar Laundry Union also formed a strong relationship with the Iron Molders' Union, donating $1,000 to the molders after they were locked out in one of the most protracted labor disputes of the era. With her husband, John Fogarty, Mullaney lived at 350 8th St in Troy; her house was designated a National Historic Landmark and marked with a plaque in 1998, and a monument was placed on her unmarked grave in St. Peter's Cemetery in Troy in 1999. She has been inducted into the National Women's Hall of Fame.

Kathryn T. Sheehan

Mumford, Lewis (*b* Flushing, Queens Co, 19 Oct 1895; *d* Amenia, Dutchess Co, 26 Jan 1990). Writer, urban planner, and cultural critic. Raised in Manhattan, Mumford graduated in 1912 from Stuyvesant High School and enrolled in City College of New York, but left in 1914 without attaining a degree after a diagnosis of tuberculosis. Mumford considered Manhattan his true university, however, and from childhood he walked, sketched, and observed New York City, and its effects can be felt throughout his writings. Starting his career as a freelance writer, Mumford published his first book, *The Story of Utopias,* in 1922. The following year he was a cofounder of the Regional Planning Association of America, which advocated limited-scale development and economic balance between cities and regions. From 1931 to 1963 he was architectural critic for the *New Yorker.* Mumford's wide-ranging works include pioneering books on American literary transcendentalism, *The Golden Day* (1926) and *Herman Melville* (1929); 19th-century American history, *The Brown Decades* (1931); and the history of technology, *Technics and Civilization* (1934). His work on urban history, including *The Culture of Cities* (1938), was profoundly influential for regional planning. In 1936 he and his wife, Sophia, moved from their home in Queens, where they had resided since 1925, and settled permanently in Amenia. Mumford was an ardent advocate for American military action against Germany as early as 1938, and World War II claimed the life of his son Geddes in 1944. He also was an early critic of nuclear weapons in 1946 and of US involvement in Vietnam in 1965. Mumford's *The City in History* (1961) received the National Book Award, and in 1964 he was awarded the Presidential Medal of Freedom. His two-volume *The Myth of the Machine: Technics and Human Development* (1967) shows in lucid detail how the modern ethos—with its materialism and unlimited technical and economic expansionism—released a Pandora's box of mechanical marvels that eventually threatened to absorb all human purposes. Mumford's multifaceted work marks him as one of the most original voices of the 20th century.

Miller, Donald L. *Lewis Mumford: A Life* (New York: Weidenfeld & Nicholson, 1989)

Mumford, Lewis. *Sketches from Life: The Autobiography of Lewis Mumford: The Early Years* (New York: Dial Press, 1982)

Eugene Halton

Municipal Art Society. A private, nonprofit membership organization with the mission of supporting urban design and planning and the preservation of New York City's history. Founded at the turn of the 20th century by a varied group of artists, architects, and civic leaders, the Municipal Art Society (MAS) grew out of the City Beautiful Movement that linked aesthetics—primarily of the Beaux Arts architectural school—with moral rectitude and civic virtue. Early members included architects Stanford White and Henry J. Hardenbergh and financiers J. P. Morgan and Jacob Schiff. MAS sought progressive change and wanted to move beyond private philanthropy to develop a voice in public policy debates. One of the society's most celebrated accomplishments was the New York City zoning ordinance of 1916, the first zoning law in the nation. In the post–World War II period, MAS became a leading advocate for both the quality of life and the economic vitality of the city's neighborhoods. Its accomplishments during this era included New York City's watershed landmarks preservation law of 1965, the preservation of Grand Central Terminal and Central Park in the 1970s, the redevelopment of Times Square in 1980s and 1990s, and support for noise-abatement regulations and antismoking laws. Society headquarters are located at 457 Madison Ave.

Gilmartin, Gregory F. *Shaping the City: New York and the Municipal Art Society* (New York: Clarkson Potter, 1995)

Leonard Benardo

Municipal Assistance Corporation for the City of New York. In the spring of 1975 the government of New York City found itself unable to sell its own bonds or short-term notes because of excessive spending, a situation that threatened City Hall's ability to meet its obligations. At the request of Gov Hugh Carey, a panel of four financial experts, led by the financier Felix Rohatyn of Lazard Freres and Co, was convened on Memorial Day weekend 1975 to submit a policy solution. On the panel's recommendation, the state in June 1975 created the Municipal Assistance Corporation, soon known as MAC or Big MAC, headed by a governing body of nine selected by the governor (four of these individuals on the recommendation of the mayor). Its duty initially was to sell $3 billion in long-term bonds, primarily to enable the city to redeem its short-term notes. MAC bonds carried a high interest rate and were excellent investments, but the initial debt offering generated little enthusiasm because of the city's shaky finances. Only when the New York City Teachers Retirement System made a last-minute purchase, on 17 Oct 1975, of $150 million in corporation bonds did City Hall avoid default. After state legislation in May 1978 MAC's mission was expanded, enabling the corporation to sell its bonds to finance new city capital projects and other activities, which City Hall did from 1979 to 1984. In 2002 the total outstanding debt for MAC bonds was approximately $2.9 billion. No longer issuing new debt, MAC's only purpose for the remainder of its existence, until 2009, is to oversee its outstanding debt, exchange this debt for lower interest rates if possible, and close its doors when the last of its bonds are redeemed at the end of 2008.

Kramer, Daniel C. *The Days of Wine and Roses Are Over: Governor Hugh Carey and New York State* (Lanham, Md: Univ Press of America, 1997)

Daniel C. Kramer

municipally owned electric companies. Although the electric utility industry was pioneered by privately owned companies in the 1880s, the Populist and Progressive reform movements of the late 19th and early 20th centuries led to demand for municipal ownership of the local electric utility in many smaller communities. The oldest surviving municipal electric utility in New York State was established in Jamestown (Chautauqua Co) in 1890. Ten additional municipal utilities were formed in the next decade, and by 1907 there were 47 in the state. While the number of municipally owned electric utilities in the nation declined by about one-third during the holding company movement of the 1920s, in New York State the number remained stable. In the early 21st century there are about 50 such firms, ranging in size from the Village of Silver Springs (Wyoming Co), with fewer than 1,000 customers and less than $300,000 in annual revenue, to the Jamestown Board of Public Utilities, with around 20,000 customers and $27 million in revenue. Only a handful of municipal utilities generate any of their own electricity; nearly all obtain their power directly from the New York Power Authority or cooperatively through the New York Municipal Power Agency.

American Public Power Association. *2002 Annual Directory and Statistical Report* (Gainesville, Fla: Naylor Publications, 2002)

Rudolph, Richard, and Scott Ridley. *Power Struggle: The Hundred-Year War over Electricity* (New York: Harper & Row, 1986)

US Department of Commerce and Labor, Bureau of the Census. *Central Electric Light and Power Stations, 1907* (Washington, DC: Government Printing Office, 1910)

William Hausman

Munnsville. Village (pop 437) in Stockbridge (Madison Co). Once noted for high-quality farm equipment (Munnsville Plow Co and predecessor companies, 1824–1920), it also produced woolen cloth, edge tools, and ironwork in 1860. Its former school buildings (vacated in 1997) house the Ferris Co, manufacturer of commercial mowers. A limestone quarry just beyond the southern limits of the village has been in operation for more than a century. Munnsville's former railroad station, now a residence, has been carefully restored.

William F. Helmer

Munsee. Most Indian people living in what is now New York City and the middle and lower Hudson regions spoke Munsee, a dialect of an Eastern Algonquian language known as Delaware. Munsee territory encompassed the northernmost portion of what present-day Delaware elders call Lenapehoking, from the Delaware words *lenape* (people) and *hoking* (land). Lenapehoking stretched across a broad swath of Mid-Atlantic upland forests and coastal lowlands between the Hudson and Delaware River valleys.

Prehistoric Archaeology

Paleo-Indian Period: 11,500–10,000 BP. Like all North American Indians, the Munsee had no written language and no recorded history. At best, they used now indecipherable petroglyphs or stick figures carved on rocks that served as mnemonics. We know them through archaeological excavations, Dutch and English archival records, and the oral tradition of their descendants. Archaeologically, they became an identifiable people only after 1,100 BP. Lenapehoking had been inhabited since Paleo-Indians arrived after the retreat of the Wisconsin glacier, a time when a park tundra environment sustained mastodon, caribou, and walrus, among other cold-adapted animals. One recognizes these hunters-gatherers from their exquisitely crafted implements: fluted spearpoints, knives, scrapers, and drills, all made from high-quality stones. Sites containing Paleo-Indian artifacts have been found on Staten Island, in Westchester Co, and at various locales in Greene and Orange Cos.

Archaic Period: 10,000–3,000 BP. As the climate warmed, glacial lakes, streams, and marshes abounded, and mixed forests covered the landscape. Nuts and berries sustained human beings and provided mast foods for deer, bear, turkeys, and other animals hunted by the earliest inhabitants. Trees provided firewood for warmth and cooking and saplings and bark for shelters; tree trunks were hollowed into dugout canoes. Heavy stone implements—including axes, adzes, and gouges—were essential for felling trees and clearing forests and were used by women as well to chop firewood, to crack bones to extract marrow, and for other domestic chores. Spears, the principal hunting weapons, consisted of spearpoints fastened to wooden shafts. These were thrust by hand or launched with a catapult-like spear-thrower. Mounted into short handles, the same points might serve as knives. Bolas, traps, snares, and deadfalls were other ways to capture game. Fish were caught in nets and weirs. Butchered animals provided meat and skins for clothing and containers, sinew and gut for sewing and binding, bones and antlers for making tools, and hooves for glue. Almost nothing was wasted. Women and children gathered up to 60% of the food: plants, seeds, roots, berries, nuts, birds' eggs, turtles, shellfish, and other edible and useful things. Nuts, seeds, and dried meats could be pulverized using milling stones and handheld mullers. Cooking pots were unknown, so most foods were eaten raw or roasted; however, water, meat, and plant ingredients enclosed in a skin or bark container could be cooked by immersing fire-heated stones into the liquid through a process called stone-boiling. About 4,000 BP, people carved stone bowls out of soapstone and talc. Such fire-resistant pots could be placed directly over a flame. Ceramic vessels also appeared about this time. Shelters made in Archaic times were probably temporary structures easily abandoned when families moved in search of food and raw materials. Where available, natural rock-shelters and caves were occupied during hunting and gathering forays.

Woodland Period: 3,000–400 BP. Early and Middle Woodland people (3,000–1,000 BP) continued the hunting-and-gathering traditions of earlier times. Most lives were prosaic, but more adventuresome cultures made extraordinary artifacts and engaged in elaborate burial rituals. Cult burials provide evidence of extensive trade networks in artifacts made from Lake Superior copper; shells from the Gulf Coast; and large, thin blades of colorful, fine-grained stones from Labrador, Ohio, the Dakotas, and other distant sources. Such cremations and burials also provide the earliest evidence of woven cloth and the use of tobacco for smoking. By Middle Woodland times the bow and arrow replaced the spear as the preferred hunting weapon.

Munsee and other Delaware Indians are usually associated with the Late Woodland period, 1,000–500 BP and forward. Garden vegetables including corn, bean, squash, and possibly sunflower supplemented foods from hunting, fishing, and gathering. The need to tend gardens caused people to settle down and build substantial houses and storage facilities. Once crops were harvested and stored, bands set out on fall hunting and nut-gathering trips. American chestnuts and certain acorns helped to sustain them throughout the winter, which was also the optimum time for hunting deer and bear. In late prehistoric times, the Munsee lived seemingly tranquil lives in small, unfortified communities. There is no evidence of harassment by the Iroquois nations, the Mohican (Mahican), or other Indians. Wigwams and round-ended longhouses were constructed on domed trellises made from saplings and covered with tree bark tied with bast fillets. Some longhouses measured 60 x 20 feet (18 x 6 m), and according to historic accounts occasionally housed 25 or more people. Wigwams were smaller and more circular. Smoke was vented through a roof opening, and a single doorway at the side provided entrance. Raised platforms overlaid with skins and furs provided seating during the day and sleeping places at night. Firewood was kept under the bunks, and tobacco, herbs, and corn were hung from roof poles. Storage pits dug at the ends of large houses provided easy access to food. Similar pits, suitably covered against rain or snow, were located outside the dwellings.

Clans and Marriages

Munsee communities dotted the landscape near streams, lakes, and seashores. With no centralized political authority and no chiefs before the coming of the Europeans, each group operated independently. There were three principal clan designations: Wolf, Turtle, and Turkey, and each may have had subdivisions. Affiliation was by birth, which served to regulate marriage and family responsibilities, among other things. For example, a Munsee woman of the Turtle lineage was admonished to marry a man from another lineage, be it Turkey, Wolf, or another subdivision of her own clan. Marriage was a simple agreement to live together. Descent was matrilineal. Members of the mothers' lineage cared for orphaned children. Initially, a couple resided in the wife's home, which was likely shared by other members of her lineage including mother, sisters, and their respective husbands and children. Work was gender specific. Women cared for the children and domestic affairs, tanned hides, made clothing, fashioned pottery vessels, tended gardens, gathered firewood, and, together with the children, foraged for edible foods and raw materials. Men hunted, fished, and did the heavy physical work. They cleared the forest, helped till garden soils, made dugout canoes, gathered saplings and bark for house construction, chipped stone tools and weapons, and made wooden bowls and utensils.

Spiritual Beliefs and Practices

The Munsee used herbal teas and poultices that were applied topically to alleviate internal disorders. Every woman knew the properties of common medications, but herbalists with special skills were highly regarded. To be effective, medicaments, whether made from plants, roots, leaves, or bark, had to be gathered in a ritually prescribed manner that placated the plants' spirit and enlisted its aid in the curative process. The Munsee believed in a single, all-powerful force whose thoughts created them. Having created the universe and all good things, this force delegated the maintenance of the system to lesser spirit beings. Of these, Mesingw, the Keeper of the Game, was especially important for safeguarding the animals while also permitting their occasional deaths to assuage human hunger and to provide skins and sinews needed for clothing, blankets, and other items. The beneficent creator provided only wholesome and useful things, but the creator's counterpart, Mahtantu, put the thorns on berry bushes and created poisonous snakes, useless plants, and undesirable things. This perverse being was not a devil in the Christian sense, for the Munsee had no conception of hell. In the afterlife, the good enjoyed a provident and peaceful place, while evildoers were barred from participation. There were no churches, no prescribed prayers, and few rituals. Individuals communicated directly with spirit beings. *—HCK*

Historic Contact

Giovanni da Verrazano in 1524 and Robert Juet's account of Henry Hudson's voyage in 1609 provide the earliest known recorded contact with the Munsee. The number of such accounts rose as colonists from several northern European nations moved to New Netherland settlements established by the Dutch West India Co during the early 1600s along the lower Hudson River, at New Amsterdam, and at Wiltwijck [now Kingston, Ulster Co]. Colonial chroniclers described a populous hunting, farming, and fishing people numbering perhaps as many as 12,000 living in bark and mat–covered frame houses scattered along the region's rivers, streams, bays, and beaches.

Small groups of Munsee houses clustered at and around the mouths of streams flowing into New York Harbor, at the Hudson River estuary, at the western end of Long Island, and at the uppermost reaches of the Delaware River. The more prominent of these locales included Canarsee, Massapequa, Matinecock, and Rockaway on Long Island; Esopus, Tappan, and Haverstraw [Rockland Co], and Wiechquaeskeck [now Dobbs Ferry, Westchester Co] along the Hudson; and the great Minisink Island town in the Delaware River [now Sussex Co, NJ]. Often referred to as band homelands, they were more properly stretches of well-drained and watered lands of families, clans, and friends linked to one another through succeeding generations of women.

Particularly astute chiefs, such as Oratam of the Hackensack and the Massapequa sachem Tackapousha, became intermediaries between Indian communities and colonists. Sachems presided over exchanges of pelts, local produce, and land for metal tools, textiles, and other European imports that grew indispensable as Munsees gave up stone tools and other traditional manufactures. Diplomacy became important as Munsee communities, devastated by new epidemic diseases, found themselves pressed between increasingly rapacious colonial neighbors and Mohawk, Mohican, and other powerful interior Indian nations.

Conflicts such as Kieft's War (1640–45) and the two Esopus Wars (1659–60, 1663–64); outbreaks of smallpox, malaria, and measles between 1633 and 1691; and emigration of dispossessed communities forced by deed or treaty to part with no less than 90% of their best ancestral lands reduced the Munsee population to less than 10% of its aboriginal level by 1700. Many Munsees moved beyond the borders of their ancient homeland to the Susquehanna Valley or farther west or north to Ohio or Canada. Those who did not move away found themselves increasingly restricted to small backcountry settlements and reservations set aside on rocky hills, swamps, pine barrens, and other lands unwanted by colonists. Unable to make their living on such poor tracts, formerly sedentary Munsees took up what colonists called a "strolling" life, wandering from place to place in and beyond the borders of their homeland in search of sustenance and security. Traveling as far as Maine, Montreal, and the Mississippi Valley, they mixed with and married European colonists, enslaved and free Africans, and Indians from other places.

Munsee people were increasingly drawn into the colonial cash economy during the 1700s. Women made money as house servants, farmhands, herbalists, and basket weavers. Some Munsee men shipped out on whalers, fishing boats, and merchantmen sailing from Oyster Bay, Huntington, and other New York harbors. Most, however, worked as trappers, guides, and laborers. Support and shelter could also be had in Protestant Indian mission settlements like Shekomeko in Dutchess Co established in and around their ancestral lands during the 1730s and 1740s. In addition, the Munsee received cash and goods in return for the sale of their remaining lands in the province, most of which were sold by 1760.

Munsee men also found employment as military auxiliaries, trackers, messengers, and porters during the four imperial wars fought between France and England between 1697 and 1763. Sir William Johnson, appointed first Crown superintendent of Indian Affairs in 1755, clothed and armed Munsee warriors willing to fight for the British while provisioning and protecting their families during the French and Indian War (1754–63). French authorities did the same for other Munsees fighting alongside their soldiers. After the war Munsees living along the upper reaches of the Chemung River around present-day Corning (Steuben Co) and Elmira joined the coalition of western Indians resisting British expansion west of the Alleghenies in Pontiac's War (1763–64). Other Munsee men were among the warriors sent by Johnson to destroy Chemung Valley towns in 1764.

Some Munsees refusing to abandon their homeland had joined Christian Indian mission communities at Schaghticoke, Conn, Stockbridge, Mass, and Brotherton [now Indian Mills, NJ] by the time Treaty of Fort Stanwix restored peace along the frontier in 1768. Others moved west beyond the Catskills to multicultural Indian towns at Unadilla [now Nichols, Tioga Co], Oquaga [now Windsor, Broome Co], and Otsiningo [now Binghamton] along the North Branch of the Susquehanna River. The Revolutionary War uprooted most of these communities. Munsees and other Indians loyal to the Crown had to move to Fort Niagara [now in Porter, Niagara Co] after rebel troops burned their Susquehanna Valley towns in 1778. Most of them ultimately joined expatriate Iroquois, accepting homes on the Six Nations Reserve established by the Crown in Canada after the Revolutionary War. Munsees who remained neutral often moved west as well, finally settling along the banks of the Thames River at Muncietown, also in Canada. Brotherton and Stockbridge Munsees who supported the victorious rebels also were dislocated by the conflict. Most were compelled to move to present-day Madison and Oneida Cos among Oneidas who supported the patriot cause between 1785 and 1802. Many of these Munsees ultimately joined Oneidas in their westward exile in the 1820s and 1830s.

Those who remained in their ancestral homeland continued to reside in remote or unwanted back lots. All but the most conservative elders gradually adopted American ways, marrying non-Indians, forgetting the Munsee language and customs, and disappearing into the population. Traditions of Indian ancestry, however, have persisted in many families.

Archaeological Sites

Some New York archaeological sites, such as the Paleo-Indian Port Mobil (Richmond Co) and Dutchess Quarry Caves (Orange Co) sites, the Archaic period shell middens at Croton Point and Piping Rock (Westchester Co), the Woodland period locales such as the many rock-shelters in the Hudson Highlands, and the village site at Clasons Point (Bronx Co), contain deposits primarily associated with particular periods of aboriginal occupation. Others, such as the Mohonk (Ulster Co) and Sylvan Lake (Dutchess Co) rock-shelters and the Bowman's Brook site (Richmond Co), preserve remains of many periods of occupation. And a very few, such as the Grapes site (preserving the pattern of an Esopus longhouse in Ulster Co), the Ward's Point National Historic Landmark (Richmond Co), and Fort Massapeag National Historic Landmark (Nassau Co), bridge the divide between the archaeological and written record of human occupation in Munsee country. —*RSG*

Funk, Robert E. *Recent Contributions to Hudson Valley Prehistory,* Memoir 22 (Albany: NYS Museum and Univ of the State of New York, 1976)

Grumet, Robert S. *The Lenapes* (New York: Chelsea House, 1989)

———. *Historic Contact: Indian People and Colonists in Today's Northeastern United States in the 16th through 18th Centuries* (Norman: Univ of Oklahoma Press, 1995)

Kraft, Herbert C. *The Lenape-Delaware Indian Heritage: 10,000 BC to AD 2000* (Elizabeth, NJ: Lenape Books, 2002)

Weslager, C. A. *The Delaware Indians: A History* (New Brunswick, NJ: Rutgers Univ Press, 1972)

Robert S. Grumet, Herbert C. Kraft

Munsell, Joel (*b* Northfield, Mass, ?14 Apr 1808; *d* Albany, 15 Jan 1880). Printer, antiquarian, and historian. The son of a wagon maker in Northfield, Munsell had little formal schooling and worked with his father from the age of 14 until being apprenticed at age 17 to a Greenfield, Mass, printing office in 1825. In 1826 he apprenticed under John Denio, who ran a Greenfield bookshop and printed the *Greenfield Gazette and Franklin County Advertiser.* Munsell came to Albany in May 1827 with his employer after Denio sold the Greenfield paper to establish a bookshop in Albany. While a journeyman printer in Albany, Munsell served as clerk for Denio, worked for Albany printer Solomon Southwick, and introduced the *Albany Minerva* (1828), an eight-page literary newspaper, on 1 Jan 1828. Munsell stopped publication in April 1828 to take a better position offered by Denio.

Munsell was a printer in several Albany shops from 1830 until 1834 when he began producing and printing the *Microscope* (1834–36) with Henry D. Stone. In October 1836 Munsell purchased a small Albany print shop at 58 State St and began printing books, pamphlets, newspapers, and ephemera as well as contract jobs for the state. He was an early leader in publishing scholarly Americana. His first significant original work was the *Outlines of the History of Printing* (1839). Among his most important works are the 10-volume *Annals of Albany* (1849–59) and the 4-volume *Collections on the History of Albany* (1865–71). Both reproduce materials relating to the history of Albany and include transcriptions of common council meetings, church records, newspaper items, and biographical materials. Munsell was a meticulous printer, renowned for his discriminating choice of paper, careful composition, and fine typography. He was a dedicated antiquarian and a prolific publisher and is responsible for preserving and making accessible countless records important to the history of Albany, New York State, and the northeast. After his death, Munsell's sons succeeded him in business until the firm was dissolved in 1895.

Edelstein, David. *Joel Munsell: Printer and Antiquarian* (New York: Columbia Univ Press, 1950)

Suzan D. Friedlander

Munsey Park. Village (pop 2,632) in North Hempstead (Nassau Co). Restaurateur Louis Sherry's 300-acre (121 ha) estate was acquired in 1922 by Frank A. Munsey, publisher of the *New York Evening Sun* and *New York Herald.* When he died three years later, he left the estate to the Metropolitan Museum of Art, which developed it and named the streets after American artists such as Peale and Copley. The village incorporated in 1930; despite the depression, its population more than tripled between 1930 and 1940. The development of the exclusive residential community was completed by 1960.

Richard A. Winsche

Munson-Williams-Proctor Arts Institute. Regional fine arts center located at 310 Genesee St in Utica and featuring an art museum, art instruction, and a performing arts program. In 1919 Maria Williams Proctor, her husband, and brother-in-law chartered the institute as a "an artistic, musical and social center." It was named after three generations of Maria's family. Her grandfather, Alfred Munson, was a notable Utica textile manufacturer. Her mother, Helen Williams, married to Utica lawyer James Williams, established the core of the family collection of decorative and fine arts and built the Italianate mansion, Fountain Elms (1850), which continues to house some of these items. The Munson-Williams-Proctor Arts Institute (MWPAI) first opened to the public in May 1936, shortly after Maria's death. In June 1941 it launched the School of Art, offering instruction to both adults and children. In 1960, to accommodate the expanding art collection, a modern gallery building, designed by Philip Johnson, opened adjacent to Fountain Elms, which then became MWPAI's Decorative Arts Department. In 1995 the Education Wing was built to join the two museum buildings. At the beginning of the 21st century, fine arts highlights of MWPAI Museum of Art include Thomas Cole's four-part painting *The Voyage of Life,* works by Frederic Church and Winslow Homer, and New York school paintings of the 1940s and 1950s. The decorative arts collection includes much fine American silver, among other items. The institute's Performing Arts Division presents more than 100 events year-round. Its School of Art has an enrollment of 2,500. A joint program with Pratt Institute enables BFA candidates to study for two years in Utica and then complete degree work at Pratt in New York City. The MWPAI is administered by 12 trustees and employed about 200 persons in 2002.

Joseph G. Schmidt

murals. The painting of architectural spaces gained recognition in New York State in the last quarter of the 19th century when builders working on projects of notable scale and cost began hiring trained artists to create equally grand interior wall decoration. Builders included the state, municipalities, and entrepreneurs of the post–Civil War economy. Mural subjects were generally scenes of history or allegory designed to celebrate or instruct. Beginning in the 1930s, abstract designs intended to soothe or distract prevailed and were intended for culturally mixed audiences experiencing the Great Depression. As with other murals, these were specifically relevant to a place, both the building and its locale, and to an idea or function. Urban renewal of the 1960s provided expanses of blank exterior wall as canvases for trained and untrained artists alike, changing mural art into an outdoor form. Between the work of community muralists and graffiti artists, unadorned walls were uncommon by the end of the 20th century.

Civil War to the Depression

Early mural examples include several in the New York State Capitol (1867–99), such as the 1878 Assembly Chamber paintings of William Morris Hunt (1824–79), *The Discoverer* and *The Flight of Night.* Other works were destroyed in the 1911 Capitol fire, including those of William de Leftwich Dodge (1867–1935) and Will H. Low (1853–1932). In the decades that followed, municipalities and businesses statewide commissioned murals as gestures of local or regional pride, education, or inspiration. When the New York City Board of Education mandated permanent artworks in new school buildings in 1901, mural painting was reinforced as community or social art. The first mural executed under this policy was *Opening the Erie Canal* by Charles Yardley Turner (1850–1919) for DeWitt Clinton High School [1905; now in the Bronx].

At Roycroft, in East Aurora (Erie Co), landscapist Alexis Jean Fournier (1865–1948) painted the wonders of the world and other subjects *ca* 1910 in his signature Barbizon style, helping define the aesthetic of the community. In 1911 Manhattan's American Museum of Natural History asked Charles R. Knight (1874–1953) to imagine and render murals of extinct animals in natural settings, the same year N. C. Wyeth (1882–1945) painted his earliest mural, now lost, on a historic theme for Hotel Utica. Wyeth received private mural commissions from the 1920s to 1945 in New York City for historic subjects that included *Life of the Pilgrims* for Metropolitan Life Insurance. Around 1927 African American artist Aaron Douglas (1899–1979) painted a mural series for the Club Ebony inspired by Harlem nightlife, an evolution in the art form away from romanticized history and allegory toward social realism, a change seen in two series of 1929–31 done by muralists of different generations: the allegorical *Frontiers Unfettered by Any Frowning Fortress* and *Talents Diversified Find Vent in Myriad Form* for Buffalo's City Hall by William de Leftwich Dodge, and the more vernacular *America Today* at Manhattan's New School for Social Research by Thomas Hart Benton.

New Deal Muralists

The work of Mexican muralists was familiar by 1930, and one of the best-known teachers and practitioners, Diego Rivera (1886–1957), was commissioned in 1933 to paint a large fresco in Manhattan's Rockefeller Center RCA Building (now GE Building). When Rivera included an image of the Soviet leader Lenin and then refused to paint it out, the mural was destroyed before he could complete it. This became a national benchmark for artistic freedom and censorship. Rivera's effort was replaced with *American Progress* by Spaniard José Maria Sert (1876–1945), glorifying Abraham Lincoln, Ralph Waldo Emerson, and the towers of Rockefeller Center itself.

During the depression dozens of muralists went to work in New York State under federal programs, best known of which is the Federal Art Project of the Works Progress Administration (1935–39; later Work Projects Administration, 1939–43, WPA]. Designed to employ artists and to bring citizens into daily contact with art, these projects hired muralists to enhance post offices, schools, and other public spaces. WPA murals survive in over 170 locales across the state, some sites with several works by one artist or more, including women and minority artists.

Lucienne Bloch (1909–99) painted *Evolution of Music* in Manhattan's George Washington High School in 1936–38; Marion Greenwood (1909–70) completed the fresco *Planned Community Life* for Brooklyn's Red Hook Houses in 1940. For post offices, Georgina Klitgaard (1893–1976) painted *The Hambletonian Stake* in Goshen (Orange Co) in 1937 and *View of Poughkeepsie about 1840* in Poughkeepsie in 1940; Amy Jones (1899–1992) completed *Recording the Victory* in Painted Post (Steuben Co) in 1939 and *The Glen Family Spared by French Indians* in Scotia (Schenectady Co) in 1941; and Victoria Huntley (1900–71) produced *Fiddler's Green* in Springville (Erie Co) in 1938.

While many WPA artists were associated with New York City—particularly the Art Students League where muralists Thomas Hart Benton and William Palmer (1906–87) taught in the 1920s and 1930s—several were born, studied, and gained regional acclaim elsewhere in the state. Pascal Scime (*fl* 1935) and Angelo Scibetta (1902–62) worked together and separately from 1934 to 1940 at 10 sites in Buffalo, Barker (Niagara Co), and Hamburg (Erie Co), producing scenes of historic and daily life. Eugene M. Dyczkowski (1899–1987) painted *Industrial Activities* and *Cultural Activities* in Buffalo's Burgard Vocational High School in 1938 and *Defending Forts* at the US Army 28th Infantry Post at Fort Niagara [now in Porter, Niagara Co] in 1939. The Fort Niagara post contains murals by several artists, including Ernst Wille (*ca* 1916–), a German World War II prisoner of war at the fort, who painted *American History ca* 1945–46. The Rochester area's most prolific muralist was Carl W. Peters (1897–1980), commissioned for *Evolution of Contemporary Commerce in Rochester* by Genesee Valley Trust bank in 1930. His WPA work included 12 murals for three high schools—Madison, 1937; West (now Joseph C. Wilson), 1938; and Charlotte, 1942—with subjects of local history, American Indian, and pioneer families, and *From Painting Man to Modern Lines, Life of Contemplation,* and *Life of Action.*

Although the majority of murals were painted for post offices, they were also done for other locations. Tom Loftin Johnson (1900–?) painted *Fifteen Decisive Battles of the World* at the US Military Academy at West Point (Orange Co) in 1934–36 and others at two other military sites. The Hempstead Fire House (Nassau Co) had six murals done by Carl Noble (*fl* 1930s) in 1938 on the subject of firefighting. Harold Lehman (1913–) painted *Man's Daily Bread* at Riker's Island Penitentiary (Bronx Co) in 1940 (destroyed 1962). James D. Brooks (1906–92) painted *Flight,* probably the state's largest single WPA mural at 12 x 235 feet (3.5 x 71.5 m) for the Marine Air Terminal at La Guardia Airport (Queens Co) from 1935 to 1942 (now painted over). Manhattan had a great variety of mural sites. Aaron Douglas did his best-known series, *Aspects of Negro Life,* for the Cullen Branch Library (now Schomburg Center for Research in Black Culture) in Harlem in 1934, four pieces beginning with *The Negro in an African Setting.* Fellow African Americans Vertis Hayes (1911–99) and Charles Alston (1907–77) produced murals for Harlem Hospital entitled *Pursuit of Happiness* (1936–37), and *Magic and Medicine* and *Modern Medicine* (1936–40), respectively. Between 1934 and 1938 Attilio Pusteria (1862–1941) and others executed more than 30 murals including "Administration of Justice," studies of contemporary and old New York, and classical subjects in Manhattan's New York County Court House. Well-known figurative artist Moses Soyer (1899–1974) painted 10 WPA murals. Reginald Marsh (1898–1954) and assistants painted scenes of New York Harbor in the rotunda of the US Custom House at Bowling Green in Manhattan in 1936–37 under the Treasury Relief Art Project.

Most WPA murals were done in stylized realism, but some abstract and modern artists worked on WPA commissions in New York City or surrounding boroughs and for the 1939 New York World's Fair. These include Hugo Gellert (1892–1985), Anton Refregier (1905–79), Ilya Bolotowsky (1907–81), and Philip Guston (1913–80).

Because WPA murals had to be proposed by artists and approved by hosting institutions, questions of content, style, and intention were always evident: rejections sometimes occurred, as did controversy. Among WPA artists, a few openly espoused socialism, communism, or Marxism. The Relief Bill of 1940 required a loyalty oath from all Federal Art Project artists. When August Henkel (1880–1961) refused to sign, his murals at Brooklyn's Floyd Bennett Municipal Airport were destroyed, an incident contributing to the cessation of the program in 1943.

Recent Decades

Mural art in New York State continued after World War II with the UN mural competition of 1955 and public and private commissions. Stuart Davis (1892–1964), an assistant to Diego Rivera in 1933 at Rockefeller Center, did a WPA mural for Brooklyn's Williamsburg Houses *ca* 1938 (now moved) and was one of the UN artists. Hans Hofmann (1880–1966) designed a mural for Manhattan's High School of Graphic Communication Arts in the 1950s. Thomas Hart Benton painted some of his last murals for the New York Power Authority under Robert Moses: *Expedition of Jacques Cartier* for its facility at

Massena (St. Lawrence Co) in 1957 and *Father Louis Hennepin at Niagara Falls* for the Niagara Power Project in Lewiston in 1958–61. Hugo Gellert produced four murals in 1959 for the United Housing Federation at Manhattan's Seward Park cooperative; they were saved by community activism in 1998. Josef Albers (1888–1976) produced two murals entitled *Growth* for the Rochester Institute of Technology in 1969. Albers and Ben Shahn (1898–1969), a WPA post office muralist *(America at Work* and *The First Amendment,* in the Bronx and Queens, 1939 and 1941), also produced wall mosaics in New York State during the 1960s. Controversy greeted the 1974 mural by Romare Bearden (1911–88) for Lincoln Hospital (Bronx Co) because it depicted bare-breasted women and emphasized African American images over Latino, unbalanced for the hospital's local population; the completed mural was not installed for several years. Renowned African American artist Jacob Lawrence (1917–2000) designed a 72 ft (22 m) mural for Manhattan's Times Square Subway Station, destined to be installed in 2001 after his death.

Murals remained a vehicle for Keith Haring (1958–90), who painted at parks, handball courts, children's hospitals, and community centers in Manhattan and at Dobbs Ferry (Westchester Co) beginning in 1983 and addressing contemporary problems of drugs and AIDS, including *Crack Is Wack* (1986) and *Don't Believe the Hype* (1988). A permanent indoor mural for Woodhull Hospital in Brooklyn was painted in 1986.

In 1982 the New York City Council passed the Percent for Art law requiring 1% of the budget for construction of certain city-owned properties be spent on artwork. Approximately 160 pieces of art have been produced through this program. A small number have been painted murals, but other forms have also been supported. A similar initiative was passed by the New York City School Construction Authority in 1989. The Adopt-a-Mural program of Manhattan's Municipal Arts Society, begun in 1991, led the country in raising public awareness of 20th-century murals, providing funds to identify and restore public murals by artists Alston, Benton, Bolotowsky, and others.

Cohen, Phyllis Samitz. *Adopt-a-Mural* (New York: Municipal Art Society, Art Commission of the City of New York, 1991)

Falk, Peter Hastings, ed. *Who Was Who in American Art, 1564–1975* (Madison, Conn: Sound View Press, 1999)

O'Connor, Francis V. *Art for the Millions: Essays from the 1930s by Artists and Administrators of the WPA Federal Art Project* (Greenwich, Conn: New York Graphic Society, 1973)

Riggs, Thomas, ed. *St. James Guide to Black Artists* (Detroit: St. James Press, 1997)

"Extant Murals and Sculptures from the Government Art Projects of the 1930s in New York State," http://lsb.syr.edu/projects/wpafolder/nyartlist.html

David F. Martin and Michael L. James

Murphy, Charles F(rancis) (*b* New York City, 20 June 1858; *d* New York City, 25 Apr 1924). Political leader. Murphy followed the traditional New York City political path of being born in a tenement district, opening a saloon, sponsoring athletic clubs, and then entering politics. In 1902 he became the leader of Tammany Hall, the New York City political machine. Murphy was, in terms of his victories, the greatest boss Tammany Hall ever enjoyed and, in his social conscience, the most progressive. A quiet man, Murphy had a knack for choosing the right person for the right position in city government, resulting in an unprecedented string of election triumphs for the Democratic Party, including the election of Mayors William J. Gaynor and John F. Hylan, and Govs John Alden Dix, William Sulzer, and Alfred E. Smith. He was the only Tammany boss to support social reform causes, backing Robert F. Wagner Sr's and Al Smith's efforts to create a fire safety code in the wake of the Triangle Shirtwaist Factory fire and, until his death in 1924, playing a leading role in Smith's efforts to become the first member of the new generation of urban immigrants to become president.

Weiss, Nancy. *Charles Frances Murphy, 1858–1924* (Northampton, Mass: Smith College Press, 1968)

Robert A. Slayton

Murray. Town (pop 4,892) in E Orleans Co. Formed in 1808 and settled in 1809, Murray was crossed by the Ridge Rd, the Erie Canal (1824), and the Niagara Falls Branch of the New York Central (1852). Medina sandstone was quarried extensively at Hulberton, and manufacturing and food processing was carried out in the village of Holley. Farming continues, and some residents commute to Rochester.

Marsha DeFilipps

Murray, William H(enry) H(arrison) (*b* Guilford, Conn, 26 Apr 1840; *d* Guilford, 3 Mar 1904). Travel writer. He graduated from Yale College in 1862 and married Isadora Hull, a woman who shared his passion for the outdoors. He went on to study at the East Windsor Theological Seminary in Connecticut and in 1868 accepted the prestigious position of pastor at Park Street Congregational Church in Boston, a leader of evangelical Congregationalism. Years before, he began vacationing on Raquette Lake in the Adirondacks. Based on his own travels, Murray wrote *Adventures in the Wilderness; or, Camp-Life in the Adirondacks.* The guidebook depicted the Adirondacks as offering abundant sport, health, and hospitable accommodations. It immediately became popular and encouraged thousands to travel to the region. A backlash of criticism, however, filled magazines and newspapers by the summer of 1869 and several years to follow. Though many vacationers, sometimes dubbed Murray's Fools, did not find the comfortable lodgings and dramatic improvements of health as promised in Murray's book, the Adirondacks grew in popularity as a vacation destination. In 1875 Murray established his own weekly newspaper, *The Golden Rule,* which printed more of his Adirondack tales, including his first fictional stories about the trapper John Norton (published in 1877 in book form as *Adirondack Tales*). After retiring from the ministry in 1879, Murray tried ranching in Texas and operated a small restaurant in Montreal before returning to the house where he was born.

De Sormo, Maitland. *The "Murray Rush" in Retrospect; or, With the Multitude in the Adirondacks* (Saranac Lake, NY: Adirondack Yesteryears, 1989)

Murray, William H. H. *Adventures in the Wilderness.* Ed. William K. Verner (1869; repr Syracuse: Syracuse Univ Press, 1970)

Strauss, David. "Toward a Consumer Culture: 'Adirondack Murray' and the Wilderness Vacation," *American Quarterly* 19 (Summer 1987): 270–86

Douglas McCombs

Museum of Modern Art (MoMA). Lillie P. Bliss, Mary Quinn Sullivan, and Abby Aldrich Rockefeller founded New York City's Museum of Modern Art in 1929 to house and display modern art exclusively. From its original core collection of paintings and sculpture, MoMA has expanded to include departments of photography, architecture and design, film and video, painting and sculpture, drawings, and prints and illustrated books. The permanent collection of nearly 100,000 works reflects many different schools of modern and contemporary art, including works by Henri Matisse, Pablo Picasso, Vincent Van Gogh, Jasper Johns, René Magritte, Jackson Pollock, and Piet Mondrian. It also has extensive collections of films, film stills, books, and documents. First housed on 57th St, the museum moved to West 53d St near 5th Ave in 1932. A new building designed in the International style by Philip Goodwin and Edward Durell Stone opened at the site in 1939. Beginning in 2001 the glass and steel building underwent extensive changes to provide almost twice the former capacity. Architect Yoshio Taniguchi's renovation plans included two new buildings framing the Sculpture Garden, with the seven-story Gallery Building displaying the main collection, the eight-story Education and Research Center containing auditoriums, classrooms, and study centers, and the Library and Archives taking up the top three floors of the new center and housing resources on more than 70,000 artists. In addition to the expanded facility in Manhattan, with a planned opening in 2005, a permanent branch of MoMA was opened in Long Island City (Queens Co) on 29 June 2002. At the beginning of the 21st century MoMA had an endowment of $400 million and received about 1.5 million visitors annually.

Barr, Alfred. *The Museum of Modern Art: Its History and Collections* (New York: Museum of Modern Art, 1981)

Museum of Modern Art, http://www.MoMA.org

Dorothy M. Browne

mushrooms. Fungi that possess large, fleshy, fruiting bodies as well as an extensive, long-lived, rootlike network of microscopic tubes, the mycelium, from which the short-lived, fruiting bodies arise each season. Single-celled spores form on the fruiting bodies and disperse in air currents to start a new generation of organisms. Many mushrooms form symbiotic relationships, or mycorrhizae, with forest trees and other plants in which nutrients are exchanged. This relationship makes mushrooms particularly important for New York State with its extensive forested lands. The state is estimated to have several thousand species of mushrooms. Some of the common edible ones are yellow morel *(Morchella esculenta)*, chanterelle *(Cantharellus cibarius)*, king bolete *(Boletus edulus)*, sulphur shelf *(Laetiporus sulphureus)*, giant puffball *(Langermannia gigantea)*, and "field mushrooms" of various types *(Agaricus)*. Some poisonous varieties include destroying angel *(Amanita virosa)*, jack-o-lantern *(Omphalotus illudens)*, fly agaric *(Amanita muscaria)*, and deadly galerina *(Galerina autumnalis)*. Common wood rot fungi are artist's conk *(Gano-*

derma applanatum), turkey tail *(Coriolus versicolor),* birch polypore *(Piptoporus betulinus),* and tinder polypore *(Fomes fomentarius).* George F. Atkinson (1854–1918) of Cornell University, William A. Murrill (1869–1957) of the New York Botanical Garden, Charles H. Peck (1833–1917) of the New York State Museum, Josiah L. Lowe (1905–97) of Syracuse University, and others have made New York State a center of the scientific study of mushrooms.

The Iroquois were and are fond of edible fungi, diced and boiled in soups. British settlers made poor use of this food source, tending to regard all mushrooms as poisonous, although immigrants from continental Europe did not. By the 1890s wild mushrooms gathered in spring and fall commanded high prices in New York City, and commercial growing operations (the technology had been developed in the sewers of Paris some years earlier) soon followed. Interest in edible wild mushrooms revived in the 1960s and composer John Cage and botanist Guy Nearing founded the New York Mycological Society, headquartered at Manhattan's American Museum of Natural History. The Central New York Mycological Society has operated from Syracuse since 1980. By 1992–93 New York State growers produced 4,500 lbs (2,000 kg) of mushrooms, mainly *Agaricus bisporus,* with a cash value of near $4 million.

Bessette, Alan E., Arleen R. Bessette, and William C. Roody. *North American Boletes: A Color Guide to the Fleshy Pored Mushrooms* (Syracuse: Syracuse Univ Press, 2000)

Phillips, Roger. *Mushrooms of North America* (Boston: Little, Brown, 1991)

John Haines

musical instrument manufacture. Though one Geoffrey Stafford reportedly made lutes and violins in Albany and Manhattan about 1700, few professional instrument makers worked in the Colony of New York before the 1770s. Sheet metal for brass instruments was scarce, and keyboard manufacture was limited to a few ambitious artisans. After the American Revolution, import embargoes and tariffs spurred local production, much of it by recent immigrants. Manufacture of instruments accelerated after 1800 as small workshops using water-powered tools sprang up around eastern New York State. Militia bands and other players depended on these shops for inexpensive flutes, clarinets, and bassoons based on British prototypes. Some producers branched out into related enterprises: William Whiteley, a Utica woodwind maker active from about 1810, published one of America's first music instruction books in 1816. Improved transport, patent protection, and increasing demand for luxury goods promoted manufacture in New York City. Flute makers William Hall and John Firth began a retail music business in 1821. In 1833 Sylvanus Pond came from Albany to join Firth and Hall, and their firm and its successors became the nation's foremost mid-19th-century music retailers. Drum making emerged after 1850 in Herkimer Co, a center for cheese production, with the same coopers presumably making both drums and drum-shaped cheese boxes.

Social upheaval in Europe in 1848 brought an influx of instrument makers and musicians. Familiar with advances in instrument design abroad and insistent upon quality, these immigrants raised standards and elevated the status of musical performance. Stringed instrument making, difficult to mechanize, was pursued by specialists such as German guitar maker Christian Frederick Martin, who immigrated to Manhattan in 1833 and moved to Nazareth, Pa, in 1838. The Gretsch company was founded in Brooklyn by German luthier Friedrich Gretsch in 1883, and the Epiphone company was founded by Greek immigrant Anastasios Stathopoulo in 1904. Les Paul made the first solid-body electric guitar in the Manhattan Epiphone factory in 1941.

Englishman John F. Browne manufactured prizewinning harps in Manhattan from about 1843, and they sold widely in the South before the Civil War. Among the state's few prominent violin makers during this period was William Sidney Mount, a painter who lived on Long Island. In 1852 Mount patented an odd-shaped violin called the Cradle of Harmony, the outcome of experiments begun in 1837. About 1900 further waves of immigration brought outstanding Italian mandolin makers to New York City. People of other ethnic groups made, and still make, distinctive folk instruments throughout the state.

Alfred G. Badger, an outstanding flute maker, worked in Utica and Buffalo before establishing himself in New York City in 1845. Badger was one of the first Americans to promote silver, Boehm-system flutes, which have become the standard; he also pioneered the use of ebonite, a durable synthetic material invented by Charles Goodyear. Theodore Berteling moved from Boston to New York City in about 1857, and many orchestral performers favored his patented woodwinds. Large-scale fabrication of trumpets, horns, and other brasses never took root in New York State, but major brass instrument retailers kept headquarters in New York City while controlling factories elsewhere. John F. Stratton started a brass instrument shop in Manhattan in 1859, and it thrived with Civil War demand.

Piano making has a long history in New York State. Labor unrest led journeymen to form the cooperative New-York Pianoforte Manufacturing Co (1837–40), but the experiment failed. Piano manufacture leaped forward when the German Henry Steinway opened a Manhattan factory in 1853. Innovative in tonal design, construction, and promotion, Steinway and Sons became world famous, and the company began moving to a large factory in Long Island City (Queens Co) around 1873. Other piano manufacturers in the state included Kohler and Campbell (1896) and Winter and Co (1903) in New York City, and the Weber Piano Co (1852) with factories in New York City and East Rochester.

George Prince and Co began manufacturing reed organs in Buffalo before the Civil War, and after the war New York State led the country in manufacturing sophisticated instruments, which were conveniently shipped by rail and water. Churches throughout the nation received pipe organs from such Manhattan firms as Henry Erben and Co, active after 1827, and Hilborne and Frank Roosevelt, who built hundreds of noteworthy organs between 1872 and 1893. Robert Hope-Jones, an eccentric English organ builder and telephone engineer, opened his Electric Organ Co in Elmira in 1907, and his inventions were incorporated into Wurlitzer theater organs, constructed in North Tonawanda (Niagara Co) beginning in 1910. Manufacturers of automatic organs and player pianos included Aeolian in Manhattan (1885) and the Q-R-S company in Buffalo (1900).

The Russian physicist Leon Theremin's eponymous theremin, produced in Manhattan and licensed to the city's Radio Corporation of America (RCA) in 1929, was a milestone in the development of electronic instruments. Theremin's work was continued by Robert A. Moog, who began manufacturing theremin kits in 1961 and synthesizers in Trumansburg (Tompkins Co) in 1965. Other advances in musical electronics occurred after 1959 at the Columbia-Princeton Electronic Music Center in Manhattan.

The Great Depression, the radio and the phonograph, and finally World War II decimated instrument manufacturers. With exceptions such as Steinway and Sons, Woodstock Percussion of Shokan (Ulster Co), and American Kazoo Co in Eden (Erie Co), by the late 20th century the state's reputation for instrument making rested with small workshops, notably of William Kramer-Harrison, Michael Tobias, and Thomas Humphrey, and crafters replicating antique instruments such as harpsichords and baroque flutes.

Groce, Nancy. *Musical Instrument Makers of New York: A Directory of 18th- and 19th-Century Urban Craftsmen* (Stuyvesant, NY: Pendragon Press, 1991)

Libin, Laurence. *American Musical Instruments in the Metropolitan Museum of Art* (New York: Metropolitan Museum of Art and Norton, 1985)

Ogasapian, John. *Organ Building in New York City: 1700–1900* (Braintree, Mass: Organ Literature Foundation, 1977)

Laurence Libin

musical theater. To American audiences, a "musical" is a play, serious or comic, whose songs, dances, and production elements are all closely integrated with its story. The musical was developed in Manhattan's theater district, which has remained its home. Over the course of the 19th century this district gradually moved uptown, from Lower Manhattan in the early decades of the century, to lower Broadway around Astor Place in midcentury, to Union Square and 14th St from 1870 to 1900. After the turn of the century, the theater district moved to the Times Square area, where it is associated with Broadway, though relatively few theaters are actually on Broadway. While the theater district is the home of most musicals, in recent decades some important musicals have originated off Broadway in different regions of Manhattan.

ORIGINS

Through ballad operas, minstrel shows, and other genres of theatrical performances with singing, New York City audiences were long accustomed to hearing musical entertainments on stage. The diverse roots of the modern musical were exemplified in 1866, when a Parisian female ballet troupe arrived in New York City to find that the theater where it was scheduled to perform had burned down. The producers of a melodrama scheduled to open at about the same time decided to help the dancers out by incorporating dancing and music into their play. *The Black Crook,* named after a shepherd's crook, opened at Niblo's Garden Theatre at Broadway and Prince St in 1866, a five-and-a-half-hour extravaganza with a far-fetched story, numerous songs, lavish sets and costumes, and lots of beautiful women in what then passed for scanty dress, with their legs partially exposed. It ran for 474 performances, unheard-of at the time, awakening theatrical producers to the possibilities of a show for mass audiences combining all of that show's elements. A similar extravaganza at Niblo's Garden was *Evangeline* (1874, revived 1885), a parody of Longfellow's popular poem. Despite the success of these and similar works in the late 19th century in New York City, American musical theater was slow to emerge as a distinct and coherent art.

The dominant genre of musical theater until the turn of the 19th century was European operetta: works by Offenbach, Gilbert and Sullivan (*The Pirates of Penzance* had its world premiere at the Fifth Avenue Theater on 31 Dec 1879), and Johann Strauss. The works of the next generation of operetta composers, notably Franz Lehar and Emmerich Kalman, were also greatly successful in English translation. Several American composers attempted to break the European lock on operetta at the turn of the century. Most had intermittent success, as did John Philip Sousa (1854–1932) with *El Capitán* (1896) and Reginald DeKoven (1859–1920) with *Robin Hood* (1890). The most successful American operetta composer before World War I was the Irish-born Victor Herbert (1859–1924). A classical cellist and conductor of the Pittsburgh Symphony, Herbert had an active concert career, which he pursued simultaneously with composing a long string of Broadway successes, including *The Fortune Teller* (1898), *Babes in Toyland* (1903), *Mlle Modiste* (1905), *The Red Mill* (1906), *Naughty Marietta* (1910), *Sweethearts* (1913), and *Eileen* (1917). After World War I the flow of imported operettas suddenly ceased, and there were more opportunities for American composers. Herbert's most important successors were Sigmund Romberg (1887–1951) and Rudolf Friml (1879–1972), who brought the Broadway operetta to flower in the 1920s. Romberg's *Blossom Time* (1921), *The Student Prince* (1924), *The Desert Song* (1926), and *The New Moon* (1928), and Friml's *Rose-Marie* (1924) and *The Vagabond King* (1925) added contemporary dance rhythms and production numbers to the romantic lushness of older operettas. All these shows were long-running successes, and most were made into Hollywood films.

There was another, more vernacular strain in New York's musical theater: homegrown musical comedies often with contents slanted toward recent immigrants. Ned Harrigan (1845–1911) and Tony Hart (1855–91) created a series of shows that often highlighted Irish life in New York City. Other shows targeted the large German and Jewish audience: the burlesque, slapstick, and dialect humor of the "Dutch comics" Joe Weber and Lew Fields were among vaudeville's biggest draws in the 1890s and early 1900s. George M. Cohan (1878–1942), who starred in a series of comic musicals that he wrote, was the most successful performer in the new vernacular style. Simple and brash in execution but definitely American in content, Cohan's shows included songs like "Give My Regards to Broadway" and "Yankee Doodle Dandy." His success helped prepare the way for a new generation of performers, including Al Jolson (1886–1950) and Fanny Brice (1891–1951). Many found a showcase in the lavish revues of producers like George White, whose *Scandals* appeared regularly from 1919 to 1939, and Florenz Ziegfeld, whose *Follies* appeared yearly from 1907 to 1932.

In the early 20th century African American composers created a series of influential shows on Broadway, culminating in Eubie Blake and Noble Sissle's *Shuffle Along* (1921) and Fats Waller and Andy Razaf's *Hot Chocolates* (1929). The black musical remained popular, whether in such adaptations of classics as *The Hot Mikado* (1939) and *Carmen Jones* (1943), or much later in *The Wiz* (1975), or in such original works (by white writers and composers) as *Cabin in the Sky* (1940), *St. Louis Woman* (1946), and *Jamaica* (1957).

The Mighty Five

By the end of the 1920s, the "Mighty Five" had emerged, a group still regarded as Broadway's greatest composers: Jerome Kern, Irving Berlin, George Gershwin, Cole Porter, and Richard Rodgers. As a group they had much in common. Four of the five were Jewish and either were native New Yorkers or were raised in the city from an early age. Their work drew from the city, both from the vernacular music styles popular early in the century, such as ragtime and Tin Pan Alley compositions, and from the city's diversity and vitality. If most of their shows through the early 1940s were, by the standard of a later generation, rather loosely constructed, the settings of their librettos (books) were contemporary and lively, often with a New York City setting.

In 1915 composer Jerome Kern (1885–1946) began a series of musicals with librettists Guy Bolton and P. G. Wodehouse to be performed at the tiny Princess Theatre on West 39th St. Light and comic, with graceful music and witty lyrics, the "Princess shows" were hailed by many critics as the antidote for heavy European operettas. The series continued until 1920 and included *Very Good Eddie, Leave It to Jane,* and *Oh, Lady! Lady!!* Kern accordingly moved on to big Broadway musicals, including the lavish *Sally* (1920) and *Sunny* (1925). Kern's musical *Show Boat* (with Oscar Hammerstein, 1927) was based on Edna Ferber's novel of the American South and was the first Broadway musical to tackle the theme of interracial unions. It included such songs as "Old Man River," "Can't Help Lovin' That Man," and "Bill," and has often been revived. Kern's subsequent musicals were less ambitious, but *The Cat and the Fiddle* (1931) and *Music in the Air* (1932) displayed his talent for graceful melody. Irving Berlin (1888–1989), one of America's most prolific songwriters, made comparatively few contributions to the book musical but wrote music and lyrics for such successful revues as *Watch Your Step* (1914), *As Thousands Cheer* (1933), and *This Is the Army* (1942). Berlin had a perfect ear for American idiom in his lyrics and an uncommon gift for simple, emotionally satisfying melodies. Berlin's *Annie Get Your Gun* (1946) and *Call Me Madam* (1950), both written late in his career for Ethel Merman, were his most successful Broadway shows. The Broadway career of composer George Gershwin (1898–1937) is inseparable from that of his brother, lyricist Ira Gershwin (1896–1983). Such Gershwin shows as *Lady, Be Good!* (1924), *Oh, Kay!* (1926), *Funny Face* (1927), and *Girl Crazy* (1930) produced strings of wonderful songs. *Of Thee I Sing* (1931), more serious and satirical, was written with George S. Kaufman, a leading Broadway playwright. A modern operetta about a presidential election in Gilbert and Sullivan style, it won the Pulitzer Prize for drama in 1932. The Gershwins' most ambitious work was an opera for Broadway, *Porgy and Bess* (1934). A failure in its initial run, it is considered by many to be one of the greatest American operas.

The odd man out among these Jewish songwriters was Cole Porter (1891–1964), scion of a wealthy midwestern family who went to Yale and spent much of 1920s among Europe's high society. Porter's first Broadway hit, *Fifty Million Frenchmen* (1929), gave notice of an unusually sophisticated talent. Its songs, notably "Let's Do It," was typical of Porter's lighthearted and carefree lyrics about sex. Porter was often inspired by unusual melodies and rhythms he heard in his world travels, and his lyrics made an art of list compiling and name-dropping. Scores for *Anything Goes* (1934), *Jubilee* (1935), *Red, Hot and Blue!* (1936), and *DuBarry Was a Lady* (1939) were exemplars of the carefree " '30s musical." After a fallow period in the early 1940s, Porter had his greatest Broadway success with *Kiss Me Kate* (1948).

Richard Rodgers (1902–79) was a successful Broadway composer by his early twenties. With Lorenz Hart (1895–1943), Rodgers wrote a series of adventurous musicals. *On Your Toes* (1936) integrated ballet sequences choreographed by George Balanchine. *Babes in Arms* (1937) was almost completely cast with theatrical newcomers. *The Boys from Syracuse* (1938)—the Syracuse in the title being the one on Sicily—was the first Broadway musical based on Shakespeare *(The Comedy of Errors),* and *Pal Joey* (1940) was the first musical to feature an antihero. The combination of Rodgers's sweet melodies and Hart's sour, disillusioned, often poetic lyrics was a potent one. Other than *Pal Joey,* their shows are seldom revived, but songs like "Manhattan", "My Funny Valentine," and "It Never Entered My Mind" have become standards. Other notable Broadway composers of this period include Vincent Youmans (*Wildflower* [1923], *No, No, Nanette* [1925], *Hit the Deck* [1927]); Arthur Schwartz (*The Band Wagon* [1931], *Revenge with Music* [1934]); Vernon Duke (Vladimir Dukelsky]) (*Cabin in the Sky* [1940]); and Harold Arlen, who was much influenced by blues and jazz (*Bloomer Girl* [1944], *St. Louis Woman* [1946]). Like Kern and Rodgers, Schwartz and Arlen were successful in Hollywood and were represented intermittently on Broadway until the early 1960s.

The Golden Age

The "Golden Age" of the book musical began 31 Mar 1943, the opening night of Rodgers and Hammerstein's *Oklahoma!* directed by Rouben Mamoulian. For all its bucolic charm, this was a revolutionary musical: a model of integration with a series of memorable songs growing naturally from the plot. Agnes De Mille's choreography made dance an integral part of the drama. Wartime audiences embraced its idealized pastoral America. Rodgers and Hammerstein's next work was *Carousel* (1945), a dark, romantic tragedy that many consider the team's finest achievement. *Allegro* (1947), their most formally experimental show, dispensed with sets and conventional storytelling. *South Pacific* (1949) and *The King and I* (1951) represent Rodgers and Hammerstein at the zenith of their popularity. Later works include *Me and Juliet* (1953), *Pipe Dream* (1955), *Flower Drum Song* (1958), and the tremendously popular *Sound of Music* (1960). Rodgers and Hammerstein's integration of book, music, lyrics, choreography, and production design with more complex characterization and more thoughtful, coherent storytelling on serious topics (such as interracial romance) became the norm for Broadway by the late 1940s. Musicals that did not share these ambitions and that continued in the older style, in which the lighthearted romance of the story provided little more than an excuse for the introduction of unconnected songs, came to be seen as flimsy or old-fashioned. Even the masters of the older, loosely constructed musical, such as Cole Porter, adopted the new Rodgers and Hammerstein style, as in his *Kiss Me Kate.*

Other innovative forces in the development of the Broadway musical included Kurt Weill (1900–1950), who escaped Nazi Germany in 1933 and ended up in New York in 1935. Weill was famous as the composer of politically slanted pieces with texts by Bertolt Brecht (*Threepenny Opera* [1928], *Rise and Fall of the City of Mahagonny* [1930]). With his first Broadway musical, the antiwar satire *Johnny Johnson* (1936), Weill showed a wide musical range and a willingness to tackle important social and political issues. Pieces like *Lady in the Dark* (1941), *One Touch of Venus* (1943), *Street Scene* (1947), and *Lost in the Stars* (1949) addressed such themes as psychoanalysis, modern marriage, and South African apartheid. One composer directly indebted to Weill was Marc Blitzstein (1905–64), whose politically charged musical *The Cradle Will Rock* (1938) created a furor at its premiere. Another successful postwar team was Alan Jay Lerner (1918–86) and Frederick Loewe (1904–88), whose *Brigadoon* (1947), *My Fair Lady* (1956), and *Camelot* (1960) were updatings of the Broadway operetta style. *My Fair Lady*'s skillful adaptation of George Bernard Shaw's witty *Pygmalion* was especially admired and popular.

Leonard Bernstein's (1918–90) *On the Town* (1944), a celebration of New York City's vitality, balanced conventional ballads and comic songs with dance music in a driving, rhythmically complex style. Bernstein's musical theater masterpiece *Candide* (1956), which was based on Voltaire, is a 20th-century light opera, a racy, inventive work in the tradition of Offenbach and Gilbert and Sullivan. *West Side Story* (1957), based on Shakespeare's *Romeo and Juliet* and set in the Hell's Kitchen area of Manhattan, is a tragedy set to dark, propulsive music. By the 1990s both works had entered the repertory of opera houses. Frank Loesser (1910–69), who wrote both lyrics and music, produced three shows that have become classics: the jazzy *Guys and Dolls* (1950), the near operatic *The Most Happy Fella* (1956), and the satiric *How to Succeed in Business Without Really Trying* (1961). The prolific Jule Styne (1905–96) wrote many tuneful, uncomplicated hits, from *High Button Shoes* (1947) to *Funny Girl* (1964). His masterpiece is *Gypsy* (1959), a frequently revived musical biography of stripper Gypsy Rose Lee. Styne excelled at tailoring shows to outgoing singer-actresses like Carol Channing, Ethel Merman, and Barbra Streisand.

Two distinguished composer-lyricist teams emerged in the 1960s. Jerry Bock (1928–) and Sheldon Harnick's (1924–) first musical, *Fiorello!* (1959), about New York City Mayor Fiorello La Guardia, won the 1960 Pulitzer Prize. Even more successful was *Fiddler on the Roof* (1964), which held Broadway's long-run record for many years. Emerging at about the same time were John Kander (1927–) and Fred Ebb (1935–), whose *Cabaret* (1966), directed by Harold Prince, was a landmark in the development of the "concept musical," which replaced the straightforward plots of the older musical with fragmented storytelling in which musical numbers often commented on the story instead of furthering it. *Cabaret* was something of a hybrid in this regard, but Kander and Ebb's *Chicago* (1975), a satirical exposé of a 1920s murder trial, which was directed, choreographed, and written by Bob Fosse, took this style much further.

Less artistically ambitious but remarkably successful were musicals by Jerry Herman (*Hello, Dolly!* [1964], *Mame* [1966], *La Cage aux Folles* [1984]) and Charles Strouse (*Bye Bye Birdie* [1960], *Applause* [1970], *Annie* [1977]). One of the biggest hits of the 1970s was Marvin Hamlisch and Edward Kleban's Pulitzer Prize–winning *A Chorus Line* (1975), based on the true stories of Broadway gypsies (show dancers). New York City itself has been a favorite subject for musicals. In the 1940s and 1950s, the city was often a backdrop for adventure and romance, an exciting, largely innocent playground (*On the Town, Guys and Dolls,* and *Wonderful Town* [1953]); later productions began to show a darker view (*West Side Story, Sweet Charity,* [1966], and *Company*). More recent musicals, such as *The Life* (1994, music by Cy Coleman) and *Rent* (1996), present the gritty realities of prostitution, poverty, drug abuse, and AIDS.

Stephen Sondheim and His Contemporaries

The dominant American figure in Broadway musicals from the 1970s through the 1990s was Stephen Sondheim (1930–). After initial success as a lyricist for *West Side Story* and *Gypsy,* Sondheim wrote words and music for *A Funny Thing Happened on the Way to the Forum* (1962); it was a great success, but Sondheim's score was not highly valued. He did not return to Broadway as a composer-lyricist until 1970, with the highly original *Company.* This was a concept musical par excellence, a plotless study of modern urban marriage. An important factor in *Company*'s success was Harold Prince's imaginative staging. This team remained together throughout the 1970s for an increasingly daring and controversial series of musicals: *Follies* (1971), *A Little Night Music* (1973), *Pacific Overtures* (1976), *Sweeney Todd* (1979), and *Merrily We Roll Along* (1981). With their unusually dramatic stories and integration of music, lyrics, and book that bordered on opera (particularly in *Sweeney Todd*), the Sondheim-Prince collaborations were the most ambitious musicals since Rodgers and Hammerstein, pushing the limits of musical theater forward.

After the failure of *Merrily We Roll Along,* Sondheim broke with Prince and eventually collaborated with the playwright and director James Lapine, who moved Sondheim in a more poetic, somewhat avant-garde direction with *Sunday in the Park with George* (1984). This unusual show starts as a sort of musical documentary about the pointillist painter Georges Seurat and ends as a moving meditation on the nature and the necessity of art. It stunned some audiences, thoroughly bored others, and won the Pulitzer Prize for drama. Sondheim and Lapine's clever *Into the Woods* (1987) scrambles a number of well-known fairy tales together to make some trenchant points about society and community. Then they wrote *Passion* (1994), a moody, operatic study of passionate love. *Assassins* (1991, with John Weidman) is Sondheim's most politically radical work, a kind of mordant, satirical revue whose characters are the murderers and would-be murderers of US presidents. Few of Stephen Sondheim's musicals have been commercially successful, but their high artistic standards, the wit and polish of his lyrics, and the emotional appeal of his often complex music ensured survival after their initial Broadway runs.

Londoner Andrew Lloyd Webber wrote spectacular musicals in "rock opera" style that were international, long-running hits: *Jesus Christ Superstar* (1972), *Evita* (1980), *Phantom of the Opera* (1987), and *Sunset Boulevard* (1994). Less demanding than Sondheim's works, Lloyd Webber's shows gave audiences dramatic excitement, lavish sets and staging, and lush, melodious scores. Two globe-trotting shows by the British team of Boublil and Schonberg, *Les Misérables* (1986) and *Miss Saigon* (1991) were just as successful, running simultaneously in major cities all over the world. The only original American musical of the 1990s that could match these British successes was Jonathan Larson's *Rent* (1996), a rock updating of Puccini's *La Bohème* to East Village bohemians.

Bordman, Gerald. *American Musical Theatre: A Chronicle* (New York: Oxford Univ Press, 1979)
Gottfried, Martin. *Broadway Musicals* (New York: Abrams, 1979)
———. *More Broadway Musicals: Since 1980* (New York: Abrams, 1991)
Green, Stanley. *Encyclopedia of the Musical* (New York: Dodd, Mead, 1976)
Lerner, Alan Jay. *The Musical Theatre: A Celebration* (London: Collins, 1986)
Traubner, Richard. *Operetta: A Theatrical History* (Garden City, NY: Doubleday, 1983)

David Raymond

music camps. The origin of summer music camps in New York State can be traced to the opening of the Ithaca Military Band School in 1929. Ernest S. Williams, a member of the Ithaca Conservatory, directed the Williams Music Camp, a 10-week program for high school and college students. Following Williams's death in February 1947, his camp director, Frederic Fay Swift, opened the New York State Music Camp that summer at Otter Lake in the Adirondacks, which, with a name change in 1994, continues as the Hartwick College Summer Music Festival and Institute in Oneonta (Otsego Co). Other camps and summer music programs include the Chautauqua Festival, which provides for a Summer Youth Orchestra; Crane Youth Music Camp at SUNY Potsdam; Eastern US Music Camp on the Colgate University campus in Hamilton (Madison Co); Fredonia Summer Music Program on the SUNY campus; Piano Camp at Houghton College (Allegany Co); Signature Band and Choir Camp and the Summer Piano Institute at Ithaca College; French Woods Festival in Hancock (Delaware Co); Long Lake Camp (Hamilton Co); Summerfame in Syracuse; Summer School of the Arts at Nazareth College in Rochester; and several programs at Saratoga Springs, including the New York Summer School of the Arts, the Skidmore Jazz Institute, and the Skidmore Summer Flute Institute. Offerings may include both instrumental and vocal private lessons, ensembles, and larger groups, such as bands, choirs, orchestras, and jazz ensembles. Several programs encompass visual arts, theater, and dance, along with athletic and recreational activities. Ages of participants generally range from 8 to 18. Tens of thousands of young people have attended the state's music camps, and many have gone on to musical careers.

Swift, Robert F. *Music from the Mountains: New York State Music Camp, 1947–1996* (Plymouth, NH: NYSMC Press, 1996)

Robert F. Swift

music publishing

New York City

New York City was always the undisputed capital of the state's music publishing industry. Gustav Schirmer, a German immigrant, established his enduring music publishing company in New York City in 1861. Vigorous promotional methods became popular in the late 19th century, and some songs sold in the millions in the 1890s. The biggest hits, such as "After the Ball" by Charles K. Harris (1892), sold 5–10 million copies. After the 1890s the business grew larger and more centralized. Leading composers of the era, including Scott Joplin and Irving Berlin, were habitués of the publishers' offices in Tin Pan Alley, and some started their own enterprises. In 1914 ASCAP (American Society of Composers, Authors and Publishers) was founded in New York City by artists including Victor Herbert and John Philip Sousa, to collect royalties on performances and recordings. In 1924 Carl Fischer, who had opened a musical instrument store in 1872 and gone into music publishing soon after, expanded his popular sheet music business to include classical music. By the end of World War I, however, recordings were economically more important than music sheets.

A tremendous wave of new talent in American popular music helped the industry in the 1920s. New York City had become the major music publishing center in the United States by the 1930s, but the sheet music industry had been eroded by radio and the phonograph. After the rise of sound films most of the large publishing houses were bought out by Hollywood studios, though Tin Pan Alley continued to be a force into the 1960s. At the beginning of the 21st century there are still several independent music publishers in New York City and a few elsewhere in the state. European classical music publishers maintaining offices in Manhattan include Boosey and Hawkes of London and, until recently, Ricordi of Milan. The meaning of "publishing" itself has changed with the decline of sheet music and now refers principally to property rights over recordings, broadcasts, and performances. In addition to a number of the largest international music conglomerates, the two licensing organizations, ASCAP and BMI (Broadcast Music Inc, established 1940), remain headquartered in Manhattan.

Elsewhere in the State

The most important center in music publishing outside of New York City, and the last to maintain some independent life, was Buffalo. Its chief publishers before the Civil War included James D. Sheppard (whose firm was renamed Denton and Cottier in the 1880s) and J. Sage and Sons. Edward H. Hulse was active in the 1880s, when Buffalo's leading publisher was August Rottenbach, formerly of the partnership Dannreuther and Rottenbach. He published the work of local German and Italian immigrant musicians and editions of works by leading European masters such as Liszt and Grieg. America lagged behind Europe in international copyright law, and it was common in the 19th century to publish bowdlerized arrangements of works by such composers, often simplified for amateur performance.

In Albany the leading publishers around 1850 were J. H. Hidley and Boardman and Gray. Hidley was still doing business 30 years later, when music publishing had dwindled in Albany but was successful in Rochester, Syracuse, and Troy (Rensselaer Co). In Rochester, by the 1870s, Gibbons and Stone were turning out a good deal of music. Henry S. Mackie was also active, and there were numerous smaller firms. T. Hough was publishing in Syracuse in the 1850s, and activity burgeoned in the 1870s, when Horace W. Coon was in business. In Troy both Edward P. Jones and Edward Hopkins published in the 1850s; H. L. Greywack, R. A. Spalding, B. H. Hidley, and numerous others published later in the 19th century. In Utica George Dutton was active in the 1830s–1850s and E. D. Buckingham in the 1870s–1880s.

Some music was published by smaller firms in Elmira in the 1850s–1880s. During the 1870s J. H. Hickock and Reed and Van Vliet published music in Poughkeepsie; O. S. Burr and the Estey Organ Co in Newburgh (Orange Co); and Thomas Bros in Catskill (Greene Co). Material published in small towns, whether in name only or actually engraved there, was necessarily printed in the nearest population center with presses. Active regional businesses were outnumbered by those that published only a few pieces. Music publishing in the state outside of New York City declined over the course of the 20th century.

Dichter, Harry, and Elliott Shapiro. *Handbook of Early American Sheet Music, 1768–1889* (New York: Dover, 1977)

US Library of Congress. "American Memory," http://lcweb2.loc.gov/ammem/

Wolfe, Richard J. *Early American Music Printing and Engraving* (Urbana: Univ of Illinois Press, 1980)

Elliott S. Hurwitt

Muttontown. Village (pop 3,412) in Oyster Bay (Nassau Co). Named for its pre-1750 use as a "great sheep district," Muttontown was incorporated in 1931 to control development pressures; nonetheless, its population has expanded considerably from the 335 residents of 1940. In 1951 former King Zog of Albania purchased Knollwood but never lived there. It is now part of the county's 550-acre (223 ha) Muttontown Preserve. The village remains an exclusive residential community with a rural character.

Tom Kuehhas

Myers, Mordecai (*b* Newport, RI, 1 May 1776; *d* Schenectady, 24 Jan 1871). Soldier and politician. The son of Hungarian Jewish immigrants, Myers settled with his family in New York City in 1787. A merchant and auctioneer, Myers exhibited a keen sense of civic duty, becoming active in many organizations, including the Congregation Shearith Israel and the state militia. Commissioned an officer in the US Army during the War of 1812, he distinguished himself in engagements against British forces on the Niagara Frontier and saved the lives of 200 shipwrecked soldiers. In 1813 he was stationed in Williamsville (Erie Co) for almost a year and is considered the earliest known Jewish resident in Western New York. Following the war he lived in New York City and served in the state assembly as a Democrat (1829, 1831–34) where his gift for oratory helped enact legislation that secured for Quakers the right to abstain from military service for Quakers and pensions for veterans of the Revolutionary War. In 1836 he moved to Kinderhook (Columbia Co), where he was elected mayor three years later. In 1851 Myers relocated to Schenectady, where he served as mayor in 1851 and in 1854.

Yetwin, Neil B. "Notable Schenectadians: Major Mordecai Myers: A Freemason of New York," *Schenectady County Historical Society Newsletter* 33 (Sept–Oct 1996): 1–2, 16

Wesley G. Balla

Myers Corner. Locality (pop 5,546) in Wappinger (Dutchess Co). It is said to have been named for an 18th-century farm family and its 19th-century hotel at the corners. Suburban development followed the 1963 opening of an IBM manufacturing facility at East Fishkill. With small manufacturing facilities, a small mall, and an apple orchard, Myers Corners is a bedroom community, and its residents commute as far as Westchester Co and New York City.

William P. McDermott

Myrick, Luther (*b* Dutchess Co, 1794; *d* Jackson, Mich, 1 Sept 1843). Religious reformer. Raised in Paris Hill (Oneida Co), Myrick was an early supporter of, and perhaps influenced, Charles Grandison Finney's combination of revivalism and reform in Central and Western New York. He was ordained as a Presbyterian minister, but his advocacy of antislavery, perfectionist theology, unsophisticated evangelistic methods, and women's religious rights troubled his fellow clergy. Tried before the Oneida Presbytery in 1834, he was suspended from the ministry for preaching doctrine contrary to Calvinist orthodoxy. Concluding that all denominational hierarchies were corrupt on the basis of their binding human minds, just as slavery bound human bodies, Myrick founded a nonsectarian Union church in Cazenovia (Madison Co) and promoted similar churches in the *Union Herald,* which he edited in Cazenovia from 1836 to 1842. Following his example on behalf of "spiritual democracy," hundreds of similar churches were established throughout the North before the Civil War. He published a political antislavery paper, the *Madison County Abolitionist* (1841), and its successors, the *Madison and Onondaga Abolitionist* (1841–42) and the *Abolitionist* (1842), before moving to Michigan in 1843.

Strong, Douglas M. *Perfectionist Politics: Abolitionism and the Religious Tensions of American Democracy* (Syracuse: Syracuse Univ Press, 1999)

Douglas M. Strong

N

NAACP. See NATIONAL ASSOCIATION FOR THE ADVANCEMENT OF COLORED PEOPLE (NAACP).

Nabokov, Vladimir (*b* St. Petersburg, Russia, 23 Apr 1899; *d* Lausanne, Switzerland, 2 July 1977). Writer. He was born to liberal, wealthy, aristocratic parents. Privately tutored until the age of 11, he voraciously read Russian, French, and English classics. After the October 1917 Revolution, the family fled to the Crimea and then to London in 1919. Nabokov studied French and Russian literature at Cambridge University. In the years following his graduation in 1922, Nabokov settled in Berlin, where he wrote plays and stories, supporting himself by teaching English, French, and Russian. He published his first novel in 1926; by 1929, when *Zashchita Luzhina* (The defense) began to appear serially, many considered Nabokov the foremost writer to emerge in the emigration. The family escaped from Berlin to France in 1937, by which time Nabokov was completing his greatest Russian novel, *Dar* (The gift). After years of trying to obtain exit visas from France and entry permits to the United States, he at last succeeded and sailed with his family into New York Harbor on 28 May 1940.

Through Vladimir's cousin, the composer Nicholas Nabokov, he was introduced to critic Edmund Wilson, who arranged for him to write reviews for the *New Republic* and the *New York Sun.* He supported himself by publishing poems and stories and by teaching and lecturing. Nabokov, a passionate butterfly collector since childhood, also carried out research at the American Museum of Natural History in Manhattan and after 1941 at the Harvard Museum of Comparative Zoology, where he quickly became the world expert on North and South American Blues. Among the butterflies Nabokov had named while working as a scientist was the subspecies *Lycaeides melissa samuelis,* which he searched for in the Northeast and at last rediscovered in the Karner Pine Barren between Albany and Schenectady. The Karner Blue, as it became known, would become the focus of a major conservation drive starting in the 1970s and, partly through Nabokov's support, a key symbol of the conservation movement.

Female Karner Blue butterfly on a lupine leaf.

In 1948 he was appointed to Cornell University as a professor of Russian literature but soon became famous on campus for his course on masterpieces of modern European fiction (published as *Lectures on Literature,* 1980). In his first years at Cornell, Nabokov completed his autobiography, *Conclusive Evidence* (1951), later revised as *Speak, Memory* (1967). At the same time, he began to be revisited by the idea for *Lolita,* whose theme—a fortyish man's intense sexual passion for 9–11-year-old girls and his fatal love for one 12-year-old—he had treated in an unpublished Russian story (*The Enchanter,* written 1939, published 1986). After beginning the novel he was on the verge of burning the manuscript in his Ithaca incinerator when his wife convinced him that he would be haunted by the idea for the rest of his life. He rescued what he had written and resumed the novel. Humbert Humbert arrives from Europe to think up and edit perfume ads in New York City, and after trying to spy on nymphets playing in Central Park, moves to the New England town of Ramsdale, where fate seems to hand him Lolita. Years later, after Lolita escapes from his clutches, he settles in a relationship with an undemanding older woman, in an apartment "with a view of gleaming children taking shower baths far below in a fountainous arbor of Central Park," before Lolita resumes contact and the novel rushes to its tragic end.

In the mid-1950s he also wrote *Pnin,* the story of a Russian émigré professor at Waindell College (a small-scale Cornell) who becomes a comic campus legend. In 1958 *Lolita,* which had been published three years earlier in Paris after being turned down by four New York City publishers, had already become famous before it was published in the United States. Shooting to the top of the best-seller lists, it allowed Nabokov to retire from Cornell in 1959.

That year the Nabokovs sailed from New York City to Europe, where their son, Dmitri, was studying to be an opera singer. They settled in Montreux, Switzerland, in 1961. Nabokov's next novel, *Pale Fire* (1962), was set in Wordsmith, New Wye, a stylized but vividly rendered Cornell and Ithaca. *Ada* (1969), his longest novel, takes place on Antiterra, a kind of mirror world, where a very recognizable New York City is known only as Manhattan, and New Hampshire joins with the Catskills as New Cheshire. Nabokov returned to New York City in 1962 for the premiere of Stanley Kubrick's film version of *Lolita,* for which he received screenplay credits, and for a last time in 1964, when he gave a reading in Manhattan to launch his translation of Alexander Pushkin's *Eugene Onegin.* The translation led to a fierce controversy the next year on the pages of the *New York Review of Books,* with Nabokov and his former friend Edmund Wilson as chief antagonists. Often considered one of the greatest novelists of the 20th century, Nabokov introduced a new fluency of perception, emotion, and imagination into the texture and structure of fiction, which allowed him, in critic and novelist Martin Amis's words, "to do all the usual things better than anyone else" and to incorporate innovation and discovery into his vivid style of storytelling.

Boyd, Brian. *Vladimir Nabokov: The Russian Years* (Princeton, NJ: Princeton Univ Press, 1990)
———. *Vladimir Nabokov: The American Years* (Princeton, NJ: Princeton Univ Press, 1991)
Nabokov, Vladimir. *Speak, Memory: An Autobiography Revisited* (New York: Knopf, 1999)

Brian Boyd

Namath, Joe [Joseph William] (*b* Beaver Falls, Pa, 31 May 1943). Professional football player. Raised in Beaver Falls, Joe Namath played quarterback for Bear Bryant at the University of Alabama. The New York Jets made Namath their first-round pick in the 1965 American Football League (AFL) draft. He signed a then record $427,000 contract and was named the 1965 AFL Rookie of the Year. In 1967 Namath became the first quarterback to pass for more than 4,000 yards in a season. The league's Most Valuable Player (MVP) for the 1968 season, Namath was also MVP of Super Bowl III (January 1969). He is remembered for guaranteeing a Jets win in that game, then leading them to a 16–7 victory over the greatly favored Baltimore Colts. In the summer of 1969 Namath announced his retirement rather than yielding to league pressure to sell his share in a New York City bar or face suspension. The episode highlighted Namath's carousing lifestyle that earned him the nickname Broadway Joe. Namath changed his mind by summer's end, selling the bar and returning to football. Troubled by knee injuries his entire career, Namath played with the Jets through 1976 and still holds most of the team's passing records. He spent a final season with the Los Angeles Rams. Namath passed for 27,663 yards in his career and was inducted into the Pro Football Hall of Fame in 1985. An immensely popular public figure, Namath began acting and doing commercial endorsements during his playing days and continued after retiring.

Ralbovsky, Marty. *The Namath Effect* (Englewood Cliffs, NJ: Prentice-Hall, 1976)

Randy Lange

Nanticoke. Town (pop 1,790) in W Broome Co. Settled in 1793, the town was formed from Lisle in 1831. Lumbering was the principal industry until the timber stand was exhausted. In the mid–19th century leather, rakes, and stoves were produced. The population declined from a peak of 1,058 in 1870 but increased after 1920. Sulfurous Nanticoke Springs attracted health seekers from 1831 until 1860, and there was speculation for oil drilling around 1866. The town remains rural and agricultural, with some suburban housing; residents commute to Whitney Point or to the greater Binghamton area. Nanticoke is the site of the 439-acre (178 ha) Greenwood Park.

Charles J. Browne

Nanuet. Locality (pop 16,707) in Clarkstown (Rockland Co). It developed on the Nyack Turnpike (1830) and around an Erie Railroad station (1841) and junction with branchlines. In 1846 it acquired a post office named Nanuet. Intensive suburban development began *ca* 1950. The Nanuet Mall (1968) is the most prominent in Nanuet's concentration of retail businesses and the largest in the county.

Naples. Town (pop 2,441) and village (pop 1,072) in S Ontario Co. At a meeting in Partridgefield,

Mass, in 1789 a company of 60 families formed to buy a township of the Phelps and Gorham Purchase, settling near an Indian village named Nundawao in 1791. Native people were living nearby as late as 1826. The town formed as Middletown in 1795, and the name was changed to Naples in 1808. In the early 1850s the Isabella grape was planted in town, and a grape industry was launched *ca* 1864; many of its workers were Germans. A regular steamboat connection to Canandaigua at the foot of the lake was inaugurated in 1867, and the railroad came to Naples in 1892. The village incorporated in 1894. Jacob Widmer established a successful winery in 1888 that is an ongoing concern in the early 21st century; D. H. Maxfield built another. An important fossil of a Devonian era tree, *Archeosigullaria primerum,* was found in town. Naples is a wine-producing town and has a tourism sector related to the industry.

Marla A. Bennett

Napoli [NA-PO-LYE]. Town (pop 1,159) in central Cattaraugus Co. Settled in 1818, it was formed in 1823 as Coldspring; the name was changed in 1828. Dairying, cheese making, sugaring, and the shipping of its apples to New York City and Buffalo drove the farm economy in the late 19th century. On the county prison farm (1918–53), prisoners raised garden produce. Farming remained the predominant land use in 2003. Enchanted Lake, an 1,100-acre (445 ha) recreational housing development begun in the 1970s, went bankrupt and was restructured in the late 1990s as the Napoli Development Corp. The Waterman Swamp, partly in New Albion, is the site of the 390-acre (158 ha) Allenberg Bog Wildlife Refuge, owned by the Buffalo Audubon Society, known for its wild orchids, liverworts, mosses, vascular plants, and thickets of wildflowers and stands of pines, black spruce, black cherry, and tamarack. The Gladden Windmill (1890) is listed on the National Register. Napoli's population almost doubled between 1960 and 2000.

Bruce D. Fredrickson and Madelynn P. Fredrickson

Nassau. Town (pop 4,818) and village (1,161) in S Rensselaer Co. In what is now Nassau, David Brainerd was a missionary to the Mohican Indians in 1743–44. Settled in 1760, the town was formed from Petersburgh, Stephentown, and Schodack in 1806 as Philipstown but the name changed to Nassau in 1808. Hoags Corners was a center of antirent activity in the 1840s. Creeks powered manufacturing, including paper mills, a foundry, a chair factory, a hoe factory, and, later, the Kosegarten Piano Action Manufacturing Co (?1904–1929). In the early 20th century a number of Jewish families from New York City took up farming in town and built a small synagogue. Totem Lodge (1922–58) on Burden Lake was a popular resort. Eastfield Village, a privately owned museum village, is located near Hoags Corners. The Village of Nassau, incorporated in 1819, straddles the Nassau and Schodack town line. Its population was swelled by German Catholics, who founded a church in 1852. In 1880 a foundry produced plows, cultivators, and straw cutters. The same year the village was the site of six card printers. In 2002 it was a small market village and home to Albany commuters.

Kathryn T. Sheehan

Nassau County (287 mi²/743 km²; pop 1,334,544). Formed from Queens Co in 1899, it borders New York City on the east and extends from Long Island Sound on the north to the Atlantic Ocean on the south. Nassau Co is divided into two cities and three towns. The latter contain 64 incorporated villages and a similar number of substantial unincorporated localities. The Village of Mineola serves as the county seat.

The county is located on the Atlantic coastal plain and is underlain by Cretaceous sedimentary rocks that dip southward and are everywhere covered with a deep mantle of glacial till deposited by the two most recent ice sheets, the Illinoian and the Wisconsinan. The older Illinoian ice sheet reached a position just north of Long Island, but outwash sand and gravel was carried south and deposited by meltwater streams. The more recent Wisconsinan ice sheet overrode the earlier deposits and advanced farther south to a line marked by the Ronkonkoma terminal moraine, a band of elevated, irregular topography consisting of unsorted boulders, sands, and gravels, that extends from Montauk Point (Suffolk Co) to Brooklyn. In the latter part of this period, the ice front on the west end of the island advanced farther south, while the front farther to the east retreated, creating the discrete Harbor Hill Moraine. The pivot point for this movement was in northwestern Nassau Co and resulted in an exceptionally wide band of irregular topography across its northern half. The area south of the terminal moraine is a flat outwash plain that slopes gently to the island's south shore.

The county's north shore consists of a series of elevated peninsulas, known commonly from west to east as Great Neck, Cow Neck, Mill Neck and Cove Neck. They were formed when north-flowing tributaries of the river that drained Long Island Sound cut deep valleys that were subsequently drowned when sea levels rose. The resulting bays are deep, steep sided, and irregular in shape. In contrast, the estuaries on the south shore are shallow, former meltwater channels that open onto island tidal flats, salt marshes, and a myriad of low islands that are themselves protected from the Atlantic Ocean by two large barrier islands. These islands, Jones Beach and Long Beach, are effectively long strips of sand that are very sensitive to wind, waves, and along-shore currents. Elevations in the county range from sea level to approximately 340 feet (104 m) near the eastern county line just south of the Jericho Turnpike (Rte 25).

Nassau Co's climate is humid-continental.

The mean July temperature is 74° (23°C), with daytime highs often exceeding 80°F (27°C) and sometimes 90°F (32°C). The mean January temperature is 32°F (0°C). The coldest recorded temperature was -5°F (-21°C). Average seasonal snowfall is 21 inches (53 cm); mean annual precipitation is 46 inches (117 cm). Drainage is divided into three primary regions. The largest consists of a series of modest, south-flowing, perennial streams that discharge into South Shore estuaries. Streams draining the northern third are generally smaller, shorter, and often intermittent.

Much of the precipitation that falls in the area between the Jericho and North Hempstead (Rte 25A) Turnpikes collects in landlocked ponds or depressions and percolates directly into the groundwater system. The same is true for much of the runoff from paved surfaces in recently developed areas, where waters are routed to artificial basins ("sumps") for groundwater recharge. The soils of the outwash plain are well-drained, medium-to-moderately-coarse textured tills and alluvium well suited for agriculture. Those of the county's northern half are also medium-to-coarse tills, but many are excessively drained. The area's primeval vegetation consisted of a central hardwood forest dominated by beech, maple, hickory, oak, elm, tulip, and chestnut except for the Hempstead Plain, a naturally occurring prairie that extends across the center of the county. It was dominated by bluestem beard grass and masses of bird's-foot violets.

American Indians and Early Settlement

Archaeological evidence indicates that Nassau Co was long inhabited before European contact. Paleo-Indians moved into the area about 12,500–8,000 years ago and established campsites along the south and north shores in the Woodland period (3000 BC–AD 1600) and had pottery, wampum, stone tools, and wigwams of trees, bark, and skins. Living in family groups, these Algonquian-speaking Indians had small settlements on watercourses or protected shore locations. They included the Matinecock along the North Shore and the Rockaway, Merrick, and Massapequa along the South Shore. At the time of initial European contact, they numbered perhaps 3,000–5,000 in the present Nassau Co. Several armed conflicts between the settlers and Indians, disease, and the pressure of colonial settlement decimated the Indians. By the end of the 1600s, the few remaining had moved to isolated Suffolk Co locations.

In 1640 a small group of English settlers led by Daniel Howe from Lynn, Mass, attempted to settle at Cow Bay near the present Manhasset under a grant from James Farrett, agent of the earl of Stirling, but the Dutch authorities forced them to relocate farther east to Southampton [now in Suffolk Co]. In 1643 some 50 families from Wethersfield and Stamford in Connecticut established a settlement at Heemstede, or Hempstead, purchasing half of "the Greate plaines" from the local Massapequa, Mericoke, and Rockaway Indians. In 1644 they received a Dutch patent incorporating the town that authorized local government and land use; it remained the basis of much later regulation. In 1648 Hempstead proprietor Robert Williams purchased a large tract from the Indians and, with a group of colonists from Massachusetts, established settlements around Oyster Bay. As in much of New England, the original settlers were each granted a home lot, meadow lot, and wood lot, and the right to the common lands, although after 1664 royal grants were made directly to some patentees. The Dutch and English colonies contested the Oyster Bay settlement, and in 1653 the first English purchase from the Matinecock Indians led to settlement at the present hamlet of Oyster Bay. Subsequent land division varied, with individuals or associated groups taking Indian deeds, while many large manorial patents were made by colonial governors.

Following the British takeover of New York Colony, Hempstead was the site of the 1655 meeting that promulgated the Duke's Laws, New York Colony's first legal code. In 1683 Long Island was divided into the three counties of Kings, Suffolk, and Queens, the latter containing the Towns of Hempstead and Oyster Bay, as well as the western localities of Jamaica, Flushing, and Newtown. From the late 1600s until the mid-1700s, Hempstead's and Oyster Bay's population rose slowly. Settlement was limited to a scattering of farms outside the Town of Hempstead, throughout Oyster Bay, and along the North Shore bays, with waterpowered grist-, saw-, and fulling mills. A large portion of the Hempstead Plain and the South Shore meadows were retained as common lands and provided forage for extensive sheep and cattle raising. Hempstead Plain was the site of the first recorded American horse race in 1665, inaugurating Nassau's later role as a major center of horse racing. Agriculture was principally for subsistence, but firewood, livestock, and orchard fruits were transported to New York City for sale. Local government took the form of town meetings. Although desire for political and religious independence motivated the English settlers to come to Long Island, they resisted the first Quaker residents in 1657. The Society of Friends, however, attracted adherents and established settlements at Jerusalem [now Wantagh and North Wantagh], Jericho, and Bethpage.

The American Revolution brought divided loyalties. Supporters of independence were in the majority on the North Shore, Quakers followed their nonviolent beliefs and remained neutral in midisland, and tories dominated the South Shore. After the Battle of Long Island and Washington's withdrawal from New York City in 1776, the island remained under British control for the duration of the war. Patriots in northern parts of Hempstead seceded from the tory southern part in 1775 to form the Town of North Hempstead (though it did not become official until 1784). British occupation forces exacted supplies and quartered troops on local farms, and raiding parties from across Long Island Sound often terrorized residents. At war's end, many tory families fled to New Brunswick and Nova Scotia, and there was renewed growth in the Long Island area. The western towns of Queens Co remained lightly settled, and by 1800 there were twice as many people in the three eastern towns of Hempstead, North Hempstead, and Oyster Bay as in the western towns.

The 19th-Century Economy

The rural economy changed in the early 1800s as new transportation methods enabled commercial farming and some industrial growth. East-west turnpikes were built, improving roads along northern, central, and southern routes. The greatest factor was the addition of rail service from Brooklyn to Hicksville in 1837. The Long Island Rail Road consolidated various smaller branches to Syosset, Hempstead, and Manhasset and along the South Shore in the 1870s and 1880s, and the system completed its last major line to Port Washington in 1898. The railroad, along with the steamboats on Long Island Sound, transported tourists to the island and residents to their jobs in the city.

In the early 1800s agriculture evolved into market gardening for the growing cities of Brooklyn and New York. Scientific farming methods were introduced, and the Queens County Agricultural Society was established in 1841, with its permanent fairgrounds built in Mineola in 1866. Wheat, corn, and oats were ground in local mills and transported by sloops to city markets. By midcentury, grain production was supplemented by crops of sweet corn, cabbage, peas, onions, carrots, turnips, cucumbers, and apples. Potatoes became a Long Island specialty; production increased from 215,000 bushels (7.6 million l) to 875,000 bushels (30.8 million l) between 1875 and 1900. Pickles were

NASSAU CO POPULATION CENSUS FIGURES

	White	Nonwhite	Total Population	Foreign-Born
1900	53,093	2,355	55,448	11,063
1910	81,541	2,389	83,930	19,396
1920	122,934	3,186	126,120	26,148
1930	294,747	8,306	303,053	63,437
1940	393,213	13,535	406,748	64,733
1950	655,008	17,757	672,765	81,677
1960	1,258,039	42,132	1,300,171	121,417
1970	1,355,754	72,326	1,428,080	118,010
1980	1,204,208	117,374	1,321,582	135,882
1990	1,116,949	170,399	1,287,348	169,311
2000	1,058,285	276,259	1,334,544	238,414

Notes: "Nonwhite" includes African Americans, Asians, American Indians, and Pacific Islanders and, for 2000, also the mixed race and other race categories. Through the 1960 census these figures primarily reflect the African American population. For 1930 and 1950, the foreign-born totals include Whites only. Other years include all foreign-born in the population.

POPULATIONS OF TOWNS AND CITIES, NASSAU CO

Town or City, Year Founded	1800	1840	1880	1920	1960	2000
Glen Cove (city), 1918	—	—	—	8,664	23,817	26,622
Hempstead, 1657[a]	4,141	7,609	18,164	70,790	740,738	755,924
Long Beach (city), 1922	—	—	—	—	26,473	35,462
North Hempstead, 1784	2,413	3,891	7,560	26,370	219,088	222,611
Oyster Bay, 1658[b]	4,548	5,865	11,923	20,296	290,055	293,925

Note: The Towns of Hempstead, North Hempstead, and Oyster Bay were part of Queens Co until 1898.

[a]Earliest town meeting minutes 1657. Called South Hempstead 1784–96.

[b]Earliest town record book started 1658.

made in Farmingdale and Wantagh. Dairy farming was concentrated in the midisland localities of Westbury, Syosset, and Hicksville, and reached a peak production of 1.4 million gallons (5.3 million l) of milk sent to the city in 1875 by special railcars. By the late 1800s, Hicks Nursery in Westbury was an innovative horticultural supplier and John Lewis Childs's Mayflower Press in Floral Park was a nationally known seed packer.

Fishing was the economic basis of the shorefront villages as both tourist and commercial fishing activities. Oyster beds were seeded in North Shore harbors as early as 1822. Shipbuilders produced the noted Seaford skiff and Roslyn yawl, and Oyster Bay hamlet became a maritime business center. There was also scattered manufacturing and craft activity with Glen Cove a major center around the Duryea Starch Works, a leading national producer from 1859 to around 1900. Other small operations included gold beating in Hicksville, A. T. Stewart's brickworks in Bethpage, East Williston cart production, and miscellaneous producers of tin toys and hammocks. Localities that developed commercially around this time included the Villages of Hempstead (inc 1853), Rockville Centre (inc 1870), Sea Cliff (inc 1883), and Freeport (inc 1892). German and Italian immigrants provided much of the new growth in the mid- to late 19th century.

Creation of the County

By the late 19th century Queens Co had become two distinct regions: the fast-growing areas adjacent to Manhattan (by 1880, comprising 60% of its population) and the more rural settings of Hempstead, North Hempstead, and Oyster Bay. Increasing economic and political differences with the more densely populated western half of Queens Co led leaders in the eastern towns to consider political separation beginning in 1859. Discontent in western Queens Co over the isolated location of the county courthouse a mile west of present-day Mineola initiated a bill for the courthouse's relocation in 1869. The eastern towns retaliated with legislation to create a new county in which they would be incorporated along with Huntington, Smithtown, and Islip (Suffolk Co). Although defeated, the latter proposal killed the new courthouse proposal, but the controversy continued. The dominant population and political strength of the western towns led to the approval and opening of a new courthouse in Long Island City (Queens Co) in 1877. North Hempstead leaders initiated new state legislation that year to create "Ocean County" from the three eastern towns plus Huntington and Babylon (Suffolk Co). The powerful Democratic leaders of western Queens defeated the measure.

After the consolidation of New York City in 1898, a new effort to create a separate county was initiated by the three Queens Co towns not included in the municipal consolidation (Hempstead, North Hempstead, and Oyster Bay). The measure established a new boundary line that removed Rockaway Peninsula, Inwood, and parts of Lawrence, Cedarhurst, and Valley Stream from the Town of Hempstead and made them part of New York City. Immediately after the creation of Nassau Co, new state legislation was passed restoring this area, except for Rockaway Peninsula, to Nassau Co.

Citizens led by banker Benjamin Hicks gathered at Allen's Hotel at Mineola in 1898 and resolved to "have a county free from any entangling alliances with the great City of New York." Later, residents agreed on the name Nassau in honor of its English and Dutch heritage, represented in William III, King of England, a member of the House of Orange and Nassau. An act to establish a new county was introduced in the New York State legislature by local Republican leaders. Despite general public support, Queens Co politicians of both parties, hoping to maintain control of the territory, opposed the measure. It finally passed with the active assistance of Thomas C. Platt, then the powerful state Republican boss. Nassau Co came into existence 1 Jan 1899. Residents elected public officers and by public referendum chose to locate the county seat within one mile of the railroad station at Mineola. Although the Classical Revival county courthouse (now a national historic landmark) was built within a short distance of the Mineola train station, the structure is actually located in the Village of Garden City.

The Gold Coast and Suburbanization

The hilly, wooded, and picturesque landscape and bays near the North Shore combined with a multitude of sport and recreational activities prompted an era of millionaire estate building beginning with the 325-acre (132 ha) E. D. Morgan property in Wheatley Hills near Westbury in the 1880s. By the 1920s about 600 major estates, along with private golf courses, yacht clubs, and other exclusive facilities, covered large parts of the North Shore of Nassau Co and extended southward to Westbury and Jericho. The lavish lifestyles associated with the area that became known as the Gold Coast were acclaimed in the magazine *Country Life in America* and other arbiters of fashion. Woodsburgh and the Hewletts in the southwestern Five Towns area became a separate enclave of costly houses. Estates were also scattered throughout the central and southern villages, but these areas, particularly those served by the Long Island Rail Road, later underwent middle-class suburbanization.

Although commuters to New York City such as William Cullen Bryant established suburban homes before the Civil War, it was A. T. Stewart who attempted to establish the first suburban village in what became Garden City in 1869; Stewart's death in 1876 stalled that vision. While slow growth occurred in the old village centers to service the increasing number of estates and the recreational interests of middle-class visitors in the late 1800s, the pivotal influence on suburban growth was the 1911 extension of through railroad service to Pennsylvania Station in Manhattan. Between 1910 and 1930, with timely and convenient commuter service, Nassau's population tripled to 303,053. On the major South Shore line, commuters from Rockville Centre increased from 589 to more than 3,000, and on the North line, Port Washington commuters increased from 100 to more than 800. Large segments around the old hamlet centers were purchased by real estate speculators such as John Randall, developer of southern Freeport, and William Gibson in Valley Stream. Movie magnate I. J. Fox initiated development of Biltmore Shores in Massapequa, and publisher Frank A. Munsey's bequest of 600 acres (243 ha) to the Metropolitan Museum of Art made possible the creation of an exclusive residential area in Manhasset.

Parks and Parkways

The automobile's imprint on Nassau Co's landscape began early. From 1904 to 1910, the world's fastest cars competed across Nassau's dirt roads in the famed Vanderbilt Cup races. The Long Island Motor Parkway, America's first modern, albeit private, toll highway, linked northern Queens Co to Lake Ronkonkoma (Suffolk Co) and provided high-speed automobile access to central Nassau Co beginning in 1908. The Sunrise Highway was completed by the state along the South Shore in the late 1920s. This new highway and improvement of existing east-west roads was still inadequate to accommodate the surge of automobile use. With motor vehicle registrations soaring in the region in the 1930s, highway development was beyond the capacity of local governments. Local leaders supported creation of a new state agency, the Long Island State Park Commission (1924) to create new parks and parkways to serve the recreational needs of the population of New York City and the island. Under the dynamic leadership of Robert Moses, the commission and associated agencies under his control reshaped the vehicular, recreational, and development patterns of Long Island.

Construction began with the Southern State Parkway (1925–49) along the south side of the island, followed by the Northern State Parkway (1931–65) along the southern fringe of the Gold Coast in mid-Nassau. Despite opposition by estate owners and South Shore villages concerned about the intrusion of city motorists, Moses persevered, and an extensive parkway system was in place before the outbreak of World War II. The commission acquired acreage in Hempstead once used as water supply properties for New York City. There it developed Valley Stream and Hempstead Lake State Parks (both in 1925) with swimming, picnic grounds, play and sport fields, and bridle paths. After Moses secured support of local Republican leaders, Town of Hempstead voters approved a transfer of common lands in 1925 that enabled creation of Jones Beach State Park and construction of the Meadowbrook (1932–55) and Wantagh State (1927–65) Parkways. Opened by Gov Alfred E. Smith in 1929, Jones Beach State Park included a 2,413-acre (977 ha) barrier beach.

Early 20th-Century Economy

Estate and real estate development had reduced the 59,353 acres (24,019 ha) of farmland in 1900 to 23,477 acres (9,501 ha) in 1930. Potatoes continued as the dominant crop until 1941 when golden nematode infestation reduced potato yields. Milk production declined to below 1 million gallons (3.8 million l), while vegetable and horticultural products still provided employment for 5,977 residents and some 3,000 horses despite increased mechanization. The suburban growth of the 1950s and 1960s further reduced farm acreage to less than 1,000 acres (400 ha) in 1980 with only a dozen family market garden operations and one vineyard.

After aviation pioneer Glenn H. Curtiss made the first sustained air flight of 16 miles (25 km) across the Hempstead Plains in 1909, other aviators followed, drawn to test their craft above this flat, open prairie that was ideal for flying. Nassau Co became the home of two nationally significant airstrips. Roosevelt Field, named in 1918 in honor of Quentin Roosevelt (son of former president Theodore Roosevelt), became a center of civilian aviation and the starting point of Charles Lindbergh's famous 1927 flight. Nearby Mitchel Field was established in 1918 as an army air base. Named for former New York City mayor John Purroy Mitchel, it was a major military field until its closure in 1961. Each airfield attracted thousands of curious onlookers. Many small aircraft manufacturing companies were also drawn to Nassau Co during this period. Curtiss Engineering established the first large factory at Garden City in 1917. In 1929 Grumman Aircraft Engineering (later Northrop Grumman) established operations at Baldwin, moving to Farmingdale in 1932, and then to Bethpage in 1937. Seversky Aircraft (later Republic Aviation) opened its plant nearby in 1934. Producing naval and army aircraft during World War II, these factories, along with instrument-maker Sperry Gyroscope at Lake Success, employed some 90,000 workers and were essential to the World War II victory.

Other manufacturing in the county was limited. By 1930 the economy was based on its 120,000 commuters to New York City. In 1910 Doubleday and Page established a publishing plant at Garden City, one of the nation's largest by 1930. Far greater was the impact of the expanding estate- and home-building industries. Local business was led by 15,905 construction and 4,678 real estate jobs, and retail and wholesale services were provided by 16,857 people.

Religion, Education, and Culture

The influx of new residents in the 20th century resulted in a significant change in the ethnic and religious composition of the county. The population migration in the early 1900s included Irish and Italian working-class families that provided staff for estates. The postwar movement from New York City attracted many residents of Italian heritage, and the Roman Catholic Church expanded to serve these residents; the Diocese of Rockville Centre was created in 1957. The Jewish population also surged, reaching an estimated 395,000 in 1980. Synagogues spread, with concentrations on the Great Neck peninsula and in the Five Towns areas. In the last two decades of the century, dramatic population decline diminished the Jewish population by nearly half and continued the decline of the Protestant community, resulting in an increase in the Roman Catholic plurality.

Since the first private and public schools in Hempstead in the early 1700s, education has been a major element. Under state legislation of 1812 and 1814, common schools were established, with some 51 districts in the present Nassau Co by the late 1800s. In 1892 Rockville Centre District No. 21 opened the first high school, and by the turn of the century, Freeport and Great Neck did the same. Private academic programs were provided by Friends Academy, opened in Locust Valley in 1876 and still operating, and St. Paul's School in Garden City, founded in 1877. The common school districts expanded with the population, and by the late 1950s most had converted to Union Free School district status with high schools and district superintendents. The postwar generation of school expansion often involved continual, controversial tax increases, but the educational systems were the pride of most communities. Economic problems have hampered the quality of schools in low-income communities, requiring state intervention in Roosevelt and Hempstead in the 1990s.

In 2003 Nassau Co had 57 independent school districts and was home to 11 colleges and universities, the largest private ones being Adelphi University in Garden City, C. W. Post in Brookville, and Hofstra University in Hempstead. There were also three SUNY campuses, including Nassau Community College, with more than 20,000 students. Locally based research institutions included Cold Spring Harbor Laboratory. The Nassau Library system provided central services to 63 public libraries.

Weekly newspapers have served some villages since the mid-1800s, and New York City dailies were delivered to the area beginning in the early 1900s. In 1940 *Newsday* was founded at Hempstead as a daily to compete with the *Nassau Daily Review Star* (1921). A tabloid, *Newsday* grew with suburbia and in 2004, published at Melville (Suffolk Co) as part of the Times Mirror chain, is among the top five daily newspapers in circulation in the United States.

Politics

Early 20th-century suburbanization prompted an unprecedented demand for increased local government as residents attempted to control development and manage local services. An initial wave of growth preceding World War I led to the creation of 14 new villages, which joined the 5 already existing. More intensive growth in the 1920s and 1930s led to the creation of 45 more villages, predominantly along the North and South Shores, leaving large unincorporated areas in the Towns of Hempstead and Oyster Bay. After 1921 Nassau was authorized by state law to reorganize its county government. This threat and the desire of many small, exclusive, wealthier areas to control their growth, limit taxes, and share new state aid to localities, climaxed with the organization of 13 more villages in 1931. The county's 1938 charter restricted villages from enacting their own zoning, removing that incentive for incorporation.

Several citizen commissions unsuccessfully proposed reforms in county government structure. In the mid-1930s, J. Russel Sprague, Town of Hempstead supervisor and astute county Republican leader, led an effort to reform county government while retaining existing towns and villages. In 1938 Nassau adopted the county executive form of government with an elected chief administrator. Centralized police, social services, health, and public works enabled it to meet the challenges of post–World War II growth.

Under Sprague's leadership the county Republican Party became one of the strongest political machines in the nation, dominating local government throughout the century. The Republican Party, bolstered by a strong local patronage system, attached a "Tammany" stigma to their Democratic opponents. Congressman Leonard Hall, an early supporter of Dwight D. Eisenhower, was chairman of the Republican Congressional Committee from 1946 to 1952 and served as National Republican chairman from 1953 to 1957). In 1961 Democrat Eugene H. Nickerson defeated the Sprague machine and became county executive, thus initiating two-party government in the county. But the new Republican chairman, Joseph Margiotta, led the party in regaining its power, electing Alfonse M. D'Amato of Island Park as US senator from 1980 to 1998. William Casey of Roslyn was a trusted advisor to Pres Ronald Reagan and served as director of the CIA from 1981 to 1986.

In recent decades county government has been involved in voting and political rights cases that led to the abolition of the county Board of Supervisors in 1996 and the creation of a county legislature. The Democratic Party, taking advantage of convictions of Republicans for corruption, regained both legislative and executive leadership. In the Town of Hempstead they also won creation of "councilmanic districts," which made council members representative of a portion of the town's residents instead of the entire town.

Recent History

In the 1920s and 1930s, Abraham Levitt and his sons William and Alfred became major custom home builders in several Nassau subdivisions. After World War II, William led the firm in establishing several experimental, mass-produced, inexpensive housing developments in North Hempstead. Beginning in 1947 Abraham Levitt and Sons transformed former Hempstead potato fields into a community of 17,447 that was acclaimed to be America's 20th-century prototype suburb. The rise of Levittown exemplified the explosive growth in Nassau Co's population, which doubled from 672,765 in 1950 to 1,300,171 in 1960. Vacant lots in older villages were filled, and entire new communities sprang up across the open central plains in the center of the Town of Hempstead, including Levittown, East Meadow, and Uniondale. Further east in Oyster Bay, the older villages of Hicksville and Farmingdale and the farm hamlets of Jericho, Syosset, Plainview, Plainedge, and Bethpage became suburban communities. South Shore meadows from Oceanside through the Massapequas that had remained undeveloped were then filled with housing tracts. County government expanded to provide sewer systems, roads, parks and natural area preservation, public hospital services, and expanded judicial and police protection.

In 1970 the county's population peaked at 1,428,838 as most of the county approached maximum development based on existing building lot regulations. The growth also transformed the character of the county's populace. More than 80% of new residents formerly lived in New York City; some 20% were of Italian heritage, 13% were of Russian ancestry, and 13% were of German ancestry. The ethnic mosaic continued to broaden during the last quarter of the century. According to the 2000 federal census Nassau Co's white population was below 79%; African Americans constituted 10% and Asians 5% of the population. In addition, 10% of the county's population is of Latino ethnicity. Substantial numbers of Asian Indian, Iranian, Columbian, Chinese, Haitian, and Korean are recent immigrants. The Elmont School District, for instance, serves children of more than 50 languages. The county has also been a testing ground for national educational and social issues. In 1962 the US Supreme Court ruled against the use of prayer in public school in a case originating in the Herricks School District.

Nassau Co's aviation industry had some difficulty adjusting to the post–World War II economy. While local firms helped lead the development of military fighter jets, it was less successful in the civilian aircraft market. In 1962 NASA awarded Grumman Aircraft Engineering Corp the contract to design and build the Apollo lunar module, a project that employed over 9,000 space technicians. Aircraft manufacturing ended in the early 1990s, dealing a severe blow to the local economy. Nevertheless, aerospace parts, electronics, and printing companies, and diversified small industrial parks continued to provide local employment.

Sperry's Lake Success plant was the first home of the United Nations (1946–51). Mitchel and Roosevelt Fields were surrounded by suburban growth and ceased operations by 1961, but provided open land for a large shopping center and an educational/recreational complex that included Hofstra University, Nassau Community College, and the Nassau Veterans Memorial Coliseum. The Cradle of Aviation Museum opened in 2002.

An expansion of office space and related service businesses of banking, legal, insurance, and accounting firms significantly changed the county's economy. By the end of the 1980s, more than 30 million ft^2 (2.8 million m^2) of office buildings provided service concentrations in the Mitchel Field area, Lake Success, Garden City, and Great Neck. Retail business expanded, and Nassau Co took the lead among the nation's largest market areas in retail sales per household based on one of the nation's highest per capita incomes (more than $46,000 in 2000). Major regional shopping centers dominate retailing, including Roosevelt Field Mall in Garden City, Broadway Mall in Hicksville, Green Acres Mall in Valley Stream, and Sunrise Mall in Massapequa. Of Nassau Co's workforce, 12% commuted to New York City in 2000, but commuting to offices and industry on Long Island has increased pressure on local highways.

Although still a preeminent suburb of New York City, Nassau Co continues to lessen its economic and cultural dependence on the metropolis by developing major cultural and recreational facilities, including the Nassau Veterans Memorial Coliseum, the Tilles Center for the Performing Arts, Museums at Mitchel, higher education facilities, and expanded university hospital complexes. Its government and business leaders are pursuing brownfield remediation, redevelopment of village downtowns and maximum utilization of undeveloped parcels, and housing initiatives to retain and provide employment for its younger generations.

The pre-suburban period is covered by *History of Queens County* (1882). An update for Nassau Co is Paul Bailey, *Long Island: A History of Two Great Counties,* 3 vols (1949). The three most important sources are *Hometown Long Island* (1999); Joann P. Krieg and Natalie A. Naylor, eds., *Nassau County from Rural Hinterland to Suburban Metropolis* (2000); and Edward J. Smits, *Nassau: Suburbia USA* (1974). Other books useful for the entire county's history include *Long Island, Our Story* (1998); Bette S. Weidman and Linda B. Martin, *Nassau County, Long Island, in Early Photographs, 1869–1940* (1981); Richard A. Winsche, *The History of Nassau County Community Place Names* (1999); and *Nassau County Data Book* (1978). Colonial period community histories include Bernice Schultz Marshall, *Colonial Hempstead* (1937); Natalie A. Naylor, ed., *The Roots and Heritage of Hempstead Town* (1994); and Van Santvoord Merle-Smith, *The Village of Oyster Bay, Its Founding and Growth from 1653 to 1700.* Comprehensive community histories include Robert R. Coles and Peter L. Van Santvoord, *A History of Glen Cove* (1967); Mildred H. Smith, *History of Garden City* (1963); *A History of the Town of Hempstead, 1644–1969* (1969); Preston Bassett, *History of Rockville Centre* (1969); Joan Gay Kent, *Discovering Sands Point* (2000); and Roy W. Moger, *Roslyn: Then and Now* (1965; rev ed. 1992).

Edward J. Smits

National Association for the Advancement of Colored People (NAACP). Founded in New York City in 1909, the organization relocated to Baltimore in 1986. Formed in the wake of a race riot in 1908 in Abraham Lincoln's hometown (Springfield, Ill), an integrated group of 53 leaders signed the Call, announcing a meeting on civil rights that began on 31 May 1909 in Manhattan. Among the prominent early leaders of the organization, known by 1910 as the NAACP, were middle-class socialist Mary White Ovington, editors William English Walling and Oswald Garrison Villard, progressive reformer Henry Moskowitz, literary critic Joel E. Spingarn, and lawyer Arthur Spingarn (brothers). The most prominent African American founder was W. E. B. DuBois, who in 1910 became founding editor of *Crisis,* the NAACP's national magazine.

The first local branch was organized in Manhattan in 1911. Early successes included a 1912 suit against a New York City theater owner who refused seats to a group of African Americans. The same year NAACP won admission to New York's Central Preparatory School for the son of Dr Owen M. Waller, a black NAACP member. Race riots during World War I gave new focus to the organization's campaign against lynching and racial violence. The NAACP sponsored a memorable silent march in New York City on 17 July 1917 to protest the vicious race riot in East St. Louis, Ill. Legal efforts by NAACP against Jim Crow had two early victories: *Guinn v United States* (1915), which outlawed the grandfather clause (a clause in southern state constitutions that prevented African American suffrage), and *Buchanan v Warley* (1917), which made it unconstitutional to exclude Blacks from residential areas. In 1940 the NAACP created a tax-exempt legal arm, the NAACP Legal and Defense Fund, headquartered in New York City, which under the direction of Thurgood Marshall would fight many landmark civil rights cases, including *Brown v Board of Education* (1954). By the time writer James Weldon Johnson became secretary of the NAACP in 1921, African Americans were more prominently represented in the organization's leadership positions. Walter White served as executive secretary from 1931 to 1955. During the depression and New Deal, the NAACP advocated including Blacks on equal footing in government programs. During World War II it pressed the military for commissioned black officers and for fair economic treatment on the home front. It was also a leading national force in the civil rights battles of the 1950s and 1960s. Roy Wilkins served as executive director from 1955 to 1977.

The NAACP established branches in counties throughout the state beginning in the 1910s. Branches oversaw local chapters, which took the lead in fighting the vestiges of legal segregation in public education and the growing problem of de facto segregation in education, and in general advocating for civil rights for local citizens. The Buffalo chapter formed in 1915 and was one of the earliest. Rochester's branch was founded in 1919. The Jamaica (Queens Co) branch was founded in 1927 with the assistance of DuBois, and its first branch leaders suppressed a Ku Klux Klan movement in the community, desegregated local movie theaters, and forced Queens General Hospital to hire black doctors and nurses. The Albany chapter formed in 1935, a time when police treated Blacks violently. Members worked to foster better police community relations, contributed to the national antilynching campaign, and pressed local department stores to hire African Americans. In Schenectady an interracial group of men and women founded a chapter in 1949 and initially targeted discrimination in housing and in hiring and promoted Blacks who worked in private industry and municipal government. During the 1950s and 1960s, with General Electric a major Schenectady employer and a strong union and a minor Communist Party presence in the city, the Schenectady branch found itself confronting employers, unions, and the NAACP's strict anticommunist membership policy. In the 1960s and early 1970s that branch noted the city's police force and schools were not hiring Blacks and therefore began to focus on public employee discrimination. Following World War II branches continued to be founded throughout the state: Syracuse/Onondaga Co, Troy (Rensselaer Co), Utica/Oneida Co, and Nassau and Suffolk Cos.

The role of the NAACP has changed since its heyday in the 1960s, but it has been active in numerous fronts, including civil rights, apartheid in South Africa, affirmative action, and, in general, the interests of African Americans. A recent episode, which generated national publicity for the Buffalo chapter, took place after the December 1995 death of Cynthia Wiggins, an African American mother killed as she crossed the street on her way to work at a suburban mall, from which city busses with predominantly African American riders were banned.

NAACP Schenectady and Albany Branches. Papers. State Univ of New York at Albany

Ross, Barbara Joyce. *J. E. Spingarn and the Rise of the NAACP, 1911–1939* (New York: Atheneum, 1972)

Wedin, Carolyn. *Inheritors of the Spirit: Mary White Ovington and the Founding of the NAACP* (New York: Wiley, 1998)

John Recchiuti

National Baseball Hall of Fame and Museum. The nation's first sports hall of fame and museum was established in Cooperstown (Otsego Co) in 1939 by local philanthropist Stephen C. Clark and National League president Ford Frick. Although there is no credence to the founding myth of the Hall of Fame—that Abner Doubleday invented baseball in the village in 1839—this has had little impact on its subsequent success. The museum explores the historical development of baseball and its impact on American culture by collecting, preserving, exhibiting, and interpreting its collections, as well as honoring those who have made outstanding contributions to baseball.

The institution is composed of the Hall of Fame itself, a gallery of plaques representing the 256 (as of 2003) elected players, managers, umpires, executives, and pioneers of the game; a 60,000 ft^2 (5,574 m^2) museum featuring exhibits on many aspects of the game's history and culture; and a research library. New museum wings were added in 1950, 1980, and 1989, when the Fetzer-Yawkey wing was opened in conjunction with the institution's 50th anniversary. The first Hall of Fame library building opened in 1968, and a major expansion and redesign of the library was completed in 1994. The new library includes the A. Bartlett Giamatti Research Center, which more than 10,000 researchers visit each year. The library holds approximately 2 million documents including books, photographs, video and audio recordings, and archival records. The Hall of Fame also features an educational outreach program, multimedia production facilities, an art gallery, a publishing program, an endowed internship program, and a museum shop.

There are over 160,000 artifacts in the museum's collection, including approximately 130,000 baseball cards. There are also historic bats, balls, gloves, uniforms, and other items related to the game or its famous personalities. Featured artifacts include the ball used in the Troy Haymakers' defeat of the New York Mutuals, 25-10, at Brooklyn's Union Grounds on 25 May 1871 and the Home Base Ball Game, an early baseball board game first published by McLoughlin Bros of New York City in 1897. As of 2003, 26 native New Yorkers have been inducted in the Hall of Fame, including Sandy Koufax (1972), Jim Palmer (1990), and Phil Rizzuto (1994). In addition, through 2003 there were 80 Hall of Fame enshrinees with at least four years' service with New York State major league teams.

Hall of Fame Weekend, which takes place in late July or early August, is the institution's major annual event. It includes the Sunday induction of new Hall of Famers and a number of related festivities. Other annual summer events include the Hall of Fame Game, an exhibition between two major league teams at Cooperstown's Doubleday Field, and the Cooperstown Symposium on Baseball and American Culture, which is cosponsored with SUNY Oneonta. Held in early June, the symposium attracts scholars from nearly every academic discipline, who present their research and play a ball game by 19th-century rules. In 2002 the museum embarked on an ambitious 10-city, five-year touring exhibition entitled Baseball as America, the first major American tour of the collections. The Hall of Fame is visited by 325,000–400,000 people annually, with 90% of visits made during the summer. Approximately 80 people are employed year-round, and the summer staff is nearly 200.

National Baseball Hall of Fame and Museum, http://www.baseballhalloffame.org

Thorn, John. *Treasures of the Baseball Hall of Fame: The Official Companion to the Collection at Cooperstown* (New York: Villard, 1998)

Tim Wiles

National Grape Co-operative Association. In 1933 Jacob "Jack" Kaplan purchased, sight unseen, the Chautauqua and Erie Grape Growers Cooperative of Brocton (Chautauqua Co). By 1935 the renamed National Grape Corp was breaking even; by 1945, it was grossing about $3 million a year. In 1945 Kaplan proposed that the growers form one large cooperative, combining many smaller ones, and that they buy his Brocton plant with profits placed in escrow until they reached $2 million, at which time he would transfer ownership to the new National Grape Co-operative Association. In 1945 Kaplan also purchased Welch Grape Juice Co and became its president. The National Grape Corp had been Welch's major competitor, but Kaplan did not intend to compete with it. Under his plan, grapes produced by the co-op were guaranteed a sale to Welch's, which leased its Brocton facility to the co-op for 3 years, and its Westfield (Chautauqua Co), Silver Creek (Chautauqua Co), and North East, Pa, plants for 21 years. Before the leases could expire, however, in 1952, the National Grape Co-operative Association voted to buy Welch's in a unique deal, of which Kaplan was the architect. Again, none of the co-op members had to risk any of their personal funds. The co-op assumed ownership of Welch's in 1956 under the terms of the contract. The two organizations maintained independent boards of directors and created a model business relationship. New products and marketing techniques were introduced with great success. In 1983 the Welch corporate offices moved to Concord, Mass. The following year the Brocton plant closed. Westfield production lines were transferred to North East, Pa. At the start of the 21st century, the co-op had 1,400 members. Under its leadership, Welch's plants have been modernized and sales have steadily increased.

Chazanof, William. *Welch's Grape Juice: From Corporation to Co-operative* (Syracuse: Syracuse Univ Press, 1977)

Pam Kirst

National Guard. See NEW YORK AIR NATIONAL GUARD; NEW YORK ARMY NATIONAL GUARD.

National Gypsum Company. Manufacturer of wallboard and related home-building materials with a presence in the Buffalo area. National Gypsum was founded in 1925 by Joseph Haggerty, Clarence Williams, and Melvin Baker. Baker convinced wealthy local residents, whose names he found from Erie Co automobile registrations, to underwrite the fledgling company and to build a plant in Clarence Center (Erie Co), where rich mineral deposits existed. The company employed 50 people when the plant began operating in 1926. By 1937 National Gypsum was listed on the New York Stock Exchange. The growth of home building in the United States during the 1920s and continuing into the postwar period contributed to the company's success, while its strategy of geographic decentralization, vertical integration, and product diversification helped it become the second largest gypsum producer in the United States. Sales grew from $2.5 million in the early 1930s to $75 million by 1950. By 1965 National Gypsum earned $257 million in sales, operated 72 plants, including four plants and three offices in New York State, and employed over 11,000 people nationally. In 1976 it moved its headquarters from Buffalo to Dallas and later to Charlotte, NC. Gold Bond Building Products, one of Gypsum's largest divisions, moved from Buffalo to Charlotte in 1978. Delcor bought the company in 1995. In 2002 the company relocated most employees from its Tonawanda (Erie Co) research center to Charlotte but continued to operate a treatment plant in Rensselaer.

Bockmon, Marc. *Turning Points: The National Gypsum Story* (Dallas: Taylor Publishing, 1990)

Howard R. Stanger

National Invitation Tournament (NIT). Created by the Metropolitan Basketball Writers Association of New York, it was the first attempt at crowning a single national intercollegiate men's basketball champion by means of a postseason play-off series. The first men's NIT, held at the end of the 1937–38 season, consisted of a six-team field and ended with Temple University as champion. Responsibility for administering the tournament, including the issuing of invitations, was shifted in 1940 to the Metropolitan Intercollegiate Basketball Committee (now Metropolitan Intercollegiate Basketball Association), the Eastern Collegiate Athletic Conference affiliate that included Fordham University, Manhattan College, New York University, St. John's University, and Wagner College. The tournament was played entirely at Madison Square Garden until 1977, when preliminary games were played at the home courts of participating teams, with only the semifinal and final rounds played at the Garden. In 1980 the field expanded to 32 teams. More than 220 schools have taken part in the tournament since 1938; St. John's University holds the record for number of appearances (25) and titles (5). Other tournament champions from New York State include Long Island University, City College, and St. Bonaventure University. Because of the NIT's success, the NCAA Championship tournament, which gained recognition as the more reliable barometer of national superiority in men's college basketball by the late 1950s, has not scheduled any of its games in New York City since 1974. In 1985 the NIT added a preseason tournament, with only the championship rounds played at Madison Square Garden.

National Invitation Tournament, http://www.nit.org

David Marc

National Organization for Women–New York State (NOW-NYS). Women's civil rights membership organization. Following the 1966 establishment of NOW nationally to obtain full partnership with men in society, chapters sprang up throughout New York State, with the first established that year in New York City. A committee to fight for legal abortions was formed in 1967. In 1974 NOW-NYS was formally established, and since 1982 the state president has been a full-time, paid position. NOW has fought for a number of issues, including those concerning reproduction, women in the workplace, lesbians, and violence against women. NOW-NYS worked from 1972 to 1988 to pass the Equal Rights Amendment (ERA) to the federal constitution. In the early 1970s a Rochester NOW lawsuit resulted in the elimination of sex-segregated employment ads. Enforcement of New York State antidiscrimination laws in the Division of Human Rights has long been an issue for NOW-NYS and the subject of contentious litigation. The *NOW-NYS Action Report* began publication in 1984 and was replaced in the mid-1990s with the *NOW-NYS Reporter.* The largest women's rights organization in the state, in 2001 NOW-NYS had approximately 14,000 members in 23 chapters.

See also ABORTION; LESBIANS, GAYS, BISEXUALS, AND TRANSGENDERED PEOPLE.

NOW-NYS Administrative History, http://library.albany.edu/speccoll/findaids/apap029.htm

Jane R. Plitt

National Park Service areas. Natural, historic, and recreation areas of national significance administered by the National Park Service (NPS), a federal bureau created in 1916.

PARKS ESTABLISHED 1933–45

The Statue of Liberty National Monument on Bedloe's Island [now Liberty Island] in Upper New York Bay, designated a national monument in 1924, was the first NPS site in New York State. This was one of many parks and monuments transferred in 1933 from the US War Department to the Office of National Parks, Buildings, and Reservations, now the NPS. In 1935 Congress authorized Fort Stanwix National Monument, now in Rome (Oneida Co) and in 1938, Saratoga National Historical Park, subject to the donation of land for the new parks. The Saratoga Park was formally established in 1948, but land for Fort Stanwix was not acquired until 1973.

Pres Franklin D. Roosevelt pressed for Vanderbilt Mansion National Historic Site (1940) in Hyde Park (Dutchess Co), just 2 miles (3 km) north of his lifelong home. He also donated his own estate to be administered as a National Park Service area. A 1939 law establishing the first presidential library at Hyde Park provided for the Roosevelt family to donate other portions of the estate to the US government at a future date. In 1944 Secretary of the Interior Harold Ickes designated the presidential home as the Home of Franklin D. Roosevelt National Historic Site.

EXPANSION INTO NEW YORK CITY

The NPS's spread into New York City between the late 1940s and the early 1960s reflected a developing alliance between the historic preservation community and the NPS. Transfer of Castle Clinton National Monument in Battery Park to the NPS in 1950 ended a decade-long conflict over the preservation of the building, which had been slated for demolition. Built 1808–11 as a defense for New York Harbor, it later functioned as a theater and opera house, as an immigration station, and as the New York Aquarium from 1896 to 1941. When the NPS acquired the partially demolished structure, preservationists considered it an important victory for historic preservation. Reconstruction, which took 25 years to complete, reflected the building's initial use as a fortification.

Subsequently, several other New York City sites managed by preservation organizations became part of the NPS system. Federal Hall National Memorial at 26 Wall St was built as a customhouse, completed in 1842, and later used as the US subtreasury. Located on the site of the first Federal Hall (demolished in 1812), where George Washington took the oath of office as president, it was designated by Secretary Ickes a National Historic Site in 1939 to coincide with the opening of the New York World's Fair. The Federal Hall Memorial Associates administered it under a cooperative agreement with the NPS until 1955, when the latter took over site ownership and administration. General Grant National Memorial, at 122 St and Riverside Drive, the largest mausoleum in the United States, was funded, constructed, and operated as a memorial site by the Grant Monument Association from 1885, when planning began, until its donation to the NPS in 1959. Theodore Roosevelt Birthplace National Historic Site at 28 East 20th St in Manhattan began as a project of the Women's Roosevelt Memorial Association in 1922. A total reconstruction, it was furnished, in part, based on the memories of Theodore Roosevelt's two sisters and his second wife, Edith Kermit Carow Roosevelt. The Theodore Roosevelt Association donated the birthplace to the NPS in 1962. Alexander Hamilton's country retreat in northern Manhattan in Harlem is preserved as Hamilton Grange National Memorial. The building was moved approximately 350 feet (107 m) southeast to its current location at 287 Convent Ave in the 1880s and acquired for the American Scenic and Historic Preservation Society in 1924. The society transferred ownership to the NPS in 1962. The site's authorizing legislation required it to be "preserved in a fitting setting."

NEW PARKS AFTER 1960

Reflecting a new social and political agenda, the NPS after 1960 added new sites intended to represent the entirety of the American experience. The agency, under Director George Hartzog, developed a plan to guide new site additions in 1972, but even before that, new site additions reflected congressional and administration efforts to expand the system, a resurgent interest in historic preservation, concern for urban recreation, and the new social history. The creation of Fire Island National Seashore in 1964 followed studies by the Mellon family foundation and the Outdoor Recreation Resources Review Commission that recommended the development of seashores. Occupying most of the 32 mi (52 km) long barrier island off the southern coast of Long Island in Suffolk Co, the park includes beaches, sand dunes, and a federally designated wilderness area that followed the passage of the Eastern National Wilderness Areas Act in 1975. Similarly, the New York Regional Plan Association's proposal for an urban park, eventuating in Gateway National Recreation Area, gained wide support in the aftermath of the urban violence of the late 1960s. More urban than Fire Island, the park encompasses 26,000 acres (10,522 ha), mostly beach and unused military properties, in three units: Jamaica Bay and Breezy Point in Brooklyn and Queens; the southeastern shoreline of Staten Island; and Sandy Hook, NJ. Congress established the park in 1972 as one of the first urban recreation areas.

The park system also benefited from the Wild and Scenic Rivers Act and the National Trails Systems Act, both passed in 1968. The Appalachian Trail, extending 2,167 miles (3,487 km)—88 miles (142 km) through New York State from Warwick (Orange Co) to Dover (Dutchess Co)—was named by the trails act as an initial component of the system and is administered as the Appalachian National Scenic Trail (1968). The Upper Delaware Scenic and Recreational River along the New York State–Pennsylvania border was designated a National Wild and Scenic River in 1978. It runs 73 miles (117 km) from Hancock (Delaware Co) to Deerpark (Orange Co). Reflecting the national trend that included many diverse cultural sites within the system, the Statue of Liberty National Monument was expanded in 1965 to include nearby Ellis Island. More recent parks included the Eleanor Roosevelt National Historic Site at Hyde Park in 1977 and the Women's Rights National Historical Park in Seneca Falls (Seneca Co) in 1980. Val-Kill, Eleanor Roosevelt's principal residence from 1945 to her death in 1962, was historically part of Roosevelt's Hyde Park estate and remained in family ownership until 1970. The site opened to the public on Eleanor Roosevelt's 100th birthday in 1984. Other sites added during this period include Sagamore Hill National Historic Site (1962), Theodore Roosevelt's home in Oyster Bay (Nassau Co); Theodore Roosevelt Inaugural National Historic Site on Delaware Ave in Buffalo (1966), where Roosevelt took the oath of office on 14 Sept 1901 as the 26th president of the United States following the assassination of Pres William McKinley; Martin Van Buren National Historic Site (1974) in Kinderhook (Columbia Co); and Saint Paul's Church National Historic Site (1978), a colonial church and site in Mount Vernon (Westchester Co) associated with freedom of the press.

RECENT DEVELOPMENTS

In the mid-1980s, the NPS undertook a $350 million restoration of the Statue of Liberty and Ellis Island largely funded by the Statue of Liberty–Ellis Island Foundation. In the 1990s the service began to provide planning and technical assistance to "heritage areas" and "affiliated areas" designated by Congress. In New York State, Congress authorized the Hudson River Valley National Heritage Area as "the landscape that defined America" (1996) and the Erie Canalway National Heritage Corridor (2000). Affiliated areas authorized were the Lower East Side Tenement National Historic Site (1998) at 97 Orchard St in Manhattan and the Thomas Cole National Historic Site (1999) in Catskill (Greene Co). The most recent expansion of the park system in New York State is Governors Island National Monument in New York Co, added in 2001. The NPS counted 16,621,375 recreational visitors to national parks in New York State in 2001.

Blumberg, Barbara. *Celebrating the Immigrant: An Administrative History of the Statue of Liberty National Monument, 1952–1982* (Boston: National Park Service, 1985)

Foresta, Ronald. *America's National Parks and Their Keepers* (Washington, DC: Resources for the Future, 1985)

Mackintosh, Barry. *The National Parks: Shaping the System* (Washington, DC: US Department of the Interior, 1991)

National Park Service. "Parks and Recreation," http://www.nps.gov/parks.html

Rettie, Dwight F. *Our National Park System: Caring for America's Greatest Natural and Historic Treasures* (Urbana and Chicago: Univ of Illinois Press, 1995)

Paul O. Weinbaum

National Technical Institute for the Deaf. Founded by Congress in 1965, the world's first technical school for the deaf was established at the Rochester Institute of Technology after a national advisory group established by Pres Lyndon Johnson selected the location in 1966. Dr Robert Frisina, a specialist in issues of childhood deafness with a doctorate in audiology from Northwestern University, agreed to leave his position as dean of the Graduate School at Gallaudet College to serve as the NTID's first director. Seventy-one students were admitted, and classes began in September 1969. The campus's main building, dedicated in 1974, is named in honor of Pres Johnson, who signed the bill establishing the school into law. In 2002 the student body numbered some 1,100. The institute offers associate, bachelor's, and master's degrees in the arts, sciences, and a variety of technical fields.

Gordon, Dane R. *Rochester Institute of Technology: Industrial Development and Educational Innovation in an American City* (Lewiston, NY: Edwin Mellen Press, 1982)

R. A. R. Edwards

National Woman's Party (NWP). Suffrage organization with substantial New York State membership. Founded by Quaker suffragist Alice Paul in Washington, DC, in 1916, the NWP revitalized the forces struggling since 1848 to achieve the vote for women. The party had its origins in a 1910 committee, soon named the Congressional Union, of the National American Woman Suffrage Association (NAWSA). Set out to achieve national woman suffrage via a federal amendment to the US Constitution, this division of NAWSA adopted an aggressive strategy of picketing and demonstrations at the White House. These tactics, patterned after Harriot Stanton Blatch's Women's Political Union campaign at Albany's State House in 1908, led NAWSA to sever ties with the militant wing in 1914. As the NWP the militants continued to demonstrate with the sole goal of promoting woman suffrage. Their White House picketing brought much publicity, particularly after demonstrators were imprisoned. New York State NWP members included Harriot Stanton Blatch, Crystal Eastman, Charlotte Perkins Gilman, Doris Stevens, and Alva Belmont, who was the group's main source of financial support. With the 1919 passage of a federal suffrage amendment, many members left the party. Those remaining debated over a new focus for the group. Belmont wanted an organization dedicated to abolishing sex discrimination in the United States. Blatch saw a need for a feminist force in the world to promote world peace and to fight communism; she also warned against alliances with other political parties. By January 1921 Belmont's views won out, and the party dedicated itself to a single purpose, the passage of the Equal Rights Amendment (ERA), which would be presented to the US Congress repeatedly from 1923 through the 1970s; New York State would ratify the amendment in 1972. From the 1920s the party's membership stayed small, and it never again achieved the glory of the suffrage years. By 1980 infighting and a lack of new blood had virtually destroyed the NWP, though in 2002 it was officially still in existence.

Lunardini, Christine A. *From Equal Suffrage to Equal Rights: Alice Paul and the National Woman's Party, 1910–1928* (New York: New York Univ Press, 1986)

Neumann, Caryn Ellen. "The National Woman's Party and the Equal Rights Amendment, 1945–1977" (MA thesis, Florida Atlantic Univ, 1994)

Caryn E. Neumann

National Women's Hall of Fame. Nonprofit educational institution in Seneca Falls (Seneca Co). The hall was established in 1969 to honor American women who have made significant contributions to society in the arts, athletics, business, education, government, the humanities, philanthropy, and science. Located on the site of the famous Seneca Falls Convention of 1848, the structure housing the organization was purchased in 1979. A renovated bank, it lies in the city's historic district, just down the street from the Women's Rights National Historical Park, and features exhibits, artifacts, offices, and a research library for women's achievements and struggles, many of which began in Seneca Falls.

Each fall the organization conducts an induction ceremony in Seneca Falls to recognize the accomplishments of outstanding women, both living and dead. Selected by a national panel of judges, the inductees have been trailblazers who have changed the paradigms for future generations and advanced society to new levels. One of the first was activist Elizabeth Cady Stanton, the principal organizer of the Seneca Falls Convention. By 2002, 195 had been inducted, many of them New Yorkers, including the country's first female medical doctor, Elizabeth Blackwell (1821–1910), who received her degree at Geneva Medical College (now Hobart and William Smith Colleges); the first female African-American federal court judge, Constance Baker Motley (*b* 1921), who was also the first black woman elected to the New York State Senate; and the first female spacecraft pilot, Eileen Collins (*b* 1956).

National Women's Hall of Fame, http://www.greatwomen.org

Margaret D. Costello

Nation of Islam. See AFRICAN AMERICANS; BLACK NATIONALISM; ISLAM.

nativism. Anti-immigrant movement. Although rooted in Protestant anti-Catholic prejudices, its emergence in the 1830s owed much to the strains and dislocations of economic modernization and rapid urbanization; these twin forces transformed the northeast and Great Lakes regions. Many native-born Protestants saw their world of independent agrarian smallholders, shopkeepers, and artisans under assault by the expanding and intensifying market economy. Urbanization disrupted traditional family and communal mechanisms for addressing deviance, indigence, and illness. The new cities brought rising rates of violence, physical and mental illness, and poverty.

A growing influx of Catholic Irish and German immigrants intensified job and wage competition to native-born workers. In New York State the Catholic population rose from 13,000 in 1815 to about 250,000 by 1855. The new arrivals often became unskilled workers in low-wage jobs. They filled jails, poorhouses, hospitals, and public relief rolls. Some native-born Protestant workers lashed out at social changes and increased economic competition by targeting Catholic immigrants. The predominantly Protestant country became increasingly hostile toward the new cities and new Americans.

In New York State organized nativist protest began in New York City, Brooklyn, and Buffalo. By July 1835 New York City activists launched a local political party, the Native American Democratic Association (NADA), to combat rising Catholic German and Irish political influence within the regular Tammany Hall Democratic machine and city government. With no Whig candidates running, NADA polled 39% of the vote in the November 1835 New York City elections. NADA nominated inventor Samuel F. B. Morse for mayor in spring 1836, but renewed Whig competition held NADA to only 6% of the vote. In 1837 NADA, with Whig support, swept the mayoral and common council elections but subsequently declined in local electoral influence.

Nativism resurged in a New York City public schools controversy in the 1840s. Antebellum state-supported public schools used anti-Catholic textbooks and based classroom lessons on the Protestant King James Bible. In response, Catholics established their own parochial schools and called for a share of state subsidies. Catholic Church leaders such as Bishops John J. Hughes in New York City and John Timon in Buffalo lobbied for these subsidies. In 1840 Whig governor William H. Seward endorsed state and local funding for both parochial and public schools. In response, nativists undermined an 1842 state law aimed at reducing Protestant sectarian influence in public schools. The state legislature replaced the Public School Society with elected local school boards, prompting nativists to elect school officials who would keep public schools Protestant in their orientation. In 1844 a new nativist political party, the American Republican Party (ARP), successfully elected James Harper as mayor in New York City. The ARP's agenda included a 21-year naturalization period and exclusion of the foreign-born from public office. ARP faded away after 1844 in the wake of violent nativist riots in Philadelphia, which undermined nativism nationally.

In the mid-1840s some nativists joined secret fraternal orders, such as the Order of United Americans (1844) in New York City, whose members pledged to vote for or nominate only native-born Protestant candidates. The explosive growth of immigration in the late 1840s and early 1850s spurred a rise in nativism's popularity. In 1854 a nativist mob in Palmyra (Wayne Co) burned a Catholic church. Nativist organizations coalesced in 1854 to form the national American (Know-Nothing) Party. Politicians such as Millard Fillmore hoped to use nativism to build a national party that could unite North and South to overcome the slavery issue. The Know-Nothing Party faded after its failure to affect the outcome of the 1856 presidential election. Nativism in other guises would return after the Civil War. The American Protective Association (APA), which sought to exclude Catholics from elected office, was founded in 1887 and was supported in Buffalo and Rochester in the 1890s. The greatest triumph of the immigration restriction movement, after decades of agitation, would be the Immigration Act of 1924, which drastically reduced immigration quotas of those not from northern European countries.

See also CATHOLICS; KU KLUX KLAN; RIOTS AND CIVIL DISTURBANCES; URBAN GANGS.

Higham, John. *Strangers in the Land: Patterns of American Nativism, 1860–1925* (New York: Atheneum, 1963)

Scisco, Louis Dow. *Political Nativism in New York State* (New York: Columbia Univ Press, 1901)

M. Stephen Pendleton and Jean Richardson

natural gas. See PETROLEUM AND NATURAL GAS INDUSTRY; POWER AND LIGHTING.

naturalists. See BOTANISTS AND NATURALISTS.

Nazareth College of Rochester. Private college in Pittsford (Monroe Co). Founded in 1924 by the Sisters of St. Joseph as a Catholic women's college. Originally located on Lake Ave in Rochester, Nazareth moved four years later to Augustine St, then to the Town of Pittsford in 1942. The college became independent of the Sisters of St. Joseph in 1971 and coeducational in 1973. In 2000 it doubled its campus to 150 acres (61 ha), featuring new Centers for International Education, Service Learning, and Teaching Excellence. In 2002–3, Nazareth offered 42 undergraduate, 37 master's, 11 postbaccalaureate, and 3 post-master's programs. Enrollment in 2002 included 1,728 full-time undergraduate students (1,287 women, 441 men) and 1,418 part-time and graduate students (1,136 women, 282 men).

Trybalski, M. Petrina. *Nazareth College of Rochester: Some Aspects of the Foundation and Development, 1924–1949* (Rochester: Nazareth College, 1969)

Joann Minor

Nazi Saboteurs (U-boat) Incident. See AMAGANSETT U-BOAT LANDING.

Negro Convention Movement. See BLACK CONVENTION MOVEMENT.

Negro Leagues. African Americans have played baseball since the creation of the modern game in the New York City metropolitan area in the decades before the Civil War. The Henson Baseball Club and the Unknown Club played on Long Island in 1859, and the following year possibly the same Unknown Club and the Colored Union Club, both made up of former slaves, played in Brooklyn. In 1869 the Brooklyn Uniques and the Philadelphia Excelsiors played in a "Championship of Colored Clubs." Elsewhere around the state all-black teams also flourished. Rochester's Unexpecteds, organized in 1866, probably included Charles Redmond Douglass, the son of Frederick Douglass. The Unexpecteds played other black clubs in Western New York, such as the Lincoln of Niagara Falls. In 1870 Charles Douglass was a member of the Alerts of Washington, DC, which played games at Lockport, Niagara Falls, Buffalo, Rochester, Utica, Canajoharie, and Troy. Cooperstown (Otsego Co), though not the birthplace of baseball, was the childhood home of Bud Fowler, likely the first professional black ballplayer. African Americans also played on New York State teams in the International Association and other professional minor leagues in Organized Baseball from 1886 to 1898, at which time the color barrier banning Blacks from competition became absolute and impermeable.

New York State is also the birthplace of professional black baseball. The Cuban Giants, who toured in 1885 as the first salaried black team, were organized in Babylon (Suffolk Co) by Frank P. Thompson. Headwaiter at the Argyle Hotel, Thompson built the team from hotel staff based on their baseball ability. Their primary competitor was the New York Gorhams (1887–91). No professional black team was playing in the state in 1905 when black café owner John W. Connor organized the Brooklyn Royal Giants. Connor sold the franchise to white booking agent Nat Strong, who played the team in the Eastern Colored League (ECL) from 1923 to 1927 before returning to independent play. An associate member of the Negro National League (NNL) in 1933, the team's quality declined after Strong's death in 1935, and it faded into obscurity. Will Tyler's Brooklyn Eagles also played in the NNL in 1935, before Tyler sold the franchise at the end of the season.

The New York Lincoln Giants emerged as the dominant team in New York City. Organized by white sports promoter Jess McMahon in 1911, the Lincoln Giants were led by shortstop John Henry Lloyd to three consecutive championships decided by series played among the East's top teams. They were challenged in 1913 by the Mohawk Giants of Schenectady, who featured ace pitcher Frank Wickware. A year later McMahon sold his team to white entrepreneur James Keenan. McMahon then organized the rival New York Lincoln Stars, which operated only three years but fielded strong teams. Keenan's Lincoln Giants, with pitcher Joe "Cyclone" Williams, became charter members of the ECL and, after the league folded, joined the American Negro League in 1929, the league's only year of existence. The next season Keenan fielded one of his strongest teams, but the franchise dissolved after losing a playoff for the Eastern Championship. During the 1930 season, a game between the Lincoln Giants and the Baltimore Black Sox, a benefit for the International Brotherhood of Sleeping Car Porters, was the first black ball game played at Yankee Stadium.

In 1931 Bill "Bojangles" Robinson and other investors organized the Harlem Stars, a transitional franchise that evolved into the New York Black Yankees the following season under the ownership of M. E. Goodson and James Semler. This team frequently played at Yankee Stadium when the New York Yankees were on the road. The Black Yankees were part of the NNL from 1936 to 1948, when the league dissolved. Afterward the franchise continued as an independent team of lesser quality. Also popular were the New York Cuban Stars, which were organized by Alejandro Pompez in 1935 and often played at the Polo Grounds. With the versatile Martin Dihigo in the lineup—he was the team's leading pitcher and hitter, as well as the manager in the team's early years—the Cubans, as they were known, reached the postseason, losing playoffs for the NNL pennant in 1935 and 1941. They finally won the Negro World Series in 1947, the same year that Jackie Robinson broke Major League Baseball's color line. When Robinson stepped on the diamond at Ebbets Field in a Brooklyn Dodgers uniform, it signaled the end of baseball's color line and the beginning of the end of the Negro Leagues. In 1996 the state legislature honored surviving Negro League players for their pioneering role in integrating New York State.

See also BASEBALL.

19th-Century African American Baseball Players in Organized Baseball on New York State Teams

Year	Player (position)	League	Team
1886–88	Grant, Frank (2b, of)	International League[a]	Buffalo
1887	Fowler, John "Bud" (2b)	International League	Binghamton
1887–88	Higgins, Robert (p)	International League	Syracuse
1887	Renfro, William (p)	International League	Binghamton
1888–89	Walker, Moses Fleetwood (c)	International Association	Syracuse
1890–91	Kelly, R. A. (if)	NY-Penn League	Jamestown
1890	Stovey, George (p)	New York State League	Troy
1898	Acme Colored Giants (entire team)	Iron and Oil League	Celeron

Source: Bob Davids, "Chronological Register of 19th-Century Black Players in Organized Baseball." In *Sol White's History of Colored Base Ball, with Other Documents on the Early Black Game, 1886–1936,* comp Jerry Malloy (1995).

[a]Known in different years as the International League or the International Association.

Mohawk Giants, Schenectady, 1913

Peterson, Robert. *Only the Ball Was White* (Englewood Cliffs, NJ: Prentice-Hall, 1970)
Riley, James A. *The Biographical Encyclopedia of the Negro Baseball Leagues* (New York: Carroll & Graf Publishers, 1994)

James A. Riley

Nelliston. Village (pop 622) in Palatine (Montgomery Co). Nelliston was crossed by the Mohawk Turnpike (1806) and the Utica and Schenectady Railroad (1836; later New York Central). After the Civil War the community grew, incorporated in 1878, but did not have a post office until 1889. Limestone was quarried, and a dairy plant served the surrounding farm. The plant was known successively as the Orange Co Milk Co, (*ca* 1880), Borden Condensed Milk Co (1903), Dairymen's League (*ca* 1920), and a farmer-owned cooperative, the Fort Plain Milk Co (1929–71). In 2002 Palatine Dairy began producing specialty cheddars and curd in a former Dairylea milk collection station. William Frederick "Bad Bill" Dahlen (1870–1950), a major league shortstop for the New York Giants and several other teams from 1891 to 1911, was a native.

James Crawford

Nelson. Town (pop 1,964) in central Madison Co. Settled in 1794, the town was formed from Cazenovia in 1807. In the mid–19th century Welsh families settled in Nelson in substantial numbers; they organized a church in 1850 and for many years preserved their language, religion, and traditions. The town was served by the Syracuse and Chenango Valley Railroad (1872–1937). The wetlands near Nelson hamlet, which furnished farmers with cedar fence posts, is now the Nelson Swamp State Unique Area, supporting endangered orchid species and other rare flora and fauna, and most of the southwest part of town is within the Tioughnioga State Wildlife Management Area. Tuscarora Lake was a feeder for the Erie Canal. The Welsh Church (1876) at East Nelson is listed on the National Register.

William F. Helmer

Nelson, Samuel (*b* Hebron, Washington Co, 10 Nov 1792; *d* Cooperstown, Otsego Co, 13 Dec 1873). State judge and US Supreme Court justice. The son of a farmer, Nelson was educated at local schools and Middlebury College in Vermont, graduating in 1813. Admitted to the bar in 1817 after clerking in the Salem (Washington Co) office of John Savage and David Woods, Nelson practiced with Woods for two years in Madison Co before establishing a solo practice in Cortland in 1817. In 1819 Nelson married Woods's daughter, Pamela, who died in childbirth three years later. Through connections to Martin Van Buren's Bucktail faction, Nelson rose quickly, being designated a presidential elector in 1820 and elected to the 1821 Constitutional Convention (he was the youngest member). He became a circuit court judge in 1823 and moved to Cooperstown, marrying Catherine Ann Russell of that community around 1825 and having three children. In 1831 Nelson was elevated to chief justice of the state supreme court, succeeding his former mentor John Savage, and was Pres John Tyler's appointee to the "New York seat" on the US Supreme Court in 1845. Nelson's 27 years on the Court reflected his prosouthern or "doughface" sentiments, commitment to following precedent, expertise in admiralty law, and capacity for hard work. His concurring opinion in the 1857 Dred Scott case found Scott a slave on the basis of Missouri law, avoiding broader constitutional issues. In his dissent in the 1863 *Prize Cases* he argued that the president could not institute a blockade without a congressional declaration of war. Nelson also served as a member of the 1871 *Alabama* Claims Commission to settle disputes relating to that English-built Confederate sea-raider. He resigned from the Supreme Court in November 1872.

Gatell, Frank Otto. "Samuel Nelson." In *The Justices of the United States Supreme Court, 1789–1969: Their Lives and Major Opinions,* ed. Leon Friedman and Fred L. Israel, 5 vols (Chelsea House, in association with Bowker, 1969–78)

Donald M. Roper

Nelsonville. Village (pop 565) in Philipstown (Putnam Co). Worker housing for the West Point Foundry in adjacent Cold Spring initiated the development of Nelsonville at the time of a foundry expansion in 1837. The village incorporated in 1855. The Fairgate Rule Co (1962; measuring tools) and Saunders Foundry Supply (1978) were early 21st-century employers. Nelsonville remains a suburb of Cold Spring, and most of its architecture dates from the Victorian period.

Charlotte B. Eaton

Nesconset. Locality (pop 11,992) in Smithtown (Suffolk Co). Nesconset, lightly populated until after the turn of the 20th century, acquired a post office in 1908. Concrete blocks and pearl buttons were manufactured. Summer cottages were built in the 1920s. With suburban development in Suffolk Co and the Nesconset Highway (Rte 347, 1950s), its population exploded from 3,000 in 1960 to 10,048 in 1970. In the early 21st century, Nesconset is primarily composed of single-family houses.

Luise Weiss

Neumann, John (Nepomucene) (*b* Prachatitz, Bohemia [now Czech Republic], 28 Mar 1811; *d* Philadelphia, 5 Jan 1860). Roman Catholic bishop and canonized saint. After attending seminaries in Budweis and Prague, Neumann immigrated to New York City in 1836 and that year was ordained into the priesthood, celebrating his first mass at the Church of St. Nicholas. He immediately made his way to Buffalo, where he began to minister, initially settling near Williamsville (Erie Co) and later at North Bush [now Kenmore, Erie Co]. With assistance, Neumann's work prospered and stations emerged at Lancaster, Tonawanda (Erie Co), and other locales around Buffalo. Despite his successes Neumann left his work to join the Congregation of the Most Holy Redeemer in Pittsburgh in late 1840. He worked under the Redemptorist order in and around Pittsburgh and Baltimore until he was named bishop of Philadelphia in 1852. Neumann is best known for his support and extension of parochial education. In 1977 he became the first American Catholic bishop to be canonized.

Curley, Michael J. *Venerable John Neumann, C.SS.R: Fourth Bishop of Philadelphia* (Washington, DC: Catholic Univ of America Press, 1952)

David B. Malone

Neutral Indians. Name given by the French to the allied Iroquoian groups who lived between the Huron and the Iroquois and were neutral in the wars between them. These tribes lived primarily in what is now Ontario between the Grand and Niagara Rivers, though some were on the New York State side of the Niagara. The Jesuits never established a mission among them but did visit the territory on a number of occasions and reported on what they saw. The few surviving documents suggest that the Neutral were a community quite similar in culture, size, and organization to the Five Nations. In 1640 the Jesuits identified 18 villages in the Neutral Nation, peopled by constituent groups known as the Attiragenrega, Ahondihronon, Andouaronon, Niagara, Kakougaga, and, until 1638, the Wenro.

In 1647 a Seneca war party interrupted its march homeward from a raid on the Huron to attack the Ahondihronon Neutrals. It was the first of a number of significant Iroquois blows against Neutral autonomy. After the collapse of the Huron in 1649 and the Jesuit mission amongst them, evidence of the Neutral becomes ever harder to find. No European observers were in a position to witness the series of attacks launched by members of the Five Nations. By 1652, most sources agree, the Neutrals had been dispersed by the much better armed Senecas and Onondagas. Some were adopted into Five Nations villages; others found shelter among neighboring native communities.

White, Marian. "Neutral and Wenro." In *Northeast,* ed. Bruce G. Trigger, vol 15 of *Handbook of North American Indians,* ed. William C. Sturtevant (Washington, DC: Smithsonian Institution, 1978)

Michael Leroy Oberg

Neversink. Town (pop 3,553) in NE Sullivan Co. Settled before the Revolutionary War but abandoned during the hostilities, it was the site of a skirmish known as the Battle of Chestnut Woods in 1778, in which a contingent of 18 colonial militiamen were all but wiped out by a band of Mohawks and tories. Resettled after the war, in part by Quakers who formed a meeting at Grahamsville in 1797 (the only such congregation in the county), the town was formed in 1798. Neversink's residents worked at lumbering, tanning, and, later, dairying. The Little World's Fair at Grahamsville has brought together farmers and vacationers since 1879. Filmmaking pioneers Fred Balshofer and Arthur C. Miller shot Western movies in Neversink in 1909; their experiences are chronicled in the book *One Reel a Week.* Although it had boardinghouses in the late 19th century, the town did not develop the huge hotels typical of adjacent towns and was a minor player in the resort industry. The construction of Rondout Reservoir (built 1937–51) and Neversink Reservoir (built 1941–53) displaced a number of valley hamlets to impound water for the New York City supply. Neversink's land remains predominantly agricultural; many nonfarm workers are employed at the prisons in Woodbourne. Neversink is the only dry town in Sullivan Co.

John Conway

New Albion. Town (pop 2,068) in NW Cattaraugus Co. Settled in 1818, the town was formed from Little Valley in 1830. The Erie Railroad came through in 1851. Dairy farming became dominant, along with fruit growing and maple sugar production; several cheese factories and creameries were organized starting 1867 along with a cheesebox factory (1876). Manufacturing firms in the Village of Cattaraugus continue to employ New Albion residents in the early 21st century. Allenberg Bog Wildlife Refuge, partly in Napoli, is a remarkable wetland environment.

Bruce D. Fredrickson and Madelynn P. Fredrickson

Newark. Village (pop 9,682) in Arcadia (Wayne Co). The settlement, originally called Miller's Basin, was founded in 1820 by Joseph Miller, a contractor who built 1.25 miles (2 km) of the Erie Canal here. Newark was incorporated as a village in 1853, subsuming the neighboring Village of Arcadia (originally Lockville, incorporated in 1839). In 1863 the oldest canning firm in the region, after 1889 called Edgett-Burnham, relocated to Newark from Oneida Co, and canning remained important until 2000. Jackson and Perkins (founded 1872, relocated 1966) made Newark a center of rose production for many years. During World War II, it was the site of a German prisoner of war camp. Furniture, tubing assemblies, electronic circuits, lithium batteries, and advanced porous ceramics were manufactured in 2003, and there were metalworking and machining firms. The village has a clock museum and a canal port adjacent to downtown.

Scott C. Monje

Newark Valley. Town (pop 4,097) and village (pop 1,071) in E Tioga Co. Settled in 1791, the town was formed in 1823 from Berkshire as Westville; the name changed to Newark in 1824 and to Newark Valley in 1862. Early industries included tanneries (1825–99) and maple-sugar making. The Southern Central Railroad (1871; later Lehigh Valley Railroad) led to the establishment of an International Harvester factory making manure spreaders (1901–12), a Borden's milk plant (?1906–62), and a Chesebro Whitman Co ladder factory (1922–93). The village, incorporated in 1894, is the terminal for Tioga Scenic Railroad excursions, originating in Owego. Dairy farming continues in town, but most residents commute to Cortland, Owego, and the Triple Cities (Binghamton, Endicott, and Johnson City in Broome Co) for work. Newark Valley is the site of the Bement-Billings Farmstead Museum. Ketchumville State Forest and parts of Jenksville and Oakley Corners State Forests are in town.

Joann Lindstrom

New Baltimore. Town (pop 3,417) in NE Greene Co. Part of the 1673 Coeymans Patent, the area was settled by the Dutch soon afterward and received an influx from Westchester and Dutchess Cos after the Revolution. The town was formed from Coxsackie in 1811. New Baltimore hamlet was surveyed in 1786 and became a shipbuilding center by 1797, with some trade conducted directly with the West Indies. Later its residents worked at ice cutting and fruit growing and in paper mills; boat building continued until the depression. In the early 21st century, most residents commute to jobs in other towns.

Field Horne

New Berlin [BERL-IN]. Town (pop 2,803) and village (pop 1,129) in NE Chenango Co. Settled in 1790 primarily from Rhode Island, the town was formed in 1807; the village incorporated in 1816. Manufacturing, including cotton, woolen, and paper mills, provided employment in the 19th century. Dairy farming was encouraged by the construction of railroad lines in 1870 and 1895, permitting shipment of fluid milk and butter. Preferred Mutual Insurance Co (1896) has become the major employer. St. Andrew's Episcopal Church and Preferred Manor are on the National Register of Historic Places. Hunts Pond State Park is in the town.

Barbara B. Avery

newborn screening. In the 1930s Dr George Jervis identified 50 patients at the Letchworth State Village School in Thiells (Rockland Co) whose mental retardation was caused by an inherited enzyme defect that prevented the breakdown of the amino acid phenylalanine, a disease known as phenylketonuria (PKU). By the 1950s a treatment aimed at reducing phenylalanine in the diet became an effective therapy and improved the cognitive outcomes for children with PKU. In the late 1950s at the Children's Hospital in Buffalo, Dr Robert Guthrie developed a new way of testing and monitoring blood levels for phenylalanine with the use of filter paper cards. Through the development of this inexpensive and accurate means, newborn screening was launched in New York State in 1965.

All infants born in New York State currently have a heel stick performed after birth in the hospital newborn nursery. Filter paper cards saturated with a small amount of blood are sent to the Wadsworth Center in Albany for laboratory processing of the newborn screen. Abnormal results are followed up at designated metabolic centers throughout the state. Since the early days of screening, additional disorders have been added to the screening panel: branched-chain ketonuria (MSUD, or maple syrup urine disease), galactosemia, homocystinuria, hypothyroidism, sickle cell disease/sickle cell trait, biotinidase deficiency, and HIV. In late 2002 three additional diseases were added: congenital adrenal hyperplasia, cystic fibrosis, and medium-chain acyl-CoA dehydrogenase deficiency (MCADD). In 2002 the laboratory at Wadsworth Center screened 252,470 newborns for a total of 485 positive diagnoses of inborn errors of metabolism and other diseases.

Koch, Jean Holt. *Robert Guthrie—The PKU Story: Crusade against Mental Retardation* (Pasadena, Calif: Hope Publishing, 1997)
March of Dimes, "Professionals and Researchers," http://www.marchofdimes.com/professionals
Wadsworth Center, New York State Department of Health, "The Newborn Screening Program," http://www.wadsworth.org/newborn

Jane M. DeLuca

New Bremen [BREE-MEN]. Town (pop 2,722) in central Lewis Co. Settled briefly by French refugees in the 1790s, it was resettled in 1821 and after 1830 German immigrants, including many Mennonites, arrived. The town was formed in 1848 from Watson and Croghan. Mills, a tannery, and a brewery were built on Crystal Creek, followed later by a potato distillery (1860), an excelsior mill, and a sash and blind shop; dairy farming developed and remains important in the early 21st century. The short-lived North Country Aggregates (1966) produced cement blocks based on crushed gravel, used in the construction of the Everson Museum in Syracuse and the Empire State Plaza in Albany. New Bremen is the site of Lewis Co's only airstrip, used primarily by a crop-dusting firm. The Mennonite Heritage Farm at Kirschnerville is open seasonally, as is the Adirondack International Speedway.

Arthur Einhorn

Newburgh. Town (pop 27,568) and city (pop 28,259) in E Orange Co. Settled in 1709 by Palatine refugees followed with a significant Scottish immigration by midcentury, it was formed as a precinct in 1762 and recognized as a town in 1788. Ferry service began in 1743. By 1767 its landing was busy with produce and livestock shipping because it was the first place north of the Hudson Highlands with a water-level shoreline. The village incorporated in 1800. After the construction of the Newburgh and Cochecton Turnpike (1801), the landing drew extensive trade from the hinterland, much of which was diverted to the Erie and Delaware and Hudson Canals when they opened, but trade was revived by the Erie Railroad branch line (1849). Local capitalists organized the Newburgh Whaling Co, which operated from the river port from 1832 to 1837. In the 19th century industrial products included cotton fabrics, brick, steam boilers, beer, agricultural implements, railroad cars and car wheels, pianos, soap, and clothing. Horatio Swift was the first US manufacturer of lawnmowers in 1852. The village incorporated as a city in 1865. The Sweet-Orr Co manufactured the nation's first individually sized work clothes and overalls from 1876 through the 1950s. The factories drew a diverse population of workers, including Irish, African Americans, Slovaks, Italians, Poles, and Ukrainians.

After World War II, Newburgh's economy was hurt by industrial decline, the growth of suburbs, the end of ferry service (1963), the closing of the nearby Stewart Air Force Base (1970), and, with urban renewal (1965–71), the demolition of some of its oldest neighborhoods. In 1961 city manager Joseph Mitchell blamed much of the city's ills on rising welfare costs. The subsequent "Battle of Newburgh" and its scarcely veiled racial overtones attracted national attention. The opening of the New York State Thruway (1954) and I-84 (1964, 1967), which intersect in Newburgh, and the Newburgh-Beacon Bridge (1963) encouraged growth of the town, the population of which doubled between 1960 and 2000 as the city's population declined 10%. The real estate boom of the late 1990s brought some retail and residential development back to the riverfront area. In the late 20th century, many Central American immigrants joined older ethnic communities. In 2000 the city's population was 33% black. In addition, people of Latino ethnicity made up 36% of the population.

In the early 21st century manufacturing in the city includes Atlas Textile (fabric dyeing), Christmas in America (artificial trees), New England Laminates (veneer), Newburgh Molded Products (plastics), Cobra Systems (razor wire), and Orange Die Cutting. Newburgh was the home of landscape architect Andrew Jackson Downing (1815–52). Washington's Headquarters, where Washington disbanded the Continental army in 1783 and the site of the Newburgh Affair (a threatened mutiny by Continental army officers), is the nation's oldest historic house museum (1850). Mount St. Mary College (1960) is located downtown, as is the Karpeles Manuscripts Library Museum. City landmarks include the Greek Revival Dutch Reformed Church (1835) designed by A. J. Davis and the 25-acre (10 ha) Downing Park (1887) designed by Frederick Law Olmsted and Calvert Vaux. The Gomez Mill House (*ca* 1714) in the Town of Newburgh is the oldest Jewish residence in the United States.

Field Horne

Newburgh Affair. Planned protest by Continental army officers over the prospect of being discharged before the Continental Congress made adequate provision for pay, pensions, and settling accounts. By late 1782 Congress had no resources to satisfy obligations to the army. States were not able to pay troops with cash, and some were opposed to pensions for officers. Peace negotiations in 1782 raised the prospect that the army would be discharged, which would deprive officers any leverage to enforce their demands on Congress.

In January 1783 Gen Alexander McDougall led a delegation from army headquarters in Newburgh (Orange Co) to Philadelphia to inform Congress that the army was angry to the point of mutiny because the government had made no commitment for compensation. Pressed by the Newburgh delegates, Congress urged Robert Morris, its financier, to provide the army some pay. He agreed to pay for January 1783 but did not have enough funds to cover the payments. After the French minister refused his request for an advance on a hoped-for loan, Morris informed Congress he would resign unless it passed a funding plan to pay all public debts. Morris's allies urged the army to unite with public creditors to pressure states to grant Congress adequate revenue powers. Rumors circulated that the army would not disband until its demands were met.

News of Morris's impending resignation reached Newburgh on 8 Mar 1783. On 10 March Maj John Armstrong Jr anonymously circulated two documents known as the Newburgh Addresses. The first invited army officers to meet and consider how best to procure justice for the army. The next day Gen George Washington interceded and scheduled a formal meeting under his auspices for 15 March. In a second address written 12 March, Armstrong implied that Washington concurred with suggestions in the first document. During Washington's 15 March meeting he diffused the threat of mutiny by persuading officers to trust Congress's desire to do the army justice and his own willingness to advocate their causes before it. After the Newburgh Affair, Congress agreed to commute officers' pensions. They received full military salary for five years funded at 6% interest. Revenue to cover costs was supposed to come from a revised impost plan that Congress submitted to the states for ratification in 1783. It was never ratified. Eventually officers were issued final settlement certificates for commutation owed them, but because Congress had no revenue the certificates depreciated and most were sold to creditors.

Ferguson, E. James, et al, eds. *The Papers of Robert Morris, 1781–1784*, vol 7 (Pittsburgh: Univ of Pittsburgh Press, 1988)

Mary A. Y. Gallagher

New Cassel. Locality (pop 13,298) in North Hempstead (Nassau Co). Before the Revolution, enslaved Blacks freed by Quakers settled in what was known as Grantsville. In 1870 real estate promoters named the area New Cassel to attract German immigrants. That attempt failed, as did a giveaway promotion by the Buchner Co, a manufacturer of chewing tobacco: 2,000 Gold Coin chewing tobacco wrappers could be exchanged for a building lot. In the early 20th century, Ukrainian, Polish, and Irish immigrants farmed in the area, and Blacks working nearby also settled. The population of New Cassel grew from 10,257 in 1990 to 13,298 in 2000, making it one of the two fastest-growing places in Nassau Co. With a historically black population core, New Cassel was more open to minority residents than many other Nassau Co localities. In 2000 New Cassel's racial composition was 47% black, and 41% of the population was of Latino ethnicity.

Richard A. Winsche

New Castle. Town (pop 17,491) in N central Westchester Co. A large part of the town was purchased from the native proprietors in 1696 and was erected into the West Patent of North Castle in 1702; it remained part of that town until 1791. It was settled by Quakers in the 1730s and was a farming town until many farms were transformed into estates around 1900. Beginning in the 1920s but especially after World War II, subdivisions of the estates, along with the Taconic Parkway (1931) and Saw Mill River Parkway (1935), made New Castle a commuter town, and its population increased 61% in the course of the 1950s. *Reader's Digest* (1939) is the largest employer.

New Castle County. See EXTINCT COUNTIES.

New City. Locality (pop 34,038) in Clarkstown (Rockland Co). Named New City as an optimistic statement regarding its potential for growth, it was designated the county seat for Orange Co in 1774. The first courthouse was built in 1784. New City became part of Rockland Co when the latter formed in 1798. Germans came to the locality in the mid–19th century. It acquired rail service from the Nanuet and New City branchline in 1875. In the early 20th century New City was the site of a farm raising guinea pigs for laboratory use, a racetrack, a fairground, and the 600-acre (243 ha) estate (1918) of Adolph Zukor (1873–1976) of Paramount Pictures. Its suburban growth came during the 1950s when its population swelled from 2,091 to 27,344. In 2000 New City was the most populous unincorporated place in the county. The county seat remains centered on a 1928 Art Deco courthouse.

Newcomb. Town (pop 481) in W Essex Co. Settled in 1816 it was formed in 1828 from Minerva and Moriah. From 1832 to 1856 iron was mined at the boomtown of Adirondac, which was then abandoned. Otherwise forest products supported its economy. In 1941 a titanium mine was opened by National Lead Co on the site of Adirondac, and the Delaware and Hudson Railroad was extended from North River to serve it. A hamlet was built for the workers and named Tahawus, which was dispersed in 1963. Mining ended in 1989. Forest products, outdoor recreation, and tourism have since provided employment. A highway monument in town marks the approximate spot where Theodore Roosevelt was when Pres William McKinley died.

Thomas A. Rumney

New Deal landscapes. The New Deal offered a range of federal programs to put people to work, to improve the social and physical landscape of the country, and to combat the economic hardships of the Great Depression. These programs included the Agricultural Adjustment Administration (AAA), Civilian Conservation Corps (CCC), Civil Works Administration (CWA), Federal Emergency Relief Administration (FERA), Historic American Building Survey (HABS), Public Works Administration (PWA), Resettlement Administration (RA), Soil Erosion Service (later Soil Conservation Service), and Works Progress Administration (WPA). Such initiatives, implemented by Harry Hopkins, Pres Franklin D. Roosevelt's federal relief administrator, did not create an identifiable landscape style. Rather, what arose was an understanding and commitment to large-scale planning and design, and an appreciation for the economic and environmental usage of native materials in design and construction. The result was forest reclamation, restoration of historic properties, and new construction of housing, government facilities, parks, roadways, schools, and waterworks.

From the early 1930s into the 1940s, New York State residents were employed on projects. Farmland was purchased and readied for reforestation or for use as wildlife sanctuaries, such as Hilltop Farm near Ithaca, which was acquired by the RA to add to timber supplies, contribute to flood control, and improve recreational and wildlife facilities. Along the coast, shorelines such as in Oak Beach and Quogue (Suffolk Co) were stabilized through reclamation of dunes, both having been undertaken by the WPA in 1939. These undertakings relied on traditional methods for reestablishing natural conditions and resulted in landscapes that exhibited little evidence of human intervention. By contrast, major waterworks projects involved extensive modifications to natural features and substantial new buildings and structures; most were built with native materials. Examples include the Harrison and Rye Water System in Rye (Westchester Co), Loudonville Reservoir in Albany, and Clearwater Reservoir in Buffalo, all WPA projects from around 1936.

State and local park facilities were improved or created through the construction of roads, trails, campsites, and buildings that complemented natural topography, vegetation, and water features. Letchworth State Park in Castile (Wyoming Co), Gilbert Lake State Park in New Lisbon (Otsego Co), and Cedar Point State Park in Clayton (Jefferson Co) incorporated materials indigenous to each location. These and other state parks were substantially transformed through the efforts of the CCC, whose program participants lived in or near the facilities in residential camps built with the same high-quality materials and skills. The WPA undertook similar improvements in municipal parks throughout the 1930s, such as those in Rochester, Schenectady, and Syracuse, where in 1938 Onondaga Creek was diverted into a channel within Syracuse's Onondaga Park. Other major recreational facilities were noticeable additions to the existing natural and built context, including the Split Rock Golf Course in Pelham Bay Park (Bronx Co). The native materials in buildings and structures tempered the contrast made by these substantial landscape projects.

Many public works of this period established precedents for future generations of sanitary, water, electrical, and road systems. Improvements to the Utica sewer system made under the WPA, for example, set standards for repairs and extensions for the following decades. Roosevelt's New Deal programs affected the state's landscape from their initiation in the first 100 days of the president's first term. A few programs remained in operation into the early 1940s, such as the CCC, which until 1942 employed nearly 220,000 men for projects that continued to include state parks improvement.

Birnbaum, Charles A., and Lisa E. Crowder, eds. *Pioneers of American Landscape Design: An Annotated Bibliography* (Washington, DC: US Department of the Interior, National Park Service, Cultural Resources Division, 1993)

Birnbaum, Charles A., and Julie K. Fix, eds. *Pioneers of American Landscape Design II: An Annotated Bibliography* (Washington, DC: US Department of the Interior, National Park Service, Cultural Resources Division, 1996)

Cutler, Phoebe. *The Public Landscapes of the New Deal* (New Haven, Conn: Yale Univ Press, 1985)

Pregill, Philip, and Nancy Volkman. *Landscapes in History: Design and Planning in the Western Tradition* (New York: Van Nostrand Reinhold, 1993)

Christine Capella Peters

Newfane. Town (pop 9,657) in central Niagara Co. Settled in 1807 by Canadian migrants, the town was formed in 1824 from Hartland, Wilson, and Somerset. The first worship service was conducted by a black Methodist minister from Canada in 1811. Ditching in the 1820s created farmland from swampland, and orchards were set out along the lake. Industries included woolen mills, a basket factory, and a foundry. Olcott was a port of entry with a customhouse. At Olcott Beach, a late 19th-century resort, the carousel and carousel building have been restored, and plans in 2003 included the restoration of other 20th-century amusement park rides. Agriculture remains the principal land use, especially orchards. Landmarks include the Van Horn Mansion (1823) and the cobblestone First Baptist Church (1849).

Nancy B. Mingus

Newfield. Town (pop 5,108) in SW Tompkins Co. Settled in 1800, it was formed from Spencer (Tioga Co) as Cayuta in 1811; it was renamed Newfield in 1822 and annexed to Tompkins Co in 1823. The town had a cloth factory (1815) and an oilcloth factory (1846). The Ithaca and Athens Railroad came through in 1871. The hamlet of Newfield was an incorporated village from 1895 to 1925. Czechs settled in Pony Hollow starting in 1905 and on Bohemian Hill in 1918. Between 1910 and 1920 a large number of Finns came and took over marginal farms. Reforestation in the 1930s resulted, in part, in the Connecticut Hill State Wildlife Management Area. Among the town's early 21st-century employers are Palisade (software), Omni (turbine parts), American Polysteel (construction), and Veteran Landstrom Gravel Co. Although the poorer farms were abandoned in the late 20th century, the growth of trailer parks (nine in 1990) has added to the population. A covered bridge (1853) over a branch of the Cayuga Inlet is a historic landmark.

Jane Dieckmann

New France. Term for the collective French colonies of North America in the 17th and 18th centuries. At this time the term Canada referred to the settlements along the St. Lawrence River in what is now Ontario and Quebec. Its western territory was the Pays d'en Haut (Upper Country), which encompassed the lands around the Great Lakes and the eastern Great Plains. Acadia included what are now Nova Scotia, New Brunswick, Prince Edward Island, and Maine. After Nova Scotia was ceded to Great Britain in 1713, Cape Breton Island became the colony of Ile Royale. The island of Newfoundland was known as Terre-Neuve. Louisiana encompassed all the lands around the Mississippi and Missouri Rivers.

In 1534 Jacques Cartier made the first claim of territory for France in what is now Canada. He made two additional trips in 1535–36 and 1541–42. During the second he explored the St. Lawrence River to what is today Montreal but in all three failed to find the Northwest Passage or quantities of gold and diamonds. Throughout the 16th century, however, another commercial

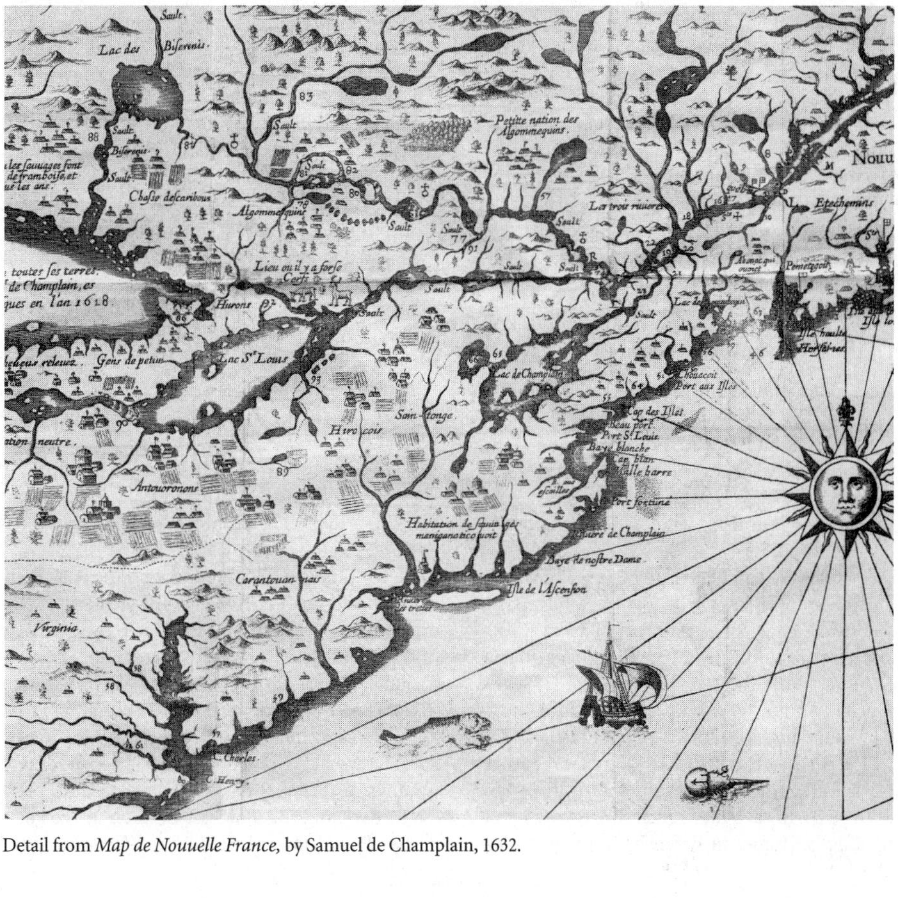

Detail from *Map de Nouuelle France,* by Samuel de Champlain, 1632.

interest was growing on the Grand Banks off Newfoundland. Basque and Portuguese fishermen made annual trips to the region for whaling and cod fishing and dominated the Canadian fisheries until the early 17th century, establishing seasonal processing camps at Lesquemin [now Les Escoumins, Que] on the north shore of the St. Lawrence River and at Red Bay along the southern shore of what is now Labrador.

New France in Iroquoia

Beginning with Henry IV in 1603, the French monarchy granted private companies a monopoly on trade, the most prominent of which was the Compagnie des Cent-Associés (1627–63). In return the companies were required to settle and develop the land. In 1608 Samuel de Champlain established a settlement at what is now Quebec City. The following year he explored the lake that would later bear his name and fought a battle with the Mohawk near Ticonderoga [now in Essex Co] in which several Mohawk were killed. This was the first of numerous military and missionary expeditions into Iroquois territory in the 17th and 18th centuries. The mission established at Ville-Marie [now Montreal] in 1642 corresponded to an increase in hostilities with the Iroquois Confederacy to the south. Slow growth and distress over Indian raids led the Crown to assume control over New France in 1663, at which time the colonies became royal provinces.

Additional exploration of the continent's interior took place with the increase of the fur trade and the travels of missionaries. Among others, René-Robert Cavelier de la Salle extended the interior boundaries of New France. Exploring parts of what is now western New York State by 1669 and establishing Fort Frontenac [now Kingston, Ont] in 1674–75, La Salle built the short-lived Fort Conti in 1679 at the mouth of the Niagara River. That same year, at a shipyard above Niagara Falls, he built the *Griffon,* which he used to explore the Great Lakes before moving on to claim the Mississippi Valley for France in 1682.

Jesuit and Sulpician missionaries played a prominent role in New France and in relations with the Iroquois in New York. They established missions among the Mohawk by the 1640s, notably at Ossernenon [now Auriesville, Montgomery Co]; among the Onondaga they founded the mission called Sainte Marie de Gannentaha in what is now Liverpool (Onondaga Co). After the 1660s Iroquois Christian converts moved to missions at Kahnawake, founded in 1667 along the St. Lawrence River near Montreal. Later missions included La Présentation at Oswegatchie [now Ogdensburg, St. Lawrence Co] in 1749 and St. Regis at Akwesasne (Saint Regis Indian Reservation) [partly loc in Franklin Co] in the 1750s. Despite these efforts, a relatively small number of Indians converted to Christianity.

For more than half its history, New France was at war with Indians, the British, and British colonists. The four major conflicts in North America, resulting from developments in Europe, included King William's War (1689–97), Queen Anne's War (1702–13)—after which Newfoundland, Acadia, and Hudson's Bay were ceded to the British—King George's War (1744–48), and the French and Indian War (1754–63). In each the French strategy was to tie up English forces in defensive measures. New York Colony was often at the center of these struggles. To ensure security in Canada, from 1665 to 1667 the Carignan-Salieres Regiment defended the colony against Iroquois raids and launched attacks against the Mohawk in February and October 1666. The militia in Canada was formally organized in 1669 and involved all men aged 16–60. In 1683 the king began sending Troupes de la Marine to serve as a permanent force of regular soldiers in the colony. The French and their Indian allies attacked the Seneca at Ganondagan [now Victor, Ontario Co] in July 1687, the settlement at Schenectady in February 1690, Mohawk villages [now in Montgomery Co] in February 1693, and the main villages of the Onondaga and Oneida [now in Onondaga and Oneida Cos] in August 1696. After King William's War, peace between the Iroquois and the French was formally established by treaty in 1701 and lasted nearly five decades. Throughout the conflicts of the 18th century, Louis-Thomas Chabert de Joncaire and his sons represented French interests among the Iroquois, primarily with the Seneca Nation.

New France was ruled by a Quebec-based governor general who dealt primarily with military and diplomatic affairs. An intendant supervised the economy and the judicial system. Each colony had its own governor and in practical terms operated separately. The French brought their form of land tenure, the seigneurial system, to New France, under which the king granted parcels of land to seigneurs, generally aristocrats or prominent members of the Catholic Church, but increasingly to members of the middle class. Seigneurs then allocated land to farmers, who paid a portion of their crop as rent. Between 1736 and 1752, 10 seigneuries were created on land around Lake Champlain, but they attracted relatively few settlers. Canada grew slowly. In 1663 there were just over 3,000 French settlers and 20 years later more than 10,000. The long peace from 1713 to 1744 was a time of prosperity and growth in Canada. By 1755 there were more than 60,000 Canadians, approximately 7,000 in Quebec and 4,500 in Montreal.

Canada produced 80% of all fur exports from North America, but French markets could not absorb the prodigious quantities and prices were kept low by the monopoly on beaver exports. In 1696 the market collapsed. A new outlet was needed, and Canadian traders found it in New York Colony. Running against the protectionist legislation of both empires, smugglers headed from Montreal to Albany. Several merchants specialized in this activity, including John Hendricks Lydius. Much smuggling was undertaken by mission Indians, particularly at Kahnawake.

The French maintained a substantial military and commercial presence in what is now New York State to protect valuable trade routes. By the early 1720s the Iroquois allowed the British to trade for furs at Oswego, angering the French for what they considered a violation of their territory. After several previous works at the mouth of the Niagara River at Lake Ontario, the French built Fort Niagara [now in Porter, Niagara Co] in 1726. The Richelieu River/Lake Champlain corridor between Montreal and Albany was fortified by 1665 at what is now Chambly, Que. Extending southward in the 18th century, they built Fort St. Frédéric in 1734 and Fort Carillon in 1755 at Crown Point [now in Essex Co] and Ticonderoga.

Military Defeat

The French and Indian War brought an end to New France, which, vastly outnumbered in population by the British colonies to the south, fell partly because its economy was overwhelmed by military expenditures. In the years leading up to this war, the colony's armed forces increased 10-fold. French victories early in the war included Oswego in 1756, Fort William Henry [now in Lake George, Warren Co] in 1757, and, outnumbered five to one, Ticonderoga in 1758. The French were defeated in the Battle of the Plains of Abraham on 13 Sept 1759, and Quebec City surrendered. Montreal fell on 8 Sept 1760, and the fate of the colony was sealed. The Treaty of Paris officially ended the conflict in 1763. The Louisiana Territory was transferred to Spain. The British retained all of the northern colonies except for the islands of Saint-Pierre and Miquelon, fishing stations off Newfoundland, which remain part of France into the 21st century. Restored forts from Lake Champlain to the Niagara remain as the monuments of the mighty struggle between New France and British North America for the control of New York Colony.

See also Fortifications; Seneca nation.

Cassel, Jay. *The Life and Death of an Army: French Forces in Colonial Canada* (Toronto: Univ of Toronto Press, forthcoming)

Dechene, Louise. *Habitants and Merchants in 17th Century Montreal.* Trans Liana Vardi (Montreal: McGill-Queen's Univ Press, 1992)

Eccles, W. J. *France in America* (New York: Harper & Row, 1972)

Fregault, Guy. *Canada: The War of the Conquest.* Trans Margaret M. Cameron (Toronto: Oxford Univ Press, 1969)

Harris, Richard C., and Geoffrey J. Matthews. *Historical Atlas of Canada,* 3 vols (Toronto: Univ of Toronto Press, 1987–93)

Jay Cassel

New Hartford. Town (pop 21,172) and village (pop 1,886) in E Oneida Co. Settled in 1788 the town was formed from Whitestown in 1827. Located along the Seneca Turnpike (incorporated in 1800; now Rte 5), New Hartford was later served by the Chenango Canal (1837–78), two lines of the Delaware, Lackawanna and Western Railroad, and the Utica-Clinton trolley (1901–36). Manufactures included at least three cotton factories during the War of 1812 era and, later, ingrain carpets, leather, woolen cloth, farm tools, knit goods, paper, and batting. The village incorporated in 1870. In 1946 the campus of Utica Country Day School (1921–41) became the site of the New York State Institute of Applied Arts and Sciences at Utica (now Mohawk Valley Community College). Intensive suburbanization followed World War II. New Hartford Shopping Center opened in the village in 1958, and Sangertown Square opened in the town in 1980. Other major employers are Utica National Insurance Co (relocated in town in 1951), Special Metals, and Par Technology.

New Haven. Town (pop 2,930) in N Oswego Co. Bounded on the north by Lake Ontario and settled in 1800, the town was formed in 1813 from Mexico. Potash produced in town was shipped to Montreal starting in 1816. Cattle, butter, cheese, and fruit, especially apples and berries, were important products. After 1865 the Rome, Watertown and Ogdensburg Railroad provided shipment to market. Dempster Grove (1875), a camp meeting ground with a large wooden tabernacle, remains in use by the Central New York Methodist Conference each August into the 21st century. Orchards continue in production, but most residents commute to work elsewhere places.

Barbara J. Dix

New Hempstead. Village (pop 4,767) in Ramapo (Rockland Co). The area was settled by Scots in 1734, and they formed the so-called English Church (Presbyterian, 1754), the second congregation in the present Rockland Co, whose building dates from 1827. Coe's Tavern was the site of two encampments by the Continental army, and it served as an alternate seat of Orange Co government. In 1983 the village was incorporated so that residents could control planning and zoning.

Newhouse, S(amuel) I(rving) (*b* New York City, 24 May 1895; *d* New York City, 29 Aug 1979). Newspaper publisher. Solomon Irving Neuhaus, son of Russian Jewish immigrants Meier Neuhaus and Rose Arenfeldt, began his newspaper experience at age 15 as advertising salesman and later manager for the *Bayonne (NJ) Times.* Having negotiated a share of the profits he created, he bought his first newspaper, the *Staten Island Advance,* in 1922. With a keen ability to discover, assess, and then purchase financially strapped papers in New York and New Jersey during the 1920s and 1930s he built the foundation of his empire. A hands-on manager, he succeeded by expanding circulation and advertising and by cutting costs. From the 1930s on he engaged in fierce and largely successful battles against unions. By the time of his death, he had built one of the country's largest communication empires, Advance Publications, whose holdings comprised 31 profitable newspapers in 22 cities, including the daily newspaper in Syracuse, the *Post-Standard, Staten Island Advance,* Sunday *Parade, Vogue,* and other magazines, as well as radio, television, and cable interests. He was the major benefactor of the S. I. Newhouse School of Public Communications at Syracuse University.

Meeker, Richard H. *Newspaperman: S. I. Newhouse and the Business of News* (New Haven, Conn: Ticknor & Fields, 1983)

W. Richard Whitaker

New Hudson. Town (pop 736) in W Allegany Co. Settled in 1817, it was formed from Rushford in 1825 as Haight; the name was changed in 1837. The Genesee Valley Canal (1856–78) provided transportation, as did the Erie and Pennsylvania Railroads. In the 1890s the 1,300-acre (526 ha) Empire City Stud Farm of William Simpson Jr of New York City was an important trotting-horse facility with its own quarter-mile covered track that employed 20 men. In the late 20th century New Hudson became home to an Amish community. It is the site of the 4,571-acre (1,850 ha) Hanging Bog State Wildlife Management Area.

New Hyde Park {New Hyde Park, village (pop 9,523) in Hempstead and North Hempstead, Nassau Co; North New Hyde Park, locality (pop 14,542) in North Hempstead}. Gov Thomas Dongan built a house in what is now Lake Success in 1688; it is believed that Dongan Manor was renamed Hyde Hall for Ann Hyde, wife of owner Lt Gov George Clarke, in 1715. Irish and German farmers came in the 19th century, the railroad came through in 1870, and its new post office was named New Hyde Park in 1871 to avoid confusion with the Dutchess Co town. Farms were subdivided in the 1920s, and the village was incorporated in 1927. Babe Ruth threw out the first ball at Barton's baseball field in 1938; Barton's was sold for retail development in 1957. Population continued to increase after World War II, peaking in New Hyde Park at 10,808 in 1960 and in North New Hyde Park at 18,154 in 1970. Village and locality are both mainly residential, with a fast-growing Asian population, which approached 15% in 2000.

Laura E. Mann

New Lebanon. Town (pop 2,454) in NE Columbia Co. Montepoole, New Lebanon's warm spring, was explored as early as 1756; settlement began in 1764. In 1771 visitors began using the spring water, which was a constant 73°F (23°C) flowing at 500 gal (1,900 l) per minute. Columbia Hall (1794–1914) was the most noted of its hotels. The six "families" of Mount Lebanon Shakers (1787–1947) produced garden seeds, brooms and brushes, baskets, and medicinal herbs. The town was formed in 1818 from Canaan. Other industries included the Kimball Thermometer Factory (1820–93), Tilden Pharmaceutical Co (1824–1963), and tinware manufacturing. New Lebanon was served by the Harlem Extension Railroad (1869–1953). After the Civil War, Clark's Bakery pioneered the wrapping of bread. In the first quarter of the 20th century, the last of New Lebanon's resort trade ended. In the early 21st century, Ceramaseal (1951) continues to produce ceramic connectors, bushings, and seals. The town was the birthplace of Samuel J. Tilden (1814–86), who won the popular presidential vote in 1876, and is the site of Darrow School (1932), the Lebanon Valley Dragway (?1959), and the Abode of the Message (1974), a Sufi retreat. Landmarks include Mount Lebanon Shaker Village, the Church of Our Saviour (1872–81), and Our Lady of Lourdes Grotto (1929).

See also SHAKERS.

New Lisbon. Town (pop 1,116) in W central Otsego Co. Settled in 1773, its pioneers were driven off in 1778, but it was resettled after the war. The town was formed in 1806 from Pittsfield as Lisbon; the name was changed in 1808. New Lisbon was a rural and isolated town, and its population declined sharply through the 19th and early 20th centuries; it is still only half of what it was in 1830. Most workers commute to jobs outside the town. The 1,500-acre (607 ha) Gilbert Lake State Park (1926) is a regionally popular facility with 38-acre (15 ha) Gilbert Lake and is the site of the New York State Civilian Conservation Corps Museum. There are several private campgrounds, including one on Crystal Lake near Garrattsville. The Lunn-Musser Octagon Barn (1885) is listed on the National Register.

Hugh C. MacDougall

Newman, Barnett (*b* New York City, 29 Jan 1905; *d* New York City, 4 July 1970). Painter, sculptor, and essayist. Newman was a son of Jewish immigrants who left Poland to escape religious persecution and economic hardship. Though his father trained him for the family clothing business, from an early age Newman planned to become an artist and as a teenager attended the Art Students League in Manhattan. In 1927 he graduated from City College of New York. In 1933 Newman ran for mayor of New York on a "cultural" ticket that lobbied for free art schools and a civic noncommercial art movie theater. In the 1940s he composed essays and curated exhibitions that appealed to artists like Mark Rothko and Adolph Gottlieb who, like Newman, would later be known as abstract expressionists. Newman's exhibits of pre-Columbian, native Northwest Coast, and oceanic objects claimed a profound similarity between modern and primitive totemic art. For Newman such primitive art was important because it was a living expression of human beings' terror before nature and embodied authentic feelings from which humankind had been alienated in a technological age.

In 1948 Newman developed his signature style with the painting *Onement I,* a 27 x 16 in (69.6 x 40.6 cm) field of rusty-red bifurcated by a brushy, brilliant orange stripe. Later that year Newman began painting large canvases, often 18 ft (5.5 m) wide, which were likewise punctuated with vertical stripes, or "zips" as he later called them. Newman's abstraction, which offered neither narrative content nor illusory three-dimensional space in which narrative could seem to take place, was meant to create an immediate impact upon the viewer. Most critics and artists disapproved of Newman's work. Only in 1959 when critic Clement Greenberg curated a show of his paintings did Newman receive substantial attention. After 1959 until his death Newman was considered one of the most influential abstract expressionists, as younger artists painted stripes and large canvases after his example.

O'Neill, John P., ed. *Barnett Newman: Selected Writings and Interviews* (Berkeley: Univ of California Press, 1990)

Temkin, Ann. *Barnett Newman.* Exhibition Catalog (Philadelphia: Philadelphia Museum of Art, 2002)

Sarah K. Rich

Newman, Pauline (*b* Papilé [now in Lithuania], ?18 Oct 1887; *d* New York City, 8 Apr 1986). Labor organizer. Newman immigrated with her family to the United States in 1901 and soon after went to work for the Triangle Shirtwaist Co in New York City. She was active in building support for the 1909 garment workers' strike of 500 New York City shirtwaist shops, traveling throughout the state to raise money for the International Ladies' Garment Workers' Union (ILGWU). Following the strike, she left her job at Triangle and became the first full-time female organizer for the ILGWU, serving from 1909 until 1913. In 1924 Newman became the ILGWU health education director, a position she held for 62 years. She was active for many decades in the New York Women's Trade Union League, which she joined in 1909. A Socialist, she ran for Congress on that party's ticket in 1918. Newman spoke on street corners, at union strike and organizing meetings, at suffrage gatherings, and in her later years at university classes about women's labor history.

Orleck, Annelise. *Common Sense and a Little Fire: Women and Working-Class Politics in the United*

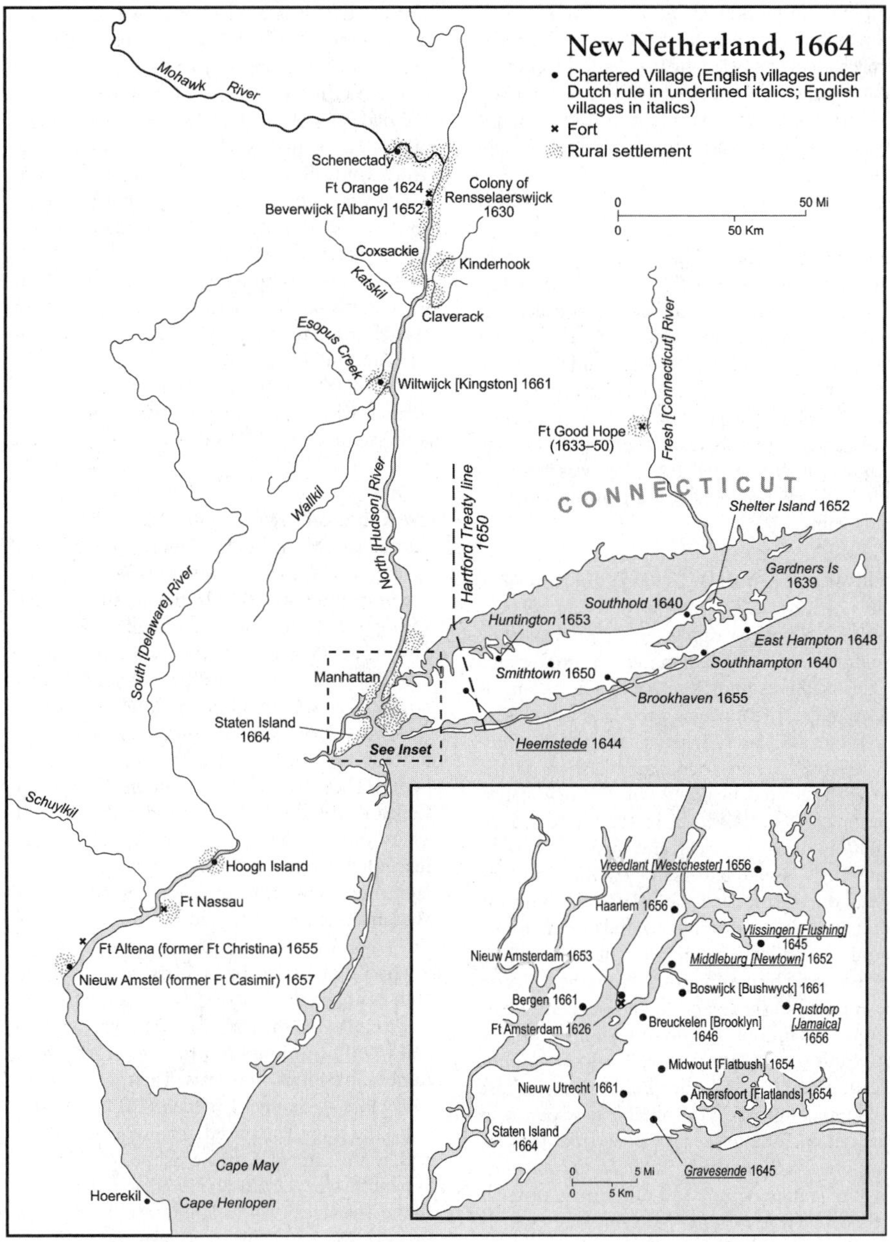

States, 1900–1965 (Chapel Hill: Univ of North Carolina Press, 1995)

Connie Kopelov

New Military Tract. An approximate 1.5 million-acre (600,000 ha) tract of central New York State set aside by the state legislature in 1782 to satisfy the state's commitment during the American Revolution to give land to those who enlisted in the Continental army. Military bounty lands served the needs of cash-poor but potentially land-rich states. Land bounties were commensurate with military rank. New Military Tract bounties ranged from 500 acres (202 ha) for the rank of private to 5,500 acres (2,226 ha) for that of major general. The survey of the territory, which did not begin until 1789, had to wait until treaties with the Onondaga (1788) and the Cayuga (1789) were struck, thereby formally ceding the majority of the land within the tract to the state. The delay forced the state legislature to designate a second military bounty tract in northern New York State in 1786; the northern lands were known as the Old Military Tract.

Consisting of what is now Onondaga, Cayuga, Tompkins, Cortland, and Seneca Cos, and parts of Oswego, Wayne, and Schuyler Cos, the New Military Tract is known for its classical township (land tract) and town (local government) names and its rectilinear survey form. In 1789–91, the tract was divided into 28 townships on the New England model; each was in turn divided into 100 rectangular lots of 600 acres (243 ha) each, which included the minimum 500-acre state military grant and soldiers' 100-acre (40.5 ha) federal right. This grid survey was one of several experiments throughout the United States in land subdivision at a time when the nation was abandoning the traditional European metes and bounds survey systems in favor of a uniform grid. This new approach was seen both as a rational method of land division and as a symbol of American democratic ideals. Ironically, speculators acquired most lands in the New Military Tract from soldiers who grew tired of waiting for their distribution or who wanted to move farther west. Because of its size, reputation, and proximity to large, privately held land schemes, the New Military Tract served as a model framework for European American postrevolutionary colonization of central and western New York State. Speculators oversaw the transfer of the majority of lands to settlers from eastern New York State, New England, New Jersey, and Pennsylvania beginning in 1791. By 1820 the New Military Tract was politically, socially, and economically integrated into New York State's maturing settlement framework. In the early 21st century evidence of the actual survey lies in the right-angles that characterize much of the region's field and road patterns.

See also SYRACUSE.

Schein, Richard H. "Framing the Frontier: The New Military Tract Survey on Central New York," *New York History* 74 (1993): 5–28

Richard Schein

New Netherland

PROLOGUE: THE DUTCH ATLANTIC EMPIRE

The Netherlands was one of the last countries of western Europe to enter the competition for colonial riches. It was not until the last two decades of the 16th century, well after the Dutch had begun their struggle for independence against Spain in 1568, that Dutch ships began to sail the oceans of the world. Two companies were formed to handle the trade that resulted: the Dutch East India Co (VOC) in 1602 and the Dutch West India Co (WIC) in 1621. Most attention was devoted initially to the East Indies, where the rich spice trade offered lucrative possibilities. For this trade the VOC combined the efforts of several private merchant companies under a government-sanctioned monopoly. The Dutch presence in Asia during the 17th century was mostly confined to small trading posts.

The situation in the Atlantic was different in many ways. The investments required to send a ship to New Netherland, Brazil, or the Caribbean were small in comparison with the large outlays necessary for East Indiamen, the large ships that sailed far greater distances. A government-sanctioned monopoly on shipping and trade to a single company was therefore initially not an essential ingredient for a successful Dutch role in the Atlantic. Before 1620 the fur trade in New Netherland and trade with the Portuguese and Spanish colonies, which consisted of bulk goods like salt, sugar, tobacco, and dyewood, remained in private hands. Dutch shipping to West Africa concentrated on more valuable return cargoes, such as gold and ivory.

The WIC, a joint-stock trading company, was organized similarly to the VOC. The continuing war with Spain, which from 1580 to 1640 also controlled Portugal, provided the impetus for its founding. Only by pooling their resources would the private concerns of the Dutch Republic be able to launch attacks on the Spanish and Portuguese colonies and thus cut off the financial basis for the Iberian war efforts in northern Europe. The Twelve Years' Truce between Spain and the Netherlands (1609–21) halted the plan's implementation. Immediately after the resumption of war with Spain in 1621, the WIC was founded. It comprised five regional chambers that contributed representatives to the governing board of directors in proportion to their financial contribution to the company. The Amsterdam

Chamber was the largest investor and had supervision of New Netherland.

The WIC, supported by government subsidies and the income from its privateering expeditions, attempted what was called the Grand Design, an all-out attack on the Portuguese Atlantic empire. This included the capture of fortifications on the West African coast and the conquest of Brazil. From 1630 to 1654 a part of northwestern Brazil was under Dutch control. The need for labor on the sugar plantations in Brazil led the WIC to import slaves from West Africa. Attacks on the Portuguese strongholds in West Africa had failed in the 1620s, but by the 1630s the Dutch finally gained footing when Portugal's Fort Elmina [now in Ghana] was taken. Other forts followed, and by the mid-1640s the WIC occupied a string of trading posts along the coast.

The Dutch Atlantic empire reached its zenith in 1645. By then it comprised New Netherland, several trading forts in West Africa, ranging from Fort Elmina to Kongo-Angola [now Republic of the Congo (Brazzaville) and Angola], a considerable portion of Brazil, several islands in the Caribbean, including Curaçao, which had been captured in 1634. Events took a turn for the worse. The investments required for maintaining the Atlantic empire far exceeded the financial rewards. As a result the WIC had to relinquish parts of its monopoly on trade and shipping, adversely affecting its financial position. After Portugal regained its independence from Spain in 1640, the Portuguese planters in Brazil began a revolt against Dutch rule in 1645. This ultimately led to the loss of Dutch Brazil in 1654. Other losses occurred in West Africa, although enough fortifications remained in Dutch hands, and they maintained an interest in the slave trade. After the loss of Brazil, Curaçao became the pivotal transit point in the smuggling of slaves to Spanish colonies in South America. It is estimated that the Dutch brought about 530,000 Africans to the New World, although this represented only 5% of the total number of people brought into slavery.

Within the Dutch imperial world, New Netherland was a relatively unimportant colony. It was too far out of the way to be of much utility within the Dutch Atlantic trading network. There was some thought of making it an agricultural colony, since it had a moderate climate, but hemmed in by more populous English colonies, its economic and social development proved precarious. Within its first half century of existence, however, New Netherland created a distinctive pattern of settlement and a way of life that would persist long after Dutch sovereignty ended.

Early Settlement, 1609–40

North America came to the attention of Dutch merchants through the voyage of Henry Hudson in his ship *Halve Maen* (known in English as *Half Moon*) in 1609. Employed by the VOC to reconnoiter the northeast passage to Asia, he decided to follow his own plan to discover a northwestern route. Sailing up the river that would later bear his name, Hudson conducted some trade in peltries, which were abundantly available. News of the prospects of a rich fur trade with the Indians soon reached Amsterdam, and several merchant companies equipped ships to sail to the area. There was fierce competition among these companies, each trying to outbid the other to obtain furs. This resulted in conflicts among the skippers on the Hudson and in litigation in Amsterdam.

As the competition caused a decrease in profit, the Amsterdam merchants united to petition the States General for exclusive trading rights to the North American coast. They pooled their resources into a single company, the New Netherland Co, which received a monopoly from the States General in 1614. Its charter, which contains the first use of the name New Netherland, covered the "newly discovered countries situate in America between New France and Virginia, the sea coasts whereof lie in the latitude of from forty to forty five degrees." With later changes, New Netherland stretched from Delaware Bay to Cape Cod. The company lasted from 1614 to 1618, during which several trading voyages were made. The States General in 1618 turned down a request to renew the charter of New Netherland Co, a decision connected to the intention to found the WIC. Two years after its founding in 1621, the WIC took over control of New Netherland from the private merchants.

For the WIC, New Netherland initially was of minor importance. However, directors soon became aware that to continue the fur trade, they needed to change the New Netherland Co practice of seasonal and occasional trading posts. To oppose English claims for New Netherland, some form of permanent settlement was required, and in January 1624 the WIC sent a scouting party with a small number of colonists to Manhattan on the *Eendracht,* under the command of Adriaen Jorisz Thienpont. A couple of months later, a second ship, the *Nieu Nederlandt,* under the command of Cornelis Jacobsz May, arrived in the colony. The two ships carried a number of Walloon colonists, mostly religious refugees from the Spanish-occupied southern Netherlands. In an attempt to maintain the Dutch claim to New Netherland, the settlers were divided among three trading posts: Fort Orange [now Albany] on the Hudson River, Fort Good Hope [now Hartford, Conn] on the Connecticut River, and Fort Wilhelmus [now Burlington Island, NJ] on the upper Delaware River. Within two years, however, all the colonists were resettled on Manhattan Island, where Fort Amsterdam would be erected. More colonists and cattle were sent in 1625 to reinforce the colony. In 1626 Manhattan was purchased from the Indians by Director Peter Minuit.

Fort Amsterdam was intended to be the main trading post in New Netherland, supported by smaller fortifications such as Fort Orange, where most of the fur trading took place. The government of the colony was initially set up similarly to that for trading posts of the VOC. Central authority rested with the director, sometimes called commander, and his council. This body held all administrative, judicial, and commercial power in New Netherland, although it had to operate within the framework of Dutch law. In the 1620s all colonists were employed by the company, which held a monopoly over the fur trade with the Indians. The trade doubled from 5,000 pelts in 1624 to about 10,000 in 1632. By 1628 the size of the colony warranted the appointment of a minister of the Dutch Reformed Church, Jonas Michaëlius, and by 1632 the European population had increased to between 200 and 300.

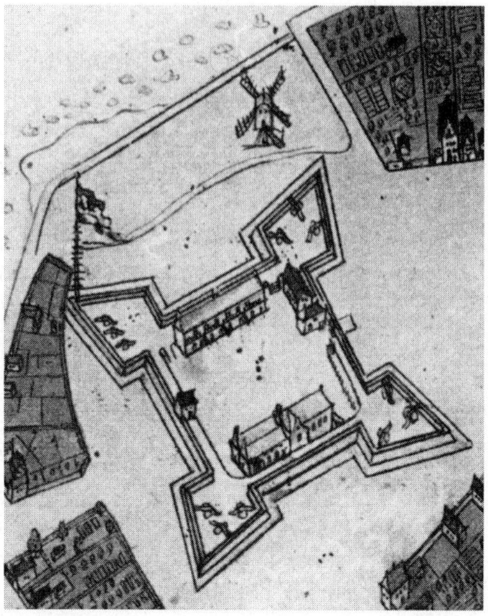

Detail of Fort Amsterdam from *Afbeeldinge Van De Stadt Amsterdam in Nieuw Neederlandt* (Costello Plan), 1660.

In the eyes of some WIC shareholders and directors, however, the progress made in the colonization of New Netherland was disappointing. In the mid-1620s a conflict arose within the Amsterdam Chamber of the WIC, which supervised New Netherland's affairs. One faction wanted the colony restricted to a few company-run trading posts that could be maintained with minimum expense and personnel. The profits from the fur trade would therefore belong solely to the WIC. Although the colony would be vulnerable to attacks from European competitors, such as England, the overall loss in the case of a takeover would be low. The opposing faction favored opening the colony to private investment in agricultural settlements, hoping that it would increase immigration. The outcome of the conflict was the patroonship plan of 1629, which allowed for privately owned colonies (patroonships) within New Netherland.

While New Netherland experienced a gradual increase in immigration, its population remained small relative to the surrounding English colonies. The Dutch erected forts throughout New Netherland to mark their claim to the area, but they found it impossible to prevent entirely the intrusion of other nations. The English in the early 1630s established themselves on the Connecticut River, taking over the local trade with the Indians. By 1640 English settlements surrounded the Dutch Fort Good Hope, but the English attempt to settle on the Delaware in 1635 was thwarted by Director Wouter van Twiller. In spring 1638 a Swedish expedition under the command of Peter Minuit landed settlers on the Delaware at what is now Wilmington, Del. The Swedish Fort Christina effectively cut off the Dutch Fort Nassau, which was located farther north on the east side of the river, opposite present-day Philadelphia. The Swedes, by establishing several trading posts, managed to dominate the fur trade with the Indians. The new director, Willem Kieft, who arrived in March 1638, issued a strong protest against Swedish intrusions that summer but was unable to put up an effective counterforce. Ultimately he joined forces with the Swedes in 1642 to prevent a second English attempt on the Delaware. The problems on New

New Netherland Political Subdivisions. In New Netherland, villages were established when there were sufficient numbers to have their own inferior court of justice, which both administered the village and adjudicated civil and minor criminal cases. The court contained a *schout* (chief law enforcement officer), appointed by the director and council of New Netherland, and the *schepenen* (magistrates), appointed by the director and council from a double number of names submitted by the sitting magistrates. New Amsterdam, the colony's only city, received a municipal charter in 1653, which gave it a government of burgomasters, *schepenen,* and *schout.* Before that date, the people were governed by the director and council.

Patroonships, such as Rensselaerswijck, were organized under individual investors called patroons but were also referred to as colonies, as was New Amstel. The latter was dissolved with the English takeover in 1664, while Rensselaerswijck lasted into the 19th century as the Manor of Rensselaerswijck. Habitation was not limited to the immediate environs of the chartered villages. Throughout New Netherland's jurisdiction, a handful of families and individuals lived in such places as Kinderhook and Claverack [now in Columbia Co] on the east side of the Hudson River, Schenectady on the Mohawk River, Coxsackie and Catskill [now in Greene Co] on the west side of the Hudson, Communipaw across the Hudson in New Jersey, Arnhem [now in Queens Co], and around Fort Altena [formerly the Swedish Fort Christina; now Wilmington, Del] on the Delaware River.

Dutch Name	Year Organized	Current Name	Current County
Villages			
Heemstede[a]	1644	Hempstead	Nassau
Gravesande[a]	1645	Gravesend	Kings
Vlissingen[a, b]	1645	Flushing	Queens
Breuckelen	1646	Brooklyn	Kings
Beverwijck	1652	Albany	Albany
Mespath/Middleburgh[a]	1652	Maspeth/Elmhurst	Queens
Amersfoort[c]	1654	Flatlands	Kings
Midwout[c]	1654	Flatbush/Midwood	Kings
Vreedlant[a]	1656	—	Bronx and/or Westchester
Rustdorp[a]	1656	Jamaica	Queens
Haarlem	1660	Harlem	New York
Wiltwijck	1661	Kingston	Ulster
Bergen	1661	Bergen	Hudson (NJ)
Boswijck	1661	Bushwick	Kings
Nieuw (New) Utrecht	1661	New Utrecht	Kings
Staten Eylandt	1664	Staten Island	Richmond
City			
Nieuw (New) Amsterdam	1653	New York City	New York
Patroonships			
Nieuwer (New) Amstel[d]	1657	New Castle	New Castle (Del)
Rensselaerswijck	1630	—	Albany, Rensselaer, and Columbia

Source: E. B. O'Callaghan, "Preface." In *Laws and Ordinances of New Netherland, 1638–1674,* trans E. B. O'Callaghan (1868)

[a]Initially settled by colonists from New England under the Dutch government.

[b]Had only a *schout* in 1645; *schepenen* were approved in 1648.

[c]Amersfoort and Midwout shared a court until granted separate courts of justice in 1661.

[d]Formerly the Dutch West India Co post Fort Casimir; ceded to the City of Amsterdam in 1657.

Netherland's southern and northeastern borders made it clear that for it to survive stronger incentives for immigration were necessary to populate and hold the land.

A Colony in Crisis, 1640–54

During the late 1630s, the States General of the Netherlands discussed with the WIC the problem of insufficient colonization to defend the province or to improve trade. The final result was the Freedoms and Exemptions of 1640, in which WIC gave up its monopoly on the fur trade and shipping to New Netherland in an attempt to promote and accelerate immigration.

Unfortunately, the 1640s were plagued with equally troublesome problems. The first were triggered by financial reverses of the WIC; between 1640 and 1645 its shares lost much of their value. To supplement the company's revenue in New Netherland, Kieft in 1639 decided to require the Indians in the vicinity of Manhattan to exchange skins and maize for the protection they were supposedly receiving from the company. This ill-fated decision triggered a vicious and bloody war with the Indians. Kieft's War lasted from 1640 to 1645 and involved many of the Munsee-speaking groups in the lower Hudson River area. An estimated 1,000 Indians were killed by the time peace was established. Although approximately 50 colonists were killed, many more fled the area, leaving the colony with a severely diminished population and an eroded economy.

The stress of war exacerbated the discontent among some elements of the European population. Supported by Minister Everardus Bogardus, many turned against Kieft. Blaming him for causing the war, they tried to persuade first the WIC and then the States General to have him recalled. Despite opposition from the Amsterdam Chamber, the States General forced the WIC in 1644 to summon Kieft back to Holland, though he did not return until after the arrival of his replacement, Petrus Stuyvesant, in 1647.

Stuyvesant, who was given the title of director general of New Netherland, Curaçao, Bonaire, Aruba, and other dependencies in the Caribbean, faced several problems upon his arrival in New Netherland. Continuing encroachments by the English and Swedes and the unstable situation with the Indians were important, but Stuyvesant's first concern was to restore good relations with the colonists. To better handle their concerns, Stuyvesant and the council asked the community, following Dutch tradition, to elect a double number of nine upstanding men to act as their representatives. From the 18, Stuyvesant and the council selected 9—3 farmers, 3 merchants, and 3 burghers (citizens)—to serve on the advisory board called the Nine Men. However, the conflict about the company's New Netherland policy flared up again in 1649. The Nine Men sent a delegation, headed by Adriaen van der Donck, to the Netherlands to persuade the States General to change the government of New Netherland. The delegation asked that Stuyvesant be recalled and that the WIC no longer govern New Netherland. They wanted the States General to have direct control and the colonists to have more say in local government. But by this time the internal political situation within the Netherlands had changed, and the delegation achieved little success. Relations between the colonists and Stuyvesant did begin to improve in the early 1650s. The policy of instituting local courts of justice, such as the Court of Fort Orange and Beverwijck [now Albany] in 1652 and New Amsterdam in 1653, played an important role in this. These courts were given administrative authority as well as civil and limited criminal powers, albeit within the framework set by the director general and council. Some tension remained, but never again would the relations between the colonists and the WIC be as problematic as they had been in the mid-1640s.

More difficult to solve were the problems with the English. Even though the Dutch felt that the eastern part of Long Island came under their jurisdiction, they had made no attempt to settle it. By 1639 the colonial council under Director Kieft had purchased only the land west of Oyster Bay [now in Nassau Co] from the Indians. However, the arrival in 1640 of a few English settlers from Massachusetts Bay Colony on Long Island near what would become Hempstead [now in

New Netherland and New England as depicted in detail from *Nova Belgica et Anglia Nova*, by Willem Janszoon Blaeu, *ca* 1635.

Nassau Co] brought swift action from Kieft. The settlers were evicted from the land, but fear that other English would try to enter Long Island illegally, coupled with the lack of sufficient Dutch to settle in the area, led Kieft to grant patents between 1644 and 1645 for three of the five English villages on Long Island: Hempstead, Gravesend [now in Kings Co], and Flushing [now in Queens Co]. Stuyvesant patented the last two English villages, Middleburgh [now Elmhurst, Queens Co] and Jamaica [now in Queens Co], in 1652 and 1656. The English settlers were subject to Dutch laws and ordinances but were given more freedom than the Dutch settlers in their town governments. Thus they did not need council approval for local laws and could nominate their own magistrates and *schout* (chief law enforcement officer). Even though the English settlers had to take an oath of allegiance to the colonial council, the WIC, and the States General, their loyalty to the Dutch government was fragile.

Although the immediate problem on Long Island was, for the moment, dealt with by the chartering of the English towns, Connecticut and the Delaware remained in contention. The WIC instructed Stuyvesant to come to a settlement with the English colonies. This eventually was achieved in the Hartford Treaty, a 1650 agreement establishing boundary lines on Long Island; the Dutch retained the land west of Oyster Bay, while the English controlled the land east. The boundary on the mainland ran north from the west side of Greenwich, Conn. Hostilities were avoided, but the treaty did not ease the Europe-based tensions between the Dutch and English. By 1650 the English Civil War had come to an end with Oliver Cromwell firmly in power. During the conflict (1642–50) the disruption of economic relations between England and its North American colonies had led to an increase in trade between New Netherland and the tobacco colonies of Virginia and Maryland. This suited the English colonies but was not to the liking of the government in London. The new English government soon issued the first of the so-called Acts of Navigation, laws that prohibited the transportation of goods to and from England and its colonies in foreign vessels. These acts were aimed at diminishing Dutch mercantile power and soon led to the First Anglo-Dutch War in 1652. New Netherland was an obvious target for an English attack, and a fleet destined for the Dutch colony had already reached New England when news of a peace settlement in Europe halted preparations for war in America.

Consolidation and Growth, 1654–64

The years between the end of the First Anglo-Dutch War in 1654 and the English conquest of 1664 were the best for New Netherland. The population grew from 1,500–2,000 around 1650 to 7,000–8,000 in 1664, spread out over New Amsterdam, 16 villages, and 2 patroonships. In comparison with the population of New England or Virginia, the Dutch colony was of modest size, but by Dutch colonial standards it was considerable. After the fall of Dutch Brazil in 1654, New Netherland was the only sizable Dutch settlement colony.

One of the reasons why New Netherland remained smaller than the surrounding English colonies was the prosperity of the Netherlands. The incentives for emigration from England were not present on the other side of the North Sea. The northern Netherlands experienced an economic boom that lasted for most of the 17th century, drawing immigrants from all over Europe. Religious toleration made the Netherlands a safe haven for many dissident refugees. On the whole there were no compelling reasons for the Dutch to seek their fortune overseas. And if they decided to do so, taking employment with the VOC seemed a wise choice, as the rich spice trade from Asia allowed for many opportunities to enrich oneself quickly.

The question, therefore, is why people were willing to settle in New Netherland at all. Many of those who came to New Netherland were immigrants to the Netherlands. The most impor-

DIRECTORS OF NEW NETHERLAND

Name	Dates of Service
Adriaen Jorisz Thienpont	1624
Cornelis Jacobsz May	1624
Willem Verhulst	1625–1626
Peter Minuit	1626–1632
Bastiaen Jansz Krol	1632–1633
Wouter van Twiller	1633–1638
Willem Kieft	1638–1647
Petrus Stuyvesant (director general)	1647–1664
Anthony Colve (governor)	1673–1674

tant patroon, Kiliaen van Rensselaer, drew his farmers, artisans, laborers, and servants from recent immigrants, though he also made use of the local population in the villages of the Utrecht and Gelderland provinces, where he owned land. The WIC Amsterdam Chamber recruited their soldiers and sailors from the large group of immigrants in Amsterdam, including many Scandinavians and Germans fleeing from the ravages of the Thirty Years War. This accounts, in large part, for why only about half of New Netherland's total population had been born in the Netherlands. Many soldiers and farmhands decided to stay in New Netherland after their contracts expired. After 1650 the WIC recruited soldiers for only a couple of years, provided for their passage to New Netherland, and hoped they would turn to farming once their contracts were up. The company also advanced the cost of the voyage for private immigrants. If the newcomers decided to leave the colony, the sum had to be refunded. The number of colonists returning from New Netherland appears to have been very low, both before and after the English takeover in 1664.

After 1650 many immigrants came over either independently or were employed by colonists who had settled earlier. Family networks played an important role in promoting immigration, not just because family members in New Netherland were the main source of information on the colony but also because they provided a rudimentary form of social security if things did not turn out as planned for the new arrivals. Another important aspect of the immigration patterns was the connection between occupational background and geographical origin. To generalize, soldiers came from Germany, sailors from Scandinavia, farmers from the eastern provinces of the Netherlands, while merchants, ministers, and high officials primarily came from the province of Holland. The people who formed the highest layers of the New Netherland society shared a common cultural heritage, and they were in a position to determine the public aspects of colonial culture.

Public culture in New Netherland was dominated by the Calvinist elite. However, full church membership was probably no higher than 20%, which was lower than the 37% average found in the Dutch Republic. Membership was more common among the elite because it was not only a requirement for magistrates but an essential ingredient of social status. In the eyes of both the colonial elite and the directors in Amsterdam, New Netherland society was to follow as much as possible the examples set in the Netherlands. In many cases the colonial government adopted regulations and institutions almost identical to those in the Netherlands. The system of greater and lesser "burgherrights" (citizens' rights), for example, was created in Amsterdam in 1652 and adopted only in the city of New Amsterdam in 1657. Under this system, shopkeepers and artisans had to purchase the small burgherright to exercise their profession, whereas the large burgherright was a requirement for magistrates and clergy in city government. Another example is the institution of "orphanmasters," who were responsible for looking after the inheritances of minors.

While emulations could be accomplished relatively easily in matters such as government, justice, religion, and economy, they were hardly enforceable in less formal facets of life. Yet even in customs surrounding birth, baptism, courtship, marriage, death, and burial, models from the Netherlands were followed in the colony. Such details of informal life can be observed in many court cases in New Netherland. For instance, those in the Dutch colony show a remarkable participation of women in public life. Roman-Dutch law allowed Dutch women a much larger freedom of action in all aspects of business, even when they were married. In many ways the women were equal partners with their husbands. Court records also provide insight into the life of slaves in New Netherland. They were used primarily on farms and in public works projects in Manhattan. Despite their low status, slaves in the colony could own property and testify in court.

While the population of New Netherland increased, the economy grew and diversified. Although the fur trade began to decline after 1657 because of intertribal wars, which limited hunting, the cultivation and export of tobacco grew considerably. The quality of New Netherland tobacco was inferior to tobacco grown in Virginia and Maryland, a portion of which was transported to Europe via New Amsterdam, but nonetheless there are indications that by 1664 the total value of exported tobacco was larger than that of fur. Other products of New Netherland included wheat, which was grown as a cash crop and exported, and lumber. Economic growth allowed the standard of living to rise, and the hardships of pioneer settlements were left behind.

Another step in the maturation process of New Netherland was the consolidation of governmental structures along Dutch lines, evident in the proliferation after 1654 of the number of villages granted a court of justice that both administered the village and dispensed civil justice. However, these courts' criminal jurisdiction was limited to minor offenses, and the provincial government had to approve their local ordinances. Thus New Netherland had a relatively centralized government, comparable more with rural provinces in the east of the Netherlands than with the cities in the province of Holland.

In ecclesiastical matters no colonial centralization is apparent. The number of ministers in New Netherland increased to six in 1664, but that was not sufficient to warrant the institution of a classis, a regional meeting of ministers and elders. Instead the ministers in the colony remained under the supervision of the classis of Amsterdam. In New Netherland, as in other Dutch colonies, the Dutch Reformed Church was the established church. Scandinavian and German colonists tried to obtain a Lutheran minister, an attempt that was forcibly suppressed by the director general and council, who considered religious pluralism a threat to the stability of colonial society. For the same reason, the colonial government tried to evict arriving Jews and Quakers. The WIC directors in Amsterdam, however, favored a more liberal stance and eventually overturned the decision.

Together with the growth of agriculture and the decline in the fur trade, population growth increased tensions with the Indian tribes along the Hudson River. In 1655 a short war erupted. Called the Peach War, it was caused by the shooting of an Indian woman caught stealing peaches from a colonist's garden in New Amsterdam. In later years troubles with the Indians were concentrated in the mid-Hudson area, where the Dutch had erected a small village at Wiltwijck [now Kingston, Ulster Co]. In 1660 and 1663 there were hostilities, resulting in a siege of the palisaded village. But, in contrast to Kieft's War, these later wars with the Indians did not threaten the existence of New Netherland as a whole.

More serious threats came from European countries. One of them was dealt with in 1655, when Director General Stuyvesant led a successful expedition to the Delaware to conquer New Sweden. The southern border of New Netherland was strengthened by the settling of New Amstel [now New Castle, Del], a patroonship granted by the WIC to the City of Amsterdam. The city-colony, started in 1657, soon suffered from failed harvests and diseases, resulting in a steady depopulation. The English colonies remained a serious problem. In the south of New Netherland, Virginia and Maryland continued

17th-century utility ware from the Netherlands of the type used at Fort Orange. *Top, from left:* chamber pot, serving dish, and pipkin; *bottom, from left:* skillet, bowl, and colander.

to covet the Delaware, whereas in the northeast, New Haven, Conn, did not relinquish its claims to the whole of Long Island, including the Dutch-governed western end. Yet the push for the final conquest of New Netherland came from England.

CONQUEST AND PERSISTENCE

In England the Restoration of 1660 brought Charles II to the throne. Charles immediately started an imperial policy aimed at obtaining more power over the North American colonies and at diminishing the mercantile power of the Netherlands by issuing a new Act of Navigation against Dutch shipping. The conquest of New Netherland was favored by the king's brother, James, Duke of York, and early in 1664 the king granted him a large part of the North American continent. Soon after, an English fleet left Portsmouth, England, and arrived at New Amsterdam in September 1664 with the first English governor, Richard Nicolls, aboard. New Amsterdam's situation was without much hope. As the Netherlands and England were at peace at the time (the Second Anglo-Dutch War was officially declared only in 1665), the attack came as a surprise. Although news of the English fleet's arrival in America had reached Stuyvesant two weeks earlier, this did not allow much time to improve the defenses. Fort Amsterdam was in bad condition due to the financial difficulties of the WIC, and reinforcements from other parts of New Netherland were not forthcoming. Once the lenient English terms for capitulation became known to the New Amsterdam population, Stuyvesant found himself under increasing pressure to surrender, which he eventually did 5 September. The capitulation was signed at Stuyvesant's bowery, though curiously not by the director general himself, a day later. The colony was retaken by the Dutch nine years later, only to be returned to the English in 1674 in the Treaty of Westminster, which brought the Third Anglo-Dutch War to an end.

English government did not lead to the rapid anglicization of the Dutch colonists. The Dutch language was used well into the 19th century, especially in rural parts of upper New York State. Most of the Dutch forms of government were abolished by the English. In New York City the government of *schout,* burgomasters, and *schepenen* was changed to sheriff, mayor, and aldermen in 1665, though this change was temporarily reversed in 1673–74 during the Dutch Restoration of New Netherland. Upstate changes came later, but by 1700 the forms of local government had been anglicized. The Dutch, however, were able to maintain some of their own customs, such as the mutual will, until the beginning of the 18th century. Also the Dutch Reformed Church remained under supervision of the Amsterdam classis until 1772. In New York City the Dutch were an ethnically distinguishable group until the 1730s. In Albany they were the most prominent group until after the American Revolution. The legacy of New Netherland lies in the persistence of Dutch culture in New York Colony, where it helped to shape the distinctive multiethnic culture.

See also AFRICAN AMERICANS; CARTOGRAPHY AND MAPPING; COURTS, STATE; DUTCH LITERATURE; FORTIFICATIONS; MILITIA; MOHICANS; NEW YORK CITY: EDUCATION IN NEW YORK CITY; WAMPUM.

Biemer, Linda B. *Women and Property in Colonial New York: The Transition from Dutch to English Law, 1643–1727* (Ann Arbor: Univ of Michigan Press, 1983)
Burke, Thomas E. *Mohawk Frontier: The Dutch Community of Schenectady, New York, 1661–1710* (Ithaca: Cornell Univ Press, 1991)
Cohen, David Steven. *The Dutch-American Farm* (New York: New York Univ Press, 1992)
De Jong, Gerald F. *The Dutch Reformed Church in the American Colonies* (Grand Rapids, Mich: Wm. B. Eerdmans Publishing, 1978)
Fabend, Firth Haring. *A Dutch Family in the Middle Colonies, 1660–1800* (New Brunswick, NJ: Rutgers Univ Press, 1991)
Goodfriend, Joyce D. *Before the Melting Pot: Society and Culture in Colonial New York City, 1664–1730* (Princeton, NJ: Princeton Univ Press, 1992)
———. "Burghers and Blacks: The Evolution of a Slave Society at New Amsterdam," *New York History* 59 (Apr 1978): 125–44
Jacobs, Jaap. *Een zegenrijk gewest: Nieuw-Nederland in de zeventiende eeuw* (Amsterdam: Samenwerkende Uitgeverijen Prometheus Bert Bakker, 1999)
Kross, Jessica. *The Evolution of an American Town: Newtown, New York, 1642–1775* (Philadelphia: Temple Univ Press, 1983)
Merwick, Donna. *Possessing Albany, 1630–1710: The Dutch and English Experience* (New York: Cambridge Univ Press, 1990)
Narrett, David E. *Inheritance and Family Life in Colonial New York City* (Ithaca: Cornell Univ Press, 1992)
Postma, Johannes. *The Dutch in the Atlantic Slave Trade* (New York: Cambridge Univ Press, 1990)
Richter, Daniel K. *The Ordeal of the Longhouse: The Peoples of the Iroquois League in the Era of European Colonization* (Chapel Hill: Univ of North Carolina Press, 1977)
Rink, Oliver. *Holland on the Hudson: An Economic and Social History of Dutch New York* (Ithaca: Cornell Univ Press, 1986)
Shattuck, Martha Dickinson. "The Dutch and the English on Long Island: An Uneasy Alliance," *De Halve Maen* 68 (Winter 1995): 80–85
Smith, George L. *Religion and Trade in New Netherland: Dutch Origins and American Development* (Ithaca: Cornell Univ Press, 1973)
Snow, Dean R., Charles T. Gehring, and William A. Starna, eds. *In Mohawk Country: Early Narratives about a Native People* (Syracuse: Syracuse Univ Press, 1996)
Sullivan, Dennis. *The Punishment of Crime in Colonial New York: The Dutch Experience in Albany during the 17th Century* (New York: Peter Lang, 1997)
Trelease, Allen. *Indian Affairs in Colonial New York: The 17th Century* (Ithaca: Cornell Univ Press, 1960)
Van Zwieten, Adriana. "The Orphan Chamber of New Amsterdam," *William and Mary Quarterly,* 3d ser, 53 (Apr 1996): 319–40
Weslager, C. A. *The Swedes and the Dutch at New Castle* (Wilmington, Del: Middle Atlantic Press, 1987)

Jaap Jacobs

New Paltz. Town (pop 12,830) and village (pop 6,034) in S Ulster Co. Twelve French Huguenots purchased much of the land that later made up the town—39,000 acres (15,783 ha)—from the Esopus Indians in 1677 and settled the tract after receiving a patent from the colonial governor. During the 17th and 18th centuries, the area's economy revolved around wheat; with the culture of the town strongly French, the Dutch and English languages did not gain ground until *ca* 1755. Beginning in 1738 it was governed by 12 trustees elected annually, a system supplemented by town government in 1785. With limited waterpower and no riverfront, New Paltz was bypassed by industry, although bricks were made from local clay during the Gilded Age. The Wallkill Valley Railroad (1869) provided modern transportation. The village incorporated in 1887, remaining relatively isolated until the New York State Thruway (1954) opened through the town. In 2002 the Mohonk Mountain House resort (1869) and SUNY New Paltz (founded as a state normal school in 1828) were important institutions that benefit the local economy. Huguenot St, with its stone houses, is a National Register district and tourist attraction.

Karen Nichols

Newport. Town (pop 2,192) and village (pop 640) in Herkimer Co. Settled in 1791, the town was formed from Herkimer, Fairfield, Norway, and Schuyler in 1806. Agriculture was its chief industry, but there was a cotton factory as early as 1808. The Herkimer Manufacturing Co (1814–*ca* 1865; iron and textiles) and a tannery (1846–89) produced goods for sale. Although most of the early settlers were from New England, Irish immigrants settled after the Erie Canal. Another employer was the lock factory, started by Linus Yale in 1835. An octagon house (1849), built for Yale's daughter, is a landmark. The village incorporated in 1857. A narrow-gauge railroad began service in 1882 and was widened to standard gauge in 1892; it became the Herkimer, Newport and Poland (later Mohawk and Malone) and was abandoned in 1971. The tannery building became a knitting mill, producing underwear and ribbed jerseys (1890–1901) and, later, a shoe factory (1941–56). The Michigan condensed-milk plant was acquired in 1916 by Borden, making condensed milk, malted milk powder, and instant coffee until 1971. A small Amish community settled beginning in 1979. In the early 21st century Newport continued to rely on dairy farming as its primary industry. Two mines of Herkimer diamonds, which are fine quartz crystals, attract tourists.

James Crawford

New Rochelle. City (pop 72,182) in S Westchester Co. Settled in ?1686 by Huguenot refugees, the territory was purchased by them in 1687–89 from John Pell, Lord of Pelham Manor; Jacob Leisler acted as their agent. A French church was formed in 1692 and became Anglican in 1709. A 1693 survey indicated that New Rochelle was divided into long, narrow farm lots. Records of town government survive from 1699. After the Revolution, Thomas Paine (1737–1809) was granted a farm by the US government and lived there for several years around 1805.

New Rochelle remained chiefly agricultural, with horticultural specialties such as blackberries, but by 1842 had become a fashionable summer resort with such facilities as the Neptune House, a hotel whose guests arrived by steamboat. The New Haven Railroad provided a modern link to New York City in 1848, after which suburban villas were built. New Rochelle incorporated as a village in 1857. Irish immigrants amounted to 21% of the population in 1855, and Germans 6%; Jews founded the first synagogue, Anshe Shalom, in 1896.

New Rochelle incorporated as a city in 1899 and became known as the "Queen City of the Sound" in recognition of its 9 mi (14.5 km) shoreline. It never was heavily industrial, although a number of small factories employed residents. The New York, Westchester and Boston Railway (1912–37, electric) ran through the less-developed north, promoting upper-income development; in 1930 the city was third wealthiest per capita in the country. The Hutchinson River Parkway (1928) in the northern part of the city and the New England Thruway (1958) near the shore became the city's arteries to New York City and facilitated its build-out after World War II. New Rochelle's downtown became an important suburban shopping district by the 1930s with notable Art Deco buildings, but it lost ground in the 1950s to neighboring shopping centers, responding with a 58-store enclosed mall (1968–93). When it closed, ambitious redevelopment plans totaling $265 million were launched. In 2000 the population was 18% black, 11% of Latino heritage, and 20% of Italian heritage.

It is the site of the College of New Rochelle (1904), Iona College (1940), and Monroe College (campus, 1983), and of the Thomas Paine Cottage and Wildcliff museums. Other features of interest are the curious silhouette welcome signs at the city's borders created in the interwar years by nine resident artists, including Norman Rockwell, whose home and studio were in New Rochelle from 1914 to 1939. Suffragist Carrie Chapman Catt (1859–1947) was another famous resident beginning 1928. George M. Cohan's musical *Forty-Five Minutes from Broadway* (1906) was set in the city, as was the television series *The Dick Van Dyke Show* (1961–66). A number of islands in Long Island Sound are within New Rochelle city limits, notably Davids Island, a military hospital starting 1862 and known as Fort Slocum until 1967, and Glen Island, a popular day resort beginning 1879 and a county park from 1929.

New School University. The founding of the New School for Social Research in 1919 in Greenwich Village in Manhattan was precipitated by a controversy at Columbia University, when in 1917 Pres Nicholas Murray Butler fired two faculty members opposed to American intervention in World War I. Historians Charles A. Beard and James H. Robinson resigned in protest, and they founded the New School as an academic institution that would guarantee academic freedom. They were joined by prominent colleagues such as philosopher John Dewey, sociologist Thorstein Veblen, and economists Alvin S. Johnson and Wesley C. Mitchell. After 1922 the New School's orientation was broadened from the social sciences to include the humanities and the arts, primarily delivered by visiting lecturers in evening courses, becoming a pioneering institution in adult education. In 1922 Johnson became president, a position he held until 1963.

Johnson was the key figure in establishing, in 1933, the University in Exile, a home for refugee scholars. During the next decade the émigré university rescued more than 170 scholars, initially from Germany and Italy and then, as fascism swept across Europe, from Austria, Spain, Hungary, Belgium, and France. In 1934 the University in Exile became the Graduate Faculty of Political and Social Science with a charter to award master's and doctoral degrees. Although the Graduate Faculty and its quarterly *Social Research* had somewhat outsider status in US higher learning, its European-based scholarly approach contributed to Pres Franklin D. Roosevelt's social and economic programs and influenced the cross-fertilization of US and European culture. During World War II the émigrés were probably the academic group most frequently consulted by US government officials for the war effort and the future postwar order after the defeat of fascism in Europe. Sometimes they were hired directly by the government; sociologist Hans Speier worked for the Office of War Information, and his colleague Gerhard Colm, an expert on public finance, worked for the Bureau of the Budget and the President's Council of Economic Advisers.

Other scholars came to the Graduate Faculty after the war from other countries of exile. Political philosophers such as Hannah Arendt, Hans Jonas, and Leo Strauss broadened their discipline and deepened its integration with the social sciences. The French émigré scholars at the Ecole Libre des Hautes Etudes, founded in 1942, included philosopher Alexandre Koyré, linguist Roman Jakobson, and ethnologist Claude Lévi-Strauss. The arts have occupied a prominent place at the New School since the 1920s; faculty members have included composers Aaron Copland and John Cage, poet W. H. Auden, and dancer Martha Graham. The Dramatic Workshop, founded in 1940 by German dramatist and director Erwin Piscator, offered training to Marlon Brando and Rod Steiger, among others.

In the late 20th century the New School expanded into further academic divisions. The Graduate Faculty as one of the key divisions continues the European émigré legacy, in part through two professorships sponsored by the German government that bring distinguished social scientists from Europe each year. The New School remained a haven for oppressed scholars, many from countries formerly dominated by the Soviet Union. The Kaplan Center for New York City Affairs was established in 1964; it became the Graduate School of Management and Urban Policy in 1975 and was later renamed in honor of trustee Robert J. Milano. The Parsons School of Design, one of the city's leading art and design schools since 1896, merged into the New School in 1970; a second campus was established in Paris in 1980. The Eugene Lang College (named the Seminar College until 1985) became a full-time, four-year undergraduate liberal arts program for students in 1978. The Mannes College of Music merged into the New School as its sixth division in 1989; the Actors Studio Drama School, founded in 1947, became the seventh division, the School of Dramatic Art, in 1995. In 1997 the New School was renamed New School University, and in 2002 it enrolled about 7,000 degree students and 20,000 nondegree students.

Krohn, Claus-Dieter. *Intellectuals in Exile: Refugee Scholars and the New School for Social Research* (Amherst: Univ of Massachusetts Press, 1993)

Rutkoff, Peter M., and William B. Scott. *New School: A History of the New School for Social Research* (New York: Free Press, 1986)

Claus-Dieter Krohn

New Scotland. Town (pop 8,626) in central Albany Co. Settled *ca* 1660 by Teunis Slingerland, the town gained its name after an influx of Scottish immigrants in the third quarter of the 18th century. Limestone was quarried for Erie Canal construction and burned for lime. Formed from Bethlehem in 1832, New Scotland was served by the Albany and Susquehanna (1863) and the Saratoga and Hudson River (1865; later West Shore) Railroads. Fodder, fruit, and hops were raised. Camp Pinnacle (1898) was the first US summer camp exclusively for girls and young women. The Bender Melon Farm was nationally known in the early 20th century. New Scotland is known for its natural beauty and includes John Boyd Thacher State Park (1914) with its Indian Ladder Trail, Five Rivers Environmental Education Center (1972), previously a state game farm, Horton Falls on Vly Creek, and caverns at Clarksville. The Onesquethaw Valley Historic District encompasses 34,100 acres (13,800 ha). In the early 21st century New Scotland is both agricultural and suburban. Indian Ladder Farms (1916), a major orchard, draws 200,000 customers during its autumn season.

Cynthia B. Childs

Newsday. Founded in the Village of Hempstead (Nassau Co) in 1940 by Alicia Patterson and Harry Guggenheim, when Guggenheim bought the defunct *Nassau Daily Journal* for his wife Alicia. After a shaky start *Newsday* flourished as Long Island's suburban population surged in the 1950s and 1960s. Daughter of Joseph Medill Patterson, editor and publisher of the *New York Daily News,* Alicia Patterson was *Newsday's* editor and publisher from 1940 until her death at 56 in 1963. She put her powerful stamp on the tabloid, taking liberal editorial positions often directly opposed to those of the more conservative Guggenheim. During Patterson's tenure the paper won its first Pulitzer Prize (1954) for an exposé on labor racketeering, and circulation reached almost 400,000. In 1970, a year before his death at 80, Guggenheim sold his controlling interest in *Newsday* to the Los Angeles–based Times Mirror, and the paper became a subsidiary in 1971. *Newsday* was published six days a week until 1971 when management added a Sunday edition. Expanding westward with a Sunday Queens edition in 1977, the paper added a daily there a few months later. It combined Nassau and Suffolk operations in its Melville (Suffolk Co) plant in 1979. In 1983 the tabloid entered the New York City print media market with *New York Newsday,* which survived until 1995.

Included among the 17 Pulitzer Prizes awarded to *Newsday* staff by 2002 were prizes for a three-year investigative series about corruption in the Suffolk Co Towns of Babylon, Islip, and Brookhaven (1970) and for a series on the international heroin trail (1974). With an editorial staff of over 800 and large teams of reporters, the paper in the late 1990s ran several in-depth series on Long Island's people and history, which were later published as coffee table books. In 2000 *Newsday* became part of the Tribune Co of Chicago when it merged with Times Mirror. *Newsday* dominates the newspaper market of Nassau and Suffolk Cos. With a combined daily and Sunday circulation of almost 1.3 million for its Nassau, Suffolk, and Queens editions in 2002, *Newsday's* estimated sales were $59.8 million.

Keeler, Robert F. *"Newsday": A Candid History of the Respectable Tabloid* (New York: William Morrow, 1990)

Newsday, http://www.newsday.com

Catherine A. McKeen

newspapers. The first New York newspapers were partisan, generally by necessity, since they relied on subventions from the government or opposition factions. The *New-York Gazette*, the first newspaper in the Colony of New York, was first published in New York City on 8 Nov 1725 by William Bradford, the government's printer. Eight years later the *New-York Weekly Journal*, sponsored by an opposition faction, started publishing. Its editor, John Peter Zenger, was arrested in 1734 on a charge of seditious libel. His landmark trial in 1735, as well as his acquittal, for publishing the truth was an important precedent for establishing freedom of the press. But despite the fireworks of the Zenger case, until the era of the Revolution, the average fare of colonial newspapers, which consisted largely of advertisements and foreign news, was rather dry. The pre-Revolutionary crisis led to greater political commentary. Patriot newspapers included John Holt's *New-York Journal*, starting in 1766; the leading tory paper was *Rivington's New-York Gazetteer; or, the Connecticut, New-Jersey, Hudson's-River and Quebec Weekly Advertiser*, first published in 1773. Early newspapers were published weekly or semiweekly. The first daily was the *New York Daily Advertiser*, established 1 Mar 1785 by Francis Childs. Most newspapers had short lives in the late 18th century amid a glut of weeklies, biweeklies, and dailies. Affiliations with political parties and factions continued to be profitable for many newspapers. In 1787 and 1788 the *Federalist Papers*, which gave their name to the political party, were written in defense of the ratification of the US Constitution in New York State and largely published in the *New York Independent Journal*. Federalist editor and future lexicographer Noah Webster edited the *American Minerva*, starting in 1793. He also edited the *Herald; a Gazette for the Country* (1794–97), which was one of the first semiweekly editions created for rural circulation and which established a model for city papers to reach a ready audience economically. By far the longest lived of the early partisan press in New York City was Alexander Hamilton's *New York Evening Post*, first published on 16 Nov 1801 and still published as the *New York Post*.

Early National Era and the Penny Press

The first newspaper published outside of New York City, the short-lived *Albany Gazette* (1771), was followed by eight others by 1788, four of them in Albany and most controlled by Federalists. The *Gazette of the United States*, originally published in New York City on 15 Apr 1789, received financial aid from the Federalists and was transferred to Albany in 1790. The *Whitestown Gazette* was the first newspaper west of Albany, issued in New Hartford [now in Oneida Co] on 11 July 1793 and transferred to Utica five years later. In Canandaigua (Ontario Co) James D. Bemis, a former bookstore owner known as the Father of the Western New York Press, made the *Ontario Repository*, first published in 1809, into an outstanding Federalist paper. Press freedom was tested and ultimately extended under the impact of the Sedition Act of 1798. The *Mount Pleasant (Westchester Co) Register* played a role in this act when its editor William Durell was fined $50 and sentenced to three months in prison for reprinting libel on Pres John Adams. After serving a small portion of his prison term Durell was pardoned by the president's only act of clemency relating to the act. In 1804 Federalist editor Harry Croswell was charged with reprint-

DAILY NEWSPAPERS PUBLISHED IN NEW YORK STATE

County	1850	1900	1950	2000
Albany	7	9[a]	3	1
Allegany	0	1	1	1
Broome	1	3	4	1
Cattaraugus	0	2	2	2
Cayuga	1	2	1	1
Chautauqua	0	5	3	2
Chemung	0	4	2	1
Chenango	0	1	1	1
Clinton	0	4	1	1
Columbia	0	2	0	1
Cortland	0	1	1	1
Dutchess	0	6	3	1
Erie	5	12[b]	5[c]	1
Franklin	0	1	2	2
Fulton	0	3	2	1
Genesee	0	1	1	1
Greene	0	1	1	1
Herkimer	0	3	2	2
Jefferson	0	2	1	1
Kings	3	5	3[d]	1
Madison	0	0	1	1
Monroe	5	6	4[e]	2
Montgomery	0	2	1	1
Nassau	0	0	3	1
New York[f]	19[g]	40[h]	33[i]	14[j]
Niagara	0	7	3	3
Oneida	4	6	3	2
Onondaga	4	4	2	1
Ontario	0	2	2	2
Orange	0	9	3	2
Orleans	0	0	1	1
Oswego	2	2	1	1
Otsego	0	3	2	1
Queens	0	1	4	4[k]
Rensselaer	3	5	2	1
Richmond	0	3	1	1
Rockland	0	2	1	0
St. Lawrence	0	2	1	2
Saratoga	2	3	1	1
Schenectady	0	3	2	1
Schoharie	0	0	0	1
Steuben	0	5	3	2
Suffolk	0	0	0	1
Tioga	0	1	0	0
Tompkins	1	4	2	2
Ulster	0	4	2	1
Warren	0	3	2	1
Westchester	0	6	9	1
Yates	0	1	0	0

Source: The New York State Newspaper Project.

Note: The following counties did not have daily newspapers in the years covered by the table: Delaware, Essex, Hamilton, Lewis, Livingston, Putnam, Schuyler, Seneca, Sullivan, Washington, Wayne, Wyoming. Bronx Co had a daily newspaper, the *Bronx Home News*, from 1922 to 1948.

[a]Includes 1 German newspaper.

[b]Includes 1 Polish and 2 German newspapers.

[c]Includes 1 Polish newspaper.

[d]Includes 1 Spanish and 1 Finnish newspaper.

[e]Includes 1 German newspaper.

[f]In 1800 there were 5 daily newspapers in New York State, all published in New York Co.

[g]Includes 3 German newspapers.

[h]Includes 1 Croatian, 2 Czech, 7 German, 1 Greek, 1 Hungarian, 3 Italian, and 2 Yiddish newspapers.

[i]Includes 1 Arabic, 3 Chinese, 1 Czech, 2 Greek, 1 Hungarian, 1 Italian, 2 Polish, 1 Russian, 1 Slovak, 1 Spanish, 1 Ukrainian, and 2 Yiddish newspapers.

[j]Includes 2 Chinese, 1 Japanese, 1 Greek, 1 Russian, and 2 Spanish newspapers.

[k]Includes 1 Chinese, 1 Greek, 1 Korean, and 1 Spanish newspaper.

Compiled by Heidi Knoblauch

ing in his *Hudson Wasp* accusations against Pres Thomas Jefferson originally published in the *New York Evening Post.* Although Croswell was found guilty (later acquitted upon appeal), Alexander Hamilton's arguments that reviewed the entire libel law situation led the state legislature in 1805 to pass a law accepting truth as a defense when publishing statements with "good motives."

Upstate cities soon developed strong daily newspapers. The *Albany Argus* was first issued as a semiweekly in 1813 and as a daily in 1824. The paper reflected the views of the Albany Regency, and under editor Jesse Buel—who doubled as state printer after 1814—the paper rose to state and national importance. Even more influential was Thurlow Weed's *Albany Evening Journal,* first published in 1830. Weed, a peripatetic newsman who had worked on nine papers in different parts of the state, was a staunch anti-Democrat and, in turn, an Antimason, a Whig, and a Republican. Among the first New York State editors to become a political force in his own right, he shepherded the career of William H. Seward from the legislature to a prospective presidential candidacy. Newspapers established in the early 19th century in other major cites in New York State include the Democratic *Utica Observer,* first published in 1817; it ranked behind only the *Albany Argus* in terms of influence outside of New York City. The *Buffalo Gazette,* the city's first paper, started as a weekly in 1811; its first daily, the *Buffalo Star,* started in 1831. Rochester's first paper, the weekly *Rochester Gazette,* was established in 1816; the *Rochester Advertiser,* begun in 1826, was the first daily published west of Albany. By the late 1830s many cities in the state had daily newspapers.

The most significant development in US journalism of the 1830s was the rise of the penny press. Written and designed for a mass audience, these papers broadened newspaper readership with compelling stories about crime, scandal, and the underside of the city. Unlike earlier newspapers, which were sold by subscription, the penny press was peddled on street corners. New printing technology, like the Hoe rotary press, facilitated ever greater pressruns. Benjamin Day started the *New York Sun* in 1833, and by 1838 its daily circulation was about 38,000. James Gordon Bennett Sr started the *New York Morning Herald* in 1835; his keen understanding of the public would make him perhaps the most successful penny press publisher. His greatest rival was Horace Greeley, whose *New York Tribune,* first appearing in 1841, used its weekly edition to extend its influence beyond the New York City area and garnered a substantial rural following in the Midwest, becoming in effect a national publication. By the eve of the Civil War, it had a circulation of 287,750 and was distributed throughout the North. A paper that rejected the penny press approach was the *New York Times,* started by Henry J. Raymond in 1851. The *Times* sought a wealthier audience that, presumably, had less appetite for sensationalism. The advent of the Civil War greatly increased the demand for news and had a marked impact on metropolitan papers throughout the state. The *Herald* and *Tribune* went from 8 to 16 pages and Sunday editions appeared. (As late as 1879, when Norman Mack started the *Buffalo Sunday Times,* successful Sunday editions were rare.) By 1850 there were 57 daily newspapers published in the state; 19 in New York City (3 of those in German), and 4 or 5 in each of the state's other large cities.

In the 1830s city papers began to seek rural subscribers. Specialized publications also proliferated; New York State was a leader in farm publications. Luther Tucker, publisher of the *Rochester Daily Advertiser,* issued the *Genesee Farmer* in 1831, and *Albany Argus* editor Jesse Buel founded the *Cultivator* in 1834. In the 1870s the *New York Tribune* weekly edition devoted a page or more to agricultural correspondence, a precursor of self-help columns. These rural beginnings in New York State led to the westward spread of agricultural journalism and even more specialized publications. A number of notable specialty publications were among those advocating women's rights. The *Lily* (1849–59) was founded by the Seneca Falls Temperance Society and edited by Amelia Bloomer, who with Elizabeth Cady Stanton made it into a women's rights monthly with 6,000 subscribers. Perhaps the best known of the feminist newspapers was the radical *Revolution* (1868–72). With suffragist Susan B. Anthony as business manager, the paper earned 3,000 subscribers. The nation's first black newspaper, *Freedom's Journal,* was started in New York City in 1827. The abolitionist *Standard and Democrat* in Utica, like others of its kind, presented a challenge to the constitutional guarantee of freedom of the press and whether that freedom would be upheld in the face of unpopularity; its offices were destroyed by mobs in 1835. Slavery opponents such as Horace Greeley and Thurlow Weed helped circulate nationally the *Elevator,* originally published in Albany in 1842. Abolitionist editor Frederick Douglass first published the *North Star* on 3 Dec 1847 in Rochester. It was the first black paper to reach a circulation of 3,000.

Era of the Press Lords

There was a new stability to the newspaper business after the Civil War. If new papers regularly emerged on the scene, established papers thrived and often expanded their reach, becoming leading civic institutions in their own right. (This development built on the foundation of smaller weekly newspapers, whose offices on village main streets from about 1800 served as the reading rooms and gathering places for civic leaders.) The headquarters of major newspapers became part of the cityscape. The era of the newspaper tower is preserved in place-names like Herald Square and Times Square in New York City. The rise of department stores afforded a more secure revenue base for the large daily newspapers, making them into vehicles for popularizing the new consumer-based culture. This in turn contributed to a gradual decline in their overt partisanship. In addition to relaying political news, daily newspapers emerged as perhaps the premier interpreters of urban life. By the end of the 19th century, a combination of aggressive mass-circulation journalism and social and political ferment set the stage for the emergence of star reporters Richard Harding Davis and Nellie Bly. The *New York Tribune* and *New York Sun* developed what became known as the human interest story. The period was also marked by the circulation wars of William Randolph Hearst and Joseph Pulitzer. Pulitzer had acquired the *New York World* in 1883, Hearst had bought the *New York Journal* in 1895, and the ensuing competition changed the face of journalism. Sensational journalism came to be known as yellow journalism (a name derived from the *Journal*'s "Yellow Kid," one of the first successful comic strips and itself an indication of how newspapers were increasingly emphasizing non-news features to draw in readers). Exposés of scandals, accounts of the seamier sides of urban life, and numerous features and Sunday supplements were the hallmarks of yellow journalism. If accompanied by lurid prose and attention-grabbing headlines, the best of yellow journalism (like its close cousin, muckraking) exposed numerous civic issues for a large audience. It also helped create a constituency for progressive reform and drew more people into the ranks of newspaper readers. An alternate but equally successful approach was developed by the *New York Times,* rescued from bankruptcy by Adolph S. Ochs in 1896. Relying on numerous foreign correspondents and solid news coverage reported in a sober and comprehensive style, the *Times* nurtured a growing ethos of "objectivity" among serious journalists.

By 1900 the daily newspaper had become a part of the lives of most New Yorkers, and before

Union News Co stand at Union Depot, Albany, *ca* 1905.

the inroads of the radio and other electronic media, it was near the apogee of its popularity. That year 192 daily newspapers were published in the state. Daily newspapers were published in 43 of the state's 61 counties and circulated widely in the rest. This included at least 21 daily newspapers published in languages other than English, countless weeklies, and other foreign language publications. These numbers grew as the immigrant population in the state, and especially in New York City, expanded; by one reckoning there were 42 daily foreign language newspapers published in 15 languages, including Croatian, Slovak, and Arabic, in New York City by 1914. Herman Ridder's *New Yorker Staats-Zeitung,* which started publication in 1834, had a daily circulation of nearly 250,000 in 1914. The Yiddish language *Forverts,* or *Forward,* began in 1897; its editor, Abraham Cahan, shaped it into a voice for socialism that also guided immigrants in their adjustment to American life. *Il Progresso Italo-Americano,* owned by Genereso Pope after 1928, was a political voice in the Italian American community. The ethnic press also included many English language newspapers. The *Irish World and American Industrial Liberator* and *Gaelic American* were only two of the many New York City–based Irish American newspapers that had a major influence on politics in New York State and Ireland. The *New York Age,* edited by T. Thomas Fortune from 1889 to 1907, and the *Amsterdam News,* after 1909, were the leading weekly newspapers for African Americans.

World War I and its repressive aftermath brought harsh military censorship to the New York State press. German language newspapers declined in numbers, in part due to harassment and in part due to lack of interest and declining foreign language skills of US-born generations. Many left-wing publications, such as the *The Masses,* were suppressed by federal censors. Tabloids, papers printed in a smaller, more convenient format, were an innovation of the postwar period. The *New York Illustrated Daily News,* the first and most successful example, premiered in June 1919 and became one of the most widely circulated papers in the United States. In 1924 Hearst and Bernarr Macfadden followed suit with the competing *New York Daily Mirror* and *New York Evening Graphic,* respectively. Improvements in photo technology and a relentless emphasis on big pictures and photos, big headlines, and sensational stories about gangsters, sports, entertainment, and society helped carve out a new readership for the tabloids.

Chains and Consolidation

By the 1920s the ethic of objectivity—of separating the facts of news from the political values of reporters and editors—was an established value in the culture of journalism. Yet the rise of objectivity and the notion of the reporter as a professional did not necessarily translate into power in the newsroom for working journalists. In 1933 *New York World-Telegram* columnist Heywood Broun spurred editorial newspaper workers to action, which resulted in the formation of the Newspaper Guild Union (now Newspaper Guild). Less than a year after its formation, it had 8,000 members and by the end of the 20th century, 31,000 nationwide. In the 1930s during the depression and the international crises that led to World War II, there was a heightened emphasis on interpretive reporting and syndicated columnists, such as the *New York Herald-Tribune*'s Walter Lippmann and Dorothy Thompson.

Newsboy, by Carl G. Hill, 1938. Hill was a student at the Harlem Community Art Center at the time this lithograph was produced. All rights reserved, The Metropolitan Museum of Art.

The syndication of columnists amplified the voices of individual journalists, but around the state economic trends in the newspaper business encouraged the growth of newspaper chains, which would elevate the power of the publisher and diminish the significance of individual editors and reporters. The great popularity of the tabloids and the growing competition from radio led to a series of consolidations among newspapers. The *Herald* and the *Tribune* merged in 1924, the *New York World* merged with the *New-York Telegram* in 1931, and subsequently it absorbed the *New York Sun* in 1950 to become the *New York World-Telegram and Sun.* As ownership became more concentrated, some publishers started to develop chains of newspapers in different cities. Frank E. Gannett began creating a newspaper chain with the *Elmira Gazette* in 1906. He then acquired newspapers in Rochester (which became his base of operations), Utica, Binghamton, Albany, and Ithaca. Gannett papers were known for their technological innovation; by 1938 the presses for his Rochester newspapers had been adapted for color printing. Hearst's papers also acquired a statewide focus. From 1922 through 1925 Hearst bought the *Syracuse Evening Telegram,* the *Syracuse Journal,* the *Rochester Evening Journal,* and the *Albany Times-Union,* adding to the newspapers he already owned in New York City. After acquiring the *Staten Island Advance* in 1927, the Queens-based *Long Island Press* in 1932, and several other papers in the New York City metropolitan area, S. I. Newhouse in 1939 purchased three Syracuse newspapers *(Herald, Journal,* and *Sunday American),* which formed the *Syracuse Herald-Journal,* and in 1942 bought the *Post-Standard.* The publishers of newspaper chains often gained considerable political power in the state; Hearst served two terms in the US Congress (1903–7) before unsuccessful bids for mayor of New York City and for governor. Gannett's political influence culminated in an unsuccessful bid for the 1940 Republican presidential nomination.

Media Competition and the Internet

The consolidation of newspapers continued after World War II. Evening newspapers and evening editions became a thing of the past. A series of disastrous newspaper strikes in New York City in the early 1960s greatly hurt local newspapers and led to the bankruptcy of four of the city's seven major dailies. In New York State there was an 8.7% loss in daily circulation between 1980 and 1990. Newspapers were increasingly part of an international communications industry. In 1976 Australian magnate Rupert Murdoch purchased the *New York Post* and successfully turned it into a mouthpiece for his conservative politics. In the early 1990s British publisher Robert Maxwell briefly owned the *New York Daily News.* In 2002 there were 79 daily newspapers published in the state, including 27 in New York City. These encompassed several trade journals and 15 newspapers in languages other than English. More than 600 weekly newspapers were also being published in the early 21st century. The *New York Times* retained its position as perhaps the most respected national and international newspaper and as the only New York State newspaper read widely around the state that regularly covered state affairs. The *Wall Street Journal,* founded in 1889, having long since outgrown its origins as a daily stock tip sheet and market forecaster, was circulated nationally, its reputation based on excellent reporting and conservative editorial opinions. Its rival as a nationally circulated newspaper was *USA Today,* started in 1982 by the Gannett Co, which had built on its upstate roots to become a most influential newspaper company. As the Internet became a recognized mass medium, newspapers began to go on-line, primarily to keep up with the times and secondarily to increase subscriptions. While going on-line served as a means to connect disparate parts of the state, it proved to be an ineffective source of revenue. At first the rise of the Internet caused many to forecast the death of the print newspaper, but at the start of the 21st century, it was apparent that the Internet had become another facet of the newspaper business in the state.

See also Advertising industry; Ethnic press; Free speech; Photography.

Emery, Michael C., Edwin Emery, and Nancy L. Roberts. *The Press and America: An Interpretive History of the Mass Media,* 9th ed (Boston: Allyn & Bacon, 2000)
Nevins, Allan. "The Newspapers of New York State 1783–1900." In *Mind and Spirit,* vol 9 of *History of the State of New York,* 10 vols, ed. Alexander C. Flick (New York: Columbia Univ Press, 1937)
New York State Newspaper Project, http://www.nysl.nysed.gov/nysnp/history.htm
Picard, Robert G., and Jeffrey H. Brody. *The Newspaper Publishing Industry* (Boston: Allyn & Bacon, 1997)
Tebbel, John. *The Compact History of the American Newspaper,* rev ed. (New York: Hawthorn Books, 1969)

Kathleen Collins

New Square. Village (pop 4,624) in Ramapo (Rockland Co). Square is an English homonym of Skvirer, the name of a Ukrainian village where New Square's Hasidic sect originated. In 1954, under the direction of Rabbi Ya'akov Yosef

DAILY NEWSPAPERS PUBLISHED IN NEW YORK STATE BY COUNTY, 2002

County	Newspaper	County	Newspaper
Albany	*Albany Times-Union*	Niagara	*Lockport Union-Sun and Journal*
Allegany	*Wellsville Daily Reporter*		*Niagara Gazette*[d]
Broome	*Binghamton Press and Sun-Bulletin*		*Tonawanda News*[e]
Cattaraugus	*Olean Times Herald*	Oneida	*Rome Daily Sentinel*
	Salamanca Press		*Utica Observer-Dispatch*
Cayuga	*Auburn Citizen*	Onondaga	*Syracuse Post-Standard*
Chautauqua	*Dunkirk Observer*	Ontario	*Canandaigua Daily Messenger*
	Jamestown Post-Journal		*Geneva Finger Lakes Times*
Chemung	*Elmira Star-Gazette*	Orange	*Middletown Times Herald Record*
Chenango	*Norwich Evening Sun*	Orleans	*Medina Journal-Register*
Clinton	*Plattsburgh Press-Republican*	Oswego	*Oswego Palladium-Times*
Columbia	*Hudson Register Star*	Otsego	*Oneonta Daily Star*
Cortland	*Cortland Standard*	Queens	*Chosun Ilbo* (Korean daily times)
Dutchess	*Poughkeepsie Journal*		*Hankook Ilbo* (Korea times)
Erie	*Buffalo News*		*Mingpao Daily News* [Chinese]
Franklin	*Adirondack Daily Enterprise*[a]		*Noticias del Mundo* [Spanish]
	Malone Telegram		*Proine/Prioni* [Greek]
Fulton	*Gloversville Leader-Herald*		*Segye Times* [Korean]
Genesee	*Batavia Daily News*		*Shi jie ri bao* (World journal) [Chinese]
Greene	*Catskill Daily Mail*	Rensselaer	*Troy Record*
Herkimer	*Herkimer Evening Telegram*	Richmond	*Staten Island Advance*
	Little Falls Evening Times	St. Lawrence	*Ogdensburg Journal*
Jefferson	*Watertown Daily Times*		*Potsdam Daily Courier-Observer*
Kings	*Brooklyn Daily Eagle*[b]	Saratoga	*Saratogian*[f]
	Daily Challenge	Schenectady	*Schenectady Daily Gazette*
Madison	*Oneida Daily Dispatch*	Schoharie	*Cobleskill Daily Editor*
Monroe	*Rochester Daily Record*	Steuben	*Corning Leader*
	Rochester Democrat and Chronicle		*Hornell Evening Tribune*
Montgomery	*Amsterdam Recorder*	Suffolk	*Newsday*[g]
New York	*Chung kuo jih pao* (China daily)	Tompkins	*Ithaca Journal*
	Daily Racing Form	Ulster	*Kingston Daily Freeman*
	El Diario–la Prensa [Spanish]	Warren	*Glens Falls Post-Star*
	Ethnikos Keryx (National herald)[Greek]	Westchester	*White Plains Journal News*
	Hoy [Spanish]		
	Hua mei jih pao (China tribune)		
	Lian he ri bao (United journal) [Chinese]		
	Mei-chou Hua chiao jih pao (Chinese free daily news)		
	New York Daily News		
	New York Journal of Commerce		
	New York Post		
	New York Sun[c]		
	Novoe Russkoe Slovo (New Russian word)		
	Qiao Bao (China press)		
	New York Law Journal		
	New York Times		
	Wall Street Journal		
	Women's Wear Daily		
	Yomiuri Shimbun [Japanese]		

Source: The New York State Newspaper Project.

[a]Published in Saranac Lake (Franklin and Essex Cos).

[b]Not to be confused with the *Brooklyn Eagle,* 1841–1955.

[c]Not to be confused with the *New York Sun,* 1833–1950.

[d]Published in Niagara Falls.

[e]Published in North Tonawanda.

[f]Published in Saratoga Springs.

[g]Published in Melville.

Compiled by Heidi Knoblauch

Twersky, the first 20 families moved from Brooklyn to a 130-acre (53 ha) farm. The village incorporated in 1961, its land area subsequently increased through annexation, and its population grew 77.5% in the 1990s. New Square combines features of an Old World Hasidic community, under the control of the rabbi, with those of an American village. New Square received unwanted publicity when four prominent rabbis were convicted of the misuse of federal education funds in 1999. They received a controversial pardon by Pres Bill Clinton on his next to last day in office in 2001. More publicity came in spring 2003, when a carp in a New Square fish store allegedly prophesied in Hebrew. Many saw it as a divine omen, and it became the talk of the Hasidic world.

Newstead. Town (pop 8,404) in NE Erie Co. Settled *ca* 1800 and now bordering the Tonawanda Indian Reservation on the northwest, the town was formed from Batavia (Genesee Co) in 1804 as Erie; the name was changed to Newstead in 1831. Discovery of limestone (1839) and gypsum (1840) added quarrying to what had been a purely agricultural economy. Two railroads (1840, 1854) crossed the town. Sheep were raised for wool, and in 1865 the town was first in the county in wool production. The New York State Thruway crossed Newstead in 1954. In the early 21st century, farming remains an important land use, and manufacturing continues, primarily in Akron.

Andrew C. Maines

New Sweden. Swedish colony (1638–55) on the Delaware River, now part of the states of Delaware, Pennsylvania, and New Jersey. The New Sweden Co was founded in 1637 with Swedish and Dutch capital. Sweden's Chancellor Axel Oxenstierna and Councillor of State Claes Fleming were the prime movers and hoped to import tobacco and furs. In March 1638 the ships *Kalmar Nyckel* and *Fågel' Grip* arrived at Delaware Bay, an area then claimed by the Dutch, and relations between New Sweden and New Netherland were often strained. Peter Minuit, former director of New Netherland and expedition leader, bought land from the Indians and built Fort Christina [now Wilmington, Del], naming it after the Swedish queen. New Sweden's fur trade expanded after 1643 under

Gov Johan Printz. Land bought by Minuit, Printz, and Peter Holländer Ridder created a Swedish region on the banks of the Delaware that extended north near present-day Trenton, NJ, and south to Cape Henlopen, Del, and Fort Elfsborg, near present-day Salem, NJ. Swedish and Finnish settlers, numbering about 350 at the colony's peak, lived in scattered settlements mainly from Fort Christina to New Gothenburg [now Philadelphia].

Sweden sent 12 expeditions to the colony, although not every ship reached that destination. Printz returned to Sweden in October 1653 after settlers complained about his authoritarian rule. Sweden's largest expedition, led by future governor Johan Risingh, reached the colony in May 1654 with the warship *Ornen.* Risingh's first act was to capture the Dutch Fort Casimir [now New Castle, Del]. He also reorganized the administration, confirmed earlier land transactions from the Indians, and bought Susquehannock land that extended New Sweden west to the northern part of Chesapeake Bay. Petrus Stuyvesant, director general of New Netherland, retaliated a year later, bringing warships from New Amsterdam and forcing the colony to surrender Fort Christina after a short siege. The colonists maintained their institutions, including their Swedish language, religion, and a local court, even after the English took the area from the Dutch in 1664. The region officially fell out of New York's jurisdiction on 24 Aug 1682, when control of Pennsylvania and present-day Delaware were transferred to William Penn.

See also MID-ATLANTIC REGION.

Dahlgren, Stellan, and Hans Norman, eds. *The Rise and Fall of New Sweden: Governor Johan Risingh's Journal, 1654–1655.* Trans Marie Clark Nelson (Stockholm: Almqvist & Wiksell International, 1988)

Hoffecker, Carol E., et al, eds. *New Sweden in America* (Newark: Univ of Delaware Press, 1995)

Johnson, Amandus. *The Swedish Settlements on the Delaware: Their History and Relation to the Indians, Dutch and English 1638–1664,* 2 vols (1911; repr Bowie, Md: Heritage Books, 1999)

Weslager, C. A. *New Sweden on the Delaware, 1638–1655* (Wilmington, Del: Middle Atlantic Press, 1988)

Hans Norman

Newtown, Battle of. Revolutionary War engagement. On 29 Aug 1779, facing an army that outnumbered them better than four to one, a mixed force of approximately 800 loyalists and Indians attempted to stop Maj Gen John Sullivan's expedition into the Iroquois homelands of western New York State. Commanded by Mohawk war chief Joseph Brant and loyalist leader John Butler, the ambuscade was located near the Delaware Indian settlement of Newtown [now Elmira] on the Chemung River. It hoped to catch Sullivan's lead element in a cross fire between warriors and loyalists hidden on a ridge along the river and a nearby second group. Once the ambush was initiated, a third group of Indians and loyalists were to fall on Sullivan's rear with the hope of destroying his wagon train and running off or killing his cattle. The expectation was that Sullivan would withdraw from Iroquoia.

Little, however, went according to plan. Sullivan's scouts spotted cooking fire smoke and soon after discovered the location of the ambuscade. Sullivan refused to allow his lead elements to penetrate into the trap and instead deployed light artillery and some of his light infantry units under Brig Gen Edward Hand to engage the positions along the ridge while sending Brig Gen Enoch Poor's brigade to flank them on the right. Poor's men encountered difficult terrain but eventually did turn the position. Realizing that certain destruction awaited them if they remained where they were, both Indians and loyalists withdrew, leaving the field to Sullivan. Loyalist and Indian casualties numbered not more than 20 killed with an undetermined number of wounded. In a report to Gen George Washington dated 30 Aug 1779 Sullivan listed 3 dead and 39 wounded. For the loyalist and Indian forces, the battle proved a complete failure and marked their last significant attempt to stop Sullivan's scorched-earth campaign of the Iroquois territory. The site of the battle is owned by New York State, listed on the National Register of Historic Places, and maintained by Chemung Co as the Newtown Battlefield Reservation and Sullivan's Monument Park. The stone monument to Sullivan first dedicated in 1879 was replaced with a granite obelisk in 1912.

Fischer, Joseph R. *A Well-Executed Failure: The Sullivan Campaign against the Iroquois, July–September 1779* (Columbia: Univ of South Carolina Press, 1997)

Joseph R. Fischer

New Windsor. Town (pop 22,866) in E Orange Co. The first settler, Col Patrick MacGregorie, established a trading post at Plum Point on the Hudson in 1685 that became an important landing for shipping produce. Glass was being made about 1753, and the town was formed as a precinct in 1762. It was the site of Continental army winter encampments, notably the final one in 1782–83. Recognized as a town in 1788, New Windsor was served by three railroads: the Newburgh Branch of the Erie (1849), the Ontario and Western (1873), and the West Shore (1883). Industries in the late 19th century included as many as six brickyards at the landing, along with textile and paper mills elsewhere in town. Stewart Air Force Base (1941) became Stewart International Airport and has attracted industry, and residential development for long-distance commuters has been substantial. It is the site of Knox Headquarters and New Windsor Cantonment State Historic Sites and the Temple Hill Memorial, all associated with the Revolutionary War. The hamlet of Little Britain was the birthplace of Gen James Clinton (1733–1812), Gov George Clinton (1739–1812), and Gov De Witt Clinton (1769–1828).

Glenn T. Marshall

New York Air National Guard. Members of the First Company Signal Corps of the New York National Guard studied ballooning at the Park Avenue Armory in 1908, moved to heavier-than-air craft in 1911, and became the progenitors of the New York Air National Guard (NYANG). The First Aero Company, New York National Guard, was organized in 1915, followed by the Second Aero Company, New York National Guard (from Buffalo) in 1916. New York National Guard training contributed pilots to the Signal Corps Reserve during World War I; afterward, the Air Service and the Militia Bureau developed plans for National Guard air units. New York's 102d Observation Squadron was federally recognized in November 1922 and continued training through the 1930s at Pine Camp (later Fort Drum, Jefferson and Lewis Cos). NYANG units delivered trained personnel to the Army Air Forces during World War II and served to maintain national security during the Korean War. Starting in 1953 in collaboration with the Strategic Air Command (SAC), the 138th Fighter Interceptor Squadron at Hancock Field (Onondaga Co) became part of an experimental runway alert force, which became a permanent 24-hour program that brought reserve units into the peacetime operation of the armed forces. The first woman in the Air National Guard (ANG), Capt Norma Parsons Erb, joined the NYANG as a nurse in October 1956. New York's 136th Tactical Fighter Squadron was deployed to Vietnam during the Tet Offensive of 1968. On 24 Aug 1990 the 137th Military Airlift Squadron at Stewart Air National Guard Base in Newburgh (Orange Co) was recalled to active duty in the Persian Gulf; many were already flying C-5 transports as volunteers. The 138th Tactical Fighter Squadron flew F-16 fighters in the air campaign against Iraqi forces in the Persian Gulf War. The 102d continued as a unit, the oldest in the ANG, based at Francis S. Gabreski Airport in Westhampton Beach (Suffolk Co) at the beginning of the 21st century. After the terrorist attack on 11 Sept 2001, NYANG units flew combat patrols over New York City.

Elliott, James C. *The Modern Army and Air National Guard* (New York: D. Van Nostrand, 1965)

Gross, Charles Joseph. *The Air National Guard and the American Military Tradition: Militiaman, Volunteer, and Professional* (Washington, DC: Historical Services Division, 1995)

Pamela Cooper

New York Army National Guard. Component of the US Army that serves both the federal government and New York State. Colonies in 17th- and 18th-century America provided for defense by imposing military service on almost all men within in their boundaries, and militiamen supplied their own weapons and equipment. Large numbers of New York militiamen served in the Revolutionary War and the War of 1812. New York's Second Battalion Second Artillery (later the wealthy Seventh "Silk Stocking" Regiment) designated itself National Guard of New York on 14 July 1825, and the name spread to other regiments. The New York State Militia maintained law during times of civil disorder, such as the fire of 1835 and the food riots during the panic of 1837. Although New York State eliminated obligatory militia service in 1846, volunteers continued to enroll. The forerunner of the later 69th Regiment was founded by Irish volunteers and accepted into the New York system in December 1849. Other ethnically identified regiments included the 79th New York "Highlanders," who wore kilts. In 1862 New York National Guard (NYNG) was officially adopted as the new name of the New York State Militia.

The NYNG provided the Union with 38,028 officers and men for short-term service during the Civil War. Its organizational structure was essential in raising and equipping the 370,232 volunteers for that war. In the late 19th century NYNG's primary mission was riot control, particularly during labor unrest, such as the Brooklyn streetcar strikes of 14 Jan–2 Feb 1895. The 71st Infantry Regiment New York Volunteers fought as part of the Fifth Army Corps at

San Juan Heights, Cuba, during the Spanish-American War. The Militia Act of 21 Jan 1903 ensured the provision of free arms and equipment to the guard from the federal government. The National Defense Act of 1916 authorized the president to federalize the guard; the NYNG formed the 27th Infantry Division under federal jurisdiction on 16 July 1917. During World War I New York State furnished 12 regiments of infantry and 2 troops of cavalry, in total 12,460 men. As part of the US Second Corps during the war, the 27th served in Flanders under British command. The division's most notable exploit was "Breaking the Hindenburg Line" on 29 Sept 1918. The African American 15th Infantry Regiment of the NYNG, the "Harlem Hellfighters," went to France, where they became the 369th US Infantry and served with the French army, earning the Croix de Guerre. The National Defense Act of 1920 increased federal control of the guard.

The guard was again federalized during World War II. The 27th "New York" Infantry Division served in the central and western Pacific and the 42d "Rainbow" Infantry Division from New Jersey, New York, and Vermont served in western and central Europe. On 23 Dec 1941 Battery F of the 105th Field Artillery Battalion engaged a Japanese submarine near Laguna, Calif. The division eventually saw action at Saipan and Tanapag Plain. The conquest of Okinawa was its last action, but it spent time on occupation duty in Japan. Upon deactivation the 27th had served longer than any other National Guard division in World War II.

During the Korean War three NYNG commands went to Korea, and others to stateside duty. NYNG units were mobilized during the Berlin Crisis of 1961 and the Vietnam War. During the Persian Gulf War, NYNG units were activated both stateside and overseas; the 244th Medical Group served with the Third Army in the Kuwaiti theater of operations. At the beginning of the 21st century, the NYNG had 82 armories and a presence in 72 communities. NYNG units assisted in emergencies such as forest fires and snow removal and replaced regular army units as they were deployed overseas from New York State facilities during the action against the Taliban terrorists in Afghanistan and during the Iraq War.

Elliott, James. *The Modern Army and Air National Guard* (New York: D. Van Nostrand, 1965)

Weigley, Russell F. *History of the United States Army* (Bloomington: Indiana Univ Press, 1984)

Robert E. Mulligan Jr

New York Bay. Formed by the division of the Verrazano Narrows into Upper and Lower New York Bays and a complex of interconnected waterways including the Hudson River, East River, Kill Van Kull, Arthur Kill, and the New York Bight. The mixing of fresh and salt waters makes the bay an ecologically productive estuary, with 4–5 ft (1–2 m) tides and salinities below seawater levels. American Indians harvested food from the bay for thousands of years, and European explorers were awestruck by its natural riches. In the late 17th century the Dutch explorer Jasper Danckaerts was amazed by the numerous swarms of small fish and by the mammals, including whales and porpoises, in the bay. Eagles and other birds of prey were common, feeding easily on the many smaller fish swimming near the surface. The bay also contained remarkably productive oyster beds. Oysters from Gowanus Creek were Brooklyn's first export to Europe; in 1880 some 765 million were gathered from all the waters around New York City.

The burgeoning population of the metropolitan region and development of the bay's port, however, led to pronounced environmental degradation in the 19th and 20th centuries, including channel dredging—soon to extend beyond 45 feet (14 m)—landfilling, destruction of salt marshes, many forms of industrial pollution, and sewage contamination. In the late 1800s New York City's household refuse was simply shoveled off barges near the mouth of the bay, creating seas of floating garbage, with much of it drifting back. By 1900 Manhattan Island's population numbered 2 million, and all of its human waste was piped untreated into its waterways. Sewage sludge blanketed the bottom in some locations 10 feet (3 m) thick, and its decomposition drove oxygen levels so low that portions of the bay became seasonally or completely uninhabitable by marine life.

Eventual initiation of primary treatment, followed by significant sewage plant improvements mandated by the federal Clean Water Act of 1972, have led to major recoveries of life in the bay; most dramatically, a return, after decades-long absences, of thousands of breeding pairs of herons, egrets, and ibis on its islands. The bay's diverse fish populations, approximately 250 species, including game fish such as striped bass, have also rebounded. Although environmental regulations have led to great reductions in chemical pollution, fishing is limited almost exclusively to recreational angling because of lingering contamination, particularly PCBs, and state health advisories on the consumption of fish and crab remain in effect. The recent environmental recovery of the bay has changed people's perception of it from being a place to be avoided to an exceptional resource to be enjoyed, and its use by anglers (including catch-and-release fishers), sailors, and kayakers has increased, as have the number of waterfront festivals and marine education programs. New government programs are striving to achieve a balance between future waterfront and port development, public access and amenities, and environmental preservation.

Kornblum, William. *At Sea in the City: New York from the Water's Edge* (Chapel Hill, NC: Algonquin Books of Chapel Hill, 2002)

Waldman, John. *Heartbeats in the Muck: The History, Sea Life, and Environment of New York Harbor* (New York: Lyons Press, 1999)

John Waldman

New York Botanical Garden. Located on 250 acres (101 ha) at the northern end of Bronx Park, the New York Botanical Garden is a leader in plant research. The grounds contain the Bronx River gorge; the last remaining part of the forest that once covered what is now New York City; and the historic Lorillard Snuff Mill, erected in 1840. In 1888 a state-mandated committee purchased land for Bronx Park, which was to include a botanical garden for New York City. Nathaniel Lord Britton (1859–1934), a professor of botany at Columbia, persuaded the state legislature to incorporate the garden in 1891. As its director from 1896, Britton presided over landscaping, planting, and construction on the grounds. The garden opened to the public in 1897. Puffed wheat and puffed rice were developed in 1902, as was the Bronx daylily, the official Bronx flower. The facilities include the largest herbarium in the Western Hemisphere, a museum, the Enid A. Haupt Conservatory, a library, and a laboratory. The Institute of Economic Botany was established at the museum in 1981, and the Institute of Systematic Botany in 1991. The garden attracts around 590,000 visitors per year.

See also SCIENTIFIC CULTURE (19TH–21ST CENTURIES).

Lloyd Ultan

New York Central College. An abolitionist and nonsectarian educational institution in McGrawville [now McGraw, Cortland Co]. Incorporated in December 1848 and opened to students in September 1849, New York Central College was sponsored by the American Baptist Free Mission Society. Cyrus P. Grosvenor served as president. The college operated on the manual labor philosophy and admitted students, male and female, rich and poor, African American, Native American, and white, on an equal footing. Students read the classics but also studied the Hebrew Bible and Greek Testament, as the Bible was considered the textbook for morals. Science and mathematics were also taught. New York Central was the first American college to have African American faculty: Charles L. Reason and William G. Allen. Controversy over Allen's 1852 marriage to a white student cost the college some of its supporters, and by 1858 the school was hopelessly in debt. Gerrit Smith purchased the property, which included a farm and a four-story main building. New York Central closed in 1859 but reopened for the 1860–61 academic term. In 1864 the premises were sold to McGrawville's Union School.

Short, Kenneth R. "New York Central College: A Baptist Experiment in Integrated Higher Education, 1848–1861," *Foundations* 5 (July 1962): 250–56

Milton C. Sernett

New York Central Railroad

BEGINNINGS

The railroad system that crossed New York State and eventually reached into the Midwest involved the merger and development of numerous railroads dating back to the 1820s. The first of many component lines began with the 1826 chartering of the Mohawk and Hudson Railroad (M&HRR), running between Albany and Schenectady from 1831. The next railroad in the Albany-to-Buffalo chain that eventually became the New York Central was the Utica and Schenectady Railroad (U&SRR). The state's third railroad, the U&SRR opened in 1836 but was barred from carrying freight until 1844 because of its proximity to the state-owned Erie Canal. By 1839 the Syracuse and Utica Railroad was completed, and two years later the Syracuse and Auburn Railroad and the Auburn and Rochester Railroad together linked Syracuse with Rochester. By early 1843 the Tonawanda Railroad and the Attica and Buffalo Railroad connected Rochester and Buffalo. It was possible to cross the state by rail but only by riding with seven railroad companies, which meant changing carriers six times.

On 31 Jan 1843 delegates from eight railroads, which included the recently completed Schenectady and Troy, met to discuss cooperation. An agreement followed, along with optimistic announcements that the 326 mi (525 km) trip from Albany to Buffalo could be made in 25 hours at a price of $10 for a first-class ticket. Yet, coordinating through traffic was a challenge because railroads in 1843 lacked telegraphs, signals, air brakes, and dining cars. Keeping tracks clear of snow during hard winters added to scheduling problems. Only the Schenectady and Troy Railroad had all-iron-rail trackage, and the strap-iron or iron-capped wood rails of the other railroads slowed train speed. In 1847 the New York State legislature mandated that all state lines convert to iron rails by 1850; with this accomplished, the fastest rail travel between Albany and Buffalo dropped to 15 hours.

Corning and Vanderbilt

In 1850 there were 29 railroads in operation or under construction in the state. The following year a single railroad finally spanned the state with the completion of the New York and Erie Railroad, chartered in 1832. A ceremonial train officially opened the 483 mi (777 km) route, which ran from Piermont (Rockland Co), 25 miles (40 km) north of New York City on the Hudson River, to Dunkirk (Chautauqua Co) on Lake Erie. Also notable in 1851 was the completion of the Hudson River Railroad from New York City to East Greenbush (Rensselaer Co) across the Hudson from Albany. The route along the east shore of the Hudson had been avoided by railroad builders, who feared rival steamboat traffic, but the new railroad became a model of high-speed passenger transportation.

Faced with competition from the New York and Erie Railroad, U&SRR president Erastus Corning began consolidating the central and western New York lines. On 2 Apr 1853 the eight railroads between Albany and Buffalo became the New York Central Railroad. By the early 1860s Cornelius Vanderbilt and his son William H. began to buy Hudson River Railroad stock, increasing their hold on the company year by year, with an eye on New York Central and westward connections. In 1867 New York Central acquired the Buffalo and Erie Railroad, further enhancing its western route. Two years later, Cornelius Vanderbilt engineered a merger between the New York Central and the Hudson River Railroads, attaching the Lake Shore and Michigan Southern Railroad to the merged system. The New York Central and Hudson River Railroad (NYC&HRRR) then offered a through connection between New York City and Chicago.

Expansion

The line to the Midwest helped New York City to keep its hold on the hinterland, first gained via the Erie Canal, and to remain the leading Atlantic port city. The city supplied much of the capital needed to build many component roads of NYC&HRRR over the following decades. In 1877, on the death of his father, William H. Vanderbilt took over leadership of NYC&HRRR until 1883. When Chauncey M. Depew became president two years later, the company operated over 740 miles (1,191 km) of mostly double-tracked route, carried over 8 million passengers per year, and nearly tripled the 1870 figure of 769,087,777 annual freight ton-miles (1,257 million MT-km). In 1889 NYC&HRRR reached the Mississippi River via the newly acquired Cleveland, Cincinnati, Chicago, and St. Louis Railroad. The company acquired other midwestern as well as eastern lines, in 1893 leasing the Rome, Watertown and Ogdensburg Railroad, which merged with NYC&HRRR 20 years later. Between 1891 and 1893 the growing company added its Adirondack Division linking Utica and the northern Adirondacks; in 1900 it leased the Boston and Albany, creating one of the largest rail systems in the nation with 23,000 miles (37,015 km) of track.

The next four decades were a halcyon era for the company, renamed New York Central (NYC) in 1916. Profits remained high as both freight and passenger service were strong. The company's famous passenger trains, Empire State Express and Twentieth Century Limited, ran regularly between New York City and Chicago.

New York Central Aerotrain, 1956.

Decline

After World War II competition from air and highway transportation, aging equipment, and investment in real estate rather than the line itself led to profit uncertainty. In the early 1950s Pres Alfred Perlman downsized, mostly cutting passenger service. These measures were unproductive, and talks soon opened regarding a merger with Pennsylvania Railroad, the other eastern giant. After a decade of discussions, a 1968–69 union and reorganization created two new companies: Penn Central Transportation Co, owner and operator of railroad routes in over a dozen states, and Penn Central Co, owner and operator of non-railroad real estate, including NYC's sizable property holdings in New York City. The marriage of NYC and Pennsylvania Railroad was short and stormy. Within two years, mismanagement and other factors forced Penn Central Transportation Co into bankruptcy. Penn Central Co with its lucrative real estate remained solvent. In 1976, six years after entering receivership, Penn Central Transportation Co became part of Conrail, the government-sponsored rail system.

See also GREAT LAKES SHIPPING LINES AND WATERCRAFT.

Hungerford, Edward. *Men and Iron: The History of New York Central* (New York: Crowell, 1938)

Saunders, Richard. *The Railroad Mergers and the Coming of Conrail* (Westport, Conn: Greenwood, 1978)

Stevens, Frank W. *The Beginnings of the New York Central Railroad* (New York: Putnam's, 1926)

F. Daniel Larkin

New York, Chicago and St. Louis Railroad. Midwestern mainline, or trunk, railway that stretched from Chicago and St. Louis through Indiana and Ohio to Buffalo. First chartered in 1881, New York, Chicago and St. Louis Railroad was known from its earliest days as "The Nickel Plate Road," probably an allusion to the company's solid financial backing and rich prospects. The Nickel Plate owned large terminal facilities in Buffalo and a rail route that ran along the south shore of Lake Erie. Between the 1880s and 1910s, Nickel Plate grew into a conglomeration of Midwestern railroads, including Lake Erie and Western, and Toledo, St. Louis and Western. The entire system was consolidated in 1923 under control of the Van Sweringen brothers of Cleveland, Ohio. While the Nickel Plate carried some passengers, it was notable for fast freight service between Buffalo and the industrial cities of the Midwest. It also achieved notoriety for operating steam locomotives into the late 1950s, long after other railroads in the region had switched to diesel power. The Nickel Plate, along with Wabash Railroad, was merged into Norfolk and Western in 1964.

Rehor, John A. *The Nickel Plate Story* (Milwaukee: Kalmbach Publishing, 1965)

Jeff Schramm

New York Chiropractic College. Nonprofit, private, professional school. Founded as the Columbia Institute of Chiropractic in Manhattan in 1919 by Dr Frank E. Dean, it merged with the Columbia College of Chiropractic of Baltimore, Md, in 1954 and the Atlantic States Chiropractic Institute of Brooklyn in 1964. In 1977 the college adopted its present name, and it moved to Old Brookville (Nassau Co) in 1980. The school moved to Seneca Falls (Seneca Co) in 1991 to the 286-acre (116 ha) former campus of Eisenhower College. While the college has traditionally offered the doctor of chiropractic (DC) degree, the curriculum was expanded in 2003 to include the bachelor of professional studies (BPS) in life sciences and master of science (MS) in both acupuncture and acupuncture and Oriental medicine. The school operates outpatient clinics in Syracuse, Depew (Erie Co), and Levittown (Nassau Co), with a postgraduate center also in Levittown. In fall 2003 the student body numbered approximately 750.

New York Chiropractic College, http://www.nycc.edu

Jeffrey Kraus

New York City (303 mi²/785 km²; pop 8,008,278). The most populated city in the United States and the largest city in area in the state, the City of New York since 1898 has included five counties within its boundaries, each of which also constitutes a borough of the city: New York Co (Borough of Manhattan; 23 mi²/60 km²; pop 1,537,195), Kings Co (Borough of Brooklyn; 71 mi²/184 km²; pop 2,465,326), Bronx Co (Borough of the Bronx; 42 mi²/109 km²; pop 1,332,650), Queens Co (Borough of Queens; 109 mi²/282 km²; pop 2,229,379), and Richmond Co (Borough of Staten Island; 58 mi²/150 km²; pop 443,728).

The complex waterways of the Hudson River estuary define the collection of islands and peninsulas on which New York City is situated. Its five counties include 128 mi² (332 km²) of surface waters and more than 770 linear miles (1,240 km) of waterfront. For a distance of 16 miles (26 km) from the city's northern boundary, the Hudson River flows past the city, separating it from New Jersey. The river empties into Upper New York Bay (Upper New York Harbor), a 3 mi (5 km) wide partially enclosed body of water that also receives the waters of New Jersey's Passaic and Hackensack Rivers via Newark Bay and Kill Van Kull. The Upper Bay is linked through the Verrazano Narrows to Lower New York Bay (Harbor), which opens into the Atlantic Ocean. The East River, a strait 16 miles (26 km) in length, connects it to Long Island Sound at the city's east and north. Manhattan is a narrow island lying north of the Upper Bay between the Hudson River, the East River, and the Harlem River, a smaller strait connecting the East River and the Hudson. Governors Island, Liberty Island, and the New York portion of Ellis Island (within the Upper Harbor), and Randall's Island, Ward's Island, and Roosevelt Island (in the East River) are administratively attached to Manhattan; Rikers Island, in the East River, is part of Queens. The Bronx, across the Harlem River on Manhattan's north and east, is a roughly square peninsula bordering Westchester Co on its north, with an arm of the East River to its south. City Island and Hart Island lie in Long Island Sound to the east.

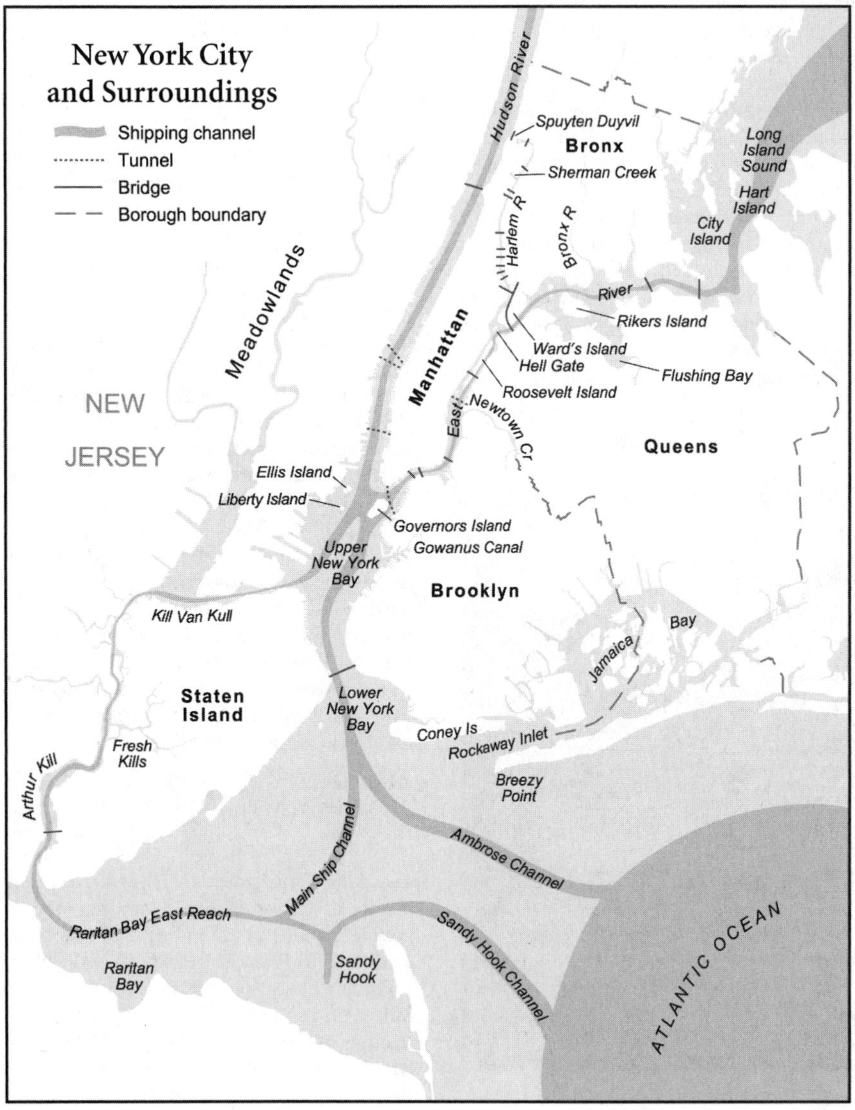

Manhattan and the Bronx form the southern tip of the Manhattan Prong of the hilly New England Upland physiographic province. Here three highly metamorphosed layers of Cambrian and Paleozoic bedrock have produced a topography of ridges and valleys running parallel to the Hudson. Valleys have taken shape where folding has exposed the relatively soft middle layer of Inwood marble to erosion; the less eroded bottom layer of Fordham gneiss and top layer of Manhattan Formation schist form ridges as exemplified by the Bronx's University Heights. The highest elevation in the Bronx is on Grosvenor Ave in Riverdale (284 ft/87 m); in Manhattan, at James Gordon Bennett Park in Washington Heights (264 ft/80 m). The Manhattan Formation schist, glittery with mica, is visible in outcrops in Central Park. It provides a firm footing for skyscrapers and rises close to the surface in Midtown and Downtown Manhattan. Glacial till from the most recent ice age covers the surface.

Separated from the Bronx and Manhattan by the East River, Brooklyn and Queens share a sharply different geologic history. These boroughs occupy the western eighth of Long Island, with Nassau and Suffolk Cos to their east and the Atlantic Ocean to their south. Long Island, a feature of the Atlantic coastal plain, was shaped by the approach and retreat of the Wisconsinan ice sheet, which reached its southernmost extent here 15,000 years ago. A terminal moraine or band of debris left by the glacier trends northeast to southwest across the island into northern Brooklyn and Queens, creating the bulge in Brooklyn's western shoreline that shelters Upper New York Bay from the ocean. Elevations on the moraine, the highest in these boroughs, range up to 265 ft (81 m) at Bennett Park in Queens and 220 ft (67 m) at Green-Wood Cemetery in Brooklyn. North of the moraine, a relatively flat region of Cretaceous age sedimentary bedrock is covered by till from the retreating glacier. To the south and east, streams flowing from the moraine formed a gently sloping outwash plain. Jamaica Bay, a roughly 25 mi² (65 km²) lagoon with numerous low-lying islands, is now part of Gateway National Recreation Area and affords refuge to migratory waterfowl. Rockaway Peninsula (10 mi/16 km), which protects wilderness from the ocean on the south, is characteristic of Long Island's south shore barrier beaches.

Across the 1 mi (1.6 m) Verrazano Narrows lies triangular-shaped Staten Island, the only borough of New York City on the west shore of the Hudson estuary. It is separated from New Jersey by Arthur Kill and Kill Van Kull. The Long Island terminal moraine crosses on to Staten Island at the Narrows and follows the island's long eastern shore. Todt Hill, where the moraine overlays a previously elevated intruded stratum of serpentinite rock, is 412 feet (126 m), the highest point in New York City. It is also said to be the highest elevation on the nation's eastern coastline south of Massachusetts. An arm of the Palisades diabase formation juts into the northern part of the island, while much of its western third is low-lying marsh that surrounds Fresh Kills Creek and is now a garbage dump and landfill.

Deep indentations in many of New York City's

shores, such as Flushing Bay in northern Queens and Eastchester Bay in the Bronx, are the result of stream erosion following the retreat of the Wisconsinan ice sheet and the subsequent flooding of the valleys when sea levels rose. The sea's rise also helped produce abundant salt marshes in Jamaica Bay, along the East River's banks, and elsewhere in the city. Human habitation and technology has visibly altered the shoreline by debris buildup and landfill operations, pushing the riverbanks outward 100–1,000 feet (30–305 m) in most parts of Lower Manhattan.

New York City lies in the humid-continental climate zone, with prevailing westerly weather patterns producing hot summers and cold winters. The ocean's moderating effect on temperature is not pronounced except at the shoreline. Average mean July temperature at meteorological stations in the five boroughs is 76°F (24°C), with average daytime highs of 84°F (29°C). Average January mean temperature is 32°F (0°C), with average nighttime lows of 26°F (-3°C). The warmest recorded temperature in Central Park since 1876 is 106°F (41°C) on 9 July 1936 and the coldest is -15°F (-26°C) on 9 Feb 1934. Mean annual precipitation is 46 inches (117 cm), and mean seasonal snowfall is 22 inches (56 cm). Observed weather conditions can vary significantly between stations within the city. At John F. Kennedy International Airport on Jamaica Bay, average annual precipitation has been 15% less and average July mean temperature a couple of degrees lower than at Central Park over the past 30 years.

Drainage in the city is now largely a function of sewers and culverts. The Bronx River, flowing southward through that borough from Westchester Co toward the East River, and the headwaters of Fresh Kills Creek and Richmond Creek on Staten Island are the only considerable above-ground freshwater streams remaining within the city limits. Sherman Creek in the Washington Heights area is the only above-ground waterway on Manhattan. Pine and beech forest is believed to have covered most of the area of the city after the glacier's retreat, but this cover was succeeded first by spruce and fir and then by a central hardwood forest principally of beech, sugar maple, basswood, oak, and chestnut. Remnants are preserved in the New York Botanical Garden in the Bronx and other parks.

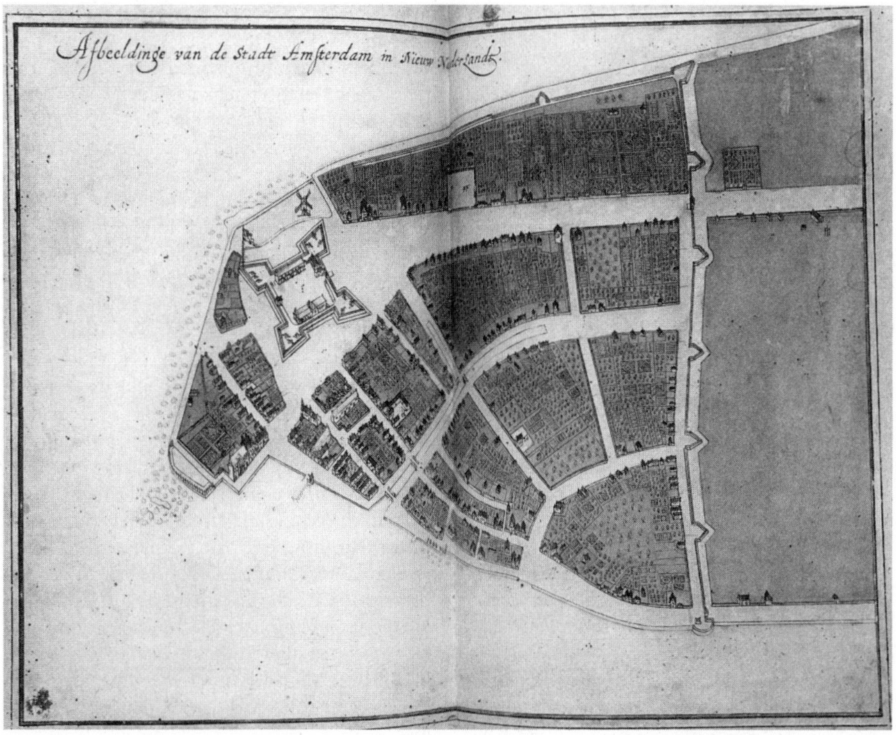

17th-century map of Lower Manhattan, *Afbeeldinge Van De Stadt Amsterdam in Nieuw Neederlandt* (Costello Plan), 1660.

Company Town (1626–64)

Despite early visits by Giovanni da Verrazano, who scouted the Upper Bay in 1524, and by Esteban Gómez, a black Portuguese pilot who the following year ventured a short distance up the Hudson in search of a water route to China, the site of modern New York City did not attract the interest of European explorers until after Henry Hudson's voyage of 1609. Hudson's report of the area's abundant supply of fur-bearing animals—and a substantial indigenous population eager to trade pelts for European goods—drew fur traders from the Netherlands in search of beaver, otter, mink, fox, and other valuable skins. A map produced in 1614 by Adriaen Block, most famous of these Dutch skippers, was the first to show Manhattan as an island as well as to use the name New Netherland for the land between the Delaware and Connecticut Rivers.

In 1614 the Dutch government chartered the New Netherland Co to regulate the intense, sometimes violent competition between the fur traders converging on this vast territory. The expiration of its charter at the end of 1617 triggered another competitive free-for-all that lasted until 1621, when the government chartered a second and much larger firm, the Dutch West India Co (WIC) and gave it a monopoly of all Dutch trade with West Africa and the Americas. In 1624 a WIC ship, the *Nieu Nederlandt*, deposited 30 families, mostly Walloons from Leyden, on Nutten Island [now Governors Island], not as independent settlers but as company employees assigned to establish and maintain fur-trading stations at sites along the Delaware, Hudson, and Connecticut Rivers. Additional colonists arrived in 1625. In 1626 the Nutten Island settlement was relocated on the southern tip of Manhattan Island, which the director of New Netherland, Peter Minuit, purchased from some local Indians for trade goods worth 60 guilders. Work began on a fort that would anchor WIC operations in the colony by controlling access to both the Hudson Valley and Long Island Sound. By the end of the year, a cluster of huts, wood cabins, storehouses, and a horse-powered mill had sprung up east and south of the site of the projected fort. The settlement, now called New Amsterdam, boasted somewhat more than 200 inhabitants. A report in 1628 put its population at 270.

When the fur trade failed to generate anticipated profits and only after heated debate among WIC's directors, the WIC began to shift its focus from trade to long-term colonization. In 1629 it offered land to individuals (patroons) who agreed to bring over settlers at their own expense, and in 1640 the company surrendered its monopoly of the fur trade. Neither measure produced the desired result, partly because relatively few inhabitants of the Netherlands had reason to emigrate. New Amsterdam's population thus grew slowly, rising from 400–500 in the early 1640s to 700–800 a decade later. New Amsterdam remained strikingly diverse and turbulent. Only a slender majority of its white population was in fact Dutch; one visitor reported that 18 different languages were spoken there in the 1640s. The population included footloose young men who had signed on with the company for adventure and a chance to strike it rich, and there were several cases of theft and assault reported. Not surprisingly, as the company's fortunes continued to dim, there was talk in Amsterdam of bringing everyone home before things got even worse. Conditions actually did get worse in the early 1640s when Director Willem Kieft ignited an Indian war that led to the deaths of 1,000 or more natives and dozens of colonists, plus the destruction of numerous homesteads on the periphery of New Amsterdam. Townsfolk were furious with Kieft, and the company soon ordered him back to Amsterdam.

Resolving to make one final attempt to salvage its investment in New Netherland, the WIC replaced Kieft with Petrus Stuyvesant, the director general whose governance also included Curaçao, Bonaire, Aruba, and other dependencies in the Caribbean. Stuyvesant reached New Amsterdam in 1647 and immediately got to work on a program of municipal improvements that over the next decade helped turn New Amsterdam into a thriving port (as well as a major problem for its English neighbors). Two public works in particular—the erection of the first municipal pier near the foot of Whitehall St and the conversion of a sluggish creek into a shipping canal that sliced into town from the East River—promoted the gradual expansion of overseas trade as local merchants sought markets in Europe and the West Indies for locally produced tobacco, grain, timber, and potash. Both the pier and the canal also helped fix New Amsterdam's orientation toward the East River waterfront and foreshadowed the increasingly ambitious construction projects that would in time transform the geography of Lower Manhattan.

The company had in the meantime launched another campaign to attract colonists. Its efforts, combined with Stuyvesant's reform program, boosted New Amsterdam's population to around 1,500 people by 1660 and pushed the built-up area several blocks north of the fort. Yet Stuyvesant's heavy-handed attempts to establish a more homogeneous, Calvinist population were also earning him a string of rebukes from his superiors in the company for suppressing Lutheran services of worship, for persecuting Quakers, and for opposing the settlement of Jewish refugees from Brazil. At the urging of New Amsterdam's burgeoning merchant community, the company ordered the creation of its first municipal government in 1653, arguably a more accurate date for the birth of New York City than either 1624 or 1626.

In 1650 Stuyvesant traveled up to Hartford [now in Connecticut] to resolve the long-standing boundary dispute between New Netherland and the New England colonies. The ensuing Treaty of Hartford recognized English control over all of Connecticut east of Greenwich and over Long Island east of Oyster Bay (not a bad deal, since the English had previously claimed sovereignty over the whole of New Netherland). But neither the treaty nor Stuyvesant's subsequent efforts to plant new villages on western Long Island and at Nieuw Haarlem on Upper Manhattan deterred land-hungry New Englanders from trying to settle in WIC territory. The likelihood of a peaceful solution diminished sharply in 1653, when war broke out between England and the Netherlands. Fearing an English attempt to seize New Amsterdam, Stuyvesant and the magistrates erected a wooden stockade across the northern edge of town, its course marked by modern Wall St. Although the immediate danger passed without incident, nobody doubted that the English on both sides of the Atlantic wanted to evict the Dutch from North America once and for all. Just how they would do it emerged soon after the accession of Charles II in 1660.

The new king's younger brother, James, Duke of York, lord high admiral, and master of vast estates in England and Ireland, was a tireless imperialist who saw the acquisition of New Netherland as an essential step to England's mastery of the Atlantic seaboard from Maine to Cape Fear off the North Carolina coast. In 1664 the duke persuaded the king to make him proprietor of all the territory between the Delaware and Connecticut Rivers—the entirety, that is, of New Netherland—and dispatched Col Richard Nicolls to seize New Amsterdam. Stuyvesant wanted to fight, but disaffected townsfolk, mindful that they were outnumbered and outgunned, compelled him to accept Nicolls's generous terms for a peaceful capitulation. On 6 Sept 1664 Stuyvesant surrendered without firing a shot. Nicolls promptly announced that in the duke's honor, both New Amsterdam and New Netherland would thenceforth be known as New York.

Imperial Port (1664–1783)

The conquest of 1664 had little or no immediate effect on New York. Nicolls reassured its residents that their lives, property, and customs were in no danger (provided they took an oath of allegiance to the king), and both he and his successors carefully nurtured the support of prominent Dutch merchants, landowners, and Reformed clergymen. Well into the 18th century, accordingly, visitors often remarked that "York City" seemed more Dutch than English. Its private houses continued to be built with the high stoops, stepped gables, and multicolored tiles characteristic of Dutch domestic architecture. Dutch remained the language of the streets and markets. Dutch holidays and festivals still crowded the calendar.

Inside this Dutch shell, however, powerful forces were reshaping the city and its people. Streams of new arrivals from England, Germany, France, and Scotland boosted the population to 3,000 by 1680, to 7,000 by 1720, and to 18,000 by 1760, at which point New York City passed Boston to become the largest urban center in British North America after Philadelphia. New residential and commercial construction pushed the built-up area farther up the island, past Wall St (the crumbling old stockade came down in 1699) toward the Common (now City Hall Park). By 1775 New York was home to some 25,000 people and could boast of a college, numerous churches, a synagogue, a new city hall, a theater, and busy public markets. Lower Broadway, well removed from the tumultuous East River waterfront, was the most fashionable neighborhood, in no small part because of the allure of Bowling Green, a "leafy little retreat" laid out in 1732.

The very topography of the city was changing as well. To meet the incessant demand for building lots, municipal authorities ran new streets through orchards and pastures, drained swamps, buried streams, and leveled hills. In the 1670s the old Dutch canal had been filled in to create an usually wide thoroughfare, Broad St, which soon became one of the town's principal commercial arteries. At its foot, the city built a new stone pier, much larger than its predecessor and protected by two great moles, or breakwaters, that arced out into the East River. But even this impressive structure could not accommodate the swelling traffic in and out of the port, so the city encouraged merchants and shipowners to construct their own wharves by filling in and building on tide lots (a solution facilitated by a new municipal charter, which gave the municipal corporation title to all land lying under water between low tide and high tide). During the 18th century, as a result, the East River waterfront began to creep beyond the island's original shoreline. The same thing occurred on the west side. Portions of Greenwich and Washington Sts were laid out and filled as early as the 1720s, and by midcentury new docks and warehouses had appeared in the blocks between Trinity Church and St. Paul's.

Crucial to this growth was New York City's trade with the West Indies, where the rising demand for sugar in Britain had created slave labor economies heavily dependent on food and raw materials imported from the North American mainland. Long Island, New Jersey, and Hudson Valley farmers sold grain, beef, leather, lumber, and other products to city merchants, who moved them down to the islands and returned with molasses and rum for the local market (including the city's numerous distilleries and refineries) or for re-export to England. Money in the pockets of merchants meant employment for the tradesmen who manufactured rope, sails, and barrels for the growing number of ships working out of the city as well as wages for sailors, cartmen, tavern keepers, and casual laborers. The extent of the city's dependence on its ties to the West Indies was emphasized by the seasonal rhythms of municipal business, which was feverish between November and January as merchants scrambled to get down to the islands in time to take delivery of the new sugar crop, then again between April and June as they raced back to port to escape hot-weather diseases and hurricanes. (They frequently brought the diseases along, with devastating results. In the summer of 1702, an epidemic of what was probably yellow fever claimed 580 lives, roughly 10% of the population. Milder outbreaks occurred so often over the next century that well-to-do residents made a point of leaving town during July and August.)

Perhaps the most visible consequence of the West Indian connection was the extraordinary concentration of slaves within and around New York. Although the West India Co had relied on slaves for construction projects in New Amsterdam—there were fewer than 400 slaves in town when Stuyvesant surrendered in 1664—slave labor would not become indispensable until after the beginning of the 18th century, when merchants took an increased interest in the slave trade and began importing multitudes of slaves for sale to area residents. Between 1700 and 1775, some 7,400 slaves arrived in the city, which was more than its entire population at the turn of the 18th century, and by 1750 African Americans made up roughly 20% of the population; New York City, with neighboring Kings Co, had the highest concentration of slaves north of Virginia. Slaves were used by merchants to fill out crews and toil on their docks, by artisans to work in their shops, and by farmers to till their fields and tend their herds. So insistent was this demand for slaves that as early as 1711 the city established a market for their purchase and lease at the foot of Wall St.

For white New Yorkers, the size and broad distribution of their servile population (roughly half the households in the city held one or more slaves) proved a source of constant anxiety. Disobedient and defiant slaves were a fact of life that required constant tinkering with local ordinances and spawned frequent rumors of revolt, typically linked to lurid accounts of slave uprisings in the Caribbean. The city's first taste of open insurrection came in 1712, when a group of slaves set fire to buildings and ambushed residents who rushed to put out the flames; two dozen slaves were eventually hanged, burned at the stake, or broken on the wheel. In 1741 fears of another uprising swept the city and led to the executions of 30 Blacks and 4 Whites. Although the extent of the 1741 conspiracy remains a matter of dispute, the panic it caused was fueled by the outbreak of war in Europe and the departure of many soldiers from the garrison for an expedition to the Caribbean.

War, too, was a fact of life in colonial New York, touching residents in myriad ways. As early as the summer of 1673, less than a decade after the conquest, England and the Netherlands were again at war, and a great Dutch fleet, 20-odd warships and 1,600 fighting men, crossed the Atlantic to attack English possessions in the Caribbean and along the coast of North America. The Dutch reached New York at the end of July and easily recaptured the city, renaming it New Orange in honor of the young Prince William of Orange, whose heroics had helped the Netherlands win battle after battle in Europe. But New Orange was a chimera created by the vagaries of war; when the conflict ended less than a year later, the Dutch returned it.

Toward the end of the 17th century, as conflict between England and France became the axis of European affairs, New Yorkers were often alarmed by the prospect of yet another invasion and surrounded themselves with defensive works: the hulking fort that still occupied the southern tip of the island, as well as gun emplacements scattered along both shores (one of which, built directly below the fort in 1693, would inspire locals to speak of the area as "the Battery"). A new palisade with gates and blockhouses would also be thrown across the width of Manhattan in 1745 when officials got word that the French were planning to descend on the city from Canada. The palisade zigzagged along a route between present-day Chambers and Canal Sts. And because the city's harbor and location made it an especially convenient station for both the army and navy, residents must often have thought themselves under more or less continued military occupation: great warships riding at anchor in the harbor, throngs of sailors on shore leave prowling the streets in search of a good time, regiments of redcoats drilling on the Common. In 1755 New York City became the headquarters of all British forces in North America, and the government initiated monthly packet service between Falmouth and Manhattan, confirmation of the city's importance in the Empire.

War and preparations for war contributed significantly to the city's economy. Provisioning His Majesty's forces required gargantuan quantities of food, clothing, shoes, rum, horses, wagons, and other materiel that meant brisk business for local merchants and artisans, who typically greeted the outbreak of a new conflict or a new campaign as a boon. For those inclined to high-risk adventure, it afforded an opportunity to obtain letters of marque and go privateering in the West Indies. In fact, more privateers would operate out of New York City during the 18th century than out of any other Atlantic port, returning home with prizes worth approximately £2 million, an immense accession of wealth and the basis of more than one family fortune.

Almost predictably, the end of the French and Indian War in 1763 brought great hardship to the city, helping to fuel the controversy that soon erupted over Parliament's attempts to tax the colonies. Between the adoption of the Stamp Act in 1765 and the outbreak of war a decade later, patriots (also known as Whigs) and loyalists (or tories) battled for supremacy in mass meetings, elections, ad hoc committees, demonstrations, and bloody riots. Initially, moderates held the upper hand, and New York was widely regarded as a weak link in the chain of opposition to Britain. By 1775, however, as colonial resistance stiffened and groups like the Sons of Liberty politicized unprecedented numbers of ordinary residents, the balance moved toward the patriots. Royal authority buckled and thousands of loyalists fled.

In the spring of 1776, anticipating a British attempt to retake New York City, George Washington brought the Continental army down from Boston and began work on the city's defenses, throwing barricades across streets, building forts, and erecting new shore batteries. He did not have long to wait. At the end of June, lookouts on the Battery spotted the initial contingents of what proved to be the largest British expeditionary force before the 20th century. All told, stationed on or near Staten Island were two great men-of-war and two dozen frigates mounting 1,200 cannon, plus 400 transport ships, 32,000 soldiers, and 13,000 seamen. The British attack began at the end of August, when 15,000 British troops crossed the Narrows to Long Island and occupied the flat southern portions of what is now Kings Co. Their goal was Brooklyn Heights, directly across the East River from New York. On the morning of 27 August, the British, fortified by the addition of another 10,000 British soldiers and 5,000 Hessians, assaulted American positions blocking the approaches to the Heights. By early afternoon they had driven the Americans from the field, killing several hundred as well as capturing 3 generals and some 90 junior officers. Although Washington managed to get the demoralized remnants of his army back to Manhattan, New York City's fate was sealed. In mid-October, the city fell, for the third time in little more than a century.

New York City lay under British occupation until the end of the war in 1783, enduring two catastrophic fires, one of which raged up the west side of town and consumed Trinity Church, as well as the widespread destruction of both public and private property. As the war came to an end and residents returned to survey the damage, many wondered how the city would recover, if at all.

Mercantile Metropolis (1783–1840)

New York not only recovered but roared back to life, and the trajectory of its rise over the next half century can be traced in Manhattan's surging population. By 1790 it was already the most populated city in the United States, although Philadelphia's metropolitan area remained larger, a distinction that was soon lost. Only 20 years later, in 1810, there were more than 96,000 people living in New York City, making it the largest urban center in the United States, and municipal officials were putting the finishing touches on a proposal, adopted the following year as the Commissioners' Plan, that anticipated the city's continued thrust up Manhattan by dividing the island above (approximately) Houston St into a neat grid of north-south avenues and east-west streets. By 1830, indeed, New York City boasted a population of more than 200,000 people. By 1840 that figure climbed to 313,000 (almost a 10-fold increase in 50 years), and the feverish tempo of residential and commercial construction pushed the northern limits of the city into streets in the twenties and thirties. It also triggered a building boom just across the East River, on the western end of Long Island. Between 1790 and 1840 the population of Kings Co surged from fewer than 5,000 inhabitants to almost 48,000, the sharpest growth coming in Brooklyn, the town and village (after 1834, the city) closest to New York City. On both sides of the river, the bulk of these increases can be attributed to a combination of high birth rates and the arrival of numerous migrants from elsewhere in the United States, especially New England. No more than 1 out of every 9 or 10 residents was foreign-born.

Behind this dramatic growth lay a number of interlocking factors. Especially striking was the ability of local merchants and ship captains to find new markets to replace those in the British West Indies (no longer open to American business after independence). An early signal of their acumen and resourcefulness came in 1784, when the *Empress of China* sailed off to Canton with a load of furs and ginseng; it returned to Manhattan 15 months later, holds bulging with tea, chinaware, silk, and other exotic wares, establishing a commercial connection with the Far East that figured importantly in the city's economy well into the next century. When the invention of the cotton gin revolutionized southern agriculture in the 1790s, New York City merchants moved just as nimbly to build the financial ties to southern planters that soon brought a commanding share of the annual crop to the East River docks on its way to the mills of Manchester and other British textile manufacturing centers (and once again hinged the city's prosperity to slave labor).

In 1792, when the French Revolution triggered a new round of war in Europe, the city's merchants moved quickly to take advantage of the sudden demand for American produce on the continent and along the way grabbed a big piece of the international carrying trade as well. The postwar stampede of settlers across Central and Western New York—the state's population ballooned from 340,000 in 1790 to 959,000 in 1810—sent a flood of agricultural goods down the Mohawk and Hudson Rivers, ready for export to Europe. City business owners thus had good reason to invest heavily in projects that quickened communication with the country's interior, most famously Robert Fulton's steamboat and the Erie Canal. In the 1830s, when the advent of the railroad threatened to divert commercial traffic away from Manhattan, local investors poured millions into the Mohawk and Hudson Railroad Co, the New York and Harlem Railroad, and other enterprises.

There were additional reasons for New York City's dynamism, including the speed with which its old commercial connections with Great Britain would be revived after the Revolution. By the early 1790s more ships were leaving Liverpool for the East River than for any other American port, and New York City had regained its former role as the American terminus of the transatlantic packets from Falmouth, which enabled city merchants to get vital mercantile information days, even weeks, ahead of their rivals elsewhere along the East Coast. With the organization of the Bank of New York in 1784 and the beginning of an active securities market in the 1790s, the city also began to build a commercial infrastructure that drew talent, capital, and commodities from all over the United States and Europe. Between 1790 and 1800 the number of merchants in town quadrupled, and by the latter year New York City could already lay claim to more banks, more insurance companies, and a greater volume of financial transactions than any other American city. It had also become the nation's principal market for the bills of exchange that were the lifeblood of international trade. Municipal authorities cooperated by improving the waterfront with new market buildings, wharves, slips, and piers, and by extending the Manhattan shoreline with landfill to create new commercial thoroughfares (work on South St began in 1798, on West St in 1810). The city likewise encouraged a new climate of entrepreneurship by dismantling many pre-Revolutionary wage and price controls; how much bakers could charge for a loaf of bread, for instance, was a restriction struck down in 1800 when the Common Council voted to let bakers charge what the market would bear.

One thing municipal authorities could not do was preserve New York City as the national capital. Congress had moved to the city in 1785, occupying quarters in the City Hall that then stood on Wall St at the head of Broad St, site of Pres George Washington's first inaugural four years later under the new Constitution. Perhaps because of an arrangement between Secretary of the Treasury Alexander Hamilton and Secretary of State Thomas Jefferson, Congress voted in 1790 to locate the Federal District on the Potomac and to move to Philadelphia for the 10 years it would take to erect the necessary buildings. Although New Yorkers cried foul, they soon came to realize that the city's prospects may well have been enhanced, not hindered, by its isolation from the national government, and from the state government, which departed for Albany in 1797.

Certainly they had no trouble fending for themselves, even in times of imminent danger. In 1794, when war with Britain seemed likely, anxious citizens headed for Governors Island to erect fortifications (the old colonial era fort on the Battery had been removed several years earlier); the same thing happened in 1798, when everyone expected war with France. Great Britain was again the probable enemy after 1800, and work began on a string of forts to protect the city from naval attack for the foreseeable future: the circular West Battery (dubbed Castle Clinton in 1815), originally built on a rocky outcropping about 200 feet (61 m) off the Battery but since enclosed by landfill); Castle Williams and Fort Jay on Governors Island; Fort Wood on Bedloe's Island [now Liberty Island]; the North Battery, which stood on the Hudson shore at Hubert St; and, further upriver, Fort Gansevoort on Gansevoort St. Though isolated, New York City could not be ignored by the federal government. The city's emergence as the nation's leading port and financial center made the New York Customs House a crucial source of federal revenue and ensured that East River shipyards played a key role in creating the nation's naval forces, which was evident as early as 1800, when construction began on the Brooklyn Navy Yard in Wallabout Bay.

The city's rapid growth in these years was accompanied by, and in varying degrees responsible for, the relentless erosion of the pre-Revolutionary social order. One early sign of change came in 1785, when a group of prominent citizens of divergent political views organized the New York Manumission Society to promote the gradual abolition of slavery. Initially, the state legislature proved unreceptive, and residents seemed devoted to the use of slave labor. By 1790 there were more slaves than ever in the city, approximately 2,400, and one-fifth of its white households owned at least one. Two-thirds of the merchants kept slaves, as did one of every eight artisans.

Over the next decade, however, support for the institution declined sharply. Although the absolute number of slaves would reach almost 2,900 by 1800, more and more of them (chiefly women) were being used as domestic servants. On the waterfront and in the shops of its tradesmen, the attractiveness of slave labor faded quickly with the expanding supply of cheap wageworkers who did not need to be housed, clothed, and fed. Concurrently, the number of free Blacks jumped from 1,100 to 3,500, a threefold increase resulting from high birth rates, migration from elsewhere in the United States, and the arrival of the "French Negroes," casualties of the revolutionary turmoil in the West Indies. Once it was a safe assumption that almost any African American in New York was enslaved, but by 1800 well over half the city's black residents were free.

The impact of this shift on the city's racial dynamics was profound. Free Blacks harbored and aided runaways, openly defied white authority, and agitated against servitude. Rumors of insurrections and plots to burn the city terrified white residents, and even the most obdurate masters must have wondered if owning one's cook or butler had not become too dangerous to be worthwhile. The General Society of Mechanics and Tradesmen, the Sail Makers Society, and other organizations representing or allied with the city's artisans meanwhile joined the Manumission Society to condemn slavery as inconsistent with the principles of both the American and the French Revolutions. Antislavery forces made little or no headway until 1799, when the state legislature adopted a bill that envisioned the emancipation of all slaves in the state on or before 4 July 1827. As a result, after 1820 the number of slaves in the city began to plunge. According to the 1820 census, New York City's population stood at 113,000 Whites and 11,000 Blacks, a mere 500 of whom still remained in bondage. Less than a decade later, for the first time in nearly two centuries, all residents of the city would be free.

The transformation of New York's racial system took place alongside equally momentous changes in the organization of labor and labor relations. A fateful convergence of circumstances—new foreign and domestic markets, surging prosperity, improved access to money and capital, a booming population—prompted the city's master craftsmen in one trade after another to restructure the process of production. Before independence, masters had relied on the labor of the apprentices they were training in the "mysteries" of their crafts, supplemented when necessary by that of skilled journeymen. During the buoyant 1790s and early 1800s, however, New York's most aggressive entrepreneurial masters began to shed these traditional relationships, simplifying and standardizing production to the point where they could jettison the paternalistic supervision of apprentices altogether and replace expensive journeymen with lower-paid, semiskilled workers. As this trend gained momentum during the second and third decades of the 19th century in cabinetmaking, tailoring, shoemaking, printing, and other key trades, masters metamorphosed into labor-employing manufacturers and apprenticeship steadily declined as a means for educating and disciplining youth. Journeymen, once able to imagine their ascension into the ranks of independent masters, now saw themselves slipping into the ranks of permanent "hirelings" in a capitalist economy: mere wageworkers, thrown into the same proletarian pot as former slaves, unskilled immigrants, servants, casual laborers, and a burgeoning corps of female "outworkers" who toiled at home for subsistence pay.

In many trades, embittered journeymen responded by organizing fraternal and benevolent societies that over time would evolve into vehicles of opposition to the masters. As early as 1785, journeyman cordwainers (shoemakers) banded together and refused to work until paid higher wages, arguably the first authentic strike or turn-out in the city's history. Such confrontations multiplied in the 1790s and became almost routine by 1820. Masters fought back with lockouts, strikebreakers, and lawsuits, keeping the journeymen on the defensive until 1829, when they joined with labor radicals and small masters to form the short-lived Working Men's Party. The party's demise several years later led, in 1833, to the creation of the General Trades' Union, a confederation of craft organizations that spearheaded nearly 40 major strikes in the city before it succumbed in the depression that followed the panic of 1837.

Commercial development along the East River waterfront had meanwhile been pushing the city's poor and laboring classes toward new plebeian precincts on the Lower West Side, in Greenwich Village, and in Five Points, a squalid, overcrowded, pestiferous slum that lay just north of the new City Hall (completed in 1812). Well-to-do residents, bemoaning the loss of what they imagined to have been, a generation or two earlier, a more decorous, less contentious city, were horrified. During the 1820s, if not earlier, they began to flee the noise and proletarian turmoil of Lower Manhattan, grimly retreating up Broadway, away from the Battery and Bowling Green toward newer, more exclusive uptown sanctuaries: Hudson Square (also known as St. John's Park), Gramercy Park, Union Square, and ultimately 5th Ave, areas where bourgeois standards of public propriety and private domesticity were less difficult to maintain. They also created a variety of educational, scientific, literary, artistic, religious, humanitarian, and philanthropic organizations to improve (according to their lights) the lives of their ever more numerous and turbulent fellow citizens.

What the prosperous and respectable classes never quite figured out was how to manage New York City's increasingly fractious public life. The expansion of popular political involvement that had begun in the 1760s–1770s accelerated after the adoption of the US Constitution in 1788 as new national parties—the Federalists, led by Secretary of the Treasury Hamilton, and the Democratic-Republicans, led by Secretary of State Jefferson—tangled bitterly over federal financial policy and the French Revolution. Before 1800, Hamilton and the Federalists generally held the upper hand in municipal affairs, partly because the city charter restricted voting in Common Council elections to freeholders owning property worth at least £20 ($50) and to residents of the city admitted as freemen. Under these rules, a mere 28% of the adult white male population qualified in 1790 to vote in municipal elections, a statistic that prompted repeated Democratic-Republican demands over the next decade to widen the suffrage and make the government more responsive to the city's working people. In 1804 the state legislature amended the charter to enfranchise white males who rented property (another change approved the use of secret ballots in municipal elections), after which the Democratic-Republicans drove the patrician Federalists out of power.

The decline of Federalism after 1800 owed much to the work of the organization originally called the Society of St. Tammany, or Columbian Order. Formed after independence as a vehicle for tradesmen and small merchants to express their fervent Americanism—hence the Indian regalia and titles like brave and sachem—the Tammany Society gradually emerged as a center of support for the French Revolution and as opposition to the pro-British Federalists. Although not formally affiliated with the Democratic-Republicans, Tammany members campaigned and voted for their candidates with such effectiveness that by the mid-1790s the two organizations were openly allied, and Tammanial Hall, the society's meeting room, functioned as the party's campaign headquarters on election day.

Over the next several decades, as the Federalists sank into oblivion and the Democratic-Republicans split into warring factions, the Tammany Society spearheaded further democratic reforms, most notably the adoption of a new state constitution in 1821 that enfranchised all white males over the age of 21 who paid taxes or served in the militia, but required Blacks to own property worth at least $250 to qualify for the suffrage. The new constitution shifted the power to appoint mayors from the governor (where it had resided for over a century) to the Common Council. Several years later Tammany fought successfully for a constitutional amendment that removed all but a simple residency requirement for male voters. In 1833, by which date the society had established itself as a bulwark of Andrew Jackson's new Democratic Party, another amendment to the state constitution empowered residents to elect mayors directly. To be sure, Tammany's appeal to the city's laboring people was openly racist, its leadership included plenty of well-off merchants and professional men whose interests did not always coincide with the aspirations of the rank and file, and it was slow to make common cause with the city's nascent labor movement. The rise of Tammany had nonetheless pushed the city's political center of gravity further toward a functioning democracy.

The Age of Industry (1840–1940)

After 1840 New York City's position as the principal western terminus of transatlantic shipping made it the destination of millions of European immigrants, who became the predominant reason for the city's ballooning population until the early 20th century. Already conspicuous were the Irish, thousands of whom had converged on the city every year during the 1830s, driven out of their homeland by poverty and grasping landlords; hundreds of thousands followed during the terrible potato famine of the 1840s. Close behind the Irish came the Germans, forced out of their native states by devastating crop failures, industrialization, and the turmoil that followed the ill-fated revolutions of 1848. Both groups grew so swiftly in the 1850s that by 1860 the city was home to 204,000 Irish and 118,000 Germans, together making up almost 40% of the city's 813,000 inhabitants. To manage this unprecedented influx, the city and state designated Castle Garden, formerly Castle Clinton, as an Emigrant Landing Depot, the first such facility in the nation. Between 1855 and 1890, at least 7 out of 10 immigrants entering the United States passed through Castle Garden, a total of 7.7 million men, women, and children. (Castle Garden is now known as the Castle Clinton National Monument.)

It is almost impossible to exaggerate the effects of such increases on New York City's economic and physical development. By 1855, German artisans were a majority of the city's tailors, shoemakers, bakers, brewers, cigar makers, and other trades people, while the bulk of its manual laborers were Irish. Fed by the seemingly endless supply of cheap immigrant labor, manufacturing bloomed so luxuriantly in Manhattan after 1840 that on the eve of the Civil War New York City had become the nation's premier industrial center. Brooklyn, whose factory district stretched from Greenpoint and Williamsburg down past the Navy Yard to South Brooklyn, was fifth overall and first in sugar refining. Except for the vast ironworks and shipyards creeping up the East River shore, most industries remained small enterprises with under 100 employees (one-half had fewer than 25) and crammed into the upper floors of warehouses and commercial buildings. Only one in five relied upon steam power. The garment industry, which accounted for a third of the city's industrial workers and produced roughly 40% percent of the nation's ready-to-wear clothes by 1860, relied upon the labor of tens of thousands of foreign-born outworkers: men, women, and children engaged as cutters, tailors, and seamstresses in their own rooms for mere pennies an hour, 16 hours a day, 7 days a week. When Isaac Merritt Singer's sewing machine appeared during the 1850s, garment manufacturers that could afford the new device began to centralize the final assembly of their products in sweatshops, employing single females between the ages of 16 and 25.

With pick, shovel, hammer, and trowel, German and especially Irish construction crews meanwhile built bridges, roads, docks, and canals in and around the city. They erected the great Croton Aqueduct (1842), which promised the booming metropolis a supply of fresh water commensurate with its needs. They ran the rail lines north and west of the city, which accelerated the flow of goods and people to Manhattan from the Mississippi Valley and points west. In the Red Hook section of Brooklyn, they drained marshes and put up breakwaters for the huge Atlantic Basin (1844–50), a complex of wharves, warehouses, and steam-powered grain elevators that became the main destination of Erie Canal boats.

Irish and German immigration continued strong through the 1870s and 1880s. The 1890 census showed more residents of the city born in Germany (211,000) then ever before, while the number of Irish-born New Yorkers (190,000) stood only slightly lower than in decades past. The 1900 census, reflecting the consolidation of Greater New York City two years earlier, raised those totals to 324,000 Germans and 275,000 Irish. But both the Germans and the Irish were about to be eclipsed by significantly larger streams from eastern and southern Europe: Jews fleeing murderous pogroms in Russia and Poland, and Italians fleeing chronic economic hardship and exploitation in southern Italy. In 1870 there were 60,000 Jews in New York; 40 years later there were well over a million, and Russian Jews constituted the city's largest immigrant community. The number of Italians exploded from a mere 800 in 1850 to 20,000 in 1880, to 145,000 in 1900, and to 341,000 by 1910. This so-called new immigration was not entirely an Italian and Jewish story. Easily overlooked were tens of thousands of others, among them Greeks, Czechs, Swedes, Norwegians, Syrians, Poles, Croats, and 2,000-odd Chinese, the latter mostly fugitives from racist violence in California, who reached New York City via the transcontinental railroad between 1870 and 1890.

When it became evident that Castle Garden could not cope with the volume of newcomers, the federal government put up a much larger installation on Ellis Island in Upper New York Bay to screen steerage passengers (first- and second-class passengers were allowed to disembark directly on Manhattan). Between 1892 and 1924, Ellis Island processed 16 million immigrants, often more than 1 million a year. Many quickly moved on to destinations elsewhere, but sufficient numbers stayed to catapult the population of Manhattan to better than 1.4 million people by 1890, a million more than had lived there a half century earlier. Immigration brought even higher rates of population growth in Kings Co (now almost completely subsumed by the City of Brooklyn), which swelled from 48,000 to 838,000 between 1840 and 1890. Regionally, the combined population of the five counties that would be consolidated into New York City in 1898 increased from 391,000 in 1840 to 2.5 million by 1890. By 1900 the addition of another 900,000 newcomers had boosted it to 3.4 million.

Like the Irish and Germans before them, the "new immigrants" found or carved out niches in the municipal economy that enabled them to survive, if only barely. Jews gravitated into the needle trades, which expanded greatly during the 1880s and 1890s to meet the rising demand for ready-to-wear women's clothing. These trades also reorganized as the introduction of new, more expensive machines quickened the shift from outwork to sweatshop. By 1895 there were reportedly 6,000 sweatshops in New York City and another 900 in Brooklyn, together employing perhaps 80,000 workers (mainly recently arrived Jews). Italian men made ends meet as casual day laborers in service jobs like barbering or in skilled trades like shoemaking, bricklaying, cabinetmaking, and stonecutting. Italian women, never so numerous as the men, found work in box factories and candy shops, or worked as finishers and artificial-flower makers for the garment industry. The Chinese, overwhelmingly men, dominated the hand laundry business; between 1877 and 1888 the number of hand laundries in New York leapt from a couple of dozen to over 2,000. Czech immigrants became identified as metalworkers, Greeks as restaurateurs, Syrians as rug merchants, Norwegians as seamen. The list goes on and on.

These successive waves of immigrants sprinkled the city with ethnic enclaves, informal and always in flux, that harbored the institutional apparatuses of survival in a strange, often hostile land: foreign language newspapers, stores, taverns, restaurants, churches and synagogues, clubs, theaters, banks, and mutual-aid societies. Thus the dilapidated and already infamous Five Points became distinctly Irish during the 1840s–1850s (only Dublin, it was said, could boast of more Irishmen), but Irish strongholds appeared as well in Hell's Kitchen on the west side of Manhattan between 34th and 57th Sts, as well as in Brooklyn around the Navy Yard, and out in Bedford (now known as Bedford-Stuyvesant). Manhattan's two principal German settlements took shape during the 1850s: Kleindeutschland (Little Germany), a 400-block district on the Lower East Side around Tompkins Square, and Yorkville on the Upper East Side below 96th St and east of 5th Ave. "Dutch Hill," a warren of shacks housing German and Irish squatters, sprawled over a promontory on 40th St and 1st Ave. Over time, more prosperous Germans moved up Manhattan to Yorkville and Harlem (above 110th St), or across the East River to the Williamsburg, Bushwick, and Flatbush sections of Brooklyn. During the 1880s and 1890s, what had been Kleindeutschland was reinvented as the Jewish Lower East Side, while a Little Italy sprang up in the blocks north of Canal St, between Broadway on the west and Mulberry St on the east.

Paralleling the "new immigration" from Europe was a significant revival of the city's African American population. Although the number of black residents actually declined from 12,600 to 10,000 between 1825 and 1865, an influx of migrants from Virginia, North Carolina, and South Carolina would reverse that trend in the 1870s and 1880s. By 1890 some 23,600 Blacks lived in the city, which was less than 2% of the total population, well below mid-18th-century levels, but in absolute numbers more than at any previous time in the city's history. By 1900 the five boroughs were home to 60,700 Blacks, more than half of whom had been born outside the state. Not unlike the Irish, Jews, Italians, and so many others, these new additions to the city's population hailed from small farms and country towns, driven out by bigotry, oppression, and terror. And like their white counterparts, they established niches in the municipal economy as domestic servants, coachmen, valets, and the like. But racism and fierce competition with European immigrants, especially the Irish, steadily weakened their access to such employment, and after the middle of the 19th century, New York's African Americans had been relegated to the city's lowest-paying menial jobs.

At the same time, and for similar reasons, the focal point of the African American community shifted from a handful of blocks in Five Points north and west to Greenwich Village, where a Little Africa emerged along Bleecker and nearby streets. In the 1880s and 1890s, as Little Italy expanded into Greenwich Village, the city's black residents moved again, this time to 8th and 9th Aves in the famous rough-and-tumble Tenderloin district of the west 40s and 50s. By the turn of the century, a second and more clearly delineated African American community had taken root along 10th and 11th Aves in the west 60s, an area dubbed San Juan Hill.

White or black, the neighborhoods of New York City supplied generations of novelists, journalists, and sociologists with examples of squalor and misery as bad or worse than they could find anywhere else in the Western world. The least fortunate residents lived in rookeries: private houses, commercial buildings, and even churches that real estate speculators had carved into tiny, often windowless rooms where multiple families slept on piles of rags (many a New York fortune would be made by packing the poor into the smallest spaces possible). In Five Points the Old Brewery, reputedly the most densely occupied structure in the city before the Civil War, sheltered around 1,200 people. Thousands of others reportedly lived in unlit basements, often ankle-deep in water that seeped through the walls from outdoor privies and underground streams. Somewhat more fortunate were those able to find accommodations in the tenements that sprouted by the thousands after midcentury. They were four-story brick buildings, 25 feet (8 m) wide and 100 feet (30 m) deep, hastily erected by enterprising landlords to accommodate four or more families per floor in rooms strung together like the cars of a train (hence "railroad flat"). Residents of the tenements brought in water from street pumps for drinking and cooking, and shared backyard washtubs and privies. Not surprisingly, they were also the first and most numerous casualties of the epidemics of typhoid fever, dysentery, typhus, and cholera that periodically scoured the 19th-century city.

Immigration was not, however, the only force revolutionizing the landscape of New York City after 1840. The arrival of the Erie and Hudson Railroads and the explosive growth of the city's overseas trade completed the transformation of downtown Manhattan from a residential neighborhood into a congested business district. In 1849 over 3,000 ships sailed or steamed into the harbor from more than 150 foreign ports, three times the number that had arrived in 1835. By 1850 a collar of piers, wharves, docks, and slips girdled Manhattan below 14th St, and new warehouses rose up along streets that only a few years earlier had been lined with private two- and three-story brick houses. Banks, insurance companies, law firms, and brokerage offices expelled the last homeowners from Greenwich, Washington, and Wall Sts, and from lower Broadway.

Horse-drawn wagons, carts, hacks, carriages, and omnibuses clogged downtown thoroughfares: 15,000 vehicles reportedly passed St. Paul's Chapel on Broadway on an average weekday in the 1850s. And the incessant clatter of iron-rimmed wheels against cobblestones, mixed with the shouts of cartmen and street vendors, ensured that the last residents of the City Hall neighborhood would soon join the uptown exodus. Although St. John's Park, Union Square, and Gramercy Park remained desirable destinations, they were no longer far enough north to escape the relentless press of commerce. St. John's Park would be torn up for a railroad depot in 1868. Monolithic department stores—a major innovation in retailing that dates from the 1846 opening of A. T. Stewart's "Marble Palace"—had meanwhile been advancing up Broadway above Canal. After the Civil War, anchored by R. H. Macy's establishment at 6th Ave and 14th Sts, so many fancy department stores congregated along Broadway and 6th Ave that the 10-block stretch between 14th and 23d Sts became known as Ladies' Mile. Along with the department stores came luxury hotels that lured business travelers, tourists, and out-of-town shoppers with such amenities as dining rooms, private baths, elevators, and, later in the century, telephones and electric lighting. Particularly notable were those along 5th Ave from the Fifth Avenue Hotel on 23d St (1859) to the Waldorf-Astoria on the block between 33d and 34th Sts (1897), and on to the Plaza on 57th St (1890).

Given the scope and intensity of New York's growth after 1840, it comes as no surprise that the ensuing 75 years would be marked by bitter ethnic, racial, and labor strife. During the 1840s and 1850s, native-born Protestants, fearing the political and economic repercussions of unrestricted Irish Catholic immigration, repeatedly called for immigration restriction, the exclusion of immigrants from public office, publicly financed schooling for immigrant children, and lengthy waiting periods of citizenship. Nativism made little headway, however, largely because of the opposition of Tammany Hall, now almost indistinguishable from the Democratic Party, which found that more was to be gained by cultivating immigrants than by opposing them. Tammany's increasingly close identification with the Irish would be confirmed in 1872 when it chose an Irishman as Grand Sachem, the first

View of Wall St in 1859, print, artist unidentified.

Wall St, view toward Broadway and Trinity Church, 1934.

of 10 Irish American bosses who indirectly governed the city until the 1920s.

In the meantime, New York was rocked by frequent clashes between Protestant and Irish street gangs, between Irish and German immigrants and the police or militia, and between Whites and Blacks. Fatalities were common. Twenty-two people died during the Astor Place Riot of 1849. In the draft riots of 1863, arguably the bloodiest event of its kind in American history, 100 or more perished (some estimates range as high as 1,000 or more) when the Irish poured Uptown from Five Points to protest a new Civil War conscription act and went on a four-day rampage, burning elite stores, assaulting police, and lynching at least 11 black men. Another eight New Yorkers died during the 1870 Orange Riots, when an Irish Catholic mob attacked a parade of Irish Protestant Orangemen; the following year, national guardsmen assigned to protect the marchers fired into the crowd, killing more than 60. As the health of New York's economy became ever more closely synchronized with the moods of national and world markets, labor unrest too became a familiar feature of municipal affairs, most notably during the succession of depressions that battered the country in the 1870s, 1880s, and 1890s. In the Tompkins Square Riot of 1874 club-wielding police charged a peaceful crowd of union demonstrators, injuring many. In 1895 rioting transit workers in Brooklyn traded gunfire with police and had to be dispersed by soldiers.

For New York's middle and upper classes, these eruptions only underscored what they had been fearing since the early decades of the 19th century: that feverish expansion and development (for which they bore no small responsibility as merchants, bankers, property owners, and civic leaders) would sooner or later tear the city apart. Handfuls of patricians, huddling in private clubs and historical societies, devoted themselves to celebrating "old New York": a quaint Anglo-Dutch village, serene and securely Protestant, that never really existed but afforded old families a comfortable vantage point from which to look down on the alien, turbulent masses of the modern city.

Much larger numbers of well-to-do citizens threw themselves into reform, though that meant different things to different people. Evangelicals thundered against irreligion, immorality, vice, and indolence, particularly among the poor, whom they regarded as the victims of their own improvidence. Physicians and social workers, arguing that better housing and healthcare would be more effective, fought to improve conditions in the tenements through stricter building codes and sanitary regulations. School reformers, contending that ignorance lay at the root of poverty and crime, established a system of free public education (1842) that offered three years of elementary school followed by four in grammar school (not compulsory until 1874 and racially segregated until the 1880s). Civic reformers won legislation creating the city's first professionalized Police Department (1845) and replacing the system of volunteer fire companies with a full-time Fire Department (1865); continued corruption and political influence in both forces helped spark movements in New York and Brooklyn to adopt the nation's first civil service regulations (1883). The city's haphazard arrangements for street cleaning and garbage collection, barely adequate at the end of the 18th century and now obviously outmoded, prompted the creation of the Board of Health (1866), later the Department of Health. Good-government groups, targeting rampant patronage, graft, and electoral fraud, launched repeated campaigns to wrest control of City Hall from the Tammany machine and to expose rampant corruption in the Police Department (NYPD). Philanthropists funded libraries and museums, and wealthy merchants and landowners urged the city to create a park grand enough to rival those of great European cities, a vision realized in 1859 with the opening of Central Park on an 840-acre (340 ha) site between 59th and 110th Sts.

In 1874, with the annexation of the Towns of Kingsbridge, Morrisania, and West Farms from Westchester Co, New York City was no longer confined to Manhattan and the smaller islands adjacent to it. Led by Andrew Haswell Green, a loose alliance of reform-minded merchants, politicians, and civic leaders campaigned for still further expansion, scoring an important victory in 1894 when the residents of Kings, Richmond, lower Westchester, and western Queens Cos agreed in a nonbinding referendum (176,170 in favor, 131,706 opposed) to join New York City. The following year the Town of Westchester, parts of the Towns of Pelham and Eastchester, and the Village of Wakefield (all Westchester Co) were duly annexed to the city. Things did not go smoothly in Kings Co, where nativist organizations like the Loyal League had cut the margin of victory to fewer than 300 votes in the 1894 referendum by circulating dire warnings that the county's traditionally middle-class, Protestant communities would be overrun by immigrant hordes pouring across the new Brooklyn Bridge (1883). Proponents of consolidation carried the day, however, with more practical arguments:

Washington Square Arch, 1909.

that 1 central municipal government would be more efficient than the 40 local jurisdictions it would replace; that it would be better positioned to develop and maintain harbor facilities, roads, utilities, bridges, and other elements of the city's infrastructure; that its expanded tax base would provide even poor, outlying communities with money for public schools, sewers, water, police, and fire protection; that the enlarged scale of public business, emphasizing professionalism and economic rationality, would eradicate Tammany-style influence peddling and corruption.

The state legislature concurred with the outcome of the popular vote and passed the necessary legislation in 1896. On 1 Jan 1898, Greater New York City was created. It consisted of five boroughs and four counties. New York Co was divided into two boroughs, the Borough of Manhattan and the Borough of the Bronx (the portions of lower Westchester Co annexed in 1874 and 1895). It was not until 1914 that the Bronx became a county in its own right. Queens Co was divided; the western towns became the Borough of Queens, and the eastern towns became (in 1899) the newly formed Nassau Co. In Brooklyn (Kings Co) and Staten Island (Richmond Co) the boroughs and counties were coextensive.

Wall St bankers, brokers, and law firms were simultaneously orchestrating a surge of mergers and takeovers around the United States that would be justified with strikingly similar (and similarly optimistic) appeals to economies of scale. This historic shift in the way the country did business ensured New York City's preeminence in the nation's financial markets and made Manhattan the preferred base of operations for a third or more of the country's biggest corporations. In addition, as always happened in periods of rising municipal power and prosperity, the city's propertied classes left a distinctive mark on the built environment, in this case with heroic Neoclassical and Beaux Arts public edifices like the New York Customs House (1907), the New York Public Library (1911), and Grand Central Terminal (1913).

More dramatic was the metamorphosis of the Manhattan skyline. Before 1890 New York had grown horizontally rather than vertically: other than the 272 ft (83 m) towers of the Brooklyn Bridge, its tallest structures remained ships' masts and church steeples. After 1890 the insistent demand for office space below Chambers St resulted in the appearance of buildings 10, 15, even 20 stories high. Full skeleton construction, an innovation in widespread use before the turn of the century, removed the height limitations of masonry or combined masonry and steel construction, liberating the new corporate moguls to erect taller and taller icons of their wealth and power. Almost overnight, Lower Manhattan thickened with clusters of 20-, 30-, and 40-story skyscrapers that served as a kind of visual shorthand for the city's economic power. The tallest of them immediately ranked among the most widely recognized structures in the world: the Flatiron Building (1903; 21 stories), the Singer Tower (1908; 47 stories), the Metropolitan Life Tower (1909; 50 stories), and the Woolworth Building (1913; 60 stories). Although the city sought to restrict the bulk and height of skyscrapers with the nation's first zoning ordinance (1916), the pace of construction accelerated through the 1920s, culminating in 1930 with the almost simultaneous completion of the Chrysler Building (77 stories) and the Empire State Building (102 stories).

Below the streets another revolution was underway, no less important than the one above. In the final decades of the 19th century, the city created a mass transit system based on elevated rail lines running above 2d, 3d, 6th, and 9th Aves. But the noisy, dirty, and slow "el" could not keep up with the booming numbers of passengers, already in the hundreds of thousands, who relied on it every day to travel back and forth from home to work in the downtown business district. Even though the solution had long been obvious—run the lines underground using electric motors—the wealthy and well-connected owners of the elevated lines held up action for years. The impasse was not cleared until 1894, when voters approved a plan to use public money for the construction of a subway under the auspices of what would become the Interborough Rapid Transit Co (IRT). The first segment of the IRT line, linking City Hall to Times Square, opened in 1904. Four years later, it boasted 22 miles (35 km) of track extending up to 242d St in Upper Manhattan, to the Bronx (via a tunnel under the Harlem River), and into Brooklyn (via a tunnel under the East River). The IRT's success prompted the Brooklyn Rapid Transit Co (BRT), which controlled surface transit in that borough, to launch a subway line of its own. In 1913, faced with the prospect of competing networks, city and state officials created the dual system that connected the two lines, set the fare at 5¢, added better than 100 miles (160 km) of track, and served 2 billion riders annually.

This privately controlled facility became a subject of heated political controversy when the owners sought to raise the 5¢ fare. (The BRT's financial woes would lead to its reorganization in the 1920s as the Brooklyn-Manhattan Transit Co, or BMT.) In 1930, hoping that competition would keep the power of the owners in check, the city launched its own line, the Independent Subway System (IND), which began running trains two years later. Fast and convenient, especially for riders in Queens and Brooklyn, the IND attracted so many riders that its rivals, already in deep financial water, soon sank into bankruptcy. In 1940 they sold out to the city, and their operations were taken over by the Board of Transportation. Although the three lines (IRT, BMT, IND) would remain distinct, they were now part of a single, municipally owned system with over 700 miles (1,130 km) of track, the longest system in the world.

The subway's ability to shuttle swarms of workers between home and office every day, cheaply and quickly, made it an essential precondition for the proliferation of corporate skyscrapers in downtown Manhattan. By the same token and in conjunction with the opening of the Manhattan Bridge (1903), the Williamsburg Bridge (1909), and the Queensboro Bridge (1909), the subway produced a bumper crop of new residential neighborhoods across the East River in the hitherto remote farmlands of Brooklyn and Queens. Between 1890 and 1940, the population of Queens jumped from 87,000 to 1.3 million, and the urbanized areas of the borough sprawled as far east as Queens Village, near the Nassau Co line. During the same 50-year period, the population of Brooklyn rocketed from 839,000 to 2.7 million, and old country villages like Gravesend, New Utrecht, and Flatbush were buzzing with new development, not always welcome. Mass transit likewise helped turn Brooklyn's Coney Island into an international prototype of commercial culture; by the 1920s, a hot summer day could draw more than a million visitors to its beaches and amusement parks. The Bronx, too, experienced a surge of residential and commercial construction to accommodate a population that climbed from 89,000 in 1890 to 1.4 million by 1940. Staten Island, isolated from the rapid transit network and lacking a vehicular connection to the other boroughs, remained the least populated and most rural of the five boroughs, but its population grew as well, from 52,000 in 1890 to 174,000 in 1940. Manhattan actually lost people, however. In 1910 its population reached an all-time high of 2.3 million then began to decline as the residents of its congested immigrant neighborhoods followed the subway lines north and east in search of better housing. By 1940 its population had fallen to 1.9 million and would fall still further over the decades to come.

Against the background of this historic shift in the distribution of its population, New York City's economy received another major boost from American participation in World War I. Between 1914 and 1918, massive quantities of food, munitions, and steel streamed through the city on their way to the European theater, while Wall St bankers floated billions of dollars of loans to sustain the Allied war effort. By 1920 European nations had bought and borrowed so much that the United States was the world's principal creditor nation and New York City rivaled London as a global financial center.

Over the next decade, buoyed by foreign money and a postwar explosion of domestic production and consumption, New York City reveled in unprecedented prosperity and cultural authority. Its newspapers, books, and magazines, nationally distributed via canal and railroad, had swayed American tastes and ideas ever since the early 1800s. But influence segued into dominance during the second and third decade of the 20th century as New York became the ebullient center of a national culture centered on consumption and mass entertainment. Madison Ave advertising agencies, 5th Ave retailers, and 7th Ave fashion houses now told Americans what to wear, drive, smoke, drink, and eat. A new generation of Manhattan-based maga-

Columbus Circle, 1912.

zines—*Time* (1923), the *New Yorker* (1925), *Newsweek* (1933), *Business Week* (1929), *Life* (1936), and myriad others—saturated the country with New York City ideas and images. New York architects and designers introduced it to the modernist Art Deco style, instantly recognizable in pictures of the Empire State and Chrysler Buildings and other city skyscrapers. Manhattan music publishers, recording companies, and radio stations effectively nationalized New York jazz, New York humor, and New York idioms, as did the new motion picture industry, another New York innovation, budding just across the East River in Queens. Greenwich Village, though weakened by the trauma of war and the Red Scare, remained the best place this side of the Atlantic to find out what was modern, avant-garde, hip.

Additionally, a recent migration of the city's black residents to Harlem had turned that middle-class white sanctuary into the premier African American community in the United States. Joined by tens of thousands of new arrivals from the deep South and the West Indies, they made Harlem a magnet for the brilliant assemblage of artists, poets, musicians, novelists, scholars, and activists whose work would be celebrated as the Harlem Renaissance.

While Europeans may have regarded New York as the beginning of America, many Americans increasingly resented New York City as the beginning of Europe. Many found the city to be alluring and enviable, but others were disquieted by its alien faces, alien accents, and alien notions. One measure of this resentment was the adoption in 1921 of the first immigration quota law, which capped the number of immigrants admissible from any foreign country at 3% of the number of persons from that country resident in the United States in 1910. Subsequent legislation lowered the limit to 2% of the number in 1890, a move clearly designed to exclude southern and eastern Europeans. Further evidence of New York City's problematic reputation emerged during the presidential campaign of 1928. Gov Alfred E. Smith, the Democratic candidate, embodied much of what the rest of the country found most troubling about the city: he was the child of immigrants, a product of the Tammany machine, pro-labor and progressive on social questions, anti-Prohibition, and Roman Catholic. In what almost amounted to a national referendum on New York City, urban voters backed Smith, but the nation as a whole gave the election to the Republican nominee, Herbert Hoover.

Smith's defeat was a blow but nothing compared with the Great Depression. The stock market crash of October 1929 unleashed a plague of unemployment and homelessness in New York City that by 1933 had deprived one in four employable residents (roughly 1.5 million people) of their livelihoods, slashed the wages of countless others (in the garment industry by as much as 50%), and spawned shantytowns, dubbed Hoovervilles, in parks and vacant lots. Men in suits stood in breadlines and sold apples on the streets. Local hospitals tracked an alarming rise in the number of suicides and deaths by starvation. Half the families in Harlem were said to be without money for food or rent. Closely tied to plunging real estate values, city revenues declined, halting work on the Triborough Bridge and numerous other municipal construction projects.

The sheer magnitude of this crisis seemed to paralyze public officials at every level of government. Their inability, or unwillingness, to take decisive action injected new life into the city's socialist movement, which had been crippled by its opposition to World War I and arcane factional squabbles in the 1920s. Morris Hillquit, a candidate for mayor in 1917 on the Socialist Party of America ticket (he also stood five times for a seat in Congress from the Lower East Side), ran again in 1933 and pulled over 100,000 votes. The city's communists, too, enjoyed a sudden burst of popularity, hosting demonstrations in Union Square, organizing rent strikes, fighting evictions, and clashing with police. It did not hurt the socialists or the communists (or the Republicans, for that matter) that Mayor Jimmy Walker was forced to resign in 1932 after a series of investigations by Judge Samuel Seabury uncovered rampant corruption in almost all branches of the municipal government.

Pulling New York City out of the depression, above all, was the new relationship between the city and the federal government established by Pres Franklin D. Roosevelt, who drove Hoover from office in 1932, and Mayor Fiorello La Guardia, who captured City Hall as an anti-Tammany Fusion candidate in the 1933 election. While New York City academics and business and labor leaders hurried down to Washington, DC, to assemble the pieces of Roosevelt's New Deal—yet another confirmation of the city's commanding presence in national affairs—La Guardia helped convince Roosevelt to combat unemployment in the city by providing billions of dollars for a massive public works program. By 1936 the federal Works Progress Administration (later Work Projects Administration) was spending about $20 million a month in New York City alone and had quickly become its largest employer; when the WPA finally ended in 1943 it had employed 700,000 city residents. How the city's share of federal money would be spent fell increasingly to one man: Robert Moses, La Guardia's choice as the city's first parks commissioner. Before the end of the decade, Moses had 80,000 WPA workers building bridges, roads, tunnels, schools, colleges, swimming pools, hospitals, parks, airports, and public housing. He kept going, project after project, until Gov Nelson A. Rockefeller forced him to retire from civil service in the late 1960s. By that time Moses had done more than any other individual before or since to change the city's appearance, the way it functioned, and how it shaped the lives of its people.

La Guardia, for his part, tore into the grafters, crooked police, racketeers, gangsters, and Tammany hacks who inhabited the city's famously freewheeling underworld. No sooner had he taken the oath of office than he ordered the arrest of Lucky Luciano, a key figure in the organized crime syndicate that fattened on bootleg liquor and beer during Prohibition, then moved into prostitution, gambling, and narcotics after repeal. Over the next half-dozen years the kinetic, peppery mayor proceeded to balance the budget, reorganize the municipal government, win the adoption of a new city charter, unify the transit system, reform the courts, straighten out the civil service, and clean up the NYPD. He smashed impounded slot machines with a sledgehammer, chased fire engines to blazes, and went on the radio to speak directly to the people of the city. Enthralled voters elected him to a second term in 1937 and to a third in 1941.

In the spring of 1939, marking the 150th anniversary of Pres Washington's first inaugural, La Guardia opened the New York World's Fair in Flushing Meadow (Queens Co). The fair's theme was the brave new urban World of Tomorrow. Its most popular attractions were the exhibits of big Manhattan-based corporations, which wowed visitors with models and drawings of the city of the future: vertiginous office towers and massive apartment buildings, elevated skywalks and aerial gardens, broad highways sprinkled with speeding automobiles, multitiered rail lines, skies crowded with flying machines and dirigibles bound for faraway places. Despite their techno-utopian bravado, however, these visions could not dispel the malaise that still gripped the city. When city radio announcers interrupted their regular broadcasts to tell the nation of the Japanese attack on Pearl Harbor on 7 Dec 1941, the unemployment rate stood at 15%. This was better than it had been in the depths of the depression but was still bad enough that appalling numbers of residents could barely make ends meet.

EMPIRE CITY (1940–2003)

What finally recharged the municipal economy was World War II. Between 1941 and 1945, New York's ordnance factories, shipyards, bases, and government offices anchored the Allied war effort and provided jobs to hundreds of thousands of city workers (75,000 in the Brooklyn Navy Yard alone, which built one-third of the navy's capital ships during the war). Not that everyone benefited. Garment makers and other small manufacturers did not work at full capacity because of shortages or restrictions on the production of consumer goods. Old racial barriers, despite the demand for labor, still excluded African Americans from many skilled trades (one of the grievances that fueled the 1943 Harlem riot, which took the lives of six Blacks, three by police gunfire). So, too, despite capturing a larger share of the workforce than ever before, women continued to be paid at significantly lower rates than men doing the same work, and fully one-third of them promptly lost their jobs after V-J Day. The soaring housing prices in the city had been a precipitating factor in the Harlem riot, and in November 1943 the federal Office of Price Administration froze the rents of 1.4 million dwellings in the city. The state government took over management of the rent control and stabilization programs in 1947.

On balance, the war ended with New York City more vigorous, more optimistic, and more assertive than at any point since the 1920s. As the most powerful urban center in the world's most powerful nation, its position was confirmed when the United Nations chose to build its headquarters on the site of an East Side slaughterhouse (after some backroom maneuvering by Moses and a hefty donation from the Rockefeller family). New York City's supremacy in global trade and finance was assured as well, partly because of the devastation in Europe and partly (perhaps mainly) because of the new American conviction that no expense should be spared, at home or abroad, to oppose the Soviet Union and the spread of international communism. Concurrently, the arrival of prominent artists, musicians, writers, and intellectuals from war-torn Europe globalized the city's cultural influence. By the middle of the 20th century, its art galleries, museums, concert halls, and universities would be as well known around the world as Wall St or the Empire State Building.

Automat at 977 8th Ave between West 57th and 58th Sts, photograph by Berenice Abbott, 1936.

As in earlier periods of prosperity and confidence, in the 1950s and 1960s sweeping changes occurred in the city's built environment, most of them conceived, planned, or approved by the autocratic Moses. Bulldozers plowed through, in the name of urban renewal, one working-class and minority neighborhood after another, clearing the way for more bridges, tunnels, and high-rise housing projects. San Juan Hill, once the West Side bastion of African American New York, was obliterated to build the Lincoln Center for the Performing Arts (1962–69), while great swaths of Brooklyn and the Bronx vanished in the construction of the Gowanus Expressway, the Cross Bronx Expressway, and other superhighways (so many, in fact, that New York could boast of more than Los Angeles). Dozens of new skyscrapers popped up around Midtown and the financial district, mostly plain glass and aluminum boxes in the then fashionable International Style. The building boom culminated in the 110-story twin towers of the World Trade Center (1973). But the cost and scale of these projects, to say nothing of their usually unimaginative design and insensitive implementation, had begun to draw fire from community activists and preservationists. In 1965, when Pennsylvania Station was demolished to make way for a complex of buildings that included a new Madison Square Garden (1968), the public outcry prompted the creation of the Landmarks Preservation Commission, a municipal agency empowered to identify and protect historically important structures and neighborhoods. Opposition to Moses had meanwhile come to a head. In 1962 Gov Rockefeller removed him from several powerful state posts, and in 1968 Moses resigned from the Triborough Bridge and Tunnel Authority, his final stronghold.

During the 1960s, moreover, New York City's prospects began to look more problematic than they had in 1945. One source of impending trouble, foreshadowed by the simultaneous departure of the Brooklyn Dodgers and the New York Giants at the end of the 1957 season, was the exodus of hundreds of thousands of middle-class Whites to the suburbs of Long Island, New Jersey, Westchester, and Connecticut. The explanation for this "white flight" lies in a combination of circumstances over which the city had little or no control. The Federal Housing Administration provided veterans with low-interest home mortgages and developers with up-front financing for new construction; on Long Island alone, the ensuing building boom produced hundreds of thousands of new single-family homes in effectively segregated communities and drove the combined populations of Nassau and Suffolk Cos from 604,000 in 1940 to 1,967,000 in 1960. Feeding this explosive rate of growth was the lure of well-paying jobs in the defense industries that settled on Long Island during the war and continued to thrive on mushrooming military budgets. There was also the new automobile-friendly transportation network that extended the range of white-collar commuters; the Long Island Expressway, begun in 1953, reached the Suffolk Co border in 1962. The Verrazano-Narrows Bridge (1964), another Moses creation, likewise siphoned thousands of Whites from Brooklyn and Queens over to Staten Island, the city's most bucolic borough. Also to be reckoned with, finally, were the heightened racial tensions that blanketed the city with hostility in the 1960s and 1970s. Major riots convulsed Harlem in 1964 and 1968, but it was day-to-day conflict along the color line (highlighted by the struggle in 1968 for control of public schools in the Ocean Hill–Brownsville section of Brooklyn) that helped persuade so many white residents to leave for the suburbs.

Suburbanization reined in the city's demographic expansion of the 19th and early 20th centuries. Between 1950 and 1970 the population stabilized at around 7.9 million people, then fell to somewhat over 7 million by 1980. (During the same 30-year period, the population of the United States grew from 151 million to 227 million, a 50% increase, and was the first time the national growth rate exceeded the city's). What was more, the racial makeup and distribution of its population was shifting rapidly. In 1950 minorities were under 15% of the residents of all five boroughs; by 1970 they made up over 40%, and one-half of the Whites present 20 years before had left. Between 1975 and 1980, another million people moved out, three-quarters of them white. To no one's surprise, the 1980 census revealed that the city's "minorities" stood only a few percentage points away from becoming the majority; by 1990 they had become the majority, non-Hispanic Whites accounting for just 43% of New York City's 7.3 million inhabitants. In Brooklyn and the Bronx, the outlines of this epic transformation were especially striking. Between 1950 and 1980, the nonwhite population of Brooklyn rose from 8% (213,000) to 44% (981,000) although the borough's total population fell by some 136,000; by 1990 Brooklyn's 1.2 million nonwhites made up 53% of its total population. In the Bronx, which lost nearly 250,000 residents between 1950 and 1990, the proportion of nonwhites jumped from 7% (99,600) to 64% (772,500) over the same period.

Alongside this reconfiguration of New York City's population was a second trend: the deindustrialization of its economy. During the 1950s, like many older manufacturing centers of the Northeast and Midwest, the city began to hemorrhage industrial jobs: 11,000 were lost every year, then flared to some 43,000 every year in the late 1960s and early 1970s. By 1975 entire industries (garment making, printing, brewing, baking) had either decamped or imploded, permanently erasing hundreds of thousands of factory positions that once afforded livelihoods for working men and women. Nor was that the only bad news. The waterfront withered in the heat of competition brought on by the creation of huge containerized shipping facilities in New Jersey in the 1950s, by the new Interstate Highway System, and by air travel. Transatlantic liners no longer crowded Manhattan's West Side piers. The federal government abandoned the Brooklyn Navy Yard in 1966. Shipping virtually disappeared from Newtown Creek, once second only to the Mississippi in total annual tonnage. Major corporations pulled out as well, often chasing their white-collar employees to the suburbs of Long Island, New Jersey, or Westchester. In 1960 better than one of every four Fortune 500 firms was headquartered in the city; 30 years later, only 55 remained. Wall St languished in the 1970s, when the Vietnam War and an increasingly unfavorable balance of trade hammered the dollar, cooled off the national economy, and knocked the bottom out of the local real estate market.

That unlucky convergence of events had dire ramifications. Not only did white flight make the

NEW YORK CITY POPULATION AS PERCENTAGE OF NEW YORK STATE (COLONY) POPULATION

Year	New York City Population	New York State (Colony) Population	City as % of State (Colony) Population
1698	4,237	18,067	23.5
1723	7,248	40,564	17.9
1746	11,717	61,589	19.0
1756	13,046	96,790	13.5
1771	21,863	168,007	13.0
1790	33,131	340,120	9.7
1800	60,489	589,051	10.3
1810	96,373	959,049	10.0
1820	123,706	1,372,812	9.0
1830	197,112	1,918,608	10.3
1840	312,710	2,428,921	12.9
1850	515,547	3,097,394	16.6
1860	813,669	3,880,735	21.0
1870	942,292	4,382,759	21.5
1880	1,206,299	5,082,871	23.7
1890	1,515,301	6,003,174	25.2
1900[a]	3,437,202	7,268,894	47.3
1910	4,766,883	9,113,614	52.3
1920	5,620,048	10,385,227	54.1
1930	6,930,446	12,588,066	55.1
1940	7,454,995	13,479,141	55.3
1950	7,891,957	14,830,192	53.2
1960	7,781,984	16,782,304	46.4
1970	7,894,984	18,236,967	43.3
1980	7,071,639	17,558,072	40.3
1990	7,322,564	17,990,455	40.7
2000	8,008,278	18,976,457	42.2

Sources: US Census; E. B. O'Callaghan, *Documentary History of the State of New York* (1849).

[a] The consolidation of New York City in 1898 accounts in part for the sharp rise in the city's population in 1900. The combined populations of New York and Kings Cos as a percentage of the state's population in the second half of the 19th century are as follows: 1860, 28.0%; 1870, 31.0%; 1880, 35.5%; 1890, 39.2%.

city poorer vis-à-vis the suburbs, as measured by median family income, but the shrinking middle class and falling real estate values cost it hundreds of millions of dollars in revenue. That led to higher taxes, layoffs, and steep cuts in essential services (education, health, police and fire protection, sanitation), which in turn drove away more middle-class taxpayers, sharpened the resentment of those who remained, and accelerated the deterioration of poor neighborhoods. Mayor John Lindsay (1965–73), a liberal Republican, tried to shore up the city's finances with a municipal income tax and heavy borrowing, although his administration soon sagged under the weight of acrimonious labor disputes, racial turmoil, another police scandal, and the embarrassing collapse of a section of the West Side Highway.

Lindsay's Democratic successor, Abe Beame (1974–77), ordered more layoffs, deferred more repairs to the city's crumbling infrastructure, and borrowed still more money. Then, over the winter of 1974–75, nervous bankers, unsure the city could continue to pay their steep interest rates, dumped over $2 billion worth of municipal securities, triggering a panic among investors that effectively barred the city from further access to capital markets. As New York City tumbled toward bankruptcy, Mayor Beame pleaded with the federal government for over $2 billion in loan guarantees, but at the end of October 1975, Pres Gerald R. Ford turned him down, a rebuff famously summarized by the *Daily News* headline "Ford to City: Drop Dead." Cornered, Beame bowed to the bankers' ultimatum: no more loans until the city surrendered control of its finances to a new Emergency Financial Control Board (EFCB), which they controlled and which (among its other broad powers) could terminate union contracts they considered too generous. At the same time, to ensure that the banks would never again have to fret about the city defaulting on loans, the state legislature set up the Municipal Assistance Corporation (dubbed Big MAC) to issue municipal bonds with a first lien on city tax revenues. Discredited by this backroom coup, Beame was defeated in the 1977 Democratic primary by Ed Koch.

Koch went on to win the first of three terms in City Hall (1977–89), earning national attention for feisty, wisecracking pronouncements on national issues and his trademark query, "How'm I doing?" New Yorkers also identified him with EFCB-style austerity budgets that imposed severe and often divisive retrenchments in education, healthcare, housing, public safety, and transportation (accompanied by generous tax concessions for powerful business and real estate interests). Many Whites, especially in the outer boroughs, hailed Koch for refusing to waste their taxes on what they saw as superfluous social programs for the city's troublesome minorities, who in turn perceived the mayor as a bigot with little or no interest in the demonstrable spread of poverty, crime, disease, and homelessness in their communities. That the polarization of the city in the Koch years did not tear completely through its social fabric can be attributed, at least in part, to Wall St's dramatic resurgence in the early 1980s. Federal deregulation of key US industries under Pres Ronald Reagan (1981–89) sparked a burst of corporate mergers and acquisitions that pumped billions into the financial markets. Bankers, brokers, lawyers, accountants, secretaries, restaurateurs, limousine drivers, messengers, parking-lot attendants—everybody downtown—seemed to be doing well as Koch's second term got underway, and it appeared there would be plenty of work to go around (between 1977 and 1983 alone, some 90,000 new jobs were created in the city's financial sector and an additional 100,000 in white-collar support services). Builders and developers put up luxury apartments, hotels, and office buildings in the whimsical Postmodern mode, a welcome change from the grim International-Style boxes of the postwar era. Old blue-collar neighborhoods like Chelsea in Manhattan and Carroll Gardens in Brooklyn became newly fashionable, attracting a range of residents from college students to eager young couples flush with six- and seven-figure annual bonuses. Rents and real estate values increased sharply, in part because of the conversion of thousands of former rental properties into owner-occupied "co-ops."

New York City's ethnic landscape evolved as well, in ways that rearranged (again) the lines of social and political conflict and blurred the effects of white flight. Already conspicuous when Koch took office was the city's rising Puerto Rican population, the upshot of an economic revolution in Puerto Rico, largely engineered by US corporations, that wrecked the livelihoods of tens of thousands of small farmers and laborers and pushed them north in search of jobs. By 1970 some 818,000 New Yorkers were either born in Puerto Rico or had a parent born there, which was three times the number in 1950 and represented somewhat over 10% of the overall population (21% in the Bronx). Puerto Ricans were not, however, the only new arrivals in the city. Nor would they prove the most numerous.

In 1965 Congress passed the Immigration and Nationality Act (commonly known as the Hart-Celler Act), which lifted the quotas adopted a half century earlier for countries in the Eastern Hemisphere and set the first limits on immigrants from countries in the Western Hemisphere. This legislation, supplemented by the Refugee Act of 1980 and the Immigration Act of 1990, triggered a rush of immigrants from over a hundred countries in Asia, Africa, the Caribbean, and Latin America. By 1980 almost a fourth of New York's population was foreign-born. Over the next 10 years about 1 million people immigrated to New York, boosting the number of foreign-born residents to nearly a third; another 800,000 would join the mix between 1990 and 2000.

This extraordinary influx balanced the loss of native-born Whites to the suburbs, and its sheer diversity (other American cities claim larger percentages of foreign-born residents, but none approaches New York City in their variety) put a certain worldly sheen on the 1980s boom. The decline of manufacturing, however, made it increasingly difficult for unskilled newcomers to find work, and the numbers of native-born residents who would never finish high school soared (by 1975 the dropout rate had reached 50%). And even if they did find work, it probably meant a low-wage, dead-end job in some nonunionized corner of the service sector where employers never troubled themselves over the health and safety of their employees.

While Wall St reveled in its good fortune, therefore, the gap between rich and poor grew ever wider. Between 1970 and 1980, the percentage of children in families living below the official poverty line jumped from one-fifth to one-half, and as Koch began his second term in office, some 900,000 New Yorkers (one out of every seven or eight) were reported to be on welfare. Neighborhoods not coveted by the new urban gentry were beset by mounting unemployment, crime, gang violence, and failing schools. By contrast, the new, high-paying jobs in finance and information technology went to graduates of the nation's top colleges, law schools, and business schools; roughly one of every five did not even live in the city but commuted to their downtown offices from suburbs. Between 1960 and 1980, indeed, the city's share of upper-income families in the Greater New York region sank from 66% to 54%, a movement of wealth that further jeopardized the city's ability to pay for essential services. As manufacturing declined, moreover, the city grew more dependent every year on three sectors of the economy often described by the acronym FIRE (Finance, Insurance, Real Estate). The consequences became readily apparent in 1987, when the bubble burst and the city plunged into another round of layoffs and cutbacks.

The 1987 crash dimmed Koch's prospects for a fourth term, as did a series of municipal scandals and his glaring lack of rapport with black, Hispanic, and immigrant voters. In the 1989 Democratic primary he narrowly lost the nomination to Manhattan Borough president David Dinkins. The subsequent victory of Dinkins over Republican Rudolph Giuliani in the general election made him New York's first African American mayor. It did not guarantee him an easy tour of duty. Played out against the background of a stubborn recession, his four years in City Hall were marred by racially charged disturbances in several neighborhoods and by rancorous relations between his administration and the NYPD. In 1993 Giuliani again challenged Dinkins, vowing to crack down on street crime, cut taxes, clean up the city, and revitalize business. This time he won, becoming New York's first Republican mayor in 28 years.

To his many admirers, numerous enough to give him a crushing margin of victory when he stood for a second term in 1997, "Rudy" made New York City livable again. His aggressive approach to policing was credited with cutting the number of homicides from 1,946 in 1993 to 633 in 1998 and with reducing auto thefts by 76% between 1990 and 2000. He incorporated the transit and housing police into the NYPD, a step toward greater efficiency in law enforcement long advocated by reformers and civic groups. He cleared the streets of panhandlers and squeegee men, pushed new zoning legislation to remove sex shops from Times Square, and eliminated thousands from the welfare rolls. Faced with a $2.3 billion budget gap at the beginning of his first term, he slashed spending by nearly $700 million, laying the foundation for a series of surpluses that grew to over $3 billion by the end of the decade and reduced taxes to boot. Business revived, construction picked up again, and the tourists returned. Even the Metropolitan Transportation Authority began to make money.

Giuliani's critics, on the other hand, saw him as a thin-skinned bully who got credit for things he did not do. It was actually the Dinkins administration, they contended, that began to bring down the crime rate by enlarging the police force, improving communications and equipment, and adopting new crime-fighting tactics; and crime rates were falling everywhere, not only in New York City. Worse, the Giuliani's overzealous war on crime seemed to have heightened police brutality in poor and minority communities, a charge that gained wider credibility in 1997 when a Haitian immigrant named Abner Louima was sexually assaulted in a police station and again in 1999 when Amadou Diallo, a Liberian immigrant, died in a hail of police bullets. Guiliani's critics likewise insisted that the city's recovery from the 1987 crash stemmed from the national economic resurgence that began in 1992. They faulted him, too, for failing to reduce New York's unhealthy dependence on Wall St, which as the new century began accounted for one-fifth of the city's personal income, a fourfold increase since 1980, and about one-third of its total payroll. Industrial jobs had in fact continued to evaporate at an alarming rate, dwindling to a mere 7% of the labor force by the end of the decade. Hundreds of thousands of new positions opened up for brokers, lawyers, accountants, and data processors, but that was cold comfort for the bulk of New York working people. One in five residents still lived below the poverty line, and the city's long-term unemployment rate had become stuck two or three percentage points above the national average. Toward the end of 2000, moreover, the great bull market of the 1990s began to lose momentum. Banks and investment firms announced massive layoffs. Major corporations shifted employees to Westchester or New Jersey. And because the mayor's tax cuts had deprived the city of more than $2 billion in revenue every year, the city once again found itself sliding into the red.

During 2001, as the effects of the slowdown rippled through the municipal economy and Giuliani's reputation lost its luster, potential successors began to gear up for the November mayoral elections. Then, on 11 Sept 2001, terrorists flew two hijacked jetliners into the World Trade Center, destroying both towers and killing over 2,750 people. The mayor's stalwart leadership during and after the attacks brought him national renown and even led to talk of suspending the elections so that he could remain in City Hall to lead the recovery effort in and around Ground Zero. That idea drew heavy criticism, however, and Giuliani eventually threw his support to Michael Bloomberg, a billionaire media executive with no prior experience in public office. Running on the Republican ticket, Bloomberg reportedly spent $50 million of his own money (a record for American mayoral contests) and edged out the Democratic candidate, Mark Green, in the November balloting.

Sworn in at the beginning of 2002, the new mayor inherited a nearly $5 billion budget deficit along with rising unemployment. A turnaround on Wall St could fix things, but after 11 Sept, which accelerated but did not create the city's fiscal woes, a turnaround appeared less likely than ever. Bloomberg initially seemed reluctant to impose the draconian cutbacks and layoffs that had been his predecessor's response to problems with the budget, and he spoke feelingly of New York City's liberal tradition: it was "more compassionate" than other cities, he declared. Dismal revenue projections nonetheless soon obliged him to hike sales, income, and property taxes, and he indicated his wish to revive the tax on suburban commuters, previously scrapped by the Giuliani administration. As early as the end of 2002 he was projecting a total budget gap for the 2004 fiscal year of roughly $6.4 billion and declaring his intention to prune expenditures by as much as $600 million. None of this went over well with voters, and in the summer of 2003 pollsters reported that only 32% approved of Bloomberg's performance, down from a high of 65% on inauguration day. He was widely acclaimed, on the other hand, for reorganizing the Board of Education to give the mayor a greater voice in school policy, long a goal of educational reformers.

One thing at least was certain: New York City's attractiveness to immigrants is undimmed. According to the 2000 census, the city's population stood at a record-breaking 8,008,000, a gain of roughly 686,000 since 1990. This was its largest gain since the 1920s and the first time since 1930 that New York led the nation's cities in population growth. In fact, taking into account the number of native-born residents who died or moved away, approximately 800,000 immigrants settled in the city between 1990 and 2000, lifting the foreign-born share of the overall population from 28% to 36%. Only Los Angeles claimed a greater percentage of foreign-born residents, but the bulk of them come from a single country, Mexico, while New York City's immigrant population is more varied. In 1910 six countries—Russia, Italy, Germany, Austria, Ireland, and England—accounted for 85% of the city's foreign-born population. In 2000 the six leading sources of immigrants were the Dominican Republic (369,000), China (262,000), Jamaica (179,000), Russia (162,000), Guyana (131,000), and Mexico (123,000), 1,226,000 in all, or just 40% of the foreign-born population. Making up the remainder are people from every continent and virtually every nation: Koreans, Indians, Poles, Haitians, Pakistanis, Filipinos, Peruvians, and numerous others. If the past is any guide, these newest additions to the already rich diversity of the city will be a source of optimism, energy, innovation, daring, and turmoil for decades to come.

Although the historical literature on New York City is vast, there have been relatively few significant general histories. Useful older histories include the monumental I. N. Phelps Stokes, *The Iconography of Manhattan Island, 1498–1909*, 6 vol (1915–28), and Bayrd Still's *Mirror for Gotham: New York as Seen by Its Contemporaries* (1956). General histories on specific topics in the city's history include Thomas Bender, *New York Intellect: A History of Intellectual Life in New York City, from 1750 to the Beginning of Our Own Time* (1987), Richard Plunz, *A History of Housing in New York City: Dwelling Type and Social Change in the American Metropolis* (1990), and Frederick Binder and David M. Reimers, *All the Nations under Heaven: An Ethnic and Racial History of New York City* (1995). Eric Homberger, *The Historical Atlas of New York City* (1994), and Paul E. Cohen and Robert T. Augustyn,

Education in New York City. Private tutors, charity, and parochial and public schools have all had a role in educating children in New York City. The issue of who had influence over the schools has been central to their evolution, as an appropriate balance has been sought between governmental and community control.

Colonial Education

The family was the main educational institution in New Netherland, covering both religious and occupational education. Trades were generally passed down through families, and children were also trained in particular skills through apprenticeships with relatives or acquaintances, a practice becoming more formalized by the 1650s. Apprenticeships provided access to positions such as merchant or physician for boys, and girls were apprenticed in domestic skills; many apprentices were also instructed in reading, writing, and arithmetic. Local schools, sponsored by the Dutch West India Co and likely held in teachers' homes, supplemented this instruction. The Collegiate School, the nation's oldest private school now located on Manhattan's Upper West Side, traces its antecedents to New Amsterdam in 1628. The school continued under local municipal control after the 1664 conquest of New Netherland by the British. In 1674 it passed into the hands of the Dutch Reformed Church, with public responsibility limited to the licensing of teachers.

With public sponsorship of schooling nonexistent under the English, private and religious auspices expanded educational opportunities. To New York City's many artisans, traders, and shopkeepers, schooling was a vehicle for economic advancement, and private schoolmasters offered for a fee such "useful" subjects as reading, writing, arithmetic, bookkeeping, surveying, and modern foreign languages. Private venture evening schools provided a basic education to apprentice youth, and wealthy merchants depended upon itinerant tutors to educate their children. For secondary level education, private academies offered a Latin grammar school curriculum. In 1764 King's College (now Columbia University) established a college preparatory grammar school. Education for poor children was provided by denominational charity schools. Most notable was the Anglican Church's Society for the Propagation of the Gospel in Foreign Parts, which in 1709 established a school affiliated with Trinity Church offering a rudimentary education at no cost to poor children and at a small fee to others. In 1704 the society opened a school for catechizing black and Indian children. Despite these endeavors the numbers of unschooled and illiterate children remained high.

Emergence of the Public School System

Although charity and private for-pay schooling continued into the early national period, there was a growing recognition of the importance of education and concern over the limited availability of schools in the city. Beginning in 1795 state educational funds were used to support public schooling statewide. New York City's Common Council, however, distributed the money to charity schools. Belief in the moral value of schooling encouraged private associations to establish schools for children not served by the denominations. In 1787 the New York Manumission Society opened the first African Free School, and in 1801 the Female Association began a school for poor girls of churchless parents. Most significant was the Free School Society established in 1805. With a board of influential citizens including De Witt Clinton, supported by private and public funds, and utilizing the Lancastrian monitorial system, which employed older students to teach younger children, the society was able to educate a large number of children at relatively low cost and to absorb a number of the city's charity schools. In 1825 the society convinced the city government to cease distributing public school funds to denominational schools. Consequently those monies were shared by the Free School Society (renamed the Public School Society in 1826), the Manumission Society, and the Orphan Asylum Society. In 1834 the seven existing African Free Schools were absorbed by the Public School Society.

At the outset of the second quarter of the 19th century new groups sought increased public support of education. Crafters, their financial and social status affected by the emerging factory system, were concerned for their children's future in light of the declining apprentice system and called for tax supported public schooling in New York City. Their short-lived Working Men's Party argued for public schools as promoters of democracy and equal opportunity. The inadequacies of the existing educational scene were further illuminated in the 1840s by the onset of the city's first great immigration wave. Not only were there not enough spaces in existing institutions for the children of German and Irish immigrants, who constituted the bulk of the wave, the curricula of public tax-supported schools were unacceptable to Irish and German Catholics. The teaching and textbooks of these supposedly nonsectarian schools projected a Protestant bias and in many instances expressed anti-Catholic sentiments. Under the leadership of Bishop John J. Hughes and with encouragement from Gov William H. Seward, Catholics petitioned the city government for a share of public school funds for their parochial schools. Twice denied, the campaign shifted to Albany, where in 1842, after a protracted battle involving issues of separation of church and state and pro- and anti-Catholic sentiment, the legislature passed a bill establishing a public school system in New York City. The law provided for an elected central board of education, but dominant control was given to ward school committees. Although the committees in Catholic wards would likely have Catholic majorities that could hire Catholic teachers, the law contained an amendment prohibiting the teaching or practicing of religious sectarian doctrines or tenets. Dissatisfied with this prohibition, Hughes subsequently turned his attention to expanding the Catholic parochial school system. The Public School Society disbanded in 1853 after transferring its schools to city control; by 1860, 153,000 students were enrolled in the city's public schools and 14,000 in Roman Catholic schools.

Centralization and Reform

In the second half of the 19th century, there was dramatic geographic and demographic expansion of the city and its public schools. By 1880 there were 228 public schools, all on the elementary level. Free textbooks were introduced in 1877, kindergartens in 1888, and the first public high school in 1897. Mandatory segregation ended in 1873, and the last "colored school" was closed by law in 1884. By the late 19th century, the system faced innumerable problems stemming from massive immigration from eastern and southern Europe; by 1898 the school-aged population had grown to half a million, over 70% of whom were children of foreign-born parents. Beginning in 1874 state child labor and compulsory education laws also increased the number of potential students, but there was not enough space to enforce attendance.

Educational reformers criticized the city's schools for being unprofessional, dirty, and overcrowded; for failing to prepare immigrants for jobs and for citizenship; and for being subject to mismanagement and corruption because of their ward-based authority. Advocates of change sought to bring efficiency and honesty to the system through centralized control. This was achieved in 1896 when the state legislature ended the ward system and established the citywide Board of Education. In 1897 the Board of Examiners was established to ensure the merit-based appointment of teachers. Under the leadership of William Henry Maxwell, superintendent of schools from 1898 to 1917, major steps toward reform were instituted: the establishment of more kindergartens and the construction of new elementary schools and of 19 large high schools.

Influenced by the progressive education movement, steps were taken to adjust the curriculum and services to the needs of immigrant children and adults. Classes for non-English-speaking students were organized according to age at entry to the schools; evening school programs were expanded to serve adults and older children; inexpensive lunches were offered; school baths and summer vacation schools appeared; and special classes for children with mental and physical disabilities were provided. Science, art, hygiene, homemaking, shop, sewing, and other "modern" and "useful" subjects entered the elementary grades; trade schools appeared as alternatives to traditional high schools. Catholic parish schools also increased during this period, adding 36 schools between 1886 and 1908; by 1920, 20% of the city's Catholic children were enrolled in parish schools and in convent schools and academies independent of the parishes.

The overcrowded classrooms of the early 20th century made it impossible for public school teachers to implement the teaching methods advocated by the leaders of the progressive education movement. Ideals such as psychological adjustment, learning through direct experience, and individualized instruction were expressed in several new private "progressive" schools established between 1914 and 1919. The public school system responded to the progressives' interest in greater efficiency. During the 1920s and 1930s, testing and tracking according to ability became hallmarks of the public schools.

The early years of the Great Depression brought hardship to all schools in New York City, but as the 1930s waned conditions improved. Federal aid, immigration restrictions, and a declining birthrate removed some of the pressure. Teaching in the public schools had become a sought-after job during high unemployment, and a large number of highly qualified people entered the profession. Students in the upper academic tracks and in such specialized academic schools as the Bronx High School of Science and Stuyvesant High School benefited immensely, as did the national reputation of the city's public schools. Few of these benefits, however, affected the schools in the city's poorer districts.

Recent History

New pressures on the city and its schools developed during the 1950s and 1960s. The immigration of rural African Americans that began during World War II continued in the 1950s, along with a massive influx of newcomers from Puerto Rico. Between 1954 and 1964 the number of schools with 90% or more black or Puerto Rican students had increased by more than 200%. The liberalized immigration law of 1965 resulted in a new wave of immigrants, most coming from Asia, Latin America, the Caribbean, and Africa. At the same time an increasing number of the city's white middle-class residents moved to the suburbs, and others transferred their children to private and parochial schools. By 1966 white children were in the minority in the city's public schools. De facto residential segregation by race and class, a declining white population, and resistance to busing frustrated attempts to comply with court directives to desegregate the schools. Education experts and minority parents saw an overcentralized school bureaucracy as a significant contributor to the high rate of academic failures and dropouts in inner-city schools.

Pressure to decentralize school control led to the establishment in 1967 of three experimental school districts governed by community school boards. In 1968 a power struggle between the United Federation of Teachers and the community leaders in the Ocean Hill-Brownsville experimental district resulted in a bitter strike. In 1969 the state legislature enacted a decentralization bill that established 32 local school districts in which elementary and junior high schools were governed by locally elected school boards. Control over high schools and over school finances remained in the hands of the central Board of Education and the system's chancellor. But decentralization proved to be no panacea. Low voter turnout led in many districts to inept school boards. In 1996 the community boards' power to hire teachers was given to the district superintendents. Power struggles between the mayors on one hand and the central board and chancellors on the other have also not enhanced the quality of education. The central board's relative independence from direct mayoral control has long been contentious. The New York City Board of Education, since 1973, has consisted of seven persons, two appointed by the mayor, and one by each of the borough presidents. Despite political struggles, the public schools have continued to experiment and innovate in their effort to effectively educate 1.1 million children. Charter schools, magnet schools, bilingual education, English as a second language, and multicultural curricula are but some examples. Curriculum innovations have also been introduced in many of the city's private and parochial schools as they strive to meet the educational needs of children and society.

In 2002 Mayor Michael Bloomberg instituted the most sweeping change in the structure of the New York City public schools in over a century. The Board of Education was abolished and replaced by a new 13-person Panel for Educational Policy, a majority of whose members serve at the pleasure of the mayor. The panel has greatly reduced powers, and authority for running the city's schools was transferred to the Department of Education. To underline mayoral control, its headquarters were transferred from its longtime home at 110 Livingston St in downtown Brooklyn to the Tweed Courthouse, adjacent to City Hall. The first chancellor of the new department was the prominent antitrust lawyer Joel I. Klein.

Cremin, Lawrence A. *American Education: The Colonial Experience, 1607–1783* (New York: Harper & Row, 1970)

——. *American Education: The National Experience, 1783–1876* (New York: Harper & Row, 1980)

——. *American Education: The Metropolitan Experience, 1876–1980* (New York: Harper & Row, 1988)

Graham, Patricia A. *Community and Class in American Education, 1865–1918* (New York: John Wiley & Sons, 1974)

Kaestle, Carl F. *The Evolution of an Urban School System: New York City, 1750–1850* (Cambridge, Mass: Harvard Univ Press, 1973)

Ravitch, Diane. *The Great School Wars: A History of the New York Public Schools* (New York: Basic Books, 1988)

Ravitch, Diane, and Ronald K. Goodenow, eds. *Educating an Urban People: The New York City Experience* (New York: Teachers College Press, 1981)

Frederick M. Binder

Manhattan in Maps, 1527–1995 (1997) are invaluable guides to the city's physical growth, while Anne-Marie Cantwell and Diana diZerega Wall, *Unearthing Gotham: The Archaeology of New York City* (2001) conveys the richness and complexity of its material record. Writing about New York City is abundantly documented in Kenneth T. Jackson and David S. Dunbar, eds., *Empire City: New York through the Centuries* (2002), and Philip Lopate, ed., *Writing New York: A Literary Anthology* (1998). John A. Kouwenhoven, *Columbia Historical Portrait of New York* (1953) is a classic essay in pictorial history.

There are hundreds of studies of neighborhoods and communities. Among the best are Tyler Anbinder, *Five Points* (2001), Jervis Anderson, *This Was Harlem: A Cultural Portrait, 1900–1950* (1981), and Christine Stansell, *American Moderns: Bohemian New York and the Creation of a New Century* (2000). Biographies of significant New Yorkers are legion. Undoubtedly the most influential is Robert A. Caro, *The Power Broker: Robert Moses and the Fall of New York* (1974). Two comprehensive, recent general historical works are Kenneth T. Jackson, ed., *The Encyclopedia of New York City* (1995), and Edwin G. Burrows and Mike Wallace, *Gotham: A History of New York City to 1898* (1999).

Edwin G. Burrows

New York City as metropolis. Since the early 19th century New York City has been the metropolis of the United States. Unlike some other leading cities, such as London or Paris, New York's role has not been anchored by political leadership; it had ceased to be the nation's capital (1790), even the state's capital (1797), well before its national economic and cultural leadership became clear. Rather, its national dominance was built on its economic function as an entrepôt—a central trading place for the goods, finances, and ideas of the American economy and nation.

Colonial Era (1624–1783)

The Dutch West India Co explicitly intended that New Amsterdam become a trading post when it was founded in 1624. The city's merchants focused on the fur trade with the natives of the Hudson Valley and the further interior, but also traded with the British colonies of New England, the Chesapeake, and the West Indies, though this trade was sometimes interrupted by the economic and military rivalry between the Dutch and the English. As a result, the British conquest of the city in 1664 facilitated local trade. New York City grew tremendously as a trading hub in the 50 years after the conquest, augmenting its transatlantic fur trade by sending grain to the West Indies once the Hudson Valley began to produce surpluses. The region's small ports relied heavily on New York City and its merchants for European imports such as textiles, tea, wine, and luxury goods. By the early 1700s, New York had become the dominant city of a region extending from southern New Jersey to Nantucket. However, a nearby rival, Philadelphia, surpassed New York City in trade and population in the 1730s and remained the leading city in the British colonies through the American Revolution.

Metropolis of the New Nation (1783–1860)

It was American independence and the development of a domestic American economy that catapulted New York City to the role of national metropolis. Like all ports, New York's trade patterns changed in the years following independence. Separation from Britain and its protected commercial empire led to more direct trade with Europe and with French and Spanish colonies in the Caribbean. After the adoption of the Constitution, domestic trade gradually increased, although its growth was masked by a trading frenzy in Caribbean goods caused by the Napoleonic Wars.

Two factors helped boost New York City's commerce in these years. First, the city became a hub for domestic commerce. Its fine harbor and proximity to New England's many small ports made it a natural center of coastal shipping. As the Napoleonic Wars drew British ships and merchants out of the transatlantic trade, New York City's merchants stepped in, particularly in channeling the trade of the South through Manhattan. Four commodities dominated the city's export trade, all from different parts of the United States: wheat from the Hudson Valley, New Jersey, and Virginia; flaxseed from southern New England; potash mainly from New York's frontier; and cotton from the South. Second, New York City had a special relationship with Britain, which quickly reemerged as the nation's most important trading partner. Unlike other American ports that focused on West Indian goods, New York handled domestic goods that Britain needed; flaxseed, potash, and cotton went primarily toward the production of British textiles. New Yorkers also had many personal and familial connections with Britain, stemming particularly from the British military's use of the city as its main North American base during both the French and Indian War and the Revolution. The city's unique ties to Britain became most apparent in 1818, when the Black Ball Line, the first scheduled transatlantic shipping line, started business; by 1822, it and its competitors had scheduled ships leaving for Liverpool once a week and for several other European destinations once a month.

With these two factors in its favor, New York City's role as a central hub quickly grew beyond the movement of goods for sale to news, capital, and people. The high volume of shipping in and out of New York City, with its large fleet and its year-round harbor, ensured that many American ports heard their news (especially news from Europe) first from a ship out of New York City. The ships that brought news and textiles from Europe also brought immigrants, and by the late 1810s the city had eclipsed Philadelphia as the nation's main immigrant port, contributing to a population boom that doubled the city's size between 1815 and 1830 to 197,112.

These activities also made New York City the center of American finance. Merchants from around the United States saw that they could conduct their financial dealings—securing or selling British exchange, investing surplus cash in government bonds, speculating in stock—more easily through New York agents than anywhere else, and that the New Yorkers' access to European news gave them a clear advantage. As more business owners found agents in New York City, more of America's business was transacted there. New York City wholesalers addressed advertisements to "Southern and Western Merchants," who often took semiannual trips to New York City to buy goods for their stores. A group of brokers organized the New York Stock and Exchange Board in 1817 to facilitate the trading of bank and insurance stocks; in 1863 the name was changed to the New York Stock Exchange. By 1825 New York was clearly the nation's central city.

The opening of the Erie Canal, its first sections in 1820 and its full length in 1825, heralded a new era for the city and ensured that Western New York would be as closely tied to the city as the Hudson Valley was. The canal made New York City the greatest grain port in the United States, and it remained the port of choice for immigrants, who found the canal an easy route to the West. As the country began to industrialize, the city's role as a trading hub also determined which industries would take root in Manhattan. Garment trade entrepreneurs found the city a perfect setting. Its access to Europe gave it the best entrée to European fabrics and fashion news; its access to the rest of the United States gave it markets for clothing; the many immigrants from New England and abroad gave it a low-cost, exploitable workforce; and its own large local market gave it a reliable base of customers. Other industries grew in New York City, such as printing, furniture making, and metalwork, for similar reasons. Newspaper publishers found it the best place to gather and sell news, and the best place from which to distribute it across the country.

The Capital of Capitalism (1860–1920)

The American Civil War transformed New York City and its role as the nation's business center. First, the disruption of the cotton trade created a long-term shift in British demand for American cotton, demoting what had long been the city's largest export and the specialty of many of its brokers. The government's enormous need for credit intensified New York City's control of the nation's finances; with Europeans unwilling to lend to an American government whose prospects were uncertain, the city's bankers underwrote much of the war's cost. The Republican Congress's efforts to pass legislation long opposed by the South also changed the American economy to New York City's benefit. Two laws in particular embodied this change. One, an 1864 amendment to the National Banking Act of 1863, brought order to the banking system in part by requiring all American banks to deposit their reserves in New York City banks. Another, the Pacific Railway Act of 1862, which authorized construction of the transcontinental railroad, symbolized the importance of railroads in the postwar economy.

The railroad industry was important to New York City because it required vast amounts of capital, and railroads were thus generally corporations that were publicly traded on New York's stock exchange, giving Wall St much control over the railroads, no matter where their lines ran or where they were headquartered. When railroads went bankrupt, as they often did, New York City bankers seized control of the companies. As other large-scale industries developed—steel, coal, oil, and heavy manufacturing—more and more of America's business took the form of publicly traded corporations in order to gain capital. In doing so, they, too, placed themselves under the control of Wall St.

Beginning in the 1880s, Wall St's bankers began to wield this control to make American corporations more profitable. In many cases, this meant making them larger, so bankers often engineered mergers to create huge corporations that dominated their industries, achieving both economies of scale and reducing competition.

NEW YORK STATE CITIES' RANKINGS AMONG 100 LARGEST US CITIES

	1800	1820	1840	1860	1880	1900	1920	1940	1960	1980	2000
Albany	17[a]	11	9	13	21	40	60	65	94		
Auburn			73	84	84						
Binghamton						93					
Brooklyn		24[b]	7	3	3[c]						
Buffalo			22	10	13	8	11	14	20	39	57
Elmira					97						
Hudson	28	33	72								
Lockport				87[d]							
Newburgh				76[d]							
New York	1	1	1	1	1	1	1	1	1	1	1
Oswego				55	92						
Poughkeepsie				60	99						
Rochester			19	18	22	24	23	23	38	57	78
Schenectady	17[a]	47	59	98			81				
Syracuse				30	32	30	37	41	53	86	
Troy		35	21	24	29	62	98				
Utica		57[b]	29	39	52	66	74	92			
Williamsburgh				23[c]							
Yonkers						79	68	61	64	73	94

Source: C. Gibson, *Population of the 100 Largest Cities and Other Urban Places in the United States 1790–1990* (1998).

[a]Tie.

[b]Includes combined populations of town and village.

[c]Annexed after this census.

[d]Estimates.

Wall St's importance led many firms that had started elsewhere to move to New York City. John D. Rockefeller and his Standard Oil Co, for example, moved from Cleveland to New York City in 1883, and James Buchanan Duke moved his tobacco firm, later to become the American Tobacco Co, from Durham, NC, to the city in 1884.

Although strong, Wall St and America's capital markets in general had always been merely an adjunct of Europe's. During World War I when Britain borrowed huge sums from the United States, this relationship began to change. In the 1920s New York City increasingly developed a reputation as the most important financial center in the world—the capital of capitalism.

THE INFORMATION AGE (1920–2003)

As important as finance was to the city, much of its influence after World War I was in the emerging world of media. Home to the nation's most influential newspapers, two news wire services, and many national magazines for years, the city was the nation's undisputed news headquarters. In 1925 *Time* magazine tried to save money by moving its offices to Cleveland but was back in Manhattan within two years, having found it impossible to succeed so far from the center of news. The presence of national magazines in New York City also made it the home of the nascent advertising industry, which soon became synonymous with "Madison Avenue."

Madison Ave also helped make the city the center of the newer media industry, radio. The two major radio networks, NBC (1926) and CBS (1927), sought to be near the advertising executives who financed radio shows. The sponsorships that advertisers could afford to pay the networks quickly gave network stations across the country an advantage over stations broadcasting only local shows; by 1943 two-thirds of all US radio stations were part of one of the New York City–based networks. After World War II, when the radio networks expanded into television, the city's influence deepened with the increased power of this medium, also financed by advertising. Only American filmmaking, which had begun largely in New York City for similar reasons as radio, left the city, attracted by the predictable and film-friendly weather of southern California.

After World War II the city's role as America's window on the world was enhanced as the United States assumed a leading role in world affairs; although not the only candidate, the city was a logical site for the new United Nations. The city also quickly became the main hub of international air travel to the United States, with its new international airport at Idlewild (later John F. Kennedy International), which opened in 1948.

Manhattan's original trade hub function began to wane in the 1950s and 1960s. The increasing importance of Asia in global commerce boosted activity at Pacific ports. Atlantic port activity grew more slowly. The containerization of oceanic freight reduced the importance of the Port of New York in general and moved what traffic remained to New Jersey, with its more spacious new terminals. When the World Trade Center was built, beginning in the late 1960s, its developer, the Port of New York Authority, intended it to be as its name implied—a center for the shipping, forwarding, and merchandising companies that moved goods in and out of New York Harbor. Instead, the twin towers came to be dominated by financial firms trading in what had long since become the city's main commodity, capital. While the world price of coffee, gold, and crude oil might have been set by the traders at the commodity exchanges of Lower Manhattan, very little of the goods themselves ever entered the harbor.

The departure of much of the city's physical trade was paralleled by its loss, particularly in the 1970s and 1980s, of many corporate headquarters. Whereas in 1955 New York was the home of 131 of the Fortune 500, by 1980 it was home to 81, and 10 years later to only 41. Ten years after that, in 2003, it had 40. Some moved to the suburbs, following General Foods, which had relocated to White Plains (Westchester Co) in 1954. Later, many chose the sunbelt, such as American Airlines, which moved to Dallas in 1979. Even the city's centrality to American news was challenged as Atlanta-based CNN grew to prominence in the 1980s. In the 1970s and 1980s New York City offered tax breaks and incentives to some of its most iconic institutions (eg, New York Stock Exchange and Madison Square Garden) to keep them from fleeing the city.

Despite these setbacks, the city's renaissance and the economic boom of the 1990s brought back economic and cultural prestige. Although California's Silicon Valley was the undisputed center of the Internet economy, New York City attracted many Internet firms, primarily because of access to the city's capital, secondarily because of its advertising and cultural communities. The increasing importance of financial markets, as a majority of American households became shareholders, focused more attention on New York City's leading industry. Even the terrorist attacks of 11 Sept 2001 horrifically emphasized the city's reputation as the center of world finance and the capital of the American economy.

See also PORT OF NEW YORK.

Aggarwala, Rohit T. "Seat of Empire: New York, Philadelphia, and the Emergence of a National Metropolis, 1776–1837" (PhD diss, Columbia Univ, 2002)

Albion, Robert G. *The Rise of New York Port, 1815–1860* (New York: Charles Scribner's Sons, 1939)

Jackson, Kenneth T. *Crabgrass Frontier: The Suburbanization of the United States* (New York: Oxford Univ Press, 1985)
Kessner, Thomas. *Capital City: New York City and the Men behind America's Rise to Economic Dominance, 1860–1900* (New York: Simon & Schuster, 2003)
Shefter, Martin, ed. *Capital of the American Century: The National and International Influence of New York City* (New York: Russell Sage Foundation, 1993)
Spann, Edward K. *The New Metropolis: New York City, 1840–1857* (New York: Columbia Univ Press, 1981)

Rohit T. Aggarwala

New York City as national capital. The city was the capital of the United States from 1785 to 1790 but was never, except in the minds of a few hopeful New Yorkers, intended to be the permanent capital. The Continental Congress had met in Philadelphia almost exclusively since its first meeting (1774), but tensions with the Pennsylvania state government had convinced most congressional leaders to establish a new capital city in which Congress alone would have jurisdiction. Quitting Philadelphia in 1783, Congress then met in Princeton, NJ, Annapolis, Md, and Trenton, NJ, but none offered enough lodgings and a larger city was clearly desirable. Congress adjourned to New York City in 1784.

It was welcomed in January 1785 by a city still recovering from a British occupation that had ended only 13 months earlier and whose society reorganized its life around Congress. Attracted to the city were foreign travelers, diplomats, and elites of all sorts, and their presence and spending provided news and gossip but also drove up the cost of living. Congress's presence helped make New York City the communications capital of the nation. The British and the new French postal sailing packets served the city in part because it was the capital. The demand for news from and visits to Congress helped develop stagecoach lines to the city. Speculation on public debt and about whether the United States would assume the states' debts from the Revolution made the city the center of the nascent bond market.

The presence of Congress influenced New York State's ratifying convention for the US Constitution in 1788. The decision on where the first Congress under the Constitution would meet had been postponed until after New York State's decision; many saw this as an implied promise that it would remain in New York City if the state ratified the constitution. Despite opposition, the first Congress stayed, and the city made physical improvements to prepare for George Washington's inauguration as president on 30 Apr 1789. The old City Hall was refurbished into Federal Hall under the direction of Pierre L'Enfant, who later designed Washington, DC. Streets were repaved, new docks were built, and the new steeple for Trinity Church, still being rebuilt after its destruction in the Great Fire of 1776, was hurriedly completed.

Nevertheless, it was clear that New York City would not become the permanent capital; even its continued temporary presence was contentious. Many sites had been proposed since the idea of a separate, new federal city had emerged in 1783; the main contenders were several sites along the Delaware or the Potomac Rivers. New York State offered Kingston (Ulster Co), Newburgh (Orange Co), and New Windsor (Orange Co) to Congress at various times; other, unofficial proposals included Morrisania [now in Bronx Co] and Brooklyn. Maneuvering in 1790, tied to Alexander Hamilton's proposal for the federal assumption of Revolutionary War debt, led to a compromise that established the capital at Washington, DC, beginning in 1800, with an immediate temporary move to Philadelphia until the new city was ready. Congress adjourned on 12 Aug 1790 to convene in Philadelphia in December, a treaty with the Creek Indians was ratified on 13 August, and George Washington left New York City on 14 August.

On 6 Sept 2002 Congress convened for the day in New York City for the first time since 1790 to honor those killed in the World Trade Center attack on 11 Sept 2001.

Bowling, Kenneth R. *The Creation of Washington, D.C.: The Idea and Location of the American Capital* (Fairfax, Va: George Mason Univ Press, 1990)

Rohit T. Aggarwala

New York City Ballet. See BALLET; BALANCHINE, GEORGE.

New York City fiscal crisis. When in 1975 financial institutions and other participants in the municipal credit market refused to purchase any more of the city's securities, New York City experienced a major fiscal crisis. This presented the municipal government with an enormous problem, because even in the best of times, it must borrow large sums of money to continue functioning. Municipal revenues—tax proceeds, state aid payments, federal aid—arrive at City Hall irregularly over the course of the year, whereas every month the city must pay its employees and meet other expenses. To ensure that it has enough cash on hand to cover these expenses, the city is authorized to sell securities, which it redeems when revenues arrive.

In early 1975, it became clear to major participants in the municipal credit markets that the securities New York City was issuing amounted to more than the revenues it could reasonably expect to collect. This meant that the municipal government would be unable to repay all the money it was borrowing. Hence, investors refused to lend additional funds to New York City. To obtain the funds the city needed to continue operating and to avoid bankruptcy, Mayor Abe Beame turned to the state and federal governments. Gov Hugh Carey helped the city secure much of the money it needed on the condition that the state government establish two fiscal monitoring agencies, the Municipal Assistance Corp and the Emergency Financial Control Board, to supervise New York City's finances and to provide investors with assurances that funds lent to the municipal government would be repaid.

To obtain the balance of the financing it needed, New York City asked the US government to extend federal guarantees to its securities, a request that Pres Gerald R. Ford initially rejected. A famous headline in New York's *Daily News* on 30 Oct 1975 summarized this exchange between the president and mayor: "Ford to City: Drop Dead." But after being pressed by several top Republican officials from New York State, Ford changed his mind, and the US Congress enacted federal loan guarantees.

New York City faced these crippling financial problems because municipal spending had regularly outpaced increases in municipal revenues for more than a decade before 1975. Large expenditure increases had been incurred to bolster the wages and benefits of municipal employees and to provide a range of social services to the city's low-income population. Those expenditures had been advocated most vigorously by municipal employee union leaders, spokespersons for racial minorities, and other liberal political forces. The fiscal crisis discredited those forces and enhanced the influence of their critics, particularly prominent business leaders who served on the city's fiscal monitoring agencies and conservative politicians, such as New York City mayors Ed Koch (1978–89) and Rudolph Giuliani (1994–2001), the two mayors who served for most of the quarter century after 1975.

Shefter, Martin. *Political Crisis/Fiscal Crisis: The Collapse and Revival of New York City* (New York: Columbia Univ Press, 1992)

Martin Shefter

New York City Housing Authority. Municipal agency created in 1934 to provide decent, affordable housing for New York City's low-income residents. It was the first public housing authority in the nation. The mayor appoints its three board members, one of whom is designated as the chair, serving at the pleasure of the mayor. Nonchair members serve five-year terms, and no more than two members of the authority may be enrolled in the same political party. Pursuant to the National Housing Act of 1937, the New York City Housing Authority (NYCHA) operates federally subsidized housing for New York City residents.

In 1936 NYCHA completed First Houses, a 123-unit complex on Manhattan's Lower East Side. While early projects were low-rise, walk-up buildings, NYCHA soon implemented high-rise designs, the first being Brooklyn's Red Hook Houses (1939). Such elevator-serviced buildings housed more people in a smaller geographic area and were less expensive to build than low-rise buildings. But in later years, the high-rises drew criticism for isolating tenants and contributing to residential segregation by race.

After World War II, the city's construction coordinator Robert Moses assumed control of the creation of new public housing. During the 1950s an average of 7,500 apartment units were built each year. Large complexes rose in Manhattan's East Harlem, in the South Bronx, and in the Bedford-Stuyvesant, Brownsville, and East New York neighborhoods of Brooklyn. During the 1960s NYCHA started to build "scatter-site" projects—located on existing residential blocks—so as not to distort the character of neighborhoods. A 1966 report by Mayor John Lindsay's Housing and Urban Renewal Task Force urged construction of scatter-site projects in middle-class neighborhoods to promote racial and economic diversity. NYCHA had completed 172,000 scatter-site units when, in 1967, it transferred responsibility for construction to the New York City Housing and Development Administration, though NYCHA continued to manage all properties. After 1968 only 10,000 units were built.

In 1971 NYCHA proposed construction of three 24-story apartment buildings to house 840 low-income families in the largely Jewish, middle-class neighborhood of Forest Hills in Queens. The Forest Hills Residents Association opposed the project, and a little-known Brooklyn lawyer named Mario M. Cuomo, acting as a mediator between the residents and NYCHA, helped to develop a compromise plan for three 12-story, NYCHA-managed buildings owned cooperatively or by tenants. Nevertheless, the resistance to the original project, as well as resistance by black, middle-class residents to a similar proposal in the Baisley Park neighborhood of Queens in 1972, ended the scatter-site program.

Reductions in federal funding during the 1980s halted new construction, and many of NYCHA's existing properties deteriorated. As late as the mid-1980s, a majority of NYCHA tenants were low-income working families. But changes in federally mandated income limits in the 1980s, as well as NYCHA policy, implemented between 1987 and 1992, giving priority to housing homeless families, reduced the proportion of low-income working families to about one-third of the 182,000 households served by 1999. The increasing proportion of highly distressed families threatened public safety in the housing projects. In 1994, to address safety concerns, the NYCHA Police Department, an autonomous law enforcement agency, merged with the New York City Police Dept (NYPD). The Housing Bureau now forms a 1,300-member command within the 40,000-member NYPD. In 1997 NYCHA estimated that it would require $7 billion to raise the bulk of its properties (325 federally funded projects) to a state of "good repair."

In 2002 NYCHA operated 346 housing developments, containing 182,000 apartments in over 2,800 buildings. Its properties provided housing for an estimated 536,000 residents; 431,000 were legal tenants while an estimated 105,000 persons lived "doubled up" with family or friends. NYCHA also administers Section 8 of the federal Leased Housing Program, which encourages rental of privately owned apartments.

Cuomo, Mario M. *Forest Hills Diary: The Crisis of Low-Income Housing* (New York: Vintage Books, 1974)
Plunz, Richard. *A History of Housing in New York City* (New York: Columbia Univ Press, 1990)

Jeffrey Kraus

New York City Marathon. A 26 mi 385 yd (42.195 km) footrace run annually in the fall, starting in Staten Island on the Verrazano-Narrows Bridge and continuing through Brooklyn, Queens, Manhattan, the Bronx, and back into Manhattan to finish in Central Park. The New York City Marathon was started in 1970 by the New York Road Runners Club (NYRRC) with 126 competitors racing within Central Park and grew to over 500 participants by 1975. In 1976, when city authorities permitted the race to travel through all five boroughs as part of the US bicentennial celebration, the New York City Marathon under the direction of NYRRC president Fred Lebow drew more than 2,000 entrants. The publicity surrounding this race, which featured Olympic competitors Bill Rodgers and Frank Shorter, increased national interest in marathon running for individuals of all abilities. In 2001 the New York City Marathon was the USA Track and Field Men's and Women's Marathon Championships as well as a major international sporting event, attracting over 30,000 runners from around the world.

Cooper, Pamela. *The American Marathon* (Syracuse: Syracuse Univ Press, 1998)

Pamela Cooper

New York City regional transportation. The New York metropolitan area is unique in size, density, and extent of transportation systems. Its approximately 20 million residents are spread across some 8,000 mi^2 (20,700 km^2) extending from Trenton, NJ, to New Haven, Conn. New York City, the nation's most densely developed city and the heart of the region, contains slightly more than a third of the population within its 320 mi^2 (829 km^2). Transportation systems have contributed to the New York metropolitan area's growth and economy and have helped to sustain high employment in the Manhattan central business district (CBD). These systems, mainly developed over the past century, continue to evolve as settlement patterns and economic conditions change.

New York City's harbor at the confluence of the Hudson and East Rivers, proximity to Europe, and access to the West by plank roads and canals triggered its 19th-century growth. Ridges, valleys, and water bodies influenced the development of communities and transport facilities. The city grew northward on Manhattan Island, and growth in surrounding areas was initially concentrated along railroad lines on the Hudson River, Long Island Sound, and New Jersey plains.

Railroads

The first railroads entered Manhattan in the early years of the 19th century, but a city ordinance soon prohibited steam trains from reaching points south of 42d St and ultimately led to the two-level Grand Central Terminal, completed in 1913. Railroads from Philadelphia and other points west and south initially terminated in Hoboken, NJ. The Pennsylvania Railroad and Long Island Rail Road tunnels under the East and Hudson Rivers and across Manhattan were completed in 1910, and Hell Gate Bridge opened in 1917. These facilities provided direct entry into Manhattan and permitted through service between the South and West and New England. Some rail lines continue to terminate at Hoboken, where Port Authority Trans-Hudson (PATH) rapid transit trains provide service to Midtown and Lower Manhattan. The region's commuter rail systems converge on Manhattan: Metro North's Harlem, Hudson, and New Haven lines enter and depart from Grand Central Terminal, while Long Island Rail Road, New Jersey Transit, and Amtrak serve Pennsylvania Station.

Rapid Transit

The 2d, 3d, 6th, and 9th Aves elevated lines were built during the 1870s, and the city's first subway line opened between Brooklyn and the Bronx in 1904. In 1940 Interborough Rapid Transit (IRT), Brooklyn-Manhattan Transit (BMT), and Independent Subway System (IND) lines were integrated into a single city system. The outer reaches of the subway and elevated lines dramatically affected urban development, especially where they penetrated vacant or largely undeveloped areas. They transformed the Bronx from farmland to high-rise apartments between 1890 and 1940 and spurred growth in Queens between 1920 and 1960. In 2001 the subway system was both mature and complex. Its 656 miles (1,056 km) of track and 468 stations served approximately 4.6 million riders each workday, with several lines crowded by passenger flows as high as 50,000 people per track per hour.

Highways, Bridges, and Tunnels

The nation's first limited-access highway, the Bronx River Parkway, opened in 1921. Its success led to the present network of expressways and parkways, originally outlined in a 1936 publication of the Regional Plan Association, a public-private partnership founded in 1929 that continues to address regional planning issues. At the beginning of the 21st century, there are about 1,900 miles (3,060 km) of limited-access highways in the region. Many expressways have spawned major shopping centers and industrial and office parks, which have created suburban traffic congestion unrelated to work trips to Manhattan. An extensive system of bridges and tunnels links the city's five boroughs with each other and with New Jersey. Brooklyn Bridge, spanning the East River, was completed in 1883, and the Williamsburg, Queensboro, and Manhattan Bridges were built over the next several decades. Holland Tunnel, linking New York and New Jersey, opened in 1927. George Washington Bridge opened in 1931 and Lincoln Tunnel in 1932. Other major river crossings include the Brooklyn-Battery Tunnel, Queens-Midtown Tunnel, Triborough Bridge, Bronx-Whitestone Bridge, Throgs Neck Bridge, Verrazano-Narrows Bridge, and Tappan Zee Bridge. Tolls are charged on several of the expressways and water crossings, with value pricing (higher tolls for peak periods) introduced on the New Jersey Turnpike and the Hudson River crossings in 2000.

Travel Patterns and Problems

In 1992 some 20 million residents of the New York metropolitan region made 60 million trips each weekday, and some 10 million registered motor vehicles aggregated 300 million miles (483 million km) of travel daily. More than three in four weekday trips are made locally within a single county. Intercounty travel is primarily to or from a neighboring county. About 55% of all trips begin in New York State counties, 31% in New Jersey counties, and 9% in Connecticut counties. Of all travel, 33% is to or from New York City, and one of every 8 trips begins or ends in Manhattan. Public transport accounts for 15% of all individual trips within the region, about 30% within New York City, and about 66% to the 9 mi^2 (23 km^2) Manhattan CBD, where almost 2 million people work. More than 600,000 people enter this area during the morning peak hour each day, 85% by public transport. From 1995 to 2001 the region's subway lines carried 4.6 million people each weekday, commuter rail lines 725,000, buses over 3.3 million, and ferries over 80,000.

A large part of the region's transportation infrastructure is old, replete with design deficiencies and operating problems, and requires substantial maintenance or rehabilitation. Imbalances between transport capacity and demand cause overcrowding on some rail lines and unduly long journey times or transfers to reach Manhattan on others; a few areas in both the city and suburbs lack nearby rail stations. Major new highway construction, necessitating major expenditures and environmental impact assessments, faces community opposition, especially in highly developed areas.

Strategic transportation problems, particularly as they relate to Manhattan, include

- an overtaxed trans-Hudson rail and road capacity, with up to one-half-hour delays entering Manhattan by car during the morning peak period;
- overcrowded subway and commuter rail lines between Queens and Manhattan;
- inadequate subway service on Manhattan's East Side;
- no direct subway service to Manhattan from several outlying parts of the city;
- no direct rail service to Manhattan from the northwest part of the region or from Staten Island;
- convergence of major roadways resulting in long peak-hour queues at "choke points," such as major river crossings;
- traffic congestion near suburban employment centers such as Princeton, NJ, White Plains (Westchester Co), and Stamford, Conn; and
- competition for limited space on Manhattan streets, many of which serve as conduits for through traffic.

THE FUTURE

Slow but steady growth is anticipated in the region's population and employment, with continued dispersion of residences and workplaces. Employment in the Manhattan CBD, which grew from about 1.7 million in 1975 to almost 2 million in 1997, will likely increase, placing greater pressures on radial roads and rail lines, especially at river crossings, and on public transit. Planners also foresee new workplaces along the Hudson River in New Jersey and expanding car ownership, with a resulting boom in suburban traffic volumes and traffic congestion. The Regional Plan Association, Metropolitan Transit Association, Metropolitan Transit Authority (MTA), and Port Authority of New York and New Jersey all favor a regional rail strategy to upgrade and expand existing rail lines, build additional rail crossings over the Hudson River, provide a new east side trunk-line subway across Manhattan and into the Bronx, improve Long Island Rail Road access to Manhattan's east side, and ultimately electrify New Jersey rail lines to permit direct entry into Manhattan. The agencies' planners view improved rail access to the region's three airports—currently underway to John F. Kennedy and completed to Newark International—as essential. Their highway strategy concentrates on rehabilitating and modernizing existing roads and bridges, alleviating bottlenecks on the expressway and arterial systems, and increasing suburban arterial road capacity. The Regional Plan Association and New York State Department of Transportation have studied plans for tunnels or platforms over highways where in-city expressways, such as Gowanus and Cross Bronx, are rebuilt.

Other contemplated changes include construction of an additional road crossing over the Hudson River and the possible restriction of cars from entering the Manhattan CBD—at least from New Jersey and Long Island—during peak periods. Value pricing of motor vehicle travel, especially on river crossings and within Manhattan, has recently received increased consideration. Some also suggest extending control of access to arterial roads to protect them from encroachments, with a highway access code similar to New Jersey's adopted by New York State and Connecticut. This would define allowable access to developments and permitted spacings between driveways. Those who wish to change the auto-oriented nature of suburban areas call for land-use controls to encourage "mixed-use" developments, with both vehicular and rail access. They advocate clustering employment and residential areas around rail stations, possibly requiring that office buildings of more than 250,000 ft^2 (23,226 m^2) locate within .25 mile (.4 km) of a rail transit station.

See also BRIDGES AND TUNNELS; LONG ISLAND RAIL ROAD (LIRR); NEW YORK CITY SUBWAY; RAILROADS; TRAFFIC MANAGEMENT.

Levinson, Herbert S. "Transportation Policy and Development in the New York City Area," *Transportation Quarterly* 46 (Summer 1992): 361–81

Herbert S. Levinson

New York City subway. A major urban public work and one of the city's best-known structures. A source of the distinctive metropolitan land-use pattern of skyscrapers and apartment buildings with high residential densities, the subways contributed to the development gap that opened between New York City and the rest of the state in the mid–19th century.

When New York City's economy began to grow rapidly in the early 19th century, transportation service became a critical need because of the city's large population and difficult geography. Urban development centered on Manhattan, a long, narrow island extending 13 miles (20.9 km) from north to south and 2 miles (3.2 km) from east to west with a total area of 22.6 mi^2 (58.53 km^2); Manhattan's developed areas were crowded and its open areas difficult to reach. In 1829 New York City acquired the first city mass transit service in the Western Hemisphere when horse-drawn omnibuses were introduced in Lower Manhattan. In 1832 the world's first horse-drawn railway entered service on the Bowery in Lower Manhattan. In 1869 the first elevated railway opened on Greenwich St. By the 1890s New York City claimed the largest and most heavily patronized urban transit system anywhere, but as vast as it was, this system was incapable of alleviating Lower Manhattan's overcrowding.

New York City's first subway, the Interborough Rapid Transit (IRT), was built to provide high-speed, high-capacity transportation. The new line was the creation of elite merchants such as Alexander Orr and Abram Hewitt who wanted to stimulate development of northern Manhattan and the Bronx; they sought to broaden the city's tax base to allow the city to pay for further commerce-enhancing public works projects. Because subway construction was so expensive, the IRT required a combination of public and private investment. A public agency, the Board of Rapid Transit Railroad Commissioners, financed and built the line, while privately owned Interborough Rapid Transit Co leased and operated it. Opened in 1904, the IRT ran from City Hall in Lower Manhattan to the Bronx. It became the fastest rapid transit railway in the world and spurred residential construction on the Upper West Side, in Harlem, and in the West Bronx.

In 1913 the municipal government authorized a second stage of subway construction to be carried out under a dual contract system involving IRT and Brooklyn Rapid Transit Co (BRT), renamed Brooklyn-Manhattan Transit Co (BMT) in 1923. Progressive reformers such as Manhattan Borough president George McAneny had designed the dual system. These reformers had supplanted the mercantile elite, as subway planners. They wanted to alleviate urban poverty by using rapid transit to disperse the poor from Lower Manhattan's slums to the city's periphery. An ambitious experiment in social planning that more than doubled the city's rapid transit mileage, to 619 single-track miles (996.2 km), the dual system extended beyond developed areas into outlying portions of the Bronx, Queens, and Brooklyn. Far more than the 1904 IRT, these new lines enabled working-class residents to move from crowded Manhattan neighborhoods such as the Lower East Side into new housing on the outskirts. After completion of the dual system in the 1920s, New York City's subway system was the longest and most heavily patronized in the world.

A third subway network, the Independent Subway System (IND), opened in stages between 1932 and 1940. Unlike the IRT and BMT, the IND was publicly owned and operated. It was conceived by Mayor John F. Hylan (1918–25),

Seventh Avenue Subway, by James W. Kerr, 1931.

GROWTH OF NEW YORK CITY SUBWAY SYSTEM

Date	Station or Line Segment
1862	Brooklyn, Bath and Coney Island Railroad (West End Line): 25th St and 5th Ave to 65th St and New Utrecht Ave opened
21 Oct 1865	Brooklyn and Rockaway Beach Railroad (Canarsie Line) opened
1867	Brooklyn, Bath and Coney Island Railroad (West End Line): 65th St and New Utrecht Ave to Coney Island opened
1 July 1868	9th Ave Elevated: Cortlandt St to Battery Place (Manhattan) opened
14 Feb 1870	9th Ave Elevated: Rector St to 30th St (Manhattan) opened
15 June 1875	Prospect Park and Coney Island Railroad (Culver Line): 9th Ave and 20th St to Gravesend (McDonald) Ave and Neck Rd (Brooklyn) opened
27 July 1875	Prospect Park and Coney Island Railroad (Culver Line): Gravesend (McDonald) Ave and Neck Rd to Culver Terminal (Surf Ave and West 5th St) (Brooklyn) opened
18 July 1877	New York and Sea Beach Railroad (Sea Beach Line): 64th St Pier to Bath Junction (62d St and New Utrecht Ave) (Brooklyn) opened
5 June 1878	6th Ave Elevated: Rector St to 58th St (Manhattan) opened
5 June 1878	6th Ave Elevated: 53d St Branch (Manhattan) opened
2 July 1878	Brooklyn, Flatbush, and Coney Island Railroad (Brighton Line): Prospect Park to Brighton Beach (Brooklyn) opened
26 Aug 1878	3d Ave Elevated: Hanover Square to 42d St (Manhattan) opened
26 Aug 1878	3d Ave Elevated: 42d St Branch (Manhattan) opened
26 Aug 1878	3d Ave Elevated: 99th St to 125th St (Manhattan) opened
9 Dec 1878	3d Ave Elevated: 67th St to 89th St (Manhattan) opened
30 Dec 1878	3d Ave Elevated: 125th St to 129th St Junction (Manhattan) opened
18 Jan 1879	9th Ave Elevated: 34th St to 42d St (Manhattan) opened
17 Mar 1879	2d Ave and 3d Ave Elevated: City Hall Spur (Manhattan) opened
9 June 1879	6th and 9th Ave Elevated: 59th St to 81st St (Manhattan) opened
17 July 1879	New York and Sea Beach Railroad (Sea Beach Line): Bath Junction (62d St and New Utrecht Ave) to Coney Island (Brooklyn) opened
21 July 1879	6th and 9th Ave Elevated: 81st St to 104th St (Manhattan) opened
17 Sept 1879	6th and 9th Ave Elevated: 104th St to 135th St (Manhattan) opened
7 Oct 1879	6th and 9th Ave Elevated: 135th St to 155th St (Manhattan) opened
1 Mar 1880	2d Ave Elevated: Canal St to 65th St (Manhattan) opened
1 July 1880	2d Ave Elevated: 34th St Branch (Manhattan) opened
6 Aug 1880	2d Ave Elevated: 65th St to 125th St (Manhattan) opened
9 Sept 1885	Broadway-Brooklyn Line: Broadway Junction to Kosciusko St (Brooklyn) opened
23 May 1886	3d Ave Elevated: 129th St Junction (Manhattan) to 143d St (Bronx) opened
27 Feb 1888	Fulton St Elevated: Sands St to Rockaway Ave (Brooklyn) opened
16 Sept 1888	Broadway-Brooklyn Line: Marcy Ave to Kosciusko St (Brooklyn) opened
29 Sept 1888	3d Ave Elevated: 143d St (Bronx) to 169th St opened
13 June 1889	Fulton St Elevated: Rockaway Ave to Atlantic Ave (Brooklyn) opened
29 Oct 1890	Fulton St Elevated: Atlantic Ave to Van Siclen Ave (Brooklyn) opened
9 Aug 1892	Fulton St Elevated: Van Siclen Ave to Linwood St (Brooklyn) opened
16 Nov 1892	Fulton St Elevated: Linwood St to Montauk Ave (Brooklyn) opened
12 June 1893	Broadway-Brooklyn Line: Broadway Junction to Cypress Hills (Brooklyn) opened
12 Dec 1894	Fulton St Elevated: Montauk Ave to Grant Ave (Brooklyn) opened
15 Aug 1896	Brooklyn and Brighton Beach Railroad (Brighton Line): Prospect Park to Sands St, via the Fulton St El opened
21 May 1902	3d Ave Elevated: 190th St–Fordham Rd to Bronx Park Junction (Bronx) opened
27 Oct 1904	Original subway line opened: Lexington Ave Line (IRT): City Hall to Grand Central/42d St Shuttle (IRT)/ Broadway (IRT) Line: Times Square to 145th St (Manhattan)
12 Nov 1904	Broadway Line (IRT): 145th St to 157th St (Manhattan) opened
23 Nov 1904	Lenox Ave Line (IRT): 96th St to 145th St (Manhattan) opened
26 Nov 1904	White Plains Rd Line (IRT): Jackson Ave to 180th St (Bronx) opened
16 Jan 1905	Lexington Ave Line (IRT): Brooklyn Bridge to Fulton St (Manhattan) opened
12 June 1905	Lexington Ave Line (IRT): Fulton St to Wall St (Manhattan) opened
10 July 1905	Lenox Ave Line (IRT): 135th St (Manhattan) to Jackson Ave (Bronx) opened
10 July 1905	Lexington Ave Line (IRT): Wall St to South Ferry (Manhattan) opened
12 Mar 1906	Broadway Line (IRT): 157th St to 215th St (Manhattan) opened
14 Jan 1907	Broadway Line (IRT): 215th St (Manhattan) to 225th St (Bronx) opened
9 Jan 1908	Lexington Ave Line (IRT): Bowling Green (Manhattan) to Borough Hall (Brooklyn) opened
25 Feb 1908	Hudson and Manhattan Tubes (now PATH): Hoboken, NJ, to 19th St (Manhattan) opened
25 Feb 1908	Hudson and Manhattan Tubes (now PATH): 19th St to 23d St (Manhattan) opened
1 May 1908	Brooklyn IRT: Borough Hall to Atlantic Ave (Brooklyn) opened
1 Aug 1908	Broadway Line (IRT): 225th St to 242d St (Bronx) opened
19 July 1909	Hudson and Manhattan Tubes (now PATH): Jersey City, NJ, to Hudson Terminal (Manhattan) opened
2 Aug 1909	Hudson and Manhattan Tubes (PATH): Hoboken, NJ, to Jersey City, NJ, opened
16 Sept 1909	Broadway-Brooklyn Line (Williamsburg Bridge tracks–BMT): Essex St (Manhattan) to Marcy Ave opened
20 Sept 1909	Hudson and Manhattan Tubes (now PATH): 6th Ave–Jersey City, NJ, connection opened
10 Mar 1910	Hudson and Manhattan Tubes (now PATH): 23d St to 33d St (Manhattan) opened
13 June 1911	Dual Contracts Plan announced
29 May 1912	New York, Westchester and Boston Railway: East 180th St (Bronx) to North Ave, New Rochelle (Westchester Co) opened
29 May 1912	New York, Westchester and Boston Railway: East 180th St to Hunts Point (Bronx) opened

GROWTH OF NEW YORK CITY SUBWAY SYSTEM (continued)

Date	Station or Line Segment
14 Mar 1913	New York State Public Service Commission approves the Dual Contracts Plan
1 Aug 1913	Centre St Line (BMT): Essex St to Chambers St (Manhattan) opened
29 July 1914	Myrtle Ave Line (BMT): Broadway to Central Ave (Brooklyn) opened
22 Feb 1915	Myrtle Ave Line (BMT): Wyckoff Ave (Brooklyn) to Metropolitan Ave (Queens) opened
22 June 1915	Flushing Line (BMT): Grand Central–42d St (Manhattan) to Vernon-Jackson (Queens) opened
22 June 1915	Sea Beach Line (BMT): 59th St to Stillwell Ave (Brooklyn) opened
22 June 1915	4th Ave Line (BMT): Myrtle Ave to 59th St (Brooklyn) opened
26 Sept 1915	Fulton St Elevated (BMT): Lefferts Blvd to City Line (Brooklyn) opened
15 Jan 1916	4th Ave Line (BMT): 59th St to 86th St (Brooklyn) opened
17 Jan 1916	Broadway-Brooklyn Line (BMT): Marcy Ave to Myrtle Ave (Brooklyn) opened
15 Feb 1916	Flushing Line (IRT): Vernon-Jackson to Hunters Point Ave (Queens) opened
24 June 1916	West End Line (BMT): 36th St to 18th Ave (Brooklyn) opened
24 June 1916	West End Line (BMT): 18th Ave to 25th Ave (Brooklyn) opened
5 Nov 1916	Flushing Line (IRT): Hunters Point Ave to Queensboro Plaza (Queens) opened
21 Dec 1916	Broadway-Brooklyn Line (BMT): Myrtle Ave to Alabama Ave (Brooklyn) opened
1 Feb 1917	Astoria Line (BMT)[a]: Queensboro Plaza to Ditmars Blvd (Queens) opened
3 Mar 1917	White Plains Rd Line (IRT): 180th St to 219th St (Bronx) opened
3 Mar 1917	White Plains Rd Line (IRT): 219th St to 238th St (Bronx) opened
21 Apr 1917	Flushing Line (IRT)[a]: Queensboro Plaza to Junction Blvd opened
28 May 1917	Jamaica Ave Line (BMT): 111th St (Queens) to Cypress Hills (Brooklyn) opened
1 July 1917	3d Ave Elevated (IRT)[b]: Bronx Park Junction to Gun Hill Rd (Bronx) opened
21 July 1917	West End Line: 25th Ave to Stillwell Ave (Brooklyn) opened
2 June 1917	Jerome Ave line (IRT): 149th St to Kingsbridge Rd (Bronx) opened
4 Sept 1917	Broadway (BMT) Line: 14th St to Prince St (Manhattan) opened
4 Sept 1917	Broadway (BMT) Line (Manhattan Bridge tracks): Prince St (Manhattan) to Myrtle Ave (Brooklyn) opened
5 Jan 1918	Broadway (BMT) Line: Prince St to Whitehall St (Manhattan) opened
5 Jan 1918	Broadway Line (BMT): Union Square to Times Square (Manhattan) opened
15 Apr 1918	Jerome Ave Line (IRT): Kingsbridge Rd to Woodlawn (Bronx) opened
1 July 1918	6th and 9th Ave Elevated (IRT): 155th St (Manhattan) to connection with the Jerome Ave Line (Bronx) opened
1 July 1918	7th Ave Line (IRT): 34th St to Wall St and South Ferry (Manhattan) opened
1 July 1918	Myrtle Ave Line (BMT): Central Ave to Wyckoff Ave (Brooklyn) opened
3 July 1918	Jamaica Ave Line (BMT): 111th St to 168th St (Queens) opened
1 Aug 1918	Pelham Line (IRT): 125th St (Manhattan) to 138th St–3d Ave (Bronx) opened
8 Jan 1919	Pelham Line (IRT): 138th St–3d Ave to Hunts Point Ave (Bronx) opened
10 Mar 1919	Culver Line elevated structure (BMT): Kings Highway to Ave X (Brooklyn) opened
16 Mar 1919	Culver Line elevated structure (BMT): 9th Ave to Kings Highway (Brooklyn) opened
16 Mar 1919	Culver Line elevated structure (BMT): Ave X to Stillwell Ave (Brooklyn) opened
15 Apr 1919	7th Ave Line (IRT): Wall St (Manhattan) to Borough Hall (Brooklyn) opened
10 July 1919	Broadway Line (BMT): Times Square to 57th St (Manhattan) opened
30 May 1920	Pelham Line (IRT): Hunts Point Ave to 177th St–Parkchester (Bronx) opened
1 Aug 1920	Broadway Line (BMT): 57th St (Manhattan) to Queensboro Plaza (Queens) opened
1 Aug 1920	Broadway Line (BMT): Whitehall St (Manhattan) to DeKalb Ave (Brooklyn) opened
1 Aug 1920	Brighton Line (BMT): DeKalb Ave to Prospect Park (Brooklyn) opened
23 Aug 1920	Eastern Parkway Line (BMT): Atlantic Ave to Utica Ave (Brooklyn) opened
23 Aug 1920	Nostrand Ave Line (IRT): Franklin Ave to Flatbush Ave (Brooklyn) opened
24 Oct 1920	Pelham Line (IRT): 177th St–Parkchester to Westchester Square (Bronx) opened
22 Nov 1920	New Lots Line (IRT): Utica Ave to Junius St (Brooklyn) opened
13 Dec 1920	White Plains Rd Line (IRT): 238th St to 241st St (Bronx) opened
20 Dec 1920	Pelham Line (IRT): Westchester Square to Pelham Bay Park (Bronx) opened
24 Dec 1920	New Lots Line (IRT): Junius St to Pennsylvania Ave (Brooklyn) opened
16 Oct 1922	New Lots Line (IRT): Pennsylvania Ave to New Lots Ave (Brooklyn) opened
6 Dec 1923	3d Ave Elevated (IRT): 42d St Branch (Manhattan) closed
16 June 1924	6th Ave Elevated (IRT): 58th St Spur (Manhattan) closed
30 June 1924	14th St–Canarsie Line (BMT): 6th Ave (Manhattan) to Montrose Ave (Brooklyn) opened
13 Oct 1925	Flushing Line (IRT): Junction Blvd to 103d St–Corona Plaza (Queens) opened
31 Oct 1925	4th Ave Line (BMT): 86th St to 95th St (Brooklyn) opened
22 Mar 1926	Flushing Line (IRT): Grand Central–42d St to 5th Ave (Manhattan) opened
14 May 1927	Flushing Line (IRT): 103d St–Corona Plaza to Willets Point Blvd (Queens) (now Willets Point Blvd–Shea Stadium) opened
21 Jan 1928	Flushing Line (IRT): Willets Point Blvd to Main St–Flushing opened
14 July 1928	14th St–Canarsie Line (BMT): Montrose Ave to Broadway Junction (Brooklyn) opened
16 Sept 1929	Second System Plan announced
14 July 1930	2d Ave Elevated (IRT): 34th St Branch (Manhattan) closed
30 May 1931	Nassau St Line (BMT): Broad St to Montague St Tunnel connection (Manhattan) opened
30 May 1931	14th St–Canarsie Line (BMT): 6th Ave to 8th Ave (Manhattan) opened
10 Sep 1932	8th Ave–Washington Heights Line (IND): Chambers St to 207th St (Manhattan) opened
1 Feb 1933	8th Ave–Washington Heights Line (IND): Chambers St (Manhattan) to Jay St–Borough Hall (Brooklyn) opened
30 Mar 1933	Smith St Line (IND): Jay St–Borough Hall to Bergen St (Brooklyn) opened
1 July 1933	Concourse Line (IND): 145th St (Manhattan) to 205th St (Bronx) opened
13 Aug 1933	Brooklyn-Queens Crosstown Line (IND): Queens Plaza (Queens) to Nassau Ave (Brooklyn) opened

continued on page 1084

GROWTH OF NEW YORK CITY SUBWAY SYSTEM (continued)

Date	Station or Line Segment
19 Aug 1933	Queens Blvd Line (IND): 53d St Line stations (Manhattan) to Roosevelt Ave–Jackson Heights (Queens) opened
7 Oct 1933	Smith St Line (IND): Bergen St to Church Ave (Brooklyn) opened
1 Jan 1936	6th Ave–Houston St Line (IND): West 4th St to 2d Ave (Manhattan) opened
9 Apr 1936	Fulton St Line (IND): Jay St to Rockaway Ave (Brooklyn) opened
9 Apr 1936	6th Ave–Houston St Line (IND): 2d Ave (Manhattan) to Jay St–Borough Hall (Brooklyn) opened
31 Dec 1936	Queens Blvd Line (IND): Roosevelt Ave–Jackson Heights to Union Tnpk–Kew Gardens (Queens) opened
24 Apr 1937	Queens Blvd Line (IND): Union Tnpk–Kew Gardens to 169th St (Queens) opened
1 July 1937	Brooklyn-Queens Crosstown Line (IND): Nassau Ave to Hoyt-Schermerhorn (Brooklyn) opened
31 Dec 1937	New York, Westchester and Boston Railway service ended; service would resume on East 180th St–Dyre Ave service on May 15, 1941, as part of the IRT
30 Apr 1939	Queens Blvd Line (IND) World's Fair Extension: 71st Continental Ave–Forest Hills to World's Fair (Queens) opened
31 May 1940	Fulton St Elevated service (BMT): City Hall and Fulton Ferry to Rockaway Ave (Brooklyn) ended
31 May 1940	5th Ave Elevated service (BMT): City Hall (Manhattan) to 65th St (Brooklyn) ended
15 May 1941	Dyre Ave Line opened as a subway line (IRT) (Bronx)
11 June 1940	6th and 9th Ave Elevated service (IRT): Battery to 155th St (Manhattan) ended
1 Oct 1941	Broadway Ferry branch of the Broadway-Brooklyn Line (BMT) (Brooklyn) closed
13 June 1942	2d Ave Elevated service (IRT): Battery (Manhattan) to Queensboro Plaza ended
1 June 1946	Fulton St Shuttle service (IND): Hoyt-Schermerhorn to Court St. (Brooklyn) ended; the Court St station would later be used as the New York Transit Museum
30 Dec 1946	Fulton St Line (IND): Rockaway Ave to Broadway–East New York (Brooklyn) opened
20 Nov 1948	Fulton St Line: Broadway–East New York to Euclid Ave (Brooklyn) opened
13 Oct 1950	Lexington Ave (Brooklyn) Elevated service (BMT) discontinued
10 Dec 1950	Queens Blvd Line (IND): 169th St to 179th St (Queens) opened
4 Aug 1952	White Plains Rd: Bronx Park Spur (IRT) (Bronx) closed
31 Dec 1953	3d Ave Elevated: City Hall Spur (Manhattan) closed
30 Oct 1954	Smith St Line (IND): Church Ave to connection with the Culver Line opened (Brooklyn)
12 May 1955	3d Ave Elevated (IRT): 149th St (Bronx) to Hanover Square (Manhattan) closed
27 Apr 1956	Fulton St Elevated service (BMT): Rockaway Ave to Grant Ave (Brooklyn) ended
29 Apr 1956	Fulton St Line (IND): Euclid Ave to connection with Fulton St El (Brooklyn) opened
28 June 1956	Rockaway Line (IND) opened: Fulton St Line connection to the Hammels "Wye" (Queens)
28 June 1956	Far Rockaway Line (IND): Hammels "Wye" to Beach 25th St–Wavecrest (Queens) opened
28 June 1956	Rockaway Park Line (IND): entire length (Queens) opened
1 Jan 1957	Dyre Ave Line connected to White Plains Rd Line (IRT) (Bronx)
16 Jan 1958	Far Rockaway Line: Beach 25th St–Wavecrest to Mott Ave–Far Rockaway (Queens) opened
31 Aug 1958	9th Ave Elevated (IRT): 155th St (Manhattan) to connection with the Jerome Ave Line (Bronx) closed
26 Nov 1967	Chrystie St connections (IND/BMT) (Manhattan)
13 May 1968	Lenox Ave Line (IRT) extended to 148th St–Lenox Terminal (Manhattan)
1 July 1968	6th Ave Line (IND/BMT): 47–50th St–Rockefeller Center to 57th St (Manhattan) opened
3 Oct 1969	Myrtle Ave Elevated service (BMT): Bridge–Jay St to Broadway (Brooklyn) closed
6 Apr 1973	Bronx segment of the 3d Ave Elevated (IRT) closed
11 May 1975	Culver Line service (BMT) (Brooklyn) discontinued
11 Sept 1977	Jamaica Ave Elevated service (BMT): 168th St to Queens Blvd (Queens) closed
15 Apr 1985	Jamaica Ave Elevated service (BMT): Queens Blvd to 121st St (Queens) closed
11 Dec 1988	Archer Ave Line: Jamaica Center–Parsons Blvd to Briarwood–Van Wyck Blvd and 121st St (BMT/IND) opened
26 Oct 1989	63d St Line (BMT/IND): 57th St (Manhattan) to 21st St–Queensbridge (Queens) opened
16 Dec 2001	63d St Line (BMT/IND): 21st St–Queensbridge to connection with the Queens Blvd Line (Queens) opened
17 Dec 2003	AirTrain JFK (Port Authority): Sutphin Blvd (Queens) to JFK International Airport to Howard Beach (Queens)

Abbreviations: IRT: Interborough Rapid Transit Co; BMT: Brooklyn-Manhattan Transit Co; IND: Independent Subway System.

[a]The Astoria Line (and to a lesser extent the Flushing Line) were built for joint BMT/IRT service.

[b]Elevated line directly built by the IRT. Other Manhattan els were not built by the IRT but rather by other companies that became the Manhattan Elevated Railway Co, which later merged with the IRT.

Compiled by Joseph Raskin

an urban populist who condemned the IRT and BMT companies for monopolistic behavior and poor passenger service. Hylan wanted the IND to compete with the private companies and thereby wrest more favorable terms from them. The smallest of the three systems, the IND was primarily confined to highly developed areas and had little effect on urban growth. The IND represented the last major phase of subway construction in New York City.

From the 1920s the subway system experienced financial difficulties. Rising costs after World War I created a crisis as the IRT and BMT companies were prohibited by contract from raising the 5¢ fare. The companies' demands for a fare hike in the 1920s met resistance from a public embittered by past transit monopolies and by poor passenger service. This emergency led to deferral of maintenance and repairs and reduction of new rolling-stock purchases. After the Great Depression threatened failure of the subways, New York City unified the three separate networks—IRT, BMT, and IND—in 1940 into a single, municipally run system under the auspices of the New York City Board of Transportation. In 1947 the fare was raised to 10¢ and in 1953 to 15¢, requiring the introduction of tokens. The same year the New York City Transit Authority (NYCTA) was created by the state to run the city's subways and buses. The NYCTA was incorporated into the Metropolitan Transportation Authority (MTA) in 1968.

By the 1930s almost all new transportation improvements in metropolitan New York were highways. The shift of transportation funding from the municipal government to the federal government in the 1930s and 1940s confirmed the preference for highways. Since the completion of the IND in 1940, the subway system

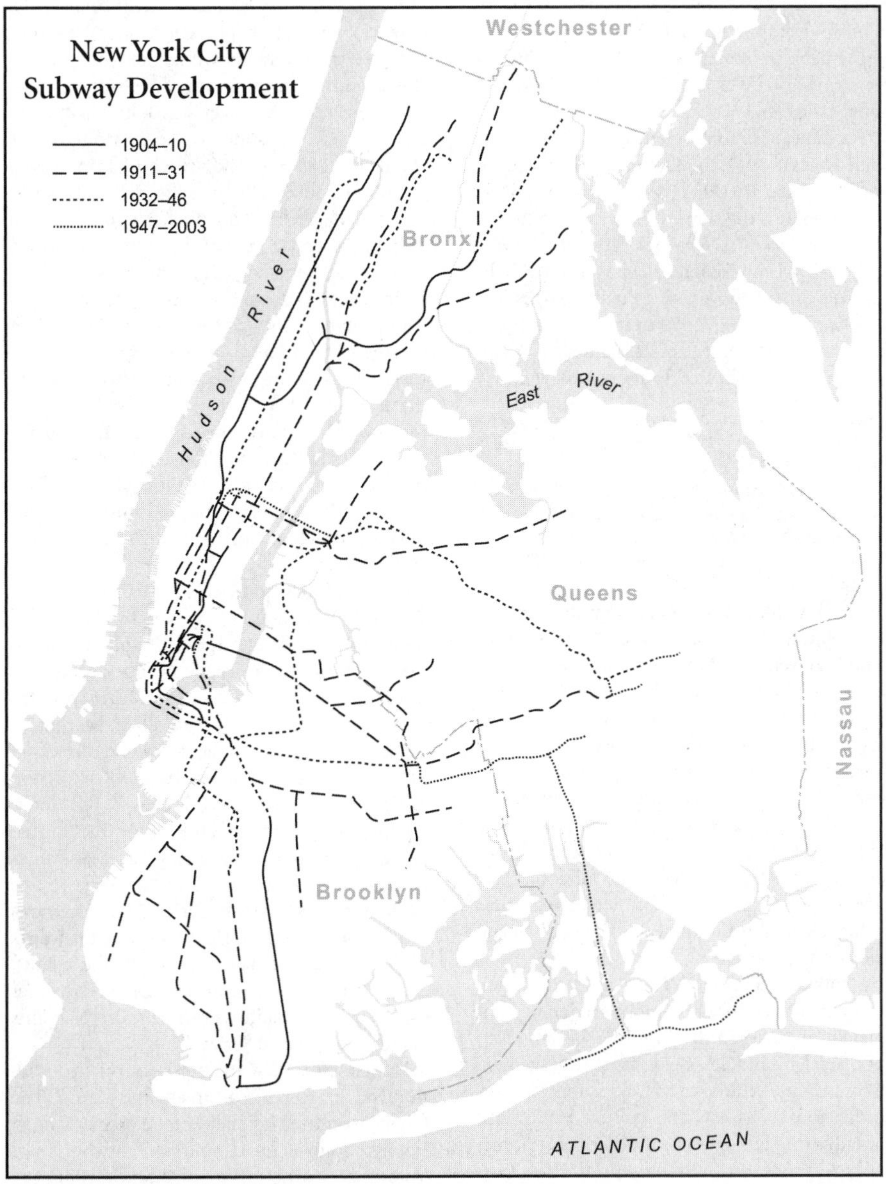

has only two entirely new routes, the Dyre Ave line (1941) in the Bronx and the Rockaway line (1956) in Queens. Ridership reached a peak of 2,051 billion riders in 1947, but unification had not solved the subways' financial problems. Political opposition to municipal subsidies, coupled with growing competition from automobiles, led to the system's decline. The long-discussed Second Ave subway in Manhattan and a new Queens line were included in a 1968 MTA plan, but financial problems halted most construction in the mid-1970s. By 1980 most of the subway system was mechanically unreliable and physically dilapidated.

The MTA began to rehabilitate the subways in 1982. Improvements included replacement or overhaul of 6,003 cars, rehabilitation of 145 of the 468 stations, and rebuilding of every mile of main-line track. In 1989 a section of the delayed Queens line—the tunnel from Manhattan's 63d St to Queensbridge—entered service. In 1994 the MTA started to replace subway tokens with electronic fare cards (Metrocards), offering discounts on the cards by 1998. These improvements, along with a strong national economy and decreasing urban crime, increased subway ridership, and in the late 1990s the authority made plans to construct the long-postponed Second Ave route. In 2001, 1,445 billion people rode the subways.

The 11 Sept 2001 attack on the World Trade Center completely disrupted transit service downtown by crushing the tunnel that carries the subway's No. 1 and No. 9 lines, and by destroying portions of the Port Authority Trans-Hudson (PATH) subway route that runs from Lower Manhattan to Jersey City, NJ. The New York City Transit Authority reopened the subway in September 2002, ahead of schedule and under budget, an engineering feat that helped Lower Manhattan recover from its economic devastation. The PATH line reopened in late 2003.

Cudahy, Brian. *Under the Sidewalks of New York: The Story of the Greatest Subway System in the World* (Brattleboro, Vt: Stephen Greene Press, 1979)
Derrick, Peter. *Tunneling to the Future: The Story of the Great Subway Expansion That Saved New York City* (New York: New York Univ Press, 2001)
Hood, Clifton. *722 Miles: The Building of the Subways and How They Transformed New York* (New York: Simon & Schuster, 1993)

Clifton Hood

New York City Technical College. Public college, part of the City University of New York (CUNY). The New York State Institute of Applied Arts and Sciences was established in downtown Brooklyn at 300 Jay St in 1946. Under Otto Klitgord, director of the institute, the first class entered on 5 Feb 1947. In 1948 the school became a unit of the State University of New York, focusing on occupational programs. As New York City's only state-assisted college of technology, the institute provided training for the military in such fields as dental laboratory technology. In 1952 the college came under the administration of the New York City Board of Estimate as New York City Community College of Applied Arts and Sciences. In 1971 it merged with Voorhees Technical Institute (founded 1881). The school became part of CUNY in 1974 and adopted its present name in 1980, when it was authorized to grant the baccalaureate as well as the associate degree. City Tech, as it is popularly known, offers career-oriented certificate and degree programs in business and management, engineering technologies, health-related occupations, human services, and liberal arts. In fall 2002 New York City Technical College enrolled 7,245 full-time and 4,454 part-time students.

Roff, Sandra Shoiock, Anthony M. Cucchiara, and Barbara J. Dunlap. *From the Free Academy to CUNY: Illustrating Public Higher Education in New York City, 1847–1997* (New York: Fordham Univ Press, 2000)

Pamela Cooper

New York Conference of Mayors and Municipal Officials (NYCOM). Organization founded in 1911, a year after 49 New York State mayors met to discuss urban health matters. Dedicated to helping local governments lobby the governor and the state legislature on local issues, the organization in 1915 hired a full-time director and established a municipal information bureau. In 1923 the organization recommended the state legislature's passage of laws to better protect state milk supplies. Typically the mayor of New York City is the best-known member of the group. During the Great Depression, New York City mayor Fiorello La Guardia pushed the state legislature, through NYCOM, for more state aid to localities. In recent decades much of the work of the organization has been devoted to monitoring changes in the state's mandates to local governments. Since 2000 NYCOM has forcefully pushed for the repeal of the Wicks Law, a state provision that requires local governments to use multiple contractors on construction projects. NYCOM is chartered by the Board of Regents to carry out training for elected officials and their staff, and it holds general meetings, training seminars, and regional conferences annually. Headquartered in Albany, in 2002 NYCOM represented 573 cities, towns, and villages in New York State.

New York Conference of Mayors and Municipal Officials, http://www.nycom.org/

Richard M. Flanagan

New York Council for the Humanities. Private, nonprofit institution dedicated to educating young people in the humanities. Organized in 1975, the council is among 56 state councils on the humanities in the United States. Based in New York City with seven full-time staff members, it receives an annual budget appropriation of $1.8 million from the National Endowment for the Humanities and donations and grants from the New York State Education Department, private foundations, corporations, and individuals. The council strongly discourages charging any admission fee for public films, lectures, and exhibits, and supports a variety of educational and professional development projects with teachers, schools, and cultural institutions. These include the annual Young Scholars Contest, an essay contest for high school students. Council grants have funded such projects as the reinterpretation of an Iroquois village on the grounds of the New York State Fair in Syracuse and an exhibit and conferences in West Park (Ulster Co) on African Americans in the mid-Hudson Valley since World War II. The annual, week-long Humanities Teacher Institute was initiated in 1990. Every October the council celebrates New York history and culture with its State Humanities Month (begun in 1998), featuring exhibitions and lectures. The Speakers in the Humanities project provides a list of over 200 lectures and topics, with subsidies available for not-for-profit institutions to present them.

New York Council for the Humanities, http://www.nyhumanities.org

Dorothy M. Browne

New York County. See MANHATTAN.

New York Daily News. First tabloid newspaper in United States. Founded by Capt Joseph Medill Patterson and Col Robert McCormick and first published 26 June 1919 as the *Illustrated Daily News.* The name was changed to its present form on 20 Nov 1920. Patterson and McCormick were both heirs to the Medill family, which owned the *Chicago Tribune,* and the *Tribune* financed the start-up. During World War I both men served in Europe, where the picture-heavy, reader-friendly tabloid format was popular, and Patterson's goal was to introduce one to this country.

After a slow start during the summer of 1919, the *Daily News* soon won favor among readers for its emphasis on photographs, crime, features, and local news; it turned a profit in 1920 after little more than a year in operation. Its front-page photograph of convicted murderer Ruth Snyder at the moment of her execution at Sing Sing Prison (Westchester Co) sparked protests and sold hundreds of thousands of copies in 1927. Popular items that regularly appeared included the "Inquiring Fotographer" column, which asked questions of average New Yorkers and printed their pictures and responses in the newspaper; color comics; and features on the annual Golden Gloves boxing competition, a *Daily News*-sponsored contest started in 1929 that continues into the early 21st century. After World War II the editorial policy became extremely conservative, although in recent decades it has moderated. The paper remains a favorite for its sensational headlines and punchy copy. In 1975, when Pres Gerald R. Ford rebuffed the city's request for financial aid, the resulting front-page headline—"Ford to City: Drop Dead"—became an instant classic. Ford later said the headline cost him New York State in the 1976 presidential election.

The *Daily News* was owned by the Tribune Co until March 1991, when British media magnate Robert Maxwell bought it. The newspaper's sale ended a violence-marred five-month strike that halted publication. But Maxwell, hailed by the unions as a savior, died mysteriously in November of that year, and the *Daily News* filed for bankruptcy protection a month afterward as his publishing empire began to collapse under staggering debt. In January 1993 Mortimer Zuckerman, who also owns *US News and World Report,* bought the *Daily News.*

The paper's circulation peaked at 2,377,000 daily copies in 1947; in March 2003 daily circulation stood at 737,030 copies, placing it sixth in the nation. It is the third most widely circulated newspaper based in New York City, with the *Wall Street Journal* and *New York Times* ahead of it. By 2004 the paper had won nine Pulitzer Prizes. The latest was awarded in 1999 to its editorial board for a series of opinion pieces aimed at saving Harlem's Apollo Theater from financial ruin.

Bessie, Simon Michael. *Jazz Journalism: The Story of the Tabloid Newspapers* (1938; repr New York: Russell & Russell, 1969)

Chapman, John Arthur. *Tell It to Sweeney: The Informal History of the "New York Daily News"* (Garden City, NY: Doubleday, 1961)

Kenneth Aaron

New York Folklore Society. Nonprofit organization founded in Albany on 6 Oct 1944 at the annual convention of the New York State Historical Association. Harold Thompson became its first president and Louis Jones the first editor of its journal, the *New York Folklore Quarterly.* The function of the society and its journal was, as Jones said, "to plow back" into the community the folklore collected by scholars and laypeople. Early issues of the journal were concerned with the collection of New York State folklore. They gave voice to then current luminaries in the field such as Benjamin Botkin, Emelyn Gardner, and Thompson and Jones.

As folklore developed as an academic discipline, the society became more academic in its orientation. In 1975 the *Quarterly* became *New York Folklore* and lessened its encouragement of community scholars and folklore enthusiasts. In the mid-1980s arts and culture institutions started hiring folklorists and other cultural specialists to research and present the folk arts and traditional ways of life of their communities. With a new constituency to serve, the society began to reestablish its connections with nonacademic folklorists, folk artists, folk arts enthusiasts, and other cultural specialists. For its service to the field of folk arts in New York State, the society was designated a "primary institution" in 1989 by the New York State Council on the Arts as being "particularly important to the cultural life of New York State, with its loss constituting a serious artistic loss to the people in the State."

In 1990 the society opened an office in Ithaca and hired its first full-time executive director. Headquartered in Schenectady since 1999, the society has become a leader as a statewide service organization for the field of folk and traditional arts, with more than 400 members worldwide in 2002. Programs and services include folk arts forums throughout the state, technical assistance programs, radio documentaries featuring folk life in New York State, and a New York State folk artists' gallery in Schenectady.

Jones, Louis. "Early Days of the Folklore Renaissance." In *Upstate Literature,* ed. Frank Bergmann (Syracuse: Syracuse Univ Press, 1958)

Ellen McHale

New York Giants (baseball). With the dissolution of the Troy (Rensselaer Co) Trojans after the 1882 season, many former Trojans formed the core of a new National League team in New York City. It was briefly known as the Gothams before acquiring the nickname the Giants in 1884. The team's first manager was John Clapp, and an early star was shortstop John Montgomery Ward. In 1885 Jim Mutrie, who had managed the Metropolitans, became the National League club's manager, bringing pitcher Tim Keefe with him. Democratic politician Andrew Freedman acquired the team in 1895; in his constant interference with his team and players, Freedman was a forerunner of sorts of New York Yankees owner George Steinbrenner. Freedman hired John McGraw as manager in 1902. Freedman sold the team in 1903 to John T. Brush, who gave McGraw control over the team's on-field operations. In 1911 the Giants moved into New York's first concrete-and-steel stadium, the new Polo Grounds (known until 1919 as Brush Stadium) at West 159th St between Coogan's Bluff and the Harlem River.

Between 1902 and 1932 McGraw's teams dominated the National League, winning the World Series in 1905, 1921, and 1922 and coming in first or second in the league 11 times. McGraw's leading players included pitchers Christy Mathewson, Joe McGinnity, and Rube Marquard, catcher Roger Bresnahan, second baseman Frankie Frisch, outfielder Mel Ott, shortstop Travis Jackson, and first baseman Bill Terry. Olympian Jim Thorpe signed a contract for the 1913 season, played in 152 regular season games over the next six seasons, and appeared in one game in the 1917 World Series. After McGraw's retirement in 1932, Bill Terry became the team's player-manager. During the 1930s the Giants, led by the home-run-hitting Ott and pitcher Carl Hubbell, would win three more pennants and the 1933 World Series.

The Giants ended the 1951 season tied with the Dodgers, forcing a three-game playoff. The Giants won the National League pennant when Bobby Thomson hit a home run, "the shot heard 'round the world," off Ralph Branca, climaxing a Giant comeback. That year outfielder Willie Mays joined the Giants and was named Rookie of the Year. The Giants won their last World Series in New York in 1954, defeating the Cleveland Indians. In May 1957 the National League authorized the Giants to begin negotiations to move to San Francisco. On 29 Sept 1957 the Giants played their last game in New York.

Graham, Frank, and Ray Robinson. *The New York Giants* (Carbondale: Southern Illinois Univ Press, 2002)

Thornley, Stew. *Land of the Giants: New York's Polo Grounds* (Philadelphia: Temple Univ Press, 2000)

Jeffrey Kraus

New York Giants (football). In 1925 the National Football League (NFL) created a New York–based team in hopes of adding credibility to the league. Tim Mara, a legal bookmaker, paid $500 for the Giants franchise that played its home games at the Polo Grounds. In 1930 Mara would turn over formal ownership of the team to his sons Jack and Wellington. The team won its first NFL championship with the best record in the league in 1927. Two more championships followed in 1934 and 1938 under head coach Steve Owen (1931–53). The 1934 championship contest is renowned as the "sneakers game" because Giants players donned basketball shoes for the second half in the icy Polo Grounds and pulled away from the Chicago Bears for a 30-13 win. The Giants returned to the championship game four more times (1939, 1941, 1944, 1946) but did not win another title until 1956, the year the team moved from the Polo Grounds to Yankee Stadium. Head coach Jim Lee Howell (1954–60) and defensive coordinator Vince Lombardi (1954–58) directed an intimidating defense featuring middle linebacker Sam Huff (1956–63). Donning sneakers again because of icy conditions, the Giants trounced the Chicago Bears (47-7) for the 1956 championship.

That would be their last NFL championship for 30 years. In 1958 New York and Baltimore battled for the title in Yankee Stadium in what is often called the greatest game ever played. The Colts prevailed in the first sudden-death overtime game in NFL history (23-17) on Alan Ameche's 1 yd run. The Giants lost the championship to Baltimore again the next year. Head coach Allie Sherman (1961–68) and quarterback Y. A. Tittle (1961–64) led the team to championship games each year from 1961 to 1963, but the Giants lost every time.

They had winning records only twice over the next 17 seasons. The highlight of the period may have been the team's 1976 move to Giants Stadium in the Meadowlands Sports Complex in New Jersey. But the Giants continued to lose, despite support from so-called diehard Giants fans who have sold out the stadium for virtually every game since their Meadowlands debut against the Dallas Cowboys. The team's poor play was epitomized by the "fumble game" late in the 1978 season: instead of falling on the ball to run out the clock, the Giants ran a play, quarterback Joe Pisarcik fumbled, and Philadelphia's Herman Edwards returned it for the game-winning touchdown. Change came with the arrival of general manager George Young (1979–97), quarterback Phil Simms (1979–93), linebacker Lawrence Taylor (1981–93), and head coach Bill Parcells (1983–90). In 1986 the Giants were 14-2 and defeated Denver (39-20) in Super Bowl XXI. New York returned to the Super Bowl in 1991, edging Buffalo (20-19) in one of the most exciting title games ever played. The following year Tim Mara, nephew of the founder, sold his 50% interest in the team to businessman Preston Robert Tisch. The 2000 Giants reached the NFL title game, losing Super Bowl XXXV to the Baltimore Ravens (34-7).

Izenberg, Jerry. *New York Giants: 75 Years* (Alexandria, Va: Time-Life Books, 1999)
Whittingham, Richard. *The Giants: An Illustrated History, from the Polo Grounds to Super Bowl XXI* (New York: Harper & Row, 1987)

Randy Lange

New York Guard. In August 1917 a homeland defense force was created by the adjutant general of New York to replace New York National Guard (NYNG) units, which had been federalized. The New York Guard (NYG) located drill units at all armories; these units retained the same numerical designations as the activated units they replaced. To guard public property, a provisional brigade headquarters at Albany and two provisional regiments were organized for active state service. The First Provisional Regiment, composed of veterans and New York City policemen who volunteered their off-duty time, guarded the New York City water supply system. The Second Provisional Regiment was responsible for the area from Troy and Albany to Niagara Falls. The NYG numbered 22,000 officers and men by January 1919. When the NYNG units returned from World War I, they assumed their old state militia designations and returned to their armories, often consolidated with the NYG units. While some NYG units continued adjacent to the returned units, the NYG as an entity ceased between the wars.

Preparing for US entry into World War II, New York State reactivated the NYG because the NYNG was federalized for training in 1940 and 1941. During the war the NYG was organized under a divisional structure with two brigades in New York City, a brigade in the Capital District, and a brigade in Western New York and Erie and Niagara Cos. NYG units guarded aqueducts, bridges, railroads, airports, and key governmental facilities. Numbering 24,722 officers and men in February 1944, the NYG developed distinctive insignias for its units, drawing on designs, devices, and campaigns associated with NYNG regiments and history. With the end of World War II and the return of NYNG units, the NYG continued as a cadre organization.

By the beginning of the 21st century the NYG had become more of a support force to the New York Army and Air National Guards, and had created a joint staff headquarters with an army division, an air division, and a civil affairs brigade. While maintaining its divisional structure, the army division now has five brigades, including two in the New York City area, one in Middle Hudson, one in the Capital District, and one in Western New York. The air division organizes air groups for support at the New York Air National Guard bases throughout the state. The civil affairs brigade has organized five regiments that provide legal services to military components throughout the state.

After the terrorist attacks of 11 Sept 2001, the NYG worked in communications and medical assistance, helped distribute emergency supplies, and guarded state armories. NYG members are not paid unless deployed and do not see service outside New York State.

Michael J. Stenzel

New York Herald Tribune. Daily newspaper created when Ogden Mills Reid, owner of the *New York Tribune,* bought the financially troubled *New York Herald* in 1924. The *Herald* had been founded in 1835 by James Gordon Bennett Sr, the *Tribune* in 1841 by Horace Greeley. The two pioneers of the penny papers, Bennett, a Democrat, and Greeley, who had helped launch the Republican Party, held each other in contempt. Evoking the epic rivalry, Greeley Square and Herald Square lie side by side at West 34th St and Broadway in Manhattan. In 1872 control of the *Tribune* was bought from Greeley's estate by Whitelaw Reid, an employee and stockholder who served as absentee publisher-editor while also minister to France and ambassador to Great Britain. His wife's fortune supported the paper for many years. The Reids' son Ogden took over the *Tribune* in 1912. The *Herald* was the more aggressive paper, not only quicker to report the news but also often more sensational. James Gordon Bennett Jr, who had become the *Herald's* editor in 1867, sent reporter Henry Morton Stanley to track down the missionary explorer Dr David Livingstone, supposedly lost in Africa; Stanley found Dr Livingstone in 1871.

The *Herald Tribune* was staunchly Republican, reporting national and world news with thoroughness rivaling the *New York Times,* its head-to-head competitor for educated readers. After Ogden Reid's death in 1946, his widow, Helen Rogers Reid, and their sons, first Whitelaw "Whitey" Reid, then Ogden "Brown" Reid, took charge until 1958, when they sold to financier John Hay Whitney. Under Whitney, *New York* magazine was started as a Sunday supplement in 1963. The "*Trib*" was known for stylish writing; its galaxy of columnists and reporters included Walter Lippmann, Joseph and Stewart Alsop, Red Smith, Dorothy Thompson, Virgil Thomson, Marguerite Higgins, Homer Bigart, Tom Wolfe, and Jimmy Breslin. Damaging strikes pushed the *Herald Tribune* and two other New York City newspapers into bankruptcy in 1966, after they unsuccessfully collaborated to publish a morning *Herald Tribune,* an afternoon *World Journal* (succeeding the *World-Telegram and Sun* and the *Journal-American*), and a Sunday *World Journal Tribune,* nicknamed the Widget. The three newspapers ended production in 1967. Ogden Reid acquired the Paris edition of the *Herald* when he bought the *New York Herald,* and the Paris-based *International Herald Tribune* is still published.

Childs, Marquis, and James Reston, eds. *Walter Lippmann and His Times* (New York: Harcourt, Brace, 1959)
Kluger, Richard. *The Paper: The Life and Death of the "New York Herald Tribune"* (New York: Knopf, 1986)
Van Deusen, Glyndon G. *Horace Greeley: 19th-Century Crusader* (Philadelphia: Univ of Pennsylvania Press, 1953)

Richard E. Mooney

New-York Historical Society. Founded in 1804 by banker John Pintard, Mayor De Witt Clinton, and eleven other New Yorkers, the New-York Historical Society (NYHS) is the state's oldest operating museum. Pintard contributed the beginnings of the library in 1807, and by 1813 the NYHS held over 4,000 books and 230 volumes of US documents. It had no permanent home until 1857, when it acquired a building at 2d Ave and 11th St, expedient for its acquisition of the entire collection of the New York Gallery of Fine Arts in 1858. The present colonnaded limestone building on Central Park West and 77th St was completed in 1908. Among the NYHS's treasures are John James Audubon's original watercolors for *The Birds of America* and an extensive collection of Louis C. Tiffany lamps and Hudson River school landscapes. The oldest research library in the United States, it has 350,000 books and pamphlets, 2 million manuscripts, and a vast collection of prints and photographs. Financial problems plagued the NYHS from the 1970s through the early 1990s. Starting in 1995 city and state grants and the directorship of Betsy Gotbaum stabilized the society's finances. In November 2000 the Henry Luce III Center for the Study of American Culture opened to assist research and to facilitate the exhibition and storage of the collection. The NYHS was the sponsor of the *Encyclopedia of New York City* (1995). In 2001 the encyclopedia's editor, Kenneth T. Jackson, became the president of the NYHS. In the early 21st century, the society has an endowment at $22.9 million and receives about 125,000 visitors annually.

New-York Historical Society, http://www.nyhistory.org

Richards, Pamela Spence. *Scholars and Gentlemen: The Library of the New-York Historical Society, 1804–1982* (Hamden, Conn: Archon Books, 1984)

Dorothy M. Browne

New York House of Refuge. The first juvenile reformatory in the nation. Opening in 1825 in an abandoned Manhattan federal arsenal, it moved to its permanent home on nearby Randall's Island in 1854. Throughout its history, it was operated by the Society for the Reformation of Juvenile Delinquents in the City of New York, a private philanthropic organization. State government was closely involved with the reformatory from the beginning, providing partial funding from legislative appropriations and from license fees on taverns and theaters. The State Board of Charities supervised the institution and helped create policies and procedures.

The House of Refuge received each year approximately 300 boys and girls under the age of 16 for indefinite terms, not to exceed the age of 21 for males and 18 for females. Most had been arrested for vagrancy or petty crimes. Initially the institution received youths from across the state, but after the Western House of Refuge in Rochester opened in 1849, it received youths only from the eastern counties. Male inmates worked eight hours a day on contract labor, producing brushes, chairs, nails, shoes, and other articles for sale. Female inmates made clothing and performed domestic chores. Inmates received four hours a day of school instruction and attended Protestant religious classes. Most eventually were indentured to work on farms, in trades, or in domestic service. Dozens of boys also were indentured to whaling ships. During the Civil War, several hundred boys enlisted directly from the reformatory into the Union army. The House of Refuge served as a model for other juvenile reformatories and became a necessary stop on tours by penal reformers.

Beginning in the 1880s political and societal changes necessitated reorganization. Indenturing and contract labor were replaced with a system of industrial education. Nonsectarian parole agents were hired in place of Protestant chaplains. Military drill became a daily routine for boys, and corporal punishment was reduced. As the benefits of rural reformatory settings gained favor, inmates were gradually transferred to new state institutions outside of New York City. Beginning in 1901 female inmates were transferred to the New York Reformatory for Women at Bedford (Westchester Co). By 1932 males under 16 were being sent to the State Training School for Boys at Warwick (Orange Co), and in 1935 those 16–19 were transferred to the New York State Vocational Institution at Coxsackie (Greene Co). Later in 1935 the society managing the House of Refuge dissolved, and the institution closed.

Golding, Elizabeth A., and Kathleen Roe. *The Greatest Reform School in the World: A Guide to the Records of the New York House of Refuge* (Albany: NYS Archives and Records Administration, 1989)

Pickett, Robert S. *House of Refuge: Origins of Juvenile Reform in New York State, 1815–1857* (Syracuse: Syracuse Univ Press, 1969)

Richard Andress

New York Institute of Technology. Private college. It was founded in 1955 by educator Alexander Schure, whose family members headed the college for 45 years. It specializes in technology and medical fields. Opening in Brooklyn in 1955, the school developed its Manhattan campus in 1958; the Old Westbury (Nassau Co) campus followed in 1964 and the Central Islip (Suffolk Co) campus in 1984. The college has eight undergraduate schools and nine graduate schools, offering degrees in more than 100 majors. A Doctor of Osteopathy degree is also offered at its New York College of Osteopathic Medicine (chartered 1977), the first school of its kind in New York State, located on the Old Westbury campus. The majority of students commute, although some student housing is available at Central Islip. In 2002 more than 10,000 students were enrolled, 7,500 of them undergraduates.

Laura E. Mann

New York intellectuals. Arguably the most influential circle of American intellectuals in the post–World War II period. From the 1940s to the 1960s this remarkable group of writers and critics helped shape literary and artistic taste in the United States, thus adding to the cultural preeminence of New York City, as well as to the transatlantic cultural prestige of the United States during the Cold War. Dubbed "the New York intellectuals" by Irving Howe in his 1968 essay of the same name, many shared a common background despite their differences. Most were first-generation Jews from New York City and emerged from the left-wing political milieu of the 1930s. They gained their reputation by forging a unique union between cultural modernism and radical politics while espousing secular, liberal, and universalist values that gave precedence to the individual, to moral complexity, and to antitotalitarianism. The most prominent among them included the writers and critics Saul Bellow, Irving Howe, Alfred Kazin, Mary McCarthy, William Phillips, Norman Podhoretz, Philip Rahv, Delmore Schwartz, Diana and Lionel Trilling; art critics Clement Greenberg, Harold Rosenberg, and Meyer Schapiro; social critics Daniel Bell, Nathan Glazer, Irving Kristol, and Dwight Macdonald; philosopher Sidney Hook; and historian Richard Hofstadter. Closely related figures included James Agee, Hannah Arendt, Kenneth Burke, John Dewey, C. Wright Mills, Reinhold Niebuhr, George Orwell, Arthur Schlesinger Jr, and Edmund Wilson.

The New York intellectuals coalesced around the group's chief periodical, *Partisan Review,* founded in 1934 by editors William Phillips and Philip Rahv. Originally one of many proletarian "little" magazines under the auspices of the Communist Party, in 1937 the magazine was reestablished by Phillips and Rahv with a commitment to independent, anti-Stalinist socialism and literary modernism. Within a decade it had become the most formidable literary magazine of its day, eventually spawning such influential publications as *Politics* (1944–49), *Commentary* (1945–), *Dissent* (1954–), the *New York Review of Books* (1963–), *Public Interest* (1965–), and the *New Criterion* (1982–).

Employing a distinctively sharp, polemical style, which Irving Howe characterized as "freelance dash, peacock strut, daring hypothesis, knockabout synthesis," the New York intellectuals waged a series of key cultural battles that continue to influence American cultural and intellectual life. The first of these was the successful campaign to discredit Stalinism and the Communist Party during the 1930s and early 1940s. The New York intellectuals attacked the Party for its subordination to the interests of the Soviet Union and the Comintern. They dissented from the Party on several key international issues, such as the Spanish civil war, the Moscow show trials, and the Hitler-Stalin nonaggression pact.

On literary matters they assailed the Party for what they perceived to be its politically expedient and corrupt practices, evidenced by the sudden and dramatic shift in 1935 from doctrinaire Marxism, which had led Party critics to chastise "bourgeois" writers like James Joyce, to building an unprincipled "popular Front" at home and championing mediocre "celebrity" writers like Howard Fast. On this literary battlefield they joined with the New Critics in replacing both the "progressive" and the traditional literary canons of the 1930s with a modernist and cosmopolitan one, championing an earlier generation of writers and contemporary European writers that included T. S. Eliot, William Faulkner, F. Scott Fitzgerald, Ernest Hemingway, James Joyce, Franz Kafka, Arthur Koestler, D. H. Lawrence, André Malraux, George Orwell, Marcel Proust, Ignazio Silone, and William Butler Yeats. Among contemporary American writers they enthusiastically endorsed William Faulkner and Ralph Ellison, and secured the ascendancy of the Jewish American novel by heaping praise on the young Saul Bellow and Philip Roth. In the visual arts Clement Greenberg, Harold Rosenberg, and Meyer Schapiro exerted enormous influence in gaining a worldwide reputation for the New York school of abstract expressionists, the first indigenous American group of painters to triumph in the international art world.

During the 1940s the New York intellectuals endorsed modernism's critical spirit and complexity as a corrective to the instrumentalism and rationalism of what Trilling called "the liberal imagination"—the attitudes and habits of mind of liberals and progressives. Gradually their unease with modernist politics (Ezra Pound's anti-Semitism, D. H. Lawrence's "blood consciousness," Jean Genet's amoralism) became more pronounced. Most, for instance, opposed awarding the 1949 Bollingen Prize to Ezra Pound for his *Pisan Cantos,* which contained several blatantly anti-Semitic passages. During the Cold War the New York intellectuals' anticommunism and gradual shift rightward from socialism (although some, such as Irving Howe and Philip Rahv, remained avowed socialists) added to their influence. McCarthyism presented both opportunities and challenges. As former communists, many knew the movement well and spoke with authority about its ideology and character. On the other hand, assessing the relative dangers of communism versus Sen Joseph McCarthy's attacks on civil liberties proved extremely difficult. As a group the New York intellectuals tended to be critical of McCarthy, but their hatred of the Communist Party made them less critical than many other liberals and leftists. During the 1950s most New York intellectuals echoed Dwight Macdonald's public pronouncement, "I choose the West" in the face of the Soviet threat. Nevertheless they continued to critique American culture, roundly condemning, for instance, the dull conformity of what they perceived to be an increasingly administered and banal mass culture.

The New York intellectuals were active supporters of the Civil Rights Movement and opponents of the Vietnam War, with varying degrees of intensity. Some only gradually came to disapprove of the war, while others, like the editors of the *New York Review of Books* and the writer Mary McCarthy, who visited Hanoi in 1967, were early and vociferous opponents. However, few of the New York intellectuals were impressed with the rebellious Beat writers of the 1950s or the New Left and counterculture of the 1960s. Many took the opportunity to attack these emerging cultural and political trends, which the New Yorker Harry Levin was the first to label "postmodern" in 1960. Some —Nathan Glazer, Hilton Kramer, William Kristol, Seymour Martin Lipset, and Norman Podhoretz—founded the neoconservative movement in the 1970s in the wake of the perceived excesses of the 1960s. In reaction to the left's alleged coarsening of cultural life and attack on democratic and entrepreneurial values, the neoconservatives fiercely upheld traditional highbrow culture and a commitment to political stability and moderation.

By the 1960s many New York intellectuals had acquired positions of influence and authority within academia and government policymaking. Since then many members of groups whose values were shaped by the movements of that decade, such as feminism, gay liberation, environmentalism, black liberation, and ethnic pride, have regarded the New Yorkers as increasingly superannuated, variously citing their disdain or indifference toward popular culture (including jazz, modern dance, theater, film, and television), Eurocentric neglect of third world and minority cultural figures, skepticism toward feminism and neglect of women writers outside their circle, gradual substitution of psychoanalysis for social analysis, contempt for academic scholarship, and general avoidance of Jewish experience, including the Holocaust.

Many of these charges, however, can be refuted. Regarding popular culture, for instance, Dwight Macdonald, Robert Warshow, and James Agee produced compelling film criticism, and Mary McCarthy wrote regularly on theater for nearly 20 years; moreover, Macdonald's corrosive analysis of mass culture, although overly critical, is to be preferred to the recent trend of celebrating the alleged subversions of even the most formulaic and tame of cultural commodities. As to their neglect of the range of minority, third world, and women writers, the New York intellectuals' record stood up well, given the standards of the time: to have presented and promoted the work of James Baldwin, Ralph Ellison, Hannah Arendt, Elizabeth Bishop, Elizabeth Hardwick, Mary McCarthy, Tess Slesinger, and Susan Sontag was no insignificant achievement. The New York intellectuals' delayed response to the Holocaust did not in fact distinguish them from the American Jewish community as a whole. Their lack of interest in religion did not prevent intellectuals like Irving Howe from contributing substantially, in his several anthologies of Yiddish literature and in his classic *World of Our Fathers,* to the understanding of Jewish history and culture. The style and sensibility of the New York intellectuals remains alive, particularly within that portion of public intellectual life that emanates from New York City in such highly influential publications as the *New York Review of Books,* and the *New Yorker.*

Bloom, Alexander. *Prodigal Sons: The New York Intellectuals and Their World* (Oxford: Oxford Univ Press, 1986)

Teres, Harvey. *Renewing the Left: Politics, Imagination, and the New York Intellectuals* (Oxford: Oxford Univ Press, 1996)

Wald, Alan. *The New York Intellectuals: The Rise and Decline of the Anti-Stalinist Left from the 1930s to the 1980s* (Chapel Hill: Univ of North Carolina Press, 1987)

Harvey M. Teres

New York in the British Empire. Initially a Dutch colony that drove a wedge between English settlements in New England and the Chesapeake Bay, New York played a central role in the development of Britain's North American empire prior to the American Revolution. This decisive role reflected not only the colony's geographic significance in the Anglo-French wars fought between 1689 and 1783 but also the development of military, religious, and political institutions in New York that served British imperial interests.

Two major water routes made the colony a battleground between the French and British. The Hudson River–Lake Champlain corridor opened a door for invasion between French Canada and the northern English colonies, and the Mohawk River–Oneida Lake corridor provided an avenue to the Great Lakes and the continent's interior. These routes met in Albany, a city fundamentally Dutch in population and culture throughout the colonial period, but one that served as a center for British military encampments, Indian diplomacy, and intelligence-gathering during the Anglo-French wars for empire.

New York Colony occupied a special place in the British governance of North America. Whenever the Crown experimented with joining colonial governments under a single administration, New York figured in its plans. During the last two years of the Dominion of New England (1686–89), New York's government was joined with that of New Jersey and the New England colonies. At various points in subsequent decades, the Crown brought other colonies under the authority of New York's royal governor, including New Jersey (1702–38), Pennsylvania (1692–94), and Massachusetts and New Hampshire (1698–1701). Treating New York as an administrative center for the northern colonies offered strategic advantages in defending them against French and Indian enemies. Favoring neutrality to promote trade between Montreal and Albany, however, such efforts were checked by the rising power that the New York Assembly claimed over the colony's treasury and its royal governor.

During the 18th century New York Colony's role in the British Empire expanded in trade and communications. The colony's shipbuilding industry facilitated intercolonial trade, and it shipped beef, flour, pork, and wheat to the West Indies to feed slaves and British troops. After the 1707 Act of Union opened the British Empire to Scotland, numerous wealthy and educated Scots emigrated to New York, including Cadwallader Colden, Archibald Kennedy, and James Alexander. These well-connected Scots also strengthened the colony's cultural ties to the British Empire by participating in transatlantic correspondence on such topics as botany, philosophy, astronomy, and medicine. As New York's significance as a military and commercial hub grew, so too did its role as a center of communication. From 1710 to 1715 it was the American terminus for packet ship service initiated by the Crown between England and the colonies. New York City also served as the principal office of the North American postal service, created by Parliament in 1711.

The need to protect Albany and the Mohawk frontier led the British to concentrate their North American military establishment in New York Colony. Before 1755 New York and South Carolina were the only mainland colonies to have British regulars stationed there. The four independent companies in New York were notoriously understaffed and ill equipped, but they garrisoned a series of posts stretching from the eastern shore of Lake Ontario to the tip of Manhattan. During the French and Indian War (1754–63), British generals made New York the base of their operations, and when the Crown decided to maintain troops in North America after the war, commander in chief Gen Thomas Gage made his headquarters in New York City. Albany and New York City also provided winter quarters for the bulk of British troops in North America between 1755 and 1775, making quartering one of the most incendiary issues in the colony's relations with England prior to the American Revolution.

New York played a central role in the British Empire's relations with American Indian. The British administration of the Covenant Chain, the intercolonial alliance with the Iroquois confederation, remained under the leadership of New Yorkers during the colonial period. It was initially supervised by the Dutch magistrates of Albany, but by 1720 an imperialist faction had emerged in the colony's government that disliked Albany's neutralist approach to the French. Led by Gov William Burnet and supported by Cadwallader Colden and Robert Livingston, those involved pushed for a more aggressive policy against Canada. This included the establishment of Fort Oswego on Lake Ontario in 1727 as a new western terminus for the colony's fur trade. During the administration of Gov George Clinton (1743–53), this faction advanced British interests by advocating reforms in quitrent and customs collections, fortification of the frontier, and centralization of Indian affairs under a royal official. It achieved this last objective in 1755, when Sir William Johnson was appointed the Crown's Indian superintendent for the northern colonies.

New York's diverse population and tenuous Indian relations made it a focal point for missionary efforts by the Anglican Church. The Society for the Propagation of the Gospel, an Anglican missionary organization, devoted considerable energy to converting the Mohawk and promoting the Anglican faith among the colony's Dutch and French inhabitants. The Anglican establishment was stunted by the influx of Scots-Irish Presbyterians in the first half of the 18th century, but New York nonetheless became the intellectual and administrative center for the Anglican Church in the northern colonies.

The Revolutionary War fractured the British Empire in North America and ended imperial rule in New York. Yet in the aftermath of independence, the United States treated New York as the same sort of geographic and political springboard for its own expansionist plans. New York City as the new nation's capital (1789–1801), the continued volatility of the New York–Canadian border, and the Erie Canal's role as a route for western trade and immigration all testify to advantages inherited from the colonial era that would earn New York State its reputation as the

"Empire State," the name perhaps in part a reflection of its former role in the British Empire.

See also FORTIFICATIONS; MILITIA.

Jennings, Francis. *The Ambiguous Iroquois Empire: The Covenant Chain Confederation of Indian Tribes with English Colonies from Its Beginnings to the Lancaster Treaty of 1744* (New York: Norton, 1984)

Kammen, Michael. *Colonial New York: A History* (New York: Charles Scribner's Sons, 1975)

Matson, Cathy. *Merchants and Empire: Trading in Colonial New York* (Baltimore: Johns Hopkins Univ Press, 1998)

Norton, Thomas Elliot. *The Fur Trade in Colonial New York, 1686–1776* (Madison: Univ of Wisconsin Press, 1974)

Timothy J. Shannon

New York Islanders. Professional hockey team. Founded by owner Roy Boe as a National Hockey League (NHL) franchise in 1972, the team plays its home games at Nassau Coliseum in Uniondale. Bill Torrey, a St. Lawrence University graduate, became the first general manager. The team won only 12 games in its first season, and with new coach Al Arbour only 19 the next. However, the Islanders steadily improved over the subsequent few seasons, with goalie Billy Smith, an original Islander, and outstanding draft picks, including defenseman Dennis Potvin, center Bryan Trottier, and forwards Clark Gillis, Bobby Nystrom, and Mike Bossy. They finished first overall in the 1978–79 regular season but lost to the New York Rangers in the Stanley Cup semifinals. The next season the Islanders won the first of four consecutive Stanley Cup championships (1980–83). With the retirement of their star players by the end of the decade, the team became just one of several playoff contenders. During that period, though, the Islanders played one of the NHL's most memorable games—a quadruple overtime playoff win over the Washington Capitals in 1987. Since the mid-1990s the team has added stars like defenseman Kenny Jonsson, centers Michael Peca and Alexei Yashin, and goaltender Chris Osgood in an effort to recapture the success of the early 1980s.

Fischler, Stan, and Tom Sarro. *Metro Ice: A Century of Hockey in Greater New York* (Flushing, NY: H & M Productions, 1999)

Wilner, Barry. *The New York Islanders: Countdown to a Dynasty* (New York: Leisure Press, 1983)

Jack A. Bucco

New York Jets. One of the eight original American Football League (AFL) teams. The Jets began as the New York Titans when Harry Wismer was granted a franchise at the AFL's first organizational meeting in August 1959. Clad in blue and gold uniforms, they played at the Polo Grounds in Upper Manhattan. In the middle of the their third season, Wismer could not meet his payroll. The league took over the team until it was sold for $1 million in March 1963 to a five-man syndicate including entrepreneur David "Sonny" Werblin and oil magnate Leon Hess. The renamed Jets, with their new green uniforms, set up training camp in Peekskill (Westchester Co) and in 1964 moved their home field from the Polo Grounds to Shea Stadium. In 1965 the Jets signed quarterback Joe Namath (1965–76), and play gradually improved. The franchise's first winning season came in 1968 with an 11-3 record. Coach Weeb Ewbank (1963–73) led the team to the AFL championship and a 16-7 upset victory over the Baltimore Colts in Super Bowl III. The Jets returned to the playoffs in 1969 with a 10-4 record but did not have another playoff appearance or winning season until 1981. The following season they reached the American Football Conference (AFC) championship game.

In 1974 the Jets established their permanent training complex at Hofstra University in Hempstead (Nassau Co). A decade later, pointing to poor conditions at Shea Stadium, the Jets moved their home field to Giants Stadium in New Jersey. Also in 1984 Leon Hess took over sole ownership. The Jets reached the playoffs in 1985 and 1986 but followed with only one winning season and one playoff appearance in the next 10 years before hiring head coach Bill Parcells (1997–99). In 1998 Parcells led the Jets to a 12-4 record, the team's first division title since 1969, and a berth in the AFC championship game, in which they lost at Denver. Hess died in May 1999, and Parcells resigned after the Jets finished at 8-8 that year. On 18 Jan 2000 pharmaceuticals heir Robert Wood Johnson IV officially purchased the team from the Hess estate for $635 million.

Eskenazi, Gerald. *Gang Green* (New York: Simon & Schuster, 1998)

Ryczek, William J. *Crash of the Titans: The Early Years of the New York Jets and the AFL* (Kingston, NY: Total Sports, 2000)

Randy Lange

New York Knickerbockers. The Knickerbockers, commonly referred to as the Knicks, were named for New York's early Dutch settlers. The team was established 6 June 1946 when Madison Square Garden received a charter franchise in the Basketball Association of America, a forerunner of the National Basketball Association (NBA). Yonkers native Joe Lapchick (1947–56) coached the Knicks to three NBA Finals (1951–53), losing to Rochester and twice to Minneapolis. Nathaniel "Sweetwater" Clifton, one of the NBA's first African American players, was part of the 1950–51 team. Other members included Huntington (Suffolk Co) native Dick McGuire (1949–57) and Harry Gallatin (1948–57), both of whom later joined Lapchick in the Basketball Hall of Fame. The Knicks failed to make the playoffs from 1959 through 1966. The team improved under the guidance of Brooklyn native and former Rochester Royals player William "Red" Holzman, who coached them from 1967 to 1982, except for the 1977–78 season. In 1970 the Knicks won the NBA championship, defeating the Los Angeles Lakers in seven games. They were led by regular-season and finals Most Valuable Player (MVP) Willis Reed (1964–74), Walt Frazier (1967–77), Dave DeBusschere (1969–74), and Bill Bradley (1968–77). All four players would later be inducted into the Hall of Fame. That club, emphasizing pressure defense and teamwork, is considered one of the best teams in NBA history. The Knicks repeated as NBA champions in 1973, defeating the Lakers in five games. Reed, the only Knick ever voted league MVP, again won finals MVP honors. Other key players were future Hall of Famers Earl "the Pearl" Monroe (1971–80) and Jerry Lucas (1971–74). The Knicks had less success in subsequent years, with 10 losing seasons between 1974 and 1988. Better play came with the drafting of center Patrick Ewing (1985–2000). During the 1990s the Knicks had only one losing season (1990–91) and reached the finals twice with Ewing, an 11-time all-star. Under Rome (Oneida Co) native Pat Riley they lost to Houston in 1994, and under coach Jeff Van Gundy, a Nazareth College graduate, they lost to San Antonio in 1999. The talent of Knicks players through the years was recognized in 1997 when the NBA's selection of All-Time 50 Greatest Players included Ewing, Reed, Frazier, DeBusschere, Monroe, and Lucas.

Kalinsky, George. *The New York Knicks: The Official 15th Anniversary Celebration* (New York: Macmillan, 1996)

Mitch Lawrence

New York Manumission Society. In January 1785 the Society for Promoting the Manumission of Slaves began operating in New York City. Formed as an advocacy group for gradual abolitionism, it became known as the New York Manumission Society (NYMS) and was the nation's second abolitionist organization. The society established schools for free blacks, aided African Americans in courts of law, and fought for an end to overseas and domestic slave-trading practices. Its membership included prominent statesmen, such as John Jay and Alexander Hamilton, but was predominately Quaker. The Society of Friends, which began questioning the legitimacy of slavery in the 1750s and 1760s, contributed more than half of the members during the society's first three decades. Inspired by American Revolutionary ideology depicting slavery as anathema to democratic society, the society's inaugural members hoped to further antislavery sentiment unleashed during America's war with Britain and to pressure both masters and governing officials to abolish slavery. Beginning in 1785, it pushed the New York State legislature to pass an emancipation decree similar to one passed in Pennsylvania. Plans were foiled several times, including a proposed bill in the mid-1790s when John Jay was governor. In 1799 a gradual New York State abolition law was finally adopted: all slaves born after 4 July 1799 were to be registered and then freed at age 25 (men) and 28 (women). Abolitionists had to defend the law over the next several years as slave owners tried to overturn it. In 1827 the legislature adopted a final emancipation decree, in no small part because of the exertions of the Manumission Society and its African American allies.

The society agitated against the domestic and overseas slave trade in and around New York City, confronting ship captains who came into port with captured Africans and helping change a law allowing slave catchers to use city jails for fugitives captured in other states. It also helped end New York City laws permitting masters to bring unruly slaves to city prisons for punishment. In perhaps their most unheralded task, NYMS lawyers gave legal aid to several hundred distressed Blacks, particularly those accused of being fugitive slaves and men and women kidnapped into the domestic slave trade. The society sponsored several African Free Schools during the early Republic, the first in 1787 and others over the next few decades. By the 1820s more than 2,000 pupils had studied at one of the schools, including some of the leading pre–Civil War black activists, such as Henry Highland

Garnet and Alexander Crummell. By the late 1820s, however, some of the city's black leaders criticized the paternalistic attitude of the society's schools, even though most instructors were black. But the society did not encourage black members to join, and black activists were often treated as less-than-equal activists. For this reason, among others, it was bypassed by younger generations of abolitionists who favored immediate emancipation, more radical attacks on masters, and a publicizing of slavery as a national problem. In 1849 it disbanded and transferred its assets to the Quaker-run Colored Orphan Asylum in New York City.

See also ABOLITIONISM.

Davis, David Brion. *Slavery in the Age of Revolution, 1770–1823* (Ithaca: Cornell Univ Press, 1976)

Hodges, Graham. *Roots and Branch: African Americans in New York and East Jersey, 1613–1863* (Chapel Hill: Univ of North Carolina Press, 1999)

Richard Newman

New York Medical College. Private health sciences university. The school was founded in 1860 as the New York Homeopathic Medical College at 20th St and 3d Ave in New York City. An affiliate, the New York Medical College and Hospital for Women, was established by Clemence Sophia Lozier in 1863. The first black female physician in the state, Susan McKinney-Steward, graduated in 1870. In 1875 Metropolitan Hospital, staffed mainly by the medical college's faculty, opened on Wards Island (New York Co). In 1889 the college built the Flower Free Surgical Hospital. The college merged with its female affiliate in 1918. In 1938 the college dropped "homeopathic" from its title and expanded to award other degrees in the health sciences. In 1972 the institution moved to Valhalla (Westchester Co). After years of financial difficulties, the college allied with the Roman Catholic Archdiocese of New York in 1978. The Graduate School of Health Sciences was founded in 1980. A new medical education center and renovation of the basic sciences building was completed in 2001. Enrollment as of 2002 was 760 in the School of Medicine, 650 in the School of Public Health, and 250 in the Graduate School of Basic Medical Sciences.

Wershub, Leonard Paul. *One Hundred Years of Medical Progress: A History of the New York Medical College, Flower and Fifth Avenue Hospitals* (Springfield, Ill: Charles C. Thomas, 1967)

Mary Anne Hansen

New York Mets. The New York Metropolitan Baseball Club was granted a National League (NL) franchise on 17 Oct 1960, filling a void left when the NL Brooklyn Dodgers and New York Giants moved to California after the 1957 season. Noted New York City thoroughbred horse owner Joan Whitney Payson was the principal owner, and the Mets appointed Casey Stengel manager on 29 Sept 1961. The team played its first game on 11 Apr 1962, losing to the St. Louis Cardinals, 11-4. Through the efforts of sportswriters, led by Dick Young of the *New York Daily News,* the press emphasized Stengel's humor rather than the players' inadequacies. The Mets record in 1962 was 40-120, the worst in 20th-century baseball history. But loyal fans at the Polo Grounds near Harlem were known as the "New Breed," and they made players such as Richie Ashburn, Choo Choo Coleman, and Marv Throneberry into folk heroes. In 1964 the Mets moved to Queens and the new William A. Shea Stadium, named after the attorney who helped bring NL baseball back to New York City.

Stengel retired on 2 Sept 1965 after breaking his hip in a fall. Losing seasons continued for the next few years. Gil Hodges, previously a popular first baseman for the Brooklyn Dodgers and an original Met, was named team manager in 1968. A year later, pitchers Tom Seaver and Jerry Koosman and outfielders Tommie Agee and Cleon Jones led the Mets to a World Series triumph in five games over Baltimore. Hodges died of a massive heart attack on 2 Apr 1972 and was succeeded by former Yankees catcher and manager, Yogi Berra. The Mets returned to the World Series in 1973, losing to Oakland in seven games. Play declined soon after, and the Mets had losing records every season from 1977 through 1983. The Payson family in 1980 sold the Mets to publishing heir Nelson Doubleday and real estate financier Fred Wilpon.

The team improved with the addition of Keith Hernandez, Gary Carter, Darryl Strawberry, and pitcher Dwight Gooden, who in 1986 all contributed to a second World Series Championship in seven games under manager Davey Johnson. The series actually turned in the sixth game when the Boston Red Sox, a strike away from their first series championship since 1918, saw Mookie Wilson's grounder go through first baseman Bill Buckner's legs. The Mets have since returned to the postseason three times: losing in the NL Division Series in 1988, losing in the NL Championship Series to the Atlanta Braves in 1999, and returning to the World Series but losing to the crosstown rival New York Yankees in 2000.

Honig, Donald. *The New York Mets: The First Quarter Century* (New York: Crown Publishers, 1986)

Koppett, Leonard. *The New York Mets: The Whole Story* (New York: Macmillan, 1970)

Maury Allen

New York Mills. Textile manufacturer located in Whitestown and New Hartford (Oneida Co), along the banks of Sauquoit Creek. In 1806 Scottish immigrant Seth Capron established a small weaving cottage industry in the area. Approximately 80 people hand carding and hand spinning at Capron's facility produced a coarse cotton yarn that was distributed to area families for handloom weaving. For this work skilled weavers earned around $1 per day, and their family members were often hired to assist with warp setup and bobbin winding at a rate of $.50 to $1.75 per week. Many of these families rented company housing. In 1817–18 power looms were introduced in the production of cotton cloth—probably the earliest instance of such looms in use in New York State—and water-power rights were acquired along the creek. By the 1870s four plants that made up the New York Mills Co, known respectively as Mills No. 1, No. 2, No. 3, and No. 4, had been established in three major locations called the Lower, Middle, and Upper Mills.

Although the company was profitable, owners Benjamin Walcott Jr and Samuel Campbell invested relatively little in its physical structures or machinery, so working conditions deteriorated drastically. Nevertheless, the labor force was sustained by an influx of immigrants, especially ethnic Poles beginning in the late 19th century. Employment at the mills stood at approximately 1,000 in 1878. A decade later some 1,600 looms were in use. Default on a loan of $1 million, however, transferred control of the company's operations to A. D. Juilliard and Co, a New York City textile selling agent, around 1906. To revitalize the mills Juilliard brought in machinery for the manufacture of pile fabrics, particularly corduroy and cotton velveteen. But little was done to improve working conditions, and labor unrest ensued. Strikes in 1912 and 1916, supported by the United Textile Workers of America, were largely successful in addressing workers' wage and safety concerns. By 1930, however, the operations were obsolete. World War II brought a reprieve, with nearly 2,000 people employed at the various plants, but decline resumed after the war. Juilliard sold off all facilities by 1953, and operations ceased altogether within a few years. Mill No. 3 has since been refurbished and is occupied by a variety of small businesses.

The Blue Book: A Pocket Directory of the Textile Manufacturers of the United States and Canada (New York: J. E. Palmer, 1888)

Pula, James S., and Eugene E. Dziedzic. *United We Stand: The Role of Polish Workers in the New York Mills Textile Strikes, 1912 and 1916* (New York: East European Monographs, 1990; distributed by Columbia Univ Press)

The Village of New York Mills: Celebrating 75 Years as a Village, 1922–1997 (New York Mills, NY: 75th Anniversary Booklet Committee, 1997)

Allen Fannin

New York Mills. Village (pop 3,191) in New Hartford and Whitestown (Oneida Co). A handweaving industry, producing cotton cloth, began in 1806. In 1809 the three-story brick Oneida factory began operations along Sauquoit Creek. It is believed to be the first to shift to power looms in 1817–18. Three other mills, all built by 1868, were known collectively as the New York Mills, the name assigned to the post office in 1832. In 1878 the combined mills employed 1,000 workers, including many ethnic Poles. The village was incorporated in 1922. All production by the mills ended in 1958. In the early 21st century the village was mostly residential, but the renovated Mill No. 3 is used by small businesses.

New York Nets. The team entered the American Basketball Association (ABA) in the league's 1967–68 inaugural season as the New Jersey Americans. After one year the franchise moved to Long Island and renamed itself the New York Nets. For the next eight seasons, the team played in Commack (Suffolk Co), Hempstead (Nassau Co), and Uniondale (Nassau Co), compiling a 338-328 regular-season record in the ABA. The Nets defeated the Utah Stars to win the 1974 league championship, and two years later beat the Denver Nuggets to reclaim the ABA title. They were led in both series by Julius Erving, a Roosevelt (Nassau Co) native and league Most Valuable Player from 1974 to 1976 (sharing the award in 1975). In 1976 the ABA merged with the National Basketball Association (NBA). Fees to enter the NBA were high, leading team owner Roy Boe to sell Erving's contract to Philadelphia because Boe claimed he could not afford to pay Erving. The team played one NBA season in New

York, winning just 22 games, before moving to New Jersey and being renamed the New Jersey Nets in 1977.

Remember the ABA: New York Nets, http://www.remembertheaba.com/New-York-Nets.html

Mitch Lawrence

New York, New Haven and Hartford Railroad. Formed on 6 Aug 1872 through the merger of the Hartford and New Haven Railroad and the New York and New Haven Railroad, this new company, commonly known as the New Haven, operated from New York City to New England via Westchester Co. At the turn of the century J. P. Morgan bought the company and set out to create a transportation monopoly in New England, with the New Haven as the centerpiece of this expanded enterprise (the company passed out of Morgan's control following his death in 1913).

Following a 1903 state law that limited the use of steam-powered locomotives in Manhattan after 1908, the New Haven became one of the first railroads to electrify. It used New York Central's third rail system between Grand Central Terminal and Woodlawn in the Bronx, and a catenary wire system for the rest of the route. The 1917 Hell Gate Bridge, constructed with the Pennsylvania Railroad, permitted a direct rail link between New York City and New England for the first time. By 1929 the New Haven had 2,131 miles (3,430 km) of track and one of the heaviest passenger loads of all the major railroads in America. However, the depression hit the railroad hard, and on 23 Oct 1935 the company entered bankruptcy. The railroad shuttered many branchlines, sold off its nonrailroad assets, and spent $283 million to improve infrastructure. On 18 Sept 1947 a leaner and more efficient railroad emerged from receivership. But its decline continued in the postwar period, and after failing to turn a profit after 1957 the New Haven entered bankruptcy for the final time in July 1961. On 1 Jan 1969 the New Haven went out of existence when the Penn Central Transportation Co absorbed all of its 1,550 miles (2,494 km) of track and rolling stock. After the Penn Central fell into bankruptcy in 1972, the New Haven was taken over by Conrail, with the Metro-North Division of the Metropolitan Transportation Authority (MTA) of the State of New York and the Connecticut Department of Transportation operating the actual commuter trains. Since 1983 the two states share joint ownership of the original New Haven passenger service.

Swanberg, J. W. *New Haven Power* (Medina, Ohio: Alvin F. Staufer, 1988)
Weller, John L. *The New Haven Railroad: Its Rise and Fall* (New York: Hastings House, 1969)

Wayne D. Drummond

New York, Ontario and Western Railway. Incorporated in 1866 as the New York and Oswego Midland Railroad, this line promised a shortcut between the Atlantic Ocean and the Great Lakes and served a transportation-starved area of the state. Communities along the route provided substantial municipal support, made possible by the General Bonding Act of 1869, which permitted municipal bond sales to finance railroad building. State senator Henry R. Low of Middletown (Orange Co) and Assembly speaker Dewitt C. Littlejohn of Oswego pushed this and other acts favorable to the Midland through the state legislature and then engaged in shameless profiteering from its construction.

Following financial support rather than the easiest route, the Midland required extensive trestlework, countless cuts and fills, sharp curves, heavy grades, and three tunnels as it negotiated much rugged, mountainous territory between Oswego and the Port of New York at Weehawken, NJ. Operating in 1871 but bankrupt by 1873, it was bought in 1880 by a group of English and American bankers and renamed the New York, Ontario and Western. Because the line bypassed centers of population and industry, the principal source of freight was farm products, especially fluid milk, and the principal source of passengers was seasonal resort traffic to the southern Catskills and to Sylvan Beach (Oneida Co). However, anthracite coal became a profitable freight commodity when the company reached the mines of northeast Pennsylvania with its Scranton division in 1890. The railroad thus enjoyed, for a time, a period of relative prosperity.

By 1937, however, with milk, coal, and passenger traffic nearly gone, the company declared bankruptcy. Trustee Frederic Lyford attempted to increase business in many ways, including the "streamstyling" (refurbishing old equipment in the streamline style) of one passenger train by prominent industrial designer Otto Kuhler (1894–1976). One economy measure was conversion from steam to diesel motive power, completed in 1948. Neither these nor other, later efforts succeeded. On 29 Mar 1957 the railroad, known to Wall Streeters as the Old Woman and to its neighbors as the Old and Weary, closed down at 541 miles (871 km) of track—the longest railroad to cease operations up to that time.

Helmer, William F. *O. & W.: The Long Life and Slow Death of the New York, Ontario and Western Railway* (1959; repr Hensonville, NY: Black Dome Press, 2000)
Mohowski, Robert E. *The New York, Ontario and Western Railway and the Dairy Industry in New York State: Milk Cans, Mixed Trains, and Motor Cars* (Laurys Station, Pa: Garriques House, 1995)
Wakefield, Manville B. *To the Mountains by Rail* (1970; repr Fleischmanns, NY: Purple Mountain Press, 1989)

William F. Helmer

New York Philharmonic. Oldest American orchestra with a continuous existence. Formed as a musicians' cooperative in 1842, its first concert was the first of three in a season that began 7 Dec 1842 and included Beethoven's Fifth Symphony. By 1870 the season had expanded to six programs, each given twice (with the first performance a public rehearsal). The first conductor to provide strong individual leadership was Carl Bergmann, a notably progressive musician (1855–76). His successor, Theodore Thomas (1877–91), was an outstanding figure who helped create an American symphonic culture. Thomas's successor, Anton Seidl (1891–97), was a European luminary; his early death in 1897 plunged the orchestra into a period of limbo. By 1900 the New York Philharmonic was an anachronism; the orchestras of Boston and Chicago, differently organized, gave many more concerts. Even in New York City, the Philharmonic's concerts represented a fraction of the city's symphonic activity.

In 1909 the orchestra was reorganized as a full-time professional ensemble whose directors pledged to ensure financial solvency, and it hired a new conductor, Gustav Mahler, who died in 1911. As of 1910–11, the season totaled 54 concerts. Of Mahler's numerous successors over the next half century, few made a lasting impression. The most notable was the galvanic but conservative Arturo Toscanini, who presided over the Philharmonic-Symphony Society Orchestra (still the orchestra's legal name). The Philharmonic merged with the New York Symphony Orchestra (founded in 1878) in 1928. Toscanini's departure in 1936 triggered another artistic hiatus. Leonard Bernstein (1958–69), the first American-born conductor of a major American orchestra, brought much needed glamour. In 1962 the orchestra moved from Carnegie Hall, its home since 1892, to Lincoln Center. Bernstein's successors as music directors of the Philharmonic were Pierre Boulez (1971–78), Zubin Mehta (1978–91), Kurt Masur (1991–2002), and Lorin Maazel (2002–). As of 2004, the Philharmonic gave 130 concerts per season.

Krehbiel, Henry, James Gibbons Huneker, and John Erskine. *Early Histories of the New York Philharmonic* (New York: Da Capo Press, 1979)
Shanet, Howard. *Philharmonic* (New York: Doubleday, 1975)

Joseph Horowitz

New York Post. Daily newspaper founded in 1801 by the Federalist Alexander Hamilton as the *New-York Evening Post.* With William Coleman as its first editor, the *Post* emphasized shipping notices and attacks on Jeffersonian Democrats. After poet and lawyer William Cullen Bryant assumed the editorship in 1829, the paper moved further from its Federalist origins and supported Andrew Jackson and the Democratic Party. Under Bryant in the 1850s the *Post* became strongly antislavery and eventually migrated from the Democrats to the emerging Republican Party.

In 1881 railroad builder Henry Villard bought the paper. Under editor Edwin L. Godkin, the *Post* opposed Tammany Hall and supported civil service reform and conservative fiscal policies. The Villard family gave up control in 1917 and the newspaper passed through the ownership of Thomas Lamont and then Cyrus H. K. Curtis. In 1934 it became the *New York Post.* In 1936 J. David Stern bought the paper and made it a bulwark of the New Deal in New York City. In 1939 Stern sold out to George Backer, husband of Dorothy Schiff, granddaughter of financier Jacob Schiff. She eventually divorced Backer and gained control of the paper. In 1942 it switched from a broadsheet design to a tabloid. Under Schiff and editor James Wechsler, it acquired a reputation for liberalism, opposition to both McCarthyism and communism, human interest stories, and a distinguished roster of columnists. Paul Sann, who took over as editor in 1961, nurtured many notable journalists and increased sports and crime coverage.

In 1976 circulation reached a low of 489,000 and Australian press magnate Rupert Murdoch purchased the financially ailing *Post* from Schiff. Murdoch pushed the paper to the right politically and ran more sensational stories. "Headless Body in Topless Bar" was one of the paper's most memorable page-one headlines. Murdoch, who owned WNYW-TV, was forced to sell the paper in 1988 to satisfy federal regulations that forbid the ownership of newspapers and televisions in the same market. In 1993 Murdoch was granted a waiver by the Federal Communications Commission and reassumed ownership. The paper remains a strong conservative voice in the city's politics and culture. In March 2003 weekday circulation was 620,080.

The New York Post. *The Post's New York* (New York: Harper Collins, 2001)

Robert W. Snyder

New York–Presbyterian Hospital. Voluntary hospital in New York City. The older member of this hospital partnership, New York Hospital, was chartered by King George III in 1771 and began admitting patients in 1791. Its psychiatric division, Bloomingdale Asylum, opened at what is now 116th St and Broadway in 1821 and moved to White Plains (Westchester Co) in 1894. In 1877 the main hospital moved from its original location on lower Broadway to West 15th St. Its future partner, Presbyterian Hospital, was established on East 70th St by James Lenox and other philanthropists in 1872.

Both New York and Presbyterian Hospitals were originally founded to provide charity care to the poor. By the early 1900s, with the wider use of modern medical technologies and a reduced danger of hospital infection, they began attracting a growing number of private patients who could pay for their care. That most doctors were entering the profession with inadequate clinical experience led millionaire Edward Harkness to offer Presbyterian a major contribution in 1910 to form a teaching affiliation with Columbia University College of Physicians and Surgeons. Two years later financier George Baker funded a similar arrangement between New York Hospital and Cornell Medical College. In 1917 the four institutions even discussed building a single medical center, but the project foundered on Columbia's insistence that Cornell Medical College become a Columbia department. Instead each of the hospitals moved with its educational partner to the complex it now occupies: Columbia Presbyterian Medical Center at 622 West 168th St (1928) and New York Hospital–Cornell Medical Center (now New York Weill Cornell Medical Center) at 525 East 68th St (1932).

During the 1990s third-party payers, including insurance companies, HMOs, and the government, began pressing hospitals to cut costs. Competing to survive in this climate by expanding market share and achieving greater economies of scale, New York Hospital and Presbyterian each built its own network of allied facilities around the metropolitan area and subsequently began plans for a merger. In 1997 the two officially became one hospital, although they maintained their separate locations and their affiliated medical schools did not combine. The merged hospital holds more than 2,300 inpatient beds and provides about 1 million ambulatory visits per year. In 2002 the New York–Presbyterian Healthcare System included 35 hospitals in New York, New Jersey, and Massachusetts.

Burlage, Robb Kendrick. "From Campus to Corporation: New York City Medical Empires, 1960–1985: Urban Planning, Regional Policy, and the Structure of Health Care Institutions" (PhD diss, Cornell Univ, 1994)

Lamb, Albert R. *The Presbyterian Hospital and the Columbia-Presbyterian Medical Center, 1868–1943: A History of a Great Medical Adventure* (New York: Columbia Univ Press, 1955)

Larrabee, Eric. *The Benevolent and Necessary Institution: The New York Hospital, 1771–1971* (New York: Doubleday, 1971)

Sandra Opdycke

New York Public Library (NYPL). Circulating library created by private philanthropy and supported by public money. In 1854 a noncirculating library was established by the will of John Jacob Astor to serve the citizens of Manhattan. The Lenox Library was incorporated in 1870 to house the rare books collected by James Lenox, while the Tilden Trust, established in 1886 by the will of Gov Samuel J. Tilden, ultimately left approximately $2 million to create a public library. Tilden trustee John Bigelow negotiated the formation of the New York Public Library, and the Astor, Lenox, and Tilden Foundations on 23 May 1895. In 1897 the city donated a site for the library on 5th Ave between 40th and 42d Sts in Manhattan. John M. Carrère and Thomas Hastings won the design competition, and foundation work began in 1900 after the Egyptian-style distributing reservoir of the Croton water system was demolished. On 23 May 1911 the $9 million Beaux Art–style building, with two lions sculpted by Edward Potter flanking the piazza before the main entrance, was dedicated by Pres William H. Taft. The ever expanding reference resources of the "people's university" brought it recognition as one of the world's greatest research libraries. New York City's financial difficulties forced staff and funding cuts between 1961 and 1980, especially in the branch libraries that were established beginning in 1901, but Pres Vartan Gregorian (1981–89) revived the institution and raised over $300 million for renewal. The catalog was computerized in 1985, more than 30 miles (48 km) of new stacks were constructed beneath adjacent Bryant Park, the facade was cleaned, and the reading room and exhibition halls were refurbished. With over 50 million items, the NYPL is among the five greatest scholarly libraries in the world. Its four research libraries include the Humanities and Social Sciences Library, the Library for the Performing Arts at Lincoln Center, the Schomburg Center for Research in Black Culture in Harlem, and the Science, Industry, and Business Library located on 34th St since 1996.

Dain, Phyllis. *The New York Public Library: A History of Its Founding and Early Years* (New York: New York Public Library, 1972)

Reed, Henry Hope. *The New York Public Library: Its Architecture and Decoration* (New York: Norton, 1986)

George J. Lankevich

New York Racing Association (NYRA). Private, nonprofit corporation based in Jamaica (Queens Co) that owns and runs New York State's three major thoroughbred racetracks. Originally the Greater New York Association, it was created in 1955 in response to a Jockey Club study recommending the consolidation of track ownership to rouse New York State racing out of its postwar slump. Later that year the group reorganized as NYRA, which is governed by a self-perpetuating board of directors ultimately answerable to the State Racing and Wagering Board over such matters as rule changes and racing dates. The new corporation purchased the privately held Aqueduct (Queens Co), Belmont (Elmont, Nassau Co), Saratoga (Saratoga Springs), and Jamaica racetracks for $20.1 million. After immediately demolishing the Aqueduct facility, NYRA built a new $33 million racing plant on its site (opened 1959) and sold the Jamaica track for housing development. Renovations also took place at Belmont from 1963 to 1968 and at Saratoga in 1965. The updated tracks were successful, drawing top horses and record crowds. NYRA tracks have hosted the Belmont Stakes, the Travers Stakes at Saratoga, and the Breeders Cup Championship at Aqueduct (1985) and at Belmont (1990, 1995, 2001).

While overall attendance and betting declined beginning in the early 1970s with the advent of off-track betting (OTB), a problem at tracks nationwide, 2,469,928 fans attended NYRA's tracks during 258 racing days in 2000, wagering $508,353,010, of which almost $16,500,000 went to the state as its cut of wagering profits. In 2003 the state attorney general indicted four parimutuel clerks and two former directors of the department, along with NYRA, on charges that clerks skimmed money from their cash drawers and had their paychecks docked, generating an unreimbursed business expense and reducing their tax liabilities. Although charged with collusion in the scheme, NYRA management cooperated with the investigation and promised reforms.

New York Racing Association. *2003 NYRA Yearbook and Media Guide* (Jamaica, NY: Author, 2003)

Elizabeth Redkey

New York Rangers. Professional hockey team founded as a National Hockey League (NHL) franchise in 1926 by boxing promoter George Lewis "Tex" Rickard. The Rangers shared the ice at Madison Square Garden with the New York Americans, founded the previous year, and a keen rivalry developed between the franchises. The 1927–28 Rangers club became the first American team to win the Stanley Cup, defeating the Montreal Maroons in the final. The championship team included forwards Bill Cook and Frank Boucher and defenseman Ivan "Ching" Johnson. The Rangers won the Stanley Cup again in the 1932–33 and the 1939–40 seasons, defeating the Toronto Maple Leafs both times. The 1939–40 team was led by the line of Neil Colville, his brother Mac, and Alex Shibicky. The Rangers struggled during the 1940s and early 1950s, though forward Buddy O'Conner (1948) and goalie Chuck Rayner (1950) were both honored as NHL Most Valuable Player. The team continued its mediocrity until 1966 when coach and general manager Emile "the Cat" Francis led the Rangers to the playoffs for the first of nine consecutive seasons, the first NHL team to accomplish this feat. Led by the line of Rod Gilbert, Jean Ratelle, and Vic Hatfield, and goalie Ed Giacomin, the Rangers reached the Stanley Cup finals in the 1971–72 season only to be defeated by the Boston Bruins. The 1978–79 team, featuring forwards Phil Esposito, Ulf Nilsson, and Anders Hedberg, also played in the Stanley Cup finals, where it lost to the Montreal Canadiens. The 1980s again proved frustrating as the Rangers repeatedly made the playoffs but could not win a championship. In 1991 the team acquired superstar center Mark Messier. With Messier and other players, including defenseman Brian Leetch, goalie Mike Richter, and forward Adam Graves, added through the draft and trades, the Rangers won the Stanley Cup in 1993–94. In 1996 the Rangers acquired the NHL's all-time leading scorer Wayne Gretzky, reuniting him with old teammate Messier for a season. At the start of the 21st century the Rangers again reshaped the team with the return of Messier and the addition of forwards Eric Lindros and Pavel Bure. More than 35 Rangers players have been inducted into the Hockey Hall of Fame, including Boucher, Cook, Gilbert, Giacomin, and Lester Patrick.

Fischler, Stan, and Tom Sarro. *Metro Ice: A Century of Hockey in Greater New York* (Flushing, NY: H & M Productions, 1999)

Meisel, Barry. *Losing the Edge: The Rise and Fall of the Stanley Cup Champion New York Rangers* (New York: Simon & Schuster, 1995)

Jack A. Bucco

New York State Agricultural Experiment Station. See GENEVA EXPERIMENT STATION.

New York State Agricultural Society. Private, volunteer membership society formed in Albany in 1832 by James Le Ray de Chaumont, Jesse Buel, and other leading agriculturalists "to improve the condition of agriculture, horticulture, and the household arts." One of the oldest agricultural societies in the United States, it was inspired by similar groups in the United States and Europe. State financial and other assistance early supported its influence and contributed to its longevity. Buel's monthly, the *Cultivator,* which has been retained as the title of the society's current newsletter, served the society's membership, as did its annual *Proceedings,* published from 1833 to 1893, which contained society business, reports of county agricultural societies and fairs, essays on agricultural tools, "scientific" techniques, crops and breeds, field-trial results, and household arts.

After reorganizing in 1841 the society planned one of the nation's first state fairs, held that September in Syracuse, and continued to hold them for the next half century, purchasing property for fairgrounds near Syracuse in Geddes (Onondaga Co) in 1890. The society also lobbied for state aid for county agricultural societies and fairs, the creation of an agricultural college, established at Cornell University, and farmer institutes, educational programs foreshadowing the Cooperative Extension Service (1914). The state assumed many of the functions of the agricultural society, including the reporting of county and state agricultural statistics and the sponsorship of the state fair, after it bought the society's fairgrounds in 1899. The State Fair Commission created in 1900 came under the jurisdiction of the Department of Agriculture (1893).

The society acquired agricultural implements in the 1850s and 1860s from inventors and manufacturers and created a museum in Albany. In 1900 numerous pieces became the basis of the agricultural collection of the New York State Museum. In 1928 the society opened the Daniel Parrish Witter Agricultural Museum on the state fairgrounds and in 1937 initiated the New York State Century Farm awards for active farms owned by the same family for 100 or more years. It first distributed "Cap" Creal awards for agricultural journalism in 1978 and New York State Bicentennial Farm awards in 2000. The society meets yearly to present these awards, conduct business, and share a forum on agricultural trends and innovations.

Neely, Wayne Caldwell. *The Agricultural Fair* (New York: Columbia Univ Press, 1935)

Kathryn A. Boardman

New York State Archives. Established in 1971 to preserve and make accessible recorded evidence documenting New York State's history, governments, events, and peoples from the 17th century to the present. The State Archives also advises local governments on the care and management of their records. Full operations began in 1978 when the organization's storage and research facility opened in the Cultural Education Center (CEC) on Madison Ave in Albany. The facility provides access to over 130 million documents relating to Dutch and British colonial rule, as well as to records from all three branches of state government. Topics covered in those records include relations with American Indians, the Erie Canal and westward expansion, industrial development, labor, rise of the modern social welfare system, public education, public health, the environmental movement, and numerous wars.

In 1987 the State Archives assumed the responsibility for overseeing management and disposition of state agency records, including management of the State Records Center in Albany. Legislation in 1988 provided for regional technical advisory services and competitive grants to historical societies, museums, libraries, and other nonprofit organizations holding historical records. A local government records law the following year required the appointment of records management officers in every county, city, town, village, and school and special district.

The organization serves students and teachers, scholarly and community researchers, government officials, the legal and business community, and the general public. It encourages students through awards, grants, and historical publications, and helps teachers use historical documents from the archives as source material in the classroom. Staff responds to over 57,000 research requests annually and makes archival services available to 62 state agencies, 4,300 local governments, and 3,000 historical records repositories statewide. Recent projects include a $7.5 million renovation of the 11th-floor public areas and records storage facilities in the CEC and a multi-institution project to create a virtual research collection that focuses on the environmental history of the Adirondack and Catskill Parks. The nonprofit Archives Partnership Trust (1992) provides support for archival activities.

See also ARCHIVES.

New York State Archives, http://www.archives.nysed.gov

Kathleen Roe

New York State Assembly. See LEGISLATURE.

New York State Association Opposed to Woman Suffrage. Established in New York City in 1895, the association oversaw the antisuffrage organizations that had formed in nearly every city and town in the state in response to the national interest in woman suffrage. The antisuffragists' opposition to the vote came from their trust in the male electorate to protect women's best interests and from their belief that gaining the vote would threaten established gender roles as well as lead to voting rights for black and immigrant women. Antisuffrage women advanced their cause by using their connections to politically powerful men and by engaging in activities that actually defied traditional gender expectations: they wrote for publication and distributed literature on the benefits of the state's existing legislation; they lectured in front of mixed audiences; they presented papers and spoke at political conventions; and they sent speakers throughout the state to inform men and women about the dangers of allowing women to vote. The association almost always lacked funds because fund-raising was considered improper for women, and usually the members themselves contributed money. Though many meetings were held in private parlors, antisuffragists made it their business to investigate any activities that related to the suffrage issue.

The wives and relatives of many political leaders, usually Republican, belonged to the organization, including Mrs William Forse Scott (Bertha Lane), the first female police officer in Yonkers; Mrs Alfred Meyer (Annie Nathan), a founder of Barnard College; Mrs Arthur M. Dodge (Josephine Jewell), a leader in the daycare movement; Mrs Abram Stevens Hewitt (Sarah Amelia Cooper), wife of the US congressman; Mrs Elihu Root (Clara Wales), wife of the US senator; and Alice Hill Chittenden, appointed by Gov John Alden Dix to a committee to investigate labor conditions. Association members, perhaps as many as 20,000, were their most organized and dynamic in 1915 during the suffrage referendum. New York City was divided into districts so that local antisuffrage clubs could be created and annexes of the state association established. The antisuffragist campaign to prevent suffrage was successful. In 1917, however, the woman suffrage referendum passed in New York State with more than 53% of the vote. Pres Woodrow Wilson's support for woman suffrage was finally made public, causing antisuffragists to feel betrayed because their work in the war effort was as diligent as the work of the suffragists. The New York State association dissolved soon after. Some members joined the Women Voters' Anti-Suffrage Party, while Chittenden helped to found the Women's National Republican Club. Others, in an effort to unify all state antisuffrage campaigns, put their energies into the National Association Opposed to Woman Suffrage, which was founded in 1911 and had shared office personnel with the New York State association. It announced the move of its headquarters to Washington, DC, in July 1917 and the election of Mrs James W. Wadsworth (Alice May), wife of the US senator from New York State, as president. Antisuffragists were vitally important to the suffrage movement because they provided an opportunity for suffragists to clarify their arguments and to step up their activities, ultimately leading to women's right to vote.

Camhi, Jane Jerome. *Women against Women: American Anti-Suffragism, 1880–1920* (Brooklyn: Carlson Publishing, 1994)

Jablonsky, Thomas J. *The Home, Heaven, and Mother Party: Female Anti-Suffragists in the United States, 1868–1920* (Brooklyn: Carlson Publishing, 1994)

Susan Goodier

New York State Bar Association. Established to provide services to and represent the interests of those in the legal profession and to maintain professional standards, the association received its charter from the New York State legislature in 1877. Its code of professional responsibility, descended from canons adopted in 1909, contains disciplinary rules that were promulgated in 1990 by the four appellate divisions of the New York State Supreme Court as joint rules governing the conduct of attorneys. Former association presidents include US Supreme Court Chief Justice Charles Evans Hughes (1917–18) and US Secretary of War and Secretary of State Elihu Root (1910–11). In 2002 the permanent staff consisted of more than 100 employees, and the membership roster numbered more than 70,000 attorneys. Staff headquarters are maintained in several adjoining historic brownstone houses in Albany.

The association serves as the primary organ through which the profession interacts with the courts, the legislature, the media, and the public. Membership is voluntary. Policy is developed through its House of Delegates, which meets four times each year, and a smaller executive committee. A president is elected for an annual term; day-to-day operations are the responsibility of a permanent executive director. Members may join any number of the association's 23 large sections devoted to various areas of practice and may also be assigned to one or more of the 70 smaller committees. The New York Bar Foundation (1950) is the philanthropic arm of the association, providing grants and assistance to law-related projects. The association offers educational programs and publications for professional advancement, comments on pending legislation and legislative proposals, and pursues projects to foster access to legal services and to encourage the growth of pro bono practice by attorneys.

Association members practicing in New York City often also belong to the Association of the Bar of the City of New York (1870) or the New York County Lawyers' Association (1908), both voluntary. These two collaborate on a lawyers' referral service that provides an array of legal services to the public, and each has played an important role in setting and maintaining standards for the legal profession. Many other bar associations in addition to the American Bar Association are active in the state, organized at the county, city, and town level, by reference to area of practice or around some other defining characteristic.

Gardner, Deborah S., and Christine G. McKay. *Of Practical Benefit: New York State Bar Association, 1876–2001* (Albany: New York State Bar Association, 2003)

William S. Helmer

New York State Board of Railroad Commissioners. Defunct regulatory agency. Railroad regulation began in 1843 with an assembly resolution mandating that all railroad corporations operating in the state submit reports to the secretary of state. An 1850 law required them to file annual reports with the state engineer and surveyor regarding finances, passenger and freight loads, and equipment operated. In 1855 a formal railroad commission was created to examine operations and review the reports. It was composed of three members: the state engineer and surveyor, who was an elected statewide official; a member nominated by the state's railroad corporations; and a member nominated by the governor with the consent of the senate. This commission was abolished in 1857 under pressure from the state's railroad corporations, and the railroads once again reported to the state engineer and surveyor.

In 1879 the Chamber of Commerce of the State of New York petitioned the assembly to reestablish a railroad board. After passing the assembly in 1880 and 1881, both houses of the legislature approved a bill in 1882 creating a new Board of Railroad Commissioners, which first convened in early 1883. The board had no powers of enforcement but was charged with reviewing annual reports, investigating grievances, and making recommendations to the state on rates and services. Its three-person membership consisted of two gubernatorial appointees and one member nominated jointly by the Chamber of Commerce, the New York Board of Trade and Transportation, and the National Anti-Monopoly League. In addition, one of the three members was required to have a background in the railroad industry. The board was granted jurisdiction over all steam railroad and electric railway companies operating in the state and published the railroads' reports in its own annual report. It continued to function this way until 1891, when a separate Board of Rapid Transit Railroad Commissioners was established to deal with the unique transportation concerns of New York City, notably rapid surface transport and subway construction.

In 1905 the legislature expanded the board membership to five, all appointed by the governor for five-year terms; one had to be experienced in the railroad business. Just two years later, Gov Charles Evans Hughes proposed that public utility regulation across the state be reorganized. With the enactment of the Public Service Commissions Law in 1907, all existing state regulatory agencies were replaced by two five-member bodies, the Public Service Commission of the First District for New York City and the Public Service Commission of the Second District for the rest of the state. The Board of Railroad Commissioners was formally abolished effective 1 July 1907, and its responsibilities transferred to the second district, which had power to investigate complaints, order improved service, establish rates, and supervise utility finances. In 1921 a single statewide agency replaced the two commissions. Railroad regulation has been handled by the New York State Department of Transportation since 1967.

New York State Board of Railroad Commissioners. *Annual Report of the Board of Railroad Commissioners of the State of New York* (Albany: Weed, Parsons, 1883–94, 1896–1906)

Jeffrey Kraus

New York State College of Agriculture and Life Sciences at Cornell University. A beneficiary of the federal Morrill Land Grant Act of 1862 that fostered higher education in agriculture, Cornell University in Ithaca has offered related subjects since its beginning in 1868, establishing the Department of Agriculture that year. In 1882 an agricultural experiment station became operative in Geneva (Ontario Co). In 1888 the department's name was changed to the College of Agriculture. In 1894 extension education by county agents was instituted. Despite free tuition, enrollment remained low, numbering no more than 107 students in 1900. Liberty Hyde Bailey, dean from 1903 to 1913 and one of the country's outstanding educators in agriculture and horticulture, contributed significantly to the college's international visibility and prestige. In 1904 the state assumed full financial responsibility for the school, which was renamed the New York State College of Agriculture. Attendance increased to 846 in 1910, and the experiment station activity proliferated, notably in animal nutrition, horticulture, and entomology. When the college became a unit of SUNY in 1948, it remained an integral component of Cornell. Adding life sciences to the college's name in 1971 recognized a post–World War II change in focus from production agriculture to basic and applied research and instruction in subjects related to biology. One of seven undergraduate colleges at Cornell, the school offers 19 major fields of study. Enrollment in 2002 was 4,210 full-time students, 55% of whom were women.

Colman, Gould. *Education and Agriculture: A History of the New York State College of Agriculture at Cornell University* (Ithaca: Cornell Univ, 1963)

Gould Colman

New York State College of Human Ecology at Cornell University. SUNY statutory college. In 1900 Cornell University in Ithaca introduced reading and correspondence courses for farm women, and the program in 1919 became the Department of Home Economics under Martha Van Rensselaer and Flora Rose. In 1925 the department received a state charter as New York State College of Home Economics and in 1949 became a partnership college of SUNY. Reflecting the expanding nature of its concerns, it adopted the current name in 1969. It is the only human ecology program in the Ivy League. Its academic programs focus on family and life-course, nutrition and health, design and technology, and economic and social well being. About 20% of the 1,400 undergraduate and 200 graduate students are men.

Stage, S., and V. B. Vincenti, eds. *Rethinking Home Economics: Women and the History of a Profession* (Ithaca: Cornell Univ Press, 1997)

Carl A. Westerdahl and Susan S. Clarke

New York State College of Veterinary Medicine at Cornell University. SUNY statutory college. From its beginning in 1868, Ezra Cornell, founder of Cornell University in Ithaca, insisted that the institution have a veterinary department. In 1894 the department received a state charter creating the College of Veterinary Medicine, funded by New York State but with Cornell determining all aspects of the academic and research programs. Significant research at the college has included vaccines for bovine viral diarrhea, bovine leptospirosis, hog cholera, and dog distemper. The college became a statutory college in the SUNY system in 1949. The only veterinary college in the state, it enrolls about 320 doctor of veterinary medicine candidates and 100 other graduate students. Changing applicant patterns have resulted in a student body that is 75% women.

Fontana, Elizabeth A. *A Centennial Celebration: 100 Years of Creating a Healthier Future for Animals and People* (Ithaca: Cornell Univ Press, 1994)

Carl A. Westerdahl and Susan S. Clarke

New York State Council on the Arts. Created in 1960 as a temporary state commission to support the arts, it was one of Nelson A. Rockefeller's first proposals to the state legislature after being elected governor. A year later, the legislature granted the agency $450,000 for its touring program, technical assistance, and administration. On 13 May 1965 the council became a permanent state agency. A major turning point occurred in 1971 when the legislature approved Gov Rockefeller's request for $20.1 million for the agency, up from $2.2 million the previous year. In addition to funding from state government, the council has, since 1966, received financial support from the federal National Endowment for the Arts. The council's Board of Directors consists of 20 members appointed by the governor with the advice and consent of the senate. Prominent New Yorkers who have served on the board include Edward Albee, Shana Alexander, Peter Duchin, Thomas Hoving, Dina Merrill, Bess Myerson, and Aline Saarinen. The council receives grant applications each year from approximately 1,300 nonprofit arts and cultural organizations throughout the state, more than 75% of which are funded with grants from hundreds to many thousands of dollars. The legislature requires the council to give funding of at least 40¢ per person for each county in the state. In 2002 the council's funding was $44 million.

Al Berr

New York State Electric and Gas (NYSEG). Investor-owned utility and since 2002 a subsidiary of Energy East Corp, a northeastern United States energy servicer and delivery company. NYSEG supplies electricity to 830,000 customers and has 250,000 gas customers in 44 of New York State's 62 counties, primarily in Western and Central New York. Founded in 1852, Associated Gas and Electric (AGEC) was a utility holding company that went bankrupt in the 1930s; it was reorganized under court supervision and broken down into smaller companies by government order. All but two of the resulting 14 subsidiary companies were located in New York State, the largest and most important of them being Ithaca Gas Light and Homer and Cortland Gas Light. Through mergers among its operating companies, the numbers were reduced to four: Homer and Cortland Gas Light, Ithaca Gas Light, Ithaca Electric Light and Power, and Norwich Gas and Electric. These were consolidated in 1916 under the name New York State Electric and Gas Corp, which was reorganized into a holding company in 1998. Energy East became NYSEG's corporate parent. As part of this reorganization, the company agreed to a Public Service Commission proposal to auction the company's electric generating plants. In 2002, when Energy East acquired RGS Energy Group, NYSEG became a wholly owned direct subsidiary of RGS, also the parent company of Rochester Gas and Electric Corp, serving Rochester and the surrounding area. NYSEG is headquartered in Ithaca and Binghamton.

New York State. Assembly. *Public Hearing on New York State Electric and Gas Corporation's Electric Restructuring Plan* (Albany: NYS Standing Committee on Energy, 1997)

Jeffrey Kraus

New York State Employees' Retirement System. Provider of retirement, disability, and death benefits to employees of participating public employers. The New York State Employees' Retirement System (NYSERS) was created by an act of the state legislature and signed into law by Gov Alfred E. Smith in 1920. It is one of two systems—the other being the Police and Fire Retirement System—administered by the New York State and Local Retirement System, a part of the Division of Retirement of the New York State Department of Audit and Control (commonly known as the State Comptroller's Office). The comptroller is administrative head of NYSERS and also trustee of its Common Retirement Fund, valued at over $112 billion in December 2001. The comptroller is assisted by two deputies with professional staffs as well as by four advisory committees: Advisory Council for the Retirement Systems, Investment Advisory Committee, Real Estate Advisory Committee, and Actuarial Advisory Committee. Participating employers include New York State as well as many local governments; New York City does not participate but operates its own systems. Through its investment program, NYSERS has directed almost $7 billion to further state development via the Affordable Housing Permanent Loan Program, New York State Mortgage Pass-Through Program, a co-lending program with Union Labor Life Insurance, and New York Venture Capital Investment Program. Benefits provided by the plan are guaranteed by Article 5, Section 7, of the state's constitution. In 2001 NYSERS had 590,959 members with 273,147 benefits-entitled dependents. From 1 Sept 1983 the system has offered a four-tier benefit plan, with employees contributing to the plan and receiving benefits according to the length of their membership. NYSERS is headquartered at 110 State St in Albany.

New York State and Local Retirement System. *Annual Report, 2001* (Albany: Author, 2002)

Jeffrey Kraus

New York State Fair

Founding and Early Years

In February 1832 the New York State Agricultural Society was founded in Albany by a group of farmers, legislators, and others to promote agricultural improvement and local fairs. In spring 1841, with the promise of an annual state subsidy, the society planned the nation's first state fair, subsequently held on 29–30 Sept 1841 in Syracuse. There an assembled 10,000–15,000 people heard speeches by notables and viewed animal exhibits, a plowing contest, and samples of manufactured goods for the farm and home. The second New York State Fair, held in Albany in 1842, ushered in an era of growth and travel for the institution. During the 1840s the fair's directors increased attendance and revenues by adding horse racing and other forms of entertainment. From 1842 to 1889 the fair traveled among 11 different cities—Albany, Auburn, Buffalo, Elmira, New York City, Poughkeepsie, Rochester, Saratoga Springs, Syracuse, Utica, and Watertown—before permanently settling in Onondaga Co in 1890.

The Permanent Site and State Control

In February 1889 Syracuse Land Co donated to the Agricultural Society a 100-acre (40 ha) tract of land in Geddes (Onondaga Co) crossed by railways that facilitated exhibit transport. This parcel has served as the fair's permanent home since September 1890. By the end of the 1890s, burdened with debt from constructing permanent buildings on the site, the Agricultural Society turned to state government for relief. New York State purchased the grounds in 1899 and took over management of the fair the next year, creating the 11-member State Fair Commission appointed by the governor. The first structure in a $2 million long-term building plan was erected in 1908, with subsequent buildings completed at intervals over the next two decades. Its building plan begun, the fair promoted revenue-enhancing attractions like automobile racing and stunt flying, dangerous endeavors that frequently resulted in performer and spectator casualties. Less hazardous and more instructive were popular Grange and Labor Day speeches and farm camps for boys and girls. The camps of the 1910s were forerunners of 4-H gatherings and competitions later managed by Cornell Cooperative Extension. During World War I the fair shared its grounds with an army training center and supply base. New York's governors appointed faithful members of their own parties to run the fair, even after administration of the event shifted to the Department of Agriculture and Markets in 1927. The opening of an Iroquois village exhibit and an agricultural museum in 1928 addressed a growing and nostalgic public interest in local history; both displays have continued to thrive into the 21st century.

Mid-20th Century

Revenue and attendance problems of the depression era brought modifications. The fair grew from six to eight days and by 1933 included activities on Sunday, with Sabbatarians appeased by an interfaith ceremony that became a tradition lasting into the 1970s. In 1934 the state created the Industrial Exhibit Authority, which supervised construction of new buildings for both farm and corporate exhibits. Exhibiting manufacturers paid fees that helped offset the cost of these improvements, originally undertaken with federal and state monies. In 1938 the fair acquired a new name—New York State Agricultural and Industrial Exposition—reflecting closer ties to industry, while an extended 14-day schedule featuring popular entertainment acts such as swing dance bands increased attendance.

No fair was held from 1942 through the fall of 1948, as the fairgrounds again became a military base (1942–46). Deterioration of the physical plant and a November 1943 flood of industrial waste from nearby Solvay Process Co raised questions about the fair's future. One postwar plan proposed a $52 million fairground at Syracuse Army Air Base (Onondaga Co), while a second advocated keeping the fair in Geddes and linking the site with a newly cleansed Onondaga Lake. The Geddes plan prevailed, though the fairgrounds were not extended to the lake, which remained heavily polluted. A truncated fair took place in 1948, with a six-day, full-scale exposition returning in 1949 to large crowds. The event grew in the 1950s, expanding to nine days and gaining an attendance of over 500,000 by decade's end. New parking lots added to the fair's acreage and held the multitude of cars that arrived via the growing highway system. Many exhibits emphasized atomic energy, civilian and national defense, and plentiful consumer goods. Fair publicists of the 1950s and 1960s touted James E. Strates Shows' midway and nationally known entertainers, both of which attracted nonagricultural families and teenagers. A short-lived (1962–66) name change to New York State Exposition reflected the diminished focus on agriculture.

Later 20th Century

The New York State Fair was so named once again in 1967. Financial pressures caused by state budget problems, stagnating attendance, and the increasing cost of entertainment prompted changes. Starting in 1976 the fair charged a separate admission for grandstand acts, while the state subsidy cut in 1977 led to a 10-day fair, sale of name franchises to corporations, and rental of the buildings off-season. State aid for operating expenses ended in 1990, although capital improvement costs were underwritten up to 2000. New political currents were also evident. In the 1970s women's programs added discussions of the Equal Rights Amendment to child welfare talks, cooking demonstrations, and lectures on home economics. In the 1980s and 1990s fair officials countered criticism of a slim minority presence by increased attention to multicultural representation and participation through gospel festivals and a Pan-African village display. The event also added sign language interpreters and made its grounds accessible to people with disabilities.

Through 2005 the budget has grown to nearly $16 million. The fair attracts over 1 million visitors to Geddes on the western edge of Syracuse during its 12-day run in late August and early September. Visitors to the fairground's 375 acres (152 ha) view exhibits and competitions in such categories as livestock, dairy products, baked goods, and artwork. These attractions and others, including the midway, a miniature state park, and concerts, make the fair a civic ritual and seasonal marker that also entertains and unites diverse New Yorkers while recalling the agricultural past. Utilization of the fairgrounds and its buildings during nonfair time draws more than 2 million additional visitors.

Hedrick, U. P. *A History of Agriculture in the State of New York* (New York: Hill & Wang, 1966)
Marti, Donald B. *Historical Directory of American Agricultural Fairs* (New York: Greenwood, 1986)
Neely, Wayne Caldwell. *The Agricultural Fair* (New York: Columbia Univ Press, 1935)
Schramm, Henry W. *Empire Showcase: A History of the New York State Fair* (Utica: North Country Books, 1985)

Chad Wheaton

New York State Geological Survey (NYSGS). Located in Albany, this state agency has operated since 1836, which makes it the oldest continuously operating geological survey after the British and French. It was formerly known as the New York State Geological and Natural History Survey.

In 1834 the state legislature ordered a four-year planned survey of the natural resources of New York and provided $26,000 annually to compile and complete an accurate geological survey of the state. James Hall, designated state geologist and state paleontologist in 1843, continued the survey's work following the end of the legislated period and remained as director until his death in 1898. In 1845 legislation established the State Cabinet of Natural History and placed it under the aegis of the State Board of Regents. In 1870 the legislature renamed the cabinet the Museum of Natural History.

The NYSGS has amassed a collection of over 600,000 rocks, minerals, and fossils, and published more than 600 bulletins, circulars, memoirs, maps, leaflets, and other special documents, as well as thousands of articles in scientific and professional journals. In 2003 the functions of the NYSGS were to provide a large number of bedrock and surficial geologic maps and research reports and offer access to unpublished open-file materials. In 2003 the staff included a chief, an associate director in charge of mineral economic studies and geologic mapping, an engineering geologist who also disseminated geologic data from the open file, and a secretary. The total budget for salaries and overhead in 2002 was approximately $380,000, and the operations and research budget was $8,500.

Socolow, Arthur A., ed. *The State Geological Surveys: A History* ([Grand Forks?, ND]: Association of American State Geologists, 1988)

Robert H. Fakundiny and James R. Albanese

New York State Historical Association (NYSHA). Established in 1899 in Caldwell [now Lake George, Warren Co] by 25 men who were primarily interested in the early history of New York State. The main activity of the association in its early years was an annual meeting at which papers were presented. In 1919 the association initiated the *Quarterly Journal of the New York State Historical Association* (from 1932, *New York History*) to present essays based on research of state subjects.

The organization's first permanent home was Hancock House in Ticonderoga (Essex Co), donated by Ticonderoga native and philanthropist Horace Moses, and it became association headquarters in 1926. Dixon Ryan Fox, historian and president of Union College, served as association president from 1929 to 1945. Fox brought to NYSHA distinguished professionals such as Julian Boyd and Clifford Lord, and stimulated the association's publication efforts, which included a 10-volume history of New York State (1933–37) and monographs of enduring significance.

In 1939 the association accepted philanthropist and collector Stephen C. Clark's offer to move to Cooperstown (Otsego Co) and occupied what is now the Village Building on Main St. In 1944 NYSHA moved to Fenimore House, a Neo-Georgian home built by Clark's late brother on the site of James Fenimore Cooper's farmhouse overlooking the Village of Cooperstown. The Fenimore House opened to the public on 24 Aug 1945 with exhibitions of important American paintings and two period rooms. Clark made significant purchases in American art for the association, including portraits (*Joseph Brant* by Gilbert Stuart), landscapes (*Last of the Mohicans* by Thomas Cole), and genre paintings (*Eel Spearing at Setauket* by William Sidney Mount). A collector of American folk art since the early 1930s, Clark began the creation of an outstanding museum collection with the purchase of 13 important pieces from the well-known collection of modernist sculptor Elie Nadelman in 1948. Folk art became an important part of the association's collection and early exhibitions in Cooperstown. Significant pieces in the collection include sculpture (*Head of a Boy* by Asa Ames), paintings (the Van Bergen Overmantel attributed to John Heaten), textiles (the Trade and Commerce Quilt by Hannah Stockton Stiles) and furniture (Mount Lebanon Shaker rocking chair).

Louis C. Jones, a leader in the promotion of folklore studies in New York State, served as the director of NYSHA between 1947 and 1973. Guided by Mary Cunningham, editor of *New York History* (1944–47, 1952–57), the Yorkers program to promote interest in state history in schools came to number several hundred Yorker clubs throughout the state. Wendell Tripp became editor of *New York History* in 1964 and held the position until 2000. Also in 1964, the Cooperstown Graduate Program in History Museum Studies, which offers a master's degree in museum studies, was cofounded with SUNY Oneonta.

The association's library acquired its own building in 1968, and it contained more than 88,000 volumes in 2003. The library collections also include thousands of diaries, journals, account books, and family letters, relating to the lives of "ordinary" New Yorkers. The association also awards endowed prizes yearly, including the Kerr History Prize (1969) for the best article published in *New York History*, the Dixon Ryan Fox Manuscript Prize (1973) for the best unpublished monograph on the state's history, and the Henry Allen Moe Prize (1983) for the best catalog of an art exhibition in the state. In 1995 the association renovated the Fenimore House, which was renamed the Fenimore Art Museum, to bring it to contemporary museum standards, and added an 18,000 ft^2 (1,670 m^2) wing, donated by Jane Forbes Clark, to accommodate the promised Eugene and Clare Thaw Collection of North American Indian Art. In 2002 museum attendance was 45,935.

Other historical programs flourished, notably Seminars on American Culture and National History Day. The publication program continued with scores of individual monographs, most recently *Art of the North American Indians: The Thaw Collection* (2000) and *Ralph Fasanella's America* (2001). NYSHA copublished two editions of David Maldwyn Ellis's standard one-volume history of New York State (1957, 1967) and its successor, the multiauthored *Empire State* (2001).

New York State Historical Association, http://www.nysha.org

Suzan D. Friedlander

New York State in television. Since the 1920s New York State has been a major force in the development of the television industry and an inspiration to countless writers and producers in the creation of programming. Once the point of origin for most prime-time programs, New York continues as the colorful setting for many of television's most popular shows and a potent symbol of American diversity and fortitude.

Early Live Television

Many of the earliest television images were produced in New York State studios. In 1928 there were five experimental stations in New York City, three in Schenectady, and one in Beacon (Dutchess Co). The first dramatic program on television, the spy thriller *The Queen's Messenger,* was transmitted by a General Electric station in Schenectady on 11 Sept 1928. After years of experimentation, television was introduced to the public at the World's Fair in Flushing Meadows (Queens Co) on 30 Apr 1939. The next day sets went on sale in New York City, as mobile television trucks covered sporting events and pageants around the city. Commercial television began on 1 July 1941 with WNBT in New York City airing the first advertisement, a 10-second spot for Bulova watches. World War II interrupted the nascent industry, however, and television did not take off until the late 1940s.

New York City was the main production center of live programming during the late 1940s and 1950s. The most popular variety series—*Texaco Star Theater* (1948–56), hosted by Milton Berle; *Your Show of Shows* (1950–54); and *Toast of the Town,* later *The Ed Sullivan Show* (1948–71)—were broadcast live each week from Manhattan, as were the noted anthology dramas *Studio One* (1948–58); *Kraft Television Theatre* (1947–58); and *Philco Television Playhouse* (1948–55), alternating weekly with *Goodyear Television Playhouse* (1951–60). Many programs dealt with New York themes: Milton Berle and Ed Sullivan each did several salutes to the Broadway heritage, and the era's most acclaimed drama, "Marty" (*Goodyear Television Playhouse,* 1953), concerned a lonely Bronx butcher. Several of the earliest situation comedies grappled with ethnic life in New York City, most notably the Jewish experience in the Bronx (*The Goldbergs,* 1949–55), and African American stereotypes in Harlem (*Amos 'n' Andy,* 1951–53). Jackie Gleason based the live sketches and filmed series of *The Honeymooners* (1952–70) on his Irish working-class adolescence in Brooklyn. During these early years of commercial television, New York City symbolized a thriving, noisy melting pot of diverse nationalities.

The Rise of Filmed Programming

Two of television's legendary icons, Lucille Ball and Rod Serling, used their childhoods in upstate New York as creative springboards for their respective series, *I Love Lucy* (1951–57) and *The Twilight Zone* (1959–64). Ironically, both were filmed in California. Although live television bustled with the energy of the Broadway stage, filmed television used the movies as inspiration, recording small-screen adaptations of familiar genres for distribution throughout the United States and later the world. Lucille Ball supplanted Milton Berle as television's most popular personality, demonstrating that filmed programs could be profitable without sacrificing creativity. As the television industry migrated to the West Coast, producers discovered that they could approximate the rhythms and atmosphere of New York life in the studios and back lots of Hollywood, even with the advent of color. In fact, the first color series, the now forgotten *Norby* (1955), focused on the comic misadventures of a banker in Pearl River (Rockland Co).

When crime dramas emerged as a popular television genre, however, producers found the best way to capture the gritty reality of New York City was to film on location there. The use of cameras on the city's streets was pioneered by the police series *Naked City* (1958–63), which each week featured one of the metropolis's "eight million stories," and carried on by *N.Y.P.D.* (1967–69), with Jack Warden. Another advantage of filming in the boroughs was the availability of theatrical actors like Dustin Hoffman and Robert Duvall to portray troubled denizens of the underworld. With the arrival of *Kojak* (1973–78), New York City detectives became just as hardened and streetwise as the criminals they pursued. Viewers observed the psyches and personal lives of New York City cops, men and women, in such tough-minded series as *Cagney and Lacey* (1982–88) and *NYPD Blue* (1993–), both filmed primarily in Los Angeles. On-location filming of New York City crime shows was revived in the 1990s with producer Dick Wolf basing his *Law and Order* franchise (1990–) on stories taken directly from current headlines. Wolf's *New York Undercover* (1994–98), set in Harlem, examined the lives of young cops, bringing the urban sounds of jazz and hip hop to prime time. Two threads have linked New York City police dramas over the decades: an emphasis on intense realism and the use of fine ensembles.

The complications and competitiveness of New York City living have been the subtexts of other dramatic series throughout the years. From the Prestons of *The Defenders* (1961–65) to District Attorney Jack McCoy and his colleagues on *Law and Order,* Manhattan lawyers on television have tackled difficult, controversial cases, including blacklisting, abortion, and affirmative action. In 1963–64 George C. Scott starred as a New York City social worker in *East Side/West Side,* investigating such problems as child abuse and the welfare system. *The Nurses* (1962–65), aired as both a prime-time and a daytime series, and the daytime serial *Ryan's Hope* (1975–89) examined the personal and professional lives of medical personnel. The artistic vitality of New York City provided the backdrop for *Fame* (1982–83), which explored the lives and ambitions of students at Manhattan's School of Performing Arts. *Felicity* (1998–2002) charted the emotional turmoil of a California college student confronting life and education in Manhattan's Greenwich Village. Other recent series have drawn on the city's reputation as a capital of glamour (*Central Park West,* 1995–96) and high finance (*Bull,* 2000; *The $treet,* 2000). *Third Watch* (1999–) deals with emergency service personnel—police officers, firefighters, and paramedics; in the wake of the 11 Sept 2001 terrorist attacks, the show ran a special episode in which cast members talked with their characters' real-life equivalents.

New York City has also been the explicit or thinly veiled setting of television superhero shows and mythic fantasies. *The Adventures of Superman* (1952–57) and *Batman* (1966–68) transformed the city into Metropolis and Gotham City, respectively. In *The Man from U.N.C.L.E.* (1964–68) super agents Napoleon Solo and Ilya Kuryakin battled international crime from their New York City headquarters. The tunnels and caverns of Manhattan were later home to lionlike Vincent in *Beauty and the Beast* (1987–90).

The Comic Side of New York City

Following the *Lucy* mold, many situation comedies set in New York City have looked at the turbulent private world of the entertainer, notably *Make Room for Daddy* (1953–64), *The Joey Bishop Show* (1961–65), and *Seinfeld* (1989–98). The behavior of the upper crust has been humorously treated in such series as *Family Affair* (1966–71), *Diff'rent Strokes* (1978–86), and *The Nanny* (1993–99). New York City comedy has anticipated many new trends in living arrangements: divorced members of the same sex living together (*The Odd Couple,* 1970–75; *Kate and Allie,* 1984–89), mixed marriages (the controversial *Bridget Loves Bernie,* 1972–73; *Rhoda,* 1974–78), and gay and straight roommates (*Love, Sidney,* 1981–83; *Will and Grace,* 1998–). Over the years the plight of the single woman in the city has been charted in series like *Private Secretary, Meet Millie,* and *My Friend Irma* in the 1950s; *My Sister Eileen* and *That Girl* in the 1960s; *Rhoda* (after the character's divorce) in the 1970s; *The Days and Nights of Molly Dodd* in the 1980s; and *Living Single* and *Caroline in the City* beginning in the 1990s. Unmarried men looking for love in the urban jungle have been the subject of such series as *My Little Margie* (1953–55), *Dream On* (1990–96), *Love and War* (1992–95), *The Single Guy* (1995–97), and *Becker* (1998–2004). Married couples too have survived the city, notably on *He and She* (1967–68), *Barefoot in the Park* (1970–71), *The Jeffersons* (1975–85), *Mad about You* (1992–99), and *Cosby* (1996–2000).

To get by in the intense, success-oriented 1990s, many comic characters found meaning and solace in their peers, and such series as *Seinfeld, Friends* (1994–2004), and *Sex and the City* (1998–2004) became the most watched and discussed programs on television. Comedic versions of the New York City cop show appeared with *Car 54, Where Are You?* (1961–63) and *Barney Miller* (1975–82), though the police humor later became more cynical and desperate in *Joe Bash* (1986) and *The Job* (2001–2). The New York City legal system was humorously exposed in *The Associates* (1979) and *Night Court* (1984–92), while other shows tweaked the city's political machine (*Spin City,* 1996–2002), a cab fleet (*Taxi,* 1978–83), publishing industry (*Just Shoot Me,* 1997–2003), social workers (*The Norm Show,* 1999–2001), and even the unemployment office (*Calucci's Department,* 1973).

The Outer Boroughs, Suburbs, and Elsewhere

A number of shows over the years have based their comedy on the cultural environment of particular New York City boroughs. In *All in the Family* (1971–79) producer Norman Lear created a Queens that was a cauldron of conflicting political and social perspectives. *The King of Queens* (1998–) brought to the borough the same working-class comedy pioneered by Gleason. *Grounded for Life* (2001–), set in Staten Island, underlines the cultural collision between parents and children. *The Bronx Zoo* (1987–88), with Ed Asner, was one of the few comedic series to make use of that locale since *The Goldbergs* and *Car 54.* Although many of America's funniest writers, including Neil Simon, Garry Marshall, and Carl Reiner, have created works about their Bronx childhoods in other media, none has revisited the borough for television. However, singer Jennifer López has developed a series based on her tightly knit Puerto Rican family in the multicultural Bronx, scheduled to debut in 2004. The demographic variety of post-*Honeymooners* Brooklyn has been on display in series like *The Patty Duke Show* (1963–66), *Welcome Back, Kotter* (1975–79), *The Cosby Show* (1984–92), and the nostalgic *Brooklyn Bridge* (1991–93).

Other counties in New York State have also provided local color for television series, especially situation comedies. Lynbrook (Nassau Co) is the setting of *Everybody Loves Raymond* (1996–2005), in which intrusive parents live across the street from their married son. Suffolk Co was presented to America on *The Pruitts of Southampton* (1966–67), which chronicled a society family fallen on hard times, and later on the prime-time soap *The Hamptons* (1983). Creator Neal Marlens fondly remembered his 1960s Long Island childhood in *The Wonder Years* (1988–93), though the network prohibited Marlens from specifying the setting for fear of alienating Middle America. Westchester Co locations featured in television sitcoms include New Rochelle (*The Dick Van Dyke Show,* 1961–66), Tuckahoe (*Maude,* 1972–78), and Peekskill (*Facts of Life,* 1979–88). Finally, Buffalo was home to an abrasive local talk-show host in *Buffalo Bill* (1983–84).

NEW YORK LIVE

Over the years television talk shows and other live-format programs have tried to capture the electricity and perpetual motion of New York City. Studio windows have been thrown open to catch the city at daybreak on *Today* (1952–) and *Good Morning America* (1975–). Other New York City–based shows are, in the morning, Regis Philbin's talk show, with cohosts Kathie Lee Gifford (1989–2000) and Kelly Ripa (2001–), and *The Rosie O'Donnell Show* (1996–2002); in the afternoon *Home* (1954–57), featuring Arlene Francis, and MTV's show for teenagers, *Total Request Live* (1998–); in the evening *The Tonight Show* in the 1950s and 1960s and *The Late Show with David Letterman* (1993–); and after midnight *Tomorrow* (1973–82), with Tom Snyder, and *Late Night,* hosted first by David Letterman (1982–93) and then by Conan O'Brien (1993–). Since 1975 *Saturday Night Live* has carried on the live tradition of weekend New York entertainment, popularizing the catchphrase, "Live from New York . . ."

Other live spectacles regularly broadcast from New York City include the 4th of July fireworks display over the East River, the Thanksgiving Day Parade, the lighting of the Christmas tree at Rockefeller Center, and the New Year's Eve celebration at Times Square. New York City will always be remembered on 11 September, when the world witnessed the destruction of the World Trade Center on television. In times of joy or tragedy, as a symbol of diversity or decadence, a beacon of cultural achievement or a sign of societal conflict, New York maintains its hold on the popular imagination through television.

Barnouw, Erik. *Tube of Plenty: The Evolution of American Television,* 2d rev ed. (New York: Oxford Univ Press, 1990)

Brooks, Tim, and Earle Marsh. *The Complete Directory to Prime Time Network and Cable TV Shows, 1946–Present,* 8th rev ed. (New York: Ballantine Books, 2003)

Castleman, Harry, and Walter Podrazik. *Watching TV: Six Decades of American Television* 2d ed. (Syracuse: Syracuse Univ Press, 2003)

McNeil, Alex. *Total Television: The Comprehensive Guide to Programming from 1948 to the Present,* 4th ed. (New York: Penguin, 1996)

Mitz, Rick. *The Great TV Sitcom Book,* rev ed. (New York: Perigee Books, 1988)

Rose, Brian, ed. *TV Genres: A Handbook and Reference Guide* (Westport, Conn: Greenwood, 1985)

Udelson, Joseph H. *The Great Television Race: A History of the American Television Industry, 1925–1941* (Tuscaloosa: Univ of Alabama Press, 1982)

Ron Simon

New York State Library. A unit of the State Education Department located in the Cultural Education Center on Madison Ave in Albany. Established by the legislature in 1818, the library was preceded only by state libraries in Pennsylvania (1816) and Ohio (1817). Gov De Witt Clinton and Chancellor James Kent were among those who supported the founding of the library and donated books for its initial collection. Originally housed in the old Capitol, it became the main library for state government. To reduce political interference, the Board of Regents was given authority over the library in 1844. In 1855 the collection moved into its own building and in 1883 transferred to larger quarters in the new Capitol. Melvil Dewey, state librarian from 1888 to 1905, guided the institution to national prominence by creating a professional staff, expanding the collections, and broadening the mandate to improve library service throughout New York State. Dewey had founded the School of Library Economy at Columbia University in 1887, which he moved to Albany in 1889 and upgraded into a graduate program in 1902. He also established specialized libraries for education, medicine, and legislative reference. He started a traveling library system in 1893 and began providing books to the blind in 1896. By the beginning of the 20th century, the institution had developed into the fifth largest library in the country.

On 29 Mar 1911 a fire in the Capitol ravaged the library's collection. Considered the greatest library disaster of modern times, more than 450,000 books and 270,000 manuscripts were destroyed. Although many of the books were eventually replaced, numerous priceless items were lost, including early Indian treaties, the papers of Sir William Johnson, and an elephant folio set of John James Audubon's *Birds of America.* Some treasures were saved, such as original drafts of Abraham Lincoln's Emancipation Proclamation and George Washington's Farewell Address. Beginning with donations from libraries throughout the country, the library gradually rebuilt its collection in the State Education Building on Washington Ave, built in 1912. By 1913 the collection reached 335,000 volumes, and by 1930 counted more than 1 million. In 2003, with more than 20 million items, including 2.5 million volumes, the institution was the only state library with membership in the Association of Research Libraries. The Talking Book and Braille Library serves 40,000 adults and children with disabilities statewide and the State Library's extensive interlibrary loan program distributes thousands of items annually. Since the 1960s the library has been in the forefront of developing information technology. Its first on-line public catalog appeared in 1978, coinciding with the move of the library to its present location.

In an effort to continue Dewey's initiatives, the Division of Library Development provides leadership and training for library personnel statewide. After World War II the State Library began regionalizing library services, partnering with local library systems. This network has expanded to serve more than 7,000 school, public, academic, and special libraries. During the 1990s the library focused on making information in electronic formats accessible to New Yorkers. By 2003 its New Century Libraries initiative had joined together over 4,300 libraries statewide in the effort. In 2003 the library employed 210 people and had a book budget of over $3 million.

Roseberry, Cecil R. *For the Government and People of This State: A History of the New York State Library* (Albany: NYS Library, 1970)

Richard Andress

New York State Museum. A unit of the State Education Department located in the Cultural Education Center, Madison Ave, Albany. The museum originated in 1836 after the legislature established the State Geological and Natural History Survey to document the state's minerals, rocks, flora, and fauna. Noted scientist James Hall directed the survey, and during a 62-year tenure served as state geologist and state paleontologist. Hall also began an ambitious publications program, which has resulted in hundreds of important studies examining New York State's natural history. Survey specimens were first collected in the State Cabinet of Natural History, housed in the State Library, and supervised by the Board of Regents beginning in 1845. In 1870

Restored Cohoes Mastodont *(center)* at the Hall of Fossil Animals in the New York State Museum in the State Education Department building, Albany, 1925.

the cabinet was renamed the New York State Museum of Natural History and relocated to its own building, Geological and Agricultural Hall.

A state botanist was hired in 1868 and a state entomologist position was established in 1881; entomological surveying started in 1847 when Asa Fitch was hired to collect insect specimens. Cultural artifacts were collected in 1848 with the acquisition of Lewis Henry Morgan's massive collection of artifacts documenting New York's native peoples. Thousands of these artifacts were tragically lost in the 1911 fire in the State Capitol. An archaeologist was hired in 1906, and the position of state archaeologist was created in 1933.

The museum became part of the new State Education Department in 1904, and between 1915 and 1975 museum exhibit halls opened in the State Education Building. The exhibits were widely known for their comprehensive geological displays and popular dioramas of native peoples. In 1945 curatorial and scientific functions were separated when the State Science Service was created and given responsibility for scientific research and assisting various state and private agencies and the public; it carried out its work in separate surveys in anthropology, biology, and geology. Service staff researched problems such as radioactive waste, acid rain, and endangered water resources.

In 1976 the Division of Historical Services was created, combining many of the functions of the Education Department's former Office of State History, which had a strong tradition in historical publications, roadside historical markers, and service to local historians. New exhibits focusing on people and their environments in the state also opened in 1976. Comprehensive exhibit halls on the Adirondacks and New York City were developed, as well as impressive dioramas including a Pleistocene mastodon and a Mohawk longhouse. Beginning in the 1980s the museum mounted an ambitious program of temporary history and art exhibits from various New York State institutions such as the Metropolitan Museum of Art. Some 4 million scientific specimens are preserved in the museum's renowned collections, including fossils, gems and minerals, rock drilling cores, plants and fungi, insects, and mammal skins. The notable collection of over 1 million historical artifacts contains prehistoric tools and pottery, New York State furniture, Shaker objects, farm implements, and Iroquois crafts. Since 1985, with creation of the Division of Research and Collections, the museum's scientific and curatorial functions have again been combined. In 2003 more than 70,000 students visited the museum.

New York State Museum, http://www.nysm.nysed.gov
New York State Museum and Science Service. *The New York State Museum: A Short History* (Albany, 1964)

Richard Andress

New York State Nurses Association (NYSNA). The first state constituent of the Nurses Associated Alumnae (now the American Nurses Association) was founded in 1901 in Albany to advance the profession of nursing and to protect the public's health. The association's first goal was to develop legislation to regulate the profession; it provided national leadership in developing a law permitting registration of nurses and creating the title "registered nurse (RN)." The New York State Nurse Practice Act was enacted in 1903, and protecting and strengthening the law has been an organizational priority throughout its history. In 1906 NYSNA supported the creation of the position of state inspector of training schools to ensure compliance with the law and worked diligently to maintain high standards of nursing education.

As the primary voice of nursing in New York State, the association has historically advocated for the healthcare consumer by elevating standards, providing a forum for developing policy on nursing practice issues, supplying expertise to nurses and regulatory agencies on nursing and health issues, and offering and approving continuing education programs for nurses. During the severe shortage of nurses in the 1940s, NYSNA began a program to attract and retain nurses through better salaries and improved working conditions by engaging in cooperative planning with hospital officials. In 1957 the program was expanded when NYSNA adopted a collective bargaining program to elevate the economic security of nurses and to improve working conditions. In the 1970s the association became the largest collective bargaining agent for nurses in the country. With the advent of new systems of managed health care in the 1990s, NYSNA lobbied for retraining funds for nurses in hospital reimbursement legislation, provided career guidance to nurses, and worked for job security in negotiated contracts. The association also works to raise the public perception of the profession through media campaigns and publishes numerous publications on nursing and health issues. The headquarters of NYSNA is located in Latham (Albany Co), with regional offices in New York City and Buffalo.

Pavri, Julie M. *Honoring Our Past, Building Our Future: A History of the New York State Nurses Association* (Virginia Beach, Va: Q Publishing, 2000)

Julie M. Pavri

New York State Office of Science, Technology and Academic Research (NYSTAR). Preceded by the New York Science and Technology Foundation, begun in 1963, NYSTAR was created as an executive branch agency in 1999. It provides grants to the 15 Centers for Advanced Technology (CATs) across the state to enhance and expand their activities, support the efforts of colleges and universities to commercialize high-tech innovations, and serve as a resource for small and start-up technology companies. NYSTAR's capital facilities program at public and private universities supports 8 Strategically Targeted Academic Research (STAR) Centers and 5 Advanced Research Centers (ARCs) based on peer review. NYSTAR is also responsible for development and oversight of the state's 10 Regional Technology Development Centers (RTDCs), which provide assistance to small- and medium-sized employers.

New York State Office of Science, Technology and Academic Research, http://www.nystar.state.ny.us

Jim Denn

New York State School of Industrial and Labor Relations at Cornell University. See School of industrial and labor relations (ilr).

New York State Senate. See Legislature.

New York State Soldiers' and Sailors' Home. Nursing home in Bath (Steuben Co) established for honorably discharged Civil War veterans. Initial funding came after a public appeal made by the Grand Army of the Republic (GAR), a national fraternal organization for Union veterans, during the 1870s, and the home was incorporated in 1876 as the Grand Army of the Republic Soldiers' Home of the State of New York. Construction began in June 1877 and the first veterans moved in the following year. Also in 1878 ownership and management was transferred from a board of trustees to the State of New York, and it was renamed the New York State Soldiers' and Sailors' Home. The facility was under scrutiny for several decades because of charges of financial irresponsibility and poor treatment of residents, and in response Lt Gov Harry Walker conducted a Moreland Act investigation of the home in 1920. Recommending the removal of Commandant Samuel Maurice Morgan and Surgeon in Chief Raymond C. Hill, he concluded that the trustees had been careless in their fiduciary responsibilities and ordered that new trustees be appointed. In 1927 the newly created Division of Military and Naval Affairs took over supervision of the home, which was renamed the State Camp for Veterans. In May 1929 the state turned the facility over to the federal government, and it became part of the Veterans Administration (VA) in 1930. In 2003 the US Department of Veterans' Affairs operated the Bath VA Medical Center on the site, as well as the Bath National Cemetery and a military and medicine museum. The Soldiers' and Sailors' Home reached its peak population of 2,143 in 1907.

New York State Soldiers' and Sailors' Home. *Annual Report of the New York State Soldiers' and Sailors' Home* (Albany: Weed, Parsons, 1880–1926)

Jeffrey Kraus

New York State Thruway. One of the most significant and readily identifiable projects of state government among New York State residents, this roadway during its construction was the largest, most expensive, and one of the most controversial public works projects in state history.

Origins and Design

The Thruway's origins lie with Abbot Low Moffat, the long-serving chairman of the Ways and Means Committee of the state assembly (1936–43). Moffat, after enduring years of driving the more than 150 miles (240 km) between his Manhattan home and Albany on the winding, two-lane US 9 with its numerous stoplights, felt that a modern highway tying the state's principal cities together had to be constructed. Ideas for such a state highway had existed for years, including a mid-1930s proposal by Triborough Bridge Authority chairman Robert Moses. Yet in the spring of 1942 it was Moffat, after consultation with the state's public works commissioner, who drew up the necessary legislation authorizing the construction of a statewide limited-access roadway, modeled on the Reichsautobahn in Germany, to be constructed at the conclusion of the war. Moffat sponsored and passed this bill through the legislature, and on 23 May 1942 Gov Herbert H. Lehman signed the bill into law. The road's name reflected the conviction of Melvil Dewey, the former state librarian

New York State Thruway in Montgomery Co.

(1889–1906) and a champion of spelling reform, that "thruway" was a more sensible term than "highway." Dewey's suggestion, while adopted in New York State, has not been widely adopted in other states.

State commercial and industrial interests strongly supported the proposed road. The Thruway plan called for a roadway rarely seen before in the United States: 427 miles (687 km) long running north from New York City, up the Hudson River valley to Albany, then west along the Erie Canal to Buffalo. Linking seven of the state's major cities, 90% of the state's population lived within a 30 mi (48 km) band of the planned road. Designed with an emphasis on safety and high-speed travel, the road's innovative features included a limited number of exits and entrances, two lanes in each direction separated by a mall of up to 1,000 feet (300 m), no sharp curves or grades, a minimum sight distance of 1,000 feet, acceleration and deceleration lanes 1,200 feet (366 m) long, and rest stops strategically placed every 30 miles (48 km). Designed for 70 mph (113 kph) traffic, the Thruway would allow drivers to cut their travel time from Buffalo to New York City from 16 to 7 hours. To win public support, the state government presented the Thruway as a means to secure a better postwar quality of life, particularly for returning veterans. Completion of the Thruway was set for 1951 with a cost estimate of $202 million.

Construction and Political Controversy

On 11 July 1946 at Liverpool (Onondaga Co), with Gov Thomas E. Dewey presiding, work officially began on the New York State Thruway. Its initial construction was plagued with delays. Labor and material costs soared after World War II, severely hampering the project. Because the road was financed only through general state revenues and not bonds, funds for the project were insufficient. By 18 Sept 1949 only 48 miles (77 km) of the Thruway had been built. It also encountered fierce political opposition from state Democrats, whose political base rested in New York City. With the Thruway outside of New York City, residents elsewhere in the state benefited disproportionately from the project. Moreover, the project's prime spokesperson was Republican governor Dewey. Democrats derided the project as "Dewey's ditch," a "luxury boulevard," a "financial Frankenstein," and an "enemy of schools." Every Democratic candidate for governor in 1946, 1950, and 1954 made attacking the Thruway an element of their campaign strategy. The Democrats' criticism of the project, however, garnered little public enthusiasm. To get the project completed, on 21 Mar 1950 Gov Dewey radically altered the project's administration by placing the Thruway project under the control of the new public New York State Thruway Authority, which was to build and administer the roadway, raising needed funds through the sale of bonds. A toll system would pay the bonds. Through his administrative and political efforts to get the Thruway finished, Dewey, more than anyone else, can claim credit for the project's completion.

On 6 Nov 1951 New Yorkers approved a state constitutional amendment to allow the state to guarantee the Thruway Authority's bonds. This amendment was approved by 82% of voters in New York City and 79% of voters outside of New York City, illustrating the great statewide popularity of the project. Flush with new cash, the Thruway proceeded rapidly after 1951, and the first major segment opened on 6 June 1954. Much of the new urgency in completing the Thruway reflected cold war imperatives. With rising tensions abroad, the roadway was now seen as vital to national security, enabling troops and material to move quickly. From 1950 to 1956 the state government launched an ambitious public relations campaign to build public support for the road and its new mission. Radio spots were aired and documentaries for television and movie theaters were shown throughout the state trumpeting the Thruway's integral link to defense; film titles included *Thruway to Tomorrow, Thruway Just Ahead,* and *On the Way.* The State Education Department even mandated that the Thruway's benefits be taught in all high school social studies classes. Heralded as "New York State's New Main Street," after 10 years of construction at a cost of $600 million, the 427 mi (687 km) main line was completed, opening on 31 Aug 1956.

Impact, Expansion, and Challenges

At its opening the Thruway was America's longest toll highway. Numerous industrial firms sited new plants along the roadway. The Thruway also spurred rapid suburbanization among all the areas it touched; for example, Rockland and Orange Cos were completely transformed from rural regions in 1956 to suburbs of New York City by the late 20th century. The Thruway's revolutionary high-speed and safety features became standard for all limited-access highways beyond New York State. After the 1956 creation of the Federal Highway Administration (FHWA), many of the Thruway's key administrators and engineers took jobs there, and Thruway chairman Bertram D. Tallamy was appointed by Pres Dwight D. Eisenhower to head the new federal agency.

Numerous additional sections of the Thruway were constructed. Some of the more notable spurs include the authority's 1957 opening of both a 3 mi (4.8 km) link to New Jersey's Garden State Parkway at Spring Valley (Rockland Co) and a 70 mi (113 km) section connecting the main line to Pennsylvania at Ripley (Chautauqua Co). This latter section was tied to a spur of the Pennsylvania Turnpike, and in 1959 the authority opened a 24 mi (39 km) section of road tying the main line to the Massachusetts Turnpike at Canaan (Columbia Co). The Thruway has remained autonomous from the federal interstate system; however, in 1958 the Thruway did adopt the interstate numbering system, designating the Buffalo-to-Albany section as I-90 and the Albany-to-New York City section as I-87. On 17 Feb 1964 the highway was renamed the Governor Thomas E. Dewey New York State Thruway in honor of Dewey's leadership on the project.

To accommodate growing traffic flows in the late 20th century, parts of the main line were expanded to three and four lanes in each direction. The Thruway Authority has also acquired existing interstates. These include the 11 mi (18 km) Cross Westchester Expressway (I-287), which connects to the main line at Tarrytown (Westchester Co), added in 1990, and I-84, a 71 mi (114 km) road, which joins the main line at Newburgh (Orange Co), added in 1991. On 3 Aug 1993 E-Z Pass, an electronic toll collection system, became operational on the Thruway. Allowing drivers to move through toll plazas with greater speed, E-Z Pass reduces traffic congestion and provides the benefit of volume discounts.

Since 1956 the Thruway has generally been free of controversy. On 5 Apr 1987, however, a bridge carrying the Thruway's main line over the storm-swollen Schoharie Creek in Glen (Montgomery Co) collapsed, killing 10 motorists. Subsequent investigation indicated that the authority had curtailed normal periodic checks of its bridges. Lucrative engineering and construction contracts have also raised political issues. Thruway contractors are often among the state's most generous political donors, the object of their largesse greatly dependent on which party controls the governor's office, which appoints the head of the Thruway Authority. In 2002, at 641 miles (1,032 km), the Thruway remains the longest toll highway system in the United States.

See also BONDED INDEBTEDNESS.

New York State Thruway, http://www.thruway.state.ny.us

Smith, Richard Norton. *Thomas E. Dewey and His Times* (New York: Simon & Schuster, 1982)

Thomas, Lowell Jackson. *The New York Thruway Story* (Buffalo: Henry Stewart Publishers, 1955)

Tod M. Ottman

New York State Thruway Authority. Independent public corporation established to finance the New York State Thruway. Although the state completed several sections of the Thruway during the 1940s, funding from normal revenues was not sufficient to complete the project. In February 1950 a special committee appointed by Gov Thomas E. Dewey recommended the establishment of an autonomous public corporation with the ability to finance the highway. A month later Dewey signed legislation creating the Thruway Authority, granting it power to acquire property by eminent domain, enter into contracts to build and maintain the highway, and collect tolls and other fees. In 1951 voters approved by a 4 to 1 margin a constitutional amendment allowing the authority to issue $500 million in guaranteed revenue bonds. Legislation in 1954 allowed the issuance of additional nonguaranteed bonds; $472 million in these bonds were eventually issued. Construction of the highway moved rapidly; the first toll section opened in 1954, and the 416 mi (669 km) New York City to Buffalo main line was completed in 1956. Bertram D. Tallamy, the authority's first chairman, left in 1957 to become Pres Dwight D. Eisenhower's federal highway administrator. The authority was widely criticized in 1961 for awarding Tallamy a lucrative consulting contract, but a bipartisan committee later cleared the authority of any misconduct. By 1970 the authority had repaid the state the entire $80 million cost of the construction completed before the authority began financing the project.

During the Cuomo administration (1982–94), the state began using the authority's bonding and revenue-producing capabilities to help alleviate budget deficits and to repair and maintain the state's deteriorating transportation infrastructure. Since 1986 the authority has issued more than $5 billion in revenue bonds to finance various state and local highway improvements. The legislature transferred several state highways to the authority, principally I-287, a route from Tarrytown to Rye in Westchester Co, and I-84, a route between Port Jervis (Orange Co) and North Salem (Westchester Co) and Brewster (Putnam Co) in 1991, effectively eliminating them from state budget obligations. In 1992 the state transferred the entire 524 mi (843 km) canal system to the authority, encouraging canal operations to be self-sufficient. That legislation created a subsidiary New York State Canal Corp to operate the system and expanded the duties of the Thruway Authority to undertake major economic development projects throughout the state's main transportation corridor. A number of unsuccessful legal challenges have criticized the expansion of the authority's original mandate, particularly its powers to bond non-Thruway projects. Other court actions have attempted, without success, to eliminate tolls from the highway. There was a general understanding that tolls would be eliminated when the original bonds were paid off in 1996, yet in that year the legislature determined that tolls would remain, primarily to ensure that the authority could issue enough bonds to meet capital expenditures.

In 1990 the authority began partnering with the Marriott and McDonald's corporations to replace and operate the Thruway's 27 travel plazas, most of which had been constructed in the 1950s. In 1993 the New York State Thruway Authority implemented the E-Z Pass electronic toll collection system, the first such system introduced in the Northeast. By 2001 nearly 5 million cars were equipped with the pass. In 2001 the authority had $648 million in expenditures and $428 million in revenues from the Thruway and canals. It is headquartered at 200 Southern Blvd in Albany.

Winders, Edward E. "Public Authorities in New York State: The Interdependent Governmental Roles of the New York State Thruway Authority" (PhD diss, SUNY Albany, 1998)

Richard Andress

New York Stock Exchange (NYSE). The dominant securities market in the United States was organized on 8 Mar 1817 as the New York Stock and Exchange Board with a constitution, a set of governing rules, and a slate of elected officers. The board at first was a call market in which each listed security was announced and bid on in turn, twice daily. Banks, insurance companies, and some foreign currency trading provided the main business for the exchange in its early years. In 1830 the Mohawk and Hudson, a line between Albany and Schenectady, became the first railroad security to trade; within a few years railroad stocks and bonds dominated the business of the NYSE and continued to do so for most of the remainder of the century.

The Civil War years brought rapid changes to New York City's securities markets. The name New York Stock Exchange was adopted on 29 Jan 1863, and the NYSE moved to its first permanent home, at the corner of Wall and Broad Sts, on 9 Dec 1865. The speculative investment market of the Civil War era saw the birth of a number of short-lived securities markets. From its founding in 1863, the Open Board of Stock Brokers rivaled the NYSE in trading volume. Along with the Government Bond Department, the two exchanges merged on 8 May 1869, giving the NYSE over 1,000 members, doubling its previous size. Starting in October 1868 membership in the exchange became a salable commodity.

In 1871 the call market was replaced by the continuous auction market, in which every listed security is traded throughout the day at a specific place on the trading floor. Industrial securities began to be traded in significant numbers in the 1890s and soon became the dominant business of the exchange. The introduction of the stock ticker in the late 1860s and the telephone in 1878 permitted expansion of the trading volume of the exchange, which experienced its first million-share day in 1886. The occasional crash or corner gave the NYSE more than its share of notoriety. The failed 24 Sept 1869 effort of Jim Fisk and Jay Gould to corner the gold market was afterward known as Black Friday. The failure of the prominent Philadelphia investment bank of Jay Cooke and Co on 18 Sept 1873 led to the closing of the exchange for 10 days. In 1901 the Northern Pacific corner saw spectacular price fluctuations, with the price of common stock rising from under $150 to over $1,000 per share in the course of a single trading session.

By the 1880s the NYSE was developing the specialist system, in which each listed security has a specific broker with the responsibility of making the market in that security. The system, with some modification, remains the way securities are traded at the NYSE. Every listed security has a designated specialist or market maker, a firm granted monopoly rights by the NYSE to hold orders by individual or institutional investors away from the current market price for these securities. Such orders are called limit and stop orders. When there are no public orders on the opposite side of the market, specialists also buy securities from individual or institutional investors or other trading firms at their "bid" price and resell these securities to purchasers at their

The Bulls and Bears in the Market, by William Holbrook Beard, 1879. The painting, with the NYSE to the left and Federal Hall to the right, is set on Broad St, the site of the outdoor curb market in securities.

higher "ask" price, thereby earning a profit on the difference. Since the late 19th century, specialist firms, each making the NYSE market for a specific and unique group of listed securities, have had no direct dealings with public customers. In return for having the exclusive right to make a market in a given security, specialist firms have an obligation to maintain a "fair and orderly market" and prevent panic selling in their assigned securities.

The NYSE moved its operations in 1903 into its current headquarters, dominated by an imposing Neo-Renaissance facade, on its old site on Broad and Wall Sts. The exchange closed down from 31 July 1914 through 11 Dec 1914 because of profound financial dislocations provoked by the onset of World War I. At the war's end the NYSE, long the dominant securities market in the United States, was now poised for a paramount position among global financial markets. Trading volume and interest in the NYSE surged during the boom of the 1920s but came to a shuddering halt after Black Tuesday, 29 Oct 1929, when more than 16 million shares (a record that would last for decades) were traded amid a more than 20% drop in the Dow Jones Industrial Average (DJIA) in a single week. As the crash lengthened into the Great Depression, both trading volume and share prices steadily dropped.

The creation of the Securities and Exchange Commission (SEC) in June 1934 marked a new era in American securities markets. The NYSE was now a self-regulating organization under the aegis of the SEC. Although the exchange retained a great deal of autonomy, many resented the intrusion of the federal government in its operations. Richard Whitney, president of the NYSE, was the leader of the opposition to the SEC, but both the power of the "old guard" and Whitney's career came to an end in 1938, when he was expelled from the exchange for embezzling funds. Whitney was replaced by William McChesney Martin Jr, whose tenure was marked by a new rapprochement with the SEC.

Throughout the 1930s and the years of World War II, the business of the exchange remained fairly anemic. Trading volume increased in the late 1940s, and efforts to convince small investors to return to the market was a dominant theme during the 1950s. By the early 1960s, however, the NYSE was increasingly dominated by large institutional investors. Technology and trading volume increased during the decade, and on 20 Dec 1966, the transmission of trade and quote data from the NYSE floor became fully automated. Nevertheless, the inability to process the increased volume, which rose from 3 million shares a day in 1960 to 15 million in 1970, led to a "paperwork crisis," caused by the inability of many small firms to deal with the new technological and financial realities. There was a consolidation of member firms, and from 1968 to 1970 about 100 went out of business. In 1971 member firms, for the first time, were allowed to incorporate. Then on 1 May 1975, "May Day," the long-established practice of fixed minimum commission ended with the introduction of the practice of negotiated commission rates between buyers and sellers of shares and their brokers. Although the exchange had long fought this innovation, it proved to be a boon, leading to rapidly increasing trading volume and further concentration of securities firms. The next year alternative listing standards were adopted to facilitate the listing of major foreign corporations on the NYSE. The first 100 million-share trading day came on 18 Aug 1982. The governance structure of the NYSE was changed on 5 June 1986 with the Board of Directors reconstituted to include only outside members, 12 drawn from the public and 12 from the securities industry.

On 20 Oct 1987 the market crashed, as the DJIA dropped 20% on record trading volume. "Circuit breaker" rules were put into effect thereafter, stopping trading in the event of extremely rapid drops in stock prices. The rules were first activated on 27 Oct 1997 as the result of the largest ever point drop in the DJIA. The next day was the first 1.2 billion share trading day. Stock trades, which since the exchange's founding had been conducted in eighths, went to sixteenths on 24 June 1997 and to decimals on 29 Jan 2001.

The NYSE underwent remarkable expansion during the bull market of the 1990s. In 2000 the NYSE set its ninth consecutive trading volume record, 262.5 billion shares, a 29% increase from the trading volume reported in 1999. Average daily share trading volume was also a record in 2000, at 1.041 billion, an increase over the 809.2 million for 1999, representing the first time that the NYSE averaged over 100 million shares traded per day for an entire year. The average daily monetary value of trading was also a record in 2000, at $43.9 billion, up from $35.5 billion in 1999. The long ebb-and-flow bull market of 1982 to 2000 brought trading volume and interest in stock trading to record levels, but when the bull market finally ended so did the unrealistic expectations for continuing profits of many who had entered the market in the preceding years.

Trading on the NYSE was suspended with the collapse of the World Trade Center on 11 Sept 2001 as the financial district lost its communications network. The NYSE did not sustain direct physical damage during the attack, although the chaotic conditions in the infrastructure of Lower Manhattan made its reopening less than a week later on Monday, 17 Sept 2001, a heroic undertaking. NYSE president Richard Grasso received much of the credit for the exchange's response to the crisis. However, two years later, in May 2003 when it was revealed that Grasso was receiving a retirement package of $139.5 million, the furor forced him to resign in September 2003. In the wake of his fall, there were calls for revamping the exchange's structure for a clearer separation of its regulatory functions from its service to member firms and listed companies.

Commission-based buying and selling of stocks had become a low-margin business as a result of the fall of commissions and the use of electronic trade matching and order routing systems. Long-term questions about the viability of the specialist system, still based on face-to-face transactions in the technological world of the early 21st century, were heightened among revelations that some specialists had placed their own financial gains above the need to find the best possible price for customers and that the exchange had failed to adequately discipline the errant brokers. In November 2003 the NYSE voted in governance changes, removing the chief executives of Wall St companies from the exchange's Board of Directors and placing them on an advisory panel; a new eight-member board was charged with management of the exchange.

See also SECURITIES INDUSTRY; SECURITIES REGULATION.

Buck, James E., ed. *The New York Stock Exchange: The First 200 Years* (Essex, Conn: Greenwich Publishing, 1992)

Editors of the *Wall Street Journal. Guide to Who's Who and What's What on Wall Street* (New York: Ballantine Books, 1998)

Geisst, Charles R. *Wall Street: A History* (New York: Oxford Univ Press, 1997)

Stedman, Edmund C., ed. *The New York Stock Exchange* (1905; repr New York: Greenwood, 1969)

Watchel, Howard M. *Street of Dreams, Boulevard of Broken Dreams: Wall Street's First Century* (London: Pluto Press, 2003)

Young, Allan E. *The New York Securities Industry: Its Contribution to New York State and City* (New York: Securities Industry Association, New York District, 1985)

Allan E. Young

New York, Susquehanna and Western Railroad (NYS&W). Established in 1881 through the merger of several smaller railway companies that linked the Pennsylvania coal regions to the industrial centers of the New York City metropolitan area. Between 1898 and 1940, the line was owned by the Erie Railroad and operated between northeastern Pennsylvania and the Little Ferry yard near Jersey City, NJ. Following bankruptcy proceedings in 1940, the NYS&W emerged as an independent company. In 1956 the directors filed to drop all passenger service, and by 1958 more than two-thirds of all passenger trains were gone; in 1966 all passenger service ended. Within the next 10 years the railroad provided service for freight customers but ultimately suffered a decline in both operations and track mileage. In 1976 the railroad once again filed for bankruptcy and four years later, in 1980, was acquired by the Delaware Otsego Corp (DO), led by Walter G. Rich, an operator of short lines in New York State and Pennsylvania. By using trackage rights on Conrail between Binghamton and Buffalo, the Susquehanna became an important bridge route for general freight and Sea-Land Corp container traffic during the late 1980s and early 1990s. It provided shippers with non-Conrail access to New York City and the container docks in northern New Jersey.

The NYS&W operates over 400 miles (644 km) of track in New York, New Jersey, and Pennsylvania. It is 286,000 lb (129,730 kg) gross weight capable on all lines and transports a wide range of commodities such as feed ingredients, lumber and other building materials, chemicals, and aggregates.

Mohowski, John E. *The New York, Susquehanna and Western Railroad* (Baltimore, Md: Johns Hopkins Univ Press, 2003)

David Babson

New York Times. Daily newspaper founded in 1851 as the *New-York Daily Times* by Henry J. Raymond, journalist and politician, with Albany banker George Jones and others. Editorially, the *Times* supported the Whigs and then the Republicans, and opposed compromise with secessionist states. It lost standing by backing Pres Andrew Johnson on postwar Reconstruction. Jones took over at Raymond's death in 1869 and abandoned Republican orthodoxy. The *Times* exposed corrupt practices of the Tweed Ring in 1871 but lost readers and advertising after endorsing Democrat Grover Cleveland for president in 1884.

After Jones died in 1891, editor Charles R. Miller and a syndicate that included J. P. Morgan bought the paper. Losses mounted in the panic of 1893, and the paper resorted to publishing cheap fiction. Miller put it into bankruptcy rather than let it be merged with another newspaper, then arranged its sale to Adolph S. Ochs, owner of the *Chattanooga Times.*

The New York Times Co was created when Ochs took over the *New York Times* on 19 Aug 1896, under a contract that gave him control after three years' profit. He created book and arts sections and an illustrated Sunday magazine, and coined the slogan All the News That's Fit to Print. Still losing circulation to the sensationalist journalism of William Randolph Hearst's *Journal* and Joseph Pulitzer's *World,* Ochs recovered by cutting his price from 3¢ to 1¢. In 1905 the *Times* moved from Park Row opposite City Hall to Long Acre Square, which became Times Square. Times Tower was circled by a band of lights, called the "zipper," spelling out news bulletins around the clock. In 1912 Ochs built an annex nearby at 229 West 43d St, eventually *Times* headquarters.

The *Times* has long been known for extensive and authoritative coverage. Early emphasis on news of science and discovery gave it an edge in covering Guglielmo Marconi's first transatlantic telegraphy in 1901, polar expeditions, the sinking of the *Titanic* in 1912, and Charles Lindbergh's flight to Paris in 1927. The paper has also won two landmark Supreme Court cases. In *New York Times Co v Sullivan* (1964), involving civil rights in Alabama, the Court limited public officials' libel claims. The decision in *New York Times Co v United States* (1971), the *Pentagon Papers* case about official deception of the public during the Vietnam War, proscribed the government's "prior restraint" of articles not yet published.

The New York Times Co acquired the classical music station WQXR in 1944, which it retained in 2004. In the 1960s it began acquiring magazines, television and radio stations, and newspapers, including the *Boston Globe.* It acquired part ownership of the *International Herald Tribune* in 1967 and full ownership in 2003.

Ochs's descendants retained control of the *Times* through a family contract. Ochs's son-in-law Arthur Hays Sulzberger was publisher from 1935 to 1961; Sulzberger's son-in-law Orvil E. Dryfoos was publisher from 1961 to 1963, and his son Arthur Ochs Sulzberger was publisher from 1963 to 1992; and Arthur Ochs Sulzberger Jr, Adolph Ochs's great-grandson, became publisher in 1992.

Among the staff that contributed to the paper's reputation were editors Clifton Daniel, Harrison Salisbury, and A. M. Rosenthal, columnists Arthur Krock and James Reston (both of whom served as head of the Washington bureau), and Tom Wicker, Russell Baker, Anthony Lewis, William Safire, and Paul Krugman. On-line publication began in 1996. In 2000 plans were announced for a new headquarters tower on 8th Ave at 41st St. In the early 21st century circulation, including the National Edition, was 1.1 million daily and 1.7 million Sunday. With a news staff of over 1,200 in more than 50 US and foreign bureaus, the newspaper and its writers won 89 Pulitzer Prizes through 2003. In May 2003 *Times* reporter Jayson Blair resigned after he was found to have committed numerous acts of journalistic fraud. In its wake, allegations of poor management forced the resignations of Executive Editor Howell Raines and Managing Editor Gerald M. Boyd.

See also SEPTEMBER 11TH, 2001.

Berger, Meyer. *The Story of the "New York Times," 1851–1951* (New York: Simon & Schuster, 1951)

Tifft, Susan E., and Alex S. Jones. *The Trust: The Private and Powerful Family behind the "New York Times"* (Boston: Little, Brown, 2000)

Turner, Hy B. *When Giants Ruled: The Story of Park Row* (New York: Fordham Univ Press, 1999)

Richard E. Mooney

New York University (NYU). Private university founded in 1831 as the University of the City of New York. While nondenominational and established on egalitarian ideals by a committee of business and professional men, the influence of evangelical Protestant clergy was initially dominant. The founders were divided over whether the education to be offered would be practical, for those entering mercantile careers, or classical, for prospective clergymen. The more conservative classical curriculum prevailed during the first few decades. In 1835 the university moved into the Gothic Revival–style University Building on Washington Square in Greenwich Village. Instruction in medicine began in 1841, and the medical department merged with Bellevue Hospital in 1898 to form the Bellevue Hospital–New York University Medical College (now New York University School of Medicine). As the curriculum expanded, a department of law, permanently established in 1858, evolved into the School of Law. In 1853 the School of Art opened and in 1873 became the first school at the university to admit women.

Two strong chancellors led the transformation of the institution into a large university. Henry Mitchell MacCracken, beginning in 1884 as vice chancellor and from 1891 as chancellor, was a major force. He inaugurated the graduate program in arts and sciences in 1886, while the School of Pedagogy (now School of Education), the first of its kind in the nation, opened in 1890. In 1894 the university moved the College of Arts and Sciences into buildings designed by Stanford White in a section of the Bronx that became known as University Heights, hoping to create a residential, academically selective undergraduate school. The School of Applied Science (1889), forerunner of the engineering program, was located on the Heights. In 1896 the school became officially known as New York University. Under MacCracken's successor, Elmer Ellsworth Brown (1911–33), NYU had one of the largest university enrollments in the country and established a separate undergraduate school, called Washington Square College, with a liberal admissions policy (1914); a university press (1916); and professional schools in business (1916), dentistry (1925), and fine arts (1928).

During the depression years of the 1930s the university drew both full- and part-time students from the entire New York City metropolitan area. In the years following World War II, the scholarship provisions of the GI Bill had a strong impact on NYU. In 1946 it had more veterans enrolled than any school in the United States (12,620), and its total student body (47,155) surpassed by several thousand the record set in 1931 for a US university. Partly in response to a financial crisis in the 1960s, NYU sold its University Heights property to CUNY and transferred the programs there to Washington Square. Under the presidency of John Brademas (1981–91), NYU began an ambitious mission to transform itself into a well-endowed and academically selective urban research university. In 1982 a major gift financed the Tisch School of the Arts, and other gifts have promoted the development of important international programs. The School of Continuing and Professional Studies, the origins of which date to 1906, has developed a constellation of professional certificate and degree programs in fields ranging from arts administration and publishing to real estate. In the early 21st century New York University has more than 150 academic departments organized into 15 schools, as well as numerous institutes and centers. In 2003 more than 50,000 students were enrolled in all programs.

See also INTELLECTUAL ÉMIGRÉS; SCIENTIFIC CULTURE (19TH–21ST CENTURIES).

Frusciano, Thomas J., and Marilyn H. Pettit. *New York University and the City: An Illustrated History* (New Brunswick, NJ: Rutgers Univ Press, 1997)

Jones, Theodore Francis. *New York University, 1832–1932* (New York: New York Univ Press, 1933)

Barbara J. Dunlap

New York, Westchester and Boston Railway. The railway began in 1872. Its planned but unbuilt route extended from a terminal on the Bronx shore of Harlem River to Port Chester (Westchester Co) with branches to Throgs Neck [now in Bronx Co] and Elmsford (Westchester Co). Part of the New York, New Haven and Hartford Railroad network since 1906, the line's name changed to the New York, Westchester and Boston Railway Co (NYW&B) after a 1910 merger. Construction on an innovative, $14,000,000 four-track suburban electric railway from Mount Vernon (Westchester Co) to the Harlem River started in 1909, and work was completed in 1912. Passengers had to transfer to the 2d and 3d Ave "el" at Harlem terminal to reach Midtown Manhattan. Another transfer occurred with the Interborough subway at E 180th St. Moving north from Mount Vernon, a two-track branch ran to Westchester Ave in White Plains (Westchester Co). The two-track main line continued to New Rochelle (Westchester Co) and extended to Port Chester in 1929. The 11,000 V, alternating current, overhead catenary line hosted 95 modern, steel, multiple-unit cars designed by L. B. Stillwell, a consulting electrical engineer for the NYW&B. The line was impressive with concrete viaducts, bridges, and large stations. Passenger volume on the NYW&B never materialized, however, as suburbanites used other lines in Westchester for a ride without transfers to Grand Central Terminal. In 1935 the New Haven went bankrupt and the NYW&B followed on 31 Dec 1937. Most of the 25-year-old line was sold for scrap, but New York City retained the four-track line in the Bronx from 180th St to Dyre Ave, and it became the northern portion of the 5 Train route.

Arcara, Roger. *Westchester's Forgotten Railway, 1912–1937: The Story of a Short-lived Short Line Which Was at Once America's Finest Railway and Its Poorest: The New York, Westchester and Boston Railway,* 3d ed. (New Rochelle, NY: I & T Publishing, 1985)

Middleton, William. *When the Steam Railroads Electrified* (Milwaukee: Kalmbach Publishing, 1974)

James Clifford Greller

New York Women's Trade Union League. Founded in 1903, the organization sought to improve women's working conditions through unionization and legislation. The members of the New York Women's Trade Union League (NYWTUL) came primarily from New York City, particularly from the International Ladies' Garment Workers' Union locals, the League of Women Workers, and the YWCA's Industrial Clubs. The NYWTUL initially modeled itself on the national Women's Trade Union League by emphasizing trade unionization. Its organizing experiences were mixed from 1903 to 1909 because of a lack of response from women workers in New York City and the hostility of male trade unions. The NYWTUL's first significant success came in the 1909–10 waist makers' strike in Manhattan. Mary Dreier, NYWTUL president from 1906 through 1914, formed an effective cross-class coalition to support the strikers with the assistance of working-class colleagues Rose Schneiderman and Leonora O'Reilly. After the Triangle Shirtwaist Factory fire in March 1911, Dreier was named a commissioner of the Factory Investigating Commission that June, and she and Schneiderman shifted the organization's focus to legislative matters. The NYWTUL lobbied the New York State legislature for fire safety measures and a 54-hour bill for working women, all of which became law in 1912. Schneiderman, NYWTUL president from 1918 to 1949, continued the focus on labor legislation, in part through her work with the Women's Joint Legislative Conference (WJLC). As a member of the WJLC, the NYWTUL successfully lobbied for a 48-hour bill in 1927 and a minimum wage measure in 1933. Schneiderman and her fellow NYWTUL colleague, Maud Swartz, also formed important friendships during the 1920s with Eleanor Roosevelt, who joined the NYWTUL and became an important fund-raiser, and with Franklin D. Roosevelt. Frances Perkins later credited Schneiderman and Swartz with alerting the future president to the need for labor legislation. When Roosevelt became president in 1933, Schneiderman established labor codes as a member of the National Recovery Administration. The NYWTUL lost its impetus after the New Deal ended in the late 1930s, although Schneiderman continued to press for labor legislation in New York State into the early 1950s. Due to a sharp decline in membership, the New York Women's Trade Union League officially ceased to exist in 1955.

Dye, Nancy Schrom. *As Equals and as Sisters: Feminism, the Labor Movement, and the Women's Trade Union League of New York* (Columbia: Univ of Missouri Press, 1980)

Orleck, Annelise. *Common Sense and a Little Fire: Women and Working-Class Politics in the United States, 1900–1965* (Chapel Hill: Univ of North Carolina Press, 1995)

John Thomas McGuire

New York Yankees. The American League (AL) baseball franchise began in 1903 when league president Ban Johnson arranged for Frank Farrell and Bill Devery to purchase the Baltimore Orioles for $18,000 and move the club to New York City. Named the New York Highlanders, the team played at Hilltop Park at Broadway and 168th St, one of the city's highest points and now the site of Columbia Presbyterian Medical Center. Newspaper editors seeking a shorter name for headlines began using "Yankees" by 1905, and the team's famed pinstripe uniforms were first worn in 1912. The name was officially changed in 1913 when the Yankees moved into the Polo Grounds in Upper Manhattan as tenants of the National League's New York Giants. In 1915 Cols Tillinghast L'Hommedieu Huston, who made his fortune in harbor improvement in Cuba, and Jacob Ruppert, a brewer and former four-term congressman, bought the Yankees for $460,000.

Through 1920 the team never won a championship, and it finished higher than fourth in an eight-team league just four times. Improvement came soon after the Yankees purchased Babe Ruth's contract from the Boston Red Sox on 3 Jan 1920. Ruth's home runs and popularity drew fans to the team in such great numbers that the Giants pressured the Yankees to leave. The team built its own field, and Yankee Stadium in the Bronx opened on 18 Apr 1923. The Yankees won six pennants that decade (1921–23, 1926–28) and three World Series championships (1923, 1927, 1928) under manager Miller Huggins (1918–29). Joe McCarthy (1931–46) managed the team to another seven World Series championships (1932, 1936–39, 1941, 1943). The Yankees in 1929 became the first team to make numbers, then corresponding with the team's usual batting order, a permanent part of the backs of their uniforms. They also started the practice of permanently retiring uniform numbers, beginning in 1939 with the number 4 worn by the critically ill Lou Gehrig. By century's end the Yankees would retire 15 numbers.

In 1945 Dan Topping, Del Webb, and Larry MacPhail purchased the Yankees for $2.8 million from the estate of Ruppert, who had bought out Huston in 1922. Under this ownership, manager Casey Stengel (1949–60) led the team to a record five consecutive World Series championships (1949–53). After the 1964 season the Columbia Broadcasting System (CBS) bought 80% of the Yankees for $11.2 million, later purchasing the remaining 20%. The Yankees finished with losing records in four of the next five seasons, and they failed to reach postseason play under CBS ownership. In 1973 a group headed by Ohio shipbuilder George M. Steinbrenner III bought the team for $10 million. Steinbrenner became renowned for meddling with the Yankees. Manager Billy Martin (1976–78, 1979, 1983, 1985, 1988) was hired and fired five times. In 1996 Joe Torre (1996–) became the 14th man to manage for Steinbrenner. The Yankees won two AL championships (1976, 1981) and six World Series championships (1977, 1978, 1996, 1998–2000), including four under Torre.

Forty players, managers, and executives with Yankees connections are enshrined in the Baseball Hall of Fame. As of 2003 the Yankees had won 39 pennants and 26 World Series championships, more than twice the number of any other team.

Gentile, Derek. *The Complete New York Yankees: The Total Encyclopedia of the Team* (New York: Black Dog & Leventhal, 2000)

Pepe, Phil. *The Yankees: An Authorized History of the New York Yankees,* 3d ed. (Dallas: Taylor Publishing, 1998)

Weinberger, Miro, and Dan Riley. *The Yankees Reader* (Boston: Houghton Mifflin, 1991)

Niagara. Town (pop 9,878) in W central Niagara Co. The town was formed from Cambria in 1812 as Schlosser and renamed in 1816. Part of Niagara Falls International Airport (1928) and Niagara Falls Air Force Base are in town. It is adjacent to and a suburb of the City of Niagara Falls. A landmark is Niagara School No. 2 (1878).

Nancy B. Mingus

Niagara County (523 mi^2/1,355 km^2; pop 219,846). Created from Genesee Co in 1808, it was named after the river that drains the four western Great Lakes and forms the western boundary of the county. Subsequent boundary changes took place with the creation of Erie Co in 1821 and the loss of Grand Island to it in 1824. Niagara Co is divided into the cities of Niagara Falls, North Tonawanda, and Lockport, the county seat, and 12 towns containing 5 incorporated villages. Elevations range from 246 feet (75

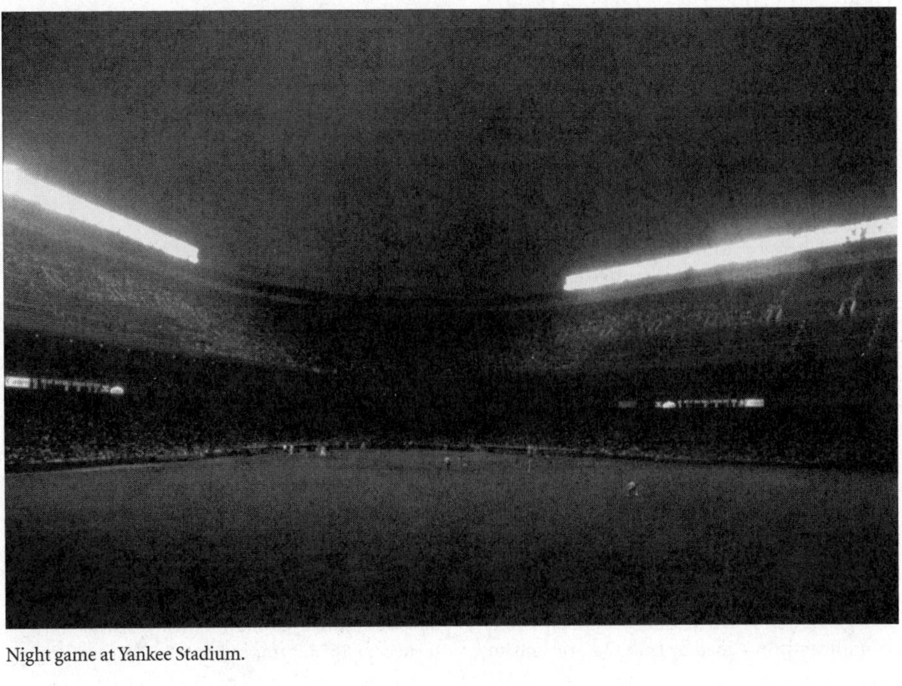

Night game at Yankee Stadium.

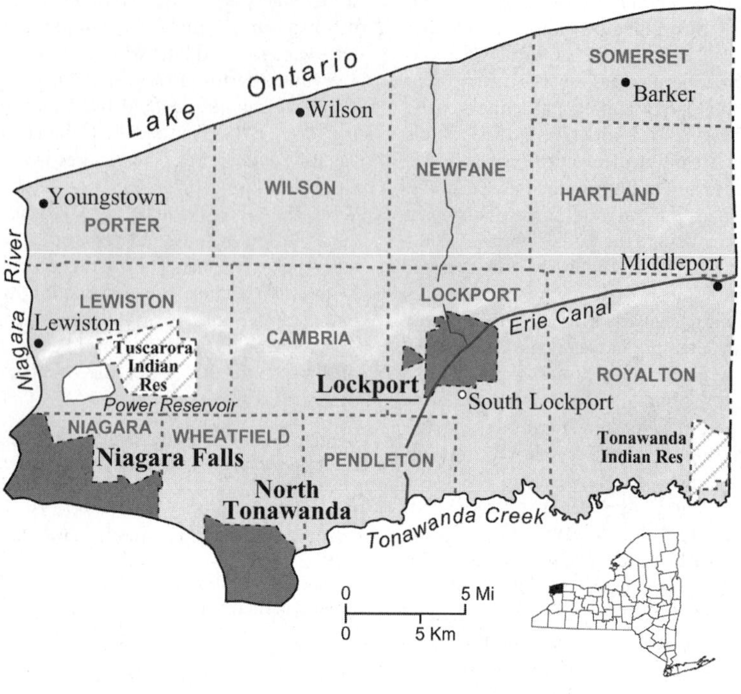

m) along the shore of Lake Ontario to 675 feet (206 m) at Bunker Hill in the Town of Royalton. The county lies entirely within the Erie-Ontario Lowland physiographic province. The steep, nearly vertical Niagara Escarpment, a north-facing cuesta, extends latitudinally across the entire county and marks the boundary between the Lake Ontario Plain subregion in the north and the Southern Ontario (sometimes called Huron) Plain subregion in the south. Bedrock north of the escarpment is Ordovician shale and siltstone; Silurian limestone, dolostone, shale, and siltstone lie to the south.

The most impressive and best-known site in the county is the 184 ft (56 m) high American Falls on the Niagara River. Capped with a layer of erosion-resistant Lockport dolomite, the falls has migrated southward during the past 12,000 years from the northern margin of the Niagara Escarpment near Lewiston to its present location, leaving the dramatic 7 mi (11 km) long Niagara Gorge in its wake. Evidence of glaciation can be found throughout the county, most commonly in till deposits that take the form of ground moraines, low drumlins, elongated till ridges, and the Barre and the Rochester-Albion terminal moraines. Arguably the most noteworthy Pleistocene feature is the former beach ridge of prehistoric glacial Lake Iroquois, rising 10–30 feet (3–9 m) above the surrounding country, that later served as an Indian trail, an early settlement trail (the Ridge Rd), and present Rte 104. The nearly flat relief of the Lake Ontario Plain results in poor surface drainage, with small, meandering streams flowing north into Lake Ontario. The land south of the Niagara Escarpment drains south into Tonawanda Creek, which in turn flows west into the Niagara River. Soil quality varies greatly throughout the county, ranging from high agricultural value to none. The most extensive areas of high-quality arable land are near the lakeshore and in the southeast quarter.

Niagara Co's climate is humid-continental and is significantly modified by Lake Ontario and, to a lesser extent, Lake Erie. Average January temperatures are 24° or 25°F (-4°C) throughout the county. The open waters of Lake Ontario keep nighttime lows from falling below 0°F (-18°C) more than once or twice each winter. Those same moderating waters limit summer temperatures of 90°F (32°C) or above and also the number of severe thunderstorms relative to more inland counties. July temperatures average near 71°F (22°C). Moderating breezes off Lake Ontario push the growing season back two weeks or more in the northern half of the county, lessening the threat of frost damage to orchard crops in the spring and fall. Average annual precipitation ranges from above 37 inches (94 cm) in the southeast to less than 33 inches (84 cm) along the lakeshore. The mean seasonal snowfall pattern is similar. The higher country south of the escarpment receives as much as 86 inches (218 cm), lakeshore areas less than 60 inches (152 cm). Primeval forest cover consisted primarily of a central hardwood community dominated by beech, sugar maple, and basswood, augmented in places by oak, hickory, and chestnut. Substantial east-west bands of wetland soils along Tonawanda Creek and the old beach lines of Lake Iroquois supported forests of elm, black ash, and hemlock.

American Indians and Early Settlement

The first known residents were the Neutral Indians, who lived in the area in the early 17th century. They were defeated by the Seneca about 1651, and the remaining Neutrals were incorporated into the social and kinship structures of the victors. The Seneca were to occupy the region over the next century. French explorers passed through as early as 1615, when Samuel de Champlain mapped all of Lake Ontario and its surrounding territory. René-Robert Cavelier de la Salle first came to the area in 1669 and built Fort Conti in what is now the Town of Porter in the following year. He returned in 1678, camping on the Niagara River at Lake Ontario. La Salle's party included Fr Louis Hennepin who, as the party's scribe, became the first to publicize the wonders of Niagara Falls. At a point above the falls at Cayuga Creek [now La Salle], La Salle constructed a ship, the *Griffon,* which was launched in May 1679 and sailed up the river to Black Rock [now in Erie Co]. On 7 August, when the weather cleared, it became the first ship to sail on Lake Erie. In 1687 Fort Denonville was built where Fort Conti had stood; like its predecessor, it was short-lived.

Also important to the region's development were Louis-Thomas Chabert de Joncaire and his sons Philippe-Thomas and Daniel-Marie. Joncaire had come to the region in the late 1600s and was captured and adopted by the Seneca, remaining among them until 1694. After his release he became an interpreter between the French and the Seneca. About 1720 Joncaire the father built a French trading post near the present Lewiston. Called Magazin Royal (King's Store), it was the chief trading post until the building of Fort Niagara [now in Porter] (1726). Joncaire died in 1739, but his sons carried on, building another post, the stone chimney of which still stands, near Niagara Falls in 1750.

In 1759 the French lost the fort and the Niagara Frontier to the British, who remained in control of the area throughout the Revolutionary War. They used Fort Niagara as a base of operations during the war and kept control of it until Jay's Treaty went into effect in 1796. The British built other forts along the Niagara River: in 1760 they built Fort Schlosser in what is now the City of Niagara Falls and, in 1764, a fort near Lewiston Heights. An important road between Fort Schlosser and Fort Niagara, the Portage Rd, was used to transport goods from Lake Ontario to the rest of Western New York. In the aftermath of the Sullivan-Clinton campaign against the Iroquois in 1779, many of the Indian allies of the British moved to the Fort Niagara area. At the war's end there were several thousand Indians in the area, many of whom later moved to the Grand River Reservation in Ontario. Since 1797 the Tuscarora Indian Reservation, and a portion of the reservation of the Tonawanda Band of Seneca, are in the county.

What is now Niagara Co became part of the Holland Land Purchase in 1792–93, and European settlement began after the Treaty of Big Tree (1797). The Holland Land Co then began subdivision into 120-acre (49 ha) parcels for resale to settlers. Despite the activity along the river, the rest of the county had remained undeveloped; it was settled rapidly between 1800 and 1810. In 1802 the county's first Holland Land Purchase sales were recorded; by the end of that decade more than 300 people had purchased land.

Perhaps no area of the United States saw as much military action during the War of 1812 as Niagara Co. With the intention of capturing Canada, a small American force assembled along the Niagara River in the summer of 1812. Americans briefly captured Queenston Heights [now in Ont] in October. On the night of 18 Dec 1813 the British took Fort Niagara, which they held until the peace treaty, and they destroyed Youngstown and Lewiston, killing many Americans and torching everything that stood along the Niagara River.

The first white settlers of Niagara Co migrated

NIAGARA CO POPULATION CENSUS FIGURES

	White	Nonwhite	Total Population	Foreign-Born
1810	8,932	39	8,971	—
1820	22,908	82	22,990	65
1830	18,380	102	18,482	589
1840	30,891	241	31,132	—
1850	41,959	317	42,276	9,000
1860	49,882	517	50,399	14,312
1870	49,989	448	50,437	13,227
1880	53,756	417	54,173	12,840
1890	62,093	398	62,491	15,031
1900	74,066	895	74,961	17,691
1910	91,199	837	92,036	24,373
1920	117,747	958	118,705	29,616
1930	147,656	1,673	149,329	35,301
1940	158,203	1,907	160,110	29,765
1950	185,232	4,760	189,992	26,196
1960	232,277	9,992	242,269	24,628
1970	223,944	11,776	235,720	17,197
1980	212,873	14,481	227,354	12,999
1990	204,812	15,944	220,756	9,270
2000	199,404	20,442	219,846	8,495

Notes: "Nonwhite" includes African Americans, Asians, American Indians, and Pacific Islanders and, for 2000, also the mixed race and other race categories. Through the 1960 census these figures primarily reflect the African American population. Foreign-born figures for 1820 and 1830 include only those not naturalized, and for 1930 and 1950, the foreign-born totals include Whites only. Other years include all foreign-born in the population.

largely from the New England states, especially Vermont, and established close-knit communities. Many transplanted New Englanders were strong opponents of slavery and, in the 1840s and 1850s, helped fugitive slaves escape to Canada. Niagara Co was also embroiled in the Patriots' War of 1837, an insurrection against the British by Quebecois and other residents of both Upper and Lower Canada. On 12 Dec 1837 the steamboat *Caroline,* which was used to ferry arms and ammunition to Canadian rebels on Navy Island, was set afire at Schlosser Landing by a British force and cut loose to drift over the falls. Some of its crew perished, and this created outrage and greater sympathy for the Canadian rebels. Ultimately the movement resulted in greater autonomy, though not independence, for the Canadian colonies.

The first large influx of Irish immigrants began in 1821, with the offer of work on the Erie Canal. As in the rest of the state, foreign immigrants poured into Niagara Co in the late 19th and early 20th centuries to work in factories and, to a lesser extent, for farmwork. In 1855 Irish-born residents were a substantial 12%, while German-born were 8.5%. Twenty years later, Irish natives had dropped to 7%, but the Germans had increased slightly to 8.7%. In 1920, 25% of residents were foreign-born.

Transportation

The Indian trail along the ridge connecting Rochester to the Niagara Frontier became a stage road in the early 19th century. Soldiers stationed at Fort Niagara built a road connecting Lewiston to Black Rock in 1803–4. Known respectively as the Ridge Rd (Rte 104) and the Military Rd (Rte 265), these arteries helped advance settlement and development all along their routes. In 1816 New York State authorized the building of the Erie Canal between Albany and Buffalo, with a section running through Niagara Co. While the canal had a negative impact on the commerce of the Niagara River communities whose economy had been based on river shipment and portage, new settlements grew up along the canal. The county's first railroads, the Lockport and Niagara Falls and the Buffalo and Niagara Falls, began service in 1836. Three more lines were completed in the early 1850s: the Rochester, Lockport and Niagara Falls (1852), Buffalo and Lockport (1853), and Canandaigua and Niagara Falls (1854). All five lines became part of the New York Central Railroad either when it was formed (1853) or within a year afterward. The northern tier of towns remained unserved until the Rome, Watertown and Ogdensburg was built in 1876.

Economic Development

Even before Niagara Falls developed as a tourist attraction, its abundant waterpower was harnessed for industry. The Joncaires established a sawmill *ca* 1750, rebuilt by an Englishman by 1779. When the falls were under American control, a sawmill (1805) and gristmill (1807) were built. After the disruption of the War of 1812, industrial development resumed. In 1824 the Cataract House, the first significant hotel in Niagara Falls, was built, and the area began to draw tourists in an organized way. From that point on its scenic beauty and its industrial potential were in competition.

In an attempt to maximize power for industry, construction on a hydraulic canal was started in 1853. When it was completed in 1874, however, its waterpower was used by a single mill. Jacob F. Schoellkopf assumed control of the canal and began generating electricity in 1881, quickly drawing large factories eager to use electric power. The Niagara Tunnel (1890–93) was subsequently built for hydropower and, in 1896, began transmitting alternating current to Buffalo. Niagara Falls became a center of electrochemical and electrometallurgical plants, as well as the home of the trademark Natural Foods Co factory (1901), maker of Shredded Wheat.

The county's second industrial center was Lockport. Because of the steep fall of water from the top of the Erie Canal locks, Lockport had become a manufacturing center by 1835, with mills, a cotton factory, boot and shoe factories, tanneries, sash and blind works, a furnace, and a plow factory. Many more plants followed, most notably Birdsill Holly's industrial complex in which he produced his patented water-supply system, which included elliptical rotary water pumps and hydrants. Nearby Middleport was a small village but had a blast furnace and paper mill.

North Tonawanda developed initially as a port handling Michigan lumber, a business that peaked in the 1890s; when that industry declined North Tonawanda became home to iron and steel, chemical, and paper manufacturing, along with the Rudolph Wurlitzer Plant (1908), which produced organs and musical machines, and the Allan Herschell Carousel Factory (1910).

Inland and along Lake Ontario, farming was dominant, and most of the small industries were tied to agriculture. The Niagara Co Farmers Club (1880) served as a lobbying, education, and marketing group. It worked in conjunction with Cornell University to convert many tillage farms between the lake and Ridge Rd to orchards by the early 1900s. In 1900 there were 4,356 farms in the county, and although the number decreased to 3,362 in 1950, most of the county's towns remained predominantly agricultural.

By the post–Civil War era, the industries and somewhat garish tourist facilities of Niagara Falls had grown to the point that many were concerned that the beauty of the falls would be ruined. Frederick Law Olmsted and other national figures led a successful campaign in 1885 to protect the area surrounding the falls by creating the Niagara Reservation. During the same period, the county's Lake Ontario shore developed a minor resort industry, particularly at Olcott and Wilson.

Religion, Education, and Culture

Many of the first visitors to Niagara Co were French and American religious missionaries. The French installed a Roman Catholic chapel in Fort Niagara (1726), but the first church building was an 1806 Presbyterian mission to the Tuscarora. In 1855 there were 24 Methodist, 11 Baptist, 10 Presbyterian, and 8 Lutheran churches in the county. Half of the latter were in Wheatfield, where a substantial German Lutheran colony had settled in 1843; it would remain a cultural enclave for nearly a century. Niagara Co's first Roman Catholic Church was formed in Lockport around 1840, and the county had 5 parishes by 1855, and 12 by 1900.

The first school in the county may have been one established in Lewiston as early as 1806. Secondary education began with the Lewiston Academy (1824). This large four-story structure

POPULATIONS OF TOWNS AND CITIES, NIAGARA CO

Town or City, Year Founded	1840	1880	1920	1960	2000
Cambria, 1808	2,099	2,267	1,596	3,661	5,393
Hartland, 1812	2,350	3,340	1,987	3,577	4,165
Lewiston, 1818	2,533	2,768	2,750	13,686	16,257
Lockport, 1824	9,125	2,847	1,833	6,492	19,653
Lockport (city), 1865	—	13,522	21,308	26,443	22,279
Newfane, 1824	2,372	3,462	3,515	8,523	9,657
Niagara, 1812[a]	1,277	7,432	4,173	7,503	8,978
Niagara Falls (city), 1892	—	—	50,760	102,394	55,593
North Tonawanda (city), 1897	—	—	15,482	34,757	33,262
Pendleton, 1827	1,098	1,730	1,175	3,589	6,050
Porter, 1812	2,177	2,278	2,682	7,309	6,920
Royalton, 1817	3,549	4,888	4,485	6,585	7,710
Somerset, 1823	1,742	2,015	2,003	2,489	2,865
Wheatfield, 1836	1,057	4,390	1,884	8,008	14,086
Wilson, 1818	1,753	3,234	2,753	5,319	5,840

[a]Schlosser until 1816.

drew students not only from the surrounding towns but from Canada as well. The public school system developed in response to 1812 and 1814 legislation; in addition to the common (one-room) schools, Union Free School districts were created by consolidation in the larger villages following 1853 legislation. During the 1920s the state pursued an initiative to centralize education. No schools were centralized in Niagara Co, however, until Barker Central School (1937), followed by Wilson (1941), Newfane (1941), Royalton-Hartland (1944), Lewiston-Porter (1947), Pendleton-Cambia (1953), and Niagara-Wheatfield (1955). North Tonawanda and Lockport continued to absorb adjacent common schools as late as 1957. The only four-year accredited college in the county is Niagara University (1856) in Lewiston. The two-year Niagara County Community College was formed in 1962; its Sanborn campus opened in 1973.

Many of the county's cultural activities are concentrated along its waterways: the Niagara River, Lake Ontario, and the Erie Canal. The county's first newspaper, the *Niagara Democrat,* was printed in Lewiston in 1821 and moved to Lockport the following year. Lewiston is also home to the Earl W. Brydges Artpark (1974), a performing arts center located in a 150-acre (61 ha) state park bordering the Niagara Gorge, and to the Castellani Art Museum (1978) at Niagara University. The southeastern part of the county contains the Tonawanda State Wildlife Management Area, bordering the Iroquois National Wildlife Refuge. There are also 30 museums ranging from house museums to a geological museum (Niagara Falls) and an Erie Canal museum (Lockport).

Politics

During and after the Civil War the Towns of Niagara, Wheatfield, Pendleton, and Royalton were Democratic territory. After its incorporation the new city of Niagara Falls joined those towns to cast predominantly Democratic votes into the first decade of the 20th century. Since that time, Niagara Co has been generally Republican. In consequence of the one person–one vote ruling, the County Board of Supervisors was replaced in 1970 with a Board of Legislators elected from 31 legislative districts. A county manager was hired to oversee day-to-day business. A new county charter was drafted in 1977, but New York law required concurrent majority approval by both city residents and town residents; the latter turned it down and it was defeated. John J. Raskob of Lockport was a close friend of Gov Alfred E. Smith and chairman of the Democratic National Committee during Smith's presidential bid in 1928. Earl W. Brydges of Niagara Falls was the majority leader of the New York State Senate from 1965 to 1972.

The 20th Century

The county's three cities, Niagara Falls, North Tonawanda, and Lockport, boomed with heavy industry in the 20th century. Power generation continued to be both beneficial and harmful. Built along the Niagara Gorge, the Schoellkopf Power Station was completed in 1924 but was rendered virtually useless by a 1956 rockslide. It was replaced in 1961 by the current Robert Moses Power Plant following a long, contentious battle with the Tuscarora Nation, which lost part of its reservation to the facility. Another facility, the Knight Generating Station (1984) in Somerset, is coal-fired.

The large industrial plants that were attracted to the area by cheap power began closing in the mid–20th century, leaving behind high unemployment and three dozen Superfund sites. The most notorious of these is Love Canal, but there are an estimated 150 polluted sites along a 3 mi (5 km) stretch of the river. Despite significant initiatives in the 1970s planned to help Niagara Falls break its dependence on heavy industry, improvements to electric transmission neutralized the city's advantage in being near hydro-electric generation, and the important Carborundum Co pulled out in 1987. The city lost nearly half its population between 1960 and 2000, plunging from 102,394 to 55,593, but heavy industry is still significant, as is tourism. The Seneca Niagara Casino opened in 2002 with much publicity, though many doubt that it will be able to turn around the sagging Niagara Falls tourist business. Niagara Falls chemical manufacturers Olin, Oxychem, and DuPont remain important employers. Lockport too remains an industrial city, with seven manufacturing firms employing 100 or more workers each, notably Delphi-Harrison Thermal Systems (1910), a General Motors subsidiary, with 6,500 on its payroll. Meanwhile, the county's southern towns have become bedroom communities to Buffalo and other places in Erie Co.

Large expanses of good farmland were taken out of production in 1942–43 when the US government acquired 7,567 acres (3,062 ha) in Porter and Lewiston for the Lake Ontario Ordnance Works, originally for TNT production. Half the land was returned to private ownership after World War II, while the rest has gone to a variety of uses, notably Model City's Chemical Waste Management landfill (1984), which remains controversial among residents.

The northern towns remain primarily agricultural and are largely fruit-producing areas with businesses that support agriculture. Most processing is done outside the county, although Mayer Bros (Somerset) bottles apple juice, Cherries Central (Newfane) packs cherries, and Sun Orchards (Newfane) packs apples. Acreage for all crops has decreased significantly. Total farmland in 1997 was 127,355 acres (51,539 ha), only 57% of the 224,687 acres (90,928 ha) in 1940. However, between 1992 and 2002 the market value of crops increased 49.8% before adjustment for inflation. The county's population, which reached a peak of 242,269 in 1960, dropped 9.3% in the 40 years that followed, largely as a result of population loss in Niagara Falls.

The standard work is *History of Niagara County* (1878). Orsamus Turner, *Pioneer History of the Holland Purchase* (1849), is indispensable for the settlement period. Later works have included William Pool, ed., *Landmarks of Niagara County* (1897); *Souvenir History of Niagara County* (1902); Frank H. Severance, *Studies of the Niagara Frontier* (1911); *An Old Frontier of France,* 2 vols (1917); Edward T. Williams, *Niagara County,* 2 vols (1921); Merton M. Wilner, *Niagara Frontier: A Narrative and Documentary History,* 4 vols (1931); and John Aiken et al, *Outpost of Empires* (1961). Robert D. Kostoff, *A History of Niagara County* (2001), is annotated but idiosyncratic in both coverage and arrangement. Unfortunately, the level of documentation for the towns in all these books combined is surprisingly limited. Several town histories, along with other topical materials, have been published as *Occasional Contributions of the Niagara County Historical Society* (1948–). Two books of the many on Niagara Falls contribute to an understanding of city history: Hamilton B. Mizer, *A City Is Born, Niagara Falls, a City Matures* (1991), and William Irwin, *The New Niagara: Tourism, Technology, and the Landscape of Niagara Falls, 1776–1917* (1996). An interesting essay on the German community in Wheatfield is Eugene W. Camann, *Uprooted from Prussia, Transplanted in America* (1991). Lockport's history has been documented in a large number of pamphlets, including John C. Shea, ed., *History of Lockport* (?1910), and Lockport Board of Commerce, *Modern Lockport* (1935).

Nancy B. Mingus

Niagara Falls. Few natural objects have attracted as much attention as the great cataract of Niagara. The contrasting realities of the falls area—nature at its most sublime, popular recreation at its most tawdry, industrial might at its most powerful—have long competed to define Niagara in the popular imagination. When reports of the falls first reached Europe in the late 17th century, Niagara quickly became an emblem of the new continent itself and remains one of North America's best-known attractions. Like the Great Lakes, Niagara Falls is a product of repeated glacial advances that scoured away less-resistant rock, leaving a steep escarpment capped by very hard dolomite. During the 12,000 years that the waters of the upper Great Lakes poured over the escarpment, the falls migrated about 7 miles (11 km) upstream, carving out the Niagara Gorge. Goat Island separates Niagara's two waterfalls, the American and the Horseshoe, which are distinguished from other great cataracts not so much by their height—about 167 feet (51 m)—as by the prodigious volume of water—over 200,000 ft^3 (5,700 m^3) per second before hydroelectric diversions—that plunges in a single drop. A rising column of mist is usually visible from a considerable distance, crowned by a rainbow when the sun is shining.

Early 20th-century postcard view of Niagara Falls in winter, American Fall and Ice Mountain.

The indigenous Iroquois, or Haudenosaunee, apparently found the falls as compelling as subsequent European visitors would. Although little evidence survives of the Neutral Nation that controlled the Niagara River region until the mid–17th century, two other Iroquoian groups, the Seneca and the Tuscarora, have maintained a continuous oral tradition that associates the falls with spiritual values. Fr Louis Hennepin, probably the first European to see the falls, was stunned by its power; his written account (1683) and print (1697) greatly exaggerate the height of the cataract. During the period of French control, until 1759, Niagara Falls remained inaccessible to all but a trickle of visitors, leaving others to imagine it as spectacularly as they pleased.

The strategic importance of the Niagara region made it highly contested. The Niagara River is an international border and the narrowest point on the entire Great Lakes–St. Lawrence River system. The first bridge to join the United States and Canada on that system was built by engineer Charles Ellet Jr across the Niagara Gorge in 1848. The east-west transportation corridor that crosses the Niagara River there is a continuation of the Hudson-Mohawk route that takes advantage of the most important gap in the Appalachian Mountains. This route meets the St. Lawrence Lowland, another path to the continent's interior, at Niagara Falls. These considerations, along with the fact that the falls is the most significant obstacle to movement on the river itself, have made the area a particularly important transportation nexus. Bloody conflict came to the region during the French and Indian War, the Revolutionary War, the War of 1812, the Canadian Rebellion of 1837, and the Fenian invasion of 1866. Tensions at the Niagara border also rose during times when Canada was a destination for escaped slaves, rumrunners, or Vietnam War dissenters.

Rock of Ages and the Cave of the Winds at Niagara Falls, early 20th century.

As a Tourist Attraction

The opening of the Erie Canal in 1825 made Niagara accessible for the first time to ordinary travelers. This coincided with the rise in the United States of a new commercial and industrial middle class with the leisure and resources to travel for pleasure. Niagara Falls became the culmination of the North American Fashionable Tour that always included the Hudson River and the Erie Canal. Many Europeans joined American travelers on this pilgrimage to the falls. Niagara became a fashionable resort for literary, artistic, and educated travelers. The first railroad reached the falls in 1842, bringing many more visitors. By the outbreak of the Civil War, Niagara had lost much of its cachet as an elite resort, but its broader appeal continued to grow. In the early 20th century the automobile further democratized and diversified Niagara's tourism. Recent estimates of the number of visitors to the falls range as high as 20 million annually.

Beginning in the 1820s local landowners gradually changed the landscape around Niagara Falls to accommodate the influx of visitors. Stairways, paths, and footbridges eased the visitor's approach to the cataract, and a stone tower provided panoramic views. Hotels, museums, peddlers, and numerous other accoutrements of the resort industry sprang up on both banks. Much of what appeared during the initial phase of tourism still characterizes Niagara Falls. Recently married couples began to arrive in the 1830s. Honeymooning at Niagara has waxed and waned since, but no place in North America is more associated with this practice. The circus atmosphere created by museums, sideshows, and daredevils has been another constant presence. In recent decades the Canadian side has claimed the lion's share of the tourist market. Niagara Falls, Ont, abounds in garish attractions, including a successful gambling casino (1996) that draws vast numbers of visitors from the United States. Advertisements and Hollywood movies such as Henry Hathaway's *Niagara* (1953), starring Marilyn Monroe, have both exploited and enhanced the allure of the falls.

In the Imagination

People have imagined Niagara Falls in a bewildering number of ways over the years. The perceived meanings of the falls have varied with the viewer's gender, class, and nationality, and often reflect a tendency to compare contemporary lowbrow tourists to the supposedly sophisticated travelers of an imagined past. Nathaniel Hawthorne, who visited Niagara Falls in 1834, was initially very disappointed, noting that many visitors were more impressed with the technological marvel of the Erie Canal than with the falls itself. From afar, people could imagine Niagara as such an overwhelming sight that many were bound to be disappointed by the reality. Many were fascinated with the idea of the falls as it would have been prior to the arrival of Hennepin and the Europeans. This may have been the impetus for the legend of the "maid of the mist"—that the spirit of the falls demanded the fairest virgin of the tribe to be sacrificed each year—a purely European American, mid-Victorian invention.

By the early 19th century, new middle-class tourists were well schooled in the aesthetics of the natural sublime, centered on the mixture of terror and joy that scenes like the falls inspired. The overwhelming and apparently limitless power in nature is attractive, they believed, because it corresponds to the viewer's own spiritual, imaginative, or rational powers. A common response to Niagara Falls throughout the century was an urge to confront and symbolically conquer it. Some expressed this desire in words, while others preferred to cross the gorge on tightropes—famously initiated by Jean François Gravelet, "the Great Blondin," in 1859—or ride the boat *Maid of the Mist* (from 1846) to the very foot of the Horseshoe Falls. Because many of Niagara's antebellum visitors saw nature itself as sacred, they often spoke of the Niagara experience as a pilgrimage. Indeed, the circus atmosphere at Niagara, matching the sacred with the profane, resembles the exotic fairs and markets that surrounded medieval Christian pilgrimage sites. Writers like James Fenimore Cooper and artists like Thomas Cole evoked a Niagara Falls in which romanticism intertwined with nationalist pride in the grandeur of the American landscape. After 1900 Niagara was rarely the focus of high literature or art, but its popular appeal continued to grow. In 1901 Annie Edson Taylor became the first person to go over the falls in a barrel and survive. Fifteen others have made the attempt since, with 10 surviving, including Kirk Jones of Canton, Mich, whose plunge on 20 Oct 2003 was the first without protective equipment. Movies, television, Broadway tunes, and other entertainment forms presented Niagara Falls as a spectacular and romantic part of the North American landscape. As photographs replaced paintings and drawings, the number of images swelled.

WATERPOWER

Perhaps the most obvious way of taming Niagara was to harness its power for industry, an idea that dates back to the late 18th century. Indeed, the people who established the first village at Niagara Falls, just before the War of 1812, named it after the greatest manufacturing city in the world, Manchester. By 1850 a few small mills clustered on the American shore in the islands of the upper rapids and along two small raceways that emptied back into the river above the crest of the falls. The first large-scale power development was a hydraulic canal that cut diagonally across the Village of Niagara Falls on the American side, creating a concentrated manufacturing district that thrived from 1875 to 1900 at the top of the gorge a few hundred feet downstream from the falls. An international movement to free the immediate vicinity of the falls from industry and private development led to the creation of the Niagara Reservation State Park (1885), New York's first state park, which was designed by Frederick Law Olmsted, and Queen Victoria Park (1887) on the Ontario side.

THE HOME OF SHREDDED WHEAT
at Niagara Falls, N.Y.

Early-20th-century postcard view of Niagara Falls.

By the 1890s momentum began to gather for a much larger power development at Niagara Falls. Many ideas were proposed. King Camp Gillette, who would later become famous for inventing the safety razor, suggested that efficiency and logic would eventually lead to a single great city where all of North America's manufacturing could be concentrated and believed there was enough power at Niagara to supply such a city. The flamboyant entrepreneur William T. Love wanted to create a utopian "Model City" by diverting water from the upper Niagara River through a power canal; 1 mile (1.6 km) of the canal was excavated when financial problems halted the project. The scheme that eventually reached fruition created enormous excitement. In 1886 Thomas Evershed suggested digging a tunnel deep under Niagara Falls on the New York side. Water from the upper river would be diverted through the tunnel, turning turbines and generating electricity. Against the advice of Lord Kelvin and Thomas Edison, the Niagara Falls Power Co decided to use Nikola Tesla's idea of alternating current for this unprecedented project. In 1896 the company successfully powered the streetlights of Buffalo in the first long-distance transmission of electricity, a phenomenon that was fully exploited and demonstrated at Buffalo's Pan-American Exposition in 1901.

Despite fears that Niagara Falls itself might be dried up, international agreements have continued to expand allowable water diversions. Regulations passed in 1950 simply require that at least 100,000 ft^3 (2,830 m^3) of water per second must go over the falls during the daylight hours of the tourist season, and at least half that amount at night and during the off-season. Therefore, at minimum, during peak daytime viewing hours the early 21st-century visitor sees about half of the volume that the 19th-century tourist observed. New power plants on both sides of the river began to operate in the 1960s. From the turn of the 20th century, electrochemical companies have concentrated at Niagara Falls to take advantage of inexpensive power. The Hooker Chemical Co used the abandoned canal from Love's utopian project as a toxic waste dump. Ironically, Love Canal finally achieved a grotesque version of the fame its creator had hoped for when harmful chemicals began to ooze to the surface in the 1970s, after the City of Niagara Falls had allowed a school and a residential neighborhood to be built there. The disaster played a pivotal role in increasing public awareness of toxic waste issues.

The series of hydropower projects has not, however, prevented urban decline from taking hold on the American side of the falls. While Niagara Falls, Ont, has benefited from a thriving tourist business, Niagara Falls, NY, has seen its industry largely disappear and its population drop from over 100,000 in 1960 to 55,000 in 2000. In recent years the American city has taken steps to emulate the success of its Canadian sister; a casino run by the Seneca Indian Nation opened on the last day of 2002. To date these revitalization efforts have been modestly successful.

See also BRIDGES OF THE NIAGARA GORGE; RESORT HOTELS.

Adamson, Jeremy Elwell. *Niagara: Two Centuries of Changing Attitudes, 1697–1901* (Washington, DC: Corcoran Gallery of Art, 1985)

Berton, Pierre. *Niagara: A History of the Falls* (New York: Kodansha International, 1997)

Dow, Charles Mason. *Anthology and Bibliography of Niagara Falls*, 2 vols (Albany: State of New York, 1921)

Dubinsky, Karen. *The Second Greatest Disappointment: Honeymooning and Tourism at Niagara Falls* (New Brunswick, NJ: Rutgers Univ Press, 1999)

Irwin, William. *The New Niagara: Tourism, Technology, and the Landscape of Niagara Falls, 1776–1917* (University Park: Pennsylvania State Univ Press, 1996)

Lane, Christopher W. *Impressions of Niagara: The Charles Rand Penny Collection of Prints of Niagara Falls and the Niagara River from the 16th to the Early 20th Century* (Philadelphia: Philadelphia Print Shop, 1993)

McGreevy, Patrick. *Imagining Niagara: The Meaning and Making of Niagara Falls* (Amherst: Univ of Massachusetts Press, 1994)

McKinsey, Elizabeth. *Niagara Falls: Icon of the American Sublime* (New York: Cambridge Univ Press, 1985)

Sears, John F. *Sacred Places: American Tourist Attractions in the 19th Century* (New York: Oxford Univ Press, 1989)

Patrick McGreevy

Niagara Falls. City (pop 55,593) in W Niagara Co. The first European known to have seen the falls was Fr Louis Hennepin in 1678; the following spring the *Griffon* was constructed within present city limits for an exploratory journey in the Great Lakes by René-Robert Cavelier de la Salle. In 1720 Louis-Thomas Chabert de Joncaire (?1670–1739), a French emissary to the Seneca, built a trading post on the Niagara River in what is now Lewiston, and his son Daniel-Marie Chabert de Joncaire (1714–1771) built a sawmill *ca* 1750 just above what is now called American Falls, but the region came under British control in 1759. The Seneca Nation granted the Mile Reserve, a tract surrounding the falls, to Sir William Johnson in 1764. By 1779 John Stedman had rebuilt Joncaire's sawmill. At the close of the Revolutionary War, the Niagara settlement was firmly in British hands and remained so until Jay Treaty took effect in 1796, but the falls quickly became an American icon when rendered in a famous engraving (*A Symbol of America*, 1800) commemorating George Washington's death.

In 1805 New York State sold the Mile Reserve to Augustus Porter and associates, who built a sawmill (1805) and a gristmill (1807); Porter moved to the area to engage in trade. A post office named Fort Schlosser, established in 1809, was changed to Manchester two years later to convey the industrial vision generated by the site's vast waterpower. The settlement was burned by the British in 1813, but in 1815 industrial growth resumed, accelerating with the 1820–23 construction of woolen, grist, and paper mills, along with a forge, rolling mill, and nail factory. At the same time, tourism expanded, thanks to the elite Fashionable Tour, a circuit of northeastern spas and scenic attractions; the post office name was changed again to Niagara Falls in 1823. The Cataract House (1824–1945) was built to accommodate the growing number of visitors, and the Erie Canal (1825) opened the region to less wealthy tourists. The Lockport and Niagara Falls Railroad (1836–51) was the first rail connection, but a link from the southeast (Buffalo and Niagara Falls Railroad in 1836) proved more enduring, as did the Canandaigua and Niagara Falls Railroad (1853). Niagara Falls incorporated as a village in 1848. The great Niagara Railway Suspension Bridge to Canada was built between 1852 and 1855, and at its location 2 miles (3 km) below the falls Niagara City developed, which incorporated as a village in 1854; its post office name was Suspension Bridge. About 1860 it became the site of extensive rail yards.

A hydraulic canal project (1853–75) was intended to provide waterpower to multiple factories but powered a single mill until sold to Jacob F. Schoellkopf in 1877. His Niagara Falls Hydraulic Power and Manufacturing Co began generating direct-current power in 1881, and by the next year six mills (grist, paper, silver-plate) had located in a new mill district by the canal basin. Factories and railroad lines within sight of the falls created deplorable conditions that threatened Niagara's primacy as a tourist attraction. What Henry James called "shops and booths and catch penny arcades" further cluttered the landscape, appealing to working-class tourists but adding to the objections of such luminaries as Frederic Edwin Church and Frederick Law Olmsted. "Save Niagara" advocacy groups demanded that the area near the falls be returned to "a state of nature," and the Niagara Reservation, one of the first American state parks, was created in 1885. The villages of Niagara Falls and Niagara City merged to form the city of Niagara Falls in 1892.

At the time it became a city, Niagara Falls was still more of a tourist area than a manufacturing center, despite its four pulp and paper mills, three flour mills, a business-forms plant, and a silver-plating factory. A plan by the Niagara Falls Power Co for industrial development based on hydraulic-generated electricity required the construction of the Niagara Tunnel, specifically for power purposes, between the upper and lower rivers (1890–93). Once the tunnel was completed, the city's manufacturing sector expanded rapidly, particularly in electrochemical and electrometallurgical fields, attracting such firms as Union Carbide Corp, Carborundum Co, and Pittsburgh Reduction Co (after 1907, Alcoa). Power production became an industry of its own when alternating current was successfully transmitted to Buffalo in 1896, transforming electricity into a commodity; from 10,000 kW at the start, generation rose to 360,000 kW in 1925. In 1901 the Natural Food Co, maker of Shredded Wheat, opened its model factory near the falls; contrasting with the city's other industries, this sparkling, progressive plant became a tourist attraction. Besides rapid industrial expansion, the state park helped revive Niagara Falls as a tourist destination, and it was a preeminent honeymoon spot in the United States throughout the first half of the 20th century.

Niagara Falls Power Co developed a model village, Echota, designed by Stanford White beginning in 1894 in the Shingle style, but most working-class housing was drab. Polish and Italian immigrants were attracted nonetheless by the burgeoning industrial employment and joined the more established Irish and German populations; in 1920, 35% of the city's residents were foreign-born, and 15% were Black. The city continued to grow rapidly, adopting a city manager form of government in 1914. After La Salle (incorporated 1897), a village of some 4,000 people just east of the city, was annexed in 1927, print media frequently proclaimed Niagara Falls "the fastest-growing city in New York State." Its 1920 population of 50,760 jumped to 75,460 a decade later, a 48.7% growth rate.

Following depression era doldrums, Niagara Falls chemical plants boomed with lucrative contracts for World War II production. Industrial decline began with the 1949 departure of Alcoa, and in the 1950s the city's industrial sector lost 10,000 jobs, although population peaked in 1960 at 102,394. Niagara Falls declined as a railroad terminal with the increase of motor vehicle traffic, which was stimulated in part by highway, parkway, and bridge construction directed by Robert Moses beginning in 1955. In 1956 two-thirds of the Schoellkopf Power Station (1924) was destroyed by a rockslide; its replacement, the Robert Moses Niagara Power Plant (1958–61), was built by the New York Power Authority just over the city line in Lewiston over strong protests by the Tuscarora Nation, some of whose land was taken.

It fell to Mayor E. Dent Lackey (1963–75) to oversee the city's shift away from dependence on heavy industry. Among the initiatives he set in motion were the Philip Johnson–designed Niagara Falls International Convention Center (1974), the Wintergarden (1977; an enclosed botanical garden designed by Cesar Pelli), the Turtle (a Native American museum and arts center), and the Rainbow Centre Mall. Environmental concerns arose during the Love Canal crisis in 1978, and deindustrialization continued in the last quarter of the century: transmission advances neutralized the city's location near hydropower, and labor costs made local production less competitive. Major losses included the Carborundum Co in 1987. In the 40 years after 1960, the population of Niagara Falls was cut almost in half. City government was again transformed by a return to a strong mayor with an administrator and a seven-member council in 1988.

In the early 21st century heavy industry continues to be significant in Niagara Falls; the largest manufacturing employers are Oxychem, DuPont, and Olin. Tourism remains a powerful economic engine, with 6–11 million visitors each year. Attractions include the Aquarium of Niagara (1965), the Niagara Gorge Discovery Center (1971), the Niagara Aerospace Museum (2002), and the Seneca Niagara Casino (2002). The city is the site of Niagara Reservation, Whirlpool, and Devils Hole State Parks.

See also CHEMICAL INDUSTRY.

Mizer, Hamilton. *A City Is Born: Niagara Falls: A City Matures*, rev ed. (Lockport, NY: Niagara County Historical Society, 1991)

Vogel, Michael N. *Echoes in the Mist: An Illustrated History of the Niagara Falls Area* (Chatsworth, Calif: Windsor Publications, 1991)

Williams, Marjorie F. *A Brief History of Niagara Falls, New York* ([Niagara Falls, NY]: Niagara Falls Public Library, 1970)

H. William Feder

Niagara Frontier. Erie and Niagara Cos form what is commonly known as the Niagara Frontier. The term frontier was applied when the area had very sparse European settlement and continued to be used because the area was seen as an economic and technological frontier. It had had a very significant American Indian population. Despite the expropriation of the large Buffalo Creek Reservation [now in Erie Co] in 1838, portions of three Indian reservations remain in the area. The region, at the juncture of Lakes Erie and Ontario, was perfectly situated to become a nexus of trade and, through the Niagara River, a center of industry and electrical production.

The 19th and Early 20th Centuries

The area developed rapidly after Buffalo became the western terminus of the Erie Canal in 1825. The canal made Buffalo the western gateway for the movement of people and goods into the upper Midwest and for the transfer of products from the interior to the coast, especially to New York City. Buffalo emerged as a leading rail hub, and the entire frontier served as a conduit for international railroad linkages with Canada. The area became a center of bridge engineering because of the need to project a span over the rapids near Niagara Falls, starting with John Roebling's Niagara Railway Suspension Bridge (1855). Technology also played an important role on Buffalo's waterfront. Joseph Dart designed the first mechanized grain elevator and storage warehouse, which went into use on the waterfront in 1842. Buffalo grain elevators would become famous worldwide and serve as an inspiration to 20th-century European urban architects.

The Niagara Frontier also led the world in the early development of electric power generation and use. In 1881 Jacob Schoellkopf's Niagara Falls Hydraulic Power and Manufacturing Co provided the first commercial application of hydroelectric power. By 1896 the world's largest and most technologically sophisticated hydroelectric project began operation at the falls, developed by the Niagara Falls Power Co. The new alternating current system was used to transmit the electricity to Buffalo almost 20 miles (32 km) south. This was the longest distance electricity had been sent from a generating plant at that time.

The City of Niagara Falls became an early center of electricity-intensive industries such as metallurgy and chemicals. At the same time Buffalo's location in the nation's railroad network and the Great Lakes shipping system made the city a rising center of heavy industry. Iron ore from Minnesota came across the Great Lakes to Buffalo. It was combined with western Pennsylvania coal to produce steel in a manufacturing complex stretching along Lake Erie from South Buffalo to Lackawanna (Erie Co). The Niagara Frontier's steel and aluminum plants provided the materials needed for an automobile industry (Pierce-Arrow, Ford, General Motors). Beginning in the 1930s and continuing through World War II, Bell and Curtiss-Wright produced thousands of aircraft in the Buffalo area.

Although the Niagara Frontier is best known for heavy industry, the area is also a center of agriculture. In 1900 the area had 12,285 farms on 876,540 acres (354,723 ha). In the late 20th century, the numbers were down, but farming was still important to the economy. In 1997 there were 1,660 farms on 270,589 acres (109,503 ha). Wheat farming after 1825 declined in the face of midwestern competition, and Niagara Frontier farmers shifted to dairy, vegetable, and fruit production to serve the region's expanding industrial cities. By the 20th century, improved food processing and shipping technologies brought larger and more distant markets for the Niagara Frontier's milk, grape, and vegetable products. However, throughout the 20th century Niagara and Erie Cos fell in statewide rankings of the value of agricultural output among state counties.

The industrial and commercial development in the Niagara Frontier attracted a number of immigrants, large numbers of whom had arrived by the mid–19th century. In 1850 the population of Erie and Niagara Cos was 32% foreign-born, percentages that remained substantial through the middle of the 20th century (24% in 1920). Most of the antebellum immigrants to the area were German and Irish and Catholic. Between the 1870s and 1920s great numbers of southern and eastern Europeans settled in the area, including Poles, Slavs, Italians, and Sicilians, the majority of whom were Catholic. Since World War II there has been a migration of Puerto Ricans and an influx of Greeks, Arabs, eastern Europeans, and Asians. The small African American population present from the early 19th century grew significantly during and after the Great Migration of the 1920s and 1930s.

RECENT HISTORY

The two main trends in the area in the second half of the 20th century were the linked phenomena of suburbanization and deindustrialization. In 1920, 74% of the population of Erie and Niagara Cos lived in the two largest cities, by 1960 only 48%, and by 2000 only 29%. The deindustrialization of Buffalo and Niagara Falls started in the immediate postwar years, rapidly accelerating after 1970 and sparking a drastic decline in urban population. By 2000 both cities had lost about half of their population from their midcentury peaks. Although there was considerable movement to the suburbs, the total population of the area declined, and between 1960 and 2000 the population of the Niagara Frontier declined 12%.

Irwin, William. *The New Niagara: Tourism, Technology, and the Landscape of Niagara Falls, 1776–1917* (University Park: Pennsylvania State Univ Press, 1996)

Shelton, Brenda K. *Reformers in Search of Yesterday: Buffalo in the 1890s* (Albany: SUNY Press, 1976)

M. Stephen Pendleton and Jean Richardson

Niagara Mohawk. Syracuse-based electricity and natural gas utility serving parts of the Capital District, the Mohawk Valley, Adirondack/North Country, Central New York, the Buffalo/Niagara region, Western New York, and the Southern Tier. The Buffalo, Niagara, and Eastern Power Corp, the Northeastern Power Corp, and Mohawk Hudson Power Corp provided power to residents of these regions through 59 subsidiary companies before Niagara Hudson Power Corp was established as a holding company in 1929. Floyd Leslie Carlisle, former president of Northeastern Power Corp and a Watertown native, was named Niagara Hudson's first chairman of the board. Seeking simplification of its corporate structure, by 1937 Niagara Hudson consolidated to 20 companies, including three principal operating companies (Buffalo Niagara Electric Corp, Central New York Power Corp, and New York Power and Light Corp), and became a world leader in electricity sales. Further consolidation came after 1942, when the federal Securities and Exchange Commission (SEC) ordered the breakup of United Gas Improvement Co (UGI), which had owned a controlling interest in Niagara Hudson. To comply with the law, UGI distributed those shares to its own shareholders, effectively ending UGI's interest in the company. Niagara Hudson was dissolved, and its three main companies merged to form Niagara Mohawk Power on 1 Jan 1950.

Commonly known as NiMo, the new company, with Earle J. Machold as its first president and director, headquartered in Syracuse. Machold, born in Ellisburg (Jefferson Co), had replaced Carlisle as president of Niagara Hudson in 1942, and his family had bought a controlling interest in Niagara Mohawk when it formed. Niagara Mohawk supplied close to 900,000 customers with electricity and almost 300,000 customers with gas in 1950. As electricity demand increased, the company began expanding existing plants, such as the Oswego Steam Station (1940), and building additional plants, such as the Albany Steam Station (1952). In 1956 a mammoth rock slide crushed part of Niagara Mohawk's Schoellkopf Station plant in Niagara Falls. One person was killed beneath the 120,000 tons (108,900 MT) of rock that destroyed the plant, one of the world's largest hydropower generators. The sudden loss of capacity pushed the state's Power Authority to build a new hydroelectric plant, the Robert Moses Generating Station, which opened on the Niagara River in 1961. At 2,400 MW, it remains the state's largest source of power in the early 21st century. With the state providing Niagara Mohawk's immediate energy needs, Niagara Mohawk began planning for nuclear power production. Although the company had already been delivering nuclear power—in 1955 the first American homes powered by nuclear energy were owned by Niagara Mohawk customers—it began producing nuclear energy after the Nine Mile Point One power plant opened in Scriba (Oswego Co) in 1969. Nine Mile Two opened at the same site in 1988. The company sold its interest in the Nine Mile reactors in November 2001 to Constellation Nuclear, leaving it with no generating facilities in its portfolio.

The nation's energy crisis of the 1970s resulted in legislation that almost bankrupted Niagara Mohawk. The so-called Six Cent Law required utilities to buy electricity from independent generators for at least 6¢ a kilowatt hour, a price much higher than what it would have cost utilities to produce the power on their own. Legislators repealed the law by 1992, but existing long-term contracts continued to hurt the company, which was paying about $400 million a year more for electricity under these contracts than it needed to in the mid-1990s. Deregulation was a growing trend. In 1995 Niagara Mohawk submitted a reorganization plan with the state's Public Service Commission that aimed to mitigate rising rates by selling its portfolio of generating assets and allowing consumers to purchase electricity directly from suppliers.

By September 1997 it had reached tentative agreement with state regulators on its restructuring plan, which allowed it to buy out its long-term contracts. The sudden return to financial health made Niagara Mohawk a takeover target. In January 2002 National Grid Group (now National Grid Transco), a British utility company, bought it for $3 billion. Niagara Mohawk was one of nine National Grid companies in the United States in 2003. As of September 2003 it served 1.5 million electricity customers and close to 550,000 gas customers across more than 24,000 mi^2 (62,160 km^2) of New York State. In 2003 it maintained approximately 8,300 miles (13,360 km) of gas main and distribution pipe and 6,000 miles (9,700 km) of electricity transmission lines, recording $4 billion in revenue. As of April 2004, Niagara Mohawk employed 4,200 employees. Its Art Deco–styled headquarters in Syracuse remains a noted architectural landmark.

Niagara Mohawk: An Uncommon History (Syracuse: Niagara Mohawk, 2001)

"SEC Scores Twice in 'Death Sentence,' " *New York Times*, 31 Dec 1942

Kenneth Aaron

Niagara Mohawk Building, Syracuse.

Niagara Movement. The first national civil rights organization of its kind founded in the 20th century (1905). Its chief architect, W. E. B. DuBois, wished to create an African American advocacy movement that would militantly push for black civil equality as an alternative to the views of Booker T. Washington. DuBois and another like-minded colleague, William Monroe Trotter, started in early 1905 planning for a meeting of black men in Buffalo that summer to launch their anti-Washingtonian organization. The Buffalo site was likely connected to DuBois's friendship with two leaders of that city's African American community, William Talbert and Mary B. Talbert. A preliminary meeting of the Niagara Movement was held at the couple's Michigan St home. Plans for a larger meeting in a Buffalo hotel were stymied through racial prejudice, and DuBois arranged at the last minute for accommodations in Fort Erie, Ont, across the Niagara River. The 29 men (women were allowed into the Niagara Movement only the following year) from 14 states met at the Erie Beach Hotel 11–14 July and issued the Declaration of Principles calling for black equality, suffrage, and an end to Jim Crow. The Niagara Movement, named for the location of its initial conference and the wish of its founders to evoke the great force of the nearby waterfall, was incorporated in early 1906. The group met annually for five years at historic locations such as Harpers Ferry, W Va, which was the site of John Brown's raid, and Faneuil Hall in Boston. At the height of its activity, the Niagara Movement had 30 branches and 400 members. But dogged by Washington's opposition, hampered by the movement's loose organizational structure and inadequate financing, and riven by internal disputes between DuBois and Trotter, the Niagara Movement soon became moribund. Many of its leaders, with the significant exception of Trotter, joined the National Association for the Advancement of Colored People (NAACP) after its founding in 1909. With the added help of influential white members and financial backers, the NAACP continued the Niagara Movement's struggle for the full realization of black civil rights.

Harlan, Louis R. *Booker T. Washington: The Wizard of Tuskegee, 1901–1915* (New York: Oxford Univ Press, 1983)

Lewis, David Levering. *W. E. B. DuBois: Biography of a Race, 1868–1919* (New York: Henry Holt, 1993)

Peter Eisenstadt

Niagara Reservation State Park. As early as 1834 visitors remarked on the commercialization of the shoreline overlooking the American side of Niagara Falls. A campaign to wrest the view of the falls and the river from private ownership and to restore its natural beauty was first discussed in 1869, at which time Frederick Law Olmsted, Calvert Vaux, and H. H. Richardson made an inspection, and Olmsted began championing the project. In 1880 he and Vaux prepared a landscape restoration plan encompassing islands and riverbank. Gov Lucius Robinson spoke in favor of protection in his January 1879 message to the state legislature. After unsuccessful legislative efforts in 1880 and 1881, the Niagara Reservation Acts of 1883 (condemnation) and 1885 (appropriation) were passed. Gov David B. Hill signed the appropriation bill on 30 Apr 1885. The park was formally presented to the people of New York State on 15 July 1885 and the last of more than 150 privately owned buildings was removed in 1908. It is considered the oldest state park in the United States, consists of 435 acres (176 ha) (296 acres/120 ha of which are under water) and includes popular features such as the Maid of the Mist, the Cave of the Winds, and the Observation Tower.

Dow, Charles Mason. *The State Reservation at Niagara: A History* (Albany: J. B. Lyon, 1914)

Irwin, William. *The New Niagara: Tourism, Technology, and the Landscape of Niagara Falls, 1776–1917* (University Park: Pennsylvania State Univ Press, 1996)

Welch, Thomas V. *How Niagara Was Made Free: The Passage of the Niagara Reservation Act in 1885.* Publications of the Buffalo Historical Society, vol 5 (Buffalo: The Society, 1902)

Vicki Weiss

Niagara River (35 mi/56 km). A link in the chain of waters connecting the Great Lakes and the Atlantic Ocean, the Niagara River extends from the northeast end of Lake Erie to the southern shore of Lake Ontario, flowing generally northward between New York State and Canada and dropping approximately 325 feet (99 m) in its brief length. Above Niagara Falls, the river is relatively broad and placid, flowing past settled landscapes and around several islands, the largest of which is Grand Island. Below the falls, it descends into a narrow gorge and races past rugged cliffs until it reaches the Village of Lewiston (Niagara Co). It was here that the falls first poured over the Niagara Escarpment at the end of the most recent ice age, perhaps 12,000 years ago. Since that time, the gorge has been steadily carved by the river, which erodes softer rock strata below the harder upper dolomite. Eventually, the upper layer collapses, thus moving the falls southward. When the French arrived, the river was the home to the Neutral Nation and the Erie, who were assimilated into the Iroquois Confederacy in the 17th century. The Tuscarora Nation entered New York in the 18th century and established itself on land along the Niagara Escarpment in the years following the Revolution.

As a boundary water, the river remained a flashpoint of conflict between the United States and British North America for most of the 19th century. After failing to seize Toronto during the 1837 rebellion, William Lyon Mackenzie retreated to Navy Island above the falls and proclaimed a short-lived provisional government of Canada. Irish Americans, known as Fenians, staged a series of major raids into British territory after the Civil War. At the same time, commercial and transportation links were being forged as the area underwent rapid industrialization. The river was first spanned by a conventional bridge joining the United States with Canada in 1848. That feat was soon eclipsed by the completion of John Roebling's railway suspension bridge in 1855. With the railroads providing easier access to the falls, tourism in the river communities increased enormously after midcentury. In the final quarter of the 19th century, manufacturers were given a new reason to locate factories along the river when the generation and transmission of hydroelectric power became a practical reality. By 1882 Jacob Schoellkopf's Niagara Falls Hydraulic and Manufacturing Co was producing electrical power for seven factories using water from the river.

From that time, a considerable portion of the natural flow of the river has been diverted above the falls and returned to the lower river after being used to generate electricity. Pursuant to international agreement, from April to October, when the tourist season is at its height, approximately 100,000 ft^3 (2,800 m^3) per second of the river's flow (approximately half of the total) is diverted to the power plants during daylight hours, and at other times approximately 150,000 ft^3 (4,200 m^3) per second is diverted. The United States and Canada have equal rights to the diverted flow. The Niagara power project at Lewiston first produced commercial power in 1961 and is the biggest power producer in New York State, generating approximately 2.4 million kW on an annual basis.

The imprint of the late 19th century can be seen along the river. Industrial facilities still dominate the shoreline above the falls, and the problematic legacy of more than a century of contamination remains in the river sediments and fish. Because of the accumulation of polychlorinated biphenyls (PCBs), mirex, and dioxin, fish consumption advisories were issued in 2003 for carp, white perch, and smallmouth bass. The New York State Department of Environmental Conservation adopted a Remedial Action Plan for the river, but achieving the set goals will require many decades of effort by public and private entities. In general, water quality in the river allows for a broad range of uses. Sportfishing is popular, and bass, muskellunge, pike, yellow perch, and other species are taken by anglers.

Jackson, John N. *The Mighty Niagara: One River, Two Frontiers* (Amherst, NY: Prometheus Books, 2003)

William S. Helmer

Niagara Ship Canal. A proposed waterway for on the American side of the Niagara River, bypassing Niagara Falls and enabling vessels to pass

Mills on American shore of Niagara River, *ca* 1900.

between Lakes Erie and Ontario. In 1798 the Niagara Canal Co was chartered by the State of New York to construct a canal capable of passing boats of 80 tons (73 MT), but this canal was never begun. Initially the project was advocated to permit navigation around the falls. After completion of the Welland Canal in Canada in 1829, which accomplished that navigational purpose, such a canal was promoted to eliminate dependence upon a foreign waterway. Numerous state and federal government surveys were conducted throughout the 19th century, and several pieces of legislation were introduced appropriating funds for construction. Some proposals included the construction of a marine railway whereby vessels would be moved by rail in floating docks or tanks. In 1900, as part of the Barge Canal project, the state engineer prepared yet another estimate. As recently as the 1950s and 1960s, the construction and operation of the St. Lawrence Seaway revived talk of an "All-American" canal. However, no serious start on this project was ever made.

Dow, Charles Mason. *Anthology and Bibliography of Niagara Falls* (Albany: J. B. Lyon, 1921)

Paul J. Bartczak

Niagara University. Private coeducational university in Lewiston (Niagara Co). Founded by the Vincentian community in 1856 as the Seminary of Our Lady of Angels, in 1883 it was chartered and became Niagara University. Located four miles from Niagara Falls on 160 acres (65 ha), the school, previously for males only, became fully coeducational in 1944. Student education continues to be influenced by the school's history of Catholic and Vincentian traditions. Niagara University offers associate, baccalaureate, and master's degree programs in four academic divisions: arts and sciences, business administration, education, and hospitality and tourism management. It had an approximate enrollment in 2002 of 3,000.

McKey, Joseph P. *History of Niagara University, Seminary of Our Lady of Angels, 1856–1931* (Niagara Co: Niagara Univ, 1931)
Niagara University, http://www.niagara.edu

David W. Sawicki

Nicaraguans. A consistent pattern of emigration from Nicaragua was not established until the late 1970s and the beginning of the 1980s, though Nicaraguans were present in New York State by the 19th century. The revolution of 1979 led to a mass exodus, mainly to Costa Rica and the United States. Emigration during the Sandinista period (1979–89) first included members of the former ruling elite but then incorporated people of varying socioeconomic backgrounds and ideological persuasions. Most Nicaraguans in New York State come from the Pacific region of Nicaragua and are predominantly Roman Catholic, but some, especially from the Atlantic region, are affiliated with various Protestant denominations, particularly the Moravian Church. Nicaraguan immigrants developed their own community organizations, such as the Comité Cívico Cultural Nicaragüense, the Comisión Hispana Pro Obra Rubén Darío, the Organización Dariana, and the Comité de Apoyo Nicaragüense (based in New Jersey but serving New York City as well). The main goals of these organizations are community support and maintenance of Nicaraguan cultural roots. Nicaraguans also gather to celebrate Roman Catholic religious festivities, such as La Gritería, which is celebrated on 7 December. According to the 2000 US census there were 10,197 foreign-born Nicaraguans living in New York State. The majority lives in New York City (8,166) and is concentrated primarily in Brooklyn (2,821) and Queens (2,128).

Logan, John. "The New Latinos: Who They Are, Where They Are," http://mumford1.dyndns.org/cen2000/HispanicPop/HspReport/HspReportPage1.html

Ana Margarita Cervantes-Rodríguez

Nichols. Town (pop 2,584) and village (pop 574) in S central Tioga Co. In 1967, during the construction of Rte 17 (I-86), over 135 Indian burials were unearthed from the Englebert site, first occupied *ca* 2000 BC and site of an Owasco culture village from AD 1100 to 1500; the human remains were to be repatriated in 2002. Settled in 1787, the town was formed from the Town of Tioga in 1824; the village was incorporated in 1903. Until the railroad came, sawmills were the only industrial enterprises. The Delaware, Lackawanna and Western Railroad operated through town from 1882 to 1965. In the 20th century there were a number of industries: creameries (1887–1971), Nichols Knitting Mills (*ca* 1900–1920), Johnson and Son Furniture Co (1908–48), and Nichols Industrial Corp (precision parts, 1952–82). A quarter-horse facility, Tioga Park racetrack, had a brief existence (1976–78).

Joann Lindstrom

Nicholson, Francis (*b* Yorkshire, England, 12 Nov 1655; *d* London, 5 Mar 1728). Soldier and royal governor. Capt Nicholson was posted to Boston in 1686, accompanying Edmund Andros, whose task was to establish the Dominion of New England by uniting the colonies of Massachusetts, Plymouth, Connecticut, Rhode Island, and eventually New York and New Jersey. In 1688 Nicholson was appointed lieutenant governor in charge of administering New York. Among his main concerns were defending the frontier and promoting Andros's policy on centralization. Nicholson alienated many colonists with his difficult personality, violent temper, and factional favoritism. In March 1689 news arrived in New York City that Catholic James II was deposed in favor of Protestant William and Mary. Although Protestant, Nicholson hesitated to recognize the new sovereigns, and New York residents grew impatient. On 31 May 1689 the New York Militia, led by Jacob Leisler, seized Fort James on Manhattan and took control of New York. A month later Nicholson departed for England but returned to North America in 1690, serving in Maryland and Virginia for several years. During Queen Anne's War (1702–13), he acted as commander of the forces in New York Colony, New Jersey, and Connecticut. He led the campaign that captured Acadia [now Nova Scotia] in 1710 and two aborted campaigns to take New France in 1709 and 1711. He served as governor of Nova Scotia from 1712 to 1714 and as royal governor of South Carolina from 1721 to 1729.

Haffenden, Philip S. "The Crown and the Colonial Charters, 1675–1688: Part II," *William and Mary Quarterly* 15 (Oct 1958): 452–66
Webb, Stephen Saunders. "The Strange Career of Francis Nicholson," *William and Mary Quarterly* 23 (Oct 1966): 513–48

Jennifer Steenshorne

Nickerson, Eugene H(offman) (*b* Orange, NJ, 6 Aug 1918; *d* New York City, 1 Jan 2002). Politician and judge. Educated at St. Mark's School in Southborough, Mass, and Harvard University, Nickerson practiced corporate law in Manhattan beginning in 1946. A resident of Roslyn Harbor (Nassau Co), Nickerson rose to prominence as the first Democrat to be elected Nassau Co executive. He served three terms (1962–70), establishing a strong record of promoting civil rights, expanding county parks, and improving the police force. The Nassau Veterans Memorial Coliseum in Uniondale was built as a result of his vision for development of the old Army Air Corps base at Mitchel Field. He served as federal judge in the Eastern District of New York from 1977 until his death, presiding over many high-profile cases involving police brutality, racketeering, and constitutional issues. His most notable trials were those of the New York City police officers charged with the assault and torture of Abner Louima, a Haitian immigrant, in 1999.

Greenhouse, Steven, "Eugene Nickerson, Ex-Nassau Politician," *New York Times*, 3 Jan 2002

Lynda R. Day

Nicolls, Matthias (*bap* Plymouth, England, 8 Apr 1626; *d* New York Colony, July 1693). Colonial government official. Nicolls was a London barrister in 1663 when King Charles II appointed him secretary to the commission to conquer New Netherland, giving him the military rank of captain. He participated in negotiations in September 1664 for the surrender of New Netherland. During New York's first English period, Nicolls served as provincial secretary (1664–73), member of the provincial council (1667–73), member and secretary of the Court of Assizes (1667–80), and on numerous special Courts of Admiralty and Oyer and Terminer. He was probably the principal writer of the Duke's Laws in 1665. He also served New York City as alderman (1668–71, 1673) and mayor (1672), and was captain of cavalry in the Long Island Militia (1671–73).

During the Dutch reoccupation of New York Colony (1673–74), Nicolls oversaw the Duke of York's American interests from Connecticut. When New York returned to English rule in 1674, Nicolls was immediately reappointed provincial secretary and council member (offices he held through 1680), and mayor of New York City (1674–75); he was also appointed vendue master (1677–80). While Gov Edmund Andros was at Albany (1677–78), Nicolls served as commander of the Long Island Militia. He was in England from 1681 to 1683, after which Gov Thomas Dongan commissioned him as Queens Co's first tax collector in 1683 and a judge of the now regular Courts of Oyer and Terminer in 1683 and the Court of Admiralty in 1686. He was elected in 1683 and 1684 to the new Colonial Assembly and was chosen as its speaker.

After Lt Gov Jacob Leisler revoked Nicolls's commissions in 1689, Nicolls retired to his estate on Cow Neck [now in Manhasset, Nassau Co] until a new council appointed him provincial vendue master on 8 Dec 1692. During service with five governors over three decades, Matthias Nicolls played an integral part in the development of New York's colonial government, laws, and court procedures.

American National Biography, sv "Matthias Nicolls"
Bailey, Rosalie Fellows. *The Nicoll Family and Islip Grange: Address before the Order of Colonial Lords of*

Manors in America, April 21, 1938 (New York: Publications of the Order of Colonial Lords of Manors in America, no. 29, 1940)

Peter R. Christoph

Nicolls, Richard (*b* Bedfordshire, England, 1624; *d* Sole Bay, England, 28 May 1672). Soldier and first governor of New York Colony. Raised in an influential family and well educated, Nicolls served in the household of James, Duke of York. In 1664 James was granted the proprietorship of former Dutch lands in North America, including New Netherland. Nicolls led the expeditionary force sent to take control of New Netherland, and transform it into an English colony. With a force of 300 soldiers and three frigates, the English arrived in America in July 1664. Faced with a superior force and promised lenient surrender terms, New Amsterdam director general Petrus Stuyvesant surrendered on 27 Aug 1664; Beverwijck [now Albany] followed on 24 Sept 1664. Nicolls was appointed governor of the colony, which was renamed New York. He restructured the government along English lines. The most significant innovation was the enactment in October 1665 of the Duke's Laws, compiled by provincial secretary Matthias Nicolls. These established civil and criminal codes for the English-speaking settlers in the colony, but most of the Hudson Valley was able to retain Dutch customs. Towns on Long Island, however, lost the right to levy taxes. Nicolls earned a reputation for fairness and honesty among the mostly Dutch residents of the colony. Resigning his office to Col Francis Lovelace in 1667 after the Second Anglo-Dutch War, he returned to England in 1668 and died in a naval battle at the beginning of the Third Anglo-Dutch War (1672–74).

Schuyler, Montgomery. *Richard Nicolls: First Governor of New York, 1664–1668* (New York: Order of Colonial Lords of Manors in America, 1933)
Webb, Stephen Saunders. *1676: The End of American Independence* (New York: Knopf, 1984)

Jennifer Steenshorne

Niebuhr, Reinhold (*b* Wright City, Mo, 21 June 1892; *d* Stockbridge, Mass, 1 June 1971). Christian social ethicist. The son of a minister in the Evangelical Synod of North America, Niebuhr studied at the denomination's Elmhurst College near Chicago, at Eden Theological Seminary near St. Louis, and at Yale Divinity School (MA, 1915). He became pastor of Detroit's Bethel Evangelical Church in 1915. From 1928 to 1960 he taught at Union Theological Seminary in Manhattan, becoming one of the pivotal figures of 20th-century liberal Protestant ethics. He was an editor of the Christian socialist *World Tomorrow* and, as a candidate of the Socialist Party, ran unsuccessfully for state senate in 1930 and for the US Congress in 1932. Rejecting what he saw as liberal Protestantism's naive optimism, Niebuhr's "Christian realism" emphasized the tendency of individuals, groups, societies, and nations to drift toward pride, hypocrisy, and self-righteousness. Niebuhr was a founding editor of *Christianity and Crisis* (1941–93), a major source of critical Christian commentary on social and political issues. In 1941 Niebuhr helped found the Union for Democratic Action, a coalition of New York City–area progressives that challenged isolationism. He then helped launch Americans for Democratic Action in 1947, a progressive national organization, within the Democratic Party. Niebuhr's liberal anti-Communist credentials were strengthened with his role in the formation of the Liberal Party in 1944. If Niebuhr's Christian realism was generally supportive of the Cold War (though hostile to McCarthyism), he was a prominent critic of the Vietnam War. He was undoubtedly the best-known Protestant theologian of his time, and his influence with non-Christians and secular liberals reached far beyond divinity school cloisters.

Fox, Richard Wightman. *Reinhold Niebuhr* (New York: Pantheon, 1985)

Michael T. Bradley Jr

Niles. Town (pop 1,208) in SE Cayuga Co. Settled in 1792, the town was formed from Sempronius in 1833. It lies between two Finger Lakes, Owasco and Skaneateles, on whose shores are hundreds of summer cottages. Slate for flagstone was quarried in the 19th century and late in that century Niles was considered the best dairy town in the county. Farming remained the primary occupation in 2003, with other residents commuting to surrounding towns. A landmark is the Frozen Ocean, the flat summit of a former quarry, which at 1,620 feet (493.8 m) is the highest point in town. New Hope Mills has been grinding grain in Niles since 1823.

Sue Stoyell

92nd Street Y (YM-YWHA). Founded in 1874 as the Young Men's Hebrew Association, it offered a wide range of educational, religious, and social activities to its clients. It has been at its current location at 1395 Lexington Ave since 1900 and in its current facility since 1930. It merged in 1942 with the Young Women's Hebrew Association and adopted its current name in 1945. The Y established a nursery school (1928), organized activities for senior citizens (1950), introduced a parenting center (1978), and created a camp for children with autism (1987). In 1962 it merged with the Clara de Hirsch Home for Working Girls (1897), a residence.

In 2001 cultural programs, health screenings, support groups, and classes are held at the Bronfman Center for Jewish Life; the Charles Simon Center for Adult Life and Learning; the May Center for Health, Fitness and Sport; the Milstein/Rosenthal Center for Media and Technology; a School of the Arts; and the Tisch Center for the Arts. The Lillian and Sol Goldman Family Center serves thousands of children in East and West Harlem public schools, adults with disabilities, and many others. Concerts and lectures are given in the 916-seat Kaufmann Concert Hall, many on Jewish themes. Beginning in 1935 what is now the Harkness Dance Center provided a venue for Martha Graham, Katherine Dunham, and other modern dance figures. Other long-term series include poetry recitals and performances by noted musicians. The Y Chamber Symphony (now New York Chamber Symphony) was formed in 1976.

Jackson, Naomi M. *Converging Movements: Modern Dance and Jewish Culture at the 92nd St Y* (Hanover, NH: Univ Press of New England, 2000)

Andrea Olmstead

Niskayuna. Town (pop 20,295) in SE Schenectady Co. Mohawks planted corn on the Mohawk River flats before Whites first settled about 1664. The town was formed from Watervliet (Albany Co) in 1809. The Erie Canal (1825) crossed the Mohawk on an aqueduct; Lock 7 of the Barge Canal remained in active use in 2004. Except for some bluestone quarrying, Niskayuna was entirely agricultural until about 1920. In the early 20th century its farmers raised broomcorn, grain, potatoes, and fruit. As Schenectady grew after World War I, suburban neighborhoods were developed in Niskayuna adjacent to the city line. General Electric established research laboratories in town beginning in 1946, including the Knolls Atomic Power Laboratory. Niskayuna is the home of the 108-acre (44 ha) Lisha Kill Preserve, an old hemlock forest administered by the Nature Conservancy.

Nissequogue [NIS-SEE-KWAG]. Village (pop 1,543) in Smithtown (Suffolk Co). The village takes its name from the Nissequogue River, which rises near the center of the island and flows northward into Long Island Sound. Richard Smith, founder of Smithtown, settled the area in 1665. In the late 19th century Nissequogue began attracting affluent vacationers and summer-home seekers, and it became an incorporated village in 1926 to maintain control over development. Its population more than tripled in the 1960s. It remains one of the most attractive, affluent communities on Suffolk Co's North Shore.

Richard F. Welch

Nixon, Richard M(ilhous) (*b* Yorba Linda, Calif, 9 Jan 1913; *d* New York City, 22 Apr 1994). US president. One of the most polarizing figures in modern American politics, Nixon was elected to Congress from his hometown of Whittier, Calif, in 1946. As a member of the House Committee on Un-American Activities (HUAC), he gained recognition for his role in pursuing allegations that Alger Hiss had spied for the Soviet Union. He was elected to the US Senate in 1950. As Republican candidate for vice president in 1952, he survived a fund-raising scandal with his Checkers speech and served two terms under Pres Dwight D. Eisenhower. After losing the close presidential election of 1960 and the 1962 California gubernatorial race, his political career seemed over. Nixon moved to New York City in 1963 and became a senior partner in the Wall St law firm now known as Mudge, Stern, Baldwin, and Todd. He rebuilt his political career and was elected president in 1968 after winning the GOP nomination over his Manhattan neighbor Gov Nelson A. Rockefeller.

As president, Nixon pursued what was called the Vietnamization of the war in Vietnam, but the war continued to exact a high toll on American troops during his presidency. Despite his two decades of staunch anticommunism, in 1972 Nixon made a historic visit to China and sought détente with the Soviet Union. He followed a moderate domestic program, taking a hard line on crime while promoting significant environmental and regulatory initiatives and some civil rights measures such as affirmative action and school desegregation. Reelected by a landslide in 1972, Nixon was engulfed by the Watergate scandal and resigned on 9 Aug 1974 just ahead of an impending impeachment. After leaving office, Nixon lived in San Clemente, Calif, until 1980 when he moved to New York City, relocating to Park Ridge, NJ, in 1981. After his presidency Nixon wrote a series of books that helped him gain a measure of respectability before his death from a stroke in 1994.

Ambrose, Stephen E. *Nixon: The Triumph of a Politician, 1962–1972* (New York: Simon & Schuster, 1989)

———. *Nixon: Ruin and Recovery, 1973–1990* (New York: Simon & Schuster, 1991)

Nixon, Richard. *In the Arena: A Memoir of Victory, Defeat, and Renewal* (New York: Simon & Schuster, 1990)

Jonathan Entin

nonprofit sector. From the time of the Revolutionary War, New York State has had one of the more interesting and complex nonprofit sectors in the United States. At the beginning of the 21st century, it defines its nonprofit sector as including religious institutions, mutual benefit associations, and private, self-governing charitable nonprofit organizations. New York State's nonprofits are distinctive in several ways: in the state's sometimes direct role in their governance, in the wide array of their state-subsidized public services, and in their international significance. New York City's foundations, nonprofit hospitals, arts organizations, and international organizations are among the largest and most important in the United States. And the state is notable for its use of nonprofit organizations to manage potentially bitter religious and ethnic conflict and for its vigorous tradition of nonprofit freedom and advocacy.

Through the 18th Century

Colonial New York did not have a significant nonprofit sector. It did have some notable churches and schools, but the Dutch Reformed Church dominated the colony of New Netherland, insisting, for example, in 1657 that settlers in Flushing [now in Queens Co] preserve religious uniformity by prohibiting the Quakers who proposed to settle in their midst the right to public worship. Despite the brief rule of Catholic governor Thomas Dongan in the 1680s and an official British policy of toleration after 1710, the Church of England held a strong position in New York Colony. As an established church (albeit with a loose and partial establishment), it received private gifts and provided some education and charity to individuals; it also served as an arm of government. The colony in the 18th century supported the Church of England with corporate charters, land grants, and access to lottery funds; it rarely supported other denominations. In 1754 Lower Manhattan's Trinity Church provided land for the new King's College (now Columbia University) on condition that its head and its chapel were Anglican, devoted to church and king. Anglicans in the colonial government accepted these conditions over the famous protest of attorney William Livingston, whose prominent family was strongly Calvinist, and others who argued for an independent college.

The Rise of Religious Nonprofits

Revolutionary New York created the state's nonprofit sector by disestablishing the Church of England and rechartering King's College as Columbia College in 1784. To supervise Columbia and to manage the founding and governance of other institutions, New York State created the Regents of the University of the State of New York, empowered to grant corporate charters to schools, colleges, orphanages, and other educational institutions, and to oversee their operations. The state legislature also continued to grant such charters. Continuing the British tradition of viewing nonprofit corporations as instruments for the provision of public services, New Yorkers quickly set up an array of nonprofit schools, libraries, medical clinics, artistic and scientific societies, and other nonprofit organizations. From early in the 19th century, the state subsidized schools, including nonpublic chartered schools, through funds assigned to the Regents. From 1828 through the Civil War, such funds provided important support to academies that served women students, as Emma Willard and other advocates of women's education urged.

Religious organizations dominated New York State's nonprofit sector through much of the 19th century. New Yorkers agreed that church and state should be kept separate but continued to view nonprofit organizations as entities created for state purposes and disagreed about the degree of freedom that should be accorded non-Protestants. The legislature and the Regents chartered many Protestant schools, missions, Bible and tract societies, and medical clinics, as well as some nonsectarian academies, libraries, and lyceums. New York City became home to the vast publishing and distribution activities of the American Bible Society and the American Tract Society. It was also home to many of the other organizations of this "benevolent empire" through which eastern Protestants sought to convert migrants to the West and immigrants, including Catholics, in the cities of the East.

Arthur and Lewis Tappan—New Englanders who built up their New York City Mercantile Agency credit-rating firm into a national business that evolved (after many changes of name) into Dun and Bradstreet—used their extensive commercial contacts and their money to promote abolitionist, but not feminist, organizations beginning in the 1830s. In Central and Western New York's Burned-over District, as well as in New York City and Brooklyn, evangelical Protestants created many churches, missions, and reforming societies. This activity served as the context for the famous 1848 convention at Seneca Falls at which Elizabeth Cady Stanton and others endorsed abolition, woman suffrage, married women's property rights, and other reforms. Quite apart from the campaign for woman suffrage, 19th-century New York State women in all religious communities used nonprofit organizations to play key civic and public roles as "friendly visitors," teachers and school principals, leaders of orphanages and clinics, and campaigners for change.

From 1807 through the mid-1840s, the Protestant Free School Society, a private charity, used state tax money (and some private donations) to provide free elementary education in New York City. In the view of many Protestant New Yorkers, the intellectual life of the state and of New York City manifested itself largely in discussions within Protestant institutions.

But others disputed Protestant claims. With the Hebrew Benevolent Society (1822) and other institutions, New York City's Jews developed a comprehensive array of community facilities. Despite opposition from some Protestants, Catholics opened parish schools in New York City as early as 1800, and the state granted a corporate charter to the New York City Roman Catholic Orphan Asylum in 1817. In 1845 the state legislature, responding to the protests of Bishop John J. Hughes, ended state support for the Free School Society and set up the city's public school system. Although the Regents awarded few corporate charters to Catholic schools (perhaps because Catholics rarely asked for them), the state legislature did charter several Catholic schools after 1846. By the late 1850s Bishop Hughes had persuaded the legislature to allow Catholic institutions to set up under hierarchical control, using "corporation sole," whereby the bishop, by virtue of his office, served as a one-man board of trustees for Catholic institutions. Protestants, meanwhile, now sought to reach the city's poor through social agencies, such as Robert Hartley's New York Association for Improving the Condition of the Poor (1843). Charles Loring Brace's Children's Aid Society (1855) added "orphan trains" to transport poor children from New York City and other eastern cities to placements in rural families, an early form of foster care.

New Civic Purposes after the Civil War

After the Civil War, New York officials multiplied the purposes of nonprofit organizations, using them to manage, if not resolve, Protestant-Catholic conflict, to develop a more comprehensive and rational approach to social welfare, and to give cities—especially New York City—civic attractions like those of the great European capitals. At the same time, as New Yorkers became more and more diverse, they sought to advance an increasingly wide variety of causes through associational and nonprofit activity.

Under William M. "Boss" Tweed's influence, state subsidies to charities and other nonprofit organizations ballooned from $200,000 or less in earlier years to $400,000 in 1869 and to $900,000 in 1871. Quite separately, the state's Central Park Commission provided substantial aid to the new Metropolitan Museum of Art and to the American Museum of Natural History in this period. The reaction against such subsidies went far beyond the 1871 ouster of the Tweed Ring. The legislature refused to pass any general charities aid bill in 1872, and revisions to the state constitution in 1874 banned state appropriations to many private charitable and educational institutions, including charity schools.

State leaders moved, through creative political compromise, to use the nonprofit sector to handle religious conflicts. The constitutional revisions of 1874 left municipalities free to subsidize orphanages and other charities. In 1875 the state adopted the remarkable Children's Law under which each orphaned, abandoned, mistreated, or vagrant child who became a ward of the state was to be sent, not to a municipal or county poorhouse, but to "an orphan asylum, charitable or other reformatory institution . . . governed or controlled by officers or persons of the same religious faith as the parents of such child, as far as practicable." Public money came with government placement of the children. In 1874, 132 private orphanages cared for 12,000 children. In 1884, more than 200 orphanages were caring for 23,000.

The Blaine Amendment adopted in the 1894 New York State Constitution confirmed these arrangements. It withheld funds from elementary and secondary schools sponsored by religious communities, a policy that remained in place for more than 100 years. Yet the amendment also allowed "payments by counties, cities, towns, and villages to charitable, eleemosynary, correctional and reformatory institutions, wholly or partly under private control."

Expansion, Nonsectarianism, Internationalism

As New York State's nonprofit sector expanded, many worked to make it more efficient, more effective, less sentimental, and less sectarian. Josephine Shaw Lowell, Louisa Schuyler, and other New York leaders of the private, nonsectarian US Sanitary Commission, which provided medical care to the Union army, sparked these efforts. The Rev Stephen Humphreys Gurteen of Buffalo introduced the British plan of a Charity Organization Society (COS) in 1877, emphasizing systematic accounting and self-help. Lowell brought the COS idea to New York City in 1882 and for 20 years directed efforts to make poor relief in the city more rational and effective, which culminated in the Russell Sage Foundation's work, between 1907 and World War II, to build an efficient, coordinated, private system of charitable organizations for the entire nation from a New York City base. Over the same period, the Carnegie Foundation worked from New York City to reform education across the United States, and the Manhattan-based Rockefeller Foundation worked to advance medical and scientific research.

Immigration had given rise to extraordinarily complex and diverse ties with other parts of the world. Accordingly, New York City also became the base, by the end of the 19th century, for a wide range of efforts to shape international developments. The Rockefeller Foundation and its associates undertook many of these efforts. Religious groups attempted others: Protestant efforts to evangelize China, India, and Africa; the building up of the Hebrew University, Hadassah Hospital, and other institutions in Israel; the rescue of Jews and others during the Holocaust; the promotion of Catholic concerns in many parts of the world. New York State–based associations also worked to advance national causes in Ireland and, during World War II and the Cold War, in Eastern Europe. These included Freedom House, the PEN American Center, US offices of Amnesty International, the American Jewish Committee, and Hadassah.

State efforts to improve access to housing, healthcare, and higher education without adding too much to tax burdens accounted for more of the nonprofit sector's expansion in New York State after the 1920s. During the middle third of the 20th century, the state made active use of nonprofit housing arrangements, promoting the use of cooperatives for unsubsidized, market-rate apartment housing, as well as for subsidized housing complexes sponsored by labor unions and religious bodies. New York State had some of the nation's leading public hospitals (Manhattan's Bellevue, Brooklyn's Downstate and Syracuse's Upstate), but it also relied to a great extent on nonprofits to provide the bulk of hospital facilities as hospitals grew quickly after the early 1920s. New York State also had some notable public colleges (City College, Brooklyn College, Queens College, and some schools that became part of the State University of New York after 1948), but throughout the 20th century, it depended more than most states on private colleges and universities to meet the demand for higher education. The state found a wide variety of ways to provide subsidies to nonprofit hospitals and colleges.

Legal Change Amid Prosperity

Despite its exceptional diversity and liberal traditions, New York State imposed significant limitations on the right to create nonprofit organizations through the middle of the 20th century. By the late 19th century, trial judges were successfully asserting that they had the right to determine the lawfulness of applications for nonprofit charters. They often ruled against charter requests on the basis of their personal political, religious, or ethnic preferences, but the Civil Rights Movement encouraged challenges to this. Judges abandoned most restrictive practices after the mid-1960s, and in 1970 the state adopted a new Not-for-Profit Corporation Law that sharply limited the judges' role and provided a more comprehensive system for classifying nonprofits. Judges still sought to deny charters to groups of which they disapproved such as those that provided services to gays, but higher courts confirmed the rights of such organizations under the First Amendment.

With the lifting of state restrictions on incorporation, the numbers of nonprofits expanded rapidly in New York after 1970, as in other states across the nation. Three other factors reinforced the expansion. From the very beginning, women performed a large share of the work of nonprofit organizations: teaching, nursing, and social reform. Before the women's movement of the 1960s, many did this work as volunteers or as workers who more or less willingly accepted salaries lower than their education and responsibilities might have warranted. Since 1970 women have increasingly demanded a fair wage, narrowing—though not closing—this wage gap. Nonprofits expanded and raised their budgets to employ women. Asserting their rights, women also founded new nonprofits that provide shelters from domestic violence, institutions relating to healthcare and education, and opportunities for artistic expression and advocacy.

Before the 1960s the federal government provided little financial support for nonprofit organizations, except in the fields of scientific and medical research (through the Defense Advanced Research Projects Agency, the National Science Foundation, and the National Institutes of Health). Pres Lyndon Johnson's Great Society programs, especially Medicare, Medicaid, grant and loan programs for college students, and job-training and community development programs, brought large amounts of federal money into the fields in which nonprofits operated, and those amounts continued to grow, nearly doubling to 4.5% of the total US economy between 1975 and 2000.

Finally, in New York State as throughout the United States the nonprofit sector grew because incomes rose sharply for most Americans after World War II. Most nonprofit organizations now sell services: education for tuition, student housing and meals for room-and-board charges, healthcare for fees, concerts for the price of the tickets. Increased income in turn allowed nonprofit organizations to serve people either unable or unwilling to pay. Organizations devoted to personal reform or religious conversion often had many such nonpaying clients.

Early 21st Century: A Snapshot

At the beginning of the 21st century, nonprofit activity accounts for perhaps 14% of New York State's economy and for more than 16% of New York City's economy. In comparison, nonprofits account for more than 17% of the economy in Massachusetts, 11% of most states' economies in the Northeast and Midwest, 6–8% in the South, and 3% on the West Coast. As elsewhere in the nation, more than half of New York State's nonprofit activity is in hospitals and other healthcare institutions, and perhaps a quarter in private schools, colleges, and universities. Much of the regional variation is because of greater southern and especially West Coast reliance on state universities and on county and (especially in the South) on profit-seeking hospitals. About 10% of New York State's nonprofit activity is in social service organizations, with 15% divided about equally among organizations devoted to the arts, to religion, and to advocacy.

In 2001 New York State was also home to an exceptional array of nonprofit organizations providing public services with state tax money. This arrangement reflected a long tradition. By 1800 the state subsidized New York Hospital and several schools. In the 1860s the New York City and Brooklyn municipal governments provided land for the Metropolitan Museum of Art, American Museum of Natural History, New York Public Library, Central Park and Bronx Zoos, New York Botanical Garden, Brooklyn Museum, and Brooklyn Botanic Garden. New York City continues to provide some operating support to these institutions. Since the 1960s the state has also provided, through "Bundy aid," a high level of unrestricted funding to private colleges and universities based on the numbers of graduates.

At the beginning of the 21st century, New York State provides significant state and local supplements to federal funding for an even wider range of efforts: cooperative and nonprofit housing facilities for families of low and moderate income and for the elderly, residential schools and homes for the mentally challenged, and organizations providing home-care attendants to the sick and infirm. The state also encourages auxiliary support organizations, research foundations for state universities, business improvement districts and community development organizations to promote economic development in many areas, "friends" groups for parks, and many similar groups. New York State's nonprofits are multifarious and surprising. For example, the nonprofit Shubert Foundation owns the Shubert Organization, which produces Broadway plays and musicals and owns and operates 16 Broadway theaters as well as theaters in other cities. And that bastion of capitalism, the New York Stock Exchange, has been a nonprofit corporation since 1971.

Dolan, Jay. *The Immigrant Church: New York's Irish and German Catholics, 1815–1865* (Baltimore: Johns Hopkins Univ Press, 1975)

Goren, Arthur A. *New York Jews and the Quest for Community: The Kehillah Experiment, 1908–1922* (New York: Columbia Univ Press, 1970)

Hammack, David C., ed. *Making the Nonprofit Sector in the United States: A Reader* (Bloomington: Indiana Univ Press, 1998)

Hough, Franklin B. *Historical and Statistical Record of the University of the State of New York during the Century from 1784 to 1884* (Albany: Weed, Parsons, 1885)
Kaestle, Carl F. *The Evolution of an Urban School System: New York City, 1870–1850* (Cambridge, Mass: Harvard Univ Press, 1973)
Klein, Milton M. *The Politics of Diversity: Essays in the History of Colonial New York* (Port Washington, NY: Kennikat, 1974)
Lannie, Vincent P. *Public Money and Parochial Education: Bishop Hughes, Governor Seward, and the New York School Controversy* (Cleveland: Case Western Reserve Univ Press, 1968)
Pratt, John Webb. *Religion, Politics, and Diversity: The Church-State Theme in New York History* (Ithaca: Cornell Univ Press, 1967)
Smith-Rosenberg, Carroll. *Religion and the Rise of the American City: The New York City Mission Movement, 1812–1870* (Ithaca: Cornell Univ Press, 1971)

David C. Hammack

Norfolk [NOR-FORK]. Town (pop 4,565) in N St. Lawrence Co. Settled in 1809, the town was formed in 1823 from Louisville. Waterpower on the Raquette River created the mill hamlets of Norfolk, Raymondville, and Yaleville, where manufactured products included bricks, woolens, leather, iron, pulp paper, starch, butter tubs, agricultural implements, furniture, and pumps. In 1974 Old Order Amish families from Michigan and Indiana purchased several farms and built a cheese factory (1977), but by 2001 the community had largely dispersed. Railroad boxcars were made by National Railway Utilization Corp (1979–89). Clay soils and large areas of wetland have made farming difficult, and relatively few active farms remain. In 2003 the Norfolk Paper Co mill (founded in 1902 by Remington-Martin Co) is an employer. The town is essentially a bedroom community for Massena and Potsdam. Norfolk resident Alex Pepin invented and piloted the *Inocrain,* an airship, in 1906. The 288 ft (87.8 m) Raymondville Parabolic Bridge (1886) is listed on the National Register.

Richard E. Mooers

Norfolk Southern Railway. Freight railway serving central and western New York State. A subsidiary of the Norfolk Southern Corp, headquartered in Norfolk, Va, the railway runs in 22 states through the Southeast, Midwest, and Northeast as well as in Washington, DC, and the Province of Ontario. In all the system operates 21,600 miles (34,762 km) of track. Norfolk Southern Railway was created 1 June 1982 from the consolidation of Norfolk and Western Railway and Southern Railway. In 1998 Norfolk Southern received permission from the US Surface Transportation Board to operate many old Conrail routes, expanding the railroad into New York State. Norfolk Southern routes cover more than 890 miles (1,430 km) in the state with a Southern Tier line from New York City to Buffalo, a line from Buffalo to Harrisburg, Pa, and spur lines to Jamestown, Geneva, and Ithaca. The railway's facilities at Buffalo include an automobile distribution terminal, an intermodal terminal (rail to truck or ship), and a bulk transfer terminal. Norfolk Southern has spent $35 million to modernize signal systems and upgrade track from Buffalo to Port Jervis (Orange Co), $6 million for new track connections at Buffalo, $3 million for improvements near Angola (Erie Co), and $16 million to upgrade New York bridges. The rail network brings New York State into contact with 13 Atlantic Ocean and Gulf of Mexico port cities and 6 Great Lakes ports. Principal commodities moving along this network are coal, paper and forest products, agricultural products, chemicals, metals, construction materials, automotive parts and finished vehicles, and intermodal trailers and containers. Norfolk Southern Corp also owns Thoroughbred Technology and Telecommunications, which maintains microwave towers and fiber-optic cable installations along many rail lines and serves areas of New York State.

Norfolk Southern Corp, "Norfolk Southern 1999 Annual Report," http://www.nscorp.com/nscorphtml/ar99/contents.html

Albert S. Eggerton Jr

normal schools. In an effort to improve the quality of New York State teachers, teacher training schools were created in the 19th century to formally prepare them. Modeled after the system of French teacher training schools called *école normale,* the American schools were known as normal schools. Public normal schools also developed as part of a broader effort to create free public education. The first one in the United States opened in 1839 in Massachusetts.

In 1844 the New York State legislature designated funds for the state's first normal school, in Albany. The New York City Board of Education opened the Female Normal School and High School (1870; now Hunter College). A number of other cities in the state opened their own teacher training schools. In 1861 school board superintendent Edward Austin Sheldon organized the Oswego Primary Teachers Training School (Oswego Co), which later became the Oswego State Normal and Training School, and its training methods were adopted throughout the country. The substantial growth of free public schools during the post–Civil War period increased the need for teachers, and the existing private and city programs could not meet the demand. Between 1867 and 1893, 10 additional state normal schools were opened, and by 1915 there were a dozen two-year city programs in New York State.

Most normal school students were young women in their late teens and early twenties enrolled in a two-year course to become grammar school teachers. Applicants had to pass basic knowledge tests and be recommended by the school district commissioner in their home communities. Young men were more likely to be enrolled in four-year degree programs that prepared them for secondary school teaching or school administration. A high school diploma was not required to enroll in the two-year program, so the first year concentrated on academic subjects the students would teach, and the second covered teaching methods and included practice teaching, which often took place in model schools within the institution. The State of New York provided free tuition and transportation to normal school students, enabling those who could not afford private schools to obtain further education, although students did pay their own room and board. Graduates were in high demand in the early part of the 20th century, when the need for teachers grew dramatically as immigration and school attendance increased.

Albany and Buffalo became baccalaureate degree–granting colleges in 1890 and 1927, respectively. In 1923 the other normal schools expanded to three-year programs and, in 1938, to four years. This change reflected the national trend to expand and standardize certification requirements for all grade levels. The normal schools were converted to state teachers colleges with four-year degree programs in 1942. These colleges became part of the SUNY system in 1948, were renamed state university colleges in 1962, and grew to include programs in the liberal arts and professions. Since the 1960s, teacher education programs have continued to be an important component of the state university colleges, but there has been competition for resources. The model schools were closed in the 1970s, and students now complete practice teaching in area public schools.

See also ACADEMIES; HIGHER EDUCATION.

Horner, Harlan Hoyt, ed. *Education in New York State, 1784–1954* (Albany: Univ of the State of New York, State Education Department, 1954)
Rogers, Dorothy. *Oswego: Fountainhead of Teacher Education* (New York: Appleton-Century-Crofts, 1961)

Christine E. Murray

North American Martyrs. Isaac Jogues (1607–47), born in Orléans, France, entered the Society of Jesus by 1626 and in 1636 began missionary and diplomatic work among Iroquoian-speaking peoples of Canada and what is now New York State, journeying into the Richelieu, Hudson, and upper St. Lawrence Rivers drainage regions. He was the first European to see Lake George, which he named Saint-Sacrement. In June 1642 Mohawk warriors captured and tortured Jogues near Trois-Rivières [now in Que]. Captured at the same time was a Jesuit brother accompanying Jogues, René Goupil (*b* 1608), who was murdered by the Mohawk on 29 September at Ossernenon [now Auriesville, Montgomery Co]. After 13 months Jogues was released with the help of the Dutch near Fort Orange [now Albany]. He returned to France through New Amsterdam, leaving behind invaluable descriptions of the Dutch colony. Jogues subsequently returned to Canada, traveling to Mohawk territory with a French-Huron peace mission in 1646. French relations with the Mohawk deteriorated, and Jogues was taken prisoner, brought to Ossernenon, and killed by a hatchet blow to the head on 18 Oct 1647. Killed with Jogues was a lay missionary, John Lalande.

In 1885 a pilgrimage shrine to Jogues, Goupil, and Lalande opened at Auriesville near the site of the former Mohawk village. The shrine ground consisted of a small chapel on 10 acres (4 ha) of land. From its beginning the shrine was a focal point for the cause of having the three declared martyrs. In 1930 the North American Martyrs—Jogues, Goupil, Lalande, and five other French missionaries killed in Canada around the same time—were canonized. The National Shrine of North American Martyrs covers over 600 acres (243 ha), is open from May to October, and contains a large open-air church able to accommodate 10,000 visitors, as well as a museum. The shrine is also venerated as the 1656 birthplace of the beatified Mohawk nun Kateri Tekakwitha.

Greer, Allan. *The Jesuit Relations: Natives and Missionaries in 17th Century North America* (Boston: Bedford/St. Martin's, 2000)

Eva C. Fognell, Daniel A. Scalberg

North Amityville. See Amityville.

Northampton. Town (pop 2,760) in NE Fulton Co. Settled near Fish House in 1762, the town was formed from Broadalbin in 1799. Its men worked largely in lumbering and maple sugaring, while many Northampton women were employed as home-workers by the glove industry. The Fonda, Johnstown and Gloversville Railroad served the town from 1875 to 1930. Begun as a camp meeting before 1875, Sacandaga Park became a railroad-operated recreational park, and after an 1898 fire it was resurveyed and rebuilt with a midway and hotels. A miniature steam train carried visitors to the Sports Island athletic fields. The inundation of the Great Sacandaga Lake (1930) closed down the railroad and the park, but farms along its shores were divided for camp lots. In the early 21st century Northampton's economy is dependent upon tourism.

North Babylon. See Babylon.

North Bay Shore. See Bay Shore.

North Bellmore. See Bellmore.

North Bellport. See Bellport.

North Castle. Town (pop 10,849) in E central Westchester Co. Significant settlement probably took place after the creation of the Ann Bridges Patent (1708), although some settlers may have arrived in the 1690s. Provincial records refer to a town government as early as 1721. The Miller House (1738) at North White Plains, now a museum, served as Washington's headquarters during the Battle of White Plains (1776). The town was recognized in 1788. In the 19th century residents farmed and worked at cottage industries such as shirt- and shoe-making, but railroads bypassed the town, and its population declined. From 1900 to 1915 granite quarrying for the Kensico Dam stimulated the economy, and Italian immigrant stonemasons settled in the town. Suburban development began in the 1920s with the establishment of country clubs and gentlemen's farms. Substantial postwar residential development was further promoted by the construction of I-684 (to Armonk, 1968; completed, 1974). The world headquarters of IBM and other corporate offices are near Armonk.

Scott C. Monje

North Collins. Town (pop 3,376) and village (pop 1,079) in SW Erie Co. Settled in 1810 by Quakers, the town was formed from Collins in 1852 as Shirley; it was renamed in 1853. Germans came in the 1830s and Italians in the late 1890s. The Buffalo and Jamestown Railroad (1874; later Erie Railroad) sped the transportation of people and produce to Buffalo. Manufactured products included handles, baskets, shale bricks, and distilled peppermint. The Western New York Preserving Co (1881), the first of a number of canneries, was among the earliest in the region, and in the 20th century another business produced frozen food. The village incorporated in 1907. In the early 21st century North Collins is a fruit-growing town, manufactures farm machinery and wire, and extracts natural gas. The 16-sided Gamel Barn (1901) is listed on the National Register.

Andrew C. Maines

North Country. The region known as the North Country is a loosely defined cultural region. In its oldest usage, the North Country included all or parts of the counties of Clinton, Franklin, Jefferson, Lewis, and St. Lawrence in various combinations. Other definitions include parts of Essex and Oswego Cos, and a growing number include all of the Adirondack Park. In its broadest conception, it encompasses all of New York State north of the Mohawk River. Its varying definitions were evident in the early 1970s when beginning geography students at SUNY Potsdam were asked over a five-year period to locate the North Country on a map of the state and to indicate their hometown's location. No two maps were alike, and the farther north the hometown, the farther north the North Country.

Settlement Patterns

Until well into the 19th century, only the very far north, the Black River Valley, and the Lake Ontario Lowland were settled north of the Mohawk Valley. The early settlers entered from the east via Vermont's far north, from the south along the lake and river valley, and from Canada. The region's early outlets for goods were in Canada (lumber and potash, by water), and its early major US market was Boston (midwestern grain and local dairy products, by rail). The far northeast was settled primarily from Vermont (there were early attempts to form a state from Vermont, northeastern New York State, and northern New Hampshire). So many Vermonters—a portion of them originating in Connecticut, Massachusetts, or New Hampshire—moved in that the eastern edge of northern New York State once was known as New Vermont, and a road and a cemetery in Warren Co bear that name. Many Francophone Canadian, Irish, Scottish, and English immigrants settled in the northern counties in the 1800s and early 1900s. The ethnic mix in the Massena (St. Lawrence Co) area was greatly enriched by Italian, Armenian, and other immigrants recruited for construction of a hydropower project in the early 20th century.

Core Regions

A North Country identity became especially strong in the northwest in St. Lawrence and Jefferson Cos. This northwest focus was first reflected in the 1900 novel by Irving Bacheller, *Eben Holden: A Tale of the North Country,* which likely included the first published use of the term for northern New York State. However, the term was in use earlier in the north of Maine, New Hampshire, and to a smaller extent Vermont, and was applied even earlier to northern England just south of Scotland. Bacheller's father moved to New York State from northern Vermont, where the term is still found today, along with the better known but geographically more specific Northeast Kingdom.

The North Country of Bacheller's day was a slender band of farmland and foothills running northeast from Lake Ontario and bordered on the north by the St. Lawrence River and the international border. Its location north of the "Great South Woods" was determined by the mountains' poorer soil, steeper slopes, and shorter growing season. For Bacheller and others in the northwest corner of the state, people symbolically left the North Country when they passed Sunday Rock in South Colton (St. Lawrence Co), which has long marked the divide between the vast forest—where it is always "Sunday" and thus one does not work—and the workaday North Country, and many northern residents still feel that way in the early 21st century. More recent writers, H. F. Landon, Chris Angus, and others, show that Bacheller's concept of a North Country in northwestern New York State remains strong.

At the same time the North Country identity also remains fairly strong in northeastern New York State, as evidenced in local usage (eg, Plattsburgh–North Country Chamber of Commerce). Northeastern New Yorkers appear to limit the scope of their definition of North Country to Clinton, Essex, and Franklin Cos, excluding areas to the west.

Canoe carry in the North Country, late 19th century.

The two North Country core regions in the northeast and northwest overlap in northern Franklin Co, an area that also sees competition for readers by the major North Country newspapers printed in Plattsburgh (Clinton Co) to the east and Watertown (Jefferson Co) to the west, and by newspapers of statewide significance in Syracuse and Albany. In the early 21st century, Franklin Co appears to be included more often with Clinton Co than with St. Lawrence when state agency regional lines are drawn.

An Expanded North Country

The North Country region has become linked (though some might say confused) with the Adirondacks through the economic development activities of the Adirondack North Country Association (covering 14 counties from an office in Saranac Lake [Franklin and Essex Cos]) and by North Country Public Radio (WSLU-FM), which has expanded from low-power coverage of the central St. Lawrence Valley to a system that reaches most of the major pockets of population in northern New York State and into Canada and Vermont through repeater stations (19 in 2003).

A survey of statewide business telephone listings in 1975 showed that the core North Country of Bacheller's time had not changed essentially, with "North Country" absent from business names in the Adirondack Mountains. "Adirondack" businesses were similarly uncommon in the old North Country, with Plattsburgh a major exception. A review of business names prepared in 2003 found that the use of "North Country" was stronger everywhere in the northern regions of the state, especially in northern Franklin and eastern Clinton Cos. However, "Adirondack" also was found in larger numbers, though mostly in the eastern portion of the old region. The growth in "North Country" naming outside the north appeared to be proportionally largest in the Champlain Valley, although the numbers were still small in absolute terms. It is clear that the New York State North Country of the early 21st century is no longer the limited, isolated, far northern region that it once was. Whatever the reason, with "North Country" usage found far and wide, the old distinction between North Country and Adirondacks is no longer as sharp as before, and in some distant time may become vestigial. A core North Country region still exists in the early 21st century, but its edges, wherever they may be, are far away from the old region's former limits.

Bacheller, Irving. *Eben Holden: A Tale of the North Country* (New York: Grosset & Dunlap, 1900)

Darlington, James. "Peopling the Post-Revolutionary New York Frontier," *New York History* 74 (Oct 1993): 341–81

Landon, H. F. *The North Country: A History, Embracing Jefferson, St. Lawrence, Oswego, Lewis, and Franklin Counties* (Indianapolis: Historical Publishing Co, 1932)

Mooers, Richard E. "Action Space, Information Space, and the Hierarchical Ecology of Folk Regions in Northern New York." In *Proceedings, New England–St. Lawrence Valley Division, Association of American Geographers* (1975)

Mosher, Howard Frank. *North Country: A Personal Journey* (Boston: Houghton-Mifflin, 1998)

Singer, Natalia R., and Neal Burdick. *Living North Country* (Utica: North Country Books, 2001)

Richard E. Mooers

North Dansville. Town (pop 5,738) in SE Livingston Co. Settled in ?1793, the town was formed from Sparta in 1846. Sweet, Faulkner and Co (1839) manufactured agricultural machinery. Two railroad lines (1872, 1882) served shippers. Fruit trees are grown in the fertile sandy bottomlands of the Genesee Valley flats, at the head of which North Dansville lies. Fifty-five nurseries shipped nationally around 1900. I-390 was built through town in 1979. In the early 21st century, small business, agriculture, and tourism support the economy.

Mary Jo Marks

North East. Town (pop 3,002) in NE Dutchess Co. Part of Little Nine Partners Patent (1706) and the Oblong, it became a precinct in 1744. It was settled in the 1730s. In 1753 the Moravians established a mission to the Indians near the Connecticut border. The area formed as a town in 1788. Iron ore was mined from the late 18th century to the mid–19th century, and pig iron was produced in the mid–19th century. The Harlem Railroad (1850) opened up New York City's fluid-milk market, making it an important dairying region. Taconic State Park occupies much of its northeastern corner.

William P. McDermott

North Elba. Town (pop 8,661) in NW Essex Co. It was settled in 1809 by Archibald McIntyre, who ran Elba Iron Works until 1815. In 1846 abolitionist Gerrit Smith offered 40-acre (16 ha) tracts in North Elba to African Americans in order to qualify them to vote, creating the community of Timbucto; in 1849 abolitionist John Brown arrived and farmed alongside them, but the experiment ended before the Civil War. The town was formed in 1849 from Keene. The villages of Saranac Lake (Franklin and Essex Cos) and Lake Placid are the most popular tourist destinations in the central Adirondacks. John Brown Farm State Historic Site and Algonquin Peak, the second highest mountain in New York State, are in the town, as are the state Adirondack Correctional Facility (1976) and a federal prison.

Thomas A. Rumney

John Brown's grave in North Elba, *ca* 1900.

North Greenbush. Town (pop 10,805) in W Rensselaer Co. Settled by Dutch farmers under Rensselaerswijck, the town was formed in 1855 from Greenbush. North Greenbush never had a strong riverfront orientation because of clay bluffs that rise steeply from the Hudson. Close to Troy and Albany markets, it supplied the cities with dairy and garden products; mills in the hamlet of Wynantskill were the only industrial enterprises. The population decreased 70% from 1880 to 1920 but grew sixfold between 1920 and 1960. In recent years suburban growth has been fueled in part by the Rensselaer Technology Park (1987) and by the expansion of Hudson Valley Community College with its Joseph L. Bruno Stadium, home of the Tri-City Valley Cats, a minor league baseball team.

Kathryn T. Sheehan

North Harmony. Town (pop 2,521) in SW Chatauqua Co. Settled in 1806 the town formed from Harmony in 1919. Ashville, named from the four asheries located there in early years, is in the southeast corner of town. In the 1850s hammer dulcimers were made in Stedman and sold nationally. The town includes farms, with residential and commercial development concentrated along the west shore of Chautauqua Lake. Stow, on the lake, is the western terminus of the ferry, in operation since 1811, and Rte 17 (I-86), completed through town in 1983, crosses on a bridge (1982) at the same point.

Michelle Henry

North Haven. Village (pop 743) in Southampton (Suffolk Co). Called Hog Neck in town records as early as 1641, the area was purchased in 1665 from Indian proprietors. North Haven is connected to the mainland of Long Island by a narrow spit, and in 1834 a toll bridge was built connecting it to Sag Harbor. By resolution of the inhabitants, the Hog Neck name was changed to North Haven in 1842. In the late 19th century it became a summer resort. The village was incorporated in 1932. In the late 20th century its residents were mostly middle class or retired, but a high-cost second-home development was built *ca* 1990.

Debra A. Willett

North Hempstead. Town (pop 226,611) in NW Nassau Co. Bounded on the north by Long Island Sound where a number of peninsulas and coves create a highly irregular waterfront, North Hempstead extends across a range of hills formed by glacial moraines into the northern reaches of the flat and, historically, treeless Hempstead Plains. Colonists from Connecticut landed and settled at the head of Hempstead Harbor in 1643; Hempstead township was chartered the next year and extended from Long Island Sound to the Atlantic Ocean. In 1775 a group of strongly loyalist dissenters in what is now North Hempstead declared their independence from Hempstead, asking for a separate town. Due to wartime conditions, action was not taken until 1784, when the state legislature recognized the new town. Farming was the principal occupation until the late 19th century when sand mining and shellfishing became economically significant. Steamboat service (1836) and railroad service (1841) brought country house owners; the opening of the Port Washington branch rail line of the Long Island Rail Road in 1898 permitted subdivision on a larger scale. Gold Coast estates were built in some locations. After World War I the use of the automobile in commutation increased; the Northern State Parkway (1931) provided improved access to the town. Between 1920 and 1960 the town experienced more than an eightfold increase in its population. By the 1950s taxes and labor shortages led to the demise of most estates, and the Long Island Expressway (1958) further encouraged development.

There are 31 incorporated villages in North Hempstead, all organized prior to 1932 in order to secure zoning powers for themselves. They include 3 of the 15 wealthiest localities on Long Island, but the town has its pockets of poverty. There are 15 town parks and beaches, including a 27-hole golf complex, as well as six private country clubs and two village-owned golf courses. Manhasset Bay, with its town dock, four yacht clubs, and eight marinas, is one of the busiest small boat harbors on the Atlantic Coast. The United States Merchant Marine Academy is located in Kings Point. Upscale stores are located in the Miracle Mile shopping area in Manhasset. Major industrial parks are located in Port Washington, New Hyde Park, and Lake Success. North Hempstead encompasses 55 miles^2 (142 km^2). Its population in 2000 was 78.9% white, 9.1% Asian, and 6.4% black, 2.9 "some other race," and 2.5 "two or more races." Additionally, 9.8% of the population was of Latino ethnicity.

Joan Gay Kent

North Hills. Village (pop 4,301) in North Hempstead (Nassau Co). An area of large estates in the 1920s, its residents incorporated as a village in 1929 so that they could enact their own zoning laws. It was home to a mere 295 people as late as 1970, though later many of the estates were turned into expensive developments and gated communities. The 1990 population of 3,453 increased by almost 25% by 2000 and became nearly 16% Asian. The county's 98-acre (40 ha) Christopher Morley Park has swimming, tennis, and a nine-hole golf course.

Richard A. Winsche

North Hornell. Village (pop 851) in Hornellsville (Steuben Co). Located immediately north of the City of Hornell and closely linked to it, North Hornell was platted in 1909, and lots were sold for residential development. Incorporated in 1924, it is primarily a bedroom community. It is the site of the Hornell Country Club and former site of Bethesda Hospital.

Virginia L. Wright and Jerry Wright

North Hudson. Town (pop 266) in central Essex Co. Dix Mountain, sixth-highest of the Adirondack High Peaks, is in North Hudson. Settled *ca* 1800, the town was formed from Moriah in 1848. There were some ironworks and tanning in the 19th century, but forest products were and are its mainstay. Frontier Town (1953–99) was a famous amusement park. The Northway (1967) has made the town more accessible for hunting, fishing, and other outdoor recreation.

Thomas A. Rumney

North Lindenhurst. See LINDENHURST.

North Massapequa. See MASSAPEQUA.

North Merrick. See MERRICK.

North New Hyde Park. See NEW HYDE PARK.

North Norwich. Town (pop 1,966) in central Chenango Co. Settled in 1792 from Dutchess Co, it acquired a post office in 1811 but was formed as a town in 1849 from Norwich. It was served by the Chenango Canal (1837–78), the Utica, Chenango and Susquehanna Valley and Ontario and Western Railroads (both 1869). Through much of the 19th century, Plasterville was the site of a plaster mill. Industries in the early 21st century include Rea-D-Pack Foods (1958), the largest US producer of bulk sauerkraut, and OSG Norwich Pharmaceuticals, successor to Norwich Pharmacal (1976). Smaller industries are located in the Warren E. Eaton Airport and Industrial Park (1990) and the Earl B. Clark Business Park (1997). The airport (1928) offers charter service and has freight service on the New York, Susquehanna and Western Railroad (1982). Much of the town remains in dairy and cropland.

North Patchogue. See PATCHOGUE.

Northport {East Northport, locality (pop 20,845) in Huntington (Suffolk Co); Northport, village (pop 7,606) in Huntington}. The area was part of the Second Purchase (1656), and the economy was based on farming, fishing, and shipbuilding. Its post office, established in 1820 as Crab Meadow, was renamed Northport in 1840. Oyster farming began in 1848 and continued until 1990, when the Long Island Oyster Farms closed down. The Long Island Rail Road reached Northport in 1867 and East Northport in 1873. The East Northport post office, established in 1896, was called Larkfield until 1909. In 1881 an oysterman established the Edward Thompson Law Book Co in Northport; it attracted young lawyers from the South, who are credited with establishing the Victorian style of the village, which incorporated in 1894. The company employed 125 in the 1890s, merged with West Publishing Co in 1935, and moved to Brooklyn. Potatoes and cucumbers were farmed in East Northport, and a pickle factory processed crops from 1892 to 1961. Sand was mined in Northport from 1923 to the 1950s. East Northport developed rapidly after World War II. East Northport is the site of the 1,000-bed Northport VA Medical Center (1928).

Robert C. Hughes

North River Steamboat. See *CLERMONT.*

Northrop Grumman Corporation. Defense contractor. The company originated as Grumman Aircraft Engineering Corp, which was founded on 6 Dec 1929 with a capitalization of $32,000. Operations began in a converted garage in Baldwin (Nassau Co). Leroy R. "Roy" Grumman, Leon A. "Jake" Swirbul, and William T. Schwendler formed the core management team. During its first months the company repaired aircraft and built floats for navy seaplanes, but in early 1931 it won a contract from the US Navy to design and produce two prototypes for what became Grumman's FF-1 fighter plane. Over the next two years, Grumman moved twice in Nassau Co seeking larger facilities, first to Valley Stream and then to Farmingdale. The navy ordered 27 FF-1s in 1932 and over 140 other fighters by 1936. In 1937 Grumman moved to Bethpage (Nassau Co) and by the end of 1939 employed over 800 workers.

The three most famous Grumman designs of World War II were the F4F Wildcat, F6F Hellcat, and TBF Avenger. Production of the F6F Hellcat fighter began in 1942, with thousands built by August 1945. The planes made a significant contribution to the Allied victory in the war, especially in the Pacific theater. The Grumman planes developed a reputation for rugged dependability that earned the Bethpage plant the nickname Ironworks, and by the end of World War II the Grumman Co employed over 22,000 workers.

Rapid demobilization at the end of the war forced Grumman to enter the civilian market with a line of aluminum products, though military contracts remained the primary source of income. In 1948 the company, sole US aircraft manufacturer to earn a profit that year, produced its first navy jet fighter, the F9F-2 Panther, soon followed by other jet models. In 1953 Grumman began construction of a second plant in Calverton (Suffolk Co) and in 1954 produced the supersonic F11F-1 Tiger. The company also pursued guided missile research and spacecraft design. In 1962 Grumman obtained the contract for the US space program's lunar landing module, and in 1969 an Apollo 11 crew landed on the moon in Grumman's LM5, known as the *Eagle.*

A major restructuring in 1969 created a parent company, Grumman Corp, and four subsidiaries, Grumman Aerospace Corp, Grumman Allied, Grumman International, and Grumman Data Systems, with a fifth subsidiary, Grumman Ecosystems Corp, created in 1971. For a time the Bethpage works continued to flourish, building many navy planes, including the F-14 Tomcat and the A-6 Intruder. But the end of the Cold War severely contracted the aerospace industry as government contracts waned. Layoffs from Grumman plants contributed to economic recession on Long Island in the early 1990s. In 1994 Grumman Corp merged with California-based Northrop Corp creating Northrop Grumman Corp, headquartered in Los Angeles. Operations on Long Island continued to shrink over the next few years, with the federal government acquiring some of the company buildings. In the first years of the 21st century, the Long Island divisions of Northrop Grumman employed 2,000 people in computer and electronics work.

Thruelsen, Richard. *The Grumman Story* (New York: Praeger, 1976)
Treadwell, Terry C. *The Ironworks: A History of Grumman's Fighting Aeroplanes* (Osceola, Wisc: Motorbooks, 1990)

Louis R. Eltscher

North Salem. Town (pop 5,173) in NE Westchester Co. Settled probably in the 1730s, it was separated from Salem [now Lewisboro] in 1784 and recognized as a town in 1788. The DeLancey House (1773) became North Salem Academy (1786–1886) and is now the town hall, a National Register landmark. In the 1840s the town was the home of June, Titus, Angevine and Co, a circus company. An area of mixed farming, it became a dairying town when the Harlem Railroad (1847) came. In the late 19th century small factories produced condensed milk, woolen goods, paper, hats, augers, machinists' tools, slates, and toys. Some of the town's best farmland was inundated for Titicus Reservoir (1896). Suburbanization was advanced by the construction of I-684 (1967) along the town's west border. In the early 21st century North Salem is an affluent suburb that appeals to equestrians. Balanced Rock, a 90-ton (81 MT) red granite boulder on five smaller limestone rocks, is a landmark. California banker Darius Ogden Mills (1825–1910) was raised in North Salem.

Richard Yakman

North Star. Established by Frederick Douglass in Rochester in 1847, it was one of the most well known and widely circulated abolitionist journals. With $4,000 from supporters in the United States and Great Britain, Douglass bought a printing press and materials, and published the first four-page, weekly issue of the *North Star* in December 1847; Douglass and Martin R. Delany, former editor of the *Pittsburgh Mystery,* were the editors of record, and William C. Nell, formerly a reporter for the *Liberator,* was its publisher. First published from the basement of Rochester's Memorial African Methodist Episcopal Zion Church, the newspaper eventually published from an office at 25 Buffalo St (now 25 East Main St). Bearing a masthead that declared, "Right Is of No Sex—Truth Is of No Color—God Is the Father of Us All, and We Are All Brethren," the *North Star* attacked all aspects of slavery and supported immediate emancipation, as well as education for African Americans and women's rights. Antislavery speeches from congressional meetings and abolition conferences were featured on the front page, often in full text, followed by editorials, poetry, literature reviews, and advertisements. Correspondents reported from Europe, the West Indies, and the United States.

Douglass's reputation as an eloquent orator and writer gave credibility to the *North Star,* which became a leading voice for free Blacks in the North; Delany, who edited the paper until 1849, toured the United States to solicit subscriptions, which eventually reached 4,000. Though its audience widened, the paper struggled against financial instability, which led Douglass to mortgage his home to ease the paper's increasing debt. Marking his support for political abolitionism, Douglass merged the *North Star* with the *Liberty Party Paper* in 1851, prompting Nell, a Garrisonian, to resign and return to the *Liberator.* Renamed *Frederick Douglass' Paper,* the newspaper published until 1860. *Douglass' Monthly,* originally a supplement to *Frederick Douglass' Paper,* was its successor; it published separately from 1859 to 1863.

Hutton, Frankie. *The Early Black Press in America, 1827 to 1860* (Westport, Conn: Greenwood, 1993)

Tripp, Bernell. *Origins of the Black Press: New York, 1827–1847* (Northport, Ala: Vision Press, 1992)

Audrey M. Wilson

North Syracuse. Village (pop 6,862) in Cicero and Clay (Onondaga Co). Settled about 1826 and known locally as Podunk, it was later called Centerville (1846) and was given the postal address of Plank Road (1846), reflecting its location on the first plank road completed in the United States. Its name was changed to North Syracuse in 1887. The village was incorporated in 1925. After World War II, residential subdivisions and shopping malls centered on US 11, the former plank road. Population doubled from its 1940 level of 3,356 to its 2000 level.

Barbara S. Rivette

North Tonawanda. City (pop 33,262) in SW Niagara Co. A military bridge was built across Tonawanda Creek in 1800–1801, and the present city was platted under the name Niagara in 1824, shortly before the Erie Canal brought it commercial potential. When Michigan forests were opened to lumbering, North Tonawanda became a lumber port, rivaling Chicago, that peaked in 1890 when it received 719 million board feet by lake and river vessels. Lumber barons built fine Victorian homes in the community. When lumber shipments declined, iron and steel, paper, and chemical manufacturing grew important, and immigrants from Poland, Italy, Germany, Hungary, and other nations made up the labor force. North Tonawanda incorporated as a village in 1865 and became a city in 1897. Several distinctive industries brought it fame: the Rudolph Wurlitzer plant (1908) made organs, radio cabinets, mechanical pianos, and coin-operated phonographs, and the Allan Herschell Carousel Factory (1910) produced amusement park equipment. When the Barge Canal (1918) replaced the Erie, North Tonawanda became its western terminus. In 1940 North Tonawanda manufactured iron and steel, spark plugs, and filing cabinets in addition to Wurlitzer and Herschell products, and the city's population more than doubled between 1920 and 1960. North Tonawanda has responded to the deindustrialization of the late 20th century with initiatives to develop historic and cultural tourism. The Riviera Theater (1926) and the Herschell Factory Complex (1910–15) are listed on the National Register.

See also CAROUSELS.

Daniel Bille

Northumberland. Town (pop 4,603) in NE Saratoga Co. Fort Miller was built along the Hudson River in 1755, but the first permanent European American settlement was in 1765. The town was formed in 1798 from Saratoga. Gen Peter Gansevoort (1749–1812) developed mills on the Snook Kill in the northern part of town, while the Champlain Canal (1823), crossing its southeastern corner, fostered such enterprises as brickmaking, ice cutting, and the Liberty Wall Paper Co (1898–1924). With limestone underlying much of the land, it remains a rich agricultural town, especially for dairying. Stark's Knob, a hill composed of a volcanic core, is a landmark in the southeastern corner.

Field Horne

Northup, Solomon (*b* Minerva, Essex Co, July 1808; *d ca* 1860). Author of a slave narrative. The free-born son of a Rhode Island-born freedman, Northup worked at various jobs on the Champlain Canal and in the resort industry in Saratoga Springs, where he was known as a fiddler. In 1841 two men tricked him into traveling to Washington, DC, supposedly for work. In Washington he was sold to slave traders and taken to New Orleans for resale. After nearly 12 years of slavery in Louisiana's Red River region, he was able to secretly send a letter to friends in Saratoga Springs, who contacted Henry Northup, the son of his father's former owner. With a legal case based on a state law of 1840, Henry traveled to Louisiana to find Solomon Northup and to secure his freedom. Assisted by David Wilson, a lawyer, Solomon recorded his experiences as a slave, published in 1853 as *Twelve Years a Slave.* It sold more than 30,000 copies over the following decade and earned him $3,000, which he used to purchase property. It remains one of the best descriptions of day-to-day slave resistance in the plantation South. His last years are obscure, and his date of death has never been verified.

Northup, Solomon. *Twelve Years a Slave.* Ed. Sue Eakin and Joseph Logsdon (Baton Rouge: Louisiana State Univ Press, 1968)

Lynda R. Day

North Valley Stream. See VALLEY STREAM.

Northville. Village (pop 1,139) in Northampton (Fulton Co). Settled in the late 1780s, the area's early industries were lumbering and tanning. A smaller industry was mitten factories, of which there were four in 1860. Tourism became important after the Civil War. The village incorporated in 1873, and in 1875 the railroad line was extended from Gloversville. A unique local industry was the small Globe Metallic Binding Co (1880; corners for oil cloth). Other factories included a knitting mill (1891) and Johnson Textile Machinery Works (1912; silk tricot-making machines). The creation of the Great Sacandaga Reservoir (1930) and the Great Depression led to decline. Tourism is the primary industry in the early 21st century, many residents commuted, some as far as the Capital District, and the only manufacturer was Adirondack Furniture (1964).

James Crawford

North Wantagh. See WANTAGH.

Northway. Limited-access superhighway stretching 176 miles (283 km) from Albany to the Canadian border at Champlain (Clinton Co) and also known as the Adirondack Northway. Proposed by Gov Thomas E. Dewey in 1954 as one of a number of such highways to connect with the New York State Thruway, its first design contracts were awarded in 1956. In 1958 the road was made part of the proposed Interstate Highway System and numbered I-87, along with the Major Deegan Expressway in the Bronx and the segment of the Thruway from the New York City line to Albany. A constitutional amendment in 1959 permitted its construction through the Adirondack Park. The first section, from Albany to Clifton Park (Saratoga Co), opened 12 Apr 1960. Bypasses were given priority: the one at Plattsburgh was completed in 1960, Glens Falls (Warren Co) in 1961, and Lake George (Warren Co) in 1965. The section from Plattsburgh to Canada was officially opened in 1962; those from Clifton Park to Lake George and Keeseville (Clinton and Essex Cos) to Plattsburgh opened in 1963; and the section from Lake George to Pottersville (Warren Co) opened in 1966. The final section between Pottersville and Keeseville opened 31 Aug 1967. The highway's final cost was $208 million, substantially below the original estimate of $275 million. Concerns were expressed as early as 1966 about urban sprawl engulfing communities along its route. The Northway made possible the intensive suburbanization of its corridor in Saratoga Co and in Queensbury (Warren Co), and has made the Adirondacks more accessible, but it did not negatively impact towns within the park, where it remains a scenic drive largely free of visual clutter.

Field Horne

Norway. Town (pop 711) in central Herkimer Co. Settled in 1786–88, the town was formed from Herkimer in 1792. Located on the State Rd (1806–8) from Johnstown (Fulton Co) to Sackets Harbor (Jefferson Co), it became a dairy farming town at an early date. The county's first large dairy farm (a "20-cow dairy") was on Dairy Hill *ca* 1810, and local cheese was a recognized product by the 1820s. Other industries included limestone quarrying and tanning; LaDew's Tannery (1853) at Gray employed 75 men. Irish Catholics settled in Norway *ca* 1850. Resident David Brainard (1856–1946) served in the ill-fated International Polar Expedition (1881–84). Norway's population reached a 20th-century low of 386 in 1940 but rebounded. In the early 21st century the town is a farming and lumbering town.

Susan R. Perkins

Norwegians. Having first settled in New Netherland in Rensselaerswijck and New Amsterdam, Norwegians remained in New York Colony through the Revolutionary War. In 1825 Cleng Peerson led a group of religious dissenters to Kendall (Orleans Co). In 1833 they moved on to the Fox River in northern Illinois, and became the nucleus of subsequent Norwegian immigration to the Midwest. In 1820s Norwegian sailors and others connected to the maritime trades began to settle in New York City in larger numbers. By 1900, 12,606 Norwegian-born lived in New York State. Of the 11,820 who lived in the New York City area, 7,969 lived in Brooklyn, first settling in larger numbers in Red Hook and then in Bay Ridge, where by 1910 an estimated 40,000 lived. There were branches of the Sons of Norway (1895), a fraternal order, and singing and gymnastics societies, affiliated with the Norwegian National Federation after 1905. The main organ was the weekly *Nordisk Tidende (Norway Times)*, founded in 1891. Since the 1980s, *Norway Times* has been published primarily in English. Most Norwegians were Lutherans. In Brooklyn they founded Our Saviour's Scandinavian Lutheran Church (1860), Norwegian Seamen's Church (1878), now in Manhattan, Trinity Lutheran Church (1890), and the Norwegian Lutheran Deaconesses' Home and Hospital, (1892), which in 1956 became the Lutheran Medical Center. The Norwegian Lutheran Church of America, formed in 1917 from the combination of three Norwegian synods, has since 1960 been part of the American Lutheran Church.

Few emigrated from prosperous Norway after World War II, and Bay Ridge slowly lost its Norwegian flavor after the children of the immigrants moved to the suburbs. By 2000, fewer than 5,000 Norwegian-born lived in New York State, mainly in New York City. Famous Norwegians include Ole Singstad, the engineer of the Holland, Lincoln, Brooklyn-Battery, and Queens-Midtown Tunnels, and Kirsten Flagstad, the noted Wagnerian soprano at the Metropolitan Opera in the 1930s and 1940s.

Mauk, David C. *The Community That Rose from the Sea: Norwegian Maritime Migration and Community in Brooklyn, 1850–1910* (Northfield, Minn: Norwegian-American Historical Association, 1997)
Norway Times, http://www.norway-times.com/index.html

Thomas Reimer

Norwich. Town (pop 3,836) and city (pop 7,355) in E Chenango Co. Settled in 1788, the town was formed in 1793 from Union [now in Broome Co] and Jericho [now Bainbridge]. The village that became the city was incorporated in 1816. When the Chenango Canal (1837–78) came through, industrial production began in earnest. Norwich Foundry (*ca* 1836; later Thompson Foundry) produced cookstoves, iron bridges, steam engines, and circular sawmills. David Maydole (1807–1882), inventor of the adze-eye hammer, founded the Maydole Hammer Factory (1840). Norwich also had the Hayes and Rider Piano Factory (1838), several tanneries, a ropewalk (1848), and eight cigar factories. In 1869 the Ontario and Western Railroad came through and established repair shops. Norwich Pharmacal Co (1885) was known for Unguentine, Pepto-Bismol, and Norwich Aspirin. The village was incorporated as a city in 1914, leaving the town government independent. Among 20th-century manufacturers were Norwich Knitting Co (1907–94; later Champion Products) and Norwich Shoe Co (1946–91). In the early 21st century nearly all industry was located in the town, including Unison (aircraft components), Quest International (fragrances and flavors), Norwich Beverage, and Wal-Mart. The city began tourism development, and a museum district was established in 2002, encompassing the Chenango County Historical Society Museum (1965), its Norwich Pharmacal Museum (1985), the Northeast Classic Car Museum (1997), and the Bullthistle Model Railroad Museum (1999). The Greek Revival courthouse (1837) is a landmark and still in use.

Dale C. Storms

Norwood. Village (pop 1,685) in Potsdam and Norfolk (St. Lawrence Co). The hamlet of Raquetteville was developed by entrepreneur Benjamin G. Baldwin (1806–73) beginning in 1846 in preparation for a station on the Northern Railroad (1850; later Rutland Railroad). It became a junction point with the Watertown and Potsdam Railroad in 1854. Its 1850 post office name was North Potsdam, but the village incorporated as Potsdam Junction in 1871 and changed its name to Norwood in 1875. Products of manufacture included lumber, leather, iron, caskets, butter tubs, starch, threshing machines, ice cream, and broom handles; a pulp and paper mill operated from 1902 to 1932. It remains the junction of the Ogdensburg Bridge and Port Authority and CSX Montreal Secondary railroad lines. It mainly is a bedroom for Potsdam and Massena. Baldwin's Italianate house (1861) is a landmark. The Norwood Brass Firemen, a nearly 100-year-old brass band, has performed at the Olympic Winter Games in Sarajevo, Bosnia (1984) and at the White House.

Richard E. Mooers

Nott, Eliphalet (*b* Ashford, Conn, 25 June 1773; *d* Schenectady, 29 Jan 1866). Educator. Nott rose from modest Calvinist beginnings. From age 9 he lived in Franklin, Conn, with his older brother Samuel, a Congregational minister who tutored him in the Scriptures and liberal arts. Nott taught in the Franklin district schools and was principal of Plainfield Academy from 1793 to 1795. In summer 1795 he studied at Rhode Island College (now Brown University) and received an MA in the fall. The next year he married Sarah Maria Benedict, was licensed to preach, and became pastor of the Presbyterian Church in Cherry Valley (Otsego Co) and principal of the Cherry Valley Academy. Nott was named pastor of Albany's prominent First Presbyterian Church in 1798. His 1804 sermon condemning dueling, after parishioner Alexander Hamilton's death, brought national stature and an offer of the presidency of Union College in Schenectady, which he accepted. Earlier that year Sarah Maria had died; he married Gertrude Peebles Tibbits in 1807 and, one year after her 1842 death, married Urania Sheldon.

Nott publicly condemned slavery beginning in 1811 and helped organize the New York State Colonization Society in 1829. He crusaded forcefully for temperance beginning in the 1830s and was an early supporter of common schools. A successful and wide-ranging inventor, he obtained 30 patents, including the anthracite-burning Nott Stove (1826–32), which created a mass market for hard coal. In the 1830s he extended his anthracite experiments to Hudson River steamboats. At Union he was a forceful administrator, adding an elective system (1827), a scientific course (1828), and a civil engineering department (1845). However, his efforts to raise funds for the college were often problematic. Beginning in 1804 he used state lottery money for the college, though accusations of fraud and mismanagement contributed to the state lottery's demise in 1833 and followed Nott to the end of his life. His mining ventures and New York City real estate speculation put the college on unstable financial footing and brought personal financial ruin by 1858. He suffered a stroke in 1859 but served as Union's president until his death.

Hislop, Codman. *Eliphalet Nott* (Middletown, Conn: Wesleyan Univ Press, 1971)
Raymond, Andrew Van Vranken, ed. *Union University: Its History, Influence, Characteristics, and Equipment* (New York: Lewis, 1907)

Jim Carl

Noyes, John Humphrey (*b* Brattleboro, Vt, 3 Sept 1811; *d* Niagara Falls, Ont, 13 Apr 1886). Founder of the Oneida Community. During his unfinished ministerial studies at the theologically liberal Yale Divinity School and his pastoral activities in New Haven, Conn, Noyes developed a radical interpretation of the perfectionist belief in the human capacity for holiness. In 1838 he married Harriet A. Holton, one of his converts. After she had one live and four still-born children, he practiced male continence *(coitus reservatus)*, a birth control method later used by members of his two communities. Between 1834 and 1847, based at his family home in Putney, Vt, he proselytized throughout New York State and New England in person and in print. Under his direction, converts living in Putney, including his wife and three of his siblings, gradually adopted communal practices and became the Putney Community. In 1848, after being driven out of Putney because he and a few others shared marriage partners, he folded the Putney group into the Oneida Community in Madison Co. Noyes taught that earthly perfection involved religious study, spiritual improvement, and communalism in all things, including sexual encounters. While central members applied these principles, Noyes presented his constantly developing ideas in Oneida Community periodicals, pamphlets, and books. Between 1834 and 1879 he oversaw publication of nine successive periodicals beginning with the *Perfectionist* and ending with the *American Socialist.* He became increasingly interested in social experiments, and in 1869 he published *History of American Socialisms,* a survey of communities using materials collected by the deceased A. J. McDonald of New York City. In the 1870s Noyes established a eugenics program during which he fathered 9 of the 58 live children born. His increased emotional detachment from the community, aggravated by serious deafness, contributed to the internal conflict that divided the community in the late 1870s. In 1879, fearing that disaffected members would bring charges of statutory rape, he left for Canada, where he offered advice but not direction to members managing the community's reorganization in 1880. His last years were spent with a few, mostly elderly followers in Niagara Falls, Ont. He is buried in the Oneida Community cemetery.

See also ONEIDA COMMUNITY.

Carden, Maren Lockwood. *Oneida: Utopian Community to Modern Corporation* (Syracuse: Syracuse Univ Press, 1998)

Kern, Louis J. *An Ordered Love: Sex Roles and Sexuality in Victorian Utopias: The Shakers, the Mormons, and the Oneida Community* (Chapel Hill: Univ of North Carolina Press, 1981)

Thomas, Robert David. *The Man Who Would Be Perfect* (Philadelphia: Univ of Pennsylvania Press, 1977)

Maren Lockwood Carden

nuclear power. Development of the Indian Point plants on the Hudson River in Buchanan (Westchester Co) was begun by Consolidated Edison (Con Edison) in the late 1950s. Indian Point 1 opened in 1962, was shut down in 1974, and never reopened. Indian Point 2 (1973) and Indian Point 3 (1976) are two pressurized light water reactors with a combined capacity of 1,950 megawatts. The New York Power Authority (NYPA) acquired Indian Point 3 in 1975 after Con Edison admitted severe financial distress. By September 2001 Entergy Corp had bought all three Indian Point nuclear facilities.

The Robert E. Ginna station in the Town of Ontario (Wayne Co), built and operated by Rochester Gas and Electric (until purchased by Constellation Energy in 2003), has been in service since 1969 and is the oldest continuously operating nuclear-generating plant in the nation. The Ginna plant has a 495 MW capacity. The largest concentration of nuclear plants in the state is in Scriba (Oswego Co), where Niagara Mohawk began development of a series of boiling water reactors in the late 1960s. Three plants, Nile Mile Point 1 (1969), Nine Mile Point 2 (1988), and James A. FitzPatrick (1975), with a combined capacity of 2,582 megawatts, were built at Nine Mile Point, together with the only cooling water tower built in connection with the state's nuclear-generating facilities. In the early 21st century, Nine Mile 1 is owned by Constellation, and the FitzPatrick plant (built by NYPA) by Entergy. Ownership of Nine Mile 2 is shared by Constellation and the Long Island Power Authority (LIPA).

In 1992 LIPA assumed ownership of Long Island's only nuclear plant, in Shoreham (Suffolk Co), solely to have it decommissioned. The nation's sole commercial facility for reprocessing nuclear fuel operated at West Valley in Ashford (Cattaraugus Co) from 1966 to 1972. Thirty years after reprocessing ceased, federal and state agencies continued to pursue a massive cleanup operation. A milestone was reached in the summer of 2003 when 125 irradiated fuel assemblies were shipped from the site by rail to Idaho.

In 2003 New York State had six commercial nuclear-generating facilities at three locations. All six plants were operated pursuant to long-term licenses issued by and renewable at the discretion of the federal Nuclear Regulatory Commission.

See also TECHNOLOGY.

Energy Information Administration, http://www.eia.doe.gov/fuelnuclear.html

William S. Helmer

nuclear weapons. Nuclear weapons were first stored in New York State in the early years of the Cold War and peaked at an estimated 1,900 devices around 1985, at the height of the Reagan-era arms buildup. The Seneca Army Depot at Romulus (Seneca Co) held 1,300 nuclear weapons, at one time the largest nuclear weapon storage facility in the world. Nearly all of the weapons held there were tactical weapons designated for shipment to Europe, including 500 neutron bombs. Arkin and Fieldhouse listed 27 New York State sites in 1985 that were part of the "nuclear infrastructure," though this number included radar units and research facilities that did not harbor nuclear weapons. The Air Force had the greatest striking power: the 416th Bombardment Wing at Griffiss AFB in Rome (Oneida Co) had B-52s—eventually fitted with cruise missiles—from 1959 to 1994; the Plattsburgh AFB had Atlas liquid-fueled intercontinental ballistic missiles (ICBMs) in the mid-1960s as well as the 380th Bombardment Wing flying the nuclear-armed B-47s (1955–65), B-52s (1966–71), and FB-111s (1971–91). Additionally the F-4C/D Phantoms of the Air National Guard's 107th Fighter/Interceptor Group at Niagara Falls International Airport and the F-106s of the 49th Fighter/Interceptor Squadron at Griffiss AFB were capable of delivering nuclear weapons. The Brookhaven National Laboratory (Suffolk Co) did nuclear research, and there were about 12 training, research, and procurement installations in the state. The number of naval nuclear weapons in the immediate New York City area was minimal, and their presence, if any, sporadic. Though contemporary estimates of the number of nuclear weapons in New York State are difficult to come by, with the closing of the Seneca Army Depot and the Plattsburgh and Griffiss AFBs in the 1990s, and the decline in the US nuclear arsenal, there are likely few, if any, in-state nuclear weapons.

Arkin, William M., and Richard W. Fieldhouse. *Nuclear Battlefields: Global Links in the Arms Race* (Cambridge, Mass: Ballinger, 1985)

Bulletin of the Atomic Scientists, http://www.thebulletin.org

Andrew D. Todd

nudism. Social nudity in nonsexual settings, also called naturism, is practiced for physical, social, and psychological benefits. Nudists desire the freedom to be nude when climate permits and where others are not unduly offended. Some enjoy private campgrounds, country clubs, or resorts developed for nude recreation; others prefer beaches and hot springs that are either secluded or sanctioned by authorities as clothing-optional. Skinny-dipping has a long history in New York State. John Humphrey Noyes's Oneida Community in Oneida Co met at secluded sites to skinny-dip in the 1850s, and others sought remote stretches of Jones Beach (Nassau Co) through the 1930s. In 1929 German immigrant Kurt Barthel (1884–1969) introduced organized nudism to the United States. He placed ads in New York City and German language magazines seeking help in forming a nudist group. On 4 Sept 1929 he met with three young couples for sunbathing and skinny-dipping at a secluded site near Peekskill (Westchester Co). On 5 Dec 1929 Barthel met with two of the three men at the Café Michelob in Manhattan and created the American League for Physical Culture (ALPC). The ALPC rented a gymnasium on upper Broadway one night per week for nude swimming and exercising, giving the United States its first nudist club. On 21 June 1930 the ALPC rented a 21-acre (8.5 ha) site near Spring Valley (Rockland Co) as a summer nudist camp and continued to rent a New York City gymnasium for the winter. Police raids at the camp and gymnasium, the ALPC's growth in membership, and an emerging intolerance toward nudism in the state forced the ALPC to seek property elsewhere. Brooklyn-born Ilsley Boone (1879–1968), a Baptist minister-turned-nudist, joined the ALPC in 1931 but quickly wrested control from Barthel. Creating his own International Nudist League (renamed the International Nudist Conference in 1932, the American Sunbathing Association in 1937, and the American Association for Nude Recreation in 1994) and publishing America's foremost nudist periodical, the *Nudist,* Boone led the promotion of US nudism through the early 1950s.

Camp Olympia on the shores of Lake Auchmoody (now Sylvan Lake) in Dutchess Co was a nudist resort run by Vincent Burke in 1932. Jan Gay, author of *On Going Naked,* took over as manager in 1933, renaming it the Out-of-Doors Club. Camp Olympia was a setting for *This Nude World* (1932), the first feature film about nudism. By 1934 over a dozen nudist groups had developed in New York State, but in 1935 former governor Alfred E. Smith convinced the state legislature to pass the McCall bill outlawing public nudity. Nudist groups began to move elsewhere. In 1972 the California Supreme Court ruled that mere nudity, without lewd intent, was not lewd. New York State nudists appealed to this ruling to defeat charges of indecent exposure. Nudists began to use portions of Jacob Riis Park (Queens Co) and Fire Island (Suffolk Co) for sunbathing and swimming while authorities looked for ways of stopping the nonlewd behavior. Local citizens and legislators were split throughout the 1970s on the issue of nudity at these sites, but in 1983 Assemblywoman Gerdi Lipschutz convinced the assembly to ban all nudity on all public lands, whether or not the conduct was lewd. The Exposure of a Person Law made it a violation to expose in a "public place" one's "private or intimate parts." New York State courts have considered nudist parks and campgrounds not to be public places in this context, making nudity at such facilities legal. In 2002 the state had seven clothing-optional parks or campgrounds that offered typical visitor amenities found at any family-oriented campground. Empire Haven Nudist Park in Moravia (Cayuga Co), founded in 1959 by George Robinson, is the state's oldest and largest existing nudist club. Enforcement of law against nonlewd nudity in public places varies unofficially depending on community standards and tradition of nude use at each site. Since the 1970s nudist advocacy groups, such as the Naturist Society, have lobbied for greater tolerance for social nudity in New York State.

A related issue involves top-free rights. The 1992 New York State Court of Appeals decision in *People v Santorelli* modified the Exposure of a Person Law so as not to include a woman with bare breasts. The judges indicated that an earlier lower court ruling convicting seven women (the Rochester Topfree Seven) for not wearing shirts at a picnic at Cobbs Hill Park in Rochester had wrongfully dismissed appeals by the defendants for equal protection under the law. The decision found the state law in violation of sexual equality protections and gave women the same right as men to be in public for recreational purposes without a shirt.

Baxandall, Lee. "New York's Nudity History," *Nude and Natural* 11 (Spring 1992)
Cinder, Cec. *The Nudist Idea* (Riverside, Calif: Ultraviolet Press, 1998)
Storey, Mark. "Naturist Clubs of New York State," *Nude and Natural* 22 (Winter 2003)

Mark Storey

numbers gambling. A type of illegal lottery where bettors wager money on a three-digit number between 000 and 999. The payoff rate is typically 500:1, with a $1 wager on a winning number netting the bettor $500 (minus 10% of the winnings, which goes to the collector/runner who accepted the wager). Organized crime groups, which employ hundreds and sometimes thousands of New York State residents in this very popular and high-volume game, have always operated the industry. Although the precise origins of numbers gambling remain uncertain, the game was first played in New York City in the early 1920s. Most early numbers gamblers were African Americans who used the proceeds from the game to finance local political organizations. West Indian gamblers such as Wilfred Brunder, Enrique Miro, and Casper Holstein most likely introduced numbers to Harlem. By the 1930s Jewish and Italian bootleggers began to move in and take over black-run enterprises. For a brief time (1932–34) the gangster Dutch Schultz centralized the Harlem numbers market, primarily through the political clout and protection he wielded through his association with Tammany Hall power James J. Hines, while Albert Anastasia of Murder Inc exerted control over numbers on the Brooklyn docks. With the help of Otto Berman, who found a complex method of fixing the winning number, Schultz's syndicate grossed about $20 million a year at its peak. The US Attorney's Office's pursuit of Schultz and a grand jury investigation of bail bonds and numbers precipitated the disintegration of the syndicate. After Schultz's murder in October 1935, much of his numbers racket was taken over by Michael "Trigger Mike" Coppola. The relatively successful law enforcement efforts of the late 1930s by New York Co district attorney Thomas E. Dewey and New York City mayor Fiorello La Guardia in attacking certain mobsters did not impede the overall operations of numbers gambling.

The New York State Commission of Investigation uncovered an extensive numbers gambling racket when it investigated law enforcement in Buffalo in 1961. A raid on four numbers "banks" (accounting centers) in 1959 had revealed gross annual numbers wagers of over $6 million. In a report on syndicated gambling in central New York State published in 1961, the commission also uncovered in Syracuse and Utica an illegal lottery similar to numbers based on the last five or six digits of US Treasury balance figures published daily. With the advent of the New York Lottery in 1967 and other forms of legalized gambling in the 1970s, including a daily numbers game that closely mimicked the illegal version, many predicted the demise of the numbers game, but it continues to flourish into the 21st century. Its resilience in the face of legal state competition may be due to the better odds offered by the illegal games and the fact that winners do not have to pay taxes on their gains.

Liddick, Donald R. *The Mob's Daily Number: Organized Crime and the Numbers Gambling Industry* (Lanham, Md: Univ Press of America, 1999)

Don Liddick

Nunda [NUN-DAY]. Town (pop 3,017) and village (pop 1,330) in SW Livingston Co. Settled in 1806, the town was formed from Angelica (Allegany Co) in 1808 and was annexed to Livingston Co in 1846. The village was platted in 1824 and incorporated in 1839. The Genesee Valley Canal (1851–78) helped the town's development by opening up vast lumber resources in Livingston and Allegany Cos for harvesting, but three railroads built between 1852 and 1882 rendered the canal obsolete. Farming, especially wheat, was also important. In 1867 mineral springs were discovered, and a water cure sanatorium was built that closed in the early 20th century. Nunda Casket Co operated from 1879 to 1979. The Foote Co (1897–1955) produced concrete mixers, and during World War II supplied Allied construction forces. In the early 21st century, Nunda is home to Nunda Mustard Co and Once Again Nut Butter Co.

Mary Jo Marks

nurses. Many colonial women nursed sick and injured family members and neighbors in their homes. Pest houses employed a minimal staff to care for victims of communicable diseases. During the American Revolution, family members, volunteers, and women hired by the military cared for the wounded. At a time when nursing was regarded as a distasteful and undesirable occupation, New York Hospital, which opened in 1791, initiated the first course of instruction for nurses in North America; the course was offered from 1798 to 1817. Little formal training for nurses was offered until the beginning of the Civil War, when Bellevue Hospital instituted an intensive four-week course to prepare nurses for military hospitals. By and large, however, Civil War wounded were cared for by untrained nurses. The need for training became evident during the war, and the involvement of upper-class women in providing care helped make nursing a more socially acceptable activity. The opening of the New York Training School at Bellevue Hospital in 1873, modeled after Florence Nightingale's famous school in London, marked the beginning of formal nurse training in the United States. In 1888 Bellevue Hospital established the Mills Training School to train male nurses.

Nursing as a Profession

Training schools for nurses quickly proliferated in hospitals throughout the state. In 1899 the hospital of the Sisters of Charity in Buffalo established a school of nursing. Other schools outside of New York City opened before 1900: the Syracuse Training School; St. Luke's Hospital Training School, Utica; and the Buffalo General Hospital Training School. In 1900 the country's first graduate education program for nurses was initiated as the Hospital Economics Course at Teachers College, Columbia University, to prepare nurses for teaching and administrative positions. By 1900 New York State had 2,500 trained nurses and 15,000 untrained nurses, and the public was largely unaware of the distinction between the two.

Believing that the large number of practicing untrained nurses was a threat to the public's health, trained nurses organized to secure legislation to provide a credentialing mechanism. New York was the first state to form a state nurses association for this purpose. The association succeeded in securing legislation in 1903 with the Nurse Practice Act, which called for registration of state residents "of good moral character" who had completed a two-year program in a training school registered by the Board of Regents and created the title "RN" for those duly registered. Although only those registered were permitted to use the title, the bill was voluntary, and anyone could legally provide nursing care. In 1904 the first State Board of Nurse Examiners was appointed to test prospective candidates for licensure, and in 1906 the first inspector of nurse training schools was appointed. The Nurse Practice Act was revised in 1938, and New York became the first state in the nation to mandate registration for "all those who nurse for hire." The 1938 law also created a second level of nursing practice, the licensed practical nurse. In 1972 New York State was first to define nursing statutorily as an independent and distinct discipline. The law identified the nursing functions of case finding, health teaching, health counseling, and providing supportive and restorative care. The licensed practical nurse performs tasks within the same framework, but under the direction of a registered nurse or other licensed healthcare provider.

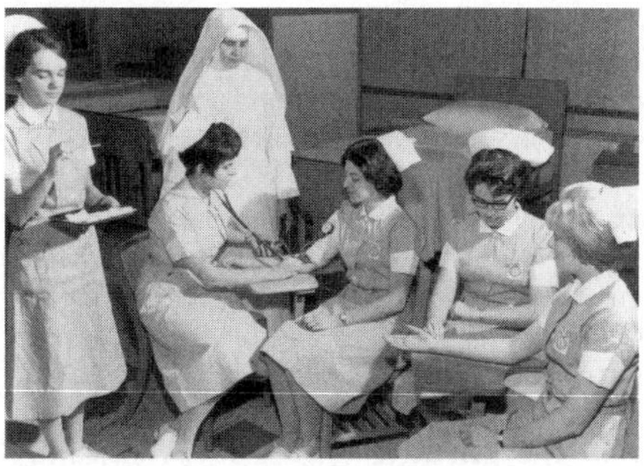

Student nurses at St. Joseph's Hospital, Syracuse, 1975.

New York nurses were at the forefront of developing the nursing profession and providing national leadership. Lavinia Dock, an 1886 graduate of Bellevue Hospital Training School was a founder of the first state, national, and international nursing organizations. She was a visiting nurse, a social activist, an author of the first thorough history of nursing, and an advocate of legislation to regulate nursing. Jane Delano was a graduate of the Bellevue Hospital Training School and later served as director of the school. She served as superintendent of the US Army Nurse Corps and as president of the American Nurses Association, and she directed the American Red Cross Nursing Service. M. Adelaide Nutting was president of the American Society of Superintendents of Training Schools for Nurses (1896, 1909). In 1907 she took charge of the hospital economics course at Teachers College, Columbia University, becoming the nation's first professor of nursing. In 1893 Lillian D. Wald founded the Henry Street Settlement, a visiting nurse service and settlement house for the poor on New York City's Lower East Side; she is considered to be the originator of public health nursing. Annie Goodrich served as the superintendent of nursing at several New York City hospitals and as the director of nurses at the Henry Street Settlement. She was the second inspector of Nurses' Training Schools in New York State and president of the American Nurses' Association (1915–18). During World War I she served as dean of the Army School of Nursing. In 1923 she became dean of the first experimental, university-based independent school of nursing at Yale University.

Adah Thoms campaigned for the acceptance of African American nurses in the American Red Cross and US Army Nurse Corps during World War I, and wrote a history of African American nurses. She was a leader in the organization of the National Association of Colored Graduate Nurses (NACGN) and served as its president (1916–23). Mabel Staupers served as both president and executive secretary of NACGN. Instrumental in securing acceptance of colored nurses into military service during World War II, Staupers guided the NACGN through its merger with the American Nurses Association.

Changes in Nursing Education

Until well after the turn of the 20th century, the majority of nurses were private-duty nurses who provided nursing care in patients' homes. Nurses who were employed by hospitals were most often administrators or teachers in the hospital's school of nursing. Hospitals depended on student nurses to provide nursing care, and hospital diploma nursing programs remained the primary supplier of nurses to the profession. As hospital use increased, many private-duty nurses provided "special-duty" nursing to hospital patients who desired additional care. Studies on the nursing profession in the 1920s and 1930s repeatedly recommended the baccalaureate degree as the minimal educational preparation for entry into the profession.

Although there were a few such programs in the state, the continuing demand for increased numbers of nurses and the dependence of hospitals on student labor interfered with the program becoming widespread. During the depression, many schools of nursing closed and hospitals hired increasing numbers of staff nurses. By World War II there were nearly as many general-duty hospital staff nurses as private-duty nurses. The demands of war created a serious shortage of nurses, and for the first time, federal programs provided funding for nursing education. The Cadet Nurse Corps program subsidized baccalaureate nursing education, and many New York collegiate nursing programs were initiated, including nursing programs at Keuka College, Adelphi University, and Alfred University.

In the 1950s an experimental two-year associate degree program in nursing, developed by Mildred Montag at Teachers College, Columbia University, was introduced in community colleges around the country. The associate degree program quickly became an accepted preparation for nursing practice, and hospital diploma nursing programs began to decline. By 1989 a majority of New York State nurses were educated in institutions of higher learning. In 1996, 34% of the RNs in the state had earned associate degrees, 31% baccalaureate degrees, 23% diplomas, and 12% master's or doctoral degrees as their highest degree. In the 1980s and 1990s, nursing programs admitted increasing numbers of men, minorities, and second-career students.

More specialization and the need for additional primary caregivers led to the development of new roles for nurses in the 1960s and 1970s. Postgraduate programs prepared nurse practitioners, clinical nurse specialists, nurse anesthetists, and nurse midwives for roles in advanced practice. New York's 1988 Nurse Practitioner Bill regulated the practice of nurse practitioners and provided for prescriptive privileges. In 2001 there were 230,866 RNs in New York State; 160,009 of those registered were employed in nursing in a wide variety of settings including hospitals, home healthcare agencies, schools, churches, private practices, and community agencies. With changes in the healthcare system in the 1980s and 1990s, hospitalized patients are sicker. At the same time, severe cost containment measures have reduced the number of nurses and increased the number of nurse-supervised, unlicensed personnel. These demands on nurses, together with exposure to new strains of infectious diseases and rapidly developing medical technology, require highly motivated, skillful, and resilient professionals.

Bullough, Vern L., Olga Maranjian Church, and Alice P. Stein, eds. *American Nursing: A Biographical Dictionary,* 3 vols (New York: Garland, 1988–2000)

Kalisch, Philip A., and Beatrice J. Kalisch. *The Advance of American Nursing,* 3d ed (Philadelphia: J. B. Lippincott, 1995)

Kaufman, Martin, ed. *Dictionary of American Nursing Biography* (New York: Greenwood Press, 1988)

Pavri, Julie M. *Honoring Our Past, Building Our Future: A History of the New York State Nurses Association* (Virginia Beach: Q Publishing, 2000)

Julie M. Pavri

nursing home scandals. In New York City the problems of inadequate and exploitative nursing homes were the focus of a 1960 investigation by the city's investigative commissioner Louis J. Kaplan. His report of that year found that, through fraud and error, operators of many of the city's homes had received hundreds of thousands of excess Medicaid dollars. Little action followed; none of the operators were prosecuted, and their names were not publicized. After 1967 the availability of Medicaid funds and the limited number of state auditors to oversee nursing homes attracted more rogue operations. In 1974 articles in the *New York Times, Village Voice,* and *Buffalo Evening News,* as well as reports on WNEW-TV, exposed more scandals.

In January 1975 Gov Hugh Carey appointed Charles J. Hynes to head the Office of the New York State Special Prosecutor for Nursing Homes, Health, and Social Services (within the year renamed Medicaid Fraud Control Unit, or MFCU) to investigate the state's nursing home industry. Also in 1975 the state legislature voted to require at least one unannounced inspection of every nursing home each year, in addition to regular inspections. From 1975 to 1979 Hynes indicted 198 individuals and convicted 120, with several operators—notably Bernard Bergman, owner of more than two dozen facilities—losing their businesses. The careers of Assemblyman Stanley Steingut, Brooklyn Dem-ocrat and 1975–78 speaker of the New York State Assembly, and of Albert Blumenthal, Republican of Manhattan's West Side, who had both aided Bergman in obtaining licenses, ended. Assemblyman Andrew J. Stein, a Democrat of Manhattan's East Side and 1968–72 chair of the Temporary State Commission on Living Costs and the Economy, which had conducted hearings on corrupt nursing homes, became Manhattan borough president in 1977 and president of the New York City Council in 1987.

By 2000 MFCU had prosecuted over 3,000 defendants for Medicaid fraud and related crime, with a 91% conviction rate; the unit had also recovered more than $326 million in government overpayments. MFCU's biggest case was the successful prosecution of nursing home owner Lawrence Friedman of Brooklyn in 2001, who was indicted for fraudulent Medicaid billings of $62 million. Following New York State's lead, most other states have established Medicaid fraud control units. The MFCU, with 75% of its activities federally funded, maintains regional offices in seven communities: Albany, Buffalo, Mineola, New York City, Pearl River, Rochester, and Syracuse.

Hynes, Charles. "The Regulation of Nursing Homes: A Case Study," *Proceedings of the Academy of Political Science* 33 (Winter 1980): 126–36

Maria Kiriakova

Nyack. Village (pop 6,737) in Orangetown (Rockland Co). It was settled in 1675, and its protected harbor at a gap in the Palisades made it the natural shipping point for inland products destined for the city, a situation enhanced by the Nyack Turnpike (*ca* 1830). Quarrying (1780–1840), boatbuilding (1805–1940s), and shoe manufacturing (1826–1900) were its dominant industries, but Nyack also produced cut flowers for city florists, woodenware, pianos, and ironwork. It became a summer resort as early as 1832 during a cholera epidemic and flourished from the 1880s to the 1920s. The Nyack and Northern Railroad served the village from 1870 to 1966. After an attempt at incorporation (1872–78), the village effectively incorporated in 1883. The retail center of Rockland Co until the development of malls, Nyack has become a tourist town and an antique center. The Tappan Zee Bridge and the New York State Thruway, opened in 1955, made it readily accessible from New York City. As early as 1865, the village was 10% black, a proportion that grew to 26% by 2000. The Edward Hopper House, birthplace of the artist (1882–1967), is open to the public. Nyack is the home of Nyack College (1897). Helen Hayes (1900–1993) lived in the village from 1932 until her death and Carson McCullers (1917–67) from 1945 until hers.

Nordstrom, Carl. *Frontier Elements in a Hudson River Village* (Port Washington, NY: Kennikat, 1973)

Jean M. Pardo

Nyack College. Four-year Christian liberal arts college. In 1880–81 Canadian-born Presbyterian minister Dr A. B. Simpson (1843–1919) left a traditional Presbyterian church on Manhattan's 13th St to form a new interdenominational evangelical ministry based mainly in public halls and serving mostly Italian immigrants. In 1883 he founded the Bible study–centered Missionary Training Institute in Manhattan, with members of his congregation as its first students. Simpson soon established a parent organization, the Christian and Missionary Alliance, to sponsor the institute, and in 1936 it was renamed Nyack College. After several moves within Manhattan, the institute relocated to Nyack (Rockland Co) in 1897. By the mid-1940s the school offered four-year courses in theology, missions, Christian education, and music, and by the mid-1960s instituted a wider curriculum and gained accreditation from state, regional, and national education associations as a four-year college. Branch campuses were established in New York City (1995), Washington, DC (2001), and Dayton, Ohio (2001). In 2003 student enrollment was 1,980. Graduate programs are available through Alliance Theological Seminary, an accredited branch campus of the college at 335 Broadway in New York City.

Cable, John H. *A History of the Missionary Training Institute: The Pioneer Bible School of America, 1883–1933* (Nyack, NY: Nyack College, 1933)
Niklaus, Robert L. *The School That Vision Built: Centennial Review of Nyack College* (Nyack, NY: Nyack College, 1982)

Jeffrey Kraus

Nyack shootout. On 20 Oct 1981 a Brinks truck was robbed at a bank in Nanuet (Rockland Co). As security guards transferred over $1.5 million to the truck, the robbers emerged from the back of a red Chevrolet van and opened fire, killing security guard Peter Paige. The police later determined that among those in the van were Jeral Wayne Williams, Cecilio "Chui" Ferguson, Samuel Brown, Samuel Smith, and Donald Weems, most of whom had ties to the Black Panthers or the Black Liberation Army. The robbers drove the van to a nearby shopping center where accomplices waited in a U-Haul truck and two other vehicles. The robbers transferred themselves and their heist to the waiting vehicles. Police stopped the U-Haul at the South Nyack/Grandview entrance to the New York State Thruway. The driver, who has never been positively identified, and a passenger got out, proclaiming their innocence. As the police went to search the rear of the U-Haul, a group of six men emerged firing, killing two of the officers, Waverly Brown and Edward O'Grady. Several of the robbers, attempting to escape in a car, plowed into a wall at 6th and Broadway in Nyack. The police then arrested the occupants of the car, David Gilbert and Judith Clark (former members of the Weather Underground) and Samuel Brown, associated with the Black Liberation Army. The police discovered that a woman who had been sitting in the passenger seat of the U-Haul was Kathy Boudin, a former leader of the Weather Underground.

Jeral Wayne Williams, whom authorities suspected was the leader of the group, was arrested in 1986 in Los Angeles after a nationwide hunt, convicted, and sentenced to 60 years. Clark, Gilbert, and Weems were tried, found guilty, and sentenced to three consecutive 25-years-to-life prison terms. Boudin pled guilty to murder and robbery charges. She expressed remorse for the loss of life before being sentenced to a 20 years-to-life term. Many people in Rockland Co, including families of the victims, expressed anger at the apparent leniency of Boudin's sentence. On 17 Sept 2003 Boudin was released from prison after serving 22 years. The Federal Bureau of Investigation identified a number of other radicals it believed had participated in the planning, execution, or aftermath of the holdup. The participants planned to use the money from the robbery to further their political aims. While some of the suspects still remain at large, the arrests and convictions of this racially mixed group of revolutionaries marked the end of a cycle of left underground political activity that began in the late 1960s in response to racial injustice and the war in Vietnam.

Frankfort, Ellen. *Kathy Boudin and the Dance of Death* (Briarcliff Manor, NY: Stein & Day, 1984)
Gado, Mark. "The Brinks Robbery of 1981,"http://www.crimelibrary.com/terrorists_spies/terrorists/brinks/4.html

Harold Jacobs

NYRA. See NEW YORK RACING ASSOCIATION (NYRA).

O

Oakdale. Locality (pop 8,075) in Islip (Suffolk Co). Dutch immigrants were instrumental in the development of the oystering industry, active beginning in 1850. After the South Side Rail Road arrived in 1868, wealthy industrialists built summer homes in Oakdale, including William K. Vanderbilt (Idle Hour, 1902). During the 1920s and 1930s some of the estates were platted in building lots, although most development did not occur until after World War II. It is the site of Dowling College (Oakdale campus, 1963) and the Connetquot River State Park. St. John's Episcopal Church (1765) is a landmark.

Eileen Effrat

Oakfield. Town (pop 3,203) and village (pop 1,805) in NW Genesee Co. The Oakfield Fort site was inhabited by Native Americans around AD 1400. Settled in 1801 the town derived its name from the "oak openings" in its territory; it was formed in 1842 from Elba. Cary Collegiate Seminary (1843–1903) was a private school. The village was incorporated in 1858. Gypsum, first discovered in the area in 1825, was mined and manufactured into wallboard by US Gypsum Co from 1902 to 1998. Agrilink and predecessor firms have operated a cannery since 1904. Labor Daze, an annual folk art festival, takes place in early September.

Susan L. Conklin

Oak Hill Country Club. Incorporated in 1901 and situated along the Genesee River in Rochester, the club in 1924 sold its property to the University of Rochester and relocated to its present site in Pittsford (Monroe Co), where renowned golf course architect Donald Ross designed its two 18-hole courses. Major golf competitions have been held on the more difficult East Course, including two US Amateur Championships (1949, 1998), three US Opens (1956, 1968, 1989), two PGA Championships (1980, 2003), a US Senior Open (1984), and the Ryder Cup (1995). The course has been redesigned over the years, but the thousands of oak trees lining its fairways remain its distinctive feature.

Sal Maiorana

oats. This Old World grain grows in cool climates with short growing seasons and from very early times formed an important part of the foodways in Scotland and Ireland. But in British North America oats were mainly used as horse fodder, with white oats most common, although black, brown, and gray varieties were also grown. The history of oats cultivation in New York State is linked with using horses rather than oxen for power, whether operating agricultural machines or moving goods and people. In frontier regions oxen were more common, largely because feeding and maintaining them was less costly. As rough settlements matured into established farms and associated rural villages, however, both horses and the oats needed to feed them became more common. Horses also grew more common in urban areas, where they were used for hauling as well as transportation. By the mid-1800s, almost all New York State farmers grew oats for their own teams and sold any surplus. The state produced 27,015,296 bushels (951,991,900 l) in 1855, with Onondaga and Montgomery Cos leading in production. Cultivation peaked at the turn of the 20th century, with the most acres in oats, 1,430,000 (578,700 ha), in 1896 and the highest production, 54,800,000 bushels (1,931,097,000 l), in 1902. The shift from horses to gasoline-powered tractors occurred across the state. Where large-scale arable farming predominated, it occurred as early as the 1920s or 1930s, but many small upland dairy farms did not make the change until after World War II. Farmers in western New York State still grow oats, though in small quantities relative to corn, or even wheat. Still fed to horses, oats are also used in the cereal industry. In 2000 New York State farms, mainly in the Southern Tier and Western New York, produced 3.9 million bushels (137 million l) of oats.

Hurt, R. Douglas. *American Farm Tools from Hand-Power to Steam-Power* (Manhattan, Kans: Sunflower Univ Press, 1982)

Jessie Ravage

objectivism. See RAND, AYN.

Oblong. Land patent in Westchester, Putnam, and Dutchess Cos. The 1664 boundary between New York and Connecticut was intended to be 20 miles (32 km) from the Hudson and parallel to its course, but was to run north-northwest from the mouth of Mamaroneck River; by 1683 it was understood this course would cross the Hudson below West Point. In that year it was agreed the colonies would retain settlements on Long Island Sound already made. Therefore, the boundary was begun at the mouth of the Byram River, running north-northwest 8 miles (13 km), then 12 miles (19 km) parallel to the Sound, after which it ran, as previously agreed, parallel to the Hudson as far as the Massachusetts line. The tract thus ceded to Connecticut was compensated for by ceding to New York an equivalent tract, thereafter called the Oblong, on the east side of the agreed-upon line, 1.75 mi (2.82 km) wide, encompassing 61,440 acres (24,864 ha). It was surveyed in 1731; in May of that year the entire tract was patented by the Crown to a group of influential Englishmen; and in June the province patented 50,000 acres (20,234 ha) to the Equivalent Land Co of 22 colonists, which soon became the de facto owner. A division survey, marking two tiers of square lots, was made in 1732, and freehold sales followed, encouraging quick settlement. Many settlers were Quakers from Rye, Long Island, Massachusetts, Connecticut, and Rhode Island. Disputes continued for decades with unauthorized settlers coming over the border from Connecticut and others who leased land under the 1731 royal patent. The granting of the Oblong also called into question the eastern bounds of the Highland and Beekman Patents and contributed to tensions that fostered the tenant revolt in 1766. Discrepancies in the boundary line were revealed by an 1860 survey using more advanced instruments. These were not settled until 1879.

Kim, Sung Bok. *Landlord and Tenant in Colonial New York: Manorial Society, 1664–1775* (Chapel Hill: Univ of North Carolina Press, 1978)
"The Oblong." In *History of Putnam County, NY,* William S. Pelletreau (Philadelphia: W. W. Preston, 1886)

Field Horne

Occom, Samson (*b* Mohegan, Conn, 1723; *d* New Stockbridge [now Stockbridge, Madison Co], 14 July 1792). Presbyterian clergyman and

Farmer threshing oats near Hobart, 1915.

teacher. He was a native Mohegan, a subgroup of the Algonquian-speaking Pequot Nation, then located on the Thames River near New London, Conn. He was converted to Christianity around 1740 during the Great Awakening and expressed a desire to become a religious teacher. In 1743 he enrolled in Eleazar Wheelock's experimental school in Lebanon, Conn, that trained young natives as missionaries among their own people. Occom was one of the first students and the model for all who attended thereafter. He adopted habits of industry and frugality, and mastered a curriculum that required knowledge of Latin and Hebrew. But his enthusiasm for study eventuated in chronic eyestrain by 1747, and this weakened state precluded further preparation for college.

In 1749 Occom was licensed as a Presbyterian preacher, and that same year he moved to Long Island, where he began work among the Montaukett Indians, conducting an elementary school and supporting himself through farming, fishing, and handicrafts. For a time the Society for the Propagation of the Gospel gave him a salary of £20. In 1751 he married Mary Fowler, a Montaukett, and together they had 10 children. After many frustrating delays, the Long Island Presbytery ordained him on 29 Aug 1759 at East Hampton (Suffolk Co). Occom had an understandable affinity with native groups and preached to them with considerable results, especially when addressing them in their language. His *Account of the Montauk Indians on Long Island*, not published until 1809, is a significant ethnographic study. Beginning in 1761 he made several journeys among the Oneida to assess the chances of mission work there, but by 1764 he had returned to his birthplace in Connecticut, where, against the advice of Wheelock, he became a strong advocate for Mohegan land claims. Encouraged by Wheelock and famous evangelists such as George Whitefield, Occom agreed to campaign in Great Britain, raising funds for more extensive Indian missions. The preaching tour lasted from 1765 to 1768 and the Native American orator was an outstanding success. Crowds in England and Scotland donated freely because of Occom's solidly cogent sermons, which he delivered with impressive elocution and great dignity. He eventually raised more than £12,000 and returned to America expecting a great expansion of mission work. However, by 1769, Wheelock had diverted most of the collected funds to establish Dartmouth College, a school for Whites instead of Indians. Occom denounced the move and entered a period of great despair. In Connecticut he continued to preach but only sporadically, living in poverty while often indulging in self-pity and excessive drinking. On 2 Sept 1772, in New Haven, Conn, he delivered a famous sermon on the sins of drunkenness at the request of Moses Paul, an Indian who was to be executed that day for a murder he committed while intoxicated.

By 1773 Occom had concluded that Indian groups in New England could not coexist peaceably with the encroaching white population. The next year he reached agreement with the Oneida Nation to obtain a tract of land for Christian Indians, which he called Eeayam Quittoowauconnock (Brothertown), where native groups could find refuge and preserve some measure of their traditional dress, language, and kinship patterns. The American Revolution delayed its opening (Occom urged Indians to remain neutral), but the town officially opened on 7 Nov 1785. By 1789 he lived at Brothertown and served as pastor, ministering to Indians there and at nearby New Stockbridge. When the Presbytery of Albany was established in 1790, Occom was accepted with full standing among fellow clergy in the region. Samuel Kirkland preached his funeral sermon. His unique career connected the plight of the two major Indian groups in late 18th-century New York State: the Algonquian-speaking Indians on Long Island and the nations of the Iroquois Confederacy in Central and Western New York.

Blodgett, Harold W. *Samson Occom* (Hanover, NH: Dartmouth College, 1935)

Love, W. DeLoss. *Samson Occom and the Christian Indians of New England* (1899; repr with introduction by Margaret Connell Szasz, Syracuse: Syracuse Univ Press, 2000)

Richardson, Leon B. *An Indian Preacher in England* (Hanover, NH: Dartmouth College, 1933)

Henry Warner Bowden

Ocean Beach. Village (pop 138) in Islip (Suffolk Co). Located on Fire Island, Ocean Beach originated with John A. Wilbur's platting of 1,000 lots in 1908, which he advertised in the *Brooklyn Daily Eagle.* Wilbur coined the slogan Where Health and Happiness Go Hand in Hand and promised to build a church when all the lots were sold; Union Free Church was built in 1913. Ocean Beach acquired a post office in 1911 and, with the adjacent Stay-A-While Beach Estates, incorporated as a village in 1921. It was supplied with water, sewer, and concrete walks, rather than roads. Electricity was available by 1938. Most of the 595 housing units in the village in 2003 were summer residences.

Geri Solomon

Ocean Hill–Brownsville crisis. Racially divisive 1968 struggle over community control of public education in New York City. During the mid-1960s, black parents who were frustrated by continued racial segregation in the New York City schools and by deteriorating educational conditions in their communities demanded control over neighborhood schools. In response the New York City Board of Education, with the support of Mayor John Lindsay and the Ford Foundation, authorized an experiment in community control of education in Ocean Hill–Brownsville, a predominantly black and Puerto Rican neighborhood in Brooklyn. Local residents in 1967 elected a governing board that quickly clashed over the extent of its powers with the largely white, mostly Jewish United Federation of Teachers (UFT), the union representing the city's public school teachers. In May 1968 the governing board created a test case by sending termination letters to 19 white, predominantly Jewish, union-affiliated educators. That summer, an administrative law judge ruled the terminations illegal, but the governing board refused to rescind them. With Lindsay unable to guarantee the teachers their jobs back, the UFT called the first of three citywide teachers' strikes on 9 Sept 1968.

The strikes divided New York City along racial, class, and geographic lines. Many white middle-class New Yorkers supported the UFT, viewing the governing board's action as a threat to labor rights, due process protections, and equality under the law. The city's black community, with support from a range of legal, academic, liberal, and business elites, backed the governing board in the belief that local control of institutions was the only way to reverse the cycle of marginalization and poverty in neighborhoods like Ocean Hill–Brownsville. A small but significant group within the UFT also opposed the strikes on these grounds. The atmosphere in the city became bitter, rife with accusations of union busting, class bias, and antisemitism from UFT supporters, and racism, labor bossism, and cultural imperialism from their opponents.

The first two strikes (9–10 and 13–29 September) were settled by agreements reached by the UFT, the Board of Education, and Lindsay to reinstate the teachers. Both broke down when the governing board refused to accept them. The third and final strike (14 October–18 November) was the longest teachers' strike ever in a major US city and ended largely on the UFT's terms. The disputed teachers regained their jobs, and the Ocean Hill–Brownsville School District was placed under state trusteeship. In 1970 when a new citywide decentralization law took effect, the Ocean Hill–Brownsville community control experiment passed out of existence. The crisis left New York City with a legacy of racial division that affected mayoral elections, labor negotiations, fiscal policies, and everyday relationships between Blacks and Whites into the 21st century.

Gittell, Marilyn, and Maurice Berube, eds. *Confrontation at Ocean Hill–Brownsville* (New York: Praeger, 1969)

Podair, Jerald E. *The Strike That Changed New York: Blacks, Whites, and the Ocean Hill–Brownsville Crisis* (New Haven: Yale Univ Press, 2002)

Jerald E. Podair

Oceanside. Locality (pop 32,733) in Hempstead (Nassau Co). Originally called Parsonage Farm because mid-17th-century residents gave land to support the minister, the land was sold by St. George's Episcopal Church between 1794 and 1826. It then became known as Christian Hook, reflecting its religious origins and a hook in its creek. By the 1860s oystering had become the main occupation; in 1864 it took the name Oceanville, changed to Ocean Side when the post office opened in 1892. As a result of a building boom in the 1920s, Oceanside had 9,744 residents in 1940; another surge in the 1950s resulted from new techniques making it profitable to build on reclaimed marshland.

Georgina Martorella

O'Connell, Daniel P(atrick) (*b* Albany, 13 Nov 1885; *d* Albany, 28 Feb 1977). Democratic Party leader. The son of a saloon keeper in Albany's South End, O'Connell attended but never graduated from Albany's public schools, dropping out in the sixth grade. He tended bar in his father's tavern and there learned to speak German with the immigrant patrons. After serving in the US Navy during World War I, he was elected city assessor in 1919. This victory signaled the end of long-standing Republican control, led by William Barnes Jr, over local office. The four O'Connell brothers, especially Daniel and Edward, worked with Edwin and Parker Corning to build a powerful Democratic organization in the city and county of Albany. In 1921 that organization succeeded in electing the city's first Democratic administration in more than two decades. O'Connell soon came to be called "The Boss" or "Uncle Dan." After the death of Edward in 1939, Dan O'Connell assumed sole control of the Albany Co Democratic organization, a position he retained until his death in 1977. Although subject to intense investigation under Gov Thomas E. Dewey, the organization survived that and other challenges, and Albany remained a Democratic stronghold in the early 21st century. The organization achieved such longevity through centralization of control in the party chair, a well-developed system of ward leaders, and effective use of patronage.

Robinson, Frank S. *Albany's O'Connell Machine: An American Political Relic* (Albany: Washington Park Spirit, 1973)

Ivan D. Steen

O'Connor, John (Joseph) (*b* Philadelphia, 15 Jan 1920; *d* New York City, 3 May 2000). Roman Catholic cardinal. O'Connor grew up in a small row house in southwest Philadelphia and attended public and parochial schools. Following graduation from high school, he studied for the priesthood and was ordained on 15 Dec 1945. After 7 years of teaching and parish work, O'Connor became a US Navy chaplain and progressed through the ranks over the next 27 years. During this time he earned a master's degree in clinical psychology and a doctorate in political science. At his retirement O'Connor was serving as chief of chaplains. In 1979 Pope John Paul II selected him to serve as an auxiliary bishop of New York with the charge to assist Terence Cardinal Cooke with the military ordinariate, the special needs of US military personnel. O'Connor became bishop of Scranton, Pa, in June 1983 and seven months later was appointed archbishop of New York, serving Catholics in a 10-county archdiocese. He was made cardinal archbishop in 1985. Comfortable with public life, O'Connor used his Sunday sermons at St. Patrick's Cathedral and his weekly newspaper column in *Catholic New York* to speak out on a wide range of controversial issues. His defense of marriage, his attacks on all forms of abortion and pro-choice Catholics, and his troubled relationship with the gay community made him a lightning rod for controversy. Yet O'Connor also was an ardent defender of unions, led ecumenical prayer services against racism, and issued a pastoral letter in 1999 apologizing to the Jews for the anti-Semitism of the Catholic Church. He established an archdiocesan office to provide food and shelter programs for the hungry and homeless and developed plans to refurbish archdiocesan housing for low-income families. O'Connor wrote several books and traveled widely. He died after a protracted battle with brain cancer.

Hentoff, Nat. *John Cardinal O'Connor: At the Storm Center of a Changing American Catholic Church* (New York: Scribner's, 1988)
O'Connor, John Cardinal, and Edward Koch. *His Eminence and Hizzoner: A Candid Exchange* (New York: William Morrow, 1989)

Timothy Walch

O'Conor [O'Connor], **Charles** (*b* New York City, 22 Jan 1804; *d* Nantucket, Mass, 12 May 1884). Lawyer and politician. Son of an Irish rebel who immigrated to New York City after 1798, O'Conor gained admittance to the bar in 1824. Early legal victories, including his defense of slaveholders in *Jack v Martin* (1834, 1835) and his representation of Catherine Sinclair Forrest in her divorce from actor Edwin Forrest (1851, 1852), reaped notoriety and earned him limited political rewards. Associated with the Hunker and later Hardshell factions, O'Conor was elected to the 1846 New York State Constitutional Convention and ran unsuccessfully for lieutenant governor (1848). He became US attorney for the Southern District of New York in 1853 and later argued for the rights of slaveholders in *Lemmon v the People* (1860). He served as former Confederate president Jefferson Davis's lawyer and obtained Davis's release by posting his bail in 1867. O'Conor prosecuted William M. "Boss" Tweed while serving as a special state deputy attorney general (1871–75). He ran for president on the Straight-Out Democratic Party ticket (1872) to protest Horace Greeley's nomination by the Democrats; he received fewer than 20,000 votes. He also represented presidential candidate Samuel J. Tilden before a special electoral commission (1877). O'Conor retired from the law in 1881 and moved to Nantucket, Mass.

Finkelman, Paul. *An Imperfect Union: Slavery, Federalism, and Comity* (Chapel Hill: Univ of North Carolina Press, 1981)

Robert D. Sampson

octagon houses. Over half of the estimated 1,000 eight-sided structures inspired by the 1848 publication of Cohocton (Steuben Co) native Orson S. Fowler's book, *A Home for All; or A New, Cheap, Convenient, and Superior Mode of Building,* were constructed in New York State. A noted phrenologist and social reformer as well as amateur architect, Fowler's intent was to make comfortable and efficient housing available to all economic classes. Because the octagon form enclosed more interior space than a square or rectangle form of equal exterior wall area, Fowler argued that octagon houses would provide improved heating efficiency and lower building costs since exterior walls are most expensive to construct. Other cost-saving ideas included building all outside walls with grout (natural cement) and constructing one's own house, points Fowler demonstrated by building his own five-story, 60-room octagon house in Fishkill (Dutchess Co). He also believed that all houses should have hot and cold running water, centralized heating, water closets, and good ventilation, all novel ideas at the time. In addition, he proposed a reorganization of domestic space, one that placed the kitchen near the center. Although built statewide, the highest concentration of eight-sided houses was in Central and Western New York, a fact not surprising given those areas' involvement with social reform in the mid–19th century.

Darlington, James. "A Home for All: Orson Fowler and the Domestic Octagon," *North American Culture* 3 (1987): 18–29

William J. Darlington

Odell, Benjamin B(arker), Jr (*b* Newburgh, Orange Co, 14 Jan 1854; *d* Newburgh, 9 May 1926). Governor and businessman. Odell attended local schools, Bethany College in West Virginia, and Columbia College in New York City before joining his father, who was active in Republican politics, in the ice business in 1875. Odell's other business ventures included utilities and transportation, and in 1887 he became a member of the Republican State Committee. He was elected to Congress—representing Orange, Rockland, and Sullivan Cos—in 1894 and 1896. He did not seek another term in 1898, the year he was chosen chairman of the Republican State Committee. His efforts to secure Theodore Roosevelt the Republican nomination for governor in 1898 reflected Odell's skills in political maneuvering. Odell himself was elected governor in 1900 and 1902. During his tenure Odell consolidated overlapping state agencies, supported tenement house reform, and repealed the direct state tax on real estate while increasing indirect taxes on corporations. He also favored enlarging the Erie Canal, and in 1903 voters approved a bond act allocating $101 million for the project. Odell's disputes with Republican political boss Thomas C. Platt on various topics, including administration of the New York City police, undercut Platt's authority. Odell did not run for reelection in 1904. He returned to Newburgh and remained active in business, and during World War I he served as state ice controller.

McCormick, Richard L. *From Realignment to Reform: Political Change in New York State, 1893–1910* (Ithaca: Cornell Univ Press, 1981)

Laura-Eve Moss

Odessa. Village (pop 617) in Catharine and Montour (Schuyler Co). The first sawmill (1799) and gristmill (1801) in present Schuyler Co were in Odessa. Streets were laid out about 1827. A post office was established in 1855, and the village was incorporated in 1903. The Lehigh Valley Railroad (1892–1976) boosted growth. Odessa had a nursery, an evaporator, and a milk station, and was home to Cotton-Hanlon (1921), a timber company that employed 170 people by World War II. In 2003 the one industry was Ron Parmenter Motors, a tire-retreading facility. Other residents commute to Elmira, Ithaca, and Corning.

Glenda Gephart

Office of General Services. Created in 1960 as part of New York State's Executive Department, the agency oversees support services for the operation of state government through four groups: Real Property Management and Development, Support Services, Information Technology and Procurement Services, and Design and Construction. A governor-appointed commissioner heads the Office of General Services (OGS). In 2002 Real Property Management and Development administered 18 million ft^2 (1.6 million m^2) of state-owned space valued at more than $3 billion and a capital projects budget of approximately $30 million. Major facilities under this group's jurisdiction include Albany landmarks: New York State Capitol, Governor Nelson A. Rockefeller Empire State Plaza, Executive Mansion, Ten Eyck and Holland Ave buildings, and W. Averell Harriman State Office Building Campus. In addition it is responsible for about 50 other buildings, including Adam Clayton Powell State Office Building in Harlem, Eleanor Roosevelt State Office Building in Poughkeepsie; Binghamton State Office Building, and Gen William J. Donovan State Office Building in Buffalo. The group also manages 11 million ft^2 (1 million m^2) of leased space and is responsible for the Empire State Plaza Art

Collection of 92 works of art—paintings, sculptures, and tapestries—sited throughout the Empire State Plaza complex.

Support Services is responsible for mail and freight services, printing, management of the state's motor vehicle fleet, and transfers of surplus government property. This group also coordinates the Government Donated Foods Distribution Program, which in 2002 received, stored, and distributed approximately $70 million in federally donated food for school districts, childcare facilities, and food pantries. Information Technology and Procurement Services provides telecommunications and information technology services. It also establishes statewide contracts for commodities, services, and technology for more than 4,000 public sector organizations. Design and Construction provides architectural, engineering, and construction management services. In 2002 the OGS, headquartered at Albany's Empire State Plaza, had about 2,000 employees.

Roseberry, Cecil R. *Capitol Story* (Albany: NYS Office of General Services, 1982)

Jeffrey Kraus

Off-Track Betting Corporation (OTB). In April 1970 Gov Nelson A. Rockefeller signed legislation into law that permitted local governments to establish public benefit corporations to administer off-track betting on thoroughbred and harness racing at the state's racetracks, lifting a 60-year prohibition against off-site wagering. These local corporations were authorized to set up "horse parlors," and local officials were empowered to appoint members to the local corporation's governing board. Under a complicated revenue formula, local corporations sent their profits to state and local governments and provided compensatory revenue to racetracks for the anticipated drop-off in track revenue.

The legalization of off-track betting came after more than a decade of lobbying by New York City officials. In 1958 New York City mayor Robert F. Wagner Jr (1954–65) established the Citizen's Commission on Off-Track Betting to study the legalization question. The commission recommended the establishment of government-run off-track betting facilities. Mayor Wagner, who strongly favored the plan as a means to raise local revenue, sponsored in 1963 a nonbinding ballot initiative in New York City calling for off-track betting; the measure won by a three to one margin. Later New York City mayor John Lindsay (1965–73) and Comptroller Abe Beame (1961–73) also backed the proposal. While most New York City officials supported the measure, state Republicans and some state Democrats were against the initiative, arguing that off-track betting promoted gambling, particularly among the poor and the elderly. Gov Rockefeller's opposition to the measure kept it locked up in the state legislature throughout the 1960s. In 1970 Rockefeller reversed course, supporting off-track betting as part of a state aid package to help New York City close a projected budget gap.

In 1971 New York City was the first local government to form a public benefit corporation. New York City's OTB is the biggest in the state. In 2000 its 2,000 employees took in $1 billion in bets at 67 branches, $32 million of which went to City Hall, $15 million to the state government, and $90 million to the racing industry. Following New York City's lead, other local governments formed compacts creating five additional regional OTBs throughout the state: Capital OTB (representing the Capital District region), Catskill OTB, Nassau OTB, Suffolk OTB, and Western New York OTB. Revenue transferred from the six regional OTBs to the state government totaled $36 million in 2000, and in 2002, 222 betting parlors operated statewide.

Important changes since OTB's creation include the 1973 formation of the New York State Racing and Wagering Board (SRWB). The SRWB oversees the operations of each of the regional OTBs as well as other gambling enterprises in the state. In 1974, over the protests of the regional OTBs, the state government instituted a 5% surcharge on all bets placed. After interest in horse racing waned and the profitability of off-track betting stagnated in the 1980s, the state legislature expanded OTB services to include simulcast studios (1986), self-service betting stations (1993), and the opportunity to place bets on racing at out-of-state tracks (1994). Since 1994 these changes have revitalized off-track betting; the total handle (bets placed) at OTB facilities hit $2.01 billion in 2001.

The regional OTBs have been dogged by continual allegations of corruption and administrative inefficiency. Local politicians and party leaders often fill the regional OTBs' administrative posts with patronage appointments. Allegations came to a head in 1997 when it was revealed that more than $750,000 had been misappropriated at Capital OTB over a six-year period. This misuse of funds took the form of lavish salaries for top Capital OTB officials and the inappropriate use of expense accounts. A 1999 investigation by State Comptroller H. Carl McCall detailed that prior to 1997 the SRWB provided little oversight of the regional OTBs, although such a function was the SRWB's principal mandate. He also documented that three of the OTB regional corporations had never prepared a formal annual budget. In the 1990s New York City mayor Rudolph Giuliani and members of the Suffolk Co legislature argued for the privatization of their respective OTBs as a solution to corruption and inefficiency. Despite the criticism, OTB generates a steady stream of revenue for government and significant patronage for politicians, and it employs a large, unionized workforce, thus ensuring its continued existence.

See also GAMBLING AND GAMING.

New York State Racing and Wagering Board. *Annual Reports* (Albany: Author)

Richard M. Flanagan

Ogden. Town (pop 18,492) in W Monroe Co. Settled in 1802, the town was formed from Parma in 1817. It produced wheat, apples and other fruits, and cabbage, shipped via the Erie Canal (1823) and the Niagara Falls Branch of the New York Central Railroad (1852). Largely rural until 1950, its population almost doubled in a decade, and it has become increasingly suburban in the intervening decades. In 1907, 200 residents organized Ogden Telephone Co. When sold to Citizens Utilities Co in 1997, it had 20,000 telephones in service.

Carolyn Vacca

Ogden, Samuel (*b* Newark, NJ, 9 Dec 1746; *d* Newark, 1 Dec 1810). Land speculator. By 1770 Ogden, a member of a prominent New Jersey family, was the owner of ironworks and considerable land at Boonton, NJ. In 1775 he married Euphemia Morris, sister of New York politician Gouverneur Morris. During the war Ogden's ironworks supplied the Continental army. Ogden served as Robert Morris's agent in the 1791 purchase of western New York State land from Massachusetts. In 1792–93 Ogden purchased the present Town of Oswegatchie and City of Ogdensburg and parts of the Towns of De Kalb and Gouverneur [now in St. Lawrence Co] from Morris and his partner Alexander Macomb. Once the British withdrew from the region in 1796, he hired Nathan Ford (1763–1824) to serve as his land agent, who evicted Canadian settlers and platted Ogdensburg. Ogden never visited the city bearing his name nor any of his New York State land holdings. His nephew David A. Ogden formed the Ogden Land Co in 1810.

Hough, Franklin B. *History of St. Lawrence and Franklin Counties* (1853; repr Baltimore: Regional Publishing, 1970)

Wheeler, William Ogden. *The Ogden Family in America* (Philadelphia: J. B. Lippincott, 1907)

Francis P. Boscoe

Ogden Land Company. Land trust. In 1810 David A. Ogden purchased the preemption (first purchase) rights for the Seneca Indian reservations in Western New York from the Holland Land Co. Ogden, a New York City attorney, assembled a private group of investors, which included his brother Thomas Ludlow Ogden and various other family members, to form the Ogden Land Co. It was an investment premised on the eventual removal of the Seneca, who proved a resilient opponent. Outspoken chiefs such as Red Jacket opposed the sale, and confusing, overlapping federal and state jurisdictions hindered the company's efforts to acquire the land through bureaucratic means. Quakers and Protestant missionaries aligned against the company. In 1826 Ogden Land Co finally profited when it purchased most of the Buffalo Creek Reservation, five smaller reservations in the Genesee Valley, and parts of the Cattaraugus and Tonawanda Indian Reservations for amounts substantially below market value; considerable bribery and deception were involved. The Buffalo Creek land was especially valuable because it adjoined the booming city of Buffalo. Setting its sights on the remainder of the Seneca territory, including the Allegany Indian Reservation, the company helped draft a removal treaty (1838), which was not enforced due to Seneca and missionary opposition. A revised treaty in 1842 allowed the company to buy the remainder of Buffalo Creek and Tonawanda, again at a substantial discount, with the Allegany and Cattaraugus Reservations remaining under Seneca control. By the late 1840s most of the original investors had died and interest in the company was waning. In 1857 the US Supreme Court voided the 1842 Tonawanda sale because the Tonawanda had not been represented in the negotiations. The Ogden claim to the Allegany and Cattaraugus Reservations was never formally resolved by legislation or litigation.

Conable, Mary H. "A Steady Enemy: The Ogden Land

Company and the Seneca Indians" (PhD diss, Univ of Rochester, 1995)

Francis P. Boscoe

Ogdensburg. City (pop 12,364) in NW St. Lawrence Co. Lying at the confluence of the St. Lawrence and Oswegatchie Rivers, Ogdensburg is a US port of entry and a deepwater port. European settlement began in 1749 when Sulpician priest François Picquet established the missionary outpost Fort La Présentation. A dam and sawmill followed in 1751. The settlement was taken over by the British, however, who renamed it Oswegatchie (1760–96). American settlement began in 1796 immediately after the British withdrew under terms of the Jay Treaty. Saw- and gristmills were in operation within two years, and the area was platted in 1798–99. It became a place of considerable trade, but business was interrupted by the 1807 embargo and subsequent War of 1812. A February 1813 battle resulted in British reoccupation until the end of the war. Ogdensburg incorporated as a village in 1817.

The Oswego Canal (1828) connected Ogdensburg with the American market, and the Welland Canal (1839) allowed ships to bypass the Long Sault Rapids and continue downstream to Montreal, but it was the Northern Railroad (1850) that initiated the most rapid growth. It transshipped lumber and grain from the upper Midwest and much of the trade from New England to the west. The Rome, Watertown and Ogdensburg Railroad linked it to the New York City area in 1862, and the Utica and Black River Railroad (1878) completed its transportation network. The village incorporated as a city in 1868.

Catholic tradition was strong because of Quebecois and Irish immigration, and the first Catholic parish was established in 1828. In 1855 the population was 30% Irish-born and 28% Canadian-born, and after 1858 separate Irish and French parishes developed. With the 1898 consecration of St. Mary's Cathedral, Ogdensburg became the see of the Diocese of Northern New York.

A diverse manufacturing sector centered on finished lumber and woodworking. An example was Skillings, Whitney and Barnes (1859–1924), which employed as many as 700 men. Other manufacturing included flour milling, foundries and machine shops, papermaking, and the Manhattan Silk Co (1905), which employed 400 in its early years. Another important employer was and is St. Lawrence Psychiatric Center (1887). Population peaked in 1940 at 16,909. The postwar period was not kind to the economy, and after 1960 population declined sharply. The opening of the St. Lawrence Seaway in 1959 and the international bridge in 1960 did not deliver the anticipated economic benefits. Ogdensburg adopted a city-manager form of government and hired a director of planning and development to meet its needs; the Ogdensburg Bridge and Port Authority developed an industrial park and had considerable success in attracting manufacturing facilities, including such Canadian firms as Mitel, Canadian Bank Note, Newbridge Networks, CompAS, Bata Shoes, and ACCO. Other successes have included tourism growth, with the Frederic Remington Museum (1923) an important attraction, and the construction of two prisons (Ogdensburg in 1981 and Riverview in 1988) that employ over 1,000 people. The Robert C. McEwen Customs House (1810) is a landmark. In 2000 Ogdensburg's population was 10% black; approximately 6% of the population was of Latino ethnicity.

Douglas B. McDonald

Ohio. Town (pop 922) in central Herkimer Co. Settled before the Revolutionary War, the town was formed from Norway in 1823 as West Brunswick; the name was changed to Ohio in 1836. Products in the 19th century included cheese, potatoes, lumber, and tanbark. In the late 1870s there was a furniture factory and a tannery at Gray. In the early 21st century Ohio is a second-home and tourist destination. Loyalist leader Capt Walter Butler (1752–1781), a leading character in Walter D. Edmonds's novel *Drums Along the Mohawk* (1936), was killed in town 30 Oct 1781 in an indecisive battle while retreating from Johnstown [now in Fulton Co].

Susan R. Perkins

oil. See PETROLEUM AND NATURAL GAS INDUSTRY.

Oil Spring Indian Reservation. One of three Seneca Nation of Indians reservations, the uninhabited tract comprises 1 mi² (2.6 km²) in Cattaraugus and Allegany Cos. It was here that a famous natural oil spring provided a balm for traditional treatment of various ailments.

At the Treaty of Big Tree in 1797, Oil Spring was inadvertently omitted from the list of Seneca reservations to be retained by the Seneca. Handsome Lake and a delegation of other prominent Senecas visited Pres Thomas Jefferson in the winter of 1801–2 to gain assurance of their ownership. During this visit Handsome Lake unsuccessfully attempted to have the Oil Spring Reservation designated as a personal grant to him with an increased 10 mi² (25.9 km²), in much the same manner as Cornplanter had earlier had personal assignments of land made to him. Handsome Lake maintained that the reservation had been given to him during the treaty negotiations at Big Tree and that celestial beings had directed that this be done at the behest of the Great Spirit. Jefferson assured the delegation that the United States would secure their ownership of Indian lands. Following the disastrous Treaty of Buffalo Creek of 1838, under which all Seneca lands in New York State were surrendered, the Compromise Treaty of 1842 restored three reservations, Allegany, Cattaraugus, and Oil Spring.

Oil Spring has been subject to legal challenges from the beginning. Gov Blacksnake, a nephew of Handsome Lake, gave testimony in 1856 at the age of 107 regarding the circumstances of Seneca ownership and substantiating their claim to the reservation. He had attended the original treaty negotiations and testified that Handsome Lake had been given a separate paper from Robert Morris recognizing the omission. He also produced a map clearly indicating Oil Spring in the list of Seneca reservations. Legal controversy continues in the early 21st century as a result of the construction of the canal system in the mid-1800s and the illegal occupation of lands by non-Seneca along the shore of Cuba Lake.

Abler, Thomas S., and Elisabeth Tooker. "Seneca." In *Northeast,* ed. Bruce G. Trigger, vol 15 of *Handbook of North American Indians,* ed. William C. Sturtevant (Washington, DC: Smithsonian Institution, 1978)

Abrams, George H. J. *The Seneca People* (Phoenix, Ariz: Indian Tribal Series, 1976)

George H. J. Abrams

Olcott, Chauncey [Chancellor John] (*b* Buffalo, 21 July 1858; *d* Monaco, 18 Mar 1932). Songwriter and actor. Olcott, the son of Irish immigrants, was educated in Buffalo's public schools and then with the Christian Brothers. He sang as a soloist at Buffalo's Academy of Music, performed in blackface with the Thatcher, Primrose and West Minstrels, and sang in a vocal quartet in *The Old Homestead* (1888). Olcott made his New York debut in 1886, starring in the Lillian Russell Opera Co's *Pepita.* Soon after, he traveled to London where he learned to speak in his trademark Irish brogue for his 1891 performance in John Wyndham's *Miss Decima.* After returning to the United States, Olcott was hired by writer and impresario Augustus Pitou in 1892, contributing songs and performing as an Irish tenor in his shows on 14th St until 1912. Olcott's first hit as a composer was the title song of Pitou's *The Minstrel of Clare* (1896). This was the first in a string of successful songs playing on the nostalgia of recent Irish American immigrants for their homeland. "My Wild Irish Rose" (from *A Romance of Athlone,* 1899), "When Irish Eyes Are Smiling" (from *The Isle of Dreams,* music by Ernest R. Ball, 1912), and "Mother Machree" (from *Barry of Ballymore,* also with Ball, 1911) have remained enduringly popular. He continued to perform until 1925 and spent most of his retirement in Monte Carlo, Monaco.

Olcott, Rita O'Donovan. *Song in His Heart* (New York: House of Field, 1939)

David Raymond

Old Bethpage. Locality (pop 5,400) in Oyster Bay (Nassau Co). Settled in 1695 and largely a Quaker community, it was known as Bethpage until 1936. The site of brickworks from the 1850s until 1981, its bricks were used to build Garden City in the 1870s. It was otherwise primarily agricultural until after World War II, when it underwent rapid development. Old Bethpage Village Restoration, a re-created antebellum Long Island community on 209 acres (85 ha), was established by Nassau Co in 1963 and opened in 1970; the Long Island Fair is held there in October. Much of the 1,475-acre (597 ha) Bethpage State Park is in Old Bethpage; the 2002 US Open was held on its Black Course, one of five golf courses in the park.

Richard A. Winsche

Old Brookville. See BROOKVILLE.

Old Field. Village (pop 947) in Brookhaven (Suffolk Co). In 1672 English settlers divided the land into lots of 3–4 acres (1.2–1.6 ha), later called Old Fields. Beginning in the 1870s wealthy New Yorkers began building summer homes. To comply with legal requirements, Old Field became a village in 1927 on the merger of three others (West Meadow, Oldfield, and Conscience Bay), which had been incorporated weeks earlier in a legal strategy that had Old Field as the end point. The village remains an exclusive residential community with two-acre zoning in effect. Landmarks include the Old Field Point Lighthouse (1868) and Flax Pond, a protected salt marsh.

Beverly C. Tyler

Old Forge. Locality in Webb (Herkimer Co). The Mohawk and Malone Railroad (1892) opened up the area for tourism. In 1903 the hamlet of Old Forge incorporated as a village, requiring expensive services for the remote village's 200 residents and creating a $100,000 debt in the early 1930s. The village dissolved in 1934. Lumbering was the first industry, but in the early 21st century winter and summer tourism dominates the area, boosting the entire county's economy. With an estimated permanent population of about 1,200, most residents are seasonal, and the population drops off at summer's end. Attractions include Enchanted Forest/Water Safari (1956), the Old Forge Arts Center, and Old Forge Lake Cruises.

Susan R. Perkins

Old Military Tract. State land grant. During the Revolution, New York State's borders were exposed and, in the absence of a functioning federal plan, the state passed a 1781 law to raise two regiments for border duty, promising them land bounty rights. Lands in Central New York were reserved for the purpose, but their availability was delayed by the war and by continuing Indian claims. As an alternative, North Country land where Indian title had already been extinguished (1,550 mi^2/4,014 km^2) was surveyed in 1786, but no part of this Old Military Tract (now western Clinton Co, eastern Franklin Co, and the northwest corner of Essex Co) was actually patented by military claimants, who correctly judged the land marginal for farming. When the central New York tract was opened for settlement, it acquired the name New Military Tract. The Old Military Tract was sold by the state commissioners to land speculators, some of them in the employ of lumber companies looking for timberlands.

Hurd, Duane. *History of Clinton and Franklin Counties, NY* (Philadelphia: J. W. Lewis, 1889)

Thomas A. Rumney

old-time music. Traditional country dance and play-party music that was the primary source of entertainment in preindustrial farm communities. Labeled old-time after World War I to signify traditional rural values in a modernizing society, the music combined British American fiddle tunes, square dance numbers, Victorian parlor songs, American and British ballads, sacred songs, minstrel songs, and play-party tunes (music at adult dances featuring singing games and rhymes). Old-time music can be traced through four periods: traditional music dating from the colonial period to the early 20th century, the hillbilly period during the second quarter of the 20th century, the country era in the three decades after World War II, and the revival and renewal age since the 1960s.

Preindustrial Era

New Englanders coming to New York State in great numbers during the late 18th and early 19th centuries brought their fiddle-tune tradition with them. Among the favorite dances were jigs, reels, contras, cotillions (forerunner of American square dances), quadrilles, minuets, and hornpipes. Commonly relying on the storehouse of British tradition, many old dance tunes were adapted to reflect the American national spirit. In 1807, for example, *A Selection of Cotillions and Country-Dances* offered the "Federal Cotillion" along with the British "Money Musk." That same year *Collection of the Most Celebrated Figures of Cotillions and Contra Dances* included "Humors of Boston," "Jefferson and Liberty," "American Fair," "Democratic Rage," and "Independence." Still the old British tunes persisted, partly because the familiarity of the tunes helped to signal the dances. This British American tradition spread throughout North America, and in New York State the music gained a stylistic stamp that distinguished it from that of the southern Appalachians. In New England and New York, quadrilles and jigs in 6/8 time, along with hornpipes and reels in 4/4 time, were especially common. New York State fiddlers typically featured light, separate bowing to produce melodies with a clear, lilting quality. The tunes were usually free of syncopation, with brief and distinct notes. Performers traditionally took away the ornamentation common to the British originals. They also regularized the beat and gave the music a bounciness in place of the drones common in many British tunes. Among the hornpipes in New York State, Durang's, Sailor's, Fisher's, Lamplighter's, Hull's Victory, and Rickett's were common; reels included Opera, Virginia, and Chicken. Among the quadrilles and jigs were "Larry O'Gaff," "Haste to the Wedding," and "Blackberry." Other standards of the old-time fiddle-tune repertoire included "Soldier's Joy," "Turkey in the Straw," "Devil's Dream," "Arkansas Traveler," "Wilson's Clog," "Rakes of Mallow," "Wind That Shakes the Barley," "Buffalo Gals," "Black Cat," "Flop-Eared Mule," and "Wake Up Susan."

The country fiddler, typically male, was the center of community entertainment throughout the 19th century. With his old familiar tunes and a style that recalled the British Isles, the American country fiddler could lead dances, lighten the load at work bees, delight the young, and raise conversation at the general store. The fiddler would be summoned to play and shout calls when a house dance, sometimes called a kitchen junket, whang, or hop, was held in a farm family's home. Accounts of some exceptional 19th-century fiddlers went beyond local reputations. Delaware Co fiddler Alva Belcher's fame lives on in a reel bearing his name. Piano accompaniment became more standard toward the end of the 19th century. Many parlors had pianos for family singing, and at dances they provided the steady rhythm the fiddler demanded. The accordion and occasionally the harmonica, or mouth organ, were brought along when no piano was available.

The best documentation of the tradition comes through the commercial recordings of John McDermott (1869–1957) from Cortland. McDermott owed much of his repertoire to "Happy" Bill Daniels (1853–1923) of Varna (Tompkins Co). By 1926 McDermott had achieved the title of State Fiddle Champion and was already claiming the world championship. Just before the end of 1926, he headed for New York City to record commercially for Brunswick. Listed on the label as a "Pioneer Fiddler and Caller," McDermott recorded "Happy Bill Daniels Quadrille," "Virginia Reel Medley," which included two traditional British American fiddle tunes, "Miss McLeod's Reel," and "Girl I Left Behind Me." Like most other New York and New England folk fiddlers, McDermott used steady bowing strokes to punch out an uncluttered and unhurried melody.

Hillbilly Period

During the early 20th century, when urban areas began swelling with rural migrants, the old-time fiddling sound could be heard increasingly in dance halls. The larger crowds demanded a bigger sound. Old-time bands added tenor banjos, guitars, and basses to the fiddles. Woodhull's Old Tyme Masters from Elmira, one of the best-known old-time music bands in New York State, was composed of Fred Woodhull, who had been active in the earlier house dance days, and his sons Floyd on accordion, Herb on tenor guitar, and John on guitar. Fred had taught his sons the old British American tunes, and to bring the music up-to-date the sons adapted new popular songs to 19th-century square dance calls. During the 1940s the band recorded several albums for Victor Records. Other well-known bands, typically with family connections, such as Ott's Woodchoppers from Ithaca and the Hornellsville Hillbillies from Hornell (Steuben Co), crisscrossed the state, still featuring the British American fiddle-tune tradition. Underscoring the changes occurring in the 20th century, the bands often dressed in hillbilly garb when performing the old tunes that had been proudly handed down from parents and grandparents. But in the modern age, the tunes and the musicians were increasingly cast as rustic and old-time.

The lone fiddler was being hailed nostalgically in state and county fairs and minstrel shows as a throwback to pioneer days. The New York State Fair in Syracuse held an annual fiddle contest, which regularly featured musicians over 60 years old. The backdrop for the contest was a log cabin that reminded fairgoers of their Yorker pioneer heritage. By the end of World War II, commercial recordings and public performances of old-time music became less frequent, but the tradition was nurtured in some families and villages. Elial Glen "Pop" Weir (1890–1965) from the North Country near Gouverneur (St. Lawrence Co) was a prominent character. Working in the lumber camps, he became adept at fiddling as well as lumbering. Pop moved his family to Otsego Co in the 1920s, and 5 of his 12 children took up instruments and performed at play-parties. In addition to dance tunes, the family sang parlor and folk songs such as "Bury Me beneath the Willow," "Frankie and Johnny," and "The Old Gray Bonnet." Pop was a fixture at old-time fiddling contests throughout Central New York and dominated them through the 1950s.

Country Era and Folk Revival

Radio and commercial country music produced in Nashville had an influence on the Yorker fiddling tradition. The pace became faster, and double-stops (the simultaneous sounding of two strings) and slurred notes entered the style of many fiddlers. The generation growing up after World War II changed the hillbilly label to avoid stereotyping by city people. The proud, adventurous western pioneer image and down-home values in country music were more appealing than the hillbilly image, and country music's pop strains moved into commercial clubs and bars. In rural Central New York these establishments were often called hotels, not because they had rooms to let but because they were leftovers from the small 19th-century inns and from Prohibition when the word "bar" was taboo. But even as the electric instruments of country musicians worked through the arrangements of contemporary country songs such as "Truck Driving Man," they typically still included a set or two of square dance tunes. During the 1950s and 1960s the best-known country band in Central New York was the Westernaires, whose instrumentation was typically electric guitars, drums, and pedal steel-guitar. They included square dances to old-time tunes such as "Irish Washerwoman" and "Girl I Left Behind Me" in public appearances until they stopped performing in the early 1980s. Other band names like the Rhythm Rangers and Driftwoods bespoke restless images. The members of many bands had been reared on the old fiddle music but were also influenced by the swing beats of Hank Williams and Lefty Frizell heard on the radio.

The folk music revival of the 1960s and 1970s, when urban youth on college campuses flocked to coffeehouses to hear old-time songs and tunes interpreted by groups such as the New Lost City Ramblers in New York City, the Putnam String County Band, and the Highwoods String Band in Ithaca inspired more efforts to recover the authentic sounds of regional and family traditions. Aging ballad singers around the state such as Sara Cleveland, Lawrence Older, and Grant Rogers were recorded on folk music labels appealing to this spirit of rediscovery. Rogers and Older also recorded fiddle tunes. Beginning in 1960 the Friends of Old Time Music in New York City promoted concerts by rural folk musicians. Elsewhere several large folk festivals drew significant audiences during the 1970s and sought homegrown talent, reviving and renewing the original fiddle tunes and old-time songs. Among these festivals were the Fox Hollow Festival in Petersburgh, Syracuse Folk Festival, Binghamton Folk Festival, Old Songs Festival of Traditional Music and Dance in Altamont, and Cornell Folk Festival in Ithaca.

Folklore courses and cultural heritage series on college campuses encouraged fieldwork in rural communities to document old-time musicians. Beginning in 1973 and continuing into the 21st century, Bill Knowlton broadcast a bluegrass and old-time music radio show from Liverpool (Onondaga Co) that featured local talent. Bluegrass music, which jazzed and sped up many old-time tunes from the southern tradition, became nationally popular, and this led many northern musicians to look for local connections to old-time music's roots. Museums, historical societies, and state and regional folk art programs sponsored special events such as Fiddlers' Conversations, Folk Artists in the Schools, and Community Days that featured old-time music as part of regional heritage. Camp Woodland in Phoenicia (Ulster Co) promoted the collection and performance of Catskills dances and songs from 1939 to 1962. Beginning in the 1980s prominent fiddler Jay Ungar and guitarist Molly Mason organized music and dance camps at Ashokan (Ulster Co), including a Northern Week with New York and New England material.

In 1981 the New York State Old Tyme Fiddlers Association established the North American Fiddlers Hall of Fame and Museum in Osceola (Lewis Co). Organizations specifically devoted to the renewal of old-time music, such as the Del-Se-Nango Olde Tyme Fiddlers Association in McDonough (Chenango Co) and the Friends of Fiddle and Dance in Saugerties (Ulster Co), have taken the lead in maintaining tradition, encouraging youth to take interest in old-time tunes and songs, and organizing scattered old-time musicians and fans into a cohesive group. The music has different functions than it had for the barn dances and work bees of earlier generations. Old-time music is often considered a participatory connection to authentic heritage, a connection to regional rural identity in a mass urban culture.

See also FOLK MUSIC REVIVAL.

Bethke, Robert D. *Adirondack Voices: Woodsmen and Woods Lore* (Urbana: Univ of Illinois Press, 1981)
Bronner, Simon J. *Old-Time Music Makers of New York State* (Syracuse: Syracuse Univ Press, 1987)
Cazden, Norman. *Dances from Woodland: Square Dances from the Catskills* (Ann Arbor, Mich: Cushing-Malloy, 1955)
Cazden, Norman, Herbert Haufrecht, and Norman Studer, eds. *Folk Songs of the Catskills* (Albany: SUNY Press, 1982)
Ungar, Jay, and Molly Mason. *The Catskill Collection* (Fiddle and Dance Records, FDCD 103, 1998)
Warner, Anne. *Traditional American Folk Songs from the Anne and Frank Warner Collection* (Syracuse: Syracuse Univ Press, 1984)

Simon J. Bronner

Old Westbury. Village (pop 4,228) in North Hempstead and Oyster Bay (Nassau Co). Settled in 1658 by Quakers, it had a post office named North Hempstead (1805), which was changed to Old Westbury in 1868. The village incorporated in 1924. Estate owners forced the Northern State Parkway (1931) to bypass the village completely but were unable to do the same with the later construction of the Long Island Expressway (1958). After World War II some of the largest estates were divided or converted to institutional use: the 550-acre (223 ha) William C. Whitney estate is now the Old Westbury Golf and Country Club and the New York Institute of Technology; F. Ambrose Clark's 650-acre (263 ha) property is the SUNY Old Westbury campus. Old Westbury Gardens, with its mansion and formal gardens, draws visitors from April through December.

Joan Gay Kent

Olean [OH-LEE-ANN]. Town (pop 2,029) and city (pop 15,347) in SE Cattaraugus Co. Maj Adam Hoops, the founder of Olean, purchased 20,000 acres (8,100 ha) from the Holland Land Co in 1803, hoping to profit from New Englanders migrating west in search of good farmland; his brother Robert settled at Olean Point in 1804. Adam Hoops laid out the community and called it Hamilton, but settlers preferred the name Olean, and the post office was given that name in 1817. The Town of Olean was formed in 1808 and was at first coextensive with what became Cattaraugus Co. Hoops did not fully achieve his dream and defaulted on his payments as travelers followed the Erie Canal rather than the Allegheny River.

Even though Olean was not on a major transportation artery, the village continued to grow. Flat-bottomed boats navigated the Allegheny River when the water was high, but the river was not dependable for transportation. The Genesee Valley Canal reached Olean in 1856 and was extended to Mill Grove on the Pennsylvania line, but it was not a financial success and closed in 1878. Industries in the 19th century included the large Conklin Wagon Works, Chamberlain Manufacturing Co (1848), makers of stump pullers and ditching plows, a number of tanneries, a pottery, and a foundry. In 1854 the village was incorporated, becoming a city in 1893.

The industrial age arrived in Olean with the railroad, beginning with local narrow-gauge lines; the Erie Railroad came through in 1851. The Buffalo, New York and Philadelphia Railroad (later Pennsylvania) was completed in 1872 and the Olean, Bradford and Warren in 1878. Olean achieved success with the discovery of oil; the Olean Petroleum Co (1874) and the Olean Oil Refinery (1877) were soon sold to Standard Oil Co. By the 1880s Olean had the largest oil storage depot in the world, and Standard Oil ran a pipeline to New Jersey. Oil-related industries appeared, such as Clark Bros, manufacturers of engines for the oil industry; the company merged with S. R. Dresser Manufacturing Co in 1937.

The oil boom ran its course, and during the middle decades of the 20th century, local entrepreneurs achieved some success. Despite the

North Union St, Olean, mid–20th century.

upgrading of Rte 17 to I-86, Olean experienced the general industrial decline found in most of western New York State and the former iron belt. In the early 21st century, industries in the city include Dresser Rand, the county's largest employer; in the town, manufacturers include Cooper Industries (electrical protective devices) and Olean Advanced Products (multilayer ceramic capacitors). Attractions include the Butterfly Ballroom, a private nature preserve, the Bartlett House, and Olean Point Museum. Higher education is offered by Olean Business Institute and Jamestown Community College.

Philip G. Payne

Olive. Town (pop 4,579) in central Ulster Co. Settled *ca* 1740, the town was formed from Hurley, Marbletown, and Shandaken in 1823. Logging and bluestone quarrying were early occupations. A tannery, woolen factory, pulp mill, and a spoke and felloe (wheel component) factory also operated at various times. In 1862 the Ulster and Delaware Turnpike Co created a 1.1 mi (1.8 km) "stone road" of bluestone slabs on an older plank road. The Ulster and Delaware Railroad crossed the town in 1870 and helped develop the summer boarding business. The Ashokan Reservoir, built between 1907 and 1917, inundated most of the town's valley farmland and required that several hamlets and many houses be moved. Olive is the site of the Ashokan campus of SUNY New Paltz (1957), an environmental education facility. The Ashokan-Turnwood covered bridge (1898, Town Lattice) is a landmark.

Ruth Piwonka

Olmsted, Frederick Law (*b* Hartford, Conn, 26 Apr 1822; *d* Belmont, Mass, 28 Aug 1903). Travel writer and landscape architect. He was primarily educated by ministers and by instructors at private schools in Connecticut. In 1837, when he was about to enter Yale College, he suffered a severe case of sumac poisoning that weakened his eyes, leading to a decade of desultory training in surveying and farming, as well as a voyage to China as a crew member. He spent 1846 studying scientific farming with George Geddes at Camillus (Onondaga Co), near Syracuse, and in 1848 purchased a farm on Staten Island that he operated for the next seven years. From 1852 to 1854 Olmsted traveled in the slaveholding South as a correspondent for the *New York Times*, writing 64 letters describing his journey. In 1855 he moved to Manhattan to become managing editor of *Putnam's Monthly Magazine* and a partner in the publishing firm of Dix, Edwards and Co.

Following the failure of the firm in 1857, his literary connections helped secure him the position of superintendent of Central Park, and later that year he joined Calvert Vaux in preparing the plan, entitled "Greensward," that in 1858 won the design competition for the park. A unique element of the plan was to sink the four required transverse roads below the surface of the park, creating broader expanses of scenery than would otherwise have been possible, and avoiding both reality and perception of danger of collision between crosstown and park traffic. The design was also remarkable for the amount of earth and rock that was moved to create the pastoral landscape of the 15-acre (6 ha) Sheep Meadow and for the profusion of vegetation and wildness of scenery in the Ramble section. Immediately following the design competition, the designers ex-

FREDERICK LAW OLMSTED'S DESIGN COMMISSIONS IN NEW YORK STATE

Project	Date	Codesigner
Albany		
Proposed park system[a]	1868	—
State Capitol[b]	1874–82	—
Auburn (Cayuga Co)		
J. Letchworth estate	1879	—
Babylon (Suffolk Co)		
Henry B. Heyde estate	1874	—
George C. Magoun estate	1882	—
Bronx		
23d and 24th Wards street and rapid transit plan	1876	J. J. R. Croes
W. B. Ogden estate (Highbridge)	1870s	—
Brooklyn		
Prospect Park[c]	1866–74	Calvert Vaux
Parade Ground	1868	—
Fort Greene Park	1867	Calvert Vaux
Carroll Park	1868	Calvert Vaux
Tompkins Park	1868	Calvert Vaux
Eastern Parkway	*ca* 1868	Calvert Vaux
Ocean Parkway	*ca* 1868	Calvert Vaux
Coney Island Jockey Club	1880	—
Buffalo		
Delaware Park	1868–74	Calvert Vaux
Delaware Park Extension	1886	—
The Front	1871	Calvert Vaux
Extension to The Front	1887–91	—
The Parade (now Martin Luther King Jr Park)	1871	Calvert Vaux
Parkways and circles including Humboldt Parkway, Lincoln, Bidwell, and Chapin Parkways, Agassiz Circle, Soldiers Place, Chapin Place, Bidwell Place, and North St Circle (now Symphony Circle)	*ca* 1871	Calvert Vaux
Niagara Square	1874, 1876	—
Lafayette Square	1870s	—
Bennett Park	1887	—
Masten Place	1887	—
Terrace Parks	1887	—
Day's Park	1887	—
South Park:		
design for lakeside site[a]	1888	—
inland site	1892	—
Cazenovia Park	1892	—
McKinley Parkway	1892	—
Red Jacket Parkway	1892	—
New York State Insane Asylum grounds	1870, 1873	—
Buffalo City Hall grounds	1875	—
Parkside residential subdivision[d]	1874	—
Villa Park Land Co, north of Parkside[a]	1885	—
J. J. Albright estate	1890	—
Edmund Hayes estate	1891	—
Depew (Erie Co)		
Residential community for J. J. Albright, Apollo Iron and Steel Co	1892	—
Geneseo (Livingston Co)		
W. A. Wadsworth estate	1874	—
Hastings-on-Hudson (Westchester Co)		
Residential subdivision	*ca* 1870	Calvert Vaux
Hudson (Columbia Co)		
James W. Ellsworth estate	1890	—

continued on page 1136

panded the separation of ways to the park's interior circulation system, creating separate ways for pedestrians, carriages, and equestrians. During the next three years, as architect in chief of the park, Olmsted directed construction of most of it below the 86th St transverse road. His reputation as a capable administrator led to his selection as general secretary of the US Sanitary Commission, a position he held during the first two years of the Civil War, during which time he created a system for inspecting the camps of volunteer soldiers in the Union army and a national system of medical and relief supplies for them.

In 1863, exhausted and disillusioned, he left the Sanitary Commission and went to California, at the behest of former mayor George Opdyke and other New York capitalists, to become manager of the extensive Mariposa Estate and its numerous gold mines. When the mining company failed in 1865, Olmsted accepted Vaux's invitation to return to New York to resume oversight of Central Park and to design Prospect Park in Brooklyn. The site for Prospect Park was the most promising and its plan, particularly the Long Meadow section, was the fullest realization of the park ideal in his entire career. The unwavering support of Prospect Park Commission president James Stranahan was essential for realizing the plan executed between 1866 and 1874. Concurrently in Brooklyn, Olmsted and Vaux designed the Parade Ground next to Prospect Park, as well as Fort Greene Park, Tompkins Park, and Carroll Park. They also developed their concept of the "park way," a 210 ft (64 m) wide boulevard containing a central drive for private carriages and separate paths for pedestrians and equestrians, all bordered by tree-lined medians, with roads on the outside for cart and wagon access to residences. Two parkways following their plan were built in Brooklyn in the early 1870s: Eastern Parkway, running northeast from Prospect Park for 3 miles (5 km), and Ocean Parkway, running the 8 miles (13 km) from Prospect Park to Coney Island.

After the Civil War, Olmsted never regained the control over Central Park that he had enjoyed as architect in chief, but the 1870s brought new opportunities with the planning of Riverside and Morningside Parks in New York City. He also drew up new plans for Union Square, with Vaux, and for Tompkins Square and Mount Morris Park. William R. Martin's ascendancy to the presidency of the New York parks board in 1876 gave Olmsted the opportunity, in collaboration with engineer J. J. R. Croes, of creating plans for the street system and parkways (officially approved and adopted by the city) and a below-grade rapid transit system (not built) in the area of Westchester Co recently annexed to New York City [now the Bronx]. Olmsted was especially interested in planning a system of curvilinear streets for the hillside facing the Hudson River in the Riverdale section, by which he hoped to create an attractive and permanent residential area. This was his only successful implemented effort to plan a suburban community area in the New York City metropolitan region. In 1870 he had written a remarkable report for Staten Island that proposed planning for residential areas and parkland on the basis of geological and ecological conditions.

The third city for which Olmsted did extensive park planning was Buffalo. Between 1868 and the end of their partnership in 1872, he and Vaux planned their only system of parks and

FREDERICK LAW OLMSTED'S DESIGN COMMISSIONS IN NEW YORK STATE (continued)

Project	Date	Codesigner
Ithaca		
Cornell University[e]	1867–73	—
Lawrence (Nassau Co)		
J. F. Schenck estate	1886	—
Manhattan		
Central Park:		
architect in chief	1858–61	Calvert Vaux
landscape architect to park board	1865–78	—
Morningside Park[a]	1874	Calvert Vaux
Morningside Park	1887	Calvert Vaux
Riverside Park	1872	—
Manhattan Square, plan for zoo	1868	Calvert Vaux
Mount Morris Park	1870s	—
Union Square, prepared plan	1872	Calvert Vaux
Tompkins Square	1875	—
Washington Heights area, proposals	1860	Calvert Vaux
Bloomingdale Asylum	1860	—
Columbia University campus	1890s	William Ware
Middletown (Orange Co)		
Hillside Cemetery	1861	Calvert Vaux (primary designer)
Millbrook (Dutchess Co)		
George H. Brown estate	1867	—
Montauk (Suffolk Co)		
Summer Colony[f]	1881	—
New Rochelle (Westchester Co)		
E. K. Collins estate	1860	—
C. Oliver Iselin estate	1889	—
Adrian Iselin estate	1892	—
Newburgh (Orange Co)		
Downing Memorial Park	1887	Calvert Vaux
Niagara Falls		
Niagara Reservation	1887	Calvert Vaux
Oakdale (Suffolk Co)		
Bayard W. Cutting estate	1886	—
Oyster Bay (Nassau Co)		
Charles A. Dana estate, Dosoris Island	1875	—
Point Chautauqua (Chautauqua Co)		
Chautauqua Point summer community	1875	—
Poughkeepsie		
New York State Insane Asylum	1867	Calvert Vaux
Queens		
Rockaway Point hotel and resort	1879	—
Rochester		
Genesee Valley Park	1890	—
Genesee Valley Parkway	1890	—
Highland Park	1890	—
Seneca Park	1890	—
Washington Square	1892	—
Franklin Square	1894	—
Plymouth Park	1893	—
Salem (Washington Co)		
Rexleigh School	1891	—

FREDERICK LAW OLMSTED'S DESIGN COMMISSIONS IN NEW YORK STATE (continued)

Project	Date	Codesigner
Saratoga Springs		
United States Hotel	1874	—
Congress Spring Hotel	1875	—
Staatsburgh (Dutchess Co)		
R. T. Ford estate	1884	—
Staten Island		
Vanderbilt Mausoleum	1886	—
Staten Island Improvement Commission	1870	—
Tarrytown (Westchester Co)		
Tarrytown Heights Land Co[a]	1870	—
William D. Rockefeller estate (Rockwood Hall)	1887	—
White Plains (Westchester Co)		
Whitelaw Reid estate (Ophir Farm)	1889	—
Bloomingdale Asylum	1892	—
Yonkers		
Bryn Mawr subdivision	1888	—
Leake and Watts Orphan House	1889	—
St. Joseph's Seminary	1891	—

Sources: C. E. Beveridge and C. F. Hoffman, *The Master List of Design Projects of the Olmsted Firm, 1857–1950* (1987); Olmsted Research Guide Online, http://www.rediscov.com/Olmsted.

Note: Single dates indicate approximate beginning of commission.

[a]Plan not carried out.

[b]Member of advisory board.

[c]Directed early construction.

[d]Not constructed according to plan.

[e]Provided advice concerning plan and served as trustee.

[f]Advised on plan; McKim, Mead and White architects.

Compiled by Charles E. Beveridge

connecting parkways. This consisted of Delaware Park with its extensive Meadow Park section and large lake, dedicated to the enjoyment of landscape; it was supplemented by the Parade, with a parade ground, refectory, and children's play area, and by the Front, designed to serve as a formal water entrance to the city with views over Lake Erie and as a venue for music concerts and athletic events. The major parkways, especially Humboldt Parkway with several separate ways and eight rows of trees, rivaled the boulevards of Paris in size and dignity. Olmsted believed that Buffalo was "the best planned city, as to its streets, public places and grounds, in the United States if not in the world."

Furthermore, Olmsted and Vaux designed the 1,000-acre (405 ha) South Park of Chicago (now Washington and Jackson Parks and the Midway Plaisance) during this time. In the 15 years after his partnership with Vaux ended, Olmsted went on to design parks on Belle Isle in Detroit and Mount Royal in Montreal, and planned several sections of the park system that he and his partners created in Boston. In 1874 he began to design the US Capitol grounds and terraces. In addition, he became a member of the advisory commission for the New York State Capitol, along with Leopold Eidlitz and H. H. Richardson.

In 1887 Olmsted returned to Buffalo to address the recreation and transportation needs of the newly developed industrial section of the city south of Buffalo Creek. He proposed a lakefront park that would provide more active recreation than planned for in Delaware Park, a viaduct over the many railroad tracks that divided the city, and a system of parkways running through many parts of southern Buffalo. Instead, city authorities decided on two smaller inland sites and a parkway connecting to each. These features, South Park, Cazenovia Park, and McKinley and Red Jacket Parkways, were designed by the Olmsted firm beginning in 1892. As a result, Olmsted was involved in the designing of more parks and parkways in Buffalo than in any other city in the state, while the presence of William Macmillan, parks superintendent throughout the years, provided a continuity of administration enjoyed by no other city.

When he returned to Buffalo, Olmsted began his four other projects for public parks and recreation grounds elsewhere in the state. Most extensive was the park system of Rochester, beginning in 1888, which emphasized the preservation of the riverside scenery of the Genesee River. Genesee Valley Park above the falls secured both banks of the river while providing an extensive meadow park, and Seneca Park along the gorge below the falls preserved that scenery while providing access to it by carriage drives and paths. The third element of the system, Highland Park, served as an arboretum for shrubs and conifers, and as a vista for views over the city. The Olmsted firm also planned several small squares in Rochester during the last years of Olmsted's practice. A companion commission of this period was the park system of Louisville, Ky, with three parks of differing landscape character and several smaller squares and parks.

As early as 1869, Olmsted had been involved in planning to set aside Niagara Falls as a public scenic reservation. After preparing the *Special Report of the New York State Survey on the Preservation of the Scenery of Niagara Falls* in 1879 with James T. Gardner, he became a leader in the campaign to create the reservation. Once the land was acquired by the state, Olmsted and Vaux were selected to draw up a plan. In their report of 1887 they emphasized the importance of the experience of the rapids that flowed through the American reservation and the richness and variety of the vegetation along the shores of Goat Island, its central land feature. The report also contained a comprehensive approach to preserving natural scenery while making it available to a large number of visitors. In 1887 Olmsted and Vaux again collaborated to design a park in Newburgh (Orange Co) as a memorial for Andrew Jackson Downing, to whom they both owed a debt of gratitude. They collaborated as well on a new plan for Morningside Park in Manhattan.

The design of public parks was Olmsted's principal accomplishment in New York State. In addition, his restorative and therapeutic landscapes became part of the treatment of the insane at state institutions in Buffalo and Poughkeepsie and at two sites for the Bloomingdale Asylum, one in Manhattan *ca* 1860 and a later one in White Plains (Westchester Co). Another notable commission was the planning of the new campus for Columbia University in 1893, which led to design work by the successor firm in 1905–6. Olmsted also planned several large private estates, the most notable being Whitelaw Reid's Ophir Farm in White Plains. In all, Olmsted carried out some 85 commissions in New York State, a substantially larger number than for any other state. His 20 years of involvement with Central Park, most of those as an employee of the city's Department of Public Parks, was his longest connection with any design project.

During the last eight years of his practice, Olmsted's principal concerns were the World's Columbian Exposition of 1893 in Chicago, for which he was site planner, the Boston park system, and the Vanderbilt estate in North Carolina, his last great undertaking. Following his retirement in 1895, his nephew and adopted son John C. Olmsted (1852–1920), his major partner since 1884, became senior partner in the Olmsted firm. In 1898 John joined with Frederick Law Olmsted Jr (1870–1957) in forming Olmsted Bros Landscape Architects. During the next 50 years the firm continued several commissions in New York State that had started during Olmsted's career and added some 400 new projects that reached at least the stage of drawing up plans. The most extensive were Fort Tryon Park, the extension of Riverside Drive in Manhattan, and the residential community of Forest Hills Gardens in Queens. The firm also created designs for Claremont Park in the Bronx; the grounds of Riverside Church in Manhattan; the

Brooklyn Botanic Garden; several parks for Kings Co, including Brooklyn Forest, Highland Park, the Shore Drive in Bay Ridge, Dyker Beach Park, and Bushwick Park; several parks in Utica, including Roscoe Conkling and F. T. Proctor Parks; and Thompson Park in Watertown. The firm also did significant planning for the Niagara Gorge below the falls. The major academic campuses planned by the firm were the US Military Academy at West Point, the University of Rochester, and Syracuse University. The firm also did extensive design work for the Rockefeller family at their estates near Tarrytown (Westchester Co).

For illustration see CENTRAL PARK (MANHATTAN).

Beveridge, Charles E., and Carolyn F. Hoffman. *The Master List of Design Projects of the Olmsted Firm, 1857–1950* (Boston: National Association for Olmsted Parks, 1987)

Beveridge, Charles E., et al, eds. *The Papers of Frederick Law Olmsted* (Baltimore: Johns Hopkins Univ Press, 1977–)

Olmsted Research Guide Online, www.rediscov.com/Olmsted

Rogers, Elizabeth Barlow, and William Alex. *Frederick Law Olmsted's New York* (New York: Praeger, 1972)

Charles E. Beveridge

Onassis, Jacqueline Kennedy. See FIRST LADIES.

Onderdonk, Benjamin Tredwell (*b* New York City, 15 July 1791; *d* New York City, 30 Apr 1861). Episcopal bishop. Onderdonk attended Columbia Grammar School and later Columbia College in Manhattan, graduating in 1809. He studied theology under the direction of John Henry Hobart, was ordained deacon in 1812, became assistant minister of Manhattan's Trinity Church in 1813, and was ordained as a priest in 1815. He was secretary of the diocesan convention (1816–30) and professor at General Theological Seminary (1821–61). In 1830 he was elected, then consecrated, as the fourth bishop of the New York Diocese. He ordained almost as many persons during the first 7 years of his rapidly growing episcopate as his predecessor had in 19 years and consecrated even more churches. He also encouraged the establishment of missions in urban New York. In 1838 the enlarged diocese was divided into two. Not a tactful person, Onderdonk often irritated people by his inability to presuppose honorable disagreement. He was a supporter of the Oxford Movement and its attempt to reintroduce Catholic thought and practice into the Episcopal Church, and in 1844 his enemies began to publicize older charges concerning Onderdonk's inappropriate comportment with women. In November 1844 he was brought to trial by three fellow bishops, all opposed to his High Church theology, for "immorality and impurity." On 3 Jan 1845 he was suspended from the ministry. His diocese remained loyal to him and would only permit a "provisional bishop" to serve them until after his death. A number of attempts were made to remove the sentence of suspension, but none were successful.

Lindsley, James Elliott. *This Planted Vine: A Narrative History of the Episcopal Diocese of New York* (New York: Harper & Row, 1984)

Robert Bruce Mullin

Oneida. City (pop 10,987) in NE Madison Co. Originally part of the Oneida Indian Nation Reservation, the area was mostly a flat cedar swamp when it was settled in 1818. In 1839 landowner Sands Higinbotham negotiated with the Syracuse and Utica Railroad for a stop to be called Oneida Depot, under which name it acquired a post office in 1842. It incorporated as a village, Oneida, in 1848. In the second half of the 19th century many factories concentrated there, including producers of cigars, caskets, lathe chucks, canned vegetables, steel pulleys, and burial vaults; many continued to operate through most of the 20th century. As business prospered, two additional rail lines, the Ontario and Western (1869) and the West Shore (1883), added Oneida stops. In 1896 the Town of Oneida was formed from Lenox, and in 1901 it became a city. In the city's outside district, the autonomous Oneida Indian Territory was created in 1922. The major employer of Oneida residents in the early 21st century is Oneida Ltd at Sherrill (Oneida Co). The A. J. Davis–designed Cottage Lawn (1849), the Oneida Community Mansion House at Kenwood, and the Oneida Nation's Shako:wi Cultural Center all attract visitors. The larger part of the US Air Force's Stockbridge Test Annex is located in the outside district.

William F. Helmer

Oneida Carrying Place. This short portage with its seasonably variable 3 mi (4.8 km) length was between the Mohawk River and Wood Creek in Central New York. The portage was an integral part of the water route that extended from the Atlantic Ocean to Lake Ontario. Situated on the best alternative route to the St. Lawrence River to access the Great Lakes, the Oneida Carrying Place was strategic for both the Iroquois Indians and later Europeans. At one time the Oneida Nation protected the De-O-Wain-Sta, an Iroquois term for the carry. They used this land bridge to control the economic and political advantages provided by the transportation route, especially the fur trade. Control of the carry was also important for military reasons, leading to alliances between Iroquois nations and the British. At the Oneida Carrying Place during the 1750s, the British constructed several forts, including Fort Bull (destroyed by the French in 1756) and Fort Stanwix (1758). After the British gained control of Canada from the French during the French and Indian War, they abandoned the eroding Fort Stanwix. It was rebuilt by the Continental army during the American Revolution and named Fort Schuyler. In 1795 the Oneidas ceded the Carrying Place and surrounding territory to New York State in a treaty of questionable legality. By 1806 the Western Inland Lock Navigation Co built a canal through the portage site at Lynchville [now Rome, Oneida Co], which was a precursor to the Erie Canal.

Luzader, John F., Louis Torres, and Orville W. Carroll. *Fort Stanwix* (Washington, DC: Office of Park Historic Preservation, National Park Service, US Dept of the Interior, 1976)

William R. D. Lange

Oneida Castle. Village (pop 627) in Vernon (Oneida Co). Situated near the site of the chief village of the Oneida and located where the Seneca Turnpike (incorporated 1800; now Rte 5) crossed Oneida Creek, the settlement acquired a post office as Oneida in 1818. The name was changed to Oneida Castle in 1833, and the village incorporated in 1841. From the 1820s through 1863, it was the site of Bronson Academy. In 2003 many residents work in Oneida (Madison Co) or Sherrill.

Oneida Community. Perfectionist religious community, 1848–80. John Humphrey Noyes (1811–86), like the more influential, less radical Charles Grandison Finney and other preachers in the northeastern United States, questioned the Calvinist emphasis upon people's sinfulness. He taught that those who accepted Christ in their hearts achieved a state of spiritual perfection and could, through prayer and constant effort, achieve behavioral perfection. Complete perfection could be achieved only in a separate communal society. Members of Noyes's first community in Putney, Vt, including his mother, three siblings, and two in-laws, lived and farmed on Noyes family property. When a few key members, following Noyes's teachings, began to share marriage partners as well as strenuous religious study, work, meals, finances, and schooling, the townspeople brought charges of adultery against Noyes, and he left Putney. In 1848 the 31 adults and 14 children who had lived in the Putney Community joined a smaller group of Perfectionists loyal to Noyes who were living in the less densely settled area of Central New York on the border between Madison and Oneida Cos.

Eventually the Oneida Community had almost 300 members. Turnover was limited to about four people a year. Most members came from rural areas and small towns in New England and New York State. The first 100 or so to join were from Congregational, Methodist, Baptist, Presbyterian, and similar denominations. Most came as young couples with children. The men's occupations included farmer, clerk, schoolteacher, printer, trap maker, architect, bookkeeper, shoemaker, storekeeper, lawyer, minister, and doctor. Although rarely wealthy, they had contributed $108,000 to Oneida by 1857. From 1848 to 1858 community members used $40,000 in capital, trying unsuccessfully to make their farm support Oneida and several of the five small branch communities scattered through the Northeast. A particularly serious drain was the Brooklyn branch (1849–55), where Noyes and 26 followers printed and distributed Perfectionist literature. By the mid-1850s Noyes had reduced expenses by closing all but the Wallingford, Conn, branch. More important to financial security, the businesses begun by Noyes's brother-in-law John R. Miller had begun to prosper. The most profitable item was an animal trap made with specially tempered steel and patented by Sewell Newhouse before he joined. Community peddlers sold these traps, along with chains, canned fruits and vegetables, sewing silk, and traveling bags, in the neighboring areas and throughout the newly settled western regions. By 1862 the community's products were in such demand that in busy seasons it employed workers from the surrounding area. By 1875 it provided transportation and housing for up to 200 men and women who worked on the farm, in the trap factory, and in the silk mill. The Perfectionists took care to treat their workers well and in general maintained good relations with these less-prosperous neighbors, holding themselves aloof and making no effort to convert them.

In 1862 the Perfectionists began constructing the brick Mansion House next to their original wooden house, to which they continued to add

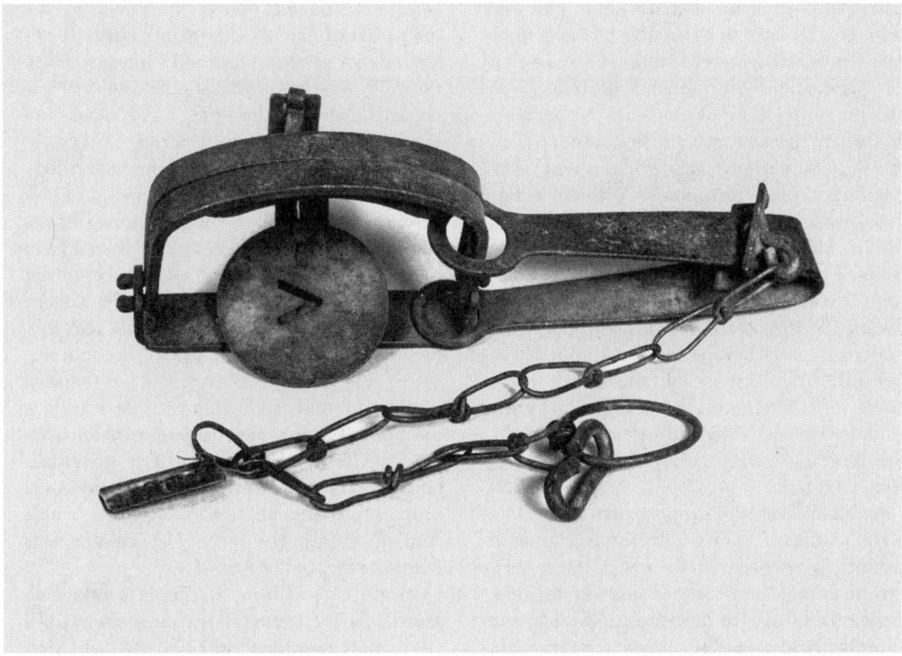

P-shaped animal trap. Animal traps were the most profitable product manufactured by the Oneida Community, and Oneida Ltd continued to make them until 1925.

until the community's last year. In design, the 475-room, 93,000 ft^2 (8,640 m^2) building exemplified the Perfectionists' emphasis upon community over the individual: public rooms were large, elaborate, and fashionable, while private and semiprivate rooms were small, simple, and sparsely furnished. Members put the group's interests over their own in all aspects of their lives. The women cut their hair unfashionably but conveniently short and wore practical calf-length dresses with their legs modestly covered by loose pantalets. To reduce kitchen labor just two meals a day were prepared. Group interests and the Perfectionist belief that women should not be confined to an excessively narrow role meant that women and men shared work in many of the community's departments, including the kitchen, dairy, printing office, trap shop, and garden. A few women cared for all of the community's infants and young children in separate children's quarters, and both men and women taught in the community school. Women were exclusively responsible for tasks like sewing and mending, and rarely headed business departments or committees like those set up to buy land, sell land, or make plans for the business. When the prosperity of later years brought more leisure time, men and women gathered for group picnics, dances, plays, and musical performances.

Each evening members gathered in the two-tiered family hall of the Mansion House to discuss all aspects of their communal life and to listen to Noyes's "home talks," which were later printed for community members and outside Perfectionist sympathizers. Sometimes Noyes explained such theological points as his conviction that Christ's Second Coming had occurred when Jerusalem was destroyed in AD 70. At other times he guided members' spiritual endeavors, detailed how to live perfectly, and criticized individual and communal lapses from perfection. For Noyes and his followers, communalism extended to social and sexual relationships. Members expressed their determination to love all equally by avoiding cliques and individual friendships. Monogamous marriage was replaced by complex marriage: men and women were expected to have intercourse with many partners, and frequent sexual contacts by any particular couple were forbidden. Spiritually superior, usually older, men and women were encouraged to have intercourse with less spiritually advanced women and men. Because only men who were skilled in *coitus reservatus* were allowed to participate, relatively few accidental pregnancies occurred. During Oneida's first 20 years, 40 children were born: 21 of these were conceived accidentally, 6 were conceived before their parents joined Oneida, and 13 were probably sanctioned by the community.

During the community's third decade, the Perfectionists conducted a eugenics program called stirpiculture. Between 1869 and 1879, 58 children were born, 44 to carefully selected couples and 14 to couples who did not participate in the stirpiculture program but conceived accidentally or intentionally. All these children were normally referred to as stirpicults. Like children born before 1869, they attended a community school which set high academic standards. But neither in school nor in the rest of their training did they receive the same rigorous religious education in Perfectionism. After their formal schooling, teenage boys and young men studied topics like algebra, zoology, humans' future victory over death, and the then fashionable phrenology. Women also studied but less extensively and systematically. During the 1870s a dozen young men studied practical subjects like medicine at Yale University, and a few women studied voice in New Haven, Conn.

A system of social control called "mutual criticism" encouraged members to accept the rigorous demands of community life. Committees composed of both central and ordinary members evaluated a particular member. They identified faults such as lack of religious and intellectual cultivation, insubordination, hardness of spirit, and lack of manners. The most common faults involved complex marriage: members were criticized frequently for forming exclusive or special attachments. Virtues such as loyalty, cheerfulness, or readiness to volunteer were noted but received less attention than faults. Those criticized confirmed the committee's evaluation in written statements, which they often read during the evening meeting. Central members also criticized people privately, and members would respond in person or with letters acknowledging their faults.

During Oneida's final decade the spiritual underpinnings of communalism weakened, and the careful balance once maintained between group and individual interests was lost. In this context several problems took on major importance: Noyes's failure to find a successor, the young people's secular interests and reduced emphasis on religion, attacks from outside clergy led by Prof John W. Mears of Hamilton College, and the issue of who should replace the aging, seriously deaf Noyes in initiating the young women into sex. Fearing accusations of statutory rape that never materialized, Noyes left for Canada in 1879. At Oneida both sides in the conflict wanted to continue complex marriage and communal life, but they could not agree how this should be done. They voted to cease complex marriage in August 1879. Married couples returned to monogamous relationships, and single members married whenever possible. The next year they voted to disband. With one exception they accepted a carefully thought-out plan of division. The community's wealth, valued at $600,000, was distributed to members as stock in proportion to the size of their original contribution and their length of membership. As future breadwinners, men received more than women. On 1 Jan 1881 the Oneida Community legally became the nonreligious joint stock company Oneida Community, Ltd. The great majority of former members stayed on in the Mansion House or nearby. They lived as traditional nuclear families with women keeping house and caring for children, and men managing the business and still supervising outside employees. For many years the Mansion House remained company property. Community descendants, their spouses, and people connected with the company occupied its private rooms, which were gradually converted into apartments. In 1988 the company, now named Oneida Ltd, donated the house to a nonprofit corporation, Oneida Community Mansion House (OCMH), which runs it as both a museum and residence. A large part of the house and its landscaped grounds are open to the public.

Carden, Maren Lockwood. *Oneida: Utopian Community to Modern Corporation* (Syracuse: Syracuse Univ Press, 1998)

Fogarty, Robert S. *Desire and Duty at Oneida: Tirzah Miller's Oneida Memoir* (Bloomington: Indiana Univ Press, 2000)

Holloway, Mark. *Heaven on Earth: Utopian Communities in America, 1680–1880* (New York: Dover, 1966)

Kern, Louis J. *An Ordered Love: Sex Roles and Sexuality in Victorian Utopias* (Chapel Hill: Univ of North Carolina, 1981)

Rich, Jane Kinsley, and Nelson M. Blake, eds. *A Lasting Spring: Jessie Catherine Kinsley, Daughter of the Oneida Community* (Syracuse: Syracuse Univ Press, 1983)

Robertson, Constance Noyes. *Oneida Community: An Autobiography, 1851–1876* (Syracuse: Syracuse Univ Press, 1970)

Maren Lockwood Carden

Oneida County (1,213 mi²/3,142 km²; pop 235,469). Created in 1798 from Herkimer Co and named after the Oneida Nation of the Iroquois Confederacy. Part of the county was lost to Clinton Co in 1801; a section of Chenango Co was annexed in 1804. Subsequent territorial loses occurred with the creation of Jefferson and Lewis Cos in 1805 and Oswego Co in 1816, and an annexation by Madison Co in 1836. Oneida Co is subdivided into 3 cities—Rome, Sherrill, and Utica—and 26 towns that contain 19 incorporated villages. Utica serves as county seat. Elevations range from under 410 feet (125 m) where the Mohawk River exits the county at Utica to 1,945 feet (593 m) on Tassel Hill in the Town of Marshall.

The county extends across five major physiographic provinces. The five southernmost towns lie almost entirely within the Susquehanna Hills subregion of the Appalachian Upland. Beginning at the base of the Helderberg Escarpment that forms the region's northern margin, elevations range from around 500 feet (150 m) to over 1,900 feet (580 m) on parts of a massif located between the Villages of Bridgewater and Waterville. Three partially contiguous subregions of the Erie-Ontario Lowland physiographic province extend into the western, central, and northeastern parts of the county. The low, flat, and in places featureless Oneida Lake Plain subregion stretches south and east from Oneida Lake to the center of the county. The Ontario Ridge and Swampland subregion lies between the West Branch of Fish Creek and the north shore of Oneida Lake. Separate and well to the northeast, the Black River Valley, the third subregion, extends like a long, narrow finger south from Lewis Co as far as Kayuta Lake. Lying between these lowland regions, the Tug Hill Upland extends across most of the county's north, sloping southward from 1,400 feet (425 m) to less than 500 feet (150 m) over a distance of 10 miles (16 km). The county's far northeast corner beyond the Black River Valley lies within the Western Adirondack Hills subregion of the Adirondack Upland. Finally the Hudson-Mohawk Lowland extends across the east-central section from Utica north to beyond Holland Patent.

Precambrian age gneisses, quartzites, and marbles underlie the Adirondack Hills. A mantle of sedimentary rock covers the rest of the county. Devonian shale and siltstone underlie the Susquehanna Hills, with limestone and dolostone along the Helderberg Escarpment farther north. Silurian limestone, dolostone, sandstone, siltstone, and shale form the floor of the Oneida Lake Plain and the southern Mohawk Valley. Ordovician sandstone and shale underlie the rest of the county, except for the Black River Valley, where limestone and dolostone of similar age are found. All of Oneida Co was glaciated, as evidenced by scoured valleys and rounded hills in the south, a variety of glacial and postglacial lake deposits including the Rome Sand Plains, and scattered ground moraine deposits.

The county straddles four major watersheds. Waters in the northeast drain north via the Black River. The remainder of the eastern half drains east through the Mohawk, except for an area in the extreme south that lies within the greater Susquehanna watershed. Waters in the western half flow primarily by way of Fish Creek and its many tributaries into Oneida Lake and ultimately the Oswego River and Lake Ontario. Oneida Co's soils are highly variable. With few exceptions those in the northern third are marginal and unable to support modern agriculture. Soils in the middle third exhibit roughly equal proportions of high- and low-quality arable land; in contrast, high-quality agricultural soils dominate the southern third.

Oneida Co's climate is humid-continental. Mean January temperatures range from 16°F (-9°C) in the northeast to 22°F (-6°C) at Utica. Below 0°F (-18°C) readings are a significant part of every winter's climate. Mean July temperatures range from 66°F (19°C) in the Adirondack Hills to 71°F (22°C) at Utica. Temperatures of 90°F (32°C) or above occur a few times every summer at the lower elevations but much more rarely in the higher areas. Normal average annual precipitation ranges from 42 inches (107 cm) at Utica to 60 inches (152 cm) at Boonville, while seasonal snowfall varies from 78 inches (198 cm) in the southeast to 218 inches (554 cm) at Boonville. With a few local exceptions, the primeval forest cover consisted of two distinct communities of northern hardwoods. The county's northern half was blanketed with an Adirondack hardwood forest dominated by beech, sugar maple, yellow birch, hemlock, and white pine, combined at the higher elevations with red spruce and balsam fir. The southern half of the county was covered by an Alleghenian hardwood forest of beech, sugar maple, hemlock, white pine, and basswood. Wetland forest covered the poorly drained lands east of Oneida Lake, while an oak-pine association of pitch pine, several species of oak, bigtooth aspen, and a shrub layer of huckleberry covered the sand plains farther north. Approximately 60% of Oneida Co is presently covered with second- or third-growth forest. The far northeastern corner is contained within the Adirondack Park.

American Indians and Early Settlement

Archaeologists believe that the region has had human settlement for about 10,000 years. Proto-Iroquoians have inhabited the region since approximately AD 1000. The Oneida Nation of the Iroquois Confederacy was in control of the region. Beginning in the 17th century, Dutch and English traders arrived primarily as traders with whom the Indians established peaceful relations. During the French and Indian War, the British government erected a series of military forts and outposts guarding the Mohawk Valley from attack, including Fort Stanwix [now Rome] and Fort Schuyler [now Utica]. After the war the eastern part of Oneida territory was divided into land grants sold to European settlers, forming the basis for a conflict between the colonial gov-

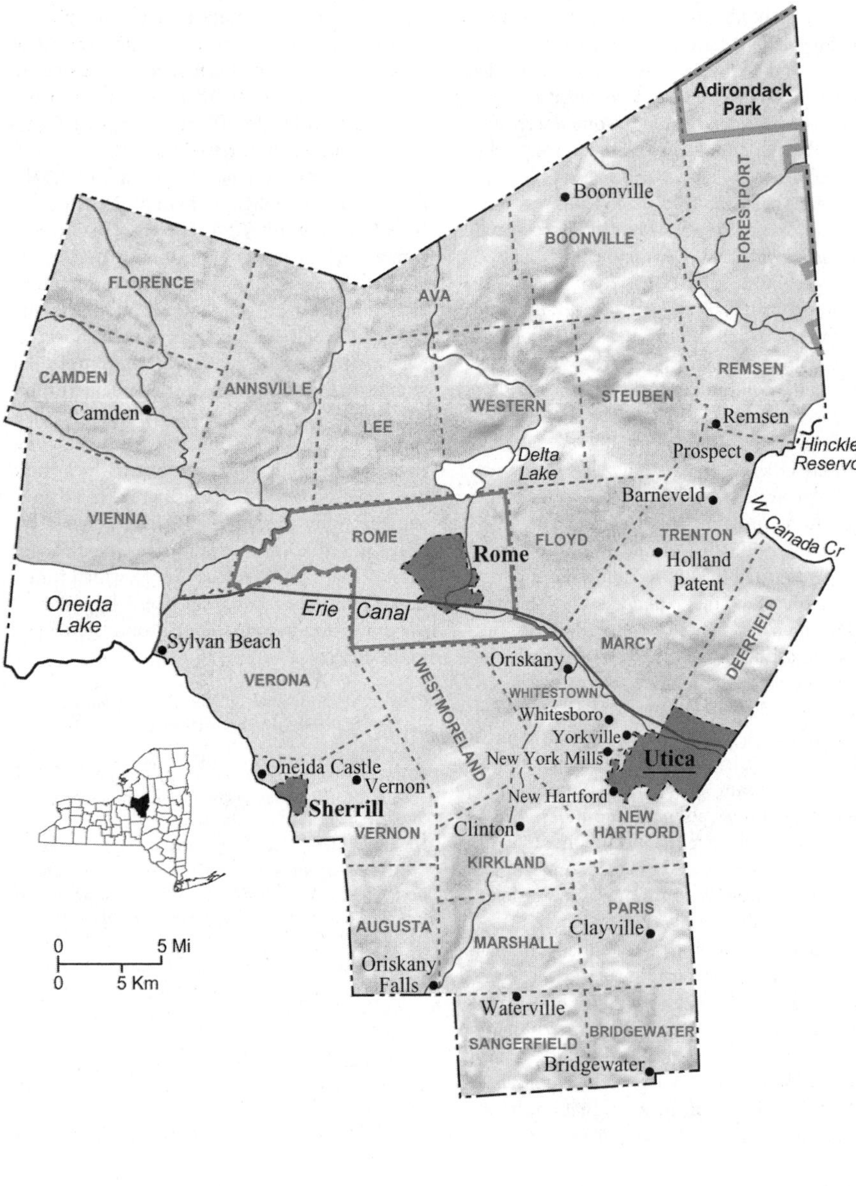

ONEIDA CO POPULATION CENSUS FIGURES

	White	Nonwhite	Total Population	Foreign-Born
1800	21,924	123	22,047	—
1810	33,581	211	33,792	—
1820	50,620	377	50,997	945
1830	70,858	468	71,326	4,373
1840	84,666	644	85,310	—
1850	98,894	672	99,566	22,711
1860	104,564	638	105,202	26,368
1870	109,358	650	110,008	25,707
1880	114,837	638	115,475	23,435
1890	122,370	552	122,922	25,255
1900	132,306	494	132,800	24,477
1910	153,476	681	154,157	33,804
1920	182,110	723	182,833	37,268
1930	197,724	1,039	198,763	34,612
1940	202,621	1,015	203,636	28,980
1950	220,317	2,538	222,855	24,539
1960	259,317	5,084	264,401	20,172
1970	264,633	8,404	273,037	13,983
1980	243,022	10,444	253,466	10,791
1990	232,335	18,501	250,836	9,057
2000	212,414	23,055	235,469	12,347

Notes: "Nonwhite" includes African Americans, Asians, American Indians, and Pacific Islanders and, for 2000, also the mixed race and other race categories. Through the 1960 census these figures primarily reflect the African American population. Foreign-born figures for 1820 and 1830 include only those not naturalized, and for 1930 and 1950, the foreign-born totals include Whites only. Other years include all foreign-born in the population.

ernment and the Oneida. As a result the Treaty of Fort Stanwix (1768) established a formal boundary between the colony and the native peoples, running from Fort Stanwix to the headwaters of the Unadilla River and south to the Pennsylvania border.

The outbreak of the American Revolution renewed the importance of the forts, especially Fort Stanwix. Situated at the Oneida Carrying Place, the fort was an important guardian of the western frontier against British advances. The area was the site of numerous engagements during the war, notably the bloody Battle of Oriskany on 6 Aug 1777. Two years later American general James Clinton again moved troops through the region to suppress border raids by natives and loyalist militias. His army destroyed villages in the region before turning its attention southward to the Susquehanna Valley.

By the end of the Revolution, much of the native population of Central New York was forced out of its traditional homeland, and the Treaty of Fort Stanwix was no longer observed. The Oneida Nation's holdings were reduced to a mere 350 acres (140 ha) in a series of treaties with New York State starting in 1785. This later formed the basis of litigation during the late 20th century. European American settlement, primarily from New England, began in earnest after the Revolution, especially along the Mohawk River. In communities located on quick-running streams, such as the Sauquoit and Oriskany Creeks, small mills sprung up to process flour, timber, and textiles, creating New York Mills, Whitesboro, New Hartford, Sangerfield, Oriskany Falls, and Oriskany. The county's two largest settlements on the Mohawk River, Utica and Rome, grew rapidly as commercial villages during this time: Rome because of its location at the Carrying Place and Utica because of its location at the eastern terminus of the Genesee Road (1794; later Seneca Turnpike).

Transportation

The strategic positions of both Utica and Rome turned the villages into major hubs for stagecoaches and river traffic. In southern Oneida Co, the Third Great Western Turnpike (1803) ran along the present-day route of US 20. In 1817 the first section of the Erie Canal was begun in Rome; it was completed to Utica in 1820. The communities of Utica, Rome, Whitesboro, and Oriskany grew dramatically as a result of proximity to the canal. The Erie was such a success that two other canals were built. The Black River Canal (1851–1924) joined with the Erie at Rome and ran to Boonville on the Black River and northward. It was never as successful as the Erie but did serve the purpose of transporting produce and, especially, timber from the Adirondack region to Rome. Starting from Utica, the Chenango Canal (1837–78) was intended to connect the Erie to northern Pennsylvania. Like the Black River Canal, the Chenango was not as successful as the Erie and in fact was never completed past Binghamton.

The main competition for the Erie Canal came from the railroads. The Utica and Schenectady Railroad arrived in 1837, followed by the Syracuse and Utica Railroad in 1839; the two merged with others as the New York Central Railroad in 1853. The arrival of the railroad ended Utica's status as a gateway city, as it became a mere stop on the main line. This was true for Rome as well. In both Utica and Rome, there were rail lines leading north or south, but they were not as successful as the main line of the New York Central. The corridor utilized by the canal and the railroads is still used by the New York State Thruway. In part because of competition with the automobile, the rail system has been by and large reduced to the main line of the New York Central (now operated by CSX Corp and Amtrak), the New York, Susquehanna and Western Railroad, and the Adirondack Scenic Railroad. The Erie Canal is now used for recreation.

Economic Development

Historically, much of Oneida Co's land has been devoted to agriculture, although there were significant timber operations in the north. Following the trend of much of the state, Oneida Co has suffered a decline in the number of farms and in acreage, from 7,232 farms spread across 657,748 acres (266,181 ha) in 1900 to only 928 farms on 216,094 acres (87,450 ha) in 1997, just under 28% of the county's land area. Nevertheless, the county remains a major agricultural producer, the largest sector being in dairy production. In 1997 over 27,000 dairy cows were raised on 397 farms.

With the arrival of the railroads in the 1830s, the county lost its status as a jumping-off point for westward migration, and by the early 1840s, its growth began to slow in comparison with other metropolitan counties. Because of the inexpensive coal brought by the Chenango Canal, factories manufacturing shoes, metalwork, textiles, and other products began to dominate the economies of communities on the canals, particularly Utica and Rome. By the 1910s Rome processed 10% of the country's copper ore, and by 1920 it was known as the Copper City. Sherrill was known as the Silver City based on the manufacturing of tableware products at Oneida Community, Ltd (now Oneida Ltd). Utica was one of the largest textile-producing regions in the world. After World War I, however, many textile companies began to leave the area in search of lower wages and a nonunion workforce, and by 1960 most had left the area or closed.

Rome's economy expanded with the construction of the US Army Air Force's Rome Air Depot, which opened in 1942. The depot's research functions were expanded, and the facility was renamed Griffiss Air Force Base in 1951. During the 1950s the area rebuilt its economy as several large defense contractors, including General Electric Co, Bendix Corp, and numerous smaller companies, either opened or expanded in Utica and Rome, replacing some but not all of the jobs lost after World War II when many of the textile firms left. Perhaps the most notable was Sperry-Rand Corp, later Unisys, in Utica, the first commercial producer of the computer (1950s). This period 1945–58 is referred to by local historians as the "loom to boom" years.

Religion, Education, and Culture

Oneida Co was part of the Burned-over District of religious revivalism during the early 19th century. Charles Grandison Finney held some of his first urban revivals in Utica in 1825–26, helping to make the county a center of evangelical Protestantism during the 19th century. Encouraged by pastors, Oneida Co became a center of abolitionist activity during the mid–19th century. Some African Americans, both slave and free, followed the initial waves of New Englanders as early as 1790. Other migrants included Palatine Germans who moved to the area from farther east in the Mohawk Valley.

POPULATIONS OF TOWNS AND CITIES, ONEIDA CO

Town or City, Year Founded	1800	1840	1880	1920	1960	2000
Annsville, 1823	—	1,765	2,554	1,353	1,635	2,956
Augusta, 1798	1,598	2,175	2,171	1,911	2,021	1,966
Ava, 1846	—	—	1,039	615	518	725
Boonville, 1805	—	5,519	3,996	3,147	3,786	4,572
Bridgewater, 1797	1,061	1,418	1,218	746	966	1,671
Camden, 1799	384	2,331	3,392	3,054	4,318	5,028
Deerfield, 1798	1,048	3,120	2,082	706	3,554	3,906
Florence, 1805	—	1,259	2,073	701	583	1,086
Floyd, 1796	767	1,742	1,115	663	2,234	3,869
Forestport, 1869	—	—	1,358	862	821	1,692
Kirkland, 1827	—	2,984	4,984	4,744	7,978	10,138
Lee, 1811	—	2,936	2,360	1,134	4,302	6,875
Marcy, 1832	—	1,799	1,413	1,191	7,024	9,469
Marshall, 1829	—	2,251	2,276	1,490	1,902	2,127
New Hartford, 1827	—	3,819	4,394	8,646	18,444	21,172
Paris, 1792	4,721	2,844	3,573	3,004	4,219	4,609
Remsen, 1798	254	1,638	1,195	969	1,128	1,958
Rome, 1796–1870	1,479	5,680	—	—		—
Rome (city), 1870	—	—	12,194	26,341	51,646	34,950
Sangerfield, 1795	1,144	2,251	3,171	1,795	2,482	2,610
Sherrill (city), 1916	—	—	—	1,761	2,922	3,147
Steuben, 1792	552	1,993	1,223	786	586	1,172
Trenton, 1797	624	3,178	3,097	2,389	3,417	4,670
Utica (city), 1832	—	12,782	33,914	94,156	100,410	60,651
Vernon, 1802	—	3,043	3,056	2,761[a]	7,146	5,335
Verona, 1802	—	4,504	5,287	3,136	5,305	6,425
Vienna, 1807[b]	—	2,530	2,834	1,544	2,896	5,819
Western, 1797	1,453	3,488	2,264	1,061	1,811	2,029
Westmoreland, 1792	1,542	3,105	2,744	1,984	4,084	6,207
Whitestown, 1788	4,212	5,156	4,498	10,183	19,185	18,635

Notes: In 1800 Oneida Co included the Towns of Mexico and Redfield [now in Oswego Co], the Towns of Leyden, Lowville, and Turin [now in Lewis Co], the Towns of Champion and Watertown [now in Jefferson Co], and the Towns of Canton, Louisville, Madrid, Massena, Oswegatchie, and Stockholm [now in St. Lawrence Co]. The Town of Sangerfield was in Chenango Co in 1800.

[a]1920 US census includes Sherrill (city) in Town of Vernon and prints population as 4,522.

[b]Orange until 1808, then Bengal until 1816.

By the mid–19th century Oneida Co was one of the main centers of Welsh population in the United States, with 4,195 Welsh-born residents in 1855, nearly 4% of the total population. In 1855 Oneida Co had no fewer than 67 Methodist churches, of which 18 were of the Calvinistic Methodist denomination, and 34 Baptist churches. Its 25 Congregational and 19 Presbyterian congregations were evidence of New England immigration. There were also 12 Episcopal and 13 Roman Catholic churches; the latter were a result of Irish canal and railroad workers settling in the county, numbering over 10.4% in 1855. Two of the county's three Unitarian churches were a result of Dutch immigration to Trenton in the 1790s.

As Utica and Rome began to industrialize after the mid–19th century, successive waves of Irish, Italian, and Polish immigrants arrived, and many settled in distinct ethnic neighborhoods. By the dawn of the 20th century, the arrival in Utica and Rome of Catholic Irish, Italian, and Polish immigrants, as well as Jewish immigrants from throughout Europe, created a distinct urban-rural dynamic in ethnic and religious matters.

Following 1812 legislation a common school system developed. Although larger communities established Union Free School districts in the late 19th century, state-initiated centralization created the county's modern educational system. The first central school district was Forestport (1926); upon the creation of the Rome Enlarged City School District (1957) the transformation was essentially complete, although scattered common schools were added to existing districts. In 2004 Oneida Co had 15 school districts, ranging in size from New York Mills, with 586 students, to Utica, with 8,474 students. The county's 37,367 public school students in 2003 attended 44 elementary, 14 middle, and 15 high schools. The Roman Catholic Diocese of Syracuse operated 4 elementary and 2 high schools, and there were a number of non-Catholic Christian private schools as well.

The first college in the county was founded by Samuel Kirkland in 1793 as Hamilton-Oneida Academy and chartered in 1812 as Hamilton College, in Clinton. In 1827 Oneida Academy was started in Whitesboro as a school that combined manual labor and education for the ministry; it was renamed Oneida Institute in 1829. After Beriah Green became president in 1833 it became one of the first institutions of higher learning in the United States to admit Blacks. After merging with the Clinton Seminary in 1845, it was renamed the Whitestown Seminary but closed before 1900. In 1896 the Utica School of Commerce was formed, followed in 1904 by the St. Elizabeth College of Nursing, both in Utica. In 1941 the Munson-Williams-Proctor Institute opened its School of Art, now affiliated with the Pratt Institute. In the period immediately after World War II, educational institutions expanded. Syracuse University opened a campus in Utica (now Utica College) in 1946. That same year, the New York State Institute of Applied Arts and Sciences (now Mohawk Valley Community College) was founded in Utica and in the early 21st century operates campuses in that city and in Rome. The SUNY Institute of Technology at Utica/Rome was founded in 1966.

Utica is home to the Munson-Williams-Proctor Arts Institute (1919), the Oneida County Historical Society (1876), and the Children's Museum (1963). Fort Stanwix National Monument (1976), a reconstruction of the original fort, is situated in downtown Rome. The county also has three centers for the performing arts—the Stanley Theater (Utica), the Capital Theater (Rome), and the Utica Memorial Auditorium—as well as several smaller venues. Utica is home to the Utica Symphony Orchestra and the Mohawk Valley Ballet. The National Distance Running Hall of Fame is located in Utica, where the prestigious Boilermaker 15 km Road Race began in 1976. Whitesboro has been the home of the Utica Curling Club (1868) since 1997. There is harness racing at Vernon Downs and automobile races at the Utica-Rome Speedway, both in Vernon.

Politics

The waves of immigrants in the cities and the relative stability in the rural areas of the county resulted in political differences between them. In the cities, and in particular Utica, political machines grew to advocate for newly arrived immigrants. The community experienced its first political machine in the 1870s in the form of the predominantly Irish Wheeler machine, which for a time controlled both political parties. By the 1880s the machine had lost control of the Democratic Party but nonetheless continued to dominate city politics until the 1920s. During the 1928 presidential election the New York City Irish Catholic Alfred E. Smith ran against Herbert Hoover. National party officials utilized anti-Catholic feeling to defeat Smith, but at the local level this alienated many Catholic Irish, Italians, and Poles. With this opening, the Democratic machine of Rufus Elefante was able to gain control of city politics, and because of its strong connection with the administration of Pres Franklin D. Roosevelt, it attracted large amounts of state and federal aid during the depression and World War II. The Elefante machine came under criticism during the late 1950s when state and federal agencies launched a series of investigations into corruption in the city that became known as the Sin City Scandals. The negative attention the scandals brought the city ended the reign of the Elefante machine.

In contrast, the rural areas of the county typically have voted Republican. There are indications of informal agreements among politicians during the Elefante years that the city was to be run by Democrats and the county by Republicans. The county is governed by an elected 29-member Board of Legislators and an elected county executive. The voters also elect a comptroller, county clerk, district attorney, and sheriff. Since 1970 the county has tended to vote

Republican in local elections, and as of 2003, 21 of the 29 county legislators were Republican.

RECENT HISTORY

Since the 1970s the county has had difficulty competing with the assets found in larger metropolitan areas, notably Syracuse and Albany, and it began a period of economic stagnation and population decline. Oneida Co's population decreased by about 15% between 1970 and 2000. The bulk of this loss was in the white population, with African American and Latino populations increasing since 1970, especially in Utica. More recently immigrants from Southeast Asia and the Balkans have further changed the composition of the county's population.

As in other metropolitan areas, both Utica and Rome suffered the effects of people and business moving to the suburbs, in particular New Hartford and Whitestown. Urban renewal programs in Utica during the late 1950s and in Rome beginning in 1964 resulted in the demolition of much of their historic downtowns, and neither city has fully recovered. The county has responded by relying on service-sector employment, such as insurance, financial services, and marketing. Major employers in 2003 included SBU Bank (1839), Bank of Utica (1927), and the public opinion firm Zogby International (1984), all in Utica, as well as Utica National Insurance (1914) in New Hartford and the Rome Savings Bank (1851).

Beginning in 1969, a series of lawsuits brought by the Oneida Nation challenged the legality of 27 treaties signed between 1785 and 1846 by which the state acquired land without the sanction of the federal government. The lawsuits culminated in a US Supreme Court ruling (*Oneida Indian Nation v County of Oneida,* 1974) in which the Oneida were awarded a land claim of 270,000 acres (109,265 ha) in Oneida and Madison Cos. There has been considerable conflict since that decision, with lawsuits initiated on both sides. As of 2003 negotiation was continuing, although no land had been returned to the Oneida; they have, however, expanded their holdings throughout the land claim area through private purchases. They also expanded business operations, starting Turning Stone Casino and Resort in Verona in 1993, a chain of service stations, and other economic concerns. In 2003 the nation employed over 3,100 people, most of whom were not Native American, making it the largest employer in the county. In 1993 Griffiss Air Force Base was targeted for closure, and by the following year only an accounting office and Rome Research Laboratory remained. Officially closed in 1998, the base has since been deeded to the county and rechristened Griffiss Business and Technology Park (1998). The park has attracted numerous companies and as of 2003 was slowly revitalizing Rome and the surrounding metropolitan area.

See also WELSH.

Oneida Co has benefited from no fewer than six county histories: Pomroy Jones, *Annals and Recollections of Oneida County* (1851); Samuel W. Durant, *History of Oneida County* (1878); Daniel Wager, ed., *Our County and Its People: A Descriptive Work on Oneida County* (1896); Henry J. Cookenham, *History of Oneida County* (1912); Nancy Bashant, ed., *The History of Oneida County* (1977), and its update, Donald F. White, ed., *Exploring: 200 Years of Oneida County History* (1998). Three communities, aside from Utica, were studied in the 19th century: A. D. Gridley, *History of the Town of Kirkland* (1874); Henry C. Rogers, *History of the Town of Paris* (1881); and Daniel E. Wager, *Our City and Its People: A Descriptive Work on the City of Rome* (1896). In the mid-20th century, two very readable books based on good scholarship were written by Howard Thomas: *The Life of a Village: A History of Prospect* (1950) and *Trenton Falls Yesterday and Today* (1951). More recent community histories include Jack Henke, *Sylvan Beach* (1975), and Virginia C. Loin, *Deerfield, NY: A Glimpse into the Past* (1998). Mary P. Ryan, *Cradle of the Middle Class: The Family in Oneida County, 1790–1865* (1981), is a classic work of social history. James S. Pula and Eugene E. Dziedzic, *United We Stand: The Role of Polish Workers in New York Mills Textile Strikes, 1912 and 1916* (1991), examines issues of ethnic identity and labor unrest in New York Mills and Utica. Allen George Noble, *An Ethnic Geography of Early Utica, NY: Time, Space, and Community* (1999), is a good overview of immigration and diversity. Alexander R. Thomas, *In Gotham's Shadow: Globalization and Community Change in Central New York* (2003), examines the social and economic changes in the Utica metropolitan area in the last half of the 20th century.

Alex Thomas

Oneida Institute. The reform and abolitionist school in Whitesboro (Oneida Co) began as Rev George Washington Gale's Oneida Academy in 1827. Two years later it was chartered as the Oneida Institute of Science and Industry, a Presbyterian-sponsored institution to provide a practical theological education for young men recruited during the revivals of Charles Grandison Finney. The school operated on the manual labor philosophy. Students worked in the shops and fields to defray the costs of their education. In 1833 Beriah Green replaced Gale as Oneida Institute's president, and the school became an abolitionist training ground. In 1836 there were 136 students. Green admitted at least 14 African Americans, including Henry H. Garnet and Alexander Crummell, an important step in breaking down the barrier of racial caste in American higher education. A few American Indians also attended the school. Green deemphasized the traditional classical curriculum, instituted during Gale's tenure, for one emphasizing moral reform and study of the biblical languages. Its radical reputation caused Oneida Institute to lose the support of conservative Presbyterians. The school closed and the property was sold to the Freewill Baptist denomination in 1844.

See also ABOLITIONISM.

Sernett, Milton C. *Abolition's Axe: Beriah Green, Oneida Institute, and the Black Freedom Struggle* (Syracuse: Syracuse Univ Press, 1986)

Milton C. Sernett

Oneida Lake (79.8 mi²/206.68 km²). Located in Oneida and Oswego Cos and bordering on Onondaga and Madison Cos, this body of water formed 12,000 years ago when melting glacial ice flooded central New York State. The state's largest inland lake, it is 20.9 miles (33.64 km) long with a mean width of 3.8 miles (6.12 km). Its maximum depth is 55 feet (16.8 m), but about 26% of the lake is shallower than 12 feet (3.7 m), making the mean depth at 22.3 feet (6.8 m). Beyond the headwaters of the Mohawk River near Rome (Oneida Co), and after a short overland carry to Fish Creek, Oneida Lake forms part of a natural corridor from the Hudson River to Lake Ontario.

The Oneida Indians called the lake Tsrioqui (white water), for the white-capped waves that lapped the sandy beaches on the west shore. In the early 1600s French explorers on their route to Lake Ontario called Oneida Lac Vert (green lake), because of the color its algae produced. The Oneida control of the lake and of the Oneida Carrying Place, a strategic portage on the water route between Lake Ontario and the Atlantic, ended in the decades after the American Revolution.

Until the 20th century the lake was classified as eutrophic, rich in nutrient concentrations such as nitrogen and phosphorus, with an abundance of fish. Within the past 50 years major changes have occurred, and the lake is now classified as mesotrophic, containing only moderate levels of nutrients. Shoreline dwellings rose from 476 in 1900 to 4,298 in 1960, resulting in increased wastewater runoff. An invasion of zebra mussels beginning in 1991 further changed the ecosystem and resulted in the extinction of six species of clams by 2000. Zebra mussels' activity in filtering out microscopic algae and organic debris has increased water clarity, which has harmed some species. In 2002 the predominant fish were yellow perch, white perch, walleye, and white suckers. Fishing remains important to the region's economy. On the south shore at Shackelton Point in Bridgeport (Madison Co), the Cornell Biological Field Station, an endowed research and teaching facility, provides long-term ecological research on Oneida Lake. The lake's Frenchman Island is an undeveloped state park.

Oneida Lake Book (Syracuse: Central New York Regional and Development Board, 2000)

John White

Oneida Lake Canals. The Oneida Lake Canal, which opened in 1835, ran both parallel to and laterally from the Erie Canal. It was a shortcut to Lake Ontario and saved Oswego-bound shippers two days over the traditional Erie Canal–Oswego Canal route when used in conjunction with Oneida Lake and the Oneida River Towing Path. The Oneida Lake Canal was 4.5 miles (7.24 km) long from its junction with the Erie Canal at Higginsville (Oneida Co) to its entry into Oneida Lake at Fish Creek [now Sylvan Beach, Oneida Co]. The popular shortcut required constant dredging, and its seven wood locks demanded considerable maintenance. The canal was built by the Oneida Lake Canal Co and purchased by the state in 1841. The locks were condemned in 1863 and disassembled for rebuilding. Before the work was completed, the state decided to relocate the line of the canal to eliminate the annual maintenance needed in the Wood Creek section. It took 4 years to select the new route and 10 years to build the new canal. The New Oneida Lake Canal, which ran 4.9 miles (7.89 km) from the Erie Canal at Durhamville (Oneida Co) to Oneida Lake's South Bay, was an engineer's nightmare. Construction of the channel and its six composite locks was fraught with such difficulties as collapsing walls, quicksand, and sections that refused to hold water. The canal was never completely filled with water. It opened for brief periods in 1877 and 1878, but it was closed completely after the walls broke and flooded the adjacent fields. The canal was doomed because its unstable banks jeopardized the Erie Canal, its water source.

Canal Society of New York State. *Field Trip Guide, May 1–3, 1998: Oneida Lake and Its Canals* ([Syracuse]: Author, 1998)

Whitford, Noble E. *History of the Canal System of the State of New York,* vol 1 of *State of New York Annual Report of the State Engineer and Surveyor Supplement* (Albany: Brandow Printing, 1906)

Bill Orzell

Oneida Limited. Tableware manufacturer headquartered in Sherrill (Oneida Co). The company is the successor to the utopian Oneida Community, which developed numerous business enterprises after the group settled in Madison Co in 1848. When the community disbanded in 1880, its leaders created a joint-stock corporation using members' assets of $600,000 to capitalize Oneida Community, Ltd, on 1 Jan 1881. In 1889 a group affiliated with the old community's spiritualist faction gained control of the board of directors. A successful proxy fight in 1894, led by Pierrepont Burt Noyes, a son of the community's founder, ushered in a new era marked by growth and consolidation. Between the community's old core in the Madison Co hamlet of Kenwood and the main plant to the north along the West Shore Railroad line, the community of Sherrill developed to accommodate the growing workforce. During World War I the company made ammunition clips, combat knives, and surgical instruments for the US armed services. With the sale of its trap business in 1925, the company concentrated on silverware production. In 1935 it shortened its name to Oneida Ltd. Noyes was assisted after World War II by his son Pierrepont T. Noyes. The latter stepped down as president in 1978 and as chairman of the board in 1981. Since then the corporation acquired and sold various subsidiaries, but by the end of the century, its energies were again concentrated on its core tableware businesses. Through several domestic and international subsidiaries, it has also offered tabletop products, including china, crystal, and glassware. Although net sales in 2002 and 2003 approached the half-billion-dollar mark, excessive debt and market factors led to a major restructuring of the company in 2004.

Carden, Maren L. *Oneida: Utopian Community to Modern Corporation* (Baltimore: Johns Hopkins Univ Press, 1969)

William S. Helmer

Oneida Nation. One of the members of the Haudenosaunee (Iroquois) Confederacy. The name is derived from *Onyota'a:ka,* meaning "People of the Standing Stone." The tradition is that a large boulder led the Oneida to where they should establish new camps or villages, and that it finally settled in upstate New York, signifying that this was to be the Oneida's permanent home. Although there were a number of Oneida villages, the main one, Kanowalohale ("Place of the Impaled Skull"), was located at what is now the City of Oneida (Madison Co). The Oneida and Cayuga are the "younger brothers" of the Iroquois League, making decisions jointly during Grand Councils. The Oneida have 9 of the 50 hereditary chiefs of the league, 3 from each of the Wolf, Turtle, and Bear Clans.

Colonial and 19th-Century History

The Oneida's history during the 17th and 18th centuries was similar to that of other Haudenosaunee. They joined in the fur trade raids against the Huron and Algonquin and in the conquest of surrounding Indian nations such as the Susquehannock and the Ottawa. To maintain their population and strength in times of war, the Oneida would often kidnap from among their enemies to replace lost family members. They also adopted many individuals or groups of people as provided in the Great Law of Peace. The largest of these were the Tuscarora, evicted from North Carolina and adopted into the confederacy in 1722, fighting with the Oneida in all battles that followed. In the 1780s the Oneida adopted the Brotherton and Stockbridge Indians.

Just prior to the Revolutionary War, a power struggle arose between the traditional and the nonhereditary (Pine Tree) chiefs. The Presbyterian minister Samuel Kirkland capitalized on this division and his friendship with Pine Tree Chief Shenandoah to influence the warriors to become Christian and pro-American. This group became known as the First Christian Party and those who followed the ancient religion the Pagan Party. These and the other parties that evolved resulted in dividing the Oneida spiritually, politically, and eventually geographically.

The Revolutionary War era was one of great upheaval for all of the Haudenosaunee. Most of the Mohawks, Onondagas, Cayugas, and Senecas fought with the British, and most of the Oneidas and Tuscaroras with the colonists. The Oneidas fought valiantly at the Battle of Oriskany and other battles. In June 1779, 12 Oneida and Tuscarora warriors were awarded captain and lieutenant commissions in the Continental army. Some Oneidas, however, did support the British. Unfortunately, those who remained loyal to the American forces lost their homes and villages at the hands of British. The village of Kanowalohale was destroyed in July 1780. About 400 Oneidas moved to Schenectady in the fall of 1780, outside the American fort, where they built makeshift huts, and many froze to death or died from starvation or smallpox. After the war, the surviving Oneidas returned to their original homelands and rebuilt their communities. The First Christian Party settled in Oneida Castle and the Pagan Party settled near Oriskany.

Before the Revolution, the original homeland of the Oneida consisted of approximately 6 million acres (2.4 million ha) stretching roughly from the Susquehanna River in Pennsylvania to the St. Lawrence River, and from near the western tip of Oneida Lake to the western foothills of the Adirondack Mountains. Despite a guarantee of their lands through the Treaties of Fort Stanwix in 1784, of Fort Harmar in 1789, and of Canandaigua in 1794, the Oneida were the first of the Iroquois to lose significant amounts of land through a series of illegal dealings. The first large land deal came on 28 June 1785, when the Oneida were coerced into selling 300,000 acres (121,406 ha) in what is now Broome and Chenango Cos to New York State when threatened with the withdrawal of the state's protection. The treaty of 22 Sept 1788, which dispossessed the Oneida of nearly 5 million acres (2 million ha) and left them only 300,000 (121,406 ha) in what are now Madison and Oneida Cos. From 1795 to 1846, more than 25 other illegal treaties were struck, leaving the Oneida with only about 350 acres (140 ha). In 1843 New York State passed legislation to allot the remaining Oneida land in severalty, which eventually led to the illegal loss of much of the remainder of their land; by the early 20th century it had been reduced to plots of 32 acres (13 ha) and 65 acres (26 ha) on Marble Hill, near Oneida.

Following Kirkland's death in 1808, Eleazer Williams, an Episcopal minister of Mohawk descent, converted most of the First Christian Party members as well as many of the Pagan Party to what became known as the Orchard Party. Williams and Chief Daniel Bread were instrumental in convincing many Oneidas that the only way to secure lands for future generations was to move out of New York State. From 1823 to 1836, 448 First Christian Party Oneidas, 206 Orchard Party Oneidas, and 44 Pagan Party Oneidas moved to a reservation near Green Bay, Wisc, forming the separate Oneida Nation of Wisconsin. Most of the Brotherton and Stockbridge Indians moved with them, eventually forming their own nearby settlements. Approximately 900 Oneidas chose to remain in New York State.

The 1838 Treaty of Buffalo Creek stipulated that all Iroquois were to move from New York to Kansas within a five-year period. Most Oneidas refused to leave. However, in 1839, 242 purchased land on the Thames River near London [now in Ont] when they were forced to sell their land in New York State. From 1840 to 1845, 410 more joined them. An 1845 state census shows that there were 210 Oneidas living in New York State, 53 of whom were in nearby Haudenosaunee communities.

The Oneidas in New York became farmers, owning livestock and making a living selling barley, oats, wheat, corn, and potatoes. Many supported themselves by fashioning crafts such as baskets, wooden artwork, and beadwork. They lived in small farmhouses, similar to their non-Indian neighbors, and tried to remain a community despite discouragement and disillusionment with the displacement of their family and friends, the trickery of government officials, and the loss of nearly all of their lands.

Oneida Land Claims and National Revival

The Oneida never accepted their loss of land as legal and have appealed to the federal government over a 200-year period to intervene, eventually leading to a number of lawsuits. In 1974 the US Supreme Court ruled that the Oneida Indians of New York, Wisconsin, and the Thames in Canada have the right to sue Madison and Oneida Cos in federal court for lands taken from them in New York State treaties. In 1985 that court further ruled that the 1795 treaty with New York State violated the 1790 and 1793 Indian Trade and Non-Intercourse Acts, which stipulated that all treaties made with American Indians must first have the consent of the federal government. This ruling provided that the Oneida receive damages for parcels owned by the counties. In 1995 the Oneida of New York opened the Turning Stone Casino in Verona (Oneida Co). They did not pay local property taxes, and local non-Indian landholders were further inflamed in 1998 when the Oneida added 20,000 private landowners as defendants to the case in the same year, though courts rejected this effort. Also in 1998 the federal government sued New York State on behalf of the Oneida and agreed to assist in compensation for the settlement of claims. In 2001 the City of Sherrill lost its case against the Oneida's sovereign immunity. The Oneida continue to negotiate with New York State for an equitable land claims settlement for the original claim for possession of 250,000 acres (101,171 ha) of land, a settlement for damages and back rent on the land. Meanwhile, the Oneida Nation has purchased approximately 15,000 acres (6,070 ha) in the land claims area.

In the early 21st century, the Oneidas who moved to Grand River, Ont, number about 4,800. They have both an elective and a traditional government, and both Christian and Traditional Longhouse religion can be found in their community. Those Oneidas who live in Wisconsin number about 14,000 and have an elective government. They are primarily Christian, though there is a growing number returning to traditional religion. They operate a casino to cover administrative operations.

The Oneidas who remained in New York maintained their rolls and organized a land claims committee that operated from about 1954 to the mid-1960s. Elections were held for nation officers until 1975, when the quasi-elective government was replaced with a traditional government. Today the Oneida Nation claims to follow a traditional government, but it has no chiefs in place and does not attend Grand Councils. This is in part because of the establishment of the Turning Stone Casino in 1995, a move that has brought the Oneida some degree of economic prosperity but has been condemned by the Iroquois Confederacy. The New York Oneidas also have both Christian and Traditional Longhouse members. Membership of the Oneida Nation in New York in the early 21st century is a little over 1,000.

Campisi, Jack. "Oneida." In *Northeast,* ed. Bruce G. Trigger, vol 15 of *Handbook of North American Indians,* ed. William C. Sturtevant (Washington, DC: Smithsonian Institution, 1978)

Campisi, Jack, and Laurence M. Hauptman, eds. *The Oneida Indian Experience* (Syracuse: Syracuse Univ Press, 1988)

Graymont, Barbara. *The Iroquois in the American Revolution* (Syracuse: Syracuse Univ Press, 1972)

Hauptman, Laurence M., and L. Gordon McLester III, eds. *The Oneida Indian Journey: From New York to Wisconsin, 1784–1860* (Madison: Univ of Wisconsin Press, 1999)

Shattuck, George C. *The Oneida Land Claims: A Legal History* (Syracuse: Syracuse Univ Press, 1991)

Vecsey, Christopher, and William A. Starna, eds. *Iroquois Land Claims* (Syracuse: Syracuse Univ Press, 1988)

Elizabeth A. Obomsawin

Oneonta. Town (pop 4,994) and city (pop 13,292) in S Otsego Co. Oneonta had some settlers before the American Revolution, but permanent settlement by Mohawk Valley Palatines and New Englanders began about 1786. The town was formed from Unadilla in 1796 as Otego and was renamed Oneonta in 1830. The village incorporated in 1848 and became a city in 1909; it has long had the nickname of Klipnockie, the etymology of which is unknown. Originally agricultural, Oneonta grew dramatically with the arrival of the Albany and Susquehanna Railroad (1865; after 1870 Delaware and Hudson), which in 1872 built its machine shops and roundhouse at Oneonta. In 1883 the Brotherhood of Railway Trainmen was founded in a caboose that is now a local landmark. The Delaware and Hudson built a large roundhouse in 1906 with stalls for 52 locomotives and a 75 ft (23 m) turntable (demolished in 1996). In 1912, 39% of the city's labor force, about 600 men, worked for the railroad. Cigar rolling (second after the railroad in employment numbers) and the trade in locally produced hops flourished prior to World War I. Other industrial products included tables (1885–94), chairs (1887–91), knit goods (1887–1900), and pianos (1891–98). By 1890 Oneonta was the largest town in Otsego Co as well as its business and transportation hub. The largely Yankee population mingled with Italians (8% of the workforce in 1910), Syrian Lebanese, and small African American populations, attracted by railroad work.

After World War II Oneonta ceased to be a rail center, and the Delaware and Hudson was acquired in 1991 by Canadian Pacific. Since 1978 most through travel is via I-88. The city remains the county's commercial hub but has its lowest per capita income. In 2003 SUNY Oneonta (1948, previously Oneonta State Normal School, 1889), with 5,600 students, and Hartwick College (1815, moved to Oneonta in 1928), with 1,400, anchored the economy. Other employers were Medical Coaches, Mold-o-matic, Corning Inc, and Fox Memorial Hospital. Oneonta is the site of the National Soccer Hall of Fame (1979) and Damaschke Field, a minor league baseball park since 1940.

Hugh C. MacDougall

onions. See MUCK FARMING.

Onondaga. Town (pop 21,063) in central Onondaga Co. Ephraim Webster, a hunter, trapper, scout, and interpreter, made camp in the present town in 1786. The town was formed in 1798 from the Onondaga and Salt Springs Reservations and from Manlius, Marcellus, and Pompey but lost territory to successive expansions of Syracuse. The county's first post office was established at Onondaga Hollow in 1794, and Onondaga Hill was platted and made the county seat the same year, keeping that status until 1830. In the 19th century blue and gray limestone was quarried for use in construction, lime and water lime (cement) were manufactured, grain cradles were made at Cradleville and brooms at Navarino. The town is abutted by the Onondaga Indian Reservation. A suburban population is clustered around hamlets and along state highways, while in the high hills and deep valleys of the southern part of town, apple growing remains important. Onondaga Community College (1962) is on a hilltop overlooking Syracuse.

Barbara S. Rivette

Onondaga County (780 mi^2/2,020 km^2; pop 458,336). Formed in 1794 from Herkimer and Tioga Cos and named after the Onondaga Indians. Territory was lost in the creation of Cayuga, Cortland, and Oswego Cos in 1799, 1808, and 1816 respectively; from these counties, part or all of seven more counties were formed. An additional boundary adjustment was made with Cayuga Co in 1828. Onondaga Co is presently subdivided into the City of Syracuse and 19 towns containing 15 incorporated villages and the Onondaga Indian Reservation. The county seat is Syracuse. Elevations range from below 360 feet (110 m) where the Oswego River exits the county in the north to over 2,060 feet (628 m) south of the Village of Fabius. The northern half of the county falls within the Erie-Ontario Lowland physiographic province, with the western portion in the Ontario Drumlins subregion and the eastern section within the Oneida Lake Plain. Additionally, areas along the Oswego Co border lie within the Ontario Ridge and Swampland

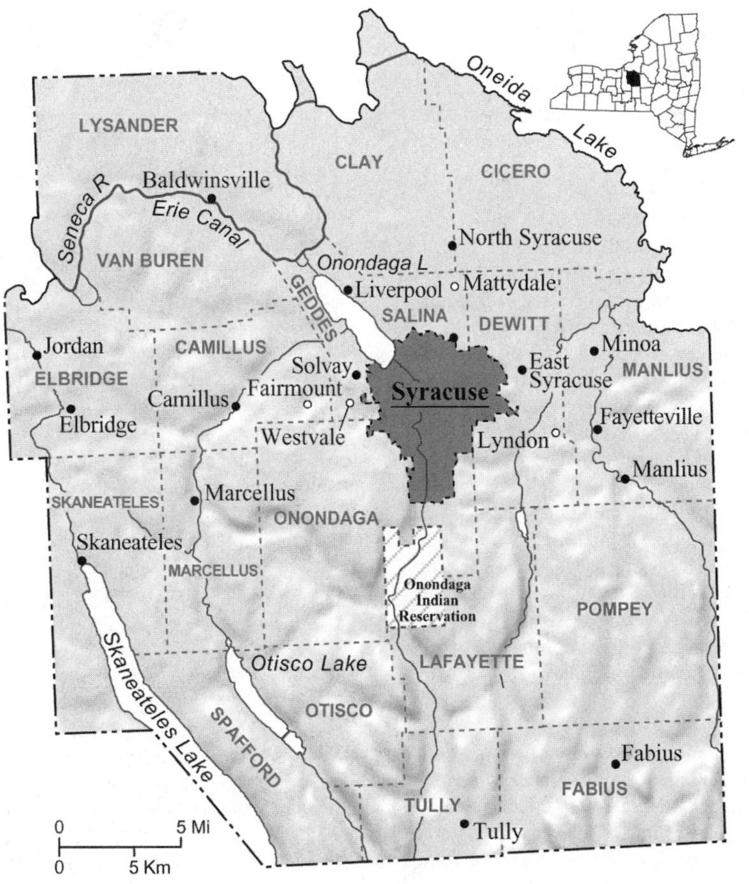

subregion. Underlying geology consists of late Silurian shale and dolomite, with some gypsum deposits and a series of exceptionally strong brine springs in and around Onondaga Lake. With the exception of the extreme southeastern corner, which is part of the Susquehanna Hills, southern Onondaga Co is part of the Finger Lakes Hills subregion of the Appalachian Upland physiographic province. Upland bedrock consists of Devonian limestone, shale, sandstone, and dolostone. The Helderberg Escarpment, composed of limestone, bisects the county along a west-east axis, passing just south of Syracuse.

The county was entirely glaciated, and prominent glacial features abound. A series of deep U-shaped valleys, trending north-south, dissect the upland; the Tully Moraine cuts across the southern part of the county. Near the northern margin of the upland, there are several substantial valleys lying east-west, along with three very large plunge pools carved by massive volumes of meltwater flowing along the ice front. A drumlin field occupies the county's northwest quarter. The lowlands contain numerous wetlands, remnants of former glacial Lake Iroquois. Onondaga Co straddles two major watersheds. Waters in the far southeast flow south to the Susquehanna. All other waters, including those of the two easternmost Finger Lakes, Skaneateles and Otisco, flow north before entering the Oswego River at Three Rivers. Soil quality varies substantially across the region. The highest concentrations of commercially viable agricultural land are found on the upland.

Onondaga Co's climate is humid-continental with cold, snowy winters and warm, wet summers. Average January temperatures range from about 23°F (-5°C) at lower elevations to the upper 10s°F (-9° to -7°C) at the highest. Readings dip below 0°F (-18°C) about six times each winter. July temperatures average around 70°F (21°C) except for higher elevations, which are several degrees cooler. Temperatures reach 90°F (32°C) or higher at least three times in a typical summer. Higher elevations have more days below 0°F and rarely reach 90°F. Average annual precipitation ranges from approximately 43 inches (109 cm) in the northwest to 46 inches (117 cm) in the southern uplands. Snowfall amounts are high everywhere, the result of both coastal storms and lake effect snows from Lake Ontario. Nevertheless, more snow typically falls in the south central uplands—about 128 inches (325 cm) around Tully—than in the northwest, where just under 84 inches (213 cm) is observed at Baldwinsville. Primeval forest cover across the north and west consisted of a central hardwood community dominated by beech, sugar maple, and basswood, augmented in places by oak and chestnut. Alleghenian hardwoods composed primarily of beech, sugar maple, hemlock, white pine, and basswood covered the southeast. Swamp forests covered significant portions of the lowland and were dominated by elm, black ash, red maple, and willow.

Native Inhabitants

There were numerous Owasco period sites (*ca* 1000–1300) in the area prior to the emergence of the Onondaga around 1400. Native peoples established villages in the hills south and east of today's Syracuse; they also made seasonal fishing camps along rivers and lakes. Archaeologists have studied more than 30 major sites, of which Furnace Brook (1300–70) in Onondaga, Kelso (1390) in Elbridge, and Pen (1700) in DeWitt have yielded extensive artifacts and data about progressive changes in culture and lifestyle. Onondaga villages increased in size in the late 15th and early 16th centuries. Onondaga land became the geographical and spiritual center of the Iroquois League. Within Onondaga Co, yet separate from it, the 9 mi² (23 km²) Onondaga Indian Reservation, just south of the Syracuse border, is home to about 1,700 Onondagas and members of related tribes. During colonial times, and since the 1840s, the Onondaga have been the keepers of the Iroquois council fire, which remains on the reservation in the early 21st century.

Settlement

In 1759, during the French and Indian War, Fort Brewerton was erected at the eastern end of Oneida Lake as part of a series of fortifications extending from the present Rome (Oneida Co) to Oswego. During the American Revolution, following Indian raids against the Mohawk Valley and Cherry Valley settlements, an expedition of 558 Continental soldiers marched south from Oneida Lake with orders to prevent the Onondaga from supplying significant aid to the British. They destroyed crops and villages along the route and, on 21 Apr 1779, the main Onondaga village.

In 1782 New York State created the New Military Tract to provide land for Revolutionary War soldiers' bounties. By that time most of the soldiers had sold their bounty rights and only a few settled on the 600 acres (240 ha) they received for their military service. Whites first made camp in what is now the Town of Onondaga in 1786 and in the present-day DeWitt and Van Buren in 1789. The New Military Tract officially opened in 1791; most towns were settled between 1790 and 1795, with Otisco the last in 1801. This influx was primarily from the Mohawk Valley, eastern New York State, and New England. The county's first village, Manlius (1813), started at the junction of the east-west Seneca and Cherry Valley Turnpikes. But most of Onondaga Co consisted of one-and-a-half-story farmhouses spaced a mile or two apart on rutted wagon tracks. Both free and enslaved African Americans came with the settlers. In the 1820 census there were 59 slaves and 195 free Blacks.

Transportation

The state's first public east-west route, the Genesee Road, later incorporated as the Seneca Turnpike (1800), stimulated settlement. The county's main north-south road followed a Native American trail that had been used by the earliest settlers. The first plank road in the world was built in 1846 from Syracuse to Central Square (Oswego Co). The section between Liverpool and Central Square operated until 1913. The Baldwinsville Canal (1807–1919) around the Seneca River rapids was the first in the county. The completion of the Erie Canal across Onondaga Co in 1819 fostered new settlements and drew trade and people from locations along the earlier roads. Hamlets developed where bridges crossed the canal: Kirkville, Manlius, Syracuse, Geddes, Amboy, Memphis, and Jordan. The Oswego Canal north to Oswego and Lake Ontario opened in 1828.

These early canals were replaced by the New

ONONDAGA CO POPULATION CENSUS FIGURES

	White	Nonwhite	Total Population	Foreign-Born
1800	7,377	29	7,406	—
1810	25,823	164	25,987	—
1820	41,213	254	41,467	99
1830	58,481	492	58,973	668
1840	67,434	477	67,911	—
1850	85,277	613	85,890	16,829
1860	90,131	555	90,686	20,048
1870	103,475	708	104,183	24,073
1880	116,999	894	117,893	23,384
1890	145,147	1,100	146,247	31,056
1900	166,978	1,757	168,735	32,227
1910	198,441	1,857	200,298	40,234
1920	239,435	2,030	241,465	42,121
1930	288,568	3,038	291,606	44,539
1940	291,780	3,328	295,108	36,055
1950	335,444	6,275	341,719	31,624
1960	408,934	14,094	423,028	30,818
1970	445,970	26,776	472,746	26,576
1980	424,786	39,134	463,920	25,187
1990	418,980	49,993	468,973	21,597
2000	388,555	69,781	458,336	25,929

Notes: "Nonwhite" includes African Americans, Asians, American Indians, and Pacific Islanders and, for 2000, also the mixed race and other race categories. Through the 1960 census these figures primarily reflect the African American population. Foreign-born figures for 1820 and 1830 include only those not naturalized, and for 1930 and 1950, the foreign-born totals include Whites only. Other years include all foreign-born in the population.

POPULATIONS OF TOWNS AND CITIES, ONONDAGA CO

Town or City, Year Founded	1800	1840	1880	1920	1960	2000
Camillus, 1799	336	3,957	2,416	2,905	18,328	23,152
Cicero, 1807	—	2,464	2,934	2,536	14,725	27,982
Clay, 1827	—	2,852	2,910	2,488	17,760	58,805
DeWitt, 1835	—	2,802	3,975	10,279	22,740	24,071
Elbridge, 1829	—	4,647	4,087	2,736	4,644	6,091
Fabius, 1798	844	2,562	2,069	1,285	1,565	1,974
Geddes, 1848	—	—	7,088	7,995	19,679	17,740
LaFayette, 1825	—	2,600	2,160	1,293	3,379	4,833
Lysander, 1794	121	4,306	4,903	4,725	10,225	19,285
Manlius, 1794	989	5,509	5,954	6,599	19,351	31,872
Marcellus, 1794	909	2,726	2,678	2,854	4,527	6,319
Onondaga, 1798	893	5,658	6,358	6,620	13,429	21,063
Otisco, 1806	—	1,906	1,558	914	1,188	2,561
Pompey, 1794	2,332	4,371	3,240	1,882	3,469	6,159
Salina, 1809	—	11,013	2,888	4,257	33,076	33,290
Skaneateles, 1830	—	3,981	4,866	4,247	6,603	7,323
Spafford, 1811	—	1,873	1,450	875	974	1,661
Syracuse (city), 1847	—	—	51,792	171,717	216,038	147,306
Tully, 1803	—	1,663	1,476	1,358	1,633	2,709
Van Buren, 1829	—	3,021	3,091	3,425	8,754	12,667

Note: In 1800 Onondaga Co included the Towns of Homer and Solon [now in Cortland Co].

York State Barge Canal (completed 1918), which made use of the natural waterways closer to the northern edge of the county. By 2000 traffic on the Erie and Oswego sections of the New York State Canal System was entirely recreational. Parts of the earlier Erie and Oswego Canals were filled to become highways. The 19th-century Erie Canal from DeWitt to Rome is part of the well-used, 30 mi (48 km) long Old Erie Canal State Park. In the west, from Camillus to Jordan, the canal is within town parks.

Each new transportation system brought different places into prominence. Syracuse became an important junction when rail lines were completed to the east (to Utica, 1839), west (to Auburn, 1840), north (to Oswego, 1848), and south (to Binghamton, 1854). Local trains carried farm produce and products from the paper, grain, and other local mills, as well as passengers. After 1872 East Syracuse became the New York Central Railroad's main freight transfer and engine repair yard. At the height of railroad dominance, nine lines served Onondaga Co, dwindling by the 1960s to the Delaware, Lackawanna and Western on the north-south axis and the New York Central on the main east-west line. In 2003 most lines, along with the intermodal railyard at East Syracuse, were operated by CSX Transportation; the exceptions were lines to Auburn, run by Finger Lakes Railroad Co, and to Binghamton, run by New York, Susquehanna and Western Railroad.

Steamboats were operated on Skaneateles and Otisco Lakes by the short rail lines that carried summer visitors. Electric trolleys later served the resorts on Onondaga and Oneida Lakes and connected the villages to each other and to the city. The first commercial airport was at Amboy from 1919 to 1949. Since then, Syracuse Hancock International Airport in Salina and DeWitt, owned by the City of Syracuse, has served the region. The William F. Walsh Regional Transportation Center (1999) in Syracuse has consolidated the rail and bus terminals.

Economic Development

The first settlers practiced subsistence farming and used a barter system until the 1820s. Gypsum was first identified in the United States in Camillus in 1792 and was quarried there starting in 1809. In Manlius and Camillus limestone became an important product, used for building, plaster, cement, and eventually to improve the soil. Limestone was also quarried in Onondaga. Abundant waterpower and thick forests led to sawmills in every part of the county.

The salt springs on the east, south, and west shores of Onondaga Lake provided the raw material for commercial salt production and attracted related trades of firewood cutting and barrel, pipe, and pump making. Tanneries were located at almost every crossroads that had waterpower in the early years. The first pottery in the county was in Manlius (1813); important potteries developed later in Baldwinsville, Jordan, and the west end of Syracuse. Syracuse Pottery (1874) manufactured flowerpots in Camillus from 1920 to 1993. Brick and drainage tile were produced in Camillus, DeWitt, and Van Buren.

Beginning in the 1820s cotton and woolen mills in Baldwinsville, Camillus, Jamesville, Manlius, Marcellus, Pompey, and Skaneateles provided employment for women outside the home. Longest lasting was the Marcellus woolen mill, which operated under various names from 1812 to 1961. Paper mills were located in Manlius, Baldwinsville, Camillus, Fayetteville, Jordan, Marcellus, and Skaneateles. The Fayetteville mill survived until 2000, and one in Marcellus remained in operation in 2003. Foundries, farm implement factories, and machine shops were found in Baldwinsville, Elbridge, Fabius, Jordan, Manlius, Marcellus, Onondaga, Otisco, and Skaneateles.

After 1830 farming expanded. Oxen continued to provide power; farmers kept about three times as many sheep as either cattle or pigs. Grain crops, hay, apples, and butter led farm production. After 1880 vegetable farming became more important. Corn, peas, tomatoes, cabbage for sauerkraut, and fruit went to the small canneries that operated in many villages until about 1920. Smaller crops included tobacco (Clay, Lysander, Manlius, Marcellus, and Van Buren), teasels (Marcellus and Skaneateles), and ginseng (Fabius). Fresh apples, raspberries, currants, and grapes were shipped by railroad to Boston and New York City. Milk amounted to more than half the total value of farm products from 1880 to 1940. After 1860 almost every town had a small cheese factory. In the 20th century many farmers operated home delivery routes for milk, cheese, butter, and eggs.

Development of railroad and trolley connections made possible resorts and summer homes on Oneida, Onondaga, Otisco, and Skaneateles Lakes and, to a lesser extent, on the Seneca River and Cross and Tully Lakes. The county's central location drew the New York State Fair to Syracuse in 1841 and 1849. The present fairgrounds in Geddes were chosen as the permanent location after 10 years of debate and opened in 1890. In the early 21st century fair buildings and exhibit space host about 1 million visitors at the end of every summer and are used for many different functions throughout the year. During wartime the fairgrounds were used by army troops.

Operating from 1884 to 1986, the Solvay Process Co (after 1920, Allied Chemical and Dye Corp) had the largest payroll in Onondaga Co and was its largest taxpayer. Located on the Erie Canal just west of Syracuse, the firm was the first US producer of synthetic soda ash, an essential chemical for glass, steel, paint, and other basic products. Solvay research developed ingredients needed to create detergents, dyes, synthetic phenols, and polyethylene foam. Company officials provided funds and impetus for the village's library and village-owned water and electric systems that continue today. From its beginning, the firm provided medical, social, and educational benefits for its workers and their families, many of whom came from the Tyrol on the border of Austria and Italy; the benefits ended soon after the company's acquisition by Allied Chemical. Other industrial products included furniture made by L. and J. G. Stickley Furniture Co in Fayetteville, willow baskets and furniture made in Liverpool, gunpowder in Marcellus in the 19th century, and cutlery in Camillus.

Religion, Education, and Culture

Churches, schools, and Masonic organizations were the earliest centers of social life for county residents. The 1855 census reported 142 religious congregations, among them 49 Methodist Episcopal, 21 Presbyterian, and 19 Baptist churches; there were also 10 Episcopal, 8 Congregational, and 6 Roman Catholic congregations, with smaller numbers of Universalist, Unitarian, African Methodist Episcopal, Swedenborgian, and Jewish congregations.

Onondaga Co was a part of the Burned-over District, a region of fervid evangelizing during the antebellum period. Evangelical-inspired reform followed. The temperance movement became widespread after 1840, when both the Carson League and Good Templars had chapters in almost every village. Antislavery sentiment was also prevalent. Abolitionists from Syracuse, such as Samuel J. May and Jermain Loguen, spoke regularly at rallies and participated in the so-called Jerry Rescue of 1851 that freed a captured fugitive slave from a Syracuse jail. The Skaneateles community (1843–46) operated on Fourierist principles on a farm near that village. The women's rights movement had many supporters: Matilda Joslyn Gage of Fayetteville, who wrote and spoke throughout the United States from 1855 until her death in 1898; Harriett May Mills (1857–1935), national organizer and speaker, was the first woman nominated on a statewide ticket when she ran for secretary of state as a Democrat in 1920; and Florence E. S. Knapp, who won the same race as a Republican in 1924.

Before the development of public high schools, advanced academic studies were offered by private academies, beginning with Pompey Academy (1811–95). Later, St. John's Academy (1869–1970), which became Manlius Military School, achieved national renown. Elbridge Central School (1928) was the county's first consolidated district; a number of common schools in DeWitt, Manlius, and Geddes were independent until after 1958. In 2003 there were 15 central and 2 Union Free School districts in the county, as well as the Syracuse City School District. Institutions of higher education include Syracuse University, which has a large graduate and research component, along with SUNY College of Environmental Science and Forestry, Le Moyne College, and SUNY Upstate Medical University, all in Syracuse. Onondaga Community College (1962), also in Syracuse, grants two-year degrees.

A necklace of 11 county parks, totaling more than 6,500 acres (2,630 ha), extends from the shores of Oneida Lake to the hills of Highland Forest (3,000 acres/1,200 ha) and provides four-season recreation. The county also operates a nature center, a fish hatchery, and a stadium that is the home of the Syracuse SkyChiefs, an International League baseball club. Three museums highlight different phases of history: Sainte Marie de Gannentaha, the Salt Museum in Onondaga Lake Park in Liverpool, and the Pioneer Museum at Highland Forest in Fabius.

Politics

From 1794 to 1961 Onondaga Co was governed by a Board of Supervisors, which until after 1900 met only once a year. Eventually its membership represented 19 towns and the 19 wards of the city of Syracuse. Town supervisors had a dual function, as the chief executive officer of the town and as a member of the county board. Towns were responsible for the location and maintenance of roads, had some control over school districts until after 1920, and maintained health and welfare programs. Counties were required to maintain property records, operate a court system, and provide law enforcement through the sheriff and deputies. The first county buildings were a jail, a courthouse, a county clerk's office, and a poorhouse. In the early 21st century the county operates the 526-bed Van Duyn Home and Hospital for the elderly and disabled on Onondaga Hill in Syracuse; Oncenter, a Syracuse convention complex; a jail; and a penitentiary.

As county responsibilities increased, a new type of government was organized under provisions of a charter approved in 1961. Beginning in 1962 county affairs were placed under centralized management with a county executive, initially elected by the supervisors and then, in 1964, by the voters. The county was divided into legislative districts based on population, and in 1968 a county legislature replaced the Board of Supervisors. Town functions such as health and welfare were also centralized. Gradually other functions became county responsibilities, such as the operation of city zoo, solid waste and sewage disposal, planning, and libraries.

Until about 1970 voters predominantly supported Republican candidates on county, state, and national levels. Two residents have been governor: Horace White (1910) and Nathan L. Miller (1921–22). Ten lawyers have served on the Court of Appeals, the state's highest court, and six have been its chief judge. Grover Cleveland, who twice was president of the United States, grew up in Fayetteville and worked there as a young man from 1841 to 1854.

Recent History

Onondaga Co's population increased 30% between 1940 and 1960, mainly because of suburban growth. The City of Syracuse reached its peak population of 220,583 in 1950 but by 2000 had only 147,306 residents. The suburbanization of the county was encouraged by two major limited-access highways. The Thruway opened its first link just north of Syracuse in 1954. The north-south I-81 opened in segments between 1955 and 1966, passing directly through the city with downtown exits. A limited-access ring surrounds the city on the north, east, and south sides. Westvale Plaza (1948) in Geddes, Valley Plaza (1950) on Syracuse's south end, and Shoppingtown (1954) in DeWitt began the trend of locating stores and services outside the downtown; the vast Carousel Center mall, however, opened within city limits in 1990. In the half century following the first shopping centers, factories and offices also sought suburban locations. Radisson, the county's only planned community, was created in Clay in 1969.

As public water and sewers became more generally available, there was rapid expansion along major roads. Since 1967 Lake Ontario, 50 miles (80 km) away, has supplied unlimited water for residents and industries that once depended on local wells and lakes. The county operates a sewage treatment system for Syracuse and the surrounding towns. The proportion of the county's residents living in Syracuse has declined from 70% in 1920 to half in 1960 and to about 32% in 2000. Manufacturing, once the backbone of the county's economy, declined 32% from 1970 to 1997. Distribution and transportation services, engineering, high-end technology, and the service economy have become the major employers. Many serve international markets and most are under out-of-town ownership. The largest segment of residents work in a concentration of hospitals and medical and eldercare services that employ more than 20,000.

Nationally known businesses with manufacturing plants include Bristol-Myers Squibb (drug research and manufacturing), Carrier Corp (air-conditioning, heating, and refrigeration), Lockheed-Martin Corp, formerly General Electric (electronic guidance and information systems), New Venture Gear (car and truck components), Stickley (furniture) and Welch Allyn (medical diagnostic instruments and portable computing products). Anheuser-Busch produces 8 million barrels of beer a year in its Baldwinsville brewery, opened in 1983. Other nationally known firms that carry local names are Camillus Cutlery Co (1894), Syracuse China Co (1871, tableware), Syroco (founded in 1880 as Syracuse Ornamental Co; plastic furniture and decorative pieces); and Will and Baumer Candle Co (1855). In the Town of DeWitt, the largest quarry in the eastern United States (3,000 acres/1,200 ha) produces stone and bituminous products.

Cast of *The Magic Toy Shop*, a locally broadcast children's television show in Syracuse in the 1960s.

Despite heavy suburban pressure, 29.5% of the county's land area remained in agriculture in 1997. In 2003 there were about 240 full-time farmers, including 125 dairy farmers with herds of from 60 to 600 cows. The Plainville Turkey Farm in Lysander is the largest grower and processor of turkeys in the Northeast, raising 500,000 birds each year. A diminishing number of farms produce eggs and field crops. Apples are the chief orchard crop, especially in LaFayette, Onondaga, and Van Buren.

In 220 years Onondaga Co has been transformed from the "perfect wilderness," as described in 1780 by a Revolutionary soldier, to a county with few acres untouched by homes or businesses. An area with primeval forest cover in Green Lakes State Park (Town of Manlius) is a permanent reminder of those earliest days.

See also STICKLEY FURNITURE; SUBURBANIZATION.

The standard histories are Joshua V. H. Clark, *Onondaga; or, Reminiscences of Earlier and Later Times* (1849); W. W. Clayton, *History of Onondaga County* (1878); Dwight H. Bruce, *Onondaga's Centennial,* 2 vols (1896); William M. Beauchamp, *Past and Present of Syracuse and Onondaga County,* 2 vols (1908); and Franklin H. Chase, *Syracuse and Its Environs: A History,* 3 vols (1924). A recent survey is Richard N. Wright, *Onondaga County: The Early Years* (1987), and *Onondaga Landmarks* (1981) is a useful guide. Roberta B. Miller, *City and Hinterland: A Case Study of Urban Growth and Development* (1979) takes an academic approach to the subject, and Roscoe Coleman Martin, et al, *Decisions in Syracuse: A Metropolitan Action Study* (1965) summarizes the history of topics such as health, water, zoning, and government organization.

There are many town and village histories, including L. Pearl Palmer, *Historical Review of the Town of Lysander* (1947); Mary E. Maxwell, *Among the Hills of Camillus* (1952); *Solvay* (1959); Jean Keough, *Water, Wheels, and Stone: Heritage of the Little Village by the Creek, Jamesville, New York* (1976); Sylvia Shoebridge, *Pompey: Our Town in Profile,* 2 vols (1976); Kathryn C. Heffernan, *Nine Mile Country: The History of the Town of Marcellus, New York* (1978); and Ruth Cominolli, *Smokestacks Allegro: The Story of Solvay* (1990). Early town and village histories include Henry C. Van Schaack, *A History of Manlius Village* (1873); *Re-union of the Sons and Daughters of the Old Town of Pompey* (1875); Israel Parsons, *The Centennial History of the Town of Marcellus* (1878); Edward N. Leslie, *Skaneateles* (1902); and George K. Collins, *Spafford* (1917). Among the more recent publications are Ralph H. Sims, *A History of Camillus* (1999); *Welcome to Clay* (1978); Jeanette R. Horner, ed., *A Stroll through Time: Elbridge* (2003); Barbara S. Rivette, *Our Town at 200: Town of Manlius, 1794–1994* (1994); *People and Places: Fayetteville, Manlius, Minoa, and Neighbors,* 3 vols (1986–2002); J. Roy Dodge, *Crossroads Town: A Photo-Biography of the Town of LaFayette* (1979); Marion Luke, ed., *Liverpool, NY: 1830–1980* (1980); and Donald H. Thompson, *The Golden Age of Onondaga Lake Resorts* (2002).

Barbara S. Rivette

Onondaga Lake (4.6 mi^2/ 11.9 km^2). Body of water notable for its salt industry and pollution legacy, formed by glacial retreat action and meltwater runoff about 10,000 years ago. Located in Onondaga Co, it is 4.5 mi (7.2 km) long and 1 mile (1.6 km) across at its widest and has a maximum depth of 64 feet (19.5 m). The lake was an early fishing site for American Indian groups, a tradition that continued among the Onondaga Nation of the Iroquois Confederacy, for whom the lake was named. Water connections to Lake Ontario and the St. Lawrence River, combined with its central location for the Iroquois, made Onondaga Lake a site for contact and exploration by 17th-century settlers from New France. The lake was ceded by the Onondaga to New York State in late 18th-century treaties.

The shoreline brine springs prompted the state to create a public reserve around the lake in 1788 to control production of salt. These sites covered hundreds of acres around the southern half of the lake until the early 20th century. Transportation improvements of the 1820s, including the opening of the Erie and Oswego Canals, helped move the salt to markets. Other modifications involved the deepening of the lake's outlet at the Seneca River in 1823, which lowered lake levels and drained shoreline swamps in what became downtown Syracuse. In 1884 the brine attracted the Solvay Process Co, America's first synthetic soda-ash plant, to the area because the company's formula required saltwater. The west shore plant helped create the lakeside village of Solvay and nurtured associated chemical manufacturing facilities.

The lakeshore's undeveloped northwest quadrant was used for private hotels, dancing pavilions, and small amusement parks after the Civil War. This resort era thrived between 1880 and 1920, with steamboats and interurban rail lines drawing patrons from Syracuse. Ice boating was a major winter pastime, followed by intercollegiate rowing in the spring. Pollution and changing transportation and recreation patterns contributed to the decline of the resorts.

The state had abandoned the Oswego Canal along the east shore by 1928, inspiring a local plan to construct a landscaped parkway. Gov Franklin D. Roosevelt's early state public works programs funded the Onondaga Lake Park and Parkway, which opened in 1933. In addition to traditional recreational facilities, the park included development of three historic sites interpreting the lakeshore's canal, salt, and colonial history. A popular bike trail was extended to sections of the northwest shore in the 1970s. When the Oswego Canal closed, the lake itself became part of the state's Barge Canal. Salt lands were filled with oil and gasoline storage tanks in the 1920s, supplied by tanker barges. The tanks, made obsolete by new pipeline distribution systems, were removed during the 1990s, and an 800-acre (324 ha) lakefront revitalization begun, anchored by the Carousel Center shopping mall with other retail, marina, and housing developments planned around the former 1918 Barge Canal terminal.

The Solvay Process plant closed in 1986 but left a legacy of heavy metal and other pollutants in and near the lake, including concentrations of calcium, sodium, and chloride. Pollutants continue to leach into the lake from acres of waste beds near the shore. These factors, combined with the long use of the lake by metropolitan Syracuse for sewage effluence, created a pollution crisis. Swimming was prohibited in 1940, and eating fish from the lake was banned in 1970. The lake came to be known as one of the most polluted in America, with high levels of phosphorus, ammonia, and mercury contaminants. Considerable public and private efforts and expense have been directed at solving Onondaga Lake's complex pollution status, with over $300 million devoted to correcting most of the sewage-related concerns.

Thompson, Donald H. *The Golden Age of Onondaga Lake Resorts* (Fleischmanns, NY: Purple Mountain Press, 2002)

Dennis J. Connors

Onondaga Nation. The Onondaga are the fire keepers and the wampum keepers of the Haudenosaunee (Iroquois) Confederacy. They call themselves Onontakeka, "The People of the Hills." The Onondaga Indian Reservation is near Nedrow (Onondaga Co) about 5 miles (8 km) south of Syracuse and is the traditional political and geographical center of the Haudenosaunee Confederacy. It continues in that role in the early 21st century and is recognized by all Haudenosaunee communities in the United States and Canada as the capital of the confederacy.

The Onondaga Nation government is composed of the council of chiefs and clan mothers chosen through a consensual selection process. The Onondaga have 14 of the 50 hereditary chiefs on the Grand Council of the Haudenosaunee Confederacy and the most clans of any other Haudenosaunee nation, including the Wolf, Bear, Turtle, Snipe, Hawk, Eel, Deer, and Beaver. Thadodaho, the most noble of the chiefs and chairman of the Confederacy, must be Onondaga and is often chosen from the Eel Clan. Chiefs from each of the Six Nations meet on a regular basis at the Onondaga Longhouse for Grand Council Meetings to discuss and make decisions on matters that affect all Haudenosaunee. As the fire keepers and keepers of the Great Law, the Onondaga convene, open, and close Grand Councils, and ratify all decisions made at these national confederacy meetings. As the wampum keepers of confederacy wampum, they keep the administration records of the Haudenosaunee Confederacy.

ONONDAGA HISTORY

Before and during early European contact, the principal villages of the Onondaga were near Onondaga Lake. As with the other Iroquois, the Onondaga were involved in trading fur throughout the 17th and 18th centuries with the French, Dutch, and British. As a gesture of peace toward the French, they allowed the French to establish several missions near their main village during the mid–17th century. However, the increased antagonism between other Haudenosaunee nations and the French led the Jesuits to withdraw their missionaries from Onondaga throughout the 1680s. In 1689 King William's War engaged the Onondaga with other Haudenosaunee nations in battle with the French until 1696, when the French led a large expedition against the Onondaga and Oneida, during which the main Onondaga village was destroyed. Peace was established with the French again in 1701. Another mission was established and burned in 1709 amid tense relations with the French. The French and English persistently interfered in each other's attempts to build forts at Onondaga in the early 18th century and neither had any lasting success. In the 1750s about half of the Onondagas moved to the French fort and mission at La Présentation at Oswegatchie [now Ogdensburg, St. Lawrence Co] because of political differences with the pro-English Onondagas. During the French and Indian War, the Onondagas at Oswegatchie fought with the French.

The Revolutionary War deeply divided the Haudenosaunee Confederacy. In 1777 the

Woman with basket and beadwork at the Onondaga Indian Reservation, 1910.

Onondaga Nation extinguished the unifying confederacy fire as a result of a plague in their villages. Although the Onondaga as a nation attempted to remain neutral and a number were pro-American, some were pro-British, especially those at Oswegatchie. In April 1779 the Onondaga villages were destroyed by Col Goose van Schaick as part of the Sullivan-Clinton campaign to destroy all Iroquois villages not friendly to the colonial cause. In response, many Onondagas joined the approximately 1,700 other pro-British Iroquois at Buffalo Creek [now in Erie Co] in Seneca territory. Those who stayed in the principal village of Onondaga for the most part remained neutral. Around 1806, under pressure from settlers, New York State ordered the Haudenosaunee to leave Oswegatchie, and the Onondagas there dispersed, many to the nearby Mohawk community at St. Regis and many to their people at the Onondaga Reservation.

At the time of the Revolutionary War, the Onondaga controlled a swath of New York stretching north to Lake Ontario and south to the Susquehanna River. At the 1784 Treaty of Fort Stanwix, the Onondaga were forced to give up about 6 mi² (16 km²) near Oswego and their claims in the Ohio Valley. Over a 34-year period, the Onondaga made five treaties with New York State. On 12 Sept 1788, the first dispossessed them of all but 100 mi² (259 km²) of 12 million acres (4.9 million ha). The second on 11 Mar 1793 left them with about 25 mi² (65 km²). The third on 28 July 1795 ceded the Salt Lake [now Onondaga Lake] and some surrounding areas in what is now Syracuse. On 25 Feb 1817, 4,320 acres (1,748 ha) were sold. On 11 Feb 1822, the last New York State transaction of 800 acres (320 ha) was completed, leaving with Onondaga Reservation with only 7,300 acres (2,950 ha).

Approximately 300 Onondagas lived at Buffalo Creek in 1790, and 100 at their traditional village. An additional 225 or so had moved to Grand River [now in Ont] shortly after the Revolutionary War, where the British government had set aside land for their Iroquois allies. Although the confederacy fire was rekindled under the protection of the Senecas at Buffalo Creek, a duplicate longhouse was established on the newly established Six Nations Reserve at Grand River, where in the early 19th century, the Onondaga resumed their role as fire keepers. By 1847, after the Buffalo Creek Reservation was lost in the 1838 Treaty of Buffalo Creek, most of the Onondagas living at Buffalo Creek had reunited with other Onondagas on the Onondaga Indian Reservation and rekindled the ancient fire. Over the years, many Onondagas from other locations returned to their original homeland. The 1890 census recorded 494 Haudenosaunee living on the Onondaga Reservation: 341 Onondagas and 86 Oneidas.

Contemporary Onondaga Life

In the early 21st century, the reservation, now referred to as a territory in acknowledgment that the land is on original Haudenosaunee lands, accommodates about 1,600 Onondagas. About 600 Onondagas live at Grand River; the rest are scattered across the United States and Canada. A number of other Haudenosaunee people also live on the Onondaga Indian Territory.

In the early 19th century most of the Onondagas accepted the teachings of the Seneca prophet Handsome Lake, or Gaiwiio, which promoted ways to maintain a traditional way of life in an non-Indian world. Today, traditional Onondaga continue to practice Gaiwiio through what some refer to as the Longhouse Religion. Gaiwiio affirms high moral codes such as abstinence from alcohol and gambling. Throughout the early 20th century, Methodist, Episcopal, and Seventh-day Adventist churches were all built on the reservations and continue to operate into the early 21st century. For many decades there were two schools on Onondaga territory, one operated by New York State and one by the Episcopal Church. In 2003 the Onondaga Indian School was the only active elementary school, and although it follows state guidelines, it is operated by the Onondaga. Most Onondaga children attend it. The Onondaga have for many years been pursuing one of the largest land claims in the United States and continue attempts to resolve it through negotiations with New York State.

Blau, Harold, Jack Campisi, and Elisabeth Tooker. "Onondaga." In *Northeast*, ed. Bruce G. Trigger, vol 15 of *Handbook of North American Indians*, ed. William C. Sturtevant (Washington, DC: Smithsonian Institution, 1978)

Fenton, William N. *The Great Law and the Longhouse: A Political History of the Iroquois Confederacy* (Norman: Univ of Oklahoma Press, 1998)

Graymont, Barbara. *The Iroquois in the American Revolution* (Syracuse: Syracuse Univ Press, 1972)

Jennings, Francis, ed. *The History and Culture of Iroquois Diplomacy: An Interdisciplinary Guide to the Treaties of the Six Nations and Their League* (Syracuse: Syracuse Univ Press, 1985)

Richter, Daniel K. *The Ordeal of the Longhouse: The Peoples of the Iroquois League in the Era of European Colonization* (Chapel Hill: Univ of North Carolina Press, 1992)

Snow, Dean R. *The Iroquois* (Cambridge, Mass: Blackwell, 1994)

Elizabeth A. Obomsawin

Ontario. Town (pop 9,778) in NW Wayne Co. Bounded on the north by Lake Ontario and settled in 1806, the town was formed from Williamson in 1807 as Freetown and renamed Ontario in 1808. The Rome, Watertown and Ogdensburg Railroad arrived in 1873. Iron ore (hematite) was discovered in 1811, and the Ontario iron industry became the county's largest employer until it suffered a collapse in 1887 because of competition from Minnesota. Some pig iron production continued until about 1918, and ore was mined for use in red paint into the 1940s. Mink were raised here from the 1930s to the 1990s. The Robert E. Ginna Nuclear Power Plant is in Ontario, and local industries manufacture optics, electronics, plastics, and metal products. Apples and other fruits are grown. Owing to its proximity to Rochester, Ontario has experienced significant suburban development; its population increased by 197% between 1950 and 2000. Monroe Community College has an extension site in Ontario, and several 19th-century buildings are preserved at Heritage Square in the north central part of town.

Scott C. Monje

Ontario County (644 mi²/1,668 km²; pop 100,224). Created in 1789 from Montgomery Co and called the "Mother of Counties" for the numerous counties of western New York State carved from its original territory. The present boundaries were finalized in 1828. Ontario Co is divided into 2 cities and 16 towns, which contain 8 incorporated villages. The City of Canandaigua serves as the county seat. The southern two-thirds of Ontario Co lies within the Finger Lakes Hills region of the broader Appalachian Plateau; the remainder is part of the extensive drumlin field that occupies part of the Erie-Ontario Lowland. The plateau is underlain by southward-dipping Devonian shales and sandstones, the lake plain by similar-trending limestones. Elevations range from 415 feet (126 m) in

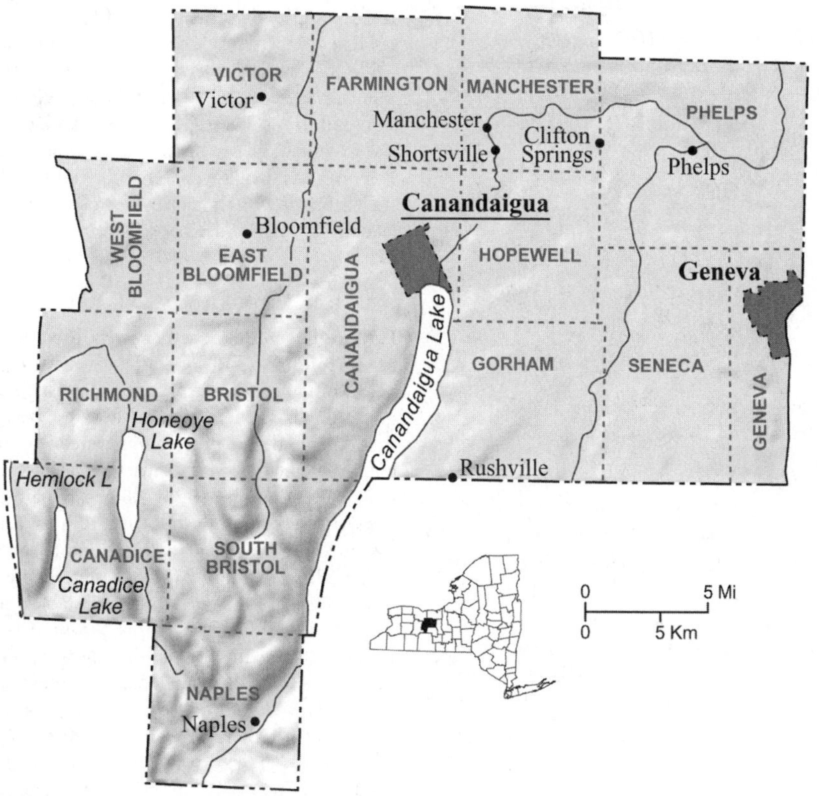

the county's far northeast corner to the 2,256 ft (688 m) Gannett Hill in South Bristol. Land surfaces rise significantly to the south, as does relief. Glaciation is evident everywhere. Most prominent are the hundreds of drumlins that dot the lake plain and a series of deep (sometimes exceeding 1,000 ft/305 m), glacially scoured valleys trending north-south across the plateau. Finger Lakes occupy four of these valleys: Canandaigua, Honeoye, Canadice (formerly Caneadea), and Hemlock. Another, Seneca Lake, borders the county on the east. All of Ontario Co lies within the Lake Ontario watershed, the principal streams being Flint Creek, Canandaigua Outlet, and Mud Creek. Soils in the southwest quarter are generally poor. Elsewhere, alluvial or glacially based limy soils provide the foundation for highly viable farm operations.

The climate is humid-continental. Mean January and July temperatures are in the mid-20s°F (-4°C) and low 70s°F (22°C) respectively. Average annual precipitation ranges from 32 to 35 inches (81–89 cm) with higher amounts in the east. Snowfall exceeds 80 inches (200 cm) at some of the higher elevations in the far south but less than 60 inches (150 cm) across the eastern half of the county. Aside from scattered pockets of wetland, primeval forest cover consisted principally of hardwoods dominated by beech, sugar maple, and basswood. Areas of shallower soil supported oak-hickory hardwood forests.

American Indians and Early Settlement

Archaeological evidence indicates the migration of native peoples from the northwest into the Genesee Valley, then east into present-day Ontario Co between AD 1250 and 1450. By the 1500s the region was the home of the Seneca, "keepers of the western door" of the Iroquois Confederacy. European contact with the Seneca is reported as early as 1632. Jesuits established missions at Ganondagan [now in Victor] and Gannongarae [now in Bloomfield] between 1656 and 1714; they were followed in 1750 by Moravian missionaries. At the height of their power, the Seneca lived across the region northwest of Canandaigua Lake and in the area of Honeoye Valley and what is now Lima (Livingston Co). A 1677 visitor reported a town consisting of 150 longhouses, but by 1700 clan housing had been replaced by cabins. Decimated by warfare, measles, and smallpox, the Seneca moved east to Ganundagwa [now Canandaigua] and Kanadesaga [now Geneva], where they remained until after the Revolutionary War.

In 1786, in accordance with the Hartford Convention, Massachusetts gained preemption rights to lands west of Seneca Lake, including all of Ontario Co. Two years later the rights were sold to a group of New England investors led by Oliver Phelps and Nathaniel Gorham, who, at a council held at Buffalo Creek [now in Erie Co], purchased the Seneca land east of the Genesee River for $5,000 and an annual annuity of $500. Though they opened a land office at Canandaigua the following year, financial difficulties forced Phelps and Gorham to sell nearly all of their landholdings to financier Robert Morris in 1790 for 8¢ an acre. A year later Morris sold the bulk of his purchase to an English syndicate led by Sir William Pulteney. The latter group, under the direction of land agent Charles Williamson, enhanced its investment by building roads and bridges, erecting mills, laying out villages, and clearing land to entice settlement. Geneva, Canandaigua, and the surrounding areas were major beneficiaries of these promotional efforts.

European settlement commenced at Geneva in 1786 and soon afterward at Canandaigua. By 1795, guided by the Genesee Road in the east and the Susquehanna River and its tributaries in the south, settlers streamed into the area, primarily from southern New England, eastern New York State, and Pennsylvania. By 1800 an estimated 10,000 people lived within 15 miles

ONTARIO CO POPULATION CENSUS FIGURES

	White	Nonwhite	Total Population	Foreign-Born
1790	1,058	17	1,075	—
1800	15,052	166	15,218	—
1810	41,521	511	42,032	—
1820	87,540	727	88,267	214
1830	39,833	455	40,288	307
1840	42,837	664	43,501	—
1850	43,319	610	43,929	4,888
1860	43,924	639	44,563	7,134
1870	44,578	530	45,108	7,350
1880	48,938	603	49,541	7,681
1890	47,989	464	48,453	7,539
1900	49,159	446	49,605	6,910
1910	51,919	367	52,286	6,864
1920	52,339	313	52,652	5,198
1930	53,968	308	54,276	5,565
1940	54,969	338	55,307	4,259
1950	59,671	501	60,172	3,730
1960	67,045	1,025	68,070	2,862
1970	77,236	1,613	78,849	2,402
1980	86,629	2,280	88,909	2,585
1990	92,434	2,667	95,101	1,960
2000	95,256	4,968	100,224	2,749

Notes: "Nonwhite" includes African Americans, Asians, American Indians, and Pacific Islanders and, for 2000, also the mixed race and other race categories. Through the 1960 census these figures primarily reflect the African American population. Foreign-born figures for 1820 and 1830 include only those not naturalized, and for 1930 and 1950, the foreign-born totals include Whites only. Other years include all foreign-born in the population.

POPULATIONS OF TOWNS AND CITIES, ONTARIO CO

Town or City, Year Founded	1800	1840	1880	1920	1960	2000
Bristol, 1796	751	1,953	1,650	896	1,002	2,421
Canadice, 1829	—	1,341	895	457	558	1,846
Canandaigua, 1790	1,153	5,652	8,363	1,858	4,894	7,649
Canandaigua (city), 1913	—	—	—	7,356	9,370	11,264
East Bloomfield, 1795[a]	1,940	1,986	2,527	1,715	2,297	3361
Farmington, 1796	633	2,122	1,978	1,465	2,114	10,585
Geneva, 1872	—	—	7,412	1,251	2,603	3,289
Geneva (city), 1898	—	—	—	14,648	17,286	13,617
Gorham, 1796[b]	476	2,779	2,521	1,936	2,664	3,776
Hopewell, 1822	—	1,976	1,894	1,339	1,822	3,346
Manchester, 1821[c]	—	2,912	3,920	5,567	6,242	9,258
Naples, 1795[d]	259	2,345	2,699	2,122	1,955	2,441
Phelps, 1795[e]	1,097	5,563	5,189	4,205	5,825	7,017
Richmond, 1796[f]	635	1,937	1,772	1,071	1,384	3,452
Seneca, 1792	1,522	7,073	2,877	2,638	2,698	2,731
South Bristol, 1838	—	1,375	1,327	696	617	1,645
Victor, 1812	—	2,393	2,804	2,319	3,295	9,977
West Bloomfield, 1833	—	2,094	1,713	1,113	1,444	2,549

Notes: In 1800 Ontario Co included the Towns of Avon [then Hartford], Geneseo, Lima [then Charleston], and Sparta [now in Livingston Co]; the Town of Northfield [now in Monroe Co]; the Towns of Palmyra and Sodus [now in Wayne Co]; and the Towns of Jerusalem and Middlesex [then Augusta; now in Yates Co]. Several towns claim earlier creation dates based on the formation of judicial districts in 1789.

[a]Bloomfield until 1833.

[b]Easton until 1806, then Lincoln until 1807.

[c]Burt until 1822.

[d]Middletown until 1808.

[e]Sullivan until 1796.

[f]Pittstown until 1808, then Honeoye until 1815.

(24 km) of the Genesee Road in the area between Geneva and the Genesee River. About 1,000 lived in Canandaigua, which at that time was the hub of a 250 mi (400 km) network of roads and navigable waterways. The community seemed destined for greatness. By the 1810s it was touted to become "the Metropolis of the Western Counties." Gideon Granger, US postmaster general (1801–14), was a prominent Canandaiguan. Elsewhere lands continued to fill up and villages expanded as the fame of the Genesee Country spread. By 1850 the county had nearly 44,000 residents, over 600 of whom were African American.

Economic Development

From the beginning, agriculture was the basis of the economy, with wheat the premier crop. The challenge was getting the bountiful harvest to market. Scheduled stage service between Canandaigua and Utica began in 1804, but cost made freight connections far more tenuous. Overland shipment to Albany was prohibitively expensive; some goods were sent south via the Susquehanna River to Philadelphia and Baltimore. Livestock was driven to eastern markets. The Ontario Bank, the county's first, opened at Geneva in 1813. Navigation improvements to the Seneca River helped some, and the Erie Canal much more. Although the canal barely touched Ontario Co soil at Port Gibson, the artificial river was near enough to benefit the farmers throughout the northern part of the county. The opening of the Cayuga and Seneca Canal in 1828 gave the industrializing locality of Geneva direct access to the state's canal system and helped further stimulate agricultural and industrial development in the county's eastern half. In 1841 the Auburn and Rochester Railroad opened, linking Geneva and Canandaigua with Rochester and later with Syracuse and points beyond, enhancing connections for growth. In 1855 the census reported 40 gristmills, 54 sawmills, 7 plaster mills, and 2 paper mills in the county.

As transportation facilities improved, competition from the Midwest forced changes in the farm economy. During the latter half of the 19th century dairy farming grew in importance, along with plant breeding and propagation and specialty crops like peppermint, grapes, and raspberries. The Agricultural Research Station at Geneva (1882) was both a spin-off from and a major contributor to the horticultural business. Geneva-based nurseries, notably W. and T. Smith and T. C. Maxwell and Bros, became major suppliers of ornamental plants and fruit stock. The county's grape and wine industry began at Naples in 1864 and continues to expand in the early 21st century. Manufacturing operations were natural offshoots of this strong agricultural base. Factories forged the implements used in the fields. The harvest was processed at canneries, breweries, wineries, and mills; put in jars, bottles, and cans produced in manufacturing plants; and shipped by rail throughout the region and beyond. Leading manufacturers included E. J. Burrall Manufacturing Co (1812–64), Geneva Preserving Co (1889–1953), and G. W. Lisk Co (1910–). In 1900 the county had 4,328 farms that averaged under 95 acres (38 ha). In 1873 the Geneva and Ithaca Railroad (after 1876 Lehigh Valley) opened, improving connections southward, while the Lehigh Valley opened a line through Manchester in 1892, making it the site of its division end, transfer yard, and shops, and a work site to which Syrians, Italians, Ukrainians, and Poles were drawn. Roads were a different matter. Ira Cribb of Canandaigua became a national leader in the Good Roads Movement in the 1890s.

Religion, Education, and Culture

Early white and black settlers were overwhelmingly Protestant, and soon after settlement they began organizing congregations. Baptists, Congregationalists, Methodists, and Presbyterians predominated, but other faiths were also present. A colony of Massachusetts Quakers settled in Farmington in 1789–90 and remained a strong presence until the late 19th century. Joseph Smith Jr was led by revelations to what he called Hill Cumorah in Manchester, where he claimed to have uncovered the gold tablets that provide the foundation for the Mormon faith. His chief lieutenant, Brigham Young, was a longtime resident of Canandaigua. An annual pageant at Hill Cumorah commemorates Smith's discovery. In 1855 there were 14 Baptist, 8 Congregational, 7 Episcopal, 28 Methodist, and 11 Presbyterian churches in the county. The first Roman Catholic parish, made up primarily of Irish immigrants, was formed in Geneva in 1832. A Jewish congregation was established in 1947.

Schools originated in log cabins in the early 1790s, and Canandaigua and Geneva Academies followed later in the decade. The Ontario Female Seminary opened in 1825. Ontario Co's public school system was established in response to 1812 legislation. Between 1930 and 1949 district schools gave way to central districts to address the changing educational needs of students in rural communities. In 2001 Ontario Co was served by seven central and two city school districts, two Catholic parochial schools, and five sectarian schools. Baccalaureate-granting Hobart and William Smith Colleges (established 1822 and 1943, respectively) share a campus and facilities in Geneva, and the Finger Lakes Community College (1967) is based in Canandaigua.

Lucius Carey published the county's first newspaper, the *Ontario Gazette and Genesee Advertiser,* at Geneva in 1797; it soon moved to Canandaigua. Dailies were usually published in Canandaigua and Geneva, weeklies in some of the villages, including Phelps, Naples, Clifton Springs, Shortsville, and Rushville. Famed newspaper publisher Frank E. Gannett (1876–1957) was born at Bristol Springs. Today Canandaigua's *Daily Messenger* and the Geneva's *Finger Lakes Times* are published daily. Radio station WEOS (public radio) broadcasts from Hobart and William Smith Colleges and WCGR and WYSL broadcast from Canandaigua.

Ontario Co has several important museums, including the Granger Homestead and Sonnenberg Gardens, both in Canandaigua. The Finger Lakes Performing Arts Center (1983), a county-owned facility also in Canandaigua, is the summer home of the Rochester Philharmonic Orchestra.

Politics

County representation in the state assembly began in 1792; at the time, political activity was centered on candidates rather than parties. Emerging social movements in the early 19th century, especially the Antimasonic movement, strengthened the political party system. The "Anti-Nebraska" movement in 1854 was instrumental in the election of Canandaiguan Myron H. Clark (1806–92) as state governor. With the exception of residents of the two cities, voters have been predominantly conservative (Whig/Republican). The county is governed by a Board of Supervisors made up of elected representatives from the 16 towns and the 2 cities. An administrator serves at the discretion of the board. In 2002 the county budget was $129.1 million, with 61¢ of each dollar expended on state-mandated programs and services.

RECENT HISTORY

Agriculture remains at the heart of Ontario Co's economy. The county leads the state in wheat production and leads the nation in sauerkraut cabbage and table beets production. Within the Ontario Co dairying ranks first and vegetables for processing second in total sales. The Geneva Experimental Station continues to aid livestock and crop management. In 1997 the county had 692 farms averaging 269 acres (109 ha), covering 45.7% of the land, the ninth-greatest percentage in the state. Agribusiness is best represented by the grape and wine industry, which links agriculture to the other economic engine, tourism. In 2003 there were approximately 225 manufacturing businesses countywide. Some of the biggest employers were food-processing firms like Seneca Foods (Geneva) and Great Lakes Kraut (Manchester/Shortsville area). Other important employers included Crosman Corp (Bloomfield), G. W. Lisk Co (Clifton Springs), Pactiv (Canandaigua), Xerox Corp (Farmington), and Zotos International (Geneva).

Ontario Co's long ties to tourism and recreation began around the sulfur waters of Clifton Springs, where a hotel was built in 1806 and a large sanatorium in 1850. Its four Finger Lakes drew tourists—and with the advent of the automobile, cottagers—to such places as Cottage City in Gorham. In recent years increasing numbers of cottages have been converted or replaced by all-season homes, and tourism has become increasingly important to the economy. Water sports are available on the four Finger Lakes, golf at eight public and four private courses, thoroughbred racing at the Finger Lakes Racetrack (Farmington), and winter sports at Bristol Mountain Winter Resort (Bristol). The Finger Lakes Performing Arts Center provides cultural offerings in season. In recent years historic tourism has become significant in Canandaigua and Clifton Springs.

Groundbreaking for the western section of the New York State Thruway took place in Victor in 1946, and its first 4 mi (6 km) section opened to the public in 1948. The limited-access highway serves the entire northern tier of the county with exits in the Towns of Phelps, Manchester, Farmington, and Victor, thereby creating prime development conditions for industry, suburban housing, and regional marketing centers. The Eastview Mall (1970) doubled in size by 1995 and draws shoppers from nearby Monroe Co as well as Ontario Co; much of the latter now falls within the expanding ambit of metropolitan Rochester. The county's total population rose over 47% during the past four decades, with the Towns of Victor and Farmington more than tripling in size. In the 1990s, however, towns and villages in the southern part of the county experienced slower population and employment growth. Ontario Co is presently served by the Norfolk Southern Railway, Finger Lakes Railway, and Ontario Central Railroad.

Although it is one of the centennial era histories, W. H. McIntosh, *History of Ontario County* (1876), concentrates heavily on the settlement period. A recent illustrated history is Valerie Knoblauch, *Ontario County: Pictorial Reflections in the Finger Lakes Region* (1989). Geneva has two solid histories: E. Thayer Emmons, *The Story of Geneva* (1931), and G. David Brumberg, *The Making of an Upstate Community* (1976). Lewis F. Fisher, *Victor: The History of a Town* (1996), is exemplary, and Frederick L. Gifford, *The Early History of the Village of Clifton Springs* (1984), is also of high quality. There are a number of specialized works: Kathryn Grover's study of Geneva, *Make a Way Somehow: African-American Life in a Northern Community, 1790–1965* (1994), is remarkably comprehensive; Lynda McCurdy Hotra, *Better Quality: An Illustrated History of the Lisk Manufacturing Co* (1987), discusses one of the county's largest industries; and William H. Siles, "A Vision of Wealth: Speculators and Settlers in the Genesee Country of New York, 1788–1800" (PhD diss, Univ of Massachusetts, 1978) provides analysis of the settlement period.

Marla A. Bennett

Oppenheim. Town (pop 1,774) in SW Fulton Co. Settled by Palatine Germans around 1750, the town was formed from Palatine (Montgomery Co) in 1808. Industries in the 19th century included a large tannery (approximately 1805–35), glove factories, and a turning mill. In the late 19th century it was an important dairy town, with seven cheese factories producing over 500,000 pounds (230,000 kg) of cheese in 1878. Part of the Village of Dolgeville's industrial complex was in Oppenheim. In the late 20th century it became home to a small community of Amish farmers from Ohio and elsewhere. Town native Mahlon Loomis, working in Virginia, demonstrated a primitive form of radiotelegraphy in 1868. The 1,500-acre (610 ha) Florence Jones Reineman Wildlife Sanctuary is the outgrowth of the lifelong work of Dorothy Richards, who began work with beaver habitats locally in 1933.

James Crawford

Oquaga (Onaquaga). Native American settlement [now Windsor and Colesville, Broome Co] extending several miles along the Susquehanna River. By the 1740s the large Oneida village at Oquaga was located near two Tuscarora villages and one of displaced Delawares and Mohicans. Oquaga and nearby Otsiningo [now Binghamton] on the Chenango River helped the Iroquois hold back European settlement in the Susquehanna Valley. From 1748 to 1777 Protestant missionaries intermittently served the Oneida mission, which had a chapel and school; among resident ministers were Revs Gideon Hawley, Ebenezer Mosely, and Aaron Crosby. Sir William Johnson, superintendent of Indian Affairs, was asked by the Oquaga to set up a trading post in 1756. In the same year he ordered a fort to be built to protect local Indian families during the French and Indian War. Joseph Brant, a Mohawk who had a farm at Oquaga, fought for the British in the Revolutionary War, in part because the Americans would not respect the 1768 Treaty of Fort Stanwix boundary line, which passed close to Oquaga. In response to Brant's raids on the frontier using forces gathered at his headquarters at Oquaga, Col William Butler, sent from Schoharie [now in Schoharie Co] in 1778, destroyed the corn, buildings, and the fort. After the war, the Oneida, allies of the Americans in the war, were pressured by New York State to sell their land at Oquaga and surrounding territory, which they did reluctantly in 1785.

Calloway, Colin G. *The American Revolution in Indian Country: Crises and Diversity in Native American Communities* (New York: Cambridge Univ Press, 1995)

Hinman, Marjory Barnum. *Onaquaga: Hub of the Border Wars* ([Windsor, NY: Author], 1975)

Shirley W. Dunn

Orange. Town (pop 1,752) in SW Schuyler Co. Settled by German families from New Jersey in 1802, the town was formed from the old town of Jersey (Steuben Co) in 1836 and became a part of Schuyler Co in 1854. In the 19th century livestock raising was the primary means of subsistence. At Monterey, rakes, shingles, and cheese were manufactured in the late 1870s. During the depression a Civilian Conservation Corps camp was located in town. The minimum security Camp Monterey (1958) became Monterey Shock Correctional Facility (1987). In 2003 about 40% of Orange was public forest, including the Sugar Hill Recreation Area.

Glenda Gephart

Orange and Rockland Utilities. Pearl River (Rockland Co) electric and natural gas utility serving the northwestern suburbs of New York City as well as Sullivan Co and neighboring areas in New Jersey and Pennsylvania. The company was founded in 1859 as the Nyack and Warren Gas Light Co. In 1899 S. R. Bradley established Rockland Light and Power Co by combining a number of local gas and electric companies, including Nyack and Warren. In 1912 Charles H. Tenney Co of Boston purchased Rockland Light and Power and in 1926 merged it with newly acquired Orange County Public Services. In 1958 Rockland Power and Light was merged with Orange and Rockland Electric Co, becoming Orange and Rockland Utilities (O&R). During the 1960s O&R embarked on an expansion program, building new generating plants and accessing power from other systems.

In 1993 scandal rocked O&R when four high-ranking executives, including the company chairman, were charged with making illegal campaign contributions, spending utility funds on personal expenses, and improperly offering gifts to New York State and New Jersey public officials, with such misappropriations totaling $3.4 million. In 1998 O&R agreed to an acquisition by the Manhattan-headquartered public utility holding company Consolidated Edison (Con Edison) for $1.5 billion in cash and assumed debt. To resolve US Department of Justice antitrust concerns raised by the merger, O&R agreed to sell all of its electrical generating plants. Although an entirely owned subsidiary of Con Edison from 1999, O&R continued to operate as a separate entity in 2003. Along with its own two subsidiaries, Rockland Electric Co and Pike Co Light and Power, it employed 1,011 people and supplied power to 280,000 electric and 124,000 natural gas customers.

Management and Operations Review of the Orange and Rockland Utilities, Inc: Final Report ([Staten Island]: Doherty Hogan, 1989)

New York State. Assembly. *Joint Public Hearing: Orange and Rockland's Electric Restructuring Plan* (Brooklyn: EN-DE Reporting Services, 1997)

Jeffrey Kraus

Orange County (816 mi²/2,113 km²; pop 341,367). Created in 1683 as 1 of the 10 original counties of the colony and named for Mary Stuart of England, and her husband William III, Prince of Orange. Boundary adjustments were subsequently made with Ulster Co (1701, 1709, 1798) and Rockland Co (1798, 1800). Orange Co is subdivided into 3 cities and 20 towns that contain 18 incorporated villages. Goshen serves as the county seat. Elevation ranges from sea level along the Hudson River shore to 1,664 feet (507 m) at Schunnemunk Mountain's summit in the Town of Blooming Grove. The county lies within three physiographic provinces trending northeast-southwest. The Hudson Highlands, including the Ramapo Mountains, occupy the eastern quarter and are a subregion of the New England Upland province. Local relief here can be as much as 1,000 feet (305 m). Bedrock consists of metamorphic gneiss and quartzite rocks extensively faulted and folded. The Wallkill Valley subregion of the Hudson-Mohawk Lowland stretches across the broad central part of the county and is composed largely of Ordovician shale. Exceptions in the north and south include small areas of Cambrian and early Ordovician limestone, dolostone, slate, and schist. The rolling topography exhibits relief, seldom greater than 150 feet (45 m). The Shawangunk Mountains subregion of the Appalachian Upland physiographic region forms the valley's west wall and transects the western part of the county. Composed of Silurian limestone, sandstone, and conglomerate, the "Gunks," many near vertical rock faces, attract technical climbers from across the Northeast. The Delaware Hills occupy the westernmost portion of the county and consist of Devonian shales and sandstones. Aside from the west wall of the Shawangunks, which rise dramatically about 800 feet (240 m) from the Neversink Valley, maximum local relief of 500 feet (150 m) is typical in the west. Orange Co was completely but moderately glaciated, as reflected by a smoothed ground surface and till deposits that cover over 85% of the land, along with outwash and lake deposits.

Primary drainage is oriented in a northeast-southwest direction. The Neversink River drains lands west of the Shawangunk divide into the Delaware River at Port Jervis. The principal drainage ways in the Hudson Hills, Woodbury and Moodna Creeks, empty into the Hudson River below Newburgh. The county's central valley is drained primarily by the Wallkill River, which flows northeast into Ulster Co, before emptying into the Hudson River. Greenwood Lake and surrounding country drain south into New Jersey. Extensive portions of the Wallkill Valley contain very productive agricultural soils, including substantial pockets of muckland. Much of the area around Pine Island was under water until the 19th century, when immigrant farmers drained the Drowned Lands and converted them to valuable farmland. Soils elsewhere have little agricultural potential.

Orange Co's climate is humid-continental. Mean January temperatures range from 24°F (-4°C) in the west to 27°F (-3°C) in the south near the intersection of the Rockland Co and New Jersey borders. The coldest temperature ever recorded was -11°F (-24°C) at West Point in 1963. Mean July temperatures range from the low 70s°F (21°C) west of the Shawangunks to 74°F (23°C) at West Point. Daytime highs can exceed 90°F (32°C) from May through September. Average annual precipitation amounts range from 44 inches (112 cm) at Middletown to 51 inches (130 cm) at West Point. Seasonal snowfall amounts vary from 31 inches (79 cm) at West Point to over 60 inches (152 cm) in the Shawangunks. Primeval forest was dominated by central hardwoods, made up of beech, sugar maple, basswood, oak, and chestnut, along with small areas of swamp forest of black ash, silver maple, and sycamore in the south and west.

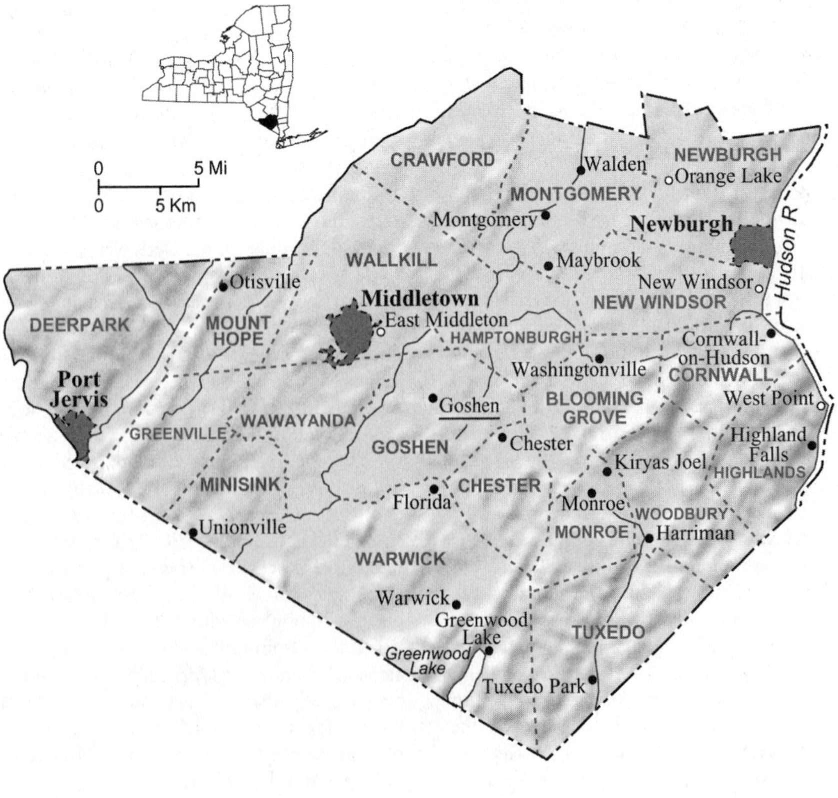

Settlement

Henry Hudson anchored off of Orange Co in September of 1609. At the time the area was inhabited by the Minisink Indians. Native American populations in the region declined in the 17th and 18th centuries as they migrated west or died from disease. Interaction between Native Americans and later settlers, therefore, was relatively rare. The first European settlement within the present limits of the county occurred in 1685, when a Scot named Patrick MacGregorie built a cabin at Plum Point [now New Windsor]. In the western part of the county, William Tietsoort settled in 1690 near present-day Port Jervis. A large award of land known as the Evans Patent, covering an area from New Paltz (Ulster Co) south to New Windsor, was granted in 1694 but revoked in 1699 and divided into smaller parcels of land that were granted at various times through 1775. The Wawayanda Patent (1703) covered much of the southern part of early Orange Co, and the Minisink Patent (1704) granted land in the west. Important groups of settlers included Palatine Germans in Newburgh and Montgomery and Huguenots in the Minisink region near Port Jervis, but English and Scottish settlers dominated. African Americans were early settlers, primarily as slaves. In 1800 there were 1,145 enslaved persons and 534 free Blacks, accounting for about 10% of all residents. The percentage of African Americans dropped to just over 3% by 1860, a level that held through the first half of the 20th century.

Revolutionary War

Orange Co played a crucial role in the Revolution, and most residents of the area supported independence. Both patriot and British generals realized that the Hudson River was a vital transportation corridor for troops and supplies. Because of the need to control the Hudson, several fortifications were built. Most notable were Forts Montgomery and Clinton [the latter now in Rockland Co], built on either side of Popolopen Creek near Bear Mountain, and fortifications at West Point. Forts Montgomery and Clinton, under the command of Little Britain natives James and George Clinton, were attacked and taken by the British in October 1777. This defeat prompted George Washington to strengthen Hudson defenses at West Point in 1778. Fort Constitution on Constitution Island [now in Putnam Co] was protected by Forts Arnold and Putnam across the river at West Point, and the "Great Chain," made from Orange Co iron, was floated across the Hudson to hamper British ships. George Washington spent considerable time in the region between 1780 and 1783 and ordered the end of hostilities from his Newburgh headquarters in April 1783. In 1788 Orange Co delegates voted against ratifying a federal constitution but supported the vote when it was ratified.

ORANGE CO POPULATION CENSUS FIGURES

	White	Nonwhite	Total Population	Foreign-Born
1790	17,325	1,167	18,492	—
1800	27,676	1,679	29,355	—
1810	32,454	1,893	34,347	—
1820	39,119	2,094	41,213	175
1830	43,143	2,223	45,366	1,153
1840	48,447	2,292	50,739	—
1850	54,681	2,464	57,145	7,715
1860	61,700	2,112	63,812	9,753
1870	78,370	2,532	80,902	14,259
1880	85,420	2,800	88,220	12,422
1890	95,286	2,573	97,859	15,231
1900	101,018	2,841	103,859	14,723
1910	112,862	3,139	116,001	19,222
1920	117,257	2,587	119,844	16,460
1930	127,196	3,187	130,383	16,832
1940	135,971	4,142	140,113	16,306
1950	146,950	5,305	152,255	15,351
1960	173,786	9,948	183,734	13,886
1970	206,351	15,306	221,657	13,575
1980	237,359	22,244	259,603	16,309
1990	273,276	34,371	307,647	22,073
2000	285,721	55,646	341,367	28,710

Notes: "Nonwhite" includes African Americans, Asians, American Indians, and Pacific Islanders and, for 2000, also the mixed race and other race categories. Through the 1960 census these figures primarily reflect the African American population. Foreign-born figures for 1820 and 1830 include only those not naturalized, and for 1930 and 1950, the foreign-born totals include Whites only. Other years include all foreign-born in the population.

Transportation

The dramatic topography of the Hudson Highlands made overland travel difficult along the eastern edge of the county and prompted the development of roads, and later railroads, that bypassed the highlands for the interior. The Old Mine Rd, built before 1664, crossed the western portion of the county and carried copper ore from New Jersey to Esopus [now Kingston, Ulster Co]. Another pre-Revolutionary road was the King's Highway, which ran from New Jersey to Albany passing through Orange Co by way of Harriman. It had two spurs, one through Newburgh to Montgomery, the other through Chester and Goshen to Montgomery. For-profit roads were built in the 19th century. One of the earliest, the Newburgh-Cochecton Turnpike, was begun in 1801 to connect the Hudson at Newburgh with Cochecton (Sullivan Co). At about the same time, the Orange Turnpike was built to connect Suffern (Rockland Co) with Goshen.

The most important early role of transportation was to move agricultural products from the interior to the Hudson River to New York City. River traffic before the early 1800s was dominated by sailing vessels known as sloops, which were largely replaced by steam-powered boats by the mid–19th century. In the 18th and early 19th centuries New Windsor and later Newburgh were important outlets for wheat from the interior, but by the mid–19th century wheat was replaced by dairy products. The opening in 1841 of the Erie Railroad connected Piermont (Rockland Co) on the Hudson with Goshen; it later extended to Lake Erie. A branch (1849) of this rail line also ran to Newburgh. Other major railroads included the New York, Ontario, and Western, with a terminus at Middletown, and the Lehigh and Hudson River, which had large rail yards in Warwick and Maybrook. The completion in 1883 of the West Shore Railroad along the banks of the Hudson allowed goods and people to get to New York City quickly all year long. In addition, it placed Orange Co at the junction of east-west and north-south lines. Other vital transportation infrastructure included the Delaware and Hudson Canal (1828–99), which passed through Port Jervis with barges carrying coal from Pennsylvania to Rondout (Ulster Co). The county has one major airport, Stewart International (formerly Stewart Airfield and Stewart Air Force Base).

The Storm King Highway (1916–22) was an engineering marvel and attracted pleasure drivers. Rte 17 (I-86), the main road to the Sullivan Co Catskills, drew increasing traffic and was expanded to four lanes in 1951–54, in time to connect with the New York State Thruway (1954) at Harriman. I-84, crossing the northern part of the county and intersecting with Rte 17 (I-86) near Middletown, was constructed between 1964 and 1972.

Economic Development

About 90% of the county's population engaged in farming in the years following the Revolution. Wheat production dominated until, by the mid–19th century, disease and insects rendered it unprofitable. Dairy farming replaced wheat production, and better railroad and steamboat transportation carried butter and milk to the exploding population in New York City. Goshen butter became world famous during this time.

Early industry centered on iron production, and numerous small forges and furnaces dotted the landscape of the highlands. The Forest of Dean mine in Fort Montgomery is estimated to have yielded over 2 million tons (1.8 million MT) of ore between 1746 and 1934. The need for charcoal to fire furnaces for the smelting process resulted in widespread deforestation until coal replaced charcoal around the time of the Civil War. Iron furnaces generally closed down by the last decades of the 19th century, and the mining of ore ended by the 1930s. There was also extensive mining of bluestone in and around Deerpark for use in paving the sidewalks of New York City. Other early industry was generally focused on sites with waterpower, such as Cornwall, Walden, and Craigville. Overall, the types of industries were quite diverse; products included textiles, carpets, glass, and knives, and their production was concentrated in the larger industrial communities, especially Middletown, Port Jervis, Newburgh, and Walden. Much of Orange Co's manufacturing slowly declined in the 20th century as the railroads died and cheaper labor sources were sought elsewhere in the United States. In the early 21st century businesses manufacture plastic and rubber goods, chemicals, fabricated metal products, and electrical components. A drive along I-84 from Newburgh to Middletown reveals several large warehouse and transshipment facilities for trucking companies. Significant employment is provided by two prisons in Mount Hope and one in Wawayanda.

The resort business began in earnest just after the Civil War, especially at Cornwall-on-Hudson and Highland Falls. Lake resorts at Orange and Greenwood Lakes followed by the 1880s, as did elite colonies at Tuxedo Park and Warwick. Tourism remains important to Orange Co, and the Woodbury Common Premium Outlets center (1985) attracts 11 million visitors annually. West Point is one of the state's primary attractions.

Religion, Education, and Culture

Dutch, English, and German settlers brought Protestant denominations. Later immigrants in the 19th and early 20th centuries brought Catholicism, and more recent immigrants have brought Islam and other religions. The census of 1860 showed Methodists and Presbyterians dominating with 35 churches each. Baptist, Episcopalian, Dutch Reformed, Catholic, Quaker, and Congregationalist denominations each had 10 or fewer churches. The Jewish presence in the area dates back to the early 18th century: the Gomez Mill House north of Newburgh, built in 1714 by Spanish merchant Luis Moses Gomez, is the oldest surviving Jewish residence in North America. Today Jewish populations remain important. Kiryas Joel, a Hasidic village settled in 1974 and incorporated three years later, was the fastest-growing community in the county during the 1990s. The village's attempt to support Hasidic schools with federal funds caused over a decade of legal battles in local, state, and federal courts.

The first newspaper in the county was the *Goshen Repository* (1788), followed by the *Newburgh Packet* (1795) and *New Windsor Gazette* (1797). The oldest continuously published newspaper is the *Goshen Independent Republican*

POPULATIONS OF TOWNS AND CITIES, ORANGE CO

Town or City, Year Founded	1800	1840	1880	1920	1960	2000
Blooming Grove, 1799	1,611	2,396	2,444	1,881	3,777	17,351
Chester, 1845	—	—	2,229	1,803	3,494	12,140
Cornwall, 1764[a]	1,648	3,925	3,833	4,259	8,094	12,307
Crawford, 1823	—	2,075	1,951	1,507	2,574	7,875
Deerpark, 1743[b]	955	1,607	11,420	1,615	2,777	7,858
Goshen, 1714[c]	2,563	3,889	4,387	5,016	6,835	12,913
Greenville, 1853	—	—	1,002	618	890	3,800
Hamptonburgh, 1830	—	1,379	1,143	1,104	1,695	4,686
Highlands, 1873	—	—	3,404	6,136	11,990	12,484
Middletown (city), 1888	—	—	—	18,420	23,475	25,388
Minisink, 1788	3,584	5,093	1,360	1,252	1,433	3,585
Monroe, 1799[d]	2,116	3,914	5,096	2,630	5,965	31,407
Montgomery, 1772[e]	4,206	4,100	4,795	8,351	11,672	20,891
Mount Hope, 1825[f]	—	1,565	1,549	1,708	2,291	6,639
Newburgh, 1762[g]	3,258	8,933	3,918	4,034	15,547	27,568
Newburgh (city), 1865	—	—	18,049	30,366	30,979	28,259
New Windsor, 1762[g]	2,001	2,482	2,576	2,984	11,908	22,866
Port Jervis (city), 1907	—	—	—	10,171	9,268	8,860
Tuxedo, 1889	—	—	—	2,355	2,227	3,334
Wallkill, 1743[g]	3,592	4,268	11,486	2,598	8,176	24,659
Warwick, 1788	3,834	5,113	5,699	7,462	12,551	30,764
Wawayanda, 1849	—	—	1,879	1,689	3,229	6,273
Woodbury, 1889	—	—	—	1,885	2,887	9,460

[a]Formed as precinct; recognized as Town of New Cornwall 1788; renamed 1797.

[b]Formed as Mamakating Precinct; recognized as town 1788 within Sullivan Co; Deer Park, comprising original precinct territory, taken off and made a town 1798.

[c]Formed as precinct at uncertain date; first reference 1722; recognized as town 1788.

[d]Cheesecocks until 1801, then Southfield until 1808.

[e]Formed as Hanover Precinct; recognized as Town of Montgomery 1788.

[f]Calhoun until 1833.

[g]Formed as precinct; recognized as town 1788.

(1813). In the early 21st century the largest newspaper in the region is the daily *Middletown Times Herald-Record.*

Schools have operated in Orange Co at least since 1745, when a Lutheran church in Newburgh began a basic education program. The first secondary school was probably Moffat's Academy (1778) in New Windsor, and the first college was the US Military Academy (1802) at West Point. Other institutions of higher education are Orange County Community College (1950) and Mount Saint Mary's College (1960).

Authors and artists have long been attracted to the beauty of Orange Co. Noah Webster, author of America's first dictionary, taught in Goshen at the end of the Revolutionary War. The chair of the Department of Drawing at the US Military Academy, Robert Weir (1803–89), was a nationally known artist who painted works for the rotunda of the US Capitol in Washington, DC. Famed etiquette expert Emily Post (1872–1960) summered in Tuxedo Park in the late 19th and early 20th centuries. Newburgh landscape architect Andrew Jackson Downing (1815–52) popularized Gothic Revival and Italianate styles of American house design with fellow architect Alexander Jackson Davis (1803–92). Filmmaking pioneer D. W. Griffith (1872–1948) used Cuddebackville as the backdrop for many of his early features from 1906 to 1915.

Politics

After its creation in 1683, Orange Co was under the care of the provincial government because its population was not deemed large enough to warrant its own. A county government was finally established by 1703. Administrative functions, such as court sessions, were originally split between Goshen and Orangetown [now Tappan, Rockland Co]. A courthouse was built at Goshen by 1737. A prominent colonial politician was Montgomery resident, anthropologist, and botanist Cadwallader Colden (1689–1776), who became New York's lieutenant governor in 1760 and later served as acting governor on five separate occasions. Orange Co resident George Clinton (1739–1812) and his nephew De Witt Clinton (1769–1828), born in Little Britain, were both long-term governors of New York State. Later governors with county connections include Benjamin B. Odell Jr from Newburgh and W. Averell Harriman from Arden.

Recent History

Orange Co changed significantly after World War II. A decline in farming from over 400,000 acres (162,000 ha) in cultivation at the beginning of the 20th century to just 95,000 acres (38,500 ha) in 1997 highlights one significant change. Dairying continues on a small number of consolidated farms in the western and northwestern towns, while vegetable farming remains a highly profitable endeavor in the Black Dirt region in Warwick, Chester, Goshen, and Minisink.

With the completion of the Thruway in 1955, Orange Co began its transformation into a suburb for New York City and Westchester Co workers. The population has more than doubled since 1950, with a 60% increase since 1970. Between 1990 and 2000 the population rose by 11%, twice the state average and the third-highest percentage in the state. Towns along Rte 17 (I-86) from Monroe to Middletown have seen much new residential housing construction for commuters. From 1960 to 2000 the African American population increased from 5,266 to 27,601, accounting for over 8% of the population, and is more widely dispersed than previously. In 2000 the Asian population stood at 5,157. Those of Latino ethnicity numbered 39,738. There have been attempts at urban renewal, but many historic but dilapidated buildings in Newburgh were torn down for green space and low-income housing. Many manufacturing jobs were lost during the economic downturn of the 1970s. Orange Co became the focus of one of the most important legal cases of the modern environmental movement after Consolidated Edison proposed building a hydroelectric facility on Storm King Mountain near Cornwall-on-Hudson. After nearly two decades of legal battles, the project was abandoned in 1981. Economic prosperity in the 1990s brought jobs back to the region, and the county's proximity to New York City and its location at the junction of major transportation routes should ensure a lasting importance in the state.

Major attractions, aside from the US Military Academy, include Goshen's Historic Track and the Trotting Horse Museum, Cornwall-on-Hudson's Museum of the Hudson Highlands and Storm King Art Center, Monroe's Museum Village, and Tuxedo's Arden House conference center.

The first countywide history was Samuel W. Eager, *An Outline History of Orange County* (1846–47). Standard references are E. M. Ruttenber and L. H. Clark, *History of Orange County* (1881) and Russel Headley, *History of Orange County* (1908). Early community histories include Charles E. Stickney, *History of the Minisink Region* (1867), John J. Nutt, *Newburgh* (1891), Daniel N. Freeland, *Chronicles of Monroe in the Olden Time* (1898), E. M. Ruttenber, *History of the Town of New Windsor* (1911), and Franklin B. Williams, *Middletown: A Biography* (1928). Several midcentury books are useful, including S. J. Levy, *Chester, NY: A History* (1947) and Elizabeth Sharts, *Land o' Goshen* (1960). More recent works are Richard W. Hull, *People of the Valleys* (1975), Doris E. Cole, *History of Minisink Township* (1976), Doris Crofut, *A Brief History of the Town of Tuxedo* (1982), Janet Dempsey, *Cornwall, NY* (1994), Elaine Flynn, *Wawayanda Our Town* (1999), and Florida Historical Society, *Florida, NY* (2002).

Jon C. Malinowski

Orange Lake. Locality (pop 6,085) in Newburgh (Orange Co). The lake itself is 400 acres (162 ha) and spring fed. Thomas Machin, designer of the chain across the Hudson during the American Revolution, operated a mint in the area that produced copper coins for the Republic of Vermont from 1787 to 1789. After the Civil War the community of Orange Lake became a resort with two racetracks, two hotels, a casino, and boardinghouses. In 1885 the Newburgh YMCA began operating one of the earliest American summer camps at Orange Lake; it is now Camp Dudley at Westport (Essex Co). Orange Lake Park (?1895–1929) was a popular trolley-company amusement park. In the late 20th century summer cottages around the lake were replaced by year-round homes. Orange Lake is noted for iceboating and as a training location for rowing crews.

Orangetown. Town (pop 47,711) in SE Rockland Co. Settled in the late 17th century, it was formed as a precinct in 1686 and organized as a town in 1788. It was chiefly agricultural, and its farms were served by four railroads built between 1841 and 1883. Through the 20th century heavy industry at Piermont and Pearl River provided employment, as did Orangeburg Fiber Conduit Co (1893–1972). In 1942–43 Camp Shanks, an army training camp, was constructed on 2,040 acres (826 ha) and used as a dispatching post; it also housed members of the Women's Army Corps and was a processing center for prisoners of war. In 1946 Camp Shanks was transformed into Shanks Village, providing housing for veterans, especially students at Columbia University. The New York State Thruway and Tappan Zee Bridge (both 1955) and the Palisades Interstate Parkway (1958) improved commuter access to Orangetown and encouraged subdivision. In 1956 housing developments replaced Shanks Village. The town is the site of Rockland Psychiatric Center (1931) at Orangeburg, Columbia University's Lamont-Doherty Earth Observatory (1948) at Palisades, and St. Thomas Aquinas College (1952) at Sparkill. A short section of the Palisades extends into the town's southeast corner in Tallman Mountain State Park.

Mary R. Cardenas

Orangeville. Town (pop 1,301) in central Wyoming Co. Settled in 1804, the town was formed from Attica in 1816. A tannery (1814) went through a large expansion in 1848. Dairying began in earnest in 1823 when a farmer began milking 20 cows and producing both butter and cheese; others soon followed. The first cheese factory was built in 1864. A map roller factory operated at Johnsonburg in the late 19th century. In the early 21st century, dairy farming remains important, and a majority of the town's nonfarm workers commute to Attica or beyond. Mary Hosford Fisher of Orangeville became the first woman to receive a degree under equal terms with men when she graduated from Oberlin College in 1841.

Orchard Park. Town (pop 27,637) and village (pop 3,294) in central Erie Co. Settled in 1803, the town was formed in 1850 from Hamburg as Ellicott; the name was changed in 1852 to East Hamburg. The Village of Orchard Park was incorporated in 1921, and in 1934 the town adopted the same name. Quakers from New England had formed a meeting by 1807 and, according to tradition, made the town an important stop on the Underground Railroad. The State Line Railroad (1872; later Buffalo, Rochester and Pittsburgh Railway) facilitated transport of products to Buffalo, but it was the electric railroad (1900–32) that initiated suburbanization. The town's population nearly doubled in the 1950s as it became a wealthy suburb of Buffalo. In 1968 Orchard Park acquired a four-lane highway connection to the Thruway and Buffalo when US 219 was rebuilt. Orchard Park is home to Erie Community College's South Campus, Ralph Wilson Stadium (1973), the Buffalo Bills, and the Burgwardt Bicycle Museum.

Andrew C. Maines

ordnance. See GUNS AND ORDNANCE INDUSTRY.

O'Reilly, Leonora (*b* New York City, 16 Feb 1870; *d* New York City, 3 Apr 1927). Labor activist and suffragist. O'Reilly's parents were politically active Irish immigrants. Her father died in 1871, and her mother worked in a garment factory to support the family. At age 11 O'Reilly went to work in a Brooklyn collar factory. She joined the Knights of Labor at 16 and was a founding member of the Working Women's Society. Its goal was to improve working women's lives through legislation and public awareness of their plight. In 1897 she organized the women shirtwaist workers to join with the United Garment Workers. A rank-and-file founder of the New York Women's Trade Union League (NYWTUL) in 1903, she inspired workers and allies to help women unionize. She was a compelling speaker concerning union, suffrage, or specific legislation. In 1909 with financial help from NYWTUL president Mary Dreier, she left work to devote herself to the NYWTUL, supporting the 1909 "Uprising of 20,000" by shirtwaist workers, organizing protests after the Triangle Shirtwaist Factory fire of 1911, and supporting Irish independence and women's suffrage. She served as president of the New York City Wage Earner's Suffrage League in 1911. By 1914 poor health and her mother's needs limited her activities.

Dye, Nancy Schrom. *As Equals and As Sisters: Feminism, the Labor Movement, and the Women's Trade Union League of New York* (Columbia: Univ of Missouri Press, 1980)

Connie Kopelov

organized crime. The proliferation of early criminal enterprises in the 1800s was linked to vice operators, the purveyors of gambling, prostitution, and liquor. Immigrant street gangs and the development of urban political machines and corrupt police forces provided additional ingredients for the growth of organized crime syndicates. One early gambling entrepreneur was Capt Isaiah Rynders, who gained power over the Five Points street gangs in Lower Manhattan in the 1830s and 1840s, which he used to control the elections and politics of the city's Sixth Ward. The street gangs of the era, such as the Dead Rabbits, Bowery B'hoys, and the Plug Uglies, have enjoyed a romanticized afterlife in the history of New York City, as in Martin Scorcese's 2002 film, *Gangs of New York.* At midcentury prizefighter and gambler John Morrissey helped establish Saratoga Springs as an elite gambling resort, becoming a Tammany leader, New York State senator, and US congressman. Another with close ties to illegal gambling was Big Tim Sullivan, a Tammany leader in Lower Manhattan at the turn of the 20th century. Two of the largest organized gangs at the turn of the century were the primarily Italian Five Pointers led by Paul Kelly and the largely Jewish gang commanded by Monk Eastman.

Prohibition greatly strengthened organized crime in New York State. Criminal syndicates provided protection to bootleggers and dispensed payments to local officials. For instance, in Elmira, Irving Wexler ("Waxy" Gordon) operated an illegal distillery that included one large still just three blocks from police headquarters. Stefano Magaddino and his brother Antonio became the most powerful criminals in western New York State, especially Buffalo and Rochester, by smuggling Canadian whiskey across the US-Canadian border. Arnold Rothstein, who had made a fortune in illegal gambling enterprises, began bankrolling bootleggers at the beginning of Prohibition. Italian Johnny Torrio is credited with centralizing the East Coast liquor trade in the late 1920s and early 1930s. Prohibition transformed the Italian mob from its insular and largely parochial roots under leaders like Giuseppe "Joe the Boss" Masseria and Salvatore Maranzano. These men were murdered in 1931 in the so-called Castellammarese War, allegedly engineered by Charles "Lucky" Luciano, a figure who is credited with Americanizing the mob, a process characterized by Italian-Jewish joint ventures and a measure of regional and intracity cooperation. This process led to the emergence of the five Cosa Nostra "families" of New York City, known by the surnames of their leaders: Gambino, Profaci, Lucchese, Bonnano, and Genovese.

Mid–20th Century

Periodic reform movements and the successes of special prosecutors made careers and altered the constitution of municipal and state politics. In New York City, Mayor Jimmy Walker resigned in 1932, his political career ruined as a result of the state's Seabury Investigations (1930–32), which uncovered widespread corruption, bribe taking, and strong links between city officials and organized crime under his administration. Appointed by Gov Herbert H. Lehman in 1935 as a special state prosecutor, Thomas E. Dewey successfully convicted a number of well-known gangsters, including Lucky Luciano in 1936. Another successful prosecutor was Brooklyn District Attorney William O'Dwyer, who was credited with breaking up the Murder Inc ring of extortionists led by Albert Anastasia and Louis "Lepke" Buchalter. In 1951 Gov Dewey established the New York State Crime Commission to investigate the relationship between organized crime and governmental units in the state. The work of the commission led to the creation in 1958 of the Temporary Commission of Investigation.

Propelled by the televised Kefauver Committee hearings in 1951 in the US Congress, organized crime became increasingly viewed as synonymous with a secret underworld organization called the Mafia. The meeting of organized criminals, including perhaps 30 from New York State, in Apalachin (Tioga Co) on 14 Nov 1957 at the home of Joseph M. Barbara, a member of the Magaddino crime family of Buffalo, fueled the idea that the Mafia was well organized and national in scope. Buffalo crime lord Stefano Magaddino is believed to have arranged the conference.

The Modern Era

Legislative initiatives such as the federal Racketeer Influenced and Corrupt Organizations (RICO) statute (1970) have targeted criminal enterprises with great success, particularly in the 1980s and 1990s. RICO allowed prosecutors to try groups of mobsters in a single prosecution while providing for hefty civil as well as criminal penalties. Law enforcement successes include the 1987 conviction of 18 mobsters involved in the "Pizza Connection" case, in which a network of American Cosa Nostra and Sicilian Mafia gangs used pizza shops from New York City to the Midwest as fronts for a $1.6 billion heroin and money-laundering enterprise. Rudolph Giuliani, US attorney for the Southern District of New York from 1983 to 1989, secured the conviction of crime boss Carmine Persico and eight other members of the Colombo crime family for racketeering in the New York City construction industry. In the 1990s Manhattan district attorney Robert Morganthau engineered important prosecutions against racketeers at the Javits Center and in the garment and waste-hauling industries. Gangsters convicted of crimes in the 1990s included Gambino crime boss John Gotti Sr in 1992, Genovese boss Vincent "the Chin" Gigante in 1997, and John Gotti Jr in 1999. While local, state, and federal law enforcement efforts have had a significant impact on New York City's Cosa Nostra families, all five groups remained intact as of 2002. The Gambino crime family is the largest Mafia group in the country, with approximately 20 capos, 300 members, and 3,000 associates, and is thought to gross some $300 million a year from various illicit activities. The Genovese family has perhaps 200 members and 1,300 associates. The Lucchese family is the third-largest Cosa Nostra group in New York City with near 125 members and 500 associates. Internecine gang warfare decimated the Bonnano crime family in the 1980s. The Colombo family was substantially weakened by a civil war in the early 1990s.

Organized crime in New York State in the 21st century is characterized by expansion into new criminal realms, increasing sophistication in methods and activities, and a growing transnational dimension to enterprises. In addition to some of the old rackets such as extortion in industries like construction and waste hauling, contemporary organized criminals involve themselves in stock frauds, cigarette smuggling, fuel tax rip-offs, and identity theft on the Internet. In recent decades Russian and Asian organized crime groups have become prominent. These are centered primarily in the New York City area, but associated drug and money-laundering activities by nontraditional organized crime networks permeate the state. Russian organized criminals have been linked to criminal counterparts in Buffalo who are involved in the transnational sex trade. High-tech surveillance equipment, state-of-the-art communications, and encryption technologies are in common use.

See also RUSSIANS; URBAN GANGS.

Block, Alan A. *East Side–West Side: Organizing Crime in New York, 1930–1950* (New Brunswick, NJ: Transaction Books, 1983)
Jacobs, James B., Christopher Panarella, and Jay Worthington. *Busting the Mob: US vs. Cosa Nostra* (New York: New York Univ Press, 1994)
Nelli, Humbert. *The Business of Crime: Italians and Syndicate Crime in the United States* (New York: Oxford Univ Press, 1976)
Potter, Gary W., and Michael D. Lyman. *Organized Crime*, 2d ed. (Upper Saddle River, NJ: Prentice-Hall, 2000)

Don Liddick

Organized Crime Task Force. Division of the New York State Department of Law established by the state legislature in 1970. The Organized Crime Task Force (OCTF) was created with the support of Gov Nelson A. Rockefeller against the backdrop of increased federal responses to the organized crime problem and the establishment of federal strike forces in cities across the country, including Buffalo and New York City. The OCTF specializes in the investigation and prosecution of multicounty, multistate, and multinational organized crime activities. The head of the OCTF is a deputy attorney general appointed jointly by the governor and the attorney general. The task force has engaged primarily in long-term investigations of narcotics trafficking, gambling, money laundering, grand larceny, official corruption, and fraud. The OCTF was reorganized in 1981 with headquarters in White Plains (Westchester Co) and field offices in Buffalo and Albany, and it became a hybrid investigative and prosecutorial agency. During its most active period in the late 1980s and early 1990s the task force employed about 20 attorneys and 50 investigators, analysts, accountants, and other professional staff. Under Director Ronald Goldstock (1981–94), OCTF personnel were responsible for the hidden microphones in automobiles that allowed agents to listen in on incriminating conversations of Lucchese family crime boss Tony "Ducks" Corallo in 1983. The surveillance resulted in an indictment of 21 individuals, including Corallo, and 16 waste-hauling firms on charges of conspiring to rig bids on commercial carting contracts and to dominate private garbage collection on Long Island. OCTF personnel were also instrumental in the surveillance of John Gotti Sr's social club in Manhattan and Gotti's 1992 conviction in federal court of racketeering conspiracy. In 2002 the OCTF consisted of 55 attorneys and investigators.

Jacobs, James B., Coleen Friel, and Robert Radick. *Gotham Unbound: How New York City Was Liberated from the Grip of Organized Crime* (New York: New York Univ Press, 1999)

Don Liddick

Oriskany. Village (pop 1,459) in Whitestown (Oneida Co). Settled in 1802 the area grew with the opening of the Oriskany Manufacturing Co in 1811, a woolen mill that operated until ?1856. Other early factories processed tobacco and malleable iron. The Erie Canal passed through Oriskany, which was visited by the Marquis de Lafayette in 1825. The village incorporated in 1914. Summit Park (1897–1926) was a trolley-owned amusement park. The Waterbury Mill has been manufacturing papermakers' felt in Oriskany since 1869. Steel Treaters was another employer in 2002.

Oriskany, Battle of. One of the fiercest engagements of the Revolutionary War in which loyalists and Indians ambushed New York militia. On 3 Aug 1777 British brigadier general Barry St. Leger laid siege to Fort Stanwix, which the Americans had renamed Fort Schuyler [now Rome, Oneida Co], at the head of the Mohawk Valley. His forces consisted of over 1,100 British regulars, Hessian troops, Canadian militia, and New York loyalists, led by Sir John Johnson and Col John Butler. Approximately 1,000 Indians, led by the Mohawk leader Joseph Brant, were also present. After capturing Fort Schuyler, St. Leger intended to take his forces to Albany to meet Gen John Burgoyne's army, advancing south from Canada. Almost 30 miles (48 km) to the east, Gen Nicholas Herkimer and 800 men of the Tryon Co Militia assembled at Fort Dayton [now Herkimer] to relieve Fort Schuyler. Leaving on 4 August, the column was joined by 60 Oneidas and encamped 8 miles (13 km) from their destination the night of 5 August.

St. Leger learned of the militia advance from Brant's sister Molly, then living at Canajoharie [now in Montgomery Co]. He dispatched approximately 500 loyalists and Indians to ambush them at a heavily wooded and swampy ravine, about 5 miles (8 km) east of the fort, near Oriskany Creek. Early on 6 August Herkimer sent a message to the fort, asking the garrison to fire three cannons on receipt of the message as a signal for the militia to make its final approach. After a long delay, Herkimer suggested that his men still wait for the signal but was goaded into advancing when his officers questioned his resolve. By mid-morning, the Americans descended into the ravine. When the ambush erupted, Herkimer turned to investigate and was shot, a musket ball shattering his left leg. Confusion reigned as the militia took heavy fire from all directions. They soon recovered, however, and fought back with Herkimer directing the fight while smoking his pipe, propped up against a tree. The general directed his men to fight in pairs so that one could provide cover while the other reloaded. After about an hour of heavy combat, much of it hand to hand, the Americans took advantage of a pause in the fighting caused by a downpour to regroup into a rough circle.

When the rain subsided, men in a loyalist detachment reversed their green jackets to confuse the militia and approached their line as if a relief column from the fort. Herkimer's men discovered the ruse at the last moment and poured a deadly volley into them as the violent fighting renewed. Brant's Indians drifted away, having suffered heavily and hearing that a sortie from the fort had looted their camps. This action from the fort was the long-delayed diversion that Herkimer had been waiting for, but it began too late to help the militia. Herkimer's column retreated, with some 500 killed, wounded, or missing. The loyalists and Indians suffered about 150 casualties. Herkimer died at his home on 17 August. St. Leger was deserted by his Indian allies and unable to force a surrender from Col Peter Gansevoort, the commander of Fort Schuyler, retreated on 23 August, fearing that Continental army reinforcements were on their way up the Mohawk Valley. The battlefield was declared a New York State Historic Site in 1927.

Watt, Gavin K. *Rebellion in the Mohawk Valley: The St. Leger Expedition of 1777* (Tonawanda, NY: Dundurn Press, 2002)
Wood, W. J. *Battles of the Revolutionary War, 1775–1781* (Chapel Hill, NC: Algonquin Books of Chapel Hill, 1990)

Michael P. Gabriel

Oriskany Falls. Village (pop 698) in Augusta (Oneida Co). Its waterpower attracted industry, including a tannery (1816), a distillery (*ca* 1825), a foundry and machine shop (1853), and a woolen factory (1865) that was shifted to yarn production in 1875. Limestone was quarried as well. The village is located on Oriskany Creek, and the Chenango Canal (1837–78) and the Utica, Clinton and Binghamton Division of the Delaware, Lackawanna and Western Railroad (1870) augmented access to the community. The Utica Knitting Co (1897) was an important employer until it closed *ca* 1950. Other firms adapted its mill, and beginning in 1998 the Kendall Corp manufactured hospital products there. The Oriskany Falls High School consolidated with Waterville in 1983. Village population declined 12% between 1990 and 2000. The

Stone Church, built in 1833 for a Congregational society, is a landmark.

Orleans [OR-LEENS]. Town (pop 2,465) in N central Jefferson Co. Part of Penet's Square, a tract given to Frenchman Peter Penet by the Oneida Nation in 1788, its title was clouded by 1806 when squatters arrived and began cutting timber. The town was formed from Brownville in 1821. John LaFarge claimed the territory by purchase in 1824 and secured clear title in 1830, which permitted the town to grow. Many lime kilns were located south of LaFargeville. St. Vincent de Paul Seminary (1838) trained Catholic priests but after two or three years was moved to Fordham [now in Bronx Co], where it became St. John's College (now Fordham University). The Clayton and Theresa Railroad (1873) made LaFargeville a shipping point for produce. Orleans includes the larger part of Wellesley Island, where the nondenominational Thousand Island Park Camp Meeting Association (1874) created a summer resort used by both Canadians and Americans. I-81 provided modern highway access beginning in 1965. The Northern New York Agricultural Museum at Stone Mills is an attraction, along with Wellesley Island, Grass Point, DeWolf Point, and Waterson Point State Parks.

Laura Lynne Scharer

Orleans County (391 mi²/1,013 km²; pop 44,171). Created in 1824 from Genesee Co and named for the French royal house of Orleans. Territory was returned to Genesee Co in 1826. Orleans Co is subdivided into 10 towns that contain 4 incorporated villages. Albion serves as county seat. Lake Ontario forms the county's northern boundary, and its shoreline is the lowest elevation at 246 feet (75 m). The highest is 742 feet (226 m) in the Town of Barre. Orleans Co is part of two subregions of the Erie-Ontario physiographic province, the Ontario Lake Plain in the north and the Southern Ontario Plain in the south. The two are separated by the Niagara Escarpment. The generally flat Ontario Lake Plain starts at the edge of 5–40 ft (2–12 m) high bluffs that border Lake Ontario's narrow, gravel-covered beaches and gradually rise in elevation southward to about 400 feet (120 m), where a former beach ridge of prehistoric glacial Lake Iroquois rises 8–30 feet (2–9 m) above the surrounding plain. The plain continues south of the ridge to the limestone and dolostone Niagara Escarpment. South of the escarpment the Southern Ontario Plain consists generally of gently rolling to flat terrain. Elevation increases southward but averages around 600 feet (180 m). Ordovician shale and siltstone underlie the Ontario Lake Plain. The bedrock under the Southern Ontario Plain consists of Silurian limestone and dolostone, along with concentrations of sandstone and shale in places, especially the far south.

Orleans Co was once entirely glaciated and contains many depositional landforms such as terraces, eskers, and kames, along with outwash deposits. The county lies entirely within the Lake Ontario watershed. Surface drainage is hindered by limited slope and, more significantly, by remnant strand lines and other depositional features. Most of the county's western half is drained by Oak Orchard Creek, the largest stream in the county. The northeast-central part is in the Marsh Creek watershed, while eastern Orleans Co is drained by Sandy Creek. Extensive areas in the south are artificially drained. A number of small streams close to the lake have cut 40–60 ft (12–18 m) deep ravines. The county contains extensive areas of arable, highly productive soil, including nearly all of the land south of Rte 104. Large acreages of black or muck soils are found in the far south.

Orleans Co's climate is humid-continental. Lake Ontario and northwest winds have a moderating effect on the temperature and delay the growing season, particularly in areas closer to the lake. Nevertheless, seasonal temperatures are surprisingly uniform across the county. Mean January temperatures hover around 24°F (-4°C), and winter lows can be expected to fall below 0°F (-18°C) once or twice every year. Mean July temperatures fall within a degree of 71°F (22°C). Daytime highs reach 90°F (32°C) a few times nearly every summer. Average annual precipitation amounts range from slightly over 30 inches (76 cm) in the southeast to 36 inches (91 cm) at Albion and areas west. Seasonal snowfall amounts vary from 67 inches (170 cm) at Albion to over 80 inches (203 cm) in the higher south. The primeval forest cover consisted of two communities: a central hardwood forest dominated by beech, sugar maple, basswood, and in places hemlock cloaked all but the wettest parts of the county, where a wetland forest of elm, soft maple, and black ash predominated.

American Indians and Early Settlement

Archaeological evidence indicates the presence of Archaic hunters in the present Orleans Co *ca* 5000 BP, and a mound near Waterport further indicates human occupation *ca* 2000–2500 BP. The only large, permanent village known is the so-called Shelby fort, dating from around AD 1500. In late pre-Contact times the Native Americans, thought to have been Neutral or Wenro, hunted, fished, and gathered in the region; after they were defeated in 1651 by the Seneca, the latter included it within their territory but used it only for hunting. Residents remembered Tonawanda Senecas on the east branch of Sandy Creek in Clarendon until 1818.

The county passed through the nominal control of the land-speculating Phelps and Gorham Co (1788) and of Robert Morris (1791) who, when settling his debts, retained a part called the Morris Reserve. He then sold the 100,000-acre (40,000 ha) Connecticut Tract, covering Clarendon, Kendall, and Murray, to the State of Connecticut and Sir William Pulteney, who held it jointly until 1811. The rest of the county passed from Morris into the hands of the Holland Land Co (1792–93). The latter firm ordered a survey in 1798, and the first settlement was on the east side of the mouth of Oak Orchard Creek in 1803. Most of the present towns were settled between 1809 and 1812, but Barre, with swampy conditions, remained unoccupied until 1815.

Transportation

Orleans Co is bisected by one of the state's finest natural roadways, the Ridge Rd, a glacial ridge standing above the surrounding land. Long known to the Indians, it was surveyed in 1798 and, by an act of 1815, the state appropriated funds for its improvement. Although its significance as east-west transportation conduit declined with the building of the Erie Canal, it remains in use as Rte 104. The county's second highway was built by the Holland Land Co in 1803 from Batavia (Genesee Co) to Manilla, a hamlet on the harbor at Oak Orchard, which was expected to become the county's port. This road, too, saw its period of greatest use prior to the canal, since the harbor was not large enough for major development. The Oak Orchard Road is now Rte 98. Construction on the Erie Canal began in 1817 and was completed across Orleans Co in 1824. It gave rise to the villages of Holley, Albion, and Medina, and made possible economical shipment of agricultural produce and stone, the county's chief exports.

A very early railroad on wooden rails, the Medina and Darien Railroad, connected Akron (Erie Co) with the canal at Medina from 1836 to *ca* 1840. The Rochester, Lockport and Niagara Falls Railroad was completed across the county in 1852, and in the following year it became the

ORLEANS CO POPULATION CENSUS FIGURES

	White	Nonwhite	Total Population	Foreign-Born
1830	17,705	27	17,732	69
1840	25,058	69	25,127	—
1850	28,393	108	28,501	2,349
1860	28,586	131	28,717	4,601
1870	27,517	172	27,689	4,243
1880	29,904	224	30,128	4,799
1890	30,608	195	30,803	6,225
1900	30,059	105	30,164	5,520
1910	31,851	149	32,000	5,804
1920	28,502	117	28,619	4,449
1930	28,697	98	28,795	4,013
1940	27,551	209	27,760	3,048
1950	29,503	329	29,832	2,397
1960	32,668	1,491	34,159	1,720
1970	35,237	2,068	37,305	1,116
1980	36,023	2,473	38,496	997
1990	38,259	3,587	41,846	899
2000	39,367	4,804	44,171	1,172

Notes: "Nonwhite" includes African Americans, Asians, American Indians, and Pacific Islanders and, for 2000, also the mixed race and other race categories. Through the 1960 census these figures primarily reflect the African American population. Foreign-born figures for 1830 include only those not naturalized, and for 1930 and 1950, the foreign-born totals include Whites only. Other years include all foreign-born in the population.

Niagara Falls Branch of the New York Central. It remains in use as a freight line under the name of Falls Road Railroad, offering service between Brockport (Monroe Co) and Niagara Falls. Another port was improved at Shadigee *ca* 1850 with the construction of a 275 ft (84 m) pier by a stock company but became less important as soon as the county's two railroads provided freight service. The Lake Ontario Shore Railroad was completed through the northern tier of towns in 1876. It was immediately acquired by the Rome, Watertown and Ogdensburg Railroad and was locally known as the Ho-Jack.

ECONOMIC DEVELOPMENT

While clearing land, the first settlers sought to produce low-bulk, high-value commodities and goods to send to distant markets. As early as 1804—the year after initial settlement—the oak stands of Carlton provided material for ladles, bowls, and rolling pins, which were sent across Lake Ontario for sale in Canada. Similarly, potash was made from felled trees, and grain was distilled into whiskey. Starting as early as 1805, brine was boiled for salt in several locations, but when Syracuse salt could be shipped by canal, the relatively inefficient operations in Orleans Co ceased.

The first settlers raised wheat for sale and other crops for subsistence, reducing their dependence on wheat after western competition affected the market. The county's first specialty crop was beans, cultivated beginning in 1837. By 1854 Orleans Co led the state in bean production, with 40,000 bushels (1.4 million l); 20 years later, though now a close second to Monroe Co, it produced 250,000 bushels (8.8 million l). The story is told that a sailor on Lake Ontario gave an apple to little Rachel Lovewell of Carlton in 1805, and from its seed grew the first apple tree in the county north of the Ridge. Gradually, especially in the northern tier of towns, orchards were planted, chiefly of apples but also pears, peaches, cherries, and quinces. In 1874 Orleans Co was sixth in the state in apple production. The fruit crop was shipped whole, dried in evaporators, processed into cider or vinegar, and later canned at a number of canneries. Six Albion canneries merged in 1919 to form New York Canners (later Snider Packing). In the 20th century advancing technology made cold storage possible, and facilities in Medina (1901), Ridgeway (1912), Waterport (1915), and Yates were constructed to serve orchard owners. The industry was supported by many cooper's shops throughout the county. The great freeze in 1934 killed many of the orchard trees, but most farmers replanted, and in 2003 there were producing orchards in every town, with many concentrated near Lake Ontario.

In each of the southern tier of towns, settlers found large expanses of swamp that promised rich farmland if drained. This was first attempted in Shelby in 1829. Draining began in Barre under state appropriations of 1865 and 1867, and by 1879 there were 4,670 acres (1,890 ha) of reclaimed land throughout the county. The most extensive creation of muck farmland took place in Barre between 1900 and 1910 under the auspices of the Western New York Farms Co, which ceased operation in 1917. In Clarendon muck farming began in the 1910s, and more land was drained in the 1930s. The muck, now privately owned by extremely large farms, is used to grow lettuce, onions, carrots, potatoes, and cabbage. Wheat, corn, hay, vegetables, and apples have been the chief farm products, with some dairy. In 1875 the county had only two cheese factories and was in the bottom quarter of the state's counties in dairy production.

Orleans Co's second industry was, historically, the quarrying of red Medina sandstone for building purposes. Discovered in the course of excavation for the Erie Canal (which also made shipment practical), it was quarried beginning in 1837. Vast stone quarries were opened near each of the canal villages (Medina, Albion, and Holley) and near Hulberton hamlet. As many as 300 quarry workers were employed at Albion late in the 19th century. The industry expanded greatly after 1890, and in 1900 there were nearly 50 quarries in operation, but labor costs, the development of Portland cement, and changes in building methods killed the business by the 1920s.

With the digging and enlargement of the Erie Canal and the boom in the quarrying industry, foreign workers arrived to work. The quarrying industry brought Polish, Italian, English, and Irish workers. By 1855 the Irish-born exceeded 8% of the population, and in 1890 over 20% of the county's population was born outside the United States.

Manufacturing, aside from the food-processing plants, was a minor part of the economy. In the 19th and 20th centuries most factories were located in the canal villages, where transportation was optimal. Shelby claims the first iron furnace west of the Genesee River (1821–22) and the first cast-iron plow; at various times there were foundries or furnaces at Albion, Holley, Medina, Lyndonville, and Waterport. Medina developed several significant industries: Bignall Manufacturing Co (1862; iron

POPULATIONS OF TOWNS, ORLEANS CO

Town, Year Founded	1840	1880	1920	1960	2000
Albion, 1875	—	5,147	5,846	6,416	8,042
Barre, 1818	5,539	2,325	1,622	1,922	2,124
Carlton, 1822[a]	2,275	2,477	1,832	2,600	2,960
Clarendon, 1821	2,251	1,797	1,139	1,659	3,392
Gaines, 1816	2,268	2,338	1,669	2,090	3,740
Kendall, 1837	1,692	1,893	1,275	1,680	2,838
Murray, 1808	2,675	2,812	3,390	3,767	6,259
Ridgeway, 1812	3,554	5,495	5,969	6,911	6,886
Shelby, 1818	2,643	3,824	3,937	5,051	5,420
Yates, 1822[b]	2,230	2,020	1,940	2,063	2,510

[a]Oak Orchard until 1825.

[b]Northton until 1823.

and brass pumps), Medina Manufacturing Co (1873; wood pumps), and Ives and Hubbard Pail Co (1875). Other 19th-century products included bricks at Lyndonville and paperware in Shelby. Oddly, agricultural implements and machinery were not made to any degree, although threshing machines were manufactured briefly in Barre from 1830 to 1834. The urban business of Orleans Co was food processing and the buying and shipping of produce by commission houses. The First Bank of Orleans was founded in 1834 at Albion.

Religion, Education, and Culture

Churches developed gradually as settlement progressed. In 1816 a Congregational Church was founded in Barre, and a Church of Christ congregation established in Murray. The first church edifice was built at Gaines in 1824. In 1855 the county had 17 Methodist, 12 Baptist, and 9 Presbyterian congregations, along with 4 Universalist and 2 Church of Christ congregations. A Quaker meeting functioned at Millville from 1818 to around 1872. Roman Catholicism was introduced by Irish immigrants who initially came with canal enlargement. The first Catholic church opened at Medina in 1850.

Although a school operated in Carlton in 1810, most of the county was barely settled when 1812 legislation authorized the development of a system of common schools. Most towns had at least one school by the decade's end, and the districts later divided until each town was dotted with one-room schools. Secondary education was first provided by Gaines Academy (1825), the first academy west of the Genesee River. By 1850 it was joined by similar schools in Albion, Millville, Lyndonville, Medina, and Holley, and by the Phipps Union Seminary in Albion, a girls' boarding school. Legislation in 1853 authorized the operation of high schools by Union Free School districts, leading to the takeover of some of the academies. Holley and Albion Academies became those villages' high schools in 1868 and 1876, respectively. Others, such as Lyndonville, which graduated its first class in 1898, grew directly from Union Free School districts. Medina Free Academy, incorporated privately in 1849, became the village's high school in 1895. In the 20th century the rural districts outside the villages and larger hamlets offered no high school program, requiring the payment of tuition by the rural district. From 1935 to 1953 Orleans Co schools formed five central districts: Kendall (1935), Lyndonville (1939), Holley (1949), Albion (1953), and Medina (1953). In the early 21st century the Albion Branch of Genesee Community College offers higher education.

The county's first newspaper was the *Gazette*, published at Gaines in 1822. Orleans Co is unusual for a rural county in having a daily, the *Medina Journal-Register* (1903). A weekly, the *Albion Advertiser* (1929), is also published. There is no radio station in the county. The first library, in Kendall, was formed in 1822 but was closed when the common schools began keeping small libraries. In 2004 there were four libraries: Swan Library in Albion (1900); Community Free Library in Holley (1946); Yates Community Library in Lyndonville (1948); and Lee-Whedon Memorial Library in Medina (1928). The county's museums are chiefly historical in content. The most important is the Cobblestone Museum at Childs, which showcases the distinctive masonry construction characteristic of the region from 1825 to 1860; seven buildings are open to the public. There are also railroad museums at Holley and Medina, the latter of which houses the largest HO (1:87 scale) model railroad in the East. The Orleans County Council on the Arts merged with the Genesee County Council on the Arts in 1993 to form GO ART (Genesee Orleans Regional Arts Council).

Recent Years

In the late 20th and early 21st centuries, agriculture remained king in Orleans Co. In 1940 its 2,200 farms covered 83% of the land area, the highest in the state. In 1997 there were 456 farms covering 57% of the county, again the state's highest. In 2003 Orleans is in the top 10 New York counties in cabbages, onions, potatoes, sweet corn, and tomatoes, and is a large producer of feed corn, wheat, and soybeans. Its orchards produce over 130 million pounds (60 million kg) of apples annually and are served by four cold storage facilities (in Holley, Yates, Medina, and Gaines). In 2003 a 15-acre (6 ha) hydroponics plant was built in Gaines to produce tomatoes for shipment throughout the East.

In addition to ongoing produce-processing industries, Orleans Co became home to a number of manufacturing operations in the mid–20th century, mostly in its villages. Medina produced chemicals, toys, shirts, furniture, and firefighting equipment, and Lyndonville made insecticides and electronics. At the beginning of the 21st century, Orleans Co's successful application for designation as an Empire Zone and its three new industrial parks have sparked a diversification of the local economy.

In the 1990s exurban population spread from Greater Rochester caused the eastern town of Clarendon to grow by 25%. The rest of the county was stable except for Albion and Gaines, which expanded because of prison populations and related employment. Many residents commute outside county boundaries for work in Rochester, Batavia, Lockport, Buffalo, and surrounding communities. Minorities make up about 10% of the county's population because of the presence of prisons in Albion.

The county has a seven-person legislature. Four members are elected from specific districts. The other three are elected at large, but each must reside in a specified section of the county (eastern, central, or western). The legislature selects the chief administrative officer.

Tourism, never a large part of the county's economy, has been growing. Lakeside Beach State Park (1968) and the limited-access Lake Ontario State Parkway (1970) have encouraged use of the county's lakeshore, especially by Rochester residents. Sportfishing for chinook salmon, brown trout, and other species is popular on Lake Ontario and its tributaries, Oak Orchard and Johnson Creeks. While the Barge Canal is no longer in use for freight, it has become a recreational and historical tourism asset. In the county's southwest, the Iroquois National Wildlife Refuge offers thousands of acres of natural habitat. The Cobblestone Society Museum and the Cobblestone Historic District, both at Childs, are significant historical tourism attractions.

Among famous Orleans Co residents are George M. Pullman (1831–97), builder of the Pullman Sleeping Car, from Albion; George Coles Stebbins (1846–1945) of Carlton, composer of many well-known hymns; and Charles W. Howard, the first Macy's Santa Claus, who ran his Santa Claus School in the Town of Albion beginning in 1937.

Arad Thomas, *Pioneer History of Orleans County* (1871), has more value to genealogists than to historians, and Isaac S. Signor, *Landmarks of Orleans County*, 2 vols (1894), has similar limitations. Useful sources are the *Historical Album of Orleans County* (1879) and *Orleans County History* (1976), which is superb despite having little discussion of the county as a whole. Other countywide works include Irene M. Gibson, *Historic Sites in Orleans County* (1979), and Delia A. Robinson, *Historical Amnesia: Forgotten Women of 19th-Century Orleans County, NY* (2000). Town histories include David Copeland, *History of Clarendon* (1889); Carol D. Gardepe and Janice D. Regester, *A History of the Town of Yates* (1976); and Alan J. Isselhard, *Images of Clarendon Past* (1985). J. Howard Pratt, *Memories of Life on the Ridge* (1978), *Saga of the Ridge* (1983), and *Life on the Ridge* (1987) are useful memoirs, and Richard Canuteson, *A Little More Light on the Kendall Colony* (1954) documents the short-lived, early Norwegian colony in that town. Delia A. Robinson, *Historic Gaines, 1809–1984* (1984), updates that town's 20th-century history.

Field Horne

orphanages. Indenture, almshouses, or the charity of neighbors were the options for orphans in New York State prior to 1806, when the Orphan Asylum in the City of New York began to shelter white Protestant orphans and give them basic education and religious training. In response to a petition for funds, the legislature authorized annual payments of $500 to the trustees of the asylum in 1811. By 1836 there were 13 orphanages in New York State, eight in New York City, and one each in Albany, Troy, Utica, Rochester, and Buffalo. Many were associated with religious groups. The Hebrew Benevolent and Orphan Asylum Society opened in New York City in 1860. The Jewish Orphan Asylum of Western New York was founded in 1881 in Rochester to care for Jewish orphans from Syracuse, Rochester, and Buffalo. The Sisters of Charity established Catholic asylums in Albany in 1832 and in Buffalo in 1848 in response to cholera epidemics. In 1857 there were 2,816 government-supported children in 26 institutions. By 1867 the number of orphanages receiving public money had grown to more than 60. The Thomas Asylum for Orphan and Destitute Indian Children operated on the Cattaraugus Indian Reservation [loc in Cattaraugus, Chautauqua, and Erie Cos] from 1855 to 1955. This institution was unique because it became a state institution on a reservation, directed by the New York State Board of Charities after 1875.

The same year, what became known as the Children's Law directed that children be removed from almshouses and placed, at county expense, with families or in private institutions of the same religious faith as the parents of the children. After 1867 the State Board of Commissioners of Public Charities supervised institutions receiving public funds, but the board almost never withheld certification based on compliance with state laws, regardless of conditions. The size of orphanages and quality of care varied; while some housed fewer than 50 children, others held up to 2,000. Some institutions provided adequate education, maintained contact with birth families, and provided loving caregivers and well-equipped buildings; others harbored uncaring or cruel keepers and poor conditions.

Most orphanages originally housed children in large buildings, but by 1910 some institutions (eg, the New York Orphan Asylum Society and the Colored Orphan Asylum) had built more homelike cottages for 30–40 children. In 1900 only 10% of the children were "full" orphans; others had one or two parents. Some parents removed children soon after admission, but some children remained until they were teenagers and able to work. By the 1920s use of family foster care and the provision of mothers' pensions and Aid to Dependent Children (later Aid to Families with Dependent Children), passed as part of the National Security Act of 1935, caused the number of children in institutions to decline. Some orphanages closed, and others became residential treatment centers for emotionally disturbed children. Most institutions were segregated by race until the 1950s. In 1974 in New York State there were 49,041 children in care away from their own homes, but only 8,753 (about 18%) lived in institutions.

By the mid-1970s the number of children in foster care diminished, and the State Board of Social Welfare closed the worst of the institutions, but when the average age of children in care increased in the late 1970s, agencies were encouraged to open special facilities, known as group homes, for older children unacceptable to foster families; they held six to eight children each. Quasi-institutional residences were also established for older children, which housed 12–20 youths. In 2003 most children who lived in group homes were at least 6 years old, and almost 25% of New York State foster children lived in institutions, group residences, or group homes.

See also CHILD WELFARE; NONPROFIT SECTOR.

Bremner, Robert H., ed. *Children and Youth in America: A Documentary History,* 3 vols (Cambridge, Mass: Harvard Univ Press, 1970–74)

Folks, Homer. *The Care of Destitute, Neglected, and Delinquent Children* (1902; repr Washington, DC: National Association of Social Workers, 1978)

Smith, Eve P. "Bring Back the Orphanages? What Policymakers of Today Can Learn from the Past." In *A History of Child Welfare,* ed. Eve P. Smith and Lisa A. Merkel-Holguin (New Brunswick, NJ: Transaction Publishers, 1996)

Eve P. Smith

Orthodox churches. Orthodoxy, the eastern branch of Christianity, has numerous denominations in New York State. These are broadly divided into autocephalous denominations (those retaining their autonomy while remaining in communion with the Church of Constantinople) and those that are independent. Some of the major Orthodox churches in New York State are from Slavic countries such as Russia, Georgia, Serbia, and Bulgaria; some are from Greece and Albania; and Arab Orthodox churches originate from Lebanon and Palestine.

Russian Orthodox Churches and Other Slavic Churches

The first East Coast Orthodox parish was established in 1870 in New York City under the Russian Orthodox Church by Fr Nicholas Bjerring, an American of Danish descent. Because the Russians were the first of the Orthodox Christians to arrive on the American continent, according to the principle of "one bishop in one city," most of the subsequent Orthodox immigrants came under the jurisdiction of the Russian Orthodox Church, even though they were not Russian themselves. Despite efforts by Archbishop Tikhon (Bellavin) in the first decade of the 20th century to organize all the Orthodox groups in the United States into a single entity, union did not happen. The large numbers of Orthodox immigrants, their linguistic and cultural differences, and, subsequently, the impact of Communism in the home countries precluded this.

The substantial Slavic immigration of people to the United States before World War I provided the main source for Russian Orthodox congregations. A sizable population came from the Austro-Hungarian Empire, particularly from the areas around the Carpathian Mountains and Galicia. The former were usually known as Carpatho-Russians (Rusyns). Many clustered in the area of Albany, Troy (Rensselaer Co), and Cohoes (Albany Co). In 1909 Fr Alexis Toth, a leader of the Rusyn community, entered the Russian Orthodox diocese and headed a group of Rusyns that wished to join it. By 1916 two-thirds of the officially Russian Orthodox parishes in the United States were located in the Northeast and consisted of Rusyn congregations consisting of former Eastern Catholics.

The most significant figure in the early history of the Russian Orthodox Church in New York State was Archbishop Tikhon, who moved the American diocesan center from San Francisco to New York City in 1905 to be closer to the parishes on the East Coast established by immigrants from Carpatho-Russia, the Ukraine, the Balkans, and the Middle East. He created many Orthodox institutions, including the St. Nicholas Russian Orthodox Cathedral on East 97th St in New York City. An advocate of Orthodox unity in America, he sought to unite the various Orthodox immigrant groups into a single church and use English in liturgical services. He returned to Russia in 1907; he became patriarch of Russia in 1917 and died under mysterious circumstances in 1925.

The Bolshevik Revolution and Russian Civil War increased the numbers of Russian Orthodox in New York State but led to a confusing situation created by the end of financial and moral support from the imperial government and by differing attitudes toward the Russian Orthodox Church in the Soviet Union. By 1933 four major Russian Orthodox jurisdictions in New York State claimed to be the rightful and legitimate successor of the Russian Orthodox Archdiocese. The World War II era concordat between the Moscow Patriarchate and the Soviet government sharpened the fault lines in the United States. The two most important Russian Orthodox denominations were the Metropolia created in 1924 and the Russian Orthodox Church Outside of Russia (ROCOR) created in 1922. The latter, unstintingly hostile to the Moscow Patriarchate, moved its headquarters to New York City in 1950. Bishops within the Metropolia began to take a more conciliatory position during World War II, and some sought reunion with Moscow. In 1970 the Metropolia, renamed the Orthodox Church in America, became an autocephalous church. The headquarters of the Orthodox Church in America are in Syosset (Nassau Co). There are over 30 congregations in New York State. Despite the fall of the Soviet Union, the Orthodox Church in America and ROCOR continue to disagree on issues such as ecumenism and the Julian calendar. New York State has been a major center of Orthodox learning and spirituality. St. Vladimir's Orthodox Theological Seminary, associated with the Orthodox Church in America, founded in New York City in 1938 by Metropolitan Feofil (Pashkovsky), moved to Crestwood (Westchester Co) in 1962. Its distinguished faculty has included Georges Florovsky, Alexander Schmemann, and John Meyendorff. The Holy Trinity Russian Orthodox Monastery (1928) in Jordanville (Herkimer Co) and Holy Trinity Seminary (1948) are associated with ROCOR.

Other Slavic Orthodox churches include the Church of Bulgaria, which organized five Bulgarian parishes in New York State into a diocese in 1938. After Bulgaria became a communist state, the diocese broke with the Church of Bulgaria in 1947, joining a new diocese under the ROCOR in 1964. The Ukrainian Orthodox Church in the United States, with about 50 parishes, was established in 1931; its headquarters are in Jamaica (Queens Co). The Ukrainian Autocephalous Orthodox Church in the United States was established in 1950 with headquarters in the Bronx; the Holy Ukrainian Autocephalic Church in Exile was organized in 1954. The Romanian Orthodox Missionary Archdiocese in America and Canada is associated with the Orthodox Church in America. The Serbian Orthodox Church in America was organized in 1940. The Serbian Cathedral of St. Sava in Manhattan is a historic building built by Richard Upjohn in 1855 and was purchased from the Episcopal Church in 1942.

Arab Orthodox Christians

Arab Orthodox Christians came to the United States in the late 19th century from Syria and from the region that became Lebanon. The Russian Orthodox Archdiocese had consecrated Bishop Raphael Hawaweeny in 1904 to care for the Arab immigrants in North America. After 1915, however, the Patriarchate of Antioch sought to draw these immigrants to itself, and the Arab community split. In 1936 two rival groups of Russian bishops consecrated Archbishop Antony (Bashir) in New York City and Archbishop Samuel (David) in Toledo, Ohio. The Patriarchate of Antioch eventually recognized both bishops and their parishes and permitted the two jurisdictions to function simultaneously. A unified Antiochian Orthodox Christian Archdiocese was established in 1975.

Greek Orthodox Churches

Significant Greek migration to the United States began during the last quarter of the 19th century and continued until 1921. Greeks from the Kingdom of Greece favored the authority of the autonomous Church of Greece, while those from Asia Minor supported the Russian Orthodox Church, which was the first Orthodox presence in North America and associated with the Patriarchate of Constantinople. The first Greek church in the Northeast, Holy Trinity, was established in New York City in 1892; by 1921 Greeks had organized 138 parishes throughout the United States. In the absence of a resident bishop, these early parishes were entirely controlled by the immigrants through elected boards of trustees. The *kinotitos,* or community council, has remained a vital and integral part of Greek Orthodox life. The general pattern of Greeks in North America was to organize a society, name it after some classical hero or ancestor, and to solicit for members and pledges. In New York City the Society of Athena established churches and provided for instruction in the Greek language.

The formal organization of Greek parishes in the United States followed the vagaries of politics in Greece, shifting between the followers of the monarchist King Constantine I and the republican Prime Minister Eleftherios Venizelos. The Greek Orthodox Archdiocese of North and South America was incorporated in 1921. Archbishop Athenagoras (Spirou) arrived in New York City on 24 Feb 1931 to assume leadership of the Greek Orthodox Archdiocese. In 1934 he proposed the establishment of an Orthodox theological seminary that would serve the needs of all the Orthodox jurisdictions in America. English was to be the language of instruction, while Greek and Church Slavonic was to be used in liturgical services. The plan foundered, and Athenagoras opened the Holy Cross Theological School on 5 Oct 1937 in Pomfret, Conn. The 10th Clergy-Laity Congress of the Greek Orthodox Archdiocese formally authorized an English language Sunday school curriculum.

Today Greek jurisdictions in New York State include the Greek Orthodox Archdiocese of America, with headquarters in New York City; the Greek Orthodox Old Calendar (Synod of Souris); the Greek Orthodox Metropolis of North and South America (reunited with the Greek Orthodox Archdiocese in 1997, with headquarters in Astoria, Queens Co); the Hellenic Orthodox Traditionalist Church of America (headquarters in Astoria); the Holy Orthodox Archdiocese of Vasiloupolis and Missionary Eparchy of America (headquarters in Woodside, Queens Co), the Holy Orthodox Church in North America (originally under the Russian Orthodox Church Abroad, now headquartered in Roslindale, Mass), and the Italo-Greek Orthodox Church in Utica.

Dedication and 40th Anniversary Jubilee (Cohoes, NY: St. Nicholas' Russian Orthodox Greek Catholic Church, 1954)
FitzGerald, Thomas E. *The Orthodox Church* (Westport, Conn: Greenwood, 1995)
Maximovitch, John, "The Russian Orthodox Church Outside Russia," *Orthodox Word* 8 (1975): 165–77
Saloutos, Theodore. *The Greeks in the United States* (Cambridge, Mass: Harvard Univ Press, 1964)
Stokoe, Mark. *Orthodox Christians in North America, 1794–1994* (Wayne, NJ: Orthodox Christian Publication Center, 1995)

Nadieszda Kizenko

Orwell. Town (pop 1,254) in NE Oswego Co. Settled in 1806 the town was formed in 1817 from Richland. The Salmon River has a 110 ft (34 m) waterfall. In 1913 a dam above the falls created the Salmon River Reservoir, providing hydroelectric power and recreation. Lumbering and wood products have always been important industries, and dairying de-veloped after *ca* 1860. Orwell is, by local option, a "dry" town, forbidding the sale of all alcohol.

Barbara J. Dix

Osborne, Thomas Mott (*b* Auburn, Cayuga Co, 23 Sept 1859; *d* Auburn, 20 Oct 1926). Prison reformer and warden. Osborne was the only son of David Munson Osborne, Auburn's leading 19th-century industrialist, and Eliza Wright Osborne. He graduated from Harvard in 1884 and was president of agricultural machinery manufacturer D. M. Osborne and Co from his father's death in 1886 until 1903, when he sold the company to International Harvester Co. In 1905 Osborne founded the *Auburn Citizen* and remained president of the newspaper until his death. Osborne held a number of public positions, including mayor of Auburn (1903–5), New York State's commissioner of forest, fish, and game (1909–11), and chairman of the New York State Commission on Prison Reform (1913). To gain firsthand knowledge of prison life, he lived for a week as an inmate in Auburn Prison. This gave him insight into the humiliations inmates suffered and their deep distrust of their keepers. His books *Within Prison Walls* (1914), *Society and Prisons* (1916), and *Prisons and Common Sense* (1924) brought Osborne worldwide recognition as an authority on prison problems. His influence put an end to the Auburn system, in which prisoners labored in small workshops in brutally enforced silence for little pay, and led to the founding of Mutual Welfare Leagues, inmate self-improvement associations within prisons. Osborne's success at initiating reforms at Auburn Prison led to his appointment in 1914 as warden of Sing Sing Prison in the Village of Ossining (Westchester Co). However, his aggressive attempts at reform based on his theories of prisoner rehabilitation rather than punishment were stymied by deeply ingrained corruption within the Sing Sing system. He was tried for misconduct, and though acquitted he resigned from Sing Sing in 1915. The following year Osborne was appointed head of the US Naval Prison at Portsmouth, NH, where his reform efforts were more successful and where he remained until 1920. As a member of a privileged class in a socially conscious generation, Osborne dedicated much of his life to improving prison conditions and changing attitudes toward prisoners and their rehabilitation. His work, particularly the spirit of the Mutual Welfare Leagues, survives in the Osborne Association, founded in 1931 to provide treatment, educational, and employment services for current and former prisoners and their families.

Chamberlain, Rudolph. *There Is No Truce: A Life of Thomas Mott Osborne* (New York: Macmillan, 1935)

Scott W. Anderson

Osceola [AH-SEE-OH-LA]. Town (pop 265) in SW Lewis Co. Settled ?1822 by squatters, the land was sold beginning in 1839 to permanent settlers from the region and from Vermont. Its rugged Tug Hill Plateau territory serves as the headwaters of the Salmon River, once a spawning ground for Atlantic salmon. The town was formed in 1844 from West Turin. Its forests were harvested for the paper mill in Lyons Falls, which closed in 2001, but lumbering remains its main occupation. Catering to snowmobilers is an important seasonal business. Osceola is the site of the North American Fiddlers Hall of Fame and Museum (1976), the creation of resident Alice Colvin Clemens, a noted fiddler.

Arthur Einhorn

Ossian [OSH-AN]. Town (pop 751) in S Livingston Co. Settled in 1804, it was formed from Angelica (Allegany Co) in 1808; it was annexed to Livingston Co in 1857. Lumbering was economically important and was succeeded by agriculture. The soil is a sandy loam suited to crops of wheat, corn, barley, and oats. In 1862, 22 residents of Bisbee hamlet who had joined the Mormon Church emigrated together to Utah. Ossian is an active dairy farming community with one 3,000-acre (1,200 ha) beef cattle farm. Most residents work in nearby communities. Part of the Rattlesnake Hill State Wildlife Management Area is Ossian.

Mary Jo Marks

Ossining. Town (pop 36,534) and village (pop 24,010) in W central Westchester Co. Originally an important river shipment point, the area was first called Hunter's Landing. The post office established in 1797 was named Mount Pleasant until 1830. The village was incorporated as Sing Sing in 1813, became the site of Sing Sing Prison in 1825, and changed its name to Ossining in 1901. The town was formed from Mount Pleasant in 1845. Industries in the 19th century included sloop and steamboat yards and Brandreth's Pills (1836), a major manufacturer of patent medicines. The Hudson River Railroad (1849) drew some trade away from river traffic. Industrial and prison jobs attracted Irish, Italians, and African Americans, and, in the late 20th and early 21st centuries, Latinos. New York City commuters also made Ossining their home. At the 2000 census Ossining was 14% black; 19% of the population was of Latino ethnicity. Landmarks include St. Mary's Church Scarborough (1851), Woodlea (1893–95; now Sleepy Hollow Country Club), and Maryknoll Center for Catholic World Missions (1920).

Oswegatchie [OS-WE-GATCH-EE]. Town (pop 4,370) in W St. Lawrence Co. The town was formed in 1802 from Lisbon. A large Irish influx created a population of 1,790 Irish-born residents in 1855, 30% of the total. In 2003 the town was an important farming area but was experiencing housing development pressure on roads leading from Ogdensburg, especially along the St. Lawrence River and Black Lake shorelines, partly because of the conversion of second homes to year-round use. Oswegatchie's population increased 60% between 1960 and 2000. Black Lake is a warm-water fishing tourist destination. Oswegatchie is home to a growing Swartzentruber Amish community.

Richard E. Mooers

Oswego. Town (pop 7,287) and city (pop 17,954) in W Oswego Co. Originally part of the Onondaga Indian homelands, the City of Oswego is located where the Oswego River flows into Lake Ontario and received its name from an Onondaga word meaning "the flowing out of waters." Simon Le Moyne, a French Jesuit missionary, led the first European expedition through Oswego in 1655. By the early 18th century, Oswego became a fur-trading site for Dutch, English, and Native American traders. The British established a settlement on the west bank of the Oswego River in 1722 and built a stone fort in 1727, their "eye on the lake." By 1755 the British had added two more forts at Oswego: Fort Ontario and Fort George. In August 1756, during the French and Indian War, the French destroyed all three forts. The British rebuilt Fort Ontario in 1759 and remained until 1796, when the United States occupied it under the Jay Treaty. Destroyed by the British during the War of 1812, the fort was rebuilt in the 1840s.

The 19th Century

After 1796, with Fort Ontario securely in US hands, European Americans began to settle near the harbor. They came from New England and eastern New York State, many of them involved in shipping salt from Syracuse to Canada and the west. The single most important event in the city's history was the completion of the Oswego Canal in 1828. Connecting with the Erie Canal at Syracuse, the Oswego Canal made Oswego a major transshipment point between New York City, Canada, and the upper Great Lakes. In 1841 an Oswego shipyard built the *Vandalia,* the first screw-propelled vessel on the Great Lakes, designed by Swedish-born inventor John Ericsson and financed by local ship captain James Van Cleve. In 1848 the Syracuse and Oswego Railroad began operating. Grain imports from Canada and the western United States made Oswego a major flour milling center. In 1848 Kingsford Starch Co became the first corn starch factory in the world. Lumber imports sustained the Wright and Boyle Sash and Blind Factory, the Goble and Doolittle shipyards, and beginning in 1896 the Diamond Match factory. Iron imports supported such industries as Ames Iron Works and Fitzgibbons Boiler Co. Cotton and wool supplied textile factories, including the Oswego Cotton Factory (1832), which later became the Conde Factory and then the Breneman Shade Cloth Factory. After tolls were removed from the Erie Canal in 1882, fewer boats came through the Oswego Canal, but industrial development continued to fuel the city's economy. The Delaware, Lackawanna and Western Railroad brought coal from Pennsylvania coalfields to Lake Ontario, Canada, and the west.

Oswego's political organization directly reflected its economic growth. First designed by New York State surveyor Simeon DeWitt in 1796, the city plan incorporated two large public squares, one on each side of the river, with streets laid out in a grid. The town was formed from Hannibal in 1818; Oswego became a village in 1828 and a city in 1848, in both cases incorporating land on the east side of the Oswego River from Scriba and on the west side from the Town of Oswego. Attracted by job opportunities, Oswego's population grew steadily. By 1850, 12,205 people lived in the city, of whom 38% (4,638) were foreign-born. Of those about 60% were Irish, with about 25% from Canada. The African American population of more than 100 included a number of freedom seekers from the South.

The city's built environment was shaped during its greatest period of population growth, from 1828 to 1920. Its residential areas incorporated blocks of working-class and middle-class houses. A few homes, such as the Richardson-Bates House (now owned by the Oswego County Historical Society), reflected the wealth of a commercial and industrial elite. Most homes featured Greek Revival or Italianate styles, with a few Gothic, Classical Revival, or Arts and Crafts designs. Major public buildings included Fort Ontario (1840s), Jonathan Walton's stone store (1828), the early city hall and market house (1836–37), city library (donated by Gerrit Smith in 1855, the oldest library building in continuous use in New York State), customhouse (1858), county courthouse (1859–60), commercial buildings on Oswego's west side (mid–19th century), city hall (1870), New York State Armory (1907), and the harbor lighthouse (1934).

Houses of worship, including the First Presbyterian Church (1844), St. Mary's Catholic Church (1926), and Temple Adath Israel (1911, congregation organized 1858), served Oswego's diverse population. Other community organizations established the Oswego Hospital (1881), the Ladies' Home (1877), the YMCA (1903), and, west of the city, the Oswego Normal School (1863; now SUNY Oswego). The school's first president, Edward Austin Sheldon, promoted object teaching based on the work of Swiss educator Johann Pestalozzi.

The 20th Century

In 1920 Oswego had 40 manufacturing plants, employing 4,800 men and 1,900 women, but the local economy received a considerable blow in 1922 when the Kingsford Starch factory closed abruptly, throwing 900 people out of work. In 1920 Oswego's population reached 23,626, with many newcomers from Poland, Italy, and eastern Europe. It declined slightly thereafter but peaked in 1970 at 23,836. The depression hit Oswego hard, and in 1935 relief costs totaled half the city's budget. At the same time the development of Niagara Mohawk's power plant (1938–40) and the increase of harbor shipping (from 73 vessels in 1931 to 650 vessels in 1941) helped sustain economic recovery. In June 1944 almost 1,000 European refugees arrived at Fort Ontario. In the 1950s the opening of the St. Lawrence Seaway led many shippers to bypass Oswego. By 1980 most of Oswego's factories had closed, leaving only a few industries just outside the city in Scriba, such as Alcan Rolled Products, Niagara Mohawk, and Sithe Energies. By 2003 tourism, based on fishing, winter sports, historic attractions, and Harborfest, a major summer festival, enhanced the economy.

See also Fort ontario; Fur trade.

Judith Wellman and Helen Moore Breitbeck

Oswego Canal. The first lateral canal to the Erie Canal, built from 1825 to 1828. Joining the City of Oswego on Lake Ontario with the Erie Canal at Syracuse, it was 38 miles (61.2 km) long, 40 feet (12.2 m) wide, and 4 feet (1.2 m) deep; its 18 stone lift locks overcame 154 feet (46.9 m) in elevation; it had six guard locks. Boats traveling the canal carried 50–75 tons (45–68 MT). Its total original cost was roughly $565,000. Between 1851 and 1862 the prism was altered to Enlarged Erie Canal dimensions of 70 feet (21.3 m) wide by 7 feet deep (2.1 m), increasing the tonnage of boats to 210–240 tons (191–218 MT). The canal's peak years for total tonnage occurred in 1860, 1862, and 1863 with roughly 1 million tons (907,000 MT) per year, while its peak toll revenue years were 1868 with nearly $165,000, 1869 with just over $160,000, and 1867 with roughly $154,000. The total revenue from tolls on the canal between 1828 and 1882, when the collection of tolls was suspended, totaled just over $3.7 million.

A second planned enlargement (1896–98) to a depth of 9 feet (2.7 m) was never completed, but the Oswego Canal was included in the state's early 20th-century Barge Canal enlargement (1905–18) that brought a canalized Oswego River with land cuts measuring from 94 to 123 feet wide (28.7 to 37.5 m) and 12 feet deep (3.7 m); river sections were 200 ft wide (70 m) by 12 ft (3.7 m). The federal government undertook another enlargement program beginning in the 1930s in response to competition from Canadian waterways on the St. Lawrence River. The project increased the canal's depth to 14 feet (4.3 m) and earth section width to 120–160 feet (36.6–48.8 m), and raised the bridges to a clearance of 21 feet (6.4 m) above low-water level from Oswego to the eastern end of the Erie Canal at the Hudson River in Waterford (Saratoga Co).

During its heyday the canal was an important grain and salt carrier and still transports an occasional load of calcium chloride. Its last regularly scheduled commodity, cement transported in the motorship *Day Peckinpaugh* between Oswego and Rome, ended in September 1994. At 24 miles (38.6 km) long, the canal provides access to the Canadian Rideau Canal and Trent-Severn Waterway as well as to the St. Lawrence Seaway and the upper Great Lakes via the Welland Canal at the western end of Lake Ontario.

Whitford, Noble E. *History of the Canal System of the State of New York* (Albany: Brandow Printing, 1906)

Thomas X. Grasso

Oswego County (1,038 mi²/2,688 km²; pop 122,377). Formed in 1816 from Oneida and Onondaga Cos, Oswego Co lies east and south of Lake Ontario and is divided into 22 towns that contain 10 incorporated villages and 2 cities, Oswego and Fulton. Organized on the half-shire system, the county has courthouses at Oswego and Pulaski. The northeastern portion of Oswego Co occupies part of the Tug Hill Upland, where the land rises to over 1,700 feet (520 m) near the Lewis Co line. The remainder of the land lies within the Erie-Ontario Lowland. The area west of the Oswego River is part of a very extensive drumlin field. With the notable exception of some sand dunes near the lakeshore, the area due east of Lake Ontario consists largely of low hills composed of glacial drift. Much of the county is poorly drained and characterized by swamps separated by low-lying ridges of glacial deposits, a topography known as Ontario Ridge and Swampland. Bedrock consists of Paleozoic sandstone and shale that dip gently westward. Aside from a limited area along the eastern margins, the land surface tilts toward Lake Ontario, whose shoreline is the lowest elevation (246 ft/75 m) in the county. All of Oswego Co lies within the Lake Ontario watershed. The largest river by far is the Oswego, followed by its tributary, the Oneida. The Salmon and Little Salmon Rivers are also significant. The western half of Oneida Lake lies in the county's southeast corner. Soils are highly variable. Shallow, acidic, nonarable soil associations dominate the eastern half; productive limy tills are scattered in parts of the south and west.

Oswego Co's climate is humid-continental. Lake Ontario significantly modifies local temperature and snowfall patterns by delaying the onset of spring, extending late summer temperatures, and supplying substantial amounts of moisture to the prevailing northwesterly winter winds, resulting in copious amounts of lake effect snow falling on large portions of the county.

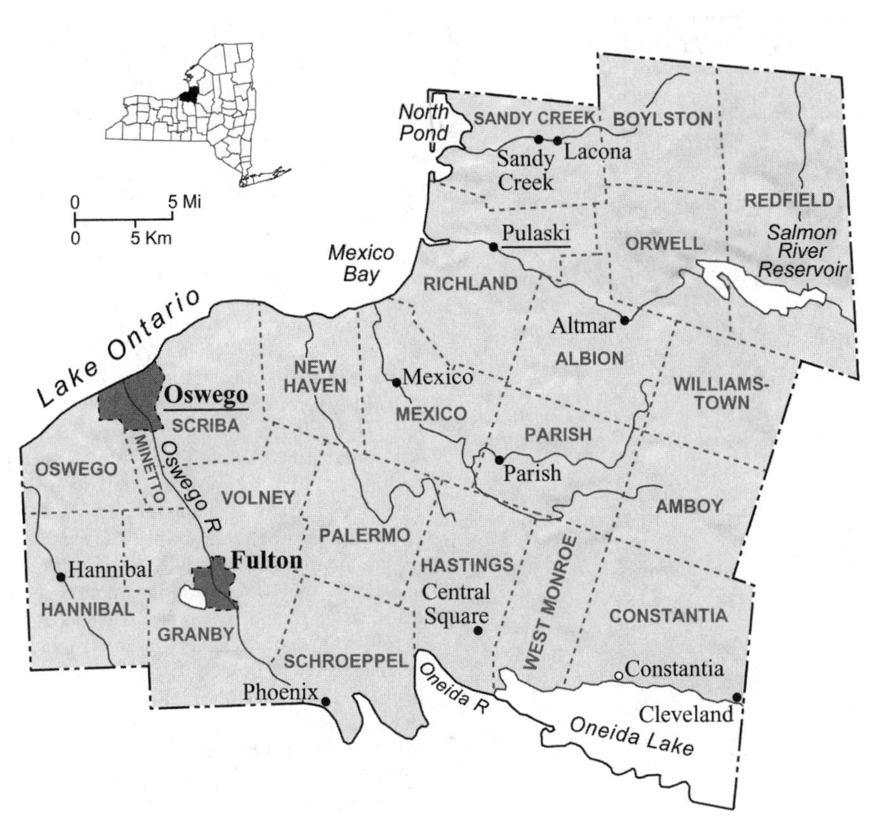

Average January temperatures range from 23°F (-5°C) along parts of the Lake Ontario shore to 17°F (-8°C) on the Tug Hill; average July temperatures are 70°F (21°C) and 67°F (19°C), respectively. Mean annual precipitation ranges from less than 34 inches (86 cm) at Oswego to approximately 50 inches (130 cm) in the highest elevations. Average annual snowfall ranges from 90 inches (229 cm) in the southwest to more than 200 inches (510 cm) in the northeast corner. Primeval forest consisted primarily of variations of central and northern hardwood communities dominated by beech, sugar maple, and hemlock in combination with white pine, basswood, and yellow birch. Exceptions include areas of wetland forest and the sand dune area east of Lake Ontario, one of only three areas in the state that cannot naturally support forest cover.

American Indians and Early Settlement

The earliest known evidence of human habitation in the county is a Paleo-Indian site in the Town of Schroeppel estimated to be 10,000 to 12,000 years old. Archaeological evidence suggests at least 10 Indian hunting and fishing camps existed at one time or another in the county, though not simultaneously. The sites are clustered along the Oswego and Salmon Rivers and the shore of Oneida Lake. By the 15th century the Onondaga were using the area for fishing and hunting. They continued to occupy the region until 1788, when they ceded the land to the State of New York.

The first Europeans to set foot in the county were French explorer Samuel de Champlain in 1615 and French Jesuits, led by Simon Le Moyne, in 1654. By the late 17th century the British were keenly aware of the strategic importance of the Oswego River system as a trade route between the Mohawk River and Lake Ontario. In 1727 they built a fort at the mouth of the Oswego River, where, with the exception of 1756–59, they would remain until 1796.

Following the Treaty of Fort Schuyler (1788), the lands that became Oswego Co were divided into three major tracts. Those west of the Oswego River were part of the New Military Tract and were surveyed in 1789–90. Lands generally north of the Salmon River were contained in the Macomb Purchase. The remaining, larger portion was purchased by New York City businessman and land speculator George Scriba, who in turn sold parcels to other speculators, including George Schroeppel, David Parish, and Alexander Hamilton. All four then sold land to individual settlers. Scriba's efforts to entice settlers are particularly notable. He established Rotterdam [now Constantia] as his principal settlement, complemented it with the port of Vera Cruz [now Texas] on Lake Ontario, and built roads, mills, and other facilities. All proved of limited effectiveness in promotion, because they could not overcome the marginal quality of the land in the eyes of many prospective settlers. By the 1790s settlers were taking up land along the Oswego River corridor, the north shore of Oneida Lake, and the areas around what are now Mexico, Pulaski, and Redfield. A few African Americans also settled in the county. Some were free, such as Henry Bakeman, a Revolutionary War veteran who settled at Oswego Falls [now Fulton]. Aside from the Port of Oswego, early population centers—Oswego Falls, Pulaski, and Mexico—grew up where streams provided abundant waterpower for milling. Central Square emerged at an important crossroads along the Old Salt Rd (now US 11) that linked Salina (Onondaga Co) with Adams (Jefferson Co). Cleveland developed around a sand deposit used for glassmaking.

Economic Development

From the time of initial settlement, strategic location, natural resources, and limited agricultural promise combined to shape the local economy. Farmers searched out, occupied, and made productive the county's arable land. Simultaneously the Oswego River system stimulated commercial development by facilitating

OSWEGO CO POPULATION CENSUS FIGURES

	White	Nonwhite	Total Population	Foreign-Born
1820	12,342	32	12,374	131
1830	26,975	144	27,119	554
1840	43,404	215	43,619	—
1850	61,983	215	62,198	9,276
1860	75,623	335	75,958	11,886
1870	77,633	308	77,941	13,255
1880	77,646	265	77,911	11,195
1890	71,725	158	71,883	9,215
1900	70,726	155	70,881	7,318
1910	71,220	444	71,664	8,101
1920	70,925	120	71,045	7,536
1930	69,557	88	69,645	5,892
1940	71,200	75	71,275	4,763
1950	77,046	135	77,181	4,047
1960	85,869	249	86,118	3,442
1970	100,349	548	100,897	2,564
1980	112,603	1,298	113,901	2,728
1990	119,897	1,874	121,771	2,138
2000	118,918	3,459	122,377	1,958

Notes: "Nonwhite" includes African Americans, Asians, American Indians, and Pacific Islanders and, for 2000, also the mixed race and other race categories. Through the 1960 census these figures primarily reflect the African American population. Foreign-born figures for 1820 and 1830 include only those not naturalized, and for 1930 and 1950, the foreign-born totals include Whites only. Other years include all foreign-born in the population.

POPULATIONS OF TOWNS AND CITIES, OSWEGO CO

Town or City, Year Founded	1800	1840	1880	1920	1960	2000
Albion, 1825	—	1,503	2,569	1,288	1,125	2,083
Amboy, 1830	—	1,070	1,244	617	524	1,312
Boylston, 1828	—	481	1,283	545	293	505
Constantia, 1808	—	1,476	3,124	1,789	2,730	5,141
Fulton (city), 1902	—	—	—	13,043	14,261	11,855
Granby, 1818	—	2,385	4,514	1,913	3,704	7,009
Hannibal, 1806	—	2,269	3,173	1,834	2,673	4,957
Hastings, 1825	—	1,983	2,866	2,153	4,457	8,803
Mexico, 1792	241	3,729	3,687	2,824	3,435	5,181
Minetto, 1915	—	—	—	913	1,290	1,663
New Haven, 1813	—	1,738	1,713	1,256	1,478	2,930
Orwell, 1817	—	808	1,550	890	663	1,254
Oswego, 1818	—	4,665	3,022	1,662	2,796	7,287
Oswego (city), 1848	—	—	21,116	23,626	22,155	17,954
Palermo, 1832	—	1,928	1,996	1,046	1,663	3,686
Parish, 1828	—	1,543	1,817	1,265	1,439	2,694
Redfield, 1800	107	507	1,294	647	388	607
Richland, 1807	—	4,050	3,991	3,738	4,554	5,824
Sandy Creek, 1825	—	2,420	2,878	2,018	2,506	3,863
Schroeppel, 1832	—	2,098	3,381	2,617	5,554	8,566
Scriba, 1811	—	4,051	2,971	1,817	2,489	7,331
Volney, 1806	—	3,155	6,588	1,995	3,785	6,094
West Monroe, 1839	—	918	1,314	782	1,417	4,428
Williamstown, 1804	—	842	1,820	767	739	1,350

Note: In 1800 the Towns of Mexico and Redfield were in Oneida Co.

the shipment of locally produced goods like cordwood and barrels to the Salina saltworks. In turn thousands of barrels of salt were shipped down the river to the Port of Oswego, where they were transferred to schooners for shipment to the Old Northwest and Upper Canada. Ties to the Onondaga Co salt industry remained strong throughout the first half of the 19th century. By 1820 three "salt roads"—present-day US 11, Rte 57, and a road from Constantia to Redfield—were constructed across the county, using salt tax revenues to facilitate the distribution of that essential commodity. Salt traffic was also a key motivating force behind the construction of the Oswego Canal, which opened in 1828 and continues, much modified, to operate as part of the state canal system. The county was the source of much cordwood used in salt production, and its workers supplied a large proportion of the barrels used to ship salt.

One of the most positive influences on early industrial growth was even further removed geographically from the county. In 1833 the Welland Canal opened, linking Lake Erie and Lake Ontario through Canadian territory and bypassing Niagara Falls. This development gave the Port of Oswego, already blessed with abundant waterpower and easy access to the Erie Canal, the opportunity to serve as a terminal and processing point for midwestern agricultural products being shipped east. Soon large flour mills, malt houses, and the Kingsford Starch Co factory (1848) crowded the river's banks. Upstream at Fulton and Minetto, textile mills produced cotton and woolen fabric for clothing and bookbindings. In the eastern half of the county forests remained the mainstay of the economy well into the 19th century. In 1855 Oswego Co ranked third in the state in numbers of tanneries and shingle mills and fourth in sawmills and cooper shops. Access to large stands of hot-burning hemlock, along with an abundant supply of impurity-free sand, supported a glassmaking industry along the north shore of Oneida Lake. The Oswego Bank, believed to be the first in the county, was established in 1831.

In 1846 the nation's first plank road was built between Syracuse and Watertown, following what had been a salt road. Within a decade a network of plank roads crisscrossed the county, including the predecessors of present Rtes 13, 49, 57, and 104. In 1848 the Syracuse and Oswego Railroad was completed. Rail service expanded further after the Civil War. The Delaware, Lackawanna and Western acquired the Syracuse and Oswego and became, along with the Ontario and Western, an important anthracite carrier, operating coal-shipping trestles at Oswego. Many farmers responded to improved transportation and heightened competition by shifting attention to dairy and fruit farming, particularly apples and strawberries. Others began raising tobacco for cigar wrapping.

Economic growth between the 1820s and World War I brought new people to the area. While the earliest settlers had come almost exclusively from New England or eastern New York State, mid-19th-century immigrants came from the British Isles (especially Ireland), Canada, and Alsace-Lorraine. By the end of the century the dominant immigrant groups were Italians, eastern Europeans, and Quebecois. Most new immigrants settled in Oswego and Fulton, although some Italians helped drain local wetlands and establish muck farms in the county's south early in the 20th century.

Religion, Education, and Culture

The first church organization, formed in Redfield in 1802, was Congregational. In 1855 there were 30 Methodist churches (including one African Methodist Episcopal congregation), but settlement by New Englanders was evident in the 20 Baptist, 9 Presbyterian, and 6 Congregational churches. The first Roman Catholic church was St. Mary's in Oswego (1848); by 1855 there were four Catholic churches in the county. Jews in the City of Oswego organized Congregation Berith Sholem in 1858.

The first school may have been one held in a log house at Oswego about 1798. Organization of the common school system followed state legislation of 1812 and 1814; in 1877 there were 289 districts in the county. The system was supplemented by private academies such as the Rensselaer Oswego Academy (later Mexico Academy), incorporated in 1828. In Oswego the academy became the high school following Union Free School legislation in 1853. The first central school was created at Mexico in 1936; the rest of the county followed by 1950, except for districts adjacent to the Oswego and Fulton city school districts, which remained independent as late as 1958. In 2003 the county was served by its original seven central districts and two city districts. The Oswego Normal School became a state teachers college in 1942, joined the new SUNY system in 1948, and became a liberal arts college in 1963, changes that brought large increases in staffing and students. In 2004 SUNY Oswego enrolled 8,500 students.

Throughout the county's history, social movements reflected both local and national trends. Conflicts over slavery split communities before the Civil War, as the area became an important site of Underground Railroad activity. The route through the county to the port at Oswego and on to Canada was used by many fugitive slaves, including William "Jerry" Henry, who passed through Mexico after his sensational 1851 rescue from a Syracuse jail. The favorable geography was bolstered by a deep commitment to abolitionism by many in Mexico, Oswego, and elsewhere in the county.

Women's literary clubs, suffrage groups, the Woman's Christian Temperance Union, and the Home Bureau (1917) complemented men's fraternal organizations. In rural areas the Grange became important. After World War I residents organized local chapters of the American Legion (1919). During the 1920s the growing Catholic presence prompted a backlash among some residents, who briefly supported the Ku Klux Klan. The county's first newspaper, the *American Farmer,* was published at Oswego before 1807. In 2003 the county was served by the *Oswego Palladium-Times* (1819), a daily, and by the *Mexico Independent Mirror, Fulton Valley News, Fulton Patriot, Phoenix Register,* and the *Pulaski Salmon River News.* Radio is broadcast by two stations in Oswego and one each in Fulton and Pulaski.

Politics

Oswego Co's unusual half-shire system, with county seats at Oswego and Pulaski, reflects regional cultural and economic ties that date from the county's creation. The northeast was closely tied to the North Country and the Tug Hill area, whereas the southern and western sections were more influenced by developments along Oneida Lake and the Oswego River. In 1971 the county's Board of Supervisors was replaced by a more equitably apportioned 25-person legislature. Day-to-day business is overseen by a county administrator appointed by the legislature. Although Democrats did well in some areas through the 1870s, Republicans have been the dominant party in county government ever since. In the early 21st century enrolled Republicans outnumber Democrats two to one across the county.

THE 20TH CENTURY

Between 1900 and 2000 Oswego Co experienced an economic transformation and a 70% increase in population. Technological changes, combined with federal government help, provided residents with improved communication and transportation facilities. Electric interurban service opened between Oswego and Syracuse in 1910. Rural Free Delivery (1902) brought mail directly to the doors of farm families. Beginning in 1916 federal government assistance augmented earlier state expenditures encouraging and subsidizing road construction. In 1900 the county boasted 6,914 farms; in 1997 there were only 605, with one-fifth of the 1900 acreage. This represented a modest 16.8% of the county's land area. Some farms were created in the early 20th century when wetlands were drained to make rich muck land available for lettuce and onion production. Increased mechanization and diminished profit margins played key roles in the agricultural transition. The average farm in 1997 was 169 acres (68 ha) compared to 71 acres (29 ha) in 1900. In 2000 dairy products outsold other farm products three to one. At the same time, the county produced one-quarter of the state's total lettuce crop.

Industrial change also began early in the century. The Kingsford Starch Co closed in 1922, putting hundreds out of work. The depression of the 1930s was felt unevenly. While half of the City of Oswego's 1935 budget was devoted to relief efforts, Fulton was called "the city the Depression missed." By the end of the decade the nation was preparing for war, and the county benefited from new manufacturing jobs. In 1944, 9,000 Oswego Co citizens were in the armed forces.

In the 1950s, 74 industries (52 of them locally owned) remained concentrated in Oswego, Fulton, and Pulaski. With the opening of the St. Lawrence Seaway in 1959, Oswego was no longer on the main water route. As a result many manufacturing plants closed, including the Diamond Match factory and all the textile mills. In 1960 almost 37% of the county's industrial workers produced food or food products, while another 20% made paper products. By 1970 the county had lost much of its early 20th-century economic base, but three other sectors—energy, education, and tourism—were growing. The Pulaski Gas and Oil Co drilled 85 wells between 1888 and 1947. Niagara Mohawk greatly expanded its production of electric power, first by enlarging its coal-fired generating station (later converted to oil) at Oswego in 1938–40 and then by building three nuclear power plants—Nine Mile Point One (1969), Fitzpatrick (1974), and Nine Mile Point Two (1987), all in the Town of Scriba. An aluminum-smelting plant was built near Oswego in 1961 to take advantage of the power supply and good transportation facilities. It was acquired by Alcan Rolled Products in 1963. Miller Brewing Co built a large plant at Fulton in 1973. The expansion of SUNY Oswego added another important economic stimulus to the area in the final decades of the 20th century. Tourism, notably sportfishing, became a major economic asset when the New York State Department of Environmental Conservation successfully reintroduced salmon into local waters. By the late 20th century, anglers from across the country traveled to Oswego Co to test their salmon-fishing skill. The growth of winter sports, especially snowmobiling and cross-country skiing, turned the long-standing liability of too much snow in places like Redfield into an asset.

After decades of modest growth or decline, the county experienced a 59% population increase between 1950 and 2000. All 22 towns grew significantly, although the cities of Fulton and Oswego lost population. One key factor in the population explosion was the northward expansion of Syracuse's commuter region, which was facilitated by the construction of limited-access highways beginning with I-81 between 1960 and 1962. Seventy-five percent of Oswego Co citizens owned their own homes. Housing demand has resulted in many acres of farmland being divided into small residential plots or in some instances into mobile home parks. Concurrently, urban renewal programs in the late 1960s and early 1970s destroyed key downtown areas in Fulton and Oswego, adversely affecting their aesthetic appeal. Large employers in 2003 included Black Clawson (coating equipment for paper and plastic), Agrilink (frozen foods), Interface Solutions (floor backing and gaskets), and Humataki (coated cardboard dairy cartons), all in Fulton; Alcan Rolled Products, Niagara Mohawk, and Sithe Energies, all in Scriba; Schoeller Technical Papers and the Fulton Co (boilers), in Pulaski; Interface Solutions in Volney; and Omega Wire in Williamstown.

Prominent residents have included Oswego's Mary Edwards Walker (1832–1919), a Civil War surgeon, dress reformer, woman suffragist, and the first woman to win the congressional Medal of Honor; Thaddeus C. Sweet (1872–1928) of Phoenix, Speaker of the state assembly from 1914 to 1920; and Edward Austin Sheldon (1823–97), who introduced Pestalozzian education to the United States at the Oswego Normal School.

The standard history is Crisfield Johnson, *History of Oswego County* (1877), updated by John C. Churchill as *Landmarks of Oswego County* (1895). The City of Oswego is discussed in two books: Charles M. Snyder, *Oswego: From Buckskin to Bustles* (1968), and Anthony M. Slosek, *Oswego: Its People and Events* (1985). There are histories of many towns, the best of which is Hope I. Marston, *Salmon River Odyssey: The Town of Richland and Its Hamlets* (2002). Elizabeth M. Simpson, *Mexico: Mother of Towns* (1949), is good despite its age, as is Evelyn L. Sauers, *The Story of Schroeppel* (1974). A comprehensive survey of the built environment is Judith Wellman, ed., *Landmarks of Oswego County* (1988).

Judith Wellman and Barbara J. Dix

Oswego River system. The Oswego River basin is a 5,115 mi^2 (13,248 km^2) watershed that includes the Seneca, Oneida, and Oswego Rivers, and the Onondaga, Oneida, Otisco, Skaneateles, Owasco, Cayuga, Seneca, Keuka, and Canandaigua Lakes, and all related tributaries. Within it are some 7,000 mi (11,265 km) of streams, 106 mi (171 km) of canals, and lakes that cover somewhat less than 6% of the total land area. The system encompasses three physiographic provinces—the Appalachian Plateau, the Tug Hill Plateau, and the Ontario Lake Plain—delineated by differences in geologic history and makeup. The basin formed during and following the last Ice Age (14,000 BP) at the same time that glaciers carved out erodable shale lying between the Lockport Dolomite bedrock and the Onondaga Limestone bedrock on the northern edge of the Appalachian Plateau. A trough formed as a result, filling with a conglomeration of clay, silt, and gravel from the receding edges of the glacier and forming a low-lying area with many miles of wetlands. The topography of the watershed, which is derived from the dolomite and limestone highland ridges and the low-lying sediment trough, dictates the runoff direction and flow rates. The Oswego River occupies the lowest points in this area and is the main outlet from the basin to Lake Ontario. The Oswego originates at the confluence of the Oneida and Seneca Rivers immediately north of Syracuse, a confluence that receives water from 96% of the Oswego River basin. This area, sometimes referred to as the Three Sisters, is also the flattest, slowest-moving reach of the Barge Canal and Oswego River basin, with inflow at times exceeding channel capacity and causing flooding. The gradient of the Oswego River, downstream of Fulton (Oswego Co), increases to 4 feet (1.2 m) per mile (1.6 km) toward Lake Ontario.

HISTORY AND GROWTH

The Iroquois established a settlement 400 years ago at the natural harbor where the Oswego River flows into Lake Ontario. The village was used for trade among the Indians but grew rapidly to encompass Europeans once they arrived. The estuarine region was crowded with aquatic biota, and the deltaic region consisted of sand, which blocked direct entry into the river from the lake. The sand was an accumulation of sediment from the entire basin, and its presence encouraged the growth of an estuarine region with well-developed spawning grounds for fish. European settlers arrived in the middle to late 1600s. In 1779 Congress designated Oswego as the first freshwater official port of entry. The port also became a major shipbuilding center, reaching its peak, of 26 vessels, in 1847.

The Oswego-Oneida-Seneca system was originally developed for navigation and power generation. In the early 1800s, entrepreneurs set up mills along the shores of the Oswego River to take advantage of its waterpower. The river was integrated into the east-west leg of the Erie Canal in 1829 and connected the Oneida and Cayuga Lakes during the early 1900s. Eight locks and dams were built to maintain enough flow to allow navigation. As an important port of entry to the Midwest, the Oswego harbor was pressured by demands from larger boats and schooners to dredge the sand split to ease access to the canal system. The harbor was first dredged in 1866, deepening it from 10 feet to 12 feet (3.1 m to 3.7 m). This split is dredged annually to allow access to the commercial harbor currently in place.

Boatyards, grain elevators, and flour mills soon developed near the mouth of the river on the east bank to promote the movement of merchandise to and from the area. Salt from Syracuse was shipped to the Midwest and grain from the Midwest was brought into New York State by the canal. The Oswego River as an economic entity suffered something of a setback after salt fields were discovered in the 1870s in the Midwest. In 1870 approximately 900,000 tons (816,000 MT) of freight was shipped on the Oswego Canal system; by 1900 the amount was about 30,000 tons (27,000 MT). In the late 1920s Niagara Mohawk Power Corp added flash guards to seven of the existing dams to provide additional storage capacity to generate hydroelectric power. Two sewage treatment plants on either side of the river opened in 1971 and discharge to the western end of the harbor. Utilities such as Niagara Mohawk discharge a portion of their cooling water into it as well.

Recent Developments

In 2002 the Oswego harbor was an active commercial port and an area for recreational boating, with storage facilities for petroleum, grain, cement, and salt. Tourism and commercial fishing are vital to the resident economy of the cities surrounding the river. However, periodic low-flow conditions near the harbor below the Varick power dam have taken a toll on wildlife habitat and fish populations. Eutrophication and reported algal blooms are attributed to excess phosphorus from municipal discharges, combined sewer overflows, and agricultural runoff. The US-Canada International Joint Commission collected data between 1976 and 1983 and concluded that the ecosystem was impaired by toxic substances contaminating the water. The New York State Department of Environmental Conservation reported the status improved with the introduction of zebra mussels in the river system. They filter the water and improve water clarity, but their metabolic activities tend to lower dissolved oxygen content necessary for fish. The 1994 Oswego River Water Quality Survey found no impairment in the harbor. Since then, however, algae have been reported in certain upstream river segment waters and associated with some of the waters directly in the locks along the river. The water drained into the Oswego River basin is treated discharge from Oswego to Canandaigua (Ontario Co) and Ithaca. In 2000 approximately 1.5 million people lived in the Oswego River drainage basin, and more than half are resident in the metropolitan area of Syracuse. The basin contains eight small cities and many villages. The health of the river system affects the roughly 1.2 million people who live in the watershed.

Managing the Water Resources of the Oswego River Basin in Central New York. Fact sheet FS 189–99 (Troy, NY: US Geological Survey, 2000)

New York State Department of Environmental Conservation. *Oswego River Remedial Action Plan: Stage 1* (Albany, Dec 1990)

Oswego River Basin, http://www.canals.state.ny.us/faq/oswego/

Samuel H. Sage

OTB. See Off-track betting corporation (otb).

Otego. Town (pop 3,183) and village (pop 1,052) in SW Otsego Co. Though early settlers arrived around 1774, Dutch from the Mohawk and Schoharie Valleys and Yankees permanently settled in 1783. The town was formed from Franklin (Delaware Co) and Unadilla in 1822 as Huntsville; the name was changed in 1830. An early source of livelihoods was the rafting of pine lumber down the Susquehanna River. After timber was depleted, farming became dominant. The Susquehanna Valley Mills (1816–1972) and the Bowe Casket Factory (1888–?1910) also provided employment. Two east-west turnpikes traversed Otego at an early date, but the Albany and Susquehanna Railroad (1866) revolutionized transport and provided employment for many residents. The population remained under 2,000 until 1960 and has since become a bedroom community for Oneonta, Unadilla, and Sidney (Delaware Co), helped by I-88 (1977). The village, incorporated 1892, is the site of the Rowland B. Hill Memorial Museum of Archaeology (1974).

Hugh C. MacDougall

Otisco. Town (pop 2,561) in SW Onondaga Co. Settled in 1801, the town was formed in 1806 from Pompey, Marcellus, and Tully. Settlement was promoted by the Skaneateles-Hamilton Turnpike (1806). Otisco Lake was made a feeder for the Erie Canal in 1863, its level raised by a dam in 1868–69 and again in 1908. Beginning around 1900 its lakeshore became a resort for summer residents. Although fanning mills were long made at Otisco Center, the town was predominantly an agricultural community and is so in the early 21st century.

Patricia Blackler

Otis Elevator. In 1852 Elisha Graves Otis, a master mechanic at a Yonkers bedstead factory, constructed a hoist that locked in position if the cable failed. This safety mechanism made the elevator acceptable for passenger use. The next year Otis opened the Union Elevator and General Machine Works Co in Yonkers and demonstrated his steam-driven safety elevator at the Crystal Palace Exposition in New York City. By 1855 there were 27 Otis freight elevators in service, most located in or near New York City. The first passenger safety elevator was installed in 1857 in a five-story retail building, E. V. Haughwout and Co, on the corner of Broadway and Broome St in New York City.

Charles and Norton Otis ran the company after their father's death in 1861 and were responsible for more than 50 elevator patents. By 1870 Otis Bros and Co revenues had surpassed $1 million. It developed the geared hydraulic elevator in 1878, which made the construction of buildings higher than five or six stories practical, and installed the first hydraulic passenger elevator at 155 Broadway in New York City. The firm introduced electric elevators (1889), pushbutton elevators (1892), and gearless traction elevators (1903–4). In 1898 the Otis Elevator Co was formed from the $11 million merger of Otis Bros and Co and 14 other elevator firms. The new company made constant improvements in elevator design and operation, introduced the escalator, acquired overseas firms, and began to offer service and maintenance contracts. By the 1950s Otis employed more than 20,000 at domestic and international sites. By 1960 net sales surpassed $500 million.

In 1976 it was sold to United Technologies Corp (UTC). The Yonkers factory was closed in 1983, in part because of increased overseas manufacturing and service. Corporate headquarters are in Farmington, Conn, with 25 manufacturing facilities in 16 countries. There are no manufacturing sites in New York State. In 2002 Otis remained a subsidiary of UTC and was the world's largest manufacturer of elevators and escalators, selling 80,000 annually with revenues of $6.8 billion.

Goodwin, Jason. *Otis: Giving Rise to the Modern City* (Chicago: Ivan R. Dee, 2001)

Suzan D. Friedlander

Otisville. Village (pop 989) in Mount Hope (Orange Co). Isaac Otis opened a store in 1816; the post office was named Otisville in 1819. The Erie Railroad served the community after 1848. An important business was the Borden Condensed Milk Co (1903). The village was incorporated in 1921. In 2003 Wessels Farm (1976) was a large greenhouse operation. The Otisville Country Fair is held each August. The major employers, located outside village limits, are Otisville Correctional Facility (1977) and the Federal Correctional Institute, Otisville (1980). Ketcham Fencing, located in the village, is a large producer of fences.

Otsego. Town (pop 3,904) in N Otsego Co. The town was formed from the Old England District in 1788, and the territory of the town was settled in 1788–89. Early manufacturing was concentrated in hamlets in Otsego's southwest. The Union Factory (1808) produced cotton at Toddsville, where there was a paper mill in later years. In 1813 a foundry was established at Fly Creek, and the hamlet produced forks, pails, agricultural implements and machinery, and ironwork in the Civil War era. Oaksville had a cotton mill beginning in 1830. As early as 1850, a resort hotel was built at Five Mile Point, and the lakeshore and the village of Cooperstown became important resorts. Visitors are drawn especially by the National Baseball Hall of Fame and Museum (1935), the Farmers' Museum (1944), and the Fenimore Art Museum (1945). SUNY Oneonta operates the Biological Field Station (1968) on Otsego Lake. Farming remains a primary land use, but Otsego has many second homes and affluent year-round residents drawn by Cooperstown's amenities.

Hugh C. MacDougall

Otsego County (1,003 mi²/2,598 km²; pop 61,676). Created from Montgomery Co in 1791 and named for 9 mi (14.5 km) long Otsego Lake. Subsequent boundary changes occurred with the creation of Schoharie (1795) and Delaware (1797) Cos. Boundary adjustments were made with Herkimer Co in 1816 and with Delaware Co in 1817 and 1822. Otsego Co is presently divided into one city, Oneonta, and 24 towns that contain 9 incorporated villages. Cooperstown is the county seat. Elevations range from just under 740 feet (226 m) in the northeast corner to over 2,420 feet (738 m) in the Town of Worcester near the Schoharie Co line. Aside from a small area in the far northeast that is part of the Helderberg Hills subregion, Otsego Co lies entirely within the Susquehanna Hills subregion of the Appalachian Upland landform province. The region is characterized by a series of highlands separated by deep narrow valleys trending northeast to southwest. The north-facing Helderberg Escarpment composed of Silurian

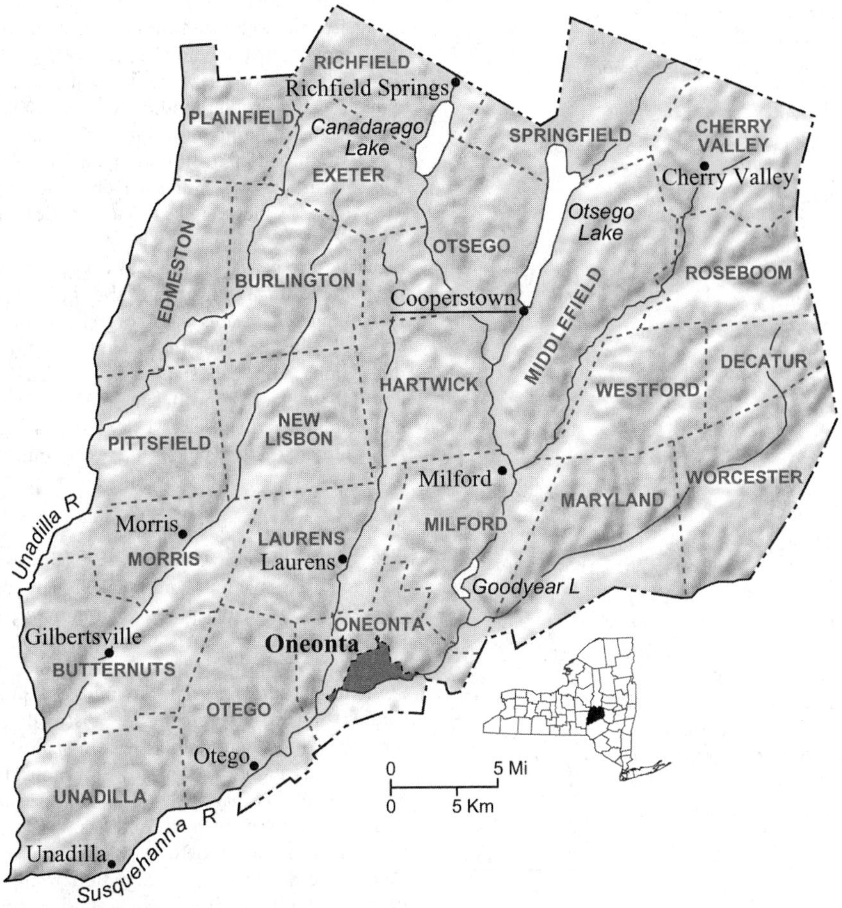

and Ordovician limestone and dolostone cuts across the county's northern margin. Here soluble limestone outcrops in layers, locally termed fissure rock, and forms characteristic karst features. Elsewhere bedrock consists of flat-lying Devonian shale and siltstone with scattered occurrences of sandstone, particularly in the southwest corner. All dip gently southward.

The county was glaciated in its entirety, as evidenced by the ridges and deep, ice-sculpted valleys that have very steep eastern slopes and more gentle western ones. Otsego Lake is the headwaters of the Susquehanna River, which along with its tributaries drains all but the northeast corner of the county, where waters flow north into the Mohawk River. The south-flowing Unadilla River serves as the county's western boundary. Otsego Co's most fertile soils are alluvial; they flank the primary streams and cover the larger valley bottoms. In the north, underlying limestone enriches the soil. Scattered patches of moderately arable soil are found in other areas, but the more prevalent upland soils are thin, acidic, and of limited agricultural value.

Otsego Co's climate is humid-continental. Mean January temperatures range from 19°F (-7°C) at Cooperstown to about 22°F (-6°C) in the lower Unadilla Valley. Mean July temperatures lie within a degree of 67°F (19°C) throughout the county. Annual average precipitation amounts vary from 39 inches (99 cm) near the southwestern border to 46 inches (117 cm) in higher elevations near Cherry Valley. Seasonal snowfall amounts range from 72 inches (183 cm) in the northwest to 117 inches (297 cm) in the northeast near Cherry Valley. The primeval forest cover consisted of two communities. Northern hardwood forest with primary species of beech, sugar maple, hemlock, white pine, and basswood dominated all but the south and southeastern margins of the county, which were covered by central hardwood forests made up of beech, sugar maple, basswood, oak, and chestnut.

Settlement

Artifacts found in the Town of Milford indicate a 11,000–12,000 year old Paleo-Indian presence, but the overall paucity of evidence suggests limited pre-Contact activity in the area. During the colonial period, present-day Otsego Co was situated along the northern edge of an extensive buffer zone between the Mohawk and various tribal groups in northern Pennsylvania. The Unadilla River and Otego Creek marked important routes between the Mohawk and Susquehanna Valleys. The area's comparative remoteness and its rough upland terrain discouraged land acquisition until after lands in the nearby Mohawk and Schoharie Valleys were partitioned. The earliest transaction involving Otsego Co territory was the Lindesay Patent in 1738. Two years later Samuel Dunlop, a Presbyterian minister, led the settlement of the Lindesay Patent by Scots-Irish families from Londonderry, NH. Other patents followed, the majority granted after 1763 when the destabilizing French presence was permanently removed. Early settlers included Palatine German descendants from the Mohawk Valley, who settled in Springfield, and Quakers from Pennsylvania and New Jersey, who took up lands in the Otego Patent [now Laurens] in 1774. Other colonial era outposts lay at Morris and Edmeston. Most settlers were bound by long leases, following the English pattern of land tenure prevalent in the colony.

The American Revolution disrupted these frontier settlements. Committee of safety records indicate that many pioneer residents supported the American cause. In response tory forces destroyed the settlement at Springfield in July 1778. That November Joseph Brant directed the destruction of the Cherry Valley settlement. In both attacks entire families were killed, and in consequence all remaining frontier settlements in the area were quickly abandoned. The following year Gen John Clinton's army passed through the Otsego and upper Susquehanna Valleys in its campaign against the Iroquois. The stability heralded by the 1783 Treaty of Paris encouraged some of the Scots-Irish, Palatine German, and Quaker settlers to reclaim abandoned lands, but by the early 1800s New England Yankees, primarily from Connecticut and Massachusetts, dominated local settlement. Others came from the Hudson Valley. A handful of wealthy families in established villages held slaves, but in general black settlement was limited, with several towns recording no African Americans whatever.

By 1800 land was being cleared in all parts of the county. The population grew rapidly over the next few decades, reaching nearly 39,000 by 1810. Growth was partly because of local land tenure conditions fostered by Judge William Cooper. Cooper sold his lands in the Town of Otsego freehold and did the same on Lutheran minister John Christopher Hartwick's 21,000-acre (8,500 ha) patent where Cooper served as agent, thereby making them more enticing to prospective settlers. In other parts of the county, tenancy coexisted with freehold status until 1846, when state legislation abolished long-lease tenancy in response to the Antirent Wars. By 1830 the county's population stood at roughly 50,000, where it was to remain until the 20th century. By the end of the second quarter of the 19th century nearly half the county's forests were felled.

Economic Development

At first the economy focused on the family farm and the production of wheat, corn, potatoes, rye, cattle, and swine, largely for home consumption. By 1810 turnpikes were operating across the northern and southern reaches of the county. The most important were the First, Second, and Third Great Western Turnpikes. They met at Cherry Valley and helped channel the flow of people, freight, and livestock across the northern part of Otsego Co between Albany and the Hudson Valley to points farther west. Farther south, turnpikes passed through Oneonta, Morris, Unadilla, and other growing towns.

The two largest communities were Cooperstown and Cherry Valley. The latter's destiny seemed especially ensured: it acquired a post office in 1794 (1 of only 35 in the state at the time), became a major turnpike junction by 1810, and was the site of one of the first banks to open west of Albany (1818). But the completion of the Erie Canal a few years later depleted traffic and dashed expectations. As the transportation system and the market economy expanded, competition from farms in Central and Western New York and beyond forced local farmers to reconsider their role in the marketplace. During the 1820s and 1830s the merino sheep craze swept

OTSEGO CO POPULATION CENSUS FIGURES

	White	Nonwhite	Total Population	Foreign-Born
1800	21,544	92	21,636	—
1810	38,595	207	38,802	—
1820	44,605	251	44,856	321
1830	51,108	264	51,372	418
1840	49,406	222	49,628	—
1850	48,463	175	48,638	1,807
1860	49,950	207	50,157	2,456
1870	48,732	235	48,967	2,733
1880	51,178	219	51,397	2,650
1890	50,623	238	50,861	2,523
1900	48,793	146	48,939	2,294
1910	47,109	107	47,216	2,332
1920	46,078	122	46,200	2,367
1930	46,567	143	46,710	2,661
1940	45,929	153	46,082	2,517
1950	50,603	160	50,763	2,735
1960	51,740	202	51,942	2,211
1970	55,743	438	56,181	1,789
1980	58,283	792	59,075	1,831
1990	59,189	1,328	60,517	1,566
2000	59,083	2,593	61,676	1,416

Notes: "Nonwhite" includes African Americans, Asians, American Indians, and Pacific Islanders and, for 2000, also the mixed race and other race categories. Through the 1960 census these figures primarily reflect the African American population. Foreign-born figures for 1820 and 1830 include only those not naturalized, and for 1930 and 1950, the foreign-born totals include Whites only. Other years include all foreign-born in the population.

across the less arable areas. Dairy farming and butter and cheese production grew in importance. By the 1860s enough farmers had turned to growing hops to make Otsego Co the biggest center of production in the country.

Abundant waterpower encouraged small-scale industrial development, and by 1800 grist- and sawmills were operating in most towns. Other industries soon followed, including a number of textile mills. The first two spinneries, where cotton from southern states was spun into thread, were erected in 1812 and 1813 in the Towns of Butternuts and Otsego, respectively.

The 1850 federal census recorded foundries in two-thirds of the county's towns. By then there were nearly 40 gristmills, over 140 sawmills, and over 4,700 farms operating. It ranked high within the state in the production of hay, oats, buckwheat, potatoes, apples, and butter, while remaining first in the nation in the production of hops, with an annual harvest of over 3 million pounds (1,360,000 kg). By 1870 one-sixth of the country's hops were grown in Otsego Co. But a decade later the situation began a rapid decline because of an infestation of blue mold and vigorous competition from West Coast growers, with Prohibition the final blow to the crop. Dairy farming prospered during most of this period as well. By the mid-1870s the county's dairy herd exceeded 40,000 head, with butter and, less significantly, cheese being the primary end products; in the late 1870s many farms near a railroad shifted to shipment of fluid milk. Unlike much of the surrounding area, Otsego Co developed a modest tourist trade in the mid-1800s. The mineral springs at Richfield Springs and to a lesser degree at Cherry Valley attracted summer tourists wishing to "take the waters," while Cooperstown touted its best-known citizen, James Fenimore Cooper, and the beauties of Otsego Lake.

The Albany and Susquehanna Railroad (later Delaware and Hudson) reached Oneonta from the state capital in 1865, but its full impact was not felt until the line was completed to Binghamton in 1869. That same year an independent line opened from Cooperstown Junction in Milford to Cooperstown. Another branch line was completed in 1870 from the Utica, Chenango and Susquehanna Valley Railroad at Waterville (Oneida Co) to Richfield Springs. A year later, rail service reached Cherry Valley from Cobleskill via Sharon Springs (Schoharie Co). Despite being served primarily by branch lines, the railroads' impact on local business was substantial. Improved transportation transformed dairy farming into a fluid-milk industry, with the railroads providing next-day delivery to large urban markets. Rail passenger service was also a boon to the resort trade at Cooperstown and Richfield Springs, where large hotels and smaller boardinghouses were built in response. The hotel staffs included African Americans, who developed small communities within the respective villages. That black population dropped by half, however, between 1890 and 1900. Contributing factors included shifts in tourist tastes and the destruction by fire of the largest hotels in Cooperstown (Cooper House) and Richfield Springs (Spring House). Smaller hotels continued the trade, and the luxury Otesaga Hotel opened in Cooperstown in 1909.

The community that benefited most directly from the railroad was Oneonta, which grew 10-fold between 1850 and 1900, largely because of extensive engine and car shops of the Delaware and Hudson, facilities that included a massive 52-stall roundhouse said to have been the nation's largest. In the adjoining rail yard on 23 Sept 1883, eight workers met in a caboose and organized the Brotherhood of Railroad Brakemen (later Brotherhood of Railway Trainmen), the first railroad labor union. In 1901 an electric interurban line connected Oneonta with the Mohawk Valley via Hartwick and Richfield Springs.

During the period of railroad expansion, almost all the small industries in the agricultural hamlets failed. The area was in overall economic decline by the late 1880s and did not attract new immigrants, although significant numbers of Irish (1840s–1850s) and Italians (1870s–1880s) had established themselves before the lack of non-railroad industry put an end to the county's draw.

Religion, Education, and Culture

Otsego Co's earliest settlers were Lutheran, Reformed, Presbyterian, and Quaker. New England migrants in the post-Revolutionary period brought other Protestant faiths. By 1810 congregations included Methodist Episcopal, Presbyterian (after the Plan of Union of 1801), Church of Christ, Baptist, and Episcopal. Of these the Baptist and Methodist Episcopal were the most numerous. Using funds bequeathed by John Christopher Hartwick (1714–96), the first Lutheran seminary in North America was chartered at Hartwick in 1816 as a seminary and classical academy. Irish immigration brought Roman Catholicism, beginning with St. Mary's Church at Cooperstown in 1847. In the early 21st century, Methodist, Baptist, Presbyterian, and Episcopal congregations are most numerous, with Roman Catholic churches in a number of communities. Oneonta's Roman Catholic parish is the largest in the county.

The Common School Act of 1812, championed by Burlington resident Jedidiah Peck, mandated primary education for all New York State children. Ultimately over 300 one-room schools dotted the county's landscape. They were supplemented by private academies, beginning with Dunlop's classical school at Cherry Valley, which opened about 1750. Oneonta built the county's first union school in 1868 following the Union Free School Act of 1853. School centralization in the 20th century began at Cherry Valley and Milford in 1927. Cooperstown Central School was the last district to centralize (1944). Otsego Co residents are currently served by 1 city school district and 10 centralized districts. BOCES provides shared services to county schools. The Otsego School (1922) is continued by Pathfinder Village (1980), a nationally known program for adults and children with Down's syndrome, located in Edmeston. Hartwick Seminary moved to Oneonta in 1929 and began granting liberal arts degrees as Hartwick College. Postsecondary education is also provided by SUNY Oneonta, founded as Oneonta Normal School in 1889, and its affiliate, the Cooperstown Graduate Program in History Museum Studies (1964). Other educational facilities include a library system that began with a Cooperstown library in 1797; all libraries in the county are members of the Four County Library System.

The *Oneonta Daily Star* is the newspaper of record. Journalism began at Cooperstown with the *Otsego Herald and Western Advertiser* (1795) and in 2004 that village had two weeklies, the *Freeman's Journal* (1800) and the *CoopersTown Crier.* The Clark family founded the renowned National Baseball Hall of Fame and Museum at Cooperstown in 1939 and the Farmers' Museum in 1942. The family was also instrumental in persuading the New York State Historical Association to move to the village during that same period. The village is also the site of the Fenimore Art Museum. The National Soccer Hall of Fame (1979) is located in Oneonta. The Glimmerglass Opera in Springfield draws major artists and has offered a varied program every summer since opening in 1974. State-maintained facilities include the Hyde Hall State Historic Site and Gilbert Lake and Glimmerglass State Parks. The Upper Catskill Council on the Arts and the Cooperstown Art Association manage ambitious cultural programs. Since 1922 residents of Cooperstown and the surrounding area have benefited from Bassett Healthcare, a not-for-profit teaching hospital with several satellite clinics.

Politics

Otsego Co government changed in 1970 from a 28-member Board of Supervisors with a representative from each town and 4 from the City of Oneonta to a 14-member Board of Representatives with 4 from the City of Oneonta and 10 representing the rest of the county. The elected chairperson serves as chief government administrator. County residents have long voted Republican in local elections. As of 2001 enrolled Republicans outnumbered Democrats by a margin of three to two.

The 20th Century

In 1900 there were 5,634 operating farms in Otsego Co but agriculture in general had passed its peak. Dairy farming remained relatively strong but the hops industry was nearing its end. The textile mills closed early in the century. In response, population declined to its lowest point in a century but stabilized and rebounded in the 1940s. The National Baseball Hall of Fame and historical institutions brought celebrity to Cooperstown, but the county's population growth occurred in and around Oneonta in the 1940s and again in the late 1950s. This was partly tied to college expansion. Conversely the railroads' role in the community declined as a result of the switch to diesel fuel and the closing of the engine and car shops. Intensive private camp development around Otsego Lake, which began in the 1870s, took place largely before World War II.

I-88 was completed along the southern margins of the county between 1976 and 1979. This helped prompt the concentration of retail along its corridor, along with a few industries (Astrocom Electronics in Milford; Corning, Inc in Oneonta) and retail warehouses. The towns have grown as well. The main rail line, now the Delaware and Hudson, remains in operation, but the spur lines are gone.

In 1997 there were only 865 operating farms in Otsego Co. Although the imprint of dairy farming remains on much of the rural landscape, the drastic decline in agricultural activity has wrought substantive economic change, most conspicuously the loss of functioning village centers, as retail trade has moved to malls both in the county and beyond. The northwestern and central areas have been hardest hit by agricultural decline, and these areas have developed few economic alternatives. As a result villages and hamlets in Hartwick, Edmeston, Burlington, Richfield, and Plainfield have lost much of their local service structure. Working farms are concentrated on limestone soils in the north and in the Susquehanna River valley. Communities and individuals now look increasingly to develop tourist-based businesses. The legend of baseball's invention in Cooperstown draws hundreds of thousands of visitors annually to the National Baseball Hall of Fame, related events, and theme camps. Cooperstown also holds the General Clinton Canoe Regatta, the longest single-day flat-water canoe race in the world. Others look simply to the county's primarily rural character to draw visitors. The largest employers include Bassett Healthcare, with a payroll of over 2,000, and the two colleges at Oneonta. A sizable segment of the population works outside the county, some as far away as Albany, Binghamton, and Utica. Economic initiatives and associated planning issues are among the most pressing concerns facing town and county boards. But despite them, during the past several decades, the area's scenic character, cultural amenities, exceptional medical facilities, and affordable and available land have enticed growing numbers of relatively affluent retirees from outside the region to move into the Cooperstown area.

POPULATIONS OF TOWNS AND CITIES, OTSEGO CO

Town or City, Year Founded	1800	1840	1880	1920	1960	2000
Burlington, 1792	2,380	2,154	1,599	999	809	1,085
Butternuts, 1796	1,388	4,057	2,036	1,383	1,352	1,792
Cherry Valley, 1791	1,550	3,923	2,260	1,400	1,156	1,266
Decatur, 1808	—	1,071	779	422	254	410
Edmeston, 1808	—	1,907	1,794	1,553	1,721	1,824
Exeter, 1799	712	1,423	1,353	814	923	954
Hartwick, 1802	—	2,490	2,340	1,648	1,400	2,203
Laurens, 1810	—	2,173	1,827	1,335	1,498	2,402
Maryland, 1808	—	2,085	2,324	1,529	1,386	1,920
Middlefield, 1797	1,044	3,319	2,726	1,547	1,376	2,249
Milford, 1796[a]	711	2,095	2,319	1,616	2,055	2,938
Morris, 1849	—	—	2,404	1,207	1,525	1,867
New Lisbon, 1806[b]	—	1,909	1,569	912	812	1,116
Oneonta, 1796[c]	4,224	1,936	4,461	1,601	4,068	4,994
Oneonta (city), 1909	—	—	—	11,582	13,412	13,292
Otego, 1822[d]	—	1,919	1,918	1,366	2,008	3,183
Otsego, 1788	1,362	4,120	4,690	4,223	4,121	3,904
Pittsfield, 1797	1,206	1,395	1,450	813	880	1,295
Plainfield, 1799	1,005	1,450	1,195	791	764	986
Richfield, 1792	1,405	1,680	2,515	2,133	2,662	2,423
Roseboom, 1854	—	—	1,515	773	518	684
Springfield, 1797	1,586	2,382	2,016	1,287	1,121	1,350
Unadilla, 1792	828	2,272	2,523	2,395	3,649	4,548
Westford, 1808	—	1,478	1,271	735	526	784
Worcester, 1797	2,235	2,390	2,513	2,136	1,946	2,207

[a]Suffrage until 1800.
[b]Lisbon until 1808.
[c]Otego until 1830.
[d]Huntsville until 1830.

America's first significant novelist, James Fenimore Cooper (1793–1851) must be counted as the county's most famous citizen. His father, Judge William Cooper (1754–1809), came to public attention through the Pulitzer Prize–winning book by Alan Taylor. Susan Fenimore Cooper (1813–94), James's daughter, was among America's first nature writers. Cooperstown native Samuel Nelson (1792–1873) served on the US Supreme Court from 1845 to 1872. Less well known is Edward Clark (1811–82), a lawyer and business partner of sewing machine inventor Isaac Merritt Singer. The Clark family fortune accrued through this wise investment has provided the Cooperstown area with museums and a hospital that aid in its overall economy and set it apart from the surrounding county.

See also ARCHITECTS AND ARCHITECTURE, MOHAWK VALLEY.

The standard county history is Duane Hamilton Hurd, *History of Otsego County* (1878), and there are several atlases, including F. W. Beers, *Atlas of Otsego County, from Actual Surveys* (1868), and Thomas F. O'Connell, *New Century Atlas of Otsego County, New York, with Farm Records* (1903). More recent accounts include Edith M. Fox, *Land Speculation in the Mohawk Country* (1949), and Jessie Ravage, *A Region of Romance* (2000). There are numerous histories of individual towns, including Kate M. Gray, *The History of Springfield* (1935); John Sawyer, *History of Cherry Valley from 1740 to 1898* (1898; repr 1997); Linda Norris, *"Time Once Past Never Returns": A History of the Town of Milford* (1996); and *Town of Pittsfield: A History* (2001). The literature on Cooperstown is voluminous, including James Fenimore Cooper, *The Chronicles of Cooperstown* (1838), and the award-winning book by Alan Taylor, *William Cooper's Town: Power and Persuasion on the Frontier of the Early American Republic* (1995). Alexander R. Thomas, *In Gotham's Shadow: Globalization and Community Change in Central New York* (2003), is a valuable study of the recent history of Cooperstown and Hartwick.

Jessie Ravage

Arthur "Putt" Telfer at Kingfisher Tower, Otsego Lake, *ca* 1910.

Otsego Lake (6.2 mi²/16.06 km²). A deep, glacier-cut lake in Otsego Co also known as Glimmerglass, from James Fenimore Cooper's *The Deerslayer* (1841). Otsego Lake has been a popular summer resort since the mid–19th century. It is 9 miles (14.5 km) long and 1.5 miles (2.4 km) wide and has a maximum depth of 168 feet (51.2 m). Shared by the Towns of Otsego, Springfield, and Middlefield and the Village of Cooperstown, Otsego Lake extends south from Mt Wellington (called the Sleeping Lion from its shape) to Cooperstown, where its outlet is the source of the Susquehanna River. The gentler west shore is lined with summer homes and camps, as well as the Fenimore Art Museum (1945), Farmers' Museum (1944), SUNY Oneonta's Biological Field Station (1968), Alice Busch Theater (1987) of Glimmerglass Opera, and Otsego Golf Course (1894), one of the oldest in the United States. The steeper, forested east shore, marked by Kingfisher Tower (1876), is largely protected from development. Glimmerglass State Park, site of Hyde Hall (1817), is at the shallower north end. Otsego Lake, though ecologically fragile, is popular for boating and fishing; the Otsego bass (a native variety of lake whitefish, now extinct) was long a nationally recognized delicacy. In 1999 the 15,000-acre (6,070 ha) Glimmerglass Historic District, comprising the lake and surrounding hills, was listed on the National Register of Historic Places.

Ravage, Jessie A. *A Region of Romance: Otsego Lake* (Cooperstown, NY: Smith-Pioneer Gallery and Otsego 2000, 1997)

Hugh C. MacDougall

Otselic [AHT-SEE-LICK]. Town (pop 1,001) in N Chenango Co. Settled in 1800, the town was formed in 1817 from German; the name is Iroquois for "Place of the Wild Plum." It was served by the Auburn Branch of the Midland Railroad. By 1855 the hamlet of South Otselic had become known for ropewalks and later became the site of Gladding Braided Products (1816), a fishing-line manufacturer that had originated south of the town line in Pharsalia; it remained in production in 2003 as a subsidiary of Wellington Leisure Products. Other 19th-century industries included a tannery (1838), the large Otselic Creamery, and a small edge-tool factory. Unproductive farmland was acquired for state forest in the 1930s, amounting to about 6,000 acres (2,400 ha). A fish hatchery was created in 1943 at South Otselic. From 1972 to about 1990, the hamlet was the site of the Gladding International Sport Fishing Museum. Grace Brown of South Otselic, who was murdered in the Adirondacks in 1906, was the subject of Theodore Dreiser's book *An American Tragedy* (1925).

Otto. Town (pop 831) in N central Cattaraugus Co. Settled in 1811, the town was formed from Perrysburg in 1823. The town had limited industry in the 19th century, including Pearce Woolen Mills (1839) and an iron foundry and machine shop, all at Waverly [now Otto hamlet]. Dairy farming became the major occupation in the mid–19th century, and factories were built to produce butter and cheese. Agriculture remains a predominant land use in the early 21st century, but second homes and recreation are growing in importance. Otto is bordered on the north by the Zoar Valley State Multiple Use Area on Cattaraugus Creek.

Bruce D. Fredrickson and Madelynn P. Fredrickson

Ovid [OH-VID]. Town (pop 2,757) and village (pop 612) in S Seneca Co. Settled in 1789, the town was formed in 1794. The village, a small part of which is in Romulus, was incorporated 1816; its government was allowed to lapse, and it was again incorporated in 1852. The original shire town of Seneca Co, Ovid has shared the county seat with Waterloo since 1822. Three brick Greek Revival buildings (courthouse, library, and jail) are known as the Three Bears because of their graduated sizes. Ovid was served by the Geneva and Ithaca Railroad, later the Lehigh Valley (1873–1960s) and by its Seneca Lake Line (1892). The Cayuga and Seneca lakeshores drew 19th- and early 20th-century vacationers; the first hotel (1852) was at Kidders, but Sheldrake Point became a noted resort with the Cayuga Lake House (1875–1909) and the Sheldrake House (1886–1939), along with many private cottages. Amish farmers from Pennsylvania arrived in the 1990s, and Ovid remained largely agricultural in 2003, dominated by grain and grapes.

Lisa Compton

Owasco. American Indian culture. The name, from nearby Lake Owasco, was given by William A. Ritchie of the New York State Museum during his 1964 excavations. He discerned three phases of Owasco, which he named Carpenter Brook (AD 950–1200), Canandaigua (AD 1200–1275), and Castle Creek (AD 1275–1350). Sites assigned to these are scattered across central New York State, from the Finger Lakes to the Mohawk Valley and the upper Susquehanna. The Owasco, it is generally accepted, were Iroquoian and evolved into the Five Nations Iroquois. Ritchie also believed that the Hunter's Home phase served as a transition between the earlier and more widespread Point Peninsula culture and early Owasco. However, the Hunter's Home phase is actually based on a misleading mixture of Point Peninsula and Owasco assemblages from separate occupations at a few sites.

The contrasts between Point Peninsula and Owasco are striking. Owasco sites feature Iroquoian longhouses, hilltop locations, palisades, maize farming, pottery, and projectile point types that are all very different from the earlier Point Peninsula culture. Most likely the early Owasco derived from the closely related Clemsons Island culture of central Pennsylvania. They expanded into central New York State from the south, displacing and partially absorbing the non-Iroquoian Point Peninsula population. The details of this long process, however, are proving to be so complex that some researchers are advocating redefining or abandoning Owasco as a meaningful archaeological culture.

See also AMERICAN INDIANS: BEFORE CONTACT.

Hart, John P., and Hetty Jo Brumback. "The Death of Owasco," *American Antiquity* 68 (2003): 737–52
Ritchie, William A. *The Archaeology of New York State* (Harrison, NY: Harbor Hill Books, 1980)
Snow, Dean R. *The Iroquois* (Cambridge, Mass: Blackwell, 1994)

Dean R. Snow

Owasco. Town (pop 3,755) in E Cayuga Co. Owasco was settled in 1792 by Dutch Americans from Orange Co who were joined by Dutch and French Huguenots from Conewango, Pa, in 1793. The town was formed from Aurelius in 1802. Lakeside Park, an amusement park at the foot of Owasco Lake, is the site of the professional Merry-Go-Round Playhouse (1975; summer musical theater) and of the 133-acre (54 ha), county-run Emerson Park. The expansion of Auburn in the 20th century resulted in a doubling of Owasco's population between 1920 and 1960; the town's northwest corner is a suburb of Auburn. But most of Owasco is agricultural, with large dairy farms growing their own corn, soybeans, and hay. It is the site of the Ward O'Hara Agricultural Museum of Cayuga County.

Laurel Auchampaugh

Owasco Lake (10.3 mi²/26.68 km²). The smallest of Central and Western New York's six major Finger Lakes. Its name derives from the Iroquoian word *wasco* (permanent river crossing), which was also the name of an important Cayuga Indian village along the Owasco Lake Outlet in Auburn (Cayuga Co). Owasco Lake fills a glacier-scoured U-shaped valley. It is 10.75 miles (17.3 km) long from north to south, an average of .9 mile (1.45 km) across from east to west, and has a maximum depth of 177 feet (54 m). Because it lies at 710 feet (216 m) above sea level, its outlet provided ample water power to spur the industrial development of Auburn in the 19th century. A number of waterworks projects that raised and stabilized the water level of the outlet have affected the lake, including the building of a permanent dam in 1835, the cutting of channels from 1852 to 1855, and the substantial dredging of the lower outlet in 1868. These works secured sufficient water resources year-round for Auburn industries and much of Cayuga Co. The zebra mussel, a nonindigenous species that clogs pipes and drains, was discovered in the lake in the 1990s. The northern end of the lake has also suffered contamination from E. coli bacteria, probably because of a growing waterfowl population. Nevertheless water from the lake won a statewide taste test in 1997. Approximately 140 acres (56.7 ha) of land along the lake's northern shore comprise Emerson Park, built in the early 1900s by trolley and shoe factory owner Frederick L. Emerson. The Emerson family donated the park to Cayuga Co in 1944. It hosts summer concert and theater series as well as the Great Race, an annual team triathlon event.

Case, Wheeler Chapin. *Along Owasco Water* (1950; repr Union Springs, NY: Tallcot, 1990)

Scott W. Anderson

Owego. Town (pop 20,365) and village (pop 3,911) in SE Tioga Co. An Onondaga settlement in what is now the village was destroyed by the Sullivan-Clinton campaign in 1779. The first Europeans settled between 1785 and 1788. The town was formed in 1791 as Union, and the name changed to Tioga in 1800 and to Owego in 1813. Lumber and shingles were rafted southward on the Susquehanna River, and there was a tannery as early as 1795. Beginning in 1808 the Ithaca and Owego Turnpike made it possible to transport goods from points north to Chesapeake Bay. The village was incorporated in 1827. Constructed over the turnpike roadbed, the second railroad in the state was completed from Ithaca to Owego in 1834, followed by the Erie Railroad (1849; its bridge shops located in the village 1850–*ca* 1890), Southern Central Railroad (1871; later Lehigh Valley Railroad), and Delaware, Lackawanna and Western Railroad (1882). Major industrial products included foundry work (*ca* 1837), pianos (1857–1918), leather (1862–1912), wagons (1880–1924), and iron bridges (1892–1927). Also, tobacco was locally cultivated, and cigars were made in small shops.

In the 20th century the village continued to grow. Stakmore Chair Co began manufacturing folding chairs in 1926. Tioga Castings operated from 1946 to 1987; IBM employed 5,000 in its Town of Owego plant from 1958 to 1994, but the numbers decreased in later years; and Endicott-Johnson Co opened a shoe factory in 1925 (closed 1986). In the 1970s the village's downtown was restored and designated a historic district. Many residents work for Owego's largest employers, Lockheed-Martin (since 1996; formerly the IBM facility) and Sanmina-SCI Corp (printed circuit boards). Suburban developments, such as Crestview Heights, serve Binghamton, Endicott, and Johnson City (Broome Co) commuters. Students of Owego Academy (1827) included industrialist John D. Rockfeller Sr; Republican political boss Thomas C. Platt (1833–1910), who celebrated electoral victories in the village's Ahwaga Hotel; and Gen Benjamin F. Tracy (1830–1915), who was secretary of the Navy (1889–93). Famous Owego residents include Gen Henry M. Robert (1837–1923), who wrote *Robert's Rules of Order Revised* here in 1915, and Belva Ann Lockwood (1830–1917), the first woman presidential candidate (1884, 1888).

Joann Lindstrom

Owenites. The socialistic ideas of Robert Owen (1771–1858), the wealthy cotton spinner of New Lanark, Scotland, attracted followers on both sides of the Atlantic. In *A New View of Society* (1813), Owen argued that proper education and environment from infancy could form superior human character resulting in a "New Moral World" of cooperation, peace, plenty, and happiness. Owen first visited New York State in November 1824 on his way to purchase New Harmony, Ind, where he attempted a working model of the New Moral World from 1825 to 1827. Dr Cornelius Camden Blatchly, who organized the New York Society for Promoting Communities in 1819, was already popularizing the creation of ideal communities as a method of social reform.

Owenites in New York formed two communities in the Hudson Valley. Forestville, also called Coxsackie, was organized on 16 Dec 1825. In 1826–27, 60 members settled 325 acres (132 ha) in the Town of Coxsackie (Greene Co). Jacob Peterson became leader after 1826 when he came in with others from the disbanded Owenite effort at Haverstraw (Rockland Co). The Forestville constitution welcomed people from all religious backgrounds, including freethinkers. Forestville operated a tannery, two sawmills, a gristmill, and a carding machine. However, disagreements ended in sale of the property in October 1827.

Owenites from New York City established the Franklin community in Haverstraw in 1826, but the community lasted only five months. Eighty members, including many farmers, tailors, and cabinetmakers, began settling in April, intending to make the 125-acre (51 ha) sawmill and rolling and splitting mill economically successful. Their secretary, George Houston, had been imprisoned in England for atheistic writings. Other prominent members included Abner Kneeland, a Universalist minister, and Robert L. Jennings, a Rationalist preacher from New Harmony. New York City attorney Henry A. Fay became director. Dissension came when Houston, Fay, and Jennings secularized the schools, established the Church of Reason, encouraged Sunday labor, and sanctioned Owen's condemnation of religion and approval of divorce. Financial mismanagement and outside objections to Franklin's radicalism accompanied the experiment's end.

When New Harmony dissolved in 1827, Owenism changed its focus from building whole communities to achieving gradual reform. Owenites in New York State became known as "free enquirers" because Owen's eldest son, Robert Dale Owen, and feminist Frances Wright brought the *New Harmony Gazette* to New York City as the *Free Enquirer*. In their Hall of Science (or Temple of Reason) on Broome St, they preached antislavery, women's rights, secularism, free public boarding schools, and political action on behalf of labor. They endorsed the New York Working Men's Party, which folded after the 1830 election. New York experienced a revival of utopian community building after 1843, inspired by Fourierism and lingering Owenite influence. Robert Owen revisited the state again and again between 1844 and 1847. Two later communities in the state bore Owenite characteristics: Skaneateles and Modern Times.

Harrison, John F. C. *Quest for the New Moral World: Robert Owen and the Owenite Movement in Britain and America* (New York: Charles Scribner's Sons, 1969)
Noyes, John Humphrey. "The Skaneateles Community." In *History of American Socialisms* (1870; repr New York: Hillary House Publications, 1961)
Stockwell, Foster. *Encyclopedia of American Communes, 1663–1963* (Jefferson, NC: McFarland, 1998)
Wunderlich, Roger. *Low Living and High Thinking at Modern Times, New York* (Syracuse: Syracuse Univ Press, 1992)

Donald E. Pitzer and Rita G. Herrington

Oxford. Town (pop 3,992) and village (pop 1,584) in central Chenango Co. The town was formed from Jericho [now Bainbridge] and Union [now in Broome Co] in 1793; Guilford was taken off in 1813 and part of Coventry was taken off in 1843. The Chenango River's mile-wide valley divides the Town of Oxford. Settled in 1790, the town quickly established Oxford Academy (1794–1895). In 1808 the center of population incorporated as a village. An elevated area in the village, known as Fort Hill, was the site of an Indian fort. The Catskill and Ithaca Turnpike (1798) was an important route for westbound settlers and eastbound produce, but the Chenango Canal (1837–78) provided the town's first commercial boost. Production included bluestone (by 1838), hoes and edge tools (1853), artificial teeth (1872), and baskets (1890). Two railroads (Utica, Chenango and Susquehanna, running north-south, and Ontario and Western, running southeast-northwest) were built in 1870. A Borden milk station (1893) served area dairy farms. In the early 21st century, Oxford residents work in surrounding communities or at the New York State Veterans Home (1897). Merritt Beardsley (1857–65), because he was afraid of the dark, asked his father for a window in his grave; it can still be seen in the Beardsley Cemetery.

Michele A. McFee

Oyster Bay. Town (pop 293,925) and locality (pop 6,826) in E Nassau Co. The town stretches from Long Island Sound to the Atlantic Ocean. Though there were earlier European settlers, the site of Oyster Bay hamlet was settled in 1653, and the northern part of the town was purchased in that year from Matinecock Indians. Town records begin in 1658. Prior to the English capture of New Netherland in 1664, the settlement was a matter of contention between the Dutch and the English. It was the Dutch who gave Oyster Bay its name, from the quantity and the quality of the oysters. The 17th-century community included Quakers, and Quaker founder George Fox visited the area in 1672. Residents engaged in farming, shipbuilding, and other maritime pursuits. The majority of the town residents were loyal to the king during the Revolutionary War, and the hamlet of Oyster Bay was a headquarters for American loyalist troops. However, one of the key members of George Washington's spy network was Robert Townsend of Oyster Bay; the family's home, Raynham Hall, is a museum. The town was recognized by New York State in 1788.

The Town of Oyster Bay remained primarily agricultural through the beginning of the 20th century, supplying produce to New York City. Asparagus and pickle cucumbers were important crops in the 19th century, and shellfishing became a major industry in the 1880s. Goods were shipped by water until the Long Island Rail Road's (LIRR's) branchlines were extended; a steamboat line began operating in 1840. Although the town acquired LIRR service in 1837, it was the rail line to Syosset (1854) that encouraged the construction of numerous mansions. Many new immigrants, particularly Irish and Italians, provided the workforce for the estates. Upon Theodore Roosevelt's presidency in 1901, Oyster Bay gained national prominence because his home at Sagamore Hill served as the "Summer White House" during his administration.

The long history of shipbuilding at Oyster Bay hamlet at the bayfront continued in the 20th century. Jakobson Shipyard (1938–93) employed as many as 600 during World War II, building ships for the US Navy. In the years leading up to and during World War II, the central part of the town, especially around Farmingdale, became home to a number of pioneering companies in the burgeoning aviation industry, employing thousands of area residents.

Many villages were incorporated in Oyster Bay in the two decades before 1938; they were intended to prevent growth, keep down taxes, and maintain political control. After World War II, rapid suburbanization transformed Oyster Bay farmland into vast residential developments consisting of thousands of private homes. The town's population rose from 42,594 in 1940 to 293,925 in 2000.

The government changed as the town grew. For much of Oyster Bay's history, town meetings were held in the spring, and all town officeholders, from supervisor to highway overseer, were elected by voice vote of the residents present. These meetings were discontinued in 1919. In 2003 a Town Board of six at-large members serving four-year terms functioned as the legislative body. A supervisor elected to a two-year term was the head of the administrative branch of town government. The town seat is the hamlet of Oyster Bay.

The area's historic buildings include the Earle-Wightman House (*ca* 1720), where the Oyster Bay Historical Society is housed. The town is the site of several state and county parks, including Bethpage State Park (1,475 acres/597 ha), Planting Fields Arboretum State Historic Park (409 acres/166 ha), and Old Bethpage Village Restoration (209 acres/85 ha). The Oyster Bay National Wildlife Refuge contains the only commercial oyster farm in New York State.

Tom Kuehhas

Oyster Bay Cove. Village (pop 2,262) in Oyster Bay (Nassau Co). Originally settled by the Youngs family, the Oyster Bay Cove grew into a small village center with its own store, church, blacksmith shop, mill, and a school attended by several of Pres Theodore Roosevelt's children. Beginning in the 1880s some of its farms were turned into estates, and in 1931 the village was incorporated in an effort to control growth. Pres Roosevelt is buried in Youngs Memorial Cemetery. The population more than quadrupled from 1950 to 2000, and it has one of the top five average household incomes in Nassau Co.

Tom Kuehhas

oysters. The species native to New York State waters is *Crassostrea virginica.* Before European settlement, oysters were ubiquitous. Laws enacted as early as 1679 to prevent the destruction of the oyster beds were for the most part unsuccessful; by the 19th century overfishing had severely depleted the natural oyster beds. During oystering's heyday in the 19th century, oysters packed in barrels were shipped by sailing vessel to New York City; some were exported to Europe. After the Civil War oysters were shipped by train and after World War I, by truck.

The waters around New York Bay and Staten Island were prime oystering locations prior to late 19th-century depletion and 1927 condemnation because of pollution. Many of the bays and inlets along Long Island's shores were also harvesting locations. Oysters were named for their locality, the most famous being the Blue Point oyster of Long Island's Great South Bay. In several areas, seed oysters from Chesapeake Bay or Connecticut were brought in and planted when the native oyster population had been exhausted.

The availability of oysters made them a highly popular dish from the 1830s on, especially in oyster bars, saloons, and cellars in major cities, particularly New York City. The 19th-century appetite for oysters would perhaps rival the current popularity of hamburgers. Like fast food, oysters were sold in informal settings suited for quick dining. The manner in which oysters have been harvested progressed from tonging from a small skiff, to dredging from a sail-driven sloop, to sucking the oysters from the bay's bottom with modern dredgers.

Early 20th-century outbreaks of typhoid traced to polluted raw shellfish, changing eating habits among Americans after World War I, and the pollution of many oyster beds caused a drastic decline in the industry. Because few localities are clean enough to allow oyster growth and harvesting, New York State's annual oyster harvest is a small fraction of what it once was. Most oysters are commercially planted and harvested. In 2002 almost 90% of the harvest came from a commercial oyster farm at Oyster Bay National Wildlife Refuge (Nassau Co). The Long Island Maritime Museum at West Sayville (Suffolk Co) houses its oystering exhibit in an old oyster shack.

Kochiss, John M. *Oystering from New York to Boston* (Middletown, Conn: Wesleyan Univ Press, 1974)

Tom Kuehhas

P

Pace University. Founded as a proprietary or for-profit business institute in 1906 by accountant Homer St. Clair Pace and his brother, attorney Charles Ashford Pace, the school first occupied rented space in the New York Tribune Building in Lower Manhattan. In addition to on-site instruction from 1909 through 1933, the institute offered correspondence courses that, from 1906 through 1921, were linked to a national network of YMCA-based classes in accounting. Rapid growth led to successive moves, first to Church St and then to 225 Broadway (1927). Incorporated as a nonprofit institute in 1935, the school received a permanent New York State charter in 1942 and five years later became a college granting bachelor's degrees. In 1951 Pace expanded in Lower Manhattan, purchasing the old New York Times Building on Park Row. The Civic Center Building opened in 1970. Pace became a university in 1973 and at the beginning of the 21st century maintains, in addition to the Lower Manhattan facility, a Midtown Manhattan center, a law school and graduate school in White Plains (Westchester Co), and undergraduate campuses in Pleasantville and Briarcliff Manor (Westchester Co). The university also offers courses at Stewart International Airport in Newburgh (Orange Co) and via the World Trade Institute, which it acquired from the Port Authority of New York and New Jersey in 1997.

Weigold, Marilyn, and David Finn. *Opportunitas: The History of Pace University* (New York: Pace Univ Press, 1991)

Marilyn E. Weigold

Paine, Thomas (*b* Thetford, England, 29 Jan 1737; *d* New York City, 8 Jun 1809). Pamphleteer. Paine lived in England with no great success as a corset maker and as an excise collector until 1774, when he moved to Philadelphia at the suggestion of Benjamin Franklin. He expected to start a school, but the Franklin connection and his natural temperament of critical protest drew him into politics and especially to political writing. In his first great work, *Common Sense* (1776), he produced a powerful argument for independence and republicanism. He also crystallized a new political language that expressed the concerns and consciousness of the ordinary people, artisans and farmers, whom the revolutionary movement brought to the center of political events. The pamphlet enjoyed the best sales in 18th-century America, with an estimated 150,000 copies produced. Although Paine donated his royalties from *Common Sense* to the Continental army, the pamphlet's success turned him into a professional writer. Paine wrote continuously throughout the Revolutionary era, most notably the series he called *The Crisis*. In 1784 the New York State legislature voted to give him a farm in New Rochelle (Westchester Co) that had been confiscated from a loyalist as a sign of its appreciation of his work.

Returning to Europe in 1787, he produced *The Rights of Man* (1791), which praised the French Revolution, and *The Rights of Man, Part the Second* (1792), which proposed the idea of a welfare state. *The Age of Reason* (1794) attacked orthodox Christianity and inspired many freethinkers, and *Agrarian Justice* (1797) advocated land reform. In England his circle included the founding conservative thinker Edmund Burke, until the two broke over the issue of the French Revolution. He also befriended the feminist writer Mary Wollstonecraft, who preceded her *Vindication of the Rights of Woman* (1792) by "vindicating" Paine's *Rights of Man* from Burke's attack upon it in *Reflections on the Revolution in France.*

Paine fled an increasingly repressive Britain for France in 1792 where his fame won him a seat in the National Convention. He fell from favor, however, when the Jacobin group replaced the Girondins, with whom he had associated himself, and he spent nearly a year in prison. He returned to the United States in 1802 by invitation of Pres Thomas Jefferson and settled on his Westchester Co farm. He moved to Greenwich Village in Manhattan in 1808 and died the following year. His remains were later exhumed and taken to England, where they were lost.

Paine's unorthodox religious beliefs alienated him from orthodox Christians, and he spent the last part of his life in obscure poverty. However, he is remembered as the foremost pamphleteer of the American and French Revolutions, and his ideas influenced New Yorkers during and long after the Revolutionary era. Just as *Common Sense* crystallized the case for independence, *The Rights of Man* inspired the Democratic-Republican societies of the mid-1790s, and *The Age of Reason* was being read and debated within the Working Men's political movement of the late 1820s and early 1830s.

Foner, Eric. *Tom Paine and Revolutionary America* (New York: Oxford Univ Press, 1976)
Keane, John. *Tom Paine: A Political Life* (Boston: Little, Brown, 1995)

Edward Countryman

Painted Post. Village (pop 1,842) in Erwin (Steuben Co). The name comes from a wooden post erected by the Iroquois to signify an important trail junction. European settlement began in 1787 with the arrival of William Harris, a trader to the native peoples. The post was subsequently replaced by a series of monuments. Streets were surveyed in 1833, and the present Painted Post post office (formerly Erwin) was named in 1840. The village was incorporated in 1893. Machine shops that built and repaired equipment for the area's sawmills led to the founding of what became Dresser Rand. In 2003 Painted Post was a village of residential streets surrounding a small business district. The Dresser Rand plant left the village in 1987 for a new facility in Erwin; in 2003 the Erwin plant was the primary employer of Painted Post residents.

Thomas Dimitroff

Pakistanis. Pakistanis started arriving in New York State in large numbers in the late 1960s, the majority from Punjab, the country's most populous province. The primary reason has been economic opportunity, and migration increased after the 1971 civil war. In the early 1970s professionals settled in the New York City area, often joined by family or friends. Pakistanis in the state are often politically and culturally active, and through hard work have quickly improved their economic status, often while supporting relatives in Pakistan. The largest communities are in the Boroughs of Queens, especially Jackson Heights, and Brooklyn, encompassing about one-third of the statewide population. Many move on to Westchester or Rockland Cos seeking better public schools and room for growing families. Many have pursued education and work in small businesses such as grocery stores, restaurants, newsstands, and auto repair shops, with a small group consisting of professionals who are pharmacists, physicians, dentists, or importers of garments and carpets from Pakistan.

Pakistani social, cultural, and religious organizations were founded and initially controlled by a few enterprising individuals. In the early 1970s the first Pakistani television program was aired; there are now at least three regular broadcasts. Prominent Urdu language weekly newspapers, several of them founded in the past decade, include the *Pakistan Post* and *Pakistan News* (both published in Jamaica, Queens Co), *Pakistan Express* and *Pakistan Calling* (Jackson Heights, Queens Co), *Sada-E-Pakistan* (Jersey City, NJ), *New York Awam* (founded in 1987 and published in Lower Manhattan), and *Urdu Times*, the first and largest Pakistani newspaper in North America (founded in the 1980s and published in a dozen US cities including New York). Musicians, actors, and pop singers visit on tour every summer, and traditional Urdu poets and writers from Pakistan frequently read their works in New York City at recitals sponsored by the New York Literary Forum, Halqa-Fun-O-Adab, and Urdu Markaz. Cricket is another passion, with games every Sunday. The next generation is gradually merging into mainstream America, and the majority of younger Pakistani Americans speak only English.

In 2000 the state was home to 51,055 Pakistanis, over 22% of the US total. More than 75% of the state's Pakistan-born residents live in New York City, with over 92% in the greater metropolitan area. In the wake of 11 Sept 2001, large numbers of Pakistanis living in New York City went to Canada or to Pakistan to avoid deportation, an exodus that affected the businesses that had thrived in their communities. However, many have continued to live throughout New York State with few or no problems.

Hassan, Nasim. "An American Experience," http://www.contactpakistan.com/Communitylibrary/general/news43.htm

Nasim Hassan

Palatine. Town (pop 3,070) in NW Montgomery Co. The town was settled by Palatine Germans; Hendrick Frey, by tradition the first settler, came to Stone Arabia *ca* 1723. Organized as Stone Arabia District in 1772 and changed to Palatine District in 1773, the town was formed in 1788. During the Revolutionary War, the area suffered several raids, particularly the 19 Oct 1780 skirmish at Stone Arabia. Dairy farming, lumbering, and quarrying occupied most residents in the 19th century. In the early 21st century most of the land remains agricultural, and much of it is farmed by an Amish community that first settled in 1986. The Palatine Church (1770) and the Reformed Dutch Church of Stone Arabia

(1787–89) are National Register landmarks. The 322-acre (130 ha) former Montgomery County Home on Rte 5 was sold to Akwesasne Mohawks in 1993 and became the Kanatsiohareke community and cultural center.

James Crawford

Palatine Bridge. Village (pop 706) in Palatine (Montgomery Co). Settled by members of the Frey family before 1739, it took its name from a covered bridge (1798), the first bridge across the Mohawk River west of Schenectady. A post office opened in 1814, and the Utica and Schenectady Railroad (later New York Central) came through in 1836. Incorporated in 1867, the village had a diverse industrial base during the 19th century, with limestone quarries, a cider factory, and other food-processing businesses. Webster Wagner (1817–82), stationmaster from 1843 to 1860, was the inventor of an early railroad sleeping car. In the early 21st century most residents work in service businesses, at Beech-Nut in Canajoharie, or in communities east or west.

James Crawford

Palatine immigration of 1709. The first sizable German group to migrate to colonial New York, the Palatines were sent to implement British mercantilist policies but ended up forging their own communities. Overpopulation, heavy taxation, and the exceptionally harsh winter of 1708–9 burdened the people living in central western and southwestern Germany, in and around an area known as the Palatinate, a region still recovering from the devastation of the Thirty Years' War and subsequent warfare. Religious persecution played little role in their desire to leave the war-torn region, but appeals to a shared Protestantism brought assistance from the English monarchy. An initial group of about 41 Palatines traveled to London to petition Queen Anne for assistance as war refugees and were then joined by 13,000 more between 1708 and 1710. A majority were Pietists and Lutherans, and about one-third were Catholics. Most were sent back to Germany. Those remaining received permission to settle on the Hudson River on the condition that they work in the production of the important naval stores of tar and pitch—vital supplies for an empire dependent upon naval commerce.

Hearing of the opportunities for land and employment, thousands of people poured into Rotterdam (Netherlands), awaiting expense-paid voyages to New York Colony via London. During the six-month voyage, over one-seventh of them died from typhus. On 13–14 June 1710, some 2,500 immigrants arrived in New York City to join the naval stores project. Fearing these much-needed workers would settle in another colony, royal governor Robert Hunter had the Palatines indentured to the Livingston estates along the Hudson. Their earnings from making naval stores were meant to reimburse the British government for its expenses. The Palatines faced difficult conditions: supplies dwindled, many of their children were apprenticed without regard to family claim, and they resented being forced to work as gang laborers. After the tory government lost interest in the project, Hunter, himself heavily in debt, withdrew his financial support in 1712.

Disgusted, over 150 Palatine families left in 1712–13, despite Hunter's protest, determined to claim the lands they believed had been promised them in the Schoharie Valley. Although the land had been returned to the Mohawk because of a spurious deed, the Indians supplied them with food and even lodged young Conrad Weiser for the winter. The Palatines founded seven villages, of which Schoharie and Middleburgh (Schoharie Co) remain today. Title disputes between royal agents, the Seven Partners—a group of British investors that claimed rights to the lands—and the settlers ensued. The Palatines clung to their land, forging the legend that Mohawk chieftains, upon seeing their miserable conditions in London, were moved by pity to promise the Schoharie Valley solely for the immigrants' use. By the 1720s and 1730s, many families left, settling in the nearby Mohawk Valley or moving south to Pennsylvania. Members of the Palatine Evangelical Lutheran Church built the Old Palatine Church [now in Nelliston, Montgomery Co] in 1770. The Palatines assimilated by intermarrying with Dutch families or joining Dutch Reformed churches but also remained a distinct ethnic group vigorously defending their rights to property against Dutch and English claimants. Today the Palatine Society, whose members are descendants of the early settlers, continue to restore the Old Palatine Church and with advance notice open it to visitors.

Knittle, Walter Allen. *Early 18th-Century Palatine Emigration* (Philadelphia: Dorrance, 1937)

Roeber, A. G. *Palatines, Liberty, and Property: German Lutherans in Colonial British America* (Baltimore: Johns Hopkins Univ Press, 1998)

Kathryn Clippinger Kosto

paleontology. See ANCIENT LIFE.

Palermo. Town (pop 3,686) in central Oswego Co. Settled in 1806 the town was formed in 1832 from Volney. Barrelheads and staves were valuable early products that were shipped to manufacturing villages. Lumbering remains important; in the early 21st century two sawmills still operate, but they are the only industry aside from farming. Most residents commute. The Anti-Slavery Methodist Episcopal Church was incorporated at Denton's Corners in 1860. It closed in 1964 and the building was demolished.

Barbara J. Dix

Palisades Interstate Parkway. Scenic 42 mi (67 km) road. The parkway runs along the west side of the Hudson River between Fort Lee, NJ, and the Bear Mountain Bridge at Harriman (Orange Co). In New Jersey, it skims the majestic 550 ft (168 m) Palisades Escarpment, and in New York it traverses the 53,463-acre (21,636 ha) naturalistic preserve of the Bear Mountain and Harriman State Parks (Rockland and Orange Cos). The parkway completed the effort to preserve the Palisades initiated by the Palisades Interstate Park Commission (PIPC) in 1900. By the 1920s the commission owned most of the cliff face and shore land that had been threatened by quarrying, but land atop the cliffs remained in private hands. With the anticipated completion of the George Washington Bridge (1927–31) linking New York City with northern New Jersey, this formerly inaccessible land was ripe for intensive suburban development. The plan to construct a scenic drive along the cliffs, developed by the Regional Plan Association and the PIPC, was intended to channel development and local/commercial traffic to the west, thus preserving the most scenic areas for public use and providing the urban population with access to thousands of acres of parkland. Securing public approval and land acquisition took 20 years but was bolstered by John D. Rockefeller Jr's donation of 60% of the land needed in New Jersey in 1935. Built from 1947 to 1961 by the New York and New Jersey departments of public works, the road followed the parkway model established in the 1920s but incorporated contemporary improvements in highway design. The traffic load for 2002 was 21 million vehicles.

See also STATE PARKS.

Perkins, George W. "References and Notes on the Palisades Interstate Parkway," 1946. Palisades Interstate Park Commission Archives, Bear Mountain State Park, NY

Kathleen LaFrank

Palmer, Erastus Dow (*b* Pompey, Onondaga Co, 2 Apr 1817; *d* Albany, 9 Mar 1904). Sculptor. Palmer moved with his parents to Utica when he was 9 years old. Until he was 29, he worked as a carpenter and joiner, crafts he learned from his father. In 1846, while living in Utica, he carved a cameo portrait of his second wife, Mary, on an oyster shell using files he had made himself. Recognizing Palmer's talent, people began commissioning cameo portraits, and for the next two years, Palmer carved more than 100 portraits. He moved to Albany in 1849 and later was familiarly called "the Albany Sculptor." Two years later, Palmer exhibited his first marble bust, *Infant Ceres,* modeled after his young daughter, at the National Academy of Design in New York City. Palmer's fame was further enhanced the same year with two bas-reliefs, *Morning* and *Evening.* Other notable sculptures include *Faith Viewing the Cross* (1852), *Indian Girl* (1853), *The White Captive* (1857–59), *Peace in Bondage* (1863), *The Angel of the Sepulchre* (1868), and *Robert R. Livingston* (1874). Palmer also created portrait busts of Alexander Hamilton, Washington Irving, and Commodore Matthew C. Perry. Unlike many American contemporaries, Palmer honed his self-taught artistic skills, as well as acquired inspiration for his sculpture in the United States rather than in Europe. Palmer visited Europe in 1873–74, only after he had attained considerable renown.

Webster, J. Carson. *Erastus D. Palmer* (Newark: Univ of Delaware Press, 1983)

Thomas A. Hunter

Palmer [née Worrall], Phoebe (*b* New York City, 18 Dec 1807; *d* New York City, 2 Nov 1874) and **Palmer [née Worrall], Sarah A. Lankford** (*b* New York City, 23 Apr 1806; *d* New York City, 24 Apr 1896). Methodist preachers. These sisters were two of the most effective leaders of the Holiness movement in 19th-century Methodism, which emphasized Christian perfectionism, sanctification, and holy living. In 1827 Phoebe married Walter C. Palmer, a New York City physician and active Methodist. Four years later Sarah married Thomas Lankford, a Virginia architect. As young women, both sisters spoke to Sunday school classes and prayer meetings. Sarah established weekly meetings in her home in 1835, which eventually attracted Methodist leaders and featured Bible study, prayer, and personal religious testimonies. In 1838 Phoebe began her career as a revival preacher, traveling extensively across the United States, Canada, and Great Britain. When Sarah and her husband moved from New York City to Caldwells Landing [now Haverstraw, Rockland Co] in 1840, Phoebe assumed the leadership of the weekly gatherings; when Phoebe was occupied with speaking engagements outside of the city, Sarah resumed as leader. Phoebe served as the editor of the *Guide to Holiness* (1864–74), the foremost publication of the Holiness movement, and was the author of several books, including *The Way of Holiness* (1843), *Faith and Its Effects* (1848), and *Promise of the Father* (1859), which is a defense of women's right to preach. Believing that ministry must be more than preaching the Christian message, Phoebe provided medical care, food, and other aid to the poor. She was an active member of the Methodist Woman's Home Missionary Society and a founder of the Five Points Mission in New York City, one of the first attempts by the church to reach out to the poor. Sarah's husband died in 1871. Two years after Phoebe's death, Sarah married Walter Palmer, moved back to New York City, took up the role of editor of the *Guide to Holiness,* and carried on a preaching ministry. In the years following Walter Palmer's death, she contributed regularly and generously to the home and overseas mission work of the Methodist Episcopal Church.

See also HOLINESS-WESLEYAN MOVEMENT.

Raser, Harold E. *Phoebe Palmer: Her Life and Thought* (Lewiston, NY: Edwin Mellen Press, 1987)
Roche, John A. *The Life of Sarah A. Lankford Palmer* (New York: George Hughes, 1898)
White, Charles Edward. *The Beauty of Holiness: Phoebe Palmer as Theologian, Revivalist, Feminist, and Humanitarian* (Grand Rapids, Mich: Francis Asbury Press, 1986)

Charles Yrigoyen Jr

Palmer, Sophia F(rench) (*b* Milton, Mass, 26 May 1853; *d* Forest Lawn, Monroe Co, 27 Apr 1920). Nurse administrator and journalist. Palmer held the position of superintendent of the Rochester City Hospital (1896–1901) and served as the first editor (1900–1920) of the *American Journal of Nursing,* the primary journal written by and for nurses. Palmer's forceful editorials advocated for statutory regulation of nursing, a united profession, and the development of nursing organizations during the profession's formative years. She was one of the founders of the American Society of Superintendents of Training Schools for Nurses (later National League for Nursing) and the Nurses Associated Alumnae (now American Nurses Association). She was instrumental in the formation of the New York State Nurses Association and worked for passage of the 1903 New York State Nurse Practice Act. In 1903 she was appointed to the state's first Board of Nurse Examiners and was elected its first president. Palmer remained an influential nursing leader until her death. As nursing evolved she championed reforms in nursing education and effective communication in the profession and, following World War I, assisted in drafting a resolution requesting military rank for nurses.

Christy, Teresa E. "Portrait of a Leader: Sophia F. Palmer," *Nursing Outlook* 23 (Dec 1975): 746–51

Julie M. Pavri

Palmer, Walter Launt (*b* Albany, 1 Aug 1854; *d* Albany, 16 Apr 1932). Painter. Son of sculptor Erastus Dow Palmer, he studied with Charles Loring Elliott, Frederic Edwin Church, and Carolus Duran. After studying in Paris with Duran during the early 1870s, he moved to New York City, where he shared a studio with Church from 1877 to 1881. He established a reputation as a follower of the Pre-Raphaelites and painted interior scenes such as *Library at Arbour Hill* (Albany, 1878) but became notable for landscapes of the Catskills and Hudson Valley. During the 1880s he embraced impressionism and painted vistas of Venice. He returned to Albany in 1881 and began painting winter landscapes. He was celebrated for using delicate tones to illustrate reflections of light and was renowned for using shades of blue to illuminate snow. In 1897 Palmer was elected to the National Academy of Design. He produced over 1,000 landscapes, including a depiction of Hudson (Columbia Co) in *Road to Olana* (1888) and the well-known *Autumn Morning Mist Clearing Away* (1892), and continued to exhibit until his death.

Mann, Maybelle, and Alvin Mann. *Walter Launt Palmer: Poetic Reality* (Exton, Pa: Schiffer Publishing, 1984)

Mary Alice Mackay

Palmyra. Town (pop 7,672) and village (pop 3,490) in SW Wayne Co. Settled in 1789 by, among others, an organized colony from Southampton (Suffolk Co), it was created as Tolland District in that year and formed as a town under its present name in 1796; Macedon was separated from in 1823. The village, incorporated 1819, was on the Erie Canal (1822) and the New York Central Railroad (1853). Joseph Smith Jr, the founder of the Church of Latter-day Saints (LDS), said he unearthed the Golden Tablets on Hill Cumorah just south of the village, and the Book of Mormon was first published in the Grandin printing shop in Palmyra in 1830. Palmyra resident Olin J. Garlock devised an improved way to seal piston rods in steam engines about 1884. In 2003 Garlock Sealing Technologies was one of the largest employers in Wayne Co and maintained facilities around the world. Palmyra was the setting for Samuel Hopkins Adams's 1944 novel *Canal Town.* The nearby LDS Hill Cumorah Pageant has been an attraction since the 1930s, and in recent years Palmyra has become a center for Mormon tourism, as the church has purchased and refurbished several sites associated with Smith, including the Smith family homestead, the print shop, and the grove where Smith encountered the angel Moroni. In 2000 the LDS opened a temple in Palmyra, the first in New York State.

See also ARCHITECTS AND ARCHITECTURE, ROCHESTER AND WESTERN NEW YORK.

Scott C. Monje

Pamelia. Town (pop 2,897) in central Jefferson Co. Settled around 1805, Pamelia was formed in 1819 from Brownville and briefly renamed Leander in 1824–25. In 1869 its industrial area along the Black River was annexed to the new city of Watertown. The rest was primarily a dairying district, specializing in Limburger and cheddar cheeses, later switching to fluid milk; there was also a brickyard (1888). I-81 was completed through town in 1965–66. Since the 1960s, and especially since the expansion of Fort Drum in the 1980s, Pamelia has become increasingly urbanized.

Laura Lynne Scharer

Panama. Village (pop 491) in Harmony (Chautauqua Co). Settled around 1818, the village incorporated in 1861. In its early years the economy centered on an ashery and a large tannery, but it lost ground when the village was bypassed by the railroads. Later it was a center of butter and cheese factories. Employers in 2002 included the school system and an insurance firm. James H. McGraw (1860–1948), founder of McGraw-Hill Publishing Co, was a Panama resident until his 1884 graduation from Fredonia Normal School. Privately owned Panama Rocks, a popular tourist attraction for over 100 years, consists of conglomerate rock formations, including caves, chasms, and passageways.

Pamela A. Brown

Panamanians. A diverse, racially mixed nation consisting mainly of Spanish- and English-speaking Antillean blacks, Panamanians are predominantly Roman Catholic, though some 15% are Protestant, and some affiliate with African Caribbean religions. Panamanians, primarily descendants of Caribbean canal workers, started migrating to New York State during the 1950s. The political unrest and uncertainty of the years just before and after Manuel Noriega's regime ended in 1989 led to significant emigration.

New York City residents from this isthmus country hold two parades in Brooklyn to celebrate national holidays. The first, which began in 1998, is held on 10 August, in celebration of the foundation of the City of Panama. The second is in celebration of their 3 November Independence Day and is typically held on Franklin Ave in Brooklyn on the second Saturday of October. Panamanians have also formed various civic groups such as the Dedicators and the Panamanian Civic Committee of New York. Well-known Panamanian New Yorkers have included baseball players Rod Carew, who moved to New York City as a teenager, and Mariano Rivera, a star pitcher for the New York Yankees; Ruben Blades, a renowned singer-songwriter who arrived in New York City in 1978. Kenneth B. Clark, the eminent sociologist, was born in the Canal Zone in 1914. Panamanian-born Waldaba Stewart, a former New York State senator, is also a prominent figure within the Panamanian community in New York State. The 2000 census indicated that the Panamanian-born population in New York State was approximately 20,055, down from 26,173 in 1990. The majority are in Kings Co (10,616), primarily in Flatbush; Queens Co (3,201); New York Co (1,120); and Bronx Co (1,585).

Logan, John. "The New Latinos: Who They Are, Where They Are," http://mumford1.dyndns.org/cen2000/HispanicPop/HspReport/HspReportPage1.html

Ana Margarita Cervantes-Rodríguez and Michael C. English

Pan American Airways. Juan Trippe, a young Yale alumnus and aviation pioneer who became involved in airline ventures in New England in the early 1920s, formed Pan American Airways on 14 Mar 1927, and this became the operating name on 2 June 1927 for the Aviation Corp of America. Based in Miami, Pan American proceeded to build an airline network throughout Latin America, expanding in 1935 across the Pacific Ocean. This was Trippe's initial step in his ambition to encircle the globe with his airline. On 18 June 1937 Pan American began a joint service, with British Imperial Airways, from Port Washington (Nassau Co) to Bermuda. Also, during 1937, survey flights were conducted across the Atlantic Ocean with the British to establish the feasibility of operating a scheduled service to Europe. These flights were based at Port Washington, where Pan American established its Atlantic Division. Scheduled North Atlantic passenger service was inaugurated in 1939 from Port Washington. The company continued to operate several routes to Europe during World War II. Operations were transferred on 31 Mar 1940 to the Marine Air Terminal at the newly opened La Guardia Airport in Queens, and this remained Pan American's base until the 1949 opening of Idlewild International Airport (now John F. Kennedy International Airport) in Queens.

The airline, which changed its name to Pan American World Airways in 1950, was a major presence in New York City throughout the postwar years until its demise. From JFK, Pan American launched first the jet age with Boeing 707s on 26 Oct 1958 and then the jumbo jet age with Boeing 747s on 22 Jan 1970. The airline had consolidated its New York image on 7 Mar 1963 when it opened headquarters in the Pan Am Building next to Grand Central Terminal. For a short period this was the rooftop site of the helicopter station of New York Airways operated in conjunction with Pan American's global network. Service opened directly from JFK to the rooftop on 21 Dec 1965 but was suspended in February 1968. Service was reopened in the spring of 1977 but abruptly terminated after a fatal accident on the rooftop on 16 May 1977. Other Pan American operations in its latter years included the New York–Washington, DC, shuttle service, opened on 1 Oct 1986, and the Pan Am Express local commuter connections to cities in neighboring states. Battling competition from both national and foreign airlines and suffering from deteriorating management leadership, the airline's fortunes declined. The airline was never the same after founder Juan Trippe retired in 1968. On 4 Dec 1991 Pan American closed its doors.

Banning, Gene. *Airlines of Pan American since 1927* (McLean, Va: Paladwr Press, 2001)
Davies, R. E. G. *Airlines of the United States since 1914* (1972; repr McLean, Va: Paladwr Press, 1998)

R. E. G. Davies

Pan-American Exposition. After a visit to the Cotton States Centennial and International Exposition in Atlanta in 1895, several Buffalonians decided their city should host an exposition to promote trade and social relations among the nations of North, South, and Central America. The latest in a series of international expositions begun in the early 1850s, it opened on 1 May 1901. The exhibit buildings and the midway, in Spanish Renaissance style, were built on a 350-acre (142 ha) site in and around Delaware Park. Because the event was in part designed to promote Buffalo by celebrating the electrical power generated at Niagara Falls, each building was outlined in lights after dark, and its most prominent structure was the Electric Tower, which rose 410 feet (125 m) from its base to the top of the *Goddess of Light* statue. Pres and Mrs William McKinley visited the fair on 5–6 September; on 6 September, as McKinley was shaking hands with well-wishers after delivering a speech in the Temple of Music, he was shot by Leon F. Czolgosz and died eight days later. The fair, despite its 8 million visitors, was a financial failure. Only one of its buildings was intended as a permanent structure; all were demolished after the fair closed on 2 November except the New York State Building, which was transformed into the home of the Buffalo Historical Society (now Buffalo and Erie County Historical Society).

Leary, Thomas, and Elizabeth Sholes. *Buffalo's Pan-American Exposition* (Charleston, SC: Arcadia, 1998)

Vicki Weiss

paper industry. The first paper mill in New York was established in 1773 by Hendrick Onderdonk in Hempstead [now in Nassau Co]. Pres George Washington visited Onderdonk's mill in 1790, expressing much interest in, and even trying his hand at, the unfamiliar process of hand papermaking. This was an arduous and time-consuming process. The rags used in it were first shredded, then mixed with water in a vat, where the rags were beaten until they formed a pulp, called stuff. A mold was dipped into the vat of stuff and then shaken to interlace the fibers and form them into a uniform thickness. The moist sheet of paper was then removed from the mold, laid on felt cloth, put in a press to eliminate excess water, and allowed to dry for several days.

Electric Tower at night, Pan-American Exposition, Buffalo, 1901.

Making 1 pound (.5 kg) of paper required 1.5 pounds (.7 kg) of rags and gallons of water. Paper was costly, often scarce, and sensitive to erratic supplies of rags. The 1810 US census reported 28 mills in New York State; workers produced 77,000 reams of paper valued at over $230,000. New York accounted for nearly one-fifth of the nation's paper production, trailing only Massachusetts and Pennsylvania. Even so, early 19th-century printers continued to buy paper from Europe, as they long had done.

Advances in Technology

In the early 1800s a series of technological breakthroughs in papermaking allowed for a vast domestic expansion of the industry. Beginning in 1804, a series of new techniques pioneered in England mechanized most of the papermaking process, increasing production and reducing costs. Bryan Donkin, an English immigrant, introduced the first of the mechanized processes, the Fourdrinier, to America in 1827 at the Beach Mill in Saugerties (Ulster Co). Most if not all paper mills during this period were along substantial rivers because water—for processing fibers, generating power, and transporting rags and finished products—was the irreplaceable lifeblood of the paper industry. The Hudson River between Albany and New York City provided a natural center for the industry until the post–Civil War advent of wood-pulp paper shifted most paper production into the Adirondacks. Another modification, the cylindrical process, was introduced in the state at the Knowlton and Rice Mill in Watertown in 1832. The cylinder machine produced lower quality paper but required less capital investment and less skilled labor and increased production.

The number of paper mills in the state grew steadily, from 77 in 1840 to 109 in 1855. The cylinder machine soon outpaced the Fourdrinier, and by 1864 the ratio was more than 100 to 17 in the state. In 1855 the state's paper mills employed 1,674 workers and consumed 19,882 tons of rags. Only 12 used steam engines; the rest relied on waterpower. There were also 37 mills, 15 in Columbia Co alone, making wrapping, board, and box paper from straw. New York State papermakers had experimented with cane, bamboo, and wire grass but became well known for their strawboard. In 1860 paper mills were located across the state from Chautauqua to St. Lawrence to Suffolk Cos. Mills could be found in 36 of the state's 60 counties. New York State's 126 mills, valued at more than $2 million, employed 1,857 workers. These mills produced 14,340 tons of wrapping paper, 8,652 tons of printing paper, 2,154 tons of strawboard, 886 tons of writing paper, and 850 tons of wallpaper, products valued in all at $3 million for that year. New York State led the country in production of wrapping paper and strawboard, with only the more heavily capitalized mills of Massachusetts ahead in the production of both writing and printing paper. —*WSP*

Wood-Pulp Revolution

A revolution in papermaking in New York State and elsewhere occurred in the late 1860s as a result of discoveries made in Europe. In 1858 an English company patented a method of producing paper from wood pulp. To make pulp, wood is treated to separate its wood fibers in one of two ways: mechanical or chemical. Ground wood pulp is made by grinding wood mechanically. In the 19th century, after the bark was removed, the wood was ground between large mill-type stones, approximately 5 feet (2 m) in diameter and 15 inches (38 cm) thick, whose movement was powered by water or steam. These were replaced by huge electric-powered mechanical grinders before the end of the century. Paper from ground wood pulp was used primarily for newsprint. The second method used chemicals, removing the lignin that binds wood fibers together and creating cellulose pulp. Chemicals were not used extensively until after 1880. These two methods were later combined in a third process.

Two brothers, German immigrants Albrecht and Rudolf Pagenstecher, founded the German language *New Yorker Staats-Zeitung* in Manhattan in 1834; in 1868 the *Staats-Zeitung* became the first newspaper in the country to use wood pulp, an innovation that transformed the paper industry and its geographic distribution. Initially, at a mill in Massachusetts, the Pagenstechers used ground poplar wood to make paper by the Fourdrinier process. After local supplies of poplar were depleted, they perfected a way of using spruce. The fibers of spruce and balsam were long enough that only a small amount of rags, to be mixed with the pulp, were needed to make newsprint. In 1868 the brothers opened a mill in the southeastern Adirondacks around the confluence of the Hudson and Sacandaga Rivers because it was near a source of spruce and offered the large quantities of water required to make pulp and paper. There, at Luzerne (Warren Co), the Pagenstechers established the Hudson River Pulp and Paper Co in 1869 and shortly after added an additional mill nearby at Palmer Falls [now Corinth in Saratoga Co].

By the early 1870s numerous pulp and paper mills were sited around the periphery of the Adirondacks, including along the Hudson River and its tributaries in the east, in the Champlain Valley to the north, and along the Black River to the west. Spruce wood-pulp production in the state rose precipitously from 60 tons annually in 1880 to 40,150 tons by 1890. By 1891 New York State had 75 pulp and paper mills, 48 in the Adirondacks. Numerous large paper firms formed in this area included International Paper Co, founded in 1898 in Corinth; Hinckley Fibre Co, organized in 1890 from several small companies located near the West Canada Creek in Herkimer Co; and St. Regis Paper Co, incorporated in 1899 from several mills in the Tupper Lake area of St. Lawrence and Franklin Cos. J. and J. Rogers of Au Sable Forks (Essex Co) began producing paper in 1894 and Finch, Pruyn and Co (1865) of Glens Falls (Warren Co) shifted from saw log to paper production in 1905. That year marked the peak of pulp production in New York State, when 294,582,420 board feet were converted to pulp.

New Chemical Processes and Industry Decline

Pulp and paper production continued to increase until 1905 and then declined dramatically as New York State's forests were depleted of their merchantable spruce. By 1910 more than half the pulp wood consumed in the North Country's mills came from Canada. To cut transportation costs, new chemical processes were pioneered that allowed other local woods to be combined with spruce to make pulp. One of these, using sulfite, blended hemlock with spruce. By 1920 half of New York State's mills used this process. For a time New York State pulp and paper mills survived using chemical processes, but gradually the number of mills began to decline through closures or consolidation. Many paper firms began to relocate out of the Adirondacks, moving to the southern and western parts of the country, where timber was more plentiful and less expensive and newer and more efficient mills could be built. In 1939 only 42 wood-pulp and paper mills remained in New York State, and by 1963 these had decreased to 18. Although newer chemical processes developed by the New York State College of Forestry at Syracuse made it feasible to mix hardwoods with spruce, they could not stem further deterioration in the state's paper industry. As a result of the decline, the population of the Adirondack region fell slightly until after World War II.

By 2003 only two integrated paper mills remained in New York State: Finch, Pruyn and Co of Glens Falls and the International Paper Co's mill at Ticonderoga (Essex Co), both of which rely on local wood and employ a total of about 1,000 unionized workers (United Paperworkers International Union Locals 18,155 and 5,497 respectively). The number of workers in the paper industry throughout New York State dropped from over 34,000 in the 1990s (3.5% of all manufacturing jobs in the state, sixth nationwide in paper production), to just over 22,000 workers in 2002. Most worked in small plants making specialty papers from fiber from southern states, Canada, and South America. An increasing amount of fiber came from recycled paper.—*BM*

Canham, Hugh O. "New York's Paper Industry," *New York Forest Owner* 39 (May–June 2001)
McGaw, Judith W. *Most Wonderful Machine: Mechanization and Social Change in Berkshire Paper Making, 1801–1885* (Princeton, NJ: Princeton Univ Press, 1987)
McMartin, Barbara. *The Great Forest of the Adirondacks* (Utica: North Country Books, 1994)
Smith, David C. *History of Papermaking in the United States, 1691–1969* (New York: Lockwood, 1970)

Barbara McMartin, William S. Pretzer

Paraguayans. Of the estimated 8,822 Paraguayans living in the United States in 2000, approximately 2,668 lived in New York State, followed by Florida (909) and New Jersey (803). In New York State they tend to concentrate in Queens Co (1,308), mainly in Jackson Heights, a community rich in South American–origin populations. As with other South American countries, military rule shaped emigration from Paraguay in the late 1980s. Political-economic restructuring, however, tends to account for most recent emigration. While they constitute only a small percentage of South American New Yorkers, Paraguayans participate in many multicultural Latin American events held in New York City. In 2000, for example, at Copa Latina, a four-week, 32-team adult soccer tournament and cultural festival, the local Paraguayan team played. Many Paraguayans in New York State celebrate their homeland Independence Day on 14 May.

International Organization for Migration. *World Migration Report: 2000* (Geneva, Switzerland: UN Publications, 2000)

Ana Margarita Cervantes-Rodríguez and Michael C. English

pardons, commutations, and reprieves. Executive clemency in New York State can take several forms. Pardons revoke a criminal conviction and nullify any related sentence; commutations shorten a criminal sentence; and reprieves postpone a sentence for the consideration of the legislature. The New York State Constitution of 1777 provided the governor power to grant pardons and reprieves to convicted offenders in all cases except murder and treason, which were reserved to the legislature. The Constitution of 1821 expanded the scope of this clemency to include murder cases, and the Constitution of 1846 granted the authority to commute sentences. Since 1938 the governor's clemency powers have been stated in Article 4, Section 4 of the constitution and require that grants of clemency be reported to the legislature each year.

The legislature retains the authority to grant clemency in cases of impeachment and treason, though the Penal Law does not specify a penalty for the latter crime. The State Board of Parole, established in 1908, reviews applications for clemency; its recommendations are advisory only. The governor retains discretionary authority to grant executive clemency, which is not subject to review by any court. However, the governor's discretion is not absolute. Pres Gerald R. Ford could pardon former Pres Richard M. Nixon prior to any indictment, but the governor of New York State can grant clemency only after a conviction.

Over time there have been progressively fewer grants of clemency. During the 19th century pardons and commutations were numerous because there was no other legal way to release prisoners before a fixed-length sentence was completed. In 1877 Gov Lucius Robinson granted 297 pardons and 169 commutations. Use of variable-length sentences, mandated for first-time adult felony offenders in 1901, resulted in a gradual decrease in the number of clemency applications and grants during the 20th century. The frequency with which governors use the clemency power continues to vary. For example, Gov Hugh Carey granted clemency 150 times between 1975 and 1983. In contrast, Gov George E. Pataki commuted sentences only 31 times between 1995 and 23 Dec 2003, most frequently for lengthy prison terms of nonviolent drug offenders sentenced under rigid laws he favored reforming. Pataki also granted New York State's first posthumous pardon in December 2003, to performer Lenny Bruce.

Commutations are preferred over pardons because the Parole Board retains supervisory powers over prisoners whose sentences are commuted and can revoke parole if its conditions are violated. Applications for commutations are usually considered only if an inmate has served at least half of the minimum sentence, and not after that minimum has been reached because the Board of Parole can then consider the case. Individuals who are granted clemency often evidence extraordinary rehabilitation while imprisoned. Reprieves are most frequently sought to delay executions in death penalty cases. No one has been executed by the state since 1963, and appeals in the five state death penalty cases were pending as of December 2003.

New York State Division of Parole. *New York State Parole Handbook* (Albany: Division of Parole, 1998)
Rothman, Meah D. "The Pardoning Power: Historical Perspective and Case Study of New York and Con-

necticut," *Columbia Journal of Law and Social Problems* 12 (1976): 149–220

Janet Kaye

Paris. Town (pop 4,609) in SE Oneida Co. Settled in 1789 the town was formed from Whitestown in 1792 and is named for Isaac Paris Jr, a Fort Plain (Montgomery Co) miller who provided grain to settlers during a 1789 famine. Following the Farmers Cotton Factory and the Friendly Woolen Co, both begun at the start of the War of 1812, a large number of cloth factories were built on the Sauquoit Creek, as were shops producing silk, scythes, and paper. The southern part of Paris was settled by the Welsh. "Burning springs" once provided gaslight for a hotel. The Utica, Chenango and Susquehanna Railroad (1869) serviced the area. The Lincoln Davies store (1890) at Paris Station is a landmark business. The Basin, a perfectly round depression 100 feet (30.5 m) deep and 850 feet (259.1 m) in diameter, is thought to be the result of a meteorite.

Parish. Town (pop 2,694) and village (pop 512) in central Oswego Co. Settled in 1803 the town was formed in 1828 from Mexico. Lumbering and wood products have dominated the town's economy; barrels for the Syracuse saltworks, shingles, and leather were early sources of income, with dairying important from about 1865. The Syracuse Northern Railroad (1871) improved shipping. The village incorporated in 1883. From the late 19th century through the early 20th century, an annual town picnic was held after harvest. I-81 (1960–62) has improved access, and tourism has become important. Many residents commute to work. A portion of Happy Valley State Wildlife Management Area lies in the northeast corner of town.

Barbara J. Dix

Parishville. Town (pop 2,049) in SE St. Lawrence Co. Settled in 1810, the town was formed from Hopkinton in 1814. Developer David Parish platted Parishville hamlet (1812) and began the development of factories that exploited the waterpower of the St. Regis River; late 19th-century products included potato starch, lumber, iron, leather, butter tubs, eaves spouts, and boats. In 2003 agriculture, though diminished, was important in the north part of Parishville, which is also within the commuting range of Potsdam. The forested southern part of town is in the Adirondack Park. Attractions include Parishville Gorge.

Richard E. Mooers

Parker, Alton B(rooks) (*b* Cortlandville, Cortland Co, 14 May 1852; *d* New York City, 10 May 1926). Judge and presidential candidate. Parker studied law in Kingston (Ulster Co) at the firm of Schoonmaker and Hardenbergh, earned a degree at Albany Law School (1873), and returned to practice in Kingston. Elected county surrogate in 1877 and 1883, he managed David B. Hill's successful gubernatorial campaign in 1885, whereupon Hill appointed him to the New York State Supreme Court. Successively higher appointments followed until he became chief justice of the New York State Court of Appeals, serving from 1898 until 1904.

Regarded as a friend of labor but also as a political and economic conservative, Parker accepted the presidential nomination in 1904 only after telegraphing his support of the gold standard to the Democratic National Convention at St. Louis. Called "the Sphinx" and "the Enigma from New York," Parker waged a very low-key campaign against the incumbent Republican, Theodore Roosevelt. He accused the Roosevelt camp of accepting large sums from corporations in exchange for protection, which later inquiries determined well founded. After his defeat—Parker garnered 42.3% of the popular vote in New York State and 37.6% nationwide and 140 out of 476 electoral votes—he practiced law in New York City. He defended the American Federation of Labor in the US Supreme Court in the Danbury Hatters' case *(Loewe v Lawlor)* in 1908 and in 1913 was counsel for the managers of the impeachment proceedings against Gov William Sulzer. From 1898 he maintained a 200-acre (81 ha) estate, Rosemount, in Esopus (Ulster Co).

Grady, John R. *The Lives and Public Services of Parker and Davis* (Philadelphia: National Publishing, 1904)
Stone, Irving. "Alton Brooks Parker." In *They Also Ran: The Story of the Men Who Were Defeated for the Presidency* (1943; repr Garden City, NY: Doubleday, 1966)

Veronica F. Towers

Parker, Arthur C(aswell) [Ga'wasowaneh] (*b* Cattaraugus Indian Reservation [loc in Cattaraugus, Chautauqua, and Erie Cos], 5 Apr 1881; *d* Naples (Ontario Co), 1 Jan 1955). Archaeologist, ethnologist, and museum director. His father was Frederick E. Parker, a Seneca, and his mother was Geneva H. Griswold, of English and Scottish descent and a teacher of the Seneca language at the Cattaraugus and Allegany [loc in Cattaraugus Co] Indian Reservations. His great-uncle was Gen Ely S. Parker, an aide to Gen Ulysses S. Grant during the Civil War and a collaborator with Seneca ethnographer Lewis Henry Morgan. In 1904 Parker was adopted into the Seneca Bear Clan at Tonawanda Indian Reservation and gained his ceremonial name, Ga'wasowaneh (Big Snowsnake). This allowed him to participate in many of the Iroquois ceremonies originally denied to him because of his European matrilineal descent.

Parker was educated at the Dickinson Seminary in Williamsport, Pa, but left in 1903 without graduating. He worked briefly as an archaeological assistant for the American Museum of Natural History in New York City and as a field archaeologist for the Peabody Museum at Harvard University. In 1904 Parker was commissioned by the New York State Department of Education to compile information and artifacts related to Seneca culture, including the work of Seneca artist Jesse Cornplanter. Two years later he was hired as the first full-time archaeologist at the New York State Museum in Albany.

In 1925 he accepted the post of director at the Rochester Museum of Arts and Sciences (now Rochester Museum and Science Center), where among other things he initiated a program in Iroquois arts and crafts. In 1935 Parker was elected as the first president of the Society for American Archaeology. He cofounded the New York State Archaeological Association in 1916 and later served as its president. His efforts to compile a state inventory of more than 400 archaeological sites within New York culminated in the 1922 publication of *The Archaeological History of New York*. This two-volume work still serves archaeologists as a vital research component in field investigations.

His other publications include *Iroquois Uses of Maize and Other Food Plants* (1910), *The Code of Handsome Lake, the Seneca Prophet* (1913), and *The Constitution of the Five Nations* (1916; the three volumes are reprinted in *Parker on the Iroquois* [1968]), *Seneca Myths and Folk Tales* (1923), *The History of the Seneca Indians* (1926), and several works for children, including *Skunny Wundy and Other Indian Tales* (1926) and *Red Streak of the Iroquois* (1950). Parker was awarded honorary doctorates from Union College (Schenectady Co) in 1940 and from Keuka College (Yates Co) in 1945. A longtime Indian activist, he cofounded the Society of American Indians in 1911 and attended the first meeting of the National Congress of American Indians in 1944. He retired from the Rochester Museum in January 1946.

Parker, Arthur C. *Parker on the Iroquois.* Ed. William N. Fenton (Syracuse: Syracuse Univ Press, 1968)
Porter, Joy. *To Be Indian: The Life of Iroquois-Seneca Arthur Caswell Parker* (Norman: Univ of Oklahoma Press, 2001)

Darrell Pinckney

Parker, Ely S(amuel) [Hasanoanda] (*b* Tonawanda Reservation [loc in Erie, Genesee, and Niagara Cos], ?1828; *d* Fairfield, Conn, 30 Aug 1895). Seneca leader and commissioner of Indian Affairs. He was descended from a notable Seneca family from the Tonawanda Reservation. While a teenager he played a central role in the attempt to save the Tonawanda Reservation from the Ogden Land Co. In Albany in 1844 he had a chance encounter with Lewis Henry Morgan, the future anthropologist who was then a young white man involved in a ritualistic fraternity called the Grand Order of the Iroquois. Soon after, the white "warriors" of the Grand Order initiated Parker into their fraternity and paid for his tuition at Cayuga Academy in Aurora (Cayuga Co). Parker changed Morgan's life by helping him learn about real Iroquois society, and through Morgan's connections, Parker obtained a series of jobs as an engineer. In 1850 Parker moved to Rochester, where he continued to help Morgan collect information about the Iroquois. The following year Parker was appointed assistant engineer on the New York canals and selected as a Seneca chief, or sachem, with the name Deyohninhohhakarawenh. While no chief possessed more authority than any other, the traditional system was in disarray. Thus, although only 23 years old, Parker was often acknowledged by both Indians and Whites—and identified himself—as "Head Sachem" and "the Chief of the Six Nations."

In the mid-1850s Parker worked as an engineer in Virginia while continuing to act on behalf of his people. In 1857 he helped take to the US Supreme Court a case contesting the right of the Ogden Land Co to force individual Tonawanda Seneca off disputed lands. When the court decided in March 1857 that only the federal government had the legitimate power to force Indians from their lands, the Tonawanda Seneca won the slender wedge they needed to save their reservation. With Parker as one of the chief negotiators, the Tonawanda Seneca were able to buy back a portion of their land from the company with money that the federal government had originally set aside for their removal.

When the Civil War began, Parker sought a commission but was turned down because he was an Indian and therefore not an American citizen. He farmed his property on the Tona-wanda Reservation until 1863, when he finally obtained an army commission on the staff of Gen Ulysses S. Grant, whom Parker had met in Galena, Ill, where Grant was a shopkeeper. Serving as Grant's military secretary and aide-de-camp, Parker eventually rose to the rank of brevet brigadier general. He acted as the scribe and wrote out the terms of surrender at Appomattox Court House in Virginia.

When Grant was elected president, Parker became the first Native American commissioner of the Office of Indian Affairs. With his ultimate goal of "humanization, civilization, and Christianization" of the Indian, he devoted himself to the administration's Peace Policy, which included an end to treaty making with Indians, a cessation of hostilities, and the settlement of Indians onto reservations. A figure of public authority representing the US government, bearded like a white man, and costumed in the clothing appropriate to his station, Parker exemplified in his own life the policies that he advocated. On 23 Dec 1867 he married Minnie Orton Sackett, a "respectable" white woman over 20 years younger than himself. Unfortunately he was also assimilated into the rings of scandal that engulfed the Grant administration. In January 1871 Parker was charged with "defrauding the government in the purchase of Indian supplies." An investigation by the House Committee on Appropriations exonerated him of any crimes but found "irregularities," "neglect, and incompetency," and even a "departure" from the law. As a result Congress passed a law that shifted the balance of power from the commissioner of Indian Affairs to the Board of Indian Commissioners. Rather than serve under these new conditions, in the summer of 1871 Parker resigned.

After leaving public service, he entered the business world. At first he was successful enough to provide himself and his wife with a genteel life in Connecticut. But he soon suffered a series of financial losses that continued until he was forced to take a job as a clerk in the New York City Police Department in 1876. Parker spent the remainder of his life in relative obscurity, comforted by his wife and Maud Theresa Parker, the daughter born to them in 1878. Exemplifying the contradictions of Parker's life, his daughter assimilated into the dominant white culture, while his bones rest beside other Tonawanda Seneca and underneath a statue of his relative, the Seneca leader Red Jacket.

Armstrong, William. *Warrior in Two Camps: Ely S. Parker, Union General and Seneca Chief* (Syracuse: Syracuse Univ Press, 1978)

Waltmann, Henry G. "Ely Samuel Parker, 1869–1871." In *The Commissioners of Indian Affairs, 1824–1977*, eds. Robert M. Kvasnicka and Herman J. Viola (Lincoln: Univ of Nebraska Press, 1979)

Daniel N. Moses

parks. See AMUSEMENT PARKS; NATIONAL PARK SERVICE AREAS; STATE HISTORIC PARKS, SITES, AND HERITAGE AREAS; STATE NATURE AREAS AND PRESERVES; STATE PARKS; URBAN PARKS.

Parks, Recreation, and Historic Preservation, Office of. State agency overseeing the administration of public lands for leisure and educational use. New York State established a Conservation Commission to supervise forest preserves in 1911. With a reorganization of state government in 1926, the administration of parks, reservations, and historic sites was moved to the Conservation Department of the Division of Parks. The responsibility for the state's 27 historic sites was moved to the Education Department in 1944, only to be returned again in 1966 with the creation of the New York State Historical Trust within the Conservation Department. The Office of Parks and Recreation was created in 1970 and began centralized management of all parks through 11 regional commissions in 1972. The office was renamed Parks, Recreation, and Historic Preservation in 1981.

In 2003 the agency operated 170 state parks, 1,350 miles (2,173 km) of trails, and 35 state historic sites. Agency staff are responsible for ensuring that the parks are in condition to host athletic events such as the Empire State Summer and Winter Games, the largest state-sponsored amateur athletic competition in the country. Parks also host the Empire State Games for the Physically Challenged and the Empire State Senior Games. The Bureau of Historic Sites, established on Peebles Island in Waterford (Saratoga Co) in 1972, was the first conservation center of any historic site program in the country. It provides interpretation, landscape conservation, preservation and curatorial services, and collections management advice and services to historic sites throughout the state. In 2002–3 the office had a budget of $246,675,000 and 1,500 full-time equivalent positions.

See also NEW YORK CITY; STATE HISTORIC PARKS, SITES, AND HERITAGE AREAS.

Office of Parks, Recreation, and Historic Preservation, http://nysparks.state.ny.us/

Sarah E. DeSanctis

parkways. In 1922 the Committee on the State Park Plan, established by the civic advocacy group New York State Association, issued *A State Park Plan for New York* recommending a statewide parkway system. George W. Perkins Sr, former president of the Palisades Interstate Park Commission, is credited with the idea for the plan. The State Council of Parks was created in 1924 as an advisory board within the New York State Conservation Commission specifically to develop and implement the parks and parkways plan. When the New York State Conservation Department was established in 1926, a new Division of Parks was created and the conservation commissioner was made chair of the Council of Parks. The council, however, retained primary responsibility for overall implementation of the parks and parkways plan.

Modeled after the Bronx River Parkway (1917–24), the new parkways were to be limited-access roads designed with smooth driving surfaces, gentle grading, natural alignments, and landscaped settings. The plan envisioned scenic routes linking each of the state's major urban areas with regional parks and connecting parks and regions to each other. Beyond ensuring a pleasant trip between home and park, parkways were independent features—elongated, landscaped parks for the automobile designed for recreational driving. Parkway systems were planned for the Long Island, Taconic, Palisades, Genesee, and Niagara State Park regions. Each was based on regional scenic attractions, landscape characteristics, and social patterns. Regional park commissions built the earliest parkways themselves before design and construction were turned over to the New York State Department of Public Works in the 1930s. Parkway funds were appropriated by the state legislature, but federal public works funds were also used, especially during the depression.

Although various parkways were completed in

Northern State Parkway at Westbury, 1949.

Genesee and Niagara, the goal of creating a scenic transportation system across the state was unrealized. However, in the southeastern area of the state, with the New York City metropolitan area as its hub, the parkway system was developed and functioned substantially as planned. State parkways, including the Taconic State Parkway (1923–63), Palisades Interstate Parkway (1947–61), Southern State Parkway (1925–49), and Northern State Parkway (1931–65), extended across Long Island and up both sides of the Hudson River. Encompassing state, metropolitan, and county parks and parkways, the connected system of Hudson Valley and Long Island state parks and parkways, along with New York City metropolitan and county parks and parkways, included more than 200 miles (320 km) of designed roads and linked thousands of acres of public parkland. State parkways in other regions include the Lake Ontario Parkway (1935) near Rochester and the Robert Moses Parkway (1960) near Buffalo and Niagara Falls. The parkway system, totaling 346.2 miles (557.17 km), was largely completed by the mid-1960s.

See also MOSES, ROBERT; STATE PARKS; SUBURBANIZATION.

Moses, Robert. *New York State Parks and Highways* (Albany: State Council of Parks, 1928)

Kathleen LaFrank

Parma. Town (pop 14,822) in NW Monroe Co. Settled in 1796, the town was formed from Northampton [now Gates] in 1808 as Fairfield, but its name changed almost immediately. In 1860 Parma had a furnace and a pump factory. Cereals were the original focus of agricultural production. Commercial orchards began in 1859 and thrived for many years, a notable product being Collamer's Twenty Ounce apple, which started as a Sport, an unintended variation. A freeze in 1934 killed nearly half the apple trees and reduced dependence on the business, but some orchards remained in 2003. Shore resorts began with the development of Manitou Beach (1888). Parma's increasingly suburbanized population grew rapidly in the decades around World War II and has more than doubled since 1960. The Braddock Point Lighthouse (1896) on Bogus Point is a landmark.

Nancy Martin

Parole, Division of. Develops and implements supervision and treatment plans for criminal offenders returning to the community from prison. The division is directed by a board of parole consisting of 19 members appointed by the governor and confirmed by the senate. The board decides which inmates serving indeterminate sentences are released on parole and under what conditions the parole is granted. The board may revoke an individual's parole if those conditions are violated. The board also makes clemency recommendations to the governor. The division's staff members at correctional facilities review inmate cases and prepare inmates for release, and field officers counsel parolees and help them obtain vocational and rehabilitative services.

Parole can be traced to an 1877 law authorizing state prison superintendents to hire agents to assist inmates with release. This function expanded in 1889 when a Board of Commissioners for Paroled Prisoners was established at each prison. In 1908 a Board of Parole for State Prisons was established to coordinate parole activities, and in 1926 a Division of Parole was formed within the new Department of Correction. In 1930 this division became an independent agency and transferred to the Executive Department. In 1971 the state's parole functions again were joined with corrections, this time in the new Department of Correctional Services. This change was short-lived, however. In the aftermath of the Attica uprising and a series of court decisions favorable to prisoner freedoms, pressures increased on the state to protect parolee rights. As a result, the Division of Parole in 1977 was again made an autonomous agency within the Executive Department.

Guidelines for parole also became more standardized in response to public perceptions of arbitrary parole decisions. In the 1980s and early 1990s, the surge of drug-related sentences led to an expansion of division duties, particularly in assisting parolees entering substance abuse treatment programs. The Willard Drug Treatment Campus, located in Ovid (Seneca Co) and staffed in part by division employees, was created as a 90-day drug and alcohol treatment program for parolees in 1995. The Sentencing Reform Act of 1998, commonly known as Jenna's Law, mandated changes in the division's function, particularly the elimination of discretionary releases for violent offenders. Although the division still makes parole determinations and sets conditions for those serving indeterminate sentences, the legislation mandated standard parole release dates and conditions for inmates with the new determinate sentences. The law also established lengthy periods of parole supervision after an inmate's release, thereby increasing demands on Division of Parole staff. Headquartered in Albany, in 2003 the division's annual budget was $198 million, and 2,351 division staff supervised 45,000 New York State parolees and another 15,000 individuals who were inmates in Department of Correctional Services work release programs, parolees from other states, or inmates awaiting release.

New York State Division of Parole, http://parole.state.ny.us

Richard Andress

Parran, Thomas, Jr (*b* St. Leonard, Md, 28 Sept 1892; *d* Pittsburgh, 16 Feb 1968). Public health leader. Following graduation from Georgetown Medical College in 1915, Parran's early public health career focused on rural populations and combating venereal disease. He was commissioned in the US Public Health Service in 1917. In 1930 Gov Franklin D. Roosevelt appointed Parran New York State health commissioner, a position from which he worked to strengthen county health departments to improve service to the rural poor during the Great Depression. A reformer who believed in aggressive government action to better public health by reducing poverty and economic insecurity, Parran was an early advocate for national health insurance and public education of venereal disease, particularly syphilis. He served on the committee that in 1935 drafted the original Social Security Act, which included significant public health and health research programs. Pres Roosevelt named him US surgeon general in 1936. Parran helped to found the World Health Organization in 1946 and retired as surgeon general in 1948 to become founding dean of the University of Pittsburgh School of Public Health.

Peter Slocum

Parsis. See ZOROASTRIANS (PARSIS).

Parsons School of Design. See NEW SCHOOL UNIVERSITY.

party system. The development of political parties in New York State has in large part followed the national pattern. In the first system of the 1790s through 1816, the Federalists and the Democratic-Republicans, later known as Jeffersonian Republicans, vied for control of the state. With the collapse of the Federalist Party, configurations became murky in the so-called Era of Good Feelings. The modern Democratic Party emerged in New York State in the 1820s, with Martin Van Buren, leader of the Albany Regency, its chief architect. Between 1834 and 1852 the Democrats and Whigs dominated the political scene. In 1856 the Republican Party emerged. It and the Democrats have since dominated the state. When the Republican and Democratic Parties emerged in the 19th century, New York City consisted of only New York Co. Democrats did well there and in the southernmost part of Westchester Co [now Bronx Co], and they generally dominated politics in the City of Brooklyn. Republicans did better in the rest of the state, and this pattern persisted for the remainder of the 19th century.

TRENDS IN THE 20TH CENTURY

Greater New York City came about in 1898 with the creation of a city with five boroughs: Manhattan, Brooklyn, Queens, Staten Island, and the Bronx. There was considerable potential to mobilize the many immigrant and poor voters by stressing their urban needs and the lack of sympathy of the rest of the state for city needs, but this did not happen until Democrat Alfred E. Smith first ran for governor in 1918. Smith made the case that government could intervene to help protect urban workers with regulations and that government could do more to help those in need. The result of his appeal was Democratic success in New York City; solidified regionalism and an overlap of region, class, and ethnicity; and partisan support. Before 1920 Democrats were regularly winning between 50% and 60% of city-based assembly seats (Fig 1). From 1920 forward, they won 80% to 90%.

Despite these victories, the influence of legislative representation from New York City was limited for much of the 20th century by the apportionment process. As the population moved to urban areas during the 19th century, the legislature gradually awarded more seats to urban counties, but not enough to make the number of seats in urban counties equal to the population in them. The 1894 state constitution limited New York City to no more than one-third of the seats in the legislature, a provision that stood until the 1960s when court rulings required that the seats be equal to population distributions. The result was that a Democratic gubernatorial candidate such as Al Smith could win a statewide majority by doing well in New York City, but that partisan success was not reflected in legislative results.

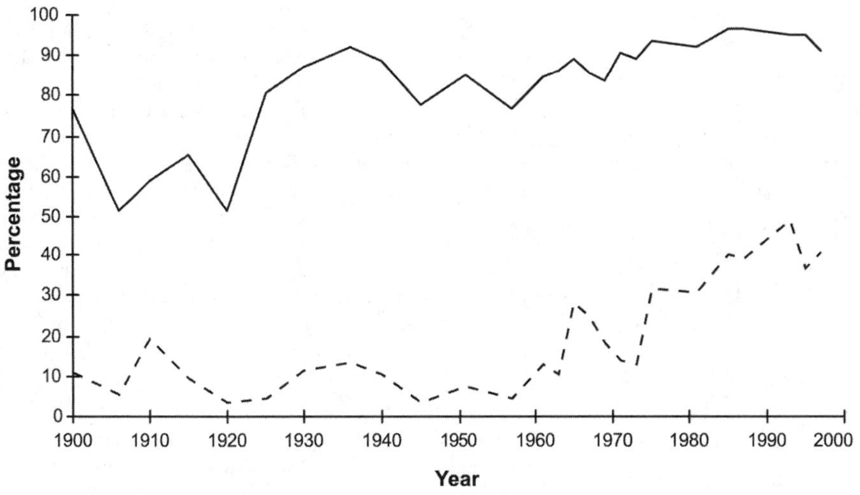

Fig 1. Democratic proportion of assembly seats by region, 1900–2000. —— NYC; – – – outside NYC.

The rest of the state remained unsympathetic to New York City and its concerns, and Democrats continued to win less than 10% of assembly seats elsewhere in the state. Although it contained pockets of enormous wealth, New York City was seen by many outsiders as being filled with immigrants and the poor, who had endless need for government assistance. Most areas outside New York City were less supportive of extensive government activity and much more Republican, though some cities, notably Albany after 1920, had a strong Democratic machine that dominated local elections, and Democrats often won in cities such as Buffalo and Utica.

The two regions—New York City and the state outside the city—provided enough voters for each party to have an electoral base of roughly comparable size from the 1920s into the 1960s, ensuring conflicts about what role government should play. Areas outside New York City were generally, though not uniformly, less supportive of taxes and government, and New York City was more supportive of higher taxes and more government programs.

The 1974 elections somewhat modified this division. Following the Watergate scandal that led to the resignation of Republican president Richard M. Nixon, the state's electorate voted heavily Democratic in many areas outside New York City. Since then Democrats have been able to win assembly seats from Nassau and Suffolk Cos, in the suburbs in Westchester and Rockland Cos, and in the urban and suburban areas around Buffalo, Rochester, Syracuse, and Albany. Extensive party resources go to retaining seats in these areas. Democratic success has also been helped along by a steady decline in once overwhelmingly Republican enrollment in many upstate counties, such as Onondaga, Chenango, and Herkimer.

Although partisan regionalism is not as pronounced in the early 21st century as it was in the mid-20th, it still has a significant impact within the state. Many policy discussions begin with a focus on how much New York City will get from the program, with Democrats advocating more aid and Republicans concerned with limiting it. Regionalism also affects levels of political competition. Many areas within the state still vote heavily Republican or Democratic, and party candidates within these partisan areas win by large margins. The majority parties in each house also draw district boundaries in some areas to make the district safer for their party members. The lack of competition is regularly criticized in newspaper editorials across the state.

Party Strength and Electoral Bases

Two distinct trends involving party registration have been evident since the 1960s: a decline in voters choosing to enroll as Republican, and an increase in those declining to choose a party (Fig 2). Several registrants filed suit in the late 1950s, arguing that they should be allowed to register without enrolling in a party. The courts ruled in their favor. At the start of the 21st century, the Democratic Party dominates with 47% of voter registrants, the Republicans have only 28%.

Although party enrollment is valuable as a guide to the relative strengths of the two major parties in New York State, party lines are often crossed in actual voting. Republican George E. Pataki was able to win the governorship in 1994, 1998, and 2002, even with many more Democrats enrolled in the state. Moreover, in New York City, Republican candidates Rudolph Giuliani (1993, 1997) and Michael Bloomberg (2001) were able to win the mayorship despite an overwhelming five-to-one Democrat advantage in party enrollment within the city.

The differences in the electoral bases of the parties at the start of the 21st century in New York State can be seen by examining how partisan success for legislative seats varies by the nature of districts (Fig 3). Democrats were much more likely to win seats with large nonwhite populations. Democrats were more likely to win in less affluent districts, while Republicans were more likely to win as income increased. Yet despite these clear tendencies, the parties are not as polarized as they may appear. Each party wins seats in areas often portrayed as belonging to the other party. Each party needs seats from these "other" areas if it is to maintain a majority in its respective house. Democrats have a majority in the assembly but must have seats outside New York City to maintain it, and Republicans are the majority in the senate but must win seats in New York City to maintain it. Thus while New York State's two parties clearly differ in constituents and policy, each needs to court some degree of support outside its core constituencies, leading to some compromise in policy.

Party Organization

County party organization dominated the process of selecting candidates until the 1960s, after which apportionment was no longer based on counties and their role diminished. Beginning in the 1960s candidates also acquired greater access to pollsters, direct mail, and consultants, and they moved from a heavy reliance on county party organizations to conduct campaigns to creating their own campaign organizations. Candidates in the early 21st century raise most of their own campaign funds and have their own campaign offices, and with the rise of unenrolled voters, they do not make their party affiliation a central issue in campaigns. This has led many to characterize contemporary campaigns as candidate centered. Although candidates have a growing inclination to operate with considerable independence, party organizations are still vital to New York State's political process and often play a significant role. The parties rely on diverse organizational arrangements to help their candidates in elections. At the county level, party organizations manage the nomination process and assist candidates in gathering signatures for petitions and in identifying and recruiting volunteers to work on campaigns. Party officials at the county level help connect candi-

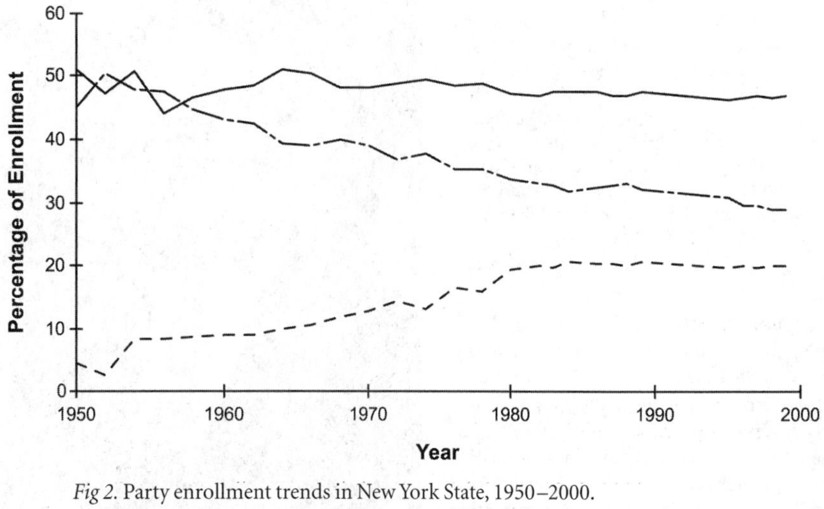

Fig 2. Party enrollment trends in New York State, 1950–2000. —— Democrat; –·–·– Republican; – – – Independent.

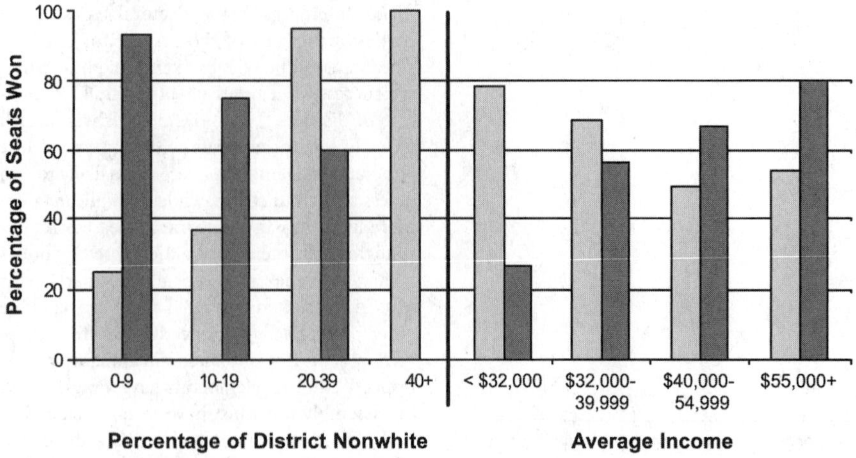

Fig 3. Pecentage of seats won by senate Republicans and assembly Democrats by race and income of district, 1996. ▒ assembly Democrats; ■ senate Republicans.

dates with likely contributors and raise money to transfer to campaigns. They also prod candidates to coordinate their campaigns when it may help all candidates. A popular mayor or county executive, for example, is often pushed to write supporting letters for legislative candidates and help them raise money.

At the state level there are several organizations. First is the official state party committee, which acts to coordinate as many activities as possible among state and local officials. Within the legislature, the parties in each house have legislative campaign committees that play a major role in organizing campaigns. The staffs of these organizations help recruit candidates, contract with companies to conduct polls to help a candidate formulate a campaign plan, and create electronic ads and written material for direct mail. The parties also raise significant funds for many of these activities. While campaigns focus on the image and positions of individual candidates rather than on party labels, party organizations at the local and state level still remain very important in bringing together resources to help candidates win.

See also APPORTIONMENT AND DISTRICTING.

Stonecash, Jeffrey M. "Political Cleavage in Gubernatorial and Legislative Elections: Party Competition in New York, 1970–82," *Western Political Quarterly* 42 (Mar 1989): 69–81

———. " 'Split' Constituencies and the Impact of Party Control," *Social Science History* 16 (Fall 1992): 455–77

Stonecash, Jeffrey M., and Diana Dwyre. "Where's the Party: Changing State Party Organizations," *American Politics Quarterly* 20 (July 1992): 326–44

Stonecash, Jeffrey M., and Sara E. Keith. "Maintaining a Political Party: Providing and Withdrawing Campaign Funds," *Party Politics* 2 (July 1996): 3–28

Stonecash, Jeffrey M., and Amy Widestrom. "Political Parties and Elections." In *Governing New York State,* 5th ed., ed. Robert F. Pecorella and Jeffrey M. Stonecash (Albany: SUNY Press, 2005)

Jeffrey M. Stonecash

Pataki, George, E(lmer) (*b* Peekskill, Westchester Co, 24 June 1945). Governor. Pataki grew up on the edge of the New York City metropolitan area, where his father worked as a farmer and postmaster. He graduated from Yale University (1967) and Columbia Law School (1970) and practiced law while entering local Republican politics. Elected mayor of Peekskill in 1981, Pataki won a seat in 1984 in the state assembly, where he served until being elected to the state senate in 1992. Running as a little-known, first-term Republican state senator, Pataki stunned American politics in 1994 by upsetting nationally prominent incumbent Gov Mario M. Cuomo, a perennial Democratic presidential prospect. Long Island and upstate were key to his victory, and he became New York State's first governor elected with Conservative Party backing. He gratified conservative supporters in 1995 by reinstating the death penalty and enacting a large tax cut, both key campaign promises. Pataki also appealed to moderates by supporting abortion rights and public funding for poor women's abortions, and backed laws that outlawed discrimination against gays.

As governor Pataki enjoyed the benefits of a booming stock market and expanding economy through 2000 and was able to cut taxes while increasing spending on education and healthcare. His embrace of such liberal policies and programs in a heavily Democratic state helped him win reelection in 1998 and 2002. He undertook major expansions of health programs for the working poor, including the development of Child Health Plus and Family Health Plus. A dedicated environmentalist, he embarked on an expansion of state parklands and wilderness areas, particularly in the Adirondack and Catskill Mountains. Pataki faced a major challenge in leading the state toward recovery after the terrorist attacks of 11 Sept 2001. The resulting economic shock, coupled with a national economic slowdown, contributed to major state budget deficits after years of surpluses. Pataki won 49% of the popular vote in the 2002 gubernatorial election (as compared to 34% for his nearest challenger), with strong union support. His 2003 budget called for substantial spending cuts, and he suffered a political setback when his veto of 119 separate budget items was overridden by a bipartisan coalition of members of the assembly and senate.

See also STATE UNIVERSITY OF NEW YORK (SUNY).

Gov George E. Pataki.

Pataki, George E., with Daniel Paisner. *Pataki: An Autobiography* (New York: Viking Press, 1998)

Peter Slocum

Patch, Sam (*b* Reading, Mass, 17 June 1799; *d* Rochester, 13 Nov 1829). Daredevil. Sam Patch worked in a cotton textile mill in Pawtucket, RI, from about age 8. Pawtucket boys amused themselves by leaping into the basin below the falls of the Blackstone River, and Patch was among the bravest. He moved to Paterson, NJ, and there in September 1827 he leaped at Passaic Falls, upstaging the celebration of an unpopular local businessman's new bridge and gardens at the falls, and then jumped again on 4 July 1828. Patch's jump on 19 July 1828 was associated with the first industrial strike in Paterson. The manufacturers announced that they would fire the ringleaders, and Sam Patch disappeared from Paterson. On 6 Aug 1828 he leaped at Hoboken, NJ, beginning his brief career as a professional daredevil. Invited by Niagara Falls hotel keepers, Patch leaped 80 feet (24 m) from the base of Goat Island on 7 Oct 1829, the first daredevil stunt at Niagara Falls. Patch jumped again at Niagara on 17 October from an apparatus that raised the jump to 120 feet (37 m). The Niagara leaps made Patch a national celebrity. He began appearing with a silk scarf at his neck, a sailor's jacket, and a tamed bear on a chain.

On his way home from Niagara Falls, Sam Patch leaped the High Falls on the Genesee River at Rochester on 6 November before a crowd of about 6,000 people. He advertised a second leap for 13 November from a platform that raised the height to 125 feet (38 m). In front of 10,000 people, he lost control during the jump and was killed. A notorious drunkard, most believed that he was intoxicated when he made his fatal leap, and some thought he had survived and was in hiding. His body was found at the mouth of the Genesee River the following March and buried in Charlotte [now Rochester]. The epitaph on his wooden marker read, "Sam Patch. Such Is Fame."

The makers of commercial popular culture wrote about Sam Patch in sentimental poetry, tall tales, almanacs, travel books, stage plays, and, later, a popular children's book. Pres Andrew Jackson named a favorite horse Sam Patch, and the name was also given to a castaway Japanese sailor who accompanied Commodore Matthew C. Perry to Japan in 1853. "What the Sam Patch" persisted as a surrogate curse phrase for many decades, and writers ranging from Nathaniel Hawthorne and Herman Melville to William Dean Howells made allusions to him. The falls at Pawtucket, Paterson, Niagara, and Rochester were popularly known as Sam Patch's waterfalls

Broadside for Sam Patch's ill-fated leap of 1829.

for a long time. A contemporary tourist boat, the *Sam Patch,* still plies the waters of the upper Genesee River in and near Rochester.

Dorson, Richard M. "Sam Patch, Jumping Hero," *New York Folklore Quarterly* 1 (Aug 1945): 133–51

Johnson, Paul E. *Sam Patch, the Famous Jumper* (New York: Hill & Wang, 2003)

Paul E. Johnson

Patchogue {East Patchogue, locality (pop 20,824) in Brookhaven, Suffolk Co; North Patchogue, locality (pop 7,825) in Brookhaven; Patchogue, village (pop 11,919) in Brookhaven}. Purchased by Gov John Winthrop Jr of Connecticut from the Unquachog (Unkechaug) Indians in 1664, it was confirmed as the Winthrop Patent (1680) but did not become part of Brookhaven until 1773. Maritime activities including fishing, shellfishing, shipbuilding, and sailmaking began in the colonial period. Settlement was encouraged by a lottery through which Humphrey Avery sold large lots in 1758. Patchogue River and Tuthill and Swan Creeks were dammed to power mills that produced flour, lumber, wrapping paper, cotton twine, carpet warp, leather goods, and woolen and linen cloth between the late 18th and early 20th centuries. Patchogue acquired its post office in 1802. The South Side Rail Road (1868) transformed the village into a commercial hub and summer resort. Justus Roe and Sons produced the steel tape measure (invented 1876, patented 1888) and a mechanical awning. Oystering employed 400 men at Patchogue in 1882. The village was incorporated in 1893. East Patchogue became a flower-growing district, with greenhouses producing roses and orchids, among other products.

The Army Corps of Engineers dredged the Patchogue River and Fire Island Inlet (1902, 1958, 1970, 1976), making Patchogue an important deepwater oil port and a shipping point for the Blue Point oyster. Patchogue's lace mill (1884–1954) produced household goods as well as silk parachutes and mosquito and camouflage netting during World War II; it employed 800 in 1940. After the war, downtown Patchogue became a regional shopping destination. When strip malls multiplied, merchants fought a decades-long decline. In the late 20th century Patchogue Theater (1923) was restored and the Suffolk County Sports Hall of Fame relocated there. The village became home to St. Joseph's (1979) and Briarcliffe (1981) Colleges.

Mark Rothenberg

patent medicines. In the 18th and 19th centuries, the names and trademarks of patent medicines were often registered or patented, but the ingredients—roots, herbs, barks, alcohol, cocaine, and opiates—remained a carefully guarded secret. In spite of exorbitant claims, some patent medicines contained little more than alcohol, laudanum, water, and flavorings, sometimes leading to drug and alcohol addictions. With no restrictions on truth in advertising or federal regulation of ingredients, these remedies reaped huge fortunes for their manufacturers. They were advertised in almanacs, through traveling medicine shows, and on broadsides and trade cards. Some recipes came directly from folk medicine and included traditional formulas that had been in domestic use for centuries. When it was first discovered, petroleum was the basis for many patent medicines.

The Shaker communities in Watervliet (Albany Co) and New Lebanon (Columbia Co) established medicinal gardens in the 1820s for dried herbs, seeds, and patent medicines and processed 75 tons (68 MT) of roots and herbs annually by the 1850s. In 1875 the Columbia Co Shaker community at Mount Lebanon made a business arrangement with A. J. White, owner of the New York City company that promoted and distributed Mother Siegel's Syrup. A. J. White and Co survived until 1957, when it was bought by Smith, Kline, and French Laboratories (in 2003 this firm was a part of the United Kingdom–based pharmaceutical conglomerate GlaxoSmithKline). Benjamin Brandreth, an emigrant from Liverpool, England, established a proprietary medicine business on Hudson St in New York City in the 1830s using his grandfather's formula for Vegetable Universal Pills. Within a few years he moved the manufacturing operation to Sing Sing [now Ossining, Westchester Co], where his purgative was successfully promoted in newspaper advertising and in his book *The Doctrine of Purgation* (1867). Henry T. Helmbold moved from Philadelphia to New York City and built a grand Temple of Pharmacy on Broadway. His patent medicine contained buchu, a sub-Saharan African shrub he promoted as a cure for diseases of the sexual organs. Other 19th-century New York City manufacturers included a firm that made Pond's Extract, which was endorsed by Andrew Dickson White, the first president of Cornell University. The William H. Comstock Co also began in New York City in 1833, later moving to Morristown (St. Lawrence Co), where it produced Comstock's Dead Shot Worm Pellets and Dr. Howard's Electric Pills.

William A. Rockefeller, the father of John D. Rockefeller Sr, was a traveling patent medicine salesman based out of various locales in Central New York in the 1840s. Willis Kilmer, known widely as the Swamp Root King, headed the advertising department for the patent medicine company founded by his uncle and his father. The firm, established in Binghamton in 1879, was best known for its Swamp Root Kidney Liver and Bladder Cure. Trained in both allopathic and homeopathic medicine, the company's founder, Dr S. Andral Kilmer, built a sanatorium at a nearby sulfur springs in 1892 where he experimented in treatments for cancer and other diseases. After Willis inherited the business, he used profits from the company to start the *Binghamton Press* (1904), the city's major newspaper.

Other patent medicine businesses were established in Schenectady, Syracuse, Rochester, Buffalo, and Poughkeepsie, where Smith Bros, the famous cough drop company was founded in 1847 and later absorbed by Warner-Lambert Pharmaceutical Co. In 1874 Ray Vaughan Pierce opened what later became known as the World's Dispensary in Buffalo. He sold his patent medicines including the famous Golden Medical Discovery. In 1877 Pierce won a state senate seat, and in the following year he also used his patent medicine profits to open Pierce's Invalids' Hotel and Surgical Institute, Buffalo's first luxury hotel. The Town of Le Roy (Genesee Co) was considered by many to be the patent medicine capital of the world. The firms here once included the Oatka Medicine Co, the Langham Medicine Co, the O. F. Woodward Medicine Co, the Shiloh Medicine Co, the Genesee Pure Food Co—all founded in the 19th century—and Pearle B. Wait and Co, which invented Jell-O in 1897. By 1900, 392 companies represented New York State's patent medicine manufacturing sector; together, they were the 13th largest industry in the state in terms of value of products sold for that year.

The decline of the patent medicine business is often traced to the passage of the federal Pure Food and Drug Act (1906), which required labeling the amount of specified dangerous drugs—alcohol, opium and its alkaloids, and others—and prohibited labels that claimed ingredients not included in the product, but this requirement applied only to drugs in interstate commerce. Other factors were attacks by the American Medical Association and by the popular press. Edward W. Bok, editor of *Ladies' Home Journal,* refused to accept advertising for patent medicines on principle. A series of articles by Samuel Hopkins Adams in *Collier's* in 1905–6 depicted the patent medicine business as "The Great American Fraud." The change in public opinion contributed to the decline, but the 1906 law was also used as a tool by better-established firms to deter competition, and many small patent medicine businesses were bought by larger firms. Some firms, including W. H. Comstock Co, survived until the 1950s by exporting patent medicines to Latin America and the West Indies. In the wake of the increasing use of complementary and alternative medicines at the start of the 21st century, however, herbal patent medicines produced in China and Southern Asia continue to find a market. And the popularity of over-the-counter remedies attests to the widespread use of patent medicines under other names.

Young, James Harvey. *The Toadstool Millionaires: A Social History of Patent Medicines in America before Federal Regulation* (Princeton, NJ: Princeton Univ Press, 1961)

Margaret Kruesi

PATH (Port Authority Trans-Hudson Corporation). Commuter rail line between Manhattan and New Jersey. The Hudson Tunnel Railroad Co, owned by De Witt Clinton Haskin, began work on the first rail tunnel from Jersey City to Manhattan in 1874. Work halted in 1891 with the tunnel 70% complete. In 1902 William Gibbs McAdoo, a New York City lawyer, revived the project by finding new financial backers and organizing several companies, later consolidated as Hudson and Manhattan Railroad Co (H&M), which resumed excavations. McAdoo opened an uptown line from 19th St and 6th Ave to Hoboken, NJ, on 25 Feb 1908 and a new downtown line from Cortlandt St through Jersey City to Hoboken the following year. In 1910 McAdoo extended service under 6th Ave to 33d St, and in 1911 from Jersey City to Newark. Known as the Hudson Tubes, H&M lines gave New Jersey residents, bound for Manhattan, a quicker alternative to the ferries and also a choice of midtown or downtown terminals. Despite the company's New York City headquarters, the tubes remained a New Jersey–oriented operation and never integrated with the New York City subway system. By the mid-1920s, the lines transported 113 million passengers annually. The opening of the Holland Tunnel in 1927 ended traffic growth, and H&M declared bankruptcy in 1954, lingering in receivership until 1962. The Port of New York Authority (PA), a bistate agency of New York and New Jersey, then took over the troubled system in an arrangement that also permitted PA to build the World Trade Center on the site of H&M's downtown terminal. PATH, which began operations on 1 Sept 1962, modernized the old lines to become the first in the metropolitan area to be wholly air-conditioned. The PATH system's World Trade Center facilities were destroyed on 11 Sept 2001.

Condit, Carl. *The Port of New York,* 2 vols (Chicago: Univ of Chicago Press, 1980–81)
Cudahy, Brian J. *Rails under the Mighty Hudson: The Story of the Hudson Tubes, the Pennsy Tunnels, and Manhattan Transfer* (Brattleboro, Vt: Stephen Greene Press, 1975)

Christopher T. Baer

patronage. See Civil service.

patroonships. Patroonships were privately financed agricultural colonies within Dutch West India Co (WIC) territories. Some directors promoted them to relieve the firm of recruiting settlers and shipping supplies. Others saw them as reducing the WIC's opportunities for profits. The WIC enacted the Charter of Freedoms and Exemptions in 1629, entitling its directors to establish private colonies and to enjoy the title of patroon. They could purchase four leagues of coastal or river shore from Indians, or two leagues on both sides of a river, and could expand their holdings as population increased and trade local products along the entire North American coast. They could choose the form of government and had power to judge capital cases, although civil cases over 50 guilders could be appealed. They were obliged to settle 50 people aged above 15 within four years and were to provide a comforter of the sick, a clergyman, and a schoolmaster. Weaving was forbidden, as was fur trading except where the company had no factor.

Three patroonships were established in New Netherland in 1630: Kiliaen van Rensselaer's Rensselaerswijck on the upper Hudson, Michiel Pauw's Pavonia, which included Staten Island, Hoboken, and Ahasimus [now Jersey City, NJ], and Samuel Godijn's Swanendael on the west side of Delaware Bay. Swanendael was destroyed by Indians before March 1632 and the title sold back to the company in 1635. Pauw, who was underfinanced, sold Pavonia back the same year. Only Rensselaerswijck succeeded, surviving under Dutch, English, and American governments for another two centuries.

Under a new charter in 1640, patroonships were instituted by Meijndert Meijndertsz van Keeren at Achter Col [now Bogota, NJ] on the west side of the Hudson between the Hackensack and Hudson Rivers, and Cornelis Melijn on Staten Island. Both were destroyed by Indians in 1643. Melijn, in partnership with Hendrick van der Capellen, restarted in 1650, but that settlement was destroyed by Indians during the 1655 Peach War. Melijn and Van der Capellen's execu-

Detail of Van Rensselaer family heraldry, *ca* 1650.

tor sold their interests back to the WIC in 1659 and 1660, respectively, as had Meijndertsz earlier. Adriaen van der Donck, in 1646, started his colony of Nepperhaem, which he called Colendonck, at present-day Yonkers.

WIC directors informed Petrus Stuyvesant in 1659 that they would no longer grant patroonships under terms similar to those recently surrendered by Melijn, for they had proved disadvantageous to the company. In fact, it did not grant any further patroonships under any conditions. An institution devised to reduce the company's expenses seemed to the directors to have reduced its income.

Bachman, Van Cleaf. *Peltries and Plantations; The Economic Policies of the Dutch West India Company in New Netherland, 1623–1639* (Baltimore: Johns Hopkins Press, 1969)
O'Callaghan, E. B. *History of New Netherland,* 2 vols (New York: Appleton, 1848)
Rink, Oliver A. *Holland on the Hudson; An Economic and Social History of Dutch New York* (Ithaca: Cornell Univ Press, 1986)

Peter Christoph

Patterson. Town (pop 11,306) in NE Putnam Co. Settled around 1731, the town was formed from the old towns of Frederickstown and Southeast in 1795 as Franklin; its name was changed in 1808. In 1766 William Prendergast led a tenant uprising, protesting the Philipse family's rents. In fall 1778 Washington's army encamped at Patterson. The Harlem Railroad (1849) provided shipping for dairy farmers. In the 20th century farms were gradually replaced by estates and subdivisions, such as Putnam Lake (1931), a summer colony. I-84 crossed a corner of Patterson in 1968–70, encouraging development; population increased 30.3% in the 1990s. Patterson is bisected by the Great Swamp and is the site of Cranberry Mountain State Wildlife Management Area and Bog Brook State Unique Area.

Sallie S. Sypher

Paulding, James Kirke (*b* Great Nine Partners Patent [now in Putnam Co], 22 Aug 1778; *d* Hyde Park, Dutchess Co, 6 Apr 1860). Writer and secretary of the navy. Raised near Tarrytown (Westchester Co), Paulding read widely in English literature though his formal education was slight. In 1796 he obtained a clerk's position in the US Loan Office in New York City, where he met William, Peter, and Washington Irving and began a career as a writer. He contributed to newspapers, magazines, and *Salmagundi* (1807–8), a series of 20 pamphlets containing poetry, prose, theater reviews, social commentary, and racy gossip. Paulding showed his ardent patriotism in satirical attacks on the British during the War of 1812, efforts noticed by Pres James Madison. In 1815 Madison appointed him secretary to the Board of Navy Commissioners in Washington, DC. There, Paulding produced sketches of travel in Virginia, *Letters from the South* (1817); a poem, *The Backwoodsman* (1818); a second series of *Salmagundi* (1819–20); and a historical novel on the settlement of Swedes in Delaware, *Koningsmarke: The Long Finne* (1823). Beginning in 1824 he served as naval agent for New York State, based in New York City, while writing more stories and sketches. In 1830 Paulding won actor James Hackett's $300 prize for *The Lion of the West,* a comedy in two acts about a Kentucky frontiersman. Two novels soon followed: *The Dutchman's Fireside* (1831) and *Westward Ho!* (1832), dealing, respectively, with Dutch settlers in New York and with life on the Kentucky frontier. A biography of George Washington for young readers (1835) and an analysis and defense of slavery (1836) preceded his appointment as Pres Martin Van Buren's secretary of the navy in 1838. Paulding returned to New York City in 1841, later moving to a farm near Hyde Park, where he continued writing on current political issues though was passed over by a new generation.

Reynolds, Larry J. *James Kirke Paulding* (Boston: Twayne Publishers, 1984)

Ralph M. Aderman

Paulists. First religious order of Roman Catholic priests in the United States. The Missionary Society of St. Paul the Apostle, popularly known as the Paulist Fathers, was founded in 1858 by Fr Isaac Thomas Hecker (1819–88). Hecker, a native of New York City, was raised a Methodist. After a period of spiritual seeking at Brook Farm and Fruitlands (transcendentalist communities near Boston) with his fellow religious pilgrim Orestes Brownson, Hecker entered the Roman Catholic Church in 1844. He was ordained into the Redemptorist order in 1849. A gifted preacher and author, his conviction that Catholicism was uniquely harmonious with the American democratic spirit led him to dedicate himself to converting Americans to Catholicism. This, Hecker felt, would require opening a new Redemptorist house specifically concerned with presenting Catholicism to a largely Protestant, and often hostile, population. His efforts to achieve this led to his dismissal from his order, and with the encouragement of Pope Pius IX, he began his own religious community in 1858. Entrusted with the care of a church in Manhattan, the Paulists built the Parish of St. Paul the Apostle as a center of operations and seminary as they continued conducting parish missions and initiated a wider outreach by launching a magazine, the *Catholic World* (1865), the Catholic Publication Society (1866), and the Catholic Book Exchange (1892), which became the Paulist Press in 1913.

In 1870 Hecker journeyed to Rome to attend the First Vatican Council. He wrote a series of controversial essays, and his views sparked a later storm of controversy known as the Americanist heresy, which ended with a papal condemnation in 1895. The Paulists pioneered the use of mass media, with radio station WLWL established in New York City in 1924 and with ventures that included numerous film and television productions. In the early 21st century their community of about 228 remains committed to its three central goals of evangelization, reconciliation, and ecumenism.

O'Brien, David J. *Isaac Hecker: An American Catholic* (New York: Paulist Press, 1992)

Kathleen L. Riley

Paul Smith's College. Private college. In 1937 Phelps Smith bequeathed Paul Smith's Hotel, a resort with over 20,000 acres (8,100 ha) on Lower St. Regis Lake in Franklin Co, to endow a college named for his father. Paul Smith's College opened in 1946 and focuses on providing career training for people living in the Adirondacks. In 1961 it purchased Hotel Saranac in Saranac Lake (Franklin Co) and used it as a training facility. In 2001 the school enrolled about 700 students. In 2002 it offered 12 associate and 3 bachelor's degrees in culinary arts and hospitality trades, tourism, recreation, and wildlife and forest technology.

Woods, James R. *Paul Smith's College, 1937–1980: A Saga of Strife, Struggle, and Success* (Burlington, VT: George Little Press, 1980)

Carl A. Westerdahl and Susan S. Clarke

Pavilion. Town (pop 2,467) in S Genesee Co. Settled in 1805 along the state road from Geneseo (Livingston Co) to Batavia (Genesee Co), the town was formed in 1842 from Covington (Wyoming Co). Oatka Creek provided power for brick, chair, and wagon factories, and mills. Natural gas was extracted beginning in 1879, and salt in 1891. The DeWitt Corp (1923) is a construction firm that has worked on state projects including Attica Prison, St. Lawrence Seaway, and Mount Morris Dam; it was sold in 1999 to Hanson Aggregates. The Woodward Tower, a five-story Ribstone silo, was built in 1926 as a party house for the son of the Jell-O promoter.

Susan L. Conklin

Pawling. Town (pop 7,521) and village (pop 2,233) in SE Dutchess Co. Part of Beekman Patent (1697), which was enlarged in 1743 by the annexation of part of the Oblong, it was settled in the late 1720s by Quakers from New England and Westchester Co, organized as a precinct in 1769, and formed as a town in 1788. The Harlem Railroad (1849) opened up the New York City market for fluid milk, and the town shifted from cattle raising to dairying. The railroad also stimulated the growth of its principal locality, incorporated as the Village of Pawling in 1893. Resort hotels, such as Mizzen Top Hotel (1880) and the Dutcher House (1884), were followed by summer homes. In the 20th century it became a weekend home destination for wealthy New Yorkers and, in the last quarter of the century, a commuter town. Some modern manufacturing was introduced after World War II, notably Pawling Rubber Co and Lumelite (plastics). Prominent residents included Edward R. Murrow (1908–65), television news commentator; Norman Vincent Peale (1898–1993), spiritual leader; Lowell Thomas (1892–1981), world traveler, author, and broadcaster; and Thomas E. Dewey (1902–71), governor. Trinity-Pawling School (1907) is a private boarding school.

William P. McDermott

Payne, Sereno E(lisha) (*b* Hamilton, Madison Co, 26 June 1843; *d* Washington, DC, 10 Dec 1914). US congressman. Payne's family moved to Auburn (Cayuga Co) when he was a boy. He attended Auburn Academy and graduated from the University of Rochester in 1864. Payne became active in Republican Party politics early, speaking at local political rallies during the 1864 reelection campaign of Pres Abraham Lincoln. Two years later he was admitted to the state bar and began a law practice in Auburn. He served as city clerk of Auburn from 1867 to 1868 and as Cayuga Co district attorney from 1873 to 1879. Elected to the US House of Representatives in 1882, Payne served his constituents until his death, with the exception of one term when Democrats gerrymandered him out of his district and he lost the 1886 election. In Washington, Payne was known as an expert on tariffs and an advocate of protectionism. He served as chair of the Merchant Marine and Fisheries (1895–99) and Ways and Means Committees (1897–1911) and as majority leader (1899–1911). Payne's ambition was to be elected Speaker of the House, but in 1903 he lost a campaign for the position when the New York congressional delegation was split behind him and Rep James S. Sherman of Utica. Rep Joseph Cannon of Illinois was elected as the compromise candidate.

See also ART MUSEUMS, COLLECTING, AND PATRONAGE.

Cuddy, Michael J., Jr. *Bicentennial Portraits: Noteworthy Sons and Daughters of Auburn, New York* (Auburn, NY: Historic Resources Advisory Board, 1993)

John David Rausch Jr

peace and antiwar movements. Before Europeans arrived, a Great Tree of Peace symbolized attempts to unify five warring Iroquois nations into a confederation called the Haudenosaunee. Although the confederacy did not end the warfare, subsequent leaders drew on the image of the tree as an ideal of extending peace among all peoples. The teachings of the early 19th century Seneca reformer Handsome Lake reinforced the Haudenosaunee vision of peace and social harmony.

Quakers arriving in New Netherland introduced European religious pacifism to the colony. Their peace testimony—repudiation of all violence and war—challenged compulsory militia service. As early as 1675, New York Colony officials fined Quakers who refused militia duty. The 1755 Militia Act provided conscientious objectors with alternatives to military service but also strictly enforced them. Many rejected the alternatives as also violating the peace testimony. Distraint or imprisonment sometimes followed. This pattern replayed itself, with variations among Quakers and other small sectarian pacifist groups such as the Shakers, from the Revolutionary through the Civil War. During the American Revolution, Quakers in New York State enlarged the peace testimony to encompass civilian issues such as opposition to war taxes and war profiteering. Quaker pacifism remained influential, and Quakers played key roles in subsequent religious and secular peace movements.

David Low Dodge (1774–1852), a New York City merchant, temperance advocate, and Presbyterian elder, believed that the Christian gospel forbade all use of violence, even in self-defense. Dodge wrote pacifist literature and, in 1815, organized the New York Peace Society (NYPS), perhaps the first such group in the world. He also helped establish the American Peace Society in 1828. Although the small NYPS membership declined after the first decade, it promoted the idea of international organizations as alternatives to war and encouraged antiwar sentiments in international conflicts in the 1830s and 1840s. By 1840 Garrisonian abolitionists also advocated nonresistant pacifism. Other peace advocates, including the NYPS, repudiated this nonresistance because it rejected human governments. With the onset of the Civil War, the core of religious pacifists turned their attention to conscientious objection.

Peace advocates began new campaigns in the 1880s to build international institutions to lessen friction and to mediate disputes. This internationalist movement attracted numerous backers in New York State. In 1895 Albert Smiley, a Quaker, held the first of 22 annual conferences on international arbitration at his Mohonk Mountain House in New Paltz (Ulster Co). In the early 20th century, New York City legal experts, Columbia University administrators and professors, and politician Elihu Root formed numerous organizations promoting international legal codes and judiciaries. Steel magnate Andrew Carnegie funded peace efforts, including a revived NYPS. The 1907 National Arbitration and Peace Congress in New York City drew 1,200 delegates from around the world. Two years earlier the Shakers had organized their own peace convention near New Lebanon (Columbia Co).

THE WORLD WARS

With the start of World War I, some internationalists shifted to advocating military preparedness, but the core of religious and secular pacifists established new antiwar and antimilitarist organizations. Many were headquartered in New York City, and some have remained central to peace advocacy into the 21st century. Peace was a key issue for many in the women's movement of the period, and the Henry Street Settlement in Manhattan served as a gathering place for peace advocates. The national Woman's Peace Party (WPP), rooted in these gatherings and Chicago meetings, emerged in 1915. Its dynamic New York City branch, under the leadership of Crystal Eastman, spawned the Women's Peace Society (1919) and the Women's Peace Union (1921). In 1919 the WPP became the Women's International League for Peace and Freedom (WILPF), still a major peace organization in 2003. In late 1915 a meeting in Garden City (Nassau Co) established the US Fellowship of Reconciliation (FOR), a key organization of religious pacifists for the rest of the century. By 1924 one FOR committee had evolved into the secular War Resisters League, headquartered in New York City. Other groups that originated in New York City included the American Union against Militarism (1915–16) and two organizations that gave legal support to conscientious objectors, the Bureau of Legal Advice (1917) and the American Civil Liberties Union (1920).

The two decades after World War I reunited, for a period of time, internationalists and pacifists. Women's groups, movements on college campuses, democratic socialists, and Jewish and Christian groups worked against war in words and in actions. In early 1932, WILPF organized a mass demonstration in Manhattan's Madison Square Garden in support of the Geneva Disarmament Conference. The largest student antiwar protests of the 1930s occurred in New York City. Those of 1934 and 1935 were dominated numerically by students striking from Columbia and New York University. There were also strikes at Syracuse University and Vassar College (Dutchess Co). In the late 1930s Abraham Johannes "A. J." Muste began his long tenure as head of FOR (1940–53) and as spiritual leader of various peace and social justice efforts, through the Vietnam War. Other key pacifists included Norman Thomas, the interwar Socialist Party candidate for governor and US president, and Oswald Garrison Villard, editor of the *Nation*.

The Catholic Worker movement, established in New York City in 1933 by Dorothy Day and Peter Maurin, introduced pacifism into the American Roman Catholic Church and enlarged the Catholic presence in the national peace movement. During World War II, pacifists again focused on conscientious objection. More than 1,100 conscripted men served in ten Civilian Public Service (CPS) units in the state as an alternative to the military. Some rejected participation in CPS and instead served prison terms. Among them was Bayard Rustin, who connected pacifism and racial justice in his work in FOR and in the Congress of Racial Equality (CORE), which was formed as an outgrowth of FOR in 1942.

SINCE 1945

Protests against the proliferation of nuclear weapons after World War II inspired numerous organizations, notably the Committee for a Sane Nuclear Policy (SANE), founded in New York City in 1957, and the Women's Strike for Peace, cofounded in 1961 by Bella Abzug, later a congresswoman from New York City. From 1964 through the mid-1970s New York City was a center of the protests against the Vietnam War. The Fifth Avenue Peace Parade Committee in New York City held its first demonstration in 1965 and organized semiannual protests (sometimes called moratoriums) through 1973. Among the most charismatic figures in the postwar peace movement were Syracuse-raised brothers Daniel and Philip Berrigan, and both were influenced by the Catholic Worker movement. The Nuclear Freeze movement of the late 1970s and 1980s, which called on the United States and the Soviet Union to halt the building of nuclear weapons, culminated in a massive rally in Central Park in Manhattan on 12 June 1982. Important contributions also came from a statewide network of peace groups, including Quaker monthly meetings, the Syracuse Peace Council, and the 1983 Women's Encampment for a Future of Peace and Justice in Romulus (Seneca Co) protesting the presence of nuclear weapons at the nearby Seneca Army Depot. Before the Gulf War in 1991 and the Iraq War of 2003, antiwar protesters in the state made known their opposition to the government's plans for war.

See also VIETNAM WAR.

Alonso, Harriet Hyman. *Peace as a Women's Issue: A History of the US Movement for World Peace and Women's Rights* (Syracuse: Syracuse Univ Press, 1993)

Brock, Peter. *Pacifism in the United States: From the Colonial Era to the First World War* (Princeton, NJ: Princeton Univ Press, 1968)

Brock, Peter, and Nigel Young. *Pacifism in the 20th Century* (Syracuse: Syracuse University Press [dist], 1999)

M. J. Heisey

Peacemaker Legend. See IROQUOIS CONFEDERACY.

Peach, Robert E. (*b* Syracuse, 9 Mar 1920; *d* Clinton, Oneida Co, 20 Apr 1971). Airline executive. Following his education in Syracuse public schools, Peach graduated with a BA from Hamilton College in 1941. He entered the University of Chicago Law School but left at the beginning of World War II to join the US Navy. Learning to fly, Peach went on to command a patrol squadron in the Pacific and to earn two Distinguished Flying Crosses and other decorations for valor. He resumed the study of law at Cornell University in 1945 and flew part-time for Robinson Aviation, a local company that offered air taxi service between Ithaca and New York City. Finding aviation more appealing than law, Peach soon dropped out of school, became a full-time employee of the rapidly expanding company, and by 1948 had risen to the positions of general manager and executive vice president. Peach guided the airline through a period of continued growth as the company added routes throughout New York State. Robinson changed its name to Mohawk Airlines on 1 Jan 1953, and Peach became the company's president the next year. Recalled by associates as arrogant and independent, Peach was a hands-on manager. By 1970 as financial losses mounted at Mohawk, Peach retired for "health reasons." In April 1971, following a decision by Mohawk's board of directors to merge the financially weakened company with Allegheny Airlines, he died of a self-inflicted gunshot wound.

Leary, William M. "Robert E. Peach and Mohawk Airlines: A Study in Entrepreneurship." In *Airline Executives and Federal Regulation: Case Studies in American Enterprise from the Airmail Era to the Dawn of the Jet Age,* ed. W. David Lewis (Columbus: Ohio State Univ Press, 2000)

William M. Leary

Peach War. While Petrus Stuyvesant, director general of New Netherland, was invading New Sweden on the Delaware River on 15 Sept 1655 with a force of 350 men, a large party of Indians from various nations attacked Manhattan Island. Landing within the city walls of New Amsterdam [now New York City] were 600 Indians in 64 canoes; they were quickly repulsed. They went on to Pavonia [now Jersey City, NJ] and Staten Island, where the damage and loss were extensive. The reason for the attack was unclear. Stuyvesant was informed by dispatch that the Swedes might have instigated the attack. Although this report cannot be verified, it is most likely that news of possible Swedish complicity was responsible for the unruly behavior of the Dutch soldiers in the Swedish settlements. Some Indians had claimed that they were looking for "Northern Indians" when they broke into houses. However, many of the Dutch were of the opinion that their true motive was revenge for the actions of several officials of New Netherland. The war's name is derived from an incident involving Hendrick van Dijck, the former fiscal (financial officer) of New Netherland who killed an Indian woman he caught stealing peaches from his garden. Although Dutch West India Co directors in Amsterdam later concluded that Van Dijck's brutal act was the primary cause of the uprising, it was probably the behavior of another official that moved the Indians to action. Refugees who flooded into New Amsterdam from Staten Island and Pavonia called for fiscal Cornelis van Tienhoven's head, claiming he was the sole cause of the attack, although no charges against the fiscal are found in the records.

The cause of the war remains unknown, but it is clear that much damage was done. Stuyvesant reported that "in less than 3 days over forty of our nation" were killed; 100 people, mostly women and children, were taken prisoner; and 28 farms were destroyed, including 500 head of cattle and 9,000 bushels (317,000 l) of grain. Although damage to Manhattan was minor, Pavonia and Staten Island were devastated. The war can be viewed as a continuation of Indian unrest begun in 1643 during the administration of Willem Kieft.

Gehring, Charles T., ed. and trans. *Delaware Papers, 1648–1664 in the New York Historical Manuscripts: Dutch Series* (Baltimore: Genealogical Publications, 1981)

———. *Council Minutes, 1655–1656 in New Netherland Documents Series* (Syracuse: Syracuse University Press, 1995)

Charles T. Gehring

Pearl River. Locality (pop 15,553) in Orangetown (Rockland Co). In 1870 Pearl River acquired a station on the New Jersey and New York Railroad and, in 1872, a post office. Julius E. Braunsdorf platted the hamlet when he began his Aetna Sewing Machine Co (1873–80). Pearl River was home to the Dexter Folder Co (1894–1983; postcard manufacturers). Lederle Laboratories (1906) dominated the community during the 20th century. The lab, a subsidiary of Wyeth Pharmaceuticals since the 1990s, employed 3,168 in 2003.

Mary R. Cardenas

Peck, Everard (*b* Berlin, Conn, 6 Nov 1791; *d* Rochester, 9 Feb 1854). Printer and publisher. Peck learned bookbinding in Hartford, Conn, and worked as a journeyman printer in Albany before settling in Rochester in 1816 to open a bookstore and bindery. In 1818 he began publishing a weekly newspaper, the *Rochester Telegraph.* He also undertook job printing, producing almanacs, school texts, and religious works. He printed the first directory of the young and growing village of Rochester in 1827. It contained a history of the community, which was also published separately. In 1825 Peck sold the newspaper to Thurlow Weed, later an influential Albany newspaper editor. Peck left his bookshop in 1831 and in the mid-1830s he became a banker, first with the Bank of Orleans in Albion (Orleans Co), then the Rochester City Bank, and finally the Commercial Bank of Rochester. He was vice president of the latter at the time of his death. Several of Rochester's benevolent groups were founded during meetings at Peck's home, including the Rochester Orphan Asylum (1837) (now Hillside Children's Center). Peck was a founding trustee of the University of Rochester in 1850.

Stern, Madeline B. "Books in the Wilderness (Part II) Some 19th Century Upstate Publishers," *New York History* 31 (Oct 1950): 414–29

Karl S. Kabelac

Peck, Jedidiah (*b* Lyme, Conn, 28 Jan 1748; *d* Burlington, Otsego Co, 15 Aug 1821). County judge and state politician. Peck grew up in Connecticut where he obtained a common school education before serving in the Revolutionary War. Settling on a farm in Burlington where he held several town offices, Peck was appointed an associate justice of the court for the newly formed Otsego Co in 1791. A tireless public campaigner among farmers, in 1798 he won a seat in the state assembly as a Democrat-Republican, serving six terms. Peck is perhaps most noted for his vocal opposition to the federal Alien and Sedition Acts of 1798, and a heated rivalry existed between him and the local supporter of the laws, Congressman William Cooper. Constantly at odds with aristocratic Federalist leaders, Peck ran successfully for the state senate in 1804 and was placed on the Council of Appointment by the Republican-controlled legislature the following year. While serving in the state senate (1804–8) he helped enact a body of legislation that advanced the economic prosperity and political rights of the state's farmers and artisans. A prominent political figure of the New York State frontier, Peck's greatest accomplishment was securing comprehensive state funding for common schools in 1812.

Taylor, Alan. *William's Cooper Town* (New York: Knopf, 1995)

Wesley G. Balla

Peckham, Rufus Wheeler, Jr (*b* Albany, 8 Nov 1838; *d* Altamont, Albany Co, 24 Oct 1909). State judge and US Supreme Court justice. Educated at Albany Academy, privately in Philadelphia, and on a year-long European tour with his brother Wheeler, Peckham studied law for two years in his father's Albany firm. Admitted to the bar in 1859, Peckham that year succeeded his father, who was elected to the state supreme court, as a partner in Peckham and Tremain. Peckham's political and social connections contributed to his election as district attorney of Albany Co (1869–72). He returned to public life in 1881 as Albany's corporation counsel, failed to get the Democratic nomination for the Court of Appeals in 1882, gained a seat on the state supreme court the following year, and won election to the Court of Appeals in 1886. Pres Grover Cleveland, after failing to perpetuate the "New York seat" on the US Supreme Court following Samuel Blatchford's death in 1893, selected his friend Peckham for the Court in 1895, and the nominee, unlike his brother Wheeler (a rejected Cleveland candidate), was perfectly acceptable to New York State Democratic boss Sen David B. Hill. Peckham in his *Lochner v New York* (1905) opinion elevated liberty of contract to a protected constitutional right, a position consistent with his work on the Court of Appeals.

Skolnik, Richard. "Rufus Peckham." In *The Justices of the United States Supreme Court, 1789–1969: Their Lives and Major Opinions,* ed. Leon Friedman and Fred L. Israel, 5 vols (New York: Chelsea House, in association with Bowker, 1969–78)

Donald M. Roper

Peekskill. City (pop 22,441) in NW Westchester Co. On the Hudson River, the site was developed as a river landing in the mid–18th century and served as the region's headquarters for the Continental army from 1776 to 1778. The village was incorporated in 1816 but never held elections and began its government functions in 1827. Beginning in 1826 Peekskill became a manufacturer of cast-iron stoves and plows, and by 1884 there were eight stove works in the village. The Hudson River Railroad arrived in 1849. Industries included Binney and Smith (1864–1902; chemicals, later the creator of Crayola crayons), Baker Underwear (1892–1924), Peekskill Hat Manufacturing Co (1895–1923), and Fleischmann's, which made yeast, vinegar, gin, and whiskey from 1900 to 1977. Among the ethnic groups drawn by industrial work were Hungarians, who came primarily to work in the hat factory. Peekskill incorporated as a city in 1940. With the opening of Beach Shopping Center

(1958) at its eastern edge, it made an early attempt to revitalize through urban renewal (1961–75), but several later initiatives such as the Riverfront Green (1976), the artists' district (1992), and artists' loft complex (2002) were more effective in creating the modern city. Famous residents have included Chauncey M. Depew (1834–1928), New York Central Railroad president and US senator. George E. Pataki (1945–) was elected mayor of Peekskill twice (1981, 1983) and governor of New York State three times (1994, 1998, 2002). Peekskill's population grew by 15% in the 1990s, one of the highest rates in the county, and in 2000, 25.5% of the population was black and approximately 21% were of Latino ethnicity.

John J. Curran

Peekskill riots. People's Artists held a concert for the benefit of the Civil Rights Congress on 27 Aug 1949 at Lakeland Picnic Grounds in Van Cortlandtville, 3 miles (5 km) northeast of Peekskill (Westchester Co). The concert was headlined by the noted African American bass Paul Robeson and folksinger Pete Seeger. Both organizations and the concert participants were closely affiliated with the Communist Party. By 1949, with the escalation of the Cold War, the American Communist Party was increasingly seen by the mainstream media as pariahs, and inflamed by an editorial in the *Peekskill Evening Star,* American Legion members and others blocked the entrance, prevented Robeson's arrival, and attacked about 200 concertgoers already there. The state troopers, who were there to monitor the concertgoers as possible subversives, did not intervene. A mass meeting was called by the Civil Rights Congress soon afterward at the Golden Gate Ballroom in Harlem (New York Co). The concert was rescheduled for Labor Day (4 September) at the former Hollow Brook Country Club, a short distance from the picnic grounds. Organizers arranged for trade unionists to act as security and were more prepared. A counterdemonstration numbering no more than 1,000 amassed on the road. A crowd estimated at 15,000–25,000 heard Seeger, Sylvia Kahn, and Robeson. After the concert ended and the 300 troopers withdrew to the road, the counterdemonstrators began throwing rocks. Anti-Semitic and racist epithets were widely heard. The exit road was blocked, and cars and buses leaving the site were attacked by troopers and others; organizers estimated 140 serious injuries. The national press denounced the incident, although many newspapers primarily regretted its effect of calling attention to the leftist sympathizers. The Peekskill riots became a rallying point for the American left. The noted folk group the Weavers released their first recording, "The Peekskill Story," in the fall of 1949.

Walwik, Joseph. *Peekskill, New York, Anti-Communist Riots of 1949* (Lewiston, NY: Edwin Mellen Press, 2002)

Field Horne

PEF. See PUBLIC EMPLOYEES UNIONS.

Pelham. Town (pop 11,866) and village (pop 6,400) in S Westchester Co. Part of a 1654 land purchase by Thomas Pell (1613–69), Pelham was established as a manor in 1687. Beginning in 1673 the Boston Post Rd served the town, which in 1776 was the site of the Battle of Pell's Point and in 1788 was formally recognized as a town. Suburban development began soon after the New Haven Railroad established a Pelhamville station (1848). In 1895 the south part of the town was annexed by New York City, becoming part of Bronx Borough three years later. The villages of Pelham and North Pelham incorporated in 1896 and consolidated in 1975. During the 1920s the town's population more than doubled, from 5,195 to 11,851. Commuter access was improved by the Hutchinson River Parkway (1928) and the New England Thruway (1958). In the early 21st century the town's two villages, Pelham and Pelham Manor, are chiefly upper-class commuter suburbs, with a small industrial area in the extreme southwest. Landmarks include Pelhamdale (*ca* 1750) and the Gothic Revival–style Bolton Priory (1838), as well as the private New York Athletic Club, which occupies most of the town's Long Island Sound shoreline.

Pelham Manor. Village (pop 5,466) in Pelham (Westchester Co). Residential development began soon after the New Haven Railroad crossed the town in 1848. Prospect Hill was platted in 1852 around Prospect and Highland Aves and Esplanade. When the New Haven line's Harlem River Branch (1873) passed through the village, real estate development accelerated with Pelham Manor and Huguenot Heights Associations. The village was incorporated in 1891. The Hutchinson River Parkway (1928) connects the village with New York City. By 1930 the village was largely built out, and in 2003 it was a commuter suburb. Landmarks include the Priory (1837–38), a private house, and Christ Church (1843), modeled after a Romantic-style English parish church.

Barbara J. Dunlap

Pembroke. Town (pop 4,530) in W Genesee Co. The town was formed from Batavia in 1812 after the area's settlement in 1804. Indian Falls was the birthplace of Ely S. Parker (1828–95), a Tonawanda Seneca who became the first Native American to serve as US commissioner of Indian Affairs. Boulder Park (1949–70), an amusement park at Indian Falls, featured a fine carousel and a miniature steam train. Kutter's Cheese Factory (1947) sells its product throughout the Northeast. A Pembroke exit of the Thruway (1954) made commuting to Buffalo and Rochester practical. The Brick House Corners Fair held each September commemorates the town's history, farms, and crafts.

Susan L. Conklin

Pendleton. Town (pop 6,050) in S central Niagara Co. Settled around 1808, the town was formed from Niagara in 1827. The Erie Canal opened through Pendleton in 1825, when the primary industry was timber. Germans settled in the southern and eastern parts of town beginning in 1832. The canal's enlargement in the 1850s made the drainage of swamplands for farming possible; in the same period, Pendleton acquired rail service (Buffalo and Lockport, 1853). By the early 1900s the timber was gone, as was most of the canal traffic. A log cabin on the grounds of the Pendleton Town Park is a landmark.

Nancy B. Mingus

Penet's Square. Land tract. Of the land the Oneida surrendered at the 1788 Treaty of Fort Schuyler, a tract 10 mi^2 (26 km^2) was allocated to Pierre Penet, a French adventurer and schemer whom the Oneida had appointed as their agent. Penet had convinced the divided Oneida Nation that, among other things, he was a confidant of the Marquis de Lafayette and an emissary from King Louis XVI. Penet's agent, John Duncan, selected land in the present towns of Orleans, Clayton, and Pamelia (Jefferson Co). Penet is believed to have sold the tract in 1790 in an unrecorded deed, but many sales and counterclaims clouded the title, and ownership of the land remained uncertain. First settled at French Creek [now Clayton] in 1799, the tract became home to squatters often called Penayers. By 1806 many believed Penet to be dead, and, because he was an alien, it was thought that ownership of his land reverted to New York State. Without a claim to the land, the squatters cut the timber and took what short-term profits they could. Because they were not taxpayers, no roads were built, no schools were established, and few improvements were made. Between 1817 and 1825 French landowner John LaFarge bought almost all of Penet's Square and cleared his title in 1830. Successful development followed under his proprietorship.

Powell, Thomas F. *Penet's Square* (Lakemont, NY: North Country Books, 1976)

Laura Lynne Scharer

Penfield. Town (pop 34,645) in E Monroe Co. Penfield was explored by René-Robert Cavelier de la Salle in 1669, 1678, and 1679, and it was the location of Fort Schuyler (1721). Waterpower from the 90 ft (27 m) drop of Irondequoit Creek attracted its first settlers in 1800. The town was formed from the old town of Boyle in 1810. Grinding wheat was an important business in early years. Penfield residents also made salt from brine (1806–?1812), operated a forge and ironworks (1822–25), woolen factory (burned 1844), and limekilns (*ca* 1855). The weekly *Penfield Extra* (1861–66, circulation 2,000) was supposedly edited and published by Nellie Williams (1849–75) starting when she was 12. A large paper mill was in operation soon after the Civil War and continued until 1916 when it moved to Perinton. In 1872 there were five nurseries in town, some continuing until the 1960s. Suburbanization began after World War II, with its population increasing from 4,847 to 12,601 over the course of the 1950s, during which time Panorama Plaza (1959) and Eastway Plaza were built. In 2002 the town, one of the fastest growing in Monroe Co, is a mixture of retail centers, subdivisions, and farms. Major industrial enterprises include Nalge Co (plastic laboratory beakers), Dolomite Products Co, and Paychex (1971, payroll and human resources services), whose CEO, B. Thomas Golisano, was an Independent candidate for New York State governor in 1994, 1998, and 2002. Penfield is the site of the William Gorse House (1835), the only mud house (rammed earth with straw) in New York State with its original exterior intact, and the Thousand Acre Swamp, owned by the Nature Conservancy.

Carolyn Vacca

Penn Central Railroad. The Pennsylvania Railroad absorbed its rival New York Central Railroad on 1 Feb 1968, taking the name Pennsylvania New York Central Transportation Co, which then changed to Penn Central Co on 8 May 1968. As a condition of the merger, the government required Penn Central to purchase the bankrupt commuter line New York, New Haven and Hartford Railroad on 31 Dec 1968. The railroad's properties were reorganized 1 Oct 1969 as Penn Central Co, a holding company, and Penn Central Transportation Co (PCT), the actual carrier. All PCT traffic from the Midwest to points east of Philadelphia traveled the former New York Central Water Level Route between Buffalo and Albany, with the Alfred E. Perlman Yard near Selkirk (Albany Co) functioning as the company's eastern traffic hub. But with Pennsylvania Railroad the senior merger partner, corporate headquarters remained in Philadelphia. Poor planning doomed the merger. Management philosophies differed, computer systems were incompatible, and government regulation hindered necessary downsizing. For some time the company balanced railroad losses with short-term borrowing and the income from nonrailroad investments. PCT collapsed on 21 June 1970 in the largest US corporate bankruptcy to that date. Bankruptcy trustees rebuilt the company, but it remained unprofitable under then existing government regulations. The federal government soon intervened, with Amtrak taking over long-distance passenger service in 1971 and state agencies, including Metropolitan Transportation Authority, assuming commuter service. The Regional Rail Reorganization Act of 1973 combined viable portions of PCT and other northeastern railroads into federally funded Consolidated Rail Corp (Conrail), effective 1 Apr 1976.

Salisbury, Stephen. *No Way to Run a Railroad: The Untold Story of the Penn Central Crisis* (New York: McGraw-Hill, 1982)

Christopher T. Baer

Pennsylvania Railroad Company. Incorporated on 13 Apr 1846, it completed its main line between Harrisburg and Pittsburgh, Pa, in 1852. As New York Central Railroad extended branches into Pennsylvania coal and steel centers, the Pennsylvania Railroad Co (PRR) moved into New York State, chiefly by acquiring existing lines. By 1875 it connected New York City with Chicago, St. Louis, the Potomac and Ohio Rivers, and the Great Lakes. In 1863 its subsidiary Northern Central Railway leased line from Williamsport, Pa, to Elmira (Chemung Co), arranging with Erie Railroad for through traffic to Buffalo. In 1872 PRR gained track from Elmira to Canandaigua (Ontario Co) from Erie Railroad and in 1884 acquired track from Stanley (Ontario Co) to Sodus Point (Wayne Co). The company used these lines to move Pennsylvania coal north to Lake Ontario and Canada. In 1900 PRR took control of Long Island Rail Road (LIRR). That same year PRR leased Western New York and Pennsylvania Railroad, embracing main lines from Buffalo to Emporium, Pa, and from Buffalo through Corry to Oil City, Pa, and from Rochester through Salamanca (Cattaraugus Co) crossing the Buffalo-Emporium line at Olean (Cattaraugus Co) to Oil City. These and other PRR lines linked Western New York, Buffalo, Niagara Falls, and the Southern Tier with Pennsylvania's oil region, Washington, DC, and points farther south and west. In 1910 PRR opened its Manhattan terminal, Pennsylvania Station, a showpiece of the rail network for the next half century. The company began losing money after World War II, and in 1966 it sold LIRR to New York State. On 1 Feb 1968 PRR merged with its principal rival, New York Central Railroad, to form the company later known as Penn Central Transportation Co.

Burgess, George H., and C. Miles Kennedy. *A Centennial History of the Pennsylvania Railroad, 1846–1946* (Philadelphia: Pennsylvania Railroad Co, 1949)
Caloroso, Bill. *Pennsylvania Railroad's Elmira Branch* (Andover, NJ: Andover Junction Publications, 1993)
Pietrak, Paul V., Joseph G. Streamer, and James A. Van Brocklin. *The History of the Western New York and Pennsylvania Railway and Its Predecessors and Successors* (Hamburg, NY: Authors, 2000)

Christopher T. Baer

Pennsylvania Station. Manhattan rail station located between 7th and 8th Aves and 31st and 33d Sts, commonly known as Penn Station. Pennsylvania Railroad Co (PRR) built Penn Station between 1902 and 1910 as part of a $100 million project that included a line running from Harrison, NJ, under the Hudson River to Manhattan and continuing under the East River to the Borough of Queens. The New York City firm of McKim, Mead and White designed the station building above track level in a grand but austere Roman style. The 7th Ave facade featured a Roman Doric colonnade; central entrances on all four sides of the structure were topped with large clocks, each framed by the allegorical figures Night and Day and flanked by rows of granite eagles. The station's Main Waiting Room, 150 ft (45.7 m) high and sheathed in warm-toned travertine marble, was inspired by Rome's Baths of Caracalla, and the Concourse featured Roman-style vaults in modern steel and glass. The station opened for Long Island Rail Road service on 8 Sept 1910 and PRR service on 27 Nov 1910. In 1945, the peak year of its use under PRR ownership, 109 million people passed through the facility.

Penn Station lacked rental space to offset expenses, and by the 1950s PRR management judged the building obsolete. Between 1963 and 1967 PRR razed the above-ground portion of the complex, which was replaced by a new Madison Square Garden and an office tower. Underground facilities remained, redecorated in shopping mall style. The razing of Penn Station led to the formation of New York City's Landmarks Preservation Commission in 1965 and helped spark an interest in historic preservation in many cities. New regulations helped save New York City's other major rail facility, Grand Central Terminal, from a similar fate. Ownership of Penn Station passed to Amtrak in 1976, and in 1991 all long-distance trains were rerouted from Grand Central Terminal to Penn Station. In 1999 the New York City and Chicago firm of Skidmore, Owings and Merrill (SOM) designed a new Penn Station, scheduled for completion in 2003, to serve mainly long-distance trains while leaving most commuter operations in the old complex. The design of the new Penn Station, like that of the old, juxtaposes steel and glass with classical architecture. Farley Post Office, another McKim, Mead and White building, forms the outer shell of SOM's complex.

Ballon, Hilary. *New York's Pennsylvania Stations* (New York: Norton, 2002)
Middleton, William D. *Manhattan Gateway: New York's Pennsylvania Station* (Waukesha, Wisc: Kalmbach Publishing, 1996)

Christopher T. Baer

Penn Yan. Village (pop 5,219) in Milo, Jerusalem, and Benton (Yates Co). Settled in 1791, it acquired its name by 1809, signifying its population mix of Pennsylvanians and Yankees. It became the county seat when Yates Co was created in 1823 and was incorporated as a village in 1833. Birkett Mills (1801), a large producer of buckwheat products, is one of New York State's oldest businesses. Penn Yan's early commerce centered on milling along Crooked Lake Canal (1833–77), whose right-of-way was replaced by a rail line in 1884; the Northern Central Railway provided direct service beginning in 1851. By the 1850s Penn Yan was home to a community of African Americans escaped from slavery. Products in the 19th century included straw paper, fruit baskets, agricultural machinery, malt, and flour; in the 20th century, Penn Yan produced shoes, clothing, buses, boats, and store fixtures. Penn Yan Boat Co (1921, later Penn Yan Marine) closed in 2000; Penn Yan Express (1949), a trucking firm with 750 trucks and 630 employees, was sold in 1983 and its local terminals closed. Penn Yan's economy was increasingly resort driven, but in the early 21st century a group of small manufacturers, including Coach and Equipment Co (buses), Iron Age Shoes, and Silgan Plastics, employs a number of residents; other residents commute to Canandaigua (Ontario Co) and Rochester.

Gwen Chamberlain

Pentecostals. Protestant Christians who believe that normative Christian experience should include a baptism of the Holy Spirit with the evidence of speaking in tongues. The connection between such baptism and tongues speech was first made in 1900 in Topeka, Kans, by independent evangelist Charles Parham. The movement that grew out of Parham's subsequent evangelistic efforts spread around the world as eager adherents convinced others to accept the movement's central tenets. Pentecostals believe that they live in the end times and that their movement is a harbinger of the imminent return of Christ.

Early in 1907 Marie Burgess (later Marie Burgess Brown), a follower of Charles Parham, established a Pentecostal mission in a storefront on West 42d St in New York City. The congregation grew quickly, became affiliated with the Assemblies of God, and in 1921 purchased the former Calvary Baptist Church on West 34th St. Burgess and her husband, Robert Brown, named this church Glad Tidings Tabernacle. In the 1930s and 1940s they added radio broadcasting and work among the military to their activities. Before World War II this congregation served as a hub for a growing number of small Pentecostal congregations scattered around the city as well as for Pentecostal missionaries en route to the field. After World War II, as new churches sprang up across the metropolitan area, the prominence of Glad Tidings waned.

Also in 1907 the Pentecostal movement found acceptance in Rochester, where five sisters, daughters of one-time Methodist minister James Duncan, established and supervised an inner-city mission, a faith home, a small publishing plant, and Rochester Bible Training School. Collectively known as Elim, these ministries became affiliated with the Pentecostal movement in the spring of 1907. They remained independent of denominational control, but the Bible school trained numerous men and women who went on to become influential Pentecostal missionaries, teachers, pastors, and denominational administrators. The sisters chose to discontinue their efforts early in the 1920s rather than turn them over to other leadership, but one of their students, Ivan Q. Spencer, reopened the Elim Bible Institute in 1924 in Hornell (Steuben Co) and in 1951 moved it to Lima (Livingston Co), where it remains the focal point for the Elim Fellowship, a network of independent Pentecostal congregations scattered throughout the state and elsewhere.

Aimee Semple McPherson was the most influential Pentecostal evangelist to work in New York State. She lived briefly in New York City in 1911, conducted evangelistic meetings in Corona (Queens Co) in 1916, and returned to Glad Tidings Tabernacle in 1927. For a brief period in 1933, McPherson performed on Broadway, preaching five times daily for a week at the Capitol Theater in ten-minute segments following vaudeville programs. McPherson's evangelistic efforts in New York City did not establish new congregations but strengthened existing churches. From 1943 until 1968 Queens served as the headquarters of a small but colorful Pentecostal denomination known as the Church of God (World Headquarters), led by Homer Tomlinson, whose political ambitions were rooted in his hope of realizing the kingdom of God on earth and whose notoriety derived from his tabernacle featuring the flags of the nations of the world, his radical claims of 30 million followers, and his fascination with Jerusalem.

As the principal site for early Pentecostals in New York City, Glad Tidings Tabernacle was an interracial congregation. By the 1930s, however, its leadership encouraged African American Pentecostals to establish their own congregations in other parts of the city. By then the Church of God in Christ, a predominantly black Pentecostal denomination, had established a few meeting places in Manhattan and Brooklyn. With their own networks and agendas, these congregations have grown up in larger cities in New York State independent of Anglo-Pentecostalism. Their pastors and parishioners have tended to be more attuned to social and political issues than have Anglo-Pentecostals. Spanish-speaking Pentecostals constitute another large group of Pentecostals in New York State, especially in urban areas. Some have affiliated with Pentecostal denominations, especially the Assemblies of God. Many more are independent or network in associations with ties to Latin America. Both Latino and African American Pentecostal constituencies have within their ranks sizable minorities known as "Oneness" or "Jesus Only" Pentecostals. The appellation derives from a controversy in Anglo-Pentecostalism in the World War I era when some denied the Trinity, adopted the practice of water baptism "in the name of Jesus," and began invoking the name of Jesus as a store of spiritual power and an object of piety.

Ethnic Denominations

Ethnic enclaves have always attracted church-planting Pentecostals. In 1925 an independent German mission in Ridgewood (Queens Co) named as its pastor Hans Waldvogel, a native of Switzerland who established the Ridgewood Pfingstegemeinde (Ridgewood Pentecostal Church) on the border of Brooklyn and Queens. This grew to include a network of churches in New York City and a camp on Brant Lake near Chestertown (Warren Co). In New York City this group of churches has made a transition to English, and especially its camp continues to attract people from around the state. The Christian Church of North America, a small Italian denomination, reaches back to the first decade of the century when Italian-speaking immigrants in the Buffalo area and New York City formed Italian language Pentecostal churches that networked with other Italian missions around the country and in Canada. Since 1961 these congregations have evangelized outside the Italian ethnic community, and their congregations now mirror the new immigrant mix of cities in New York State. The Church of God (Cleveland), a Pentecostal denomination based in Tennessee, sponsors Romanian congregations in New York City. The Assemblies of God work among Korean immigrants, and earlier they had Italian, German, and Hungarian branches that established small congregations in the state wherever these language groups were numerous. Scattered throughout New York City and Buffalo are evangelistic efforts to Korean- and Chinese-speaking immigrants. Pentecostal congregations abroad also sponsor outreaches among their immigrants.

At the turn of the 21st century, the Brooklyn Tabernacle on Flatbush Ave was perhaps the best-known Pentecostal congregation in the country. A racially mixed and thriving independent congregation, it began in the late 1960s as a modest effort by an independent-minded Swedish Pentecostal named Claire Hutchins. Focused on prayer and the person and work of Christ rather than on spiritual gifts, the congregation has outgrown its quarters and sponsors aggressive church planting throughout New York City. It has succeeded as an urban congregation by confronting the enormous spiritual and economic challenges of inner-city life. The Brooklyn Tabernacle Choir has received several Grammy Awards. This congregation may best model the potential of Pentecostalism for urban religious renewal in the new millennium.

Anderson, Robert Mapes. *Vision of the Disinherited: The Making of American Pentecostalism* (Peabody, Mass: Hendrickson Publishers, 1992)

Blumhofer, Edith L. *Aimee Semple McPherson: Everybody's Sister* (Grand Rapids, Mich: Eerdmans Publishing, 1993)

———. *Restoring the Faith: The Assemblies of God, Pentecostalism, and American Culture* (Urbana: Univ of Illinois Press, 1993)

Edith L. Blumhofer

peppermint. Perennial herb *(Mentha piperita)* grown for its menthol and oil, used for pharmaceuticals and flavoring. After discovering how well suited the rich alluvial flats of the Canandaigua Outlet were for peppermint culture, emigrants from Ashfield, Mass, who settled near Vienna [now Phelps, Ontario Co] and Lyons [now in Wayne Co] became the first peppermint producers in New York State around 1816. They lacked reliable markets until 1837, when Hiram Gilbert Hotchkiss (1810–97), a Vienna merchant, began accepting peppermint oil as payment. He first shipped consignments to Europe in 1839. In 1841 he relocated to Lyons to be nearer the Erie Canal, established the H. G. Hotchkiss Essential Oils and a bank, and was on his way to becoming America's peppermint king.

New York State's peppermint growers were concentrated in Wayne Co and some adjacent areas of Seneca and Ontario Cos, with a secondary center in Lewis Co. There were 44,500 pounds (20,185 kg) of peppermint oil manufactured in the state in 1846, triple the combined output of competitors in Michigan (10,000 lb/4,536 kg), Ohio (3,000 lb/1,361 kg), and Indiana (700 lb/318 kg). After discovering European demand to be only 12,000 pounds (5,443 kg), Hotchkiss paid growers in 1847 to sell him set amounts for two years, while destroying all surpluses. This temporary monopoly gave him control of the market and of crop quality and elevated peppermint oil prices. After winning prizes in London (1851) and New York City (1853), Hotchkiss bought only from New York State growers to maintain quality, allowing Albert May Todd of St. Joseph Co, Mich, to win control of that state's more cheaply produced peppermint. The A. M. Todd Co and the renamed H. G. Hotchkiss International Prize Medal Essential Oil Co vied for dominance of the American peppermint industry from the 1870s through the 1890s, even as the center of its cultivation moved to more fertile and cheaper lands in the Midwest, and as New York State peppermint farmers shifted to higher-priced crops. From 1910 through the 1920s Beech-Nut Packing Co, a top manufacturer of American candy and chewing gum, made major purchases of peppermint. It merged with Life Savers Corp in 1956 and controlled that brand, including the popular Pep-O-Mint flavor. Life Savers was a part of Kraft Foods in 2003.

Hotchkiss's peppermint oil company, whose records are at Cornell University Library, remained in the family until 1982, when it was sold to the William Leman Co of Bremen, Ind, which operated the Lyons facility until 1990. The village of Lyons has held annual Peppermint Days celebrations since 1989. At the end of the 20th century, Oregon and Washington grew more peppermint than any other states. New York State's crop was so minimal that it did not appear in the 1997 US Department of Agriculture census of state agriculture.

Landing, James E. *American Essence: A History of the Peppermint and Spearmint Industry in the United States* (Kalamazoo, Mich: Kalamazoo Public Museum, 1969)

Scott C. Monje

peppermint pig. Candy tradition begun around 1880 in Saratoga Springs, where confectioners made peppermint pigs of peppermint-flavored candy for the Christmas season. After the holiday meal families and friends broke the pig and shared the pieces, inviting good health and luck for the new year. The pig as a symbol of prosperity lay in Western European beliefs. The pigs were originally handmade by placing a globule of very hot candy on the flat side of a broom handle–shaped piece of wood and forming it into the shape of a pig. By the early 1900s candy makers began using lead butter molds to shape the candy and pure peppermint oil, or wintergreen by 1910, for flavor. After the original Saratoga confectioners died, peppermint pig candies disappeared in the 1930s, and the molds were lost. Saratoga Sweets of Halfmoon (Saratoga Co) revived the tradition in 1987, producing solid pink peppermint pigs in various sizes; the 8 oz (226.8 g) pig is packaged with a red pouch and a tiny hammer. Available only from October through December, the patented pigs are sold in Saratoga Co and around the world through mail order.

"Food," Vertical File, Saratoga Room, Saratoga Springs Public Library

Saratoga Sweets, http://www.saratogasweets.com

Ellen M. deLalla

PepsiCo. The company traces its history to Caleb Bradham, a pharmacist from New Bern, NC, who invented a drink, pepsi-cola, in 1898 with claims that it cured dyspepsia. Initial ingredients included sugar, kola nut extract, vanilla, and rare oils. Bradham developed a bottling franchise system but, after stockpiling sugar to hedge against rising costs, was forced into bankruptcy in 1923 by declining sugar prices. He eventually sold his business to the Loft Candy Co in 1931. Located in the Empire State Building in Manhattan, headquarters moved to Long Island City (Queens Co) in 1935. Six years later, Loft merged with its Pepsi subsidiary and became the Pepsi-Cola Co, introducing one of the earliest national radio jingles. In 1948 corporate headquarters moved to Midtown Manhattan. The company acquired Mountain Dew in 1964 and merged with the Frito-Lay Co in 1965 to become PepsiCo. At that time the company reported 19,000 employees and $510 million in sales.

In 1970 the company moved to new corporate headquarters in Purchase (Westchester Co). The 144-acre (58 ha) complex, designed by Edward Durell Stone, includes the Donald M. Kendall Sculpture Gardens, where works by Auguste Rodin, Henri Laurens, Henry Moore, and others are exhibited. PepsiCo has expanded considerably in the years since, purchasing Pizza Hut (1977) and Taco Bell (1978). In 1979 the PepsiCo Research and Technical Center opened in Valhalla (Westchester Co). The company purchased Kentucky Fried Chicken in 1986 and spun off its $10 billion fast-food unit as TRICON Global Restaurants in 1997. That year it purchased Borden Food Co's Cracker Jack Snacks and the next year acquired Seagram Co's Tropicana Juices. The firm completed purchase of a majority share in South Beach Beverage Co and merged with the Quaker Oats Co in 2001. PepsiCo had revenues of $27 billion with approximately 143,000 employees in 2002.

Stoddart, Bob. *Pepsi: 100 Years* (Los Angeles: General Publishing Group, 1999)

J. Brooks Flippen

Perinton. Town (pop 46,090) in SE Monroe Co. The area was settled around 1790, the town formed from the old town of Boyle in 1812. The Erie Canal (1822) created Fairport as a commercial and political hub. Potatoes and cattle were early farm products. At the end of the 19th century cabbages, onions, canned asparagus, tomatoes, sweet corn, peas, cherries, berries, and other fruit were shipped. Comstock Canning operated until 1982, Rand's Powder Mill operated at Bushnell's Basin from 1853 to 1910, Crystal Rock Mineral Spring Water Co shipped bottled water (*ca* 1895), and the Salter Bros Nursery (1885) raised carnations and violets. Small-scale development began with a trolley line (1906), though it was not until the 1960s and 1970s that extensive suburbanization took place, giving Perinton an upper-middle-class quality. Beginning in the late 1950s Perinton experienced commercial growth with office parks like Corporate Crossings and shopping facilities like Country Club Plaza (1957). There were eight canal breaks in the 19th century, but the worst occurred in 1974, when a break in the Barge Canal destroyed 41 homes and caused millions of dollars of damage.

Carolyn Vacca

Perkins, Frances [Fannie Coralie] (*b* Boston, 10 Apr 1880; *d* New York City, 14 May 1965). Secretary of labor and reformer. She graduated from Mount Holyoke College in 1902 and moved to New York City, where she came under the tutorage of reformer Florence Kelley. She attended graduate school at Columbia University, graduating in 1910. That year she became the executive secretary of the Consumers' League of the City of New York, a position that put her at the center of New York City reform. After the Triangle Shirtwaist Factory fire in 1911, just blocks from her house, Perkins worked closely with the Factory Investigating Commission, which included rising national political figures Robert F. Wagner Sr, the commission's chair, and Alfred E. Smith, the vice chair. By 1915 she was a leading expert in industrial policy. She married Paul Caldwell Wilson, a fellow urban reformer, in 1913, keeping her birth name. In 1918 her husband suffered a breakdown and lived in and out of institutions until his death in 1952. In 1918 Gov Alfred E. Smith appointed Perkins to the Industrial Commission of New York State. She was one of the first women appointed to a position of significance in state government, and she was the highest paid woman on a state payroll at the time. Perkins was the director of the Council on Immigrant Education (1921–22). From 1923 to 1929 she was a member of the state's Industrial Board, serving the last three years as chair. In 1929 newly elected Gov Franklin D. Roosevelt appointed her industrial commissioner, the top position in the State Labor Department. As industrial commissioner she developed key relationships with labor unions and labor leaders in New York. When Roosevelt became president in 1933, Perkins was appointed secretary of labor, a position she held until 1945, becoming the first female cabinet member in US history and an effective labor secretary. She served on the Civil Service Commission from 1945 to 1953. In 1946 she wrote *The Roosevelt I Knew,* an impassioned biography of her political hero. She began a new career in 1957 teaching labor relations at the New York State School of Industrial and Labor Relations at Cornell University.

Martin, George Whitney. *Madame Secretary: Frances Perkins* (Boston: Houghton Mifflin, 1976)

Richard A. Greenwald

Perry. Town (pop 4,876) and village (pop 3,945) in E Wyoming Co. Settled in 1806, the town was formed in 1814 from Leicester (Livingston Co). The village, which is partly in the Town of Castile, was incorporated in 1830. In the 19th century Perry produced cloth (starting in 1827), leather, spokes, ax helves, and hames, and had a foundry and an oil mill. Wyckoff, Tuttle and Olin manufactured the Royce Reaper, and the Perry Salt Co (1886–1909) produced salt. The Silver Lake Railroad connected Perry to Gainesville and beyond in 1872. Starting in 1903, Poles and Italians came to work in the Perry Knitting Co (1882–1969), which employed over 1,000 and caused a population spurt between 1900 and 1920. Other 20th-century industries included Robeson Cutlery Co (1898–1974), Tempest Knitting Co (1907; later Wyckoff Knitting, 1916–34, and Duracraft/Champion, 1935–98), Kaustine Co (1915–1990s, chemical toilets), Borden's powdered milk plant (1919–59), and Archway Bakery (1953; now Perry Baking Co). Dairy farming remains important. Pioneer Credit Recovery, based in Arcade, opened a new facility in 2002 to house 350 workers. Perry is home of the Arts Council for Wyoming County and the Wyoming County International Speedway for stock cars. Pres Chester A. Arthur lived in Perry from 1833 to 1837.

Perrysburg. Town (pop 1,771) and village (pop 408) in NW Cattaraugus Co. The town was formed from Olean and Ischua [now Franklinville] in 1814 as Perry and was renamed Perrysburg in 1818. The first settlers arrived in 1815. Lumbering was succeeded by dairying and grape culture. The Erie Railroad crossed the town in 1851. At Versailles, on Cattaraugus Creek, the steam-powered Versailles Botanic Mills (late 1850s) prepared roots, barks, and herbs for market, and the Versailles Tannery (1861) processed hides. Chapman's 20-acre (8 ha) market garden raised vegetables to sell in McKean Co, Pa. The Perrysburg Agricultural Works (1866) made cradles, stave baskets, cheeseboxes, grain measures, and butter firkins, and Sprague and Ticknor (1869) produced barrels, baskets, and snaths. The J. N. Adams Sanitarium (1909) served tuberculosis victims until midcentury and was later a developmental facility; the building was vacant in 2003. In the early 21st century vineyards and dairy and stock farms are important to the economy. The Cattaraugus Indian Reservation of the Seneca Nation of Indians adjoins the town on the north and east.

Bruce D. Fredrickson and Madelynn P. Fredrickson

Persia. Town (pop 2,512) in NW Cattaraugus Co. Settled in 1810, the town was formed from Perrysburg in 1835. The Erie Railroad crossed Persia in 1851. In the mid–19th century dairy farming became the main occupation. The hamlet of Hidi was named as a pun to contrast with nearby Lodi and was annexed by the Village of Gowanda in 1878. The Gaensslen Brothers' Tannery employed 30 people in its Hidi tannery (1853) and glue factory (1874), and Charles Kengott also operated a glue factory (1869). In the early 21st century, farming continues, but much land has been reforested and is used for recreational activities. The town is bordered on the north by Cattaraugus Creek and the Zoar Valley Gorge, which contains an old-growth forest that includes some of the nation's tallest trees. The Zoar Valley State Multiple Use Area is a destination for white-water rafters, canoeists, and kayakers.

Bruce D. Fredrickson and Madelynn P. Fredrickson

Persian Gulf War. Conflict between the Allied Coalition Against Iraq (29 nations following US leadership) and Iraq precipitated by the 2 Aug 1990 invasion of Kuwait by Iraqi forces. Among the first US troops to deploy were more than 100 nurses and medical personnel from the 137th Aeromedical Evacuation Squadron at Stratton Air National Guard Base (ANGB) (Schenectady Co) and C-5 Galaxy cargo planes from the 105th Airlift Wing at Stewart ANGB (Orange Co). On 22 August Pres George H. W. Bush ordered the activation of 46,703 National Guard and Reserve personnel, the first since the Vietnam War. Among New York Army Reserve and National Guard units deployed were military police and medical, maintenance, civil affairs, intelligence, and transportation units. The 174th Tactical Fighter Wing from Hancock Field (Onondaga Co), dubbed the "Boys from Syracuse," deployed 18 of their F-16A Falcons and took part in the first sorties on 17 Jan 1991. In addition to army and air units, several naval reserve hospital units and Marine Corps reservists were deployed. Popular efforts supported the troops. Based in Albany, Operation Mustard Seed sent packages of sun block, games, and personal items, and a Rochester mall held National Guard Day to honor those deployed. By the time of the 3 Mar 1991 cease-fire, an estimated 2,100 Army and Air National Guard members from the state were activated, among which 16 casualties were recorded. New Yorkers paid tribute to returning troops at a ticker-tape parade through Lower Manhattan on 10 June 1991.

The Guard Times, Jan–July 1991

Martin Bannan

Perth. Town (pop 3,638) in SE Fulton Co. Settled ?1772 by Scots tenants of Sir William Johnson, the town was formed from Amsterdam (Montgomery Co) in 1838. German farmers came to Perth, followed by Poles after *ca* 1890. In addition to farming, its residents worked in tanneries and produced gloves and mittens. From 1824 to 1848 there was a linseed oil mill at West Galway. In the early 21st century large farms coexist with suburban residences and a commercial strip along Rte 30. At West Perth, Tryon School for Boys (1966) is operated by the New York State Office of Children and Family Services; its girls school dates from 1974.

Peru. Town (pop 6,370) in SE Clinton Co. It was settled in 1772 and resettled in 1785. The town, bounded on the east by Lake Champlain, formed in 1792 from Willsboro (Essex Co) and Plattsburgh. A naval battle of the Revolution was fought in the channel west of Valcour Island on 11 Oct 1776. In early years white pine was shipped from Port Jackson [now Valcour] by raft to lumber markets in Montreal and Quebec and, beginning in 1823, to Albany. Aside from an ironworks, a lumber mill, a cloth factory, and a starch factory, Peru has been a farming town. In the early 21st century it has dairy farms and apple orchards, along with housing for workers who commute to Plattsburgh via the Northway (1967).

Thomas A. Rumney

Peruvians. Although Peruvians came to New Jersey in the 1910s and 1920s as a cheap source of skilled labor for the state's textile companies, their arrival in New York State became more visible in the late 20th century. Immigration became more significant in the late 1980s, when political violence escalated and large segments of the population were trapped in a growing spiral of social and economic insecurity. In New York State most settled in Queens, with the overwhelming majority living in Jackson Heights. Nassau, Suffolk, and Westchester Cos have also attracted many immigrants. According to 2000 census data, 43,753 foreign-born Peruvians were living in New York State; 26,719 were in New York City, and of those, 18,697 (70%) lived in Queens. Elsewhere in the metropolitan area, 6,087 resided in Westchester Co, 4,821 in Nassau Co, and 2,744 in Suffolk Co. The majority of Peruvians are Roman Catholic, and religious holidays are important events in New York State's Peruvian communities. El Mes Morado is celebrated in October, when Peruvians wear purple and attend masses and processions honoring El Señor de los Milagros, a religious brotherhood. They honor two Peruvian saints, Santa Rosa de Lima and San Martín de Porres, with special festivities in New York City. Patriotic holidays, including Peru's Independence Day on 28 July, are also celebrated.

Peruvian Americans have established their own civic and professional organizations, including the Club Peru de Nueva York, Capítulo de la Asociacíon Institucional Peruana en los Estados Unidos, the Peruvian American Chamber of Commerce, and the Peruvian American Medical Society, which operate largely in New York State. Peruvian Americans have recently begun to make inroads in state politics; a Peruvian American candidate ran for City Council in the 25th District of Queens in 2001. The Queens television program, *Viva el Pueblo,* is one of the media outlets serving the growing Peruvian population.

Logan, John. "The New Latinos: Who They Are, Where They Are," http://mumford1.dyndns.org/cen2000/HispanicPop/HspReport/HspReportPage1.html
Sheahan, John. *Patterns of Development in Latin America: Poverty, Repression, and Economic Strategy* (Princeton, NJ: Princeton Univ Press, 1989)

Ana Margarita Cervantes-Rodríguez and Deborah Woeckner Saavedra

Petersburgh. Town (pop 1,563) in E Rensselaer Co. Two small Dutch farming settlements from *ca* 1740 were broken up by French and Indian raiders in 1754. Settled after the Revolutionary War by Rhode Islanders, the town was formed in 1791 from Stephentown. Lumbering and farming predominated, but dairying was encouraged when the Harlem Extension Railroad (1869–1953; later Rutland Railroad) came through town. Shirtmaking developed as a home industry around 1850, and a cooperative laundry for the finishing of work had formed by 1887. Tourism developed slowly after the Taconic Trail (1920) provided better east-west access. The Taconic Range offers spectacular views, and near its crest is a natural curiosity, the Snow Hole, which often remains snow covered throughout the summer. Petersburgh was the site of the nationally known Fox Hollow Festival (1966–80).

Kathryn T. Sheehan

Peterson, Roger Tory (*b* Jamestown, Chautauqua Co, 28 Aug 1908; *d* Old Lyme, Conn, 28 July 1996). Ornithologist. Raised by European immigrant parents, Peterson began his passionate interest in birds when his seventh-grade teacher organized a Junior Audubon Club. After graduating from Jamestown High School, Peterson went to New York City to study drawing at the Art Students League (1927–28) and the National Academy of Design (1929–31). While teaching at the Rivers School in Brookline, Mass, Peterson began publishing magazine articles on bird identification for amateurs. He also wrote and illustrated *A Field Guide to the Birds, Including All Species Found in Eastern North America* (1934), a breakthrough publication for nature guides. Previous books of this type were academic in tone, used primarily by scientists and researchers. But Peterson's guide was intended for a mass audience, with simple illustrations that grouped birds by easily identifiable characteristics. Peterson's work helped make birdwatching a national pastime and contributed significantly to public interest in environmental conservation. From 1934 to 1943 Peterson served as the education director for the Audubon Society in New York City and served concurrently as the art editor for its magazine *Audubon.* After serving in the US Army (1943–45), Peterson became editor of the Field Guide series, which eventually included over 50 titles, many of which he coauthored and illustrated. From 1960 to 1964 Peterson served as the secretary of the National Audubon Society. In 1986 he founded the Institute of Natural History in Jamestown to promote nature study in schools. A tremendous success, his first field guide, *A Field Guide to the Birds,* was issued in four editions during Peterson's lifetime and sold over 5 million copies, making Peterson one of the most famous individuals in the history of ornithology.

Devlin, John C., and Grace Naismith. *The World of Roger Tory Peterson* (New York: Times Books, 1977)

Darwin Stapleton

petroleum and natural gas industry. During the Devonian geologic period, a shallow sea covered much of central and western New York State. Over millions of years organic deposits from marine life were converted into petroleum and natural gas, producing deposits small by national standards. In 2001 New York State had fewer than 5 million barrels in proven oil reserves, 0.01% of the national total, and 318 billion ft^3 (9 billion m^3) in proven natural gas reserves, about 0.2% of the national total. New York State's oil is of high quality, however, valued for specialized lubrication products.

The Seneca and other Indians were familiar with petroleum, using it as a curative for rheumatism and arthritis. One of their principal sources was the Seneca Oil Spring on the Oil Spring Indian Reservation [loc in Allegany and Cattaraugus Cos]. A 1 mi^2 (2.6 km^2) area centered on this spring was retained by the Seneca at the Treaty of Big Tree in 1797. The spring inspired the naming of nearby Olean (Cattaraugus Co) after the Latin word for oil, *oleum,* in 1804. Whites recognized petroleum's potential as a lighting source but, in the absence of any significant supply, relied on whale oil and gas manufactured from coal. In 1855 Yale chemist Benjamin Silliman Jr reported on the potential economic value of petroleum in northwest Pennsylvania. Four years later Edwin Drake drilled the first oil well near Titusville, Pa, establishing a new industry and thus very likely saving sperm whales from extinction. By the 1870s kerosene, a petroleum product, was the most common source of domestic illumination for the American working class.

Oil Exploration and Production

Entrepreneurs tried without success to extend Pennsylvania's oil boom into New York State. The first well in the state was dug in Rushford (Allegany Co) in 1860 on the site of small oil seeps, but little oil was found. Wells dug on the Oil Spring Reservation were similarly unproductive. The first successful New York well was dug by Job Moses, a manufacturer of patent medicine based in Rochester and New York City. His well, dug in 1865 near the Village of Limestone (Cattaraugus Co), was only marginally productive by Pennsylvania standards but profitable enough to allow him to dig additional wells in the vicinity. Eventually he became the principal landowner in nearby Carrollton, with large holdings in neighboring towns and Pennsylvania. Between 1865 and 1875 other small operators, through trial and error, defined Cattaraugus Co's major oil-producing area as the southern halves of Carrollton, Allegany, and Olean. Many early unsuccessful wells proved to be just hundreds of yards from later successful ones, underscoring the role of random luck in oil exploration. Oil was sought on the Allegany Indian Reservation [loc in Cattaraugus Co] as early as 1860, for example, but not found until 1897.

The other major oil field in New York State is in Allegany Co, covering much of the Town of Bolivar and extending into Alma, Scio, and Wirt. In 1879 Orville P. Taylor, a tobacconist, drilled the first commercially successful well in the county in the southeastern corner of Scio and 40 miles (64 km) east of the nearest productive well. The boomtown that arose near the site was dubbed Petrolia. Another significant discovery was made in 1881 in the Village of Richburg. Crandall Lester, a local shop owner, led a group of partners in digging a well that yielded oil of higher quantity and quality than any previous, though still modest by Pennsylvania standards. The Allegany oil boom drove New York State's all-time peak annual oil production of 6.7 million barrels in 1882. Oil production declined sharply by the 1890s, followed by a resurgence after waterflooding was legalized in 1919. In this technique water is injected into abandoned wells to force oil from pores in the surrounding soil and drive it into a producing well. During the 1920s–1940s annual production of 4 million barrels was typical. Oil production declined steadily to 426,000 barrels in 1991 and a modern low of 183,000 barrels in 2001.

Oil Refining and the Standard Oil Trust

Kerosene was the petroleum product of greatest impact in the 19th century, but many other useful products were developed, including gasoline, machinery oils, lubricants, chemicals, and pharmaceuticals. Petroleum jelly was developed by Brooklyn chemist Robert Chesebrough after he observed that a gooey material that clogged wells was useful in soothing cuts and burns. He patented the product in 1872 under the trade name Vaseline. To create products from petroleum it first had to be refined. Beginning in 1861 small refineries were built in Olean and other towns in New York's oil region but most refining business accrued to cities such as Buffalo, Cleveland, Pittsburgh, and Baltimore.

John D. Rockefeller Sr, a native of Richford (Tioga Co), saw that controlling oil refining and transport rather than production was the key to controlling the entire industry. Rockefeller built his first refinery in Cleveland in 1863; by 1877 his company, Standard Oil, controlled 90% of the US refining market. The company used many aggressive tactics, the most notorious being secret rebates to railroads to ensure that nearly all crude petroleum was delivered to the company's refineries. In 1879 Standard Oil purchased a controlling interest in Rochester-based Vacuum Oil Co (1866), which held patents to a number of useful products derived from kerosene residues, including oils used for softening harnesses and lubricating machinery. Standard Oil Trust was formed in 1882 to administer the dozens of companies Rockefeller controlled and was the target of much public outcry and antitrust legislation, even though retail prices dropped and new petroleum-based products were developed under its management.

Opposition reached a fever pitch in 1902 when Manhattan-based *McClure's Magazine* began a lengthy exposé of the company, popularizing the term "muckraking." Pres Theodore Roosevelt became known as the "trust buster" when he went after the conglomerate. A 1911 US Supreme Court ruling broke the company into its constituent parts including Vacuum and the Standard Oil Co of New York, or Socony, both of which developed international profiles as oil was discovered in other parts of the world. When the two merged to form Socony-Vacuum in 1931 the company had offices and refineries in Europe, South Africa, Indonesia, and Iraq. Socony-Vacuum renamed itself Socony Mobil in 1955, then simply Mobil in 1966. In 1998 the company merged with Exxon Corp, previously Standard Oil of New Jersey. The global company maintains a significant retail presence in New York State in the early 21st century.

Oil Pipelines

The first oil pipelines were laid in Pennsylvania in the early 1860s to connect oil from wells outside Titusville to refineries in town. Teamsters repeatedly sabotaged the lines, delaying until the mid-1870s widespread use of pipelines in the industry. New York State's first oil pipeline was built in 1875, linking Carrollton and Olean. Two years later this line was purchased by United Pipe Line Co, a Standard Oil subsidiary and the company that subsequently built or took over other pipelines in the vicinity. In 1880, for example, a group of Buffalo capitalists wishing to remain independent of Standard Oil tried to build a pipeline from the Cattaraugus Co fields to their refinery in Buffalo but had great difficulty crossing Standard Oil–affiliated railroads, where they were subject to sabotage. After protracted court hearings the pipeline was completed, at which point Standard Oil simply bought both the line and refinery. Standard Oil built the first long-distance pipeline in New York State in 1881, which ran from Olean to Bayonne, NJ, paralleling the Erie Railroad. The line was patrolled by pipeline walkers who covered the 28 miles (45 km) between pumping stations in two days, reporting trouble by telegraph. One such walker, Marshall Calkins of Catatonk (Tioga Co), traversed 62,500 miles (100,580 km) in his career. This pipeline was eventually linked to oil fields in the Midwest, Texas, and Oklahoma, and became the major route by which oil was brought to eastern seaboard refineries. Eventually it proved cheaper to route oil via tanker from the Gulf of Mexico, and the line ceased operations in 1927.

Manufactured Gas

The heating of coal produces a flammable gas composed mainly of hydrogen and carbon monoxide. In the late 18th century European inventors devised ways to use this gas as a source of artificial light. Baltimore became the first American city with manufactured gas lighting in 1816. In 1823 the New York Gas Light Co was chartered to provide lighting to Manhattan: the density of gas lights along Broadway earned it the moniker "The Great White Way." Pine tar was originally used as a substitute for coal, because coal supplies were limited before the Pennsylvania anthracite region was developed in the 1830s–1840s. Manufactured gas remained an important source of lighting until electricity arrived in the late 19th century. As electricity gained prominence, the manufactured gas industry shifted its focus to domestic heating and cooking. The New York City metropolitan area used manufactured gas for these purposes almost exclusively until the 1950s, when it was displaced by cleaner, more efficient natural gas. Coal-tar waste pits from former manufactured gas plants remain a significant environmental problem in the early 21st century. As of 2002 the New York State Department of Environmental Conservation had identified 194 former manufactured gas plant sites requiring cleanup.

Natural Gas

The difficulty of storing and transporting natural gas hindered its development. The Village of Fredonia (Chautauqua Co) harnessed natural gas springs for streetlights and interior lighting in the 1820s, but this was an isolated phenomenon. During the oil boom of the 1860s natural gas was seen as a promising indicator of oil, but otherwise useless. An enormous natural gas discovery in West Bloomfield (Ontario Co) in 1865, for example, was abandoned after no oil was found. Five years later an attempt was made to pipe this gas via wooden line to Rochester, but few furnaces were capable of burning the gas and the pipeline was prone to leak. In the 1880s Pittsburgh became the first city to use significant amounts of natural gas. By 1886 National Transit, part of Standard Oil Trust, controlled the natural gas industry in Pittsburgh as well as in New York State. Several national holding companies controlled the industry by the 1920s, known collectively as the Power Trust. The largest, Cities Services Co, controlled the lower midwestern market from its headquarters in New York City at a time when the metropolis itself had no natural gas service. The holding companies were broken up through legislation passed in the 1930s as utilities came under federal regulation.

Periodic coal strikes between the 1920s and 1940s helped expand natural gas use, although coal and railroad interests helped keep natural gas out of New York City until 1951, when Transcontinental Gas Pipe Line Co constructed a line from Texas to Manhattan. Manufactured gas companies in New York City, the largest of which was Consolidated Edison, found adapting to natural gas cheaper than continuing to burn coal and undertook a major initiative to convert the appliances of all city residents during the early 1950s. Nationally, failure to develop new natural gas reserves in the 1950s and 1960s, combined with the international oil crises of the early 1970s, led to chronic natural gas shortages. These peaked in the winter of 1976–77 when Gov Hugh Carey declared a state of emergency in order to maintain heat for New York State residents. Deregulation in the 1980s led to industry consolidation and corporate structures that were compared to the monopolistic holding companies of the 1920s. In New York State in 2001, 16 gas utilities served 4.2 million residential customers, 360,000 commercial customers, and 6,000 industrial customers through a network of over 48,000 miles (77,200 km) of pipeline.

Natural gas production in New York State peaked in 1938 with a volume of 39.4 million ft^3 (1.1 million m^3). Historically, Chautauqua Co was the leading producer in the state. In the late 1990s, however, discovery of large natural gas reserves in Steuben and Chemung Cos, 2 miles (3 km) beneath the surface in the Trenton–Black River Formation, moved that area into the lead as of 2001 and caused much excitement in the industry. Statewide production rose from 16.8 million ft^3 (475,700 m^3) in 1999 to 27.8 million ft^3 (787,200 m^3) in 2001, the increase largely because of the Trenton–Black River output. These wells accounted for only 32 of the nearly 6,000 active wells statewide, but 55% of the state's total production.

See also POWER AND LIGHTING.

Castaneda, Christopher J. *Invisible Fuel: Manufactured and Natural Gas in America, 1800–2000* (New York: Twayne Publishers, 1999)

Clark, James A. *The Chronological History of the Petroleum and Natural Gas Industries* (Houston: Clark Book, 1963)

Herrick, John P. *Empire Oil: The Story of Oil in New York State* (New York: Dodd, Mead, 1949)

New York State Department of Environmental Conservation. Division of Mineral Resources. *New York Oil, Gas, and Mineral Resources.* Annual Report (1984–)

Paleontologic Research Institution. "Proved Reserves: Northeastern US as of 2001," http://www.priweb.org/ed/pgws/backyard/sections/northeast/northeast2.html

Tarr, Joel A. "Transforming an Energy System: The Evolution of the Manufactured Gas Industry and the Transition to Natural Gas in the United States, 1807–1954." In *The Governance of Large Technical Systems,* ed. Olivier Coutard (London: Routledge, 1999)

Francis P. Boscoe

pharmaceutical industry. The discovery, development, and marketing of drugs and related products led to the founding of a number of New York State firms, some of which became and remain industry leaders. The state also serves as the corporate headquarters for companies that developed elsewhere.

During the 18th and early 19th centuries, pharmaceuticals were primarily plant-based drugs, often prepared by householders in their kitchens and administered without the supervision of a physician. The early drug industry involved the distribution of local or imported raw materials, frequently as part of the grocery or spice trade, though the large common market of the United States soon encouraged specialization. New York City was home to several large drug houses, including W. H. Schieffelin, established in 1794, and Olcott and Robbins, established in 1833 and becoming McKesson and Robbins in 1853. They sold their wares to doctors, druggists, and householders locally and nationwide, and exported American botanicals to the rest of the world.

Ethical Manufacturers

In the early 19th century, after scientists used techniques not available to householders to extract the active ingredients from traditional plant drugs, a number of druggists and wholesalers such as Schieffelin added pharmaceutical manufacturing to their activities. Despite the potency of new drugs such as morphine from opium and quinine from cinchona, self-treatment remained an important part of American life. Many respectable manufacturers found it both practical and profitable to provide consumer-ready tinctures, elixirs, and pills, which they sold to physicians and public alike. The majority of companies catered to local or state customers, but a few established national, even international, markets. Nevertheless, they tended to remain family businesses with small staffs, enjoying modest success. The Tilden Co of New Lebanon (Columbia Co), established in 1824, with connections to the Shaker sect, and the Charles Pfizer Co of Brooklyn, established in 1849, are examples.

Self-prescribing remained common and legal for most of the 19th century, but as the American medical profession became better educated and more highly regarded, some drug manufacturers began to serve physicians exclusively. These "ethical" manufacturers provided only standard (public domain), doctor-approved items and declined to advertise to the public. Dr Edward R. Squibb (1819–1900), a Quaker naval surgeon, had improved the production of ether and chloroform while supervising the Brooklyn Naval Hospital laboratory, setting up his own company in 1856. Squibb rejected patents and excessive profits as immoral; his signature on the label was his guarantee of quality. The Brooklyn concern, which became E. R. Squibb and Sons in 1895, was recognized as the model of an ethical firm.

By the 1880s about 40 pharmaceutical companies in New York State were carrying almost identical, public-domain products, competing vigorously for doctors' business; 36,500 different items were available from these firms. Among them were such companies as the Norwich Pharmacal Co, founded in 1885 in Norwich (Chenango Co); the New York Quinine and Chemical Co, founded by D. C. and Charles Robbins of McKesson and Robbins in Brooklyn in 1885; and the Clinton Pharmaceutical Co, founded in Clinton (Oneida Co) in 1887, which became Bristol-Myers in 1899. They sometimes improved manufacturing methods and developed new formulas, but they did not engage in much scientific research. Some were indistinguishable from the patent-medicine sellers of this era, but the more respectable firms concentrated on pure, standardized products and quality control.

Scientific Drug Production

Developments in medical sciences led to new vaccines and antitoxins unsuitable for self-treatment. In 1906 New York City commissioner of health Ernst J. Lederle created Lederle Antitoxin Laboratories in Pearl River (Rockland Co) to produce diphtheria antitoxin on a large scale. Lederle had earned a doctorate in chemistry from Columbia University, and his company emphasized the scientific knowledge of its staff. Progress in chemistry led to medicines derived from coal tar, powerful new drugs designed to cure disease. Unlike traditional medicines, these pharmaceuticals were completely artificial, created by university research and production scientists under highly controlled conditions in huge German chemical factories such as Bayer, Schering, Hoechst, and Merck. Pure, reliable, and efficacious, these ethical pharmaceuticals were also private property, protected by patents, trade names, and other devices. Few American drug manufacturers were able to produce the new items, especially the synthetics, which were German inventions. German companies such as Schering and Merck operated in the United States through sales agents in New York City. The US patent for Salvarsan, the "magic bullet" against syphilis developed in Germany in 1909 by Paul Ehrlich under contract to Hoechst, was held by New York City businessman Herman A. Metz, who represented Hoechst in the United States. Americans complained bitterly, accusing the Germans of placing profits above the public welfare, as their monopoly tactics prevented US firms from making synthetics except under license and forced Americans to pay high prices.

Botanicals remained crucial to medical practice; S. B. Penick and Co was founded in New York City as a botanical supplier in 1914. But the German drugs presaged the future of the industry. The solution came with entry of the United States into World War I, when German real and intellectual property was confiscated and Americanized. Bayer, owner of a number of valuable pharmaceutical patents, had established a factory in 1903 in Rensselaer, where it made aspirin. In late 1918 Bayer (and aspirin) was auctioned to Sterling Products, a West Virginia proprietary firm that then relocated to New York City. After World War I research laboratories, mass production techniques, dynamic marketing tactics, and aggressive protection of intellectual property became central features of the pharmaceutical industry worldwide.

Corporate Growth

The New York State pharmaceutical industry in the interwar period was characterized by mergers, acquisitions, and partnerships on a national and international scale; for example, American Cyanamid of Niagara Falls, a fertilizer manufacturer, acquired Lederle Laboratories in 1930. American Home Products, headquartered in the Whitehall building in Lower Manhattan, acquired a Philadelphia pharmaceutical firm, John Wyeth and Brother, in 1931. Companies sought to acquire patentable products, a respected brand name, the best production methods, or profitable sidelines such as toiletries, agricultural chemicals, medical instruments, and drugstore chains. These strategies helped the pharmaceutical industry successfully weather the depression. Moreover, the distinction between ethical (now meaning prescription-only) and proprietary (over-the-counter) firms blurred, as did regional distinctions; subsidiaries and divisions were created around the nation and the globe to discover, produce, and market a vast range of products. For instance, Sterling also owned the Bayer Aspirin plant in Canada and was active in the Latin American market; its ethical subsidiary Winthrop Laboratories sold the latest products created by Bayer in Germany.

Cooperation between pharmaceutical firms and academic research institutions brought a number of significant new products to market. Under the direction of Dr George Hoyt Whipple, the Department of Pathology at the University of Rochester collaborated with Eli Lilly and Co to develop and test liver extracts in the hope of finding a cure for pernicious anemia. The two institutions entered a contract on 1 Jan 1931 that brought years of significant funding to the University of Rochester School of Medicine; in 1933 Lilly introduced Lextron, a successful treatment for anemia. In 1942 Pfizer's Brooklyn plant introduced deep-tank fermentation methods to produce the large quantities of penicillin for the injured of World War II; within two years the firm was the foremost producer of penicillin in the world. Penicillin was avail-able only to the armed forces until 1946, when Pfizer began to manufacture the antibiotic for the public.

RECENT DEVELOPMENTS

The New York State pharmaceutical industry continued to expand as a result of postwar innovations in steroids, psychotropics, antihypertensives, antivirals, and various biotechnologies. Researchers at Lederle Labs produced synthetic B vitamins in 1947. Pfizer's scientists discovered the broad-spectrum antibiotic oxytetracycline, which was marketed as Terramycin in 1950. The industry has welcomed new companies such as Sanofi-Synthelabo, with commercial headquarters in New York City, and Stiefel Laboratories, which established the August C. Stiefel Research Institute at Oak Hill (Greene Co). Albany Molecular Research, incorporated in 1991, engages in research and development of chemistry-based drugs, working in cooperation with SUNY Albany, seeing the products through commercial manufacturing. American Cyanamid was acquired in 1994 by American Home Products, founded in 1926 in Delaware but with links to Sterling. Sterling's saga is arguably the most ironic; sold to the Rochester-based Eastman Kodak Co in 1988, its pharmaceutical properties were reacquired by German Bayer in 1994, and "Bayer Aspirin" is once again a German-owned trademark in the United States.

New York State is corporate headquarters for five international pharmaceutical firms, including global conglomerates Bristol-Myers Squibb and Pfizer. At the beginning of the 21st century, 130 pharmaceutical firms were located in New York State, directly providing 26,300 jobs and creating nearly 100,000 jobs over all, producing about $1 billion in tax revenues for municipalities and the state.

Haynes, Williams. *The American Chemical Industry: A History,* 6 vols (New York: Van Nostrand, 1945–1954)

Liebenau, Jonathan. *Medical Science and Medical Industry: The Formation of the American Pharmaceutical Industry* (Baltimore: Johns Hopkins Univ Press, 1987)

Liebenau, Jonathan, Gregory J. Higby, and Elaine C. Stroud, eds. *Pill Peddlers: Essays on the History of the Pharmaceutical Industry* (Madison, Wisc: American Institute of the History of Pharmacy, 1990)

Mahoney, Tom. *The Merchants of Life: An Account of the American Pharmaceutical Industry* (New York: Harper, 1959)

Swann, John. *Academic Scientists and the Pharmaceutical Industry: Cooperative Research in 20th-Century America* (Baltimore: Johns Hopkins Univ Press, 1988)

Jan R. McTavish

Pharsalia [FAR-SAIL-YAH]. Town (pop 542) in NW Chenango Co. Settled in 1797, the town was formed from Norwich in 1806 as Stonington and renamed in 1808. The predecessor of Gladding Braided Products (1816) made rope and fishing line in Pharsalia, relocating to South Otselic late in the 19th century. Pharsalia was primarily a dairy-farming town, but marginal land was acquired by the state in the 1930s for state forest. At the same time the federal government established a Civilian Conservation Corps camp that became a minimum security prison, Camp Pharsalia, in 1956, teaching inmates construction and forestry skills and operating a pheasant farm.

Dale C. Storms

Phelps. Town (pop 7,017) and village (pop 1,969) in NE Ontario Co. Settled in 1788, the town was formed as Sullivan in 1795 but was renamed Phelps in 1796. The Auburn and Rochester Railroad came through in 1841; a station was established for Vienna, which incorporated as the Village of Phelps in 1855. Although Phelps had a woolen factory as early as 1812–15, a plaster mill, other enterprises, and an early thrashing machine invented by Ezra Goodell, industrialization followed the Civil War when many mills were built. The European and American Oil Depot (1832–76) distilled peppermint oil. In 1904 the Empire State Pickling Plant was constructed, launching Phelps as a center of sauerkraut production. The modern economy is based on canning, milling, and farm implement sales. Ontario Co leads the United States in sauerkraut cabbage production, and Phelps holds an annual Sauerkraut Festival in early August.

Marla A. Bennett

Phelps, Oliver (*b* Poquonock, Conn, 21 Oct 1749; *d* Canandaigua, Ontario Co, 21 Feb 1809). Land developer and public official. At the age of 21, after serving an apprenticeship, Phelps entered the mercantile business in Granville, Mass. Brilliant and energetic, he served in a series of provincial offices from 1777 to 1786, superintending military purchases during the Revolutionary War. In 1787 he assembled the Phelps and Gorham Co to buy lands in western New York State claimed by Massachusetts. In 1788 the company secured a preemption right to buy 6 million acres (2.4 million ha) from the Indians and completed the purchase of 2.6 million acres (1.1 million ha). Phelps supervised a survey of the purchase, approved the plan of Canandaigua (Ontario Co) as a market center and county seat, and backed the creation of Ontario Co in 1789. In 1790, unable to meet the first payment for the purchase, the company returned two-thirds of the land to Massachusetts. Phelps moved to Canandaigua in 1802. From there he was elected to the US Congress, serving from 1803 to 1805. In 1804 he ran for the lieutenant governorship in New York State on the Republican ticket with Aaron Burr but lost.

Siles, William H. "Wilderness Investment: The New York Frontier during the Federal Period." In *World of the Founders,* ed. Stephen L. Schechter and Wendell Tripp (Albany: NYS Commission on the Bicentennial of the US Constitution, 1990)

William H. Siles

Phelps and Gorham Purchase. In the Hartford Treaty of 1786 Massachusetts settled its colonial charter dispute with New York State. New York retained sovereignty and jurisdiction, and Massachusetts gained the preemption right to buy the land from the Indians and then sell it. The tract, about 6 million acres (2.4 million ha) occupied by the Seneca Nation, lay between Seneca Lake and Lake Erie. To pay its Revolutionary War debts Massachusetts sold its right to these lands in March 1788 to the Phelps and Gorham Co for 300,000 Massachusetts pounds. Noted members of the company were Oliver Phelps, a former member of the Massachusetts senate; Nathaniel Gorham, then a member; and other New England and New York investors.

On 8 July 1788, in an agreement known as the Treaty of Buffalo Creek (the earliest of three by the name), Phelps and Gorham purchased from the Seneca and the chiefs of the Five Nations a tract of land bounded roughly by Seneca Lake, the Genesee River, Lake Ontario, and the northern border of Pennsylvania, an area of about 2 million acres (810,000 ha). The firm also acquired some 600,000 acres (242,000 ha) northwest of the Genesee River, between Braddock Bay [now in Monroe Co] and Caledonia [now in Livingston Co]. The Senecas were to be paid $5,000 plus a $500 perpetual annuity. The other nations also received payments. In 1788–89 the company surveyed its purchase into townships usually 6 mi^2 (15.5 km^2), established Canan-daigua as trading center and seat of the newly created Ontario Co, built a few roads, and commenced selling the land. The company quickly sold 46 of 92 townships east of the Genesee, 2 of the 8 on the west side, plus parts of 5 others. Total profits from these sales amounted to about 60,000 Massachusetts pounds.

In 1790 the value of Massachusetts currency suddenly rose when Secretary of the Treasury Alexander Hamilton proposed his funding plan for state war debts, whereby the federal government would redeem state notes at par. The value of Massachusetts pounds went from 37¢ to $1.25, and the company was unable to make its payment to the state. In March 1790 the company conveyed back to Massachusetts the lands that it had not yet purchased from the Seneca, about two-thirds of the total, in return for a reduction of its debt to that state.

In November 1790 Phelps and Gorham sold about 1.2 million acres (486,000 ha) of unsold lands, lying mostly in the northern and southern portions of its purchase east of the Genesee River, to land speculator Robert Morris. He, in turn, sold those lands to a group of London investors headed by Sir William Pulteney. Phelps and Gorham had sold about half the lands they had acquired from the Seneca. The firm's investors in 1791 sold its original preemption right acquired from Massachusetts back to that state and liquidated the company. In its brief, three-year existence, Phelps and Gorham yielded a profit of 90,000 Massachusetts pounds for its shareholders.

Siles, William H. "Pioneering in the Genesee Country: Entrepreneurial Strategy and the Concept of a Central Place." In *New Opportunities in a New Nation*, ed. Manfred Jonas and Robert V. Wells (Schenectady: Union College Press, 1982)

Turner, Orsamus. *History of the Pioneer Settlement of Phelps and Gorham's Purchase* (Rochester: William Alling, 1851)

William H. Siles

Philadelphia. Town (pop 2,140) and village (pop 1,519) in N central Jefferson Co. Settled in 1802, its most influential settlers, a company of Quakers from Pennsylvania and New Jersey, began arriving in 1804. The town was formed from Le Ray in 1821. Development was retarded by the Quaker Hicksite controversy (1828) and some antirent activities (1835–44). In the late 1830s an iron mine, furnace, and forge were opened, remaining important until *ca* 1880. The town was then almost entirely agricultural and was known for Limburger cheese, made beginning in 1878. The Rome, Watertown and Ogdensburg Railroad came through in 1855, and later railroads, completed 1872–73, connected to Clayton, Carthage, and Theresa. The village was incorporated in 1872. With the expansion of Fort Drum in the 1980s, the town's population grew and the village's population doubled. Besides 801 military housing units, senior citizen and subsidized housing has been built. Philadelphia was the birthplace of Cassius Marcellus Coolidge (1855–1934), painter of the familiar pictures of anthropomorphic poker-playing dogs.

Laura Lynne Scharer

philanthropy. New York State's philanthropies reflect both its diversity and its central position in the nation's economic, religious, and intellectual life. New Yorkers have given money and time for many reasons: to fulfill religious obligations, to repay institutions that helped them, to help others, to advance causes, to win fame, to celebrate their success, to dominate, to create a more ideal world. State policy and state court decisions have influenced New York State donors as well, as have the views and actions of those who received donations.

Colonial Times to the Late 19th Century

Both Dutch and British colonial officials forced donors to serve imperial interests. British policy, despite becoming more liberal toward other Protestant sects after 1720, discouraged all non–Church of England charities. After the Revolutionary War, New York State made it much easier to create charities for many purposes, long maintaining the colonial view that charity was a close concern of government and that government should provide key gifts. From the 1800s to the 1840s, New York State supported the private Public School Society of New York City, as well as Protestant and, from the 1840s, Catholic orphanages.

As soon as New York City became the nation's financial capital in the 1820s, some of its wealthiest citizens began to make large gifts intended to persuade people to share their own values and also to help themselves. During the 19th century, gifts went to religious causes, colleges, universities, libraries, music and art schools, technical institutes, and high schools. Like other colleges before the Civil War, Union College (chartered 1795) relied on many small donations such as those attracted by its dynamic early leader, Eliphalet Nott. New York City donors also sent money elsewhere. Yale won significant New York donations in the 1820s. The American Bible Society (1816), the American Tract Society (1825), and other Protestant reform organizations built prominent Manhattan offices for their national campaigns to raise money, often from small donations, to provide Bibles and tracts for westerners and the poor, to educate African Americans and Indians, and to support home and foreign missions. From 1826 each artist elected to New York City's National Academy of Design donated a work of art to support its educational programs. In 1849 John Jacob Astor bequeathed $400,000 for a Manhattan library; 10 years later glue magnate Peter Cooper endowed Lower Manhattan's Cooper Union; in 1861 Poughkeepsie brewer Matthew Vassar donated about $500,000 to found a college for women.

After the Civil War

New Yorkers made more large donations to large institutions. Ties between government and charitable organizations remained close as the state provided tax funds to orphanages, schools, and museums. During the Civil War, New Yorkers led the private, federally chartered US Sanitary Commission, whose nurses and field hospitals, funded by thousands of donors, cared for Union soldiers. In 1865 telegraph pioneer Ezra Cornell's offer of a $500,000 endowment helped persuade the state legislature to concentrate federal Morrill Act funds on Cornell University. Private donations helped make New York City collections to rival those of European princes; city funds paid for buildings to house the collections, including the Metropolitan Museum of Art (private collection founded 1870; move to public building, 1880) and the American Museum of Natural History (1869; building, 1877).

In 1872 Louisa Lee Schuyler set up the New York State Charities Aid Association to oversee efforts to help the poor through both government and private agencies. A year later Anthony Comstock received federal authority for his privately funded, New York City–based Society for the Suppression of Vice to open and inspect mail suspected of containing discussions of birth control or abortion. Between 1886 and 1917 Andrew Carnegie contributed millions from his Manhattan office for over 1,600 public libraries in more than 1,400 towns and cities across the United States on the condition that each town vote a permanent tax to support the facility.

Seth Low, as mayor of Brooklyn in the 1880s, sought to cut municipal poor relief and to encourage the able-bodied poor to work. Many of his contemporary philanthropists worked for this end as well. Low's neighbor and kinsman A. T. White invested his mercantile inheritance to provide Tower and Home Apartments (1877), intended to enable the poor to live orderly, productive lives. In 1885 Western New York business leaders founded the Mechanics Institute, which evolved into the Rochester Institute of Technology. Brooklynite Charles Pratt founded the Astral Apartments in 1886 and the Pratt Institute in 1887. Manhattan banker Jacob Schiff and others joined with Germany's Baron Maurice de Hirsch in 1889 to build the Educational Alliance (to help eastern European Jewish immigrants become self-sufficient) on New York City's Lower East Side. And Wall Street financier John S. Kennedy built the United Charities Building near Manhattan's Gramercy Park in 1892 to help Josephine Shaw Lowell promote self-help.

Andrew Carnegie, industrialist and philanthropist. Photograph from *The Autobiography of Andrew Carnegie* (1920).

Foundations

In the late 1880s distant relatives of former governor Samuel J. Tilden used longstanding rules limiting charitable bequests to break his will, which had left his fortune to a new public library. Following a national outcry against the diversion of Tilden's bequest, in 1893 the state legislature passed new laws friendly to philanthropy. Some of Tilden's relatives honored his wishes: combining about $2 million of his fortune with the resources of the older Astor and Lenox Libraries (1876), they helped launch the New York Public Library (1895; new city-supported building, 1911).

The new charity laws made foundations possible. In 1880 Pittsburgh's Andrew Carnegie and Cleveland's John D. Rockefeller Sr had moved to Manhattan to direct their vast business operations; from there, they carried on their famous discussions of ways to conduct large-scale philanthropy. In 1907 Margaret Olivia Sage, working with attorney Robert W. deForest, used her late husband's fortune to create the Russell Sage Foundation near the United Charities Building. As the first modern American foundation, it devoted the income from significant wealth to general purposes. Several Carnegie and Rockefeller foundations, the Harkness Fund, the Milbank Memorial Fund, and others joined Russell Sage. From the 1920s into the 1950s, the Russell Sage Foundation organized social work; the John Simon Guggenheim and Harkness Foundations evaluated applications for fellowships in the arts and medicine; Carnegie worked to systematize education; Rockefeller sought excellence in medical and scientific research and in public health in the American South and abroad; and the Samuel H. Kress Foundation supported art museums. The Ford Foundation moved to Manhattan after World War II, reinforcing the city's place at the center of large-scale philanthropy.

Since the Mid–20th Century

In New York State as elsewhere, Catholic philanthropy took many forms over the years. Until well into the 20th century, many families encouraged at least one child to enter a Catholic religious order, providing priests, brothers, and nuns to staff Catholic churches, schools, hospitals, and orphanages. The greatest expansion of Catholic schools, colleges, and hospitals, made possible by thousands of often unpublicized gifts, came in the 30 years after World War II. Gifts also helped Jewish institutions expand in the wake of the Holocaust, as Yeshiva University, the Mount Sinai School of Medicine, many small schools, and other institutions grew with remarkable vigor.

After World War II New York State became especially noted for its modern art museums, including Manhattan's Museum of Modern Art (1929; 53d St building, 1939) and Whitney (1931; Madison Ave building, 1966) and Solomon R. Guggenheim (1939; Frank Lloyd Wright building, 1959) Museums as well as Buffalo's Albright-Knox Art Gallery (modern addition, 1962). Philanthropy also brought international distinction to other New York City museums, including Manhattan's American Folk Art Museum (1961; new building, 2001); the Jewish Museum (1904; expansions 1963, 1993); the Metropolitan Museum of Art (major additions named for donors and honorees Robert Lehman in 1975, the Sackler family (including Arthur M. Sackler) in 1978, Michael C. Rockefeller in 1982, and Lila Acheson Wallace and Henry R. Kravis in 1987); and the Brooklyn Museum of Art. These benefited from very large donations. Others, such as El Museo del Barrio in Upper Manhattan (1969; permanent building, 1977), benefited from grassroots efforts.

Over the course of the 20th century, many donors gave New York State an exceptional group of research and community hospitals. In the 1960s Mary Lasker and others fought to launch a national "war on cancer," and in the 1990s the Aaron Diamond Foundation created its leading AIDS Research Center. Once bastions of a Protestant establishment, elite hospitals, universities, and colleges began to welcome students from all backgrounds in the 1960s; by the 1990s substantial donations from grateful Jewish, Catholic, and Protestant donors helped maintain their quality.

Some charities and national associations moved to Washington, DC, after the Kennedy, Johnson, and Nixon administrations opened the floodgates of federal funding in health, education, and human services. In the 1980s Protestant charities such as the American Tract Society moved to Dallas and other cities in the middle of the nation. But the Foundation Center Library remained in New York City, providing definitive information on foundation giving for the entire nation.

Since the 1930s philanthropy, together with finance, publishing, communications, and the United Nations, has made New York City a leading international center for human rights advocacy. Individual gifts, small and large, support such characteristic New York City organizations as the American Civil Liberties Union, Freedom House, Amnesty International's US office, the Committee to Protect Journalists, Human Rights Watch, the International Rescue Committee, the Lawyers Committee for Human Rights, MediaRights.org, and the Open Society Institute. UNICEF and other organizations that work with the United Nations or that seek to influence the UN base themselves in New York. So, too, do philanthropic organizations concerned with many other parts of the world, especially the parts closely tied to New York through human migration: Ireland, Israel, Italy, southeastern Europe, Africa, and Asia.

In 2000 New York foundations gave away more money than those of any other state. The incomes of hospitals, colleges, and other recipients of philanthropy more than tripled from the 1960s to the beginning of the 21st century. Because donations did not grow as a share of income, gifts became less important to most nonprofit organizations over these years, and nonprofit leaders have had to pay more attention to the government agencies and paying "customers" that provide more of their resources. Some New York philanthropists have responded by demanding more influence, by insisting on "enterprise" philanthropy, not entirely a new idea. Members of the Rockefeller family, for example, had worked very closely with the leaders of Lincoln Center, Memorial Sloan-Kettering Cancer Center, and other institutions they supported. In the 1990s New York City's Eugene Lang encouraged one approach by offering mentorship and college scholarships to poor children who stayed in school, thus updating a long-standing philanthropic emphasis on helping people help themselves. Sanford I. Weill took a strongly entrepreneurial approach in his support of the Cornell University Medical College and Carnegie Hall, just as Peter B. Lewis provided advice as well as very substantial financial support to the Guggenheim Museum of Art. At the same time, other donors saw the past achievements of New York philanthropy as reason to change more slowly.

Bonomi, Patricia U. *A Factious People: Politics and Society in Colonial New York* (New York: Columbia Univ Press, 1971)

Brown, Dorothy M., and Elizabeth McKeown. *The Poor Belong to Us: Catholic Charities and American Welfare* (Cambridge, Mass: Harvard Univ Press, 1997)

Dolan, Jay. *The Immigrant Church: New York's Irish and German Catholics, 1815–1865* (Baltimore: Johns Hopkins Univ Press, 1975)

Hammack, David C., and Stanton Wheeler. *Social Science in the Making: Essays on the Russell Sage Foundation, 1907–1947* (New York: Russell Sage Foundation, 1994)

Lagmann, Ellen Condliffe, ed. *Philanthropic Foundations: New Scholarship, New Possibilities* (Bloomington: Indiana Univ Press, 1999)

Rosner, David. *A Once Charitable Enterprise: Hospitals and Health Care in Brooklyn and New York, 1885–1915* (Princeton, NJ: Princeton Univ Press, 1982)

Sills, David L. *The Volunteers: Means and Ends in a National Organization* (Glencoe, Ill: Free Press, 1957)

Waugh, J. *Unsentimental Reformer: The Life of Josephine Shaw Lowell* (Cambridge, Mass: Harvard Univ Press, 1997)

David C. Hammack

Philipsburg Manor. Estate of approximately 52,000 acres (21,000 ha) owned by the Philipse family in the 17th and 18th centuries in what is now Westchester and Bronx Cos. Frederick Philipse I, with Thomas Delavall and Thomas Lewis, made the first land purchase in 1672 of a part of Adriaen van der Donck's patroonship in what is now northern Yonkers (Westchester Co). Philipse made seven additional land purchases (1680–86) from the Wiechquaeskeck and the Sinsink Indians. Philipse eventually bought his original partners' shares and acquired an additional parcel of Tappan meadowlands, on the west side of the Hudson River. The estate's borders were Spuyten Duyvil [now in Bronx Co] (south), Croton River (north), Hudson River (west), and Bronx River (east). In 1693 a royal charter was granted for the Manor of Philipsburg; Frederick Philipse I became the first lord of the manor. After his death (1702), the manor was divided: Adolph Philipse, the second son, was given the Upper Mills property, from Dobbs Ferry [now in Westchester Co] to the Croton River, while Frederick Philipse II, Frederick I's grandson, was given the Lower Mills at the confluence of the Saw Mill and Hudson Rivers. The entire estate was reunited briefly under Frederick II in 1750 and finally in 1751 under his son Frederick III, who became third lord of the manor.

The Philipses developed both the Upper and Lower Mills as agricultural centers. Enslaved Blacks built the original structures at the Upper Mills. Two gristmills were built, one at the natural shelf on the Pocantico River, in the hope of attracting settlers to the manor. A stone manor house, wharf, cooperage, and bake house supported the manor's economic focus. The Old Dutch Church of Sleepy Hollow was part of the original construction on the manor, completed by 1697. At the Lower Mills, a sawmill was renovated, and a gristmill and manor house were built on the north side of the Neperhan River.

An ethnically and racially diverse population lived and worked on the manor. The original cohort of enslaved Africans was most likely from Kongo-Angola [now Republic of the Congo (Brazzaville) and Angola]. Twenty-three slaves representing different African cultures lived at the Upper Mills by 1750. Tenant farmers who settled on manor lands came from England, Holland, France, Germany, and other areas of North America. By the time of the American Revolution, the tenant population had increased from 200 in 1702 to about 1,000.

Frederick Philipse III was a loyalist. In 1779 the family was attainted for treason by New York's revolutionary government. All manor property was confiscated and sold at public auction to 287 people. The largest segment, 750 acres (304 ha) at the Upper Mills, was sold to Gerard G. Beekman Jr. In subsequent years, the Upper Mills parcel passed to several owners. In 1951 the property was acquired by Sleepy Hollow Restorations (now Historic Hudson Valley). With the assistance of John D. Rockefeller Jr, some 20 acres (8 ha) of Upper Mills property have been restored as an historic site, Philipsburg Manor. At the Lower Mills, the Philipse Manor Hall became the Yonkers City Hall in 1872. Now a state historic site, it is also a National Historic Landmark.

See also Manor system.

Haley, Jacquetta M. "Philipsburg Manor Tricentennial, 1693–1993." Research report, Historic Hudson Valley, Tarrytown, NY, 1992

Judd, Jacob. "The Philipse Castle Land and Structures, 1680–1956." Reseach report, Sleepy Hollow Restorations, Tarrytown, NY, 1956

Wheeler, Robert G. "A Report on the Archaeological Findings, the Research and the Reconstruction of the Manor House at the Philipsburg Upper Mills, Tarrytown, NY." Report prepared for Sleepy Hollow Restorations, Tarrytown, NY

Dennis J. Maika

The Mill-Dam at "Sleepy Hollow," depicting 19th-century view of Philipsburg Manor grounds, by Currier and Ives.

Philipse family {Philipse, Frederick, I (*b* Bolswaert, Netherlands, 1626; *d* New York City, Nov 1702); Philipse, Adolph (*bap* New York City, 15 Nov 1665; *d* New York City, Jan 1750); Philipse, Frederick, II (*b* Barbados, 1695 or 1698; *d* New York City, 26 July 1751; Philipse, Frederick, III (*b* New York City, 12 Sept 1720; *d* Chester, England, 30 Apr 1786)}. Merchant, landowning, and slaveholding family. Frederick Philipse I arrived in New Amsterdam *ca* 1650 as a carpenter and architect-builder for the Dutch West India Co. He quickly began his career as a merchant during New Amsterdam's boom years of the 1650s and 1660s. By exporting furs and tobacco, importing goods from Europe, and speculating in wampum, Frederick became one of the wealthiest men in the province by 1674. In later years he also began to ship grain and foodstuffs to the West Indies and to import slaves from Africa. By the 1690s Frederick was heavily invested in the Madagascan slave trade. His commercial success led to prominent political positions. He was elected New York City alderman in 1674 and was appointed to the governor's council, where he served from 1676 to 1688 and from 1691 to 1698, when he and seven other council members were removed by the Board of Trade for questionable trading activities. Frederick used profits from his commercial ventures to buy land in Manhattan, New Jersey, and the Hudson Valley. In 1672 he bought most of the old Van der Donck patroonship and thereafter made additional purchases from the Wiechquaeskeck and Sinsink Indians in present day Westchester Co. In 1693 this estate was given a royal charter as the Manor of Philipsburg, with Frederick as lord of the manor. He married Margaret Hardenbroeck (widow of Pieter Rudolphus de Vries) in 1662 and adopted her daughter Eva and had four other children. A merchant in her own right, Margaret contributed to the expansion of the Philipse family fortune. After her death, Frederick married Catherine van Cortlandt (widow of John Darvall) in 1692.

The second son of Frederick and Margaret, Adolph Philipse, followed his father as a merchant entrepreneur. He represented the family's business in Europe from 1685 until 1691, when he returned to New York City. In the 18th century Adolph conducted a diversified trade in the Atlantic basin but profited especially from the West Indian trade in sugar, slaves, and foodstuffs. Adolph enhanced his economic position with land purchases in Manhattan and the Highland Patent in the Hudson River valley in 1697. He inherited one-half of Philipsburg Manor Upper Mills upon the death of his father; the other half went to Frederick Philipse II (son of Philip Philipse, first son of Frederick I, who died ca 1700). Adolph served on the New York governor's council from 1705 until 1721, when he was dismissed at the request of Gov William Burnet. The following year, he was elected to fill Westchester's seat in the Colonial Assembly. Elected New York City's representative in 1725, Adolph became Speaker of the assembly, serving in that position from 1725 to 1737 and from 1739 to 1745, when he retired. He never married.

Frederick Philipse II, the second lord of the manor, was more committed to a political career than to a mercantile one. In 1719 he was elected New York City alderman, a position he held for 14 years, and also served as a justice of the peace. He simultaneously held positions in the assembly (representing Westchester Co from 1726 until his death), and on the New York Supreme Court; he was one of three presiding justices in John Peter Zenger's 1735 trial for seditious libel. Frederick II married Johanna Brockholst in 1719 and had 10 children.

Frederick Philipse III became third lord of Philipsburg Manor in 1751 upon the death of his father, Frederick II. He married Elizabeth Williams (widow of Anthony Rutgers) in 1756 and had 10 children. Unlike his Dutch Reformed ancestors, Frederick III supported the Anglican faith. He was elected to the assembly in 1751, replacing his father as Westchester's representative, and served until 1775. More concerned with his role as a landed aristocrat, he attended the sessions of the assembly irregularly. His voting record shows that he generally supported the royal prerogative. Throughout the Revolutionary crisis, Frederick III supported the Crown. In spring 1777 he moved with his family from the manor to British-occupied New York City. The Philipses were attainted for treason by the New York State legislature in 1779, and all Philipse land was confiscated and sold. For his loyalty, Philipse was awarded a royal pension in 1782. At the end of the war in 1783, Frederick III and his family left New York for England.

Bielinski, Stefan. *An American Loyalist: The Ordeal of Frederick Philipse III* (Albany: NYS Parks and Recreation, 1976)

Haley, Jacquetta M. "Philipsburg Manor Tricentennial, 1693–1993." Research report, Historic Hudson Valley, Tarrytown, NY, 1992

Judd, Jacob. "Frederick Philipse III of Westchester County: A Reluctant Loyalist." In *The Loyalist Americans: A Focus on Greater New York,* ed. Robert A. East and Jacob Judd (Tarrytown, NY: Sleepy Hollow Restorations, 1975)

Maika, Dennis J. "Philipse Family Commerce, 1650–1750." Research report, Historic Hudson Valley, Tarrytown, NY, 1997

Dennis J. Maika

Philipstown. Town (pop 9,422) in W Putnam Co. Formed as Philips Precinct in 1772, it was recognized as a town in 1788. It is along the rocky ridges of the Hudson Highlands on the east bank of the Hudson, including Anthonys Nose (900 ft/274 m). Industry in the 19th century, concentrated in and around Cold Spring, included iron mining and foundry production, brickmaking, and granite quarrying. The Hudson River Railroad (1849; later New York Central) helped create a district of estates at Garrison. Topography and relative inaccessibility have retarded intensive development. It is the site of the 4,000-acre (1,619 ha) Hudson Highlands State Park and of the Constitution Marsh Audubon Center and Sanctuary. The Catskill Aqueduct (1907) and the Appalachian Trail (1923) cross the town. Landmarks include Graymoor Monastery (1898), Dick's Castle (1904–11), Boscobel (1808, moved and restored 1961), and Manitoga (1942), the home of Russel Wright, industrial designer.

Charlotte B. Eaton

Philmont. Village (pop 1,480) in Claverack (Columbia Co). Although wool carpet was produced in the village by 1818, industry did not begin in earnest until 1845, when George P. Philip built a large dam and cut a hydraulic canal through rock, providing waterpower for woolen (1847) and paper (*ca* 1855) mills. The Harlem Railroad provided service beginning in 1852, and later industries included Philmont Machine Works (*ca* 1860; paper and woolen mill machinery), Philmont Hosiery Mills (1861), Connelly Needle Factory (1876), and Philmont Scale Works (1877). The village was incorporated in 1892. In the 1920s the High Rock Knitting Co employed up to 750 workers but closed in the late 1960s. In the early 21st century Philmont has no large manufacturers.

Phoebe Snow. Celebrated streamliner or lightweight steel train of the Delaware, Lackawanna and Western Railroad (DL&W). On 15 Nov 1949 Phoebe Snow replaced the older-style heavy-weight Lackawanna Limited. Diesel-powered Phoebe Snow made daylight runs between Hoboken, NJ (connected by ferry to Manhattan) and Buffalo. It drew a dining car and observation lounge as well as luxury passenger coaches. The train's name recalled an earlier advertising icon of DL&W. Known as the Road of Anthracite, DL&W hauled hard coal from eastern Pennsylvania and also burned the coal in its steam locomotives. From 1900 the railroad's advertisements featured white-gowned Phoebe Snow, a "Maiden all in Lawn (fine white linen)," who rode the DL&W and arrived at her destination unsoiled by the soot and cinders of soft-coal-burning locomotives. Phoebe Snow touted her clean, fast, and scenic journeys in illustrated verses that appeared on "car cards" aboard railway coaches and elsewhere until 1917. The Phoebe Snow survived DL&W's 1960 merger with the Erie Railroad but was discontinued on 27 Nov 1966. No trains have traveled Phoebe Snow's former route since 1970.

Zimmermann, Karl R. *Erie Lackawanna East* (New York: Quadrant Press, 1975)

Karl Zimmermann

Phoenix. Village (pop 2,251) in Schroeppel (Oswego Co). Settled in 1801 at a portage around the rapids on the Oswego River, it grew with boatbuilding shops on the Oswego Canal from 1828 through 1873. Salt-related industries such as barrel making and charcoal making were also important. Later in the century paper and silk mills were operating. The village incorporated in 1848. The completion of the railroad through the village (1885) and the arrival of the trolley (1909) advanced transportation. A 1916 fire destroyed the village center. The county industrial park and several pattern shops employ residents, but most commute to Syracuse or Oswego.

Barbara J. Dix

photography. Prephotographic means of capturing images were used in New York as early as 1827, when Capt Basil Hall of the British navy composed a drawing of the major buildings of Rochester with the aid of a camera lucida, a portable device containing a prism fitted with a viewfinder, through which an easily traceable image was cast onto a sheet of drawing paper. "The Village of Rochester" was published in 1829, along with 39 other etchings made from sketches that Hall drew in North America with the aid of the camera lucida.

The Daguerreotype

The daguerreotype entered the United States via New York City shortly after its published announcement in France in January 1839. In April of that year the *New York Observer* printed a letter from American inventor Samuel F. B. Morse (then in Paris) describing the remarkably detailed city views that Louis Jacques Mandé Daguerre had captured and fixed on polished, chemically prepared and developed metal plates. The technique caught on quickly, and early daguerreotypes were produced in New York City in late 1839 by Morse, John W. Draper, and D. W. Seager. At its outset the daguerreotype seemed unsuited to portraiture, as the process required extremely bright light, exposures of 20 to 40 seconds, and an absolutely still subject. Nevertheless a daguerreotype portrait industry developed in New York City and other American centers during the 1840s, spurred by improved sensitizing techniques and equipment, and by the persistent desire to possess the likeness of loved ones. John Johnson and Alexander Wolcott opened the first American daguerreotype studio in New York City in 1840. Ten years later there were over 70 studios in the city, mostly on lower Broadway. The most famous were those of Mathew B. Brady, Martin W. Lawrence, and Jeremiah Gurney. Rivaling these luxury Broadway galleries were important studios like the outdoor operation run by Platt D. Babbitt at Niagara Falls during the 1850s, where clients could pose with the falls in the background. Thomas Mercer opened Rochester's first daguerreotype studio in 1842; he worked for a while with Edward T. Whitney, who gained a national reputation. Studios also flourished in Buffalo and Albany, while itinerant daguerreotypists visited various parts of New York State.

Stereography

During the 1850s the daguerreotype was replaced by the more economical collodion wet-plate process, a negative-positive technique that yielded multiple prints on albuminized paper. At the same time that the established studios switched to making paper prints, a new pictorial format was becoming immensely popular: the small twin-imaged stereographic card that, when viewed through a lensed apparatus called a stereoscope, offered the illusion of a three-dimensional view. Most stereographic imagery was travel related. Large houses such as E. and H. T. Anthony and Co in New York City commissioned, produced, and distributed over 70,000 single images. The cards were purchased by government agencies, libraries, schools, and the general public. Series titles included Niagara, The Catskills, Broadway, Central Park, and Public Buildings in New York City and Brooklyn. By the 1870s many professionals, like Adirondack photographer Seneca Ray Stoddard, made their own stereographic views. George Barker's stereographs of Niagara Falls made him one of the most famous photographers in the country, and Barker soon expanded his subjects and formats to include large prints of city views, including a photographic series of Buffalo. Stereographic photography survived the introduction of dry-plate and paper negative processes.

Kodak and Its Consequences

Increasingly simple, inexpensive photographic equipment and processes became available to amateurs in the 1880s and 1890s, spurred by the film camera and photo finishing process invented by George Eastman, a dry-plate maker in Rochester. Eastman's small, handheld Kodak camera, sold loaded with sensitized film, required no special skill or patience from the photographer. The cost of the camera included film development by the company, whose slogan You Press the Button, We Do the Rest caught on quickly. Middle-class consumers could now take their own photographs, and these uncomposed "snapshots" brought a new informality to photography. Amateur snapshot photography had an enormous impact on the representation of private life. Henceforth the activities and rituals of families and intimates would be defined by homemade photographs destined for albums. The market for professional portrait photography declined at this time, yet the demand for mass-produced views continued to grow, as recreational travel became increasingly accessible. Postcards and souvenirs bearing photographic images became lucrative items beginning around 1900. Serious amateurs, many of them expert technicians, established clubs that flourished in the late 19th century. A notable example was the Buffalo Camera Club, which was formed in 1888 and launched annual lantern-slide presentations that year. The club began to mount print exhibits in 1892 and exchanged prints with members of similar clubs in Albany and Syracuse.

Art Photography and Modernism

Partly in response to photography's popularization, an aggressive photography-as-art movement took shape in the United States at the turn of the 20th century. During this period art photography meant pictorialism, a practice that espoused painterly effects in photography through various focusing, developing, and printing techniques. Amateur clubs like the New York Camera Club, headed by Alfred Stieglitz from 1897 to 1902, disseminated pictorialism as a coherent movement through traveling slide shows, exhibitions, and publications. Most influential was Stieglitz's Photo-Secession group (1902–17), whose journal, *Camera Work,* and art gallery in Manhattan promoted photography in the same context as modern painting and sculpture by European masters. New York City–based photographers who thrived in this environment include Gertrude Kasëbier, Edward Steichen, and Alvin Langdon Coburn. Coburn made frequent trips to Western New York and was close to the Photo-Pictorialists of Buffalo, a group that broke off from the Buffalo Camera Club.

In the decades between the world wars, the soft, timeless air of pictorialist photography was replaced by the straight lines and dynamic viewpoints of modernist aesthetics, which favored urban and industrial subjects and tended toward formal abstraction. In addition to Stieglitz's vehicles, various New York City venues featured modernist photography, including the galleries of art dealers J. B. Neumann, Erhard Weyhe, and Carl Zigrosser; the salon of Walter and Louise Arensberg; and multimedia exhibitions such as the *Machine Age Exposition* in 1927 at Steinway Hall on 57th St, and *Cubism and Abstract Art* and *Fantastic Art, Dada, and Surrealism,* both at the Museum of Modern Art in 1936. Paul Strand, Charles Sheeler, Morton Schamberg, and Man Ray were among the influential modernist photographers who worked in New York City.

Social Documentation

The first American social reformer to make extensive use of a camera was Jacob Riis, who began his career in the 1870s as a reporter. While working in the Mulberry St area of Manhattan, Riis wrote a series of columns for the *New York Tribune* describing the wretched tenement and sweatshop conditions endured by recent immigrants. In 1890 Riis published *How the Other Half Lives,* an exposé of the Lower East Side slums, illustrated with halftone reproductions of his photographs. From 1904 to 1909 Lewis Hine, a teacher at the Ethical Culture School in New York City, took approximately 200 photographs of recent immigrants at Ellis Island. His aim was to counter prejudice against these new Americans by portraying them as distinct individuals. Hine also documented child labor, mostly while working as staff photographer for the National Child Labor Committee between 1907 and 1917. His images include children stringing and shipping beans in Buffalo and tending machines at a Niagara cannery. Interest in photography as a social document declined in the 1920s but was revived in the 1930s, helped by sponsorship from the Photo League and the Works Progress Administration. Hine, Berenice Abbott, and Margaret Bourke-White were commissioned to photograph newly erected skyscrapers, and Abbott's *Changing New York,* with text by journalist Elizabeth McCausland, extensively chronicled the dynamism and ruptures in the rapidly changing cityscape. In addition to documenting rural poverty for the federal Resettlement Administration in the mid-1930s, Walker Evans recorded images of subway passengers and other vernacular subjects in Manhattan.

News Photography

Photographs of contemporary news events date to the beginnings of the medium. Photographer George Barnard's 1853 daguerreotype "Burning Mills, Oswego, New York" is one of the earliest extant news photographs. Both Barnard and Mathew Brady were leading photographers of the American Civil War. While the first decades of photography correspond with the rise of illustrated New York news journals such as *Harper's Weekly* and *Frank Leslie's Illustrated Newspaper,* these were illustrated with wood engravings; photographically illustrated newspapers had to await the perfection of the halftone plate in the 1890s, which could print in relief with the type on high-speed magazine presses. A key contribution to the process was made by Frederic E. Ives, who began to develop the halftone screen while working at the photography laboratory of Cornell University in the 1870s. The simultaneous introduction of small, handheld cameras, dry-plate, and flexible, sensitized film allowed the instantaneous recording and mass dissemination of news events with photography.

New York City, home of Henry Luce's *Life* and *Fortune* magazines, had become the center of photojournalism by the early 1930s. First published in 1936, *Life* portrayed the social and political developments of a complex world in ways that invoked the reader's compassion. The great demand for pictures attracted leading American and European photographers such as Bourke-White, Robert Capa, Andreas Feininger, W. Eugene Smith, and Alfred Eisenstaedt. By mid-century urban photojournalism was often associated with a sensational style originated by Weegee (Arthur Fellig), whose stark photographs of crime scenes appeared in the *New York Daily News.* Photographic agencies like Magnum, which was formed in New York City in 1947, send photographers to areas discussed in the news and supply media outlets, publishers, and individuals with images.

Since World War II

After World War II photographs became ever more pervasive and varied. As the illustrated weekly magazine continued to flourish and compete for readers, new techniques in color, and high-speed, aerial, and abstract photography became familiar to a mass audience. The photograph as social document was increasingly viewed as a potentially artistic image, and photographs began to appear more frequently in art galleries and museums. The Museum of Modern Art in New York City officially established its Department of Photography in 1940. In 1949 the International Museum of Photography at George Eastman House opened in Rochester. Though not the first museum of photography, it possesses the largest and most comprehensive collection of international photography, photographic equipment, and cinema, and is the leading center of photographic education in the United States.

New York City–based photographers in the postwar era explored the social scene in snapshots of urban street life. The social sympathies evident in earlier decades of documentary photography gave way to a more detached view of contemporary environments and anonymous people in photographs by Walker Evans, Louis Faurer, Roy DeCarava, Helen Levitt, and William Klein, among others. Various aspects of postwar US society—forms of leisure, consumerism, spectacle, and class—were viewed somewhat critically in the work of European-born photographers Lisette Model and Robert Frank, and in the unsettling figures of Diane Arbus. Many of these photographers produced work for commercial outlets while pursuing independent projects. In the 1960s and 1970s photographers like Garry Winogrand created provocative social landscapes by juxtaposing people and things in an apparently "objective" or uninflected manner. Others such as Bruce Davidson used the camera to report on the social struggles of this era while working on assignment and independently.

Avant-garde artists in New York State have used photography in a variety of ways since the 1960s. In the silk-screened prints and paintings of Andy Warhol, photography is a means of processing images for consumers rather than a way to capture a reality that exists independently of the photograph. The power of photography to shape as well as to document social roles has been explored in many photo-based art practices since the 1970s, including the work of Cindy Sherman. Other New York City–based artists, such as Nan Goldin, have used the photograph as a portal into subcultures that would otherwise be inaccessible to most viewers. A continuing strategy of artist-photographers is to use the photograph as a point of departure for retelling or reclaiming history, as in the influential work of Syracuse- and Brooklyn-based photographer Carrie Mae Weems.

See also Art, adirondacks and north country; Art, buffalo and the niagara frontier; Eastman kodak company; Iroquois art.

Bannon, Anthony, with C. Robert McElroy. *The Photo-Pictorialists of Buffalo* (Buffalo: Albright-Knox Art Gallery, 1981)
Hales, Peter Bacon. "American Views and the Romance of Modernization." In *Photography in 19th-Century America,* ed. Martha A. Sandweiss (New York: Abrams, 1991)
Livingston, Jane. *The New York School: Photographs, 1936–1963* (New York: Stewart, Tabori & Chang, 1992)
Newhall, Beaumont. *The Daguerreotype in America,* 3d ed. (New York: Dover, 1976)
Rosenblum, Naomi. *A World History of Photography,* 3d ed. (New York: Abbeville Press, 1997)
Sobieszek, Robert, Joan Pedzich, and Philip Condax. *Rochester: An American Center of Photography* (Rochester: International Museum of Photography at George Eastman House, 1984)

Amy Kurlander

Phyfe, Duncan (*b* Loch Fannis, Scotland, 1768; *d* New York City, 16 Aug 1854). Cabinetmaker. Perhaps the most famous of New York State's fine furniture craftsmen of the Federal period (1790–1825), Phyfe came to Albany about 1784. Little is known of his early years. The son of a Scottish cabinetmaker, he evidently completed an apprenticeship in Albany before moving to New York City about 1790. In 1795 he opened his New York City cabinetmaking shop that would become highly successful. Phyfe led the way in furniture design until his retirement in 1847. His classical designs were based on French Directoire and Empire forms via English cabinetmaking tradition. Influenced by archaeological excavations in Greece and Rome, the elements of this new style were often copied directly from ancient forms such as klismos and curule chairs, tripod stands, and other forms found on ancient vases. Favorite motifs were winged and caryatid supports, lions' or dogs' paws, lyres, palmettes, lotus leaves, griffins, and rams' heads.

Phyfe's former employees spread this new style when they went to work for other cabinetmakers or started their own shops. Many of his competitors copied his interpretation of English Regency forms. Some of New York State's wealthiest families ordered his furniture. To accommodate them and his other customers, he employed as many as 40 workmen. Phyfe's furniture designs were so fashionable they were copied as Revival styles long after his death, and his influence is still found in furniture stores and homes. Today, the name Duncan Phyfe is synonymous with the popular style he created. He was not accustomed to labeling his furniture, and his work is largely identified through documentation, receipts, and comparison with the designs and quality of work known to come from his shop. Original pieces are found in museums including the Metropolitan Museum of Art, the Museum of the City of New York, the Merchant's House Museum, and Delaware's Winterthur Museum. His tool chest is preserved at the New-York Historical Society.

Cornelius, Charles Over. *Furniture Masterpieces of Duncan Phyfe* (New York: Doubleday, Page, 1922)
Montgomery, Charles F. *American Furniture: The Federal Period* (New York: Viking Press, 1966)
Scherer, John L. *New York Furniture: The Federal Period, 1788–1825* (Albany: NYS Museum, 1988)

John L. Scherer

physicians. Since the colonial era, New York State has been central to the development of medical science, practice, and theories, and has pioneered in the areas of alternative medicine, professional standards, education, and research.

Competing Philosophies of Medicine

In the Colony of New York, folk medicine shared the stage with the latest European medical controversies. Cadwallader Colden received his MD at Edinburgh in 1705, immigrated to Philadelphia around 1710, but came to New York in 1718 at the invitation of Gov Robert Hunter, eventually serving as lieutenant governor from 1760 to 1775. The regular, or allopathic, medicine practiced by Colden and others was violent. Methods such as cupping, bleeding, leeching, purging, inducing emesis, chilling, steaming, and scarifying were typical. Patients' abhorrence and distrust of these methods led to the rise of gentler means of therapeutics. In the 19th century regular medicine competed with botanic medicine, homeopathy, hydropathy, phrenology, eclectic medicine, and other medical systems.

The Boston-born, Danish-trained physician Hans Burch Gram brought homeopathy to the United States when he established practice in New York City in 1825. The homeopaths he trained expanded the influence of homeopathic thought across New England and the Midwest. It was especially popular among the literati of New York City. William Cullen Bryant served as president of the New York Homeopathic Society. In the mid–19th century a Central New York botanic healer, Cyrus Thomson, tried to alleviate suffering by prescribing various foodstuffs (mostly of vegetable origin) and steam baths to keep the patient warm, stabilize body heat, and restore the balance of body fluids. Preaching the gospel of "every man his own physician," he strove to educate his patients, auditors, and readers in that direction. The son of Samuel Thomson, founder of Thomsonian medicine, he extended his father's principles and to a degree supported them with the medical philosophy of Benjamin Rush. Wooster Beach, a former Thomsonian, founded eclectic medicine in New York City in the 1830s and then moved to Ohio in 1845. Eclectic medicine flourished throughout New York State for many decades. Rochester Eclectic Medical College and two institutions in Syracuse, Stephen Hollister Potter's Syracuse Medical College and Central Medical College of New York, were bastions of eclectic medical education in the 1840s and 1850s.

Much impetus for the nationwide hydropathy or "water-cure" fad in the mid–19th century came from New York State. Russell Thatcher Trall and Joel Shew opened their hydropathic spa in Lebanon Springs (Columbia Co) in 1845. Trall's two-volume *Hydropathic Encyclopedia,* which went through several editions in the early 1850s, and Shew's *Hydropathic Family Physician* (1854) contributed significantly to that movement. Beginning in the 1830s the diagnostic pseudoscience of phrenology became popular for a few decades in the United States. Founded by Lorenzo Niles Fowler, Lydia Folger Fowler, Orson S. Fowler, and Samuel R. Wells in 1844 and specializing in phrenological works, Fowler (sometimes Fowlers) and Wells in New York City was the leading American publisher of alternative medicine in the 19th century.

In the wake of the discoveries of anesthesia, antisepsis, surgical hemostasis, germ theory, and other scientific developments, dramatic therapeutic improvements led to a qualified triumph of allopathy over alternative philosophies of medicine in the late 19th and early 20th centuries. In the late 20th century, patients' reactions against the coldness of scientific, allopathic medicine created a resurgence in the popularity of alternative therapies, which continued into the 21st century. Some methods that were once mainstream later became alternative. At the end of the 20th century, nonlicensed healers in eastern European ethnic communities in New York City and isolated rural areas of New York State still practiced traditional cupping.

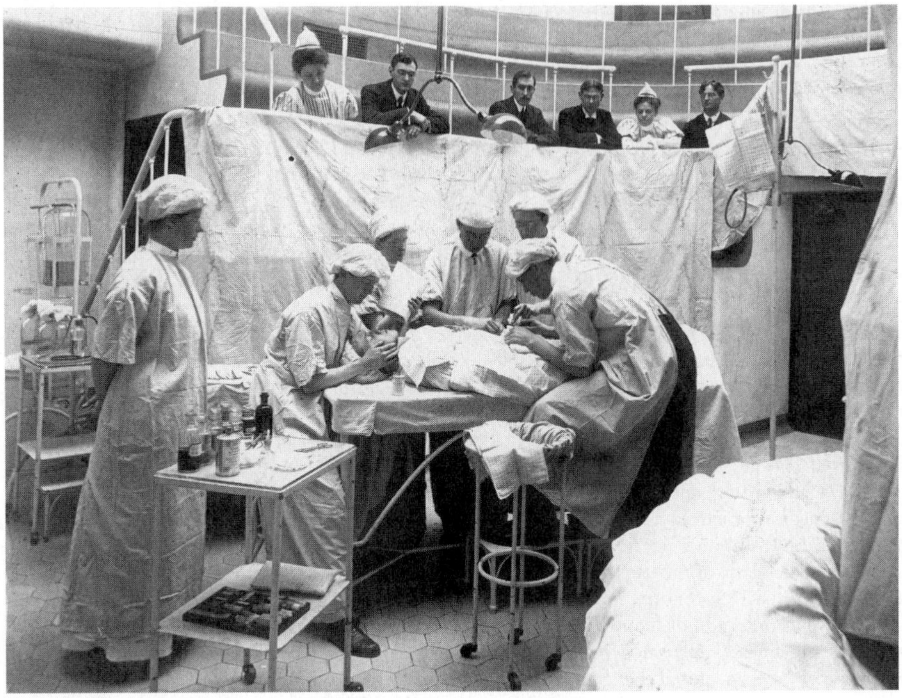

Observing an operation at the Hospital of the Good Shepherd, Syracuse, *ca* 1906.

Women and Minorities

New York State, along with Switzerland, was a world leader in fostering the earliest women physicians. Geneva Medical College graduated Elizabeth Blackwell, the world's first woman with a regular medical degree, on 23 Jan 1849. Other first-generation women physicians who received their degrees in New York State include Lydia Fowler, Sarah Marinda Fraser, Clemence Sophia Lozier, Susan McKinney-Steward, Sarah Van Tuyl, and Mary Edwards Walker. The first hospital founded by women for women was the New York Infirmary for Women and Children (later Beekman Downtown Hospital), which opened in 1857 with Elizabeth Blackwell as director, Emily Blackwell as chief of surgery, and Marie Zakrzewska as chief resident. Many superior women physicians, including Mary Putnam Jacobi, S. Josephine Baker, Emily Dunning Barringer, Karen Horney, and Patricia J. Numann, built their careers in New York State. Numann became the first woman surgeon at SUNY Upstate University Hospital in 1970. She founded the Association of Women Surgeons in 1981.

The first licensed African American physician, James McCune Smith, was born in New York City around 1813 and made his medical and pharmaceutical career there until his death in 1865. Because African Americans were denied admission to American medical schools even in the northern states in the 1830s, Smith studied at the University of Glasgow, in Scotland, where he received his MD in 1837. Some medical schools in New England, Philadelphia, and the Midwest began admitting people of color in the 1840s, but there were no black medical students in New York State until the late 1850s. Thereafter New York State was generally active in removing hurdles for minorities and women seeking to become doctors. McKinney-Steward and Fraser were two of the first four African American women physicians.

Professional Organizations and Publications

The Medical Society of the State of New York (MSSNY) was founded in 1806. Many of the local and county medical societies predated it, and throughout the 19th century the state society was frequently at odds with over 100 of these smaller societies about ethics, polity, and especially licensing. Many statewide societies arose to promote particular medical specialties and interests. Among the most prominent were the New York Dermatological Society, founded in 1869 by Faneuil D. Weisse; the New York Society of Tropical Medicine, founded in 1933 by Ralph Welty Nauss and other physicians; and the Academy of Family Physicians in New York State, founded in 1948 by William Buecheler and 11 others. The Women's Medical Society of New York State began as the merger of four women's medical organizations in 1907 to honor Sarah Read Adamson Dolley, who received her MD from Central Medical College in 1851.

Some societies encouraged the medical humanities; the first in New York State was the Literary and Philosophical Society (1814–34). John Wakefield Francis, Valentine Mott, John Stearns, and Isaac Wood created the New York Academy of Medicine in 1847 as a reformist organization. The Charaka Club, the foremost American medical literary society, was founded by neurologists Charles Loomis Dana and Bernard Sachs and two other prominent physicians at Dana's home in New York City in 1898. Its *Proceedings,* published irregularly in 11 volumes from 1902 to 1947, contain many classic papers in the medical humanities.

New York State has been headquarters for many important medical periodicals since the first American medical journal, the *Medical Repository,* appeared in 1797 in New York City.

In 1845 Austin Flint founded the *Buffalo Medical Journal,* which showed his early support for women in medicine by publishing Elizabeth Blackwell's medical dissertation, *Ship Fever,* in February 1849. The *Bulletin of the New York Academy of Medicine* shifted its main focus from the broader medical humanities in 1998 and became the *Journal of Urban Health.*

MEDICAL LEGISLATION AND ETHICS

New York Colony enacted a law in 1684 restricting the practice of medicine to qualified individuals. New York City required licensing of physicians in 1760. New York State required licensing in 1797 and empowered several nonmedical kinds of officials to grant licenses. In 1809 the New York State Board of Regents first authorized colleges to award the MD degree. State laws attempting, and generally failing, to regulate medical practice were passed in 1806, 1813, 1827, 1844, and 1872. The MSSNY adopted its first code of medical ethics in 1823. For much of the 19th century, most states, including New York, did not require medical degrees as prerequisites for practicing medicine. Most practitioners acquired the status of "doctor" merely by passing examinations arranged by "censors" of their local medical societies. Alternative and unregulated practitioners prospered. The 1823 code was very liberal in its acceptance of alternative medicine. As a result, jurisdictional conflicts arose. Attempts by one organization to suppress alternative or unorthodox practitioners usually failed because candidates could get licenses from other organizations. When the Orange County Medical Society refused in 1843 to license a homeopath, he immediately founded a local homeopathic medical society and licensed himself. In 1880 the New York State legislature abolished the right of county medical societies to license practitioners and reduced the number of authorized licensing organizations from over 150 to 8 "regular," 2 homeopathic, 2 eclectic, and 1 unaffiliated.

Since its founding in 1847, the American Medical Association (AMA) fought to restrict both its own membership and medical practice in general to "regular" practitioners with MD degrees. In 1880 the Richmond Co and New York Co medical societies each tried to get the other expelled from the AMA on the grounds that the other had admitted alternative practitioners into its membership. After 1882 open warfare existed between the AMA and the MSSNY because the MSSNY refused to toughen its 1823 code. In 1884 a splinter group from the MSSNY formed the New York State Medical Association (NYSMA) to support the AMA. The issue was not resolved until 1903, when the respective ethics codes of the MSSNY, the NYSMA, and the AMA had become compatible. In 1905 the NYSMA dissolved and rejoined the MSSNY. Cornelius Rea Agnew was a prime mover in this battle over the development of medical practice standards in New York State. At the beginning of the 21st century the New York State Office of Professional Medical Conduct, a branch of the State Health Department, was responsible for monitoring the ethics of physicians and other health care professionals.

INNOVATIONS

New York State physicians and hospitals have been in the forefront of medical innovation for the past two centuries. Bellevue Hospital in Manhattan led the nation in introducing new medical and surgical techniques from Europe: Valentine Seaman used Edward Jenner's vaccine in 1800, David Hosack ligated the femoral artery in 1808, and Lewis A. Sayre resected the hip in 1854. The Bureau of Medical and Surgical Relief for the Outdoor Poor, America's first outpatient department, was created at Bellevue in 1867, and in 1869 Edward L. Dalton created the world's first hospital-based ambulance service in 1869.

The state's research pioneers include William Beaumont, who founded the science of gastric physiology in Plattsburgh in 1833 by publishing the results of his experiments on Alexis St. Martin, a man whose stomach, as a result of a hunting accident, was partially open to investigation. John Call Dalton brought Claude Bernard's physiological research methods to the United States in the 1850s. At midcentury Frank Hastings Hamilton made important breakthroughs in orthopedic surgery at the University of Buffalo and Long Island College Hospital, and at Bellevue Hospital Medical College, Austin Flint was a pioneer in heart and lung surgery.

In the 20th century New York University (NYU) Medical School alumni include Walter Reed and William Crawford Gorgas, who conquered yellow fever; Joseph Goldberger, who discovered the control of pellagra; and Jonas Edward Salk and Albert Bruce Sabin, who created polio vaccines. NYU Medical School faculty member Saul Krugman in 1980 developed a vaccine against hepatitis B. Largely because of the results of pathologist Simon Flexner, the Rockefeller Institute for Medical Research (now Rockefeller University) achieved a reputation for excellence soon after its founding in 1901. David Ho of the Aaron Diamond AIDS Research Center, associated with Rockefeller University, was named *Time* magazine's Man of the Year in 1996 for his innovations with combination antiretroviral therapy that dramatically reduced AIDS morbidity rates.

See also ABORTION; BIRTH CONTROL.

Blau, Saul. "Origins of Dermatology in New York," *New York State Journal of Medicine* 76 (July 1976): 1174–76

Cameron, Cyril T. M., Edward W. Gilmore, and Edward L. McNeil. "History of Emergency Medicine in New York State," *New York State Journal of Medicine* 76 (July 1976): 1176–78

King, Lester S. *Transformations in American Medicine from Benjamin Rush to William Osler* (Baltimore: Johns Hopkins Univ Press, 1991)

Santilli, Veronica C. "Perspectives on Women Physicians in New York State: Past, Present, and Future," *New York State Journal of Medicine* 90 (June 1990): 317–21

Walsh, James Joseph. *History of Medicine in New York: Three Centuries of Medical Progress* (New York: National Americana Society, 1919)

Wheatley, George M. "Brief History of Pediatrics in New York," *New York State Journal of Medicine* 76 (July 1976): 1197–1200

Eric v. d. Luft

Pierce, Ray Vaughan (*b* Stark, Herkimer Co, 4 Aug 1840; *d* St. Vincent's Island, Fla, 4 Feb 1914). Physician and patent medicine entrepreneur. Pierce attended local schools and graduated from the Eclectic Medical Institute in Cincinnati, Ohio, in 1865. After establishing a medical practice in Pennsylvania, specializing in "private and female diseases," Pierce moved to Buffalo in 1867. In 1874 he opened a downtown office, which became known as the World's Dispensary, where his famous Golden Medical Discovery and other patent medicines were manufactured and bottled. He also opened Buffalo's first luxury hotel, Pierce's Invalids' Hotel and Surgical Institute, also known as Pierce's Palace, in 1878. Pierce authored *The People's Common Sense Medical Adviser in Plain English; or, Medicine Simplified,* which sold more than 4 million copies in 100 editions between 1875 and 1935. His popularity, enhanced through advertising in national magazines, won him a state senate seat (1877–79) and a stint in Congress (1879–80), both on the Republican ticket. In 1909 Pierce purchased an island off the Florida coast where he remained until his death from a brain hemorrhage. His wife, the former Mary J. Smith, and three sons survived him. He is buried in Buffalo's Forest Lawn Cemetery.

Allen, Luella. "Ray Vaughan Pierce, MD, 1840–1914: Buffalo's Common Sense Medical Adviser." In *Medical History in Buffalo: 1846–1996,* ed. Lilli Sentz (Buffalo: School of Medicine and Biomedical Sciences, SUNY at Buffalo, 1996)

Howard R. Stanger

Pierce-Arrow Motor Car Company. Founded in Buffalo in the 19th century as the George N. Pierce Manufacturing Co, a producer of metal consumer products, the company turned to high-quality bicycles in the 1890s and began experiments with automobiles at the turn of the century. From the first production in 1901, a one-cylinder runabout, the model line quickly moved to large, upscale autos with deluxe components including cast-aluminum body parts and 6-cylinder (later 8- and 12-) engines. The cycle and automobile operations split in 1906, with the Pierce family soon selling its interest in the automobile enterprise, which was renamed the Pierce-Arrow Motor Car Co. A large factory complex was erected on Elmwood Ave. During the 1910s the company employed several thousand workers. However, the consolidation of the auto industry with a limited market for luxury cars produced a financial squeeze. The Studebaker Corp purchased Pierce-Arrow in 1928, but five years later, during the depression, Studebaker declared bankruptcy, prompting the sale of Pierce-Arrow in 1933 to a group of Buffalo entrepreneurs. Experiencing its own financial difficulties, the company was reorganized as the Pierce-Arrow Motor Corp in 1935 and produced its last cars in 1938. Travelodge trailers were also manufactured, but trucks had been discontinued in 1932. The Pierce-Arrow Society was founded in 1957.

Brierley, Brooks T. *There Is No Mistaking a Pierce-Arrow* (Coconut Grove, Fla: Garrett & Stringer, 1986)

Hendry, Maurice D. *Pierce-Arrow* (New York: Ballantine Books, 1971)

Geoffrey N. Stein

Piercefield. Town (pop 305) in SE St. Lawrence Co. Settled in 1858, the town was formed from Hopkinton in 1900. An International Paper Co mill operated from 1892 to 1935. Mountains include Mt Matumbla (2,688 ft/819 m), highest point in the county, and Mt Arab (2,549 ft/777 m), with a restored fire observer tower and cabin. Piercefield Flow is a largely undeveloped lake formed in the Raquette River by a hydroelectric dam at Piercefield hamlet. The town, mainly a bedroom community for nearby Tupper Lake (Franklin Co), includes the former

Pierce-Arrow convertible coupe, 1937.

sawmill hamlets of Conifer and Childwold, where the Conifer Park Hotel operated from 1889 to 1909.

Richard E. Mooers

Piermont. Village (pop 2,607) in Orangetown (Rockland Co). A river landing from the time of settlement, Piermont grew beginning in 1832 around the Erie Railroad pier, built to provide an eastern terminus connecting with river shipping. It acquired a post office in 1839. Irish immigrants followed shortly thereafter. The village was incorporated in 1850, one contemporary source claimed, "to keep the Irish in subjection and compel them to keep houses and yards clean." In 1859 the Erie completed a Jersey City terminal, and the village lost half its population within three years. The roundhouse and shops were closed in 1869, but it was later served by the Nyack and Northern Railroad (1870–1966). Piermont Paper Co (1902), later the Robert Gair Co, employed 450 workers in 1927. It was sold to Continental Can in 1956 and closed in 1971. Other firms operated the mill until the mid-1980s. Another early 20th-century factory was the Meisch Manufacturing Co, a maker of silk ribbon, which closed in 1976 after nearly 70 years. Piermont's industrial sites were redeveloped beginning in 1989 as condominiums and commercial spaces. The hand-operated Sparkill Creek Drawbridge (1880) is a local landmark.

Pierrepont [PEER-POINT]. Town (pop 2,674) in E central St. Lawrence Co. Settled in 1806–7 and boosted by the St. Lawrence Turnpike (1812), the town was formed from Russell in 1818. An early potato starch factory (1845, converted to cornstarch 1858) operated until 1861. In 2003 some farming continued, but the town was mainly a bedroom community for Canton and Potsdam, especially Hannawa Falls hamlet. Famous residents have included Leonora Kearney Barry (1849–1930), pioneer woman labor activist who served as general investigator of the Knights of Labor. Natives included polar explorer Albert Crary (1911–87) and Irving Bacheller (1859–1950), author of *Eben Holden* (1900) and other novels, many with a North Country setting. Pierrepont's historic district includes a schoolhouse (1826), the town hall (1847), and the Union Church (1885). The Gardner Cox House (1838) at Hannawa Falls is listed on the National Register of Historic Places.

Richard E. Mooers

Pike. Town (pop 1,086) and village (pop 382) in SE Wyoming Co. Settled in 1806, the town was formed from Nunda (Livingston Co) in 1818. The village was incorporated in 1846. A very early dam on Wiscoy Creek that powered mills has survived into the 21st century. Nineteenth-century industries included a furnace, a foundry, a woolen factory, a paper mill, and several quarries. In the early 21st century, milk and potatoes are produced on Pike farms, gravel is quarried, and residents commute to Arcade, Attica, and other nearby towns, as well as to Buffalo and Rochester. Pike is site of the Wyoming County Fair, held each August, and of the Genesee Valley Rotary Camp (1963) for young people with disabilities.

Pinckney. Town (pop 319) in NW Lewis Co. Settled ?1803, the town was formed in 1808 from Harrisburg. Population reached 1,152 in 1880, but many farms were abandoned by the mid–20th century; much of that land was reforested. Pinckney receives some of the highest snowfall east of the Rocky Mountains (in 1977, 537 in/1,364 cm). The 1960s emergence of the snowmobile as a recreational vehicle brought snowmobile clubs and winter camps. At the end of the 20th century, some abandoned farmland was put to use for deer and elk farms; the producers market the meat to gourmet restaurants and the antlers to the Chinese apothecary trade.

Arthur Einhorn

pineapple cheese. During the 1700s in England Cheshire cheeses were sometimes pressed into cone shapes and called pineapple cheeses. These were first made in the United States in Goshen, Conn, in 1808 by dairyman Lewis M. Norton, who secured a patent for the form in 1810. Cheddar cheese curds were pressed in pineapple-shaped molds and hung in net bags to imprint a diamond design on their rinds. The rind was then toughened and often varnished, giving these attractive cheeses an exceptionally long life. They usually weighed from 10 to 40 ounces (284–1,134 g). To serve, the top was cut off, usually in decorative notches, and pineapple cheese spoons, narrow and long handled, were used to remove the cheese. Norton's son Robert later moved production to Rushford (Allegany Co) to take advantage of rail transportation when the Erie Railroad opened in that county. In 1850 Rushford produced 35 tons (32 MT) of the delicacy. Norton Pineapple Cheese was produced in Rushford until 1883, when Eugene Norton, Robert's nephew, moved the business to Attica (Wyoming Co) to take advantage of better transportation facilities. In 1904 Wilbert W. Norton, a grandson of Lewis, transferred the last of the manufacturing out of Goshen and into Delta (Oneida Co). Other pineapple cheese producers in New York State included Oscar A. Weatherly, who moved his Norwich (Chenango Co) factory to Milford (Otsego Co) in 1900. There it produced 500 cheeses daily before moving to Wisconsin in 1955. In the 1940s government regulations required a substitute shellac for the shell, and World War II shortages slowed production. Pineapple cheese is no longer produced in the United States.

Stamm, Eunice R. *The History of Cheese Making in New York State* (Endicott, NY: Lewis Group, 1991)

Suzan D. Friedlander

pine barrens. Areas supporting rare or imperiled natural upland communities with sparse canopies of pine trees. Pine barrens occur in pockets of limited extent throughout the state on poor soils of dunes, glacial till, or outwash plains, on thin soils of rocky ridge tops and summits, and on shallow soils over noncalcareous bedrock (ie, a substratum lacking in calcium or limestone). Pitch pine is the dominant tree in most of the state's barrens, with jack pine prevalent in some northern barrens. Scrub oak, black huckleberry, blueberry, sweet fern, and sheep laurel are common understory shrubs. These plants and the ground layer grasses and herbs are adapted to the dry, acidic, infertile, and sandy or gravelly soils of pine barrens and the periodic fires that maintain some of them. Unusual and rare plants and animals occur in many of New York State's barrens. The poor soils and tendency toward frequent fire prevented early agricultural development on pine barrens. Prior to the middle of the 20th century, these areas were often considered barren wastelands and are still called barrens in both popular and scientific literature. However, some barrens served as hunting grounds, as sources of lumber, firewood, and sand, or as transportation corridors, and the fires set intentionally or unintentionally by hunters, loggers, and railroad trains are thought to have contributed to the development and maintenance of some barrens. Fire suppression policies initiated early in the 20th century and scarcity of other undeveloped lands for the mid-century suburban boom led to housing, commercial, and industrial development in some. Environmental awareness and activism during the last third of the 20th century resulted in efforts to preserve the state's best remaining pine barrens as nature preserves and open space for recreational activities, including nature study, hiking, cross-country skiing, and rock climbing. Agencies authorized by the state legislature in 1988 and 1993 oversee preservation of approximately 2,600 acres (1,050 ha) of the Albany Pine Bush and 55,000 acres (22,300 ha) in Long Island's Central Pine Barrens. Pine barrens communities in the Shawangunk Mountains, Rome Sand Plains, Clintonville Pine Barrens in the Adirondacks, and other areas are also being preserved through the combined efforts of various private and public entities.

See also ENVIRONMENTAL LAW.

Reschke, Carol. *Ecological Communities of New York State* (Latham, NY: New York Natural Heritage Program, 1990)

Jeffrey K. Barnes

Pine Plains. Town (pop 2,569) in N central Dutchess Co. Part of Little Nine Partners Patent (1706) that was partitioned in 1744, it was settled in the 1740s by Palatine Germans. In 1740 a Moravian mission for American Indians was established at Shekomeko, growing into a 65-member church before the religious and political hostility of nearby settlements resulted in its expulsion, and the community moved in 1745 to Bethlehem, Pa. From 1780 to 1864 there was a scythe factory at Hammertown. Pine Plains was formed as a town in 1823 from North East. It remains in part agricultural.

William P. McDermott

Pinkster. The Dutch celebration of Pentecost, or Whitsunday, occurring the seventh Sunday after Easter and commemorating the descent of the Holy Ghost on Christ's disciples. Occurring in the springtime, a time of renewal, it was both a religious and a secular celebration that the Dutch brought with them to New Netherland. In general, on Pinkster the Dutch attended church services as well as visited neighbors and baked special breads while children colored eggs.

Initially a Dutch holy day, Pinkster was celebrated in New York State and New Jersey mainly as an African-Dutch festival. Each region of New York Colony had its own Pinkster grounds that drew people from the surrounding area for the entertainment. Revelries were in part a social safety-valve in which mingling and recreation were intended to mitigate the harshness of life in bondage. For Blacks in New York Colony, celebratory traditions inherited from Africa were grafted onto Pinkster celebrations, and it became the most significant black celebration in New York and New Jersey from colonial days until well into the 19th century. It was reminiscent of first fruit harvest celebrations for the mainly Congo and Gold Coast agricultural peoples of New York's black population.

Pinkster began on Whitsunday or Whitmonday. Although the celebration might last for days, Tuesday was traditionally the most significant frolic day, when people of all races, classes, ages, sexes, and conditions gathered at the Pinkster grounds to observe activities or engage in the revelry. Events included competition sports such as wrestling, boxing, and gymnastics; gambling at cards and cockfights; drinking booths offering cider, rum, and ale; food stands; storytellers; singing; and dancing. The latter often included Congo dances, among them the "breakdown," the "jig," and the "Toto Dance." Musicians playing drums, fifes, fiddles, tabors, and lyres accompanied singing and dancing. Blacks attributed deeper meanings to Pinkster than mere entertainment. Enslaved couples rarely lived together and their barely weaned children were routinely sold or bequeathed to white family members in other households and communities. At Pinkster enslaved Blacks had an opportunity to see spouses, children, and friends.

Above all, Pinkster symbolized freedom. The highlight of the Pinkster celebration was the appearance on the Pinkster grounds of the African Pinkster king. The 1803 Pinkster ode by "Absalom Aimwell," written in Albany, reveals the importance of black leadership, role reversal, and particularly the king as a personification of liberty. That year's king, African-born King Charles, was described as "A slave whose soul was always free." The ode stated:

Tho' torn from friends beyond the waves,
Tho' fate has doom'd us to be slaves,
Yet on this day, let's taste and see
How sweet a thing is Liberty.

James Fenimore Cooper's novel *Satanstoe* (1845), set around the time of the French and Indian War (1756–63), provides a fascinating account of Pinkster as a sacred, secular, and ethnic holiday in New York City. Cooper believed that what distinguished Pinkster from other fairs and merrymaking was its Africanness. Although Cooper acknowledged that during his time few Blacks were of African birth, he insisted that Pinkster's traditions and uses remained originally African rather than European. Pinkster declined among Blacks after 1827, when northern emancipation celebrations emerged.

Cohen, David Steven. "In Search of Carolus Rex: Afro-Dutch Folklore in New York and New Jersey," *Journal of the Afro-American Historical and Genealogical Society* 5 (1984)
Hodges, Graham. *Slavery and Freedom in the Rural North: African Americans in Monmouth County, New Jersey, 1665–1865* (Madison, Wisc: Madison House, 1997)
Williams-Myers, A. J. *Long Hammering: Essays on the Forging of an African American Presence in the Hudson Valley to the Early 20th Century* (Trenton, NJ: African World Press, 1994)

Margaret Washington

piracy and privateering. Piracy, the illegal seizure of vessels and cargoes on the high seas, and privateering, the officially sanctioned assault or capture of enemy shipping by privately owned vessels, were widely practiced in the waters off New York from the 17th century through the War of 1812. To augment their standing navies during the series of colonial wars, the contending nations issued official commissions, called letters of marque and reprisal, to privateers. Pirates were attracted to the valuable goods moving along the Atlantic and Caribbean seaways; the vessels carrying them seemed easy targets due to slow communication, spotty naval presence, and inconsistent government attitudes.

Long Island, especially its east end, was the center of piracy in New York during its peak period (*ca* 1690–1710). One governor denounced Long Island as the pirates' "rendezvous and sanctuary." As early as 1654 the towns on Long Island discussed common measures against pirates and robbers, but the practice grew rather than declined. The island's many inlets, bays, and satellite islands provided excellent landing and storage places for those involved in illicit trade, and the profits could be substantial. Evidence suggests that many residents of the region, including members of the Colonial Assembly and the lord of the manor of Gardiners Island, were familiar with some of the pirates and handled, guarded, or traded their goods. Gov Benjamin Fletcher was widely reputed to protect pirates and their onshore partners for a cut of the spoils. New York lawyer James Emott sometimes served as intermediary between Fletcher and those who needed protection from dutiful local officials. In 1698, after Richard Coote, Earl of Bellomont succeeded Fletcher as governor, the government took a more active interest in suppressing piracy. In 1699 Bellomont reported "about 30 pirates come lately into the East end of Nassau Island [Long Island] and have a great deal of money with them," which led to their being "cherished by the inhabitants." Bellomont succeeded in arresting William Kidd, Joseph Bradish, and a number of lesser-known figures, after which the practice seems to have declined. Nevertheless, in 1728, Spanish pirates raided Gardiners Island.

Privateers fitted out from the American colonies during the colonial wars of the 18th century. American privateers attacked British shipping during the Revolutionary War, but after the Battle of Long Island and British occupation of New York, none sailed from New York waters. The last era of American privateering probably occurred during the second war with Britain (1812–15). While Baltimore and New England ports were most active in the enterprise, New York State commissioned 102 privateers and at least one privateering ship was built in Sag Harbor. However, the increasingly tight British blockade rendered privateering unprofitable. The privateers would have to slip the blockade to conduct operations and run it in reverse to bring their captures back to an admiralty court as required by law to collect their share. The United States abandoned the practice of privateering after the War of 1812.

Chidsey, Donald Barr. *The American Privateers* (New York: Dodd, Mead, 1962)
Rattray, Jeanette Edwards. "Some Pirates in Long Island Waters, 1699–1933," *Journal of Long Island History* 3 (Fall 1963): 40–49
Ritchie, Robert C. *Captain Kidd and the War against the Pirates* (Cambridge, Mass: Harvard Univ Press, 1986)

Richard F. Welch

Pitass, Jan (*b* Deutsch Piekar [now Piekary Śląskie, Poland], 3 July 1844; *d* Buffalo, 11 Dec 1913). Roman Catholic priest. After studying at the Gregorian University in Rome, he moved to the United States in May 1873 and settled in Buffalo. That year he was ordained and appointed founding pastor of St. Stanislaus, Bishop and Martyr Parish, the first Polish parish in the state, where he served as pastor for 40 years. Pitass collected funds and worked tirelessly as his own contractor, building a church, convent, hall, and rectory. He founded the first Polish school in Buffalo (1874), brought the Sisters of St. Felix of Cantalice (Felicians) to teach (1881), and organized a cemetery (1891). Under Pitass's leadership the parish peaked at 30,000 parishioners. Drawn to the church and school, the Polish community established itself on the east side of Buffalo, growing to 100,000 by the early 20th century. In addition to creating 20 Polish churches in the diocese, Pitass taught, arbitrated disputes, provided food and clothing to the needy, found homes and jobs, and beginning in 1886 published the newspaper *Polak w Ameryce* (The Pole in America). In 1894 Bishop Stephen

Ryan named Pitass dean of all Polish churches in the diocese. Pitass hosted two successful Polish Catholic Congresses in Buffalo (1896, 1901) to work for church unity, equality of clergy in the hierarchy, and educational standards.

Farkas, Robert L. *St. Stanislaus Bishop and Martyr Parish, 1873–1998: 125 Years of Glory, Praise, and Wisdom* (Buffalo: St. Stanislaus Parish Committee, 1998)

Wanda Slawinska

Pitcairn [PIT-C'RN]. Town (pop 783) in S St. Lawrence Co. Settled in 1824, the town was formed in 1836 from Fowler. Part of it is within the Adirondack Park. There is a small population on the border with the Village of Harrisville (Lewis Co), but the only population center is Pitcairn hamlet. A county forest at Greenwood Falls and the Boy Scout's Camp Portaferry are in town.

Richard E. Mooers

Pitcher. Town (pop 848) in W Chenango Co. Settled in 1791, the town was formed in 1827 from German and Lincklaen. Industrial products in the 19th century were leather, hames, hoes, forks, and woolen cloth. At Pitcher Springs a sulfureted hydrogen spring attracted health seekers; a boardinghouse was built in 1833. The area became more developed with three hotels, two bathhouses, and two bowling alleys, but by 1880 all resort business was gone. In 2003 seven families continued dairy farming alongside several beef and heifer operations, but most residents commuted to Cortland and Norwich. The Baptist and Methodist churches are listed on the National Register of Historic Places.

Pitcher, Nathaniel (*b* Litchfield, Conn, 30 Nov 1777; *d* Sandy Hill [now Hudson Falls, Washington Co], 25 May 1836). Assemblyman, congressman, and acting governor. By 1786 his family had moved to Kingsbury (Washington Co), where Pitcher farmed and built on his rudimentary education to study law. From 1802 to 1812 he advanced from justice of the peace of Kingsbury to surrogate of Washington Co. A Jeffersonian Republican assemblyman in 1806, Pitcher was reelected in 1814 and 1816 as a supporter of the war. He endorsed De Witt Clinton's gubernatorial nomination in 1817 but soon joined the Bucktail opposition. Pitcher served in Congress (1819–23) and as delegate to the state's 1821 Constitutional Convention. He married Anna B. Merritt in 1823, eight years after the death of his first wife, Margaret Scott. In 1825 Pitcher became one of three commissioners to survey an east-west road across the southern Central New York region. Pitcher's work earned him the 1826 Bucktail nomination for lieutenant governor. Elected to that position, he became acting governor upon Clinton's death in 1828. The Albany Regency thwarted Pitcher's nomination as Martin Van Buren's running mate in 1828, maintaining that Pitcher, a Freemason, would run poorly in western New York State. In 1830 he was nominated by an anti-Regency county "Coalition Convention" and won reelection to Congress (1831–33). Thereafter he remained active locally as a Whig.

Cole, Donald B. *Martin Van Buren and the American Political System* (Princeton, NJ: Princeton Univ Press, 1984)

Hammond, Jabez D. *The History of Political Parties in the State of New-York from the Ratification of the Federal Constitution to December, 1840,* 2 vols (Albany: Van Benthuysen, 1842)

Craig and Mary L. Hanyan

Pittsburg, Shawmut and Northern Railroad. Railway created in 1899 to link the Shawmut coalfields near Brockway, Pa, with the Delaware, Lackawanna and Western Railroad at Wayland (Steuben Co). Pittsburg, Shawmut and Northern (PS&N) was made up of Central New York and Western Railroad, dating from the early 1870s, and four Pennsylvania roads. At its peak in 1912 PS&N controlled a 171 mi (275 km) main line from Brockway through St. Marys, headquarters of the road, to Coryville, Pa, Olean (Cattaraugus Co), and Wayland, with a 10 mi (16 km) branch to Hornell (Steuben Co). In 1904 a 9 mi (14 km) branch was built from Paine, south of St. Marys, to Weedville, Pa, on Pennsylvania Railroad (PRR). Pittsburg and Shawmut Railroad (P&S), a 57 mi (92 km) extension from Brockway through Brookville to Mahoning, Pa, was built in 1908 and leased to PS&N. Further access to Pittsburgh was via PRR. In 1905, with the decline of timber and coal resources, PS&N became bankrupt and remained so until its demise in 1947. Passenger service between Brockway and Wayland ended in 1935. P&S survives as a wholly owned subsidiary of Genesee and Wyoming Inc.

Drury, George H., ed. *The Historical Guide to North American Railroads* (Waukesha, Wisc: Kalmbach Publishing, 1985)

Pietrak, Paul. *Pittsburg, Shawmut and Northern Railroad Company* (North Boston, NY: Author, 1969)

Edward T. Dunn

Pittsfield. Town (pop 1,295) in W Otsego Co. Settled about 1792, the town was formed from Burlington in 1797. Population peaked in 1845 at 1,730. The Arkwright Cotton Factory (1832–47) at the hamlet of Hoboken was succeeded on the same site by the large Borden Condensed Milk Co (1899–1920). Former slave James Parish founded a small African American community (1830–1962) on Shacktown Mountain. The former resort cottages at Silver Lake are now year-round homes. The town is economically linked to New Berlin (Chenango Co) across the Unadilla River.

Hugh C. MacDougall

Pittsford. Town (pop 27,219) and village (pop 1,418) in SE Monroe Co. Settled in 1789, the town was formed from the old town of Smallwood in 1814. The village was the site of Monroe Co's first schoolhouse (1794), first library (Northfield Library Co, 1803), and first newspaper (*Gospel Herald,* 1815), and was incorporated in 1827. As a result of the Erie Canal (1822), canal warehouses were rapidly built. The canal, along with the Auburn and Rochester Railroad (1840; later New York Central), fostered commercial development in the village while the town remained largely agricultural, with suburban development after 1950. It is the site of Nazareth College, St. John Fisher College, and the Pittsford Plaza mall. Graflex (1957) formerly manufactured cameras, tape recorders, and projectors. The Village of Pittsford, with a developed landing on the Erie Canal, has retained many historic 19th-century buildings, especially in its retail center. Pittsford's Greenprint (1996), a plan to preserve 67% of the town's farmland and other undeveloped land, has received national recognition as a model for other communities.

Carolyn Vacca

Pittstown. Town (pop 5,644) in N Rensselaer Co. Patented as a township in 1761 and settled soon afterward, Pittstown was made part of Schaghticoke District in 1772. The town was formed in 1788. In the mid–19th century flax was grown extensively, supplying local linen mills. Manufactured goods included cordage, paper, cotton bags, and axes made by the American Edge Tool Co (1859–1906) of Johnsonville; shirtmaking provided home work for farm women. Tomhannock Reservoir (1902–5) flooded valley farms to provide water for Troy, and the Johnsonville Dam (1906) generates waterpower for Niagara Mohawk. The town remains a mix of farms and limited suburban development.

Kathryn T. Sheehan

pizza. This dish, originally a specialty of the peasants of Naples, Italy, was introduced to New York State by emigrants from that area who arrived in New York City in the late 19th century. Made for home use in commercial bakers' ovens, pizza began to appear in bakeries in Italian neighborhoods. Gennaro Lombardi opened a grocery store in New York City's Little Italy in 1897 and started making pizzas in the bakery oven in 1905, later adding tables to his store, thus establishing the country's first pizzeria. His descendants continue to make pizzas at Lombardi's, now just a few blocks from its original location on Spring St. Lombardi went on to train many of New York City's best-known *pizzaioli* (pizza makers), several of whom opened their own pizzerias, including Totonno's and Grimaldi's. In these shops the New York style of pizza was born: crust thin in the center but puffy and breadlike on the outer edges, topped with mozzarella cheese, fresh tomatoes or tomato sauce, and perhaps toppings such as sausage and roasted peppers or other vegetables. The fresh dough and ingredients were cooked in coal-fired ovens at extremely high temperatures on a stone or rack but no pan. Little Italy's *pizzaioli* modified the traditional recipe in various ways, such as using cow's milk mozzarella instead of the water buffalo variety favored in Naples. The New York pizzas were also much larger than their Neopolitan counterparts.

By the 1920s pizzerias could be found in Italian enclaves in cities throughout New York and other northeastern states, but pizza was still eaten mainly by Italian immigrants and their children. Following World War II, however, pizza started to gain popularity outside the ethnic neighborhoods, as soldiers who had spent time in Naples returned home with fond memories of the specialty. Greek Americans, who began operating pizzerias in significant numbers during the 1950s, discovered ways to prepare dough in advance, which allowed pizza to become a fast food market item. Franchised pizza chain restaurants spread across New York State and the country in the 1960s. Pizza emerged as a grocery store item, with companies such as Totino's and Kraft Foods developing and distributing frozen pizzas, and began to lose its ethnic associations, becoming instead an essential component of American cuisine. Today chain pizzerias and privately owned pizza shops can be found in every city and town in New York State, and grocery stores carry a wide variety of frozen pizza, but these little resemble the original pies served in Little Italy's bakeries and pizzerias. There has been in recent years, however, a resurgence of interest in pizzas as created by the Neopolitan immigrants of a century ago, making "New York–style" pizza distinctive.

Asimov, Eric. "New York Pizza, the Real Thing, Makes a Comeback," *New York Times,* 10 June 1998

Gabaccia, Donna. *We Are What We Eat: Ethnic Food and the Making of Americans* (Cambridge, Mass: Harvard Univ Press, 1998)

Levenstein, Harvey. *Paradox of Plenty: A Social History of Eating in Modern America,* rev ed. (Berkeley: Univ of California Press, 2003)

Cindy R. Lobel

place-names. As people from New York State and elsewhere migrated west, they often looked to the East Coast for inspiration in naming their new towns, giving some locales familiar New York State names. Not all were named for similar New York communities: some "Hudsons" were named for people such as explorer Henry Hudson (Hudson Co, NJ), Daniel Hudson (Hudson, Mich), or David Hudson (Hudson, Ohio). But the frequency with which New York State names appear nationwide (outside of New York State) is striking: Brooklyn, 160 places, Albany 130, Manhattan 108, Saratoga 105, Rochester 101, Utica 87, and Syracuse 34. In many cases there are direct links between the spread of these names and New York origins. The name New York itself identifies 138 places beyond the state's borders.

Auburn, used for 317 other places nationwide, was named for the 1770 Oliver Goldsmith poem "The Deserted Village." The line, "Sweet Auburn, loveliest village of the plain" provided the inspiration for this growing Cayuga Co community in the early 1800s. Auburn, Calif, was named directly for New York State's Auburn by men from Central New York who arrived at a mining camp in 1849. Auburn, Iowa, and Auburn, Ky, were also named directly from New York's Auburn. Other names that came from New York State include Geneseo, Ill; Moscow and Lansing, Mich; Oneonta Park, Calif; Bronx, Wyo; Genesee Park and Gowanda, Colo; Niagara, Ky; and Oneida, Tenn. The name Saratoga appeared in Kentucky, Nebraska, Utah, and Wyoming. Some of these places no longer exist, but New York State directly influenced their initial naming.

In some instances, New Yorkers who attained fame affected the naming of places outside the state. Theodore Roosevelt's name was used in a number of places that he visited or influenced because of his land conservation policies (the Dakotas, Louisiana, Montana), and his distant cousin Franklin D. Roosevelt also was a source of naming. There are 558 place-names starting with Roosevelt outside of New York State. In Tennessee Clinton was named for De Witt Clinton or George Clinton, both New York State governors.

Another fertile source of place-names has been Indian nations located in New York State, especially the names Seneca (used for 209 places) and Mohawk (160 places). New York State places and people have also been assigned to sites outside the United States. There is a Brooklyn Island off the coast of Antarctica, and at greater distances there is an Albany Crater on Mars. A crater on the Moon was named after Albany scientist Joseph Henry, and one on Venus named after Rochester suffragist Susan B. Anthony.

CLASSICAL PLACE-NAMES IN NEW YORK STATE

Locality (County)	Derivation
Apulia (Onondaga)	District of ancient Italy
Arcadia (Wayne)	Province of ancient Greece
Athens (Greene)	Greek city-state
Attica (Wyoming)	Alternative name for Athens
Aurelius (Cayuga)	Probably Marcus Aurelius, Roman emperor, AD 121–180
Brutus (Cayuga)	Probably Marcus Junius Brutus, assassin of Julius Caesar, 85–42 BC
Camillus (Onondaga)	Marcus Furius Camillus, Roman commander, ?454–365 BC
Carthage (Jefferson)	Ancient North African city
Cato (Cayuga)	Probably Marcus Porcius Cato, Roman politician and general, 95–46 BC
Ceres (Allegany)	Roman goddess of agriculture
Cicero (Onondaga)	Marcus Tullius Cicero, Roman politician and author, 106–43 BC
Cincinnatus (Cortland)	Lucius Quinctius Cincinnatus, Roman consul and general, ?519–439 BC
Corfu (Genesee)	Island in Ionian Sea
Corinth (Saratoga)	Greek city-state
Delphi Falls (Onondaga)	Greek Oracle site
Etna (Tompkins)	Sicilian volcano
Euclid (Onondaga)	Greek mathematician, *fl* 300 BC
Fabius (Onondaga)	Fabius Maximus Cunctator, Roman general, 303–203 BC
Galen (Wayne)	Claudius Galenus, Greek physician, 129–?199 AD
Greece (Monroe)	Name of country
Hannibal (Oswego)	Carthaginian general, 247–183 BC
Hector (Schuyler)	Hero of Trojan War
Homer (Cortland)	Greek epic poet, *fl* ?8th century BC
Ilion (Herkimer)	Alternative name for ancient Troy
Ionia (Ontario)[a]	Ancient name for western Turkish coast
Ithaca (Tompkins)	Greek island and legendary home of Odysseus, hero of *The Odyssey*
Junius (Seneca)	Probably Lucius Junius Brutus, a founder of the Roman Republic, *fl* late 6th century BC
Lysander (Onondaga)	Spartan naval commander, *d* 395 BC
Macedon (Wayne)	Greek kingdom
Manlius (Onondaga)	Possibly Marcus Manlius Capitolinus, Roman consul, *fl* early 4th century BC
Marathon (Cortland)	Ancient Greek battle site
Marcellus (Onondaga)	Marcus Claudius Marcellus, Roman general, ?268–208 BC or Marcus Claudius Marcellus, Roman general, 43–23 BC
Medusa (Albany)	Mythological monster
Milo (Yates)	Probably Titus Annius Papianus Milo, Roman tribune, 95–48 BC
Minerva (Essex)	Greek goddess of wisdom
Mycenae (Onondaga)	Ancient Greek city

The trend of assigning Greco-Roman names to places started in New York State in 1789 with the choice of the name Troy for a town on the Hudson River in what is now Rensselaer Co. In 1790 commissioners of the New York State Land Office were charged with naming and dispensing of the New Military Tract in Central New York, land reserved as payment for veterans of the Revolutionary War. The tract had been surveyed into 25 sections, each of which was made into a town and identified. The choice of classical names was credited to Simeon DeWitt, surveyor general of New York State, but he later denied it, as did the land commissioners themselves. It seems a deputy secretary of state, Robert R. Harpur, penned Greco-Roman names on the map the land commissioners were given to use in their task of land divestment.

The tract names were initially those of military men: Lysander, Hannibal, Cato, Camillus, Cicero, Manlius, Marcellus, Scipio, Sempronius, Tully, Fabius, Aurelius, and Romulus; then came various poets, philosophers, and other warriors: Ovid, Homer, Solon, Hector, Ulysses, Virgil, Junius, Brutus, and Cincinnatus. The names of these towns opened the way to using classical names in the rest of the state. What might be considered the "classical belt" extends through Cayuga, Cortland, Onondaga, Oswego, Seneca, Tompkins, and Wayne Cos. Using classical names let the settlers of New York State show Europeans that this new frontier was populated by learned, genteel folk who knew their history and culture, not by barbaric adventurers. This movement provided the state with names like Ithaca, Syracuse, Rome, Utica, Ilion, Attica, Delphi Falls, Marathon, Pompey, and Milo.

Harder, Kelsie B., ed. *Illustrated Dictionary of Place Names: United States and Canada* (New York: Facts on File, 1985)

Stewart, George Ripley. *Names on the Land* (New York: Random House, 1945)

———. *American Place-Names* (New York: Oxford Univ Press, 1970)

Ren Vasiliev

Plainedge. Locality (pop 9,195) in Oyster Bay (Nassau Co). It was known as Turkeyville for one of its farm products. By 1814 the name of Plainedge had been adopted for its location on the eastern edge of the plains. Poultry, pasturage, and hay remained important during the 19th century, but cabbage for sauerkraut and cucumbers for pickling assumed importance late in the

CLASSICAL PLACE-NAMES IN NEW YORK STATE (continued)

Locality (County)	Derivation
Niobe (Chautauqua)	Mythological princess
Ovid (Seneca)	Publius Ovidius Naso, Roman poet, 43 BC–AD 18
Penelope (Cortland)	Wife of Odysseus
Pharsalia (Chenango)	From Pharsalus, ancient Greek city
Phoenicia (Ulster)	Ancient Mediterranean kingdom
Plato (Cattaraugus)	Greek philosopher, 428–347 BC
Plutarch (Ulster)	Greek biographer and historian, AD ?46–120
Pomona (Rockland)	Roman goddess of fruit
Pompey (Onondaga)	Gnaeus Pompeius Magnus, Roman general, 106–48 BC
Rome (Oneida)	Italian city
Romulus (Seneca)	Mythological founder of Rome
Scio (Allegany)	Ancient Greek seaport
Scipio (Cayuga)	Publius Scipio Africanus, Roman general, 237–183 BC
Sempronius (Cayuga)	Tiberius Sempronius Gracchus (163–133 BC) and Gauis Sempronius Gracchus (153–121 BC), Roman tribunes and agrarian reformers
Seneca Lake[b]	Roman consul and playwright, 4 BC–AD 65
Smyrna (Chenango)	Ancient Greek seaport
Solon (Cortland)	Athenian politician and lawgiver, ?638–?558 BC
Sparta (Livingston)	Greek city-state
Syracuse (Onondaga)	Ancient Sicilian city
Troy (Rensselaer)	Ancient city in Asia Minor
Tully (Onondaga)	Marcus Tullius Cicero, Roman politician and author, 106–43 BC
Ulysses (Tompkins)	Roman name of Odysseus
Utica (Oneida)	Ancient North African city
Varna (Tompkins)	Ancient Black Sea port
Vestal (Broome)	Roman priestess of the goddess Vesta
Virgil (Cortland)	Publius Vergilius Maro, Roman poet, 70–19 BC

Sources: W. R. Farrell, *Classical Place Names in New York State: Origins, Histories, and Meanings* (2002); G. R. Stewart, *Names on the Land: A Historical Account of Placenaming in the United States* (1982); and G. R. Stewart, *American Place-Names: A Concise and Selective Dictionary for the Continental United States of America* (1970).

Note: This table does not include names derived from a common source and is limited to place-names from Greco-Roman antiquity.

[a]Also a locality in Onondaga Co.

[b]The oldest "classical" place-name in New York State, in use before the end of the 18th century, though probably derived from the European name for the westernmost Iroquois nation and not the Roman literary figure. Also used in the name of a county (Seneca) and a town (Seneca Falls).

century before being hit by a blight early in the 20th century; potatoes became an important crop but were also hit by a blight in the 1940s. After World War II the area rapidly developed, and its population peaked at 11,072 in 1960.

Richard A. Winsche

Plainfield. Town (pop 986) in NW Otsego Co. Settled in 1793, the town was formed from Richfield in 1799. Always predominantly agricultural, it had some small enterprises, including an early oil mill and cloth factory and a hoe factory (*ca* 1860). Population peaked at 2,940 in 1814. Hamlets in town are Unadilla Forks, at the meeting of the east and west branches of the Unadilla River, and Plainfield Center, site of a small Welsh settlement (1853) and the Shiloh Congregational Church (1861–1941). Plainfield remained a farming town; 11% of its workers engaged in agriculture in 2000, and most others commuted.

Hugh C. MacDougall

Plainview. Locality (pop 25,637) in Oyster Bay (Nassau Co). The Matinecock Indians originally called the area Manetto Hill. In 1837 the arrival of the railroad at nearby Hicksville made New York City an easy market for its farmers. In 1886 the new post office took the name Plainview from the clear view of the adjacent Hempstead Plains. Potatoes and cucumbers were the principal crops, but both were hit by blights in the early 20th century, after which farmers began to sell out to developers. The population grew from 527 in 1940 to 31,695 in 1970 but has aged and declined moderately since then. Chiefly residential, Plainview has a large Jewish community.

Laura E. Mann

Plandome {Plandome, village (pop 1,450) in North Hempstead, Nassau Co; Plandome Heights, village (pop 971) in North Hempstead; Plandome Manor, village (pop 838) in North Hempstead}. The Plandomes lie on the east shore of Manhasset Bay, just north of the locality of Manhasset. Plandome Manor's land once belonged to Matthias Nicolls, mayor of New York City in 1672; his house was demolished in 2000. Development began shortly after the Long Island Rail Road was extended to Port Washington in 1898; a group of New Yorkers purchased 90 acres (36 ha) in what is now Plandome, and in 1905 the land was subdivided into lots, many of which were sold to teachers. More affluent buyers, including dancers Irene and Vernon Castle, soon followed, and author Frances Hodgson Burnett lived in Plandome for two decades before her death in 1924. The Village of Plandome was incorporated in 1911; its name is from the Latin *planus domus* (plain home). Development of Plandome Heights began in 1909 when tobacco heir Benjamin Duke purchased the land from the American Bible Society and formed the Plandome Heights Corp. The bluffs along the shore were sold to Gallagher Sand and Gravel Co. During the 1920s Plandome Heights grew rapidly as the Manhasset Hill Realty Co sold building lots to New York City executives; it incorporated in 1929 and expanded in 1949 by annexing the 92 brick houses of Chester Hill. Plandome Manor, now the site of the Long Island Science Museum, incorporated as a village in 1931. The only public building in Plandome Heights, which has 320 houses, is Manhasset Baptist Church (1956).

Joan Gay Kent

plank roads. Wooden-surfaced toll roads popular in many states between 1846 and 1860. Constructed of transverse planks laid on longitudinal stringers, the smooth road surface eliminated mud and pothole problems, increased the speed and efficiency of draft animals, and decreased wear and tear on wagons. With plentiful wood supplies, plank roads were as much as 50% cheaper than macadam roads. New Yorkers borrowed the plank road concept from Canada and completed the first American plank road between Salina (Onondaga Co) and Central Square (Oswego Co) in 1846. Over the next seven years, New York became the leading plank road state with over 3,500 miles (5,630 km) of road built by 350 companies. Plank roads were built in all areas of the state except the Catskills and Adirondacks. Most mileage was concentrated in a rough quadrilateral defined by Utica, Marcellus (Onondaga Co), Oswego, and Ogdensburg (St. Lawrence Co), where it facilitated the growth of dairy farming. Plank roads also radiated from all major cities. Local investors built plank roads both as profit-making ventures and to improve the beds of old turnpikes. Most plank roads stretched less than 20 mi (32 km) and linked farms, mills, and mines with the nearest market town, canal port, or railroad station. They provided cheap, efficient access for areas bypassed by state canals and the first railroads. Promoters thought that plank roads would last eight years and pay annual dividends of as much as 20% of initial investment. Experience revealed that wood set in earth rotted in half that time and that few roads earned even 10%. As a result the plank road boom collapsed around 1854. Some roads were converted to dirt, gravel, or macadam toll roads or turnpikes, but most reverted to toll-free, common dirt roads over the next decade. Only 32 plank road companies filed for reincorporation after 30 years.

Kingsford, William. *History, Structure, and Statistics of Plank Roads in the United States and Canada* (Philadelphia: A. Hart, 1851)

Klein, Daniel B., and John Majewski. "Plank Road Fever in Antebellum America: New York State Origins," *New York History* 75 (Jan 1994): 39–65

Majewski, John, Christopher Baer, and Daniel B. Klein. "Responding to Relative Decline: The Plank Road Boom of Antebellum New York," *Journal of Economic History* 53 (Mar 1993): 106–22

Christopher T. Baer

planning and regional planning associations. As New York City grew northward after the Revolutionary War, it was consistently (al-

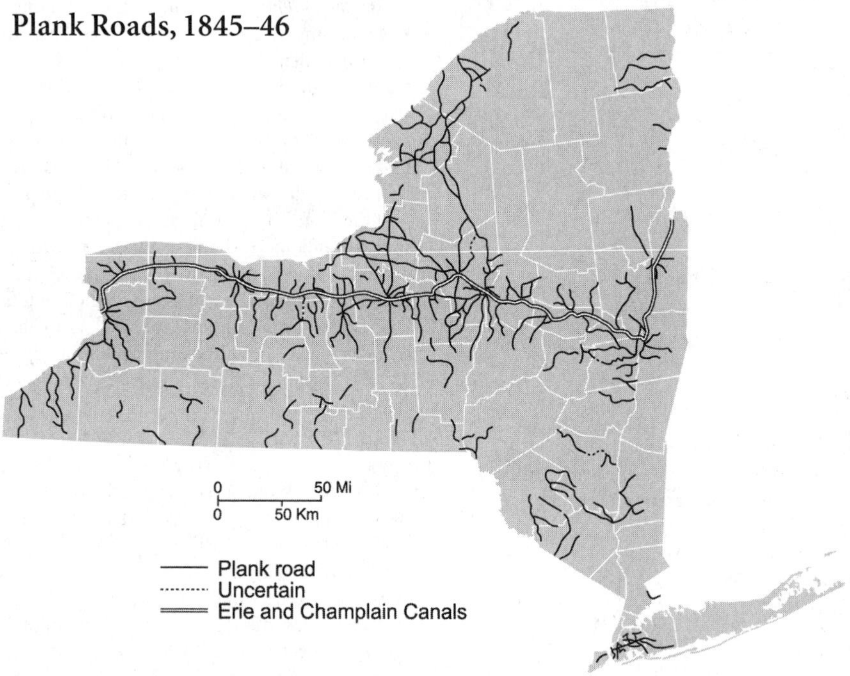

SOURCE: Adapted from J. Majewski, et al, "Responding to Relative Decline," *Journal of Economic History* 53 (1993).

though not uniformly) laid out in a rectangular form. By 1801 the New York State legislature had granted power to New York City to "regulate buildings and street lines" and in 1807 granted further power to "lay out the leading streets and great avenues." Although controversial, the 1811 Commissioners' Plan of New York City imposed a gridiron pattern from North St [now Washington Square] to 155th St, a pattern that still exists. Although Philadelphia originated the American gridiron pattern, as New York City became the dominant economic city in the country, its layout had a profound influence on street patterns and thus on land use in New York State and across the country. The gridiron approach had its negative aspects. A narrow focus just on economic issues, specifically the "buying, selling and improving of real estate," at the expense of aesthetics and practicality resulted in unhealthy, unsafe, and sometimes dangerous land uses in adjoining or nearby locations. As the 18th century wound down, such conditions became intolerable and led to the accession to power in New York City of reform-minded individuals who eventually brought about the country's first zoning regulations in 1916.

Formal Land-Use Regulation

Land-use regulation and control has been part of development and growth in America since colonial times. Community-wide public health and safety and rapid urban growth pushed the need for controls. Building codes, block ordinances, city plans, and nuisance regulations were promulgated in various places, but inevitably as cities grew land use on adjoining or proximal parcels conflicted with each other. There was a need to create so-called zones, in which some zoning became a powerful and effective land-use control. Although the zoning battle was fought on several urban fronts over several different land-use conflicts, it was in New York City that this issue was decided. Recommendations in 1913 by the New York City Commission on the Height and Arrangement of Buildings stated that "height, area, and use" be regulated in the interest of public health and safety, and that the regulations be "adopted to the varying needs of different districts." A comprehensive zoning code, adopted on 25 July 1916 for the entire city, was criticized for not including a planning component, by having no "forecast for future land use demand" to make it effective. Despite shortcomings, the ordinance regulated, for the first time, not just individual buildings but whole districts by imposing different regulations within different zones. It is regarded as the first comprehensive zoning ordinance in the world.

New York State soon addressed planning issues statewide. Although early zoning legislation lacked an overt planning component, it became the linchpin in subsequent planning legislation. In the 1920s the legislature passed the Statute of Local Governments and the Municipal Home Rule Law. Both granted authority to cities, villages, and towns to regulate, at their option, land development and use for "promoting the health, safety, morals, or general welfare of the community." Cities are thus enabled to create an official map, master plan, and planning board. They may modify zoning ordinances, conduct site plan review, issue variances, and review subdivision proposals. Villages are similarly empowered, as are towns, except within villages. Such regulations are usually based on a comprehensive land-use plan. These powerful regulatory tools enable a community to "encourage the most appropriate use of land throughout the municipality."

Municipal regulatory powers over planning and land use have been through many legal challenges in New York State courts. Land-use regulations are entrenched in most, but not all, municipalities in the state. A 1999 survey by the New York State Legislative Commission on Rural Resources found that only 59% of municipalities have a comprehensive plan, 77% have zoning regulations, 70% have subdivision regulations, 64% conduct site plan review, and 86% have a formal planning board. Percentages are higher in cities (where land-use pressures are greatest) and lower in towns and villages. Some would argue that the more distressed landscapes are to be found in municipalities where land-use regulation, and thus formal planning, are nonexistent.

Regional Planning

Of the many kinds of planning practiced in New York State, regional planning is perhaps the most challenging. The purpose of local planning can be defined as establishing a future-oriented agenda that sets objectives and outlines a course of action and organizational structure for development within a particular municipality. Regional planning has a similar purpose but with priorities on issues that have a potential impact on several municipalities, such as a regional highway, sewer system, water delivery system, and waste management. By being multijurisdictional, achieving objectives can sometimes be a daunting task.

Regional planning is practiced at many government levels. Along the border between New York State and Canada (in both western and northern New York State), cooperative agreements exist for such things as recreation, power production, water-level regulation, and immigration. Not all of these relationships are classic regional planning examples, but they all include regional planning considerations and all have an impact on extensive regions. The International Joint Commission (1909) manages lakes and rivers that either cross borders or are crossed by the border between the United States and Canada, such as the Niagara River, Lake Ontario, and the St. Lawrence River.

New York State participates in numerous interstate regional planning efforts. The Regional Plan Association (1922) creates long-term plans in the 31-county New York State–New Jersey–Connecticut metropolitan area. New York is a charter member (1965) of the multistate Appalachian Regional Commission. The planning arm of the commission includes several regional planning boards in the Southern Tier counties of New York State implementing commission programs. The Port Authority of New York and New Jersey and its predecessor, the Port Authority of New York, have been prominent players in the regional planning of the metropolitan area since at least the 1920s. The Port Authority has been the major developer and operator of practically all the major transportation facilities in the region, ranging from the Holland Tunnel and the George Washington Bridge to John F. Kennedy International and La Guardia Airports. Although many of the regional planning boards around the state may have had locally influential members, no one approaches the influence and lasting effect of Robert Moses on land use and planning throughout the state. Beginning in the 1920s and extending into the 1970s, his name, or fingerprints, could be found in the planning and implementation of hundreds of public works projects from Montauk to Massena.

Intrastate Planning

Although many states have statewide comprehensive plans, New York State is not among them. Some New York State agencies do include an element of regional planning, and some state governmental responsibilities such as transportation, environmental conservation, and economic development are organized into formal regions. The Department of Economic Development provides an annual strategic plan for the state in consultation with other state departments and agencies. Although the administrative regions participate in some interagency planning, such activity tends to be isolated by agency and is not considered comprehensive regional planning.

The Adirondack Park Agency (1971) administers a 6 million-acre (2.4 million ha) multijurisdictional area covering parts of 12 counties in northern New York. It is responsible for a comprehensive land-use and development plan for all private and public land within the large forested and mountainous area delineated by the famous Blue Line (on many maps of New York State). There are numerous towns, villages, and hamlets included within the park, and local land use and projects are subject to review and approval by the agency. The park has existed as a large state preserve since 1892.

Other state-created organizations are involved in a regional approach to land use and planning. There are regional organizations such as the Lake George Park Commission (1961) and the Tug Hill Commission (1972). The Lake George Park is entirely within the Adirondack Park, and the commission is responsible for 300 mi^2 (777 km^2) of land and water. The Tug Hill Commission has planning responsibilities within 41 towns and 21 villages in parts of four counties. Additionally there are numerous public authorities and public benefit corporations, development authorities, industrial development agencies, and resource recovery and solid waste disposal authorities throughout the state. Many of them play roles in regional land-use decisions in different areas.

REGIONAL PLANNING COUNCILS AND BOARDS

In 2002 there were nine regional planning councils or boards within New York State representing 45 of the 62 counties. The first boards were established in the 1960s, authorized and funded by the federal government. Later they were restructured under New York State General Municipal Law, particularly Section 239B. Among the early and still functioning boards were the Central New York Regional Planning and Development Board (1966) and the Capital District Regional Planning Commission (1967). Others, such as the Black River–St. Lawrence Regional Planning Board, have disbanded. In the interest of intermunicipal cooperation and comprehensive regional planning New York State also passed legislation in 1960, 1992, and 1993 authorizing municipalities to negotiate intermunicipal agreements and/or to create regional planning boards. Not all regions continue to participate.

Municipalities may enter into cooperative agreements to accomplish their land-use goals and into an intermunicipal agreement for any function they can perform alone. Within the state there are several examples in which intermunicipal agreements have been made. In 1982 the Town and Village of Lowville (Lewis Co) established a joint planning board and a joint zoning board of appeals. In 1994 the Town and Village of Castile and the Village of Perry (Wyoming Co) amended their respective zoning regulations to coordinate development and preservation efforts within the three municipalities. In 1994, 10 villages and towns in Westchester Co created an intermunicipal agreement to improve local economic development in their portion of the Hudson River watershed. There are also examples of situations in which several years of discussion and negotiation have not resulted in an agreement. The City and Town of Ithaca, Village and Town of Lansing, Village of Cayuga Heights, and Town of Dryden (Tompkins Co), after negotiating the details of an intermunicipal sewer project for six years, had not as of late 2003 come to a final agreement.

Regional planning boards attempt to reflect the legislature's intent to bring comprehensive planning to appropriate regional alliances. The boards are empowered to conduct surveys and studies, create a comprehensive plan for their region, and participate in some municipal land-use decisions as appropriate. The regional comprehensive plans consider many topics in a regionwide context, including land-use intensity, agriculture, historic and cultural resources, environmental issues, population trends, transportation, infrastructure, and public facilities. An important component of the finished comprehensive regional plan is a strategy for implementation.

Significant geographical areas are not part of any formal regional planning, and many intrastate regional planning organizations are limited in that they cannot exercise direct, statutory governing authority. While dealing with regional issues, the constituent members often report back to other units of government or make nonbinding recommendations. Thus there is often the challenge of a regional planning organization trying to convince local and independent constituent governments to cooperate in the best interests of the larger area. There is no shortage of available planning tools or statutes in New York State. In 2002 over 40 special land-use tools exist by law, along with nearly 400 state statutes on land-use planning, regulation, and development.

Cullingworth, J. Barry. *The Political Culture of Planning: American Land Use Planning in Comparative Perspective* (New York: Routledge, 1993)
Makielski, S. J., Jr. *The Politics of Zoning: The New York Experience* (New York and London: Columbia Univ Press, 1966)
Meck, Stuart. *Growing Smart Legislative Guidebook: Model Statutes for Planning and the Management of Change* (Chicago: American Planning Association, 2002)
New York State Legislative Commission on Rural Resources. *Land Use Planning and Regulation in New York State Municipalities: A Survey* (Albany, 1999)
Nolon, John R. *Well Grounded: Shaping the Destiny of the Empire State, Local Land Use Law and Practice* (White Plains, NY: Pace Univ School of Law, 1998)
Reps, John W. *The Making of Urban America: A History of City Planning in the United States* (Princeton, NJ: Princeton Univ Press, 1965)
So, Frank S., Irving Hand, and Bruce D. McDowell. *The Practice of State and Regional Planning* (Washington, DC: International City Management Association, 1986)

Douglas B. McDonald

Plan of Union. An 1801 agreement between the General Assembly of the Presbyterian Church and the General Association of Congregational Churches in Connecticut (soon endorsed by other New England Congregational bodies) to cooperate in establishing churches in Central New York and on the western frontier. Since many clergy of both churches were trained at Yale, Princeton, and Andover Theological Seminary and moved easily between Congregational and Presbyterian churches, the partnership was the practical extension of a long-standing relationship. After 1826 it was administered by the newly formed American Home Missionary Society. Although the plan was never intended as a means of denominational merger, Congregationalists believed it undermined their growth as many new churches affiliated with presbyteries. Presbyterians worried that Congregationalists were less than orthodox in their Calvinism; the Old School Presbyterian Church repudiated the plan after the 1837 New School–Old School split. Congregationalists terminated it at the 1852 Albany Convention.

Walker, Williston. *The Creeds and Platforms of Congregationalism* (1893; repr New York: Pilgrim Press, 1991)

Charles E. Hambrick-Stowe

plate tectonics. See GEOLOGY AND PLATE TECTONICS.

Platt, Jonas (*b* Poughkeepsie, 30 June 1769; *d* Peru, Clinton Co, 22 Feb 1834). Lawyer, politician, and judge. Platt read law in Richard Varick's New York City office and was admitted to the bar in 1790. He married Helen Livingston the same year. He practiced in Poughkeepsie before moving to Whitesboro [now in Oneida Co], serving as county clerk of Herkimer Co and then Oneida Co until 1802. Platt simultaneously practiced law, served as county clerk, and was a Federalist assemblyman (1795). In Congress (1798–1801) he defended the 1798 Sedition Act and supported Aaron Burr in the House vote of 1801. During the first decade of the 19th century, Platt continued his law practice and remained politically active. In 1810 he lost the gubernatorial election to Daniel D. Tompkins but began the first of three consecutive terms in the state senate. An early supporter of a western canal, Platt feared his Federalist identity would harm the cause and yielded leadership of the canal campaign to De Witt Clinton. Platt supported Clinton's presidential candidacy in 1812, and Clintonians joined Federalists in securing Platt's nomination to the New York State Supreme Court in 1814. Platt's nine-year judicial career was not particularly notable. In one dissent he urged that Congress delegate authority to state courts, yet in another opinion he maintained that militia were protected by state sovereignty and not subject to the president. At the 1821 Constitutional Convention, Platt was generally in the minority opposed to change and watched the convention legislate him out of office. A move by Gov Joseph C. Yates to appoint him to the new court was defeated, and his move to private practice in New York City, where he had never previously practiced, was not a happy one. His last years were marred by ill health.

Roper, Donald M. "The Elite of the New York Bar as Seen from the Bench: James Kent's Necrologies," *The New-York Historical Society Quarterly* 56 (July 1972): 199–237

Donald M. Roper

Platt, Thomas C(ollier) (*b* Owego, Tioga Co, 15 July 1833; *d* New York City, 6 Mar 1910). US senator and representative. Platt worked as a druggist, newspaper editor, and bank president in Tioga Co before he entered politics full time. He was elected clerk of Tioga Co in 1859 and later became chair of the county Republican committee. With the support of Roscoe Conkling, Platt served two terms in the US House of Representatives (1873–77) and joined Conkling in the US Senate in 1881. Following his mentor, Platt resigned almost immediately in a struggle over patronage, thereby earning the nickname Me Too Platt. With Conkling he sought vindication in a new election, but he withdrew his name in the deadlock that followed in the state legislature. Unlike Conkling, Platt regained his power in New York politics, eventually consolidating his control over patronage and developing friendships with powerful business leaders. By the 1890s Platt's Republican "machine" ruled much of New York State. He served as a US senator again from 1897 to 1909, but New York State politics remained his primary interest. Platt's nonthreatening style and appeal to a wide range of citizenry earned him the sobriquet the Easy Boss. He was largely responsible for the election of Theodore Roosevelt as governor in 1898. But following Roosevelt's independent actions as governor, Platt helped push him into what Platt expected to be an uneventful term as vice president in 1900. Platt's power waned in his last years with the ascendancy of Roosevelt to the presidency, Charles Evans Hughes's rise to power in New York, and the extension of civil service.

Gosnell, Harold. *Boss Platt and His New York Machine* (1924; repr New York: Russell & Russell, 1969)
McCormick, Richard L. *From Realignment to Reform: Political Change in New York State, 1893–1910* (Ithaca: Cornell Univ Press, 1981)

Jon Sterngass

Plattekill [PLAT-TE-KILL]. Town (pop 9,892) in SE Ulster Co. Settled in the early 18th century, the town was formed in 1800 from Marlborough. Many of its settlers were from Westchester Co, some of them Quakers. In the 19th century, apple and grape growing became important; grape culture ended around 1930, but cultivation resumed after 1960. The town was served by the Central New England Railroad (1889–1983). In the 1930s hotels serving Spaniards created the largest Latino resort in the East, which peaked in the 1960s with the arrival of Cubans and Puerto Ricans but faded after the 1970s. By the 1980s many residents commuted to work in Orange and Dutchess Cos.

Ruth Piwonka

Plattsburgh. Town (pop 11,190) and city (pop 18,816) in E Clinton Co. Located where the Saranac River empties into Lake Champlain, the Ramezay-la-Gesse seigneury (1749) was granted by the French but never settled. In 1769 the British government granted land near the mouth of the Saranac to Charles de Fredenburgh, a British army officer of German Swiss birth, who built a house and sawmill but left in 1775. In 1784 New York State granted 33,000 acres (13,355 ha) to Zephaniah Platt and 32 others, 12 of whom settled on the tract beginning in 1785. The town was formed in that year and became the county seat in 1788. Migrants from the Hudson Valley, Quebec, Vermont, and elsewhere in New England were drawn by available land, the excellent harbor, and mill sites on the Saranac. Industries developed to process the natural resources of the Saranac watershed, including fulling, carding, and dyeing mills, sawmills, gristmills, oil mills, tanneries, asheries, and distilleries. The first forge (1798) used the Saranac's waterpower to process ore from Monkton, Vt, and later from Port Henry (Essex Co). Located near the Canadian frontier, Plattsburgh was exposed to raids during the War of 1812 and in September 1814 was the site of both a land engagement, in which part of the village was burned, and a decisive naval battle. Four British ships surrendered and their army retreated. The US Military Reservation (703 acres/284 ha) was created in 1813; many of its buildings date from 1838.

The village incorporated in 1815. The opening of the Champlain Canal (1823) connected Plattsburgh and its entire trading region to national and international markets through the Hudson River. Plattsburgh expanded as a banking and mercantile center. With the 1829 creation of a canal to further harness the Saranac's waterpower, milling increased as well. The failure of the Papineau rebellion (1837–38) in Quebec resulted in the migration of Francophone Canadians southward, where they joined the earliest Irish immigrants to organize St. Peter's Church in 1853. As late as 1940 half of Plattsburgh's population was reckoned to be of French descent. Plattsburgh's mercantile character attracted Jews who, in 1861, incorporated the earliest synagogue in New York State north of Albany. The excellent lake transportation tended to retard investment in rail lines. Plattsburgh was connected to Montreal in 1852, but it was not until 1875 that a line to Whitehall (Washington Co) linked it to Albany. In 1876 a direct line to Rouses Point created an improved route to Montreal; rails were also laid to Dannemora in 1879 and to Au Sable Forks (Essex Co) in 1894.

Plattsburgh's first school, underwritten by mill owners, opened in 1786. In 1811 an academy was organized, and a union school (1867) provided public secondary education. Founded in 1889 Plattsburgh Normal School produced teachers for many North Country schools. Late in the 19th century, marble sawing and ice cutting were added to Plattsburgh's industrial mix; the latter employed 5,000 men seasonally in its heyday from about 1890 to about 1940. Plattsburgh incorporated as a city in 1902. In addition to marble and ice, 20th-century products included ironwork, furniture, clocks, sewing machines, typewriters, shirts, razor blades, dynamite, paper, and the Lozier Automobile (1906–14). Pre–World War I military preparedness for college students and businessmen at the Military Reservation in 1915 and 1916 became nationally known as the Plattsburgh Idea and was a forerunner of the Reserve Officer's Training Corps (ROTC). During Prohibition, Plattsburgh was a depot for the transshipment of illegal alcohol from Canada. The Military Reservation was turned over to New York State and became the site of the short-lived Champlain College (1946–53), a liberal arts institution for veterans. It closed when the federal government reacquired the land for the Plattsburgh Air Force Base (1955). Its economic effect on the city and town was considerable. The city also became more accessible for tourism and business when the Northway opened to Canada in 1965 and to points south in 1967. Plattsburgh Normal School had become a teachers college and then a state university college in 1948; in the early 21st century it is SUNY Plattsburgh, graduating over 1,000 students annually with bachelor's and master's degrees in education, business, and the liberal arts.

The air base closed in 1995, causing an outflow of people and resources: the city lost 11% of its population between 1990 and 2000, while the town lost 35%. Since the closing, however, the community has recovered by attracting new retail businesses, new industrial and service firms, especially Bombardier Transportation (rail and subway cars), Pratt and Whitney (aircraft engines), and other enterprises on the former air base land.

Everest, Allan S. *Briefly Told: Plattsburgh, NY, 1784–1984* (Plattsburgh: Clinton County Historical Association, 1984)

Thomas A. Rumney

Plattsburgh, Battle of. American victory during the War of 1812. Also known as the Battle of Lake Champlain, the engagement occurred near Plattsburgh. In early 1814, after more than a year of naval skirmishes and the refitting of existing vessels, American and British navies began a shipbuilding race at their respective shipyards at Vergennes, Vt, and Isle-aux-Noix, Que, an island in the Richelieu River north of Lake Champlain. The completed American fleet, under the command of Master Commandant Thomas Macdonough, consisted of the 26-gun, 143 ft (43.6 m) ship *Saratoga*, the 17-gun, 120 ft (36.6 m) schooner *Ticonderoga*, the 20-gun, 117 ft (35.7 m) brig *Eagle*, and the 9-gun sloop *Preble*, along with six galleys and four gunboats.

On 31 Aug 1814 British troops began pouring across the Canadian border. By 6 Sept 1814, 8,200 British troops reached Plattsburgh, with 2,100 additional soldiers stationed at outposts between the town and the border. Plattsburgh quickly fell to British control, but British commander Gen Sir George Prevost delayed an attack on Forts Scott, Brown, and Moreau, just south of Plattsburgh, until the British fleet arrived from Isle-aux-Noix. He later suggested that his plan was to use Plattsburgh as a base for an attack on the Vergennes naval yard.

On the morning of 11 Sept 1814 Capt George Downie entered Plattsburgh Bay with the British fleet made up of the flagship *Confiance*, the *Linnet*, *Chub*, and *Finch*, and 12 gunboats. Downie prematurely anchored the *Confiance* at a distance from the *Saratoga* after having two anchors shot away and immediately commenced firing with a double-shotted broadside. Fifteen minutes after the action had begun, Capt Downie was killed when a shot from the *Saratoga* struck a cannon aboard the *Confiance*, throwing it completely off its carriage into him. He died instantly. Late in the battle Macdonough's starboard cannons were nearly all damaged. By a prearranged plan, the *Saratoga*'s stern anchor was disengaged and the bow cable cut, allowing the flagship to be turned end to end so that fresh guns could be brought into action. By then the *Confiance* had been torn to pieces. When the British flagship attempted to duplicate the turning maneuver, it became stranded with its bow facing the *Saratoga.* A short time later the commanding officer surrendered the *Confiance,* and at 11:20 AM Capt Daniel Pring surrendered the *Linnet.*

During the course of the naval battle, American brigadier general Alexander Macomb's vastly outnumbered troops successfully defended the three forts on the south side of the Saranac River. Prevost began a massive artillery assault on the forts coordinated with the start of the naval battle. Some of his troops were able to ford the Saranac, but they did not have time to attack Forts Scott, Brown, and Moreau before the surrender of the British fleet. On hearing of the surrender, Prevost halted the attack on the forts and then ordered the army to return to Canada. The Treaty of Ghent was signed on Christmas Eve 1814, ending the war. The American success at Plattsburgh has often been called, notably by Sir Winston Churchill, the most decisive victory of the War of 1812.

Bellico, Russell P. *Sails and Steam in the Mountains: A Maritime and Military History of Lake George and Lake Champlain,* 2d ed. (Fleischmanns, NY: Purple Mountain Press, 2001)
Crisman, Kevin J. *The Eagle: An American Brig on Lake Champlain during the War of 1812* (Shelburne, Vt: New England Press, 1987)
Everest, Allen S. *The War of 1812 in the Champlain Valley* (Syracuse: Syracuse Univ Press, 1981)

Russell P. Bellico

Plattsburgh Air Force Base (AFB). Plattsburgh Barracks was established as a military site in 1814 when the federal government bought 200 acres (81 ha) of land on the shore of Lake Champlain near the Saranac River in Clinton Co and stationed troops there. The first permanent stone barracks were built in 1838. From 1946 until 1953 the facility was used for Champlain College for returning World War II veterans. Plattsburgh AFB, authorized in 1953, consisted of a 3,200-acre (1,295 ha) expansion of Plattsburgh Barracks from the Saranac River on the north to the Salmon River on the south. Plattsburgh AFB was a Strategic Air Command (SAC) bomber base from 1955 to 1991, home to the 380th Bombardment Wing. The location was suitable for SAC polar routes, initially using B-47s, then B-52s starting in 1966, and FB-111s starting in 1971, as well as KC-135 air refueling tankers. In the 1960s the base was also home to the 56th Strategic Missile Squadron, which brought the Atlas F, the first operational intercontinental ballistic missiles (ICBMs) fitted with nuclear warheads, to Plattsburgh in October 1961. The Atlas F was removed from alert in June 1965. In 1991 the base was reassigned to the 380th Air Refueling Wing as part of the Air Mobility Command. The base was officially closed 30 Sept 1995. In 2000 aircraft manufacturer Pratt and Whitney established an airplane design and testing facility on the grounds.

Yenne, Bill. *SAC: A Primer of Modern Strategic Airpower* (Novato, Calif: Presidio Press, 1985)

Michael J. Stenzel

Plattsburgh Movement. US Army general Leonard Wood established the Business Man's Training Camp for civilian military training in 1915 at Plattsburgh Barracks. The program intended to provide basic military skills, promote leadership, and enlist popular support for American intervention in the European Great War, later called World War I. Attendees of the camp included New York politicians, professors, journalists, and celebrities; among them were New York City mayor John Purroy Mitchel, *New York Times* general manager Julius Ochs Adler, Quentin Roosevelt, and Theodore Roosevelt. Financed privately by Bernard Baruch and promoted by prominent men such as Theodore Roosevelt and by industrialists and university presidents, the civilian training camp produced affirmative press for the army and encouraged the idea of war preparedness.

Because of controversy over America's position of neutrality and the future of America's military forces, Gen Wood faced opposition to his plans for expansion of the Plattsburgh camp until upheaval in Mexico in 1916 led to American intervention. Gen John Pershing led troops across the border, yet the addition of militias from several states was insufficient if the conflict escalated to war. In response Congress passed the National Defense Act of 1916, which was critical to the success of the Plattsburgh Movement. This authorized federal funding for training camps for professional men, the recruitment of a volunteer army in times of war, and the creation of the Reserve Officer's Training Corps (ROTC). Under the terms of the National Defense Act, Grenville Clark began conversion of the Business Man's Training Camp into a military training facility for officers, and the War Department authorized the creation of 15 other training camps. Based on the Plattsburgh model, they were known as Citizens' Military Training Camps. Each camp had nine infantry companies, one or two cavalry troops, three field artillery batteries, and one engineering company. Each location accepted 2,500 candidates for a three-month training program that collectively produced over 27,000 commissioned officers for service in World War I. The Plattsburgh Movement initiated a new format for war with the reserve system, national training standards, and military and industrial collaboration. The Citizens' Military Training Camps were maintained through 1940. The army ROTC program commissioned a minimum of 5,000 officers each year until 1940. After World War II ROTC became the armed forces primary source of officers.

Allen-Hanks, Kristen. "The First 10,000: War Preparedness and the Plattsburgh Training Camp Movement," *Antiquarian* 18 (Fall 2001): 7–15.
Clifford, John. *The Citizen Soldiers: The Plattsburgh Training Camp Movement, 1913–1920* (Lexington: Univ of Kentucky Press, 1972)
Kington, Donald. *Forgotten Summers: The Story of the Citizens' Military Training Camps* (San Francisco, Calif: Two Decades Publishing, 1995)

Kristen L. Allen-Hanks

Plattsburgh State University. See SUNY PLATTSBURGH.

Pleasant Valley. Town (pop 9,066) in central Dutchess Co. Part of Great Nine Partners Patent (1697), it was settled in the late 1720s. In 1777 a group of armed loyalists "from the lower part of the county" [now Putnam Co] skirmished with the militia. A cotton mill (1809) and other textile factories stimulated growth of the Village of Pleasant Valley (incorporated 1814–1926). The town was formed from Clinton in 1821. When the Poughkeepsie and Eastern Railroad was built through the village in 1871, business increased. Today the town is a suburb of Poughkeepsie.

William P. McDermott

Pleasantville. Village (pop 7,172) in Mount Pleasant (Westchester Co). Originally called Clark's Corners, the present name was chosen for the post office (1828) and railroad station (1846). It grew as a market hamlet with some shoemaking and shirtmaking. The home of Moses Pierce (1816–86) is documented as an Underground Railroad stop. By 1886 Pleasantville had commuters to New York City; it quickly became a commuter village, incorporating in 1897. *Reader's Digest* began in the village in 1922 and continues to use Pleasantville as its postal address even though its offices moved to nearby Chappaqua.

Field Horne

Plum Island. Island in Southold (Suffolk Co). This 840-acre (340 ha) island lying 1.5 miles (2.4 km) east of Orient Point was named for the beach plums that grow along its shores. It was purchased from Native Americans in 1669; until the late 19th century its residents were largely devoted to farming and cattle raising. The first lighthouse on the island was erected in 1826; the present structure was built in 1869. From 1897 to 1948 the War Department maintained Fort Terry on the island. In 1952 the Army Chemical Corps established the animal disease research laboratory but transferred it to the Department of Agriculture in 1954. Since 1991 the lab has been operated under contract by LB&B Associates of Maryland. A division of the Agricultural Research Service, Plum Island Animal Disease Center can be reached only by special ferry. It is the only site in the United States permitted to study foot-and-mouth disease; other infectious diseases, including African swine fever, are also investigated. Safety is a major priority, and no pathogen under study has ever escaped from the island. The work of Plum Island has figured into the plots of contemporary thrillers such as Thomas Harris's *The Silence of the Lambs* and Nelson DeMille's *Plum Island.* In 2003 jurisdiction over Plum Island and its facilities was transferred to the Department of Homeland Security.

Plum Island, http://www.usda.gov/plum

Richard F. Welch

Plymouth. Town (pop 2,049) in central Chenango Co. Settled in 1794 by several French families, the town was formed from Norwich in 1806. Plymouth Reservoir (1855) was created to increase the waterpower of the Canasawacta Creek for mills. In the 19th century butter and cheese, along with some hops, were the chief products. The town was served by the short-lived Auburn Branch of the Midland Railroad; its depot has been restored by the Plymouth Historical Society. Plymouth Days is an annual July event.

Dale C. Storms

Plymouth Church, Brooklyn. Congregational church established in Brooklyn Heights in 1847 by leaders of Brooklyn's Church of the Pilgrims and Broadway Tabernacle, and made famous by the pastorate of Henry Ward Beecher (1847–87). It first occupied a former Presbyterian building, but after an 1849 fire, a 2,800-seat meetinghouse was constructed to accommodate the crowds. At the center of the abolition movement in the 1850s, the church came to embody the fashions and values of Victorian American culture. Progressive religious journalist Lyman Abbott (1888–99) succeeded Beecher. Other notable pastors included Newell Dwight Hillis (1899–1924), former Howard University president J. Stanley Durkee (1926–41), and L. Wendell Fifield (1941–55). Church attendance declined in the early 20th century as affluent families moved away, and in 1934 Plymouth Church merged with the Church of the Pilgrims, pastored by Richard Salton Storrs, to form Plymouth Church of the Pilgrims. Services were held at the Plymouth Church site, which was modernized and expanded for the 1946–47 centennial. Restoration work began again in 1997 as the church, with a small congregation, continued its independent Protestant ministry in multicultural Brooklyn.

Fifield, L. Wendell, et al. *A Church in History: The Story of Plymouth's First Hundred Years* (Brooklyn: Plymouth Church of the Pilgrims, 1949)

Charles E. Hambrick-Stowe

Poestenkill. Town (pop 4,054) in central Rensselaer Co. Settled *ca* 1755, the town was formed in 1848 from Sand Lake. Small industries grew up along its creeks, and a mineral spring was developed for visitors, but its bath- and boardinghouses were swept away in a freshet in 1814. James A. Garfield, later US president, taught in Poestenkill hamlet in 1855–56 while a student at Williams College in Williamstown, Mass. Camp Rotary (1923) for Boy Scouts is an East Poestenkill landmark. The town is mostly residential with some farming but in 2003 had a number of manufacturing plants, including Duffers Scientific (computer components), Saint-Gobain Corp (fluid systems), and Interstate Laminates (counter tops).

Kathryn T. Sheehan

point-shaving scandal. In New York City, which emerged as a hotbed of men's college basketball in the 1930s, gambling-related scandals occurred as early as 1945, when two Brooklyn College students confessed to taking $500 each to keep point totals down. Similar incidents were exposed at Manhattan College (1951) and Long Island University (1951). The most infamous involved the City College of New York (CCNY) team, which had won both the National Collegiate Athletic Association (NCAA) championship and the National Invitation Tournament (NIT) during the 1949–50 season. On 18 Feb 1951 New York Co district attorney Frank S. Hogan announced that CCNY players Ed Roman, Al Roth, and Ed Warner had been charged with accepting gamblers' bribes in return for point shaving during the previous and current seasons; four more CCNY students, Floyd Lane, Herb Cohen, Irwin Dambrot, and Norman Mager, were eventually charged, but their coach, Nat Holman, was never implicated. The students pleaded to the lesser charge of conspiracy, and only Warner received jail time (six months). The *New York Journal-American*'s Max Kase won a Pulitzer Prize in 1952 for the investigative articles that broke the case.

Several college sports figures, including University of Kentucky head coach Adolph Rupp, blamed the low moral character of New Yorkers, read in some quarters as African Americans and Jews because of the team's makeup, for the stain on American collegiate sports. Eventually, however, the scandal was discovered at other schools, including the University of Kentucky, where five players were indicted. In total, 32 players from seven colleges were named in indictments for fixing 86 games between 1947 and 1951. The scandal ruined the students' basketball careers and damaged the New York City college basketball scene, which was tainted further after the New York City Board of Education revealed that 14 players' high school records had been tampered with to make them eligible for admission to CCNY and other municipal colleges. The New York City men's college basketball scene never really recovered. The city's NIT was displaced as the premier men's collegiate basketball tournament by the late 1950s, while almost all New York City colleges (with the exception of St. John's) ceased to play basketball at the highest collegiate level.

Cohen, Stanley. *The Game They Played* (1977; repr New York: Carroll & Graf Publishers, 2001)

David Marc

Poland. Town (pop 2,467) in SE Chautauqua Co. Settled in 1805 the town formed from Ellicott in 1832. Poland was covered with forests of pine and hardwood, the pines of such outstanding quality that "Poland Quality" distinguished high-grade lumber; a large commercial sawmill was built by Dr Thomas Kennedy of Meadville, Pa, in the year of first settlement. The forests have been replaced by dairy farms, the chief industry of the town. Rte 17 (I-86) was opened through town between 1967 and 1971. Residents work in Jamestown and Falconer.

Michelle Henry

Poland. Village (pop 451) in Newport and Russia (Herkimer Co). In the early and mid–19th century Poland was a significant manufacturing hamlet, producing scythes, mill gears, small box stoves, hollowware, cotton cloth, yarn, candlewicking and batting, rubber boots, cheese and cheese boxes, fanning mills, bootjacks, ladders, and leather. It was served by the Herkimer, Newport and Poland Narrow Gauge Railway (1881; Mohawk and Malone Railroad after 1892). The village incorporated in 1890. Industries in the 20th century included the Jamestown Veneer Corp (1926–69) and Perfex Corp, maker of brooms, mops, and brushes, which remained in business in 2003. The largest employer is Poland Central School.

Susan R. Perkins

Poles. One of the earliest Polish settlers in what would become New York State was Alexander Carolus Curtius (Kurczewski), a Polish Lithuanian hired as the schoolmaster at the first Latin school in New Amsterdam in 1659. Curtius was a Protestant, but later immigrants were predominantly Catholic. Immigrants in the 18th century included the surveyor Casimir Goerck (*d* 1798) and Thaddeus Kosciuszko, who distinguished himself at the Battle of Saratoga in 1777, served as chief engineer for the construction of West Point, and contributed in other ways to American independence. Several hundred refugees arrived following failed insurrections against Poland's partitions in 1831, 1846, 1848, and 1863. Most settled in New York City, with a few venturing north to Albany, Troy, and the small mill towns along the Erie Canal as far as Buffalo. In the Civil War, New York City supplied Polish recruits for Maj Alexander Raszewski's Company C of the 31st New York Volunteer Infantry and Col Wladimir Krzyzanowski's 58th New York Volunteer Infantry, known as the Polish Legion. To support the 1863 Polish insurrection, New York City Poles founded the Democratic Society of Polish Exiles in America and *Echo z Polski* (Echo from Poland, 1863–65), the first US Polish language weekly.

Immigration and Settlement

Mass migration of Poles to the state began in the early 1870s, primarily for economic reasons but also because of political and cultural repression in Prussian and Russian Poland. Most intended to return to Poland. Estimates of the number of ethnic Poles arriving in the United States between 1870 and 1920 vary from about 1.7 to 2.4 million. In 1900 there were 69,636 Polish-born in New York State; by 1930 there were 350,383, with the largest concentrations in Buffalo and New York City. This figure included large numbers of Jews who immigrated from historically Polish lands. Although they often cultivated their ties to Europe, they generally did not consider themselves ethnic Poles and had a separate community life. Most of the early Polish communities in New York City, Brooklyn, and Buffalo were founded by Poles from German Poland, while smaller communities elsewhere were generally founded by those from Austrian and Russian Poland. Early Polish parishes were established in Buffalo (1873), Dunkirk (1875), Amsterdam (1888), Rochester (1889), Schenectady (1890), Elmira (1891), Syracuse (1892), and Albany (1893).

Mass immigration ceased with World War I and the restrictive quotas of the 1920s. During World War II, refugee scholars came to New York State, and after the war over 250,000 Polish refugees came to the United States rather than return to a Poland dominated by the Communists. Their ranks included veterans of the Polish armed forces and displaced people, including many Jewish Holocaust survivors. Post–World War II arrivals tended to be better educated than pre–World War I immigrants. By 1960, after various federal acts to admit displaced persons, there were 139,591 Polish-born residents in the state. Following the relaxation of restrictions in 1965, approximately 242,500 Poles emigrated to escape oppression and limited opportunity. Another wave arrived after the end of Communist rule in 1991. The 2000 US census listed 93,187 Polish-born New York State residents, with more than 60% in Brooklyn and Queens combined, and another 11% on Long Island. The count of New Yorkers reporting Polish ancestry was 986,141, with Erie Co accounting for over 18%. Brooklyn remains home to major Polish enclaves, especially Greenpoint. Outside the New York City and Buffalo metropolitan areas, there are large Polish American communities in Syracuse, Utica, Rochester, the Albany-Schenectady area, and Binghamton.

Social Life

The family, the parish, and the community were the main institutions of Polish American life from the late 19th century. The extended fam-

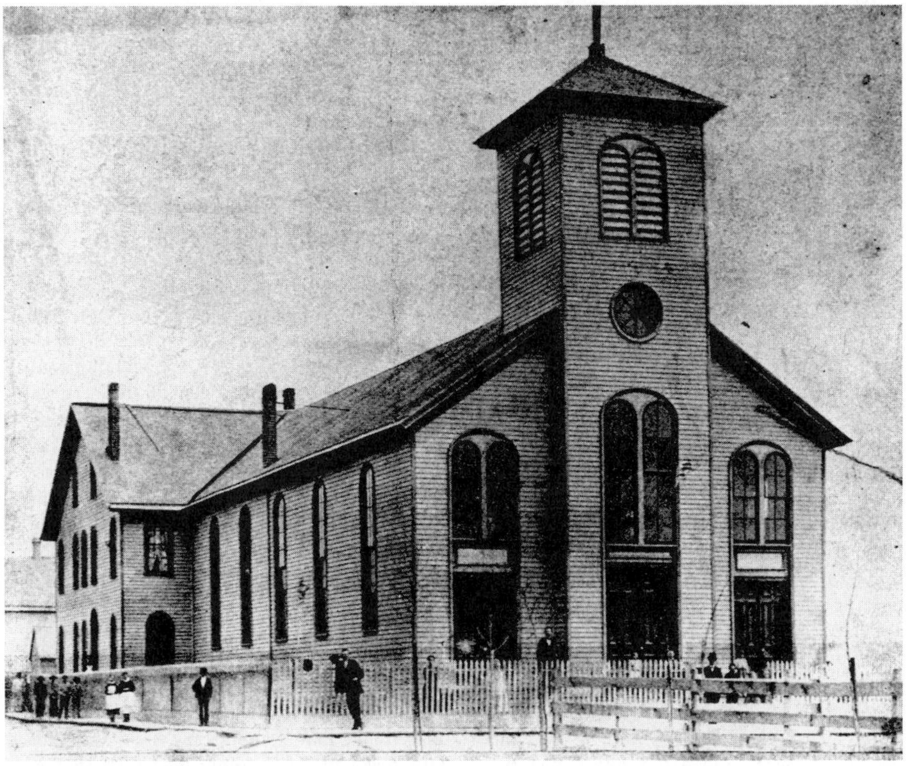

St. Stanislaus Church, Buffalo.

ily was most important, often living in a single household unit or in close proximity. The Roman Catholic Church tied Polish communities together, encouraging stable family structures and a high rate of endogamous marriage. Polish Americans closely identified with their home parishes, telling those who inquired that they were from Stanislawowo (St. Stanislaus's) or Wojciechowo (St. Adalbert's). This identification implied not merely a church but an entire neighborhood. Polish American social life revolved largely around the celebration of religious and national holidays. Social control occurred through peer pressure and religious rules enforced by the local parish priest.

During the second half of the 19th century, as self-help organizations became popular in Poland, Polish immigrants in America also created fraternal associations. New York State Poles grew resentful of Chicago's dominant nationwide influence, which was exercised through the Polish National Alliance and the Polish Roman Catholic Union, and formed their own organizations such as Rev Dominic Majer's Polish National Union (1890). A dispute between officers from the Buffalo and Pennsylvania chapters eventually led the group to split into the Polish Union of the United States, with headquarters in Wilkes-Barre, Pa, and the Polish Union of America, long headquartered in Buffalo and presently in West Seneca (Erie Co). A further secession was led by wealthy New York City businessman Erazmus Jerzmanowski, forming the Polish National Alliance of Brooklyn (1903). Nearly all sizable communities had local chapters of the Polish National Alliance, Polish Roman Catholic Union, Polish Singers' Alliance, Harcerstwo (Polish scouts), Falcons (a group stressing physical training), arts groups affiliated with the American Council for Polish Culture, and the Polish Legion of America Veterans (for veterans of the US armed forces) or Polish Army Veterans Association (for veterans of the Polish armed forces). The insurance fraternal society, a response to the challenge of industrial America, eventually became a primary agency of "communal capitalism." The earliest societies usually provided death benefit insurance to immigrant families living on marginal income, later expanding their activities to health insurance, community service, building and loan funds, and fund raising for the parish or homeland.

The Polish language press was a pillar of Polish American life. More than 150 Polish language newspapers were published in the United States by the 1920s. The number published in New York State varied; during the 1920s there were about a dozen. Most were local, such as the weekly *Gazeta Tygodniowa*, published in Schenectady from 1908 to the late 1940s. Among the more influential newspapers in the state were the daily *Polak w Ameryce* (The Pole in America, 1887), a Roman Catholic publication founded by Rev Jan Pitass in Buffalo; the weekly *Robotnik Polski* (The Polish worker, 1896), which was founded in Chicago but moved to New York City in 1907; *Nowy Swiat* (New world, 1919–*ca* 1973), the New York City organ of the Polish Socialist Alliance in America; the independent *Nowy Dziennik* (Daily news, 1971) of New York City, which today enjoys a national audience; and the English language monthly *Polish-American Journal* of Buffalo (founded as *Zorza* [The dawn] in Pennsylvania, 1911).

Through World War II, Polish Americans tended to be insular. Suspicious of American public education as antireligious and anti-Polish, they supported Polish parish schools as guardians of their traditional values. Most early parochial schools offered education only to the sixth or eighth grade, used a curriculum heavy with religion and Polish history, and generally taught classes in Polish, with English as a foreign language. Although parochial education dramatically increased literacy rates among the second generation, the lack of practical courses hindered economic and social advancement. After World War II, Polish Americans enrolled to a much greater extent in public schools. Church attendance remained high among Polish Americans in the post–World War II generation, but the Polish character of many parishes declined as migrations and changing demographics reduced the Polish presence in many urban neighborhoods. By 1970 many of the smaller parishes were conducting services in English and catering to new ethnic groups.

Economic Life

Until the late 1860s most Polish immigrants were educated people who obtained positions as soldiers, government officials, merchants, professionals, or teachers. After the 1860s most male immigrants had been peasant farmers in the Old World but became urban industrial workers in the United States. A small minority were farmers on Long Island, in the lower Hudson Valley, and in Central New York, but the majority worked as laborers in manufacturing, the garment industry in Manhattan, the textile mills between Albany and Buffalo, the leather industry in the Gloversville (Fulton Co) area, shoe factories in Endicott and Johnson City (Broome Co), or the steel industry in the Buffalo area. Poles were heavily recruited to work in the iron and steel mills of Lackawanna (Erie Co), constituting over one-third of the city's population in 1910. (Erie Co would retain the most heavily Polish American percentage of population of any county in the country into the late 20th century.)

Harsh working conditions led Polish Americans to join labor unions beginning in the period between 1910 and 1917. The United Textile Workers of America was the first to hire Polish organizers and print union materials in Polish. Polish workers struck successfully in Auburn (Cayuga Co, 1912), Little Falls (Herkimer Co, 1912), New York Mills (Oneida Co, 1912 and 1916), Utica (1919), and elsewhere. Other strikes followed in later periods. Because of the low wages paid to unskilled male laborers, Polish women worked as domestics, factory operatives, and service workers. Many Poles took in boarders and removed their children from school early to help support their families. Despite the later closing of many New York State factories, opportunities provided by the GI Bill and the social legislation of the 1960s facilitated a significant improvement in the livelihoods of Polish Americans. Recent studies show relatively high incomes among Polish Americans, with the professions well represented.

Culture and Politics

In 1942 refugee scholars in New York City, led by historian Oskar Halecki, founded the Polish Institute of Arts and Sciences in America to spread knowledge about Polish culture and foster scholarly contacts between Poland and America. It remains a major center for Polish American intellectual life and publishes the *Polish Review*. In 1943 another group in New York City founded the Jozef Pilsudski Institute of America for Research in the Modern History of Poland, which maintains a reference library, archives, photographic collection, films, and other historical materials. The Polish American Historical Association, founded in New York City in 1942 as part of the Polish Institute and now located in Utica, publishes *Polish American Studies.*

The Polish community has been strongly aligned with the Democratic Party and the labor movement. A few Polish Americans joined the leftist American Slav Congress, but it was criticized for supporting the Soviet Union, and most members withdrew from the organization between 1943 and 1945. Polish New Yorkers overwhelmingly supported organizations that stood behind the London-based Polish government in exile. Refugees from Nazism were succeeded by those fleeing Communism, with an influx of Solidarity supporters in the 1980s.

The Kosciuszko Foundation was founded in New York City in 1925 to promote cultural exchange and education. Numerous organizations sustain Polish traditions including music, folk dancing, and traditional cuisine. The Polish American Museum (1977) is in Port Washington (Nassau Co). The Pulaski Day parade, held in Manhattan every 11 October, draws more than 100,000 people annually. Notable writers in New York State have included Isaac Bashevis Singer, novelist Jerzy Kosinski, and playwright Janusz Glowacki. Prominent musicians have included Artur Rodzinski, music director of the New York Philharmonic (1943–47) and Metropolitan Opera star Marcella Sembrich. Casimir Funk, the doctor who discovered vitamins, immigrated in 1915. Other immigrants or children of immigrants achieving fame in New York City have included film producers Samuel Goldwyn and Harold and Jack Warner; fashion and cosmetics innovators Max Factor, Helena Rubinstein, and Oleg Cassini; and artist-illustrators Wladyslaw Benda, Jules Feiffer, and Maurice Sendak.

See also ETHNIC PRESS.

Bukowczyk, John J. *And My Children Did Not Know Me: A History of the Polish Americans* (Bloomington: Indiana Univ Press, 1987)

———, ed. *Polish Americans and Their History: Community, Culture, and Politics* (Pittsburgh: Univ of Pittsburgh Press, 1996)

Pula, James S. *Polish Americans: An Ethnic Community* (New York: Twayne Publishers, 1995)

Pula, James S., and Eugene E. Dziedzic. *United We Stand: The Role of Polish Workers in the New York Mills Textile Strikes, 1912 and 1916* (New York: Columbia Univ Press, 1990)

Urbanic, Kathleen. *Shoulder to Shoulder: Polish Americans in Rochester, NY, 1890–1990* (Rochester: Monroe Reprographics, 1991)

James S. Pula

Poletti, Charles (*b* Barre, Vt, 2 July 1903; *d* Marco Island, Fla, 8 Aug 2002). Governor. The son of working-class Italian immigrants, Poletti was educated at Harvard College, the University of Rome, and Harvard Law School, from which he graduated in 1928. He cultivated ties with the Democratic Party when he joined the Wall St law firm of John W. Davis, the 1924 Democratic presidential candidate. Poletti was legal counsel to Gov Herbert H. Lehman from 1933 to 1937, when he was elected a justice to the state supreme court. He also chaired the committee that prepared the Poletti Report with materials for use at the state's 1938 Constitutional Convention, to which he was a delegate. Poletti was elected as Lehman's lieutenant governor in November 1938. He became governor on 2 Dec 1942 and served the last month of Lehman's term after Lehman resigned to direct foreign relief efforts. As governor Poletti continued his work of directing the state's civil defense and other wartime programs. He served in the army from 1943 to 1945, rising to the rank of colonel while administering Allied military relief operations in Italy. Poletti then resumed the practice of law in Manhattan. He served as a trustee of the New York Power Authority from 1955 to 1960 and was vice president for international relations for the 1964–65 World's Fair in New York City before moving to Florida in 1965.

Public Papers of Charles Poletti, 50th Governor of the State of New York, 1942 (Albany: Williams Press, 1947)

Laura-Eve Moss

police unions. Formed originally as benevolent associations by police officers to provide financial aid to sick and disabled members and to families of deceased officers. After abortive organizing efforts in the 1840s and 1880s, an influenza epidemic in 1894, which caused the deaths of a number of New York City officers, led to the founding of a group making contributions for death benefits and fraternal purpose. The group incorporated on 30 Mar 1894 as the Patrolmen's Benevolent Association (PBA), the oldest continuous association in the state. Similar groups soon sprang up elsewhere, including the Erie Club in Buffalo in 1895, the Troy Police Benevolent and Protective Association (Rensselaer Co) in 1903, and the Rochester Police Locust Club (named for the wood used to make nightsticks) in 1907.

The associations quickly achieved influence over working conditions and salaries. New York City's PBA was particularly successful. Following the lead of police officers, on 5 Mar 1899 supervisors in the New York City Police Department (NYPD) formed the Police Sergeants Endowment and Benevolent Association. The PBA was successful in Albany in preventing passage of the Lexow bills in 1895, which would have given the police board the power to dismiss officers without a hearing. The associations were officers' responses to changes in policing after the Civil War, when cities attempted to remove police from local political control by introducing paramilitary rank structures and by instituting civil service regulations to maintain discipline and to foster a less transient workforce. Job stability gave police a stake in their working conditions and allowed them to protest without fear of reprisal.

The associations were also emblematic of the discontent that led to the trade unionism of the period. One of the first police strikes in the nation occurred on 16 Apr 1889, when Ithaca's five patrolmen refused to work after their wages were reduced from $12 to $9 a week. The officers, who withheld their services for a week, were victorious in having the reduction reversed. A police strike in Boston in 1919 effectively ended sustained efforts by national unions to organize police departments. Many departments followed the lead of the NYPD, which in 1924 added provisions to the department's rules that prohibited officers from joining a variety of outside organizations, including unions.

FROM ADVOCATES TO UNIONS

Early steps to unionization took place in New York City in March 1953, when Mayor Robert F. Wagner Jr issued Executive Order 49 (the Little Wagner Act), which continued to exclude the police from formal labor negotiations. In 1961 the PBA won dues checkoff rights, allowing it to collect dues from employees through voluntary deductions from their paychecks, and recognition as the sole negotiating entity for patrolmen. Statewide developments followed on 1 Sept 1967, when Gov Nelson A. Rockefeller signed the Taylor Law, which prohibited strikes by public employees but granted state workers, including police, the right to join unions and bargain collectively. The New York State Police PBA, which incorporated in 1944, won a representation fight to become the bargaining agent for troopers, sergeants, and investigative personnel up to the rank of lieutenant, and signed its first contract effective 1 Apr 1969. Other PBAs also achieved union status, and many, including Buffalo and Troy, signed their first contracts starting in 1969. By the 1970s smaller cities also recognized PBAs. In 1969 the Buffalo PBA (an outgrowth of the Erie Club formed in 1895) became the first municipal union in Buffalo to invoke the mediation provisions of the Taylor Law to win a 20% pay increase. In May 1970 police officers in Rochester undertook a one-day strike after being placed on a mass standby for the day shift after rumors circulated about the possibility of racial unrest. In 1971 25,000 members of New York City's PBA (85% of the membership) engaged in a five-day "sick-out," which led to wage, benefit, and pension improvements. In 1975 the Nassau County PBA was fined $60,000 under Taylor Law provisions when officers called in sick with cases of what became known as the "blue flu."

Many battles between the associations and their municipalities have been over attempts to diversify the race and sex of department employees. In New York City and in Buffalo the unions successfully fought against federally financed exams in the 1970s that would have been open only to residents of designated areas as a way to increase the numbers of black and Hispanic officers. The PBAs of Schenectady, Nassau Co, and the State Police tried to preserve height, weight, physical agility tests, and seniority rules. A quota system had been established in the NYPD in April 1978 as part of an agreement between the department and the Policewomen's Endowment Association, which resolved a sex discrimination suit that had been filed by female officers with the city's Human Rights Commission. The New York City PBA excluded women from membership until 1968 and voted not to change its name to Police Benevolent Association in 1998.

Unions in New York City and Rochester were particularly active in fights against civilian review boards. These became a public issue in the wake of accusations of widespread police brutality, especially against minorities. In 1966 the New York City PBA succeeded in getting Mayor John Lindsay's Civilian Review Board placed before the voters as a citywide referendum, and voters defeated the board by an almost two-to-one majority. Its successor, the Civilian Complaint Review Board, first consisted solely of police department employees, but since 1993 it has had a civilian majority. Rochester's Police Locust Club also fought a civilian review board, arguing that it would interfere with officers in the course of their work. The union prevailed when the city abolished the board in 1969. Review boards and questions of police brutality continue to be controversial. The defense of alleged perpetrators of police brutality by police unions sometimes can directly involve the union in legal proceedings, as happened to the PBA in the case of Abner Louima, who was attacked in a Brooklyn police station in 1997. Benevolent associations remain concerned primarily with local issues, such as salaries, benefits, and working conditions, including attempts to alter civil service provisions of their contracts or to open departments to civilian review.

Halpern, Stephen C. *Police-Association and Development Leaders: The Politics of Co-Optation* (Lexington, Mass: Lexington Books, 1974)

Kirwan, William E. *The New York State Police: History and Development of Collective Negotiations* (Albany: NYS Police, 1969)

Levi, Margaret A. *And the Beat Goes On: Patrolmen's Unionism in New York City* (Cambridge, Mass: MIT Operations Research Center, 1974)

Riccucci, Norma M. *Women, Minorities, and Unions in the Public Sector* (Westport, Conn: Greenwood, 1990)

Dorothy Moses Schulz

policing

Colonial Period to the American Revolution

In the Dutch West India Co's colony of New Netherland, the government's law enforcement officer and prosecuting attorney was the *fiscaal*, who was a member of the provincial council. He was responsible for enforcing company laws, such as those regulating trade and navigation or selling liquor to the Indians, and for apprehending and prosecuting those who contravened the laws. At the village level, law enforcement and prosecution was handled by the *schout*, who was appointed by the director and council. An exception was Rensselaerswijck [now in Albany, Columbia, and Rensselaer Cos], where the patroon appointed the *schout*. New Amsterdam [now New York City], though chartered in 1653, did not have its own *schout* appointed until 1660, before which time the *fiscaal* acted in that capacity. *Schouts* were occasionally assisted by a deputy to help keep the peace, arrest suspects, and gather information for prosecuting criminal cases. Only minor criminal infractions were handled by the local courts, while major crimes were referred to the colonial council. In at least the two largest towns, Beverwijck [now Albany] and New Amsterdam, rattle watches were established for nighttime policing. In Beverwijck two men were hired in September 1659 for night watch duty. They made rounds of the town every hour from 9 PM to 4 AM—sounding their rattles and calling out the hour—and watched for fires and thieves, whom they could arrest. New Amsterdam established a rattle watch of eight men who began patrolling in October 1658. In 1665, less than a year after the Dutch surrendered the colony to the English, Gov Richard Nicolls replaced the Dutch municipal government of burgomasters, *schepenen*, and a *schout* with the English form of mayor, aldermen, and a sheriff.

Residents of New York City in 1682 created day and night watches, which were often supplemented or replaced by the militia. In 1734 it paid day and night watchmen to maintain a fire watch and to keep the streets free of vagrants and strangers. The job was part-time, the quality of personnel was low, and the day and night patrols viewed one another as competition. Although the watchmen, called leatherheads because of the protective leather helmets they wore, were an improvement over earlier systems, they were frequently fired to save money and then rehired when fears of crime or warfare intensified. These men patrolled the streets, particularly at night, to ensure that strangers and criminals (often viewed as one and the same) were arrested, watched, or asked to leave the town limits. The myriad other roles included serving warrants, securing town meetings and elections, checking harbors, keeping reservoirs free from obstruction, transporting the ill, dying, or dead to hospitals and morgues, and removing animals and other obstructions from streets. Thus police were not so much crime fighters as they were guardians of the public peace, authorized to maintain order and to ensure that law-abiding citizens would not be hampered in their daily activities. At the same time that policing was only beginning to become organized, the sheriff was a powerful officer of the court. In 1735, for example, New York Co sheriff, Henry Beekman Jr, a member of the mercantile family whose mansion was located in what is now New York City's Beekman Place, chose the jury for the trial of John Peter Zenger.

Postindependence to the Civil War

The practice of the governor appointing sheriffs continued until after the American Revolution and was incorporated into the first constitution adopted in New York in 1777. In the 1821 Constitutional Convention, the office was made elective. Prior to 1821 a sheriff could be appointed for four successive terms, but when the office was made elective, the term of office was set at three years and it was specified that sheriffs could not succeed themselves. In 1935 the restriction against sheriffs succeeding themselves was repealed by referendum; the term of office was extended from three to four years in 1985.

Although a few towns, such as New Windsor and Wallkill (Orange Co), hired peace officers prior to independence from England in 1783, police departments were rare until the mid-1840s, when crime, disorder, and fear increased in cities, due largely to societal changes associated with industrialization and urbanization. After much political maneuvering, Democratic mayor William F. Havemeyer on 23 May 1845 signed legislation creating the Municipal Police—forerunner of the New York City Police Department (NYPD). Composed of between 800 and 900 men, it was the first 24-hour department in the United States, modeled on the quasi-military force created by Sir Robert Peel in London in 1829. The Municipal Police was a major source of patronage. Officers, often immigrants, served at the pleasure of local politicians. Both Democrats and Whigs sought control of the Municipals, particularly since officers supervising polling places were known to ensure the victory of those who would guarantee their continued employment.

When the Republicans controlled the state legislature in 1857, they were able, despite objections from New York City and Brooklyn citizens and Democratic politicians, to merge the police departments of New York, Kings, Richmond, and Westchester Cos into what came to be known as the Metropolitan Police. In 1860 parts of present-day Queens Co were added. Some of the Municipals remained active and loyal to local politicians, leading to a battle between the two forces when, later in June 1857, the Metropolitans tried to arrest Democratic mayor Fernando Wood in front of City Hall. After the National Guard's Seventh Regiment ended the conflict, both forces patrolled the streets for several weeks. Although the Municipals were soon disbanded, by 1870 police power was returned to the local level.

Civil War to World War I

Activities by two of the state's best-known politicians of the post–Civil War years indicate the continuing influence of the sheriff's office and its importance as a source of political power. In New York City William M. Tweed, who gained notoriety as "Boss" of New York City's Tammany Hall, ran for sheriff in 1861 but was defeated. Grover Cleveland, who first achieved elective office as Erie Co's sheriff in 1871, was more successful than Tweed in using the position of sheriff as a stepping-stone to higher office. The sheriff was responsible for the jail and its lodgers prior to the creation of the separate State Commission of Prisons (now Commission of Correction) in 1895. Cleveland was also one of a small number of sheriffs who fulfilled the duty of hanging those sentenced to death before that task was turned over to the state prison system in 1888. Cleveland personally sprang the trap twice in 1872.

As communities grew in the postwar years, the number of police forces increased substantially. Thus Warwick (Orange Co) incorporated as a village in 1867 and appointed four police officers. In 1871 Yonkers established a 25-person police force, and the Village of Frankfort (Herkimer Co) hired officers to patrol on foot, inspect buildings, and make arrests. Rochester's police force followed a progression similar to the NYPD, beginning as a night watch in 1826, reorganizing into a police force with a paid chief in 1853, donning uniforms in 1865, and forming the Bureau of Public Safety in 1899. In 1872 Peekskill (Westchester Co) uniformed its officers in part because riders of the Hudson River Railroad were frightened to detrain at the depot at the sight of plainclothes policemen they mistook for criminals.

In Buffalo a small state-administered force was developed in 1866 but was frequently reduced in size. In 1872 the state returned to the city the power to organize and administer its own police force. Similar to New York City, Buffalo police were administered by a board of leading citizens while the police superintendent, often a member of the force, had little real power. Tenure was uncertain before 1915, when the city adopted the commission form of government and eliminated the police board. By 1915 the Buffalo Police Department (BPD) had grown to more than 900 officers, close to its size in 2002. According to the 1890 census, one-half of the police in New York City were born outside the United States; in Buffalo the figure was one-third. In both cities most of the foreign-born were Irish, whose dominance of the NYPD continued into the 1960s.

In New York City increased enforcement of gambling, prostitution, and liquor laws created enhanced opportunities for corruption. The first of what would become recurring, 20-year cycles of investigations began in 1894 with the Lexow Committee, named for its chairman, Clarence

Lexow of Nyack (Rockland Co). This state senate committee investigated allegations of police protection of vice establishments connected to corruption in Tammany Hall. Its findings led to Tammany's defeat and selection of Theodore Roosevelt as president of the New York City Police Commission in 1895 during the reform administration of Mayor William L. Strong. The city created the commission in 1854 in an attempt to provide less overtly political administration of the police force; it was eliminated in 1901, when a single police commissioner became the officer in charge. Roosevelt instituted many reforms during his two-year tenure, including disciplinary rules, firearms instruction and inspection, and annual physical exams. He created a bicycle squad to assist horse-mounted officers in controlling traffic, and he reorganized the detective division, which included the adoption of a criminal identification system. Many of his reforms were short-lived; the state legislature's Curran Committee hearings in 1912 and the Seabury Commission's findings in 1932 confirmed that corruption remained widespread within the department. Fear of labor unrest and the growing tramp population traveling on the expanding railroad network led the police into increased involvement with vagrants. To enforce many of the tramp acts passed in the Northeast, railroads began to establish their own police forces, which, although privately employed, were recognized as state-authorized police officers. Local police departments were often faced with the problem of lodging transients. In 1895 the NYPD recorded more than 65,500 overnight lodgers. One of Roosevelt's few lasting changes was to remove sleeping facilities from precinct houses. He also was instrumental in increasing the number of matrons in the NYPD, the first of whom had been hired in 1891, after 10 years of lobbying by women's groups. Brooklyn, Buffalo, and Rochester had hired matrons in 1887, even before passage of a New York State law in 1889 that directed all cities with 30,000 or more inhabitants to appoint police matrons.

In 1883 Buffalo's police were placed under civil service regulations, followed a year later by New York City's police. By 1892 civil service protected many officers in the state, and it was another tool that reformers hoped would eliminate politics from policing and would create a professional outlook among officers. Also by the late 1880s, police departments had armed their officers. By the 1930s the .38 caliber revolver had become the most common firearm and would remain so until the 1980s and 1990s, when departments began to equip officers with 9mm semiautomatic weapons.

World War I to World War II

Concerned about urban criminals flooding their areas and fearing labor unrest, rural elites called for the creation of the New York State Police (NYSP), which formed in 1917. Organized labor fought its creation and won support from Democratic Party politicians. Some Republicans also opposed the measure because of its cost. A coalition of rural and suburban legislators overcame the opposition by inserting into the bill limitations on the use of State Police within city limits to suppress riots and disorders, and the legislation narrowly passed. The NYSP were introduced at the New York State Fairgrounds later that year. Troopers were appointed for two years subject to approval of the superintendent. It was a misdemeanor to quit without the superintendent's consent until 1938, when appointments became permanent. Troopers lived in barracks and needed permission to marry. In 1935, as a result of fears caused by Prohibition violence, the rise of organized crime, and the increasing mobility of criminals, the legislature authorized creation of a crime laboratory and the Bureau of Investigation (now Bureau of Criminal Investigation), both now located at the NYSP's Albany headquarters. Progressives succeeded in changing the role of women in policing. Although their responsibilities sometimes overlapped, matrons generally searched female arrestees and cared for women in police custody, while policewomen, usually better educated than the matrons, investigated cases involving women and juveniles. Rochester in 1913 appointed the first policewoman in the state to be covered by civil service.

Police during and immediately after World War I expanded automobile patrol. The Monroe Co Sheriff's Office may have been the first in the state to rely on a car for patrol in 1908. That same year the New Rochelle Police Department (Westchester Co) began using motorcycles. In 1913 Rochester created a traffic squad, with motorcycles replacing bicycles. The NYPD added motorcycles in 1911 to counter traffic problems and turned to marked, radio-dispatched patrol cars in 1917. The Endicott Police Department (Broome Co) acquired a vehicle in the 1920s after a sergeant on a foot patrol was forced to commandeer a vehicle to chase a car fleeing the scene of a gas station robbery. Resembling a scene that would become a staple of movies and television programs, he shot out the tire of the fleeing car while standing on the sideboard of the one he had ordered to assist him. Glens Falls (Warren Co) officers began to rely on vehicles during Prohibition, when they were involved in a number of high-speed chases on US 9, "The Bootleg Trail," between New York City and Canada. Officers in these patrol cars could receive messages but not transmit them until the 1930s, when two-way communications became available to many police departments. By 1932 the NYSP was able to broadcast information to most troops on its own AM radio transmitters; by the end of the decade the entire state was covered.

The Seabury Commission (1931–32), named for its chief counsel, Samuel Seabury, was created by the state legislature to investigate corruption in the court system. Its findings included testimony by New York Co's sheriff Thomas M. Farley that he had deposited $360,000 in banks even though his net income over the previous six years had been $120,000. His statements confirmed that the New York Co sheriff's position was a lucrative one. Fiorello La Guardia, elected New York City mayor in part because of the Seabury Investigation, ushered in a number of policing changes, including the creation of the Transit Police Department in 1936. In 1942 La Guardia also consolidated the city's five county sheriffs into the office of New York City Sheriff and placed it under civil service regulations. On 12 July 1990 the New York City sheriff became a mayoral appointee.

Officer Charles Diesend directing traffic on 5th Ave in New York City, 1920s.

Motorcycle squad in Rochester. Photograph by Albert R. Stone, 1916.

World War II to the 21st Century

Many of the changes in policing instituted before and since World War II separated the police from the public. Strategies moved from order maintenance and crime prevention through patrol to crime fighting through rapid deployment and after-the-fact investigative techniques. Reliance on vehicle patrol and responses to calls that police received from a dispatcher rather than directly from citizens encouraged a change in orientation from peacekeeper to crime fighter. This change would become almost total by the 1960s and 1970s, when the emergency 911 response system became prevalent throughout the state. While this provided the appearance of greater control by police managers over both their officers and the criminal population, and also curtailed some of the most obvious forms of corruption, it fostered animosity toward the police.

In the 1960s there was greater attention to increasing the number of minorities in police ranks. The first African American known to have served as a police officer in the state was Wiley G. Overton, appointed to the Brooklyn Police Department in 1891. Shunned by colleagues, he resigned a year later. In 1914 Samuel J. Battle, who had been rejected three times based on a medical evaluation, became the first African American in the NYPD. Although he was initially hazed and ignored, he served for 35 years and achieved promotions as the first black sergeant and then first black lieutenant in the department. In 1896 George Garcia became the first Latino officer. The department formally recognized the Guardians, a fraternal association of black police officers in 1949, and the first association of Latino officers was formed in 1957. In 1964 Lloyd Sealy became the first black precinct commander, assigned to the 28th Precinct, in central Harlem (New York Co). In 1984 Benjamin Ward became the first black police commissioner in the city and in the state. When Ward became commissioner, 10.2 % (just under 2,400) of the NYPD's more than 23,400 officers were black and 7.2% (about 1,700) were Latino. By 2000, 34.7% of all officers in the NYPD were black or Latino. Elsewhere there has been less progress in the hiring of minorities. In 1999, of Schenectady's 158 officers, 2 were African American and 3 Latino, while Troy (Rensselaer Co) had 1 African American recruit in training at the time but none yet sworn among its 109 personnel. In the City of Newburgh (Orange Co), where more than 70% of the population is either black or of Latino ethnicity, 3 of the 90 police officers in 2002 were black and 8 were Latino. Women were not integrated into all aspects of police work until the 1970s. In 1972, primarily in response to passage of Title VII of the 1964 Civil Rights Act, which extended provisions of the original act to public agencies, the NYPD and other police departments changed the titles "patrolman" and "policewomen" to "police officer" and began to assign women tentatively to uniformed patrol. In 1973 the NYSP graduated the first female troopers from its academy in Albany. By mid-2003 there had been at least five women chiefs in the state, all in relatively small departments. No county to that point in time had elected a woman sheriff.

Rising crime rates undercut police claims of greater professionalism and resulted in the 1980s in the introduction of a more collaborative style of policing, called first "problem-oriented policing" and then "community policing." One of the initial steps toward community policing was team policing, which involved decentralizing the police organizational structure and giving officers wider geographical range beyond beats and wider discretionary roles in solving problems as members of a patrol team, usually four to six officers and a sergeant. The Troy Police Department began an experiment in team policing in summer 1978; the Nassau County Police Department (NCPD) instituted a team policing program in 1979. Community policing gained greater currency in New York City with the appointment of Lee P. Brown as New York City's police commissioner in 1990. Concurrent with this trend, some departments turned to enforcement of public order under the label of "quality-of-life" or "zero-tolerance" policing. These styles rely on aggressive street patrol by uniformed and plainclothes officers. The techniques have been applied to curtailing major crimes, particularly after the NYPD successfully enhanced its use of crime analysis through a process instituted by Police Commissioner William Bratton in 1994 called Compstat. Named for the book in which crime activity information was assembled and disseminated after computer statistical analysis, Compstat was soon implemented in Mount Vernon (Westchester Co) and was modified in 2000 in Rochester to focus specifically on investigations. Much like community policing, the phrase has come to mean different things in different agencies. While these proactive strategies gained support from property owners and members of racial and ethnic majorities, by the 1990s they had resulted in claims of bias based on social or financial status and of racial profiling of minority groups.

In 2002 about 70,000 sworn officers were employed in approximately 550 law enforcement agencies within New York State. These included municipal, county, and state police, members of special-purpose police forces, and sheriff's officers and deputies. More than 450 of the agencies were local police departments. By mid-2002 the NYPD contained almost 37,000 members, reduced from a high of 40,000 in 2000 but still by far the largest municipal police department in the United States. The force included the approximately 5,000 members of the Transit and Housing Police Departments that had been merged into the NYPD in 1995. The state's second largest policing agency is the NYSP, with more than 4,000 officers assigned throughout the state. The third and fourth largest agencies are the countywide departments in Nassau Co, which established its police department in 1925, and Suffolk, which organized a department on 1 Jan 1960. As of late 2002 the Suffolk County Police Department had almost 2,700 officers, and Nassau Co had just over 2,600. Both rank among the country's 15 largest police departments. Buffalo Police Department had close to 1,000 officers in 2002. Sheriff's departments are larger than most small town and village police departments, but far smaller than the large city or county departments. As of October 2001 state statistics put the number of sworn personnel in all sheriff's departments at just over 3,500. The only departments with more than 200 officers (some part-time) were Monroe Co (344), Onondaga Co (238), and Erie Co (202).

Astor, Gerald. *The New York Cops: An Informal History* (New York: Charles Scribner's Sons, 1971)

Harring, Sidney L. "The Buffalo Police—1872–1915: Industrialization, Social Unrest, and the Development of the Police Institution" (PhD diss, Univ of Wisconsin, 1976)

Reppetto, Thomas A. *The Blue Parade* (New York: Free Press, 1978)

Richardson, James F. *The New York Police: Colonial Times to 1901* (New York: Oxford Univ Press, 1970)

Schulz, Dorothy M. *From Social Worker to Crimefighter: Women in United States Municipal Policing* (Westport, Conn: Praeger, 1995)

Shelton, Pamela T. *History of the New York State Police, 1917–1987* (Dallas: Taylor Publishing, 1987)

Sullivan, Dennis. *The Punishment of Crime in Colonial New York: The Dutch Experience in Albany during the Seventeenth Century* (New York: Peter Lang Publishing, 1997)

Dorothy Moses Schulz

Polish National Catholic Church of America (PNCC). The Catholic Church in 19th-century America, dominated by Irish bishops, attempted to assimilate Polish immigrants and eliminate their culture and language. Higher church authorities strictly controlled local parishes, demanding title to all parish property, assigning priests, and denying lay participation in decision making. In Poland, gentry families who endowed a parish might nominate its pastor, and immigrants in America funding Polish parishes expected the same prerogatives and the appointment of Polish bishops. While most Poles remained in the Catholic Church despite frustration, others joined new independent Polish parishes. A controversy at St. Hedwig's in Chicago in 1894–95 led to the establishment of the Independent Polish Catholic Church of America under Rev Antoni Stanislaus Koz-lowski. Buffalo's first independent Polish Catholic parish was formed in 1895, and an independent synod elected Rev Stefan Kaminski of the Holy Mother of the Rosary in Buffalo bishop of the Polish Independent Church of America in 1896. That year the first Polish Catholic Congress convened in Buffalo; some delegates advocated schism, but the convention's leader, Rev Jan Pitass, counseled patience. Kozlowski was consecrated bishop in 1897, entering into communion with the Old Catholic movement in Europe; Kaminski was consecrated in 1898 and began publishing the weekly *Warta* (The watch).

The PNCC was founded in 1897 by the Rev Franciszek Hodur, who established a new parish, later named St. Stanislaus, in Scranton, Pa. In 1901 a second congress in Buffalo discussed the appointment of Polish-speaking auxiliary bishops in strongly Polish American dioceses. Petitions to the Vatican were ignored, and in 1903 Buffalo congressman Rowland B. Mahaney and Rev Waclaw Kruszka of Wisconsin went to Rome in an unsuccessful appeal. The PNCC officially seceded from the Catholic Church in 1904. After Kozlowski's death in 1907, his former rival, Kaminski, became the dominant figure of the Polish Catholic independent movement, claiming leadership of 23 parishes with more than 75,000 followers nationwide. That same year Hodur succeeded Kozlowski as bishop when he was consecrated by the Dutch Old Catholic Church, formally establishing the PNCC as an official church and freeing it from dependence on Europe. In the years following Kaminski's death in 1911, the parishes loyal to Kaminski and Kozlowski gradually united under Hodur's leadership.

The church retained many Roman Catholic traditions and beliefs but added feast days commemorating events in Polish history; adopted Polish as the language of the Mass; allowed its clergy to marry; and though maintaining a hierarchical church organization, stressed parishioner control over parish affairs and the selection of local pastors. Over the next generation, parishes were created in many Polish communities throughout New York State, but membership never rose above 5% of Polish Americans. In 1946 the PNCC entered intercommunion with the Episcopal Church, splitting from it in 1977–78 over the issue of Episcopalian ordination of women. Since the 1990s a general rapprochement with the Vatican has occurred and may eventually lead to intercommunion with Roman Catholicism. Today there are approximately 10,000 parishioners in 16 PNCC parishes throughout the state, in Buffalo, Lackawanna, and Lancaster (Erie Co); Niagara Falls (Niagara Co); Latham (Albany Co); Rome and New York Mills (Oneida Co); Johnson City (Broome Co); Amsterdam (Montgomery Co); East Meadow (Nassau Co); Little Falls (Herkimer Co); Rochester; Schenectady; Syracuse; and Brooklyn.

Kubiak, Hieronim. *The Polish National Catholic Church in the United States of America from 1897 to 1980* (Kraków, Poland: Pastwowe Wydawnictwo Naukowe, 1982)

Wlodarski, Rev Stephan. *The Origin and Growth of the Polish National Catholic Church* (Scranton, Pa: PNCC, 1974)

James S. Pula

polka. Dance form in 2/4 meter, common among central and eastern European ethnic groups, especially Polish Americans. As an American dance form, the polka is a hybrid of eastern European folk melodies and popular music influences, especially Dixieland jazz. It is a celebratory music of the working class, common at weddings, anniversaries, and social functions. The Polish American polka falls into two major classes, both still popular: the older, quick-tempo Eastern style and the slower Chicago style.

One of the first Buffalo-area bandleaders to gain national recognition was Matt Pajakowski, who toured the Northeast in the 1930s. Eastern-style bands from the Buffalo area include Joe Macielag's Pic-A-Polka Band, the New Yorkers, the Jumping Jacks, and the Eddie Olinski Orchestra. The pioneer of Chicago-style bands in the area was Big Steve (Krzeminski) and the Belares. In recent decades bands include the Krew (Krupski) Brothers, and the Dyna-Tones. Dyna-Tone frontman Dave "Scrubby" Seweryniak, is a Polka Music Hall of Fame member and award-winning vocalist. Many New York State–born musicians have toured with national polka acts. Among them are Buffalo natives James "Whitey" Ryniec, brothers John and Tom Karas, Joseph Magnuszewski, Mark Trzepacz, and David "Nigel" Kurdziel.

Dana Publishing (1940s–2000) of New York City and Stella Music in New Jersey were among the most prolific producers of polka sheet music. From the early 1950s through the mid-1960s, Dana Publishing (later Dana Records) came to dominate the market for polka recordings, though national labels recruited talent from Polish American communities across the state. The company, founded by Walter Dana (Wladyslaw Danilowski; 1902–2000), a classically trained Polish pianist and composer turned jazz musician, launched the careers of hundreds of bandleaders and orchestras. Bernie "Wyte" Witkowski, the son of a Polish immigrant bandleader who settled in Brooklyn, led the Silver Bells, one of the most successful polka bands. They played New York City's finest hotels for more than three decades starting in the early 1930s and prestigious dance halls such as Roseland Ballroom.

Probably the best-known figure in contemporary polka is Jimmy Sturr of Florida (Orange Co). From the mid-1960s on, he has led his orchestra to 11 Grammy Awards. Of Irish and Polish heritage, Sturr continues to introduce new audiences to his polka sound, and his popularity continues to grow. Albany's Kosek Brothers and the Syracuse-born Al Piatkowski, Bernie Witkowski, and the Krakowska Melodiers in Binghamton have all been leading polka performers for several decades. Polish communities in New York City, Buffalo, Syracuse, Binghamton, Utica, and Dunkirk, among other places, have hosted numerous polka events in the state, usually under the auspices of Polish fraternal societies or churches. With guidance from the Polish Community Center of Buffalo, the New York State Council on the Arts produced several polka recordings, including *Polkas for Children* (1987) and *The Immigration Story* (1992), both written by New York State recording artists Larry Trojak and Mark Kohan, and *Kolberg Sampler* (1989). Albums from Buffalo-based Sunshine Records and Ethnic World Records have received a number of national awards. In an effort to compile the names of all the musicians who have recorded polkas in the United States, Steve Litwin, editor of the *Polka Magazine* of the *Polish American Journal* in Buffalo, began the Polka Musicians Database in 1999, which as of 2003 contained more than 600 entries.

Green, Victor. *A Passion for Polka: Old Time Ethnic Music in America* (Berkeley: Univ of California Press, 1992)

Keil, Charles, Angeliki V. Keil, and Dick Blau. *Polka Happiness* (Philadelphia: Temple Univ Press, 1992)

Litwin, Steve. Polka Musicians Database, http://www.polamjournal.com/polka/pmd.html

Mark Kohan and Steve Litwin

Pollock, (Paul) Jackson (*b* Cody, Wyo, 28 Jan 1912; *d* East Hampton, Suffolk Co, 11 Aug 1956). Artist. Pollock, the youngest of five brothers, grew up in the rural Southwest and attended Manual Arts High School in Los Angeles. He dropped the name Paul in 1930 when he moved to New York City to study at the Art Students League. Under the guidance of Thomas Hart Benton, a leader of the regionalist movement, which emphasized American scene subject matter and representational imagery, he learned his craft and posed for figures in his teacher's murals at the New School for Social Research. There he saw frescoes by the Mexican muralist José Clemente Orozco, whose expressionist style and apocalyptic themes affected him deeply. In 1936 another Mexican painter, David Alfaro Siqueiros, introduced him to the use of fluid paint. European modernists, especially Pablo Picasso, Surrealism's exploration of the unconscious, and the pictography of Native American art are among the other influences he synthesized while working for the easel division of the Works Progress Administration's Federal Art Project from 1935 to 1943. His artistic development was hampered by emotional problems and alcoholism, for which he sought treatment, including Jungian psychotherapy that validated the abstract, symbolic direction his art was taking. Several of the paintings in his first solo exhibition in November 1943 were praised by critics, and *The She-Wolf* was purchased by the Museum of Modern Art. In spite of this recognition, or perhaps because of it, his drinking and mood swings threatened to derail his fledgling career. In October 1945 he married painter Lee Krasner, and the following month the couple left New York City and settled in the Springs, a rural hamlet in East Hampton on eastern Long Island, removed, but not remote, from the art world.

Krasner, an active member of New York's abstractionist vanguard, recognized Pollock's potential and gave him crucial encouragement throughout his career.

One of the 20th century's leading abstract painters and the first American artist to be recognized internationally as an innovator, Pollock made his breakthrough in the late 1940s to "direct painting," using liquid pigment applied to canvas laid on the studio floor. By 1947 he was creating spontaneous, poured-paint compositions that earned both positive and negative reviews. Writing in *Horizon* in October 1947, art critic Clement Greenberg, one of Pollock's most ardent supporters, maintained that he was "the most powerful painter in contemporary America." His radical breakthrough was followed by a period of sobriety from 1948 through 1950 when he painted some of his most lyrical masterpieces, including *Arabesque: Number 13A* (1948), *Out of the Web: Number 7* (1949), *Lavender Mist: Number 1, Autumn Rhythm: Number 30,* and *One: Number 31* (all in 1950). But in late 1950 he began drinking again and abandoned nonobjective imagery in favor of abstracted references to human and animal forms. For the next few years he struggled to solve his drinking problem while his art underwent a series of revisions. By 1955 he had stopped painting altogether. Pollock died when, driving while intoxicated, he ran his car off the road and crashed. His grave, marked by a huge glacial boulder, is in Green River Cemetery in the Springs.

Landau, Ellen G. *Jackson Pollock* (New York: Abradale Press, 2000)
Naifeh, Steven, and Gregory White Smith. *Jackson Pollock: An American Saga* (New York: Clarkson N. Potter, 1989)
O'Connor, Francis V., and Eugene V. Thaw, eds. *Jackson Pollock: A Catalogue Raisonné of Paintings, Drawings, and Other Works* (New Haven, Conn: Yale Univ Press, 1978)

Helen A. Harrison

polls. Opinion polls are used by politicians, news media, advocacy groups and others to help measure and shape voter sentiment. Newspapers and other New York State–based publications were among the pioneers in using nationwide surveys to gauge voter support of presidential candidates. Although newspapers in various parts of the country took straw polls beginning around 1824, in 1904 the *New York Herald* led a group of newspapers in one of the first efforts to conduct nationwide polls in advance of presidential elections. The New York City–based *Literary Digest* accurately predicted Herbert Hoover's landslide victory for the presidency over Gov Alfred E. Smith in 1928 and, four years later, Gov Franklin D. Roosevelt's defeat of Hoover. New Yorkers were also involved in some of the most noteworthy errors in early opinion polls. After its two successful predictions of presidential victories, the *Literary Digest* inadvertently helped launch the career of a young competitor, George Gallup, with its badly mistaken projection of an Alf Landon victory over Pres Roosevelt in 1936. Perhaps the best-known poll disaster came in 1948, when surveys showed Gov Thomas E. Dewey easily beating Pres Harry S. Truman for the presidency, but the incumbent won an upset victory.

Independent state-level polls developed first in Texas, Iowa, Minnesota, and California in the 1940s. The first to make extensive and regular use of polls in New York State politics was Thomas E. Dewey, doing so to help gauge public opinion on the state government in 1942 when he made a successful bid for the governor. Routine use of polling in state politics had to wait until the governorship of Nelson A. Rockefeller (1959–73). Since Rockefeller, almost all candidates for statewide office, the legislature, and top posts in major local governments regularly use polls to shape their campaign messages in ways reflecting voter attitudes. Political parties also use polls to assess whether to support potential candidates. Polling strategists routinely serve as top advisers to elected officials in major offices, such as governor.

In 1935 George Gallup set up headquarters at the Institute for Public Opinion at 114 Nassau St in Manhattan for his Gallup poll, and today the Gallup organization employs more than 2,000 specialists at 40 offices in 20 countries around the world, with headquarters in Princeton, NJ. Zogby International of Utica and the Marist College Institute for Public Opinion in Poughkeepsie regularly conduct polls on New York State politics and policy matters. In addition to Zogby, several national media polling operations—including the CBS/*New York Times,* and NBC/*Wall Street Journal*—are also based in New York City.

Moore, David W. *The Super Pollsters: How They Measure and Manipulate Public Opinion in America* (New York: Four Walls Eight Windows, 1992)

Robert B. Ward

pollution. New York State's cities, towns, and villages enjoyed the legal right to establish their own sanitary regulations well into the 19th century. Early pollution resulted from the by-products of slaughterhouses, tanneries, breweries, distilleries, and households. The first pollution law in the state dates to 1866, when the legislature created the Metropolitan Board of Health to control unsanitary conditions in New York City that might be considered "dangerous or detrimental to life or health." In 1880 the first Public Health Law was enacted to provide the state with specific authorities regarding nuisances, and in 1881 the newly formed State Board of Health made its first public statements on the implementation of the new law and issued to local authorities "a proposed form of sanitary regulations" instead of mandating any particular requirements.

Water Quality

The New York Rivers and Harbors Act of 1888 prohibited the disposal of pollutants into the Hudson River and its tributaries. The legislature codified public health laws in 1893, elevating the state's authority on sanitation matters, but there was still no formal pollution law to deal with growing industrialization. By 1900 pollution problems were becoming evident in New York City, along the Erie Canal system and the Hudson River, and on the Niagara Frontier. The New York State legislature passed the first general antipollution law in 1903 under the Public Health Law. Its most promising provisions were a prohibition on discharges of sewage and waste in quantities sufficient to injure public health and the new authorities it gave to the state health commissioner to make such a determination. Over time the legislature passed new laws protecting fish, forests, and watersheds that in 1913 were consolidated into a general conservation law. Also in 1913 the Department of Health acquired new powers with the creation of the Public Health Council, which was given the authority to devise the new Sanitary Code.

The state conservation commissioner began comprehensive pollution studies in 1918, and the Joint Legislative Committee in Reference to the Pollution of Waters in the State began its own work on policy recommendations regarding sewage disposal in 924. Starting that year sewage was disposed of 12 nautical miles (22 km) offshore, where the Atlantic Ocean was about 88 ft (27 m) deep; the practice continued until 1987. In 1926 another joint legislative resolution expanded the committee's mandate to include industrial pollution. The recommendations focused on the most severely polluted rivers, especially those in New York City as well as the Hudson and Mohawk Rivers. A 1935 joint legislative resolution created the Committee on Interstate Cooperation with a mandate of controlling the pollution of interstate waters; it also had an important role in the development of environmental policy within New York State. The Joint Legislative Committee on Natural Resources (JLCNR) assumed the responsibility of developing environmental legislation in the 1950s, but their activities were mostly limited to sewage disposal matters. New requirements for water treatment facilities created tensions between the state government and municipalities over the financing of these public works projects. But water pollution remained a serious problem. For instance, in 1965 the US Military Academy at West Point was found to be disposing of partially treated sewage into the Hudson River at the rate of 1.2 million gallons (4.54 million l) per day.

Chemistry professor Bruce McDuffie of SUNY Binghamton brought one of the consequences of water pollution to international attention in the fall of 1970, when his investigation of canned supermarket tuna revealed it contained 0.75 parts per million (ppm) of mercury (a heavy metal that can cause blindness and death), which is 50% greater than the Food and Drug Administration (FDA) limit. McDuffie's investigation of commercially available swordfish revealed even higher concentrations of mercury. On 23 June 1976 the barge *Nepco,* grounded in fog at Wellesley Island, discharged a 30 mi (48 km) long slick on the St. Lawrence Seaway, from Wellesley Island (Jefferson Co) to Morristown (St. Lawrence Co), endangering or killing wildfowl, fish, and semiaquatic mammals. Lakes and rivers have also been threatened by the introduction of phosphorus compounds, which cause the overgrowth of plants, depriving fish of oxygen. In 1979 Suffolk Co issued one of the first bans on laundry detergents that contained phosphorous compounds.

Air Pollution

Both stationary sources (eg, industries) and mobile sources (eg, automobiles) contribute unwanted emissions to the atmosphere. Nitrogen dioxide (NO_2), carbon monoxide (CO), and sulfur dioxide (SO_2), as well as hydrocarbons, result from fossil fuel combustion. In 1952 the JLCNR began a four-year investigation into New York

Protest banner at Onondaga Lake, 1991.

State air pollution. At that time complaints about air pollution mainly concerned smoke and odors; dust, soot, ash, and gases were of lesser concern. A pollution episode in New York City 17–23 Nov 1953, marked by high levels of SO_2, resulted in widespread complaints of eye irritation, respiratory distress, and increased mortality. Only New York City and Buffalo/Niagara Falls were interested in developing a broad program of air pollution control. The JLCNR investigation resulted in the Air Pollution Control Act of 1957. By 1959 Albany, Binghamton, Buffalo, New York City, Niagara Falls, Rochester, Schenectady, Syracuse, Utica, and Yonkers, as well as a nonurban station at Tibbett Point in Cape Vincent (Jefferson Co), were participating in the National Air Sampling Network. State legislation passed in August 1966 directed the New York Air Pollution Control Board to regulate automobile emissions within the parameters of federal guidelines.

When gasoline vapors and hydrocarbons react with sunlight, they form ground-level ozone and peroxyacetyl nitrate. Breathing ground-level ozone can cause throat irritation and chest pain, and that ozone is also damaging to crops and other vegetation. Peroxyacetyl nitrate causes stinging, tearing eyes. Ground-level ozone, peroxyacetyl nitrate, and particulate matter are the major components of smog. During the Thanksgiving weekend of 1966 a temperature inversion held a stagnant mass of air over the Northeast coast for five days, causing Gov Nelson A. Rockefeller to declare an air-pollution emergency in New York City. Statistical analysis attributed 168 deaths to this episode, and such episodes brought recognition of the threat of photochemical smog to New York State. In January 1967 a federal study disclosed that New York City's high level of SO_2 presented a health threat. In 1970 the United States passed the Clean Air Act, which set pollution level standards for NO_2, CO_2, SO_2, ozone, and particulates, and described asbestos as a "hazardous air pollutant." Asbestos, a natural fibrous silicate mineral, was required as fireproof insulation in newly built schools and in schools undergoing renovation since 1940. Particles of asbestos, released into the air through construction activity, can be inhaled and cause serious, often fatal, lung disease. Schools abandoned the use of asbestos insulation in 1973; the EPA banned the installation of asbestos in all new buildings in 1975.

Hazardous Chemicals

The US Environmental Protection Agency (EPA) and the New York State Department of Environmental Conservation (DEC) were created in 1970. A renewed public interest in ecology stimulated environmental activism and led to new laws dealing with water quality, waste disposal, and air quality. Anaconda Wire and Copper Co had been disposing of oil and solvents into the Hudson River in Hastings-on-Hudson (Westchester Co). In 1971 the company was charged with violating the federal Refuse Act of 1899, which prohibited disposing of any waste except sewage and runoff into navigable rivers. The Western New York Nuclear Service Center, a commercial nuclear reprocessing plant in West Valley (Cattaraugus Co), was shut down in 1972. It had been in operation for six years and left 2.4 million ft^3 (68,000 m^3) of solid radioactive waste, 600,000 gallons (2,270 m^3) of liquid radioactive waste, and 170 tons (154 MT) of depleted nuclear fuel rods. By the late 20th century, the site was co-managed by the New York State Energy Research and Development Authority and the US Department of Energy, which are overseeing the remediation.

Developments in the chemical industry led to the emergence of persistent organic pollutants (POPs), such as polychlorinated biphenyls (PCBs), which were marketed as fire-resistant insulators for electrical components. POPs tend to stay in the environment and accumulate as they move higher in the food chain. Starting in 1946 General Electric (GE) plants that manufactured electric capacitors at Fort Edward and Hudson Falls (Washington Co) discharged over 30 pounds (14 kg) of PCBs per day into the Hudson River. State officials recorded levels of PCBs over the limits set by the FDA in bass and salmon taken from the river near industrial sites in 1975. The *New York Times* took up the issue and the federal Toxic Substances Control Act of 1976 banned the manufacture of PCBs. Dumping of PCBs by the Hudson Falls and Fort Edward plants finally ended in 1977. Other POPs include organochlorinated insecticides such as DDT (dichlorodiphenyltrichloroethane) and BHC (benzene hexachloride, or hexachlorocyclohexane).

The discovery of toxic contamination, including the carcinogen 2,3,7,8-tetrachlorodibenzo-p-dioxin (TCDD), at Love Canal in Niagara Falls (Niagara Co) had enormous implications for environmental policy and politics locally, but also became a national concern. A 7 Aug 1978 presidential declaration made Love Canal the first man-made environmental disaster to become a federal emergency. The Comprehensive Environmental Response, Compensation, and Liability Act of 1980 (CERCLA), known as the Superfund, was enacted in response to the situation at Love Canal. CERCLA provides for the identification and remediation of toxic waste sites. The Superfund is supported by taxes on the industries that produce toxic wastes and by funds collected through litigation against polluters. As of year-end 2000, DEC had investigated 1,714 potentially contaminated sites across New York State; 624 revealed no hazardous wastes on-site, and 401 were remediated. Of the latter, 231 were closed and the contaminants contained, and 170 were removed from the registry subsequent to contaminant removal or destruction. Sediment sampling of the Hudson River extending 40 miles (64 km) north from Albany began in August 2002 to prepare for dredging to remove over 150,000 pounds (68,000 kg) of PCBs; the EPA expects GE to pay the $460 million anticipated costs of the dredging project.

Radon was widely recognized as an indoor air pollution danger beginning in 1985, when high levels of it were documented in homes in the Reading Prong, a uranium-enriched granite formation underlying part of southern New York as well as parts of Pennsylvania and New Jersey. The product of the decay of uranium into radium, radon 222 is a colorless, odorless, inert radioactive gas with a half-life of 3.8 days. It decays to nongaseous radioactive products that can be inhaled when attached to dust or other particulate matter; these radioactive particles can be a significant cause of lung cancer. Radon can accumulate in poorly ventilated houses built on the granite and dark shales common in New York State. The regions with the highest potential for radon are the Middle Hudson, the Capital District, the Mohawk Valley, Central New York, Western New York, Buffalo/Niagara, and the Southern Tier, as well as Washington Co.

Consequences of Antipollution Legislation

Because the practice of disposing of solid waste in landfills can contaminate an aquifer (the porous, water-bearing layer of rock that supplies wells), in June 1983 Gov Mario M. Cuomo signed legislation to phase out disposal of solid waste in New York State landfills by 1990. Concerns over public health and waste disposal garnered national attention in 1987, when the Town of Islip (Nassau Co) arranged with United Marine Transport Services to ship 3,200 tons (2,900 MT) of baled municipal refuse to North Carolina, where Alabama-based contractor Lowell Harrelson expected to turn the trash into methane fuel. On 22 Mar 1987, the tugboat *Break of Dawn* left New York Harbor towing the barge *Mobro 4000.* Rumors that its cargo was contaminated with hospital waste preceded the "Garbage Barge," and it was denied acceptance at Morehead City, NC. Attempted landings at Louisiana, Texas, Florida, Mexico, the Bahamas, and Belize were similarly aborted. The *Mobro 4000* returned to New York Harbor under police escort on 16 May 1987. In accordance with the judgment passed at Kings County Supreme Court on 27 July 1987, the trash was inspected for hazardous materials before it was burned in the Southwest Brooklyn incinerator. The resultant 430 tons (390 MT) of ash were buried at the Islip landfill.

New York State industries continue to generate pollution, but federal "community right-to-know" regulations make this information available to the public as well as government regulators. The US Toxic Release Inventory (TRI) reports releases and transfers of over 640 individually listed chemicals and chemical categories. According to EPA data available for industrial releases of toxic chemicals, 737 industries in New York State were responsible for 60.5 million pounds (27.4 million kg) of toxic chemical releases and transfers into the environment in 2000. This was a 15.7% decrease from 1999 and a 43% decrease since 1988, when the reporting requirements were first established. Actual reductions are more significant given that more industries are required to report emissions at present than was the case in the early years of the program. In 2000, 53% of the reported chemicals, 32.6 million pounds (14.8 million kg), were released into the atmosphere through stack emissions. This was a 9.3% decrease from 1999 and a 68% decrease since 1988. Other air emissions from diffuse sources (fugitive emissions) increased by 3.8% to 3.9 million pounds (1.8 million kg), accounting for 6.4% of total releases. Surface-water discharges accounted for 14.9% of total chemical releases, amounting to 9 million pounds (4.1 million kg) in 2000. This involved an 8.6% decrease from 1999 and a 260% increase since 1988. On-site land disposal made up 9.6% of pollution releases in 2000, amounting to 5.8 million pounds (2.6 million kg), a 6.5% decrease from 1999 and a 9.4% decrease since 1988. Off-site shipments of toxic waste to treatment, storage, and disposal facilities accounted for approximately 16.5% of the state's industrial pollution releases in 2000, totaling 10 million pounds (4.5 million kg), a 0.7% decrease from 1999 and a 65% decrease since 1988. The facilities with the largest emissions in 2000 were located in Chautauqua, Erie, Essex, Monroe, Niagara, Orange, Rockland, Saratoga, St. Lawrence, Warren, and Yates Cos.

Even though vehicle miles traveled since 1970 have doubled, DEC's air quality program has achieved impressive decreases of 100% in airborne lead, 55% in volatile organics, 40% in carbon monoxide, and 20% in particulates through 2000. It also controls vehicular emissions by regulating fuels and testing and researching exhaust emissions. Two principal air pollution difficulties remain for New York State: acid deposition and ground-level ozone. The regulation of acid deposition is complicated because most of it derives from coal-fired utilities in the Ohio Valley. Acid deposition is also caused by mobile sources, as is ground-level ozone. The current EPA standard for ground-level ozone is 0.08 ppm averaged over an eight-hour period. Levels less than 0.065 ppm are considered good, levels from 0.065 to 0.084 ppm are considered moderate, and levels greater than that are considered unhealthy by state and federal regulators. The worst problems occur from mid-May to mid-September, and the highest levels in New York State occur in the New York City and Buffalo metropolitan areas. The 11 Sept 2001 terrorist attacks on the World Trade Center caused the combustion of approximately 200,000 gallons (757,000 l) of fuel and oil, releasing the fossil fuel pollutants into the air. The massive destruction of office buildings and equipment, plastics, paper products, and wood, released such toxic atmospheric pollutants as dioxins and furans as well as asbestos and lead.

See also Fishing, recreational (freshwater); Genesee river; Lake Champlain; Lake Erie; Lake Ontario; Love Canal; Oswego river system; Sanitation and sewage.

Berton, Pierre. *Niagara: A History of the Falls* (Toronto: McClelland & Stewart, 1992)
Boyle, Robert H. *The Hudson River: A Natural and Unnatural History* (New York: Norton, 1979)
Dow, Charles M. *The State Reservation at Niagara: A History* (Albany: J. B. Lyon, 1914)
Martin, Roscoe C. *Water for New York: A Study in State Administration of Water Resources* (Syracuse: Syracuse Univ Press, 1960)
Mavor, James. *Niagara in Politics: A Critical Account of the Ontario Hydro-Electric Commission* (New York: Dutton, 1925)
Meinig, D. W. "Geography of Expansion." In *Geography of New York State,* ed. John H. Thompson (Syracuse: Syracuse Univ Press, 1977)
New York State Department of Environmental Conservation. *New York State Inactive Hazardous Waste Disposal Site Remedial Plan: 2000 Report* (Albany, 2000)
US Environmental Protection Agency. "Toxics Release Inventory (TRI) Program," www.epa.gov/tri/

Thomas Fletcher

polo. A sport played on horseback in which two teams, each with four players, attempt to hit a ball between goal posts set at each end of a 10-acre (4 ha) grass field. Polo was imported to the United States from India, where it had become popular with British soldiers, by James Gordon Bennett, publisher of the *New York Herald,* in 1876. The first match was played at an indoor riding academy in Manhattan, and shortly afterward Bennett formed the Westchester Polo Club.

The sport's popularity grew swiftly, with an 1879 match at Prospect Park in Brooklyn between the Westchester and Queens Co clubs drawing 10,000 spectators. The same year North America's most famous club, the Meadowbrook Polo Club, was established and played in Old Westbury [now in Nassau Co]. By the turn of the century Long Island had become the center for the American game. Other clubs formed in the state, including the Oyster Bay Polo Club [now in Nassau Co], organized in 1890 by Theodore Roosevelt, and the Saratoga Polo Club in 1898, with the game reaching western New York State in 1904 when James Wadsworth formed a club in Geneseo (Livingston Co). By 1910 clubs had formed in Buffalo, Albany, and Otsego. In 1883 one of the first outdoor polo grounds in the United States, just north of Central Park in Manhattan, was the home of the New York Giants baseball team. When the team moved to Coogan's Bluffs in Upper Manhattan in 1891, the new field retained the name Polo Grounds, although polo was never played.

Polo's popularity crested in the decades between the world wars when Tommy Hitchcock Jr (1900–1944), probably the greatest of all American players, played for the Meadowbrook Polo Club and lived for several years in Old Westbury. Crowds in excess of 30,000 were typical at Old Westbury matches; the Westchester Cup, one of the oldest and most prestigious international competitions, was frequently held there. After World War II, however, the game rapidly declined in New York State. In the early 1950s the Meadowbrook Club moved to Jericho (Nassau Co) when the construction of the Long Island Expressway (I-495) forced a relocation; the club never recovered its preeminent position.

Since the 1960s there has been both a nationwide and a statewide resurgence of the sport. In 2003 there were 17 polo clubs in New York State affiliated with the US Polo Association, including college clubs at Cornell, Skidmore, and Vassar; 14 of the clubs were founded after 1970. Long Island has four clubs, including Meadowbrook; Orange and Schenectady Cos each have three; Saratoga and Tompkins Cos each have two, and Dutchess, Erie, and Onondaga Cos each have one.

Milburn, Frank. *Polo: The Emperor of Games* (New York: Knopf, 1994)

Eric L. Kline

Polytechnic University. Private university. The second-oldest independent engineering and technical university in the country, the Brooklyn Collegiate and Polytechnic Institute opened in 1854 in downtown Brooklyn. It conferred its first bachelor of science and bachelor of arts degrees in 1871 and changed its name to the Polytechnic Institute of Brooklyn in 1889. Master's degrees were added in 1901, and the school awarded its first BA degree to a woman, Anna Erdman, in 1907. The following year the liberal arts program was dropped from the curriculum. Coeducational study was also discontinued but reinstated on both graduate and undergraduate levels in

1958. The school entered into a merger agreement in 1973 with New York University, which agreed to transfer the charter of its own Bronx-based School of Engineering and Sciences to the Brooklyn school, forming the Polytechnic Institute of New York. It became Polytechnic University in 1985. The undergraduate program remains centered in downtown Brooklyn on a 16-acre (6.5 ha) campus adjacent to the Brooklyn Bridge. Graduate centers are located in Melville (Suffolk Co), Hawthorne (Westchester Co), and Manhattan. Degrees are offered at the bachelor's, master's, and doctoral levels in engineering and the sciences, computer science, and information management. Polytechnic enrolled 1,525 undergraduates in 2003.

Marianne Rahn-Erickson

Pomfret. Town (pop 14,703) in NW Chautauqua Co. Settled in 1804 the town formed from Chautauqua in 1808. More than 30 factories were built in early years using the waterpower of Canadaway Creek. The shipping of grape roots became an important industry *ca* 1875 and was continued in the 21st century. Lily Dale, a camp meeting ground of Spiritualists, was organized in 1879 and is still extant. Newton Memorial Hospital (1920–58) treated tuberculosis cases; since 1977 its site has been the Cassadaga Job Corps Center. The New York State Thruway was completed through town in 1957. With the growth of SUNY Fredonia, the population has continued to increase into the early 21st century.

Michelle Henry

Pomona. Village (pop 2,726) in Haverstraw and Ramapo (Rockland Co). Camp Hill Rd was the site of American troop encampments in the Revolutionary War. The name of Pomona, the Roman goddess of fruit, was given to its new post office in 1876 in recognition of the area's orchards. During their marriage from 1944 to 1949, Paulette Goddard and Burgess Meredith built a house in Pomona where they also opened an antiques shop. Frederick Loewe and Alan Jay Lerner later wrote *My Fair Lady* in the Goddard-Meredith house. Pomona was incorporated in 1967 to control zoning and prevent overbuilding.

Pompey [POM-PEE]. Town (pop 6,159) in SE Onondaga Co. Settled in 1791, the town was formed in 1794. Its residents founded Pompey Academy (1811–95), the first in Onondaga Co. Nineteenth-century industries included the Ten Eyck woolen factory (1812–53), one of two in town, the Salisbury (1823–?1890s) edge-tool factory, and brickmaking. Irish farmers settled in town and the first Catholic mass was said in 1857. The 306-acre (124 ha) Pratts Falls County Park includes a 137 ft (41.8 m) waterfall. Among the town's famous natives were sculptor Erastus Dow Palmer (1817–1904), Gov Horatio Seymour (1810–86), financier Leonard Jerome (1817–91), and Sarah J. Clarke (1823–85), who wrote Victorian novels under the name Grace Greenwood. Dairy farming dominated the town through most of the 20th century and continues as an important land use. Housing developments in the northern part consume a relatively small area, but many new home plots are scattered throughout Pompey.

Sylvia Berry Shoebridge

poorhouses. See ALMSHOUSES AND POORHOUSES.

Poospatuck (Poosepatuck) Indian Reservation [Unkechaug Nation]. The Unkechaug, an Algonquian-speaking people, lived along the southern shore of eastern Long Island for thousands of years before the Europeans arrived. As the European settlements expanded and the traditional hunting grounds were taken over for farms, the Indian communities dispersed. By the end of the 17th century, European diseases had disrupted communities and had taken a frightful toll on Indian life. The Unkechaug and other Long Island Indians found themselves marginalized wanderers in their ancient homelands. In 1700 Col William Smith, who had received a large land grant on the south shore of Long Island in what is now the Town of Brookhaven (Suffolk Co), sought to alleviate the situation in the local area by granting a 175-acre (71 ha) reservation to the Unkechaug. Poospatuck Indian Reservation lies on the bank of the Forge River where it runs into the tidal wetlands near Mastic. The place was known to the Indians as Poospatuck, a word some believe means "where a little river flows into tidal water." The Unkechaug were joined by remnants of other Long Island Algonquian-speaking communities and by African Americans who married tribal members.

During the later decades of the 17th century, many Unkechaug men were employed as whalers. They hunted the Right whales, which migrated along the coast of Long Island from November to March. White owners formed whaling companies and hired Indians to do the dangerous work of hunting the whales in small cedar boats carrying crews of six men. Within a few decades the Right whales in the area were nearly eliminated, forcing a major adjustment in the whaling enterprise. Large ships were sent out on whaling expeditions to distant waters, with only a few of the Indian whalers on them. Most of the men instead found employment in the English communities as day laborers, and the women worked as domestics.

When New York State replaced the colonial government, the Poospatuck reservation attained de facto recognition. Christian missionaries often visited the reservation in the 18th century. Two, Samson Occom and Peter John Cuffee, were Indians who preached to many small Indian communities throughout Long Island. In 1812 a Methodist church was built on the reservation. The church became the center of community activity until it was displaced by a Presbyterian church in the 20th century. In 1875 New York State established a public school on the reservation. At the end of the 19th century a tribal government consisting of an elected chief and a council of three elders was established. In the 19th and early 20th centuries, parcel after parcel of the original reservation was taken over by Whites in highly questionable land grabs, leaving only 50 acres (20 ha), and in 1935 an attempt was made to evict the Poospatuck from their reservation. In a lengthy court case the judge ruled in favor of the Poospatucks and changed their de facto status to full state recognition. Beginning in the 1980s tax-free tobacco stores on the reservation have provided a significant source of income to several tribal members. Although they adapted to several European lifeways, the Unkechaug retain many of their ancient customs. One of the most significant communal ceremonies is the annual June Meeting, which can be traced back to an aboriginal celebration of the spring season. The children learn about tribal customs in an after-school program at the community center on the reservation. At the beginning of the 21st century, about 250 people live in very crowded conditions. In 1994 the tribe elected a new tribal chief, Harry Wallace, who is committed to expanding community self-help projects and to reaffirming traditional culture; Chief Wallace was reelected for five straight years by a large majority.

Gonzales, Ellice, B. *From Unkechaug to Poospatuck* (Patchogue, NY: National Park Service, Fire Island National Seashore, 1984)

Strong, John A. *"We Are Still Here!" The Algonquian Peoples of Long Island Today,* 2d ed (Interlaken, NY: Empire State Books, 1998)

John A. Strong

Popular Front culture. During the 1930s and 1940s, New York City was a center for cultural activities expressing the political perspective of a broad left wing tied to the labor movement, the Roosevelt wing of the Democratic Party, and the social world of the Communist Party, which after 1934 worked more closely with "bourgeois" culture and left-leaning political parties. By 1936–37, this social movement was known as the Popular Front. Its culture was rooted in the immigrant left, the African American community, the Congress of Industrial Organizations (CIO), and the New Deal. It emphasized the rights and dignity of organized labor and a democratic vision of racial harmony and ethnic diversity. Popular Front culture was marked by tensions among social democrats, Communists, and former Communists; while New York City was the center of Communist Party membership, social democrats dominated the trade unions. Although conflicting ideological and aesthetic agendas often pitted New York intellectuals and modernists against working-class activists, the Popular Front movement shared many points of convergence with proletarian culture.

Eastern European Jews were heavily represented in radical culture with theater companies, folk orchestras and dance troupes, socialist and Communist Yiddish language newspapers, literary journals, and a Communist humor magazine, *Der Hammer.* In the post–World War I period there was an unprecedented explosion of African American cultural production, with Harlem Renaissance writers such as Langston Hughes and Claude McKay confronting social issues. The Scottsboro case, starting in 1931, increased black sympathy for the left. This trend culminated in the election of Communist Ben Davis as Harlem's City Council member in 1943. Established and new writers, including John Dos Passos and Ralph Ellison, published in journals such as Michael Gold's *New Masses* (1926); *Partisan Review* (1935), which had an anti-Stalinist editorial policy after 1937, and a profusion of literary and political "little magazines." The first and largest chapter of the John Reed Club was in New York City; in 1933 it was instrumental in organizing unemployed artists and writers, which led to the formation of the Artists Union and the Writers Union. The American Writers' and Artists' Congresses held in New York City in 1935–37 brought many new talents into the fold.

The Composers' Collective was formed in the early 1930s by Charles Seeger, Ruth Crawford,

Aaron Copland, Earl Robinson, Marc Blitzstein, Elie Siegmeister, and Wallingford Riegger to promote new American concert music. Several of its members taught at the Downtown Music School and organized workers' choruses. Folksongs including Appalachian ballads, blues, and spirituals were popularized by Paul Robeson, Lead Belly, Woody Guthrie, the Almanac Singers, and Pete Seeger. Jazz was another musical genre closely associated with Popular Front culture, as reflected in John Hammond's groundbreaking 1938–39 Spirituals to Swing concerts at Carnegie Hall and performances at Barney Josephson's Café Society (1938–48) by Billie Holiday, Teddy Wilson, Hazel Scott, Josh White, Lena Horne, and Sarah Vaughan. The blend of jazz, blues, and political cabaret songs at the Café Society, a racially integrated nightclub where in 1939 Holiday sang "Strange Fruit" (a song protesting southern lynching), had a lasting influence on American popular music. Many painters turned their attention to portrayals of working-class life and social struggle. The American Contemporary Art Gallery and the Downtown Gallery were important venues for such artists as Ben Shahn and Jacob Lawrence.

Communist Party members were among those active in projects funded by the Works Progress Administration (WPA) for the relief of unemployed artists, writers, musicians, and theater workers. The WPA sponsored art classes and murals, and employed writers to create a series of state guidebooks. Its most ambitious and successful effort in the arts was the Federal Theatre Project (FTP). Directed by Hallie Flanagan and administered from New York City, the FTP sponsored hundreds of regional and local productions nationwide, with the largest unit in New York City employing over 5,000 people. Its innovative and controversial plays included a critically acclaimed all-black *Macbeth* staged by Orson Welles and John Houseman in 1936, and the Living Newspaper series, a new form of social theater addressing topical issues.

The perceived left-wing bias of some productions led to congressional hearings charging that the FTP was dominated by the Communist-affiliated Workers' Alliance. Funding was eliminated during a 1937 national steel strike on the eve of the premiere of Blitzstein's pro-labor musical *The Cradle Will Rock*. In one of the most famous opening-night events in the history of American theater, after the initial venue was shuttered, Welles and Houseman led the audience up Broadway to a rented theater in Columbus Circle, where cast members performed the show from the house seats. Blitzstein's work had a successful run and led to the formation of the Mercury Theatre. Popular Front culture's biggest public success came in 1937 with the labor revue *Pins and Needles*, sponsored by the International Ladies' Garment Workers' Union (ILGWU). Featuring workers who were theater amateurs in musical sketches and political satire, it attracted a working-class audience and ran for over three years, then a record for a Broadway musical. Many other theater companies were at the forefront of Popular Front culture, notably the Group Theatre, which introduced the plays of Clifford Odets, and the American Negro Theatre. The New Deal and the struggle against fascism made many Popular Front figures more mainstream, with such popular entertainers as Frank Sinatra lending their talents and fame to creative projects. The Hitler-Stalin pact of 1939 marked the ebbing of the Popular Front, and after it was revived during the years of US-Soviet collaboration during World War II, it came to an end in the early years of the Cold War, though many of its leading figures went on to enjoy long and successful careers.

Denning, Michael. *The Cultural Front* (New York: Verso, 1997)

Dunaway, David K. "Unsung Songs of Protest: The Composers Collective of New York," *New York Folklore* 5 (Summer 1979: 1–19)

Flanagan, Hallie. *Arena: The History of the Federal Theatre* (1940; repr New York: Proscenium Publishers, 1985)

Nekola, Charlotte, and Paula Rabinowitz. *Writing Red: An Anthology of Women Writers, 1930–1940* (New York: Feminist Press, 1987)

North, Joseph. *New Masses: An Anthology of the Rebel Thirties* (New York: International Publishers, 1969)

Paul C. Mishler

Poquott. Village (pop 975) in Brookhaven (Suffolk Co). Originally called George's Neck, it divides Port Jefferson and Setauket Harbors. By 1917 it was divided into 25 estates. The village was incorporated in 1931. It has both luxury homes on the Long Island Sound waterfront and modest houses and bungalows to the south and east, many of them converted from summer cottages.

Beverly C. Tyler

Portage. Town (pop 859) in SW Livingston Co. Settled in 1814 and formed from Nunda in 1827, Portage was annexed to Livingston Co in 1846. The Genesee River's rocky ravines and scenic waterfalls extend along most of the town's western boundary, and east of the river is rolling farmland. The Buffalo Division of the Erie Railroad (1852) replaced the Genesee Valley Canal (1840–78) as the major commercial route; the Pennsylvania Railroad later served the town until the 1960s. The Cascade House (1853) developed as a resort at the eastern end of an extraordinary wooden railroad bridge (1852–75), some 800 feet (244 m) long and 235 feet (72 m) high, later replaced by a iron bridge that still stands. A part of Letchworth State Park (1907) lies within town limits.

Mary Jo Marks

Port Authority of New York and New Jersey. Founded by the states of New York and New Jersey on 30 Apr 1921, its jurisdiction encompasses a 25 mi (40 km) radius from the Statue of Liberty, consisting of New York City, portions of Nassau, Westchester, and Rockland Cos and portions of nine New Jersey counties. The Port Authority (called the Port of New York Authority until 1 July 1972) has a 12-member board of commissioners, 6 appointed by each state governor. Since 1926 the governors have had the right to veto the authority's actions. Traditionally the chairman of the board has been from New Jersey, and the executive director has been from New York. The chief architect of the Port Authority, Julius Henry Cohen, Authority General Council from 1921 to 1942 and a Manhattan Democratic progressive, developed the idea of the bistate compact to alleviate tensions arising from the need for most area rail freight to be unloaded at New Jersey ports and ferried to New York City docks. The chief mandate of the new authority was to reorganize the freight system in the metropolitan area, but the railroad companies balked, and the authority had neither the power nor the funds to implement its ambitious plans. One consequence was a new interest in improving interstate vehicular transportation. In 1925 the authority agreed to build four vehicular bridges. Three of the spans connected Staten Island to New Jersey: the Goethals Bridge (1928), the Outerbridge Crossing (1928), and the Bayonne Bridge (1931). The fourth, the George Washington Bridge, spanned the Hudson River and connected Manhattan to New Jersey. Opened in 1931, the George Washington, designed by Othmar H. Ammann (who headed the authority's engineering department until 1939), was the longest suspension bridge in the world. In 1930 the authority gained control of the Holland Tunnel (opened in 1927) and the Holland Tunnel Commission and then built the first tube of the Lincoln Tunnel in 1937; additional tubes were added in 1945 and 1957.

The Hudson River crossings gave the authority a steady flow of revenue and made the authority a model on which future authorities, such as the federal Tennessee Valley Authority, were based. At the same time, the Great Depression cut deeply into revenue and future plans, bringing retrenchment to the authority. Austin Tobin, a Brooklyn lawyer who served as executive director from 1942 to 1972, set the authority on a new course of expansion. Besting Robert Moses in a battle of bureaucratic titans, the authority assumed management of the New York City airports, both the fledgling Idlewild Airport (now John F. Kennedy International Airport) and La Guardia Airport in 1947, and added Newark International Airport in 1949. The authority defeated Moses again in 1950 with the construction of one of Manhattan's most famous landmarks, the Midtown Port Authority Bus Terminal. Another bus terminal, the George Washington Bridge Terminal, was built in 1963. In 1956 the authority pioneered cargo containerization with the construction of Port Newark. Containerization is now the industry standard for maritime freight movement, and the authority now maintains seven container facilities, making the ports of New York and New Jersey among the world's largest.

The building of the World Trade Center required a delicate balancing of New York State and New Jersey interests. At New Jersey's insistence, the authority reluctantly acquired the Hudson and Manhattan Railroad Co (H&M) (now PATH, Port Authority Trans-Hudson Corp), a small commuter line connecting New Jersey with Manhattan, as the price for building the center. Located in Manhattan's Financial District, the center consisted of a massive seven-building complex with two 110-story towers, completed in 1972–73. Other projects include the Newark Legal Center (1989), the Staten Island Teleport, and various other industrial parks and facilities. In 2001 the authority had a budget of $4.6 billion, a total net worth of $35 billion in facilities, and 7,200 employees. Under Tobin, the authority reached its height of bureaucratic independence from its two state masters; in recent decades it has been kept on a shorter leash. The Port Authority has always been controversial. From its inception, politicians in New York State and New Jersey were often suspicious of its prerogatives and powers and their lack of oversight of its activities. In recent years New York City mayor Rudolph Giuliani attacked the authority for its alleged bias toward New Jersey and called for it to be broken up; New York State governor George E. Pataki has also tried to curb its independence.

The worst day in the history of the Port Authority was 11 Sept 2001, when a terrorist attack on the World Trade Center resulted in the destruction of the seven-building complex, including the toppling of both twin towers and the collapse of the PATH station located beneath the site. The Port Authority's headquarters, located at the center, was destroyed. Of the approximately 2,000 Port Authority employees who worked at the complex, 74 lost their lives, including 37 members of the authority's police department.

See also BONDED INDEBTEDNESS.

Doig, Jameson W. *Empire on the Hudson: Political Power and Progress at the Port of New York Authority* (New York: Columbia Univ Press, 2000)

Port Authority of New York and New Jersey. *Annual Reports* (New York: Author)

Thomas A. Birkland

Port Authority Trans-Hudson Corporation. See PATH (PORT AUTHORITY TRANS-HUDSON CORPORATION).

Port Byron. Village (pop 1,297) in Mentz (Cayuga Co). A post office named Mentz was established in 1816 and renamed Port Byron in 1824. A woolen mill was established in 1821. The Erie Canal (1819) transformed the community into one of the state's principal grain centers. To service this trade, a large dry dock, now part of the Canal Park, was constructed. One of the state's largest flouring mills (1828–57) operated in the village, and later in the century such enterprises as a foundry, planing mill, and sash and blind factory were also present. The village was incorporated in 1837. The New York Central Railroad came through in 1853, and the West Shore Railroad in 1884. In the mid–20th century the principal industry was the H. C. Gutchess Co, mincemeat makers. The Erie House operated as a saloon along the canal from 1894 to 1917 and was a canal museum in 2002.

Penny Helzer

Port Chester. Village (pop 27,867) in Rye (Westchester Co). Known by 1732 as Saw Pit, it began as a minor landing on Long Island Sound at which some small lots were surveyed in 1741. The shipment of grain, beef, and pork from inland farms became an increasingly important business beginning in 1798 but declined in the 1830s. The name Port Chester was adopted in 1837. It moved toward manufacturing, including the Eagle Foundry (1840–1920) owned by Abendroth Brothers, and the Russell, Burdsall and Ward Bolt and Nut Co (1882–1973), among many others. The village was incorporated in 1868. Among its 20th-century employers was Beech-Nut Life Savers (1920–85, originally Mint Products Co). As an industrial village it has drawn many immigrants and, in 2003, it is home to families of Irish, Italian, and Polish ancestry, with Latino and black families in the downtown core. The William E. Ward House (1876), the first concrete house in the United States, is a landmark. Television personality Ed Sullivan (1902–74) grew up in Port Chester.

Port Dickinson. Village (pop 1,697) in Dickinson (Broome Co). The Old State Rd from Catskill terminated at Port Dickinson, which grew as a canal port after the Chenango Canal opened in 1837. In the 19th century it had a number of factories that produced paper, plaster, barrels, whips, cotton batting, and brooms; Carman's Binghamton Pickling and Preserving Works and Stow's Flexible Shaft Works were large industries. The village incorporated in 1876, the year the canal closed, and is now primarily residential.

Charles J. Browne

Porter. Town (pop 6,920) in NW Niagara Co. René-Robert Cavelier de la Salle built Fort Conti in 1678, but it burned soon afterward. The French later built what is now called Old Fort Niagara (1724). This was transferred by the British to the United States in 1796. Civilian settlement began in 1801, and the town was formed from Cambria in 1812. A short-lived railroad brought passengers from Niagara Falls to Youngstown in the 1850s, but the Rome, Watertown and Ogdensburg Railroad (1876) made Ransomville, the only station in Porter, a thriving agricultural center. Many of the town's enterprises were related to agriculture, such as the Excelsior Elevator (1877), Ransomville Basket Co (1896–1941), an apple-drying plant (1901–27), and a cold-storage plant (1916). Orchards remained an important land use in 2003. The federal government took 7,000 acres (2,830 ha) in 1942–43 for TNT production, then *ca* 1945 for anti-aircraft equipment; in 2003, the site served as an US Air Force test site and a National Guard training area. Old Fort Niagara was given up by the government in 1963, became a state park, and is now the area's main attraction. It and Four Mile Creek State Park border the Robert Moses State Parkway.

Nancy B. Mingus

Porter, Cole. See MUSICAL THEATER.

Porter, Peter B(uell) (*b* Salisbury, Conn, 4 Aug 1773; *d* Niagara Falls, 20 Mar 1844). Attorney, politician, military commander, and state canal commissioner. A graduate of Yale College (1791) and Litchfield Law School, Porter settled in Canandaigua (Ontario Co) in 1795 and practiced law. He became involved in politics as a clerk of Ontario Co (1797–1804) and state assemblyman (1802). In 1806 he founded, with his brother Augustus and Benjamin Barton, the trading firm Porter, Barton and Co, in Black Rock (Erie Co), which controlled the transportation business around Niagara Falls. He took up residence in Black Rock in 1810. Porter served in Congress (1809–13) and as quartermaster general of the New York State Militia prior to the War of 1812. A major general of New York Volunteers (1812–15), he distinguished himself in actions against British troops at Black Rock in 1813 and Fort Erie, Ont, in 1814. Returning to Congress (1815–16) Porter successfully sought federal compensation for war losses on the Niagara frontier as well as federal funds to improve roads there. Appointed to the state's Canal Commission in 1810, he advocated a canal route from the Hudson River to Lake Ontario, with a second canal connecting Lakes Ontario and Erie, around Niagara Falls, terminating at Black Rock. Both proposals failed: the legislature in 1817 approved a canal route connecting the Hudson River to Lake Erie, and in 1823 it decided to place the canal terminus at Buffalo. Though Porter's hopes for the development of Black Rock were not realized, his efforts ultimately benefited all of western New York State. He remained active in public service, returning to the assembly (1828) and serving as a regent of the University of the State of New York (1824–30), US secretary of war (1828–29), and Whig presidential elector (1840).

For illustration see WAR OF 1812.

Grande, Joseph A. *Peter B. Porter and the Buffalo–Black Rock Rivalry* (Buffalo: Buffalo and Erie County Historical Society, 1982)

Paul J. Bartczak

Port Henry. Village (pop 1,152) in Moriah (Essex Co). Port Henry became an important ironwork center with the opening of its first blast furnace in 1824, when iron was shipped by barge on Lake Champlain and then by the Delaware and Hudson Railroad (1874). The village incorporated in 1869. Starting in the mid-1890s Irish workers were joined by Italians, Hungarians, Lithuanians, Poles, and Russians. Labor unrest and unfulfilled promises resulted in a prolonged strike in 1913. The last iron operation, Republic Steel, closed in 1971, causing economic hardship and out-migration of much of the village's population. Every August Port Henry stages a whimsical celebration for Champ, Lake Champlain's mythical sea monster.

Thomas A. Rumney

Port Jefferson. {Port Jefferson, village (pop 7,837) in Brookhaven, Suffolk Co; Port Jefferson Station, locality (pop 7,527) in Brookhaven}. Port Jefferson began shipbuilding in 1797, an industry that continued until after World War II, shipped cordwood cut inland, and milled flour. The post office was established as Satucket in 1801 and renamed Drown Meadow in 1810 for its tidal marshes and then Port Jefferson in 1836. Later in the 19th century a pump factory, a molding shop, and the Effingham Tuthill carriage factory (1855) provided employment. Port Jefferson was a port of entry from 1852 until the 1880s. Steam ferry service to Bridgeport, Conn, began in 1872 and continues in the early 21st century. The Long Island Rail Road arrived at Port Jefferson Station in 1873; the line was extended in 1895, but the extension was abandoned in 1938. Port Jefferson Station industries included the short-lived manufacture of a one-cylinder automobile, the Only (1909–13), and the Thomas Wilson and Co lace-making factory (1921–1980s). Sand mining was carried out in the early 20th century. Improvements to the Nesconset Highway opened Port Jefferson Station to development in the late 1950s. Port Jefferson incorporated as a village in 1962. Tourism, once important but less so since the mid–20th century, is again significant in the early 21st century. Port Jefferson also serves as an oil port, with large tanks on the waterfront.

Luise Weiss

Port Jervis. City (pop 8,860) in W Orange Co. Having originated as Carpenter's Point, a Delaware River landing for timber raftsmen, Port Jervis was renamed in 1830 after becoming a port on the Delaware and Hudson Canal (1828–98). It was made a division point of the

Erie Railroad (1848) and the site of the Erie yards and maintenance facilities. It soon acquired a number of industries, including a foundry, machine shop, planing mill, and saw factory. Germantown, its western extension, centered around glass factories. Port Jervis incorporated as a village in 1853 and as a city in 1907, its territory taken from the Town of Deerpark. In 1908, 82 industrial establishments employed 1,000 workers producing glassware, saws, silk, gloves and mittens, shirts, and ladies' collars. The railroad yards and shops remained a significant presence until the 1960s. Major firms in 2003 included Kolmar Laboratories (cosmetics), OAS Swimwear, A and W Products (office supplies), Future Home Technology (modular homes), Wilder Manufacturing (food service equipment), and Gillinder Glass. In the early 21st century most residents work in the New York City metropolitan region, and tourism is becoming an important aspect of the economy. Port Jervis was home of painter and illustrator John N. Howitt (1885–1958) and the boyhood home of author Stephen Crane (1871–1900). Fort Decker, a 1793 stone house on the site of a Revolutionary War blockhouse, and the Erie Railroad Station (1892) are listed on the National Register.

Peter Osborne

Portland. Town (pop 5,502) in N Chautauqua Co. Settled in 1805 the town formed in 1813 from Chautauqua. Resident Elijah Fay is credited with planting the first grapevines in Chautauqua Co in 1818, though grapes did not become economically significant until the 1850s. The Brotherhood of the New Life, a communitarian experiment, raised grapes and made wine on 2,000 acres (809 ha) near Brocton from 1867 to 1881. When it failed the Brocton Land Improvement Co bought 500 acres (202 ha), parceling them out in small vineyard tracts. The Buffalo and State Line Railroad improved access in 1852, as did the New York State Thruway in 1957. Population increased 14% in the 1990s. The town lies along Lake Erie, where 20–30 ft (6–9 m) high bluffs line the shore. It is the site of Lake Erie State Park.

Michelle Henry

Port Leyden. Village (pop 665) in Leyden and Lyonsdale (Lewis Co). Settled in 1796, Port Leyden grew as a result of the Black River Canal (1851–1924) and the Rome, Watertown and Ogdensburg Railroad (1867), but it did not incorporate until 1871. Tanneries, sawmills, and iron foundries dominated the economy in the 19th century, giving way to a pulp mill (1896–1950s) and a knitting mill (1907–1990s). Spruce gum, chemicals, and excelsior have also been produced. The population has dropped steadily since 1950 because of limited economic opportunities. Most residents commute.

Arthur Einhorn

Port of Buffalo. At the eastern end of Lake Erie and the head of the Niagara River, Buffalo's port has been a major factor in the history and development of the city, Erie Co, and the state. It was the most easterly port on the Great Lakes, it was the practical location for commerce to flow from the fast-growing Midwest and such places as Cleveland, Detroit, and Chicago. The prevailing southwest winds are aligned with the 241 mi (387.9 km) length of Lake Erie, resulting in severe storm action at Buffalo and requiring an extensive breakwall system. A storm effect known as a seiche results in water-level fluctuations as great as 15 feet (4.6 m). Ice may close navigation on the lake from December to March or later. The rise of the port can be traced to two main factors: Buffalo's strategic position on Lake Erie, where the 327 ft (99.7 m) Niagara Escarpment hindered navigation onto Lake Ontario, and the opening of the Erie Canal in 1825, which permitted water travel from the Great Lakes to the Hudson River and New York City.

Development of the Port Facilities

The early development of the Buffalo area was promoted by the Holland Land Co, which owned much of western New York State. Before the building of the Erie Canal, the nearest port was downstream at the adjacent community of Black Rock, where access to Lake Erie was made difficult by a 5 ft (1.5 m) drop in the Niagara River and the resulting swift current. The goods passing through the port required a portage around Niagara Falls or overland transport to the Hudson River on nearly impassable roads. It was reportedly cheaper to ship freight eastward by sending it down the Mississippi River to New Orleans and then via sailing ship to New York City. The decision in 1817 to build the Erie Canal promised to open a major trade route, but a harbor would be needed for its western terminus. Buffalo and Black Rock competed energetically for the honor. Because neither had an adequate natural harbor, Buffalo built a 1,200 ft (366 m) pier out into Lake Erie and removed an obstructing sandbar, while Black Rock built a 8,750 ft (2,667 m) pier that separated its harbor from the Niagara River, with a dam and lock to access the river. Although Black Rock's efforts were comparatively far greater, its location limited its harbor potential and ability to supply water to the canal, and Buffalo was awarded the terminus.

Gov De Witt Clinton officially opened the canal in Buffalo in 1825. The original canal ended at Little Buffalo Creek, which flowed into the Buffalo River. Little Buffalo Creek was deepened and realigned, and was named the Canal Basin [later Commercial Slip]. As traffic on the canal increased, extensive additions were made to the port, including an inland network of accessory canals. In 1833 the pier was extended to 1,720 feet (524 m) and a stone lighthouse built; from 1869 to 1902 a 3.2 mi (5.15 km) breakwall was built in the lake between Buffalo and what is now Lackawanna to the south, forming the port's outer harbor, and the inland canal network was extended to total 17 miles (27.4 km); by 1945, 5.5 miles (8.85 km) of the Buffalo River were deepened to 22 feet (6.7 m). Buffalo's shipbuilding industry also expanded dramatically as a result of the canal, with the construction of marine railways, dry docks, and repair facilities. Later improvements included a new federal lock at Black Rock (opened 1913) and the deepening in 1960 of the south entrance to the seaway depth of 29 feet (8.8 m).

Freight and Passenger Traffic

The Erie Canal was the first efficient trade route to breech the Appalachian Mountain barrier and resulted in a freight rate reduction of over 90%. Throughout the 19th century grain was the main commodity handled at the port. In the canal's early years grain was transferred from lake boats to canal boats manually, a backbreaking job. The mechanized grain elevator was introduced in 1842. They soon lined the Buffalo River, facilitating explosive growth in the grain trade. Capacity soared from 1.8 million bushels (64.9 million l) in 1841 to 58.4 million bushels (2.1 billion l) a century later. Because the elevators were not on the canal system of towpaths, specially designed tugs shuttled boats between canal and harbor.

Lake freighter entering Buffalo harbor, *ca* 1900.

When the grain elevators were filled, some lake boats would spend the winter in the harbor, to be unloaded as space became available. In 1924 this "winter fleet" comprised 118 boats, with 27 million bushels (951 million l) on board. The last winter fleet, in 1977, was a single vessel. The completion of the fourth Welland Canal in 1932 allowed some cargo to be diverted to Lake Ontario, making Ogdensburg (St. Lawrence Co) and Oswego important points of grain transfer to railroads, smaller boats, and the Erie Canal. Nevertheless, grain traffic at Buffalo continued to rise, peaking in 1945 at 314 million bushels (11 billion l). Buffalo's reign ended in 1959, however, with the opening of the St. Lawrence Seaway, which gave the largest lake boats direct access to the Atlantic. By 1998 Buffalo grain volume had dropped to 12.9 million bushels (454.6 million l), mostly for use in local flour mills.

Iron ore, coal, and stone became important freight items with the rise of the iron and steel industries in the Buffalo area around 1900. The transmission of cheap electric power from Niagara Falls beginning in 1896 also stimulated the growth of local flour-milling and cement-manufacturing industries. Movement of goods through the port was overwhelmingly west to east. There was considerable trade in anthracite coal and, at various times, in automobiles. With the end of transshipping on the Erie Canal and the departure of the steel, malting, oilseed crushing, and animal feeds industries, freight traffic at the port declined steeply, from 23,663,000 tons (21,466,700 MT) in 1955 to 2,341,000 tons (2,123,700 MT) in 1998. Nevertheless, the port continues to handle such commodities as coal for power generation, petroleum, salt, cement, sand, and stone.

Waves of immigrants and American-born migrants traveling west on the Erie Canal transferred to lake boats at Buffalo. In the 1850s railroads took over the canal traffic, but lake traffic continued, evolving into regular scheduled service to Cleveland, Detroit, Chicago, and Erie, Pa, and to amusement parks in Ontario and Grand Island (Erie Co). Weekly tourist service operated from Buffalo to Duluth, Minn, and points in between until *ca* 1970, when boat travel was completely superseded by plane, train, and automobile. In the early 21st century only an occasional cruise ship visits the port.

Redevelopment

Of the 17 miles (27.4 km) of dug canals that once made up the harbor's inland network, only 8.5 miles (13.68 km) remain. Canals built for small boats have been completely filled in except for 2.1 miles (3.38 km) incorporated into the Black Rock Canal. I-190 covers 4 miles (6.4 km) of the Erie Canal main line. Two miles (3.2 km) of the City Ship Canal are now part of the Tifft Nature Preserve. The Union Ship Canal, once lined with blast furnaces and ore docks, is to become a small boat harbor and marina. With the port's decline, miles of frontage are available for redevelopment. The Canal Basin has been converted to a marina and is partly lined with condominiums and office buildings. There are plans to develop the remaining areas with public and commercial facilities, parks, beaches, trails, historic restorations, restaurants, and living space. Grain elevators with a combined capacity of 31.5 million bushels (1.1 billion l) stand idle or abandoned. Ideas for their reuse include conversion to hotels, condominiums, restaurants, museums, offices, and even fish hatcheries.

Barrick, Paul. *Buffalo's Waterways: A History of the Port of Buffalo and Related Matters* (Buffalo: City Planning Board, 1970)

US Army Corps of Engineers. *The Port of Buffalo, New York.* Lake Series, no. 1, rev ed. (Washington, DC: US Government Printing Office, 1940)

Vogel, Michael N., and Redding, Paul F. *Maritime Buffalo* (Buffalo: Western New York Heritage Institute, 1990)

Henry H. Baxter

Port of New York. After almost two centuries of fairly equal status with the ports of Boston, Philadelphia, and Charleston, in the second quarter of the 19th century, the Port of New York began to handle more trade than the other three combined. By the mid–19th century it handled more than all other ports in the country combined and by about 1912 was the busiest port in the world, a position it held for more than half a century. It remained the busiest in North America until late in the 20th century.

Early Development

Prints of the mid-1600s reveal the port's beginnings on the east side of Manhattan Island a short distance from the island's southern tip. A basin had been created north of the future Broad St, with a pier and a small breakwater, to serve small, local craft and the boats bringing passengers and cargo ashore from ships at anchor. Prints of the early 18th century show the East River shoreline of Manhattan as far north as the future South Street Seaport Historic District lined with piers and slips large enough to accommodate ships. North of the pier and slip area was a stretch of shoreline where ships were built or repaired.

Manhattan's East River side was favored during the sailing ship era because of its shelter from prevailing westerly winds and Hudson River ice. From 1715 to 1815 landfilling moved this shoreline steadily eastward, allowing the layout of a succession of waterfront streets: first Water, then Front, and, finally, South St. In the process, most slips indenting the shore were eliminated; some, such as Burling Slip and Peck Slip, left their names on wide streets. The first major pier on the Hudson River side of Manhattan was built at the foot of Albany St in 1797.

The Port of New York was the scene of the first successful experiment in using steam to power vessels. Robert Fulton inaugurated service on the Hudson with his 1807 *North River Steamboat* (often called *Clermont*). Larger boats designed for Long Island Sound and ferryboats for service to Brooklyn and New Jersey soon followed. Early experiments with steam propulsion on the open sea, in both the coastal and transoceanic trades, proved unsuccessful; not until the late 1830s did steam engines become sufficiently economical in both use of fuel and creation of fresh water for boilers on these routes. Sailing ships would dominate trade on the North Atlantic until the 1840s and on the longest routes, to the Pacific and the Far East, until late in the century.

In 1815 a group of New York City merchants originated a system of scheduled sailings between their home port and Liverpool. The success of these earliest liners, popularly known as packet ships, was one factor that drew capital and managerial talent to the Port of New York. But the overwhelming factor in New York's advantage as a seaport was its access via the Hudson River to the interior of the continent, an ever expanding hinterland supplying commodities for export, and a growing market for imports. Navigable for almost 150 miles (240 km), the Hudson passes through the Appalachian Mountains in the highlands around West Point and, beginning in the mid-1820s, met the termini of the Erie and Champlain Canals at Watervliet (Albany Co). The Erie Canal linked the Hudson River with the rich farmlands of central and western New York State and, through the Great Lakes, with much of the interior of the continent. It allowed goods shipped from Buffalo to reach the port in eight days, instead of the pre-1825 time of 20 days, and at a cost of $15 per ton instead of the pre-1825 cost of $100 per ton. The Champlain Canal provided a similar water road accessing northern New York and Canada. In 1826 the booming canal traffic led to the start of

South St from Maiden Lane, 1828, by Samuel Hollyer, *ca* 1913.

work on the Harlem River Ship Canal linking the Hudson and East Rivers. Improvements on the Harlem River would continue on and off through 1938.

Steamboats and Clippers

After regular transatlantic steamer service was established in 1838, Manhattan's Lower West Side developed rapidly and became New York City's steamship waterfront. By the 1850s the Collins Line, the most successful American-flag transatlantic company before the Civil War, was operating out of a pier at the foot of West Canal St. Other West Side companies ran steamships to Panama and Nicaragua, providing a sea route to the California gold fields. The earliest ocean steamships were wooden-hulled side-wheelers, the majority produced by East River shipyards. Port of New York shipbuilding remained active throughout the Civil War, during which a Greenpoint (Kings Co) builder produced the revolutionary, ironclad warship USS *Monitor,* designed by John Ericsson. After the war New York shipyards went into decline as the center of iron hull construction, in favor from the early 1870s, shifted to the Delaware River, and wooden hull construction concentrated in New England.

Over this same period, the sailing ship flourished before it was eclipsed by steam. In 1846 the *Rainbow,* the world's first clipper ship, launched from the Port of New York. The clippers were the largest sailing vessels of the era and, with their sharp and graceful hulls and towering rigs, were designed to be the fastest. The high profits of the Chinese tea trade stimulated their creation, but the discovery of gold in California just two years later created an even greater demand. Their era was brief, with the last extreme clipper in terms of hull form launched in 1857. Through the third quarter of the 19th century, Manhattan's East River waterfront continued to be the center of port activity. Growth of the pier area northward had driven shipbuilding and ship repair to a stretch of shoreline between Corlears Hook and East 14th St, with shipyards also established across the East River in the communities of Williamsburg and Greenpoint in Brooklyn.

Sailing vessels built for carrying capacity rather than for speed continued to be built until the end of the century and to rest at piers along South St into the early years of the 20th century, but the center of port activity gradually shifted to the West Side of Manhattan in the latter decades of the 19th century. During the same period, the first large-scale cargo terminals, Atlantic Basin and Erie Basin, were built in Brooklyn's Red Hook.

By the 1860s steamboats resembling giant multidecked floating palaces operated on the Hudson River and on Long Island Sound. From piers on the Hudson River side of Manhattan, Hudson River Day Line provided daytime service to Albany, while People's Line and Citizens' Line provided overnight service to Albany and Troy. Overnight steamers running out of piers on both sides of Lower Manhattan linked the Port of New York with cities in southern New England. In 1876 and 1885, reefs were blasted out of East River's Hell Gate to allow safer passage for these boats.

Additional Modes of Transportation

By the 1880s, 11 major railroads had terminals in what is now New York City with other lines terminating on the New Jersey shore. Before the first trans-Hudson tunnels were built in the early 20th century, all these companies used ferries and lighterage vessels (barges) to move passengers and cargo onto Manhattan, Staten, and Long Islands; many continued to do so through the mid-1950s. Thus a multitude of craft, including huge barges carrying entire trains, crisscrossed the port in this era.

While sailing ships berthed at open piers along South St, steamship companies favored covered piers with better weather and theft protection for cargos. During the 1890s construction began on the Chelsea Piers, a series of large piers with two-story sheds south of West 23d St. The dredging of the Ambrose Channel at the port's entrance accommodated the first giant liners of the 20th century, vessels such as White Star Line's *Olympic* and Cunard Line's *Lusitania* and *Mauretania. Olympic*'s sistership *Titanic* was bound for one of these piers when she was lost in 1912.

In 1921 state lawmakers in both New York and New Jersey created the Port of New York Authority (from 1972, Port Authority of New York and New Jersey) to improve freight traffic flow. Their immediate success was limited because of resistance from railroad companies, and the authority turned instead to building vehicular bridges and tunnels. In the early 1930s still larger piers were built between West 48th and West 52d Sts to berth the liners *Normandie, Queen Mary,* and *Queen Elizabeth.* Most West Side piers were built with "head houses" at the street that extended to meet their neighbors on either side, blocking views of the Hudson. New piers also rose along much of the Brooklyn waterfront facing the East River and Upper Bay, on parts of the Hoboken, NJ, waterfront, and along the north shore of Staten Island. When activity in the harbor reached its peak during World War II, there were enough berths in the port to accommodate 600 ships and enough space in the anchorages for another 400.

Developments since World War II

In the second half of the 20th century, new systems for the transportation of goods brought change. By the 1950s two decades of bridge, tunnel, and highway construction plus the advent of air travel had almost ended the port's old steamboat and railroad-related traffic. The Interstate Highway System and the rise of the trucking industry, in particular, eliminated much railroad freight handling, and most railroad-owned facilities in the harbor were abandoned. Containerized cargo was introduced around 1960, and its standardized 40 ft (12.2 m) units transferred easily across road, rail, water, and air transportation systems. Old port facilities of covered piers and warehouses, by then in need of rebuilding, became obsolete because the new steel containers adequately protected their contents from environmental damage or theft and needed only large open spaces for storage and handling. In the 1970s three large piers between West 48th and West 52d Sts were modernized to create the New York City Passenger Ship Terminal, used primarily by cruise ships.

Terminals designed to handle containers were built on the Upper Bay in south Brooklyn and south Jersey City and on adjoining Newark Bay at Elizabethport, NJ. These facilities have maintained the Port of New York as one of the most active in the country, but this activity is not apparent in the historic heart of the port, Manhattan Island, where most old piers and ferry terminals have been converted for new uses or replaced by shoreline promenades and parks. Among the earliest such developments were the South Street Seaport Historic District on Lower Manhattan's East Side and Battery Park City on its West Side, both begun in the late 1960s. At the beginning of the 21st century, passenger ferries have experienced a revival. In addition to the long-standing route between Manhattan and Staten Island, new services are reaching the other boroughs and many New Jersey communities. Recreational use of New York City's harbor is also growing, with commercial traffic limited to tugs and barges handling building materials and petroleum products.

Adams, Arthur G. *The Hudson through the Years* (New York: Fordham Univ Press, 1996)

Albion, Robert Greenhalgh. *The Rise of New York Port (1815–1860)* (1939; repr New York: South Street Seaport Museum, 1984)

Doig, Jameson W. *Empire on the Hudson: Political Power and Progress at the Port of New York Authority* (New York: Columbia Univ Press, 2000)

Writers' Program of the Works Progress Administration of the City of New York. *A Maritime History of New York* (Garden City, NY: Doubleday, Doran, 1941)

Norman Brouwer

Portuguese. Although a small population of Sephardic Jewish refugees of Portuguese ancestry arrived in New Amsterdam in 1654, a more substantial population dates to the mid–19th century when Portuguese men found work on American whaling vessels and ultimately settled in the Long Island seaport communities of Cold Spring Harbor and Sag Harbor (Suffolk Co). The most significant Portuguese immigration to New York State occurred between 1880 and 1930. Like other southern Europeans coming to the United States during this era, most Portuguese sought to escape poverty, although some emigrated to avoid mandatory military service. During the 1880–1930 period, Portuguese emigrants sailed from the Azores, Madeiras, and Cape Verde Islands as well as from continental Portugal. Although more than 75% of these migrants went to Brazil, thousands chose to settle in the United States, on both the East and West Coasts.

In 1880 New York State was home to 295 foreign-born Portuguese, more than half of whom resided in Manhattan and Brooklyn. By 1920 there were 1,404 Portuguese living in the state, and by 1930, 5,106; almost 70% lived in New York City. In Manhattan, they resided in the vicinity of Bleecker and Varick Sts, while those living in Brooklyn clustered about Court and Columbia Sts. Outside New York City, sizable Portuguese communities developed in Yonkers and Mount Vernon (Westchester Co). On Long Island, Portuguese settled in Mineola (Nassau Co) and in parts of Suffolk Co. In Western New York, smaller settlements sprouted in Rochester and Corning (Steuben Co) as Portuguese immigrants from Erie, Pa, moved to these cities in search of work. Although their compatriots in other parts of the nation were employed in fishing and agriculture, most of New York State's Portuguese served as unskilled labor in industrial plants and small businesses, particularly in the New York metropolitan area. On arrival, new immigrants relied on mutual aid societies, the Roman Catholic Church, and the family unit to help them adjust to life in New York.

The passage of restrictive US immigration acts in the early 1920s and the depression curtailed Portuguese migration into the United States. In 1959 Portuguese Americans in New York City founded the American Portuguese Society to promote Portuguese culture and a positive relationship between the United States and Portugal. A second wave of Portuguese immigration followed in the 1960s and 1970s as a result of changes in US immigration laws and a series of submarine volcanic eruptions that caused hardship in Portugal's island region, the Azores. Some of the new immigrants settled in established Portuguese enclaves in New York State. After Cape Verde achieved independence in 1975, its nationals appeared as Cape Verdeans on US immigration records. In 2000 an estimated 40,000 people of Portuguese ancestry resided in New York State. Most lived in New York City and in Westchester, Nassau, and Suffolk Cos. John Dos Passos, the novelist and author of *Manhattan Transfer* (1925), was the son of a Portuguese immigrant who became an eminent corporate lawyer.

Mira, Manuel. *The Forgotten Portuguese* (Franklin, NC: Portuguese American Historical Research Foundation, 1998)
Pap, Leo. *The Portuguese-Americans* (Boston: Twayne Publishers, 1981)

Nicholas P. Ciotola

Portville. Town (pop 3,952) and village (pop 1,024) in SE Cattaraugus Co. Settled in 1809, the town was formed from Olean in 1837. It established sawmills, shingle mills, and other wood-related businesses early on, using the Allegheny River to transport goods to Pennsylvania and Ohio markets as well as to Louisville, Ky. Portville was the site of one of the region's largest tanneries, begun in 1849, and in the late 1870s, as Wright, Wheeler and Co, it employed 150 people. Portville was located on the short-lived Genesee Valley Canal Extension (1861–78) and the Buffalo, New York and Philadelphia Railroad (1873). The village was incorporated in 1895. In the early 21st century Portville village is noted for its stately homes, and many residents commute to Olean. The 188-acre (76 ha) Pfeiffer Nature Center (1998) includes 85 acres (34 ha) of old-growth forest. Sprague's Maple Farm and Pancake House produces maple syrup on site and is known for the turkeys raised and served there.

Bruce D. Fredrickson and Madelynn P. Fredrickson

Port Washington. Locality (pop 15,215) in North Hempstead (Nassau Co). Settled around 1676 as Cow Neck, it was occupied by British forces during the Revolution. Steamboat service to New York City (1836) made it more accessible. Its name was changed to Port Washington when it acquired a post office in 1859. Shellfishing and sand mining became important around the time of the Civil War; later, Italians and Poles were drawn by jobs in those industries and by work on nearby great estates. It became the terminus of a Long Island Rail Road branch in 1898, opening it up for commuters. A seaplane factory operated here beginning in 1929. Efforts to incorporate Port Washington as a city around 1930 failed as the constituents of water, sewer, and various other special districts did not want to give up sovereignty and political clout. Hispanic and Asian immigrants have made the community more diverse in recent years. Port Washington is site of the Town Dock and has two boatyards, three yacht clubs, an industrial park, and a downtown business district.

Joan Gay Kent

Port Washington North. Village (pop 2,700) in North Hempstead (Nassau Co). The settlement grew up around Mill Pond in the 19th century. Another neighborhood developed adjacent to the estates of Sands Point to the north and drew many Italian and Polish families. The village incorporated in 1932. After World War II Soundview Village houses and apartments were sited on a reclaimed sand mine, and the village population nearly quadrupled between 1960 and 1970. There is an extensive commercial/industrial section with two shopping centers and subscription sweepstakes originator Publisher's Clearing House. Model boat regattas, with many out-of-state participants, are held on Mill Pond in the warm months.

Joan Gay Kent

Post, Isaac (*b* Westbury [now in Nassau Co], 26 Feb 1798; *d* Rochester, 9 May 1872) and **Post [née Kirby], Amy** (*b* Jericho [now in Nassau Co], 20 Dec 1802; *d* Rochester, 29 Jan 1889). Social reformers. Isaac Post, raised a Quaker on Long Island, married Hannah Kirby in ?1822 and moved to Scipio (Cayuga Co) in 1823. She died in 1827, and Isaac married her sister Amy Kirby the following year. In 1836 they moved to Rochester, where both were active in numerous reform movements. Amy Post attended the Seneca Falls Convention in 1848 and signed the Declaration of Sentiments, and helped organize the follow-up Rochester Woman's Rights Convention in August 1848. Deeply involved in abolition as well, the Posts assisted in the founding of the Western New York Anti-Slavery Society in 1842 and later helped persuade Frederick Douglass to relocate to Rochester. Although they resigned from the Quakers in 1845 because they believed the Friends too ambivalent on abolitionism, they remained committed to the Quaker testimony on peace. The Posts sanctioned social relations between Blacks and Whites and welcomed African Americans in their homes as guests. Participants in the Underground Railroad, they also frequently housed fugitive slaves, including Harriet Ann Jacobs, in their Rochester home. Isaac Post was an avid spiritualist, having been converted to it in 1848 by Margaret Fox. He published his communications with the departed spirits of, among others, Benjamin Franklin and Martha Washington in *Voices of the Spirit World* (1852).

Hewitt, Nancy A. *Women's Activism and Social Change: Rochester, New York, 1822–1872* (Ithaca: Cornell Univ Press, 1984)

R. A. R. Edwards

postal service. Provision for delivery of mail in New Netherland dates to an ordinance of June 1660 that called for letters to be deposited in a box in the provincial secretary's office in New Amsterdam. In 1673 Gov Francis Lovelace created the first regular intercolonial postal service with monthly mail deliveries via post riders between New York City and Boston. Mail was delivered along the Boston Post Rd; modernized portions of that route remain in use in New York City and Westchester Co. During the late colonial period, the Office of Comptroller for the colonies in New York City served as headquarters for the colonial post office. Following the American Revolution the postal system, designed to meet federal postal regulations, began to provide more regular delivery: three times a week stagecoaches made the 22-hour trip between New York City and Philadelphia on post roads—those routes designated by Congress for the carriage of mails.

The best-known post road in the state was the Old Albany Post Rd, which developed along the stage route between Albany and New York City. Many parts of this historic road have become main driving routes and retain the name Post Rd; a 6.6 mi (10.62 km) remnant in Philipstown (Putnam Co) is one of the oldest unpaved roads in the country still in use. Until 1792 mail delivery reached only as far north and west as Albany. By the 1830s stagecoach service gave way to newer, faster modes of transport. In 1837 a route agent began accompanying railway mail between Albany and Utica, and rail transport of the mail quickly spread, enduring until 1977. Part of Railway Mail Services' history includes Owney, a dog that crawled into the Albany Post Office in 1888 searching for food, became the agency's mascot, and spent the rest of his days riding around the country on the rails.

New York State's significance as a postal center peaked during the 19th century. Between 1825 and 1860 its postal receipts made up 22% of the national total. The City Despatch Post, a private New York City mail service, introduced adhesive postage stamps in the United States in 1842. The stamps were engraved by the New York City firm of Rawdon, Wright, and Hatch. In 1845 some postmasters began issuing their own stamps, known as postmasters' provisionals, and in 1847 Rawdon, Wright, Hatch and Edson printed the first US government-issued stamps. The state also influenced the mails' content during this period. New York City resident Anthony Comstock, a self-appointed crusader against obscenity, lobbied Congress to pass what became known as the Comstock Law. Approved in 1873, it forbade the movement of obscene materials through the mails.

During the 1840s private express companies that delivered packages, which the postal service did not carry, were also used to deliver letters to avoid the federal Post Office's high prices. The Post Office responded by establishing several express routes, including one running between Albany and New York City and one between New York City and Boston. Competition from express companies for carriage of letters declined after 1845, when Congress decreased postal rates. In 1848 the US Mail Steamship Co began a transatlantic mail service from New York City, which had an important role moving mail, though the venture lasted less than 10 years. There were 2,440 post offices in the state in 1876 and 3,394 in 1899. Establishment of a post office was often the first official recognition of a locality's existence, and many communities adopted the name of their post office. From 1897 to 1953 a unique mail delivery system in New York City, pneumatic tubes, handled 55% of the city's letter mail. Installed underground, compressed air moved letters and parcels between central business districts. The first delivery of mail by automobile went from a downtown Buffalo post office to the Pan-American Exposition grounds outside of the city in 1901. The first sanctioned airmail flight traveled between Garden City and Mineola (Nassau Co) in September 1911, and regularly scheduled airmail service between New York City and Washington, DC, began in May 1918.

Several impressive post offices have been built in New York City, such as the massive Second Empire–style post office in City Hall Park built by Alfred B. Mullet in 1875 (since demolished) and the General Post Office on 8th Ave and 33d St by McKim, Mead and White in 1913. Many New York State post offices were bestowed beautiful artwork from the mural project of the Works Progress Administration in the 1930s, including the main post offices at Boonville, the Bronx, Clyde, Dolgeville, Ellenville, Honeoye Falls, Poughkeepsie, and Scarsdale. Management reorganization, automation, and competition brought changes to the postal system throughout the 20th century, particularly after 1960. To combat deficit and to improve its overall operation, the US Post Office Department in 1970 became a government-owned corporation named the US Postal Service, allowing private mail companies to compete.

Kay, John L., and Chester M. Smith Jr. *New York Postal History: The Post Offices and First Postmasters from 1775 to 1980* (State College, Pa: American Philatelic Society, 1982)

Palmer, Richard F. *The "Old Line Mail": Stagecoach Days in Upstate New York* (Lakemont, NY: North Country Books, 1977)

Kimberly McCray

potash and pearl ash manufacturing. Potash (potassium carbonate) is a salt that can be derived from the boiling and baking of wood ashes; pearl ash is its further refined counterpart. Both were used for cleaning wool before it was woven into textiles, and for making soap, saltpeter, dyes, and other products. North American potash and pearl ash were in demand in Europe from the 17th until the early 19th century; by the 20th century, potash was synthesized chemically. In the 21st century the term potash is commonly used for several potassium-based salts and minerals, some of which exist naturally and are mined (the main use of mined potash is for fertilizer).

Ashes were a byproduct of frontier settlement—forest was generally burned to clear the land for farming, and the 60–100 bushels (2,100–3,500 l) of ash from an acre (.4 ha) of burned hardwood were worth $3.25–$6.25 locally in the 1790s. Refining these ashes into potash made them compact and light for their value, making it economical to transport them from the frontier to Atlantic ports. During New York State's rapid settlement in the colonial period and the early republic, potash and pearl ash were among its most important commodities. In 1765 it exported only 423 barrels (a potash barrel held approximately 530 lbs [240 kg]), but by 1774 that number had increased 10-fold. Production continued to increase and in 1792 was about 20,000 barrels. The manufacture of potash was relatively easy, mainly requiring only large kettles for the boiling. These were often provided by landowners eager to see their settlers producing goods with immediate cash value or were owned and operated by asheries that bought the ashes from settlers and produced the potash themselves. Wood ashes were mixed with lime, and then water was run through them; the resulting dark brown water would then be boiled for hours to reduce it, and the gray mass was afterward left to cool and solidify.

Potash from New York State was generally exported via either New York City or Montreal. Between 1809 and 1812 the bulk went through New York City, one observer estimating 40,000–50,000 barrels annually; fewer than 10,000 barrels went through Montreal. After the War of 1812, these positions were reversed, with New York State's exports averaging 25,000 barrels in the 1820s and Montreal's exceeding 50,000. This movement reflected not only the development of the Canadian frontier and its own potash production but also the westward movement of the frontier in New York State to areas closer to Lake Ontario and away from the Mohawk River and New York City. Nevertheless, potash continued to be valuable: in 1815–16 the 18,877 barrels of pearl ash and potash exported from New York City were worth $1.3 million, approximately 10% of the state's total exports. After the opening of the Erie Canal, New York City's potash exports included significant amounts of potash from the Midwest. American potash exports peaked in the mid-1820s and then declined in significance.

Aggarwala, Rohit T. "Seat of Empire: New York, Philadelphia, and the Emergence of a National Metropolis, 1776–1837" (PhD diss, Columbia Univ, 2002)

White, Philip L. *Beekmantown, New York: Forest Frontier to Farm Community* (Austin: Univ of Texas Press, 1979)

Rohit T. Aggarwala

potatoes. A tuber *(Solanum tuberosum)* requiring sandy or well-drained soils and ideally suited to New York State's climate. First brought to Europe from Peru in the mid-1500s, potatoes were carried by Scots-Irish immigrants to New England in the late 1710s. Peter Kalm reported their being grown at Albany in 1749. In the early 1800s, demand for potatoes as a cheap foodstuff began to grow among New York City's working class, which depended on imports from New England until the opening of the Erie Canal enabled Central New York's "Chenango" potatoes to capture the metropolitan market. In 1839 New York State produced more than 30 million bushels (1.1 billion l), almost one-third of America's potato crop, with Oneida Co and Long Island potatoes particularly noted for their quality.

In 1843, the fungal disease late blight *(Phytophthora infestans)*, or potato rot, first struck the United States. New York State's yields declined from 300 bushels (10,600 l) an acre (0.4 ha) to 90 bushels (3,200 l) by 1845. That year the blight also reached Europe, possibly from New York State, particularly devastating Ireland and sending waves of immigrants to New York City. This sharpened the demand for potatoes, and rising prices kept the crop profitable despite lower yields. In 1853 Rev Chauncey Enoch Goodrich (1801–64) of Utica purchased from South America blight-resistant Rough Purple Chile stock, the ancestor of most later American varieties. Later in the century, starch manufacturing further increased the demand for potatoes in the state. By the late 1800s the growers in Washington, Rensselaer, Saratoga, Jefferson, and Franklin Cos were the nation's leading producers, and in 1899 New York State's potato harvest of 38 million bushels (1.3 billion l) led the nation. In the 20th century yields continued to improve, but many growers shifted to dairying or ceased farming altogether, and in the 1920s Maine overtook New York State as America's top potato producer.

In the 1990s niche markets developed for exotic varieties and patented heirloom potatoes. Scientists at Cornell University and elsewhere have engineered better blight- and pest-resistant varieties and developed a potato that functions as an edible vaccine. State potato output peaked in 1909, and total acreage fell substantially in the second half of the 20th century, especially on Long Island, where the pressures of suburban development were rising. Still, potatoes were grown in more than 45 counties, according to the 1997 census of agriculture, with Suffolk, Steuben, Wayne, Wyoming, and Livingston Cos the leading producers. In the early 21st century, about 40% of the state's crop is processed, mostly for potato chips (invented by George Crum in Saratoga Springs in the early 1850s). The state's 2002 crop was 275,000 tons (249,500 MT), making New York State the 11th most productive potato-growing state in the nation.

Hedrick, U. P. *A History of Agriculture in the State of New York* (1933; repr New York: Hill & Wang, 1966)

Scott C. Monje

Potsdam. Town (pop 15,957) and village (pop 9,425) in central St. Lawrence Co. Settled in 1803, largely from Vermont, the town was formed in 1806 from Madrid. The Union from 1804 to 1810 and now at Unionville was probably the first secular cooperative experiment in US history. The Village of Potsdam, which developed around falls on the Raquette River, incorporated in 1831. The Northern Railroad (1850; later Rutland Railroad) and, in the village, the Potsdam and Watertown (1854) provided service. Potsdam was St. Lawrence Co's richest agricultural town and ranked third in the state in butter production in both 1855 and 1865 and in maple sugar in 1875. It also had huge gang sawmills at Hewittville and Sissonville, and produced cutlery (1863), woolens (1874), and paper (three mills, 1892, 1902, and *ca* 1905). Three quarries produced sandstone from 1877 to 1922. In the early 21st century the town's rural land use remains predominantly agricultural. The Potsdam Paper Co mill at Unionville and a glass recycling plant are industrial employers. Potsdam is the most populous town in the county because of SUNY Potsdam (1869), including its Crane School of Music (1886), and Clarkson University (1896). Potsdam's strong business district, known for its red sandstone buildings, is consciously Victorian; the Market Street Historic District, with 27 buildings from the 19th century, is listed on the National Register.

Richard E. Mooers

Potter. Town (pop 1,830) in N central Yates Co. Settled in 1789, the town was formed from Middlesex in 1832. Pennsylvania Germans were early settlers, followed by Alsatians (*ca* 1815–60). The

Round Stone Schoolhouse (1838–1920) was a unique structure built of fieldstone faced with cobblestone. Flint Creek's slow passage created Potter Swamp, muckland drained *ca* 1945–60 and now cultivated for onions and a variety of other produce. A community of Groffdale Conference Mennonites began settling in Potter in the late 1970s.

Gwen Chamberlain

pottery. See CERAMICS AND POTTERY.

Poughkeepsie [PUH-KIP-SEE]. Town (pop 42,777) and city (pop 29,871) in E central Dutchess Co on the east bank of the Hudson River. The city, the county seat since 1717, is surrounded by the town, which was primarily agricultural until it became the city's first suburb in the 1930s. Settled by Albany Dutch from around 1693 to 1695 on parcels of land granted to Pieter Schuyler and other Albany residents in 1688, the area had several good river landings and became the county's commercial center by the mid–18th century; it became a precinct in 1737 and a town in 1788. A portion of the town was incorporated as a village in 1799 and became a city in 1854. It served briefly as the state capital (1777–79) during the Revolution and was the site of the New York State convention that ratified the US Constitution in 1788. During the first quarter of the 19th century, textile and other factories, banks, insurance companies, newspapers, and related businesses were established. During the 1830s prominent businesses, working within a newly formed, local Improvement Party, developed the village's infrastructure and supported new enterprises such as whaling, hardware, stovemaking, and silk and carpet manufacturing. Business failures following the Panic of 1837 interrupted this process.

During the 1840s Irish and German immigration helped expand the village population from under 8,000 to approximately 11,500. Initially adding stress to the village's economic recovery, these immigrants became the labor force for newly established industries such as agricultural implement manufacturing, glass and iron works, shipbuilding, pottery making, piano manufacturing, shoemaking, and quarrying. The Hudson River Railroad, a cross-county railroad network completed in 1872 connecting Poughkeepsie to New England commercial centers, ran through the village beginning in 1849, and the Poughkeepsie Bridge rail link (1888) contributed to the city's economic growth. By the end of the 19th century the city population reached 24,000.

Harvey Eastman (1832–78), a Poughkeepsie mayor, and entrepreneur-philanthropist Matthew Vassar (1792–1868) each established a nationally recognized college, Eastman National Business College (1859–1932) and Vassar College (1861). In 1960 a former Catholic seminary became Marist College, a liberal arts institution. After reaching a high of 41,000 residents in 1950, the City of Poughkeepsie's population declined to under 29,000 in 1990. The neighboring towns of Wappinger, an emerging suburban area, and East Fishkill provided new employment and shopping malls and siphoned off some of the city's population. Fueled in part by incoming Latino residents starting in the late 1980s, the city's population grew slightly during the last decade of the 20th century. The downtown area, once the county's primary retail center, is occupied by small service businesses and professional offices that benefit from convenient access to courts and municipal offices. The loss of retail and other small businesses downtown resulted in unemployment and poverty among residents unable to work in the suburbs because of a lack of transportation. African Americans moved to the city after World War II, and Asians arrived more recently. These changes, together with employees relocating from other urban areas, altered voting patterns. Town residents, a majority of whom were Republican in prior decades, crossed party lines in local elections in the early 21st century. An elected mayor, an appointed city administrator, and eight city council members manage the city government.

During the last quarter of the 20th century the city, town, and county's economy, highly dependent on IBM (since 1948), several smaller manufacturing establishments, and the Hudson River State Hospital (1871) for employment, was vulnerable when these employers downsized. A near complete recovery at the end of the century resulted in a more diversified economy based on small-scale businesses. Famous residents have included Samuel F. B. Morse (1791–1872), artist and promoter of the telegraph, and James J. McCann (1880–1969), feed and coal dealer who made a fortune in the stock market and established the McCann Foundation, which funds cultural and educational institutions. The Bardavon 1869 Opera House, the Hudson Valley Philharmonic, the Mid-Hudson Civic Center, three nearby colleges, and a waterfront development draw county residents to the city. The once blighted core of the city is being rejuvenated.

See also BEER AND BREWING; IBM.

Griffen, Clyde, and Sally Griffen. *Natives and Newcomers: The Ordering of Opportunity in Mid-19th-Century Poughkeepsie* (Cambridge: Harvard Univ Press, 1978)

William P. McDermott

Poughkeepsie Railroad Bridge. It reaches across the Hudson River between Poughkeepsie and Highland (Ulster Co). When opened on 1 Jan 1889, it became the first bridge to be built over the Hudson River between New York Harbor and Albany. Built in what was the newly popular cantilever style, the bridge is 212 ft (64.6 m) above the water, higher than the Brooklyn Bridge. At 6,767 feet (2,062.6 m) it was one of the longest bridges in the world. Philadelphia investors built the bridge primarily to carry Pennsylvania coal to New England, avoiding the congestion of metropolitan New York and the uncertainties of ferry crossings. From 1899 it was owned by the Central New England Railway, which strengthened it for heavier traffic, and from 1927 by the New York, New Haven and Hartford Railroad, which used it as its primary freight route from the South and West into New England. Regular passenger traffic over the bridge ended by 1930. Freight traffic became heavy during World War II. Afterward, as the use of trucks increased and manufacturing in the Northeast declined, traffic on the bridge diminished. When Penn Central acquired the bridge in 1968, it favored the Selkirk Bridge, a newer railroad bridge just south of Albany. After a fire closed the Poughkeepsie Railroad Bridge in 1974, efforts to find state, federal, or private funds to restore it to railroad use failed. In 1998 a private group acquired the bridge, hoping to open it to the public as a walkway.

Mabee, Carleton. *Bridging the Hudson: The Poughkeepsie Railroad Bridge and Its Connecting Rail Lines* (Fleischmanns, NY: Purple Mountain Press, 2001)
O'Rourke, John F. "The Construction of the Poughkeepsie Bridge," *Transactions of the American Society of Civil Engineers* 18 (June 1888): 199–216
"Poughkeepsie, The Bridge and Its Connections," *Poughkeepsie Eagle*, souvenir number, Oct 1889

Carleton Mabee

poultry and eggs. Chickens, turkeys, ducks, and geese have been part of the agricultural scene since the Dutch first settled New Netherland in the 17th century. Mainly in small flocks of several to a few dozen, fowl did not assume the economic importance of cattle, horses, sheep, and goats, but they did provide meat, eggs, and feathers for use on the home farm. Women and children typically tended the flock, receiving goods or income from the occasional barter or sale of poultry products.

Poultry keeping changed little during the 17th,

Poughkeepsie Railroad Bridge, early 20th century.

18th, and early 19th centuries, remaining a small-scale ancillary activity on most farms. The number of farms increased, nonetheless, and the growth of New York City, Albany, and other urban areas along the Hudson and Mohawk Rivers created expanding markets for poultry products. According to the 1840 census, the value of poultry production in New York State, $1.1 million, was the highest in the country. The bulk of the production occurred along the Hudson River and on Long Island. The availability of grain from New York State farms and technological developments such as artificial incubation allowed poultry to be raised in ever increasing numbers. By the late 1800s farms having poultry or eggs as their main products began to appear near cities. Counties surrounding New York City and those near Albany, Buffalo, Rochester, Syracuse, and Binghamton became important regions of egg, chicken, and turkey production. Eastport (Suffolk Co) became a major center of duck farming after the introduction of the Pekin duck from China in 1873. The improvement of rail links spurred the development of dozens of duck farms in the area in subsequent decades.

Poultry production in New York State reached a peak at mid–20th century. Farmers kept about 14 million laying hens and produced 2.5 billion eggs annually in 1950. Turkey and broiler production peaked at greater than 950,000 turkeys in 1955 and about 15 million broilers in 1956. Approximately 7.5 million ducks were raised in 1959. All of these sectors of poultry production declined from 1960 through the early 1990s in response to economic factors, population pressures, and competition from farms in other states. In 1993 the laying hen population averaged 3.8 million; about 1 million broilers, 2 million ducks, and .5 million turkeys were raised in the state. The US Agricultural Census of 1997 recorded 1,842 farms in New York State with laying hens, 306 with broilers and other meat-type chickens, 313 with turkeys, 242 with ducks, 391 with geese, and 403 with miscellaneous poultry, such as pheasants, quail, and pigeons.

In 2001 a population of 4 million hens produced 1.1 billion eggs in New York State. About 2.3 million broilers, 2.25 million ducks, and 510,000 turkeys were raised the same year. Large farms account for most of the poultry production, with the biggest egg farms having at least several hundred thousand hens. One farm in Onondaga Co produced more than 90% of the turkeys in New York State. In 2001 the eggs and poultry produced in the state were estimated to be worth about $76.5 million, with eggs accounting for 70%, ducks 17%, broilers 7%, and turkeys 6%. New York ranks 20th among all egg-producing states. In 2003 the leading counties in egg production were Erie, Wayne, Onondaga, Sullivan, and Clinton.

Hedrick, U. P. *A History of Agriculture in the State of New York* (New York: Hill & Wang, 1966)

Richard E. Austic

Pound Ridge. Town (pop 4,726) in E Westchester Co. Although part of Turner's Purchase (1640), settlement began only in the 18th century. It was governed by North Castle town officers through 1746, despite not being part of it, after which it functioned independently. British troops under Lt Col Banastre Tarleton raided Pound Ridge hamlet in 1779. The town was recognized in 1788. Basket making, especially for the Long Island Sound oyster industry; shoemaking; and dairy farming were significant in the 19th century, but all had largely died out by the next century, and the population dropped from 1,486 in 1850 to 515 in 1920. Hiram Halle, a New York City entrepreneur, renovated over 30 old houses (1929–44), attracting writers, artists, and musicians seeking seclusion, and, in the early 21st century, celebrities. Most of Ward Pound Ridge Reservation (4,315 acres/1,746 ha), Westchester's largest county park, lies in the town and is home to more than 1,000 species of plants, insects, birds, and animals. In 2003 it was declared a biodiversity reserve.

Scott C. Monje

poutine. Popular in Clinton, Essex, Franklin, and St. Lawrence Cos as well as all across Quebec, this dish, generally eaten with a fork, consists of hot french fries topped with a layer of cheese curds and covered with gravy hot enough to melt most of the cheese, leaving just a few large blobs. The proper ingredients for the gravy are a matter of intense debate, with some favoring beef and some chicken. Poutine originated in the 1950s in a restaurant in Warwick, Que, called Le Lutin Qui Rit (The Laughing Imp). A customer suggested the combination to innkeeper Fernand Lachance, who described it with the French Word *poutine* (funny mixture).

Lynn Ekfelt

poverty. The federal government's definition of poverty—inadequate food, shelter, and clothing—specifies a financial threshold qualified by family size, with figures adjusted annually for inflation. Many people, however, who meet or surpass this threshold still cannot provide for themselves and their families.

Early New York

Helping the poor in colonial New York was primarily directed to the "deserving poor": widows, orphans, the aged, and the infirm, who could not reasonably be expected to provide for themselves adequately in a mainly agricultural society where livelihood often depended on physical strength. The deserving poor might also include those only temporarily in reduced circumstances because of adversity. The undeserving poor were considered such when their plight was determined to be the result of a moral failure such as intemperance or laziness. "Outdoor relief"—food, clothing, firewood, even cash or tools provided to the poor in their own homes—was the most common form of assistance, although Beverwijck [now Albany] had a poorhouse by 1652 and New Amsterdam [now New York City] had similar facilities by 1653. In 1700 there were about 35 permanent poor counted by church officials in New York City; between 1691 and 1748 about 1,400 people received some public assistance. In Westchester Co and on Long Island, only a few depended on charitable support. Aid was distributed through religious organizations or as a community obligation to those in temporary distress; the municipal government and private charity organizations later took a share of the burden, supplemented by committees formed to aid victims of specific situations. As immigration increased, ethnic groups created aid societies; the Scots Charitable Society, for example, founded in 1744, provided both outright aid and work relief. New York State legislated relief in 1784, when each locality was determined responsible for the aid of its own poor.

Revealing commonly held 19th-century opinions on the causes of poverty in the midst of an economic depression in 1821, the New York Society for the Prevention of Pauperism (1816) commented, "No man who is temperate, frugal, and willing to work need suffer or become a pauper for want of employment." The Yates Committee, appointed by the New York State legislature in April 1823 to determine the expenses and systems involved in caring for the poor, reported a total of 22,111 paupers; this included the aged, the infirm, and 8,753 children. About 12,270 paupers lived in the more densely populated counties bordering the Hudson River or the Atlantic Ocean. The result of this investigation was the Act to Provide for the Establishment of County Poor-Houses, passed 27 Nov 1824, mandating a poorhouse in every county.

New York State piloted the creation of organizations devoted to addressing poverty, such as the New York Association for Improving the Condition of the Poor, founded in 1843. The Children's Aid Society, founded in 1853, transported large numbers of children, many with destitute parents, to the Midwest on "orphan trains." An 1857 investigation revealed deplorable conditions in the state's county poorhouses, leading to post–Civil War efforts on behalf of the poor. Starting in the 1860s the Catholic Church became an important source of aid to the urban needy. Louisa Schuyler formed the State Charities Aid Association in 1872 to monitor county residential institutions and to assist in the administration of charitable organizations. Some Civil War veterans, unable to readjust to civilian life, traveled the cities and countryside as tramps and subsisted on handouts, day labor, and petty pilferage; they usually found aid at state veterans' homes. The depression of 1873 was credited with increasing the number of tramps, both male and female. The work of New York City photojournalist Jacob Riis documented conditions of the urban poor, bringing increased attention to their plight and spurring on reform at the end of the 19th century.

Unemployment peaked during the depression of the 1890s, and in 1897, 19% of New York State residents were considered impoverished. The unprecedented numbers of jobless workers demonstrated the effect of the fluctuating labor market on poverty to public officials and charity administrators. Often the first agencies directly involved were police departments, which had since the mid–19th century offered shelter to the vagrant poor. Although 85,567 people spent some time in county and municipal poorhouses during 1900, most 19th-century public relief in New York State was given as aid to peeople in their own homes.

Views of Poverty in the 20th Century

Robert Hunter's *Poverty,* published in 1904 when Hunter was head worker at the first settlement house in the United States (New York City's University Settlement), was a seminal work in defining poverty in terms of a standard of living. Under the aegis of the New York State Conference of Charities, Columbia University doctoral student Robert Chapin produced a study of New York standards of living, which was published by the Russell Sage Foundation in

1909. These investigations became the models for other determinations of the parameters of poverty.

As poorhouses increasingly became refuges for the chronically ill or mentally incompetent, progressive reform reinstated outdoor relief with the 1929 New York State Public Welfare Act. The decreased incomes of New York State's elderly were acknowledged in the Old Age Security Act of 1930. The State Unemployment Relief Act, otherwise known as the Wicks Act, was enacted in 1931. New York thus became the first state in the nation to provide such legislation to assist the unemployed. The bill created the Temporary Emergency Relief Administration (TERA) to administer aid by furnishing employment, food, clothing, and shelter for persons in need who had been state residents for two years prior to 1 Nov 1931. Pres Franklin D. Roosevelt's administration adopted the New York State prototype, instituting the Federal Emergency Relief Administration (FERA) in 1933. The New York State Constitution asserted that "the aid, care and support of the needy are public concerns and shall be provided by the state and by such of its subdivisions" through Article 17, Section 1, incorporated in 1938.

The prosperity of the 1950s drew migrants from the South to northern states such as New York, where the number of blue-collar jobs for the unskilled was already declining. Resentment of the new arrivals' use of public relief was manifest in Newburgh (Orange Co) in the summer of 1961, when the city government tried to impose a number of welfare restrictions, including a limit of three months of aid per year to all except the elderly and disabled. In December 1961 the courts ruled against the Newburgh restrictions, but the case revealed widespread hostility toward groups such as unwed mothers on welfare and Blacks. In 1981 the *New Yorker* published a number of articles by Ken Auletta on the plight of African American youth in New York City enrolled in supported work programs. These articles were later published as a book, *The Underclass* (1982), the title becoming a popular term for the homeless poor increasingly visible on city streets. New York City spent $6.8 million on shelters in 1978; by 1989, this expenditure was $320 million. Approximately 80,000–100,000 people slept on the streets or sought places in shelters during the early 1990s, according to the New York State Department of Social Services. By the early 1990s Aid to Families with Dependent Children (AFDC), financed by the federal and state governments, was extended to nearly 1 million residents of New York State, 90% of them women and children.

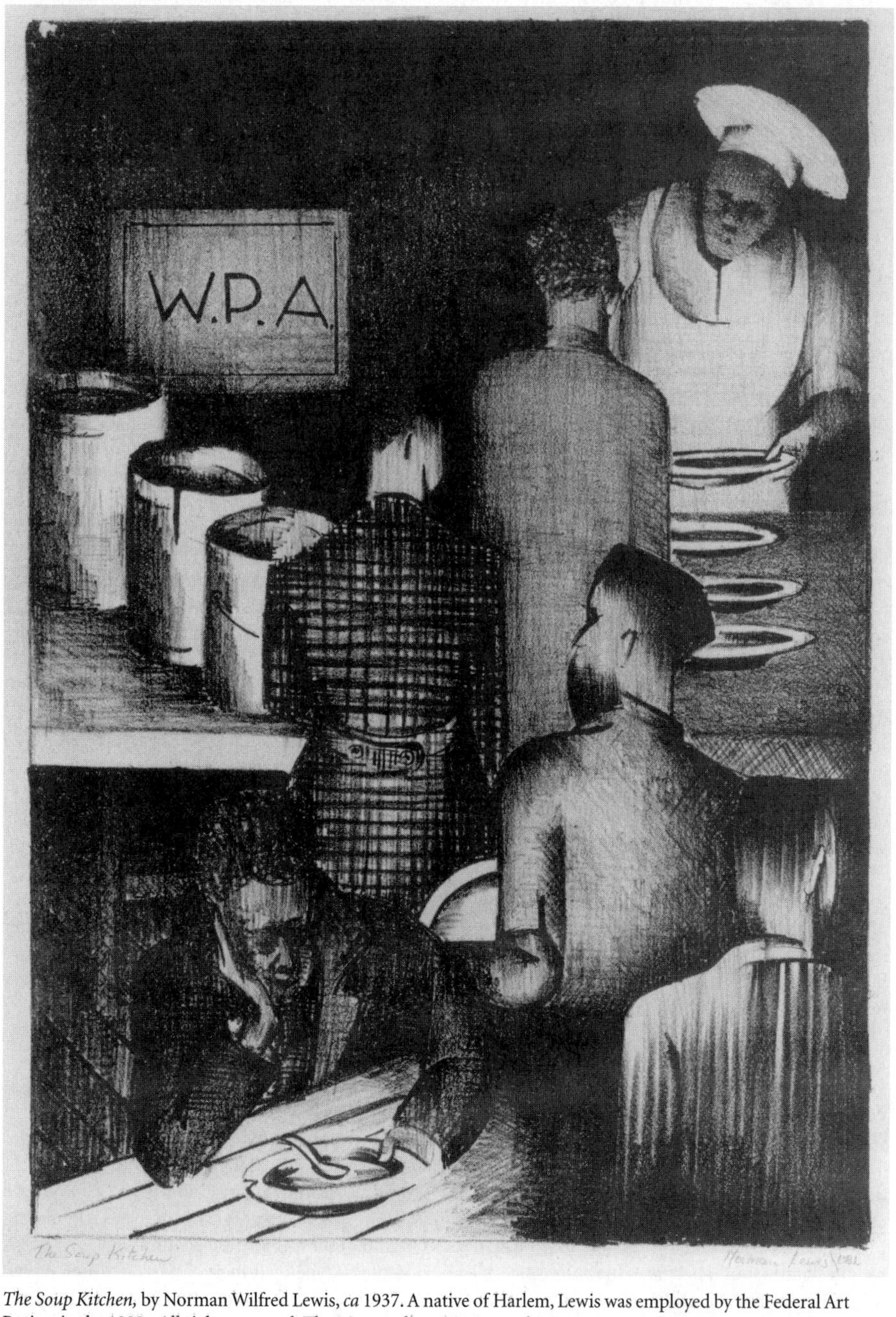

The Soup Kitchen, by Norman Wilfred Lewis, *ca* 1937. A native of Harlem, Lewis was employed by the Federal Art Project in the 1930s. All rights reserved, The Metropolitan Museum of Art.

Conclusion

At the end of the 20th century, poverty was unevenly distributed throughout the state. More than 80% of its poor lived in urban centers in 1999, but significant pockets of poverty were scattered across rural areas. A full 61% of the most impoverished lived in New York City, another 5% in Nassau and Suffolk Cos, and upward of 15% in central counties of metropolitan areas such as Erie and Monroe. The state's highest rates of poverty were in the Bronx (30.7%), Brooklyn (22.7%), and Manhattan (20.5%), but a number of rural areas, St. Lawrence and Tompkins Cos, for example, were not much lower (16.9% and 17.6%, respectively). Four of the five next poorest—Allegany (15.5%), Cattaraugus (13.7%), Chautauqua (13.8%), and Steuben (13.2%)—were in the relatively rural Southern Tier.

With the advent of federal welfare reform in 1996 and the creation of Temporary Assistance for Needy Families (TANF), with its time limitations, to replace AFDC, New York State established a constitutional mandate to continue to help support the needy, even after their TANF assistance expired. Its legislature created the Article 17 Safety Net Program to assist those not eligible under any of the categorical aid programs.

Among New York State residents, 14.6% fell below the poverty threshold in 1999. The poverty rates of minorities are generally more than double those of Whites, who accounted for 68% of New York's population but only 46% of its poor. For Blacks and Latinos, the poverty rates were approximately twice their proportion of the population. The 2000 census data indicate that approximately 15.6% of New Yorkers are poor, compared with 13.3% for the country as a whole. For children, although the national rate is nearly one out of five (19.9%), in New York State it is closer to one out of four (24.7%).

See also Almshouses and poorhouses; Homelessness.

Beard, Rick, ed. *On Being Homeless: Historical Perspectives* (New York: Museum of the City of New York, 1987)

Brown, Dorothy, and Elizabeth McKeon. *The Poor Belong to Us: Catholic Charities and American Welfare* (Cambridge, Mass: Harvard Univ Press, 1997)

Galie, Peter J. *The New York State Constitution: A Reference Guide* (Westport, Conn: Greenwood Press, 1991)

Ingalls, Robert P. *Herbert H. Lehman and New York's Little Deal* (New York: New York Univ Press, 1975)

Katz, Michael B. *The Price of Citizenship: Redefining the American Welfare State* (New York: Metropolitan Books, 2001)

Mohl, Raymond. *Poverty in New York, 1783–1825* (New York: Oxford Univ Press, 1971)

Newman, Katherine S. *No Shame in the Game: The Working Poor in the Inner City* (New York: Knopf, 1999)
Trattner, Walter I. *From Poor Law to Welfare State: A History of Social Welfare in America,* 5th ed. (New York: Free Press, 1994)

Alejandro Garcia and Vincenza Rose Marash

Powell, Adam Clayton, Jr (*b* New Haven, Conn, 29 Nov 1908; *d* Miami, Fla, 4 Apr 1972). Congressman. The son of the famous pastor of the Abyssinian Baptist Church in Manhattan's Harlem, Powell attended Colgate University, graduating in 1930. Ordained as a minister, he took an assistant pastorship at Abyssinian and in 1937 rose to the head of the church. In 1941, after several years as a political activist and occasional columnist for the *New York Amsterdam News,* Powell won election to the New York City Council, the first Black to serve in that body. Powell soon became a gadfly, challenging racist practices in city housing and education policies. In 1945 he became the state's first African American congressman, and his confident, undeferential, and highly flamboyant style made him a hero to many Blacks. Although probably the most visible national African American leader for almost two decades, his erratic personal and political style made many enemies. Unhappy with the Democratic Party's pusillanimity on civil rights matters, Powell endorsed in 1956 Republican president Dwight D. Eisenhower for reelection and Republican Jacob K. Javits in New York's senatorial race. An attempt by local Democrats to unseat Powell in 1958 failed.

Powell's most notable legislative achievements were the introduction of amendments, dubbed "Powell amendments," to social legislation that forbade the distribution of federal funds to segregationist organizations. Although his amendments failed to pass, they raised awareness about racially discriminatory federal policies. In 1967 Powell was denied his seat by his colleagues for misuse of committee funds and for his conviction of contempt of court charges a year earlier relating to a civil suit lodged against him. However, Powell won reelection to his seat in a special 1967 election and in the general election of 1968. The US Supreme Court ruled in 1969 that his exclusion from the US Congress two years earlier was unconstitutional, but Powell lost his seat to Charles B. Rangel in the 1970 election. Powell's last years were spent in retirement at his vacation home in the Bahamas.

Hamilton, Charles V. *Adam Clayton Powell, Jr: The Political Biography of an American Dilemma* (New York: Collier Books, 1991)

Richard M. Flanagan

Powell, Colin (Luther) (*b* New York City, 5 Apr 1937). US military officer and government official. Powell was born in Harlem to Jamaican immigrants and raised in the racially mixed Longwood section of the Bronx. He has described his youth as "directionless," although he was active in the local Episcopal church as an acolyte and a subdeacon. He attended City College of New York in Upper Manhattan from 1954 to 1958. At college he joined the US Army Reserve Officer's Training Corps, finding direction and a sense of belonging. After graduation he was commissioned in the regular army and served in Vietnam (1962–63, 1968–69). Powell later occupied several ranking military and government positions. He was the first black American to serve as national security adviser to the president (1987–89); as chairman of the Joint Chiefs of Staff (1989–93), a position he held during the Persian Gulf War; and as US secretary of state (2001–). Powell briefly considered a run for the US presidency in 1996.

Powell, Colin L., with Joseph E. Persico. *My American Journey* (New York: Random House, 1995)

Scott C. Monje

power and lighting. In the early 21st century gas and electricity are the main sources of residential, commercial, and industrial power for New York State residents, while electricity provides the only meaningful source of artificial lighting. Network industries have three basic segments: production, transmission, and distribution. The gas and electricity distribution industries in New York State are intertwined, with one company usually offering both services. The electric utility industry comprises an array of firms, including large, vertically integrated, investor-owned utilities; specialist electricity-generating firms; state-owned producers and wholesale distributors; small municipal distributing utilities; and a few rural cooperatives. Both gas and electric industries are subject to numerous regulations by government agencies at the state and federal levels.

MANUFACTURED GAS, 1820S–1950S

The early history of the gas industry is the history of manufactured gas, which was produced by distilling bituminous coal in heated, anaerobic vessels known as retorts. After the product was treated, it could be stored or delivered immediately to mains for distribution to nearby customers. Manufactured gas was initially used for street lighting, but it eventually came to be used in homes and factories. The first gas-lighting company in the United States was founded in Baltimore in 1816. The New York Gas Light Co, the first in the state and the ancestor of Consolidated Edison (Con Edison), was formed in 1823 to serve part of New York City. It was joined in 1830 by the Manhattan Gaslight Co and, over the course of the 19th century, by several dozen other companies. Not all pioneering gas companies were successful. The Brooklyn Gas Light Co was founded in 1825 but failed before delivering any gas. It was not until 1849, when the company was revived and renamed Brooklyn Union Gas (now part of KeySpan Energy) that Brooklyn's streets were illuminated with gas. Other present gas and electric utilities can trace their origins to this period. Rochester Gas Light Co (now Rochester Gas and Electric) and the Ithaca Gas Light Co (now New York State Electric and Gas Corp [NYSEG]) were founded in 1848 and 1852, respectively. Both are subsidiaries of Energy East early in the 21st century. By 1860 the state had 71 manufactured gas companies, more than any other in the nation. Despite a merger movement in the industry around the turn of the century and competition from electricity in the lighting market, in 1909 New York still led the nation, with 141 manufactured gas companies.

Although new techniques for manufacturing gas were developed, manufactured gas was superseded by cheaper natural gas in the 1950s as interstate pipelines connected New York State to the productive gas fields of the Southwest. The last manufactured gas plant in the state ceased operation in 1972. Today the New York State Department of Environmental Conservation investigates and oversees cleanup of contamination associated with these plants. Of the 194 sites identified up to 2002 (of an estimated 300 in the state), most are the responsibility of the successor utilities of the early manufactured gas companies.

NATURAL GAS, 1820S–1950S

New York State played a prominent role in the early history of the natural gas industry in the United States. The basic properties of natural gas, which rose from springs, had been known since ancient times, but William Hart, a gunsmith of Fredonia (Chautauqua Co), is credited as the first person to harness natural gas and to deliver it to customers. The Fredonia gas springs were discovered around 1821, and Hart's 27 ft (8.2 m) well was probably supplying streetlights or buildings by 1825. Around 1829, with a contract from the US government, Hart tapped a gas spring at Westfield (Chautauqua Co) and used a half-mile pine-log pipeline to supply 144 burners in the Barcelona lighthouse on Lake Erie, the world's first navigational beacon lighted with natural gas.

The primary problem facing the natural gas industry was primitive pipeline technology. In 1870 a gas deposit was discovered near West Bloomfield (Ontario Co), about 25 miles (40 km) from Rochester. The Rochester Natural Gas Light Co was formed, and a wooden pipeline was completed in 1872. Although gas was delivered, the pipeline was unreliable and the company quickly failed. The first successful metal pipeline was constructed also in 1872. In 1886 the United Natural Gas Co (later National Fuel Gas Co of Buffalo) constructed an 87 mi (140 km) wrought-iron transmission line that connected the gas fields of Pennsylvania to Buffalo; at the time this was the longest natural gas pipeline in the world. By the 1930s natural gas was making headway in some parts of the state. Standard Oil and Columbia Gas and Electric owned a small pipeline that originated in the Appalachian gas fields, extended from Olean (Cattaraugus Co) through Binghamton along the southern border of the state, with a branch to Syracuse, and ended at Tappan (Rockland Co).

New York City remained one of the last metropolitan areas in the Northeast not connected to natural gas. The "Big Inch" and "Little Big Inch" pipelines connecting the oil fields of Texas with northern New Jersey were converted to natural gas immediately after World War II, but the terminus was diverted to Philadelphia. About the same time, the Transcontinental Gas Pipe Line Co (now Williams) applied to the Federal Power Commission (now Federal Energy Regulatory Commission) for permission to construct a gas pipeline from Texas to New York City. This ultimately was granted over the opposition of vested coal and railroad interests. The first natural gas was supplied to the New York City on 16 Jan 1951, and by the end of the decade natural gas had replaced manufactured gas.

ELECTRICITY, 1880S–PRESENT

Although preceded by several arc-lighting systems, Thomas Edison is usually given credit for initiating the modern era of electricity. On 4 Sept 1882 he switched on incandescent lights in a section of Lower Manhattan using direct current (DC) electricity produced by a dynamo installed several blocks away on Pearl St. Central station electric service spread quickly to the towns and cities of New York. This pioneering era involved direct competition in many cities, where the awarding of multiple franchises was the norm; for example, 6 companies formed between 1880 and 1893 in Rochester, a community of under 150,000 people, while nearly 100 were created in New York City, Brooklyn, and neighboring areas. Smaller towns tended to be served by a single utility, and some municipalities established their own electric utilities. There were also major technological innovations; most significant was the introduction of alternating current (AC), which permitted long-distance transmission and greatly increased the optimal scale of electrical systems. When the Niagara Falls Power Co began high-voltage transmission of power to Buffalo in 1896 using a Westinghouse AC system, it was clear that alternating current was destined to become the industry norm.

By 1902 there were 256 commercial and municipal electric utilities and 96 electric railway companies in the state, but a dramatic consolidation movement was under way. Within a few years most cities were served by a single electric utility that was often also the sole supplier of gas. The public and politicians reacted by demanding some kind of control over these monopolies. In 1905 the state legislature appointed a joint committee, with Charles Evans Hughes as counsel, to investigate gas and electric rates and service in New York City. The committee recommended a reduction in rates and the creation of a commission to regulate gas and electric companies. The Commission of Gas and Electricity was formed in 1905, but its powers were limited. In the state gubernatorial campaign of 1906, the Democratic nominee, William Randolph Hearst, ran on a platform advocating public ownership of utilities, while Hughes, his Republican opponent, favored comprehensive regulation of all utilities. Hughes was elected, and in 1907 the legislature enacted the Public Service Commissions Law, which created two district commissions, one for New York City and another for the rest of the state, with powers to regulate rates, capitalization, and security issues. The districts were combined in 1921.

Niagara Mohawk's steam station in Oswego, 1965.

Electrification spread in the 1920s, rapidly in urban areas and modestly in rural ones, and companies consolidated regionally. This was the heyday of a frenzied holding company movement. By the end of the decade, most of New York's regional electric and gas utilities were controlled by multistate holding companies, the exception being Consolidated Gas Co (1884) in the New York City area. The United Corp, the largest utility company in the United States in 1929, not only controlled the Niagara Hudson Power Corp, itself a holding company, and Columbia Gas and Electric, but also had an interest in Consolidated Gas. The Associated Gas and Electric Co had extensive holdings in the state, including companies such as Rochester Gas and Electric and much of what later became NYSEG. The stock market crash of 1929, the ensuing collapse of many holding companies, and the passage of the federal Public Utility Holding Company Act of 1935 caused the divestiture of most holding company properties, creating the basic corporate structure that survived until the late 20th century.

Another restructuring of the electric utility industry occurred in the 1990s. One utility, Long Island Lighting Co, ceased to exist because of a disastrous investment in the Shoreham Nuclear Power Plant (Suffolk Co). Several companies have merged, and many utilities are divesting themselves of generating capacity, the sector where competition is most vigorous, to focus on distribution. Between 1990 and 1999 the share of electricity generated by utilities declined from over 90% to below 70% as nonutility generators exempt from traditional utility regulation expanded. Some independent power producers, such as the Bronx Zoo, supply only their own needs, while wholesale generators like Oswego Harbor Power—the largest nonutility generator in the state, with a capacity of 1,800 megawatts—supply utilities under long-term contracts. In 1998 the New York Independent System Operator (NYISO), a nonprofit entity, was created to administer the state's wholesale market for electricity and its transmission system. Several electric utilities have been reorganized or purchased by domestic or foreign utilities. By 1999 the five largest electric utilities in the state, accounting for 86% of total sales, were Niagara Mohawk Power Corp (acquired in 2002 by National Grid plc), Con Edison, Long Island Power Authority (LIPA), New York Power Authority (NYPA), and NYSEG. Two of these, LIPA and NYPA, are state owned.

The 21st Century

Electric utilities and nonutility generators in the state use a well-balanced combination of fuels for generation: in 2000, 28% of the electricity generated in New York State came from natural gas, 23% from nuclear energy, 18% from coal, 18% from hydropower, 11% from oil, and 2% from renewable sources. The state imports over 98% of its natural gas but still has nearly 8,000 operating gas wells.

The biggest change for consumers of both gas and electricity in coming years will be the ability to choose suppliers. The energy crisis of the mid-1970s stimulated federal legislation culminating in the Energy Policy Act of 1992, which sought to bring more competition to bear in these industries, in part by separating the production, transmission, and distribution functions. However, markets for gas and, especially, electricity were slow to change, leading states to identify specific policy goals for their energy industries. In 1998 the New York State Energy Planning Board issued a plan, updated in 2002, that focused on increasing consumer choice, ensuring nondiscriminatory access to transmission and distribution systems, allowing freedom of entry and exit of firms while safeguarding system reliability, and promoting energy conservation and a clean environment. The state energy plan will be periodically updated in response to events. The Public Service Commission believes competition will result in lower rates than would have been obtained under the old system of regulation. But the experience of states like California indicates that restructuring in the electricity industry may create opportunities for manipulation and uncompetitive practices. It remains to be seen whether the system can be operated fairly and efficiently for the benefit of both producers and consumers.

See also Niagara Falls (city); Petroleum and Natural Gas Industry; St. Lawrence Seaway; Technology.

Adams, Edward Dean. *Niagara Power: History of the Niagara Falls Power Company, 1886–1918,* 2 vols (Niagara Falls, 1927)

Castaneda, Christopher J. *Invisible Fuel: Manufactured and Natural Gas in America, 1800–2000* (New York: Twayne Publishers, 1999)

Jonnef, Jill. *Empires of Light: Edison, Tesla, Westinghouse, and the Race to Electrify the World* (New York: Random House, 2003)

New York Independent System Operator, http://www.nyiso.com

New York State Public Service Commission. *Utility Regulatory Bodies in New York State, 1855–1953* (Albany: Author, 1953)

US Department of Energy, Energy Information Administration. "Electricity Profile, New York," http://www.eia.doe.gov/cneaf/electricity/st_profiles/new_york/ny.html

William Hausman

Power Authority of the State of New York. Established in 1931 to develop the hydroelectric potential of the St. Lawrence River as a natural resource in the public interest. As early as 1906, New York City business concerns (which were later backed by the Democratic Party) enthusiastically endorsed the state developing its rich hydropower resources, lured by the benefits of cheap electricity. However, Republicans and state business interests outside of New York City, often closely tied to private utilities, were opposed. In 1921 Republican governor Nathan L. Miller created the State Water Power Commission to grant leases to private companies to develop sites along the St. Lawrence and Niagara Rivers. Before private plants could be built, Democrat Alfred E. Smith was elected governor in 1922. Smith, who supported a public power policy, abolished Miller's commission in 1927 but facing a Republican-controlled legislature was unable to do more. Taking advantage of the crisis atmosphere of the Great Depression, Democratic governor Franklin D. Roosevelt achieved a breakthrough for public power advocates in April 1931 when the legislature passed the Power Authority Act, calling for the construction of public hydropower plants. For many years thereafter litigation initiated by private utilities, including the Niagara Hudson Power Corp (a predecessor of Niagara Mohawk) hamstrung the new authority. The deadlock was broken in 1953 when Republican governor Thomas E. Dewey, a strong public power advocate, won over private interests and began construction the following year of a plant along the St. Lawrence River in Massena (St. Lawrence Co) under the auspices of the Power Authority.

To get the project moving quickly, in 1954 Dewey chose Robert Moses, the head of the Triborough Bridge and Tunnel Authority (TBTA), as the new chairman of the Power Authority. As head of the TBTA and numerous other state commissions and authorities, Moses had a wealth of political, financial, and labor connections in the state and had a reputation for completing large-scale construction projects on time. The leadership of Moses was critical to the fledgling Power Authority. With an impeccable reputation on Wall St as a protector of bondholder interests, Moses enabled the authority to make an initial bond offering in 1954 of more than $1 billion. The issue sold in just four days and was the largest revenue bond offering in state history at that time. With financing in hand Moses completed the St. Lawrence project in 1959. Built jointly with Canadian authorities, the facility was named the St. Lawrence–Franklin D. Roosevelt Power Project. While construction was underway at the Massena site, Moses began construction of another hydroelectric facility in 1957 located along the Niagara River in Lewiston (Niagara Co). To build the project, the Power Authority used the state's powers of eminent domain to condemn 1,350 of the 6,300 acres (546 of the 2,550 ha) of the Tuscarora Indian Reservation. The Tuscaroras sued to stop the action. Moses was undeterred, moving the project forward regardless of the legal challenges; the Tuscaroras lost their case in the US Supreme Court in 1960. When the facility opened in 1961 it had a maximum generating capacity of 2.4 million kW of power, making it one of the world's largest hydroelectric facilities. The power plant had been named in honor of Moses the preceding year as construction began to wind down.

In 1962 Moses abruptly resigned as Power Authority chairman when Gov Nelson A. Rockefeller tried to curb Moses's influence in state government. The last major hydroelectric facility built by the authority was the Blenheim-Gilboa Pumped Storage Power Project (Schoharie Co); opened in 1973, this plant draws upon the waters of Schoharie Creek. With most of New York State's hydropower opportunities now tapped, the authority turned to other power sources, including nuclear generation. In 1975 it opened the James A. FitzPatrick Nuclear Power Plant in Scriba (Oswego Co) and the Indian Point Nuclear Power Plant 3 in Buchanan (Westchester Co) the following year. Both of these nuclear facilities were sold in 2000 to subsidiaries of Entergy Corp as part of New York State's electrical deregulation policy. The authority also owns and operates fossil fuel plants in Astoria (Queens Co) and Holtsville (Suffolk Co).

In 2002 the authority operated five major power plants, five small hydroelectric plants, and 11 small natural-gas turbines located in Queens, the Bronx, Brooklyn, Staten Island, and Brentwood (Suffolk Co) to help alleviate electrical generation shortages in New York City and Long Island. The authority's electricity is sold at a price based upon cost of production to public utilities, to private utilities that are obligated to resell the power at cost to customers, to private industries that commit to remain in New York State, and to commuter trains and subways in the New York metropolitan region and in Buffalo. The Power Authority also operates an extensive high-voltage electrical transmission system, consisting of 1,400 miles (2,253 km) of power transmission lines and ancillary facilities. The authority's two most notable power lines run from Massena to Marcy (Oneida Co) and from Marcy to East Fishkill (Dutchess Co). The latter line, known as Marcy-South, was highly controversial; after it went into service in 1988, lawsuits continued over claims, first voiced in 1982, that high-voltage power lines could cause cancer and reduce property values. At a significant additional cost the line was rerouted away from ecologically sensitive areas, including the Catskill Park. A five-member board of trustees appointed by the governor and confirmed by the senate governs the authority. As a nonprofit entity, the authority's costs of operation and construction are financed solely through its own revenues and by bonds backed by its revenues. The Power Authority's rates and practices are not subject to the jurisdiction of the State Public Service Commission. In 2000 the authority provided 35.5 billion kW hours, or 22%, of the electrical power used by New Yorkers. In the same year, its total revenues were $2,034 million, with a net revenue of $170 million.

Caro, Robert. *The Power Broker: Robert Moses and the Fall of New York* (New York: Vintage Books, 1974)
Peterson, Raymond Edward. *Public Power and Private Planning: The Power Authority of the State of New York* (New York: NYS Power Authority, 1990)

Thomas A. Birkland

Practical Bible College. Private, nondenominational Christian college. Evangelist John A. Davis founded Practical Bible Training School in 1900 on Harrison St in Lestershire [now Johnson City, Broome Co], near Binghamton, as an outgrowth of his popular Bible classes. Coeducational since its inception, the school's mission was to provide a Bible-centered education within the conservative evangelical Christian tradition. It emphasized the inerrancy of the scriptures and used the Bible as its core curriculum. Courses were initially held in the evenings, during the summer months. In 1906 the school instituted a two-year study program with a traditional academic schedule and in 1911 moved to the site of the former White City Amusement Park on Riverside Drive, overlooking the Susquehanna River. A US post office was established there that same year, giving the school its official address of Bible School Park. A three-year program was added in 1912. The school became known as Practical Bible College in 1993 and began granting associate of applied science (AAS) and bachelor of religious education (BRE) degrees. The three-year diploma program is still offered, as is a one-year course in Bible study. Enrollment in 2003 was 308.

Barackman, Floyd Hays. "A History of Practical Bible Training School" (Bible School Park, NY: Practical Bible College, 1994)

Marianne Rahn-Erickson

pragmatism. A uniquely American philosophy that justifies experience, knowledge, and thought by their usefulness in actualizing individual goals, furthering ethical interests, and promoting social values. Conceived by Charles Sanders Peirce in Cambridge, Mass, during the 1870s, its best-known exponent was William James of Harvard University. New York City became a center for pragmatism in 1904 when John Dewey arrived at Columbia University. Dewey called his strain of pragmatism "instrumentalism" and argued that the value of any concept is determined by its experienced function. For Dewey and his adherents, truth always has a social context, and knowledge is a tool or instrument for the betterment of society, especially through education. Horace M. Kallen, a disciple of James who taught at the New School for Social Research from 1919 until his death in 1974, was a prime formulator of the theory of cultural pluralism, which argued for the importance of ethnic identity in the formation of a democratic society. Sidney Hook, a doctoral student of Dewey who taught at New York University from 1927 to 1968, published many works on pragmatism including *The Metaphysics of Pragmatism* (1927) and *Pragmatism and the Tragic Sense of Life* (1975). His *Toward the Understanding of Karl Marx* (1933) offered a Deweyian perspective on Marx. Always opposed to communism, Hook later became a leading neoconservative. Four of Dewey's doctoral students had long and distinguished careers as philosophy professors at Columbia: Irwin Edman (1918–54), Herbert Schneider (1918–57), John Herman Randall Jr (1920–70), and Ernest Nagel (1931–70). In the late 20th century, the two main exponents of pragmatism at Columbia were Isaac Levi and Sidney Morgenbesser. Pragmatism has been well represented on SUNY campuses, frequently by Columbia graduates: Thomas Martland and Naomi Zack at SUNY Albany, Peter Hare and Paul Kurtz at SUNY Buffalo, Stephen David Ross at SUNY Binghamton, Milton Mayeroff at SUNY Cortland, and Justus Buchler (after many years at Columbia) at SUNY Stony Brook.

Menand, Louis. *The Metaphysical Club: A Story of Ideas in America* (New York: Farrar, Straus & Giroux, 2001)
Morris, Charles. *The Pragmatic Movement in American Philosophy* (New York: Braziller, 1970)

Pratt, Zadock (*b* Stephentown, Rensselaer Co, 30 Oct 1790; *d* Bergen, NJ, 6 Apr 1871). Tanner. Pratt learned the tanning trade in his family's small farm tannery alongside his father and brothers. In 1816 he formed a partnership with his two brothers to operate a tannery in Lexington (Greene Co). After five years Pratt struck out on his own. He built the foundation for one of New York State's best-known tanneries in 1824 when he began building a tannery on the banks of the Schohariekill at what became Prattsville (Greene Co). Through his own self-promotion, Pratt became one of the 19th century's most recognizable tanners. His Prattsville Tannery, with a capacity to tan 55,000 sides of sole leather annually, was reportedly the nation's largest. Writing in trade and scientific journals as well as in the popular media, Pratt was widely known as a tanner and successful artisan-entrepreneur. He served as a justice of the peace in 1824 and was elected to the New York State Senate in 1830. He represented the state as a Democrat in the US Congress twice (1837–39, 1843–45), and he reportedly enjoyed reenacting historic battles. As the Catskills became deforested in the decade before the Civil War, Pratt pioneered the expansion by tanners into Pennsylvania, providing the capital for two tanneries. He was not so much an innovator in the leather industry as he was a successful implementer of other tanners' technical improvements and business strategies. Pratt married five times; his only son, George, followed him into the leather trade before dying in the Civil War. While most monuments to New York's tanners consist of crumbling ruins along mountain streams, Pratt had his autobiographical tribute carved into a Prattsville mountainside, known today as Pratt Rock.

Millen, Patricia E. *Bare Trees: Zadock Pratt, Master Tanner and the Story of What Happened to the Catskill Mountain Forests* (Hensonville, NY: Black Dome Press, 1995)

David S. Rotenstein

Pratt Institute. Private university. It was founded in Brooklyn in 1887 as a technical secondary school by Charles Pratt, an associate of John D. Rockefeller Sr. The institute's library, opened in 1887, was the first free library in Brooklyn and helped support the liberal arts and sciences program that began the following year. In 1890 the institute opened its Library School (now School of Library and Information Science), while the high school program closed in 1905 and the kindergarten training school closed in 1917. The institute awarded its first bachelor's degree in 1938, and graduate studies opened in 1950. In 1954 the School of Architecture formed as a separate entity from the Art School, and the Center for Continuing and Professional Studies offers programs in graphics and design. Pratt combined with the Munson-Williams-Proctor Institute in Utica in 2000 to establish an extension campus in Utica. Pratt enrolled 4,000 students in 2002.

Sarah E. DeSanctis

Prattsburgh. Town (pop 2,064) in NE Steuben Co. Settled in 1801, the town was formed in 1813 from Pulteney. The Kanona and Prattsburgh Railroad connected the Village of Prattsburgh (chartered in 1848, dissolved in 1972) to the Rochester Division of the Erie Railroad in 1882. In the 19th century Prattsburgh had a foundry and a tannery. In an area of muckland in the town's southeast, onions and other vegetables are cultivated. In 2003 industries included McConnell Manufacturing Co (1961; farm equipment) and Air-Flo (early 1960s; farm and heavy equipment). The birthplace of Narcissa Prentiss Whitman (1808–47), a town native who journeyed to Oregon Territory in 1836 as a missionary, is operated as a seasonal museum.

Virginia L. Wright and Jerry Wright

Prattsville. Town (pop 665) in NW Greene Co. Located in the upper Schoharie Valley, it was settled from the lower Schoharie Valley before 1757. In 1824 Zadock Pratt established a tannery reputed to be the largest in the world. It used local tanbark and Latin American hides, closing in 1845 when the hemlock woods were depleted. Pratt's vision helped the town make the transition to a dairy economy. The hamlet of Prattsville was an incorporated village from 1883 to 1900. Initial plans for the Schoharie Reservoir were to drown the hamlet, but ultimately Gilboa Dam (1927) flooded only a small tract within the town. The Shandaken Tunnel, part of the New York City water supply aqueduct, was constructed from 1917 to 1924.

Field Horne

Preble. Town (pop 1,582) in NW Cortland Co. Settled in 1796, it formed from Tully (Onondaga Co) in 1808. The land is hilly with a wide valley formed by the west branch of the Tioughnioga River, holding very productive soil. There are several kettle lakes in town. The completion of the railroad in 1854 gave farmers access to wider markets for their produce and encouraged dairying; the first cheese factory was built in 1863–64. I-81 further improved access when completed in 1966. Farming remains significant. Saulsbury Fire Fighting Apparatus Co was called on to build a large number of fire trucks to replace those lost by the New York City Fire Department on 11 Sept 2001. Preble is the site of Song Mountain Ski Area.

Cathy A. Barber

Preemption Line. After an agreement was struck between Massachusetts and New York State in 1786, a boundary line was drawn from the 82d milestone on Pennsylvania's northern border to Sodus Bay on Lake Ontario, marking the eastern edge of lands disputed in the 1780s and 1790s. The states of New York and Massachusetts both claimed over 6 million acres (2.4 million ha) of fertile land in central and western New York State based on colonial charters. Representatives from the states meeting in Hartford, Conn, agreed on 16 Dec 1786 that New York State held political sovereignty over lands west of the surveyed line, but Massachusetts had title to the lands, giving them the right to preemption and the ability to purchase land titles from the Iroquois nations and then sell that land for a profit. Massachusetts eagerly sought buyers for the acreage and in 1788 sold the tract to a group of New England investors represented by Oliver Phelps and Nathaniel Gorham. The land west of the Preemption Line and east of the Genesee River became known as the Phelps and Gorham Purchase. After a complex series of transactions, most of the remaining land was controlled by the Holland Land Co by 1793.

The legality of the treaties with the Iroquois nations necessary to extinguish the native title to the land, largely complete by the 1797 Treaty of Big Tree, has long been debated. The first survey incorrectly veered the line westward, excluding the burgeoning community of Geneva (Ontario Co) from Massachusetts's holdings and the line was redrawn in 1792. The new line nearly bisected Geneva, running along what is now Preemption St.

Mau, Clayton C. *The Development of Central and Western New York,* rev ed. (Dansville, NY: F. A. Owen, 1958)

Kathryn Clippinger Kosto

prehistoric archaeology. Prehistoric archaeology in New York State is the study of material remains of Native American cultures that predate the arrival of Europeans.

Establishing the Discipline

Published descriptions of archaeological objects or sites pertaining to New York State are rare until the beginning of the 19th century. Antiquarian collecting typified much 19th- and early 20th-century archaeological activity: sites were mined for objects with little regard for the context. In the mid–19th century prominent scholars of New York State archaeology included Henry Rowe Schoolcraft, Joshua V. H. Clark, and Ephraim G. Squier. Lewis Henry Morgan collected archaeological artifacts and ethnographic objects for what was to become the New York State Museum and published a report on the collection in 1849. Most of the materials he collected were destroyed in the 1911 State Capitol building fire in Albany.

Around the turn of the 20th century, the Rev William Beauchamp published New York State Museum bulletins about chipped stone, polished stone, earthenware, and other artifact types. In 1900 he also published *The Aboriginal Occupations of New York.* This synthesis of site locations across the state was further elaborated by Arthur C. Parker in 1922 as *The Archaeological History of New York.* Parker was hired by the New York State Museum in 1906 as its first permanent full-time archaeologist. His excavation that same year at the Iroquoian Ripley site (Chautauqua Co) and subsequent report in 1907 set a high standard for its day. Under his leadership the State Museum played a major role in New York State archaeology during the first quarter of the 20th century. In 1924 Parker became director of the Rochester Museum of Arts and Sciences (now Rochester Museum and Science Center). Soon after his arrival William A. Ritchie became a staff archaeologist at the museum. Through his directorship, Parker championed the systematic excavation of sites that resulted in large archaeological collections being housed in both the State Museum and the Rochester museum.

In 1916 the New York State Archaeological Association was founded, being composed of both avocational and professional archaeologists. Its journal, the *Bulletin,* focuses on the archaeology of New York State. During the early years of the 20th century Frederick Houghton, an educator who was also associated with the Buffalo Museum of Science, synthesized available information on the archaeological record of western New York State. During this same period, the American Museum of Natural History in New York City sponsored a series of excavations by Alanson Skinner and Mark R. Harrington, including sites on Manhattan and Staten Island and at Armonk (Westchester Co). The Heye Foundation, now part of the Smithsonian's National Museum of the American Indian, also sponsored archaeological work. Reginald P. Bolton, Foster Saville, and James Finch were active avocational archaeologists in the New York City and Long Island areas. Their work was later synthesized and expanded by Carlyle Smith in *The Archaeology of Coastal New York* (1950).

An Expanded Chronology for State Prehistory

Despite some stratigraphic excavations, how long humans had occupied New York State was seriously underestimated until radiocarbon dating began to be used in the 1950s and 1960s. Ritchie categorized the growing body of archaeological data in the 1940s. His numerous excavations included the artifact-rich sites of Brewerton (Onondaga Co) and Lamoka Lake (Schuyler Co). The material recovered from these sites was used in formulating the Brewerton and Lamoka cultures, which Ritchie characterized as part of an Archaic hunting-and-gathering way of life. His use of the term "Archaic" was borrowed by other North American archaeologists and today refers to a general stage of cultural development characterized by the use of a wide range of natural resources. Subsequent research established the range of the Archaic to be from 8,100 BC to 1,000 BC and has revealed a diversity of sites, artifacts, and resources exploited by Archaic peoples.

In 1949 Ritchie moved from Rochester to Albany to become state archaeologist. In 1965 he published *The Archaeology of New York State,* a synthesis that made use of radiocarbon dates unavailable when he published a similar volume in 1944. Robert Funk was hired as Ritchie's assistant in 1960; he became state archaeologist in 1973. That same year he and Ritchie published *Aboriginal Settlement Patterns in the Northeast,* an update of Ritchie's 1965 synthesis. Funk published contributions on the archaeology of the Hudson Valley, the upper Susquehanna Valley, and the Paleo-Indian occupation of the Dutchess Quarry Caves (Orange Co), among others.

Iroquoian Archaeology

Parker and other early 20th-century archaeologists assumed that Iroquoians had migrated into New York State and displaced Algonquian speakers. Such a migration was seen as explaining the change from pre-Iroquoian to later Iroquoian artifact styles. In the 1940s James B. Griffin cautioned that migration might not be the explanation for this change. Then in the early 1950s Richard MacNeish formulated a series of ceramic types and used these to demonstrate continuities between pre-Iroquoian and later Iroquois sites, or a development of Iroquois traditions within what is now New York State. The in situ model of Iroquoian development has been widely accepted, but it has recently been challenged by Dean Snow. Sequences of Iroquoian village movement were worked out by Marian White for the Niagara Frontier Iroquoian (Erie/Neutral/Wenro), Charles Wray for the Seneca, Mary Ann Niemczycki for the Cayuga, James Tuck for the Onondaga, and Peter Pratt for the Oneida. More recent refinements have been provided by Nancy Herter for the Erie/Neutral/Wenro, Martha Sempowski and Lorraine Saunders for the Seneca, Kathy Allen for the Cayuga, James Bradley for the Onondaga, and Dean Snow for the Mohawk.

Arrowhead made of Onondaga chert (a type of limestone), found in Chili.

Recent Trends

Avocational members of the New York State Archaeological Association continue to make important contributions to the state's archaeological database. Early and Middle Archaic sites, once considered rare, have increasingly been identified. Professional research includes reconstruction of past landscapes, settlement systems, and human demography and often involves interdisciplinary cooperation. The development of sedentary communities and horticulture is being documented. There is interest in both the earliest occupations and the impact of Europeans on American Indians.

In the last three decades of the 20th century, there was widespread archaeological survey and excavation in the state as a consequence of the passage of both federal and state legislation designed to protect archaeological resources. In the 21st century the majority of archaeologists in New York State are involved in contract archaeology or cultural resources management (CRM) projects. These activities are overseen by various state agencies including the New York State Museum's Anthropological Survey and the Office of Parks, Recreation, and Historic Preservation. In 1972 Marian White, Bert Salwen, and other professional archaeologists formed the New York Archaeological Council (NYAC) to promote professional standards in the conduct of contract archaeology in the state.

Passage in 1990 of the federal Native American Graves Protection and Repatriation Act (NAGPRA) requires the inventory of American Indian skeletal remains and sacred objects by institutions holding such material. The New York State Museum, the American Museum of Natural History, and the Rochester Museum and Science Center all have extensive holdings of remains and materials subject to this legislation. These institutions and others are in the process of returning both skeletal material and material objects to American Indian groups claiming them.

See also Munsee; Owasco.

Engelbrecht, William. *Iroquoia: The Development of a Native World* (Syracuse: Syracuse Univ Press, 2003)
Funk, Robert E. "An Introduction to the History of Prehistoric Archaeology in New York State," *Bulletin* 113 (1997)
Kuhn, Robert D. "The New York State Historic Preservation Office Archaeology Program, 1990 to 2000: A 10-Year Retrospective," *Bulletin* 117 (2001)
Ritchie, William A. *The Archaeology of New York State,* rev ed. (Garden City, NY: Natural History Press, 1969)
Ritchie, William A., and Robert E. Funk. *Aboriginal Settlement Patterns in the Northeast* (Albany: Univ of the State of New York, 1973)

William Engelbrecht

Presbyterians. Protestant denomination. The first strain of Presbyterianism in New York Colony developed from New England migrants to the Puritan congregations on eastern Long Island in the 1640s. The first Presbyterian minister was Francis Doughty, a Puritan who came to Long Island from New England in 1642 because of differences over the practice of infant baptism. Doughty represents the dominant strain of Presbyterianism in New York Colony's history, heavily influenced by Puritanism and its practical Christian devotion. The other important strain, the Scots-Irish component of New York Presbyterianism, emerged in 1707 when the Philadelphia minister Francis Makemie (1658–1708) preached without a license to a small private gathering and was arrested. Makemie was eventually acquitted, but the case became one of the first contests of religious liberty in colonial America. In 1719 Presbyterians worshiped for the first time in a church building of their own but did not have sufficient numbers to create a presbytery until 1738. Even then the Presbytery of New York needed assistance from congregations in northern New Jersey. The Scots-Irish version of the Protestant faith was less introspective and more formal than New England Puritanism, and this tension gave New York Colony a role in American Presbyterian history that would have repercussions for Presbyterians nationwide.

A third group, Scottish Presbyterians, also contributed to the colony's Presbyterian diversity. The Associate Presbyterians emerged in Scotland in the 1730s as part of an effort to recover the central truths of Calvinism. By the 1760s they had migrated to New York Colony and formed a congregation in Cambridge [now in Washington Co]. The Reformed Presbyterians, also Scots, were called Covenanters because of their adherence to national covenants of 1638 and 1643, and they refused to participate in any civil government that did not acknowledge Christ as king. Covenanters settled in Salem [now in Washington Co] in the 1760s. The Associate and Reformed Presbyterians would not compete in numbers or influence with the mainstream denomination, the Presbyterian Church in the United States of America (PCUSA), which was founded in 1789. Presbyterian laity were active in politics during the late colonial period and took a leading role to limit the influence of the Anglican Church in education and politics, and many, such as William Livingston and Alexander MacDougall, were leading patriots.

Revivalism and National Influence

At the time of the Presbytery of New York's founding, American Presbyterianism was becoming increasingly polarized between those who stressed correct procedure and teaching, the Old Sides, and those who favored the zeal and devotion attending revivals, the New Sides. When the church split in 1741 along these lines, Presbyterians from New York Colony at first tried to stay neutral, but their affinities to the New England tradition of experiential piety prevailed. Presbyterians from New York Colony were leaders in the establishment of the Synod of New York in 1745, a court of appeal higher than presbytery, which was composed of the presbyteries of New York and New Brunswick, NJ. When these pro-revival Presbyterians founded the College of New Jersey in 1746 (now Princeton University), they ensured a steady stream of ministers ever alert to the importance of stirring up strenuous piety among the faithful. Revivals would continue to mark the character of New York Presbyterianism into the first half of the 19th century. The leading figure in the Second Great Awakening, Charles Grandison Finney (1792–1875), was born in Connecticut and reared in Kirkland (Oneida Co). Finney's controversial methods first gained attention during revivals he promoted during the 1820s in Central and Western New York, sometimes known as the Burned-over District because of the frequency of revivalistic fervor that marked the region. Finney's successes alarmed New England Congregationalists who had entered with Presbyterians into the Plan of Union (1801), a strategy allowing cooperation between both groups in the task of planting churches in the West. But by 1837 the revivalism and abolitionism in Western New York led to another split, this time into Old School and New School denominations, and New York State was at the center of the division. The Old School, which drew its strength once again from southeastern Pennsylvania and the South, voted to abrogate the Plan of Union and to remove from its rolls the Synods of Utica, Geneva, and Genesee, all areas where Finney had been successful and where Presbyterians and Congregationalists had worked together.

By 1837 Presbyterians had two seminaries, Auburn (Cayuga Co), founded in 1821, and Union, founded in New York City in 1836 by New School Presbyterians. These institutions would help check conservative forces after the reunion in 1869 between Old and New School branches of the northern PCUSA. However, the heresy trial of Union Theological Seminary professor and Presbyterian minister Charles Briggs (1841–1913) for denying the authority of Scripture culminated with both Briggs and Union Theological Seminary leaving the Presbyterian fold.

The 20th Century

In many respects the fundamentalist controversy of the 1920s in the PCUSA was the fruit of New York State Presbyterianism's tolerance of religious modernism. In 1923 the Auburn Seminary drafted the Auburn Affirmation, which urged theological diversity. In 1924 the Presbytery of New York ordained two ministers who would not affirm the doctrine of the Virgin Birth of Christ. In 1925 at the General Assembly, conservatives affirmed the Virgin Birth as an essential doctrine. Observers believed this ruling would force Presbyterians in New York State to secede, but the General Assembly appointed a committee to study the controversy, and their report appeased New York State Presbyterians while pressuring conservatives to accept theological diversity. As the headquarters of the Federal Council of the Churches of Christ in America (1908), which would become the National Council of Churches (NCC) in 1950, New York City emerged in the 1940s and 1950s as the capital of Protestant ecumenism. The NCC arguably gave New York State Presbyterians an influence disproportionate to their numbers. In 1971 the PCUSA moved its headquarters from Philadelphia to New York City. This move was short-lived. In 1983 the southern and northern branches of the Presbyterian Church healed their split dating to the Civil War, and Presbyterian headquarters moved to Louisville, Ky. In 1998 the PCUSA counted approximately 720 congregations in New York State, compared to the smaller and more conservative denominations, including the Presbyterian Church in America (25), the Orthodox Presbyterian Church (9), Associate Reformed Presbyterian Church (5), and the Reformed Presbyterian Church of North America (2).

See also Burned-over district; Scots; Scots-Irish.

Alexander, S. D. *Presbytery of New York, 1738–1888* (New York: Anson D. F. Randolph, 1887)

Longfield, Bradley J. *The Presbyterian Controversy: Fundamentalists, Modernists, and Moderates* (New York: Oxford Univ Press, 1991)

Nichols, Robert Hastings, and James Hastings Nichols. *Presbyterianism in New York State.* Ed. James Hastings Nichols (Philadelphia: Westminster Press, 1963)

Savage, Theodore Fiske. *The Presbyterian Church in New York City* (New York: Presbytery of New York, 1949)

D. G. Hart

presidential elections. New York State has traditionally played an important role in US presidential elections because of both its large population and its prominent economic and social leadership role. The state has produced the most major party presidential candidates of any state, six presidents, and nine unsuccessful contenders. In the first 210 years of the US presidency, a New Yorker was in the White House for about 38 years; Martin Van Buren (Democrat, 1837–41), Millard Fillmore (Whig, 1850–53), Chester A. Arthur (Republican, 1881–85), Grover Cleveland (Democrat, 1885–89, 1893–97), Theodore Roosevelt (Republican, 1901–9), and Franklin D. Roosevelt (Democrat, 1933–45). Fillmore, Arthur, and Theodore Roosevelt succeeded to the office after the deaths of their running mates. Although not included in these totals, Dwight D. Eisenhower and Richard M. Nixon both claimed state residence when they won office. New York's unsuccessful nominees include De Witt Clinton (1812), Rufus King (1816), Horatio Seymour (1868), Horace Greeley (1872), Samuel J. Tilden (1876), Alton B. Parker (1904), Charles Evans Hughes (1916), Alfred E. Smith (1928), and Thomas E. Dewey (1944, 1948).

New Yorkers dominated the vice presidency in the opening decades of the 19th century, with four Democratic-Republican, Jeffersonian Republicans, or Democrats serving as a junior partner to a southern president: Aaron Burr (1801–5), George Clinton (1805–12), Daniel D. Tompkins (1817–25), and Martin Van Buren (1833–37). In addition to the vice presidents who later became president, there have been four other New Yorkers who served as vice president, all Republicans: William A. Wheeler (1877–81), Levi P. Morton (1889–93), James S. Sherman (1909–12), and Nelson A. Rockefeller (1974–77). Unsuccessful major party candidates for vice president from the state, besides Franklin D. Roosevelt in 1920, include the last three New Yorkers on national tickets; William E. Miller (Republican, 1964), Geraldine A. Ferraro (Democrat, 1984), and Jack Kemp (Republican, 1996).

New York State's size and its partisan leanings account for its importance in presidential elections. Between 1812 and 1968, it had more electoral votes than any other state, making it the most important win in the contest. From 1972 until 2000 it maintained the second-largest electoral total after California. After the 2000 reapportionment it dropped to third in electoral votes (31), behind California (55) and Texas (34).

From 1868 to 1892 a New Yorker was the Democratic nominee in every election except for 1880. Between 1900 and 1948, a New Yorker was on the national ticket in every election. During this run of New York State candidates, twice both major party candidates were New Yorkers: Alton Parker and Theodore Roosevelt in 1904, and Thomas Dewey and Franklin D. Roosevelt in 1944. Since the Civil War, the Democratic Party has dominated the state's urban areas, particularly New York City, and the Republican Party the counties of the rest of the state. Calvin Coolidge, in 1924, was the most recent Republican presidential candidate to carry New York City. Democratic candidates won New York State in 18 of the 34 contests held between 1868 and 2000. Yet since 1932, Democrats have won 12 of 18 presidential contests within the state. Political machines, which have historically held great power in New York State, have been important in shaping presidential contests. Democratic presidential nominee Al Smith's 1928 campaign was damaged in part by his close association with the Manhattan centered Tammany Hall political machine.

Since the 1970s the Democrats have maintained an extensive lead in statewide voter registration, causing many national Republicans to bypass the state. In the 2000 election, an extremely close contest between Republican George W. Bush and Democrat Al Gore, there was almost no presidential campaigning in the state, despite its 33 electoral votes. With polls showing the state firmly in Gore's column, the candidates concentrated instead on both large and small swing states. Gore won 59% of New York State with a 1.7 million vote margin.

Ragsdale, Lyn. *Vital Statistics on the Presidency: Washington to Clinton* (Washington, DC: Congressional Quarterly, 1996)

Stonecash, Jeffrey, ed. *Governing New York State,* 4th ed. (Albany: SUNY Press, 2001)

Robert J. Spitzer

presidents. Four US presidents were born and raised in New York State. Martin Van Buren (1782–1862) was born in Kinderhook (Columbia Co), where he worked as a lawyer. Millard Fillmore (1800–1874) was born in Locke Township [now Summer Hill, Cayuga Co] and practiced law in Buffalo before being elected to the New York State Assembly, the US House of Representatives, and eventually the vice presidency in 1848. Born in New York City, Theodore Roosevelt (1858–1919) held various public offices in the state, including governor and New York City police commissioner. He made his home at Sagamore Hill in Oyster Bay (Nassau Co). Franklin D. Roosevelt (1882–1945) was born in Hyde

PRESIDENTIAL ELECTIONS

1828	**Andrew Jackson** **John C. Calhoun** (Jackson Dem)	John Q. Adams Richard Rush (Nat Rep)		Total
New York and Kings Cos	16,784	10,691		27,475
Rest of State	122,628	120,872		243,500
Total State	139,412	131,563		270,975
1832	**Andrew Jackson** **Martin Van Buren** (Jackson Dem)	Henry Clay John Sergeant (Nat Rep)		Total
New York and Kings Cos	19,761	13,770		33,531
Rest of State	148,736	141,126		289,862
Total State	168,497	154,896		323,393
1836	**Martin Van Buren** **Richard Johnson** (Dem)	William H. Harrison Francis Granger (Whig)		Total
New York and Kings Cos	19,737	18,214		37,951
Rest of State	147,054	120,321		267,375
Total State[a]	166,791	138,535		305,326
1840	Martin Van Buren Richard Johnson (Dem)	**William H. Harrison** **John Tyler** (Whig)	James G. Birney Thomas Earle (Liberty)	Total
New York and Kings Cos	25,092	24,251	177	49,520
Rest of State	187,641	201,750	2,632	392,023
Total State	212,733	226,001	2,809	441,543
1844	**James K. Polk** **George Dallas** (Dem)	Henry Clay Theodore Frelinghuysen (Whig)	James G. Birney Thomas Morris (Liberty)	Total
New York and Kings Cos	32,944	31,492	194	64,630
Rest of State	204,642	200,989	15,618	421,249
Total State	237,586	232,481	15,812	485,879
1848	Lewis Cass William O. Butler (Dem)	**Zachary Taylor** **Millard Fillmore** (Whig)	Martin Van Buren Charles Adams (Free Soil)	Total
New York and Kings Cos	23,855	36,564	5,920	66,339
Rest of State	90,464	182,019	114,577	387,060
Total State	114,319	218,583	120,497	453,399
1852	**Franklin Pierce** **William King** (Dem)	Winfield Scott William Graham (Whig)	John Hale George Julian (Free Soil)	Total
New York and Kings Cos	44,847	31,602	272	76,721
Rest of State	217,236	203,280	25,057	445,573
Total State	262,083	234,882	25,329	522,294
1856	**James Buchanan** **John Breckenridge** (Dem)	John Fremont William Dayton (Rep)	Millard Fillmore Andrew Donelson (Amer)	Total
New York and Kings Cos	56,087	25,617	28,569	110,273
Rest of State	139,791	250,387	96,035	486,213
Total State	195,878	276,004	124,604	596,486
1860	Stephen Douglas Herschel Johnson (Dem)	**Abraham Lincoln** **Hannibal Hamlin** (Rep)		Total
New York and Kings Cos	82,876	49,173		132,049
Rest of State	229,634	313,473		543,107
Total State	312,510	362,646		675,156

continued on page 1242

PRESIDENTIAL ELECTIONS (continued)

1864	George B. McClellan George Pendleton (Dem)	**Abraham Lincoln** **Andrew Johnson** (Union)[b]		Total
New York and Kings Cos	99,435	57,519		156,954
Rest of State	262,552	311,217		573,769
Total State	361,987	368,736		730,723

1868	Horatio Seymour Francis Blair Jr (Dem)	**Ulysses S. Grant** **Schuyler Colfax** (Rep)		Total
New York and Kings Cos	148,154	75,445		223,599
Rest of State	281,729	344,443		626,172
Total State	429,883	419,888		849,771

1872	Horace Greeley Benjamin G. Brown (Lib Dem)[c]	**Ulysses S. Grant** **Henry Wilson** (Rep)	Other	Total
New York and Kings Cos	115,922	88,043	10	203,975
Rest of State	270,357	342,712	1,444	614,513
Total State	386,279	430,755	1,454	818,488

1876	Samuel Tilden Thomas Hendricks (Dem)	**Rutherford Hayes** **William Wheeler** (Rep)	Other	Total
New York and Kings Cos	170,086	97,627	342	268,055
Rest of State	351,863	391,580	4,005	747,448
Total State	521,949	489,207	4,347	1,015,503

1880	Winfield S. Hancock William English (Dem)	**James A. Garfield** **Chester Arthur** (Rep)	Other	Total
New York and Kings Cos	184,077	133,481	1,152	318,710
Rest of State	350,434	422,063	12,738	785,235
Total State	534,511	555,544	13,890	1,103,945

1884	**Grover Cleveland** **Thomas A. Hendricks** (Dem)	James G. Blaine John A. Logan (Rep)	Other	Total
New York and Kings Cos	202,486	143,611	8,071	354,168
Rest of State	361,669	418,394	33,938	814,001
Total State[d]	564,155	562,005	42,009	1,168,169

1888	Grover Cleveland Allen G. Thurman (Dem)	**Benjamin Harrison** **Levi Parsons Morton** (Rep)	Other	Total
New York and Kings Cos	245,242	176,974	4,506	426,722
Rest of State	390,723	473,364	28,939	893,026
Total State	635,965	650,338	33,445	1,319,748

1892	**Grover Cleveland** **Adlai Stevenson** (Dem)	Benjamin Harrison Whitelaw Reid (Rep)	Other	Total
New York and Kings Cos	275,427	169,472	16,470	461,369
Rest of State	379,441	439,878	56,105	875,424
Total State	654,868	609,350	72,575	1,336,793

1896	William Jennings Bryan Arthur Sewall (Dem)	**William McKinley** **Garret A. Hobart** (Rep)	Other	Total
New York and Kings Cos	212,506	265,494	23,908	501,908
Rest of State	338,863	554,344	28,761	921,968
Total State	551,369	819,838	52,669	1,423,876

PRESIDENTIAL ELECTIONS (continued)

1900	William Jennings Bryan Adlai Stevenson (Dem)	**William McKinley** **Theodore Roosevelt** (Rep)	Other	Total
NYC	309,524	280,343	17,715	607,582
Downstate Suburban	30,496	42,021	1,927	74,444
Upstate Urban	92,894	119,270	7,072	219,236
Upstate Nonurban	245,548	380,379	20,854	646,781
Total State	678,462	822,013	47,568	1,548,043

1904	Alton B. Parker Henry G. Davis (Dem)	**Theodore Roosevelt** **Charles W. Fairbanks** (Rep)	Other	Total
NYC	326,900	289,345	35,829	652,074
Downstate Suburban	34,416	47,543	2,735	84,694
Upstate Urban	86,527	132,520	8,933	227,980
Upstate Nonurban	236,138	390,125	26,754	653,017
Total Upstate	683,981	859,533	74,251	1,617,765

1908	William Jennings Bryan John W. Kern (Dem)	**William H. Taft** **James S. Sherman** (Rep)	Eugene V. Debs Benjamin Hanford (Soc)	Other	Total
NYC	284,760	300,998	25,965	30,551	642,274
Downstate Suburban	33,043	54,771	1,380	3,710	92,904
Upstate Urban	103,264	137,404	4,077	4,196	248,941
Upstate Nonurban	246,401	376,897	7,029	23,904	654,231
Total State	667,468	870,070	38,451	62,361	1,638,350

1912	**Woodrow Wilson** **Thomas Marshall** (Dem)	William H. Taft Nicholas Butler (Rep)	Theodore Roosevelt Hiram Johnson (Prog)	Eugene V. Debs Emil Seidel (Soc)	Other	Total
NYC	312,426	126,582	188,896	33,239	2,730	663,873
Downstate Suburban	40,352	28,267	29,400	2,017	924	100,960
Upstate Urban	84,443	72,685	56,453	10,777	3,264	227,622
Upstate Nonurban	218,352	227,953	115,344	17,401	16,810	595,860
Total State	655,573	455,487	390,093	63,434	23,728	1,588,315

1916	**Woodrow Wilson** **Thomas Marshall** (Dem)	Charles Evans Hughes Charles Fairbanks (Rep)	Allan Benson George Kirkpatrick (Soc)	Other	Total
NYC	353,235	316,933	31,788	2,358	704,314
Downstate Suburban	43,778	66,386	1,312	640	112,116
Upstate Urban	106,095	147,474	5,147	3,772	262,488
Upstate Nonurban	256,318	348,445	7,697	14,927	627,387
Total State	759,426	879,238	45,944	21,697	1,706,305

1920	James Cox Franklin D. Roosevelt (Dem)	**Warren Harding** **Calvin Coolidge** (Rep)	Eugene V. Debs Seymour Stedman (Soc)	Other	Total
NYC	345,271	785,959	130,927	17,422	1,279,579
Downstate Suburban	50,564	147,025	8,445	2,103	208,137
Upstate Urban	120,643	279,329	32,345	6,236	438,553
Upstate Nonurban	264,760	658,854	31,484	17,146	972,244
Total State	781,238	1,871,167	203,201	42,907	2,898,513

1924	John Davis Charles Bryan (Dem)	**Calvin Coolidge** **Charles Dawes** (Rep)	Robert LaFollette Burton Wheeler (Soc/Prog)	Other	Total
NYC	489,199	626,131	281,470	7,625	1,404,425
Downstate Suburban	60,950	174,225	26,298	1,607	263,080
Upstate Urban	133,180	306,295	82,206	4,468	526,149
Upstate Nonurban	267,467	713,407	84,939	4,472	1,070,285
Total State	950,796	1,820,058	474,913	18,172	3,263,939

continued on page 1244

PRESIDENTIAL ELECTIONS (continued)

1928	Alfred E. Smith Joseph T. Robinson (Dem)	**Herbert Hoover** **Charles Curtis** (Rep)	Norman Thomas James H. Maurer (Soc)	Other	Total
NYC	1,167,971	714,154	51,006	12,001	1,945,132
Downstate Suburban	150,271	237,885	9,366	549	398,071
Upstate Urban	317,294	369,569	20,080	1,077	708,020
Upstate Nonurban	454,327	871,736	26,880	1,460	1,354,403
Total State	2,089,863	2,193,344	107,332	15,087	4,405,626

1932	**Franklin D. Roosevelt** **John Garner** (Dem)	Herbert Hoover Charles Curtis (Rep)	Norman Thomas James Maurer (Soc)	Other	Total
NYC	1,455,176	584,056	122,565	30,821	2,192,618
Downstate Suburban	207,333	245,501	11,508	1,056	465,398
Upstate Urban	349,641	349,630	20,774	2,823	722,868
Upstate Nonurban	522,809	758,776	22,550	3,595	1,307,730
Total State	2,534,959	1,937,963	177,397	38,295	4,688,614

1936	**Franklin D. Roosevelt** **John Garner** (Dem/Amer Labor)	Alfred Landon Frank Knox (Rep)	Norman Thomas George Nelson (Soc)	Other	Total
NYC	2,041,347	665,951	38,520	31,952	2,777,770
Downstate Suburban	246,747	293,191	9,903	932	550,773
Upstate Urban	432,417	378,827	13,938	1,330	826,512
Upstate Nonurban	572,711	842,701	24,536	1,395	1,441,343
Total State	3,293,222	2,180,670	86,897	35,609	5,596,398

1940	**Franklin D. Roosevelt** **Henry Wallace** (Dem/Amer Labor)	Wendell Willkie Charles McNary (Rep)	Norman Thomas Maynard Krueger (Soc)	Other	Total
NYC	1,966,083	1,247,624	12,394	1,317	3,227,418
Downstate Suburban	232,035	410,307	1,321	220	643,883
Upstate Urban	454,925	448,015	2,344	404	905,688
Upstate Nonurban	598,875	921,532	2,891	1,309	1,524,607
Total State	3,251,918	3,027,478	18,950	3,250	6,301,596

1944	**Franklin D. Roosevelt** **Harry S. Truman** (Dem/Amer Labor/Lib)	Thomas Dewey John Bricker (Rep)	Norman Thomas Darlington Hoopes (Soc)	Other	Total
NYC	2,042,500	1,271,287	5,693	10,970	3,330,450
Downstate Suburban	230,771	419,469	1,115	557	651,912
Upstate Urban	460,267	438,750	1,903	1,186	902,106
Upstate Nonurban	570,700	858,141	1,842	1,639	1,432,322
Total State	3,304,238	2,987,647	10,553	14,352	6,316,790

1948	**Harry S. Truman** **Alben W. Barkley** (Dem/Lib)	Thomas E. Dewey Earl Warren (Rep)	Henry A. Wallace Glen H. Taylor[e] (Amer Labor)	Norman Thomas Tucker P. Smith (Soc)	Other	Total
NYC	1,596,545	1,108,288	422,355	25,997	3,885	3,157,070
Downstate Suburban	208,343	457,541	26,630	5,989	446	698,949
Upstate Urban	449,973	429,061	25,220	3,812	474	908,540
Upstate Nonurban	525,343	846,273	35,354	5,081	599	1,412,650
Total State	2,780,204	2,841,163	509,559	40,879	5,404	6,177,209

1952	Adlai E. Stevenson John Sparkman (Dem/Lib)	**Dwight D. Eisenhower** **Richard M. Nixon** (Rep)	Other	Total
NYC	1,854,930	1,495,493	111,283	3,461,706
Downstate Suburban	297,829	686,232	13,307	997,368
Upstate Urban	443,756	612,238	12,400	1,068,394
Upstate Nonurban	508,086	1,158,852	21,648	1,688,586
Total State	3,104,601	3,952,815	158,638	7,216,054

PRESIDENTIAL ELECTIONS (continued)

1956	Adlai E. Stevenson Estes Kefauver (Dem/Lib)	**Dwight D. Eisenhower** **Richard M. Nixon** (Rep)		Other	Total
NYC	1,617,701	1,548,132		55,345	3,221,178
Downstate Suburban	333,707	846,118		10,608	1,190,433
Upstate Urban	373,991	700,458		11,491	1,085,940
Upstate Nonurban	425,370	1,245,632		18,855	1,689,857
Total State	2,750,769	4,340,340		96,299	7,187,408
1960	**John F. Kennedy** **Lyndon B. Johnson** (Dem/Lib)	Richard M. Nixon Henry Cabot Lodge (Rep)		Other	Total
NYC	1,936,323	1,145,205		62,254	3,143,782
Downstate Suburban	575,924	748,568		12,378	1,336,870
Upstate Urban	601,390	529,150		10,487	1,141,027
Upstate Nonurban	716,448	1,023,496		18,452	1,758,396
Total State	3,830,085	3,446,419		103,571	7,380,075
1964	**Lyndon B. Johnson** **Hubert H. Humphrey** (Dem/Lib)	Barry Goldwater William Miller (Rep)		Other	Total
NYC	2,183,643	801,877		90,710	3,076,230
Downstate Suburban	853,084	568,475		22,227	1,443,786
Upstate Urban	793,593	301,490		17,235	1,112,318
Upstate Nonurban	1,082,836	571,717		30,699	1,685,252
Total State	4,913,156	2,243,559		160,871	7,317,586
1968	Hubert H. Humphrey Edmund S. Muskie (Dem/Lib)	**Richard M. Nixon** **Spiro T. Agnew** (Rep)	George C. Wallace S. Marvin Griffin (Courage)	Other	Total
NYC	1,582,681	886,959	121,781	128,448	2,719,869
Downstate Suburban	612,091	790,351	89,307	33,010	1,524,759
Upstate Urban	555,791	459,840	58,761	20,945	1,095,337
Upstate Nonurban	627,907	870,782	89,015	34,021	1,621,725
Total State	3,378,470	3,007,932	358,864	216,424	6,961,690
1972	George S. McGovern R. Sargent Shriver (Dem/Lib)	**Richard M. Nixon** **Spiro T. Agnew** (Rep/Cons)		Other	Total
NYC	1,342,996	1,259,873		94,409	2,697,278
Downstate Suburban	575,455	1,082,829		28,452	1,686,736
Upstate Urban	467,328	674,928		22,130	1,164,386
Upstate Nonurban	565,305	1,175,148		34,618	1,775,071
Total State	2,951,084	4,192,778		179,609	7,323,471
1976	**Jimmy Carter** **Walter F. Mondale** (Dem/Lib)	Gerald Ford Robert Dole (Rep/Cons)		Other	Total
NYC	1,423,380	706,663		101,177	2,231,220
Downstate Suburban	732,958	838,698		25,419	1,597,075
Upstate Urban	511,849	572,679		20,622	1,105,150
Upstate Nonurban	721,371	982,751		30,695	1,734,817
Total State	3,389,558	3,100,791		177,913	6,668,262
1980	Jimmy Carter Walter F. Mondale (Dem)	**Ronald Reagan** **George H. W. Bush** (Rep/Cons)	John B. Anderson Patrick Lucey (Lib)	Other	Total
NYC	1,052,178	719,278	113,845	127,863	2,013,164
Downstate Suburban	522,960	847,481	118,329	48,896	1,537,666
Upstate Urban	505,588	448,065	92,066	33,277	1,078,996
Upstate Nonurban	647,646	879,007	143,561	59,178	1,729,392
Total State	2,728,372	2,893,831	467,801	269,214	6,359,218

continued on page 1246

PRESIDENTIAL ELECTIONS (continued)

1984	Walter F. Mondale Geraldine Ferraro (Dem/Lib)	**Ronald Reagan** **George H. W. Bush** (Rep/Cons)	Other	Total
NYC	1,343,875	852,317	143,989	2,340,181
Downstate Suburban	616,904	1,026,527	22,735	1,666,166
Upstate Urban	526,964	601,977	17,149	1,146,090
Upstate Nonurban	631,866	1,183,942	32,583	1,848,391
Total State	3,119,609	3,664,763	216,456	7,000,828

1988	Michael S. Dukakis Lloyd M. Bentsen (Dem/Lib)	**George H. W. Bush** **Dan Quayle** (Rep/Cons)	Other	Total
NYC	1,340,795	665,407	120,216	2,126,418
Downstate Suburban	666,839	910,453	32,674	1,609,966
Upstate Urban	573,744	507,681	19,698	1,101,123
Upstate Nonurban	766,504	998,330	33,956	1,798,790
Total State	3,347,882	3,081,871	206,544	6,636,297

1992	**Bill Clinton** **Al Gore** (Dem/Lib)	George Bush Dan Quayle (Rep/Cons/RTL)	H. Ross Perot James Stockdale (Independent)	Other	Total
NYC	1,458,784	509,423	141,510	101,756	2,211,473
Downstate Suburban	744,463	677,946	245,029	37,485	1,704,923
Upstate Urban	509,021	390,559	255,826	19,169	1,174,575
Upstate Nonurban	732,182	768,721	448,356	39,202	1,988,461
Total State	3,444,450	2,346,649	1,090,721	197,612	7,079,432

1996	**Bill Clinton** **Al Gore** (Dem/Lib)	Bob Dole Jack Kemp (Rep/Cons/Freedom)	H. Ross Perot Pat Choate (Reform)	Other	Total
NYC	1,512,248	339,537	64,617	111,611	2,028,013
Downstate Suburban	824,852	543,444	113,157	47,601	1,529,054
Upstate Urban	575,595	361,593	99,174	32,124	1,068,486
Upstate Nonurban	843,482	688,918	226,510	54,666	1,813,576
Total State	3,756,177	1,933,492	503,458	246,002	6,439,129

2000	Al Gore Joseph Lieberman (Dem/Lib/Wrkg Family)	**George W. Bush** **Richard Cheney** (Rep/Cons)	Other	Total
NYC	1,703,364	398,726	166,412	2,268,502
Downstate Suburban	935,456	655,665	86,671	1,677,792
Upstate Urban	597,432	432,744	73,411	1,103,587
Upstate Nonurban	871,445	916,239	122,650	1,910,334
Total State	4,107,697	2,403,374	449,144	6,960,215

Sources: ICPSR Election Returns for New York; *Manual for the Use of the Legislature of the State of New York; New York State Board of Elections; New York Red Book.*

Notes: Winners' names appear in bold. Regional designations are as follows: NYC: Bronx, Kings (Brooklyn), New York (Manhattan), Richmond (Staten Island), Queens Cos; Downstate Suburban: Nassau, Rockland, Suffolk, Westchester Cos; Upstate Urban: Albany, Erie, Monroe, Onondaga Cos; Upstate Nonurban: remainder of counties.

[a] Source data totals are not correct.

[b] The Republican candidate ran under the Union Party ticket.

[c] Elsewhere the Greeley/Brown party is listed as "Democratic and Liberal Republican."

[d] Source data totals are not correct and sources do not agree.

[e] Henry Wallace ran on the Progressive Party ballot nationally, but in New York State he appeared on the American Labor Party ballot.

Park (Dutchess Co), attended Columbia Law School, withdrew in 1907, and practiced law in New York City before winning a seat in the state senate in 1910.

Two other presidents, Chester A. Arthur (1829–86) and Grover Cleveland (1837–1908), spent much of their early life and careers in the state and are generally thought of as New Yorkers. Arthur graduated from Union College in Schenectady in 1848 and practiced law in New York City. He held the position of quartermaster general of the State of New York during the Civil War and was the collector of the Port of New York from 1871 to 1878. Cleveland was raised in Fayetteville (Onondaga Co) and Clinton (Oneida Co). In 1855 he moved to Buffalo, where he practiced law and served as mayor of Buffalo before moving on to higher political office and working as a lawyer in New York City between his two presidential terms.

Early Presidents

A number of early presidents were associated with New York State. George Washington (1732–99) arrived in New York as commander of the Continental army in 1776 and fought several battles of the Revolution on New York soil. In

1789 he established residence at the new capital, New York City. John Adams (1735–1826) served as Washington's vice president and then as president from 1797 to 1801. He and his wife Abigail rented Richmond Hill, an elegant mansion about a mile north of the city in what is now Greenwich Village. Thomas Jefferson (1743–1826) served in Washington's administration as secretary of state and rented a small house at 57 Maiden Lane in New York City, though he stayed in the city less than six months, from March through September 1790. In the summer of 1791, however, Jefferson and James Madison (1751–1836) explored the Hudson Valley as far as Lake George and Lake Champlain, visiting Revolutionary War sites and hunting and fishing. When their journey took them to Long Island, Jefferson visited a Poospatuck Indian settlement in Suffolk Co, where he transcribed about 200 words of the Unquachog language. Madison had first explored the western frontier of New York State soon after the Revolution and traveled to New York City as a delegate to the Confederation Congress in 1787. After the Constitutional Convention in Philadelphia that year, Madison was a contributor to what become known as the *Federalist Papers,* a series of 85 articles supporting the ratification of the proposed Constitution, published in New York State newspapers.

Virginian James Monroe (1758–1831) had fought with Washington's army in New York during the Revolution and partnered with Madison to buy a 900-acre (364 ha) tract of land north of the Mohawk River, both being impressed with the fertility of the area. He served in the Confederation Congress in New York City, where he married society beauty Elizabeth Kortright in 1786. Although they soon moved back to Virginia where he made his career, after her death in 1830 he returned to New York City to live with his daughter Maria Hester and son-in-law Samuel Gouverneur, and he died there the following year.

In 1860 Abraham Lincoln (1808–65) delivered a significant speech at Cooper Union in New York City arguing that the founding fathers had supported the regulation of slavery in US territories. After his assassination in 1865, Lincoln's coffin was carried through the streets of New York City in a solemn funeral cortege and his body lay in state overnight in Albany. Ulysses S. Grant (1822–85) attended West Point from 1839 to 1843 and moved to New York City in 1877 after he left the White House. In 1881 he became a partner in the Wall St brokerage firm Grant and Ward, but the firm failed in May 1884. The failure ruined his financial position and caused him to turn to writing as a way to rebuild his family fortunes when he was diagnosed with throat cancer. Grant completed his memoirs at Mount McGregor (Saratoga Co), now a state historic site, four days before his death. He and his wife, Julia, are buried in Grant's Tomb, a large memorial on Riverside Drive in New York City that was dedicated in 1897. Pres William McKinley (1843–1901) died in Buffalo of gangrene after being shot in the stomach by Leon F. Czolgosz at the Pan-American Exposition on 6 Sept 1901.

Presidents since the Early 20th Century

Although no native New Yorker has been elected as president since Franklin D. Roosevelt, most recent chief executives have spent portions of their lives in the state. For example, after leaving the White House in 1933, Herbert Hoover (1874–1964) and his wife Lou Henry Hoover retreated to Suite 31-A at the Waldorf Towers in New York City. Although born in Kansas, Dwight D. Eisenhower (1890–1969) ran for president as a resident of New York State. Eisenhower attended West Point from 1911 to 1915 and returned to the state to become the president of Columbia University in 1948. Although he took a leave of absence to command NATO in 1950, he and his wife, Mamie, maintained their home in the university's presidential residence on Morningside Drive until the national election of 1952. John F. Kennedy (1917–63) was connected to the state during his youth. He moved with his family to Riverdale (Bronx Co) in 1927, then to Bronxville (Westchester Co) in 1929, and attended Riverdale Country Day School until he was sent to boarding school at the age of 13.

Richard M. Nixon (1913–94) moved to New York City after losing the California gubernatorial race of 1962. He joined a Wall St law firm that later merged with Caldwell, Trimble and Mitchell, where he met John Mitchell, his future attorney general. The Nixons purchased a large apartment at 810 5th Ave, in the same building as Nelson A. Rockefeller, and the family lived out of the political limelight until he entered the 1968 presidential race and eventually moved into the White House. Nixon returned to New York City in 1980 because Patricia Ryan Nixon, his wife, wanted to be closer to their children. He maintained an office in New York City after relocating to Saddle River, NJ, in 1982. George H. W. Bush lived in New York City from 1970 to 1972 while serving as ambassador to the United Nations. As a naval officer, Jimmy Carter studied reactor technology and nuclear physics at Union College (1952–53). In 1976 Carter was nominated by a Democratic convention in Madison Square Garden. After leaving the presidency, Bill Clinton established a home base with his wife, Senator Hillary Rodham Clinton, in Chappaqua (Westchester Co), as well as an office at 55 West 125th St in Harlem.

Brant, Irving. *The Nationalist, 1780–1787,* vol 2 of *James Madison* (Indianapolis: Bobbs-Merrill, 1948)
Kane, Joseph Nathan, Steven Anzovin, and Janet Podell. *Facts about the Presidents: A Compilation of Biographical and Historical Information,* 7th ed (New York: H. W. Wilson, 2001)
Malone, Dumas. *Jefferson and the Rights of Man,* vol 2 of *Jefferson and His Time* (Boston: Little, Brown, 1951)
Oates, Stephen B. *With Malice toward None: The Life of Abraham Lincoln* (New York: Harper & Row, 1977)

Susan Ingalls Lewis

Preston. Town (pop 928) in central Chenango Co. Settled in 1787, the town was formed from Norwich in 1806. The county poorhouse (1840) was Preston Manor, which became a county-run skilled nursing facility in the 21st century. Slate was quarried, and a cheesebox factory was in operation in 1875, but dairy farming predominated. Preston was the site of a Civilian Conservation Corps camp starting in 1933. In the early 21st century, agriculture still dominates the town's economy, primarily dairy and "custom crop" hay, although many residents are employed in Norwich.

primary elections. Inspired by Progressive era ideals, reformers argued that direct primaries would weaken the power of party bosses and open the candidate nomination process to rank-and-file party members. The New York State legislature passed the direct primary law in 1911, and primaries were first used to nominate candidates for offices filled by voters of the entire state in 1913. New York State adopted "closed" primaries, meaning only voters enrolled in a party may participate in primary elections. Primaries, however, did not increase party member participation in elections, and the high cost of primary campaigns kept party bosses involved in the process. Moreover, minor party candidates did not hesitate to run in primary elections. The legislature discontinued primaries for statewide offices in 1921 yet retained them for the nomination of candidates for local, county, and party offices. A 1959 law made primaries optional when there was only one candidate.

Growing concern about accountability led New York State to reintroduce primaries in 1967 for statewide offices. Under this law, first used in 1968, party organizations acquired the legal authority to make preprimary endorsements of candidates. A majority vote of a quorum of the state party committee is necessary for endorsement. Party members also have a say in the nomination process because the 1967 law established a challenge system of primaries. Any person receiving at least 25% of the committee's vote may challenge the party's endorsed candidate in a primary. A party member who does not receive 25% of the committee vote may still gain ballot access for statewide office by collecting the signatures of at least 15,000 or 5% of all registered party members. These signatures must come from at least half of the state's US congressional districts, and a minimum of 100 or 5% of a party's voters in each of these districts must sign the petition.

A party member who wants to run for any public office other than one filled by statewide vote must also circulate petitions to gain a position on the primary ballot. The signature requirement is generally 5% of a party's enrolled voters in any political unit. Only voters enrolled in the party may sign and witness petitions. A special provision applies to primaries for the New York City offices of mayor, comptroller, and public advocate. If no candidate receives 40% of the vote in these New York City primaries, then the two front-runners participate in a runoff primary. To vote in a primary, a New York State resident must register at least 25 days before the election.

New York State. State Board of Elections. *State of New York 2003 Election Law* (Charlottesville, Va: Matthew Bender, 2003)
———, http://www.elections.state.ny.us/

Gary Bugh

Princetown. Town (pop 2,132) in central Schenectady Co. Settled *ca* 1700, the town was formed from Schenectady in 1798. In the 19th and early 20th centuries, its economy was based on dairy, hay, and grain, and in the early 21st century the land remains predominantly agricultural. The Plotterkill Preserve (632 acres/256 ha) encompasses two waterfalls.

Stephanie Przybylek and Christopher Hunter

printing industry. The first printer to set up a press in New York Colony was William Bradford. Trained in London, Bradford originally immigrated to Philadelphia but moved his press to

Manhattan in 1693. Gov Benjamin Fletcher appointed him the colony's official printer upon his arrival. Bradford's shop on Manhattan's Pearl St opened in June 1693, and he served as the royal printer from that year until 1742 (with the exception of 1723–24). In 1725 he established the first newspaper in the colony, the *New-York Gazette.* John Peter Zenger, Bradford's German-born apprentice, partner, and later competitor, was the colony's second printer. Zenger opened his Manhattan press in 1726 and began publishing the *New-York Weekly Journal* in 1733. Zenger was not a distinguished printer or editor but is associated with the most famous libel case in British America. Imprisoned in early 1734 for publishing material critical of the colony's autocratic governor, William Cosby, he was guilty of seditious libel under British law. At Zenger's trial, 4 Aug 1735, his attorney argued that Zenger was not guilty because the articles were true and thus any law that prohibited truthful public criticism of government was a threat to liberty. After a few minutes of deliberation the jury called for acquittal. The Zenger case established a victory for a free press and for limitations on governmental power to control the press.

Revolutionary War and Early National Period

Two of New York's most prominent and prolific printers of the American Revolutionary era, Hugh Gaine and James Rivington, both based in Manhattan, remained loyal to the Crown. Gaine had been appointed royal printer to the colony in 1768 and, about the same time, the official printer to the City of New York. Though at first a patriot, Gaine shifted quickly and edited his *New-York Gazette and Weekly Mercury* as a loyalist publication until the war's end in 1783. His early indecision, however, left him forever suspect in the minds of British authorities, and Rivington (who published the *Royal Gazette* during the British occupation of New York City, 1776–83) was made the colony's royal printer in 1777 by British general Sir William Howe.

The printing trade grew slowly beyond Manhattan between the Revolution and the 1820s. Brothers Alexander and James Robinson, Scottish immigrants and die-hard loyalists, began publishing the *New York Chronicle* in Manhattan in 1769. Two years later they moved to Albany and published the state's first newspaper outside of New York City, the *Albany Gazette.* Samuel Loudon, who as a patriot left Manhattan when British military forces approached the city in August 1776, established the second press outside of the city in Fishkill (Dutchess Co). A year later, John Holt, another Manhattan printer and patriot, also fled the city, moving his press to Kingston (Ulster Co). Holt later moved to Poughkeepsie, making it the state's fourth town to host a press. Printing offices were founded in the 1780s in Hudson (Columbia Co), Lansingburgh [now in Rensselaer Co], and Goshen (Orange Co), and in 1791 the first press on Long Island appeared in Sag Harbor (Suffolk Co). In the 1790s offices appeared in Catskill [now in Greene Co] and Newburgh (Orange Co), finally moving farther north to Schenectady in 1794 and Ballston Spa (Saratoga Co) in 1797. Only in 1799 was a press established in Brooklyn.

As for the deeper interior of New York State, printers moved with the population as settlers followed the rivers in making their way north and west. Thus, by 1800 the northernmost printing office was in Rome (Oneida Co) on the Mohawk River, and the westernmost office was in Bath (Steuben Co) on the Cohocton River. Between 1800 and 1810, new offices were located in places like Owego (Tioga Co), Watertown, and Batavia (Genesee Co). Always financially strapped, these printers published small newspapers that produced revenue from subscriptions, commercial advertisements, and legal notices. Most offices also relied on commercial printing and the selling of books and stationery for support. By 1820 printers operated in some 30 communities in the state, principally on Long Island, along the Hudson and Mohawk River valleys, and as far north as Plattsburgh.

The 19th Century

By the 1820s Manhattan had developed into a major commercial and manufacturing center with a vibrant printing and publishing trade, finally having surpassed Boston and Philadelphia in the volume of printing. Economic specialization and technological change over the next generation divided the trade into three distinct branches: books, newspapers, and job or commercial printing. A subsector included allied trades such as stereotyping, engraving, and bookbinding. In smaller towns and rural areas, the separation was less important and offices produced various types of work. The wooden handpress gave way to the iron handpress in the 1830s for all-purpose work in small shops. The introduction of a cylinder press in 1825 (an English invention) allowed New York City press builder R. Hoe and Co to make successful copies and to double the speed of newspaper printing. In 1847 Hoe developed the type-revolving press, which revolutionized the newspaper industry. In the 1830s small foot-powered presses were developed specifically for the commercial and job printer. Type continued to be set by hand until the end of the century. However, the introduction of stereotyping (making a metal printing plate from a papier mâché mold) in the 1820s permitted the replication of pages of type for reprinting, and electrotyping (making a duplicate printing plate through the electroplating process) in the 1840s permitted the mass production of fine illustrations.

Outside of New York City, Albany became the state's most important printing center because the state government contracted for an immense amount of printing. The Albany firm of Weed and Parsons grew into one of the largest printing offices outside of Boston, Philadelphia, or New York City, and scholar-printer Joel Munsell contributed much to Albany's reputation. In addition to commercial printing, Munsell produced more than 2,000 titles between 1828 and 1870, including literature and chapbooks, textbooks, law reports, directories, almanacs, and book catalogs. He wrote or compiled several books on the history of printing and papermaking and printed limited editions of well-designed works on special paper.

By the 1850s there were 2,000 people directly employed in the printing trade in New York City. By the end of the decade, the city accounted for 33% of the nation's printed output and half of all books produced in the country. By 1890 there were 658 book and job offices in New York City employing 10,228 workers, and 497 newspaper and periodical offices employing 7,345. Book and job offices produced work worth nearly $20 million. Newspaper and periodical offices printed material valued at over $34 million.

New York City's printers, workers and employers alike, pioneered in organizing the trade. As early as 1795 and again in 1799, 1809, and 1832 short-lived typographical societies were established to promote stable wages and the trade's well-being. In 1852 New York City journeymen printers gathered again to organize a true trade union, which they called the New York Typographical Union. When the National Typographical Union formed in 1865, the New York City local was given the number six, and "Big Six" evolved into one of the largest and most influential locals in the United States. Given the dispersed nature of printing, it is not surprising that by the 1860s typographical unions existed in Albany, Brooklyn, Buffalo, Newburgh, Oswego, Poughkeepsie, Rochester, Syracuse, Troy, and Utica. In 1862 master printers in New York City established their own organization, the Typothetae of New York. In 1887 a national association, the United Typothetae, was formed with New York City master printer Theodore Low DeVinne as president. The local Typothetae merged in 1916 with its rival, the Printers' League, to form the New York Employing Printers Association, forerunner of the late 20th-century trade group the Association of the Graphic Arts.

The introduction of Ottmar Mergenthaler's Linotype machine in 1886 transformed typesetting and revolutionized the trade in New York State. Four times faster than hand composition, the machine did not so much displace workers as allow for the increase in printed matter. Instead of setting individual pieces of type by hand, journeymen printers operated the keyboard to assemble individual letter matrices into a mold of an entire line of text. The machine then cast the entire line in type metal. The Linotype operator then assembled another line of type. Makeup men assembled the individual lines of type, called "slugs," into columns and then into pages. As the International Typographical Union struggled to control who worked the machine, it changed its internal rules on seniority and negotiated a 40-hour workweek for compositors. The Linotype machine symbolized the success of machine over hand labor and contributed to a concerted effort to improve the aesthetic quality of printed works.

The Modern Era

A number of early 20th-century New York State printers, type designers, and illustrators contributed to fine book printing epitomized by the arts and crafts movement in Great Britain and the United States. From the Roycroft shops in East Aurora (Erie Co), Elbert Hubbard produced volumes with Art Nouveau borders and ornaments in embossed chamois leather bindings. Dard Hunter trained with Hubbard in the 1910s, and in 1913 he set up a small paper mill in Marlboro-on-Hudson (Ulster Co). Hunter designed and hand cast type, made fine paper by hand, and became America's preeminent paper historian. In the 1920s designer Bruce Rogers produced exquisitely designed books at the printing firm of William Edwin Rudge in Mount Vernon (Westchester Co), considered one of the best-equipped printing offices in the United States. In a campuslike setting of low buildings, Rudge's office included racks of type for handsetting, Linotype and Monotype machines, offset presses, small job presses for four-color relief printing, middle- and large-sized cylinder presses, and an excellent hand bindery. Rudge also printed books by the foremost American type designer, Frederic W. Goudy. Goudy himself taught lettering at the Art Students League in Manhattan and operated a small type foundry in an old stone mill also in Marlboro-on-Hudson from 1923 to 1938. With matrix-cutting and typesetting equipment Goudy cut and cast his own designs, thus ensuring what he called their "vitality and personality."

Throughout the first half of the 20th century, nearly one in four employees in the American printing trade worked in New York State. For instance, in 1935 it was home to 2,377 (22%) of the nation's 10,961 book and job offices, employing 38,000 salaried and wage earners producing $187 million in product, or 26% of America's production of book and job work. In that same year, 17% of all wage earners and 30% of all salaried workers in newspaper and periodical printing in the nation worked in New York State. Slightly more than 30% of the nation's 387 lithographic offices and 22,000 lithographic workers producing more than 32% of the annual national production of $92 million were found in New York State. The printing industry continued to be affected by technical and economic changes in the 20th century. The introduction of computerized typesetting led to the end of the Linotype era in the late 1970s, with the *New York Times* shutting down its last Linotype machine in 1978. In the mid-1990s the *Times* built a massive, new fully computerized and automated color printing facility at College Point (Queens Co). Traditional letterpress printing now accounts for less than 15% of all printing. Newspapers are increasingly produced by offset lithography and flexography (printing from flexible plastic or rubber plates). Catalogs and magazines are produced by gravure processes, while flexography is increasingly used for books and commercial printing. Economic pressure on the news industry has resulted in the consolidation of newspapers so that most of the state's cities that once supported several daily and weekly papers now commonly support only one, or two at the most. In the 1890s, for example, Albany supported 11 dailies, by the 1920s only 7, and by 2003 just 1.

The local demand for commercial printing and local news means that most New York State towns and cities continue to support printing offices. In the mid-1990s, 5,400 printing offices were found in New York State, second in number only to California's 8,600 offices and well ahead of Illinois with 4,800. In 2001 New York State's printing industry employed 6% (50,800 total employees, including 36,000 production workers) of the national printing workforce. New York State produced $6.4 billion worth of printing and related support activities. Printing remained one of the top five of the state's manufacturing industries in terms of employment and value of product, and printed material remained one of the its major exports to the rest of the nation and the world.

See also COLONIAL INTELLECTUAL CULTURE; NEWSPAPERS; PRINTS AND PRINTMAKING.

Gustafson, Eric W. "Printing and Publishing." In *Made in New York: Case Studies in Metropolitan Manufacturing*, ed. Max Hall (Cambridge, Mass: Harvard Univ Press, 1959)

Hamilton, Milton W. *The Country Printer: New York, 1785–1850* (New York: Columbia Univ Press, 1936)

Kelber, Harry, and Carl Schlesinger. *Union Printers and Controlled Automation* (New York: Free Press, 1967)

McMurtrie, Douglas C. *A History of Printing in the United States* (New York: R. R. Bowker, 1936)

Stevens, George. *New York Typographical Union No. 6: Study of a Modern Trade Union and Its Predecessors* (Albany: J. B. Lyon, 1913)

Wilentz, Sean. *Chants Democratic: New York City and the Rise of the American Working Class, 1788–1850* (New York: Oxford Univ Press, 1984)

William S. Pretzer

prints and printmaking. Reproducing art on paper using processes such as woodcuts, engraving, etching, lithography, intaglio, and silkscreen.

COLONIAL ERA TO 1825

Printmaking between the 17th and early 19th centuries in New York State was confined to New York City. Immigrants from England and occasionally native-born Americans engraved images on wood and metal almost exclusively for commercial purposes. In the earlier years, many illustrations in books and newspapers were anonymously produced and often copied from British sources. Small relief cuts appeared in early newspapers, almanacs, and children's books, and on currency. In the middle of the 18th century, several copperplate engravers, such as Henry Dawkins and John Hutt, emigrated from England. They produced such items as maps, military commissions, book illustrations, and advertisements. Elisha Gallaudet advertised that he would engrave six prints of Indian warriors in 1759; no copies, however, survive. Michael de Bruls advertised four views of New York City and a map in 1762; again, no copies are known to have survived. Because of the fragility of prints and the absence of many early collectors, impressions of early American prints are scarce.

Shortly after the Revolutionary War, several English engravers, including David Edwin, William S. Leney, and William Rollinson, immigrated to New York City, where they found employment in the book trades, producing engravings for books and periodicals. By this time, several Americans had learned the trade as well. Alexander Anderson, Peter Maverick, and Cornelius Tiebout all began to work in the 1780s and 1790s producing book and periodical illustrations, advertisements, and separate prints for a market that increasingly wanted images. Eventually, a sufficient demand for separately published American prints, particularly depictions of events, city views, and portraits, created additional work for these engravers. Previously, importers served the market for prints for decorative purposes. By 1825 handsome portrait prints of political and military leaders, depictions of historical events, and views of the city were available for purchase in New York City.

FROM 1825 TO 1900

In the last three-quarters of the 19th century, the publishing industry concentrated itself in New York City, and firms such as Harper and Bros, begun in 1817 as a printing firm, and organizations such as the American Tract Society, formed in 1825 to produce religious books, dominated book and, later, periodical publication. In conjunction, wood engraving became a substantial industry, and in the middle of the century hundreds of men and women found employment making relief cuts for large publishers. Some of these illustrations were fine enough to be framed and displayed in homes.

Lithography, a printmaking process of drawing on limestone with a special crayon developed at the end of the 18th century, became a commercially successful method to reproduce the works of artists. The lithography firms of Anthony Imbert, George and William Endicott, and Currier and Ives flourished in New York City. Henry R. Robinson published most of the separate political cartoons in the middle of the 19th century. Currier and Ives also sold prints through vendors who traveled throughout the country. With a shop on Nassau St and a factory on Spruce St, the company sold over 1 million copies of prints (with over 7,500 different titles), including disaster scenes, pets, winter scenes, famous racehorses, sentimental images, politics, and hunting scenes, some in editions of thousands of copies, until it closed in 1907. Currier and Ives prints were inexpensive and appealed to diverse markets, including French Catholics, Irish immigrants, patriotic Americans, and advocates of temperance. Recognized artists such as George Catlin, Eastman Johnson, Arthur F. Tait, and Fanny Palmer executed many of the company's images.

PICTORIAL PRINTING IN ALBANY, ROCHESTER, AND BUFFALO

In the years following the Revolutionary War, letterpress printing became available in most communities large enough to support a weekly newspaper. Newspaper printers usually served as job printers, producing advertisements, broadsides notices, letterheads, invoices, and other printed materials. Many of these items were illustrated with cuts, either made by crafters in the printing shop or purchased through vendors of stereotypes. Specialists in pictorial printing emerged in Albany, Rochester, and Buffalo.

Albany was the state capital, and the state government produced illustrated state documents, which nurtured the development of pictorial printing. Foremost among those who worked in Albany was Richard H. Pease, who received his early training in Connecticut and Philadelphia and arrived in Albany about 1836. His son, Harry E. Pease, joined him in business. Among the Pease firm's projects for the state were contributions to the *Natural History of New York State,* a multivolume publication printed throughout the second half of the 19th century. Initially, all of the plates were produced in New York City, most by the Endicott lithography firm. In the 1850s, however, Richard Pease's name began to appear on some of the engraved and lithographed illustrations. In 1858 John E. Gavit merged seven companies into the American Banknote Co, initially located on Wall St, which produced what are reputed to be the most beautiful steel engravings ever produced for banknotes, bond and stock certificates, and stamps. It produced work for both domestic and international markets. Two other firms, Van Benthuysen and Phil Ast, produced lithographs that appeared in the 1870s and 1880s, including maps and images of natural history and Civil War subjects.

Pictorial printing in Rochester developed because of the nursery and seed industry that began in the 1830s. Although some tradesmen issued early seed catalogs without illustrations, the practice of illustrating the many varieties of plants available through each grower soon developed. In the second half of the 19th century, Rochester became one of the leading American nursery centers and was known as the Flower City. The firm of Dellon Marcus Dewey, founded in the mid-1850s, was the first to promote the use of color plates depicting fruit and flowers, which helped sell plants of all types. In the 1870s it offered over 2,300 color plates for sale. Through the 1860s hand-colored prints were the norm, and in the 1870s Charles F. Muntz and Co introduced chromolithography (the complex printing of lithographs in color) to Rochester. There were almost 20 different firms in Rochester specializing in this business in the second half of the 19th century.

The third major printmaking center was Buffalo, which became an important commercial center because of its location at the end of the Erie Canal on Lake Erie. The various printing trades that grew along with the city's commerce produced sheet music, posters for the seed trade and theatrical performances, and railroad maps. They also crafted prints of railroad disasters, which were popular collectors' items of the day.

Fine printmaking, however, remained confined to New York City. In the 1820s and 1830s, John Hill and William J. Bennett produced elegant aquatints that were distributed nationally. These were a form of etching in which sections of a metal plate were covered with an acid-resisting powdered resin that would then dissolve the uncovered areas of the plate, ultimately creating a soft-toned print. Engravings of patriotic, military, and bucolic scenes published by the American Art Union and Goupil and Co in the 1840s and 1850s also had national distribution. Beginning in the 1870s, as etching rose in popularity, artists like Robert Swain Gifford, Samuel Coleman, and Thomas Moran turned to printmaking. Painters learned to etch their own metal plates and to create prints for which a market arose among New York City's elite. Publishers and print dealers in New York City, such as Frederick Keppel and White, Stokes, and Allen, published elegant books containing etchings made from steel-faced plates. The New York Etching Club, formed in 1877, was also an important factor in the public appreciation of this art, sponsoring exhibitions until 1893. Many of the artists who experimented with etching tried lithography as well. The National Academy of Design had been established in 1826, and though some its early members were printmakers, it did not formally offer training in printmaking until 1893. That year James David Smillie began offering classes in etching.

The 20th Century

George Bellows came to New York 1904 and learned to paint in the Ashcan style. He also installed a lithography press in his studio and became a master lithographer, producing prints from 1916 until his death in 1925. Although most of his work focused on gritty urban realities, in 1918 he produced a series of 14 lithographs entitled *War (The Tragedies of the War in Belgium)*, depicting the ghastly atrocities of World War I. In the early 20th century, lithography became firmly established as fine art in the hands of artists such as Edward Hopper and John Sloan. From 1935 to 1941 graphic arts workshops were established under the Works Progress Administration's (WPA's) Federal Art Project. The first was established in New York City in February 1936 and became the country's largest, producing 75,000 prints, one-quarter of which was produced nationwide. Technical innovations such as Carborundum printing processes and silk screening emerged from the Great Depression. Artists such as Louis Lozowick, Saul Kovner, and Kyra Markham were employed in New York's WPA workshops. In the mid–20th century the field was represented by Andy Warhol, Helen Frankenthaler, Robert Indiana, and Ellsworth Kelly. Late 20th-century artists such as Tatyana Grosman and Jasper Johns pushed the technical limits of traditional printmaking by experimenting with the commercial offset lithography process, substituting lead plates for sheets of paper, and their work explored the resulting shades of gray.

See also Art, Adirondacks and North Country.

Bruhn, Thomas. *American Etching: The 1880s* (Storrs, Conn: William Benton Museum of Art, 1985)

Davis, Elliot Bostwick. "The Currency of Culture: Prints in New York City." In *Art and the Empire City, New York, 1825–1861* (New York: Metropolitan Museum of Art, 2000)

Kabelac, Karl Sanford. "19th-Century Rochester Fruit and Flower Plates," *University of Rochester Library Bulletin* 35 (1982): 93–113

Peters, Harry T. *America on Stone* (Garden City, NY: Doubleday, Doran, 1931)

Tatham, David F., ed. *Prints and Printmakers of New York State* (Syracuse: Syracuse Univ Press, 1986)

Georgia B. Barnhill

prisoner of war facilities. In early North American conflicts, prisoners of war were generally detained long enough to be traded back in exchanges with the opposing side. Some exceptions were made, such as with the British prison ships moored in Wallabout Bay, off the shore of Kings Co, during the American Revolution. Prisoner exchange continued during the first two years of the Civil War, when the practice changed to internment. There were several facilities in New York State. Fort Lafayette, on an island in the Narrows, held prisoners of war from July 1861 through the end of the war. The Elmira Prison Camp in Chemung Co began receiving prisoners in May 1864 and soon gained notoriety for subjecting its inmates to overcrowding, inadequate shelter, starvation, disease, and public ridicule. Presented in 1863 by Dr Francis Lieber of Columbia University, the Lieber Code was the first articulation of rights later guaranteed to prisoners of war by the Geneva conventions of 1929 and 1949, but it was not acted on during the Civil War.

Prisoner of war camps reappeared in the state during World War II, when Italian prisoners arrived in 1943, followed by Germans in 1944. Housed in facilities at Fort Niagara, Halloran Army Hospital (Richmond Co), Camp Popolopen (now Camp Natural Bridge on US Military Academy reservation in Orange Co), and Pine Camp (Jefferson Co), the prisoners provided needed labor. As the War Department made every effort to follow the Geneva convention of 1929, prisoners of war enjoyed unprecedentedly good conditions, which included movies, canteen privileges, and free education. Many camps were located at former Civilian Conservation Corps facilities and military barracks; others were newly constructed. Prisoners of war at Fort Niagara transferred to smaller subcamps in Geneseo, Attica, Dunkirk, Letchworth State Park, Rochester, Oswego, and other places where labor was needed. They often worked on farms and at food-processing plants; prisoners at Camp Popolopen cleared forests for training and recreation facilities. All prisoners of war were paid, either in scrip redeemable at the

At the Webster Canning Co plant, Italian prisoners of war react jubilantly to Italy's declaration of war against Germany in October 1943.

canteen or in savings to be issued on their release. As World War II ended, efforts were made to educate prisoners of war on democracy and the American way of life. At a camp in the Town of Van Etten (Chemung Co), anti-Nazi prisoners of war worked with Americans to publish a German language newspaper entitled *Der Ruf (The Call),* aimed at fostering democratic ideals in prisoners' minds. After the war many former prisoners of war returned to make the United States their home.

Mazuzan, George T., and Nancy Walker. "Restricted Areas: Prisoner-of-War Camps in Western New York, 1944–1946," *New York History* 59 (Jan 1978): 55–72

Martin Bannan

prison industry and labor. New York State initiated development of an economically self-sufficient and custodially secure model of prison management. This model, which replaced individual handicraft work with industrial production, would dominate correctional institutions nationwide by the late 1880s. From 1797 the state had supplied raw materials to inmate workers and then sold all finished goods, but in 1817 the New York State legislature abolished this "state-account" method, allowing entrepreneurs to bring raw materials to the prison, pay fixed charges for the use of inmate labor, and market the finished goods at their own risk. In 1819 the officers of Cayuga Co's Auburn Prison introduced the "congregate system" of inmate labor. Unlike the system of employment then current in Pennsylvania prisons, in which inmates worked at individual tasks in separate cells, the Auburn system permitted inmates to work together in prison shops or factories during the day, as well as to eat together, and confined them to cells only for sleep. In the congregate as in the separate system severe corporal punishment enforced a rule of silence. But the Auburn system implemented further measures of discipline as well: striped uniforms and the lockstep, a type of close-order, single-file marching.

By 1826 Auburn had dozens of manufacturing contracts for shoes, rifles, tools, textiles, and ready-made clothing, and from 1830 to 1837 reported annual profits of about $29,000. Westchester Co's Sing Sing Prison opened eight years after Auburn; its principal industry was stonecutting. Contracts were usually let for five years and required 10-hour workdays, excluding time spent at meals, though with fewer hours in winter. Daily, per inmate prison receipts averaged 36¢ in 1852, increasing to 60¢ in 1882. In 1843 Sing Sing's total earnings from contracts were $47,000 and in 1854 reached $95,000. In 1886 Sing Sing reported a profit of $75,000. Until the late 1880s inmates received nothing for their labor, although in theory, industrious inmates received any wages, in excess of their upkeep costs, on release.

As early as the 1830s the contract method had attracted opposition from artisans and unionized workers, who demanded protection from unfair competition. Their increasingly successful opposition, together with prison reformers' criticism of the repressive nature of the congregate system, led to a sharp reduction of prison industry beginning in the 1890s. The Prison Law of 1894 placed prison labor under the supervision of the New York State Department of Correctional Services' Division of Industries (from the 1970s, Corcraft) and prohibited contracts with private manufacturers and the distribution of prison-made goods on the open market. The Hawes-Cooper Act of 1929 and the Ashurst-Sumners Act of 1935 reinforced these prohibitions on the federal level.

In 1979 the federal Prison Industry Enhancement Act eased restrictions on interstate sales and allowed private companies into prison industries, when permitted by state law. Additional federal legislation of 1984 and 1990 further fostered private use of prison labor, but New Yorkers opposed this trend, retaining their ban on such arrangements. In 1989 Corcraft reported sales of $9 million and a profit of $1 million, in 1997, sales of $60 million and a profit of $7.1 million. In the latter year, Corcraft employed 2,500 inmates in 16 adult correctional facilities, supplying products and services to federal and state agencies at competitive prices. Corcraft inmates contribute to prison upkeep and security and learn marketable skills and good work habits; they typically work 7 hours per day, 5 days a week, and receive 16–45¢ per hour. Inmates of federal prisons in New York State work for Federal Prison Industries (FPI; also known as UNICOR), founded in 1934.

Klein, Philip. *Prison Methods in New York State: A Contribution to the Study of the Theory and Practice of Correctional Institutions in New York State* (New York: AMS Press, 1969)

Lewis, W. David. *From Newgate to Dannemora: The Rise of the Penitentiary in New York, 1796–1848* (Ithaca: Cornell Univ Press, 1965)

Maria Kiriakova

Making boots and shoes, Randall's Island, *ca* 1900.

prisons, federal. Prior to 1929 New York State had no federal prisons or jails. Prisoners awaiting trial or serving sentences passed in New York's federal courts were housed in state, county, or municipal prisons and jails, with some serving time in New Jersey prisons. In New York City, short-term federal prisoners were sent to Raymond Street Jail (also known as Brooklyn City Prison, closed in 1963), Suffolk County Jail at Riverhead, Eastview Penitentiary in Westchester Co, and the Hudson County Jail in New Jersey. Those with sentences over one year were sent to the US Penitentiary in Atlanta. During the 1920s New York State's prison population soared, leading to riots within state prisons. In 1927 the state commissioner of corrections informed federal authorities that he would accept no more federal prisoners in New York City jails. In response the US government constructed the first federal correctional facility in the state, Manhattan's West Street Jail, which opened in March 1929. Fort Wadsworth, a work camp on Staten Island for prisoners serving short sentences, operated from 1930 to 1931. The Federal Bureau of Prisons was created in 1930 and thereafter administered federal correctional institutions nationwide.

The West Street Jail was used to house male prisoners of the federal Southern District who were awaiting trial or serving sentences of less than a year. The facility operated until 1975, when the high-rise Metropolitan Correctional Center (MCC) in Lower Manhattan opened. The MCC holds around 700 male and female prisoners at a variety of security levels. The Metropolitan Detention Center, opened on the Brooklyn waterfront in 1994 and significantly expanded in 2000, holds around 2,500 male and female inmates. The state's two other federal prisons are low-rise, campus-style complexes in rural areas. The medium security Otisville Correctional Facility (Orange Co), completed in 1980, was intended to house 665 male inmates, with an additional 100 at an adjacent low security camp. In 2001 the prison population at Otisville was 988, with 121 camp residents. Before opening as a medium security prison for men, Ray Brook Prison was used to house athletes competing in the 1980 Winter Olympics at Lake Placid (Essex Co).

Johnston, Norman. *Forms of Constraint: A History of Prison Architecture* (Chicago: Univ of Illinois Press, 2000)

McShane, Marilyn D., and Frank P. Williams, eds. *Encyclopedia of American Prisons* (New York: Garland Publishing, 1996)

Ellen Sexton

prisons and jails. Until the late 18th century, institutions of incarceration in New York Colony often had overlapping functions with other governmental facilities. Under the Dutch, the Stadt Huys in both Beverwijck [now Albany] and New Amsterdam [now New York City] served as council chamber, courthouse, and jail. Under the English, City Hall in New York City remained a place of confinement. In other counties, civic buildings such as the 1772 courthouse and jail in Johnstown [now in Fulton Co] served the same purpose. By the early 19th century counties were building separate jails, such as the one in Canandaigua (Ontario Co) built in 1789, with one door, two small windows, a couple of chains to which prisoners were fastened, and straw on the floor for bedding. It was common for sheriffs to charge fees to inmates for their custody, a practice gradually discontinued in the second half of the 19th century. Imprisonment for debt, a common reason for incarceration in jails, was eliminated in 1831.

Development of Penal Institutions

Thomas Eddy and other social reformers seeking to make the criminal justice system more humane—by banning corporal punishment and reducing the number of offenses mandating capital punishment—won the legislature's approval in 1796 for establishing in Manhattan's Greenwich Village the state's first penitentiary. Opened in 1797 as the State Prison of the City of New York, the institution soon became known as Newgate. At Newgate Eddy promoted religious services, sound nutrition, inmate schooling, and family visits for good-conduct convicts. Although noble in concept, the prison soon revealed flaws. Eddy had designed most cells large enough to sleep eight. The arrangement triggered problems involving inmate discipline and violence exacerbated by overcrowding. To relieve Newgate's excess numbers, the state's second penitentiary was established at Auburn (Cayuga Co) in 1816. What became known as the New York or Auburn system evolved over several years. The goal had shifted from personal rehabilitation to societal obedience. The "break-to-retrain" regime included two other Auburn innovations: the striped suit and the lockstep. The Auburn system became America's standard prison model because of its effectiveness as an economic engine. Its leading practitioner, Warden Elam Lynds, rejected programs to educate and reform inmates. He believed prison should be so terrifying and degrading that no sane man surviving it would dare risk returning. The "congregate system" of inmate labor was introduced at Auburn in 1819 with prison shops where items such as shoes, textiles, and tools were made.

In 1825 Lynds supervised the transport of 100 Auburn Prison inmates to the Village of Sing Sing [now Ossining, Westchester Co] to begin construction of Newgate's replacement. Established in 1826 as Mount Pleasant Prison, the facility was renamed Sing Sing in 1848. Mount Pleasant Female Prison opened in 1839, and its chief matrons enjoyed considerable autonomy in day-to-day management. Overcrowding forced it to close as a female prison in 1877, and county and city jails were mandated to keep women sentenced to incarceration, both felony and misdemeanor terms. The state's third oldest prison, Clinton, established in 1845, emerged from tension with the private sector over the state using inmate labor to defray prison costs. Private companies and their workers had protested the unfair competition posed by the lower prices of inmate-made goods, including some made for private contractors. In response, the legislature passed a compromise bill in 1835 that protected domestic manufactures by limiting the number of shop inmates except for those making articles usually imported from abroad. Competition with foreign labor was encouraged, and an 1844 act approved a prison in Clinton Co, where inmates could mine iron, a product largely imported to the United States. The prison mining operation proved uneconomical, ceasing in 1877, and the inmates shifted to manufacturing items for use in state prisons.

The nation's first juvenile reformatory, the New York House of Refuge, opened in 1825 at a former federal arsenal in Manhattan, moved to Randall's Island in 1854, and remained open until 1935. Operated by the Society for the Reformation of Juvenile Delinquents, the facility housed vagrants and juvenile offenders aged 16 and younger. The house managers had control over males until they reached age 21 and females until 18. In 1849 the Western House of Refuge opened in Rochester for male felons under 18 years of age from Central and Western New York. It is considered the first state-managed reformatory in the country. The reformatory concept received significant endorsement at the 1870 National Congress on Penitentiary and Re-

ADULT CORRECTIONAL FACILITIES IN NEW YORK STATE, 2002

Correctional Facility	County	Established	Security Level	Sex	Capacity
New York State					
Adirondack	Essex	1972	Medium	Male	713
Albion	Orleans	1893	Minimum/Medium	Male	1,399
Altona	Clinton	1983	Medium	Male	560
Arthur Kill	Richmond	1976	Medium	Male	995
Attica	Wyoming	1931	Maximum	Male	2,240
Auburn	Cayuga	1816	Maximum	Male	1,818
Bare Hill	Franklin	1988	Medium	Male	1,722
Bayview	New York	1974	Medium	Female	323
Beacon	Dutchess	1981	Minimum	Female	257
Bedford Hills	Westchester	1901	Maximum	Female	972
Butler	Wayne	1989	Minimum	Male	300
Butler ASACTC[a]	Wayne	—	Medium	Male	250
Cape Vincent	Jefferson	1988	Medium	Male	1,122
Cayuga	Cayuga	1988	Medium	Male	1,202
Chateaugay	Franklin	1990	Medium	Male	250
Clinton	Clinton	1845	Maximum	Male	2,959
Collins	Erie	1981	Medium	Male	1,307
Coxsackie	Greene	1935	Maximum	Male	1,074
Downstate	Dutchess	1979	Maximum	Male	1,234
Eastern	Ulster	1900	Medium/Maximum	Male	1,037
Elmira	Chemung	1876	Maximum	Male	1,856
Fishkill	Dutchess	1892	Medium	Male	2,253
Five Points	Seneca	2000	Maximum	Male	1,422
Franklin	Franklin	1986	Medium	Male	1,730
Gouverneur	St. Lawrence	1990	Medium	Male	1,082
Gowanda	Erie	1994	Medium	Male	2,119
Great Meadow	Washington	1911	Maximum	Male	1,692
Green Haven	Dutchess	1949	Maximum	Male	2,170
Greene	Greene	1984	Medium	Male	1,821
Groveland	Livingston	1982	Minimum/Medium	Male	1,331
Hale Creek ASACTC[a]	Fulton	1990	Medium	Male	400
Hudson	Columbia	1976	Minimum/Medium	Male	643
Lakeview Shock Incarceration	Chautauqua	1989	Minimum	Male/Female	1,192
Livingston	Livingston	1991	Medium	Male	881
Lyon Mountain	Clinton	1984	Minimum	Male	162
Marcy	Oneida	1989	Medium	Male	1,522
Mid-Orange	Orange	1977	Medium	Male	750
Mid-State	Oneida	1983	Medium	Male	1,754
Mohawk	Oneida	1989	Medium	Male	1,305
Monterey Shock Incarceration	Schuyler	1958	Minimum	Male	300

ADULT CORRECTIONAL FACILITIES IN NEW YORK STATE, 2002 (continued)

Correctional Facility	County	Established	Security Level	Sex	Capacity
Moriah Shock Incarceration	Essex	1989	Minimum	Male	300
Mt. McGregor	Saratoga	1976	Medium	Male	551
Ogdensburg	St. Lawrence	1982	Medium	Male	685
Oneida	Oneida	1988	Medium	Male	1,215
Orleans	Orleans	1984	Medium	Male	1,322
Otisville	Orange	1977	Medium	Male	771
Queensboro	Queens	1977	Minimum	Male	610
Riverview	St. Lawrence	1988	Medium	Male	1,122
Shawangunk	Ulster	1985	Maximum	Male	575
Sing Sing	Westchester	1826	Medium/Maximum	Male	1,813
Southport	Chemung	1988	Maximum	Male	948
Sullivan	Sullivan	1985	Minimum/Maximum	Male	834
Summit Shock Incarceration	Schoharie	1961	Minimum	Male	70
Taconic	Westchester	1973	Medium	Female	502
Ulster	Ulster	1990	Medium	Male	882
Upstate	Franklin	1999	Maximum	Male	1,500
Wallkill	Ulster	1932	Medium	Male	608
Washington	Washington	1985	Medium	Male	1,090
Watertown	Jefferson	1982	Medium	Male	753
Wende	Erie	1983	Maximum	Male	962
Willard Drug Treatment Center	Seneca	1995	Administrative	Male/Female	906
Woodbourne	Sullivan	1935	Medium	Male	981
Wyoming	Wyoming	1984	Medium	Male	1,806
Federal					
Metropolitan Detention Center, Brooklyn	Kings	1975	Administrative	Male/Female	2,176[b]
Metropolitan Correctional Center, New York	New York	1994	Administrative	Male/Female	882[b]
Federal Correctional Institution, Otisville	Orange	1980	Administrative	Male	771
Federal Correctional Institution, Ray Brook	Essex	1981	Medium	Male	1,156

Source: American Correctional Association, *2002 Directory of Adult and Juvenile Correctional Departments, Institutions, Agencies, and Probation and Parole Authorities.*

Note: This table does not include the state's adult community residential facilities that house selected inmates transitioning to life after incarceration.

[a] Alcohol and Substance Abuse Correctional Treatment Center.

[b] Average daily population.

formatory Discipline in Cincinnati. Additionally, the National Prison Association (renamed American Correctional Association in 1954) was formed at the 1870 meeting. The New York State Reformatory at Elmira opened in 1876 under penologist Zebulon Reed Brockway. At Elmira Reformatory, first-time felons aged 16–30 had opportunity to earn early release through behavior reflecting their "reformation" by educational and moral uplift programs. Elmira overcrowding prompted authorization in 1892 for a second men's reformatory. Situated in Napanoch (Ulster Co), the Eastern New York Reformatory opened in 1900. In 1921 Eastern was transformed into the State Institution for Male Defective Delinquents. A decade after Napanoch's mission change, the women's prison at Albion (Orleans Co) was converted into the Institution for Mentally Defective Delinquent Women. In 1935 the Woodbourne Institute for Defective Delinquents (Sullivan Co) opened, relieving Eastern's overcrowding.

The reformatory approach was considered particularly appropriate for young female convicts. In 1876 Josephine Shaw Lowell, the first female commissioner named to the State Board of Charities monitoring institutions for the needy, made reformatories run by women for women a priority goal. She and Abigail Hopper Gibbons took the fight directly to the legislature and to the public. The state's first women's reformatory opened in Hudson (Columbia Co) in 1887 and soon became overcrowded. The Western House of Refuge for Women opened in 1893 in Albion. A third such facility opened in 1901 in Bedford Hills (Westchester Co).

The New York City Department of Correction originated in 1895 when the Department of Public Charities and Correction, successor to the Almshouse Department (which operated institutions housing the poor on various islands of the city), was divided into two agencies with the Department of Correction administering the city's penal facilities. Blackwell's Island [now Roosevelt Island] in the East River was the site of the city's main correctional operations until 1935, when its penitentiary and workhouse were abandoned and their inmates transferred to the newly built City Penitentiary on Rikers Island in the East River.

The legislature authorized a separate institution, the State Lunatic Asylum for Insane Convicts, erected on Auburn Prison grounds in 1859. It sought to treat its inmates' mental conditions rather than inflict punishment. By the 1880s it was overcrowded. Matteawan State Hospital (Dutchess Co) was built in 1892, allowing the Auburn Asylum to close. In 1899 Dannemora State Hospital (Clinton Co) opened next to the penitentiary. Run separately, it housed and treated male "insane convicts," whereas Matteawan held and treated males ruled insane prior to trial and females in both categories. Although mental deficiency as grounds for imprisonment went out of fashion after World War II, institutionalization of the mentally ill continued as a common practice until the 1970s, when in response to high hospital costs and legal rulings the pendulum swung toward deinstitutionalization, sending patients to community health centers providing mind-stabilizing drugs. The prison hospitals of Dannemora and Matteawan, which housed about 3,000 inmate patients in the mid-1960s, closed in 1972 and 1977, respectively.

Progressive Penal Reform

In 1944 John W. Edmonds, president of the Board of Inspectors of Sing Sing, initiated formation of the Prison Association of New York (renamed Correctional Association of New York in 1961) to ameliorate prison conditions, improve prison discipline, and help former convicts find honest livelihoods. With encouragement from Isaac T. Hopper, a founder of the Prison Association, his daughter Abigail Hopper Gibbons and other women formed a Female Department of the association in 1845, visiting prisons and seeking to improve conditions. The first Hopper Home was established in 1845 in Manhattan to shelter and train released female convicts for domestic employment. In 1853 the Female Department separated and became the Women's Prison Association. Both organizations remain involved in prison reform and rehabilitation services.

Each state prison operated under its own set of managers until the 1846 Constitution established a single Board of Prisons to oversee them all—initially Auburn, Sing Sing, and Dannemora. In 1876 the legislature replaced the board with the Office of Superintendent of State Prisons. The following year that superintendent was empowered to appoint agents at the prisons to help prerelease inmates find suitable homes and jobs. Separate prison parole boards were replaced in 1901 by the State Commission of Prisons, created in 1894 to inspect penal institutions and to promote their humane and efficient administration. Its members served as a board of commissioners for paroled prisoners. Their duties were transferred in 1908 to yet another parole board that consisted of the superintendent and two members named by the governor. In 1915, under New York City Correction Commissioner Katherine B. Davis, the nation's first municipal parole commission was initiated. Until 1967 it made early release decisions on inmates serving sentences up to three years in city correctional facilities. The city parole panel ceased when a limit of a year was set as the maximum sentence (misdemeanor time) that could be served in the municipal correction system, as had been the practice in all other localities of New York State. Felony sentences of incarceration (more than a year) are served in the state's prisons.

The Office of Superintendent of State Prisons administered the prisons until it was replaced in 1926 by the Department of Correction, which operated under the direction of a commission named by the governor. The new department also took on management of correctional-type institutions, such as certain reformatories previously under the State Board of Charities. Among the Department of Correction's four divisions were Parole and Probation, now separate from the prison agency. In 1970–71 the Department of Correctional Services (DOCS) was formed.

On 4 June 1888 Gov David B. Hill signed the law that made electrocution the method for carrying out death sentences for capital crimes committed after 1 Jan 1889. The first "electrical execution" anywhere in the world took place under Auburn warden Charles F. Durston's supervision 6 Aug 1890 when William Kemmler of Buffalo was executed. New York State abolished the death penalty in 1965 except for the murder of a police officer or a murder committed by a prisoner serving a life sentence. The legislature restored the death penalty to criminal statutes for certain murder categories in 1995 but adopted lethal injection as the method. Although several prisoners have been sentenced to death under the new laws, as of the end of 2003 no prisoner has been executed in the state since 1963.

Attica and Post-Attica Reforms

Beginning with Newgate, almost all of the state's prisons have experienced inmate disturbances, some turning into full-scale riots. There were riots at Auburn in 1819, 1820, 1857, and 1929; Sing Sing in 1843, 1855, and 1857; and Clinton in Dannemora in 1861 and 1929. Prison violence tends to come in cycles, and overcrowding, inadequate services, and an unsettled political and racial climate contributed to the state's three prison riots in 1970 at the Manhattan House of Detention for Men (commonly known as the Tombs), Auburn Correctional Facility, and Attica Correctional Facility (Wyoming Co). In the first two, hostages were taken, but the disturbances were quelled fairly quickly. These riots were a prelude to the bloodiest prison riot in the nation's history—at Attica in September 1971—which culminated in the deaths of 32 inmates and 11 hostages.

The riots profoundly changed prison architecture, moving it away from hard-to-control large cellblocks with hundreds of inmates to smaller, more manageable modules with 50 or so prisoners. Highly restrictive "supermax" prisons such as Upstate Correction Facility in Malone (Franklin Co) evolved to segregate disruptive or violent inmates. Opened in 1999, Upstate became the first maximum security facility built after the 1988 opening of Southport Correctional Facility (Chemung Co). Attica era unrest also sparked renewed interest in pushing programs to engage the minds and hands of inmates. Prison boot camps—combination military drills, remedial schooling, and group therapy—were established. Monterey (Schuyler Co), one of several youth camps created in the 1950s on Department of Environmental Conservation land for "reorientation" of inmates aged 16 to 21, became the site in 1987 of a pilot DOCS shock incarceration program stressing education and substance abuse treatment in addition to military-style training. The intensely rigid six-month program, offering participants the incentive of early release, proved such a success that shock incarceration camps for youths were opened at Summit (Schoharie Co); Moriah (Essex Co); and Lakeview (Chautauqua Co), which offers separate versions for females and males. The recidivism rate is reported lower among graduates than comparable general population inmates.

Modeled on shock incarceration camps is the Willard Drug Treatment Campus in Ovid (Seneca Co), opened in 1995 and operated by DOCS, in partnership with the Division of Parole and the State Office of Alcohol and Substance Abuse Services. Its residents are parolees whose drug abuse relapses could result in their being returned to regular prison except for the second chance being offered by the three-month program. New York City has run a 61-day High Impact Incarceration program on Rikers Island since 1990. It has a somewhat similar female inmate program. Both draw voluntary participants from among nonviolent crime parolees who have violated certain technical rules of their parole and who may avoid returning to prison if they successfully complete the program. Also in the wake of the Attica era riots, the need for increased professionalism among staff became obvious, in part because of the recognition that inmate organizers use increasingly sophisticated techniques and strategies. The US Department of Justice–sponsored National Institute of Corrections, an educational resource center for correctional agencies and personnel, was founded in 1974 as a direct result of a national conference held in December 1971 specifically to address Attica-related issues.

These changes in prison operations took place amid a rapidly expanding prisoner population. Gov Nelson A. Rockefeller sponsored legislation in 1973 that mandated sentences of as much as 25-years-to-life imprisonment for convictions of selling or possessing specified quantities of illegal drugs. The state's prison count expanded from 13,437 in 1973 to 70,044 in 1998, and from 33 facilities in 1979 to 69 by 1994. Drug-related felonies have come to constitute the leading category of crime among those sentenced to prison, with almost 30% of state prison inmates committed for drug offenses in 2002. Courts were authorized to compel certified addicts to undergo treatment for up to three years as a civil commitment and for up to five years if the commitment stemmed from a criminal case. For a variety of reasons, including a desire to reduce the burden on taxpayers, a general consensus emerged in the early 2000s that the drug law violation penalties needed some downward revision, but the extent and kind of changes remain issues hampering agreement.

Against this backdrop emerged New York State's own drive to upgrade facilities and staff operations to standards of penal excellence. Thomas A. Coughlin III, state corrections commissioner from 1979 to 1994, initiated performance-measuring programs as well as educational and vocational opportunities, with every prison accredited by the American Correctional Association. About the time that the state prison system was moving onto an accreditation track, the county jail systems were also being moved in that direction. Participating jointly in that process has been the New York State Sheriffs' Association and the Commission of Correction. The commission promulgates minimum standards for state, city, and county correctional facilities and inspects them to ensure adherence. The commission also has oversight responsibilities for numerous lockups as well as juvenile detention facilities. In 1993 the commission joined and enhanced a State Sheriffs' Association–initiated accreditation program for county correctional facilities begun the previous year. In July 1994 the Ontario County Correctional Facility became the first county jail to receive the joint commission/sheriffs association accreditation.

The Sentencing Reform Act of 1998, also known as Jenna's Law—named after Jenna Grieshaber of Camillus (Onondaga Co), a Russell Sage College nursing student slain 6 Nov 1997—went into effect 1 Sept 1998. It extended to first-time violent felons the no-parole strictures that the Sentencing Reform Act of 1995 had imposed on violent felony repeaters by requiring that first-time violent felons serve at least six-sevenths of their sentence. The 1995 and 1998 laws are examples of the trend away from parole in particular and progressive penology generally. They removed discretionary release for all violent felony offenders while mandating court-imposed periods of post-release supervision of up to five years that the offender must serve after completing the period of incarceration imposed by the court.

In recent years the total prison and jail population in New York State has ranged from 105,388 in March 1999 to 95,296 in December 2001. About two-thirds of the inmates are in state correctional facilities, with the remaining divided almost evenly between New York City and the other 57 counties combined. In early 2003, with approximately 96,850 inmates in the state, the New York City jail system accounted for about 14,720, the majority housed in 1 of 10 facilities on Rikers Island; the combined other counties, approximately 15,570; and the state prison system, about 66,560. DOCS operates 71 prisons throughout the state; the average time served in the state correctional facilities is 43 months; and men make up 95% of prisoners. The operating budget for the state prison system in fiscal year 2000–2001 was $2.25 billion.

Federal Prisons in New York State

In 1929, a year before the Federal Bureau of Prisons (BOP) was established, the US Justice Department opened the state's first federal correction facility, the House of Detention, commonly known as the West Street Jail, in Manhattan near the Hudson River. The West Street Jail closed in 1975, replaced by the Metropolitan Correction Center situated in Lower Manhattan. Other federal prisons in New York State are the Metropolitan Detention Center in Brooklyn, Otisville Correctional Facility (Orange Co), and Ray Brook Prison (Essex Co).

See also Capital punishment.

Eisenhauer, Paul Robert. "Organizing Discipline: Prison Organization and Penal Theory in 19th-Century New York" (PhD diss, Univ of Pennsylvania, 1988)

Glenn, Myra C. *Campaigns against Corporal Punishment* (Albany: SUNY Press, 1984)
Lewis, Walter David. *From Newgate to Dannemora: The Rise of the Penitentiary in New York, 1796–1848* (Ithaca: Cornell Univ Press, 1965)
New York Correction History Society, http://www.correctionhistory.org/
Reich, Ilan K. *A Citizen Crusade for Prison Reform: The History of the Correctional Association of New York* (New York: The Association, 1994)

Thomas C. McCarthy

prison ships. After the American defeats at the Battle of Long Island in Brooklyn and the fall of Fort Washington on Manhattan in 1776, the British held thousands of Continental soldiers as prisoners of war. Soon realizing that their prisons on land could not contain the growing number of captives, they began to use old warships and transports as prisons. These vessels were stripped of almost all rigging and anchored in Wallabout Bay in the East River, near what is now the Fort Greene section of Brooklyn. Under the command of Provost Marshal William Cunningham, the prison ships became known for their brutal living conditions. Prisoners were kept below decks most of the time; food and water were grossly inadequate; yellow fever, typhus, dysentery, and smallpox accounted for most deaths. Approximately 11,000 civilians and combatants lost their lives aboard British prison ships in New York, more than twice the number of Americans killed on the battlefield during the entire war. The first prison ship in New York City was the *Whitby*, but more than two dozen followed, including the notorious *Jersey*. Cunningham later confessed that, in addition to the thousands of prisoners who died of disease and starvation, more than 200 had been executed. The dead were often buried along the shore in Wallabout Bay. For many years after the war, prisoners' bones were either uncovered or washed up in Brooklyn. As a memorial and final resting place for the remains, the New York Tammany Society constructed a vault in the early 19th century at the present location of Vinegar Hill in Brooklyn. After falling into disrepair, the vault was replaced in 1873 with a large stone crypt in what is now Fort Greene Park in Brooklyn. In 1908 this was replaced by the 148 ft (45.1 m) Prison Ship Martyrs' Monument, designed by architect Stanford White and bearing the inscription, "They shall not be forgotten." It too soon fell into disrepair. In the early 21st century there were plans for restoring the monument.

Cray, Robert E., Jr. "Commemorating the Prison Ship Dead: Revolutionary Memory and the Politics of Sepulture in the Early Republic, 1776–1808," *William and Mary Quarterly* 56 (July 1999): 565–90
Dring, Thomas. *Recollections of the Jersey Prison Ship, from the manuscript of Capt Thomas Dring.* Ed. Albert G. Greene (1829; repr Bedford, Mass: Applewood Books, 1987)

Jennifer Steenshorne

privateering. See PIRACY AND PRIVATEERING.

probation. System under which a convicted person, in lieu of incarceration, is permitted to remain within the community under the supervision of an officer of the court. Probation sentences are generally used for nonviolent crimes and are fixed by the state legislature for terms of 1 year (Class B misdemeanor), 3 years (Class A misdemeanor), 5 years (certain felony offenses), and lifetime probation (certain drug felonies). Probation is also assigned for terms of 6 years (misdemeanors) or 10 years (felonies) to sex offenders who will remain in the community. Probation officers monitor the person through regular meetings, occasional home visits, and telephone or electronic monitoring systems. The most common sentence imposed by New York State judges in both juvenile and adult criminal court, probation can be revoked after a court hearing because of new criminality or a violation of the restrictions on behavior such as ignoring a curfew, carrying a weapon, failing a drug test, associating with known felons, or quitting work or school. A second or persistent adult felon is not eligible for probation.

John Augustus helped pioneer the idea of probation in Boston during the 1840s and 1850s when he persuaded the courts to release young offenders into his care instead of prison. Probation was first officially authorized as a possible sentence by the New York State legislature in 1901. In 1907 the New York State Probation Commission was formed and became the Division of Probation in 1927 within the Department of Correction. In 1970 the Probation Division became a separate state agency within the Executive Department, and in 1984 the Classification/Alternatives Law gave the newly named Division of Probation and Correctional Alternatives expanded authority. The department oversees the operation of 58 local government agencies and more than 160 diversion and alternative-to-detention or incarceration programs, some of which are run by nonprofit community organizations.

Probation officers monitor their clients' activities but also refer them to job training, drug treatment, and other rehabilitative services. Initially probation officers were volunteers or part-time employees, usually social workers, police officers, or court personnel who combined the role of law enforcer with that of counselor. Today probation officers are required to hold a master's degree in the social/behavioral sciences or a bachelor's degree with two years' experience in a social service or criminal justice agency. Annually they complete 21 hours of training on the state or local level; they are also peace officers under the New York State Penal Code and have certain law enforcement responsibilities, including mandatory training in the use of firearms and deadly force. Probation departments assist judges by carrying out presentence investigations that focus on the defendant's prior record of arrests and convictions, lifestyle, and mental and physical condition, and by providing advisory sentencing recommendations. Many probation departments suffer from chronic underfunding, excessive caseloads, staff shortages, and high officer turnover rates. As of 2003 more than 200,000 adult and juvenile offenders were supervised under the probation system annually.

Jones-Brown, Delores, Elsie Chandler, and Susan Decker. *Criminal Justice in New York* (Boston: Allyn & Bacon, 2000)

Charles Lindner and Andrew Karmen

Progressive Party. Three separate, short-lived political organizations of the same name, formed in 1912, 1924, and 1948. The first and most politically significant was the instrument of former Republican president Theodore Roosevelt, dissatisfied with the pace of reform under his successor, William H. Taft. At its convention in Syracuse in 1912, the Progressive Party called for legislation to prevent industrial accidents and occupational diseases and to promote workers' compensation, public control of utilities, woman suffrage, the end of child labor, and fair pay for working women. Minorities and women played a major role in supporting the party. Reformer Frances Kellor ran its main strategy and information hub, the Progressive Service, in Manhattan. Although Roosevelt, in hopes of gaining white support in the South, banned black delegates from the Deep South at the party's national convention, they played a role at the New York State convention.

The Bull Moose Party, as it was also known, with its standard bearer a native New Yorker and the party headquarters in Manhattan, had a strong presence in the state. In 1912 it ran candidates for assembly and senate in almost every state district, and contenders generally finished a respectable second or third. In the fall elections Roosevelt captured 25% of the state's presidential vote, and the party's gubernatorial candidate, Oscar S. Straus, a former secretary of commerce (and the first Jew to be nominated for statewide office in New York State by a major party) received 24% of that vote. There were some electoral successes. Walter M. Chandler was elected to Congress from Manhattan (and reelected as a Progressive in 1914), as was a state senator (also from Manhattan), and three assemblymen (two from Manhattan, one from Brooklyn). By 1914 the Progressive Party's electoral fortunes were ebbing, garnering a mere 3% in that year's gubernatorial contest. In 1916, at both state and national levels, it folded into the Republican Party.

Robert LaFollette revived the party in 1924. He was dismayed, like many liberal Republicans, by the conservative candidates nominated by the two major parties. Many were distressed when the Democrats did not nominate New York State governor Alfred E. Smith as candidate, choosing, after 104 ballots, the far more conservative Wall Street lawyer John W. Davis. LaFollette received 414,913 votes for president in New York State, about 15% of the state's presidential tally. The party had not run candidates for other offices and ceased to exist after the election.

It was revived once more in 1948 when former vice president Henry A. Wallace, dismayed by the growth of the Cold War, broke from the Democratic Party and ran an independent campaign for president. In New York State the core of Wallace's support, the Progressive Party, ran under the aegis of the American Labor Party. Wallace received 509,559 votes for president in the state that year, 422,355 of those from New York City. Although this was only 8% of the New York State total, it was 44% of Wallace's. This Progressive Party fared no better than its predecessors and ceased to exist after a few years.

See also WORLD WAR I.

Culver, John C. *American Dreamer: The Life and Times of Henry A. Wallace* (New York: Norton, 2000)
Gable, John A. *The Bull Moose Years: Theodore Roosevelt and the Progressive Party* (Port Washington, NY: Kennikat, 1978)
MacKay, Kenneth Campbell. *The Progressive Movement of 1924* (New York: Columbia Univ Press, 1947)

John Recchiuti

progressivism. New York State was in many ways at the center of the national progressive movement in the early 20th century. Most progressives in the state shared a commitment to increasing the role of the government in public life as a way to control large corporations and trusts and to improve the lives of average citizens. Although New York State was the home of Theodore Roosevelt, the national leader of the progressive movement and the head of the era's short-lived Progressive Party, he represented just one strand of progressive politics.

His was connected loosely to the abolitionist tradition of high-minded Republicans trying to right society's ills through moral campaigns. Most early 20th century progressives, however, unlike 19th-century abolitionists, were decidedly less concerned with the rights of African Americans. The main issues engaging Rooseveltian progressives were civil service reform, efficiency in government, and conservation; they opposed urban machines, usually controlled by the Democrats. Roosevelt brought these concerns to his single term as governor beginning in 1899, and Gov Charles Evans Hughes, elected in 1906, pursued a similar agenda. Hughes had come to prominence investigating fraud in New York City's life insurance industry in 1905. Like Roosevelt, Hughes believed in an expansive role for government, and among his innovations was establishing the forerunner of the Public Service Commission to control utility rates.

Democrats also became major supporters of progressivism, though with a different focus: factory labor, organized labor, and immigrants. New York City politicians such as Alfred E. Smith and Robert F. Wagner Sr were Tammany stalwarts, but the success of Republican progressivism and catastrophic episodes like the 1911 Triangle Shirtwaist Factory fire in New York City, in which nearly 150 young female factory workers were killed, catalyzed Democratic politicians into propounding reform. They sponsored legislation for commissions to investigate factory conditions, bills for workers' compensation, child labor laws, and other landmark legislation designed to safeguard citizens' health and welfare. New York State's efforts in progressive legislation were a model for the rest of the nation. Smith was elected to the first of his four terms as governor in 1918 on a progressive platform of making government a more positive force in the lives of citizens. As governor he greatly expanded the role of the executive branch, creating parks and housing and supporting labor; his progressive credentials were critical in his winning the 1928 Democratic presidential nomination.

There was also a distinct feminist strand of progressivism that received its fullest expression in New York State. Feminist progressives were in the forefront of the settlement house movement and developed their perspective in a variety of labor, housing, and social welfare organizations. Notable among them in New York State were Lillian Wald, innovator in providing community healthcare and founder of what is now the Visiting Nurse Service of New York; National Association for the Advancement of Colored People (NAACP) cofounder Mary White Ovington; Eleanor Roosevelt, the politically formidable wife of Franklin D. Roosevelt; Frances Perkins, later the first female member of a presidential cabinet; and Belle Moskowitz, close political advisor to Al Smith. Outside of New York City prominent female progressives included Martha Van Rensselaer, one of the founders of the School of Home Economics at Cornell University and a strong voice for farm families, and, in Buffalo, Mary Burnett Talbert, a prominent leader of African American women through organizations like the National Association of Colored Women's Clubs and the NAACP.

Strands of progressivism also appeared in fields like philosophy and law. At Columbia University, for example, John Dewey developed a social and political philosophy in large part premised on the progressive principles; it maintained that the searches for epistemological truth and for social justice in a democratic society were related. Benjamin Cardozo, who served nearly two decades as a judge (and chief judge) of the New York State Court of Appeals, developed a national reputation for advocating a progressive approach to jurisprudence. In particular, Cardozo emphasized taking social realities into account in legal decision making rather than relying simply on legal precedents.

Progressive principles continued to influence New York State well after its national heyday ended after 1920. Among those decisively shaped by its principles were New York City mayor Fiorello La Guardia and the two long-term Republican governors, Thomas E. Dewey and Nelson A. Rockefeller. Democratic governor and US senator Herbert H. Lehman was another important product of progressive politics. But undoubtedly the most important legacy of progressivism in New York State was the work of Franklin D. Roosevelt, Smith's successor as governor in 1929 and president of the United States for 12 years. Many of Roosevelt's leading advisors, including Frances Perkins, Harry Hopkins, and Roosevelt's wife Eleanor, were products of the New York State progressive tradition. In Roosevelt's career as governor and president, many of the diverse strands of New York State's progressivism were merged and expanded. National programs such as unemployment insurance, social security, and labor legislation were all built on New York State precedents.

Baker, Paula. *Gender, Politics, and the State in Rural New York, 1870–1930* (New York: Oxford Univ Press, 1991)
Nelson, William E. *The Legalist Reformation: Law, Politics, and Ideology in New York, 1920–1980* (Chapel Hill: Univ of North Carolina Press, 2001)

Peter Eisenstadt

Prohibition

Background and Local Option

The first temperance society in the United States was established in Moreau (Saratoga Co) in 1808 by Presbyterian physician Dr Billy J. Clark and promoted voluntary abstinence. Though nearly defunct after 1821, Clark's group provided a model for the New York State Temperance Society founded in 1829 and boasting a membership of 40,000 a year later. In 1836 representatives of the New York State society met with others in a national convention of the American Temperance Society in Saratoga Springs. There, they discarded the notion of voluntary abstinence for teetotalism, a philosophy that called for abstinence from all alcohol and an end to government liquor licensing.

On 14 May 1845, after a compromise in the New York State Senate exempted New York Co, the state legislature passed its first local option law, empowering towns either to license liquor sales within their borders or to forbid such sales. On 27 Apr 1846, 728 of 856 towns voted against licensing. But in May 1847, after liquor dealers won approval for a second election, over half of the no-license towns voted for licensing, and in 1847 the legislature repealed the option law. This action reinstated state regulation and the power of town and city excise boards to issue liquor licenses. Maine's statewide prohibition of alcohol in 1851 reenergized New York's temperance advocates, who secured legislative approval of a similar statewide law in 1854, which Gov Horatio Seymour, a Democrat, refused to sign. When Whig Myron H. Clark became governor, the legislature enacted a prohibition ordinance 9 Apr 1855, though the State Court of Appeals then ruled it unconstitutional.

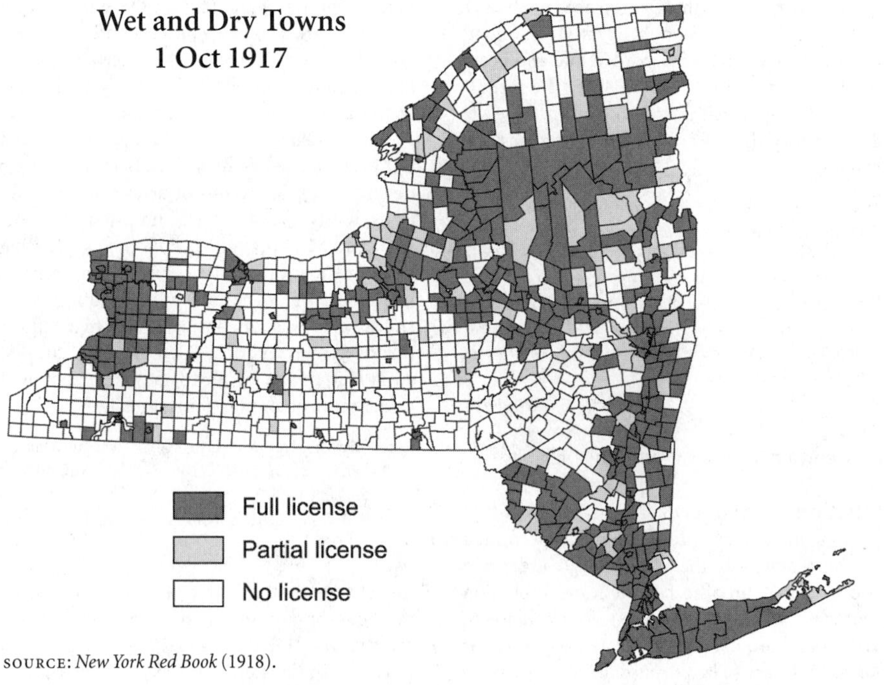

SOURCE: *New York Red Book* (1918).

Destruction of confiscated liquor in Rochester during Prohibition. Photograph by Albert R. Stone, *ca* 1921.

Following the Civil War, revitalized anti-alcohol campaigns led to New York State's adoption of a new local option law on 23 Mar 1896. By 1916, 498 of 933 towns were no-license towns, and New York Co's licensed saloons had decreased by 43%. In 1918 a modified option law allowed cities to put the license question before voters, with 18 of the 39 cities holding such special elections voting against licensing. After the United States entered World War I, the federal War Prohibition Act of November 1918 banned the manufacture and sale of beverages of more than 2.75% alcohol for the duration of the war and demobilization. On 29 Jan 1919 the New York State legislature ratified the 18th Amendment, which prohibited the manufacture, sale, or transportation of alcoholic beverages throughout the nation beginning 16 Jan 1920. The ratification, by a vote of 27 to 24 in the senate and 81 to 66 in the assembly, marked the culmination of a 110-year struggle by New York State advocates of temperance or abstinence from alcohol. Two months later, the 18th Amendment was ratified by enough states (36 including New York) for adoption.

Political Resistance to Prohibition

The New York State legislative session that ratified the 18th Amendment also defeated a bill requiring New York State voter approval of all US Constitutional amendments. Democratic Gov Alfred E. Smith then proposed a referendum on the 18th Amendment, but federal courts ruled that ratification could not be revoked after passage by the legislature. Undeterred, in 1920 anti-Prohibitionists passed the Walker-Gillett beer bill, which provided for the sale of beer in restaurants and declared beer containing 2.75% alcohol nonintoxicating. This same year the US Supreme Court overturned an act preventing state legislatures from setting their own definitions of an intoxicating beverage.

In 1921 newly elected Republican governor Nathan L. Miller, with the assistance of the Anti-Saloon League, enacted the Mullan-Gage law, a state version of the federal Volstead Act, which provided for enforcement of the 18th Amendment. Over three years of operation, 88% of the 6,902 Mullan-Gage cases presented to grand juries were dismissed. After regaining the governorship, Al Smith repealed Mullan-Gage in June 1923, assuring his critics that state officers would enforce the Volstead Act. Despite the assurances, the state police only arrested 6,071 Volstead Act violators and obtained 1,658 convictions after 1923.

Bootleggers

The Quebec liquor industry, the sparsely guarded New York–Canadian border, and the overall economics of prohibition undermined enforcement. Thousands of individuals entered New York State undetected as customs stations were understaffed, not located directly on the border, and closed at midnight. Bootleggers used farms, hotels, garages, and mountain camps as liquor storage depots and transfer stations, and employed pilot cars to protect liquor convoys, paying youths to note the whereabouts of patrol officers. Off Long Island speedboats carrying Canadian liquor from the West Indies outmaneuvered the US Coast Guard, and on the state's western frontier, boats crossed Lake Erie and regularly made their way past unsuspecting or corrupt customs officials in Buffalo. A $55 case of Scotch and a $5 case of beer purchased in Canada sold for $125 and $25, respectively, in New York City.

In 1921 Quebec's government took control of the liquor industry and prohibited liquor stores from selling more than one bottle per person, though many stores circumvented the new law. From 1921 to 1924 the Quebec Liquor Commission made $54.7 million as Canadian establishments profited from Americans coming to drink legally and to purchase alcohol for home consumption. Over 35,000 people crossed the border at Rouses Point (Clinton Co) in November 1929. If detected, one- and two-bottle smugglers usually faced only a $5 fine and confiscation of their alcohol, and an epidemic of such smugglers strained customs. But revenues from fines and sales of seized vehicles led state and local authorities to control the liquor trade, not to eliminate it, as records of other fines reveal: from 1900 to 1919, 368,750 people were convicted for public intoxication; from 1920 to 1927, 106,590 were convicted of this misdemeanor, along with 205 found guilty of liquor law violations. Fines and raids served as a quasi-excise law and controlled the proliferation of speakeasies in border counties, appeasing "dry" advocates while adding to local revenues. Speakeasies usually operated out of back rooms and basements, protected by locked doors with peepholes as well as payoffs to law enforcement. They mainly served liquor, not beer, at high prices to a middle-class clientele of men and women. Local leaders and citizens tolerated the underground economy of Prohibition as long as disorderly conduct, destruction of property, and the use of firearms were controlled.

Repeal

A New York State referendum of 2 Nov 1926 that modified the Volstead Act to allow light wines and beers, with 1,763,070 voters supporting change and only 598,484 opposing it, reenergized the campaign for repeal. An increase in deadly violence as enforcement shifted from local to federal authorities further eroded support for Prohibition. Five of seven Prohibition-related deaths in the North Country occurred between 1923 and 1933, with violence reaching a high after the 1929 implementation of the Jones Act, which made it a felony to violate the Volstead Act. Between 1929 and 1932 the number of violators sent to jail doubled, and the federal prison population rose from 5,000 to 12,000. A *Literary Digest* poll of 1930 showed that residents of rural Clinton Co, which had voted against licensing for 10 of its 14 towns in 1917, favored repeal by a 2 to 1 margin. By 1931 prominent New Yorkers such as Nicholas Murray Butler, an elder statesman of the Republican Party, began to criticize Prohibition, and anti-Prohibition organizations gained in prestige and financing as the Du Ponts, formerly supporters of Prohibition, and other New York metropolitan area industrialists lent their support to repeal. Federal officials also encouraged repeal efforts by asserting that effective enforcement in New York State would require several thousand additional agents. The state legislature responded in 1931 by passing the Culliver bill, which called for a constitutional convention to overturn Prohibition. On 20 Feb 1932 the US Congress approved the 21st Amendment, mandating repeal. New York became the eighth state to ratify the measure on 27 June 1933, with New Yorkers voting 1,946,532 to 247,450 in favor of repeal. The amendment was ratified 5 Dec 1933 and went into effect immediately.

See also Beer and brewing; Organized crime; Temperance movement; World war I.

Clark, Norman. *Deliver Us from Evil: An Interpretation of American Prohibition* (New York: Norton, 1976)

Everest, Allan S. *Rum across the Border* (Syracuse: Syracuse Univ Press, 1978)

Hamm, Richard F. *Shaping the 18th Amendment: Temperance Reform, Legal Culture, and the Polity, 1880–1920* (Chapel Hill: Univ of North Carolina Press, 1995)

Moore, Sean T. "National Prohibition in Northern New York," *New York History* 77 (Summer 1996): 177–206

Sean T. Moore

Prospect. Village (pop 330) in Trenton (Oneida Co). Settled in 1794 at a 24 ft (7.3 m) waterfall on the West Canada Creek, Prospect acquired a post office in 1834 and was incorporated as a village in 1890. Three limestone quarries and a tannery (1825–87) provided work, as did hotels for tourists such as Union Hall (1827). Welsh settlers came to Prospect by 1825. The village was served by the Black River and Utica Railroad (1855), although the station was a mile from the center of the village. Limestone was quarried from 1852 to 1967. It was the home of Nellie Thurston Squire, the first woman to make a public solo ascension in a balloon from Poughkeepsie in 1871. A hydroelectric dam was built by Niagara Mohawk from 1957 to 1959. In 2003 many Prospect residents commute to Utica and Rome for employment. Since 1946 softball's Prospect Invitational Fast Pitch Tournament has been an annual event.

prostitution. One of the most significant seaports in colonial America, New York City, had a sizable trade in prostitution by the late 1600s. In the following century prostitution grew in conjunction with the port's own expansion, and "disorderly houses" appeared all along Manhattan's waterfront. Commercial sex further accelerated with the British army's long occupation (1776–83) of the metropolis during the American Revolutionary War. Prostitution also flourished in most of the state's other urban areas and was an accepted practice of city and town life. In 1785 the port of Hudson [now in Columbia Co] had 18 inns that were all used by prostitutes. Municipal officials throughout New York State generally tolerated prostitution as long as it occurred in discrete areas; if prostitutes were caught working outside those areas they could face minor charges, such as disorderly conduct or vagrancy. Social attitudes that denied "respectable" women's sexuality while viewing sexual expression as essential to men served to promote an uneasy acceptance of prostitution. Citizens might object to these enterprises and, in times of social stress, express their objections with attacks upon their working women, as in 1793 and 1799 when residents burned a number of Manhattan brothels. In calmer times, however, prostitution was simply a part of life.

Reform and the "Tenderloin"

With the industrial revolution of the early 19th century the casual world of courtesans, camp followers, and waterfront whores gave way to an increasingly commercialized sex industry. At the same time, the occasional derision of moralists began to give way to coordinated efforts to reform and regulate prostitution. Because of its ability to engender deep emotion, the debate on prostitution encapsulated many of the social changes in the 19th and 20th centuries. Some reformers challenged prostitution because it offered women financial independence, while others viewed it as a symptom of women's dependence on men. In 1831 John McDowall, a Presbyterian minister, formed the New York Magdalen Society for reformed prostitutes. The New York Female Moral Reform Society, founded in 1834 by a group of New York City women, saw prostitutes as innocent victims of male lust. Similar societies were formed throughout the state in an effort to assist prostitutes in abandoning their work. The sensational trial for the 1836 murder of New York City prostitute Helen Jewitt brought great attention to this problem of female dependence. In 1848 the state legislature passed two bills aimed at criminalizing prostitution. In 1859 a local ordinance outlawing gambling and prostitution was passed in Hudson. At the same time, the notion that prostitution should be regulated for health reasons emerged. In 1867 the state legislature debated regulation, but the proposed bill was defeated, as was every comprehensive attempt at regulation thereafter; the purity campaigns did little to curb the growth of the sex industry.

During the antebellum period most prostitutes worked along main thoroughfares. In New York City, Broadway was a notorious street for prostitutes, particularly around the area of City Hall Park, including a male homosexual trade. Starting in the 1820s, however, prostitutes in New York City increasingly worked out of brothels. Much of this change was spurred by landowners who generally preferred to rent to prostitutes instead of families because sex workers had a better reputation for paying their rent on time. Following the American Civil War prostitution continued to flourish, generally tolerated in a "tenderloin" neighborhood that existed in nearly every city in the state. New York City's some 600 houses of prostitution, which had been originally been scattered among downtown neighborhoods, by 1860 moved uptown. By the Gilded Age these disorderly houses came to congregate between 5th and 8th Aves, and 23d and 34th Sts, now the neighborhoods of Madison Square and Chelsea. In Elmira more than a dozen brothels and 120 prostitutes were documented working in the city's center in 1913. That same year a similar district existed in Syracuse, within a half-mile radius of the Soldiers' and Sailors' Monument. Twenty-seven houses of prostitution operated in Syracuse, employing approximately 160 sex workers. Normally a weekend trade primarily serving Syracuse University, the city's vice trade swelled to a 24-hours-a-day, 7-days-a-week business during the New York State Fair, which was held directly outside the city every September. To accommodate fairgoers, additional prostitutes came from New York City, with prices doubling. Albany also had a discrete neighborhood of prostitution. Known as the Gut, now the South End, this district was in convenient walking distance of the city's train station and the state capitol.

Progressivism and Political Corruption

By the turn of the century Progressive reformers viewed prostitution and the trade's interconnections to public health with increasing concern. A 1901 investigation revealed that 80% of all women imprisoned for charges relating to prostitution at the Bedford Hills State Reformatory (Westchester Co) had venereal diseases. There was also the sense that in its wake prostitution was trailed by corruption and payoffs to the police, and a host of lesser vices. For some antiprostitution campaigners in New York City the issue offered a chance to express genuine moral outrage and to place Tammany Hall on the defensive. Charles Parkhurst, the pastor of New York City's Madison Square Presbyterian Church, was perhaps the most famous antivice reformer in state history. Starting in 1892 Parkhurst led a long fought campaign against the city's sex trade and its connections with Tammany and the police department; a singular organization in his view, which he dubbed the "organized municipal criminality," Parkhurst and others went undercover into brothels to document this relationship. Parkhurst's exposés led the state legislature to launch the Lexow Committee (1894–95), which documented a structured system of payoffs between the Tammany-controlled police and disorderly houses. A public sensation, these investigations (headed by state senator Clarence Lexow, a Republican from Rockland Co), culminated in the 1894 election of reformer William L. Strong as mayor of New York City and in an 1895 state-created board, led by Theodore Roosevelt, to oversee the city's police department.

Beyond Parkhurst other private citizens responded with vice commissions, such as the Committee of Fifteen organized in New York City in 1900; similar groups were also founded in Syracuse and Elmira in 1911. New York City's Committee of Fifteen comprised a diverse array of state reformers, including conservatives like Theodore Roosevelt and liberals like Alvin S. Johnson, and was perhaps one of the most successful grassroots organizations in state history. With upward of 35,000 prostitutes estimated in New York City alone, the Committee of Fifteen pushed hard for state legislation in Albany to help roll back prostitution, achieving impressive victories with the establishment of a women's night court (1907), the Page Law (1910)—later overturned by the State Court of Appeals this act required a medical examination of all individuals found guilty of prostitution—and a law (1914) penalizing landowners attached to the sex trade. After 1915 the Committee of Fifteen was replaced with a similar organization known as the Committee of Fourteen, which tried to restrict the trade through regulation rather than ban it outright, which was now seen as unrealistic. The association of Tammany Hall with prostitution was documented again in 1930–32 by the Seabury Investigations, revealing that the New York City Police Department and municipal courts regularly received bribes from houses of prostitution, and again in 1936, when New York State special prosecutor Thomas E. Dewey convicted Charles "Lucky" Luciano of running what was likely New York City's largest prostitution ring. Antivice reformers such as Republicans Dewey and Mayor Fiorello La Guardia, and Democrat governor Herbert H. Lehman all used the issue during the Great Depression to weaken Tammany Hall's grip on city affairs and to advance themselves politically.

After World War II a combination of political, technological, and demographic changes, including the automobile, telephones, and suburbanization, led to a geographical dispersal of prostitution; most of New York State's long tolerated red-light districts closed, the fate suffered by the tenderloins of Elmira and Syracuse. In July 1950 a New York State Police raid shuttered the brothels in Hudson for good, and in the next decade the houses in Albany's Gut locked their doors forever. At the same time some tenderloins found new uses. New York City's Times Square, long home to massage parlors that generally included prostitution as a service, transformed in the 1960s into a diverse commercial sex district that included adult novelty stores and bookstores, and pornographic movie theaters. However, the old discourse about "sex and the city" remained. Like the antiprostitution reformers of old, in the late 1990s New York City mayor Rudolph Guiliani was widely celebrated for "cleaning up" Times Square and for eliminating the visible signs of the sex industry. If history is any guide, it will not be the last time politicians in New York State battle urban prostitution and commercial sex.

Cohen, Patricia Cline. *The Murder of Helen Jewitt: The Life and Death of a Prostitute in 19th-Century New York* (New York: Knopf, 1998)
Gilfoyle, Timothy J. *City of Eros: New York City, Prostitution, and the Commercialization of Sex, 1790–1920* (New York: Norton, 1994)
Hall, Bruce Edward. *Diamond Street: The Story of the Little Town with the Big Red Light District* (Hensonville, NY: Black Dome Press, 1994)
Stolberg, Mary M. *Fighting Organized Crime: Politics, Justice, and the Legacy of Thomas E. Dewey* (Boston: Northeastern Univ Press, 1995)

Tod M. Ottman

Providence. Town (pop 1,841) in NW Saratoga Co. It was settled *ca* 1785 and formed from Galway in 1796. Its land, rough and infertile, lies partly in the Adirondack Park. Historically logging, woodenware shops, and tanneries provided employment. An aqueduct that feeds the Amsterdam (Montgomery Co) water supply, in operation since 1892, occupies a tenth of Providence's land area, including Ireland Vly. A county tuberculosis hospital, the Homestead, opened in 1914; it was used as the county nursing home from 1961 to 1979. Town population was at its lowest in 1950, at 369. Logging, summer cottages, and limited suburban development remain important land uses.

Field Horne

provincial congresses. During the early months of the American Revolution, New York was ruled by a series of four provincial congresses, or legislatures. Their rule lasted from the break with royal authority in May 1775 until the implementation of the first New York State constitution in 1777. The congresses were entirely extralegal, as the first was called popularly and convened without the imprimatur of the colonial government. New York's voters sanctioned four such congresses: the first met 22 May–4 Nov 1775; the second, 6 Dec 1775–13 May 1776; the third, 22 May 1776–30 June 1776; and the fourth, 9 July 1776–13 May 1777. While several prominent revolutionary firebrands served in the provincial congresses, representatives from the district of Vermont—home of the most radical figures in New York politics—were absent. Several members of the manorial families did participate, though their tenants had no representative of their own. The congresses consistently were dominated by wealthy, prestigious, moderate Whigs, who prevented the congresses from becoming too radical. The most significant of these men were Gouverneur Morris, Robert R. Livingston Jr, and John Jay. Chief among their concerns were the various facets of the war effort: raising and equipping military units, suppressing domestic resistance to the patriot cause, and appointing New York's representatives to the Continental Congress. When the Fourth Provincial Congress convened in White Plains (Westchester Co) on 9 July, it changed its name to Convention of the People. Chronically in military danger, members fled from town to town and building to building, depending on the latest British military deployments and the availability of physical facilities. Still, this group managed to draft a moderate, republican constitution that neither adhered unthinkingly to old ways nor abandoned all of New York's political traditions. The convention promulgated the constitution on 20 Apr 1777, and it dissolved three weeks later after making arrangements for implementing the new constitution.

See also CONSTITUTIONS AND CONSTITUTIONAL CONVENTIONS.

Countryman, Edward. *A People in Revolution: The American Revolution and Political Society in New York, 1760–1790* (Baltimore: Johns Hopkins Univ Press, 1981)
Mason, Bernard. *Road to Independence; The Revolutionary Movement in New York, 1773–1777* (Lexington: Univ of Kentucky Press, 1966)

K. R. Constantine Gutzman

Provoost, Samuel (*b* New York City, 26 Feb 1742; *d* New York City, 6 Sept 1815). Episcopal bishop. Provoost graduated from King's College (now Columbia University) in its first commencement in 1758. He received an MA in 1761, then traveled to England, entering St. Peter's College, Cambridge, as a fellow commoner. Ordained deacon, then priest in 1766, he returned to New York City, becoming assistant minister of Trinity Church in the same year. By 1769 his relations with the Trinity vestry soured, and they attempted to dismiss him, officially because of a lack of funds, but his theological criticism of Methodism and support for critics of British rule were more likely the reason, as he was probably the city's only pro-patriot Anglican cleric. The attempt to dismiss him failed, but he resigned in 1771, retiring to a farm in East Camp [now Germantown, Columbia Co]. Largely inactive in the ministry, he studied botany and languages, and he was cut off from his family's city income during the British occupation of New York City. Though supporting independence, he declined any public political role. In November 1783, just before the departure of British forces, the vestry of Trinity Church elected Benjamin Moore, a tory, as rector. Laypersons calling themselves Whig Episcopalians argued that the vestry's action was illegal and that Provoost should be made rector. The city's common council sided with the Whigs, and Provoost became rector on 21 Apr 1784. In 1785 he was appointed chaplain of the Continental Congress in Philadelphia. In 1786 he was elected first bishop of the Episcopal Diocese of New York and was consecrated in England in 1787. Because of ill health and family tragedies he resigned in 1801. With the election of John Henry Hobart as assistant bishop in 1811, Provoost attempted to reassert his office to block Hobart's High Church agenda but was unsuccessful.

Norton, John. *Life of Bishop Provoost of New York* (New York: General Protestant Episcopal Sunday School Union, and Church Book Society, 1859)

Robert Bruce Mullin

public authorities. See PUBLIC BENEFIT CORPORATIONS.

public baths. Over the course of the 19th century, homes of well-to-do New Yorkers increasingly included bathing facilities, but homes of the poor did not. To remedy this situation, middle-class reformers lobbied for the construction of public bathhouses. The Association for Improving the Condition of the Poor (AICP) initiated the state's first effort to provide bathing facilities for the poor when it opened a public bathhouse on Manhattan's Mott St in 1849. This provided laundry facilities as well as baths, but during the summer months only, and there was a charge of 3¢ an hour to use the laundry and 5–10¢ per bath, significant sums at the time. In the 1870s New York City created free outdoor bathhouses along the waterfront. They were also open only during the warm summer months, and concerns soon arose about the quality of the river water utilized.

Many reformers, increasingly impressed by the new germ theories of disease, worried that the squalid housing conditions of New York State's growing immigrant population created the risk of epidemics. Convinced that "cleansing" immigrants would help them adapt to US customs as well as reduce the risk of disease, public bathhouse proponents, led by New York City physician Simon Baruch, urged the construction of indoor bathhouses that could be open year-round. At the time, few residents of US cities had access to bathing facilities; fewer than 20% of urban residents in one 1887 survey reported access to a bathtub or shower. Citing public baths constructed in Europe as models, Baruch and other reformers successfully convinced the AICP to build the People's Bath on Manhattan's Lower East Side in 1891. It was an enormous success, attracting more than 100,000 patrons a year. Male and female patrons lined up at different entrances and paid 5¢ for a towel and a piece of soap and access to the baths. (Colgate Co had donated 80 lb [36 kg] of free soap to the institution.) The concrete and iron structure, which had the phrase "Cleanliness Next to Godliness" carved over its entryway, featured showers rather than tubs and thus was easy to keep clean.

By the 1890s the public bathhouse movement had spread to other cities in the state, and in 1895 the state legislature enacted a law requiring communities with populations of 50,000 or more to build free bathhouses. Over the next six years, municipal public baths were constructed in Albany, Buffalo, New York City, Rochester, Syracuse, Troy, Yonkers, and other cities across the state. Municipal public bathhouses typically included showers, laundries, swimming pools, and occasionally gymnasiums.

By the early 20th century, legislation required landlords to install running water and bathtubs in working-class housing; this signaled the end of the public bathhouse era. During the 1930s and 1940s, many bathhouses were torn down or converted to other uses. Most of the state's municipal bathhouses had closed by the end of World War II, although several remained open until the mid-1980s. Fear that patrons were spreading AIDS through sex at municipal bathhouses caused New York State lawmakers to allow local health officials to close them in 1985.

DeForest, Robert, et al, eds. *The Tenement House Problem* (1903; repr New York: Arno Press, 1970)
Williams, Marilyn Thornton. *Washing "The Great Unwashed": Public Baths in Urban America, 1840–1920* (Columbus: Ohio State Univ Press, 1991)

Stephen Long

public benefit corporations. Under New York State law, a public benefit corporation is a corporation organized to construct or operate a public facility totally or partially within the state, with any profits dedicated to the state. Such corporations typically are assigned the name "authority" in their respective enabling statutes. Public authorities in the United States date to an 1889 commission in Massachusetts. The first New York State public authority was the Port of New York Authority (now Port Authority of New York and New Jersey), created in 1921 by an interstate compact enacted by the state legislatures of New Jersey and New York, with the consent of the US Congress. Public authorities created during the 1920s and 1930s were concerned primarily with marine ports and bridges, and the Dormitory Authority (1944) and Thruway Authority (1950) were dedicated to developing other aspects of the state's infrastructure.

Most New York State authorities, like these early agencies, were created for a special purpose. More than 50 state public authorities and their subsidiary corporations exist to meet transportation and energy needs; some support the financing, construction, and operation of public facilities, and others promote education, public health, the arts, and economic development. There also are numerous local government public authorities responsible for parking facilities, public housing, and urban renewal. The governor often appoints the members of each state public authority board, subject to the advice and consent of the state senate, and designates the chairperson. In some cases board members are appointed by the legislature or by local governments. Public authorities submit annual reports to the governor, legislature, and state comptroller.

To assist the establishment of public authorities, the state legislature often makes a first-instance appropriation (ie, a loan) subject to repayment from the proceeds of securities issued by the corporation or from revenues generated by operations. The legislature has forgiven several loans made to deficit-incurring authorities. The legislature also determines the powers of each public authority to borrow funds by issuance of debt instruments. Only a few public authorities—the Port Authority of New York and New Jersey (via rolling stock), the Job Development Authority, and the Thruway Authority—have the right to issue bonds that have the "full faith and credit of the state." But since full-faith bonds require the approval of voters in a referendum, most early public benefit corporations issued revenue bonds with the principal and interest paid by user fees, for which no voter approval was required. Following from this logic, a major reason for the sharp increase in the number of state public authorities created during the governorship of Nelson A. Rockefeller (1959–73) was the desire to obtain financing for major programs through bond issues not submitted to the electorate.

Creation of the Housing Finance Agency in 1960 led to invention of the moral obligation bond, which establishes a procedure by which an authority whose reserve fund falls below the amount prescribed in the bond indenture must notify the governor. The governor in turn informs the legislature, which is expected to honor the enabling statute's stipulation that "the legislature shall apportion" the necessary funds to replenish the reserve fund. They generally carry a higher interest rate than bonds issued with a full-faith guarantee. In 1975 the Urban Development Corp (UDC) defaulted on $135 million in moral obligation bonds. Since the UDC's default the state legislature has been reluctant to invest authorities with broad discretionary powers. In 1976 the five-member Public Authorities Control Board (PACB) was created, which currently receives applications from 11 public authorities for the financing of projects. Moral obligation bonds are still issued although on a more restricted basis.

The pace of creation of new authorities began to decline in the 1980s, and only four new state authorities were created during the 1990s. Authorities created since 1980 generally are smaller and serve more specialized purposes, such as promoting the horse-racing industry and managing entities like the New York State Theatre Institute and the Roswell Park Cancer Institute. In 2000 the ten largest state public benefit corporations had assets totaling nearly $92 billion and annual operating revenues exceeding $12 billion. Despite their utility, critics have alleged that the creation of public authorities on an ad hoc basis fragments responsibility for solving regional and statewide problems, since each authority typically operates independently of other authorities, state departments, and local governments.

New York State Comptroller's Annual Report, 1998–1999: The Results of Audits at State Agencies and Public Authorities (Albany: Office of the State Comptroller, 2000)

Temporary State Commission on Coordination of State Activities. *Staff Report on Public Authorities under New York State* (Albany: Williams Press, 1956)

Underground Government: Preliminary Report on Authorities and Other Public Corporations. (New York: State of New York Commission on Government Integrity, 1990)

Winders, Edward E. "Public Authorities in New York State: The Interdependent Governmental Roles of the New York State Thruway Authority" (PhD diss, SUNY Albany, 1998)

Joseph F. Zimmerman

public broadcasting (radio and television). New York City was a hotbed of radio broadcasting experimentation in the early 20th century. WNYC, owned by the City of New York, went on the air July 1924. Originally for emergency communications, it was the first municipally owned noncommercial radio station in the country. A radio club at Columbia University operated a noncommercial radio frequency in the mid-1930s, which eventually became WKCR-FM. WNYE radio, the New York City Department of Education station, received a broadcast license in 1938. In 1940 the Federal Communications Commission (FCC) reserved 5 of the original 40 national radio broadcast channels for noncommercial educational radio stations and in 1952 reserved 242 channels nationally for noncommercial educational television. In 1953 the New York State Board of Regents secured FCC permits for seven educational television (ETV) channels on ultrahigh frequency (UHF) channels and asked the commissioner of education to establish a process through which New York community groups could gain access to ETV broadcasting, ultimately granting charters to educational groups to incorporate. The first was to the Mohawk-Hudson Educational Television Council in June 1953. Their station, WMHT-TV, began broadcasting from the Riverside School in Schenectady 26 Mar 1962, the second ETV station in the state, and moved to its Rotterdam (Schenectady Co) facility in 1969. The first ETV signal in New York State originated from WNED-TV Buffalo on 30 Mar 1959. The first ETV station serving New York City was WNDT, now Thirteen/WNET, which signed on 16 Sept 1962.

Over the next 25 years, all of the Regent's FCC construction permits were transferred to local organizations that became licensees of ETV stations, and since 1977 noncommercial "public" television signals have been available statewide. Each station operates as an independent entity. The television stations have always had a close working relationship with the State Department of Education, which in the early 1970s provided aid to schools for equipment to use the educational programming the stations broadcast. In the 1960s the stations charged the schools $1 per student to help finance the cost of acquiring and producing instructional programs. SUNY created a microwave interconnection system in October 1967, the New York Network (NYN), that allowed the stations to share programming easily and essentially established an informal state ETV network. This system lasted until December 1994. NYN now operates as a satellite distribution system and still provides some services to the Public Broadcasting Service (PBS) stations.

Growth of Public Broadcasting

The Carnegie Corp of New York established the Carnegie Commission on Educational Television in 1965 to study public broadcasting and in January 1967 issued "Public Television, A Program for Action." There was no mention of radio, and advocates lobbied for its inclusion. On 7 Nov 1967 the US Congress passed the Public Broadcasting Act, amended to include radio, to develop noncommercial television and radio, and authorizing federal aid to stations through a new agency, the Corporation for Public Broadcasting (CPB). CPB and PBS, which incorporated on 3 Nov 1969, are prohibited from owning broadcast stations or producing programs. PBS is a membership organization and provides services to the stations, such as aggregating program funds, program distribution, and promotion. National Public Radio (NPR), founded in 1970, is different from PBS in that it is permitted to produce programs, a function central to its purpose. Each public broadcasting station licensee is independent and autonomous from CPB, NPR, and PBS, and though there is a high degree of coordination among stations, the industry as a whole is decentralized.

ETV received state funding as early as 1956. In 1973 the nine public television stations receiving New York State funding established an association to represent their interests, the Association of Public Television Stations of New York (now Association of Public Broadcasting Stations). There is no counterpart for New York's public radio stations. In 1978 the legislature passed Chapter 236 of the State Education Law, which provided significant operational and capital funds to public television and radio stations, using a formula that combined base grants and incentives. Television stations were required to devote at least 20% of their state funds to educational programs for their local schools. State law was amended by the Public Television and Radio Act of 1981, which permitted funding.

SELECTED PUBLIC BROADCASTING RADIO STATIONS

Call Letters	Channel	Licensee	Location
WAMC-FM	90.3[a]	Northeast Public Radio	Albany
WSQX-FM	91.5	WSKG Public Telecommunications Council	Binghamton
WSKG-FM	89.3	WSKG Public Telecommunications Council	Vestal (Broome Co)
WFUV-FM	90.7	Fordham University	Bronx
WNYE-FM	91.5	New York City Board of Education	Brooklyn
WBFO-FM	88.7	State University of New York	Buffalo
WNED-AM	970	Western New York Public Broadcasting Assn	Buffalo
WNED-FM	94.5	Western New York Public Broadcasting Assn	Buffalo
WSLU-FM	89.5[a]	St. Lawrence University	Canton (St. Lawrence Co)
WNYC-AM	820	WNYC Foundation	Manhattan
WNYC-FM	93.9	WNYC Foundation	Manhattan
WRVO-FM	89.9[a]	State University of New York	Oswego
WXXI-AM	1370	WXXI Public Broadcasting Council	Rochester
WXXI-FM	91.5	WXXI Public Broadcasting Council	Rochester
WMHT-FM	89.1[a]	WMHT Educational Telecommunications	Schenectady
WPBX-FM	88.3	Long Island University	Southampton (Suffolk Co)
WCNY-FM	91.3	Public Broadcasting Council of Central New York	Syracuse
WAER-FM	88.3	Syracuse University	Syracuse

Source: Corporation for Public Broadcasting, http://www.cpb.org/radio/stations/.

[a]Main channel of licensee, which also owns other stations.

Compiled by Howard Lowe

Most public radio and television stations rely on a funding mix of federal, state, and private sources. To better represent their interests, in 1979 PBS television stations nationally formed a lobbying group, America's Public Television Stations. Both radio and television stations have since the 1980s increased their focus on raising money from private sources, especially listeners, viewers, and corporate underwriters. WBAI in New York City, with a history of supporting left-wing political causes, is the only noncommercial listener-supported radio station without corporate sponsorship in New York State. Fund-raising or "pledge drives" use on-air, mail, and Internet membership appeals. New York State initially administered ETV and radio support through the Bureau of Mass Communications, beginning in 1965. In 2003 funding to New York State public stations flowed through the State Education Department (SED) budget. The state budget allocated public radio and television $13.8 million in fiscal year 2003–4, the same amount received the previous year. The remaining funding comes from federal and private sources. The Office of Educational Television and Public Broadcasting, a department of the Cultural Education Division of SED established in 1990, provides oversight of the annual station grants, acts as a liaison to the stations, and participates in planning station services to the schools.

Recent History

Over the years, public television stations have remained close to their educational roots but have significantly diversified their programming to provide an alternative to commercial television. The PBS stations have been leaders in developing high-quality children's, "how to," science, public affairs, and cultural programs. Increasing competition from specialty channels on cable and satellite has cut into all broadcasters' audiences. Public television's national audience reached a high point in 1986–87, when on an average night over 2.3 million households tuned in during prime time. An estimated 1.7 million households watched public television nightly in 2002. Many of the New York State stations produce programs seen on PBS. Thirteen/WNET in New York City is one of the largest such producers, and its series have included *NET Playhouse* (1966), *Sesame Street* (1969), and *The Robert MacNeil Report* (1975; now *The NewsHour with Jim Lehrer*). Other stations with PBS series include WXXI (Rochester), *Assignment: The World* (1959), WNED (Buffalo), *Reading Rainbow* (1985), and WPBS (Watertown), *Rod and Reel* (1985).

In 1997 the City of New York sold WNYC-TV to a commercial network, and the AM and FM stations to the WNYC Foundation. In 2001 licensees of the Long Island public television station WLIW Channel 21 and Thirteen/WNET agreed to consolidate their operations; WLIW became a part of Thirteen/WNET in 2003, when the agreement was finalized. Many public broadcast licensees own radio and television stations, called "joint licensees." These are in Rochester, Syracuse, Schenectady, Buffalo, and Binghamton. New York City, Long Island, Plattsburgh, and Watertown licensees operate only television stations. In addition to the radio stations operated by joint licensees, there are several public radio networks and individual stations in New York State, such as North Country Public Radio at St. Lawrence University in Canton (St. Lawrence Co). Every New York State citizen can receive a public radio signal. The national audience of public radio has grown steadily nearly every year since 1970 and reached more than 22 million listeners each week in 2003 via more than 680 stations. Each public radio station in New York State produces programs for its local audience. In September 1995 PBS Online debuted on the Internet. Public radio and television also use the Internet for program information, event promotion, viewer interaction, a station store, and children's activities. All public television broadcasters were mandated by the FCC to broadcast a digital and an analog signal by May 2003. The target date Congress set for the transition to digital television (DTV) is 31 Dec 2006. DTV allows multicasting, or the broadcast of several simultaneous channels, each offering audio, video, graphics, and text data. DTV can be broadcast in high definition, which offers extremely crisp wide-screen pictures and CD-quality sound. The first noncommercial New York State television station to broadcast a digital signal was WNYE in Brooklyn in 2001.

See also Broadcasting (radio and television); Television, cable.

PUBLIC BROADCASTING TELEVISION STATIONS

Call Letters	Channel	Licensee	Location
WSKG-TV	46	WSKG Public Telecommunications Council	Binghamton
WNYE-TV	25	New York City Department of Education	Brooklyn
WNED-TV	17	Western New York Public Broadcasting Association	Buffalo
WNET-TV	13	Educational Broadcasting Corporation	New York City
WLIW-TV	21	Educational Broadcasting Corporation	Plainview (Nassau Co)
WCFE-TV	57	Mountain Lake Public Telecommunications	Plattsburgh
WXXI-TV	21	WXXI Public Broadcasting Council	Rochester
WMHT-TV	17	WMHT Educational Telecommunications	Schenectady
WCNY-TV	24	Public Broadcasting Council of Central New York	Syracuse
WPBS-TV	16	St. Lawrence Valley Educational Television Council	Watertown[a]

Source: Corporation for Public Broadcasting, http://www.pbs.org/.

[a]Also operates WNPI-TV, Channel 18, in Norwood (St. Lawrence Co).

Compiled by Howard Lowe

Halligan, William J. *Historical Note: Educational Television (ETV) and the State Education Department* (Albany: Office of Educational Television and Public Broadcasting, NYS Education Department, Feb 1995)

Jaker, Bill, Frank Sulek, and Peter Kanze. *The Airwaves of New York* (Jefferson, NC: McFarland, 1998)

Witherspoon, John, et al. *A History of Public Broadcasting* (Washington, DC: Current Publishing Committee, 2000)

Howard Lowe

public education. In the late 18th century, Gov George Clinton and other proponents of state-supported mass education argued that the new republic could survive only if it had an educated citizenry. In 1789 the New York State legislature authorized the Board of Regents of the University of the State of New York to oversee state funding to private academies. In 1795 it offered state funds and land grants as incentives to organize common schools providing instruction in basic reading, writing, and mathematics. These schools were optional, often run by churches, and open to all children in the district.

Organization of School Districts

After early plans failed to stimulate widespread growth of common schools, the legislature enacted the Common School Act of 1812, which created a state superintendent of common schools, detailed the creation and operation of local school districts across the mostly rural state, and promised annual state aid to those schools. The law was a major success; the number of school districts rapidly expanded from 2,756 in 1815 to 10,769 by 1843. In a separate act in 1813, the legislature promised state funds to private and church-run charity schools in New York City to act as the city's common schools. In both cases, the legislature demonstrated little interest in regulating these schools or in creating a state administrative body to oversee them.

Left largely to their own devices, city and town districts elected trustees, hired teachers, chose textbooks, paid for schoolhouses out of their own pockets, and settled ideological differences internally, only rarely appealing to the state for help. In densely populated areas, the common school system did not clearly differentiate between public, private, and religious schooling. For example, Elmira, Troy, Poughkeepsie, Ogdensburg, Niagara Falls, and at least six other cities and towns operated explicitly Catholic public schools. Local control did have problems, however. Rural education was disorganized, unprofessional, and inequitable, increasingly lagging behind cities in the quality of teachers, facilities, and resources. Many rural common schools charged partial tuition if their state grant ran out before the end of an academic term, a practice the legislature banned in 1867. City schools of the common school era failed to serve a significant percentage of children, particularly immigrants and the poor. Statewide, women could not vote in school district elections until 1880, and Blacks faced legal segregation until the 20th century.

Common schools gradually developed into recognizably modern public schools. In 1842, as a result of Catholic Church challenges to New York City's privatized and overtly Protestant model of common schools, the legislature reformed the city's system to resemble the model used elsewhere in the state. In 1854 the legislature created a formal Department of Public Instruction to assist the state superintendent of public instruction with the collection and publication of statistics, the adjudication of disputes, the enforcement of state law, and the disbursement of state funds. The legislature passed a compulsory attendance law 20 years later, though most districts did not enforce it. In an attempt to stamp out local arrangements between church and state, the state constitution of 1894 prohibited public money to church schools and prohibited public schools from offering sectarian instruction. In 1904 the legislature consolidated the Board of Regents and the Department of Public Instruction, renaming it the State Education Department. Increasing state regulations on curriculum and teacher certification, revised compulsory attendance laws, and a new system of state aid to school districts in 1902 fundamentally changed how leaders understood the relationship between the state and the public school. The change was exemplified by Superintendent Andrew S. Draper's declaration in an 1897 appeals decision that "The common school system of the State is a State and not a local system."

Reform in the 20th Century

Not until the early 20th century did the state's publicly funded primary and secondary schools match the modern conception of a public school—free of charge, secular, and state regulated. In several major waves of change, 20th-century reformers targeted the diversity of the public that public schools were designed to serve. Progressive era reformers such as Nicholas Murray Butler, Andrew Draper, and William Henry Maxwell attempted to redress 19th-century failures of common schools for working-class, poor, and immigrant children. They applied the business model of scientific management to school administration, making schools more centralized and efficient. While nearly all incorporated cities in the 1870s and 1880s ran their schools through ward-based trustees and the weak central boards of education they comprised, by 1904 progressive reformers in all major cities had abolished ward control over schools, and only 7 of the state's 45 cities maintained any ward system at all. These new central boards of education redesigned and expanded school curricula. From 1898 to 1916, New York City school superintendent William Henry Maxwell spearheaded a major overhaul of the city's schools: vastly increasing seating capacity (even running double sessions) to accommodate children who had previously been turned away; expanding school curricula to include vocational and industrial training; and offering special classes for children with disabilities, night schools for youth and adults who worked, and medical inspections.

While New York State never forbade children of African descent from attending public schools, a state law in 1841 formally allowed what had already been common practice: local policies of segregation. Throughout the 19th century, Blacks fought against separate schools at the local level, often with success. Finally, in 1900, a coalition of black activists, including Elisabeth Cisco, M. R. Poole, and William H. Johnson, and of white progressives, including Republican senator Nathaniel Elsberg and Gov Theodore Roosevelt, successfully pressed the legislature to pass Chapter 492, which repealed the 1841 state law allowing segregated schools and guaranteed that "no person shall be refused admission into or be excluded from any public school in the state of New York on account of race or color." The law left a legal loophole for Union Free School districts, however, that permitted segregated schools if most of a district's residents wanted them. In 1938 a state commission on the social conditions of Blacks recommended that the legislature repeal the loophole, which it did that year. The US Supreme Court's 1954 landmark decision in *Brown v Board of Education* that segregated schooling was unconstitutional touched off a decades-long struggle in cities across the state to achieve equal educational opportunity for minority students, who attended increasingly homogeneous urban schools as Whites moved out of urban centers, by attempting to integrate schools through busing, redistricting, and magnet schools. In the final decades of the century, urban school reformers also targeted poverty as another unaddressed form of diversity in the public system. Beginning with *Levittown v Nyquist* (1978, 1982), advocates of state aid reform launched a series of political and legal challenges to the state's system of aid to schools.

Recent Developments

In 2001 New Yorkers spent over $26 billion, or $12,000 per pupil, on the state's system of public pre-kindergarten, primary, and secondary schools, ranking among the highest rates per pupil in the nation. The State Education Department reaches into the lives of all school-aged

South Side Grammar School, Jamestown, early 20th century.

children, even those who do not attend public schools. The state regulates private schools and also maintains some of the nation's most stringent requirements for home schooling, in both cases insisting that these educational alternatives follow a parallel path to the public school curriculum. Current reform efforts pull public schools in different directions at once, revealing deep-seated differences of opinion about the purpose of public education. The charter school movement seeks to undo the bureaucracy and size of public schools, allowing them to operate under special charters within the public system but outside its standard set of regulations. In fall 2001 there were 32 operating in New York State. Standards advocates hope to expand Regents testing and emphasize traditional academic subjects. Critics of state aid to schools hope to reform the reliance on local property taxes to fund public education. Finally, voucher advocates seek to end the separation between private and public education with voucher programs to provide taxpayer funds for parents who wish to send their children to private or parochial schools. Reformers targeting the challenges of inner-city, minority students have moved from integration toward equalized state aid and often espouse broader movements like charters, vouchers, and standards.

See also AMERICAN INDIANS: POLICIES SINCE 1776; LIBRARIES; MENTAL RETARDATION AND DEVELOPMENTAL DISABILITIES; STATE GOVERNMENT AND SERVICES.

Finegan, Thomas E. *Judicial Decisions of the State Superintendent of Common Schools, State Superintendent of Public Instruction, State Commissioner of Education from 1822 to 1913* (Albany: Univ of the State of New York, 1914)

Mabee, Carleton. *Black Education in New York State from Colonial to Modern Times* (Syracuse: Syracuse Univ Press, 1979)

Randall, Samuel S. *The Common School System of the State of New York* (Troy, NY: John & Davis, Steam Press Printers, 1851)

Ravitch, Dianne. *The Great School Wars: New York City, 1805–1973* (New York: Basic Books, 1974)

Benjamin Justice

Public Employees Federation (PEF). See PUBLIC EMPLOYEES UNIONS.

public employees unions. One of the most important sectors of the unionized workforce. The slow pace of the civil servants' unionization can be attributed to a "white-collar" mentality on the part of many and, of probably greater significance, to government's great reluctance to enter into collective bargaining with public employees or to countenance job actions. Public employees did form mutual benefit associations, such as the Patrolman's Benevolent Association formed by members of the New York City Police Department as early as 1894. Teachers, transportation and sanitation workers, social workers, healthcare professionals, firefighters, and police officers formed similar organizations in many cities in the state in the early decades of the 20th century. Some of these organizations took pains to distinguish themselves from unions, however, and few engaged in collective bargaining with governmental authorities.

In 1910 New York State employees seeking to improve working conditions formed the Association of State Civil Service Employees, which became the Civil Service Employees Association (CSEA) after 1946. The organization lobbied for improvement of the civil service administration, protection of career tenure, adequate salaries, and retirement provisions under the leadership of its first president, William M. Thomas of the Department of Law, who served until 1918. Successful CSEA lobbying continued into the 1920s with the New York State Retirement System being signed into law by Gov Alfred E. Smith in 1920. Notable policies instituted during the 1930s include the first State Employee Credit Union, sick leave, and abolition of the 72-hour workweek for institutional employees. In 1937 the Feld-Hamilton Act defined a state salary plan with provisions for appeals, and campaigns in the 1940s and 1950s established pension plans for state employees in the military and overtime pay and extra pay for hazardous work.

Despite much progress, the CSEA still lacked several notable union prerogatives. It did not have the right to enter into collective bargaining agreements with New York State, although few public employee unions in the state did. In New York City, Mayor Fiorello La Guardia (1933–45) permitted workers to join unions but refused to allow formal bargaining, even after the city acquired the strongly unionized private subway lines in 1940. It was not until 1958 that the right was granted. CSEA members and other public employees also had no right to strike or have job actions. This restriction was reinforced by the Condon-Wadlin Act of 1947, which prohibited public sector strikes and mandated the firing of striking workers. It had been passed in the wake of the federal Taft-Hartley Act of the same year and a rash of strikes, sympathy strikes, and threatened strikes in the immediate postwar years, including the Rochester General Strike of 1946. But Condon-Wadlin's draconian provisions proved unenforceable, and after strikes by New York City teachers and especially by its transit workers in 1966 that closed the subways, it was replaced in 1967 by the Taylor Law, which put in place steep fines rather than mandatory firing and for the first time permitted state employees to engage in collective bargaining. It also created the Public Employment Relations Board (PERB), which works to facilitate union recognition and labor-management contract negotiations and to arbitrate any unresolved disputes.

Union activity swelled in the late 1960s and early 1970s. Other large unions began to represent state workers. The Public Employee Federation (PEF) is the second-largest public employee union in New York State, representing 55,000 professional, technical, and scientific employees; it includes private sector jobs and local government agencies such as the Albany County Probation Department, Albany Housing Authority, and the New York State Canal Corp. The United University Professions (UUP), founded in 1973, is the organization that faculty and nonteaching professions of the State University of New York (SUNY) use to bargain collectively. In the late 1970s CSEA became the largest affiliate of the American Federation of State, County, and Municipal Employees (AFSCME), creating a powerful partnership that protected CSEA from rival unions. In 2003 New York State membership in CSEA totaled 265,000, including private sector employees and retirees.

CSEA Local 1000 AFSCME, AFL-CIO, http://www.csealocal1000.org/

Public Employees Federation, AFL-CIO, http://www.pef.org/

Stieber, Jack. *Public Employee Unionism: Structure, Growth, Policy* (Washington, DC: Brookings Institution, 1973)

Amybeth Gregory

Public Employment Relations Board. Independent agency established by the New York State legislature in 1967 as part of the Public Employees' Fair Employment Act, commonly known as the Taylor Law. The law granted public

Civil Service Employees Association march in Syracuse, *ca* 1989.

employees throughout the state the right to join unions and required state and local governments to bargain with unions regarding the terms and conditions of their members' public service. Although the Taylor Law permitted collective bargaining, it continued the prohibition on strikes by state employees. The Public Employment Relations Board (PERB) has three major functions. First, it provides dispute resolution services to the more than 4,300 collective bargaining units that, as of 1 Jan 2002, represented the state's public employees. Services include impasse resolution, arbitration, mediation, and the handling of grievance procedures. Second, PERB certifies and decertifies bargaining agents for public service workers, also determining the eligibility of specific job classifications for collective bargaining representation. Third, PERB prosecutes cases arising from the Taylor Law prohibition on public employee strikes before administrative law judges (ALJs). ALJ recommendations are then forwarded to PERB's Board for a final determination. The Board consists of three members appointed by the governor to six-year terms, subject to confirmation by the New York State Senate. The governor designates one member as chair, and no more than two board members may be from the same political party. The Board sets policy and procedures, issues final agency rulings, assigns penalties, and maintains a panel of neutral labor relations experts to provide mediation, fact-finding, and arbitration services. An executive director heads the agency's Office of Administration; a deputy chairman serves as the Board's chief legal advisor, responsible for the Office of the Counsel and Office of Public Employment Practices and Representation; there is also a director of the Office of Conciliation. In 2002 PERB had 42 employees. The agency assisted in negotiating 335 state and local contracts, conducted 14 union certification elections, and wrote 271 decisions in negotiation and employment cases. PERB is headquartered in Albany with regional offices in Buffalo and Brooklyn.

Jeffrey Kraus

public health. Early public health efforts in the United States revolved around controlling epidemic disease and sanitation. The prevailing notion from colonial times to the mid–19th century was that unknown airborne substances, identified by their noxious odors, caused sickness. Ordinances were frequently passed, if not always enforced, in New York City and other places, calling for the elimination of garbage and animal droppings, drainage of stagnant puddles and pools, eviction of livestock living within town limits, and covering up privy stench with liberal amounts of lime. Lodgings of disease victims were fumigated with sulfur. Temporary hospitals, often called pest houses, were established to isolate the sick so that their exhalations would not infect others. Although New York Colony in 1754 established quarantine regulations to guard against the introduction of epidemics, major outbreaks of deadly disease, including smallpox (1679–80, 1689–90, 1702, 1731) and yellow fever (1702, 1731, 1742, 1743), were regular occurrences throughout the colonial period.

Other than establishing institutions for the custodial care of people with severe disabilities, New York's state government had little to do with the health of its citizens in the early post-Revolutionary years. Public healthcare was primarily a local issue, and municipalities took it seriously only when threatened. With New York City's growth as an ocean port visited by many potentially disease-carrying vessels, the state legislature in 1796 allowed the city to establish local sanitation laws. As inland settlements grew into villages, towns, and cities, they followed suit whenever epidemics of yellow fever (erupting nearly every year from 1791 to 1822), smallpox, or other contagions loomed. Ports along Lakes Ontario and Erie enacted quarantine ordinances to prevent sick immigrants, entering the heartland via Quebec and Montreal, from infecting those on shore; officials of canal ports adopted similar regulations in the 1820s. As railroads reached across the state in the 1830s, growing towns and villages likewise took protective measures, particularly with the concurrent emergence of cholera as an ongoing health threat. Outbreaks of cholera in 1832 and 1849 killed thousands. Typically, however, local boards of health were underfunded and hostage to political and economic interests. In many cases, they dissolved as soon as the threat of contagion passed.

From 1827 practicing physicians were required to belong to county medical societies, which had been established by state statute in 1806 to examine and license those who claimed to be doctors. However, disputes and competition among the various schools of medicine—"regulars," Thomsonians, homeopaths, and others—diluted the power of many of the societies, and several ceased regulating the practice of medical professionals in their jurisdictions. In many communities benevolent societies, supported by philanthropists and church congregations, often responded more actively to community illness than did local governments. City-appointed physicians, paid a small stipend for their services, regularly visited the homes of the impoverished, identified those needing medical assistance, notified city physicians, and hired nurses for in-home care when needed. For the "undeserving poor"—the ne'er-do-wells, vagrants, alcoholics, and other undesirables—counties established infirmaries within their poorhouses.

From 1860 to 1933

The germ theory of disease, popularized in the late 19th century, held out hope that contagious disease could be controlled. For the first time there was reason to believe that the deadliest diseases—cholera; malaria; yellow, scarlet, puerperal, and typhoid fevers; diphtheria; typhus; and tuberculosis—might some day be prevented. Although accurate indices of morbidity and mortality were not available until well into the 20th century, vital statistics were reported at central municipal locations from the mid–19th century, revealing patterns that prompted officials to take a more active role in public health work. Equipped with the new scientific procedures and determined to increase the life span of their citizens, larger metropolitan health bureaus began to test water sources, milk, and the condition of dairies. Slowly, municipal reservoirs replaced backyard wells, and sewers and indoor water closets replaced privy vaults, whose drainage often contaminated well water. Ordinances prevented farmers from feeding their cows brewery sludge, required pasteurization, culled tubercular cows from herds, and closed unclean dairies for careless handling of milk.

The rapid progress in public health that these advances made possible is exemplified in the careers of George W. Goler and Ernest Wende. The industrious Goler, Rochester's chief health officer from 1896 to 1932, enforced sanitary regulations for dairy and other food products, established milk distribution stations for low-income mothers (1897; succeeded in the 1910s by child welfare clinics), modernized the sewer and waste removal systems, mitigated a 1902 smallpox outbreak with free vaccinations, created hygiene education programs for immigrants, opened public dental clinics (1905, 1910), and launched an antituberculosis campaign that led to the creation of a sanatorium (1910). Wende, as Buffalo's first health commissioner (1892–1902, 1907–10), initiated many similar reforms, promoting epidemiological research, reducing typhoid morbidity through sewer improvements, and alerting the public to the dangers of unsanitary baby bottles.

Physicians of the "regular" school embraced the new science of bacteriology immediately, and their reputations soared. Having won the competition among conflicting theories of disease, they reorganized county societies. In 1880 the New York State Board of Health (now Department of Health) was organized, its membership consisting of reputable physicians from across the state. A minuscule budget allowed for little more than the collection of vital statistics, laboratory investigations of substances for impurities and adulterations, field explorations arising from complaints about contagious diseases, examinations into ventilation and sanitation of public buildings, and analyses of polluted streams. But the real impetus for change was a sensitizing of the public to the plight of the impoverished immigrant. Exposés of the deplorable hovels in which huge numbers of newly arrived foreigners lived and revelations about abusive factory conditions in industrialized communities, such as Jacob Riis's *How the Other Half Lives* (1890), energized social activists and sparked an increase in philanthropy.

New York City was a pioneer in applying the breakthroughs in bacteriology and other fields toward improvements of public health. The Metropolitan Board of Health, created in 1866 after a cholera epidemic, was broadly empowered to deal with disease and potential contagious situations. Hermann M. Biggs opened the first municipal bacteriological laboratory in the county in 1892, introduced diphtheria antitoxin in 1894, and established a number of controversial institutions where tuberculosis sufferers could be sequestered, involuntarily if necessary. He was state commissioner of health from 1914 to 1923. His colleague Homer Folks, New York commissioner of Public Charities (1902–3), was instrumental in passing the state's Public Health Law (1913) and Public Welfare Law (1921), and in the opening of the East Harlem Health Center (1921), the first neighborhood health center in the city. Lillian Wald's Henry Street Settlement and mobile nursing service (1893), forerunner of the Visiting Nurse Service of New York, made nurses a permanent presence in impoverished Lower East Side communities.

These innovations spread rapidly to other cities, where the poor continued to be the focus of public health efforts. Progressive organizations established milk stations where impoverished mothers could buy a wholesome product at cost and where trained nurses instructed them about keeping their babies, their families, and themselves healthy. District and visiting nurses entered homes and taught good health practices to mothers and toddlers. Settlement houses offered classes in hygiene, lent their facilities to groups trying to improve working conditions, and opened backyard playgrounds for children who had grown up on unhealthy city streets. Physicians gave free medical and dental examinations in New York State's schools, and health education entered the curriculum, taught by school nurses. Clinics opened for the removal of diseased adenoids and tonsils. The public pediatric health mission became two-pronged: not only to cure the sick child but to ensure that the child would grow into a healthy adult through preventative medicine and education.

From 1933 to the Present

When the massive unemployment of the depression years threatened the health of the state's residents, the New York State legislature joined with the federal and local governments to provide health-related relief to its citizens, passing the Wicks Act in 1933. Not only were municipalities able to open soup kitchens and provide free health services to the needy, but public health workers increasingly began to serve rural populations. These efforts in part explain the relative good health of World War II recruits, in contrast to the high percentage of malnourished or sick men rejected for service in World War I. The intragovernmental partnership has continued, with the federal government supporting state and local public health initiatives, Medicare and Medicaid (1965) being the most obvious examples, and the state benefiting from federal research.

Since World War II sulfonamides and penicillin have all but eliminated the most dreaded diseases of the 19th century. Poliomyelitis, a virus-borne crippler of children and young adults throughout the first half of the 20th century, was rendered insignificant in the 1950s with the Salk and Sabin vaccines. Since 1981 the AIDS epidemic has spawned a dramatic public health effort, including the closing of public bathhouses on the grounds that they were sources of infection, and the formation of organizations such as the New York City–based Gay Men's Health Crisis (1981). In 2000 the state legislature created ESAP (Expanded Syringe Access Demonstration Program), a syringe distribution and safe disposal program designed to reduce AIDS transmission through needle sharing. Tuberculosis, formerly controlled by a series of antibiotic shots, threatens to return in a more resistant form. With global travel growing, exotic diseases like Ebola, SARS (Severe Acute Respiratory Syndrome), and dengue fever, for which there are not yet effective treatments, may invade the United States at any time.

With increased good health supported by the efforts of public health advocates, workers, and officials, New Yorkers are living longer. Thus, since the end of World War II, the focus of public health has increasingly shifted to the chronic diseases of aging, such as heart disease, arteriosclerosis, diabetes, and arthritis. The EPIC (Elderly Pharmaceutical Insurance Coverage) program, launched in 1987, subsidizes prescription drug purchases for seniors. The centerpiece of the state's vigorous antismoking campaign, the Clean Indoor Air Act (1989, expanded 2003), bans smoking in public areas and workplaces, including bars and most restaurants. In the aftermath of the 11 Sept 2001 terrorist attacks in New York City and Washington, DC, bioterrorism has become a significant public health issue, prompting efforts by the Health Department to educate citizens on the symptoms, transmission, and treatment of biological agents such as anthrax, botulinum toxin, plague, and smallpox. New York State has been a national leader in promoting traffic safety. The state was the first to enact laws requiring motorists to wear seat belts (1984) and prohibiting use of handheld cell phones while driving (2001).

See also Environmentalism; Pollution; Rights; State government and services; Tobacco industry and smoking; Water supply and use (non–New York City watershed).

Duffy, John. *A History of Public Health in New York City*, 2 vols (New York: Russell Sage Foundation, 1968–74)
Epstein, Beryl. *Lillian Wald: Angel of Henry Street* (New York: Messner, 1948)
Lehr, Teresa K., and Philip G. Maples. *To Serve the Community: A Celebration of Rochester General Hospital, 1847–1997* (Virginia Beach, Va: Donning, 1997)
Ravenel, Mazyck, ed. *A Half Century of Public Health: Jubilee Historical Volume of the American Public Health Association* (New York: American Public Health Association, 1921)
Rochester Health Bureau. *50 Years of Health in Rochester, New York, 1900–1950* (Rochester: Author, 1950)
Rosner, David, ed. *Hives of Sickness: Public Health and Epidemics in New York City* (New Brunswick, NJ: Rutgers Univ Press, 1995)
Rosner, David, and Amy Fairchild. "Historical Perspectives on New York City Health," *International Journal of Mental Health* 28 (Winter 1999–2000)
Trattner, Walter I. *From Poor Law to Welfare State: A History of Social Welfare in America*, 6th ed. (New York: Free Press, 1999)
Williams, Ralph Chester. *The United States Public Health Service, 1798–1950* (Washington, DC: Commissioned Officers Association of the US Public Health Service, 1951)

Teresa K. Lehr

Public Security, Office of. A cabinet-level agency established under an executive order by Gov George E. Pataki on 10 Oct 2001. As a response to the terrorist attack that destroyed the World Trade Center on 11 Sept 2001, the office was charged with coordinating and enhancing efforts to identify terrorist threats and to prevent terrorist attacks within the state. It served as liaison with the federal Office of Homeland Security (now Department of Homeland Security) and with its counterparts in other states. It was granted no powers of arrest. The founding director was James K. Kallstrom, former assistant director in charge of the FBI's New York field office. There was considerable turnover in leadership, and new directors were appointed in 2002 and 2003 while Kallstrom continued as an unpaid senior adviser to the governor. In its first months, the office was credited with developing national models for the protection of airports, nuclear power plants, and other key facilities. It also created the computerized Counter-Terrorism Network, which disseminates information to local law enforcement officials and state and local task forces on subjects such as bioterrorism. The office assisted in the elaboration of a security plan, implemented in 2003 during the Iraq War, which called for dispatching National Guard troops and state police to bolster security on the Canadian border. It also allowed Connecticut and New Jersey authorities to help patrol commuter trains from those states. The office's headquarters are located on 3d Ave in New York City. In 2004 the office had a budget of $14.8 million and a full-time staff of 25. Plans were announced that year to create, by statute, an Office of Homeland Security to supersede the Public Security Office.

New York State Office of Public Security, http://www.state.ny.us/security

Scott C. Monje

Public Service, Department of (Public Service Commission). Established in 1907 as two commissions, one to regulate utility services in New York City (Commission for the First District) and the other to regulate such services elsewhere in the state (Commission for the Second District). The Public Service Law adopted that year and signed by Gov Charles Evans Hughes was one of the first instances of a state moving from municipal to statewide regulation of utilities. The commissions were responsible for setting just and reasonable rates and regulating services. As technology and the economy grew, so did the scope of jurisdiction. Telephone and telegraph services were added in 1910 and steam service in 1913. The two commissions were united in 1921 and became known as the Public Service Commission. Transportation services were added in 1926, water companies in 1931, and cable television in 1996. The commission has been a national leader in the area of utility regulation. It was the first to regulate accounting practices, which led to the National Uniform System of Accounts in 1934, and to require competitive bidding for the underwriting of utility securities (1944), rate-making adjustments to protect consumers from holding company abuses (1966), and competition among natural gas commodity suppliers (1985).

Since 1970, the Public Service Law has provided that no more than a bare majority of the commissioners may be members of the same political party. In the last half of the 1990s, the commission introduced competitive options for the state's retail electric, natural gas, and telephone customers and oversaw the licensing of new electric-generating facilities aimed at meeting increasing demand for power. The commission consists of five members, serving staggered six-year terms, each appointed by the governor and confirmed by the senate. The governor can increase the number to seven at the request of the commission. The chair of the commission heads the sitting boards that review applications for licensing of major generating and transmission facilities and is the chief executive officer of the Department of Public Service, which is staffed by state employees who assist the Public Service Commission in its work.

Ward, Robert B. *New York State Government: What It Does, How It Works* (Albany: Rockefeller Institute Press, 2002)

William S. Helmer

Public Service Commission. See Public Service, Department of (Public Service Commission).

publishing industry. Trade group that embraces book publishers and associated companies and individuals, including book wholesalers and retailers—of both new and used editions—literary agents, authors, and critics.

Foundation

The first printing press in America was established in Cambridge, Mass, in 1638. Some 55 years later, in 1693, New York City acquired its first printer and book retailer when William Bradford opened his shop, staying active for 50 years. Boston and Philadelphia were the earliest publishing centers, but all 13 colonies had presses by the mid–18th century. Most early printing was of documents, pamphlets, and religious materials, with books mainly imported from Great Britain until the Revolutionary War era. By 1800 New York City had passed Philadelphia in book production, allowing its early publishers to produce books of more than local interest. Included were publishers such as Hugh Gaine, from 1752 a printer of almanacs, children's books, and classics; James Rivington, from 1773 a printer of poetry, sermons, music, law, and popular British works; and Thomas and James Swords, from 1785 printers of literary, religious, and college texts and of children's books.

From at least the 1770s, New York City's location and size had made it a market for books printed elsewhere, and such books were sold through the city's printers' bookshops through subscriptions, by traveling salesmen, and at public auctions. Hugh Gaine's noted Bible and Crown bookstore operated from 1751 until at least 1800. In 1802 the city's first literary fair took place, and in 1804 Samuel Wood opened its first used or secondhand bookstore on Manhattan's Pearl St. Beginning in 1812 the Manhattan-based Wiley family (from 1875 John Wiley and Sons) published literary works, quickly expanding into medical, professional, college, technical, and other scientific books. From 1807 Charles Wiley, the patriarch of the family, had also operated a bookstore at 6 Reade St, and soon many publishers became booksellers or vice versa.

By 1815, printer-publishers were established throughout the United States as printing presses, ink, and paper had become available and relatively inexpensive and town populations had grown large enough. Joel Munsell (1808–80), who began publishing in Albany about 1828, was opposed to modern typeface and was highly knowledgeable on the histories of paper and US printing. He had published at least 2,000 different titles by 1870, including an annotated 1874 version of Isaiah Thomas's *History of Printing in America.* Rochester's William Alling was a prolific publisher from the late 1830s through at least the 1860s. Lawyers Cooperative Publishing, one of the country's premier legal publishers, was founded in Newark (Wayne Co) in 1882 and moved to Rochester in 1885. By the late 1950s it had about 600 employees. In 1989 it was bought by West Publishing, based in Minnesota, a part of Canadian media giant Thomson Corp. Cornell University Press in Ithaca, founded in 1869, claims to be the oldest continuously operating university press in the United States.

Dominance of New York City

In 1816 the Manhattan-headquartered American Bible Society, which has remained in Manhattan and is active into the 21st century, began publishing plain, nonannotated Bibles. A year later, Harper and Bros commenced a long life, assisted both by innovative marketing techniques, such as the publication of series or "libraries" of books, and by new production technologies. Harper would become an early convert to steam printing, rotary printing, stereotyped plates, electrotyped illustrations, and cloth-covered boards. Trade sales or publishers' auctions held for retailers and wholesalers were first developed in 1825 and were soon regularly scheduled in New York City and other eastern cities, remaining important through the Civil War era.

In addition to Wiley and Harper and Bros, there were a number of other pre-1850 publishers that quickly became major forces with lengthy and usually diverse booklists. These included Daniel Appleton (1830; from 1948, Appleton, Century, Crofts); Dodd Mead (1839); George Palmer Putnam (1847; from 1872, G. P. Putnam's Sons); Charles Scribner's (1846; from 1878, Charles Scribner's Sons), an especially powerful publisher of the late 1920s; and David Van Nostrand (1848).

In the area of retail sales, August Brentano started a newsstand on Broadway in 1853 and owned a bookstore by the 1870s, the genesis for the long-lived Brentano's chain. In the 1850s the Astor Library's opening prompted new bookstores to move to Astor Place and used bookstores to move to 4th Ave, between Astor Place and 14th St. In 1866 Frederick W. Leypoldt and Henry Holt started a foreign language publishing house, and on the breakup of this partnership, Leypoldt and Richard Rogers Bowker launched *Publishers Weekly* (1871) and *Library Journal* (1876). At the beginning of the 21st century, both Leypoldt-founded publishing houses survive as Henry Holt and Co and R. R. Bowker. In 1869 the religious publisher E. P. Dutton (founded in 1858) moved from Boston to New York City, and in the same year British publisher Macmillan opened a New York City branch.

By 1900 New York City book publishers had expanded into magazines, and newspaper and magazine publishers printed and sold books. Universities published books as well, and academic presses proliferated in Manhattan: Columbia University Press (1893), Oxford University Press branch (1896), Teachers College Press (1904), and New York University Press (1916). Numerous new commercial publishers prospered at the turn of the century. In 1898, the founding year of the *New York Times Book Review,* Alexander Grosset and George Dunlap started the company bearing their names. Frank Nelson Doubleday joined with magazine publisher J. S. McClure to found Doubleday, McClure (1899); Walter Hines Page replaced McClure as partner, creating Doubleday, Page. In 1910 the company set up headquarters in Garden City (Nassau Co), and soon 700 employees were turning out 6,500 books a day. McGraw-Hill (1909) quickly became an important publisher of textbooks and treatises on economics, engineering, and other professional subjects. From 1913 E. P. Ettinger's Prentice-Hall published books on business and finance, and in 1915, Alfred A. Knopf and his wife Blanche left Doubleday to start their own firm, specializing in a range of high-quality books. More and more, the city was a leader in bookstores, new and used, with 4th Ave below 14th St forming an entire used-bookstore neighborhood. Barnes and Noble, established in 1917 in New York City, opened its flagship store at 105 5th Ave in 1932.

Flowering of the 1920s

While Boston, Philadelphia, and Chicago remained regional publishing centers, new publishing giants in the New York City metropolitan area joined the long list of publishers already in business. Publishing's modern period started during and shortly after World War I, as Horace Liveright and Albert and Charles Boni launched Modern Library (1917), which reprinted classic works as a way to subsidize riskier, new literature. From 1919 Liveright continued to facilitate the 1920s literary renaissance through his own company, Horace Liveright and Co. In 1919 former Holt employees Alfred Harcourt and Donald Brace founded Harcourt, Brace, and two years later George Delacorte established Delacorte Press (from 1942, Dell Books).

From the 1920s women played an increasingly important part in publishing, particularly for books directed to women and children. In addition to the key role played by Blanche Knopf at Knopf, Helen Meyer became an important editor at Dell Books, as did Louise Sherman Bechtel at Macmillan and May Massee at Doubleday. Also starting in the 1920s, improvements in technology and economies of scale allowed publishers to sell full-color, well-illustrated children's books for low prices. W. W. Norton was launched in 1923 and quickly developed a long list of excellent books; and the *New York Herald Tribune*'s books section, the *New York Post*-originated *Saturday Review of Books,* and Simon and Schuster began in 1924. Richard L. Simon and M. Lincoln Schuster's company (from 1957 owned primarily by Leon Shimkin) produced many best-sellers and revolutionized book marketing. In 1925 Liveright editor Bennett A. Cerf, with Donald S. Klopfer, took over Modern Library and by 1927 changed its name to Random House. In 1926 new publishers included William Morrow; Viking Press, founded by Harold K. Guinzburg and George S. Oppenheimer; John Day, founded by Richard Walsh; Vanguard Press, directed by James Henle; and—following Harry Scherman's 1926 purchase of Doubleday—the Book-of-the-Month Club. In 1927 Doubleday merged with Doran, becoming Doubleday and Co in 1935. Booming publisher Doubleday would soon run numerous book clubs and start a chain of bookstores. In 1929 George Macy originated the Limited Editions Club, producing finely bound books for collectors, and John Farrar and Stanley and Frederick Rinehart founded Farrar and Rinehart, publisher of high-quality books.

Challenges of the 1930s–1960s

The Great Depression caused many small publishers to merge or fold, but the major companies survived, including the old Harper and Bros and Holt. A few new companies also entered the field. In 1932 Robert de Graff started Pocket Books with 10 titles. Pocket Books, together with the 1940 invasion of British-published Penguin Books, revived the 19th-century market for paperbacks. In 1936 Nat Wartels and Robert E. Simon bought Outlet Books, relaunching it as Crown Publishers, and James Loughlin started New Directions Press to publish avant-garde fiction and poetry.

During the World War II years, a near-avalanche of new New York City–based paperback publishers followed the lead of Pocket Books, including Fawcett World Library (1941), New American Library (1941), the Hearst Corp's Avon Books (1941), Hayward Cirker's Dover Publications (1942), Dell Books (1942), Popular Library (1942), and Bantam Books (1945). Also during the 1940s, German Jewish émigrés Helen and Kurt Wolff started Pantheon Books (1942), and Simon and Schuster created its popular and inexpensive Golden Books (1942) for children.

In the postwar period, Salman Schocken, another German Jewish émigré, started Schocken Books (1946) with John Farrar (who had split with Frederick Rinehart in 1944), which became the 21st century's Farrar, Straus and Giroux. Penguin editors Victor Weybright and Kurt Enoch launched the popular New American Library of World Literature (1947); Cambridge University Press opened a New York City office (1949); Harry N. Abrams founded his house (1950); London-based Macmillan launched the New York City–headquartered St. Martin's Press (1952); and Ian Ballantine initiated Ballantine Books (1952). Doubleday's Anchor Books (1953) and Alfred A. Knopf's Vintage Books (1954), both lines of quality paperbacks, were popular in college bookstores. New York City's 4th Ave secondhand book district reached its apogee, about 25 stores, in these immediate postwar years.

In 1955 William Jovanovich gained control of Harcourt Brace (from 1960, Harcourt, Brace and World; from 1970, Harcourt Brace Jovanovich; and from 1991, Harcourt General). In 1957 Alfred A. Knopf Jr and Simon M. Bessie started the independent Atheneum Books, and two years later, Time-Life Books appeared, achieving quick success and buying Book-of-the-Month Club in 1966. From this era, New York City dominated book-publishing trade organizations and trade publications, though some were or would be located in Washington, DC, the Boston area, and Chicago. *Literary Marketplace,* founded in New York City in 1940, would be in New Providence, NJ, by 2001. The American Booksellers Association would be in Tarrytown (Westchester Co) in 2001.

The period since the 1960s has primarily been one of steadily increasing sales and of hundreds of mergers and acquisitions, increased corporatization, and an intense focus on profit margins, often to the exclusion of authorial and editorial values. By the mid-1990s about a dozen mass media corporations, mostly multinational, owned dozens of New York City publishers. For example, between 1980 and 1988 brothers S. I. and Donald Newhouse acquired Random House, Knopf, Pantheon, Vintage, Times Books, Schocken Books, Crown Publishers, and others through their Advance Publications Co. The Newhouses have sold some properties, among them Random House, to Germany's Bertelsmann for more than $1 billion in 1998.

The 1990s brought additional changes. The convergence of numerous technological advances meant books could be written, edited, agented, marketed, and printed—not to mention shipped and sold—from almost anywhere, in one form or another. Authors could live anywhere in the country or world, and many could no longer afford to live in New York City. The availability of books on the Internet, CD-ROM, and audiotape even meant that not all books required printing. With the increased costs of maintaining old buildings and of business in general, few secondhand stores remained on the old 4th Ave "Book Row," or "Booksellers' Row," with many moving to Broadway or going out of business in the 1980s. New York City–based Barnes and Noble revived the idea of retail bookstores as leisure-time destinations through superstores offering vast stocks, coffee shops, and reading or performance areas, with such stores existing nationwide. Additionally, of the thousands of new, small presses fostered by technological change, relatively few were located in New York City. Amazon.com, founded in 1994, is the world's largest Internet-based book retailer and chose Seattle for its headquarters. Despite these changes, at the opening of the 21st century New York City remains the headquarters for major publishers and most agents and is viewed by many as the US—if not the world—publishing capital.

As the US book-publishing industry consolidated in a relatively small group of cities (New York City, Boston, Chicago, and a few others), the only major publisher left upstate was Lawyers Cooperative Publishing. However, by the turn of this century, Cornell University Press was publishing about 150 titles per year, State University of New York (SUNY) Press was publishing about 200 titles per year, and Syracuse University Press was still strong and modernizing. Small publishers were proliferating, such as Purple Mountain Press (1973) in Fleischmanns (Delaware Co); Black Dome Press in Hensonville (Greene Co); and Utica's North Country Books and Nicholas K. Burns Publishing. Many small publishers were aided by the Book Bus, a mobile bookstore and distributor started in Rochester in 1974. In 1980 it moved into a permanent location and became the nationally recognized Writers and Books center, which hosts working writers, writing conferences, and readings and meetings with writers for readers.

See also AGRICULTURAL PUBLISHING; MUSIC PUBLISHING; PRINTS AND PRINTMAKING.

Bonn, Thomas L. *Under Cover: An Illustrated History of American Mass-Market Paperbacks* (New York: Penguin, 1982)

Coser, Lewis A., Charles Kadushin, and Walter Powell. *The Culture and Commerce of Publishing* (New York: Basic Books, 1982)

Davis, Kenneth C. *Two-Bit Culture: The Paperbacking of America* (Boston: Houghton Mifflin, 1984)

Hall, David D., and John B. Hench, eds. *Needs and Opportunities in the History of the Book: America, 1639–1876* (Worcester, Mass: American Antiquarian Society, 1987)

Joyce, William L., et al, eds. *Printing and Society in Early America* (Worcester, Mass: American Antiquarian Society, 1983)

Madison, Charles A. *Book Publishing in America* (New York: McGraw-Hill, 1966)

Dane S. Claussen

Puerto Ricans. Puerto Ricans, a Spanish-speaking, racially mixed, and mostly Catholic population, date back to the mid–19th century in New York State.

THE EARLY *COLONIAS:* 1860S–1898

During this period, the island's repressive political environment led to the exile of many Antillean creole liberals, who advocated for reforms or a larger degree of self-government, and separatists, who clamored for complete independence from Spain. Puerto Rican exiles found refuge in New York City and other major cities in the United States and Europe. Their early settlements were called *colonias.* Among the Antillean expatriates were prominent political and intellectual leaders, students, artisans, and factory workers. Their influx to New York State intensified after 1868, when an armed rebellion broke out in the island. Puerto Rico's Grito de Lares (Cry of Lares) uprising of 23 Sept 1868, which marked its first declaration of independence from Spain, was crushed by the Spanish army only a few days after it began.

Other frequent sojourners to the United States during this period included merchants involved in the sugar and tobacco trade and the island's creole elite, who saw the United States as the model of democracy and modernity in the Americas. Cigar making also linked Puerto Rico with the United States after tobacco shops and factories were established in several cities, including New York, beginning in the mid-1800s. The industry's *tabaqueros* (cigar makers) were an enlightened artisan sector of the working class. They initiated their own newspapers, and there were many prominent political and literary writers among them.

Through newspapers and organizations founded in New York City in the second half of the 19th century, Puerto Rican expatriates continued to labor on behalf of Puerto Rican independence and reform. As early as 1865, Antillean separatists initiated the Sociedad Republicana de Cuba y Puerto Rico (Republican Society of Cuba and Puerto Rico) in New York City. Among its leaders was Puerto Rican physician José Francisco Basora. The same year, the newspaper *La Voz de América* (The voice of America) was founded in New York City to promote activities that would end Spanish domination in the Americas. Several other separatist newspapers and organizations were initiated in the decades that followed, particularly in the 1880s.

Other prominent Puerto Rican separatists, both from the creole propertied class and the working class, arrived in New York State during this period. They included journalist typographers Sotero Figueroa (1851–1923) and Francisco "Pachín" Marín (1863–97), the poet Lola Rodríguez de Tió (1843–1924), and writer and educator Eugenio María de Hostos (1839–1903). Figueroa started his own press and collaborated with José Martí in the publication of the separatist newspaper *Patria* (1898–1901). Rodríguez de Tió wrote several memorable revolutionary poems and assisted in the movement's fundraising efforts. A prolific writer and educator, Hostos traveled all over Latin America fostering support for Puerto Rican independence. After the conclusion of the Spanish-Cuban-American War, Hostos, who had returned to New York State, established the Liga de Patriotas (Patriots' League) to persuade the US government to hold a plebiscite and allow the Puerto Rican people to decide their own political future. Hostos Community College in the Bronx, founded in 1968, bears his name and is recognized as the first institution serving Hispanics in New York State.

An Afro-Puerto Rican apprentice typographer, Arthur A. Schomburg (1874–1938), arrived in New York City in 1891 and joined the separatist movement. He became secretary of the separatist Las Dos Antillas club aimed at obtaining financial assistance and support for the independence effort. Schomburg's involvement with the separatist movement ended with the Spanish-Cuban-American War of 1898. Schomburg became a leading figure in the Harlem Renaissance. His extensive collection of books and other materials on African, Caribbean, and African American topics served as the foundation for what is now the Schomburg Center for Research in Black Culture.

Demographics, 1898–Present

Puerto Rican labor migration to New York State began to increase after the 1898 US takeover of the island but not significantly. North American authorities in Puerto Rico promoted policies that facilitated the migration of agricultural and industrial workers by allowing companies to recruit from among the large impoverished island population. The majority came to New York City to work in manufacturing and service occupations; Puerto Rican women were highly represented in the garment industry. Agricultural workers were actively recruited for migrant camps in Ravena (Albany Co) and Dunkirk (Chautauqua Co). Steamship travel from San Juan to New York State was frequent, and although Puerto Ricans were not US citizens until passage of the 1917 Jones Act, their relationship with the United States and their status as colonial migrants allowed them easy access to the state. After the US Congress made Puerto Ricans US citizens, an increased migration pattern between the island and the continent developed; this pattern continues into the early 21st century. For many decades, the majority of the US Puerto Rican population was concentrated in New York City. Communities developed around the Brooklyn Navy Yard area, the Chelsea area of Manhattan, and East Harlem (later known as El Barrio, or Spanish Harlem).

The growth of the Puerto Rican population in other New York State cities and towns occurred mostly after World War II. A reduction in the manufacturing sector in New York City that began in the 1970s pushed many working-class migrants, including Puerto Ricans, to look for work in other cities. The growth is also partly because of La Gran Migración (the Great Migration) that took place between 1946 and 1964. The Great Migration (the first massive airborne migration to the United States) resulted from the US-led industrialization of Puerto Rico that began with the implementation of the Operation Bootstrap (Operación Manos a la Obra) economic development program between 1947 and 1951. Industrialization led to a major displacement of the island's agricultural workforce. Once again, US and Puerto Rican government officials promoted migration to the United States to reduce island unemployment and poverty and, at the same time, to satisfy the needs of mainland agricultural and manufacturing industries for low-wage labor. Many US industries actively recruited workers from the island, and inexpensive airfares between San Juan and New York City facilitated movement.

During this period, other Puerto Rican settlements grew in the Lower East Side; in the Williamsburg section of Brooklyn; in Bronx neighborhoods such as Mott Haven, Longwood, Melrose, and Morrisania; and in Brentwood (Suffolk Co). Out of the 3.4 million Puerto Ricans recorded in the 2000 US census, slightly fewer than 1 million lived in New York City, down from 1,046,896 in 1990. Despite the decline, Puerto Ricans are still the most numerous Latino nationality in New York City.

The largest concentrations of Puerto Ricans in the state outside of the New York City metropolitan area are in Rochester (21,897), Buffalo (17,250), and Albany (4,805). These areas saw increases in population after the 1970s. The desire for a better quality of life and education in environments less plagued by high crime rates, overcrowded schools, a lack of affordable quality housing, and racial discrimination, also prompted Puerto Rican families to leave major urban areas like New York City.

Culture and Activism in the 20th Century

Puerto Rican New Yorkers made important literary and journalistic contributions in the 20th century. Two migrants from Cayey, Bernardo Vega (1885–1965) and Jesús Colón (1901–74), wrote frequently for newspapers in New York City, giving voice to the concerns of a primarily working-class community during its formative years. Vega, a socialist *tabaquero* who came to the United States in 1916, and Colón, who arrived in New York City in 1918 and who was also deeply influenced by the socialist ideology of the *tabaqueros,* helped establish organizations such as the Liga Puertorriqueña e Hispana (Puerto Rican and Hispanic League) and La Hermandad Puertorriqueña (Puerto Rican Brotherhood of America), which served the cultural, social, and political needs of New York State's Puerto Ricans. Colón's books include *A Puerto Rican in New York and Other Sketches* (1961). Vega's memoirs, written in the 1940s but not published until 1977, provide meticulous details about individuals, events, names of newspapers, and community organizations, and offers a working-class perspective of the experiences and survival struggles of Puerto Rican migrants. There is also a substantial body of creative literature about the migrant experience written by US Puerto Rican authors such as Piri Thomas and Nicholasa Mohr.

Puerto Ricans are still low on the socioeconomic scale when compared to the non-Latino white population, but they continue to combat racism and discrimination and to work toward improving their status. Organizations such as Aspira, founded in 1961, have been at the forefront of educational and civil rights issues. ASPIRA was founded in New York City by Antonia Pantoja, who was awarded the Presidential Medal of Freedom in 1996 in recognition of her many contributions to the New York State community, especially her commitment to the educational training and advancement of Puerto Rican and other Latino youth. Other important organizations providing support to the Puerto Rican community include the Puerto Rican Legal Defense and Education Fund (PRLDEF), the Puerto Rican Public Policy Institute, the Puerto Rican Forum, and the Center for Puerto Rican Studies at Hunter College, CUNY. In 1959 the New York City Puerto Rican community initiated the celebration of El Desfile Puertorriqueño (the Puerto Rican Day Parade), which is now an annual summer tradition that promotes unity and cultural affirmation.

Increased political participation has resulted in the election of Nydia Velázquez (1992–) and José Serrano (1990–) to represent New York City districts in the US Congress. Fernando Ferrer, Bronx borough president (1987–2001), ran for the Democratic nomination for mayor of New York City in 2001. Dennis Rivera, president of the 1199 National Health and Human Services Employees Union in New York State, has emerged as perhaps the most powerful labor leader in the state; he played a crucial role in Gov George E. Pataki's successful reelection campaign in 2002.

In the late 1960s documenting the history and contributions of Puerto Ricans was facilitated by the emergence of Puerto Rican studies programs at colleges and universities within the CUNY and SUNY systems. The Center for Puerto Rican Studies (Centro) was established at Hunter College in 1973 under the leadership of prominent scholar Frank Bonilla. The Centro led the way in creating a valuable library and archives currently located at Hunter College. In 1969 the Museo del Barrio (Barrio Museum) was established to promote the artistic work of Puerto Ricans and other Latinos such as Juan Sánchez and Marina Gutiérrez and to bring art-related programs to the community.

Puerto Ricans play a prominent role in the state's musical culture. Tito Puente (1923–2000), born in East Harlem, was a pioneer of Latin jazz and one of the Mambo Kings at the Palladium Hall in the 1950s, and his popularity continued for many decades. During the 1960s several Latino performers from New York formed the Fania recording label, which was responsible for introducing new hybrid musical beats, such as the *pachanga, bugalú,* and salsa, which reflected a combination of Latino musical genres with jazz, rock, and rhythm and blues. Other Puerto Rican mambo and salsa musicians from New York City include Ray Barretto, Rafael and Victoria Hernández, Eddie Palmieri, and Tito Rodríguez. Chita Rivera (1933) has been a leading Broadway singer and dancer since the 1950s. She created the part of the Puerto Rican character Anita in the original production of Leonard Bernstein's *West Side Story* (1957). The role was later reprised in film by Puerto Rican Rita Moreno, who won a supporting actress Oscar for her performance. A more recent Puerto Rican singer-dancer, Jennifer López, born in the Bronx in 1970, has been one of the most popular film and recording stars of the past decade. The Bronx rapper Big Pun (1972–2000), born Christopher Ríos, brought recognition to Puerto Ricans in hip hop and was a pioneer of rapping in Spanish.

According to US census data, the socioeconomic and educational status of the New York State Puerto Rican population has been improving since the 1990s. Educational and socioeconomic indicators no longer place them at the bottom of the scale, and they fare better than several other Latino nationalities and minority groups. However, when compared to non-Hispanic Whites, Puerto Ricans are far from enjoying the same levels of equality and prosperity. The work of scholars, activists, writers, and other artists are reflections of a vital community and contribute to dispelling some of the myths and stereotypes about Puerto Ricans that prevail in US society.

See also Latin music.

Acosta-Belén, Edna. "The Building of a Community: Puerto Rican Writers and Activists in New York City (1890s–1960s)." In *Recovering the US Hispanic Literary Legacy,* ed. Ramón Gutiérrez and Genaro Padilla (Houston: Arte Público Press, 1993)

Acosta-Belén, Edna, et al. *"Adiós, Borinquen querida": The Puerto Rican Diaspora, Its History, and Contributions* (Albany: CELAC, 2000)

Centro de Estudios Puertorriqueños, History Task Force. *Labor Migration under Capitalism: The Puerto Rican Experience* (New York: Monthly Review Press, 1979)

Flores, Juan. *Divided Borders: Essays on Puerto Rican Identity* (Houston: Arte Público Press, 1993)

Rivera-Batiz, Francisco, and Carlos E. Santiago. *Puerto Ricans in the United States: A Changing Reality* (Washington, DC: National Puerto Rican Coalition, 1994)

Sánchez Korrol, Virginia. *From Colonia to Community: The History of Puerto Ricans in New York City (1917–1948)* (1983; repr Berkeley and Los Angeles: Univ of California Press, 1994)

Edna Acosta-Belén

Pulaski [PUH-LASK-EYE]. Village (pop 2,398) in Richland (Oswego Co). Located on the Salmon River, the village site offered abundant waterpower and was settled in 1804. The 1816 legislation creating Oswego Co designated both Pulaski and Oswego as "shire towns," or county seats; a courthouse was built in the former in 1819. Though Pulaski lost the designation of county seat in 1853, some court sessions are still held here. A foundry manufacturing stationary engines was established in 1832; by the time of the Civil War there were tanneries and various mills processing lumber, paper, and grain. Pulaski acquired rail service in 1863 and ultimately was the junction of two lines. Later industries attracted by excellent transportation included a fancy box factory (1864) and a manufactory of housedresses (1891). Large employers early in the twenty-first century include Schoeller Technical Papers, with over 350 employees, and the Fulton Co, a boiler manufacturer with over 230. Salmon fishing is a major tourist attraction.

Barbara J. Dix

Pulitzer, Joseph (*b* Makó, Hungary, 10 Apr 1847; *d* Charleston, SC, 29 Oct 1911). Publisher. Arriving in the United States in 1864 to enlist in the Union army with the First Regiment, New York (Lincoln) Cavalry of Kingston (Ulster Co), he went to St. Louis, Mo, after the Civil War. Hired in 1868 as a reporter on the German language *Westliche Post,* Pulitzer became part owner in 1871, began buying other newspapers, and was admitted to the Missouri Bar in 1876. Two years later he bought the nearly defunct *St. Louis Evening Dispatch,* which after a merger became the *St. Louis Post-Dispatch.* Retaining the *Post-Dispatch* he moved to New York City in 1883, bought the *New York World,* and gave it a sensational, popular style. He began the *Evening World* edition in 1887. For a time the *World* was the world's best-selling daily. William Randolph Hearst's rival *New York Herald* copied the style of the *New York World,* and both papers tried to be the first to sell a million copies a day. In the late 1890s they both claimed to be the authentic home of the early "Yellow Kid" comic strip, causing critics to label their sometimes exaggerated style "yellow journalism." The *World*'s sports and social pages, its use of engravings, and its aggressive stance of representing the city's immigrants were seen favorably by many journalists as heralding a "new journalism." Many turn-of-the-century editors imitated Pulitzer's colorful, crusading, working-class populism. One successful newspaper crusade of the *World* was to raise enough funds by mid-1885 to build a base for the Statue of Liberty in New York Harbor. Pulitzer died aboard his yacht in Charleston's harbor in 1911, and by 1931 when heirs sold the *World* it had been weakened by the depression and by the competition among dailies in New York City; the *St. Louis Post-Dispatch* continued to thrive. The Pulitzer Prizes, first awarded in 1917, became the nation's most prestigious awards in journalism and the arts.

Brian, Denis. *Pulitzer: A Life* (New York: Wiley, 2001)

Eric Newton

Pulteney. Town (pop 1,405) in NE Steuben Co. Settled in 1797, the town was formed from Bath in 1808. It is bounded on the east by Keuka Lake, whose shore is lined with summer cottages in 2002. Both the climate and the terrain are well suited for vineyards. Grapes were first planted in town in 1836, and the first commercial vineyard was established in 1853. The first jinricksha, the prototype of the Japanese two-wheeled cart, was built in Pulteney. Jonathan Goble (1827–98) and Francis Pollay (*d* 1912) were serving on the USS *Mississippi* in 1853 when Commodore Matthew C. Perry opened trade relations with Japan. Goble and his wife returned to Yokohama as missionaries; in 1870 Goble wrote and asked Pollay, a Pulteney wagonmaker, to build a lightweight human-powered cart for his invalid wife. In 2002 many of the growing areas of Bully Hill Vineyards (1970), which produced 200,000 cases of wine in 2000, lay within the town limits.

Virginia L. Wright and Jerry Wright

Pulteney Purchase. Noncontiguous tracts of land lying mostly east of the Genesee River and west of the Preemption Line. Also known as the Williamson Tract, the lands were acquired by Charles Williamson for London investors Sir William Pulteney, Patrick Colquhoun, and John Hornby, collectively known as the Pulteney Association, or Pulteney Associates. Williamson bought the largest tract, about 1.2 million acres (485,000 ha), from Robert Morris in 1791–92 for £75,000 sterling; it consisted of all the unsold lands of the Phelps and Gorham Co. Williamson acquired additional tracts in central, northern, and western New York State. Until 1798 New York State law prohibited direct foreign ownership of land within the state, and therefore Williamson, a Scot, became a naturalized American citizen, holding the Pulteney lands in trust. The lands bought from Morris included 52 townships in what are now Livingston, Steuben, Allegany, Ontario, Monroe, Schuyler, and Yates Cos. Williamson planned to develop these lands around commercial centers near strategic transportation links to major urban markets. Beginning in 1792 he laid out settlements, including Williamsburgh on the Genesee River, Bath on the Cohocton River, Lyons on the Clyde River, Geneva on Seneca Lake, and Sodus Point on Lake Ontario, in an effort to attract merchants and artisans who would, it was hoped, establish trade links with Philadelphia, Baltimore, Albany, New York City, and Montreal. Settlers were expected to follow onto these lands.

Williamson relied heavily on promotional pamphlets to advertise his lands, a conventional approach of the time. He spent lavishly on his settlements, built roads, bridges, mills, dwellings, and hotels, and started a theater and newspaper at Bath [now in Steuben Co]. Fairs, including horse races, were held at Williamsburgh [now in Groveland, Livingston Co] and Bath to attract wealthy gentlemen investors. Williamson's heavy spending and modest returns led the Pulteney Association to dismiss him and to turn the land agency over to lawyer Robert Troup of New York City in 1801. The land offices at Bath and Geneva were managed by subagents.

After Sir William Pulteney's death in 1805, his property passed to his heirs in the Pulteney and Johnstone families. The Colquhoun interest was sold off by 1837 and the Hornby property by 1875. Settlers resented the illiberal sales policies of what became known as the Pulteney Estate. Public protests in 1830 resulted in reduction of land prices. Several legal challenges to the Pulteney-Johnstone title occurred between the 1820s and 1860s, but the title was repeatedly upheld. Over 80% of the Pulteney-Johnstone lands were sold off by 1840, but as late as 1850 about $100,000 was remitted to British investors annually. More aggressive collection efforts by the Bath land office commenced in 1860–61 and resulted in a decade of organized, occasionally violent resistance by poor farmers in Steuben and Livingston Cos. The few remaining Pulteney lots were sold in 1903.

Pulteney Purchase

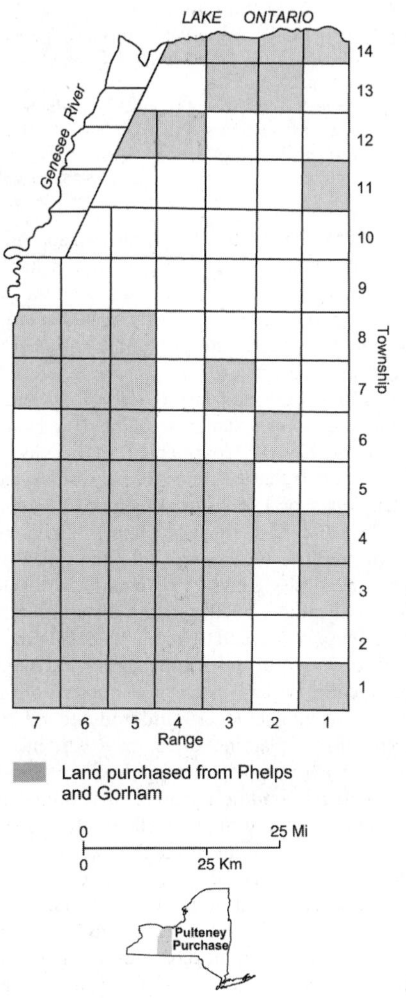

Cowan, Helen I. *Charles Williamson: Genesee Promoter, Friend of Anglo-American Rapprochement* (1941; repr Clifton, NJ: A. M. Kelley, 1973)

Folts, James D. "The 'Alien Proprietorship': The Pulteney Estate during the 19th Century," *Crooked Lake Review* (Fall 2003): 32–47

Tripp, Wendell E., Jr. "Robert Troup: A Quest for Security in a Turbulent New Nation, 1775–1832" (PhD diss, Columbia Univ, 1973)

William H. Siles

pumpkins. Early settlers in New England and New York encountered the pumpkin, a hard-shelled, orange squash, in the American Indian diet. They quickly adopted this nutritious, easy-to-grow crop and interplanted it with corn, bringing the practice to Central New York by the late 1700s. Cooperstown's (Otsego Co) Susan Fenimore Cooper, daughter of novelist James Fenimore Cooper, commented in her *Rural Hours* (1850) that everyone, even livestock, ate pumpkins. Local cooks used them for pudding and pie and dried them like apples; cattle ate them raw. The 1865 census cited the values of small quantities grown in six counties: Albany, $700; Chemung, $300; Otsego, $94; Broome, $89; Allegany, $72; and Chautauqua, $20. Pumpkins' decline probably resulted from increased production of hay, grain, and apples—other sources of animal fodder—and from the shift to seed drills and planting corn in rows, without accompanying pumpkins. Pumpkins have a long nonfood folk tradition as well. In Washington Irving's "Legend of Sleepy Hollow" (1819), the headless horseman hurls one at Lower Hudson Valley–dweller Ichabod Crane, who believes it is the horseman's head. Still symbols of a plentiful harvest, pumpkins grace Thanksgiving tables into the 21st century. In 2000 cultivation in New York State was concentrated in counties near New York City and Rochester, suggesting that most of the state's 114 million lb (51.7 million kg) production become jack-o'-lanterns for nearby city and suburban residents rather than processed, canned pumpkin pie filling.

Cooper, Susan Fenimore. *Rural Hours* (1850; repr Athens: Univ of Georgia Press, 1998)

Jessie Ravage

Purchase College. See SUNY PURCHASE.

purchase of Manhattan. Every schoolchild has heard how Dutch traders bamboozled American Indians into selling Manhattan Island for $24 worth of trinkets, a figure based on the 19th-century exchange rate for the 60 guilders reportedly paid. Writers have hailed the bargain as the greatest real estate deal in history and condemned it as a monumental swindle. Some have suggested it was made by Indians having no rights to the land; others have claimed one site or another as the historic landmark where the deal was struck. Little concrete evidence of the transaction exists, however. Several Dutch documents, most notably a 1651 description of colonial boundaries, refer to the Dutch West India Co transaction. No copy of the deed is known, though the existence of such a document was suggested when Dutch authorities looking into an Indian claim for land in Harlem made on 9 Apr 1670 found "ye Records shews it [Manhattan] was bought and paid for 44 yeares agoe." A letter addressed to the Dutch States General dated 5 Nov 1626 contains the only contemporary reference to the purchase. Announcing the arrival of the ship *Arms of Amsterdam* at its home port following a 42-day transatlantic voyage, the letter enumerated the cargo of furs and timber, summarized the status of the colonists, and reported that "they have purchased the Island Manhattes from the Indians for the value of sixty guilders; is 11,000 morgen [10,000 ha] in size." All other reconstructions of the event remain products of conjecture, folk tradition, or local belief.

Gehring, Charles T. "Peter Minuit's Purchase of Manhattan Island: New Evidence," *de Halve Maen* (Spring 1980): 6–7, 17

Grumet, Robert S. "The Selling of Lenapehoking," *Bulletin of the Archaeological Society of New Jersey* 44 (1989): 1–6

Robert S. Grumet

Putnam. Town (pop 645) in N Washington Co. Lying on a peninsula formed by Lake Champlain and Lake George, Putnam was settled ?1782 and formed as a town from Westfield [now Fort Ann] in 1806. The Delaware and Hudson Railroad was built along the Champlain shore in 1875. The town's limited valley land has been chiefly agricultural throughout its history, and the rest is hilly upland. Along Lake George are the lakefront cottage communities of Glenburnie and Gull Bay. The town lies entirely within Adirondack Park.

R. Paul McCarty

Putnam County (231 mi²/598 km²; pop 95,745). Separated in 1812 from Dutchess Co and named for Gen Israel Putnam, a veteran of the Revolutionary and the French and Indian and Wars. Putnam Co is subdivided into six towns that contain three incorporated villages; the unincorporated community of Carmel serves as county seat. Elevations in this ruggedly hilly county range from sea level along the Hudson River shore, which is the county's western border, to over 1,540 feet (470 m) on nearby Scofield Ridge in the Town of Philipstown. Putnam Co lies in the Hudson Hills subregion of the New England Upland physiographic province, a belt of hills and low mountains that extends northeastward from Pennsylvania to Massachusetts. Within the county a number of summits in the west and far northeast well exceed 1,000 feet (300 m). Elsewhere hilltops tend to be several hundred feet lower, although the country remains rugged and broken. Proterozoic age metamorphosed bedrock (gneiss, marble, and schist) underlies most of the county and forms the highlands that are the eroded and glacially scoured remnant of ancient mountains. A pattern of parallel ridges and valleys (some filled by elongated lakes) is a result of both faulting and variable erosion of the bedrock. Cambrian age carbonaceous bedrock is found in small scattered areas of the south, northeast and northwest.

Putnam Co's landscape was profoundly affected by continental glaciation, which left behind complex till and drift deposits as evidenced by numerous marshes and lakes. Putnam Lake, Lake Carmel, and several reservoirs lie along the south-flowing East and West Branches of the Croton River that joins the Hudson south of the county line. Canopus Creek, also a part of the Lower Hudson watershed region, flows south to the Hudson via a narrow valley into Westchester Co. For 9 miles (14.5 km) the Hudson River flows southward along the county's western boundary through a dramatic narrow, ice-carved fjord. Soils throughout the county are generally poor and, with the exception of some pastureland, not conducive to modern agriculture.

The county's climate is humid-continental. The mean January temperature is 25°F (-4°C) with lows dropping to 0°F (-18°C) or below a few times most winters. The mean July temperature is 72°F (22°C) with summer daytime highs reaching 90°F (32°C) or above 20 or more times in a typical year. Average annual precipitation averages approximately 50 inches (130 cm); seasonal snowfall averages 38 inches (97 cm). The county's primeval forest cover consisted of a central hardwood community dominated by beech, sugar maple, basswood, oak, and chestnut, except for a small area of Alleghenian hardwood forest (beech, sugar maple, hemlock, white pine, and basswood) located in the northwest corner. Approximately 70% of Putnam Co is now forest covered.

American Indians and Early Settlement

The area's first inhabitants were the Algonquian-speaking Wappinger Indians. Among their several settlements was Wiccopee, possibly in what is now northwest Kent. In spring and summer they grew corn, beans, and squash and fished in the Hudson estuary and swamps; in fall and win-

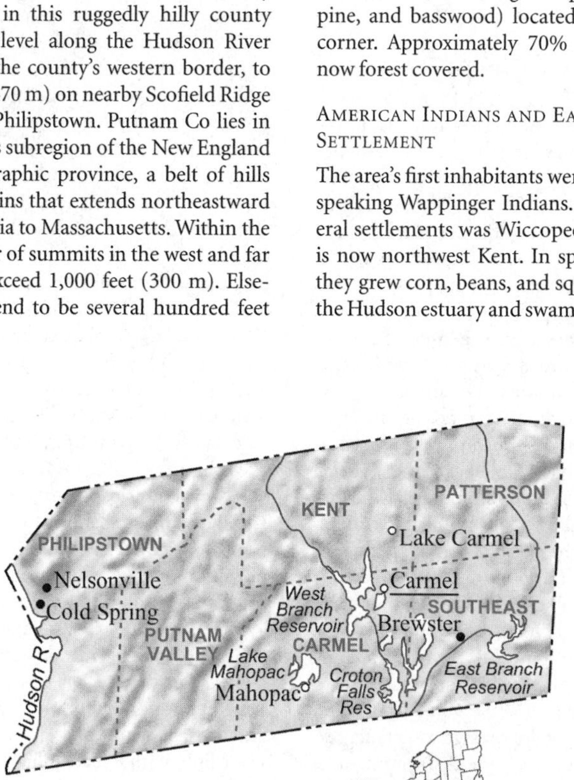

PUTNAM CO POPULATION CENSUS FIGURES

	White	Nonwhite	Total Population	Foreign-Born
1820	11,053	215	11,268	39
1830	12,464	164	12,628	65
1840	12,657	168	12,825	—
1850	14,000	138	14,138	1,507
1860	13,819	183	14,002	1,432
1870	15,300	120	15,420	2,451
1880	14,994	187	15,181	2,233
1890	14,645	204	14,849	2,631
1900	13,669	118	13,787	2,119
1910	14,473	192	14,665	3,265
1920	10,732	70	10,802	1,441
1930	13,621	123	13,744	2,024
1940	16,405	150	16,555	2,171
1950	20,210	97	20,307	2,837
1960	31,572	150	31,722	3,468
1970	56,339	357	56,696	4,755
1980	76,091	1,102	77,193	6,245
1990	81,686	2,255	83,941	5,670
2000	89,876	5,869	95,745	8,420

Notes: "Nonwhite" includes African Americans, Asians, American Indians, and Pacific Islanders and, for 2000, also the mixed race and other race categories. Through the 1960 census these figures primarily reflect the African American population. Foreign-born figures for 1820 and 1830 include only those not naturalized, and for 1930 and 1950, the foreign-born totals include Whites only. Other years include all foreign-born in the population.

ter they hunted. There were no known European settlements in the area during the 17th century, but the Wappinger had regular contacts with the Dutch, with whom they traded beaver pelts for various goods. Two Dutch traders purchased a strip of land along the Hudson from the Wappinger in 1691, soon selling to wealthy merchant Adolph Philipse. In 1697 Philipse obtained a royal patent for land extending 16 miles (26 km) eastward from the Hudson, the Highland Patent. In 1731 a dispute between the colonies concerning the Oblong Patent on the Connecticut border was settled, and the tract was patented in the following year to the Equivalent Land Co, which made sales to settlers, many of them New Englanders. In 1737 the Colonial Assembly designated the Highland Patent and the adjacent portion of the Oblong as the South Precinct of Dutchess Co, and Philipse began leasing land in his patent to immigrants, primarily from New England. After his death in 1750, the patent was divided into nine lots among three Philipse heirs. The Wappinger warriors who fought with the British during the French and Indian War returned to the Highlands to find the Philipses appropriating their hunting lands and evicting tenants holding Indian leases. Hoping to regain their lands, the Wappingers challenged the patent and the Philipse leases. Their sachem Daniel Nimham argued with considerable justification that they had been cheated, but the provincial council upheld the Philipse title.

In a parallel dispute with the Philipses, William Prendergast led the Settlers' Revolt in 1766 against the system of tenancy and the denial of justice in court for yeoman farmers. When the mob stormed the Poughkeepsie jail, royal governor Henry Moore summoned first the militia and then British regulars to quell the insurrection and to defend the landlords. Following a skirmish in Fredericksburg [now Patterson] in which three redcoats were wounded, the regiment put down the rebellion with great severity. Most rebels fled to Connecticut, but 60 surrendered.

Revolutionary and Early National Period

The Hudson Highlands were the key to Britain's strategy of dividing the rebellious colonies by controlling the Hudson-Champlain corridor. From 1776 to 1781 South Precinct was the site of several fall and winter encampments. In 1777 patriot storehouses and barracks at Continental Village were raided and burned. In September 1778 George Washington came to Fredericksburg with more than 7,000 troops, remaining in present-day Patterson and Pawling (Dutchess Co) until November, when they dispersed to winter quarters at Continental Village, Fishkill (Dutchess Co), New Jersey, and Connecticut. In 1780 Benedict Arnold was staying across from West Point (Orange Co) in Philipstown when his treachery was discovered; he fled to the waiting *Vulture.* The South Precinct was also the site of the extraordinary night-long ride of 16-year-old Sybil Ludington in April 1777. The daughter of Col Henry Ludington, she roused her father's militia regiment to defend Ridgefield and Danbury, Conn, then being raided by the British. Col Ludington easily exceeded his militia quota in the South Precinct, where patriot sentiment was relatively strong. The Wappinger Indians sided with the American cause during the war, and many—including Daniel Nimham and his son—were killed in battle at Kingsbridge [now in Bronx Co] in 1778. Although forfeited lands of the Philipses and other loyalists were granted to European settlers, Wappinger lands were not returned. They left the area, finally settling in Wisconsin and Ontario.

The flight and forfeiture of the loyalists created opportunities both for Philipse tenants and for immigrants into southern Dutchess Co. A wave of new settlers entered from New England and Westchester Co, mostly of English Protestant heritage, along with some Huguenots. Because the area lacked the wealth of its neighbors to the north and south, its white settlers had few enslaved or free black servants. In 1790 there were 96 slaves and 47 free blacks, 1.6% of the total population.

By 1812 the inconvenience of travel to court at Poughkeepsie, the threat of moving the courthouse even farther north, and the failure to improve roads in the county's southern towns convinced residents that Dutchess Co was indifferent to their interests. The Clintonian votes of the southern towns were swamped by the Federalists elsewhere in the county. In 1812, on the eve of a Federalist takeover of the state legislature, the outgoing Clintonian majority granted the southern towns their independence from Dutchess, creating Putnam Co with its own board of supervisors, courthouse, and jail.

Economic Development

The Hudson River provided a good, cheap means of transporting people and goods. Ferry

POPULATIONS OF TOWNS, PUTNAM CO

Town, Year Founded	1800	1840	1880	1920	1960	2000
Carmel, 1795	1,979	2,263	2,811	2,299	9,113	33,006
Kent, 1795[a]	1,661	1,830	1,361	696	3,924	14,009
Patterson, 1795[b]	1,546	1,349	1,579	1,231	2,853	11,306
Philipstown, 1737[c]	2,754	3,814	4,375	3,272	5,918	9,422
Putnam Valley, 1839[d]	—	1,659	1,555	704	3,070	10,686
Southeast, 1788[e]	1,956	1,910	3,500	2,600	6,844	17,316

Note: In 1800 the Towns of Carmel, Kent, Patterson, Philipstown, and Southeast were part of Dutchess Co.

[a] Frederick until 1817.

[b] Franklin until 1808.

[c] Formed as South Precinct 1737; by division 1772 became Philips Precinct; recognized as Town of Philipstown 1788.

[d] Quincy until 1840.

[e] Boundaries redrawn 1795.

service between Garrison and West Point began in 1821. Sloops, which had dominated the river for nearly 200 years and could carry more than 100 tons (90,000 kg) of goods as well as passengers, were gradually replaced by steamboats after 1807. Sloops could not compete with steamboats for capacity, speed, or reliability. While steamboats gave local farm produce, livestock, and iron products access to wider markets, they also brought competition from western goods transported by the Erie Canal.

For all its advantages, the river was useless for winter or inland travel. The Highland Turnpike Co (1804) built a toll road parallel to the Albany Post Rd, while the Philipstown Turnpike Co (1815) was formed to build a toll road from the Village of Cold Spring to Connecticut. It carried manufactures inland and farm produce and Highland iron ore to Cold Spring. Inadequate tolls made the venture unprofitable for the investors, who abandoned it in stages between 1829 and 1857, but the road survived as the only east-west corridor within the county; it comprises parts of Rte 301 and Rte 311. The improved road connected Milltown [now Farmers Mills] in Kent to the river, and Milltown became a business center with mills, other small industries, a bank, and stores.

Encouraged by the federal government in the wake of the War of 1812, Putnam's most famous industry, the West Point Foundry, was established in Cold Spring in 1817 to manufacture ordnance. The location opposite West Point was ideal, having river transportation, waterpower, iron ore from nearby mines, and fuel from local charcoal burners. The foundry's need for workers, skilled and unskilled, brought Putnam's first influx of immigrants directly from the British Isles, including many Catholics from Ireland.

The industrial and transportation revolutions of the mid–19th century radically altered the county. The New York and Harlem Railroad reached Brewster in 1849, and the Hudson River Railroad reached Cold Spring in the same year, producing prosperity, booming businesses, and hotels catering to wealthy summer residents.

The "Big Woods" was an area on either side of what is now Rte 301 in Philipstown, Putnam Valley, and Kent. It was extremely rocky and steep and unsuitable for agriculture, except some sheep pasturage. Its trees were cut for charcoal and for timber, and some of the county's 19th-century industries probably used lumber from them as well. From the late 18th century to the end of the 19th century, iron ore, primarily magnetite, was mined, smelted, forged, and cast in Putnam Co. Rich ore deposits were found in linear belts in the Highlands and Southeast and at scattered sites in Carmel and Kent. Ore from the Sunk and Canada Mines in Putnam Valley was shipped by horse- and mule-drawn, narrow-gauge rail and wagon to the furnaces or dock in Cold Spring. But transportation in the Highlands was primitive and difficult. Elsewhere, better transportation by rail from the Croft, Mahopac, Tilly Foster, and Croton Magnetic Mines made the industry profitable until the 1890s. Ultimately these mines failed too, because of the cost of rail transportation to smelters, mine accidents, and competition from midwestern ore. Beginning in 1892 Mesabi Range ore was shipped from Duluth, Minn, and Putnam mining ended.

While agriculture remained the county's primary economic activity, the nature of farming changed during the second half of the 19th century. Acreage under the plow decreased as marginal and depleted land was taken out of production and many farmers moved west for better soil. The raising of sheep and swine declined precipitously. As railroads provided speedy and reliable transportation for fresh produce, apple, poultry, and egg farming grew considerably, and dairy farming increased in importance and profitability, especially in the eastern part of the county.

The Irish famine and political unrest on the continent brought workers to fuel this new prosperity. Immigrants from Ireland, Great Britain, Germany, and Switzerland came to Putnam as foundry workers, smiths, and shopkeepers, or, like Putnam's few African Americans, as laborers and servants, particularly in the Towns of Southeast and Philipstown. In 1855 and 1875 over 9% of the population was Irish-born. The 1860 census for the first time shows women working outside the home in significant numbers, notably 186 Irish domestics. Nativism was evident in the 1854 state elections when, in the towns with the most immigrants, the American Party ticket outpolled its opponents.

Even on the eve of the Civil War, voters overwhelmingly opposed the equal franchise for African Americans by a vote of 1,372 to 104. A third of Putnam's men between 15 and 55 served in the military. The county flourished during the war: Cold Spring's iron businesses, especially the foundry, worked around the clock; Putnam Valley's mines sold all the ore they extracted; sheep farmers profited because of the scarcity of southern cotton; Gail Borden's Brewster factory (1864) processed fresh milk from local farmers into condensed milk for the army. Even the resort business at Lake Mahopac fared well.

After the Civil War many parts of the economy declined. The iron mines and the West Point Foundry were unable to compete with ore from the Midwest and iron manufacturing in Pennsylvania. Following the panic of 1873, most mines shut down and the miners went west, moved to cities, or found other jobs. The Tilly Foster Mine in Southeast, which had employed Irish, Swedes, and Italians, closed soon after an 1895 cave-in that killed 13 miners. Jacob Stahl's cigar factory in Patterson closed in 1903, and his German and Bohemian employees left. Many hardscrabble farmers gave up working exhausted land and joined the movement west. Although the railroads provided employment for many and stimulated small businesses in Brewster, towns without railroads were unable to market their products economically.

The need for drinking water turned New York City's attention to the upper Croton River. Many immigrants, especially those from Italy, found employment on water projects, from the construction of Boyd's Dam in Kent in 1866 until the filling of the last reservoir in 1911. But much of the county's best land was inundated, and farmers bought out by New York City took their money and went elsewhere. Borden's milk condensery lost its supply of fresh milk. With no railroad and with the waterpower to its mills no longer reliable because of the water supply system, once-thriving Milltown withered. The demands of the reservoir system also extinguished mills at another Milltown hamlet (in Southeast), at Red Mills [now Mahopac Falls], and at the old hamlet of Mahopac. The population, which had been declining steadily since 1875, fell precipitously between 1910 and 1920, largely because of the closings of Cold Spring's foundry and Brewster's milk plant; in 1920 there were fewer inhabitants than a century earlier.

Economic distress had some long-term benefits, however. The abandonment of mines and farms, the creation of reservoirs, and the preservation of watershed as open space all enhanced the county's rural attractiveness. The older railroads and the New York Central's Mahopac Branch (1871) and Putnam Division (1880) brought more vacationers. New hotels, inns, and boardinghouses around Lake Mahopac, Oscawana Lake, and many other lakes made Putnam Co a vacation mecca for New York City.

Religion, Education, and Culture

The first churches were organized about 1745 at present-day Dykemans and Tilly Foster and were congregational in structure. The first Roman Catholic church formed at Cold Spring in 1834. In 1875 the county had 12 Methodist churches and 11 Baptist churches, along with smaller numbers of Presbyterian, Episcopal, and Roman Catholic congregations.

There has never been a college or university in Putnam Co; however, a well-regarded private secondary school for girls opened in Carmel in 1850. Drew Seminary and Female College—named for railroad magnate Daniel Drew (1797–1879), who rescued the struggling institution in 1866—attracted young women from many states and nations until its 1952 closing. Public schools developed in response to 1812 state legislation. Schools centralized between 1933 (Haldane Central School) and 1946 (Brewster Central School). Common (one-room) schools, including those at Manitou, Towners, and Haviland Hollow, were still operating as late as 1958. In 2003 the county's central school districts were Haldane (Cold Spring), Putnam Valley, Mahopac, Carmel, and Brewster. Garrison remained a Union Free School district, sending its high school students to Haldane or to Highland Falls (Orange Co). Parts of Putnam Valley and Philipstown were included in the Lakeland Central School District (Westchester Co).

Although there were several attempts to publish newspapers in the early 19th century, none lasted until the *Putnam Democrat* began weekly publication at Carmel in 1841; it was renamed the *Putnam County Courier* in 1852. The *Putnam Free Press* (1858), the *Cold Spring Recorder* (1866; now *Putnam County News and Recorder*), and the *Brewster Standard* (1871) followed. The Carmel and Cold Spring papers were still published in 2003. Putnam Co has had no daily newspaper.

The 20th Century

The automobile transformed Putnam Co early in the 20th century. The movement for better highways accelerated in the 1920s and 1930s when county planners succeeded in getting many of the dirt roads paved. In 1931 the Taconic State Parkway reached Putnam Co. Designed for leisurely driving to parks, such as the newly created Clarence Fahnestock Memorial State Park (1929), it also made access to Putnam easier for vacationers and weekenders. Bungalow rentals in small colonies became available, and cheap vacant land was laid out in large developments of inexpensive summer cottages like those in Lake Carmel, Lake Peekskill, and Putnam Lake. The population doubled during the summer months, and the year-round population also began to grow after 1920. The explosion in the summer population stimulated the construction trades and service industries and continued through the depression. Putnam Co had only one defense plant during World War II, but many residents worked in others nearby. Despite the shortage of labor, the county's chief contribution to the war effort was egg production. Bond drives consistently exceeded their quotas, and a bomber was named *County of Putnam* in recognition.

In the 1950s Putnam began to evolve from a rural county into an outer suburb. Returning veterans and workers in New York City and lower Westchester Co found they could live in Putnam and commute on excellent highways and railroads. The Taconic State Parkway became a heavily traveled, high-speed commuter road. Between 1967 and 1970 interstate highway connections were completed to Connecticut, New York City, and the west side of the Hudson, promoting commercial development and shopping malls in the eastern part of Putnam and resulting in more in-migration, commuting, congestion, crowded schools, and higher housing costs. The county experienced a housing boom of new single-family homes and the rapid conversion of summer cottages to year-round use. These conversions provided affordable housing for many but at a cost to the environment, since many of the lots were too small to support water wells and septic systems in year-round use.

Between 1960 and 2000 the county's population tripled. The minority population, below 1% as recently as 1970, rose to over 6% by 2000. Of that, 1.6% was African American and 1.2% Asian. Those of Latino ethnicity increased from 2.7% to 6.4% during the 1990s and included many day laborers from Guatemala and Mexico. One brake on development has been New York City's stringent environmental regulations, adopted to protect its reservoir watershed. The Croton watershed is affected by these rules, which together with the enormous expansion of state parks and other dedicated open space have helped to preserve for the 21st century many of the attributes that attracted vacationers to the area more than a century ago.

Among the well-known residents of Putnam Co have been the Warner sisters, who lived on Constitution Island in Philipstown from 1836 to 1915. Susan (1819–1885), a highly successful novelist, was the pseudonymous author of *The Wide, Wide World* (1850), while her sister Anna (1824–1915), a poet and hymnodist, wrote "Jesus Loves Me." An even more famous hymnodist, Fanny J. Crosby (1820–1915), lived in Southeast; blind since childhood, she wrote thousands of verses, including "Safe in the Arms of Jesus" and "Blessed Assurance." Other prominent residents have included jurist James Kent (1763–1847); circus pioneer Seth B. Howes (1813–1901); Civil War generals Gouverneur Kemble Warren (1830–82), Daniel Butterfield (1831–1901), and Darius N. Couch (1822–97); mystery writer Rex Stout (1886–1975); and actress Jane Alexander (1939–).

One of the state's earliest county histories was William J. Blake, *History of Putnam County* (1849); it was succeeded by William S. Pelletreau, *History of Putnam County* (1886). The only 20th-century survey was Willitt C. Jewell, "Putnam County," in *Southeastern New York,* 3 vols (1946). *Thirty Years of Early History [of] Cold Spring and Vicinity* (1886) is a small pamphlet packed with detail. Abba Laura Howe, et al, eds., *Brewster through the Years* (1948), though outdated, is quite good. Late 20th-century publications include Margaret Brutting and Betty M. Light Behr, eds., *Town of Kent: An Historical Biographical Profile* (1976); Charles A. Raymond, *Historic Carmel, Mahopac, Mahopac Falls* (1976); and Susanne F. Truran, ed., *The Town of Southeast, 1788–1988* (1990).

Sallie S. Sypher

Putnam Valley. Town (pop 10,686) in W Putnam Co. The land consists of narrow valleys, including that of Peekskill Hollow Brook, between steep, rocky ridges. It was settled under the Philipse Patent beginning around 1745. The town was formed from Philipstown as Quincy in 1839 and the name became Putnam Valley in 1840. In the 19th century iron ore was mined in town; two paper mills provided employment at times between 1864 and 1902. Farming declined after *ca* 1900, and a variety of summer resorts and vacation homes appeared. Part of the 11,000-acre (4,500 ha) Fahnestock State Park is located in the northern part of town. Since World War II, suburban development has accelerated, and residents commute to jobs outside of town.

Field Horne

Puzo, Mario (*b* New York City, 15 Oct 1920; *d* Bay Shore, Suffolk Co, 2 July 1999). Novelist. Born in Hell's Kitchen on Manhattan's West Side, Puzo was the son of immigrant Neopolitan parents and graduated from Commerce High School at the age of 18. After service in World War II, he stayed in Germany as a public relations liaison for the US Army Air Force, returning to New York City in the late 1940s, where he studied at the New School for Social Research and Columbia University. His first two books were *The Dark Arena* (1955) and *The Fortunate Pilgrim* (1964), the latter a semi-autobiographical book about Italian immigrants in depression era New York City. Neither book was a financial success, though both received good reviews. In 1969 Puzo published *The Godfather,* about the roots of the Mafia, violence, corruption, and honor. Most of the story was set in New York City and Long Island. The novel became an international sensation, eventually selling more than 21 million copies. The film version won the Oscar for Best Picture in 1972 as *The Godfather Part II* did two years later. Puzo wrote the screenplay for both films, for which he received two Academy Awards, and also wrote the screenplay for *The Godfather Part III* (1990). His other books, many with a Mafia-related theme, include *Fools Die* (1978), *The Sicilian* (1984), *The Fourth K* (1990), *The Last Don* (1996), and *Omerta* (2000).

Puzo, Mario. *The Godfather Papers and Other Confessions* (New York: Putnam's, 1972)

Brett Forman

Q

Quakers. See SOCIETY OF FRIENDS (QUAKERS).

Quartering Act. Complex and often misunderstood parliamentary act regulating the quartering of British troops in the American colonies. First passed in 1765 with the official title of Mutiny Act, the law did not authorize putting soldiers in private houses but required a province where troops were stationed to provide firewood, bedding, and other minor articles for their comfort and health. Provincial compliance was spotty, and New York in particular objected to the law as a form of taxation. For two years the elected Colonial Assembly resisted direct compliance by offering money to the army without mentioning the act. In response Parliament suspended the assembly with the New York Restraining Act in 1767. A compromise was soon reached, however, that involved a "voluntary" appropriation of New York funds for the required supplies. Parliament soon amended the law to make this form of compliance an option for all the colonies. A later amendment, aimed at Massachusetts resistance to British rule, was part of the Coercive, or Intolerable, Acts of 1774.

Shy, John W. *Toward Lexington: The Role of the British Army in the Coming of the American Revolution* (Princeton, NJ: Princeton Univ Press, 1965)
Tiedemann, Joseph S. *Reluctant Revolutionaries: New York City and the Road to Independence, 1763–1776* (Ithaca: Cornell Univ Press, 1997)

John Shy

Queen Anne's War. In 1702, five years after the end of King William's War, another broke out. Known in Europe as the War of the Spanish Succession, its North American component is known as Queen Anne's War. The primary issue was French expansion into the Great Lakes, Midwest, and Mississippi Valley. For a variety of reasons, New York Colony remained relatively inactive during the conflict. The treaties of 1701, which established Iroquois neutrality, spared the New York frontier from French and Indian raids. The factionalism resulting from Leisler's Rebellion in 1689 was now aggravated by the divisive governorship of Edward Hyde, Viscount Cornbury. Finally, a lucrative illegal trade between New York and New France required neutrality to survive.

New England absorbed the brunt of the war in raids and in 1708 complained bitterly of New York Colony's inaction to the Board of Trade, the administrative body in London that supervised colonial affairs. Barring a significant commitment from England for troops and resources to invade Canada, New York's commercial and political elite were determined not to participate in the war. In February 1709 a Scottish-born Boston merchant named Samuel Vetch convinced British authorities to cooperate with the provincials in a two-pronged attack against Quebec and Montreal. With royal support assured, New York lieutenant governor Richard Ingoldsby began war preparations and Col Francis Nicholson mustered New York's forces for the overland attack. Peter Schuyler convinced many Iroquois warriors to join the campaign, despite their official neutrality. The British forces never arrived, however, and the attack was called off.

Schuyler still hoped to launch the invasion. To strengthen Britain's resolve, he took four pro-British Indian chiefs, three Mohawk and one Mohican (Mahican), to London in 1710. The chiefs were guests of honor at numerous feasts, had their portraits painted, and implored the queen for military assistance. In June 1711 a British fleet arrived in Boston harbor to support another invasion. As part of the combined overland and naval operation, Nicholson was again responsible for organizing about 2,000 New Yorkers and Iroquois warriors to march against Quebec. Rear Adm Hovenden Walker called off the naval invasion when several ships were lost because of bad weather and poor knowledge of the St. Lawrence River; the land invasion was called off soon after. Defeated and disillusioned, the northern colonies retreated into inactivity for the remainder of the war, which ended with the Treaty of Utrecht on 11 Apr 1713. The treaty ceded Hudson's Bay, Newfoundland, and Acadia [now Nova Scotia] to Great Britain. France also recognized the Iroquois Confederacy as subjects of the British Crown. This gave England an advantage in terms of colonial policy, though the Iroquois continued to assert their sovereignty. Exhausted after 25 years of almost constant warfare, New France, British North America, and the Iroquois Confederacy observed a truce that lasted nearly 30 years.

Leach, Douglas Edward. *The Northern Colonial Frontier, 1607–1763* (New York: Holt, Rinehart & Winston, 1966)
Peckham, Howard H. *The Colonial Wars, 1689–1762* (Chicago: Univ of Chicago Press, 1964)
Steele, Ian K. *Warpaths: Invasions of North America* (New York: Oxford Univ Press, 1994)
Waller, George. "New York's Role in Queen Anne's War," *New York History* 33 (1952): 42–53

Daniel A. Piazza

Queens [Queens County] (109 mi²/282 km²; pop 2,229,379). Created as Queens Co in 1683 as one of the original counties of New York Colony. The Towns of Flushing, Jamaica, Newtown, and Long Island City, and the Rockaway Peninsula, previously part of the Town of Hempstead, lost

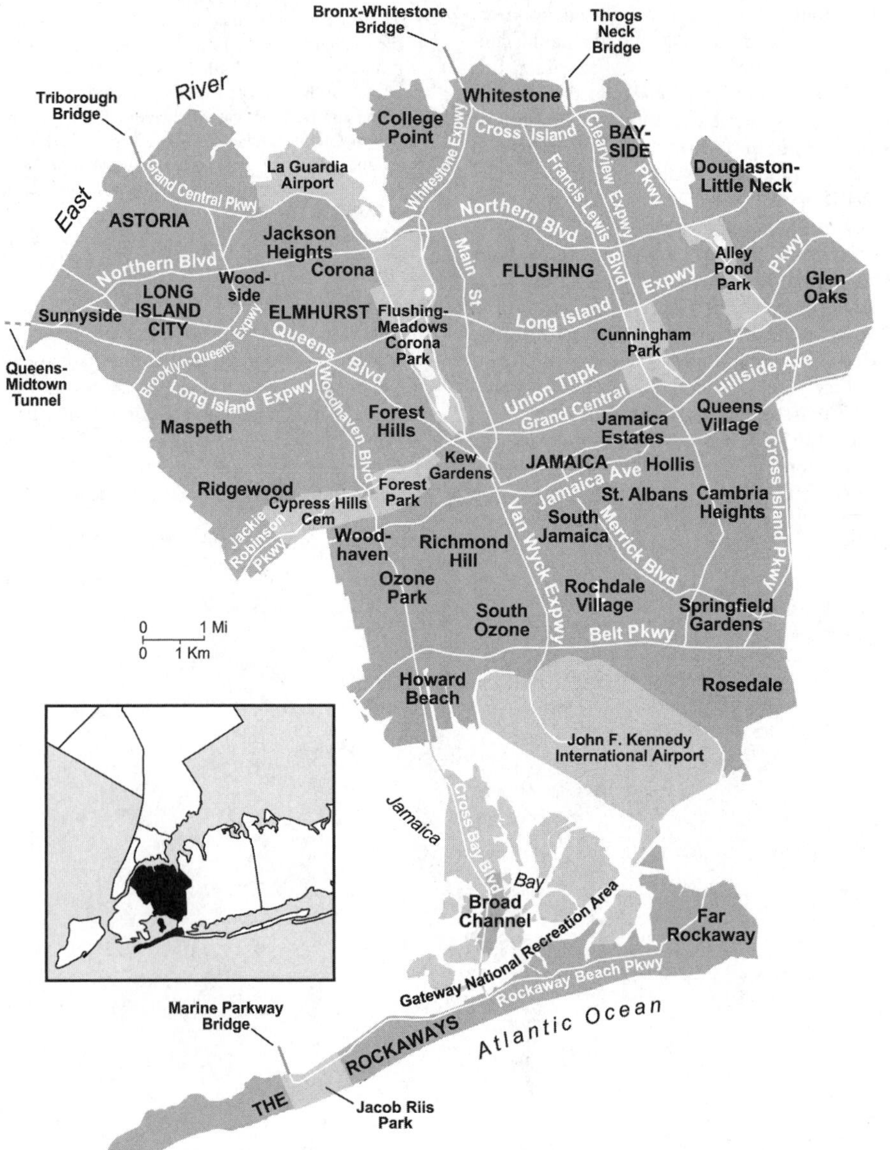

their separate political status and joined together on 1 Jan 1898 to form the Borough of Queens, one of the five boroughs of New York City. The three eastern towns of Queens Co that did not become a part of the borough (Hempstead, North Hempstead, and Oyster Bay) formed Nassau Co in 1899.

Queens, the largest in area of the boroughs, is nearly 14 miles (23 km) east-west and 15 miles (24 km) north-south. Newtown Creek separates Queens from Brooklyn; from it the border ran straight toward Jamaica Bay, but the imposition of the street grid in the early 1900s meant the line cut through houses, so it was shifted to follow the streets. Indenting the north shore are Bowery Bay, Flushing Bay—originally reaching the expanse of wetlands that served as the historic boundary between Flushing and Newtown (now Flushing Meadows–Corona Park)—and Little Neck Bay. The terminal moraine stretches from Brooklyn through Forest Park; Grand Central Parkway runs along the ridge.

Settlement

In 1639 Director Willem Kieft purchased much of what became Queens Co from the Indians, and in 1640 Canarsee chief Penhawitz sold lands around Jamaica Bay, giving all of western Long Island to the Dutch West India Co (WIC). Although the land was part of New Netherland, the settlers were English. Rev Francis Doughty established the first settlement, Maspeth, at the head of Newtown Creek in 1642. It was abandoned the next year during Kieft's War. A second settlement, farther inland, was established in 1652 as Middleburg, renamed Newtown [now Elmhurst] by the English. The First Presbyterian Church of Newtown was founded in 1652. Vlissingen [now Flushing] received its charter in 1645, granting the right to self-government and "free liberty of conscience according to the custom and manner of Holland, without molestation or disturbance from any magistrate." Englishmen from Hempstead founded Rustdorp [now Jamaica] in 1656.

During Director General Petrus Stuyvesant's administration, residents of Flushing, Jamaica, and Newtown resisted the WIC's efforts to prohibit public worship by those not of the Reformed persuasion. The 1657 Flushing Remonstrance protested his edict against the Quakers. In 1662 Stuyvesant deported John Bowne for failing to pay a fine levied for holding Quaker meetings in his Flushing home; vindicated by the WIC in Amsterdam, Bowne returned a year later. The Bowne House (1661) is maintained as a shrine to religious freedom. The nearby Quaker Meeting House (1694) remains in use. The first Anglican congregation was St. George's in Flushing (1702). The first Roman Catholic mass was held in a Flushing storefront in 1826; St. Monica's in Jamaica (1838; dedicated 1840) was the first Catholic church in the county.

During the American Revolution the majority of the population remained loyalist, but that did not prevent the ravages of the seven-year British occupation, which took a serious toll on woodlands, livestock, and agricultural resources. The occupiers often used Presbyterian churches and Quaker meeting houses as prisons, hospitals, stables, and barracks. No major battles were fought in Queens during the war, but occasional raiding parties sailed over by whaleboat from Connecticut. The last British troops marched out of Jamaica on 8 Dec 1783.

Economic Development and Transportation

Many householders used enslaved Africans for agricultural and domestic labor in the colonial era, and the institution persisted until statewide abolition in 1827. The slave population grew from 6% around 1700 to over 20% on the eve of the Revolution, the second-highest percentage in the province although significantly smaller than that of Kings Co. While there were no open revolts, there were incidents in which slaves murdered their masters or burned property, and in 1775 several were jailed in Jamaica on suspicion of conspiracy. The Quakers were a significant voice for abolition and the education of Blacks.

Agriculture was the primary economic activity, both for export and for domestic consumption by the growing populations of New York City and Brooklyn. The nursery business thrived in Flushing from the establishment of the Prince family nursery in 1732 through the 19th century. Samuel Parsons brought a weeping beech from Belgium and planted it in his nursery in 1847; that magnificent specimen, the first tree designated a city landmark, died in 1998. The legacy of another nursery is still evident in Kissena Park. After the Erie Canal opened, farmers shifted from grains to fruit, vegetables, and flowers. (The Queens County Farm Museum in Floral Park was founded on a truck farm which thrived into the 1920s.) The Wallabout Market opened near the Brooklyn Navy Yard in 1884 for Long Island's farmers, who trekked before dawn along Metropolitan, Myrtle, and Jamaica Aves. By the mid–20th century, most farms were sold for housing. The 2-acre (.8 ha) Klein Farm in Fresh Meadows, the borough's last, was sold in 2002.

Transportation problems limited the county's growth in the 19th century. Private turnpikes offered the only relatively smooth route to the East River ferries from the south shore; the last toll road, Jamaica Ave, stopped charging in 1897. The East River was the most efficient route from the north shore, particularly after steam ferries appeared. The Brooklyn and Jamaica Railroad Co completed a railroad from the foot of Atlantic Ave in 1836 and leased it to the Long Island Rail Road (LIRR), which extended the line to Hicksville [now in Nassau Co] in 1837 and to Greenport (Suffolk Co) in 1844. Injuries to pedestrians, damage to wagons, and complaints about pollution (the railroad carried manure from the cities to Long Island's farms) forced the LIRR to abandon Brooklyn and open a new terminal in Hunters Point in 1861. Hunters Point grew rapidly as a transportation hub where commuters changed from streetcars and railroad to the ferry. Rival railroads, including the Flushing Railroad (1854) and the South Side Rail Road (1861), operated on parallel routes, making railroading a cutthroat and unprofitable business. In 1876 College Point industrialist Conrad Poppenhusen united all the lines on the island under a single ownership, but his empire collapsed during the panic of 1877. Austin Corbin bought the railroad, which passed to Pennsylvania Railroad ownership in 1896. The Pennsylvania electrified the line and built the East River tunnels

QUEENS (QUEENS CO) POPULATION CENSUS FIGURES

	White	Nonwhite	Total Population	Foreign-Born
1790	12,897	3,117	16,014	—
1800	13,934	2,959	16,893	—
1810	16,173	3,163	19,336	—
1820	18,312	3,207	21,519	52
1830	19,352	3,108	22,460	107
1840	26,815	3,509	30,324	—
1850	33,382	3,451	36,833	6,261
1860	54,004	3,387	57,391	14,090
1870	70,007	3,796	73,803	19,075
1880	86,743	3,831	90,574	22,001
1890	124,477	3,582	128,059	35,146
1900	150,235	2,764	152,999	44,812
1910	280,691	3,350	284,041	79,237
1920	463,661	5,381	469,042	111,937
1930	1,059,680	19,449	1,079,129	266,150
1940	1,270,731	26,903	1,297,634	278,937
1950	1,497,126	53,723	1,550,849	288,197
1960	1,654,959	154,619	1,809,578	335,623
1970	1,695,288	291,185	1,986,473	416,887
1980	1,335,805	555,520	1,891,325	540,818
1990	1,130,320	821,278	1,951,598	707,153
2000	982,725	1,246,654	2,229,379	1,028,339

Notes: "Nonwhite" includes African Americans, Asians, American Indians, and Pacific Islanders and, for 2000, also the mixed race and other race categories. Through the 1960 census these figures primarily reflect the African American population. Foreign-born figures for 1820 and 1830 include only those not naturalized, and for 1930 and 1950, the foreign-born totals include Whites only. Other years include all foreign-born in the population. The former Queens Co towns of Hempstead, North Hempstead, and Oyster Bay were erected into Nassau County in 1898.

POPULATIONS OF FORMER TOWNS, QUEENS (QUEENS CO)

Town	Years in Existence	1790	1800	1810	1820[a]	1830	1840	1850	1860	1870	1880	1890
Flushing	1645–1898	1,607	1,818	2,230	—	2,820	4,124	5,376	10,188	14,650	15,906	19,803
Jamaica	1656–1898	1,675	1,661	2,110	—	2,376	3,781	4,247	6,515	7,745	10,088	14,441
Long Island City	1870–98	—	—	—	—	—	—	—	—	3,867	17,129	30,506
Newtown[b]	1652–1898	2,111	2,312	2,437	—	2,610	5,054	7,208	13,725	20,274	9,804	17,549

[a] 1820 census did not include population figures for towns of Queens Co.

[b] Renamed Elmhurst in 1896.

(1910), bringing the LIRR into the new Pennsylvania Station in Manhattan. Improved service encouraged suburbanization along the lines.

Horsecar lines began operating in the 1860s, converging on the East River ferries in Williamsburg [Kings Co] and Hunters Point. Trolleys began running on Jamaica Ave in 1887, the first electric streetcars in the metropolitan area. Business on the street railways was especially brisk on Sundays, when families visited the rural cemeteries and picnic grounds. Expansive cemeteries had opened in Newtown after the 1847 Rural Cemeteries Act banned graveyards in Manhattan. In 1848 Catholics established Calvary Cemetery along Newtown Creek, and a Jewish burial ground opened near Cypress Hills; four years later, Lutheran Cemetery was laid out in Middle Village.

Industrialists discovered Queens before the Civil War. Poppenhusen relocated his India Rubber Comb Co from Williamsburg to College Point in 1854. He supported the families of his workers who fought for the Union in the Civil War and gave the community the Poppenhusen Institute, with a theater, classrooms, a bank, and the first kindergarten. In Astoria in 1871 the Steinway family opened a factory that still produces handmade pianos. William Steinway built housing for his workers and donated a library and other facilities. The Sohmer Piano Co opened a factory along the East River in 1886. The Lalance and Grosjean tinware factory opened in Woodhaven in 1863; it too built company housing. Breweries, stables, and associated businesses located in Ridgewood (formerly East Williamsburgh).

With no local regulation, Queens attracted industries driven out of Manhattan and Brooklyn by the congestion, high costs, and complaints about pollution. Astoria, incorporated as a village in 1839, was a summer refuge for New York merchants; Edith Wharton spent summers there at her grandfather's house. Stately homes dotted the East River shore from Ravenswood to Bowery Bay, but by the mid-1880s the area had industrialized. Newtown Creek attracted oil refineries, distilleries, varnish works, and bone boilers. The Laurel Hill Chemical Works opened there in 1866, and production continued until the successor corporation, Phelps Dodge, ceased operations in 1983. By the early 20th century, Newtown Creek was one of the busiest waterways in the nation, carrying more tonnage than the Mississippi River, and had Queens been a separate city, it would have ranked among the top 15 in manufacturing.

Leisure

Proximity to New York City and Brooklyn made Queens an ideal playground. The Rockaways emerged as a resort in the first decade of the 19th century. A hotel, the Marine Pavilion, opened in 1833, and railroad service to Far Rockaway began in 1869. In the last decades of the 19th century, the Rockaways attracted great summer colonies, ranging from the impressive Victorian homes of Far Rockaway and Arverne (devastated by fire in 1922), to row after row of tents rented by the week or the season. Along the boardwalk arose hotels and amusement parks; the last, Rockaway Playland, closed in 1986. In 1886 William Steinway and George Ehret, owner of the Hell Gate Brewery in Yorkville, opened Bowery Bay Beach, soon renamed North Beach, with picnic grounds, dance halls, rides, and a swimming pool. It closed in the early 1920s, a victim of Prohibition; La Guardia Airport was built on the site. Picnic parks, beer gardens, and ball fields dotted the western Queens landscape, attracting Sunday visitors openly flouting unenforceable blue laws.

Consolidation

Queens had a weak county government. The Towns of Jamaica and Flushing incorporated their cores as villages, in 1814 and 1837 respectively. The Town of Newtown never contained an incorporated village and was renamed Elmhurst in 1896 following the wishes of developer Cord Meyer, who wanted to disassociate the place from malodorous Newtown Creek. The original county courthouse was at the geographical center on Jericho Turnpike in North Hempstead [now in Nassau Co] in 1789. In 1870 Long Island City, extending from Newtown Creek to Steinway, seceded from Newtown and received a city charter. The county seat moved there in 1872, reflecting the shift in population, power, and wealth from the rural eastern towns. By 1890 Long Island City, Newtown, Flushing, and Jamaica had almost twice the population of the rest of the county. In the nonbinding referendum of 1894, 61% of Queens Co voters supported consolidation within a larger New York City, Long Island City voting overwhelmingly in favor and only Flushing rejecting the measure. Hempstead, North Hempstead, and Oyster Bay were excluded from the vote and the consolidated city.

After consolidation Queens rapidly urbanized. The Williamsburg Bridge (1903) spurred development in Ridgewood, Middle Village, and other communities abutting Brooklyn. The Queensboro Bridge (1909) and the extension of rapid transit lines to Long Island City in 1915, to Astoria and Corona in 1917, and to Flushing in 1928, opened up the northern sections. Between 1900 and 1930 the borough grew from 153,000 to almost 1.1 million, a 750% increase. In 1930 an astounding 45% of the families owned their own homes. Moving from older immigrant neighborhoods, the majority were Catholic, but Protestants and Jews came to Queens as well. Astoria and Ridgewood were heavily German; Sunnyside and Woodside were Irish.

Queens has several historically significant planned communities. The Russell Sage Foundation funded Forest Hills Gardens (1912), a suburban enclave along the Long Island Railroad considered the finest example of the form. Jackson Heights (1914), the earliest example of garden apartments, featured the first cooperative ownership plan in the city, originally with a private golf course and other upper-middle-class amenities. Sunnyside Gardens (1924) by Clarence Stein and Henry Wright followed the example of the English garden city movement; Lewis Mumford was an early champion and a resident. A local firm, G. X. Mathews Co, erected hundreds of model flats from Astoria to Ridgewood and exhibited the design at the 1915 Panama-Pacific Exposition in San Francisco. The three-story Mathews flats are distinguished by striking yellow and orange brickwork, a design element that was used again in a group of Art Moderne houses built in Elmhurst in the 1930s. In the early 1920s the Metropolitan Life Insurance Co built model tenements in Astoria, Woodside, and Sunnyside designed by the architect of Jackson Heights. While it was home to significant achievements in planning, Queens might be considered the prototype for suburban sprawl, particularly the hundreds of identical wood-frame houses built in the 1920s in places like Rego Park.

Depression and Midcentury

The boom ended abruptly in 1929, and within a year employment in the borough declined by 20%. During the Great Depression tens of thousands of families went on relief, and thousands lost their homes to foreclosure. In Sunnyside Gardens over half of the residents lost their homes, some forcibly evicted by city marshals. The New Deal, however, was especially generous to the borough, and much of the infrastructure for postwar growth was built in an astonishing six years. New York City began building the Triborough Bridge in 1929 but ceased work as financial conditions deteriorated. Robert Moses secured Public Works Administration funding, and the bridge opened in 1936. Other projects built in the 1930s and 1940s included Grand Central, Interboro, and Cross Island Parkways, the Bronx-Whitestone and Marine Parkway Bridges, the Queens-Midtown Tunnel, La Guardia Airport, the Queensbridge and South Jamaica public housing projects, the IND (Independent Subway System) Queens Blvd line, Queens Borough Hall, Queens Hospital Center,

Triborough Hospital for Tuberculosis, neighborhood health centers, sewage treatment plants, libraries, schools, numerous parks and playgrounds, and of course, the infrastructure for the 1939 World's Fair. Moses endorsed the fair as the means to create Flushing Meadows–Corona Park, which was later the site of the 1964 World's Fair.

The tradition of innovative planning made visible in the 1910s and 1920s continued after World War II. Planned communities included Glen Oaks (1946); Parkway Village (1946), which was built for employees of the United Nations; and Fresh Meadows (1947), which Mumford called "perhaps the most positive and exhilarating example of large-scale planning in the country." Between 1945 and 1970 Queens was built out, and the population rose to just short of 2 billion. Eastern sections, hitherto inaccessible by mass transit, sprouted automobile suburbs with access from parkways and the Long Island Expressway, the first section of which opened in 1955. Jamaica Ave, with branches of Macy's and other Manhattan department stores, remained a thriving shopping destination through the 1950s until competition from new suburban malls drew away customers. The racial composition changed as Whites moved to the suburbs and Blacks moved into such neighborhoods as Jamaica, Cambria Heights and Springfield Gardens. From the late 1940s through the 1960s large public housing projects were completed from Astoria to the Rockaways, accounting for nearly half of the new residents.

RECENT HISTORY

During the 1970s the fiscal crisis brought cuts in services and a pronounced decline in the quality of life. The population dipped, but by the early 1980s the borough was rebounding, a delayed effect of the Immigration Act of 1965. Richmond Hill attracted South Asians and Guyanese, and Flushing became home to Chinese and Koreans. Central and South Americans moved into Corona, Elmhurst, and Jackson Heights; Russian and Central Asian Jews settled in Rego Park and Forest Hills; and Muslims moved to Greek Astoria. No neighborhood became an exclusive ethnic enclave, and significant diversity exists within each. Some schools cope with students speaking over 30 different languages. Queens finally topped 2 million inhabitants in 2000, though the census undoubtedly missed many thousands of undocumented immigrants. In the 2000 census, the racial composition of the borough was 44% White, 20% African American, and 18% Asian. In addition, 25% were of Latino ethnicity.

Major cultural institutions included the Queens Museum of Art, located in the New York City Building from the world's fairs (the main attraction being the panorama of the city from the 1964 fair); the Hall of Science, in another building from that fair; the Isamu Noguchi Museum in Long Island City; the Queens Historical Society in the Kingsland Homestead (*ca* 1785) in Flushing; the Queens County Farm Museum; Project Studios 1 (1976), contemporary galleries and studios in a former Long Island City school building; King Manor, home of senator and diplomat Rufus King; the American Museum of the Moving Image in the former Paramount Studios; and Socrates Sculpture Park along the East River in Astoria.

Major newspapers included the dailies *Long Island Press* (1821–1977), originally the *Farmer;* the *Long Island City Star,* which became the *Star Journal* (1866–1968); and the *Newtown Register* (1873), which continues as the *Queens Ledger.* The borough lacks a daily of its own, but there are many weeklies, including the *Queens Tribune.* And while Walt Whitman belongs to Brooklyn and Manhattan, Queens can take pride in Bloodgood Haviland Cutter (1817–1906), the "Long Island Farmer Poet," dubbed by Mark Twain the "Poet Lariat" in *Innocents Abroad* for his "barbarous rhyme."

The City University of New York has five branches in the borough: Queens College (1937), Queensborough Community College (1958), York College (1966), La Guardia Community College (1971), and the CUNY School of Law (1983). St John's University abandoned downtown Brooklyn for a new campus on the former Hillcrest Golf Club in 1956. The Queens Borough Public Library (QBPL), founded as the Long Island City Public Library in 1896, has boasted the highest circulation in the nation. With 62 branches and a Central Library in Jamaica, the QBPL offers literacy and English language classes, as well as career centers and cultural events reflecting the borough's diverse population. Shea Stadium at Flushing Meadows–Corona Park was built in conjunction with the 1964 fair; it has been home to the New York Mets and, until 1983, the New York Jets. The West Side Tennis Club in Forest Hills hosted the US championship from 1915 to 1977; known as the US Open since 1968, the tournament moved in 1978 to a site near Shea Stadium, where the Arthur Ashe Tennis Stadium opened in 1997. The Works Progress Administration–built Astoria Pool hosted the 1936 Olympic swimming and diving trials. Queens once had many famed golf courses, including the 1887 Old Country Club in Flushing, the Fresh Meadows Golf Club, and the Pomonok Country Club, site of the 1939 PGA (Professional Golfers' Association) tournament. Most were developed for housing in the 1930s and 1940s. Horse racing has been associated with Queens Co since the 17th century. The Union Course (1823) racetrack in Woodhaven was the most famous course of its time. When Jamaica Race Track (1903–59) was torn down, it was replaced by Rochdale Village (1964), at the time the largest cooperative housing project in the United States. The borough's thoroughbred racing tradition is maintained by Aqueduct Racetrack (1894), named for its proximity to the Brooklyn water system.

Queens came to national attention in an unfortunate way in 1964 with the murder of Kitty Genovese in Kew Gardens. Dozens of her neighbors heard her screams for help, but none called the police because they "didn't want to get involved." The borough has been the setting for several television shows. Norman Lear's *All in the Family* began a 12-year run on CBS in 1971, and Archie Bunker entered the national vocabulary as the very personification of the blue-collar borough. *Everyone Loves Raymond* is also set in Queens. More recent cultural products include the prominent hip hop stars Run-DMC and LL Kool J. To attempt to characterize what is arguably the most diverse community on earth by any one symbol is impossible, except perhaps the Unisphere, a Queens landmark remaining from the 1964 World's Fair.

See also AIRPORTS; CENTRAL ASIANS; LONG ISLAND RAIL ROAD (LIRR).

Early histories include *History of Queens County* (1882); George Von Skal, *Illustrated History of the Borough of Queens, New York City* (1908); and Henry I. Hazelton, *The Boroughs of Brooklyn and Queens, Counties of Nassau and Suffolk, Long Island, New York, 1609–1924* (1925). A recent popular work is Vincent F. Seyfried, *Queens: A Pictorial History* (1982), while Jon Peterson and Vincent Seyfried, *A Research Guide to the History of the Borough of Queens* (1987) offers a brief essay, chronology, and bibliography. Modern scholarship on the borough includes Jessica Kross, *The Evolution of an American Town: Newtown, NY, 1664–1775* (1983), and Jeffrey A. Kroessler, "Building Queens: the Urbanization of New York's Largest Borough," (PhD diss, CUNY, 1991). Local histories include those by Vincent Seyfried in the Queens Community Series: *The Story of Queens Village* (1974), *300 Years of Long Island City* (1984), *The Story of Woodhaven and Ozone Park* (1985), *Corona: From Farmland to City Suburb, 1650–1935* (1986); *Elmhurst: From Town Seat to Mega-Suburb* (1995); and *Flushing in the Civil War Era, 1837–1865* (2001).

Jeffrey A. Kroessler

Queensbury. Town (pop 25,441) in the SE Warren Co. The 1762 Queensbury Patent was sold to and settled by Quakers in 1763. The colonial town authorized by the patent was formed in 1766 and confirmed by the state in 1786. Residents lived by farming and lumbering, but tourism began early; the Trout Pavilion, an inn, was built on the Lake George shore in 1810. Queensbury's business center was Glens Falls until 1908, when the city incorporated. Floyd Bennett Field (1928) was replaced by Warren County Airport in 1943. Suburbanization began after World War II. The Great Escape/Splashwater Kingdom (1982), succeeding Storytown USA (1954) became one of the Adirondacks' best-known attractions. The Northway (1961) and Quaker Rd (1961), an east-west bypass north of Glens Falls, drove development of new suburban housing and of shopping centers, such as Aviation Mall (1975). In 1963 Adirondack Community College began developing its Queensbury campus, and in the same year, the county offices were moved to town. Queensbury's population increased 154% from 1960 to 2000. The Adirondack Balloon Festival is held in September. The town was the home of 10-term congressman Gerald Solomon (1930–2001).

Marilyn J. Van Dyke

Queens College. Public college, part of the City University of New York (CUNY). Its first freshman class on its Flushing campus at Long Island Expressway and Kissena Blvd was admitted in 1937. Pres Paul Klapper designed the curriculum, basing it on programs offered at the University of Chicago. In 1945 Queens College underwent a major expansion that included a science building, a new library, and a recreation center. The Benjamin Rosenthal Library at Queens College is the repository for the Louis Armstrong archives, which include recordings, photographs, and papers. The Aaron Copland School of Music, with a 491-seat concert hall as well as studios and offices, is the most recent addition to the college. Queens College is known for its prolific teacher-education program. In fall 2002 Queens College enrolled 7,690 full-time and 4,322 part-time undergraduates, and 396 full-time and 4,196 part-time graduate students.

Roff, Sandra Shoiock, Anthony M. Cucchiara, and Barbara J. Dunlap. *From the Free Academy to CUNY: Il-*

lustrating Public Higher Education in New York City, 1847–1997 (New York: Fordham Univ Press, 2000)

Pamela Cooper

Quidor, John (*b* Tappan, Rockland Co, 26 Dec 1801; *d* Jersey City, NJ, 13 Dec 1881). Painter. At the age of 10, Quidor moved with his parents to New York City, where in 1818 he was apprenticed to the portraitist John Wesley Jarvis. In 1822, frustrated by his teacher's neglect, Quidor successfully sued Jarvis for breach of indenture. From 1827 to 1836 Quidor was listed in the *New York City Directory* as a portrait painter, yet no portraits by him are extant. He is instead known for his eccentric, colorful, and humorous scenes based on the writings of Washington Irving and James Fenimore Cooper. These works include *Ichabod Crane Flying from the Headless Horseman* (1828), *Return of Rip Van Winkle* (1829), and *Leatherstocking's Rescue* (1832). From 1837 to 1849 Quidor spent time in Illinois, where he speculated in land, farmed, and painted. After returning to New York City, Quidor began to produce more simplified compositions, such as *Wolfert's Will* (1856). In the 1860s he created a series of paintings illustrating Irving's *Knickerbocker History of New York* (1809), including *The Vigilant Stuyvesant's Wall Street Gate* (1863). Monochromatic and hazy, these works were less popular than his earlier paintings. He retired to Jersey City in 1868 where he remained until his death.

Baur, John I. H. *John Quidor, 1801–1881* (New York: Brooklyn Institute of Arts and Sciences, 1942)
Sokol, David M. "John Quidor: His Life and Work" (PhD diss, New York Univ, 1971)

Dana Pilson

Quids. The Clintonian faction of the Republican Party applied the term derisively to Gov Morgan Lewis and his supporters for acting with the Federalists, beginning with the chartering of the Merchants' Bank in 1804–5. The term had been used nationally earlier by Virginian John Randolph of Roanoke, after his break with the Jefferson administration, to identify his followers as "*tertium quids*" (third somethings), neither Federalists nor Republicans, and was analogously applied to the Lewisite faction. While the Lewisite-Federalist arrangement existed, the Federalists profited with some political patronage, including a state supreme court seat. The struggle within the Republican Party culminated in the gubernatorial election of 1807, when Clintonian candidate Daniel D. Tompkins successfully challenged Lewis. The term was still used at the Constitutional Convention of 1821, although its reason for existing had long since passed.

Alexander, DeAlva Stanwood. *A Political History of the State of New York*, 4 vols (1909; repr Port Washington, NY: I. J. Friedman, 1969)
Hammond, Jabez D. *The History of Political Parties in the State of New-York from the Ratification of the Federal Constitution to December, 1840*, 2 vols (Albany: Van Benthuysen, 1842)

Donald M. Roper

Quill, Michael J(oseph) (*b* Gortloughera, Ireland, 18 Sept 1905; *d* New York City, 28 Jan 1966). Labor leader. He played an active role in the Irish Republican Army before immigrating to the United States in 1926, eventually gaining employment with New York City's subway system. Popular with the largely Irish workforce, he was recruited by left-wing union organizers on the transit system. In 1935 he was elected the first president of the Transport Workers Union of America (TWU), a position he held until his death. As a New York City Council member (1937–39, 1943–49), generally as the candidate of the American Labor Party, he represented labor's interests in the city and state. In 1948 Quill broke with the left faction in the TWU, purging them from the union. A vice president of the Congress of Industrial Organizations (CIO), he initially opposed merging with the American Federation of Labor (AFL) in 1955. Known for his cutting wit and charming personality, Quill pioneered the use of radio and television to promote the union. During his tenure the TWU became a national union with branches in all areas of transportation. In 1966, shortly before his death, Quill led the TWU's first citywide transit strike.

Freeman, Joshua. *In Transit: The Transport Workers Union in New York City, 1933–1966* (New York: Oxford Univ Press, 1989)

Robert Wechsler

quilting. Textile art based on the craft of stitching together layers of fabric, usually with a filling, or batting, between them. Quilting was, and is, used for clothing, such as petticoats and vests, and household items, such as women's work pockets and potholders, but the end product has typically been a bed quilt or decorative covering. Today's quilters also make wall hangings and a range of other decorative pieces, and some modern artists have built on the vibrant traditions of quilt making to create complex yet accessible works of art. New York City's early prominence as a center of both overseas trade and domestic commerce ensured that the state's quilting tradition would be rich and varied. Its diverse ethnic makeup, relatively ready access to European fabrics and fashions, and, later, its concentration of cloth manufacture and distribution all provided women (and some men) with quilt-making materials and a wealth of patterns and techniques.

Developing Patterns and Styles

Few firm generalizations can be made about the history of quilts in New York State. New Yorkers were quite mobile and took their quilting traditions with them wherever they settled. Patterns were widely shared, by hand, by letter, and through regional events such as expositions and fairs, some of which offered premiums for prizewinning quilts. Then, as now, prizewinners were copied. These trends only strengthened over the 19th and into the 20th century, as cottons and then silks and velvets became more affordable and as ladies' magazines, syndicated newspaper columns, and books brought quilt making fashions within the reach of most everyone.

In 1987 the New York Quilt Project of the New York City–based Museum of American Folk Art (now American Folk Art Museum) undertook a broad survey of quilts made in New York State up to 1940, including, insofar as possible, quilts made in the state but since dispersed. The project's *New York Beauties: Quilts from the Empire State* was published in 1992, and research and documentation continued. The earliest surviving quilt identified by the project as having been made in what is now New York State is dated 1753 and was probably made in Rye (Westchester Co). Some evidence emerged of direct ties to European quilting traditions. A "whitework" cradle quilt made in New York about 1830 by a woman of Dutch ancestry, for example, displays a technique of stuffing with overlaid embroidery, which was traditional in the Zaam River region of the Netherlands.

As elsewhere, English influences were carried over in an early penchant for medallion-style quilts, both whole-cloth and cut-out chintz-style appliqués with a sequence of borders; block-style construction and "conventional" appliqués were generally later developments. Patterns were known by multiple names, and their geographical diffusion is difficult to trace. For the most part it is uncertain what pattern names were used before the names began to be fixed by commercial publication. The pattern usually called New York Beauty, for example, apparently originated in the mid–19th century and was known to the early 20th-century quilt historians Rose Kretsinger and Carrie Hall as Rocky Mountain Road, Crown of Thorns, and New York Beauty. Its common modern name was popularized after 1930 by the Stearns and Foster Co (makers of Mountain Mist brand batting). Nevertheless, the New York Quilt Project located few New York Beauty quilts actually made in the state.

Although no "typical" patterns or strong regional styles were found to prevail among New York quilts, patterns and techniques occasionally attained some local or regional popularity. In the later 19th century, quilters often used the pattern Chimney Sweep for friendship or album quilts, especially in central New York State; certain other patterns, such as Caesar's Crown, and pieced sampler-style alphabet quilts are found in New York and only a handful of other states, mostly nearby. Chosen by New York quilters at least since 1775, stars proved to be the most popular design motif, followed by log cabin variations and basket motifs (both of which emerged in the mid–19th century) and the early 19th-century pattern of pieced hexagons called Honeycomb or, commercially, Grandmother's Flower Garden.

After World War II quilting fell into decline. But in the early 1970s a revival began, sparked by the influential *Abstract Design in American Quilts* exhibit at New York City's Whitney Museum in 1971 and by the period preceding the US Bicentennial, which gave quilts prominence as art and as traditional craft. Many of the state's very active quilt guilds were formed at that time. New York State had become the home of the first American quilt study group, the Genesee Valley Quilt Association, in 1936.

Quilts and the Community

Interest in quilting was also stimulated by the Hudson River Quilt, made in Croton-on-Hudson (Westchester Co) from 1969 to 1972 with the intention of raising the public's consciousness of the river as a priceless resource in ecological peril. Groups of quilters had often used quilts to raise money for their churches or for causes such as temperance or Civil War relief; more than 26,400 quilts had been donated to the New York State branch of the US Sanitary Commission during the Civil War years to raise money for care of the Union wounded. Taking up this altruistic idea and drawing on the commemorative and album quilt traditions, the makers of the Hudson River Quilt were among the first of a wave of groups to use quilts and

Hudson River Quilt, by Irene Preston Miller and the Hudson River Quilters, Croton-on-Hudson, 1969–72, 95¼ x 80 in. Photograph by Matt Hoebermann.

their symbolism to build broad public support for a cause as well as to raise funds for it. After being displayed in museums around the world for nearly two decades, the Hudson River Quilt was auctioned for the benefit of regional educational institutions; eventually it was donated to the Museum of American Folk Art.

Earlier efforts chiefly used quilts directly as a means to an end, donating or selling them outright (as many individuals, guilds, church groups, and other organizations continue to do today), but many modern projects have followed the path of the Hudson River Quilt and retained and exhibited the quilt as a symbol. The most famous example is the AIDS Memorial Quilt, formally organized in San Francisco in 1987. The New York State chapters of its sponsoring NAMES Project Foundation are located in Albany and New York City. Similar organizations have sprung up nationwide.

Numerous local guilds and regional guild associations host annual quilt shows, many competitive. The Quilters Consortium of New York State, an organization of guilds, mounted the state's first state-level show, *NYQuilts!,* in 1996; held at Russell Sage College in Troy (Rensselaer Co), it has become an annual event. Quilts remain among the highlights of each year's New York State Fair in Geddes (Onondaga Co), and the winning quilts are donated to charity. The state's quilters have recognized excellence among their peers not only by emulation but in more formal ways, notably through the Catskill Mountain Quilters Hall of Fame, founded in 1982 by four Catskill-area guilds and now housed at the Catskill Mountain Foundation in Hunter (Greene Co).

For another illustration see FOLK ART.

Atkins, Jacqueline M., and Phyllis A. Tepper. *New York Beauties: Quilts from the Empire State* (New York: Dutton Studio Books, 1992)

Hoare, Steve. *The Unbroken Thread: A History of Quilt-making in the Catskills* (Hensonville, NY: Black Dome Press, 1996)

Hoffmann, Lynn T. *Patterns in Time: Quilts of Western New York; Highlights from the Collection* (Buffalo: Buffalo & Erie County Historical Society, 1990)

Warren, Elizabeth V., and Sharon L. Eisenstat. *Glorious American Quilts: The Quilt Collection of the Museum of American Folk Art* (New York City: Penguin Studio, 1996)

Veronica F. Towers

Quimby, Harriet (*b* ?Michigan, 11 May 1875; *d* Quincy, Mass, 1 July 1912). Aviator and photojournalist. She left Michigan in 1888, moving to California and then to New York City in 1902–3. She worked as a drama critic and editor for *Leslie's Illustrated Weekly* from 1903 to 1912, publishing over 250 articles. One of the earliest female screenwriters, she wrote scripts for D. W. Griffith at the Biograph Co. Quimby attended the first class of the Moisant Aviation School at Mineola (Nassau Co), becoming the country's first licensed female pilot on 1 Aug 1911. That year she flew monoplanes at exhibitions for the Richmond County Fair, won $600 at the Nassau Blvd air meet, and became one of the first women to fly in Mexico. She also became the first woman to pilot her own airplane across the English Channel on 16 Apr 1912. Quimby and her passenger fell to their deaths over Dorchester Bay, Mass, during the Boston Aviation Meet. She is buried in Kensico Cemetery at Valhalla (Westchester Co).

Koontz, Giacinta Bradley. *The Harriet Quimby Scrapbook: The Life of America's First Birdwoman, 1875–1912* (Encino, Calif: Little Looper Press, 2004)

Giacinta Bradley Koontz

quiz show scandal. Seeking to adapt successful radio programs for a new medium, CBS executives brought the quiz show to prime-time television in 1955 with the *$64,000 Question,* a more lucrative version of radio's *$64 Question.* Its success spawned spin-offs and imitators, including the *$64,000 Challenge, Tic Tac Dough, Dotto,* and *Twenty One.* Promoted by the networks as geniuses, the quiz shows' money winners became celebrities, the most popular of whom was Columbia University English instructor Charles Van Doren. After appearances on NBC's *Twenty One* in 1956 and 1957, the telegenic Van Doren received sacks of fan mail, appeared on the cover of *Time,* and became a *Today Show* commentator. By 1958 charges of cheating, including the coaching of contestants and the fixing of outcomes by producers, caused quiz show ratings to decline sharply.

Among the accusers was Herb Stempel, a City College of New York student from Forest Hills (Queens Co) who had been "defeated" by Van Doren in 1957. Stempel attempted to disclose fraudulent quiz show practices publicly, but newspapers, including the *New York Post,* refused to print the story after network executives denied the accusations. In 1958 New York Co district attorney Frank S. Hogan convened a grand jury to investigate Stempel's charges, but Judge Mitchell J. Schweitzer sealed all testimony by exercising an obscure legal statute. Historians speculate that threats by television executives to move production facilities and corporate headquarters out of New York City influenced Schweitzer's decision. Irrefutable proof of fraud came when a congressional investigation, convened in October 1959, uncovered a time-stamped registered letter that *Twenty One* contestant James Snodgrass had sent to himself; it contained the questions for an episode telecast after he mailed it. After repeated denials, Van Doren eventually confessed to deception in a November 1959 appearance before a congressional subcommittee.

The revelation hastened the demise of New York City as the national center of broadcast production. Proclaiming their innocence, network officials blamed the Madison Ave advertising executives who pressured program producers for higher ratings. To prevent future problems, they planned to keep the two groups apart, a task made easier by concentrating production in southern California. In 1999 the big money quiz show returned to prime-time television with the premiere of *Who Wants to Be a Millionaire?*, a program telecast live from New York City.

Anderson, Kent. *Television Fraud: The History and Implications of the Quiz Show Scandals* (Westport, Conn: Greenwood, 1978)

David Marc

Quogue [KWAG]. Village (pop 1,018) in Southampton (Suffolk Co). Purchased from the Shinnecock Indians in 1659, Quogue was an early port for whaling ships that carried many American Indians as hands. Before its post office was established in 1828, mail was deposited in a hollow oak known as the Old Box Tree, destroyed by fire in 1893. The Long Island Rail Road provided service beginning in 1869, making a resort industry possible, celebrated in the 1917 song by Jerome Kern and P. G. Wodehouse, "Let's Build a Little Bungalow in Quogue." The village was incorporated in 1928. The Episcopal Church of the Atonement (1884), with its Tiffany windows, is a landmark. Quogue remains a resort area in the early 21st century.

Debra A. Willett

R

radicalism. See ANARCHISTS; COMMUNISTS; POPULAR FRONT CULTURE; SOCIALISTS; TROTSKYISTS.

radio broadcasting. See BROADCASTING (RADIO AND TELEVISION; PUBLIC BROADCASTING (RADIO AND TELEVISION).

Radio City Music Hall. Largest indoor theater in the United States. One of the finest Art Deco theaters in the world, it is one of two theaters in the original Rockefeller Center complex in Manhattan. Radio City Music Hall cost $8 million to construct. The joint creation of financier John D. Rockefeller Jr, designer Donald Densky, and impresario Samuel "Roxy" Rothafel, the theater opened on 27 Dec 1932 with a vaudeville show that ran a lengthy four hours. Nevertheless, enthusiastic crowds marveled at the mirrored grand foyer featuring Lalique chandeliers and the *Fountain of Youth* mural above the grand staircase. Elegant lounges were decorated with art such as Stuart Davis's *Men without Women* and Witold Gordon's *History of Cosmetics*. A huge proscenium curtain combined with a gilded ceiling to create a glorious sunset effect; all three balconies enjoyed unobstructed views. The theater's 144 ft (44 m) wide stage was lighted by Rothafel's most sophisticated lighting system, and its three-stage elevator system later became a model for aircraft carriers. An orchestra and two Wurlitzer organs accompanied performances by the resident Corps de Ballet and the famed Rockettes dancers. The music hall initiated a combined movie-stage show arrangement; *King Kong* (1933) was its first big hit. After Rothafel resigned in January 1934, managing director William George Van Schmus and vice president and chief producer Leon Leonidoff made the operation profitable. It drew over 50 million visitors in its first decade. Badly deteriorated by the 1970s, Radio City Music Hall faced demolition until its interior obtained landmark status from the city and designation on the National Register of Historic Places (1978). Reopened as a concert and special events venue in 1979, Radio City Music Hall underwent a $70 million renovation in 1999. Its nearly 6,000 seats are filled with over 2 million people each year.

Balfour, Alan. *Rockefeller Center: Architecture as Theater* (New York: McGraw-Hill, 1978)

Loth, David. *The City Within a City: The Romance of Rockefeller Center* (New York: William Morrow, 1966)

George J. Lankevich

radon. See POLLUTION.

ragtime. A style or genre of syncopated music that flourished from 1890 to 1925. Ragtime evolved primarily from older rural African American styles, particularly the syncopated banjo picking of minstrelsy and folk music. The music originated in the Midwest, especially the rough, swaggering saloon culture of St. Louis and smaller Missouri cities such as St. Joseph and Sedalia, in the early 1890s. A peppy and slangy music, ragtime juxtaposes ragged rhythms over a steady beat, generally in a duple meter; in piano rags, typically the left hand maintains a square march-tempo beat while the right hand plays the raggy syncopated melody, and additional harmony notes are divided between the two. The best-known form of ragtime today is the solo piano rag, but during its heyday there was a good deal of ragtime for instrumental ensembles ranging from banjo duos to brass bands. Around 1900 "coon songs" were the most commercially successful ragtime pieces. Often these songs dwelt on negative stereotypes of African American society in both lyrics and sheet music covers.

Ragtime was introduced to New York City in 1896 when songwriter Ben R. Harney (1871–1938) arrived from Louisville, Ky, and made a sensation in vaudeville, with ragtime songs such as "You've Been a Good Old Wagon but You Done Broke Down." The first published piano rag, "Harlem Rag," by St. Louis saloon keeper Tom Turpin, appeared in 1897. Scott Joplin (1868–1917), the leading ragtime composer, moved to New York City in 1907 in a futile attempt to find a producer for his opera *Treemonisha* (published 1911). He made valuable contacts among the leading black musicians in the city and added about 20 pieces to his catalog over the next decade, including "Pine Apple Rag" (1908) and "Solace: A Mexican Serenade" (1909), one of his masterpieces. Joplin's publisher John Stark moved to New York City in 1905, and Tin Pan Alley became a center of ragtime publishing.

The center of black musical life was in west Midtown, and musicians congregated at the Marshall Hotel on West 53d St and, beginning in 1910, the nearby Clef Club headquarters. Ragtime was played and enjoyed in all the leading entertainment neighborhoods. Venues for ragtime downtown included Mike Salter's Pelham Café in Chinatown and the Green Gates on 6th Ave. In the Tenderloin district were Ike Hines's club (West 27th St) and Barron Wilkins's Savoy Club (West 35th St). Further uptown along Broadway were Rector's and Reisenweber's, well-known venues for vaudeville and early jazz performers. These cabarets were key in the development of the new ragtime dances, such as the turkey trot and the one-step, around 1915. The Jungles Casino was on West 62d St in a neighborhood that came to be known as "the Jungles." Harlem was home to the Alamo on 125th St and Leroy's on 135th. The former employed white musicians as entertainers, and the latter was exceptional in not allowing Whites as patrons. In the 1910s the uptown venues gradually replaced the older ones downtown.

Ragtime was popular throughout the United States by 1910. A new generation of ragtime pianists appeared on the New York City scene around 1915–20. Most, like Eubie Blake (1883–1983) and Luckey Roberts (1887–1968), were from elsewhere. Those from New York City included Fats Waller (1904–43), Rube Bloom, Pauline Alpert, Muriel Pollock, Harry Jentes, and Mike Bernard. Also from the area were composer Joseph Lamb (1887–1960) and James P. Johnson (1894–1955), known as the father of the stride piano; both were from New Jersey. Some notable ragtime pianists and composers came from other parts of New York State: Willie "the Lion" Smith (1897–1973) from Goshen (Orange Co), George L. Cobb from Mexico (Oswego Co), and William F. Wirges from Buffalo. Practically all eventually settled in New York City; Blake and Lamb lived in Brooklyn for many years. Apart from Joplin and Lamb, most evolved from ragtime into newer styles: Blake was a crucial figure in 1920s musical theater, and Johnson, Smith, and Waller became the giants of Harlem stride piano, an outgrowth of ragtime. Bloom became a songwriter and jazz pianist, Jentes a vaudevillian, and Alpert and Pollock wrote "novelty" piano pieces, another successor style to ragtime.

Berlin, Edward A. *Ragtime: A Musical and Cultural History* (Berkeley: Univ of California Press, 1980)

Jasen, David A., and Trebor Tichenor. *Rags and Ragtime: A Musical History* (New York: Dover, 1978)

Elliott S. Hurwitt

railroad grade crossings. As railroads became the dominant form of intercity transportation, their tracks generally crossed roads and streets at grade, or street, level. Sometimes trains and automobiles even shared rights-of-way, for example, the New York Central Railroad track in the center of Syracuse's Washington St. Cities made initial efforts to eliminate these crossings or to alleviate the danger. From 1888 to 1908 Buffalo eliminated 65 crossings, generally by tunneling under streets or by carrying streets over tracks on viaducts. The state's 1894 Constitution included a provision for the elimination of grade crossings; under New York's first state-funded law for that purpose, adopted in 1897, affected railroads bore 50% of costs, affected municipalities 25%, and the state 25%. Annual appropriations were small, though, suggesting elimination might take 400 years. By 1910 gates, bells, or flagmen protected only 282 of the state's 9,065 highway grade crossings, and the State Public Service Commission noted 56 fatalities and 100 additional injuries in the previous two and a half years at the 457 street crossings by steam railroads in New York City alone.

As motor vehicle traffic grew, so did appeals for separation. Of 719 crossing accidents, with 91 fatalities, in 1923, one particular incident catalyzed action: following the abandonment of an automobile on a crossing at Forsyth (Chautauqua Co), nine people died as one section of a New York Central passenger train crashed into another. Voters in 1925 approved a bond issue, the $300 million Grade Crossing Elimination Amendment to the constitution, to pay for crossing elimination. Implementation in 1926 continued the 50%, 25%, and 25% fiscal responsibilities of the previous law, but now the state could front entire costs and be repaid by the relevant parties at a later time. Another referendum led to a 1928 law assigning to the state 40% of project costs, the counties 10%, and the railroads 50%. The mix was changed again in 1929, with the state paying 49% and the counties 1%. A 1931 law directed spending of the bond money: no more than $85 million in New York City, $28 million in Syracuse, and $17 million in Buffalo. A municipal transit commission in New York City, special grade crossing commissions in Buffalo and Syracuse, and the State Department of Public Works (now Department of Transportation [DOT]) elsewhere supervised projects designated by the Public Service Commission.

Railroads were responsible for design and construction within their rights-of-way. In general, rails were elevated with street traffic remaining at grade.

While federally funded projects in the 1930s required that railroads contribute only 17% of costs, the state, via another constitutional amendment and the 1939 Wicks bill, took total fiscal responsibility. Railroads were liable only up to 15% for incidental improvements to their properties. But the impetus for crossing removal had abated. A 1941 constitutional amendment diverted $60 million of bond act money to road construction. With the onset of World War II, warning bells and flashing lights became Public Service Commission policy for grade crossing safety. At the end of 1942, 912 crossings had been eliminated under the Grade Crossing Act of 1926 and 578 under the previous Railroad Law. Some 6,041 crossings remained outside New York City. Many would be eliminated by track abandonment over the next several decades.

In 1970, with some 4,500 public crossings remaining, the DOT assumed all responsibility for grade crossing projects. By January 2003 the number had declined to 2,927, many eliminated by the abandonment of rail lines. Closing of redundant crossings, instead of separation of rails and roads, has become the key to removal. The state receives approximately $6 million from the Federal Railroad Administration for crossing work each year. With separations costing about $3 million each, the DOT prefers to upgrade safety measures at active crossings. Railroads performing such safety work are reimbursed by the state.

New York State Public Service Commission. *Annual Report* (Albany: Author, 1907–70)
Railway Age (1876–)
Stein, Geoffrey N. "The Railroad Crossing Elimination Projects in Elmira," paper prepared for the Chemung County Historical Society, Elmira, 1998
———. "Grade Crossing Elimination Projects of the 1930s in Elmira and Elsewhere" (NYS Museum and the Chemung County Historical Society, in progress)

Geoffrey N. Stein

railroad marine operations. New York City's immense success as a seaport from the 1830s led to its becoming the major rail hub of the eastern United States by the 1870s, despite one serious disadvantage: that the island of Manhattan is separated from the mainland by several waterways, including the wide lower Hudson River, which was a formidable barrier. There were no railroad bridges south of the Albany area until the one at Poughkeepsie, 90 miles (145 km) north of New York City, was built in 1889. The New York Central, with its route down the east shore of the Hudson, had trackage extending onto Manhattan Island, but many of the dozen major rail lines linking New York City with the west during the 19th century did not have tracks on the island. Freight tunnels only began operating under the river when Pennsylvania Station was completed in 1910.

From the 1830s New York State railroads seeking access to the Port of New York included the Erie and the Ontario and Western. In 1851 the Erie, originally required by the state legislature to stay within state boundaries, established its eastern terminus at Piermont (Rockland Co) on the Hudson and ferried passengers and goods downriver. In 1889 Ontario and Western established a cargo-handling facility at Cornwall Landing (Orange Co). By the 1880s both railroads had acquired rights-of-way into northern New Jersey and built terminals in communities across the Hudson from Manhattan's West Side. Other lines approaching the port from the west built similar facilities, including the Pennsylvania, Central Railroad of New Jersey, Lehigh Valley, Philadelphia and Reading, Baltimore and Ohio, and Delaware, Lackawanna and Western. An 1881 merger with an intended rival line down the west side of the Hudson, the West Shore Railroad, gave the New York Central a passenger terminal and extensive freight yards in Weehawken, NJ.

From the 1870s through the mid-1950s nearly all of the ferryboats taking people across the Hudson to the city were operated by railroads whose terminals were scattered along the West Side of Manhattan. From 1877 to 1910 the Pennsylvania Railroad, based in Jersey City, also had an "annex" ferry service to the foot of Fulton St in Brooklyn. To create freight yards, the railroad companies filled in a series of coves along the New Jersey shore of the Hudson River and the Upper Bay. Corresponding freight yards were established on the shores of the New York City boroughs of Manhattan, Brooklyn, and the Bronx, served by car floats that either sent freight cars ashore to loading docks and warehouses or retained them onboard while stevedores transferred the contents of the cars to waterside sheds.

The railroads also operated covered lighter barges carrying bagged cargoes, hold barges carrying commodities in bulk, derrick scows for heavy goods, stock barges for livestock, and steam lighters for special cargoes such as mail. The total fleets of some railroads—including ferryboats, steam lighters, barges, car floats, and the tugboats needed to move them—numbered over 300 vessels. Railroad marine operations remained fully active into the 1950s. During the 1960s additional bridges and tunnels, the Interstate Highway System, a growing trucking industry, and containerization of cargo led to their rapid demise. By the close of the century one vestige survived, a tug and car float operation between the old Pennsylvania Railroad Greenville yards in South Jersey City and points on the waterfront of South Brooklyn.

See also STEAMBOATS.

Doig, Jameson W. *Empire on the Hudson: Political Power and Progress at the Port of New York Authority* (New York: Columbia Univ Press, 2000)

Norman Brouwer

railroads. In the early 19th century New York State earned fame for its Erie Canal, harbinger of the canal craze, but it also quickly emerged as a leader in railroad construction. One of America's pioneer carriers was Mohawk and Hudson Railroad, incorporated in 1826 to replace stagecoaches running between Albany and Schenectady. When the railroad opened in 1831, it caused a national sensation, and most Americans knew of DeWitt Clinton, its first locomotive. The Empire State remained in the national spotlight with the advent of the 6 ft (1.8 m) wide, broad-gauge New York and Erie Railroad (from 1895 to 1960, Erie Railroad), which opened in 1851. It cut an Atlantic Ocean–to–Great Lakes route across the state's Southern Tier and received widespread recognition as the longest rail artery in the world under single management. But the nature of this project differed radically from the building of most lines elsewhere in New York State during the formative years of railroading. Rather, small companies, often designed to connect an inland community with a navigable waterway or canal, dominated.

By the mid–19th century, system building had begun to fuse short lines into regional, even interregional networks. A prime example of this occurred in 1853 with the consolidation of several small companies—Auburn and Rochester; Mohawk and Hudson; Rochester, Lockport and Niagara Falls; Syracuse and Utica; and Tonawanda—into New York Central Railroad. It would be New York Central, not Erie, that emerged as the dominant force in New York State railroading, largely through the efforts of

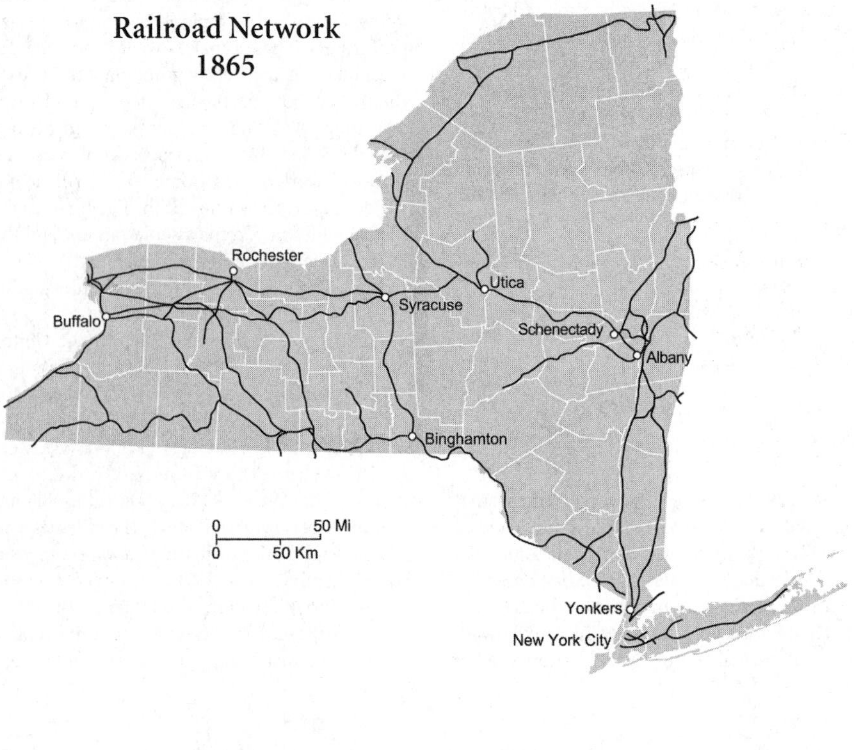

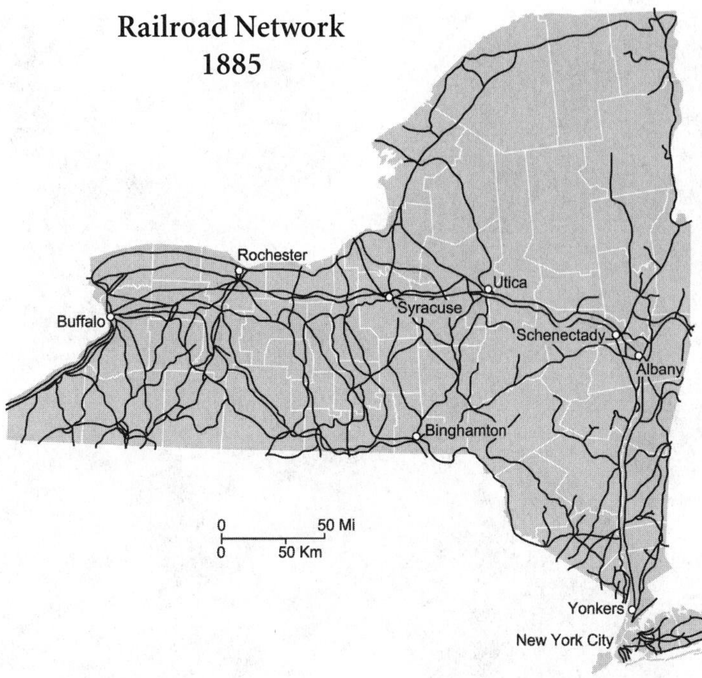

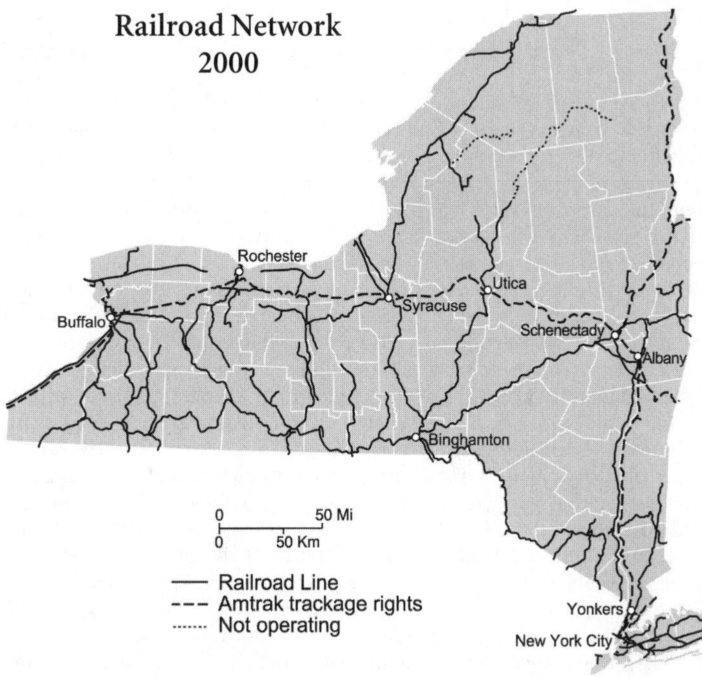

Cornelius Vanderbilt (1794–1877). He gained control of New York and Harlem Railroad in 1857, not long after it opened between New York City and Albany, and of Hudson River Railroad five years later. Together the lines paralleled the Hudson River from New York City to East Greenbush (Rensselaer Co), on the east bank of the river opposite Albany. In 1867 Vanderbilt acquired New York Central and two years later consolidated it with Hudson River to form New York Central and Hudson River Railroad. His oldest son, William H. Vanderbilt (1821–85), and his sons then made the map of the state's New York Central routes resemble a spider's web, with routes extending into and crisscrossing nearly every region. By the late 19th century the company, then known as New York Central System, included Rome, Watertown and Ogdensburg; Lake Shore and Michigan Southern; New York, West Shore, and Buffalo; and Boston and Albany Railroads. By the 1920s New York Central was the largest of the eastern trunk systems in mileage and second only to Pennsylvania Railroad in revenue.

While New York Central reigned supreme, other companies also served the state. By the turn of the 20th century, important carriers included Buffalo, Rochester and Pittsburgh, which linked the cities of its corporate name and formed part of the Baltimore and Ohio system; Delaware, Lackawanna and Western, which served Binghamton, Buffalo, Ithaca, Oswego, and Utica; Delaware and Hudson, whose main line connected Albany with Montreal and also linked Schenectady, Binghamton and Owego; Lehigh Valley Railroad, reaching Buffalo, Camden, Cortland, Fair Haven, Ithaca, and Rochester; and New York, Ontario and Western, which crossed the state from Weehawken, NJ, through Middletown to Oswego. Other railroads with an important presence were New York, Chicago and St. Louis, nicknamed Nickel Plate; Lehigh and Hudson River; New York, New Haven and Hartford; and Rutland. In 1900 the Pennsylvania Railroad gained control of the Long Island Rail Road. In 1910 Pennsylvania Station was completed in Manhattan, allowing a direct rail connection between New Jersey and New York City and enabling the Pennsylvania to compete directly against the New York Central.

Just as New York State was a locus for construction of broad-gauge railways like the Erie—converted to standard gauge, 4 feet 8.5 inches (1.4 m), in the early 1880s—it was also a locus of the narrow-gauge phenomenon of the late 19th century. Proponents of these slim-gauge pikes of 3 feet (.9 m) or 3 feet 6 inches (1 m) held that they were easier and cheaper to construct, maintain, and operate than standard-gauge roads. Of the approximately 12,000 miles (19,312 km) of narrow-gauge lines built nationally between 1871 and 1883, several hundred were constructed in New York State, the largest concentrations serving the Catskill Mountains and the New York–Pennsylvania oil fields. By the early 20th century, most of the state's narrow-gauge operations had ended, with lines either abandoned or widened to standard gauge and economically viable trackage commonly ceded to established carriers. In one example, in 1901 the 73 mi (117 km) Chateaugay Railroad, which dated from the late 1870s, became a branch of the Delaware and Hudson.

By the eve of World War I, New York State's railroads had reached their zenith in terms of size (more than 9,000 route miles/14,484 km), importance to the public, and economic strength. Following a brief, disruptive episode from 1917 to 1920 when, because of the war, most carriers were placed under control of the US Railroad Administration, industry leaders anticipated a bright future for rail transportation. But beginning in the 1920s, more and better intercity roads carrying rapidly increasing numbers of automobiles, buses, and trucks siphoned off freight and passenger business just as the state's 1,100 miles (1770 km) of electric interurban railways had done earlier in the century. Railroad officials wisely focused on long-distance carload freight and passenger traffic, with the latter carried by such crack New York Central trains as the Lake Shore Limited, the Twentieth Century Limited, and the Empire State Express.

Limited by World War I, ravaged by the Great Depression, and invigorated by World War II, railroads in New York entered the postwar era with evident assets. An accelerating process of technology replacement, best represented by the diesel-electric locomotive, boosted corporate profits. Railroads also remained important employers in such places as Albany, Binghamton, and Hornell (Steuben Co). But construction of the New York Thruway and other high-speed interstates made possible by the National Defense Highway Act of 1956 hurt the state's carriers and forced some to consider mergers.

Neither dieselizing nor merger saved one historically significant railroad, the 541 mi (871 km) New York, Ontario and Western, known as the Old Woman, from being abandoned on 29 Mar 1957. Declining coal production in Pennsylvania's anthracite region and the changeover

Last trains on Washington St in downtown Syracuse, 1936.

of milk traffic to trucks ended the road's operations, despite efforts to save the company that included a $1 million aid bill passed by the New York legislature. The closure was the longest route totally abandoned in American railroad history to that date and a precursor for what was to come. Initially mergers offered hope, such as the October 1960 union of the Erie and the Delaware, Lackawanna and Western into the Erie Lackawanna; by 1964 the new company appeared financially strong. But in 1968 New York Central merged with the Pennsylvania, creating the 19,000 mi (30,578 km) Penn Central Transportation Co, and in less than two years it failed. Poor management, increasing competition from highways, and inflation doomed the struggling giant, and in 1970 it declared bankruptcy. The firm's trustees proposed liquidation, informing a federal court that the railroad could not be reorganized on an income-producing basis.

Other railroads serving the state faced severe financial problems as well. In 1970 Lehigh Valley Railroad collapsed, with Erie Lackawanna and Lehigh and Hudson River doing the same two years later. These failures, most notably Penn Central's, led to federal intervention. In 1973 the US Congress passed the Regional Rail Reorganization Act, which provided the framework for formation in 1976 of Consolidated Rail Corp (Conrail). This quasi-public entity assumed control of Penn Central, Erie Lackawanna, Lehigh Valley, and several other bankrupt carriers. Another federal measure, the Staggers Act of 1980, also had a major impact on the state's railroads. It brought about partial deregulation of the industry, allowing railroads greater freedom in setting rates and thus enabling them to compete more effectively with motor carriers.

During this period the federal government entered the passenger business; it made some of the state's few remaining intercity trains part of the quasi-public National Railroad Passenger Corp (Amtrak)—which debuted on 1 May 1971—and canceled others. Amtrak service was limited to Penn Central trackage, with trains calling daily at New York City, Albany, Utica, Syracuse, Rochester, and Buffalo. Rail commuter service continued in the New York City metropolitan area; the majority of trains were operated by Long Island Rail Road.

Over the next several decades, Amtrak maintained its original service in New York State and added trains to the former Delaware and Hudson route between Albany and Montreal. At the same time, major changes occurred with the freight roads. Corporate transformations such as "mega-mergers" and other restructuring, together with regulatory changes, led to abandonment or sale of unwanted trackage. As a result a number of new short lines appeared, such as Ontario Midland Railroad Corp, based in Sodus (Wayne Co), which began service in October 1979. Monroe and Wayne Cos own Ontario Midland's trackage, with the operating company controlled by shippers located along the former New York Central line. New York State's railroad map continues to change. In August 1998 Conrail disappeared; its lines were sold to CSX and Norfolk Southern, with CSX acquiring most of the former New York Central trackage. At the beginning of the 21st century, mileage of major or Class 1 carriers in the state is less than 2,000 route miles (3,219 km).

See also Canada; Great lakes shipping lines and watercraft; Interurban railways; Labor; New york city as metropolis; Street railways; Suburbanization.

Carson, Robert B. *Main Line to Oblivion: The Disintegration of New York Railroads in the 20th Century* (Port Washington, NY: Kennikat, 1971)

Drury, George H., ed. *The Historical Guide to North American Railroads* (Milwaukee: Kalmbach Books, 1985)

Stover, John F. *American Railroads* (Chicago: Univ of Chicago Press, 1997)

H. Roger Grant

rail trails. Abandoned railroad grades used as recreational trails for hiking, running, bicycling, cross-country skiing, snowshoeing, horseback riding, and driving all-terrain vehicles and snowmobiles. In 1986 Rails-to-Trails Conservancy (RTC), a nonprofit group advocating establishment of recreational trails throughout the United States, was founded in Washington, DC. By 1996 there were 40 RTC trails in New York State totaling 295 miles (475 km), including Wallkill Valley, Harlem Valley, and Mohawk Hudson Trails. A portion of the former Ulster and Delaware line between Grand Gorge and Stamford (Delaware Co) became a recreational trail *ca* 2000. In the Adirondacks many abandoned grades have become recreational trails informally, without the assistance of RTC or any such organization. Examples are Malone–Lake Clear Junction Snowmobile Trail, Bloomingdale Bog Trail, used largely for nature study, and High Falls Truck Trail from Wanakena (St. Lawrence Co), now used for hiking.

Trailblazer (Rails-to-Trails Conservancy) (1986–99)

Michael Kudish

Ramapo. Town (pop 108,905) in W Rockland Co. The town formed as New Hampstead in 1791 from Haverstraw, and the name changed to Hempstead in 1797 and to Ramapo in 1828. Industry developed because of abundant waterpower, timber, and iron ore in Ramapo. The J. G. Pierson and Bros Iron Works (1796–1851) employed 500; in 1815 it produced 1 million pounds (450 MT) of nails. A cotton mill and screw factory were added. Dater's ironworks began operating south of what is now Sloatsburg around 1800, and the Ramapo Works was in operation by 1807, when a post office was established. The town grew as a result of the Nyack Turnpike (?1830) and the Erie Railroad (1841). In the rugged Ramapo Mountains in the north, hoop poles, cordwood, wooden scoops, and splint baskets were the chief products until the early 20th century. Between 1950 and 1970 rapid suburbanization increased the population 273% from 20,584 to 76,702. The population in 2000 was 17% black, with the largest African American concentrations in Spring Valley, Hillcrest, and Hillburn. Ramapo is the site of Rockland Community College (1959), and a large part of town is in Harriman State Park.

Ramapo Mountain People. A population of approximately 1,500 racially mixed people living primarily in Hillburn (Rockland Co) and Ringwood and Mahwah, NJ. The origin of the Ramapo Mountain People is complex and controversial. One theory holds they are descendants of culturally Dutch free Blacks living in and near New York City in the late 17th century. Many have Dutch surnames. Another widely held theory is that they are descendants of Native Americans, including local Lenape bands and Tuscarora Indians who migrated to and through the area in the 18th century. A triracial origin is very likely, in which the free black and Indian ancestors, as well as some white ancestors, intermixed. There are numerous records of persons of Indian and African American descent in the Ramapo Mountain area dating to the middle of the 18th century. The Ramapo Mountain People led fairly insular lives, speaking a variant of the

Jersey Dutch dialect into the late 19th century. They were often shunned by their neighbors and subject to racial discrimination. In Hillburn they attended the last legally segregated public school in New York State, not closed until 1943. In 1978 the Ramapough Mountain Indians, the name of their tribal group, sought official recognition from the Bureau of Indian Affairs. In 1993 their claim was denied, though many scholars and advocates continue to contest the lack of an Indian designation. An earlier name for the group, Jackson Whites, is now considered offensive.

Cohen, David Steven. *The Ramapo Mountain People* (New Brunswick, NJ: Rutgers Univ Press, 1974)

Ramones. Punk rock group. Formed in Forest Hills in Queens, the Ramones, consisting of Joey Ramone (*b* Jeffrey Hyman, 1951–2001), Johnny Ramone (*b* John Cummings, 1951–2004), and Dee Dee Ramone (*b* Douglas Colvin, 1952–2002), began to perform in 1974, later joined by Tommy Ramone (*b* Tom Ederlyi, 1952), the group's manager and the first of several drummers. The group achieved acclaim at CBGB's in Manhattan's East Village. A precursor of punk rockers, they played stripped-down, fast, three-chord rock in such songs as "Blitzkrieg Bop" (1976) and "Gimme Gimme Shock Treatment" (1977). After the peak of their popularity in the late 1970s, the Ramones toured until disbanding in 1996. The group was inducted into the Rock and Roll Hall of Fame in 2002.

Bessman, Jim. *Ramones: An American Band* (New York: St. Martin's Press, 1993)

Hugh W. Foley Jr

Rand, Ayn [Rosenbaum, Alissa Zinovievna] (*b* St. Petersburg, Russia, 2 Feb 1905; *d* New York City, 6 Mar 1982). Novelist and philosopher. She earned a degree in history from Leningrad University in 1924. A passionate foe of both communism and religion, she immigrated to the United States, arriving in New York City in February 1926. She began working in Hollywood in September 1926 mainly as a screenwriter, and in 1951 she returned permanently to New York City, whose skyscrapers she admired as a triumph of human achievement. There she resided in the Murray Hill section of Manhattan until her death. Rand was a controversial and influential thinker, the founder of objectivism, and the author of the novels *We the Living* (1936), *Anthem* (1938), *The Fountainhead* (1943), and *Atlas Shrugged* (1957) and several nonfiction collections. According to the philosophy of objectivism, the world exists independently of what human beings think or feel; reason is the only valid means of human knowledge; and rational self-interest is the highest ethical ideal. Rand celebrated the creative individual and saw laissez-faire capitalism as the only social system consonant with individual rights. Objectivism emerged as a bona fide movement as a result of regular meetings held in Rand's New York City residence in the 1950s. After the publication of *Atlas Shrugged,* Nathaniel Branden, Rand's closest follower, formed the Nathaniel Branden Institute (NBI) with Rand's approval. In later years NBI opened its headquarters in the Empire State Building. The organization became the chief means of spreading Rand's philosophy through live and taped lectures, a book service, and social events. The institute folded in 1968 after Rand and Branden ended their professional and personal relationship. Other close associates of Rand included Alan Greenspan, who wrote for Rand's *Objectivist* magazine and was later appointed chairman of the Federal Reserve Board, and Leonard Peikoff, heir to the Rand estate, who founded the Ayn Rand Institute (now in Marina del Rey, Calif) in 1984, two years after Rand's death. In 1989 David Kelley founded the Institute for Objectivist Studies (now the Objectivist Center) with headquarters in Poughkeepsie. Among the periodicals influenced by Rand are *Aristos,* a journal on the arts based in New York City, and *Navigator,* produced by the Objectivist Center. Rand is buried in Kensico Cemetery in Valhalla (Westchester Co).

Sciabarra, Chris Matthew. *Ayn Rand: The Russian Radical* (University Park: Pennsylvania State Univ Press, 1995)

Chris Matthew Sciabarra

Randolph. Town (pop 2,681) and village (pop 1,316) in W Cattaraugus Co. Settled in 1820, the town was formed from Conewango in 1826. Conewango Creek provided a means for early settlers to raft lumber to market. The Central Medical College of New York (1848) operated only briefly before moving to Syracuse. The Randolph Academy and Female Seminary (1850; after 1866, Chamberlain Institute) was a teacher training school. The Atlantic and Great Western Railroad (1860) provided freight transportation to eastern and southern cities. The village incorporated in 1867. Dairying replaced lumbering as the major industry, but several handle factories operated in the 1870s. The Western New York Home for Homeless and Dependent Children (1877) became the Randolph Children's Home for young people with special needs and remained in operation in 2003. Rte 17 (I-86) was built through town in 1966–68. Agriculture remains an important land use, while manufacturing includes Randolph Dimension Corp (furniture) and Metallic Ladder Manufacturing Co along with its Alumidock Division. The Alcoa plant, located in a 1907 Borden milk plant, closed in 2003. Randolph's large Amish community also attracts tourists.

Bruce D. Fredrickson and Madelynn P. Fredrickson

Randolph, A(sa) Philip (*b* Crescent City, Fla, 15 Apr 1889; *d* New York City, 16 May 1979). Labor organizer and civil rights activist. Randolph moved to Harlem in Manhattan in 1911 and took night classes at City College that introduced him to socialism. He became known as a street-corner orator. With Chandler Owen, Randolph established and edited the *Messenger,* which, owing to its trenchant socialism and activist cast, was deemed by the US Department of Justice in 1919 as "the most able and the most dangerous of all the Negro publications." Randolph organized the Pullman Co's railroad sleeping car porters in 1925. Throughout 12 years of prolonged struggle and a company policy of personal retaliation, it was Randolph's perseverance and the critical, albeit qualified, support of the American Federation of Labor (AFL) that enabled the Brotherhood of Sleeping Car Porters (BSCP) to endure. New Deal labor legislation enabled the BSCP to gain recognition as the porters' legitimate bargaining agent, and the union signed its first contract with Pullman in 1937.

Early in 1941 Randolph proposed an African American march on Washington, DC, to compel the government to end racial discrimination in government services and the defense industry. To avert this march, scheduled for July, Pres Franklin D. Roosevelt in late June created the Fair Employment Practices Committee by executive order. Randolph sought to build upon this signal achievement a permanent, centrally organized, nonviolent mass movement, but the momentum of the march on Washington movement could not be sustained. After World War II he advocated a campaign of civil disobedience specifically targeting service in the segregated military. In response, Pres Harry S. Truman signed an executive order desegregating the US armed forces in July 1948. Through the 1940s and 1950s, Randolph was often called as a mediator as the Civil Rights Movement fractured. He was one of only two African American members in a new executive council arising from the 1955 merger between the AFL and the Congress of Industrial Organizations (CIO). Although Randolph was censured by the AFL-CIO for his outspokenness, he was branded insufficiently militant by factions within his Negro American Labor Council (NALC), founded in 1960. As its president, however, he issued a new call for a march on Washington. Coordinated by Bayard Rustin, the march on 28 Aug 1963 drew some 250,000 participants. A triumph of coalition building, it was the culmination of Randolph's career.

Randolph's support for Pres Lyndon Johnson in the 1964 election drew sharp criticism, but Randolph remained committed to coalitions, especially with labor, and pragmatic strategies. In 1964 the A. Philip Randolph Institute was founded in New York City to forward his pursuit of economic and social justice and to give his protégé Rustin an organizational base. In failing health, Randolph retired from his public career in 1968. He moved at that time from his home of 35 years in Harlem's Dunbar Apartments to the Penn South housing complex in Manhattan's Chelsea section owned by the International Ladies' Garment Workers' Union, where he spent his last decade.

Anderson, Jervis. *A. Philip Randolph: A Biographical Portrait* (1973; repr Berkeley: Univ of Calif. Press, 1986)
Kornweibel, Theodore. "The Most Dangerous of All the Negro Publications." In *Seeing Red: Federal Campaigns against Black Militancy, 1919–1925* (Bloomington: Indiana Univ Press, 1998)
Pfeffer, Paula F. A. *Philip Randolph: Pioneer of the Civil Rights Movement* (Baton Rouge: Louisiana State Univ Press, 1990)

Veronica F. Towers

rape laws. In the 19th century under New York State law, a man who had "sexual intercourse with a female not his wife, against her will" was guilty of first-degree (forcible) rape. Sexual intercourse with or without force with a "female not his wife under the age of 10" was second-degree (statutory) rape. After reformer lobbying, the "age of consent" for second-degree rape was raised to 16 (1892) and then to 18 (1895). In 1950 some same-age sexuality was decriminalized: perpetrators under 21 could not be charged with statutory rape—that is, sex with a minor.

The 1965 Penal Code revision created three gradations of statutory rape in New York State and made the age of consent 17. First-degree rape also covers rape by forcible compulsion. All three degrees are felony offenses.

Feminist lobbying has been behind most changes to rape laws. The requirement that a witness corroborate the victim's testimony was repealed in 1974. In 1982 the language defining the requirement of "forcible compulsion" as overcoming a woman's "earnest resistance" was repealed. Forcible compulsion has been redefined as force or threat that instills fear of death or physical injury. The "marital exemption" that prevented a man from being charged with raping his wife was struck down by the New York State Court of Appeals in *People v Liberta* in 1984. In the same case the Court overturned the law's gender-specific language to make rape a gender neutral crime. The reach of rape laws was extended in 1995 through the Sex Offender Registration Act. Modeled after New Jersey's Megan's Law, it required sex offenders to register with the state for at least 10 years. If the risk of repeat offense is designated "high," the offender must continue to register annually beyond 10 years unless a court decides otherwise, and his or her address and photograph can be disseminated to the community. All of these changes, along with some changes in cultural beliefs about female sexuality, have enabled increases in rape prosecutions and convictions. The crime is probably still underreported, but the number of reported forcible rapes in New York State more than doubled between 1965 and 1985 before slowly declining.

Governor's Task Force on Rape and Sexual Assault. *Rape, Sexual Assault, and Child Sexual Abuse: Working Towards a More Responsive Society* (Albany, 1990)
McKinney's Consolidated Laws of New York Annotated. Penal Law (Bk 39), Article 130—Sex Offenses. Practice Commentaries, William C. Donnino (St. Paul, Minn: West Publishing, 1998)

Carolyn E. Cocca

rap music. See HIP HOP.

Rapp-Coudert Committee. See COLD WAR AND MCCARTHYISM.

Raskob, John J(akob) (*b* Lockport, Niagara Co, 19 Mar 1879; *d* Centerville, Md, 15 Oct 1950). Businessman, financier, and Catholic philanthropist. After attending Clark's Business College in Lockport, he became a bookkeeper for the Johnson Co in Lorain, Ohio, and later personal secretary to its manager, Pierre Du Pont. Raskob assisted Du Pont in expanding and modernizing his family business, the explosives manufacturer DuPont, and became its treasurer in 1914. With Du Pont, Raskob shrewdly invested in General Motors Corp (GM) and from 1915 served on the automaker's board of directors, which Du Pont chaired. By 1928 he was a vice president at both GM and DuPont.

During the 1920s Raskob's investments grew into a $100 million fortune. An internationalist, he joined the League of Nations Non-Partisan Association in 1923 and endorsed American membership in the World Court. Domestically he was active in Republican politics, supporting the presidential campaigns of Warren G. Harding and Calvin Coolidge and contributing to other party causes between 1920 and 1927. However, Raskob became friends with Democratic New York State governor Alfred E. Smith, a fellow Catholic and opponent of Prohibition, and supported Smith's presidential bid in 1928. Smith named Raskob chair of the Democratic National Committee (DNC) that year over the objections of party leaders. Raskob reorganized the DNC into an ongoing body, applied efficient business strategies to operations, raised $3.2 million by persuading the rich to contribute to Smith's campaign, and fought unsuccessfully against rising anti-Catholicism.

In 1929 Raskob headed a group of investors intent on building the world's tallest building on the site of the old Waldorf-Astoria Hotel in New York City. Opening in 1931, the Empire State Building failed to find enough tenants to turn a profit, given the depression, but became a New York City icon. Although initially an enthusiastic supporter of Franklin D. Roosevelt's presidency, Raskob soured on the New Deal and was instrumental in organizing and financing the anti-Roosevelt American Liberty League in August 1934. The reelection of Roosevelt in 1936 killed the league and Raskob's role in politics. Remaining active in business, he kept his connections with GM and DuPont until 1946 and contributed to Catholic charities until his death.

Lopata, Roy Haywood. "John J. Raskob: A Conservative Businessman in the Age of Roosevelt" (PhD diss, Univ of Delaware, 1975)
Rudolph, Frederick. "The American Liberty League, 1934–1940," *American Historical Review* 56 (Oct 1950): 19–33
Slayton, Robert. *Empire Statesman: The Rise and Redemption of Al Smith* (New York: Free Press, 2001)

Harvey Strum

Rathbone. Town (pop 1,080) in S central Steuben Co. Settled in 1793, the town was formed from Addison, Cameron, and Woodhull in 1856. Lumbering was an important enterprise during the 19th century. The Erie Railroad (1850) facilitated shipment of farm products: butter was shipped beginning in 1860, and a cheese factory was built in 1876. The town is home to the 126-acre (51 ha) Helmer Creek Wildlife Management Area. Many residents commute to jobs in nearby communities.

Virginia L. Wright and Jerry Wright

ratification convention. See UNITED STATES CONSTITUTION RATIFICATION.

Rauschenbusch, Walter (*b* Rochester, 4 Oct 1861; *d* Rochester, 25 July 1918). Baptist clergyman and theological educator. Rauschenbusch's father, August, a German immigrant, was a widely respected Baptist pastor and professor of general studies and taught the Bible in the German department at the Rochester Theological Seminary. Walter attended the gymnasium in Gutersloh, Germany, from 1879 to 1883, after which he graduated from the University of Rochester (1884) and Rochester Theological Seminary (1886).

He went to New York City to serve as a pastor at Second German Baptist Church (1886–97). His congregation was near Hell's Kitchen, a Manhattan immigrant neighborhood with widespread poverty. Rauschenbusch's environment forced a major revision in his social awareness and theological system. Under the influence of Henry George, Richard Ely, and Christian socialist writers and thinkers, Rauschenbusch became an advocate for the Social Gospel, a movement that combined a commitment to realizing the Kingdom of God within society, a critique of unchecked capitalism, and support for public ownership of utilities and trade unions. In 1889 he developed profound deafness from a neurological disorder that limited his potential in the local church ministry. In 1892 he helped organize the Brotherhood of the Kingdom, a group of religious progressives dedicated to social change, which lasted until the early 1910s, when many of its members joined with the Federal Council of the Churches of Christ in America. A sabbatical to Europe in 1891 further acquainted him with European social reformers.

In 1897 he moved to Rochester to take up his father's chair in the German department of Rochester Theological Seminary, and four years later he also took the chair in church history. With the endorsement of seminary president Augustus H. Strong, Rauschenbusch pushed ahead to advocate and publish his views. He wrote *Christianity and the Social Crisis* (1907), which rocketed him to fame, and his reputation established the Rochester Theological Seminary as a center of social Christianity. In Rochester Rauschenbusch was active in a variety of social efforts, working with the YMCA to produce a comprehensive investigation of the city's social problems, campaigning to lower the rates of Rochester Gas and Electric, and reforming local government and the public schools. In 1908 he cofounded the People's Sunday Evening, a popular lecture series for working people that attracted crowds of over 30,000 and lasted until 1916. He had a great impact on the theological direction of the Northern Baptist Convention, assisting it to form a Social Service Commission, but less upon his own German Baptist Conference, which thought him too liberal. World War I left him disillusioned with the prospects for serious social change.

Hudson, Winthrop S., ed. *Walter Rauschenbusch: Selected Writings* (New York: Paulist Press, 1984)
Minus, Paul M. *Walter Rauschenbusch: American Reformer* (New York: Macmillan, 1988)
Sharpe, Dores. *Walter Rauchenbusch* (New York: Macmillan, 1942)

William H. Brackney

Ravena [RA-VEE-NAH]. Village (pop 3,369) in Coeymans (Albany Co). At the junction of the Saratoga and Hudson River Railroad (1865) and the West Shore Railroad (1883), Coeyman's Square became known as Coeyman's Junction, acquired a post office in 1886, and was renamed Ravena in 1893. It became a shipment point for local produce to urban markets and the site of a rail yard and shops for the West Shore. The village was incorporated in 1914. Although the rail yards were moved to nearby Selkirk in 1924 after consolidation into the New York Central Railroad system, many Ravena residents commuted the short distance to the new yard, and the village remained a residential and commercial center for the surrounding rural area.

Wesley G. Balla

Raymond, Henry J(arvis) (*b* Lima, Livingston Co, 24 Jan 1820; *d* New York City, 18 June 1869). Journalist and politician. Raymond contributed to Horace Greeley's *New-Yorker* weekly while a University of Vermont undergraduate, went to work at the paper after graduating in 1840, and helped Greeley start the *New York Tribune* in 1841. Raymond joined the *Courier and Enquirer* in 1843 and married Juliette Weaver the same year. In 1846 Raymond and Greeley debated in print, with Raymond sharply criticizing Greeley's advocacy of utopian socialism. Elected to the New York State Assembly as a Whig in 1849, Raymond became Speaker in 1851 and was elected lieutenant governor in 1854. With Albany banker George Jones and others, he launched the *New-York Daily Times* on 18 Sept 1851, setting higher standards than the dominant *Tribune* and *Herald.* Sometimes called the Republican Party's godfather, Raymond was keynote speaker of the 1856 national convention, played key roles in subsequent presidential campaigns, and became chairman of the party's national committee. Elected to Congress in 1864, Raymond doomed his political career by prematurely advocating postwar leniency toward southerners and supporting Pres Andrew Johnson, but he remained involved with editing the *Times.*

Brown, Francis. *Raymond of the Times* (New York: Norton, 1951)
Turner, Hy B. *When Giants Ruled: The Story of Park Row* (New York: Fordham Univ Press, 1999)

Richard E. Mooney

Reader's Digest. The magazine was the brainchild of William Roy DeWitt Wallace (1889–1981) and his wife, Lila Acheson Wallace (1887–1984). DeWitt Wallace had long held that much American journalism was too verbose and that too many interesting stories were escaping public attention because they appeared in small, specialized magazines. He believed there might be a market for a digest-sized magazine that both reprinted and condensed articles originally published elsewhere. After failing to interest any publisher, the couple decided to put out the magazine themselves and printed 5,000 copies from their Greenwich Village apartment. The first issue of *Reader's Digest* appeared in February 1922. The following fall the operation moved to Lila Wallace's hometown of Pleasantville (Westchester Co). In 1929 the magazine, which had been sold exclusively by mail, first appeared on newsstands, and circulation reached 62,000.

The magazine's circulation grew steadily, reaching 1,457,500 in 1935. In 1939 the Wallaces moved the business into new headquarters in Chappaqua (Westchester Co). During the 1940s and 1950s the company expanded circulation to Latin America and Europe and in 1950 launched the Reader's Digest Condensed Books division. The magazine began to include advertising only in 1955 and has never accepted ads for tobacco products; alcoholic beverage advertising was permitted as of 1979. In 1973 the Wallaces ended their management of the business. The company was publicly traded as of 1980. Subscriptions peaked at 17.5 million in 1985. The magazine underwent a stylistic makeover in 1998, adding more photographs and artwork and moving the table of contents off its traditional place on the front page. In 2002 the magazine had 12 million subscribers and the Reader's Digest Association had revenues of $2.4 billion. There are approximately 1,000 workers at the global headquarters in Chappaqua.

Canning, Peter. *American Dreamers: The Wallaces and "Reader's Digest": An Insider's Story* (New York: Simon & Schuster, 1996)

J. Justin Gustainis

Reading. Town (pop 1,786) in N Schuyler Co. Bordered on the east by Seneca Lake and settled in 1798, Reading was formed from Fredericks-town [now Wayne, Steuben Co] in 1806 and served by the Syracuse, Geneva and Corning Railroad (1877). Agriculture has always been dominant, especially grape culture. In 2002 there were several wineries, including Lakewood Vineyards, and one of Schuyler Co's two salt-brine extraction plants.

Glenda Gephart

Real Property Services, Office of. An independent agency within the Executive Department responsible for overseeing and helping to improve the local administration of the property tax, establishing equalization rates, and carrying out the policies of the State Board of Real Property Services. The first State Board of Equalization was established in 1859 to oversee the fair distribution of the state property tax among counties. Equalization to a common basis of market value was required to impose a common tax because of varying levels of assessment among counties. Through 1959 the expanded authority to make equalization rates for each city, town, and village, and the authority to assess special franchise (the right of railroads and utilities to occupy public rights-of-way) were granted successively to various agencies. Although the state property tax was terminated in 1928, equalization rates continue to be used for school and county tax distribution as well as for determination of tax and debt limits.

In 1960 the legislature reconstituted the State Board of Equalization and Assessment as a permanent agency (it had been created as a temporary commission in 1949). The State Division of Equalization and Assessment, with responsibility for implementing the programs of the state board, was designated an independent agency within the Executive Department in 1975. The division was renamed the State Office of Real Property Services in 1995. Since the Annual Aid Program was enacted in 1999 to encourage municipalities to comply with state law by keeping assessments current each year, the number of reassessments has tripled annually. In 2000 property tax in New York State generated more than $26 billion. Office headquarters in 2002 were in Albany; regional offices were in Batavia (Genesee Co), Newburgh (Orange Co), Syracuse, and Albany, with satellite offices in Saranac Lake (Franklin Co) and Melville (Suffolk Co). The agency had a budget of $52.4 million and employed 403 people. As of January 2003, more than one-quarter of the state's municipalities had inequitable assessments because of a lack of reassessment activity.

Kilmer, Robert F. "Introduction to the Real Property Tax Law." In *McKinney's Consolidated Laws of New York Annotated.* Real Property Tax Law (Bk 49-A) (Brooklyn: Edward Thompson Co, 1960)

reapportionment. See APPORTIONMENT AND DISTRICTING.

Reason, Charles L(ewis) (*b* New York City, 21 July 1818; *d* New York City, 16 Aug 1893). Educator and abolitionist. Born to Haitian immigrants, Reason grew up in New York City and excelled at the African Free School, becoming a math instructor there at the age of 14. Rejected from the city's General Theological Seminary because of his race, Reason quit the Episcopal Church in disgust and studied at New York Free Central College in McGrawville [now McGraw, Cortland Co]. An active poet in the 1830s, Reason was published in the *Colored American* and wrote the acclaimed poem "Freedom" in 1847. While pursing a teaching career, he became a prominent abolitionist and an advocate for rights of fugitive slaves, and in 1840 served as secretary for the New York State Convention for Negro Suffrage. An opponent of the American Colonization Society, he campaigned for the creation of a black industrial college, which led to the founding of the state-sponsored Society for the Promotion of Education for Colored Children (1847). Reason taught at Public School 2 in New York City in 1849, the same year he became the first African American professor at an American college, teaching literature, mathematics, and French at New York Free Central College. After a term as principal of the Institute of Colored Youth in Philadelphia (1852–55), Reason returned to New York City, where he worked as a public school teacher and administrator and became a national advocate for civil rights, education, and labor. In July 1853 he served as secretary to the Colored National Convention in Rochester and after the Civil War as vice president of the New York State Labor Union. In 1873 Reason spearheaded a movement to outlaw segregation in New York State schools. When he retired in 1892, Reason had dedicated 60 years to public education. Although he is known to have married three times, details on his personal life are scant.

Sernett, Milton. *North Star County: Upstate New York and the Crusade for African American Freedom* (Syracuse: Syracuse Univ Press, 2002)

Graham Russell Hodges

recreational boatbuilding. In the mid–19th century urban vacationers flocked to watery regions like the Adirondacks, the Thousand Islands, the Finger Lakes, and Long Island Sound, and area boatbuilders adapted local types of boats for pleasure use. Artisans such as Xavier Colon of Clayton (Jefferson Co) and George Smith of Long Lake (Hamilton Co) were typical, and by the 1870s boatbuilders such as James Everson in Williamsburg (Kings Co), George Ruggles in Rochester, and J. Henry Rushton in Canton (St. Lawrence Co) catered to this new market. On Long Island Sound yards turned out sailing yachts for the growing affluent class of the New York City metropolis.

By the early 20th century boatbuilding increasingly was taken over by firms that standardized production, combining quality with volume and marketing widely. Technological innovations also affected the industry. The popularity of motorboats by the 1920s meant that builders needed more capital, more specialized labor, and access to transportation networks. The Fay and Bowen Engine Co in Geneva (Ontario Co), the Charles L. Seabury/Gas Engine and Power Co (later Consolidated) on the Harlem River, and the Lozier Motor Co in Plattsburgh were among the companies building motorboats, and smaller craft were produced by the Penn Yan Boat Co (Yates Co) and the Thompson Boat Co in Cortland. By the 1930s powerboat production had shifted to the Midwest and some builders simply closed, but others relocated, such as John L. Hacker, who became one of the great names in the industry after he moved from Albany to Michigan around 1914.

Because of the economic depression of the 1930s, the rapid development of the pleasure boat market, and the introduction of fiberglass and aluminum technology after World War II, many boat companies went out of business. Some New York State companies, such as Penn Yan, attempted to adapt by switching from wood to fiberglass, but the transformation of the industry spelled the end for many others. Grumman Aircraft Engineering Corp assumed industry leadership in the years following World War II with facilities in Bethpage (Nassau Co) and later Marathon (Cortland Co) and quickly became the most successful builder of small craft in the state and the nation. Although today most recreational boat types are primarily manufactured by large national firms, New York State is home to a number of small shops that cater to pleasure boaters looking for traditional designs or types.

Bond, Hallie E. *Boats and Boating in the Adirondacks* (Syracuse: Syracuse Univ Press, 1995)

Hallie E. Bond

recycling. See SANITATION AND SEWAGE.

Red Creek. Village (pop 521) in Wolcott (Wayne Co). Settled before 1811, Jacksonville was renamed Red Creek in 1836 for the high iron content in its water, and the village was incorporated in 1852. Red Creek originally developed as a crossroads trading point. Early industries included a woolen factory, a furnace, and a tannery. Construction of the Rome, Watertown and Ogdensburg Railroad began in Red Creek 1873, proceeding east and west to Oswego and Lewiston. The railroad spurred the food-processing and -packing industries, especially fruit evaporators. Agrilink operated a cannery there until 2002.

Scott C. Monje

Red Cross. Medical relief organization. The organization that would become the International Committee of the Red Cross was founded by Swiss businessman Henri Dunant in 1863. Clara Barton (1821–1912) founded the American Red Cross in 1881 while she was living in Dansville (Livingston Co). The village was the site of the first local organization, which was formed in August 1881 to provide money and supplies and to organize local relief efforts. Later that year Rochester and Syracuse also started Red Cross societies. Barton played a key role in persuading the US government to ratify the Geneva convention, which recognized battlefield aid workers as noncombatants, in 1882. In 1893 the New York Red Cross Society, a branch of the national organization, was founded in Manhattan, and from 1893 to 1914 the chapter operated the Red Cross Hospital and Training School for Sisters (nurses) in Manhattan.

While the New York organization continued to grow in size and resources, Barton's Washington-based American National Red Cross was plagued by financial irregularities and eccentricities that alienated potential philanthropists, and Barton was forced out of leadership in 1904. The national organization carried out a reform program in 1905 that included the creation of state branches supported by local chapters. The New York State headquarters was opened in Manhattan in May 1905.

During World War II the Red Cross cooperated in a Plasma for Britain program and helped collect over 1 million units (pints). However, in 1941 the director of the newly formed Blood Donor Service in New York City resigned after the Red Cross agreed to the US armed forces' demand that nonwhite donors be excluded from a military plasma collection program. The following year the organization began accepting donations from African Americans, but the blood was labeled with the donor's race. In January 1948 Rochester opened a Red Cross Regional Blood Center and held the first Red Cross blood drive collecting specifically for civilian use.

After World War II the organization faced a steep decline in volunteerism and an increased need for services. The 1950s became known as the Decade of Disasters. Beginning with the Korean conflict, when New York sent 400,000 units of blood overseas, the organization was called to service in 3,100 major relief operations in that decade. A reorganization in 1959 created the American Red Cross in Greater New York. In the 1990s State Service Councils were created by the national organization to share resources and coordinate services. The New York–Penn Blood Services Region, formed in 1994 and headquartered in West Henrietta (Monroe Co), was the only Red Cross blood services organization operating in the state in 2003.

In addition to its wartime efforts, the Red Cross in New York State has administered relief in the aftermath of disasters for more than 100 years. The organization responded to such events as the Triangle Shirtwaist Factory fire (1911), the sinking of the *Titanic* (1912), the 1947 smallpox outbreak in New York City, hurricanes and severe storms (1955, 1960, 1992), the explosion of TWA Flight 800 (1996), and the terrorist attacks on the World Trade Center (1993, 2001). Following the 11 Sept 2001 bombings, the American National Red Cross ran a fund-raising campaign called the Liberty Disaster Fund, which became controversial when it was revealed that much of the money would not go directly to the victims of the 11 September terrorist attacks. Subsequent pressure from Congress and the public persuaded the Red Cross to narrow the focus of the fund and to use the money exclusively for victims of those attacks. In 2003 there were 36 active Red Cross chapters in New York State, the largest of which was the Greater New York Chapter. During the fiscal year ending in June 2003, this chapter responded to 1,855 multifamily disaster situations, with 45,413 volunteers aiding 8,216 families.

American Red Cross in Greater New York. "The History of the Red Cross in New York," http://www.nyredcross.org/organization/history/index.htm

Dulles, Foster Rhea. *The American Red Cross: A History* (New York: Harper & Bros, 1950)

Pryor, Elizabeth Brown. *Clara Barton: Professional Angel* (Philadelphia: Univ of Pennsylvania Press, 1987)

Ellen Sexton

Albany volunteers make bandages for Red Cross distribution, 1917.

Redfield. Town (pop 607) in NE Oswego Co. Settled in 1795 by Connecticut migrants, its New England village green known as Center Square was laid out in 1800, and the town was formed from Mexico in the same year. Located on the military road to Sackets Harbor (Jefferson Co), it produced and shipped forest products, including lumber, the oils of wintergreen and other plants, and spruce gum. The northern half of town was taken off in 1843 as Greenborough but returned to Redfield in 1848. Salmon River Reservoir (1914) flooded valley lands in town but created sites for outdoor recreation and generated waterpower. The town includes Edrington Park, a hunting and fishing preserve, and Little John State Wildlife Management Area. Much of the town is used for hunting, fishing, and other outdoor sports. Most residents commute to work.

Barbara J. Dix

Red Hook. Town (pop 10,408) and village (pop 1,805) in NW Dutchess Co. Called Roode Hoeck by Dutch mariners because of red berries growing on the hillsides, it was patented to Pieter Schuyler in 1688 and settled in 1712 by Palatine Germans and New York Dutch. The town was formed from Rhinebeck in 1812, and the village was incorporated in 1894. Before the Hudson River Railroad (1851), produce was freighted on the river. Livingston family members built substantial estates along the Hudson, as did wealthy New York City families, such as the Astors. Cigars were made throughout most of the 19th century at the Red Hook Tobacco Factory. It remains a fruit farming town, celebrating an apple blossom festival in May (begun 1995). It was the home of St. Stephens College (1860), which was renamed Bard College in 1934. The local economy is supported largely by commuters to Poughkeepsie and Kingston (Ulster Co).

William P. McDermott

Red House. Town (pop 38) in SE Cattaraugus Co. White settlement began in 1827 and the town, named for a house on the banks of what is now Red House Creek, was formed from Salamanca in 1869. Lumbering has always predominated over farming. One of the largest enterprises was Bay State Lumber Co (?1853–1875); other related industries, one a handle factory (1873), also operated. The Atlantic and Great Western (1860) and two other railroads served the town. A number of federal and state actions during the course of the 20th century effectively dropped the population until Red House was, in 2000, the least populous town in the state. In 1921 the state appropriated 32,160 acres (13,015 ha), 80% of the town's area, for Allegany State Park; in 1965 the federal government created Allegheny Reservoir for flood control, swallowing the hamlet of Red House; also in 1965, Rte 17 (I-86) was built through town. In 2003 only 14 landowners remain. The state has first claim to buy their land to expand the park. The Allegany Indian Reservation of the Seneca Nation divides the town's territory.

Bruce D. Fredrickson and Madelynn P. Fredrickson

Red Jacket [Sagoyewatha] (*b* Canoga, [now in Seneca Co], ?1758; *d* Buffalo Creek Reservation, [now in Erie Co], 20 Jan 1830). Seneca orator and diplomat. He spent his early years in Central New York and probably moved with other Seneca to Buffalo Creek in 1780. During the Revolution, he was an ally of the British, who presented him with a red coat, the basis of his English name. Nevertheless, his military role was controversial, and he was ever after dogged with accusations of cowardice by his political enemies. From the 1780s to the 1820s, he participated in nearly all significant councils of the Seneca with Whites and other Indian nations in New York State, Canada, and the Ohio Country. He was the spokesman for the Seneca in the negotiations leading up to the Treaty of Canandaigua (1794), which still defines the basic relationship between the US government and the Iroquois living in New York State. Red Jacket was also an important figure in negotiations concerning the sale of Seneca lands and played a controversial role at the Treaty of Big Tree (1797); some Whites who participated in the treaty charged him, probably unfairly, with supporting the sale privately while opposing it in public. After 1805 Red Jacket became famous from the wide publication of his speeches opposing Christian missionaries and any additional sale of Indian land; his "Reply" to the missionary Jacob Cram, originally delivered at Buffalo in 1805, proved popular and was widely reprinted.

Red Jacket's position among the Iroquois rested largely on his highly valued oratorical skill, but he never earned the status of a league chief and was only one of several important chiefs at the Buffalo Creek Reservation. Although he was eloquent in defense of Indian religious values, he was hostile to the Seneca religious leader Handsome Lake. He initially opposed Seneca involvement in the War of 1812, but he later served as an officer with the New York State Indians who joined the American army. After 1815 the Seneca in Western New York were increasingly factionalized into the so-called Christian and Pagan Parties, and Red Jacket became the most publicly visible leader of the Pagan Party at the Buffalo Creek Reservation. In the 1820s he opposed any missionary presence on the reservations and any proposals to move the New York Indians to the West. In 1827 the Christian Party at Buffalo Creek, with the implied backing of the US government, attempted to depose him. Reconciled in the final two years of his life to the existence of Christians among the Seneca, he sought to work with his former political enemies. Red Jacket was buried in 1830 at the Mission Cemetery on the Buffalo Creek Reservation.

Red Jacket at Niagara Falls, wearing the peace medal he received from Pres George Washington in 1792. Painting by Robert W. Weir, 1828.

Densmore, Christopher. *Red Jacket: Iroquois Diplomat and Orator* (Syracuse: Syracuse Univ Press, 1999)
Parker, Arthur C. *Red Jacket: Last of the Seneca* (New York: McGraw-Hill, 1952)

Christopher Densmore

Red Oaks Mill. Locality (pop 4,930) in Poughkeepsie and La Grange (Dutchess Co). A crossroads with a mill on Wappinger Creek until the mid–20th century, the area slowly grew into a Poughkeepsie suburb. With employment nearby at IBM beginning in 1948, the community expanded with tract housing and a small shopping center.

William P. McDermott

Red Scare. See World war i.

referendums. Questions on public issues passed by the state legislature or state constitutional convention and submitted to the people for their approval or rejection. Generally only a simple majority is required. State referendums usually relate to whether or not to hold a convention to amend the New York State Constitution, revise it, or authorize the state to borrow funds. A local government in New York State may use referendums to resolve any issue, provided there are particular grounds for them in the state constitution or in state law. Generally local governments are required to use referendums on proposed changes in the form or structure of government.

In 1821 the New York State legislature, for the first time, passed a bill requiring a referendum on the question of whether to convene a constitutional convention. It also required the convention, if materialized, to submit its work to the people. The voters at the time voted to hold a constitutional conventional and then in 1822 ratified the result. The Constitutional Convention of 1846 proposed a referendum (among other reforms) mandating that, starting in 1866 and every 20 years thereafter and at other intervals designated by the legislature, a referendum be offered asking the people whether a convention should be held to revise and amend the state constitution; it was later approved by the voters. Even when a revised constitution is rejected by the voters, some of the constitutional provisions often reappear as separate referendums. Although the 1915 proposed constitution was rejected, in 1925 the short ballot consolidation amendment was passed as a referendum, and in 1927 the executive budget amendment also won popular approval. The 1938 Constitutional Convention also issued significant referendums, this time approved by the voters; enacted during the depression these referendums included state guarantees to the rights of labor and the responsibility of the state government to the poor. In 1967 the revised constitution was rejected by the voters, and in 1977 and 1997 referendums on whether to hold a constitutional convention were rejected. Despite several attempts, most recently in 1995, voters have consistently rejected efforts to circumvent the constitutional requirement that bond issues be subject to statewide referendum (bond issues regularly appear on the statewide ballot). Although few significant constitutional issues have been approved by voters in recent decades, voters in 2001 approved an amendment that eliminated gender-specific language in the state constitution.

Galie, Peter J. *The New York State Constitution: A Reference Guide* (Westport, Conn: Greenwood, 1991)

Bernard Hirschhorn

Reform Democrats. Neighborhood political clubs formed in New York City after World War II to challenge control of the preexisting Democratic Party organizations. The initial impetus came mainly from returning veterans impatient with the one-man rule of existing clubs that bestowed office on the basis of seniority. The old clubs also excluded women from full membership. Reform clubs, in contrast, were committed to grassroots participation and included many female activists. Club officers and candidates were chosen through democratic votes of an open membership. The first enduring reform club, the Lexington Democratic Club, was established in 1949.

Volunteers for Adlai Stevenson's 1956 bid for the US presidency formed a new generation of reform clubs. The largest were the Riverside Democrats and the Village Independent Democrats (VID). They challenged Manhattan Democratic leader Carmine DeSapio. By 1958 these clubs received the backing of such influential state political figures as Eleanor Roosevelt and former governor Herbert H. Lehman. By 1960 Riverside Democratic leader William Fitts Ryan defeated an incumbent US congressman, mostly by linking him to DeSapio and bossism. The next year, Mayor Robert F. Wagner Jr decided to run against bossism, though he himself had run twice before as the candidate of the county leaders. He swept to victory along with VID candidate James I. Lanigan, who defeated DeSapio for district leader, thereby depriving him of his Tammany leadership as well. DeSapio made three subsequent comeback attempts and was defeated each time by Ed Koch. Despite these victories the reformers never really managed to gain control of the Manhattan Democratic leadership until Koch was elected mayor in 1977.

Koch's mayoralty intensified divisions in the reform movement between moderate and left liberals. Moderate liberals generally supported his programs, but by his second term some had begun to question his combative political style, especially on racial issues. Reform clubs played a leading role in Koch's 1989 defeat by David Dinkins, New York City's first black mayor. Despite many local political successes and the election of Charles Schumer of Brooklyn to the US Senate in 1998, reform clubs have been largely on the sidelines of citywide politics under Republican mayors Rudolph Giuliani (1995–2001) and Michael Bloomberg (2002–).

McNickle, Chris. *To Be Mayor of New York* (New York: Columbia Univ Press, 1993)

Jonathan Soffer

Reformed Churches. Three of the main Reformed Churches, those emerging from the Calvinist rather than the Lutheran wing of the Reformation on the Continent, came to New York Colony in the 17th and 18th centuries: the Dutch, French, and German Reformed. Of these, the Dutch was the most significant.

Dutch Reformed Church

The Dutch Reformed Church dates its beginnings in New Netherland to 1628. Its doctrinal cornerstones are the Belgic Confession, the Heidelberg Catechism, and the Canons of the Synod of Dort (1618–19). Its form of government is presbyterian. A consistory, made up of the minister and the elders and deacons, governs the local congregation. Over time, consistories came to report to semiannual classes, mediating institutions between the local churches and the General Synod, the main judicatory body of the denomination, which meets annually.

As the only church sanctioned by the Dutch West India Co in New Netherland, the Dutch Reformed Church served people of many ethnic and religious backgrounds. Ministers and congregations of all Calvinist backgrounds (English, Scottish, French, and German) were welcomed by the Dutch Reformed clergy, as they were by the authorities of New Netherland, but both church and state discriminated against those not conforming to Dort. Full membership in the Dutch Reformed Church in its early centuries required a thorough acquaintance with the Heidelberg Catechism, memorization of various prayers, psalms, and creeds, and a public profession of faith.

Toleration for all religions came with the English takeover of New Netherland in 1664. Under the Articles of Surrender, the Dutch were allowed to continue the public practice of their religion. But at the end of the 17th century, the Dutch Reformed Church began to be threatened by efforts on the part of the English to further the Anglican Church. Hampered also by a shortage of Reformed ministers and by a rift in the laity over the Anglicizing tendencies of the New York Reformed Dutch clergy, the Reformed Church entered the 18th century in a weak state. Its difficulties were exacerbated by a major internal controversy in the 1720s and 1730s over Pietist preaching and principles. At midcentury, dissension arose over the use of English for preaching, accompanied by conflicts between the "coetus" and "conferentie" factions over the relationship of the American body to its mother church in the Netherlands. After achieving ecclesiastical independence from Amsterdam in 1772, with a Plan of Union for future harmony, the Reformed Church agreed upon a new constitution (published in 1793) accentuating individual liberty of conscience while adhering to its traditional standards of faith.

In the 19th century, notwithstanding progress toward internal unity, the Reformed Dutch Church continued to have its share of controversies. These had to do with the ongoing process of Americanization, which now required (or so it seemed to progressives within the church) new styles of worship compatible with a rapidly changing society and with the spirit of evangelical piety that filled the air. Conservatives resisted change and so-called heart religion, and especially any reinterpretations of doctrine received at Dort. Progressives, however, welcomed opportunities to broaden the denomination's appeal, which they believed was hampered by its "foreign" image and its insistence on the theology of the 16th and 17th centuries. Innovations such as the revival meeting, the Sunday school, missionary activity, women's societies, participation in moral-reform and benevolent associations, and ecumenical action proved the progressives right in the long run, for the Reformed Dutch Church in New York State thrived after adopting them. Its period of greatest growth was from 1850 to 1880. After this, especially in New York City, the Reformed Church went into a decline for some decades.

Pulpit made in the Netherlands and installed in the Dutch Reformed Church of Beverwijck, 1656.

Its fortunes revived after World War II, with concerted efforts to start up new congregations, support lagging older ones, expand programs for youth, engage in domestic mission, oppose apartheid in South Africa, support conscientious objectors to the war in Vietnam, and admit women to church office for the first time. The main thrust in the last quarter of the 20th century was toward diversity and new ways of relating to urban communities. As the 21st century began, Reformed Church congregations in New York State counted not only a strong African American element but also worship in a number of languages other than English, including Spanish, German, Taiwanese, Korean, Japanese, Mandarin, Ghanaian, Indonesian, and Thai. A Chair of Metro-Urban Ministry at the denomination's theological seminary in New Brunswick, NJ, endowed in 2000 by the First Reformed Church of Schenectady, ensures the future of this trend.

French and German Reformed Churches

The Revocation of the Edict of Nantes by Louis XIV in 1685 produced a surge of about 800 French Protestants, or Huguenots, in New York Colony and the organization of French Reformed congregations in Manhattan, Staten Island, New Rochelle (Westchester Co), and New Paltz (Ulster Co). However, because of their small numbers, intermarriage with those of other Reformed faiths, and similarities between French Reformed doctrine and polity and that of the Dutch, Scottish, and English Reformed Churches (which allowed for comfortable assimilation), the French Reformed Church did not flourish beyond the colonial period. In addition, many Huguenots joined the Anglican Church.

Huguenot refugee merchant Elias Neau started an important school in New York City for African slaves and became well known for his deeply pious letters and tracts written from Marseilles, France, where he had been imprisoned for six years for his Protestant beliefs. Back in New York City in 1699, his conversion to Anglicanism dealt a severe blow to the French Reformed Church there, as did the subsequent conformity of that church to the Church of England.

German Reformed Churches were formed by Palatine refugees in early 18th-century New York Colony, notably in the Hudson, Schoharie, and Mohawk Valleys. In 1747 the German Reformed Church organized its first synod. After experiencing all of the same growing pains as the Reformed Dutch Church, it adopted a constitution in 1793 and changed its name to the Reformed Church in the United States. In 1934 this body, which accepted Lutheran as well as Reformed components, merged with the Evangelical Synod of North America to form the Evangelical and Reformed Church. Organized on presbyterian lines, it accepted both the Heidelberg Catechism and Luther's Catechism, as well as the Lutheran Augsburg Confession. In 1957 it merged with the General Council of Christian Churches to form the United Church of Christ.

See also DUTCH.

Brumm, James Hart, ed. *Equipping the Saints: The Synod of New York, 1800–2000* (Grand Rapids, Mich: Eerdmans Publishing, 2000)

Butler, Jon. *The Huguenots in America: A Refugee People in New World Society* (Cambridge, Mass: Harvard Univ Press, 1983)

De Jong, Gerald F. *The Dutch Reformed Church in the American Colonies* (Grand Rapids, Mich: Eerdmans Publishing, 1978)

Fabend, Firth Haring. *Zion on the Hudson: Dutch New York and New Jersey in the Age of Revivals* (New Brunswick, NJ: Rutgers Univ Press, 2000)

Firth Haring Fabend

Regents examinations and state testing. Tests used to maintain instructional standards in New York State. In 1865 the New York State Board of Regents distributed the first "preliminary" examinations for entry into secondary schools and developed a testing system based on high scholastic standards accompanied by curriculum, syllabi, and teachers' guides. In 1877 a statute authorized the Regents to give academic examinations as a standard for high school graduation and college admission. In 1921–22 the exams were made optional for schools under city and village superintendents, allowing the use of College Entrance Examination Board tests or local exams approved by the New York State Education Department. By 1925 Regents high school exams were given in 68 different subjects. Studies conducted during the 1920s and 1930s indicated that high scores on Regents exams could be good predictors of success in college; however, the complexity and expense of the exam system was a concern. In 1927 one-third of the high school exams were discontinued, and consolidation of Regents exams continued through the 1960s.

Although academic subjects were the primary focus of state testing, Regents exams were offered for some commercial, vocational training, and domestic science courses beginning in 1898. General high school education for young adults was also provided in evening sessions beginning in the late 1920s. Special state aid was provided for adult secondary education programs beginning in 1945. The state-administered high school equivalency exam for the General Education Diploma (GED) became available in 1947 and was revised in 2000. Since 1940 the State Education Department has also issued standardized reading and math progress tests for middle and upper grades. New state tests were developed under Title I of the federal Elementary and Secondary Education Act, and funds made available in 1965–66 led to the development of Pupil Evaluation Program (PEP) tests to measure reading, writing, and math skills for grades three, six, and nine.

The 1984 Regents Action Plan required the demonstration of competency in English, mathematics, science, global studies, and US history and government for high school graduation. Districts were required to report the results of student assessments in the Comprehensive Assessment Report that was used as a state accountability and registration review for all districts. In 1991 the Regents approved the appointment of a State Curriculum and Assessment Council to assist in a comprehensive revision of the state assessment system based on higher learning standards. Incorporating the recommendations of the council, the Regents approved a plan in 1994, implemented in 1996, establishing the Regents exams as the general testing standard for high school graduation for all districts in New York State, including the large cities. Also in 1996 the Regents approved a policy to phase out Regents Competency Tests developed in the 1970s as the minimum standard for the local high school diploma, making the Regents exams the sole criteria for graduation for students beginning with those entering grade nine in 1996. A State Assessment Panel was appointed in 1997 to review alternative tests that could be used in lieu of the revised Regents examinations. Alternative tests are sometimes accepted by the Regents but are required to hold students to the same high standards adopted by the New York State Board of Regents in 1996. The increasing rigor of the Regents examinations created controversy in 2003 when very low passing rates in the Math A test forced the state commissioner of education to provide alternative scoring options. In 2003 all New York State high school students were required to pass examinations in comprehensive English, mathematics, global history and geography, US history and government, and science in order to graduate. The Regents examinations remain unique in the nation.

Folts, James D. *History of the University of the State of New York and the State Education Department, 1784–1996* (Albany: NYS Education Department, 1996)

Barbara Shay

Regional Plan Association (RPA). Formed in 1922 under the leadership of influential urban planner Charles Dyer Norton and a committee of businessmen, architects, engineers, and planners, and with funding from the Russell Sage Foundation. The organization's mission is to improve quality of life in the 31-county New York–New Jersey–Connecticut metropolitan area by creating long-term comprehensive plans and by promoting their implementation across political boundaries. As a nonprofit organization, RPA is governed by a 60-member board of directors and advisory state and local committees that set policy and priorities. The staff is based in Manhattan with three additional offices in the region. RPA takes positions on public policy issues in its published plans and then works cooperatively with the public and private sectors regarding implementation.

RPA's First Plan in 1929 provided the blueprint for transportation improvements, which resulted in the construction of the George Washington, Whitestone, and Verrazano-Narrows Bridges and the Henry Hudson Parkway. The First Plan also helped to create open space networks that included new parks at Orchard Beach (Bronx Co), Flushing Meadows (Queens Co), and the Palisades in New Jersey and New York State. The Second Regional Plan, published in 1968, was instrumental in restoring the region's deteriorating mass transit, preserving threatened natural resources, and revitalizing urban centers. Seaport and airport development around Newark Bay and the creation of NJ TRANSIT and the Metropolitan Transportation Authority were on that agenda. Additionally, local governments acquired 210 mi^2 (544 km^2) of new parkland, including area on Fire Island (Suffolk Co), Sandy Hook, NJ, and Breezy Point (Nassau Co).

The 1996 Third Regional Plan focused RPA's efforts on improving the region's economy, environment, and social equity. Transportation improvements, such as the 2d Ave Subway, the connection of the Long Island Railroad to Grand Central Terminal, and a one-seat ride from Manhattan and Brooklyn to John F. Kennedy International Airport are the centerpiece of its ongoing economic generation program. Environmental successes include Sterling Forest State Park (Orange Co) and a 1997 plan for Governors Island, published with a coalition of civic groups, that was instrumental in the state's acquisition of the island from the federal government. In 2001 RPA formed the Civic Alliance to Rebuild Downtown New York, a coalition of regional leaders, which, in conjunction with the Lower Manhattan Development Corp, has been working to prepare a civic agenda for the redevelopment of Lower Manhattan in the aftermath of the World Trade Center disaster.

Regional Plan Association, http://www.rpa.org

———. *Regional Plan of New York and Its Environs*, 8 vols (1929; repr New York: Arno Press, 1974)

Ann L. Buttenwieser

regional planning. See PLANNING AND REGIONAL PLANNING ASSOCIATIONS.

Reinstein family. Dr Anna Mogilova Reinstein (1866–1948) came to Buffalo from Switzerland in 1891. Her husband, Boris Isaevich Reinstein (1865–1947), joined her in 1892 after fleeing a conviction for plotting to assassinate the czar. They were both ardent socialists, and Boris became a leader of the Socialist Labor Party. He returned to Russia in 1917, and working for the Soviet government, he distributed relief from American supporters. He died there and was buried in the Kremlin Wall. Anna had a long and distinguished career as Buffalo's first female gynecologist. Their son, Victor (1894–1984), practiced medicine and later earned a law degree. In the interwar years, he and his mother purchased large tracts of land, which they sold for suburban development after 1945, becoming quite wealthy. Victor and his wife, Julia Boyer (1906–98), gave land and money for two public libraries, helped organize the central school system, and donated land for a town park and a nature preserve. A Cheektowaga library and a building at the Buffalo and Erie County Historical Society are named in Julia Boyer's honor. Another Cheektowaga library is named in Anna's honor.

Reinstein, Victor. Papers. Cheektowaga Public Library, Cheektowaga, NY

William H. Siener

released time. A religious education program begun in the early 20th century that provides church-sponsored weekday religious instruction to children enrolled in public schools. Public schools have historically supported the practice in various ways, offering course credit, meeting spaces, and transportation, and modifying the school schedule to release children early to allow religious study in classes on campus (released time) and off campus (dismissed time). The idea had early antecedents, including a weekday after-school program at Christ Lutheran Church in New York City in 1906, but did not gain notoriety until Gary, Ind, schools adopted the practice in 1914. By 1922, 50 towns and cities in New York State offered some released or dismissed time for religious instruction.

The issue caused considerable legal controversy in New York State and nationally. In 1948 the US Supreme Court in *McCollum v Board of Education of Champaign County* (Ill) declared released time for in-school programs unconstitutional because it established religion in state schools. Dismissed time was more legally acceptable. In 1927 the New York State Court of Appeals decided that a dismissed-time program in White Plains (Westchester Co) did not violate the state constitutional prohibition against denominational instruction. The State Supreme Court took a similar view of New York City's dismissed-time program in 1948 in *Zorach v Clauson*. It was appealed in 1952, but the US Supreme Court upheld the state court decision, ruling that the program did not violate freedom of religion or constitute the establishment of religion by the government. The Supreme Court stipulated, however, that the program could not be held on public property and could not be supported by public money. Initially enrollments in released-time programs climbed in response to the *Zorach* decision but then began a long, steady decline in the 1960s. New York State does not currently collect statistics on scheduling arrangements between public schools and religious organizations, although they continue to be legal in the terms described in *Zorach*.

Cope, Henry F. *Week-Day Religious Education: A Survey and Discussion of Activities and Problems* (New York: George Doran, 1922)

Gorham, Donald. "A Study of the Status of Weekday Church Schools in the United States" (PhD diss, Univ of Pennsylvania, 1934)

Zimmerman, Jonathan. *Whose America? Culture Wars in the Public Schools* (Cambridge, Mass: Harvard Univ Press, 2002)

Benjamin Justice

religion. New York State's religious diversity, which has arisen through a variety of processes of migration, conversion, and innovation, has produced significant differences in the religious makeup of different parts of the state. In 2003 the New York City metropolitan area had major concentrations of a variety of world religions, with particularly large Roman Catholic and Jewish populations. Cities across the Mohawk corridor generally had a strong Roman Catholic presence but a wide variety of other groups as well. In rural areas, Roman Catholics dominated in Northern and Western New York and Protestants in Central New York.

Colonial Religion

Religious and spiritual questions were central to American Indian identity and played a huge role in defining society, clan, and family structure. Indian religious practices were transformed by European contact, in part through missionaries seeking converts to Christianity and in part through exposure to European social structure. The large Indian population in New York State was a spur to missionary activity, and in the early 17th century French Catholic missionaries began to expand their work from Canada into what is now New York State. Efforts were limited by political and military conflict during the colonial period and by the sharp decline in the Indian population from war and disease, but many Indians converted to Christianity. Some, under the influence of the French, became Roman Catholic, like the beatified 17th-century Mohawk nun Kateri Tekakwitha. Others, like the Mohegan Congregationalist minister Samson Occom, who preached to the Montaukett and the Oneida, were Protestant. Some Iroquois creatively dealt with the crisis to Indian civilization by reviving, in somewhat altered form, their traditional religion, notably the 1799 code promulgated by the Seneca chief Handsome Lake.

The Dutch attempted to create a Calvinist enclave in New Amsterdam and the Hudson Valley. In establishing New Netherland, the Dutch West India Co intended the Reformed Church to be the dominant religious institution but generally allowed adherents of other religious groups to worship in private, though conflicts arose over how other Christian groups were to hold worship services and over the admission of Jews to the colony. By the time the English took control in 1664, the colony was diverse, including, in addition to the Reformed Church, Congregationalists, Presbyterians, Lutherans, Quakers, Roman Catholics, and Jews. This diversity was concentrated primarily in New York City, with the Reformed Church remaining particularly dominant in the more rural Hudson Valley, still one of America's largest concentrations of Dutch Reformed churches.

During the period of English rule, changing patterns of immigration especially influenced the religious composition of New York City, the Hudson and Mohawk Valleys, and Long Island. As English immigration increased, Anglican churches were established throughout these settled areas but were less numerous than in most of the other non–New England colonies, and Anglicans remained a religious minority in New York Colony. Although Anglicanism was the established faith, it was weakly established and limited to New York, Richmond, Westchester, and Queens Cos. The colony's policy of tolerance toward Protestant churches also allowed the spread of dissenting groups from England, such as the Baptists and Quakers. During the 1700s New York Colony experienced a significant increase in immigration from continental Europe and Northern Ireland. As the German population in New York grew, so did the number of Lutheran churches, particularly in the Hudson and Mohawk Valleys. German Reformed churches also began to appear in these areas, and French Huguenots established a number of Reformed churches in the lower Hudson Valley. Scots-Irish immigrants reinforced the presence of Presbyterianism in the lower Hudson Valley and on Long Island. The tolerance granted to Protestant churches did not extend to Roman Catholicism, however, which had almost no institutional presence in New York during the colonial period, though some Catholics did settle in the region. New York City also contained a small Jewish community. Three distinctive religious regions thus developed in colonial New York: a comparatively cosmopolitan New York City; Long Island, dominated mainly by British adherents of Reformed denominations; and the more diverse Hudson and Mohawk Valleys, dominated by the Dutch Reformed Church and other religious groups from continental Europe.

The 19th Century

Following the Revolutionary War, the religious geography of the state gradually became more complex. Through the early national period it remained heavily Protestant. Migration from New England and occupied areas of the state were key to settlement of the state's frontier during the late 1700s and early 1800s. Evangelism and revivalism played an important role in shaping the state's religious character in the early and middle 1800s, a trend that coincided with the nationwide growth of several evangelical Protestant denominations, particularly in newly settled areas with no established religious institutions. As a result, the Methodists and Baptists, and to a lesser extent the Presbyterians, saw rapid increases in membership. The Methodists were the most successful of these in New York State and by midcentury had more than 1,200 churches established; Baptists had nearly 800 and Presbyterians nearly 700.

Central and Western New York underwent a series of revivals and awakenings from the 1820s through the Civil War; the area was called the Burned-over District. Charles Grandison Finney sparked revivals in Rochester and Utica that had far-reaching influence. Upstate New York emerged as a center of religious innovation, giving rise to the Latter-day Saints in 1830 and the beginnings of the Adventist and Spiritualist movements in the 1840s. The state also continued to attract a variety of smaller Christian sects, such as the Shakers, who arrived from England in the late 1700s and established several communities near Albany.

The rapid expansion of European immigration in the 19th century contributed to the religious diversity. New York State was a key destination for Irish emigrants fleeing the devastation of the potato famines of the 1840s. Arriving with little wealth and little interest in resuming an agricultural way of life, Irish immigrants generally settled in urban areas close to their port of arrival. Important Irish communities developed in New York City, Albany, Troy, and other cities, where they contributed significantly to a growing Roman Catholic presence. Emigration from Germany during the early to mid-1800s was more varied and included Protestants, Catholics, and Jews. In rural New York, immigrants tended to have less impact on the religious composition. An important exception developed in the counties along the St. Lawrence River, where the Roman Catholic Church grew with Francophone Canadian immigration.

The 20th Century

As the 19th century ended, changing patterns of immigration transformed the religious character of the state. Most important, the spread of economic and political change in southern and eastern Europe brought about a significant increase in the immigration of Roman Catholics and Jews. Roman Catholics became the state's

Depiction of a religious revival at the Jane Street Methodist Church, New York City, from *Frank Leslie's Illustrated Newspaper,* 11 Feb 1888.

largest religious community, accounting for a third of the population by 1906. Although spread widely throughout the state, their predominance remained most pronounced in New York City and other urban centers, the major destinations for immigrants at the time, but their numbers also increased in the borderlands of northern New York with migration from French Canada. Jewish immigrants escaping persecution and political instability in Europe were even more heavily urbanized than Roman Catholics. New York City became the primary focus of Jewish settlement in the country and by 1920 had the world's largest Jewish population. A further consequence of this immigration was the emergence of distinct ethnoreligious neighborhoods within larger cities, especially New York City. This trend had begun earlier but accelerated as the diversity of immigration increased in the decades before World War I. Neighborhoods identified with a particular ethnoreligious group—for example, Russian Jews, Hungarian Jews, Italian Catholics, and Polish Catholics—became an important feature of urban social geography.

The history of African American religion dates to the 17th century. The African Methodist Episcopal Zion (AMEZ) Church, founded in 1796 in New York City by black members of the Methodist Episcopal Church, organized as a national body in 1821. The Abyssinian Baptist Church, the first black Baptist congregation in the state, was founded in New York City in 1808. Black churches played an important role in the abolitionist struggle and in serving as centers of African American political and spiritual life. The massive migration of Blacks from the rural South to the industrial North during the first half of the 20th century had a major impact on cities in New York State and yielded a resurgence of urban growth in evangelical Protestantism, particularly in Baptist and AME and AMEZ denominations.

At the same time, many newcomers were members of independent churches associated with the Holiness and Pentecostal movements, which provided alternatives to established forms of evangelical Christianity, and found many converts in New York, at first primarily in urban centers but later in rural areas as well. Within the African American community, the effects of religious innovation in movements like Father Divine's Peace Mission, and the Nation of Islam, both non-Christian religious forms that achieved great popularity in black communities, was especially felt in Harlem in Upper Manhattan. Migration from Puerto Rico and from other Spanish-speaking Caribbean counties exerted more significant influence on religious patterns by midcentury, particularly in the New York City area, bringing, along with more Catholicism, various syncretistic religions that had developed in the Caribbean, such as Santeria and Espiritismo, and in recent decades a wave of Pentecostalism and Holiness.

Since the 1960s changes in American immigration law have led to much higher levels of immigration from non-European places, particularly Latin America and Asia. Because New York has continued to be a principal immigrant destination within the United States, it has experienced rapid growth in the various world religions, including Islam, Hinduism, Buddhism, and Sikhism. The New York City metropolitan area was again the center and by the end of the 20th century ranked among the world's most religiously diverse cities. Beyond it, the educated immigrants favored under current immigration law have also contributed to the spread of Islam, Hinduism, and other Asian religions to upstate urban areas, especially those with large universities or technology-oriented industries such as Troy, Albany, Syracuse, Rochester, and Buffalo.

See also BURNED-OVER DISTRICT; NONPROFIT SECTOR.

Ahlstrom, Sydney E. *A Religious History of the American People* (New Haven, Conn: Yale Univ Press, 1972)

Balmer, Randall Herbert. *A Perfect Babel of Confusion: Dutch Religion and English Culture in the Middle Colonies* (New York: Oxford Univ Press, 1989)

Carnes, Tony, and Anna Karpathakis. *New York Glory: Religions in the City* (New York: New York Univ Press, 2001)

Cross, Whitney R. *The Burned-over District: The Social and Intellectual History of Enthusiastic Religion in Western New York, 1800–1850* (Ithaca: Cornell Univ Press, 1950)

Des Grange, Jane. *Long Island's Religious History* (Stony Brook, NY: Suffolk Museum, 1963)

Dolan, Jay P. *The Immigrant Church: New York's Irish and German Catholics, 1815–1865* (Baltimore: Johns Hopkins Univ Press, 1975)

Gaustad, Edwin S., Philip Barlow, and Richard W. Dishno. *New Historical Atlas of Religion in America* (New York: Oxford Univ Press, 2001)

Johnson, Curtis D. *Islands of Holiness: Rural Religion in Upstate New York, 1790–1860* (Ithaca: Cornell Univ Press, 1989)

Perciaccante, Marianne. *Calling Down Fire: Charles Grandison Finney and Revivalism in Jefferson County, New York, 1800–1840* (Albany: SUNY Press, 2003)

Ward, William Ralph. *Faith in Action: A History of Methodism in the Empire State, 1784–1984* (Rutland, Vt: Academy Books, 1986)

Roger W. Stump

Remington. See GUNS AND ORDNANCE INDUSTRY; TYPEWRITER INDUSTRY.

Remington, Frederic (Sackrider) (*b* Canton, St. Lawrence Co, 4 Oct 1861; *d* Ridgefield, Conn, 26 Dec 1909). Painter and sculptor. Raised in Canton, Remington moved with his family in 1873 to Ogdensburg (St. Lawrence Co). He worked at several jobs in Albany, including an 1880 clerkship in the office of the governor, Alonzo B. Cornell, and at the Albany *Morning Express.* In 1881 he made his first trip west to the Montana Territory and subsequently sold his first sketch of cowboys to *Harper's Weekly.* On 1 Oct 1884 he married Eva Adele Caten of Gloversville (Fulton Co). Remington traveled in

Coming through the Rye, bronze sculpture by Frederic Remington, 1902.

Arizona and New Mexico and in 1885, determined to try working as an illustrator, settled in Brooklyn. His sketch *The Apache War—Indian Scouts on Geronimo's Trail* appeared on the cover of *Harper's Weekly* on 9 Jan 1886, launching Remington's successful career illustrating for publications such as *Outing, Century Magazine, Harper's Weekly, Harper's Monthly,* and *Collier's.*

To gain knowledge of his subjects, Remington began a pattern of annual trips to the West. He also took vacations in New York State's North Country, spending time in Canton and Cranberry Lake (St. Lawrence Co) in the Adirondacks, which inspired his portrayals of woodsmen and the vigorous outdoor life. He moved to Manhattan in 1887 and, aspiring to be a fine-arts painter, began submitting his work to major exhibitions. Theodore Roosevelt suggested that Remington illustrate his Western essays, compiled as *Ranch Life and the Hunting-Trail* in 1888. In 1890 Remington and his wife moved to New Rochelle (Westchester Co). The National Academy of Design elected him an associate member the following year. Remington produced his first sculpture, *The Broncho Buster,* in 1895 and began his mastery of the bronze medium. In 1900 he purchased Ingleneuk, a St. Lawrence River island, as a summer retreat and studio. The artist made his last trip to the West in 1908 and moved to his final home in Ridgefield the following year. During his life Remington became the best-known artist of the American West. A man of tremendous energy, Remington produced over 3,000 paintings, drawings, and watercolors, and 22 bronze sculptures (cast in editions); he also wrote over 100 articles, several short stories, and two novels. By using photographs he made notes for use in his art and studied figures in motion, becoming known for his portrayal of action and movement, especially of horses. His early works were naturalistic, but later in his career his paintings incorporated an impressionistic style. His works can be seen in the Frederic Remington Art Museum in Ogdensburg, the Metropolitan Museum of Art in New York City, and the Rockwell Museum in Corning (Steuben Co).

Greenbaum, Michael D. *Icons of the West: Frederic Remington's Sculpture* (Ogdensburg, NY: Frederic Remington Art Museum, 1996)

Hassrick, Peter H., and Melissa J. Webster. *Frederic Remington: A Catalogue Raisonné of Paintings, Watercolors, and Drawings* (Cody, Wyo: Buffalo Bill Historical Center, in association with Univ of Washington Press, 1996)

Sarah E. Boehme

Remsen. Town (pop 1,958) and village (pop 531) in NE Oneida Co. Settled in 1792 the town was formed from Norway (Herkimer Co) in 1798. Welsh settlers first arrived in neighboring Steuben in 1795; by 1878 all but two families in the Village of Remsen were, at least in part, of Welsh ancestry. Remsen benefited from good transportation, as it was located on the road (chartered 1803) from Johnstown (Fulton Co) to Sackets Harbor (Jefferson Co) and the turnpike (completed 1812) from Utica to Sackets Harbor. Early industries produced wood products such as butter tubs and cheese boxes. The village, incorporated in 1845, is partly in Trenton and was on the Black River and Utica Railroad (1855) and the Mohawk and Malone Railroad (1892), now the Adirondack Scenic Railroad, which stops at Remsen's reconstructed depot. Most residents commute to work in 2003, many to Utica by way of Rte 12, rebuilt in 1948–49 as a superhighway. The village is known for the Remsen Barn Festival of Art, held every September since 1980, during which a *gymanfa ganu* (Welsh hymn-singing festival) is held. A landmark is the Capel Cerrig (1831), a Welsh stone church.

Rensselaer [REN-SA-LUR]. City (pop 7,761) in W Rensselaer Co. It was settled ?1628, and a ferry across the Hudson was established in 1642. In 1755 British army surgeon Richard Shuckbergh wrote the words to "Yankee Doodle" at what is now Fort Crailo State Historic Site. The city, incorporated in 1897, was formed from three distinct localities: Bath-on-the-Hudson, platted in the early 1790s and incorporated as a village in 1874; Greenbush, platted speculatively in 1810 and incorporated as a village in 1815; and East Albany, which grew up around the Western Railroad (1841) depot and the shops of the Boston and Albany Railroad (1848). Relatively limited waterpower hampered industrial growth until the steam era. The Huyck Felt Mill (1894–early 1980s), which produced felt lining for papermakers, created a pioneering sick benefit and pension plan (1911). Bayer aspirin was first produced in the United States in 1903 at the former Hudson River Aniline and Color Works. The German-owned company was seized during both world wars and ultimately was sold to Sterling-Winthrop Laboratories, which continued as a major employer until 1993. J. R. Smith's Jew's harp factory was a small but distinctive industry until it closed in the 1960s. The Albany rail passenger station moved to Rensselaer in 1968, and a new $52 million intermodal station opened in 2002. Major employers are Amtrak, Organichem (drug production), and the State Office of Children and Family Services. In 2003 the city was addressing its future with a variety of initiatives, including plans for use of its undeveloped waterfront, a connection to the Hudson River Valley Greenway, and mixed-use condominiums. Greenbush was the birthplace in the 1840s of Edmonia Lewis, the most prominent African American sculptor of the 19th century.

Kathryn T. Sheehan

Rensselaer County (654 mi²/1,694 km²; pop 152,538). Created from Albany Co in 1791 and named for the landholding Van Rensselaer family. Additional territory was annexed from Washington Co in 1822, but Havre Island [now Peebles Island] was surrendered to Saratoga Co in 1888. Rensselaer Co is divided into the Cities of Rensselaer and Troy and 14 towns that contain 6 incorporated villages. Troy is the county seat. The oblong-shaped county lies between the Hudson River and the state border. Elevations range from sea level along the banks of the Hudson River south of Troy to 2,818 feet (859 m) at the summit of Berlin Mountain near the Massachusetts state line. Rensselaer Co's central and eastern portions are part of the Taconic Mountain subregion of the New England Upland physiographic province. Here the folded and thrust-faulted bedrock reflects the action of the Taconic mountain-building event of 450 million years ago, which compressed and sometimes metamorphosed Proterozoic and Ordovician sedimentary rocks and slid them westward over older bedrock. Graywacke, shale, and sandstone underlie the undulating hills of the centrally located Rensselaer Plateau. The higher Taconics along the state border are composed of phyllite and green schist.

The western third of the county lies within the Hudson Valley subregion of the Hudson-

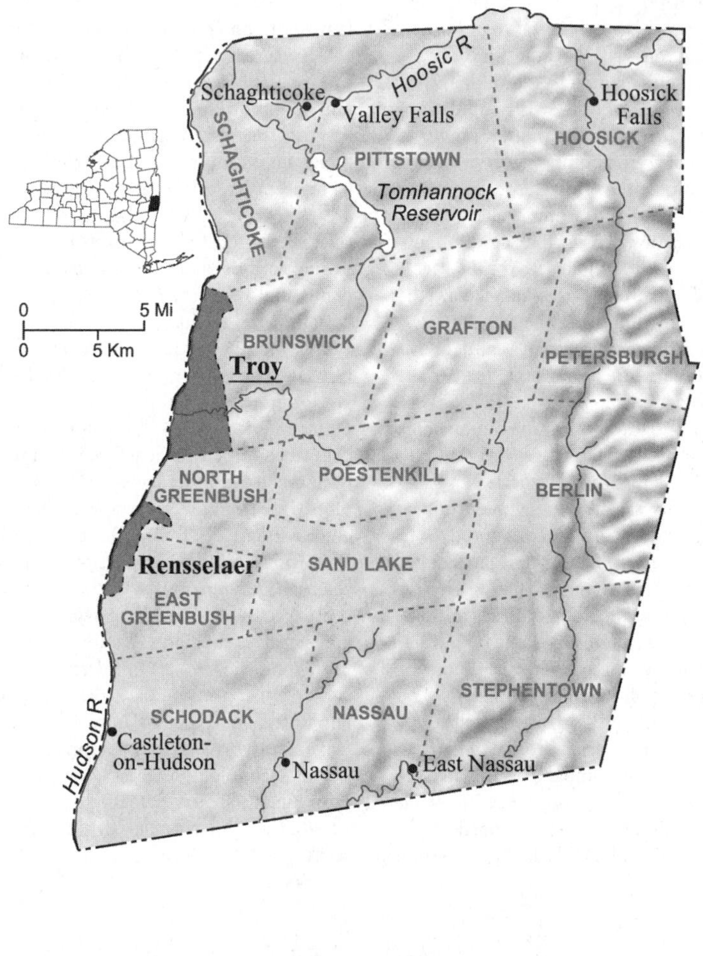

Mohawk Lowland physiographic province. Here bluffs rise as high as 300 feet (90 m) above the Hudson's narrow floodplain and tidewater. Streams have carved deep gullies into the predominantly shale bedrock. Continental glaciers completely covered the county during the most recent ice age. As a consequence its eastern two-thirds are covered with a mantel of glacial till that subdues the relief, especially in the central plateau. Kames and eskers are present in the uplands as well. Outwash deposits cover portions of the western third, which is also studded by numerous drumlins. The entire county lies in the watershed of the Hudson River, which serves as its western boundary. Fed from the slopes of the Taconics, the Little Hoosic River rises near the county's eastern margin and flows north before joining the Hoosic River, which enters the county from Vermont. Poestenkill drains the central region, while the southern hills are drained by Kinderhook Creek, which drops into Columbia Co before emptying into the Hudson. Soils are generally poor and of marginal modern agricultural value. Little of the Rensselaer Plateau is arable, while soils near the Hudson River tend to be sandy and in places excessively drained.

Rensselaer Co's climate is humid-continental. Average January temperatures hover around 22°F (-6°C). Below 0°F (-18°C) readings occur every winter, most frequently in the higher elevations. Average July temperatures range from 68°F (20°C) at Grafton in the more elevated interior to 73°F (23°C) at Troy along the Hudson. Daytime highs of 90°F (32°C) or above occur every summer, except in the highest elevations. Average annual precipitation, just under 38 inches (97 cm) at Troy, rises to 46 inches (117 cm) at Grafton. Snowfall can be heavy, reaching a seasonal average of 82 inches (208 cm) in the interior, though Troy averages only 41 inches (104 cm). The primeval forest cover for much of the county consisted of a hardwood community of beech, sugar maple, basswood, hemlock, and white pine, mixed with oak and chestnut in the Hudson Lowland and with spruce and fir in the Taconic Mountains. A dwarf oak and pine forest covered the sandy area in the extreme northwest corner. About 60% of the county is presently covered by second- or third-growth forest.

Native Inhabitants

Rensselaer Co was territory of the Algonquian-speaking Mohicans (Mahicans). Schotak [now Castleton-on-Hudson] was an important village during the fur trade era, which began in 1611. Remnants of the tribe remained near Schotak in the mid–19th century. Another important village was Schaghticoke, probably occupied around 1628 in the course of Mohican withdrawal from their lands west of the Hudson following conflict with the Mohawk. At the end of King Philip's War in 1676, remnants of New England tribes were encouraged to settle at Schaghticoke to provide a buffer of loyal and peaceful Indians between the Albany area settlements and hostile French Canadians and Canadian Indians. Population pressure resulted in groups of Schaghticoke Indians removing to the western Mohawk Valley (1703), Wyoming, Pa (1730), and on the shore of Missiquoi Bay in what is now Vermont (1754).

Colonial and Revolutionary History

The county's riverfront was settled slowly, beginning in 1628. In 1630 Kiliaen van Rensselaer purchased most of what became Rensselaer and Albany Cos, and received a patent from the Dutch West India Co for the patroonship of Rensselaerswijck. In the 17th century the present Rensselaer, Schodack, East Greenbush, North Greenbush, and Troy were occupied by manorial tenant farmers. Back from the river, Brunswick was settled by Palatine Germans (1742), Petersburgh by Dutch Americans (*ca* 1740), Poestenkill (*ca* 1755), Nassau (1760), Stephentown (?1765), and Sand Lake (1767), all as Van Rensselaer tenant holdings. French and Indian raids resulted in the breaking up of two small settlements in Petersburgh's Little Hoosic Valley in 1754, but the region was later resettled. The last town to be occupied was Grafton, settled by New Englanders around 1779.

The towns in the county's north were patented under the English colonial government. First was Hoosick (1682); it was settled by Dutch Americans in ?1724. Schaghticoke, purchased by the corporation of Albany from the Mohicans to grow wheat for the city, was settled by Albany colonists in 1709. Pittstown was patented to English settlers as a town in 1761. Until the 19th century Blacks were the only noticeable minority in Rensselaer Co. At the time of the 1790 census, most were enslaved and living in white households; a few farms housed as many as 13–14 slaves. Only 19 free Blacks then lived within what became the county, nearly all of them in two households in Hoosick.

During the Revolution there was relatively little loyalist sentiment. The white population of the region was, except in Pittstown, over 95% Dutch and German and had no ancestral loyalty to the British Crown. Further, landlord Stephen Van Rensselaer served as a general on the American side. An important engagement took place in the extreme northeast. An American army expedition to acquire horses set off from Saratoga for the Connecticut Valley; at Walloomsac it encountered and defeated British forces on 16 Aug 1777 in what became known as the Battle of Bennington.

Immigration and Ethnicity

Waterpower potential on the rapid streams flowing into the Hudson attracted postwar development. Troy's site was surveyed in 1786, and industrial development began immediately. Unlike previous settlements nearby, it was dominated by New Englanders seeking business opportunities. The Irish arrived as laborers for canal construction and for Troy industries, and were holding Roman Catholic services by 1818; St. Peter's Church was built in 1827. In 1855 there were 14,109 Irish-born county residents, or 17.8% of the population. They were concentrated in Troy but with significant numbers in Greenbush [now Rensselaer] and Hoosick.

In 1834 a group of Bavarians immigrated to Berlin, where many of them became charcoal burners. Other Germans came to Nassau by 1852 and to Castleton-on-Hudson *ca* 1875, joined later by immigrants from the Netherlands. German Jews were holding services in Troy by 1851. A Jewish agricultural colony developed in Nassau and Schodack beginning in 1894; it numbered 200 families in the 1920s.

A small but vibrant black community formed in Troy. There, in succeeding decades, abolitionism was supported by such leaders as Rev Henry Highland Garnet and by such institutions as the Liberty Street Presbyterian Church, as well as by enlightened whites. The play *Uncle Tom's Cabin* premiered in Troy in 1852, and the city was a way station on the Underground Railroad. In 1860 it

RENSSELAER CO POPULATION CENSUS FIGURES

	White	Nonwhite	Total Population	Foreign-Born
1800	29,439	1,003	30,442	—
1810	35,197	1,112	36,309	—
1820	39,049	1,104	40,153	165
1830	48,388	1,036	49,424	1,418
1840	59,069	1,190	60,259	—
1850	72,344	1,019	73,363	14,498
1860	85,270	1,058	86,328	21,324
1870	98,765	784	99,549	25,621
1880	114,381	947	115,328	26,373
1890	123,709	802	124,511	27,706
1900	121,005	692	121,697	22,982
1910	121,462	814	122,276	21,156
1920	112,401	728	113,129	16,002
1930	118,989	792	119,781	14,936
1940	121,089	745	121,834	11,993
1950	131,347	1,260	132,607	9,764
1960	139,962	2,623	142,585	7,800
1970	148,210	4,300	152,510	6,292
1980	146,213	5,753	151,966	6,429
1990	146,049	8,380	154,429	5,915
2000	139,002	13,536	152,538	5,709

Notes: "Nonwhite" includes African Americans, Asians, American Indians, and Pacific Islanders and, for 2000, also the mixed race and other race categories. Through the 1960 census these figures primarily reflect the African American population. Foreign-born figures for 1820 and 1830 include only those not naturalized, and for 1930 and 1950, the foreign-born totals include Whites only. Other years include all foreign-born in the population.

was the site of the rescue of Charles Nalle, an escaped slave.

The Van Rensselaers were benevolent landlords, and the majority of Rensselaerswyck farms were still leaseholds in the early 19th century. Rent collection was often lax. When Stephen Van Rensselaer (1764–1839), called the Good Patroon because of his patience in such matters, died, his heirs immediately sought to collect arrears. Many tenants asked to buy out their leases but were turned down. The resistance escalated into the antirent wars (1839–46). The Van Rensselaer heirs sold their interest in Rensselaer Co lands in 1854 to Walter A. Church, who pursued a policy of foreclosing on and then selling tenant land. In 1858 about half the land in Berlin and Petersburgh consisted of leaseholds; Grafton, Nassau, Schodack, East and North Greenbush, and Brunswick were about two-thirds leased; and Stephentown was still almost entirely tenant holdings. The land was sold quickly, however, and by the 1880s most farms were freeholds.

Staats house, built *ca* 1695. Oldest house in Rensselaer Co, occupied by members of the Staats family since construction.

Transportation

Early residents used the Hudson River as much as possible. A ferry was established from Albany to the present city of Rensselaer in 1642. The Kings Highway from New York City to Albany, authorized in 1703, passed along the river in the southwest. Steam travel on the Hudson River began in 1812, when the *Fire-Fly* began offering scheduled service from Troy to Albany. The Rensselaer and Columbia Turnpike (chartered 1798) to Lebanon Springs (Columbia Co) was one of the nation's first; the Northern Turnpike (chartered 1799) ran from Lansingburgh northeasterly to Vermont. The first bridge crossing the Hudson opened in 1804 between Lansingburgh and Waterford (Saratoga Co).

Troy's economy was propelled by the construction of the Champlain and Erie Canals in the mid-1820s. Both terminated across the river from Troy. Railroad service began with the tourist-oriented Rensselaer and Saratoga Railroad (1835). Rail lines were built across Rensselaer Co: from Albany to West Stockbridge, Mass (1841), Troy to Greenbush (1845), and Troy to Vermont (1852). The Hudson River Railroad (1851) supplemented the water route to New York City. The marginal Harlem Extension Railroad (1869–1953) ran through the Kinderhook and Little Hoosick Valleys. Horse-drawn street railroads began operating in Troy in 1863. Electrification began in 1889, at which time lines were being constructed to such rural towns as Sand Lake and East Greenbush, encouraging limited suburbanization. "Auto stages" (buses) appeared by 1910, and the rural electrics were supplanted by bus service in 1925.

Economic Development

Early farmers primarily grew grains, but in the 19th century grazing and dairying became dominant, especially in the eastern towns. Fluid milk was produced in close proximity to Troy markets; in 1875 it was an important product of East Greenbush, North Greenbush, and Brunswick. The Harlem Extension Railroad's milk train (1869) carried fluid milk to New York City, especially from Berlin, also the source of 70% of the county's output of maple sugar. Garden farming for Troy was concentrated in North Greenbush and in Brunswick; the latter's huge potato fields amounted to 17% of the town's land area in 1875. Environmental conditions favored fruit growing in Schodack.

With so much poor land in the county, extractive industries were widespread. Glass was produced in Sand Lake by Scots and Germans beginning in 1802. Most of the eastern and central towns exploited local forests; for example, Grafton produced wood, tanbark, charcoal, brush blocks, and handles. Before the Civil War Berlin and Stephentown exported charcoal. In the 1870s, 1,000 men in Castleton were employed seasonally to cut ice.

Manufacturing concentrated in Troy and Lansingburgh, whose brushes, clothing, shirts, collars and cuffs, iron and steel, and surveyors' instruments were nationally known throughout the 19th and early 20th centuries. Rensselaer, where waterpower had less potential, developed its industries with steam power, most notably Huyck Felt Mill (1894; linings for papermaking) and Bayer Co (1903; aspirin). Large mills also supported Schaghticoke, Valley Falls, and Hoosick Falls, and there were small factories in Brainard, Castleton-on-Hudson, Hoosick, Nassau, Pittstown, and Sand Lake. Their products included woolen, cotton, and linen cloth, paper and paper products, piano components, agricultural tools and machinery, cordage, iron goods, and gunpowder. Shirtmaking as a home craft in Grafton, Petersburgh, and Pittstown supported the Troy factories. Sanforization, a process for preventing the irregular shrinking of textiles, was developed in Troy and revitalized that city's shirtmaking industry in the 1930s.

Tourism was never a large business. A mineral spring in Poestenkill was briefly a resort with a hotel, but the facilities were never rebuilt after being swept away in a freshet in 1814. The Burden Lake House in Sand Lake was a resort from the 1840s. Some towns drew summer boarders in the late 19th century, and trolleys from Troy reached Sand Lake. Two of the early named motor routes crossed the county: the Taconic Trail (Rte 2, 1920) attracted motorists with its spectacular scenery, and the Mohawk Trail ran from Troy along Rtes 7 and 346. In Grafton, one of Rensselaer Co's few summer colonies developed at Babcock Lake (1925).

Religion, Education, Culture, and Politics

Rensselaer Co settlers, many of whom lived relatively close to the Reformed Church across the Hudson at Albany, were slow to form churches. The Reformed Church at Schaghticoke organized in 1714, and those at North Hoosick and Schodack in the mid–18th century; Brunswick's German Palatines founded Gilead Evangelical Lutheran Church in ?1757. Most churches organized after the Revolution with the influx of New Englanders; the county had 33 Methodist, 19 Presbyterian, and 17 Baptist churches in 1855, though its Dutch and German heritage was still evident in 10 Reformed and 8 Lutheran churches. Roman Catholics built a Troy church in 1827, followed by others in Hoosick Falls (1833) and Schaghticoke (1842). In 1855 there were 7 parishes, increasing to 19 two decades later. Troy's large Catholic population ultimately supported a number of ethnic parishes, including St. Mary's (Irish), St. William's (German), and St. Jean Baptiste (Francophone Canadian). Jews formed Troy's Congregation Berith Sholom in 1866 and, in the early 20th century, supported three rural synagogues in Nassau and Schodack, of which one remained in 2004.

Troy was a leader in education, building its first grammar school with state funds in 1795 and a public high school in 1854. Its most important institutions were for women (Emma Willard School, 1821; Russell Sage College, 1916) and engineers (Rensselaer Polytechnic Institute [RPI], 1824). Hudson Valley Community College (1953) has a strong reputation among technical colleges, and SUNY Albany maintains its

POPULATIONS OF TOWNS AND CITIES, RENSSELAER CO

Town or City, Year Founded	1800	1840	1880	1920	1960	2000
Berlin, 1806	—	1,794	2,202	1,305	1,329	1,901
Brunswick, 1807	—	3,051	3,402	2,812	9,004	11,664
East Greenbush, 1855[a]	—	—	2,127	1,558	9,107	15,560
Grafton, 1807	—	2,019	1,676	733	1,009	1,987
Greenbush, 1784–1897[b]	3,472	3,701	6,743	—	—	—
Hoosick, 1772[c]	3,141	3,539	7,914	6,858	6,490	6,759
Lansingburg, 1807–1900	—	3,330	7,759	—	—	—
Nassau, 1806[d]	—	3,236	2,629	2,015	3,721	4,818
North Greenbush, 1855	—	—	4,131	1,408	8,161	10,805
Petersburgh, 1791	4,412	1,901	1,785	1,066	989	1,563
Pittstown, 1761[e]	3,483	3,784	4,095	2,342	2,973	5,644
Poestenkill, 1848	—	—	1,672	1,002	2,493	4,054
Rensselaer (city), 1897	—	—	—	10,823	10,506	7,761
Sand Lake, 1812	—	4,303	2,550	1,916	4,629	7,987
Schaghticoke, 1772[c]	2,352	3,389	3,591	2,177	5,269	7,456
Schodack, 1795	3,688	4,125	4,319	3,992	8,052	12,536
Stephentown, 1784	4,968	2,753	1,986	1,109	1,361	2,873
Troy, 1791–1816	4,926	—	—	—	—	—
Troy (city), 1816	—	19,334	56,747	72,013	67,492	49,170

[a]Formed as Clinton 1855; renamed 1858.

[b]Informally considered district of East Manor from before 1767; formed as Rensselaerwyck District 1784; recognized as town 1788; renamed 1792.

[c]Formed as district; recognized as town 1788.

[d]Philipstown until 1808.

[e]Patented as township 1761; formed as town 1788.

East Campus in East Greenbush. The public school systems outside Troy are largely the result of 1812 legislation establishing common schools. Centralization of rural schools took place between 1928 and 1956, creating Averill Park, Berlin, Brunswick, East Greenbush, Hoosic Valley, Hoosick Falls, and Schodack Central School Districts. In 2003 Rensselaer and Troy operated city school districts, but Lansingburgh, part of Troy, had its own central school district. Wynantskill operates a Union Free School district through eighth grade, and the Williams District in North Greenbush continues a K–2 common school.

With its considerable industrial wealth, Troy was a city of culture, evidenced by the Troy Music Hall (1875) and its resident Troy Chromatics concert series (1894). Its first newspaper, the *Northern Centinel and Lansingburgh Advertiser,* was published in 1787–88; in 2003 the *Troy Record* was the county's only daily. The *Press,* published in Petersburgh, reported on the eastern towns. Rensselaer Co was a pioneer in radio, having the first college station licensed for broadcasting (WHAZ, 1914); today the college-run WRPI is the only station in the county.

The rural towns produced two of America's most important folk painters, Joseph H. Hidley (1830–72) and Grandma Moses (1860–1961). Moses lived in Washington Co but was closely associated with Hoosick Falls. Elijah Galusha (1804–71) of Troy was nationally recognized for furniture design in the mid–19th century. Edmonia Lewis, the leading 19th-century African American sculptor, was a native of Greenbush. Critic Granville Hicks lived for many years in Grafton and explored its social structure in *Small Town* (1946). Important institutions in the early 21st century include the Arts Center of the Capital Region (formerly Rensselaer County Council for the Arts, 1962); Rensselaer County Historical Society (1927); Rensselaer County Junior Museum (1954); Eastfield Village (1971), a privately owned outdoor museum in Nassau; and Fort Crailo State Historic Site. The 4,500-seat Joseph L. Bruno Stadium at Hudson Valley Community College opened in 2002. The county's cultural contributions include the song "Yankee Doodle," thought to have been written at Fort Crailo in 1755, and the figure of Uncle Sam, based on Troy's Samuel Wilson (1766–1854).

Rensselaer Co was formed with seven towns; their supervisors composed the legislative Board of Supervisors. With the incorporation of Troy in 1816 and of Rensselaer in 1897, supervisors from the cities' wards were added until there were 34 members. A county legislature based on population was created in 1970. It in turn hired the first county executive in 1973. Rensselaer Co has generally voted Republican since the Civil War, but there is a significant Democratic presence in Troy.

Recent History

In the second half of the 20th century, Rensselaer Co became increasingly dependent on the automobile. Rail service declined after World War II and Troy's Union Station was demolished in 1958, but the important Albany station was relocated to Rensselaer in 1968 and a new intermodal station opened in 2002. I-90 was completed from Rensselaer to the Berkshire Spur of the New York State Thruway between 1969 and 1976, encouraging suburban development in East Greenbush, Schodack, and other towns. Similarly, the Collar City Bridge (1984) improved Capital District connections to Rte 7 leading eastward.

Since much of the county is not good farmland, agriculture has declined substantially. In the areas of better soil, however, it continues unless crowded out by suburbanization, as in most of East Greenbush, North Greenbush, and Schodack. In the eastern tier of towns, only the narrow valleys of Kinderhook Creek and the Little Hoosick River support dairy and related farming. Brunswick and the northern tier remain largely agricultural despite suburbanization and the loss a century ago of much of Pittstown's best land for Tomhannock Reservoir (1902–05). In 1997 there were 459 farms in Rensselaer Co covering 23.6% of the land.

The loss of heavy industries in Troy and Rensselaer created economic distress and, along with suburbanization, eviscerated Troy's once grand retail shopping district. Troy's urban renewal program (1966) created the unsuccessful Uncle Sam Mall (1978) downtown but also led to Riverside Park (1982), which brought a renewed focus on Troy's waterfront. RPI leadership, with government funding, created Rensselaer Technology Park (1987) in North Greenbush and incubator space in downtown Troy. The largest employers in 2002 were the healthcare, government, and education sectors. Manufacturing and technology are represented in the early 21st century by such young firms as Mapinfo, Taconic, Organichem, and Albany International. Production of goods continues in Troy and in small operations in Berlin, Hoosick Falls, and Poestenkill. Workers now commute from all the towns, especially the western and central ones, to Albany Co; from the southeast to Pittsfield, Mass; and from the northeast to Bennington, Vt. In the late 20th and early 21st centuries, Rensselaer Co politics was dominated by Troy's Joseph L. Bruno, majority leader of the state senate and a strong advocate for Rensselaer Co.

The standard histories are Nathaniel B. Sylvester, *History of Rensselaer County* (1880), and Rutherford Hayner, *Troy and Rensselaer County, NY: A History* (1925). A modern, illustrated book is Rachel D. Bliven, ed., *A Resourceful People: A Pictorial History of Rensselaer County* (1987). Scholarly research has included the important book by Daniel J. Walkowitz, *Worker City, Company Town: Iron- and Cotton-Worker Protest in Troy and Cohoes, NY, 1855–1884* (1978), along with R. Beth Klopott, "The History of the Town of Schaghticoke, NY, 1676–1855" (PhD diss, SUNY Albany, 1981), and Richard J. Miller Jr, "Patroons of Modernization: The Economic Elite of Rensselaer County, New York, 1800–1860" (BA thesis, Williams College, 1986). Philip Lord Jr has produced two remarkable works exploring the Rensselaer Co landscape in history: *Mills on the Tsatsawassa: Techniques for Documenting Early 19th Century Water-Powered Industry in Rural New York* (1983) and *War over Walloomscoick: Land Use and Settlement Patterns on the Bennington Battlefield* (1989). The standard history of Troy is Arthur J. Weise, *Troy's 100 Years* (1891). Among the many local history booklets, *Farming in Poestenkill* (1998) stands out for its focus on agricultural change as experienced in one partially suburbanized town.

Field Horne

Rensselaer Falls. Village (pop 337) in Canton (St. Lawrence Co). The Tate, Chaffee and Co forge (1839), located at a 6 ft (1.8 m) fall on the Oswegatchie River, was the nucleus of the village, which was platted in 1846 and acquired a post office in 1851. The Rome, Watertown and Ogdensburg Railroad (1862) provided service. Besides iron, village products included chairs and cheeseboxes. Incorporated in 1912, the village is primarily a bedroom community for Canton in the early 21st century.

Richard E. Mooers

Rensselaer Polytechnic Institute. Founded as the Rensselaer School in Troy (Rensselaer Co) in 1824 by itinerant science lecturer Amos Eaton and philanthropist Stephen Van Rensselaer, the curriculum focused on teaching children of farmers and mechanics how to apply science to everyday life. The first school, located on River and Middleburgh Sts in a former bank building, developed into a leading engineering and technology college by the 1830s. Early students included James Hall and Ebenezer Emmons, leaders in the state's geological survey, and Asa Fitch, the first state entomologist. In 1833 the school was renamed the Rensselaer Institute and emphasized civil engineering. Pres Benjamin Franklin Greene (1847–59) aimed to model the college after European polytechnic schools. The school was renamed in 1861 to Rensselaer Polytechnic Institute (RPI). By 1896 the campus consisted of six main structures along Troy's Eighth Ave.

Pres Palmer C. Ricketts (1892–1934) restructured curriculum and incorporated more degree programs, establishing a graduate school and departments in science, business administration, architecture, and the arts. After a fire destroyed the main building in 1904, 13 new structures were built, changing the environment to an extensive campus. Enrollment grew from 200 students in 1900 to 1,700 by 1930, and in 1942 women were admitted. After World War II Pres Livingston Houston (1943–58) began collaborations with the US Navy to educate servicemen in engineering. By 1949, 4,600 students were enrolled, and a graduate affiliate was established in Hartford, Conn. Graduates include George M. Low of the NASA Apollo program and Nancy Deloye Fitzroy, the first woman to head the American Society of Mechanical Engineers. Low served as president from 1976 to 1978 and initiated programs with private industry and the state. To encourage technologically based businesses, he helped establish the George M. Low Center for Industrial Innovation (dedicated 2002), the Rensselaer Technology Park in North Greenbush (Rensselaer Co) (1983), and the Rensselaer Incubator Center in Troy (1980). Shirley Ann Jackson, past chair of the Nuclear Regulatory Commission, became president in 1999; she is the first African American woman to lead a major technological university. In 2002 the school enrolled more than 5,200 undergraduates and over 2,000 graduate students, and offered degrees in architecture, engineering, humanities and social science, management and technology, and information technology.

Phelan, Thomas, D. Michael Ross, and Carl A. Westerdahl. *Rensselaer: Where Imagination Achieves the Impossible* (Troy, NY: Rensselaer Polytechnic Institute, 1995)

Carl A. Westerdahl

Rensselaerswijck. New Netherland's only successful patroonship was established by Kiliaen van Rensselaer, who was granted the privileges and title of patroon by the Dutch West India Co (WIC) in 1629. The next year he sent settlers and an agent who purchased land from Mohicans (Mahicans) along the Hudson River. Uncertainty about boundaries was largely settled by further purchases in 1631, 1652, and 1661 to encompass 27 miles (43 km) from the mouth of the Mohawk River south and 27 miles both east and west of the Hudson. The WIC's Fort Orange was thus completely surrounded by Rensselaerswijck, which even claimed the land under the fort.

Following Van Rensselaer's death in 1643, his heirs appointed a director for Rensselaerswijck, Brant van Slichtenhorst, who encouraged settlers to build around the fort, cutting it off from the fur trade. New Netherland's director general, Petrus Stuyvesant, seized the area around the fort, had the nearest buildings removed, and, in 1652, created the town of Beverwijck [now Albany] beginning a few hundred feet north of the fort.

The second patroon, Kiliaen van Rensselaer's son, Johannes, appointed as the next two directors his brothers Jan Baptist in 1652 and Jeremias in 1658, the first members of the family to go to New Netherland. Jeremias died in 1674; his brother Nicholas van Rensselaer, who had arrived in New Netherland the same year, was appointed director in 1676. At Nicholas's death in 1678, Stephanus van Cortlandt was named director, but Maria van Rensselaer, Van Cortlandt's sister and Jeremias's widow, managed daily operations. She refused to provide the European Van Rensselaers with an accounting because they wanted to sell off the patroonship, and she rebuffed claims by Robert Livingston, who had married Nicholas van Rensselaer's widow, Alida Schuyler. Another brother, Richard, did manage to sell a few prime parcels.

Johannes's son Kiliaen, the third patroon, came to America in 1684 to sell Rensselaerswijck. Instead he married Maria's daughter, Anna, and thereafter joined the American Van Rensselaers in opposing the alienation of Rensselaerswijck. Since the English takeover of the colony in 1664, the Van Rensselaers had sought confirmation of their land title, which included Albany, from successive English governors, who balked at surrendering the city. In 1685 the patroon and his wife's brother, Kiliaen, ceded title to Albany and an access route from there northwest to Schenectady. In return, Gov Thomas Dongan granted not only title confirmation but also made Rensselaerswijck a manor and the patroon a manor lord with a seat in the general assembly and freedom from taxation.

In 1687 the manor lord died and was succeeded by Maria's son (and his wife's brother) Kiliaen as second lord (and fourth patroon, the title now merely honorific). Maria died in 1689, and in 1696 her four children settled their accounts with the Van Rensselaer family in the Netherlands, renouncing their interest in the European estate in exchange for full title to Rensselaerswijck.

The patroonship had been unprofitable for its first half century, settlers finding short-term leases unattractive. Kiliaen now offered lifetime leases, which included the privilege of voting in colonial elections and the right to sell a leasehold or subdivide it among heirs, with Rensselaerswijck providing buildings, equipment, and livestock. The patroon's benefits were a small annual fee and a quarter of the price if the property was sold. The population of the manor grew rapidly thereafter.

Kiliaen was succeeded as manor lord by his sons Jeremiah in 1719 and Stephen in 1745, grandson Stephen Jr in 1747, and great-grandson Stephen III in 1769. After the Revolutionary War Stephen III increased leaseholds sixfold to more than 3,400 at the time of his death. Following his death in 1839, tenants on the poorest farms refused to pay rent, resorting both to violence and intimidation in the antirent movement (1839–52) and to the courts. The state supreme court and court of appeals in 1858 and 1863 confirmed the Van Rensselaers' title to the farms, which the sons of Stephen III were already turning over to land agents. Most of the farms were sold during the 1860s, though some paid rents well into the 20th century.

See also MANOR SYSTEM.

Christoph, Peter R. "Worthy, Virtuous Juffrouw Maria van Rensselaer," *de Have Maen* 70 (Summer 1997): 25–40

Nissenson, S. G. *The Patroon's Domain* (1937; repr New York: Octagon Books, 1973)

Colonial era cannon from Rensselaerswijck.

Van Laer, A. J. F. *Van Rensselaer Bowier Manuscripts* (Albany: Univ of the State of New York, 1908)
Venema, Janny. *Beverwijck: A Dutch Village on the American Frontier, 1652–1664* (Albany: SUNY Press, 2003)

Peter R. Christoph

Rensselaerville [REN-SA-LUR-VIL]. Town (pop 1,915) in SW Albany Co. First settled at Preston Hollow in 1770, the town was formed from the old town of Watervliet in 1790. The hamlet of Rensselaerville, at the end of the Albany and Delaware Turnpike (1805), had a concentration of tanneries, iron furnaces (1833–*ca* 1900), and woolen manufacturers (1854–79). Rensselaerville's other hamlets had tanneries and mills as well. At the terminus of a highway (1905) that became Rte 85, the largely agricultural town became in the 20th century a residential retreat for Albany commuters and vacationers. It is the site of the 1,400-acre (567 ha) Edmund N. Huyck Nature Preserve (1931) and the Institute on Man and Science (1963). Chicago merchant and developer Potter Palmer (1826–1902) was a native.

Wesley G. Balla

rent control and stabilization. New York State regulatory programs that seek to protect tenants in privately owned buildings from excessive rent increases and to provide them with other guarantees. Rent control concerns tenants without leases. It limits the amount an owner may charge for rent according to a maximum base rent (MBR) system and places restrictions on tenant eviction. It applies to apartments—generally in residential buildings constructed before February 1947—where a tenant, or his or her legal successor, has lived continuously since before July 1971. Rent stabilization concerns tenants with leases. It curbs rent increases on buildings with six or more units built between February 1947 and January 1974 according to rulings of local Rent Guideline Boards, which meet annually. At the beginning of the 21st century, rent stabilization is the larger and more important of the two regulatory plans.

A form of rent regulation first appeared in the state during a post–World War I housing shortage; during the 1920s the New York State legislature passed laws allowing tenants to challenge rent increases in magistrates' court. While these laws lapsed in 1928, another measure, the Minkoff Law (1939), forbade rent increases in old buildings not in compliance with a housing code (the Multiple Dwellings Law) of 1929. More far-reaching regulation began in 1943 with a federal initiative prompted by another severe wartime housing shortage. Three months after a rent-related riot in Manhattan's Harlem district in August 1943, the US Office of Price Administration (OPA) froze the rents of 1.4 million dwellings in New York City, allowing 15% increases only in cases of landlord hardship. The OPA relinquished control of this program in 1947; henceforth, 1947 became an important cutoff date in rent regulation. After a rather confused three-year transition, New York State began to oversee rent control with the inception of the Temporary State Housing Rent Commission in 1950. In 1962 New York City launched its own program, and two years later the New York State Division of Housing and Community Renewal (DHCR) began to administer rent control in municipalities outside New York City. Beginning in 1969 New York City also operated a rent stabilization program in response to the sharply rising rents of that era in post–World War II buildings. In 1974 the state legislature passed the Emergency Tenant Protection Act (ETPA), which provided for a stabilization system in Nassau, Rockland, and Westchester Cos.

At the beginning of the 21st century, there are over 1 million regulated units in the state, with approximately 960,000 in New York City, of which perhaps 50,000 are rent controlled. In New York City, MBR establishes a maximum rent figure for each rent-controlled apartment every two years. Owners can raise rents as much as 7.5% each year until the MBR limit is reached, and tenants can challenge the increases. When a rent-controlled apartment becomes vacant, it either becomes rent stabilized or is removed from regulation. Starting with 1997, two provisions, commonly known as "vacancy decontrol" and "luxury decontrol," have steadily reduced the number of rent-regulated apartments. The first provision allows deregulation if the rent can be raised legally to $2,000 or more per month upon vacancy; the second allows deregulation if the tenant's household income exceeds $175,000 per annum for two consecutive years. Outside of New York City, DHCR determines maximum rates of rent increases. A total of 51 municipalities have rent control, including New York City, Albany, and Buffalo, as well as parts of Erie, Nassau, Rensselaer, Schenectady, and Westchester Cos.

Since the inception of rent-regulation programs, debate has raged over their advantages and liabilities. Tenant groups support extending them, often on the grounds that affordable housing is a right. Landlords and others argue that it distorts the housing market, limits the overall supply of housing, and leads to deterioration of existing housing stock. New York State's rent-control ordinance must be renewed every two years and has become bitterly controversial.

Plunz, Richard. *A History of Housing in New York City* (New York: Columbia Univ Press, 1990)

Leonard Benardo

reprieves. See PARDONS, COMMUTATIONS, AND REPRIEVES.

reptiles. See AMPHIBIANS AND REPTILES.

Republican Party. The breakup of the Whig Party over the issue of slavery during the 1850s, and especially the controversy over the Kansas-Nebraska Act in 1854, led to the creation of a new national party that opposed the extension of slavery in the territories. The party developed in a fairly spontaneous fashion in several places more or less simultaneously in 1854. The opponents of the Kansas-Nebraska Act drew on several political streams to form the new party: many Whigs, but also antislavery Democrats and former Free Soilers.

The Republican Party organized slowly in the state. In July 1854 a New York City committee opposed to the Kansas-Nebraska Act invited opponents of the act of any party to gather for a meeting. After selecting delegates at the county level, they convened at a state convention at Saratoga in August. Calling themselves Republicans, the delegates adopted an antislavery platform but adjourned without forming a cohesive political party. At a second convention in Auburn (Cayuga Co) in September 1854, the Free Democrats (remnants of New York State's Free Soil Party of 1848) and some Whig factions coalesced around mutual candidates. Myron H. Clark, generally known as a Fusion Republican though no formal party fusion had occurred at Auburn, won a confusing four-way race for governor by a mere 309 votes of 469,431 votes cast.

Some powerful Whigs, such as *Albany Evening Journal* editor Thurlow Weed, had held back from supporting fusion with Republicans in 1854. But in 1855 Weed backed such a coalition, and his support also attracted some members in the Barnburner faction of the Democratic Party, such as Preston King and Reuben E. Fenton. On 26 Sept 1855 the dying Whig Party and the nascent Republican Party met simultaneously in Syracuse for their respective state conventions. Whig endorsement of a fusion with the Republicans marked the end of the Whigs as an effective party. The new Republican Party was greatly aided by Horace Greeley's pro-fusion *New York Tribune* and by the backlash against the Democratic administration of Pres Franklin Pierce over the Kansas-Nebraska issue.

At the Republicans' first national convention in 1856 some delegates tried unsuccessfully to nominate former governor and sitting US senator William H. Seward for president. In the state elections of 1856, however, the Republicans elected their first governor, John A. King, and captured the state assembly. By 1860 the Republicans controlled most of New York's statewide offices. At the Republican National Convention that year the New York State delegation again attempted to nominate Seward for president. Unsuccessful in that venture, the state delegation backed the eventual Republican nominee, Abraham Lincoln. During the war years the Republican Party candidates ran on the Union Party ticket, emphasizing their patriotic commitment to the Union cause.

The Postwar Decades

The rise of the Republican Party brought a shift in politics outside of New York City. Where before the Civil War Whigs and Democrats often vied for power, exchanging control regularly, those regions now became solidly Republican, especially outside of urban areas. This contrasted with the usually solid Democratic voting pattern of New York City and provided to many perhaps the strongest confirmation of an enduring "upstate-downstate" tension at the heart of the state's politics and culture. If the Republican Party had emerged from the debate over slavery, in the postwar era, especially after Reconstruction, its ideological fervor slaked. It became identified with the interests of business, generally in support of tariffs, sound money, and maintenance of the gold standard, and in New York State, the interests of farmers and rural traders in opposition to the position of urban dwellers and immigrants. And if the Republicans did not control the politics of New York City, their influence in business, finance, and public and private organizations gave them great prominence and cultural clout, and the ability, if running a fusion candidacy with independent Democrats, to wrest power in the city away from Tammany Hall, the organization of the regular Democrats.

The relative stability of both major parties

after the Civil War made it a time of entrenched hierarchies and political bosses. The Republicans dominated the state legislature, significantly aided by its apportionment, which unequally favored rural districts over New York City. For example, between 1859 and 1900 the Republicans controlled the assembly for 33 sessions compared to the Democratic majority's 8 sessions. Similar situations existed in the state senate. The Republicans exercised a great influence over the drafting of state laws including those that governed the operations and charters of municipalities; that granted certain industry networks dominance over railroad, banking, insurance, and commerce; and that controlled broad tax policy. They also dominated the selection of US senators from the state until 1913, when the position became popularly elected. Their legislative dominance did not extend to other political arenas. From 1865 to 1900 Republicans had only a slight lead, 5 to 4, in presidential election totals in the state, and Democratic governors were in office for 21 of those 35 years.

The split between the two parties often centered more on the acquisition of patronage than on philosophy or state or national political party platforms. As a check on the power of the Democratic city organizations, the Republicans, via state legislation, often enacted laws to curb the power of their chief political rivals in local governments. Federal patronage was the ultimate plum, and the Republicans, who were in the White House for all but eight years between 1865 and 1900, had far more to dispense, especially appointments at the lucrative Port of New York and the hundreds of US post offices throughout the state. Chester A. Arthur, a former collector of the Port of New York and a loyal Republican, would serve as president of the United States (1877–81). But the dominant figure in Republican politics in the postwar decades was Roscoe Conkling, who resigned his seat as US senator (1867–81) in protest over Pres James A. Garfield's handling of federal patronage in New York City. After Conkling resigned in 1881 and his power diminished, Thomas C. Platt, known as the Easy Boss, succeeded to the leadership of the state Republican Party. Platt also resigned from the US Senate in protest in 1881 but was politically active until his death in 1910. Platt generally tried to avoid intraparty disputes and was reelected to the US Senate in 1896 and 1902.

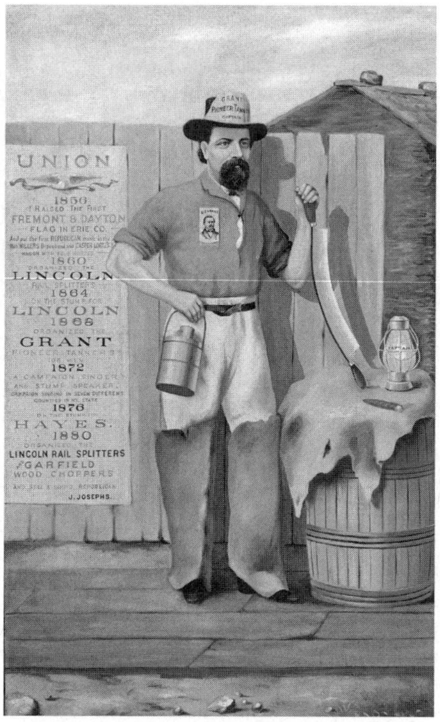

Joe Josephs or Elephant Joe, Pioneer Tanner Captain, self-portrait, late 19th century.

Progressive Era, 1896–1940

The close ties between business and the Republican Party created the appearance, and often the reality, of corrupt and unseemly influence on the political process. This was apparent as early as 1872, when Horace Greeley openly split with the Republicans over the first Grant administration and ran for president as a Liberal Republican and Democrat. The Liberal Republicans, or as they were increasingly called, Mugwumps, were badly defeated that year, but fear of political corruption remained. Civil service was a dominant issue in the 1880s, and the first semblances of civil service reform in New York State was championed by Republican assemblyman Theodore Roosevelt in 1883. Roosevelt emerged as one of the leaders, in the state and nation, of the Progressive movement. Roosevelt's commitment to creating efficient government, ending boss rule, and regulating the power of industry would become the hallmarks of Progressive reform. The presence of Theodore Roosevelt as governor (1898–1900) and later as president (1901–9) diminished the power of political boss Platt, who Roosevelt bypassed in distributing patronage. Platt was eventually replaced as state leader by Gov Benjamin B. Odell Jr (1901–4).

In the early 1910s the state Republican Party was run by Thurlow Weed's grandson, William Barnes Jr, a newspaper publisher who settled in Albany. Barnes was a national leader in the Republican Party and active in the state and local party until he lost control of his home base of Albany Co in the 1920s. Those in the Roosevelt wing of the party included Joseph H. Choate, a Mugwump who was president of the 1894 State Constitutional Convention, and Gov Charles Evans Hughes (1907–10). Hughes made great progress in implementing a variety of initiatives, such as tighter control of utility services and rates. Relative conservatives such as Elihu Root, president of the 1915 State Constitutional Convention, retained great influence in party affairs, as did James W. Wadsworth Jr, a US senator from 1915 to 1927 and one of the Senate's leading opponents of women's suffrage. The tension between the progressive and conservative wings was a precipitating factor in the decision of Roosevelt to leave the Republican Party and run for president as a candidate of the newly formed Progressive Party in 1912. In the aftermath of Roosevelt's defection, the conservatives were strengthened. Gov Charles S. Whitman (1915–18) was a moderate conservative, and the next Republican governor, Nathan L. Miller (1921–22) of Syracuse, would be the last truly conservative governor of the state, with the possible exception of George E. Pataki, through the early years of the 21st century.

Miller's defeat by Alfred E. Smith in 1922 ushered in a period of 20 consecutive years of very liberal Democratic governors in New York State. Democrats also controlled the state's US Senate seats, with no Republicans elected to that body from the state between 1922 and 1946. As Al Smith strengthened the executive powers of the governor, longer tenures for party leaders in the legislature gave new power to the Speaker of the Assembly and Majority Leader in the senate. The Republicans in the legislature were led by a series of leaders from the state's rural areas, including Assembly Speakers Thaddeus Sweet of Phoenix (Oswego Co) from 1914 to 1920, H. Edmund Machold of Ellisburg (Jefferson Co) from 1921 to 1924, and Joseph A. McGinnies of Ripley (Chautauqua Co) from 1925 to 1934. Republican Majority Leaders in the senate during this era were Elon R. Brown of Watertown from 1915 through 1918, J. Henry Walters of Syracuse from 1919 through 1920, Clayton Lusk of Cortland from 1921 through 1922, and John Knight of Arcade (Wyoming Co) from 1925 through 1931. These men, primarily conservative in outlook, were generally strong supporters of Prohibition, very concerned about raising taxes, and suspicious of many of the gubernatorial reform initiatives, which they were often able to blunt or block.

Liberal Republicans, 1940–75

Some in the state party wished to engage more positively the liberal trends in state and national politics, especially after the advent of the New Deal in 1933. Maverick Republican Fiorello La Guardia, mayor of New York City from 1933 to 1946, was an ardent New Dealer who depended on Democratic as much as Republican votes. Other Republican leaders felt that a moderately liberal stance and candidate could return them to power in Albany and perhaps in Washington. J. Russel Sprague, longtime leader of the powerful Republican Party organization in Nassau Co, saw in New York Co district attorney Thomas E. Dewey an ideal candidate who would attract a good deal of support from New York City. Dewey was elected governor in 1942, the start of a 32-year period in which Republicans served as governor for all but 4 years. Dewey, who would remain in office until 1954, ran for president twice during that period. Other liberal Republicans who came to power in Albany during those years were Oswald D. Heck of Schenectady, Speaker of the Assembly from 1937 to 1959; Assemblyman Abbot Low Moffat (1929–43) of New York City; and Irving M. Ives of Norwich (Chenango Co), who served two terms in the US Senate (1947–58).

Central concerns for Dewey and other liberal Republicans were the steady expansion of state services, as in the creation of the State University of New York (1948) and the New York State Thruway (1954), the latter now officially named in Dewey's honor. The Dewey administration's commitment to civil rights was realized with passage of the 1945 Ives-Quinn Law, the first law passed in any state banning racial discrimination. Republican control of the assembly and senate gave Dewey an almost veto-proof legislature; Dewey used this edge to his advantage by vetting most of his programs prior to submission to ensure passage and implementation.

The era of liberal, downstate Republicanism continued under Nelson A. Rockefeller, governor from 1959 to 1973, along with US senator Jacob K. Javits (1957–81) and state attorney general Louis J. Lefkowitz (1957–78). John Lindsay, who tested the outer limits of Republican liberalism, was elected mayor of New York City as a Republican in

1965, was reelected on the Liberal Party line in 1969, and ran briefly and ineffectively as a liberal Democrat for the 1972 presidential nomination. During the Rockefeller administration New York State continued its expansion of government and services, along with the corresponding taxes to pay for them, such as the state's permanent sales tax in 1965, much to the dissatisfaction of Rockefeller's more conservative critics. Perhaps the high-water mark of Republican liberalism occurred in 1970 when New York State became the first state in the nation to legalize abortion, with the bill winning passage, albeit narrowly, in the Republican-controlled senate and assembly and signed into law by Gov Rockefeller.

Resurgent Conservatism

Not all Republicans were pleased with the liberal direction of the Republican Party under Rockefeller. Starting in the late 1950s, conservative Republican ire at Rockefeller grew. This was especially evident during the expansion of state and federal spending under Pres Lyndon Johnson's Great Society programs, in which New York State was a willing participant. There was also a tremendous building program of colleges, hospitals, and state offices under Rockefeller, including his signature project, the 98-acre (40 ha) South Mall office complex in Albany, now fittingly known as the Governor Nelson A. Rockefeller Empire State Plaza. Conservatives were also increasingly concerned by the financing of these projects through sophisticated circumvention of state constitutional limits on debt and borrowing.

Dissatisfied Republicans began forming the Conservative Party in 1961. It gained impetus with Rockefeller's refusal to support the conservative 1964 Republican presidential candidate, Barry Goldwater. Goldwater's running mate was William E. Miller, a conservative Republican congressman from Niagara Co. The Conservative Party received more attention when political commentator William F. Buckley Jr ran against Lindsay in the 1965 New York City mayoral campaign.

In 1964 Democrats won control of the state assembly and senate for the first time since 1935. In 1966 reapportionment finally ended rural overrepresentation in the legislature, stopping the long-term Republican advantage. Since 1974 Democrats have controlled the assembly, and Republicans have controlled the senate, making it difficult for either party to have unfettered control of the political process. The social disturbances of the 1960s and economic downturn of the 1970s marked the end of Rockefeller liberal Republicanism, and in his last years a somewhat chastened Rockefeller cut back on new building projects and endorsed conservative social legislation, notably the draconian drug laws of 1973. From 1975 to 1994 the leading state Republicans were the senate leaders, Warren M. Anderson (1973–88) of Binghamton and Ralph J. Marino (1989–94) of Syosset (Nassau Co). Perry B. Duryea Jr of Montauk (Suffolk Co), who served as Speaker of the Assembly from 1969 through 1974, was the last Republican to hold that position in the 20th century. New York City's fiscal crisis of 1974 seemed to many Republican leaders a grim confirmation of the consequences of profligate liberal ways. Despite that sentiment, state Republicans were instrumental in persuading Pres Gerald R. Ford to back away from his intention of letting the city default on its obligations without providing federal assistance.

The growing rightward tenor of the state's Republican Party was demonstrated in 1980 when the conservative and little-known Hempstead (Nassau Co) town supervisor Alfonse M. D'Amato defeated four-term US senator Javits in the Republican primary. D'Amato would go on to win the general election and become the dominant figure in the state's Republican Party for the next 15 years. He was a mentor of Republican state senator Pataki of Peekskill (Westchester Co), who in 1994 was elected governor, with strong backing from the Conservative Party. As governor, Pataki reinstituted the death penalty (1995) and undertook a massive tax-cutting program. Nevertheless, Pataki, who favors abortion rights and works closely with many labor unions, would be considered by the increasingly conservative guidelines of the national party a moderate Republican. Much the same can be said about New York City's two-term Republican mayor, Rudolph Guiliani (1994–2001), who was highly praised for his handling of the World Trade Center terrorist attacks on 11 Sept 2001. He was succeeded by Republican Michael Bloomberg. Pataki has worked closely with Joseph L. Bruno of Brunswick (Rensselaer Co), Majority Leader of the senate since 1995, though Bruno joined with his counterparts in the assembly to override Pataki's 2003 budget veto because the proposed tax cuts (and service cuts) were considered too severe.

Chris Dupras, president of Syracuse University's College Republicans chapter, posing before statue of Abraham Lincoln in 1982.

In November 2003 there were 3,069,153 voters enrolled as Republicans in the state. There were five registered Democrats for every three registered Republicans. Despite being outnumbered in terms of formal voter affiliation, the Republican Party seemed in strong shape at the start of the 21st century, having, as of 2002, won three straight elections for governor and New York City mayor.

See also Apportionment and districting; Civil war; Italians; Progressivism; United states house of representatives; United states senate.

Alexander, DeAlva Stanwood. *A Political History of the State of New York,* 4 vols (1906–9, 1923; repr Port Washington, NY: Ira J. Friedman, 1969)

Benjamin, Gerald, and T. Norman Hurd, eds. *Rockefeller in Retrospect: The Governor's New York Legacy* (Albany: Nelson A. Rockefeller Institute of Government, 1984)

Booraem, Hendrik. *The Formation of the Republican Party in New York: Politics and Conscience in the Antebellum North* (New York: New York Univ Press, 1983)

Eager, Robert Crosby. "Governing New York State: Republicans and Reform, 1894–1900" (PhD diss, Stanford Univ, 1977)

McCormick, Richard L. *From Realignment to Reform: Political Change in New York State, 1893–1910* (Ithaca: Cornell Univ Press, 1981)

New York Republican State Committee, http://www.nygop.org

Rosen, Hy, and Peter Slocum. *From Rocky to Pataki: Character and Caricature in New York Politics* (Syracuse: Syracuse Univ Press, 1999)

Stein, Judith. "The Birth of Liberal Republicanism in New York State, 1932–1938" (PhD diss, Yale Univ, 1968)

John Evers

Republic Aviation Corporation. A manufacturer of military aircraft, it originated as Seversky Aircraft Corp, headquartered in New York City. In 1931 Alexander Prokofieff de Seversky (1894–1974), former ace pilot of the Czarist Russian Air Force and US Army Air Corps major, founded the company with Alexander Kartveli, another Russian émigré, who became chief engineer at Seversky Aircraft. The first Seversky aircraft were fabricated at the College Point (Queens Co) facilities of Edo Aircraft Corp. By 1936 the company acquired its own factory at Farmingdale (Nassau Co) and relocated its headquarters there as well. Serious financial problems in 1939 forced a complete reorganization: the company's board forced out Seversky and renamed the business Republic Aviation Corp. Existing facilities and personnel were retained, along with several aircraft designs then in production or under development. Kartveli designed the most important of these planes, the P-47 Thunderbolt, which was rated one of the best fighter planes of World War II. From 1940 through 1945 the Farmingdale plant turned out 9,006 airframes for P-47s. After the war Republic Aviation struggled to adjust to the peacetime economy but by 1946 began production of a series of jet fighters, beginning with the F-84 Thunderjet, a mainstay of the US Air Force during the Korean War. In 1958 the company launched a research and development program into advanced aeronautics, missiles, and astronautics, but financial reverses forced a merger with Maryland-based Fairchild Hiller Corp in September 1965. In 1971 the company was renamed Fairchild Republic Co. After the merger the Farmingdale plant built its last fighter, the Vietnam era F-105 Thunderchief. All aircraft production ceased in 1987 when the US government canceled a contract for the company's last design, the T-46 trainer. The Long Island facilities closed the same year. An adjacent airfield, Republic Airport, still carries the old company name. Fairchild, now located in Virginia, manufactures communication equipment.

Stoff, Joshua. *The Thunder Factory: An Illustrated History of the Republic Aviation Corporation* (Osceola, Wisc: Motorbooks, 1990)

Louis R. Eltscher

reservoirs. See DAMS AND RESERVOIRS.

resort hotels. First established during the early 19th century, resort hotels were located in the most scenic areas throughout the state. They were built along the route of the Fashionable Tour, a major travel route that passed through the Hudson River valley, Albany, and Lakes George and Champlain. The first large hotel built was the 120-room Sans Souci (1803) at Ballston Spa (Saratoga Co). Along the edges of the Catskill and Adirondack Mountains many hotels were established. These included the Catskill Mountain House (Greene Co), erected in 1823 overlooking the Hudson River, and the Lake House on Lake George (Warren Co), which opened as a hotel in 1828. Erected in the Federal and Greek Revival styles, early hotels were meant to look like fashionable country houses. They catered to a wealthy clientele; less well-off visitors preferred cheaper taverns, inns, and boardinghouses.

Spa Hotels and Cure Institutes

The completion of the Erie Canal in 1825 provided an alternative travel tour from Albany to western portions of the state. In the late 1820s most resorts were designed and established near spas catering to health and self-improvement. From 1820 to the 1920s Saratoga Springs had the largest concentration of resort hotels in the state, with 26 major hotels, including Congress Hall, the Pavilion, and the United States. By the 1850s towns and villages in western New York State copied the style of Saratoga Springs but on a smaller scale. Avon (Livingston Co) had five large hotels, Clifton Springs (Ontario Co) had several hotels near a cure institute, and hotels had a passing existence in places such as Breesport (Chemung Co). Niagara Falls, despite its reputation for beautiful scenery, had notably fewer hotels because the village government concentrated more on perfecting waterpower to create an industrial center. In the 1830s the Cataract House and Eagle House were established at the falls but were open only seasonally. Most visitors to Niagara Falls were on one-day excursions, so resort hotels did not develop. Most hotels were located on the Canadian side of the falls.

A new type of hotel, the cure institute, began appearing in the 1850s and was run by a doctor. Typically, the physician prescribed a schedule, diet, and hydrotherapy tailored for each guest. The largest institute in the state was located in Dansville (Livingston Co) under the proprietorship of Dr James C. Jackson. A complex of four-story hotels, it flourished in the pastoral setting from 1858 to 1872 under the name Our Home on the Hillside. In the first half of the 19th century the profitability of all resort hotels was precarious: their season was limited to the summer, they were expensive to build and maintain, and constant plumbing upgrades were required for the springs to flow indoors adequately. A few hotels attracted the serious investment of promising industrial enterprise. For example, in 1855 a New York City joint-stock company financed and built the Fort William Henry Hotel at the southern end of Lake George, indicating that resorts were considered profitable enough to attract outside capital.

Grand Hotels

After the 1876 centennial vast Second Empire- and Queen Anne–style hotels were erected to serve vacationers, who now included more middle-class people. Visitors had mixed reactions to the new type of hotel. The public rooms and porches were elegant, but the chambers were tiny, drafty, and scarcely furnished, often preventing visitors from getting a decent night's sleep. Food, while plentiful, was poorly prepared and served, with everyone sitting at long tables in family style and manners disappearing in the scuffle to get a portion of a favored dish. In the 1870s the Grand Union and United States Hotels in Saratoga Springs were the largest in the state, with 824 and 768 rooms respectively. Somewhat more modest but with a spectacular setting was the Mohonk Mountain House in New Paltz (Ulster Co). In 1869 Quakers Alfred Smiley and Albert Smiley converted a 10-bedroom tavern into a 450-guest complex that stretched along Lake Mohonk. Its purpose was to improve health through exercise, temperance, and a variety of techniques, including electrical treatments. In the western part of the state was the Athenaeum Hotel (1881), built in the midst of the Chautauqua Institution on Chautauqua Lake. With a name reflecting the institute's need to improve the mind, the Athenaeum's cottages, guesthouses, and tents were top of the line. To fill rooms in these vast hotels, the middle class was welcomed. At the same time, the wealthy began to shun grand hotels and instead bought private cottages or camps in the Adirondack Mountains.

The Adirondacks and Catskills

Interior Adirondack and Catskill regions were mountainous and barely accessible. Major hotels were thus not built in either region until the end of the 19th century, after the railroads arrived in the 1870s. Most early hotels in the Adirondacks were modest log structures, but Frederick C. Durant completed the six-story Prospect House at Blue Mountain Lake (Hamilton Co), which opened in the summer of 1882. It was the world's first hotel to equip each of its 300 bedrooms with an electric light. In 1883 the Queen Anne–style Sagamore Hotel opened on Lake George's Greene Island, the result of Philadelphia investors. The Lake Placid Club (Essex Co) was first developed in 1895 and formed a complex of clubhouses and cottages on the east shore of Mirror Lake. The hotel helped bring the Winter Olympics to Lake Placid in 1932. As its name suggests, however, it was a club only for members and their guests. At one time membership exceeded 100,000.

Most of the elite resorts discriminated against racial and religious minorities, and Catholics, Jews, and Blacks were generally unable to visit major resort hotels like that at Lake Placid. These groups often formed their own resorts. As early as the 1870s, there were "Jewish" resorts, such as Fort William Henry and smaller hotels in Lake Luzerne (Warren Co). In the late 19th and early 20th centuries, a network of resorts, designed especially for a Jewish clientele, developed in the lower Catskills, mainly in Ulster and Sullivan Cos, and many of them originated in the early years of the 20th century as glorified dairy farms. The Nevele in Ellenville (Ulster Co) kept its herd until 1938. After World War I the classic Catskill resort was created and centered around a hotel that had separate bungalows or cabins for families, a kosher menu, a variety of recreational and educational activities, and golf courses. The leading hotels, jewels of the borsht belt, were located in Sullivan Co and included Grossinger's in Liberty, Kutsher's Country Club in Monticello, and the Concord in Lake Kiamesha, which attracted big-name entertainment and sports figures from New York City.

The Seaside

The Long Island seaside was developed with only limited presence of large hotels. As early as 1824 the Coney Island House attracted fashionable visitors to the south shore of Kings Co. After the 1870s the area became a mass tourist destination when thousands of New York City residents took the train or later the subway to Coney Island, where attractions included carousels, roller coasters, the first frankfurters, and three monumental amusement parks. Because working-class crowds could return to their homes in the evening, the hotel did not figure prominently in the mix. The exception was the development east of Coney Island at Brighton and Manhattan Beaches. Brighton was developed by businessmen who copied the famous English resort, which in 1878 became the Hotel Brighton. The Coney Island Improvement Co, a consortium of business owners and politicians who bought waterfront property, developed Manhattan Beach. They built up the area and its beaches, and erected the Brooklyn, Flatbush, and Coney Island Railroads to attract more families. In 1877 both the Manhattan Beach Hotel and the Oriental Hotel were built and captivated a wealthy clientele, in part because of the nearby racetracks, but their heyday was brief and did not outlast the closing of the racetracks around 1910. There were some resort hotels further east on Long Island. Starting in 1880, with the opening of the Long Beach Hotel, the south shore locality of Long Beach (Nassau Co) tried to build itself into a fashionable resort, with some success through the depression. Babylon and Shelter Island (Suffolk Co) also built grand hotels during the same period.

Decline

Resort hotels declined in most places in New York State after World War II, becoming casualties of improved roads that provided access to more remote locations, proliferation of motels and roadside cabins, and increased popularity of lakeside cottages for purchase by the middle class. There were some exceptions to this downturn. An innovation in the 1950s was the dude ranch, which offered a popular rustic experience and horseback riding. The ranches were most concentrated in the Lake Luzerne area, where the Roaring Brook Ranch and Tennis Resort (1946) still operated in 2003. The Jewish resorts of the Catskills reached their peak in the 1940s and 1950s. But here, too, there was a decline in popularity after 1970, and by the 1990s virtually all of the major Catskill resort hotels had closed. Casino gambling has helped restore the concept of the resort. Turning Stone in Verona (Oneida Co), a casino resort managed by the Oneida Indian Nation, is successful and looms as the model to revive Catskill resorts. In 2003 numerous inns offered many of the comforts and services the old hotels had once offered. A few of the original resort hotels continue to have a summer season, such as the Otesaga (1909) in Cooperstown (Otsego Co). In 2003 the only year-round, first-class resort hotels in the state were the Sagamore on Lake George and the Mohonk Mountain House.

See also ANTI-SEMITISM; BORSCHT BELT; CATSKILLS; SARATOGA SPRINGS.

Brown, Phil. *Catskill Culture* (Philadelphia: Temple Univ Press, 1998)

Corbett, Theodore. *The Making of American Resorts: Saratoga Springs, Ballston Spa, Lake George* (New Brunswick, NJ: Rutgers Univ Press, 2001)

Kasson, John. *Amusing the Million: Coney Island at the Turn of the Century* (New York: Hill & Wang, 1978)

Morrison, Theodore. *Chautauqua: A Center for Education, Religion, and the Arts in America* (Chicago: Univ of Chicago Press, 1974)

Sears, John. *Sacred Places: American Tourist Attractions in the 19th Century* (New York: Oxford Univ Press, 1989)

Theodore Corbett

Revere Copper Products. Headquartered in Rome (Oneida Co), this company traces its origins back to America's first successful copper rolling mill, established in 1801 by Paul Revere in Canton, Mass. Between 1801 and 1929 the firm experienced a series of mergers, eventually becoming Revere Copper and Brass in the latter year. With Rome having a long history of metal production, the company's largest manufacturing units were centered there. By the late 1930s the firm employed approximately 4,000 at Rome, processing at that site 10% of all the copper ore in the United States. In 1937 the copper-clad cookware Revere Ware, which the firm has been associated with ever since, was invented at Rome. Reorganized in 1980 as Revere Copper Products, it became an employee-owned company nine years later. The company is a world-leading copper fabricator, making such products as roofing shingles and electrical and telecommunications components. In 2002, the firm operated a rolling and extrusion mill in Rome, employing approximately 500 workers in the city, plus 125 employees at its facility in New Bedford, Mass.

Marcosson, Isaac F. *Copper Heritage: The Story of Revere Copper and Brass Incorporated* (New York: Dodd, Mead, 1955)

Edith J. Steblecki

Revival of 1857–58. Interdenominational religious awakening. On 23 Sept 1857 New York City missionary Jeremiah Lanphier began noon-hour prayer meetings for businessmen at the North Reformed Protestant Dutch Church, known as the North Dutch Church or the Fulton Street Church, in the heart of the city's business and financial district. Attendance grew steadily, in tandem with the financial panic of October–December 1857. Many Protestants turned to prayer in response to business losses and uncertainties. By January–February 1858 religious weekly newspapers in New York City, including the *Examiner* (Baptist), the *New York Observer* (Old School Presbyterian), and the *Christian Advocate and Journal* (Methodist), printed reports of local revivals. By 27 Feb 1858, 600 people, mostly men, were crowding the Fulton St prayer meeting; similar meetings, often organized by the Young Men's Christian Association (YMCA), had proliferated in many city churches, including the historic John Street Methodist Church. Towns and villages throughout New York State were affected as well. Meetings were reported in over 40 sites, including Fort Edward (Washington Co), Woodville (Jefferson Co), and Newburgh (Orange Co). During March, New York City Methodist Holiness teacher Phoebe Palmer served as revival speaker in various locations, including Owego (Tioga Co) and Binghamton. These and other localized expressions of religious fervor coalesced into a national awakening, the Great Revival, through coverage in widely circulated newspapers such as the *New York Tribune* and the *New York Herald.*

During the three years (1857–59) that included the beginnings and aftershocks of the revival, nearly half a million people joined Protestant churches throughout the United States, more than twice as many as during the preceding three-year span. The revival helped to shape the entrepreneurial, middle-class character of modern American evangelicalism. In addition it indirectly fanned the religious intensity surrounding sectional conflicts that led to the Civil War; it gave new life to the floundering YMCA and inspired the women who would help found the Young Women's Christian Association (YWCA). The events of 1857–58 lent momentum to Protestant mission work, and in many ways marked a severing of connections between revivalism and social reform movements that had characterized the first half of the century. If the revival of 1857–58 helped to shape American evangelism for the next century, New York City was critical in giving shape to the revival itself.

Long, Kathryn Teresa. *The Revival of 1857–58: Interpreting an American Religious Awakening* (New York: Oxford Univ Press, 1998)

Kathryn T. Long

Revolt of 1837. See *CAROLINE* AFFAIR AND THE CANADIAN REBELLION OF 1837.

Rhinebeck. Town (pop 7,762) and village (pop 3,077) in NW Dutchess Co. Bounded on the west by the Hudson River and patented to Gerrit Aertsen, Hendrick Kip (1686), Henry Beekman Sr (1697), and others, it was settled in 1688 by one or two Dutch families and in 1713 by a colony of Palatine Germans. At an early date, riverfront estates were created by heirs of the Beekman and Livingston families and later by New York City residents, including the Astors. The town was formed in 1788. The village was laid out in lots in 1792 on a 44-acre (17.8 ha) gift from Henry Beekman Jr and incorporated in 1834. Rail service to New York City was established in 1851 and to Connecticut in 1875. In the early 21st century the village is a busy commercial center and tourist destination, home to Northern Dutchess Hospital, Dutchess County Fair, and Old Rhinebeck Aerodrome. It was the home of New York governor Levi P. Morton (1824–1920) and birthplace of John A. Quitman (1799–1858), governor of Mississippi.

William P. McDermott

R. H. Macy. In 1858 Rowland Hussey Macy opened a "fancy" dry goods store in New York City after four unsuccessful attempts in the 1840s–1850s to operate stores in Massachusetts and California. He used a low-price strategy and aggressive advertising to develop a fast-growing business at the store on 6th Ave between 13th and 14th Sts. In 1874 Macy rented basement space to his china, glass, and silverware supplier, Lazarus Straus, whose sons Isidor and Nathan became partners with Macy's successor after Macy's death in 1877 and the death of three other partners shortly thereafter. Becoming partners in 1888 the Strauses became sole owners in 1896. The Straus family moved Macy's to Herald Square (34th St and Broadway) in 1902. The company became well known for its innovations in marketing and sales, including one of the first in-store employee training programs in 1914 and its renowned executive training program, in place into the 21st century, in 1919. With completion of an addition on 7th Ave in 1924, Macy's became the largest store in the world at that time. That same year it held its first Thanksgiving Day parade, which ran from 145th St to the Herald Square store. Organized by store employees, many of whom were first-generation immigrants, the parade has become an annual holiday tradition. Macy's became a public corporation in 1922 and expanded outside of New York State over the next few decades. In the state it expanded first into Queens, then Long Island. After 1950 Macy's gradually became a fashion merchant rather than a price-driven retailer; it began targeting the more affluent customer rather than the more moderate; the merchandising focus shifted to apparel. In 1986 Macy's executives bought the company in a leveraged buyout, using debt to buy stock. The large debt, however, forced the company into bankruptcy in early 1992. Two years later Federated Department Stores acquired control of Macy's and consolidated other Federated stores, creating the divisions of Macy's East, headquartered in New York City, and Macy's West, headquartered in San Francisco. Macy's East, which now included the venerable Brooklyn-based Abraham and Straus department store, formed a retailing division with $4.8 billion in sales and 30,400 employees. In 2002 Macy's East had 31 stores in New York State, accounting for 30% of sales and concentrated in metropolitan New York.

Hower, Ralph M. *History of Macy's New York, 1858–1919: Chapters in the Evolution of the Department Store* (Cambridge, Mass: Harvard Univ Press, 1943)

International Directory of Company Histories, vol 30 (Chicago: St. James Press, 2000)

Trachtenberg, Jeffrey A. *The Rain on Macy's Parade: How Greed, Ambition, and Folly Ruined America's Greatest Store* (New York: Times Business, 1996)

Jerry R. N. Brisco

Richardson, H(enry) H(obson) (*b* St. James Parish, La, 29 Sept 1838; *d* Brookline, Mass, 27 Apr 1886). Architect. An 1859 Harvard graduate, Richardson studied architecture at the Ecole des Beaux-Arts in Paris and worked for two Paris architects before settling in 1865 in New York City, working there and in Boston. He moved to Brookline in 1874, but he retained his New York City office until 1878. Richardson was an innovative, influential architect whose unique style came to be known as Richardsonian Romanesque. As exemplified in Boston's Trinity Church (1872–77), the mature architect adapted and combined the styles of French Romanesque with an unwavering functionalism; a love of mass, open space, asymmetry, texture, and materials (especially natural stones and masonry); and an allover unfussy approach foreshadowing the Modern movement.

Richardson's buildings in New York State include Arrochar, his Staten Island residence (1868), a wooden house related to the American Stick style, and the mansard-roofed Dorsheimer House in Buffalo (1868–71) in French Second Empire style. The New York State Insane Asylum (1869–95; later Buffalo State Hospital and Buffalo Psychiatric Center) featured 10 connecting pavilions and a central administration building faced with reddish-brown Medina sandstone and brick; it was landscaped in 1876 by Frederick Law Olmsted, with whom Richardson later often collaborated. Leopold Eidlitz, Olmsted, and Richardson formed an architectural firm called Eidlitz, Richardson and Co in 1876 to take on construction of the New York State Capitol in Albany (the three had been named to serve on an advisory committee for the proposed building a year earlier). Richardson completed the capitol (1867–99; Richardson's involvement 1875–86) with Eidlitz. Richardson's contributions include the designs of the Great Western Staircase and, with the assistance of Stanford White, the Senate Chamber (1876–81). The Senate Chamber's oak-beamed ceiling over 50 feet (15 m) high, lower walls sheathed in granite, marble, and onyx, arches of Siena marble and arcade columns in red-brown granite, and specially designed furniture and its subtle touches of foliate ornament throughout make the chamber the most immense, elegant, and quietly powerful interior that Richardson ever created. Albany City Hall (1880–82) and Albany's Sard House (1882–83; now part of State Street Tower Apartments) are also credited to him.

Pittsburgh's Allegheny County Courthouse and Jail (1883–88) and Chicago's Marshall Field Store (1885–87; demolished) are chief among Richardson's other prominent works. Frail health and overwork contributed to his early death, but despite a short professional career Richardson influenced a generation of architects such as Charles Follen McKim, John Galen Howard, George Shepley, Louis Sullivan, and Frank Lloyd Wright.

Meister, Maureen, ed. *H. H. Richardson: The Architect, His Peers, and Their Era* (Cambridge, Mass: MIT Press, 1999)

Ochsner, Jeffrey Karl. *H. H. Richardson: Complete Architectural Works* (Cambridge, Mass: MIT Press, 1982)

O'Gorman, James F. *Living Architecture: A Biography of H. H. Richardson* (New York: Simon & Schuster, 1997)

Patricia Bayer

Richburg. Village (pop 448) in Wirt and Bolivar (Allegany Co). Settled in 1819, it was a busy but small mill hamlet until the oil boom of 1881. Its population went from 150 to 3,000 in a matter of months, and Richburg was incorporated as a village. Large buildings, including an opera house, were built, but frontier conditions prevailed, including many saloons and as many as 40 brothels. In May 1882 the Cherry Grove strike in Warren Co, Pa, drew most of Richburg's roughnecks, and the local oil business ultimately centered a few miles away at Bolivar. Richburg had Allegany Co's first consolidated school in 1926, which in 1994 merged to become Bolivar-Richburg Central School. In 2003 the village has a library, housed in a *ca* 1840 hotel, and a historical society, housed in the former Seventh Day Baptist Church.

Richfield. Town (pop 2,423) in N Otsego Co. Although settlers arrived before the Revolutionary War, permanent settlement was not achieved until 1787; the town was formed from Otsego in 1792. Transformed by the discovery of the Great White Sulphur Spring in 1820 and the subsequent development of Richfield Springs, the town was a nationally known health and summer resort approximately between 1850 and 1930. Its waters were bottled and shipped, and farmers found a ready market for produce. There was little manufacturing, although matches were produced at Brighton Corners starting *ca* 1845, using mechanized dipping. Richfield was an important cheese-making town, producing double the quantity of any other Otsego Co town in 1860. Hops were also grown in quantity. With the decline of the town as a resort, many residents have had to commute for employment, although Otsego Co has organized Richfield Business Park to attract employers. The Baker Octagon Barn (1882) is listed on the National Register.

Hugh C. MacDougall

Richfield Springs. Village (pop 1,255) in Richfield (Otsego Co). Beginning in 1820 Horace Manley developed the springs, and in 1823 Samuel Chase built a hotel known as the Spring House. The village, incorporated in 1861, briefly achieved a minor place in the 19th-century watering-place circuit, especially after a railroad link to Utica was completed in 1870. Although it attracted an international clientele, including a large number of Cubans in the years after World War I, the lack of modern hotels, the changing attitudes toward mineral waters, and the rise of automobile touring transformed Richfield Springs into a small regional market town. A fountain in Spring Park still provides sulfur water for the curious.

Richford. Town (pop 1,170) in NE Tioga Co. Settled by 1808, the town was formed from Berkshire in 1831 as Arlington; the present name was adopted in 1832. The village square, surveyed in 1821, was the center of the community until it was destroyed when Rte 38 was built in the 1950s. Richford found itself on an important east-west turnpike, now Rte 79. Lumber and tanbark were early industries. Cigar making was a local trade in the third quarter of the 19th century. The Southern Central Railroad came through Richford in 1871 and was acquired by the Lehigh Valley Railroad in 1887. Although poultry farming and Clark Seed Farms (1941–*ca* 1972) are gone, some farming continues. John D. Rockefeller Sr (1839–1937) is the town's most famous native son. Richford is the site of Michigan Hill, Turkey Hill, and Robinson Hollow State Forests.

Joann Lindstrom

Richland. Town (pop 5,824) in N Oswego Co. Settled in 1801 the town was formed in 1807 from Williamstown. The Salmon River flows through the town and empties into Lake Ontario at Port Ontario, where a city was projected in the 1830s. A lighthouse at Port Ontario, built in 1838 and in active service until 1858, is on the National Register of Historic Places. The Civilian Conservation Corps (CCC) constructed Selkirk Shores State Park on Lake Ontario during the Great Depression. Salmon were originally found in large numbers in the Salmon River but disappeared; efforts to restock them have been successful, and Richland is now a sportfishing center. I-81 (1962) renders the town easily accessible to tourists and vacationers. The Village of Pulaski is its population and business center.

Barbara J. Dix

Richmond. Town (pop 3,452) in SW Ontario Co. Settled in 1790, the town was formed in 1796 as Pittstown, renamed Honeoye in 1808 and Richmond in 1815. In 1814 a cooperative "mercantile association" was formed but, having bought a large stock of goods at war prices, it failed when prices dropped. Saw- and gristmills were built on Honeoye Creek, the outlet of Honeoye Lake. In 1865 Richmond was the leading wool-producing town in New York State. In the late 1860s drain tiles and earthenware were manufactured. Honeoye Park, a lakeshore resort, was surveyed in 1924 but never developed. In 2003 Richmond was a farming town, with much sheep raising.

Marla A. Bennett

Richmond County. See STATEN ISLAND [RICHMOND COUNTY].

Richmondville. Town (pop 2,414) and village (pop 786) in W central Schoharie Co. First settled in 1764, Richmondville village was burned by Joseph Brant's Mohawks and tory forces during a 1778 raid. Although much of the town is hilly upland, the alluvial soils of the Cobleskill and its tributaries have made it a productive agricultural region for two centuries. The town, formed from Cobleskill in 1849, was a thriving manufacturing center early on; the arrival of the Albany and Susquehanna Railroad (1865) (later Delaware and Hudson) boosted the production of straw paper (1865–83), woolen cloth (1872), and ironwork. The village incorporated in 1881 and was strengthened as a secondary retail center in 1980 by the opening of I-88.

Peter Johnson and Dawn Johnson

Rich Products. Vegetable-based and frozen foods manufacturer founded in Buffalo in 1945 by Robert E. Rich Sr. Early major products were a nondairy soybean whipped topping for desserts and a nondairy coffee creamer. The company expanded in the Buffalo area through the 1960s and acquired a number of frozen food and seafood companies in the 1970s and early 1980s. In 1975 sales were $100 million. Robert E. Rich Jr became president of the firm in 1978. Its major innovation in 1979, Freeze-Flo, was a process that froze food without crystallization and allowed food to be eaten without defrosting. In 2002 the firm made 2,300 products in 70 countries, with sales of $1.6 billion and employed 1,400 at its world headquarters in metropolitan Buffalo and 802 plant workers in the Buffalo area.

"The Riches of Rich Products," *Buffalo Courier-Express Magazine,* 4 Nov 1979

Kenneth S. Mernitz

Richville. Village (pop 274) in De Kalb (St. Lawrence Co). Settled in 1804, the village was incorporated in 1880. Beginning in 1850 a community of Welsh, mostly from Cardigan in West Wales, settled in and around the Richville. A lime kiln active in the 1870s produced 30,000 bu (1 million l) of lime annually. The Welsh Congregational Church (1859) is a landmark and is maintained by the Welsh Society of Richville (1974), which organizes an annual service and other cultural events. Richville is essentially a distant suburb of Gouverneur.

Richard E. Mooers

Rickard, Clinton (*b* Tuscarora Indian Reservation [loc in Niagara Co], 19 May 1882; *d* Buffalo, 14 June 1971). American Indian rights leader. Raised on the Tuscarora Reservation, in 1901 Rickard enlisted in the US Army at Fort Niagara, was assigned to the 11th Cavalry, and saw service in the Philippines during the Philippine insurrection. After his discharge from the army in 1904, he returned to the reservation, married Ivy Onstott, and became a farmer. His wife died in 1915, and he later married Elizabeth Patterson. His interest in American Indian rights activity began in the early 1920s when he attended hearings in Albany for Assemblyman Edward Everett's report concerning Indian rights and the historic confiscation of Indian land in New York State. At about this time he was chosen sachem chief of the Tuscarora Beaver Clan to replace the ailing Chief Marcus Peters, who had resigned. On 1 Dec 1926 Rickard and his Indian friends organized the Indian Defense League of America. He was active throughout the rest of his life in various Indian causes protecting Indian rights and promoting Indian education and advancement. His wife Elizabeth died in 1929. In 1931 he married Beulah Mt. Pleasant, who survived him.

Rickard, Clinton. *Fighting Tuscarora: The Autobiography of Chief Clinton Rickard.* Ed. Barbara Graymont (Syracuse: Syracuse Univ Press, 1973)

Barbara Graymont

Rickard, William (*b* Tuscarora Indian Reservation [loc in Niagara Co], 6 Aug 1918; *d* Niagara Falls, 18 Sept 1964). Indian rights leader. The eldest son of Clinton Rickard and Elizabeth Patterson Rickard, William developed an interest in perpetuating American Indian culture, which led to his breeding an early-maturing variety of Indian corn that could be harvested before the killing frosts. He distributed the seed widely to Iroquois farmers in New York State and Canada, where it is now grown both for traditional foods and for religious ceremonials. He was a member of the Indian Defense League of America, serving as president of the Niagara District in the early 1950s, and belonged to the Longhouse League of North American Indians, a national traditionalist group. From 1957 to 1960, along with others of the Tuscarora Nation, he participated vigorously in the protest against the New York State Power Authority's movement to confiscate a large part of their reservation for a reservoir and became an eloquent national spokesman for his people. At the American Indian Chicago Conference in 1961, he was an active proponent of the sovereignty of Indian nations and of those Indian groups east of the Mississippi River whom western Indians had hitherto ignored. In keeping with traditionalist Iroquois teaching, he claimed that Indians were treaty people who were citizens of their own sovereign nations, allies of the United States but not subjects. He therefore rejected enforced US citizenship for Indian people. Rickard's message of Indian nationalism formed the foundation of what would later be known as the Red Power movement.

Rickard, Clinton. *Fighting Tuscarora: The Autobiography of Chief Clinton Rickard.* Ed. Barbara Graymont (Syracuse: Syracuse Univ Press, 1973)
Hauptman, Laurence M. *The Iroquois Struggle for Survival: World War II to Red Power* (Syracuse: Syracuse Univ Press, 1986)
Lurie, Nancy Oestrich. "The Voice of the American Indian: Report on the American Indian Chicago Conference," *Current Anthropology* 2 (Dec 1961): 478–500

Barbara Graymont

Ridge. Locality (pop 13,380) in Brookhaven (Suffolk Co). Settled in 1728 by Stephen Randall, it was first known as Randallville. The region was used for pasture and farmland, and cordwood was cut and shipped on Long Island Sound. A post office was established in 1949. The William Floyd Parkway (1959) gave it better automobile access. Beginning in 1970, developers constructed planned retirement communities at Ridge, including Leisure Village, Leisure Knoll, and Leisure Glen. Ridge is the site of the Middle Island State Game Farm and of Longwood, a 35-acre (14 ha) farm operated by the Town of Brookhaven that includes the Smith Homestead (*ca* 1790) and the former Ridge School (1872–1952).

Suzanne Johnson

Ridge Road. A natural highway in western New York State that ran atop a gravel ridge parallel to the south shore of Lake Ontario from Sodus Bay (Wayne Co) to Lewiston (Niagara Co) and constituted the shore of a larger, prehistoric lake. As an Indian trail it first came to the attention of white settlers about 1798. In the early 19th century, the road was important in bringing settlers to the western part of the state and for transporting goods in both directions. Because of its location along the ridge, the road had a reputation (which it may not have always deserved) as one of the best in the state: elevated 15–20 feet (4.6–6.1 m) above the surrounding countryside, entirely level, and always dry. Nevertheless, the going could be slow, which gave rise to closely placed taverns. The stretch between the Genesee and Niagara Rivers averaged one every mile.

In 1813 the state legislature appropriated $5,000 to improve the path and to bridge streams between the Genesee and Niagara Rivers, thus establishing it as a military road to aid in the defense of the Niagara Frontier. It became a thoroughfare for troops moving to and from the frontier and, when the British burned Lewiston, an escape route and sometimes a temporary home for refugees.

To extend the route eastward, the Oswego Falls and Sodus Bay Turnpike Co was incorporated in 1817, and the Sodus Bay Bridge Co in 1819. The route was used by tourists visiting Niagara Falls, although John Fowler, a British visitor in 1830, dismissed the road itself as "beyond comparison the most uninteresting 80 miles of ground I have passed over in the country." The significance of the road was reduced, except during the winter months, by the completion of the Erie Canal in 1825. It received yet a greater blow from the coming of the railroads, which linked Albany and Buffalo in 1842. The development of the automobile, however, made it useful again. The Good Roads Movement prompted improvements beginning in 1901, and it was completely resurfaced by 1926. Today portions of the Ridge Road are followed by Rte 104 (formerly US 104).

Cowles, George W. *Landmarks of Wayne County, New York* (1895; repr Salem, Mass: Higginson Book, 1997)
Green, Walter Henry. *History, Reminiscences, Anecdotes, and Legends of Great Sodus Bay, Sodus Point, Sloop Landing, Sodus Village, Pultneyville, Maxwell and the Environing Regions, The Ridge Road, and the Four-Horse Post Coaches of Pioneer Days* (Sodus, NY: 1947)
Merrill, Arch. *The Ridge: Ontario's Blossom Country* (Rochester: Louis Heindl, 1944)

Scott C. Monje

Ridgeway. Town (pop 6,886) in W Orleans Co. Settled in 1810, the town was formed in 1812 from Batavia (Genesee Co). Its major village, Medina, was located on both the Erie Canal (1824) and the Niagara Falls Branch of the New York Central Railroad (1852). Discovered during the digging of the canal, Medina sandstone was quarried beginning in 1837. Fruit drying and storage were important industries. Early 21st-century industries include Brunner International (castings), Finney Tool and Die, and Ontario Harvest. The Cobblestone Inn (1817) is a landmark restaurant. Ridgeway has the only road in New York State that passes under the Erie Canal.

Riga. Town (pop 5,437) in SW Monroe Co. Settled in 1806 by a group largely from Massachusetts, the town was formed from Pultney in 1809. Its farms produced cereals until they were succeeded by apple orchards. The 742-acre (300 ha) Churchville County Park (1928) has a public golf course. There has been suburban development since the 1960s, and in 2002 the town is a mixture of subdivisions and farms. It is the site of Monroe Co's Mill Seat Landfill, which opened amidst controversy in 1993. I-490 (1964) passes through Riga, but there is no exit within the town's limits.

Carolyn Vacca

***Riggs v Palmer,* 115 NY 506 (1889).** A case regarding estate law in which the New York State Court of Appeals considered whether a man who murdered his grandfather to prevent the elder from changing his will was still entitled to receive the inheritance. Francis B. Palmer had a substantial estate, in which his grandson Elmer E. Palmer would have a share. Francis remarried in March 1882 and intended to have his estate pass to his new wife. Later that same year Elmer, then 16 years old, poisoned his grandfather to prevent the will change and claimed his property. The court found that Elmer was not entitled to the estate. The opinion of the court, authored by Judge Robert Earl, became well known for its holding that no one should profit from their own fraud or crime. The Riggs principle that wrongdoers should not benefit from the fruits of their crime was eventually incorporated into the state's 1977 "Son of Sam" law.

Mitchell C. Newton-Matza

rights. New Yorkers, by virtue of being New Yorkers, have been protected by a variety of rights that date back to the colonial period and continue to evolve. These rights emanate from several sources, including the common-law tradition, the state constitution, and state laws. In many cases these rights mirror those guaranteed to all US citizens through the federal Constitution and federal statutes, but in some cases state rights offer even more protection than those guaranteed at the federal level.

New York State's tradition of protecting and promoting personal liberty is rooted in the colonial period. Several factors contributed to this tradition, including the colony's diversity, early tolerance of religious worship, and a well-developed legal profession. The existence of charters and a commitment to self-government would provide models for subsequent constitutions adopted by the citizens. Significantly, New Yorkers' understanding of constitutionalism embodies the notion that written constitutions attempt to place effective restraints on the exercise of political power.

Common-Law Rights

A provision of New York State's 1777 Constitution (as amended, current Art 1, §14) made the English common law in force as of April 1775 part of the law of the new state, subject to alterations by the legislature. Excluded were those parts of the common law concerning the establishment of any particular religious denomination, those concerning allegiance to the sovereignty and prerogatives claimed or exercised by the king, and any others "repugnant to this constitution." This provision ensured continuity and stability as the state moved from colony to independence, and preserved the personal rights and principles that were the distinguishing features of the common law. Although the 1777 Constitution had no formal bill of rights, the common law's vast store of substantive liberties and procedural rights was viewed by New Yorkers as their natural heritage and shield.

Although Article 1, Section 14 of the state constitution places responsibility for alteration of the common law with the legislature, the state's judiciary has played an important role in expanding common-law principles. In *Scholendorff v Society of New York Hospital* (1914), Court of Appeals judge Benjamin N. Cardozo relied on common-law principles in ruling that "every human being of adult years and sound mind has a right to determine what shall be done with his own body." Later, in *Rivers v Katz* (1986), the court relied on that same common-law rule in holding that an involuntarily committed mental patient has a fundamental right to refuse antipsychotic medication. In the *Matter of Fosmire v Nicoleau* (1990), the court permitted an adult Jehovah's Witness to refuse a blood transfusion both prior to and after delivering her baby.

The common law has had its greatest impact in the area of criminal procedure rights. Appellate courts in New York State have shaped rules governing the examination of witnesses, hearsay exceptions, and the taking of guilty pleas. The court has invoked the common law to define the appropriate levels of suspicion for official questioning of passengers in train and bus terminals, adopting a more protective standard than the federal floor established in *Terry v Ohio* (1968). The decision in *People v Conyers* (1981), which held that a prearrest silence could not be used to impeach the accused's trial testimony, relied on a "judicially created rule of exclusion" designed to exclude evidence whose prejudicial effect outweighs its probative value.

A striking example of the court's use of the common law was the 1996 case of *Brown v State.* The Court of Appeals concluded that damage claims for violations of equal protection and search and seizure provisions of the state constitution could be entertained, because the rights guaranteed by those provisions have common-law antecedents and a damage remedy is consistent with the purposes underlying the duties they impose.

Various statutory and constitutional privileges exist under New York State and federal law that originated in the common law. These include attorney-client and husband-wife (marital) privileges, and protection against self-incrimination, which are all included in the New York Civil Practice Laws and Rules (CPL). New York State has also provided statutory protection for physician-, dentist-, and nurse-patient privileges not recognized in the common-law tradition or in federal law. An 1829 law made New York the first state to protect physicians from compulsory disclosure of information obtained while treating their patients. This privilege has been extended to psychologists, social workers, and rape counselors and their clients. These privileges have not been recognized in federal law. A provision of the New York State Civil Rights Law, commonly known as the Shield Law, grants journalists absolute protection from contempt citations for refusing to disclose information obtained confidentially or for refusing to name their sources. There is no comparable federal shield law, and whatever privilege there is in federal courts derives from media-friendly readings of *Branzburg v Hayes* (1972).

Constitutional Rights

The New York State Constitution contains its own Bill of Rights, as well as other provisions aimed at protecting social and economic rights. The state's first constitution included provisions guaranteeing the free exercise of religion and trial by jury. Such rights were consolidated into Article 7 of the 1821 Constitution, and since 1846 the Bill of Rights has comprised the first section of the state constitution. Though many provisions are duplicated in the state and federal Bills of Rights, the New York State Court of Appeals has interpreted the comparable provisions of the state's constitution more broadly than the US Supreme Court has interpreted the national Bill of Rights. New York State's Bill of Rights also includes protections not present in the federal Bill of Rights.

Freedom of Speech and Press. Article 1, Sections 8–9 of the state constitution protect the freedom of speech, press, and assembly. The Court of Appeals has not created an independent state-based jurisprudence for free speech, but it has been especially protective of the freedom of the press. This tradition derives from the expansive language of the guarantees and the formation and adoption of constitutional standards prior to the application of the First Amendment to the states beginning with *Gitlow v New York* (1925).

In the realm of free speech, mainly linked to freedom of the press, the state constitution has been interpreted to provide a number of protections. *People v Calbud* (1980) required a statewide standard for determining what is obscene, rather than the local community standards permitted under federal law. Refusing to follow the US Supreme Court in *Miller v California* (1973), the Court of Appeals held that topless dancing is protected speech under the state constitution's free speech clause. *People ex rel Arcara v Cloud Books* (1986) ruled that a nuisance statute authorizing closure of offending establishments could not be enforced against a "concededly" offending bookstore, as bookselling is protected expression. Freedom of speech and the press was also at the core of *People v P. J. Video* (1986), a case involving unreasonable search and seizure of allegedly obscene materials. The Court of Appeals placed a more demanding standard than the federal courts for obtaining a warrant for materials that "presumptively enjoyed First Amendment protection."

The decisions of the Court of Appeals regarding libel law and reporter's privilege also reflect the court's attention to the freedom of the press. While most states have chosen negligence as the standard of liability necessary for private parties to win a libel suit, New York has adopted the more demanding, and press-friendly, gross irresponsibility standard. On remand from the US Supreme Court, the Court of Appeals in *Immuno A. G. v J. Moor-Jankowski* (1991) rejected the federal test for separating factual statement from nonactionable statements of opinion, adopting a standard more likely to immunize publications from libel judgment. On a related matter, *O'Neill v Oakgrove Construction* (1988) held that journalists' nonconfidential sources enjoy a qualified protection from disclosure under the state freedom of press clause. As of 2003 a similar protection for confidential or nonconfidential sources had yet to be definitively provided by the US Supreme Court. As the Court of Appeals has observed, New York State "has long provided one of the most hospitable climates for the free exchange of ideas."

Unreasonable Search and Seizure. Although Article 1, Section 12 of the state constitution parallels the Fourth Amendment, the state's high court has determined that the protections it provides extend beyond those of its federal counterpart. For example, when the US Supreme Court during the 1980s carved out a good-faith exception to the federal exclusionary rule (stating that evidence seized in violation of the Fourth Amendment may not be used against a criminal defendant at trial), the Court of Appeals allowed no such exception and also limited the use of the inevitable-discovery exception to secondary evidence.

The judiciary has been particularly active on the question of the scope of a search incident to a lawful arrest. After the US Supreme Court ruled that a police search of an automobile incident to a traffic stop to read the vehicle identification number did not violate the Fourth Amendment, the Court of Appeals in *People v Class* (1986) held that such a search violated the state constitution. With regard to searches incident to a lawful arrest not involving vehicles, New York State law has established the rule that closed containers are not automatically searchable in the absence of exigent circumstances involving the safety of the officers or destruction of evidence. The principle was extended in *People v Torres* (1989). In the *Matter of Patchogue-Medford Congress of Teachers v Board of Education* (1987), the court struck down a school district's program of compulsory urine testing of all probationary teachers, ruling the policy a violation of the state constitution's guarantee against unreasonable searches and seizures. The Court of Appeals has consistently upheld what it called in *People v Scott* (1992) "New York's tradition of tolerance of the unconventional and of what may appear bizarre or even offensive."

Right to Counsel and Protection from Self-Incrimination. Statutory guarantees for assigned counsel appeared in 1877, and the Court of Appeals, in *People v Price* (1933), held that regardless of the statutory distinction between capital and noncapital cases, when a defendant appears without counsel and requests same, the court must comply. The US Supreme Court did not reach that position until 1963. A long line of cases in New York State has established that once formal proceedings have commenced, suspects may not waive their right to counsel or to remain silent in the absence of counsel, even if an attorney is neither retained nor requested. In New York State the issuing of an arrest warrant automatically initiates criminal proceedings; this means protections for the accused may be activated sooner than under federal provisions.

A second line of cases in the last decades of the 20th century has established that an individual in custody without charge, having retained or requested counsel, may not be questioned in the absence of counsel. The interpretation of the right to counsel, especially the no-waiver, absent-counsel rule, provides significantly greater protection for the right against self-incrimination than does the comparable federal position. Another area in which the state offers expanded protection concerns confessions given prior to a Miranda warning. Although New York State followed the voluntary standard prior to the federal *Miranda v Arizona* (1966) ruling, the state's strong right-to-counsel tradition provided protections similar to those mandated by Miranda. The case of *People v Harris* (1991) illustrates the effects of this expansive counsel protection. In Harris police entered a suspect's house illegally and obtained a confession. The US Supreme Court found no violation of the Fourth Amendment. Under New York State law, however, the right to counsel attaches when an arrest warrant is issued, and under the state's indelible right-to-counsel rule, suspects may not be questioned in absence of an attorney. Since police cannot interrogate a person arrested with a warrant, they have every reason to arrest a suspect without a warrant and thus attempt to circumvent the accused's indelible right to counsel. The Court of Appeals in Harris refused to rest its decision on this reading, because to do so would subvert the indelible right to counsel guaranteed by the state constitution.

Due Process. Due process rights come in two forms, procedural and substantive. Procedural due process requires that the government follow fair and nonarbitrary procedures before depriving a person of life, liberty, or property. The heart of due process is the notion of fundamental fairness expressed in the requirements of notice, reasonable definiteness in the law, and a hearing appropriate to the nature of the case. The Court of Appeals has relied on Article 1, Section 6 of the state constitution to extend the reach of the state due process clause beyond the federal protections.

The interplay between constitutional and statutory protections is illustrated by the right to a speedy trial. This right, protected by the Sixth Amendment to the US Constitution, is not mentioned in the state constitution, but is guaranteed by CPL §30.30. The Court of Appeals, under the state's due process clause, extended the protection beyond the Sixth Amendment and statutory requirements, holding that a lengthy, unjustifiable delay may require dismissal, even if no prejudice has been shown and the defendant is not formally accused or incarcerated. In a challenge to the imposition of a more severe sentence upon retrial, the Court of Appeals established a rebuttable presumption of invalidity stemming from institutional "vindictiveness," even when a different judge presides at the second trial. In justifying these greater protections, the court pointed to its longstanding "special vigilance" concerning appellate review of sentences.

The Court of Appeals provided more expansive due process protection in noncriminal proceedings in *Sharrock v Dell Buick-Cadillac* (1978), holding that even privately conducted lien sales violated due process if property owners were not first afforded the opportunity to be heard. This position had already been rejected by the US Supreme Court on the grounds that such sales did not trigger state action. The Court of Appeals relied on the history and language of the state due process clause to find "a more flexible State involvement requirement."

Substantive due process refers to the substance of the law or regulation that deprives a person of life, liberty, or property. Under substantive due process review, courts attempt to ensure that laws are not unreasonable or arbitrary. While courts in New York State have generally followed federal standards, the state due process clause has provided some enhanced protection for liberty and property interests. *Cooper v Morin* (1979) voided a regulation restricting inmates' visits with family members because it infringed on the fundamental right to "marriage and the family." In *McMinn v Town of Oyster Bay* (1985), a town ordinance restricting occupancy of housing units to single families based on biological or legal relationships was found to lack any rational relationship to the goals set forth by the village. *Barr v Town of Brookhaven* (1989) extended New York State's protection of nontraditional "families" when it invalidated an ordinance limiting the number of unrelated individuals who could live in the same household as a single family, the US Supreme Court holding to the contrary.

Examples of statutory protection in the criminal procedure area include the right of individuals to appear and testify before a grand jury (CPL §190.50 [5]) and the right of defense lawyers to be present in the grand jury room to advise a client who has waived immunity (CPL §190.52). The right to a speedy trial guaranteed by the Sixth Amendment is given specifications and teeth in the state's Criminal Procedure Law, which requires the People to be ready for trial within six months of the commencement of a felony case. The constitutional right of defendants to be present during all material stages of the proceedings against them was extended on statutory grounds to include the right to be present at any sidebar discussions.

Statutory Rights

In addition to the protections granted by the national and state constitutions, New York State provides significant protections in its statutory law. These statutes implement constitutional protections and, more importantly, add dimensions to rights protection not found in the state or federal constitutions.

Discrimination. New York State's adoption of the Ives-Quinn Law in 1945 made it the first state to enact an antidiscrimination law. That law now forms part of an omnibus statute banning discrimination in employment, housing, credit, places of public accommodation, and nonsectarian educational institutions. The New York State Human Rights Law, among the most comprehensive statutes of its kind in the nation, declares that the state has the responsibility to act to ensure that every denizen "is afforded an equal opportunity to enjoy a full and productive life and that the failure to provide such equal opportunity . . . menaces the institutions and foundation of a free democratic state and threatens the peace, order, health, safety and general welfare of the state and its inhabitants." The protected categories include, among others, age, race, disability, creed, color, national origin, sex, marital status, and sexual orientation.

The state's Human Rights Law provides the broadest remedy in the country for discrimination on the job. New York State was among the first jurisdictions to recognize the concept of sexual harassment and prohibited disability discrimination in 1974, more than a decade before Congress passed the Americans with Disabilities Act (ADA). Further, state law defines disabilities more broadly than federal law, meaning New Yorkers have protections not available under the ADA.

Going beyond the antidiscrimination coverage of federal law, the New York State Executive Law applies to martial status, genetic predisposition or carrier status, and arrest records. To this list of protected categories New York State Labor Law adds discrimination on account of lawful consumption of alcohol or tobacco or participation in lawful recreational activities on an individual's own time, and requires employers to provide leave for the adoption of a child if such leave is provided for the birth of a natural child. Moreover, a 1977 amendment to the Workers' Compensation Law requires that disability benefits must be provided for pregnancy leave. New York State is one of a handful of states whose Short-Term Disability Benefits Law provides a mandatory floor of benefits for those who have a non-job-related injury.

Privacy. New York was the first state to recognize a right to privacy. A 1903 statute prohibited the use of a person's name or picture without their consent for advertising or business purposes. The New York State Penal Law, which protects all conversations from intentional mechanical eavesdropping, gives worker privacy broader protection than the federal eavesdropping statute. The 1984 Personal Privacy Protection Law (Public Officers Law, §91 ff) establishes rules governing the collection, maintenance, and safeguarding of records to ensure the privacy of those records consistent with lawful disclosure. The 1999 Video Consumer Privacy Act (General Business Law, §672 ff) protects individuals from undue intrusion into legitimate activities such as videotape rentals. Section 520(a) limits merchants' access to their customers' credit card information and social security numbers (General Business Law, §518a). New York, along with a handful of other states, protects the identity of sex crime victims and the personnel records of police officers, firefighters, and corrections officers (Civil Rights Law, §50a–b).

Healthcare. A number of protections relating to HMOs are provided under New York State law. These include a right to receive emergency care, information, child immunization, and continuing care, and to challenge decisions and obtain information from one's doctor. Cumulatively, they provide a "Managed Care Bill of Rights" for New Yorkers. Additionally, the state's Public Health Law requires that every nursing home or facility providing health-related services shall adopt and post the rights and responsibilities of its patients. These include, among others, the rights to noninfringement of civil or religious liberties, to communicate privately with physicians and any other persons, to present grievances without fear of reprisal, to manage their own financial affairs, and to enjoy privacy in treatment and care for personal needs. Similar protections are provided for hospital patients. Although there is much overlap in federal and state law in protecting patients' rights in hospitals, residential healthcare facilities, and HMOs, federal law applies only to Medicare and Medicaid recipients, whereas New York law applies to all residents of the state.

Housing and Social Welfare. An extensive statutory network and an elaborate social service bureaucracy have been created to implement Articles 17 and 18 of the state constitution, which were adopted in 1938. Article 17 makes the aid, care, and support of the needy public concerns to be provided by the state and thus creates a social right that requires affirmative action on the part of the government. As the Court of Appeals noted in *Tucker v Toia* (1977), this provision "unequivocally prevents the legislature from simply refusing to aid those whom it has classified as needy." The courts have given considerable leeway to the legislature in fulfilling this mandate but have reacted aggressively when benefits have been provided in a discriminatory manner. Differential Medicaid eligibility requirements for resident aliens were struck down as inconsistent with the provision, as was a state statute mandating reduced payments of home relief (general assistance) benefits to new residents based on benefits paid in their previous state. Article 18 makes it the duty of the legislature to provide housing for low-income groups, and the state has responded with large-scale projects in this area.

New York State's Social Services Law includes extensive provisions for social welfare. Although sweeping changes in welfare programs have taken place—such as those brought by the State Welfare Reform Act of 1997, which emphasized personal responsibility and reduction in dependency on government programs—the state's commitment to providing support services is noteworthy. Unlike a number of states that have no programs for singles or childless couples or for those who have "timed out" under the 1996 federal act's mandated five-year limit on eligibility, New York, consistent with its state constitution, mandates that care be provided for all categories of the needy. When eligibility limits are reached, those in need are switched from cash aid to other benefits, such as vouchers for utilities and/or landlords.

New York State's Public Housing Law of 1939 initiated the country's first state-subsidized public housing program. Unlike earlier federal legislation, the state law admitted elderly and single persons and barred discrimination on the basis of "race, color, creed or religion." No other state at that time prohibited discrimination in public housing. Under a variety of statutes, the State Department of Housing and Community Renewal is responsible for the supervision, maintenance, and development of affordable low- and moderate-income housing. In addition to the early antidiscrimination provision and extensive federal and state protection against most forms of discrimination, the legislature has adopted extensive protections for tenant rights. These include warranties of habitability and a landlord's duty of repairs, as well as a variety of measures aimed at protecting tenants from criminal harm. Tenants also possess personal rights under these provisions, among which are a right to organize, a right to privacy, and protection against retaliation (Real Property Law, §§223b, 228, 230).

Conclusion

In the last decade of the 20th century the Court of Appeals was not as active in expanding state-based rights protection and in some cases retreated from that protection, particularly in the area of criminal procedure rights. However, the court has not relinquished its rights-expanding role entirely. In the landmark decision *Campaign for Fiscal Equity, Inc v State of New York* (2003), the Court of Appeals held that the state had failed to provide a sound basic education to students in New York City as required by the state constitution. Moreover, state legislation continued to provide a variety of consumer-rights protections, ranging from the state's "lemon laws" to the Sexual Orientation Non-Discrimination Act of 2002, which added sexual orientation to the list of characteristics protected against discrimination in public accommodations, employment, housing, and education. At a time when security and national defense concerns continue to receive high priority from the national government, the state remains active in ensuring a balance between protecting security and promoting liberty and equality.

See also LESBIANS, GAYS, BISEXUALS, AND TRANSGENDERED PEOPLE.

Bonventre, Vincent M. "State Constitutionalism in New York: A Non Reactive Tradition," *Emerging Issues in State Constitutional Law* 2 (1989): 31–59

———. "State Constitutional Recession: The New York Court of Appeals Retrenches," *Emerging Issues of State Constitutional Law* 4 (1991): 1–16

Bonventre, Vincent M., and Amanda Hiller. "Public Law at the New York Court of Appeals: An Update on Developments, 2000," *Albany Law Review* 64 (2001): 1355–403

Galie, Peter J. "State Constitutional Guarantees and the Protection of Defendants' Rights: The Case of New York, 1960–1978" *Buffalo Law Review* 28 (1979): 157–94

———. *The New York Constitution: A Reference Guide* (Westport, Conn.: Greenwood Press, 1991)

Kaye, Judith. "Dual Constitutionalism in Practice and Principle," *St. John's Law Review* 61 (1987): 399–429

———. "Foreword: The Common Law and State Constitutional Law as Full Partners in the Protection of Individuals Rights," *Rutgers Law Journal* 23 (Summer 1992): 727–52

Pitler, Robert M. "Independent State Search and Seizure Constitutionalism: The New York State Court of Appeals' Quest for Principled Decisionmaking," *Brooklyn Law Review* 62 (1996): 1–331

Peter J. Galie

Right to Life Party. Single-issue political party devoted to the abolition of abortion. The party developed from a book study group of Merrick (Nassau Co) housewives. The group became politically active during New York State's consideration of a liberalized abortion law in 1968 and 1969. Subsequent enactment of this law in 1970, coupled with the Supreme Court's ruling in *Roe v Wade* (1973), accelerated their electoral efforts to curtail abortions. The party was strongest on Long Island and in rural areas.

Party cofounder Ellen McCormack ran in the 1976 Democratic presidential primaries, and in 1978 cofounder Mary Jane Tobin ran for New York State governor on the new Right to Life Party (RTLP) line, winning over 132,000 votes. The RTLP used its line on the ballot to bargain with candidates, offering the line in exchange for support of pro-life issues and threatening to run its own candidates to draw votes away from opponents. The party's influence peaked in the early 1980s when the country's conservative mood coincided with hostility toward abortion rights and Ronald Reagan was elected to the presidency. The party's endorsement of US Senate nominee and abortion foe Alfonse M. D'Amato (Republican) provided critical votes in his narrow 1980 victory.

The party's unwillingness to compromise or broaden its concerns alienated it from the National Right-to-Life Committee and damaged its position in the state. The party refused to endorse Reagan in 1980 and 1984, endorsing McCormack instead in 1980. She appeared on the ballot in three states and garnered 32,000 votes. RTLP's insistence on absolute single-issue purity, however, alienated potential allies. New York State's prevailing sentiments at the time were pro-choice, and the RTLP endorsement came to be viewed as a liability, with some local parties even forbidding their candidates to accept the RTLP designation. The party lost its automatic ballot line in New York State after the November 2002 election, when it failed to garner the required minimum 50,000 votes. Ironically, its enrollment peaked in 2002 at 49,116.

Spitzer, Robert J. *The Right to Life Movement and Third Party Politics* (New York: Greenwood Press, 1987)

Stonecash, Jeffrey M., ed. *Governing New York State,* 4th ed. (Albany: SUNY Press, 2001)

Robert J. Spitzer

Riis, Jacob (August) (*b* Ribe, Denmark, 3 May 1849; *d* Barre, Mass, 26 May 1914). Journalist, social reformer, and photographer. Riis, the third of 15 children, worked as a carpenter in Copenhagen before he immigrated to the United

States in 1870. After arriving in New York City he worked a number menial jobs, from which he gained firsthand knowledge of poverty. In 1877 he became a crime reporter for the *New York Tribune* and later the *New York Evening Sun.* His journalism in the 1880s focused on reporting the harsh conditions in which impoverished immigrants and their families lived in New York City. Riis became a pioneer in documentary photography during this period, using his photographs to illustrate his exposés on slums and tenements, many of which were taken late at night with flash technology he helped invent. His work in this area led to the publication of *How the Other Half Lives* (1890), a groundbreaking indictment of poverty and the overcrowded living conditions of the poor on the Lower East Side.

A critical voice in the campaign for housing reform that led to the Tenement House Law of 1901, Riis was an advocate for improving the city's public schools, establishing a fresh-air fund for the city's youth, and many other social causes. He convinced Theodore Roosevelt, then head of New York City's Police Commission (1895–97) and a sometime companion of Riis on his investigative forays into the poorest neighborhoods of the city, to close the squalid lodging houses in police stations, an abuse on which Riis had written eloquently. In 1888 he founded one of the first settlement houses in the Lower East Side, which would be named in his honor in 1901, offering among other things healthcare, sewing classes, and citizenship classes. The same year he published his autobiography, *The Making of an American.* In his later years Riis continued to write books. A longtime resident of Richmond Hill in Queens, Riis moved to Barre, Mass, in 1913.

Alland, Alexander. *Jacob A. Riis: Photographer and Citizen* (Millerton, NY: Aperture, 1974)

Brett Forman

riots and civil disturbances. In New York State popular disorder followed the patterns established elsewhere in the United States. Most colonial and Revolutionary period rioters publicly displayed their grievances and destroyed property, but deemphasized violence. Beginning in the 19th century violence became more common, until the mid–20th century, when violent collective action diminished.

Colonial and Revolutionary Period

Leisler's Rebellion (1689–91) included rioting when Jacob Leisler took control of the colonial government and when he was deposed. But as in other colonies, such moments joining riot and rebellion were both rare and limited to the 17th century. Given New York State's polyglot nature, ethnic and religious differences were sometimes expressed in the 17th and 18th centuries through popular disorder. As early as 1667, 60 Dutch settlers of Esopus (Ulster Co) rioted in a dispute between a brewer and the local English commander. Disagreements over the control of local churches broke into disturbances in Fordham [now in Bronx Co] in 1688, Flatbush (Kings Co) in 1711, and Jamaica (Queens Co) in 1715. In New York City mobs also harassed Jews in 1743 and 1749. The most extensive religion-related disturbances were the processions held on Pope Day, a November 5th holiday originally celebrated as Guy Fawkes Day in England, during which New York City crowds paraded with effigies of the Pope, the Pretender (the Stuart claimant to the throne), and the devil beginning by 1748. On several occasions New Yorkers sought to regulate their community though the use of mobs. In New York City there was an attack on prostitutes released from the workhouse in 1753 and a massive demonstration over the revaluation of coinage to the disadvantage of the poor in 1754. As fearsome as these crowds may have appeared—the coinage mob had been "armed with Clubs and Staves"—they perpetrated little real violence. The same could be said for most of the land riots and anti-impressment riots of the 1750s and 1760s, but occasionally there was greater violence, sometimes even leading to fatalities.

Riots increased dramatically during the Revolutionary period, though crowds generally emphasized communal solidarity rather than physical violence. Massive demonstrations against the Stamp Act began on 1 Nov 1765, just as the law was to go into effect. The crowd borrowed its ritual directly from the Pope Day celebrations by marching through New York City with effigies of the Pope, the devil, and Lt Gov Cadwallader Colden. The procession stopped in front of Fort George, burned carriages belonging to Colden, destroyed other property, and created much uproar. Throughout the Stamp Act crisis, mobs controlled New York City's streets, preventing the enforcement of the hated British tax. There was also a Stamp Act riot in Albany in January 1766 when a mob defaced the house of a suspected stamp distributor, destroyed some of his furniture, and burned his winter carriages. From 1766 through 1770 a series of confrontations between British soldiers and civilians over New York City's Liberty Pole occasionally erupted into brawls, but these usually focused on the flagstaff that became a symbol of the colony's resistance movement. The most serious confrontation, known as the Battle of Golden Hill, occurred on 18 Jan 1770, when New Yorkers and British soldiers exchanged blows. Crowds elsewhere in the colony did not get as involved with the resistance movement. During 1766, however, there was an upsurge of riotous activities between landlords and tenants on the Hudson River estates. The squatters failed in an attempt to ally themselves with the resistance movement and were ultimately suppressed by British troops.

During the Revolutionary War and its immediate aftermath, mobs followed the same patterns of collective action. In 1775 and 1776 New Yorkers intimidated loyalists by riding them on rails and practiced other traditional crowd rituals. A Dutchess Co mob tarred and feathered a judge for speaking out against the work of the local committee on 16 Sept 1775, and a crowd in Huntington (Suffolk Co) paraded and blew up an effigy of George III on the reading of the Declaration of Independence. During the war itself, shortages led to several riots over food in several towns, including Kingston (Ulster Co), Fishkill (Dutchess Co), New Windsor (Orange Co), and Poughkeepsie. Usually such crowds seized a food item in short supply and distributed it to the crowd or sold it at an uninflated price. New York Federalist and Antifederalist crowds demonstrated in Albany and New York City in 1788, and New York City mobs rioted against grave robbing in 1788 and against bawdyhouses in 1793 and 1799.

The 19th and Early 20th Centuries

After 1800 patterns of rioting began to change, with violent confrontations increasing with the rise of equality. Like Americans elsewhere, New Yorkers lost the attachment to a single community uniting all of society and began to identify with a variety of interest groups competing with one another. An ethnic clash took place in 1806 when a group calling itself the Highbinders harassed a Catholic church service on Christmas Eve in New York City. The following day the Highbinders invaded an Irish neighborhood and fought with its residents. When the police appeared, they were attacked by the Irish as intruders, and one watchman was killed. In June 1812 sailors and Hispanics brawled along New York City's waterfront, leading to one death. Within a few decades such ethnic confrontations were occurring frequently. Sometimes groups of laborers from different parts of Ireland fought, as in the battle between the "Downers" and "Corkeans" who worked on the railroad near Port Jervis (Orange Co) in 1847. At other times fighting was between different ethnic groups, like German and Irish laborers in May 1847 in Brooklyn. Most often nativist Americans attacked immigrants and their institutions, as when a Palmyra (Wayne Co) mob burned a Catholic church in July 1854. The largest nativist disturbances occurred in 1870 and 1871 when Catholic Irish New Yorkers objected to an Orange parade in New York City on 12 July. In the 1870 riot the Catholic Irish drove members of the Orange order off, killing three. In 1871 the military offered protection to the Orange order and opened fire on the Irish Catholic crowd. Fifty-four civilians and two policemen were killed.

Typically, in race riots of the 19th century and early 20th century, Whites attacked Blacks and their institutions. The New York City antiabolitionist riot of July 1834 quickly spread from a protest against abolitionists to an assault on the black community. The New York City draft riots, 13–17 July 1863, one of the greatest civil cataclysms in American history, grew from a complaint against an unfair draft to an attempt to purge the city of Blacks. Mobs beat Blacks mercilessly, stringing some up from lamp poles. Troops used cannon to clear the streets. Total casualties remain unknown, but at least 120 died, including 11 Blacks. A draft riot also took place in Troy (Rensselaer Co) about the same time, and in Buffalo Irish stevedores attacked Blacks several times during the Civil War. Similar riots occurred intermittently after 1865, including a disturbance in New York City that lasted several days in August 1900 when Whites injured almost 80 Blacks after a policeman had been killed in a racial confrontation. Though not typical, other less violent race-related disturbances garnered significant attention during this period, including one that broke up a meeting of statewide abolitionists gathered at Utica's Bleecker Street Presbyterian Church in 1835, and another in Syracuse where some 2,000 black and white opponents of the Fugitive Slave Act freed escaped slave William "Jerry" Henry from federal custody in 1851.

There were two types of riots reflecting economic class divisions. First, there were those riots that represented the antagonisms between the rich and the poor, such as the Astor Place riot of 10 May 1849. On that night the Astor Place Theater, which entertained affluent patrons, had booked English performer William C. Macready. The Bowery Theater, which served less-affluent patrons, featured American Edwin Forrest. The rivalry between the actors erupted into violence after Bowery supporters disrupted Macready on stage. The military and police in the street outside the theater were bombarded with stones and debris by a crowd numbering into the thousands. Besieged, the military fired into the mob. When the shooting stopped, 22 people had been killed and scores wounded. The other type of class-based riot was more directly connected to the labor movement. At the time the forces of law and order sided with the owners of the means of production during strikes. On 5 Aug 1850, when striking tailors ransacked a nonunion shop, the police interceded, killing 2, wounding several others, and arresting 32. In winter 1895 about 7,000 militiamen were mobilized during a Brooklyn trolley work stoppage because crowds of strike sympathizers had prevented nonunion trolleys from running. In the series of confrontations that followed, several people on both sides were wounded, and one man was killed. Soldiers also killed a striking dam worker in Mamaroneck (Westchester Co) in April 1900 during a riot. Labor unrest in New York State also included actions by dairy farmers protesting low prices paid to them for milk. At the so-called Battle of Boonville on 1 Aug 1933, state troopers teargassed and clubbed local farmers protesting in the Oneida Co town.

To the 21st Century

This cycle of violence only began to be broken in the mid–20th century, when a combination of factors changed the conditions for rioting. First, the power of the state increased, providing instruments of law and order that could effectively block collective violence. Second, media attention made every collective action public; no longer could a community riot in isolation. Finally, many of the interest groups that had been excluded from politics and that had turned to violence or had been the victims of violence now became a part of the legitimate political order. Despite these developments, riots, though less violent, continued to occur. The Harlem riots of 1935, in which black residents responded to the rumored police shooting of a shoplifting suspect, and of 1943, in which they reacted to the police shooting a black serviceman, helped to establish a new pattern of disturbance. In both cases, black rioters responded to injustice by looting and burning property within their own neighborhood. Most casualties in these disturbances were inflicted by the forces of law and order against perceived disturbers of the peace. This type of rioting swept the nation in the mid-1960s, including riots in Rochester (1964), New York City (1964, 1965), Troy (1966), Buffalo (1967), Albany (1967), and Syracuse (1967). So ritualized had this form of disturbance become that during a blackout in New York City in July 1977 rioters poured into the streets shouting "It's Christmas time" as they looted stores. Even when Whites attacked Blacks, the most prominent type of race rioting before the transition to new forms of popular disturbances in the 20th century, the violence was minimal. On 27 Aug and 4 Sept 1949, white vigilantes sought to stop a Paul Robeson concert in Peekskill (Westchester Co) by throwing stones and bottles at the mixed-race left-wing crowd of concertgoers on the way to the venue. Several people were injured, but no one was killed.

The increase in immigration at the end of the 20th century contributed to hostility between groups such as Jews, Blacks, and Asians. African American youths beat three Asian men in Brooklyn on 13 May 1990, and tension between Hasidic Jews in Brooklyn and nearby Blacks and Puerto Ricans flamed into violence several times. The legitimization of the labor movement has led to more peaceful strikes, though occasionally there have been some attacks on scabs, as occurred during a newspaper delivery strike in 1991. An upsurge of political rioting occurred in the 1960s and 1970s, as several college campuses erupted into disorder, with students protesting the Vietnam War and asserting a new left perspective. Most of the protests, especially on the campuses of SUNY Buffalo, Columbia University, Brooklyn College, and Cornell University, entailed the destruction of property or the occupation of buildings. Other political issues also spawned collective violence. Claiming that a police raid on a gay bar was a form of antigay harassment, a group of New York City homosexuals attacked police during the Stonewall riot of 27 June 1969. Since the 1970s other political demonstrations have turned into rioting, including actions by the antinuclear, women's rights, and antiabortion movements.

By the beginning of the 21st century, riots seldom included tremendous personal violence. A rock concert, sport victory, and other gatherings of large numbers of people have become disorderly. Often these disturbances seem epiphenomenal—moments of disorder in which a crowd seizes an opportunity to misbehave and destroy or loot property—such as in the Woodstock riot of 1999. Although recent collective violence is less frequent and less intense, the long history of American rioting reveals how easily divisions within society can turn lethal.

See also Attica uprising; Columbia University in the City of New York.

Bernstein, Iver. *The New York City Draft Riots: Their Significance for American Society and Politics in the Age of the Civil War* (New York: Oxford Univ Press, 1990)

Brandt, Nat. *Harlem at War: The Black Experience in WWII* (Syracuse: Syracuse Univ Press, 1996)

Gilje, Paul A. *The Road to Mobocracy: Popular Disorder in New York City, 1763–1834* (Chapel Hill: Univ of North Carolina Press, 1987)

———. *Rioting in America* (Bloomington: Indiana Univ Press, 1996)

Gordon, Michael A. *The Orange Riots: Irish Political Violence in New York City, 1870 and 1871* (Ithaca: Cornell Univ Press, 1993)

Headley, Joel Tyler. *The Great Riots of New York, 1712–1873* (1873; repr Indianapolis: Bobbs-Merrill, 1970)

United States. Kerner Commission. *The Kerner Report: The 1968 Report of the Advisory Commission on Civil Disorders* (New York: Pantheon, 1988)

Paul A. Gilje

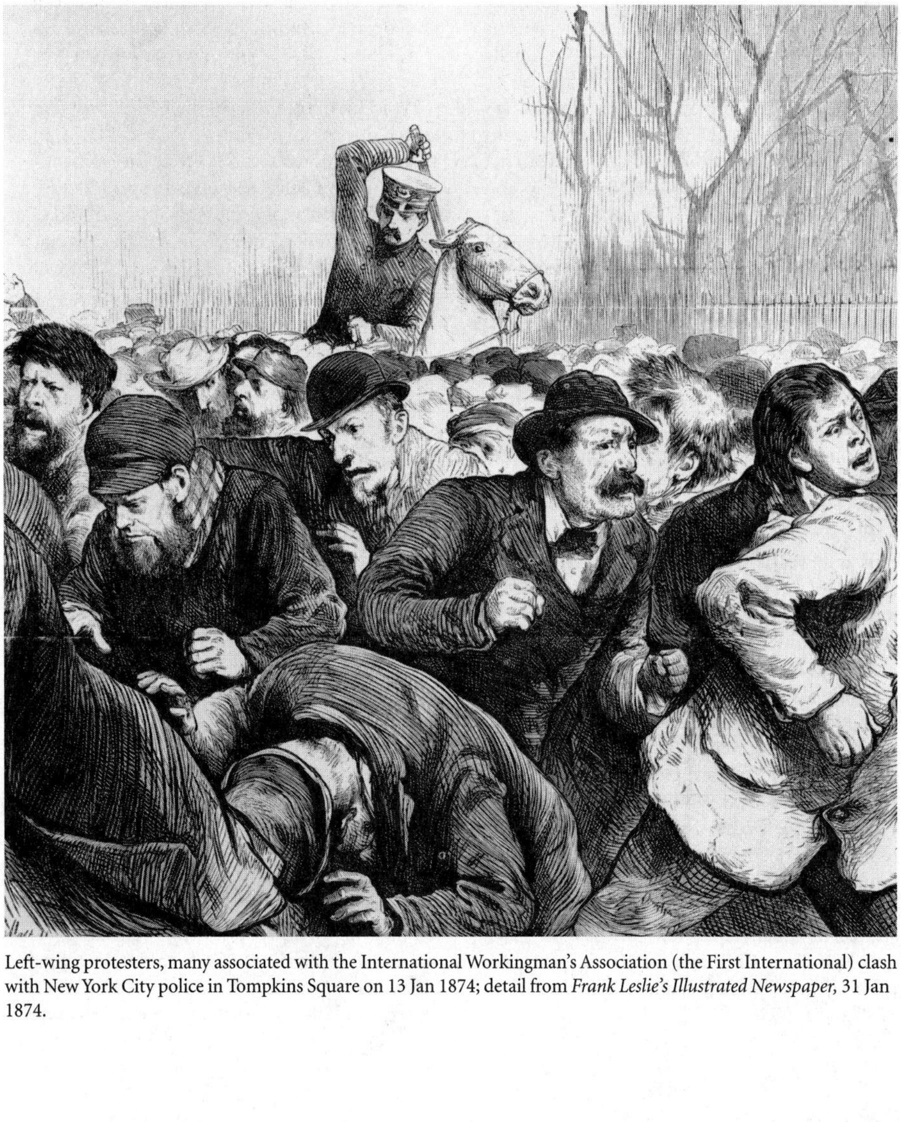

Left-wing protesters, many associated with the International Workingman's Association (the First International) clash with New York City police in Tompkins Square on 13 Jan 1874; detail from *Frank Leslie's Illustrated Newspaper,* 31 Jan 1874.

Ripley. Town (pop 2,636) in W Chautauqua Co. The area was settled around 1804, and the town was formed in 1816 from Portland. It lies between Lake Erie and the Allegheny foothills, the heart of the Concord grape belt. The first mechanical grape picker was invented here. From the 1880s to 1937, eloping couples from other states created a marriage industry for the town, which ended with a change in New York State law. Ripley is the western terminus of the Thruway, which was constructed through town in 1957. Grapes continue to be the mainstay crop. Ripley was the birthplace of B. F. Goodrich (1841–88).

Marie McCutcheon

Rip Van Winkle. Title character in short story by Washington Irving (1783–1859) published in *The Sketch-Book of Geoffrey Crayon, Gent.* (1819). He lives an idle existence, frequenting the tavern in an unspecified Catskill Mountain farming community late in the English colonial period. One day, accompanied by his dog and gun, he rambles into the mountains where he has a mysterious encounter with a group of solemn men who wear antiquated Dutch dress. They are playing a game of ninepin (an early form of bowling), and each roll of the ball produces a loud peal of thunder along the mountains. After drinking their liquor, Rip falls asleep on the hillside and wakes up alone, his dog vanished and his gun rusted. He returns to the village, where everything is strange yet familiar. Twenty years have passed in a single night. The Revolutionary War has been fought and won while he slept. The face of King George III on the tavern sign has been replaced by that of George Washington, and all discussion is now of politics and parties. The community to which Rip returns exemplifies not quiet colonial life but the busy, forward-looking world of the new American republic.

"Rip Van Winkle" offers a myth of the birth of the independent American nation. The tale purports to have been discovered posthumously among the papers of Diedrich Knickerbocker, the fictional historian of Irving's *History of New York* (1809). Irving also ties the story to the German legend of Emperor Frederick Barbarossa, who fell asleep in the Kyffhäuser Mountains awaiting the time when he would make his nation the world's most powerful. Irving likely borrowed the name of his character from Rip van Dam (*ca* 1660–1749), colonial merchant and politician. Irving never claimed a specific setting for his tale, although several Catskill localities have vied for the honor, among them Palenville (Greene Co), which he visited several times.

Subsequent treatments of the character include Hudson River school artist Asher B. Durand's 1838 painting of Rip being introduced to Henry Hudson's crew. Joseph Jefferson (1829–1905), one of the most popular comedians of the 19th century, became famous for his starring role in a theatrical version (1859), appearing in more than 3,000 performances. These inspired a series of sculptures of Rip, beginning in 1869, by popular sculptor John Rogers (1829–1904). The most substantial monument to Irving's character is undoubtedly the Rip Van Winkle Bridge (1935), a 5,040 ft (1,536 m) cantilever bridge crossing the Hudson between Catskill (Greene Co) and Greenport (Columbia Co).

Irving, Washington. *The Sketch-Book of Geoffrey Crayon, Gent.* Ed. Susan Manning (New York: Oxford Univ Press, 1998)
Young, Philip. "Fallen from Time: The Mythic Rip Van Winkle," *Kenyon Review* 22 (1960)

Susan Manning

Rivera, Oscar Garcia (*b* Mayagüez, Puerto Rico, 6 Nov 1900; *d* Mayagüez, 1969). Elected official and political activist. Born to a prosperous family in Puerto Rico, Rivera visited New York City after his high school graduation and became concerned with the plight of the city's poor and working class. He returned to New York City in 1926 and entered law school at St. John's University. While in law school, he worked in the City Hall Post Office and organized Puerto Rican employees, encouraging them to become active in the Postal Clerks' Union of America. After graduating law school, he practiced law in New York City, providing many Latino residents with legal services at no charge. Hoping to improve conditions for the 20,000 residents of Spanish Harlem particularly hard hit by the Great Depression, Rivera successfully ran for the New York State Assembly in 1937. He was the first Puerto Rican elected to public office in the continental United States and served two terms in the state legislature, achieving a distinguished record of service related to labor, children, and other issues. In February 2002 a post office in East Harlem was renamed the Oscar Garcia Rivera Post Office in honor of Rivera's service to the local community.

Moore, Joan, and Harry Pachon. *Hispanics in the United States* (Chicago: Pearson Education, 1985)
Wakefield, Dan. *Island in the City: The World of Spanish Harlem* (New York: Arno Press, 1975)

Barry Mowell

Riverbank State Park. Located in Manhattan at West 145th St and Riverside Drive, this 28-acre (11 ha) multilevel landscaped facility opened in 1993. The plan for the park was adopted from Japanese rooftop designs. Rising 69 feet (21 m) above the Hudson River, the park entertains visitors with recreational facilities as well as a view of the Palisades and the George Washington Bridge. There are five major buildings within the park housing a pool, skating rink, amphitheater, athletic complex, and restaurant. The outdoor facilities include lap and wading pools; tennis, basketball, handball, and paddleball courts; a softball field; and a running track with an artificial turf field for football and soccer. The park is also home to the Totally Kid Carousel created by New York City artist Milo Mottola and 37 young children. The carousel's creatures are the fiberglass manifestations of animal sketches drawn by the youths. The park is constructed on top of the North River Wastewater Treatment Plant, at 137th St in West Harlem, which opened in March 1986. The park hosts an average of 2.5 million visitors annually, but the plant often exuded noxious smells. In 1992 the New York City Department of Environmental Protection allocated $55 million to ameliorate the smell, and the project was completed in 1997.

New York State Parks and Recreation. "Riverbank State Park," http://www.nysparks.state.ny.us/cgi-bin/cgiwrap/nysparks/parks.cgi?p+146

Samuel H. Sage

Riverhead. Town (pop 27,680) and locality (pop 10,513) in E central Suffolk Co. Settled around a 1659 sawmill at the headwaters of the Peconic River, the hamlet became the county seat when a courthouse was built in 1728 and formed as a town from Southold in 1792. It acquired the Suffolk post office in 1794 and was renamed Riverhead in 1856. Industry in the 1800s included farming, shipbuilding, timbering, fishing, and cigar making. The Perkins Woolen Mill (1828) was famous for its waterproof cloth. Irish workers came in the 1840s and Polish farmers later in the century. In the 20th century farming cen-

Rip Van Winkle's Return from the Mountains, Tompkins Harrison Matteson, 1860.

tered initially on potatoes and ducks, then developed initiatives designed to encourage horse breeding, horticulture, and vineyards. Golf courses and retail outlet shops also bolstered the economy. A large part of the town's west end was occupied by the Calverton Naval Weapons Industrial Reserve Plant (1952–94). Open space preservation has been an important concern, and Riverhead is the site of the large Otis Pike Preserve and the 769-acre (311 ha) Wildwood State Park. Late 19th-century agriculture is interpreted at the Hallockville Farm and Folklife Center. Riverhead is also the site of the Railroad Museum of Long Island, the Suffolk County Historical Society, and the Calverton National Cemetery. The former Naval Weapons tract is now Calverton Enterprise Park (1998), home to a number of growing businesses. The Riverhead Country Fair and the Polish Town Festival are annual events in Riverhead hamlet, which has two notable halls, the Vail-Leavitt Music Hall (1881) and the Art Deco–style Suffolk Theatre (1930s).

Bronwyn Hannon

Riverkeeper. Privately funded nongovernmental environmental group. Founded in New York State in 1966 by members of the Hudson River Fishermen's Association, Riverkeeper adopted a mission of protecting the waters of the Hudson River system from the Adirondacks to Long Island Sound. Robert Boyle, author of *The Hudson River: A Natural and Unnatural History,* which documents the region's past industrialization and contemporary environmental problems, modeled the organization on British riverkeepers who looked after private trout and salmon streams. Riverkeeper has publicized the pollution of the Hudson and worked with the state and federal governments to promote legal remedies. In 1977 the US Environmental Protection Agency (EPA) required General Electric to eliminate its PCB discharges after contamination was discovered in the sediments of the upper and lower Hudson River; at the beginning of the 21st century, the cleanup of PCBs from the Hudson River bed is still in progress.

In 1983 John Cronin became the first full-time Hudson riverkeeper. In 1994 the group successfully sued the EPA to set new pollution standards for power plants such as those located on the Hudson River. Another Riverkeeper success was the installation of $25 million worth of equipment on the water intakes of the Indian Point Nuclear Power Plant; this technology saves fish that would otherwise be killed or maimed in an estuary that is also a breeding ground for numerous freshwater species. By 1998 the group had filed over 150 successful legal challenges to polluters, and as a result the Hudson River has made a dramatic recovery. In 2000 Alex Matthiessen succeeded Cronin as Hudson riverkeeper and executive director. In the early 21st century there are 63 local programs in watersheds across North and Central America, each a member of the Waterkeeper Alliance headed by Robert F. Kennedy Jr. As codirector of the Pace Environmental Litigation Clinic, Kennedy supervises students from the Pace University School of Law who represent the organization in court proceedings and other legal matters.

Boyle, Robert H. *The Hudson River: A Natural and Unnatural History* (New York: Norton, 1979)

Cronin, John, and Robert F. Kennedy Jr. *The Riverkeepers: Two Activists Fight to Reclaim Our Environment as a Basic Human Right* (New York: Scribner's, 1997)

Thomas Fletcher

Riverside. Village (pop 594) in Corning (Steuben Co). Settled in 1795 and originally known as Centerville, the locality contained the region's first store (1795), a station for stagecoaches connecting to Bath, Elmira, Watkins, and Pennsylvania, and the original Painted Post post office (1800). Incorporated as the Village of Riverside in 1922 and located between the City of Corning and the Village of Painted Post, its character was dramatically altered with the 1995 completion of the Rte 17 (I-86) bypass; a Riverside exit (1989) brought new retail growth serving local needs. Most residents work in Corning and Painted Post.

Thomas Dimitroff

Rivington, James (*b* London, 17 Aug 1724; *d* New York City, 4 July 1802). Loyalist printer and suspected patriot spy. After going bankrupt, Rivington left England and opened bookstores in Philadelphia, New York City, and Boston. By 1765 he consolidated his presses and operated chiefly out of New York City. His *Rivington's New-York Gazetteer* was founded in 1773 and became a tory vehicle; Rivington claimed it had 3,600 subscribers. The Sons of Liberty (May) and a mob (November) destroyed his presses in 1775, forcing him to sail for England. In 1777, after being appointed the king's printer, he returned to New York City and established *Rivington's New-York Loyal Gazette,* later changed to *Royal Gazette* (1777–83). Despite his loyalist wartime activities, Rivington was allowed to remain in New York City after 1783, in part because many believed he had been a spy for the patriots. After the British evacuated New York City, Rivington changed the name of his paper to *Rivington's New-York Gazette and Universal Advertiser.* He was imprisoned for debt in 1797, paid his creditors, and was released in 1801, but died a year later still bankrupt.

Crary, Catherine Snell. "The Tory and the Spy: The Double Life of James Rivington," *William and Mary Quarterly,* 3d Series, 16 (January 1959): 61–72

Jennifer Steenshorne

roads. The public highways of New York State have evolved over the course of several centuries from a loose aggregation of well-trod but poorly maintained pathways into a cohesive system of hard-surfaced roads. Responding to a broad range of social changes, New Yorkers developed the political capacity during the 20th century to produce an innovative transportation infrastructure. Within the context of perennial political division caused by differences in wealth, demography, and cultural geography, the state oversaw this mammoth public works program, the sheer size of which constitutes an impressive contribution to the built environment. The state, however, struggled to sustain the system it had created, an automobile-dependent system that, indelibly transformed New York State.

Early Roads

Private road construction in the early 19th century provided New Yorkers with a system of toll roads that was both integrated and in competition with the other major transportation initiatives of the era, canals and railroads. Thinly capitalized turnpike companies strained under high maintenance costs, and new road construction declined after midcentury with the waning of state promotional activity. Overland transport devolved onto the heavily subsidized private railroads, leaving the public roads to continual neglect.

The public roadways of early New York State were defined by town governments' local interests. Town commissioners of highways, who received and adjudicated petitions for new roads, also appointed local overseers, or pathmasters, to administer the public roads, each of whom was allotted a set number of labor days to maintain their short stretch of road. Labor was assessed against each male town resident between the ages of 21 and 70, with each eligible resident working at least one day and the remainder of the days apportioned by assessed property value. Labor could be commuted at the rate of $1 per day, but most rural New Yorkers chose to work out their tax. Those who lived in incorporated areas, by contrast, were exempt from these taxes; city and village residents paid for urban improvements by special assessments but contributed little to the rural, intercity road system.

This decentralized brand of road administration, with its less-than-rigorous repair schedule, yielded a highly segmented jumble of unimproved highways. Moreover, inadequate engineering, especially regarding road drainage, left state roads rutted and muddy, cracked and dusty, pitted and overgrown, or completely washed out, depending on the season. Traveling under these conditions ranged from uncomfortable to nearly impossible. As 19th-century New Yorkers focused their energy on more modern transportation innovations—the Artificial River and the Iron Horse—they saw the unimproved condition of public roadways as largely inevi-

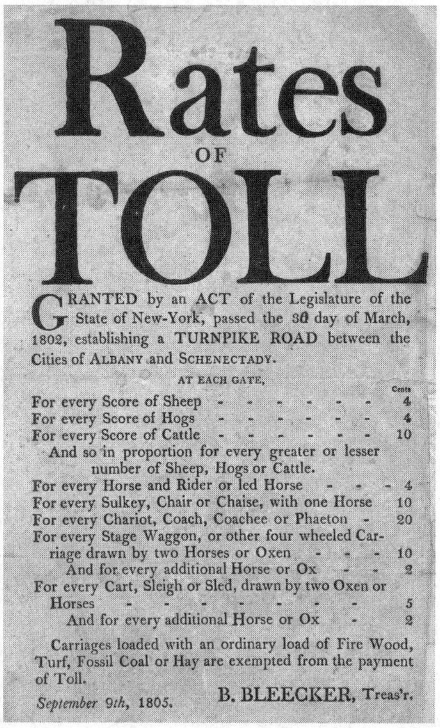

Rates

OF

TOLL

GRANTED by an ACT of the Legislature of the State of New-York, passed the 3d day of March, 1802, establishing a TURNPIKE ROAD between the Cities of ALBANY and SCHENECTADY.

AT EACH GATE,

	Cents
For every Score of Sheep - - - - - - -	4
For every Score of Hogs - - - - - - -	4
For every Score of Cattle - - - - - - -	10
And so in proportion for every greater or lesser number of Sheep, Hogs or Cattle.	
For every Horse and Rider or led Horse - - -	4
For every Sulkey, Chair or Chaise, with one Horse	10
For every Chariot, Coach, Coachee or Phaeton -	20
For every Stage Waggon, or other four wheeled Carriage drawn by two Horses or Oxen - - -	10
And for every additional Horse or Ox - -	2
For every Cart, Sleigh or Sled, drawn by two Oxen or Horses - - - - - - - -	5
And for every additional Horse or Ox -	2

Carriages loaded with an ordinary load of Fire Wood, Turf, Fossil Coal or Hay are exempted from the payment of Toll.

September 9th, 1805. B. BLEECKER, Treas'r.

Broadside listing toll rates for the Albany and Schenectady Turnpike, 1805.

table; the roads had become part of the common landscape and conformed to the unique particularities of the local communities they served.

The Decline of Local Control

During the last quarter of the 19th century, the Good Roads Movement emerged as a force for improving roads and reforming the nation's highway administration. The League of American Wheelmen (LAW), founded in 1880 to promote bicycling interests, was best organized. Especially strong in New York State, the group increasingly criticized the local system of road administration, especially the position of pathmaster, which was seen more as a bestowal of political patronage than as an acknowledgment of civil engineering skill. It also objected to the labor system, perceiving it as inefficient and more as a "neighborhood picnic" than as a serious attempt to maintain important thoroughfares. Reformers argued that improved highways would decrease hauling costs, bring New York State produce into tighter competition with the West, increase land value, and stem the outflow of rural men and women to urban centers. But they still encountered resistance from rural populations that endorsed only marginal changes: some towns adopted the money system, requiring payment in cash rather than labor; some centralized road control through county supervision; and some purchased labor-saving road machinery.

The New York State division of the LAW called for both state and federal involvement in road building by 1888. Members prompted the creation in 1893 of the small and underfunded federal Office of Road Inquiry, which after several reorganizations became the Bureau of Public Roads (BPR) in 1918. They achieved greater success at the state level, promoting state control of highway administration, finance, and construction. New York State road reformers won their first victory with the 1898 passage of the Higbie-Armstrong Act, which provided for state construction of highways upon petition from a county board of supervisors. Costs were split 50–35–15 among the state, county, and town, respectively. Since all construction was contingent upon a county's request for assistance, this provision was heralded as a brake on runaway state spending. The Fuller-Plank Act, passed the same year, provided state funds to any town that adopted the money system. Both acts worked toward better coordinating the state's highways while still containing elements of local control.

Petitions for state assistance quickly outpaced the legislature's meager annual appropriations, and Good Roads advocates began lobbying for large bond issues to support an extensive construction program. In 1905 state voters overwhelmingly ratified a constitutional amendment authorizing the legislature to create a $50 million bonded debt to improve state highways. Cost-apportionment provisions allowing poorer localities to pay less than the standard proportion often led the state to cover as much as three-quarters of all highway costs. In response to this shortfall, the legislature issued another $50 million bond in 1912, making New York State by far the nation's leading road builder.

State road-building authority was originally lodged with the Office of State Engineer and Surveyor, but charges of political jobbery prompted several administrative reorganizations during the first two decades of state highway construction. A bipartisan state highway commission was created in 1908 and reorganized (under a single head) in 1911 and 1913 in attempts to insulate the body from party politics.

The State in Ascension

Two developments in the late 1910s drastically changed the scope of highway construction in New York State. The rapid increase in the use of motor vehicles as a popular mode of transportation pointed to the need for more and better roads. The 1916 Federal Aid Road Act provided matching road-building grants-in-aid to states, based on size, population, and road mileage, on the condition that they create state highway departments to oversee the construction. New York, like most states, took advantage of the program. Although the BPR set construction and material standards, conducted extensive research, and dispersed the federal government's significant largess, road-building authority remained within the state.

The wartime emergency and postwar depression forestalled extensive construction until the early 1920s, but soon the state's road-building program made significant strides in new construction, repair, and maintenance. The damage caused by convoys of heavy military trucks emphatically demonstrated the need for a better grade of construction. The state's first macadam roads, built under the Higbie-Armstrong Act but before the ascension of the automobile, could not stand the increased motor traffic. New York State motor vehicle registrations, which had increased from 234,000 in 1915 to 683,000 in 1920, jumped to 2,347,000 in 1930. From 1923 to 1931, highway expenditures tripled in an effort to keep apace of mounting construction and reconstruction costs.

Col Frederick S. Greene, former Army Corps of Engineers member, guided state highway construction through these expansionary years. Appointed in 1919 by Gov Alfred E. Smith, Greene purged the office of "soft political berths" and oversaw the state's highway administration through several reorganizations, including the creation of the expanded Department of Public Works (DPW) in 1923. He fought tirelessly to bring engineering principles to the planning and construction of the state highway system. In the early 1920s he successfully opposed the legislature's effort to authorize a state highway map riddled with pet local projects. Later in the decade Greene worked to bring town and county highways more tightly within the orbit of state power.

During these boom years, Greene oversaw numerous other changes at all levels of highway activity. In public finance, the state adopted the motor fuel tax, a move that brought millions of dollars to the annual highway budget. In planning and construction, the DPW built limited-access parkways, like Long Island's Northern and Southern State Parkways, in conjunction with the State Council of Parks. In the field of safety, the DPW engaged in a $300 million railroad grade crossing elimination program and in 1925 instituted an early system of route numbering and warning signs. By 1929 the state had nearly completed the system of US routes within its borders as well as its own larger system of primary state highways. Construction peaked in 1931, and the DPW envisioned a new reconstruction program that would include straightening, widening, and strengthening the state's highways to meet the needs of faster, heavier, and more diverse traffic.

Road Building in Depression and War

By the early 1930s New York State sank deeper into the Great Depression, and the state's highway program was dominated by the need to increase employment. To spread jobs as widely as possible, moneys from federal emergency grants, the Works Progress Administration, and

State Paved Highway System 1926

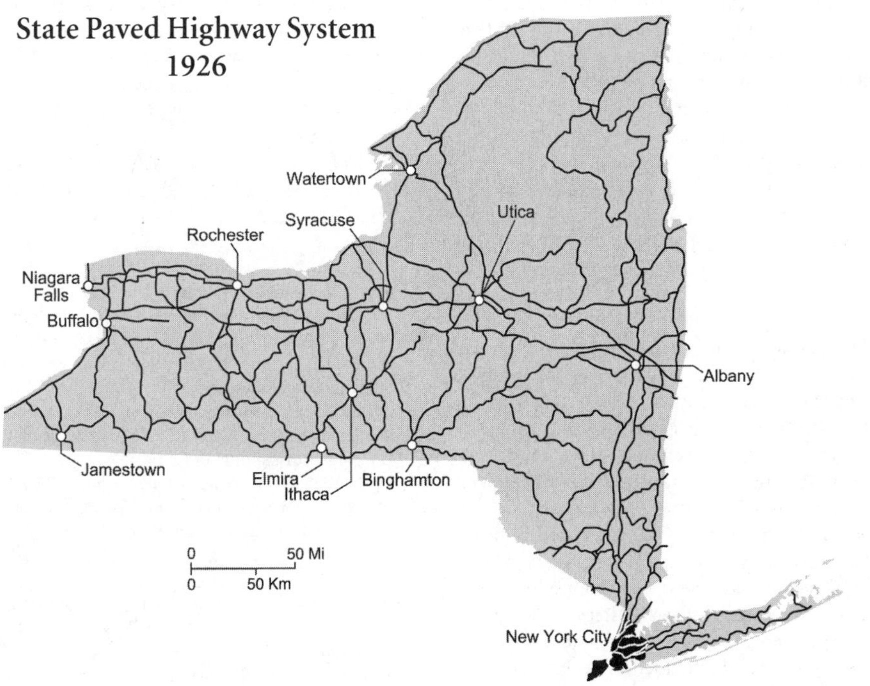

SOURCE: Adapted from *Rand McNally Auto Road Atlas of the United States* (1926).

the Public Works Administration were directed to work programs on the state's secondary road system. Farm-to-market roads, a low priority for most of the state's road-building history, began receiving attention. Emergency appropriations were also allocated for urban arterial highways, which had previously been outside the parameters of state control.

Despite these new initiatives, road construction waned. Maintenance costs grew with the construction of each new mile, and it became impossible to keep up under depression era budgeting. Slowed by the late 1930s, the building program halted during the war. Shortages of men and materials confined new plans to paper. As the war neared an end, however, the DPW prepared to enter a new era of road building.

Thinking Big

In 1946 the DPW unveiled its proposal for a 535 mi (861 km) express highway connecting New York City, Albany, and Buffalo to each other and to neighboring states and Canada. The New York State Thruway would be, as the state billed it, the "Greatest Highway in the World." Nearly 80% of the state's population would live within 20 miles (32 km) of it. Gov Thomas E. Dewey broke ground at Liverpool (Onondaga Co) in 1946, and the first major portion of the multilane expressway opened in 1954. The self-supporting project, ultimately costing close to $1 billion, was financed by the New York State Thruway Authority, a quasi-independent public agency established in 1950 whose bonds were backed by the state's credit. Though other states had previously initiated toll roads, the scale of the Thruway far surpassed them in expense and mileage.

The postwar expansion of the 1940s and 1950s fostered other new construction as New York State sought to catch up on 15 years of delayed work. As travel in and out of cities increased correspondingly with suburban growth, the state in 1946 created a new branch of the DPW devoted to urban arterial route planning and construction. That same year, rural road building received new attention when the state began work on its Federal Aid Secondary Highway System, a system of rural roads designated under the Federal-Aid Highway Act of 1944. And the state took on even more traditionally local responsibilities. While counties had been responsible for securing rights-of-way since 1898, the refusal or inability of some counties to secure the land necessary for new route alignment prompted the state to reverse its policy in 1942 and to take more direct action in acquiring property.

Interstates and Beyond

The passage of the 1956 Federal-Aid Highway Act ensured the continuation of the postwar construction boom. Almost 1,300 (2,090 km) of the 41,000 mi (65,980 km) of the Interstate Highway System ran through the State of New York, 90% of which was funded by the federal government. This new express highway system, into which the Thruway was integrated, radically transformed the pace and pattern of New Yorkers' lives. Yet these new roads continued to rest upon the state highway system: older roads groaned under the increased car and truck traffic that was dumped onto them from the new highways, and maintenance costs continued their steep climb.

Gov Nelson A. Rockefeller sustained this expansionary momentum, administering an unprecedented $1 billion program during the late 1950s and 1960s. But the costly and expansive nature of the postwar program, which cut through urban and rural communities alike, heightened opposition to new road building. Management demands linked to previous expansion led to the DPW's reorganization in 1967. Road-building authority was vested in the Department of Transportation (DOT), a central agency created to oversee the state's land, air, and waterborne transportation networks. During the 1970s, however, broad concerns over new roads' environmental and community impact prompted a backlash against highway construction. This hostile response to new development, coupled with the state's financial crisis, severely limited the DOT's highway program at this time.

As the interstate system neared completion in the last decades of the 20th century, New York State faced the tremendously difficult task of creating a balanced, manageable highway infrastructure that served the needs of its citizens. The modern highway system had already produced serious social consequences: it furthered the decline of historic downtown districts, allowed for unchecked suburban growth, and increased the amount of time New Yorkers spent on the roads. But there seemed no going back. As commercial truck traffic and average commuting time rose, the DOT responded in 1984 with another major building campaign to address increased congestion. This program, however, aimed to improve the existing system through the rehabilitation of local and supporting roads rather than to focus solely on controversial new construction. Road maintenance, now the largest of the DOT's divisions, also received new attention following the tragic collapse of the Thruway's Schoharie Bridge in 1987.

One hundred years of highway construction had generated an extensive, and expensive, transportation network. Once a purely local concern, highway administration now demanded continuous, innovative management. As the state entered its second century of modern road building, it embarked on a $12.6 billion capital program to improve and maintain its 111,000 miles (178,640 km) of highway and 17,000 bridges over which 100 billion vehicle miles are driven annually.

See also Automobile landscapes; Cartography and mapping; Interstate highways; New York State Thruway; Traffic management; Turnpikes.

Baker, Paula. *The Moral Frameworks of Public Life: Gender, Politics, and the State in Rural New York, 1870–1930* (New York: Oxford Univ Press, 1991)
Barron, Hal S. "And the Crooked Shall Be Made Straight: Rural Road Reform and the Politics of Localism." In *Mixed Harvest: The Second Great Transformation in the Rural North, 1870–1930* (Chapel Hill: Univ of North Carolina Press, 1997)
Curtiss, William M. *The Development of Highway Administration and Finance in New York* (Ithaca: Department of Agricultural Economics and Farm Management, NYS College of Agriculture, Cornell Univ, 1936)
Jackson, Kenneth T. *Crabgrass Frontier: The Suburbanization of the United States* (New York: Oxford Univ Press, 1985)
Lewis, Tom. *Divided Highways: Building the Interstate Highways, Transforming American Life* (New York: Viking, 1997)
New York State Department of Public Works. Annual Reports. NYS Archives, Albany
New York State Department of Transportation. Annual Reports. NYS Archives, Albany
Rose, Mark. *Interstate: Express Highway Politics, 1939–1989* (Knoxville: Univ of Tennessee Press, 1990)
Seely, Bruce E. *Building the American Highway System: Engineers as Policy Makers* (Philadelphia: Temple Univ Press, 1987)

Michael R. Fein

roadside attractions. The rapidly spreading popularity of the automobile in the United States spawned the development of a new kind of roadside commerce in the first half of the 20th century. As a center of American commercial activity and a northeastern crossroads, New York State saw the rise of many homespun efforts to pull motorists curbside to spend money. As roads were improved and speed increased, many of those efforts took outsized and fanciful forms. Prime examples of these attractions have survived despite the development of the interstate highway system. One of the state's notable roadside amusements capitalized on the newfound interest in dinosaurs. In 1938 the Petrified Creatures Museum, a primitive kind of Jurassic Park, opened in Richfield Springs (Otsego Co) along US 20 and still operates, despite the death of its founder, John Mlecz, in 1997. Nearby, the 40 ft (12.2 m) tall TePee beckons the same stream of motorists in Cherry Valley. The TePee is an excellent example of programmatic architecture, a building designed to indicate its purpose, which in this case is selling Native American–inspired gifts and novelties to tourists. In Buchanan (Westchester Co) motorists would easily identify the Gallon Measure Service Station as a place to buy gasoline. Travelers can also buy ice cream at the Twist-o-the-Mist in Niagara Falls, or fresh duck and eggs at the Big Duck in Flanders (Suffolk Co). Additionally large fiberglass statues that once simply served to advertise local merchants have become attractions in their own right. Albany's Big Nipper, a 25 ft (7.6 m) fiberglass construction of the RCA Victor mascot, sits high above Broadway. The Amoco Man in Elmsford (Westchester Co) is one of many fiberglass statues otherwise known as muffler men or Paul Bunyan statues, made by International Fiberglass. They stand 20 feet (6.1 m) tall and hold the merchant's signature product. In the 1950s roadside features declined because more people traveled on newly developed highways and because sign and billboard advertising replaced programmatic architecture.

Liebs, Chester. *Main Street to Miracle Mile* (Baltimore: Johns Hopkins Univ Press, 1995)

Randy Garbin

Robertson, Constance Noyes (*b* Niagara Falls, Canada, 27 Sept 1897; *d* Kenwood Heights, Madison Co, 10 Mar 1985). Author. The granddaughter of John Humphrey Noyes, who founded the Oneida Community (1848–79), Constance graduated in 1916 from Dana Hall in Wellesley, Mass. She then attended the University of Wisconsin but withdrew to marry Miles E. Robertson in 1918. The couple lived abroad until 1921. From 1925 to 1930 Robertson edited a small magazine, the *Community Quadrangle,* owned by the Oneida Community, Ltd. She published her first novel in 1931. Many of her works were carefully researched historical novels and several were set in New York State, among them *Fire Bell in the Night* (1944), a story of the Underground Railroad and the state's abolitionists, and *The Unterrified* (1946), which concerned New York State Peace Democrats during the Civil War. *Seek-No-Further* (1938) is a historical novel about American communal life. She also wrote three nonfiction works that deal directly with her family's connection to the Oneida Community: *Oneida Community: An Autobiography, 1851–1876* (1970), *Oneida Community: The Breakup, 1876–1881* (1972), and *Oneida Community Profiles* (1977).

"Constance Robertson." *Contemporary Authors,* vol 29–32 (Detroit: Gale Research, 1972, 1978)

John R Deitrick

Robertson, James (*b* Burntisland, Scotland, 29 June *os*/10 July *ns* 1717; *d* London, 4 Mar 1788). British general and royal governor of New York. The son of George Robertson, a laird, and Christian Dundas, he enlisted as a private in a marine regiment, was commissioned a second lieutenant in 1739, and by the dint of hard work rose to lieutenant general in 1780. While fighting in the Scottish Highlands in 1745–46, he made the acquaintance of John Campbell, Earl of Loudoun, who became his patron. In 1756 Robertson followed Loudoun to America and became deputy quartermaster general in 1758. British commander in chiefs in America found the ever efficient Robertson indispensable. After persuading Gen Thomas Gage and the ministry of the need for the Quartering Act (1765), he also served as barrackmaster general (1765–76). In 1776 he persuaded Gen William Howe to start the invasion of New York by landing on Staten Island instead of Long Island. In September 1776 Howe appointed him military commandant of New York City, in which capacity he served until May 1778. In May 1779, at the behest of Lord George Germain, he appeared before Parliament to support the ministry's new policy of conciliation. Appointed governor of New York that year, he was to institute that policy by restoring civil government in the province. Although he served until April 1783, he did not restore the government. He declined to end martial law when offered that opportunity, partly because of his own corrupt dealings. This failure hurt the British cause and made the American victory more acceptable to New York neutrals and loyalists.

Klein, Milton M., and Ronald W. Howard, eds. *The Twilight of British Rule in Revolutionary America: The New York Letter Book of General James Robertson, 1780–1783* (Cooperstown, NY: NYS Historical Association, 1983)

Joseph S. Tiedemann

Roberts Wesleyan College. Private, liberal arts college. Founded in Rochester as Chili Seminary (1866), renamed Chesbrough Seminary (1885), Roberts Junior College (1945), and Roberts Wesleyan College (1949). The school shares a campus with Northeastern Seminary (1998) on land purchased by the founder, Rev Benjamin Titus Roberts. Ousted from the Methodist Episcopal Church in the 1850s as a leader of the Holiness-teaching Nazarites, Roberts was the first general superintendent of the Free Methodist Church, which he founded in 1860. From its inception the school has been coeducational and affiliated with the Free Methodist Church. The first catalog stated the school would combine "the benefits of mental, moral, and religious culture." Instruction was at the academy level, including a program for preparation of clergy. A junior college curriculum was added in 1923. The first bachelor's degree was awarded in 1951 and master's-level programs began in 1992. Enrollment as of 2002 was 1,800.

Pfouts, Neil E. *A History of Roberts Wesleyan College* (Rochester: Roberts Wesleyan College, 2000)

Charles H. Canon III

Robins Island. Island in Southold (Suffolk Co). This 2 mi (3 km) long island in Great Peconic Bay off New Suffolk on Long Island's North Fork derives its name from the Dutch word for seal. In the 18th century Robins Island was owned by the Wickham family, but they lost it because of their loyalist sympathies. The island's remarkable state of preservation is largely due to its use as a hunting preserve throughout most of the 20th century. In 1993 Louis Moore Bacon purchased the island for $10.5 million. The new owner signed an agreement with the Nature Conservancy to manage the island in an environmentally sensitive manner, continuing its use as a hunting preserve. The conservancy has carried out several projects to protect threatened species, including ospreys and eastern mud turtles, and to restore environmentally degraded areas.

Mackay, John W. *Robins Island* (Smithtown, NY: Exposition Press, 1984)
Wells, Betty Tuthill. *Robins Island Reflections: 1639–2001* (Sevierville, Tenn: Insight Publishing, 2001)

Richard F. Welch

Robinson, Jackie [**Jack Roosevelt**] (*b* Grady Co, Ga, 31 Jan 1919; *d* Stamford, Conn, 24 Oct 1972). Professional athlete and civil rights activist. The son of sharecroppers in the rural South, Robinson was raised by his mother in Pasadena, Calif. He excelled in athletics at the University of California, Los Angeles, starring in football, basketball, track and field, and baseball. Drafted by the army in 1942 and commissioned as a lieutenant, he was court-martialed, though subsequently acquitted, in a case deriving from his refusal to accept Jim Crow regulations. He played professional baseball for the Kansas City Monarchs in the Negro Leagues in 1945 before signing with the Brooklyn Dodgers that fall, and after a season in the minor leagues he joined the parent club in 1947, becoming the first African American to play major league baseball in the 20th century. Despite suffering harassment from fans, opposing players, and umpires, as well as enduring segregation in several major league cities, Robinson was a stellar player and a source of pride and inspiration for many African Americans. He finished his 10-year career, playing mainly as a second baseman, with an impressive .311 batting average, and many observers credited his base running with revolutionizing the game. Robinson was elected to the Baseball Hall of Fame in 1962.

Robinson's role in the struggle for racial equality extended beyond baseball. In 1949 he testified before the House Un-American Activities Committee that African Americans were indeed loyal to the United States, denying the claim of radical Paul Robeson that Blacks would not fight a war against the Soviet Union. As the Civil Rights Movement strengthened in the 1950s and early 1960s, Robinson, a strong proponent of integration and interracial harmony, became a prominent spokesperson and fund-raiser for mainstream civil rights groups, such as the National Conference of Christians and Jews and the NAACP. He also assisted NAACP voter registration drives, participated in civil rights demonstrations, and routinely tried to raise awareness of racial matters through his newspaper columns, first in the *New York Post* and later in the *New York Amsterdam News.* By the mid-1960s, though, Robinson came under increasing attack from more radical African American figures, including Malcolm X, who denounced him as a puppet of white society.

Robinson took a keen interest in Republican politics. He worked as an unpaid volunteer in Richard M. Nixon's 1960 presidential campaign. Four years later he campaigned for Gov Nelson A. Rockefeller's unsuccessful attempt for the Republican presidential nomination. Deeply alarmed that Barry Goldwater's triumph signaled that the Republican Party was being taken over by segregationists, Robinson, like many liberal Republicans, supported Democrat Lyndon Johnson that fall. Gov Rockefeller appointed Robinson as a special assistant for community affairs in 1966. Robinson also traveled the state that year helping Rockefeller win reelection. By 1968, however, Robinson had grown more disillusioned with the Republican Party: Rockefeller failed again to win the party's presidential nomination, and Robinson had become greatly alarmed at nominee Nixon's overtures to white southerners.

Robinson also devoted time to numerous business ventures in New York City. In 1957 he became head of personnel for Chock Full O'Nuts, a restaurant chain. He was involved in real estate, insurance, radio, television, and fast-food franchising, and played important roles in the founding of the Freedom National Bank in Harlem and the establishment of the Jackie Robinson Construction Corp, an enterprise to foster low-income housing projects.

Rampersad, Arnold. *Jackie Robinson: A Biography* (New York: Knopf, 1997)
Tygiel, Jules. *Baseball's Great Experiment: Jackie Robinson and His Legacy,* enlarged ed. (New York: Oxford Univ Press, 1997)

Timothy N. Thurber

Robinson, Lucius (*b* Windham, Greene Co, 4 Nov 1810; *d* Elmira, 23 Mar 1891). Governor. Educated in public schools, Robinson studied law at Delhi Academy (Delaware Co) and was admitted to the bar in 1832. After practicing law in Catskill (Greene Co), he became district attorney of Greene Co in 1837 and was master of chancery in New York City from 1843 to 1847. Robinson, a Democrat, was a prominent member of the 1848 Free-Soil Convention, and his strong antislavery views led him to join the newly formed Republican Party in 1856. He was elected to the state assembly in 1860 and as state comptroller in 1861 and 1863. Robinson returned to the Democratic Party after the Civil War. Voters elected him comptroller in 1875 and governor in 1876. A believer in budgetary frugality, Robinson's overriding concern was easing the tax burden. The state general debt was paid off in 1878, leading to the lowest state tax rate in 16 years. Unhappy with cost overruns on the new capitol building in Albany, Robinson approved only enough funds to complete the legislative and gubernatorial chambers. On 7 Jan 1879 he became the first governor to give his annual message to the legislature in the new building. After losing his bid for reelection later that year, Robinson retired to his farm outside Elmira.

Lincoln, Charles Z., ed. *Messages from the Governors,* vol 7 (Albany: J. B. Lyon, 1909)
Robinson, Col David C. "Life of Lucius Robinson." In *The Democratic Party of the State of New York,* vol 2, ed. James K. McGuire (New York: US History Co, 1905)

Gerald Horton

Rochester. City (pop 219,773) in Monroe Co. Situated at the mouth of the north-flowing Genesee River, Rochester's site featured fertile soil deposited by glaciers, waterways left by the receding ice pack, and hardwood trees, as well as nearby deposits of natural gas and oil, salt, gypsum, and building stone, all of which attracted settlers. Waterways that provided transportation and energy enabled Rochester to become a boomtown at an early date. The Seneca Nation inhabited the area, but there were no permanent villages on the present city site, though there were seasonal hunting and fishing camps. French fur traders established an outpost nearby at Fort des Sables [now Irondequoit] in 1716, and Anglo-Dutch fur traders did the same at Fort Schuyler [now Penfield] in 1721.

Settlement

In 1788 Oliver Phelps and Nathaniel Gorham purchased 2,600,000 acres (1,050,000 ha) in Western New York from the Seneca, who also agreed to grant them a 12 x 20 mi (19 x 32 km) tract to be used as a mill lot. In return the partners promised to provide sawmill and gristmill services to the Seneca. Phelps and Gorham gave Ebenezer "Indian" Allan land to build and operate the mills on what came to be known as the 100-Acre Tract, the nucleus of downtown Rochester, but Allan soon abandoned the site.

The Genesee Country was just opening to settlement when partners Col Nathaniel Rochester, Maj Charles Carroll, and William Fitzhugh, all from Maryland, visited during a land purchase tour and were impressed with the waterpower available at the ruins of Allan's mills. In 1803 the men purchased the 100-Acre Tract, leaving it idle until 1811, when, in the aftermath of the Embargo and Non-Intercourse Acts, merchants at the mouth of the Genesee River sent goods through Canada. The tract had competition. Six other settlements on the Genesee River (Charlotte, McCrackenville, Carthage, Castletown, Frankfort, and the Johnson and Seymour Tract) all had advantages their founders hoped would make their site the economic hub of the Genesee River valley. The federal government designated the mouth of the river a port in 1805, drawing shipping from shallow Irondequoit Bay to Charlotte. When war ended in 1814 settlement accelerated, and three years later the 100-Acre Tract and Frankfort, with the most powerful millrace in the valley, joined together to incorporate as the Village of Rochesterville. A bridge was built in 1812 to carry the state road across the river, in 1821 the new county of Monroe erected a courthouse, and in 1823 an aqueduct was planned to carry the Erie Canal across the river. The falls were advantageous for industry but prevented shipment between the canal and Lake Ontario. In 1832 investors formed the horse-drawn Carthage Railroad to connect the canal with the landing at Carthage, siphoning business from Charlotte. International trade tended to be channeled through New York City as a result of the Erie Canal, while the Canadian trade continued across Lake Ontario.

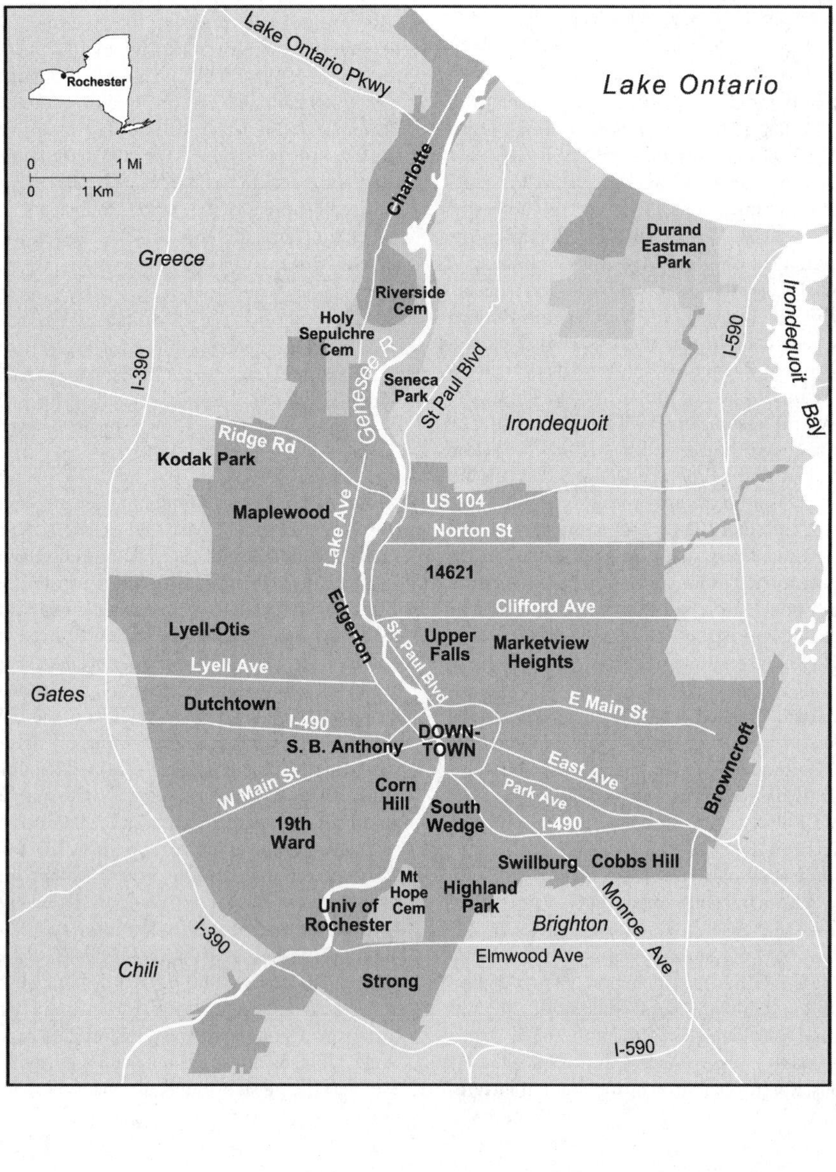

Economic Development in the 19th Century

Rochester was incorporated as a city in 1834, the direction of growth set by its New England founders and Pennsylvania German settlers. Beginning in the 1830s flour milling dominated local industry. Despite giving Rochester its first nickname, Flour City, milling directly employed relatively few people, though support industries such as barrel making, canalboat building, and forwarding employed hundreds. By 1856–58, when an infestation by the wheat midge destroyed the crops, the grainfields and related milling had moved farther west.

New trades emerged, including tobacco, woodworking, gear manufacturing, precision-instrument making, the beginnings of the shoe and clothing industries, and a large nursery industry. William Kimball (1837–95), who came to Rochester in 1858, was the most creative of the businessmen, buying up patents and underwriting the improvement of such inventions as the cigarette-cutting machine, which made him a nationally competitive cigarette maker. By the 1880s he was manufacturing a million cigarettes a day and was the city's largest employer, mostly of women and children. Kimball and H. H. Warner formed the Chamber of Commerce in 1887 to promote the growing industrial and business diversity of the city. Warner became the chamber's first president and a wealthy patent medicine king, promoting his tonic through contests and by underwriting astronomer Lewis Swift's observatory. Daniel Powers and Samuel Wilder competed to run the largest bank, while James Cutler, Claude Bragdon, and Harvey Ellis designed some of the period's most brilliant examples of commercial and residential architecture.

Ethnicity and Immigration

By the late 19th century Rochester was a city of immigrants. The Irish began arriving in large numbers in the 1840s and 1850s, many to work as laborers on the expansion of the Erie Canal and, later, building the distinctive cobblestone houses peculiar to Western New York. In 1826 Henry O'Reilly became the editor of Rochester's first daily newspaper, the *Rochester Daily Advertiser,* and later was its first historian. Irishman Patrick Barry joined with German immigrant George Ellwanger to establish the Ellwanger and Barry Nursery. Despite anti-Irish sentiment, the

Rattlesnake Pete [Gruber, Peter] (b Oil City, Pa, 1857; d Rochester, 11 Oct 1932). Snake collector. Gruber was raised by Bavarian immigrant parents who were saloon keepers. One of Rochester's more colorful citizens, Gruber arrived in that city in 1893 and operated a combination saloon and museum of unusual and curious items at 8–10 Mill St. The establishment housed a variety of oddities ranging from a pipe owned by the actor and presidential assassin John Wilkes Booth to the corpse of a petrified female. Gruber's most renowned attraction, however, was his live collection of caged reptiles, most notably the rattlesnakes that he caught himself during his celebrated snake hunts. Gruber extracted the venom and promoted and sold it as a medicinal curative. Various accounts of cures for goiter, snakebites, and other assorted disorders added to his fame. Attired in a hat and suit made from rattlesnake skin, Gruber attracted attention wherever he went.

McKelvey, Blake. "Historic Antecedents of the Crossroads Project," *Rochester History* 26 (Oct 1964): 15

Mary E. Gabriel

Irish secured jobs as policemen and took an active part in politics, electing John Allen as the city's first Irish-born mayor (1844). The Irish formed their own Rochester militia unit during the Civil War, the 140th Regiment. Col Patrick O'Rorke's heroism while defending Gettysburg's Little Round Top marked a turning point in respect given the Irish. The children of Irish immigrants distinguished themselves in industry; for example, James Gleason manufactured gears and James Cunningham produced wagons and later cars.

Germans were the largest immigrant group in 19th-century Rochester, their ranks including Protestants, Roman Catholics, and Jews. Between 1845 and 1855, the German-born population grew from 1,316 to 6,678. The nativism that briefly appeared in the city caused the Irish and Germans to unite their political strength. In 1852 Bernard Schoeffel was elected to the Chamber of Commerce, and six years later two Germans were elected aldermen. Temple B'rith Kodesh, founded in 1848, became the first of many Jewish congregations in the city. Musical and drama societies, militias, sports and gymnastic organizations, public performances and benefits exposed the citizens to German traditions, some of which, like the Christmas tree, were widely adopted. The Civil War was an opportunity for Germans to demonstrate patriotism. The 13th New York State Regiment, formed of several local militias, had one unit commanded by Capt Adolph Nolte, the editor of *Beobachter.* Other Germans joined the 108th or 140th New York Regiments. Germans were active in the brewing and shoe industries, as well as in gear and precision-instrument manufacturing. German Jewish industrialists dominated Rochester's nationally known men's clothing industry. During World War I there was considerable repression of German cultural and political activities. The number of German-born city residents decreased from 17,000 in 1890 to 10,000 in 1920.

The Italian-born population increased nearly 10-fold between 1900 and 1910 and reached a high of nearly 24,000 by 1930. Most Italian immigrants were dependent on construction or manufacturing work arranged by *padrones* who contracted their services. The Italian Civic and Educational League worked to ensure fair treatment of Italians in courts as well as the press. In 1915 Clement C. Lanni became the first Italian to graduate from the University of Rochester. He merged two Italian weeklies into *La Stampa* and provided news to the Italian community in both English and Italian. Italians became politically active and through the decades successfully elected supervisors and council and assembly members. In 1961 Henry E. Gillette became the city's first Italian mayor.

Cityscape

Just as Rochester absorbed successive waves of immigrants, so it took in the settlements, mostly along the Genesee River, that once each vied for economic supremacy. The merging of Frankfort and the 100-Acre Tract as Rochesterville ended the competition, as the new village became the center of industrial power and the seat of both business and government. The Erie Canal and the Main St bridge both solidified the village as the core. Other settlements were reduced to neighborhoods within Rochester. Carthage, overlooking the Lower Falls of the Genesee, swelled with new immigrants. New arrivals took their places in the older housing as second-generation Rochesterians moved.

East Ave, the main route between Rochester and Pittsford, is lined with trees and large, beautiful mansions (almost all now used by public institutions) built by executives of the successful early 20th-century businesses. Charlotte, the last of the independent settlements, became part of the city in 1914 but retains its identity. The once busy commercial port is popular with pleasure boaters, and its waterfront has been revitalized. A new port building and dock, as well as walkways, piers, and restaurants, attract tourists and residents. Elevation of the railroad tracks in the late 19th century stimulated residential and commercial construction northward along Lake and St. Paul Sts on both sides of the river as the city's population swelled.

Rochester's 1984 sesquicentennial inspired neighborhood associations to form and record their history. Some neighborhoods, such as Browncroft, Susan B. Anthony neighborhood, Cobb's Hill, and Brown Square, focus on the preservation of their historical buildings. Corn Hill, the residential center of the 100-Acre Tract, retains some of the architecture of the wealthy milling families. Other areas, such as Maplewood, South Wedge, and Park Avenue, emphasize the development of distinctive neighborhood lifestyles.

Reform

The rapid growth of Western New York, particularly after the Erie Canal opened, sparked a struggle to retain the old values brought by the first settlers from New England. Petty crime, rough characters, heavy drinking, and large numbers of foreigners disturbed their Protestant culture, providing fertile ground for religious turmoil. The idle entertainment exemplified by Sam Patch's fatal jump from the High Falls of the Genesee River in 1829 was, for many, a sign that Rochester was immersed in sinfulness. The revival meetings of Rev Charles Grandison Finney in 1830, 1842, and 1855 electrified the nation and set an enduring model for urban evangelism. Heterodox spirituality also flourished in Rochester and its environs; the Fox sisters demonstrated their "spirit rappings" in Roch-ester in 1848, giving birth to the modern Spiritualist movement.

The evangelical temperament in Rochester had a broader agenda than the mere saving of souls. Many prominent reform movements, notably temperance, antislavery, and women's rights, had deep roots in the city's religious culture. Over the next two decades, the influx of the Irish followed by German brewers strengthened the resolve of temperance societies. Antislavery societies grew in number. Frederick Douglass was Rochester's best-known abolitionist, having arrived in 1847 to publish his abolitionist newspaper, the *North Star,* later called *Frederick Douglass' Paper.* Douglass became internationally known as a fiery orator on women's rights as well as on antislavery issues, and worked closely with Susan B. Anthony. Rochester's location on the border of free Canada, at the head of a north-flowing river, and on the major route from Elmira made it an important stop on the Underground Railroad. On the day abolitionist John Brown was hanged for treason in Virginia in 1859, a few bold sympathizers, including Susan B. Anthony, stood vigil at Rochester City Hall. The outbreak of the Civil War in 1861 gave Blacks the opportunity to form their own military units, though they were not accepted until 1863. Until her death in Rochester in 1906 Anthony remained an unflinching supporter of woman suffrage and other women's causes, including equal pay for equal work, higher education, property rights, and a mother's right to custody of her children following divorce. She was instrumental in getting the University of Rochester to admit women in 1900.

Labor

Sheer numbers opened Rochester's factories to union activity early in the 19th century. The old journeymen's associations took an aggressive stance as the city's booming economy created rapid change and demand for workers. The first union action, in 1831, was brought by boat caulkers; it was rebuffed by the press and by the boatyard. A raise to $2 a day, followed by a demand for a 10-hour day, was considered unreasonable. Masons and coopers also protested wages and hours, but the economic slump of the late 1830s brought only weak protest against due bills and company scrip, for many workers were glad to have a job.

Mechanization of many trades sparked union organizing throughout the 1840s and 1850s as shoemakers, garment workers, machinists, cigar makers, and ironworkers sought to prevent job losses, raise wages, and reduce hours. The introduction of sewing machines prompted female workers in shoe and clothing shops to organize the Women's Protection Union in 1848. Numerous trades unionized in the 1850s, the most successful of which were printers, masons and bricklayers, and carpenters and joiners.

The Civil War drew many experienced workers into the army, and those who remained hesitated to make demands until 1862, when due bills again were issued by employers unable to meet payroll. The Typographical Union launched an unsuccessful strike, but the sympathetic response of other unions led to the formation of the nation's first central trades council, the Workingmen's Assembly of Rochester (1863), which organized boycotts to support strikers, raised a strike fund, networked with unions in other cities, and within a year formed five new unions. Strikes called during the 1860s were largely unsuccessful. Nevertheless, Rochester became a popular venue for state and national labor conventions. The Rochester Trades Assembly supported the National Labor Union's campaign for an eight-hour day and, when the NLU disbanded, Rochester invited its successor, the National Industrial Congress, to meet in the city in 1874. During this period labor picnics (through 1874) and parades (beginning 1870) served as promotional events.

Labor unrest was endemic in Rochester for the remainder of the 19th century. The depression of 1873 and 1877 brought a series of wage cuts and weakened the unions. Unrest among workers mounted through the 1870s. By 1880 the shoe and clothing industries had grown so large that Rochester became a national battleground for unions. The Knights of Labor put employers on notice when its secret order of workingmen paraded in force with unions of bricklayers, plasterers, and stonemasons in 1881. Significant strikes by the Knights included one at the Cunningham Carriage Factory in 1882, which was settled by arbitration.

In 1882 the Knights' strength was challenged when the shoe workers' unions' demand for a wage increase was rejected, setting off a series of strikes, union organizing, and sometimes violent unrest so extensive that the *Rochester Democrat and Chronicle* ran a column devoted to strike issues. The Knights struggled for credibility and distanced themselves from some strikes while losing control of others. The Knights lost much of their power as employers hired cheaper immigrant labor and replaced workers with machinery. In 1888–89 unions such as the Central Trades Council, the Building Trades Council, the Boot and Shoemakers Assembly, and the Boot and Shoe Workers International pulled membership from the Knights. Strikes and unrest continued into the 20th century, particularly in the garment industry. Modern equipment replacing experienced workers, cheaper labor among immigrants, and alleged sweatshop conditions fed the unrest. In a particularly bitter strike in 1912 the United Garment Workers beat at the doors of a factory and frightened the armed owner, who then fired into the crowd, killing Ida Braiman, a 17-year-old Russian Jewish immigrant garment worker.

Early 20th-Century Economy

By the turn of the 20th century the nursery and flower industry was waning as the western United States became more cultivated. The Ellwanger and Barry Nursery donated 20 acres (8 ha) of land that in 1888 became the nucleus of the city's parks system. By 1918 Rochester's internationally known horticulture business was gone. In the early 20th century the shoe and clothing industries were among the city's largest. German Jews, who began to arrive in Rochester in the 1840s, dominated the ownership of the men's ready-made clothing industry, while Russian Jews and Italians supplied much of its labor. L. Adler Bros and Co; Michaels, Stern and Co; Hickey-Freeman Co; and other clothiers built worldwide markets. In the early 1900s Kimball sold out to the American Tobacco Co. Another major employer was the company started by German immigrants John Jacob Bausch and Henry Lomb in 1853 as a daguerreotype parlor; an exclusive patent for rubber eyeglass frames gave Bausch and Lomb the edge to build a worldwide market. Gleason Tool Co perfected gear-cutting machines; its innovative head, Kate Gleason, suggested shifting from tools to gears, a market it dominated for years.

Rochester entered the 20th century with a diversified economy, producing shoes, clothing, optics, and other manufactured goods. But the greatest sensation at the turn of the century was introduced by George Eastman, who started the Eastman Dry Plate and Film Co in 1884. Eastman's 100-frame, film-loaded Brownie camera (1890) was readily accepted by a public eager to record images of everyday life. Eastman's creative marketing of the unusual name Kodak and his slogan, "You press the button, we do the rest," proved successful. Eastman avoided labor unrest and kept unions at bay by offering generous employee benefits, bonuses, and community support. In a growing city, Eastman's financial largesse continued the paternalism of early 19th-century employers. Eastman formed the Community Chest of Rochester (predecessor of the United Way); built Eastman Theatre, the Eastman School of Music, and a dental dispensary for poor children; and gave millions to the Mechanics Institute (now Rochester Institute of Technology) and the University of Rochester. Few philanthropists have shaped one city as thoroughly as Eastman refashioned Rochester.

The Great Depression profoundly affected Rochester. Alarmed by rising numbers out of work, estimated at 10,000–24,000, the Council of Social Agencies met on 22 Jan 1930 to assess the employment problem. City Manager Stephen Story reopened an employment bureau that had closed at the end of World War I. Although there was some new construction and the opening of a General Motors plant with 900 new jobs, the job situation in general was bleak, and there was a massive rally of unemployed workers at Washington Square on 5 Mar 1930. The seriousness of the economic outlook led numerous social and civic organizations to join together to form the Civic Committee on Unemployment. Federal work relief payments began in 1932. Many people left the city for the security of farm country. The New Deal brought construction, art, and conservation projects to employ workers. Marion Folsom, Kodak's representative on the Council of Social Agencies, complained about make-work projects and favored the unemployment insurance system he developed at Kodak. Pres Franklin Roosevelt invited him to Washington, DC, to serve on a committee on social security.

Depression era public works projects undertaken with federal funds included the Rundel Memorial Library, the Veterans Memorial Bridge, and the second deepening of the Genesee River for downtown flood control. Foreign contracts for war materials increased manufacturing in the late 1930s, and anticipation of US involvement in World War II brought a readiness to move from peacetime to wartime production. Bausch and Lomb, Gleason Works, Eastman Kodak, and others began manufacturing lenses, cameras, film, tank parts, radios, airplanes, and automobiles. Manufacturers, all of whom worked to earn awards for meeting production goals, also made clothing and military gear. Women, Italians, and Blacks found new opportunities in factories, taking the place of those who left for the battlefield. Women made significant advances in employment and education but lost most of their gains when they gave up their jobs to returning soldiers after 1945.

Postwar Rochester

The return to peacetime industry brought an increase in the production of automotive parts, precision instruments, film and cameras, optics, and other high-tech products. It was also a time of remarkable labor action. In the Rochester General Strike of 1946, hundreds of city employees were fired for organizing, and 5,000 workers struck, paralyzing Rochester for 22 hours and

Pavilion at Highland Park, Rochester, early 20th century.

forcing the reinstatement of the city employees. The Haloid Co (1906) purchased the patents to xerography in 1947 and renamed itself Xerox in 1962.

After the war construction of highways and the availability of new housing through the GI Bill led to suburbanization. The general prosperity of Rochester and its suburbs and the dominance of the corporate cultures of Kodak and other large companies led some to dub Rochester "Smugtown USA," after a controversial 1957 book. The city reached its peak population of 332,488 in 1950. As white families moved to new suburban developments, African Americans migrating from the South began to move into many city neighborhoods. Some, like Corn Hill and the 19th Ward, remained racially diverse, but others, especially in the city's northeast quadrant, became overwhelmingly African American. The rapid migration of African Americans to the city taxed the school system and available housing. Adding to the low-income housing shortage was the gentrification of downtown neighborhoods. Hanover Houses (1952), the city's first public housing project, helped alleviate the housing shortage.

Although some government officials and settlement house workers noted the needs of the new arrivals, response was too slow. In July 1964 a riot erupted; for three days sporadic unrest, fires, and looting disrupted black neighborhoods, and the National Guard was called in. Four were killed and hundreds arrested. Response was prompt from both the black community and corporations. The Inner-City Ministry of the Rochester Council of Churches invited noted organizer Saul Alinsky to organize the city neighborhoods in 1964. The following year a black organization, FIGHT (Freedom, Integration, God, Honor and Today) formed. Kodak, Xerox, and Bausch and Lomb worked to increase the number of African Americans employed and promoted.

The Inner Loop (constructed 1953–74) surrounding the downtown area was designed to relieve traffic congestion as people traveled in and out of the city to work, while the Outer Loop offered easy access to downtown from the Thruway. By 2000 public housing efforts focused on demolition of deteriorated housing and reconstruction of single-family homes. Public housing complexes were mixed with low- and moderate-income apartments and owner-occupied homes. Under Mayor William A. Johnson Jr (1994–), Rochester's first African American mayor, the city was divided into 10 sectors, each with a NET (Neighborhood Empowerment Team) office. Many strong neighborhood associations worked with the city to improve and augment housing. Efforts to create more downtown housing are underway, with old factories being converted to loft apartments and condominiums, attracting residents who work nearby, and accessible entertainment such as live theater, nightclubs, and symphonies. In cooperation with the federal government the city has assisted neighborhood regeneration in areas like the Susan B. Anthony neighborhood.

Politics and Culture

Mayors were chosen annually by the Rochester Common Council from 1834 until 1840, when a charter revision authorized election of the mayor by popular vote and provided for a stronger mayoralty and weaker council. Veto power won by the mayor in a later revision caused stalemates between council and mayor, leading some to advocate government by state-appointed commissions. In 1871 a charter amendment doubled the mayoral term to two years, which allowed the mayor to establish a reputation and further reduced the council's power. In 1876 the creation of the Executive Board diminished the influence of both council and mayor, though the mayor could appoint three of the board's six members. Only four years later charter revision reduced the board to three elected officials, whose mostly administrative duties freed the mayor to attend to the needs of the city.

George W. Aldridge won a seat on the Executive Board in 1883 and became its chairman in 1891. In 1891 he opposed the movement to abolish the Executive Board and to create a strong mayor with power to appoint most officials. Elected mayor in 1894, he resigned the following year to become state superintendent of public works, but he established boss party control during his administration and extended influence over most mayors until his death in 1922. On his resignation the Good Government League formed to improve the schools and government. In 1900 the "White Charter," drafted by a legislative commission headed by Horace White, abolished the Executive Board and gave the mayor full executive powers, checked by an independently elected comptroller, treasurer, and Common Council. The mayor held appointive power over all departments, while the Board of Education remained independent. Hiram Edgerton was a popular mayor (1908–22) who gave more freedom of decision to the health office, police chief, city engineer, and park commissioner.

In 1915 George Eastman led the movement for responsible government by establishing the Rochester Bureau of Municipal Research (now Center for Governmental Research), modeled after a similar institution in New York City. It conducted independent studies to inform citizens and city planners. The bureau recommended a city manager form of government as more effective than one relying on a strong mayor. Aldridge, who still wielded great influence in naming department heads through his favored mayoral candidates, opposed the city manager plan, but with Eastman and the Women's City Club in support, the Common Council reluctantly drafted a new charter, and in 1928 Rochester adopted a council/manager form of government, briefly accomplishing the objective of reformers to remove partisan politics from the city. Party chairs soon regained their influence, however. The strong mayoralty did not reappear until 1984, when Thomas P. Ryan Jr, a mayor under the council/manager system, became mayor by popular election. He retired after 18 years in 1994.

American Music Festival in Brown Square Park with Eastman Kodak Building in background, Rochester, 1995.

Rochester has three colleges or universities and branches of six others, including Colgate Rochester Divinity School, Nazareth College, St. John Fisher College, and the University of Rochester (including music, medical, and dental schools and the Memorial Art Gallery), Rochester Institute of Technology, National Technical Institute for the Deaf, Monroe Community College, Rochester Business Institute, and SUNY Empire State College. Museums include the Memorial Art Gallery of the University of Rochester, Rochester Museum and Science Center, Susan B. Anthony House, Rochester Historical Society, and Strong Museum, a noted children's museum. The public library system in Rochester comprises 11 branches.

Recent History

Rochester's three major international businesses, Kodak, Xerox, and Bausch and Lomb, declined in the world market during the final three decades of the 20th century. Battling stiff competition and rising labor costs, some Rochester companies began a series of layoffs and relocations of some operations to foreign countries where labor was cheaper. As digital cameras and computer printing captured much of the commercial and home photographic markets, Kodak experienced a dramatic reduction in the profit margin it had enjoyed for more than half a century as a world leader in the photographic film industry.

Although Rochester's productivity is diversified, rapid downsizing by major employers has been unsettling to the population. However, medical research, education, and technology employ thousands, while the single grocery established by Robert Wegman in 1921 has grown to a Rochester-based firm with stores in three states. Paychex, a payroll services company started by B. Thomas Golisano in 1971, employs more than 1,000 people in the Rochester area and several thousand others nationwide.

In 2000 Rochester had 219,773 residents (about two-thirds of its 1950 population): 48% were white, 39% black, and 2% Asian, with over 1,000 persons of American Indian ancestry. Those of Latino ethnicity made up 13% of the population. The ethnic mix of Rochester continues to change. By 1980 Puerto Ricans represented a significant group, as did South Asian Indians, Chinese, and Southeast Asians. In 2003 construction was underway for the city's downtown riverfront development, including housing, small business space, and entertainment venues. Condominiums and apartments have stabilized the area where the railroad once ran. A new baseball

Education in Rochester. As one of the state's five largest urban school districts, Rochester's schools have been challenged to meet the needs of a diverse student population. Rochester has become known for its educational innovations, which have often gained national attention. The area's first property owners, William Fitzhugh, Charles Carroll, and Nathaniel Rochester, demonstrated their concern for education early in the city's history by giving the Village of Rochesterville land for a school. In 1813 the first school was built, and parents could send their children there for a fee, paid with money, wood, or service to the school. With the completion of the Erie Canal in 1825, Rochesterville became a boomtown and was incorporated as a city in 1834. During these years the first private high school and many private elementary schools were opened. The growing number of public schools made up six small districts within the city. In 1841 the Rochester City School District was organized with a board of education made up of 10 citizens, 2 from each of the 5 political wards; 16 schools, including a separate school for black children, enrolled 4,246 pupils. Funding was based on enrollment, so larger schools could afford longer school years than smaller ones.

In 1850 the state legislature passed a new school law that guaranteed free schooling from ages 5–16 and equalized resources for each school. The school for black children was closed in 1857, allowing all children to attend neighborhood schools. This same year Rochester opened its first public high school, Rochester Central High School. In 1859 the city held districtwide examinations for all students above third grade. The grammar school program was increased from seven to nine years in 1869, reflecting a strong commitment to public education. Citizens became increasingly dissatisfied with the political control of the schools that resulted from the ward system. In 1900 the city revised its charter to reduce the Board of Education to five members elected for four-year terms in citywide elections. Charles B. Gilbert was appointed superintendent, shifting control of schools from the ward system to trained educational administrators.

From 1900 to 1910, five new schools were built, including two high schools, with a total enrollment of 25,710 in 1910. The requirements for teachers were increased from one year of training to two, with many educated at Rochester's own training program (1883–1931). The curriculum was expanded to include evening schools and English language instruction, partly to serve a large and growing immigrant population. Programs for students with special educational needs began in 1906. From 1911 through 1933, Herbert S. Weet served as superintendent. Under his administration, junior high schools were created, a new concept that received national attention. Weet also oversaw the development of programs in health education, music, art, home economics, and industrial arts. More changes came during the depression, as the district had to respond to the large number of students who remained in school because jobs were scarce. In 1930, 43,470 students were enrolled. Junior highs were eliminated, and schools were reorganized into elementary schools that included grade 7 and secondary schools for grades 8–12. The school district also provided social services for needy children.

Classroom in Rochester School 26, *ca* 1915.

Enrollment dropped during World War II and then rebounded in the postwar years with an increasing birth rate and a renewed interest in education. Schools were overcrowded, and new buildings were added to meet the demand. Despite the economic boom of the 1950s, teachers' salaries did not keep pace. Teachers became increasingly dissatisfied and began to press for unionization. In addition to the district's fiscal problems, concern about addressing de facto segregation became a central issue during the 1960s. The Rochester Teachers Association, formed in 1894, supported desegregation by endorsing a districtwide school reorganization plan and by supporting a school boycott in 1970 when the Board of Education refused to accept the plan. While not wholly successful, this action demonstrated the growing power of the teachers' union.

In the 1980s the Rochester City School District received national attention for an innovative contract that increased teachers' salaries by 40% and adopted major reforms. Rochester has continued to be recognized for its efforts to enhance the professional status of teachers. The Career in Teaching program was developed to provide new teachers with a mentor teacher, and Lead Teacher programs gave experienced teachers the chance to take on new roles, including mentoring new teachers, enhancing professional development, and writing curriculum. Goals included giving teachers more choice in the method of their evaluation, with the option of being evaluated by their peers, and the decentralization of school governance, with major decisions made by school-based planning teams made up of administrators, teachers, staff, and parents. Secondary school teachers were expected to communicate more effectively with students' families and assume responsibility for monitoring students' overall progress.

Implementing these changes was more challenging than expected. The most successful reform, widely emulated, is the mentor teacher program. Students' performance on state tests has improved, but large numbers of students remain unsuccessful. In the 1990s initiatives to promote student achievement included increased preschool education, summer school, and a new comprehensive reading program. In 2000 the enrollment in the Rochester City School District was 59,137 students: 65% African American; 17% Hispanic; 16% white; and 2% Asian, American Indian, or East Indian. The district has 43 pre-kindergarten sites, 39 elementary schools, 7 middle schools, and 8 high schools.

McKelvey, Blake. "Rochester's Public Schools: A Testing Ground for Community Policies," *Rochester History* 31 (April 1969): 1–28

Murray, Christine E. "Teaching as a Profession: The Rochester Case in Historical Perspective," *Harvard Educational Review* 62 (Winter 1992): 494–518

Christine E. Murray

stadium and the remodeled Community War Memorial attract crowds to the downtown, while loft apartments in former factories encourage plans for downtown living and revitalized commerce. Docks, walkways, and street reconstruction have stimulated private investment and improved the lakefront in anticipation of rapid ferry service between Rochester and Toronto.

See also AFRICAN AMERICANS; BOTANICAL GARDENS; EASTMAN KODAK COMPANY; GARMENT INDUSTRY; NUDISM; OLMSTED, FREDERICK LAW; POLICING; SUBURBANIZATION; WATER SUPPLY AND USE (NON–NEW YORK CITY WATERSHED).

Hewitt, Nancy E. *Women's Activism and Social Change: Rochester, New York, 1822–1872* (Ithaca: Cornell Univ Press, 1984)
Husted, Shirley Cox, and Ruth Rosenberg-Naparsteck. *Rochester Neighborhoods* (Charleston, SC: Arcadia, 2000)
Johnson, Paul. *A Shopkeeper's Millennium: Society and Revivals in Rochester, New York, 1815–1837* (New York: Hill & Wang, 1978)
McKelvey, Blake F. *Rochester: Water Power City, 1812–1855* (Cambridge, Mass: Harvard Univ Press, 1945)
———. *Rochester: The Flower City, 1956–1890* (Cambridge, Mass: Harvard Univ Press, 1949)
———. *Rochester: The Quest for Quality, 1891–1925* (Cambridge, Mass: Harvard Univ Press, 1956)
———. *Rochester: The Emerging Metropolis, 1925–1962* (Rochester: Christopher Press, 1961)
———. *Rochester on the Genesee,* 2d ed. (Syracuse: Syracuse Univ Press, 1993)
McKelvey, Blake, and Ruth Rosenberg-Naparsteck. *Rochester: A Panoramic History* (Sun Valley, Calif: American Historic Press, 2001)
Rochester History, http://www.rochester.lib.ny.us/~rochhist/index.html

Ruth Rosenberg-Naparsteck

Rochester. Town (pop 7,018) in central Ulster Co. Settled *ca* 1680, the town was patented in 1703 and recognized as a town in 1788. Crossed by the Delaware and Hudson Canal (1828–98), it was known for bluestone and millstone quarrying, for wintergreen oil distilling, and for huckleberry harvesting (1860–1930). Alfred Smiley made Rochester a resort with the Lake Minnewaska Mountain Houses (Cliff House, 1879; Wildmere House, 1887) at the summit of the Shawangunk Mountains; the site of the hotels is now part of Minnewaska State Park. In 1902 the town was crossed by the Ontario and Western Railroad and became the site of many Jewish boardinghouses and hotels, including the Granit (now Hudson Valley Resort). In 2003 it was home to self-employed people and long-distance commuters. The 1,000-acre (400 ha) Schoonmaker Farm, producer of vegetables and fruit, was operated by the 10th- and 11th-generation descendants of its 17th-century founder.

Ruth Piwonka

Rochester, Nathaniel (*b* Westmoreland Co, Va, 21 Feb 1752; *d* Rochester, 17 May 1831). Businessman and land speculator. He was born to a family of small landowners on a Virginia farm dating back to 1689. His mother, widowed in 1754, took the family to North Carolina in 1759. When he entered the military in the North Carolina line in August 1775, he had received no formal education. Col Rochester served in various political, military, and business positions in North Carolina and Maryland. In 1800 he visited the western part of New York State with Col William Fitzhugh and Maj Charles Carroll. The trio purchased what was known as the 100-Acre Tract [now downtown Rochester] at the falls of the Genesee River in 1803. Moving to Dansville [now in Livingston Co] in 1810, then East Bloomfield (Ontario Co) after five years, Rochester engaged in milling while surveying his lands to the north and in 1818 settled in the village that would take his name. Instrumental in establishing Monroe Co, he also served as first president of the Bank of Rochester in 1824. In 1829 he established the Rochester Athenaeum, one of the forerunners of Rochester Institute of Technology.

Nathaniel Rochester Family. Papers. Rush Rhees Library, Univ of Rochester

David Minor

Rochester Academy of Science. Educational organization promoting research in natural sciences. Founded in 1879 as the Rochester Microscopical Society, the group consisted of academics and science enthusiasts interested in anthropology, geology, botany, ornithology, and astronomy. In 1881 it became the Rochester Academy of Science. Early members included some of Rochester's most influential businessmen, such as George Eastman, John Jacob Bausch, and Henry Lomb, and the academy provided a significant forum in western New York State for the discussion of intellectual and scientific development. Since its founding the academy has maintained close ties to New York State colleges. The academy has officers and members affiliated with the University of Rochester, Nazareth College, St. John Fisher College, and Rochester Institute of Technology, and research grants often go to students at these schools. Although the only qualification for membership is an interest in science, many academy members are professors. The academy, which had 400 members in 2003, publishes original articles by members and stores more than 15,000 research papers at the University of Rochester.

See also SCIENTIFIC CULTURE (19TH–21ST CENTURIES).

Rochester Academy of Science, http://www.rasny.org

Matt Leingang

Rochester Americans. Minor league hockey team. The team joined the American Hockey League (AHL) in 1956, jointly owned by the National Hockey League's (NHL) Montreal Canadiens, Toronto Maple Leafs, and local investors. Because of its affiliation with the Canadiens, Rochester's squad was named to reflect its national identity, though it is commonly known as the Amerks. The team consistently outdrew the National Basketball Association's Rochester Royals at the new War Memorial Auditorium (now Blue Cross Arena at the War Memorial) until 1957, when the Royals moved to Cincinnati. Toronto became the Americans' sole owner in 1963. Under coach and general manager Joe Crozier and featuring goalie Gerry Cheevers, winger Dick Gamble, center Bronco Horvath, and defenseman Al Arbour, the team won the Calder Cup in three (1965, 1966, 1968) of four straight finals appearances. After its 1966 championship the franchise was purchased by local investors, who sold the team to the Vancouver Canucks in 1968. The worst stretch of hockey in team history followed; from 1968–69 to 1971–72 their record was 71-114-36. In 1972 local investors purchased the struggling franchise, which remained independent for the 1972–73 season because it was too late to affiliate with an NHL team. Lured from the high school coaching ranks, former team captain Don Cherry assembled a roster of veterans and discards, including wingers Bob "Battleship" Kelly and Barry Merrell, and earned an improbable playoff berth. Rochester became the farm team of the Boston Bruins in 1974 before affiliating with the Buffalo Sabres in the 1979–80 season. In 1982 Buffalo purchased the Americans, who won the Calder Cup under Coach Mike Keenan a year later. Their 1987 Calder Cup came under John Van Boxmeer, who, with a 333-282-75 record in nine seasons, became the team's all-time winningest coach. In 1995 local investors, headed by Steve Donner, bought the Americans from Buffalo, with which the team maintained a working agreement. Coach John Tortorella led the Amerks to another Calder Cup (1996) during winger Jody Gage's 11th and final season. With 351 goals and 377 assists in 653 games, Gage remains Rochester's all-time leading scorer; while the team's general manager, he was named AHL Executive of the Year (1999). Rochester entered the 2002–3 season with a regular season record of 1711-1426-384 and had .500 or better records in 34 of 46 years.

American Hockey League, http://www.theahl.com
Rochester Americans, http://www.amerks.com

Bob Matthews

Rochester Democrat and Chronicle. The newspaper's origins trace back to the *Balance,* a weekly newspaper established in Rochester in 1833. After several name changes, the paper became the *Daily Democrat* in 1840. Despite its name its politics supported the Whigs and thereafter was a staunch backer of the Republican Party. In 1868 Lewis Selye, a Republican dissatisfied with the city's party leadership, started his own daily, the *Chronicle.* But in 1870 Freeman Clarke, concerned that competing Republican dailies would interfere with his election to Congress, bought controlling interests in both papers and combined them as the *Democrat and Chronicle.* The newspaper published its first Sunday edition in 1879.

In 1928 the paper was purchased by Frank E. Gannett, who had already purchased two other Rochester dailies, the *Union and Advertiser* and the *Rochester Evening Times,* and combined them in 1918 into the *Times-Union,* an afternoon daily. In the 1920s the Hearst chain made several offers to purchase Gannett's Rochester newspapers, but Gannett rejected them. His papers briefly supported Franklin D. Roosevelt in the 1930s but soon returned to backing Republican positions. The *Democrat and Chronicle* remained a Republican paper until shortly after Gannett's death in 1957, when it became nonpartisan. For more than four decades, the Gannett chain maintained its headquarters in the same building as the *Democrat and Chronicle* and *Times-Union,* at 55 Exchange Blvd. In 1977 the Gannett corporation's headquarters were moved to another location in downtown Rochester and then to Arlington, Va, in 1985.

In 1992 Gannett combined the editorial staffs of the *Democrat and Chronicle* and the *Times-*

Union, and in 1997 the *Times-Union* ceased publishing, leaving the *Democrat and Chronicle* as the only daily newspaper in Rochester. The paper opened a new production plant in suburban Greece in 1997, although editorial offices remained downtown. Like most other Gannett newspapers, the *Democrat and Chronicle* is the only daily published in its primary circulation market and emphasizes local rather than national or international news. At the beginning of the 21st century, the paper averages a Monday-to-Saturday circulation of 175,000 and a Sunday circulation of 240,000.

Coates, Hilda A. "Some Aspects of Rochester Journalism in the 1890's," *Rochester History* (Jan 1951): 1–23

Williamson, Samuel T. *Imprint of a Publisher: The Story of Frank Gannett and His Independent Newspapers* (New York: Robert M. McBride, 1948)

Martin Naparsteck

Rochester Gas and Electric (RG&E). Energy company serving residential and business customers in a nine-county area around Rochester. The company's origins date to 1848 with the creation of the Rochester Gas Light Co, which supplied gas in the city. This company consolidated with the Citizens' Gas Co (1872) and Municipal Gas Light Co (1880) to form the Rochester Gas Co in 1889. Electric power arrived in Rochester in 1879 with the formation of the Rochester Electric Light Co, later joined by the Brush Electric Light Co (1881), and the Edison Illuminating Co (1886). The gas and electric companies were consolidated in 1892 with the formation of the RG&E. This became the Rochester Railway and Light Co in 1904 and passed into the control of the New York Central Railroad, which intended to use it to help electrify its lines. The Rochester Railway and Light Co left the railroad business by 1919, when it reverted to the name RG&E; the New York Central sold the company in 1928. RG&E opened the Robert E. Ginna Nuclear Power Plant in 1969 in Ontario (Wayne Co). In 1999 the RGS Energy Group, a holding company, became the parent company of RG&E. Energetix, a subsidiary, sells electricity, natural gas, appliance warranty contracts, and energy services, and owns Griffith Oil Co, the latter selling liquid fuels, primarily propane and oil, in New York State, Pennsylvania, and Vermont. In 2002 Energy East Corp, an Albany-based energy company, acquired the RGS Energy Group. RG&E in 2002 provided electricity to 350,000 customers and gas to 280,000; Energetix and Griffith Oil served 230,000 customers.

Rosenberg-Naparsteck, Ruth. "The Development of Gas and Electricity in Rochester," *Rochester History* 51 (Fall 1998): 1–24

Waxman, Jan Lamartina. "Rochester Gas and Electric Corporation." In *The Image of Rochester,* ed. G. Dalmath, G. R. DeFranco, and J. L. Waxman (Memphis: Tower Publishing, 1997)

Martin Naparsteck

Rochester General Hospital. Chartered in 1847 as Rochester City Hospital, the goal of the institution was to care for poor people. Local opposition and apathy delayed its opening until 1864. With the help of funds raised by the Rochester Female Charitable Society, a four-story hospital was built on West Ave (now West Main St) with a superintendent and a Board of Lady Managers overseeing daily operations. Private physicians admitted their own patients and treated ward patients for free, and regular staff included a physician, informally trained nurses, and maintenance workers. New wings were added in 1865 and 1871, and a training school for nurses was established in 1880. Early support came from voluntary contributions, city subsidies, and federal payments for treating Civil War soldiers. Community groups like the Twigs, the first of which was organized in 1887, sewed linens and sponsored social events to raise money. Children often donated food from home and pennies toward bricks for new buildings.

The original structures were replaced in 1909, thanks to George Eastman's $500,000 gift, and in 1911 the institution was renamed Rochester General Hospital. During the 1918–19 Influenza Pandemic the hospital formed one of the country's earliest hospital volunteer aide organizations, and it became a national model. Medical staff made up the major complement of Base Hospital 19, which worked in Vichy, France, during World War I, and the 19th General Hospital unit, which served in Le Mans, France, during World War II. A second hospital complex opened on Portland Ave in northeastern Rochester in 1956, and services from both sites centralized there 10 years later. In 1963 the Isabella Graham Hart School of Practical Nursing superseded the school for registered nurses, which closed in 1964. The hospital, a major tertiary care institution in Rochester, with 500 beds in 2002, has been recognized for its work in the field of cardiothoracic medicine.

Lehr, Teresa K., and Philip G. Maples. *To Serve the Community: A Celebration of Rochester General Hospital, 1847–1997* (Virginia Beach, Va: Donning, 1997)

Teresa K. Lehr

Rochester General Strike. On 28 May 1946, at a moment when America's railroad workers and coal miners had shut down their industries in national walkouts, Rochester labor staged its own general strike. Rochester city employees had begun to organize into a local of the American Federation of State, County and Municipal Employees. Unable to deter them, City Manager Louis B. Cartwright on 15 May discharged 489 workers, notifying them at home by special messenger. The next day the fired workers and their supporters attended a protest meeting at Carpenters Hall, then marched to City Hall to address the City Council. That night the central labor bodies of both the American Federation of Labor (AFL) and the Congress of Industrial Organizations (CIO) held emergency meetings. On 18 May pickets blocked all Rochester Department of Public Works (DPW) stations. Drivers were fired for refusing to take out ash wagons, and sewer and bridge workers walked out in sympathy.

Police arrested 264 pickets near the main DPW garage between 21 and 23 May. The pickets, though demonstrating peacefully, were charged with disorderly conduct, held several hours, and released on $100 bond posted by the AFL's Central Trades and Labor Council. On 23 May, Teamsters Local 398 stayed out "on holiday" in support of Alphonse A. Capone, their business agent and president of the AFL council, who had been arrested. Their action brought deliveries and construction work to a standstill, while a mass meeting was held in Washington Square Park that evening to protest the arrests.

The general strike began when the city manager refused to negotiate with a joint AFL and CIO strategy committee. Transportation was paralyzed when bus and cab drivers went out, pickets appeared throughout the city, and 50,000 workers went on strike. After 22 hours the strike resulted in complete victory for labor: the discharged workers regained their jobs, charges against those arrested were dropped, and the City of Rochester recognized municipal workers' rights to organize, though later refusing to negotiate a contract.

Hardisky, David L. "The Rochester General Strike of 1946" (PhD diss, Univ of Rochester, 1983)

Rochester Democrat and Chronicle, 16–30 May 1946

"Strike Anniversary Celebrated," *Rochester Democrat and Chronicle,* 29 May 1996

Jonathan Garlock

Rochester Institute of Technology. Private college in Henrietta (Monroe Co) that originated in two 19th-century institutions. The Athenaeum, a reading and discussion society, was established in 1829 by a group of prominent citizens who elected Nathaniel Rochester, the city's preeminent founder and namesake, as its first president. The Mechanics Institute was started in 1885 by a group of city businessmen to teach drawing and other studies for industrial pursuits. The two merged in 1891 to form the Rochester Athenaeum and Mechanics Institute (RAMI). The Athenaeum, which brought its members into contact with Ralph Waldo Emerson, Oliver Wendell Holmes, and other distinguished orators of the day, provided a liberal arts legacy. The Mechanics Institute emphasized the importance of adequately preparing students for the world of work. In 1912 RAMI began the cooperative education program, which allowed students to gain on-the-job experience as part of their educational curriculum. In 1944 the school was renamed Rochester Institute of Technology (RIT) and in 1968 moved from downtown Rochester to a new 1,300-acre (526 ha) campus in Henrietta. RIT consists of eight colleges: Applied Science and Technology, Business, Imaging Arts and Sciences, Liberal Arts, Science, the B. Thomas Golisano College of Computing and Information Sciences (the largest comprehensive computing college in the nation), the Kate Gleason College of Engineering, and the National Technical Institute for the Deaf (the first and largest technical college in the world for deaf and hard-of-hearing students). RIT was the first school in the country to offer a PhD in imaging science, with the first graduate in 1993. In fall 2002 RIT enrolled 12,938 undergraduate and 2,374 graduate students, with a 2 to 1 male to female ratio. The cooperative education program includes more than 1,300 employers and 2,500 students.

Gordon, Dane R. *Rochester Institute of Technology, Industrial Development and Educational Innovation in an American City* (New York and Toronto: Edwin Mellen Press, 1982)

Joann Minor

Rochester Labor Council, AFL-CIO. Rochester's central labor council, dating from the 1850s, is one of the oldest such organizations in the United States. Central labor bodies were first formed in 1834, when General Trades'

Unions developed in several cities, including New York City, Brooklyn, and Poughkeepsie. These bodies furthered the interests of workers through boycotts and strikes, promotion of union-made goods, labor journals, agitation for shorter hours, safety regulations, convict labor laws, and support for reform parties. By 1863 the new Workingmen's Association of Monroe County was established, and city directories indicate its presence from "about 1855." Members participated in Rochester's first labor parade in 1870, and delegations were sent to the 1873 and 1874 meetings of the national Industrial Congress. Following a disruption, the association was succeeded by the Rochester Trades Assembly, chartered in 1888 by the American Federation of Labor (AFL), in turn replaced in 1900 by the Rochester Central Trades and Labor Council, which included 103 unions with 13,000 members at its founding. This council continued until 1958.

During the 1880s parallel labor organizations emerged. The Knights of Labor in 1888 formed District 44, representing 20 Local Assemblies with 6,000 members. From 1884 through 1897 it ran central labor bodies dominated by their members. In 1888 Rochester's building trades unions formed their own council, which continues into the 21st century. The founding of the Congress of Industrial Organizations (CIO) in 1938 divided Rochester's unions between the CIO's Council of Rochester and Vicinity, with 18 unions and 22,000 members (1938), and the AFL's Central Trades and Labor Council, with 85 locals and 30,000 members (1946). The two bodies cooperated, however, in conducting Rochester's 1946 General Strike, and following the national merger, they joined in 1958 to become the Rochester and Vicinity Labor Council, AFL-CIO. During the 1980s the council expanded its membership to over 100 affiliated unions representing more than 50,000 members. At the same time the council reinvigorated its programs and its role as labor's voice in the community. In 2001 the Rochester Labor Council joined the Chemung and Steuben labor councils as well as Auburn and Genesee-Wyoming unions to form the Rochester and Genesee Valley Area Labor Federation, representing 183 unions and 100,000 members.

Gleason, Alan H. "The History of Labor in Rochester: 1820–1880" (MA thesis, Univ of Rochester, 1941)
Hawley, Natalie F. "The Labor Movement in Rochester: 1880–1898" (MA thesis, Univ of Rochester, 1948)
McKelvey, Blake. "Organized Labor in Rochester before 1914," *Rochester History* 25 (Jan 1963): 1–24

Jonathan Garlock

Rochester Museum and Science Center (RMSC). Nonprofit educational institution comprising a history and science museum, planetarium, nature center, and school. The City of Rochester Municipal Museum opened in 1912 as part of the city's centennial celebration of the first white settlement in the area. The original museum was located in Exposition Hall in Edgerton Park. It moved to its East Ave location in 1942 and was renamed Rochester Museum of Arts and Sciences. Seneca anthropologist Arthur C. Parker, museum director from 1925 to 1946, was one of the first Native Americans to lead a major cultural institution, and he collaborated closely with Iroquois peoples, especially in the Indian Arts and Crafts Project. In 1968 the RMSC adopted its current name and became a private nonprofit institution. The Strasenburgh Planetarium opened next door to the museum the same year. The RMSC also administers the 900-acre (360 ha) Cumming Nature Center in Naples (Ontario Co). A new wing, the Elaine Wilson Hall, opened in 1988.

See also PREHISTORIC ARCHAEOLOGY.

Focus (1984–)
Rochester Museum and Science Center, http://www.rmsc.org

Martin Naparsteck

Rochester Red Wings. Baseball team. Professional baseball in Rochester dates to 1877. In its formative decades the team used a variety of names, like the Live Oaks, Jingoes, Bronchos, Hustlers, Colts, Brownies, Champs, Chiefs, Beau Brummels, Hop Bitters, and Tribe. Except in 1890, when the Hop Bitters joined the major league American Association, all of Rochester's teams have been minor league franchises. Rochester played annually in the Eastern League from 1895 and remained a member when it became the International League (IL) in 1912. In 1928 the National League St. Louis Cardinals purchased the Rochester club and made it their top player-development affiliate. The team was renamed Red Wings, a sobriquet still used, and the Cardinals built a new ballpark, Red Wing Stadium on Norton St in northwest Rochester, to replace the rickety, wooden Baseball Park on Bay St. The franchise quickly found success, finishing the regular season in first place for four consecutive years (1928–31). The 1930 Wings, managed by Billy Southworth (1928–32, 1939–40) and featuring seven starting players who batted above .300, is considered the best team of the Cardinals era. The Red Wings later slumped through six losing seasons (1942–47) before recapturing the pennant in 1950. Four years later, Thomas Edison Alston became the team's first African American player.

The future of baseball in Rochester was uncertain after 1956 when the Cardinals decided they would drop the Red Wings from their farm system. Local businessman Morrie Silver led a community stock drive to save the financially strapped team and purchase the stadium, which in 1968 was renamed Silver Stadium. The Red Wings continued a loose affiliation with the Cardinals through 1960 before contracting to be a minor league franchise of the American League Baltimore Orioles.

The teams of the 1960s included power hitters Luke Easter (1959–64) and John "Boog" Powell (1961). In 1971 Joe Altobelli managed the Wings (1971–76) to the IL championship (the Governors' Cup) and Junior World Series title with a roster that included future major league stars Bobby Grich (1970–71) and Don Baylor (1968, 1970–71). The most memorable game for the Wings took place at McCoy Stadium in Pawtucket, RI, in 1981 when Rochester and the Pawtucket Red Sox played for 33 innings, the longest game in professional baseball history. It began on 18 April, when the teams played for 32 innings before play was suspended, and concluded on 23 June with the Red Sox winning 3-2.

Notable baseball figures having ties with the Red Wings include George Sisler (1931), Stan Musial (1941), Bob Gibson (1958, 1960), Jim Palmer (1967–68), Eddie Murray (1976), Cal Ripken Jr (1981), and manager Earl Weaver (1966–67). Other renowned Wings include Ron Shelton (1970–71), later an Academy Award–nominated screenwriter and producer whose credits include the baseball film *Bull Durham,* and Dan Boone, a descendant of the famous frontiersman who pitched a no-hitter in 1990.

In 1997 the Wings moved into Frontier Field, a red-brick 12,000-seat downtown stadium across the street from the world headquarters of the Eastman Kodak Co. The $37.3 million stadium was built after years of often rancorous public debate and was funded by the state, Monroe Co, the City of Rochester, and the team. The Wings established team attendance records, attracting more than 500,000 fans in each of their first two seasons at the new park, and they hosted the 2000 Triple-A All-Star Game. In the 20th century the Red Wings garnered 10 Governors' Cup titles, the last in 1997. The team became affiliated with the Minnesota Twins in September 2002.

Mandelaro, Jim, and Scott Pitoniak. *Silver Seasons: The Story of the Rochester Red Wings* (Syracuse: Syracuse Univ Press, 1996)

Scott Pitoniak

Rochester Royals. Professional basketball team. Lester Harrison, who owned a vegetable business in Rochester, purchased the Rochester Royals in the infant National Basketball League (NBL) in summer 1944 for $500. The Royals played their first professional game in 1945. The team moved to the Basketball Association of America (BAA) in 1948, and the NBL merged with the BAA the next year to form the National Basketball Association (NBA). In 1946 Harrison signed the NBL's first African American players: Dolly King, from Long Island University, and Pop Gates. On the court the Royals, led by guards Bob Davies and Al Cervi, won NBL titles in 1946 and 1947. In 1951 forward Arnie Risen teamed with Davies to defeat the defending champion Minneapolis Lakers in the Western Division Finals and lead the Royals to the NBA Finals against the New York Knicks. In the best-of-seven series, Rochester won the first three games and the Knicks won the next three. The championship game was played in Rochester at the Edgerton Park Sports Arena on 21 Apr 1951, and the confident Knicks reportedly brought celebratory champagne with them. Rochester took a 16-point lead, then watched the Knicks rally for a 2-point lead. Two Davies free throws clinched a 79-75 Rochester victory. The Royals had winning seasons for the next three years but then posted losing records in the franchise's final three seasons in Rochester. The Royals had the first pick in the 1956 NBA draft but passed over future star center Bill Russell in favor of guard Sihugo Green, who averaged nine points throughout his NBA career. As losses increased, attendance dropped, despite the move to play in the Rochester War Memorial subsequent to its opening in October 1955. After the 1956–57 season Harrison, who had coached the Royals from 1945 to 1955, moved the team to Cincinnati. A year later he sold the Royals for $200,000, and the franchise has since evolved into the Sacramento Kings. In nine NBA seasons the Rochester Royals compiled a record of 357-263. Davies, Cervi, Risen, and Harrison have been elected to the Basketball Hall of Fame.

Ramsey, David. *The Nats: a Team, a City, an Era* (Utica: North Country Books, 1995)

David Luke Ramsey

Rochester Subway. Built between 1922 and 1927 by the Scott Bros Co of Rome (Oneida Co), which transformed the bed of the Erie Canal and the Genesee River aqueduct into a partially covered subway, with overhead catenary structure, below-grade platforms at intersecting streets, and ramps to connect to the interurbans and local trolley lines. At a total cost of $12 million the Rochester Subway opened on 1 Dec 1927. Arguments about whether the city should be given direct control over the subway or if New York State Railways, which operated surface transit, should control the line preceded its construction. The railways were chosen on the basis of universal transfer privileges, an ability to maximize use of rush hour transit surface cars, and service-at-cost arrangements.

By 1928, 125 cars entered the subway at Winton Rd, and a $3.6 million extension south to the Rochester and Eastern interurbans crossing into Brighton (Monroe Co) was approved. In 1929 Dewey Ave streetcars were diverted into the subway to improve and speed up service to Kodak Park, indirectly connected by surface car lines. The last Rochester-area interurban line was abandoned in 1931 after the bankruptcy of New York State Railways and other integral electric railroad companies. Acquired by Rochester Transit Corp (RTC), the subway operated as a single-line urban mass transit system with transfers to local buses. It connected downtown with the Kodak plant and, after 1937, with the large General Motors plant at the line's western end. Although primarily a bus system, RTC managed to increase its subway passenger load from 1.5 million in the 1930s to its peak of 5.1 million in 1946–47, as the Office of Defense Transportation ruled in 1943 that bus service was to be curtailed by 20% because of World War II.

Subway ridership declined as local automobile use increased after the war. Sunday and holiday service ended in 1952. In 1955 the state legislature approved converting the subway's eastern end into a connector road to the New York State Thruway from the inner loop (a short controlled-access expressway surrounding downtown Rochester). On 30 June 1956 Rochester became the only city in the United States to abandon a mass transit system, ending 29 years of service on America's smallest urban subway.

Amberger, Roy, Dick Barrett, and Greg Marling. *Canal Boats, Interurbans, and Trolleys: The Story of the Rochester Subway* (Rochester: National Railroad Historical Society, 1985)

Gordon, William Reed. *94 Years of Rochester Railways* ([Rochester?]: Author, 1975)

David Babson

Rockaway Indians. Local records document the presence of Rockaway Indian communities along a stretch of Long Island's southern shore extending from East Rockaway (Nassau Co) west to Far Rockaway and the east end of Jamaica Bay (Queens Co) throughout the colonial era. The name Rockaway probably derives from the Munsee term for sandy place, an accurate description of the area. The locale (Reckouw Hacky) was first mentioned in the 1639 Indian deed of land to the Dutch. Although Rockaways were among those accepting a peace agreement on 4 Mar 1643, many Rockaway warriors angered by the sale of their lands on 13 Nov 1643 to Hempstead settlers joined the war against the colonists. Devastated by subsequent Dutch attacks, the Rockaway allowed Massapequa sachem Tackapousha to sign the peace treaty ending hostilities on their behalf on 30 Aug 1645. The Rockaway, led by two sons of Tackapousha, Waumitampack (*fl* 1655–69) and Monguamy (*fl* 1655–81), struggled to hold onto lands claimed by persistent Hempstead and Jamaica townsfolk. Ultimately unable to prevent the loss of their lands, they managed to gain the right to camp on unfenced land at Rockaway in exchange for their acknowledgment of English claims. Reasonably near New York City on unwanted marshlands considered wastelands by neighboring colonists, Rockaway became a regular stop for Indians traveling across Long Island in search of work. Today, most people tracing descent from Rockaway Indian ancestors continue to make their homes on Long Island.

Grumet, Robert S. *Native American Place Names in New York City* (New York: Museum of the City of New York, 1981)

Strong, John A. *The Algonquian Peoples of Long Island from Earliest Times to 1700* (Interlaken, NY: Empire State Books, 1997)

Robert S. Grumet

Rockefeller, John D(avison), Sr (*b* Richford, Tioga Co, 8 July 1839; *d* Ormond Beach, Fla, 23 May 1937). Businessman. A descendant of German Palatines, Rockefeller was raised in various locales in Central New York, and in 1852 he attended the Owego Academy (Tioga Co). When Rockefeller was 14, he and his family moved to Ohio, and in 1855 he was hired as a bookkeeper at a wholesale firm. Eight years later he and two partners built an oil refinery to make kerosene in Cleveland. In 1864 Rockefeller married Laura Celestia Spelman. With his brother William and several other investors, Rockefeller formed the Standard Oil Co in 1870 and embarked on an acquisition campaign that gave them control of Cleveland's oil-refining business in 1872. He also turned his attention to acquiring pipelines and railcars to ship kerosene to the Atlantic coast. By 1879 Standard Oil was a virtual monopoly, controlling 90% of American refining capacity, as well as a dominant player in the distribution of petroleum products.

Rockefeller and his family moved from Ohio to New York City in 1883, and Standard Oil opened new headquarters in the city at 26 Broadway in 1885. Rockefeller's tremendous success—through his fierce competitiveness and cutthroat business tactics—led him to have many enemies. Beginning in the 1870s a series of court challenges and government inquiries were launched against Standard Oil. One of the earliest investigations was in New York State in July 1879, when Assemblyman A. Barton Hepburn, a Republican representing St. Lawrence Co, led an assembly investigation into railroad management abuses. Part of Hepburn's probe explored alleged rate collusion between Standard Oil and state railroads. In response to the findings, the legislature and Gov Alonzo B. Cornell created the New York State Board of Railroad Commissioners in 1882. On the federal level Rockefeller's close relationship with railroads provided some political impetus for the US Congress's 1887 creation of the Interstate Commerce Commission. In response to these challenges, Rockefeller created in 1882 the Standard Oil Trust (America's first modern trust) as a legal means to operate and protect his monopoly. The Ohio-based company held all the stock of Rockefeller's companies. In 1892, after the Ohio Supreme Court annulled Standard Oil's charter, the trust moved to New Jersey. Subsequently journalists Henry Demarest Lloyd and Ida Tarbell published scathing exposés of Standard Oil's and Rockefeller's excesses and ruthlessness. In 1911 the US Supreme Court found that Standard Oil was a monopoly and ordered it divided into 38 separate companies.

After the development of the gasoline-powered automobile in the early 1900s, Rockefeller became the world's richest businessman. His wealth peaked in 1913 at $900 million. A devout Baptist throughout his life, Rockefeller gave away over half his fortune. In New York City he created both the Rockefeller Institute for Medical Research in 1901 (renamed Rockefeller University in 1965) and 12 years later the Rockefeller Foundation, the first global philanthropic organization. He made numerous gifts to New York State–based educational and charitable organizations, including Vassar College in Poughkeepsie, Rochester Theological Seminary, and the Seamen's Church Institute in New York City. The Rockefeller family home, Kykuit, built between 1905 and 1913 and originally located on 5,000 acres (2,020 ha) in Pocantico Hills (Westchester Co), is owned by the National Trust for Historic Preservation and is a popular tourist attraction. His son, John D. Rockefeller Jr, was the primary developer of Rockefeller Center in Manhattan; his grandson, Nelson A. Rockefeller, was a four-term governor of New York State.

Chernow, Ron. *Titan: The Life of John D. Rockefeller, Sr.* (New York: Random House, 1998)

Darwin Stapleton

Rockefeller, Nelson A(ldrich) (*b* Bar Harbor, Maine, 8 July 1908; *d* New York City, 26 Jan 1979). Governor and US vice president. The third of six children of John D. Jr and Abby Aldrich Rockefeller, Nelson was a grandson of John D. Rockefeller Sr, the founder of the Standard Oil Co and the nation's first billionaire. Raised primarily at his family's estate in Pocantico Hills (Westchester Co) and in Manhattan, he attended the Lincoln School of Teachers College of Columbia University (1917–26), and in 1930 he received a BA from Dartmouth College and married Mary Todhunter Clark. Divorcing her in 1962, he married Margaretta Fitler "Happy" Murphy a year later.

Early Life

Rockefeller's early career was built within his family's enterprises and shaped by family influences. He was a member of the board of directors of Rockefeller Center (Manhattan) for more than a quarter of a century (1931–58), serving twice as chairman (1938–45; 1948–51). As a board member of Creole Petroleum (1935–40), a subsidiary of Standard Oil of New Jersey, he gained experience in Latin America. The creation of the Rockefeller Brothers Fund with his brothers in 1940 was an early venture in philanthropy. Interest in the arts, encouraged by his mother, was manifest in almost four decades on the board of the Museum of Modern Art (1932–79; as president 1939–41, 1946–53). In 1957 he founded the Museum of Primitive Art to provide a venue for art created by the indigenous cultures of Africa, Oceania, and the Americas. This collection was transferred to the Metropolitan Museum of Art in 1976. The Rockefeller family's long Republicanism notwithstanding, Pres Franklin D. Roosevelt made Rockefeller coordinator of the Office of Inter-American Affairs, the US Department of State's center of anti-Nazi efforts in Latin America during World War II. After the war Rockefeller was instrumental in helping bring the United Nations headquarters to New York City. Following the national Republican victory in 1952, he first served as the founding undersecretary of the federal Department of Health, Education, and Welfare and then, in 1954, became White House special adviser to Pres Dwight D. Eisenhower.

Governor

Rockefeller was nominated by his party for the New York State governorship in 1958 because Republican prospects against an incumbent Democrat did not seem promising, because he could finance his own campaign, and because he was able to win the early backing of key Republican leaders in his home county of Westchester. With wealth neutralized as an issue in a "battle of millionaires," Rockefeller prevailed against Gov W. Averell Harriman (1955–58) and became New York State's 49th governor. Rockefeller was elected to four successive four-year terms, serving almost 15 years before his resignation on 18 Dec 1973; only George Clinton, the first governor, served longer.

More than any Republican governor before or since, Rockefeller was able to draw Democratic and independent support. In politics and government he displayed enormous personal energy, magnetism, confidence, tenacity, and toughness. Reelection in 1962 and 1970 was relatively easy. He almost certainly squeaked through in a difficult four-way race in 1966 because of votes drawn from the Democratic candidate, Frank D. O'Connor, by the Liberal Party candidacy of Franklin D. Roosevelt Jr. Rockefeller became governor at a time when New York State was still the nation's commercial and industrial engine, and citizens' belief in government as a positive force was strong. His approach as governor was to identify big problems, gather the best minds to craft solutions, have these solutions enacted into law, and then implement them on a large scale. In this way he fashioned the crown jewel of his legacy, the SUNY system, while reassuring New York State's powerful, prestigious independent colleges and universities—secular and religious-based—with the highest level of state assistance for nonpublic higher education in the nation. In the year before Rockefeller became governor, New York State budgeted $44.5 million for the state university. In 1973, Rockefeller's last year in office, SUNY state purposes budget was $464.4 million. In addition, direct state aid to private colleges and professional schools totaled $69.6 million. Moreover, much of the $88.7 million in scholarship support provided by the state government indirectly flowed (as intended) to these institutions.

Gov Nelson A. Rockefeller with Princess Beatrix of the Netherlands at the Hudson-Champlain Ball, Albany, 1959.

Other massive building projects throughout the state—among them the Empire State Plaza (1978) later named for him in Albany, Lincoln Center (1962), and the World Trade Center (1970) in New York City—cemented Rockefeller's relationship with labor unions and other traditionally Democratic constituencies. At first Rockefeller used a classic Republican pay-as-you-go financing for the state's capital projects, though previously authorized debt was issued. During his second term in 1965, voters were asked, as required by the New York State Constitution, to approve full-faith-and-credit borrowing. By 1973 voter-authorized debt ($3.65 billion) was four times as great as when Rockefeller took office in 1959 ($897 million). Even before 1965, "back door" borrowing techniques were invented by the Rockefeller administration to finance his programs. Their use was expanded when voters failed to approve additional full-faith-and-credit borrowing at the polls. Rockefeller's first budget as governor totaled just over $2 billion; his last $8.7 billion. The rate of spending increase in New York State during his tenure far exceeded that for the other industrial states. In 1972 New York's combined state and local taxes were one and one-half times the national average; per capita state taxes were seven times their 1957 level. The accumulated negative effects of Rockefeller's taxing and borrowing to support his approach to government began to be felt late in his third term. Certainly the burdens created by his policies deepened the difficulties New York State faced as a result of dramatic shifts in the national and world economies during the 1970s. But the governor received his greatest contemporary criticism for his handling of the Attica prison uprising in 1971, which resulted in 43 deaths.

To achieve his goals Rockefeller relied on the decisive, sometimes ruthless, use of the wealth, status, prestige, and private power inherent in being a Rockefeller in combination with his public power as governor. For much of his tenure the state legislature was controlled by his party, and he used his role as party leader to dominate it. Even in brief periods of Democratic control of one or both houses, Rockefeller had his way. In fact, the movement for legislative independence from the executive that flowered soon after his departure from Albany in 1973 was in substantial measure a reaction to his dominance. Rockefeller is widely regarded not only as one of the most important American governors of the 20th century, but also as a major national advocate for the states in the federal system.

Seeking the Presidency

A liberal Republican for much of his public career in the mold of his predecessor and two-time nominee for the US presidency, Gov Thomas E. Dewey (1942–54), Rockefeller failed in several attempts to capture that nomination himself. The extraordinarily hostile reception he received at the 1964 Republican convention marked the decisive rightward shift of the national Republican Party in the final third of the 20th century. A last-minute effort to gain the nomination in 1968 following the withdrawal of the incumbent Democrat, Pres Lyndon Johnson, from the race proved fruitless. On 19 Dec 1974, after he was nominated by Pres Gerald R. Ford and after stormy confirmation hearings in both houses of the US Congress, Rockefeller became the first vice president appointed under the provisions of the 25th Amendment. Vehemently opposed by the Republican Party's conservative wing, Rockefeller was not renominated for vice president in 1976. He returned to private life and in 1978 started a company to market reproductions of items from his vast art collection.

See also ATTICA UPRISING; BONDED INDEBTEDNESS; EXECUTIVE BRANCH; LIBERALISM; STATE PARKS; STATE UNIVERSITY OF NEW YORK (SUNY).

Connery, Robert, and Gerald Benjamin. *Rockefeller of New York: Executive Power in the Statehouse* (Ithaca: Cornell Univ Press, 1979)

Kramer, Michael, and Sam Roberts. *"I Never Wanted to Be Vice President of Anything"* (New York: Basic Books, 1976)

Persico, Joseph E. *The Imperial Rockefeller* (New York: Simon & Schuster, 1982)

Reich, Cary. *The Life of Nelson Rockefeller: Worlds to Conquer* (New York: Doubleday, 1996)

Rockefeller Archive Center, http://archive.rockefeller.edu/

Gerald Benjamin

Rockefeller Center. National Historic Landmark of 19 buildings on 22 acres (8.9 ha) in Midtown Manhattan. The site, originally city common land, held the Elgin Botanic Garden between 1801 and 1811 before being acquired by Columbia University, which used the land for its new home and for rental purposes. In the late 1920s Otto Kahn, believing the land perfect for the Metropolitan Opera's (the Met's) new home, convinced John D. Rockefeller Jr to secure a long-term, multimillion dollar lease on the property. Tenements, speakeasies, and theaters began to be cleared, and ultimately over 4,000 people were relocated, but the Met deserted the project after the stock market crashed in October 1929. Left holding the property, Rockefeller ordered his architectural consortium, led by John Todd and Raymond Hood, to create a commercial center both beautiful and profitable. Constructed in the midst of economic depression, the center was a symbol of Rockefeller's faith in capitalism. He confidently participated in the planning, insisting that 15% of the space be devoted to gardens and plazas and that natural light reach the ground.

An army of 75,000 workers, aided by over 100,000 fabricators outside the city, labored without any major labor disputes. The first two buildings were completed by 1932. In 1933 the center of the complex, the 70-story RCA Building (since 1988 the General Electric Building) at 30 Rockefeller Center, opened for business, including the Rockefeller family offices. At the base of "30 Rock," the plaza originally intended as an entryway to underground shops became instead the site of a wintertime ice-skating rink and a summertime outdoor restaurant; atop was an observation deck and the Rainbow Room, which opened in 1934 and remains one of Manhattan's most elegant nightspots. In 1939 Rockefeller drove the last of 10 million rivets, completing his dream that, at the insistence of his son Nelson, was given the family name. The project cost over $120 million. It included Radio City Music Hall as well as the British Empire Building and La Maison Française, separated by the Channel Gardens, islands of greenery that slope downward into the plaza where Paul Manship's 1934 gilded *Prometheus* reigns. Rockefeller Center is famed for an innovative underground delivery system, communication and shopping arcades, artwork, and its annual Christmas tree.

Architectural critics dealt harshly with the project during its construction, but the complex is now praised as extraordinary planning. Nelson A. Rockefeller helped obtain tenants in the 1930s and within a decade it was highly profitable. By 1973 the architectural firm Harrison and Abramovitz had added four skyscrapers to the complex, including Time-Life Building, completed in 1960, the first to cross 6th Ave, where elevated trains once operated. In 1985 the Rockefellers purchased the underlying land from Columbia for $400 million; the family's financial interest in the complex ended in December 2000 when it was sold for $1.85 billion.

Karp, Walter. *The Center: A History and Guide to Rockefeller Center* (New York: American Heritage Publishing, 1982)

Loth, David. *The City within a City: The Romance of Rockefeller Center* (New York: William Morrow, 1966)

George J. Lankevich

Rockefeller Drug Laws. Harsh mandatory prison terms for drug crimes, signed into law 8 May 1973 by Gov Nelson A. Rockefeller, who pressed the legislature to enact them. The laws, which led the nation in a mandatory sentencing movement, required fixed-term prison sentences for anyone caught possessing even small amounts of narcotics, with longer terms for those convicted of selling drugs. An individual convicted of selling 2 ounces (57 g) of cocaine received the same mandatory minimum sentence (15 years to life) that applied to murder. The laws were a reaction to rising drug-related violent crime in the state's major cities, which years of drug treatment programs had failed to stop. Many nonviolent, low-level drug runners were incarcerated under the laws because the mandatory minimum provisions permitted no exceptions based on an individual's history or circumstance. Other states and the federal government adopted similar fixed-sentencing laws, struggling to respond to rising crime rates and drug abuse, which led to a rapid expansion in the prison population nationwide.

New York State was forced to build dozens of new prisons in the last quarter of the 20th century, and the inmate population grew from approximately 14,000 in 1973 to more than 70,000 in 2000, the sharpest rise in state history. By 1996, nearly half (46%) of all inmates sent to prison were drug offenders (most sentenced under the Rockefeller laws), up from 11% in 1980. In the same period the percentage of inmates sent to prison for violent crimes declined from 60% to 29%. Supporters of the laws argued that many drug-related prisoners had likely committed other violent crimes for which they were never convicted. The laws had a disproportionate impact on Blacks and Latinos in the state; only 6% of those sentenced for drug crimes in 2000 were white. Governors routinely granted clemency to a small number of nonviolent drug couriers, usually young women, at Christmas. Political support for major reforms to the laws grew in the 1990s and early 21st century, and the legislature responded in December 2004 with a vote to reduce some mandatory sentences.

Rosen, Hy, and Peter Slocum. *From Rocky to Pataki: Character and Caricatures in New York Politics* (Syracuse: Syracuse Univ Press, 1998)

Peter Slocum

Rockefeller University. Private research institution and graduate school of medicine. It was established by John D. Rockefeller Sr in 1901 as the Rockefeller Institute for Medical Research in New York City with the mission to study infectious diseases. After two years in rented space, the institute moved in 1906 to the corner of York Ave and 66th St in New York City. The Rockefeller Institute Hospital, opened in 1910, was the first clinical research hospital in the United States. In 1954 the school's charter was changed to award doctor of philosophy and doctor of medical science degrees, with the first such degrees awarded in 1959. The name was changed to Rockefeller University in 1965, and in 1972 the school began collaboration with Cornell University to offer graduate students a joint MD-PhD program. Rockefeller faculty and former students include 22 Nobel laureates and 11 recipients of the National Medal of Science. In 2003 the university had 340 postdoctoral investigators, 140 PhD students, and 35 MD-PhD students.

See also SCIENTIFIC CULTURE (19TH–21ST CENTURIES).

Hanson, Elizabeth. *The Rockefeller University: Achievements: A Century of Science for the Benefit of Humankind, 1901–2001* (New York: Rockefeller University Press, 2000)

Sarah E. DeSanctis

Rockland. Town (pop 3,913) in N central Sullivan Co. Settled in 1789, largely from Massachusetts, its lumber exports to Philadelphia began in 1798. The town was formed in 1809. Its land was owned by the Livingston family, which leased or sold farms. The resort trade was made possible by the Ontario and Western Railway (1872–1953). Sullivan Co's first golf course (1897) was at Trout Valley Farm on the Beaverkill. Industrial products included leather from a large tannery at Debruce; Spalding baseball bats, which were all made at Livingston Manor from 1877 to 1900; bowling pins; and wood acid and other hardwood distillates from six acid factories. The first Jewish hotel keepers arrived in 1908, and the area became a center of the borscht belt. A poultry plant operated at Livingston Manor from 1950 to the 1990s. Two streams in town, the Beaverkill and the Willowemoc, are regarded as destinations for eastern fly fishers; Livingston Manor is the site of the Catskill Fly Fishing Center and Museum, and the Catskill State Fish Hatchery is at Debruce. The Roscoe Diner is a famous eatery on Rte 17 (I-86), and Roscoe is home to the only mother-son Olympians in US history: Alice Arden Hodge (1936 high jump) and Russell Arden "Rusty" Hodge (1964 decathlon).

John Conway

Rockland County (174 mi²/451 km²; pop 286,753). Created in 1798 from Orange Co, with a subsequent boundary adjustment in 1800. Rockland Co is subdivided into 5 towns and 19 incorporated villages. The unincorporated locality of New City serves as county seat. Elevation ranges from sea level along the Hudson River to 1,283 feet (391 m) at the summit of Rockhouse Mountain. The county straddles two physiographic provinces. The western third lies within the Hudson Hills subregion of the New England Upland, known locally as the Hudson Highlands and the Ramapo Mountains, and is largely contained within the Harriman State Park, which occupies over 25% of the county's area. The uplands are geologically complex but moderate in relief. Middle Proterozoic granite, gneiss, and schist underlie the Hudson Hills. The Ramapo fault line runs along the southern foot of the Ramapo Mountains. The Palisades, an extensive and imposing basaltic rock formation stretching along the west bank of the Hudson River, was formed when molten lava was forced upward through rifts in the overlying Newark sandstone deposits. The county's eastern two-thirds belong to the Triassic Lowland, whose topography consists of broad, gentle valleys punctuated by occasional ridges. Shale, soft sandstone, and hard lava lie under the Triassic Lowland, the only region of New York State where dinosaur fossils can be found; tracks of a coelophysis were discovered at Blauvelt in 1972.

Continental glaciation left behind a complex mix of till and outwash deposits and contributed to the formation of numerous lakes and marshes. Unconsolidated glacial deposits are more than 500 feet (150 m) thick in places. Rockland Co lies within the watersheds of the Hudson, Hackensack, and Passaic Rivers and their tributaries. The Mahwah, Ramapo, and Hackensack Rivers drain the southern two-thirds of the county into Newark Bay. The eastern margin and the north drain into the Hudson. The soils vary substantially in character. Very little land is used for agriculture; about half of the soils are well suited for urban land use.

Rockland Co's climate is humid-continental. Mean January temperatures range from 27°F (-3°C) or lower in the north and west to 30°F (-1°C) in the southeast. Mean July temperatures range from 73°F (23°C) at Suffern and slightly cooler in the higher elevations to 75°F (24°C) in the southeast along the Hudson. Average annual precipitation is about 50 inches (125 cm). Seasonal snowfall amounts vary from approximately 25 inches (65 cm) in the southeast to around 30 inches (75 cm) in the higher elevations near the northwestern border. Rockland Co's primeval forest cover was a central hardwood community

dominated by beech, sugar maple, basswood, oak, and chestnut. Approximately one-third of the county is presently covered by forest.

American Indians and Early Settlement

The present Rockland Co was inhabited by Munsee-speaking Indians prior to European contact. The best-known were the Hackensack, the Haverstraw, the Minisink, and the Tappan. The first attempted (albeit unsuccessful) settlement, Vriessendael, near Tappan Slote [now Piermont], was begun by David Pietersz de Vries in 1639. It was broken up after the Indians burned all its buildings except de Vries's house during Kieft's War in February 1643. Although some American Indians remained through the colonial period, only a few were present by 1800.

The mountainous, rocky landscape of the Ramapo Mountains and the riverfront barrier of the Palisades were responsible for gradual settlement and small farms. The earliest European settlers were Dutch and English, while Scots settled at New Hempstead and Chestnut Ridge. Among the land patents in the county were the DeHarte (1666) and Crom (1685) Patents in what is now Haverstraw and the Tappan Patent (1686) in Orangetown. Others were the Mattasink (1694), Quaspeck (1694), Kakiat (1696), and Chesecock (1707) Patents. Most early settlers were farmers, although the Hasenclever iron mine [now in Harriman State Park] was in operation as early as 1766. During the Revolution the mine supplied iron for cannonballs and for the great chain that was stretched across the Hudson at Fort Montgomery. Tappantown [now Tappan] was the Orange Co seat from 1683 to 1773, although after 1738 county court sessions alternated with Goshen (Orange Co). In 1774 the locality of New City was made county seat, and a courthouse was built in 1798–99.

Slavery was introduced to Rockland Co by settlers on the Tappan Patent. The first census of Rockland Co in 1800 recorded 551 slaves and 68 free Blacks, about 10% of the county's population. Skunk Hollow, near the state line in Orangetown, was an African American settlement during most of the 19th century. The Ramapo Mountain People, who have lived near Hillburn on both sides of the state line since the 18th century, have a mixed African American and American Indian ancestry.

Revolutionary and Early National Period

The Revolutionary War divided residents in their loyalties. The Continental army encamped for a time in Haverstraw Precinct [now Pomona and New Hempstead]. There were American fortifications at Sidman's Fort at Suffern, a blockhouse at Palisades, and larger forts at Stony Point, Fort Clinton, and Fort Montgomery in Orange Co. The British captured Forts Clinton and Montgomery in October 1777. The King's Ferry in Stony Point and the Dobbs Ferry in Sneden's Landing were links on an important route from New England to New Jersey and the southern colonies. The Americans, under the command of Gen "Mad" Anthony Wayne, stormed Stony Point in July 1779 in one of the most brilliant actions of the war, recapturing the fort from the British. George Washington was headquartered at Tappan for several months in 1780, and on 2 Oct 1780 Maj John André, Benedict Arnold's co-conspirator, was hanged on what became known as Treason Hill. On 5 May 1783 Washington received the British commander, Gen Guy Carleton, at the DeWindt House in Tappan, which still stands, to discuss the terms for peace.

Transportation

Improvements in transportation spurred development in the first half of the 19th century. Steamboats gradually replaced river sloops, with the steamboat *Orange* beginning daily service between Nyack and New York City in 1828. After much debate about routes, the Nyack Turnpike opened between Nyack and Suffern in 1830. The Erie Railroad (1841) was the county's first rail link; its eastern terminus was constructed over the marshes at Piermont to the end of a 500 ft (150 m) pier. In the 1870s several short lines were built, providing north-south links to New Jersey port terminals, and the West Shore Railroad (1883) established long-distance service along the Hudson to Albany and Buffalo. While highways were not well developed until after World War II, the Bear Mountain Bridge (1924) in the Town of Stony Point was the first vehicular bridge across the Hudson below Albany.

Economic Development

Abundant wood and waterpower encouraged the processing of grain, cider, and lumber from colonial times. By the early 19th century the county had evolved into a farming district that shipped dairy products, apples, and garden produce to the New York City market. The lumber industry provided wood for shipbuilding and pilings, and fuel for mills, foundries, and brickyards. The mining industry was important to American defense during the Revolution. Timber and iron ore in Ramapo supplied the J. G. Pierson and Bros Iron Works (1796–1851), which employed 500; Dater Iron Works (*ca* 1800); Ramapo Iron Works (1881); and the Ramapo Wheel and Foundry Co. Beginning in 1815 the clay deposits of Haverstraw were used to manufacture brick shipped to New York City. That industry declined in the early 1900s, and the last brickyard ceased production in 1942.

Quarrying and ice cutting also served the New York City market. Red and gray sandstone and granite were quarried through the mid–19th century. Both quarries and brickyards operated at Grassy Point and Tompkins Cove from 1830 to 1930. Brownstone was quarried at Grand View-on-Hudson, and sand and gravel at Mount Ivy. Limestone is still quarried in the early 21st century, and many traprock companies in the county provide stone for general and road construction. Ice was harvested beginning in 1831; the leader, Knickerbocker Ice Co in Clarkstown, employed about 1,000 workers at its height, cutting ice on Rockland and Hessian Lakes. Boatbuilding (1805–1940s) and shoe manufacturing (1826–1900) were dominant industries in Nyack, which was also a river port for the shipping of inland products destined for New York City. Tanneries supplied leather for shoes and harnesses. Cigars were made in Wesley Hills in the late 19th and early 20th centuries. Textile manufacturing began with cotton factories in Sloatsburg and near Spring Valley during the War of 1812; twine, mosquito netting, and briar smoking pipes were later manufactured. Clothing factories and knitting mills, concentrated in Spring Valley and West Haverstraw, supplied dresses, suits, underwear, hats, and leather goods to New York City in the early 20th century, while Piermont's Meisch Manufacturing Co produced silk ribbon. In 2003 Pearl River's Wyeth-Ayerst Laboratories, which began as Lederle Antitoxin Laboratories in 1906, employed 3,168; Pearl River was also home to the Aetna Sewing Machine Co (1873–80) and the Dexter Folder Co (1894–1983). The Robert Gair Co produced folding cartons at its Piermont plant, employing 450 in 1927. California Perfume Co was formed in Suffern in 1897 and renamed Avon Products in 1939; it remained an important employer in 2003.

ROCKLAND CO POPULATION CENSUS FIGURES

	White	Nonwhite	Total Population	Foreign-Born
1800	5,734	619	6,353	—
1810	7,150	608	7,758	—
1820	8,301	536	8,837	55
1830	8,937	451	9,388	52
1840	11,543	432	11,975	—
1850	16,366	596	16,962	3,569
1860	21,943	549	22,492	5,073
1870	24,484	729	25,213	5,350
1880	26,874	816	27,690	4,993
1890	33,900	1,262	35,162	7,442
1900	36,238	2,060	38,298	7,249
1910	45,324	1,549	46,873	9,719
1920	44,057	1,491	45,548	6,981
1930	57,266	2,333	59,599	9,128
1940	71,038	3,223	74,261	11,636
1950	84,668	4,608	89,276	11,441
1960	129,651	7,152	136,803	13,758
1970	215,625	14,278	229,903	20,422
1980	232,666	26,864	259,530	29,205
1990	223,045	42,430	265,475	38,798
2000	220,538	66,215	286,753	54,766

Notes: "Nonwhite" includes African Americans, Asians, American Indians, and Pacific Islanders and, for 2000, also the mixed race and other race categories. Through the 1960 census these figures primarily reflect the African American population. Foreign-born figures for 1820 and 1830 include only those not naturalized, and for 1930 and 1950, the foreign-born totals include Whites only. Other years include all foreign-born in the population.

Rockland Co grew slowly, its population increasing from 6,353 in 1800 to only 38,298 a century later. By the middle of the 19th century Irish and Germans arrived to work in industry. Brickmaking drew many Irish families to Haverstraw and Stony Point, and they also settled in Piermont. Germans moved to Clarkstown, New City, and Blauvelt. Later, Italians and Bohemians settled in Clarkstown, while Francophone Canadians, Poles, Italians, Hungarians, and Austrians moved to Stony Point in the late 19th century.

Religion, Education, and Culture

In 1694 a Dutch Reformed church was organized in Tappan, followed by other congregations in New Hempstead and West Nyack. The first Roman Catholic church, St. Peter's in Haverstraw, opened in 1847; German Catholics were in Blauvelt by 1853, building St. Catharine's Church in 1869. In 1855 Rockland Co had 13 Methodist, 9 Reformed, and 8 Presbyterian churches. The Jewish Society of Nyack formed in 1870, later becoming Congregation B'nai Israel (1890), and was followed by Haverstraw's Congregation Sons of Jacob (1877). Upper Nyack is the national headquarters of the interdenominational pacifist organization, the Fellowship of Reconciliation. In 2003 the Jerrahi Mosque (1990) in Chestnut Ridge served as the US headquarters of Sufi Islam's Jerrahi Order. Upper Nyack's Old Stone Church (1813), originally Methodist and now nondenominational, is the oldest church building in Rockland Co.

The first school within the county's current borders was associated with the Tappan Reformed Church in 1711. Education was advanced by state legislation of 1812, which authorized common schools. By 1829 there were 34 school districts. The Rockland Female Institute and other private schools in Nyack were housed in resort hotels out of season. A Union Free School district in Nyack was founded by legislation in 1859. In the 20th century eight central school districts consolidated; Edwin Gould Academy in Spring Valley operated as a Union Free School district, housing and educating up to 200 at-risk youth.

Education and sustainable agriculture were the original purposes of Threefold Community (1926), based on the ideas of Rudolf Steiner; it now encompasses the Green Meadow Waldorf School (1950) in Chestnut Ridge. In Montebello the School for the Living (1934–45) and Bayard Lane Community (1936–45) were "Back to the Land" experiments founded by Ralph Borsodi, as was Van Houten Fields (1937–45) near West Nyack. The first institution of higher education in the county was Rockland College (1876–?1892) in Nyack; later the village was the site of the short-lived Rockland Junior College (1932–35). In the early 21st century colleges include Nyack College (1897), founded as the Missionary Training Institute; St Thomas Aquinas College (1952) at Sparkill; Dominican College (1952) at Blauvelt; Rockland Community College (1959) at Viola; and Sunbridge College (1986) at Chestnut Ridge. Cultural institutions include Columbia University's Lamont-Doherty Earth Observatory (1948) at Palisades and the NASA-designed Challenger Space Science Center (1999) at Airmont, which provides services to school systems. History is interpreted by the Stony Point Battlefield State Historic Site, which includes the Stony Point Lighthouse.

The county's first newspaper was the *Palladium* (1812) at Warren [now Haverstraw]. The *Matilda Ziegler Magazine for the Blind* (1907) was published at Monsey from 1927 to 1967. In 2003 the county's daily was the *Journal News,* while weeklies *Rockland County Times* at Nanuet and *Rockland Review* at West Nyack provided in-depth coverage.

Politics

From the late 19th century through the first half of the 20th century, the Republican Party dominated Rockland Co, with the exception of the traditional Democratic stronghold in Haverstraw. In 2003 the Democratic Party had the most registrants, but neither party dominated. From its beginning the county government was managed by a Board of Supervisors composed of the supervisors of the five towns; in 1972 the board was replaced by a county legislature. In 1984 voters authorized the position of county executive. Rockland's most famous politician was James A. Farley of Grassy Point, who managed the 1932 and 1936 presidential campaigns of Franklin D. Roosevelt and served as chair of the state Democratic Party from 1933 to 1940.

The 20th Century

The rugged, spectacular terrain of Rockland Co has been ideal for parks and nature preserves and, consequently, a frequent battleground between preservationists and developers. About 30% of the county is parkland. The 1910 establishment of Harriman State Park was an important step preserving the county's natural resources. Bear Mountain State Park was saved from becoming the site of a prison through public efforts and a gift of land by Mary Williamson Averell Harriman. High Tor Mountain was preserved from quarrying in the 1930s, in part through Maxwell Anderson's play *High Tor* (1936), a response to the efforts of the New York

POPULATIONS OF TOWNS, ROCKLAND CO

Town, Year Founded	1800	1840	1880	1920	1960	2000
Clarkstown, 1791	1,806	2,533	4,378	7,317	33,196	82,082
Haverstraw, 1719[a]	1,229	3,449	6,973	9,027	16,632	33,811
Orangetown, 1686[b]	1,337	2,771	8,077	14,284	43,172	47,711
Ramapo, 1791[c]	1,981	3,222	4,954	11,709	35,064	108,905
Stony Point, 1865	—	—	3,308	3,211	8,739	14,244

[a]Formed as precinct; recognized as town 1788.

[b]Patented as township; recognized as town 1788.

[c]New Hampstead until 1797, then Hempstead until 1829.

Traprock Co to quarry the mountain. The land was purchased by the Hudson River Conservation Society and acquired by the Palisades Interstate Park Commission in 1943.

Standard Oil Co built rows of oil storage tanks near Piermont in the 1920s, but founder John D. Rockefeller ordered them destroyed in 1932; the site is now part of Tallman Mountain State Park. The county's parks were primarily day-use areas for the New York City metropolitan area, but Monsey and Spring Valley were significant Jewish summer resorts from the 1920s until about 1960, when suburbanization forced an end to the era of boardinghouses and cottage colonies. Through the 20th century Rockland Co was the site of two large and important state institutions: the State Rehabilitation Hospital (since 1974 Helen Hayes Hospital), founded at West Haverstraw in 1900, and Letchworth Village (1907–96), a residential facility for people with developmental disabilities at Thiells.

During World War II Camp Shanks at Orangeburg was the largest army port of embarkation on the East Coast, with some 1.3 million soldiers passing through en route to North Africa and England. The Rockland Psychiatric Center was used by Camp Shanks as a field hospital; after the war it became Shanks Village, the largest veterans' housing complex in the nation. From 1946 to 1971 the US Navy housed the "Mothball Fleet" of decommissioned vessels at Iona Island, now under Palisades Interstate Park Commission jurisdiction.

The completion of the Palisades Interstate Parkway (1953–58), which connects the Bear Mountain and Harriman State Parks to the George Washington Bridge and New York City, began the rapid suburbanization of the county, a process greatly accelerated by the opening of the Thruway and Tappan Zee Bridge (1955). The population nearly tripled between 1950 and 1970, and many communities incorporated during those decades to control zoning and to prevent overbuilding. The waterfront at Piermont has been successfully redeveloped with businesses and residences since 1989. Following much controversy centered on traffic and quality-of-life issues for adjacent West Nyack neighborhoods, the Palisades Center Mall opened in 1998 with 3.5 million ft^2 (325,150 m^2) of shopping space.

In recent decades the African American, Asian, and Latino populations have increased dramatically; in 2000 the population was 21.3% black and 10.6% Asian. Those of Latino ethnicity made up 20%. Puerto Ricans have been an important part of Haverstraw's population since 1945, joined by Dominicans in the 1960s; there is a large Haitian population of almost 25,000 centered in Spring Valley. Hasidim have created two villages: New Square (1961) and Kaser (1990), homes of the Skviver and Visnitz sects, respectively. There is a large Orthodox Jewish population in Monsey and Spring Valley. In 1997 only 21 farms remained in the county, producing vegetables and orchard crops on 561 acres (227 ha). Rockland is characterized by slowing population growth and rising housing prices. Traffic problems and overcrowding are exacerbated by the Tappan Zee Bridge because of its disrepair and inability to accommodate high traffic.

The standard histories are three: David Cole, *History of Rockland County* (1884); Frank B. Green, *History of Rockland County* (1886); and Linda Zimmerman, ed., *Rockland County: Century of History* (2002). Carl Nordstrom, *Frontier Elements in a Hudson River Village* (1973), studies economic and social relationships in Nyack, while Jacquetta Haley, *Rockland County in the 1790s* (1997), concentrates on a single decade. Robert Binnewies, *Palisades* (2001), covers the geography and history of the county's southeast, and *Palisades Interstate Park, 1900–1960: 60 Years of Park Cooperation* (1960), provides excellent documentation of the transformation of the north and west. There have been a number of well-done village studies in recent years, including Daniel de Noyelles, *Within These Gates* (1982), a history of Haverstraw; Alice Munro Haagensen, *Palisades and Snedens Landing* (1986); *Piermont Three Centuries* (1996); and *Nyack in the 20th Century* (2000). Arthur Adams, *The Hudson River Guidebook* (1996) and *The Hudson River through the Years* (1996) have extensive information on Rockland Co. A superb documented history of an aspect of the county in the mid–20th century is Scott E. Webber, *Camp Shanks and Shanks Village: A Scrapbook* (1991). Jerome R. Mintz, *Hasidic People: A Place in the New World* (1992), has several chapters on Rockland Co's Hasidic enclaves.

rock music. The popular music that came to be known as rock and roll and rhythm and blues (R&B) developed in the late 1940s and 1950s from a number of diverse roots, among them big-band jazz, urban blues, and gospel vocal groups. Different forms of these were primarily African American entertainment and were embraced from the mid-1950s by the general white public, especially teenagers. New York City's role in the 1940s as one of the core cities of the recording and entertainment industry (with Los Angeles) ensured that the city would play an important role in this transition. Many of the genres of early rock and roll, such as jump jive, doo-wop, and later folk roots, have strong ties.

By the end of World War II, a new style of big-band jazz known as "jump" had become increasingly popular, characterized by simple, danceable rhythms, popular song structures, and often lyrics about the humor in African American life. New York City–based big bands such as Lionel Hampton's helped introduce the style; Illinois Jacquet's tenor saxophone solo on Hampton's "Flying Home" (1942) was a model for hundreds of R&B "honking" sax solos to come. Buddy Johnson and Lucky Millinder were other 1940 New York City band leaders whose music crossed over into R&B. However, the most prominent of the New York City jump bands was Louis Jordan and his Tympany Five. Jordan's catchy tunes and sardonic songs, which featured a small ensemble that performed with a minimum of improvisation, remained immensely popular through the 1950s.

Doo-Wop, the Brill Building, and Girl Groups

The early rock style most associated with New York City is doo-wop, characterized by strong lead vocals, rich harmonies, and often minimal instrumentation. Contrary to legend, doo-wop evolved not out of street corner entertainment but rather from sophisticated popular black vocal groups like the Mills Brothers and the Ink Spots. Among the earlier New York City groups to feature this style were the Red Caps (also known as the Toppers); the Ravens, the first of the "bird groups" and featuring the first bass lead in the style, Jimmy Ricks; the Larks; the Dominoes, featuring the soaring tenor lead solos of Clyde McPhatter, who would later perform with the first incarnation of the Drifters; and the Crows. Black vocal music crossed over from the R&B chart to the pop chart with such records as "Sh-Boom" (1954) by the Chords. The Bronx-based group was also one of the first to suffer the questionable flattery of a cover version issued by less-talented white imitators. Notable recordings by New York City artists of the era included "Why Do Fools Fall In Love" (1955) by Frankie Lyman and the Teenagers and "Speedo" (1956) by the Cadillacs. Other doo-wop groups included the Bop-Chords, the Crests, the Cellos, the Cleftones, the Elegants, the Heartbeats, the Jive Five, and Little Anthony and the Imperials. Significant white doo-wop groups soon appeared as well, often with predominately Italian personnel, like the Capris. Dion DiMucci, leader of Dion and the Belmonts, hailed from the Belmont Ave area of the Bronx.

The rise of rock and roll in the late 1940s and 1950s coincided with the growth of independent record labels, many of which recorded doo-wop and R&B performers. New York City area labels included Savoy and Apollo, but the most successful independent was Atlantic Records, which got its start in 1947 under the direction of Ahmet Ertegun. Atlantic recorded artists such as Joe Morris, Ruth Brown, the Clovers, and the Drifters. A group of talented young songwriters in the late 1950s and early 1960s worked at Manhattan's Brill Building at 1619 Broadway and other offices along Broadway from 49th to 53d Sts. Producer Don Kirschner and his Aldon Music helped catalyze the Brill Building sound; its songwriters, many of whom became performers and producers as well, included Gerry Goffin, Carole King, Cynthia Weil and Barry Mann, Neil Sedaka, Neil Diamond, Ellie Greenwich, and Phil Spector. A style often associated with Brill Building pop was that of the girl groups, one of the earliest being the Chantels ("Maybe," 1957). Other prominent representatives from the New York City area included the Angels, the Crystals, Reparata and the Delrons, the Shangri-Las, the Chiffons, the Ronnettes, the Shirelles, and solo performer Lesley Gore. Soul music in the 1960s had relatively few native New York State performers, and the Apollo Theater in Harlem was a key venue and the site of many recordings, such as *James Brown Live at the Apollo* (1962).

Folk Rock

While the tunesmiths in Midtown Manhattan were crafting music for the pop market, folksingers congregated downtown in Greenwich Village. Attracted by the neighborhood's political and cultural freedom, musicians like Woody Guthrie and Ramblin' Jack Elliott established the neighborhood as the center of a nationwide folk revival, inspiring many New York youths to take up folk music and attracting hundreds of aspirants from elsewhere. One newcomer was Bob Dylan, who in 1964 and 1965 led the transition from acoustic to electric instruments. Other New York City folk rockers with different balances of folk and rock included Phil Ochs, Joan Baez, Mimi and Richard Fariña, Al Kooper, the Mamas and the Papas, the Blues Project, the Lovin' Spoonful, and the Fugs. Folk rockers (Paul) Simon and (Art) Garfunkel, who had begun singing together while in elementary school in Forest Hills in Queens, reached stardom with "Sound of Silence" (1965) and had a series of hits until splitting up in 1970. Simon would go on to a successful solo career. Other New York City performers in a somewhat similar mode included Harry Chapin, Janis Ian, Carly Simon, and Phoebe Snow.

By the mid-1960s Woodstock (Ulster Co) had become a rural refuge for many of the folk rock artists who were coming to prominence in New York City. The Woodstock Music and Art Fair, arguably the best known rock music event in history, actually took place in Bethel (Sullivan Co), some 90 miles away. Held in a farm field 15–17 Aug 1969, the festival attracted as many as 400,000 people for "Three Days of Peace and Love." Several recording studios were established in the Woodstock vicinity in the years that followed, and in 2002 the area continued to attract prominent rock musicians.

In addition to folk rock, in the 1960s the city remained a center of a more mainstream brand of rock and roll. The focal point of the twist craze in the early 1960s was the Peppermint Lounge, immortalized in Joey Dee's "Peppermint Twist" (1961). Other venues for rock included the Paramount Theater in Brooklyn and the Fillmore East in the East Village in Manhattan. Undoubtedly no rock-related event in the 1960s received more attention than the arrival of the Beatles from Britain in 1964 to appear on the *Ed Sullivan Show.* Their arrival was endlessly hyped by prominent New York City disc jockeys (DJs), notably Murray the K (Murray Kaufman) and Cousin Brucie (Bruce Morrow). After the breakup of the Beatles in 1970, John Lennon lived in New York City, despite the best efforts of the federal government to deport him from the United States. His assassination on Central Park West on 8 Dec 1980 at the hands of a deranged fan is a sad moment in New York City's rock history. Perhaps the "British invasion" limited the success of New York City groups. Jimi Hendrix, who was playing New York clubs mostly as a sideman in R&B and soul groups, was persuaded to move to England in 1966 to record his first album. Some of the more commercially successful groups in the late 1960s were the soul-oriented Young Rascals and the psychedelic Vanilla Fudge.

Punk and the 1970s

Punk evolved in the East Village in the early 1970s. Its model was the Velvet Underground. Formed in 1964 and led by Lou Reed, the Velvet Underground combined a bleak view of modern society with graphic lyrical treatment of sex, violence, and drug addiction. One of its protégés, the New York Dolls, crafted an outrageous transvestite stage persona and a raucous sound that came to be known as glitter rock. Others soon followed and by the mid-1970s the structures of a new scene were in place. Clubs like Max's Kansas City, Club 82, and CBGB's were booking punk bands. Independent labels recorded local bands, locally produced fanzines chronicled the scene, and a fan base rapidly formed, especially in the low-rent districts of Lower Manhattan. Many fans were soon onstage themselves. Among them were Patti Smith, a poet turned rock star, and the Ramones, perhaps epitomizing the New York punk scene with simple, fast, and loud songs. Other acts included Television, Wayne County, the Plasmatics, and the Cramps.

Donald Fagen and Walter Becker formed Steely Dan in Manhattan around 1970, using talented jazz sidemen to shape a number of sophisticated and highly successful studio albums throughout the decade. Long Island native Billy Joel, an unabashed champion of his home state, rose to become one of the nation's most prominent stars, launching a career that would span the next several decades with such songs as "New York State of Mind" (1976). The outlandishly costumed hard rock band KISS also emerged in New York City in the 1970s with several successful albums and would have a resurgence of popularity in the 1990s. Other popular New York hard rock acts during this period included Mountain, Blue Oyster Cult, Foreigner, and Billy Squier.

Underground dance clubs, such as the Loft, emerged in the early 1970s. Influenced by emerging hip hop scenes in the Bronx, DJs played funk and R&B mixes to huge crowds, sparking a national disco dance craze from about 1975 to 1980. Groups and artists included the Village People, who gently mocked the gay scene in Greenwich Village, and Brooklyn-born Barry Manilow. Disco's most famous club, Studio 54, opened in 1977, attracting a celebrity clientele and several high-profile drug raids. *Saturday Night Fever* (1977), set in New York City, was disco's definitive cinematic treatment.

The 1980s and After

Several of CBGB's mainstays found commercial success as founding members of the so-called new wave genre. Blondie was an early breakout from the punk scene, scoring a series of number one hits in the late 1970s and early 1980s. The Talking Heads also found some measure of commercial success with their eclectic, danceable sound. Others from the punk scene moved toward hardcore, playing fast, distorted, often politically charged music in bands like the False Prophets and the Undead. The Beastie Boys, originally a hardcore band, became one of the first white groups to incorporate hip hop styles. Sonic Youth, formed in 1981, influenced many of the popular 1990s alternative rock bands with their noisy no-wave sound. Pat Benatar and Scandal were commercially successful in the 1980s. Heavy metal bands included Twisted Sister, White Lion, Winger, Living Color, Dio, White Zombie, Anthrax, and Helmet. Guitar virtuosos Steve Vai and Joe Satriani are both from Long Island. The new music-video medium was crucial to the success in the early 1980s of several artists, including Madonna (Ciccone), who emerged from Manhattan's postdisco dance-club scene to become a defining figure in US pop culture for the next several decades, and Cyndi Lauper. Other acts of the 1980s were the rockabilly-tinged Stray Cats, formed in Massapequa (Nassau Co) in the early 1980s, the folk pop group They Might Be Giants, and the Zen Tricksters. In the 1990s two Buffalo-based acts that developed substantial followings were Ani DiFranco, whose unique sound has been described as folk punk, and the Goo-Goo Dolls, a hard-edged alternative rock act.

See also Folk music revival; Woodstock festival.

Aquila, Richard. *That Old Time Rock & Roll: A Chronicle of an Era, 1954–1963* (New York: Schirmer Books, 1989)

Barnard, Stephen. *Rock: An Illustrated History* (New York: Schirmer Books, 1986)

Gillett, Charlie. *The Sound of the City : The Rise of Rock and Roll* (New York: Da Capo Press, 1996)

Graves, Steven M. "A Historical Geography of the Music Industry" (PhD diss, Univ of Illinois, 1999)

Wade, Dorothy, and Justine Picardie. *Music Man: Ahmet Ertegun, Atlantic Records, and the Triumph of Rock and Roll* (New York: Norton, 1990)

Steve Graves

Rockville Centre. Village (pop 24,568) in Hempstead (Nassau Co). Michael DeMott built a gristmill in 1710, and the post office (1849) was named in honor of Methodist minister Mordecai "Rock" Smith. Building lots were surveyed in 1851, the railroad established a station stop in 1867, and the South Shore's first commercial bank opened in 1891. The village incorporated in 1893. Major development followed the construction of a municipal power plant in 1898 and continued through the post–World War I boom. Rockville Center became a commuter suburb of New York City, with 22,362 inhabitants in 1950, a population that peaked in 1970. A heavily Catholic community, it is the site of Molloy College (1955) and St. Agnes Cathedral, the seat of the diocese of Rockville Centre (1957), sixth largest in the nation in 2003 with a congregation of 1.5 million in Nassau and Suffolk Cos.

Georgina Martorella

Rocky Point. Locality (pop 10,185) in Brookhaven (Suffolk Co). In the 18th century Rocky Point was the terminus of a "landing road" by which Brookhaven cordwood cutters drove loads to the landing to be shipped to New York City and, later, Haverstraw (Rockland Co). A post office was established in 1872. George Hagerman developed Grand View Park, a summer resort, in 1890. Rocky Point acquired a station on the Long Island Rail Road when the Port Jefferson branch was extended in 1895, but service ended in 1938. In 1921 RCA created the world's largest and most powerful wireless transmission station in Rocky Point. New York State bought the decommissioned facility in 1978 for $1 and created a 5,000-acre (2,020 ha) pine barrens preserve. In 1925 the *New York Daily Mirror* offered building lots for summer cottages as premiums with newspaper subscriptions. When eastern Long Island began to suburbanize, many Rocky Point cottages were winterized and the locality's population began to increase.

Suzanne Johnson

Rodgers and Hammerstein. See Musical theater.

Rodman. Town (pop 1,147) in SE Jefferson Co. Settled in 1801, the town was formed from Adams in 1804 as Harrison and renamed in 1808. Except for its distillery (1828) and large tannery (*ca* 1840), it was almost entirely agricultural and boasted the first Limburger cheese made in the United States (1853). Since the 1950s dairy farms have consolidated into a few large ones, including Jefferson Co's largest. In 1992 a solid waste management facility opened, serving Jefferson, Lewis, and St. Lawrence Cos; it was operated by the Development Authority of the North Country. Residents work in Watertown and Syracuse. Rodman was the birthplace of department store founder Frank W. Woolworth (1852–1919).

Laura Lynne Scharer

Roebling family {Roebling, John (Augustus) (*b* Muhlhausen, Germany, 6 June 1806; *d* Brooklyn, 22 July 1869); Roebling, Washington A(ugustus) (*b* Saxonburg, Pa, 26 May 1837; *d* Trenton, NJ, 21 July 1926); Roebling [née Warren], Emily (*b* Cold Spring, Putnam Co, 23 Sept 1843; *d* Trenton, NJ, 28 Feb 1903)}. Bridge builders. In 1826 John graduated from the Royal Polytechnic School in Berlin. He and his family immigrated to the United States in 1831. He became the leading suspension bridge builder in the country, building four aqueducts for the Delaware and Hudson Canal in Highland (Sullivan Co) in 1848, and bridges over the Allegheny and Monongahela Rivers in Pittsburgh, as well as the internationally renowned Niagara Railway Suspension Bridge on the Niagara River in 1855. The Niagara Bridge proved that suspension bridges could be designed to carry the heavy loads of locomotive traffic. John's eldest son Washington graduated from the Rensselaer Institute in Troy in 1857. Washington fought in the Civil War, achieving the brevet rank of lieutenant colonel. With his father, he subsequently built the Ohio River Bridge between Cincinnati and Covington, Ky, the longest suspension bridge in the world, with a main span of 1,057 feet (322.2 m) when finished in 1867.

In 1867 John Roebling was named chief engineer for the construction of the Brooklyn Bridge over the East River. Washington, as chief assistant engineer, went to Europe to learn about pneumatic caissons. In July 1869, while John was surveying for the bridge, his foot was crushed in a ferry accident. He died from lockjaw induced by the accident, and Washington became chief engineer. One of the most important aspects of the bridge's construction was the sinking of caissons that acted as the bridge's foundation. Washington closely supervised the work done inside the highly pressurized caisson work space. The effects of moving in and out of high-pressure environments were not understood at the time, and Washington contracted caisson's disease (nitrogen narcosis), which left him physically disabled. Washington's loss of mobility necessitated his wife Emily's involvement in the project. While Washington oversaw the project from a nearby Brooklyn window, his wife initially relayed information to her husband, but as construction continued, she gained significant knowledge of engineering and handled many of the details, decisions, and meetings about the bridge independently. The bridge opened in 1883, the last engineering project Washington Roebling directed.

McCullough, David. *The Great Bridge: The Epic Story of the Building of the Brooklyn Bridge* (New York: Simon & Schuster, 1972)

Steinman, David B. *The Builders of the Bridge: The Story of John Roebling and His Son* (New York: Harcourt, Brace, 1945)

Frank E. Griggs Jr

Rogers' Rangers. Colonial scouts in the British service commanded by Robert Rogers in the French and Indian War (1754–63). Based primarily on Rogers' Island at Fort Edward (Washington Co) and serving in the Hudson River–Lake George–Lake Champlain corridor, they were formed in 1756 at Fort William Henry as an alternative to Indian scouts, whom the British found unreliable and difficult to recruit. Initially two companies (about 60 men) under Capt Rogers were formed, but this was increased to nine companies (about 600 men) by 1758 under Rogers, now a major. Rangers performed invaluable service in long-range reconnaissance and raiding throughout the war and after in Pontiac's War of 1764, making surprise attacks on French and Indian detachments that were on similar missions. On one such mission on the west side of Lake George (Warren Co) on 13 Mar 1758, a patrol of 184 men under the command of Rogers successfully ambushed about 95 French and Indians but were themselves immediately ambushed and surrounded by another party of about 200 French and Indians who had run toward the gunshots. Rogers returned with only 52 men from this winter "Battle on Snowshoes," but the Rangers were able to recover, participating in the captures of Fort Ticonderoga and Crown Point (Essex Co) in July of 1759. They continued their raids and patrols, including an attack launched from Crown Point on the Abenaki village of St. Francis [now Odanak, Que] in October 1759 that may fairly be called a massacre, because the Rangers made no distinction between warriors and women and children. The "Plan of Discipline" and "Standing Orders" that Rogers formulated for his Rangers are considered classics in the literature of irregular warfare.

Loescher, Burt Garfield. *The History of Rogers' Rangers*, 4 vols (1946; repr Bowie, Md: Heritage Books, 2001)

Edward H. Knoblauch

Rohlfs, Charles (*b* Brooklyn, 15 Feb 1853; *d* Buffalo, 29 June 1936). Furniture designer. The son of a Danish cabinetmaker of German descent, Rohlfs was born and raised in a working-class neighborhood near Prospect Park in Brooklyn. From an early age he aspired to become an actor, an ambition his father discouraged. Although the death of his father in 1865 forced the 12-year-old to enter the workforce and contribute to the family's survival, Rohlfs was determined to continue his education. Upon graduation from grammar school he enrolled in night classes at the Cooper Union School of Science, where from 1867 to 1871 he studied chemistry and physics. By 1869 he was working for local foundries and by 1872 was promoted to designer of stoves and furnaces. He embarked upon a career in the theater in 1877 but after disappointing engagements accepted a foundry position in Taunton, Mass, in 1881. In 1884 he married the author Anna Katherine Green. The couple returned to Brooklyn in 1885, and Rohlfs again found work as a stove and furnace designer. He expanded his interests to inventing, and a series of his patents attracted the attention of the Jewett Stove Co of Buffalo, which offered him a position. The family relocated to Buffalo in the summer of 1887. Rohlfs began producing furniture for their new home and accepting design commissions from acquaintances. By 1897, after an ultimately unsuccessful return to the stage, demand for his idiosyncratic designs allowed Rohlfs to venture into a third career and open a workshop. He combined a variety of influences—including Gothic Revival and Art Nouveau—into bold, often whimsical pieces of superior artisanship that sought a perfect harmony of form and function. He quickly achieved an international reputation as an artist of great originality and skill: his participation in the Pan-American Exposition of 1901 in Buffalo led to an invitation to exhibit at the 1902 International Exposition of Decorative Modern Art in Turin, Italy, and to his induction into the Royal Society of Art in London. His accomplishments, however, were obscured by his strict adherence to the philosophy of the Arts and Crafts movement, which opposed mass production and aggressive marketing. By 1910 changing tastes led to the decline of his business and reputation. He closed his shop in 1930.

Major Robert Rogers, by Thomas Hart, 1776.

James, Michael L. *Drama in Design: The Life and Craft of Charles Rohlfs* (Buffalo: Burchfield Art Center/Buffalo State College Foundation, 1994)

Ellen Prokop

Rom. See Gypsies.

Romanians. Because of changing national boundaries in Europe during the 19th and 20th centuries, ethnic Romanian immigrants to New York State were often recorded as Austrian, Hungarian, or Russian. In the Civil War, ethnic Romanian captain Nicolae Dunca of New York's Volunteer Infantry was killed in 1862 at the Battle of Cross Keys in Thomas "Stonewall" Jackson's Shenandoah Valley campaign. After 1870 Romanian Jews immigrated from Bessarabia (Moldavia) and Bukovina. Many were crafters and merchants with families who settled in New York City. From 1895 to 1920 some 145,000 Romanians came to the United States, mostly peasants from Transylvania and the Banat. Many earned money as laborers, then returned home. By 1920 the US Romanian-born population was about 85,000, and a middle class of entrepreneurs, professionals, and skilled workers began to emerge. Romanians founded St. Dumitru Church in Manhattan, newspapers, and fraternal organizations. They opposed Hungarian attempts to regain Transylvania but were divided on relations with the fascist government of Ion Antonescu during World War II and the Communist regime that followed.

After World War II refugees and exiles settled in New York City. In 1952 the Romanian Orthodox Episcopate of America split from the Communist-affiliated Romanian Orthodox Missionary Episcopate in America. Anticommunist newspapers included the Romanian National Committee's monthly *Romania* (1951–67), *Dreptatea* (Justice, 1973), and *Lumea Libera Romaneasca* (Free Romanian world, 1987). The Orthodox Jewish First Romanian-American Congregation Synagogue opened in 1988 on Manhattan's Lower East Side.

A new wave of immigrants came after the 1989 fall of the Communist dictatorship. The 2000 US census reported 25,059 Romanian-born New York State residents, with over 46% in Queens and over 85% in the New York City area. New Yorkers claiming Romanian ancestry numbered 51,380. Over 60% live in New York City, and nearly half of those are in Queens. In 2002 New York State was home to an estimated 21% of all Romanian Americans, more than any other state. The majority live in northern Manhattan, Astoria, Sunnyside, Ridgewood, and Long Island. Most non-Jewish Romanians in the United States belong to the Romanian Orthodox Church; others are Catholics, Baptists, Seventh-day Adventists, or Pentecostals. There are more than 32 Romanian American organizations in the state; most, including the Romanian Cultural Center (1980), the Iuliu Maniu American Romanian Relief Foundation, *Romanian Journal* (1997), the weekly *ZIUA USA* (1999), *Zum Magazine, Romanian Voice TV,* and *Dacia TV,* are in New York City. Romanians and Romanian Americans contributing to cultural life include Cornell University psychiatry professor Valer Barbu, Metropolitan Opera soprano Stella Roman, theater director Andrei Serban, tennis player Ilie Nastase, and artists Elie Cristo-Loveanu and Saul Steinberg.

Diamond, Arthur. *Romanian Americans* (New York: Chelsea House, 1988)

Galitzi, Christine Avghi. *A Study of Assimilation among the Roumanians in the United States* (1929; repr New York: AMS Press, 1968)

Wertsman, Vladimir. *The Romanians in America, 1748–1974: A Chronology and Fact Book* (Dobbs Ferry, NY: Oceana Publications, 1975)

James S. Pula

Rome. City (pop 34,950) in central Oneida Co. Located at the 3 mi (4.8 km) carry between the Mohawk River and Wood Creek, its site was strategically important, and a number of forts were built between 1755 and 1758 when they were supplanted by Fort Stanwix. According to local tradition the Stars and Stripes were first flown during a battle at Fort Stanwix on 3 Aug 1776. The fort was destroyed in 1781, and the settlement dispersed. In both 1768 and 1784 important treaties with the Indians were signed at Fort Stanwix; each had the effect of opening the western country to white settlement.

Resettlement commenced in 1784. In 1796 Dominick Lynch (1754–1825) platted what he called Lynchville, attracting settlers to his city lots with permanent leases. In the same year a post office named Rome was established, and the town was formed from Steuben. In 1797 a canal was dug between the Mohawk River and Wood Creek, and it was improved in 1806 by the Western Inland Lock Navigation Co. A woolen factory, the first major industry, was built between 1810 and 1812. The first section of the Erie Canal, originally half a mile south of the community, was completed in 1819, and the village was incorporated in the same year. Later the New York Central Railroad (1839), the Rome, Watertown and Ogdensburg Railroad (1850), and the Black River Canal (1851) served Rome; railroad shops (1863) were an important employer. In 1844 the canal was relocated to the village, benefiting Rome. In 1851 Jesse Williams of Rome developed a factory system for cheese manufacturing that revolutionized the dairy industry in the village and everywhere in dairy country. By the Civil War, Rome was an important trading center for the cheese industry. In the late 19th century, Rome was a highly diversified manufacturing city producing shoes, brick, brooms, cement pipe, cigars, ironwork, knit goods, pumps, shirts, silverplate, soap and candles, soda water, packed pork, and canned goods. The Rome Iron Works (1866), which became Rome Brass and Copper Co (1891) and, in a large nationwide merger, Revere Copper and Brass (1929), produced railroad iron but added brass in 1878 and copper in 1887. By the 1910s Rome firms processed 10% of the nation's copper ore.

The Town of Rome incorporated as a city in 1870 with 72.66 miles^2 (188.19 km^2); outside the urbanized Inside District, the city's territory was rural and remained so in 2003. It had many German and Welsh residents, but it was not until the end of the 19th century that the city's dominant group, the Italians, began to arrive. Other industries developed, including the cable industry, starting with Electric Wire Works (1883). Later Rome Electrical Co (1904), maker of insulated wire, became General Cable Corp in 1927. In 1940 iron, steel, knit goods, sporting goods, and lumber, along with the large copper industry, provided employment. The city was also the site of the Rome State School (1893), whose campus became Oneida Correctional Facility (1988) and Mohawk Correctional Facility (1989), and of the New York State School for the Deaf (1875), which continued to educate young people in 2003.

As heavy industry began to decline, Rome received a boost with the construction, beginning in May 1941, of the US Army Air Force's Rome Air Depot; it opened in February 1942 on 2,488 acres (1,007 ha) within city limits. It employed up to 4,000 military personnel and 9,000 civilians. In 1951 it was transformed into a major research facility for the newly constituted Air Force and renamed Griffiss Air Force Base (AFB). An unusually destructive urban renewal program demolished most of the historic downtown beginning in 1964. Its original conception was a central mall with circumferential traffic and parking. In the demolition stage, however, the site of Fort Stanwix was uncovered, and it was reconstructed as Fort Stanwix National Monument, which opened in 1976. Another historic attraction, Erie Canal Village (1967), created an 1840s canal community on the site of the 1817 groundbreaking. These two institutions initiated development of a tourist industry.

Griffiss AFB closed between 1993 and 1998, causing the loss of 5,000 jobs. The city's population, in consequence, dropped 9,400, or 21.2%, between 1990 and 2000. The remaining components of the base, the Air Force Research Laboratory's Information Directorate and two other military units, were the center of the new Griffiss Business and Technology Park. Revere Copper Products, Rome Cable Co, and Rome-Turney Radiator Co continued the city's metals industries into the 21st century. The city's Outside District is the site of the Rome State Fish Hatchery and the Rome Sand Plains State Unique Area. Part of Oriskany Battlefield State Historic Site is also within city limits.

Field Horne

Rome, Watertown and Ogdensburg Railroad. In 1832 the New York State legislature chartered the Rome and Watertown Railroad. Construction was deferred until the links in the chain of railroads stretching from Buffalo to the Hudson River neared completion in the late 1840s. Work finally began in 1848, but the line only reached Watertown and its original termi-

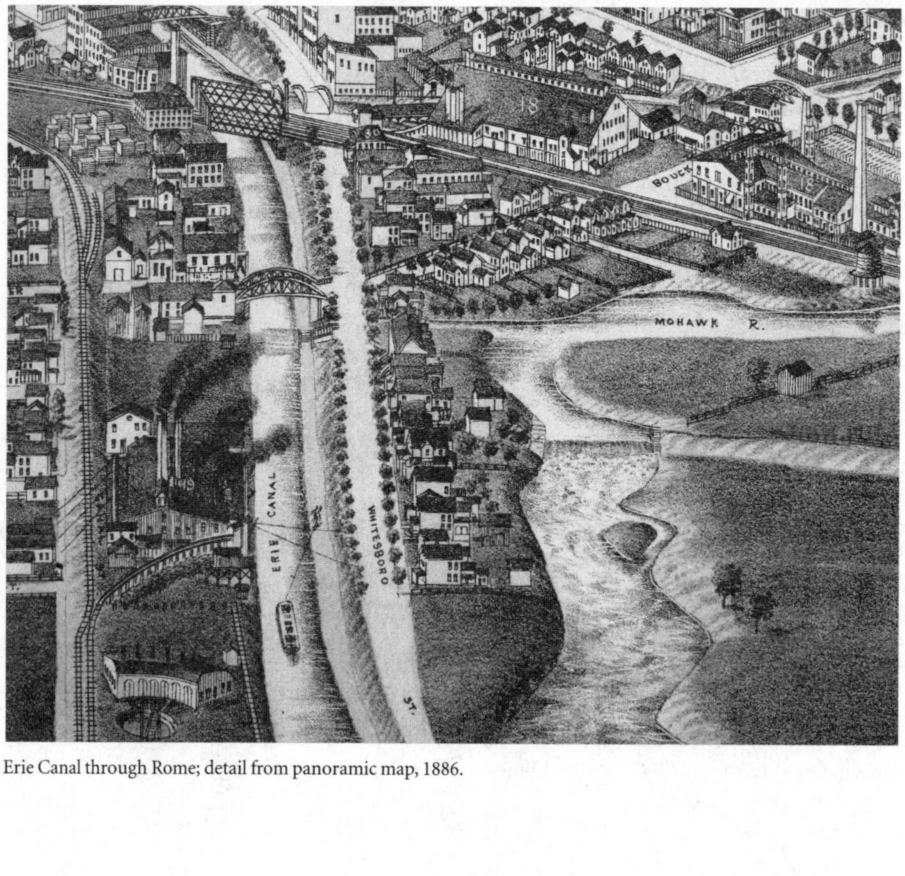

Erie Canal through Rome; detail from panoramic map, 1886.

nus at Cape Vincent (Jefferson Co) on Lake Ontario in 1851. By that time the Northern Railroad had already connected Ogdensburg (St. Lawrence Co) with northern Vermont and New England but had passed to the north of the Village of Potsdam (St. Lawrence Co). The need for a connection between the two trunk lines was obvious to the commercial interests of St. Lawrence Co, and the Potsdam and Watertown Railroad began operations in 1857. A northward spur was extended to Ogdensburg in 1860, and the Potsdam line was acquired by the Rome and Watertown in the following year. Known thereafter as the Rome, Watertown and Ogdensburg Railroad, the line formed a crucial commerce bridge linking the St. Lawrence Valley with the rails, turnpikes, and canals that crossed New York from east to west. Local industry and agriculture benefited from the easier access to metropolitan markets.

Following the Civil War the railroad entered a period of expansion, reaching Oswego in 1866 and Syracuse in 1875. In 1876 it completed a line following the shore of Lake Ontario between Oswego and Lewiston (Niagara Co). By 1886 it had enough strength to take over its North Country rival, the Utica and Black River Railroad. By the end of the decade, the Rome, Watertown and Ogdensburg extended from Niagara Falls to Massena (St. Lawrence Co) with important connections all along its 643 miles (1,035 km) of track. The line was vital to the economic life of northern New York. When the New York Central and Hudson River Railroad acquired the railroad in 1891, the appearance of the Central's top two officials, Cornelius Vanderbilt II and Chauncey M. Depew, at a series of North Country meetings was required to reassure the public that local interests would not be subordinated to larger corporate policies. Most of the lines operated by the Rome, Watertown and Ogdensburg were abandoned and torn up in the following century, but in the early 21st century the freight service that connects Montreal and Syracuse uses part of the right-of-way first acquired by the railroad in 1847.

Hungerford, Edward. *The Story of the Rome, Watertown and Ogdensburg Railroad* (New York: Robert M. McBride, 1922)

William S. Helmer

Romulus. Town (pop 2,036) in central Seneca Co. Settled in ?1789, the town was formed in 1794. The New York State College of Agriculture (1860–61), the state's first, had campuses in town and in Ovid; the first was appropriated by the Willard Asylum for the Chronic Insane (1869; later Willard State Hospital). In the 1940s Willard had over 3,000 psychiatric patients, but the facility declined due to pharmacological advances and became a jail and drug treatment center. Seneca Army Depot (1941–2000) employed more than 2,500 civilians in 1945 and occupied 10,932 acres (4,424 ha) in Romulus and Varick; adaptation to new uses was underway in the early 21st century, including Five Points Correctional Facility (2000), Seneca Woods Youth Residential Treatment Center (2000), and an eBay warehouse (2002). Sampson Naval Training Station (1942) provided basic training for 35,000 sailors at any one time; it was used for the veterans' Sampson College (1946–49), an air force base (1951–55), and finally (1960) Sampson State Park (1,852 acres/749 ha). The town has four wineries and raises grain in support of the dairy industry.

Lisa Compton

Rondeau, Noah John (*b* near Au Sable Forks, Essex Co, July 1883; *d* Lake Placid, Essex Co, 24 Aug 1967). Adirondack hermit. Rondeau ran away from home as a teenager and then worked as a barber and laborer in Lake Placid. Uncomfortable with society, he began guiding and trapping, learning woodcraft from Abenaki Indian Daniel Emmett. Rondeau's conviction that advanced civilization was fundamentally flawed led him to settle along the Cold River in Essex Co in 1929. He called his camp Cold River City (pop 1), elected himself mayor, and built the Town Hall (his residence) and a Hall of Records. Rondeau later said of the years 1930–1940 "I dodged the American labor failure at which time I could not get enough in civilization to get along even as well as I could at Cold River under hard circumstances in the back woods." In 1943 he responded to critics who claimed he was dodging the war (he was almost 60 when the United States entered World World II) by saying, "What I'm doing toward the war effort looks like nothing, but that's all I can do and I'm doing it and it is this—I'm self sustained." Hunters, fishers, and hikers brought supplies and enjoyed his hospitality, poetry, and fiddling. A 1946 article by Clayton Seagears in the *New York State Conservationist* portrayed Rondeau as a colorful Adirondack character, and he began appearing at sportsmen's shows and tourist attractions. He left the woods in 1950, his fame fading after several years.

De Sormo, Maitland C. *Noah John Rondeau: Adirondack Hermit* (Saranac Lake, NY: North Country Books, 1969)

O'Hern, William J. *Life with Noah: Stories and Adventures of Richard Smith with Noah John Rondeau* (Utica: North Country Books, 1997)

William M. Healy

Ronkonkoma [RON-KON-KO-MA] {Lake Ronkonkoma, locality (pop 19,701) in Brookhaven and Smithtown, Suffolk Co; Ronkonkoma, locality (pop 20,029) in Brookhaven and Islip, Suffolk Co}. The localities are centered on the 243-acre (98 ha) Lake Ronkonkoma, the largest freshwater lake on Long Island. A glacial creation, its porous banks make it an indicator of Long Island's water table. Claimed by the Townsend family under a colonial patent, the lake's ownership was in dispute until the Townsends' Middle Island Land and Water Co won a court case *ca* 1930. The area was served by the Long Island Rail Road beginning in 1844. Lakeland post office opened in 1851 and became Ronkonkoma in 1870. Around the turn of the 20th century Lake Ronkonkoma hamlet became a site of working-class summer boardinghouses and, later, of recreation pavilions and an amusement park; a separate post office opened in 1905. In 1908 it became the terminus of the Long Island Motor Parkway. By the 1970s both the lake and the hamlet were eyesores, but major rehabilitation efforts took place in the 1980s. Suburbanization was accelerated by the Long Island Expressway and by the 1988 establishment of the terminus of electric express rail service, which reduced a two-hour Manhattan commute to 67 minutes. The Ronkonkomas are the site of the 223-acre (90 ha) Lake Ronkonkoma County Park, of the annual Hungarian Grape Festival (1923), and of the historic Agnew and Taylor Hardware Store (1888), which was still in operation in 2003.

Luise Weiss

Roosevelt. Locality (pop 15,854) in Hempstead (Nassau Co). Originally known as Rum Point for its taverns, it had become Greenwich Point by 1860. When a post office was established in 1902 it took the name of the sitting president. With improved transportation, including a trolley line, suburbanization took off in the 1920s, its population reaching 8,248 in 1940. Roosevelt's population was 20% African American in 1957 and 40% in 1967, largely of middle-class, first-time homeowners. The integration of the Roosevelt school system in 1966 led to a white exodus, which was abetted by blockbusting tactics by unscrupulous realtors. Though it remains a middle-class locality, Roosevelt had to deal with overcrowding, absentee landlords, and a troubled school system, though local leaders continue in attempts to improve conditions. It has become a center of African American life in Nassau Co. In 2000 the population of Roosevelt was 79% black; ethnically 16% were Latino. It is the home of the United Cerebral Palsy Center and the hometown of athlete Julius Erving, comedian Eddie Murphy, radio personality Howard Stern, and author David Halberstam.

Richard A. Winsche

Roosevelt, (Anna) Eleanor (*b* New York City, 11 Oct 1884; *d* New York City, 7 Nov 1962). Political leader. Roosevelt had an unhappy childhood. Her emotionally distant mother, Anna Hall, and her alcoholic father, Elliott Roosevelt, were both dead by the time she was 10. The orphaned girl and her baby brother went to live at the home of her stern grandmother, Mrs. Valentine Hall, in Tivoli (Dutchess Co). In 1899 Roosevelt was sent to Allenswood, a progressive girl's boarding school outside London. She remained at Allenswood for three years. Under the influence of the headmistress, Marie Souvestre, who instructed the young Eleanor and traveled through Europe with her on vacations, Roosevelt developed an interest in social conditions and leadership. Following her return to the United States, Roosevelt endured her "coming out" year, during which her time was divided between parties and debutante functions and teaching in a settlement house on Manhattan's Lower East Side. During this period she began seeing Franklin D. Roosevelt, her fifth cousin once removed, who was impressed by her intelligence and social conscience. The two were engaged in 1904 and married in March 1905; the bride's uncle, Pres Theodore Roosevelt, escorted her to the altar. In the 12 years after her marriage, Roosevelt had 6 children, one of whom died in infancy. Under the influence of her strong-willed mother-in-law, Sarah Delano, she withdrew from settlement work and occupied herself with social and family activities. Her political involvement was limited to acting as a hostess for her husband during his service as state senator and then as assistant secretary of the navy.

Political Leadership and Activism

In 1918 Eleanor Roosevelt began to seek a more independent role. Following the US entry into

World War I, she organized a Red Cross canteen for soldiers and absorbed herself in hospital reform. Meanwhile she discovered that her husband had been carrying on a sexual liaison with her social secretary, Lucy Mercer. Devastated by the discovery, she agreed to remain in the marriage, but its character changed from a relationship of romantic intimacy to a partnership of political interests and shared ideals. In 1919 Roosevelt accompanied her husband on a postwar inspection tour of Europe and the following year joined his unsuccessful cross-country vice presidential campaign tour. In August 1921, shortly after leaving public office, Franklin D. Roosevelt suffered a crippling attack of polio. Eleanor Roosevelt devotedly nursed him and cared for him. In the months that followed, she joined forces with her husband's political advisor Louis Howe to encourage her husband not to retire and to prepare his return to public life.

Her husband's confinement actually allowed her to create an independent public role for herself. With Howe's guidance she became active in New York State politics in 1921–22, ostensibly to keep the Roosevelt name active. She made a series of speeches and became active in the Women's Division of the New York State Democratic Committee. Meanwhile she joined organizations such as the National Consumers League and the Women's Trade Union League to lobby for progressive legislation. Eleanor Roosevelt's rebirth as an independent figure was complete by 1924, when she campaigned throughout the state in support of Democratic governor Alfred E. Smith's reelection. In the four years that followed, she assumed the editorship of a monthly political journal, the *Women's Democratic News,* and wrote editorials for it; raised money to support the Women's Trade Union League; and began publishing magazine articles. With her friends Nancy Cook and Marion Dickerman, she purchased and taught at the Todhunter School, a progressive girl's school in Manhattan. Using land on the Roosevelt estate in Hyde Park (Dutchess Co) donated by Franklin D. Roosevelt, the three women also built a furniture factory, Val-Kill, and an adjoining cottage in which to live. In 1928 Eleanor Roosevelt helped direct Al Smith's unsuccessful presidential campaign against Herbert Hoover. Through the campaign she gained a network of contacts beyond New York State. In 1928 Franklin D. Roosevelt was elected governor. Although Eleanor Roosevelt was forced as the governor's wife to curtail some of her activities, such as resigning her post at the *Women's Democratic News,* she continued her school teaching and magazine writing. She also went on a number of inspection tours of state government facilities, including hospitals and prisons, and served as an investigator for the wheelchair-bound governor. During this period Eleanor Roosevelt cemented close relationships with state reformers such as Frances Perkins and Harry Hopkins, who would become important figures in the later New Deal.

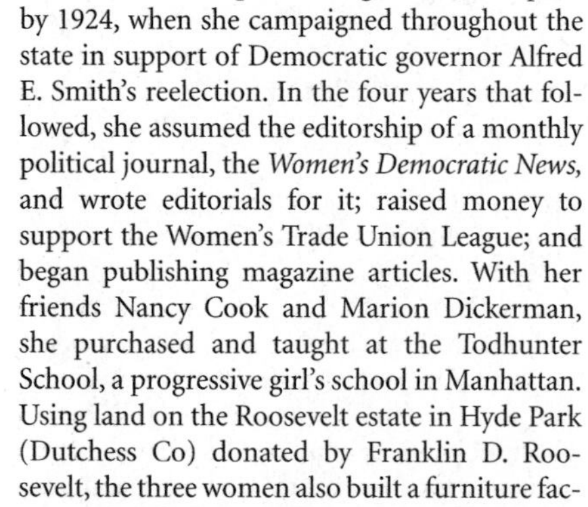

Detail from a photograph of Eleanor Roosevelt in Chazy, 1931.

The First Lady

In 1932 Franklin D. Roosevelt was elected president of the United States. Although Eleanor Roosevelt was initially apprehensive of being relegated to the ceremonial role of first lady, she soon seized the chance to assert her independence. Through endless inspection tours, behind-the-scenes lobbying of government officials, and weekly press conferences, Roosevelt acted as unofficial administration intermediary, intervening with administration officials on behalf of citizens and pushing for progressive reforms in fields such as housing, education, civil rights, and equality for women. In addition Roosevelt was able to disseminate her views and earn money for charities through sponsored radio broadcasts, books, and magazine articles. In 1935 she began a widely syndicated newspaper column, "My Day." During World War II Roosevelt traveled on extended inspection trips to US military facilities both in England and in the South Pacific. She remained active in New York State throughout her career as first lady and diplomat, and frequently used an apartment she maintained in Manhattan's Greenwich Village for meetings and sleepovers. She remained involved with the Val-Kill furniture business until its demise in 1937, after which she transformed the factory building into a cottage for herself.

The Final Years

In 1945, following the president's death, Roosevelt settled permanently at Val-Kill and in New York City. The following year she was appointed a US delegate to the United Nations (UN). She attended General Assembly meetings in New York City, as well as sessions in London and Paris. In 1948 Roosevelt was named chair of the UN commission appointed to draft the Universal Declaration of Human Rights. She spent several months directing the creation of the document and lobbying for its adoption by UN member states. Her efforts were crowned with success in December 1948. Roosevelt remained a delegate to the UN until her resignation in 1953. In the decade that followed she remained active in journalism and political organizing, both in New York State and on the national level. Within New York State she promoted the unsuccessful 1954 gubernatorial candidacy of her son, Franklin D. Roosevelt Jr. She also played a leading role in the New York Reform Democratic Party, which challenged Tammany Hall's significant power in the state party. Roosevelt was active in the national Democratic Party, and her support of Adlai Stevenson was crucial in his nomination as the Democratic candidate for president in 1952 and 1956. Eleanor Roosevelt's career is commemorated in a wing of the Franklin D. Roosevelt Library at Hyde Park, and her home at Val-Kill has been transformed into a museum.

See also WOMEN'S RIGHTS AND FEMINISM.

Black, Allida M. *Casting Her Own Shadow* (New York: Columbia Univ Press, 1995)

Cook, Blanche Wiesen. *Eleanor Roosevelt,* 2 vols (New York: Viking Press, 1992, 1999)

Roosevelt, Eleanor. *The Autobiography of Eleanor Roosevelt* (New York: Harper & Bros, 1961)

Greg Robinson

Roosevelt, Franklin D(elano) (*b* Hyde Park, Dutchess Co, 30 Jan 1882; *d* Warm Springs, Ga, 12 Apr 1945). Governor and US president. Raised on his family's estate at Hyde Park, Roosevelt's parents were James, a gentleman farmer, and Sara Delano, a dominating figure who closely supervised her only child. His boyhood was spent in privileged surroundings. Roosevelt was educated by tutors at home and during frequent trips to Europe, and then at Groton School and Harvard University in Massachusetts. In 1903 Roosevelt became editor of Harvard's student newspaper, the *Crimson,* which inspired him toward a career in public service, as did the example of his distant cousin, Pres Theodore Roosevelt. In the years following his 1904 graduation from Harvard, Roosevelt lived in New York City, attended Columbia Law School, and was later hired as a junior associate at a law firm. In March 1905 Roosevelt married his fifth cousin once removed, Eleanor Roosevelt.

Early Political Career

In 1910 Roosevelt ran as the Democratic Party's nominee for the state senate in the 26th District (which included parts of Putnam, Dutchess, and Columbia Cos). Although no Democrat had been elected from the district for over 30 years, Roosevelt campaigned hard, using a rented car, and won handily. In Albany he associated himself with reform elements and gained wide publicity for opposing the nomination of William Sheehan, a Tammany Hall nominee for US senator. Roosevelt easily won reelection in 1912 but resigned his seat shortly afterward to become assistant secretary of the US Navy; he remained at the post for seven years and distinguished himself as an advocate of naval rearmament. With help from his advisor Louis Howe, Roosevelt remained interested in state politics. In 1914 he sought the Democratic nomination for US senator from New York but was soundly defeated by a Tammany-backed candidate.

In 1920 Roosevelt was selected as the vice presidential running mate to Democratic presidential nominee James Cox. He resigned his navy post and campaigned on a platform of American membership in the League of Nations; the Cox and Roosevelt ticket lost that November. Roosevelt returned to New York City, where he resumed practicing law. In August 1921 he suffered a crippling attack of polio and spent much of the following years attempting unsuccessfully to regain the use of his legs. During this period he became an outstanding supporter of progressive New York State governor Alfred E. Smith. In 1924 Roosevelt began his political comeback with his now famous Happy Warrior speech at the Democratic National Convention, nominating Smith for president. In 1928 he again nominated Smith for president. After Smith secured this nomination, he pressed Roosevelt hard to run as the Democratic candidate for governor of New York. Although Roosevelt wished to continue his rehabilitation efforts, he agreed to run. Throughout fall 1928 Roosevelt campaigned actively, laying to rest doubts about his physical ability to handle the governorship. In November

1928, although Smith lost the presidential election, Roosevelt was narrowly elected governor.

Governor

A two-term governor (1928–32), Roosevelt faced throughout his years in Albany both a Republican-controlled legislature opposed to his policies and a state treasury drained by the onset of the Great Depression. Nevertheless, Roosevelt extended Al Smith's progressive reforms into areas the former governor never covered, particularly programs that benefited rural New Yorkers. He adroitly countered legislative resistance to his initiatives by appealing for voter support in radio broadcasts. During his first term Roosevelt concentrated on administrative reform, most notably in confirming executive authority over the budget, which gave the governor control over the disposition of funds voted by the legislature. In November 1930 Roosevelt was reelected by a 725,000-vote margin. His second term was largely devoted to meeting the massive relief needs triggered by the depression. Roosevelt became the first state governor to advocate openly for a federal old-age pension system and in 1930 passed through the legislature a bill creating old-age insurance for New Yorkers over 70 years of age. In 1931 Roosevelt created the Temporary Emergency Relief Administration, a bureau dedicated to providing assistance to the state's unemployed. Roosevelt also signed into law the Power Authority Act, which provided for public development of the state's waterpower resources. Roosevelt's years in the Executive Mansion were also dominated by a wide-ranging political scandal. In 1929 corruption charges arose in the New York City government controlled by Tammany Hall. Wary of his administration becoming ensnared in the scandal, Roosevelt did not address the issue with the straightforwardness that characterized his response to the depression. At first he resisted an investigation, but public outrage was too strong. The state probe, known as the Seabury Investigations and opened by Roosevelt in 1931, uncovered extensive fiscal improprieties ultimately leading to the resignation of Jimmy Walker, mayor of New York City.

President

Roosevelt's gubernatorial record made him an attractive national candidate, and in 1932 he was elected president of the United States. Roosevelt served 13 years (1933–45) in the White House. During his first two terms, he concentrated on fighting the Great Depression through a battery of reforms, which he named the New Deal. Among the New Deal's lasting innovations were the creation of the Federal Deposit Insurance Corp, which guaranteed bank deposits; the Securities and Exchange Commission, which regulated the financial markets; the Social Security Act, which provided unemployment insurance and old-age pensions; and the Wagner Act, which guaranteed labor unions the right to collective bargaining. A number of New Deal programs, such as the Federal Emergency Relief Administration and the Social Security Act, grew out of programs developed in New York State. A number of Roosevelt's close advisors, notably Frances Perkins, Harry Hopkins, and Samuel Rosenman, had first worked for Roosevelt in his administration in Albany. Although the New Deal did not cure the nation's economic ills, it did provide jobs and inspiration to millions of people. After 1939 Roosevelt's attention was increasingly drawn to foreign affairs. During 1940–41, he championed the cause of American rearmament and aid for Great Britain against Nazi Germany. Once the United States entered the war on 7 Dec 1941, Roosevelt joined the country with Great Britain, the Soviet Union, and China in a grand alliance to coordinate military and political strategy that by 1945 led to the total defeat of the Axis powers.

Franklin D. Roosevelt at his desk in Albany.

The Final Years

Roosevelt remained a New Yorker throughout his presidency. He traveled frequently to his Hyde Park home, and he never lost his interest or influence in state politics via his lieutenants James A. Farley (state Democratic Party chair) and Edward Flynn (Bronx Co Democratic Party chair), and through his alliance with New York City mayor Fiorello La Guardia. To help bolster his support at the ballot box in 1936, Roosevelt, with the cooperation of labor leaders, formed a third state party, the American Labor Party (ALP). The ALP brought under one umbrella socialist and Jewish voters who were inclined to vote for Roosevelt but did not because of Irish Catholic domination of the state Democratic Party. Once formed the ALP provided over 400,000 extra state votes for Roosevelt in the 1940 and 1944 elections. The president's influence in state politics, however, did not always help the Democrats. In 1942 Roosevelt and Farley, by then fierce adversaries, sharply disagreed over who would be the Democratic gubernatorial nominee that year. Farley's choice, John J. Bennett Jr, won out over Roosevelt's, leading the president to refuse to endorse Bennett, who lost to Republican Thomas E. Dewey. His love of his local roots was reflected in his prolific efforts as an active amateur historian, and he published several works on the architecture and local history of Dutchess Co. Conscious of his place in history, in 1939 Roosevelt donated his personal papers to the US government and directed the building of the Franklin D. Roosevelt Library on the grounds of his Hyde Park estate. The library and the Roosevelt home, which opened to the public following Roosevelt's death in 1945, remain a popular state tourist attraction.

Bellush, Bernard. *Franklin D. Roosevelt as Governor of New York* (New York: Columbia Univ Press, 1955)
Freidel, Frank. *Franklin D. Roosevelt: The Triumph* (Boston: Little, Brown, 1958)
Ward, Geoffrey C. *A First Class Temperament: The Emergence of Franklin Roosevelt* (New York: Harper & Row, 1989)

Greg Robinson

Roosevelt, Franklin Delano, Jr (*b* Campobello Island, NB, 17 Aug 1914; *d* Poughkeepsie, 17 Aug 1988). Politician. Born the third son of Franklin D. and Eleanor Roosevelt, his life was defined by the hovering shadow of his famous parents. He attended Groton (1933) and Harvard University (1937) and earned a law degree from the University of Virginia in 1940. The following year he joined the navy; after his discharge in 1946, he returned to New York State and became an influential figure in state Democratic politics. A moderate liberal, he supported civil rights and championed large state public works projects like the St. Lawrence Seaway. In 1949 Roosevelt won a US congressional seat from Manhattan. He was, however, a critic of Tammany Hall, and as a result the machine successfully blocked Roosevelt's attempt to secure the 1954 Democratic gubernatorial nomination. After that defeat Roosevelt resigned his congressional seat and made a bid for state attorney general that same year, an election he lost to Republican Jacob K. Javits. From 1963 to 1965 Roosevelt served as US undersecretary of commerce and then chaired the new federal Equal Employment Opportunity Commission (1965–66). In 1966 he ran as the Liberal Party candidate for governor but finished a disappointing fourth; thereafter he retired to his farm in Millbrook (Dutchess Co).

Lash, Joseph P. *Eleanor and Franklin* (New York: Smithmark, 1971)

Erik van den Berg

Roosevelt, Theodore (*b* New York City, 27 Oct 1858; *d* Oyster Bay, Nassau Co, 6 Jan 1919). Governor and US president. The son of Theodore Roosevelt Sr, a merchant and philanthropist, and Martha Bulloch Roosevelt, Theodore Roosevelt was a sickly child who had asthma and was unable to attend school regularly. Through exercise and willpower he built himself into a powerful outdoorsman and leader. He graduated magna cum laude from Harvard College in 1880, the same year he married Alice Hathaway Lee.

Early Career

Elected as a Republican to the New York State Assembly in 1881, at 23 Roosevelt was the youngest member of that body. He served three terms, 1882–84, and was minority leader in 1883. As a reformer, Roosevelt was instrumental in enacting legislation outlawing the manufacture of cigars in tenements (later declared unconstitutional by the courts) and in creating the first state civil service law in the United States. His bill to inflict corporal punishment on wife beaters did not pass. On 14 Feb 1884 Roosevelt's mother and his wife, who had given birth two days earlier, died in the same house in New York City. Grief-stricken, Roosevelt completed his assembly term and then went to his ranch in what is now North Dakota, where he stayed for two years.

In 1886 Roosevelt returned east because he had become engaged to childhood friend Edith Kermit Carow. In November he finished third in New York City's mayoral race and the following month married Edith. In 1887 the couple took up residence at Sagamore Hill in Oyster Bay. Edith raised Roosevelt's daughter, Alice, and their own five children: Theodore Jr, Kermit, Ethel, Archibald, and Quentin. In 1887 and 1888 Roosevelt devoted himself to writing, publishing four books in two years and starting his four-volume history of the frontier, *The Winning of the West.* From 1889 to 1895 Roosevelt was a US civil service commissioner in Washington, DC. He served as president of the Board of Police Commissioners of New York City from 1895 to 1897, seeking to professionalize and modernize the New York Police Department. Roosevelt replaced political appointment with the civil service system, set physical and educational standards, employed medical and written exams, began systematic training, and encouraged the adoption of new identification, communications, transportation, and weapon technologies for police work.

Appointed assistant secretary of the navy in 1897, Roosevelt moved to prepare it for the war he foresaw with Spain over Cuban independence. When Spain declared war on the United States in April 1898, Roosevelt resigned his post and became lieutenant colonel and later colonel of the First US Volunteer Cavalry Regiment, popularly known as the Rough Riders. On 1 July 1898 they became the heroes of the battle for Kettle Hill and San Juan Heights. After the regiment was mustered out in September 1898, Roosevelt was nominated for governor of New York State by Republicans who believed that, as a popular war hero, he offered the party its only chance for victory because the incumbent Republican administration was discredited by corruption. The Republican state machine, ruled by Sen Thomas C. Platt, mistrusted Roosevelt as a reformer but accepted his assurances that he intended to cooperate with them. Roosevelt waged a dynamic campaign and narrowly defeated Democrat Augustus Van Wyck.

Governor

In his inaugural address Roosevelt made it clear that he was both practical and partisan, but he also gave a reformer's view of parties and the polity, declaring that the needs of the people should be put above partisan interest. During his term Roosevelt acknowledged the power of the Republican machine and consulted regularly with Platt, without whose support many of his reforms would not have passed, while using his public popularity to assert his independence from the party leadership. Roosevelt's unprecedented twice-daily press conferences provided him a means to communicate his message. Using tact and compromise he mixed politics and reform and, although unable to accomplish all that he wanted, frequently saw his views prevail. He obtained legislation improving the civil service system, raising teachers' salaries, setting wage and hour standards for state employees and those working on government contracts, outlawing racial segregation in public schools, and placing a franchise tax on corporations controlling public utilities. In conservation, he expanded the state's Forest Preserves, reformed the fish and game service, established the Palisades Interstate Park, and outlawed the use of bird plumage in the manufacture of women's apparel.

Theodore Roosevelt on a hunting trip in the Adirondacks.

The reputation of the Republican Party in New York State was restored, and Sen Platt and the Republican machine, unhappy with much of Roosevelt's legislative program and political appointments, preempted a second gubernatorial term by joining with western Republicans and others in nominating Roosevelt in 1900 as vice president to Pres William McKinley, who was running for reelection. The McKinley-Roosevelt ticket won in a landslide, and Roosevelt was sworn in as vice president on 4 Mar 1901. Following McKinley's assassination in Buffalo, Roosevelt became president on 14 Sept 1901. At 42 he was the youngest president in US history.

President

Roosevelt transformed the presidency and placed it center stage in the drama of American democracy. Seeking a "Square Deal" domestically, he broke up trusts and regulated big business; started the first federal irrigation projects under the Newlands Reclamation Act of 1902; protected consumers through federal meat inspection and the Pure Food and Drug Act of 1906; provided labor with some compensation for workplace injuries with the Federal Employers' Liability Act of 1908; and saved over 230 million acres (93 million ha) of parks, forest reserves, national monuments, and wildlife refuges. In foreign affairs Roosevelt pushed for a vigorous American presence overseas; his policy was summed up by a West African proverb he was fond of quoting, "Speak softly and carry a big stick." His 1904 corollary to the Monroe Doctrine, defining the role of the United States as a police officer in Latin America, was highly controversial, as were his dealings with Colombia and Panama in connection with construction of the Panama Canal, which he began that same year. In 1906 Roosevelt won the Nobel Peace Prize for mediating the conclusion of the Russo-Japanese War. His "big stick" was the US Navy, which he greatly expanded and sent on a famous world tour from 1907 to 1909. While in office Roosevelt escorted his niece, Eleanor Roosevelt, down the aisle for her marriage to the president's fifth cousin, future president Franklin D. Roosevelt. Roosevelt announced after his electoral victory in 1904 over Alton B. Parker, chief judge of New York State Court of Appeals, that he would not run for a third term in 1908. His presidency ended on 4 Mar 1909.

Later Years

After leaving office Roosevelt led an expedition to Africa sponsored by the Smithsonian Institution, followed by a triumphal tour of Europe in 1910. Upon his return to the United States he found the Republican Party, both in New York State and nationwide, bitterly split between progressives and "standpatters," or conservatives. His handpicked successor, Pres William H. Taft, had sided with the conservatives. Taking up the progressive cause, Roosevelt became a candidate for chairman of the Republican State Convention in 1910. After defeating Taft's vice president, James S. Sherman of Utica, for the position, Roosevelt engineered the nomination of respected attorney Henry L. Stimson for governor, but Stimson lost the election. In 1912 Roosevelt opposed Pres Taft for the Republican presidential nomination. Although Roosevelt won the primaries, many Roosevelt delegates from nonprimary states were denied seats at the convention and the Taft forces prevailed. Charging theft of the nomination, Roosevelt and his supporters bolted the Republican Party and founded the Progressive Party, nicknamed the Bull Moose Party after its robust leader. Roosevelt was the party's nominee for president, and Progressive Party candidates ran for office in most states. In the popular and electoral vote Roosevelt came in ahead of Taft but behind Democrat Woodrow Wilson. In New York State Roosevelt and Progressive Party gubernatorial candidate Oscar S. Straus both finished third.

After traveling to South America in 1913 and leading an expedition in the jungles of Brazil in 1914, Roosevelt led the Progressive campaign in that year's state and congressional elections. After unsuccessfully working for a merger with the Republicans in New York State, he campaigned for Frederick M. Davenport, the Progressive candidate for governor. Davenport was badly defeated, as were most Bull Moose candidates. During the campaign New York State Republican chairman William Barnes Jr launched a libel suit against Roosevelt for declaring that Barnes regularly made deals with corrupt Tammany Hall Democrats. The case came to trial in 1915 in Syracuse, and the jury found in favor of Roosevelt. As World War I raged in Europe Roosevelt spoke out vigorously against Pres Wilson's neutrality policies and urged military preparedness. In 1916 Roosevelt declined a second Bull Moose nomination for president, backing Republican Charles Evans Hughes against Wilson. The Progressive Party disbanded that same year. Roosevelt refused to run for governor in 1918 but was regarded as the favorite for the Republican presidential nomination in 1920, an event precluded by his death.

Roosevelt was a prolific writer. His historical writings include a biography of Gouverneur Morris (1888) and a history of New York City (1891), and he was the author of several well-regarded accounts of his outdoor adventures. The state's official memorial to Roosevelt is the entrance hall of the American Museum of Natural History in New York City. A statue of Roosevelt on horseback stands in front of the museum. The National Park Service administers the Theodore Roosevelt Birthplace at 28 East 20th St in Manhattan, Roosevelt's Long Island home Sagamore Hill, and the Theodore Roosevelt Inaugural National Historic Site in Buffalo.

See also ENVIRONMENTALISM. For other illustration see LEGISLATURE.

Chessman, G. Wallace. *Governor Theodore Roosevelt: The Albany Apprenticeship, 1898–1900* (Cambridge, Mass: Harvard Univ Press, 1965)

Hagedorn, Hermann, ed. *The Works of Theodore Roosevelt,* memorial ed., 24 vols (New York: Charles Scribner's Sons, 1923–26)

Harbaugh, William H. *The Life and Times of Theodore*

Roosevelt, rev ed. (New York: Oxford Univ Press, 1975)
Morison, Elting E., ed. *The Letters of Theodore Roosevelt,* 8 vols (Cambridge, Mass: Harvard Univ Press, 1951–54)
Morris, Edmund. *The Rise of Theodore Roosevelt* (New York: Coward, McCann and Geoghegan, 1979)
———. *Theodore Rex* (New York: Random House, 2001)
Naylor, Natalie A., Douglas Brinkley, and John Allen Gable, eds. *Theodore Roosevelt: Many-Sided American* (Interlaken, NY: Heart of the Lakes Publishing, 1992)

John Allen Gable

Roosevelt Field. Historic airfield in East Garden City (Nassau Co). The Hempstead Plains Airfield or Aerodrome, nearly 1,000 acres (405 ha) east of Clinton Rd, was established in 1911. The US Army renamed it Hazelhurst Field in 1917. The present name was adopted in 1918 for the eastern section in honor of Lt Quentin Roosevelt, son of Pres Theodore Roosevelt, who trained there and was later killed in aerial combat over France. The western section became Curtiss Field in 1920. Charles Lindbergh began the first solo, nonstop flight across the Atlantic from Roosevelt Field on 20 May 1927. In 1929 the two sections were united as Roosevelt Field. During the 1930s it was considered the most technologically advanced airfield in the United States and was the largest and busiest commercial airport in the country. The eastern airfield was sold in 1935, and Roosevelt Raceway opened there in 1940; the western airfield continued until 1951, when it was sold to developers. In 1956 Roosevelt Field Mall, one of the first shopping centers on Long Island, was opened on the site. In 2002 the mall had about 250 stores. The eastern section is the site of Fortunoff's and Merchants Concourse.

Dade, George C., and Frank Strnad. *Picture History of Aviation on Long Island, 1908–38* (New York: Dover, 1989)
Stoff, Joshua. *The Aerospace Heritage of Long Island* (Interlaken, NY: Heart of the Lakes Publishing, 1989)
———. *Roosevelt Field: World's Premier Airport* (Terre Haute, Ind: SunShine House, 1992)

Laura E. Mann

Root. Town (pop 1,752) in S central Montgomery Co. Jacob Diefendorf was the first settler, sometime before the Revolution. In 1781 his family and others at Currytown were attacked, the settlement burned, and three killed during Doxtater's Raid. The town was formed in 1823 from Canajoharie and Charleston; its population peaked at 2,979 in 1840, then declined in response to rent increases by landlords. In 1822 the Erie Canal opened, and Daniel Spraker built one of the most famous Erie Canal stores at Sprakers; by the 1850s it was operated by the Cohen family, who remained the owners for many years. Tanneries operated at Leatherville [now Rural Grove] beginning in 1828. The West Shore Railroad (1883) served the town. In the early 21st century, Root's land remains predominantly agricultural.

James Crawford

Root, Elihu (*b* Clinton, Oneida Co, 15 Feb 1845; *d* New York City, 7 Feb 1937). Lawyer and US senator. Raised in Clinton, he graduated from Hamilton College (1864) and New York University School of Law (1867). He then practiced law in New York City, primarily representing industrialists and financiers in civil matters. From 1883 to 1885 he served as US attorney for the Southern District of New York. Root became associated with Theodore Roosevelt in 1886 while chairing the Republican County Committee during Roosevelt's bid for mayor of New York City. He later acted as Roosevelt's legal adviser. Root was the majority floor leader of the New York State Constitutional Convention of 1894 and subsequently served as US secretary of war (1899–1904), US secretary of state (1905–9), and US senator (1909–15). He was awarded the Nobel Peace Prize in 1912 and was president of the state's 1915 Constitutional Convention. After 1909 Root, an advocate of order and stability, supported the more pro-business Taft Republicans in party disputes with Roosevelt. Opposed to the popular election of senators, he refused to run for reelection to the US Senate in 1914. As president of the Carnegie Endowment for International Peace (1910–25), he led a special diplomatic mission to the new provisional government of Russia in 1917, but he had little impact on events. In his later years, he played the role of an elder statesman, advocating activism for the United States in world affairs.

Jessup, Philip C. *Elihu Root,* 2 vols (1938; repr New York: Dodd, Mead, 1964)
Leopold, Richard W. *Elihu Root and the Conservative Tradition* (Boston: Little, Brown, 1954)

Scott C. Monje

Root, Erastus (*b* Hebron, Conn, 16 Mar 1773; *d* New York City, 24 Dec 1846). Politician. Upon graduating from Dartmouth College in 1793, Root briefly taught school while preparing for the law and published *An Introduction to Arithmetic for the Use of Common Schools* in 1796. That same year he settled in Delhi [now in Delaware Co], where he lived the rest of his life and which provided his solid political base. Starting with his 1798 election to the state assembly as a Jeffersonian Republican, Root served in that body, the state senate, and the House of Representatives in nonconsecutive terms totaling 10, 8, and 8 years, respectively. He was a member of the 1821 Constitutional Convention, where, always vigorous in his political positions and generally a radical, he fought for universal white male suffrage. He served one term as lieutenant governor (1823–24). For much of his career he was affiliated with Martin Van Buren's Bucktail faction of the Republican Party and then the successor Jacksonian Democrats. In the early 1830s Root broke with the latter group and became a Whig for several reasons, including what he believed were Pres Andrew Jackson's dictatorial tendencies, the question of the national bank (which Root considered a lesser evil than Democratic banks), and Van Burenites' thwarting of his efforts to be governor or US senator. Always supportive of his constituents in the Catskill Mountains, Root's final rhetorical stand was in the 1840s for the antirenters in their struggle for justice for yeoman tenant farmers. Root and his wife Elizabeth Stockton had five children.

Hammond, Jabez D. *The History of Political Parties in the State of New-York from the Ratification of the Federal Constitution to December, 1840,* 2 vols (Albany: C. Van Benthuysen, 1842)

Donald M. Roper

Rose. Town (pop 2,442) in central Wayne Co. Settled in 1805, Rose was formed from Wolcott in 1826. Marshes were drained in the 19th century to produce fertile farmland. With the arrival of the Rome, Watertown and Ogdensburg Railroad in 1873, North Rose developed as a depot with several large produce warehouses. A local religious group, known as the Neversweats, arose briefly in the 19th century; forswearing all organization, creed, and ceremony, they held fervent meetings and spoke in tongues well before the rise of Pentecostalism. A significant back-to-the-land colony developed in the 1970s. Rose remains predominantly agricultural, with about 10% of its population living on farms, the highest proportion in the county. Dairy products, fruit, and field crops are produced. The Olga Fleischer Ornithological Foundation established Huckleberry Swamp as a nature preserve in western Rose in 2002.

Scott C. Monje

Roseboom. Town (pop 684) in E Otsego Co. From 1830 to 1912 Roseboom hamlet was the terminus of a short plank road from Cherry Valley. The town was formed from Cherry Valley in 1854. A tannery and a rake factory at South Valley provided employment after the Civil War. The hilly terrain remains agricultural, and residents either farm or commute. Roseboom has the county's largest amount of reforested land held in state forests.

Hugh C. MacDougall

Rosenberg, Julius, and Ethel Rosenberg. See COLD WAR AND MCCARTHYISM.

Rosendale. Town (pop 6,352) in central Ulster Co. Settled around 1680, the town was formed in 1844 from Marbletown, New Paltz, and Hurley. The 1825 discovery of natural hydraulic cement at Bruceville, initially used in constructing the Delaware and Hudson Canal (1828), had enormous significance for the town, whose many cement companies produced half the nation's output. Natural hydraulic cement was largely replaced by Portland cement after 1900, and by 1920 the town's population dropped from 6,278 to 1,959. In 1929 a new mill at Lawrenceville was built to produce masonry cement (a mixture of hydraulic and Portland), operating until about 1970. Rosendale hamlet was an incorporated village from 1890 to 1977, and Catherine O'Leary was elected as mayor in 1957, becoming the first woman mayor in New York State. In the early 21st century, the abandoned cement mines have found a use for records storage. The International Pickle Festival is held in November. The Snyder Estate Natural Cement Historic District and Perrine's covered bridge (1844, Burr arch) are landmarks. A colonial family from Binnewater was slandered by Richard Dugdale's flawed eugenics treatise, *The Jukes: A Study in Crime, Pauperism, Disease, and Heredity* (1877).

Ruth Piwonka

Roslyn {Roslyn, village (pop 2,570) in North Hempstead, Nassau Co; Roslyn Estates, village (pop 1,210) in North Hempstead; Roslyn Harbor, village (pop 1,023) in North Hempstead and Oyster Bay, Nassau Co; Roslyn Heights, locality (pop 10,665) in North Hempstead}. Roslyn was the first European-settled place in the present North Hempstead Town (1644). Known by 1709 as Head of Hempstead Harbor, after the body of water on which it is located, its post office was changed to Roslyn in 1844. It was a commercial and industrial center in the 18th and 19th centuries; its paper mill (1773) was the first on Long Island. Roslyn incorporated in 1932. Population grew dramatically from 1945 to 1960 and again in the 1990s (an increase of 31%), when over 30 new homes were built. Landmarks include the Van Nostrand–Starkins House (1680), oldest in the county and now a museum; a gristmill (*ca* 1730, on site of an earlier mill); the Bryant Library (1878); the Ellen E. Ward Clock Tower (1895); and Trinity Episcopal Church (1907), designed by Stanford White. The Main Street Historic District (1962) and the Roslyn Village Historic District (1967) placed dozens of buildings on the National Register of Historic Places. The business district, housed in historical buildings along Old Northern Blvd, serves as the center of the greater Roslyn area.

Roslyn Estates is composed of 263 acres (106 ha) of private homes. The first residential development was begun in 1906; five years later its residents formed the first residents association in the area. The village incorporated in 1931. Roslyn Estates was the home of author Christopher Morley (1890–1957) after 1920; his studio, the Knothole, lies in Christopher Morley Park in North Hills. The village is entirely residential; its population doubled in the 1950s.

In the 19th century Roslyn Harbor was the site of a steamboat dock, a small industrial area, and farms. Beginning in 1843 it was the home of William Cullen Bryant, whose home, Cedarmere, is operated as a house museum by Nassau Co. In the late 19th century it became an area of great estates; the former Lloyd Bryce/Childs Frick mansion is now the Nassau County Museum of Art. The village incorporated in 1931; its population more than doubled in the 1950s.

The Glen Cove branch of Long Island Rail Road arrived at the present Roslyn Heights in 1864, creating a commercial district around the station. Residential development began in 1899; initially divided into Roslyn Highlands and Roslyn Heights, it became known as the Heights. A post office was established in 1913, and the Roslyn High School was erected 1925 and replaced in 1971. Roslyn Heights, an area of mixed commercial and residential use, underwent substantial population growth from 1945 to 1960. Author Michael Crichton grew up in Roslyn Heights.

Myrna Sloam

Rossie [RAW-SEA]. Town (pop 787) in SW St. Lawrence Co. Settled in 1807, the town was formed in 1813 from Russell. Scottish settlers arrived between 1818 and 1832. Iron mining began in 1812, and the first blast furnace in northern New York State operated intermittently from 1815 to 1867. Lead mining began in 1837, and a foundry operated from 1848–49 to 1887. Railroad service was provided by the Potsdam and Watertown (1854). Woolens were produced by a Wegatchie mill in the late 19th and early 20th centuries. Mining ended in the early 20th century. Rossie remains largely covered by farmland and forest. The old stone mill buildings in Rossie hamlet, at the Indian River falls, are built of attractive yellow sandstone. The Yellow Lake State Multiple Use Area is in town.

Richard E. Mooers

Roswell Park Cancer Institute. On 29 Apr 1898 Dr Roswell Park (1852–1914), an outstanding surgeon of the late 19th and early 20th centuries, with the political help of *Buffalo Evening News* founder and publisher Edward H. Butler, received a $10,000 grant from New York State to establish a cancer research institute at the University of Buffalo, to be known as the New York State Pathological Laboratory. Park improved on traditional cancer treatment by providing an organized effort to investigate the nature of cancer and to pursue treatment in a devoted institutional setting through multidisciplinary research involving the fields of biology, chemistry, physics, and medicine. Park's revolutionary approach led the state government to support a cancer institute and to recognize that cancer was a growing public health problem. In 1911 the institute became a state institution known as the New York State Institute for the Study of Malignant Diseases, changing its name in 1946 to Roswell Park Memorial Institute. Other states and countries (England, Germany, Russia, France, and Japan) followed the lead of the Roswell Park Memorial Institute, which became the blueprint for modern-day comprehensive cancer centers, particularly those developed since the passage of the National Cancer Act (1971). The institute's current name was adopted in 1992, and, with a staff of more than 2,400, the institute is internationally recognized. In 1998 the institute ended its association with the New York State Department of Health and became a New York State public benefit corporation.

Mirand, Edwin A. *Legacy and History of Roswell Park Cancer Institute, 1898–1998* (Virginia Beach, Va: Donning, 1998)

Edwin A. Mirand

Rotterdam. Town (pop 28,316) in SW Schenectady Co. Settled by 1658, the town was formed from Schenectady in 1820. Broomcorn was once an important crop, introduced to Rotterdam farmers by nearby Shakers. The first railroad through town was the Utica and Schenectady (1836). Rotterdam Junction was later both the freight center for railroads including the New York Central, the West Shore, and the Boston and Maine, and the site of Locks 8 and 9 of the Barge Canal. Most of the manufacturing facilities of the General Electric Co complex were in Rotterdam. Commercial development increased in town after World War II; shopping complexes were built in the 1960s and 1970s. Commercial operations in Rotterdam include the headquarters and warehouse facilities for the Golub Corp (Price Chopper supermarkets), Rotterdam Industrial Park, and Rotterdam Square Mall (1988). The Jan Pieter Mabee House (*ca* 1700) was under restoration in 2003.

Stephanie Przybylek and Christopher Hunter

Round Lake. Village (pop 604) in Malta (Saratoga Co). Founded in 1868 as the Round Lake Camp Meeting Association of the Methodist Episcopal Church, the community evolved into a summer religious, cultural, and educational center. The timber-frame auditorium, the association's spiritual center, was built in 1885 and housed a Ferris tracker organ (1847), installed in 1888. Begun as a communal tent site, Round Lake evolved into a resort of private cottages that declined in the early 20th century. The business district, known as the Arcade, burned in 1917 and the Round Lake Hotel (1878, various names) burned in 1933, but the Northway (1963) made the village accessible for commuters. In 1968 the association dissolved and leaseholders were given the option to exchange shares for deeds. Incorporated as a village in 1969, Round Lake experienced a renaissance as a bedroom community of Albany, and many of its houses were restored.

Jon Sterngass

Rouses Point. Village (pop 2,277) in Champlain (Clinton Co). Settled in 1783 by Jacques Rouse, it became a lake port and commercial center after 1800. It was the site of repair shops and depots connected with the Northern Railroad (later Rutland Railroad) after 1854. The village incorporated in 1877. Today it is a commercial center, the home of Wyeth Pharmaceuticals (1934), an important port of entry on the international border, and the site of many warehouses and import-export businesses engaged in international trade.

Thomas A. Rumney

Ironworks ruins at Rossie.

Route 5. State highway from Albany to Buffalo. With the beginning of road improvements to facilitate development and commerce in western New York State, a series of turnpikes were built linking the state capital with Black Rock [now in Erie Co] on Lake Erie. The first to incorporate was the Albany and Schenectady Turnpike in 1797 (built 1802–5). It was linked by a long wooden bridge over the Mohawk River to Scotia [now in Schenectady Co] and the start of the Mohawk Turnpike, which ran to Utica, connecting there with the Seneca Turnpike to Canandaigua (Ontario Co); both those roads incorporated in 1800. The Ontario and Genesee Turnpike (incorporated 1807) completed the link from Canandaigua to Black Rock soon after the War of 1812. These four turnpikes formed one of the most important migrant routes westward but came under competition from the Erie Canal (1825) and, especially, from the completed railroad system a few decades later. By that time the unprofitable turnpikes had reverted to public ownership. Under the Good Roads Movement at the beginning of the 20th century, selected roads were paved; among the first were sections of the present Rte 5 as early as 1904–5 in Colonie (Albany Co). In the 1920s, the 299 mi (481 km) route was designated the Iroquois Trail, but the numbered system became dominant. In 1954 the Thruway diverted most of Rte 5's long-distance traffic, but it remains a heavily traveled route, especially in the major cities it traverses.

Route 9. See US 9.

Route 17 and Interstate 86. Limited-access highway from Mina (Chautauqua Co) to Suffern (Rockland Co). At Harriman (Orange Co) it connects to the New York State Thruway. In Waverly (Tioga Co) the highway crosses briefly into Pennsylvania, and beyond Mina the road continues in Pennsylvania connecting with I-90 east of Erie. The original Rte 17 was constructed in the late 1920s over existing roads, including Rte 4 near Liberty (Sullivan Co), Rte 434 in Binghamton, and Rte 417 west of Corning (Steuben Co). Calls for expanding the road into a modern, limited-access highway grew in the late 1940s. The New York State Thruway Authority, fearing competition from the toll-free east-west route across the state, blocked three attempts (1958, 1962, 1968) to have the road included in the Interstate Highway System. Nevertheless, the state went ahead in stages, expanding Rte 17 (known informally as the Quickway east of Binghamton and as the Southern Tier Expressway west of Binghamton) as far west as Tioga Co between 1951 and 1969. Several battles raged over its expansion in the 1960s and 1970s. Fly fishing enthusiasts unsuccessfully tried to reroute the road away from the Beaver Kill in Delaware Co. The Apalachin Marsh in Tioga Co was preserved by construction of the road: the eastbound and westbound lanes form boundaries for the fragile ecosystem. In Cattaraugus Co the highway passes through the Allegany Indian Reservation, whose residents fought New York State over its location for 17 years. When the road was finally built through the reservation in 1981, the state compensated the Seneca Nation of Indians by providing adjacent land equal in size to the land used in road construction. In 1998 the final four-lane segment was built, completing the Rte 17 Expressway (389 mi/626 km; 8 mi/13 km are in Pennsylvania). In 1997 US senator Daniel Patrick Moynihan led the drive to designate it as I-86. The first part was so designated from Mina to Corning in 1999. After further improvements to at-grade intersections, the rest of the road will become part of I-86 by 2012.

See also ARCHITECTS AND ARCHITECTURE, MOHAWK VALLEY.

Quickway, http://www.nycroads.com/roads/I-86_NY/

Joann Lindstrom

Route 20. See US 20.

rowing and crew. Boat racing in small craft with one to eight rowers. Rowed races in New York State date at least to the colonial period; unofficial competition led to organized racing in specialized boats by the early 19th century. One of the earliest documented races was between two New York City Whitehall boats, 12–24 ft (3.7–7.3 m) rowboats used for harbor navigation and named for their origin at Whitehall St in Manhattan. In 1811 the Whitehall fours *Knickerbocker* and *Invincible* raced from Harsimus, NJ, to the Battery in Manhattan. Whitehall boats were used in several important events, including the 1824 race between the Whitehall *American Star* and the British *Dart* in New York Harbor. *American Star* soundly defeated *Dart* in a 4 mi (6.4 km) race before 20,000–50,000 spectators and claimed the $1,000 purse. The most successful Whitehall boat was the six-oar *Wave*, victorious in the three regattas held from 1835 to 1837 by the Castle Garden Amateur Boat Club Association at New York Harbor.

Six-oar boat racing between Newburgh (Orange Co) and Poughkeepsie began in 1837, and Saratoga Lake and Lake George hosted numerous amateur and collegiate races. One of the most publicized was the Great Saratoga Boat Race of 1874, when nine principal US colleges, including Cornell and Columbia, sent their best six-oar boats for a 3 mi (4.8 km) race. Columbia won over such rowing powers as Harvard and Yale, and a parade up 5th Ave to the college welcomed the crew on its return. Cornell won the next year. The annual championship at Saratoga Regatta was a major sporting event—even inspiring the Saratoga Regatta Waltzes for piano—at least until 1879, when several schools boycotted the race to protest betting on collegiate rowing. As rowing participation increased, hull design evolved from the elongated working rowboat, such as the Whitehall form, to a sleek, lightweight shell. Wood hulls dominated, though between 1868 and 1901 Waters and Sons of Troy (Rensselaer Co) made experimental boats of laminated paper, the precursors to modern composite construction.

By the late 19th century the Hudson River had eclipsed New York Harbor as the site of big regattas. Crews from Columbia, Cornell, and the University of Pennsylvania established the Intercollegiate Rowing Association (IRA) in 1895, with Columbia winning the first IRA Regatta, a 4 mi (6.4 km) race held on the Hudson River at Poughkeepsie on 24 June 1895. The event, also known as the Poughkeepsie Regatta, moved to the Ohio River in 1950 but returned to New York State in 1952 to Onondaga Lake in Syracuse, where it was held until 1995. Collegiate rowing declined in the early 20th century, except at large institutions such as Columbia, which held the IRA National Championship title in 1914 and 1929, and Cornell, where the varsity eight had six wins at the IRA Regatta between 1955 and 1962. After 1970 there was a resurgence of interest in college rowing. Colgate formed a club in 1974. Syracuse won the IRA varsity eight championship in 1978 and the varsity four in 1980. Women's varsity crew started in the late 20th century at New York State schools. Syracuse women's varsity eight finished sixth at the 2001 NCAA Rowing Championship. At least 22 New York State schools fielded crew teams in 2002. Saratoga Springs continues to host well-known races, including the annual Head of the Fish Regatta, one of the larger events in the Northeast. The University of Rochester and the Rochester Institute of Technology host the annual Stonehurst Capital Invitational Regatta on the Genesee River in the fall.

Adelman, Melvin L. *A Sporting Time: New York City and the Rise of Modern Athletics, 1820–70* (Urbana: Univ of Illinois Press, 1990)
Chapelle, Howard I. *American Small Sailing Craft* (New York: Norton, 1951)
Mendenhall, Thomas C. *A Short History of American Rowing* (Boston: Charles River Books, 1979)

Daria E. Merwin

Roxbury. Town (pop 2,509) in E Delaware Co. Settled in 1786, the town was formed from Stamford in 1799. In the 19th century it became primarily a dairy-farming community, noted for butter and cheese products that were later shipped on the Ulster and Delaware Railroad (1872–1976). Summer boarders arrived starting in the 1870s. When farming declined in the mid–20th century, Roxbury focused on tourism. Ski Plattekill opened in 1950. Roxbury was the birthplace of railroad financier Jay Gould (1836–1892) and essayist John Burroughs (1837–1921). Burroughs's writing cabin, Woodchuck Lodge (1910); Gould Memorial Church; Helen Gould's retreat, Kirkside Park; and Roxbury's Main St are all listed on the National Register. The Catskill Scenic Trail has a terminus at Roxbury.

Dorothy Kubik

Royalton. Town (pop 7,710) in SE Niagara Co. Settled in 1803, the town was formed from Hartland in 1817. Gasport, a hamlet, was named for natural gas issuing from a spring, but the gas was never made commercially viable. The Erie Canal was completed through town in 1824; railroad service began with the Niagara Falls Branch of the New York Central Railroad (1852). Gasport gained a station on the line by removing neighboring Orangeport's station, with the railroad's permission but against the wishes of Orangeport residents, who pelted the Gasporters with rotten eggs to show their displeasure. Wolcottsville was settled 1852–53 by 75 families from Germany; cigars were made there in the late 1870s. The Friend Manufacturing Co in Gasport manufactured gas-driven sprayers between 1901 and 1930. Farming, particularly fruit growing, remains the principal industry. Part of the Tonawanda Indian Reservation and the Tonawanda State Wildlife Management Area are located in town. Belva Ann Lockwood (1830–1917), the first woman admitted to practice before the Supreme Court, was a native.

Nancy B. Mingus

Roycroft. Arts and crafts community. Founded in 1895 by Elbert Hubbard (1856–1915) in East Aurora (Erie Co), the Roycroft Press published books and magazines loosely modeled on the arts and crafts style of William Morris's Kelmscott Press in England. The name Roycroft honored 17th-century London printers/bookbinders Thomas and Samuel Roycroft, and its insignia was modeled on that of Cassiodorus, a 14th-century monk and bookbinder. Less socialist than his British models, Hubbard paid a minimal wage, provided healthful and pleasant working conditions with good ventilation and light, and instituted an eight-hour working day. He also built a library and playgrounds for the workers and established a lecture series that presented a wide variety of speakers. Every June a Roycroft Convention widened the audience for the community's work. The Roycroft Inn (1903) with its 50 guest rooms was established to accommodate the many visitors to the campus. The rooms are unnumbered but bear the names of famous people, exhibiting the eclectic tastes of the founder. Alexis Jean Fournier (1865–1948), the "Roycroft court painter," painted huge murals depicting the human-constructed wonders of the world, the times of day, and the seasons.

With the success of his publications, Hubbard expanded the community in 1897 to include furniture and leather work. Books were typically bound in either tooled leather or chamois suede; the pages were handmade paper, beautifully decorated with borders and hand-illuminated initials. Hardwood furniture was constructed with pins, pegs, and mortise-and-tenon joints. No furniture was individually signed. In 1903 he established the Copper Shop, which produced hand-hammered copper vases, trays, bowls, candlesticks, lighting fixtures, and numerous other household objects. All these products were aimed at a middle-class market. Roycroft employed machine-assisted artisanship while maintaining an arts and crafts standard of good design.

Around 1910, at the height of its production, Roycroft employed over 500 artists and workers. Master artists included William Denslow (1856–1915), best known for his illustrations for L. Frank Baum's *Wonderful Wizard of Oz;* Dard Hunter (1883–1966), a European artist and a specialist in paper who brought the influences of Vienna, Glasgow, and Germany to his work; Samuel Warner (1872–1947), an English illustrator who produced work largely influenced by British arts and crafts; and Karl Kipp (1882–1954), a bookbinder who eventually took over the running of the Copper Shop. The Roycroft Fraternity consisted of dues-paying members who had access to the community's workshops. The Creed, sent to each member upon joining, stated the community's purpose: "A belief in working with the Head, Hand, and Heart, and mixing enough Play with the Work so that every task is pleasurable and makes for Health and Happiness." In 1912 the Roycroft shops received their largest commission: to supply furnishings for the new 152-room Grove Park Inn, a resort hotel in Asheville, NC. Designed in an arts and crafts style by architect Edwin Wiley Grove and his son-in-law Fred Seely, it opened in 1913.

Hubbard and his second wife, Alice, went down with the *Lusitania* off the coast of Ireland in 1915. His son Elbert Hubbard II carried on the business, selling furniture through retail stores, but the community never fully recovered from the death of its founder. In 1938 the campus finally shut down. In 2003 the old Furniture, Leather, and Book Bindery houses the Roycroft Potters and the Foundation for the Study of the Arts and Crafts Movement at Roycroft, which sponsors a variety of ongoing programs. The print shop is now the home of Cornell Cooperative Extension offices. The Roycroft Inn remains open to the public, complete with its original Roycroft furnishings, and is included in the National Register of Historic Places.

Via, Marie, and Marjorie R. Searl, eds. *Head, Heart, and Hand: Elbert Hubbard and the Roycrofters* (Rochester: Univ of Rochester Press, 1994)

Kammen, Michael. "A Little Journey: Elbert Hubbard and the Roycroft Community." In *American Places: Encounters with History.* Ed. William E. Leuchtenberg (New York: Oxford Univ Press, 2000)

Nancy E. Green

running. See MARATHONS AND RUNNING.

rural education. Prior to New York State's first short-lived involvement with educational funding from 1795 to 1800, rural schools were generally associated with religious congregations, which continued to maintain them when state funding ceased. With the passage of the Common School Law of 1812, they were slowly incorporated into the state school system. From the colonial period into the mid-1800s, schools emphasized literacy and mathematics while occupational skills were learned at home through apprenticeship in the family business and engagement in household tasks. Cultural knowledge and moral attitudes were developed jointly by church, home, and school, and rural schools have had consistently high enrollment throughout their history.

New York State's rural economy matured in the first half of the 19th century with the development of the Erie Canal, new roads and railroads, and the rapid settlement of the western portions of the state. In this period of religious revivalism, the geographically defined common schools adopted a generalized Protestant curriculum. The maturing economy also brought increased industrialization and economic opportunity for rural youth. Many parents now worked for others, and home apprenticeships were often no longer possible. Schools started teaching social and vocational skills and worked to inculcate morals and to develop a common culture. Throughout the 19th century, academies—sometimes called seminaries, literary institutes, or people's colleges—served rural areas as equivalents to modern high schools, vocational schools, and community colleges. Combining practical and classical instruction, these schools were generally nonsectarian in instruction though denominational in organization and support. After passage of the Union Free School Law of 1853, many of these joined the emerging system of public high schools. Others gradually developed into colleges or universities, such as Syracuse University.

During the latter half of the 19th century, legislators and state education officials worked to build a truly statewide school system. In 1895 responsibility for the maintenance and support of a system of free schooling became part of the state constitution. The State Education Department (SED) was created in 1904 to oversee and administer common and high schools. By the first decades of the 20th century, farming, mining, and timber centers had shifted to the West

Roycroft sideboard, East Aurora, *ca* 1903–15.

and Midwest. Industrialization and immigration shifted the balance of political power, and rural economies and population declined while urban populations boomed. The number of common school districts, a good indicator of rural community vitality, peaked in 1865 at 11,780 and dropped to 9,950 by 1925. Starting in the 1890s numerous research studies focused on problems in rural schools and communities. In 1911 the US Country Life Commission proposed scientific agriculture, farm associations, and schooling focused on farm skills and rural life as solutions. The SED set about to create a centrally administered system of comprehensive schools to take advantage of perceived economies of scale. The number of school districts dropped from 11,000 in 1900 to 705 in 1998, and during the same period, the number of schools went from almost 13,000 to less than 4,000. Almost all of these reductions reflect fiercely resisted consolidation of rural schools and districts. Rural supporters of large-scale agriculture and modernization of the economy generally supported consolidation. Small-scale farmers and rural citizens who emphasized local democratic control and community identity over administrative efficiency and training better suited for urban areas generally opposed consolidation.

The Cole-Rice Law of 1925 boosted consolidation efforts by providing significant building and transportation aid for consolidating districts. The initial round of consolidations created central school districts, typically formed from 8 to 30 common school districts and 1 or more union free districts. This round received the most support as it took advantage of state aid to build new schools and improve the educational program while keeping existing patterns of relationships between villages and outlying areas. In the 1940s the focus shifted to consolidating central schools, as laid out in the 1947 *Master Plan for School District Organization* and its 1958 revision. The state substantially subsidized new buildings and renovations, but rejected all proposals from districts that did not conform to the 1958 plan. With local pride and economy attached to the central school, resistance often lasted decades until the need for buildings or improvements led voters to approve consolidations. For a time in the 1960s, the state pursued "super consolidations," districts roughly the size of counties. The 1,292 districts in 1960 were reduced to 705 by 1999. Rural districts and schools have still not reached the size the SED sought, but Boards of Cooperative Educational Services (BOCES), approved in 1948, have largely provided the level of services desired. Ironically, when rural schools succeed, students often leave their communities to seek education, careers, and cultural opportunities unavailable locally.

See also PUBLIC EDUCATION.

Pugh, Thomas J. "Rural School Consolidation in New York State, 1795–1993" (PhD diss, Syracuse Univ, 1994)

Stern, Joyce D., ed. *The Condition of Education in Rural Schools* (Washington, DC: US Department of Education, Office of Educational Research and Improvement, 1994)

Thomas J. Mauhs-Pugh

Rush. Town (pop 3,603) in S Monroe Co. Settled in 1788, the town was formed from Avon [now in Livingston Co] in 1818. Among early settlers were a colony of 16 Baptist families from Hartford, Conn (1804) and a community of free Blacks. Farms produced wheat, which was succeeded by potatoes and cabbage. The New York Central Railroad (1853) and the Genesee Valley Railroad (1854) crossed at Rush Junction. Later the town was also served by the Lehigh Valley Railroad (1892). I-390 (1980) facilitated commutation to Rochester, although the town is largely rural in 2002. It is home to the Rochester and Genesee Valley Railroad Museum (1971), the New York Museum of Transportation (1975), and the Industry School (1907), a detention school for boys. The Oak Openings State Unique Area contains 131 acres (53 ha) of prairie-like land.

Carolyn Vacca

Rushford. Town (pop 1,259) in NW Allegany Co. Settled in 1808, the town was formed in 1816 from Caneadea. A woolen factory (1840–73) employed 15–20 hands; a foundry (1844) manufactured "cheese factory furnishing goods" in the 1870s. In the mid–19th century East Rushford was home to a foundry, tannery, chair factory, and a melodeon factory. Rushford was the first place in the state to make pineapple cheese. In 1861 the state's first test well was drilled for oil, and Rochester Gas and Electric Corp created Rushford Lake (1927) to generate hydroelectric power. A resort community, Hillcrest, was created on its south shore. Author Philip Wylie (1902–71) was a summer resident of Rushford.

Rushton, J(ohn) Henry (*b* St. Lawrence Co, 9 Oct 1843; *d* Canton, St. Lawrence Co, 1 May 1906). Boatbuilder. Rushton was a schoolteacher and lumber millworker prior to building light sporting boats in Canton beginning in 1873. His first boats were open canoes and lapstrake rowboats, whose construction entailed each plank overlapping the one below it. By the late 1870s he was building decked cruising canoes for sail and paddle. At the time of his death his shop in Canton had 25 employees working year-round to produce pulling boats and canoes for racing, cruising, pleasure paddling, fishing, and livery use, along with steam and gasoline launches and sailboats. Rushton was known for his fine craftsmanship, lightweight construction, and innovative business practices such as mail-order marketing and cost accounting. The Rushton boat shop went out of business during World War I, unable to compete with better capitalized enterprises like the Old Town Canoe Co, particularly in the production of canoes using the new technology of wood and canvas construction.

Manley, Atwood, with Paul F. Jamieson. *Rushton and His Times in American Canoeing* (Syracuse: Syracuse Univ Press, 1968)

Hallie E. Bond

Rushville. Village (pop 621) in Potter (Yates Co) and Gorham (Ontario Co). First known as Federal Hollow, it acquired in 1812 a post office called West River, which was renamed Rushville in 1819. The village incorporated in 1876. The Middlesex Valley Railroad (later Lehigh Valley Railroad) came through in 1892, and Rushville became a railroad and market village for the surrounding country. During World War II the village housed detained Italian prisoners of war. In the 20th century it had a creamery and a cannery. In the early 21st century its most important facility is the Rushville Health Center.

Gwen Chamberlain

Russell. Town (pop 1,801) in S central St. Lawrence Co. Settled in 1804, the town was formed in 1807 from Hopkinton. In the mid–19th century Russell had a forge, a furnace, and an axe factory, becoming a dairy town and a large producer of maple sugar after the Civil War, ranking fourth in the state in 1875. An Adirondack foothills town, Russell lies between the farmland of the St. Lawrence Valley and the deep forest of the northwest Adirondacks, with nu-

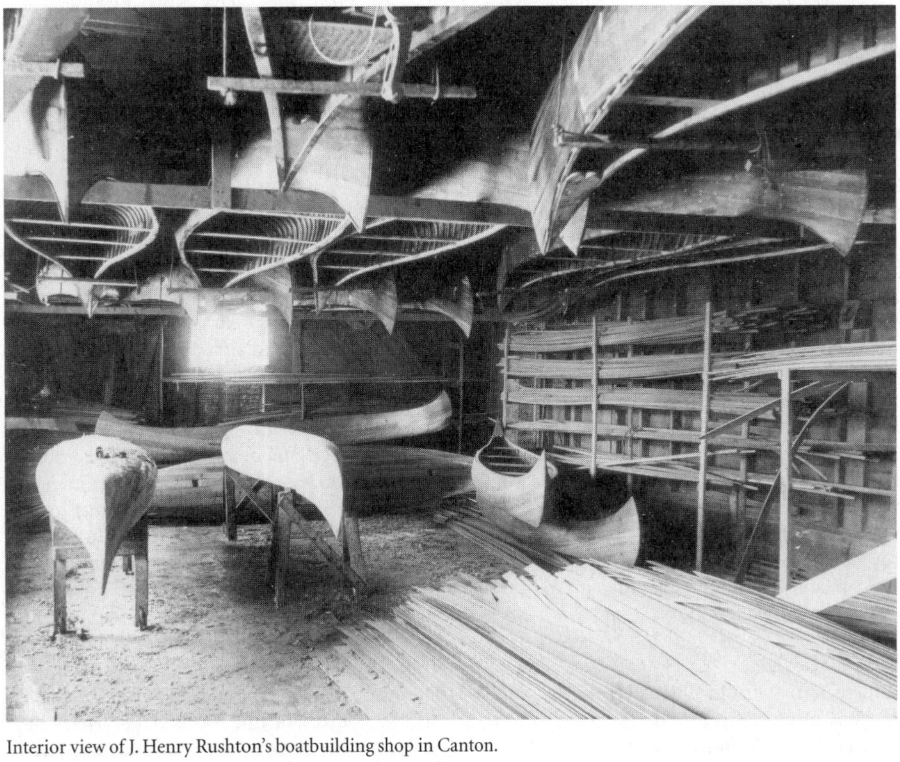

Interior view of J. Henry Rushton's boatbuilding shop in Canton.

merous falls and rapids on branches of the Grass River. Many residents work in nearby Canton.

Richard E. Mooers

Russell Gardens. Village (pop 1,074) in North Hempstead (Nassau Co). In 1924 Capt Frederick Russell sold 60 acres (24 ha) of his estate on Northern Blvd to developer Francis H. Knighton, who after acquiring additional acreage and with the help of landscaper J. J. Levison, created Russell Gardens, totaling 135 acres (55 ha). The village, incorporated in 1931 with the same boundaries as the development, is entirely residential.

Laura E. Mann

Russell Sage College. See SAGE COLLEGES.

Russia. Town (pop 2,487) in central Herkimer Co. Settled in 1792, the town was formed from Norway in 1806 as Union, changing its name to Russia in 1808. It was crossed by the State Rd (1806–8) from Johnstown to Sackets Harbor (Jefferson Co). Lumbering was the primary industry with gang mills, such as the Hinckley and Ballou (1848), employing hundreds of men. Between the Villages of Poland and Cold Brook was a cluster of other industries: an axe factory (1832), a saw set factory (1835), and a saw and plane handle factory. Trenton Falls on the West Canada Creek at the west end of town was a tourist destination from 1822 until the end of the 19th century. Russia's farms were cheese and butter producers. Hinckley Dam (1915) inundated one-third of the hamlet of Hinckley and 1,700 acres (690 ha) of the town's valley land. The dam was originally built to provide water for the Barge Canal and to control downstream flooding, and in 1986 the New York Power Authority installed a power plant at the dam, later named the Gregory P. Jarvis Plant after the astronaut from Mohawk (Herkimer Co) who died in the 1986 Challenger explosion. In the early 21st century there is still some farming but no industry, making the town chiefly a bedroom community.

Susan R. Perkins

Russian Orthodox churches. See ORTHODOX CHURCHES.

Russians. Russians came to New York State in significant numbers only from 1870 on. The successive "waves" of Russian immigration have varied in their cultural background, religion, and reasons for coming. The strength of these variations makes Russians unique among ethnic groups in the state: despite a shared original language, a dedication to maintaining a sense of Russianness, and being considered equally Russian by American society, the major waves of population and their descendants still dispute each other's claim to Russianness and have little contact among one another. Moreover "Russian" has often been used to refer to immigrants from the Russian Empire and the Soviet Union who were not ethnically Russian, such as Belarusians, Rusyns, and Jews. This entry concentrates on those people for whom being Russian was their primary cultural identity.

PRE-SOVIET SETTLEMENT

Settlement patterns for Russians resemble those of many other ethnic groups: the ports of New York City were often the first entry points, and New York City remains both the primary settlement point and the center of a community that has dispersed all over the state. Over 2 million Jews came to the United States between 1880 and 1920, the vast majority from the Russian Empire. Most settled in New York City, almost 1.5 million by 1914, though a substantial Russian Jewish population moved to other New York cities such as Rochester and Buffalo. Their primary language was Yiddish—though most spoke Russian—and they were fleeing difficult conditions in the Russian Empire and did not set for themselves the goal of maintaining Russian identity in any form. Nevertheless, their Russian cultural lineages were evident in their diet, which included such staples of Russian cuisine as borscht, pickles, bagels, and kasha (buckwheat groats); their music, indebted to Russian dance forms; and even their penchant for socialist and left-wing politics, formed in large part by their participation in radical movements in the Russian Empire.

The Russian Orthodox Christians who came at the same time had a far stronger identification with Russia partly because Orthodox Christianity was the official religion of the Russian Empire, and Orthodox parishes provided a focus for expressing and maintaining Russian identity. The first Russian Orthodox parish in the state was organized in 1870 in New York City at 941 2d Ave. Services were held in both Slavonic and English. Russian immigration to New York State continued in large numbers to the beginning of World War I, when it was estimated that about 50,000 non–Jewish Russian immigrants had settled in the United States. Most of these came because of precarious economic conditions and tended to be of peasant or working-class backgrounds. As a result they found themselves competing with other immigrants for low-paid, strenuous physical work, and many returned to Russia. There were enough educated Russians, however, for Russian language activities to take root. The Russian Symphonic Orchestra was established in New York City in 1906. *Novoe Russkoe Slovo,* the oldest Russian American newspaper in existence, was founded in New York City in 1910. The Rev Alexander Horovetzky organized the St. Nicholas Russian Orthodox Cathedral Choir, which was sponsored by the millionaire Charles R. Crane.

FIRST WAVE

The back-and-forth pattern of migration came to an end after the Bolshevik Revolution of 1917. It was during this time that the so-called first wave of Russian immigrants came to New York State, numbering approximately 70,000. Because the "Red Terror," first aimed at members of the upper and middle classes, this was an elite group—nobility, army officers, landowners, clergy, professionals—often fleeing for their lives. Although millions went to Europe, thousands came to New York City. Their high level of education defined the organizations they formed. In New York City the Russian Collegiate Institute supported higher education for the immigrants, and the Fund for the Relief of Russian Writers and Scientists sponsored lectures and concerts. Prominent immigrants included pianists Sergei Rachmaninov and Vladimir Horowitz, and choreographers Michael Fokine and George Balanchine. Boris Bakhmeteff, the former Soviet ambassador who became a successful American industrialist, created a fund at Columbia University to expand its Russian studies program. The Tolstoy Foundation was established in New York City by Alexandra Tolstoy, the daughter of the writer, to aid refugees; it later moved to Reed Farm in Valley Cottage (Rockland Co). The monastic community at Jordanville (Herkimer Co) and St. Vladimir's Orthodox Theological Seminary in Crestwood (Westchester Co) came into being. A small minority, including a number of Russian Jews, supported the Bolshevik Revolution and helped to form the American Communist Party. *Novyi Mir* (New World), an influential radical journal founded in 1911, briefly included among its editors, in exile in New York City, the future Soviet leaders Leon Trotsky and Nicolai Bukharin.

SECOND WAVE

In 1947 the so-called second wave of Russian immigrants started to come to the United States. It consisted of over 20,000 former war prisoners, slave laborers, refugees in Germany during World War II who were not forcibly repatriated, and first-wave Russians from Europe fleeing Nazism and Communism. Most had to work in locations all over the United States, but they eventually returned in large numbers to New York State to work primarily in industry, construction, and factories. Russians from this group tended to cluster around New York City, Nyack and Spring Valley (Rockland Co), Poughkeepsie, and industrial cities along the Erie Canal, including Albany, Schenectady, Utica, Syracuse, Rochester, and Buffalo, where Orthodox parishes and church schools opened. Although some members of the first wave mistrusted those of the second, a shared antipathy for Communism and a shared Orthodox Christianity allowed them to mingle. Together they fostered Russian national identity for their children through summer camps in both the Catskills (Ellenville, Ulster Co) and the Adirondacks (Northville, Fulton Co). They also formed the Congress of Russian Americans, a political and cultural organization that successfully protested against the media identification of "Russian" with "Soviet." Such initiatives as the seminars and conferences sponsored by the Russian Orthodox Church Musicians' Foundation, organized by Nicolas Schidlovsky in preparation for the commemoration of the millennium of Christianity in Rus', became effective means of transmitting Russian liturgical tradition.

Prominent Russian Americans who came to New York State at this time include the writer Vladimir Nabokov, who taught at Cornell University, the widely published scholars Nina Berberova, Pitirim Sorokin, Wassily Leontief, Michael Florinsky, and Michael Rostovtzeff; and Vladimir Zworykin and Igor I. Sikorsky, respectively the inventors of the television and the helicopter. According to the 1970 US Census, 334,615 Russian Americans declared Russian as their mother tongue. Today the cultural orientation of the first and second waves partly reflects church affiliation. The Orthodox Church of America based in Syosset (Nassau Co), which received its independence from the Moscow Patriarchate in 1970, has largely moved to using the English language in services. The Russian Orthodox Church Outside Russia (ROCOR), based in New York City, continues to use Slavonic and the Julian calendar, and to dispute the authority of the Moscow Patriarchate to call itself the "Russian Church."

SINCE 1970

The third wave of emigration from the Soviet Union began in the 1970s. It was predominantly Jewish, because the Jackson-Vanik Amendment to the 1974 Trade Act had linked most-favored-nation status and trade credits to the emigration of Jews from the USSR. During the second half of the 1970s nearly 110,000 Soviet Jews emigrated to New York State, representing the largest Jewish migration to the United States since World War II. They automatically received refugee status and federal aid consisting of such programs as food stamps, Medicaid, and job placement. With a five-year interruption between 1982 and 1987, this wave resumed in 1987. Between January 1989 and December 1991, 106,667 Soviet Jews emigrated to the United States. By 1996 another 156,901 had come, well over a quarter of a million people in six and a half years. More than half chose to stay in the New York City metropolitan area, settling in many of the city's historically Jewish communities: Rego Park and Forest Hills in Queens; Washington Heights in Manhattan; Kings Highway, Boro Park, Midwood, and, above all, Brighton Beach in Brooklyn. The last quickly became known as Little Odessa, and by 1980 it was the largest Soviet émigré outpost in the world. Most Soviet immigrants came to these enclaves through the assistance of private Jewish resettlement agencies, the most important of which is the New York Association of New Americans (NYANA).

Even if they speak only Russian, residents of Russian ethnic enclaves in the New York City area can find jobs, purchase food and clothing, seek medical care, and attend cultural events. In Brighton Beach, Russian restaurants and nightclubs serve as important public gathering spaces where a sense of group identity is forged and reinforced. They serve cuisines from different areas of the former Soviet Union, reflecting a growing sense of pan-Soviet identity among immigrants. Brighton's Russian language bookstores and video stores, movie houses, concert venues, and theaters have revitalized Russian cultural life in New York State. Many Russian language books, CDs, and cassettes are actually easier to find in Brighton Beach than they are in Moscow. Most of the third-wave Jews speak Russian, rather than Yiddish, as their native language and identify themselves with Russian culture. Probably the best known of all Soviet Jewish émigrés to the United States is the poet Joseph Brodsky (1940–96), who, like Nabokov, began to publish in English after emigrating. In 1987 he was awarded the Nobel Prize for literature and was appointed poet laureate of the United States in 1991. Another less salubrious aspect of the recent Russian immigration is the role of organized crime, primarily Ukrainian Jewish gangsters who had learned their trade in the port city of Odessa. Several organized crime syndicates have made their headquarters in Brighton Beach. Evsei Agron and Marat Balagula have been two of the most notorious leaders of the Brighton Beach "Russian Mafia." This underside notwithstanding, Brighton Beach still functions as a cultural home base for Soviet Jews across the New York City area.

In another continuation of earlier Russian Jewish immigration to New York State, the third wave has patronized the same summer retreats—the old Borscht Belt in the Jewish Catskills. These hotels, which had their heyday in the 1950s and 1960s, are once again enjoying full occupancy. Similarly, recent émigrés are reviving an even older Jewish tradition: renting the bungalow cottages in White Lake (Sullivan Co) and Monticello (Sullivan Co) that were the summer refuge of Jewish immigrants from the 1920s to the 1940s. They have given new life to these resort ghost towns, as they have to many fading Jewish institutions of an earlier era, like the Ocean Parkway Jewish Center in Brooklyn. But the American tradition of assimilation continues; in every city with a large Soviet Jewish population, the move to the suburbs has already begun.

See also BALLET; ORTHODOX CHURCHES.

Markowitz, Fran. *A Community in Spite of Itself: Soviet Jewish Emigrés in New York* (Washington, DC: Smithsonian Institution Press, 1993)
Orleck, Annelise. *The Soviet Jewish Americans* (Westport, Conn: Greenwood, 1999)
Wortsman, Vladimir. *The Russians in America, 1727–1970* (Dobbs Ferry, NY: Oceana Publications, 1977)

Nadieszda Kizenko

Russo, Richard (*b* Johnstown, Fulton Co, 15 July 1949). Writer. Raised in Gloversville (Fulton Co), he received his BA, MA, and PhD in American literature from the University of Arizona. After teaching at several colleges, he devoted himself to writing fiction. Working in the serious but humorous tradition of Sherwood Anderson and Sinclair Lewis, he is known for his vivid portrayals of working-class characters and life in small towns facing deindustrialization and economic decline. His novels *Mohawk* (1986) and *The Risk Pool* (1988) take place in the imaginary setting of Mohawk (based on Gloversville), a New York State leather town coping with unemployment and pollution as its tanneries are closed down. *Nobody's Fool* (1993) is set in the fictional locales of North Bath (modeled after Ballston Spa [Saratoga Co]), a former resort town whose mineral springs have dried up, and the thriving Schuyler Springs (based on Saratoga). Other novels are *Straight Man* (1997) and *Empire Falls* (2001), winner of the 2002 Pulitzer Prize for fiction. Russo has co-written several screenplays, including film adaptations of *Nobody's Fool* (1994) and *Empire Falls* (slated for release in 2005).

Stuart Smyth

rustic furniture. Outdoor/indoor furniture made from tree parts, usually with no modification, especially in the Adirondack and Catskill Mountains. Stylistic antecedents include 10th-century Chinese garden furniture and 18th-century English furniture. Early makers were largely anonymous and worked seasonally. Rustic garden houses and furniture appeared in American parks and resorts during the 1840s, at the same time as the Gothic Revival originated by Alexander Jackson Davis (1803–92) and Andrew Jackson Downing (1815–52). Adirondack artisans elevated the craft to a more refined and permanent level between the 1870s and 1920s, making one-of-a-kind pieces with elaborate and fanciful designs, some of them patterned after high-style furniture. The furniture is considered rustic because of a craftsman tradition that continues to the present day in the Adirondacks and other forested areas. Cottage furniture designed for rustic or country living, especially Craftsman furniture made by Gustav Stickley (1858–1942) and factory-made Mission Oak and Old Hickory, is also considered rustic.

Gilborn, Craig. *Adirondack Furniture and the Rustic Tradition* (New York: Abrams, 1987)

Caroline M. Welsh

Ruth, Babe [George Herman] (*b* Baltimore, Md, 6 Feb 1895; *d* New York City, 16 Aug 1948). Professional baseball player. Raised at St. Mary's Industrial School for Boys in Baltimore, Ruth pitched for the minor league Baltimore Orioles in 1914 before his contract was sold to the Boston Red Sox later that year. A winning pitcher in Boston, Ruth was coveted by the New York Yankees for his offensive skills. They purchased Ruth's contract, and he played 15 seasons in New York (1920–34). Credited with saving baseball after the 1919 Black Sox gambling scandal, Ruth's mammoth home runs became the game's biggest attraction. Ruth set a major league record with 29 home runs in 1919, surpassed it with 54 the next season, and hit 60 home runs in 1927. He finished his career with 714 home runs, a record that endured for 39 years. "The Bambino" helped the Yankees win seven American League pennants and four World Series championships (1923, 1927, 1928, 1932). Released by New York, Ruth played a portion of the 1935 season with the Boston Braves before retiring. Though Ruth's uninhibited life off the field often led to unflattering headlines, he remained an idol for US youth and was widely praised for volunteer work with children. He coached for the Brooklyn Dodgers in 1938 but never realized his wish of managing in the major leagues. Ruth died of cancer at age 53, still fondly remembered as the Sultan of Swat.

Creamer, Robert W. *Babe: The Legend Comes to Life* (New York: Simon & Schuster, 1992)

Rutland. Town (pop 2,959) in E central Jefferson Co. Settled in 1799 by New Englanders, the town was formed from Watertown in 1802. The Rutland Woolen Manufacturing Co operated at Tylerville (1811–*ca* 1850), and three paper mills at Black River and one at Felts Mills operated for over a century. Rutland was also a dairying town, producing over 1 million pounds (450,000 kg) of cheese in 1877. In the early 21st century, most residents work in Watertown or at Fort Drum. The construction of modern infrastructure, including water lines, sewers, and a new Black River bridge, is expected to draw new residents and businesses.

Laura Lynne Scharer

Rutland Railroad. Primarily a Vermont corporation, the railway carried freight and passengers and had two extensions into New York State. The Chatham line, known as the Corkscrew Division due to its curving alignment, extended 57 miles (91.7 km) south from Bennington, Vt, through eastern Rensselaer Co to Chatham (Columbia Co). Chartered in 1851 as the New York and Bennington Railroad and the Lebanon Springs Railroad in 1852, the Bennington and Rutland

Railroad leased it in 1870. The line was reorganized in 1899 as the Chatham and Lebanon Valley Rail Road Co and purchased by the Rutland Railroad in 1901. The line was abandoned in December 1952. The northern New York division extended 118 miles (189.9 km) from Rouses Point (Clinton Co) west to Ogdensburg (St. Lawrence Co). Chartered as the Northern Railroad in 1845, the line opened in 1850. It became the Ogdensburg Railroad in 1858 and finally the Ogdensburg and Lake Champlain Railroad in 1864. Leased by Vermont Central Railway from 1870 to 1898, it was purchased by the Rutland Railroad in 1901. The line is credited with the invention of the refrigerated railroad car in 1851 to ship butter to Boston. The line was abandoned from Rouses Point to Norwood (St. Lawrence Co) in 1963. The 25 mi (40.2 km) Norwood-to-Ogdensburg line is owned by the Ogdensburg Bridge and Port Authority and operated by the Vermont Rail System.

Shaughnessy, Jim. *The Rutland Road,* 2d ed. (1981; repr Syracuse: Syracuse Univ Press, 1997)

Jim Shaughnessy

Bathing pavilion at Rye Beach, early 20th century.

rye. A multipurpose wheatlike grain that grows well in poor soil. Rye was grown to some extent on nearly every farm in colonial times, its flour used to make bread and its straw as livestock fodder and bedding. The greatest demand, however, may have been by distilleries for the manufacture of alcohol. Rye became an especially important grain crop as wheat cultivation in the state dropped in the early 19th century. In 1840 New York State produced 2,979,000 bushels (104,977,000 l) of rye, second only to Pennsylvania. By 1850 inexpensive wheat flours from the West were readily available, and the excessive consumption of spirits was discouraged, leading to a nationwide decline in rye cultivation. In 1855 and 1875 Columbia, Rensselaer, Dutchess, and Ulster Cos led the state in rye production. New York State remained a principal producer even as the grain became less important in the United States. Rye straw, which was as profitable as the grain, was used in urban livery stables as bedding. It was also used as coarse packing, in upholstery, and to make mats, hats, and other articles. In the 21st century rye in the United States is principally grown as a cover crop to prevent soil erosion and to suppress weed growth, and it may be harvested or plowed under to add nutrients to the soil. It is used as a cover crop for corn in New York State. In 2002 the state produced 350,000 bushels (12,333,650 l).

Bidwell, Percy Wells, and John I. Falconer. *History of Agriculture in the Northern United States, 1620–1820* (New York: Peter Smith, 1941)

Suzan D. Friedlander

Rye. Town (pop 43,880) and city (pop 14,955) in SE Westchester Co. First settlement was on Manursing Island in 1660 by Connecticut migrants. The town was formed in 1665 and surviving minutes begin in 1672. Located on Long Island Sound, Rye was a major trading center of agricultural products and manufactured goods between the Westchester hinterland and New York City throughout the 18th and early 19th centuries, until the New Haven Railroad (1848) made it suitable for country estates for wealthy New Yorkers, as well as a resort. The American Yacht Club, a group of steam yacht owners, established itself in Rye in 1887. Between 1880 and 1920 the population surged 292% with the growth of a commuting population. Playland, a Westchester Co amusement park, opened on the waterfront in 1928. The southern half of the town incorporated as a city in 1942. The New England Thruway (1958) cut through the edge of the city's downtown but improved commuter access. In the early 21st century Rye is an affluent commuter suburb. The Square House (*ca* 1730) and the Peter A. Jay House are landmarks.

See also AMUSEMENT PARKS.

Rye Brook. Village (pop 8,602) in Rye (Westchester Co). The area, part of a 1640 land purchase, was settled from Greenwich, Conn. It retained its agricultural character well into the 20th century, but its population quadrupled in the decades right after World War II. Making up the last unorganized portion of the Town of Rye and roughly corresponding to the Blind Brook School District, Rye Brook was incorporated in 1982 to avoid annexation by Port Chester. It is an affluent community with several corporate office parks, a conference center, and two shopping centers but no central business district. It is served by the Hutchinson River Parkway (1937) and the Cross Westchester Expressway (I-287, 1960).

Scott C. Monje

S

Sabbatarianism. The belief that a divine commandment obligates humans to devote one day a week to rest and spiritual edification. In the 17th century English Puritans revitalized the doctrine of the Sabbath, transferring the Saturday Sabbath of the Jews to Sunday, the Lord's Day. Strict Sabbath keeping was seen as an index to religious vitality, and on eastern Long Island, to which many New England Puritans migrated after 1640, the Sabbath was strictly observed.

The Reformed religion was established in New Netherland from the beginning, and in 1625 a rule of the Dutch settlement held that the Sabbath not be violated. Despite this the Sabbath was probably not well observed. In 1647 Gov Petrus Stuyvesant promulgated ordinances that made attending divine service on Sunday afternoons and forenoons compulsory and forbade the sale of liquor on Sunday, except to travelers, before 2 PM or 4 PM, depending on whether there was afternoon preaching, and after 9 PM. The law also prohibited all tapping (selling of drink), fishing, hunting, ordinary occupations, and trading during divine service; violations resulted in stiff monetary penalties. In 1656 a new Sabbath law protected all of Sunday from desecration. Religious diversity prevented the state from compelling church attendance.

In 1664 English forces took possession of the province, and a year later the Duke's Laws prohibited Sabbath breaking and declared it one of the abominable sins. In 1685 and again in 1695, the Colonial Assembly passed a bill that condemned and penalized Sabbath breaking, and these laws persisted with little change during the 18th century. In 1788 and again in 1813 the state legislature drew on the 1695 precedent, prohibiting all secular occupations, games, and pastimes on Sunday. The rise of evangelical Protestantism in 19th-century New York State intensified the concern with protecting Sabbath observance. The opening of the Erie Canal in 1825 provoked a debate over the propriety of Sunday travel on the canal, and some canal and stage lines, such as Josiah Bissell's Pioneer Line, suspended operations on Sunday. This was a failure as a business strategy but was widely applauded by the clergy. Many New Yorkers also opposed the practice of Sunday mail delivery. One element behind the renewed Sabbatarianism in the state was an effort by the clergy and others to restrict the perceived disorders among the working class on Sundays, though for most workers, Sunday was their only rest day. The class tensions in Sabbath restrictions were heightened by the growing presence of large numbers of working-class Roman Catholic immigrants in the state, especially from Ireland and Germany, who tended to see Sunday as a day of mirth and celebration, often with alcoholic beverages. By the late 19th century many people devoted Sundays to travel, trade, servile labor, recreations, or worldly pursuits, and Sunday newspapers multiplied. Still most Sabbath restrictions remained in place. It was not until 1919, for instance, that Major League Baseball was permitted in New York State on Sunday.

The influx of Jews from eastern Europe who observed the period from sundown Friday night to Saturday night as their Sabbath accentuated the problem of protecting the faith of the majority and the rights of the minority. As early as 1881 the state legislature addressed the issue by permitting those who observed a Saturday Sabbath to engage in servile labor on Sundays if they did not disturb persons who observed the Christian Sabbath. The courts of New York interpreted the exemption strictly and did not permit merchants to open their commercial establishments on Sundays. The law was gradually broadened to allow Saturday keepers to perform any kind of work on Sundays. Jewish organizations challenged such blue laws on constitutional grounds, alleging that they denied Jews free expression of their religion. The issue was carried to the US Supreme Court, and in *McGowan v Maryland* and *Braunfeld v Brown,* both decided in 1961, the prevailing opinion of a divided court declared that Sunday laws may have been designed originally to aid religion, but currently they fulfilled other purposes, and that they should not be invalidated even if their original purpose no longer prevailed. Nevertheless in the 1970s and 1980s most of the remaining blue laws regulating the sale of food and other items, permissible hours for sports and other pastimes, and labor on Sundays were gradually relaxed, with the notable exception of Sunday hours for liquor stores. This exception was removed in May 2003, after the state passed legislation allowing businesses to sell wine and liquor on any six days of the week, including Sunday. Tradeoffs between diverse religious and secular groups have resulted in a hodgepodge of laws. For many the increasingly pluralistic and secular climate has made blue laws increasingly irrelevant. For other New Yorkers, however, observance of a weekly day of rest, spiritual edification, and gatherings with family and friends add a meaningful dimension to their lives.

Hyman, Melvin, "Sabbatarians and the Sunday Blue Laws Controversy in New York State" (PhD diss, New York Univ, 1973)

Solberg, Winton U. *Redeem the Time: The Puritan Sabbath in Early America* (Cambridge, Mass: Harvard Univ Press, 1977)

Winton U. Solberg

Sacandaga Lake. See GREAT SACANDAGA LAKE.

Sackets Harbor. Village (pop 1,386) in Hounsfield (Jefferson Co). Founded in 1801, it acquired a post office in 1807 and was incorporated in 1814. It was designated a customs port in 1803, and federal troops were stationed there in 1808 to control massive smuggling during the Embargo of 1807. During the War of 1812, the village was the major military post, naval base, and shipbuilding center on the northern frontier; two battles were fought in the harbor. It became the terminus of the state road from Rome (1813). Just after the war a permanent army base, Madison Barracks, was completed; there was also a small naval station.

Sackets Harbor was a commercial port and civilian shipbuilding center during much of the 19th century. The *Oneida* (1818–32), the first steamer on Lake Ontario, was built in the village. Other industries included an early cotton factory and a foundry (1843). The village was served by the short-lived Sackets Harbor and Ellisburgh Railroad (1853–62) and by the Utica and Black River Railroad (1875).

Madison Barracks was abandoned by the army in 1945. After World War II businesses included oil storage, dog food production, and fruit packing, but the village needed economic revitalization. By the 1970s it was recognized that history was Sackets Harbor's greatest asset. Zoning laws (1973), the placement of Madison Barracks and the battlefield on the National Register (1974), and the formation of a historical society (1975) were the beginning of restoration. The village was designated an urban cultural park (1982) and joined the Local Waterfront Revitalization Program (1986); its Main St business district was added to the National Register in 1983. Grant projects and private investment made Sackets Harbor one of the most viable villages in Jefferson Co.

In the early 21st century, attractions include Sackets Harbor State Historic Site, the Pickering-Beach Museum, the Sackets Harbor Visitors Center (1995), and the Seaway Trail Discovery Center (1999). Madison Barracks has been adapted for quality housing, and Main St is lined with flourishing restaurants and shops. Sackets Harbor was much in the news in 2003 when Funny Cide, a thoroughbred owned by a group of high school friends from the village, was a strong Triple Crown contender.

Laura Lynne Scharer

Sackets Harbor, Battle of. Failed British assault in War of 1812. In May 1813, with the American fleet at the western end of Lake Ontario, British governor Gen Sir George Prevost decided to attack the American shipyards at Sackets Harbor (Jefferson Co). Prevost left Kingston [now in Ont], 35 miles (56 km) north, on 27 May with approximately 900 British regulars and Canadian militia and nine ships, but their landing was delayed by light winds. The following day he captured 140 soldiers heading for Sackets Harbor but was still unable to land. Meanwhile Brig Gen Jacob Brown arrived in Sackets Harbor with approximately 300 militia to reinforce the town's 550-man garrison, which had detected Prevost's approach. On 29 May at 6:00 AM, British troops landed on Horse Island, a half mile west of Sackets Harbor, and crossed a causeway to the shore. Brown met them with 500 militia, but most of his command ran after the first shots. The British then marched toward the town, steadily driving back a detachment of regulars and volunteers, who retreated into fortified barracks and Fort Tompkins, located on the west side of the harbor and shipyards. Prevost's men repeatedly attacked the position but made no progress in the face of heavy fire. British naval gunfire was ineffective because only one warship was able to enter the harbor. After several hours and with casualties mounting, Prevost ordered his troops to withdraw. As they did so, Brown threatened their flank with militia he had rallied but was unable to cut off the retreat. The Americans suffered from 21 killed, 85 wounded, and 51 missing, in addition to those captured the previous day. An American officer also burned $500,000 worth of provisions when he mistakenly thought the battle was lost. British casualties were 48 dead, 195 wounded, and 16 missing. The American defense of Sackets Harbor preserved it as the most important naval base and shipyard on Lake Ontario for the War of 1812.

Morris, John D. *Sword of the Border: Major General Jacob Jennings Brown, 1775–1828* (Kent, Ohio: Kent State Univ Press, 2000)

Quimby, Robert S. *The US Army in the War of 1812: An Operational and Command Study* (East Lansing: Michigan State Univ Press, 1997)

Michael P. Gabriel

Saddle Rock. Village (pop 791) in North Hempstead (Nassau Co). This village on the Great Neck peninsula has an area of only 0.2 mi^2 (0.5 km^2) and was developed from a single estate subdivided into building lots. It was named for a curiously shaped rock in Little Neck Bay. The tide-powered Saddle Rock Grist Mill was constructed no later than 1702; it is on the National Register of Historic Places and is a county museum property. Saddle Rock was incorporated as a village in 1911, though it had a population of only 33 in 1950. Most of its elegant housing was built subsequently, and its population peaked in 1960 at 1,109.

Richard A. Winsche

Sage [née Slocum], **(Margaret) Olivia** (*b* Syracuse, 8 Sept 1828; *d* New York City, 4 Nov 1918). Philanthropist. She graduated in 1847 from Emma Willard's Troy Female Seminary (Rensselaer Co) with a teaching degree and taught in Syracuse. By 1857 her father was in financial ruin after being swindled by his business partner, Russell Sage. Her father's problems prompted Olivia to teach in West Troy [now Watervliet, Albany Co], where she became reacquainted with Sage, a recent widower whom she married in 1869. She moved to New York City and for 30 years advocated for the advancement of women and worked for benevolent organizations. After her notoriously stingy husband died in 1906 she inherited $75 million, which she donated to charity and women's causes. In 1907 she gave her largest donation, $10 million, considered the largest gift in the world at the time, to establish the Russell Sage Foundation in New York City; it remains one of the most important social science research foundations in the nation. A major supporter of higher education and a noted benefactor of women's colleges such as Vassar, she provided an endowment to establish Russell Sage College for women in Troy in 1916. In her will she left instructions to distribute $49 million to institutions that promoted education, charity, women, or the environment, and an additional $5 million to Russell Sage College.

Crocker, Ruth. "Margaret Olivia Slocum, Mrs. Russell Sage: Private Griefs and Public Duties." In *Ordinary Women, Extraordinary Lives: Women in American History*, ed. Kriste Lindenmeyer (Wilmington, Del: Scholarly Resources, 2000)

Tricia A. Barbagallo

Sage Colleges. Private postsecondary educational institution, comprising Russell Sage College (Troy, Rensselaer Co), an undergraduate women's college; Sage College of Albany, a coeducational undergraduate school of applied studies; and Sage Graduate School (Troy and Albany). Margaret Olivia Slocum Sage, widow of financier Russell Sage, established Russell Sage College with a $250,000 endowment in 1916. Initially a women's vocational college, the institution offered a core curriculum of secretarial studies, household economics, and industrial arts. By the late 1920s liberal arts, nursing, and education were added. Tied by its original charter to the Emma Willard School, whose former downtown Troy campus it occupies, Russell Sage College was formally rechartered as a separate institution on 17 May 1928. Between 1946 and 1952 it operated a nonresidential men's division, providing two years of education for returning veterans.

In 1949 Pres Lewis Froman created a coeducational adult education unit in Albany, the Evening Division (later Sage Evening College), which offered associate degree programs and a master's degree in education. After discussions with Albany mayor Erastus Corning 2d, Froman established in 1957 an administratively independent two-year college, Sage Junior College of Albany (JCA), offering day classes. The Evening Division began an adult education program at Coxsackie Correctional Facility (Greene Co) in 1974 and for the next 20 years offered courses at four correctional facilities in New York State. In 1989 the division's functions were split between Sage Evening College and Sage Graduate School, and the board of trustees designated the two units, along with the women's and two-year colleges, collectively as the Sage Colleges. Pres Jeanne Neff merged the units' faculties and academic departments in 1996–97. The faculty's attempt to unionize was rejected by the National Labor Relations Board in 2001. Sage Evening College and JCA were restructured in 2001–2 as Sage College of Albany, offering two- and four-year degrees with an emphasis on professional education. In 2002–3 the Sage Colleges enrolled approximately 3,200 full- and part-time students: about 700 at Russell Sage College, 1,400 at Sage College of Albany, and 1,100 at Sage Graduate School.

Paratore, Coleen, ed. *Sage Stories: Essays on the Third Quarter Century, 1966–1991* (Troy, NY: Sage Colleges, 1991)

Spears, George. *Russell Sage College: The Second Quarter Century, 1941–1966* (Troy, NY: Birkmayer Press, 1966)

Harvey Strum

Sag Harbor. Village (pop 2,313) in Southampton and East Hampton (Suffolk Co). A port on Gardiners Bay, it was founded in 1730 on the site of the Indian village Wegwaganok and takes its name from *sagabon*, a native groundnut cultivated by both Indians and colonists. Its first wharf was built in 1761. It was under British control during the Revolution and was raided by Connecticut patriots in 1777; the British raided it in 1813. Sag Harbor was a major participant in the American whaling boom of the mid–19th century. Between 1820 and 1850, 490 whalers landed in the port, bringing cargoes valued at over $15 million, and Sag Harbor whalers hunted the marine mammals around the globe. It was a Sag Harbor mariner, Capt Mercator Cooper, who supplied the charts that aided Matthew C. Perry in his voyage that opened Japan to the outside world. In 1845 the population reached its peak of 3,600, and it incorporated as a village in 1846. The population decreased with the decline of whaling. Later industries included cotton and flour mills, a watch case factory (1882–1931), the Alvin Silver Co (1890–1925), and the Bulova Watch Co (1937). One positive result of Sag Harbor's backwater status was the survival of a large number of structures dated between 1770 and 1850, contributing to the village's distinctiveness; its historic district is on the National Register of Historic Places. Since the 1970s much of Sag Harbor has been gentrified, elevating real estate prices. The Sag Harbor Whaling Museum and the Customs House (1795) are attractions, and the Bay Street Theater offers professional productions in the summer. The village includes Eastville and the planned resort communities of Azurest and Nineveh, where black professionals have maintained vacation homes since the mid–20th century. Literary figures associated with Sag Harbor include John Steinbeck, whose *Winter of Our Discontent* (1961) is set there, and James Fenimore Cooper.

Richard F. Welch

Sainte Marie de Gannentaha. The first Jesuit mission among the Iroquois located on Lake Gannentaha [now Onondaga Lake] in what is now Liverpool (Onondaga Co). After the peace of 1654 ended hostilities between the Iroquois and French, the Onondaga and Mohawk competed to host a mission in their country for the diplomatic and trade benefits it would provide. That fall Fr Simon Le Moyne journeyed to Onondaga Nation territory, where he encountered a "captive church" of Christian Hurons who had been adopted by the Iroquois. This discovery prompted Fr Pierre Joseph Marie Chaumonot and Fr Claude Dablon to follow the next year. The Onondaga requested a permanent mission, and Dablon returned to Quebec in 1656 to seek assistance for the endeavor. That same year the governor of New France, Jean de Lauson, sent four priests, two brothers, and 50 workers to erect a mission-fort among the Onondaga. In July 1656 they selected a site on the bluffs overlooking the east shore of the lake because of its central location among the League of the Iroquois, accessibility by canoe, and proximity to a salt spring.

The Jesuits named the site Sainte Marie, after the Huron mission they had abandoned in 1649 in what is now Midland, Ont. Using the mission as a base, Fr Chaumonot and Fr René Ménard ministered to the Seneca and Cayuga. Although the Jesuits reported many conversions to their superiors, Sainte Marie became the focus of discontent for many in the League of the Iroquois, who viewed the Jesuit presence as capitulation to the French. Learning that the Mohawk intended to attack Sainte Marie, the priests fled on the evening of 20 Mar 1658. After a renewed peace in 1661, Jesuits resumed their work in Iroquoia but did not reoccupy Saint Marie. In the 1930s the federal government rebuilt the mission as part of the Public Works Administration, but by the 1970s the buildings had deteriorated. Sainte Marie underwent a second and more accurate reconstruction, which included archaeological investigations, and reopened as a living history museum in 1991. It was forced to close its doors in 2003 because of financial constraints in Onondaga Co, but it reopened in 2004.

Campeau, Lucien. *Gannentaha: Première mission Iroquoise, 1653–1665* (Montreal: Editions Bellarmin, 1983)

Metz, Elizabeth R. *Sainte Marie among the Iroquois: A*

Living History Museum of the French and the Iroquois at Onondaga in the 17th Century (Syracuse: Friends of Historic Onondaga Lake, 1995)
Thwaites, Reuben Gold, ed. *Jesuit Relations and Allied Documents: Travels and Explorations of the Jesuit Missionaries in New France, 1610–1791,* 73 vols (Cleveland: Burrows Bros, 1896–1901)

James Paxton

Salamanca [SAL-A-MANK-A]. Town (pop 544) and city (pop 6,097) in S central Cattaraugus Co. White settlement began in 1815, and the town was formed from Little Valley in 1854 as Bucktooth, changing its name to Salamanca in 1862. Lumbering was the chief economic pursuit, and the town supported a number of furniture factories through the mid–20th century. The Erie (1851) and the Atlantic and Great Western (1860) were the first of several railroads to come through the area. Their repair shops, built in 1865 and 1864 respectively, along with stockyards, encouraged the development of Salamanca. The Rochester and State Line Railroad was completed in 1878, as was the United Pipe Line from Bradford, Pa, which had loading racks in Salamanca's rail yard. Salamanca incorporated as a village in 1878 and as a city in 1913. Its combined population peaked at near 10,000 in 1930. Salamanca's role as a rail center declined when the diesel engine replaced coal- and wood-powered steam engines. Modern highway access came with Rte 17 (I-86), built in 1965–68.

Approximately 85% of the city had been built on Seneca Indian Nation land on long-term leases, assigned at terms not at all favorable to the Indians. After decades of agitation, in preparation for the expiration of most leases in 1991, the Seneca Nation Settlement Act (1990) authorized new 80-year leases at adjusted terms. Salamanca capitalizes on its American Indian heritage with the Seneca-Iroquois National Museum, shops, and an annual powwow. Its transportation history is celebrated in the Salamanca Rail Museum. A large antique mall in the city and Seneca Gaming and Entertainment, which offers high-stakes bingo and gaming machines, also attract visitors. The Falling Leaves Festival is held in September. Songwriter Ray Evans (1915–), known for such songs as "Mona Lisa," was a native. In 2000, 12% of the population of the City of Salamanca was of American Indian descent.

Bruce D. Fredrickson and Madelynn P. Fredrickson

Salamanca lease controversy. Approximately 85% of the City of Salamanca lies within the Seneca Nation's Allegany Indian Reservation [loc in Cattaraugus Co]. It is one of the few municipalities in the United States situated on a reservation. In the mid–19th century, timber and railroads brought white settlers to the area. After the Erie Railroad was completed in 1851 non-Indians leased land from both the tribe and individual Senecas. These leases were declared illegal in 1873 by the New York State Supreme Court because the lessees had failed to acquire the required federal approval. In 1875 Congress, against the objections of the Seneca government, validated what the state court had invalidated. The new leases had 5-year terms with 12-year renewals and encompassed one-third of the reservation. Salamanca was incorporated as a village in 1878. The leases were renewed again for 99-year terms in 1892. Salamanca incorporated as a city in 1913.

Since the 1870s the lessees had tried to acquire title to the leased lands via allotment, although the General Allotment (Dawes) Act of 1887 specifically excluded Seneca and a few other tribal lands, with the Ogden Land Co's right to preemption blocking any such allotment of Seneca territory. There were several attempts to purchase this right, but all failed. Arrearage had become a serious problem in the early 1900s. In 1939, because one-quarter of all the leases were in default, the tribe canceled 839 of them, a move supported by the US Department of Justice. The test case on the matter was *United States v Forness,* which the Senecas won in the US Circuit Court of Appeals for the Second Circuit in 1942. The ruling affirmed the tribe's right to cancel leases and evict delinquent lessees. None of the lessees were evicted, however, and approximately 75% of the canceled leases were renegotiated at 2.5% of 1939 assessed land values.

Leasing as an issue went dormant until 1969, when New York State authorized the creation of the Salamanca Indian Lease Authority (SILA) to negotiate a new lease when the 99-year leases expired in 1991. In 1977 the Senecas won an Indian Claims Commission award of $600,000 for past inequities up to 1946 because the 1892 leases did not provide for rent increases and a majority of them stipulated the 1892 lease rates (approximately $1 per year). By the 1980s negotiations had faltered. After the issue was heard in Washington, DC, by the House Committee on Interior and Insular Affairs, Congress approved the Seneca Nation Settlement Act (1990), which extended the leases for 80 years and included a $60 million payment for past inequities. New York State contributed $25 million toward settlement. A significant proportion of the lessees protested the new agreement; about 600 lessees unsuccessfully challenged the 1990 settlement in *Fluent v Salamanca Indian Lease Authority,* a decision affirmed by the US Second Circuit in 1991. Also that year, the Salamanca City Council defaulted on its annual lease payment in protest until the 1992 *Yehl v Salamanca* decision mandated payment. There were four separate signing periods, and all but 16 homeowners signed the new lease agreement, which expires in 2071 and stipulates an average payment of approximately $200 a year. By 1998 the delinquent owners were evicted and lost their homes.

Hauptman, Laurence M. "The Historical Background to the Present-Day Seneca Nation–Salamanca Lease Controversy." In *Iroquois Land Claims,* ed. Christopher Vecsey and William A. Starna (Syracuse: Syracuse Univ Press, 1988)

Randy A. John

Salem. Town (pop 2,702) and village (pop 964) in E central Washington Co. Massachusetts migrants who arrived in 1764 to settle the area were soon joined by Scots-Irish immigrants from Ballibay, Ireland. Camden Valley, at the eastern end of town, was granted to soldiers in 1770 and was the last home of Methodist pioneer Philip Embury (1728–73). Salem became the county's half-shire town in 1786, was served by the Northern Turnpike (1799), and was incorporated as a village in 1803. Sheep raising predominated until the mid–19th century, followed by dairy farming and potato growing. The railroad came through in 1852, bringing summer vacationers by the late 1870s. The Salem Shirt Factory (1885) became the Manhattan Shirt Co (1899–1938), and its building served other garment factories until 1989. Other 20th-century manufacturers were Acme Road Machinery Co (1924–36) and Gotham Tissue Co (1941–68). In the early 21st century, Salem attracts tourists with the Fort Salem Theater (1971), and the hamlet of Shushan has the Batten Kill Railroad (1994), the Shushan Covered Bridge Museum (1975), and the Georgi Museum (1991). Mettawee Valley Theater Co (1975) produces original drama using giant puppets. In 2003 agriculture predominated.

R. Paul McCarty

Salina. Town (pop 33,290) in central Onondaga Co. Settled in the early 1790s on the lakeshore in Liverpool, the town was formed in 1809 from Manlius and Onondaga. Salt making, barrel making, and farming were dominant in the early years. The town was crossed by the Oswego Canal (1828). From 1852 until the 1920s willow baskets and other willowware were manufactured. The 1940 population of 11,168 grew rapidly after 1942 with the development of the Mattydale Bomber Base of the Army Air Force and reached 19,125 in 1950 and approximately 30,000 by 1960. Salina became a transportation hub with the New York State Thruway (1954) and I-81 (1959). Industries include Lockheed-Martin (housed in former General Electric facilities), Syracuse China, Will and Baumer Candle Co, and high-tech firms. It is the site of the county-operated Onondaga Lake Park (1932) and Salt Museum (1934).

Barbara S. Rivette

Salisbury. Locality (pop 12,341) in Hempstead (Nassau Co). The name derives from a course Gov Richard Nicolls established for horse racing in 1668 on the "Little Plains" near Hempstead. Originally part of the northeast section of East Meadow (and within that school district), Salisbury's residential development began in the 1950s. From 1960 through 1980 it was in part designated as South Westbury by the census, but its mailing address has remained Westbury. Asians made up 9% of the population in 2000 and Latinos 8.6%.

Salisbury. Town (pop 1,953) in E Herkimer Co. Settled before the Revolutionary War, the town, located on the State Rd (1806–8) from Johnstown to Sackets Harbor (Jefferson Co), was formed from Palatine (Montgomery Co) in 1797 and annexed to Herkimer Co in 1817. Iron ore was mined, and lumber, leather, and cheese were important products. In 1855 the town ranked fourth in the state in cheese production. A shoepeg factory at Salisbury Center and a paper mill at Paper Mill Corners operated in the latter half of the 19th century. The northern part of Salisbury, where the ore was mined, lies within the Adirondack Park. The town has the county's only surviving covered bridge (1875), an arch and truss structure, and holds the Covered Bridge Festival the first weekend in June.

Susan R. Perkins

Saltaire. Village (pop 43) in Islip (Suffolk Co). Located on Fire Island, Saltaire was begun in 1910 when lots were sold for summer homes. The lots were larger than most others on Fire Island, and restrictions were placed on construction and architecture to preserve the original intent of an upper-class summer retreat. The village acquired a post office in 1913 and was incorporated in 1918. The main forms of transportation remain wagons and bicycles. In 2003 there were 401 housing units, mostly summer homes.

Geri Solomon

salt industry. Salt is the common name for the mineral halite (sodium chloride). An estimated 4.3 trillion tons (3.9 trillion MT) of rock salt underlie approximately 10,000 mi^2 (26,000 km^2) of Central and Western New York within the Salina Group of Upper Silurian aged rock stratum. Deposits range from 3 to 800 feet (1–240 m) thick, at a depth of 500–4,000 ft (150–1,200 m). Besides being a human and livestock dietary supplement, salt was historically vital in preserving meat and other foods before the advent of artificial refrigeration. Beginning in the late 19th century, salt has served as a major raw material in the chemical industry. Since the mid–20th century it has been used as a road deicer in winter. Salt was a relatively scarce and highly valued commodity away from coastal areas of the continent before salt mining was introduced in the later part of the 19th century. Salt deposits were first indicated by the saline or brine springs that extend in an arc across New York State from Delaware Co north to Montgomery Co and west to Niagara Co. The largest and most saturated of these, indeed the most saline and prolific in the eastern United States, was a series of springs scattered around the margins of Onondaga Lake near Syracuse. Another far less significant but still productive deposit was at nearby Montezuma (Cayuga Co).

Onondaga Salt Springs

The European discovery of these springs came in 1654 when French Jesuit missionary Simon Le Moyne visited the Onondaga Indians. He showed them how to manufacture salt, and in following years traders would sometimes carry salt along with furs to Albany for exchange. Significant salt production did not begin until 1795, after the Onondaga ceded most of their lands to the State of New York and a small vanguard of white settlers moved into the area. Early production techniques involved boiling brine in a large cast-iron potash kettle suspended between two forked poles over an open fire. Salinity varied from spring to spring but 45 gallons (170 l) were reported to produce one bushel (35 l) of salt. A more efficient manufacturing facility was soon developed. Known as a salt block, the structure consisted of a series of masonry arches that supported multiple kettles over an enclosed fire, all housed within a wooden shell.

Concerned that production could result in a monopoly if left in private hands and perceiving a promising revenue source, the state legislature established the Onondaga Salt Springs Reservation (OSSR) in 1797. The bill directed that the surveyor general survey a tract surrounding Onondaga Lake to be set aside as state land. Part of the resulting 15,000-acre (6,070 ha) reservation was subdivided into a series of manufacturing lots around the most promising springs, along with associated marsh and pasture lots. The lots were leased to manufacturers. The rest of the reservation was intended to be a renewable source of firewood. The following year the surveyor general laid out what became the village sites of Salina (commonly known as Salt Point and later part of Syracuse) and Liverpool (sometimes called Ireland). The OSSR also contained the privately surveyed future village site of Geddesburg [now Geddes]. The act of 1797 also specified that the salt was to be packed and shipped in barrels and that the maximum selling price be 60¢ per bushel. It further authorized appointment of a superintendent to oversee the distribution of brine, inspect all manufactured salt, collect a 4¢ duty on every bushel produced, and serve as general administrator.

In 1798 more than 59,000 bushels (2.1 million l) of salt were inspected. By 1800 the demand was such that, in addition to the market in the state north of New York City, Onondaga salt was being shipped as far as Pittsburgh, Cleveland, Detroit, and Upper Canada [now Ontario], sometimes by a rather circuitous route. Production continued to rise. Salt revenues were used to pay for the construction of a series of "salt roads" that radiated out from Salina to Oswego, Adams (Jefferson Co), Norwich (Chenango Co), and other surrounding localities.

Solar salt vats along the shore of Onondaga Lake, Syracuse, early 20th century.

Getting Onondaga salt to market was a major argument used to promote building the Erie Canal. When the state legislature passed the bill authorizing the construction of the canal in 1817, it also passed legislation increasing the duty on salt from 4¢ to 12.5¢ per bushel to help pay for the waterway's construction. The canal passed just to the south of Onondaga Lake through Geddesburg, and salt traffic was anticipated to be so significant that a mile-long branch canal, the Salina Cut, was made part of the original canal construction. True to expectations salt production soared from roughly 500,000 bushels (17.6 million l) in 1823 to over 1 million bushels (35.2 million l) in 1828, and to over 3 million (105.7 million l) in 1841. Wood consumption was huge, amounting to an estimated 2,500 acres (1,000 ha) or 4 mi^2 (10 km^2) of prime woodland for every million bushels of salt produced. By 1820 the OSSR timber stand was largely depleted, and no effort was made to replant. As a consequence the state surveyed much of the reservation into farm lots and sold them. Concern over the depletion of the wood supply prompted the state to encourage experimentation in alternative methods of production. Not until 1841, however, were significant quantities of salt produced by an alternative method, namely solar evaporation, a method that eventually dominated local production. By 1848 the industry comprised 170 saltworks employing over 2,400 workers, the majority being Irish immigrants. The local German immigrant community focused on barrel making.

Production reached an all-time high in 1862 when a little over 9 million bushels (317.2 million l) were produced (approximately 7 million by boiling, 2 million by solar evaporation). By the 1870s rising competition from Michigan began to cut sharply into extensive western markets, while a halving of the federal tariff on foreign salt in 1872 undermined eastern markets. The state government joined the effort to stave off the local industry's collapse and for a time it worked, but by the mid-1880s business entered a period of rapid decline from which it never recovered. The state bowed out of the industry in 1908. A handful of manufacturers continued until 1926, when the last, Thomas Gale, closed his salt yard on the north shore of Onondaga Lake.

Salt Mining

Although long known to exist in the region, subsurface salt beds were not actually discovered until 1878 in the course of oil exploration near Warsaw (Wyoming Co). Within a decade other salt strata were also discovered in Schuyler and Tompkins Cos. Commercial salt mining began at Warsaw in 1883. Within four years production exceeded that of the OSSR. By 1900 significant quantities of salt were being mined in Livingston, Genesee, Onondaga, Wyoming, Tompkins, and Schuyler Cos. Two distinctly different mining methods were used. Solution mining techniques, used by mine operations in Wyo-ming, Livingston, Schuyler, Tompkins, Steuben, and, in modified form, Onondaga Cos, involve pumping water down to the salt strata to dissolve the mineral. The resulting brine is forced back to the surface, where it is evaporated, leaving crystalline salt. Annual production within the state using this method presently exceeds 2.6 million tons (2.4 million MT). Hard-rock mining involves the extraction of solid rock salt and is the method used at operations in Tompkins, Genesee, and Livingston Cos. In 1994 a portion of the ceiling of the Retsof Mine near Geneseo (Livingston Co) collapsed, flooding what at the time was considered the largest salt mine in North America. In response a new mine was opened by the American Rock Salt Co near Hampton Corners (Livingston Co) to supply highway deicing salt for New York and adjoining states. In 2000 New York ranked third among states in salt production, with 13% of the 49.6 million ton (45.0 million MT) national total.

Kappel, William M. "Salt Production in Syracuse, New York ('The Salt City') and the Hydrogeology of the Onondaga Creek Valley." US Geological Survey Fact Sheet FS 0139–00, NYUSGS, 2000

Laws of New York, 20th Session, Chapter 40, An Act Concerning the Salt Springs in the County of Onondaga, 1797

Murphy, Joseph Hawley. "The Salt Industry of Syracuse: A Brief Review," *New York History* 30 (1949): 304–15

Werner, Charles J. *A History and Description of the Manufacture and Mining of Salt in New York State* (Huntington, NY: Author, 1917)

James W. Darlington

salt potatoes. Small potatoes boiled in salted water and flavored with butter. A regional delicacy, the dish is steeped in a tradition that holds that 19th-century workers in the salt yards north of Syracuse dropped potatoes into boiling pots of brine as a treat for lunch. Newspaper accounts in the 1940s reported that salt potatoes first became a menu item at John J. "Sport" Keefe's saloon on Syracuse's north side in the 1890s as part of a free lunch board. Sport was said to get buckets of brine from nearby yards and boil potatoes in the salty water until the jackets fell off. More recently, salt potatoes have been a staple at Hinerwadel's Grove, a clambake business in North Syracuse, where the owners claim to have served them since the 1910s. Local grocery stores sell bags of potatoes supplied with packets of salt for homemade salt potatoes, as does Hinerwadel's, and salt potatoes are served throughout the state.

"First Salt Boiled Raised on Bar," *Syracuse Herald American,* 15 Aug 1948

Dick Case

Salvadorans. A few Salvadoran miners are recorded in Essex Co at the turn of the 20th century, and a trickle of Salvadorans arrived in the New York City area in the 1960s. In 1980 about 7,000 mainly middle-class Salvadorans lived in and around New York City. The vast majority of the estimated 170,000 Salvadorans living in New York State arrived in the 1980s and 1990s, fleeing the long civil war in their homeland (1979–92). The US government denied them refugee status and political asylum, leaving most Salvadorans without authorization to live and work in New York State. American involvement in the civil war and the treatment of refugees led to a long protest campaign by American human rights activists through organizations such as CARECEN (Central American Refugee Center). Because of their illegal status, Salvadorans rarely supported these political activities publicly. The post-1980 Salvadorans in New York were mainly peasants from the poorer eastern sections of El Salvador. Since 1990, when they were granted "temporary protected status" from deportation, many Salvadorans have been able to legalize their status, but many others have not. Most Salvadorans do unskilled work. Population centers include Jamaica (Queens Co), Wyandanch and Brentwood (Suffolk Co), Yonkers and Port Chester (Westchester Co), and especially Hempstead (Nassau Co). Here dozens of Salvadoran businesses have appeared since the 1980s, particularly remittance agencies, so that immigrants can send money to their families in El Salvador, and restaurants *(pupuserías).* Soccer is the most popular recreational activity, and women sell Salvadoran foods at the games just as they did in their homeland. They are predominantly Roman Catholic, but during the civil war many converted to a variety of evangelical Christian denominations. There are branches in New York City of the Salvadoran-American National Network (SANN), a nationwide federation of Salvadoran organizations, and on Long Island there are a few associations that collect relief for their hometowns in El Salvador.

Mahler, Sarah J. *Salvadorans in Suburbia: Symbiosis and Conflict* (Boston: Allyn & Bacon, 1996)

Sarah J. Mahler

Salvation Army. Evangelical and charitable organization. On 10 Mar 1880 the first official missionaries sent to the United States by the British-based Salvation Army disembarked at Castle Garden in Lower Manhattan. The eight emigrants promptly dropped to the ground and claimed America for God. For the next several days, the seven women soldiers led by George Scott Railton proselytized throughout the city, marching from uptown street corners to downtown missions. New York City's national prominence, as well as its importance as a business and communications hub, made it the optimal site for the Army's American headquarters. Though New Yorkers were unprepared for the organization's colorful style and raucous preaching, which evoked many column inches in the city's dailies, authorities were aware that the Salvationists' sensationalism had caused street fights in England, and they worried about the group's potential to be disruptive. Municipal ordinances allowed only ministers licensed to preach by their churches to obtain a permit to hold outdoor services. This posed a problem for the Salvation Army, which at that time did not ordain clergy. Accordingly the Army's presence in New York City was small until 1883, when it returned in force from its temporary headquarters in Philadelphia.

The Salvationists' zeal to save souls was a strong stimulus for outreach. One or two officers, as Army clergy are called, were dispatched to small cities and towns to set up corps (churches). Once a local group was started, the officers moved on. In this manner the Army "invaded" the rest of New York State, opening corps in cities including Poughkeepsie (1883), Syracuse (1883), Buffalo (1884), Rochester (1884), and Albany (1884). Many New Yorkers, however, thought Army practices such as female preachers, military music, and rollicking revivals were antithetical to Christianity. But the movement appealed to young people, especially women who, eager for service and adventure, saw it as an alternative to restrictive notions of feminine behavior.

Although the Salvation Army was foremost an evangelical mission, its leaders soon realized the difficulty of reaching people whose desperate physical needs drowned out the message of salvation. In 1890 Army founder William Booth's *In Darkest England and the Way Out* proposed "social salvation" to complement religious outreach. In New York City Salvationist leaders were also moving in this direction, setting up a "rescue home" for fallen women (1886), a "Cellar, Gutter and Garret Brigade" (1889) to minister to Manhattan slum dwellers, and a men's hostel and soup kitchen (1891). The success of these ventures encouraged the Army to develop more, and by the Great Depression it was a leading national social welfare provider. By early 1933 Salvationists were giving New York City's needy 100,000 meals and 25,000 lodgings free of charge each week. When the city ran out of beds, it asked the Army to provide more, and when coffee stations were needed around town, municipal leaders turned to the Army for help.

While the staff of the Army's national headquarters left New York City in 1982, the Army's landmark Art Deco building on West 14th St remains the hub for New York City activities in the early 21st century. Salvationist programs are firmly established throughout New York State and are divided into the Greater New York Division, covering 14 counties in New York City, Long Island, and the Hudson Valley, and the Empire Division with jurisdiction over the rest of the state. Since 1990 the Army's eastern territorial headquarters has been located in West Nyack (Rockland Co). Services include emergency disaster relief; holiday assistance with food baskets and toy and clothing drives; homeless services including shelters, meals, summer camps, and job training; addiction counseling and recovery programs; social services for children; educational programs for adults and seniors; youth programs; and spiritual enrichment, including Bible study classes and retreats. In 2000 there were 224 officers, 6,450 soldiers, and 102 corps serving 1 million New Yorkers.

McKinley, Edward H. *Marching to Glory: The History of the Salvation Army in the United States, 1880–1992,* 2d ed. (Grand Rapids, Mich: Wm. B. Eerdmans Publishing, 1995)

Winston, Diane. *Red-Hot and Righteous: The Urban Religion of The Salvation Army* (Cambridge, Mass: Harvard Univ Press, 1999)

Diane Winston

Sammis [née Bunce], **Ida Florence** (*b* Cold Spring Harbor, Suffolk Co, 8 Oct 1865; *d* Ogdensburg, St. Lawrence Co, 3 June 1943). Suffragist and assemblywoman. In 1890 she married Edgar A. Sammis, a Huntington (Suffolk Co) merchant; they had a son in 1897. Fascinated by politics, she took a keen interest in women's rights and established Suffolk Co's first women's suffrage club, the Huntington Political Equality League, in 1911. Like many suffragists, Sammis was also an avid supporter of Prohibition. Women earned the right to vote in New York State two years before the 19th Amendment was passed in federal court. In 1918, the first election year in which New York women could vote and a year after her husband died, Sammis ran for a seat in the New York State Assembly from Suffolk Co on a Prohibition platform. She defeated Henry Murphy, a four-term incumbent. She was the first Republican woman to serve in the assembly and the first woman to introduce a bill into law in New York State. Although newspaper accounts would minimize her accomplishments, 10 of the 15 bills she proposed during her tenure were enacted. An intraparty squabble led to her reelection defeat in 1920. Back in Huntington, she continued working for women's rights and Prohibition but was never again elected to public office.

Mathews, Jane. "The Woman Suffrage Movement in Suffolk County, New York: 1911–1917: A Case Study of the Tactical Differences between Two Prominent Long Island Suffragists: Mrs. Ida Bunce Sammis and Miss Rosalie Jones" (MA thesis, Adelphi Univ, 1986)

Donna L. Halper

Sampson Naval Training Station. This naval training facility of 2,535 acres (1,026 ha) on Seneca Lake in Romulus (Seneca Co), adjacent to the west side of the Seneca Army Depot, opened in October 1942 and trained 411,429 naval recruits during its three and one-half years of operation. The base was divided into training stations for 5,000 recruits and was developed around a parade ground and drill field of 14 acres (6 ha). Housing and administrative areas for each station included 22 barracks to house 228 men each; Sampson had five of these stations when completed. Supporting facilities included a service school, auditorium, laundry, bakery, cold storage center, and two chapels. The 1,000-bed Sampson Naval Hospital served the training base. Sampson was redesignated a separation center on 15 Sept 1945, discharging over 65,000 service persons until it closed in early April 1946. The hospital, which had about 900 tuberculosis patients, was transferred to the Veterans Administration, but it closed on 1 July 1946 and was transferred to Willard State Hospital in October 1946. The base was reactivated in 1950 as Sampson Army Airfield, training air force recruits until it closed in June 1955. Starting in 1957, 449 acres (182 ha) on the lakeshore were transferred to the Seneca Army Depot, and in 1960, 1,265 acres (512 ha) of the station were sold to New York State for Sampson State Park. The former hospital was operated as a state school until 1971.

Watrous, Hilda R. *The County between the Lakes: A Public History of Seneca County, New York, 1876–1982* (Waterloo, NY: Seneca Board of Supervisors, 1982)

Michael J. Stenzel

Sand Lake. Town (pop 7,987) in central Rensselaer Co. Settled by 1767, the town was formed in 1812 from Greenbush and Berlin. In early years the region supplied cordwood, charcoal, and tanbark to Albany and Troy. The Rensselaer Glass Factory (1802–52) employed Scottish and German glassblowers. Later industries included several hosiery mills, a cotton mill, and a palm-leaf paper mill; the last important textile factory was the Faith Knitting Co (1897–1962). The town also developed as a resort; the Burden Lake House dates from the 1840s. A trolley line (1885–1925) from Troy brought summer boarders, day trippers to Crystal Lake Park, and suburbanites to lots created by the Averill Park Land Improvement Co (1895). After World War II, Sand Lake's proximity to Troy and Albany made it increasingly a suburban town, and its population almost doubled between 1960 and 2000.

Kathryn T. Sheehan

Sands Point. Village (pop 2,786) in North Hempstead (Nassau Co). It was settled in 1676, but the village's namesake, John Sands, came in 1691. Wealthy New York City businessmen established country homes in the 1890s. Among the owners of the estates that flourished until World War II were John Philip Sousa and William Randolph Hearst. The village was incorporated in 1910. Postwar development filled it in as a residential village with a few institutional properties, including the Helen Keller National Center for Deaf-Blind Youths and Adults, the Sands Point Preserve (the former Daniel Guggenheim estate), and the Village Club of Sands Point (the former Solomon Guggenheim estate). The Sands Point Lighthouse is a landmark.

Joan Gay Kent

View of Glass Lake, by Joseph H. Hidley, *ca* 1855.

Sandy Creek. Town (pop 3,863) and village (pop 789) in N Oswego Co. Settled in 1803 the town was formed in 1825 from Richland. The War of 1812 probably had greater effect upon this town than any other town in the county due to its position between the harbor at Oswego and Sackets Harbor (Jefferson Co); Sandy Creek residents participated in engagements. Col Thomas S. Meacham organized in 1835 the production of a 1,400 lb (635 kg) cheese, which was shipped to Washington, DC, as a gift for Pres Andrew Jackson. Meacham also built a giant agricultural hall; later the county fair was established in town. The village was incorporated in 1878. Sandy Pond, an arm of Lake Ontario, is the largest indentation on the lakeshore in Oswego Co and includes Sandy Island Beach. I-81 (1962) makes the town easily accessible, and most residents commute to Watertown, Oswego, or Syracuse.

Barbara J. Dix

Sanford. Town (pop 2,477) in SE Broome Co. Settled in 1787, the town was formed from Windsor in 1821. The important Lenape settlement of Cokeose is now the site of the Village of Deposit. Lumbering and leather tanning dominated in the early years and were succeeded by dairy farming. The Erie Railroad came through in 1848. Bayliss and Berkalow produced wood acid at McClure (1881–?1907). Oquaga Lake (post office, 1884) is a resort area. The town remained rural with a few farms operating in 2003; hardwood lumbering is on the rise, as is bluestone quarrying. Sanford is the site of Oquaga Creek State Park.

Charles J. Browne

Sanford, Nathan (*b* Bridgehampton, Suffolk Co, 5 Nov 1777; *d* Flushing, Queens Co, 17 Oct 1838). Legislator, jurist, and US senator. Admitted to the bar in 1799, Sanford opened a practice in New York City and became active in politics through the Tammany Society. He combined law with politics while a US commissioner in bankruptcy (1802), US district attorney in New York City (1803–15), assemblyman (1808–9, 1811) and speaker (1811), and state senator (1812–15). Sanford served as US senator (1815–21) until losing the seat to Martin Van Buren. At the 1821 Constitutional Convention, Sanford led the effort to expand suffrage by ending property qualifications for white voters. He was appointed a chancellor of the Court of Chancery in 1823 but resigned in 1826 to serve again as US senator (1826–31). He retired from active politics in 1831 and resumed his legal practice in Flushing. A loyal but uncontroversial Jeffersonian Republican and later a Jacksonian Democrat, Sanford supported a range of orthodox party positions during his career, from the Embargo Act (1807) to Pres Andrew Jackson's attack on the Second Bank of the United States (1832–36). He died after a long illness.

Alexander, DeAlva Stanwood. *A Political History of the State of New York,* 4 vols (1906; repr Port Washington, NY: I. J. Friedman, 1969)

Jerome Mushkat

Sanger [née Higgins], **Margaret (Louise)** (*b* Corning, Steuben Co, 14 Sept 1879; *d* Tucson, 6 Sept 1966). Birth control advocate. The 6th of 11 children, Margaret Higgins was determined to escape her mother's fate of frequent childbirth, poverty, and premature death. She attended Claverack College and Hudson River Institute in Claverack (Columbia Co), and in 1900 she enrolled in White Plains Hospital's nursing program (Westchester Co) but left in 1902 to marry architect William Sanger. They settled in Hastings [now Hastings-on-Hudson, Westchester Co] and had three children. By 1911 the couple had moved to New York City, where Sanger worked as a visiting nurse among Manhattan's immigrant communities and witnessed women's struggles from unwanted pregnancies and abortions. Convinced their salvation lay in having access to contraceptive information, in 1914 she challenged federal and state Comstock Laws banning the dissemination of such information by advocating birth control in *The Woman Rebel* and publishing explicit contraceptive methods in *Family Limitation.* Indicted for violating federal law, Sanger fled to England to avoid prosecution. She returned in 1915 ready to face the charges only to have the government drop the case.

Sanger was arrested in 1916 for violating state law by opening the nation's first birth control clinic in Brooklyn, and in 1917 she served 30 days in the Queens County Penitentiary. A 1918 ruling by the state's Court of Appeals upheld Sanger's conviction but interpreted the law to allow physicians to prescribe contraceptives to women when medically indicated. In 1921 Sanger founded the American Birth Control League (ABCL) in New York City to push for legislative reform and clinics. Following her divorce from William Sanger, she married oil magnate James Noah H. Slee in 1922.The next year she opened the Birth Control Clinical Research Bureau in New York City, where licensed female physicians provided gynecological and contraceptive services. Over the next decade Sanger unsuccessfully lobbied the state and federal governments for a bill giving physicians exclusive right to dispense contraceptives. When she mounted a judicial challenge, however, the decision of the US Court of Appeals for the Second Circuit in the *US v One Package* (1936) effectively established a physician's right to import and prescribe contraceptives. In those years Sanger's rationale for the birth control movement emphasized the public health and socioeconomic benefits of birth control. She sought alliances with upper- and middle-class women, the medical profession, and the eugenics movement by emphasizing the importance of birth control to strengthen the human race, advocating sterilization of those with genetically transmitted mental or physical disabilities, and supporting immigration restriction. Although Sanger's positions on eugenics were neither extreme nor rigid, her associations with the movement have continued to cloud her legacy.

In 1939 Sanger's bureau and the ABCL merged into the Birth Control Federation of America, renamed the Planned Parenthood Federation of America in 1942. Sanger was disheartened by its lack of interest in women's empowerment and by 1942 had gone into semiretirement, dividing her time between Fishkill (Dutchess Co) and Tucson. After World War II, concerns about overpopulation and global stability propelled Sanger back into action. She helped found the International Planned Parenthood Federation (1952) and supported the research that led to the marketing of the first birth control pill in 1960.

For illustration see BIRTH CONTROL.

Chesler, Ellen. *Woman of Valor: Margaret Sanger and the Birth Control Movement in America* (New York: Simon & Schuster, 1992)

The Margaret Sanger Papers: Collected Documents Series. Ed. Esther Katz with Peter C. Engelman and Cathy Moran Hajo (Bethesda, Md: University Publications of America, 1996)

The Margaret Sanger Papers Microfilm Edition: Smith College Collections Series. Ed. Esther Katz with Peter C. Engelman and Cathy Moran Hajo (Bethesda, Md: University Publications of America, 1995)

Esther Katz

Sangerfield. Town (pop 2,610) in SW Oneida Co. Settled in 1789, the town was formed from Paris in 1795 and was part of Chenango Co until 1804. Hops, introduced *ca* 1830, became the dominant crop in town, peaking around 1880 but declining after World War I. In the 20th century dairying and potato growing were complemented by crops such as broccoli, brussels sprouts, asparagus, and snap beans. Modern industries included Wickes Building Supply (1960–late 1990s), and the Agway (1970) and Allied (1973) feed mills. Titan Homes (1973) manufactures modular houses; in 1998 it employed 185. The Nine Mile Swamp, which covers a large part of Sangerfield, was the hideout of the infamous Loomis Gang, a group of horse thieves who raided the surrounding country in 1865–66.

sanitation and sewage. From the colonial period, some of New York's refuse materials were reused, with food scraps fed to animals, animal bones boiled to make soap and candles, and manure spread on fields, cast into lowlands and water bodies, or accumulated in heaps. There were no significant waste management problems in the state until Manhattan's explosive growth in the early 19th century made apparent the health dangers associated with high concentrations of waste. The city began to experience major yellow fever and cholera epidemics as the population of a few square miles of Lower Manhattan climbed from 60,000 in 1800 to 268,000 in 1840. By midcentury fear of disease, revulsion against unsightly materials on the streets, and class antagonism toward scavengers sparked a sanitary reform movement.

Reform of Refuse Disposal

Both institutions and technologies evolved to address the refuse problem. The first significant institutional response was the creation by New York City's chief sanitary officer, Inspector Alfred White, of the modern waste management business model. White's plan, developed between 1849 and 1852 endorsed by the state legislature in 1850, made it illegal to dispose of animal wastes within city limits and authorized the city to contract with a private firm to remove waste. White was soon revealed as a secret owner of the company awarded the garbage-removal monopoly. This would not be the last instance of corruption, both within New York City and elsewhere in the state, involving municipal sanitation contracts. The 1852 facility White and his partners set up on Barren Island in the Kings Co portion of Jamaica Bay stayed in operation, with a few modifications, through 1916. The technology of White's "reduction" facilities on Barren Island differed little from the kind of bone boiling used for centuries to make candles.

Sewage Systems

In 1842 the construction of Croton Aqueduct, advocated by such sanitary reformers as John H. Griscom since 1824, solved the problem of New York City's polluted drinking water. But the success of the Croton system exacerbated sewage problems. The privy or cesspit system, which had functioned poorly in Manhattan's sodden soils even before construction of the new aqueduct, was overwhelmed by the output from thousands of new water closets, resulting in flooded basements and muddy streets. The sewers then in place were open-planked channels or crude street culverts created to drain rainfall to the nearest river. They were not intended to carry sewage, and it was forbidden for households to connect house drains to them. But the pressure of the Croton waters suggested a new sewage solution: using the flow of outgoing water to carry away excrement through a pipe network. The timely development of vitrified clay pipe about 1850 dramatically reduced the costs and logistical problems of laying sewers. In 1857 Brooklyn created the Board of Sewer Commissioners to design and construct an integrated sewer system from specifications of Julius W. Aam derived from those of an 1843 piped system in Hamburg, Germany. In 1865 Manhattan followed suit, creating sewer districts and an integrated network of pipes that drained each downtown street into collecting mains strung along the waterfront. By the early 1890s, New York City had 464 miles (747 km) of sewers, more than any European or American city except Chicago.

Evolving Technologies

H. A. Fleishman built the nation's first "modern" reduction plant—which employed the Merz process originally tested in Vienna, Austria—in Buffalo in 1886. Under contract to the city, the Buffalo Reduction Co received garbage that the city had collected separately from ashes and other dry rubbish. It then separated out the valu-

Street sweeper in Buffalo during the Influenza Pandemic, 1918–19.

able grease using naptha and dried the remaining residue to serve as fertilizer. This process produced a noxious runoff water that caused many complaints. The company, renamed Buffalo Sanitary Co, built a second plant in Cheektowaga (Erie Co) that handled 50–140 tons (45–127 MT) of garbage a day, depending on the season.

In 1895 similar technology was introduced on Barren Island to process garbage from Manhattan, the Bronx, and Brooklyn, and the same year Rochester Fertilizer and Reduction Co began to collect and process all garbage, "night soil" (human waste), and dead animals. The Genesee Reduction Co acquired the Rochester contract in 1906. In 1899 Syracuse Reduction Co had agreed to process that city's estimated 10,000 tons (9,100 MT) of garbage per year for a annual charge of $26,000. One of New York State's last reduction plants was constructed in 1916 on Staten Island, at the future site of the Fresh Kills landfill.

Alternatives to reduction, which was economically suitable only for the largest cities, were incineration and landfills. The nation's first permanent incinerator was built by the US Navy on Governor's Island in New York Harbor in 1885. Early New York State incinerators were located in Coney Island (1888), Buffalo (1891), Yonkers (1894), Troy (1894), Flatbush (1895), New Brighton (1895), Syracuse (1896), Elmira (1906), and Schenectady (1908). The early incinerators did not recover the heat energy released by combustion. Some exceptions were a Buffalo plant (1903) that provided steam power to a sewage-pumping station and a New York City facility (1905) that provided electricity to light the Williamsburg Bridge.

Though ocean dumping of refuse was outlawed by a federal statute in 1888, for much of the period until 1934, when the US Supreme Court ordered a halt, municipal employees of some New York City boroughs continued to dump significant proportions of their boroughs' waste into the Atlantic Ocean. The first facility in the country to treat sewage with chemical precipitation was built in Coney Island in Brooklyn in 1887. Similar facilities soon followed in other New York State cities. Disinfection with chlorine was first used in Brewster (Putnam Co) in 1892.

THE MODERN ERA

Incineration as a method of waste disposal reached its height in New York State before World War II. The use of municipal incinerators declined thereafter until 1973, when the oil crisis stimulated interest in waste-to-energy incineration. Ten such source-recovery facilities operated in 2002 in Babylon, Islip, Huntington, Volney, Peekskill, Hempstead, Hudson Falls, Niagara Falls, Poughkeepsie, and Syracuse. American Ref-Fuel Co owns and operates two of the three largest: the 1989 Hempstead plant with a capacity of 2,505 tons (2,272 MT) per day and the 1996 Niagara Falls plant with a capacity of 2,250 tons (2,041 MT). Renewable Energy Services Co (RESCO) owns and operates the 1984 Peekskill plant, which has a capacity of 2,250 tons (2,041 MT). These mass-burn, waterwall-type facilities have spray-dry adsorbers, fabric filters, and selective noncatalytic reduction air-pollution control systems. The Niagara and Peekskill plants also feature activated-carbon injection emission controls. All sell electricity to local utilities, and the Niagara facility also supplies 269,000 pounds (122,000 kg) of steam per hour to Occidental Chemical Corp. All recover ferrous metals from the ash residue following combustion.

Landfills served as New York State's primary waste disposal method throughout the 20th century. This mode offered a less expensive alternative to incineration and became more widespread in the 1930s with the introduction of new waste burial techniques. In 1934 as many as 89 landfills operated in New York City, and in that year Robert Moses, New York City's parks commissioner and head of the Triborough Bridge Authority, began to use landfill to construct numerous city parks and highways. In 1948 Moses began construction of the world's largest landfill, Fresh Kills, on Staten Island. In 1964 perhaps 1,600 landfills operated in the state as a whole, excluding New York City. Prior to the 1977 Department of Environmental Conservation (DEC) mandate of liners to prevent the release of polluted water, virtually all landfills were unlined, open dumps. In 2000 only 28 municipal solid waste landfills remained in the state, and all had liners or other water control systems. Fresh Kills closed in March 2001, though it was briefly reopened by Gov George Pataki's order to bury debris from the World Trade Center after 11 Sept 2001.

The growing environmental movement and new state and local regulations led to increased recycling, beginning in the 1970s. The Solid Waste Management Act of 1988 required New York State localities to make "best efforts" to reduce waste streams by 8% to 10%, to recycle 40% of wastes, to process some in waste-to-energy facilities, and to put only the remainder in landfills. In 1992 the DEC ordered localities to institute source-separation recycling programs. By the 1990s composting was also gaining recognition as an important waste management technique in New York State. In 2001 all of New York City's unrecycled refuse, about 5.6 million tons (5.1 million MT), plus 1.5 million tons (1.4 million MT) from elsewhere in the state, was exported to landfills and incinerators in other states, the bulk going to Pennsylvania and Virginia. In 2002 New York State exported more waste than any other state, and it was of a greater quantity than was put into New York State landfills.

Funding from the federal Public Works Administration had quadrupled development of sewage treatment plants in the state during the 1930s and 1940s, with seven built in New York City—the first opening in Coney Island in 1937—and one in Buffalo. But until 1986, when the North River Wastewater Treatment Plant opened, Manhattan's West Side still flushed its toilets directly into the Hudson River. While ocean disposal of refuse ended in 1934, 40% of the state's sewage sludge (New York City's share) continued to be dumped in the ocean until 1992, when a US government order ended this practice. Since then about 50% of the sewage from the state's 584 publicly owned sewage treatment plants is put to beneficial use by application to agricultural or other lands after composting, heat drying, or chemical stabilization. About 30% of the treatment plants' product is incinerated and about 15% placed in landfills.

Melosi, Martin V. *The Sanitary City: Urban Infrastructure in America from Colonial Times to the Present* (Baltimore: Johns Hopkins Univ Press, 2000)
Miller, Benjamin. *Fat of the Land: Garbage in New York, the Last Two Hundred Years* (New York: Four Walls Eight Windows, 2000)
Moehring, Eugene P. *Public Works and the Patterns of Urban Real Estate Growth in Manhattan, 1835–1894* (New York: Arno, 1981)

Benjamin Miller

Santa Clara. Town (pop 395) in central Franklin Co. Settled *ca* 1830 on one of the two roads from Lake Champlain to Hopkinton (St. Lawrence Co), the town was formed from Brandon in 1888. The Saranac Inn (1859), a resort hotel with cottages, brought vacationers to the region. Industrial development was initiated by John Hurd and his Santa Clara Lumber Co, along with three other syndicates. Hurd built a railroad to Tupper Lake in 1886–89 to ship cordwood, hemlock bark, and charcoal. To justify the cost of the railroad, he built larger mills and introduced the practice of sawing the lumber rather than chopping it. William Rockefeller developed a private park at Bay Pond beginning in 1896. Santa Clara's population, after dropping from 541 in 1920 to 158 in 1960, has rebounded, increasing by 27% between 1990 and 2000.

Thomas W. Perrin

Santa Claus. See ST. NICHOLAS.

Santaella, Irma Vidal (*b* New York City, 4 Oct 1924). New York State Supreme Court justice. Santaella was raised in Puerto Rico. She attended college there and in New York City, graduating from Hunter College (BA, 1959) and Brooklyn Law School (LLB, 1961; JD, 1967). In 1961 she became the first Puerto Rican woman to be admitted to the bar in New York State. Santaella set up practice in the Bronx and became involved in politics and civil rights issues. From 1963 to 1966 she served as deputy commissioner for the New York City Department of Correction. She founded the Legion of Voters in 1962 and chaired it until 1968, helping to draft federal legislation abolishing English language literacy tests for voters. In 1968 she joined the New York State Human Rights Appeal Board, which she chaired from 1975 until her election to the State Supreme Court in 1983. She served as justice for the 12th Judicial District (Bronx Co) until reaching the mandatory retirement age of 70 in 1994.

Edgar, Julia. "Irma Vidal Santaella." In *Notable Hispanic American Women,* ed. Diane Telgen and Jim Kamp (Detroit: Gale Research, 1993)

Ellen Sexton

Santería and Voudon. Caribbean belief systems based on West African religions and influenced by Catholicism. Voudon, which originated in Haiti, is also known as Voodoo, Vodou, or Voudoun. Santería, which originated in Cuba, is also known as Lucumí, Ifa, or Orisha. Both developed in the 18th and 19th centuries and, after substantial 20th-century Caribbean immigrations to New York City, became widely practiced in New York State. The first known Santería priest in the United States, Pancho (Francisco) Mora, arrived in New York City in 1946.

In both Santería and Voudon a priest or priestess, called *santero* or *santera* in Santería and *houngan* or *mambo* in Voudon, initiates new members, called godchildren, into the religion.

Each priest is responsible for the spiritual development of his or her godchildren, and each member is obligated to the priest who initiated him or her. Priests serve as leaders, folk psychiatrists, and healers. Although a priest may hold ritual celebrations for only the godchildren, often several groups assemble for ritual events. Initiation is one of the most important rituals in both of these religions. Until the Cuban Revolution, *santeros* took their godchildren to Cuba for initiation, and most Voudoists take theirs to Haiti today. Although Voudon has been slow to spread beyond the Haitian community, Santería includes Americans from all ethnic and national backgrounds. The major activity in both religious traditions involves physical, psychological, and emotional healing. Conflicts with outsiders tend to arise from the groups' use of animal sacrifice in rituals. Both religions have a history of persecution, both on their home islands and in the United States, and therefore tend to secrecy. Tolerance has increased, however, as more non-immigrants become involved and as the religions spread beyond urban areas. Today approximately 8% of all Haitians in the United States live in the New York City area, and the majority of these serve the Voudon spirits. Although there are substantial Santería communities outside New York City, Voudon has been slower to expand outside the metropolitan area.

Brown, Karen McCarthy. *Mama Lola: A Vodou Priestess in Brooklyn* (Berkeley: Univ of California Press, 1991)

Curry, Mary Cuthell. *Making the Gods in New York: The Yoruba Religion in the African American Community* (New York: Garland Publishing, 1997)

Mary Ann Clark

Sarah Lawrence College. Private liberal arts college. In 1926 William Van Duzer Lawrence, who developed the art colony of Bronxville (Westchester Co), founded Sarah Lawrence College to honor his wife, Sarah Bates Lawrence. Reflecting its founder's philosophy, the college incorporated the creative and performing arts as an integral part of a liberal arts education. It added an experimental early childhood center in 1937 and master's degrees in the liberal arts in 1949, followed by graduate programs in the performing arts, creative writing, human genetics and inheritable disorders (1969), women's history (1972), health advocacy (1980), and education (1985). The Center for Continuing Education (1962) helps mature women returning to college. At first limited to women, the school became coeducational in 1968. There are no formal undergraduate majors, and each student's program is unique. In 2000 the college enrolled 1,139 undergraduates and 310 graduate students. About 30% of the students were men.

Sarah Lawrence College, http://www.slc.edu

Carl A. Westerdahl and Susan S. Clarke

Saranac. Town (pop 4,165) in W Clinton Co. Settled in 1802 the town formed from Plattsburgh in 1824. Having excellent waterpower, Saranac was the site of forges and other ironworks beginning in 1826 and peaking from 1842 to 1846, and of the Redford Crown-Glass Works (1831–51). Other 19th-century industries included lumbering, a starch factory, and a tannery. Saranac serves in part as a bedroom community for Plattsburgh.

Thomas A. Rumney

Saranac Lake. Village (pop 5,041) in Harrietstown (Franklin Co) and St. Armand and North Elba (Essex Co). Settled in 1828, Saranac Lake had acquired its first hotel by 1849 and was popularized by William H. H. Murray's 1868 guidebook to the mountains. Beginning with the founding of the Trudeau Institute by Dr Edward Livingston Trudeau in 1882, Saranac Lake was a center for the treatment of tuberculosis. The introduction of streptomycin in 1944 rendered the institute unnecessary and it closed in 1954, but Trudeau's legacy continues at an independent research institute dedicated to the study of immune systems, the Trudeau Institute, which became the home of the American Management Association. The village, a resort town, serves as a significant retail and cultural center for the Adirondack Park and was awarded the All-America City Award in 1998 for its historic preservation and environmental rehabilitation efforts. Saranac Lake is the home of North Country Community College (1967). Hotel Saranac (1927), operated by Paul Smith's College, is a landmark. Saranac Lake holds the oldest winter carnival in the United States.

Thomas W. Perrin

Saratoga. Town (pop 5,141) in E Saratoga Co. It was settled by Bartel Vroman in 1689 on land granted as the Saratoga Patent (1684). Mills were built on Fish Creek from 1709 to 1710, but a village of 30 families there was destroyed by an Indian raid in 1745. It was resettled from 1763 to 1775 by Dutch and New Englanders. Formed as a district in 1772, Saratoga was recognized as a town in 1788. Though the Battle of Saratoga took place in adjacent Stillwater, the Saratoga Monument (1877) and the Schuyler House, both at Schuylerville, are associated sites in town. After the 1823 opening of the Champlain Canal, manufacturing expanded rapidly in the village of Schuylerville and later in Victory. The rest of town is a farming district, including dairy, fruit, and vegetable farms. Horse farms are an important part of the economy, as are the summer cottages on Saratoga Lake. The 373-acre (151 ha) Saratoga National Cemetery opened in 1999 along the southern border.

Field Horne

Saratoga, Battles of. American capture of an entire British army at the turning point of the Revolutionary War. In 1777 Great Britain planned to conquer New York State and isolate New England from the rest of the colonies by having three armies converge at Albany. One of these forces, composed of 7,800 British and German regulars, loyalist militia, and Indians under Gen John Burgoyne, left Canada in June and advanced south along Lake Champlain. A second force under Gen William Howe was to move up the Hudson River from New York City. A third force, under the command of Gen Barry St. Leger, was to arrive at Albany via Lake Ontario and the Mohawk River. On his move south, Burgoyne captured Fort Ticonderoga [now in Essex Co] on 6 July and defeated an American rear guard at Hubberton [now East Hubberton, Vt] on 7 July. Nevertheless, he lacked adequate provisions and lost over 900 soldiers on 16 August after the American victory at the Battle of Bennington, fought at what is now Hoosick (Rensselaer Co). One week later (and unknown to Burgoyne), St. Leger was forced to abandon his siege of Fort Schuyler [now Rome, Oneida Co] at the head of the Mohawk River and return to Canada. Although he was informed of the northern campaign, Gen Howe did not receive his orders to support Burgoyne before leaving New York City in July 1777 with his own plan to attack Philadelphia.

In September 1777 American general Horatio Gates blocked Burgoyne's advance by entrenching 7,000 men near Bemis Heights [now in Saratoga Co]. On 19 September Burgoyne sent 4,200 troops in three columns against the American position. Benedict Arnold, Gates's aggressive subordinate, attacked the western column near a clearing at the Freeman's Farm. The heavily forested, broken terrain was ideally suited for American riflemen and light infantry and prevented the British from full use of their artillery. As more American units arrived on the field, they struck the center column and inflicted heavy casualties, up to 83% in the 62d Regiment of Foot. The British center was nearing collapse when German general Friedrich von Riedesel arrived with troops from the eastern column and repelled the American advance. As darkness fell, the Americans broke off the engagement, known as the first Battle of Saratoga, or the Battle of Freeman's Farm, having suffered approximately 300 casualties. British losses included 160 dead, 364 wounded, and 42 missing.

Over the next several weeks, Burgoyne erected fortifications while waiting for relief forces from the south. On 3 October Gen Henry Clinton advanced up the Hudson River with 3,000 troops to create a diversion for Burgoyne. The action

Trudeau Sanatorium, Saranac Lake, 1930.

was too late to assist, however, as they only reached Esopus [now Kingston, Ulster Co]. Meanwhile, militia continued to swell Gates's ranks to 11,000. On 7 October Burgoyne sent a 1,500-man reconnaissance force to probe the American left. The Americans again took the initiative, however, and attacked, driving them back toward their entrenchments. The British managed to rally until Gen Simon Fraser, one of their principal officers, fell mortally wounded. Arnold, relieved from command after a dispute with Gates several days earlier, rode onto the field without orders and led a series of charges against the British works. These were repelled, so Arnold shifted to the redoubt anchoring the British right. He was seriously wounded in the leg as his men carried the position. They were unable to exploit this success because of the lateness of the day but still won a significant victory. During this second Battle of Saratoga, or the Battle of Bemis Heights, the Americans inflicted another 894 casualties at a cost of 130 lives of their own men.

Burgoyne retreated slowly but was encircled by the growing American force. Faced with dwindling supplies, heavy casualties, and increasing desertions, he surrendered near the heights of Saratoga [now Schuylerville, Saratoga Co] on 17 October. The Americans captured 5,721 soldiers, including 7 generals, 27 cannons, and thousands of muskets. The American victory boosted morale greatly and prompted France to sign a military alliance with the new nation. The battlefield and its environs became a state historic site in 1927 and a national historic park in 1938.

Ketchum, Richard M. *Saratoga: Turning Point of America's Revolutionary War* (New York: Henry Holt, 1997)

Mintz, Max M. *The Generals of Saratoga: John Burgoyne and Horatio Gates* (New Haven, Conn: Yale Univ Press, 1990)

Michael P. Gabriel

Saratoga and Schenectady Railroad. New York State's second railroad, Saratoga and Schenectady (S&SRR) was incorporated 16 Feb 1831 with Churchill C. Cambreleng of New York City as president. John B. Jervis built the company's line between Saratoga Springs and Schenectady with the same 4.75 ft (1.45 m) track gauge used on the state's first railway, Mohawk and Hudson. The S&SRR road also featured the then common strap rails—wooden rails capped with thin strips of iron—supported by wooden crossties instead of by twice-as-costly stone blocks. All but 3 miles (4.8 km) of track rested on ties; this was S&SRR's most significant design advance. When completed on 12 July 1832 at a cost of $217,201, the line permitted a three-and-a-half-hour rail trip between Albany and Saratoga via the Mohawk and Hudson to Schenectady. The company was the fourth in the United States to use steam locomotives, and S&SRR relied exclusively on six-wheeled locomotives that had the four front wheels supported by a swivel truck to guide it into curves. The railway maintained a brisk passenger business for 18 years. In January 1851 Rensselaer and Saratoga, a Troy (Rensselaer Co)-based railroad, leased S&SRR's track and rolling stock for a period of 15 years to access Saratoga Springs. On 1 July 1860 S&SRR president L. G. B. Cannon signed away the last vestige of his company's independence when he agreed to a permanent lease. Delaware and Hudson Railroad absorbed the old lines when it took over Rensselaer and Saratoga in the late 1870s.

Larkin, F. Daniel. *Pioneer American Railroads: The Mohawk and Hudson and the Saratoga and Schenectady* (Fleischmanns, NY: Purple Mountain Press, 1995)

F. Daniel Larkin

Saratoga County (772 mi²/1,999 km²; pop 200,635). Created from Albany Co in 1791, with modest boundary adjustments in 1801 and 1888. The name is derived from a Native American term for the area along its eastern border, though the etymology is obscure. Saratoga Co is subdivided into 2 cities, Mechanicville and Saratoga Springs, and 19 towns that contain 9 incorporated villages. Ballston Spa serves as county seat. Elevations range from Tenant Mountain at 2,777 feet (846 m) in the Town of Day to less than 20 feet (6 m) at the confluence of the Hudson and Mohawk Rivers. The county lies within two physiographic regions: the southern and eastern portions occupy the Hudson Valley subregion of the Hudson-Mohawk Lowland, while the northwest quadrant is part of the Adirondack Low Mountains subregion of the Adirondack Upland. The rolling topography of the lowland area builds through the increasingly imposing, northeast-trending ridges of the Palmertown and Kayaderosseras Ranges to the mountainous General Edwards Range in the northwest, rising 1,000–2,000 feet (300–600 m). The eastern and southern parts are underlain primarily with Ordovician sandstone and shale. These are bounded on the northwest by Cambrian limestone and dolostone, which in turn are bounded by Precambrian crystalline rocks of metamorphic and igneous origin, including hornblende, gneiss, schist, and granite.

The county's most significant geological feature is the range of mineral springs that emerges along a fault line running from Ballston Spa through Saratoga Springs into the Towns of Saratoga and Wilton. Associated primarily with Gailor dolostone, these naturally carbonated waters are believed to originate in the county's eastern area and adjoining Washington and Rensselaer Cos, and were recognized by the late 1780s for their therapeutic character. The entire county was once glaciated, and the middle and western parts are covered with glacial till of varying quality and thickness. Surficial deposits in the eastern third are generally finer and are tied to past meltwater features, most notably prehistoric Lake Albany.

The Hudson River serves as the county's eastern and part of its northern boundary. The Mo-

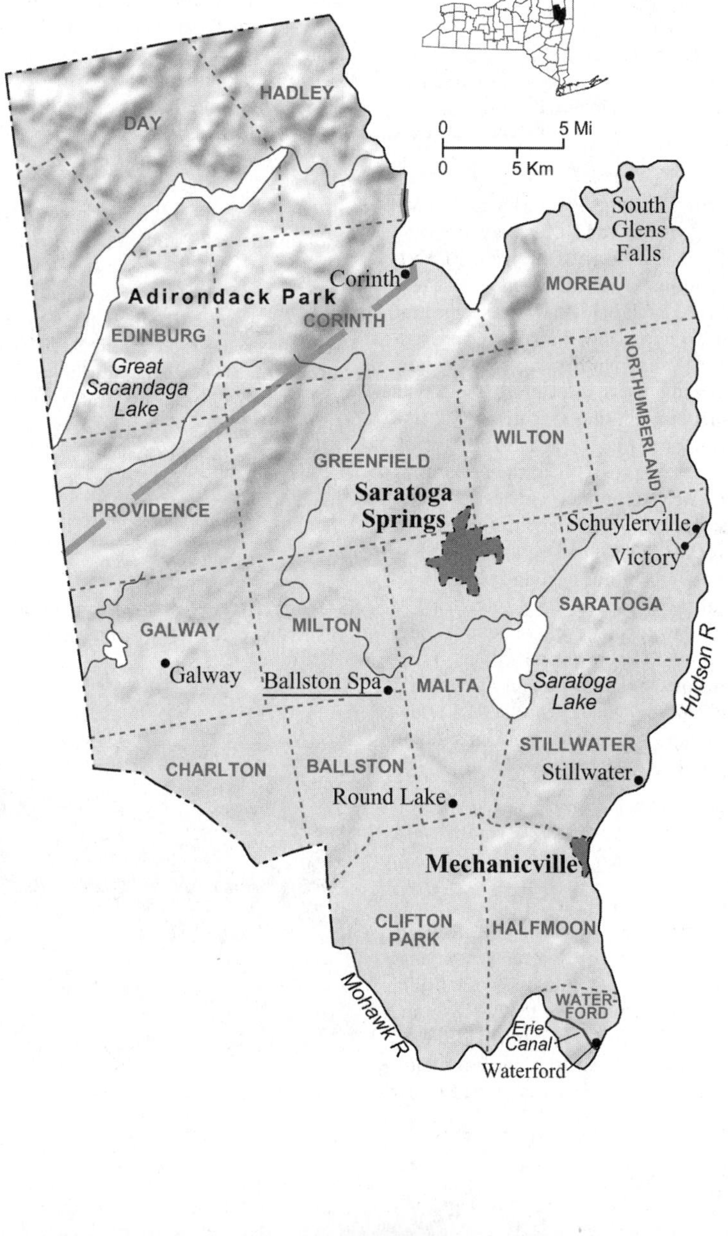

hawk River forms half of its southern boundary. Internal drainage is dominated by four stream systems that channel three-quarters of the area's surface waters into the Hudson: the Sacandaga River, which drains the Adirondack Upland region; Snook Kill; the system comprising Kayaderosseras Creek, Saratoga Lake, and Fish Creek; and the Ballston Lake, Round Lake, and Anthony Kill system. Smaller streams drain the southernmost area into the Mohawk or Hudson. Quality farmland is confined to areas east and south of Saratoga Springs. The rest of the county is by modern standards nonarable.

The climate is humid-continental. Mean January temperatures range from 19°F (-7°C) in the northern higher elevations to 23°F (-5°C) in its southern reaches. Temperatures below 0°F (-18°C) are expected every winter. Mean July temperatures range from 73°F (23°C) in the far south to 68°F (20°C) or lower in the northwest. Higher elevations aside, daytime temperatures above 90°F (32°C) occur every summer. Normal annual precipitation ranges from below 40 inches (100 cm) in the extreme southeast to 47 inches (119 cm) or more in the higher northwest. Average seasonal snowfalls vary from 90 inches (229 cm) or more in the high elevations of the extreme northwest to just over 40 inches (100 cm) in the far southeast. Primeval forest cover was diverse. Moving from east to west, oak-pine forest covered the Hudson intervale, followed by a central hardwood community of beech, sugar maple, basswood, oak, and chestnut, and then an Alleghenian hardwood community of beech, sugar maple, hemlock, white pine, and basswood. Lower Adirondack elevations were covered by spruce-fir forest and higher areas by an Adirondack hardwood community of beech, sugar maple, yellow birch, hemlock, and white pine. In the early 21st century, approximately two-thirds of the county is covered by forest. None is virgin.

American Indians and Early Settlement

The territory of what is now Saratoga Co was not heavily populated before European settlement. The eastern half of the county was a part of the Mohican (Mahican) homeland, as evidenced by archaeological sites, especially along Fish Creek. Mohican relations with the Mohawk to the west became markedly more hostile in the 17th century; in 1628 the Mohican were attacked and defeated by the Mohawk and removed eastward. The Mohawk knew of the local mineral springs, guiding Sir William Johnson to them in 1771.

The first European settlement is believed to have been that of Dutch traders at Halfmoon Point [now Waterford] in the mid–17th century. Purchases of land from the native proprietors began with the Saratoga Patent (1684; confirmed in 1708), the Van Schaick Patent in Waterford and Halfmoon (1687), and the Clifton Park Patent (1703). Dutch settlers established small farms on the north bank of the Mohawk River and, beginning in 1689, at Old Saratoga [now in or near Schuylerville] on the Hudson. The Kayaderosseras Patent (1708; confirmed in 1768) covered most of the county, and uncertainty about its title inhibited settlement until just after the end of the French and Indian War. Between 1762 and 1774 the present Towns of Stillwater, Malta, Ballston, Northumberland, Charlton, and Galway were first settled, mostly from the older, heavily populated districts of coastal New England, particularly Connecticut and Rhode Island. Organized colonies came from Canaan, Conn; Bedford (Westchester Co); Freehold, NJ; and the Galloway district of Scotland during this period.

Revolutionary and Early National Period

With the exception of the Dutch Schuyler family, there were no large land proprietors resident in the county at the outbreak of Revolution. The farming population was also largely Dutch, and few settlers harbored loyalist sympathies. But the location of the county, on the two great waterways from the English-controlled St. Lawrence Valley and backed by a trackless wilderness, placed the settlements in jeopardy. The Battle of Saratoga originated in a strategic plan by British forces to combine their armies from Lake Ontario, Quebec, and New York City. The Quebec force under command of Gen John Burgoyne arrived on 13 Sept 1777 and engaged in several battles with American forces under Gen Horatio Gates, but the other British forces failed to arrive. On 8 October Burgoyne began a retreat but was surrounded by American forces at Bemis Heights and surrendered on 17 October. After that important American victory, only isolated skirmishes and raids, notably one at Ballston on 16 Oct 1780, disturbed the inhabitants.

Settlement of the districts already occupied resumed after warfare ended; the towns in the mountainous northwest were first settled between 1785 and 1788 (except Day, settled in 1797) by New Englanders, who took available land in the older towns as well. Some African Americans came as slaves; all were freed by 1827. Work opportunities, especially seasonal hotel employment, drew Blacks to Ballston Spa and Saratoga Springs in large numbers. Irish immigrants arrived with railroad work in 1832 and after 1848. Francophone Canadians sought work in the same industries, and Italian immigrants working on later railroad projects began settling about 1880. Jews from Germany and eastern Europe were drawn primarily by business opportunities after the Civil War. They came to dominate many of the hotels in Saratoga Springs from the 1920s to the 1960s, when ethnic resorts were popular. With the opening of southern sections of the Northway (1960), south-central Saratoga Co became a "bedroom" for the Capital District.

Transportation

The Hudson and Mohawk Rivers were principal means of transportation until the 1830s. Most Saratoga Springs–bound travelers' accounts before the railroad describe journeys by horseback or coach from Waterford, Schenectady, or Schuylerville. The Sacandaga River was also navigable, except for the falls in the Town of Hadley. Recognizing its superb position in east-west trade, the State of New York acted quickly to build the Champlain Canal (completed 1823) and the Erie Canal (completed 1825). The Erie passed through the southernmost part of the county; the Champlain followed the course of the Hudson as far as Fort Edward (Washington Co). Both carried large numbers of people and goods and created business opportunities such as dry docks and warehouses at the canal villages.

The mineral springs were directly responsible for the earliest rail lines. A rail link from Albany to Saratoga Springs was completed in 1832–33 by the Saratoga and Schenectady Railroad; two

SARATOGA CO POPULATION CENSUS FIGURES

	White	Nonwhite	Total Population	Foreign-Born
1800	24,052	431	24,483	—
1810	32,475	672	33,147	—
1820	35,425	627	36,052	258
1830	38,087	592	38,679	415
1840	39,904	649	40,553	—
1850	45,028	618	45,646	4,914
1860	51,038	691	51,729	6,682
1870	50,839	690	51,529	7,709
1880	54,404	752	55,156	7,586
1890	56,877	786	57,663	8,105
1900	60,228	861	61,089	7,881
1910	61,183	734	61,917	9,007
1920	59,383	646	60,029	7,409
1930	62,673	641	63,314	7,219
1940	64,962	644	65,606	5,942
1950	74,152	717	74,869	5,343
1960	88,210	886	89,096	4,355
1970	120,358	1,321	121,679	3,941
1980	151,277	2,482	153,759	4,674
1990	176,866	4,410	181,276	4,646
2000	192,579	8,056	200,635	6,188

Notes: "Nonwhite" includes African Americans, Asians, American Indians, and Pacific Islanders and, for 2000, also the mixed race and other race categories. Through the 1960 census these figures primarily reflect the African American population. Foreign-born figures for 1820 and 1830 include only those not naturalized, and for 1930 and 1950, the foreign-born totals include Whites only. Other years include all foreign-born in the population.

POPULATIONS OF TOWNS AND CITIES, SARATOGA CO

Town or City, Year Founded	1800	1840	1880	1920	1960	2000
Ballston, 1772[a]	2,099	2,044	2,035	2,206	5,752	8,729
Charlton, 1792	1,746	1,933	1,474	914	3,024	3,954
Clifton Park, 1828[b]	—	2,719	2,454	1,983	4,512	32,995
Corinth, 1818	—	1,365	1,737	3,696	5,167	5,985
Day, 1819[c]	—	942	1,238	473	466	920
Edinburg, 1801[d]	—	1,458	1,523	595	602	1,384
Galway, 1792	2,310	2,412	1,902	1,101	1,746	3,589
Greenfield, 1793	3,073	2,803	2,448	1,481	2,548	7,362
Hadley, 1801	—	865	1,095	581	982	1,971
Halfmoon, 1772[a]	3,851	2,631	3,102	1,534	4,120	18,474
Malta, 1802	—	1,457	1,234	1,152	2,223	13,005
Mechanicville (city), 1915	—	—	—	8,166	6,831	5,019
Milton, 1792	2,146	3,166	5,565	5,294	7,114	17,103
Moreau, 1805	—	1,576	2,555	3,222	8,406	13,826
Northumberland, 1798	2,007	1,672	1,583	1,048	1,353	4,603
Providence, 1796	1,888	1,507	994	462	556	1,841
Saratoga, 1772[a]	2,491	2,624	4,539	3,680	3,515	5,141
Saratoga Springs, 1819–1915	—	3,384	10,820	—	—	—
Saratoga Springs (city), 1915	—	—	—	13,181	16,630	26,186
Stillwater, 1788	2,872	2,733	3,412	3,882	4,416	7,522
Waterford, 1816	—	1,824	4,328	4,552	7,231	8,515
Wilton, 1818	—	1,438	1,118	826	1,902	12,511

[a]Formed as district; recognized as town 1788.

[b]Clifton until 1829.

[c]Concord until 1827.

[d]Northfield until 1808.

years later the Rensselaer and Saratoga Railroad built another line from Troy (Rensselaer Co). The Saratoga and Washington Rail Road (1848–49) ran from the termini of the first two lines to Whitehall (Washington Co), where lake steamers departed for Montreal. The Adirondack Railroad (1863–71) was organized to connect Saratoga Springs to Lake Ontario via the Adirondacks but was completed only to North Creek (Warren Co), providing transportation for logging and paper mills. The county's only east-west link, the Boston, Hoosac Tunnel and Western Railroad (later the Fitchburg, still later the Boston and Maine), connected Boston with Mechanicville and Saratoga Springs. From 1912 its rail yards at Mechanicville were among that city's largest employers. Passenger service through Saratoga Springs continued, with a brief interruption, under Amtrak and in recent years has been increasing slowly.

Despite the chartering under state law of a number of turnpikes and plank roads, improved roads were a low priority because of excellent railroads and canals. Among the few roads of any historical importance was the plank road from the Mount Pleasant glassworks to Saratoga Springs in the 1850s and 1860s. Electric railroads ("trolleys") were first constructed between Saratoga Springs and two of its suburbs from 1889 to 1892; within a decade these lines were part of an elaborate interurban system connecting the Capital District to the south with most of the county's major towns, with Glens Falls (Warren Co), and with the string of manufacturing hamlets along the Kayaderosseras between Ballston Spa and Rock City Falls. However, the rapid development of automobile transportation began extinguishing the system within a decade.

Bicycles and rural free delivery provided the impetus for building better roads; a state law of 1898 authorized county highways by cost sharing, and roads were built from Saratoga Springs to Glens Falls (1901) and from Waterford to Mechanicville. A state law of 1908 created trunk routes, and a 1925 law numbered US highways. Under these laws US 9, passing north-south through Saratoga Co from Cape May, NJ, to the US border south of Montreal, became an important route. The 1944 Federal-Aid Highway Act provided for interstates, and in 1950 the Thruway was begun. The Northway was completed within the county between 1960 and 1963, setting in motion many of the forces that created modern Saratoga Co.

Economic Development

The construction of the first hotels to accommodate visitors to Ballston Spa (1792) and Saratoga Springs (1802) established tourist economies, although Ballston Spa lost its tourist base after 1830 and made a transition to manufacturing. Forest products dominated the economy of the mountainous northwest from first settlement until the rise of a second-home economy after 1930. Tanbark for tanneries was an important early product, along with potash and lumber, in the early 19th century. Later, woodenware shops provided employment, and after 1869 wood pulp was turned into paper at Corinth and other mills. Large sawmills helped drive the South Glens Falls economy late in the century. Overcutting killed many of the industries, but in the 20th century scientific forestry has created a sustainable return from the woods.

Wheat farming was significant from earliest settlement. When the Erie Canal flooded eastern markets with Genesee Valley, and later, midwestern wheat, Saratoga Co farmers shifted to mixed farming, which protected against low prices and crop failure, spread the labor need over more of the year, and helped maintain soil fertility. In 1910, 40% of county farmers' income came from livestock, 38% from field crops, 12% from market gardening, 4% from orchards, and 6% from other sources. Dairy became dominant after railroad access permitted quick shipment of fluid milk. By 1870 industrial production was significantly greater than agricultural production, but both the number of farms and acreage peaked in 1880. Dairy farming, while still important, declined sharply after the Northway opened the county for extensive suburban development in 1963. In 2002 there were still more than 200 full-time farms, with total annual production valued at $32 million. Principal crops were beef, dairy, corn, hay, alfalfa, silage, and vegetables.

Also important to the county's early economy were waterpowered milling operations. The Kayaderosseras Range in Milton and Greenfield was lined with good mill sites, and many small factories located there before railroads improved access. Waterford's hydraulic canal (1829) created a local boom. While the county had several important textile mills, notably at Victory, papermaking was more widespread, especially after the pulp process came into common use at the end of the 1860s. However, the largest manufacturer in the region, General Electric Co (GE) at Schenectady, overshadowed all county employers in the 20th century. The labor shortage of World War II encouraged commuting to GE as well as to Watervliet (Albany Co), Troy, Glens Falls, and other industrial communities on the county's periphery. Since the late 1970s Saratoga Co, through its Economic Development Commission, has effectively recruited light manufacturing and other significant employers. In 2003 the major manufacturers were Stewart's Ice Cream in Greenfield; GE Silicone Division and Mohawk Paper Mills in Waterford; Quad/Graphics, Ball Metal Container Group, Espey Manufacturing and Electronics Corp, and Ellsworth Ice Cream Co in Saratoga Springs.

Religion, Education, and Culture

Along the Hudson and Mohawk Rivers the earliest settlers were chiefly Dutch from elsewhere in the colony and founded a number of Reformed churches. Quakers gathered a meeting at Quaker Springs before the Revolution. The post-Revolutionary population pressure from Rhode Island sent many settlers to Saratoga Co, and the its oldest Baptist churches are a result. Its first Episcopal church was founded at Ballston Center in 1787. Churches of other denominations followed, especially Methodist, which ultimately were present in every hamlet. With an influx of Irish laborers and, slightly later, Francophone Canadian millworkers, the first Roman Catholic churches were established at Saratoga Springs (1839), Waterford (1843), Mechanicville, and Schuylerville (1845). Jews first came as peddlers and later opened stores, primarily in Saratoga Springs. The first synagogue organized about 1911.

Public schools were organized following enabling legislation in 1812. Private schools for boys and girls were especially prevalent in Saratoga Springs; the most famous, run by Emma Willard, was founded in Waterford in 1819 and operated there for several years before moving to Troy. Public high schools developed in the larger villages, beginning with Saratoga Springs in 1867. Consolidation into central school districts began after World War I but was not completed in some rural districts until the 1950s. Although towns had the usual small academies, only Skidmore College (1922) provided advanced study until the founding of Empire State College (1971), a distance-learning branch of SUNY based in Saratoga Springs. There is also a satellite of Adirondack Community College in Wilton. The first newspaper, the *Ballston Journal,* was published in 1798. The large number of sophisticated tourists in Saratoga Springs, starting around the turn of the 19th century, encouraged music, theater, publishing, and debate in and around the resort. However, the city did not have a free public library until 1950. Its building was converted in 1997 to a home for the Saratoga County Arts Council after completion of a modern library facility. The artists' colony Yaddo (1926) and the Saratoga Performing Arts Center (1966) solidified the community's position in the arts.

Politics

When first organized, the county was governed by four supervisors, one from each town. The sessions of the county board were originally held in November and December and transacted little business other than approving charges and auditing accounts. The number of supervisors increased with the division of towns; the chartering of Mechanicville and Saratoga Springs as cities in 1915 brought the total to 21. In 1968 a weighted representation plan was begun and additional supervisors were authorized, including a second for Saratoga Springs and, in 1971, another for Clifton Park. The first full-time county administrator took office in 1973. The county government has generally been Republican since the Civil War and exclusively so since 1902. Its administrative responsibilities have grown in the 20th century, largely in response to legislative mandates, such as those relating to infrastructure and welfare programs.

Recent History

The most critical event of the late 20th century was the construction of the Northway, which opened for traffic in the county between 1960 and 1963. It ignited a suburbanization trend, particularly in the Clifton Park area, where hundreds of acres of level farmland were subdivided and houses built; the town's population exploded from 4,512 in 1960 to 32,995 in 2000, a 733% increase. By the end of the 1960s subdivisions were scattered throughout Saratoga Co's southern half. Saratoga Springs had been in eclipse since World War I, and following the suppression of gambling in 1950 its economy bottomed out, sustained only by horse racing, the college, and a handful of industries. With the opening of the Northway, the city sought to attract light industry, beginning with a General Foods plant (1960). But it was the city's commitment to preserving its historic architecture, exemplified by the Saratoga Springs Preservation Foundation (1977), that earned Saratoga Springs national recognition as both a tourist destination and a desirable place to live.

By the 1990s suburban development was significant in all the towns reached by the Northway. Retail shopping concentrated early in that decade in the south part of the Town of Wilton near Exit 15. The Wilton Mall (1990) became such a force that it eliminated the Saratoga Mall (1973) and siphoned business from the Clifton Country Mall, which had primarily served the southern towns. The new mall was followed by a group of giant warehouse-style stores, including the county's first Wal-Mart. Through it all Saratoga Springs maintained its healthy downtown retail economy, sustained in part by tourism. New light industries in Saratoga Springs' industrial park, the North Atlantic regional office of State Farm Insurance in Malta, and Ace and Target distribution warehouses in Wilton added many jobs during the last two decades of the 20th century, while traditional manufacturing gradually declined. When the county's last large pulp paper mill, International Paper Co's Corinth facility, closed late in 2002, the shift from heavy industry to the service and retail sectors was substantially complete.

The literature on Saratoga Co, and especially of Saratoga Springs, is immense and includes travel literature, guidebooks, picture books, and fiction; however, scholarly or even antiquarian works are few. The standard history is Nathaniel B. Sylvester, ed., *History of Saratoga Co* (1878; repr 1979). A bicentennial volume by Violet B. Dunn, ed., *Saratoga County Heritage* (1974), has little original material aside from a superb chapter on Saratoga Springs by Beatrice Sweeney. Paul Loatman, "The History of Mechanicville" (PhD diss, SUNY Albany, 1974) and Earl F. Soper, "History of South Glens Falls and Town of Moreau" (MA thesis, New York State College for Teachers, 1943) explore single communities, while Myra B. Young Armstead, *Lord, Please Don't Take Me in August* (1999) studies African Americans at Saratoga Springs and Newport, RI. A few older community histories are useful, especially Edward F. Grose, *Centennial History of the Village of Ballston Spa* (1907), but also Arthur J. Weise, *History of Round Lake* (1887), and Sydney E. Hammersley, *The History of Waterford* (1957). Newer works are Field Horne, *The First Respectable House: Brookside and the Growth of Ballston Spa* (1984), and John J. Bennis, *Edinburg: A Town Divided* (1998). Three books document the built environment of Saratoga Springs: Beverley Mastrianni et al, eds., *George S. Bolster's Saratoga Springs* (1990), James K. Kettlewell, *Saratoga Springs: An Architectural History* (1991), and Robert Joki, *Saratoga Lost* (1998). Three scholarly books dealing in part with Saratoga Springs are Theodore Corbett, *The Making of American Resorts* (2001), Jon Sterngass, *First Resorts* (2002), and Thomas Chambers, *Drinking the Waters* (2002). Bruce M. Manzer compiled a comprehensive (6,600-entry) bibliography, *Saratoga County, New York, 1757–1995,* 3d ed (2004).

Field Horne

Saratoga Patent. A patent in the upper Hudson Valley, comprising nearly all of the Towns of Saratoga and Stillwater (Saratoga Co) and Easton (Washington Co), and parts of Schaghticoke (Rensselaer Co) and other towns. It was purchased in 1683 by four Dutch colonists, including Pieter Schuyler, from the Mohawk sachems, with renunciation of rights by the Mohican (Mahican). The patent was confirmed in 1684 by Gov Thomas Dongan and a new patent issued in 1708 by Gov Edward Hyde (Lord Cornbury). The tract ran along both sides of the Hudson for 22 miles (35 km) and 6 miles (10 km) east and west from the river. The first European settlement in the patent was on the west shore in 1689.

Field Horne

Saratoga Performing Arts Center (SPAC). A 1960 state-commissioned master plan identified Saratoga Spa State Park as an underused facility and recommended a performing arts center as the cornerstone of park redevelopment. With an offer from Gov Nelson A. Rockefeller for planning and site-development costs, a planning group of Saratoga Springs residents formed in 1961 to raise construction funds. Ground was broken in January 1965 for the 5,100-seat, 10-story amphitheater. With the Northway completed that summer, its opening the following year stimulated tourism in the region. SPAC is the summer home of the Philadelphia Orchestra and the New York City Ballet, and presents a full schedule of rock and popular music concerts. SPAC also encompasses the Spa Little Theater, the Summer School of Arts, the National Museum of Dance, and its educational program in schools. Attendance at all programs was 350,000 in the summer of 2000.

"Arts Center Will Complete Spa 'Emerald,'" *Saratogian,* 29 June 1962, 13

Vollmer, Arnold. "Who Really Built SPAC?" *Saratogian,* 26 Dec 1993, 1D

Field Horne

Saratoga potatoes. Despite inadequate documentation the invention of the potato chip is accepted as having taken place in or near Saratoga Springs. The earliest published account was found in the *Hotel Gazette,* 27 Aug 1885, quoted by Hugh Bradley in *Such Was Saratoga* (1940); the tale did not circulate widely until the 1930s. Most accounts credit the invention to African American and Stockbridge Indian George (Speck) Crum (*d* 1914) or his sister Catherine (Speck) Wicks, who were cooks for noted restaurateur Carey B. Moon. Most 20th-century accounts date it to 1853, a date that seems to have been taken from the opening of Moon's Lake House; but *Hotel Gazette,* quoted by Bradley, ascribes it to Montgomery Hall in the village, which Moon leased through the year 1852. First mentioned in print in 1868–70, the potatoes were always called Saratoga chips. Snack-food industry journals in the 1970s published increasingly popular versions of the story that, having noted that Moon often catered to Commodore Cornelius Vanderbilt, identified Vanderbilt as the "disgruntled patron" who, in some versions, sent his fried potatoes back to the kitchen to be sliced ever thinner until the new treat was discovered. In consequence, Mrs (Marylou) Cornelius Vanderbilt Whitney based her 1977 annual racing season party on Commodore Vanderbilt and the potato chip, igniting a brief but rancorous debate over historical accuracy with the county historian, Violet Dunn.

Fox, William S., and Mae G. Banner. "Social and Economic Contexts of Folklore Variants: The Case of Potato Chip Legends," *Western Folklore* 42 (May 1983): 114–26

Field Horne

Saratoga Race Course. The oldest major sports venue in the United States dates to 14 Aug 1847, when it opened as Saratoga Trotting Course just outside Saratoga Springs, then the country's leading watering place. A crowd of 5,000 saw the famous trotter Lady Suffolk win the inaugural race. A month later Lady Digby won the first thoroughbred race staged there.

Dirt track and grandstand at the Saratoga Race Course.

Saratoga's first meeting devoted entirely to thoroughbred races was held in 1863 on the slightly redesigned trotting track. The meet was organized by John Morrissey, a boxing champion from Troy (Rensselaer Co) and a New York City gambling house operator. Lizzie W., ridden by an ex-fugitive slave jockey named Sewell (his first name was not recorded), won the first race. The meeting so impressed Morrissey's backers, especially steamboat and railroad magnate Cornelius Vanderbilt, that they formed the Saratoga Association to operate a new track, which opened across Union Ave in 1864. Saratoga Race Course now continues on both sides of the avenue.

Saratoga is one of the world's outstanding racing centers, featuring the Travers Stakes, America's oldest major professional sporting event, and other stakes including the Hopeful, the Alabama, and the Whitney Handicap. Interruptions to these events have been rare. The track closed in 1896 because of financial problems and in 1911–12 because of state antigambling legislation. It shifted its schedule to New York City–area tracks for three years during World War II. Among its 20th-century stars were horses Man o' War, Gallant Fox, Whirlaway, Native Dancer, and Secretariat, and jockeys Earl Sande, Eddie Arcaro, Jerry Bailey, and Gary Stevens.

In 1955 the track was bought out by the Greater New York Association, soon renamed the New York Racing Association (NYRA). One of the major industries of northeastern New York, Saratoga has thrived despite off-track betting, which since the 1970s has allowed fans to wager on the races in betting parlors run by OTB, a public benefit corporation. Open during part of July, all of August, and sometimes into September, Saratoga frequently records the largest on-track daily attendance in the nation. Although it was designed for a capacity of 25,000 people, it set a record one-day attendance in 2002 with a crowd of 69,523, many of those attending for free souvenirs. NYRA's Saratoga franchise currently extends until 2007.

Hotaling, Edward. *They're Off! Horse Racing at Saratoga* (Syracuse: Syracuse Univ Press, 1995)
Manning, Landon. *The Noble Animals: A Look into the Past Events of the Turf* (Saratoga Springs: Author, 1973)

Edward Hotaling

Saratoga Spa State Park. Developed 1933–35, this 2,200-acre (890 ha) park in Saratoga Springs owes its origin to the pumping of mineral springs to extract carbonic-acid gas for carbonation beginning around 1890. Within a decade the flow of many springs had been compromised. Local activists secured passage of the Anti-Pumping Act of 1908. When it was challenged in court, state senator Edgar T. Brackett and others sought state ownership and secured passage of a bill establishing the 1,100-acre (445 ha) State Reservation in 1909. Bathhouses were constructed, but in 1929 Gov Franklin D. Roosevelt, a frequent user of hot springs for his polio, proposed intensive development of a state-operated European-style health spa. The legislature authorized the new Saratoga Springs Commission as a planning agency. The new spa included hotel, laboratory, bottling plant, bathhouses, golf courses, swimming pool, and theater. With expansion, and a gradual decline in use after a 1946 peak, the park was identified by Gov Nelson A. Rockefeller as underutilized. It was consequently redeveloped between 1960 and 1966, during which time the Saratoga Performing Arts Center (SPAC), a second pool, picnic grounds, and other facilities were added.

Swanner, Grace Maguire. *Saratoga, Queen of Spas* (Utica: North Country Books, 1988)

Field Horne

Saratoga Springs. City (pop 26,186) in central Saratoga Co. Located at the southeast edge of the Adirondack Mountains, it lies on a geological fault from which issue numerous mineral springs. High Rock Spring, first described by Sir William Johnson in 1771, began to attract health seekers, and in 1783 Philip Schuyler cut a 10 mi (16 km) path from the present Schuylerville. Primitive lodgings were built, and in 1802 Gideon Putnam opened Union Hall, a three-story hotel near Congress Spring, and platted a village along a broad main street. In 1811 Putnam began another hotel, Congress Hall, and competitors erected the Columbian (1809), Pavilion (1819), and United States (1824) Hotels. The Town of Saratoga Springs was formed in 1819 from the Town of Saratoga. John Clarke, a New York City entrepreneur, bought Congress Spring in 1823 and marketed its water throughout the country and abroad. Beginning in 1829 he began development of Congress Park as an exercise ground for those who took water at the spring.

The availability of inexpensive steamship service on the Hudson in the 1820s and the completion of the Erie Canal in 1825 made Saratoga Springs a feature of the Fashionable Tour. The increasingly urban center of the town was incorporated as a village in 1826. The Saratoga and Schenectady Railroad (1832–33), the second in New York State, greatly enhanced its accessibility. Close to 50,000 visitors a year visited antebellum Saratoga Springs. The village was especially popular with southerners fleeing their plantations in the summer. At Saratoga Springs they encountered free African American workers in substantial numbers (3–4% of the village's summer population). The seasonal, service-based economy also provided work for Irish immigrants and for women. The hotels grew ever larger, with enormous public spaces: parlors, dining rooms, and verandas. While some visitors came purely for therapeutic purposes, Saratoga Springs drew the curious and, increasingly, pleasure seekers. In consequence, dances and amusements became central to its image early on, gambling was introduced by 1835, and sporting events developed gradually beginning with harness racing in 1847.

The Civil War cut Saratoga Springs off from its southern clientele, but under the influence of sportsman John Morrissey, the resort entered into an even greater period of prosperity and fame. Morrissey opened a gaming house in 1862 and joined with three New York City turfmen to offer a thoroughbred race meeting the following year. It was a great success, and in 1864 they began development of the present Saratoga Race Course, the oldest horse-racing venue in the United States, and launched the Travers Stakes, America's oldest stakes race. The racetrack's thriving condition enabled Morrissey to expand his operations; he bought land adjacent to Congress Park and, built the Italianate Club House (1870–71), a gambling casino. Department store magnate A. T. Stewart bought Union Hall in 1872 and remodeled it on a luxurious scale as the Grand Union Hotel. Congress Hall and the United States Hotel were also rebuilt, the latter in 1872–74 with 768 rooms, a dining room of more than 10,000 ft^2 (930 m^2), a half mile (0.8 km) of verandas, and 1,000 rocking chairs. No American resort could present such a conglomeration of hostelries; among them, the three largest hotels could accommodate 5,000 guests. Visitors to Saratoga Springs could browse in attractive shops, visit an Indian encampment, attend a circus, hire rigs for pleasure drives, or patronize bowling alleys or shooting galleries. In 1875, 1876, and 1879 Morrissey promoted rowing meets on Saratoga Lake, and the first such regatta was one of the most newsworthy events of its day. Politicians and generals continued to visit the springs; in 1885 Ulysses Grant, dying of cancer, came to Mt McGregor, 8 miles (13 km) north of Saratoga Springs, to finish his memoirs.

In 1893 Richard Canfield bought the Club House, renamed it the Casino and, in 1902, added a spectacular dining room. Despite national economic recession, the 1890s was one of the most glittering periods for Saratoga Springs, but the era came to the end when the Casino closed in 1907 and the state legislature passed the Agnew-Hart Bill, which prevented race wagering in 1911 and 1912.

Both tourism and industry benefited from the construction of two additional railroad lines. The Adirondack Railroad (1865–71, later Delaware and Hudson) connected Saratoga Springs to the central Adirondacks; the Saratoga Lake Railroad (1881–82) provided connections to Boston. The Saratoga line was built largely by Italian laborers, and those who remained in the area were the start of a thriving Italian neighborhood on the West Side. Some industrial development also began. While inconsequential alongside the tourist industry, it provided year-round employment. Chief among the firms were G. F. Harvey Co (pharmaceuticals) and Baker and Shevlin (metal castings). Clark Textile Co began producing gloves in 1906; its successors, the Van Raalte Co (1919) and Saratoga Knitting Mill (1975), produced knit goods until 1986.

Saratoga Springs waters retained their popularity throughout the 19th century and became even more valuable when, in the 1880s, a method was devised to extract carbonic gas from them to carbonate bottled beverages. Gas companies, seeking greater profits, pumped more than 150 million gallons (568,000 l) of spring water, and the aquifer's water level dropped almost 100 feet (30 m). In 1908 the state legislature passed an antipumping act (upheld by the US Supreme Court in 1911), and beginning in 1909 New York State acquired more than 100 springs to prevent their commercial exploitation and consequent destruction. Modest bathhouse development by the state soon followed. An elaborate new resort and therapy complex opened in 1935, funded in part by federal money from the Reconstruction Finance Corp, but never succeeded in rivaling the great European spas or the village's 19th-century heyday.

Saratoga Springs, incorporated as a city in 1915, seemed to be in decline, but the racecourse had reopened in 1913 and maintained a high standard of racing. Although the Casino had closed, other gambling houses opened, mostly along Saratoga Lake, within city limits but 3.5 miles (5.6 km) from the city center. Boxers such as Jack Dempsey and Gene Tunney followed, and the city retained its raffish reputation from its association with the sporting life. Yet, Yaddo (1893), a mansion with gardens, opened in 1926 as a retreat for writers, artists, and composers.

The growth of automobile touring after World War I undercut the custom of an extended vacation in one place; visitors to Saratoga Springs complained of outmoded sanitary facilities, badly ventilated rooms, and the idleness of traditional hotel life. A Jewish clientele expanded substantially in the new century as immigrant families acquired the time and money for vacations, but hotel owners converted only small and midsized hotels for their use; the United States Hotel was razed in 1945–46, and the Grand Union followed in 1952–53. In 1951, following police raids and extensive publicity from the Kefauver Commission, authorities ended public gambling. Much distinguished architecture was allowed to fall into ruin. Just when it seemed the city might go altogether to seed, however, the Northway was built though Saratoga Springs (1963). The 5,100-seat Saratoga Performing Arts Center (SPAC) opened in 1966, offering both classical and popular entertainment. Skidmore College's expansion on a new campus from 1963 to 1971 increased its economic impact on the city and helped prepare Saratoga Springs for the historic preservation movement, which began locally in 1977 and restored the Spa City's attractiveness to tourists and new residents.

Saratoga's racetrack survived all the ups and downs; daily track attendance in the 1990s exceeded 20,000 horseplayers for an enlarged six-week season, and events such as the Fasig-Tipton yearling auction and the annual National Thoroughbred Racing Hall of Fame induction ceremony continue to dominate the summer calendar. Saratoga's reputation as a distinctive American cultural expression has been disseminated in such disparate works as Edith Wharton's unfinished *The Buccaneers* (1938), Edna Ferber's *Saratoga Trunk* (1941), and E. L. Doctorow's *Billy Bathgate* (1989). Beginning with the 1959 opening of an industrial park, the city has sought to diversify its economy. Major manufacturers in 2003 included Stewart's Ice Cream Co, Quad/Graphics (printing), Ball Metal Container Group, Espey Manufacturing and Electronics Corp, and Ellsworth Ice Cream Co. Saratoga Springs is a bedroom community for Albany, and benefits from the presence of Skidmore College (1903), Empire State College (1971), and many museums, including the National Museum of Racing (1950), the National Museum of Dance (1986), and the New York State Military Museum (2002). Its permanent population increased almost 40% between 1960 and 2000. Summer tourism, however, continues to be its bread and butter, augmented by a thriving year-round convention business.

Armstead, Myra. *"Lord, Please Don't Take Me in August": African Americans in Newport and Saratoga Springs, 1870–1930* (Urbana: Univ of Illinois Press, 1999)

Chambers, Thomas. *Drinking the Waters: Creating an American Leisure Class at 19th-Century Mineral Springs* (Washington, DC: Smithsonian Institution Press, 2002)

Horne, Field. *With the Strength of the Adirondacks: A History of the Adirondack Trust Company, 1901–2001* (Saratoga Springs: Adirondack Trust, 2002)

Kettlewell, James. *Saratoga Springs: An Architectural History* (Saratoga Springs: Lyrical Ballad Bookstore, 1991)

Sterngass, Jon. *First Resorts: Pursuing Pleasure at Saratoga Springs, Newport, and Coney Island* (Baltimore: Johns Hopkins Univ Press, 2001)

Waller, George. *Saratoga: Saga of an Impious Era* (Englewood Cliffs, NJ: Prentice Hall, 1966)

Sardinia. Town (pop 2,692) in SE Erie Co. Settled in 1809, the town was formed from Concord in 1821. A woolen factory, built *ca* 1840, operated for most of the 19th century, toward the end of which cheeseboxes were manufactured. The Buffalo, New York and Philadelphia Railroad (later Pennsylvania Railroad) came through in 1872 and the Springville and Sardinia in 1878. In 1883 a cannery began operations in the hamlet of Protection. In the early 21st century farming, especially dairy farming, remains important.

Andrew C. Maines

satanic panic. In the days leading up to Friday, 13 May 1988 in Chautauqua, Cattaraugus, and Allegany Cos and in large parts of nearby Pennsylvania, there was a widespread fear of attacks by satanists. The media in Buffalo reported the panic as occurring in Jamestown (Chautauqua Co), but this was merely the largest population center in the area of the rumor-panic. The central rumor asserted that a secret satanic cult planned to kidnap and murder a blond, blue-eyed virgin as a ritual sacrifice on Friday the 13th. Other rumors made claims about the killing and hanging of cats and dogs, of secret cult ritual meetings in wooded areas, and of black roses placed in student lockers to threaten potential victims. Though this rumor spread over a wide area, people in each small town did not know that the same rumor-panic was occurring in nearby towns. People in each locality believed that some local circumstance had triggered the panic. In response to the rumor, over 100 cars gathered at a wooded area near Jamestown thought to be a secret cult meeting site and were stopped by police barricades. Several young men with baseball bats wandered around downtown Jamestown, presumably looking for satanists. Some teenagers were falsely accused of being satanists. About a dozen teenagers having a countercultural appearance received telephone death threats at their homes. Fortunately there were no reports of harm done to anyone, although there was some damage to property. This largest incident of satanic panic in New York State was part of a series of satanic cult rumor-panics in the United States and Canada during the 1980s and early 1990s, almost all of which took place in small towns and rural areas.

Victor, Jeffrey S. "A Rumor-Panic about a Dangerous Satanic Cult in Western New York," *New York Folklore* 15 (1989): 23–49

Jeffrey S. Victor

Saugerties. Town (pop 19,868) and village (pop 4,955) in NE Ulster Co. Although there is record of a sawyer living in the area by 1663, only two families are believed to have been in town until 1710, when Palatine Germans settled at West Camp. The town was formed from Kingston in 1811. Industry dominated town and village, and involved sawmilling, gunpowder, paper, ironwork, brick, white lead, bluestone and limestone quarrying, and ice cutting. Principal factories were Ulster Iron Co (1828–88), Laflin Powder Co (?1832–?1874), and Martin Cantine Co (1888–1977). The village was incorporated in 1831 as Ulster and renamed Saugerties in 1855. The first railroad was the West Shore in 1883. When the ice-cutting business became obsolete, some of the large icehouses were used to grow mushrooms. The Knaust Cannery (1918) brought nearly 1,000 people displaced by World War I to Saugerties. The New York State Thruway (1954) provided modern highway access. Ferroxcube Corp (1950; television components) was succeeded by Philips Components, which closed in 1999; the facility is used by Clearly Tech (candles). Vertis, a commercial printer, employed 430 in 2003. The Mum Festival in October and the Hudson Valley Garlic Festival in September are annual events, while Woodstock 1994 was a one-time festival. Saugerties is the site of Opus 40 (1938), a 6-acre (2.4 ha) outdoor sculpture garden, the Quarryman's Museum, the Saugerties Lighthouse (1868), and Bristol Beach State Park.

Ruth Piwonka

sausage makers. Colonial and early 19th-century farmers of Dutch and German ancestry living in New York State made sausages, but their product was only a small part of the American diet until the decades after the Civil War and the introduction of refrigerated railroad cars. The first sausage factories were founded by Germans, but other ethnic groups—notably Italians, Poles, and eastern European Jews—soon followed. By the late 19th century, New York City was a center for medium-sized sausage makers. In the 1880s and 1890s, Charles Feltman sold frankfurters in buns at Coney Island. "Hot dogs" were a popular snack, and the nickname was first recorded in 1895. In 1916 Feltman's employee Nathan Handwerker founded the still existing Nathan's to make kosher hot dogs. Elsewhere, J. J. Schneck in Albany manufactured bologna sausages in wholesale quantities in the 1880s. Rochester sausage makers included Frederick Porschet, Casper Wenck's Sons, and the still extant John Zweigle Co (1880), which is famous for its "Red Hots" (beef) and "White Hots" (pork). The Hoffmann Sausage Co (1879) in Syracuse is known for its "snappys," or short wieners. In Buffalo, Christian Klinck's butcher shop of the late 1850s grew into the Christian Klinck Meatpacking Co by 1868; it also made sausages in bulk. In 1872 Jacob Dold opened a meatpacking and sausage-making plant in eastern Buffalo that had 2,000 employees in 1923. But Dold acquired a meatpacking plant in Kansas City in 1892, and production gradually moved out of state.

There are few sausage makers left in New York State as of the early 21st century. Hebrew National, founded in 1905, moved its production from Queens to Indianapolis in 1986. In New York City, remaining sausage makers include Karl Ehmer in Ridgewood (Queens Co), founded in 1932, and Schaller and Weber in Astoria (Queens Co), founded in 1937. Other ongoing producers include Fritz Helmbold and Levonian Bros (1947) in Troy, the White Eagle Packing Co (1921) in Schenectady, the Bilinski Sausage Manufacturing Co (1929) in Cohoes (Albany Co), and the smaller Rolf's Pork Store in Albany (founded in 1886 as Wiesel's Meat Shop). Gianelli's (1946) still operates in Syracuse, and Frank Wardynski and Sons (1919) and Mineo and Sapio (1920) have remained in Buffalo. In 2002 New York State production of sausages was $135 million, or about 2.1% of the national production of $6.4 billion.

Dold Quality: One Suggests the Other (Buffalo: Jacob Dold Packing, 1899)

2002 Economic Census. Industry Series. Meat Processed from Carcasses (Washington, DC: US Department of Commerce, Bureau of the Census, 2004)

Thomas Reimer

Savannah. Town (pop 1,838) in SE Wayne Co. About half the town is taken up by the Montezuma Marsh; Crusoe Lake is at its center. The first settlers came to build the Galen Salt Works (1808–11). The Montezuma Turnpike, completed in the area about 1820, gave some impetus to settlement. The town was formed from Galen in 1825. The principal settlement, also called Savannah, was founded in 1854 as a railroad depot on the New York Central; it was an incorporated village from 1867 to 1979. Coarse grass from the marsh in the southwest part of town was used to make paper in nearby Clyde until 1869. Savannah's rich mucklands are well suited for potatoes, onions, and other crops, and a potato festival is held each October. The Crusoe Conservation Center offers recreational, educational, and research opportunities.

Scott C. Monje

savings banks. These depository institutions specialize in the issuance of relatively small, demand, or short-term financial liabilities (deposits) and the purchase of relatively large, long-term financial assets collateralized by real estate (mortgages). In 1819, with support from De Witt Clinton and the Society for the Prevention of Pauperism, the New York State legislature chartered the Bank for Savings in Manhattan. The Albany Savings Bank was chartered in 1820, and the Troy Savings Bank (Rensselaer Co) was chartered in 1823. Early savings banks were organized as mutual companies in which depositors rather than stockholders owned the assets. Philanthropists ran these banks in accordance with charters mandating that depositors' funds be conservatively invested. Savings banks at first invested in securities such as federal and state bonds and bank stock; the Bank for Savings became an important financier of state projects, most notably the Erie Canal. By 1825 the Bank for Savings had amassed more assets than all of the other 14 savings banks in the nation combined.

Early New York State savings banks accepted deposits from the wage-earning working poor, teaching them the habit of thrift by providing a safe place for their savings where they could also earn modest interest. Established in 1829 the Seamen's Bank for Savings in Manhattan originally served only those who made their living on the sea. New York's mutual savings banks did not make private loans until mortgage loans were legalized in 1830. The Poughkeepsie Savings Bank, founded in 1831 reportedly at the request of a servant from New York City who had made deposits at the Bank for Savings, made mortgage loans on real estate. Devoid of stockholders interested in high profits and run by salaried business owners constrained from speculation by law, the early savings banks were conservatively operated. Most banks' losses were few and returns steady at 4–5% per annum, just a point or two below much riskier investments. The Bank for Savings accounted for 34% of all deposits and 42% of all customers in 1835, when there were 51 savings banks in the United States. Building and loan associations, the precursors of savings and loans, were set up specifically for household finance. Members of associations such as the Brooklyn Building and Mutual Loan Association, founded in 1836, pooled their savings and received mortgage loans. Building and loans were unincorporated term organizations; when the last loan was repaid and the shares matured, the association was dissolved.

Home Savings Bank, Albany, *ca* 1955.

New York State's savings banks were so well run that they continued to attract depositors in large numbers, and new banks were organized to serve new constituencies. The Dry Dock Savings Institution was established in 1848 for workers connected with the East 11th St dry dock. The Emigrant Industrial Savings Bank, for recent Irish immigrants, was incorporated in 1850 at the height of the potato famine. The overall economic importance of New York's savings banks probably peaked around 1860, when their combined assets were over six times greater than those of life insurance companies and when three of the nation's ten largest businesses were Manhattan savings banks: the Bank for Savings, Bowery Savings Bank, and Seaman's Bank for Savings. By 1892 savings bank deposits in the state totaled over $629 million. The provisions of savings banks' contracts helped them weather the Panic of 1907, when New York City savings banks decided to enforce their prerogative of postponing passbook payments for 30 or 60 days, protecting the assets of both the banks and the depositors. The management of savings banks remained largely unchanged during the 1920s, and their conservative investment strategies proved helpful during the depression years. Manhattan's dominance in mutual savings bank activity persisted despite the Great Depression. In 1936 New York State was home to 135 of the nation's 566 savings banks and to about half of national savings bank assets, an increasing percentage of which was invested in consumer mortgages. In 1933 the Federal Deposit Insurance Corp (FDIC) was created to guarantee bank deposits. In 1934 savings and loans received federal deposit insurance under the Federal Savings and Loan Insurance Corp (FSLIC).

As late as 1969, 9 of the nation's 10 largest mutual savings banks were located in New York City. Financial instability in the late 1960s and throughout the 1970s, with increasingly volatile interest and exchange rates, hurt savings institutions as depositors withdrew funds for investments with higher rates of return. Savings banks, especially following the 1980 Depository Institutions Deregulation and Monetary Control Act (DIDMCA), followed more aggressive strategies of profit maximization, moving away from home mortgages into commercial real estate and other more speculative investment strategies. Savings banks merged with the expectation that combined resources would make them more competitive with commercial banks. In 1981 the Metropolitan Savings Bank and the Brooklyn Savings Bank merged to create an institution with assets over $3.9 billion. In 1982 the Buffalo Savings Bank, established in 1846, absorbed the venerable New York Bank for Savings to create an institution with assets of $8.1 billion. The Garn-St. Germain Depository Institutions Act of 1982 gave savings banks the option of joint-stock status, and many savings banks converted to stock ownership to raise capital in the equity market.

Questionable and highly speculative banking practices in 1984 triggered a widespread failure of savings and loans institutions. The Financial Institutions Reform, Recovery, and Enforcement Act of 1989 created the Resolution Trust Corp to respond to the insolvent savings and loans; losses were estimated at $147 billion by 1990. As of 1995 savings and loans were guaranteed under the FDIC. In some ways the crisis helped the savings bank industry by weeding out poorly run banks and by forcing the creation of what may prove to be a better regulatory regime. Savings bankers adopted better strategies; for example, by the late 1990s it was common practice for savings bankers to reduce their interest rate risk by bundling and selling fixed-rate mortgages to institutional investors. As of 7 Nov 2002 there were 75 savings institutions in New York State.

Kidwell, David S., Richard Peterson, and David Blackwell. *Financial Institutions, Markets, and Money,* 7th ed. (New York: Harcourt College Publishers, 2000)

Olmstead, Alan. *New York City Mutual Savings Banks, 1819–1861* (Chapel Hill: Univ of North Carolina Press, 1976)

Welfling, Weldon. *Savings Banking in New York State: A Study of Changes in Savings Bank Practice and Policy Occasioned by Important Economic Changes* (Durham, NC: Duke Univ Press, 1939)

Savona. Village (pop 822) in Bath (Steuben Co). Settled in 1793 and connected to the railroad in 1851, the village was incorporated in 1883. In the 1890s the village had a "patent sluice" factory, a sash and blinds works, a planing mill, and a cigar factory. In 1922 Savona native Elmer "Slim" Faucett (1891–1960) became the first pilot to fly over the Andes Mountains in Peru. By 2002 most residents commuted to jobs in Bath or Corning.

Virginia L. Wright and Jerry Wright

sawmills. New York's first sawmills were set up in the lower Hudson Valley in the early 1600s. These crude mills were water powered and quite slow, producing only a few boards per hour, but they were essential to the development of the country. They were often the first manufacturing plant built in a locality. Although trees were heavy, hard to move, and difficult to process into lumber, labor was relatively cheap and plentiful. Softwoods were preferred due to the ease with which they could be machined and used for construction. White pine, plentiful throughout much of the state, was the major species utilized during the colonial era. Red spruce was also used, cut into lumber and for wood pulp. Hardwoods such as maple, cherry, and oak were harvested but were more difficult to saw in the early, slow mills.

The number of sawmills grew and spread as settlement progressed. By 1840 there were more than 6,000 sawmills in the state. Larger mills were built in the foothills of the Adirondacks, where lumber for export was the most important product for the local economy. In 1850 New York State led the nation in lumber production, probably employing about 12,000 men and producing more than 1.6 billion board feet, about 20% of the national total. Production dropped from this high point as the wave of first harvests of primeval forest moved to the Great Lakes states and then on to the western United States. By 1905 there were about 2,300 New York State sawmills employing around 7,500 men, with production still high at around 1.3 billion board feet.

Many changes came to the sawmill industry in the 20th century. Steam engine–powered mills began to arrive in the 1850s, replacing the earlier water-powered mills. By the 1940s, diesel and electric power had succeeded steam energy. The number of sawmills declined to approximately 1,000 facilities, and lumber production to approximately 175 million board feet per year during the depression years of the 1930s. From this point, production increased, and at the beginning of the 21st century, about 450 mills generated 550 million board feet annually and employed 2,100 persons.

Labor is now the expensive commodity, with machines and technology doing most of the cutting, shaping, and moving of lumber. Modern mills also employ kilns to dry lumber within weeks; from the 1800s into the early 1900s, much lumber was air dried at the sawmill for up to a year. Perhaps the greatest change in the operation of the state's sawmills across the 20th century and into the 21st has been in species of woods processed. In 1900, 80% of lumber production was softwoods (mainly pine and spruce) and 20% hardwoods. In 2000 production was 80% hardwoods (sugar maple, red maple, black cherry, red oak, basswood, white ash, yellow birch, hickory, beech, and other species) and only 20% softwoods. Another major change has been in utilization of residues. During the 18th and 19th centuries, sawdust, bark, and other waste trimmings were often used; for example, sawdust was a cleaning agent and an insulator in icehouses and hemlock bark was a source of tannin for tanneries. During most of the 20th century, sawmill wastes were burned or piled on vacant land, but at the beginning of the 21st century, all such by-products are again being used, with sawdust employed for animal bedding or in cleaning products and bark for garden mulch. The tons of wood chips produced from trimmings are often shipped to northeastern paper mills and made into high-quality paper. New York State's sawmills face an uncertain future with competition from other regions and countries, rising costs of labor and energy, and more restrictions on log movement and disposal of residues.

Canham, Hugh O., and George R. Armstrong. *Long-Term Trends in New York State's Timber Industries and Their Implications* (Albany: NYS Office of Planning Coordination, 1968)

Canham, Hugh O., and Kevin S. King. *Just the Facts: An Overview of New York's Wood-Based Economy and Forest Resource* (Albany: Empire State Forest Products Association, 1998)

Hugh O. Canham

Sayville {Sayville, locality (pop 16,735) in Islip, Suffolk Co; West Sayville, locality (pop 5,003) in Islip}. In the early 19th century residents fished and supplied cordwood to New York City. Sayville acquired a post office in 1837 and West Sayville in 1891. The South Side Rail Road came through in 1868. An influx of Dutch fishermen to West Sayville began in 1849, and by 1910 there were 1,200 in the insular Dutch community. They developed the oyster and clam fishery; the Bluepoints Co (1912 2003) of West Sayville produced and shipped oysters. A related industry was the Virginia Barrel Factory. A powerful wireless station was built in 1911–12 by Germany's Telefunken Communications Co; taken over by the US military in 1917, it was used by the Federal Aviation Administration until 1995. George Baker Jr (?1877–1965), better known as Father Divine, moved his ministry to Sayville in 1919; his interracial community raised local ire, and in 1933 he moved it again, to Harlem. In the early 21st century, West Sayville's commercial fish-processing businesses thrive, and its community dock remains active. The Sayvilles are the location of Islip Grange, a 12-acre (4.9 ha) historic farm operated as a museum; of the Suffolk County Maritime Museum, with its restored oyster house; and of St. Ann's Episcopal Church (1887), notable for its Tiffany windows.

Joan Ryan, CSJ

Scarsdale. Coextensive town and village (pop 17,823) in central Westchester Co. The town, named for the Manor of Scarsdale, to which Caleb Heathcote received a land grant in 1701, first elected officers in 1783 and was confirmed as a town in 1788. It remained entirely rural until after the Harlem Railroad came through in 1844. By 1860 it was a town of country estates and its pre-railroad population of 255 had doubled. An influx of the upper-middle-class people followed about 1890; a working-class development was started in 1891 by the Arthur Suburban Home Co. In 1908 the town was targeted for annexation by White Plains, and in 1915 the village was incorporated to prevent this from happening. During the 1920s the population grew 176%, partly because of the Bronx River Parkway (1924) and Hutchinson River Parkway (1928), which created arterials for New York City–bound commuters. After World War II, developers "built out" the town, and the predominant Anglo-American population was joined by a growing Jewish minority. The 1960 Holly Ball at the Scarsdale Golf Club exposed anti-Semitism in the village. Famous residents have included Daniel D. Tompkins and James Fenimore Cooper. Scarsdale was also the office location of Herman Tarnower (1910–80), the "Scarsdale Diet Doctor," who was murdered by his former lover Jean Harris in his nearby Purchase home. Scarsdale's growing Asian population made up 12.5% of the population in 2000.

Scenic Byways Program. Established in 1992 to recognize portions of the highway system notable for significant scenic, historic, recreational, cultural, natural, and archaeological intrinsic qualities. The State Department of Transportation supervises the New York State Scenic Byways Advisory Board and is charged with forming a comprehensive statewide system of scenic byways. These corridors offer alternative travel routes and tell thematic stories about New

York State's cultural and natural character. The board advises the commissioner of transportation on the organization and operation of the program, including additional designations. Byways are locally managed to protect their outstanding character and to encourage economic development through tourism and recreation. The benefits of designation include economic development, tourism publicity, and roadway improvements. The legislation encourages communities to make nominations to the board.

When the program was initiated by the state legislature, numerous previously designated roads automatically became scenic byways. These include 45 scenic roads named by the State Department of Conservation, such as Woods Rd (Greene Co) and the Susquehanna Turnpike (Greene Co); 14 state parkways (9 on Long Island), with the Taconic State Parkway (104 miles/167 km) as the longest. The list also includes several North Country touring routes and the 454 mi (730 km) Seaway Trail that borders Lakes Erie and Ontario and the St. Lawrence and Niagara Rivers. The Seaway Trail is the state's only nationally designated byway. In 2003 there were 79 state-designated scenic byways in New York State totaling 2,267 miles (3,649 km). These include the Adirondack Trail, 188 miles (303 km) through the Adirondack Park from Fonda (Montgomery Co) to Malone (Franklin Co); Scenic Route 90, 50 miles (80 km) in the Finger Lakes region from Homer (Cortland Co) to Montezuma (Cayuga Co); the Revolutionary Trail, 158 miles (254 km) from Port Ontario (Oswego Co) to Albany; and the Lakes to Locks Passage, 190 miles (306 km) from Waterford (Saratoga Co) to Rouses Point (Clinton Co), designated an All-American Road, the highest level of national byway.

New York State Scenic Byways Program, http://www.dot.state.ny.us/scenic/scenic.html

David H. Fasser

***Scenic Hudson Preservation Conference v Federal Power Commission*, 354 F 2d 608 (1965).** Landmark environmental law case. In 1962 the Consolidated Edison Co of New York (Con Edison) announced a plan to build a colossal 2,000 MW pumped-storage hydroelectric facility at Storm King Mountain near Cornwall (Orange Co) on the Hudson River. The plan prompted environmental activists to form the Scenic Hudson Preservation Conference in 1963, which opposed the facility on the grounds that it would spoil the scenic beauty of the region and harm the fisheries. Con Edison received a license to construct the facility from the Federal Power Commission (FPC) in March 1965. This action was overturned later that year by the Second Circuit Court of Appeals in *Scenic Hudson Preservation Conference v Federal Power Commission.* More than a decade of legal conflict ensued during which a second license was issued by the FPC in 1970 only to be surrendered by Con Edison in 1981. The 1965 decision was a landmark for the environmental movement, representing the first occasion on which grassroots activists were granted legal standing on an environmental issue. In addition, the decision paved the way for the development of a system of environmental law that requires federal agencies to take environmental issues into consideration.

Talbot, Allan R. *Power along the Hudson: The Storm King Case and the Birth of Environmentalism* (New York: Dutton, 1972)

William S. Helmer

Schaff, Philip (*b* Chur, Switzerland, 1 Jan 1819; *d* New York City, 20 Oct 1893). Theologian and historian. Educated at the universities of Tübingen, Halle, and Berlin, Schaff immigrated to the United States in 1844 and taught at the Mercersburg Seminary in Pennsylvania, where he and John W. Nevin crafted a Protestant theology that emphasized liturgy, historicism, and ecumenism. Feeling the need to live in a larger population center, he moved to New York City in 1863, serving as secretary of the New York Sabbath Committee until 1870 and thereafter as professor at the Union Theological Seminary, where he became world renowned. Through his efforts the 1873 international meeting of the Evangelical Alliance in the city was a great success. Schaff was president (1870–85) of the American Committee of Bible Revision, which produced the American Revised Version of the Bible, and he supervised the famous multivolume edition of the *Nicene and Post-Nicene Fathers.* He is the author of the seven-volume *History of the Christian Church* (1856–92), and in 1888 he became the founder and first president of the American Society of Church History. On 25 Sept 1893 shortly before his death, he delivered a paper, "The Reunion of Christendom," at the World's Parliament of Religions in Chicago, filled with his ideas about evangelical Catholicism and Christian unity. Subject to two heresy trials early in his career, this pioneer visionary dreamed of Christian ecumenism.

Schaff, David. *The Life of Philip Schaff* (New York: C. Scribner's Sons, 1897)
Shriver, George H. *Philip Schaff: Christian Scholar and Ecumenical Prophet* (Macon, Ga: Mercer, 1987)

George H. Shriver

Schaghticoke. Indian settlement. In 1676 Gov Edmund Andros invited New England Indian refugees from King Philip's War to live at Schaghticoke [now in Rensselaer Co]. In 1685 a second group, of more than 150 Western Abenaki, arrived and became the dominant faction. Albany's 1686 charter granted the city the right to purchase Indian land at Schaghticoke. A gradual loss of land resulted through land sales by unauthorized Indians and encroachment by colonial farmers. As a buffer against the French and their Indian allies, the Schaghticoke settlement helped to protect Albany during King William's War in the 1690s. Some Schaghticokes served with Mohicans (Mahicans) at the fort at Half Moon on the west side of the Hudson River north of Albany. At the invitation of the Mohawks, a group of Schaghticokes moved to Mohawk territory in 1703. Despite loss of land and harassment by traders and farmers, the Indian village at Schaghticoke persisted until 1754, when between 50 and 60 Schaghticoke men, women, and children departed, with French help, for Canada.

Dunn, Shirley W. *The Mohicans and Their Land, 1609–1730* (Fleischmanns, NY: Purple Mountain Press, 1994)
Kloppett, R. Beth. "The History of the Town of Schaghticoke, New York, 1676–1855" (PhD diss, SUNY Albany, 1981)

Shirley W. Dunn

Schaghticoke [SKAT-EE-COKE]. Town (pop 7,456) and village (pop 676) in NW Rensselaer Co. In 1676 the Schaghticoke Indians, composed of remnants of five New England tribes, were encouraged by the colonial governor to settle in the area as a barrier for the colony, but they left in 1754. European settlement began in 1709 with tenants growing wheat for the City of Albany; rent was collected for over a century. Schaghticoke formed as a district in 1772 and was recognized as a town in 1788. Large-scale industrial development began with the Rensselaer Woolen and Cotton Manufacturing Co (1810), followed by other woolen, cotton, linen, paper, iron, shirt, and agricultural tool manufacturing. The most notable operations were the Schaghticoke Powder Mills (1812–49) and the Cable Flax Mills Co (1871–1929). The village incorporated in 1867 as Harts Falls and was renamed in 1882. Its industrial base disappeared in the 20th century, and in the early 21st century the town has a mix of dairy, vegetable, and specialty farms, and suburban homes. The Knickerbocker Mansion is open to the public in the summer, and the Rensselaer County Fairgrounds (1922) is located in town.

Kathryn T. Sheehan

Schechter Poultry Corp v United States. See *A. L. A. SCHECHTER POULTRY CORP V UNITED STATES.*

Schenectady. City (pop 61,821) in Schenectady Co. Proud of its industrial heritage, Schenectady was known in the early 20th century as "The City That Lights and Hauls the World" because of its prominence in the electrical and locomotive industries.

Settlement and Economic Development

In 1661 the Mohawk sold to 15 proprietors, represented by Arent van Curler, the land extending 3 miles (5 km) above and below the present site of Schenectady. Settlement began by 1662 in what is known as the Stockade, at the beginning of navigation on the Mohawk River. Director General Petrus Stuyvesant assented to the purchase in appointing a surveyor in 1664, shortly before the colony surrendered to the English. Because Beverwijck [now Albany] leaders were concerned that the settlement would usurp its Iroquois fur trade, Stuyvesant forbade the settlers to trade with the Indians and restricted their economic activities to farming. A charter was granted in 1684, expanding Schenectady's boundaries but prohibiting activity in the lucrative but declining fur trade.

The original settlers were primarily Dutch but included Germans, Scots, and Norwegians. The palisaded Schenectady community had grown to more than 130 people by February 1690 when it was burned by a force of French soldiers and their Indian allies. Sixty people were killed and 27 captured. With assistance from the Mohawks, the residents rebuilt. Culturally it remained overwhelmingly Dutch, but during the French and Indian War, British influences began to be evident. Boatbuilding shops and warehouses developed to serve the military effort. During the Revolutionary War, the Schenectady militia (officially the Second Regiment, Albany Co Militia) participated in the battles of Saratoga and in defense of the Schoharie and Mohawk Valleys from

Abraham Yates House, located in the Stockade district, built *ca* 1700.

loyalist raids. After the war, Schenectady became an important gateway to the West as settlers migrating to western New York State and the Old Northwest passed through.

Schenectady was chartered as a borough town in 1765, one of only two in the colony, along with Westchester [now in Bronx Co]. This gave it a government with a mayor and aldermen, and the right to send a representative to the provincial assembly. It was recognized as a town in 1788, and at the time of the first census in 1790, its population was 2,520. It received a city charter in 1798.

Schenectady's importance as a river landing declined after a fire in 1819 destroyed the warehouses and boatbuilding shops, but the Erie Canal (1825) soon replaced the Mohawk River as the major water route. In 1831 the debut of the DeWitt Clinton locomotive on the Mohawk and Hudson Railroad and the first regular service from Albany helped move Schenectady into the industrial age. In 1848 locomotive production began at the Schenectady Locomotive Engine Manufactory; its successor firm was part of the 1901 merger that created the American Locomotive Co (ALCO). The city grew slowly throughout the first three-quarters of the 19th century (from 4,258 in 1820 to 13,655 in 1880) until the Edison Machine Works relocated to a site at the border between Schenectady and the Town of Rotterdam in 1886.

Ethnicity, Immigration, and Religion

By the 1850s Irish, German, and Jewish immigrants began arriving. The Germans remained the largest immigrant group until the end of the century, when they were supplanted by large numbers of Polish and Italian immigrants. More than 5,000 Polish immigrants initially settled in neighborhoods adjoining General Electric (GE) and ALCO, moving into areas farther from the plants by 1905, including Mont Pleasant and the Eastern Ave neighborhood east of City Hall. They established Roman Catholic churches (St. Mary's in 1892 and St. Adalbert's in 1902) and schools, as well as social organizations to maintain their Polish identity.

A large influx of Italian immigrants followed. Primarily from the southern regions of Italy, they moved into the Polish neighborhoods near the two industrial plants, eventually concen-trating in Mont Pleasant and the North Side. They also established Catholic churches but maintained their cultural identity through mutual-aid societies and social organizations. Immigration continues to alter the cultural composition of Schenectady. Recent arrivals have included Latino, Pakistani, Afghani, and East Asian immigrants. In 2001 Guyanese natives living in Queens Co began to arrive, attracted by inexpensive real estate and a relatively peaceful setting.

Schenectady has a rich, diverse ecclesiastical history. Several of its most notable landmarks are churches. The First Reformed Church in Schenectady was founded in 1684; its first building was destroyed in the Schenectady Massacre of 1690. St. George's Episcopal Church is the oldest church building, erected in 1759, three years after the parish was formed. The sanctuary of the First Presbyterian Church, which was organized in 1770, dates to 1809. In 2003 Schenectady had nearly 150 churches and religious societies.

Politics

The first mayor of Schenectady, Joseph C. Yates, was appointed by Gov John Jay to the first of his 12 one-year terms in 1798. Yates became the seventh governor of New York State in 1822. The mayoralty was made elective in 1840, its term expanded to two years in 1861 and to four years in 1936, the year the city adopted a city manager form of government. The city manager position was abolished in 1979 on the election of Frank Duci as the first "strong" mayor in over 40 years. The city council originally consisted of members elected from residents of the city's four wards; growth in the early 20th century necessitated expansion to 14. Since 1936 council members have been elected at large.

Republicans have historically dominated city and county politics. George R. Lunn, Schenectady's only Socialist mayor, was elected in 1911 in response to the failure of the major parties to react to the problems associated with the city's growth. The famous engineer and scientist of GE, Charles P. Steinmetz, was appointed by Lunn as president of the Board of Education and was subsequently elected president of the Common Council. In 1915 Lunn was reelected mayor as a Democrat and later served in the US Congress. In 1958 Samuel S. Stratton was elected to the US House of Representatives, where he would serve for 30 years; he was the first Democrat to serve from Schenectady in 42 years. Karen Johnson became the city's first woman mayor in 1983. Changes in the late 20th century altered Schenectady's political structure. Although the county is still primarily Republican, the city has become increasingly Democratic, with that party holding a 6–1 advantage on the city council in 2002.

Cityscape and Economic Development

The development of the city has been closely tied to its economic success. Although GE manufacturing was mainly outside city limits, most of its employees lived in Schenectady. Until the opening of the Edison Machine Works in 1886, the city was essentially confined to the 21st century's downtown area, with narrow built-up strips along the main roads to Albany and Troy. The growth of the city from 13,655 in 1880 to 95,692 in 1930 resulted in the annexation of land from the Town of Rotterdam and the development of several new neighborhoods, including Mont Pleasant, Hamilton Hill, Bellevue, Woodlawn, the GE Realty Plot, and the North Side.

The neighborhoods nearest the industrial plants of ALCO and GE became predominantly Polish and Italian by 1900. The former residents of those neighborhoods moved to Hamilton Hill, which had been rural through the 1890s with the county fairgrounds and summer homes. Mont Pleasant developed after 1905 when a trolley line opened, linking it to Hamilton Hill and the city center.

In downtown Schenectady, State St was transformed from a mix of residences and small businesses into part of the urban core. The towers of the Edison Hotel and Hotel Vendome loomed over the city into the 1930s. Schenectady's Union Station opened in 1908. Movie theaters operated downtown and in each neighborhood. In 1926 Proctor's Theatre opened as a combination vaudeville house and silent movie palace. Since its 1979 restoration, Proctor's has been one of Schenectady's most valued institutions. City Hall (1929–31) is a Federal Revival building designed by the noted architectural firm of McKim, Mead and White. The Stockade neighborhood contains one of the largest concentrations of 18th-century houses in the nation and became New York State's first historic district in 1962. The city's other historic districts include the GE Realty Plot, Union Triangle, Union Street Corridor, and Morris Avenue.

Culture

Schenectady, through GE, played an important role in the development of broadcast radio and television. The first radio drama, "The Wolf," was aired on radio station WGY in 1922. Schenectady television station WRGB traces its roots to the first public demonstration of television in the home, which took place in the residence of GE engineer E. F. W. Alexanderson (1878–1975) on 13 Jan 1928. The first television drama, "The Queen's Messenger," premiered over WRGB in the summer of 1928 and was followed by the first theater demonstration of television at Proctor's in 1930. Since the first newspaper, the *Mohawk Mercury,* was published in 1796, Schenectady has had a number of daily and weekly newspapers, now represented by the *Daily Gazette* (1894). Schenectady is the home of Union College (1795) and Schenectady County Community College (1968).

Natives and residents have included Pres Chester A. Arthur (1829–86), inventor and industrialist George Westinghouse (1846–1912), industrialist and Stanford University founder Leland Stanford (1824–93), filmmaker John Sayles (1950–), MTV cofounder John Sykes (1955–), basketball player and coach Pat Riley (1945–), original *Today Show* host Dave Garroway (1913–82), female drag racer Shirley Muldowney (1940–), and architect Edward Tuckerman Potter (1831–1904).

Recent History

Schenectady's population declined substantially in the postwar decades, from 91,785 in 1950 to

61,821 in 2000, caused in part by the city's shrinking industrial base. ALCO closed in 1969, and GE decentralized and eliminated many jobs. Suburbanization in adjacent towns also played a role, as did the completion of the I-890 bypass in 1968. The city's major department stores—H. S. Barney's, Wallace's, W. T. Grant's, and S. S. Kresge's—all closed within three years of the opening of Mohawk Mall in Niskayuna in 1970. The last major store, Carl Co, closed in its centennial year, 1991.

As in many cities, there was an increase in the minority population in the postwar decades. The African American community, a presence since colonial times, increased substantially as many moved from New York City in search of jobs. The Hamilton Hill neighborhood became the center of Schenectady's African American population, served by volunteer organizations including Hamilton Hill Arts Center and the Carver Community Center. In 2000 the racial composition of Schenectady was 77% white, 15% black, and 2% Asian. Approximately 6% of the population was of Latino ethnicity.

Downtown Schenectady has been affected in the last 50 years by a series of urban renewal projects that eliminated parking on State St, demolished several landmarks, including Union Station, and leveled residential neighborhoods adjacent to downtown, including a 22-block area east of City Hall targeted for redevelopment after World War II. Little of the planned redevelopment took place. Recent construction has included headquarters for Mohawk Valley Health Plan (MVP) and the New York Lottery, and a regional office for the New York State Department of Transportation. It has been challenging in recent years to encourage new development in downtown Schenectady while protecting its historic character.

See also ARCHITECTS AND ARCHITECTURE, MOHAWK VALLEY; BROADCASTING (RADIO AND TELEVISION); DEINDUSTRIALIZATION.

Christopher Hunter and Stephanie Przybylek

Schenectady County (206 mi²/534 km²; pop 146,555). Created in 1809 from Albany Co, its name derives from a Mohawk word meaning "beyond the pine plains." The county is divided into one city, Schenectady, and five towns that contain two incorporated villages. Schenectady serves as county seat. Elevations range from 200 feet (61 m) at the county's easternmost reach along the Mohawk River to 1,456 feet (444 m) at a location in Duanesburg. Schenectady Co lies within the Hudson-Mohawk Lowland physiographic province. The eastern third is part of the Hudson Valley and is characterized by gentle relief. The remainder falls within the Mohawk Valley subregion, where relief is more pronounced. The Mohawk River has incised itself into a relatively restricted inner valley; elevations rise most noticeably in the south, where the land rises to meet the Helderberg Hills section of the Appalachian Plateau, whose margin lies just south of the county line. Bedrock consists of Ordovician shale interbedded with sandstone, along with a small area of limestone and dolomite in the far north. Evidence of glaciation is present throughout the county. A mantle of till cloaks nearly the entire county. In the east it is covered by lake-laid materials associated with prehistoric Lake Albany, elsewhere by outwash deposited by glacial meltwaters. Present-day Mariaville Lake is the remnant of a glacial lake. The Mohawk drains most of the county, either directly or via Schoharie Creek. A small area in the southeast drains directly into the Hudson River via Normans Kill. Except for alluvial flats along the Mohawk and a few scattered areas of moderately arable land, the soils are considered poor by modern agricultural standards.

Schenectady Co's climate is humid-continental. Mean seasonal temperatures are comparatively uniform. January temperatures average around 22°F (-6°C). Every winter, lows can be expected occasionally to fall below 0°F (-18°C). The mean July temperature is 70°F (21°C) in the lower elevations, a degree or two cooler in the higher areas. Daytime highs reach 90°F (32°C) or more at least a few days every summer. Average annual precipitation is 37 inches (94 cm) at Schenectady and slightly more in the higher surrounding country. Seasonal snowfall amounts vary from 63 inches (160 cm) in the southeast to approximately 75 inches (191 cm) in the north and west. The primeval forest cover consisted of three communities. Alleghenian hardwood forests consisting of beech, sugar maple, hemlock, white pine, and basswood prevailed at the higher elevation; oak-pine forest occupied the sand plains in the east; and central hardwoods—beech, sugar maple, basswood, oak, and chestnut—were dominant along the Mohawk.

The county's major waterway is the Mohawk River, which flows from west to east. Schenectady, the starting point for westward navigation on the river, became known as the "Gateway to the West" in recognition of the Mohawk's role in the westward development of the United States. Warehouses and boatbuilding facilities were created along the river in the present city during the French and Indian War. The Mohawk bends at Schenectady and was fordable in colonial times. A long wooden bridge connected the city and Scotia beginning in 1808. The county features several small natural and artificial lakes, including Mariaville Lake; though only 2 miles (3.2 km) in circumference, it is the largest lake in the county.

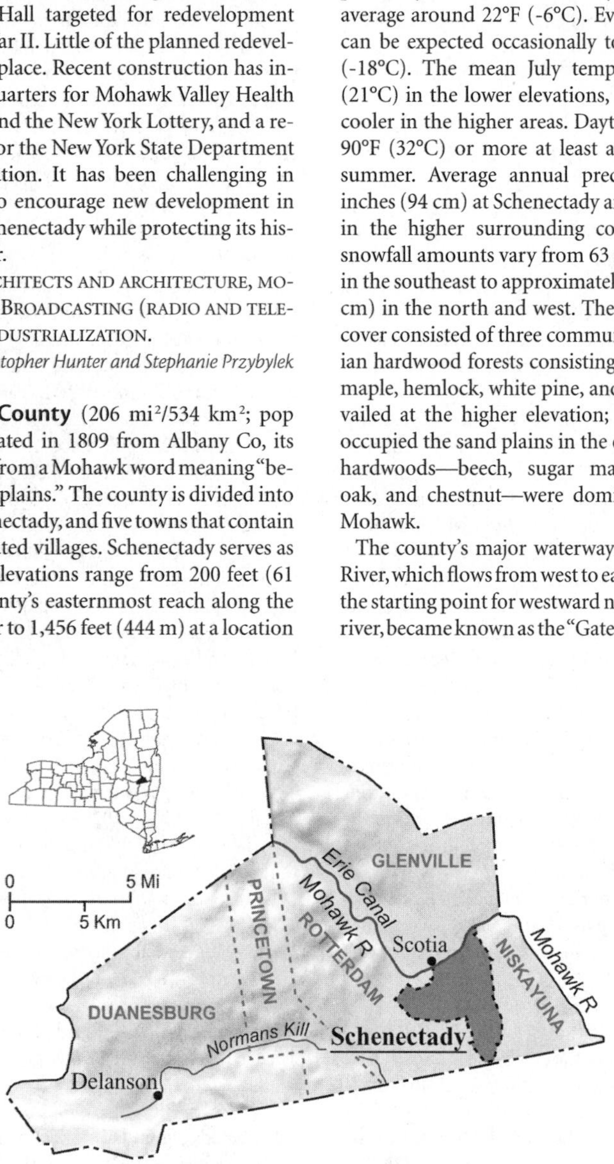

SETTLEMENT AND ETHNICITY

Schenectady Co was part of the homeland of the Mohawk Nation, whose villages were a few miles to the west of the present county during the Contact period. In 1661 the Mohawk sold land around what is now the City of Schenectady to a group of 15 farmers of Dutch, German, Scottish, and Norwegian origins; settlement began in 1662. The community was destroyed by a French and Indian raid in 1690 but rebuilt; by the mid–18th century the original European population of Dutch extraction were joined by British.

The first African Americans came to Schenectady Co as the slaves of settlers and worked at farming and domestic chores. In the 1690 Schenectady Massacre, 11 slaves were killed and another 5 were captured by the French. Slavery continued in Schenectady Co until abolished statewide in 1827. As late as 1820, 102 slaves (along with 454 free Blacks) lived here. By 1830 the total number of Blacks had dropped below 200 and remained below the 1820 level until the 1930s. Underground Railroad activity occurred around the Quaker settlement in Duanesburg and possibly within the city. Although Schenectady had an African Methodist Episcopal (AME) church and a separate school by 1837, only about 60 black families lived in the city at the time of the Civil War, most of them working as servants.

By the mid–19th century, Irish, German, and Jewish immigrants arrived, with the Germans leading in numbers until the end of the century, when large numbers of Poles and Italians formed strong communities in the city. Over the course of the 19th and early 20th centuries, Schenectady developed as a transportation and manufacturing center, so its percentage of the county's population increased, reaching 83% by 1910. In 1920 the county was 23% foreign-born; of these, 26% were Italian and 21% Polish.

ECONOMIC DEVELOPMENT

Until Thomas Edison moved his machine works to Schenectady in 1886, agriculture was the county's major industry. Wheat was the primary agricultural product, followed by potatoes and corn. Farmers also raised cattle and sheep. In the 1850s Schenectady Co was widely known for broomcorn: farms in Rotterdam and Glenville produced 727 tons (660 MT) in 1854, nearly half the state's crop. The Midwest supplanted Schenectady's production in the 1870s. Other characteristic crops were oats and apples. By the early 20th century dairy farming dominated the county's agriculture.

The city's shipping and boatbuilding industries were destroyed by an 1819 fire and were not rebuilt because of the construction of the Erie Canal, which entered Schenectady Co in Niskayuna at the Rexford Aqueduct, passed through the city along the present Erie Blvd, and continued through Rotterdam into Mont-

SCHENECTADY CO POPULATION CENSUS FIGURES

	White	Nonwhite	Total Population	Foreign-Born
1810	9,695	506	10,201	—
1820	12,320	761	13,081	194
1830	12,043	304	12,347	168
1840	16,977	410	17,387	—
1850	19,666	388	20,054	2,985
1860	19,761	241	20,002	3,792
1870	21,179	168	21,347	3,686
1880	23,375	163	23,538	3,744
1890	29,648	149	29,797	5,569
1900	46,659	193	46,852	9,689
1910	87,887	348	88,235	21,055
1920	108,859	504	109,363	23,175
1930	124,302	719	125,021	24,401
1940	121,773	721	122,494	19,595
1950	140,962	1,535	142,497	16,885
1960	150,538	2,358	152,896	13,920
1970	156,776	4,203	160,979	11,720
1980	143,439	6,507	149,946	9,170
1990	139,407	9,878	149,285	7,432
2000	128,631	17,924	146,555	7,811

Notes: "Nonwhite" includes African Americans, Asians, American Indians, and Pacific Islanders and, for 2000, also the mixed race and other race categories. Through the 1960 census these figures primarily reflect the African American population. Foreign-born figures for 1820 and 1830 include only those not naturalized, and for 1930 and 1950, the foreign-born totals include Whites only. Other years include all foreign-born in the population.

gomery Co. Only one lock, number 23 in Rotterdam, was located within the county limits after the 1841 canal enlargement. Following the opening of the Barge Canal in 1918, locks were located in Niskayuna (Lock 7) and Rotterdam (Locks 8 and 9). Railroad service began with the Albany and Schenectady Railroad (1831); direct connections followed in short order to Saratoga Springs (1832), Utica (1836), and Troy (Rensselaer Co, 1842).

In 1820 county industry included 16 gristmills, 28 sawmills, 1 paper mill, 2 cotton and wool factories, 2 breweries, 6 tanneries, and 1 small ironworks. The latter, along with machine shops, supplied the needs of agriculture. By the 1850s, as farm equipment became increasingly complex, machine shops produced small engines. The Westinghouse Co, producer of agricultural machines and implements, moved to Schenectady from Schoharie Co in 1850. The Schenectady Locomotive Engine Manufactory first opened in 1848, passing through a change of ownership and becoming Schenectady Locomotive Works in 1851. The cyclical nature of the locomotive industry complemented the county's focus on agriculture. When the economy slowed and work stopped at the locomotive works, workers returned to the farms. The Schenectady Locomotive Works consolidated with six other companies in 1901 to form the American Locomotive Co (ALCO). Economic growth demanded the creation and expansion of banks. The first was the Mohawk Bank (1807) which, along with Schenectady Savings Bank (1832), was part of Fleet Bank in 2003. The Schenectady Trust Co (1902) became Trustco Bank. Other important financial institutions included Schenectady Savings and Loan (now part of Hudson River Bank) and the First National Bank of Scotia.

The county's population grew rapidly after the Edison Machine Works, producer of power generation and transmission equipment, relocated from New York City to Schenectady in 1886. The company, which through consolidation became Edison General Electric Co in 1889 and General Electric Co (GE) in 1892, built factories on the Schenectady city boundary with Rotterdam. The development of an electric street railway system in 1891 facilitated continued growth. Edison's 300 original workers grew to more than 3,300 in 1900, and GE supplanted the Locomotive Works as the county's largest employer. By 1905 the two companies provided 90% of the city's industrial jobs.

This industrialization changed the character of the county. The city annexed land from Rotterdam that became its Mont Pleasant and Bellevue neighborhoods. The rural population in Duanesburg and Princetown declined as people moved to the city to work for GE. In 1902 trolley service was extended to Scotia, which incorporated as a village two years later. A trolley line completed in 1905 fostered the development of Mont Pleasant. Lines controlled by the Schenectady Railway Co ran to Albany and Troy, permitting development to extend into the Town of Niskayuna. In 1904 alone the railway carried 10 million passengers on 160 streetcars over 124 miles (200 km) of track. With a large industrial population, Schenectady became important in the development of labor unions. The Industrial Workers of the World (IWW) formed a union at GE in 1905 and held the nation's first sit-down strike in 1906.

Religion, Education, and Culture

The First Reformed Church (1684) was Schenectady's earliest, joined after the British influx by St. George's Church (Episcopal, 1758) and First Presbyterian (1770). In 1855 the county, still strongly Dutch in background, was dominated by Dutch Reformed churches, of which there were 10, with one or more in every town. By contrast, the Methodist Church, the next largest, had only four congregations. There was a single Roman Catholic parish at that time, but many additional parishes, some of them ethnic, were founded half a century later. Sha'ave Shamayin (1854) was the first Jewish congregation.

Common schools were established in response to 1812 legislation. The private Lancaster School and Schenectady Female Academy and Lyceum provided secondary education until 1854, when the Schenectady Union Free School District was formed and a public high school established. Elsewhere in the county the common schools served until centralization began with Mariaville in 1927. The last district to consolidate was Mohonasen in 1956. In 2003 there were five central school districts in addition to the Schenectady City School District. Rev Dirck Romeyn (1744–1804) of the Dutch Reformed Church led the movement to create the Schenectady Academy, a college preparatory school. The efforts of Romeyn and members of the local Presbyterian and Episcopal churches resulted in the founding of Union College in 1795. It was the county's only institution of higher education until Schenectady County Community College began operating in 1969.

The county's first newspaper was the *Mohawk Mercury* (1796). In the early 21st century the *Daily Gazette* (1902), an independent newspaper, serves a six-county region. The City of Schenectady pioneered in broadcasting and continues to have several radio and television stations, including the acclaimed public station WMHT. Important cultural institutions include Proctor's Theatre, the Schenectady Museum, and the Schenectady County Public Library.

Politics

When the county formed in 1809, Gen William North of Duanesburg was appointed the first chairman of the six-member Board of Supervisors. Each ward of the city and each town elected a supervisor. Schenectady's growth to 14 wards in the early 20th century gave it a disproportionately large voice on the board. In 1965 the county

Hoffman's Ferry on the Mohawk River in Schenectady County.

POPULATIONS OF TOWNS AND CITIES, SCHENECTADY CO

Town or City, Year Founded	1800	1840	1880	1920	1960	2000
Duanesburg, 1765[a]	2,787	3,357	2,995	2,115	3,070	5,808
Glenville, 1820	—	3,068	2,746	7,036	25,707	28,183
Niskayuna, 1809	—	693	990	3,149	14,032	20,295
Princetown, 1798	812	1,201	826	487	912	2,132
Rotterdam, 1820	—	2,284	2,326	7,853	27,493	28,316
Schenectady (city), 1684[b]	5,289	6,784	13,655	88,723	81,682	61,821

Note: In 1800 the City of Schenectady and the Towns of Duanesburg and Princetown were in Albany Co.

[a]Patented as township 1765; formed as district 1772; recognized as town 1788.

[b]First municipal charter 1684; charted as borough 1765; incorporated as district 1772; recognized as town 1788; city charter 1798.

charter was amended by referendum to create a 15-member Board of Representatives (now the County Legislature), which employs a county manager. For the election of representatives, the city is divided into two districts; Niskayuna and Glenville make a third district, and Rotterdam, Princetown, and Duanesburg a fourth. Reflecting the recent growth of the towns, city representation in the County Legislature has declined from eight members to six.

THE 20TH CENTURY

By the 1920s the population of the towns was increasing relative to the city because of the increasing availability of the automobile. After a fallow period for labor in the 1920s, a new union, Local 301 of the United Electrical, Radio, and Machine Workers of America (UE), emerged at GE's Schenectady Works in 1936. The GE and ALCO plants reached their employment peak during World War II, with 45,000 and 10,000 workers, respectively. Schenectady was vital to the war effort, with tank production at ALCO and a wide variety of products and research at GE. Large strikes in January 1946 at both GE and ALCO regained concessions made by the unions during the war. The beginning of the Cold War and anticommunist sentiment hindered the effectiveness of the UE, and in 1954 the 20,000-member Schenectady local voted to join the rival International Union of Electrical, Radio, and Machine Workers (IUE).

Excessive dependence on the two major manufacturers hurt the county when those companies' presence in Schenectady declined after the war. Movement to the towns accelerated after World War II, and Glenville, Niskayuna, and Rotterdam became popular suburbs. Schenectady benefited from modern superhighway connections with the New York State Thruway (1954) and I-88 (1982). Despite the decline in the City of Schenectady's population after World War II, the overall county population continued to increase until 1970, peaking at 160,979. The closing of ALCO in 1969 and the decline of GE affected the city's and county's populations.

In the early 21st century, GE, despite continued decentralization and downsizing since 1970, remains the county's largest employer, with about 4,700 workers at its steam turbine plants in Schenectady and Rotterdam and the Global Research Center (formerly GE Research Laboratory) in Niskayuna. Regional grocery chain Price Chopper in Rotterdam is the largest company headquartered in the county, with approximately 6,200 employees in a six-state area. In 2000 the towns constituted 56% of the county's population. The African American population of Schenectady increased in the 1950s as Blacks migrated from the South in search of manufacturing jobs, and the increase accelerated after 1980 as rising housing costs pushed Blacks from New York City. By 2000 the black population of Schenectady had climbed to 9,132 (almost 15% of the city's total population); many were concentrated in the Hamilton Hill neighborhood. There is a substantial Asian population in Niskayuna and a small but growing number of Guyanese in the city.

See also ARCHITECTS AND ARCHITECTURE, MOHAWK VALLEY.

The standard histories are Jonathan Pearson, *A History of the Schenectady Patent* (1883); George R. Howell, *History of the County of Schenectady* (1886); Austin A. Yates, *Schenectady County, New York: Its History to the Close of the 19th Century* (1902); and Willis T. Hanson, *A History of Schenectady during the Revolution* (1916; repr 1988). A scholarly study of the early years is Thomas E. Burke Jr, *Mohawk Frontier: The Dutch Community of Schenectady, NY, 1661–1710* (1991). Robert V. Wells, *Facing the "King of Terrors": Death and Society in an American Community, 1750–1990* (2000) uses Schenectady as its case study. Robert R. Pascucci, "Electric City Immigrants: Italians and Poles of Schenectady, NY, 1880–1930" (PhD diss, SUNY Albany, 1984), is an excellent study of immigration. The first volume of Susan Staffa's *Schenectady Genesis: How a Dutch Colonial Village Became an American City*, 2 vols, appeared in 2004. The small number of town histories includes *Glenville's Past and Present* (1970), and Irma Mastrean, *Princetown: Portrait of a Town* (1990). Larry Hart, who wrote for the *Daily Gazette*, published nine books on Schenectady, including *Schenectady: Changing with the Times* (1988).

Christopher Hunter and Stephanie Przybylek

Schenectady Massacre. On the night of 8 Feb 1690, more than 200 French troops and their Indian allies destroyed Schenectady. It was part of a three-pronged attack against English settlements in New York and New England at the beginning of King William's War (1689–97). The governor of New France, Comte de Frontenac, originally contemplated an attack on Albany, but Schenectady was chosen on the presumption that it would be more vulnerable. The invaders arrived about midnight and found the settlement's gates open and unguarded. In the wake of Leisler's Rebellion and the factions that developed in New York, Schenectady officials had ignored advice from Albany magistrates to post sentries. Almost all of the village's 80 buildings were leveled and nearly 100 inhabitants were killed or captured. Many of Lt Enos Tallmadge's detachment of 24 militiamen, on loan to the town from Connecticut, also perished or were captured. Across the Mohawk River from Schenectady, Capt John Glen and his family were spared because of past kindnesses toward French captives. Despite the murder of his son and a gunshot wound in his thigh, Simon Schermerhorn escaped and carried news of the disaster to Albany. Mohawk warriors chased the retreating invaders almost to Montreal, without any significant engagement. Several literary, theatrical, and artistic works commemorate the attack.

O'Callaghan, Edmund B., ed. "Papers Relating to the Invasion of New York and the Burning of Schenectady by the French, 1690." In *The Documentary History of the State of New York* (Albany: Weed, Parsons, 1849–51)

Peckham, Howard H. *The Colonial Wars, 1689–1762* (Chicago: Univ of Chicago Press, 1964)

Daniel A. Piazza

schepen. See NEW NETHERLAND: POLITICAL SUBDIVISIONS.

Schneiderman, Rose (*b* Saven [now in Poland], 6 Apr 1882; *d* New York City, 11 Aug 1972). Labor activist and suffragist. In 1890 Schneiderman and her family immigrated to the United States, settling in New York City's Lower East Side. At age 13 she started working in a department store but in 1898 got a better-paying job in a cap factory. In 1903 she and her co-workers organized the first women's local of the Cap Makers' Union. After a 1905 strike of her union she joined the Women's Trade Union League (WTUL). Through the New York branch of the WTUL she was active in support of the 1909 "Uprising of 20,000" strike. NYWTUL's first paid organizer, she served as the group's president (1918–49) and national president (1926–50). During the WTUL's early years, it focused on organizing women workers into unions. Later it pressed for legislation important to working women. An ardent suffragist, the International Ladies' Garment Workers' Union and the New York Wage Earners Suffrage League sent her to speak at suffrage meetings in New York and other cities from 1911 to 1912. Schneiderman was an influential friend of Franklin D. and Eleanor Roosevelt. In 1933 Pres Roosevelt appointed her to the National Recovery Administration Labor Advisory Board, the only woman to serve on that committee. She also served as the state's secretary of labor (1937–43). The national WTUL disbanded in 1950 and the New York branch in 1955. She then worked on her autobiography, *All For One* (1967). She spent the last five years of her life in the Jewish Home and Hospital for the Aged in New York City.

Dye, Nancy Schrom. *As Equals and As Sisters: Feminism, the Labor Movement, and the Women's Trade Union League of New York* (Columbia: Univ of Missouri Press, 1980)

Connie Kopelov

Schodack [SKO-DAK]. Town (pop 12,536) in SW Rensselaer Co. Originally the chief council seat of the Mohican (Mahican) tribe and settled under Rensselaerswijck *ca* 1630, the town was formed in 1795. First accessible by road on the King's Highway (1723), Schodack has always been crossed by main transportation routes; in the 19th century these included the Boston and Albany Turnpike (1800), the Albany and West Stockbridge Railroad (1841, later Boston and Albany), and the Hudson River Railroad (1851). The town was the site of brickyards and factories in the Village of Castleton-on-Hudson and of a Knickerbocker Ice Co icehouse (1872) on Schodack Island. The Berkshire Spur of the New York State Thruway (1958) and I-90 (1976) encouraged suburban connections to Albany, but parts of town remain agricultural in the early 21st century.

Kathryn T. Sheehan

Schoellkopf, Jacob F(rederick) (*b* Kirchheim unter Teck, Germany, 15 Nov 1819; *d* Buffalo, 15 Sept 1899). Entrepreneur. Arriving in Buffalo in 1844, Schoellkopf opened a small leather store and soon constructed five tanneries in Buffalo and the Midwest. He built several flour-milling operations in Buffalo and Niagara Falls and in 1877 bought the rights to the bankrupt Hydraulic Canal in Niagara Falls and the waterpower rights of the American side of the Niagara River for $71,000. In 1879 he erected in Buffalo the first US coal-tar dye plant, the Schoellkopf Aniline and Chemical Co (now Buffalo Color Corp), which blossomed under the direction of sons Jacob Jr (1858–1942) and C. P. Hugo (1862–1928) when they returned from their German education in chemistry in 1880 and 1885 respectively. Schoellkopf was the first in 1881 to develop electrical power successfully at the falls, and his Niagara Falls Hydraulic and Manufacturing Co supplied waterpower to seven factories by 1882. Schoellkopf's six sons and one daughter continued their father's businesses and expanded into banking, investment firms, real estate, and local public service. Arthur (1856–1913) partnered with his father in the hydraulic and electrical enterprises, founded the Power City Bank, and was mayor of Niagara Falls in 1896. Jacob Jr and C. P. Hugo built the dye firm and after 1918 led the family electrical business, which eventually became Niagara Mohawk Power Corp.

Glynn, Diane. *The Schoellkopfs, 1842–1994: A Family History* ([Niagara Falls, NY]: Niagara Falls Memorial Medical Center Foundation, 1995)

Kenneth S. Mernitz

Schoharie. Town (pop 3,299) and village (pop 1,030) in NE Schoharie Co. Settled late in 1712 by Palatines as Brunnen Dorf, Schoharie was made a district of Albany Co in 1772 and a town in 1788. With the formation of Schoharie Co in 1795, it became the county seat. The rich alluvial soils of the Schoharie and Fox Valleys have sustained intensive agriculture, such as the successful Guernsey Nurseries (1889), for almost three centuries. The Schoharie Valley Railroad operated from 1867 to 1942. In the early 21st century light manufacturing and quarrying are among Schoharie's principal economic activities. The village is home to two museum organizations, Schoharie County Historical Society and Schoharie Colonial Heritage Association, that operate the Old Stone Fort (1772), the Lutheran Parsonage (1743), and the railroad depot (1891). The Easter Egg Museum is privately owned. Schoharie was the site of the first open-air movie on 7 June 1917.

Peter Johnson and Dawn Johnson

Schoharie County (625 mi²/1,619 km²; pop 31,582). Created in 1795 from Albany and Otsego Cos, it was named for Schoharie Creek, its principal stream. The name was derived from an Iroquoian word for wood drift, a reference to log and brush piles that collected along the stream, especially near present-day Middleburgh. The county is divided into 16 towns that contain 6 incorporated villages; the Village of Schoharie is the county seat.

The county sits astride three of the principal subregions of the Appalachian Upland physiographic province: the Catskill Mountains, extending into the southern portion of the county with elevations ranging from 2,000 to 3,400 feet (610–1,040 m); the lower stretches of the Helderberg Hills in the north and northeast; and the Susquehanna Hills in the center and west. The county's highest elevation is 3,423 ft (1,043 m) Huntersfield Mountain on the border with Greene Co; the lowest is 510 feet (155 m) above sea level in the northeast corner where Schoharie Creek exits the county. Bedrock consists of Devonian shale, sandstone, limestone, and conglomerates. The area around Cobleskill, underlain by middle Devonian limestones, contains the most extensive cave complex in the northeastern United States. The extreme northern portions of the county lie in the lowlands of the Mohawk River. Here the bedrock consists of Ordovician and Silurian rocks. Throughout Schoharie Co the bedrock strata dip gently southward, resulting in steep north-facing escarpments and long, gentle southern slopes. Evidence of continental glaciation is found in topography and soil composition. Schoharie Creek traverses the entire county, flowing north from its source on Hunter Mountain (Greene Co). Important tributaries include Fox, Cobleskill, and Manorkill Creeks. Catskill Creek, the West Branch of the Delaware, and tributaries of the Susquehanna also rise in the county.

The climate is humid-continental, with cold snowy winters and cool wet summers. Mean January and July temperatures range from 20 to 22°F (-7 to -6°C) and 68 to 70°F (20 to 21°C), respectively, with the lower temperatures in the higher elevations. Precipitation averages 36–42 inches (91–107 cm) annually. Seasonal snowfall averages range from approximately 45 inches (114 cm) in the Schoharie Valley to over 120 inches (305 cm) in some of the higher elevations in the south. Soils range from productive limey clay loams in the north to thin clay and sandy loams in upland areas and fertile alluvial soils along the Schoharie Creek. Commercially viable farmland is largely limited to the northwest quarter of the county and to the Schoharie Valley. Primeval vegetation varied. Aside from the Schoharie Valley, the northern portions of the county contained an Alleghenian hardwood community composed primarily of beech, sugar maple, hemlock, white pine, and basswood. The Schoharie Valley held a central hardwood forest dominated by beech, sugar maple, basswood, oak, and chestnut. In contrast, higher elevations in the south supported a spruce-fur forest community. In the early 21st century over 65% of the county is forested, including approximately 20,000 acres (8,000 ha) in the southern reaches replanted in red pine.

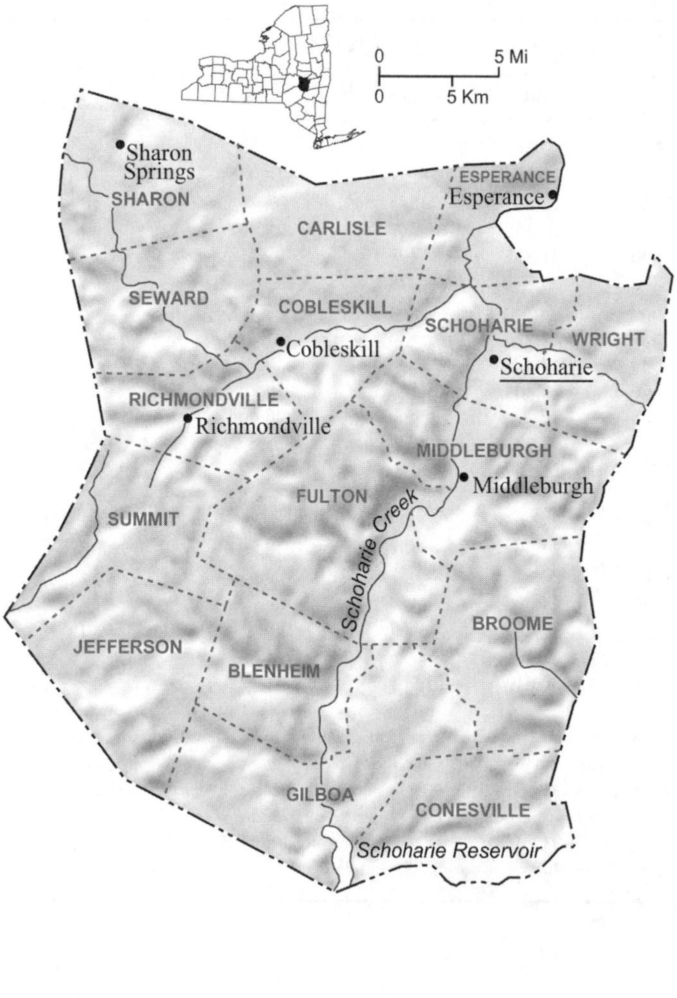

American Indians and Early Settlement

Native groups may have entered the area during the early postglacial period (*ca*11,000 BP); artifacts from all subsequent phases of human culture have been found in sites throughout the valley. In the Late Woodland period (AD 1000–1500), a more complex, sedentary culture of agriculturists emerged who raised maize, beans, and squash, and supplemented their diets through hunting, fishing, and gathering. These Owascans lived in permanent villages, produced beautiful ceramics, and buried their dead in carefully prepared graves. By the early 1600s the Schoharie Valley marked the boundary between Algonquian-speaking Mohicans (Mahicans) and Delawares to the east and the expanding Iroquois Confederacy to the west. The Dutch explored the Schoharie during the 1620s and, based at Fort Orange [now Albany], later developed the fur trade controlled by the Mohawk. A century later the first permanent European settlers entered the area and encountered the Schoharie tribe, a mix of Delaware, Mohican, Mohawk, Oneida, and Tuscarora people, living in small villages between Middleburgh and Schoharie and totaling perhaps 300 people. Years of amicable relations, including the "sale" of land to white settlers, ended with the American Revolution. Many Indian tribes sided with the British, and years of savage raiding by both sides ensued. The war and infectious diseases, especially smallpox, eliminated Native Americans from the county by the mid-1780s.

In late 1712 approximately 200 German Palatines entered the Schoharie Valley; they were part of the more than 3,000 indentured servants brought to the mid-Hudson region in 1710 to produce naval stores for the British navy. When that project failed a contingent moved to Schoharie to occupy land they believed the British Crown had promised them. Although many left within a few years, this migration marked the first permanent European penetration into the upland country west of the Catskills. They established several *dorfs* (villages), including present-day Schoharie and Middleburgh. Dutch settlers followed soon after, with approximately 700 people living in what became the Towns of Schoharie and Middleburgh. A few settlers of English descent also migrated into the area by midcentury, well in advance of the flood of New England immigration that began in the mid-1780s. By exploiting the valley's fertile soils these settlers made the Schoharie a breadbasket of the Revolution, supplying 80,000 bushels (2,820,000 l) of grain to patriot forces by 1780.

The British practice of granting land patents to well-connected men complicated the process of settlement in Schoharie. Scott's Patent, the Blenheim Patent, and more than 40 others, many of which overlapped, covered almost all the future county's productive land. Some patentees sold their land outright, but the Livingston family, among others, retained ownership and leased it on onerous terms. As population increased and settlement spread after the Revolution, the hamlets of Schoharie and Middleburgh grew in size and several others—Breakabeen, Cobleskill, Esperance, Gilboa, Sharon Springs, and Richmondville—were established.

The Dutch brought the first African slaves into the valley by the late 1720s. The 1790 census enumerated 152 slaves out of a total population of 2,073. That number rose to 302 by 1820, along with a smaller number of freedmen. A black enclave at Schoharie hamlet supported a separate school from the 1850s until 1903, when its students were integrated into the village's new 12-grade school. An African Methodist Episcopal (AME) church was established in Schoharie in 1856 and continued as a separate congregation until the 1930s. Sixty African Americans from the county volunteered for the Union army during the Civil War. The 2000 Census gave a total of 403 Blacks, 1.3% of the population.

In the 1770s Schoharians filled both loyalist and patriot ranks as the Revolutionary crisis intensified. Patriots formed Committees of Safety that recruited soldiers and built fortifications to secure the valley's essential foodstuffs for American forces. Many others sided with the British Crown. Although no major battles were fought, the first recorded cavalry charge by American troops took place at the Battle of the Flockey in Blenheim in 1777. Tory and Iroquois forces repeatedly raided the valley, killing or capturing local residents and destroying homes and crops. The Johnson-Brant Raid combined with the local commitment to supply American forces made 1780 a year of particularly great hardship.

SCHOHARIE CO POPULATION CENSUS FIGURES

	White	Nonwhite	Total Population	Foreign-Born
1800	9,443	365	9,808	—
1810	18,394	551	18,945	—
1820	22,581	573	23,154	58
1830	27,335	567	27,902	20
1840	31,865	493	32,358	—
1850	33,070	478	33,548	963
1860	33,985	484	34,469	951
1870	32,914	426	33,340	901
1880	32,427	483	32,910	742
1890	28,834	330	29,164	678
1900	26,554	300	26,854	659
1910	23,631	224	23,855	651
1920	21,137	166	21,303	620
1930	19,550	117	19,667	822
1940	20,705	107	20,812	1,105
1950	22,594	109	22,703	1,507
1960	22,527	89	22,616	1,158
1970	24,567	183	24,750	888
1980	29,247	463	29,710	1,040
1990	31,136	723	31,859	911
2000	30,514	1,068	31,582	749

Notes: "Nonwhite" includes African Americans, Asians, American Indians, and Pacific Islanders and, for 2000, also the mixed race and other race categories. Through the 1960 census these figures primarily reflect the African American population. Foreign-born figures for 1820 and 1830 include only those not naturalized, and for 1930 and 1950, the foreign-born totals include Whites only. Other years include all foreign-born in the population.

Economic Development

From the beginning of white settlement, agriculture has been the county's dominant economic activity. The fertile alluvial soils yielded bumper crops of barley, wheat, and corn. In the 1780s settlement spread beyond the principal valleys and into the adjoining uplands. Population increased to almost 28,000 by 1830, much of it in villages where the tradesmen, merchants, bankers, and lawyers serving the larger agricultural community had settled. Schoharie was home to the county's first bank, the Schoharie County Bank (1852).

Farmers sold their surplus grains in Albany and Schenectady and sometimes further afield. Transportation improvements, such as the Great Western, Lunenburg, and Susquehanna Turnpikes, facilitated this process and provided improved access to the county for immigrants. Accessibility to the outside world proved to be a mixed blessing, however. By the 1830s the Erie Canal placed Schoharie Co farmers under increasing competitive pressure in the grain markets from Genesee Country farmers and later from those in the Midwest. The initial adjustment was from wheat to barley production. Local rail connections such as the Albany and Susquehanna Railroad—completed through Cobleskill in early 1865 with a branch to Sharon Springs and beyond in 1870—and a railroad from Central Bridge to Middleburgh, completed in 1869, improved farmers' position, but by then local agriculture had shifted away from grain to specialty crops such as broomcorn, apples, plums, and hops. When these crops in turn lost market share, farmers shifted to dairying. This process continued through the 20th century until the early 1960s, when as much as 90% of the more than $50 million in the county's annual agricultural sales came from the production of eggs, cheese, butter, and whole milk.

The shift from crops to dairying reflected deeper changes. The county's population peaked at 34,469 in 1860 and began a long slow decline to just over 22,000 in 1960. Mirroring trends in the longer-settled parts of New York State,

POPULATIONS OF TOWNS, SCHOHARIE CO

Town or City, Year Founded	1800	1840	1880	1920	1960	2000
Blenheim, 1797	783	2,725	1,191	516	345	330
Broome, 1797[a]	1,078	2,404	1,636	743	517	947
Carlisle, 1807	—	1,850	1,720	861	900	1,758
Cobleskill, 1797	1,765	3,583	3,370	3,798	4,964	6,407
Conesville, 1836	—	1,621	1,127	652	593	726
Esperance, 1846	—	—	1,378	890	1,232	2,043
Fulton, 1828	—	2,147	2,683	1,227	1,008	1,495
Gilboa, 1848	—	—	2,040	1,541	782	1,215
Jefferson, 1803	—	2,033	1,636	1,065	800	1,285
Middleburgh, 1797[b]	1,831	3,843	3,376	2,109	2,437	3,515
Richmondville, 1849	—	—	2,082	1,378	1,746	2,412
Schoharie, 1765[c]	1,696	5,534	3,350	2,132	3,063	3,299
Seward, 1840	—	2,088	1,734	1,193	1,210	1,637
Sharon, 1797	2,655	2,520	2,591	1,494	1,405	1,843
Summit, 1819	—	2,010	1,405	871	704	1,123
Wright, 1846	—	—	1,591	833	910	1,547

[a]Bristol until 1808.

[b]Middletown until 1801.

[c]Formed as district; recognized as town 1788.

Schoharians moved west to farm better land or migrated to the cities of the Hudson-Mohawk corridor, leaving the county with one of the highest levels of native-born residents in the state: 95.6% in 1875 and close to 90% in 2000. The number of farms and the amount of land devoted to agriculture declined as a result, from just over 4,000 farms and 280,000 improved acres (113,300 ha) in 1875 to 518 farms and 110,000 acres (44,500 ha) in 1997. Even so, the absolute value of the county's agricultural production increased over the same period.

Manufacturing has been less important. In the 19th century six of the county's towns produced paper, cotton and woolen cloth, ironwork (especially farm implements), clothing, boots, hats and gloves, and cigars. Gilboa, for example, was home to a large textile mill (1840–?1869). In the 20th century Cobleskill was the site of knitting mills, refrigerator manufacturing, and limestone and shale quarries for Portland cement production. Early in the 21st century, Schoharie has two quarries and a small company that manufactures plastic for Department of Defense contracts.

The mineral springs at Sharon Springs have been known for two centuries, and a summer resort developed beginning in 1825. Its heyday was from the 1920s to the 1950s, when more than 60 hotels catered to an Orthodox and Conservative Jewish clientele. The village declined dramatically in the late 20th century, but in 2003 some of the old hotels had reopened or were being restored. Farther south, New York City purchased part of the Town of Gilboa in 1911 to create the Schoharie Reservoir (completed 1926). Gilboa hamlet was inundated and some agricultural land lost. The New York State Power Authority completed the Blenheim-Gilboa Pumped Storage Power Project in 1973 to generate hydroelectric power. Although some marginal farmland was lost, the project created jobs and recreational opportunities.

Religion, Education, and Culture

A Dutch Reformed congregation organized at Schoharie in 1728 and Lutherans established a congregation in 1743. New Englanders founded Methodist, Presbyterian, and Baptist congregations prior to 1800; the county's first Roman Catholic congregation, St. Ann's Gilboa, was organized in 1844, followed by a mission at Sharon Springs in 1854. In 1855 Schoharie Co had 31 Methodist and 15 Baptist congregations, while its Dutch and Palatine roots were evident in 14 Lutheran and 12 Dutch Reformed churches. Mainline Protestant churches dominated the county's religious life at that time and continue to do so today. In recent years many evangelical Christian churches have appeared, as well as a sprinkling of non-Western and nontraditional groups. In 2003, 22 distinct denominations, most of them Protestant, worshiped in the county.

Shortly after 1740 German language schools appeared in the vicinity of Schoharie hamlet, followed by Dutch language counterparts. During the 19th century one-room schools operated in the county, and a number of academies appeared, including ones in Jefferson (1812) and Schoharie (1835). A Methodist conference operated a seminary in Charlotteville from 1850 to 1875, the largest of a number of short-lived boarding schools. In the 20th century both state legislation and increased state aid encouraged consolidation into seven central school districts, starting with Sharon Springs in 1928. All were in operation by 1936, but annexation of outlying common school districts continued until the 1960s; in 1993 two of the original central districts, Cobleskill and Richmondville, merged. The SUNY Regents selected Cobleskill as the site for a school of agriculture, which began operating in 1916; it is now the State University College of Technology at Cobleskill.

Deiderick Van Veghten published Schoharie's first newspaper, the *American Herald,* in 1809. This broadsheet appeared for only a few years and encountered immediate competition from Thomas Tillman's *True American,* which also ceased after a short period. Van Veghten founded the *Schoharie Republican* (1819), which became the influential organ of the county's Democratic Party until well after the Civil War. Peter Mix established the *Schoharie Patriot* (1838–63) as a forum for Whig and later Republican ideas. For much of the 20th century residents depended on papers published in nearby cities. Charles L. Ryder bought the faltering *Cobleskill Times* in 1919 and used it as the basis for a remarkable newspaper empire serving much of the Catskill region until his death in 1973. In 2003 the *Times Journal* is published weekly in Cobleskill.

While it is unclear when the first public library was founded, lending libraries appeared in Schoharie, Middleburgh, Gilboa, and many of the smaller settlements by the mid–19th century and continue to serve the population. Opera houses operated in both Gallupville and Sharon Springs in the 19th and early 20th centuries. The immense Howe Caverns complex in Howes Cave first opened in the 1950s and welcomes more than 200,000 visitors annually. Other important museums and historic sites include the Old Stone Fort and the Palatine House in Schoharie, the Iroquois Indian Museum in Howes Cave, Lansing Manor in Blenheim, and the Landis Arboretum in Esperance.

Politics

Schoharie was Antifederalist during the debate over ratification of the Constitution, objecting to the creation of a strong central government, and became a Democratic bastion in the early 1800s. Divisions between tenant farmers and landlords dominated politics for much of the antebellum period, especially in southern and eastern towns. Opposition to the rigid enforcement of leases and the hard economic times following the panic of 1837 led to the violent antirent wars (1837–45) and eventually to the dissolution of the leasehold system. While Free Soil arguments gained some adherents, most voters remained loyal to the conservative wing of the Democratic Party; John C. Breckinridge won the county's presidential vote in 1860 and George B. McClellan narrowly defeated Abraham Lincoln in 1864. Although more than 1,000 Schoharie men fought for the Union (the 134th New York Volunteer Infantry consisted mainly of Schoharians), there was a strong undercurrent of opposition to the war, to the granting of rights to African Americans, and to the growing centralization of national political power. Democrats retained control of the county well into the 20th century; a Republican first won a countywide election in 1909. Beginning in the 1920s the major political parties became more evenly balanced on the local level and have shared power in recent years. Like many rural counties with an agriculturally based economy and an overwhelmingly white population, Schoharie has voted for Republican candidates and policies in recent years.

The 16-member Schoharie County Board of Supervisors, with one elected representative from each town, managed county affairs until 1975. At that time, under pressure from the US Supreme Court's one person–one vote ruling, the board adopted a weighted voting formula but maintained representation by town. The representative from Cobleskill wields the largest number of votes on the board but does not control a majority. The chair of the board is the administrative head of the county. A county treasurer and a county clerk are elected every four years on an at-large basis.

Winter in Schoharie Co, by Beverly T. Lavick.

RECENT HISTORY

While agriculture, still dominated by dairy farming, remains the county's most important economic sector, responsible for about 30% of annual income, tourism and a diverse array of small manufacturing and service industries have also emerged. Sales tax revenues nearly doubled between 1990 and 2000 ($4.7 to $8.7 million) while the rate remained stable, suggesting that this new mix of economic activities may have produced the basis for a more sustainable development. The recent growth in population to a level not seen since the mid–19th century also signals a new trajectory. SUNY Cobleskill, a Wal-Mart distribution center in the Town of Sharon, and a number of major tourist attractions, including Howe Caverns, Secret Caverns in Howes Cave, and the Iroquois Indian Museum, have given the county an important economic boost. The completion of I-88 (1980) across the northern part of the county and its direct connection to the Thruway (1982) increased the potential for residential and commercial development by putting much of the county within comfortable commuting distance of the Capital District. This proximity, along with the county's rural ambiance and natural beauty, present an attractive alternative to urban life, raising the possibility that Schoharie might become a "bedroom community" for the Albany area. The major problem facing the county in the early 21st century is how to develop economically while preserving its rural character and quality of life.

Prominent county residents include Revolutionary War hero Timothy Murphy (?1751–1818); Daniel Shays (?1747–1825), leader of Shays's Rebellion; David Williams (1751–1834), one of the captors of Benedict Arnold's British co-conspirator Maj John André; Gov William C. Bouck (1786–1859), born in Fulton; inventor George Westinghouse (1846–1914), born at Central Bridge; and Gail Shaffer (*b* 1949), secretary of state under Gov Mario M. Cuomo.

See also ARCHITECTS AND ARCHITECTURE, MOHAWK VALLEY.

Schoharie Co has had a wide range of histories published, including perhaps the state's earliest, John M. Brown, *A Brief Sketch of the First Settlement of the County of Schoharie* (1823), as well as Jeptha R. Simms, *The History of Schoharie County and Border Wars* (1845). The standard work, William E. Roscoe, *History of Schoharie County* (1882), is unfortunately very weak. In the late 20th century a decent history for young readers was published, Marion T. Noyes, *A History of Schoharie County* (1954), as well as a short history, Lester E. Hendrix and Anne W. Hendrix, *Sloughter's Instant History of Schoharie County, 1700–1900* (1988). There are few good town histories, although the *Official History of the Town of Cobleskill* (1937) is one example. A single geological feature has been nicely studied: Vincent J. Schaefer, *Vrooman's Nose: Sky Island of the Schoharie Valley* (1992). Fred Lape, *A Farm and Village Boyhood* (1980), is a memoir of growing up in Esperance between 1902 and 1917 by an intelligent and literate chronicler. Between 1912 and 1917 a pioneer folklorist, Emelyn E. Gardner, collected the county's traditions, publishing them as *Folklore from the Schoharie Hills* (1937). Henry Z. Jones, *The Palatine Families of New York* (1985), and subsequent books by the same author provide exceptional documentation of the county's Palatine settlers and settlement. The *Schoharie County Historical Review* has been published semiannually since 1937.

Peter Johnson and Dawn Johnson

Schomburg, Arthur A(lfonso). (*b* San Juan, Puerto Rico, 24 Jan 1874; *d* Brooklyn, 10 June 1938). Historian and bibliophile. He called himself *Afroborinqueño*, or black Puerto Rican, and was the son of an unwed black midwife Maria Josefa; he believed his father to be Carlos Schomburg, a merchant of German descent. He was educated in St. Thomas, Virgin Islands, and moved to a Cuban Puerto Rican enclave in the Lower East Side of New York City in 1891. His association with Cuban patriots José Martí and Ramón Betances during the Spanish-American War period made him an activist for Cuban independence and cofounder of the political club Las Dos Antillas in 1892. His growing interest in his African heritage led him to become a founding member of the Negro Society for Historical Research (1911), which collected documents relating to black culture and history. His famous essay, "The Negro Digs Up His Past," was first published in *The New Negro* (1925) and suggested that historical analysis of black culture created a pride in race, which was an antidote for prejudice. He devoted his life to acquiring manuscripts on black history and by 1925 acquired 5,000 items, including slave narratives and abolitionist documents. The New York Public Library purchased his collection in 1926 and made them available at Harlem's 135th St branch, which became a major educational center for black history and culture. He was curator of the Harlem Library manuscripts from 1932 to 1938, and in 1940 the collection was named in his honor. In 1972 it was designated a New York Public Library Research Library and named the Schomburg Center for Research in Black Culture. The collection has over 5 million items including sound recordings, art objects, and photographs.

Sinnette, Elinor Des Verney. *Arthur Alfonso Schomburg: Black Bibliophile and Collector: A Biography* (New York: New York Public Library, 1989)

Tricia A. Barbagallo

school aid. See STATE AID TO SCHOOLS.

school districts. Colonial New York had many locally run schools but no laws governing education and no special districts operating schools with government support. The Board of Regents of the University of the State of New York, established in 1784 to supervise higher education, urged the legislature to establish and endow a system of public schools. A 1795 law authorized spending £20,000 annually for five years to support schools, but the amount proved inadequate to meet the need, and the appropriations were not renewed. In 1805 the legislature set up a common school fund for the support of public schools; proceeds of state land sales were designated for the fund. In 1812 a landmark law authorized establishment of self-governing common school districts and provided aid to each district from the common school fund. Town and city officials were empowered to lay out school districts; the voters in each district elected trustees to operate schools, generally one per district. State aid was distributed according to the number of residents aged 5 to 15 but only to those districts holding school at least three months a year. The district was required to match the state aid with town or city tax revenues. Any additional operating expenses were met by charging tuition (or rates) as itemized in rate bills. An 1814 amendment required the establishment of school districts statewide. The 1812 and 1814 school acts made the common schools a state function under state control and the funding of common schools a joint state-local responsibility, with the school district—not the county or the town—the administrative unit for public education.

FREE PUBLIC SCHOOLS AND HIGH SCHOOLS

Rate bills prevented many poor children from attending school, which prompted concerned

OPERATING SCHOOL DISTRICTS IN NEW YORK STATE

Type of District	1905–6	1935–36	1965–66	2002–3
Independent Superintendencies				
City districts[a]	45	59	62	62
Union free school districts[b]	31	94	100	86
Central school districts[b]	—	2	73	192
Dependent Districts				
Common school districts	9,935	6,626	56	10
Union free school districts	614	629	103	79
Central school districts	—	158	394	268
Central high school districts	—	5	4	4
Total School Districts	10,625[c]	7,573	792	701
Other Districts				
School commissioner districts	113	—	—	—
Supervisory districts	—	203	71	38

Sources: State Education Department, *Annual Report* (1905, 1907, 1937); State Education Department, *Annual Education Summary* (1966); State Education Department, unpublished data (2002–3); *State Education Department Glossary of Terms* (1961).

[a]Figures for 1965 and 2002 are the total city school districts (population 125,000 or more), enlarged city school districts (population 10,000 to 125,000), and city central school districts (population under 10,000).

[b]Figures for 1905 and 1935 include independent village districts (population 4,500 or more in 1905, or 5,000 or more in 1935). Figures for 1965 and 2002 include all independent noncity districts (population 4,500 or more). Sometimes termed "village superintendencies," these supervisory units do not necessarily have an incorporated village within their boundaries.

[c]Includes an unknown but very small number of nonoperating districts, which either had no children of school age or contracted with a neighboring district.

Compiled by James D. Folts

educators and parents to lobby for free common schools. An 1849 statute made state and local funding available for tuition-free schools, subject to statewide voter approval. The free school law was approved in two successive referendums, but the Court of Appeals declared the referendums illegal. In 1851 the legislature imposed a statewide real property tax for schools to supplement other revenues and to make free common schools fiscally possible. Superintendent of Public Instruction Victor M. Rice led the fight for free schools, and a law providing the necessary funding was finally passed in 1867. The Constitution of 1894 declared that "the Legislature shall provide for the maintenance and support of a system of free common schools, wherein all the children of this State may be educated."

By the 1850s, New York State had nearly 12,000 school districts. However, small districts were insufficient for burgeoning municipal areas. Ward or district schools operating inside city limits were combined by special statutes into citywide districts in Buffalo (1837), Utica (1842), Albany (1844), Syracuse (1848), Troy (1849), Brooklyn (1850), Rochester (1850), and Schenectady (1854). Gradually, other cities were constituted as school districts, and they were all placed under a uniform law in 1917. In New York City a citywide board of education was established in 1842 and a city superintendent of schools appointed in 1851, but the ward schools with their own officers persisted in the city until 1896. A general law passed in 1853 authorized one or more common school districts outside of cities to form into a union free school district. Boards of education managed the property and finances of the city and union free districts and hired superintendents to run the schools. The new city and union free school districts soon established "academic departments," or high schools, which were tuition free. Private nonchurch academies generally could not compete with these free public high schools, and most ceased operation or transferred their property to union free school districts.

Fiscal Problems and District Consolidation

After 1850 most state aid to schools was allocated by an intricate system of quotas that set predetermined amounts of money for each district, regardless of district size or affluence. Following the calculation of the quotas, the remainder of a district's state aid was based on the number of its school-age inhabitants and their average daily attendance. This complex system of state aid covered less and less of the cost of public education each year. In the late 19th century the statewide expansion of city and village school facilities and programs was largely financed by increases in local property taxes. The declining state aid hurt rural school districts with shrinking enrollments and stagnant tax bases. State school officials for decades had called for consolidation of small country districts, which were considered fiscally and educationally weak. In 1917 the legislature eliminated all common school districts and combined them into more than 900 "township" units. Because the new system did not equalize taxes between village and farm properties, school taxes soared, taxpayers complained, and after one year the experiment was discarded.

Inflation during World War I and the agricultural depression of the 1920s caused a crisis in school finance. The quota system of state aid could not respond to rapid inflation and deflation, and it was little help to poorer districts. The richer city districts were constrained by the constitutional limit on municipal indebtedness. During the 1920s major studies of school finance by the Friedsam Commission and other groups concluded that the system of state aid to schools required fundamental revision. The crisis was resolved by using aid as a powerful incentive to consolidate rural school districts, by increasing state aid to public schools from under 10% to about 27% of total costs, and by setting standard factors for distribution of aid. After 1925 average daily attendance was made the major factor in calculating state school aid, and an equalizing factor was introduced to bring per pupil expenditures up to a statewide minimum, though wealthy districts could and did spend more.

The Cole-Rice Law (1925) provided fiscal incentives for the creation of central rural school districts, first authorized in 1914. The liberal building and transportation aid formulas encouraged centralization, particularly throughout the depression of the 1930s. The State Education Department promoted (some said it coerced) the centralization of rural schools. However, the Regents' Inquiry into the Character and Cost of Public Education (1935–38) criticized the department's gradual approach and the small size of many of the new central schools. In response, centralization measures were systematized, and a Temporary State Commission on the State Education System (Rapp-Coudert Commission, 1941–47) created a master plan for school consolidation. Statutes approved in the 1950s allowed consolidation of small city districts and adjoining common school districts, and by the 1960s centralization of common and union free school districts in rural and upstate suburban areas was essentially complete. About 170 union free districts, most of them in the New York City suburbs, continue to function.

Town, city, and county officials supervised public schools until 1856, when the elective office of commissioner of schools was established (one or more in each county). These commissioners handled local administration for the state superintendent of public instruction. Since 1912 the local agents of the commissioner of education, the head of the State Education Department (formed in 1904), have been the locally appointed district superintendents of schools. The number of supervisory districts decreased from 207 in 1912 to 38 by 2003. The district superintendent also administers programs of the local Boards of Cooperative Educational Services (BOCES). School districts in cities and larger villages have always had their own superintendents. While all city districts and many central and union free school districts are "independent," "dependent" districts are subject to detailed oversight by a district superintendent of schools. In 1978 the chief administrator in each school district was designated superintendent. The title principal is now used for the supervisor of a school building.

Since the early 1950s, smaller city school districts (population under 125,000) have had fiscal and political autonomy from municipal government. A 1996 law gave voters in city school districts—except for the "Big Five" of New York,

Yonkers, Syracuse, Rochester, and Buffalo—the right to vote on school budgets, as is already the case in other districts. In union free school districts, starting in 1864, and in central school districts as they were established, voters approve or disapprove a statement of estimated expenditures, or budget. If the voters reject the budget, a contingency budget is implemented with limited discretionary spending.

See also PUBLIC EDUCATION.

Finegan, Thomas E. *Free Schools: A Documentary History of the Free School Movement in New York State*, vol 1 of *Annual Report* (1919), New York State Education Department (1921; repr New York: Arno Press, 1971)

Fitch, Charles E. "A History of the Common Schools in New York." In *Annual Report* (1902–3), Department of Public Instruction (Albany: NYS Department of Public Instruction, 1904)

New York State. Legislature. Joint Legislative Committee on the State Education System. *Master Plan for School District Reorganization in New York State*. Legislative Doc no. 25 (1947) (Albany, 1947; rev ed 1958)

James D. Folts

school lands. See GOSPEL AND SCHOOL LANDS.

School of Industrial and Labor Relations (ILR). Founded in 1945 as the New York State School of Industrial Relations at Cornell University, it was the first program in an academic setting that was designed specifically to study the changing American workplace. It was in large part the creation of Irving M. Ives (1896–1962), a state assemblyman (1929–46) and senator (1947–59) who supported pro-union, pro-labor legislation. Ives served as ILR's first dean in 1945–46. In 2003 ILR remained the only US institution to offer four-year undergraduate degrees (BS) in industrial and labor relations. It also offered graduate degrees, including master's degrees in industrial and labor relations, professional studies, and science, and a PhD in philosophy, at Cornell campuses in Ithaca and New York City. ILR has programs at extension offices in Albany, Buffalo, Ithaca, Long Island, New York City, and Rochester. In 2003 ILR enrolled 720 undergraduate and 150 graduate students and employed 52 faculty members.

Campbell, Ralph N., and Elizabeth R. Knowlton. *Business Leadership in Air Transportation; Report on American Airlines–Cornell University Cooperation in a Management Development Program* (Ithaca: NYS School of Industrial & Labor Relations, 1960)

Report of the ILR Review Panel (Ithaca: NYS School of Industrial & Labor Relations, 1987)

Jeffrey Kraus

School of Visual Arts. Private college. Founded in 1947 and located on a 1-acre (.4 ha) campus on East 23d St in Manhattan, the school is the largest independent college of art in the country. It offers a bachelor of fine arts degree in eight fields of study: advertising and graphic design, animation, computer art, film and video, fine arts, illustration and cartooning, interior design, and photography. Master's degrees are offered in art therapy, computer art, design, fine arts, illustration as visual essay, and photography and related media. Enrollment in 2003 stood at 3,379 students.

Marianne Rahn-Erickson

schout. See NEW NETHERLAND: POLITICAL SUBDIVISIONS.

Schroeppel [SCREW-PEL]. Town (pop 8,566) in S Oswego Co. Settled in 1800 the town was formed in 1832 from Volney. It is located in the northeast angle formed by the Oneida and Oswego Rivers. The Oswego Canal was constructed in 1828, providing waterpower and good transport facilities. Lumbering and barrel making were the early industries, with an experiment in salt making at Gilberts Mills (1864). Diversified farming and dairying followed, along with a variety of manufactures, including silk thread, knives, plaster, sliding doors, and shutters. Later there were five paper mills; the last, making carbonless carbon paper, closed in 1978. Some residents work at the county industrial park, but most commute, especially to greater Syracuse.

Barbara J. Dix

Schroon [SKREWN]. Town (pop 1,759) in S Essex Co. Settled prior to 1800 the town formed in 1804 from Crown Point. Lumbering was underway *ca* 1820, peaking from 1830 to 1845; there was iron mining, ironworks, and, in the 1850s and 1860s, tanneries. Hotels were built after the Adirondack Railroad (1872), with a terminus nearby at North Creek (Warren Co), made the town more accessible. In the early 20th century a "sleepaway camp" for Jewish boys led to Schroon Lake becoming a center of camps and resorts catering to a Jewish clientele; it closed in the 1960s and 1970s. The Northway (1967) provided improved access for tourism and outdoor recreation, especially at Schroon and Paradox Lakes.

Thomas A. Rumney

Schumer, Charles (Ellis) (*b* Brooklyn, 23 Nov 1950). US senator. One of three children of Abraham and Selma Schumer, owners of an exterminating business, Schumer attended public schools in Brooklyn, graduating from James Madison High School in 1967. He received BA and law degrees from Harvard University. In 1974 he was elected to the state Assembly from the 45th District (Brooklyn), where he chaired the Subcommittee on City Management and Governance (1977–78) and the Committee on Oversight and Investigation (1979–80). In 1980 Schumer was elected to the House of Representatives from New York State's 9th Congressional District. During his 18 years in the House, Schumer championed consumers' rights, access to abortion, and gun control. In 1998 he defeated three-term Republican incumbent Alfonse D'Amato to become a US senator from New York State. After the 11 Sept 2001 attack on the World Trade Center, Schumer helped to secure Pres George W. Bush's pledge of $20 billion to rebuild Lower Manhattan.

Newfield, Jack. "An Interview with Senator Charles Schumer," *Tikkun* 14 (Spring 1999): 55

Jeffrey Kraus

Schuyler [SKY-LER]. Town (pop 3,385) in W Herkimer Co. The first European occupants, from about 1764 until the Revolutionary War, were German potash makers working for Peter Hasenclever, whose iron manufacturing took place near the New Jersey–New York border. The town was formed from Herkimer in 1792. A railroad along the Mohawk River (1836) became the main line of the New York Central in 1853. Schuyler became a dairy farming town in the 19th century. North of West Schuyler, Polish farmers settled *ca* 1900. The Thruway opened in 1954 with a rest area, but no exit, in Schuyler. Dairy farming remains important to the economy in the early 21st century.

James Crawford

Schuyler, George S(amuel) (*b* Providence, RI, 25 Feb 1895; *d* New York City, 31 Aug 1977). Journalist. Raised by his parents George Schuyler and Eliza Fischer in a racially diverse area of Syracuse, Schuyler claimed he was a descendant of Gen Philip Schuyler. He enlisted in the army at 17 and wrote for a military newspaper, the *Service*, rising to the rank of first lieutenant by the end of World War I but ending up dishonorably discharged due to racial bias. By 1918 Schuyler moved to New York City and worked as a journalist. In 1923 he initiated a lively column, "Shafts and Darts: A Page of Columny and Satire," in the *Messenger*, a New York City–based African American socialist magazine. His 1926 essay "Negro-Art Hokum," a caustic look at the Harlem Renaissance, established his reputation as a Menckenesque iconoclast.

Schuyler began a lifetime association with the *Pittsburgh Courier* in 1923. He married Josephine Cogdell, a white Texan, in 1928. They had a daughter, Phillipa, a musical child prodigy, concert pianist, composer, and journalist. During the early 1930s he served as a correspondent for the *Courier* in Africa, a modern first for a black American. In 1931 he penned an acclaimed novel, *Black No More*, about a black man who invented a chemical technique able to change black skin to white. In 1931 he published a second novel, *Slaves Today*, about forced labor in Africa. Also in the 1930s, Schuyler led the drive to banish the popular radio show *Amos 'n' Andy* from the airwaves. He took a highly unpopular isolationist position in World War II and used his column to question, on the basis of continuing segregation and a claim that Americans treated Blacks like Germans treated Jews, whether Blacks owed the United States support. The FBI criticized Schuyler's pro-Japanese statements. From 1946 to 1960, Schuyler ran the New York City desk of the *Courier*. His growing conservatism, suspicion that the Civil Rights Movement was Communist-led, and caustic criticisms of Martin Luther King Jr led to his isolation from the black press. His well-known autobiography, *Black and Conservative* (1966), summarizes his later thinking. After the death of his daughter in Vietnam in 1967 and the suicide of his wife in 1969, Schuyler lived his remaining years very quietly.

Peplow, Michael W. *George S. Schuyler* (Boston: Twayne Publishers, 1980)

Graham Russell Hodges

Schuyler, Philip (John) (*b* Albany, 10 Nov 1733; *d* Albany, 18 Nov 1804). Landowner, politician, and Continental army officer. After the death of his father John Schuyler in 1741, Philip Schuyler was raised by his mother, Cornelia van Cortlandt, and grandfather, Johannes Schuyler. From 1748 to 1751 he studied with Rev Peter Stouppe at New Rochelle (Westchester Co), where Schuyler began to suffer from "rheumatic gout," which frequently interrupted his later life.

MILITARY CAREER

During the French and Indian War (1754–63) Schuyler was commissioned to raise a militia company for an assault of the French at Lake George. This was interrupted by his marriage on 7 Sept 1755 to Catharine van Rensselaer, daughter of prominent landowner Johannes van Rensselaer and Engeltie Livingston. Later in the war Schuyler served in the commissariat with British colonel John Bradstreet, with whom he developed a strong friendship, and later acquired thousands of acres along the Mohawk River. Schuyler concentrated on developing family lands at Saratoga [now Schuylerville, Saratoga Co] after the war and built several mills, including the colony's first water-driven flax mill. He was eventually forced to replace the house and mills after the British destroyed this estate in 1777.

Illness prevented Schuyler from attending the First Continental Congress in 1774, but he served as a delegate to the second congress in 1775 and was appointed a major general of the Continental army under Gen George Washington. As commander of the Northern Department, he recruited and provisioned an army for the invasion of Canada in 1775–76. Further illness forced him to appoint Gen Richard Montgomery as field commander, who captured Montreal before the campaign's ultimate failure. In 1776 Schuyler ordered Gen Benedict Arnold to construct a fleet for the defense of Lake Champlain. Although he was defeated by Gen Guy Carleton at the Battle of Valcour Island on 11 Oct 1776, his action helped delay the British invasion until the following year.

Schuyler quarreled with Gen Horatio Gates over their jurisdictions within the Northern Department. Gates was assigned to Fort Ticonderoga [now in Essex Co] in March 1777 with orders that appeared to make him Schuyler's successor. Schuyler's command was reaffirmed, but Gates refused a subordinate role, conspiring with members of Congress from New England to replace Schuyler and managing to get himself appointed commander of the Northern Department just prior to the Battle of Saratoga in October 1777. Before his removal, Schuyler contributed to the American victory at Saratoga by strengthening American defenses and obstructing British general John Burgoyne's invasion through scorched-earth tactics. He dispatched forces under Arnold to relieve Fort Stanwix [now Rome, Oneida Co] from Col Barry St. Leger's siege, eliminating the second element of Burgoyne's campaign. Despite his contributions, he was accused of neglect of duty in the loss of Fort Ticonderoga to Burgoyne. At his own request, to clear his name, Schuyler was court-martialed in October 1778 and won acquittal with the highest honor. His status led the British to make several kidnapping or assassination attempts, including one raid in August 1781 on his Albany house.

Philip Schuyler.

POLITICIAN AND LANDOWNER

Schuyler's political career began with service on the Albany City Council (1756–58). On his election to the Colonial Assembly in 1768, he became embroiled in the partisan struggles between his DeLancey cousins and the Livingstons. In 1779–80 he again served in the Continental Congress and subsequently served in the New York State Senate (1780–84, 1786–90, 1792–97), as state surveyor-general (1781–84), and as a regent of the University of the State of New York (1784–1804), playing a leading role in chartering Union College. He was also a member of the US Senate (1789–91, 1797–98). An advocate of a strong national government, Schuyler became an ardent supporter of the US Constitution and of Alexander Hamilton's fiscal policies. Schuyler was a determined foe of Gov George Clinton and the Antifederalists, eventually helping to defeat Clinton's reelection in 1795.

BUSINESS CAREER AND PERSONAL LIFE

Schuyler had been interested in canal construction since a visit to England in 1761–62. Decades later this led him to promote similar projects in New York State when he became president of the Western and Northern Inland Lock Navigation Cos in May 1792. Western Inland Lock Navigation was successful in improving the navigation of the Mohawk River and was the precursor of the Erie Canal. Northern Inland Lock Navigation's efforts were minimal but paved the way for the Lake Champlain and Hudson Waterway. His efforts to further the work of the canal companies remained the primary focus of his public service until his death. He was also one of New York's wealthiest landholders. His estates included between 9 and 27 slaves from 1775 to 1790; after purchasing 4 more in 1797, he apparently freed or sold all of them by 1803.

Schuyler and Catharine van Rensselaer had 15 children, 8 of whom survived to adulthood. Of their daughters, Elizabeth married Alexander Hamilton, Angelica married John Barker Church, later a member of parliament, and Margaret married Stephen Van Rensselaer, the last Rensselaerswijck patroon. A statue of Schuyler stands at the entrance of the Albany City Hall. His Albany home became a state historic site in 1917, and his home in Schuylerville is part of the Saratoga National Historic Park.

Gerlach, Don R. *Philip Schuyler and the American Revolution in New York, 1733–1777* (Lincoln: Univ of Nebraska Press, 1964)

———. *Proud Patriot: Philip Schuyler and the War of Independence, 1775–1783* (Syracuse: Syracuse Univ Press, 1987)

Don R. Gerlach

Schuyler, Pieter (*b* Beverwijck [now Albany], 17 Sept 1657; *d* Albany, 19 Feb 1724). Politician, trader, and Indian agent. He followed his father, Philip Pietersz Schuyler, in the fur trade and acquired extensive land in Albany Co and the Mohawk River valley, and he obtained shares in the Saratoga and Schenectady patents. He was the first mayor of the City of Albany (1686–94) and was colonel of the Albany Militia during King William's War. In 1691 he led an attack on La Prairie (near Fort Montreal in Montreal). In 1692 he was appointed to the governor's advisory council. Schuyler headed the Albany Commissioners for Indian Affairs, and because of his trading experience and familiarity with Native American languages, he became a leader in frontier diplomacy. Indians referred to him as Quidor, or Brother. In 1710 he accompanied the "Four Iroquois Kings" to London to lobby Queen Anne's court for funds to support a Canadian invasion. When he returned, Schuyler continued his service as Indian commissioner, was president of the governor's council, and was acting governor in 1719–20. He also was royal emissary until 1721. Schuyler was the patriarch of Albany's leading family and established his base of operations at the family's farm, called the Flats or Schuyler Flats, near the northern border of Menands (Albany Co).

New York State Museum. "Pieter Schuyler," http://www.nysm.nysed.gov/albany/bios/s/pischuyler61.html

Stefan Bielinski

Schuyler County (329 mi²/852 km²; pop 19,224). Created in 1854 from parts of Chemung, Steuben, and Tompkins Cos and named after Philip Schuyler. The county is divided into eight towns containing four incorporated villages. Watkins Glen serves as county seat. Schuyler Co lies at the head of Seneca Lake, which bisects the northern portion of the county. The county is within the Finger Lake Hills region of the Appalachian Upland landform province. The bedrock is southward-dipping Upper Devonian sandstone, shale, and siltstone. Entirely glaciated during the most recent ice age, the county is dominated topographically by rolling hills and narrow valleys, whose walls are interrupted in places by deep, narrow, water-carved gorges. Valley Heads Moraine, which lies south of Seneca Lake, formed a natural dam that held back the meltwaters of glacial Lake Hall. County elevations range from 2,080 feet (634 m) at Sugar Hill to 445 feet (136 m) along the shores of Seneca Lake. Seneca Lake is the primary drainage basin via Catharine Creek and its tributaries. The Chemung River drains the west and southwest of the county as well as Cayuta Lake in the southeast, one of the three minor lakes within the county. The best arable lands are scattered throughout the eastern half. Hilltop soils are generally thin and poor.

The climate of Schuyler Co is humid-continental. The mean July temperature is 69°F (21°C), and the mean January temperature is 22°F (-6°C), with upland temperatures slightly warmer in summer and colder in winter. The county receives 36 inches (91 cm) of precipitation in a typical year, ranging from 2 inches (5 cm) in January to 4 inches (10 cm) in November. Snowfall ranges from 55 inches (140 cm) in the larger valleys to more than 80 inches

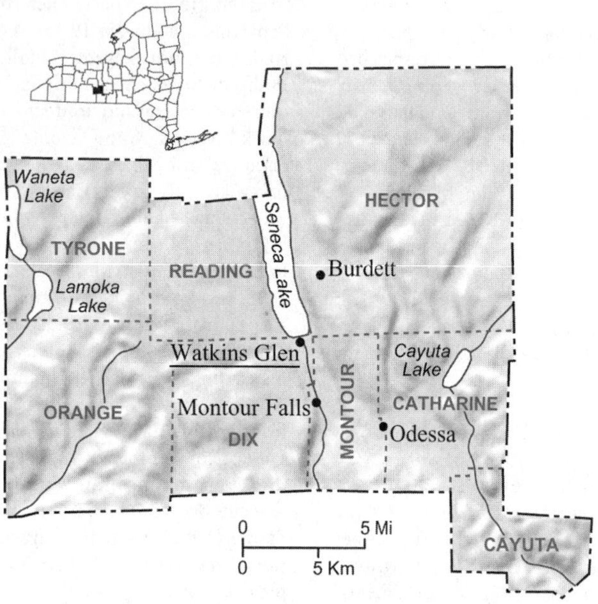

(200 cm) in the higher elevations. Seneca Lake generates a noticeable microclimate within its valley. Two hardwood communities made up the primeval forest cover. Central hardwoods consisting mainly of beech, sugar maple, and basswood dominated the valleys; Alleghenian hardwoods, primarily hemlock, beech, sugar maple, white pine, and basswood, prevailed at the higher elevations. More than 59% of the county is forested in the early 21st century. Roughly a third of Schuyler Co consists of federal- and state-owned lands, the most significant being Finger Lakes National Forest and Connecticut Hill State Wildlife Management Area. Watkins Glen State Park attracts more than 1 million visitors annually.

American Indians and Early Settlement

The earliest known settlement site in Schuyler Co is near Lamoka Lake and dates from 2500 BC. The Seneca inhabited the area at the time of contact, having migrated into the area around the 14th century. In 1779 the Sullivan-Clinton campaign against the Iroquois destroyed the Seneca village of Catharine's Town, located near what is now Montour Falls. The Seneca made no concerted effort to reoccupy the area after the war.

An agreement between Massachusetts and New York in 1786 established the Preemption Line, west of which Massachusetts might authorize purchases from the native inhabitants; this included the western third of the present Schuyler Co. East of the Preemption Line was the New Military Tract, granted to veterans, which included the present-day Hector, and the Watkins and Flint Purchase, covering the rest of the present county. The Massachusetts lands went ultimately to English speculator Sir William Pulteney, who sold lots through an agent to individual settlers and minor speculators. The first permanent European settlers arrived in 1788 and occupied land near Catharine's Town. Some were veterans of the Sullivan-Clinton campaign; most came from southern New England, particularly Connecticut, and from eastern New York State, although significant numbers also came from New Jersey and Pennsylvania.

Overall, the population grew slowly. Nevertheless by 1800 Whites were living in all of the towns of what would become Schuyler Co. African Americans, both enslaved and free, arrived within the first decade of settlement. The 1825 census lists 50 African Americans among the 13,773 persons residing in the area that became Schuyler Co. Located along a significant north-south transportation corridor, Schuyler Co became a link in the Underground Railroad. Sheltering sites have been identified in the Villages of Burdett and Watkins Glen, the hamlet of Mecklenburg, and the Towns of Reading and Montour.

Economic Development

Schuyler Co's early economy centered on agriculture. Turnpikes, such as the Newtown Turnpike linking Watkins [now Watkins Glen] with Newtown [now Elmira, Chemung Co], provided a means of carrying produce to market. Seneca Lake served as the early traffic artery northward, especially for freight. Navigation improvements on the Seneca River beginning in 1818, followed by the opening of the Cayuga and Seneca Canal in 1829, gave residents the most efficient connections to eastern markets. An all-water link between Seneca Lake and the Chemung River and the greater Susquehanna watershed to the south was discussed in the 1790s or earlier; the Seneca and Susquehanna Lock Navigation Co was incorporated by the state legislature in 1815, but its canal was never built. Finally, the Chemung Canal was authorized by the legislature in 1829 and opened in 1833. Conceived as a coal and salt carrier, the canal never lived up to expectations, in part because of poorly designed locks. Canal construction attracted Irish laborers, some of whom remained to load coal barges or build railroads, and to work as stone masons; later they found work as resort hotel staff. Railroad service followed the canal-building era, beginning with the Chemung Railroad (1849) from Elmira to Watkins and the Corning and Canandaigua Railroad (1851) from Watkins to Canandaigua (Ontario Co); both were leased by the Erie Railroad and later became part of the Northern Central Railway. The Syracuse, Geneva and Corning Railroad opened in 1877. The Seneca Lake Line of the Lehigh Valley was completed in 1892 through Havana [now Montour Falls] and northward along Seneca Lake's eastern shore.

Despite improved transport facilities, the county remained focused on agriculture. Grains had been the leading agricultural product until the expansion of markets with the opening of the Erie Canal. The soil was, however, better suited for pasturage than tillage. A shift to sheep raising resulted in Schuyler Co becoming one of the leading wool-producing areas of central New York State until well into the 20th century. By 1900 there were 2,103 farms operating, encompassing 196,718 acres (79,609 ha). As the wool industry waned, dairy farming, mainly producing fluid milk, became predominant, along with grape, apple, and peach crops. The two largest villages,

SCHUYLER CO POPULATION CENSUS FIGURES

	White	Nonwhite	Total Population	Foreign-Born
1860	18,740	100	18,840	979
1870	18,803	186	18,989	1,048
1880	18,647	195	18,842	898
1890	16,491	220	16,711	751
1900	15,631	180	15,811	706
1910	13,802	202	14,004	620
1920	12,972	126	13,098	662
1930	12,800	109	12,909	735
1940	12,891	88	12,979	568
1950	14,117	65	14,182	616
1960	14,934	110	15,044	442
1970	16,603	134	16,737	401
1980	17,508	178	17,686	440
1990	18,322	340	18,662	298
2000	18,548	676	19,224	230

Notes: "Nonwhite" includes African Americans, Asians, American Indians, and Pacific Islanders and, for 2000, also the mixed race and other race categories. Through the 1960 census these figures primarily reflect the African American population. For 1930 and 1950, the foreign-born totals include Whites only. Other years include all foreign-born in the population.

POPULATIONS OF TOWNS, SCHUYLER CO

Town, Year Founded	1800	1840	1880	1920	1960	2000
Catharine, 1798	266	2,424	1,617	1,178	1,605	1,930
Cayuta, 1824	—	835	601	282	538	545
Dix, 1835	—	1,990	4,168	3,486	3,916	4,197
Hector, 1802	—	5,652	5,025	3,030	3,209	4,854
Montour, 1860	—	—	1,771	1,967	2,182	2,446
Orange, 1813[a]	—	1,824	2,020	889	1,047	1,752
Reading, 1806	—	1,541	1,581	1,166	1,410	1,786
Tyrone, 1822	—	2,122	2,059	1,100	1,137	1,714

Notes: In 1800 the Town of Catharine was part of Tioga Co. In 1840 the Towns of Orange, Reading, and Tyrone were part of Steuben Co; the Town of Hector was part of Tompkins Co; and the Towns of Catharine, Cayuta, and Dix were part of Chemung Co.

[a]Jersey until 1836.

Havana and Watkins, developed a number of small manufacturing facilities. The Bank of Havana, the first within the present county lines, was organized in 1851. A year after the county formed in 1854, the population was 18,777.

The economy broadened in the latter 19th century with the 1863 opening of the Watkins Glen gorge to the public and associated resort industry development; Havana Glen opened in 1867 in Montour. Visitors toured the parks and made use of Watkins Glen's mineral springs, around which the resort hotels were built. One of the largest, the Glen Springs Hotel (1890–1942), welcomed dignitaries and global celebrities, such as Franklin D. and Eleanor Roosevelt, John D. Rockefeller, and Prince Otto of Austria. In 1878 efficient rail competition prompted the state, to abandon all but the northernmost 4 miles (6.4 km) of the Chemung Canal, a section that still connects Montour Falls with Seneca Lake. Although the presence of salt was long suspected, it was not until 1892 that a major salt deposit was discovered while searching for natural gas and oil. Salt mining using the brine extraction method was begun on a commercial scale in 1893 by the Glen Salt Co (now US Salt) in the Town of Reading. A second mining facility was built at the head of the lake by Watkins Salt Co in 1898. The salt industry, along with the railroads, drew recent Italian immigrants. As the men established themselves, they were joined by family members and compatriots.

Religion, Education, and Culture

The earliest religious organization was the Methodist Episcopal society in Catharine (1805), which built a church in 1809. The first Roman Catholic church was established at Jefferson [now Watkins Glen] in 1846 by Irish immigrants who had settled in Tyrone some years earlier. By 1860 there were 51 churches, with Methodist, Presbyterian, and Baptist congregations predominating.

Children were instructed as early as 1791 by surveyor John Livingston in a private house near Peach Orchard in Hector. Districts were formed following state legislation in 1812. School consolidation began in 1928 when districts in the Town of Orange were included in the formation of Bradford Central School District in adjacent Steuben Co. The Odessa Central School District (now Odessa-Montour Central School District) and Watkins Glen Central School District formed in 1936 and 1950, respectively. Seven other school districts overlap county borders. People's College, incorporated in 1854, began operations at Montour Falls in 1864 but closed the following year. Its buildings became the site of Cook Academy, a private preparatory high school, from 1873 to 1943. The New York State Academy of Fire Science occupied the buildings in 2003.

The county's first newspaper was the *Tioga Patriot,* published in Havana in 1828. Rival papers existed in Watkins Glen and Montour Falls with varied longevity, each reflecting its political leaning. The *Watkins Express* (1854) and *Watkins Review* (1896) merged in 1988. The county's first library, chartered by the state legislature in 1817, was in the Town of Catharine. It opened with 35 books and closed about the time of the start of the Civil War. The Watkins Glen Public Library, established in 1870 as the Ladies Library, is the oldest still in operation.

Politics

Efforts to create a new county began in 1830, prompted by dissatisfaction with travel distances to public offices. The location of the county seat became the subject of a protracted legal battle between Havana and Watkins. Each erected buildings to serve as county offices. From 1854 through 1971, county government was administered by a Board of Supervisors. In 1860 the Town of Montour was created so that residents of Havana, the population center of the new town, would gain political power through their own representative to the board. Watkins was finally confirmed as the Schuyler Co seat 18 years later. A countywide vote for reapportionment in 1971 established a county legislature. It is composed of eight legislators elected from three districts. Voters are predominantly registered Republicans, though Democrats and members of other parties have been on occasion elected or appointed to significant offices, including chair of the county legislature.

Recent History

Agriculture went into decline in the early 20th century; extensive tracts of marginal farmland in the Towns of Catharine and Orange and along the Hector Backbone went out of production and were acquired by the state. The popularity of the resorts and spas faded during the first half of the 20th century, but tourism remains a strong industry. The wine industry, important to both the agricultural and the tourism sectors, increases its production each year.

While the natural beauty of the county attracts thousands of visitors annually, motor sports put Watkins Glen in the international limelight during the second half of the 20th century. Cameron R. Argetsinger, a Cornell University law student, broached the idea of an automobile race through the streets of Watkins Glen and the roads of surrounding towns. The initial race in 1948 was the first post–World War II road race in the United States. After 1952 the race was moved to a site in the Town of Dix. The road course hosted international Formula 1 events from 1961 to 1980. The NASCAR Winston Cup series debuted at Watkins Glen International raceway in 1986; it draws crowds of more than 200,000, the largest attendance for a one-day sports event in the state. Racing and other motor sports at the track have a major positive impact on the economy. The two salt plants remain among the county's major employers. In the early 21st century about 300 farms are in operation; rail service is provided by the Norfolk Southern Railway and the Finger Lakes Railroad Co. A high percentage of residents depend on employment outside the county, despite efforts by planners and developers to stimulate and expand the local economy. In 1998 per capita personal income stood at 55% of the statewide figure of $32,108. In 1999, 37% of the county's firms were in the service sector, 35% in the wholesale/retail trade, and 8% in manufacturing. The population continues to grow at a respectable rate, a trend that went effectively uninterrupted from 1940 to 2000. It is expected to continue, but the growth of the employment base remains a concern of county planners. Prominent Schuyler Co natives include David B. Hill (1843–1910), born in Havana, who served as New York State governor (1885–92) and as a US senator (1892–97), and Jane Delano (1862–1919), born in Townsend, president of the Army Nurse Corps.

Little has been published on the history of Schuyler Co. The standard work is [Henry B. Peirce and D. Hamilton Hurd], *History of Tioga, Chemung, Tompkins and Schuyler Counties* (1879). A relatively recent work updates it in part: Louise V. Stillman, *Schuyler Around and About* (1994). Of the few town histories published, one of particularly high quality, though dated, is Mary Louise Catlin Cleaver, *The History of the Town of Catharine* (1945); also excellent is Wayne E. Morrison Sr, *Early History: The Village of Havana.* A comprehensive description of the county's physical environment is found in Paul S. Puglia et al, *Soil Survey of Schuyler County, New York* (1979).

Glenda Gephart

Schuyler Falls. Town (pop 5,128) in central Clinton Co. Bounded on the north by the Saranac River, the area was settled in 1794 and the town was formed in 1848 from Plattsburgh. Farming and lumbering were its mainstay in the 19th century, with some manufacturing, including a foundry and a starch factory. In the 1950s Schuyler Falls became a rural suburb for Plattsburgh. Macomb Reservation State Park is located in town.

Thomas A. Rumney

Schuyler family. The first representative of this distinguished Dutch family in colonial New York to arrive in the New World was Philip Pietersz (1628–83), a gunstock maker from Amsterdam who was in Fort Orange [now Albany] by 1650. His brother David (1636–90) followed around

1656. Their father, Pieter Tjercksz, had no family name (Pietersz was their patronymic), so they took the family name of their mother, Gertruyt Phillips van Schulyder. It is uncertain whether her family was Dutch or German.

Both brothers were major fur traders and investors in large tracts of land in the Hudson and Mohawk Valleys. As leaders in the community, Philip Pietersz Schuyler served as magistrate on the local court for two terms during Dutch rule; David also served for one term and under English rule was an alderman (1686–90). The prominence of the Schuylers in local government continued into the next generation when Philip's son Pieter became the first mayor of Albany in 1686, serving until 1694. Philip's youngest son, Capt Johannes Schuyler, served as mayor from 1703 to 1706, followed by David's son David (1669–1715). Another of David's sons, Capt Myndert Schuyler, served two terms as mayor in the 1720s. The Schuylers managed an international and intercolonial trade through family members in several locations. Philip's sons settled in Albany, New York City, and Bergen, NJ. David's son David spent extended periods in Montreal. His nephew David (1688–1764), son of Pieter, owned land in Rensselaerswijck and in Surinam as well as a home on the Van Horn Patent next to the Mohawk village at Indian Castle, having been able, as a trading partner of the Indians, to purchase the land on behalf of the Van Horn partnership.

The Schuyler family connections in business and politics and through marriage linked members to several other prominent families. Shortly after Philip's arrival in Fort Orange, he married Margareta, daughter of Brant van Slichtenhorst, director of Rensselaerswijck. Marriages of their children included Geertruy to Stephanus van Cortlandt; Alida first to Nicolaes van Renssealaer and then to Robert Livingston; Peter to Maria van Rensselaer, daughter of Jeremias; Brant to Cornelia van Cortlandt, daughter of Olaf; and Philip to Elizabeth de Meyer, daughter of New York City mayor Nicolas de Meyer.

The English conquest of New Netherland in 1664 led some of the Schuyler family to establish close English ties to have access to British markets. In the 18th century, Gen Philip Schuyler (1733–1804) spent several years in England, as did his brother Cortlandt (1735–73), who married there. Many of the family were prominent in colonial politics. Mayor Pieter Philipse Schuy-ler also served on the provincial council (1692–1720). Some of the family who served in the colonial General Assembly included Brant (1696–98), Johannes (1705–07, 1710–11), Myndert (1701–9, 1713–14, 1724–27), Nicholas (1727), and Philip Jr (1728–47, 1750–51). Stephen J. served in the state assembly (1777–78), the first of many in the family to do so. Gen Philip Schuyler, whose daughter Elizabeth married Alexander Hamilton, was a major general in the Revolutionary War. He also served in the Colonial Assembly (1768–75), in the state senate (1780–84, 1786–89, 1792–97), and in the US Senate (1789–91). His nephew Peter also served in the state senate (1787–92).

In the 19th century, the Schuyler family remained active. Some branches continued to play a role in political and military matters. Eugene Schuyler (1840–90) was a diplomat; his major assignments were to Russia and Egypt. George Lee Schuyler (1811–90) served as a Civil War colonel and was a noted yachtsman and one of the original owners of America's Cup. Other family members pursued business and other professions. Some in Oswego and Jefferson Cos, such as Abraham Schuyler (1797–1865) at Sackets Harbor, were pioneers of the Great Lakes trade. William Cushing Schuyler (1810–79), son of Peter P. Schuyler (1776–1825), was a surgeon, lawyer, and justice of the peace in Saratoga Co. A number of female family members were active in religion and reform. Among the great-granddaughters of Gen Philip Schuyler were Louisa Lee Schuyler (1837–1926), who helped form the State Christian's Aid Association, which led a state campaign for the care of the insane; Sarah Schuyler (1823–1911), who was New York vicar of the Society of the Sacred Heart (Roman Catholic) and oversaw the founding of convents and schools; and her sister Catharine (*d* 1853), an Episcopal nun in the Order of the Holy Communion.

Christoph, Florence A. *Schuyler Genealogy,* 2 vols (Albany: Friends of Schuyler Mansion, 1987–92)
Schuyler Family Papers, 1650–1907; microfilm of originals in the possession of Schuyler Cornthwaite, Ballston Spa, NY, NYS Library, Albany
Schuyler, Phillip John, 1733–1804. Papers. New York Public Library, New York

Florence A. Christoph

Schuylerville [SKY-LER-VIL]. Village (pop 1,197) in Saratoga. The site of the colonial settlement called Saratoga centered on Schuyler's Mills (1709–10) and was destroyed in a 1745 Indian raid. It was renamed Schuylerville in 1820 and expanded rapidly after the opening of the Champlain Canal (1823). It incorporated as a village in 1831 and soon gained a foundry. The Bullard paper mill was built 1863. Both the pre-Revolutionary Schuyler House, a landmark in the village, and the Saratoga Battle Monument (1877), located in the adjacent village of Victory, are operated by the National Park Service. Moribund local manufacturing leads residents to find employment in Saratoga Springs and elsewhere, while tourism contributes modestly to the village's economy.

Field Horne

Schwab, Francis X(avier) (*b* Buffalo, 14 Aug 1874; *d* Buffalo, 23 Apr 1946). Mayor of Buffalo. The eldest of seven children, Schwab attended parochial school in Buffalo until he was 13. He then began to help support his family, working at a tin shop, a millwright shop, and the Wagner Palace Car Co. In his 20s Schwab worked for several brewing companies in Buffalo and ran his own liquor store before becoming president of Buffalo Brewing Co. With the advent of Prohibition in 1919, he merged Buffalo Brewing Co and Cooperative Brewing to form Mohawk Products Co, which produced near beer. Elected as a Republican running on an anti-Prohibition platform in 1921, Schwab was the first Roman Catholic mayor of Buffalo. During his tenure (1922–29), he pushed for the rapid completion of the $4.5 million Peace Bridge (1925–27), oversaw the building of the $1 million Neoclassical Buffalo Museum of Science (1929) and of more than a dozen schools, and initiated construction in 1929 of the $6.8 million Art Deco City Hall (1932). Many of the city's residents saw Schwab as the mayor of the "plain people." His establishment of the Hotel de Gink, a shelter for homeless people in Buffalo, was controversial but demonstrated his generous concern for those in need. In his attempt for a third mayoral term, Schwab ran as a Democrat but was defeated by the Republican Charles Roesch. Schwab returned to his beer business, which improved after 1933, and was unsuccessful in various attempts to return to elective office.

Mike Rizzo, ed. "Through the Mayor's Eyes," http://www.buffalonian.com/history/industry/mayors/Schwab.htm
"Buffalo's 20th Century Club: The Far-Sighted Men and Women Who Shaped Our Past and Set a Course for the Future," *Buffalo News,* 28 Nov 1999

Joseph Golombek Jr

Schweizer Aircraft Corporation. Flying their first glider in 1930, brothers Ernie and Paul A. Schweizer founded Schweizer Metal Aircraft Co in Peekskill (Westchester Co) to build gliders in 1938, moving to Elmira Heights (Chemung Co) the following year. Schweizer Aircraft Corp (SAC) was formed in December 1939, and Bill Schweizer joined his brothers. SAC delivered the first US military glider in June 1941. Military training glider production ceased in 1943, and SAC moved to Big Flats (Chemung Co) and switched to making aircraft components for other companies and commercial glider production. In 1946 the company started the Schweizer Soaring School at the Chemung County Airport (now Elmira-Corning Regional Airport) in Horseheads. In the early 1980s, orders for agricultural airplanes and gliders were greatly reduced, and in 1983 Hughes Aircraft licensed SAC to produce the Model 300C helicopter, and three years later the company bought the entire 300C program. SAC also developed surveillance airplanes from their sailplane designs and subcontract work. Sailplane manufacturing stopped in 1983. Employment as of 2001 was 444 with annual sales of $45,000,000.

Schweizer Aircraft Corp, http://www.sacusa.com
Schweizer, Paul A. *Wings Like Eagles* (Washington, DC: Smithsonian Institution Press, 1988)

Paul A. Schweizer

science fiction. If modern science fiction has a founding figure, it is Luxembourg immigrant Hugo Gernsback (1884–1967), who after moving to New York City published several electronics magazines, including *Modern Electrics* (1908–13), the first radio magazine, in which he serialized his technologically prescient novel, *Ralph 124C 41+* (1911–12). In 1926 he started to publish *Amazing Stories,* the first of several magazines he devoted to "science fiction," a term he coined in 1929. The next generation of science fiction was ushered in by John W. Campbell Jr (1910–71), editor of *Astounding Stories* (from 1961, *Analog*) in New York City from 1937 to 1971. Campbell's demand for well written, logical stories based on real science helped improve the overall quality of the field and brought to prominence such authors as Isaac Asimov, Arthur C. Clarke, Theodore Sturgeon, A. E. Van Vogt, Lester Del Rey, Jack Williamson, and Robert A. Heinlein, the magazine's focal author. Other important magazines included *Galaxy* (1950–80), which promoted socially oriented science fiction and was edited first by H. L. Gold and then by Frederik Pohl (1961–69), and the *Magazine of Fantasy and Science Fiction* (1949), edited by Anthony Boucher and J. Francis Mc-

Comas. The latter, together with *Analog* and *Asimov's SF Magazine,* were the most prestigious markets for stories in 2001, while the *New York Review of Science Fiction* was the premier critical journal.

Authors and Conventions

Among the most prominent writers of science fiction from New York State have been James Blish, Raymond Z. Gallun, John Kessel, Damon Knight, Avram Davidson, Nancy Kress, George Zebrowski, Pamela Sargent, Judith Merril, Cyril M. Kornbluth, Frederik Pohl, Donald A. Wollheim, and Robert F. Young. Isaac Asimov (1920–92) came to New York City as a young child from the Soviet Union. A remarkably prolific author, he wrote 500 books of science and science fiction. Kurt Vonnegut (1922–), who worked for General Electric in Schenectady after World War II, used the city, fictionalized as Ilium, as a setting for *Player Piano* (1952), as well as in *Cat's Cradle* (1963) and *Hocus Pocus* (1990). The science fiction writer Kilgore Trout, a recurring fictional character in Vonnegut's work, is often depicted as living in nearby Cohoes (Albany Co). New York City–born Samuel L. Delany (1942–) has written both science fiction and nonfiction, including a remarkable autobiography, *The Motion of Light in Water: Sex and Science Fiction Writing in Greenwich Village, 1960–1965* (1988). The 2000 *Directory of the Science Fiction and Fantasy Writers of America* lists 107 active or associate members living in New York State.

In 1934 Hugo Gernsback created the Science Fiction League and issued charters to groups of fans all over the country. Many of these fan organizations soon rebelled against Gernsback's centralized authority and formed their own independent groups. Perhaps the most important was New York City's Futurian Society (1938–45). By 2001 many fan organizations hosted annual conventions with guest authors and artists. These include the Buffalo Fantasy League (Eeriecon), the Latham-Albany-Schenectady-Troy Science Fiction Association (Albacon), the Lunarians (New York Science Fiction Society) (Lunacon), the Rochester Fantasy Fans (Astronomicon), and SUNY Stony Brook Science Fiction Forum (I-Con).

New York City as Science Fiction Subject

Among outstanding works of fiction set in New York City or State are Jack Finney's *Time and Again* (1970), which views 1882 Manhattan through a time traveler's eyes; Alfred Bester's *The Stars My Destination* (1957), which includes a key scene in the basement of the old St. Patrick's Cathedral; Edgar Pangborn's *Davy* (1964), set in upstate New York, probably near Schoharie Co, after a nuclear war; Thomas M. Disch's *334* (1972), a collection of near-future stories in a New York City apartment building; Frederick Pohl's *Years of the City* (1984), a future history of New York City; Jack Womack's *Ambient* (1987); and Harlan Ellison's story "The Whimper of Whipped Dogs" (1973), based on the 1964 Kitty Genovese murder.

Orson Welles's *Mercury Theater on the Air* broadcast for Halloween 1938 of the *War of the Worlds,* in which Martians landed in Grover's Mill, NJ, before destroying Manhattan is undoubtedly the best-known science fiction account of the annihilation of New York City, but there are many others. New York City is targeted for destruction or destroyed in books like Robert Burchard's *Thirty Seconds over New York* (1970), Basil Jackson's *The Night Manhattan Burned* (1979), Irwin Lewis's *The Day New York Trembled* (1967) and *The Day They Invaded New York* (1964), and Charles Einstein's *The Day New York Went Dry* (1964), and in films including *Zeppelin Attack on New York* (1917), *High Treason* (1929), *Exterminators* (1965), *Fail Safe* (1964), *King of the Rocket Men* (1949), *Rocket Attack, USA* (1961), *Meteor* (1979), and *Independence Day* (1996). A postapocalyptic Manhattan is the setting for parts of *Planet of the Apes* (1968) and *AI* (2001).

Clute, John, and Peter Nicholls, eds. *The Encyclopedia of Science Fiction* (New York: St. Martin's Press, 1995)
Knight, Damon. *The Futurians* (New York: John Day, 1977)

David E. Lunde

scientific culture (17th–18th centuries). In the 17th and 18th centuries, science was not yet a widespread way of thinking about the natural world. For most colonists in New Netherland and New York, nature was a world they knew through direct experience and through biblical and popular lore. In the 17th century colonists worked to transform what they saw as a dangerous wilderness into an orderly landscape like that of Europe. In the 18th century, some New Yorkers pursued formal studies in astronomy, botany, electricity, and medicine. But many were reluctant to adopt the new scientific learning emerging from Europe for political and religious reasons. Yet, technological improvements, modest as they were in a world of iron, wood, and sail, were adopted more readily.

Views of Nature

Most colonists understood the natural world as permeated by unseen forces, often predictable but sometimes not. The movements of the sun, moon, and planets, for example, were believed to affect natural processes on earth. Almanac makers, who began to publish in New York Colony in 1694, calculated the movement of heavens to predict the weather. Farmers adjusted agricultural work to allow for the influence of heavenly bodies on plants and animals. Like people in the areas of Europe from which they came, 17th- and 18th-century New Yorkers believed that the human body was composed of four "humors," fluids whose balance was affected both by human activity, like one's diet, and by external influences such as the positions of the planets. Because this understanding of the human body was so widely shared, colonists only occasionally relied on the help of doctors, whose understanding of illness was largely developed through apprenticeship or self-training.

Disruptions in everyday patterns were often attributed to "Providence," the actions God took to send messages to believers. Sometimes these were warnings to repent of one's sins, as New York's Gov Robert Hunter (1710–19) explained to the Iroquois when they told him of a smallpox epidemic raging among them in 1717. At other times, they were signs of God's benevolence, as the sea captain Joseph Bailey reminded readers in his account of his rescue from a shipwreck in the Caribbean in 1749. Alternatively, individual oddities might simply be accounted as a "wonder," an anomaly that was difficult to explain. Such was the mastodon tooth dug up in Claverack [now in Columbia Co] in 1705 and sent by Gov Edward Hyde, Viscount Cornbury (1702–8) to the Royal Society in London, a scientific organization.

While many colonial New Yorkers acknowledged the power of God and natural forces, they had a guarded optimism about their own ability to manage the natural world productively. "Improvement" was key to such management. Like other European colonists along the Atlantic coast, early settlers learned to grow maize from the Algonquian-speaking peoples in the area, as well as where to fish and to gather shellfish. However, they brought with them the agricultural techniques of the Netherlands and over the 17th century developed productive farms throughout the colony. During the 18th century, farmers adopted new orchard and field crops, continually diversifying New York's agriculture. By the 1740s almanacs and newspapers published in New York City increasingly printed advice on agricultural improvements. In the 18th century iron mines were developed at Livingston Manor in what is now Ancram (Columbia Co), Sterling Forest in Warwick (Orange Co), and Cortlandt (Westchester Co).

Scientific Investigation

Only a few colonists in New Netherland and New York before the middle of the 18th century were interested in formal investigation of the natural world. However, Jacques Cortelyou (*ca* 1625–93), who arrived in 1652 and settled in New Utrecht [now in Kings Co], was an early exception. Educated at the University of Utrecht and interested in the natural philosophy of René Descartes, he put his skill as a mathematician to use as the colony's surveyor. After the English conquest of 1664, the colony's governors sent a number of reports to authorities in London describing the natural resources in colonial New York. In the early 18th century, some New Yorkers, like the wealthy Lewis Morris (1671–1746) of Morrisania [now in Bronx Co] collected "cabinets of curiosities" made up of interesting natural history specimens. James Alexander (1691–1756), a member of the governor's council and educated at the University of Glasgow, sent for the latest issues of the *Transactions of the Royal Society* to keep up with scientific developments and made astronomical observations in New York in the 1740s.

The most prominent New Yorker in the sciences was Cadwallader Colden (1689–1776), the colony's surveyor general and a member of the governor's Council. Educated at the University of Edinburgh, Colden moved to New York Colony in 1718. In the 1720s he wrote a number of useful government reports and a diplomatic history of relations with the Iroquois. In 1728 he and his wife moved to a 2,000-acre (810 ha) farm located on land in what is now Coldenham (Orange Co). In the winter of 1741–42, Colden read the works of a young Swedish botanist, Carl Linnaeus. Struck by the simplicity of Linnaeus's classificatory system, Colden began to apply it to plants that grew around his home. The result was the first flora describing plants in the Hudson Valley, *Plantae Coldenghamiae,* which Linnaeus published in parts in a Swedish learned journal between 1743 and 1750. Through his botany

Colden developed a circle of correspondents that stretched from Britain and the Netherlands to Pennsylvania and South Carolina. Colden, who had worked as a doctor in London and Philadelphia before moving to New York Colony, also published articles on local epidemics and on a local cure for cancer.

Colden's most ambitious effort involved extending the theory of celestial mechanics proposed by Sir Isaac Newton. To this end Colden published a brief description of his own theory in New York City in 1746. He sent copies to correspondents in Europe and, encouraged by the response, wrote a full exposition, *The Principles of Action in Matter,* which was published in London in 1751. It was, however, a failure because he had mastered neither the astronomy nor the mathematics necessary to address Newton's theory. He did encourage two of his children to take up similar interests. His fourth child, Jane, learned Linnaean botany from him and became a more accomplished botanist than her father, writing her own flora of plants of the mid–Hudson Valley. His youngest child, David, took up electrical experimenting and published a report in support of Benjamin Franklin's theory of electricity.

Colden was politically unpopular in New York Colony, and thus his embrace of formal science did little to encourage other New Yorkers to imitate him. Yet by the mid–18th century, some scientific activities, such as collecting unusual plants, stargazing, and perusing illustrated natural history books, had become fashionable among the upper and middle classes throughout the British Atlantic. In the 1740s booksellers in New York City began advertising popular books on natural history and natural philosophy. Itinerant lecturers traveling through the colonies offered demonstrations of new theories in optics and electricity in New York City. In 1754 the first college in the colony, King's College (now Columbia University), opened in New York City with the new sciences as part of its curriculum, and a medical school was added in 1767. A handful of young men were sent to Europe for a university education, like Samuel Bard of New York City; he earned a medical degree from the University of Edinburgh and returned to become a corresponding member of a scientific society in Philadelphia. In the Mohawk Valley, Sir William Johnson (?1715–74), a wealthy Indian trader and colonial official, laid out a fashionable garden with exotic plants at his home, Johnson Hall [now Johnstown, Fulton Co], and collected oddities of nature for his own curiosity cabinet.

Many New Yorkers remained strongly suspicious of the new learning, because it was associated with claims about the nature of God. Almanacs in New York, for example, stuck to asserting the old earth-centered universe of Ptolemy into the 1740s, and in 1767 the almanac maker "Frank Freeman" complained that many readers disdained his description of the sun-centered Copernican universe. The older picture of the universe matched understandings both of how the movement of heavenly bodies affected the weather, plants, and animals, and of a theology of an active, often wrathful, God. In 1769 the appearance of a comet led to a heated debate in New York newspapers. Some people argued that the comet was a warning sent by God to call a sinful world to repentance. Others asserted that the comet showed a harmonious universe of natural laws set up by a benevolent God. Such debates about the meaning of the comet or of the natural world more generally were not easily settled in a colony so religiously and ethnically diverse.

TECHNOLOGY

Technological innovations prompted fewer debates than explanations for the natural world did and so more easily adopted. In 1732 residents of Morrisania and Jamaica (Queens Co), facing a spreading smallpox epidemic, tried the new procedure of inoculation with considerable success. In each succeeding epidemic more and more New Yorkers submitted to smallpox inoculation, one of the few effective medical innovations of the 18th century. From the 1730s on, mathematical instrument makers like Anthony Lamb (1703–84) of New York City sold an increasingly sophisticated variety of surveying and navigational instruments. In the 1760s Philip Schuyler (1733–1804) of Albany erected flax mills on land he owned around Saratoga, and Thomas Young of Oyster Bay [now in Nassau Co] and William Prince (?1725–1802) of Flushing (Queens Co) opened commercial nurseries. In the last decade of the colonial period, the adoption of such technological innovations came to have political significance.

In 1764, in response to conflicts with Britain over trade and taxation policies, a group of New York City merchants formed the Society for the Promotion of Arts, Agriculture and Economy. Their object was to increase the New York Colony's economic independence by developing innovations like indigo cultivation and cloth manufacture. While the society had some modest success in encouraging local development, divisions over responses to British economic policies led to the society's demise in 1770. However, an organization devoted to the improvement of navigation, the New-York Marine Society for Promoting Marine Knowledge, was founded in 1770 to support such improvements as better navigational charts of the West Indies, a region of great importance to New York City–based traders.

Scientific investigation and technical improvements for the most part took a backseat to politics during the years of the American Revolution. But in the new nation, there was a renewed interest in science. In 1797 the polymath and future US senator Samuel Latham Mitchill founded the *Medical Repository* in New York City, the first scientific journal in the United States. New York State took an expansive view of its role in furthering all forms of education, including scientific research, with the 1784 founding of the State Board of Regents and the corporate identity as the University of the State of New York.

See also BOTANISTS AND NATURALISTS; WILDFLOWERS.

Allen, David Yehling. *Long Island Maps and Their Makers: Five Centuries of Cartographic History* (Mattituck, NY: Amereon House, 1997)

Bedini, Silvio A. "At the Sign of the Compass and Quadrant: The Life and Times of Anthony Lamb," *Transactions* (American Philosophical Society) 74 (1984): 1–84

Burch, Wanda. "Sir William Johnson and 18th-Century Medicine in the New York Colony." In *Medicine and Healing,* ed. Peter Benes (Boston: Boston Univ, 1992)

Eisenstadt, Peter. "Almanacs and the Disenchantment of America," *Pennsylvania History: A Journal of Mid-Atlantic Studies* 65 (1998): 143–69

Gronim, Sara Stidstone. "Ambiguous Empire: The Knowledge of the Natural World in British Colonial New York" (PhD diss, Rutgers Univ, 1999)

Sara Stidstone Gronim

scientific culture (19th–21st centuries). Science in pre-1850 New York was the vocation of few individuals. There was little need for scientists and scant financial support. Most of those for whom science was an avocation turned to wealthy patrons for support or, failing that, simply devoted whatever resources they had in any spare time. At midcentury the situation began to change. The expanding education system, federal- and state-sponsored projects and expeditions, and industry needed the services of scientists. There were new means of learning about science. The weekly *Scientific American* magazine, launched in New York City in 1845 and under the ownership of Alfred Ely Beach, Orson Desaix Munn, and Simon H. Wales from 1846 until the end of the 19th century, put the latest information about scientific discovery within reach of laypeople. The Cooper Union for the Advancement of Science and Art opened in New York City in 1859 to provide a scientific education for artisans and mechanics.

Organizations such as the Lyceum of Natural History of New York (1817) in New York City enabled persons interested in science to join with the like minded to share ideas. To better reflect the increased presence of science, the name of the lyceum was changed in 1876 to the New York Academy of Sciences. In 1879 the Rochester Microscopical Society formed, with Samuel A. Lattimore, chemistry professor at the University of Rochester, as president. In 1881 the name was changed to the Rochester Academy of Science, and Rev Myron Adams Jr, pastor of Plymouth Congregational Church, served as the first president. The purpose of the group was to promote scientific study and research as well as knowledge of the natural history of the region. Since 1891 the academy has published on an irregular schedule the *Proceedings,* containing natural science articles by authorities in their fields. Changes in economic conditions and the attitude of the wealthy led to previously unknown philanthropy. One direct result was the creation of the American Museum of Natural History in New York City, funded by the city and private donations; it took a leading role in science once inaugurated in 1874.

Beginning in the 20th century, as scientific research became an important part of the business world, industry became involved in research funding. General Electric Co (GE), one of the first to conduct research, established its laboratory at Niskayuna (Schenectady Co) in 1900. The Eastman Kodak Co established an industrial research laboratory in Rochester in 1912. Xerox Corp's research center dealing with imaging science, physics, chemistry, and materials has been in operation at Webster (Monroe Co) since 1960. Also in the 20th century the government assumed the role of the wealthy patron. This was especially true following World War II, when scientific research took on broader dimensions because of government funding. Contracts meant secure financial futures, growth, and research in new directions. Brookhaven National Laboratory at Upton (Suffolk Co) opened in 1947. Operated by the Brookhaven Science Associates for the US Department of Energy (DOE), the laboratory's mission in part has been research and training new scientists.

Geology and Botany

Until the 1820s, botany was an area of study in the field of medicine. New Yorker David Hosack studied medicine in Great Britain in the early 1790s and was a frequent visitor to a botanical garden in London. When teaching medicine at Columbia College in 1796, his subjects included materia medica. Like his predecessors, he felt hampered by the lack of a botanical garden, and the following year he petitioned the college's trustees to fund a small garden where plants useful in medical instruction could be grown. Undaunted by their refusal, Hosack used his own funds to purchase 20 acres (8 ha) far from the center of the city, at what is now Rockefeller Center, to establish the Elgin Botanic Garden in 1801. A greenhouse was built, walls erected, seeds collected, and trees and shrubs planted. Expected public support for the completed garden was not forthcoming. Expenses increased, reaching $100,000 in 1810, when Hosack sold the land to the state. Four years later the property and the abandoned garden were transferred to Columbia College.

The crusade for a botanical garden was taken up again in 1888 by the Torrey Botanical Club (named after State Botanist John Torrey) at the suggestion of Nathaniel Lord Britton, professor of botany at Columbia. Rationale for it included its scientific and educational value, its pharmaceutical and horticultural uses, and its importance as a place of public pleasure and relaxation. In 1891 the state legislature approved the use of 250 acres (101 ha) for a New York Botanical Garden in Bronx Park. The city agreed to fund $500,000 if $250,000 in private funds was raised. The effort was a success, with funds coming from wealthy individuals such as Andrew Carnegie, J. P. Morgan, and Cornelius Vanderbilt.

Geological surveys were one of the earliest state-funded scientific undertakings. However, the first survey took place under the patronage of wealthy landowner Stephen Van Rensselaer III. In 1821 he paid Amos Eaton to survey Rensselaer Co. His motives were strictly monetary; survey results described soil, crops suitable to the region, and farming methods, all information useful to Rensselaer. Rationale for state-funded inspections differed little from those conducted under private sponsorship. The state's resources (and therefore natural wealth) were of foremost interest. Using plans formulated by the Lyceum of Natural History, four geologists were each assigned an area of the state in the first survey of 1836. The information they compiled made it one of the most significant surveys of the 19th century. Most notable of the surveyors was longtime State Geologist James Hall, who was named state paleontologist in 1843. By the end of the 19th century the US Geological Survey assumed many previously state responsibilities. At the beginning of the 21st century, the New York State Geological Survey is the oldest ongoing survey in the nation.

Biology

New York has been particularly active in the field of biological sciences. Physician Cornelius Hoagland endowed one of the first laboratories for medical investigations. The Hoagland Laboratory (1881) in Brooklyn was devoted to bacteriological research. It survived as an independent laboratory until the mid-1890s, when it became part of the Long Island Medical College. John D. Rockefeller Sr made possible a similar but much more comprehensive laboratory with the founding of the Rockefeller Institute for Medical Research in New York City in 1901. Charged with advancing medicine through research, its laboratories and conditions offered complete intellectual freedom. Beginning in 1906 scientists and physicians worked without teaching duties or regular patients and were free to pursue any investigations they chose. The importance of their discoveries was not always immediately evident, as in the case of the identification of ribonucleic acid in 1910; only in the early 1960s was its role in genetic inheritance understood. Although not intended as a place of instruction, the Rockefeller Institute grew to assume some of the best characteristics of a university; in 1954 it began granting graduate degrees, and in 1965 the name was changed to Rockefeller University.

What began as a fish hatchery for the New York Fisheries Commission at Cold Spring Harbor (Suffolk Co) in 1881 eventually became one of the leading biological laboratories in the nation. The Brooklyn Institute of Arts and Sciences located its biological laboratory there in 1890 for the summer training of teachers. Ten years later its science courses included marine biology. In 1904 the Carnegie Institution came to Cold Spring Harbor and opened its Experimental Evolution laboratory devoted to genetic research. In 1924 the Long Island Biological Association assumed sponsorship of the biological lab, which during the 1930s was a refuge for a number of scientists who fled totalitarian Europe. By the end of World War II these experimentalists had devised the new field of molecular biology. Directors sought to secure the laboratory's financial future with a progressive intellectual course, and in 1968 research centered on how viruses cause cancer. Taking advantage of broad public and governmental support for such work, the lab, with its new focus, was in a position to receive federal research funding. By the 1990s the Cold Spring Harbor Laboratory was like a small university and its DNA research was significant enough to establish a learning center in 1988. At Columbia University Thomas Hunt Morgan began work in 1904 in genetics. His breeding studies of the fruit fly *Drosophila melanogaster* were seminal in the field of genetics, and he received the Nobel Prize in physiology or medicine in 1933.

Physics

The most prominent 19th century scientist and the one who set a high standard for those who followed was Joseph Henry. An 1822 graduate of Albany Academy, Henry taught mathematics and natural philosophy at the academy and conducted research on electromagnetic phenomena. In 1831 he devised an electromagnet of unparalleled power. His work attracted the attention of other scientists and established his position as a leading physicist, although he was largely self-taught in the subject. In 1824 the Albany Lyceum of Natural History and the Society for the Promotion of Useful Arts were brought together to form the Albany Institute. The institute provided a forum for intellectual exchange, and Henry, curator of the Natural History Department, was an active participant.

In the late 19th and early 20th centuries, physics researchers were highly skilled practical experimenters, and an increasing number were university trained professionals. Nikola Tesla, an immigrant from Smiljan [now in Croatia], had little formal scientific training. After coming to New York City in 1884, he worked briefly for Thomas Edison and then set up his own laboratory, where he worked as an electrical inventor. Vibrating currents were of special interest to him, and his research resulted in the Tesla coil, in which low-voltage at high frequency could be raised to very high voltages. Physicist and inventor Michael Pupin, an émigré from Serbia, graduated from Columbia College in 1883 and began working there as a teacher of mathematical physics in 1888, becoming a professor of electromechanics in 1901. Pupin's patents for electrical inductance coils (Pupin coils) and for electrical circuitry were lucrative commercial successes. Although a contemporary of Tesla, his training was typical of the physicists who followed. By the 1930s physics was being researched only by the most highly trained.

New York State universities attracted some of the leading figures in 20th-century physics, and in the 1930s their work moved into new territory. Hans Bethe, a refugee from Nazi Germany, joined the staff of Cornell University and in 1937 was made professor of physics. His work included many aspects of atomic research, and his 1947 explanation of the Lamb shift in the hydrogen spectrum proved essential to the later development of quantum electrodynamics. Bethe was awarded the Nobel Prize in physics in 1967 for his contributions to the theory of nuclear reactions. Physicist I. I. Rabi, who joined Columbia University in 1929, worked on radio frequency spectroscopy and was influential on the future direction of experimental physics. In 1944 he received the Nobel Prize in physics for work on magnetic resonance. Rabi and his colleagues played a significant role in founding the Brookhaven National Laboratory. The Physics Department at Columbia University continued its outstanding work during the 1950s when professor T. D. Lee received the Nobel Prize in physics in 1957 for his investigation of the parity laws that led to discoveries about elementary particles.

Chemistry

As science encompassed an ever increasing number of subjects during the 19th century, there was a movement toward specialization. Science as a profession and career gave rise to professional societies where ideas and information could be exchanged. Societies catering to specialists in mathematics, botany, microscopes, and minerals were joined in 1876 with the founding of the American Chemical Society, established in New York City as a national society. Irving Langmuir, affiliated with GE in Schenectady, was awarded the Nobel Prize in chemistry in 1932 for his discoveries and investigations in surface chemistry. In 1934 Harold C. Urey, affiliated with Columbia University, won the Nobel in chemistry for his discovery of heavy hydrogen. At the beginning of the 20th century, Simon Flexner, the first director of the Rockefeller Institute for Medical Research (1901–35), was one of the leading proponents of chemistry in medical research. In 1946 John Northrop and Wendell Stanley of the Rockefeller Institute shared the Nobel Prize in chemistry for their preparation of enzymes and virus proteins in a pure form, along with James Sumner of Cornell University, who discovered that enzymes can be crystallized. William H. Stein and Stanford Moore of Rockefeller University shared the prize in 1972 for their contribution to the understanding of the connection between chemical structure and catalytic activity of the active center of the ribonuclease molecule.

Anthropology and Psychology

Rochester was the home of Lewis Henry Morgan, one of the earliest researchers in anthropology during the 1850s. Although trained in law, his scholarly writing on the Iroquois and kinship made him a pioneer in the nascent field of anthropology. His rational techniques for investigation made them useful tools for answering questions about human development and helped legitimize the subject as a field of scientific study. He was elected to the leadership of the National Academy of Sciences in 1875.

Psychologist James McKeen Cattell joined the staff of Columbia University in 1891. His most significant contribution was the inspiration he provided later investigators for testing and for the use of applied psychology. Cattell is best known for the scientific journals he edited and published, including *School and Society* in Garrison (Putnam Co). His pronouncements and experimentation helped set the course for psychology during the first half of the 20th century.

Franz Boas, a professor of anthropology and cultural relativist, began teaching at Columbia University in 1899. He believed that learned behavior explained differences among human groups. Sometimes considered the father of modern anthropology, he criticized prevalent notions of racial inheritance. He had an enormous impact on his associates and students. Among the latter were Ruth Benedict and Margaret Mead. Benedict, an assistant professor of anthropology at Columbia, published her most influential book, *Patterns of Culture* in 1934. In it she suggested that 20th-century Americans were shaped by their cultural patterns and that these were not fixed. Mead held beliefs similar to Boas's regarding human development. Like Benedict, she was a culture-and-personality theorist. Mead demonstrated how the young are taught to conform to social norms. Her books *Coming of Age in Samoa* (1928) and *Growing Up in New Guinea* (1930) were popular successes, and they argued that American sexual mores and taboos were often not universal and were not necessary for healthy personal and sexual development. Taking advantage of her notoriety, she assumed the mantle of educator of the public on anthropology. She directed the Columbia University Institute for Contemporary Cultures between 1948 and 1952 and was a long-time curator at the American Museum of Natural History.

John B. Watson left the academic world of psychology in 1920 for the realm of commercial advertising psychology with the J. Walter Thompson Co in New York City. His revolutionary behaviorist theory held that individuals could be taught to be and do anything and were not preordained by background, hence its usefulness in advertising. Fellow behaviorist Edward Lee Thorndike was a student of Cattell. By 1940 Thorndike's 41-year career as a professor of educational psychology at Teachers College, Columbia University made him one of the most influential figures in shaping school curriculums, teacher training, and teaching methods in the United States.

Mathematics and Computing

New York University (NYU) was the site of important contributions in the area of mathematical research, and Richard Courant was its most famous practitioner. Courant left Germany in 1933, and when given a professorship at NYU in 1936, he was challenged to build a graduate school of mathematics. By 1938 his Graduate Center for Mathematics was a reality and modeled after the Mathematics Institute in Göttingen, Germany. In 1941 Courant sought to expand the center with an Institute for Applied Mathematics. During World War II funding for the institute came from government contracts for mathematical studies. The name was changed to the Institute for Mathematics and Mechanics in 1947 and then to the Institute of Mathematical Sciences in 1952. NYU was one of the recipients of an Atomic Energy Commission (AEC) UNIVAC computer in 1953. AEC research provided work at the university for almost 20 years. In 1964 the Institute of Mathematical Sciences had it own high-rise building, and two years later the institute was renamed the Courant Institute of Mathematical Sciences.

Commercial enterprises also had researchers in mathematics. In 1937 George Stibitz of the Bell Telephone Laboratories in New York City constructed a demonstration binary adder (with the digits 0 and 1) using telephone relays. This was a first step in developing a calculating device that eventually led to the binary computer. Computer-related fields remain the primary focus of IBM's Thomas J. Watson Research Center, established in Yorktown Heights (Westchester Co) in 1961 and expanded to a facility in Hawthorne (Westchester Co) in 1984.

Conclusion

At the beginning of the 21st century, science is a vital element of the state's culture and enterprise. Some form of it is taught in all of New York State's 263 colleges and universities. Organizations such as the New York Academy of Sciences offer research training programs for students, give teacher workshops, and cosponsor an annual New York City Science and Engineering Fair, a competition for city high school students.

See also Botanists and naturalists; Fish; Flora and vegetation.

Allen, Garland E. *Thomas Hunt Morgan: The Man and His Science* (Princeton, NJ: Princeton Univ Press, 1978)
Baatz, Simon. *Knowledge, Culture, and Science in the Metropolis: The New York Academy of Sciences, 1817–1970* (New York: New York Academy of Sciences, 1990)
Corner, George W. *A History of the Rockefeller Institute, 1901–1953: Origins and Growth* (New York: Rockefeller Institute Press, 1964)
Dubos, Rene J. *The Professor, the Institute, and DNA* (New York: Rockefeller Univ Press, 1976)
James, Mary Ann. *Elites in Conflict: The Antebellum Clash over the Dudley Observatory* (New Brunswick, NJ: Rutgers Univ Press, 1987)
Moyer, Albert E. *Joseph Henry: The Rise of an American Scientist* (Washington, DC: Smithsonian Institution Press, 1997)
Reid, Constance. *Courant in Göttingen and New York: The Story of an Improbable Mathematician* (New York: Springer-Verlag, 1976)
Reingold, Nathan, ed. *Science in 19th-Century America: A Documentary History* (New York: Hill & Wang, 1964)
———. *Science in America since 1820* (New York: Science History Publications, 1976)
Robbins, Christine Chapman. *David Hosack: Citizen of New York* (Philadelphia: American Philosophical Society, 1964)
Soderstrom, Mary. *Recreating Eden: A Natural History of Botanical Gardens* (Montreal: Vehicule Press, 2001)
Watson, Elizabeth L. *Houses for Science: A Pictorial History of Cold Spring Harbor Laboratory* (Plainview, NY: Cold Spring Harbor Laboratory Press, 1991)

William E. Worthington Jr

Scio. Town (pop 1,914) in S central Allegany Co. Settled in 1805, the town was formed in 1823 from Angelica. It was named for an island off the Turkish coast where, in 1822, the Greek Orthodox population was massacred by the Ottoman Turks in reaction to the Greek move for independence. Lumber and wood products fueled the town's economy through the 19th century. The Erie Railroad (1851) benefited Scio hamlet's growth. Maj Peter Keenan (1834–1863), an Irish immigrant who lived in Scio from 1851 to 1858, was killed while leading a heroic charge at Chancellorsville and is buried in Scio's Catholic cemetery. Riverside hamlet was the site of the Riverside Seminary (1873–88), a collegiate institute. The Triangle No. 1 oil well (1879) was the county's first productive commercial well; it created a "mushroom city" known as Petrolia. In the early 21st century many of Scio's residents work in nearby Wellsville.

Scipio [SIP-ee-oh]. Town (pop 1,537) in S central Cayuga Co. Settled in 1790, the town was formed in 1794. Jethro Wood (1774–1834) of Scipio patented the first iron moldboard plow, produced by a foundry in the nearby town of Moravia. Scipio was crossed by the Southern Central Railroad (1870) along Owasco Lake and was the terminus of short lines to Ithaca in the late 19th and early 20th centuries. A jelly factory processed local apples from 1871 to 1936, and the Ensenore Glen House (1874) was a resort hotel on the lake. Scipio's main industry in 2003 was agriculture, chiefly engaged in by crop farmers with several large dairy farms. Sherwood was the home of Emily Howland (1827–1929), abolitionist and suffragist, and a station on the Underground Railroad; her home is now the Howland Stone Store Museum.

Virginia L. Koon

Scofield, C(yrus) I(ngerson) (*b* near Clinton, Mich, 19 Aug 1843; *d* Douglaston, Queens Co, 24 July 1921). Reference Bible editor. Raised in Tennessee, C. I. Scofield served in the Confederate army. After the war he practiced law in Missouri and Kansas, served in the Kansas state legislature, and was a US district attorney. Following a conversion to Christianity at age 36, Scofield was ordained a Congregationalist in 1883, and he served in pastorates in Texas (1882–95) and Massachusetts (1895–1902). In 1901 Scofield helped to initiate the Sea Cliff Bible Conference, which existed for 10 years on the north shore of Long Island. John T. Pirie, a New York City businessman, owned an estate on Hempstead Harbor, as well as a park in the center of Sea Cliff (Nassau Co). Pirie erected a tent in the park and invited Scofield to use it for the conference. It was during the first two conferences that Scofield expressed his desire to produce a reference Bible. Pirie and Alwyn Ball Jr, a New York City real estate broker and lawyer, became his financial sponsors. In 1908 Scofield transferred his ordination and ministerial connection to the Presbyterian Church. Residing in Douglaston, Scofield started a correspondence school, the New York Night School of the Bible, in New York City in 1908. He also opened the Philadelphia School of the Bible with L. S. Chafer, founder of Dallas Theological Seminary. Oxford University Press released the Scofield Reference Bible in 1909 and within two years published 2 million copies, the single most influential publication in fundamentalism's early history.

Beale, David. *In Pursuit of Purity: American Fundamentalism since 1850* (Greenville, SC: Bob Jones Univ Press, 1986)

Gaebelein, Arno C. "The Story of the Scofield Reference Bible," *Moody Monthly* (Oct 1942-Mar 1943)

Trumbull, Charles G. *The Life Story of C. I. Scofield* (New York: Oxford Univ Press, 1920)

David Beale

Scorsese, Martin (*b* Flushing, Queens, 17 Nov 1942). Filmmaker. Scorsese's parents worked in the garment district, and he spent his youth in Manhattan's Little Italy, graduating from Cardinal Hayes High School in the Bronx and receiving his BA (English, 1964) and MA (film, 1966) from New York University. His New York City films exude an inner-city edginess and energy and often have autobiographical aspects. His work frequently explores the rituals of male bonding and camaraderie, guilt over living in perpetual states of sin, and the issues of loyalty and betrayal. Scorsese came of age surrounded by the small-time hoods he later etched in *Mean Streets* (1973), the film that established his reputation, and *GoodFellas* (1990). He depicted inarticulate and frighteningly angry New York City loners in *Taxi Driver* (1976) and *Raging Bull* (1980), the latter about prizefighter Jake La Motta, the "Bronx Bull." His representation of the complexities of life in New York City has not been limited to a single social class or a single historical era. *The Age of Innocence* (1993) was set among the city's elite at the turn of the 20th century. Mid–19th century street toughs rumbled in Manhattan's notorious Five Points slum in *Gangs of New York* (2002). In 2002 he cofounded the Tribeca Film Festival.

Brunette, Peter, ed. *Martin Scorsese: Interviews* (Jackson: Univ Press of Mississippi, 1999)

Scotia. Village (pop 7,957) in Glenville (Schenectady Co). Named for Scotland in recognition of Scottish founder Sander Leendertsz Glen, it was a broom manufacturing area in the mid–19th century. In 1902 the extension of trolley lines connected Scotia to Schenectady, making Scotia a bedroom community for General Electric's factory and professional workers. The village incorporated in 1904. In 1925 the Great Western Gateway Bridge opened, directing most westbound road traffic through Scotia. The Glen Sanders Mansion (1658, expanded in 1713), home of the families of Alexander Glen and John Sanders, was a restaurant and inn in 2003. The historic Flint House (1735) features an exhibition on broom making.

Stephanie Przybylek and Christopher Hunter

Scots

Colonial Period

Scots had arrived in New Netherland by the 1630s. Sander Leendertsz Glen, a native of Dysert in Fife, was on the Delaware by 1633 (he later settled Schenectady) and William Teller, a Shetland Islander, was at Fort Orange in 1639. Major settlement began in 1669, when the English Privy Council authorized Scottish vessels to trade and fish in New York City. The first attempt ended in shipwreck, but soon prisoners, indentured servants, dissidents, and religious exiles—such as Gypsy prisoners in 1682 and Covenanters in 1684—were being sent. Many in the colony were from Ulster, and most from Scotland proper were Lowlanders. The combination of excess population and the attempt, after 1680, to restructure the Scottish economy on an English model created economic distress. The Union of 1707 permitted Scots to settle and work in the colonies without restriction. Most went to the heavily Scottish colonies of East Jersey and the Carolinas.

In 1735 Gov William Cosby offered New York land to loyal Protestant Highlanders. When 472 Argyllshire Presbyterians arrived in 1738–40, the colony refused to honor the claims, and they settled in scattered locations, especially in Orange Co. In 1764 many of the same families secured a grant of 47,450 acres (19,202 ha), known as the Argyle Patent, in Argyle, Fort Edward, and Greenwich [now in Washington Co]. Highland regiments including the 42d (Black Watch) fought in the French and Indian War. Some veterans received land grants near Ticonderoga and encouraged other Scots to emigrate. Sir William Johnson sought tenants among Scottish immigrants for his land in present Fulton Co and in 1773 invited a colony of more than 400 Roman Catholic Highlanders (from Glengarry, Glenmoriston, Glen Urquhart, and Strathglass) to his land. In 1775, after his death and in the midst of political unrest, they relocated to the present Ontario. Galway (Saratoga Co) was settled in 1774 by Scots immigrants, and there were other such communities. One estimate calculated that 7% of the New York population in 1790 was Scottish.

Leaders in education, medicine, and religion, Scottish immigrants exerted a strong influence on colonial New York. Eight colonial governors, including Cadwallader Colden, a graduate of the University of Edinburgh, were of Scottish birth or descent. The founder of the Livingston dynasty, Robert Livingston (1654–1728), from Ancrum, Roxburghshire, came to Albany in 1674–75. At one time Livingston employed the privateer and later notorious pirate William Kidd. Although legend identified Kidd as the son of a minister from Greenock, Renfrewshire, he was in fact the son of a sailor from Dundee. In 1688 Kidd settled in New York City, where he recruited many of his crew before embarking on his piracies. In 1707 the Scots-Irish Rev Francis Makemie, visiting New York City, was imprisoned by Anglican authorities for preaching to Presbyterian immigrants. Supporters organized for his trial, and after his acquittal they founded the First Presbyterian Church in 1716. At John Peter Zenger's famous libel trial in 1735 he was ably defended by Scottish-born lawyer Andrew Hamilton. A schism between Scots and English in the Presbyterian congregation in New York City led to the creation of the Second Presbyterian Church in 1756. Newly arrived Scottish traders established Albany's First Presbyterian Church in 1762; led by missionaries William Hannah and Andrew Bay, many were loyalists, and the church temporarily shut down during the Revolutionary War. One of the leaders of the patriot cause in New York State was the half-Scottish Alexander Hamilton, the son of a trader from The Grange, Fifeshire, born out of wedlock on the Caribbean island of Nevis. Evidence of Scottish consciousness in the colony is the founding of the St. Andrew's Society in New York City in 1756, based on the Scots society founded 12 years earlier.

Federal Period to World War I

By 1775 there were 30–40 Scottish and Scots-Irish settlements in New York Colony and an estimated 25,000 people of Scottish ancestry. Scots fought on both sides in the Revolutionary War. Numerous loyalist settlements were abandoned or destroyed, and large numbers of settlers emigrated to Canada. In the 19th century, desperate economic conditions and the highland clearances sparked another wave of emigration from Scotland. Immigrants worked as farmers; factory, mill, and iron workers; carpenters; and skilled tradesmen. For much of the 19th century, hundreds of Scottish weavers lived in Manhattan around 17th St between 6th and 7th Aves, an area known as Paisley Place. Scottish immigration to the United States increased 10-fold to 38,331 in the 1850s and continued to grow. Many new immigrants were young single women who came to work in textile mills and the garment industry. Large Scottish communities thrived in Schenectady, Albany, Elmira, Buffalo, Syracuse, Brooklyn, and New York City. The Scottish immigrants of New York's 79th Cameron Highlanders (NYSV) were some of the best fighters in the Civil War.

Scottish Americans were prominent publishers, merchants, manufacturers, capitalists, philanthropists, railroad and shipping magnates, bankers, lawyers, politicians, doctors, scientists, educators, engineers, inventors, artists, and architects. Among the many famous figures of the Federal period were author Washington Irving, cabinetmaker Duncan Phyfe, and chief Erie Canal engineer James Geddes. James Gordon Bennett, born in Keith, Banffshire, settled in New York City in 1823 and in 1835 founded the *New York Herald,* a leader of the penny press. Newspapers for Scots readers included Archibald Stewart's *Scottish-American* (1857–1925) and its competitor, *The Scotsman* (1869–86). Businessmen of Scottish descent included Archibald Kennedy, Robert Bruce, James Lenox, and Archibald Gracie. The best-known industrialist and philanthropist of the late 19th and early 20th centuries, Andrew Carnegie, was born in Dunfermline, Fifeshire in 1835 and moved to the United States in 1848; in his late years he was a New York City resident.

Since 1914

Between the world wars new immigrants came mostly from Glasgow and central Scotland. In the 1920s a new wave of migration sent about 15,000 people a year to the United States; in 1923 three times as many rushed in ahead of restrictive quotas. The majority were young single urban adults: skilled tradesmen and artisans, professionals, and laborers, especially joiners, engineers, and miners. More than 200 laborers from the Isle of Lewis lived in Buffalo, working on construction projects in Niagara Falls and elsewhere. They met Hebridean wives through church and secular associations. Harlem was a gathering place for Hebrideans, with Gaelic dances regularly drawing crowds of 400 in the 1930s. By 1930 there were 354,323 foreign-born Scots in the United States; from 1940 to 1970 New York had the most of any state. In the 2000 census some 212,275 New York State residents claimed Scottish ancestry, with Erie, Monroe, New York, and Suffolk Cos having the largest number. Popularly organized Scottish activities include Robert Burns poetry nights, genealogy, heraldry, wearing of kilts and clan tartans on ceremonial occasions, highland games, country dancing, and Scottish music, notably piping and drumming, marching bands, highland reels and flings, art songs, and ballads. Organizations such as St. Andrew's Society, the New York Caledonian Club, and numerous piping societies have thriving memberships, as do various lodges and fraternal organizations. The Central New York Scottish Games have been held in the Syracuse area since the 1940s. Tartan Day festivals in New York City, Schenectady, and other places feature bands, parades, games, and dancing.

Cage, R. A., ed. *Scots Abroad: Labour, Capital, Enterprise, 1750–1914* (London: Croom Helm, 1985)
Dobson, David. *Scottish Emigration to Colonial America, 1607–1785* (Athens: Univ of Georgia Press, 1994)
Harper, Marjorie. *Emigration from Scotland between the Wars: Opportunity or Exile?* (New York: Manchester Univ Press, 1998)
MacDougall, D., ed. *Scots and Scots' Descendants in America* (New York: Caledonian Publishing, 1917)

Thomas Ross Miller

Scots-Irish. The term Scots-Irish derived from the 17th-century move of Lowland Scots into northern Irish counties, a colonizing movement that established a robust Presbyterian presence throughout Ulster. Repressive Anglican political dictates, fallout from the Cromwellian Wars, and severe economic hardships led 150,000 Scots-Irish to seek fresh opportunities in America during the 18th century.

Early Settlement

Scots-Irish immigration from Belfast, Coleraine, Londonderry, Larne, Newry, and Portrush to New York Colony and the Middle Colonies crested in 1717–18, 1725–29, 1740–41, 1754–55, and 1771–75. Estimating the numbers is complicated by undercounting, undocumented passage from smaller ports, and a lack of distinction in Irish emigration records for Ulster Presbyterians, Anglicans, and Catholics. Although most Scots-Irish settled in the less densely populated and more Dissenter-friendly areas of Pennsylvania and the Shenandoah Valley after 1725, New York City was a gateway for their immigration. Donegal-born minister Rev Francis Makemie was arrested and later acquitted in 1707 by New York Colony's governor Edward Hyde, Viscount Cornbury for unlicensed preaching. Makemie weathered the storm and established the city's flagship Presbyterian Church. Antrim-born minister Rev William Tennent achieved a strong church foundation in Westchester Co during the 1720s before departing for Pennsylvania.

Outside the city, contingents of Scots-Irish followed pioneering Scots Presbyterians first to Orange and Ulster Cos, then toward the area of modern Warren, Saratoga, Fulton, Washington, Sullivan, and Otsego Cos, and to select lands in what are now Albany, Schenectady, and Rensselaer Cos. Among the 1729–30 settlers in Little Britain (Orange Co) was Charles Clinton (1690–1773) of Scottish ancestry from County Longford, whose son George and grandson De Witt Clinton became governors of New York State. Difficulties in generating accurate settlement statistics abound, but Presbyterian Church establishment patterns reveal an influx of several thousand Scots-Irish into the larger urban centers and along the western frontier region by 1725; this population gradually dissipated as Pennsylvania and the Lower Colonies absorbed increasing numbers. Despite the limited market for indentured servants in Dutchess, Putnam, Rockland, and Orange Cos, significant Scots-Irish communities developed throughout, particularly in Goshen (Orange Co) and beyond in Warrenbush [now Florida, Montgomery Co] and Wallkill (Ulster Co). Land agents William Gilliland, David Waugh, and Henry Caldwell attracted immigrants to New York from Armagh and Antrim. For example, the 300-strong contingent from Ballybay in Monaghan led by Scottish-born Dr Thomas Clark settled during 1764 in Albany, Salem [now in Washington Co], and Stillwater [now in Saratoga Co].

By the 1740s Otsego Co's Cherry Valley and other Scots-Irish frontier communities served as buffers against Indian hostility and bases of support for a burgeoning revolutionary sensibility. Among others, Gen Richard Montgomery, who came from County Donegal, and Gen John Stark influenced Scots-Irish participation on the American side of the Revolutionary War. This was especially evident in the Battle of Bunker Hill in 1775 and in the Battles of Saratoga in 1777, although a minority retained loyalist sympathies.

Period of 1783–1900

Localized farming, cottage industries, and church-based activities defined rural New York State's Scots-Irish culture. These characteristics facilitated community assimilation into the English-speaking, Protestant-dominated, early national period population base. By 1812 improved economic circumstances and repressive shipping regulations combined to decrease immigration levels significantly. Scots-Irish culture defined perceptions of Irish identity in New York State. As yeomen farmers and Freemasons, merchants and craftsmen, Scots-Irish fared well. One of the most successful was the self-made wholesaling tycoon A. T. Stewart (1803–76).

In the mid–19th century, Scots-Irish identity became increasingly distinct from Irish Catholics. Through the 1840s the Scots-Irish participated with Catholic Irish during Saint Patrick's Day parades and within the Friendly Sons of Saint Patrick. With the huge increase in the Irish Catholic population, however, Scots-Irish developed an identity with a self-conscious separationist impulse. They affiliated with nativist and anti-Catholic groups, and they commemorated the victory on 12 July 1690 of the Protestant King William III in Ireland at the Battle of the Boyne over the deposed Catholic King James II. The Orange Order, or the Loyal Orange Institution in the United States, grew out of Ireland's Orange Order of the late 18th century. A fraternal organization akin to Freemasonry in form and structure, the Orange Order prospered in New York City after the early 19th century. The New York City parades celebrating the Battle of the Boyne in 1870 and 1871 turned into bloody riots, resulting in several dozen fatalities. A renowned pastor of the Fifth Avenue Presbyterian Church from 1867 to 1898, Armagh-born Rev Dr John Hall (1829–98) sought to promote Scots-Irish identity in an era of mass (and multiethnic) immigrant influx as a founding member of the 1889 Scotch-Irish Society. The New York City branch remained active until 1900.

After 1900

The majority of 20th-century migrants to areas with strong Scots-Irish cultural roots settled in Canada and mainland Britain. However, the Orange Order continues to link New York State's larger metropolitan centers with Ulster since the last public 12th of July parade in New York City in 1919. Orange Order members sustain their historic loyalty to the British Crown and to Ulster as a symbol of pride and identity in modern times. The political troubles in Northern Ireland have strengthened the connection between New York State's residents of Scots-Irish descent and their historic homeland into the 21st century. The Scotch-Irish Society of America, the Orange Order, and the Scots-Irish residents of New York State rallied to the Ulster Unionist (supporters of allegiance to British governance of Northern Ireland) cause during the 1990s. This interest preserves a direct connection between Scots-Irish New York State residents and the source of their heritage. In the 2000 census 138,344 New Yorkers identified themselves as having Scots-Irish ancestry. The lower Hudson Valley, New York City, and Long Island contained the most significant populations, and large communities were also located in Erie, Monroe, and Albany Cos.

Blethen, H. Tyler, and Curtis W. Wood, eds. *Ulster and North America: Transatlantic Perspectives on the Scotch-Irish* (Tuscaloosa: Univ of Alabama Press, 1997)
Chepesiuk, Ronald. *The Scotch-Irish: From the North of Ireland to the Making of America* (Jefferson, NC: McFarland, 2000)
Lehmann, William C. *Scottish and Scotch-Irish Contributions to Early American Life and Culture* (Port Washington, NY: Kennikat, 1978)
Leyburn, James G. *The Scotch-Irish: A Social History* (Chapel Hill: Univ of North Carolina, 1962)

Mary C. Kelly

Scott. Town (pop 1,193) in NW Cortland Co. The first resident of European ancestry was a Francophone Canadian trapper *ca* 1795, followed by New England settlers in 1799. The town, formed from Preble in 1815, has two long, narrow valleys running through it, one ending at the southern tip of Skaneateles Lake, the lowest elevation (880 feet/268 m) in Cortland Co. Dairying became important starting in the mid–19th century. Many residents commute to Cortland and Syracuse, while others continue the town's agricultural economy. Scott's population doubled between 1960 and 1990.

Cathy A. Barber

Scott, Blanche Stuart (*b* ?Greece, Monroe Co, ?4 Apr 1885; *d* Rochester, 12 Jan 1970). Pioneer aviator. In 1910 former finishing school student Blanche Stuart Scott, accompanied by a woman reporter, drove a Willys-Overland automobile from New York City to San Francisco. Though billed by Willys-Overland as the first woman to drive coast to coast, it is possible that another woman preceded her. Curtiss Exhibition Co offered Scott flying lessons, over initial objections by company founder Glenn H. Curtiss. Her first solo flight took place sometime during August or September 1910, and most consider her the first American woman pilot. But the indistinct date of her feat gives Bessica Raiche, who piloted her first flights on Long Island, a claim to the title. Scott flew her first exhibition flights at Fort Wayne, Ind, in November. Leaving Curtiss soon after, she worked for other exhibition teams. In 1911, by some reports, Scott set a record for a long-distance flight by a woman, making a 60 mi (98 km) loop from Mineola (Nassau Co). The next year she became the first woman test pilot by flying prototype aircraft for the Glenn L. Martin Co of Los Angeles. She retired from professional flying in 1916, complaining that she drew crowds as a freak rather than as a skilled pilot. She worked as a screenwriter and actor in Hollywood before returning in the 1930s to Rochester, where she wrote and performed for radio and television. From 1954 she also served as a public relations agent for the USAF Museum in Dayton, Ohio. The US Postal Service issued a commemorative airmail stamp in her honor on 20 Dec 1980.

Mitchell, Charles R., and Kirk W. House. *Flying High: Pioneer Women in American Aviation* (Charleston, SC: Arcadia, 2002)
Roseberry, C. R. *Glenn Curtiss: Pioneer of Flight* (Garden City, NY: Doubleday, 1972)

Kirk W. House

Scottsville. Village (pop 2,128) in Wheatland (Monroe Co). It was settled in 1790, and a post office was established in 1820. Mills were built on Oatka Creek. In 1836 residents incorporated the Scottsville and Genesee River Canal, which was completed in 1837, to facilitate shipping wheat on the Erie Canal. The Scottsville and Le Roy Railroad (incorporated 1836) was built to Mumford in 1837 and to Caledonia in 1838. An 1895 fire destroyed the mills. The Scottsville Agricultural Works operated from the 1870s to 1899. The village was incorporated in 1914. The library, formerly Windom Hall (1892), is on the National Register of Historic Places, along with many buildings of the Greek Revival style in the heart of the village.

Carolyn Vacca

Scrantom, Hamlet (*b* Durham, Conn, 1 Dec 1773; *d* Rochester, 19 Apr 1851). Early settler. Son of an American Revolutionary War soldier, Scrantom grew up in Durham. In 1805 he moved with his wife to Turin (Lewis Co), where he worked as a land agent and served as town supervisor in 1811. In 1812 the family continued farther west to become the first permanent settlers of what is now Rochester. They resided near the present-day corner of West Main St, State St, and Exchange Blvd, where Scrantom operated a sawmill owned by Enos Stone. Over the years he operated other mills, made land investments, and worked as a grocer, boardinghouse keeper, and church sexton. He also was involved as sales agent for Oliver Culver's construction company in the building of the Erie Canal. Scrantom relocated to the faster-growing city of Buffalo in 1835. He returned to Rochester in 1838 and was elected president of the newly formed Pioneer Association in 1847. Scrantom's son Hamlet D. served Rochester as mayor in 1860 and another, Edwin, became an editor, publisher, historian, auctioneer, and merchant in that city.

McKelvey, Blake. *Rochester, the Water Power City, 1812–1854* (Cambridge, Mass: Harvard Univ Press, 1945)

Joann Minor

Scriba. Town (pop 7,331) in N central Oswego Co. Bounded on the north by Lake Ontario, the town, settled in 1798 largely from Herkimer Co, was formed in 1811 from Fredericksburgh [now Volney, Oswego Co]. The Oswego Canal (1828) and two railroads (1865, 1869) opened the town to the markets. Scriba mucklands were drained to produce onions, lettuce, and similar crops; beginning *ca* 1905 it became an important agricultural sector. Upland Scriba farms produce apples, strawberries, and other fruits as well as grain, potatoes, vegetables, and dairy products. Scriba has three nuclear power plants: the James A. FitzPatrick Nuclear Power Plant (1975) and Nine Mile Point One (1969) and Two (1988). A cogeneration plant, Sithe Energies, and Alcan Rolled Products are also located in town. Residents work at the plants or commute to Oswego or Syracuse.

Barbara J. Dix

Scriba's Patent. Land tract. Originally known as the Roosevelt Purchase, it was sold by John and Nicholas Roosevelt in 1792 to German immigrant George Scriba (1752–1836) and patented to him in 1794. It consisted of much of the present Oswego Co: over half a million acres (200,000 ha) between Oneida Lake and Lake Ontario, bounded by Wood Creek and the Salmon River on the east and the Oswego River on the west. Scriba hoped that the Oneida Lake–Mexico Harbor route would become a main route to Lake Ontario and attempted to develop Rotterdam [now Constantia] as a projected city and Mexico as a port. He invested heavily in the land, building a road from Mexico to Rotterdam as well as a store, houses, mills, and other buildings. Surveyor Benjamin Wright served as one of his land agents. The tract settled slowly, and the rival town of Oswego became the main port in the region. The project bankrupted Scriba, in part because for most of the 1790s he was an absentee landlord and could not control several of his agents. The unsold lands in the patent were distributed among his creditors between 1811 and 1822 in settlement for his debts.

Scriba, George. Papers. New York State Library, Albany
Simpson, Elizabeth M. *Mexico: Mother of Towns* (Buffalo: J. W. Clement, 1949)

Rohit T. Aggarwala

sculpture, public. Aside from ship figureheads and tombstone carvings, sculpture was not common in colonial America. A relatively expensive endeavor, sculpting required quarries, foundries, trained assistants, and a receptive audience—a difficult undertaking for the fledging colonies. Sculptors had little or no formal training, like John Frazee (1790–1842), who operated a marble-cutting business in Manhattan and a marble quarry in Eastchester (Westchester Co). Another self-taught artist of the period was Erastus Dow Palmer (1817–1904) of Pompey (Onondaga Co), who helped define American Neoclassicism with marbles such as *The White Captive* (1858, Metropolitan Museum of Art) and *Peace in Bondage* (1863, Albany Institute of History and Art), as well as the *Monument to James H. Armsby* (1879, Washington Park, Albany) and *Angel of the Sepulchre* (1868–69, Albany Rural Cemetery).

It became increasingly popular, especially between 1825 and 1850, for aspiring sculptors to study in Italy. One such artist was Randolph Rogers (1825–92) of Waterloo (Seneca Co), who is best known for creating the Columbus Doors at the Capitol in Washington. The arrival of Henry Kirke Brown (1814–86) in Brooklyn in 1848 signaled an earnest attempt to create inherently American sculpture, and though he had studied in Rome, Brown advised sculptors to explore American subjects and themes. His important works include *De Witt Clinton* (1852, Green-Wood Cemetery, Brooklyn) and the equestrian statue *George Washington* (1855, Union Square), both financed through public subscription. *Indian Hunter* (1866), by Brown's longtime assistant John Quincy Adams Ward (1830–1910), reflected a bold move toward realism and varied surface textures and was the first sculpture by an American placed in Central Park. Ward's 12 major public commissions in Manhattan, including a monument to a Troy (Rensselaer Co) steel manufacturer, *Alexander Lyman Holley* (1889, Washington Square Park), make him one of the most well-represented sculptors in the city.

From the 1860s to 1920

After the Civil War public demand grew for memorials that expressed the nation's collective sense of mourning and its fervent desire to honor its heroes. Ward's *Seventh Regiment Memorial* (1869, Central Park) honored the first of New York's regiments to rally for the Union cause. Subjects for memorials would include abolitionists, such as *Henry Ward Beecher* (1891, Cadman Plaza, Brooklyn) by Ward, and military heroes, such as *Admiral David Farragut* (1880, Madison Square Park) by Augustus Saint-Gaudens (1848–1907). Sally James Farnham (1876–1943) created sculpture dedicated to the armed services with her *Soldiers and Sailors* monuments located in her native Ogdensburg (St. Lawrence Co) and in Rochester.

The American renaissance, fueled by the national pride elicited by its centennial in 1876, paradoxically signaled a shift away from the notion of a purely American form of sculpture. Americans of means developed a taste for the French Beaux Arts style, characterized by the harmonious integration of architecture and sculpture, evident in such lavish spectacles as the 1901 Pan-American Exposition in Buffalo. Daniel Chester French (1850–1931), best known for the *Lincoln Memorial,* also created the *Spencer Trask Memorial* (1915, Saratoga Springs) and *Alma Mater* (1903, Columbia University, New York City). He completed *General Philip Henry Sheridan* (1916), a sculpture that was begun by Ward before his death in 1910 and is now at the Capitol in Albany. In Rochester *Frederick Douglass* (1898), by Sidney W. Edwards, is one of the first monuments dedicated to an African American.

New York City offers a wide range of sculpture throughout its public parks and buildings. Among Central Park's many sculptures are *Angels of the Water Fountain* (1868, Bethesda Terrace), by Emma Stebbins (1815–82) and *Alice in Wonderland* (1959, overlooking the Conservatory Water), by José de Creeft (1884–1982). One of the most recognizable sculptures in New York City is the bronze *Statue of Liberty* designed by French sculptor Frédéric-Auguste Bartholdi (1834–1904). It was completed in France in 1884 and arrived in New York Harbor in 1885 at Liberty Island and, though 10 years late, was meant to celebrate the country's centennial. In 1892 a 70 ft (21 m) marble statue of *Christopher Columbus* (1892) by Gaetano Russo was unveiled at Columbus Circle to commemorate the 400th anniversary of the arrival of Columbus in the New World. Edward Clark Potter (1857–1923) created the pair of marble lions that grace the entranceway of the New York Public Library (1911).

From the 1920s

As modernism began to take hold in the second decade of the 20th century, Beaux Arts monuments soon seemed incapable of expressing the concerns of the Machine Age. Monuments to World War I flourished, such as Sally James Farnham's *Like Hell They Can* (1927) in Fultonville (Montgomery Co) and the *Father Francis P. Duffy Monument* (1936, Times Square) by Charles Keck (1875–1951). Commissions for public sculpture dwindled during the Great Depression, the notable exception being those at Rockefeller Center, such as the colossal *Prometheus* (1934) by Paul Manship (1885–1966), commissioned by John D. Rockefeller Jr. As architecture streamlined into skyscraping glass facades, private corporations began to commission minimalist or other abstract sculpture that served an aesthetic rather than a memorializing purpose. Abstract sculptor Isamu Noguchi (1904–88) crafted the *Chassis Fountain* at the Ford Motor Co's pavilion at the 1939 New York City World's Fair and *News* (1938–40), a 9-ton stainless-steel relief sculpture for the entrance of the Associated Press building in Rockefeller Center.

State commissions under Gov Nelson A. Rockefeller were considerable, including Clement Meadmore's (1929–) *Verge* (1972) and *Geometric Mouse, Variation I* (1968) by Claes Oldenburg (1929–), both located at Empire State Plaza in Albany. Federal projects such as the Art-in-Architecture program promoted the placement of public sculpture, one of the most controversial being Richard Serra's (1939–) *Tilted Arc* (1981, Manhattan, Federal Plaza), an enormous curved wall of Cor-Ten steel, dismantled in 1989. Figurative monuments and memorials still abound, including the *Vietnam Veterans Memorial of Greater Rochester* (1996, Highland Park) by Wayne Williams and *New York Fallen Firefighters Memorial* (1998, Empire State Plaza, Albany) by Robert J. Eccleston. The attack on the World Trade Center on 11 Sept 2001 has led to a competition for a permanent memorial. *The Sphere* by Fritz Keonig was one of the few sculptures left from the World Trade Center, having been placed in the plaza as a monument to peace in 1971. Although severely damaged, it has been restored by Keonig and placed in Battery Park.

See also Art, New York City Area; War Memorials.

Bogart, Michele H. *Public Sculpture and the Civic Ideal in New York City, 1890–1930* (Chicago: Univ of Chicago Press, 1989)

Gayle, Margot, and Michele Cohen. *Manhattan's Outdoor Sculpture: The Art Commission and the Municipal Art Society Guide* (New York: Prentice Hall, 1988)

Senie, Harriet F. *Contemporary Public Sculpture: Tradition, Transformation, and Controversy* (New York: Oxford Univ Press, 1992)

Tolles, Thayer, ed. *American Sculpture in the Metropolitan Museum of Art*, 2 vols (New York: Metropolitan Museum of Art, 1999–2001)

Voorsanger, Catherine Hoover, and John K. Howatt, eds. *Art and the Empire City: New York, 1825–1861* (New Haven: Yale Univ Press, 2000)

Brian Edward Hack

Seabury Investigations. A series of sensational investigations spearheaded by Samuel Seabury, a former judge of the State Court of Appeals (1930–32), that uncovered widespread municipal corruption in New York City and would eventually force the resignation of the mayor of New York City, Jimmy Walker. The murder of organized crime figure Arnold Rothstein at the Park Central Hotel in Manhattan on 2 Nov 1928 exposed links between Rothstein and leading politicians and judges in New York City. The slow pace of the investigation led to charges of a police cover-up. Gambler Thomas McManus was tried for the murder but acquitted, and as a result the reputation of the city's law enforcement organizations suffered. In the 1929 mayoral campaign, Republican candidate Fiorello La Guardia railed at Tammany Hall, citing Rothstein's loan to Albert Vitale, a state magistrate judge, as just one example of the Democratic Party's ties to the underworld. Under intense political pressure from the city's reform and civic organizations and from tabloids throughout the state, Democratic governor Franklin D. Roosevelt reluctantly launched an investigation. Roosevelt feared that his ambitions for the presidency might be ruined if he entered into a battle with Tammany Hall, since the organization had the potential power to block his nomination at the Democratic National Convention in 1932.

At the request of Gov Roosevelt, the Appellate Division of the New York State Supreme Court that covered New York and Bronx Cos appointed Seabury as referee of New York City's Magistrates' Courts (the lower criminal courts) in August 1930. Seabury was a distinguished jurist who had run for governor in 1916 on the Democratic ticket and had served as president of the New York County Lawyers' Association. The investigation forced the resignation of six judges and the dismissal of numerous police officers involved in extortion schemes. Heeding the pleas of city and state reformers, and with the ambition of positioning himself as a reform Democrat, Gov Roosevelt appointed Seabury on 10 Mar 1931 as state commissioner charged with investigating the Manhattan District Attorney's Office. Seabury's ongoing investigation of the Magistrates' Courts raised questions about the competency of the district attorney, Thomas C. T. Crain. On 31 Aug 1931, Seabury reported to Roosevelt that Crain's actions did not merit removal from office, despite his failure to investigate racketeering cases.

On 23 Mar 1931, Seabury signed on as counsel to the Hofstadter Committee, a joint state legislative committee headed by state senator Samuel H. Hofstadter, a Republican from Manhattan, and created to investigate corruption charges in New York City government agencies. The committee exposed many unethical and illegal relationships, including allegations against Thomas Farley, sheriff of New York Co, which culminated in his removal from office by Gov Roosevelt. Farley's explanation about how he had amassed $400,000 in savings while serving in office—a "wonderful" tin box that mysteriously filled with money—earned him the nickname "Tin-Box Tom" in the press. The charges with the most far-reaching impact, however, were leveled against the sitting mayor, Jimmy Walker: that a secret account established for his benefit accumulated $1 million in deposits from 1926 to 1931. Other charges against Walker included allegations that executives at Equitable Coach, a business that held contracts with New York City, had paid bribes to Walker. Seabury's work was a source of political discomfort for Roosevelt, who would have preferred a slow investigation that would wrap up after the Democratic National Convention in summer 1932. On 8 June 1932, Seabury transmitted to Gov Roosevelt his findings that Mayor Walker was unfit to continue in office. Although Roosevelt did not believe that Walker's actions merited removal from office, he felt compelled to demonstrate his independence from Tammany Hall. On 11 Aug 1932 Roosevelt exercised his power to hold hearings to determine if Walker's actions merited removal. Roosevelt presided over hearings, broadcast on radio, at which Seabury, Walker's lawyer, and Walker himself provided testimony. Walker, bowing to the inevitable, resigned from office on 1 Sept 1932. With the adjournment of the Hofstadter Committee in December 1932, Seabury faded from public view, although he was later a valued advisor to Mayor Fiorello La Guardia.

The impact of the scandal on New York State politics was considerable. The uneasy peace between reform and regular Democrats that had been enforced by former governor Alfred E. Smith was shattered. Soon after Walker's resignation, La Guardia enjoyed a three-term reign (1934–46) as a Republican–City Fusion mayor. During La Guardia's tenure, Tammany Hall's influence on New York City politics declined precipitously.

Mitgang, Herbert. *Once Upon a Time in New York: Jimmy Walker, Franklin Roosevelt, and the Last Great Battle of the Jazz Age* (New York: Free Press, 2000)

Stolberg, Mary M. *Fighting Organized Crime: Politics, Justice, and the Legacy of Thomas E. Dewey* (Boston: Northeastern Univ Press, 1995)

Richard M. Flanagan

Sea Cliff. Village (pop 5,066) in Oyster Bay (Nassau Co). It was known as Carpenterville after its first owner. In 1871, 240 acres (97 ha) were purchased by the Sea Cliff Grove and Metropolitan Camp-ground Association of New York and Brooklyn, which built a 5,000-seat auditorium, a boardwalk, and a steamboat pier, and surveyed tent sites to be a summer assembly place for Methodists. Some campers became permanent residents within a decade; the village incorporated in 1883. The 300-room Sea Cliff Hotel helped transform it into a summer resort in the 1890s. After World War I the village became home to czarist refugees; starting in 1969 it has drawn working artists. Many of its Victorian buildings are on the National Register of Historic Places.

Joan Gay Kent

Seaford. Locality (pop 15,791) in Hempstead (Nassau Co). Capt John Seaman purchased the land from the Massapequa Indians in 1643, patenting it as Jerusalem, a tract consisting of a 2 x 5 mi (3.2 x 8.1 km) area of prairie, woodland, and salt marsh. The post office established in 1838 was called Jerusalem South but was renamed Seaford in 1868. Throughout the 19th century, the main occupation was fishing, and baymen navigated the marshes using the flat-bottomed Seaford skiff. German farmers shipped produce to New York City. A railroad station (1899) and the Sunrise Highway (1928–29) encouraged suburban growth; the population grew more than sixfold between 1940 and 1970, much of it from Brooklyn, before leveling off. Located on East Bay on the South Shore, Seaford is a favorite of sportfishing enthusiasts and is the site of the county's Cedar Creek Park and Tackapausha Museum and Preserve and of the town's Seaman's Neck Park.

Georgina Martorella

Searingtown. Locality (pop 5,034) in North Hempstead (Nassau Co). Named for the family of John Searing, who settled in 1716, it remained a small farming community until after World War II, when it was developed as a residential neighborhood. It has a growing Asian population, amounting to almost 26% in 2000, and an increasing Orthodox Jewish presence. Searingtown was the site of the first meeting of the North Hempstead Town Board (1784) and of the Searingtown Methodist Church (1785), now the Searing-Roslyn United Methodist Church in nearby Albertson, the first Methodist church edifice (1788) in present-day Nassau and Suffolk Cos.

Laura E. Mann

Sears, Isaac (*b* Cape Cod, Mass, *ca* 1730; *d* at sea, near Chinese coast, 1786). Revolutionary leader and privateer. Sears, the son of an oyster catcher, moved to New York City and became a privateer during the French and Indian War (1754–63). He then became a merchant, trading primarily to the West Indies, and was very involved in organizing crowd action from the time of the Stamp Act crisis in 1765 to the outbreak of the American Revolution a decade later. He returned to privateering during the war, operating out of Boston. He entered the state legislature in 1784, representing New York City, and in 1786 he helped to organize the first American trading voyage to China, where he died. He is buried on an island in Guangzhou harbor.

Christen, Robert Jay. "King Sears: Politician and Patriot in a Decade of Revolution" (PhD diss, Columbia Univ, 1968)

Maier, Pauline. "Isaac Sears and the Business of Revolution." In *The Old Revolutionaries: Political Lives in the Age of Samuel Adams* (New York: Knopf, 1980)

Edward Countryman

Seaver, Tom [George Thomas] (*b* Fresno, Calif, 17 Nov 1944). Baseball pitcher. Raised in Southern California where he played college baseball, Seaver signed a professional contract with the Atlanta Braves in 1966, but it was voided for violating rules relating to college players. The New York Mets obtained rights to Seaver that April in a lottery drawing with the Cleveland Indians and Philadelphia Phillies. Seaver was National League (NL) Rookie of the Year in 1967 with a record of 16-13 and a 2.76 earned run average (ERA). Two years later "Tom Terrific" was 25-7 with a 2.21 ERA, leading the Mets to their first World Series. Seaver also won the first of three Cy Young Awards (1969, 1973, 1975) as the NL's best pitcher. A bitter contract dispute in 1977 caused the Mets to trade Seaver to Cincinnati, and he pitched a no-hit game for the Reds against St. Louis in 1978. The Mets traded to get Seaver back in 1983, but they left him unprotected in a player draft after the season and Seaver was claimed by the Chicago White Sox. He earned his 300th career win with Chicago in a game against the New York Yankees at Yankee Stadium on 4 Aug 1985. He finished his major league career sitting on the bench with the Boston Red Sox as the Mets won the 1986 World Series. Seaver was elected to the Baseball Hall of Fame in 1992 with a 311-205 record and a 2.86 ERA. He returned to Fresno, where he grew grapes for California wines. He also broadcast baseball with the New York Yankees and New York Mets, and he remains one of the Mets most celebrated players.

Schoor, Gene. *Seaver: A Biography* (Chicago: Contemporary Books, 1986)

Maury Allen

secession movements. Differences between the interests of New York City and New York State, as well as between New York State and the rest of the nation, have given rise within the state to a number of movements for secession. The only successful secession from New York State occurred in 1777, when Vermont, which had been within the judicial jurisdiction of the Colony of New York since 1764, broke away and formed an independent republic. Vermont joined the Union as the 14th state in 1791 after paying New York State $30,000 in compensation for its lost lands.

Secession for New York City was the question of the day in January 1861 when Mayor Fernando Wood, facing the prospects of the Civil War, proposed that the city secede from both New York State and the Union. New York City would become a "free city of itself" called Tri-Insula, encompassing Manhattan, Staten Island, and Long Island. This plan in part reflected the growing interest of New York City, then limited to Manhattan Island, in absorbing the surrounding metropolitan area. Mayor Wood, a pro-southern Democrat, feared that national division would damage New York City's economic foundation and threatened secession to discourage Republican politicians leading the country down the path to war. He believed that a free New York City could maintain trade with both the North and South and avoid the economic distress that the war was likely to cause. This dodgy plan was thwarted and then dropped when in March 1861 the Confederacy announced import duties that favored southern cities. Some prominent southern ideologists, such as George Fitzhugh, praised Wood's scheme, arguing that New York City would be well rid of the abolitionist strongholds in the remainder of the state.

Although New York City's secession from the rest of the state would occasionally be suggested over the next century, it would not be until 1969 that it would become the subject of a significant political campaign. In 1969 novelist Norman Mailer ran in the Democratic primary for mayor of New York City on a platform emphasizing the benefits of an independent New York City with a campaign focusing on the tension and differences between people living in New York City and those in more rural regions of the state. His primary concern was that New York City paid a disproportionate share of federal and state taxes in relation to the aid it received. Independence from New York State and a position as the 51st state, Mailer declared, would be the only way to make the city endure as an intellectual and cultural beacon. He finished fourth out of five, but the idea remained popular. Secession talk is occasionally heard during budget negotiations, although it usually reflects more passing ire than any serious political position. In 2003 New York City Council member Peter Vallone Jr called for it, claiming that the city did not receive a fair share of the state's revenue. Other parts of the state have made similar claims. On its web site in 2003 the Center for a Free and Independent New York called for a New York City–less state to be called either West York, Central York, or North York.

There are also secession movements that try to redraw boundaries of the state's counties and cities. Staten Island became an issue when that state senator, John J. Marchi, introduced legislation that would have allowed Staten Island to separate from leave New York City in 1984. The idea was pushed farther in 1989, when the New York City charter was changed and the borough's influence reduced. In 1993 Staten Island voters, by a 2 to 1 margin, voted to create a charter for the City of Staten Island. In addition, in 1996, 70% of the voters of the five eastern towns of Suffolk Co voted to support a nonbinding referendum to form Peconic County. Both proposals soon died in the state legislature, however, and have little chance of success.

Countryman, Edward. *A People in Revolution: The American Revolution and Political Society in New York, 1760–1790* (Baltimore: Johns Hopkins Univ Press, 1981)

Mills, Hilary. *Mailer: A Biography* (New York: McGraw-Hill, 1984)

Mushkat, Jerome. *Fernando Wood: A Political Biography* (Kent, Ohio: Kent State Univ Press, 1990)

Jennifer Steenshorne

Second Great Awakening. See BURNED-OVER DISTRICT.

secretary of state. One of the oldest offices in state government, established 13 Mar 1778 with the appointment by the Council of Appointment of John Morin Scott, an organizer of the Sons of Liberty and member of the Continental Congress. The position was anteceded by the colonial offices of secretary of the Province of New Netherland under the Dutch and of secretary of the Province or Crown, established by the English in 1664. Appointing authority for the secretary of state was transferred to the legislature in 1821. The office was made elected in the Constitution of 1846. Christopher Morgan of Auburn (Cayuga Co), a former congressman, became the first elected secretary of state in 1848, serving until 1851.

For much of the early history of New York State, there were few specialized state departments or agencies. The secretary of state's office served as the administrative center for state government, responsible for a range of custodial, ministerial, ceremonial, and regulatory functions. As governmental functions grew in size, complexity, and importance, as new theories of organization emerged, or as new leaders took office, the work of the agency shifted. As a result of a constitutional amendment adopted in 1828, the secretary served as superintendent of common schools until the creation of the position of state superintendent of public instruction in 1854. New York's strong political parties often used nominations for secretary of state to give geographic, ethnic, and gender balance to their statewide tickets. Longtime New York Co Republican leader Samuel Koenig was the first Jewish person to hold the office (1909–10). Florence E. S. Knapp (1925–27), also a Republican, was the first woman to hold statewide elective office in New York and the last elected secretary of state.

Motor vehicle registration, which was a major function of the secretary of state's office since 1901, was divested in 1921 to the State Tax Commission. The secretary became a gubernatorial appointee with the adoption of a constitutional amendment in 1926. Gov Alfred E. Smith's first appointee was Robert Moses (1927–28), one of his key advisers in the decades-long effort to restructure New York government. State land management, a historic function of the secretary of state's office, was moved to a newly created Office of General Services as a result of the major reorganization of state government under Gov Nelson A. Rockefeller in 1960. In 1975 Gov Hugh Carey abolished the Office for Local Government and moved responsibility for liaison with local governments to the Department of State.

The secretary of state still conducts the governor's inauguration, swears in legislators and other state officers, is the custodian of the state seal and statutes, and publishes the state constitution. The secretary also serves on a number of statewide boards and sometimes acts as a troubleshooter for the governor or surrogate on ceremonial occasions. Since the position's return to appointed status, governors have usually chosen secretaries of state from the ranks of party leaders who were instrumental in their election or important to their reelection, with an eye also to achieving geographic, racial, and gender balance in their administrations. Basil Paterson (1979–83) was the first African American secretary of state. In addition to their governmental responsibilities, holders of this office have often played important statewide political roles. But with the exception of Mario M. Cuomo, who served in the office between 1975 and 1978 and later became lieutenant governor and governor, secretaries of state have not gone on to high elective office.

At the turn of the 21st century, the Department of State was organized into two major divisions: local government and community services, which focuses on training, technical assistance, code promulgation, and enforcement and administration of intergovernmental grant programs; and business and licensing services, which focuses on chartering and keeping records of corporations, licensing and regulating certain businesses as specified in law, administering the Universal Commercial Code, and receiving and publishing administrative regulations. The office also provides an administrative home for the State Athletics Commission, the Ethics Commission, the Lake George Park Commission, the Tug Hill Commission, and the Committee on Open Government.

New York State. Secretary of State. *201 Years of Serving the Citizens of New York State: A Brief History of the Secretary of State* (Albany: Office of the Secretary of State, 1979)

New York State Department of State, http://www.dos.state.ny.us/

Gerald Benjamin

securities industry. Since the early days of the republic stock trading, enterprise underwriting, and other aspects of the securities industry have developed into one of New York City's largest and most profitable businesses.

Origins of Stock Trading

Informal trading sessions consisting largely of government bonds and bank stocks began around 1790. There were several attempts to organize the nascent market in the next few years, the best known instance being the so-called Buttonwood Agreement of 17 May 1792, when 24 brokers set forth a loose agreement about preference in their dealings with one another and the establishment of minimum commission rates. The agreement—so-named because of its alleged, though unlikely, signing beneath a sycamore or buttonwood tree on Wall St—did not survive long beyond the market crash in summer 1792, and its connection to the 1817 founding of the New York Stock and Exchange Board (after 1863, New York Stock Exchange [NYSE]) is tenuous at best. With the New York Stock and Exchange Board, stock traders and commission brokers had a permanent institutional home. Other trading institutions grew and prospered as well; for example, during the Civil War a number of short-lived exchanges were formed, including the Open Board of Stock Brokers, which merged with the older exchange in 1869. A curb market in securities, trading primarily in the open air on Broad St in Lower Manhattan, dates to the middle of the 19th century.

Investment bankers or underwriters originate, underwrite, and distribute newly created securities from the issuing entity, reselling them to the investing public. Since the beginning of investment banking activity in the United States in the 1820s, New York City has been the home of almost all of the country's important investment banks. Investment banks in the 19th century often relied on connections to European capital for their ability to underwrite and distribute securities issues. This European connection proved crucial for the two best-known 19th-century investment banks, J. P. Morgan (1843) and Kuhn, Loeb (1867). The latter was one of the many important New York City German Jewish investment banks whose ranks also included Lehman Bros (1865) and M. Goldman (1869, predecessor of Goldman, Sachs). The first underwriting syndicate, in which a group of investment banks agreed to jointly underwrite and distribute a securities issue, dates to about 1870. By the last decade of the 19th century, the focus of investment banking shifted from railroad to industrial securities. Through their influence on corporate and government investment decisions, investment banks have played a decisive role in shaping the economy.

Workings of the Industry

Firms that trade in securities principally for their own account also earn considerable profits on margin loans (loans to customers to buy securities) and from short sales (the sale of securities not yet owned by an investor). Since the earliest days of organized securities markets, traders in securities operated under self-imposed rules, which eventually evolved into the rules and regulations of the NYSE and other market places for securities. Until the 1970s all trading firms were partnerships. Their inability to raise external capital in significant amounts kept the size of most modest in comparison to commercial banks, life insurance companies, and similar financial institutions.

In 1908, after decades of informal association, the New York Curb Market Agency, the forerunner of the New York Curb Market, was organized. The "over-the-counter" trading in securities was carried on for many years by means of an inexact listing of dealer quotes known as the pink sheets. Until the early 20th century relatively few securities firms emphasized retail brokerage activity. Among the first was Merrill Lynch, organized in 1915. The New York Curb Market moved indoors in 1921 and was renamed the American Stock Exchange in 1953.

World War I was a significant turning point in US financial history as the country shifted from being a debtor nation to a creditor nation. With this change also came the recognition of New York City as the world's deepest and most liquid market for securities trading and underwriting. The market crash of 1929 and the Great Depression helped create a climate in which the structure of investment banking would be fundamentally altered through changes such as the Glass-Steagall Act (1933), which required the separation of commercial and investment banking. This led to the division of some traditional firms. The highly prestigious investment bank of J. P. Morgan chose to become a commercial bank when several partners left to form the investment bank Morgan Stanley. The Glass-Steagall Act also created a business and regulatory environment in which a relatively small number of modestly capitalized securities firms could dominate the market for securities underwriting for many decades. By the 1940s Merrill Lynch was the largest and one of the most successful securities firms, with a national network of offices.

The securities industry has undergone massive changes over the past several decades. The "paperwork crisis" of the late 1960s, brought on by rapidly increasing stock market volume handled by antiquated data-processing equipment, started a shakeout among poorly capitalized firms, which were unable to afford the vast capital expenditures required by new technology. In 1971 the primary self-regulatory agency in the over-the-counter segment of the securities industry, the National Association of Securities Dealers (NASD), inaugurated an automated system of over-the-counter securities trading known as the National Association of Securities Dealers Automated Quotation System, or Nasdaq. In terms of both importance and trading volume the Nasdaq now rivals and at times exceeds its older competitor, the NYSE. It was not until 1970 that NYSE member firms were allowed to be publicly traded entities. Donaldson, Lufkin, and Jenrette was the first NYSE member firm to do so, on 9 April 1970. Merrill Lynch followed on 27 July 1971, and within a few years almost all of the large investment banks became public corporations, thereby greatly assisting the capital-raising ability of the securities industry.

On 1 May 1975 the fixed minimum commission schedule, which NYSE member firms had to maintain, was abolished in favor of negotiable commission rates. The immediate effect was a dramatic decrease in institutional commission rates, which were artificially high because of the computation of commissions based upon a multiple of the round lot rate. Commission rates for small investors, however, increased slightly for a while, until the advent in the 1980s of commission discounters and deep discounters. These trends brought on a period of numerous industry mergers and acquisitions as large institutional customers were sought.

Retail Brokers and Full-Service Firms

Another effect of these conditions was the full-service firm, securities houses that retain a significant presence in each of the major activities in which the securities industry operates. The largest of them, with a total capital in 2002 about $101 billion, was Merrill Lynch. It had 12,943 financial consultants, over 9 million client accounts, and 667 offices worldwide. Another was Morgan Stanley, the product of the 1997 merger between Morgan Stanley Group, an elite investment bank, and Dean Witter, Discover and Co, a large retail broker. This firm was just below Merrill in size, with total capital in 2002 about $77 billion. Morgan Stanley had 12,035 brokers, 5.2 million clients, and 482 offices worldwide. The product of recent merger activity, Citigroup Global Markets Holdings, formerly Salomon Smith Barney Holdings, was also a full-service giant. This firm had 13,662 brokers and strong operations in stock trading and municipal bond sales. Others included UBS Financial Services, formerly UBS PaineWebber, the result of the 2000 merger of the Swiss banking firm UBS AG with PaineWebber; and Prudential Securities, the result of Prudential Insurance Co's 1981 purchase of Bache and Co. Large trading firms included Bear Stearns, which had about $30 billion in capital in 2002. Lehman Bros was another, with 2002 capital about $48 billion. In recent years consolidation has extended to the specialists firms that make markets in NYSE-listed securities; many have been acquired by the large investment banks.

Banks

Banks become directly involved in the securities industry by extending margin loans for the purchase of securities, operating as registrars or transfer agents for public corporations, acting as clearing agencies for trading activity, issuing American Depository Receipts (which enable foreign securities to trade in the United States on a basis similar to domestic securities), or engaging in other such activities. Direct trading, underwriting, and advisory activities are also common to such banks. While many carry on some portion of these activities, only a few engage in most of them to a considerable extent. In 1987 J. P. Morgan and Bankers Trust were among a select group of banks permitted to underwrite corporate debt as well as publicly traded stocks. Bankers Trust was acquired by the German financial giant Deutsche Bank in 1999. J. P. Morgan merged with the Chase Manhattan Corp in 2000 to form J. P. Morgan Chase and Co.

The recent explosive growth of investment banks has not been without its problems. One of the most powerful investment banks of the 1980s, Drexel Burnham Lambert, which pioneered financing through noninvestment grade "junk bonds," collapsed in 1990 because of the effects of complex insider trading schemes. The push to underwrite new companies through initial public offerings (IPOs) during the technology boom of the 1990s was subject to a number of abuses. Superior positions in IPOs were often highly prized, and underwriters sometimes surreptitiously made them available to favored clients. There were many reports of collusion between underwriting and stock touting by investment banks, leading to circumstances in which reports on forthcoming IPOs or recent issues were less than candid. Many of these instances were revealed and later prosecuted by New York State attorney general Eliot Spitzer, who became perhaps the most aggressive prosecutor of the financial misdeeds of the late 1990s and 2000 bull market. In late 2003 he revealed that many mutual funds had been illegally trading for their own accounts and favored customers instead of protecting the fiduciary interests of the bulk of their clients.

An increase in the concentration and size of investment banking firms at the end of the 20th century resulted from the growing capital needs of the underwriting firms, the elimination of the Glass-Steagall barrier between investment and commercial banking in 1999, and the need for expensive new data-processing and telecommunication technology. Innovations like shelf registration, where corporations comply with registration requirements early to enable a quick offering when conditions are favorable, have led to the increase in the size of the average underwriting issue. In the early 21st century, technological advances have made very real the possibility that the securities industry of the future will need neither a physical presence nor any geographic location.

See also New york city as metropolis; New york stock exchange (nyse).

Editors of the *Wall Street Journal. Guide to Who's Who and What's What on Wall Street* (New York: Ballantine Books, 1998)
Geisst, Charles. *Wall Street: A History* (New York: Oxford Univ Press, 1997)
Kessner, Thomas. *Capital City: New York City and the Men behind America's Rise to Economic Dominance, 1860–1900* (New York: Simon & Schuster, 2003)
Young, Allan E. *The New York Securities Industry: Its Contribution to New York State and City* (New York: Securities Industry Association, New York District, June 1985)

Allan E. Young

securities regulation. This body of law governs transactions in securities, the most important types of which are usually called stock, shares of ownership in a corporation, and bonds, shares of the debt owed by a business or a government. Securities trading is an efficient method of channeling capital from investors to those who need investment. Although regulators have always wished to promote this function, securities trading has long been perceived to pose dangers greater than those posed by other kinds of commerce, particularly the dangers that inexperienced participants in the market will be deceived about the value of what they are buying or selling, and that too much speculation may be harmful to speculators and to the economy as a whole. Because of this tension, the aim of securities regulation, in New York State as elsewhere, has been to deter deceitful or overspeculative trading without hindering the normal operation of the market. Because New York City has been the nation's financial center since the late 18th century, the securities regulation in the state has been important in shaping the nation's financial market.

Common Law and Securities Statutes

Common law is created by judges in the course of deciding cases, as distinct from statutes enacted by legislatures. Much of the common law that New York inherited from England concerned property. Because securities are a kind of property, common law was an important source of their regulation from the beginning of significant trading in the early 1790s. The common law doctrine of fraud, for instance, was used to protect purchasers of securities who had been deceived about their true value. Securities tend to fluctuate in price more than most other kinds of property, which caused uncertainty in early years over whether speculative transactions were void under the common law, either as gambling or as usury, but the courts eventually rejected such challenges. By the middle of the 19th century, it was clear that the common law governing securities transactions was scarcely different from that governing other kinds of commercial contracts.

Much of the state's securities regulation has come from statutes specifically targeted at transactions. In 1792, after the first stock market crash in American history, the New York State legislature enacted the nation's first significant securities statute, which became popularly known as the Stockjobbing Act. The statute aimed to end a speculative practice common both then and now by declaring void all sales of securities in which sellers did not own the securities at the time they agreed to sell them. These transactions were agreements to sell securities at a designated time in the future. Sellers expected to be able to purchase them in the market from someone else before they were obliged to sell them to the buyer, hoping the price would decline between the contract date and the transfer date. The Stockjobbing Act was modeled closely on Sir John Barnard's Act, an English statute of 1734. New York's statute remained in effect until it was repealed in 1858. By rendering a common transaction unenforceable in court, the statute had the effect of encouraging New York City's stockbrokers to develop their own enforcement mechanism by refusing to trade with those brokers who failed to comply with their contracts.

The New York Stock Exchange

Ever since the formation of the New York Stock and Exchange Board in 1817, which changed its name to the New York Stock Exchange (NYSE) in 1863, the brokers themselves have been an important source of securities regulation. From its inception the NYSE has promulgated a variety of rules governing the behavior of its members and the conduct of trading, rules that in the 19th century were probably of greater consequence than those provided by the legal system. The sanctioning power of the NYSE was limited to fines and expulsion, the only tools at its disposal, but to be expelled from the NYSE implied a significant loss of income, so it has always had considerable leverage over its members' conduct.

As the securities market grew, the role of statute grew. In the early 20th century, New York and virtually every other state passed a "blue sky law" (so called because of allegations that some of the stock being sold was as worthless as lots in the blue sky), which placed conditions on the issuance of corporate stock. While the blue sky laws of some states established regulatory commissions to evaluate the soundness of new stock issues, the securities industry was powerful enough to keep such a provision out of New York's statute. The state's blue sky law only required registration and barred deceitful sales. Although the blue sky laws are still in effect, they have been gradually superseded by a series of federal securities statutes, the first two enacted in 1933 and 1934, in response to the crash of 1929. The federal statutes established the powerful Securities and Exchange Commission, which has since promulgated rules governing nearly every aspect of securities trading. By the end of the 20th century, lawyers specializing in securities regulation attended primarily to federal statutes and rules and only secondarily to the other sources of law.

See also NEW YORK STOCK EXCHANGE (NYSE).

Banner, Stuart. *Anglo-American Securities Regulation: Cultural and Political Roots, 1690–1860* (Cambridge, England: Cambridge Univ Press, 1998)

Cowing, Cedric. *Populists, Plungers, and Progressives: A Social History of Stock and Commodity Speculation, 1890–1936* (Princeton, NJ: Princeton Univ Press, 1965)

Seligman, Joel. *The Transformation of Wall Street: A History of the Securities and Exchange Commission and Modern Corporate Finance* (Boston: Houghton Mifflin, 1982)

Stuart A. Banner

seed companies. The Shakers of New Lebanon (Columbia Co) were the first in the United States to grow seed for sale in 1789 or 1790, and Shakers would continue to sell seeds commercially throughout the 19th century. The first commercial seed house in New York State was established in New York City in 1805 by the Scottish immigrant Grant Thorburn. In the mid–19th century seed businesses began emerging in Rochester. English immigrant James Vick had transformed his avocation of growing flowers into a business selling flower seeds by 1860; Western Union Telegraph Co founder Hiram Sibley established a seed business in 1878; and farmer Joseph Harris established his business and began distributing a catalog in 1879.

With the opening of the New York State Agricultural Experiment Station in Geneva (Ontario Co) in 1882, the development of new varieties and seed testing would pass to university-trained chemists and biologists. New York State reached its peak as a seed production and distribution center during the 1880s; it had 96 listings for individuals and firms in the *Nurseryman's Directory* of 1883, more than any other state. At that time the American Seed Trade Association (ASTA) was formed to organize wholesalers and retailers nationally and to deal with problems such as postal rates and truth in labeling. Two Rochester seedsmen served as president of ASTA in its early years, C. W. Crosman in 1885 and S. E. Briggs in 1895. The western states, especially California, with a temperate climate more suited for growing seed stock, would surpass New York State.

During the 20th century the seed business moved from family firms to national and global corporations. W. Atlee Burpee of Philadelphia bought out James Vick's business in the 1920s. Joseph Harris's company continued under family control until 1979, when it was acquired by Celanese Corp; during the 1990s it was consolidated as Harris Moran Seed Co with corporate offices in Modesto, Calif. Harris Seeds Garden Trends, based in Rochester, is the distributor of the firm's product line in the East. Several other seed companies have facilities in New York State in the early 21st century. Formed in 1975, Bentley Seeds is a retail garden seed business in Cambridge (Washington Co). Seedway, since 2002 a subsidiary of Growmark, a midwestern agricultural cooperative, operates a facility in Hall (Ontario Co). Stokes Seeds, a Canadian supplier to commercial truck farmers and greenhouse growers, maintained a distribution branch in Fredonia (Chautauqua Co) for a number of years before moving to Buffalo in 2002.

Aeberli, William I., and Margaret Becket. "Joseph Harris: Captain of the Rochester Seed Industry," *University of Rochester Library Bulletin* 35 (1982): 69–83

Paine, Laura. "Hands to Work, Hearts to God: The Story of the Shaker Seed Industry," *HortTechnology* 3 (Oct/Dec 1993): 375–82

Paul Grebinger

Seeger, Pete(r) (*b* New York City, 3 May 1919). Performer and composer of folk songs, political and environmental activist. The son of musicologist and composer Charles Seeger and musician Constance de Clyver Edson, Seeger attended boarding school and Harvard College (1936–38). His father introduced him to leftist political and musical influences as well as vernacular southern music as a child, and he learned to play the five-string banjo and other instruments. After Harvard he went to New York City, where he met Alan Lomax, Aunt Molly Jackson, and Lead Belly (Huddie Ledbetter). He joined the Vagabond Puppeteers in mid-1939, appearing in performances in support of the Dairy Farmers Union strike. Also in 1939 he briefly joined Lomax at the Archive of American Folk Song at the Library of Congress in Washington, DC, cataloging and transcribing songs. He traveled the country with folksinger Woody Guthrie before he moved to Manhattan's Greenwich Village in late 1940; there he met Lee Hays and Millard Lampell, with whom he formed the Almanac Singers in 1941. Over the next two years, at times joined by Bess Lomax, Agnes "Sis" Cunningham, Woody Guthrie, Josh White, and others, they performed political and folk songs and recorded a few albums.

After a tour of duty in the army, Seeger returned to Greenwich Village in late 1945 and quickly helped launch People's Songs, a national topical songs organization that lasted until 1949. He had a solo performance and recording schedule until forming the Weavers with Lee Hays, Ronnie Gilbert, and Fred Hellerman in 1948. The group reached a peak of national popularity in 1950–52, but political pressure forced it to disband until late 1955. Despite being generally blacklisted through much of the 1950s, Seeger carried on a hectic schedule of performances while recording dozens of albums for New York City–based Folkways Records. By 1960, as the political climate thawed, he had become a key influence on the folk music revival that burgeoned into the mid-1960s. Although Seeger was banned from network television until 1967, his numerous recordings for Columbia Records, performance schedule, and political activities supporting the civil rights and antiwar movements kept him in the public eye nationally and internationally.

He and his family moved to Beacon (Dutchess Co), overlooking the Hudson River, in 1949. He built the sloop *Clearwater* and launched it in 1969 to publicize the river's degradation. Clearwater music festivals and increasing publicity helped fund the river cleanup, while stimulating a growing national environmental movement. By the 1970s Seeger was no longer a political pariah as he continued his frenzied musical and political life. His many songs include "If I Had a Hammer" (with Lee Hays, 1949), "Turn, Turn, Turn" (1954), "Abiyoyo" (1952), and "Where Have All the Flowers Gone?" (1955). Formal national recognition came in 1994 with a Kennedy Center Award followed by induction into the Rock and Roll Hall of Fame in 1996 and a Grammy Award the following year. As the 20th century ended, Seeger continued to be a vital influence on American musical and political life.

See also FOLK MUSIC REVIVAL.

Dunaway, David. *How Can I Keep from Singing: Pete Seeger* (New York: McGraw-Hill, 1981)

Seeger, Pete. *Where Have All the Flowers Gone: A Singer's Stories, Songs, Seeds, Robberies* (Bethlehem, Pa: Sing Out!, 1993)

Ronald D. Cohen

Seguin, Edward [Edouard] (*b* Clamency, France, 20 Jan 1812; *d* New York City, 28 Oct 1880). Educator and physician. When Edward Seguin emigrated from France to the United States, probably in 1850, American reformers like Hervey B. Wilbur, the first superintendent of the New York State Asylum for Idiots, had already read reports of what Seguin called his "physiological method" for educating intellectually disabled people. By training the dormant senses (or physiology) of so-called idiots, Seguin showed what educators had not thought possible—that the "feebleminded" could learn. Although he settled in Ohio, Seguin made visits to the asylum's first location in Albany and, beginning in 1855, to its permanent home in Syracuse. There he advised Wilbur on teaching methods and institutional management. Around 1860 Seguin moved to Mount Vernon (Westchester Co), and in 1861 he received an MD from the Medical Department of the University of the City of New York (now New York University). In 1863, he helped organize the School for Defectives on Randall's Island off Manhattan. His most important book in English, *Idiocy and Its Treatment by the Physiological Method* (1866), added a neurological foundation to his earlier French writings on educational methods. Besides his contribution to education, Seguin championed the use of the thermometer in the diagnosis of medical conditions, and he advocated for the metric system as a common measure in medicine. In the year of his death he founded a private school for children with disabilities in Manhattan. His widow, Elsie Mead Seguin, operated the facility, moving it to East Orange, NJ, in 1894.

Talbot, Mabel E. *Edouard Seguin: A Study of an Educational Approach to the Treatment of Mentally Defective Children.* TC Series in Special Education (New York: Teachers College, Columbia Univ, 1964)

Trent, James W., Jr. "Edward Seguin and the Irony of Physiological Education." In *Inventing the Feeble Mind: A History of Mental Retardation in the United States* (Berkeley: Univ of California Press, 1994)

James W. Trent Jr

Seidl, Anton (*b* Pest, Hungary, 7 May 1850; *d* New York City, 28 Mar 1898). Opera conductor. A protégé of Richard Wagner, in whose household he lived as a young man, Seidl came to New York in 1885 and remained until his early death. A confirmed American, he spoke English, took American citizenship, bought a summerhouse in the Catskill Mountains, and championed American composers. His greatest influence was at the Metropolitan Opera, where he was principal conductor during the German language seasons from 1885 to 1891. As the central figure in American Wagnerism, he set performance standards previously unknown in the United States and maintained a German ensemble comparable to any abroad. After 1891 the Metropolitan was no longer a German house, and Seidl appeared less frequently. As conductor of the New York Philharmonic (1891–98), he guided a period of steady growth and achievement, including the premiere of the symphony *From the New World,* on 16 Dec 1893, by his friend Antonín Dvořák. In Brooklyn Seidl conducted winter concerts at the Brooklyn Academy of Music; in summer, he conducted 14 times per week at Brighton Beach on Coney Island. The repertory for these inexpensive seaside concerts overwhelmingly stressed Wagner and Franz Liszt.

Seidl's American protégés included Victor Herbert, who was often his principal cellist and assistant conductor, and the composer-writer Arthur Farwell, who wrote that Seidl's presence "tinged the atmosphere and consciousness of [New York City] with a peculiarly individual and glowing quality of feeling such as it has not known before or since . . . [I]t was downright affection, rather than admiration or awe, that New York returned to him." His inculcation of the Wagner canon made him the most influential of all opera conductors in the United States.

Horowitz, Joseph. *Wagner Nights: An American History* (Berkeley: Univ of California Press, 1994)

Joseph Horowitz

Selden. Locality (pop 21,861) in Brookhaven (Suffolk Co). Built along the Middle Country Rd and known for cordwood cutting for the New York City market, the hamlet was called Westfield until its post office opened in 1852. Around Selden are 55 sumps that hold water in wet seasons. Telescope Hill, at 333 feet (101.5 m), was the site of a fire tower from 1919 to 1960. Selden was given primarily to chicken raising, vegetable farming, and garden seed production until the 1950s and had a population in 1950 of 1,743. The Schwencke Land and Development Co platted lots for summer bungalows in 1932, but most of the locality's growth took place in the 1960s. Selden is site of the main campus of Suffolk County Community College (1960).

Luise Weiss

Sempronius. Town (pop 893) in SE Cayuga Co. Settled in 1793, the town was formed in 1799. The Glen Haven Water Cure and Summer Resort (1846–1911) on Skaneateles Lake consisted of 18 buildings and housed as many as 200 patients. Most of Sempronius was reforested when the state bought a large number of small farms in the 1930s to create the 3,316-acre (1,342 ha) Bear Swamp State Forest.

Georgianna Tracy

Seneca. Town (pop 2,731) in E Ontario Co. The Town of Seneca was formed in 1792, and the Town of Geneva (including the present city of the same name) was taken from it in 1872. The state road from Utica to Avon (authorized 1794) passed through Seneca. John Scott Chubb (1875–1934), a syndicated cartoonist of Hall, drew "Ol' Joel Baggs," with characters based on townspeople. Clifford Kunes Jr of Seneca Castle perfected a cabbage-harvesting machine that was manufactured and marketed by Castle Harvesting (1969–81). Seneca remains a farming town, producing especially snap beans, sweet corn, red beets, and dairy products.

Marla A. Bennett

Seneca Army Depot. The Army Ordnance Depot in Romulus (Seneca Co) was started in 1941 as an 11,500-acre (4654 ha) ammunition depot on the east shore of Seneca Lake. Two General Services Administration warehouses were built in 1953 and 1954 to accommodate remaining munitions from World War II as well as those from the Cold War. The North Depot Activity was developed in 1956, principally for the storage and maintenance of special weapons, including nuclear weapons, for the Griffiss AFB. The presence of nuclear weapons was disclosed in 1981 by the Center for Defense Information, an independent group that monitored defense activities and spending. In summer 1983 thousands of women protested US nuclear policies at the Seneca Women's Peace Encampment, an adjacent 52-acre (21 ha) farm purchased by the protest organizers. The encampment remained active, addressing other political and social issues. In 1992 Seneca's special weapons mission ended. The North Depot was vacated upon closure of the Griffiss AFB in 1993 and is now the 750-cell Five Points Correctional Facility. The main depot was put into closure operations by the 1995 Base Closure and Realignment Commission, and the Department of Defense's Installation Restoration Program has addressed contamination from hazardous materials at the site.

Krasniewicz, Louise. *Nuclear Summer: The Clash of Communities at the Seneca Women's Peace Encampment* (Ithaca: Cornell Univ Press, 1992)

Watrous, Hilda R. *The County between the Lakes: A Public History of Seneca County, New York, 1876–1982* (Waterloo, NY: Seneca Board of Supervisors, 1982)

Michael J. Stenzel

Seneca Carrying Place. As the major canoe portage in the Niagara River corridor between Lakes Erie and Ontario, it was an area of great strategic significance in the colonial and Revolutionary War periods. The Seneca Indians entered the region as an expanding power in the 17th century. As early as 1718, they had firmly established themselves along the portage route around the great falls at Niagara and occupied a settlement there. The Seneca exerted political and diplomatic influence through the Niagara corridor, and although they objected to the building of Fort Niagara by the French in 1726, they took advantage of the trade created by the outpost and became the major labor force carrying packs around the falls. They even at times determined which Indians could or could not enter into trade with the French at Fort Niagara. By the 1740s the region was being referred to as the Seneca Carrying Place in a map reprinted by Cadwallader Colden in his history of the Five Nations. The Seneca presence in this area continued well into the 19th century.

Colden, Cadwallader. *The History of the Five Indian Nations Depending on the Province of New York in America* (1727, 1747; repr Ithaca: Cornell Univ Press, 1969)

Kalm, Peter. *Peter Kalm's Travels in North America* (1937; repr New York: Dover, 1987)

Laurence M. Hauptman

Seneca County (325 mi²/842 km²; pop 33,342). Created in 1804 from part of Cayuga Co and named after the Seneca Nation, whose name means "great hill people." Subsequent territorial adjustments were made with the creation of Tompkins (1817) and Wayne (1823) Cos. Area was gained from Tompkins in 1819 and from Ontario and Yates Cos in 1828. In 1946 the county surrendered jurisdictional rights to Seneca Lake to Yates Co. Seneca Co is subdivided into 10 towns that contain 5 incorporated villages, and a small part of the City of Geneva. Waterloo serves as county seat.

Elevations range from 382 feet (116 m) along the shore of Cayuga Lake to over 1,640 feet (500 m) on the Schuyler Co line in the south. Bordered on the east and west by Cayuga and Seneca Lakes, respectively, the county lies within two major landform provinces: the northern half is part of the Ontario Drumlins subregion of the Erie-Ontario Lowland, the southern half within the Finger Lakes Hills subregion of the Appalachian Upland.

All the county's territory was glaciated during the most recent ice age. The Finger Lakes Hills exhibit a rolling topography except along the lakeshores, where slopes are steep and cut by small but deeply entrenched streams. The lowland to the north exhibits an assortment of features linked to the Pleistocene. From south to north these include a till plain, a lacustrine plain along the Seneca River, and part of a much more extensive drumlin field. In addition, sand hills, remnants of a delta deposited in glacial Lake Newberry, occupy part of the county's northwest corner. The Montezuma (Cayuga) Marsh in the northeast corner is a sediment-filled section of the Cayuga Lake valley. Devonian limestone underlies the Seneca River valley. Beds of gently southward-dipping shale and siltstone form the bedrock elsewhere: Silurian in the north, Devonian in the south. The Seneca River flows eastward across the county, linking the northern ends of Cayuga and Seneca Lakes. The county is well endowed with highly arable soil capable of

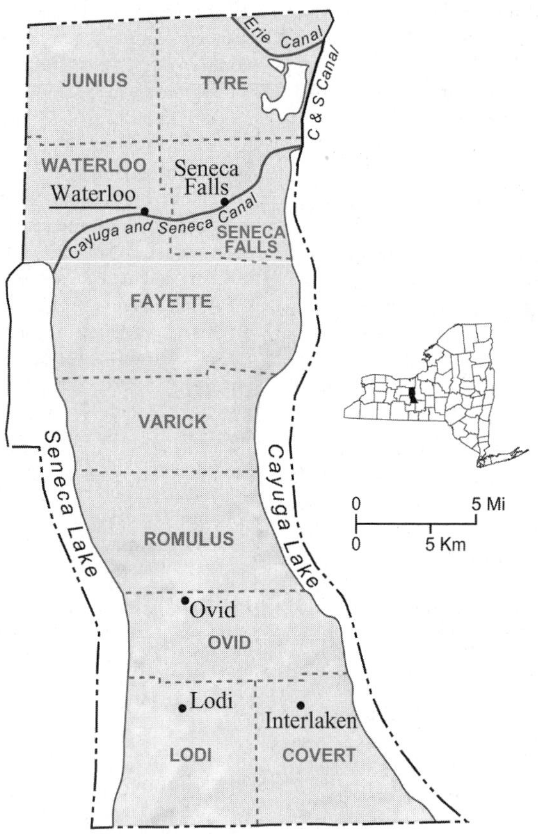

supporting modern commercial agriculture. The better agricultural land tends to be located south of the Seneca River and inland from the lakes.

Seneca Co's climate is humid-continental. Temperatures are moderated somewhat by the two bordering lakes. Mean January temperatures across the entire county are around 23°F (-5°C), while mean July temperatures cluster around 70°F (21°C). Temperatures of 90°F (32°C) or more are expected at least a few times every summer. Similarly, the temperature drops to 0°F (-18°C) or below several times most winters. Annual average precipitation ranges from 34 inches (86 cm) at Waterloo in the north to over 36 inches (91 cm) in the far south. Seasonal snowfall amounts range from 49 inches (124 cm) along the Seneca River to over 60 inches (152 cm) in the south. Primeval forest cover consisted primarily of a central hardwood community dominated by beech, sugar maple, and basswood, with varying proportions of oak and hickory. The Montezuma Marsh region in the northeast corner supported a swamp forest of hemlock and black ash and an area of cattail marsh. A substantial portion of this wetland, once much larger, makes up the Montezuma National Wildlife Refuge.

Native Inhabitants

The Iroquois culture that emerged in the area around the 14th century built on earlier Indian cultures, especially the Owasco (*ca* 900–1350). In historic times both the Seneca and the Cayuga occupied parts of what became Seneca Co, though their largest settlements were traditionally maintained to the west and east of Seneca Co. During the period of European contact, however, villages and hamlets became smaller and more scattered, and a number of such sites existed within the county. In 1779 a force under the command of Gen John Sullivan invaded the present Seneca Co and points west as far as the Genesee River, attacking those Iroquois who had allied themselves with the British. Sullivan's army destroyed crops, orchards, and houses in the villages found on their route, greatly diminishing the Indian presence in the area. After the war, in lieu of pay, veterans were granted land in what became known as the New Military Tract, which stretched from Syracuse to the western boundary of Seneca Co. The allotments were distributed by lottery in 1790; because of the long delay many veterans sold their shares to speculators. Until 1807 parts of Seneca Co's northeastern towns—Tyre, Seneca Falls, Fayette, and Varick—were Cayuga Reservation lands. In treaties of 1795 and 1807, the Cayuga ceded all of their aboriginal territory to New York State.

Settlement

When the New Military Tract opened for white settlement, Seneca Co was quickly occupied. In most towns, the clearing of farms began in 1789 and 1790; Junius and Tyre, in the north, and Covert, in the southeast, were settled later, between 1794 and 1796. The ethnic makeup and geographic origin of its European American settlers differed from that of neighboring counties. A mixture of Dutch and other ethnic groups from New Jersey settled throughout the county, with the strongest concentration in the three southernmost towns of Ovid, Covert, and Lodi. Settlers in Fayette were mainly Pennsylvania Germans. The four northern towns were settled by people from eastern New York, New Jersey, and Pennsylvania, and included a Quaker colony in Junius (1815–63). Few of the early settlers were of New England origin. Although some Irish came to Seneca Falls as early as 1827, foreign-born residents were rare before 1850. In 1870 nearly 14% of the population was foreign-born; most came from Ireland and Germany. A few Italian immigrants arrived in the 1890s, but

SENECA CO POPULATION CENSUS FIGURES

	White	Nonwhite	Total Population	Foreign-Born
1810	16,464	145	16,609	—
1820	23,355	264	23,619	37
1830	20,864	177	21,041	72
1840	24,675	199	24,874	—
1850	25,260	181	25,441	2,109
1860	27,925	213	28,138	3,876
1870	27,584	239	27,823	3,845
1880	29,035	243	29,278	3,964
1890	28,039	188	28,227	3,700
1900	27,979	135	28,114	3,355
1910	26,848	124	26,972	3,528
1920	24,616	119	24,735	2,932
1930	24,845	138	24,983	2,778
1940	25,610	122	25,732	2,369
1950	29,026	227	29,253	2,556
1960	31,609	375	31,984	1,971
1970	34,547	536	35,083	1,611
1980	33,113	620	33,733	1,134
1990	32,676	1,007	33,683	742
2000	31,682	1,660	33,342	816

Notes: "Nonwhite" includes African Americans, Asians, American Indians, and Pacific Islanders and, for 2000, also the mixed race and other race categories. Through the 1960 census these figures primarily reflect the African American population. Foreign-born figures for 1820 and 1830 include only those not naturalized, and for 1930 and 1950, the foreign-born totals include Whites only. Other years include all foreign-born in the population.

POPULATIONS OF TOWNS, SENECA CO

Town or City, Year Founded	1800	1840	1880	1920	1960	2000
Covert, 1817	—	1,563	2,166	1,661	1,965	2,227
Fayette, 1800[a]	863	3,731	3,316	2,215	2,825	3,643
Junius, 1803	—	1,594	1,356	829	871	1,362
Lodi, 1826	—	2,236	1,947	1,137	1,267	1,476
Ovid, 1794	2,169	2,721	3,569	2,855	3,097	2,757
Romulus, 1794	1,025	2,235	2,765	2,754	3,509	2,036
Seneca Falls, 1829	—	4,281	6,853	7,179	9,264	9,347
Tyre, 1829	—	1,506	1,168	798	815	899
Varick, 1830	—	1,971	1,739	1,020	1,480	1,729
Waterloo, 1829	—	3,036	4,399	4,287	6,891	7,866

Note: In 1800 the Towns of Ovid, Romulus, and Fayette were in Cayuga Co.

[a]Washington until 1808.

the major migration did not begin until the early decades of the 20th century.

African American slaves accompanied the earliest white settlers to all parts of the county. In 1803 Virginian Robert Selden Rose brought 37 slaves to his Fayette farm, Rose Hill. In 1820 there were 135 free Blacks and 84 slaves in the county, accounting for a little less than 1% of 23,619 residents. Over half the free Blacks resided in Fayette.

Transportation

The Villages of Waterloo and Seneca Falls are located on the outlet of Seneca Lake. This waterway, along with Seneca and Cayuga Lakes, profoundly affected the economic development of the county. From the earliest period of European settlement, improvements were made to the outlet for both navigation and waterpower. The Seneca Lock Navigation Co (1813) had improved the outlet by 1818, building a small canal to circumvent the waterfalls at Seneca Falls. Further improvements completed by the state in 1828 opened it for navigation from Geneva to the Erie Canal at Montezuma, a distance of 20 miles (32 km). Seneca Falls grew from 265 to 3,000 between 1827 and 1835. Improvements to the canal begun in 1909 drastically changed the character of Seneca Falls. Lowland near the canal, known as the Flats, was crowded with industrial buildings and working-class housing. Two large locks and an artificial lake were created, flooding the Flats to a depth of 60 feet (18 m). Although the project was completed, rapid changes in transportation after World War I reduced the volume of commercial traffic on the canal, and since that time it has been used for recreational purposes. Seneca Co was served by three main railroad lines. The Auburn and Rochester (1841) provided east-west service and became part of the New York Central in 1853; it continues in freight service. After the Civil War two lines were built to provide north-south service: the Geneva and Ithaca Railroad (1873–1960s; later Lehigh Valley) and the Seneca Lake Line of the Lehigh Valley (1892–1976).

Economic Development

In Seneca Falls seven flour mills processed 85,000 barrels of flour in 1835. Several sash and blind factories, a clock factory, numerous sawmills, and a 4,000-spindle cotton factory were also in operation. Waterloo experienced similar growth, with distilleries, tanneries, and a boatyard leading the list of local industries in early years; later, it also produced wool cloth, wagons, and organs. In the 1840s a shift began in Seneca Falls from milling to manufacturing; products included paper, woolen cloth, yeast, scythes, globes and rules, buttons, machinery, and, especially, water pumps and fire engines. By 1890 the population of Seneca Falls had reached 6,500, and several of the pump and fire engine manufacturers were dominant forces in the community. Among these was Downs, Mynderse and Co (1848), which later became Goulds Manufacturing Co. Goulds employed over 650 workers by the turn of the 20th century and sold its products worldwide. A third, much smaller, manufacturing village was Farmer [now Interlaken], which produced fruit baskets, metal goods, cleaning products, hardware, axe handles, and baseball bats at various periods in the late 19th and early 20th centuries.

Farming was central to the economy in the 19th century, with grain, fruits, vegetables, and dairy predominating. John Johnston, a Scottish immigrant living in Fayette, introduced field tile drainage to the United States in 1835 and wrote extensively for farm periodicals on agricultural improvements. The land between the lakes was ideal for hay, which provided a cash crop until demand was reduced by the growing use of automobiles and tractors. County farmers then moved into orchard and vineyard crops, small dairy farms, and beef cattle. The Montezuma Marsh, long a source of rushes, cooper's flag, and hay, was partially drained around 1920–25 for vegetable farming. Some observers were concerned about the consequent sharp decline in the waterfowl population, but a 1935 flood wiped out many of the growers and in 1938 a large part of the former swampland became Montezuma National Wildlife Refuge. Another federal acquisition during the depression was Finger Lakes National Forest, partly in Lodi and Covert and composed of land reforested from marginal farms. Seneca Co also developed a modest tourist economy, beginning with a resort hotel at Kidders in 1852. The Burroughs Hotel at East Varick welcomed visitors from the early 1860s to 1909; the chief resort was at Sheldrake Point, anchored by the Cayuga Lake House (1875–1909) and Sheldrake House (1886–1939). Somewhat later, cottages were built at many places along the two lakeshores.

Religion, Education, and Culture

The ethnic diversity of the county is reflected in the history of its religious institutions. Various German Lutheran and Dutch Reformed denominations established congregations during the first half of the 19th century. The county's concentration of Dutch Reformed worshipers was the highest in Central and Western New York, with 7 congregations and 1,100 regularly attending services in 1855. However, Methodism, with 15 churches, was by far the largest single denomination in the county at that time. Roman Catholicism grew from a tentative local presence in 1835 to become the largest denomination by 1890. Mormons formally organized in the area at an 1830 meeting in Fayette.

Seneca Co had various small private schools during the first years of settlement. The first academies were at Ovid (1826), Seneca Falls (1832), and Waterloo (1842). These schools attracted students from surrounding counties as well. In 2004 the county encompassed Seneca Falls (1950), South Seneca (1964), Romulus (1938), and Waterloo (1950) Central School Districts. The New York State Agricultural College was established in Ovid and Romulus in 1860 but soon closed because of the Civil War. The campus became Willard State Hospital for the Insane in 1869. The first newspaper in Seneca Co was the *Seneca Patriot* (1815) at Ovid. A Democratic newspaper was published under various titles, including the *Waterloo Observer*, from 1828 until 1961. In the early 21st century there is no daily paper published in Seneca Co, but weekly newspapers include the *Reveille/Between the Lakes* and the *Ovid Gazette*, both published at Ovid, and the *Interlaken Review*.

Reform

Various religious and social reform movements found strong support in Seneca Co. In 1848 Hicksite Quakers from the Junius Monthly Meeting split with their less radical brethren and were vocal in their support of abolition and individual religious choice. On 19–20 July of the same year the first Woman's Rights Convention was held in Seneca Falls; it was attended by 300 people, 100 of whom signed the Declaration of Sentiments, its guiding document. Their demand for social and political rights is generally seen as the beginning of the modern movement for women's rights in the United States. Antislavery sentiment was strong. In the 1830s and 1840s county citizens sent many petitions to Congress on the subject. Mary Ann and Thomas McClintock, Philadelphia Quakers, moved to Seneca Falls and, along with other county residents, were among the founding members of the Rochester-based Western New York Anti-Slavery Society (1842).

Politics

Seneca Co has historically followed the half-shire system, with two county seats. Ovid and Waterloo have fought for the honor since the county's inception. A courthouse was built in Ovid in 1806, but the courts were moved to Waterloo in 1809. An effort to move them back to Ovid in 1822 resulted in state legislation requiring court to be held alternately in each village. The controversy continued through the 19th century and most of the 20th century, with some county offices located in each place. A judge

60th anniversary of Seneca Falls Convention, 1908.

ruled in 1964 that the laws creating a two-court system in the county were still in effect. This remains the case, though in practice Waterloo is the site of nearly all county offices.

The county is governed by a Board of Supervisors consisting of 14 members; weighted voting has been in effect since 1978. The position of county manager was established in 1996. A majority of towns were Democratic in the Civil War era, but Republicans gained strength by the century's end, and by the World War I era it was solidly Republican, as it continues to be in the early 21st century. Five Seneca Co residents have served in the US House of Representatives: Silas Halsey (1805–7), Jehiel H. Halsey (1829–31), Samuel Birdsall (1837–39), Jacob P. Chamberlain (1861–63), and Norman Gould (1914–23).

Recent History

World War II brought major changes. In July 1941 the federal government began construction of the Seneca Army Depot for munitions storage. Over 11,500 acres (4,650 ha) of land in the center of the county were acquired, displacing 150 farm families with very short notice. More than $11 million was expended and 9,000 workers employed to build the depot's 500 large "igloo" storage facilities. Construction was completed in November 1941. The project brought jobs, but it also brought public health and safety problems, since the county was ill prepared to cope with the sudden influx of workers and their families. Housing and sanitation were inadequate, and the county did not have the resources to meet the health and education needs of this new population.

In 1942 the navy appropriated 3,000 acres (1,200 ha) as a temporary recruit-training center. Some 6,000 workers completed Sampson Naval Training Station in nine months at a cost of $56 million. During the station's three years of operation, 411,429 recruits were trained there. Again, the county's housing, sanitation, and public health needs were taxed. The New York State Thruway opened through the county's northern towns in 1954, with an exit in Tyre serving all points. It made long-distance commuting possible; in the early 21st century much of Seneca Co's working population is employed in Rochester or Syracuse. The Thruway was the direct stimulus for the tourist-oriented Waterloo Premium Outlet Mall (1995) in Junius, with its 112 stores.

Throughout the second half of the 20th century, new uses were found for old institutions. The Seneca Army Depot expanded and became an important source of work, employing 800 in 1982. In the 1990s, however, the base closed and the space was converted to other uses, such as Five Points Correctional Facility (2000), a 1,500-bed maximum security prison; and an eBay warehouse (2002). Willard State Hospital closed in 1995 and was converted to a Department of Correctional Services drug treatment facility. The former Sampson Naval Training Station provided space for Sampson College for veterans (1946–49), an air force base (1951–56), Sampson State School for the people with developmental disabilities (1960–71), and Sampson State Park (1964–). The campus of Eisenhower College (1967–82) near Seneca Falls was acquired in 1991 by the 800-student New York Chiropractic College, relocated from Long Island. Goulds Pumps, which merged with ITT Industries in 1997, is the largest pump manufacturer in the world and the largest employer in the county.

The county's best-known cultural institutions are in Seneca Falls. The National Women's Hall of Fame was established there in 1969. In 1980 congressional legislation created Women's Rights National Historical Park to commemorate and preserve the sites of the first Woman's Rights Convention; it attracts 18,000 visitors a year. Also in Seneca Falls are the Seneca Museum of Waterways and Industry and the Seneca Falls Historical Society. The Terwilliger Museum of local history and the Memorial Day Museum are in Waterloo, and Sampson State Park hosts naval and air force museums.

Seneca Co remains an important farming region. It ranks 24th in the state in total cropland but leads in total sales of soybeans and ranks 6th in wheat and 7th in oats and corn. The county also ranks first in hog sales and inventory. Dairy products account for nearly 40% of total agricultural sales and grain 30%. The remainder is divided evenly between fruit, vegetable and nursery products, and livestock sales. Seneca Co is home to 18 wineries. Mennonites, who came to Fayette from Pennsylvania in 1976, and Amish, settling in Ovid and Varick in the 1990s, have strengthened the farming sector, which covers 56% of the county's land and increased 2% during the 1990s—this despite extensive landholdings taken out of agriculture in the 1940s. Empire Farm Days in August is the largest farm equipment trade show in the Northeast.

The standard reference is *The History of Seneca County* (1876), but two books by Hilda R. Watrous help to bring it more up to date: *The County between the Lakes: A Public History of Seneca County, New York, 1876–1982* (1982), consisting of 10 topical essays on public works, and *The County between the Lakes: Life and People to Be Remembered, Seneca County, New York, 1895* (1988), which focuses on the year 1895. Town and village histories include Diedrich Willers, *Centennial Historical Sketch of the Town of Fayette* (1900); John E. Becker, *History of the Village of Waterloo* (1949); Elsie W. Robinson, *Sheldrake, 1789–1962: A History* (1962); Agnes McGrane, *A History of Varick* (1975); Wayne Morrison, *Town and Village of Ovid: Early History* (1980); and Clarence Gravelding, *Romulus Remembered, 1915–1930* (1990). The best is probably Maurice L. Patterson, *Between the Lakes* (1976), a history of Covert. *Soil Survey, Seneca Co, New York* (1972) covers agriculture and land use, and J. Norman Carls and Walter W. Ristow, "The Industrial Geography of Seneca Falls, New York," *Economic Geography* 12 (July 1936): 287–93, addresses Seneca Falls manufacturing.

Anne M. Derousie

Seneca Falls. Town (pop 9,347) and village (pop 6,861) in NE Seneca Co. Part of the town was included in the Cayuga Reservation ceded by the Cayugas between 1789 and 1807. Settled permanently in 1790, Seneca Falls was formed from Junius in 1826, and the village incorporated in 1831; both were named for the 40–42 ft (12–13 m) drop in the Seneca River over a series of rapids. Waterfalls were created during the 19th century to harness the waterpower for industry. The Seneca Lock Navigation Co (1813) opened canal transport through Seneca Falls in 1816 and was improved by the state as the Cayuga and Seneca Canal (1828). The Auburn and Rochester Railroad (1841) sped up the movement of freight. The first Irish workers came in 1827, and their numbers grew quickly. They were joined in the 1890s by Italians, now the predominant ethnic group. The mills and factories of Seneca Falls produced paper, cotton and woolen cloth, clocks, flour, yeast, scythes, globes and rulers, buttons, machinery, and pumps. In 1895, four firms manufactured pumps and fire engines and employed 800 workers. In the early 21st century Goulds Pumps (1848), always the leader among the village's pump firms, is a subsidiary of ITT, employs 1,500 people in research and development, and produces pumps for industry. In the 20th century, Sylvania produced cathode ray tubes. The first Women's Rights Convention (1848) was held in Seneca Falls, organized in part by resident Elizabeth Cady Stanton. Women's Rights National Historical Park (1980) maintains several associated sites, and the National Women's Hall of Fame (1969) is also in Seneca Falls; both contribute to the village's increasing tourist traffic. Empire Farm Days, the largest farm show in the Northeast, is held in August. Cayuga Lake State Park (1928) is on the site of a former trolley line amusement park established in 1886.

Lisa Compton

Seneca Falls Convention. The first women's rights convention in the United States (originally known as the Woman's Rights Convention) was held at the Wesleyan Methodist Church in Seneca Falls (Seneca Co) on 19–20 July 1848. This formal public meeting on behalf of women's social and political equality was sparked by the politicization of women in the abolition movement, long-standing discussions of equality among New York State reformers, and an emerging determination among the first women's rights activists to redress gender inequality.

The state's reformers had considered issues of equality for about 20 years before the Seneca Falls Convention. A belief in absolute human equality prompted abolitionists to oppose slavery. Women abolitionists' egalitarianism, experience with gender discrimination, and emerging awareness of their own enslavement led them to question the condition of women. Legal reformers' challenges to state laws prohibiting married women from owning property also sparked discussions of equal rights. By 1848 questions of egalitarianism had become a divisive issue within some New York State political and religious communities, as seen in the departure of Free Soil Democrats from the larger Democratic Party and of egalitarian Hicksite Quakers, many of whom lived in Rochester and Waterloo (Seneca Co), from the main body of their denomination. Nearby Seneca Falls was a community riven by these fault lines.

Seneca Falls was also the home of emerging women's rights activist Elizabeth Cady Stanton. Introduced to abolitionists' ideas of gender equality through her friendship with Quaker orator Lucretia Mott, Stanton had done some work for women's property rights reform in the early 1840s. By 1848, as her husband Henry B. Stanton stumped the state for the Free Soil Party, Stanton grew increasingly frustrated with staying at home raising small children. News of Mott's visit to dissident Quakers in Waterloo incited her to act. In early July Stanton persuaded Mott, Martha Coffin Wright, and Mary Ann McClintock to help her call the convention and to draft its Declaration of Sentiments, a manifesto appropriating the language of the Declaration of Independence to describe women's oppressed condition. Challenging current definitions of citizenship and the purported democracy arising from the American Revolution, the Declaration of Sentiments asserted women's equality based on their natural and constitutional rights and identified political rights as the remedy for inequality.

On the first day of the convention nearly 300 participants heard speeches, the Declaration of Sentiments, and 11 resolutions proclaiming the natural equality of all people and declaring illegitimate all laws and social customs that subordinated women. On the second day the participants discussed the Declaration of Sentiments before it was signed by 68 women and 32 men, most of whom lived locally and had connections to either the legal reform community, dissident Quakers, or the Free Soil movement. Next the convention discussed the resolutions, which passed unanimously except for the radical ninth resolution proposing women's enfranchisement. After speeches in its defense by both Stanton and abolitionist Frederick Douglass, the suffrage resolution was narrowly adopted. The convention concluded with calls for further action. It reconvened some two weeks later on 2 Aug 1848 at the First Unitarian Church of Rochester and its principles were reconfirmed before a larger audience. Subsequent meetings over the next few years culminated in a movement that eventually transformed women's legal, social, and political status.

Isenberg, Nancy. *Sex and Citizenship in Antebellum America* (Chapel Hill: Univ of North Carolina Press, 1998)

Proceedings of the Woman's Rights Conventions Held at Seneca Falls and Rochester, N.Y., July and August, 1848 (1870; repr New York: Arno and New York Times, 1969)

Wellman, Judith. "The Seneca Falls Women's Rights Convention: A Study of Social Networks," *Journal of Women's History* 3 (Spring 1991): 9–37

Laura E. Free

Seneca Lake (66 mi²/171 km²). The largest of the Finger Lakes, Seneca Lake is 36 miles (58 km) long, 3 miles (5 km) wide at Dresden (Yates Co), and 634 feet (193 m) deep near Lodi (Seneca Co). The lake flows north from the vicinity of Watkins Glen (Schuyler Co) to the Seneca River at Seneca Lake State Park. Keuka Lake to the west is also a major feeder. The Lamoka culture settled about 2500 BC near Geneva (Ontario Co) at the north end of the lake. The Seneca were established by AD 1400 but after 1779 no longer retained land holdings near the lake.

Water transport provided access and industrial and commercial opportunities around the lake. The Erie (1825), Chemung (1833), and Crooked Lake (1833) Canals made the lake commercially accessible from the north, south, and west. Barges, ferries, and steamboats were all important to settlement and development until the dominance of rail following the American Civil War. By 1878 Chemung and Crooked Lake Canals were closed. The Erie Canal, as part of the New York State Barge Canal System after 1918, carried commercial cargo until 1994. In 2003 Cargill Salt and US Salt Corp had facilities in Watkins Glen to harvest glacially formed salt deposits. First settled in 1794 as a transportation and commercial hub, Watkins Glen also depends on tourism; there is a state park, and the community enjoys worldwide fame as an automobile racing center. The east shore of Seneca Lake is recreational and agricultural, with peach, cherry, and apple orchards and vineyards. In 2003 there were 40 vineyards and wineries around the lake. Willard Psychiatric Center in Willard (Seneca Co) closed in 1995 after 125 years as a state-run institution. The facility housed a Department of Corrections drug rehabilitation center in 2003.

The formerly marshy north end of Seneca Lake is dominated by the Cities of Geneva, a commercial hub since 1830, and Waterloo (Seneca Co), a commercial hub from 1828 to the 1940s. Geneva's parklike waterfront, built mostly on fill, has discouraged shoreline development, but new projects include the 2002 rehabilitation of Geneva's Long Pier. The west shore of Seneca Lake is dotted by stately homes, summer cottages, and many vineyards. In 2003 AES Corp operated an electric power plant, Greenidge Station, near Dresden. Hobart and William Smith Colleges share a campus in Geneva, and their 65 ft (20 m) research vessel, the *William Scandling*, has monitored the ecology of the lake since 1976. Flooding and water levels, the growth of weeds and algae, pollution, and population pressures remained challenges in 2003.

Sisler, Carol U. *Seneca Lake: Past, Present, and Future* (Ithaca: Enterprise Publishing, 1994)

Douglas B. McDonald

Seneca Nation. The westernmost nation of the Iroquois League. As the "keepers of the western door," the Seneca traditionally occupied the region between Canandaigua Lake and the Genesee River, south of what is now Rochester. By the 18th century, because of their economic and military expansionist policy, Seneca territory and influence extended west to the shores of Lake Erie and southwest into the Ohio Country.

By the time the Iroquois League was founded in the middle to late 16th century, the Seneca were separated into an eastern and western group and lived in two large, main towns rather than in smaller villages. According to archaeological evidence, the first of these appeared in the west near Honeoye Lake. Approximately every 10 to 20 years, as local resources declined, they moved their principal settlements northward. In 1687 the eastern town was located at what is now the Ganondagan State Historic Site in Victor (Ontario Co); the western group reached what is now Honeoye Falls (Monroe Co).

European Contact

The impact of European contact reached the Seneca territory before the Europeans themselves. Epidemics of several different European diseases had horrific consequences. In the 1640s a smallpox epidemic killed thousands and devastated the Iroquois League, including the Seneca. European material items have been found on Seneca archaeological sites that predate the first European excursions into the Seneca territory. The first recorded instance of a European in Seneca territory is that of a young Frenchman, Etienne Brûlé, who was briefly a Seneca captive in 1615. In 1656 Jesuit missionary Fr Pierre Joseph Marie Chaumonot made a recorded visit to the Seneca, traveling from the recently established mission Sainte Marie de Gannentaha [now Liverpool, Onondaga Co]. Jesuits made numerous trips into Seneca territory for the rest of the 17th and early 18th centuries, establishing several missions among the Seneca and other Iroquois tribes.

European trade had a major economic and cultural impact on the Seneca. Among the Iroquois nations, the Seneca were closest to the

Seneca moose or elk antler effigy comb, late 17th century.

available western fur-trapping grounds claimed by western neighbors but the farthest removed from the centers of European trade at what are now Albany and Montreal. Throughout the 17th century, periods of conflict and peaceful relations occurred between the Seneca and the French and their Indian allies. Some competition may have developed between the Mohawk and Seneca, as it was in the Mohawks' interest to keep Iroquois trade focused on the Dutch, and later the British, on the Hudson River. On several occasions, the Seneca encouraged the French to establish direct trade in their territory, allowing René-Robert Cavelier de la Salle to establish a short-lived trading post at the mouth of the Niagara River [now Porter, Niagara Co] in 1679. Within a decade hostilities with the French returned as warfare against surrounding nonconfederacy nations also increased. In 1687 more than 3,000 French troops under Marquis de Denonville, governor of New France, landed at Irondequoit Bay [now in Monroe Co] and marched overland to attack the Seneca town of Ganondagan and burned its substantial store of corn. Denonville then burned the western Seneca town at what is now Honeoye Falls. After these attacks and eventual peace with the French, the Seneca no longer used large palisaded towns and dispersed throughout the western Finger Lakes and Genesee Valley in smaller, unfortified villages, still roughly aligned in western and eastern groups.

In the Treaty of 1701 the Iroquois established peaceful relations with the French that would last for more than five decades. Influential in the talks that led to this treaty was Louis-Thomas Chabert de Joncaire, at one time a Seneca captive, who became an important agent for French interests among them. Chabert de Joncaire and his two sons maintained the neutrality between the French and the Seneca while expanding the fur trade at Niagara. They secured permission for the construction of Fort Niagara in 1726 at the same location used by La Salle. The British were negotiating with the Mohawk, Oneida, and Onondaga to establish a post at Oswego and to maintain its supply line through Iroquois territory.

Conflicts in the 18th Century

By the French and Indian War (1754–63), the westernmost Seneca were pro-French. Prominent Mohawk Valley trader Sir William Johnson effectively maintained the support, or at least the neutrality, of most other Iroquois for the British cause. Following the French defeat in the war, some Senecas participated in Pontiac's War and his siege against British-held Detroit during the summer of 1763. Seneca warriors attacked and destroyed supply wagons traveling from Fort Schlosser [now in Niagara Falls] to Fort Niagara on 14 Sept 1763. Two companies of British regulars sent in support of the supply wagons were also routed. This Seneca military success is commonly referred to as the Devil's Hole Massacre. Pontiac's War ended unsuccessfully, and as British superintendent of Indian affairs, Johnson was in a position to force a concession from the Seneca for their attack. They ceded land along the Niagara River to the British in March–April 1764.

At the outbreak of the Revolutionary War, many Iroquois tried to remain neutral. Eventually the Oneida and Tuscarora supported the Americans, and the other confederacy nations, to varying degrees, supported the British. The first Seneca participation was during Gen John Burgoyne's campaign in 1777, the western component of which was to move through Oswego and the Mohawk Valley to take Albany. After the aborted siege of Fort Stanwix and the Battle of Oriskany in August 1777, most Iroquois abandoned the campaign. Under Chief Cornplanter, Senecas participated in the Wyoming Valley, Pa, and Cherry Valley [now in Otsego Co] attacks in 1778, which influenced Gen George Washington's decision to attack the Seneca-Cayuga territory in 1779. The Sullivan-Clinton expedition through the Finger Lakes and Genesee Valley and the Brodhead expedition up the Allegheny River from Fort Pitt burned 40 Iroquois settlements and destroyed a vast quantity of food stores. The expedition served to bolster Iroquois support for the British. The Seneca participated in numerous raids out of Fort Niagara for the rest of the war. The Treaty of Paris in 1783 made no provision for Britain's Indian allies, but Canadian governor Frederick Haldimand acquired land for the Iroquois along the Grand River on the Niagara Peninsula [now Six Nations Reserve, Ont]. Some pro-British Senecas followed Mohawk chief Joseph Brant and his followers there, but the majority stayed in New York State.

Treaties and the 19th Century

After American independence came a series of treaties between the individual and collective Iroquois tribes and the United States and the State of New York, all of which entailed a loss of tribal lands for the Indians. The treaties and disruption of traditional Seneca culture led to increasing dissatisfaction and lack of confidence in Seneca leaders. The 1784 Treaty of Fort Stanwix forced the Seneca to cede all claims to their land in the Ohio Country. The treaty and its primary Seneca representative, Cornplanter, were greatly criticized within the tribe. The boundaries of Seneca territory in New York State were not negotiated until the Treaty of Canandaigua in 1794; Seneca reservation lands were delineated three years later in the Treaty of Big Tree, near what is now Geneseo (Livingston Co). The largest included the Allegany Reservation [loc in Cattaraugus Co], the Cattaraugus Reservation [loc in Erie, Chautauqua, and Cattaraugus Cos], the Buffalo Creek Reservation [now in Erie Co], the Canadaway Reservation [now in Chautauqua Co], and the Tonawanda Reservation [loc in Erie, Genesee, and Niagara Cos]. Among numerous smaller reservations, six were established in the Genesee Valley: Caneadea, Squawky Hill, Little Beard's Town, Big Tree, Canawagus, and Gardeau.

The Seneca prophet Handsome Lake, Cornplanter's half-brother, provided a new religious philosophy in the early 19th century that ultimately led to what is now the traditional Longhouse religion. Coming from visions he had during illness, Handsome Lake preached Gaiwiio (good news, good word). Not without some controversy, Handsome Lake admonished against the use of alcohol and encouraged a return to sacred rituals and family stability and an end to negative spirits or witchcraft. Annual recitations of what is known as the Code of Handsome Lake began in the mid–19th century and continue today. The Tonawanda Reservation is considered the center of the Longhouse religion.

The question of removal became a major political issue that also divided the Seneca in the early 19th century, with the first formal inquiry into possible removal to the west occurring in 1810. After 1819 groups of Seneca and other Iroquois were already settled in the Ohio Country, living on two reservations granted to them by the federal government. A reservation had been established in Kansas to accommodate the removal of all Iroquois from New York State, but this reservation was eventually traded for land in Indian Territory (Oklahoma). A contingent of primarily Cayuga from the Six Nations Reserve joined the Seneca in Indian Territory in the 1870s. Descendants of these groups constitute the Seneca-Cayuga tribe of Oklahoma today.

Ongoing pressure for Seneca land and resources in New York State led to a series of disastrous treaties in the first half of the 19th century. Disagreements arose over who had authority to sign treaties as the legitimate representatives of the Seneca and over false or corrupt chiefs. The fraudulent Treaty of Buffalo Creek (1838) sold all of the remaining Seneca lands in New York State, but the so-called Compromise Treaty of 1842 returned some reservations to the Seneca, not including Buffalo Creek or Tonawanda.

In the mid–19th century the distribution of annuities derived from treaties began to create political disruption and resentment among the Seneca. These annuities had been under the control of the chiefs, and there was growing support to have direct distribution to heads of families. On 4 Dec 1848, the Seneca Nation of Indians (SNI) was formed at the Cattaraugus Reservation. The SNI adopted a formal written constitution abolishing the office of chief and establishing a tripartite form of government similar to that of New York State and the federal government. Political unrest among the Iroquois had been growing for some time, and the meeting at Cattaraugus was attended by representatives of the various Seneca communities and of the other tribes of the Iroquois Confederacy. By establishing this republic the SNI was removed from the Iroquois Confederacy and formed a new government representing three Seneca reservations of the time, Allegany, Cattaraugus, and the 1 mi^2 (2.6 km^2) Oil Spring Indian Reservation [loc in Allegany and Cattaraugus Cos].

The Tonawanda chiefs were present at the Cattaraugus Reservation in December 1848, but the Senecas of the Tonawanda Reservation did not join in forming the SNI. Although the Tonawanda Seneca were sympathetic to the need for governmental reform, they had unique legal concerns related to efforts to buy back their reservation that could have been jeopardized by abandoning the system of hereditary chiefs. The creation of the SNI thus marks the division into two Seneca tribal governments in New York State. The Tonawanda Senecas were ultimately successful in buying back a portion of their former acreage, although at a vastly inflated price per acre totaling $100,000, on 5 Nov 1857. Ely S. Parker, later a confederacy chief and a brigadier general for the Union during the Civil War, played a key role in negotiating the purchase.

Present Government

The present SNI government is made up of executive, legislative, and judicial branches. The executive branch consists of the president, clerk, and treasurer. Those serving as president and clerk represent either the Allegany or Cattaraugus Reservation, but the treasurer must represent the opposite reservation. At the following election the representation is reversed so that control of the executive branch is shared and the office holders are not eligible to succeed themselves. The legislative branch consists of a tribal council formed of 16 councilors, 8 from Cattaraugus and 8 from Allegany; Oil Spring Reservation has no separate representatives. The president of the Seneca Nation presides over tribal council sessions and may cast a tiebreaking vote. The judicial branch is composed of two court systems, the surrogate's and the peacemaker's, dealing primarily with issues of inheritance, property disputes, marriage, and adoption. The tribal council is the ultimate court of appeal for any judicial decision.

Elections within the SNI occur in November of even numbered years. The president, treasurer, and clerk are elected every two years. Four tribal councilors from the Cattaraugus Reservations and four councilors from the Allegany are elected for four-year terms every two years. Elections have proven to be rather tumultuous. Recent political issues involved casino gambling, taxation, sovereignty, and internal governance matters. Only enrolled SNI tribal members 18 years and older are eligible to vote, and there is no absentee voting. Following many years of political activism, Seneca women gained the right to vote in the 1964. Two years later women gained the right to hold office in the SNI.

The Tonawanda Senecas maintain a traditional system of government, which is administered by 16 chiefs and additional officers. The chiefs (8 chiefs and 8 subchiefs) are selected by the Tonawanda Seneca women.

The Seneca Today

In the early 21st century the population of the SNI is over 7,200, all of whom are enrolled members, half of whom live on the reservations. The Tonawanda Senecas have about 1,200 enrolled members, of whom 700 live on the reservation. Tribal membership and clan affiliation in the SNI is determined via matrilineal descent. Membership in one of the eight Seneca clans continues to be important. The Seneca language, while still spoken primarily by the elderly, is being taught in the local public schools that are attended by Seneca children, and culture classes of various subjects are also offered.

The construction of the New York State Thruway through the Cattaraugus Reservation in the late 1950s was accompanied by negotiation and highway blockages. For the Seneca one of the most contentious issues of the 20th century was the construction of the Kinzua Dam (Warren, Pa) on the Allegheny River in the 1960s. Seneca activists argued that it was a violation of the Treaty of Canandaigua. Approximately 10,000 acres (4,050 ha) on the Allegany Reservation and the former Cornplanter Grant in Pennsylvania were affected when the dam was completed in 1965. The completion of US 219 through the Allegany Reservation was, in the beginning of the 21st century, being negotiated with the State of New York. The renegotiations of the lease arrangement between the SNI and the City of Salamanca created a still unresolved animosity between the parties. Although the lease has been renegotiated more favorably for the Seneca, local non-native antagonism has not disappeared.

Current SNI tribal enterprises include casinos in Niagara Falls and Salamanca. In addition, there are tribal bingo establishments on both Cattaraugus and Allegany Reservations, along with tribal gas and cigarette outlets. The Seneca-Iroquois National Museum is located on the Allegany Reservation, and both the Allegany and Cattaraugus Reservations have branches of the Seneca Nation Library.

See also American Indians in literature: indigenous authors; Morgan, Lewis Henry.

Abler, Thomas S. "Factional Dispute and Party Conflict in the Political System of the Seneca Nation, (1845–1895): An Ethnohistorical Analysis" (PhD diss, Univ of Toronto, 1970)

Abler, Thomas S., and Elisabeth Tooker. "Seneca." In *Northeast,* ed. Bruce G. Trigger, vol 15 of *Handbook of North American Indians,* ed. William C. Sturtevant (Washington, DC: Smithsonian Institution, 1978)

Abrams, George H. J. *The Seneca People* (Phoenix: Indian Tribal Series, 1976)

Brandão, José Antùnio. *"Your Fyre Shall Burn No More": Iroquois Policy toward New France and Its Native Allies to 1701* (Lincoln: Univ of Nebraska Press, 1997)

Fenton, William N. *The Great Law and the Longhouse: A Political History of the Iroquois Confederacy* (Norman: Univ of Oklahoma Press, 1998)

Hauptman, Laurence M. *Conspiracy of Interests: Iroquois Dispossession and the Rise of New York State* (Syracuse: Syracuse Univ Press, 1999)

Hayes, Charles F., III, ed. *The Charles F. Wray Series in Seneca Archaeology,* 3 vols (Rochester: Rochester Museum & Science Center, 1987–2001)

Parker, Arthur C. *An Analytical History of the Seneca Indians.* Researches and Transactions of the New York State Archaeological Association, vol 6 (Rochester, 1926)

Richter, Daniel K. *The Ordeal of the Longhouse: The Peoples of the Iroquois League in the Era of European Colonization* (Chapel Hill: Univ of North Carolina Press, 1992)

George H. J. Abrams

Seneca River Towing Path. See Baldwinsville Canal and Seneca River Towing Path.

Sennett. Town (pop 3,244) in central Cayuga Co. Settled in 1794 and formed from Brutus in 1827, the town was first reached by the Great Genesee Rd in 1799. The Auburn and Syracuse Railroad (1838) and the Southern Central Railroad (1870) modernized transport. In 2002 Sennett was one of the prime agricultural towns in the county, but on the northern and eastern edges of the nearby city of Auburn are malls and big-box retailers, along with a Miller Brewing bottling plant and the Buckeye Pipeline. Residents who do not farm either work in Auburn or commute to Syracuse.

Laurel Auchampaugh

September 11th, 2001. The worst terrorist attack ever to occur on US soil took place on this date when 19 members of Al Qaeda, a fundamentalist Islamic group, commandeered four jetliners, intending to crash them into prominent targets in New York City and Washington, DC. Two airplanes crashed into and destroyed the World Trade Center (WTC) in New York City. Another smashed into the Pentagon in Arlington, Va, destroying a wing of the building. It is believed that the fourth hijacked airplane was headed for the White House or US Capitol but, instead, crashed into a field near Shanksville, Pennsylvania. In all, nearly 3,000 people were killed, of whom about 2,750 died in the collapse of the WTC towers.

The Fall of the Towers: 102 Minutes

The sequence of events on September 11th unfolded with a terrifying rapidity. American Airlines Flight 11 and United Airlines Flight 175 left Boston's Logan Airport at 7:59 AM and 8:14 AM, respectively, bound for destinations in California. Shortly into the flights, both planes were commandeered by hijackers, who took over the controls of the planes and changed their course to Lower Manhattan. At 8:46 AM American Airlines Flight 11 crashed into the WTC's North Tower, ripping a huge hole in the facade and igniting a fire. Although many observers suspected terrorism from the outset, others wondered if the crash was a horrible accident. But only minutes later, at 9:03 AM, when United Airlines Flight 175 smashed into the South Tower, all doubts that this was part of a coordinated terrorist attack were erased.

Firefighters and police rushed to the scene. Mayor Rudolph Giuliani arrived to consult with emergency personnel. The city had recently established an emergency command center in the WTC itself, which was now useless. Officials scrambled to set up temporary headquarters nearby. The order to evacuate both towers was issued over public address systems after the first plane struck the North Tower, and most people were able to exit the buildings after climbing down emergency stairwells. In several instances, people carried disabled co-workers down dozens of flights of stairs. Other disabled or injured people were unable to escape, and some people were trapped in elevators. A few delayed leaving the South Tower after hearing a confusing announcement telling them to remain in their offices.

Almost everyone who was on the floors where the planes hit perished instantly. Most people who were on floors above the impact were trapped and unable to access stairwells to escape. As the smoke and fire drew closer, some of them jumped from the towers, falling to their deaths. Others tried to make their way to the roofs of the towers, unaware that the doors were locked. On

One of the last images of the World Trade Center, 10 Sept 2001. A replica of the *Half Moon* sails on the Hudson River in front of the towers. Photograph by Woody Woodworth.

the ground, some pedestrians were hit and killed by falling debris. Below ground, the shopping concourse located in the basement of the WTC was evacuated. All New York City and PATH (Port Authority Trans-Hudson) subway stations in the vicinity were rapidly cleared of passengers and trains.

Concerned that other planes might have been hijacked, the Federal Aviation Administration (FAA) closed all US airspace for the first time in history. All planes were instructed to land. Two planes taken over by hijackers remained aloft. At 9:37 AM, American Airlines Flight 77 out of Washington, DC, crashed into the Pentagon, destroying part of the building and killing or fatally injuring 126 on the ground. All 64 people on the plane perished. Fearing that other planes might be headed toward the White House and the US Capitol, the federal government closed and evacuated all of its offices.

At 9:59 AM, less than an hour after the plane hit the WTC's South Tower, intense fires caused the failure of its structural steel and the building collapsed on itself in 10 seconds. People in streets and buildings nearby fled a massive cloud of dust and debris. Firefighters, police, Port Authority employees, other rescuers, and civilians who were still in the building were killed. Throughout New York City, offices and businesses began to evacuate their employees. In New York State, all over the United States, and in many places worldwide, regular business came to a halt as news of the attacks spread and people clustered around televisions, radio, and the Internet. The local and national tragedy was from the beginning the focus of world attention.

The fourth hijacked airplane, United Airlines Flight 93 out of Newark, NJ, was headed to Washington, DC. Passengers who had managed to make cell phone calls to relatives learned of the attacks on the WTC. Based on accounts of these calls and on the plane's black box recording, it is believed that some of the passengers attempted to overpower the terrorists. At 10:03 AM, the plane crashed in a field in Somerset Co, Pa, killing everyone on board.

At 10:28 AM, an hour and a half after the plane crashed into the WTC's North Tower, the steel failed and the building collapsed, killing rescuers and others still trapped inside, and unleashing another avalanche of debris that roared through the streets of Lower Manhattan. Once again, pedestrians (including Mayor Giuliani, who had just finished a press conference at Chambers St and West Broadway) fled for their lives.

Within a few short minutes, the New York City skyline had been transformed. The towers were gone, leaving only a few skeletal walls and a huge, burning funeral pyre whose smoke could be seen and smelled for miles. Streets near the WTC were covered with a thick layer of ash. A vast cloud of paper and other combustible material was released in the collapse, and some documents from the WTC floated for miles before alighting in central Brooklyn and other places far from the disaster site. Pulverized concrete, twisted steel, and other remains filled a rubble field spanning 16 acres (6.5 ha). Destroyed along with the towers were WTC 3 (the Marriott Hotel) and the tiny Greek Orthodox St. Nicholas Church. Later in the afternoon, WTC 7 crumbled from intense fire, without further loss of life. All remaining buildings in the WTC complex were severely damaged and later had to be demolished. Many other nearby buildings suffered heavy damage, and despite initial fears, there were no other major building failures.

The Response in New York City: The First 48 Hours

The streets and bridges of the city were full of people fleeing the disaster. An estimated 14,000–16,500 persons who had been in the WTC at the time of the attacks had been able to make their way out of the towers before their collapse, and they were joined by people exiting nearby buildings. Lower Manhattan resembled a war zone, with heavy ash covering all surfaces and fire raging. But even as the dust was still settling and the nearly incomprehensible scope of the tragedy was becoming known, others rushed toward the ruins to search for survivors. Thousands of ordinary citizens joined firefighters, police, Emergency Medical Services (EMS) workers, and construction workers and began digging through the smoldering rubble, sometimes by hand. By nightfall, many others appeared with supplies of food and clothing for the rescuers. Other volunteers rushed to nearby hospitals, such as St. Vincent's and New York University Downtown Hospital, which began making preparations to receive massive amounts of casualties. The American Red Cross and local hospitals were flooded with members of the public wanting to donate blood.

But few survivors were found. Seventeen were rescued on the first day, and the last survivor, an injured woman trapped in the rubble, was rescued on September 12. It was feared that as many as 10,000 had been killed in the crashes and the collapse of the towers. Over the coming days and months, this number was revised downward many times. By early January 2004, the official tally of victims in New York City was 2,749, not including the hijackers of the two planes. Remains of the victims were difficult to recover; by the end of 2003 only 1,541 had been identified by the New York City Medical Examiner's Office. Some of the most staggering losses were borne by companies headquartered in the WTC. Cantor

Fitzgerald, a brokerage firm, lost 658 employees; Marsh and McLennan, another financial services provider, lost 295. Also losing their lives were 343 New York City firefighters, 84 Port Authority employees, and 23 New York City police officers.

Government agencies, elected officials, nonprofit organizations, and media outlets responded quickly to events. Gov George E. Pataki postponed primary elections, which had been underway when the attacks occurred. On the afternoon of the disaster, he arrived in New York City and, together with Mayor Giuliani, held press conferences, both men overcoming their own shock in an attempt to reassure the public that authorities were doing their best to gain control over the situation. "We're going to rebuild," Giuliani promised on 12 September. "We're going to come out of this stronger than we were before. Emotionally stronger, politically stronger, economically stronger." The mayor's response to this great emergency fit his strong personality, as did his ability, in word and deed, to capture the anger, sadness, and determination of the city's residents. Many in New York City and across the nation, including many of his former critics, spoke admiringly of his courage and took solace in his resoluteness.

The state National Guard was deployed in Lower Manhattan. Schools were closed and almost all public events were canceled. Groups such as New York Cares, the Red Cross, and the Salvation Army provided feeding stations and clothing for rescue workers; set up hotlines to provide information to families of the missing; distributed emergency relief checks to victims and their families; and provided shelter for those evacuated from buildings near the disaster site and for rescue workers. The Red Cross and the city administration established the Compassion Center (now Family Assistance Center) for families to register their missing loved ones and receive grief counseling. The American Society for the Prevention of Cruelty to Animals (ASPCA), the Humane Society, and other animal rescue organizations convinced authorities to allow them into Lower Manhattan to rescue abandoned and trapped pets.

Telephone service was disrupted for several days, in part because of an overwhelming volume of calls from persons wishing to get in touch with friends or family. The loss of the broadcast antenna atop the WTC's North Tower forced some television and radio stations to scramble to arrange alternate means of broadcasting. For several days, major television networks canceled all regular programming, broadcast nonstop coverage of events without commercial interruption, and shared video with each other. The staff of the *Wall Street Journal,* forced to evacuate its offices, which were across the street from the WTC, worked from home or in borrowed offices to produce a 12 September edition of the newspaper.

Lower Manhattan was sealed off. All bridges and tunnels were closed, and no cars or pedestrians were allowed to enter the "frozen zone" below 14th St without the permission of police or the National Guard. Most New York City subways and buses, however, resumed service by late afternoon on September 11th. (Service in Lower Manhattan, however, was disrupted for months.) Commuter railways, such as Metro-North and the Long Island Rail Road, also kept running after a brief interruption of service. Airports remained closed. Airline passengers were stranded in whatever airport their planes had been suddenly ordered to land. Everywhere, the skies were silent and empty. In Manhattan, the silence was tempered by the sound of fighter jets patrolling the skies. The United States had been placed on high alert within an hour after the attacks. Two aircraft carriers were stationed in New York Harbor. On the afternoon of September 11th, Pres George W. Bush declared New York City a federal disaster area.

The tragedy of September 11th was mourned by people throughout New York State. Victims came from almost every region of the state. In every county, people jammed lines at Red Cross stations to donate blood, and groups gathered food and clothing at spontaneously established collection centers. In many communities there were candlelight vigils, and churches, synagogues, and mosques held special services. Fire companies from around the state volunteered in rescue operations. On the Friday following the attacks, ceremonies were held statewide. At Cornell University some 14,000 persons gathered at the quad. Special concerts were held; for example, the Rochester Philharmonic Orchestra offered a special performance of Mozart's Requiem. During the months ahead, there were special programs that reminded New Yorkers of the economic, political, and spiritual ties between all the state's citizens. One example was the solemn ceremony in fall 2002 at the New York State Fallen Firefighters Memorial at the Empire State Plaza in Albany, at which the 343 names of firefighters who had perished at the WTC were added to the list of 1,882 firefighters who had died in the line in duty in New York State since 1811.

Ground Zero

In the days, weeks, and months after September 11th, New York City struggled to resume as normal an existence as possible. Public attention, however, remained focused on the ruins of the WTC, commonly referred to as Ground Zero, a term previously used to describe the point of impact of a nuclear weapon. (The most common terms for the attacks themselves became 9/11 and September 11th.) The rescue operation became a clean-up operation and a mission to recover the remains of the victims.

The work to clear away more than 1.5 million tons (1.4 million MT) of rubble was carried out under the supervision of the Department of Design and Construction (DDC), a little-known city agency not ordinarily involved in emergency response work. The DDC assumed this role because its top officials took charge within the first few hours of the disaster, before other city and federal agencies (such as the Federal Emergency Management Agency [FEMA] and the Army Corp of Engineers) were able to mount an organized response. The city ignored its own organizational charts and Office of Emergency Management (OEM) plans and allowed the DDC to continue to manage the work. The OEM, Port Authority, and many other government agencies; engineers from the private firms Thornton-Thomasetti and LERA (Leslie E. Robertson Associates); and four large construction firms, AMEC Construction Management, Bovis Lend Lease LMB, Tully Construction Co, and Turner/Plaza Construction Joint Venture also played major roles in the cleanup. Hundreds of police and firefighters, devastated by the losses within their ranks, worked at the site clearing away rubble, determined to recover the bodies of their fallen comrades.

Comparatively few victims' bodies were found intact. Instead, the Medical Examiner was forced to base its identification of the dead on the DNA testing of small fragments. Debris from Ground Zero was carefully checked for human remains before being transferred on barges to the Fresh Kills landfill on Staten Island, where it was sifted once again. The removal of debris to a former garbage dump was protested by the families of the slain firefighters and by other survivors. Federal emergency funds paid for much of the clean-up work. Demolition of the remains of the WTC was hazardous. There was constant danger of being hit by debris. Engineers feared that remaining foundation walls would collapse and cause massive flooding. There was concern that dangerous gases trapped in the ruins of the complex's cooling plant might explode. Regulations about the wearing of respirators were not enforced, and as a result many workers developed (possibly long-term) health problems.

In November 2001 tensions between firefighters and police erupted into a fracas during a demonstration by firefighters protesting the city's decision to reduce their presence at Ground Zero. There were accusations, angrily denied by firefighters and their supporters, that firefighters and other workers were looting goods from ruined offices and stores. Meanwhile, the former site of the WTC became a place of pilgrimage. In December the city set up a viewing platform overlooking Ground Zero. On the six-month anniversary of the disaster in March 2002, a temporary memorial to the disaster was installed: twin beams of blue light that rose high above the city every night for a month.

Overcoming many obstacles, the recovery operation at Ground Zero proceeded quickly, reflecting the determination of state and city officials to rebuild on the site as soon as possible. By May 2002, the recovery and clean-up effort was officially declared complete. William Langewiesche wrote, "Less than a year after the attack, the World Trade Center and its burned and pulverized contents lay under bare earth, absorbed, like so much else of New York's past, into the man-made hills of Fresh Kills." — *RN*

Cultural Responses

The fires in the rubble of the WTC were still burning when New Yorkers began to mourn the dead, honor rescuers, and grapple with the meaning of the greatest human tragedy in their state and city's history. In a metropolis that suffered a loss so deep, no single cultural response could repair the damage to the city's fabric or heal its many wounds. But as the initial hours of the assault passed, people across the city and state gave form and voice to their many sorrows and questions.

In the media, September 11th was documented by professional journalists and ordinary people. Images from New York City, an international communications capital, created a shared sense of the disaster among millions of people and amplified the terrible impact of the attack. The unimaginable became real for anyone who watched television footage or looked at a photograph. For all the concentration of major media institutions in New York City, some of the most

Ephemera of September 11th. Ephemera commemorating the attack on the World Trade Center (WTC) began to appear within days of the event. Widely available at peddlers' stands, souvenir shops, and novelty stores in New York City, these buttons, pins, bumper stickers, posters, postcards, baseball caps, and t-shirts, allowed New Yorkers and tourists alike to express their feelings about the tragedy and to begin to formulate the ways in which it would be remembered. Indeed, the commercially produced ephemera reflect many of the emotions and themes that emerged after the attack.

The most common theme was patriotism, and simple American flag buttons and lapel pins were probably the most commonly worn emblems. Flags appeared on many homes, even in liberal New York City neighborhoods not previously known for nationalistic fervor. For a time, the flag became an important fashion accessory as well, emblazoned on sweatshirts, blouses, scarves, purses, and hats. Often, the flag was combined with patriotic slogans, most commonly the United We Stand slogan that seemed to emerge as the public's favorite. In the first days after the attack, buttons that had been produced in support of the Gulf War a decade earlier were retrieved from warehouses and put back on the market, sometimes with homemade alterations to update them.

Civic pride was another important theme. The I♥NY slogan, famous in the 1970s, made a strong reappearance, often amended to read I♥NY More Than Ever or depicted with the addition of a black wound on the red heart. One new development was the juxtaposition of New York City and American patriotism, which would have been considered unusual before the attacks. The city's symbols—the big apple, the Empire State Building, and the twin towers—were often paired with American flags and patriotic slogans. Very little humor appeared on commemorative items, but one business organization issued boosterish buttons exhorting New Yorkers to "Fight Back" by going shopping, eating out, and staying over.

Many New Yorkers felt a visceral pain over the destruction of the towers and the loss of life in the attack and sought to express that pain through the commemorative items they purchased and wore. Buttons, pins, hats, and shirts bearing the date of the attack, an image of the twin towers, and some indication that the wearer would "never forget" were common. Some buttons simply bade the towers a wistful "goodbye" or stated that the wearer "missed them," as if they were people. Shortly after the attack, when emotions were at their rawest, the old civil rights slogan We Shall Overcome was pressed into service. But this soon gave way to more explicitly patriotic sentiments.

The heroism of the New York City's fire and police departments received ample representation on 9–11 memorabilia. Many people wore baseball caps with the NYPD or FDNY logo, items that remained popular in the years after the attack. The iconic picture of the firemen raising the flag at the site was also common, while other items paid tribute to those members of the uniformed services who lost their lives. Another way of marking the important role of the uniformed services in the event came in the form of miniature badges with the addition of an American flag and the date of the attack. The widely admired leadership of Mayor Rudolph Giuliani and, to a lesser extent, of Pres George Bush and Gov George Pataki was also noted.

Anger found its expression in representations of Osama Bin Laden in the crosshairs of a rifle—or bomb—sight, or on a wanted poster. The latter sometimes bore the inscription, "Wanted Dead, Not Alive." Some buttons expressed support for Operation Enduring Freedom, the US retaliatory strike in Afghanistan. Antiwar buttons also appeared. The slogan Our Grief Is Not a Cry for War was popular, but most antiwar buttons lacked specific reference to the attack on New York City. One prominent exception was a button issued by the New York Friends School that featured the towers as the upright line in the peace symbol.

Many of the items drew on common genres of tourist souvenirs. In fact, simple pre-attack renditions of the New York City skyline with the twin towers took on added meaning, and rather than being pulled from the shelves, they remained on the market. The availability of the ephemera in souvenir shops, especially near the site of the towers, further indicates New York City's new status as a patriotic pilgrimage site. Visitors came to the city to view the site and marked their visit with a pin, sweatshirt, or hat. By the summer after the attack, some souvenirs no longer memorialized the event itself but instead celebrated the wearer's visit to Ground Zero. While some local residents continued to wear commemorative pins and buttons, these were increasingly available only in shops catering to tourists.

Daniel Soyer

arresting accounts of the day were made possible by eyewitnesses using camcorders, cameras, and cell phones.

Until the moment of the assault, New Yorkers had exceptional reasons to feel safe. With the end of the Cold War, the city was no longer the presumed target of Soviet missiles. Dramatic declines in crime in the 1990s made residents feel much safer than they had felt during previous decades. All of this was compounded by a special sensibility present because so many New Yorkers are immigrants or the descendants of immigrants or migrants, who found in the city a place of refuge. September 11th shook that sense of refuge.

In the hours and days after the attack, the very public nature of New Yorkers' responses was unmistakable. At prominent intersections and on blank walls, at rescue facilities, and at hospitals, people quickly posted photocopied fliers with descriptions of the missing. Inscribed with intimate details—appearance, occupation, distinguishing birthmarks—they first appeared in efforts to find people who were missing. As days passed and the likelihood of finding the missing alive diminished, the fliers commemorated the dead and expressed the grief of survivors.

Residents appropriated the walls, streets, fences, pavements, and signposts of their city in a massive expression of public mourning. At firehouses, police stations, and the homes of the dead, and in public parks and squares, shrines to the slain were erected. In a city that is an art capital, many of the memorials took the form of sculpture or painting. Others combined devotional candles, photographs, flowers, messages from survivors, flags, religious offerings, and personal items. In a memorial to messengers, a bicycle chained to a signpost was decked with plastic flowers, written messages, and a Mexican flag. Municipal workers turned to the physical materials of their jobs, in one case bricks, and arranged them in a memorial pyramid.

Flags and patriotic symbols were prominent at sidewalk memorials after September 11th, but they were complemented by personal mementoes and messages. Even as the display of the national flag was revived in New York City on a scale not seen since World War II, the personal and the individual were always put forward.

At sidewalk shrines, New Yorkers commemorated the dead according to their myriad religions. Jewish *yarzheit* candles, candles from botanicas, Roman Catholic Mass cards, a typewritten prayer from a Muslim cleric, and more were displayed alongside each other in public and amounted to a collective education in mourning. Some people left words: prayers, letters to lost loved ones, political slogans, and messages of solidarity. Some left personal objects: a Yankees cap to recall a fan's enthusiasm. Others left visual symbols: a sea of candles at the south end of Union Square that gave flickering form to the dead.

On television the most prominent public expressions of solidarity in the city and in the suburbs outside it were in the funerals for police, firefighters, and rescue workers. With the visual impact of the sea of uniforms of police and firefighters and of bagpipe bands, these rites have long been a staple of television news. In the days and weeks after September 11th, they were a powerful presence in the New York area's media.

It was not all consensus, though. Crowds gathered in Union Square recovered the park's old status as a site of dissent and argued out the appropriate response to the attacks. Signs reading "Our Grief Is Not a Cry for War" coexisted with red, white, and blue memorabilia. For many, there was intense anger at the perpetrators of the highjackings, much of it personified through attacks on Osama Bin Laden, the leader of Al Qaeda. Expression of the love of country could be debased into jingoism and bigotry against Muslims. Newspapers reported verbal abuse of Muslims in New York City. On Long Island, a man tried to run down a Pakistani woman with his car. Bomb threats, arson, and telephoned threats raised fear at mosques, Arab communal institutions, and businesses owned by Arabs and Muslims. Police guarded mosques in New York City. Muslim taxi drivers stayed home, as did Muslim women who feared being visible and vulnerable in their *hijab* (head scarves). Middle Eastern parents kept their children home from school. Malice against Muslims and Arabs was compounded by attacks on individuals who were neither Muslim nor Arab (eg, Sikh men in turbans) because their dress and appearance had hostile associations.

The city's formal observances were firmly interreligious. Mayor Giuliani, whose unwavering performance on September 11th and the days after revived his mayoralty, condemned all acts of bigotry in the city. A Prayer for America, a memorial service at Yankee Stadium held 23 Sept 2001, included Hindu, Protestant, Sikh, Jewish, Muslim, and Roman Catholic devotions. In organized civic culture, Islam gained a greater presence.

It was the newspaper, the city's oldest mass medium, that provided explicitly local dimensions of news. Particularly prominent in the press were eyewitness accounts, presented with little mediation by reporters, of individuals who had narrowly escaped the collapse of the WTC. In a disaster whose broad outlines were so widely witnessed, these stories offered specific, human dimensions to the tragedy. They also provided counterpoints of escape, rescue, and courage on a day that was otherwise defined by disaster. Notes of mourning and commemoration were not confined to the news pages. Full-page advertisements were taken out in mourning. The most famous updated Milton Glaser's famous I♥NY design; after September 11th, Glaser produced a new design with a singed heart, reading "I♥NY More Than Ever."

Newspapers also emphasized the individual identities of the lives lost on September 11th. Within days of the disaster, the *New York Times* launched its "Portraits in Grief" section, which published short pieces on the dead, each one animated by details that made each person distinct. Other papers in the metropolitan area published similar collections. What was especially striking about "Portraits in Grief" was the willingness of the *Times* to devote sustained attention to those who were, in general, not the sort of famous people who generally appeared in its pages.

The egalitarian tendencies seen in the profiles of the dead were matched by a rediscovery of the city's working class. The decline of New York City's industrial sector and the rise of Wall St and financial services had erased older images of New York City as a seaport union town with a strong manufacturing economy. After September 11th numerous acts of heroism on the part of ordinary people were widely credited and discussed. In media accounts and public observances, the heroes of September 11th came from the older New York: uniformed municipal workers like firefighters and police officers, maritime workers who ferried people from Lower Manhattan, and ironworkers who searched for survivors amid the rubble of the towers.

A photograph of firefighters raising an American flag in the ruins of the WTC, taken by photographer Thomas E. Franklin of the *Record*, a northern New Jersey newspaper, quickly became an icon; it was photocopied and hung in New York shop windows alongside Joe Rosenthal's picture of Marines raising the US flag over Iwo Jima in World War II. For many, the two photos seemed to define heroism and faith in ultimate American victory.

The emphasis on working-class heroes who traced their roots to an older New York was part of a general tendency to look back to the 1930s and 1940s, to the New York City of Fiorello La Guardia, the New Deal, and World War II. In the days after September 11th, two works of literature from this period became prominently associated with the tragedy. W. H. Auden's poem "September 1, 1939," written in New York City to mark the German invasion of Poland that began World War II, was read on National Public Radio. It also circulated widely on the Internet. Its general sense of a world on the brink of terrible change and its line "The unmentionable odour of death / Offends the September night" fit the circumstances of New York City after September 11th. In a similar spirit, people circulated E. B. White's post–World War II essay *Here Is New York,* which was written for *Holiday* magazine and gained a reputation as a classic meditation on New York City and urban culture. "The subtlest change in New York is something people don't speak much about but that is in everyone's mind. The city, for the first time in its long history, is destructible. . . . The intimation of mortality is part of New York now: in the sound of jets overhead, in the black headlines of the latest edition."

The events of September 11th, succeeded by the anthrax scare of October and the war in Afghanistan, passed quickly into realms of history and memory. The communal feeling that suffused metropolitan New York in the immediate aftermath of September 11th gave way to more complex and contentious emotions. What should be done with the WTC site? What should the national response to terrorism be? Did errors in planning and procedure take the lives of municipal rescue workers? How should the city commemorate the dead? Answers to all of these questions and more provoked strong debate and anguished feelings. So did attempts to give form and meaning to the tragedy of September 11th. Was a documentary too formulaic? Was this book or that essay insensitive? All of these questions reverberate in discussions of September 11th.

Succeeding generations of New Yorkers will look back on September 11th, 2001 and on the cultural reactions to the attack on the WTC to find lessons that meet the needs of their own time. As the immediate memory of that terrible day ebbs, there is much that will be remembered. Ordinary people stepped forward in the face of unimaginable violence and destruction to help save others. As Chris Byrne wrote in "Gates of Hell," his song of September 11th, "Now there's a whole new canyon of heroes / Full of people who seem like me and you." As New Yorkers grieved and mourned together in public, they found different routes to common experiences. Many realized that for all their differences, each contained something of the other: a Jew's injunction to remember; a Roman Catholic's sense of communalism; a Muslim's sense of fear in a familiar city that suddenly looked threatening; and a Baptist's faith that the city would rise again. —*RWS*

After September 11th: Institutional Responses

Federal, state, and city agencies all responded to the crisis of September 11th, though sometimes in a confusing and overlapping fashion. Both the city and state governments knew that the impact of September 11th on the city's economy and the subsequent rebuilding efforts would be enormously expensive and looked to the federal government for assistance. A few days after the attacks, the Bush administration pledged $21.4 billion in emergency aid to New York City. Almost a year later, it was revealed that only $4.5–$5 billion had been received. Federal officials were criticized for not honoring their promises; state and city officials were accused of allowing funds to go unclaimed because of inaction and indecision. FEMA, responsible for disbursing $8.8 billion, was blamed for failing to publicize the availability of funds and for turning away deserving aid applicants. As it was, the $21.4 billion in promised aid fell far short of the economic losses suffered by New York City, which by some accounts totaled more than $83 billion. But Congress repeatedly refused requests for more aid by New York State's congressional delegation. Local officials complained that it was unfair for New York City to bear such a lion's share of the burden incurred by what had been an attack on the United States as a whole and that New York was being shortchanged given the disproportionate share of federal tax revenues generated by the city and state. By the end of 2003, New York City had still not received all of the promised $21.4 billion.

New York City and New York State also had their differences to resolve. Because of the gubernatorial control of the Port Authority, Gov Pataki had an enormous say in development plans for the WTC site. The city and state established several programs aimed at stimulating the economy in Manhattan below Canal St (in an area designated as the Liberty Zone) in conjunction with plans to rebuild on the site of the WTC. Tax benefits were made available to businesses, and other programs provided financial incentives to retain and create jobs and move businesses and residences to the area.

One of the defining memories of the aftermath of September 11th is the acrid odor that lingered around Ground Zero and could be smelled for over a month throughout large areas of New York City. In the summer of 2003 the Environmental Protection Agency (EPA) came under attack when its inspector general released a report claiming that the White House had pressured it to issue assurances about the safety of air quality in Lower Manhattan before the completion of adequate testing. Not long afterward, the New York City Department of Health and Mental Hygiene, the Agency for Toxic Substances and Disease Registry, and FEMA launched the World Trade Center Health Registry, a comprehensive health survey aimed at monitoring the health of people directly exposed to debris from the WTC collapse and from the subsequent clean-up efforts.

Victim compensation was another major task facing government agencies. In late September 2001, Congress established a September 11th Victim Compensation Fund under the direction of Special Master Kenneth Feinberg, for relatives of those killed in the attacks and for those who had been injured. In exchange, the recipients would forgo their rights to sue for damages in civil court. During its first year and a half, the fund was sharply criticized by survivors, lawyers, and public officials, including New York State attorney general Eliot Spitzer, for unfairly excluding many victims from participating in the fund and for providing inadequate compensation to other victims. After the rules were amended in March 2002 to broaden eligibility requirements and to eliminate some sources of outside income as a basis for calculating award amounts, criticism diminished. By the deadline of 22 Dec 2003, 95% of the eligible families had applied for the funds.

In the weeks following the attacks, special victims' funds established by nonprofit organizations raised millions of dollars from the general public. Some of these initiatives were later criticized for operating without adequate oversight or for not disbursing all of the collected funds to the intended recipients. For instance, the American Red Cross came under furious attack in October 2001 when it was revealed that it was intending to put aside $200 million of funds raised for September 11th victims for other purposes. In addition a number of other funds, public and private, were established to aid survivors, but it was not always clear that those who most needed the funds were receiving them.

In the wake of the 1995 Oklahoma City bombing, public awareness of the effects of post-traumatic stress disorder had grown. Reflecting this concern, a great deal of attention was paid to the mental health of survivors of September 11th. In the days, weeks, and months after the attacks, a number of organizations and agencies offered counseling to survivors and others traumatized by the event. For example, the *New York Times* 9/11 Neediest Fund donated more than $1 million in grants to several trauma treatment programs, including COPE (a program of mandatory mental health screenings for all employees of the New York City Police Department) and several projects to provide counseling to schoolchildren. As late as December 2003, the New York City Department of Health and Mental Hygiene's Lifenet program was still offering free referrals to people whose "lives have become a lot more complicated since 9/11."

Documenting the Tragedy

Arthur Danto, writing in the *Nation* about the impact of September 11th, referred to "those months when we thought or talked about nothing else, and the enormity of our shared experiences flooded consciousness." The need to bear witness was urgent and universal. Soon after the attacks, New York State archivists and librarians launched efforts to document the events and to safeguard historical collections located in Lower Manhattan. Under the leadership of the New York State Archives and the State Historical Records Advisory Board, a World Trade Center Documentation Task Force was organized to coordinate and track documentation. The task force established a web site (http://www.nyshrab.org/WTC/wtc.html) that provided information about documentation projects, status reports on the conditions of archives and libraries near Ground Zero, and a list of government agencies (such as the Department of Transportation, the Department of Taxation and Finance, and the Port Authority) whose records were destroyed in the attack.

On the first anniversary of the disaster, several exhibits opened, among them *The Day Our World Changed: Children's Art of 9/11,* at the Museum of the City of New York; *September 11: Bearing Witness to History,* September 2002, at the Smithsonian Institution in Washington, DC; and *The World Trade Center: Rescue, Recovery, Response,* a permanent exhibit at the New York State Museum in Albany, which included a fire truck crushed at the WTC site. The New-York Historical Society launched a new initiative, History Responds, a series of collecting projects, exhibitions, and public programs devoted to the events of September 11th.

Some of the most striking documentation projects are web sites. The September 11 Digital Archive (http://911digitalarchive.org), a project of the American Social History Project at the City University of New York Graduate Center and the Center for History and New Media at George Mason University, collects firsthand accounts of the attacks and the aftermath, as well as related e-mails and digital images. The September 11 Web Archive (http://september11.archive.org) is an archive of Internet responses to September 11th organized by the Library of Congress. One of the more unusual web sites is National Public Radio's Sonic Memorial Project (http://sonicmemorial.org), a collection of audio traces of the World Trade Center. The web site includes tapes of weddings, recordings of the buildings' elevators, and voice-mail messages from people who worked in the buildings. Many of the September 11th projects are characterized by an unprecedented degree of collaboration between the general public and archivists, librarians, and curators. September 11th marks the first time that the Internet has been widely accepted as a legitimate medium for preserving the historical record and is also the first major event in world history for which e-mail messages and voice-mail recordings were seriously collected as documentation.

It is too early to write in any definitive way of the impact of September 11th on the arts. Perhaps inevitably, many of the early works have been collaborations, such as the short story collection *110 Stories: New York Writes after September 11* (2002) or the film *September 11* (2003), in which 11 filmmakers from 11 countries each contributed a segment exactly 11 minutes and 9 seconds long. A number of musical works have appeared, ranging from Bruce Springsteen's album *The Rising* (2002) to John Adams's composition *On the Transmigration of Souls,* which opened the 2002 New York Philharmonic season and included, like many of the tributes, a recitation of some of the names of victims. —*RN*

Reconstruction

The rebuilding of the WTC site will be among the most closely watched and widely debated construction projects in the nation's history, and one in which the general public has had, if not a vote, certainly a voice. As of the end of 2003, some progress was made, and several architects have been named, but controversy and disagreement still cloud the site's future. Contributing to the uncertainty surrounding the project are the size of the site, 16 acres, the involvement of several branches of government, the complexity of ownership claims, the status of insurance reimbursements, the potential for improvements including new parkland and a transit center, the requirements of an appropriate memorial, and, not least, the emotions of millions of people, especially the relatives of the disaster's victims.

Reconstruction of the site officially falls under the jurisdiction of the Lower Manhattan Development Corp (LMDC), a public benefit corporation created in the fall of 2001 and a subsidiary of the Empire State Development Corp. Half the members of the LMDC board are chosen by the governor, half by the mayor of New York City. While the Port Authority of New York and New Jersey is the owner of the site, the leaseholder, Larry Silverstein, holds the insurance policy on the destroyed WTC. Silverstein and his insurers are in dispute over the value of the claim, not resolved at the end of 2003, which will be either \$3.5 or \$7 billion, based on whether it is legally determined that the coordinated attack by two planes constitutes one or two "occurrences." Dozens of public and private interest groups have expressed strong opinions about the future of the site, including groups representing New York City's architecture and design community, nonprofit urban design advocacy organizations, and local planning bodies. Countless meetings and forums have been devoted to soliciting public input on the best possible future use of the site, and many thousands of people have offered ideas and opinions.

The initial proposals put forward by the LMDC during the summer of 2002—a series of designs featuring a group of office towers surrounding some kind of memorial green space—provoked much criticism for being a bland and uninspired group of towers and for focusing too much on re-creating as much office and commercial space as possible, for a site that seemed too important to relegate to standard office-park design. The designs were withdrawn and a search undertaken for an architect or architects who could best plan the future of the site. In December 2002, six proposals were unveiled. On 27 Feb 2003, and following the direct intervention of Gov Pataki, LMDC chose the master plan of Studio Daniel Libeskind, most recently famous for its design for Berlin's Holocaust Museum. As announced in early 2003, the plan called for five new skyscrapers to rise in a spiral culminating in a proposed 1,776 ft (541 m) high Freedom Tower at the northwest corner of the site; a two-square-block park to the south, bounded by Liberty, Greenwich, Cedar, and West Sts; and a museum and below-ground memorial area incorporating parts of the now exposed foundation walls of the WTC. At the same time, however, Larry Silverstein retained architect David Childs, of the firm of Skidmore, Owings and Merrill. Libeskind's concept has gradually evolved to meet Silverstein's requirements. Also planned are a new Fulton Street Transit Center and a new PATH terminal on the WTC site, the two connected via an underground concourse. In deference to a key demand of the victims' relatives, none of the new commercial development will rise over the footprints of the twin towers.

Much of the reconstruction project remains to be determined, including the identities of many of its designers. Spanish architect Santiago Calatrava has been selected to be the architect for the transportation hub, but the architects of the individual towers had not yet been chosen by December 2003. The competition for the memorial drew 5,201 entries. A 13-member jury in January 2004 chose Michael Arad, architect, to work with Peter Walker, landscape architect, and Daniel Libeskind, master planner for the LMDC. The memorial, called Reflecting Absence, includes twin voids that mark the location of the twin towers, with lush landscaping, and an underground center, reached by ramp, housing artifacts from the attack. *—AR*

REPERCUSSIONS

The shock waves of September 11th were felt not only in New York City but throughout the United States and the world. While it is still too soon to determine the lasting impact of the event on US and world history, some of its more immediate effects can be identified.

New York City suffered immense economic losses. Despite a federal antiterrorism insurance program, the cost and availability of insurance in Manhattan became problematic for many small and large businesses. Newly needed security measures placed great strain on public and private budgets. There was a drop in tourism. Companies began to question whether it might be safer and cheaper to move their offices out of Manhattan. Federal regulators pushed financial institutions to set up redundant facilities outside the city. But by the time of Mayor Michael Bloomberg's annual budget address in January 2004, in which he projected a \$1.4 billion surplus for fiscal year 2004–5, it appeared that the city's economy had begun to recover.

On the national level, Americans experienced a new sense of vulnerability. US airports were ordered to put new, more stringent security measures into place. Among the other responses of the federal government to the attacks were the creation of the cabinet-level Department of Homeland Security in October 2001, charged with coordinating the protection of the United States against future terrorist attacks, and the passage of the USA Patriot Act in the same month, which greatly expanded the powers of law enforcement to conduct searches and to access information about individuals. The law also allows suspects to be held for long periods of time without judicial review. Some observers worry that the Patriot Act violates the Constitution and that it may lead to the loss of civil liberties for both US citizens and immigrants. Immigration policies were also tightened: it became more difficult for people from countries with large Muslim populations to enter the United States, and more stringent review of visa status led to the deportation of many Muslims.

In July 2003 the Senate Select Committee on Intelligence and the House Permanent Select Committee on Intelligence released a report that found the Central Intelligence Agency (CIA), Federal Bureau of Investigation (FBI), and National Security Administration had not shared information with each other and therefore had missed important clues that planning for the attack was underway. The National Commission on Terrorist Attacks upon the United States (also known as the 9-11 Commission), an independent, bipartisan commission created by congressional legislation in late 2002, released its report in July 2004.

After September 11th, the United States government proclaimed that it would fight a "War on Terrorism." The first major campaign of this war, which began on 7 Oct 2001, was the invasion of Afghanistan, the main stronghold of the fundamentalist Al Qaeda movement. US forces quickly toppled Afghanistan's fundamentalist Taliban regime, but many members of Al Qaeda escaped. In early 2004 Al Qaeda leader Osama Bin Laden, believed to have been the mastermind of the September 11th attacks, was still at large.

The next theater in this war was Iraq. In the spring and summer of 2002, the US government intensified its arguments that the Ba'athist government of Saddam Hussein in Iraq presented a terrorist threat to the United States as well as an impediment to a stable Middle East by asserting the presence of weapons of mass destruction in Iraq, ties between Hussein and Al Qaeda, and the totalitarian nature of the Iraqi regime. In March 2003 the United States invaded Iraq, and within a month Hussein had been overthrown. The establishment of an American occupation government did not, however, end resistance, and by the end of 2003, 478 US soldiers had been killed in combat in Iraq. In the prelude to the invasion, the United States clashed bitterly over policy toward Iraq with the United Nations and some of its closest NATO allies, especially France and Germany. At the end of 2003, the future of Iraq and the Middle East, and the status of the NATO alliance and the United Nations were unclear. The destruction of the World Trade Center has already irrevocably altered the course of international politics, and September 11th will be remembered as a major watershed in world history. *—RN*

Gillespie, Angus Kress. *Twin Towers: The Life of New York City's World Trade Center* (1999; rev ed. New Brunswick, NJ: Rutgers Univ Press, 2001)

Glanz, James, and Lipton, Eric. *City in the Sky: The Rise and Fall of the World Trade Center* (New York: Times Books/Henry Holt, 2003)

Langewiesche, William. *American Ground: Unbuilding the World Trade Center* (2002; rev ed. New York: North Point Press, 2003)

Levitas, Mitchel et al. *A Nation Challenged: A Visual History of 9/11 and Its Aftermath* (New York: Times Books, 2002)

The 9/11 Commission Report: Final Report of the National Commission on Terrorist Attacks upon the United States (New York: Norton, 2004)

September 11: Bearing Witness to History, http://americanhistory.si.edu/september11/

September 11 Digital Archive, http://911digitalarchive.org/

Sonic Memorial Project, http://sonicmemorial.org

Roberta Newman, Anthony Robins, Robert W. Snyder

Serbians. Because of changing national boundaries in Europe during the 19th and 20th centuries, it is impossible to tell how many Serbians immigrated to the United States. Most came between 1880 and 1914 from Bosnia-Herzegovina, Croatia, Vojvodina, and Montenegro. In New York State they lived primarily in Manhattan on 9th and 10th Aves from 21st to 40th Sts and in the Buffalo area. Predominantly of peasant origin, they worked as industrial laborers trying to make enough money to better their lives in Europe. United Serbs, a fraternal aid organization, was established early on in New York City. During World War I, patriots formed Srpska Narodna Odbrana (Serbian National Defense) to recruit Serbians for military service in Europe and to raise funds for their support; relatively few of those who fought returned the United States. After World War II, highly educated refugees and displaced persons came from urban areas of Serbia proper to escape the restrictive Yugoslavian government of Josip Broz Tito. Many settled in New York City. A reported 2,687 Bosnian Serb refugees from the wars of the 1990s that tore apart the former Yugoslavia were resettled in the New York City area in 1998–99. The 2000 US census distinguished those born in Bosnia-Herzegovina from those born in Yugoslavia but did not include Serbian-born as a category; of the 25,688 New Yorkers enumerated as born in Yugoslavia an indeterminate but undoubtedly significant percentage are Serbian. New Yorkers claiming Yugoslavian ancestry numbered 30,519, and 4,997 claimed Serbian ancestry.

Orthodox Christian parishes provided the basis of religious and secular community life. In 2003 there were three Serbian parishes in the state: St. Sava Serbian Orthodox Cathedral on West 26th St in New York City, St. Stephen Church in Lackawanna (Erie Co), and St. Sava Serbian Orthodox Church in Scarsdale (Westchester Co). Important celebrations are St. Sava's Day (27 January), in honor of the founder of the Serbian Orthodox Church; St. Vitus's Day (28 June), commemorating the Battle of Kosovo in 1389; and for males the patron saint's day, called *slava.* Community institutions include the Belgrade Club in New York City, the radio station Drina Broadcasting–Voice of American Serbs in Ridgewood (Queens Co), and the Tesla Memorial Society in Lackawanna. Serbian Americans who rose to prominence in New York City include actors Karl Malden and John Malkovich, director Peter Bogdanovich, playwright Steve Tesich, poet Stephen Stepanchev, novelist and publisher William Jovanovich, and inventors Michael Pupin and Nikola Tesla. In 1976 the Serbian community dedicated a statue to Tesla at the Goat Island power station in Niagara Falls.

Gakovich, Robert P., and Milan M. Radovich. *Serbs in the United States and Canada: A Comprehensive Bibliography,* 2d ed. (St. Paul: Immigration History Research Center, Univ of Minnesota, 1992)

Kisslinger, Jerome. *The Serbian Americans* (New York: Chelsea House, 1990)

James S. Pula

Serling, Rod(man Edward) (*b* Syracuse, 25 Dec 1924; *d* Rochester, 28 June 1975). Television writer and producer. Serling earned a reputation as one of live television's "bright young men" with a remarkable string of socially conscious dramas and then became one of the medium's most recognizable writers as host and creator of the groundbreaking science fiction/fantasy series *The Twilight Zone.* He grew up in the small-town atmosphere of Binghamton, whose idyllic charms lingered in his imagination. After graduating from Antioch College in Yellow Springs, Ohio, Serling worked as a radio and television writer for a local station. He also began to freelance, selling scripts to such respected anthology series as *Hallmark Hall of Fame* and *Kraft Television Theatre.* In 1954 Serling moved his family to

Rod Serling, *ca* 1960.

Westport, Conn, to be closer to New York City, the network center of live production. He set an unofficial record by writing more than 20 teleplays in 1955, including his classic exploration of corporate competitiveness in the Big City, "Patterns," a film version of which was released the following year. Serling contributed a number of provocative dramas to the California-based series *Playhouse 90,* including "Requiem for a Heavyweight" (1956) and "The Comedian" (1957). With television production moving west, Serling relocated to the Los Angeles area in 1957. There he also became more active in the motion picture industry. *Requiem for a Heavyweight* became a movie in 1962, and Serling went on to write screenplays for such films as *Seven Days in May* (1964), *Assault on a Queen* (1966), *Planet of the Apes* (1968), and *The Man* (1972). Despite a busy Hollywood schedule he relished spending summers around Cayuga Lake.

Often at odds with the networks and sponsors about political themes in his live work, Serling created a filmed anthology series, *The Twilight Zone* (1959–64), whose eerie and fantastic story concepts allowed him to write without censorship. In addition to hosting and serving as executive producer, Serling wrote more than 90 episodes, bringing an unsettling reality and social concern to his uncanny worlds. Several episodes, including "Walking Distance" (1959) and "A Stop at Willoughby" (1960), were personal ruminations on his upstate childhood. Serling's later series, *The Loner* (1965–66) and *Night Gallery* (1970–73), did not achieve the popularity of *The Twilight Zone.* He served as president of the National Academy of Television Arts and Sciences (1965–66), exhorting the industry to strive for excellence. In the 1970s he taught dramatic writing at Ithaca College, living part of the year in nearby Interlaken (Seneca Co). Serling suffered a heart attack while working in his garden and died two months later during heart surgery at a Rochester hospital. He is remembered for his tremendous creativity and social conscience, which vitalized television storytelling for more than two decades.

Engel, Joel. *Rod Serling: The Dreams and Nightmares of Life in the Twilight Zone* (Chicago: Contemporary Books, 1989)

Sander, Gordon F. *Serling: The Rise and Twilight of Television's Last Angry Man* (New York: Dutton, 1992)

Ron Simon

Setauket {East Setauket, locality (pop 13,069) in Brookhaven, Suffolk Co; Setauket, locality (pop 2,862) in Brookhaven}. The area, on Long Island Sound, was bought from the Setalcott Indians in

Eel Spearing at Setauket, by William Sidney Mount, 1845.

1655, and a mill was built in 1668. Setauket was a headquarters for American spies from 1778 to 1783. Coastal shipping and shipbuilding (1820–79) were important trades at East Setauket's protected harbor. Piano manufacture began in 1839, and the best-known factory was Robert Nunns and Sons Co (1861–67). A series of rubber factories (1876–*ca* 1920) employed up to 500 workers, many of them Russian and Hungarian Jews. Suburban development, some by the Levitt organization, began in 1964. Setauket is the site of Caroline Church (1729, Episcopal) and of the rebuilt millpond and dam (1936). The Setaukets are considered part of the Three Village area.

Beverly C. Tyler

Seton [née Bayley], **Elizabeth Ann** (*b* ?New York City, 28 Aug 1774; *d* Emmitsburg, Md, 4 Jan 1821). Roman Catholic saint. The second daughter of Dr Richard Bayley and Catherine Charlton Bayley, she was raised Episcopalian. In 1794 she married the merchant William Magee Seton. In the first years of marriage, Elizabeth and William were socially prominent in New York City society, and they soon had five children. William Seton's virulent tuberculosis led them to sail to Italy in an effort to restore his health, but he died in Pisa in 1803. While in Italy, Elizabeth received consolation and support from the Filicchis, a devout Roman Catholic family. Impressed by their faith she began to consider conversion after returning to New York City. When she decided to convert to Catholicism, she consulted with her spiritual advisor and friend Episcopal priest John Henry Hobart, who vehemently tried to dissuade her from converting. This led to nine agonizing months of reading and praying, but in March 1805 she made her profession of faith at St. Peter's Church in Lower Manhattan. Because of anti-Catholic attitudes prevalent in New York City's high society, she faced social, economic, and religious rejection from many friends and family members. In 1808 she accepted an invitation to begin a girls school in Baltimore, and the women who joined her became the nucleus of the Sisters of Charity of Saint Joseph's, organized in Emmitsburg on 31 July 1809. Elizabeth was named first superior and held that position until her death. When Pope Paul VI canonized Elizabeth Seton on 14 Sept 1975, she became the first American-born saint of the Roman Catholic Church.

Seton, Elizabeth Bayley. *Collected Writings,* 3 vols, ed. Regina Bechtle and Judith Metz (Hyde Park, NY: New City Press, 2000–)

Kathleen Flanagan

Elizabeth Ann Bayley Seton, print by Charles B. J. Févret de Saint-Mémin, 1797.

settlement houses. In late 19th-century England, a few wealthy, educated young men took up residence in urban slums. They wanted to uplift the people living there, not by dispensing charity but by conveying middle-class customs and ideals in a neighborly way. The first settlement house was Toynbee Hall, opened in London in 1884. Early settlement workers were animated by a cluster of religiously inspired social ethics later termed the Social Gospel. The novelty of the settlement house idea was its attempt at nonsectarianism; this distinguished it from religious mission houses.

The first US settlement was Neighborhood Guild (renamed University Settlement in 1891) founded on Forsyth St on the Lower East Side in 1886 by a young philosophy student, Stanton Coit after his short residence at Toynbee Hall. College Settlement on the Lower East Side's Rivington St, launched by seven Smith College women in 1889, was probably the nation's second. Upper Manhattan's East Side House opened in 1891, and Henry Street Settlement on the Lower East Side, the nurses' settlement made famous by pioneering public health worker Lillian D. Wald, began in 1893. By 1910 there were 413 settlement houses in the United States; New York State had the largest number, 119, with 3 in Albany, 8 in Buffalo, 2 in Rochester, 1 in Syracuse, 1 in Yonkers, and about 66 in New York City. Houses in Central, Northern, and Western New York were more likely to have forthright religious connections, such as Buffalo's Jewish-affiliated Zion House (1893), Unitarian-affiliated Neighborhood House (1902), and Episcopalian-affiliated Watson House (1902), and Syracuse's Jewish-affiliated Marshall Memorial Home (1907). Other notable settlements included Social Settlement of Rochester (1901); Elmira's Women's Federation (1908); Hoosick Falls's (Rensselaer Co) Neighborhood House (1908); Buffalo's Colored Social Center (1910), operated by an integrated board; and Erie Co's Lackawanna Settlement, founded in 1910 with the support of steel industry officers. Through the 1930s settlement houses were supported by wealthy individuals—in 1913 one supporter quipped that it cost $5,000 to sit next to Lillian Wald at dinner—and by small fees for services.

Unlike in England, where a settlement's neighbors were poor but for the most part native citizens, settlements in the United States served immigrants of different races, languages, and cultures, many of whom were new both to life in a democratic society and to life in an urban setting. They lived and worked in appalling conditions, which were famously documented in photojournalist Jacob Riis's *How the Other Half Lives* (1890) and in settlement worker Robert Hunter's *Poverty* (1904).

Social Action

Settlements attempted to fill many social welfare needs. They provided public baths, clubs of many kinds, literacy programs, childcare, gyms and playgrounds, children's summer camps, health programs, penny savings banks, libraries, theaters, concerts and music programs, pure milk dispensaries to prevent typhoid, and whatever else might help a particular neighborhood. Numbers of upper-class women, including debutante Eleanor Roosevelt, volunteered as settlement workers. These workers often believed that if society as a whole knew of slum conditions, society would create remedies and conciliation across class lines. Thus they investigated, marshaled statistics, wrote and published reports, testified before commissions and boards, and rallied support for reform positions and candidates. The settlement workers were reformers of the Progressive movement, but they often addressed issues in a slightly different way from other Progressives; the workers spoke from firsthand knowledge of social distress, and their focus was always the neighborhood.

Professionalization

Settlement houses promoted the professionalization of the social sciences, of social work, and of nursing. Investigation and data gathering—such as Union Settlement's 1895 census of its neighborhood's people, saloons, factories, churches, and schools—provided the raw materials and the credibility for the emerging discipline of sociology. Data on working conditions collected by Florence Kelley while a resident at Henry Street supported Boston attorney Louis Brandeis's brief in favor of a maximum hours law in *Muller v Oregon* (1908). Another famous survey was NAACP founder Mary White Ovington's of African Americans, begun while she was a resident at Greenwich House on Jones St in Manhattan in 1904 and published as *Half a Man* in 1911.

Settlement work, one of the few independent careers for late 19th- and early 20th-century college women, was closely associated with the beginnings of professional social work. As women flocked to settlement work, they needed training, performance standards, and certification. The precursor to Columbia University's School of Social Work began in 1898, and a placement service that opened in New York City in 1911 would become the American Association of Social Workers in 1921.

Wald's nursing cadre at Henry Street (92 nurses by 1913) established the profession of public health nurse and paid for the first public school nurses. As they combated poor nutrition and hygiene, along with the scourges of typhoid, tuberculosis, cholera, pneumonia, whooping cough, and measles, they showed New York City's Health Department the way toward needed reforms.

Transformation

The years from the Progressive Party's campaign for the presidency in 1912 through World War I (1914–19) are often cited as the height of the settlement era. Thereafter, settlement work was transformed for a number of reasons. In some cases, municipalities began to assume more services. By the 1920s, for instance, College Settlement's neighborhood had a Carnegie library, a public bath, two public parks, and a Penny Provident Bank. Also, beginning in 1917, restrictive immigration laws stemmed the tide of immigrants. At the same time, Freudian theory burst on the social science scene, causing social workers to turn from neighborhood problems and a concern with community relations to problems of individual adjustment; they began to address target populations through casework. During the 1920s and 1930s, the first generation of resourceful, socially connected settlement leaders retired, and the new leaders no longer lived in the settlements. Community Chest funds, drawn from private gifts but communally pooled, replaced individual donors, and uniform standards replaced buoyantly hopeful trial programs.

In the 1940s urban renewal often meant loss of the settlement house or its removal to rooms in a high-rise project, with its program often tilted toward a specific purpose, such as managing a federal grant to combat juvenile delinquency. When southern Blacks moved into settlement neighborhoods in large numbers during the 1940s and 1950s, white settlement workers could do little to resolve the chief social problems facing the new population: de facto school segregation and job discrimination. In the 1960s Pres Lyndon Johnson's War on Poverty demanded "maximum feasible participation" of community members in new federally funded social programs, bringing numbers of African Americans into professional social work positions. This definitively changed ideals of community leadership, in the words of one scholar, from "mother power to civil rights."

Descendants of the settlement idea in New York State are called community centers or neighborhood houses. While numbers of organizations maintain community centers of widely ranging types, in 2003 the United Neighborhood Centers of America (prior to 1979, National Federation of Settlements and Neighborhood Houses) listed 36 centers in New York City, 3 in Syracuse, 2 in Rochester, and 1 in Ballston Spa (Saratoga Co). Programs continue to be valuable, extending aid primarily through educational, cultural, and recreational activities for children, young adults, and the older population.

Barbuto, Domenica M. *American Settlement Houses and Progressive Social Reform: An Encyclopedia of the American Settlement Movement* (Phoenix: Oryx Press, 1999)

Fabricant, Michael, and Robert Fisher. *Settlement Houses under Siege: The Struggle to Sustain Community Organizations in New York City* (New York: Columbia Univ Press, 2002)

Lasch-Quinn, Elisabeth. *Black Neighbors: Race and the Limits of Reform in the American Settlement House Movement, 1890–1945* (Chapel Hill: Univ of North Carolina Press, 1993)

Trolander, Judith A. *Professionalism and Social Change: From The Settlement House Movement to Neighborhood Centers, 1886 to the Present* (New York: Columbia Univ Press, 1987)

Janice K. Dunham

Seven Years War. See French and Indian war.

sewage. See Sanitation and sewage.

Seward. Town (pop 1,637) in NW Schoharie Co. Settled by Palatines in 1754 as part of New Dorlach, Seward was formed from Sharon in 1840 as a result of Whig gerrymandering and named for the state's governor. Seward had railroad service from 1870 to 1956 on the Sharon Springs branch of the Delaware and Hudson Railroad. Since the early 19th century the soils on this hilly upland have supported general farming, hops production, dairying, and, since the late 1980s, some organic vegetable farming; in 2003 most residents are still directly engaged in agriculture.

Peter Johnson and Dawn Johnson

Seward, William H(enry) (*b* Florida, Orange Co, 16 May 1801; *d* Auburn, Cayuga Co, 10 Oct 1872). Governor, US senator, and US secretary of state. The fourth of six children, Seward attended academies in Florida and Goshen (Orange Co) before graduating from Union College in Schenectady in 1820. After studying law in Goshen and New York City, he joined Judge Elijah Miller's legal practice in Auburn in 1823 and married the judge's daughter, Frances, a year later; four of their five children lived to adulthood. On a trip through Rochester in 1824, Seward met Thurlow Weed, who became a lifelong friend and political booster. With Weed's political backing, Seward won election as an Antimasonic Party state senator in 1830. As the influence of the Antimasons waned, Seward and Weed helped build the state's Whig Party, which ran Seward as its gubernatorial candidate in 1834. Unsuccessful, Seward served as an arbitrator/land agent in Westfield (Chautauqua Co) for the Holland Land Co before running for governor again. He won election as the state's first Whig Party governor in 1838.

While governor, Seward found himself split between enforcing the law and supporting policies he opposed. During the "Helderberg War" of 1839, Seward, though sympathetic to the antirent cause, used the state militia to enforce foreclosure notices at the same time he advocated legislative relief for the aggrieved farmers. Like most Whigs, Seward supported infrastructure growth. His policy of bond financing for canal and railway improvements was a controversial departure from that of his predecessors, who had used surplus canal profits for improvement initiatives. He promoted education, prison reform, and temperance, and refused to honor requests from the southern states for the extradition of fugitive slaves and those who assisted them. After winning reelection in 1840, Seward proposed spending public monies for immigrant schools, a move embraced by the Catholic diocese of New York City, which sought a parochial school system, but derided by the state's nativists. At the end of his second gubernatorial term in 1842, Seward returned to the practice of law. In 1846 he represented William Freeman, an Auburn resident of black and American Indian descent accused of murder, arguing that Freeman's insanity should exculpate his actions. Although the insanity defense failed to sway the jury, Seward's defense was reprinted and widely circulated by capital punishment reform groups.

Daguerreotype of William H. Seward, *ca* 1852.

In 1849 the Whig-dominated legislature elected Seward to the US Senate, where he established himself as a leader in the national antislavery movement. During debates on the Compromise of 1850, Seward argued in favor of California's admission to the Union but against the Fugitive Slave Act. He chided his proslavery listeners that there was a "higher law" than the Constitution. Seward argued against the 1854 Kansas-Nebraska Act, fearing that it would inflame sectional tensions, and, in an 1858 speech in Rochester, predicted that the disparities between a slave economy and one based on free labor could only result in an "irrepressible conflict." He and Frances befriended Harriet Tubman, settling her on land in Auburn in 1859, and used their home as a safe house on the Underground Railroad.

By 1860 Seward, by then a Republican, was considered one of the front-running candidates for the party's presidential nomination. His antislavery activism, however, proved too controversial. Convention delegates sought a more moderate candidate and chose Abraham Lincoln. Although disappointed, Seward accepted the secretary of state's position within Lincoln's cabinet. Seward attempted to negotiate a peaceful end to the siege of Fort Sumter and defused the uproar over the *Trent* Affair. In 1862 he advised the president on the proper time to announce the Emancipation Proclamation, and he wrote the 1863 presidential proclamation establishing a formal Thanksgiving Day. On 14 Apr 1865, the night of Lincoln's assassination, Seward was brutally stabbed in his Washington, DC, home by Lewis Powell, an accomplice of John Wilkes Booth.

Although savaged by fellow Republicans for supporting Pres Andrew Johnson, Seward returned to the State Department after his recovery and concentrated on foreign affairs. In 1866 he pushed Napoleon III to withdraw French support of Maximilian of Mexico. He negotiated with Denmark to purchase the Virgin Islands in 1867, only to see the treaty rejected by the Senate. Seward annexed Midway Island in 1867 and attempted unsuccessful negotiations with Spain for Santo Domingo and Haiti in 1869. On 30 Mar 1867 he negotiated a treaty with Russia for the purchase of the Alaska Territory for $7.2 million; Radical Republican and Democratic press dubbed the purchase "Seward's Folly." Retiring from the State Department in 1869, Seward began to travel. He visited California and Alaska in 1869 and completed a world tour from July 1870 to April 1872. Following his return to Auburn, he contracted pneumonia and died. His Auburn home, named a National Historic Landmark in 1964, is a museum.

See also Civil war.

Seward, Frederick William, and William Henry Seward. *Seward at Washington as Senator and Secretary of State. A Memoir of His Life with Selections from His Letters, 1846–1872*, 2 vols (New York: Derby & Miller, 1891)

Seward, William Henry, and Frederick William Seward. *William H. Seward: An Autobiography from 1801 to 1834. With a Memoir of His Life, and Selections from His Letters* (1877; repr New York: Derby & Miller, 1891)
Taylor, John M. *William Henry Seward: Lincoln's Right Hand* (New York: Harper Collins, 1991)
Van Deusen, Glyndon G. *William Henry Seward* (New York: Oxford Univ Press, 1967)

Peter A. Wisbey

sexually transmitted disease (STD). Before the 20th century public and health professionals considered venereal disease—sexually transmitted illnesses such as gonorrhea and syphilis—as a moral problem, not as a health problem, and little was done to prevent transmission. The connection between venereal disease and prostitution exacerbated this neglect. During the mid–19th century the most common place for treatment was New York City's Penitentiary Hospital, which treated venereal disease at an increasing rate in the later 1800s. The Metropolitan Board of Health began registering prostitutes and brothels and examining prostitutes for disease in 1867. Examinations for prostitutes became mandatory with the 1910 Inferior Courts Act (Page Law). Although this requirement was ruled unconstitutional the following year, many women arrested for prostitution continued to be examined for venereal disease. During the Progressive era New York City participated in antivice campaigns as part of a broader national program of social hygiene; the campaigns had minimal success because of their emphasis on public morality. During the 1920s the state experienced a steady rise in the number of cases of venereal disease: the New York State Department of Health counted 145,000 cases of venereal disease in the state, excluding New York City. In 1927 doctors treated 12,936 cases of syphilis, and by 1930 the number rose to 15,732.

Responding to this increase, the state in the early 1930s became a pioneer of antivenereal policies and campaigns. The 1929 sanitary code required all health professionals to report syphilis and gonorrhea to local health authorities. Three years later the state provided free treatment for all infected people unable to pay. The 1931 Public Health Law also gave the state the right to force people suspected of infection to undergo examinations. Private activities also helped control the venereal disease problem in New York State, exemplified by the Milbank Memorial Fund's support for a 1930 public education campaign. Through the distribution of pamphlets to homes and public meetings and films, the campaign targeted 150,000 residents of New York City and spoke in frank, scientific language about the dangers of venereal disease. With the help of factories, schools, and the postal system, the campaign succeeded in reaching many people. The Milbank Memorial Fund supported a similar campaign in Syracuse.

In the early 20th century the cure for venereal diseases required a long period of sexual abstinence and numerous treatments. Treatment for syphilis by the drug Salvarsan could take years. During World War II, as in World War I, antivenereal disease programs were administered by the federal government and the army. Penicillin, first used to combat venereal disease in 1943, proved quick and effective, and its use largely solved for several decades New York State's venereal disease problem. But changes in the patterns of sexual activity among New Yorkers brought both a resurgence of the traditional STDs and the appearance of new diseases that could not be treated with antibiotics. (Beginning in the 1980s the term STDs commonly was used to refer to diseases transmittable through either sexual or nonsexual contact.) Acquired immune deficiency syndrome (AIDS) was first diagnosed in New York City in 1981. During the early years of the AIDS epidemic, about half of the cases in the United States were reported from New York State. While this percentage has since declined, in 2001 the state maintained the largest number of AIDS cases in the nation. Between 1980 and 2000 doctors diagnosed over 139,000 New Yorkers, mostly residents of New York City, with human immunodeficiency virus (HIV), the viral cause of AIDS. Older STDs also remained a problem statewide. In 2000, for example, the State Health Department recorded 8,445 cases of gonorrhea, including 4,062 cases in Buffalo and Rochester. To combat such diseases, the department provided STD screenings and confidential examinations, while laws required schools to provide information to children about abstinence and other methods of preventing STDs.

Brandt, Allan. *No Magic Bullet: A Social History of Venereal Disease in the United States since 1880* (New York: Oxford Univ Press, 1987)
Duffy, John. *A History of Public Health in New York City, 1625–1866* (New York: Russell Sage Foundation, 1968)
Gilfoyle, Timothy. *City of Eros: New York City, Prostitution, and the Commercialization of Sex, 1790–1880* (New York: Norton, 1992)

Evan Lampe

sex work. See PROSTITUTION.

Seymour, Horatio (*b* Pompey Hill, Onondaga Co, 31 May 1810; *d* Utica, 12 Feb 1886). Governor and presidential candidate. Educated at Geneva Academy (now Hobart College), Seymour studied law in Utica, was admitted to the bar in 1832, and moved to Albany in 1833. He served as mayor of Utica (1842) and served three terms in the state assembly (1841, 1844, 1845), as Speaker in his last term. Seymour returned to private life until an unsuccessful run for governor in 1850 and a successful one in 1852. A conservative Democrat, Seymour, as governor, strongly opposed nativism and vetoed a prohibition bill, leading to his defeat for reelection in 1854, after which he moved to a farm in Deerfield (Oneida Co). He advocated popular sovereignty as a solution to the slavery question in the 1850s and gave only lukewarm support to the northern war effort.

Reelected governor in 1862, Seymour became an outspoken critic of the Lincoln administration, questioning the constitutionality of the Emancipation Proclamation and the wartime limits on press freedom and other civil liberties. He supported voluntary enlistments but opposed federal conscription as a violation of states' rights. His speech after the draft riots of July 1863, in which he addressed the rioters as "my friends," was widely viewed as tantamount to treason and led to his defeat in 1864. After the war Seymour supported Andrew Johnson's administration and opposed what he perceived as the excesses of the radical Republicans. In 1868 a deadlocked Democratic National Convention in New York City nominated Seymour as a compromise candidate. He ran an energetic campaign against Reconstruction. In many places the Democratic Party ran on a platform of what was very nearly white supremacy. Despite carrying New York State and drawing 47% of the popular vote, Seymour won only 80 electoral votes. After the defeat he became an elder Democratic Party statesman.

See also CIVIL WAR.

Mitchell, Stewart. *Horatio Seymour of New York* (Cambridge, Mass: Harvard Univ Press, 1938)
Silbey, Joel. *A Respectable Minority: The Democratic Party in the Civil War Era, 1860–1868* (New York: Norton, 1977)

Jon Sterngass

Shakers. This religious community, transplanted to America under the leadership of the English prophet Ann Lee, has a history centered in New York State. Lee and a handful of followers left England and arrived in New York City in 1774. Several years later these religious sectarians emerged from obscurity and relocated to Niskayuna [now Watervliet, Albany Co], where they established a communal society under the direction of Lee. Members, sometimes called Shaking Quakers because they often shook during worship, shared their resources and accepted the practice of celibacy based on Lee's teachings. These early Shakers encountered opposition from neighbors because, as pacifists, they refused to support the American Revolution. Nevertheless between 1780 and 1784 the young society successfully attracted hundreds of American converts in eastern New York State and throughout New England. In the decades following the death of Lee in 1784, these Believers, as they called themselves, gathered into local communities. In New York State the Shakers organized villages at Watervliet and New Lebanon (Columbia Co).

The Watervliet village enjoyed special status among the Believers because of its close association with Lee, who was buried there. In 1790 the federal census reported 54 Shakers resident there; the number peaked at 304 in 1840. The Watervliet community occupied more than 2,500 acres (1,000 ha) on which they pursued a variety of agricultural activities. The New Lebanon village, however, assumed increasing prominence because it became the headquarters of the society's leaders, known as the Central Ministry. Joseph Meacham and Lucy Wright, two of the first American converts, directed the Shakers from this location between 1787 and 1821. New Lebanon also quickly surpassed Watervliet in size and importance. The federal census reported 221 Believers in 1790 and 550 in 1860. In 1805 the Central Ministry sent missionaries into the Ohio Valley to spread the Shaker gospel. Believers at the New York State villages and other eastern locations supplied an immense amount of resources—personnel, capital, provisions, livestock, and other movable goods—in support of the western initiative. New Lebanon also provided the communal model for other villages. The community was divided into multiple "families," each with elders and eldresses. Believers followed a distinctive way of life, including the rejection of marriage, sexual relations, and traditional family arrangements. The notion of spiritual brotherhood and sisterhood accompanied the commitment to celibacy.

Written regulations known as the Millennial Laws governed virtually all aspects of public and private life in the community.

Western New York, a region that experienced repeated evangelical revivals during the opening decades of the 19th century, was the site of a third Shaker community in the state. The opening of the Erie Canal in 1825 brought commerce, exchange, and prosperity to the region. The Believers used the canal to travel between eastern and western villages. Word of the Shaker gospel spread among the residents of the region, including members of the Pelham family living near Lyons (Wayne Co). Awakened religiously in the revivals, they asked for instruction from the society. Believers from the east came to assist them, and in 1826 a new village was established at Sodus (Wayne Co). Ten years later that community, which was never large, sold its 1,450 acres (587 ha) of land and moved near Sonyea (Livingston Co), establishing the Groveland community.

The economic success enjoyed by the society in the pre–Civil War years was the result of a vigorous work ethic. Ann Lee reportedly urged "hands to work, hearts to God"; all members were to be productive. The Shakers gained a reputation for their agricultural products and manufactured goods. Watervliet, for example, sold seeds, herbs, and domestic products, such as bonnets. New Lebanon marketed seeds, herbal extracts, medicinal products, chairs, and carpet. Groveland raised and processed grains. Economic success brought advantages but also such perils as misuse of funds, bad investments, and poor economic decisions about the use of resources. The first half of the 19th century was also a period when Shaker religious art was thriving. The artistic expressions of the Believers arose from their religious life and experience. Dances and marches in worship meetings attracted both curiosity and condemnation from outsiders. During the 1830s and 1840s the society experienced an outpouring of extraordinary spiritual gifts, often received in the context of ecstasy, resulting in drawings that depicted Shaker values and traditions, including the ideal of simplicity and the continuing spiritual presence of Ann Lee, known fondly as Mother Ann. New songs and visionary revelations also abounded. This period of heightened religious activity began in 1837 among young females at Watervliet and spread throughout the society.

By the Civil War, evidence of the society's numerical decline was mounting. The 1870 federal census reported 196 Believers at Watervliet and 348 at New Lebanon, a Shaker village known as Mount Lebanon since 1861. Decline was even more striking at Groveland, where only 41 Believers remained in 1880; when that community disbanded in 1895, the remaining Shakers moved to Watervliet. Despite this downturn the leadership at Mount Lebanon's North Family, including Frederick Evans and Antoinette Doolittle, gained national prominence for participation in progressive causes, including women's rights and the peace movement. In the 20th century the pattern of retreat and closings accelerated throughout the society. Local villages experienced economic problems exacerbated by the failure to attract new converts, by declining numbers of males, and by the general aging of the society. In 1938 the South Family, the last family at Watervliet, dissolved, and the remaining Believers moved to Mount Lebanon. Finally Mount Lebanon succumbed to these forces, and in 1947 that community also closed, the last sisters moving to Hancock, Mass, one of three remaining Shaker villages at the time. It is estimated that Mount Lebanon had been home to more than 3,200 Shakers during its 160 years of existence. The legacy of the Shakers is visually evident in New York State today at two historic sites and several museums. The Shaker Heritage Society occupies part of the Watervliet site in Albany. Mount Lebanon Shaker Village maintains a portion of the former community as a museum. The Shaker Museum and Library in Old Chatham (Columbia Co) and the New York State Museum in Albany possess outstanding collections of Shaker material culture.

See also FOLK ART.

Andrews, Edward Deming. *The People Called Shakers: A Search for the Perfect Society,* 2d ed. (New York: Dover Publications, 1963)

Brewer, Priscilla J. *Shaker Communities, Shaker Lives* (Hanover, NH: Univ Press of New England, 1986)

Kirk, John T. *The Shaker World: Art, Life, Belief* (New York: Abrams, 1997)

Richmond, Mary L. *Shaker Literature: A Bibliography,* 2 vols (Hanover, NH: Univ Press of New England, 1977)

Stein, Stephen J. *The Shaker Experience in America: A History of the United Society of Believers* (New Haven, Conn: Yale Univ Press, 1992)

Stephen J. Stein

Shandaken. Town (pop 3,235) in NW Ulster Co. Settled in the 1770s and the site of Fort Shandaken (1779–83), the town was formed in 1804 from Woodstock. Lumbering, tanning, charcoal burning, and shingle making were livelihoods before the railroad; tourism began early, with the Mountain Inn (1848–1903) at Pine Hill. A company town, Chichester, was centered around a chair factory (?1863–84), which was succeeded by the Schwarzwaelder office furniture factory (1893–1939). At one time, 500 workers wove cane chair seats at home, and a pillbox factory and pulp mill operated at Mount Pleasant. The Ulster and Delaware Railroad (1870–1976) made the shipment of quarried stone feasible and opened up its line for summer resorts, especially the huge Grand Hotel (1881–1960s) at Highmount. The Stony Clove Railroad (1881–1940) connected the line with Greene Co resorts to the north. The Phoenicia Ski Center (1935–79) inaugurated a winter tourist season and was joined by the Highmount Ski Center (1947–94) and Belleayre Mountain State Ski Center (1949). More recently, tubing on Esopus Creek has become popular. Oliverea is a German resort, and the Big Indian Mountain Club (1934) is a private park with 28 cottages. The Catskill Mountain Railroad (excursions) and the Empire State Railway Museum are attractions.

Ruth Piwonka

Shanker, Albert (*b* New York City, 14 Sept 1928; *d* New York City, 22 Feb 1997). Labor leader. The son of staunch trade unionists, Shanker was raised in the Long Island City section of Queens and educated in public schools, at the University of Illinois, and at Columbia University. While teaching mathematics in New York City high schools between 1952 and 1959, he became active in the democratic socialist and teachers unionization movements. In 1960 Shanker helped bring together over 75 of the city's teacher representation organizations to form the United Federation of Teachers (UFT). The UFT won a collective bargaining representation election in 1961 and signed its first contract with the New York City Board of Education in 1962. Elected UFT president in 1964, Shanker led strikes for higher wages and reduced class size in 1967 and for teacher due process rights during the racially divisive 1968 Ocean Hill–Brownsville controversy. In an effort to create a statewide union of teachers, in 1971 Shanker became the first president of the United Teachers of New York, which merged with the New York

SHAKERS near LEBANON state of N YORK.
their mode of Worship.

Several rows of Shakers performing a step dance in the meeting hall at New Lebanon Community, *ca* 1830.

State Teachers Association (NYSTA) in 1972 to become the New York Congress of Teachers, renamed New York State United Teachers in 1973. Thomas Y. Hobart Jr and Shanker were the first co-presidents. From 1974 onward he served as president of the American Federation of Teachers (AFT). Though he worked primarily in the AFT headquarters in Washington, DC, Shanker maintained homes in Mamaroneck (Westchester Co) and New York City. During the 1980s and 1990s he called for higher standards and accountability for both teachers and students. Shanker was one of the labor movement's most prominent spokesmen, and the AFT placed his "Where We Stand" column in each Sunday's *New York Times* from 1970 to 1997.

Taft, Philip. *United They Teach: The Story of the United Federation of Teachers* (Los Angeles: Nash, 1974)

Jerald E. Podair

sharecroppers. See TENANT FARMING AND SHARECROPPERS.

Sharon. Town (pop 1,843) in NW Schoharie Co. First settled in 1754 by Palatines as part of New Dorlach, area settlement continued after the Revolution with people from nearby valleys and the New England states. Formed from Cherry Valley (Otsego Co) as Dorlach in 1792, it was annexed to the town and county of Schoharie in 1795, and formed again as a town in 1797. It lies on a large limestone ridge overlooking the Mohawk Valley and has good soils, conducive to general and specialty farming. The First Great Western Turnpike (now US 20) and the Lunenburg Turnpike (now Rte 145) met at Sharon hamlet by 1811, bringing travelers and goods through town. Sharon Springs began developing as a spa in 1825. Throughout the 19th century, town farmers cultivated hops as their principal cash crop. A branch of the Delaware and Hudson Railroad provided rail service in 1870. The Wal-Mart Distribution Center, the town's largest employer, opened in 1995. Much of the land is still agricultural.

Peter Johnson and Dawn Johnson

Sharon Springs. Village (pop 547) in Sharon (Schoharie Co). In 1825 David Eldredge opened the area's first boardinghouse; in 1835 New York City merchants bought the property and built the Pavilion Hotel, with a spectacular view of the Mohawk Valley. H. J. Bangs purchased the Magnesia Spring and built Congress Hall (1860) to rival the Pavilion and the Magnesia Temple (1863), an exquisite ironwork Renaissance Revival springhouse. Sharon Springs acquired rail service in 1870, and the village was incorporated in 1871 but by the 1880s was quiet enough to be termed the "invalid's resort." Its prime market shifted to German Jews beginning in the 1890s, and by World War I, boarders were mostly Jews from eastern and central Europe. The 150-room Hotel Adler was built in 1929, but business was affected by the depression and the end of rail passenger service in 1933. The Pavilion Hotel was taken down in 1941. Although demand made 1946 the resort's biggest year ever, activity declined afterward except for a new audience of Holocaust survivors. The Thruway (1954) superseded US 20 as New York State's main east-west highway, cutting business even more. In the late 1950s the village as a resort was especially popular among Brooklyn's Satmar Hasidim. Natural and arson fires took many of the old hotels, but a revival began in the 1990s. The Roseboro Hotel, closed in 1968, is slowly being renovated, and the American Hotel reopened in 2001.

Blumin, Stuart, and Hansi Durlach. *The Short Season of Sharon Springs: Portrait of Another New York* (Ithaca: Cornell Univ Press, 1980)

Sharpton, Al(fred Charles), Jr (*b* 3 Oct 1954, Brooklyn). Minister and activist. During his youth Sharpton preached in churches in Brooklyn and Queens. Ordained a Pentecostal minister at age 10, he preached with ministers in Buffalo, in the Hudson River valley, and on Long Island. While attending Tilden High School, Sharpton became youth director for the New York branch of the Southern Christian Leadership Conference's Operation Breadbasket (1969). In 1971 he founded the National Youth Movement (now United African Movement) and served as president until 1986. Sharpton came to wide attention in the 1980s as a vociferous advocate for African American causes. In 1984 he led protests against Bernhard Goetz, a white man who shot four black teenagers on a Manhattan subway, and in 1986 he led a march after racial violence in Howard Beach in Queens. The Tawana Brawley case was the most controversial episode of his career. In 1987 the Wappingers Falls (Dutchess Co) black teenager accused several white men, including local police officers, of attacking her. Sharpton and his colleagues led an incendiary campaign against New York State officials. Many believe Brawley's accusations were fabricated. Sharpton also led protests against police who brutalized Haitian immigrant Abner Louima (1997) and against police who killed unarmed Ghanaian immigrant Amadou Diallo (1999). In 1991 he founded and became president of the National Action Network. He has unsuccessfully sought elective office, running for the US Senate (1992, 1994), for mayor of New York City (1997), and in the Democratic presidential primary (2004). He has been a major, and polarizing, force in New York City politics for more than 20 years.

Sharpton, Al, and Anthony Walton. *Go and Tell Pharaoh: The Autobiography of Al Sharpton* (New York: Doubleday, 1996)

Graham Russell Hodges

Shavelson, Clara Lemlich (*b* Gorodok, Ukraine, 1886; *d* Los Angeles, 25 July 1982). Labor and community activist and feminist. The daughter of Orthodox Jewish parents, Lemlich's family fled the pogroms in 1903 for England. At 15, she arrived with her family in New York City and found work in the garment industry. In 1906, she joined Local 25 of the International Ladies' Garment Workers' Union. She is best remembered as inspiring a massive strike in the ladies' shirtwaist trades of New York City with a speech to garment workers at Cooper Union on 22 Nov 1909. The strike—the "Uprising of 20,000"—began the following day. This was the largest strike by women in the United States and marked a turning point for labor, especially for women workers. Fired after the strike, Lemlich worked in the suffrage movement and became active in the Socialist Party.

In 1913, she married Joseph Shavelson, a Socialist printer, and became a community organizer in her Brooklyn neighborhood. During the 1930s she was active in the antifascist, unemployment, and communist movements in Brooklyn. In 1944, after her husband's death, she returned to the garment shops. From 1944 until her death, she remained active in the Emma Lazarus League of the International Workers' Order and involved in women's rights, Jewish women's history, and world peace.

Scheier, Paula. "Clara Lemlich Shavelson: 50 Years in Labor's Front Line." In *The American Jewish Woman: A Documentary History*, ed. Jacob Marcus (New York: KTAV Publishing, 1981)

Richard A. Greenwald

Shawangunk [SHAWN-GUM]. Town (pop 12,022) in S Ulster Co. Settled by the Dutch between 1680 and 1700, Shawangunk was formed as a precinct in 1743 and recognized as a town in 1788. The town was served by the Wallkill Valley Railroad (1869). In the 19th century industries included a paper mill, an agricultural implement factory, a Borden Condensed Milk Co plant (1880), and the James B. Crowell and Son brick mold mill (1872). In the 20th century there was a men's hat factory (closed 1951), and the Borden plant was used by the General Slicing Machine Co (*ca* 1945). The wall-less Wallkill Correctional Facility (1932) farms 450 acres (182 ha), operates a highly productive prison optical program (1965), and a facility of the Thoroughbred Retirement Foundation (1984); the neighboring Shawangunk Correctional Facility (1985) is maximum security. In 2003 Fair-Rite Products (electrical components) employed 197. The Bruynswyck Reformed Church (1752–55) is a landmark.

Ruth Piwonka

Shawangunk Mountains. Part of the Appalachian mountain range in New York State extending from Rosendale (Ulster Co) southwest through Sullivan and Orange Cos to the Delaware River at Port Jervis (Orange Co), bracketed by the valleys of Rondout Creek and Wallkill River. These mountains, whose name probably derives from the Algonquin term for white rock, were created during the Taconic and Appalachian mountain-building episode about 280 million years ago. The base is composed largely of Martinsburg shale. Atop this base, which is as thick as 2,000 feet (609.6 m) in some places, sits the thinner Shawangunk conglomerate. This caprock is composed of fused quartz sand and pebbles and is highly resistant to erosion. The entire formation is folded and faulted and is dotted with fissures. In general the range slopes gently down in a southwest direction. Surfaces show evidence of glaciation, including the existence of wetlands, glacial debris, and five "sky lakes."

Geological differences divide the Shawangunk Mountains into two regions. The northern Shawangunks extend for 20 miles (32 km) from Rosendale to Ellenville (Ulster Co), and the southern Shawangunks stretch further south for 30 miles (48 km). The northern Shawangunks are wider and higher, with widths up to 6 miles (10 km) and elevations ranging from 1,000 feet (305 m) to more than 2,200 feet (671 m) above sea level. The northern region also features a more continuous caprock layer, which extends for miles as vertical white cliffs in northern

Ulster Co. These cliffs, known as the Gunks, are renowned for their rock-climbing opportunities. Soil and topographical variations in the Shawangunks make the mountains ecologically diverse. Pitch pine and various heath-type shrubs thrive at higher elevations, where soils are more acidic. At lower elevations, white oak, birch, maple, and hemlock trees flourish.

The diverse conditions supported different economic activities during the 18th and 19th centuries, including huckleberry and blueberry harvesting, conglomerate quarrying, and the harvesting of hemlock bark, hardwood for charcoal, and timber. Tourism is the primary industry in the Shawangunks in the 20th and 21st centuries. An 1859 inn at Paltz Point became the Mohonk Mountain House, which transformed into the region's most famous resort with the advent of Erie Railroad service to New Paltz (Ulster Co) in 1870. Lake Minnewaska Mountain House was created nearby in 1879 and destroyed by fire in 1978. Meanwhile, at Cragsmoor (Ulster Co), the first of three hotels was built in 1858, and a community developed around an art colony founded by E. L. Henry after he built a cottage there in 1882; it peaked between 1900 and 1935 but continues as a quiet cottage park. Most summer visitors to the region in 2002 lodged in Cragsmoor, although the Mohonk Mountain House was still open and the Shawangunks' best-known resort. Ice Caves Mountain, a commercial attraction opened in 1967, remained in operation in 2002.

Fried, Marc B. *Shawangunk: Adventure, Exploration, History, and Epiphany from a Mountain Wilderness* (Gardiner, NY: Author, 1998)

Karen Nichols

Shea, Jack [John A.] (*b* Lake Placid, Essex Co, 7 Sept 1910; *d* Lake Placid, 22 Jan 2002). Olympic speedskater. He started skating at age 3 and won his first international championship by age 10. He continued winning championships and setting records before attending Dartmouth in 1930. He competed in the 1932 Winter Olympics at Lake Placid, becoming the first athlete to win two Winter Olympic gold medals (1,500 and 500 meters). Favored to win speedskating events at the 1936 Olympics, Shea boycotted because of Hitler's anti-Semitism. The depression limited job opportunities, and he managed his family's stores. He later became justice of the peace, served from 1974 through 1982 as the supervisor of North Elba (Essex Co), and successfully lobbied to bring the Olympics back to Lake Placid in 1980. His son Jim became an Olympic skier in 1964. In 2002 his grandson Jim Jr became an Olympic skeleton sledder, making the Sheas the first three-generation Olympic family. One month before Jim Jr won a gold medal in the 2002 Winter Olympics, Jack Shea's car was hit by a drunk driver. Shea died the next day from internal injuries.

Dimeo, Sam. "Farewell to a Giant," *Plattsburgh Press-Republican,* 26 Mar 2002
"The Life of Jack Shea," *Plattsburgh Press-Republican,* 23 Mar 2002

George W. Garner

Sheen, Fulton J(ohn) (*b* El Paso, Ill, 8 May 1895; *d* New York City, 9 Dec 1979). Roman Catholic archbishop, author, and radio and television preacher. Sheen received a Thomistic education and was ordained in 1919. He attended Catholic University of America in Washington, DC, and the University of Louvain in Belgium; his dissertation was published as *God and Intelligence in Modern Philosophy* in 1925, the first of nearly 70 books.

After serving briefly as an assistant parish priest in Peoria, Ill, he taught theology and philosophy at the Catholic University of America from 1926 to 1950. He won a national reputation as a Catholic apologist and lecturer, most prominently as a regular Lenten preacher at St. Patrick's Cathedral in New York City from 1930 to 1952. In 1930 he was the featured speaker on the NBC radio network's *Catholic Hour Broadcasts.* He gradually gave up his academic career for his calling as an "intellectual popularizer," serving religion, education, and democracy, and crusading against communism and for social reform and justice. He broke down many walls of anti-Catholic prejudice, and his popularity and personal magnetism enabled him to convert several prominent figures, including Rep Clare Booth Luce and the former communist editor Louis Budenz.

He became a monsignor in 1934 and an auxiliary bishop of New York City in 1951. In 1950 he moved to New York City when he was appointed national director of the Society for the Propagation of the Faith. For the next 16 years, he raised millions of dollars for Catholic missions worldwide and wrote two syndicated newspaper columns, "Bishop Sheen Writes" and "God Loves You." He wrote two national best-sellers, *Peace of Soul* (1949) and *Life of Christ* (1958), and his television series *Life Is Worth Living* (1952–57) attracted an audience of over 30 million. Sheen won an Emmy Award in 1952 and appeared on the cover of *Time* magazine in 1954. In the aftermath of Vatican Council II, Sheen was appointed bishop of Rochester in 1966. Determined to implement the council's reforms, his stormy tenure was marked by controversy and innovation. He called for the withdrawal of US troops from Vietnam and focused attention on the plight of the poor in the inner city. In 1968 he donated a parish and its land for the construction of affordable housing but had to withdraw the offer amidst protests and bad publicity. He resigned in 1969 and spent his final decade writing and reflecting on his life. The greatest evangelizer in the history of the Catholic Church in the United States, Sheen sought to bridge the gap separating the church from the modern world. Bishop Sheen was buried in the crypt of St. Patrick's Cathedral.

Riley Fields, Kathleen. "Bishop Fulton J. Sheen: An American Catholic Response to the Twentieth Century" (PhD diss, Univ of Notre Dame, 1988)
Sheen, Fulton J. *Treasure in Clay: The Autobiography of Fulton J. Sheen* (Garden City, NY: Doubleday, 1980)

Kathleen L. Riley

sheep. During the colonial and early national period, New York farmers raised sheep for meat and wool, but until the early 1800s, sheep husbandry and breeding were haphazard. The embargos on British trade during Thomas Jefferson's presidency (1801–9), however, made domestic textile production a patriotic activity, with Horatio Gates Spafford's *Gazetteer of the State of New York* (1813) proudly noting that some state residents wore clothing entirely of their own making. With the import of several hundred pairs of merinos—noted for their fine, long, crimped wool—from the royal flock of Spain in the early 1800s, quarter- and half-crossings with generic American stock precipitated the merino craze of the late 1810s, 1820s, and 1830s. Through the 1830s the bulk of New York State's improved merino-mix wool was carded at local waterpowered mills before being spun, dyed, and woven into domestic textiles for blankets and coverlets at home. Even so, in 1832 New York State wool mills, located mainly in the Hudson River valley, wove 274,308 yards (250,827 m) of woolen broadcloth and 6,000 yards (5,486 m) of wool carpet. Some families continued to make yardage for clothing at home into the 1850s, although such yardage returned to mills to be blocked and texturized, a process known as fulling. In 1855 the state claimed 184 woolen factories, 13 of which were in Oneida Co. Sheep were also raised, mainly near cities, for meat; rural people regarded lamb as a summer meat, to be eaten when beef and pork were not available. Many New York State farmers continued to keep flocks of 20–100 sheep through the second quarter of the 19th century, but census statistics show a decline after an 1867 peak of 4 million statewide; at that time large-scale sheep raising moved to newly opened ranch lands in the West. But individual New York State farmers, many of whom were experimenting gentleman practitioners, continued to breed prize stock, mainly from British breeds. In 2001 the state population was 60,000 head, with 24,000 in Central and Western New York. That year 47,000 head were shorn, producing 320,000 pounds (145,150 kg) of wool, and 22,900 head were slaughtered commercially.

Bidwell, Percy, and John I. Falconer. *History of Agriculture of the Northern United States: 1620–1860* (Washington, DC: Carnegie Institute, 1925)
Schlebecker, John T. *Whereby We Thrive: A History of American Farming, 1607–1972* (Ames: Iowa State Univ Press, 1975)

Jessie Ravage

Shelby. Town (pop 5,420) in SW Orleans Co. Settled in 1810, it was formed in 1818 from Ridgeway and crossed by the short-lived Medina and Darien Railroad (1836–*ca* 1840). Shelby was the site of the first iron furnace, where plows were cast, west of the Genesee (1821–22). Later, in the 1870s, Gifford and Schermerhorn manufactured paper goods. The town's southwest is part of Tonawanda Swamp, the draining of which was first attempted in 1829. The swamp was incorporated into Iroquois National Wildlife Refuge in 1958. In the early 21st century, large farms and small home businesses occupy Shelby's residents.

Lou Fuller

Sheldon. Town (pop 2,561) in W Wyoming Co. Settled in 1804 along Big Tree Rd from the Genesee River to Lake Erie, the town was formed from Batavia (Genesee Co) in 1808. Germans began settling in 1823, forming the county's first Catholic Church in 1840. By 1850, 60 Belgians were living near Sheldon Center, and other residents came from France, Germany, and Luxembourg. The Strykersville Brewery operated from before 1861 until 1909, and shoe pegs and drain tile were manufactured in the late 19th century. The Marzolf Manufacturing Co in Strykersville patented an egg-washing machine in 1953.

Dairying remains important, while many residents commute to Rochester or Buffalo.

Shelter Island. Town (pop 2,228) in E Suffolk Co. The town consists of an irregularly shaped island (11.5 miles^2/29.8 km^2) of the same name, between the North and South Forks of Long Island and bounded by Gardiners Bay on the east and Shelter Island Sound on the south and west. Its numerous peninsulas create 45 miles (72 km) of coastline. Mashomack Preserve (owned by the Nature Conservancy since 1980) on the southeastern third of the island has a variety of ecosystems, including salt marshes, upland forests, and an unusual pine swamp. Four English merchants purchased the island in 1651 to provision their sugar plantation in Barbados, but Nathaniel Sylvester was the only one to settle on the island; he arrived in 1652 and became the sole proprietor in 1673. Most residents farmed or fished and raised sheep. Menhaden fish factories produced oil and fertilizer from 1850 to 1900. Resort development followed the Civil War. The Shelter Island Grove and Camp Meeting Association created a Methodist camp meeting ground [now Shelter Island Heights] in 1871–72, including the Prospect Hotel. The 1872–73 Manhanset House was across the harbor. In the early 21st century, the population is five times greater in the summer, and many summer residents retire to the island. Ferries connect to Greenport and to North Haven near Sag Harbor. Landmarks include the James Havens House (1743), a windmill (1810), and the Union Chapel (1875) in Shelter Island Heights.

Natalie A. Naylor

Shenandoah, Joanne (*b* Syracuse, 23 June 1957). Vocalist, composer, lyricist, and arranger. An American Indian of the Oneida Nation, Shenandoah was born into the Wolf Clan, of which her mother is a traditional leader. She has uniquely incorporated aspects of her people's traditions and melodies into contemporary popular music. A passionate advocate for her people, the Haudenosaunee, and for all American Indians, her performances have been a vehicle to present their struggles. Shenandoah performed at Woodstock 1994 and at both inaugurals for Pres Bill Clinton. *Peacemaker's Journey* was nominated for a Grammy Award in 2001 in the category of Best Native American Music Album. In 2002 Syracuse University awarded Shenandoah an honorary doctorate in music.

Joanne Shenandoah, http://www.joanneshenandoah.com

Arthur Einhorn

Sherburne. Town (pop 3,979) and village (pop 1,455) in NE Chenango Co. A horseshoe-shaped earthwork four miles (6 km) north of the village is believed to be an Indian cultural site. Settled in 1792 by familes from Kent, Conn, the town was formed from Paris [now in Oneida Co] in 1795, and the village incorporated in 1830. The Chenango Canal (1837–78) encouraged industry such as Hart Pottery (1841) and the Ross and Co Steam Cotton Mill (1862–1953; later Utica Knitting Co). Irish canal workers, joined by famine immigrants, founded St. Malachy's Church (1848). Later the town was served by the Utica, Chenango and Susquehanna Valley Railroad (1869, 1872). The Canasawacta Mill (1887–*ca* 1928) along with Utica Knitting attracted Lebanese immigrant millhands in the early 20th century. Nationally known Gaines Dog Food (1920) has evolved into Chenango Valley Pet Foods. Technical Appliance Co (1950s–1980s; television antennae and dishes) and Chesebrough-Ponds (1966–90; hospital supplies) are gone, but in 2003 Kenyon Press and Mid-York Press (industrial packaging) were employers. The Sherburne Pageant of Bands is an annual June event. Rogers Environmental Education Center (1909) devotes 600 acres (243 ha) to wildlife conservation, picnic areas, hiking and cross-country skiing trails. At Rexford Falls, site of sulfur springs and the Spring House hotel (1883), a 78 ft (23.8 m) Whipple arch-truss bridge by Sheldon and Ross of Norwich remains a landmark after more than a century.

Dale C. Storms

Sheridan. Town (pop 2,838) in NE Chautauqua Co. Settled in 1804, the town was formed in 1827 from Pomfret and Hanover. In 1851 the Erie Railroad was completed through Sheridan, allowing farmers to ship crates of fruit and grape cuttings. The main occupation is farming, but Chadwick Bay Industrial Park, near the Dunkirk Municipal Airport, the Thruway (1957), and the CSX railroad, has been developed to encourage industry. In 2002 there were two wineries.

Jean Strawser

Sherman. Town (pop 1,553) and village (pop 714) in SW Chautauqua Co. Settled in 1823 the town was formed from Mina in 1832. Butter making as a cash product was replaced by sales to a condensery (1908). Hammer dulcimers made in Sherman in the 1850s were sold nationally. The village was incorporated in 1890. Shiloh Community (1942), a Christian commune, moved to Sulphur Springs, Ark, in 1968. Rte 17 (I-86) was completed through town in 1983. The main industry is dairy farming, and the town has a large Amish population that maintains traditional farming practices. In the early 21st century, an important business is Victor Kent and Sons, a commission sales stable that is a successor to Norvel Reed and Sons. The Yorker Museum, composed of six restored buildings on the village common, was developed by a club of young historians beginning in 1947.

Michelle Henry

Sherman, James S(choolcraft) (*b* Utica, 24 Oct 1855; *d* Utica, 30 Oct 1912). US vice president. Educated in the Utica area, Sherman graduated in 1878 from nearby Hamilton College, earning an LLB degree there a year later. He began practicing law in his native city but soon turned to politics. A member of a prominent Democratic family, he became a Republican and was elected mayor of traditionally Democratic Utica in 1884. A genial politician popularly known as Sunny Jim, he had two tenures as a member of the US House of Representatives (1887–91, 1893–1909). Although he was not an extremely active legislator, he held a number of powerful positions, notably on the Indian Affairs Committee, where he made a number of statements in support of American Indians. Working effectively as a manager behind the scenes, he earned the confidence of powerful Republican congressional leaders. While in Congress he became an influential Oneida Co businessman, taking over his late father's role as head of the New Hartford Canning Co and starting the Utica Trust and Deposit Co in 1900. In 1908 Pres Theodore Roosevelt, declining to run, selected William H. Taft as the Republican presidential nominee. Party members in Congress chose the popular Sherman as Taft's running mate, and the ticket won the election. A gifted parliamentarian, Sherman presided over the US Senate with distinction as the 27th vice president. He was again nominated for vice president in 1912 but died of chronic illness before the election.

James Schoolcraft Sherman, Late Vice President of the United States, Memorial Addresses Delivered at a Joint Session of the Senate and the House of Representatives of the United States, February 15, 1913 (Washington, DC: Government Printing Office, 1913)

Frank K. Lorenz

Sherrill. City (pop 3,147) in SW Oneida Co. Sherrill grew to house the supplementary workforce for the industries of the Oneida Community, whose members lived communally across the county border in Madison Co. In 1864 the Oneida Community built a brick factory on the present site of Sherrill and began manufacturing traps, adding silk thread two years later. It became a joint-stock corporation in 1881, and its tablewares factory moved to Sherrill in 1914. Sherrill incorporated as a city in 1916. The silk thread business was sold in 1913, and the trap business in 1925. Oneida Ltd concentrates on tableware and in 2002 employed 2,500 workers. Conde Milking Machine Co began operations in 1939; now known as Westmore Ltd, in 2002 it employed over 20 workers, manufacturing vacuum pumps, compressors, and milking machines.

Shinnecock and Peconic Canal. Navigation canal linking Great Peconic and Shinnecock Bays in Suffolk Co on Long Island. Construction of such a canal was first discussed in the 1826 report of Holmes Hutchinson, state engineer, to the New York State canal commissioners. Two private companies incorporated in 1828 and 1848 to build the canal were unable to accomplish any work of significance, and the State of New York commenced construction in 1884. By 1892 the canal was completed at a cost of $98,000 with a length of about 4,000 feet (1,200 m), a width of 40 feet (12.2 m) at the bottom and 58 feet (17.7 m) at the surface, and a depth of 4.5 feet (1.4 m) at low tide. A single lock allowed boats to negotiate the tidal difference, approximately 2 feet (.6 m), between the two bays. The canal enabled navigation between the bays and revived the shellfishing industry in Shinnecock Bay by permitting the movement of water into what had become a landlocked basin. In 1895 the New York State legislature authorized another part of this project, a cut through the barrier island separating Shinnecock Bay from the Atlantic Ocean. An 1896 excavation failed, but the great hurricane of 21 Sept 1938 created the channel, permitting vessels in Great Peconic Bay to enter the Atlantic Ocean without the lengthy voyage around Shelter Island, Gardiners Island, and Montauk Point. The channel was stabilized in 1955 with rock jetties, and larger locks were placed in the canal to accommodate bigger boats.

Whitford, Noble E. *History of the Canal System of the State of New York, Together with Brief Histories of the Canals of the United States and Canada*, vol 1 (Albany: Bandow Printing, 1906)

Paul J. Bartczak

Shinnecock Hills Golf Club. Organized in Southampton (Suffolk Co) in 1891, the nation's first incorporated golf club was built on land formerly inhabited by the Shinnecock Indians. Local Indians helped build the original 12-hole course, and Shinnecock men have continuously been employed as groundskeepers and caddies. In 1894 the club expanded the playing area to create one of the nation's first 18-hole layouts, and it became a founding member of the United States Golf Association. That year Shinnecock Hills became the first club to let women play regularly. At the 1896 US Open, two of the club's caddies, an African American and a Shinnecock Indian, were allowed to compete over the strong protests of tournament regulars. Shinnecock Hills also helped shape the concept of the club professional during Scotsman Charlie Thom's 55-year tenure in that position (1906–61). The club's links-style course has hosted numerous competitions, including four US Open Golf Championships (1896, 1986, 1995, 2004), the 1896 US Amateur, the 1967 Senior Amateur, the 1977 Walker Cup, and the 1990 Women's Amateur.

Sal Maiorana

Shinnecock Nation. American Indian group on the South Fork of Long Island. Their domain once stretched from Eastport (Suffolk Co) on the west to Sagaponack (Suffolk Co) on the east, and from Peconic Bay to the Atlantic Ocean, close to the current bounds of the Town of Southampton (Suffolk Co). They were maritime-oriented fishers, gatherers, and hunters who spoke a variant of the Algonquian language family. Judging from artifacts, their belief system was congruent with the larger Algonquin cosmology. Prehistoric artifacts from the area indicate American Indian habitation from about 10,000 years ago. The Shinnecock were first noted historically by Dutch settlers Isaak DeRasieres in 1627 and Nicolaes van Wassenaer, who described in 1621–32 Pieter Barentsen's trade with the "Sinnecox," one of two great principal tribes. The English settlers who founded Southampton in 1640 pressured the Shinnecock, through numerous land purchases, into the western Shinnecock Hills area. Previously, the Shinnecocks' principal seat had been the Sebonac area fronting on Peconic Bay, now part of the Shinnecock Hills Golf Club. Records indicate that two "forts," or palisaded enclosures, from the 1630s were located in this area as part of the network of native forts on Long Island. With the coming of the Long Island Rail Road through the Shinnecock Hills, Southampton proprietors forced the exchange of this area for Shinnecock Neck through an act passed by the state legislature in 1859; Shinnecock Neck is home to the current reservation of about 800 acres (320 ha). Contrary to the 1790 Federal Trade and Nonintercourse Act, in 1861 the proprietors procured the land in Shinnecock Hills that was sold for the railroad right-of-way. The 1790 act stipulated that all Indian land alienation must be approved by the US government.

In the 18th and 19th centuries, most Shinnecock men pursued a maritime livelihood as clammers, hunting guides, decoy makers, seamen, whalers, and salvors of shipwrecks. It was a dangerous livelihood: 10 men were lost salvaging the wreck of the *Circassian* in 1876. Others were lost whaling. By the turn of the 20th century, work as greens keepers at local golf clubs was another major occupation. Women provided services like spinning, needlework, midwifery, nursing, and laundry to the settlers from the colonial period to the mid–20th century. Since World War II Shinnecocks have worked in a wide range of public, business, technical, and professional jobs. The nation is governed by three trustees elected annually, a practice initiated at the behest of Southampton officials in 1792. Shinnecock women were granted the right to vote for trustees at a 1993 tribal meeting. The 2000 population of around 500 people did not include the many Shinnecock who lived throughout the United States. The reservation is recognized by the state, and at the start of the 21st century the Shinnecock Nation was seeking federal recognition. It administers several federally funded programs and in 1990 received a three-year federal grant to plan a tribal museum and cultural center, which was completed in 2001.

DeRasieres, Isaak. "New Netherland in 1627. Letter of Isaak DeRasieres to Samuel Blomnaert." In *Collections of the New York Historical Society*, ed. H. C. Murphy, 2d ser, vol 2 (New York: Van Norden, 1849)
Stone, Gaynell, ed. *The Shinnecock: A Culture History* (Stony Brook, NY: Suffolk County Archaeological Association, 1983)

Gaynell Stone

Shirley. Locality (pop 25,395) in Brookhaven (Suffolk Co). Although bungalow communities arose in the area after World War I, it was the 1946 development of Mastic Acres by Walter T. Shirley (1896–1963) that was significant to the development of the locality. In 1949 Shirley renamed it, and a post office opened in 1952. Many Italian Americans made Shirley their home. Crossed by the William Floyd Parkway (1959), the community is the site of the 2,400-acre (970 ha) Wertheim National Wildlife Refuge (1947), the Shirley Industrial Park (1960s), and a memorial to the dead of TWA Flight 800 (1996). In 1987 citizens held a nonbinding referendum seeking a name change to Floyd Harbor, which many considered absurd given that the community has no harbor. The 1970 population of 6,280 had quadrupled by the turn of the 21st century.

shoe manufacturing. See BOOT AND SHOE MANUFACTURING.

shopping centers and malls. Well into the 20th century the term "shopping center" could refer to retail activity on almost any scale and in nearly every kind of place. Beginning in the 1920s in Kansas City, Mo, however, real estate developer J. C. Nichols redefined it as an integrated business development, planned and designed as a unified entity, owned and operated by a single party, and containing a predetermined mix of tenants. Nichols also pioneered what later became known as neighborhood shopping centers, which offered up to about 20 stores. During the interwar decades, designing a shopping center around a parking lot was a key innovation. The first notable example was the Park and Shop in Washington, DC (1930). Few could be found in New York State, although by 1940 the Buffalo-based firm of Guelich and Boebel gained some attention for similar shopping centers it had built in that metropolitan area.

Postwar Evolution

After World War II, shopping centers became the preferred form of retail development throughout the nation. The underlying reason was the rise of suburban living and the mobility afforded by routine automobile use. The distance of the suburbs from congested, expensive downtown business centers and a strong, expanding national economy contributed to the trend. Shopping centers promised merchants competitive advantages over unplanned development, and consumers flocked to them because they were convenient, informal, and family oriented.

The shopping center concept was applied on several scales. The largest example, the regional center, was anchored by a major department store and reinforced by 40 or more smaller stores targeted to a clientele of several hundred thousand. Community centers averaged between 20 and 40 stores, with a large variety store (Woolworth's, Kresge's) and/or a junior department store (Penney's, Grant's) as anchors. Neighborhood centers continued to have food stores and drugstores and perhaps a small variety store as the primary units. Off-street parking was an added convenience; by the early 1950s an area three times that occupied by the stores was recommended for customers' cars.

Nonurban shopping centers of all three kinds abounded on the perimeter of New York cities and large towns between 1945 and 1960. Neighborhood and community centers were by far the most numerous, but regional centers emerged in some number around Buffalo, Rochester, and New York City. Indeed, the New York City metropolitan area (including northern New Jersey) ranked second only to Los Angeles in the number of regional shopping centers during that period. A pioneering example was the Cross County Shopping Center, fully opened in 1955, in Yonkers, which was among the first in the nation conceived with two large department store anchors (Wanamaker's and Gimbel's), a pedestrian mall as a connecting "spine," and a location along a high-speed, limited-access highway. All these features would become commonplace by 1960. The Roosevelt Field Shopping Center in Garden City (Nassau Co), which opened in 1956, also drew considerable attention for its suave design and immense Macy's store, one of the largest branches in the East at that time.

The Rise of the Pedestrian Mall

With such successful developments, the mall became a widespread variant. The strategy was to divorce consumers from their cars and encourage pedestrian circulation in a relatively compact, informal open space, seen as conducive to longer visits and impulse buying. This idea was not always embraced, however. Developers working where open land was available long maintained a preference for stretching stores around the parking lot, even when these complexes reached epic proportions, as with Buffalo's Thruway Plaza (begun 1952). Eventually, though, the mall concept became standard, especially after its economic viability was demonstrated in other parts of the country. Enclosing the pedestrian walkway to form a great interior passage—the Walt Whitman Mall in Huntington

(Suffolk Co) that opened in 1962 being an early example—not only bolstered patronage during periods of hot, cold, and inclement weather but also proved efficient to maintain.

New regional malls continued to proliferate into the early 1980s. For much of this period, the largest structures rose two or even three levels around grand, skylit passages, a configuration inspired by the 19th-century European arcades. Expansive malls like the Colonie Center outside Albany (1965–66) and the Seneca Mall outside Buffalo (1968–69) became retail showplaces in most urban areas. Regional malls also were erected in smaller communities, serving towns and rural areas over a radius of 25–30 miles (40–48 km) or more, as with the Newburgh Mall (1979–80) in Orange Co and Champlain Center North (1986–87) in Plattsburgh. In many cases, too, complexes that began as community-sized centers were enlarged and reconfigured, often in several stages. One such example is the Shoppingtown Mall in Syracuse, which was begun in 1953–54.

The mall was conceived as a means to reinvigorate social interaction in the marketplace, and to a large degree that objective was met, especially with fully enclosed complexes. Families, teen-agers, and senior citizens all gravitate to the mall for both passive recreation and shopping. Malls also serve as settings for special events, but mall owners have generally discouraged demonstrations and other activities that might drive shoppers away.

DEVELOPMENT AND FINANCING

Regardless of size, the creation of shopping centers has generally been the work of real estate developers, though the larger regional centers were often undertaken by, or in cooperation with, major department store companies and seldom proceeded without securing most tenants. While neighborhood and community shopping centers could be financed through banks and other lending institutions, regional centers required unusually large sums of capital. Large department store ownership groups such as the St. Louis–based May Co could undertake such ventures, but financing often came from insurance companies, whose executives saw the regional center as a potentially lucrative investment. By the 1970s large mall development and management companies that could command extensive amounts of capital for construction, such as Wilmorite in the Rochester area and Pyramid in the Syracuse area, were beginning to emerge.

From 1980 to 2000 changes in growth and strategy occurred in shopping center development. The market for regional malls reached the saturation point in most places during the 1980s. New complexes carved out previously underserved territory; the Carousel Center in Syracuse (1988–90), for example, positioned itself to serve local residents as well as those from outlying areas. But far more activity focused on upgrading existing facilities and on constructing more specialized types of shopping venues. Many shopping centers were built for an assemblage of high-volume chain companies. Outlet malls such as Woodbury Common in Central Valley (Orange Co) (1994–95) and the Waterloo Outlet near the Thruway west of Syracuse, located in quasi-rural areas on the metropolitan periphery, became major destinations, altering the nature of retailing in the process.

See also SYRACUSE.

Cohen, Lizabeth. "From Town Center to Shopping Center: The Reconfiguration of Community Marketplaces in Postwar America," *American Historical Review* 101 (Oct 1996): 1050–81

Crawford, Margaret. "The World in a Shopping Mall." In *Variations on a Theme Park: The New American City and the End of Public Space,* ed. Michael Sorkin (New York: Hill & Wang, 1992)

Gillette, Howard, Jr. "The Evolution of the Planned Shopping Center in Suburb and City," *Journal of the American Planning Association* 51 (Autumn 1985): 449–60

Hanchett, Thomas. "US Tax Policy and the Shopping-Center Boom of the 1950s and 1960s," *American Historical Review 101* (Oct 1996): 1082–110

Longstreth, Richard. *City Center to Regional Mall: Architecture, the Automobile, and Retailing in Los Angeles, 1920–1950* (Cambridge, Mass: MIT Press, 1997)

———. "The Diffusion of the Community Shopping Center Concept during the Interwar Decades," *Journal of the Society of Architectural Historians* 56 (Sept 1997): 268–93

Richard Longstreth

Shoppers at Roosevelt Field Mall, Garden City, *ca* 1960.

Shoreham {East Shoreham, locality (pop 5,809) in Brookhaven, Suffolk Co; Shoreham, village (pop 417) in Brookhaven}. Known as Swezey's Landing and later as Woodville Landing in the 19th century when it was a shipping point for cordwood, Shoreham originated with the 1,400-acre (567 ha) Wardenclyffe summer colony created by the J. S. Warden Co in 1895. A Wardenclyffe post office opened in 1901, changing its name to Shoreham in 1906. The village was incorporated in 1913; its population in 1920 was only 20. The locality was served by the extension of the Port Jefferson branch of the Long Island Rail Road from 1895 to 1938. It was the site of the Stanford White–designed laboratory (1902–15) of Nikola Tesla; it became Peerless Photo Products in 1939. Growth followed the opening of the nearby Brookhaven National Laboratory (1947) and Grumman Aerospace Flight Test Facility (1953). In 1965 planning began for the nuclear-powered Shoreham plant of Long Island Lighting Co, but after decades of protest, the plant was decommissioned in 1994 without ever having operated.

Chris Kretz

Shoreham Nuclear Power Plant. In 1966 the Long Island Lighting Co (LILCO) announced that it intended to build a 540 MW nuclear electricity-generating station on a 900-acre (364 ha) site in Shoreham (Suffolk Co) by 1973 at a cost of about $75 million. Local officials and residents greeted this with enthusiasm. Responding to high growth rates in electricity demand, LILCO obtained a construction permit in 1973 for a larger 820 MW plant with expected completion in 1977 at a cost of $506 million. However, the heavily modified 850 MW plant was completed in 1984 for $5.5 billion. Management failures, equipment breakdowns, shoddy workmanship, an unproductive labor force, and new regulations following the 1979 Three Mile Island nuclear power station accident in Pennsylvania were significant factors in the cost overruns.

Despite the early enthusiasm, mounting costs led to increasing opposition from local residents, who faced escalating electricity rates. The residents used education, political pressure, and regulatory intervention to question the Shoreham plant and to stop plans for additional nuclear plants. Subsequently, activist groups from outside the area opposed to nuclear power in general coalesced around the struggling plant in 1979 after Three Mile Island, using demonstrations, sit-ins, and civil disobedience to make their message heard. Suffolk Co residents voted out county legislators supporting Shoreham in the 1981 elections. In May 1983 Gov Mario M. Cuomo attempted to mediate the conflict by forming the Shoreham Commission; its report, issued 14 Dec 1983, found that although nuclear power was not inherently unsafe, LILCO had erred in its decision to build the plant and was technologically unprepared to manage it. By 1984, 63% of Long Island residents said in a *Newsday* poll that the plant should not open. To resolve the Shoreham problem and to stabilize electricity rates on Long Island, the state legislature in 1986 established the Long Island Power Authority (LIPA).

The US Nuclear Regulatory Commission (NRC) granted a full operating license in April 1989. However, Gov Cuomo and LILCO, under political and economic pressure, respectively, had signed an agreement on 28 Feb 1989 to transfer the Shoreham plant to LIPA for $1 in exchange for LILCO allowances to recoup most of its costs from customers. LIPA took possession of the Shoreham plant for decommissioning in February 1992, and work was completed on 12 Oct 1994 at a cost of $181 million. In 2003 the plant, empty of its radioactive components and unused, still stands.

Axelrod, Regina S., and Hugh A. Wilson. "Citizen Participation and Nuclear Power: The Shoreham Experience," *Journal of Energy and Development* 11 (Spring 1986): 311–31

Thomas C. Haley

Shortsville. Village (pop 1,320) in Manchester (Ontario Co). The first settler, Theophilus Short, built a gristmill in 1804, the year he arrived. Paper and woolen mills followed. The Auburn and Rochester Railroad came through in 1841. By 1876 Shortville was producing grain drills, paper, hay forks, and plows, and employing 1,500 millworkers. The village incorporated in 1889. Papec Machine Co (1909–81) was a large manufacturer of farm machinery. In 2003 Shortsville's economy was based on manufacturing and agriculture, especially cabbage for sauerkraut.

Marla A. Bennett

Shubert brothers {Shubert, Lee [Levi] (*b* ?Neustad, Poland, 25 Mar 1871; *d* New York City, 25 Dec 1953); Shubert, Sam S. (*b* ?Neustad, Poland, 27 Aug 1878; *d* Harrisburg, Pa, 13 May 1905); Shubert, J(acob) J. (*b* ?Neustad, Poland, 29 Aug 1879; *d* New York City, 26 Dec 1963)}. Theatrical managers and producers. The offspring of poor eastern European Jewish immigrants, the brothers grew up in Syracuse, where their father was a peddler, and began their career by managing theatrical touring companies. They leased their first theater in 1897, the Bastable, in Syracuse and by the end of the decade also operated theaters in Buffalo, Rochester, Utica, Troy, and Albany. In 1900 they leased the Herald Square Theatre in New York City. After the death of Sam in a train crash, the two surviving brothers continued building and operating theaters on Broadway and in major cities around the country. In 1913 they opened Broadway's Shubert Theatre on 44th St and the Booth Theatre on 45th St, and later the Broadhurst Theatre (1917) on 44th St and the Barrymore Theatre (1928) on 47th St. The Shuberts owned more than 100 theaters across the country by the late 1920s.

The Shuberts staged a cornucopia of productions, from operettas and revues to dramas and musicals, and introduced countless star performers to the American public. While they staged Shakespeare, Sean O'Casey, and Gilbert and Sullivan, they catered primarily to popular taste. The musical comedies *Chinese Honeymoon* (1902), *Winsome Winnie* (1903), *The Babes and the Baron* (1905), and *The Dancing Duchess* (1914) were early Shubert productions. In 1906 Lee Shubert staged *Pioneer Days*, featuring Indians, cavalry, baby elephants, and chorus girls. *The Passing Show* (1912–24), a yearly musical revue, rivaled Florenz Ziegfeld's *Follies*. Beginning with *The Blue Paradise* (1915), they presented nostalgic, romantic Sigmund Romberg musicals. The Shuberts survived myriad changes in commercial taste and the economic crisis caused by the Great Depression, during which they primarily produced less-elaborate musicals and plays. The company was reorganized in 1972 as the Shubert Organization, controlled by the Shubert Foundation. In 2003 the Shubert Organization was the largest Broadway theater owner, operating 16 venues. The space alongside the outside walls of the Shubert and Booth Theatres comprises Shubert Alley, a Midtown Manhattan landmark.

Hirsch, Foster. *The Boys from Syracuse: The Shuberts' Theatrical Empire* (Carbondale: Southern Illinois Univ Press, 1998)

Sibley [née Farr], Georgianna (*b* Mountain Station, NJ, 30 May 1887; *d* Sharon, Conn, 10 June 1980). Civic leader. Farr's family had homes in Manhattan and New Jersey. She began her schooling in New Jersey and at age 15 entered Miss Spence's School for Girls in Manhattan. She graduated in 1905 and made her debut that season. In 1908 she married Harper Sibley, grandson of Western Union Telegraph Co cofounder Hiram Sibley. The couple moved in 1924 to his hometown of Rochester. A devout Episcopalian, she maintained a lifelong involvement with church-related causes. She worked with Eleanor Roosevelt on the National Women's Committee of the 1933 Mobilization of Human Needs and led Rochester organizations ranging from the Council of Churches to the World Peace Committee to the Urban League. A much sought-after speaker, she was equally comfortable giving a traditional Thanksgiving address or criticizing the House Committee on Un-American Activities hearings of the 1950s. Racial equality was a particular concern of Sibley. In 1946 she chided her city for its "psychological block" on low-rent public housing. She was best known for her efforts as a conciliator during Rochester's race riots of 1964. As president of the Rochester Area Council of Churches, she became a key mediator, using her mansion as a negotiation center and her own skills to convince deadlocked factions to talk—first to her, then to each other. Gradually, Sibley cut back on her civic activities, and in 1979 she went to live with a daughter in Millbrook (Dutchess Co).

Roosevelt, Felicia Warburg. "Mrs. Harper Sibley." In *Doers and Dowagers* (Garden City, NY: Doubleday, 1975)

Joann Minor

Sickles, Daniel E(dgar) (*b* New York City, 20 Oct 1819; *d* New York City, 3 May 1914). Politician, soldier, and diplomat. A prominent lawyer and Democrat, Sickles was elected to the state assembly in 1847 and appointed corporation counsel of New York City in 1853, serving as well in the state senate (1855–57) and in the US House of Representatives (1857–61). Married in 1852 to Teresa Bagioli, he soon gained notoriety for his extramarital affairs. Nevertheless, when in 1859 he discovered his wife's own adulterous relationship with Philip Barton Key, US attorney for the District of Columbia and son of Francis Scott Key, Sickles fatally shot Key and was later acquitted of murder on grounds of temporary insanity. During the Civil War, Sickles, appointed brigadier general in 1861, organized the Excelsior Brigade, a five-regiment brigade of New York State troops. Participating in several eastern campaigns, Sickles rose to the rank of major general and again gained notoriety, this time military, when he moved his troops at Gettysburg without orders from Gen George Gordon Meade. This insubordination nearly cost the Union the battle, and Sickles lost his right leg from a severe wound received during the fighting. In 1865 Sickles assumed command of Reconstruction in South Carolina and the following year in North Carolina as well. He was relieved of his duties in 1867 for defying a federal court order that freed men accused of killing Union soldiers. Now a Republican, Sickles campaigned for Ulysses S. Grant and served as minister to Spain (1869–74). Returning to New York City in 1879, Sickles resumed his law practice and served as New York Co sheriff in 1890. He chaired the Civil Service Commission (1888–89) and Monuments Commission (1886–1912), and served again in Congress (1893–95). In 1897 he received a congressional Medal of Honor for courage at Gettysburg during the Civil War.

Brandt, Nat. *The Congressman Who Got Away with Murder* (Syracuse: Syracuse Univ Press, 1991)
Swanberg, W. A. *Sickles the Incredible* (1956; repr Gettysburg, Pa: Stan Clark Military Books, 1991)

Bernadette Zbicki Heiney

Sidney. Town (pop 6,109) and village (pop 4,068) in NW Delaware Co. Settled in 1770, the town was formed from Franklin in 1801. The Susquehanna Turnpike (1802) stimulated development. The Albany and Susquehanna Railroad (1866; later Delaware and Hudson) and the Ontario and Western Railroad (1870–1957) contributed significantly to the growth of Sidney, especially the village, which incorporated in 1888 and became the site of many factories, including the Sidney Silk Mill (1893–1906). Twenty French families worked in a French cheese factory (1901–7), which became Phoenix Cheese in 1908, closing in 1921. A Swiss company, Scintilla Magneto (1926), employed 8,600 during World War II to manufacture airplane parts; by 2003 it operated under the name Amphenol. Keith Clark (1946; now At-A-Glance Group of Mead Westvaco) manufactures calendars and other time-management materials. These firms, along with the Mirabito Fuel Group (1927) and Unadilla Laminated Products (1963) are major employers. East Sidney Dam, constructed in the 1950s to control the floodwaters of Ouleout Creek, also serves as a recreational area.

Dorothy Kubik

Siena College. Private Catholic college. In 1937 the Franciscan friars of the Province of the Most Holy Name founded a liberal arts college for men in Loudonville (Albany Co). Following World War II former servicemen made up 75% of the student body; Quonset huts and other prefabricated structures were built to accommodate the increase in enrollment by 1948. Women gained admittance in 1968. In addition to Siena Hall, constructed in 1938, early expansion included a friary, dormitories, townhouses, a dining hall, and an athletic complex on the 155-acre (62.7 ha) campus. The college added a multimillion-dollar science center, student union, residence hall, and library between 1999 and 2002. Among the school's prominent alumni are author William Kennedy, Archbishop Roberto Gonzalez of San Juan, Puerto Rico, and former governor of California George Deukmejian. Enrollment in 2002 stood at approximately 3,000 with 47% men and 53% women. Most students attended full time and resided on campus.

Chmura, Catherine Welsh. *Siena College: The First Fifty Years* (Loudonville, NY: Siena College, 1987)

Elizabeth K. Allen

Sikhs. Sikhism shares certain elements with bhakti (devotional Hinduism) and Islam, but it has its own distinctive beliefs and traditions. By 1917 the US Congress, influenced by a rising wave of anti-Asian immigrant sentiment, had moved to disqualify almost all Asians from naturalization. In 1923 Bhagat Singh Thind (1892–1967), a Sikh who had studied in California and enlisted in the US Army during World War I, maintained that he and other Asian Indians were "Caucasians." The US Supreme Court ruled that Thind was nonetheless ineligible to become an American citizen, but he stayed in the country and later received US citizenship in New York State, where he published books based on Sikh philosophy.

The majority of Sikh immigrants came after the Immigration Act of 1965, and many settled in Queens Co. The Sikh Cultural Society was founded in 1965 with a congregation that practiced devotional singing, first in homes and then at a school in Flushing. In 1972 the group purchased a defunct 19th-century church in the Richmond Hill area and converted it into the northeast's first *gurdwara* (Sikh temple, literally "door to the guru"). Two smaller *gurdwaras* later opened in Flushing, the Sikh Center of New York (1974) and Gurdwara Singh Sabha (1985). The Richmond Hill *gurdwara* was destroyed in a fire in 2002, most likely because of a gas leak; the society planned to rebuild. *Gurdwaras* are crucial institutions in the Sikh community. The prospect of an independent Sikh state to be known as Khalistan is frequently debated in political discussions around election time at *gurdwaras*.

Men often wear the symbols of tradition known as the *panj kakke* (five Ks): *kes* (uncut hair), *kangha* (comb), *kara* (steel bangle), *kirpan* (short ceremonial dagger), and *kacch* (undershorts). Many Sikh men also cover their heads with turbans. Perhaps because of their relatively small numbers and distinctive appearance, Sikhs have often been targets of hostility; a rash of hate crimes and bias attacks followed 11 Sept 2001, when some Sikhs were mistaken for Arab Muslims. Many American Sikh men cut their hair to fit in, but most still wear a *kara* on the wrist. Some Sikh children let their hair grow and take Punjabi classes at *gurdwaras*, but more second- and third-generation youths shun the strident separatism of their fathers. They cut their hair while holding onto one very popular cross-cultural product of the Punjab, *bhangra* (Punjabi folk music, traditionally for weddings and festivals, which has acquired a more modern sound). Less political displays of Sikh pride are evident at the annual Sikh Day Parade in New York City, held every April since 1987.

Estimates of the New York Sikh population range widely, from the conservative figure of 3,400 Sikhs in New York City and 5,000 in New York State to the rather unlikely figure of 150,000 in the New York–New Jersey–Connecticut area. Many Punjabi Hindus attend *gurdwaras* because of a shared regional linguistic tradition and family ties. There are more than 20 *gurdwaras* in New York State: 14 in the New York City metropolitan area, and others are in Buffalo, East Greenbush, Fishkill, Central Square, Penfield, Rochester, Syracuse, and Williamsville. A smaller number of Sikhs are converts to the Healthy, Happy, Holy Organization of Sikh Dharma, founded in Los Angeles in 1969.

See also INDIANS AND SOUTH ASIANS.

Hawley, John Stratton, and Gurinder Singh Mann. *Studying the Sikhs: Issues for North America* (Albany: SUNY Press, 1993)
Khandelwal, Madhulika S. *Becoming American, Being Indian: An Immigrant Community in New York City* (Ithaca: Cornell Univ Press, 2002)
Singh Mann, Gurinder. "Sikhism in the United States of America." In *The South Asian Diaspora in Britain, Canada, and the United States*, ed. Harold Coward, John R. Hinnells, and Raymond Brady Williams (Albany: SUNY Press, 2000)

R. Scott Hanson

Sikorsky, Igor I(vanovich) (*b* Kiev, Ukraine, 25 May 1889; *d* Easton, Conn, 26 Oct 1972). Aircraft engineer and designer. In 1913 in St. Petersburg he built the world's first successful multiengine aircraft, which introduced long-range passenger travel and was used during World War I for strategic bombing and reconnaissance missions on behalf of the Imperial Russian Airforce. The Bolshevik Revolution in 1917 forced Sikorsky to leave Russia. He arrived in New York City in 1919 and for a short time made a living teaching mathematics at a school for Russian immigrants in Manhattan's Lower East Side. He settled in College Point (Queens Co), where he built a number of aircraft, culminating in an advanced series of amphibians—land or water aircraft that pioneered commercial passenger service for Pan American World Airways. He also worked at the pioneering aviation plant near Roosevelt Field (Nassau Co). In 1923 he founded Sikorsky Aero Engineering Corp, which later merged with United Aircraft Corp. In 1938 Sikorsky returned to his dream of building a successful helicopter, and the following year his VS-300 helicopter flew for the first time. In 1941 it set the world's durational records for helicopter flight. Following the VS-300, a series of helicopter models was developed by Sikorsky Aircraft, the company for which he served as engineering manager from 1935 to 1957 and as engineering consultant from 1957 to 1972. Sikorsky is widely accepted as the father of the helicopter industry.

Delear, Frank J. *Igor Sikorsky: His Three Careers in Aviation* (New York: Dodd, Mead, 1976)

Igor I. Sikorsky Jr

Sills, Beverly [Silverman, Belle] (*b* Brooklyn, 25 May 1929). Operatic soprano and arts administrator. Beverly Sills made her singing debut at age 3 as "Bubbles" Silverman on a radio children's program, then performed as a teenager in touring operetta productions. She joined the New York City Opera in 1955 and became one of its star sopranos. Her big breakthrough came as Cleopatra in a 1966 production of Handel's *Giulio Cesare*. She was hailed throughout the 1970s for her performances and recordings of coloratura soprano roles in such operas as Massenet's *Manon*, Donizetti's *Lucia di Lammermoor*, and Offenbach's *Tales of Hoffmann*. Her warm, ingratiating personality and sense of humor also made her a popular TV performer and host. Sills retired from singing in 1980 but remained a very public figure as director of the New York City Opera (1979–89) and later as artistic director of Lincoln Center (1994–2002).

Sills, Beverly. *Beverly: An Autobiography* (New York: Bantam, 1987)

David Raymond

Silver, Sheldon (*b* New York City, 13 Feb 1944). Democratic political leader. A product of the Lower East Side Jewish community in New York City, Silver attended Jewish day schools and graduated from Yeshiva University (1965) and Brooklyn Law School (1968). In 1976 he was elected to the state assembly, where he rose to important posts and chaired a series of key committees, including those on election law, codes, and ways and means. He was elected Speaker in January 1994, and when Republicans recaptured the governorship later that year Silver became the most powerful Democratic official in the state. He skillfully used the political tools of office to solidify Democratic control over the assembly, maintaining a 2-to-1 edge into the 21st century, and also extended his influence over the entire state Democratic Party. A more conservative Democrat than his predecessors, he supported restoration of the death penalty in 1995. Silver also authored a state program to institute full-day kindergarten at public schools statewide and was a strong advocate for expanded health-care programs and funding.

Peter Slocum

Silver Creek. Village (pop 2,896) in Hanover (Chautauqua Co). Settled in 1803 it began as a lake port with shipbuilding and lumbering. A black walnut tree with a diameter of 10 feet (3.05 m) was believed to be the largest tree in the state; when it blew down in 1822, it was hollowed out, used as a store annex, and later put on tour of the state as a curiosity. The village incorporated in 1848. The Buffalo and State Line Railroad (later New York Central) provided service from 1852. Silver Creek firms produced milling and grain-cleaning machinery for mills around the world. The first such manufacturer, S. Howes Co (1856), remains important in the early 21st century, as does Excelco Developments (1947), a manufacturer of aerospace and titanium technology. Silver Creek sponsors an annual Festival of Grapes.

Michelle Henry

Silver Grays. The faction of New York State's Whig Party that supported the Compromise of 1850. At the 1850 state Whig convention in Syracuse, a minority of delegates walked out followed by silver-haired Francis Granger, the convention chair from Canandaigua (Ontario Co), because the majority opposed the compromise. Mobilization of the Silver Grays reflected intensified resentment of the Wooly Heads, the dominant faction led by William H. Seward and Thurlow Weed, who favored appeals to abolitionists, immigrants, and antirenters to expand the party's appeal. The Silver Grays viewed such tactics as threats to the state's social, commercial, and economic stability and believed that the antislavery movement imperiled the Union. Leading Silver Grays included, besides Granger, Pres Millard Fillmore, Ogden Hoffman, James Beekman, Solomon Haven, Thomas Foote, and Nathan Hall; their newspaper voice was the *Albany State Register.* Support came principally from commercial elites in cities spread across all regions of the state. Despite efforts to paper over the breach, rival factionalists withheld support from each other's candidates, weakening the party. Tension further escalated when the state delegation to the Whig National Convention in 1852 repudiated the compromise. In 1855 the *Register* declared the party dead and urged Silver Grays who had not already done so to join the American (Know-Nothing) Party.

Warner, Lee H. "The Perpetual Crisis of Conservative Whigs: New York's Silver Grays," *New York Historical Society Quarterly* 57 (1973): 212–36

Phyllis F. Field

silversmithing. See GOLDSMITHING AND SILVERSMITHING.

Silver Springs. Village (pop 844) in Gainesville (Wyoming Co). The village was served by the Erie Railroad (1852) and the Rochester and State Line Railroad (1877). The first salt well was drilled in 1883 by the Duncan Salt Co, which became the Worcester Salt Co in 1894. Its Silver Springs plant developed the process of crystalizing salt in enclosed vacuum pans. The village incorporated in 1895. The Silver Springs Manufacturing Co (1900–*ca* 1965; later Lucas Rule Co) produced rulers and yardsticks. Since 1943 the salt operation has been part of the Morton Salt Co.

Sinclairville. Village (pop 665) in Charlotte and Gerry (Chautauqua Co). It is named for Maj Samuel Sinclear, who erected a mill in 1810; the spelling was changed when the post office was founded in 1869. With a station on the Dunkirk, Allegheny Valley and Pittsburgh Railroad (1871), Sinclairville became a small industrial village producing cheese, rakes, carriages, and brooms in the center of dairy country. The first cooperative cheese factory in the state was opened in Sinclairville in 1865. The village incorporated in 1887. Although the local school districts were consolidated in 1938, Sinclairville retained an elementary school. Residents commute to Jamestown, with smaller numbers to Buffalo and Olean (Cattaraugus Co).

Michelle Henry

Singer, Isaac Bashevis (*b* Leoncin, Poland, 14 July 1904; *d* Surfside, Fla, 24 July 1991). Writer. The son of a poor Hasidic rabbi, Singer moved with his family to Radzymin, a small Jewish village in Poland, in 1907. He enrolled in the Tachkemoni Rabbinical Seminary in Warsaw in 1921 but dropped out after only one year, and in 1923 he took a proofreader position at *Literarishe Bletter,* a Warsaw Yiddish literary magazine. In 1935 he immigrated to New York City and freelanced for the *Forverts (Forward),* which later serialized several of his novels. His American tales focus on the dislocation of Jewish immigrants and are frequently set in New York City or the Catskill Mountains of the Hudson Valley. Singer's eastern European work was realistic but often featured mystics and was tinged with eerie and supernatural elements. It was also, for Yiddish fiction of the time, quite sexually explicit. He captured critical recognition when his *Family Moskat* was translated into English in 1950. Singer was extraordinarily prolific, publishing at least 12 collections of short stories, 13 children's books, and numerous memoir collections during his lifetime. Among his works with New York State settings are *Enemies: A Love Story* (1972) and *Shadows on the Hudson* (1999). In 1978 he became the first, and very likely the only, Yiddish writer to receive the Nobel Prize for literature.

Hadda, Janet. *Isaac Bashevis Singer: A Life* (New York: Oxford Univ Press, 1997)

Mark Noon

Singer Sewing Machine Company. Manufacturer of the first technically and commercially successful sewing machine, with headquarters in New York City since 1853. Company founder Isaac Merritt Singer (1813–75), the son of German immigrants, lived his first 12 years in Oswego before running away to join a band of traveling stage players. From his early teens he worked in machine shops while continuing to appear on the stage. In 1850 Singer developed a sewing machine that—unlike earlier models employing wooden operating parts and curved needles that emulated hand motions—featured precision metal working parts and a straight needle that moved vertically. In August of 1850 he established Singer Sewing Machine Co in Boston and soon faced patent infringement charges from the creator of an earlier sewing machine, Elias Howe. Singer hired attorney Edward S. Clark to represent him in the lawsuit with Howe; in return, Clark gained a partnership in Singer's fledgling company. On 1 Jan 1851 Clark and Singer renamed the company I. M. Singer and Co and on 12 Aug 1851 obtained a patent for Singer's invention. In 1853 the company located its main office and a manufacturing facility on Manhattan's Mott St.

In May 1854 I. M. Singer and Co—already the world's largest sewing machine makers—settled the Howe lawsuit. Freed from this encumbrance, the company expanded, opening branch offices that eventually extended throughout Europe and South America. Clark's pioneering marketing techniques, such as installment purchases, trade-in policies for old machines, and regular service support at all branches, spurred this growth. In 1857 the company moved its headquarters and showroom to 458 Broadway in Manhattan and within the year opened three New York City plants that made 20,000 machines annually. During this period Isaac Singer's research produced 22 additional sewing machine patents resulting in enhanced models, such as the No. 1, No. 2, and No. 3 Standards, the Turtle Back, the Grasshopper, the Letter A, and the New Family sewing machines.

In 1863, following Isaac Singer's involvement in scandal (his wife and daughter sued him for assault), Clark forced the inventor from any leadership role in the company, which boasted capital assets of $550,000 that year. Over the next decade, the company opened its first overseas manufacturing facility in Glasgow, Scotland, and built another large plant in Elizabethport, NJ. By 1880 the company's worldwide annual production surpassed 500,000 units; it had become the first successful multinational manufacturing company. In 1904 it regained its old name, Singer Sewing Machine Co and two years later completed construction of a 47-story headquarters building at 149 Broadway, briefly the world's tallest building. By 1913 sales peaked at 3 million machines a year, and the company employed 100,000 persons in 125 countries. Sales declined during World War I, the depression years, and World War II, with Singer retooling most of its operations to produce war matériel in both world conflicts. In 1957 the company sold 1.9 million machines.

In 1961 executive offices relocated to Manhattan's 30 Rockefeller Plaza, and soon afterward the company became simply Singer Co. Home sewing declined in the United States, and Japanese competitors further diminished Singer's sewing machine business. In the early 1960s Singer diversified into the aerospace industry, becoming one of the largest US aerospace companies. Diversification-related financial troubles of the 1970s led to a takeover by corporate raider Paul Bilzerian in 1988, subsequent looting of Singer's assets, and bankruptcy in 1989. That year Hong Kong businessman James H. Ting acquired a controlling interest in Singer Co, divested the aerospace holdings, and revitalized the sewing-related portion of the business. Following a further bout of financial trouble, Singer Co reincorporated in 1999 as Singer N.V., headquartered in the Netherlands Antilles, though its operating company, Singer Corp, maintains a headquarters at 915 Broadway in Manhattan. Singer was in many ways the first successful US-based multinational company.

Bissell, Don. *The First Conglomerate: 145 Years of the Singer Sewing Machine Company* (Brunswick, Maine: Audenreed Press, 1999)
Brandon, Ruth. *A Capitalist Romance* (New York: J. B. Lippincott, 1977)
Davies, Robert Bruce. *Peacefully Working to Conquer the World: Singer Sewing Machines in Foreign Markets* (New York: Arno Press, 1976)

Don Bissell

singing schools. The singing school, early America's most important musical institution, was a brief course in musical sight reading and choral singing, taught by a singing master according to traditional methods with the aid of printed tunebooks containing instructions, exercises, and sacred choral music. Singing schools arose from British antecedents around 1700 as part of an effort to reform congregational singing in colonial churches. In New England the movement grew quickly and culminated in the first school of American composers and in the publication of hundreds of sacred tunebooks from 1770 to 1810 and the establishment of singing schools nationwide. Singing schools, held during slack agricultural seasons, attracted children and young men and women and were among the few amusements attended by both sexes, and hence were long associated with courting.

In New York State, hundreds of singing masters, most born in New England, were active in every part of the state, rural and urban. Some, like Ishmael Spicer (1760–1832) and Stephen Jenks (1772–1856), were itinerant, teaching for a season in one community and then moving on. Others, such as Lewis Edson (1748–1820) of Mink Hollow (Ulster Co) and Timothy Olmsted (1759–1848) of Whitestown (Oneida Co), became permanent or long-term residents of their towns. Although they were the first musical professionals in many areas, most singing masters pursued other occupations as well. The humorous figure of singing master and schoolmaster Ichabod Crane in Washington Irving's "Legend of Sleepy Hollow," though fictional, represents a typical Yankee stereotype in a Dutch Hudson Valley village.

Lowens, Irving. *Music and Musicians in Early America* (New York: Norton, 1964)

David Warren Steel

Sing Sing Correctional Facility. The state's second-oldest and second-largest prison, located 33 miles (53 km) from New York City, in the Village of Sing Sing [now Ossining, Westchester Co]. Originally named Mount Pleasant Prison, it was renamed Sing Sing Prison in 1848. Construction began in May 1825 to replace aging Newgate Prison in New York City. One hundred convicts were brought from Auburn Prison (Cayuga Co) to begin building the new institution from the marble deposits on the site. Auburn's warden, Elam Lynds, oversaw the construction and became Sing Sing's first warden. Mount Pleasant Female Prison operated as part of the prison from 1839 until 1877, when overcrowding forced the state to place female inmates in county penitentiaries.

Lynds perfected the ruthless discipline he began at Auburn, using enforced silence, the lockstep, striped uniforms, frequent floggings, as well as cruel techniques such as the yoke and the water bath. Brutality at Sing Sing was encouraged by contract labor agreements, through which prison officials profited as inmates made boots, barrels, and brushes under the pain of the whip. While there were a number of investigations into abuse at the prison, most New Yorkers believed the prevailing corrections philosophy that harsh discipline was necessary to ensure penitent inmates. The Village of Sing Sing changed its name in 1901 to Ossining, so that products could be distinguished from those made in the prison.

Much of the harsh treatment of prisoners was abandoned by the turn of the century; the lockstep was abolished in 1900, the striped uniforms, in 1904, and the rule of silence, in 1914. Thomas Mott Osborne, warden from 1914 to 1915, instituted a clinic where inmates were examined and classified according to mental and psychological characteristics. He also created Mutual Welfare Leagues, self-improvement associations for prisoners, making Mott popular among inmates and social critics. Yet Mott's reforms served to alienate many in the prison hierarchy, who forced his retirement after only one year at Sing Sing, although his reforms proved longer lasting. Lewis E. Lawes served as warden from 1920 to 1941, championed fewer punishments, criticized the death penalty, and oversaw the expansion and modernization of the prison's physical plant. Lawes wrote a number of popular books, including *Life and Death in Sing Sing* (1928) and *20,000 Years in Sing Sing* (1932). During the 1970s the original cellblocks were closed and later placed on the National Register of Historic Places to help preserve the prison's history. Inmate disturbances, including a 1966 prisonwide strike and a 1983 hostage crisis, have led to additional reforms, including converting the death house into space for vocational programs. A new visiting room and indoor recreation area were added, and in 1998 the original 1877 wall was replaced with a modern perimeter fence. Renamed Ossining Correctional Facility in 1970, it became Sing Sing Correctional Facility in 1985.

First popularized by visitors such as Alexis de Tocqueville and Charles Dickens during the 1830s, the prison has long been iconic. Convicts in New York City were "sent up the river" to Sing Sing, a phrase popularized in the 1930s. Much of the image of Sing Sing is linked to prisoner executions. Beginning in 1891, 614 criminals were electrocuted in Sing Sing's death house, including eight in one day in 1912. After 1914 all executions in New York State took place at Sing Sing. Those electrocuted included crime boss Louis "Lepke" Buchalter (1944), "Lonely Hearts Killer" Martha Beck (1951), and convicted spies Ethel and Julius Rosenberg (1953). The last execution at Sing Sing took place in 1963.

A number of books written by staff and former inmates have kept the prison in the public eye. These include *A Voice from Sing Sing* (1833), an exposé of the prison's brutal conditions by former inmate Levi Burr; *Life in Sing Sing State Prison* (1860) by Chaplain John Luckey; *I Was Condemned to the Chair* (1934) by Edward McGrath; and *Newjack: Guarding Sing Sing* (2000) by Ted Conover. The institution also became known through movies like *The Big House* (1930) and *Angels with Dirty Faces* (1938). In 2001, 704 correctional officers and 268 staff worked at the facility, which had a population of approximately 2,300 men in the maximum security prison and the medium security Tappan annex built in 1973.

Prisoners lined up at Sing Sing Prison.

Christianson, Scott. *Condemned: Inside the Sing Sing Death House* (New York: New York Univ Press, 2000)
Conover, Ted. *Newjack: Guarding Sing Sing* (New York: Random House, 2000)

Richard Andress

Sisters of Charity Hospital at Buffalo. The city's first public hospital founded by three Sisters of Charity in August 1848 to provide "relief of the sick and destitute" of all faiths. Antebellum hospitals were chiefly for those who could not afford home care, and physicians provided their services gratuitously. The opening of the 100-bed hospital proved timely because a cholera epidemic struck Buffalo in 1849. The mortality rate at Sisters Hospital was far lower than for those who stayed home or were admitted to the county's emergency ad hoc facility. The institution was the first teaching hospital for the University of Buffalo Medical College (1848–83) and its later short-lived rival Niagara Medical School (1883–98). Sisters Hospital opened Buffalo's first emergency ward in 1883, which became Emergency Hospital in 1884. The facility has been continuously owned and operated by the sisterhood and in the 21st century specializes in women's health care for seniors and treatment of alcohol and substance abuse. In 2002 the hospital had 413 beds.

Richardson, Jean. "Catholic Religious Women as Institutional Innovators: The Sisters of Charity and the Rise of the Modern Urban Hospital in Buffalo, NY, 1848–1900" (PhD diss, SUNY Buffalo, 1996)

Jean Richardson

Skaneateles [SKAN-EE-AT-LES]. Town (pop 7,323) and village (pop 2,616) in SW Onondaga Co. Settled in 1794, the town was formed in 1830 from Marcellus, and the village incorporated in 1833. The Skaneateles Community (1843–45) was a communal experiment. The Village of Skaneateles and the hamlets of Mottville and Skaneateles Falls became industrial centers before 1850, producing wool cloth, mill machinery, carriages, sleighs, paper, bricks, ironwork, and farm implements. The industries were served by the Skaneateles Railroad (1840–50, 1867–1971). Canoes, motor launches, and sailboats were manufactured in town from 1876 to 1953. The town's most distinctive agricultural product was teasels, marketed by factories in the village until 1960. In the early 21st century, Welch Allyn employs 965 workers, manufacturing medical and bar-code scanning products. Tourism is a mainstay of the economy; Skaneateles Lake and the village's historic district (1985) are the chief attractions, along with the Skaneateles Festival (1980; chamber music) and Dickens Christmas, an annual event. Landmark businesses are the Sherwood Inn (1807, rebuilt 1872) and Krebs Restaurant (1899).

Patricia Blackler

Skaneateles Community. Founded in 1843 on a 350-acre (142 ha) tract of land in Mottville in the Town of Skaneateles (Onondaga Co), it was one of the many utopian experiments in the Burned-over District between 1800 and 1860. The Society for Universal Inquiry and Reform, organized in Ohio in 1842, established the Skaneateles Community as one of a projected series of communities in which coercive law and religion and competitive economics would give way to nonresistance and the government of God, whereby human government is replaced by God's laws. John A. Collins (1810–90), a well-known abolitionist with ties to William Lloyd Garrison, emerged as the community's leader. In its three years of existence, about 100 residents, mostly abolitionists and Hicksite Quakers from all over New York State as well as from New England and Pennsylvania, embraced vegetarianism and women's rights, repudiated evangelical religion, and sought to show the superiority of cooperative principles over economic competition. They also endorsed common property, divorce, agnosticism, and education for all. They supported themselves through farming and sawmill work. Families shared living quarters, with many residing in a large farmhouse that still stands at the site of the community. Other buildings included the sawmill, a woodworking shop, and a print shop for the publication of the community organ, the *Communitist.* Undermined by internal dissension and Collins's disillusionment, the community dissolved in May 1846.

Hamm, Thomas D. *God's Government Begun: The Society for Universal Inquiry and Reform* (Bloomington: Indiana Univ Press, 1995)

Noyes, John Humphrey. "The Skaneateles Community." In *History of American Socialisms* (1870; repr New York: Hillary House Publications, 1961)

Wells, Lester Grosvenor. *The Skaneateles Communal Experiment* (Syracuse: Onondaga Historical Association, 1953)

Thomas D. Hamm

Skaneateles Festival. Summer chamber music festival. The festival takes place each August in the town of Skaneateles (Onondaga Co), located southwest of Syracuse. The festival was founded in 1980 by the pianist and composer Robert Weirich, who retired in 1999; he was succeeded by another notable pianist and chamber musician, Diane Walsh. In its quarter century of existence, the Skaneateles Festival has grown into a month-long festival that has attracted many notable regional musicians (from Syracuse, Rochester, and Binghamton) and such famous soloists as violinist Hilary Hahn, bassist Edgar Meyer, and pianist Garrick Ohlsson. Besides chamber music concerts, the festival includes special weekday morning concerts for children and weekly outdoor orchestral concerts at nearby Brook Farm. All are enhanced by the natural beauty of Skaneateles Lake and the surrounding hills. The Skaneateles Festival has won several ASCAP (American Society of Composers, Authors and Publishers) Awards for adventurous programming of contemporary music.

David Raymond

Skaneateles Lake (13.8 mi²/35.74 km²). The fourth largest of the Finger Lakes of Central New York. The lake is located in the Oswego River Drainage Basin in Onondaga and Cortland Cos, and at its northernmost point is approximately 20 miles (32 km) southwest of Syracuse. At the north end of the lake is the Village of Skaneateles (Onondaga Co). Cottages were built on the lakeshores beginning in 1881, and in 2002 there were over 1,000 residences. The lake is 16 miles (25.8 km) long, .75 mile (1.21 km) wide, with a maximum depth of 300 feet (91.4 m) and a mean elevation of 863.27 feet (263.12 m) above sea level. It was formed during the Pleistocene era from glacial ice that moved south across the region, carving long and thin "fingers" in the ground. The watershed is steeply sloped and the basin spans 59.3 miles² (153.59 km²) through Onondaga, Cortland, and Cayuga Cos. The geomorphology of the basin is responsible for the lake's extremely pure water. The City of Syracuse has depended on the lake as its primary drinking-water supply since 1889, and it also supplies water for the Towns of Skaneateles, DeWitt, Onondaga, Geddes, Camillus, and Salina (Onondaga Co). The lake has an AA water purity rating, and the New York State Department of Health allows its use as a drinking-water supply without filtration. The Skaneateles Lake Watershed Land Protection Program encourages conservation easements, paying landowners to protect their property from development permanently and to manage it in a way that maintains high water quality.

Samuel H. Sage

Skidmore College. Private, liberal arts college. Founded on 31 Aug 1911 in Saratoga Springs as Skidmore School of Arts for Women through a gift from Lucy Skidmore Scribner, daughter-in-law of the publisher Charles Scribner. Widowed after two years of marriage, Scribner devoted herself to creating practical education opportunities for women in Saratoga Springs. The school became Skidmore College in 1922, chartered by the State Board of Regents to grant four-year degrees. In the 1930s the college included 20 buildings in downtown Saratoga, and by 1957 the campus had extended to 80 buildings. A new campus was built in the 1960s on the outskirts of Saratoga Springs. In 1971 the college began enrolling men and also started University without Walls, a nontraditional and nonresidential program that allows students to self-direct their studies (with advisor consultation) to define their own BA or BS degree. The curriculum includes both traditional liberal arts and preprofessional disciplines. In 1993 an MA in Liberal Studies was also offered at the college. Recent construction has included the renovation and expansion of Scribner Library (1995), an addition to Dana Science Center (1996), and the building of Tang Teaching Museum and Art Gallery (2000). Enrollment in 2002 was 2,200 with 59% female and 41% male.

Lynn, Mary C. *Make No Small Plans: A History of Skidmore College* (Saratoga Springs: Skidmore College, 2000)

Mary Anne Hansen

skiing. Cross-country skiing, brought to America by 19th-century Norwegian immigrants, was an established sport when Melvil Dewey organized a resort near Lake Placid (Essex Co) in 1895. The Lake Placid Club opened for winter recreation in 1904 and in 1920 hired Norwegian Henrik Jacobsen as the first paid instructor at a US ski school. The exclusive Lake Placid Club gave skiing an aura of glamour. The Reforestation Law of 1929 and the Hewitt amendment of 1931 authorized the Conservation Department to use land acquired for reforestation for recreation as well. When enthusiasts such as Melvil Dewey's son Godfrey brought the 1932 Winter Olympics to Lake Placid, then a village of fewer than 4,000, an estimated $1 million was injected into the community to provide facilities for the games, including downhill skiing paths, the Intervale ski jump, and the 31 mi (49.9 km) cross-country ski trail from the Olympic Stadium to Clifford Falls, Hart Lake, and back to the stadium.

Cross-country skiing and ski jumping were the traditional Nordic skiing activities, but the Alpine pursuits of downhill and slalom were gaining favor. Although only rope tows were available, and skiing depended on daylight and natural snow, growing interest in the sport produced new venues such as Gore Mountain in Warren Co. Otto Schniebs founded a ski school at Lake Placid in 1936; Schniebs was a student of Hannes Schneider, who developed the Arlberg technique, a method of teaching Alpine skiing, as well as the distinctive Arlberg crouch. In 1938 Charles Minot Dole, vice president of the Amateur Ski Club of New York, became chairman of the new National Ski Patrol System, which prepared skiers for volunteer rescue work. For many

THEY LIKE WINTER IN NEW YORK STATE
THE STATE THAT HAS EVERYTHING

WPA poster touts skiing in New York State, by J. Rivolta, *ca* 1940.

decades the ski jump at Bear Mountain State Park was one of the premier venues in the Northeast.

New York City merchants contributed to the popularity of skiing, despite their "ski slopes" being carpeted indoor slides topped with crushed ice or borax. Madison Square Garden hosted an International Ski Meet and Winter Sports Show in 1936, drawing 80,000 people to see ski demonstrations and spend over $200,000 on sports paraphernalia. Mt Peter in Orange Co was founded in the 1930s by investors affiliated with Macy's department store. Saks, Wanamaker's, and Macy's attracted shoppers with in-store ski-jumping performances on fabricated ski runs, and a fashionable style of clothing developed around skiing activities. In 1939 Otto Lang premiered *Ski Flight* at Radio City Music Hall, the debut of American ski theater. New York City society embraced downhill, turning skiing into a component of sophistication. In 1950 Lake Placid hosted the national ski-jumping competition. The Winter Olympics returned to Lake Placid in 1980, renewing awareness of skiing as a major industry. In 1989 New York State passed the Safety in Skiing Code promoting safety in the Alpine ski industry and presenting detailed codes of conduct for downhill skiers and for ski area operators.

As the young adults of the post–World War II baby boom entered the recreation market, they swelled the ranks of Alpine skiers and initiated the practice of snowboarding. Early snowboards were difficult to control, but safer snowboards came on the market in the 1970s, and within a decade ski resorts began accepting snowboarders. Over 40 locales across the state provide opportunities for skiing. Skiers from Albany, Utica, Rome, and Syracuse flock to sites in the North Country and Adirondacks, such as McCauley Mountain in Herkimer Co, Gore Mountain in Warren Co, and Whiteface Mountain in Essex Co. Venues in the Catskill Mountains, such as Hunter Mountain in Greene Co and Belleayre Mountain in Ulster Co, attract skiers from New York City, the lower Hudson Valley, and western Connecticut. Central New York skiers are served by a number of ski areas, such as Greek Peak Mountain Resort in Cortland Co, which draws additional skiers from the New York City metropolitan area and Pennsylvania. Snow Ridge Ski Area in Turin (Lewis Co) promotes its location on the Tug Hill Plateau as the source of the heaviest snowfall in the East. The appealing ski terrain of western New York draws skiers from the Midwest and Canada to locales such as Bristol Mountain in Ontario Co and Holiday Valley Resort and HoliMont in Cattaraugus Co. By the 21st century the ski industry had a direct economic impact of over $250 million on New York State and employed over 10,000 workers, with ancillary services for skiers creating another 10,000 jobs.

Allen, E. John B. *From Skisport to Skiing: 100 Years of an American Sport, 1840–1940* (Amherst: Univ of Massachusetts Press, 1993)

Crowder, Robert C. *The Alpine Ski Industry in New York State, 1985–86* ([Albany]: NYS Department of Commerce, 1987)

R. Jake Sudderth

skyscrapers. The skyscraper evolved as a building type in the 19th century, mainly to accommodate business. By the end of the 20th century, skyscrapers existed throughout the state and were clustered in cities but also punctuated the atmosphere in suburban and even rural areas. It was in New York City that the building type would achieve its greatest fulfillment. Indeed, with the exception of Chicago, no place in the world would prove more important in the development of the skyscraper than New York City.

The Tall Building Emerges

The building type, first known simply as the tall building, began to proliferate around the time of the Civil War as New York City's economy expanded and Lower Manhattan, especially along Broadway, became densely developed. It was engendered in part by technological innovations, particularly Elisha Graves Otis's safety passenger elevator. New York City's first passenger elevator equipped with a safety device was put into use in 1857 when the cast-iron-clad Haughwout Store on lower Broadway was completed. Prosperous businesses, including insurance companies and enterprises focused on communications and media, sought to build large, impressive headquarters that would serve not only as efficient buildings but also as powerful advertisements for their owners. Completed in 1870, the Equitable Building, designed by Gillian and Kendall with George B. Post, at seven and a half stories high was the first office building in the world to be designed with passenger elevators. Within five years, several 10-story structures were completed in New York City, including the New York Tribune Building (1872) by Richard Morris Hunt and the Western Union Building (1875). The Tower Building (1889, Bradford L. Gilbert), 11 stories tall, pioneered skeleton construction. Since the building's metal frame supported floors and walls, exterior walls were thinner than those of conventionally constructed masonry buildings.

Located just east of City Hall Park, Newspaper Row was the first precinct in New York City to be developed with a cluster of tall buildings, realizing the potential of the building type to produce an identifiable and memorable skyline. The ensemble included Post's New York World, or Pulitzer Building (1889), which incorporated a highly visible gilded dome. At 309 feet (94.2 m) the building was the tallest in the city and the first to surpass the 284 ft (86.6 m) steeple of the city's Gothic-style Trinity Church (1846, Richard Upjohn). With this accomplishment the skyscraper gained new authority as a symbol of corporate strength, and it became an indelible feature of the state's built environment.

The Race for Height

In the 1890s, as skeleton construction became common and the term skyscraper came into vogue, both commercial demand and popular taste for tall buildings increased. Louis Sullivan's only New York City building, the Bayard-Condict Building (1899), incorporated piers terminating in depictions of angels with outstretched arms. Daniel Burnham's 21-story Flatiron Building (1903) was located at the southwestern corner of Madison Square Park. At 307 feet (93.8 m) the building memorably filled the triangular site formed by the intersection of two of the city's most important streets, Broadway and 5th Ave. Though the building's official name was the Fuller Building, it was widely know as the Flatiron, a comical reference to its distinctive shape. Along with the Brooklyn Bridge and the Statue of Liberty, the Flatiron became a sensation and was one of the city's most popular postcard images.

Despite skyscrapers' appeal, their height and bulk affected the amount of light and air reaching the streets below, causing widespread concern. Architect Ernest Flagg hypothesized that regardless of height a skyscraper would not exert a negative impact on the surrounding area if it occupied only 25% of a site. Above a full-site base, Flagg's 612 ft (186.5 m) Singer Tower (1908) was a slender shaft, which elegantly illustrated his theory and established another new record for height. In 1909 Napoleon Le Brun's 50-story Metropolitan Life Insurance Tower, also a base-and-tower composition with the tower modeled after the Campanile of San Marco, Venice, became the world's tallest building at 700 feet (213.3 m). Cass Gilbert's brilliantly romantic Gothic-inspired Woolworth Building was completed in 1913 and was 792 feet (241.4 m); it remained the world's tallest building for nearly three decades. Dubbed a "cathedral of commerce" by Brooklyn minister Rev Samuel Parkes Cadman, the building's steel frame was clad in masonry and terra-cotta. Gilbert employed decorative forms inspired by medieval cathedrals and intended to emphasize the building's vertical dimension.

Despite the aesthetic and urbanistic success of tower-like skyscrapers, buildings that all but filled their sites continued to be built in New York City. The Equitable Life Assurance Society Building (1915, E. R. Graham) rose up 38 stories without a single setback. Detractors claimed that the behemoth cast four-block-long shadows at noon. Reaction to the building spearheaded the city to pass the nation's first zoning law limiting a building's bulk and height. Ratified in 1916 the law created a so-called zoning envelope and stipulated that upper floors should be set back from those below. A tower of unlimited height could occupy a maximum of 25% of the site. The law stimulated the design and construction of "wedding cake"-style buildings.

The Boom Years

During the 1920s and early 1930s there was a dramatic increase in skyscraper construction. Prosperity and favorable financial terms sparked real estate speculation, which in turn drove up land prices and motivated builders to build ever higher. Many of the best-known office buildings in New York City were completed in this period, among them the 1,048 ft (319.4 m) Chrysler Building (1930, William Van Alen) and the 1,250 ft (381.0 m) Empire State Building (1931, Shreve, Lamb, and Harmon). Both adopted a modernistic architectural vocabulary popularly known as Art Deco. The Chrysler Building was distinguished by ornamental forms derived from car design in direct reference to the owner's products; the circular forms on a frieze evoked hubcaps, while immense gargoyles in the shape of eagles looked like car hood ornaments. The triangular forms of the building's signature pinnacle reminded many observers of the spokes of a wheel. The rooftop observation deck of the Empire State Building became one of the city's chief tourist attractions, particularly after the 1933 movie *King Kong* immortalized the building.

Prewar Decline and the Post-1950 Surge

Skyscraper construction was almost nonexistent throughout the latter half of the 1930s and much of the 1940s, with the important exception of Rockefeller Center in Midtown Manhattan. Designed by a team of architectural firms collectively known as the Associated Architects, with Raymond Hood playing a principal role in the overall design, the complex of 19 buildings was designed and built between 1929 and 1939. It contained a wide variety of facilities, including the 70-story RCA Building (now General Electric Building), Radio City Music Hall, and numerous outdoor public spaces, one of which could function as an ice-skating rink. The center demonstrated the potential of the skyscraper type to create a compelling urban ensemble, a virtual city within a city. Following World War II, advances in metal-and-glass curtain-wall construction, as well as air-conditioning, fostered the advent of inhabitable glass boxes. Among the earliest of these were the UN Secretariat Building (1950, Wallace K. Harrison, director of planning) and Lever House (1952, Skidmore, Owings and Merrill [SOM]). The Seagram Building (1958, Ludwig Mies van der Rohe, Philip Johnson, and Kahn and Jacobs) set a new standard for architectural excellence and broke with the building wall of Park Ave, setting itself back on an elegantly spare plaza.

In 1961, inspired in part by the positive critical response to the pioneering Modernist buildings of the 1950s, New York City leaders adopted radical revisions to the zoning laws for the first time since 1916. New legislation established that a building's maximum volume was to be based on a multiple of its lot's size; this formula became known as the floor area ratio (FAR). The inclusion of public amenities and spaces allowed a developer to add additional floors. These zoning resolutions had a profound influence on skyscraper development in the state and elsewhere. The zoning encouraged a tower-set-amidst-a-plaza formula that was seen throughout New York City and particularly in the redevelopment of 6th Ave, which included skyscrapers designed by Wallace K. Harrison. In the 1980s shifts in architectural fashion led some practitioners to move away the glass-box paradigm. In New York City, Philip Johnson's American Telephone and Telegraph Building (1984, now Sony Building) used masonry cladding, as well as ornament and historical reference, recalling the towers of an earlier generation. The structurally innovative World Trade Center (1973, Minoru Yamasaki, and Emery Roth and Sons) was 110 stories high. Unprecedented in size, the Twin Towers held the title of the world's tallest buildings for less than a year before being supplanted by the Sears Tower (1974, SOM) in Chicago. The towers were destroyed in a terrorist attack on 11 Sept 2001. The attack raised questions about the viability of the skyscraper type in the 21st century. Many of the entrants in the international design competition for buildings' replacement, including the winning design by Daniel Libeskind, demonstrated the continuing vitality of the skyscraper form.

Skyscrapers outside of New York City

Although New York City has long been an epicenter of the skyscraper type, other cities in the state have hosted tall buildings as well. The state's first significant skyscraper outside New York City was Buffalo's Guaranty Building, designed by Louis Sullivan and Dankmar Alder and completed in 1896. The imposing 13-story building celebrated verticality with uninterrupted piers culminating in graceful arches. Highly intricate terra-cotta decoration, for which Sullivan was known, enlivened the facades. The first tall building in Rochester was the Romanesque Wilder Building (1888, Andrew Jackson Warner, J. G. Cutler, and William Brockett) at 170 feet (51.8 m), followed by Warner's Powers Building (1891) at 175 ft (53.3 m). Syracuse's Romanesque City Hall (1889) was 150 feet (45.7 m) and for a long time the tallest building in the city. In 1901 Buffalo's Electric Tower, a temporary structure built for the Pan-American Exposition, dazzled nighttime viewers with its array of electric lights and its 386 ft (117.7 m) height. The structure served as the inspiration for the 294 ft (89.6 m) octagonal tower designed by August Esenwein and James A. Johnson, the General Electric Tower (now Niagara Mohawk Building) erected in Buffalo in 1912. The 23-story Liberty Building, designed by Alfred Bossom, was completed. In 1931 City Hall, designed by Dietel and Wade in Art Deco style, at 378 ft (115.2 m) became Buffalo's tallest building.

Many cities built high-rise structures for local businesses. In 1913 architect Howard Cutler completed Rochester's most famous skyscraper the Eastman Kodak Building. The 366 ft (111.6 m), 19-story structure had a steel skeleton and a terra-cotta facade. An aluminum tower was added in 1931 above the 19th floor. In Albany, a center for transportation, the most important skyscraper of the era was the Delaware and Hudson Building (1918), the railroad's headquarters, and is now the administrative headquarters of the SUNY system. The Neo-Gothic design and Flemish style was the work of Marcus T. Reynolds. Although the main structure had only 5 main floors, the towers made it the city's tallest structure; the center tower was 13 stories high. It was also an impressive 660 feet long (201.2 m). Hotels throughout the state also adopted the new high-rise style. Hotel Utica (1912), at 150 feet (45.7 m), had 112 rooms and was the city's tallest building. Abandoned for decades it was renovated and reopened in April 2001.

Every major city in the state built a number of structures in Art Deco style during the 1920s and 1930s, including Rochester's Genesee Valley Trust Building/Times Square Building (1930), at 260 feet (79.3 m), Syracuse's State Tower (1928), 315 feet (96.0 m), which had 22 floors, and Albany's Alfred E. Smith State Office Building (1930, Sullivan Jones and William Haugaard), which was 388 feet (118.3 m) with 34 floors.

In the 1960s and 1970s many International-style high-rises, including corporate headquarters, were built throughout New York State. Rochester, followed by Buffalo, has the most skyscrapers outside of New York City early in the 21st century. Between 1960 and 1976 more than 20 skyscrapers were built in Rochester, including the city's tallest structure, the Xerox Tower (1968, Welton Beckett Associated), at 443 feet (135.0 m), and Chase Tower (1973), at 392 feet (119.5 m), and celebrated since it wings out at the base. Designed by SOM, the precast-concrete the Marine Midland Building (now HSBC Building) was completed in Buffalo in 1970 and is 529 feet (161.2 m). Syracuse's notable MONY, or Carrier, Towers were completed in 1966, at 268 feet (81.7 m), and the Toomey Abbott Towers, at 229 feet (69.8 m), were completed in 1968. In the outskirts of Albany, four skyscraper dormitories called the University Towers (1965–71) were built for SUNY Albany, and each was 286 feet (87.2 m). Wallace K. Harrison had designed four identical skyscrapers by 1974, each 22 stories, which were agency buildings in the Empire State Plaza in Albany. Harrison's Mayor Erastus Corning 2d Tower (1973) is 589 feet (179.5 m) and the tallest structure in the state outside of New York City. While the skyscraper remained the single most iconic expression of corporate America throughout the post–World War II era, at the Empire State Plaza, Harrison sought to utilize the skyscraper to express a sense of governmental authority and civic pride.

Goldberger, Paul. *The Skyscraper* (New York: Knopf, 1982)

Landau, Sarah Bradford, and Carl W. Condit. *Rise of the New York Skyscraper: 1865–1913* (New Haven, Conn: Yale Univ Press, 1996)

Reisem, Richard O. *Classic Buffalo: A Heritage of Distinguished Architecture* (Buffalo: Canisius College Press, 1999)

Stern, Robert A. M., Gregory Gilmartin, and John Massengale. *New York 1900: Metropolitan Architecture and Urbanism* (New York: Rizzoli, 1983)

Stern, Robert A. M., Gregory Gilmartin, and Thomas Mellins. *New York 1930: Architecture and Urbanism between Two World Wars* (New York: Rizzoli, 1987)

Stern, Robert A.M., Thomas Mellins, and David Fishman. *New York 1960: Architecture and Urbanism between the Second World War and the Bicentennial* (New York: Monacelli Press, 1995)

———. *New York 1880: Architecture and Urbanism in the Gilded Age* (New York: Monacelli Press, 1999)

Thomas Mellins

slavery. Slavery was common in New York Colony and the state from the inception of white settlement in the 1620s until state legislation extinguished it in 1827. Forms of bonded servitude existed among Native American bands and nations, in African regions from which enslaved peoples were imported to New York, and in similar forms among the English, Dutch, French, and German peoples who migrated to New York. Even after 1827 the effects of human bondage weighed heavily on the state's African American population and affected the political attitudes of Whites. The nature of slavery in New York Colony was significant in all sections settled by Whites. There were varying conditions of slavery in Long Island and New York City, in the Hudson Valley from Westchester to Columbia Co, in Albany and Schenectady Cos, and the western regions. Many factors influenced the conduct of slavery in the different regions, including the ethnicities of Whites and Blacks, religion, demography, the slave trade, slave uprisings and individual resistance, work, and international politics.

In New Netherland

Although slavery did not exist in the Netherlands, the Dutch entered the Atlantic slave trade in the early 17th century by preying on Portuguese and Spanish traders. Dutch privateers captured Africans from the slave ships of other nations then brought captured people to New Amsterdam, where the Dutch West India Co (WIC) employed them mainly in agricultural work. Since New Amsterdam initially failed to at-

ENSLAVED PERSONS AND FREE BLACKS IN NEW YORK STATE

	1790		1800		1810		1820	
County	Enslaved Persons	Free Blacks	Enslaved Persons	Free Blacks	Enslaved Persons	Free Blacks	Enslaved Persons	Free Blacks
Albany	3,722	171	1,808	353	772	866	413	858
Allegany	—	—	—	—	21	0	17	12
Broome	—	—	—	—	23	30	25	63
Cattaraugus	—	—	—	—	—	—	2	4
Cayuga	—	—	53	19	75	86	48	191
Chautauqua	—	—	—	—	—	—	3	10
Chenango	—	—	16	40	13	76	7	189
Clinton[a]	16	16	58	62	29	32	2	96
Columbia	1,633	52	1,471	490	879	850	761	1,053
Cortland	—	—	—	—	0	2	3	48
Delaware	—	—	16	30	55	77	56	82
Dutchess	1,864	431	1,609	931	1,262	1,124	772	1,685
Essex[a]	—	—	—	—	0	3	3	28
Franklin	—	—	—	—	3	0	0	0
Genesee	—	—	—	—	11	14	35	82
Greene	—	—	520	59	367	371	134	637
Hamilton	—	—	—	—	—	—	1	1
Herkimer	—	—	61	8	64	77	72	188
Jefferson	—	—	—	—	0	40	5	135
Kings	1,482	46	1,479	332	1,118	735	879	882
Lewis	—	—	—	—	4	25	0	43
Madison	—	—	—	—	35	177	10	182
Montgomery	588	41	466	8	712	365	349	571
New York	2,373	1,119	2,868	3,499	1,686	8,137	518	10,368
Niagara	—	—	—	—	8	31	15	67
Oneida	—	—	50	73	81	130	9	368
Onondaga	—	—	11	18	50	114	59	195
Ontario	10	6	57	109	212	299	0	727
Orange	961	201	1,145	534	966	927	1,125	969
Oswego	—	—	—	—	—	—	0	32
Otsego	—	—	48	44	74	133	16	235
Putnam	—	—	—	—	—	—	49	166
Queens	2,308	819	1,528	1,431	809	2,354	559	2,648
Rensselaer	—	—	890	113	750	362	433	632
Richmond	755	127	675	83	437	274	532	78
Rockland	—	—	551	68	316	292	124	412
Saratoga	—	—	358	73	107	565	123	504
Schenectady	—	—	—	—	318	188	102	454
Schoharie	—	—	354	11	316	235	302	264
Seneca	—	—	—	—	101	44	84	180
St. Lawrence	—	—	—	—	5	17	8	14
Steuben	—	—	22	0	87	29	46	130
Suffolk	1,105	1,131	886	1,016	413	1,373	323	1,166
Sullivan	—	—	—	—	43	11	69	33
Tioga	—	—	17	33	61	39	104	32
Tompkins	—	—	—	—	—	—	6	66
Ulster	2,914	161	2,257	336	1,437	1,066	1,523	597
Warren	—	—	—	—	—	—	7	10
Washington	46	3	80	119	315	2,815[b]	150	254
Westchester	1,416	358	1,259	482	982	948	205	1,638
Total	21,193	4,682	20,613	10,374	15,017	25,333	10,088	29,279

Sources: US Census; Inter-university Consortium for Political and Social Research (ICPSR).

Notes: Only counties created by 1820 are shown. Many counties did not have their present boundaries. Census takers often mistakenly enumerated free Blacks as slaves. The 1830 federal census counted 75 slaves in New York State: Albany Co, 2; Chenango Co, 3; Montgomery Co, 26; New York Co, 17; Oneida Co, 15; Putnam Co, 4; and Washington Co, 8. It is likely all of these people were free Blacks.

[a]In 1800 data for Clinton and Essex Cos were combined.

[b]This anomalous figure appeared as such in the original census data.

tract a significant number of Europeans, the WIC used Africans as employees to build the forts in New Amsterdam and Fort Orange [now Albany]. Slaves constructed housing and worked to build roads and in 1644 were used as soldiers in Kieft's War. As a reward for faithful service, about 30 Africans were emancipated between 1644 and 1664 and were given small plots of land north of New Amsterdam, near Collect Pond in Lower Manhattan. This constituted the first free black class in the colony, and Blacks lived in the area for the next 200 years. Their presence was soon superseded by imports of Africans enslaved for life.

After the initial difficulties attracting Europeans and following complaints about company policy from those who did come, the WIC entered the Atlantic slave trade more assiduously. As an incentive to lure more farmers to the colony, the company promised to sell slaves to immigrants for farm labor. Since many émigrés were young families they needed bonds people to help create farms, making slaves essential for the success of the colony. Although manumission of slaves was possible, many Blacks remained enslaved for life.

Dutch commerce in slaves to New Netherland never matched the large shipments to the West Indies and South America, but Dutch traders sold Africans to local residents, New Englanders, or Virginians. By 1664 ownership of enslaved Africans spread throughout New Netherland. When the English conquered the Dutch colony in 1664, there were an estimated 800 Africans living in New Netherland, with 375 in New Amsterdam, of whom about 75 were probably free. While slavery did not exist as colonial law it had become a social reality.

The English Era

In the 60 years after the English takeover of the colony, English governors and their administrators hammered out a local code noir (black code), which attempted to restrict the freedoms of Africans and to identify the status of slaves. Local laws prohibiting sales of liquor to slaves were instituted throughout the province in the 1680s. Court cases determined that Native Americans could also be enslaved. Anxious about fugitives fleeing into Indian territories and New France, the legislature in 1705 passed a law mandating the death penalty to any slave found 50 miles (80 m) north of Albany.

The number of enslaved Africans soon outnumbered free people of color. The Royal African Co rarely sent cargoes of slaves to New York, but local merchants commissioned slave ships to purchase human chattel in Madagascar or bought enslaved people on small-lot consignments from the West Indies. Censuses in 1698 and 1703 showed over 2,000 slaves in the Province of New York. Up to 700 slaves lived in New York Co and marked increases occurred in Albany, Kings, Queens, and Westchester Cos. Overall one of every nine residents of New York Colony was an enslaved African.

There were three principal residential patterns for slaves. In urban environments, they lived in the households of the middle and upper classes in units of 3 to 5 slaves, with occasionally larger numbers up to 20. In the countryside the majority of slaves lived in similar small size units on tiny farms where they often made up the majority of a master's wealth. Few in number but important were plantations, which were owned by wealthy merchant-farmers such as the Philipse family in Westchester Co, where 50 to 60 enslaved Africans toiled. In all three areas, African males and females had multiple skills. The term "domestic" served to describe many functions from farmhand to butler. Via a thriving internal slave trade, enslaved Africans had to expect frequent changes in ownership. New York had become at least a "society with slaves," and in some sectors of society such as small farms, where enslaved Africans were the principal laborers, the colony approximated the social orders of southern slave societies.

European religions and ethnicities complicated the status of African slaves in New York. The Society for Propagation of the Gospel in Foreign Parts (SPG), the missionary wing of the Church of England, attempted to catechize and convert slaves in the colony. Dutch Reformed and Huguenot congregations (New Paltz in Ulster Co and New Rochelle in Westchester Co) feared conversion would emancipate Christian slaves and opposed the SPG. In 1706 Elias Neau, the chief Anglican missionary to African slaves, convinced the legislature to pass a law that kept baptized and converted slaves in bondage. Unconvinced and generally suspicious of the English, Dutch and Huguenot masters kept their slaves away from Neau. Angry Blacks viewed such efforts as unlawful hindrances to gaining religious and secular freedom, which also caused many Africans to remain outside the influence of European theologies.

Not all cultural interactions between Blacks and Whites were religious. A lively slave culture centered on work, but a tavern society and culture had emerged in the late 18th century. Weekly gatherings, nighttime excursions, and annual celebrations by Blacks at Shrove Tuesday and Pinkster (Pentecost) Sunday alarmed white authorities. Although the legislature passed draconian measures in 1706 to stop the gatherings, the frequency with which such laws were affirmed is testament to their failures. Other black actions directly attacked the slave system. Slaves ran away, sued their masters for freedom, fought them bitterly, and engaged in outright rebellion. After several decades of murders, slaves in New York City conspired against their masters in 1712. Under the cover of a fire, slaves killed nine Whites coming to quell the blaze. After the rebellion was suppressed, convicted participants were tortured and 21 slaves were executed. In the following two years, angry legislators drafted a full slave code, which sharply restricted chances for emancipation. Among other hindrances, it mandated that masters pay a costly £200 bond for each slave they freed, which limited emancipation.

Over the next three decades, slavery became the dominant mode of labor in New York. The census of 1731 counted 7,231 enslaved Africans. In Queens Co, where only 200 slaves toiled in 1700, census takers enumerated 1,264 enslaved people of color. Albany Co had more than 1,200, while over 1,500 lived in New York City. In New York and Albany Cos black women outnumbered men; in rural areas, the imbalance was reversed. Family fragmentation caused by small-lot slavery meant that reproduction of African people was possible only by sizable imports. Over 6,000 Africans came by direct importation into New York Colony between 1712 and 1760. The difficulties of child rearing and the impact of the slave trade suggest that black society in New York was more African than African American. Those who survived still faced tough conditions. Although enslaved Africans in New York Colony did not suffer the barbarism extant in Barbados and Jamaica, yellow fever and smallpox epidemics recurred frequently in the colony and disproportionately affected the black population. Analysis of the skeletons unearthed in the African Burial Ground in lower New York City has revealed the effects of bad diet, starvation, beatings, and plagues, all of which served to shorten enslaved people's life expectancies. Spiritual salvation administered by the Anglican Church lagged after Elias Neau's death in 1722. Slaves were limited socially, too, throughout the colony since local ordinances were harsh. In Kingston (Ulster Co) slaves were restricted from being in groups of more than three. Albany required slaves to carry a lantern at night and forbade slaves to interact with Indians. Westchester towns did not allow slaves to hunt, while in Smithtown (Suffolk Co) slaves could not travel more than 1 mile (2 km) without a pass. New York City slaves could not be buried after dark, and funerals were limited to 10 people. In all, conditions in the colony fostered biological frustration, social alienation, and deep anger among African slaves.

Enslaved persons worked in all sections of the economy. In cities and towns they assisted artisans, were semiskilled laborers, worked on wharves and ships, and in homes were multiskilled domestics. In rural Hudson River valley communities, they toiled as unpaid partners on small farms, where they performed tasks ranging from clearing land for settlements to planting and harvesting crops, herding animals, or running errands. On large plantations, there was a division of labor with slaves working at particular tasks. Most slaves were sold several times in their lifetimes, which meant they eventually learned most facets of the slave economy. On innumerable sales notices, sellers noted their chattel were capable of working in either town or country. There was little sexual division of labor in the countryside, though females tended to dominate the domestic economy, while males practiced skilled work in cities and towns. The thriving internal slave trade lessened any feelings of affection or reciprocity toward masters and mistresses.

Feelings of racial hatred spawned the infamous "Negro Plot" of 1741. The conviction of several slaves for arson after the destruction of Fort George at the foot of Manhattan Island set off a wave of investigations and forced confessions that revealed plans to overthrow English authority, burn the city, and turn it over to the Spanish. During the summer and fall of 1742, dozens of slaves were executed or exiled to West Indian colonies. Court Recorder Daniel Horsmanden's compilation of slave testimony, running over 300 pages, is considered the fullest guide to the slave culture as it was manifested in tavern oaths, gang actions, and conspiracies.

Despite the clear dangers signified by the conspiracy, New York Colony remained tied to slavery. Its black population by 1756, almost wholly enslaved, rose to 13,500. New York, Albany, and Queens Cos each had over 2,000 slaves. Only 356 slaves lived in Ulster Co in 1737, but 20 years later that total was over 1,500. Large increases in the slave population were also evident in rural Dutchess and Orange Cos. By 1771 nearly 20,000 enslaved Blacks lived in the colony, with over half of them located north of New York City. Albany and Westchester Cos had more slave inhabitants than New York City, indicating slavery flourished in rural regions. One rural slave, Jupiter Hammon, who handled accounts for his master in Queens Village [now Lloyds Neck, Suffolk Co], became the first published African American author in 1760. A deeply pious man, his poems and sermons concerned the necessity for Christian conversion and did not directly attack the institution of slavery but conveyed deep concern for his fellow Africans in bondage.

Resistance to servitude continued to fester and manifest in many ways. Enslaved Africans ran away singly, in groups, or in concert with indentured servants. Few were recaptured. A number of notorious cases note slaves attacked their masters. Other slaves used legal means to secure freedom. Over 50 so-called Spanish slaves, captured during the War of Jenkin's Ear (1739–41), sued for freedom once peace was restored between England and Spain. John Kempe, Britain's attorney general, agreed with their pleas and set them free. By the onset of the American Revolution, a tiny free black class emerged in New York Colony. At the same time a nascent antislavery movement grew in the colony, especially among the Society of Friends.

During the Revolutionary War

As New York Colony citizens split between tory and patriot, few gave much thought to the futures of the enslaved population. Although slaves commonly took part in the riots against British taxes and other repressive laws, few patriots regarded them as fellow citizens. The new state constitution of 1777 specifically reaffirmed colonial laws governing slaves. Many loyalist New Yorkers held tightly to their chattel even as their landed property was confiscated. Military actions transformed slavery in New York Colony, at least during the war itself. New York was the cockpit of the American Revolution and the site of military actions throughout the conflict. After the British navy bombarded New York City in August 1776, many urban slave owners fled north to the Hudson Valley to the patriot lines with their chattel. Tory masters and mistresses went into the city for protection. Many slaves, denied any access to the political revolution, quickly took advantage of the military chaos to secure their own liberties. A number joined the English army as "followers of the flag" or semi-organized military units and worked as soldiers, wagoners, holsterers, spies, or servants. Female slaves ran away infrequently during the colonial era, but many women emancipated themselves during the war. While some male slaves occupied blockhouses along the Hudson River, most self-emancipated Blacks went behind the British lines in New York City. Over the years they were joined by hundreds of escaped bonds people from southern states. In 1779 Albany slaves were jailed for promoting insurrection and for recruiting slaves to join the British. At the close of the war in 1783, over 3,000 African Americans left by boat with other loyalists bound for Nova Scotia. In 1791 one-third of this group, known as the Black Loyalists, decamped for Sierra Leone (named Freetown in 1787), Africa, where they founded a new nation.

After the War

Slaves who remained in New York State after the American Revolution initially faced few prospects of liberty. Although the majority of attendees at the 1777 Constitutional Convention favored the abolition of slavery, nothing was done until 1781, when slaves who served the patriot forces were freed by the legislature. In New York City the Common Council quickly reinstated the colonial slave code. Most patriots in the city regarded Blacks as dangerous property and resented their siding with the British. In 1785 Aaron Burr unsuccessfully headed movements in the state assembly to end slavery. His first proposals were saddled with clauses that severely restricted black civil rights, and the state senate rejected the entire package because of these injunctions. The state government passed legislation in 1785 and 1788 that restricted imports and exports of slaves for sale but not for personal use. This clause remained in effect for decades. In 1788 the state removed the £200 bond previously required of masters to free slaves. Other new laws gave rights of trial by jury to slaves in all cases and ended the practice of special slave courts to try capital crimes.

The abolition of slavery in New York State was a laborious and slow process. Reasons included masters' demands to be compensated in some way for their loss of property and Whites' fear that former slaves would become charity wards. Free Blacks, unable to secure loans to purchase farms and businesses, were often reduced to labor as cottagers on the property of their erstwhile masters or as domestics in households, which also contained slaves. The elite New York Manumission Society (NYMS) made the best efforts to end slavery and included, among others, John Jay, Alexander Hamilton, J. Hector St. John de Crèvecoeur, and Philip Schuyler. Founded in 1785, the society helped slaves sue for freedom, acted as a depository for freedom papers, led action to halt the practice of whipping slaves at the local jails, and attempted to stop the return of fugitive slaves to their masters. To promote education of Blacks, the Episcopal Church established an African Free School in New York City in conjunction with the NYMS. Historians have been critical of the society because members owned slaves themselves.

African Americans were also effective agents for ending chattel bondage in New York State. Blacks sued their masters, negotiated terms of emancipation, and occasionally purchased themselves and their families. They ran away when displeased and burned their masters' homes if angered. Still, more Blacks than ever were free. Some prospered, such as freed slave Prince Taylor, who owned a 250-acre (101 ha) farm near Ticonderoga (Essex Co) and employed white farmhands as indentures. Along with the efforts of the NYMS and the Society of Friends, the actions of African Americans meant that by 1790 there were over 1,000 free Blacks in New York City, nearly one-quarter of the state's total and an unimaginable number for the colonial period. The system of slavery endured, however, and in some counties actually increased after the Revolutionary War. In 1790 there were still over 21,000 slaves in the state. Masters in counties such as Ulster, Kings, Albany, Columbia, and Richmond had freed a tiny fraction of bonds people. Albany Co, with 3,722 slaves and 171 free Blacks, had the highest number of slaves in the state, followed by Ulster Co, with 2,914 slaves and 161 free Blacks. Born into slavery in Ulster Co around 1797 was Isabel Van Wagenen, who would later adopt the name Sojourner Truth. Her written accounts of her life as a slave in the Hudson Valley were as harrowing as any from the plantation South.

Slaveholding remained strongest among the wealthiest Whites, but middle-class trades people and petty merchants accounted for more than one-third of owners. Slaves were owned by even the poorest taxpayers in New York State in 1790, and slavery was found statewide. In 1798, 35 slaves worked on large Plattsburgh farms. As early as the 1750s there had been slaves in Central New York, many trafficked in by Sir William Johnson, but slavery became more prevalent in the region during the 1790s. A number of Virginia slave owners, concerned about abolitionist efforts in their states, moved north in 1795 into the Genesee Country of Western New York accompanied by sizable contingents of slaves. These masters attempted to set up southern-style plantations on the frontier, but their efforts occurred at the wrong time in history.

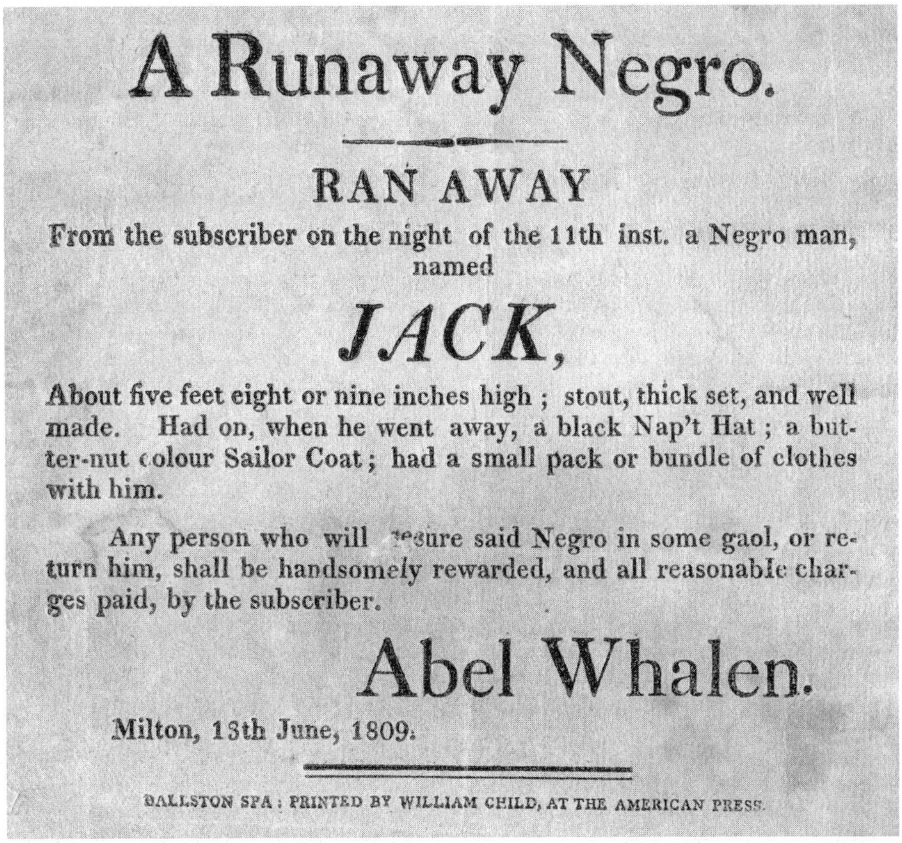

A Runaway Negro.

RAN AWAY

From the subscriber on the night of the 11th inst. a Negro man, named

JACK,

About five feet eight or nine inches high ; stout, thick set, and well made. Had on, when he went away, a black Nap't Hat ; a butter-nut colour Sailor Coat; had a small pack or bundle of clothes with him.

Any person who will secure said Negro in some gaol, or return him, shall be handsomely rewarded, and all reasonable charges paid, by the subscriber.

Abel Whalen.

Milton, 13th June, 1809.

BALLSTON SPA: PRINTED BY WILLIAM CHILD, AT THE AMERICAN PRESS.

Broadside offering reward for an escaped slave, Ballston Spa, 1809.

The cause for abolition lagged during the 1790s, although some evidence has been found that artisans in the cities supported it more frequently. In the countryside, support for slavery remained very strong, and farmers were the most vocal opponents of abolition. After several failed attempts to end slavery, the legislature reached a compromise in 1799. The gradual emancipation act stipulated that all enslaved peoples born before 4 July 1799 would remain in bondage unless otherwise emancipated, but all black persons born enslaved after that date had to serve their mother's master until they were 28 (males) or 25 (females). The new law allowed masters to collect a stipend if they freed enslaved infants a year after their birth. As paupers, children were later bound out by the overseers of the poor to their old masters, who were paid a monthly maintenance fee of $3.50. By 1804 the state had paid over $20,000 for the program, but this massive drain on the state budget caused the legislature to revoke the law. Slave owners retained the right to buy and sell young enslaved Blacks right up until their dates of freedom. Masters advertised for runaways and continued to administer private punishments for infractions by slaves. Southern masters were allowed to bring their chattel into New York State without fear of any judicial actions. Such limitations slowed emancipation to a crawl. The 1810 census shows that slaves heavily outnumbered free Blacks in most New York counties. Every new county formed between 1790 and 1810 was the home of at least a few slaves. In 1810 Geneva (Ontario Co) and Sodus (Wayne Co) had more slaves than freed Blacks. Blacks did not benefit substantially from the opening of the democracy in the Jeffersonian era. A survey of 1806 laws governing slaves shows that beyond the gradual emancipation measures, laws favoring masters included the right to bring slaves into the state for six months without penalties. Slaves could not testify in trials and were not permitted to purchase alcohol. Still, new state laws allowed slaves to legalize their marriages, and state laws in 1810 freed slaves brought north by Virginia masters who settled in the Genesee territory in the 1790s.

The slow pace of emancipation meant that slavery could have existed in New York State long into the future without additional reform. The extinction of slavery was a significant political issue between the Republican and Federalist Parties from the 1780s until 1817, when Gov Daniel D. Tompkins pushed a law that emancipated all slaves after 4 July 1827. Although the numbers of slaves in the Hudson Valley Dutch farm counties remained high in 1820, over the next few years more Blacks were free than enslaved as the date of the end of slavery loomed. On 5 July 1827 African Americans and their sympathizers all over the state celebrated Emancipation Day as the death of slavery.

Aftermath

Because few masters offered assistance to their former slaves, black economic advancement in rural areas lagged. In the cities, rising racism and the transformation from crafts to industrial capitalism hurt black artisans. Few had the capital to compete or were allowed to join the ranks of industrial laborers. Blacks also lacked any real political power in the new democracy. Black poverty worsened after the close of slavery, causing self-serving white observers to conclude that enslavement had been better for New York's African Americans. Among many Whites, nostalgia for the orderly days of servitude expanded into a favorable portrait of the state's past system of slavery. At the same time, black activism, which was undergirded by a strengthening religious and educational nationalism, made New York State among the leaders in the fight against slavery in the South and against the denial of civil rights to the descendants of slavery in the North. In New York City, in particular, a combination of locally born Blacks, former fugitive slaves from the South, and migrants from New England made the city a hub of antislavery. These antislavery activists worked unceasingly to rid the state and nation of the legacies of servitude.

Burke, Thomas E., Jr. *Mohawk Frontier: The Dutch Community of Schenectady, New York, 1661–1710* (Ithaca: Cornell Univ Press, 1991)

Day, Lynda R. *Making a Way to Freedom: A History of African Americans on Long Island* (Interlaken, NY: Empire State Books, 1997)

Goodfriend, Joyce D. *Before the Melting Pot: Society and Culture in Colonial New York City, 1664–1730* (Princeton, NJ: Princeton Univ Press, 1992)

Grover, Kathryn. *Make a Way Somehow: African-American Life in a Northern Community, 1790–1965* (Syracuse: Syracuse Univ Press, 1994)

Hodges, Graham Russell. *Root and Branch: African Americans in New York and East Jersey, 1613–1863* (Chapel Hill: Univ of North Carolina Press, 1999)

McManus, Edgar J. *A History of Negro Slavery in New York* (Syracuse: Syracuse Univ Press, 1966)

Rawley, James A. *The Trans-Atlantic Slave Trade* (New York: Norton, 1981)

White, Shane. *Somewhat More Independent: The End of Slavery in New York City, 1770 to 1810* (Athens: Univ of Georgia Press, 1991)

Graham Russell Hodges

slave transit. In 1799 New York State passed a gradual abolition statute that prohibited the importation of slaves into the state and provided that the children of all slaves would be born free, although subject to indenture. Slaves could not be imported into the state, but the law provided that visiting masters, known in legal terms as masters in transit, could bring slaves into the state and keep them there for up to nine months, recognizing the need to provide for interstate comity for citizens of slave states. Slavery was abolished for all permanent residents of New York State in 1827, but the provision relating to slaves from out of state remained in effect until 1841, when the New York legislature repealed the "nine-months law," as it had come to be called, as a result of growing antislavery sentiment in the state. William H. Seward, the state's new governor, who soon became a leader in antislavery politics, signed the repeal into law, which meant that slaves would become free the moment they were brought into New York State by their masters. The law did not affect fugitive slaves, whose status was controlled by the US Constitution.

The new legal regime, immediately emancipating slaves who were brought into the state, followed a venerable legal tradition that began with the English case of *Somerset v Stewart* (1772) and included a Massachusetts case, *Commonwealth v Aves* (1836), decided by Chief Justice Lemuel Shaw, the most important state jurist of the era. In 1852 a trial court judge in New York City enforced the new law in *People v Lemmon*, freeing eight enslaved African Americans who Jonathan and Juliet Lemmon had brought into the city while on their way by boat from Virginia to Texas. The fastest route for their travels was from Virginia to New York and then directly to New Orleans. Thus the Lemmons argued that as US citizens they should have the right to pass through New York State with their property. The court disagreed, freeing the "eight colored Virginians," as the judge called them. Business owners in New York City raised $5,000 to compensate the Lemmons, who returned to Virginia, where they remained as nonslaveholding farmers. The Virginia government, however, appealed the decision to two levels of New York courts. In *Lemmon v the People* (1860) the New York Court of Appeals upheld the interpretation of the 1841 repeal. The case might have been brought to the US Supreme Court had Virginia's secession in 1861 not removed that possibility.

US Supreme Court Justice Samuel Nelson, born in Hebron (Washington Co), raised the issue of slave transit in his concurring opinion in *Dred Scott v Sandford* (1857), strongly suggesting that the Supreme Court would support a right of transit with slaves when such a case reached the court. Abraham Lincoln raised this issue in his House Divided speech in 1858, warning that the Supreme Court would make slavery legal in the free states. In the published version of his 1860 Cooper Union address, delivered before the New York Court of Appeals had decided the case, Lincoln specifically noted that the Lemmon case raised the specter of a nationalization of slavery by the courts. Other politicians, such as Horace Greeley and Salmon P. Chase of Ohio, also saw *Lemmon* and the issue of slave transit as a threat to freedom in the North.

Finkelman, Paul. *An Imperfect Union: Slavery, Federalism, and Comity* (Chapel Hill: Univ of North Carolina Press, 1981)

Paul Finkelman

Sleepy Hollow. Village (pop 9,212) in Mount Pleasant (Westchester Co). Frederick Philipse I erected a mill, manor house, and church beginning in 1682 on his land at the mouth of the Pocantico River. After the Philipse lands were confiscated in 1779, Gerard G. Beekman Jr purchased most of the present village. It remained largely undeveloped until in 1835 his widow ordered a plat prepared and named Beekmantown. The railroad came through in 1849. Village industry products in the 19th century included bricks, tinsmith's tools, silk (1866–75), buttons, and rock-drilling equipment made by the Rand Drill Co (1885–98). The village was incorporated as North Tarrytown in 1874. In the 1890s John D. Rockefeller Sr created a vast estate partly in the village's northeast. A riverfront factory produced steam-powered (1900–1903) and gas-powered automobiles (1904–96). It was sold to Chevrolet Motor Co in 1914; after 1918 it was a part of General Motors, where the corporation built almost 12 million vehicles between 1915 and 1996. As late as 1992 it employed 4,000 workers. Philipse Manor was platted by a syndicate of English and Scots investors in 1903, and home construction was underway by 1909; it remains an elegant suburban neighborhood. The historic downtown is home to an ethnically diverse population. The name of the village was changed to Sleepy Hollow by vote of its residents in 1996. Historic sites include Kykuit (1893), the

Rockefeller mansion; Philipsburg Manor Upper Mills (restoration and reconstruction, 1968); the Old Dutch Church of Sleepy Hollow (*ca* 1685); and Sleepy Hollow Cemetery (1849).

Henry Steiner

Slide Mountain (4,204 ft/1,281.4 m). The highest mountain in the Catskill range and the first to be included in the state's Catskill Forest Preserve (1885). Slide Mountain lies within the 47,500-acre (19,223 ha) Slide Mountain Wilderness Area in northwest Ulster Co. Sitting within a cluster of nine mountains due west of the Ashokan Reservoir, Slide Mountain derives its name from a gulf on the north face produced by a mass slump of rock *ca* 1820. The summit is characterized by stunted conifers and is generally snow-covered through late spring. Mountain guide James Dutcher built the first trail up the mountain from Winnisook Lake in 1870. His trail was abandoned because it crossed private land, but in 1891 the first public funds allocated by the state for Forest Preserve trail development were used to build a replacement. Spectacular views from the summit and an extensive trail system draw more hikers than any other area within the Catskill region.

Haring, Harry A. *Our Catskill Mountains* (New York: G. P. Putnam's Sons, 1931)

Karen Nichols

Sloan. Village (pop 3,775) in Cheektowaga (Erie Co). Sloan became a post office in 1891, and the Buffalo, Bellevue and Lancaster Electric Railway began operating in 1892. This easy access into Buffalo allowed city residents, primarily Germans and Poles, to move to Sloan. The village was incorporated in 1896, and growth continued in the early 20th century, its population tripling between 1910 and 1930. The $7.5 million electronic rail yard of the Erie Lackawanna was sited in Sloan in 1962, and at the end of the 20th century it acquired the $13 million Norfolk Southern rail yard.

Nancy B. Mingus

Sloan, Samuel (*b* Lisburn, Ireland, 25 Dec 1817; *d* Garrison, Putnam Co, 22 Sept 1907). Railroad executive. When Sloan was one year old, his family moved to New York City, which remained his primary home. After his father died, Sloan left Columbia College Preparatory School to help support his family. In 1831 he began work with McBride and Co, a linen-importing firm, and became a partner in 1844. That year he married Margaret Elmendorf and moved to Brooklyn. In 1852 Sloan was made a supervisor of Kings Co. He became president of the Hudson River Railroad in 1855. He was elected as a Democrat to a two-year term (1856–58) in the New York State Senate. From 1865 to 1867 he was commissioner of the Trunk Lines Association for the Middle Atlantic States. In 1867 he became president of the Delaware, Lackawanna and Western Railroad, a coal road serving the anthracite region of Pennsylvania and several cities in New York State. He remained president until 1899 and served as president of many other railroads, including the Watertown and Ogdensburg Railroad. As president of the Lackawanna he oversaw the costly change of gauge from 6 ft (1.8 m) to the standard gauge of 4 ft, 8.5 in (1.44 m).

Cochran, Thomas C. *Railroad Leaders, 1845–1890* (Cambridge, Mass: Harvard Univ Press, 1953)

George M. Jenks

Sloatsburg. Village (pop 3,117) in Ramapo (Rockland Co). In 1753 Stephen Slot settled on 1,000 acres (405 ha) straddling the Ramapo Pass; two years later he built a house and a tavern. A cotton mill (1815) brought prosperity to the community, enhanced by the coming of the Erie Railroad in 1841. The mill, which produced twine after 1846, closed in 1878 and was destroyed in a 1903 flood; it was rebuilt *ca* 1906 and remained a major employer until it burned in 1955. The village was incorporated in 1929. Its isolation, because of topography, has retarded suburbanization. The New York State Thruway (1954) passes through the village with a major service area but without an exit.

Kathy Goldman

sloops. See *Clearwater* sloop; Hudson river sloops.

Sloughter, Henry (*b* ?; *d* New York City, 23 June 1691). Provincial governor. Col Henry Sloughter was appointed governor on 4 Jan 1690, replacing Jacob Leisler's revolutionary regime. He departed England about the same time as Capt Richard Ingoldsby, commander of an infantry company stationed in New York; Ingoldsby arrived first, on 30 Jan 1691. Leisler insisted on dealing directly with the new governor and at one point fired on Ingoldsby's men. Sloughter arrived on 19 March and had Leisler and his council arrested and charged with treason. All were pardoned, save for Leisler and his son-in-law, Jacob Milbourne. Sloughter considered granting them clemency, but Leisler's regime had many enemies. In a letter to the assembly dated 11 May 1691, Sloughter noted "great disquiet and dissatisfaction amongst the people" over the delayed executions. The governor's own council pressured him to carry out the sentences. Bowing to public opinion, Sloughter ordered them hanged on 16 May. The remainder of his brief tenure was spent reassuring the Iroquois League of England's and New York's desire to prosecute King William's War vigorously. He died suddenly on 23 June 1691; Ingoldsby served as acting governor until Benjamin Fletcher arrived in August 1692.

Lincoln, Charles Z. *Messages from the Governors* (Albany: J. B. Lyon, 1909)
McCormick, Charles Howard. *Leisler's Rebellion* (New York: Garland Publishing, 1989)

Daniel A. Piazza

Sloughters. A derogatory term referring to some residents of Schoharie Co. William Roscoe, in *History of Schoharie County, New York* (1882), stated that a Sloughter was a person "whose morality was lost long ago, and not inheriting any principle, they have failed to find it." Emelyn Gardner, in *Folklore from the Schoharie Hills, New York* (1937), made note of the derogative epithet as referring to a resident of "Sloughter Hill" (West Middleburgh). The origin of the term is uncertain. One theory holds that it is a term of opprobrium directed at the followers of Col Henry Sloughter, royal governor of New York Colony in 1691, who was responsible for the beheading of his predecessor, Jacob Leisler, for treason. The Leislerians and anti-Leislerians sparred in the colony for several decades thereafter, and when Nicholas Bayard, one of the most prominent anti-Leislerians, attempted to gain control of the area that would later become Schoharie County in the early 18th century, a riot ensued in which the epithet "Sloughter" was used.

An alternative explanation, given the traditional associations of the term with low status, is that it is a family name, Sloughter or Slaughter, and refers to a group of persons of mixed American Indian or perhaps triracial (European, Indian, and African) ancestry. Frederic Cassidy's *Dictionary of American Regional English* (1985) defines Sloughters as a term referring to a group of people "of supposedly Indian ancestry," though little is known about a possible connection to a specific Indian group.

While the derogatory sense remains in use, in recent decades Sloughter has lost its sting, and it has become an affectionate colloquial expression for someone who is native to Schoharie Co. Numerous Sloughter jokes have entered oral tradition; culinary creations such as Sloughter potpie are included in local cookbooks. "Will the last Sloughter to leave the Valley please turn out the lights?" is a popular bumper sticker in Schoharie Co.

See also Triracial groups.

Hendrix, Lester, and Anne Whitbeck Hendrix. *Sloughter's Instant History of Schoharie County, 1700–1900* (Schoharie, NY: Schoharie County Historical Society, 1988)

Ellen McHale

Slovaks. The first Slovak immigrants came to New York City in the 1840s, driven by poverty and cultural oppression from what was then part of Hungary. Mainly uneducated peasants, they worked as laborers and hoped to return home with savings. By the 1880s small Slovak neighborhoods formed on the eastern side of Central Park in Manhattan and in Long Island City, Astoria, and Sunnyside in Queens. Ethnic Slovaks were generally Catholic, with a small Lutheran and Calvinist minority. Early churches in Manhattan were the Catholic St. Elizabeth (1891), St. John Nepomucene (1895), and Holy Family (1895), and the Lutheran Holy Trinity Evangelical (1902). The immigrants joined organizations such as the fraternal Slovak League and founded a few labor unions, gymnastic clubs, and other societies, often on a Catholic foundation. Slovak newspapers included the weekly *Slovak v Amerike* (1889–), which was for some time a daily, and the daily *New Yorksky Dennik* (1895–1974). There were also communities in Syracuse, Binghamton, Schenectady, Johnstown, and Granville, where many Slovaks worked in the slate mines. Immigration restrictions after World War I ended large-scale immigration.

After World War I Slovakia became a part of the new country of Czechoslovakia. Slovak independence split the Slovak community during most of the 20th century until Slovakia became independent again in 1993. After World War II Slovak refugees fleeing the Beneš (1945–48) and Communist (1948–89) regimes came mainly to New York City. The new arrivals, politicized and better educated than earlier immigrants, founded new associations such as branches of the World Slovak Congress and the Slovak American Cultural Center (1967) to advocate Slovak independence, and others joined Czechoslovak associations that downplayed Slovak ethnicity. In 2004 there was a trickle of new Slovak immigration. The new arrivals lived throughout New York City, but there was a concentration in Astoria. St. John Nepomucene on East 66th St still held one weekly service in Slovak, but most Slovak associations vanished. The Slovak Catholic Sokol, a nationwide fraternal society, had a few branches in the Bronx and Brooklyn and two in Westchester Co. In 2000 the census counted 13,246 people born in the former Czechoslovakia, which includes Slovaks. An estimated 100,000 New Yorkers have Slovak ancestry.

Maăr, Imrich, comp. *A History of the Binghamton Slovaks: Over a Period of 40 Years, 1879–1919.* Ed. Wilhelmina Maăr Satina (Phoenix: Via Press, 2003)

Shelley, Thomas J. *Slovaks on the Hudson: Most Holy Trinity Church, Yonkers, and the Slovak Catholics of the Archdiocese of New York* (Washington, DC: Catholic Univ of America Press, 2002)

Thomas Reimer

smallpox. A highly contagious disease spread between humans. The virus, *Variola major,* becomes highly contagious 12–14 days after it enters the body, as the symptoms of fever, fatigue, and back and stomach pain appear. Smallpox pustules can disfigure or lead to complications causing blindness, and the disease can be fatal. A Dutch settlement at Fort Orange [now Albany] may have introduced smallpox to the Mohawk around 1624, and in 1649 Dutch historian Adriaen van der Donck estimated that about nine-tenths of the American Indian population of New Netherland had died of smallpox. Colonists tried to control the virus with isolation. East Hampton [now in Suffolk Co] issued a quarantine order in 1662 to stop the spread of smallpox from nearby native settlements, and New York City ordered a maritime quarantine in 1690 when a ship brought smallpox-infected slaves from the West Indies. An epidemic arose near Albany in 1689–90, during King William's War, and a 1702 epidemic compelled the New York provincial assembly to meet on Long Island.

Healthy individuals sometimes received inoculations of the contents of smallpox pustules in the hope of gaining immunity by developing a milder form of smallpox. New York City officials used inoculation to control the 1731 smallpox epidemic, which sickened half the population and killed about 700, but inoculation was controversial because it could cause the illness and death. A 1745 epidemic ravaged the Onondaga. During the French and Indian War, the combatants and major cities endured almost yearly smallpox epidemics. Trinity Episcopal Church in Fishkill (Dutchess Co) was turned into a convalescent hospital for troops who had contracted smallpox during the American Revolution.

English physician Edward Jenner used the contents of cowpox pustules to develop a vaccine in 1796. Drs David Hosack and Valentine Seaman first offered this safer form of protection in New York City in 1801, though outbreaks continued to occur. Nearly 1,000 New York City residents died of smallpox during 1853–54, and another 425 died in an 1858 epidemic. During the Civil War the United States conducted widespread vaccinations of its own troops and Confederate prisoners, yet smallpox struck the inmates at Elmira Prison Camp in December 1864, killing 10 within the first week. An 1874 smallpox epidemic convinced Syracuse authorities to establish the City Hospital for Communicable Diseases, which changed location but continued as a facility for infectious diseases through the 1970s. Because New York was a city of immigrants, smallpox remained a problem there through the 19th century. Smallpox hospitals set up on Blackwell's Island [now Roosevelt Island] in 1828 and on North Brother Island in 1880 reduced the rate of infection by separating contagious individuals from the general population.

The last smallpox outbreak in New York City began with an American returning home in March 1947 after living for years in Mexico City. Admitted to Willard Parker Hospital for Contagious Diseases, he infected two other patients. On 5 Apr 1947 Health Commissioner Israel Weinstein established free vaccination centers, and the program reached about 5 million people in less than three weeks. Routine vaccination for smallpox in the United States ended in 1972. In 1980 the World Health Organization declared smallpox eradicated, although the United States and Russia retained samples of the virus in storage.

Fenn, Elizabeth. *Pox Americana: The Great Smallpox Epidemic of 1775–1782* (New York: Hill & Wang, 2001)

Hopkins, Donald R. *Princes and Peasants: Smallpox in History.* Frwd by George I. Lythcott (Chicago: Univ of Chicago Press, 1983)

Pamela Cooper

Smith, Alfred E(manuel) (*b* New York City, 30 Dec 1873; *d* New York City, 4 Oct 1944). Governor.

Early Years

Born on the East Side of Manhattan to parents with Italian German and Irish ancestry, he lived most of his life in that crowded tenement district. He enjoyed a typical immigrant's city childhood, watching the construction of the Brooklyn Bridge from his living room windows and attending a local parochial school at St. James Roman Catholic Church. Smith was an ordinary student, but he had to leave school in the seventh grade when his father died in 1885. Smith held a series of jobs, most notably at the Fulton Fish Market—of which he would always say he was a graduate—and he acted in amateur productions at the church. He also gravitated to the local Tammany Hall chapter, and this became his social club as well as a springboard to politics. Smith's first political job was process server for the office of the commissioner of jurors. In 1903 he was nominated for the New York State Assembly and won handily in the machine-controlled district.

State Politics

At first Smith neither understood nor had much to add to the work of the state assembly, which at the time was dominated by tradition, patricians, and upstate Republicanism. He considered returning to New York City politics but decided to stay and make a success of his legislative career. Instead of falling into the comfortable role of reliable machine assemblyman, he mastered the work of the legislature, reading every bill and then checking and cross-referencing each item until he intimately knew the workings of state government. This, combined with his actor's ability to memorize vast amounts of information easily, made him a formidable member of the lower house, and in 1913 he served as speaker of the assembly. Smith became vice chair, under Sen Robert F. Wagner Sr, of the Factory Investigating Commission established in 1911 after the Triangle Shirtwaist Factory fire. His work on the commission exposed him to the horrors of industrial life, and as a result Smith joined the ranks of progressive reformers, a position he would hold for most of his political career. Smith and Wagner pushed through a host of bills that created the modern system of fire safety by enacting measures such as sprinklers, fire drills, illuminated exit signs, and panic bars on doors.

The high point of Smith's legislative career came during the 1915 Constitutional Convention, where he displayed his unmatched knowledge of the workings of state government. Elihu Root commented that of all the men in the convention Smith was "the best informed" on the business of New York State. Smith served as sheriff of New York Co (1915–17) and as president of the New York City Board of Aldermen (1917–18).

Governor

In 1918 Smith ran for governor and won. His major accomplishment during that term was creating a reconstruction committee to plan for post–World War I society and economy. In 1920 Smith lost his bid for reelection and became a businessman, running the US Trucking Co. Two years later Smith ran again and won, as he did in 1924 and 1926. In the 20th century only Nelson A. Rockefeller would match this record of four victories. The period of 1922–28 was when Smith made his greatest mark on New York State.

Smith's record as governor was achieved in two major fields: administrative and social reform. Because he had been a newcomer in the legislature, Smith had little appreciation for outmoded procedures. When he became governor, there were 189 state government departments and commissions, all of roughly the same status, with no clear hierarchy or decision-making apparatus. The budget was put together by the few legislative leaders and clerks who understood its complicated workings. Smith created a system of departments headed by secretaries who form the governor's cabinet, a structure still used in modified form. He enacted an executive budget, whereby the governor's office prepares a carefully compiled statement that is submitted to the legislature for approval. Getting these reforms passed was far from easy, but Smith managed because he was a great campaigner and a formidable speaker. He took his causes directly to the people, clarifying complex issues and urging his audience to pressure their legislators to back reform.

In social reform, he vastly expanded the state's support for housing, healthcare, and parks. In the field of education, he increased the state budget from $7 million in the 1918–19 fiscal year to $70 million in the 1926–27 fiscal year. During this period, teachers' salaries doubled in the state. He was one of few politicians to argue that urban immigrants were part of the American body politic.

Political Decline

In 1928 Smith ran for president but lost badly because of prejudice against his Roman Catholic faith and his city background. Voters were warned that if Smith won, all Protestant marriages would be annulled and their children would henceforth be illegitimate. They were warned that the pope would come over and run the White House. Thousands of photos of the Holland Tunnel construction were circulated, with the captions stating that it was the secret passageway being built to bring the pope from Rome. After Smith's loss, his fortunes took a turn for the worse. He accepted a position as president of the Empire State Building, which had been planned in prosperity but opened in depression. Smith presided over the building's financial disaster and lost much of his own financial reserves in the crash of 1929. He joined the right-wing American Liberty League and bitterly turned on Franklin D. Roosevelt and the New Deal, denouncing them in a famous speech on 25 Jan 1936. In the last years of his life, Smith returned to his core values, speaking vigorously against fascism and Nazism and supporting Roosevelt when the president spoke out against tyranny and led the effort to win World War II. Smith died seven months after the death of his beloved wife, Catherine.

See also BONDED INDEBTEDNESS.

Finan, Christopher. *Alfred E. Smith* (New York: Hill & Wang, 2002)

Handlin, Oscar. *Al Smith and His America* (Boston: Little, Brown, 1958)

Josephson, Matthew, and Hannah Josephson. *Al Smith: Hero of the Cities: A Political Portrait Drawing on the Papers of Frances Perkins* (Boston: Houghton Mifflin, 1969)

Slayton, Robert. *Empire Statesman: The Rise and Redemption of Al Smith* (New York: Free Press, 2001)

Smith, Alfred E. *Up to Now* (New York: Viking Press, 1927)

Robert A. Slayton

Smith [née Berry], **Amanda** (*b* Long Green, Md, 23 Jan 1837; *d* Sebring, Fla, 25 Feb 1915). Evangelist and temperance leader. Born into slavery on a farm north of Baltimore, she grew up free in southeastern Pennsylvania, was widowed during the Civil War, and left Philadelphia with her second husband after the war. In 1865 she moved to Greenwich Village in Manhattan where about one quarter of New York City's black population then resided. Separated from her husband, she supported herself, a daughter, and an infant son by taking in washing and ironing; two other sons had died soon after their birth. She joined Bethel African Methodist Episcopal (AME) Church on Sullivan St, but in September 1868 experienced what she called the "second blessing" of sanctification while listening to Holiness leader John Inskip preach at Green Street Methodist Episcopal Church. Widowed in 1869 she began attending Holiness camp meetings, accompanying wealthy families as their maid to pay her expenses. She became attracted to the perfectionist teachings of Phoebe Palmer, whose weekly meetings Smith regularly attended. During open testimony sessions at meetings held at Round Lake (Saratoga Co), Sing Sing [now Ossining, Westchester Co], and Sea Cliff (Nassau Co), and at Ocean Grove, NJ, Smith gained acclaim for her religious fervor, singing, and speaking ability.

In her attitudes, she was a precursor to Holiness and Pentecostal thinking, and helped lay the foundation for subsequent women to be ordained. She was the first woman and first African American member of the National Association for the Promotion of Holiness. In 1875 she joined the Brooklyn branch of the Woman's Christian Temperance Union (WCTU) and in 1878 traveled throughout England on a speaking tour. In 1880 she joined Methodist missionaries in India, and from 1882 until 1889 she worked in Liberia, organizing temperance societies and helping establish Christian schools. In 1890 she returned to the United States, moved to Chicago, and completed her autobiography. She then embarked on a speaking tour, raising money to establish an orphanage for black children. In June 1899 the Amanda Smith Industrial Orphan Home opened in Harvey, Ill, a suburb of Chicago. In 1912 Smith retired to Sebring, Fla.

Israel, Adrienne. *Amanda Berry Smith, from Washerwoman to Evangelist* (Lanham, Md: Scarecrow Press, 1998)

Smith, Amanda. *An Autobiography: The Story of the Lord's Dealings with Mrs. Amanda Smith the Colored Evangelist* (Chicago: Meyer & Bros Publishers, 1893)

Taylor, Marshall William. *The Life, Travels, Labours, and Helpers of Mrs. Amanda Smith: The Famous Negro Missionary Evangelist* (Cincinnati: Cranston & Stowe, 1886)

Adrienne M. Israel

Smith, Buffalo Bob [Schmidt, Robert] (*b* Buffalo, 27 Nov 1917; *d* Flat Rock, NC, 30 July 1998). Entertainer. At age 15 Schmidt began singing on a Buffalo radio station and later worked in vaudeville. By 1947 he had changed his name to Smith and moved to New York City, working as a disc jockey for National Broadcasting Co (NBC) affiliate WEAF. From 1947 to 1960 Smith was host of the *Howdy Doody Show,* one of the most popular children's television programs in the history of the medium. Broadcast live from NBC studios at 30 Rockefeller Plaza, the show, called *Puppet Playhouse* until 1949, was one of the first sponsored programs geared for children and the first show NBC produced in color. It featured the wooden marionette Howdy Doody, who looked like a freckle-faced little boy. Other residents of Doodyville included Clarabell the Clown, Chief Thunderthud, and Princess Summerfall Winterspring. Each show began with Buffalo Bob calling out, "Say, kids, what time is it?" prompting the response from children in the Peanut Gallery, "It's Howdy Doody time!" In the late 1950s ratings began to decline, and the show went off the air 30 Sept 1960. Smith moved to Florida, where he bought and managed several radio stations.

Smith, Buffalo Bob, and Donna McCrohan. *Howdy and Me: Buffalo Bob's Own Story* (New York: Dutton/Plume, 1990)

J. Justin Gustainis

Smith, David (Roland) (*b* Decatur, Ind, 9 Mar 1906; *d* near Bennington, Vt, 23 May 1965). Sculptor. At 17 Smith took a correspondence course in cartooning, then studied art at Ohio University in Athens. In 1925 he became a welder and riveter at the South Bend, Ind, Studebaker factory. He joined the finance department and was transferred to Washington, DC, and then to New York City in 1926. He studied at the Art Students League with John Sloan, Kimon Nicolaides and Jan Matulka. In 1929, still residing primarily in New York City, he purchased a farm in Bolton Landing (Warren Co). He made his first all-metal sculptures in 1933. A year later he rented work space at Terminal Iron Works, a factory in Brooklyn, and in 1940 he named his farm Iron Works. On a 1935 trip to Europe, Smith was introduced to modernists, including Stanley William Hayter, by painter John Graham. In 1937 he began two years of work for the Works Progress Administration and showing his works with the American Abstract Artists group.

Smith's first one-man show at the Marian Willard Gallery (1939) and the completion of the bas-relief *Medals of Dishonor: Propaganda for War* (1937–40) thrust him into the forefront of avant-garde art. By 1940 he was living full-time in Bolton Landing, where he made bird-like forms, glyphic abstractions, and large open pieces on pastoral themes. From 1940 to 1942 he lived in Schenectady, studied welding at Union College, and at night assembled tanks and locomotives at the American Locomotive Co. He taught at Sarah Lawrence College in Bronxville (Westchester Co) from 1948 to 1950 and received Guggenheim Fellowship Grants (1950–51), enabling him to create increasingly large sculpture. After 1951 his work appeared at many international exhibitions. In 1962 in Voltri, Italy, he produced 27 works in 30 days. Often grouped with abstract expressionists, he was appointed to the National Council of the Arts in 1965.

Marcus, Stanley E. *David Smith: The Sculptor and His Work* (Ithaca: Cornell Univ Press, 1983)

Miriam Steinhardt Soffer

Smith [Ward], **Elinor Patricia** (*b* New York City, 17 Aug 1911). Aviator. Known as Elinor Ward in childhood, she adopted her vaudevillian father's stage name, Smith, in her teens. At age 15 she soloed in her father's Waco biplane from an airfield near her Freeport (Nassau Co) home. The flight earned Smith US Pilot's License no. 3178, the 34th license for an American woman. She earned a transport license at age 18 and in 1928 performed a daring stunt, flying under four East River bridges in New York City. On 30–31 Jan 1929 Smith set the record for a woman's solo and nonrefueled landplane endurance flight with a time of 13 h 16 min 45 s at Garden City (Nassau Co); she broke the record in April with a time of 26 h 21 min 32 s at Mineola (Nassau Co). That November Smith and Bobbi Trout set an endurance record for a refueled flight in California, becoming the first women to refuel in the air. During the 1920s and 1930s she flew as a test pilot for aircraft manufacturer Giuseppe Bellanca, based in Staten Island [now New Castle, Del]. On 10 Mar 1930 Smith set a world women's altitude record of 27,418 feet (8,357 m) and later that year was named Best Woman Pilot in America. She set additional records, including raising the women's altitude record to 32,576 feet (9,929.2 m) in 1931, flew as a commercial pilot, sold airplanes, and wrote on aeronautic topics. She married Patrick Sullivan in 1933 and retired from flying to rear their four children but later returned to the field and was still flying monthly in 2001.

Mitchell, Charles R., and Kirk W. House. *Flying High: Pioneer Women in American Aviation* (Charleston, SC: Arcadia, 2002)

Smith, Elinor. *Aviatrix* (New York: Harcourt Brace Jovanovich, 1981)

Kirk W. House

Smith, Gerrit (*b* Utica, 6 Mar 1797; *d* New York City, 28 Dec 1874). Abolitionist, philanthropist, and social reformer. The son of Peter Smith, a wealthy land speculator and fur trader, and his wife Elizabeth Livingston, Gerrit Smith was raised in Peterboro (Madison Co). In 1818 he graduated from Hamilton College and in January 1819 married Wealtha Backus, who died less than a year later. At age 21 Gerrit became one of the state's largest landowners when he took over his father's business. In 1822 Gerrit married Ann Carroll Fitzhugh, with whom he had eight children (only two survived to adulthood). A Presbyterian by background, Smith experienced a religious awakening in 1826 and subsequently dedicated himself to numerous local and national reform causes. He supported the temperance movement and voluntary agencies such as the American Bible Society and the American Tract Society, gave to the poor, set up an orphanage in Peterboro, and advocated women's rights, prison reform, land reform, international peace, and progressive education.

Smith was perhaps best known as an abolitionist, having broken with the African Colonization Society in 1835 after hosting the organizing convention of the New York State Anti-Slavery Society in Peterboro. He supported the Oneida Institute and the New York Central College. In the late 1840s he gave away approximately 120,000 acres (48,560 ha) of land, mostly in the Adirondacks, to Blacks who were poor and not addicted to alcohol. Appalled by the failure of America's denominations to embrace abolitionism, Smith joined the "comeouter" church movement—churches composed of abolitionists who separated from congregations where radical antislavery voices were silenced—and sponsored the abolitionist Free Church in Peterboro. His religious views later shifted to the "religion of reason." He came to doubt such orthodox doctrines as the divinity of Christ and the supreme authority of an inerrant Bible.

Smith took an active part in establishing the Liberty Party, the Liberty League, and, after 1855, the American Abolition Society. A candidate for president of the United States on various party tickets in 1848, 1856, and 1860, he was elected to Congress in 1852 by a group of abolitionists and moderate reformers but resigned before his term was over. Freedom-seeking African Americans found shelter and aid at Smith's Peterboro mansion. Black abolitionists corresponded with him in large numbers and considered him a friend. Smith helped organize the Cazenovia Fugitive Slave Convention in 1850 and had a role in the 1851 rescue of William "Jerry" Henry in Syracuse. Smith gave money to free-state fighters in Kansas Territory, among them John Brown of Harpers Ferry fame. After Brown's capture in 1859, Smith was accused of being part of a criminal conspiracy; he had, in fact, given support to Brown before the raid. Smith exhibited symptoms of manic-depressive emotional illness and spent seven and one-half weeks in the New York State Lunatic Asylum at Utica.

During the Civil War Smith sided with the Lincoln administration, though he argued that Republicans should transform the conflict into a war of liberation. When the war ended Smith called for reconciliation and national healing; he signed the bail bond of Jefferson Davis. In his last years Smith remained interested in reform, especially with regard to black suffrage, temperance, and the peace movement. Known as a forceful and eloquent speaker, Smith disparaged his own writing abilities, but he authored numerous essays and published circulars, sermons, and other materials.

Guide to the Microfilm Edition of the Peter Smith Papers, 1763–1850, and Gerrit Smith Papers, 1775–1924 (Glen Rock, NJ: Microfilming Corp of America, 1974)

Harlow, Ralph Volney. *Gerrit Smith, Philanthropist and Reformer* (1939; repr New York: Russell & Russell, 1972)

Stauffer, Jon. *The Black Hearts of Men: Radical Abolitionists and the Transformation of Race* (Cambridge, Mass: Harvard Univ Press, 2002)

Milton C. Sernett

Smith, James McCune (*b* New York City, 18 Apr 1813; *d* New York City, 17 Nov 1865). Physician, writer, and activist. Born bonded to his mother's owner, he worked as a blacksmith and attended New York City's African Free School No. 2, where he excelled as a student—he was chosen to deliver the welcoming speech for the Marquis de Lafayette when he visited the school in 1824—and graduated with honors in 1828, a year after becoming free. The medical schools at Columbia College and Geneva College (Ontario Co) rejected him because of his race, and in 1832 he enrolled at the University of Glasgow, from which he swiftly earned three degrees: a BA (1835), an MA (1836), and an MD (1837). The first African American to receive a medical degree, he returned to New York City, where he opened a practice and pharmacy, joined the American Anti-Slavery Society, and became active in other reform and philanthropic causes dedicated to uplifting the position of Blacks. Smith, whom Frederick Douglass considered his most influential black colleague, was venerated for his intellect and his skills as an orator and writer. He participated in the black convention movement, served as a trustee for abolitionist Gerrit Smith's 120,000-acre (48,600 ha) Adirondack land grant to free Blacks, published essays, such as *A Lecture on the Haytien Revolutions* (1841), and edited and contributed to various African American newspapers in the 1850s and 1860s. In his writings he countered racist arguments, touted the value of education and industry, and opposed emigration.

Smith was a slow convert to political abolitionism, which he supported after 1848. He chaired the Radical Abolition Party convention in Syracuse in 1855 and was nominated in 1857 by the party to run as New York's secretary of state. Through his speeches and pamphlets, in 1860 he became a leader in the unsuccessful fight to remove, through a referendum, the property qualification imposed on the state's black voters. Though he accepted a professorship in anthropology at Ohio's Wilberforce College in 1863, Smith never moved there because of health problems. He died of heart disease in 1865.

Blight, David W. "In Search of Learning, Liberty, and Self Definition: James McCune Smith and the Ordeal of the Antebellum Black Intellectual," *Afro-Americans in New York Life and History* 9 (1985): 7–25

Stauffer, John. *The Black Hearts of Men: Radical Abolitionists and the Transformation of Race* (Cambridge, Mass: Harvard Univ Press, 2002)

Hadley Kruczek-Aaron

Smith, Joseph, Jr (*b* Sharon, Vt, 23 Dec 1805; *d* Carthage, Ill, 27 June 1844). Religious leader. Smith moved with his parents to Palmyra (Wayne Co) in 1816 and by the end of the decade was farming near Manchester (Ontario Co), part of the Burned-over District of western New York State then rife with religious revivalism. His vision of God and Jesus in spring 1820 was typical of early 19th-century revivalists, who often publicized their visions of deity. Like huge numbers of post-Revolutionary Americans, his unchurched parents read the Bible, pondered dreams, trusted faith healing, saw portents in nature, revered "second sight," feared diabolical influences, and merged informal religiosity with folk-magic amulets, charms, rites, rods, and astrology. His family possessed ceremonial parchments and a dagger with inscriptions from Ebenezer Sibly's *Occult Sciences* (1784) and Francis Barrett's *Magus* (1801). Smith developed a reputation as a treasure hunter and finder of lost objects, and he led treasure quests with "seer stones" in Wayne, Ontario, Seneca, Broome, and Chenango Cos. By 1823, and probably earlier, young Smith had undertaken summer excursions to hunt for treasure along the Susquehanna River. In 1825 he boarded at the house of Isaac Hale in South Bainbridge (Chenango Co) while working as a treasure digger. In the following year he was brought to trial locally as a "glass looker." He eloped with Hale's daughter Emma in 1827.

None of this was extraordinary. Dozens of treasure seers searched in Western New York, hundreds statewide. But Smith stunned neighbors by announcing that in 1823 an angel had revealed to him the location of gold plates buried on a drumlin Smith called the Hill Cumorah in Manchester, recording in "reformed Egyptian" a narrative of America's ancient Israelite inhabitants; he was, however, prohibited from removing the plates until 1827. Although a torrent of negative newsprint resulted, Smith published his translation, a 500-page volume of scripture called the *Book of Mormon,* in Palmyra in March 1830. The following month, at the home of Peter Whitmer in Fayette (Seneca Co), he organized a new faith, to become the Church of Latter-day Saints. Nicknamed "Mormons," Smith's followers proclaimed him a "prophet, seer, and revelator."

In the summer of 1830 Smith twice faced trial for disorderly conduct and exorcism. He was acquitted in both cases, but by year's end constables were seeking his family for unpaid debts. Unable to remain in New York State, Smith moved his headquarters in 1831 to Kirtland, Ohio, where convert Sidney Rigdon, a former minister, had receptive followers. From 1831 to 1837 the movement flourished. Smith established various communal enterprises, a temple, and a "School of the Prophets" providing basic adult education and instruction in theology, Greek, and Hebrew. The national depression of 1837 devastated his enterprises, however. Disaffected followers and lawsuits forced him to flee to Far West, Mo, in 1838. Controversy followed the church there, with Smith and Rigdon's increasing militancy resulting in civil war across four counties and the expulsion of thousands of Mormons from the state. Smith was arrested and spent six months in prison before escaping to Illinois in 1839.

The community's fortunes improved considerably in Illinois, where bloc-voting Mormons held the balance of political power. Given a liberal charter from the state legislature, the church's headquarters of Nauvoo became a city-state, with Smith as mayor, chief justice, land agent, and general of a 5,000-man militia. He even formed a theocratic council that anointed him king and appointed ambassadors to Europe. While an independent candidate for US president in 1844, he was arrested for destroying an anti-Mormon news press. Before trial, a mob killed him in his Illinois jail, creating a martyr for Mormonism. Historic sites associated with Smith, such as his family's log home near Palmyra and the Hill Cumorah, dot the Finger Lakes region. Twelve of his more than 30 wives were from New York State.

Bushman, Richard L. *Joseph Smith and the Beginnings of Mormonism* (Urbana: Univ of Illinois Press, 1984)
Hill, Donna. *Joseph Smith: The First Mormon* (1977; repr Salt Lake City, Utah: Signature Books, 1999)
Quinn, D. Michael. *Early Mormonism and the Magic World View,* 2d ed. (Salt Lake City, Utah: Signature Books, 1998)

D. Michael Quinn

Smith, Melancton (*b* Jamaica, Queens Co, 7 May 1744; *d* New York City, 29 July 1798). Merchant and politician. Smith clerked for a Poughkeepsie merchant and later established a store. He represented Dutchess Co at the First Provincial Congress in 1775. During the Revolutionary War he served in the Continental Line Regiment and was captain of Rangers for the Dutchess Co Minutemen. He served on the Commission for Detecting and Defeating Conspiracies, where he gained fame for successfully expelling loyalists from New York Colony, prompting his appointment as sheriff of Dutchess Co (1777–78). In 1785 Smith moved to New York City and expanded his mercantile business. He served in Congress (1785–88) and attended the state's 1788 convention to ratify the US Constitution. An Antifederalist, he was a major opponent of the US Constitution and felt it would allow the elite to monopolize government. Smith is believed to have authored at least a few of the *Letters from the Federal Farmer,* 18 essays opposing the proposed Constitution that appeared in many state newspapers from 1787 to 1788. A supporter of George Clinton, Smith served one term in the state assembly (1791). He died from yellow fever.

Matson, Cathy. "Politics of the Middling Sort: The Bourgeois Radicalism of Abraham Yates, Melancton Smith, and the New York Antifederalists." In *New York in the Age of the Constitution: 1775–1800,* ed. Paul A. Gilje and William Pencak (Rutherford, NJ: Fairleigh Dickinson Univ Press, 1992)
Webking, Robert H. "Melancton Smith and the Letters from the Federal Farmer," *William and Mary Quarterly,* 3d ser, 44 (July 1987): 510–28

Chris Brooks

Smith, Richard (*b* England, ?1613; *d* Smithtown, Suffolk Co, 7 Mar 1692). Founder of Smithtown. An immigrant to Massachusetts Bay by 1640, he was in Southampton [now in Suffolk Co] by 1643. An educated man, he became a town official but was banished in 1656 for insulting the magistrates, and he subsequently moved his family to nearby Setauket. In 1663 Lion Gardiner sold him a large tract of land that later became Smithtown. Smith patented it two years later but spent the next 12 years engaged in court battles over previous claims and boundary disputes. According to folklore, Smith made an agreement with local Indians to keep whatever land he could circle in a single day riding a bull; on the longest day of the year he is said to have traced the present border of Smithtown in this manner. When he died, his will divided his land among his children. Now commonly known as Richard "Bull" Smith, the name Bull was applied to his family as a nickname and became a middle name in the 19th century.

Smith, Edward H. L., III. "The Identity of Sarah, Wife of Richard Smith of Smithtown, Long Island," *New York Genealogical and Biographical Record* 121 (1990): 19–22
Smith, Frederick Kinsman. *The Family of Richard Smith of Smithtown, Long Island* (Smithtown, NY: Smithtown Historical Society, 1967)

Georgina Martorella

Smith, Stephen (*b* Spafford, Onondaga Co, 19 Feb 1823; *d* Montour Falls, Schuyler Co, 26 Aug 1922). Surgeon and public health administrator. He studied medicine privately with Caleb Green, attended Geneva Medical College (Ontario Co) and the University of Buffalo Department of Medicine, and received an MD in 1850 from the College of Physicians and Surgeons in New York City. He spent his entire career (1851–1911) on the surgical staff of Bellevue Hospital in New York City in addition to teaching surgery and anatomy at Bellevue Hospital Medical College (1861–72). He promoted antisepsis in surgery and wrote two standard textbooks, *Hand-Book of Surgical Operations* (1862) and *Manual of the Principles and Practice of Operative Surgery* (1879). A champion of sanitation and vaccination, he pushed for passage of the Metropolitan Health Bill (1866), which became a guide for public health reforms in New York City and throughout the country. Smith founded and became the first president of the American Public Health Association (1872), served on the Metropolitan Board of Health (1868–75), and in 1878 lobbied for creation of the National Board of Health. As state commissioner of lunacy (1882–88), he shifted responsibility for care of the insane from counties to the state. He served on the New York State Board of Charities from 1918 until his death.

Brieger, Gert H. "Smith, Stephen." In *Dictionary of American Medical Biography* (Westport, Conn: Greenwood, 1984)

Eric v. d. Luft

Smith, William (*b* Newton Bromswold, England, 2 Feb 1655; *d* Setauket, Suffolk Co, 18 Feb 1705). Manor lord. Smith served as the last mayor of the British Crown colony of Tangier, Morocco, in 1682–83. In 1686 he sailed to New York with his wife and family and soon purchased large tracts of land in the Town of Brookhaven (Suffolk Co). In 1689 he settled at Little Neck, now Strongs Neck. In 1693 Gov Benjamin Fletcher granted Smith a patent creating the Manor of St. George. From 1691 to 1705 Smith was a member of the provincial governor's council; he became chief justice of the supreme court of the province (1692, 1701–3) and in 1693 was commissioned as colonel of the Suffolk Co militia. He is commonly referenced as William "Tangier" Smith; he did not use the appellation Tangier, but it was adopted by his descendants.

Eberlein, Harold Donaldson. "The Manor of St. George." In *Manor Houses and Historic Homes of Long Island and Staten Island* (Philadelphia: J. B. Lippincott, 1928)
Smith, Ruth Tangier, and Henry Bainbridge Hoff. *The Tangier Smith Family: Descendants of Colonel William Smith of the Manor of St. George, Long Island, New York* (New York: Order of Colonial Lords of Manors in America, 1978)

Laura E. Mann

Smith, William (*b* Tyler Hill, England, 2 Sept 1818; *d* Geneva, Ontario Co, 6 Feb 1912). Nurseryman and philanthropist. Smith emigrated from England in 1843 with his brothers Edward and Thomas. In 1846 they established W. T. and E. Smith Nurseries in Geneva, which became a leading national wholesaler of fruit and ornamental trees after the Civil War. William was responsible for plant propagation. In addition to the nursery, he helped organize and served as president of the Standard Optical Co and was a director of the First National Bank of Geneva. Notable among his philanthropies was Smith Observatory, built on the nursery grounds, from which astronomer William A. Brooks identified 14 new comets between 1888 and 1906. In 1893–94 he built the Romanesque Smith Opera House in Geneva. Through a gift of $475,000 he established William Smith College for women in Geneva, which opened in 1908 and operates as a coordinate institution with Hobart College for men.

Grebinger, Paul, and Ellen M. Grebinger. *To Dress and Keep the Earth: The Nurseries and Nurserymen of Geneva, New York* (Geneva, NY: Geneva Historical Society, 1993)

Paul Grebinger

Smith, William Jr (*b* New York City, 25 June 1728; *d* Quebec, 3 Dec 1793). Lawyer and author. Smith graduated from Yale College in 1745 and practiced with his father before being admitted to the bar in 1750. He became a leading counsel in the mayor's court, supreme court, and the Court of Admiralty. In 1752 Smith and his partner, William Livingston, authored *Laws of New York from the Year 1691 to 1751.* With John Morin Scott and Livingston, he published and wrote for New York City's *Independent Reflector* (1752–53) and *Occasional Reverberator* (1753). Although somewhat inaccurate and politically biased, *The History of the Province of New York, from the First Discovery to the Year 1732* (1757) was his most important literary work. In 1763 Smith was appointed chief justice and in 1767 served on the provincial council. He cofounded the Moot, an association for prominent New York City attorneys in 1770. As the Revolutionary War commenced, Smith sided with the British and was sent to live on Livingston Manor. In 1778 he moved to British-occupied New York City. When the British left in 1783 Smith went to England and in 1786 moved to Quebec City to serve as chief justice of Canada.

Upton, Leslie F. *The Loyal Whig: William Smith of New York and Quebec* ([Toronto]: Univ of Toronto Press, 1969)

Mark G. Spencer

Smithfield. Town (pop 1,205) in central Madison Co. Originally part of the Oneida territory, Smithfield was bought by Peter Smith of New

York City, an associate of John Jacob Astor, and settled in 1795. The town was formed from Cazenovia in 1807. Its hamlet of Peterboro was the site of Smith's land office (1804), which sold land in 54 counties in the state. Two glass factories operated at Peterboro in the early 19th century; in 1813 a steel hay fork was patented and later manufactured at Mile Strip, a former locality in Smithfield's northwest. Because of the activism of Peter Smith's son Gerrit (1797–1874), an abolitionist and philanthropist, Peterboro became a center of reform activity. It was home to a temperance hotel (1827) and the nonsectarian Free Church of Peterboro (1843), and attracted numerous refugees from slavery, some of whom settled in the village. Gerrit's grandson Gerrit Smith Miller imported quality Holstein-Friesian cattle from Holland in 1869 to reintroduce and renew the breed in America and initiated the Holstein-Friesian registry. Civil War Days are held at Peterboro every summer. The Peterboro Land Office is a museum, part of the Gerrit Smith Estate, which was named a National Historic Landmark in 2001. In 2003, 58% of Smithfield's land was agricultural.

William F. Helmer

Smithtown. Town (pop 115,715) and locality (pop 26,901) in NW Suffolk Co. Richard Smith acquired land from Lion Gardiner in 1663 and received a patent for it in 1665; settlement followed. The town government was in operation by 1715, the year of the first surviving minutes. Dams on the Nissequogue River, which runs north through the center of the town, provided power for grist-, saw-, and fulling mills, supporting agriculture. Smithtown residents backed independence and suffered under British occupation during the Revolution. The Long Island Rail Road crossed town in 1872, making summer residences at Kings Park, Smithtown, Smithtown Branch, and St. James possible. Kings Park State Hospital opened in 1895, serving the mentally ill until 1996; it drew Irish, Jewish, and Italian workers. Nearby, Nesconset was developed starting in 1908 and the newspaper *Il Progresso* platted the hamlet of San Remo in 1922, attracting Italian Americans. Fort Salonga in Huntington and Head of the Harbor and Nissequogue in Smithtown developed with substantial houses on larger lots. Smithtown had little industry through most of the 20th century aside from concrete blocks and pearl buttons made at Nesconset. The town's population was 20,993 in 1950. Smithtown was crossed by the Long Island Motor Parkway (1911), but the Northern State Parkway (1952) and the Long Island Expressway (1962–66) were the roads that spurred the demand for commuter housing. The population exploded to 116,663 in 1980 as farmland was transformed into suburb, the change most dramatic around previously rural Hauppauge. In the early 21st century Hauppauge is the site of the Vanderbilt Industrial Park (with over 1,350 companies, the country's second largest) and of county and state office buildings. Smithtown is the site of Gov Alfred E. Smith/Sunken Meadow, Nissequogue River, and Caleb Smith State Parks. The St. James General Store (1857), still operating, is a landmark.

Smithville. Town (pop 1,347) in W Chenango Co. Settled in 1797, the town was formed from Greene in 1808. Sawmills, asheries, and stone quarries were prevalent at first as settlers dammed the Genegantslet Creek for power. Smithville's high ranges and narrow valleys were suited to dairying, and after the Civil War a creamery and a cheese factory were built. Tarbell Farms was a showplace dairy (1899–1963). Hansmann's Mills, today a national manufacturer of pancake mixes headquartered in Binghamton, began in Smithville in 1832 as Tanners Mill. In the early 21st century, Smithville is a rural home for retirees and city transplants, and a bedroom community for people working in Greene.

Michele A. McFee

smog. See POLLUTION.

smoking. See TOBACCO INDUSTRY AND SMOKING.

Smyrna. Town (pop 1,418) and village (pop 241) in N central Chenango Co. Settled in 1792, the town was formed in 1808 as Stafford but changed almost immediately to Smyrna. The village, on the Fourth Great Western Turnpike (1805), was incorporated in 1829. Several tanneries operated in the mid–19th century, as did an axe factory at Upperville. The town was served by the Ontario and Western Railroad (1869). In the early 21st century some families farm on a larger scale than in the past, and Bailey Lumber Co is a large hardwood mill. Charlie Palmer (1959–), restaurateur, chef, and cookbook author, is a native; his flagship restaurant, Aureole, is in Manhattan.

snowmobiles and snowmobiling. The first power-driven sleds of the 1930s were large, clumsy, slow-moving machines designed to carry numerous people over deep snow. Early models were utilitarian rather than recreational and used for forestry, rescue, and construction purposes. Snowmobiles continue to be used, to a significant degree, by search-and-rescue workers, emergency and medical personnel, farmers, loggers, law enforcement officers, public utility workers, and a wide variety of others who need reliable transportation in deep snow. With the development of smaller gasoline engines in the 1950s and the design of one- or two-passenger lightweight snowmobiles in the 1960s, however, the recreational use emerged. Snowmobiling is a major winter recreational activity across New York State and a significant factor in increased winter tourism in the snowbelt of Tug Hill, which offered 500 miles (800 km) of groomed trails in 2002, and the Adirondack region, with 800 miles (1,300 km).

Total direct spending by snowmobile users for trip expenditures and equipment and by snowmobile clubs and equipment dealers during the 1996–97 season in New York State was estimated at $238 million by a SUNY Potsdam study. In 2002 there were more than 146,000 registered snowmobiles in New York State and 8,500 miles (13,700 km) of trails in the statewide trail system across public and private lands. The state ranks fourth in the nation for the number of registered snowmobiles. Municipalities partner with more than 170 snowmobile clubs and their nearly 20,000 members to maintain and groom the trails in the state system. Funding for trail maintenance is provided by a state snowmobile trail fund from snowmobile registrations and by snowmobile club fund-raising and volunteer activities. In 2001 New York State awarded $1 million for snowmobile trail maintenance to 58 communities, administered by the New York State Office of Parks, Recreation, and Historic Preservation.

New York State Office of Parks, Recreation, and Historic Preservation. *Statewide Comprehensive Outdoor Recreation Plan 2003* (Albany: Author, 2002)

Chad P. Dawson

snow removal. Annual snow accumulation across New York State is 90–200 inches (225–500 cm) in the Lake Erie and Lake Ontario region, increasing to 300 inches (762 cm) on the Tug Hill Plateau and decreasing to 30 inches (72 cm) along the Atlantic coast of Long Island. During the coldest months, typically November through April, the state is also subject to frost, freezing rain, and sleet. The combination of these conditions and heavy traffic volumes make winter road maintenance a formidable task for New York State's various local, county, and state governmental entities that control snow and ice removal on the state's 250,000 lane miles (402,000 km) of public roadways. In the average winter more than 2.5 million tons (2.3 million MT) of salt are used to prevent or break up ice and hard-packed snow on public roads.

Over the course of the 19th and 20th centuries snow removal evolved into a major civic function and expense. Snow was largely shoveled by hand until after the Civil War, and horse plows did not become common until the 1880s. Snow and ice control progressed from horse-drawn plow snow removal (1880s–1920s) to removal plus heavy use of abrasives and salts (1930s–1970s) to prevention of the bonding of ice, clearing snow and ice cover, and reduction of ice and snow depth with less application of salts and abrasives (1980–present).

In Rochester various "good government" administrations at the turn of the 20th century prided themselves on their commitment to good snow removal. The city's practice of sending out snow removal teams while the storm was still ongoing was a much-copied innovation, and it was among the first to introduce motorized snow plows (1917). While municipalities across New York State have made substantial investments in snow removal equipment, inadequate removal can become a political issue. An 18 in (45 cm) snowfall on New York City in February 1969 left the streets in parts of the city impassable for almost a week, in part because plows had been buried in their storage lots. Not only were the city and surrounding suburbs forced to hire nearly 10,000 workers and shovelers to clear the streets, but the storm also created a large political problem for Mayor John Lindsay and was a contributing factor to his loss in the Republican primary later that year.

The New York State Department of Transportation (DOT) runs the largest snow and ice control operation in the state, responsible for a total of 43,000 lane miles (69,200 km) of state roads, with maintenance of 9,000 miles (14,500 km) of this contracted out to about 180 municipal entities. DOT also maintains the interstate highway system, while the New York State Thruway Authority maintains only portions of I-84, I-87, and I-90. In the early 21st century the DOT owns 1,330 heavy plow trucks and 49 driving snowblowers. Data from sophisticated weather information systems aid DOT in snow and ice control decisions, with the Internet and other data clearinghouses improving information sharing and efficiencies among authorities.

DOT plow-truck allocations are based on average snow rates of 1.1 inches (2.8 cm) per hour. During blizzard conditions, when visibility is extremely low, service may be temporarily curtailed for safety reasons, such as during the December 2001 storm that dropped 6.8 feet (2.1 m) of snow on Buffalo. Snow and ice control is typically triggered when greater than 0.5–1.5 inches (1.3–3.8 cm) of accumulation have been forecast or have occurred, launching a 24-hour response. Early response helps prevent the bonding of frozen precipitation to the pavement. Typical salt applications are 115–270 pounds (52–122 kg) per lane mile, with liquid brines applied at 20–50 gallons (76–189 l) per lane mile; the higher rates are used for lower temperatures and higher-moisture events. Liquid performance enhancers may be added to the salt, especially at pavement temperatures below 20°F (-7°C). When chemical treatment is inadequate for very cold roads with low traffic volumes or steep grades, abrasives such as sand may be spread at rates of 600–900 pounds (270–400 kg) per lane mile, with higher rates for hills, curves, and intersections.

Plow-truck cycles run from one to two hours; the trucks travel about 15–35 mph (24–56 kph), carry loads of 7–10 yd^3 (5.4–7.6 m^3) of sand and salt, and treatment targets of 20–45 lane miles (32–72 km) of road. Additional work includes clearing snow from drainage structures, catch basins, and culvert inlets to prevent flooding in thaw; protective storage of sand and salts to prevent environmental contamination; placement of snow stakes at curbs and fire hydrants; use of snow fences and tree shelterbelts to reduce snow drift; and regular calibration of automatic spreaders.

From 1995 to 2001 DOT reduced sand use from 650,000 to 30,000 tons (590,000 to 27,000 MT) annually because of its negative impacts: on human health when churned into an airborne powder; on road infrastructure when carried by meltwater to clog catch basins; and on aquatic habitats when choked by sand deposits. Road salts, which tend to accumulate in soil, also have negative environmental effects. Salt injuries to trees and soil include leaf damage from salt spray, root damage from osmotic imbalance, root toxicity, and clumping of salt-heavy soils. Both visual and laboratory methods are used to detect injury to the roadside ecosystem; visually, deeper green-colored leaves indicate sodium enrichment of the soil, while burned leaf tips indicate chlorine enrichment. DOT uses empirical formulas to identify safe salt application rates. Recent research in nearby Ontario, Canada, found that nearly 51% of woody roadside plants are sensitive to road salts but that oak species, which are well adapted to other urban pollutants and the New York State climate, are salt tolerant.

McKelvey, Blake. *Snow in the Cities: A History of America's Urban Response* (Rochester: Univ of Rochester Press, 1995)

———. "Snowstorms and Snow Fighting: The Rochester Experience," *Rochester History* 27 (1965), 1–24

Theodore A. Endreny and Joseph Doherty

soaring and gliding. Gliding is done with a simple motorless aircraft that steadily loses altitude along its glide path; soaring involves a more efficient motorless aircraft, using up currents to gain height and soar. The first practical gliders were developed in the late 19th century. By 1911 Orville Wright set the American record for motorless flight with a time of 9 min 45 s at Kitty Hawk, NC. During the 1920s Wolfgang Klemperer, a Goodyear engineer and soaring pioneer from Akron, Ohio, was given responsibility for finding a place where a national soaring contest could be held. He settled on the Chemung Valley region because of its many ridges, which face the prevailing wind directions, the abundant hayfields for safe landings, and the interest of the community. At that time gliders were launched with a rubberized rope from the tops of mountains or ridges so that they could soar in the deflected upward air currents from the winds striking the ridges. After a successful trial of soaring conditions in July 1930 by Jack K. O'Meara, a test pilot for a glider company in Akron, the first national soaring contest was held that September. Using the Caton Avenue Airport (now Southport Correctional Facility) in Chemung Co as a base, many flights, including one by Wolf Hirth, a famous German soaring pilot, were made from South Mountain and other ridges in the area. With enthusiastic community support a national soaring contest was held in the Elmira area every year from 1930 to 1947. Since then they have alternated with other sites around the country. Beginning in 1934 the contests were held at Harris Hill in Big Flats (Chemung Co), and the Elmira region became known as the Soaring Capital of America. By 1937 permanent soaring facilities, including two hangars, an administration building, and cabins, had been built at Harris Hill by the Works Progress Administration. It was operated by the nonprofit Elmira Area Soaring Corp (EASC).

During World War II the Germans effectively used troop-carrying gliders in their invasion of Belgium, Holland, and Crete. The US Army Air Force started its own glider program in 1941, buying its first training gliders from Schweizer Aircraft Corp in Elmira Heights (Chemung Co) and teaching glider pilots at Harris Hill. EASC moved the training program to Alabama to provide year-round instruction and operated the program until it was canceled in 1943. In 1967 EASC became the Harris Hill Soaring Corp (HHSC), and paved runways were installed at the Harris Hill flying field. Since 1946 the Schweizer Soaring School has operated at the Chemung County Airport (now Elmira-Corning Regional Airport) in Horseheads, and the HHSC continues to operate Harris Hill. In 1969 the Soaring Society of America (SSA) selected Harris Hill as the site for the National Soaring Museum, which includes a library and archives as well as a large collection of motorless aircraft. The SSA had nearly 20,000 members as of 2001 with numerous clubs throughout New York State.

National Soaring Museum, http://www.soaringmuseum.org

Schweizer, Paul A. *Wings Like Eagles* (Washington, DC: Smithsonian Institution Press, 1988)

Paul A. Schweizer

Snowblowing rural roads in Onondaga Co, mid–20th century.

soccer. Association football, or soccer, was first played in the United States and New York State in the second half of the 19th century, especially by newcomers from the British Isles, most of them working class. At first the difference between what emerged as American football and soccer was not that apparent. In 1873 Columbia College and three other eastern colleges met in New York City to set up rules for competitions that closely resembled association football. But this proved to be abortive, and the version of football played by eastern colleges was increasingly differentiated from soccer. One of the first true soccer games played in the United States was played in Central Park in 1886. Around 1890 a club known as the Thistles in Churchville (Monroe Co) helped to popularize the sport in Western New York.

Soccer was primarily played by amateur teams sponsored by ethnic clubs and by companies.

The Metropolitan Association Football League (1905) was the first league formed to coordinate play; the National Challenge Cup was won by the Brooklyn Field Club in 1914. In 1921 the professional American Soccer League (ASL) formed, including such well-known teams as the New York Giants, Brooklyn Wanderers, Indiana Flooring, New York Nationals, and Hakoah All-Stars. The New York State teams of the ASL included many international stars, and attendance at games sometimes exceeded 20,000. The German-American Soccer League formed in 1923; leading clubs include the German-Hungarian Sport Club (Brooklyn) and the Eintract Sport Club (Astoria, Queens Co). It has expanded over time to include teams of other ethnicities, and in 1977 became the Cosmopolitan Soccer League; in 2002 it included 82 teams.

The New York Generals played in the newly formed North American Soccer League (NASL) in 1968, but the New York Cosmos was the more enduring NASL franchise, playing from 1970 to 1984, and featured a roster of mature superstars including the world-famous Brazilian player Pelé and European greats Giorgio Chinaglia and Franz Beckenbauer. The Cosmos won the NASL championship five times before the league folded in 1984. The Rochester Lancers moved from the ASL to the NASL, playing under it from 1970 to 1980. After 1984 New York State lacked a major professional soccer representative until 1996, when Major League Soccer (MLS) brought the New York/New Jersey Metrostars to the Meadowlands Sports Complex (East Rutherford, NJ). The A-League, formed in 1990 as the American Professional Soccer League (APSL), featured a number of New York State teams, including the short-lived Long Island Rough Riders and the Staten Island Vipers, and the Rochester Raging Rhinos (1996), its champion in 1998, 2000, and 2001. The Women's United Soccer Association (WUSA), which began play in 2001, includes the New York Power, whose home field is at Uniondale (Nassau Co).

Soccer has become a sport of choice for some 200,000 New York State youth through several organizations, such as the recreational American Youth Soccer Organization (AYSO), the United States Youth Soccer Association (USYSA), the YMCA, the Young Men's Hebrew Association (YMHA), and various city parks and recreation programs. Thousands more play for public and private school teams. New York State is also home to some of the finest collegiate programs; Hartwick College won the 1977 NCAA Division I championship, and St. John's University won in 1996. Notable performances by New Yorkers in the soccer World Cup include that of Joseph Gaetjens, a Columbia University student of Haitian descent who in 1950 scored the only goal in the astonishing upset of England by the United States, and Brooklyn-born Bruce Arena, who coached the US World Cup team to the quarterfinals in 2002. The National Soccer Hall of Fame is located in Oneonta (Otsego Co) and includes a new museum facility.

Markovits, Andrei, and Steven L. Hellerman. *Offside: Soccer and American Exceptionalism* (Princeton, NJ: Princeton Univ Press, 2001)

Heidi Solberg Viar

Social Gospel. A movement within late 19th- and early 20th-century Protestantism that applied Christian principles to the solution of contemporary social problems. Part of a larger international interest in social Christianity, the Social Gospel in the United States emerged in continuity with the 19th-century social reform impulse and in conjunction with the development of ecumenism. It was bolstered by current theological trends, such as an emphasis on the ethical teachings of Jesus, affirmation of God's involvement in history, and the kingdom of God as a righteous social order on earth. Responding to social inequities, Social Gospel adherents advocated amelioration of conditions in slums and factories, and generally supported the rights of workers, women, and children, often through grassroots efforts to influence public opinion, political lobbying, and the establishment of settlement houses, hospitals, social betterment organizations, and "institutional churches."

Walter Rauschenbusch, a professor at Rochester Theological Seminary, was widely acknowledged as the movement's leading figure. He helped popularize the Social Gospel through such books as *Christianity and the Social Crisis* (1907) and helped stimulate reform efforts in Rochester and elsewhere. Rauschenbusch was a founder of the Brotherhood of the Kingdom, a group of pastors and scholars who met annually for this purpose in Marlborough (Ulster Co) from 1892 to 1915. In Buffalo prominent Christian socialist William D. P. Bliss helped found and became president of the National Social Reform Union, an effort to unify the nation's reform parties and disseminate educational information. Nearby the Chautauqua Institution often featured speakers advocating a Social Gospel perspective.

New York City was one of the centers of the movement, where its leaders included Lyman Abbott, who became editor in chief of the *Outlook* in 1876 and succeeded Henry Ward Beecher as pastor of Brooklyn's Plymouth Church (1888–99). Josiah Strong, author of the influential reform tract *Our Country* (1885), was general secretary of the Evangelical Alliance for the United States (1886–98). By 1889 the alliance had formed local branches in Binghamton, Rome, Watervliet, and Kingston, in addition to its New York City headquarters. In 1898 Strong founded and became president of the League for Social Service (renamed the American Institute for Social Service in 1902) in New York City, an office he held until his death in 1916. The leading African American figure in the movement, Reverdy C. Ransom, editor of the *AME Church Review*, was pastor of Bethel African Methodist Episcopal Church in New York City (1907–12).

The practical effects of Social Gospel advocacy were considerable. In 1900, 112 churches in New York City reported that they were employing "institutional" methods for social betterment. University Settlement, established as the Neighborhood Guild on New York City's Lower East Side in 1886 and renamed in 1891, became the nation's first social settlement—an urban residence designed to provide opportunities for social uplift. By 1906, 48 social settlements were reported in the state: 33 in New York City, 7 in Brooklyn, 6 in Buffalo, 1 in Albany, and 1 in Rochester. In 1900 and 1905 conferences sponsored by the Open and Institutional Church League met in New York City, which resulted in the founding of the Federal Council of the Churches of Christ in America (now National Council of Churches) in 1908. The Religious Citizenship League, designed for ordinary citizens who wished to apply their faith to social and political issues, was organized in New York City in 1914 with an initial concentration on the problem of unemployment. The statewide presence of Social Gospel advocates was an important factor in making New York State a center of progressive reform.

Luker, Ralph E. *The Social Gospel in Black and White: American Racial Reform, 1885–1912* (Chapel Hill: Univ of North Carolina Press, 1991)

White, Ronald C., Jr, and C. Howard Hopkins. *The Social Gospel: Religion and Reform in Changing America* (Philadelphia: Temple Univ Press, 1976)

Wendy J. Deichmann Edwards

Socialist expulsion. In 1920 the New York State Assembly expelled five members who were representatives of the Socialist Party of America (SP). This was part of a broader national effort by both Republicans and Democrats, in the wake of the Bolshevik revolution in Russia and the subsequent Red Scare in the United States, to isolate socialism and left-wing politics. The five expelled Socialists represented immigrant districts in New York City: Louis Waldman and August Claessens represented districts in Manhattan; Samuel A. Dewitt and Samuel Orr, the Bronx; and Charles Solomon, a district in Brooklyn. Dewitt was a freshman member; Waldman, Orr, and Solomon were returning for their second term; and Claessens was returning for his third term. On 7 Jan 1920, after all assembly members were sworn into office, Speaker of the Assembly Thaddeus Sweet (R-Oswego) called the five to the front of the chamber and condemned socialism and its supposed allegiance with Soviet revolutionaries. Assembly Majority Leader Simon Adler (R-Monroe) introduced a resolution to suspend the five pending a judiciary committee inquiry to determine their right to their seats. Socialists had been present in the state legislature since 1916; there were 10 in the assembly during the previous session. Illustrating the political consensus for removal, with a 110/35 Republican/Democratic split in the assembly, the five Socialists were suspended together by a bipartisan vote of 140-6; the 6 ballots cast against removal included those of four of the five Socialists (Waldman refused to vote) and two Democrats.

Much of the state press, including the *New York Times,* initially supported the expulsion. The head of New York City's Board of Aldermen, Fiorello La Guardia, strongly praised the assembly's actions, adding for good measure his conviction that, if expelled, the five should be shot. On the other side, the *Albany Knickerbocker* and the *New York World* had from the start chastised the assembly, and the *World* even helped raise money to pay for the five's legal costs. Some prominent Republicans condemned the expulsion, notably former governor Charles Evans Hughes. Democratic governor Alfred E. Smith criticized the action also but was uncharacteristically subdued in his condemnation.

In 1920 the assembly's Judiciary Committee held hearings. At issue was whether the five had pledged support to the SP constitution. If so, they were to be expelled because the interests of socialism were in accord with the Soviet movement and therefore inimical with American democracy. At the hearings' start Hughes gave an impassioned opening statement for the defense, arguing that no assembly members could be expelled for their political opinions and that the actions being contemplated were in violation of the New York State and US Constitutions. After more than two months of deliberation, during which all other assembly business ground to a halt, on 30 March the divided Judiciary Committee released its report, which found the members guilty and recommended their expulsion, with seven members (six Republicans, one Democrat) voting to expel, and six (equally divided between Republicans and Democrats) voting against expulsion. On 1 April the entire assembly took up debate on the matter. The debate lasted all day, and voting took place only the following morning. On 2 April all five Socialists were expelled with similar bipartisan votes. The vote against Waldman was typical: 115 for expulsion (98 Republicans, 17 Democrats); 28 opposed (11 Republicans, 17 Democrats). The small group of Republican and Democratic assembly members who voted against expulsion were largely from New York City, Long Island, Schenectady, and Buffalo.

The New York State Assembly's expulsion of its Socialist members is unique in the history of American state legislatures; never before or since has a legislature removed a complete party delegation from its body. Although much of the press had initially been behind the expulsion, by spring 1920 most of the state media had turned against the Socialists' removal. Nevertheless, when a September election for a special legislative session reelected all five Socialists, the assembly refused to seat three of them, and the other two refused to take their seats. In the regular November elections of 1920 the SP captured only three assembly seats: Samuel Orr (Bronx), Charles Solomon (Manhattan), and the newly elected Henry Jager (Brooklyn). On the assembly's opening day in 1921 resolutions were reintroduced to expel the Socialists. The matter was referred to the Judiciary Committee, but with the broader Red Scare by then receding, the issue died permanently in committee.

Jaffee, Julian F. *Crusade against Radicalism: New York during the Red Scare, 1914–1924* (Port Washington, NY: Kennikat Press, 1972)

New York State. Assembly. *Proceedings of the Judiciary Committee of the Assembly in the Matter of the Investigation by the Assembly of the State of New York as to the Qualifications of Louis Waldman, August Claessens, Samuel A. Dewitt, Samuel Orr, and Charles Solomon, to Retain Their Seats in Said Body*, by Louis M. Martin, chairman. Assembly Doc no. 35, 3 vols (1920)

Tod M. Ottman

Socialist Labor Party (SLP). Founded in 1877 primarily by German immigrants, it was the first significant socialist political party in the United States. The SLP had many chapters, but its greatest strength was in New York City. The party's peak coincided with the Great Railroad Strike of 1877. That same year the SLP launched a daily newspaper in several major cities, including New York City. The party witnessed modest success in electing state and local officials. Many New York City residents, particularly Jewish garment workers on Manhattan's Lower East Side, were attracted to the SLP. In 1886 the SLP assisted the New York City mayoral campaign of the single-taxer Henry George. In the 1880s–1890s the SLP became increasingly critical of conservative unionism and eventually assumed a more revolutionary tone, foreshadowing the Industrial Workers of the World. After 1890 the organization came under the influence of Daniel DeLeon, a Westchester Co schoolteacher, but split 11 years later over DeLeon's autocratic style. After DeLeon's death in 1914 the SLP lost most of its membership and influence. Through the decades the SLP has continued to promote socialism, however, and was on the official New York State ballot from 1906 to 1934 and from 1962 to 1974. As of 2002 the SLP still exists despite low membership and publishes its newspaper, the *People.*

Seretan, L. Glen. *Daniel DeLeon: The Odyssey of an American Marxist* (Cambridge, Mass: Harvard Univ Press, 1979)

Mark Noon

socialists. Advocates for communal society and public ownership of production emerged in New York State in the early 19th century, largely as a reaction to the perceived inequities of industrialization. The state was a center for advocates of European utopian socialism, followers of Robert Owen and Charles Fourier, who organized numerous short-lived communal experiments, primarily in the central and western parts of the state. Many of these experiments had a religious inspiration; the best known was the Oneida Community, led by John Humphrey Noyes, whose *History of America Socialisms* (1870) remains an important guide to the era. Prominent figures in the movement included Robert Dale Owen, Albert Brisbane, and Fanny Wright, who spent extensive time in New York City advocating socialism and a variety of other reforms. Labor groups, especially the Working Men's Party in New York City in the 1820s, had socialist elements. German socialists immigrated to New York City after 1840, including Wilhelm Weitling and Joseph Weydemeyer, who arrived from Germany in 1851. Weydemeyer and Friedrich A. Sorge founded in 1857 the Communist Club in New York City, an organization that 10 years later was the first American branch of the International Workingmen's Association (IWA). Spilling well beyond immigrant German branches, the IWA came to be a force in New York City, Buffalo, and Rochester in the early 1870s and was the most successful American socialist grouping for a number of years. Factional disputes led to its demise.

Socialist Labor Party

The IWA's successor, the Workingmen's Party, gave way by 1877 to the Socialist Labor Party (SLP), which ushered in the first sustained period of organized socialist presence in New York State and the nation. In municipal elections that year, the SLP garnered 6,000 votes in Buffalo and 1,800 in New York City, rising to 4,000 the next year; despite some initial success, however, it was confined mainly to its base among New Yorkers of German heritage until the late 1880s. The SLP was revived in the state by an influx of new immigrants, most notably Jewish garment workers organized into the United Hebrew Trades. It acquired the outstanding leadership of the Curaçao-born Daniel DeLeon, a Westchester Co educator, under whom the SLP appealed to English speakers as well as German and Jewish immigrants. Increasingly, DeLeon insisted on revolutionary purity and the exclusive dominance of his own thought. His followers, notably labor unionists, began to desert the SLP, and in 1899 a group of former loyalists, including Morris Hillquit and Meyer London bolted.

Socialist Party of America

The dissident SLP held its convention in Rochester in 1900 and in 1901 merged into the newly founded Socialist Party of America. New York State accounted for 10% of that membership before World War I, doubling to 20% by 1920. The Socialists had some electoral successes in New York State. In 1911 and 1913 in Schenectady, they elected the mayor, 8 of the city's 13 aldermen, and the first Socialist to the state assembly. In New York City by 1912 they garnered 11% of the total municipal vote, rising to 22% in 1917, and in 1914 elected Meyer London, who served three terms, to the US Congress. The high-water mark of Socialist electoral activity came in 1917. In Buffalo Socialists garnered 30% of the vote, in Schenectady 24% (despite no candidates elected), in Rochester 20%, in Gloversville (Fulton Co) 19%, and in Syracuse 12%. They also polled significantly in Olean (Cattaraugus Co) and Albany. Also in 1917 New York City elected 10 Socialists to the state assembly, 7 aldermen, and 1 municipal court judge. Rochester elected three Socialist constables, two aldermen, and two city supervisors. In 1919 in Buffalo Socialists took 25% of the vote. Party branches were founded throughout the state, and Socialist newspapers were published in Jamestown (Chautauqua Co), Schenectady, Utica, Rochester, New York City, the Ozone Park section of Queens, and Williamsburg in Brooklyn.

Culture

Socialist culture permeated various ethnic communities, which developed a network of educational and social services. German organizations, such as the Workers Sick and Death Benefit Fund of the United States of America (1884) had 50,000 members by 1937, with a recreation farm and rest-home facilities for the elderly in Fosterdale (Sullivan Co). German American socialists also founded workers' education associations with socialist schools for children and adults (12 in New York City in 1890). Socialist associations also founded large labor lyceums; that in Brooklyn had a membership of 4,000 in 1889. The socialist needle trades unions were involved in political education efforts through the Rand School of Social Science from 1906 and Unity House, both at Union Square in Manhattan. The largest socialist newspaper, the Yiddish language *Forverts (Forward),* had a circulation of 200,000 by 1917 and an enormous influence on New York City's immigrant Jewish population. In Manhattan's Harlem there were two black socialist newspapers by 1918, and a solid 25% of the neighborhood's vote went for Socialist candidates despite racism within the party. Among Italian immigrants, socialists and syndicalists came together in the needle trades unions in New York City, Buffalo, and Rochester, and after 1920 in the New York Chamber of Labor, soon to be the spearhead of the antifascist movement in the United States. In the 1920s and 1930s, the Amalgamated Clothing Workers and International Ladies' Garment Workers offered social democratic benefits to members, including unemployment insurance, cooperative housing, labor banks, and consumer cooperatives. Socialists also influenced the arts through journals like the *Masses,* a monthly magazine published from 1911 to 1917 in New York City.

Decline

World War I, internal party splits caused by reactions to the Bolshevik Revolution in Russia, political repression during the Red Scare of 1919–21, and investigations by the state legislature's Lusk Committee in 1919–20 all helped to reduce socialism as a force in New York State. The new intolerance was highlighted by the refusal of the New York State Assembly in 1920 to seat its five elected Socialist members. Party membership declined precipitously in the 1920s, though up to 1930 it still had more members than its chief rival, the Communist Party. After 1926 Norman Thomas became the leader of the Socialist Party; he was a former Presbyterian minister in New York City who led the party for several decades. The party remained an important perspective on the anticommunist left. An influential socialist in New York State in recent decades was Michael Harrington, who lived and worked in New York City and did his best to hold the party together from the 1950s to the 1980s. He is most noted for his book *The Other America* (1962), which called upon Americans to renew their commitment to eradicating poverty. Harrington was a cofounder of successors to the Socialist Party, including the Democratic Socialist Organizing Committee, established in New York City in 1973, and the Democratic Socialists of America founded nine years later in Detroit. Despite the efforts of Thomas, Harrington, Max Schachtman, and others, socialism as a political force was in terminal decline throughout the Cold War, sustained primarily by small groups with little public influence. The rise of the socialist-influenced New Left in the state's public and private colleges and universities in the 1960s proved short-lived. Since the early 1980s the Socialist Scholars Conference in New York City has been one of the largest annual gatherings of left-wing academics.

See also Jews and judaism; Labor; World war I.

Isserman, Maurice. *The Other American: The Life of Michael Harrington* (New York: Public Affairs, 2000)

Leinenweber, Charles. "Socialists in the Streets: The New York City Socialist Party in Working Class Neighborhoods, 1908–1918," *Science and Society* 41 (1977)

Weinstein, James. *The Decline of Socialism in America, 1912–1925* (New York: Vintage, 1967)

Stephen Burwood

Social Services, Department of. See Family assistance, department of.

Social Welfare, Board of. State government body responsible for monitoring programs that serve disadvantaged and dependent children and adults in New York. The main function of the board has been to inspect public and private welfare institutions like orphanages and nursing homes. The board is authorized by the state constitution to review, report on, and make recommendations concerning the policies and programs carried out by state and local agencies. It comments on proposed legislation and regulations and encourages new programs or improvement in programs operated by public and private agencies. It holds public hearings and undertakes investigations, including studies requested by the governor, and appears as a friend of the court in relevant legal proceedings. The board is composed of 15 members appointed by the governor with the consent of the senate.

Created in 1867 as the Board of Commissioners of Public Charities, it was the first unit in New York State created to supervise public welfare programs; public assistance had been the responsibility of counties and towns. Renamed the State Board of Charities in 1873, its powers were extended to oversee public and private institutions for the insane along with charitable, correctional, and reformatory institutions (except prisons). The supervision of insane asylums was transferred to the Commission in Lunacy in 1889. In 1896 the legislature repealed many of the state's poor laws and expanded the board's supervision of local public welfare officials. The reorganization of state government in 1925 and 1926 transferred the board's supervision of correctional and mental health facilities to new state agencies, creating the Department of Charities in 1926, with the Board of Charities acting as its executive arm. The new department assumed the board's functions, except for visitation and inspection, which the board continued. In 1929 the Board of Charities was renamed the Board of Social Welfare and the department renamed the Department of Social Welfare.

The board's membership increased in 1936 from 12 to 15 members, and it was given authority to develop state welfare policies and advise local welfare officials. In 1940 the Public Welfare Law and the State Charities Law were combined, retaining the board as the executive body of the Department of Social Welfare and expanding its authority in the areas of policy and supervision. In 1971 many of the board's functions that had been added since the 1930s were removed, and the board was established as a separate agency within the Executive Department as part of the restructuring of its powers. Its authority to supervise local public assistance was transferred to the Department of Social Services and its direct supervision of child and adult care institutions was taken over by other state agencies, primarily the Department of Mental Hygiene and the Division for Youth. A 1977 law further delineated the public welfare responsibilities of these agencies and eliminated overlapping regulatory powers. All direct administrative functions were removed from the board to ensure that it focused on its primary constitutional role of independent monitor of the quality of New York's public and private welfare agencies and programs.

See also American Indians: policies since 1776.

Richard Andress

social work. Social workers, who are paid to provide social services and counseling to those in need, descended from the usually female paid agents and friendly visitors of 19th-century charitable societies. In New York City the New York Association for Improving the Condition of the Poor (1845) was the first organization in the nation to use male volunteers or "paternal guardians." Buffalo, which after Boston (1851) established the nation's second YMCA (1854) and its first Charity Organization Society (1878), was the first city where paid agents placed dependent children in families. In 1907 the Hawthorne School for Delinquent Boys (Westchester Co), begun by the Jewish Protectory and Aid Society, pioneered psychiatric social work.

At the turn of the century, elite women volunteers, so-called Lady Bountifuls, dominated voluntary societies, providing services that mostly amounted to moralizing among the poor. New York City led the way with the professionalization of the occupation: with 27 students in attendance, the New York Charity Organization Society (1882) inaugurated the first formal training program in social work at its Summer School of Philanthropy in 1898. Renamed the New York School of Philanthropy in 1903, by 1919 it had become the New York School of Social Work and in 1963 the Columbia University School of Social Work. In 1916 New York City counted 3,968 social workers in 368 organizations, mostly in the private sector. They included settlement house residents and playground workers, visiting nurses, medical and psychiatric social workers, as well as industrial social workers who oversaw the social lives of employees for companies such as the Metropolitan Life Insurance Co. Approximately 72% were women, and only 162 had any formal social work training.

In the 1920s social workers moved to establish their professional standing in order to raise their status and pay and to differentiate themselves from unpaid volunteers. The new professional association, the American Association of Social Workers (1921), required formal training for admission. The activism and moral reform orientation of the settlement houses and the moralizing zeal of the older charities was replaced by an image of the caseworker as an objective, neutral investigator trained in casework and increasingly in Freudian theory. When the depression placed new pressures on social workers and clients, the Freudian shift from an emphasis on social conditions to therapeutic diagnosis divided the profession, especially in New York City, where a radical presence was strong.

The depression saw a vast expansion of the public sector and the development of a trade union movement in social work, with New York City leading the nation in both. A rank-and-file movement, inspired by the Communist Party's class and race analysis of the depression, galvanized many New York City social workers. Federation of Jewish Philanthropies of New York (1917) social workers constituted the largest and most active membership of the left-wing United Office and Professional Workers of America (1937), a branch of the Social Service Employers Union (SSEU). Social workers in New York City's Department of Welfare (DW) formed the United Public Workers (1946), similarly distinguished by their advocacy for and identification with clients. These unions and the work of social workers would suffer, however, from an anticommunist purge of Congress of Industrial Organizations (CIO) unions in 1950 as work became more routinized and the focus shifted to social worker productivity. Supervisors encouraged midnight raids to find "men under the beds" in the homes of women who would then be removed from the welfare rolls. At the same time, reduced staff was expected to manage "efficiently" increased caseloads.

New Left insurgents within welfare agencies would revitalize New York City's SSEU in the 1960s. These left-wing social workers lent their support to an emergent national welfare rights movement, and in January 1965 some 8,000 DW workers went successfully on strike on behalf of client services and a union contract. Following a series of unsuccessful 1967 strikes, New York City's public sector social workers moved into the less militant District Council 37 of the AFL-CIO-affiliated American Federation of State, County and Municipal Employees (AFSCME).

After 1970 the introduction of computers into offices and the conservative backlash against Great Society programs shaped social work in New York City. Computers relegated public service workers to deprofessionalized clerical workers or welfare-service aides, which were unskilled jobs that paid little more than relief checks. Women remained at approximately 70% from 1940 to the end of the century. Most were white, and many began using a master's in social work as an entry degree, seeking to become therapists. Men were more likely either to become administrators or to leave the field, and increasing numbers of minority women took the new clerical jobs. In 1998 New York State had 33,840 licensed social workers registered to practice, of whom 13,951 were in New York City (6,618 in Manhattan alone). Over 40% of the state total were clinically trained mental health workers, either psychiatric social workers or therapists. Ironically the new social worker jobs as therapists and welfare-service aides found themselves constrained as the century drew to a close, while the traditional family and child caseworkers continued to staff child welfare and private agencies. Congressional passage of the Personal Responsibility and Work Opportunity Reconciliation Act (1996) and federal efforts to contain rising health insurance costs reduced payments to social worker therapists at the end of the century, and welfare jobs contracted.

Freeman, Joshua B. *Working-Class New York: Life and Labor since World War II* (New York: New Press, 2000)

Katz, Michael B. *In the Shadow of the Poorhouse: A Social History of Welfare in America* (New York: Basic Books, 1986)

Walkowitz, Daniel J. *Working with Class: Social Workers and the Politics of Middle-Class Identity* (Chapel Hill: Univ of North Carolina Press, 1999)

Daniel J. Walkowitz

Society for the Promotion of Useful Arts. Created by an act of the New York State legislature on 2 Apr 1804, it replaced the Society for the Promotion of Agriculture, Arts and Manufactures after its charter had expired. Like its predecessor, the Society for the Promotion of Useful Arts was a learned society that created an institutional base for intellectual activity. It was geared toward promoting the improvement of agricultural practice and domestic productivity in New York State through scientific inquiry and useful knowledge. The society maintained a close relationship with the legislature, its activities supported by state funds as well as by the provision of a meeting room and library in the State Capitol Building. Merchants, landed gentry, attorneys, physicians, scientists, and educators from around New York State were the founding members of the society, with an average of 20 new members elected each year until membership peaked at 169 in 1815. Elected councilors representing the membership held meetings throughout the year; published *Transactions,* which contained notes and essays discussing practical methods of improving agricultural production; and awarded premiums for the best quality of wool cloth manufactured in the state. In 1810 members resolved to collect and preserve mineral specimens from around the state. Revised bylaws adopted by the membership in 1815 signaled a more formal shift to the role of a scientific society. After the War of 1812 legislative patronage declined as public interest in the presentation of scientific papers about agricultural improvements and the awarding of premiums waned.

The society's efforts to promote improved agricultural practices were eventually superseded by the creation of a State Board of Agriculture on 7 Apr 1819. Continuing its promotion of science, core members from the Albany area continued to meet sporadically until 1824, when the society merged with the Albany Lyceum of Natural History and formed the Albany Institute, eventually becoming the Albany Institute of History and Art in 1926. Members of the society included Dr Samuel Bard, who was personal physician to George Washington, and Chancellor Robert R. Livingston, who served as the society's president.

Oleson, Alexandra, and Sanborn C. Brown, eds. *The Pursuit of Knowledge in the Early American Republic: American Scientific and Learned Societies from Colonial Times to the Civil War* (Baltimore: Johns Hopkins Univ Press, 1976)

Wesley G. Balla

Society for the Propagation of the Gospel in Foreign Parts (SPG). Founded in 1701 by Thomas Bray of Maryland, its avowed goals were to reinvigorate missionary efforts among the American Indian tribes, slaves, and free Blacks; build catechetical schools; institute poor relief; and improve conditions for Anglican clergy in the colonies. By increasing clerical salaries, recruiting better-educated ministers for impoverished and neglected parishes, and reinforcing discipline, Bray hoped the SPG would eventually strengthen economic and political ties between England and its American colonies. SPG missionaries arrived in New York soon after the society's founding. The colony was of particular concern to the SPG, which concentrated on converting the Iroquois nations north and west of the Hudson River as a barrier to French Catholic influence and territorial expansion, as well as generating a higher Anglican profile in the religiously diverse colony. The SPG's efforts to Christianize the Mohawk and other Iroquois nations met with frustration, and the majority of the missionaries who worked with the Indians deemed them unfit for conversion because of their bemusement with Western ways and rejection of Christian claims. Thus the conversion of "white heathens" and Blacks became the SPG's primary concern. The success of the SPG in bringing Anglican ministers to New York and winning converts from among other churches alarmed the non-Anglicans, who perceived the SPG's true purpose as the eradication of dissent. SPG missionary Elias Neau roused popular opposition when he opened a catechetical school for Blacks in New York City in 1704. John Thomas and William Urquhart, SPG missionaries on Long Island in the 1720s, were concerned about resistance to their efforts from Congregationalists and Presbyterians, who perceived the SPG's mission as a threat to their existence, and urged moderation. A widely known Anglican campaign for the appointment of a bishop in America fueled suspicion of the SPG's motives. As relations with Britain soured in the 1760s and 1770s, the SPG was seen as an instrument of British oppression despite defenses by pamphleteers like Charles Inglis, rector of Trinity Church in New York City and president of King's College (now Columbia University). The American Revolution brought the SPG's mission in America to an end, though as the United Society for the Propogation of the Gospel (USPG), its missionary efforts continue around the world.

Bridenbaugh, Carl. *Mitre and Sceptre: Transatlantic Faiths, Ideas, Personalities, and Politics, 1689–1775* (New York: Oxford Univ Press, 1967)

Klingberg, Frank J. *Anglican Humanitarianism in Colonial New York* (Philadelphia: Church Historical Society, 1940)

Woolverton, John Frederick. *Colonial Anglicanism in North America* (Detroit: Wayne State Univ Press, 1984)

John Howard Smith

Society of Friends (Quakers). The Religious Society of Friends, commonly known as the Quakers, arose as a distinct sect in Britain in the 1640s and 1650s. Seventeenth-century Quakers were noted for their distinctive mode of worship and their religious and social testimonies, including pacifism, refusal to take oaths, plainness of speech and dress, and recognition of women as ministers.

Colonial Beginnings

Quaker missionaries arriving in New Netherland in 1657 found a ready audience among the English-speaking religious dissenters in the Long Island towns of Gravesend, Jamaica, Hempstead, Newtown, and Flushing. The early Quakers on Long Island were threatened with fines and imprisonment for their beliefs and practices. In 1657 residents of Flushing prepared a remonstrance calling for freedom of worship for Quakers. In 1662–63 John Bowne made a successful appeal for religious toleration to the Dutch West India Co. After England conquered New Netherland in 1664 the persecution of Quakers ended, though they continued to be fined and occasionally imprisoned for noncompliance with militia laws into the 19th century. In the 1670s local Quaker meetings, which began on Long Island in the late 1650s, evolved into a structured system of local, monthly, quarterly, and yearly meetings. The New York meetings were part of New England Yearly Meeting until 1695, when the first session of New York Yearly Meeting was held at Flushing. The boundaries of New York Yearly Meeting derived more from Quaker migration patterns than from political boundaries. The earliest Quaker meetings in northern New Jersey were part of New York Yearly Meeting, and as Quakers migrated northward along the Hudson River beginning early in the 18th century they established meetings west of the Connecticut River in Connecticut, Massachusetts, and Vermont as part of New York Yearly Meeting.

Antislavery and Quaker Reform

Antislavery had not been among the early testimonies of the Society of Friends, but by the 1670s individual Quakers were speaking and writing against slavery. In the 18th century New York State Quakers first prohibited their members from involvement in the buying and selling of slaves and by the 1770s prohibited Quakers from owning slaves under any circumstance. Though Quakers were often wary of becoming involved in "worldly affairs" with non-Quakers, New York State Quakers were the chief organizers and later operators of the New York Manumission Society (1785) and established the African Free School (1787) in New York City. New York State Quakers' concern with American Indians was manifest by the late 1790s in educational and agricultural efforts by New York Yearly Meeting among the Oneida, Brotherton, Stockbridge, and Onondaga Nations, and among the Seneca by Philadelphia Yearly Meeting, which established a boarding school in Cattaraugus Co at Tunesassa (Quaker Bridge) next to the Allegany Reservation. The school continued until 1938; the site of the school is now partially under the waters of the Allegheny Reservoir. At the invitation of the Six Nations of the Iroquois Confederacy, Quaker delegations were present at the Treaty of Canandaigua (1794), and in the 1830s and 1840s a joint committee representing four Hicksite Yearly Meetings worked to overturn the 1838 Treaty of Buffalo Creek. New York and Philadelphia Meeting Quakers continue to be concerned with legal and land ownership issues involving the Indians of New York State.

By the late 18th century Quakers were increasingly concerned with education, both of their own members and others. They established Friends Seminary (1781) in Manhattan, Nine Partners Boarding School (1796) in Millbrook (Dutchess Co), and numerous primary schools and academies for Quaker children. Quakers in and around New York City were the major force behind the establishment of the New York Public School Society (1805), which laid the groundwork for public education in city. At the collegiate level New York State Quakers were involved in the creation of Haverford (1833) and Swarthmore Colleges (1864) in Pennsylvania, the Howland School (1863–*ca* 1881) in Union Springs (Cayuga Co), and Friends World College (1965) at Westbury (Nassau Co), which later merged with Long Island University. Some of the current Quaker or Quaker-associated schools in New York State are Brooklyn Friends School (1867), Oakwood School (1858) in Poughkeepsie (Dutchess Co), and Friends Academy (1877) in Locust Valley (Nassau Co). Influential New York State Quaker educators include Lindley Murray (1745–1826), whose *English Grammar* (1795) and *English Reader* (1799) were standard textbooks in 19th-century America. English Quaker educational reformer Joseph Lancaster (1778–1838), founder of the Lancasterian system of education for poor children, lived in New York City from 1818 until his death.

Quakers were divided about the appropriateness of joining with non-Friends in the reform movements of the first half of the 19th century. Nevertheless, despite the reservations of some conservative Friends, New York State Quakers were disproportionately represented in the abolitionist movement in New York State and the early women's rights movement. Women's rights advocate Susan B. Anthony (1820–1906) was raised a Quaker, as were four of the five women who organized the 1848 Seneca Falls Convention.

Hicksite-Orthodox Separation

After 1800 Friends in North America became increasingly divided over questions of biblical authority and religious belief. Opposition to the testimony of Long Island Quaker Elias Hicks (1748–1830) caused a separation of meetings into Hicksite and Orthodox branches beginning in Philadelphia in 1827. Although both Hicksite and Orthodox Friends followed traditional Quaker forms of worship, the Orthodox stressed the adherence of Friends to Protestant understandings of the atonement of Christ, the trinity, and the authority of the Bible. Hicksites resisted the imposition of creedal statements of belief on these matters. The split reached New York Yearly Meeting the following year. Before the separation, the number of Quaker meetings and members had expanded rapidly in the state from the mid–18th century to reach approximately 20,000 members in 1828. New York Yearly Meeting continued to expand. The first meeting in Upper Canada [now Ont] was established in 1798, and when Friends from New York State migrated to Michigan in the 1830s, their new meetings were attached to New York. The vast extent of New York Yearly Meeting made it difficult for Quakers in the northern and western regions to attend the annual sessions in New York City. In 1834 Hicksite Friends in Central and Western New York, Upper Canada, and Michigan established Genesee Yearly Meeting and held the first session in Farmington (Ontario Co). After 1830 membership in New York State declined gradually for a variety of reasons: internal controversies, migration of Quakers out of New York State to Canada and the West, disownments for infractions of Quaker discipline, and the decision of many Quakers to join other denominations.

The Hicksites themselves were divided in the 1830s and 1840s by several issues, including Quaker involvement with non-Quakers in the increasingly public and sometimes confrontational abolitionist movement. Activist Quakers were deeply angered when New York Yearly Meeting (Hicksite) disowned Quaker abolitionist and Underground Railroad agent Isaac T. Hopper (1771–1852) and others for public criticisms of Quaker inactivity on the abolition issue. In 1848 radical Hicksites, many closely identified with the Garrisonian wing of the antislavery movement, established new yearly meetings of "Progressive" Friends in Waterloo (Seneca Co) and Michigan. Similar groups, sometimes called Friends of Human Progress, were formed in Milton (Ulster Co) and North Collins (Erie Co). Continued controversy among Orthodox Friends resulted in a minor split (1848–53) within the branch, with small groups of conservative Wilburite Friends separating from the main body of Orthodox Friends. Wilburite strength in New York State was centered in the Finger Lakes region. The Orthodox branch of New York Yearly Meeting created Canada Yearly Meeting, which opened in 1867, and two years later transferred their Michigan meetings to Ohio Yearly Meeting. In the years after the Civil War, the Orthodox (sometimes called Gurneyite) branch of the New York Yearly Meeting became increasingly influenced by the evangelical and revival movements. In the 1870s revivals were held in New York State, and some Orthodox meetings began to adopt forms typical of Protestant churches—organs, choirs, increased emphasis on biblical studies, and paid pastors. Despite dwindling numbers in both branches of New York Yearly Meeting and the New York State portion of Genesee Yearly Meeting beginning in the 1830s, there were local gains in membership during the 1870s and thereafter.

Unification

After 1900 new Quaker meetings were established in urban areas and college towns. Many of these newer meetings tended to be liberal, strongly interested in Quaker testimonies on peace and racial justice, and not concerned with the theological controversies of the 19th century or with the distinction between the various branches of Quakerism. Quakers of different branches began cooperating on projects and participating in organizations such as American Friends Service Committee (1917), concerned with international peace, race relations, and relief efforts both in the United States and abroad. This slow process of reunification culminated in the merger of the Orthodox and Hicksite branches of New York Yearly Meeting in 1955, and the remaining New York State portion of Genesee Yearly Meeting rejoined New York Yearly Meeting. The Wilburite Friends had already "laid down" their meetings in the early 1950s and rejoined New York Yearly Meeting as individuals. The merged New York Yearly Meeting, drawing from the Orthodox, Hicksite, and Wilburite Quaker traditions, represents a spectrum of Quaker belief and practices. In the 20th century New York State Friends worked as individuals with non-Quaker groups and on projects sponsored by Friends meetings, participating in the Civil Rights Movement, the pacifist antiwar and antimilitarism movements, and prison reform. Rachel Davis DuBois (1892–1993) advocated intercultural education and dialogues. Black civil rights activist and Quaker Bayard Rustin (1912–87) was a conscientious objector during World War II and later a key organizer of the 1963 March on Washington. In 2000 New York Yearly Meeting had 3,788 members in 64 monthly meetings, primarily in New York State but also in western Connecticut and northern New Jersey. As a faith community New York Yearly Meeting seeks to nurture the religious life of members and nonmembers who attend Friends meetings. Individually and as a group, Friends maintain a strong commitment to the traditional Quaker testimonies of peace, nonviolence, and social justice, sponsoring worship groups in prisons and programs for teaching alternatives to violence.

Barbour, Hugh, et al, eds. *Quaker Crosscurrents: 300 Years of Friends in the New York Yearly Meetings* (Syracuse: Syracuse Univ Press, 1995)

Cox, John, Jr. *Quakerism in the City of New York, 1647–1930* (New York: Author, 1930)

Worrall, Arthur J. *Quakers in the Colonial Northeast* (Hanover, NH: Univ Press of New England, 1980)

Christopher Densmore

Sockman, Ralph W(ashington) (*b* Mount Vernon, Ohio, 1 Oct 1889; *d* New York City, 29 Aug 1970). Methodist preacher. He spent his entire ministerial career (1916–61) at Christ Church (formerly the Madison Avenue Methodist Episcopal Church) in Manhattan. A widely known radio preacher, he appeared weekly on NBC's *National Radio Pulpit* (1928–62) and subsequently hosted a television series. He was the author of numerous books including *Live for Tomorrow* (1939), *The Higher Happiness* (1950), and *The Meaning of Suffering* (1961).

Hibbard, Robert Bruce. "The Life and Ministry of Ralph Washington Sockman" (PhD diss, Boston Univ, 1957)

Charles Yrigoyen Jr

Sodus. Town (pop 8,949) and village (pop 1,735) in N central Wayne Co. The town is bounded on the north by Lake Ontario. The name Sodus is derived from *assorodus,* believed to be a Cayuga word meaning silver waters. It was formed in 1789 as the Sodus District, one of the original subdivisions of Ontario Co. The first settlers arrived in 1794 at Sodus Point, and the town was formed in 1799. The village, located on the old Ridge Road, was settled in 1809 and incorporated in 1918. A Shaker community established in 1826 on the southwest side of Sodus Bay moved to Groveland (Livingston Co) in 1837, and the site was later used briefly (1844–46) by a Fourierist group. Two railroads came to town in the early 1870s, providing shipping for goods and making resort development possible. There are numerous summer cottages along the bay and lake shores. The Village of Sodus Point is a popular summer boating resort, and Beechwood State Park opened to the public in 2002. In the early 21st century, apples, cherries, and other fruits are grown, and food processing is a significant industry; Heluva Good distributes dairy products throughout the eastern United States and Canada. Shipboard communication, navigation, and switching systems are designed and manufactured by Dynalec Corp in the village, and Sodus-based PACE Electronics manufactures electronic components in China.

Scott C. Monje

Sodus Bay. An inlet of Lake Ontario in northern Wayne Co, approximately 5 miles (8 km) long. It is partially separated from the lake by Sodus Point, on which lies the Village of Sodus Point, and Crescent Beach, a sandbar. Known to the French as the Bay of the Cayugas, Sodus Bay was within the hunting and fishing range of the Iroquois but was not settled by them. A settlement on Sodus Point was begun in 1794 by Charles Williamson, the agent of the Pulteney Estate who anticipated the bay becoming a major trade center, but settlement and commerce gravitated to the Genesee Valley. In June 1813 a British raiding party burned the settlement, but it was rebuilt. The opening of the Erie Canal in 1825 then diverted considerable trade away from the Ontario–St. Lawrence route; nevertheless, piers constructed in 1835 spurred commerce by allowing deep-keeled schooners and steamers to dock. The Sodus Point and Southern Railroad (later Pennsylvania Railroad) opened in 1872, and trains unloaded coal from Pennsylvania onto ships in the bay until 1967. The bay's shore has been dotted with summer homes since the arrival of the railroad, and the region supports orchards.

Lighthouse at Sodus Point, built 1825.

Cowles, George Washington, ed. *Landmarks of Wayne County, New York* (Syracuse: D. Mason, 1895)
Green, Walter Henry. *History, Reminiscences, Anecdotes, and Legends of Great Sodus Bay, Sodus Point, Sloop Landing, Sodus Village, Pultneyville, Maxwell, and the Environing Regions, the Ridge Road, and the Four-Horse Post Coaches of Pioneer Days* (Sodus, NY, 1947)

Scott C. Monje

Sodus Point. Village (pop 1,160) in Sodus (Wayne Co). Charles Williamson laid out a city here in 1794, but it grew slowly; it was incorporated as a village in 1957. A port of entry, it has had two lighthouses, one on a bluff above Lake Ontario (1825–1901; present structure, 1871, now a museum) and one at the entrance to Sodus Bay (since 1834; present structure, 1938). In the early 19th century there was a community of about 80 African Americans at Sodus Point, some of whom came from Maryland in slavery in 1803 and were subsequently freed. Docks, a coal trestle, a malt house, and grain elevators were built in the 19th and early 20th centuries. The village's development as a summer resort began with the construction of the Sodus Point and Southern Railroad (1872, later Pennsylvania Railroad). Visitors also arrived later by trolley and excursion boat from Rochester. There was a German prisoner of war camp during World War II. The present economy caters largely to summer residents and recreational boaters and fishers.

Scott C. Monje

Solomon R. Guggenheim Museum. Solomon Guggenheim created the Solomon R. Guggenheim Foundation in 1937 to display his and his wife Peggy's collection of contemporary art in a museum setting. The Museum of Non-Objective Painting opened in 1939 and was renamed the Solomon R. Guggenheim Museum in 1952. The Guggenheim offers an array of late 19th-, 20th-, and 21st-century art representative of such styles as abstract, postimpressionist, and surrealist. Frank Lloyd Wright designed the collection's permanent home, an inverted spiral pyramid structure on 5th Ave between 88th and 89th Sts, its soaring design aimed to counter the relentless New York City grid system. The building was completed after Wright's death in 1959, and a tower was added during the 1992 renovation. Temporary exhibitions are hung along the spiral stairway, and the permanent collection, featuring works by Wassily Kandinsky, Amadeo Modigliani, Piet Mondrian, Marc Chagall, Paul Klee, and Pablo Picasso, is displayed in the tower. The Solomon R. Guggenheim Foundation has established museums in Venice, Berlin, Las Vegas, and Bilbao, Spain, and is creating the Guggenheim Museum Rio de Janeiro. At the beginning of the 21st century the Guggenheim has an endowment of $44 million, and the New York City branch received about 1 million visitors annually.

Art of This Century: The Guggenheim Museum and Its Collection (New York: Solomon R. Guggenheim Foundation, 1993; distributed by Rizzoli International)
Guggenheim.org, http://www.guggenheim.org

Dorothy M. Browne

Solon. Town (pop 1,108) in central Cortland Co. Settled in 1794, the town was formed from Homer in 1798. The land is broken by a number of small valleys with a ridge on the eastern border. Early on, maple sugaring supplemented farm incomes. In the 1840s a community of Irish farmers gathered there, and St. Bridget's Church (1849) was Cortland Co's first Roman Catholic parish. The Irish were followed, beginning in 1898, by a Lebanese community. Solon acquired a cheese factory in 1874 and a furniture factory in 1876. A 4-H camp (1952) now serves as both camp and outdoor education center. Agriculture remains the primary industry, with close to half the land area of town dedicated to it.

Cathy A. Barber

Solvay. Village (pop 6,845) in Geddes in Onondaga Co. This industrial village incorporated in 1894 and was named for the Solvay Process Co (later Allied Chemical), the primary impetus behind the growth of the residential area. Sharing a boundary with the City of Syracuse, Solvay has always prided itself on a distinct and separate identity. The earliest residents were predominantly Irish, who were soon joined by South Tyrolians and Poles. By 1910 an electrical wiring device company (Pass and Seymour), a foundry (Frazer and Jones), and Iroquois Pottery had also been established. The paternalistic philosophy of Solvay Process Co is reflected in a Carnegie library, a municipally owned electric utility company, and historically exceptional municipal services. Allied Chemical closed in 1986, imposing a substantial fiscal hardship that has since been partially offset by the creation of a successful industrial park, where Solvay Paper Board is the largest employer. In recent years there has been a substantial influx of Ukrainians.

James W. Darlington

Solvay Process. See ALLIED-SIGNAL.

Somers. Town (pop 18,346) in N central Westchester Co. Settled probably in the 1730s, the town was formed from Van Cortlandt Manor in 1788 as Stephentown; the name was changed to Somers in 1808. By that year, Somers resident Hachaliah Bailey (1775–1845) had acquired an African elephant he named Old Bet, which became the nucleus of a touring menagerie business. The town and its neighbors became home base of many menageries and circuses until midcentury. Bailey built the Elephant Hotel (1820–25) and erected a wooden statue of an elephant (1827) in memory of Old Bet; the building is Somers's town hall. A cattle-raising region, Somers lost good farmland first to Croton (1842) and then to Amawalk (1894), Muscoot (1903), and New Croton (1904) Reservoirs. Bypassed by the railroad in 1847, the town's population peaked in 1840 and declined through 1920, although it acquired two minor rail lines (Mahopac Branch, 1871–1950, and Putnam Division, 1881–1961), which provided transportation for its milk and apples. Its only significant industry was the Empire Sewing Machine Co (1864–85). Three lake communities (Lincolndale, Purdy, and Shenorock) in 1924 developed cottage properties that eventually became year-round homes. Gradual population growth through 1960 became more rapid with suburban development. The Baldwin Place Shopping Center opened in 1966. In 1975 the vast Heritage Hills condominium development was begun, with 3,100 homes on 1,100 acres (445 ha). With better access via I-684 (1967), the town also acquired corporate facilities: Guerlain (1969), PepsiCo (1986), and IBM (1988). The county-run Muscoot (1975) and Lasdon (1985) Parks and Lincoln Hall (1909), a school for troubled youth, are in town.

Terry Ariano

Somerset. Town (pop 2,865) in NE Niagara Co. Settled in 1810, the town was formed from Hartland in 1823. Railroad service was provided by the Rome, Watertown and Ogdensburg Railroad (1876); in 2003 the short-line Somerset Railroad connected the town with Lockport. The town is the site of 320-acre (130 ha) Golden Hill State Park (1963). The primary industry remains agriculture, especially orchards. Kintigh Generating Station (1984), a 675 MW coal-fired plant, was sold to AES in 2002, and its name changed to AES Somerset. The cobblestone Babcock House (1848) is a landmark, and the Thirty Mile Point Lighthouse, which operated from 1875 to 1958, is on the National Register.

Nancy B. Mingus

Sonnenberg Gardens. Queen Anne–style mansion and 50 acres (20 ha) of gardens in Canandaigua (Ontario Co). Sonnenberg (German for "sunny hill") was built in 1887 as the summer home of Canandaigua benefactors Frederick Ferris Thompson and Mary Clark Thompson. The gardens demonstrates the latter's interest in gardening and showcases items collected throughout Europe and Asia. The Lord and Burnham Conservatory (1903–15) overlooks the formal gardens (1902–19). Designed by John Handrahan, they include the Italian, Japanese, Sub Rosa (Secret), Pansy, Moonlight, Blue and White, and Old-Fashioned Gardens. The Rose Garden encompasses more than 2,500 pink, red, and white Jackson and Perkins roses. The Rock Garden (1916) combines the Wild, Lily, and Rock Gardens. Sonnenberg Gardens was acquired by a nonprofit corporation in 1973, and the Butterfly Garden has since been added. Annual visitation is 65,000, and the budget is $1.2 million. In 2002 it was discovered that embezzlement of a large sum of money by the director had bankrupted the institution; it was placed in the hands of a bank. Efforts were under way in 2003 to reorganize it and put it on sound financial footing.

Marla A. Bennett

Sons of Liberty. Extralegal organizations of American activists that spearheaded resistance to British imperial policies in the 1760s and early 1770s. Taking their name from the British term celebrating freeborn men who defended their rights under the English constitution, they were also called Liberty Boys. Typically, gentlemen worked cooperatively with their peers in other colonies and more privately with the mechanic and artisan leaders of urban mobs that achieved their ends through intimidation.

The Colony of New York's first Sons of Liberty group apparently organized in New York City in October and November of 1765 in an attempt gain control of the mob violence that greeted the Stamp Act of 1765, but they did not declare themselves publicly until 7 Jan 1766 and were led Isaac Sears, John Lamb, Gershom Mott, William Wiley, and Thomas Robinson. Because of the group's secretive nature, little is known about its members and activities, but the association supported early on ideas from the rank and file. The organization promoted action through public discussion, pamphlets, and newspaper essays, and sometimes through limited but forceful protests.

Faced with the threatened enforcement of the Stamp Act by British troops in New York City, the Sons of Liberty played a key role in the loose organization of Sons of Liberty groups from other colonies. On 25 Dec 1765, for example, two New York City Sons met with Connecticut Sons in New London, Conn, and agreed to a working alliance, an early move toward intercolonial resistance. It appears that two other New Yorkers traveled to Boston around the same time and secured a mutual-aid agreement with the Boston organization. Within New York, other Sons of Liberty groups formed in early 1766, including those in Albany and Schenectady by January and in Oyster Bay [now in Nassau Co] and Huntington (Suffolk Co) in February. The New York City Sons urged these groups to form committees of correspondence to maintain communications with other Sons of Liberty organizations in a continental system of cooperation. Men signing the constitution of the Albany Sons were generally younger members of the dominant Dutch families and included Dr Thomas Young, Jeremiah Van Rensselaer, and Goose Van Schaick; John Sloss Hobart was a member of the Huntington Sons.

The New York City group dissolved after official news of the repeal of the Stamp Act arrived in May 1766, but it reorganized in 1769 under John Lamb, Isaac Sears, and Alexander McDougall to fight the Townshend Revenue Act of 1767 with nonimportation of British goods. All of the Townshend duties were repealed, except for that on tea, in April 1770. By the time of the Tea Act of 1773 and the 1774 "Intolerable Acts," the Sons of Liberty generally favored armed resistance and independence. But the New York City group, officially styled the Association of the Sons of Liberty by 1773, hung back. The more conservative Mechanics Committee and Merchants Committee won over the populace after 1774, and the Sons of Liberty lost their previous political influence in the city.

Many of them went on to fight in the Revolutionary War, but little is known about their organized activity during the conflict. After the war the Sons of Liberty ideology gave rise to other political societies, including the Democratic-Republican societies and the later antirent movement.

Champagne, Roger J. "The Sons of Liberty and the Aristocracy in New York Politics, 1765–1790" (PhD diss, Univ of Wisconsin, 1960)
———. *Alexander McDougall and the American Revolution in New York* (Schenectady: NYS Bicentennial Commission, with Union College Press, 1975)
Maier, Pauline. *From Resistance to Revolution: Colonial Radicals and the Development of American Opposition to Britain, 1765–1776* (1972; repr New York: Norton, 1991)

Brad L. Utter

Sound Beach. Locality (pop 9,807) in Brookhaven (Suffolk Co). In 1928 the *New York Daily Mirror* platted building lots at Sound Beach, offering them as a premium with subscriptions. Owners started by living in tents and then erected bungalows. A post office opened in 1946. After World War II many of the summer homes were converted for year-round use.

Suzanne Johnson

South Americans. With the exception of the first large wave of Colombians who arrived during the 1950s and 1960s to escape "La Violencia" and the majority of Chileans who arrived during the military dictatorship of Augusto Pinochet, the overwhelming majority of South Americans began arriving in New York State in large numbers after 1980. As with the earlier Colombian exodus, civil strife and violence and the search for greater economic opportunities have prompted many of these departures. Emigration from South America has proven to be one of the most diverse in Latin America, involving all social classes. Though relatively small in number compared to the larger Latin American community, South Americans mark their presence in New York State through their religious, cultural, and professional organizations.

According to the 2000 census, New York State is home to the largest South American community (518,251) in the United States. The largest groups are Guyanans (142,154), followed by Ecuadoreans (139,226), and Colombians (111,727), and the smallest are the Bolivians (5,681), Uruguayans (3,366), and Paraguayans (2,668). Of those in New York State, approximately 74% live in the five boroughs of New York City. The largest Latino group in Queens Co, they settle primarily in Jackson Heights and Flushing. Smaller populations live in both the Upper East and Upper West Sides of Manhattan. Ecuadoreans have considerable populations in the Bushwick area of Brooklyn and in Upper Manhattan.

See also countries by name.

Jones-Correa, Michael. "Different Paths: Gender, Immigration and Political Participation." *International Migration Review* 32 (Summer 1998): 326–49

Ana Margarita Cervantes-Rodríguez and Michael C. English

Southampton. Town (pop 54,712) and village (pop 3,969) in E Suffolk Co. Lynn, Mass, householders purchased "eight miles square" from the Shinnecock Indians and from the grantor, the Earl of Sterling, in 1640; they settled in an Indian meadow where animal grazing could begin immediately. Town government minutes begin in the following year. The settlers first engaged in "drift whaling," cutting up beached whales, but by 1650 shore whaling developed, and about 1760 residents began going on deep-sea whaling trips, based in the port of Sag Harbor, an industry that continued until the growth of the petroleum industry.

After the Civil War wealthy urbanites arriving by steamboat found Southampton ideal for summer residences, which they built on infertile unoccupied land near the ocean. The railroad reached Southampton in 1869, expanding the summer colony even further. Beginning in 1881 the summer residents began to "colonize" what became the Village of Southampton, planting trees along streets, changing place-names, and building cultural institutions. In the same years, artists discovered the light of the East End and began painting in Southampton; led by William Merritt Chase they established the Shinnecock Summer Art School (1891). The village incorporated in 1894. Farmers, some of them Polish, cultivated potatoes on the fertile Bridgehampton loam or started duck farms along Moriches Bay's tidewater coves. Patrician socialites who created a Southampton image in the 1920s were largely replaced by celebrities in the 1960s. By the 1980s much of Southampton's farmland was converted to vineyards or summer estates, but development rights to thousands of acres have been purchased to preserve its open country ambience.

Southampton is the site of the Southampton Campus of Long Island University and the renowned Parrish Art Museum (1897). Hildreth's Department Store (1842) claims to be America's oldest. Landmarks include the Good Ground windmill (1807) and St. Andrew's Dune Church (1851), a lifesaving station made into a church featuring Tiffany windows. Bridgehampton was the childhood home of baseball great Carl Yastrzemski (1939–), son of potato farmers. The Shinnecock Indian Reservation is surrounded by the town's territory. Open space holdings in Southampton include the Conscience Point Refuge and Elizabeth A. Morton National Wildlife Refuge.

Sherrill Foster

South Bristol. Town (pop 1,645) in SW Ontario Co. Settled in 1789, the town was formed from Bristol in 1838. Cider making provided a means of marketing the apple crop beginning 1812–14. The west part of South Bristol was and is an area of general farming; the east part was given over to vineyards after 1875. Summer hotels were built on the shore of Canandaigua Lake beginning in the late 19th century. Seneca Point Glen is a natural area near the lake; Bristol Mountain Ski Area (1964) attracts winter sports enthusiasts. South Bristol is the site of the Cumming Nature Center, operated by the Rochester Museum and Science Center, and the Ontario County Park.

Marla A. Bennett

South Corning. Village (pop 1,147) in Corning (Steuben Co). Settled in 1790 by Peleg Gorton, South Corning developed in the early 20th century as a result of traffic between Elmira and the Town of Caton. The interurban Elmira, Corning and Waverly Railway (1911) maintained its storage and repair facilities in South Corning; because of a local ordinance, all freight was unloaded there and taken to Corning by wagon. In 1920 the localities of Brown's Crossing and Mossy Glen incorporated as the Village of South Corning. In 2003 the main thoroughfare (Rte 225) was the site of several large retail businesses. Many village residents worked in Corning.

Thomas Dimitroff

South Dayton. Village (pop 662) in Dayton (Cattaraugus Co). Laid out on the Buffalo and Southwestern Railroad in 1875 and incorporated in 1915, South Dayton is the home of Constable Foods (1902; began as Sheppard Canning Co) and the former home of Carnation Milk Co (1923–93). In the early 21st century shops specializing in antiques, quilts, and Amish-made products attract tourists, while the New York and Lake Erie Railroad provides freight service, along with excursions from South Dayton to Gowanda.

Bruce D. Fredrickson and Madelynn P. Fredrickson

Southeast. Town (pop 17,316) in SE Putnam Co. Good farmland, freehold tenure, and abundant waterpower drew New Englanders beginning in 1731. Formed from Southeast Precinct in 1788, it was largely redrawn in 1795. The Harlem Railroad (1849) created a fluid-milk market for Southeast's farmers. Tilly Foster Mine (1853–1897) and other iron mines drew immigrants from Britain, Ireland, Sweden, and Italy. Its best farmland was inundated, beginning in 1878, to create four reservoirs for New York City's water supply. I-84 (1967) and I-684 (1967) helped attract light manufacturing, office parks, and commercial development, making Southeast increasingly suburban. The town was the birthplace of Chancellor James Kent (1763–1847), the home of blind hymnist Fanny J. Crosby (1820–1915), and the site of Green Chimneys Farm and Wildlife Conservation Center.

Sallie S. Sypher

Southeast Asians. The term Southeast Asians usually refers to people from the countries of Vietnam, Cambodia, and Laos; they can be ethnic Vietnamese, Cambodian (Khmer), and Laotian, but also Hmong, Mien, Khmu, Thai Dam, and ethnic Chinese. The majority of Southeast Asians came to the United States as refugees, with an initial wave fleeing the turmoil that followed the Communist victories in South Vietnam, Laos, and Cambodia in 1975. Many in this first wave had worked with the United States in Southeast Asia. A second wave of refugees from the late 1970s to the early 1980s, after fighting broke out between China, Vietnam, and Laos, included ethnic Chinese from Vietnam, while some Cambodians escaped the infamous "killing fields" of the Khmer Rouge regime, which killed up to 3 million Cambodians.

In 2000 about 30,000 people of Southeast Asian origin lived in New York State. About 24,000 are from Vietnam, 4,000 are from Cambodia, 1,300 are Lao, and 700 are Hmong. They were relocated by the federal government and nonprofit organizations (including churches) and are concentrated in the New York City area and in Central New York. The Bronx, especially around Fordham Rd, is home to a significant Cambodian community. A substantial number of Vietnamese live in Oneida and Broome Cos. Southeast Asians differ greatly in their cultural and religious practices. Most Cambodians and Vietnamese are Buddhist, with a minority of Vietnamese Catholics; small minorities of Southeast Asians practice other Christian faiths. The Hmong adhere to an animist religion in which shamanism and spirits play an important role. Most Southeast Asians have great respect for older family members and deceased ancestors.

Lao and Hmong were farmers before moving to the United States, and a significant proportion of Vietnamese were merchants, government officials, or military officers with better training for life in a modern, urban society. Many Lao and Hmong, and a smaller but significant percentage of Vietnamese and Cambodians, remain in poverty. For first-generation immigrants, English language skills are often a significant barrier. Because of their varied ethnic background, Southeast Asians have few common organizations. There are multiservice community centers such as St. Rita's Center at 2342 Andrews Ave near Fordham Rd in the Bronx, and Pan-Asian advocacy groups such as the Coalition for Asian American Children and Families (CACF) at 50 Broad St in Manhattan.

Hein, J. *From Vietnam, Laos, and Cambodia: A Refugee Experience in the United States* (New York: Twayne Publishers, 1995)

Irene Bloemraad

Southern Tier. A loosely defined region of New York State, commonly including those counties that border Pennsylvania, from Delaware on the east to Chautauqua on the west; sometimes Schuyler, Tompkins, Chenango, and Otsego are included as well. A narrower definition includes only the four border counties that cannot be considered Central New York: Steuben, Allegany, Cattaraugus, and Chautauqua.

Forming part of the Appalachian Plateau, the land is drained by the Allegheny, Canisteo, Chemung, Cohocton, Genesee, Susquehanna, and Tioga Rivers, and is tucked between rolling hills and fertile countryside. In Chautauqua, Cattaraugus, and Allegany Cos, the region has most of the state's oil and natural gas fields. Before the Revolutionary War, this region was a center of American Indian life. The Battle of Newtown (1779), near the present Elmira, marked the beginning of successful patriot efforts to force American Indians from the area. Nevertheless, three Indian reservations (Allegany, Cattaraugus, and Oil Spring) remain in the Southern Tier. The area was settled in the late 18th and early 19th centuries primarily by settlers from Pennsylvania and New England, and tall-steepled churches and town squares created by the first New England settlers still anchor many of the smaller places. Even some of the larger, more notable cities, such as Corning (Steuben Co), Watkins Glen (Schuyler Co), Owego (Tioga Co), and Ithaca, retained commercial storefronts along historic main streets at the start of the 21st century. Many of the Southern Tier's residents are descendants of the New England settlers, along with later settlers of French, Irish, Italian, Swedish, and Polish descent.

The building of the Erie Canal helped define the region's identity in an unusual way. When the canal bypassed the Southern Tier, it meant the area would not experience the urbanization of places along the canal route like Syracuse, Rochester, and Buffalo. Although the region was rich in timber forest and its soils were fertile, problems with viable transportation routes slowed economic development. In 1906 historian Noble E. Whitford referred to the Southern Tier region as several inland counties south of the Erie Canal that lacked easy access to the canal's ports. Southern Tier communities dug their own canals to connect with the Finger Lakes and eventually north to the Erie Canal. However, just as the region's Chemung, Chenango, Junction, and other canals were completed in the mid-1800s, the faster, more powerful railroad arrived. Begun in 1835, the Erie Railroad promised to create the same economic boom in the Southern Tier as the Erie Canal had done in the north. The project took 17 years to complete and was plagued both by politicians like Martin Van Buren and those of the Albany Regency (Bucktails), who wanted no competition for the Erie Canal, and by a $23 million price tag, more than three times the cost of the canal. In the end, the 450 mi (724 km) track connected the western city of Dunkirk (Chautauqua Co) to Piermont (Rockland Co). Although the end points were not major ports, the Erie Railroad and several other rail lines did lead to substantial industrial growth. At the beginning of the 20th century, the Delaware, Lackawanna and Western Railroad (DL&W) launched its Phoebe Snow advertising campaign, promoting its use of clean-burning anthracite coal. By the mid–20th century, the region had a new transportation artery, Rte 17. A four-lane highway, it runs east from Jamestown through Olean, Wellsville, Corning, Elmira, and Binghamton, and continues through the Catskills. In 1999 the highway as far east as Chemung Co was designated I-86, with most of the remainder to be so designated later.

The Southern Tier is primarily rural. The eight counties from Delaware to Chautauqua Co constitute 4% of the state's population; the four counties from Steuben Co westward, only 2%. All of the Southern Tier, however it is defined, falls with the official US government definition of Appalachia, a region defined by its rugged terrain, rural conditions, and historically high levels of poverty. It would, however, be a mistake to think of it as exclusively rural. There are two substantial metropolitan areas, the Tri-Cities (Binghamton, Endicott, and Johnson City) in Broome Co and Jamestown in Chautauqua Co, along with sizable urbanized areas around Olean (Cattaraugus Co), Corning, and Elmira. Roughly 35–40% of the people in the Southern Tier live in either urban or suburban settings. Large companies historically in the region have included the shoemaker Endicott Johnson, the photographic equipment and film maker GAF, and IBM, which remained one of the largest employers in Broome Co at the beginning of the 21st century. Corning Inc has been headquartered in the Southern Tier for almost 150 years. Other major employers in 2003 included Lockheed Martin, Toshiba Display Devices, Dresser Rand, Ethan Allen, the larger hospitals and regional healthcare centers, school systems, and timber-related companies. Dairy farming and apples, corn, and grapes also contribute significantly to the Southern Tier economy.

See also Tanning industry.

Merrill, Arch. *Southern Tier* (New York: American Book-Stratford Press, 1954)
Southern Tier East Regional Planning and Development Board, http://www.steny.org
Southern Tier Economic Growth, http://www.steg.com
Southern Tier West Regional Planning and Development Board, http://www.southerntierwest.org

Margaret D. Costello

South Farmingdale. See Farmingdale.

South Floral Park. Village (pop 1,578) in Hempstead (Nassau Co). Begun as a development called Jamaica Square in 1905, it was incorporated in 1925 and changed its name to South Floral Park in 1931 to avoid confusion with Jamaica (Queens Co) and to identify more closely with neighboring Floral Park. It became one of the first racially integrated communities on Long Island, the black population growing from 6% to 23% from 1960 to 1970. It remains diverse; according to the 2000 census, 59.1% was black and 13.6% was of Latino ethnicity.

Laura E. Mann

South Glens Falls. Village (pop 3,368) in Moreau (Saratoga Co). Located on the south side of the Hudson River, it acquired the Moreau post office in 1835 (renamed in 1852) and was surveyed in streets and lots in 1837. Using waterpower from the falls on the Hudson it produced sawn marble, flagstone, and limestone and, later, was the site of large paper mills and sawmills. The village incorporated in 1895 to establish a dependable drinking water supply. A Quaker community has existed since the mid–19th century. Syrians organized an Eastern Orthodox church in 1908. The economy is oriented toward commercial and industrial development in Glens Falls and Queensbury (Warren Co).

Field Horne

South Hill. Although never a government-recognized entity, this region is a distinct area on the south side of the City and Town of Ithaca. Bounded by Sixmile Creek to the east and the upper portions of Buttermilk Falls State Park on the west, it was settled early in the 1820s. Its early community, the Klondike, was established on farmland leased about 1900 to railroad workers, mainly single men from Italy who left after World War I. Important businesses have included the Morse Chain Co (1906–75, now Borg-Warner Automotive in Lansing); Allen-Wales Adding Machine Co (1931, National Cash Register after 1943), Rubin-Apple Co (1935–60, leather handbags), and Therm Electric Motor Co (1935, turbine blades). South Hill's skyline is marked by two high-rise dormitory towers on the Ithaca College campus, which were built 1960–65. The college has a student population of about 6,000, and many students occupy rental houses on South Hill.

Jane Dieckmann

South Lockport. Locality (pop 8,552) in Lockport and Pendleton (Niagara Co). Located south of Lockport on Rte 78, the area began to develop during the late 1960s with the construction of malls, trailer parks, light industries, and commercial enterprises. Its social center is the South Lockport Volunteer Fire Co. The community has had a housing boom and now contains a sports complex, a small airport, a large drive-in movie theater complex, and the headquarters of First Niagara Bank. Author Joyce Carol Oates (1938–) lived in South Lockport during her childhood.

Bruce D. Fredrickson and Madelynn P. Fredrickson

South Nyack. Village (pop 3,473) in Orangetown (Rockland Co). Settled in the 17th century, South Nyack was the site of boatyards and quarries in the 19th century, and produce from Rockland Co farms was shipped from its docks. The village was incorporated in 1878. The Tappan Zee Bridge and the New York State Thruway opened in 1955. In the early 21st century, South Nyack is racially diverse: 16% black and 6% Asian. Latinos make up 7% of its population.

Myra Starr

Southold. Town (pop 20,599) in NE Suffolk Co. Occupying most of Long Island's North Fork, it is 23 miles (37 km) long but only 4 miles (6.4 km) wide; it includes Robins, Plum, Great and Little Gull, and Fishers Islands. The town was settled in 1640 when New Haven Colony magistrates bought the land from the Corchaug Indians and the settlers organized a church. Town records begin in 1651. As trade with New England and the West Indies developed, flax and tobacco farming flourished. After the English Restoration, residents unwillingly severed ties with Connecticut and became subject to the Duke of York, receiving a new patent in 1676. During the Revolutionary War the town was occupied and plundered by British and Hessian troops; in 1777 continental troops under Lt Col Return Jonathan Meigs crossed Long Island Sound in a raid upon British ships at Southold and Sag Harbor. Ezra L'Hommedieu was an influential patriot and a member of the state assembly (1777–83) and senate (1784–1809).

Southold remained a farming and fishing town. In 1844 the Long Island Rail Road was completed to Greenport, providing a direct route from New York City to Boston. The railroad brought laborers, especially Irish and Germans, who remained to work on farms. After the Civil War summer visitors began to patronize hotels and boardinghouses. Menhaden fisheries, oystering, and scalloping replaced the whaling industry. Yankees sold their farms to Irish and Germans, who later sold to Polish, Lithuanian, and Russian immigrants. Two large brickyards on Peconic Bay attracted Italian workers. Boom times at Southold's shipyards during the two world wars were followed by economic decline in that industry. After World War II, the automobile brought both first and second homeowners and an enormous tourist industry, which threatened open space. By the 1970s vineyards, nurseries, and horse farms began to replace potato, cauliflower, and brussels sprout fields on Southold farms. Hargrave Vineyard (1973; now Castello di Borghese) was the first of many wineries. Solid waste management, open land preservation, and planning have become major concerns of town residents. Southold is the site of the Custer Institute (1927), an observatory; of the Southold Indian Museum; and of Orient Beach State Park, which is reckoned at 360 acres (146 ha) and has 10 miles (16 km) of beachfront.

Antonia Booth

Southport. Town (pop 11,185) in SW Chemung Co. Settled in 1787, the town was formed from Elmira in 1822. A plank road (1848) through

Southport connected Elmira with Pennsylvania, as did a rail line completed in 1854. Lumbering was important in the Southport's earliest years, followed by dairying and tobacco growing. Woolen cloth was manufactured beginning in 1820, and two tanneries (1848, 1852) produced leather. The Northern Central Railway shops (1866), LaFrance Manufacturing (1873; fire engines), Payne Iron Works, and Kellogg Bridge Co were in Southport until the expansion of Elmira in 1890. In the 20th century, Willys-Morrow produced motor parts and Remington Rand typewriters. Southport's 1940 population of 5,774 doubled between 1940 and 1960 as suburbs grew. Southport Correctional Facility (1991) is an important employer.

Heather A. Wade

South Valley. Town (pop 302) in SW Cattaraugus Co. The town was formed from Randolph and Cold Spring in 1847 and based its economy on lumbering until late in the 19th century. In 1890 the old town of Elko was taken off South Valley. In the early 21st century, the town is heavily forested and there is no farming. The Onoville Marina, a large recreational facility with 394 dock slips, is located on Allegheny Reservoir, formed in 1965 by flooding caused by the Kinzua Dam project.

Bruce D. Fredrickson and Madelynn P. Fredrickson

South Valley Stream. See VALLEY STREAM.

Southwick, Solomon (*b* Newport, RI, 25 Dec 1773; *d* Albany, 18 Nov 1839). Editor and politician. After stints as a seaman and apprenticed baker, Southwick moved in 1791 to New York City. The son of a newspaper editor, he took a job with the *Albany Register,* working ultimately as a liaison between New York and Albany. He married Jane Barber in 1795, sister to John Barber, publisher of the *Register.* When his brother-in-law died in 1808, Southwick, having moved to Albany, assumed control. South defined himself as a Jeffersonian Republican, and his influence peaked during the War of 1812, which he favored. A quarrel with Gov Daniel D. Tompkins over a charter for a Bank of America led to charges against Southwick in 1812 for bribery of Speaker of the Assembly Alexander M. Sheldon. Although there was incriminating evidence, he was acquitted. The resulting animosity led to Southwick's loss of the government printing contract to the *Albany Argus.* The *Register* ceased publication (1813), and Southwick pursued other options. He was postmaster in Albany (1816–17) and ran unsuccessfully for state senate in 1814 and 1819 and for governor in 1822, switching between Clintonian, Federalist, Jacksonian, and Adamsite factions.

Impoverished by 1823, he edited religious periodicals, operated a lottery, and worked at the *Albany National Democrat.* In 1826 Southwick, a Mason, experienced a religious conversion and became a leader in the Antimasonic movement. That same year Southwick became the editor of the *Albany National Democrat,* which was renamed the *Albany National Observer.* Under his editorship, the paper became the state organ for the Antimasonic movement. In 1828 he ran unsuccessfully as an independent candidate for governor. He continued to advocate "genuine republicanism" as the editor of the *Albany National Observer* until his retirement in 1830.

Brackney, William H. *Religious Antimasonry: The Genesis of a Political Party* (Ann Arbor: Univ Microfilms International, 1976)

William H. Brackney

Spackenkill. Locality (pop 4,756) in Poughkeepsie (Dutchess Co). A residential suburb of the City of Poughkeepsie, it grew rapidly after 1950 to accommodate employees at the IBM manufacturing facility. The first shopping mall in Dutchess Co, Poughkeepsie Plaza, opened in the community in 1958. Oakwood Friends School (1858) built its Spackenkill campus in 1920. The Spackenkill Union Free School district (1859) serves the community.

William P. McDermott

Spafford. Town (pop 1,661) in SW Onondaga Co. Settled in 1794, the town was formed in 1811 from Tully and named in honor of one of the pioneer scholars in the study of New York State, Horatio Gates Spafford (1778–1832), author of the first state gazetteer. The town is bounded on the west by Skaneateles Lake and on the east by Otisco Lake, and in the early 21st century, it remains primarily agricultural. On the southeastern Skaneateles Lake shore, summer residents began building cottages in the late 19th century. Ripley Hill, at 1,982 feet (604.1 m) is the highest point in the town.

Patricia Blackler

Spafford, Horatio Gates (*b* Tinmouth, Vt, 18 Feb 1778; *d* Lansingburgh, Rensselaer Co, 7 Aug 1832). Author and inventor. As a young man, Spafford moved to Canaan and Rayville (Columbia Co), where he married Hannah Bristol in 1800. Following publication of his textbook *General Geography* in 1809, Spafford began work on a *Gazetteer of the State of New York,* which, aided by a loan from the state legislature, appeared in 1813. Rather than relying on published information, Spafford used questionnaires and local agents to collect new data. The *Gazetteer* also included many personal observations, usually found only in travelers' journals. After editing the short-lived *American Magazine,* Spafford devoted more time to inventing. He issued a pamphlet proposing an improved design for wheel carriages in 1815 and the following year delivered a paper outlining a new technique for steel production. In 1817 he published, under pseudonyms, the novel *The Mother-in-Law* and the pamphlet *Hints to Emigrants on the Choice of Lands,* the latter based on his brief experience homesteading in the Pennsylvania wilderness. In the early 1820s Spafford edited an agricultural journal, the *Ballston Spa Gazette and Saratoga Farmer,* and after moving to Troy (Rensselaer Co), completed the *Pocket Guide for the Tourist and Traveller* for users of the state's new canal system. He published a massive revised edition of the *Gazetteer* in 1824 and an updated version of his geography text in 1825. Spafford worked on mechanical inventions and agricultural improvements until his untimely death from cholera.

Boyd, Julian Parks. *Horatio Gates Spafford: Inventor, Author, Promoter of Democracy* (Worcester, Mass: American Antiquarian Society, 1942)

Warren F. Broderick

Spaniards. Sephardic Jewish refugees of Spanish ancestry were in New Amsterdam as early as 1654, but it was not until the late 19th century that the city emerged as a major destination for Spanish immigrants. By 1880 in New York City there were 669 Spanish-born residents. Spaniards who settled in New York State left their native country to escape the same agricultural disorder and rural poverty that plagued other southern and eastern European nations during this period. Most emigrating Spaniards hailed from the Canary Islands and the mainland regions of Galicia, Andalusia, the Basque country, and Catalonia.

Although sizable communities developed in present-day Bronx and Brooklyn, New York City's largest Spanish colony was situated on the Manhattan's West Side. In 1868 Spaniards in Manhattan founded the Spanish Benevolent Society, La Nacional, one of the first Spanish organizations in the city. Like other Spanish societies of the time, it provided support and mutual protection for immigrants adjusting to life in New York. Reflecting the inherent regionalism of the Spanish people, membership in many such mutual aid societies was limited to those coming from specific regions in Spain. The Roman Catholic faith, which maintained holidays and cultural traditions, was another important pillar in the lives of Spanish Americans. Many found employment in the city's cigar-manufacturing industry. New York City also served as chief embarkation point for Spaniards traveling to other areas of the United States and New York State. Between 1880 and 1920, small communities grew in Erie and Niagara Cos in Western New York. Yet in 1920 almost 11,000 Spaniards—88% of the state's overall Spanish-born population—resided in New York City. The earliest arrivals of this period were single males between the ages of 18 and 25 in search of economic opportunities.

The Spanish influx to the United States slowed to a trickle after the US government passed a series of laws restricting immigration in the early 1920s. But the trickle included a high proportion of writers and artists fleeing Spain's political upheaval of the 1920s and later the Spanish civil war of the 1930s. Their ranks included Federico García Lorca, who in 1929–30 wrote the sequence *Poeta en Nueva York* (A Poet in New York). Except for a short-lived wave in the 1960s, Spanish immigration to the United States never again reached the magnitude of earlier years. At the beginning of the 21st century, rapidly growing communities of Puerto Ricans, Mexican Americans, and immigrants from Central and South American countries have overshadowed the Spanish presence in New York City. In 2002 Spanish ancestry was claimed by 13,017 New Yorkers, almost all residents of New York City, which has the largest concentration of Spanish Americans in the nation.

Colahan, Clark. "Spanish Americans." In *Gale Encyclopedia of Multicultural America* (Detroit: Gale, 1999)
Gómez, R. A. "Spanish Immigration to the United States," *The Americas* 19 (Summer 1962): 59–77

Nicholas P. Ciotola

Spanish-American War. Cuban colonial revolution that escalated into a global war between the United States and Spain. An 1895 uprising in Cuba prompted Spain to institute a *reconcentrado* (concentration camp) system in which military officials confined Cubans in centrally located garrison towns. The nationalistic press, also known as the "yellow press" from the yellow ink used to print the popular "Yellow Kid" cartoon strip, of William Randolph Hearst's *New-York Journal* and Joseph Pulitzer's *New York World* dramatized the Cuban cause and aroused the public sentiment. On 9 Feb 1898 the *Journal* published a private letter written by the Spanish minister in Washington and stolen by Cuban patriots in New York that contained derogatory remarks about Pres William McKinley. When a mysterious explosion sank the USS *Maine,* a battleship built at the Brooklyn Navy Yard, in Havana harbor on 15 Feb 1898, killing 260, war frenzy swept the nation. Congress responded to Spain's declaration of war on 24 Apr 1898 with a US war declaration retroactive to 21 Apr 1898. Secretary of War Russell Alger called on New York State on 26 Apr 1898 to furnish 12 infantry regiments and 2 cavalry troops for a two-year term.

Fighting began in the Spanish-held Philippines; at Manila Bay on 1 May 1898, Adm George Dewey destroyed an overmatched Spanish fleet. The USS *Yankee,* crewed almost entirely by men from the First Naval Battalion New York, arrived at Santiago, Cuba, on 3 June 1898 and within four days successfully bombarded coastal batteries and cut Cuba's transatlantic cable lines. Maj Gen William Shafter's Fifth Army Corps, including the 71st Regiment Infantry New York Volunteers, arrived at Santiago by 20 June 1898 and engaged the enemy on 1 July 1898 along San Juan Heights, forcing the undermanned Spanish force to retreat. The First US Volunteer Cavalry, called the Rough Riders, with deputy commander Lt Col Theodore Roosevelt and 90 New York State residents, assisted in the attack with a heralded charge at Kettle Hill. After the Spanish forces capitulated on 17 July 1898 in Santiago, Maj Gen Nelson Miles sailed to Puerto Rico, where his expedition, including Troop A and Troop C, New York Volunteer Cavalry, advanced on San Juan but stopped when word came that Spain had agreed to an armistice.

Tropical disease and other illness had caused 5,462 American deaths, far more than the 345 from enemy fire. With Shafter fearing a yellow fever outbreak, the Fifth Army Corps had begun leaving Cuba in August for a quarantine camp, Camp Wikoff at Montauk Point in Suffolk Co, where 22,000 troops garrisoned in the fall of 1898. On 30 Sept 1898 a grand parade to honor Adm Dewey and the victorious American army, which included nearly 30,000 New Yorkers, stretched from 122d St to Washington Square, with an estimated 3 million in attendance. *New York Tribune* publisher Whitelaw Reid was among the five members of the US delegation to the peace conference. The Treaty of Paris, signed by Spain and the United States on 10 Dec 1898, granted Cuba independence, ceded Puerto Rico and Guam to the United States, and allowed the United States to purchase the Philippines for $20 million.

New York State Adjutant General's Office. *New York in the Spanish-American War, 1898: Part of the Report of the Adjutant-General of the State for 1900,* 3 vols (Albany: J. B. Lyon, 1900)

New York State Historian. *New York and the War with Spain: History of the Empire State Regiments* (Albany: Argus, 1903)

Post, Charles Johnson. *The Little War of Private Post: The Spanish-American War Seen Up Close* (Lincoln: Univ of Nebraska Press, 1999)

Christopher Morton

Sparta. Town (pop 1,627) in SE Livingston Co. Settled in 1794, the town was formed in 1796. In the early 19th century its land attracted German families from Pennsylvania. Capt Daniel Shays (1747–1825), leader of Shays's Rebellion in western Massachusetts in 1786, lived in Scottsburg hamlet after 1814. The economy was based first on lumbering and farming and later on large dairy farms and nurseries. The railroad came through in 1882. In the early 21st century Sparta is a rural residential community, and farming remains a significant land use.

Mary Jo Marks

spas. In the 18th century spas attracted the wealthy, especially those who had experienced watering places in Europe. Such places extracted charged mineral water for drinking and had a variety of bath applications to cure rheumatic and nervous disorders, circulatory problems, and general problems associated with aging. Early spas in New York Colony were located in isolated areas, and their accommodations were spartan. Lebanon Springs (Columbia Co) was an early yet rudimentary spa and like many natural springs had been used by American Indians. Jonathan Hitchcock discovered Lebanon's spring in 1756. In 1771 a bath was built there, but it was no more than a rustic bathhouse in the woods. Smaller baths include Saratoga's Chalybeate Spring [now High Rock Spring, Saratoga Springs], which was used privately by Philip Schuyler; a bathhouse was built there in 1787. Stephen Van Rensselaer established a public bath in Bath [now Rensselaer] in the 1790s.

The first fashionable spa was established at Ballston [now Ballston Spa, Saratoga Co], where a hotel and the Ballston spring were developed beginning in 1787. Six years later capital for a grander establishment came from New York City entrepreneur Nicholas Low, who designed Ballston Spa in urban form and built a home for himself, a bathhouse, and ultimately in 1803 the famed 160 ft (48 m) Sans Souci Hotel. Ballston's springs lacked flow and quality compared to its neighbor in the north, Saratoga Springs, which rivaled and surpassed Ballston's popularity by 1830 and became the most famous spa in the country.

In the 19th century spas were resorts established for health or self-improvement and were rarely if ever used for recreation or relaxation because such activities were deemed too hedonistic. Smaller springs were developed in western and central New York State. Both a sulfur and a saline spring were developed *ca* 1800 in the Village of Union Springs (Cayuga Co). In 1806 a spa was developed in Clifton Springs (Ontario Co), and White Sulphur Springs in Sharon Springs (Schoharie Co) was opened in 1825. The Richfield Springs (Otsego Co), which were baths and spas, were established near the sulfur springs in 1820. Hotels were built in Sharon Springs by 1835, and the Magnesia Spring was developed there after 1860. Entrepreneurs in Avon (Livingston Co) developed a spring in 1821, and bath spas also developed in places where they had a fleeting existence, like Breesport (Chemung Co) in 1886.

Mineral water was believed to cure many ailments, and the concept and business of spas continued to grow and became popular among the middle class. The water cure was appealing as a form of self-medication that made a physician's attention unnecessary. Spas fit the temperance movement's philosophy, which emphasized cleansing and abstinence from liquor. Water cures also satisfied concerns for physical fitness. Walking to spas, drinking the waters, and bathing in cold springs were considered investments in physical well-being. Sick people visited spas after other treatments failed, and healthy visitors were interested in using the waters as a preventive.

Detail from a stereoscopic view of High Rock, Saratoga Springs, *ca* 1875.

Restrictions on physicians' licenses became more lenient in the early 1850s, allowing doctors to open hotels and cure institutes within spas, which were essentially the forerunners of health clinics. The earliest institute in Saratoga Springs operated in 1855 as the Remedial Institute of physicians Sylvester S. and Sylvester E. Strong, and offered hydrotherapy. Its strict water cure routine was tempered by the availability of luxuries like meat or vegetarian specialties and included music as a means of spiritual regeneration. Another facility called the Water Cure, opened in Clifton Springs in 1850. By the late 1800s this sanatorium served 3,000 patients annually. The Massena Spring (St. Lawrence Co) was developed and became a major spa and resort by the 1870s.

In the 20th century the number and quality of spas declined with the public's waning faith in hydrotherapy. Saratoga Springs had an additional problem in that commercialization threatened the use of springs for health. In the 1890s the proliferation of spring outlets to extract pure carbonic acid gas, used to make soda, depleted springs by the early 1900s. Because village government was weak, the leading citizens of Saratoga Springs deemed it would be wise to involve the state government to preserve the natural resources of the springs. In 1909 a state reservation was established to regulate and limit the exploitation of every spring. Over the next 25 years, with funds from the state legislature, the state acquired the city's springs and many were capped. A few were developed for the public, including High Rock, Congress, and Geyser Springs and Lincoln Parks; the latter contained the Lincoln Baths, in 1930 one of the world's largest spas under one roof. State intervention became the basis for establishing the European-style spa that became the Saratoga Spa State Park in 1935, a true spa where doctors studied and practiced hydrotherapy. After World War II the park was developed for entertainment and in 1960–66 the Saratoga Performing Arts Center and a golf course were built, leading to a decline in the use of the wellness facilities. By contrast, most of the commercial spas that proliferated at the end of the century did not use mineral waters, emphasizing beauty and pampering rather than health. There have been some efforts, in places like Sharon Springs, for example, to restore some of the historical spas to a modicum of their former stature.

Corbett, Theodore. *The Making of American Resorts: Saratoga Springs, Ballston Spa, Lake George* (New Brunswick, NJ: Rutgers Univ Press, 2001)
Saratoga County Historical Society. *In a Pleasant Situation* (Ballston Spa, NY: Author, 1986)
Swanner, Grace. *Saratoga, Queen of Spas* (Utica: North Country Books, 1988)

Theodore Corbett

Spaulding, Elbridge Gerry (*b* Summer Hill, Cayuga Co, 24 Feb 1809; *d* Buffalo, 5 May 1897). Congressman and banker. The son of farmers, Spaulding was raised in Alexander (Genesee Co). He received a common school education and in 1829 went to Batavia (Genesee Co) to read law with the firm of Fitch and Dibble. He completed his studies in 1832 in Attica (Genesee Co) and was admitted to practice. He moved to Buffalo in 1834. Elected as mayor of Buffalo in 1847 as a Whig, he favored harbor improvements and paving and lighting the streets. As a member of the New York State Assembly in 1848 he was chairman of the committee on canals. He served a term in Congress from 1849 to 1851. In 1852 Spaulding brought the Farmers and Mechanics Bank from Batavia to Buffalo when he acquired most of its stock, and he served as president from 1852 until shortly before his death. He was appointed treasurer of New York State for 1854–55. Spaulding won election to two terms in Congress as a Republican, serving from 1859 to 1863. He was instrumental in the drafting and passage of the Legal Tender Act in 1862, which delivered the nation back to financial stability and established paper money, or greenbacks, as legal tender.

Hansen, Shirley A. "Preliminary Inventory of the Papers of Elbridge Gerry Spaulding," *Niagara Frontier* 13 (1966): 64

Varney Spaulding Greene

special education. See BOARDS OF COOPERATIVE EDUCATIONAL SERVICES (BOCES).

Speculator. Village (pop 352) in Lake Pleasant (Hamilton Co). Philip Rhinelander Jr (1788–1830) came in 1815 to his family's landholdings at Elm Lake, developing a stock farm and building a mansion. The post office was initially known as Lake Pleasant (1848–59) and Newton's Corners (1864–96). The village incorporated in 1925 to provide municipal electricity and water; its boundaries follow old school district lines and include a noncontiguous tract of wilderness to the north end. By the mid-1920s the village had developed facilities for skiing, hockey, and tobogganing and became famous for winter sports. It became even more well known when prizefighters, including Gene Tunney (1926–28), trained there. Speculator remains a busy summer and winter resort. Among its facilities are Oak Mountain Ski Area (1948) and the large, interdenominational Camp-of-the-Woods (1914).

speech and dialects. The geographical territory of New York State has historically hosted a variety of American Indian languages and, since the 17th century, numerous colonial and immigrant languages from Europe, Africa, and later Asia and Latin America. Prior to European colonization Iroquoian and Algonquian languages dominated much of the area. During the 17th century Dutch was spoken in what would become New York City and in the Hudson Valley. In the early 21st century, however, Dutch survives only in place-names and a handful of loanwords, while the few thousand remaining speakers of Indian languages are concentrated in reservations in the western and northern parts of the state. Although New York City is multilingual, English continues to be the dominant language statewide. However, the English spoken in the state varies in a number of ways.

New York City

Probably most noticeable to both natives and visitors is the distinction between the English of metropolitan New York City and that of the rest of the state. The distinctiveness of New York City speech has been widely recognized for most of the 20th century, parodied in movies and literature. While the rest of the country has mistakenly labeled the New York City dialect as "Brooklynese," it is confined neither to Brooklyn nor even to New York City, since it is heard in northern New Jersey as well. Varieties of this dialect have been used by most New York City residents for at least a century, although since World War II it has become associated with the white working class.

The most obvious difference between the dialects of New York City and the rest of the state is in the pronunciation of *r* after vowels. Outside of New York City, *r* after a vowel *(father, bird)* is a fully constricted consonant, with the back of the tongue drawn well back in the mouth. In the speech of New York City, the *r* is replaced with a vowel, so that *father* ends with something like an 'ugh' sound rather than an 'er'. "*R*-lessness," of course, is not a feature unique to New York City dialect. In the United States, it is also found in the speech of the Deep South, although rapidly disappearing there among Whites; in Boston and other parts of eastern New England, where, again, it is becoming archaic; and in African American dialects, many of which are also spoken in New York City. Around 1900 *r*-lessness was a prestige feature in New York City and elsewhere on the East Coast; the *r*-less dialect was taught to aspiring actors and frequently heard in American films made before World War II. Since the war, however, it has become stigmatized and is now mainly a working-class feature.

Other features of New York City speech include the raising of the stressed vowels in words like *coffee* and *office,* so that these words have a diphthong beginning with the vowels of *blue* and *push*, respectively. The appearance of *t* or *d* in *th*-words—so that *taught* and *thought* sound alike, and *this* and *that* become *dis* and *dat*—has become stereotyped and ridiculed to such an extent that it is avoided by educated or socially ambitious residents. Again, this feature is not unique to New York City but appears wherever English has been influenced by immigrant languages.

New York City speech also includes terms and expressions like *stand on line* (most Americans use *in* rather than *on*), *hero* for a submarine sandwich, and Yiddish borrowings like *schlep, kvetch,* and *kibbitz,* although these terms have to some extent spread to other parts of the country. Not all New York City residents, however, speak this dialect. It exists alongside Inland Northern (the dialect of New York State exclusive of the city), African American English, and a variety of other Englishes influenced by immigrant languages such as Spanish, German, and Yiddish.

Inland Northern

Another misconception is that the English spoken in other parts of the state is somehow *not* a dialect. In fact, New Yorkers outside the New York City area speak what linguists call Inland Northern (as distinct from eastern New England dialects), a dialect that arose in western New England and spread westward into New York State. It is not unique to New York and New England, for by the end of the 18th century, settlers carried it to the Western Reserve of Ohio and subsequently—especially after the opening of the Erie Canal in 1825—to the rest of the Great Lakes region, where it became the speech of the rising middle classes in Detroit, Cleveland, Akron, Chicago, and Milwaukee, as well as smaller cities, towns, and rural areas. Although it is often called General American, Inland Northern is not as general as many think. In most of Pennsylvania, for example, the dialect spoken is not Inland Northern but Midland, differing in the use of *quarter till* (the hour) instead of Inland Northern *quarter to* or *quarter of,* and condoning expressions like *the car needs washed* without an infinitive. New York State residents also pronounce the names *Don* and *Dawn* with different vowels; in western Pennsylvania, the names sound identical.

It is true that the pronunciation of some Inland Northerners, including many people in New York State, is very close to what is found in recent dictionaries and speech manuals of American English. This is partly because J. S. Kenyon, a pronunciation authority who was consultant to the authoritative *Webster's Second New International Dictionary,* mistakenly assumed his own Inland Northern dialect to be a general one. It is also partly because many of the Inland Northerners who settled the Great Lakes area from New York and Vermont acted and thought like missionaries, seeking to teach their own dialect and their own brand of Christianity. A group of Presbyterian and Congregational settlers from Oneida Co, for example, founded Knox College and the City of Galesburg in Illinois to train frontier ministers among what at the time was a largely Kentuckian population. Some of the newcomers deplored the speech of their neighbors and tried to purge it of non–Inland Northern features.

Moreover, Inland Northern is not itself a uniform dialect but has its own variant, even within New York State. The most noticeable manifestation of this variant is what linguists call the Northern Cities Shift, in which the vowel of *hat* tenses and raises until the word sounds something like *hit*, but with a diphthong: "HEE-uht." Some speakers do not raise the vowel quite as much, so that *bat* sounds like *bet*. Meanwhile, the short *o* vowel moves forward in the mouth and becomes short *a*, so that *hot* begins to sound like *hat* and *sock* like *sack*. This vowel shift was first recorded in Ithaca during the late 19th century. Today it appears to be centered in Western and Central New York and around Buffalo. It is not predominant in the Hudson or Mohawk Valleys.

This division within Inland Northern was even more pronounced earlier in the 20th century, when it affected vocabulary and grammar. Many speakers in Central and Western New York, as well as in the North Country, at one time used *sit* in the past tense, while residents of the Hudson and Mohawk Valleys preferred *sot*. Most of New York State shared the nonstandard past tense *see* with eastern New England, but some speakers in Western New York and the North Country shared *seen* with Pennsylvania. Western New York was also linked with Pennsylvania by vocabulary: *spouts* for the eaves troughs on a house and *skillet* for a frying pan. The presence of these terms points to early settlement by Pennsylvanians in the Genesee Valley. Similarly, the North Country was to some extent distinguished by its proximity to Canada, especially in its use of the word *shivaree* for a noisy wedding celebration, apparently a borrowing from Canadian French; it is also found in formerly French areas of the Mississippi Valley. Finally, the Hudson Valley at one time reflected its Dutch history in borrowings like *pot cheese* (from Dutch *pot kees*), *kill* for a small stream *(Catskill, Schuykill)*, and *kip!* (a call to chickens). While most of these have become obsolete, *stoop*, for a small porch by the front door, has spread beyond the Hudson Valley to most of the Inland Northern dialect area. Although some distinctive vocabulary has disappeared, spoken English in New York State remains far from uniform.

Atwood, E. Bagby. *A Survey of Verb Forms in the Eastern United States* (Ann Arbor: Univ of Michigan Press, 1953)

Hubbell, Allan F. *The Pronunciation of English in New York City: Consonants and Vowels* (1950; repr New York: Octagon Books, 1972)

Kretzschmar, William, Jr. "Linguistic Atlas of the Middle and South Atlantic States," http://us.English.uga.edu/lamsas/information.html

Labov, William. The Social Stratification of English in New York City (1966; repr Washington, DC: Center for Applied Linguistics, 1982)

McDavid, Raven Ioor, Jr. "The Folk Vocabulary of New York State." In *Dialects in Culture: Essays in General Dialectology*, ed. William Kretzschmar Jr (Tuscaloosa: Univ of Alabama Press, 1979)

———. "Midland and Canadian Words in Upstate New York." In *Dialects in Culture: Essays in General Dialectology*, ed. William Kretzschmar Jr (Tusca loosa: Univ of Alabama Press, 1979)

Timothy Frazer

speedskating. Formalized rules for racing on ice skates developed in Scotland in the 17th century and were brought to America by immigrants. New York City had a speedskating club shortly after the first such club was organized in Philadelphia in 1849. The predecessor of the Saratoga Winter Club was organized in 1888. Newburgh (Orange Co) is considered "the cradle of speedskating in the United States." In 1889 Joseph Donoghue of Newburgh became the first American to win a world championship. Charles Jewtraw of Lake Placid (Essex Co) won the 500 m speedskating event to take the first gold medal of International Sports Week 1924 in Chamonix, France, retroactively named the First Winter Olympics.

When Lake Placid hosted the 1932 Winter Olympics, Lake Placid native Jack Shea became the first person to win two gold medals. Irving Jaffee of New York City won the 5,000 m and 10,000 m events, during the same Olympics. Women's speedskating was included as an exhibition sport, and Catherine "Kit" Klein of Buffalo was the first woman to win an Olympic women's speedskating race, taking first in the demonstration 1,500 meter. In 1960 women's speedskating became an official Olympic sport, and Jeanne Ashworth, later of Wilmington (Essex Co), won a bronze medal in the 500 meter. Through 2002, 20 New York State residents have earned Olympic medals in speeds kating, and the state hosts a number of championship races. Newburgh hosted the Middle Atlantic Championship races from 1922 through 1972, and Saratoga Springs hosted the Eastern States Championships from 1931 through 2003. One of the three official US Olympic speedskating training facilities is in Lake Placid. Newburgh hosted the Amateur Speedskating Union's Hall of Fame from 1960 until 1999. In 2000 Saratoga Springs became the home of the new National Speedskating Museum and Hall of Fame. In 2003 there were 12 speedskating clubs operating in New York State and 189 competing skaters.

Houghton, Bill, ed. *US Speedskating Handbook 2002* (Westlake, Ohio: US Speedskating, 2002)

George W. Garner

Spellman, Francis (Joseph) (*b* Whitman, Mass, 4 May 1889; *d* New York City, 2 Dec 1967). Catholic cardinal. Spellman graduated from Fordham University in the Bronx before entering the seminary at the Urban College of Propaganda in Rome, where he was ordained in 1916 for the Archdiocese of Boston. In 1925 he was appointed to the Vatican secretariat of state and in 1932 named auxiliary bishop to William Cardinal O'Connell in Boston. In 1936 he arranged for his friend Eugenio Pacelli, cardinal secretary of state and the future Pope Pius XII, to meet Pres Franklin D. Roosevelt in Hyde Park (Dutchess Co). In 1939 he became archbishop of New York, which included the office of military ordinary. This brought him into frequent contact with Roosevelt and his successors, and in 1939 he was influential in having Roosevelt appoint a "personal representative" to the pope, a substitute for formal diplomatic relations. In 1943 he visited troops in North Africa and went to Rome. In his books *Action This Day* (1943) and *No Greater Love* (1945) and his poem "The Risen Soldier" (1944), he virtually identified the Allied cause with Christianity. In 1945 Spellman held the first Alfred E. Smith Dinner to help fund an addition to St. Vincent's Hospital, but he then made it an annual event to fete and influence national and world leaders. Named a cardinal in 1946, he became a dominant force in American Catholicism. Focused on national influence, he preached at St. Patrick's Cathedral less than a dozen times during his episcopate, usually to arouse people on moral or political issues. His chancery office was known as the "Powerhouse" because of Spellman's influence on public officials and his centralized, rigid, administrative style.

Responding to postwar migration, Spellman sent roughly half of his newly ordained priests to Puerto Rico to learn Spanish, and instead of establishing ethnic parishes, he integrated Puerto Ricans into existing parishes. In 1949 he had seminarians replace striking gravediggers, whom he pressured to sever ties to the Congress of Industrial Organizations, which he considered communist inspired. In the 1950s he publicly supported Sen Joseph McCarthy's campaign to weed out communists, and his support for the Vietnam War placed him at odds with a growing Catholic antiwar movement and with the Vatican's own position. Although a conservative in theology, he defended progressive biblical scholars before the Second Vatican Council (1962–65) and played a major role in gaining approval for its Declaration on Religious Liberty.

Cooney, John. *The American Pope: The Life and Times of Francis Cardinal Spellman* (New York: Times Books, 1984)

Gannon, Robert I. *The Cardinal Spellman Story* (Garden City, NY: Doubleday, 1962)

Gerald P. Fogarty, SJ

Spencer. Town (pop 2,979) and village (pop 731) in NW Tioga Co. Settled in 1794, the town was formed from Owego in 1806. The site of the village was the county seat from 1811 to 1822. The Wyoming Conference (Methodist) camp meeting ground was in town from 1865 to 1886–87. Spencer was on two railroad lines (Utica, Ithaca and Elmira Railroad [1869] and Ithaca and Athens Railroad [1874; later Lehigh Valley]), but manufacturing was limited to small operations: a marble factory, sash and blind shop, brickyard, and glove factory (1899–*ca* 1915). Spencer Springs became a minor resort, and a hotel was built *ca* 1880, but it lost favor. More recently Spencer Lake has attracted vacationers. The village was incorporated in 1886, and the annual Spencer Picnic began two years later, becoming a weeklong celebration in 1906. A large Finnish population settled in Spencer beginning about 1908; the town had saunas, Finnish dances, and a Finnish cooperative store (1928–94). Dairying has been the agricultural focus since the railroads came, and poultry farming was significant before the middle of the 20th century. Many residents commute to Ithaca. Part of Danby State Forest is in Spencer.

Joann Lindstrom

Spencer, Ambrose (*b* Salisbury, Conn, 13 Dec 1765; *d* Lyons, Wayne Co, 13 Mar 1848). Politician and judge. He graduated from Harvard College in 1783 and in 1784 eloped with Laura Canfield of Sharon, Conn, the daughter of his preceptor in the law. Spencer was admitted to the Columbia Co Bar in 1788 and became clerk of Hudson a year later. He won a seat in the 1794 assembly, served as an assistant attorney general from 1796 to 1801, and from 1796 to 1802 sat in the state senate, where he worked for debtor relief and reform of the penal code. In 1797 Spencer struck up a friendship with John Armstrong, who was tied to the Livingston family and the Jeffersonian Republican Party. The following year Spencer switched from Federalist to Jeffersonian Republican allegedly because he had been denied the office of comptroller. He became state attorney general in 1802 and advanced to the state supreme court in 1804. Spencer's influence with local judges and justices made him a valuable ally of De Witt Clinton. After Laura's death in 1807, he married, successively, Clinton's sisters Mary and Catharine in 1807 and 1809. Spencer broke with Clinton over political and banking issues in 1812 but backed him for governor in 1817 and became chief justice of the Supreme Court in 1819. As a judge, Spencer, dissenting, emphasized legislative authority in *Dash v Van Kleeck* (1811), squatter and tenant rights in his dissents in *Jackson v Todd* (1804) and *Jackson v Brownson* (1810), and the importance of religion to moral order in *People v Ruggles* (1811) and *Jackson v Gridley* (1820). After defending property qualifications for voters in the 1821 Constitutional Convention, he lost office under the new constitution. Spencer served as mayor of Albany from 1824 to 1825 but failed election to the US Senate in 1825. Subsequently, he acted as counsel in occasional cases. Elected to Congress in 1828 as a supporter of John Quincy Adams, he opposed Andrew Jackson's Indian removal policy. Denied reelection in 1830 and 1832, Spencer expressed outrage at Jackson's 1832 veto of the bill to recharter the Bank of the United States and remained an opponent of the Democratic Party. He also committed himself to the temperance movement, agricultural improvement, and the Episcopal Church. After moving to Lyons in 1839 to farm, he concluded the 1842 Seneca Supplemental Treaty of Buffalo Creek and chaired the 1844 Whig National Convention.

Cornog, Evan. *The Birth of Empire: DeWitt Clinton and the American Experience, 1769–1828* (New York: Oxford Univ Press, 1998)

Hanyan, Craig, with Mary Hanyan. *De Witt Clinton and the Rise of the People's Men* (Montreal: McGill-Queen's Univ Press, 1996)

Craig and Mary L. Hanyan

Spencer, John C(anfield) (*b* Hudson, Columbia Co, 8 Jan 1788; *d* Albany, 17 May 1855). Lawyer and politician. The capable but abrasive eldest son of Ambrose Spencer and Laura Canfield graduated from Union College (1806) before becoming Gov Daniel D. Tompkins's private secretary (1807). After passing the bar (1809), he opened practice in Canandaigua (Ontario Co). Discharged from military service during the War of 1812, he served as Canandaigua postmaster (1814), New York State assistant attorney general and state district attorney for the 10th District (1815), US congressman (1817–19), assemblyman (1820–22, 1831–33) and speaker (1820), state senator (1825–28), commissioner to revise state statutes (1827–28), special prosecutor to investigate William Morgan's disappearance (1829–30), and New York's secretary of state (1839). As a legislator Spencer championed public education, the state canal system, an end of imprisonment for defaulting debtors, and a bankruptcy program fair to creditors and debtors. First a Clintonian Republican, he became active in the Antimasonic Party before helping to found New York State's Whig Party. Spencer was the chief state supporter of Pres John Tyler, who named him secretary of war (1841–43) and secretary of the treasury (1843–44) before nominating him as an associate Supreme Court justice (1844). The US Senate rejected Spencer's nomination. After breaking with Tyler over the annexation of Texas and retiring from politics in 1844, he resumed practice in Albany until his death.

Alexander, DeAlva Stanwood. *A Political History of the State of New York*, 4 vols (1906; repr Port Washington, NY: I. J. Friedman, 1969)

Jerome Mushkat

Spencerport. Village (pop 3,559) in Ogden (Monroe Co). The Erie Canal (1823) created this entrepôt with warehouses and hotels; later the Niagara Falls Branch of the New York Central Railroad (1852) provided rail transportation. The village was incorporated in 1867. Late 19th-century industries included sash-and-blind manufacturing and fruit drying. The construction of the Barge Canal (1912–18) attracted new businesses and reinvigorated old companies. There was a vanilla factory in the 1930s. The Antonelli Fireworks Co shifted to the production of bombs and grenades during World War II, making deficient products that led to a 1943 sabotage charge. In 2002 it is a retail center. It was once the home of *Ziegfeld Follies* and Broadway star Claire Luce.

Carolyn Vacca

Sperry, Elmer A(mbrose) (*b* Cincinnatus, Cortland Co, 21 Oct 1860; *d* Brooklyn, 16 June 1930). Inventor and entrepreneur. The Sperry family owned a farm several miles outside of Cortland but moved into the community when Elmer Sperry was 10. Educated at Cortland Normal School (now SUNY Cortland), he spent his early life working on a variety of inventions. Sperry established companies in several states before moving to Brooklyn in 1905. Many of his inventions were based on the principle of feedback, which was instrumental in his developing, from 1907, gyrostabilizers, gyrocompasses, and autopilots for ships and airplanes. In 1910 he founded Sperry Gyroscope Co in Brooklyn and in 1912 made the first installation of his gyrostabilizer system in the USS *Worden*. He made various improvements, integrating the gyrocompass into a system of ship and gunnery controls. Sperry served on the Naval Consulting Board of the United States during World War I, and, with his son Lawrence Sperry (1892–1924), designed the aerial torpedo in 1917–19. In the 1920s Sperry traveled extensively, visiting Europe and Japan, and held leading appointments in various engineering societies. Over his lifetime he was granted more than 350 patents. A dedicated philanthropist he gave more than $1 million to the Brooklyn and Queens chapters of the Young Men's Christian Association.

Hughes, Thomas Parke. *Elmer Sperry: Inventor and Engineer* (1971; repr Baltimore: Johns Hopkins Univ Press, 1993)

Andrew D. Todd

Sperry Corporation. Cortland Co–raised inventor Elmer A. Sperry moved to Brooklyn in 1905 and began work on his most notable invention, the gyrocompass. Five years later he founded Sperry Gyroscope Co in Brooklyn to produce gyrostabilizers, which stabilized ships from rolling at sea. Later Sperry Gyroscope produced other equipment for the US Navy, including a high-intensity searchlight, fire control systems for naval guns, and a gyrostabilizer for aircraft. In 1929 Sperry sold his firm to North American Aviation Co. In 1933, three years after Elmer Sperry's death, North American Aviation formed the Sperry Corp with Sperry Gyroscope as its principal subsidiary.

During World War II Sperry Corp produced gyrostabilizers for the United States and the Allies as well as aerial bombsights, automatic piloting systems for airplanes, ball turrets for bombers, and microwave technologies for radar. To accommodate its wartime workforce, which eventually grew to 32,000 employees, Sperry Corp opened in February 1942 a massive new 32-acre (13 ha) manufacturing facility in Lake Success (Nassau Co). During the Cold War the Sperry Corp continued as a military contractor of electronics for guided missiles for both the Nike program of the US Air Force and the US Navy's Polaris and Poseidon class nuclear submarines. In 1955 Sperry Corp merged with Remington Rand (an office equipment maker) to create Sperry Rand, which produced among other products computer systems for the Mercury and Apollo space programs. In 1986 Sperry Rand merged with Burroughs to found Unisys Corp, an information technology firm based in Blue Bell, Pa. After the creation of Unisys, the Marine Systems Division of the original Sperry Gyroscope was spun off, and after being owned by a series of defense contractors, Marine Systems came to rest in 2001 as a division within Northrop Grumman Corp, the defense conglomerate of Los Angeles.

Sperry Rand Corp. *A History of Sperry Rand Corporation* (New York: Author, 1964)

Tod M. Ottman

spiedie [SPEE-DEE]. A meat snack popular in, and largely limited to, the Binghamton area and surrounding counties. The spiedie is a skewer loaded with marinated meat and cooked over hot coals. Italian immigrants most likely brought the spiedie to the Binghamton region during the early part of the 20th century. In the Abruzzi province of Italy, *spedini* (derived from *spiedo,* meaning spit) were prepared by cutting lamb, pork, or goat into small cubes and marinating them in a mixture of red wine vinegar, olive oil, oregano, and other traditional Italian spices. Augustine Iacovelli is credited with introducing the food to the Southern Tier. Iacovelli, who came to Binghamton in 1929 from Civitella in Abruzzi, opened Augie's Restaurant in Endicott (Broome Co) in 1939. He served marinated lamb sprayed with a sauce he called "zuzu." In recent decades the spiedie has grown in popularity though, with few exceptions, is limited to the Southern Tier. Since 1983 the annual Speidie Fest has been held in August in Dickinson (Broome Co), including a spiedie cook-off. Contemporary speidies are made from a variety of meats, including chicken and venison, and are served on fresh Italian bread or a roll. Lupo's Deli and Char Pit in Endicott is the most famous local eatery for spiedies, and Salamida's State Fair Spiedie Sauce (first made 1976) is available throughout the country for home use.

"Don't Call It Shish Kebab: In Binghamton, It's Heaven," *New York Times*, 16 Jan 1991

Joann Lindstrom

Spiritualism. Religious movement. In 1848 Kate and Margaret Fox, daughters of a farmer in Hydesville (Wayne Co), claimed to hear mysterious knockings that responded to their questions. Steeped in local supernatural folklore, the Fox family and others concluded that the knockings were caused by a human spirit. These beliefs seemed to provide a dramatic confirmation of the possibility of communication with the dead. Demonstrations by the Fox sisters in Rochester, New York City, and other northeastern cities, coupled with favorable coverage in the *New York Tribune*, made Spiritualism a national sensation. It was affirmed by some prominent religious thinkers, such as Andrew Jackson Davis of Poughkeepsie, whose philosophy of harmonialism was a personal mélange of mesmerism and the teachings of Swedish mystic Emanuel Swedenborg and French utopian Charles Fourier. Some attention was negative. Charges of fraud were fueled by the conclusions of a group of University of Buffalo Medical School professors who investigated mediumship in 1851, and critics concerned that Spiritualism promoted free love seized upon an 1858 sex scandal involving medium John Murray Spear and his Spirit Springs community in Kiantone (Chautauqua Co). Still, by 1890, about 45,000 Americans were affiliated with Spiritualist societies. Spiritualism appealed across lines of race and class, though its leadership was generally white and middle class. It proved particularly attractive to Quakers, Swedenborgians, Universalists, and Unitarians, and it became intertwined with several contemporary reform movements, particularly abolitionism and women's rights.

New York City and Western New York became important centers of Spiritualist activity, with about 300 circles in New York City in the mid-1850s. New York City was Davis's headquarters and the location of Partridge and Brittan, the most prominent Spiritualist publisher of the 19th century. Forty-five Spiritualist periodicals were published in the state in the 19th century, with some 27 of them in New York City, which also was an epicenter for a major rupture within the movement. Concerned that Davis emphasized Spiritualism's "modern revelations" to the neglect of the Bible, the city's leading "Christian Spiritualists" sought in 1854 to organize a biblically oriented Society for the Diffusion of Spiritual Knowledge. The society quickly folded, but it was the movement's first attempt at national organization, and the division that prompted it remains salient. The society's collapse reflected the early resistance of Spiritualists to formal organization, which was at first largely confined to the level of the private circle.

Spiritualists began holding public Sunday services in New York City during the early 1850s, held a large camp meeting in Chautauqua Co in 1858, and organized a Spiritualist church in Genesee Co by 1860. New York was second only to Massachusetts in Spiritualist church strength throughout the late 19th- and early 20th centuries, peaking around 1926 with 90 churches and over 6,500 members. In 1879 Spiritualists founded the Cassadaga Lake Free Association in Chautauqua Co, which by 1890 had more Spiritualists (3,000) than any other county in the nation. By 1906 the association, now renamed Lily Dale, had become the nation's leading Spiritualist center. Although Lily Dale declined by the 1930s, it remains headquarters for the National Spiritualist Association of Churches, the nation's largest Spiritualist organization. While many believers are not members of specifically Spiritualist churches, in 2002 there were Spiritualist churches in Lily Dale, Schenectady, Clifton Park, East Aurora, Smithtown, Patchogue, Elmont, Rochester, Binghamton, and New York City.

See also BURNED-OVER DISTRICT.

Carroll, Bret E. *Spiritualism in Antebellum America* (Bloomington: Indiana Univ Press, 1997)

Moore, R. Laurence. *In Search of White Crows: Spiritualism, Parapsychology, and American Culture* (New York: Oxford Univ Press, 1977)

Bret E. Carroll

Split Rock explosion. An accidental detonation in 1918 of nearly a ton of TNT at a munitions plant near Syracuse. The Semet-Solvay chemical company, based in Solvay (Onondaga Co) made TNT for the Allied effort during World War I. It established a manufacturing complex in 1915 for TNT and picric and nitric acid on a portion of an unused limestone quarry at Split Rock, in the Town of Onondaga (Onondaga Co). On the evening of 2 July 1918 an overheated gear in a mixing machine ignited a fire in the Number 1 TNT building. The resulting explosion shook buildings and frightened people in downtown Syracuse, 6 miles (10 km) away. Despite the presence of nearly 400 tons (363 MT) of stored TNT near the site, rescuers rushed to remove the injured and fight continuing fires. At least 50 male employees were killed, many horribly burned and dismembered, and another 50 were injured. Fifteen bodies were never completely identified and are buried in a mass grave in Syracuse's Morningside Cemetery. Production at the site ceased a few weeks after World War I ended.

Foley, Jasena R. *The Night the Rock Blew Up* (1973; repr Onondaga, NY: Town of Onondaga Historical Society, 1991)

Dennis J. Connors

sportswriting and sportswriters. The emergence and growth of sport as entertainment and New York City's development as the nation's entertainment center have been shaped by those who write about the subject. James Fenimore Cooper's vivid account of the memorable 1823 horse race between regional champions American Eclipse and Henry in Queens Co, witnessed by at least 25,000 spectators, is perhaps the first instance of sportswriting in New York State. During the 19th century a variety of publications, such as the *Spirit of the Times, New York Clipper, United States Sporting Magazine, National Police Gazette, New York Herald, Brooklyn Daily Eagle,* and *Sunday Morning Visitor* (which in 1897 became *Morning Telegraph*), helped lead to the professionalization and commercialization of sport, principally baseball, boxing, and horse racing. In this tradition New York City's first sports department came into being in 1883 when Joseph Pulitzer, realizing the need to appeal to male readers, appointed turf expert H. G. Crickmore as sports editor of the *New York World.* The circulation war between the *World* and William Randolph Hearst's *New-York Journal* led to Hearst's paying adventure writer Richard Harding Davis $500 in 1895 to cover the Princeton-Yale football game. The 19th century's most influential sportswriter was Henry "Father" Chadwick, a transplanted Englishman who championed baseball rather than cricket as America's "national pastime."

Initially sports coverage emphasized results and crowd descriptions, especially if unruly, and except for the warring tabloids, appeared without bylines. The burgeoning world of sports after World War I experienced the fruition of the seeds Pulitzer had planted, with sportswriters gravitating to New York City to sell sport and themselves. Grantland Rice's heyday coincided with sportswriting's Golden Age. As one of the foremost practitioners of the "gee whiz" school of sportswriting, Rice coined such phrases as the "Galloping Ghost" and christened Notre Dame's 1924 backfield the "four horsemen" of the Apocalypse. Rice (from Nashville via Cleveland), Damon Runyon (from Kansas via Colorado), and Red Smith (from Green Bay, Wisc, via Milwaukee, St. Louis, and Philadelphia) were just a few of the sportswriting luminaries drawn to New York City.

Sportswriters' great influence coincided with the predominance of countless daily newspapers and the designation of the tabloid back pages, complete with banner headlines, to sports. The profession peaked in the post–World War II era with *Herald Tribune* sports editor Stanley Woodward's staff of uniformly knowledgeable, urbane, and pungent writers such as Red Smith. Well behind the times on integration, New York City sportswriters in general avoided taking stands on controversial issues, although Max Kase's 1951 exposure of college basketball scandals in the *New York Journal-American* was a notable exception. In 1954 New York City's role as a center for national sports magazines climaxed with the creation of Henry R. Luce's trendsetting *Sports Illustrated.* The *Herald Tribune*'s demise in the mid-1960s reflected a drop in sportswriting's influence and that of newspapers in general, although the tabloid back pages remained sacrosanct. Nevertheless, influential and significant sportswriters in recent decades include the *New York Daily News*'s Dick Young and Mike Lupica, the *New Yorker*'s Roger Angell and Herbert Warren Wind, and authors Dick Schaap and Roger Kahn. As commercial technology such as sports talk radio station WFAN and the all-sports ESPN television channel have pushed aside sports journalism, the surviving newspapers have made significant adjustments, including, for example, more intimate coverage of athletes' personal lives.

Sportswriting in New York State is not confined to professional sportswriters, nor is reporting on major sports entirely dominated by writers in the New York City metropolitan region. Children's authors like John R. Tunis have been among the best-known American sportswriters. Coverage of the Saratoga racing season by newspapers in the Capital District is one exception. Still, the dominance of New York City's professional teams has shaped the role of sportswriters in smaller communities. In the state's larger cities, writers like Buffalo's Cy Kritzer have been responsible for acquiring major league franchises. More important, while depending on national syndication for major league coverage, writers in smaller communities have been responsible for sustaining amateur sport from Little League to senior golfers.

Berkow, Ira. *Red: A Biography of Red Smith* (New York: Times Books, 1986)
Fountain, Charles. *Sportswriter: The Life and Times of Grantland Rice* (New York: Oxford Univ Press, 1993)
Orodenker, Richard, ed. *Twentieth-Century American Sportswriters,* vol 171 of *Dictionary of Literary Biography* (Detroit: Gale Research, 1996)
———. *American Sportwriters and Writers on Sport,* vol 241 of *Dictionary of Literary Biography* (Detroit: Gale Research, 2001)

Donald M. Roper

Sprague, J(ohn) Russel (*b* Inwood [now in Nassau Co], 24 Dec 1886; *d* Lawrence, Nassau Co, 16 Apr 1969). County political leader. Sprague attended Cornell University, earning an LLB in 1910, and the following year he opened a law practice in Lawrence. In 1913 Sprague entered Nassau Co politics, rising to county Republican leader by 1935. As the county developed into one of America's premier suburbs, Sprague built his organization—a political hybrid that combined newer elements of government efficiency with older elements of patronage and personal loyalty—into one of the strongest Republican machines in the nation. As the Nassau Co executive (1938–51) and the Nassau Co Republican Party chairman (1935–59), Sprague had tremendous influence within the state and national Republican Party, which rested on his ability to deliver overwhelming Republican majorities from his county. He was an early backer of and critical adviser to Gov Thomas E. Dewey. Sprague helped Dewey secure his initial gubernatorial nomination in 1938, as well as Dewey's 1944 and 1948 Republican presidential nominations. Sprague also was one of the chief architects of Dwight D. Eisenhower's victory at the 1952 Republican National Convention and played a major role in selecting Richard M. Nixon as the vice presidential nominee. In 1951 Sprague retired as county executive. Two years later he faced allegations of improperly using his influence in that position to profit from business enterprises at Roosevelt Raceway in Westbury (Nassau Co). Although Sprague denied any wrongdoing, the public uproar that followed led to his complete retirement from politics by 1959.

Smith, Richard Norton. *Thomas E. Dewey and His Times* (New York: Simon & Schuster, 1982)

Tod M. Ottman

Springdale. The fictitious name given to Candor (Tioga Co), the subject of *Small Town in Mass Society* (1958), a classic work in the sociology and American community studies literature, written by sociologists Arthur Vidich and Joseph Bensman. The book was based on a research project sponsored by a Cornell University study of the small town of Candor (population 2,500) in the 1950s. The study examined the political and social structure of the town—and by extension, much of small town America—at a decisive moment of transition when a declining traditional order confronted the agencies and institutions of modern life. At the time, Vidich was an assistant professor and director of field research at Cornell. For the purposes of the study, he resided in the community of Candor for two and a half years.

Candor is shown to be a structural hybrid, containing features of both traditional and more modern cultural institutional patterns, although the latter were frequently unrecognized, disregarded, or sometimes strenuously avoided by residents who attempted to uphold ideological images of their town as embodying 19th-century populism and agrarian democracy. The book offers a detailed account of how Candor residents contended with external forces over which they had no control and of which they were often only dimly aware. Although the town's residents perceived their community to be staunchly self-reliant, Vidich and Bensman claimed it was heavily influenced by mass culture and increasing intervention from the state and federal governments. By examining the reactions, resistance, avoidance techniques, and coping strategies of the residents, Vidich and Bensman presented an analysis of social change in American society that emphasized the resilience of American tradition and the structural and cultural tendencies that undermine it. In this sense, one can find in 1950s Candor many of the social and cultural sources for what in the past several decades have been labeled America's "culture wars."

The book occasioned much discussion within the academic community over the ethics of ethnographic research in situations where subjects can be expected to read the final work and where it is difficult to ensure true anonymity. Specific concerns were raised regarding informed consent, invasion of privacy, violation of trust between participant and researcher, and responsibility of a researcher to the data. The townspeople also reacted with vitriol; the authors were burned in effigy and were depicted atop a manure spreader in the July 4th parade. Much of the debate is published in recent editions of the book.

Vidich, Arthur J., and Joseph Bensman. *Small Town in Mass Society* (1958; rev ed. Urbana: Univ of Illinois Press, 2000)

Michael W. Hughey

Springfield. Town (pop 1,350) in N Otsego Co. The first settlers were Palatine Germans who arrived north of the present East Springfield in 1762 but were burnt out by Indians in 1778. Resettlement, largely from New England, came after the end of the Revolutionary War. The town was formed from Cherry Valley in 1797 and was located on the Third Great Western Turnpike (1808). In 1860 it produced more hops than any other town in the county. Cheese making, at home and in factories, was also significant until fluid milk began to be shipped beginning *ca* 1895. Hyde Hall (1817–33), which lies in Glimmerglass State Park on the north end of Otsego Lake, was designed by Philip Hooker as the home of the George Hyde Clarke family; restored in the early 21st century, it is operated as a state historic site. On the west shore of the lake are many summer cottages, the Otsego Golf Course (1894, one of the nation's oldest), and the Alice Busch Opera Theater (1987), home to the internationally renowned Glimmerglass Opera. Approximately 18% of Springfield residents are engaged in agriculture in the early 21st century. Amish began buying farms in Springfield in 2000 and had established a substanital community by 2003. Natural curiosities include the Chyle, a sink into which an underground stream flows, and Summit Lake, whose waters flow both north and south in high water.

Hugh C. MacDougall

Springport. Town (pop 2,256) in SW Cayuga Co. At Great Gully Brook, at the town's south border, was an Indian village. It was later the site of the second Roman Catholic chapel within what is now New York State, ministered by a French missionary priest from 1656 to 1658 and again from 1668 to 1684. The town, settled by Europeans in 1790, was formed from Scipio and Aurelius in 1823. Limestone outcrops were discovered *ca* 1810 and later quarried by Birdseye Limestone. The Cayuga Lake Railroad ran between 1873 and 1974. Rolling land sloped toward the lake, producing in 2002 large harvests of corn and other small grains.

Springs. Locality (pop 4,950) in East Hampton (Suffolk Co). Settled around 1649, this small blunt neck of land girded by Three Mile Harbor and Gardiners Bay takes its name from freshwater springs that flow into Accabonac Creek and was originally prized for its salt hay. The waters around the springs later supported many fishers and shellfishers. With East Hampton's growth as a resort, Springs residents earned a living in the service trades. After World War II some of the artists seeking houses in the Hamptons, including Jackson Pollock, Lee Krasner, and Willem de Kooning, settled in Springs; the Pollock-Krasner House and Study Center preserves their house and studio. In the early 21st century Springs is a mix of suburban developments, estates, and nature preserves.

Richard F. Welch

Spring Valley. Village (pop 25,464) in Ramapo and Clarkstown (Rockland Co). It had its beginnings when dairy farmers petitioned for an Erie Railroad (1841) stop. A post office named Monsey opened in 1846, and it was changed to Spring Valley in 1848. Cotton, woolen, and silk mills produced goods in the 19th century. By the early 20th century, Spring Valley was the Town of Ramapo's commercial center. It incorporated as a village in 1902. Briarcraft manufactured pipes for smokers from 1932 to 1960. In the 1940s and 1950s about 50 summer resort hotels catered to a Jewish clientele. With 4,500 permanent residents in 1950, its population grew rapidly with suburbanization. Haitians began settling in the village in the mid-1960s. Over half of the village's residents are racial minorities, with 44% of the total population being African American. Spring Valley is Rockland Co's most populous and most densely settled village.

Springville. Village (pop 4,252) in Concord (Erie Co). Settled in 1807, it was known as Fiddlers Green from *ca* 1815, but a post office named Springville opened in 1820, and the village was incorporated in 1834. In 1860 products included woolen cloth, leather, lumber, wood turnings, sawn stone, and ironwork. The Buffalo, Rochester and Pittsburgh Railway (1872; later Pennsylvania Railroad) connected the village to Buffalo. In 1971 Springville produced gloves, plastics, cutlery, canned goods, and glass, and in the early 21st century, plastics, machinery, and lightning protection products. A winter sports destination, the village is also the birthplace of Glenn Scobey "Pop" Warner (1871–1954), who revolutionized American football. Ralph B. Waite (1871–1964) invented novocaine in Springville.

Andrew C. Maines

Springwater. Town (pop 2,322) in SE Livingston Co. Settled in 1807, the town was formed from Sparta and Middletown [now Naples, Ontario Co] in 1816. Lumbering and shingle making were early sources of income, succeeded by farming. The Buffalo, Corning and New York Railroad (later Erie Railroad) came through in 1852–53. In 1880 agricultural implements, plows, and wooden goods were manufactured; 20th-century products included earphones (1919 to mid 1960s) and metal fishing lures (1929–70). In the early 21st century, Springwater's farms produce potatoes, dairy products, and trees. It is mainly a rural residential community; the terrain is hilly, and the descent into Springwater hamlet from all directions is a scenic attraction.

Mary Jo Marks

Squakie [Squawky] Hill Reservation. In 1797, at the federal treaty with the Senecas at Big Tree, north of present-day Cuylerville (Livingston Co), the US government recognized the Squakie Hill Reservation, a 2 mi² (5 km²) parcel of land on the west side of the Genesee River in what is now Mount Morris (Livingston Co). It was inhabited by the descendants of Midwestern Fox Indians (also known as Mesquakie, Muskwaki, or Outagamie Indians) who moved to Iroquoia in different migrations from 1712 to 1730 at the urging of British officials, settling in several places along the upper Susquehanna, Allegany, and Genesee Rivers. During Pontiac's War in 1763–64, a number of other Fox Indians fled to the Seneca village at Big Tree. Squakie Hill was destroyed by Gen John Sullivan during the American Revolution in 1779, but the Fox, led by their chief, Stump Foot, returned to their Genesee lands no later than 1791. Described as the "Squawkey tribe," they continued to live on the Genesee at Da-yo-it'-gä-o (the Seneca name for the village). There they remained until 1826, when the Seneca were dispossessed by the Ogden Land Co in a fraudulent treaty that was never ratified by the US Senate.

Hunter, William A. "Refugee Fox Settlements among the Senecas," *Ethnohistory* 3 (Winter 1956): 11–20

Laurence M. Hauptman

Stafford. Town (pop 2,409) in E Genesee Co. Settled in 1798 with the construction of the Holland Land Co storehouse, it had a strong influx of English people beginning in 1817, including a colony from Devon. The town was formed from Le Roy and Batavia in 1820. Silk production was attempted in 1839. During the last half of the 19th century, Morganville Pottery produced drain tile, flowerpots, and glazed wares. Part of the 1984 movie *The Natural,* starring Robert Redford, was filmed in the countryside. The Rochester Zen Center built a Buddhist retreat facility in 2000.

Susan L. Conklin

stagecoach lines. Stagecoach service between New York City and Philadelphia began in 1757, but lines generally stopped short of entering New York Colony because they remained on the New Jersey side of the Hudson and transferred their passengers and bags to a ferry. The first long-distance stage within the state began in 1785 between New York City and Albany, running on the east side of the Hudson. Operated by tavern keepers Isaac Van Wyck of Fishkill (Dutchess Co), John Kinney of Kinderhook [now in Columbia Co], and Talmadge Hall of New York City, who had a state-granted monopoly, it ran three times per week in the summer and twice per week in the winter. Although faster and more reliable than the Hudson River sloops, after 1810 the stagecoaches lost business to the steamboats and became local and winter carriers. The first service on the western shore was between New York and Goshen (Orange Co) in 1797; the first through service was in 1803 between Hoboken, NJ, and Albany via Goshen, Kingston (Ulster Co), and Catskill (Greene Co).

As the gateway to the interior and the northern terminal of most steamboats, Albany became the state's greatest stagecoach hub and one of the most important nationwide. This dominance began in 1789, with a line to Troy (Rensselaer Co); service to the west began soon afterward, extending to Geneva (Ontario Co) in 1797 and to Buffalo by 1811. By 1818 Albany had twice-daily service to Utica and Buffalo and frequent service to places like Montreal, Boston, and Hartford and New Haven, Conn, as well as many New York State towns. Troy and Utica were also significant stagecoach centers.

Stagecoaches were not displaced by the canals. Travel via canals was slow, and they froze for several months out of the year. Mail contracts also helped keep the stagecoaches running. Still, stagecoaches were not fast; in 1806 the Albany-Troy stage took two hours. The winter offered the greatest speeds of the year, when runners replaced wheels for a smooth, fast ride over snow-covered roads and frozen lakes and rivers.

New York State's demand for stagecoaches also prompted their manufacture, and "Albany coaches" and "Troy coaches" were used throughout the nation. In Albany, James Goold and Co produced coaches from 1813 into the 1850s. In Troy, Charles Veazie built coaches between about 1815 and 1836. Another major employer, Orsamus Eaton, began coach building in about 1820; he took on a partner, Uri Gilbert, and in 1844 their company became Eaton, Gilbert and Co. In the 1850s New York coach building declined, in part because of competition from the more famous Concord coach, built in New England and boasting a superior suspension system. Some firms, such as Eaton, Gilbert and Co, moved into building railroad cars; Eaton left the company in 1862, and in the 1880s it became known as the Gilbert Car Co.

Beginning in the 1840s, stagecoaches were displaced from long-distance service by the railroad, but they remained important for local routes throughout the 19th century. Some of the last coaches connected railroad stations and ferry terminals to resort hotels, which had begun in the 1820s with the construction of the first Catskill hotels, some of which were developed by stagecoach operators such as Erastus and Charles L. Beach of Catskill. The last stagecoaches were replaced by automobiles and buses in the early years of the 20th century.

Holmes, Oliver W., and Peter T. Rohrbach. *Stagecoach East: Stagecoach Days in the East from the Colonial Period to the Civil War* (Washington, DC: Smithsonian Institution Press, 1983)

Rohit T. Aggarwala

Stamford. Town (pop 1,943) and village (pop 1,265) in NE Delaware Co. Settled in 1773 but abandoned during the American Revolution, the area was resettled in the 1780s at New Stamford [now Township]. The Town of Stamford was formed from Woodstock (Ulster Co) in 1792. Butter production and wool manufacture were prominent during the 19th century. The village, first called Head of the Delaware, grew along the Susquehanna Turnpike (1802), was incorporated in 1870, and now lies partly in the Town of Harpersfield. In 1872 the Ulster and Delaware Railroad reached Stamford, initiating an influx of tourists and summer guests and the construction of grand hotels and many boardinghouses. A tower on the summit of Utsayantha Mountain attracted visitors from 1882 to 1926. The Rexmere Hotel (1898; now Frank W. Cyr Center) is home to Otsego–Northern Catskills BOCES and includes a gallery and exhibit space. Edward Zane Carroll Judson (1823–86), the dime novelist who wrote under the name Ned Buntline, was a native of Stamford.

Dorothy Kubik

Stamp Act crisis. In March 1765 the British Parliament enacted the Stamp Act, which levied an impost, to be paid in specie (gold or silver coin), on such printed matter as newspapers, broadsides, pamphlets, and commercial and legal documents. The act would go into effect on 1 November. Cases involving the act could be tried in common-law courts, with juries, or in admiralty courts, without juries. In New York the act was opposed by both major political factions—Livingstons and DeLanceys, named after the elite families that headed them—and most economic groups that suffered through hard times. Both factions sought its repeal peacefully through petitions, boycotts, and protests. The act produced another political force, however: the Sons of Liberty. Led by upwardly mobile Isaac Sears, John Lamb, and Alexander Mc-

Broadside detail from advertisement of stagecoach service between Albany and Whitehall, 1831.

Dougall, the Liberty Boys, who were prone to violence and intimidation, were supported by artisans, shopkeepers, and seamen. New Yorkers complained that the act endangered American property and rights and that Americans were taxed without representation in violation of their natural rights. After news of the act arrived in mid-April, John Holt's *New-York Gazette; or, The Weekly Post-Boy* published incendiary articles decrying British tyranny and defending American rights. In August a fearful James McEvers resigned as the colony's stamp collector. The Stamp Act Congress, an intercolonial body called to consider ways to obtain repeal, met in New York City from 7 to 25 October. Among the colony's representatives were Robert R. and Philip Livingston, both of whom helped draft the Congress petitions.

Stamped paper arrived in New York City on 23 October and was placed for safety in the British-garrisoned Fort George. On 31 October, merchants voted to boycott British goods; shopkeepers agreed not to purchase them; and roving mobs shouted liberty. The next day a mob threw stones at Fort George's soldiers; Lt Gov Cadwallader Colden, the act's staunchest supporter, was burned in effigy; and a mob terrorized a British major who had threatened to collect the tax by force. Because stamped paper was not issued, the courts and port were closed.

Sir Henry Moore, the new governor, arrived on 13 November. Realizing he could not enforce the act, he dismantled the field fortifications in front of Fort George to appease the populace. Soon after, the Liberty Boys asked the Colonial Assembly to repeal the act locally and to order the resumption of business without stamps, but the assembly's two elite family factions refused. When the Liberty Boys tried to open the courts, lawyers and judges resisted, although DeLanceys, trying to prevent violence, supported the Liberty Boys in this endeavor. With DeLanceys' assistance, the Liberty Boys got the port opened early in January 1766, giving employment to discontented seamen. Such actions decreased the threats of violence.

In December 1765 and January 1766 New York City's Liberty Boys signed agreements with their counterparts in New London, Conn, and Boston, promising to march to one another's aid. In January Albany's Liberty Boys sacked the stamp distributor's house. By March Liberty Boys in New York City, Oyster Bay [now in Nassau Co], and Huntington (Suffolk Co) had adopted resolutions indicating their willingness to risk their lives and property to protect their liberties. In April New York City's Liberty Boys made various radical demands, such as the abolition of admiralty courts and trade restrictions. On 18 March Parliament repealed the Stamp Act. When official news reached New York City on 20 May, bells were rung, cannon and firearms were discharged, and toasts were made. The crisis had made the Sons of Liberty a political force; the populace had become politically active; and ruling elites now had to share power with more popular factions.

McAnear, Beverly. "The Albany Stamp Act Riots," *William and Mary Quarterly,* 3d ser, 4 (Oct 1947): 486–98

Morgan, Edmund S., and Helen M. Morgan. *The Stamp Act Crisis: Prologue to Revolution* (Chapel Hill: Univ of North Carolina, 1953)

Tiedemann, Joseph S. *Reluctant Revolutionaries: New York City and the Road to Independence, 1763–1776* (Ithaca: Cornell Univ Press, 1997)

Gaspare J. Saladino

Stanford. Town (pop 3,544) in NE Dutchess Co. Part of the Great Nine Partners Patent (1697), it was settled in the early 1740s and formed from Washington in 1793. A woolen mill (1812) was followed by paper, edge tool, and axle manufacturing in the mid–19th century. The nearby Harlem Railroad (1851) encouraged farms to specialize in dairy; later, three railroads (completed 1869–89) passed through town. Native-born James Tallmadge Jr (1778–1853) served in the House of Representatives (1817–19) and was president of New York University (1831–46). Horse farms and second homes of wealthy New York City residents have replaced a once thriving dairy industry.

William P. McDermott

Stanton, Elizabeth Cady (*b* Johnstown, Fulton Co, 12 Nov 1815; *d* New York City, 26 Oct 1902). Women's rights leader. The daughter of Margaret Livingston Cady and Daniel Cady, an attorney, judge, and state legislator, as well as future state Supreme Court justice and one-term congressman, Elizabeth Cady was educated at the Johnstown Academy. When her elder brother, the family's only surviving son, died shortly after his graduation from Schenectady's Union College, she vowed to ease her father's sadness by becoming all that he had hoped for his son. Cady devoted herself to mastering horseback riding and academics and read extensively in her father's legal texts. While her sex prohibited her from attending college, she enrolled in Emma Willard's Troy Female Seminary, where she received the equivalent of a college education. While in Troy (Rensselaer Co) the young girl underwent a conversion experience and sank into depression, only recovering when she rejected the passionate Christianity of the Second Great Awakening and embraced rationalism and scientific skepticism. After completing her education she engaged in the social and familial activities of young unmarried women of her class, which included frequent visits to her wealthy abolitionist cousin, Gerrit Smith, in Peterboro (Madison Co). There Elizabeth Cady was introduced to New York State's radical reform community and in 1839 to abolitionist orator Henry Brewster Stanton.

Marriage, Abolition, and Women's Rights

Despite her family's disapproval she married Henry Stanton on 1 May 1840, and they honeymooned at the World's Anti-Slavery Convention in London. Elizabeth Cady Stanton, witnessing the convention's rejection of some American delegates because they were women, began a friendship with one of them, Quaker abolitionist Lucretia Mott, who exposed Stanton to emerging ideas on women's equality. Despite bearing three sons between 1842 and 1845, Stanton circulated petitions and—while visiting her parents in New York State—lobbied in Albany for married women's property rights. In 1847 the Stantons left Henry Stanton's Boston law practice and moved to Seneca Falls (Seneca Co), where Henry hoped to make a name in party politics. Cut off from her urban reform circle and confined domestically, Elizabeth turned to activism. In summer 1848 in Seneca Falls, acting on ideas that were circulating within multiple reform communities, Stanton, Lucretia Mott, and a group of local women organized the first women's rights convention in the United States. Stanton drafted the convention's treatise, the Declaration of Sentiments, to demand social, religious, economic, professional, and political equality for women. After the convention Stanton returned to domestic life, giving birth to four more children between 1851 and 1859 and rarely speaking in public during the 1850s. Then prodded by Susan B. Anthony, a young temperance organizer who would become Stanton's lifelong reform partner, Stanton began to use her pen to articulate a theory of women's equality based on the political philosophy of natural rights. She also advocated dress reform, temperance, divorce reform, coeducation, married women's property rights, and woman suffrage.

War, Universal Suffrage, and Schism

As the Civil War began, Stanton moved to New York City, and she would live in this area for much of the remainder of her life. During the conflict she joined other activists in setting aside women's rights for abolition. Convinced that their antislavery efforts would be reciprocated with Republican and abolitionist support for woman suffrage, Stanton and Anthony formed the Women's Loyal National League and gathered 400,000 petition signatures to secure the 13th Amendment's passage. After the war Stanton, Anthony, Lucy Stone, and other abolitionists formed the American Equal Rights Association (AERA), which sought suffrage for all Americans regardless of gender or race. Although denied the right to vote, Stanton ran for Congress as an Independent from New York City's Eighth District in 1866, receiving only 24 votes. In 1867 she and Anthony petitioned the New York State Constitutional Convention for woman suffrage. After the New York defeat and with abolitionist and Republican hostility to woman suffrage, Stanton and Anthony accepted the help of an eccentric, racist millionaire, Democrat George Francis Train, in stumping Kansas for woman suffrage. Many friends and allies blamed this association with Train for the defeat of both the woman and black suffrage referenda in Kansas on the November ballot. Stanton further alienated other reformers by opposing the 15th Amendment, which granted the vote to black men, because it did not enfranchise women. At this period she employed racist arguments to justify suffrage for white women, particularly in editorials in her short-lived newspaper, the *Revolution,* funded by Train; later in the century she would return to a more egalitarian rhetoric. In May 1869 Stanton and Anthony left AERA to form the National Woman Suffrage Association, while 15th Amendment supporters like Lucy Stone formed the American Woman Suffrage Association.

Radicalism and Religion

Stanton continued to advocate for women's social, religious, and political equality through the remainder of her life. Increasingly independent of her husband, adult children, and Anthony, Stanton spent the 1870s on lecture tours using her wit and maternal demeanor to mask her speeches' controversial focus on the necessity for women's legal, physical, sexual, and spiritual autonomy. Despite Stanton's frequent absences she and Anthony shared leadership of the National Woman Suffrage Association. In the 1880s–1890s, after a decade of separate endeavors, Stanton and Anthony collaborated on a series of joint projects: writing the massive three-volume *History of Woman Suffrage* (1880–86); uniting women's rights movements across the globe in the International Council of Women (1888); and again petitioning a New York State Constitutional Convention to enfranchise women (1894). This spirit of unity extended to rival US organizations that merged as the National American Woman Suffrage Association (NAWSA) in 1890. To please Anthony the younger suffragists elected Stanton president of the association for two years, even though she disapproved of its conservative focus on suffrage alone. Notwithstanding these collaborations Stanton increasingly pursued her own religious interests. Believing that religion was largely to blame for women's oppression, she published *The Woman's Bible* in 1895. Part biblical commentary, part women's rights polemic, and shockingly controversial in challenging biblical and clerical authority, it was publicly denounced by NAWSA in 1896. Radical to the end Stanton was the first philosopher of the women's rights movement and its most eloquent writer and speaker. Among her seven children was Harriet Stanton Blatch, who also became a national leader of the suffragist movement.

Banner, Lois W. *Elizabeth Cady Stanton: A Radical for Woman's Rights* (Boston: Little, Brown, 1980)
DuBois, Ellen Carol. *Feminism and Suffrage: The Emergence of an Independent Women's Movement in America, 1848–1869* (Ithaca: Cornell Univ Press, 1978)
Griffith, Elizabeth. *In Her Own Right: The Life of Elizabeth Cady Stanton* (New York: Oxford Univ Press, 1984)
Stanton, Elizabeth Cady. *Eighty Years and More: Reminiscences, 1815–1897* (1898; repr, frwd Ellen Carol DuBois, Boston: Northeastern Univ Press, 1993)

Laura E. Free

Starin, John H(enry) (*b* Sammonsville [now in Fulton Co], 27 Aug 1825; *d* New York City, 21 Mar 1909). Entrepreneur. The son of Myndaert Starin, a factory owner who developed Fultonville [now in Fulton Co] and ran boats on the Mohawk River, and Rachel Sammons Starin, John received an academy education at Esperance (Schoharie Co). After studying medicine in Albany, he opened a drugstore in Fultonville, where he was also postmaster (1848–52). In 1856 he moved to New York City to manufacture medicines but soon shifted to the transportation of goods, acquiring a large fleet of harbor and river vessels. He was a major contractor for the movement of troops and supplies through the Port of New York during the Civil War. In the 1860s Cornelius Vanderbilt hired him to organize lighterage of goods for the New York Central Railroad. A Republican, he served two terms in the House of Representatives (1877–81). By the 1880s Starin had the nation's largest privately owned fleet of working vessels, including car floats for moving freight cars, and handled goods within New York Harbor for most major railroads.

During this era Starin also entered the excursion business, acquiring steamboats and barges capable of transporting thousands, as well as shoreside picnic grounds on Staten Island and along Long Island Sound. Most celebrated was internationally themed Glen Island Park in New Rochelle (Westchester Co), which featured a "Chinese" pagoda, a "Dutch" windmill, and "Little Germany's" stone castles. At the beginning of the 21st century, New Rochelle owns and manages Glen Island Park and continues to maintain the castles. Starin was president of Fultonville National Bank for more than 25 years and a member of the New York City Rapid Transit Commission.

Norman Brouwer

Stark. Town (pop 767) in SE Herkimer Co. Settled before the Revolutionary War, the town was formed from Danube in 1828. In the 19th century its economy centered on grain, hops, and dairy farming. At Van Hornesville were a number of small industries, including a furnace (1827), a cotton factory (1836) of 900 spindles, and a cigar factory. Owen D. Young (1874–1962), chairman of the board of General Electric and *Time* magazine "Man of the Year" in 1929, was a native of Van Hornesville and considered it his home. Owen D. Young Central School (1926) was among the early wave of school consolidations in New York State. Stark is home to the Van Hornesville State Fish Hatchery. In the early 21st century dairy farming remains the predominant land use.

Susan R. Perkins

Starkey. Town (pop 3,465) in SE Yates Co. Settled in ?1797, the town was formed from Reading (Schuyler Co) in 1824. Although there were several woolen factories and a shop producing carriages, sleighs, and threshing machines, farming always predominated, with a barley market at the Starkey Station malt house and both large and small fruit grown along the lake. Starkey was served by the Northern Central (1851) and Fall Brook (1877) Railroads and by Seneca Lake steamboats. In 1894 there were 65 vineyards. The hamlet of Glenora was then a resort for Elmirans. Starkey Seminary (1842–1936) was a preparatory school that reopened as Lakemont Academy in 1939. In 1981 Fletcher Brothers, pastor of Gates Community Chapel, purchased the campus and began development of Freedom Village, a home for troubled youth. Glenora Wine Cellars (1977) was the first winery opened in the state under the 1976 farm winery bill. In the early 21st century, Starkey is home to a large number of Groffdale Conference Mennonites.

Gwen Chamberlain

St. Armand. Town (pop 1,321) in NW Essex Co. Settled in 1829 the town was formed in 1844 from Wilmington. Lumbering reached its peak in the 1850s but declined by 1880 after the best timber had been harvested. The residents turned to farming, tourism, and sanatorium and service work. As of 2002 some farming and extensive outdoor recreational businesses are the area's economic bases.

Thomas A. Rumney

state aid to schools. New York State provided funds for public education beginning with the approval of grants for private academies (1789) and common schools (1795), although the latter policy failed after five years for lack of sufficient funds and political support. In 1805 the legislature planned a series of lotteries to build up a large state endowment, the interest of which could allow annual appropriations for common schools. By 1812 the fund had grown sufficiently to enable the passage of the Common School Law, which promised annual disbursement of state aid from a large, permanent school fund, including a requirement that school districts levy local property taxes to equal the state grant. In separate legislation that year, the state sent block grants to private and church organizations that operated poor schools in New York City.

While common schools spread rapidly across the state in the early 19th century, from 2,756 districts in 1815 to 10,769 in 1843, the state and local districts made no provision for economic disparities among districts or among students. Not only did each district have to pay for its own school buildings, because the state fund could be used for instruction only, but in rural districts the state grant often could not fund a full 10-week academic term even when met halfway by local tax. When the money ran out, districts either closed schools or charged tuition, called rate bills, on a per diem basis. Advocates of free schooling complained that tuition kept poor children away from schools, and the legislature banned rate bills in 1867. Inequities among districts with high tax bases and low tax bases remained, however, requiring residents of districts with low property values to pay high tax rates for poor-quality schools.

In the 20th century, the legislature made three major attempts at redressing inequities in funding for public education. In 1902 the Department of Public Instruction moderately increased the rate of aid to districts it classified as having low tax bases (assessed valuation of $40,000 or less), adding $25 to the base state grant of $125 per district. In 1925 the legislature enacted the Cole-Rice Law, which set a minimum acceptable per-pupil expenditure, initially $44 for an elementary pupil and $73 for a secondary pupil, and promised that the state would enable all districts making the required tax effort to meet that target. The legislature overhauled Cole-Rice in 1962, replacing it with a sliding scale of state aid based on the ratio of a district's wealth to the state average, offering state aid for 25–75% of a district's expenditures.

State aid continues to follow the pattern developed in the 1960s. The State Education Department distributes aid to schools in three categories. The first, general aid, considers a district's ability to pay per-pupil expenses and allocates funds in an attempt to equalize spending differences among districts. The second category makes flat allocations for students with disabilities. The third targets a variety of fiscal priorities, such as grants for students with limited English proficiency, textbooks, talented and gifted programs, and incentives to reward low-wealth districts that impose high property taxes on themselves. State aid still remains lower than local property tax, however, and constituted 46% of all sources of revenue for New York State public schools in the 2000–2001 school year. Districts identified as low wealth receive as much as five times the per-pupil state aid as wealthy districts but still manage to spend much less per pupil because their tax bases are so low. In 2000 the per-pupil expenditure in New York State was nearly $11,000. Even with state aid, large cities and "high need" rural areas spent about $10,000 per pupil, while wealthy "low need" districts spent $13,000 per pupil.

In 1997 New York State spent $26.565 billion for elementary and secondary public schools. Local funding covered 55% of that amount, the state 39%, the federal government 5%, and private sources 1%. Of those state funds, in 1998, 90% came from the general fund (income and sales tax) and 10% from the special revenue fund (financed by the state lottery). That money was disbursed as unrestricted general aid (61%), categorical aid (24%), and aid for students with disabilities (15%).

Since the 1970s state aid has faced strong challenges in court. In 1976 Levittown (Nassau Co) and 30 other districts in New York State filed a complaint in state court, charging that the state system of school finance failed not only to provide equal educational services for districts of low wealth but to address the challenge of high-cost education in urban schools. Despite a favorable 1978 state supreme court decision, the *Levittown v Nyquist* plaintiffs lost on appeal in 1982. The Court of Appeals argued that the state constitution, approved in 1894, had not envisioned educational equity as a feature of public education but had instead intended only that each district meet a minimum standard. That interpretation was challenged in January 2001 when a state judge declared in *Campaign for Fiscal Equity, Inc v State of New York* that the education provided by New York City fell below the constitutional minimum and pointed to state actions as a major cause. Advocates have continued to seek state aid reform, but each of the three most feasible options—taking money from affluent suburbs, raising statewide taxes, or making cities themselves pay more—faces strong political challenges.

Berke, Joel S., Margaret E. Goertz, and Richard J. Coley. *Politicians, Judges, and City Schools: Reforming School Finance in New York* (New York: Russell Sage Foundation, 1984)

New York State Education Department, State Aid Work Group. *Improving the Formulas to Help Students Meet State Learning Standards: The Regents Proposal on State Aid to School Districts for School Year 2002–2003* (Albany, 11 Dec 2001)

Benjamin Justice

state borders. Approximately 1,430 miles (2,300 km) of land and water boundaries enclosing New York State's distinctive configuration evolved from numerous disputes with neighbors whose colonial charters gave rise to conflicting territorial grants. Boundary controversies were settled by royal commissions during the colonial period and by joint commissions after the US Constitution (Art 1, §10, permitted states (only with congressional consent) to enter into agreements and compacts.

EARLY CLAIMS, THE WEST, AND CANADA

Early European claims to the ultimate territory of New York State appeared in the first charters of Acadia (1603) and Virginia (1606). New Netherland was bounded by the watersheds of the Fresh (Connecticut), South (Delaware), and North (Hudson) Rivers. Under the 1629 Charter of Freedoms and Exemptions, patroons could extend their holdings 4 leagues (19 km) along one side of a river or 2 leagues (10 km) on both sides and could move farther inland as far as population allowed. Charles II's 1664 grant to his brother James, Duke of York, assumed the Dutch claim. It also included the Maine coast from Pemaquid to the St. Croix River (Cornwall Co, ceded to the Dominion of New England in 1686) and Nantucket, Martha's Vineyard, and adjacent islands (Dukes Co, ceded to Massachusetts in 1691). After a 1684 treaty with the Iroquois, New York Colony claimed the inhabited lands and hunting grounds of the Iroquois and their tributary peoples, potentially stretching to the Mississippi and Tennessee Rivers. A royal decree in 1763, following the French and Indian War, established the northern border at 45° N. Gov William Tryon in 1774 specifically claimed the lands between 42° and 45° N, west to the Detroit River, a 650 mi long (1,050 km) rectangle that included southern Ontario.

In 1781 New York ceded to Congress all its land claims beyond the western extremity of Lake Ontario (which American surveyors determined in 1789 was at 79°45'54" W), retaining claims to the Niagara peninsula and lands north to 45° N. The Treaty of Paris (1783), ending the Revolutionary War, established the US-Canadian border through the St. Lawrence and Niagara Rivers and Lakes Ontario and Erie, nullifying New York State's claims to the Niagara Peninsula and other parts of Ontario. East of the St. Lawrence, the border remained at 45° N. American authorities discovered in 1818, however, that a 1774 survey had put the eastern end of that line 4,200 feet (1,280 m) too far north (45°0'42" N), placing the new US Fort Montgomery at Rouses Point (Clinton Co) in Canada. The Webster-Ashburton Treaty (1842) between the United States and Britain corrected the error.

SOUTHERN AND EASTERN BOUNDARIES

Although having no legal claim to lands west of Delaware Bay, the duke of York claimed the area by right of conquest as it had been occupied and surrendered to him by the Dutch. In 1682 he ceded these claims to William Penn's Colony of Pennsylvania. Penn's 1681 charter put the border at the Delaware River and 42° N latitude straight west to Lake Erie. After New York ceded its western claims, Congress sold the Erie Triangle (north of 42° N and west of 79°45'54" W) to Pennsylvania, giving it a port on the Great Lakes.

In 1664 the duke of York conveyed to two joint proprietors the portion of his grant between the Hudson and Delaware Rivers, which became known as New Jersey. He set the land boundary along a straight line from the Hudson at 41° N latitude to the northernmost branch of the Delaware at 41°40' N. Because the designated branch did not extend that far, a royal commission in 1769 ruled that the river, not the latitude, was the intended border, setting the western point at 41°21'37" N. Later surveys determined it was 41°21'22.6" N. On the east, New Jersey was bounded by the Hudson River and the ocean, and it unsuccessfully claimed Staten Island as being between itself and the ocean. In 1806 New Jersey renewed its claim to Staten Island and to jurisdiction over a portion of the Hudson. The two states agreed in 1834 to a border that ran through the Hudson, Upper New York Bay, Kill Van Kull, Arthur Kill (Staten Island Sound), and Raritan Bay, with each controlling the fisheries and land under the water on its side and with New York retaining the islands and waters of the Hudson River and New York Bay up to the low-water mark on the western shore, except wharves, docks, improvements, and vessels attached thereto. New York quarantine law applied on Kill Van Kull and Arthur Kill north of Woodbridge Creek. New Jersey had sole jurisdiction over the waters of Raritan Bay and Arthur Kill south of Woodbridge Creek, except wharves, docks, improvements, and vessels attached thereto on Staten Island. The US Supreme Court in *State of New Jersey v State of New York* (1998) granted New Jersey the landfill additions made to Ellis Island after 1834, which constituted most of the island.

Charles II granted Connecticut land west to the Pacific Ocean. The duke of York's proprietary extended east to the Connecticut River, sparking continual disputes and arrests of each other's settlers and officials. In 1683 the two colonies agreed in principle to a boundary running 20 miles (32 km) east of the Hudson River, and New York Colony ceded 61,440 acres (24,864 ha) on Long Island Sound (the "Panhandle"), already settled by New Englanders in return for a comparable strip along the border to the north (the "Oblong"). The duke's grant also included Long Island, which Connecticut had previously claimed, and specific islands in Long Island Sound, including Fishers Island off New London, Conn. On that basis, New York State asserted a claim to all the islands and waters up to the Connecticut shore. Connecticut ceded the islands specifically granted but claimed the northern waters of Long Island Sound for itself. In 1880 the two states divided the Sound's waters between them. Massachusetts's west-to-the-Pacific claim also caused trouble in the mid-1700s. Commissioners appointed by Congress settled the border in 1785, following the Connecticut precedent, at a line 20 miles east of the Hudson. The Hartford Treaty (1786) settled the claims of Massachusetts to land in western New York State. In 1853 Massachusetts ceded Boston Corner [now in Columbia Co], a tract in Mount Washington adjacent to New York State but separated from the rest of Massachusetts by a mountain. After the French and Indian War, New Hampshire and New York claimed Vermont, leading to armed clashes among rival titleholders. When Vermont declared independence in 1777, it claimed both shores of Lake Champlain and land west to the Hudson River. In 1790, to ease its entry into the union, it, too, accepted the Connecticut precedent of a line 20 miles east of the Hudson and ran the border through the lake. New York State and Rhode Island divided Block Island Sound in 1887 and reconfirmed the partitioning in 1944. The US Supreme Court in *United States v Maine et al* (1985), however, limited state jurisdiction to waters west of a line from Montauk Point (Suffolk Co) to Watch Hill Point, RI, leaving most of Block Island Sound in federal jurisdiction or open seas.

French, J. H. *Gazetteer of the State of New York* (1860; repr Port Washington, NY: Ira J. Friedman, 1969)

State of New York. *Report of the Regents of the University on the Boundaries of the State of New York,* 2 vols (Albany: Argus, 1874, 1884)

Van Zandt, Franklin K. *Boundaries of the United States and the Several States* (Washington, DC: Government Printing Office, 1966)

Scott C. Monje

State Capitol Building. Albany was designated the state capital in 1797, but because no state-owned building existed at the time, the legislature convened in City Hall, also called the Stadt Huys. The first official capitol building was designed by Philip Hooker, completed by 1809, and owned by the city. Albany's common council, the state supreme court, assembly, and senate used the building. Called State Hall, it had a library room and an arts society. It featured a front portico, was referred to as Grecian-Roman composite in style, and had a cupola ornamented with a wooden statue of Themis, the Greek goddess of justice. Construction was a joint expenditure of the city, county, and state. In 1829 the city sold the building to the state for $17,500. In 1831 the city government moved out. As state government became more diverse, Hooker's structure was inadequate, and state leaders often conducted their business in Congress Hall and the Delevan House, two Albany hotels. State Hall was demolished in 1883.

Construction of a larger state capitol began in 1867 and was completed in stages by 1899 at a cost of more than $25 million. Thomas Fuller served as the first architect. He planned an Italian Renaissance structure, but after nine years completed only two floors and was discharged. The state commissioned H. H. Richardson, Frederick Law Olmsted, and Leopold Eidlitz to carry on design. Because of engineering and financial problems, the capitol project often stopped. Binghamton architect Isaac Perry took over management in 1883. The structure has five stories and is built of gray granite. Because the designs changed with each architect, the exterior styles are French Renaissance, Italian Renaissance, and Romanesque.

The largest room, the Moorish Gothic assembly chamber, opened in 1879. Its vaulted 56 ft (17 m) groined sandstone ceiling was lowered in 1888 after rock fell, nearly hitting an assemblyman. The western staircase is the most significant interior feature. Called the Million Dollar Staircase, it was designed by Richardson and took 14 years to complete. It features pink-hued Corsehill sandstone imported from Scotland. Seventy-seven faces were carved into the stairs, including those of Susan B. Anthony, George Washington, and James Fenimore Cooper. Richardson designed the senate chamber, which has paneled, carved golden oak and paneled mahogany walls. Over 1,000 flags are encased in the Flag Room, from the Civil War to the World War II era. A fire on 29 Mar 1911 damaged the staircase and the skylight and destroyed irreplaceable archival documents housed in the library. In 1971 the building was listed on the state historic register, and in 1979 it was designated a National Historic Landmark. In 1998 the New York State Commission on the Restoration of the Capitol oversaw exterior masonry restoration. In 2000 an $8.23 million project to restore the terra-cotta roof and skylight got underway. Other restoration projects include renovations in the legislative law library, a lighting project, and the preservation of paintings.

New York State. Assembly. *Tour of the Capitol* (Albany, 2002)

Waite, Diana S., ed. *Albany Architecture* (Albany: Mount Ida Press, 1993)

Tricia A. Barbagallo

state debt. See BONDED INDEBTEDNESS; MORAL OBLIGATION DEBT.

State Emergency Management Office (SEMO). Coordinates emergency management services with other federal and state agencies to support county and local governments and provides administrative and program support to the Disaster Preparedness Commission, the governor's policy management group for the state's emergency management program. SEMO's origins date to the New York State Defense Emergency Act of 1951, which led to the creation of the Office of Natural Disaster and Civil Defense Preparedness, with a focus in its early years on preparation for nuclear attack. In 1973 the agency became the Office of Disaster Preparedness, a response to Hurricane Agnes (1972), which highlighted the need for a more comprehensive emergency preparedness program. The renaming in 1983 to State Emergency Management Office reflects the broader focus of preparing for and responding to all natural, technological, and human-generated hazards affecting New York State.

SEMO routinely assists local governments, volunteer organizations, and private industry through a variety of emergency management programs. These programs involve hazard identification, loss prevention, planning, training, operational response to emergencies, technical support, and disaster recovery assistance. In times of emergency or disaster, SEMO coordinates the response of all state agencies, ensuring that the most appropriate resources are dispatched to the impacted area. State agencies, such as State Police, Departments of Transportation and Health, and National Guard, are activated in accordance with the State Comprehensive Emergency Management Plan. From 1995 to early 2002, SEMO coordinated the response and recovery efforts in 20 federally declared emergencies or disasters, including the January 1998 ice storm and the terrorist attack on the World Trade Center on 11 Sept 2001. At the height of the World Trade Center response, more than 30 state agencies and nearly 17,000 agency personnel and volunteers were involved. SEMO helped coordinate the flow of information from the scene, working closely with New York City, and provided that information to the governor and the governor's Office of State Operations. SEMO coordinated the completion of more than 800 requests for state assistance from New York City and developed and initially managed the massive donated goods program to support the specific needs of the city at Ground Zero and other locations. In the 2001–2 fiscal year, SEMO had a budget of $19.4 million and a staff of approximately 100 people. Headquartered in Albany, it has five regional offices, located in Hauppauge, Newark, Poughkeepsie, Queensbury, and Syracuse.

New York State Emergency Management Office, http://www.nysemo.state.ny.us

Dennis J. Michalski

state flag. See STATE SEAL AND STATE FLAG.

state government and services. The government structure in New York State is shaped by the state constitution, which defines the powers of government and those who may exert its authority. The state's first constitution, promulgated in 1777, placed sovereign authority in the people, declaring "that no authority shall, on any presence whatever, be exercised over the people or members of this State but such as shall be derived from and granted by them." The sovereignty of the people remains the political theory underlying the exercise of power in the state. Government power is exerted at a number of levels: federal, state, county, city, borough, town, and village.

The New York State government, like the federal government, separates power among executive, legislative, and judicial branches, each of which has its own responsibilities but has some authority to check, or limit, the powers of the other branches. Unlike the federal government, which has only one elected head of the executive branch (the president), New York State's executive branch has multiple, independently selected executives: governor, attorney general, comptroller, and commissioner of the Education Department. The legislative structure is bicameral, and the legislature is composed of an assembly (lower house) and senate (upper house). The judicial branch includes courts at both the local and state levels, and the Court of Appeals is the state's highest court. Public authorities, or benefit corporations, are created by the legislature to administer distinct functions such as maintenance of the New York State Thruway or economic development projects.

Evolution of Services

At the time of the American Revolution, New York State outside of New York City was sparsely populated and predominately agrarian. State government provided few services directly affecting citizens that are associated with it since the 20th century. One recognizable service was defense, as provided through existence of the state militia. The state's role in shaping the landscape and providing internal improvements also significantly affected New Yorkers. From 1777 the state surveyor general was responsible for surveying lands vested in the state after the American Revolution. State funding for the Erie and other canals in the early and middle 19th century and subsidies to railroad corporations notably, if often indirectly, shaped the lives of residents. But much of the work of state government through the 19th century was focused on regulation, such as supervising banks operating in the state from the 1820s, and administration, such as chartering corporations established in the state or operating the canals that state funds had helped build.

For most of the century following the American Revolution, though, local governments had sole responsibility for such basic public services as police protection, fire prevention, public health, and welfare. By the end of the 19th century, the larger city governments were seriously challenged to keep pace with their burgeoning populations and increasingly manufacturing-dominated market economies. The New York City government, for example, could not satisfy the demands of its residents for protection against crime, for clean streets, and for the regulation of markets and wharves. The state government responded to an array of such problems by expanding its own scope of services to urban and rural areas statewide.

Services in the Progressive Era and New Deal

The 1911 Triangle Shirtwaist Factory fire in New York City was the catalyst for pathbreaking state legislation regulating hours and working conditions in textile plants, garment shops, and other industries, and providing workers' compensation for victims of industrial accidents. These reforms were shepherded through the legislature by Sen Robert F. Wagner Sr and Assemblyman Alfred E. Smith, who led a commission to investigate the Triangle Shirtwaist fire. While later serving as governor, Smith promoted restructuring of the executive branch, changes, including creation of an executive budget, that ultimately strengthened the governor's position in proposing and executing the state's policy agenda. Wagner, who was elected to the US Senate in 1926, went on to champion labor reform legislation for protection of workers at the national level.

New York State's social welfare legislation also became a model for national programs. Franklin D. Roosevelt, elected governor in 1928 and 1930, strongly endorsed such reforms as state government responsibility for relief for "state poor" (homeless paupers), county welfare districts (to supersede town and city) to administer income transfer payments ("home relief"), and a system of contributory old-age insurance. The first two reforms were adopted by the state legislature in 1929. As president during the depths of the Great Depression, Roosevelt successfully persuaded the Congress to adopt the Social Security Act of 1935. This act not only expanded on the 1929 New York State law by establishing national responsibility for poor families in the Aid to Families with Dependent Children (AFDC) program, it also incorporated an old-age insurance system similar to the one Roosevelt had earlier endorsed. The New York State Constitutional Convention of 1938 further strengthened the state's responsibility for meeting the social welfare needs of New Yorkers. Thereafter, Article 17 of the state constitution mandated the affirmative duty of the state to provide for the "aid, care, and support of the needy."

Direct Services since 1945

The New York State government assumes primary responsibility for a broad range of services including state police and state prisons, the state university system, registration of motor vehicles, drivers' licensing, highway maintenance, and tax collection and enforcement. Such services are delivered to residents in two distinct ways. The first is by state employees, such as faculty of the State University of New York (SUNY), guards in the state's prisons, and nurses and therapists in the state's psychiatric hospitals and institutions for people with developmental disabilities. The second is by nonprofit or for-profit agencies under contract with such state agencies as the Office of Mental Retardation and Developmental Disabilities to operate residential homes and the Department of Labor to provide job-training programs.

Approximately one-third of the total state budget is allocated for direct state services, a proportion that has been fairly steady since the 1970s. "State Operations," as they are categorized in the annual budget document, are used to fund both line and staff agencies in the executive branch. Line agencies deliver services, directly or through nonprofit organizations, while staff agencies perform control functions. The Department of Correctional Services, with responsibility for the secure confinement of convicted felons in more than 70 facilities, is a line agency. So, too, is the Department of Taxation and Finance, which estimates revenues generated by personal income, business income, sales, and other state taxes, administers those taxes, and manages the State Treasury. The Division of the Budget and the Department of Civil Service are staff agencies; their roles cut across all executive branch agencies. The Division of the Budget, because it is responsible for ensuring that agencies spend funds allocated to them for specified purposes and for monitoring revenue and expenditure projections of all executive agencies, is at the very center of executive branch operations. The Department of Civil Service, charged with maintaining the merit system of personnel selection and promotion that pertains to both state and local government in New York State, is also a key staff agency. In sum, the services solely funded and administered by the state government to New Yorkers are numerous and diverse. Such services, however, pale in comparison to those delivered by local governments.

Eastern facade of the State Capitol, Albany, early 20th century.

State and Local Services since 1945

New York State's local governments are the major delivery units of public services to residents. Their service obligations, higher than those of most states, together with state mandates and restraints, explain why the state's local tax burden is heavy. State mandates, which are legal orders that emanate from the state constitution, state laws, or regulations, cover such policy areas as environmental protection, employment, and civil rights. State restraints, such as tax limits and competitive bidding requirements, constrain local governments from undertaking or continuing certain actions. Thus, the types of services local governments provide and the costs they bear for those services are framed by mandates and restraints. Counties (outside of New York City), for example, are required to administer and partially fund local welfare, social services, and health programs. Towns, cities (other than New York City), and villages are restrained from providing those services. However, counties, towns, cities, and villages are all permitted under state laws to provide public safety, solid waste disposal, parks, and transportation services. Special-purpose local governments such as school, water, sewer, and fire protection districts are limited to the performance of a single public service function.

The provision of local services is further complicated by the existence of many different service delivery and financing arrangements in the state. Nassau Co, Monroe Co, and the Port Authority of New York and New Jersey offer examples of countywide and regional approaches to service delivery. Since 1925 Nassau Co has provided the full range of police services to most of the county's cities, villages, and towns. Monroe Co, which includes Rochester, has assumed full responsibility since 1947 for financing and delivering 22 services—ranging from pure water to zoos to emergency communication to a public library—formerly provided by the Rochester city government. The Port Authority, the first agency in the nation created by interstate compact (1921), operates airports, a bus terminal and marine terminals, a mass transit system, and bridges and tunnels in the New York City metropolitan area.

In contrast, the Metropolitan Regional Planning Council, endorsed by New York City mayor Robert F. Wagner Jr in 1956 as a voluntary vehicle for coordinated planning land use among 21 counties in New York State, New Jersey, and Connecticut, failed to attain permanent status. The promising start of the council's work was overcome by assertions of local autonomy and fear of New York City domination. A 1964 proposed interlocal agreement for formal legal status for the council, including revenues from local property assessments, was doomed when New York City and Nassau, Suffolk, and Westchester—the largest counties in the region—failed to ratify it.

The single, largest public service expenditure in New York State is elementary and secondary education. Nearly 3 million children were enrolled in the state's public elementary and secondary schools in fall 2002 at a total cost of more than $35 billion. New York State's 701 local school districts (as of 2002–3) play a primary, though not exclusive, role in educational financing, administration, and policy making. Subject to authority delegated by the state and within policy parameters established by the State Board of Regents, local districts have power to determine curriculum, employ and evaluate teachers, select textbooks, collect taxes, incur debt, and provide transportation. Local districts, acting through boards of education, are directly accountable to voters (in the case of fiscally independent school districts) or to city governments (in the case of fiscally dependent school districts). Depending on the size of the city, the voters or city governments are empowered by state law to approve annual operating and capital budgets, including the determination of local property tax rates.

In 1998–99, 53% of public elementary and secondary education revenues came from local sources (nearly exclusively the property tax), 43% from the state government, and 4% from the federal government. Although these school aid proportions fluctuated annually during the 1990s, they were almost the same at the end of the decade as at the beginning. However, when state government reimbursements to local school districts for foregone revenues from state-enacted property tax relief (the STAR program) were included, the state contribution increased in 2002 to 46% of local district expenditures, and the local contribution decreased to 50%.

New York State's school districts vary widely in terms of student need and local property tax capacity. The average statewide expenditure per student in 1998–99 was about $10,000, but this average masked a range among districts of less than $8,000 to more than $14,000. New York City and the large city districts of Buffalo, Rochester, Syracuse, and Yonkers (the Big Five) have the highest concentrations of low-income children. Poor children are less likely to attend good preschool programs and to perform well in school, and more likely to drop out, become teenage parents, and be unemployed. The Big Five school districts have the fewest fiscal resources, and their teachers have the weakest credentials. In contrast, rural and urban-suburban (in metropolitan areas) school districts have fewer children living in poverty and higher per student property tax bases. The State Department of Education has demonstrated that students in these districts perform better on standardized tests, are more likely to earn Regents diplomas, and more likely to attend college. It is clear that the inverse relationship between student need and district fiscal resources compromises the ability of local school districts to perform effectively their historical role of providing elementary and secondary education.

Federal-State Relations since 1945

At the start of the 20th century, most government activity in the United States was funded and administered at the local level. By 1950 the federal government had become the dominant provider, at 60% of total general administrative expenditures. Federal spending continued to dominate at the end of the century. The extent of that dominance, however, has varied by policy area. For example, responsibility for national defense, foreign policy, postal service, and space research has always been the exclusive province of the federal government. State and local governments have consistently assumed the major share of public education, highways, and public safety costs. Funding for welfare, health, housing and urban renewal, and highway programs, however, gradually shifted during the 20th century from exclusive state and local responsibility to partnership, with the national level as the "senior partner." Using intergovernmental grants-in-aid as incentives, the federal government induced state and local governments to establish or expand programs in all of these policy areas. The increased federal role is evident from the perspective of federal intergovernmental grants-in-aid as a proportion of total state and local government expenditures. In 1955, 10% of state and local government spending came from federal sources; by 2000, the percentage had tripled to 31%.

In 2000 the federal government spent $110 billion in New York State, which was 7% of its total expenditures in all 50 states. Given that 18.9 million New York State residents accounted for 7% of the nation's population in 2000, the state, overall, received a fair share of federal spending. In fact, since the mid-1970s per capita federal expenditures in New York State have been very close to the national average. The pattern of federal spending within New York State, however, is dramatically different from that of the nation as a whole. Direct federal spending for procurement and contract awards and for salaries and wages of federal employees in the state, including armed forces personnel, is consistently lower than the national average. Indirect spending, in contrast, through grants to state and local governments, is consistently higher. In 2000, for example, New York State ranked close to the bottom among the states in federal per capita spending for salaries and wages. At the same time, it was among the top states in federal per capita spending for grants to state and local governments, a ranking largely driven by Medicaid spending.

Medicaid, a federal-state health insurance program, was a major component of the Great Society programs. Enacted by Congress in 1965 to meet the healthcare needs of the poor, Medicaid by the end of the 20th century had been divided into four programs: health insurance for children and adults in low-income families, long-term care for low-income elderly persons receiving nursing home or community-based services, health insurance for low-income persons with disabilities who do not have Medicare coverage, and supplementary insurance to Medicare.

Unlike many states, New York already had a well-established set of publicly funded health programs in place in 1965. For example, the state legislature had established the Metropolitan Board of Health to regulate public sanitation in New York City 100 years earlier; rural health departments were authorized in the 1920s; nonprofit hospitals were transformed into publicly funded municipal acute-care institutions during the Great Depression; and local governments began to subsidize group health insurance costs for municipal employees in New York City in 1944 under Mayor Fiorello La Guardia.

Immediately after Medicaid became law, Gov Nelson A. Rockefeller urged the legislature to approve New York State's participation in this national program. He viewed Medicaid as the vehicle with which to expand health services for New Yorkers and to procure larger amounts of federal aid than were available to New Yorkers under the prior public health programs. New York State differs from other states—where the state government alone bears the nonfederal share of Medicaid (as well as welfare and social services)—with Medicaid spending shared by federal, state, and local governments. The federal share has historically been 50%, the state share about 35%, and the local share about 15%. The federal government matches each state and local dollar expended on this entitlement program.

Medicaid is the largest single federal grant-in-aid program in New York State, accounting in 2000 for 53% of all federal grant dollars to its state and local governments. New York has long led the nation in both absolute and relative spending for Medicaid, spending $32.5 billion on 3.1 million recipients in 2001. In contrast, California, with 80% more recipients (5.6 million), spent $25.7 billion. In per recipient terms, New York State has long spent twice the average of the rest of the states on Medicaid. The state's Medicaid expenditures are high for several reasons, including the state's above-average share of the aged, the disabled, and persons with AIDS and drug-abuse problems, higher costs for healthcare practitioners (except physicians), and compliance with state regulations. The high expenditures are also related to its policy choices of generous income eligibility levels and a much wider array of optional or nonmandated services than those offered in most other states.

The interplay of government jurisdictions shapes an array of other government services. The sorting-out of federal, state, and local responsibilities following Republican control of the Congress in 1994 has been called the Devolution Revolution. New York State's 57 county governments along with that of New York City, for example, were directly affected by the Personal Responsibility and Work Opportunity Reconciliation Act of 1996, the federal welfare reform initiative. These governments are mandated to administer income maintenance programs and to share the costs with the state government. Counties assume 25% of benefits paid to federal TANF (Temporary Aid to Needy Families) recipients and 50% of those for Safety Net (state-local) recipients. County and New York City governments have almost no discretion over eligibility for cash programs and amount of benefits, but they do have substantial flexibility in program design. By reorganizing the welfare bureaucracy and tailoring programs to meet local workforce needs under welfare reform, these bodies have exercised considerable autonomy in enforcing the law's work requirements and other rules affecting the behavior of TANF recipients.

Services in the 21st Century

During the 1990s the state's financial condition was strong. Multiple-year tax cuts, initiated by Gov George E. Pataki after taking office in 1995, and increased spending by the state government for education, corrections, and Medicaid were offset by revenues generated by a strong economy. The events of 11 Sept 2001 changed the fiscal situation dramatically. The terrorist attacks on the World Trade Center resulted in great human loss and extensive property damage and economic harm. Because the national economy had already been slowing at the time the attacks occurred, the consequences were intense for state and local (particularly New York City) governments. A significant drop in revenues from state personal taxes compounded the difficulties of meeting ongoing state government commitments, of responding to federal pressure to increase spending on elementary and secondary education to comply with the "No Child Left Behind Act" (2001), and of implementing homeland security stipulations.

Spending cuts, state employee layoffs, and one-time actions such as use of reserve funds and tobacco settlement securitization were proposed by Gov Pataki to solve the state's budget gap in 2003. In response, the legislature restored spending for education, hospitals, nursing homes, and localities, and increased state taxes to pay for these services. Subsequently, in actions historic for the state, the legislature overrode all 119 vetoes by the governor. The crisis in state and local government finance at the outset of the 21st century is considered to be at a modern high, with budget gaps predicted even when the national economy improves.

See also CEMETERIES; CITY GOVERNMENT; COUNTY GOVERNMENT; HOME RULE; NONPROFIT SECTOR; POVERTY.

Benjamin, Gerald, and Henrick N. Dullea, eds. *Decision 1997: Constitutional Change in New York* (Albany: Rockefeller Institute Press, 1997)
Liebschutz, Sarah F. *Bargaining under Federalism: Contemporary New York* (Albany: SUNY Press, 1991)
———. *New York Politics and Government: Competition and Compassion* (Lincoln: Univ of Nebraska Press, 1998)
New York State Education Department. *New York, the State of Learning* (Albany: Univ of the State of New York, 2001)
Stonecash, Jeffrey M., ed. *Governing New York State*, 4th ed. (Albany: SUNY Press, 2001)
Ward, Robert B. *New York State Government: What It Does, How It Works* (Albany: Rockefeller Institute Press, 2002)

Sarah F. Liebschutz

state historian. The appointment of the first New York State historian in 1895 followed decades of state-sponsored historical activity. In 1839 the state legislature authorized New York City attorney John Romeyn Brodhead to gather European documents bearing on New York's history. Edmund Bailey O'Callaghan and Berthold Fernow, employees of New York's Department of State, edited these materials to produce the 15-volume *Documents Relative to the Colonial History of New York,* published in 1856–87. In 1881 the state's historical records were transferred to the New York State Library, and in 1895 the legislature created the executive-branch position of state historian to oversee the holdings. The first state historian, Hugh Hastings, renewed the program of editing, and between 1898 and 1904, he and his successors published the papers of Govs George Clinton and Daniel D. Tompkins. Historian Victor Hugo Paltsits functioned primarily as an archivist, resigning in 1911 to become director of the New York Public Library after the Board of Regents took control of the state historian's office. James Sullivan and Alexander Flick, whose combined terms extended from 1916 to 1939, continued to edit historical materials, with their work culminating in the publication of Sir William Johnson's papers in 1921–65. In 1919 the legislature directed the appointment of 1,565 city, town, and village historians, under the supervision of the state historian, to assist in documenting New York's communities during World War I. The state historian in 1929 assumed responsibility for roadside historic markers, which were intended to increase public awareness of local history and in 1932 instituted positions for county and borough historians. After World War II, State Historian Albert Corey assisted Regents-chartered museums and incorporated historical societies and associations; he helped to found the American Association for State and Local History. Louis Leonard Tucker focused on the New York State American Revolution bicentennial. Paul Scudiere boosted statewide services, offering training for local government historians and regional seminars on New York State history, among other programs. From 1994 to 2001, the acting state historian, Joseph Meany, initiated a series of research programs for local government historians on the impact of the Irish famine on immigration into the state, the role of New Yorkers in the American migration westward, and other topics. In 2002 the future of the office was in doubt.

Hamilton, Milton. *The Historical Publication Program of the State of New York* (Albany: Univ of the State of New York, 1965)

Joseph F. Meany Jr

state historic parks, sites, and heritage areas. The New York State Office of Parks, Recreation, and Historic Preservation, through its Bureau of Historic Sites and various regional State Parks, Recreation, and Historic Preservation offices, operates and maintains 32 state historic sites and four State Historic Parks, extending from Long Island to the Niagara River. Groups of interested citizens and supportive friends have organized themselves for a number of the historic parks and sites. Private nonprofit organizations operate several historic sites under management agreements as partnerships with the state. The bureau also administers the New York State Heritage Area Program.

EARLY EFFORTS

The State Historic Sites Program, with its focus on the preservation and interpretation of places and events in the history of New York State, can be traced to efforts by Washington Irving and others in the 1830s and 1840s to preserve Washington's Headquarters in Newburgh (Orange Co). The state loan commissioners, after acquiring the property in 1849, took steps to preserve it as a historic site. Washington's Headquarters became the first publicly owned historic property in the nation in 1850. Initially the City of Newburgh administered the site, but in 1874 responsibility was transferred to a separate board of trustees appointed by the governor. By this time, other historic buildings were attracting attention. In 1869 Charles Ruggles Westbrook acquired the Abraham van Gaasbeek House in Kingston (Ulster Co), where the first popularly elected state senate convened in 1777. In 1883 he published a booklet about its history, and in 1887 his daughter and son-in-law sold the house to the state, making it New York's second state historic site. The third site, however, was not associated with the American Revolution. Early in 1889 a state law established jurisdiction over the Drexel cottage on Mount McGregor in Saratoga Co, where Gen and Pres Ulysses S. Grant died in 1885. The cottage was to be preserved exactly as it was the day Grant died as "a trust in behalf of the surviving comrades in arms of General Grant and of the whole American people."

The progressive spirit that seized the nation by 1890 included a popular interest in historic preservation. The state acquired the Saratoga Battle Monument (Saratoga Co) and John Brown Farm (Essex Co) in 1895 and Stony Point Battlefield (Rockland Co) in 1897. The state comptroller took custody of the Saratoga Battle Monument, and the State Fisheries, Game and Forest Commission administered the John Brown Farm. The Trustees of Scenic and Historic Places, founded in 1895, had jurisdiction over Stony Point Battlefield. The trustees were reestablished as the American Scenic and Historic Preservation Society in 1901. With the society taking a leading role, a remarkable period of acquisition by the state of historic sites began. Between 1900 and 1918, at least 15 historic sites were acquired, including Johnson Hall (Fulton Co) in 1906, Philipse Manor Hall (Westchester Co) in 1908, Crown Point (Essex Co) in 1910, Schuyler Mansion (Albany Co) in 1911, and Herkimer Home (Herkimer Co) in 1914. Sites acquired by the state were placed in the society's custody.

Acquisitions continued during the 1920s with the approach of the sesquicentennial of the American Revolution. These included Knox's Headquarters (Orange Co) in 1922, Fort Crailo (Rensselaer Co) in 1924, Saratoga Battlefield (Saratoga Co) in 1926, Oriskany Battlefield (Oneida Co) in 1927, and the site of the southeast bastion of Fort Stanwix (Oneida Co) in 1927. When the State Council of Parks was created in 1924, the state owned 41 different properties of "scenic, historic, scientific or practical value," designated collectively as State Parks and State Monuments. These included 10 historic buildings. The State Council of Parks was created to coordinate centrally the administration of these varied properties, with the exception of those under the State Conservation Commission. In 1926 the commission was made responsible for the acquisition and development of Revolutionary War battlefields and historic sites.

SITE MANAGEMENT ISSUES

In 1928 at least 17 "historic sites and scientific places" were assigned to the Division of Lands and Forests in the newly formed Conservation Department. Other properties were placed under the jurisdiction of the regional park commissions, while some sites were managed by boards of trustees or by the American Scenic and Historic Preservation Society. This arrangement proved unsatisfactory, prompting the director of the State Museum to warn in 1929 that these sites "require the latest museum technic, both scientific and historic, in order to prevent the deterioration of the textiles, papers, objects of leather, wood and metal which compose these historic objects." Nevertheless, the state continued to acquire sites during the depression years under different jurisdictions, with acquisitions such as the Steuben Memorial (Oneida Co) administered by the Division of Lands and Forests and other sites such as Sackets Harbor Battlefield (Jefferson Co) and Mills Mansion (Dutchess Co) overseen by park regions. By 1938 the Division of Lands and Forests was responsible for 24 state historic sites, one of which, Saratoga Battlefield, was later made part of the National Park System.

In 1944 the jurisdiction of 27 state historic sites was transferred to the Education Department; these included 13 sites that had been administered by Lands and Forests. Crown Point Reservation (Essex Co) and Lake George Battlefield Park (Warren Co), however, remained with the Division of Lands and Forests, while Stony Point Battlefield (Rockland Co), Newtown Battlefield (Chemung Co), and Niagara Reservation (Niagara Co) remained under the Division of Parks. Following World War II two historic sites, Old Fort Niagara (1948) in Niagara Co and Fort Ontario (1949) in Oswego Co, were transferred from the federal government to the Education Department. In 1952 eight historic sites, including Fort Stanwix, were eliminated from the Education Department system, while the John Brown Farm was transferred to Education from the Conservation Department in 1953. Later in the 1950s Walt Whitman Birthplace (Suffolk Co) and John Jay Homestead (Westchester Co) were acquired. By 1960 the Education Department operated 23 state historic sites, while 7 were under the Conservation Department. Meanwhile, additional sites, such as Clermont (Columbia Co) and Hyde Hall (Otsego Co), came into the state park system in the early 1960s.

Historic preservation and museum philosophies nationwide developed and improved rapidly during the 1960s. In 1966 Gov Nelson A. Rockefeller created the New York State Historic Trust to consolidate all historic preservation initiatives within a single agency and to reintegrate the state historic sites with the park system. The Historic Trust was under the director of state parks in the Conservation Department, and the jurisdiction of all state historic sites held by the Education Department was transferred to the Historic Trust. The Historic Trust also served as the State Historic Preservation Office, as mandated by the new federal historic preservation legislation of 1966. There was a new focus on the identification, preservation, and possible acquisition of threatened sites. A major preservation achievement of 1966 was the acquisition of Olana State Historic Site (Columbia Co). In addition, Crown Point was placed under the Historic Trust's management.

BUREAU OF HISTORIC SITES

The Historic Trust rapidly developed its programs in the late 1960s and early 1970s. In 1970 the Division of Parks was upgraded to an independent agency (the newly created Office of Parks and Recreation) within the Executive Department. In 1972 the Historic Trust became the Division for Historic Preservation within this new office. As the bicentennial of the American Revolution neared, the division developed a balanced, dedicated program for the state historic sites, which included collections care and conservation, archaeology, historical research, interpretation, architectural research, restoration, security, and landscape preservation. Professional standards for site staff, systematic procedures for collections acquisitions and management, and programs for architectural and archaeological research and cultural resource management were established. In 1975 conservation labs and offices for the staff of the Division for Historic Preservation's new Bureau of Historic Sites (1974) were established in the former Cluett, Peabody and Co bleachery complex at Peebles Island State Park in Waterford (Saratoga Co).

Under the bureau, the historic sites system has continued to develop and to expand its services to the public. A few sites have been transferred to local groups or other government agencies; for example, the Saratoga Battle Monument was transferred to the National Park Service in 1980. Other sites have been developed. Ganondagan (Ontario Co), a 17th-century village site of the Seneca, opened to the public in 1987. Most recently, Fort Montgomery State Historic Site (Orange Co), which includes actual ruins of a Revolutionary War fort built in 1776 and destroyed following a battle in 1777, has been developed with trails and interpretive signs. Initially opened to the public in 2001, it had a second "official" opening in 2002, attended by the governor, to recognize the 225th anniversary of the battle.

Planting Fields Arboretum (Nassau Co) was the first of the four state historic parks to be so designated. This category for Planting Fields was proposed in 1993 because of "the great diversity of its natural and physical assets and the variety and scope of experiences available to visitors." The other state historic parks are Caumsett (Suffolk Co), Old Croton Aqueduct (Westchester Co), and Old Erie Canal (Onondaga Co) State Historic Parks. The bureau and its predecessor, the Historic Trust, have carefully documented all of their work for the benefit of present as well as future scholars, producing scores of detailed historic structure reports, master plans, archaeological reports, bibliographies, environmental impact statements, furnishing plans, collections conservation assessments, cultural landscape reports, and other scholarly reports and publications about each of the state historic sites and historic parks.

The bureau also administers the New York State Heritage Area Program on behalf of the Office of Parks, Recreation, and Historic Preservation. Originally named the Urban Cultural Park Program when created by the New York State legislature in 1977, the Heritage Area Program includes 17 state-designated heritage areas encompassing over 400 communities throughout the state. The purpose of the program is to identify, preserve, and promote the state's natural and cultural resources as an expression of the state's heritage. The program includes small communities such as the Sackets Harbor Heritage Area (Jefferson Co), as well as large regions such as the eight-county Mohawk Valley Heritage Corridor. The state works in partnership with local governments, regional entities, and the private sector to administer the program.

See also STATE PARKS.

Iachettta, Stephen A. "The New York State Historic Sites System: Problems, Strengths, and Opportunities" (MA thesis, Cornell Univ, 1985)

Johnson, Ken. "Renewing Links with the Past," *New York Alive* (Nov–Dec 1985)

New York State Office of Parks, Recreation, and Historic Preservation, http://nysparks.state.ny.us

Paul R. Huey

State History Interest Project (SHIP). A program for students in grades 6–12 interested in the exploration of local, state, and national history. Built on the tradition of the New York State Historical Association's Yorker program, SHIP, established in 1999, complements classroom activities and meets the State Education Department's requirement that all students take a course in New York State and American history. As of 2001 SHIP membership was around 3,000 students. Members receive the *SHIP News*, membership cards, and achievement awards. They may choose to travel, participate in local community service, contribute to the *SHIP News*, develop leadership skills, and showcase their talents in the SHIP Participation Projects and Portfolio Activities at the annual spring convention held in cities around the state. The program is supported by the New York State Council for the Social Studies, the New York History Net, and the New York State Association of Public Historians.

New York History Net, http://www.nyhistory.com/SHIP

Mark C. Van Sluyters

State Liquor Authority. See ALCOHOLIC BEVERAGE CONTROL, DIVISION OF.

state nature areas and preserves. The protection and preservation of natural resources on state lands began most notably with the creation of the Forest Preserve in the Adirondacks in 1885 and its constitutional protection in 1894. The rationale for protecting watersheds and forest resources on public lands resulted from the extensive harvesting of forest resources and from public perception of declining environmental conditions. During the 1920s public interest in outdoor recreation was combined with preservation and conservation efforts, and the state park system was instituted in 1924. Preserving natural landscapes and resources for public enjoyment has been recognized as important in the state and has been supported by its citizens for over 100 years.

FOREST PRESERVE, STATE FOREST, MULTIPLE-USE, AND UNIQUE AREAS

The Department of Environmental Conservation (DEC) managed almost 4 million acres (1.6 million ha) of state land in 2002, including the Forest Preserve lands in the Adirondack and Catskill Parks. Forest Preserve lands are designated and protected as wilderness, wild forest, primitive, canoe, intensive-use, and historic areas, and as wild scenic and recreational rivers, travel corridors, and state administrative areas. Outside the Forest Preserve counties, 11 areas are also protected by the state constitution as state nature and historical preserves and managed by DEC for their exceptional natural character or geological, ecological, and historical significance. Examples include the Dr. Victor Reinstein Woods Nature Preserve (292 acres/118 ha), which protects forest and wetlands in suburban Cheektowaga (Erie Co), and the Rome Sand Plains (Oneida Co) (3,875 acres/1,568 ha), protecting one of the nation's few remaining inland pine barrens.

In the 1920s and 1930s, as marginal agricultural lands were abandoned across the state, the DEC acquired substantial areas as state forest and reforestation lands. The 472 state forests in 2002 included 715,000 acres (289,350 ha) managed for watershed protection, for production of timber and wood products, and for public recreation. State forests are outside the Forest Preserve, and about 85% are designated reforestation areas, with the remaining classified as multiple-use areas and unique areas. Multiple-use areas, such as the Zoar Valley in Cattaraugus Co, are used for outdoor recreation, including camping, fishing, hunting, boating, and winter sports. Unique areas have unusual ecosystems, rare plants, special landscape features, or historical significance. Examples include Nelson Swamp (831 acres/336 ha) in Madison Co, with white pine trees more than 350 years old and endangered or threatened plant species; Split Rock (32 acres/13 ha) in Onondaga Co, with a historic rock quarry and endangered plant species; and Sandy Island Beach (126 acres/51 ha) in Oswego Co, with sand dunes and endangered plant species. The state's Environmental Quality Bond Acts (1972, 1986) provided some funding to acquire unique areas.

Wildlife Management Areas

The DEC managed 85 wildlife management areas (WMAs) in 2002 for the conservation of fish and wildlife. Acquisition of land for WMAs began in the early 1900s. State bond acts, licensing fees for sports enthusiasts, and the federal tax on guns and ammunition fund a large portion of land purchased for WMAs. These areas are used for fishing, hunting, and trapping as well as hiking, cross-country skiing, birdwatching, and enjoying nature. In 2002 WMAs comprised 200,000 acres (80,937 ha), one-quarter wetland and the remaining upland and forests. Examples include Connecticut Hill WMA (11,045 acres/4,470 ha) in Tompkins and Schuyler Cos, which has been a study area for reestablishing turkey and ruffed grouse habitat; Northern Montezuma (6,304 acres/2,551 ha) in Cayuga and Wayne Cos adjoining the federally owned Montezuma National Wildlife Refuge; and Tivoli Bay WMA (1,722 acres/697 ha) in Dutchess Co, part of the Hudson River estuary. Five nature and environmental education centers are managed by DEC to encourage stewardship of natural resources and public awareness and knowledge of environmental quality. These include Five Rivers Environmental Education Center in Delmar (Albany Co), 400 acres (162 ha) of wetlands and old farm fields, and Quogue Wildlife Refuge (Suffolk Co), 305 acres (123 ha) of pine barrens representative of the historic forest cover of Long Island.

New York State Office of Parks, Recreation, and Historic Preservation. *Statewide Comprehensive Outdoor Recreation Plan 2003* (Albany: Author, 2002)

Chad P. Dawson

Staten Island [Richmond County] (58 mi²/150 km²; pop 443,728). Richmond Co was created in 1683 as one of the 10 original counties of New York Colony, named after the Duke of Richmond, brother of James, Duke of York, the colony's proprietor. Since its creation Richmond Co has been coterminous with Staten Island, a triangular island on the west side of New York Bay, roughly 14 miles (23 km) north to south, and 7 miles (11 km) east to west. It contains the southernmost point in New York State. On 1 Jan 1898, its four town and five village governments were disbanded to form the Borough of Richmond, one of the five boroughs of New York City and the smallest in population. In 1975 it was renamed the Borough of Staten Island and has no internal political subdivisions.

American Indians and Early Settlement

Evidence of human habitation reaches back perhaps as far as 10–12,000 years; artifacts of the Lamoka culture date from approximately 5,500 BP. When the Europeans arrived, Algonquian-speaking bands occupied the island, which they called Aquehonga. They engaged in hunting and fishing, particularly exploiting the prolific shellfish beds, and in subsistence agriculture, raising corn, squash, and beans. Giovanni da Verrazano, sailing the *Dauphine* for the king of France, anchored off Staten Island in April 1524. In 1630 the Dutch West India Co granted Michael Pauw a patent on Staten Island, or "Staten Eylandt" (named for the States-General in the Hague), in absentia; apparently he never took possession of it. Capt David Pietersz de Vries established the first settlement in January 1639 at the Watering Place [now Tompkinsville], named for the spring where outbound ships took on fresh water. The settlement was wiped out in September 1641 when settlers accused the Indians of stealing their pigs and the dispute escalated. Cornelius Melyn established a new settlement of about 40 people near the Narrows in 1642 but abandoned it a year later amid renewed warfare. Indians destroyed a third settlement (1650) during the Peach War of 1655. In 1661 the Dutch established a permanent settlement at Oude Dorp [now South Beach]. In 1670 the Indians finally sold the island to the English, marking the transaction by handing over soil and twigs from every type of tree growing on Staten Island except, according to legend, the ash and hickory; they retained rights to those trees for basketry.

The population in 1698 numbered 727, including about 70 slaves; by 1776 the number approximated 3,000, 10% of whom were slaves. The institution of slavery on Staten Island was typical of the province, with human property engaged in farming and domestic tasks but not in large-scale plantation agriculture. Benjamin Perine, born into slavery on Staten Island on 2 Dec 1796, died there on 3 Oct 1900 and was the island's last living link to slavery.

Four precincts, Castleton, Northfield, Southfield, and Westfield, were created for administrative purposes; they were recognized as towns by state legislation of 7 Mar 1788. Middletown was formed in 1860 from parts of Castleton and Southfield to eliminate tie votes in the county Board of Supervisors. The first seat of government was at Stony Brook [now New Dorp], relocating to Coccles Town [now Richmondtown] in 1729. The Huguenots erected the first church about 1698. Rev Aeneas Mackenzie established the first Anglican parish, St. Andrew's, in 1705 and erected its first sanctuary at Richmondtown in 1712. A Dutch Reformed church went up in Port Richmond in 1716.

Revolutionary and Early National Period

During the Revolution Staten Islanders remained generally loyalist, especially the English adherents of the Church of England; Dutch and

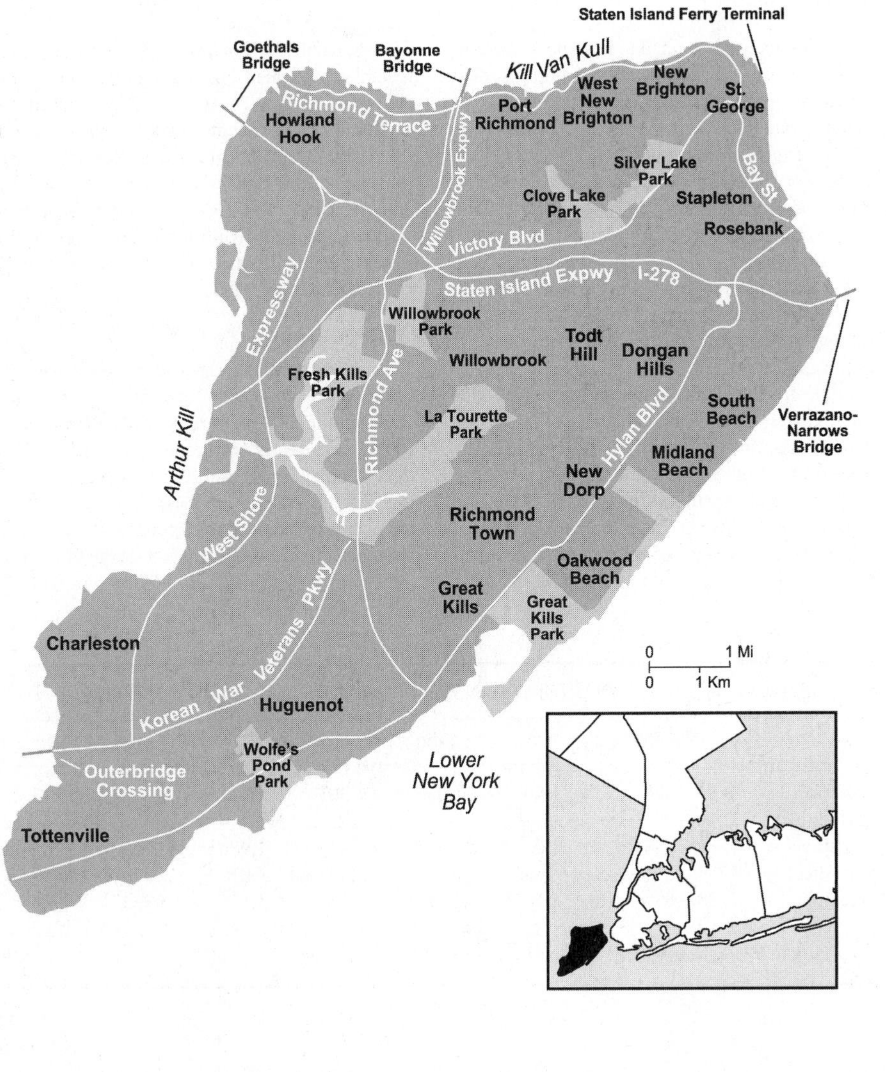

STATEN ISLAND (RICHMOND CO)
POPULATION CENSUS FIGURES

	White	Nonwhite	Total Population	Foreign-Born
1790	2,949	886	3,835	—
1800	3,805	758	4,563	—
1810	4,636	711	5,347	—
1820	5,525	610	6,135	5
1830	6,530	552	7,082	30
1840	10,482	483	10,965	—
1850	14,471	590	15,061	3,063
1860	24,833	659	25,492	8,575
1870	32,242	787	33,029	10,113
1880	38,054	937	38,991	10,961
1890	50,712	981	51,693	14,779
1900	65,863	1,158	67,021	18,687
1910	84,756	1,213	85,969	24,339
1920	114,953	1,578	116,531	31,612
1930	155,594	2,752	158,346	39,520
1940	170,875	3,566	174,441	35,318
1950	185,936	5,619	191,555	30,487
1960	211,738	10,253	221,991	25,428
1970	277,604	17,839	295,443	26,695
1980	313,534	38,587	352,121	34,514
1990	322,387	56,590	378,977	44,550
2000	344,319	99,409	443,728	72,657

Notes: "Nonwhite" includes African Americans, Asians, American Indians, and Pacific Islanders and, for 2000, also the mixed race and other race categories. Through the 1960 census these figures primarily reflect the African American population. Foreign-born figures for 1820 and 1830 include only those not naturalized, and for 1930 and 1950, the foreign-born totals include Whites only. Other years include all foreign-born in the population.

Huguenot residents tended to join the American cause. In early July 1776 British troops landed for the invasion of New York City. Despite the demonstrated loyalty of Staten Islanders, the 30,000 troops soon denuded the place of livestock, food stores, and woodlands. On 22 August most of the army crossed the harbor in preparation for the Battle of Long Island. On 11 Sept 1776 Benjamin Franklin, John Adams, and Edmund Rutledge met Lord Richard Howe and Sir Henry Strachey at the home of tory Christopher Billopp in Tottenville (built *ca* 1675, now known as the Conference House) to discuss ending the revolution. The British offered "clemency and full pardon to all repentant rebels," but the Americans rejected the terms. No major battles occurred on Staten Island, but the Americans sent raiding parties over from New Jersey throughout the British occupation.

Commerce revived swiftly after the Revolution, but the busy harbor also brought epidemics, particularly yellow fever, to the city. The federal government opened the first quarantine station at Seguine Point in 1799, causing much distress among residents as several outbreaks on the island resulted. Long the object of protest, the quarantine station was finally burned by Staten Islanders in 1858; it was reestablished on Hoffman and Swinburne Islands off South Beach. The Swinburne station closed in 1928, Hoffman Island in 1937.

Transportation

The earliest regular ferry across the Narrows to Long Island began in 1713; regular ferry service between the north shore and Manhattan also started in the early 18th century. Cornelius Vanderbilt, born on the island in 1794, began ferrying passengers to New York City while in his teens (hence his title, commodore). In 1886 the ferry began running from St. George to Whitehall St in Manhattan. Erastus Wiman purchased waterfront property from George Law and promised to "canonize" him by naming the area at the landing St. George. The city took over operation of the Staten Island ferries in 1905. The ferry from 69th St in Brooklyn stopped when the Verrazano-Narrows Bridge opened in November 1964. The Staten Island Ferry between St. George and Whitehall St has been free since 1997.

In 1816 Gov Daniel D. Tompkins, who had founded Tompkinsville two years earlier, organized the Richmond Turnpike Co to shorten travel between New York and Philadelphia; the road is now Victory Blvd. The company also bought the steam ferry *Nautilus,* operating it between Tompkinsville and Whitehall St beginning in 1817. In 1860 Staten Island Rapid Transit (SIRT) began running from Vanderbilt's Landing [now Clifton] to Tottenville; in 1883 it became associated with the Baltimore and Ohio Railroad (B&O), which inaugurated freight and passenger connections to New Jersey over the Arthur Kill in 1889. SIRT expanded passenger service along the north shore to Arlington and to South Beach in 1886. Inauguration of trolley lines in 1895 pushed SIRT into bankruptcy, and the B&O bought it in 1899. SIRT was electrified in 1925, acquired by the MTA in 1971, and renamed the Staten Island Railway. Freight service on the North Shore rail line continued until the Proctor and Gamble plant closed.

The B&O built what was, at the time, the world's longest lift bridge, across the Arthur Kill in 1928. The Port of New York Authority (now Port Authority of New York and New Jersey) built three automobile bridges to New Jersey: the Goethals Bridge (named for Gen George Goethals, engineer for the Panama Canal) and the Outerbridge Crossing (named for Staten Islander Eugenius H. Outerbridge, first chairman of the Port Authority), both opened in 1928 and span the Arthur Kill; the 1931 Bayonne Bridge, the world's longest steel arch span at the time, crosses the Kill Van Kull. The Verrazano-Narrows, the longest suspension bridge in the world at the time and the last great project of the Triborough Bridge and Tunnel Authority under Robert Moses, opened in 1964, as did the Staten Island Expressway, cutting across the island from the Verrazano to the Goethals. The West Shore Expressway opened in 1976. As the population has grown, the borough has struggled with traffic congestion for many of its roads, including Arthur Kill, Amboy, Clove and Richmond Rds; all date from the early 18th century.

Economic Development

The first census in 1790 counted 3,835 persons, nearly a quarter of whom were Black. By 1890

POPULATIONS OF FORMER TOWNS, STATEN ISLAND (RICHMOND CO)

Town	Years in Existence	1790	1800	1810	1820	1830	1840	1850	1860	1870	1880	1890
Castleton	1788–1898	805	1,056	1,301	1,527	2,216	4,275	5,389	6,778	9,504	12,679	16,423
Middletown	1860–98	—	—	—	—	—	—	—	6,243	7,589	9,029	10,557
Northfield	1788–1898	1,021	1,377	1,595	1,980	2,162	2,745	4,020	4,841	5,949	7,014	9,811
Southfield	1788–1898	855	932	1,007	1,012	971	1,619	2,709	3,645	5,082	4,980	6,644
Westfield	1788–1898	1,151[a]	1,198	1,444	1,616	1,733	2,326	2,943	3,985	4,905	5,289	8,258

[a]As printed in 1790 census; total of columns is actually 1,154.

the population had reached 51,693 but less than 2% were Black. Even in the mid–19th century, the population was largely descended from colonial settlers or migrants from neighboring states; by that time Staten Island was also attracting immigrants, mostly German, Irish, and English. The Italian patriot Giuseppe Garibaldi stayed with his friend Antonio Meucci in 1850 and 1851. By the 1880s the number of immigrants, including many Italians, began a steady increase with growing industrialization. The foreign-born population reached 30% in 1910.

Most residents engaged in agriculture or fishing, particularly oystering. There were 290 farms on Staten Island in 1900, covering 11,724 acres (4,745 ha), many of the farms raising produce for the New York City market. In the 1830s free black oystermen from Virginia and Maryland settled Blazing Star, or Sandy Ground (between Charleston and Rossville), with their families. They established the Mount Zion African Methodist Episcopal Zion Church in 1850 and probably operated a station in the Underground Railroad. When natural beds were fished out in early 19th century, baymen turned to cultivation, seeding oysters in private plots. By 1900 the waters around Staten Island yielded about 200,000 bushels (7 million l) annually, but the city closed the Arthur Kill shellfish grounds in 1917 because of pollution.

Shipbuilding and support industries thrived in the 19th century and continued into the mid–20th century, mainly along Kill Van Kull. The industrial heritage of the island dates from the establishment of a textile dyeing and printing works along the north shore in 1819, around which grew Factoryville [now West New Brighton]; by 1835 it was the largest dye works in the state. Germans established breweries on the island in the 1850s, most prominently Bechtel's, Bachmann's, and Rubsam and Horrmann's Atlantic Brewery, the only one to survive Prohibition; it closed in 1963. Drawn to Staten Island by the abundant clay pits along the Arthur Kill, Balthazar Kreischer opened his brickworks in 1854, producing glazed brick. (During World War I, Kreischerville became Charleston.) The Atlantic Terra Cotta Works opened in Tottenville in 1897 and produced materials for the Woolworth Building and other landmarks. In 1873 the nation's first linoleum factory opened at Long Neck; it closed in 1931, and Linoleumville was renamed Travis. The S.S. White Dental Manufacturing Co operated in Princes Bay from the 1860s to 1972. Proctor and Gamble created Port Ivory in 1907, producing Ivory soap and related products there until 1990.

Religion, Education, and Culture

Until the mid–19th century, Staten Island was overwhelmingly Protestant. In addition to Dutch Reformed and Episcopal congregations, there were Presbyterian (mid-1700s), Moravian (1763), Baptist (1785), Methodist (1787), and Unitarian (1851) churches. St. Peter's, the first Catholic parish, was founded in 1839. The influx of Germans and Scandinavians resulted in the first Lutheran congregation in 1852. By 1900 there were 10 Catholic churches, and 25 more opened by the late 1920s. Congregation B'nai Jeshurun, the first Jewish body, organized at Tompkinsville in 1888.

The *Richmond Republican* (1827) was the county's first newspaper, though it was printed in Manhattan for a decade. Weekly or twice-weekly papers begun in the 19th century, including several in German, were generally short-lived. The *Staten Island Advance,* founded as the weekly *Richmond County Advance* in 1886, is the indispensable source for local news. It became the island's first successful daily in 1918 and was sold to S. I. Newhouse in 1922.

Cultural institutions include the Staten Island Institute of Arts and Sciences at St. George (1881), the Staten Island Zoo (1936), and the Jacques Marchais Museum of Tibetan Art (1947). The Staten Island Historical Society (1856) opened the Historical Museum at Richmondtown in 1935; this became Historic Richmond Town, incorporating 11 buildings on the original site, including the Voorlezer's House (1696), the oldest school building in the state. Beginning in the 1960s other colonial era structures were moved there.

Sailors' Snug Harbor opened as a retirement home for seamen in 1831; after the last residents moved out, the city transformed it in 1976 into a cultural center; it is home to the Noble Maritime Collection, featuring the works of John A. Noble, who documented the working waterfront in the mid-1900s. The Staten Island Botanic Garden opened on 50 acres (20 ha) at Snug Harbor in 1977, and in 1999 the Chinese Scholars Garden opened there. The Alice Austen House honors the life and work of a pioneering photographer of the late 19th and early 20th centuries. In sports, the Staten Island Stapletons played in the National Football League from 1929 to 1932. A Class A affiliate of the New York Yankees, the Staten Island Yankees, began playing on Staten Island in 1999; its new ballpark at St. George opened in 2001.

Recent History

The opening of the Verrazano-Narrows Bridge ushered in the era of rapid urbanization. The population rose from 221,991 in 1960 to 352,121 in 1980, many of the newcomers (a large number of them Italian American) arriving from Brooklyn. Staten Island was the only borough to gain population during the 1970s. During the 1990s it was the fastest-growing county in the state, rising by 17% to 443,728 by 2000. In recent years the pressures of population growth have consumed the last open spaces, causing the demolition of older single-family homes and the construction of multi-family dwellings in their place. New York City has been hard-pressed to provide services to the growing population, especially in the southern part of the island. Efforts to control growth by protecting mature trees, prohibiting construction on hillsides, and requiring builders to certify the availability of school seats for each unit constructed have done little to slow growth.

With less than a 5% minority population in 1960, Staten Island still has the smallest percentage of minority residents of the five boroughs (22% in 2000), though there is a growing number of new immigrants, particularly Mexicans, South Asians, and Muslims. The north shore is the most diverse, with Whites making up barely half the population; the southern part of the island is 89% white. The Housing Authority operates 11 developments on the island that were built between the 1940s and the 1960s, totaling 4,860 apartments. Almost all public housing is in the northern third of the borough.

Politically, Staten Island is generally more conservative than the rest of the city, though Democrats do outnumber Republicans. John J. Marchi was elected to the state senate in 1956 and has served in that body for over 45 years, reelected most recently in 2002. He was the Republican candidate for mayor in 1969 and 1973 and a key player in resolving the fiscal crisis of the mid-1970s. Democrat Elizabeth Connelly was elected to the assembly in 1973 and was the first woman elected to office on Staten Island. Republican Guy Molinari served as borough president from 1990 until 2001. Molinari's daughter Susan served in the City Council and was elected to US Congress in 1990 to fill her father's seat, resigning in 1997.

In 1971 Sen Marchi proposed the South Richmond Plan to control development; the Rouse Co would have built suburban communities with all the necessary infrastructure while preserving open space. The plan floundered because of opposition by the Conservative Party and environmental concerns about the massive landfill proposed off Great Kills for apartment buildings. Special zoning imposed after the final rejection of the plan proved largely ineffectual in controlling development. In the late 1960s and early 1970s Staten Islanders successfully blocked the Richmond and Willowbrook parkways, which were to run along the ridge in the middle of the island, and created instead the 2,800-acre (1,130 ha) Greenbelt, a series of parks and nature preserves including golf courses, hiking trails, ponds, and streams. Great Kills Park is part of Gateway National Recreational Area.

In the early 1970s the Willowbrook scandal gave Staten Island much unwanted attention. The Willowbrook State School had been completed in 1941 for children with developmental disabilities, but during World War II it housed wounded soldiers. Beginning in 1947 the veterans were moved out, and the school opened in 1951. By the late 1960s conditions had deteriorated badly. In 1972 television reporter Geraldo Rivera brought his camera into Willowbrook, exposing the wretched conditions. Parents filed a lawsuit in 1972, resulting in the 1975 Willowbrook Consent Decree, which ordered the closing of the institution and placement of residents in group homes.

A second notorious feature of the island was the Fresh Kills landfill, which opened in 1948. By the 1980s it was allegedly the largest in the world and a constant cause of complaint by residents, particularly as more homes were built nearby. The dump was closed in March 2001, enforced by legislation; it reopened that September to receive debris from the World Trade Center, then closed again.

As one of the five boroughs, Staten Island had one vote on the New York City Board of Estimate from 1901 to 1990. In 1982 the New York Civil Liberties Union filed suit, claiming the system violated the principle of one person–one vote. This spurred a secession movement. Sen Marchi introduced legislation in 1984 permitting the county to secede; in 1993 the island's voters adopted a proposed charter for a city of Staten Island by a 2-1 margin. The drive effectively died when Sheldon Silver, Speaker of the assembly, declared he would not permit a vote on the charter until the city formally requested the legislature to do so via a home rule message.

Wagner College, founded in Rochester as a Lutheran seminary, moved to Staten Island in 1918. St. John's University has had a satellite campus on the island since the 1930s and acquired Notre Dame College of Staten Island in 1971. Staten Island Community College, the first public institution of higher education on the island, was established in 1956; Richmond College was founded in 1965 as an upper-division college intended for community college graduates. In 1976, during the fiscal crisis, the institutions merged into the College of Staten Island and became part of the CUNY system. The college moved to the grounds of the former Willowbrook State School in 1993.

Contemporary Staten Island retains an Italian American flavor, but demographics are destined to change as new waves of immigrants discover the place. Efforts to preserve historic neighborhoods, old homes, and open space by the Preservation League of Staten Island and the Friends of Pine Oak Woods are gaining ground in the race with developers, though landmark designations and rezoning perhaps come too late to preserve what is left of old Staten Island.

Several comprehensive multivolume works cover Staten Island, but the most recent dates from 1929. Richard M. Bayles, *History of Richmond County* (1887) covers geology, history, and such topics as religion, industry, and transportation. Another early work, J. J. Clute, *Annals of Staten Island* (1877), includes both documented history and local lore. Ira K. Morris, *Morris' Memorial History of Staten Island* (1898) is an encyclopedic two-volume history through the consolidation, with substantial coverage of the Revolution. The best work is the five-volume *Staten Island and Its People: A History, 1609–1929* (1929). Other general histories include Henry G. Steinmayer, *Staten Island, 1524–1898* (1950), and Dorothy V. Smith, *Staten Island, Gateway to New York* (1970). Edna Holden, *Holden's Staten Island: The History of Richmond County* (1964) was compiled for public schools and was recently updated by borough historian Richard Dickenson. Charles Sachs, *Made on Staten Island* (1988), is a well-illustrated survey of agriculture and industry. Brian J. Cudahy, *Over and Back: The History of Ferryboats in New York Harbor* (1990), and David Rothman and Sheila Rothman, *The Willowbrook Wars* (1984) are important topical works.

Jeffrey A. Kroessler

Staten Island Ferry. In 1817 the ferry ran from Tompkinsville in Staten Island to Whitehall St and was operated by the Staten Island Rapid Transit. On 29 Nov 1817 the first steam ferry, *Nautilus,* crossed the harbor; the fare was 25¢. A new Staten Island location was selected by entrepreneur Erastus Wiman, who foresaw the future connection of Staten Island with New York City and transferred the central ferry station to St. George, with service beginning in 1886, and shortly thereafter the 5¢ fare was established. In 1900 the Staten Island population was 67,021, and nearly 10,000 made the daily commute to the Whitehall St terminal. The ferry has been a municipal service from 1905 and is operated by the New York City Department of Transportation.

In 1972 the fare was raised to 10¢, in 1975 to 25¢, and in 1990 to 50¢. On 4 July 1997 the foot passenger fare was eliminated. In the early 21st century, the ferry provides 24-hour service between St. George Ferry Terminal at Richmond Terrace and Bay St on Staten Island and Whitehall and South Sts in Manhattan. Approximately 19 million people ride the ferry, and more than 33,000 trips are made annually. The ferry ride is approximately 25 minutes and covers 5.2 miles (8.4 km). The fleet consists of seven ferries. On 15 Oct 2003, 10 people were killed when the *Andrew J. Barberi* rammed into a pier near the St. George Terminal.

Staten Island Ferry.

Scull, Theodore. *Staten Island Ferry* (New York: Quadrant Press, 1982)

Leonard Benardo

State of New York Mortgage Agency (SONYMA). Public benefit corporation established by the New York State legislature in 1970 to provide increased availability of residential mortgage funds to low- and moderate-income first-time home buyers. In 1978 SONYMA's mission expanded to include issuance of mortgage insurance to help stabilize neighborhoods throughout the state. SONYMA's mortgages are designed for single-family homeowners, and the mortgage insurance program targets multifamily housing under construction in economic development zones or areas suffering disinvestment. SONYMA is overseen by a nine-member board of directors consisting of the state's comptroller, superintendent of banks, director of the budget, commissioner of the Department of Housing and Community Renewal, and five appointees of the governor. The appointees include the majority leader of the New York State Senate and the Speaker of the New York State Assembly. The president and chief executive officer of SONYMA also serves as head of the Housing Finance Agency. Since its creation in 1970, SONYMA has provided more than $7.6 billion in financing for more than 124,000 homes through its Single Family Programs and Financing Division. SONYMA issues both tax-exempt and taxable bonds to finance the mortgages. Participating lenders provide the loans to qualified applicants. In January 2002 SONYMA's Mortgage Insurance Fund portfolio of insured mortgages exceeded $1.5 billion. SONYMA is funded by mortgage income, application fees, insurance premiums, and investment proceeds. The agency is headquartered in New York City, with additional regional offices in Albany and Buffalo.

State of New York Mortgage Agency. *Annual Report 2000* (New York: Author, 2001)

Jeffrey Kraus

state parks

EARLY HISTORY

The history of the New York State park system is tied to changes in demographics and land use that began to alter the landscape of the state after the American Civil War. The depletion of natural resources such as forests and farmland, the decline in the rural population, massive immigration, industrialization, and the unprecedented growth of cities left New York State with a surplus of endangered or unproductive land and an overcrowded and needy urban population. The state's first large-scale conservation activities date to 1885, with the creation of the 700,000-acre (280,000 ha) Adirondack and Catskill Forest Preserves and the state reservation at Niagara Falls, New York's first state park. These initiatives were significant in establishing the state's mandate to protect its wild and scenic lands. From the beginning, however, public demand for access to these preserves compelled the state to balance conservation with recreation.

The initiative that proved most influential in the development of the New York State park system was the Palisades Interstate Park Commission (PIPC). The PIPC was formed by the New York and New Jersey legislatures in 1900, when both states combined efforts to acquire and protect the 550 ft high (168 m) Palisades Escarpment, which defines the southwestern Hudson River shoreline. Members included George W. Perkins Sr, J. DuPratt White, and Franklin W. Hopkins. Although this commission was a notable example of interstate cooperation, it was financial support from some of the Hudson Valley's wealthiest families, including the Harrimans, Rockefellers, Morgans, and Perkinses, that ensured its success. By 1920 the PIPC held a 14 mi (23 km) stretch of cliff and shoreline between Fort Lee, NJ, and Piermont (Rockland Co) and an inland preserve of more than 30,000 acres (12,000 ha) in Rockland and Orange Cos.

The Palisades were acquired for conservation; enormous public interest, however, motivated the PIPC to develop recreational facilities and to provide public transportation to the formerly inaccessible preserve. Influenced by Progressive era ideas, the PIPC turned stewardship of the immense Bear Mountain–Harriman State Parks just outside New York City into an opportunity for social reform, committing its resources to developing a vast playground for the urban population, particularly the lower and middle classes. By 1920 the PIPC was serving nearly 2 million patrons a year, operating camps for the poor and disadvantaged; swimming, hiking, and camping facilities for the middle class; and nature education programs for all. The PIPC established principles that became the foundation of the state park program. These included the state's obligation to provide recreational opportunities for its citizens, the mission to connect urban patrons with regional parks, and the determination to link recreational and transportation planning. The success of the PIPC also demonstrated the importance of public/private partnerships in large-scale efforts to acquire scenic land for public benefit.

A STATE PARK PLAN FOR NEW YORK

The plan for a comprehensive system of state parks was a product of Gov Alfred E. Smith's efforts to reform state government and implement Progressive era social programs. In 1918 governor-elect Smith appointed a commission, chaired by Robert Moses, to develop a reorganization plan for state government. In 1920 the New York State Association, a civic group advocating the reform agenda, established the Committee on the State Park Plan. With Moses as secretary, the committee included both well-known park benefactors (Ansley Wilcox, Francis R. Masters, Wolcott J. Humphrey, William Church Osborne, et al) and engineers (William A. Welch and Jay Downer). Expanding on ideas promoted by George W. Perkins Sr, first president of the PIPC, this committee developed a scheme for a statewide system of parks connected by scenic parkways and boulevards. Although often credited with the plan itself, Moses played perhaps a more important role by developing the political and legal mechanisms to implement it. Among his most important achievements was defining park development as an official function of state government, thus ensuring parks a legitimate place in the state's long-term budget and planning process.

A State Park Plan for New York (1922) was one of the first comprehensive state park plans in the country. The first regional park system had been developed in the Boston metropolitan area in 1893; however, New York was the first state to develop a detailed park planning philosophy, a comprehensive plan, and an administrative structure to carry it out. Far ranging in ambition and scope, the plan provided a template for New York's public recreational programs and became a model for other states. *A State Park Plan* represented an application of progressive thinking to the needs of 20th-century citizens. Drawing on national trends in conservation, recreation, and social welfare, the plan assessed the relationships between population and scenic features, identified the land that was most available and/or endangered, and outlined the best uses of different types of land. Dividing the state into regions, the report analyzed needs, noted current parks, and proposed new facilities. It affirmed the state's responsibility to protect natural resources and ensure the health and welfare of citizens. Finally, the plan balanced the organizational and financial advantages of centralized statewide planning with the benefits of local administration, leaving specific program development to regional administrators with an intimate knowledge of their regions.

Among the committee's priorities was ensuring public access to parks, especially as new demographic patterns pushed parks and patrons further apart. By conceiving a plan premised on movement, planners embraced the imminent transition to an automobile-based society. To achieve their goals, park developers would have to plan and build roads as well as parks, or, even better, parkways, roads that were themselves parks. The state's advocacy of recreational driving had the potential to expand recreational opportunities significantly: now the experience could begin and perhaps even end with the trip itself. These concepts informed the state's commitment to building scenic roads and its insistent role in transportation planning.

New York State Park System

In 1924 the State Council of Parks (SCP) was created, and voters approved a $15 million bond to develop a state park system. The council, chaired by Moses, began with a division of the state into components and an acknowledgment of regional differences. One of the goals of the park plan was consolidation of a diverse group of recreational areas governed by a variety of different public entities. These ranged from vast preserves, such as Allegany State Park at Salamanca (Cattaraugus Co) in the southwestern corner of the state, to historic sites and monuments, such as Washington's Headquarters in Newburgh (Orange Co). Among them was a chain of large, exceptionally scenic holdings near the state's major population centers: Niagara Reservation (1885) and Allegany (1921) near Buffalo, Letchworth (1907) in the Rochester area, and Bear Mountain–Harriman (1910) just outside New York City. These became the backbone of the new state park system, anchoring the major regional divisions.

Additional regions were identified based on the relationships that could be established between urban areas and significant scenic features. For example, the Long Island region capitalized on the geography of the long, narrow island with extensive access to water and its proximity to the New York City metropolitan area. Scenic parkways were laid out to follow east-west routes across the island and to link parks at graduated distances from New York City. Parks were located to take advantage of notable attractions, such as ocean beaches, as well as to preserve open space ahead of rapidly developing suburbs. Similarly, plans for a Finger Lakes region recommended improved state highways linking a group of small cities and villages to Watkins Glen State Park (1906) in Schuyler Co, the region's major scenic attraction, and 11 new parks located near the spectacular gorges and waterfalls around the five scenic lakes. The distribution of parks within each region was based on current holdings and those that might be acquired, the means of transportation to parks, both existing and planned, and the needs of regional users. Transportation systems were designed both to facilitate regional park connections and to link regions to each other.

The development of regional programs reflected the thought given to the needs of specific park patrons and the feasibility of developing parks and transportation systems in various parts of the state. For example, the Palisades regional parks were ideally situated to serve the New York metropolis. However, because the targeted users (working classes, needy children) lacked adequate transportation, the PIPC acquired its own fleet of boats and buses. In contrast, in the rural eastern Hudson Valley, which lacked a singular outstanding scenic destination, land was relatively inexpensive and anticipated patrons were middle-class citizens with cars and leisure time; thus, the Taconic State Park Commission developed its regional recreational program around a scenic parkway, offering a spectacular drive and access to new state parks along the route. So, although the plan outlined a unified park system, implementation accommodated variables such as economics, geography, and opportunity. Although parks and parkways took decades to develop, the SCP actively promoted the idea of automobile access to parks before the first state parkway was completed. The council's first guide, *New York State Parks and Highways* (1928), consisted of maps and directions to existing parks via completed and soon to be improved state highways. The guide suggested that by the late 1920s most New Yorkers with cars could visit outstanding scenic attractions within 90 mi (145 km) of home.

Letchworth State Park.

Administration

The SCP was created as an independent board within the New York State Conservation Commission. Members representing each of the regional state park commissions established policy, coordinated regional park plans, and submitted an annual budget to the legislature. The first council included representatives from each of the five established commissions (Palisades Interstate Park Commission, Allegany State Park Commission, New York State Reservation at Niagara, American Scenic and Historic Preservation Society, and Westchester County Park Commission) and two new ones (Finger Lakes State Parks Commission and Long Island State Park Commission), as well as Alexander MacDonald, conservation commissioner, and John M. Clarke, director of the state museum. In 1925 the council created three additional commissions (Central New York State Parks Commission, Taconic State Park Commission, and Erie County Park Commission). Although all 10 of these bodies were represented on the SCP, the American Scenic and Historic Preservation Society was a private organization that administered Letchworth State Park for the state, while the Erie and Westchester County Park Commissions were authorized to act as agents of the state only for the purposes of developing specific state-funded park proposals. By 1930 Letchworth was absorbed into a new state park region (Genesee), and the county-operated state facilities were turned over to regional state park commissions. Palisades regional parks, however, are still administered by the interstate commission formed by New York and New Jersey in 1900, an arrangement formalized by a 1937 compact.

The SCP struggled with the issue of regionalization versus centralization from its inception. Although the Committee on the State Park Plan had envisioned a unified park system with central oversight, it had not intended to cede control to a state agency. Nevertheless, the council's independence was threatened almost immediately when Moses, in his zeal to develop a park and parkway system on Long Island, exceeded the authority to appropriate land authorized by the new parks law, prompting an attempt to place the park system under an established state agency or office. This threatened loss of control to officials without park expertise was averted through the combined political influences of the regional park commissioners, Gov Smith, and Moses himself.

The council's autonomy was again threatened by the creation of the New York State Conservation Department in 1926. In the new department, the conservation commissioner became the statutory head of the SCP with authorization to compile a single state parks budget request. Without the authority to develop and submit an independent budget, the council was essentially subservient to the Conservation Department. A 1928 amendment returned to the SCP the right to choose its own chair and develop a budget; however, the conservation commissioner retained final approval of the submission to the legislature. This compromise delegated planning of the park system to the council, while limiting its ability to develop and fund programs independently. Even within the council itself, control of the park program remained contentious. The council's budget request to the Conservation Department was largely controlled by its chair, a position Robert Moses occupied for nearly four decades. Again and again the delicate balance between regional administration and centralized planning conflicted with Moses's iron-fisted control over state parks spending. Over the next 38 years, regional representatives struggled to secure approvals and funding for park programs without losing control of them, and Moses remained both an asset and a liability. His powerful position ensured the park program a well-funded place in state government but posed a continual threat to the structure upon which the program was founded.

In 1960, during Gov Nelson A. Rockefeller's administration, a government reorganization commission recommended abolishing the SCP and consolidating state parks administration in the Conservation Department. Although the proposal was not enacted, the ensuing tension between Rockefeller and Moses signified a struggle for control of the state park program that culminated in Moses's resignation from the SCP in 1963. At the end of the Rockefeller era, the transition to a centralized parks administration was finally accomplished through a series of state government reorganizations, beginning with creation of the Department of Environmental Conservation (DEC) in 1970. While DEC generally absorbed the old Conservation Department, the state park system was placed under the Office of Parks and Recreation, a new agency also established during the reorganization, under the Executive Department. This change marked the formal separation of the state's conservation and recreation programs. New York State's late 19th-century commitment to conservation of the Forest Preserves and the public's demand for recreational access to them had proved catalysts for the state park program. Nearly a century later, the preserves remained under the stewardship of DEC, while most of the state parks were turned over to the new agency.

In 1972 changes to the Parks and Recreation Law delegated sole responsibility for state parks to the commissioner of parks and recreation. With this change, the regional commissions relinquished control over park development and operation, and the SCP ceded its authority to the central administrative office. In 1981 the agency was renamed the Office of Parks, Recreation, and Historic Preservation (OPRHP) in recognition of its additional role as the state historic preservation office (SHPO). The state's contemporary role in historic preservation commenced (under the Conservation Department) with passage of the National Historic Preservation Act in 1966 and was expanded with enactment of the State Historic Preservation Act in 1980. With these laws, which declared historic preservation to be federal and state government policy, OPRHP assumed the administration of programs such the State and National Registers of Historic Places, cultural resources surveys, preservation grants, and environmental reviews.

Expansion of the System

Between 1924 and about 1949, the actions of the SCP were informed by the state park plan and the principles for park development that the council had established in its first year. Acquisition policy focused on enlarging, adding to, and connecting the original holdings to create the comprehensive system of parks and parkways envisioned in the plan. The council defined a state park as a large area with both scenic and recreational value located in a rural area and near a large population center. In addition to their environmental qualities, parks were developed based on their potential accessibility by automobile. Although the council noted that the value of a park would be enhanced by historical significance, the marriage of recreation and history was strained from the beginning. The state's historic sites had been among the resources inherited by the SCP; however, Moses and others saw a distinction between developing outdoor recreation programs and caring for historic sites. Eventually, in 1944, the state historic sites were transferred to the New York State Department of Education. Two decades later, with the birth of the modern historic preservation movement and the nascent idea of heritage tourism, this distinction was erased, and in 1966 the sites were returned to the Conservation Department (and later transferred to OPRHP).

Among the notable parks developed in the early years were Jones Beach (1927), Montauk Point (1924), Devil's Hole (1924), Buckhorn Island (1935), Chittenango Falls (1926), Chenango Valley (1927), Taughannock (1925), Buttermilk Falls (1924), Tallman Mountain (1928), Clarence Fahnestock Memorial (1929), Hamlin Beach (1938), and Grass Point (1926). During the same years, construction commenced on major parkways in the Long Island, Westchester, Taconic, and Niagara regions.

Although acquisition and development of the park system slowed during the depression, state and federal work relief programs such as the Temporary Emergency Relief Administration (TERA) and the Civilian Conservation Corps (CCC) funneled millions of dollars into state park projects between 1932 and 1941. Relief labor was often used to supplement road-building crews or to develop infrastructure; significant building programs were completed at a number of parks, including Gilbert Lake in Laurens (Otsego Co) and Chenango Valley State Park in Fenton (Broome Co). World War II halted new development and delayed maintenance of existing facilities. After the war, as park attendance surged, the council focused on rehabilitating deteriorated infrastructure. By 1949 the state park system had grown to include 170,000 acres (69,000 ha) of land, 78 parks, and 160 miles (258 km) of parkways.

In the early 1950s substantial population increases, rapid development, the proliferation of automobiles, and middle-class migration to the suburbs changed the needs and expectations of park patrons. Whereas urban growth and its social effects had once motivated the state to acquire, preserve, and provide access to endangered scenic lands, outward migration posed a threat to open space in general and created increased demands that challenged the resources of existing parks. This decade culminated in a significant expansion of the state park system under the leadership of Gov Rockefeller. Rockefeller, whose family was among New York State's largest benefactors of public park land (especially noteworthy for its support of the PIPC), had an interest in parks and a propensity for building that rivaled Moses's own. Rockefeller responded to the effects of explosive postwar growth on land use and recreational needs by reinterpreting the goals and objectives of the 1922 park plan to address the needs of his own day. With his brother Laurance S., a nationally known conservationist, as chair of the SCP following Moses's departure, Rockefeller developed a far-reaching land acquisition program and won public support for three substantial bond acts between 1960 and 1966. These bonds made more than $300 million available for the acquisition of park and forest preserve land and the development of recreational facilities in state parks. Between 1961 and 1971, 47 new parks and historic sites were added to the state park system, more than under any previous governor and the largest number since the park system was created under Alfred E. Smith. During the Rockefeller years, two new park regions were added, Capital District (now Saratoga-Capital) and New York City, bringing the number of regions to 12.

New York State began to embrace nontraditional parks and programs. Beginning in 1974 the new federal Land and Water Conservation Fund, under the Bureau of Outdoor Recreation, awarded matching grants to states for dissemination to municipal park projects. This approach marked a shift from establishing state-owned and -operated recreational facilities. A major state incentive was the 1972 Environmental Quality Bond Act, which allocated $68 million to new parks, reserving a significant portion for municipal park projects. In the next few decades, OPRHP responded to the effects of social and economic changes (such as the decline in leisure time) by bringing parks closer to patrons, especially those in urban areas. Roberto Clemente State Park in the Bronx (1972) was New York City's first state park. Concurrently, OPRHP diversified its programs to include parks that combined recreation with art, such as Earl W. Brydges Artpark (1974) near Niagara Falls; with history, such as the Susquehanna Urban Cultural Park (1977; now Susquehanna Heritage Area) in Binghamton; or with environmentalism, such as the Taconic Outdoor Education Center (1984) at Cold Spring (Putnam Co).

New challenges at the end of the 20th century echoed those faced by conservationists a century earlier. With relentless development threatening New York's scenic resources, the state's concern

NEW YORK STATE PARKS

Park Name	Location	Date Acquired	Acres (Hectares)	Features
Allegany Region				
Allegany SP	Salamanca, South Valley, Red House, Cold Spring, Carrolton, and Great Valley (Cattaraugus Co)	1921	64,800 (26,200)	New York State's largest state park; naturalistic preserve; old-growth forest
Cuba Lake Reservation	Cuba (Allegany Co) and Ischua (Cattaraugus Co)	1926	696 (282)	Originally Genesee Valley Canal reservoir
Lake Erie SP	Portland (Chautauqua Co)	1928	355 (144)	High bluffs overlooking Lake Erie; *ca* 1935 bathhouse
Long Point on Lake Chautauqua SP	Ellery (Chautauqua Co)	1956	360 (146)	Former Minturn estate
Central Region				
Battle Island SP	Granby (Oswego Co)	1938	235 (95)	On Oswego River; early 20th-century public golf course
Betty and Wilbur Davis SP	Westford (Otsego Co)	2000	191 (77)	Scenic views
Bowman Lake SP	McDonough (Chenango Co)	1962	653 (264)	Wilderness preserve
Canadarago MP	Richfield (Otsego Co)	1960	4 (2)	Fishing; boat launch
Chenango Valley SP	Fenton (Broome Co)	1927	1,137 (460)	Chenango River; lakes; stone-and-wood park buildings; designed landscape
Chittenango Falls SP	Cazenovia (Madison Co)	1926	193 (78)	Waterfalls; stone park buildings; designed landscape
Clark Reservation SP	DeWitt (Onondaga Co)	1926	377 (153)	Glacial lake; stone park buildings
Delta Lake SP	Western (Oneida Co)	1968	400 (162)	Lakefront peninsula; Black River Canal features
Frenchman Island SP	Constantia (Oswego Co)	1974	26 (11)	Undeveloped
Gilbert Lake SP	New Lisbon and Laurens (Otsego Co)	1926	1,584 (641)	Designed landscape; stone-and-wood park buildings; CCC era features
Glimmerglass SP	Springfield and Middlefield (Otsego Co)	1963	593 (240)	Otsego Lake; Hyde Hall SHS
Green Lakes SP	Manlius (Onondaga Co)	1928	1,756 (711)	Glacial lakes; golf course; CCC era features; designed landscape
Helen L. McNitt SP	Cazenovia	1999	134 (54)	Cazenovia Lake; 1,300 ft (400 m) shoreline; deeply forested
Hudson-Mohawk Trail	Little Falls (Herkimer Co)	1980		2.6 mi (4.18 km) trail length; Mohawk River trail
Hunts Pond SP	New Berlin (Chenango Co)	1962	235 (95)	Pond; ferns
Lehigh Valley Trail	Canastota to Chittenango Falls (Madison Co)	1975		16.7 mi (26.88 km) trail length; follows Canastota Creek
Lennox Forest Demonstration Area	Kortright (Delaware Co)	1971	172 (70)	Forest preserve
Mexico Point SP	Mexico (Oswego Co)	1986	122 (49)	Lake Ontario; fishing, boat launch
Mexico Point MP	Mexico	1964	20 (8)	Little Salmon River off Lake Ontario
Old Erie Canal Recreationway	East Verona (Oneida Co) to Green Lakes SP (Onondaga Co)	1968	973 (394)	Erie Canal features
Oquaga Creek SP	Sanford (Broome Co) and Masonville (Delaware Co)	1968	1,385 (560)	Catskill Mts; interpretive nature trail
Pixley Falls SP	Boonville and Western (Oneida Co)	1967	375 (152)	Adirondack foothills; Black River Canal features
Selkirk Shores SP	Richland (Oswego Co)	1926	980 (397)	Scenic bluffs overlooking Lake Ontario; 1920s–30s log park buildings
State Fair at the Park	Geddes (Onondaga Co)	1975	3 (1)	Core of original New York State Fairgrounds
Verona Beach SP	Verona (Oneida Co)	1944	1,735 (702)	Oneida Lake; Black Lake; sand beach; aquatic and bird habitats
Finger Lakes Region				
Allan H. Treman MP	Ulysses (Tompkins Co)	1969	91 (37)	Cayuga Lake inlet wetland; forest
Beechwood SP	Sodus (Wayne Co)	1999	172 (70)	Lake Ontario views
Black Diamond Trail	Buttermilk Falls SP to Allan H. Treman MP	1984		15 mi (24.1 km) trail length; Cayuga Lake vistas; connects four state parks
Bonavista SP	Romulus (Seneca Co)	1992	251 (102)	Seneca Lake; golf course
Buttermilk Falls SP	Ithaca	1924	793 (321)	Buttermilk Gorge; 1920s–30s stone park buildings; 19th-century farmhouse
Canandaigua Lake MP	Canandaigua (Ontario Co)	1969	15 (6)	Sucker Brook; boat launch
Catharine Valley Trail	Watkins Glen SP to Mark Twain SP	1997		30 mi (48.3 km) trail length; follows Catharine Creek; railroad and Chemung Canal features

continued on page 1462

NEW YORK STATE PARKS (continued)

Park Name	Location	Date Acquired	Acres (Hectares)	Features
Cayuga Lake SP	Seneca Falls (Seneca Co)	1927	141 (57)	Cayuga Lake; 1930s bathhouse
Chimney Bluffs SP	Huron (Wayne Co)	1962	597 (242)	Bluffs overlooking Lake Ontario; historic farmsteads
Deans Cove BL	Seneca Falls	1968	10 (4)	Cayuga Lake; Hicks Gully; fishing
Fair Haven Beach SP	Sterling (Cayuga Co)	1928	823 (333)	Bluffs overlooking Lake Ontario; 1930s–40s stone-and-frame park buildings
Fillmore Glen SP	Moravia, Locke, and Summerhill (Cayuga Co)	1925	941 (381)	Gorge; designed landscape; 1920s–30s park buildings; *ca* 1880 log cabin associated with Pres Millard Fillmore
Harriet Hollister Spencer RA	Canadice (Ontario Co)	1978	678 (274)	Views of Honeoye Lake and surrounding lowlands
Honeoye Lake MP	Richmond (Ontario Co)	1959	9 (4)	Honeoye Lake; fishing
Keuka Lake SP	Jerusalem (Yates Co)	1961	621 (251)	Ravines; boat launch
Lodi Point MP	Lodi (Seneca Co)	1962	12 (5)	Seneca Lake; boat launch
Long Point SP	Ledyard (Cayuga Co)	1963	272 (110)	Cayuga Lake; boat launch; fishing
Mark Twain SP	Veteran (Chemung Co)	1990	469 (190)	Catharine Creek; Horseheads marshland; golf course
Newtown Battlefield Reservation	Elmira and Ashland (Chemung Co)	1914	372 (151)	Site of 1799 Battle of Newtown; African American CCC camp
Pinnacle SP	Addison (Steuben Co)	1978	715 (289)	Levi Pond; Canisteo River; panoramic views; historic cemetery
Robert H. Treman SP	Enfield and Ithaca (Tompkins Co)	1920	1,075 (435)	Enfield Creek Gorge; designed landscape; CCC era features and camp; Enfield mill and mill owner's house
Sampson SP	Romulus	1960	1,905 (771)	Seneca Lake; American Indian burial grounds; settlement era farms; World War II Military Museum
Seneca Lake SP	Waterloo (Seneca Co)	1958	141 (57)	Seneca Lake; marina canal
Stony Brook SP	Dansville (Steuben Co)	1928	568 (230)	Stony Brook Gorge; woodlands; late 1930s park buildings
Taughannock Falls SP	Ulysses	1925	746 (302)	Taughannock Creek Gorge; Cayuga Lake; *ca* 1840 residence; *ca* 1930s park buildings
Watkins Glen SP	Watkins Glen and Dix (Schuyler Co)	1906	776 (314)	Glen Creek Gorge; Seneca Lake views; designed landscape; 19th-century suspension bridge; *ca* 1910 pavilion, 1928–30s park buildings
Genesee Region				
Braddock Bay SP	Greece (Monroe Co)	1961	387 (157)	Lake Ontario wetlands; bird conservation area
Canal Park–Lock 32	Pittsford (Monroe Co)	1978	9 (4)	Erie Canal features
Conesus Lake MP	Livonia (Livingston Co)	1960	3 (1)	Conesus Lake; boat launch
Darien Lakes SP	Darien (Genesee Co)	1965	1,845 (747)	Eleven Mile Creek Gorge; mineral springs; natural gas wells
Durand Eastman ROW	Irondequoit (Monroe Co)	1985	19 (8)	Lake Ontario; Irondequoit Bay; undeveloped
Genesee Valley Greenway	Genesee Junction (Monroe Co) to Letchworth SP	1984		46 mi (74.0 km) trail length; Genesee Canal features
Hamlin Beach SP	Hamlin (Monroe Co)	1938	1,287 (521)	Lake Ontario; Devil's Nose bluff; World War II POW camp
Irondequoit Bay MP	Webster (Monroe Co)	1970	35 (14)	Lake Ontario; Irondequoit Bay; boat launch; fishing
Isaac Property SP	Irondequoit	1985	35 (14)	East shore of Irondequoit Bay
Lake Ontario State Parkway	Rochester to Lakeside Beach SP	1935		35 mi (56.3 km) parkway length; along Lake Ontario; connects four state parks
Lakeside Beach SP	Carlton (Orleans Co)	1962	744 (301)	Lake Ontario; steep shoreline bands
Letchworth SP	Leicester, Mount Morris, and Portage (Livingston Co); Castile and Genesee Falls (Wyoming Co)	1907	14,345 (5,805)	Genesee River Gorge; designed landscape; American Indian commemorative sites; railroad and canal features; Glen Iris Inn; 1912–40s park buildings
Oak Orchard MP	Carlton	1964	81 (33)	Lake Ontario; wetland; boat launch; prehistoric resources

NEW YORK STATE PARKS (continued)

Park Name	Location	Date Acquired	Acres (Hectares)	Features
Rattlesnake Point SP	Irondequoit	2001	41 (17)	Genesee River; undeveloped
Silver Lake SP	Castile (Wyoming Co)	1963	776 (314)	Lake views; wetlands
Long Island Region				
Gov Alfred E. Smith/ Sunken Meadow SP	Smithtown (Suffolk Co)	1926	1,288 (521)	Long Island Sound; glacial cliffs; salt marshes; 1930s park buildings; boardwalk
Bay Parkway	Meadowbrook Parkway to Wantagh Parkway	1930		1.5 mi (2.41 km) parkway length; within Jones Beach SP
Bayard Cutting Arboretum	Islip (Suffolk Co)	1936	690 (279)	Connetquot River; 1886 estate house; Frederick Law Olmsted–designed arboretum
Belmont Lake SP	Babylon (Suffolk Co)	1926	463 (187)	Early 20th-century estate buildings and landscape; 1930s park buildings
Bethpage SP	Oyster Bay (Nassau Co); Huntington and Babylon (Suffolk Co)	1934	1,477 (598)	Former estate; five 1930s–40s golf courses (including historic Black Course); 1930s park buildings
Bethpage State Parkway	Southern State Parkway to Bethpage SP	1934–36		2.4 mi (3.86 km) parkway length; provides access to Bethpage golf courses
Brookhaven SP	Brookhaven (Suffolk Co)	1972	1,589 (643)	30 mi (48.3 km) of trails
Caleb Smith SP Preserve	Smithtown	1963	546 (221)	Nissequogue River; 19th-century private club incorporates early 19th-century community
Camp Hero SP	East Hampton (Suffolk Co)	1974	454 (184)	Atlantic Ocean; wetlands; World War II coastal defense features
Captree SP	Babylon and Islip (Suffolk Co)	1954	340 (138)	Fire Island Inlet; fishing; boating
Caumsett SP	Lloyd Harbor (Suffolk Co)	1961	1,520 (615)	Long Island Sound; wetlands; woodlands; former estate buildings
Cold Spring Harbor SP	Huntington	2000	45 (18)	Views of harbor and Long Island Sound
Connetquot River SP	Islip	1963	3,473 (1,405)	Prehistoric resources; 18th-century mill; 1890 trout hatchery; former Southside Sportsmen's Club
Gilgo Beach SP	Babylon	1928	1,223 (495)	Atlantic Ocean; Great South Bay; surfing; fishing
Heckscher SP	Islip	1924	1,657 (671)	Great South Bay; former estate buildings; designed landscape; 1930s park buildings
Heckscher State Parkway	Southern State Parkway to Heckscher SP	1959		7.8 mi (12.55 km) parkway length; eastern extension of Southern State Parkway
Hempstead Lake SP	Hempstead (Nassau Co)	1925	727 (294)	Wetlands; historic carousel; former New York City water supply
Hither Hills SP	East Hampton	1924	1,755 (710)	Napeague Bay; Atlantic Ocean; dunes; historic cemetery
Hither Woods SP	East Hampton	1987	557 (225)	Ponds; coastal walks; bridle path
Jones Beach SP	Hempstead	1927	2,413 (977)	Atlantic Ocean barrier island; beach; dunes; 2 mi (3.22 km) boardwalk; theater; 1920s–30s park buildings; water tower; Theodore Roosevelt Nature Center
Key Span Property SP	Riverhead and Southold (Suffolk Co)	2003	533 (216)	Long Island Sound; sand dunes
Loop Parkway	Lido Beach (Nassau Co) to Meadowbrook Parkway	1934		2.7 mi (4.35 km) parkway length; connects Nassau Co barrier beach communities to Jones Beach SP
Meadowbrook Parkway	Northern State Parkway to Jones Beach SP	1932–56		12.8 mi (20.60 km) parkway length; intersects Southern State Parkway
Montauk Downs SP	East Hampton	1978	171 (69)	Lake Montauk; scenic views; golf course
Montauk Parkway	Montauk Point SP to Hither Hills SP	1934		1.6 mi (2.56 km) parkway length; connects six state parks
Montauk Point SP	East Hampton	1924	862 (349)	Atlantic Ocean; Block Island Sound; Montauk Lighthouse
Napeague SP	East Hampton	1977	1,364 (552)	Napeague Bay; Atlantic Ocean; wetlands
Nissequogue River SP	Smithtown	2000	153 (62)	Long Island Sound; former Kings Park Psychiatric Center

continued on page 1464

NEW YORK STATE PARKS (continued)

Park Name	Location	Date Acquired	Acres (Hectares)	Features
Northern State Parkway	Carle Place (Nassau Co) to Commack (Suffolk Co)	1931–65		29.1 mi (46.83 km) parkway length; intersects Meadowbrook, Wantagh, and Sunken Meadow Parkways
Ocean Parkway	Jones Beach SP to Captree SP	1930–34		15.9 mi (25.59 km) parkway length; traverses Gilgo SP
Orient Beach SP	Southold (Suffolk Co)	1929	364 (147)	Long Beach; Little and Gardners Bays; wilderness beach; bird sanctuary
Planting Fields Arboretum	Oyster Bay	1972	409 (166)	Former estate buildings; farm landscape; arboretum
Robert Moses Parkway and Causeway	Sagtikos Parkway to Robert Moses SP	1930		8.1 mi (13.04 km) parkway length; intersects Southern State Parkway
Robert Moses SP	Babylon and Islip	1893	875 (354)	Atlantic Ocean; Fire Island Inlet; ocean beaches; Fire Island Lighthouse
Sag Harbor SP	East Hampton	1997	341 (138)	Golf course
Sagtikos State Parkway	Sunken Meadow Parkway to Robert Moses Parkway	1950–52		4.9 mi (7.89 km) parkway length; connects Northern and Southern State Parkways
Sanctuary SP	East Hampton	1997	339 (137)	Prairie habitat; trails
Shadmoor SP	East Hampton	2000	99 (40)	Atlantic Ocean; wetlands; bluffs; World War II coastal defense features
Southern State Parkway	North Valley Stream (Nassau Co) to Heckscher State Parkway	1925–49		25.9 mi (41.68 km) parkway length; connects four state parks; intersects Meadowbrook, Wantagh, Sagtikos, and Robert Moses Parkways
Sunken Meadow Parkway	Sagtikos Parkway to Alfred E. Smith SP	1929–57		6 mi (9.7 km) parkway length; access to Long Island Sound
Trail View SP	Cold Spring Harbor SP to Bethpage SP	2002	400 (162)	Linear park extends 7.4 mi (11.91 km); follows northern ROW for Bethpage State Parkway
Valley Stream SP	Hempstead	1925	97 (39)	Environmental trails
Wantagh State Parkway	Northern State Parkway to Jones Beach SP	1927–38		13.6 mi (21.89 km) parkway length; intersects Southern State Parkway; first parkway to Jones Beach
Wildwood SP	Riverhead (Suffolk Co)	1925	767 (310)	Long Island Sound; 19th-century estate buildings; 1930s park buildings
New York City Region				
Bayswater Point SP	Queens	1987	21 (9)	Jamaica Bay; tidal wetlands
Clay Pit Ponds SP	Staten Island	1979	258 (104)	19th-century farm; archaeological resources; wetlands
East River SP	Brooklyn	2000	9 (4)	Riverfront walkway
Empire-Fulton Ferry SP	Brooklyn	1978	9 (4)	East River; scenic views; 1880s warehouses; archaeological resources
Graniteville Quarry SP	Staten Island	2001	4 (2)	Unusual geologic formations
Hudson River SP	Manhattan	1998	550 (223)	Access to Lower Manhattan waterfront; lawns; gardens; piers; walkway
Riverbank SP	Manhattan	1988	28 (11)	Hudson River; scenic views; sports facilities; developed on wastewater treatment plant
Roberto Clemente SP	Bronx	1972	22 (9)	Harlem River; sports facilities
Niagara Region				
Amherst SP	Amherst (Erie Co)	2000	77 (31)	Ellicott Creek; orchards; woodlands
Beaver Island SP	Grand Island (Erie Co)	1935	952 (385)	Niagara River; golf course; 19th- and early 20th-century estates
Big Six Mile Creek Marina	Grand Island	1978	19 (8)	Niagara River; scenic views; boat launch
Buckhorn Island SP	Grand Island	1935	895 (362)	Niagara River; nature sanctuary
DeVeaux Woods SP	Niagara Falls	2000	51 (21)	Old-growth forest; 19th-century college for orphans
Devil's Hole SP	Niagara Falls	1924	42 (17)	Niagara River; gorge; designed landscape; American Indian resources

NEW YORK STATE PARKS *(continued)*

Park Name	Location	Date Acquired	Acres (Hectares)	Features
Earl W. Brydges Artpark	Lewiston (Niagara Co)	1974	155 (63)	Performing arts center; American Indian resources; 18th-century fortifications
Evangola SP	Brant and Evans (Erie Co)	1954	733 (297)	Lake Erie; woodlands, wetlands, meadows, low cliffs
Fort Niagara SP	Porter (Niagara Co)	1947	504 (204)	Lake Ontario; War of 1812 cemetery; Old Fort Niagara SHS; former army bases; lighthouse and keeper's residence
Four Mile Creek SP	Porter	1961	248 (100)	Lake Ontario; scenic views; 1759 British encampment
Golden Hill SP	Somerset (Niagara Co)	1962	510 (206)	Lake Ontario; Thirty Mile Point Lighthouse
Joseph Davis SP	Lewiston (Niagara Co)	1963	388 (157)	Niagara River; fishing; golf course
Knox Farm SP	Aurora and Elma (Erie Co)	2000	633 (256)	Cazenovia Creek; working farm breeds racehorses and Aberdeen Angus cattle
Niagara Gorge Trail	Artpark to Niagara Reservation SP	1933		7 mi (11.2 km) trail length; follows Niagara River; connects five state parks
Niagara Reservation SP	Niagara Falls	1885	435 (176)	New York State's first state park; Niagara Falls; Frederick Law Olmsted–designed landscape
Reservoir SP	Lewiston	1964	132 (53)	Power authority reservoir
Robert Moses State Parkway	Niagara Reservation SP to Four Mile Creek SP	1960		18.4 mi (29.61 km) parkway length; connects six state parks
South Parkway	Beaver Island SP to NYS Thruway	1935		2.7 mi (4.38 km) parkway length; Grand Island; intersects West River Parkway
Strawberry Island SP	Tonawanda (Erie Co)	1989	5 (2)	Niagara River island; views of Buffalo; fish and wildlife habitats
West River Parkway	Beaver Island SP to Buckhorn Island SP	1952		8.5 mi (13.70 km) parkway length; Grand Island along Niagara River
Whirlpool SP	Niagara Falls	1933	109 (44)	Niagara River; whirlpool; gorge; Olmsted Bros–designed landscape; trail
Wilson-Tuscarora SP	Wilson (Niagara Co)	1965	425 (172)	Lake Ontario; bird habitat; wetland fauna
Woodlawn Beach SP	Hamburg (Erie Co)	1996	106 (43)	Lake Erie; wetlands; dunes; nature boardwalk
Palisades Region				
Bear Mountain SP	Stony Point (Rockland Co) and Highlands (Orange Co)	1910	5,067 (2,051)	Hudson Highlands; Hudson River; Bear Mountain Inn; Trailside Museum; includes Iona Island SP and Perkins Memorial Parkway and Tower
Blauvelt SP	Orangetown (Rockland Co)	1913	590 (239)	Long Path; undeveloped preserve
Bristol Beach SP	Saugerties (Ulster Co)	1967	165 (67)	Hudson River; ravines, bluffs
Goose Pond Mountain SP	Chester (Orange Co)	1962	1,558 (631)	Seeley Brook; Indian Caves
Harriman SP	Highlands, Woodbury, and Tuxedo (Orange Co); Stony Point, Haverstraw, and Ramapo (Rockland Co)	1910	46,616 (18,865)	Hudson Highlands; Appalachian Trail; designed naturalistic landscape; organized group camps; furnace and mine sites; early rustic park buildings
Haverstraw Beach SP	Haverstraw and Clarkstown (Rockland Co)	1938	73 (30)	Hudson River; stone park buildings
High Tor SP	Haverstraw and Clarkstown	1943	565 (229)	Long Path; Hudson River views; former estate; vineyard; Revolutionary War site
Highland Lakes SP	Wallkill (Orange Co)	1963	3,116 (1,261)	Ponds; model airstrip; 19th-century farms
Hook Mountain SP	Clarkstown	1911	696 (282)	Hudson River; historic quarry site; inclined railroad
Lake Superior SP	Bethel (Sullivan Co)	1967	1,409 (570)	Lake Superior; Chestnut Ridge Lake; wetlands
Minnewaska SP	Rochester, Wawarsing, and Gardiner (Ulster Co)	1971	11,990 (4,852)	Shawangunk Mts; lakes; steep cliffs; resort hotel sites; historic farm sites

continued on page 1466

NEW YORK STATE PARKS (continued)

Park Name	Location	Date Acquired	Acres (Hectares)	Features
Nyack Beach SP	Clarkstown	1938	61 (25)	Hudson River; historic quarry site
Palisades SP	Orangetown	1904	20 (8)	Hudson River; contiguous with New Jersey Palisades SP
Palisades Interstate Parkway	Fort Lee, NJ, to Bear Mountain Bridge (Orange Co)	1947–61		42 mi (67.5 km) parkway length; skirts Palisades Escarpment and traverses Bear Mountain/Harriman SP; Hudson River views
Rockland Lake SP	Clarkstown	1958	1,133 (459)	Former resort; remnants of historic ice business; golf courses
Schunnemunk Mountain SP	Blooming Grove, Woodbury, and Cornwall (Orange Co)	2003	2,450 (991)	Hudson Highlands; scenic overlooks
Sterling Forest SP	Warwick, Tuxedo, and Monroe (Orange Co)	1998	18,113 (7,330)	Iron mines; streams; watershed conservation project
Storm King SP	Cornwall (Orange Co)	1917	1,884 (762)	Hudson River views; Storm King Highway scenic drive
Tallman Mountain SP	Orangetown	1928	687 (278)	Hudson River; historic quarry; marsh; woodlands; 19th-century estate
Saratoga-Capital Region				
Athens BL	Athens (Greene Co)	1964	3 (1)	Hudson River; tidal marshes
Cherry Plain SP	Berlin and Stephentown (Rensselaer Co)	1962	175 (71)	Black River Pond; 1930s CCC dam; charcoal pits
Coxsackie BL	Coxsackie (Greene Co)	1964	4 (2)	Hudson River; tidal waters
Grafton Lakes SP	Grafton (Rensselaer Co)	1968	2,357 (954)	Lakes; wetlands; trails
Hudson River Islands SP	Stockport (Columbia Co) and Coxsackie	1976	235 (95)	Hudson River Estuarine Preserve
Hudson-Mohawk Trail	Cohoes (Albany Co) to Schenectady and Amsterdam (Montgomery Co)	1982		36.6 mi (58.90 km) length; Mohawk River Trail (two sections)
John Boyd Thacher SP	Guilderland, Berne, Knox, and New Scotland (Albany Co)	1914	1,348 (546)	Helderberg Escarpment; Indian Ladder Trail; caves; limestone cliffs
Lake Lauderdale SP	Jackson (Washington Co)	1968	117 (47)	Early 20th-century rustic cabin
Max V. Shaul SP	Fulton (Schoharie Co)	1959	70 (28)	Panther Creek; Toe Path Mountain
Mine Kill SP	Blenheim (Schoharie Co)	1973	500 (202)	Overlooking Blenheim-Gilboa Reservoir; Devil's Bowl
Moreau Lake SP	Moreau (Saratoga Co)	1967	4,110 (1,663)	Hudson River views; rocky ridges; hardwood forests; duck migration route
Peebles Island SP	Waterford (Saratoga Co)	1973	142 (57)	Island at confluence of Hudson and Mohawk Rivers; marshes; Revolutionary War encampment; former bleachery complex
Saratoga Lake MP	Saratoga	1964	3 (1)	Saratoga Lake
Saratoga Spa SP	Saratoga Springs	1909	2,200 (898)	Mineral springs; geyser; 1930s Beaux Arts park buildings; baths; golf courses; Gideon Putnam Hotel; Saratoga Performing Arts Center; Little Theater
Schodack Island SP	Schodack (Rensselaer Co); Kinderhook (Columbia Co); New Baltimore (Greene Co)	1974	1,052 (426)	Hudson River Estuarial Sanctuary; wetlands; Native American council fire
Thompson's Lake SP	Knox	1961	308 (125)	Helderberg Mts; 1933 CCC camp; hardwood forests
Washington Country Trail	Salem to Granville (Washington Co)	1990		23.6 mi (37.98 km) trail length; includes Vermont section
Taconic Region				
Clarence Fahnestock Memorial SP	Philipstown and Putnam Valley (Putnam Co)	1929	11,150 (4,512)	Lakes; CCC and WPA ski area; Taconic Outdoor Education Center; includes Roaring Brook SP (1928)
Franklin D. Roosevelt SP	Yorktown (Westchester Co)	1958	761 (308)	Lake; pond; stone park buildings; originally Mohansic SP (1922)
Harlem Valley Rail Trail	Amenia (Dutchess Co) to Copake (Columbia Co)	1989		20 mi (32.1 km) trail length; follows railroad ROW
Hart's Brook Nature Preserve and Arboretum	Greenburgh (Westchester Co)	1999	123 (50)	Former estate; carriage trails; Revolutionary War encampment
Hudson Highlands SP	Philipstown; Cortlandt (Westchester Co)	1967	5,550 (2,246)	Panoramic Hudson River views; trails; wildlife habitat
Hudson BL	Hudson (Columbia Co)	1970	3 (1)	Hudson River

NEW YORK STATE PARKS *(continued)*

Park Name	Location	Date Acquired	Acres (Hectares)	Features
James Baird SP	LaGrange (Dutchess Co)	1939	590 (239)	Golf course; sports facilities
Lake Taghkanic SP	Gallatin and Taghkanic (Columbia Co)	1929	1,569 (635)	Beaches; stone park buildings; water tower; CCC era features and camp
Margaret Lewis Norrie SP	Hyde Park (Dutchess Co)	1934	330 (134)	Hudson River; tidal wetlands; stone-and-wood park buildings; CCC era features
Ogden and Ruth Livingston Mills SP	Hyde Park	1938	637 (258)	Hudson River; includes Mills Mansion SHS; Hoyt House
Old Croton Aqueduct SP	Greenburgh	1968	216 (87)	Follows route of 19th-century aqueduct
Rockefeller Park Preserve	Mount Pleasant (Westchester Co)	1983	948 (384)	Pocantico River; carriage roads; American Indian settlements
Taconic SP (includes Copake Falls and Rudd Pond sections)	North East (Dutchess Co); Ancram and Copake (Columbia Co)	1924	3,988 (1,614)	Part of proposed Tri-State Park; Copake includes iron works; trails; CCC era features; Rudd Pond includes site of 1880s iron ore production
Taconic State Parkway	Bronx River Parkway (Westchester Co) to I-90 (Columbia Co)	1931–63		105.3 mi (169.46 km) parkway length; connects four state parks; Hudson Highlands, Catskill Mts, and Taconic Mts views; developed as part of state park program and now owned by NYS Department of Transportation
Wonder Lake SP	Patterson (Putnam Co)	1998	794 (321)	Hiking; skiing; fishing
Thousand Islands Region				
Black Lake BL	Morristown (St. Lawrence Co)	1968	3 (1)	Black Lake
Black River Trail	Watertown to Black River (Jefferson Co)	1988		4.5 mi (7.24 km) trail length; follows railroad ROW along riverbank
Burnham Point SP	Cape Vincent (Jefferson Co)	1898	12 (5)	St. Lawrence River; 1940s park buildings
Canoe Picnic Point SP	Clayton (Jefferson Co)	1898	70 (28)	St. Lawrence River; Eel Bay; hilly terrain; sandy shoreline
Cedar Island SP	Hammond (St. Lawrence Co)	1898	10 (4)	St. Lawrence River island; historic pavilion
Cedar Point SP	Cape Vincent	1897	48 (19)	St. Lawrence River; stone park buildings
Chaumont BL	Lyme (Jefferson Co)	1968	27 (11)	Three Mile Bay
Coles Creek SP	Waddington (St. Lawrence Co)	1958	1,800 (728)	St. Lawrence River; wooded areas
Crab Island SP	Plattsburgh	1988	40 (16)	Lake Champlain island; 1814 military burial site
Croil Island SP	Louisville (St. Lawrence Co)	1934	796 (322)	St. Lawrence River island; waterfowl
Cumberland Bay SP	Plattsburgh	1934	350 (142)	Lake Champlain; dunes; forests
DeWolf Point SP	Orleans (Jefferson Co)	1898	13 (5)	St. Lawrence River; Lake of the Isles; rock knolls; heavily forested
Eel Weir SP	Oswegatchie (St. Lawrence Co)	1967	16 (6)	Oswegatchie River; 1930s park buildings
Galop Island SP	Lisbon (St. Lawrence Co)	1969	675 (273)	St. Lawrence River island
Grass Point SP	Orleans	1926	114 (46)	St. Lawrence River; 1930s–40s park buildings
Great Chazy BL	Champlain (Clinton Co)	1968	7 (3)	Lake Champlain
Higley Flow SP	Colton (St. Lawrence Co)	1968	1,115 (451)	Raquette River; rugged terrain; sandy beach; nature center
Jacques Cartier SP	Morristown	1957	461 (187)	St. Lawrence River; wooded terrain
Keewaydin SP	Alexandria (Jefferson Co)	1962	241 (98)	St. Lawrence River; granite outcroppings; former estate features and landscape elements
Kring Point SP	Alexandria	1898	61 (25)	St. Lawrence River; Goose Bay; narrow peninsula with rocky shoreline; 1930s–40s stone park buildings
Long Point SP	Lyme	1913	23 (9)	Lake Ontario; Three Mile Bay; Chaumont Bay; peninsula; 1920s–30s park buildings
Macomb Reservation SP	Schuyler Falls and Peru (Clinton Co)	1957	600 (243)	Salmon River; Davis Pond; wooded; stone park buildings; former farmhouse

continued on page 1468

NEW YORK STATE PARKS (continued)

Park Name	Location	Date Acquired	Acres (Hectares)	Features
Mary Island SP	Alexandria	1898	13 (5)	St. Lawrence River island; wooded; rock ledges; river views
Point Au Roche SP	Beekmantown (Clinton Co)	1975	856 (347)	Lake Champlain; woodlands; fields
Point Au Roche BL	Beekmantown	1978	9 (4)	Lake Champlain
Robert Moses SP	Massena (St. Lawrence Co)	1958	2,322 (940)	St. Lawrence River; seaway canal; views of St. Lawrence Power Project; Eisenhower Lock
Rock Island Lighthouse	Orleans	1976	4 (2)	St. Lawrence River island; beach; 1847 lighthouse complex
Southwick Beach SP	Ellisburg (Jefferson Co)	1966	464 (188)	Lake Champlain; wetlands; hardwoods; old fields
St. Lawrence SP	Oswegatchie	1968	316 (128)	Cedar groves; rock outcroppings; historic farmhouses and barn
Stony Creek BL	Henderson (Jefferson Co)	1968	23 (9)	Lake Ontario
Waterson Point SP	Orleans	1898	6 (2)	St. Lawrence River; river and island views; *ca* 1930 pavilion
Wellesley Island SP	Orleans	1951	2,636 (1,067)	St. Lawrence River; Eel Bay; wooded; rocky knolls; marsh
Wescott Beach SP	Henderson	1945	319 (129)	Lake Ontario; Henderson Bay; high plateau; forests
Whetstone Gulf SP	Martinsburg, West Turin, and Turin (Lewis Co)	1968	2,100 (850)	Whetstone Creek and Reservoir; 3 mi (4.8 km) gorge; mountain valley; steep vertical cliffs
Wilson Hill BL	Louisville	1968	4 (2)	Lake St. Lawrence

Sources: NYS Office of Parks, Recreation, and Historic Preservation (NYSOPRHP), "State Park Profiles, 2001"; NYSOPRHP, *New York State Statewide Comprehensive Outdoor Recreation Plan for 2002–2007* (2003); NYSOPRHP, Field Services Bureau, Statewide Historic Resources Survey; NYSOPRHP, Bureau of Resource and Facility Planning, Albany.

Note: Locations given for state parks and reservations indicate all minor civil divisions in which the park has a presence. Locations given for parkways, trails, and other linear features indicate start and end points only, not civil divisions through which the feature extends.

Abbreviations: BL: boat launch; MP: marine park; RA: recreation area; ROW: right of way; SHS: state historic site; SP: state park.

Compiled by Kathleen LaFrank

with the preservation of endangered land extended beyond parks and preserves to include shorelines, water bodies, agricultural landscapes, wetlands, and other public open spaces. A shared concern for environmental protection brought DEC and OPRHP together in 1990 to collaborate on the state's first open space plan. Notably, the plan advocated the protection of open space using measures other than state acquisition, including zoning, tax incentives, easements, and the creation of agricultural districts. The open space program was supported by the creation of the Environmental Protection Fund ($125 million annually) in 1993 and passage of the Clean Water/Clean Air Bond in 1996. The latter allocated $150 million to open space projects, including parks, forest preserves, and farmland protection. New York State also negotiated new public/private partnerships to preserve open space and create new parks. Notable examples include Sterling Forest, where private, state (New York and New Jersey), and federal funds stemmed intensive development of 19,000 acres (7,700 ha) of forest habitat and watershed in Orange Co; Moreau Lake State Park (Saratoga Co), where 3,200 acres (1,290 ha) in the Adirondacks were acquired with help from the Open Space Institute; and Nissequogue River State Park in Kings Park (Suffolk Co), a significant bird and wildlife habitat acquired through transfer from the New York State Office of Mental Health. Between 1995 and 2002, 15 new state parks were added to the system, which expanded to include 300,000 acres (121,000 ha) and 167 parks.

Recreation

Drawing on Romantic ideas about the American wilderness expressed by 19th-century writers such as James Fenimore Cooper, painters such as Thomas Cole, and landscape designers such as Frederick Law Olmsted, New York's state park program was premised on the idea that society could be improved by providing every citizen with the opportunity to experience the beneficial effects of nature. At the end of the 19th century, recreational activity was defined as the enjoyment of scenic beauty, prompting park administrators to develop programs for patrons, especially disadvantaged urbanites, to participate in wilderness living and nature education programs. So strong was the belief in the transformational effects of exposure to nature that park programs often combined these activities with instruction in the social graces, as if facilitating self-improvement in a natural setting would itself engender social stability.

However, New York State's commitment to automobile-accessed state parks in 1924 signaled the beginning of a shift in focus to the recreational needs of middle-class suburban residents. Suburbs were designed to give each family a private park to return to each evening. Thus, suburbanites looked to state parks to provide settings not for quiet contemplation but for active "play," family-centered activities outside the limits of the backyard. Park patrons increasingly expected to find amenities such as swimming pools, boat launches, and ski facilities. This change was acknowledged by the SCP after World War II, when it broadened its definition of a state park to include areas with opportunities for a variety of recreational activities, especially water-related pastimes. In the same period, the SCP undertook a significant expansion of the state parkway system so that increasingly mobile patrons could travel to parks more efficiently. Throughout the 1950s and 1960s, active outdoor recreation remained a program priority; however, the concept of recreation subsequently expanded to include activities that combined a variety of experiences, such as the appreciation of cultural heritage, the enjoyment of nature, and environmental education, with opportunities to engage in traditional outdoor activities. This trend is reflected in recent initiatives to link diverse public and private resources associated with historic and/or environmental themes in linear systems, complex undertakings usually developed and administered by federal, state, and local partners. OPRHP is an active partner in examples such as the Hudson River Estuary/Greenway, the Genesee Valley Greenway, and the Erie Canalway National Heritage Corridor.

In the late 20th century, OPRHP again turned its attention to the needs of urban neighborhoods threatened by poverty and decay. Riverbank State Park, opened in 1993, was constructed atop a wastewater treatment plant in Harlem. The emphasis on sports at Riverbank, which boasts playing fields, basketball courts, and organized team sports, was intended to create a safe and supportive environment for urban youth within the endangered urban landscape itself.

In 2003 almost half of the state's population was concentrated in urban areas, which occupy only 1% of its land, and the 2003 Statewide Comprehensive Outdoor Recreation Plan (SCORP) identified areas with high population density as a priority for new recreational services. SCORP also acknowledged the continuing needs of low-income urban populations, which often have little open space in their own communities and few opportunities to venture outside them. The agency has adopted a mandate to protect and expand neighborhood open space. OPRHP remains committed to the idea that contact with nature enhances the well-being of citizens and that even small-scale features such as community gardens increase the amount of open space in urban areas. Under the Inner City/Underserved Community Park program, facilities such as Gantry Plaza, which will provide access to the East River waterfront in Queens, and the Eastern District Terminal, a waterfront recreation/sports facility in the Williamsburg section of Brooklyn, are being developed. Despite nearly a century of change, the goals of the New York State park program remain consistent with those established by the PIPC, and the keystone of the state park program remains the conservation of land for public benefit.

See also MOSES, ROBERT.

Caro, Robert A. *The Power Broker: Robert Moses and the Fall of New York* (New York: Vintage Books, 1974)
Nelson A. Rockefeller Institute of Government. *Preserve and Protect: Challenges Facing New York's State Park System* (Albany: Author, 1993)
New York State Council of Parks. *First Annual Report to the Governor and the Legislature of the State of New York* (Albany: Author, 1925)
New York State Office of Parks, Recreation and Historic Preservation. *50 Years, New York State Parks, 1924–1974* (Albany: Natural Heritage Trust, 1975)
———. *New York: Statewide Comprehensive Outdoor Recreation Plan 2003* (Albany: Author, 2003)
New York State Association. Committee on the State Park Plan. *A State Park Plan for New York*, 2d ed. ([New York?]: 1924)

Kathleen LaFrank

State Police, Division of. Statewide police agency established by the New York State legislature in 1917, under Republican governor Charles S. Whitman, to provide law enforcement in rural parts of the state. The controversial measure passed by one vote in the senate. The previously organized Pennsylvania state police had a reputation for strikebreaking in the coal mines, and labor was opposed to the new agency. Additionally, sheriffs and constables did not condone increased competition. The first recruits were trained at a National Guard camp in Manlius (Onondaga Co), and on 17 Sept 1917, 232 troopers reported for duty at the New York State Fairgrounds near Syracuse. The first troopers were stationed at Batavia (Genesee Co), Oneida (Madison Co), Colonie (Albany Co), and White Plains (Westchester Co). In 1921 the New York State School for Police was organized in the Troy (Rensselaer Co) YMCA. The State Police Department became a unit of the Executive Department in 1927 and was renamed the Division of State Police. In 1935 the Bureau of Investigation was created as a plainclothes detective branch; in 1936 it was renamed the Bureau of Criminal Investigation (BCI), and a State Police crime laboratory opened in Schenectady.

The first state troopers patrolled rural areas on horseback, but by 1948 mounted patrols ended and the focus shifted to highway traffic. After the opening of the New York State Thruway in 1954 the State Police assumed sole responsibility for its policing, and the number of troopers increased from 899 to 1,201. Beginning in the 1950s, illegal drug trafficking became a target of State Police action. Division headquarters at the Gov W. Averell Harriman State Office Building Campus in Albany were built in 1964, and the crime lab was relocated to this site. The State Police Academy in Albany was completed in 1970. In the 1960s three new troops were authorized: Troop T, which became the official designation for the Thruway detail (1961); Troop E, which began operating from its new headquarters in Canandaigua (Ontario Co) in 1967; and Troop F, which began operations in Middletown (Delaware Co) in 1968. Computerization and communications improvements, such as high-band radios, occurred in the 1970s, and in 1971 the New York Statewide Police Information System was put into service. A regional crime lab was opened in Newburgh (Orange Co) in 1978, and another lab opened near Binghamton in 1979. In the 1980s and 1990s the division increased its technological capabilities, set up a regional crime lab in Olean (Cattaraugus Co) in 1985, established violent crime investigative teams (1993) to work with local authorities, created the Forensic Investigation Center (1996), and otherwise streamlined its operations to meet new demands.

From time to time outside observers have argued that the division has exceeded its proper police bounds. Governors have used the State Police as a political tool, notably Gov Thomas E. Dewey in the 1940s and early 1950s, and covert files not related to criminal matters have been kept. Gov Dewey required that every state job paying over $2,500 per year be filled only after an investigation by the State Police. For this purpose—as well as others—a special investigative unit was established under prominent judge and prosecutor William B. Herlands. A controversial noncriminal investigative unit that shadowed dissidents, anti-Vietnam War protestors, and other "political militants" as a kind of state FBI was disbanded in the 1970s. Additionally, the State Police have been criticized for excessive use of force in the Attica Correctional Facility uprising of 1971 when prisoners seized control of the Wyoming Co prison. Acting on orders from Gov Nelson A. Rockefeller to retake the prison, at least 200 state troopers stormed the facility on 13 Sept 1971 and in the ensuing battle, 32 inmates and 11 hostages, including 7 correctional officers, were fatally wounded by gunfire. A commission consisting of nine members appointed by the chief judge of the New York Court of Appeals and the presiding justices of the four Appellate Departments conducted an extensive investigation of the event. The resulting McKay Commission report noted that State Police superintendent William Kerwin was not present at Attica, leaving planning for the assault to the local commander. Numerous accounts of the assault from prisoners and prosecutors involved have not resolved the controversy surrounding it.

The division, best known for patrolling roads and highways outside major urban centers, also provides specialty and investigative police services throughout the state. The division is headed by a superintendent appointed by the governor. Headquarters are in Albany and 11 troops are stationed throughout the state. Two principal branches, the Uniform Force and the BCI, handle cases requiring intensive investigation or involving felonies. The division in 2002–3 had 5,257 employees, including 1,148 in criminal investigation activities and 2,816 in patrol activities; the remaining are involved in administration, Indian gaming, policing the Thruway, technical police services, and vehicle

State police monitoring traffic on I-81 in North Syracuse, 1991.

dimension and weight enforcement activities. Uniformed officers who have died during the course of duty are shown on the Honor Wall at the New York State Police Academy. In 2001 the division reported 796,627 vehicle and traffic arrests, 116,693 criminal cases, 10,583 BCI investigations, and 305,723 noncriminal investigations.

See also COMMUNISTS; POLICING.

Shelton, Pamela T. *History of the New York State Police, 1917–1987* (Dallas: Taylor Publishing, 1987)

Keith Henderson

state recreation areas. New York State–owned recreation lands provide opportunities for a spectrum of activities, such as swimming, skiing, golfing, camping, wildlife observation, biking, picnicking, boating, hiking, hunting, relaxing at a park or beach, fishing, and sightseeing. In 2002 the state owned the largest area of developed land for recreation, 1.3 million acres (526,100 ha), but only 6% of the developed recreation sites in the state. A larger number of smaller sites are owned and operated by commercial and private concerns as well as by town and local governments. The Office of Parks, Recreation, and Historic Preservation (OPRHP) and the Department of Environmental Conservation (DEC) manage most state recreation areas. Some of the popular areas include Niagara Reservation State Park (1885) in Niagara Falls, Jones Beach State Park (1929) in Wantagh (Nassau Co), and Belleayre Mountain Ski Center (1949) in Highmount (Ulster Co).

In 2002 OPRHP administered 165 state parks and 35 historic sites on over 300,000 acres (121,000 ha) that included 66 campgrounds, 27 golf courses, 52 swimming pools, and numerous waterway access facilities. The DEC managed 715,000 acres (289,350 ha) in 472 state forests, unique areas, and multiple-use areas as well as 2.9 million acres (1,173,600 ha) in the Adirondack and Catskill Forest Preserves for purposes including recreation. These OPRHP and DEC lands were acquired over more than 100 years through direct purchase, gifts, donations, payment of back or unpaid taxes, and land exchanges. Additional public recreational use and open space has been acquired on private lands through purchase or donation of recreation access easements and conservation easements that restrict development.

State lands are managed for recreation and multiple purposes ranging from reforestation, watershed protection, preservation of scenic and historic areas, to conservation of natural resources. Some of these lands, such as Enfield Gorge at Robert H. Treman State Park (1920) in Ithaca, were originally purchased by wealthy landowners seeking to protect unique scenic areas and later acquired for state ownership, while other lands were obtained by state programs for reforestation following the abandonment of marginal farmlands starting in the 1890s. The public purchase of lands has been supported by legislation such as the State Reforestation Act (1929), the Park and Recreation Land Acquisition Act (1960), the Environmental Quality Bond Acts (1972, 1988), and the Clean Water/Clean Air Bond Act (1996). Annual appropriations are available to support states through federal programs such as the Land and Water Conservation Fund (1964). Over 75% of all New York residents participated in various types of outdoor recreation on public and private lands in 2002.

Early version of the state seal; detail from Gansevoort flag, attributed to Ezra Ames, *ca* 1790–97.

New York State Office of Parks, Recreation, and Historic Preservation. *Statewide Comprehensive Outdoor Recreation Plan 2003* (Albany: Author, 2002)

Chad P. Dawson

state seal and state flag. The great seal of New York State was initially devised in 1777, with a modification in 1778 that included the arms and seal. The seal is kept in the custody of the secretary of state and has been used for all official matters issued under it since 16 Mar 1778. The design has been revised three times, most recently in 1882 under Gov Alonzo B. Cornell.

The seal is a round piece of metal 2.5 inches (6.4 cm) in diameter on which the device (coat of arms) of New York State is engraved. The device shows a shield at center, on which is a ship and sloop on a river with a mountain range in the background and the sun rising behind it. Above the shield is a globe showing the Atlantic Ocean and its two shores. An eagle perched on the globe is looking toward the right, considered to be a good omen. To the right of the shield (on the observer's left) stands the figure of Liberty, clothed in a flowing blue gown and red robe, with pearls in her hair. In her left hand is a staff holding a gold Phrygian cap of the sort that was awarded as a sign of freedom to a Roman slave upon emancipation and was a symbol of liberty. At the left foot of Liberty is a royal crown, which illustrates the diminished power of the English monarchy. To the left of the shield stands the figure of Justice, clothed in gold with a blue and red belt. She is blindfolded and holds a sword in her right hand and scales in her left, representing the impartiality that is required for bestowing just rewards and punishments. The state motto, Excelsior (Ever Upward), is inscribed in black type on a silver scroll beneath the shield. The whole device is surrounded by the legend "The Great Seal of the State of New York."

The state seal is the basis for the New York State flag, which is defined by law as an image of the seal centered against a dark blue background. The flag was officially adopted on 2 Apr 1901, though an earlier version had been in use since 8 Apr 1896 and included a buff-colored field. The flag is flown every day of the year, weather permitting, and at night if it is illuminated.

OFFICIAL NEW YORK STATE SYMBOLS

Category	Symbol	Year Adopted
animal	beaver	1975
beverage	milk	1981
bird	bluebird	1970
fish	brook or speckled trout	1975
flower	rose	1955
fossil	*Eurypterus remipes*	1984
fruit	apple	1976
gem	garnet	1969
insect	ladybug	1989
muffin	apple muffin	1987
shell	bay scallop	1988
tree	sugar maple	1956

Source: New York State Department of State, "New York State Symbols," http://www.dos.state.ny.us/kidsroom/nysfacts/stfacts.html.

Compiled by Hannah M. Springer

Gebhart, John Robert. *Your State Flag* (Philadelphia: Franklin Publishing, 1973)
New York State Department of State. "The Great Seal of the State of New York," http://www.dos.state.ny.us/kidsroom/nysfacts/seal2.html

Hannah M. Springer

State University Construction Fund. Public benefit corporation established by Chapter 251 of the Laws of 1962 and responsible for design, construction, and facility management at 34 SUNY campuses. The State University Construction Fund (SUCF) has no involvement with the campuses of technical and community colleges, which are locally funded. The SUCF is governed by a board of three trustees appointed for five-year terms by the governor; one trustee must also be a SUNY trustee. The board reviews and approves all construction projects, employing consultants to plan, design, and bid the projects. Capital expenditures in excess of $20,000 are awarded by public bid to the lowest bidder. The SUCF aided expansion of the state's university system during the 1960s and 1970s by constructing the campuses of SUNY Albany and SUNY Purchase and the Amherst (Erie Co) campus of SUNY Buffalo and by expanding campuses at Brockport, New Paltz, and Oswego, among other major projects. Until 1989 SUCF projects were financed through bonds issued by the Housing Finance Agency and after that date through bonds issued by the Dormitory Authority. In 1998 the state legislature approved a $2 billion, five-year capital plan for SUNY, emphasizing facility maintenance and upgrades. In 2001–2 irregularities in contract awards—the SUCF was charged with ignoring its own bidding rules in an Albany case and favoring a relative of Gov George E. Pataki in an Old Westbury (Nassau Co) case—led to establishment of a new procurement unit and new bidding guidelines. In 2002 the SUCF had 86 projects valued at $319 million under design, 13 projects valued at $44 million in the bid award process, and 116 projects valued at $448 million under construction. At its headquarters in SUNY's central administration building at State University Plaza in Albany, 113 staff members work in five offices: construction management, design management, operational support services, administration services, and counsel.

Jeffrey Kraus

State University of New York (SUNY). When New York State established a state university system in 1948, it was the last of the contiguous 48 states to do so. Since the mid–19th century, the state's private colleges and universities had blocked efforts to establish public colleges and universities, claiming they adequately provided for the liberal arts and graduate education of New Yorkers. Until the postwar period, the New York State Board of Regents, which had jurisdiction over higher education in the state, agreed with the private colleges. As late as 1942 New York State ranked second to last in total state budgetary expenditures for higher education.

FOUNDING

Pressure to establish a state university system grew after World War II. The 1944 federal Serviceman's Readjustment Act (the GI Bill) offered free higher education to every qualified returning veteran. Many doubted that New York State's private colleges would be able to meet the resulting demand. In addition, old questions about the fairness of private colleges' admissions policies were raised anew. The American Jewish Congress and other groups cited evidence that discriminatory admissions practices kept Jews, African Americans, and Roman Catholics out of many private schools and called for the state to establish a public university system. In response, Gov Thomas E. Dewey and the state legislature created the Temporary Commission on the Need for a State University in April 1946. Headed by Owen D. Young, former chair of General Electric, the commission called for the creation of a state university system and the passage of legislation mandating that all colleges and universities admit students without regard to race, religion, or ethnicity. The commission's report identified substantial economic, geographic, academic, racial, and religious barriers to higher education within the state's private college system. The commission's findings were reinforced in 1948 by the report of the President's Commission on Higher Education, which called for the substantial expansion of higher education throughout the nation. Dewey was reluctant to support the creation of a state university system, but his presidential ambitions and the popularity of the GI Bill made him reconsider. He assented to his commission's recommendations and openly supported the 1948 Fair Education Practices Act, which prohibited race- and religion-based discrimination in college admissions. The act creating the State University of New York was signed by Dewey on 4 Apr 1948 and became effective on 1 July 1948. The system's initial units were the 30 state-operated institutions of higher learning that had been established in upstate New York: 11 teachers colleges, 6 agricultural and technical institutes, 6 two-year institutes of applied arts and science, 6 public "land grant" colleges managed by private institutions, and the New York

STATE UNIVERSITY OF NEW YORK (SUNY)

Institution	Year Founded (Joined SUNY)	Full-Time Students	Part-Time Students
University Centers			
Albany	1844 (1948)	12,632	4,119
Binghamton	1946 (1950)	10,923	1,550
Buffalo	1846 (1962)	17,302	4,629
Stony Brook	1957	13,403	4,105
University Colleges			
Brockport	1830 (1948)	6,026	2,498
Buffalo State	1867 (1948)	7,972	3,427
Cortland	1868 (1948)	5,606	1,572
Empire State College	1971	2,146	5,863
Fredonia	1826 (1948)	4,531	536
Geneseo	1867 (1948)	5,106	371
New Paltz	1830 (1948)	5,485	2,238
Old Westbury	1965	2,322	673
Oneonta	1889 (1948)	5,176	408
Oswego	1863 (1948)	6,515	1,634
Plattsburgh	1885 (1948)	5,262	891
Potsdam	1816 (1948)	3,676	555
Purchase	1971	3,138	939
Health Science Centers			
Downstate Medical Center (Brooklyn)	1860 (1950)	1,075	395
Health Science Center at Buffalo	1846 (1962)	2,422	477
Health Science Center at Stony Brook	1970	1,586	830
Upstate Medical University (Syracuse)	1834 (1950)	933	163
Colleges of Technology			
Alfred	1908 (1948)	2,488	247
Canton	1906 (1948)	1,673	453
Cobleskill	1916 (1948)	2,144	159
Delhi	1913 (1948)	1,866	285
College of Technology at Farmingdale	1912 (1948)	3,009	2,036
Morrisville	1908 (1948)	2,625	408
Specialized Colleges			
College of Environmental Science and Forestry	1911 (1948)	1,397	352
Maritime College	1874 (1948)	641	135
College of Optometry	1971	289	0
Institute of Technology (Utica/Rome)	1966	1,360	1,300

continued on page 1472

State Maritime Academy at Fort Schuyler (Bronx Co). New York City's municipal liberal arts colleges were not incorporated into the system.

The enabling legislation for SUNY called for a 15-member board of trustees to govern the new system, and it transferred operating authority over the state teachers colleges and other public institutions from the Board of Regents to the SUNY trustees. The act also authorized the acquisition of two medical schools, the Long Island College of Medicine in Brooklyn and the College of Medicine at Syracuse University, and the opening of up to 22 community colleges. To stave off the opposition of the Regents, the act provided that the Regents, not the governor, would control SUNY's budget. Dewey also promised the private colleges that SUNY would open no liberal arts colleges for a decade. However, SUNY did acquire two existing liberal arts colleges in 1950: Triple Cities College (later Harpur College) in Endicott (Broome Co) and Champlain College in Plattsburgh; the latter closed in 1953 when the US Air Force reclaimed the site. In 1957 SUNY opened an additional state teachers college at Oyster Bay (Nassau Co). Dewey appointed Oliver Carmichael, president of the Carnegie Foundation for the Advancement of Teaching, as first chairman of SUNY Board of Trustees. In turn, Carmichael recruited Alvin Eurich as SUNY's first president (1949–51). Frank C. Moore, Dewey's lieutenant governor, subsequently chaired the SUNY board (1954–66). An indifferent Gov W. Averell Harriman ignored frequent calls for SUNY's expansion during his 1955–59 term. The publication of a report in 1957 calling for opening a research campus led to the dismissal of Eurich's successor, Frank Carlson (1951–57).

STATE UNIVERSITY OF NEW YORK (SUNY) (continued)

Institution	Year Founded (Joined SUNY)	Full-Time Students	Part-Time Students
Statutory Colleges			
College of Agriculture and Life Science at Cornell University	1868 (1948)	4,084	0
College of Ceramics at Alfred University	1900 (1948)	783	43
College of Human Ecology at Cornell University	1925 (1949)	1,572	0
School of Industrial and Labor Relations at Cornell University	1945 (1948)	907	1,122
College of Veterinary Medicine at Cornell University	1896 (1948)	422	0
Community Colleges			
Adirondack	1961	1,692	1,459
Broome	1947 (1953)	3,281	2,382
Cayuga County	1953	1,302	1,196
Clinton	1969	978	719
Columbia-Greene	1966	810	788
Corning	1957	2,035	2,771
Dutchess	1958	2,863	3,719
Erie	1946	6,396	3,611
Fashion Institute of Technology	1944 (1951)	6,256	4,557
Finger Lakes	1968	2,189	2,478
Fulton-Montgomery	1964	1,256	629
Genesee	1967	2,144	2,377
Herkimer County	1967	1,913	678
Hudson Valley	1953	4,837	4,467
Jamestown	1950	1,965	2,078
Jefferson	1963	1,848	1,804
Mohawk Valley	1946	3,099	1,993
Monroe	1962	7,342	7,973
Nassau	1959	12,131	7,684
Niagara County	1963	2,953	1,688
North Country	1967	719	367
Onondaga	1962	3,759	4,089
Orange County	1950	2,531	2,843
Rockland	1959	3,472	2,790
Schenectady County	1969	1,731	1,742
Suffolk County	1960	8,786	9,258
Sullivan County	1963	987	565
Tompkins-Cortland	1968	1,551	1,123
Ulster County	1961	1,417	1,254
Westchester	1946 (1948)	4,663	6,156

Source: New York Red Book (2001–2).

Note: Unless otherwise noted, year founded is the same year the school joined SUNY.

Rockefeller Years

In the 1950s SUNY's growth was relatively slow. By 1950 the system had 25,225 full-time students; by 1959 this number had increased to 38,642. However, the demand for higher education and the impending influx of baby boomers would rapidly outstrip available space. Gov Nelson A. Rockefeller recognized that SUNY's growth would educate constituents, provide construction projects, and employ many workers in predominantly Republican areas outside of New York City. In December 1959 he appointed the Commission on Higher Education, chaired by Henry T. Heald, president of the Ford Foundation and former president of New York University, to study SUNY's organization, finances, and expected growth. The commission's report, issued in 1960, set forth a program for the expansion of the SUNY system. Still facing opposition from the Regents and private colleges but strengthened by the favorable recommendations made by the Heald Commission, SUNY negotiated a compromise agreement with the private colleges and universities during the presidency of Thomas H. Hamilton (1959–62). SUNY would grow according to approved master plans. The State University Construction Fund, established in 1962, would issue the necessary bonds; the private colleges could borrow capital funds from the New York State Dormitory Authority. Beginning in 1963 SUNY, which had not charged tuition, would charge $400 per year to offset capital costs. Needy SUNY and private college students could receive Scholar Incentive Awards. Control of SUNY's budget would now be directly under the supervision of the governor, not the Board of Regents. These understandings were embodied in the 1961 Higher Education Act.

In the 1960s SUNY grew rapidly. In 1962, 10 of the state teachers colleges, now renamed state university colleges, started new undergraduate liberal and professional divisions. Two new state university colleges in the New York City metropolitan area, Old Westbury (Nassau Co) and Purchase (Westchester Co), were opened in 1965, and more than half of SUNY's 30 community colleges were established during the decade. With the 1971 opening of Empire State College, an institution for adult education with more than 40 regional centers, and the College of Optometry, one of two SUNY branches in Manhattan, SUNY reached its current complement of 64 separate colleges. Almost every county in the state hosted at least one SUNY campus. With 138,027 full-time students in 1967, the SUNY system had tripled its enrollment in less than a decade. In the early years of SUNY's existence, many envisioned that a single research university situated in Westchester Co would serve as the flagship of the system. By the early 1960s, however, SUNY trustees identified politically and geographically strategic locations for four university centers. In 1962 the state assembly speaker facilitated the founding of SUNY at Stony Brook (Suffolk Co), an outgrowth of the state teachers college at Oyster Bay. The state senate majority speaker facilitated the 1962 acquisition of the University of Buffalo, a financially troubled private university emphasizing professional education, and its reorganization as SUNY Buffalo. Two members of the Board of Regents lived in Binghamton, near where SUNY Binghamton (now Binghamton University) emerged from Harpur College. At the behest of Gov Rockefeller, SUNY Albany grew from Albany State Teachers College. Between 1962 and 1964, J. Lawrence Murray served as acting president of SUNY. Samuel Gould (1964–70), Murray's successor, oversaw the extensive construction program financed by the construction fund. Ernest Boyer followed Gould and continued the SUNY construction program. The rapid growth of the SUNY system made the state's private colleges increasingly worried about their future. To protect the private colleges and to ensure a support base as wide as possible for SUNY, Rockefeller and the state legislature in June 1968 enacted the "Bundy Aid" law, which adopted the recommendations made by a committee chaired by Ford Foundation president McGeorge Bundy and directly awarded state aid to private colleges for each degree recipient.

Crisis and Transformation

By the early 1970s, the heyday of SUNY's growth was over. Student demonstrations in the late 1960s led to growing public disillusionment with higher education. SUNY was a good target for budget cuts during the economic recession of the early and mid-1970s. By 1973 the state was also contributing heavily to the budget for the City University of New York (CUNY), further straining the state's educational budget. Rockefeller concluded in 1973 that SUNY was overbuilt and implemented a series of budget cutbacks. Tuition was increased and further expansion curtailed or eliminated. In 1973 several tenured SUNY faculty were dismissed, resulting in SUNY's censure by the American Association of University Professors. SUNY continued to retrench and consolidate during the administrations of Govs Hugh Carey and Mario M. Cuomo. SUNY chancellors during the Carey and Cuomo years included Clifton R. Wharton Jr (1978–88) and D. Bruce Johnstone (1988–94). In the 1980s and 1990s, the administrations of Govs Cuomo and George E. Pataki made SUNY, which had in the past been a state-supported system, a state-assisted system; state support decreased from 90% of SUNY's budget in 1988 to 45% in 1996. To compensate for lost state revenue, SUNY annual tuition rates rose from $1,350 in 1989–90 to $3,400 in 1995–96, just below the Northeast regional average. This partial "privatization" of SUNY resulted in the increasing independence of the individual colleges, a trend underscored by the SUNY trustees' 1998 decision to allow the colleges to keep tuition and fee revenues instead of sharing them with the SUNY system as a whole. Some critics fear that this change will eventually lead to the closing of some SUNY colleges.

Thomas Bartlett (1994–96) resigned as SUNY chancellor to protest the trustees' austerity policies and was replaced by John Ryan (1996–99). However, tax revenues generated by the economic boom of the late 1990s have reversed some earlier funding cutbacks. In 1998 Gov Pataki announced a $2 billion capital improvement and construction plan for SUNY campuses, and further state aid to enable the colleges to maintain undergraduate tuition at its current levels. A tuition increase for 2003–4 ended nine years of steady tuition. Robert L. King, former budget director of New York State in the Pataki administration, was appointed SUNY chancellor on 14 Dec 1999. Under King, SUNY moved to performance-based budgeting and to requiring completion of a core curriculum by all students.

In 1998 the 64 SUNY colleges included the 4 university centers, medical centers in Brooklyn, Buffalo (1962), Stony Brook (1970), and Syracuse; 4 specialized colleges; 13 arts and sciences colleges; 6 agricultural and technical institutes; 5 statutory colleges; and 30 community colleges. The system employed over 15,000 faculty members. United University Professions (UUP), an American Federation of Teachers (AFT) affiliate, is the bargaining agent for faculty at the universities, the four-year colleges, and several community colleges. The Civil Service Employees Association (CSEA) represents nonteaching staff at the university centers; the Graduate Student Employees Union (GSEU) represents graduate and teaching assistants throughout the SUNY system. The state chapter of the National Education Association (NEA–New York) bargains for faculty and staff at 18 two-year colleges. SUNY's enrollment, which had been increasing each year since 1997, peaked at more than 410,000 students in fall 2003. In the early 21st century, SUNY, which had graduated more than 1.9 million students, offers 1,587 associate, 1,504 baccalaureate, 956 master's, 313 doctoral, and 16 advanced professional programs.

Carmichael, Oliver, Jr. *New York Establishes a State University* (Nashville: Vanderbilt Univ Press, 1958)
Glazer, Judith. "Nelson Rockefeller and the Politics of Higher Education in New York State," *History of Higher Education Annual* 9 (1989)
Office of University Affairs and Development. *Sixty-Four Campuses: The State University of New York to 1985* (Albany: Office of Univ Affairs and Development, 1985)
Wechsler, Harold S. *The Qualified Student: A History of Selective College Admission in America, 1870–1970* (New York: Wiley-Interscience, 1977)

Harold S. Wechsler

Statue of Liberty. Monument on Liberty Island in Upper New York Bay. During an 1865 dinner party, Frenchman Edouard-René de Laboulaye, a historian and antislavery activist who feared that his country's liberty was slowly being extinguished under the authoritarian rule of Napoleon III, suggested that a monumental gift from the French people to the United States could laud American freedom. Alsatian sculptor Frédéric-Auguste Bartholdi was selected to undertake the commission and by 1870 produced a small model of "Liberty Enlightening the World." In 1871 Bartholdi traveled to the United States and selected the 10.7-acre (4.33 ha) Bedloe's Island in New York Harbor, the site of the antiquated Fort Wood, as the statue's home.

The Franco-American Union was formed in 1875 to finance construction of the 151 ft (46 m) statue while the United States prepared the site. The statue's hand and torch were displayed at the Philadelphia Centennial Exposition in 1876 and later in New York City to raise money, while the head was featured at the Paris Universal Exposition in 1878. Alexandre Gustave Eiffel built the internal iron structure that would support 100 tons (91 MT) of copper repoussé sheeting. Although Congress agreed in 1877 to accept the gift, most funding to construct a suitable pedestal came from a campaign initiated by the Union League Club of New York City. The last $102,000 was given by 121,000 ordinary citizens, primarily New York City residents, responding to an appeal by Joseph Pulitzer's *New York World.*

Statue of Liberty illuminated for the Hudson-Fulton Celebration, 1909.

The huge poured-concrete foundation for the 89 ft (27 m) pedestal was designed by Richard Morris Hunt. "Liberty" arrived in the United States in 214 crates in June 1885. The reconstructed statue, a virtual skyscraper that bends in the wind, was dedicated by Pres Grover Cleveland on 28 Oct 1886.

Only in the early 20th century did the Statue of Liberty become the "Mother of Exiles" welcoming immigrants: Emma Lazarus's poem "The New Colossus" was auctioned in 1883 as a fund-raising ploy and was placed on a plaque below the statue in 1903. Future Mt Rushmore sculptor Gutzon Borglum redesigned the torch for a 1916 renovation. Bedloe's Island was renamed Liberty Island in 1956, and a museum of immigration, which later moved to Ellis Island, operated in the statue's base from 1972 to 1991. The Statue of Liberty is administered by the National Park Service, but a private foundation raised $295 million to carry out the $87 million restoration between 1982 and 1986. A torch rebuilt to Bartholdi's original design, new crown windows, and approximately 1,800 stainless steel armature bars replacing Eiffel's originals were installed; even the 4 ft 6 in (1.37 m) nose was repaired. The statue's rededication on 4 July 1986 celebrated a national icon, the inspiration for four postage stamps, two Broadway plays, and a dozen scholarly volumes. In 2001 the Statue of Liberty appeared on the reverse of New York State's entry in the state quarter series, along with the inscription "Gateway to Freedom."

Hayden, Richard Seth, and Thierry W. Despont, with Nadine M. Post. *Restoring the Statue of Liberty: Sculpture, Structure, Symbol* (New York: McGraw-Hill, 1986)
Moreno, Barry. *The Statue of Liberty Encyclopedia* (New York: Simon & Schuster, 2000)

George J. Lankevich

statutes and statutory revision. Statutes enacted by the New York Colonial Assembly or the state legislature and approved by the governor have been periodically amended, compiled, revised, and consolidated, resulting in an ever changing body of law.

Dutch and English Colonial Laws

The director and council of New Netherland promulgated ordinances for the colony. In 1665 the first governor of New York Colony, Richard Nicolls, replaced those ordinances with the Duke's Laws, selected from English law and the codes of Massachusetts and Connecticut. With no printing press available, the early laws issued by the Dutch and English governments were recorded by the provincial secretaries and proclaimed at public meetings. New York Colony's first real statutes were passed by the assembly of 1683. The Duke's Laws were not operative after 1691. Official printers, starting with William Bradford in 1693, published in pamphlet form the acts passed at each assembly session, as well as several compilations of those acts. The laws in force were compiled by William Livingston and William Smith Jr in 1752 and 1762 and by Peter Van Schaack in 1774 and were published by New York City printers. These compilations, though officially sanctioned, were not systematically arranged, and they were not comprehensive because some English statutes were recognized in the province.

Early State Laws and the Revised Statutes

The Constitution of 1777 declared that the English statute and common law and assembly acts in force on 19 April 1775 (the day of the Battle of Lexington) continued as New York law if they conformed to the constitution and until they were altered by the legislature. In 1787–88 key English statutes concerning real property and judicial proceedings were enacted into New York law and all English statutes declared inoperative. In 1828 all remaining colonial acts were repealed. New York State has produced an enormous body of statute law (almost 135,000 chapters enacted in legislative sessions between 1778 and 2002). The need to make the law in force available in compact form was recognized early. Official editions of the session laws began to be published in 1782. Samuel Jones and Richard Varick made a retrospective compilation of the session laws, published in 1789. In 1800 the legislature directed James Kent and Jacob Radcliff to organize by topic the session laws that were in force; their compilation was published as the Revised Acts in 1802. A similar compilation by William Van Ness and John Woodworth appeared as the Revised Laws in 1813. In 1824, as requested by Gov Joseph C. Yates, the legislature appointed three commissioners to revise the session laws again, to conform to the Constitution of 1822.

Inspired by the successful Napoleonic Code and the writings of English legal theorist Jeremy Bentham, New York City lawyers such as William Sampson, Theodore Sedgwick, and Gulian Verplanck called for a comprehensive legal code. Such a code would establish the law according to a scientific, orderly system and thus eliminate the confusion resulting from the mounting number of statutes and court decisions. Proponents of the common law argued that it was flexible and was based on carefully considered judicial decisions and reliable tradition. In addition, judges and lawyers were accustomed to working within the common-law system. In 1825 Gov De Witt Clinton and the legislature endorsed a complete revision of the laws. Two of the three commissioners, Benjamin F. Butler and William Duer, were authorized to organize the statutes into a systematic whole and to propose substantive changes. A more cautious commissioner, Erastus Root, resigned and was eventually replaced by John C. Spencer. In 1827 and 1828 the commissioners submitted their drafts to the legislature, which enacted them largely as proposed. The Revised Statutes of the State of New York were published in three volumes in 1829. In just three years the commissioners had produced the first systematic compilation of statute law in any English-speaking country. The revisers followed the general organization of the esteemed *Commentaries on the Laws of England* by Sir William Blackstone. But the Revised Statutes were a distinctly American product; most notably, they rationalized the law of real property, eliminating the last vestiges of feudal tenure. The Revised Statutes incorporated some judicial decisions where appropriate but were not a full, true codification supplanting the statutes and the common law.

David Dudley Field and the Codification Movement

Because of the initial success of the Revised Statutes, further codification efforts focused on the courts. Civil and criminal procedure, as well as court organization, largely followed English models; they had been little changed by the

TITLES IN THE NEW YORK CONSOLIDATED LAWS, 2003

Law	Current Chapter Enacted	Chapter No.
Abandoned Property Law	1943	1
Agriculture and Markets Law	1922	69
Alcoholic Beverage Control Law	1934	3-B
Alternative County Government Law	1952	11-B
Arts and Cultural Affairs Law	1983	11-C
Banking Law	1914	2
Benevolent Orders Law	1909	3
Business Corporation Law	1961	4
Canal Law	1939	5
Civil Practice Law and Rules Law	1962	8
Civil Rights Law	1909	6
Civil Service Law 1909; generally recodified	1958	7
Cooperative Corporations Law	1951	77
Correction Law	1929	43
County Law	1950	11
Criminal Procedure Law	1970	11-A
Debtor and Creditor Law	1909	12
Domestic Relations Law	1909	14
Economic Development Law (formerly Commerce Law)	1944	15
Education Law	1947	16
Election Law	1976	17
Eminent Domain Procedure Law	1977	73
Employers' Liability Law	1921	74
Energy Law	1976	17-A
Environmental Conservation Law	1972	43-B
Estates, Powers and Trusts Law	1966	17-B
Executive Law	1951	18
General Associations Law	1909	29
General Business Law	1909	20
General City Law	1909	21
General Construction Law	1909	22
General Municipal Law	1909	24
General Obligations Law	1963	24-A
Highway Law	1936	25
Indian Law	1909	26
Insurance Law	1984	28
Judiciary Law	1909	30
Labor Law	1921	31
Legislative Law	1909	32
Lien Law	1909	33
Limited Liability Company Law	1994	34
Local Finance Law	1942	33-A
Mental Hygiene Law	1972	27
Military Law	1909	36
Multiple Dwelling Law	1946	61-A
Multiple Residence Law	1952	61-B
Municipal Home Rule Law	1963	36-A
Navigation Law	1941	37
New York State Printing and Public Documents Law	1917	58
Not-for-Profit Corporation Law	1969	35
Parks, Recreation and Historic Preservation Law	1972	36-B
Partnership Law	1919	39

TITLES IN THE NEW YORK CONSOLIDATED LAWS, 2003 (continued)

Law	Current Chapter Enacted	Chapter No.
Penal Law	1965	40
Personal Property Law	1909	41
Private Housing Finance Law	1961	44-B
Public Authorities Law	1939	43-A
Public Buildings Law	1909	44
Public Health Law	1953	45
Public Housing Law	1939	44-A
Public Lands Law	1909	46
Public Officers Law	1909	47
Public Service Law	1910	48
Racing, Pari-Mutuel Wagering and Breeding Law	1982	47-A
Railroad Law	1910	49
Rapid Transit Law	1941	48-A
Real Property Law	1909	50
Real Property Actions and Proceedings Law	1962	81
Real Property Tax Law	1958	50-A
Religious Corporations Law	1909	51
Retirement and Social Security Law	1955	51-A
Rural Electric Cooperative Law	1942	77-A
Second Class Cities Law	1909	53
Social Services Law	1940	55
Soil and Water Conservation Districts Law	1940	9-B
State Law	1909	57
State Administrative Procedure Act	1975	82
State Finance Law	1940	56
State Technology Law	1999	57-A
Statute of Local Governments	1964	58-A
Surrogate's Court Procedure Act	1966	59-A
Tax Law	1909	60
Town Law	1932	62
Transportation Law	1967	61-A
Transportation Corporations Law	1926	63
Uniform Commercial Code	1962	38
Vehicle and Traffic Law	1959	71
Village Law	1973	64
Volunteer Ambulance Workers' Benefit Law	1988	64-B
Volunteer Firefighters' Benefit Law	1956	64-A
Workers' Compensation Law	1922	67
Court Acts[a]		
Court of Claims Act	1939	
Family Court Act	1962	
New York City Civil Court Act	1962	
New York City Criminal Court Act	1962	
Uniform City Court Act	1964	
Uniform District Court Act	1963	
Uniform Justice Court Act	1966	

[a]Considered part of the Unconsolidated Laws.

Compiled by James D. Folts

Revised Statutes. The Constitution of 1846 required the legislature to appoint commissioners to "revise, reform, [and] simplify" court rules, pleadings, and forms, primarily to facilitate the constitutional merger of the Court of Chancery (equity jurisdiction) into the supreme court (common-law jurisdiction). Commissioners David Dudley Field, David Graham, and Arphaxed Loomis prepared what was called the Code of Civil Procedure, enacted in 1848 and amended in 1849. Field, a New York City lawyer, would be a relentless partisan of codification for nearly 50 years. The 1848 code abolished the distinction between common-law actions and equity proceedings and substituted a single civil action. All the technical intricacies of common-law actions and pleading were discarded. The New York Code of Civil Procedure became a model for similar reforms in many other states. However, the legislature in 1850 rejected a proposed code of criminal procedure and a revised code of civil procedure.

The Constitution of 1846 also required the appointment of commissioners to "reduce into a written and systematic code" all the laws of the state. This mandate to codify New York's laws largely failed. Most members of the legislature preferred to revise the statutes again not to adopt a comprehensive code. A code commission appointed in 1847 did practically nothing. Another code commission was appointed in 1857. The most prominent commissioner was Field. The commissioners dutifully prepared, but the legislature failed to adopt, a political code (1860) on the structure and functions of state and local government, a book of legal forms (1861), a civil code on property rights and personal rights and obligations (1865), and a penal code outlining crimes and their punishments (1865). Still another commission was appointed in 1870 to fulfill the codification mandates of the 1846 Constitution. Led by Montgomery Throop, the commission drafted and the legislature enacted in 1877 a voluminous, intricate Code of Civil Procedure, replacing the short, simple 1848 code. In 1881 the legislature and the governor at last approved the code of criminal procedure and the penal code, mostly as drafted years before. But the state still had no comprehensive legal code.

The recurring debates about codification resulted in gross delays in another comprehensive statutory revision. Eight other unofficial editions of the Revised Statutes of 1829 were commercially published through 1896. These ill-organized compilations were bulked up with numerous amendments and even omitted some statutes in force. Still other commercial publications, such as *Statutes at Large* (1863), edited by John W. Edmonds, and *Revised Statutes, Codes and General Laws* (1889–90), edited by Clarence F. Birdseye, were better organized and included ample notes and indexes.

The General Laws and the Consolidated Laws

Recognizing the growing inconsistency, ambiguity, and prolixity of the often amended Revised Statutes, in 1889 the legislature authorized and Gov David B. Hill appointed a Statutory Revision Commission. Because the Revised Statutes were intricately organized, the new commissioners sensibly decided to organize the statute law by topic and to call it the General Laws of New York to distinguish it from the Revised Statutes. Between 1890 and 1899 the commissioners produced and the legislature approved 46 chapters on subjects ranging from agriculture to villages. Not all topics were covered, and many statutory inconsistencies and ambiguities remained. Although the Statutory Revision Commission was disbanded in 1900, three unofficial versions of the General Laws were published between 1896 and 1901, as well as an official version in 1900, edited by Edward L. Heydecker.

After more years of debate, a new Board of Statutory Consolidation was established in 1904. Chaired by Adolph J. Rodenbeck, the board conducted an exhaustive analysis of every session law back to 1778. The Consolidated Laws, enacted in 1909–10 and published by the state, were the first comprehensive reorganization and revision of the statutes since 1827–28. All existing statutory law of general, not local or special, impact was distributed into 64 chapters arranged by topic. Hundreds of obsolete laws were repealed. A separate Civil Practice Act of 1920 replaced the 1877 Code of Civil Procedure. The Consolidated Laws of 1909–10, with innumerable amendments and many added and some deleted chapters, continue to be New York's official statement of general statutory law. Many chapters of the Consolidated Laws have been totally revised and reenacted; for example, the Insurance Law in 1937 and 1984 and the Civil Practice Law and Rules in 1962. The Consolidated Laws are not a self-contained legal code; the session law remains the primary source, and documentation of legislative intent and court decisions may guide the interpretation of a statutory provision.

The state published just one edition of the Consolidated Laws of New York, in 1909–10, but it continues to publish the annual session laws. Commercial publishers have issued both annotated and unannotated versions of the Consolidated Laws. Starting in 1916 William McKinney edited and the Edward Thompson Co of Brooklyn published *The Consolidated Laws of New York* with extensive annotations, case citations, and regular updates. Generally known as McKinney's, this edition is now published by the West Group. Included in McKinney's are the constitution, the Consolidated Laws, and the court acts, as well as other special and miscellaneous laws known as the Unconsolidated Laws. Another annotated edition is *The New York Consolidated Laws Service* (CLS), which the Lawyers Co-Operative Publishing Co of Rochester began publishing in 1950 and which is now published by LexisNexis.

See also COURTS, STATE.

Cook, Charles M. *The American Codification Movement: A Study of Antebellum Legal Reform* (Westport, Conn: Greenwood, 1981)
Gibson, Ellen M. *New York Legal Research Guide,* 2d ed. (Buffalo: William S. Hein, 1998)
Van Ee, Daun. *David Dudley Field and the Reconstruction of the Law* (New York: Garland Publishing, 1986)

R. Allan Carter and James D. Folts

St. Bonaventure University. Private university in Allegany (Cattaraugus Co). It was founded by the Franciscan Friars in 1858 as a college and seminary to educate and serve the Irish Catholic population. In 1942 the school became coeducational and in 1950 attained full university status and offered graduate classes. The university's Friedsam Library has a rare books collection on Franciscan history, manuscripts from the late Middle Ages, and early printed books. The New York City–based National Shakespeare Co has its summer residency in the university's Rigas Family Theater. The school offers 35 undergraduate and 28 graduate programs. Enrollment in 2002 was 2,164 undergraduate and 546 graduate students, with 54% female and 46% male.

Angelo, Mark V. *The History of St. Bonaventure University* (St. Bonaventure, NY: Franciscan Institute, 1961)

Mary E. Gabriel

steamboats. New York State offered tremendous opportunities for commercial steam navigation, but its broad, often tempestuous rivers, lakes, bays, and ocean channels intimidated inventors with their small models and prototype steamships. Most early experiments took place elsewhere on more sheltered waters. In 1796 John Fitch (1743–98) tested small screw-propelled steamboats on Manhattan's Collect Pond, while operating commercial steam-driven carriers on the Delaware River in Pennsylvania and New Jersey. In 1794 Samuel Morey (1762–1843) sailed a small sidewheel steamboat from Hartford, Conn, to Manhattan and back.

Four years later, Col John Stevens (1747–1838), Nicholas Roosevelt (1767–1854), and Charles Staudinger built a small steamboat, *Polacca,* at Belleville, NJ, and sailed it on the Passaic River and Newark and Upper New York Bays to Manhattan and back. Stevens's brother-in-law, Robert R. Livingston (1746–1813), a wealthy and prominent New Yorker, was a passenger. In 1802 Stevens built a tiny, 25 ft (7.6 m) screw steamboat, *Little Juliana,* at Hoboken, NJ, and sailed it to Manhattan; in 1811 he built the sidewheel *Juliana* for his trans-Hudson ferry service to run from Manhattan's Vesey St to Hoboken. Livingston had meanwhile joined with inventor Robert Fulton (1765–1815) in building experimental steamboats in France. Patron and inventor moved their operations to the Hudson River in 1807 and built *North River Steamboat,* commonly called *Clermont* after Livingston's estate at Clermont (Columbia Co). It was successfully tested on 17 Aug 1807 between New York City and Albany and entered commercial service between the two points on 4 Sept 1807, carrying passengers and freight with comfort and dependability. Fulton and Livingston retained a legal monopoly on steam navigation on New York State waters until 1824, after which many other operators began service, and by 1840 there were over 100 steamboats on the Hudson River alone.

Steamboat development and subsequent decline followed a common pattern on all the major waterways in the state. Initially they were the fastest and most comfortable, dependable, and economical transportation along navigable waterways; they connected with the few post roads and turnpikes. Major canals—Champlain (1819), Erie (1825), Welland (1832)—built to link important waterways further encouraged steamboat development. When primitive railroads were built to major ports—New York Central to Buffalo (1840), New York and Erie to Dunkirk (1851), Northern Railroad to Ogdensburg (1850), and New York, Ontario and Western to Oswego (1871)—they stimulated development of steamboat lines on the St. Lawrence River and Lakes Ontario and Erie that operated westward to Chicago and Duluth on the upper Great Lakes.

Frequently the railroads ran large steamboat lines themselves and built parallel to the waterways. The Hudson River Railroad linked Manhattan with Albany in 1851; Lake Shore Railroad connected Buffalo with Toledo in 1857; and New York and Canada Railroad (now Delaware and Hudson Railroad and Canadian Pacific Railroad) joined Albany with Montreal in 1875. These rail lines operated throughout the year at greater speeds and at increasingly lower costs, siphoning off the most lucrative freight and passenger traffic and leaving the steamboats only less profitable bulk commodities as well as the business of towing barges with steam towboats. On the Great Lakes, principal freight commodities were grain and iron ore moving east and coal moving west. Massive fleets of bulk carriers operated to the New York State ports of Dunkirk, Buffalo, Rochester, Sodus Point, Oswego, and Ogdensburg. The railroads ran most of these fleets until 1915, when operations were suspended to comply with provisions of the Panama Canal Act of 1912, which forbade railroads from owning transport lines running parallel with their rail lines. But many independently operated grain ships continued to serve Buffalo and Rochester, and independent ore carriers served Buffalo and shipped coal from Sodus Point. Most New York State steamboats were sidewheel steamers, burning wood in the early years and coal and oil in later years. Screw propellers were used primarily on routes extending into the open Atlantic waters or rougher upper Great Lakes or for bulk carrier freighters.

Steamboat passenger business changed and flourished from 1870 to 1930 with construction of fast, luxurious, giant liners plying the state's sounds, rivers, and lakes, as well as the Great Lakes cruise ships and other river and lake excursion boats. Much of the new business was seasonal, catering mainly to tourists and vacationers, but several major routes between well-spaced population centers served all classes of travelers throughout the year. Overnight liners operated on Lake Erie from Buffalo to Cleveland, Toledo, and Detroit, on the Hudson River from New York City to Albany and Troy, and on Long Island Sound from New York City to southern New England cities. These lines carried express freight and frequently were both more pleasant and more economical than overnight train travel on parallel routes.

The Great Depression, labor problems, and World War II—not automobile or rail competition—destroyed the lines' profitability. In later years remaining business was largely of the excursion type. The last Great Lakes cruise boat, SS *South American* of the Georgian Bay Line, sailed from Buffalo in 1966. The last Long Island Sound liner, belonging to the Colonial Line, traveled between New York City and Providence, RI, in 1942. Regular steamship service along the length of Lake Champlain ended with the sidewheeler *Ticonderoga* of the Champlain Transportation Co in 1953. The last steamboat on the Hudson River was the Hudson River Day Line's sidewheeler *Alexander Hamilton,* launched in 1924 and retired in 1970; Hudson River Day Line maintained limited operations with a new diesel ship until 1987. At the beginning of the 21st century, Lake Champlain boasts cross-lake diesel-powered ferries. Lake George Steamboat Co, founded in 1817, built the sternwheel steamboat *Minne-Ha-Ha* in 1969; the company still operates the dieselized former steamboat *Mohican II* (1908) and intends to construct another. Other operators plan a return of steam excursion boats to the Hudson River and Lake Champlain.

See also *GIBBONS V OGDEN;* GREAT LAKES SHIPPING LINES AND WATERCRAFT; HUDSON RIVER FERRIES; HUDSON RIVER STEAMBOAT LINES; LAKE GEORGE STEAMBOAT COMPANY; LONG ISLAND SOUND STEAMBOAT LINES; PORT OF NEW YORK.

Adams, Arthur G. *The Hudson through the Years* (New York: Fordham Univ Press, 1996)
Morrison, John H. *History of American Steam Navigation* (New York: W. F. Stametz, 1903)
Ringwald, Donald C. *Hudson River Day Line: The Story of a Great American Steamboat Company* (New York: Fordham Univ Press, 1990)

Arthur G. Adams

steel industry. See IRON AND STEEL INDUSTRY.

Steingut, Stanley (*b* Brooklyn, 20 May 1920; *d* New York City, 8 Dec 1989). Legislative and political leader. Son of former assembly speaker Irwin Steingut, he attended Union College and St. John's University School of Law. A Democrat, he was elected to the legislature in 1952 from the Crown Heights section of Brooklyn. While serving as assembly minority leader from 1969 to 1974, he built a political organization that seized power in 1974 and maintained solid Democratic control of the assembly into the early years of the 21st century. The builder of a strong staff to challenge the gubernatorial dominance that had lasted 50 years, he helped create the modern legislative political system that raised money and selected and managed candidates and campaigns. As Speaker (1975–78) Steingut played a prominent role in bringing state aid to New York City during its 1975–76 fiscal crisis and in staving off bankruptcy. He was defeated by a relative unknown in a 1978 primary election and practiced law until his death.

Benjamin, Gerald. *The Modern New York State Legislature: Redressing the Balance* (Albany: Nelson A. Rockefeller Institute of Government, 1991)

Peter Slocum

Steinmetz, Charles P(roteus) [Karl August Rudolf] (*b* Breslau, Germany [now Wroclaw, Poland], 9 Apr 1865; *d* Schenectady, 26 Oct 1923). Electrical engineer. His father, Heinrich Steinmetz, was employed as a lithographer for the Upper Silesian Railway. Having inherited hunchbacked dwarfism from his father, the young Steinmetz soon learned to compensate for his physical limitations by excelling intellectually. He early distinguished himself in academics, receiving the highest marks in mathematics and science in his gymnasium graduating class as well as numerous awards in math, physics, and chemistry at the University of Breslau, which he attended from 1883 to 1888. At that university Steinmetz became interested in socialism, joining a local Socialist Party. In Bismarckian Germany, socialism was an outlawed movement, and in 1888 Steinmetz was forced to flee his country to avoid arrest, first to Switzerland and then to the United States, arriving in New York City on 1 June 1889. Steinmetz found employment at the Yonkers firm of Eickenmeyer and Osterhud, headed by German socialist émigré Rudolph Eickenmeyer. Steinmetz and Eickenmeyer established a close rapport, and the latter strongly supported and encouraged the former's research into losses of efficiency in alternating current (AC) electrical apparatuses due to alternating magnetic fields and the tendency of materials to resist being magnetized (hysteresis). In the course of attempting to calculate the hysteresis loss of efficiency in AC motors, Steinmetz's law of hysteresis, developed in 1891, was a major breakthrough.

In 1892 the newly formed General Electric Co (GE) purchased Eickenmeyer and Osterhud and immediately hired Steinmetz to serve in its Calculating Department. When the department was moved from Lynn, Mass, to Schenectady in 1893, Steinmetz followed; within a year he became the department's new director. At GE, Steinmetz soon developed a method of using complex numbers to analyze AC currents. His derived formulas predicted AC electric motor performance based on specific material and design characteristics, and thus laid the foundation for the AC revolution of the 20th century—a revolution that transformed lighting, transportation, and communications (replacing less reliable direct current [DC] power generation and transmission technologies). His most famous research initiatives included the study of transient phenomena (surges) in AC currents, the production of artificial lightning, and the analysis of the dielectric characteristics (electrical insulating property) of air. As director of the Calculating Department, Steinmetz also anticipated and laid the groundwork for the first modern American research laboratory, founded at GE's Schenectady works in 1900, with which he was associated for the rest of his life.

Yet Steinmetz needed and protected his independence as a scholar and a scientist. Very soon after joining GE, he was made a consulting engineer, a position and title he held until his death. This permitted him the freedom to pursue projects, problems, and duties that interested him in his laboratory, built behind his home in Schenectady. It also allowed him to join the faculty of Union College in Schenectady in 1902. There, for a decade, he contributed greatly to the college's engineering curriculum and strengthened its ties to GE. Steinmetz's sense of civic responsibility led him to serve Schenectady in countless ways, most energetically in the field of education. When a popular municipal socialist movement swept through Schenectady in the early 1910s, Steinmetz returned to the Socialist Party—and to political and social reform. He was appointed by recently elected Socialist mayor George R. Lunn to the local Board of Education and filled two terms as its president. Soon afterward he was elected president of the Common Council. By 1916, however, Steinmetz began to withdraw from politics. Growing opposition to local Socialists, due to their vocal antiwar stance and suspected pro-German sentiments (many local Socialist Party members were ethnic Germans), Steinmetz's alienation from Mayor Lunn, and a growing factionalism among local progressive forces made it difficult for Steinmetz to continue to envision and implement the corporate socialist dreams he held for the city. By the time of his death, Steinmetz had made countless contributions to science and engineering, acquiring over 200 patents for his inventions.

Kline, Ronald R. *Steinmetz: Engineer and Socialist* (Baltimore: Johns Hopkins Univ Press, 1992)

Gerald Zahavi

Stengel, Casey [Charles Dillon] (*b* Kansas City, Mo, 30 July 1890; *d* Glendale, Calif, 29 Sept 1975). Professional baseball player and manager. Casey Stengel abandoned dental studies for baseball, playing for five teams, including the Brooklyn Dodgers and New York Giants, in 14 seasons (1912–25). An above-average outfielder Stengel was better known for pranks such as doffing his cap and having a bird fly out. He managed in the minor leagues and then in the majors, leading the Dodgers (1934–36) and Boston Braves (1938–43) with little success. Stengel returned to the minors, where he managed the Oakland Acorns to a pennant in 1948. A year later he was chosen to manage the New York Yankees. His teams won 10 pennants (1949–53, 1955–58, 1960) and 7 World Series championships (1949–53, 1956, 1958) in 12 years, but "the Old Professor" was fired following the 1960 season. Two years later Stengel became the first manager of the New York Mets, where his colorful personality—especially his gleefully fractured syntax, often called Stengelese—was increasingly on display, in part a calculated effort to distract attention from the team's woeful play. A broken hip forced his retirement in 1965. Elected to the Baseball Hall of Fame the following year, Stengel had the distinction of either playing or managing for all of the modern era major league clubs in New York City. In his postmanagerial years Stengel lived in California, occasionally returning to New York City, as in 1969, when his "Amazin' Mets" won the World Series.

Creamer, Robert W. *Stengel: His Life and Times* (1984; repr. Lincoln: Univ of Nebraska Press, 1996)
Stengel, Casey, and Harry T. Paxton. *Casey at the Bat: The Story of My Life in Baseball as Told to Harry T. Paxton* (New York: Random House, 1962)

Stephentown. Town (pop 2,873) in SE Rensselaer Co. Settled ?1765, chiefly from Rhode Island, Stephentown was formed as a district in 1784 and was recognized as a town in 1788. Charcoal burning was important before the Civil War. The Harlem Extension Railroad's milk trains (1869–1952; later Rutland Railroad) encouraged dairying. In recent years, calling itself "The Only Stephentown on Earth," it has remained a rural town, and many residents commute to Albany, Pittsfield, Massachusetts, or elsewhere.

Kathryn T. Sheehan

Sterling. Town (pop 3,432) in N Cayuga Co. Settled in 1805, the town was formed from Cato in 1812. The Southern Central Railroad (1871) provided service. Formerly a farming community, the town is a resort area in the early 21st century and the site of the 862-acre (349 ha) Fair Haven Beach State Park, the Sterling Nature Center, and Springbrook Greens Golf Course (1995). Since 1978 the Sterling Renaissance Festival has been held in July and August.

Hallie A. Sweeting

Stettheimer, Florine (*b* Rochester, 19 Aug 1871; *d* New York City, 11 May 1944). Artist and designer. Born into a well-to-do German Jewish family in Rochester, Stettheimer lived in Europe with her family during much of her youth. In 1892 she enrolled in the Art Students League of New York, and upon graduating in 1895 she returned to Europe. In 1914 she came back to Manhattan, determined to create a new art form reflecting the vitality of modernist New York City. Her idiosyncratic style combined the bright colors of Henri Matisse, the theatricality of Diaghilev's Ballets Russes, and the miniaturizing qualities of Persian miniatures. In 1916 she held a one-person exhibition at Knoedler's Art Gallery in New York City. Although the exhibition received a fair critical reception, none of the paintings sold, and thereafter she exhibited only in group shows. Stettheimer's well-received quasi-autobiographical compositions often included portraits of friends and well-known public figures. She participated in the Harlem Renaissance with works such as *Asbury Park South* (1920) celebrating an African American resort. She often designed plaster frames and furniture to match her paintings. With her sisters and mother, Stettheimer entertained the most celebrated members of New York's avant-garde circles, from Marcel Duchamp to Cecil Beaton, in their West 76th St apartment. In 1934 Stettheimer received public acclaim for her costume and stage designs for the Virgil Thomson/Gertrude Stein opera *Four Saints in Three Acts.* She moved to her studio at the Beaux-Arts Building, 80 W 40th St, after her mother's death in 1935. There she continued to paint, most notably her *Cathedral* series of urban New York life, and to entertain eminent cultural figures. Two major retrospectives of Stettheimer's work have appeared in New York City at the Museum of Modern Art in 1946 and at the Whitney Museum of American Art in 1995.

Bloemink, Barbara. *The Life and Art of Florine Stettheimer* (New Haven, Conn: Yale Univ Press, 1995)

Barbara J. Bloemink

Steuben. Town (pop 1,172) in NE Oneida Co. The first settler came in 1789 to build a house on land that New York State granted to Baron Friedrich Wilhelm von Steuben (1730–94) in 1786. Steuben spent the summers on his farm from 1790 to 1793 and moved to it shortly before his death. The town was formed in 1792 from Whitestown. Welsh settlers arrived in 1795 and soon became the dominant ethnic group; after 1915 many Polish farmers moved to town. In 1871 Steuben was reburied on his farm, a monument was erected, and later a replica of his house was constructed. The site is now part of a 55-acre (22 ha) state park. The town's farming emphasized sheep grazing until about the World War I era and then cattle grazing. In 1998 the town had 14 dairy farms and one horse farm; many residents worked elsewhere.

Steuben, Friedrich Wilhelm von (*b* Magdeburg, Prussia [now in Germany], 17 Sept 1730; *d* Steuben [now in Oneida Co], 28 Nov 1794). Revolutionary War general. Steuben served in the Prussian army of Frederick the Great from 1746 until 1763, rising to the rank of captain. Discharged from the army soon after the French and Indian War, he moved into a court position in the German state of Hohenzollern-Hechingen. In 1777 he sailed to America and offered his skills in drilling troops to the Continental army, which, unlike the Prussian army, had never received much formal training, as seen in the disastrous 1776 campaign in New York. Steuben arrived at Valley Forge, Pa, in February 1778, only months after he landed at Portsmouth, NH, having received permission from Gen George Washington to begin training his troops. In May 1778 he was asked to serve as inspector general of the army. The benefits of Steuben's disciplined training showed immediately when the Continentals engaged the British at the Battle of Monmouth, NJ, in June 1778. In the winter of 1778–79 he wrote his famous guide to training and drill instruction that was used for new recruits throughout the war and for decades after.

In November 1780 Steuben became the commanding Continental officer in Virginia, where he quarreled with Gov Thomas Jefferson over allocation of the state's resources. In September–October 1781 he commanded one of Washington's three divisions in the siege of Yorktown, Va, which culminated in the British surrender. After the war Steuben remained in the United States, settling first in New York City and later moving to a 16,000-acre (6,500 ha) tract granted to him by New York State in June 1786. Much of this land is part of Steuben, the town eventually named for him. Steuben Co is also named for him. A lifelong bachelor, he lived extravagantly and often found himself in financial trouble, despite a pension granted him by Congress. His home and grave are maintained as a state historic site.

Palmer, John McAuley. *General von Steuben* (New Haven, Conn: Yale Univ Press, 1937)

Richard Hite

Steuben County (1,408 mi^2/3,647 km^2; pop 98,726). Formed from Ontario Co in 1796, Steuben Co was named for Baron Friedrich Wilhelm von Steuben, inspector general of the Continental army during the Revolutionary War. Major boundary changes occurred with the establishment of Allegany Co (1808) and Schuyler Co (1854). Other adjustments were made with Cayuga (1801, 1804), Ontario (1814), Livingston (1822), Yates (1826), and Tompkins (1828) Cos. Steuben Co is presently subdivided into 2 cities and 32 towns that contain 15 incorporated villages. Bath is the county seat, but county courthouses are also maintained at Corning and Hornell. Elevations range from 2,401 ft (732 m) Call Hill in the Town of Hartsville to 715 feet (218 m), the water level at Keuka Lake.

Steuben Co straddles two physiographic subregions of the Appalachian Upland, or Allegheny Plateau. The Finger Lake Hills occupy the county's northern half, the Cattaraugus Hills the southern. Bedrock throughout consists of Devonian sandstones, shales, and, in the extreme southwest, conglomerates, all of whose strata dip gently southward. Rock deformations dating from the Alleghenian orogeny resulted in pockets of natural gas. These gas fields were exploited beginning in the 1930s and after depletion became gas storage reservoirs. Gas fields discovered later were tapped starting in 1969.

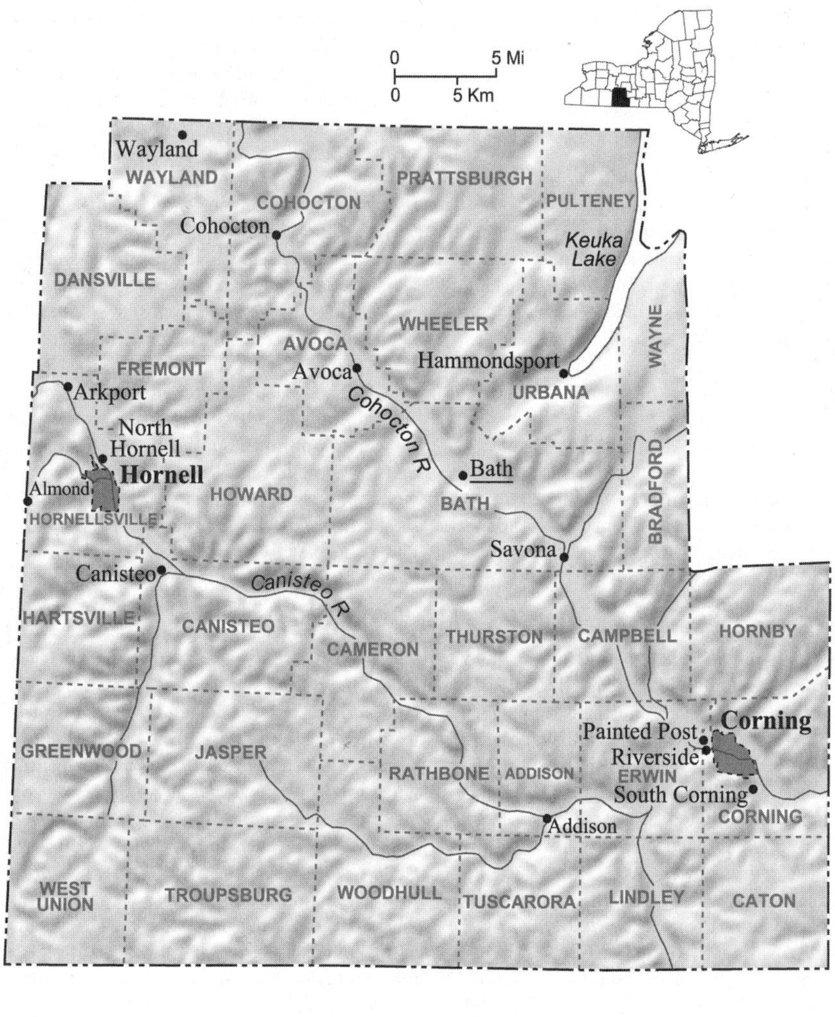

Multiple glaciations helped sculpt landforms throughout the county. Ice rounded the hilltops and gouged out the Keuka Lake basin and the larger steep-sided valleys like the Cohocton, Canisteo, Tioga, and Chemung, which later functioned as meltwater channels and hence contain substantial alluvial deposits. Glacial till covers most other areas, and remnants of the Valley Heads Moraine form an arc across the county's northeastern quarter. Remnants of the preglacial drainage system are discernible in places. Most of Steuben Co lies within the greater Susquehanna River watershed. Particularly disastrous floods occurred in 1817, 1857, 1889, 1935, 1946, and 1972. The far northwest drains into the Genesee River, while the Keuka Lake basin is within the Oswego River watershed. Soil quality varies greatly. High-quality arable land is concentrated in the northwest and in the Cohocton and lower Canisteo and Tioga River valleys. Most upland and hillside soils are unsuitable for modern agriculture.

Steuben Co's climate is humid-continental. Mean January temperatures range from 21°F (-6°C) to 24°F (-4°C). Variation is largely dependent on the local elevation, topography, and slope. Below 0°F (-18°C) readings typically occur 5–10 days during the winter. Mean July temperatures range from 67°F (19°C) to 70°F (21°C). Lower elevations normally experience 10 or more days of 90°F (32°C) or higher temperatures every summer, higher elevations 3–5 days. Annual average precipitation ranges from 31 inches (79 cm) in the far northwest to 38 inches (97 cm) around Prattsburgh in the northeast and in the higher southwest. Average seasonal snowfall amounts vary considerably from 75 inches (191 cm) or more in the high country south of Hornell to 40 inches (102 cm) in the Tioga River valley. The primeval forest cover consisted of two communities. Central hardwoods, made up primarily of beech, sugar maple, basswood, oak, and chestnut, occupied the major river valleys and some eastern uplands. Alleghenian hardwoods dominated by beech, sugar maple, hemlock, white pine, basswood, and in some places oak and chestnut colonized the remainder.

American Indians and Early Settlement

Paleo-Indian fluted projectile points found along the Canisteo River, dating from 10,000 to 8,000 BC, are the earliest known pieces of evidence of human presence in present Steuben Co. The traditional hunting territory of the Seneca Indians included present-day Steuben Co. The Seneca village of Canisteo dated probably from the early 18th century. After the outbreak of the French and Indian War in 1754, the Seneca permitted refugee Munsee and Unami Delawares from the mid–Susquehanna Valley to settle at Assinisink [now Corning Northside] and along the Canisteo River. These settlements sent war parties to the frontiers of the Delaware-Catskill region. In retaliation, Sir William Johnson in 1764 dispatched a force of Mohawks to burn the Chemung and Canisteo communities. During the Revolutionary War loyalists from Pennsylvania relocated to the Chemung Valley as far north as Painted Post, a staging point for raids on the American frontiers. Detachments from Gen John Sullivan's army destroyed these settlements in September 1779. Some Tuscaroras moved into the lower Canisteo and Cohocton Valleys after the war but left after European settlers arrived. Indians from Seneca reservations came to Steuben Co to hunt and fish as late as the 1850s.

Steuben Co lay within the huge tract purchased by Oliver Phelps and Nathaniel Gorham in 1788. After surveying the tract into townships and selling nine of them in what became Steuben Co, Phelps and Gorham conveyed their unsold lands (about 1 million acres/405,000 ha) to Robert Morris of Philadelphia in 1790. Morris then sold the property to Charles Williamson, agent for Sir William Pulteney and other British investors. To encourage settlement, Williamson founded the Village of Bath in 1793, opened a road linking the Susquehanna and Genesee Rivers, subsidized the construction of taverns and mills and established a newspaper, the *Bath Gazette* (1796). Most land sales were to speculators, producing little revenue, and in 1800 Williamson was replaced as land agent by Robert Troup. The Pulteney family's stringent fiscal policy burdened local settlers with debt and impeded economic development. In 1830 settlers' protests resulted in a lowering of prices of lots under contract for sale, and most Pulteney lands were deeded or contracted by 1840. Anti–land office sentiment, legal challenges to the Pulteney title, and isolated incidents of violent resistance continued until around 1870.

The county's settlers came mostly from eastern New York State, Pennsylvania, and New Jersey, although many were of New England descent. A few came from Virginia and Maryland, bringing slaves with them (Bath later had a small community of free Blacks). The principal river valleys provided convenient transportation routes and determined the location of the more significant, sometimes competing population centers. In the 1830s numerous Catholic and Protestant Germans began settling farms in the northwest, and Catholic Irish in the southwest. By midcentury the county had six incorporated villages and numerous crossroads hamlets.

STEUBEN CO POPULATION CENSUS FIGURES

	White	Nonwhite	Total Population	Foreign-Born
1800	1,766	22	1,788	—
1810	7,130	116	7,246	—
1820	21,813	176	21,989	155
1830	33,643	208	33,851	63
1840	45,850	288	46,138	—
1850	63,400	371	63,771	4,822
1860	66,215	475	66,690	6,170
1870	67,330	387	67,717	5,884
1880	77,118	468	77,586	6,477
1890	80,981	492	81,473	7,081
1900	82,321	501	82,822	6,041
1910	83,000	362	83,362	5,703
1920	80,320	307	80,627	4,784
1930	82,313	358	82,671	4,449
1940	84,644	283	84,927	3,878
1950	90,931	508	91,439	3,580
1960	96,872	819	97,691	2,881
1970	98,470	1,076	99,546	2,014
1980	97,635	1,582	99,217	2,027
1990	97,150	1,938	99,088	1,663
2000	95,198	3,528	98,726	1,845

Notes: "Nonwhite" includes African Americans, Asians, American Indians, and Pacific Islanders and, for 2000, also the mixed race and other race categories. Through the 1960 census these figures primarily reflect the African American population. Foreign-born figures for 1820 and 1830 include only those not naturalized, and for 1930 and 1950, the foreign-born totals include Whites only. Other years include all foreign-born in the population.

Economic Development

Before the Civil War Steuben Co's economy was based on mixed farming and lumbering of white pine and hemlock. A 1798 statute made the main rivers public highways, and for several decades lumber and log rafts and "arks" carrying farm produce were floated downriver each spring to the Chesapeake Bay and Baltimore. The Lake Erie Turnpike operated between Bath and Angelica (Allegany Co) from 1808 to 1832. County residents gained water access to the Erie Canal via Keuka Lake and the Crooked Lake Canal in 1831. A feeder of the Chemung Canal was completed close to Painted Post in 1833. The communities of Hammondsport and Corning profited the most from canal traffic. Steamboat service began on Keuka Lake in 1835 and continued until 1922. By the 1840s steam-powered sawmills began supplanting small waterpowered facilities; the largest was the Gang Mills near Painted Post. John Magee of Bath and partners founded the Steuben County Bank (1832) and operated stagecoach lines through much of the Southern Tier. The Corning and Blossburgh Railroad opened in 1839 to carry coal from Pennsylvania to the canal terminus. The Erie Railroad was completed through the county in 1851. Hornellsville [Hornell after 1906 thrived because the Erie's major repair shops were located there. The Buffalo, New York and Erie Railroad was constructed up the Cohocton Valley in 1853 and soon merged into the Erie. The railroads prompted land values to jump and agriculture temporarily to prosper.

After the 1870s dairy farming became into the county's agricultural mainstay, although sheep raising remained important for several decades. Farmers hauled milk to small cheese factories and later to creameries built near the railroads. Exploiting favorable soils and climate, farmers in northwestern Steuben Co began specializing in potato growing. Grape growing in the temperate Keuka Lake valley had begun in the 1820s. Table grapes were a major product between the 1850s and the 1910s. Sparkling wines produced by the Pleasant Valley Wine Co (established 1860, Great Western label) and the Urbana Wine Co (1865, Gold Seal label) became nationally famous. The Taylor Wine Co (1886) grew to become the largest local wine and champagne producer.

Steuben Co's population and economy expanded in the late 19th century. Numerous Irish and Italians arrived as railroad laborers. Farm and town residences, churches, and rural schoolhouses were largely rebuilt. Corning and Hornell and the larger villages boasted new brick commercial blocks. Silk mills opened in Hornellsville in the late 1880s and, by 1912, employed 1,300 people. Corning had several factories making blown and cut glass. Addison manufactured window sashes and doors; Avoca, wooden wheels; Bath, harnesses; Canisteo, buttons and leather; Cohocton, buckwheat flour; and Wayland, Portland cement. Yet prosperity was elusive; all of these factories eventually closed.

Private investment extended public transportation and utilities. The Erie Railroad's high freight rates fell after a second trunk line, the

POPULATIONS OF TOWNS AND CITIES, STEUBEN CO

Town or City, Year Founded	1800	1840	1880	1920	1960	2000
Addison, 1796[a]	174	1,920	2,534	2,122	2,645	2,640
Avoca, 1843	—	—	1,843	1,888	2,041	2,314
Bath, 1796	452	4,915	7,396	7,317	11,978	12,097
Bradford, 1836	—	1,547	937	570	558	763
Cameron, 1822	—	1,359	1,611	779	587	1,034
Campbell, 1831	—	852	1,881	1,032	2,471	3,691
Canisteo, 1796	510	941	3,694	2,901	3,652	3,583
Caton, 1839[b]	—	797	1,642	688	1,359	2,097
Cohocton, 1812	—	2,965	3,346	2,585	2,451	2,626
Corning, 1796[c]	262	1,674	7,402	2,857	6,732	6,426
Corning (city), 1890	—	—	—	15,820	17,085	10,842
Dansville, 1796	—	2,725	1,788	1,031	1,125	1,977
Erwin, 1826	—	785	2,095	3,086	5,829	7,227
Fremont, 1854	—	—	1,277	645	779	964
Greenwood, 1827	—	1,138	1,386	941	839	849
Hartsville, 1844	—	—	1,015	545	479	585
Hornby, 1826	—	1,048	1,209	700	1,383	1,742
Hornell (city), 1888	—	—	—	15,025	13,907	9,019
Hornellsville, 1820	—	2,121	9,852	1,829	3,413	4,042
Howard, 1812	—	3,247	2,131	1,127	929	1,430
Jasper, 1827	—	1,187	1,806	943	1,008	1,270
Lindley, 1837	—	638	1,563	1,024	1,313	1,913
Prattsburgh, 1813	—	2,455	2,349	1,663	1,448	2,064
Pulteney, 1808	—	1,784	1,660	1,062	1,106	1,405
Rathbone, 1856	—	—	1,371	761	726	1,080
Thurston, 1844	—	—	1,366	674	619	1,309
Troupsburg, 1808	—	1,171	2,494	1,406	1,074	1,126
Tuscarora, 1859	—	—	1,544	854	1,043	1,400
Urbana, 1822	—	1,884	2,318	2,300	2,592	2,546
Wayland, 1848	—	—	2,591	3,004	3,385	4,314
Wayne, 1796[d]	258	1,377	827	516	715	1,165
West Union, 1845	—	—	1,271	781	430	399
Wheeler, 1820	—	1,294	1,424	808	766	1,263
Woodhull, 1828	—	827	1,963	1,343	1,224	1,524

Note: In 1800 Steuben Co included the Towns of Orange, Reading, and Tyrone [now in Schuyler Co].

[a]Middletown until 1808.

[b]Wormly until 1840.

[c]Painted Post until 1852.

[d]Frederickstown until 1808.

Delaware, Lackawanna and Western, was constructed through the county in 1881–82. Several branchlines were built to serve local markets. Some towns in southern Steuben Co bonded themselves to pay for "paper railroads" that were never built. A telegraph line reached the county in 1848. Local telephone service commenced in the late 1870s and long-distance service in 1895. The Cities of Corning and Hornell had electric power plants by 1890, and the villages followed in a few years. The Steuben Rural Electric Cooperative and other systems completed rural electrification by the early 1950s.

Religion, Education, and Culture

Most of the 100 churches in 1855 were Methodist, Baptist, or Presbyterian. Antebellum religious revivals and reform movements were most prominent in Prattsburgh. Since the 1930s Catholics have made up nearly half of the county's religious adherents; Methodists, Presbyterians, Baptists, and Episcopalians are the most numerous Protestant denominations.

Academies at Prattsburgh (1824), Addison (1849), and Rogersville (1853) supplemented the 350 district schools established by the 1850s. During the late 19th century, the county's two cities and larger villages constructed new school buildings (without state aid) and offered high school courses. Fifteen central school districts were established (with generous state aid) between 1928 and 1950, and the enlarged city school districts of Corning–Painted Post and of Hornell followed in 1954 and 1956. The Steuben County Board of Cooperative Educational Services (BOCES) was formed in 1954. Corning Community College opened in 1958 and later joined the SUNY system.

Other public facilities and services were modest during the 19th century but expanded during the 20th. A county poorhouse was opened, belatedly, in 1833; ramshackle dormitories burned, with tragic death tolls, in 1838, 1859, and 1878. The New York State Soldiers' and Sailors' Home opened at Bath in 1878 and was operated by the US government after 1930. As the Bath VA Medical Center, it now includes a hospital and a large national cemetery. A county tuberculosis sanatorium opened in 1916, and public nurse service started in 1928. Cultural and recreational facilities expanded in the late 19th century and into the 20th. The annual Bath Fair commenced in 1853. Most communities had public halls for entertainment events. Baseball teams and brass bands were ubiquitous. Libraries were founded at Hornell in 1868, Bath in 1869, and Corning in 1873. Early in the 21st century, the county has 15 public libraries, 2 reading centers, and several historical societies. Significant architecture is recognized with 10 districts and 26 structures listed on the State Register of Historic Places. Numerous cultural programs are offered by the Corning Museum of Glass, opened as the Corning Glass Center in 1951, and the Hornell Area Arts Council. Resort hotels were built on Keuka Lake and Loon Lake in the 1870s, and today those lakes are lined with cottages and homes. Stony Brook State Park near Dansville was established in 1927, and Pinnacle State Park near Addison in 1976. The county operates four smaller parks.

Steuben Co's first modern deer season was in 1938, and the annual deer take has long been the largest of any New York State county. The state fish hatchery near Hammondsport was established in 1893. The Cohocton River is noted for trout and bass, but pollution has harmed the fishing. The Woodhull Raceway (stock cars and modifieds) and the annual motorcycle hill climb in Howard attract racing enthusiasts.

Politics

Steuben Co residents generally voted Democratic until 1856, when it shifted to the new Republican Party. During the depression Republican county officials accepted state and federal relief funds but worried about red tape and welfare. (In 1938, 14% of county residents were receiving some form of public assistance.) An unwieldy 38-seat county board of supervisors had legislative, executive, and audit responsibilities. A 1966 court challenge led to the county's reapportionment, and the board was replaced by a 17-member county legislature in 1984, when a county administrator was hired. Enrolled Republicans outnumber Democrats by a margin of two to one.

Recent History

In 1900 Steuben Co contained 8,179 operating, mostly dairy, farms. High-yield Holstein cows were introduced, first in southern Steuben, soon after 1900. Most of the cheese factories and creameries subsequently closed, leaving large dairy plants at Campbell and Arkport and a cheese factory at Woodhull. In 1900 and 1910 the county was first in the state in potato production and second in the nation. As soils wore out, potato yields and profits fell. Starting in 1938 immigrant farmers from Maine practiced intensive potato cultivation, long promoted by county agricultural extension agent William F. Stempfle and some local farmers. Black migrant workers from Jamaica and later from Florida worked in the potato harvest from the 1940s until mechanization in the 1970s. Steuben Co continues to be a major producer of potatoes for chips. Vegetables are grown on mucklands at Arkport and Prattsburgh. In 1997 only 1,295 farms remained in operation, yet harvested cropland (mostly of hay and corn) has stabilized at just over 200,000 acres (81,000 ha) since the 1940s. Frequently depressed dairy and potato prices in recent decades make the future of agriculture in Steuben Co uncertain. Taylor Wine Co ended operations in Hammondsport in 1994. During the 1950s and 1960s Charles Fournier and Konstantin Frank, immigrants from France and Ukraine, respectively, succeeded in growing European hybrid and vinifera grapes, transforming New York State's wine industry. The Hammondsport area has 7 wineries and about 60 grape growers in the early 21st century.

Most of the county's larger remaining industries have endured for nearly a century or more: Stern and Stern in Hornell (1888; industrial textiles), Ingersoll-Rand (now Dresser Rand) at Painted Post (1899; compressors), the Gunlocke furniture factory at Wayland (1902), W. W. Babcock Co at Bath (1905; wooden ladders), and Mercury Aircraft Co at Hammondsport (1921; metal components). Corning Inc (1868) is the county's largest employer. Two multinational corporations have acquired local facilities: Alstom builds and refurbishes railcars in Hornell, and the Phillips plant in Bath produces lightbulbs.

Steuben Co's population increased only modestly during the 20th century. The ethnic composition shifted slightly; by 2000 the minority population had risen to 3%. With the advent of state highway aid, the county mapped a road system in 1903 and appointed a highway superintendent in 1909. The initial network of hard-surfaced state highways was completed by 1917 and rebuilt with concrete pavements between the 1920s and the 1940s. The Genesee Expressway (I-390 after 1971) was completed between 1968 and 1976, and the Southern Tier Expressway (Rte 17; I-86 after 1999), between 1968 and 1973. The county has 3,146 miles (5,063 km) of highways. Norfolk Southern and two short lines continue to provide rail freight service.

Retail business has been transformed. The county had 1,200 retail establishments in 1950 and just 400 in 1997. Chain stores on the outskirts of Hornell, Bath, and Corning, and regional malls near Elmira and Rochester have eclipsed the old downtowns. In 1945 the county had 20 locally owned banking institutions; in 2003 only five retained their corporate identities. The county had 21 newspapers in 1900. A century later, only the *Hornell Tribune* (1851), the *Corning Leader* (1857), and the *Bath Courier-Advocate* (1816) continued to publish. Early in the 21st century, the hospitals at Hornell (1890), Corning (1900), and Bath (1915) are major employers. Three industrial development agencies and several other public and private agencies in Steuben Co attempt to promote economic growth.

See also AVIATION; CORNING INC.

The county's early years are covered in Orsamus Turner, *History of the Pioneer Settlement of Phelps and Gorham's Purchase, and Morris' Reserve* (1851), and in Guy H. McMaster, *History of the Settlement of Steuben County* (1853). The standard reference is W. W. Clayton, *History of Steuben County* (1879), which was followed by Harlo Hakes, *Landmarks of Steuben County* (1896), and Irvin W. Near, *History of Steuben County* (1911). Earlier community histories include Charles H. Erwin, *History of the Town and Village of Painted Post and of the Town of Erwin* (1874) and Irvin W. Near, *Early History of Hornellsville* (1890). Several town histories were published for bicentennials, of which two are prominent: Thomas P. Dimitroff and Lois S. Janes, *History of the Corning Painted Post Area* (1977), and James D. Folts, *Bicentennial History of Cohocton* (1994). Updating the town histories is *Steuben County, the First 200 Years: A Pictorial History* (1996), which does not look at the county's history as a whole.

James D. Folts

Warwick bowl made by Frederick Carder, *ca* 1932. All rights reserved, The Metropolitan Museum of Art.

Steuben Glass In 1903 Thomas G. Hawkes and Frederick Carder, an English glassmaker, opened Steuben Glass Works on Denison Parkway in Corning (Steuben Co). Hawkes funded Steuben Glass Works to supply the blanks he needed to produce cut glass. Carder, who designed the glass and supervised production and sales, initially produced blanks for Hawkes, as well as glassware of his own design, including golden and blue iridescent glasses he named Aurene. During his 30 years as designer and supervisor at Steuben, his repertoire included hundreds of transparent and opaque colors and many decorating techniques, which he used on a range of expensive artistic glassware and lighting glass. Corning Glass Works acquired the company in 1918, but Carder continued to run what became the Steuben Division of Corning Glass Works until 1933, when division heads decided to use a new formula for a brilliant colorless glass and to phase out production of his colored glassware. Under Arthur Houghton Jr's direction, the division, which became Steuben Glass in 1933, produced a range of heavy glasses influenced by 18th-century English glass and contemporary Swedish glass. A hallmark of many designs was elaborate copper-wheel engraving, which created a matte gray finish that stood out from the colorless glass. Responsible for design in the 1930s and 1940s, Sidney Waugh often created stylized designs, like the Gazelle bowl. James Houston, Steuben Glass's most prominent designer in the 1960s and 1970s, was known for naturalistic designs often showing human figures and animals. British artist Peter Aldridge, whose work is abstract and geometric, left Steuben in 2001 after overseeing design during the 1980s and 1990s. In 2002 Steuben Glass had 138 employees.

Madigan, Mary J. *Steuben Glass: An American Tradition in Crystal* (New York: Abrams, 1982)

Jane Shadel Spillman

Steward, Austin (*b* Prince William Co, Va, 1793; *d* Canandaigua, Ontario Co, 15 Feb 1869). Abolitionist and businessman. Born a slave, he moved to New York State with his owner in the early 1800s. They eventually settled in Bath (Steuben Co), where Steward and his family were hired out as laborers. Steward taught himself to read using a spelling book he had bought. Escaping to Canandaigua about 1814 and aided by the New York Manumission Society, he resisted reenslavement by claiming it was illegal for out-of-state emigrants to keep slaves for more than a few months in New York State. Steward labored on area farms, attended Farmington's Academy (Ontario Co), and moved to Rochester about 1817. There he started a meat supply business and then a grocery, offered Sunday school classes, and became an abolitionist. Vice president of the black national convention meeting (1830) in Philadelphia, Steward became an agent of the Wilberforce settlement in Upper Canada [now Ontario] in 1831. He returned to Rochester in 1837. During the 1840s and 1850s, he served as a subscription agent for the *National Anti-Slavery Standard,* attended black conventions throughout the state, and helped stage antislavery demonstrations in communities like Canandaigua, where he had been teaching at a school for African American children since about 1842. Steward returned to Rochester after publishing his autobiography in 1857.

Steward, Austin. *22 Years a Slave and 40 Years a Freeman* (1857; repr, ed. Graham Russell Hodges, Syracuse: Syracuse Univ Press, 2002)

Richard Newman

Stewart, A(lexander) T(urney) (*b* Lisburn, Ireland, 12 Oct 1803; *d* New York City, 10 Apr 1876). Merchant. Raised by his maternal grandfather in Ireland, he moved to New York City in 1818. Stewart revolutionized the US retail industry by merchandising high fashion dry goods to women. Accepting a New York City store in 1823 as payment for a debt, he began importing unusual goods that other stores did not carry. Stewart opened increasingly larger shops, including the "Marble Palace" on the corner of Broadway and Chambers St in 1848 and the "Iron Palace" on the corner of Broadway and 10th St in 1862, at the time the largest retail store in the world. Stewart was a major supporter of the Republican Party and one of the richest and most astute entrepreneurs of his time. In 1869 Pres Ulysses S. Grant nominated him as secretary of the treasury, but a federal law prohibiting business people from holding that office prevented Stewart from serving. Stewart in 1869 bought the land for what became Garden City [now in Nassau Co] and spent the rest of his life developing the property toward what he envisioned as a model city for New Yorkers of moderate means.

Elias, Stephen N. *Alexander T. Stewart: The Forgotten Merchant Prince* (Westport, Conn: Praeger, 1992)

Jerry R. N. Brisco

Stewart, Alvan (*b* South Granville, Washington Co, 1 Sept 1790; *d* New York City, 1 May 1849). Lawyer and abolitionist. After graduating from the University of Vermont (1813), Stewart moved to Cherry Valley (Otsego Co) to study and practice law, gaining, because of his oratorical abilities, a reputation as a top-rank attorney. He married Keziah Holt, with whom he had five children, and served as mayor of Cherry Valley. Disassociating himself from the Democrats over differences with Andrew Jackson's tariff policies, he became a Whig and in 1832 moved to Utica and embraced the temperance and antislavery campaigns. After joining the American Anti-Slavery Society in 1834, he abandoned his legal career and took up abolitionist campaigns in western and central New York State. He was a founding member of the New York State Anti-Slavery Society, a group that formed in 1835 in Peterboro (Madison Co) during the aftermath of the Utica antiabolitionist riot in October that year. A controversial leader, he argued that local funds should be used for local reforms. Stewart joined the American and Foreign Anti-Slavery Society in 1840 and became an advocate of political abolitionism. He was the Liberty Party candidate for governor in 1840 and 1844. Constant travel for antislavery weakened his health, however, and he died moderately young.

Sorin, Gerald. *The New York Abolitionists* (Westport, Conn: Greenwood, 1971)

Graham Russell Hodges

Stewart Manor. Village (pop 1,935) in Hempstead (Nassau Co). Part of the town common lands purchased by A. T. Stewart in 1869, it was developed beginning in 1925 by Realty Associates as Sunrise Gardens, but it was renamed Stewart Manor in 1926. The village incorporated in 1927. By 1960 the upper-middle-class locality was largely developed, and its population peaked at 2,422. In the early 21st century, it remains a residential community of only .2 mi^2 (.5 km^2).

Richard A. Winsche

St. Francis College. Private liberal arts college. St. Francis Academy was opened in 1859 on Baltic St in Brooklyn by the Right Reverend John Loughlin, first bishop of Brooklyn. The academy served boys within the diocese; its goal was to improve access to education for the burgeoning numbers of immigrants entering the city. It remains the oldest Catholic institution of learning in Brooklyn. In 1884 the academy became St. Francis College, awarding its first bachelor's degree in 1885. In 1926 the college moved to Butler St. By 1960 the school had purchased two buildings on Remsen St in Brooklyn Heights from Brooklyn Union Gas. The school became coeducational in 1969 and purchased additional property, allowing the campus to be expanded to its present 1-acre (0.4 ha) size and site near the Brooklyn Heights Promenade. It offers BA and BS degrees as well as associate degrees in applied science, science, and arts. The school is nonsectarian, although it retains the Franciscan traditions of scholarship and community service. There were 2,300 students at the college in 2003.

Corry, Emmett. *History of the Franciscan Brothers of Brooklyn in Ireland and America* (Brooklyn: St. Francis College, 2003)

Marianne Rahn-Erickson

Stickley furniture. Gustave Stoeckel (1857–1942), oldest of six brothers, was born in Osceola, Wisc. His German-born parents Americanized the surname to Stickley, and he dropped the final "e" in his first name around 1904. He trained with his stonemason father. In the mid-1870s his family moved to Brandt, Pa. There Stickley went to work for a maternal uncle who made chairs. With brothers Charles and Albert, Gustave in 1884 set up business in Binghamton, making unremarkable reproduction furniture. In 1899 he formed the Gustave Stickley Co in Eastwood (Onondaga Co), making Revival-type furniture for two years before commencing production of his Craftsman furniture and in 1901 adopting the name United Crafts for his firm. On two prior visits to England (1895 and 1896), as well as through various American and European publications, Stickley had been exposed to the output of various artisans and guilds of the Arts and Crafts movement, which in turn inspired him to produce simple, functional, well-built, handsome, and comfortable furniture. The style was almost without historical precedent in America; it became known as Arts and Crafts, Mission, or Craftsman, the last term being the one Stickley used.

United Crafts, employing woodworkers, metalsmiths, and leatherworkers, was modeled after William Morris's London firm, and its output was first shown in 1900 at the Grand Rapids Furniture Fair in Michigan. In October 1901 Stickley's monthly publication, the *Craftsman* debuted, becoming an important instrument for the dissemination and discussion of the Arts and Crafts style. From 1903 it featured metalware, lighting fixtures, and house designs to complement Stickley furnishings. Tabourets, library tables, sideboards, stools, armchairs, settles, music racks, magazine cabinets, and glass-doored bookcases were included.

The company name was changed to Craftsman Workshops in 1904, and a year later Stickley moved his executive and editorial divisions to New York City. In 1908 he bought land in New Jersey, where two years later he built a log-cabin home and set up a crafts community (now Craftsman Farms in Parsipanny, NJ, a National Historic Landmark). In 1913 he bought a large Manhattan building to serve as showrooms, office, and restaurant. By 1915, however, the taste for Arts and Crafts was ebbing and the firm declared bankruptcy. The *Craftsman* ceased publication in 1916. For a short while production continued on a few modern furniture lines, but in 1918 Stickley sold what was left of the business to his brothers Leopold (1869–1957) and John George (1871–1921) and retired to Syracuse.

The finest years of Craftsman Workshops were in the first decade of the 20th century, when the well-known Mission Oak line—thick boards of quarter-sawn white oak, unhidden mortise-and-tenon joinery, and hammered and cast metal hardware, mostly iron and brass—was introduced. The talented Rochester-born designer Harvey Ellis (1852–1904) lent his fine aesthetic sense to the firm from April 1903 through January 1904, creating a line of inlaid furniture that blended the subtle decorative aspects of contemporaneous English, Scottish, and Austrian design with the outstanding American craftsmanship for which Stickley was known. Ellis's designs and influence were reflected in Craftsman Workshops' output years after his death, and subsequent Stickley pieces tended to be lighter, taller, and more elegant and refined.

Gustav's brothers Leopold and John George were among those making Craftsman-style furniture modeled after Gustav's early efforts. In 1902 they joined to form L. and J. G. Stickley, of Fayetteville (Onondaga Co), also known as the Onondaga Cabinet Shops, and in early 1904 the company incorporated, its name shortened to Onondaga Shops. When Mission designs fell out of favor around 1915, the company tried other styles. Soon after the acquisition of Craftsman Workshops in 1918, the brothers stopped making Craftsman furniture and turned to reproduction colonial pieces, such as the Cherry Valley Collection, which was introduced in 1922. The Fayetteville business weathered the Great Depression by building desks and chairs for educational facilities and was equally flexible in securing navy contracts during World War II. In 1956 Leopold Stickley was awarded the title Revered Dean of Cabinet Makers by several trade magazines. He died in 1957 and the business, under the stewardship of his widow Louise, declined.

In 1974, with only 22 employees and less than $250,000 in annual sales, it was sold to Aminy and Alfred Audi. The factory was moved from Fayetteville to Manlius (Onondaga Co) in 1985, and since then the privately owned company has expanded several times; by 2001 it had 1,255 employees and $137 million in sales. In 2002 a new showroom opened in Fayetteville under the name Stickley, Audi, and Co. With the renewed interest in the Arts and Crafts style in the third quarter of the 20th century, the company in 1989 revived the historic Mission Oak Collection, its biggest seller, comprising designs by both Gustav and L. and J. G. Stickley. It also manufactures the French-inspired Directoire Collection, the Williamsburg Collection, the more modern Metropolitan and 21st Century Collections, and the Stickley Fine Upholstery Collection. An upholstery plant and showroom are located in High Point, NC, but all the furniture continues to be made in New York State. In 2003 the original Stickley factory became the home of the Fayetteville Free Library and the Stickley Museum.

Bartinique, A. Patricia. *Gustav Stickley—His Craft* (Parsipanny, NJ: Craftsman Farms Foundation, 1992)
Cathers, David M. *Furniture of the American Arts and Crafts Movement: Furniture Made by Gustav Stickley, L. & J. G. Stickley, and the Roycroft Shop,* rev ed. (Philmont, NY: Turn of the Century Editions, 1996)
———. *Gustav Stickley* (London: Phaidon, 2003)
Clark, Michael E., and Jill Thomas-Clark. *The Stickley Brothers: The Quest for an American Voice* (Salt Lake City, Utah: Gibbs Smith, 2002)

Patricia Bayer

Stieglitz, Alfred (*b* Hoboken, NJ, 1 Jan 1864; *d* New York City, 13 July 1946). Photographer. The prosperous and cultured Stieglitz family moved to Manhattan in 1871. In the following years the family toured scenic resorts in New York State, including Lake George in the Adirondacks, where they returned each summer when not in Europe. Stieglitz studied for a year at the City College of New York before embarking for Germany with his family in 1881. There he studied engineering and first became interested in photography. He had already achieved some renown in photographic circles by the time he returned to New York City in 1890. Over the next 20 years the immensely talented, charismatic, and opinionated Stieglitz played a key role in advancing the practice of pictorialism, the soft-focus art photography that reigned in Europe and the United States at the turn of the 20th century. Stieglitz's technically impeccable cityscapes, portraits, and figure studies established an unprecedented visual standard for photography before World War I, and his promotion of modern art and photography placed him at the center of the nation's most ambitious art activities during this period. As editor of *Camera Notes,* the journal of the Camera Club of New York, from 1897 to 1902 and as founder and leader of the Photo-Secession, the dominant art photography society of the time, he wrote articles and organized exhibitions that led to the acceptance of photography as an art form. From 1903 to 1917 Stieglitz published the Photo-Secession's journal *Camera Work*, an influential photographic publication that also promoted avant-garde painting and sculpture by European and American artists. In 1905 Stieglitz, with the help of photographer Edward Steichen, opened the Little Galleries of the Photo-Secession at 291 5th Ave, soon called 291. A public forum for Stieglitz's views on photography, 291 was also a place to see original works by European modern masters. In 1910 Stieglitz organized an enormous retrospective, the *International Exhibition of Pictorial Photography*, for the Albright Art Gallery (now Albright-Knox Art Gallery) in Buffalo.

Stieglitz closed 291 in 1917. Thereafter he concentrated on his own photography, which had become less "pictorial" and lofty, more "modern": precise, objective, and focused on common subjects close at hand. These later works included an ongoing, cumulative portrait of painter Georgia O'Keeffe (approximately 173 images between 1918 and 1923); they married in 1924. During this period he also produced photographs of New York City skyscrapers, taken from high windows, and photographs of intimates and the landscape at Lake George. In 1922 he began a series of technically exacting pictures of clouds and sky, which he later called *Equivalents*. Stieglitz also ran two other New York City galleries: the Intimate Gallery (1925–29) and An American Place (1929–46). Both were venues for Stieglitz's own photographs as well as for the work of modernist painters like O'Keeffe, John Marin, Charles Demuth, Arthur Dove, and Marsden Hartley, often referred to as the Stieglitz Group. He continued producing photographs into the late 1930s.

Greenough, Sarah, and Juan Hamilton, eds. *Alfred Stieglitz: Photographs and Writings*, 2d ed. (Washington, DC: National Gallery of Art, 1998)
Norman, Dorothy. *Alfred Stieglitz: An American Seer*, 2d ed. (New York: Aperture, 1990)
Szarkowski, John. *Alfred Stieglitz at Lake George* (New York: Museum of Modern Art, 1995)

Amy Kurlander

Stillwater. Town (pop 7,522) and village (pop 1,644) in E Saratoga Co. The area was settled by European Americans in the mid–18th century. A church colony arrived in 1762 from Canaan, Conn. The northern part of town was the site of the first Battle of Saratoga (19 Sept 1777). The town formed in 1788. The village site, originally called Upton, had an ashery, a tannery, a brewery, and various shops. It acquired a post office in 1797 and incorporated in 1816. With the Champlain Canal (1823) the village expanded rapidly and manufactured flannel, knit goods, wallpaper, and strawboard. A bridge across the Hudson River was built in 1832. Farming, especially in the western and northern parts of town, coexists with suburban development.

Field Horne

Stirling, Lord. See ALEXANDER, WILLIAM.

St. James. Locality (pop 13,268) in Smithtown (Suffolk Co). Named for St. James Episcopal Church (1854), a post office was opened in 1856. The Long Island Rail Road reached St. James in 1872 and made it attractive for summer residences. Flowerfield, a large nursery, was developed in the 1920s. After World War II suburban development accelerated. The St. James General Store (1857) is still in operation early in the 21st century.

Noel J. Gish

St. John Fisher College. Private college. Founded in 1948 by the Basilian Fathers, a religious congregation of Catholic priests, with funds raised from the Rochester community, the school is named for St. John Fisher, the bishop of Rochester, England, who was martyred in 1535 for his opposition to Henry VIII's break with Rome. In 1968 the board of trustees, once composed only of Basilian Fathers, was enlarged and diversified so that today the college is governed by an independent board of trustees that includes persons of diverse faiths and is broadly representative of the business, professional, cultural, and academic communities of the area it serves. The college began to admit women in 1971 and since then has steadily expanded its curriculum, student body, and physical plant. Maintaining a strong liberal arts tradition, it offers 28 academic majors, 9 pre-professional programs, and 12 graduate programs. The campus consists of 18 buildings on a 140-acre (57 ha) site. Enrollment in 2003 was 2,200 full-time students and 900 part-time students, with 45% men and 55% women.

St. John Fisher College, http://www.sjfc.edu

William S. Helmer

St. John's University. Private university. A Catholic institution founded in 1870 by the Vincentian Fathers and incorporated as St. John's College, Brooklyn, in 1871. In 1906 it was granted university status with a revised charter but did not change its name to St. John's University, Brooklyn, until 1933, when the first doctoral students were accepted. Women were admitted to classes beginning in 1913. The university purchased the former Hillcrest Golf Course in Jamaica (Queens Co) in 1934, but ground was not broken for a new campus until 1953. The school's name changed to St. John's University, New York, in 1954, in anticipation of the move to Queens the following year. The original campus on Lewis Ave continued until 1958 and the Schermerhorn St (Brooklyn Center) campus until 1972. The university opened a Staten Island campus in 1971 after acquiring the former Notre Dame College of Staten Island and established a campus in Rome, Italy, in 1995. The LaSalle Center in Oakdale (Suffolk Co) was purchased in 1999 to expand programs on Long Island, and in 2001 St. John's merged with the College of Insurance to create the School of Risk Management, its first campus in Manhattan.

Schools within the university, offering a variety of undergraduate and graduate programs, include the College of Liberal Arts and Sciences (1870); the Graduate Division (1913); the School of Education (1908, originally the School of Pedagogy); the School of Law (1925); the Peter J. Tobin College of Business (1927; originally the School of Accounting, Commerce, and Finance); the College of Pharmacy and Allied Health Professions (1929); and the College of Professional Studies (1962). St. John's has a storied athletic tradition, especially in basketball and in 2003 participated in 21 NCAA Division I sports. In 1999 the first residence halls opened on the Queens campus. Notable alumni include former New York State governors Hugh Carey and Mario M. Cuomo, Congressman Charles B. Rangel, and Anthony Cardinal Bevilacqua of Philadelphia. One of the largest Catholic universities in the country, St. John's enrolled 11,602 undergraduate and 4,138 graduate students in 2002.

The Story of St. John's University (New York: St. John's Univ, 1945)

Patrick Ziegler

St. John's University men's basketball. One of the nation's oldest and most successful college basketball programs. The school experienced only 11 losing seasons during the 20th century, including its first season in 1907. The 1910–11 team had a 14-0 record—St. John's only undefeated season—and was declared national champion by the Helms Athletic Foundation in the era before postseason tournaments. James "Buck" Freeman coached the Redmen, as the team was known for more than 80 years, from 1927 to 1936. His unit, known as the Wonder Five, compiled an 89-8 record in its four seasons (1928–32). Joe Lapchick (1937–47, 1956–65) coached St. John's to four National Invitation Tournament (NIT) titles (1943–44, 1959, 1965) and won 334 games. Frank McGuire coached for just five seasons at St. John's (1947–52) but led the team to its first NCAA Final Four appearance in 1952, where the Redmen lost to Kansas in the national championship game. Lou Carnesecca (1965–70, 1973–92) is the winningest coach in school history with 526 victories in 24 seasons, all of which ended with postseason appearances (18 NCAAs, including a Final Four berth in 1985; 6 NITs, including the title in 1989). Carnesecca, a colorful and charismatic figure who switched from traditional shirt-and-tie coaching garb to brightly colored sweaters during the 1980s, was one of the original coaches in the powerful and prestigious Big East Conference, which St. John's joined as a charter member in 1979. The team's many outstanding players include Chris Mullin, the career scoring leader; Mark Jackson, the career assists leader; George Johnson, the career rebounding leader; Walter Berry; Malik Sealy; David Russell; Sonny Dove; Harry Boykoff; Tony Jackson; Bob McIntyre; Bob Zawoluk; Dick and Al McGuire; Alan Seiden; and Gus Alfieri. The school changed its nickname to the more politically sensitive Red Storm in 1994. In 1998 St. John's hired Mike Jarvis as the basketball program's first black head coach; he led the team to NCAA tournament appearances in his first two seasons. Home games are played at Alumni Hall in Queens or Madison Square Garden in Manhattan.

Carnesecca, Lou, and Phil Pepe. *Louie: In Season* (New York: McGraw-Hill, 1988)
St. John's University Media Guide, 1999–2000 (Jamaica, NY: 1999)

Robert H. Herzog

St. Johnsville. Town (pop 2,565) and village (pop 1,685) in NW Montgomery Co. The present town was settled by Palatine Germans, probably in the 1720s. A battle fought in 1780 at Klock's field was the last engagement between tories and the Tryon Co Militia. The town was formed from

Oppenheim [now in Fulton Co] in 1838. The Erie Canal opened on the south side of the Mohawk River in 1822, but it was the Utica and Schenectady Railroad (1836, later New York Central) that created a manufacturing center. The village was incorporated in 1857 and hosted a wide variety of factories: Clark's Fork Factory (1850s); St. Johnsville Agricultural Works (1867; threshers, steam engines); Roth and Englehardt (1889–1930s; player pianos); Union Mills (1892; knit underwear); and Little Falls Footwear (1919). Pianos, ironwork, paper, condensed milk, cigars, and dyed silk were also produced by various companies. In the early 21st century, St. Johnsville has light industry and service industries; Sentinel Products Corp (packaging) is the largest manufacturer, and the quarries of Rifenberg Construction and Hanson Aggregates produce crushed stone. Fort Klock, dating from the 1740s, is a museum.

James Crawford

St. Joseph's College. Private, coeducational college. It was founded in 1916 in Brooklyn as St. Joseph's College for Women. In 1934 the school opened a laboratory preschool, which aided the college's reputation in the field of child development. Under Pres Sister Vincent Therese Tuohy (1956–69), a library (1965) and the Dillon Child Study Center (1968) were completed. In 1970, under Pres Sister George Aquin O'Connor (1969–97), the college became coeducational and began an extension program (1971) at a site in Brentwood (Suffolk Co). In 1979 the program, which had expanded to a four-year curriculum, moved to a 27-acre (11 ha) campus in Patchogue (Suffolk Co). Construction on the Suffolk campus has added a library building (1989), an athletic center (1997), and a business/computer science building (2002). The Brooklyn campus added a five-story brownstone at 256 Clinton Ave (1998) and purchased the former St. Angela Hall Academy (2001) at 256 Washington Ave. Enrollment on both campuses totaled approximately 5,000 for the 2003 academic year.

Leonard, S. Joan deLourdes. "Fifty Years of SJC, 1916–1966." MS, St. Joseph's College Archives

St. Josephs's College, http://www.sjcny.edu

Joan Ryan, CSJ

St. Joseph's Seminary. The theological seminary of the Archdiocese of New York, located on 38 acres (15 ha) in the Dunwoodie section of Yonkers. Its main building was constructed from 1891 to 1896 at a cost of $1 million by Michael Corrigan, the third archbishop of New York. The school formally opened in 1896, and until 1906 the seminary was administered by a religious community, the Society of St. Sulpice, and thereafter by the diocesan clergy. During its first decade the seminary enjoyed a reputation for academic excellence that was evidenced by its publication between 1905 and 1908 of the *New York Review,* the premier Catholic theological journal in the United States at that time. The faculty included Fr Francis P. Duffy, who won fame as the chaplain of the New York 69th Regiment in World War I.

The Modernist Crisis of 1907, with its severe papal condemnation of heterodox theological opinions, led to a period of intellectual retrenchment, and budgetary cutbacks resulted in a deterioration of the physical plant in the 1920s and 1930s. Beginning in the late 1940s, Francis Cardinal Spellman modernized and expanded the facilities, revitalized the faculty, and introduced professional educational standards. In 1961 St. Joseph's Seminary was accredited by the Middle States Association of Colleges and Secondary Schools. In 1970 the preliminary two years of philosophical studies were transferred to a new off-campus facility, with the seminary retaining the four-year theology program leading to ordination. The Archdiocesan Catechetical Institute (later the Institute of Religious Studies) was established in 1977 under the seminary's auspices to provide a master's degree for lay students. On 6 Oct 1995 St. Joseph's Seminary was visited by Pope John Paul II, who celebrated vespers and preached in the seminary chapel. Peak enrollment occurred in 1932 with 303 students; in recent years the number of students enrolled in programs at Dunwoodie has hovered around 40. Since 1896 the seminary has trained almost 2,500 priests, of whom approximately 2,100 were ordained for the Archdiocese of New York.

Shelley, Thomas J. *Dunwoodie: The History of St. Joseph's Seminary* (Westminster, Md: Christian Classics, 1993)

Thomas J. Shelley

St. Lawrence County (2,686 mi²/6,957 km²; pop 111,931). Formed in 1802 from Clinton Co and named after the river that serves as its northern boundary, St. Lawrence Co is divided into 1 city, Ogdensburg, and 32 towns that contain 13 incorporated villages. Canton serves as county seat. It is the largest county in land area in New York State. Elevation ranges from 158 feet (48 m) along the banks of the St. Lawrence River in the far northeast to 2,688 feet (819 m) atop Mt Matumbla in Piercefield in the county's southeast corner.

The St. Lawrence Marine Plain and the St. Lawrence Hills subregions of the St. Lawrence–Champlain Lowland occupy the northern two-fifths of the county. The marine plain runs immediately south of the St. Lawrence River and is characterized by low ridges that parallel the waterway. The southern portion of the lowland offers rolling topography and elevations reaching 500 feet (150 m) above sea level. Bedrock throughout consists of layers of Ordovician limestone and sandstone that dip gently northward. The Adirondack Upland physiographic province occupies the rest of the county. The southeast corner, which exhibits the strongest relief, is part of the Adirondack Low Mountains subregion, while the rest belongs to the Western Adirondack Hills. The Adirondack region is underlain by a complex of highly resistant and severely folded and faulted Precambrian metamorphic rock linked to the Canadian or Laurentian Shield by a low arch known as the Frontenac Axis, which is the basis for the Thousand Islands (Jefferson Co) recreational area. This area is famous among mineral collectors. It has also supported the mining of iron ore (magnetite), zinc, lead, and silver ores, in addition to talc, feldspar, marble, and tremolite. Sandstone is quarried in the lowland region.

During the most recent ice age, St. Lawrence Co was completely covered by glacial ice, perhaps as much as 2 miles (3 km) thick. A mantle of glacial till covers most of the county. Its uneven deposition in the form of a series of low ridges disrupts the drainage across the lowland, resulting in numerous swales. Extensive beach sand deposits running across the central section mark the prehistoric shoreline of glacial Lake

Iroquois. Surface drainage flows north to the St. Lawrence via one or another of four river systems: from west to east, the Oswegatchie, the Grass, the Raquette, and the St. Regis. The county is also dotted with a number of natural lakes, the largest being Black Lake, and several artificial ones, notably Cranberry Lake on the Oswegatchie and Carry Falls Reservoir on the Raquette. Each of the four rivers powers at least one hydroelectric installation. Aside from the area extending from Gouverneur and Canton north to Black Lake, a stretch that includes some quality dairy farm country, the Adirondack Upland has almost no agricultural potential; soils are thin and acidic, and rock outcrops abound. Lowland soils also vary greatly in their suitability for agriculture. Areas of moderate to highly viable farmland are concentrated between Waddington and the Jefferson Co line.

St. Lawrence Co's climate is humid-continental. Average July temperatures range from 65°F (18°C) at Wanakena to 70°F (21°C) in the northeast. Daytime highs sometimes reach 90°F (32°C) or above. Winters are long and cold. Mean January temperatures vary from 16°F (-9°C) in the northeast to less than 14°F (-10°C) at Wanakena. Temperatures below 0°F (-18°C) are a significant part of every winter. On occasion a local community will earn the dubious distinction of recording the nation's lowest daily temperature. Normal annual precipitation varies from 36 inches (91 cm) at Massena to 44 inches (112 cm) at Wanakena. Seasonal snowfall totals normally range from as low as 65 inches (165 cm) along the St. Lawrence to over 160 inches (406 cm) in some higher elevations in the far south. Primeval forest cover consisted primarily of northern hardwoods. An Alleghenian hardwood community of beech, sugar maple, hemlock, white pine, and basswood covered an approximately 5 mi (8 km) wide band along the St. Lawrence River. The rest of the county, aside from some patches of wetland forest, was covered with Adirondack hardwoods composed of beech, sugar maple, and yellow birch, in addition to hemlock and white pine, with increasing amounts of red spruce, balsam fir, and paper birch to the southeast. In the early 21st century about 75% of the county is forested. Roughly a third of St. Lawrence Co lies within the Adirondack Park.

American Indians and Early Settlement

The pre-Contact history of St. Lawrence Co is sketchy. Certainly Iroquoian and Algonquian-speaking peoples contested the area and traveled the St. Lawrence, encamping seasonally and perhaps living for longer periods on its shores and major tributaries. Oral and archeological evidence is scant, however. French exploration of the St. Lawrence between 1535 and 1543 revealed that the region was occupied by St. Lawrence Iroquois, although they had disappeared by the early 17th century. Christian Onondaga were recruited by Abbé François Picquet (1708–81) to live at Fort La Présentation beginning in 1749. After the conclusion of hostilities with France in 1763, the English garrisoned the locale and renamed it Oswegatchie. The British garrison withdrew in 1796, and permanent American settlement at the site began immediately.

New York State created the St. Lawrence Ten Towns parallel to the St. Lawrence River in 1787; each town was intended to cover 64,000 acres (25,900 ha). They were sold at auction as the Towns of Cambray [now Gouverneur], Canton, De Kalb, Hague [now Morristown], Lisbon, Louisville, Madrid, Oswegatchie, Potsdam, and Stockholm. The rest of the county, aside from lands reserved to the Mohawk Nation, was sold by the state in the Macomb Purchase (1792).

The long trip to the Clinton county seat at Plattsburgh on primitive roads made transacting public business difficult. On petition, the legislature formed St. Lawrence Co on 3 Mar 1802, and Oswegatchie [now Ogdensburg] was selected as county seat. Partly because of the locality's perceived defensive vulnerability—the county jail had been damaged by the British in the War of 1812—the county seat was moved to Canton in 1828.

Successful settlement was often the result of active recruiting. There was no general land rush to northern New York, even after War of 1812 veterans were paid off in land bounty rights. Early promoters included Nathan Ford, acting for Samuel Ogden in the Ogdensburg area; Benjamin Raymond, acting for the Clarkson family in Potsdam; William Cooper in De Kalb; and David Parish in the Parishville area. The pattern of settlement reflected the environmental challenges of each area. The St. Lawrence Valley was generally settled before the foothills: Massena, Ogdensburg, Waddington, and Morristown were peopled between 1792 and 1799. The rest of the county outside what is now the Adirondack Park was settled before the War of 1812, except for Brasher, Pitcairn, and Colton. Development of the mountainous region had barely begun when the bottom essentially fell out of the northern land market with the opening of the Old Northwest. Clifton was not settled until 1866 as mining company town.

In the early years immigration was heaviest from northern New England, supplemented by an influx of Scots to Edwards, Hammond, Madrid, and Waddington; of Welsh to De Kalb; of French to Fowler; and of Irish (many coming via Montreal) to Brasher, Lisbon, Ogdensburg, and Oswegatchie. By 1855 significant numbers of Irish and Canadian natives were living in the county, roughly 8% of the county's population in each case. The African American population has historically been fairly minuscule. In its first census of 1810, St. Lawrence Co reported 5 slaves and 17 free Blacks.

ST. LAWRENCE CO POPULATION CENSUS FIGURES

	White	Nonwhite	Total Population	Foreign-Born
1810	7,863	22	7,885	—
1820	16,015	22	16,037	990
1830	36,294	60	36,354	3,859
1840	56,671	35	56,706	—
1850	68,578	39	68,617	13,713
1860	83,630	59	83,689	17,588
1870	84,746	80	84,826	18,219
1880	85,866	131	85,997	15,412
1890	84,948	100	85,048	13,903
1900	88,997	86	89,083	13,829
1910	88,863	142	89,005	13,239
1920	87,771	350	88,121	16,055
1930	90,586	374	90,960	11,600
1940	90,829	269	91,098	8,477
1950	98,747	150	98,897	6,927
1960	110,923	316	111,239	6,512
1970	111,330	661	111,991	4,895
1980	112,997	1,257	114,254	4,513
1990	108,242	3,732	111,974	3,867
2000	105,782	6,149	111,931	3,800

Notes: "Nonwhite" includes African Americans, Asians, American Indians, and Pacific Islanders and, for 2000, also the mixed race and other race categories. Through the 1960 census these figures primarily reflect the African American population. Foreign-born figures for 1820 and 1830 include only those not naturalized, and for 1930 and 1950, the foreign-born totals include Whites only. Other years include all foreign-born in the population.

Transportation and Economic Development

Early overland transportation was very difficult, especially in summer, because of the thick forest and extensive wetlands. True roads to the county's south and east were not built for decades following settlement. The earliest settlers took the path of least resistance, shipping black salts (potash), produced from the wood cut when clearing their farms, to Montreal via the St. Lawrence. The earliest state roads connected Canton to Chester (Warren Co) and Ogdensburg to the Black River Valley. The Russell Turnpike was built inland, parallel to the St. Lawrence River, to provide a relatively safe route when river transport was threatened by British attack in the War of 1812. Economic development has generally reflected the regional transportation system. Many believe that the lack of a four-lane highway connecting northern New York to the national interstate system is at least partly to blame for chronic high unemployment in St. Lawrence and Franklin Cos.

While much of the St. Lawrence Lowland and Foothills areas were settled in oxcart days, eco-

POPULATIONS OF TOWNS AND CITIES, ST. LAWRENCE CO

Town or City, Year Founded	1840	1880	1920	1960	2000
Brasher, 1825	2,118	3,578	1,922	2,536	2,337
Canton, 1805	3,465	6,275	6,497	8,935	10,334
Clare, 1880	—	—	152	87	112
Clifton, 1868	—	71	1,573	1,306	791
Colton, 1843	—	1,974	1,299	1,195	1,453
De Kalb, 1806	1,531	3,027	2,419	2,137	2,213
De Peyster, 1825	1,074	1,194	806	759	936
Edwards, 1827	956	1,082	1,497	1,366	1,148
Fine, 1844	—	893	1,459	2,391	1,622
Fowler, 1816	1,752	1,590	1,310	1,722	2,180
Gouverneur, 1810	2,538	4,165	5,762	6,757	7,418
Hammond, 1827	1,845	1,860	1,507	1,076	1,207
Hermon, 1830[a]	1,271	1,634	1,505	1,255	1,069
Hopkinton, 1805	1,147	1,922	1,244	1,032	1,020
Lawrence, 1828	1,845	2,483	1,588	1,785	1,545
Lisbon, 1801	3,508	4,297	2,673	3,040	4,047
Louisville, 1810	1,693	2,019	1,364	2,520	3,195
Macomb, 1841	—	1,731	1,055	881	846
Madrid, 1802	4,511	2,145	1,390	1,623	1,828
Massena, 1802	2,726	2,739	8,975	17,730	13,121
Morristown, 1821	2,809	2,186	1,719	1,776	2,050
Norfolk, 1823	1,728	2,471	3,066	4,590	4,565
Ogdensburg (city), 1868	—	10,341	14,609	16,122	12,364
Oswegatchie, 1802	3,193	2,881	2,156	2,836	4,370
Parishville, 1814	2,250	2,384	1,453	1,473	2,049
Piercefield, 1900	—	—	1,454	420	305
Pierrepont, 1818	1,430	2,494	1,425	1,523	2,674
Pitcairn, 1836	396	790	646	647	783
Potsdam, 1806	4,473	7,610	8,794	14,045	15,957
Rossie, 1813	1,553	1,709	866	649	787
Russell, 1807	1,373	2,403	1,757	1,588	1,801
Stockholm, 1806	2,995	3,441	2,437	3,465	3,592
Waddington, 1859	—	2,608	1,742	1,972	2,212

Note: In 1800 the Towns of Canton, Louisville, Madrid, Massena, Oswegatchie, and Stockholm were in Oneida Co.

[a]Depau until 1834.

nomic potential arrived by rail. The first lines were the Northern Railroad (1850) and the Potsdam and Watertown (1857) with its Ogdensburg Branch (1862). These lines enabled St. Lawrence Co milk, cheese, and other products to reach Boston and New York City. The Adirondacks, though, remained largely unsettled because of the more severe climate and considerably less developed transportation system. In the 1880s and afterward, with expansion of both mining and logging to the southernmost towns, shorter rail lines were built to haul raw materials to mills and to market.

The 19th-century economy of St. Lawrence Co rested on farming and the extraction of minerals and forest products, with a smaller but not insignificant amount of manufacturing. The northern and western sections are level and have some good soils, so farms were successful during the first half of the 19th century, producing diversified crops. The advent of the Northern Railroad encouraged a shift to dairy farming. Potsdam ranked third in the state in butter production in 1855 and 1865. Cheese, which had been laboriously produced on the farm, was increasingly made in cheese factories, which were scattered throughout the county in the late 19th and early 20th centuries. Beginning in the 1840s potato starch was produced in the northeastern towns, with small factories processing the potato crops of surrounding farms. In 1875 St. Lawrence Co was by far New York State's largest producer of maple sugar, with 1,469,867 pounds (666,720 kg), or 16% of the state total. Stockholm, Potsdam, and Russell ranked first, third, and fourth in the state, respectively. At the turn of the 20th century St. Lawrence Co had 8,353 farms, the most of any county in the state, on 1,068,798 acres (432,527 ha). Some 62% of the county's area was farmland.

While forest product extraction began with potash, the vast southeastern forestlands, on soil not suitable for farming, were lumbered extensively in the late 19th century. Rich mineral deposits were exploited, beginning with iron ore in the early 19th century. It was extracted in a variety of forms, including hematite (in Fowler and Hermon) and bog ore (in Brasher and Madrid). Somewhat later, lead, talc, zinc, and graphite were mined; quarries produced building stone of Potsdam sandstone and Gouverneur marble.

Manufacturing played a lesser role in the county's 19th-century economy, but many hamlets had small factories, while Canton, Potsdam, Ogdensburg, Massena, and Norwood had diversified industrial production. The first paper mill was established in Waddington in 1826, but with the development of pulp-paper technology after the Civil War, pulp mills of considerable size and with large workforces were built in many locations. Other 19th-century products were agricultural implements, pumps, leather, furniture, iron castings of various kinds, edged tools and cutlery, and woolen cloth. Rushton canoes made in Canton and patent medicines from Morristown were widely known.

Tourism had a limited impact on St. Lawrence Co in the 19th century. Massena Springs developed as a minor mineral water resort beginning in the 1820s. Despite the county's position between the Adirondacks and the St. Lawrence River, the more accessible wilderness lakes were in counties to the south, and the Thousand Islands were to the west in Jefferson Co. The county's potential for tourism was largely unrealized until the mid–20th century.

Religion, Education, and Culture

In 1855 St. Lawrence Co had 36 Methodist churches and, because of its New England roots, 20 Congregational churches. Baptists and Presbyterians were each represented by 16 congregations, and there was a substantial cluster of 10 Universalist churches. The county was only partially settled in 1812, when state law authorized common schools. They remained the norm until further legislation in 1853 allowed some of the larger villages to form Union Free School districts to provide public high schools. Centralization began in 1927 with the creation of Madrid Central School District and was largely complete with the formation of Massena Central School District in 1955. In the early 21st century there are 16 central school districts in the county. Higher education is provided by St. Lawrence University (1856) in Canton, SUNY Potsdam (1869), Clarkson University (1896) in Potsdam, SUNY Canton (1906), and the SUNY-ESF Ranger School (1912) at Wanakena.

St. Lawrence Co's contributions to the culture of the state and nation have included one of America's greatest artists, Frederic Remington (1861–1909), and an important regionalist author, Irving Bacheller (1859–1950) of Pierrepont. Its folk culture has been rich, with such recognized tradition bearers as Colton storytellers Hamilton Ferry (1904–94) and Bill Smith (1936–); Smith is also acknowledged as the Adirondacks' finest living pack-basket maker. Traditional Arts of Upstate New York, an effective nonprofit organization, is based in Canton. The county's most important cultural institution is arguably the Frederic Remington Art Museum (1923) in Ogdensburg, and the four colleges in Canton and Potsdam offer considerable breadth in the fine and performing arts.

The 20th Century

Agriculture in St. Lawrence Co has historically meant dairy farming and dairy processing. Prior to 1960 most farms were small to medium in both size of herd and acreage. Many farms shipped milk directly to small, nearby cheese plants. As manufacturing began to consolidate in fewer but larger plants, quality standards were imposed requiring the use of bulk storage and delivery systems. Within a few years many hundreds of small farms went out of production, while some began expansion. The process is ongoing: the current trend is to consolidate farms and to maintain herds of 600 or more milking cattle, plus replacement stock. The farms still are owned by families or small family corporations rather than by off-premises corporations. A number of small farmers who no longer have dairies have converted to beef cattle, and some raise goats, bison, or sheep instead. Off-farm income is important to maintaining many farm families. The amount of land in production is much less than it was in the late 19th century but is still substantial. In 1950, 5,091 farms occupied 886,855 acres (358,897 ha); in 1997 there were 1,363 farms working 396,406 acres (160,420 ha), 23.1% of the county's area.

The county has two large, state-certified agricultural districts, each approximately 250,000 acres (100,000 ha). Cheese production continues in three factories in Heuvelton and at Canton's Kraft Foods plant. The preservation of the dairy sector has been aided by the influx, beginning in 1974, of Amish families who bought farms and developed small industries, including cheese making. Mostly of the Swartzentruber community, they live in De Kalb, De Peyster, Macomb, Morristown, and Oswegatchie, and their community continues to grow because of high birth rates and in-migration. A separate community in Norfolk has now dispersed.

Extractive industries continue to be important. Zinc and talc are mined, and marble is quarried in Gouverneur, and in St. Lawrence Co's Adirondack Park towns, modern scientific lumbering operations remain by far the largest users of land. The old manufacturing sector went through dramatic changes in the 20th century. Paper mills, once ubiquitous, have decreased dramatically in number, although papermaking continues at APC Paper of New York at Norfolk and Mead Corp at Potsdam. Hydropower generation replaced water-driven mills in various locations, but especially at Massena, where hydro for aluminum reduction began in 1902 under the company that developed into Alcoa and where electricity generation for the St. Lawrence Seaway project began generating in 1959. In the early 21st century, manufacturing is centered in industrial parks at Massena and Ogdensburg, attracting, among others, Canadian firms wishing to do business on the US side. There is also a Corning Inc plant at Canton.

Like the North Country generally, St. Lawrence Co has become increasingly hospitable to state institutions, which make few tax demands and provide dependable paychecks. The St. Lawrence Psychiatric Center (originally St. Lawrence State Hospital, 1900) at Ogdensburg was the first such institution, while three correctional facilities—Ogdensburg (1981), Riverview (1988), and Gouverneur (1990)—have been established in recent decades. Since the 1960s the county's population has been quite stable numerically, but it is aging. While some towns close to population centers gain, smaller villages shrink. The county's modest economic development has left the significant Victorian architecture of most of the villages largely intact. Canton and Potsdam in particular have made efforts to retain these assets through regulation and economic incentives. Massena has a different look, as its major industrial growth took place after 1900. In spite of its healthy economy, the downtown has been struggling, partly because of the construction of a cluster of shopping centers east of the village. Ogdensburg lost a good deal of its architectural character through urban renewal in the early 1970s but has had some success in rebuilding the downtown economy.

In the early 21st century about three-quarters of the population lives in or near one of the larger population centers of Ogdensburg, Canton, Potsdam, and Massena. Agriculture and industrial forestry, which require large landholdings, remain important to the economy; consequently the overall county population density is very light, with only about 10 families per square mile. Although the minority population has increased 10-fold since 1970, in large part because of the student and prisoner populations, the overall population is still 95% white.

One of the earliest competent county histories is Franklin B. Hough, *History of St. Lawrence and Franklin Counties* (1853), expanded by Samuel W. Durant, *History of St. Lawrence County* (1878). Three town histories appeared in the early 20th century: Carlton E. Sanford, *Early History of the Town of Hopkinton* (1903), *Centennial Souvenir History of Gouverneur* (1905), and P. S. Garand, *The History of the City of Ogdensburg* (1927). Notable among the relatively few local histories published in the last quarter of the 20th century are *Colton, New York: Story of a Town, II*, rev ed. (1993) and William G. McLoughlin, *Lake Ozonia: An Informal History* (1997). A unique reference work is Kelsie B. Harder and Mary H. Smallman, *Claims to Name: Toponyms of St. Lawrence County* (1992). Compensating in part for the limited recent literature is an excellent journal, the *St. Lawrence County Historical Association Quarterly* (1955–). Douglas Harper, *Changing Works: Visions of a Lost Agriculture* (2001), provides an extraordinary examination of the transformation of farming in the county since World War II.

Richard E. Mooers

St. Lawrence River (535 mi/861 km). Originating in Lake Ontario and flowing northeast into the Atlantic Ocean, the St. Lawrence River extends from Kingston, Ont, to Father Point on the Gulf of St. Lawrence, dropping about 245 feet (75 m) in its descent to the ocean. For the first 120 miles (193 km) downstream of Lake Ontario, it flows along the northern border of New York State and the southern border of the Canadian province of Ontario. It passes through the Thousand Islands region before reaching the City of Ogdensburg (St. Lawrence Co) and what was known as the International Rapids section of the river (extending from Ogdensburg to Cornwall, Ont). The last 3 miles (5 km) of the New York shore is part of the St. Regis Indian Reservation.

The river was created approximately 10,000 years ago when the outflow of Lake Iroquois, formed by the meltwater of the retreating Wisconsinan ice sheet, shifted to the north of the Adirondack massif into the St. Lawrence plain. There is evidence of an early American Indian presence in the valley, and the river served as a primary transportation corridor between the Atlantic Ocean and the interior for thousands of years before the arrival of the French expedition commanded by Jacques Cartier in 1534. In the 16th and 17th centuries, the northern shore was home to the Huron, the Montagnais, and the Algonquin, and the southern shore was controlled by the Iroquois Confederacy as far north as the mouth of the Richelieu River.

European settlement began under Samuel de Champlain in the early 17th century. The French settled downstream. Important foundations were laid in the 18th century at what is now Ogdensburg by the Sulpician missionary Fr François Picquet, who built Fort La Présentation on the south bank of the river. Following the American Revolution the population expanded rapidly, stimulating agriculture, shipbuilding, and other industrial activities. Beginning in the latter part of the 19th century, the tourist industry burgeoned in the stretch of the river between Lake Ontario and Ogdensburg.

Projects designed to foster commercial navigation and to harness the force of the flowing water were proposed and rejected or undertaken in piecemeal fashion until 1953, when the Eisenhower administration committed itself to the colossal international St. Lawrence Seaway project. Most directly affected was the International Rapids section, where a impoundment, christened Lake St. Lawrence, was created behind the International Power Dam linking Barnhart Island with the Canadian mainland. The American portion constitutes the St. Lawrence–Franklin D. Roosevelt Power Project and is operated by the New York Power Authority. Vice Pres Richard M. Nixon and Queen Elizabeth II inaugurated the jointly owned and operated International Power Dam in 1958. The dam generates approximately 900,000 kilowatts of electricity annually for American use and the same for Canadian. The rate of flow throughout the river is managed according to a regulation plan administered by the International Joint Commission, granted authority by the Boundary Waters Treaty Act of 1909. The St. Lawrence River closes to navigation late in the year when the ice forms and reopens with the spring thaw.

Industrial pollutants including polychlorinated biphenyls (PCBs) and heavy metals have been detected in some sediments in the river. Because of the accumulation of PCBs, mirex, and dioxin, fish consumption advisories were issued in 2003 for trout, channel catfish, salmon, white sucker, and American eel. The New York State Department of Environmental Conservation has adopted a remedial action plan for the Massena section of the river, and industrial concerns such as Alcoa and General Motors have made significant progress in land- and river-based cleanup efforts. In general, water quality in the river allows for a full range of recreational uses. Sportfishing is popular, and catfish, bass, muskellunge, pike, walleye, perch, and other species are taken by anglers.

In 2003 the Federal Energy Regulatory Commission issued a new 50-year license for the St. Lawrence–Franklin D. Roosevelt Power Project. As a result of various settlements agreed to by the New York Power Authority contingent on the license approval, more than $100 million will be

Long Sault Dam, built 1957–58, is used to control water levels on the St. Lawrence River.

spent on improving wildlife habitat, aquatic life scientific research, parks, and local governments and school districts.

See also BRIDGES AND TUNNELS; FISH; NEW FRANCE; THOUSAND ISLANDS RESORTS.

Mallaus, Alida. *Blue Water Boundary* (New York: Hastings House, 1960)

William S. Helmer

St. Lawrence Seaway. An improvement of the natural waterway from the Great Lakes to the Atlantic Ocean, via the St. Lawrence River. A joint engineering project of the United States and Canada, it was one of the largest waterway engineering projects in the world when it opened in 1959.

History and Construction

The early European settlers dreamed of improving the waterway connection between the Great Lakes and the Atlantic Ocean, and gradually canals were dug around the major impediments such as the Niagara Falls and the St. Lawrence rapids. By the 1850s small ships could sail from the Atlantic to Lake Superior. But as ships kept getting larger, only a few of them were able to pass through the canals. In the 1890s populist protests about railway rates helped to persuade the United States and Canada to support a joint study for a modern seaway that would allow a substantial proportion of oceangoing ships to enter the Great Lakes. A long struggle over creating the seaway ensued. From William H. Taft on, all American presidents supported the proposal. For many years all New York State governors, regardless of party, opposed it out of fear that the state's railroads and the Port of New York would suffer. Gov Franklin D. Roosevelt, however, supported the seaway because of the electric power it would incidentally produce; in 1931 he helped create the Power Authority of the State of New York to ensure that the power would be state owned and distributed. In 1932 Canada and the United States agreed to build the seaway, but in 1934 the US Senate rejected it. Among the factors that finally led to the decision to build the seaway were the discovery of iron ore in 1948 on the Labrador-Quebec border; the urgent need for electric power in both New York State and Ontario; an agreement by the United States and Canada to pay for constructing the seaway by charging tolls on ships using it; and Canada's decision in 1951 to build the seaway alone if necessary. Finally in 1954 the US Congress passed the Wiley-Dondero Act providing for American participation.

The seaway was one of the largest construction projects ever undertaken and meant employing as many as 22,000 persons at a time in locations stretching from Montreal to Niagara Falls. The construction of over 45 miles (72 km) of dikes and 69 miles (111 km) of channel required moving over 200 million yd^3 (153 million m^3) of earth and pouring over 6 million yds^3 (5 million m^3) of concrete and coordinating the efforts of four construction companies, the American Seaway Development Corp, the Canadian Seaway Authority, the Hydro-Electric Power Commission of Ontario, and the Power Authority of the State of New York. Buildings, highways, and rail lines had to be removed, bridges lifted, channels deepened, land flooded, and dikes, locks, and dams built. Land expropriated for the project included territory from the Mohawk Indian reservations at Kahnawake [loc in Quebec] and Akwesasne (St. Regis Indian Reservation) [partly loc in Franklin Co]. A painful and bitter controversy was the flooding in the region near Massena, which forced relocation of about 1,100 permanent residents in New York State and about 6,500 in Ontario. When the seaway was finished, Pres Dwight D. Eisenhower and Queen Elizabeth II attended its opening ceremonies on 26 June 1959. From its opening, both Canada and the United States charged tolls for the use of the seaway to pay for its construction. The US charges were discriminatory because the United States did not require users of other American waterway improvements to pay for their construction. In 1986, when seaway traffic was decreasing, the United States adopted a system of rebates by which, in effect, it stopped charging tolls. Canada, however, continued to charge in 2003.

Locks and Cargo

To avoid rapids and waterfalls, a ship passing from the Atlantic Ocean to Lake Superior must pass through 16 locks. Of these, seven are on the St. Lawrence River, five of which are in Quebec and Ontario, and two in the United States. The distance from the Atlantic Ocean via the seaway to Duluth, Minn, at the head of Lake Superior, is 2,342 miles (3,769 km), or eight and one-half sailing days. The seaway locks and channels are at least 27 feet (8 m) deep. In 1994 the seaway increased the length of vessels allowed into its locks from 730 feet (223 m) to 740 feet (226 m). In 1996, 41% of the world's merchant fleet could transit the seaway locks.

In its first year of operation, the seaway carried cargoes of about 20 million tons (18 million MT) a year. Cargoes reached their peak in 1979 at over 74 million tons (67 million MT). Since then, the seaway has been losing market share to other routes, such as rail routes to the Pacific and Atlantic coasts and the Mississippi River water route to the Gulf of Mexico. From 1994 the seaway has carried about 50 million tons (45 million MT) a year and has continued to have a major impact on the North American economy. Grain, iron ore, and coal account for almost two-thirds of seaway cargo. Great Lakes ships, called lakers, especially built to be as large as the seaway locks allow, often take grain from the western Great Lakes to the lower St. Lawrence for transshipment overseas, and return with Labrador iron ore in the form of pellets for Great Lakes steel mills. Coal originating in US Appalachian mines typically moves by lakers from Ohio ports through the Welland Canal into Lake Ontario to Canadian power-generating plants and steel mills (as at Hamilton, Ont), or for export to Europe. The number of loaded oceangoing ships using the seaway exceeded the number of loaded lakers for the first time in 1998.

In 1976 New York State's seaway ports were estimated to handle cargo second only to Ohio's in tonnage, but because the cargo was largely mechanically handled bulk cargo rather than labor-intensive general cargo, its economic value to the ports was less than that in the ports of several other seaway states. In 1998 New York State's seaway cargo was low in both tonnage and value, mostly in bulk and inbound, relative to the seaway cargo handled in other seaway states. That year Ogdensburg (St. Lawrence Co), on the St. Lawrence River, handled 110,293 tons (100,056 MT) of seaway cargo; Buffalo, on Lake Erie, handled 190,527 tons (172,843 MT); and Oswego, on Lake Ontario, handled 556,250 tons (504,621 MT).

Controversies and Future Prospects

The St. Lawrence Seaway was meant to provide the incidental benefit of hydroelectric power. The Robert Moses–Robert H. Saunders Power Dam, located on the seaway between Massena and Cornwall, Ont, was built both to assist shipping and to produce more hydroelectric power. It was built jointly by the Power Authority and the Hydro-Electric Power Commission of Ontario, and was named for the chairmen of the two agencies. It is one of the largest power dams in the world with its capacity to produce 1 million kilowatts of electricity. The Power Authority distributes more than half of the American share of the electricity to hungry, low-labor-intensive industries in the immediate vicinity of the dam, such as an Aluminum Co of America plant and a General Motors (GM) plant.

The overall, long-term economic impact of the seaway on St. Lawrence Co and the surrounding area has been relatively slight, and the region continues to have an unemployment rate well over the state average. Yet there are positive economic effects for the region: both Aluminum Co of America and GM continued to operate in 2003, and tourists have been drawn not only by the nearby locks and power dam, but also by the accompanying 30 mi (48 km) Lake St. Lawrence and parks as well as the region's rural charm.

A fundamental concern about the seaway has been whether the erosion of its cargo market share can be stopped. In the effort to stem the decline, technological improvements have been made, such as a computerized communication system linking ships, coast guard stations, bridges, and locks to speed the movement of ships. The United States continues to administer its share of the seaway through a government agency. In 1998 Canada, with hopes to improve the seaway's operating efficiency, changed the nature of the administrative agency from a government entity to a private not-for-profit corporation. Expensive improvements have been proposed for the seaway, notably enlarging it to accommodate the ever larger ocean ships being built, and extending the season when the seaway locks are open (because of ice, the locks in the St. Lawrence section have usually been closed from late December to late March). More modest proposals include reducing tolls and fostering passenger cruise shipping, which, once moribund, has been reviving by the late 1990s.

Great Lakes Seaway Review (1970–)
Mabee, Carleton. *The Seaway Story* (New York: Macmillan, 1961)
St. Lawrence Seaway Authority (Canadian). *Annual Report*, 1954–97
St. Lawrence Seaway Development Corp (American). *Annual Report*, 1954/55–
St. Lawrence Seaway Management Corp (Canadian). *Annual Report*, 1998–

Carleton Mabee

St. Lawrence Seaway Development Corporation. Federal government corporation under the authority of the US Department of Transportation. In 1954 the US Congress enacted the Wiley-Dondero Act, more commonly known as the St. Lawrence Seaway Act. It authorized the creation of the corporation and directed it to acquire land for, build, operate, and maintain the section of the proposed St. Lawrence Seaway that lay within US territorial limits. Its Canadian counterpart is the St. Lawrence Seaway Management Corp. The corporation's mission is to operate and maintain a safe, reliable, efficient, and environmentally responsible deep draft waterway in cooperation with its Canadian counterpart. In addition, the corporation is charged with encouraging the development of trade in the Great Lakes–seaway system. Of the 15 locks between Lake Erie and Montreal, the corporation is responsible for the Bertrand Snell and Dwight D. Eisenhower locks in Massena (St. Lawrence Co). The corporation also owns and participates in the operation of Seaway International Bridge that links Cornwall, Ont, and Rooseveltown (St. Lawrence Co). Access to all US territory facilities north of the seaway, including the Robert Moses State Park and the St. Lawrence–Franklin D. Roosevelt Power Project, as well as to the corporation's visitors' center, is through a tunnel passing under Eisenhower lock. The corporation's budget in 2003 was $14.6 million. Headquarters were in Washington, DC, with an operational office in Massena. The corporation is managed by a five-member advisory board that functions as the federal equivalent of a corporate board of directors. Board members are nominated by the president of the United States and confirmed by the US Senate.

Becker, William H. *From the Atlantic to the Great Lakes: A History of the US Army Corps of Engineers and the St. Lawrence* (Washington, DC: Government Printing Office, 1984)

William S. Helmer

St. Lawrence Ten Towns. Land partition in St. Lawrence Co. In 1787 the New York State Board of Land Commissioners established the Ten Towns tract from a section of Great Tracts 2 and 3 of the Macomb Purchase. The Ten Towns included 10 sections, each 10 mi^2 (25.9 km^2). The towns were southeast of the St. Lawrence River, were prime real estate, and included fertile plains and the Indian, Grass and Raquette Rivers. The original towns were Louisville (Town 1), Stockholm (2), Potsdam (3), Madrid (4), Lisbon (5), Canton (6), De Kalb (7), Oswegatchie (8), Hague [now Morristown] (9), and Cambray [now Gouverneur] (10). Macomb went bankrupt by 1792 and sold the Ten Towns to pay debts. Major patentees included Gouverneur Morris, Samuel Ogden, William Constable, and David Parish. In the early 1800s New Englanders, New Yorkers, and Canadians settled the towns. In 2002 only Potsdam, Canton, Lisbon, and De Kalb retained their original Ten Towns boundaries.

Durant, Samuel W. *History of St. Lawrence County New York, 1749–1878* (1878; repr Interlaken, NY: Heart of the Lakes Publishing, 1982)

Tricia A. Barbagallo

St. Lawrence University. Private nondenominational liberal arts institution. Founded in 1856 as a seminary by the Universalist Church in Canton (St. Lawrence Co), it is one of the oldest coeducational schools in the state. The first bachelor of divinity was awarded in 1861 and the first bachelor of arts in 1865. A graduate program in education was introduced in the early 20th century. The seminary closed in 1965 after the merger of the Universalist and the Unitarian Churches. The university, enrolling about 1,800 undergraduate and 100 graduate students, offers liberal arts and sciences undergraduate programs, including a program in Canadian studies.

Blankman, E., T. Cannon, and N. Burdick. *The Scarlet and the Brown* (Canton, NY: St. Lawrence Univ, 1987)

Carl A. Westerdahl and Susan S. Clarke

St. Nicholas. The modern image of St. Nicholas, or Santa Claus, derives largely from a series of inventions by New York City antiquarians and popular writers in the 19th century.

In traditional German and Dutch celebrations, St. Nicholas brings presents to good children and punishment to bad ones on his 6 December feast day. Only scant evidence shows how that celebration may have been observed in the American colonies. Pennsylvania's colonial Germans held St. Nicholas feasts, and colonial New Yorkers likely did the same. The term "St. a Claus" appeared in *Rivington's New-York Gazetteer* on 23 Dec 1773, and Dutch-descended New York City residents held St. Nicholas feasts in December 1773 and 1774, though not on the sixth day.

John Pintard, an influential New York City merchant and antiquarian, transformed the St. Nicholas legend. He first published an almanac in 1793 that mentioned St. Nicholas, and his diary entry for 6 Dec 1797 notes the feast day. In 1810 Pintard published a broadside of St. Nicholas along with the poem "Sancte Claus goed heylig man" (Saint Claus, good holy man). He designated St. Nicholas as patron saint of New York City and of the New-York Historical Society, which he helped found in 1804, and sponsored St. Nicholas Day dinners with the society before 1820. For most New Yorkers, New Year's Day had been the primary midwinter holiday. In a significant shift, Pintard in 1827 moved his celebration to a family-centered holiday on Christmas Day. That year, for the first time, Pintard mentioned in his diary a Christmas visit by "St. Claas," and in 1828 he described his grandchildren setting out hay for the horses of St. Claas, who came during the night and placed toys, bonbons, and oranges in stockings by the chimney. By 1831 he would speak of it as an ancient custom.

It is likely that it was Pintard who moved both the Santa Claus gift-giving traditions from St. Nicholas Day and the family feasting and conviviality of New Year's Day to the religious holiday of Christmas. In doing so, he created an appealing holiday with a greater emphasis on family, especially children, than had previously existed on any of the three days. Pintard boosted the nascent idea of a child-centered Christmas and of St. Nicholas's symbolic role in that celebration.

Author Washington Irving also contributed to this new image of Santa Claus. In his 1809 satiric *Knickerbocker's History of New York,* Irving depicted St. Nicholas riding over treetops in a horse-drawn wagon with presents for children, mentioned smoke from his pipe spreading like a cloud overhead, and described his gesture of laying a finger beside his nose. Irving's *History* is an obvious source for the 1822 poem "An Account of a Visit from St. Nicholas," which General Theological Seminary professor Clement Clarke Moore claimed to have written for his children. (An alternative tradition attributes authorship to Poughkeepsie landowner Maj Henry Livingston, Jr.) The poem was first published, according to Moore, without his knowledge or permission in the *Troy Sentinel* in 1823, and it was reprinted in newspapers and almanacs nationwide. The author may have been influenced by a poem published in the 1821 book *The Children's Friend.* There for the first time St. Nicholas appears on Christmas Eve. He also travels in a sleigh pulled by a single reindeer, perhaps borrowed from Norse legend: Odin traveled with reindeer and sleigh to distribute gifts. The eight named reindeer were among Moore's original contributions.

Moore's St. Nick is a nonthreatening figure: the size of an elf, he brings only presents, not punishment as he did in Dutch tradition. Rather than being a slender Dutch bishop, this soot-covered Santa Claus dresses in fur, perhaps inspired by the German (and Pennsylvania German) Pelz-Nickel ("Fur-Nicky"), looks like a peddler, and smokes a workman's stub of a pipe. A ruddy, portly, neighborhood Dutchman purportedly served as Moore's model. Soon after publication of the poem, St. Nick's image appeared in commercial advertisements to promote merchants' products for Christmas and New Year's gifts. By the 1840s he had become a standard figure in sales promotion. His appearance varied greatly at midcentury, sometimes appearing young and unbearded. New York City artist Robert Weir in 1837 dressed St. Nick in a red cape with white fur lining and high black boots and in 1844 added a floppy cap. Illustrator Thomas Nast drew a Santa in 1863 that resembled Moore's peddler, but within a few years he had spruced him up and Santa was no longer a begrimed, elfin workman. By 1881 Nast's Santa had evolved into a jolly, fat, white-bearded figure that would vary little in later artwork.

Foster, Don. *Author Unknown: On the Trail of Anonymous* (New York: Henry Holt, 2000)
Jones, Charles W. *Saint Nicholas of Myra, Bari, and Manhattan: Biography of a Legend* (Chicago: Univ of Chicago Press, 1978)
Nissenbaum, Stephen. *The Battle for Christmas* (New York: Knopf, 1996)
Pintard, John. *Letters from John Pintard to His Daughter Eliza Noel Pintard Davidson, 1816–1833,* 4 vols. Ed. Dorothy C. Barck (New York: New-York Historical Society, 1940)

Peter R. Christoph

St. Nicholas, by Thomas Nast, published in *Harper's Weekly,* 1862.

Stockbridge. Town (pop 2,080) in E Madison Co. Originally part of the Oneida Reservation, the land was given by the Oneida in 1786 to the Stockbridge Indians, who gave the town its name, first called New Stockbridge, and built the first saw- and gristmills in the area. The Oneida also welcomed a colony of freed slaves from the Mohawk Valley who settled New Guinea hamlet *ca* 1800. Indians remained until the mid-1820s, when they removed to Wisconsin. Settled by Whites in 1791, the town was formed from Vernon and Augusta (Oneida Co) and Smithfield and Lenox in 1836. Stockbridge has numerous small limestone caves, and limestone and gypsum were quarried extensively. Agricultural pursuits predominate in the valley. In the late 19th century it was second in Madison Co for hops, but by the early 21st dairying prevails. The Stockbridge-Munsee band of Mohicans acquired land at Munnsville in 2002.

William F. Helmer

Stockholm. Town (pop 3,592) in E St. Lawrence Co. Settled in 1802, the town was formed in 1806 from Massena. At West Stockholm, a woolen factory (*ca* 1830) and a foundry (1846) provided employment. The Northern Railroad (1850; later Rutland Railroad) provided service. After the Civil War the town turned to dairy farming and in 1875 was the largest producer of maple sugar (164,208 lb/74,483.4 kg) in the state. In the early 21st century agriculture remains important, but abandoned farms are common. Many parts of the town have extensive wetlands. Stockholm is also a bedroom community to Massena and Potsdam.

Richard E. Mooers

stock market. See NEW YORK STOCK EXCHANGE (NYSE); SECURITIES INDUSTRY.

Stockport. Town (pop 2,933) in W Columbia Co. Settled in 1654 by Abraham Staats, the town was formed from Ghent, Hudson, and Stuyvesant in 1833. Beginning in 1809, four hamlets in the town developed as mill towns. Stockport hamlet produced woolen cloth, calico, looms, paper, husk mattresses, knit goods, and cornhuskers; Columbiaville made cotton cloth, tobacco products, bricks, surgical instruments, and cotton mill machinery; Stottville manufactured woolen cloth (employing nearly 1,000 at one time) and, in the 20th century, ice cream; and Rossman had a paper mill. Stockport, served by the Hudson River Railroad (1851) and the Kinderhook and Hudson (1890), had extensive brickyards that attracted Italians and African Americans as workers. Dairying predominated after the railroad, and in 1874 Stockport produced 36% of the county's grapes. Columbia White Sulphur Springs at Stottville was the site of the Columbia Springs Hotel (1855–1920). In the 20th century Atlantic Mills (1910–53) and L and B Products (?1940s; hotel furniture) were large employers at Stottville. The town is the site of Stockport Creek State Wetland Preservation Area and Hudson River Islands State Park.

Stockton. Town (pop 2,331) in central Chautauqua Co. Settled in 1810 the town formed in 1821 from Chautauqua. Marl for cement was quarried near Cassadaga by the Chautauqua Cement Co, organized *ca* 1890. Cassadaga and Bear Lakes attract recreational users, but in the early 21st century the town's main industry remains dairy farming. Residents commute to Jamestown, Dunkirk, and Buffalo for employment.

Michelle Henry

Stoddard, Seneca Ray (*b* Wilton, Saratoga Co, 13 May 1843; *d* Glens Falls, Warren Co, 3 May 1917). Photographer. Trained as a decorative painter, he began work in 1862 for the Gilbert Car Co in Watervliet (Albany Co), ornamenting railroad cars with scenic landscapes. Within two years he set out on his own and by 1867 advertised as a photographer in Glens Falls. He began photographing scenes on Lake George by 1868, the year he married Helen Augusta Potter. During the 1870s and 1880s, using the difficult glass-plate technology of the era, he created hundreds of images of the Adirondack region, capturing not only the landscape but also the hotels and middle-class vacationers who bought his prints and stereographs as souvenirs. His photographs show the influence of the Luminist movement in painting and aim at revealing the divine in nature. Low horizons, placid waters, and an attention to atmosphere are typical features. In 1874 Stoddard published a popular guidebook, *The Adirondacks Illustrated,* which was reprinted almost annually through 1893 and then less frequently until 1913. In 1880 he completed his *Map of the Adirondacks,* which, along with the guidebooks, boosted tourism in the region. In the 1880s he took some of the earliest successful nighttime photographs, perfecting a magnesium chloride "flash" invented sometime earlier in Germany. In 1892 he played a role in the establishment of the Adirondack Park by presenting state legislators with a dramatic lantern-slide show of his Adirondack images. From the late 1880s through the first years of the 20th century, he also traveled and photographed in the American South and West, Alaska, Europe, and the Near East, and gained his living by presenting "illustrated" lectures on the different regions. Late in life he published *Stoddard's Northern Monthly* (later *Stoddard's Adirondack Monthly*) between 1906 and 1908. The short-lived magazine, whose first issue featured an unusual composite photograph of Stoddard's own face and arm emerging from the trunk of a tree, advocated the conservation of Adirondack timber, waters, and wildlife.

For illustration see TICONDEROGA.

Adler, Jeanne Winston. *Early Days in the Adirondacks: The Photographs of Seneca Ray Stoddard* (New York: Abrams, 1997)

Horrell, Jeffery L. *Seneca Ray Stoddard: Transforming the Adirondack Wilderness in Text and Image* (Syracuse: Syracuse Univ Press, 1999)

Douglas McCombs

Stone, Edward Durell (*b* Fayetteville, Ark, 9 Mar 1902; *d* New York City, 6 Aug 1978). Architect. Raised in Arkansas, Stone attended but did not graduate from the Massachusetts Institute of Technology. An adherent of the International style, Stone established his practice in New York City in 1936 and quickly emerged as one of the nation's leading Modern architects. Much of Stone's work was executed in New York State, including many of his early designs, which both faithfully epitomized the Modernist trend toward clean lines and lack of ornamentation and pioneered the use of new materials, including steel, concrete, and floor-to-ceiling glass walls. Examples of Stone's early work include the Richard H. Mandell House in Mount Kisco (Westchester Co) in 1935 and the A. Conger Goodyear House in Old Westbury (Nassau Co) three years later. Stone also codesigned the Museum of Modern Art in 1937, the first significant building of the International movement in New York City. Although he still worked with the same physical materials, after World War II Stone changed his approach, designing in an idiosyncratic style that blended the asceticism of the International school with traditional Gothic and Muslim forms. Stone's most popular work used this blended style: the General Motors Building in New York City in 1968, the State University of New York campus in Albany that same year, and the headquarters of PepsiCo in Purchase (Westchester Co) in 1970. Stone's work often had a mixed reception. For his highly controversial design of the Huntington Hartford Museum of Modern Art (1962) in New York City, many critics derided the building's clumsy ornamentation, while supporters applauded Stone's attempt to move to less stark forms with greater visual interest. Stone's later works were primarily outside of New York State and included perhaps his most famous design, the John F. Kennedy Center for the Performing Arts (1971) in Washington, DC.

Stone, Edward Durell. *Recent and Future Architecture* (New York: Horizon Press, 1967)

Thomas A. Birkland

Stone, Harlan Fiske (*b* Chesterfield, NH, 11 Oct 1872; *d* Washington, DC, 22 Apr 1946). Chief justice of the US Supreme Court. An 1894 graduate of Amherst College, Stone earned a degree from Columbia Law School in 1898, teaching school to help pay his expenses. He married Agnes Harvey in 1899 and had two sons. Both an academic and corporate lawyer, Stone taught at Columbia before resigning to practice privately full time but returned as dean in 1910. In 1923 he was named head of the litigation department of the prestigious Wall St firm Sullivan and Cromwell. In April 1924 Amherst classmate Pres Calvin Coolidge, seeking to clean up the scandal-ridden Justice Department, named Stone US attorney general and in 1925 appointed him to the Supreme Court. As a key figure in the "constitutional revolution" of 1937, Stone vigorously opined against judicial lawmaking and for judicial restraint. In *US v Carolene Products Co* (1938), he enunciated the important doctrine of preferred rights—that legislatures should be given wide latitude, but that laws concerning fundamental rights should be held to close scrutiny. Promoted to chief justice by Pres Franklin D. Roosevelt in 1941, Stone's tenure was made difficult by the contentiousness of the extremely able new justices on the Roosevelt court and his own weaknesses as a court manager.

Mason, Alpheus T. *Harlan Fiske Stone: Pillar of the Law* (New York: Viking Press, 1956)

Donald M. Roper

Stone Arabia Patent. Land grant of 12,700 acres (5,140 ha) in Palatine and Mohawk (Montgomery Co), situated several miles north of the Mohawk River between Cayadutta and Caroga Creeks. The provincial government issued the grant in 1723 to promote European settlement further into the Mohawk Valley and to facilitate the relocation of Palatine German families dissatisfied with conditions at their settlement in Schoharie. The grant was made to 27 men, 25 of whom were Palatine German. The new settlers immediately formed a joint Lutheran and Reformed congregation, which split into separate churches by 1743; both remained active in 2003. The name of the patent is most likely from the Dutch *steen raapje,* literally "stone turnips" but figuratively "stony fields," an indication of the Dutch settlers' unfamiliarity with such soil conditions. The term, spelled variously, has been found as a toponym in Lansingburgh (Rensselaer Co), Oneonta (Otsego Co), and in New Jersey.

Burch, Wanda E. "History of Stone Arabia, 1711–1792" (MA thesis, SUNY Oneonta, 1974)

Dillenbeck, Rev Andrew Luther. *Lutheran Trinity Church of Stone Arabia, NY* (St. Johnsville, NY: Enterprise & News, 1931)

Francis P. Boscoe

Stone-Campbell Movement. See CHRISTIAN CHURCHES (STONE-CAMPBELL MOVEMENT AND CHRISTIAN CONNEXION).

Stoneman, Kate (*b* Lakewood, Chautauqua Co, ?1 Apr 1841; *d* Albany, 19 May 1925). Lawyer and teacher. An 1866 graduate of the New York State Normal School in Albany, she taught drawing, penmanship, and legal topics there from 1866 until 1906 or 1907. An early supporter of women's right to vote, Stoneman played a leadership role in the Women's Suffrage Society of Albany, formed during the successful 1880 legislative campaign to allow women to vote in school board elections. After working as a lawyer's clerk, she passed the New York State Bar exam in 1886 but was denied admission by the State Supreme Court based on the Code of Civil Procedure's designation that only "male citizens" were eligible. Stoneman and supporters lobbied for amending the code, and Gov David B. Hill signed the legislation on 19 Apr 1886. Admitted to the bar three days later, Stoneman became the state's first female lawyer. In 1896 she was accepted into the previously all-male Albany Law School. Enrolled as a "special student," she earned an LLB in 1898, becoming the school's first female graduate. Stoneman practiced law in Albany until the early 1920s and worked for woman suffrage, prohibition, and world peace.

Morello, Karen B. *The Invisible Bar: The Woman Lawyer in America 1638 to the Present* (New York: Random House, 1986)

Williams, Geoffrey P., and Carol Novak. "A Woman Who Wouldn't Take No for an Answer," *Albany Law School Magazine,* Spring 1992

Geoffrey P. Williams

Stony Brook. Locality (pop 13,727) in Brookhaven (Suffolk Co). Settled in 1655, the hamlet developed around a mill on Stony Brook Creek (1699). Its harbor was a port for coastal schooners, and farming and shipbuilding were major industries. The Long Island Rail Road (1873) facilitated the onset of a summer resort industry. Ward Melville (1887–1977) created a Federal-style shopping center in 1941 to revitalize the hamlet; he also restored many buildings and provided the land for the 1962 permanent campus of SUNY Stony Brook (1957). Stony Brook is the site of the Long Island Museum of American Art, History, and Carriages (1935) and of the Museum of Long Island Natural Sciences (1973). It was the home of artist William Sidney Mount (1807–68). All Souls Church (1889), designed by Stanford White, is a landmark. Stony Brook in 2000 was 7% Asian.

Beverly C. Tyler

Stony Brook University. See SUNY STONY BROOK.

Stony Creek. Town (pop 743) in SW Warren Co. Settled in the late 18th century, the town was formed from the extinct town of Athol in 1852. Its mountainous wilderness was not attractive to settlers, but lumbermen sent logs to Glens Falls on the Hudson River. Industries included potash production, a broom factory, and John P. Bowman's large tannery (1852–1900). Products included excelsior, broom handles, and brush blocks. The Wesleyan Methodist Church helped run the Underground Railroad through town. A major forest fire in 1908 caused depopulation, and the state acquired half of Stony Creek's acreage. In the early 21st century dude ranches and summer recreation provide the principal sources of livelihood.

Marilyn J. Van Dyke

Stony Point. Town (pop 14,244) in NE Rockland Co. The Stony Point Battlefield State Historic Site (1946) celebrates the July 1779 battle when troops under Gen "Mad" Anthony Wayne successfully attacked a British fort on the peninsula during a midnight assault. The historic site also includes the Stony Point Lighthouse, which operated from 1826 to 1926. The town was formed from Haverstraw in 1865. Its hilly terrain discouraged farming, but Tomkins Cove and Grassy Point quarries and brickyards (1830–1930) employed large numbers of workers. The industries drew Irish workers around 1835, Francophone Canadians in the 1870s, and Poles, Hungarians, Austrians, Italians, and African Americans around 1900. The US Navy acquired Iona Island in 1900 for a magazine, and from 1946 to 1971 it was the site of the Mothball Fleet of decommissioned navy vessels. In the late 20th century Martin Marietta Aggregates was still quarrying limestone at Tomkins Cove, an industry since 1838. The Palisades Interstate Parkway (1953) provides access to Harriman State Park, whose 45,333 acres (18,345.6 ha) lie partly in town. Town native James A. Farley (1888–1976), son of a Grassy Point brickyard owner, served as Pres Franklin D. Roosevelt's campaign manager and as postmaster general. The 2,257 ft (687.9 m) Bear Mountain Bridge (1924) at the town's northernmost point was the first public bridge over the Hudson south of Albany.

Stony Point, Battle of. Last major battle of the American Revolution in the Hudson Highlands. On 31 May 1779 British lieutenant general Sir Henry Clinton, with about 6,000 British and Hessian troops, gained control of two small American posts and the King's Ferry crossing of the Hudson River between Verplanck Point (Westchester Co) and Stony Point [now in Rockland Co]. Capturing Fort Lafayette on Verplanck Point, the British labored to improve the works. At Stony Point, on its western shore, they seized the site of a burned American blockhouse and added earthworks and rows of defensive barriers as a prelude to what Clinton hoped would be a decisive battle in the Hudson Highlands with Gen George Washington's Continental army.

Surveying the fortification himself on 6 July from nearby Buckberg Mountain, Washington and Brig Gen Anthony Wayne planned an attack to retake Stony Point. On 15 July Wayne led his corps of light infantry of about 1,200 against the British garrison of about 600 men commanded by Lt Col Henry Johnson. After an eight-hour march from Sandy Beach near Fort Montgomery in Orange Co, Wayne organized his force into three columns at the Springsteel farm west of Stony Point. The columns began their attack at midnight, led by 21-man "forlorn hopes," soldiers armed with axes to clear the defensive works. Monetary rewards were offered to the first five men to enter the fort, from $500 for the first man down to $100 for the fifth. Two flanking columns using only bayonets penetrated the northern and southern ends of the fort's outer works, while the third column effectively created a diversion with musketry at its center. The diversion worked, and both assault columns penetrated the inner works. By 2 AM on 16 July Wayne's soldiers captured the garrison at a cost of 15 men killed and 83 wounded; they killed at least 20 and wounded 74 British soldiers. Deciding not to maintain the fort, Washington ordered it destroyed and abandoned. The British reoccupied and refortified it on 19 July but abandoned it and the Highlands for good in October 1779. The Stony Point Battlefield State Historic Site, first opened to the public in 1897, commemorates the engagement.

Johnston, Henry P. *Storming of Stony Point on the Hudson: Midnight, July 15, 1779* (1900; repr New York: Da Capo Press, 1971)

James M. Johnson

Storm King Mountain controversy. In September 1962 Consolidated Edison Co (Con Edison) and Central Hudson Gas and Electric announced plans to construct a 1.3 million kW pumped-storage hydroelectric plant at Storm King Mountain in Cornwall (Orange Co) on the Hudson River. The world's largest electrical generation plant yet planned, the proposal called for flooding the land between White Horse Mountain and Mt Misery to create an 8 billion gal (30.3 billion l) reservoir and boring a 2 mi (3.2 km) tunnel through Storm King Mountain, which would deliver this water to drive turbines to be installed at the base of the mountain on the river shoreline. Electric lines leading east under the river would also be laid, joining with existing lines serving New York City.

In March 1963 Con Edison and Central Hudson applied to the Federal Power Commission (FPC) for the necessary license to build the plant. A majority of Cornwall residents supported the project because they anticipated a significant increase in the local tax base. The plan drew sharp criticism from conservationists, commercial fishers, and sports clubs, however, who argued that once operational the project would increase the river's salinity and destroy fisheries. Most important, these opponents argued, was that the plant would spoil the scenic beauty of the Hudson Valley by destroying Storm King Mountain, one of the river's most beautiful promontories. The utilities, whose supporters included Gov Nelson A. Rockefeller, countered that the plant was necessary to help alleviate the New York City metropolitan region's electrical generation shortage. In 1964 the project's opponents formed the Scenic Hudson Preservation Conference to stop the FPC from issuing the license.

In the spring of 1965 the FPC granted the license. That December, however, a federal appellate court set the license aside and returned the matter to the FPC for further review in *Scenic Hudson Preservation Conference v Federal Power Commission* (1965). For the remainder of the 1960s and throughout the 1970s Scenic Hudson, joined by other groups, including the Hudson River Fishermen's Association, continued to oppose the licensing. Under the 1981 Hudson River Settlement Agreement the utilities abandoned the Storm King project for 10 years in exchange for environmentalists dropping their demands that the utilities make significant alterations (specifically closed-cycle cooling) to their existing Hudson River plants to reduce fish kills. Although the agreement expired in 1991, as of 2003 the utilities gave no indication of restarting plans to build a generation facility at Storm King Mountain; environmentalists' demands that the utilities adopt closed-cycle cooling remained unresolved.

Talbot, Allan R. *Power along the Hudson: The Storm King Case and the Birth of Environmentalism* (New York: E. P. Dutton, 1972)

Richard Wojtowicz

stove manufacturing. Cast-iron stoves were produced throughout New York State for most of the 19th and early 20th centuries, primarily in the Albany and Troy (Rensselaer Co) area. Warner Daniels cast the first stoves in Albany in 1808. The James and Cornell Stove Factory made the first stove, the Baltimore Cookstove, in Troy in 1815. The Albany-Troy region had unique advantages of waterpower, Rensselaer Polytechnic Institute (founded in 1824), access to resources (iron ore, limestone, sand, charcoal, and coke), and strategic transportation networks, as well as inventive and creative designers. Distinctive Franklin-type, box, parlor, pyramid, Shaker-designed, dumb, soapstone, toy, and base-burning heating and cooking stoves were produced in the heyday from 1830 to 1870. Notable contributions were made by Eliphalet Nott (1826 and 1832), Jordan L. Mott (1833), and D. G. Littlefield (1851) with successive improvements to anthracite coal base-burning stoves; Philo P. Stewart (1838) through innovative cooking stoves; and Ezra Ripley (1843) with decorative designs in patternmaking. Many stove foundries were relatively small operations, but some foundries, such as the Ransom and Rathbone Stove-Works (1840–44) in Albany and the Fuller and Warren Co (1882–1932) in Troy, had extensive operations. Scattered facilities also operated in other areas of the state, particularly in parts of Westchester Co and sections of New York City; the Lenox Furnace Co (Madison Co), founded in 1811, cast an early prototype of the Franklin stove. Census data show that by 1870 there were 63 stove manufacturers statewide that employed 3,853 workers in making stove products worth $6,741,000. The Albany-Troy area in the same year employed 2,678 workers of mainly Irish descent in 24 stove-making firms producing $4,767,916 worth of goods, about 70% of the statewide total. Stove mounters, polishers, patternmakers, and finishers formed unions around the mid–19th century in the Albany-Troy area for economic and social betterment. After 1890 the New York State stove industry rapidly declined because of midwestern advantages in expanding markets and resources for stove production; new stove products based on alternative gas, oil, and electric technologies; and local labor strife. Albany's last stove foundry closed in 1925 and Troy's in 1936. Rapid closure of the remaining cast-iron stove foundries followed after World War II.

Groft, Tammis K. *Cast with Style: 19th Century Cast-Iron Stoves from the Albany Area* (Albany: Albany Institute of History & Art, 1984)

Edward T. Howe

St. Patrick's Cathedral. Located at 50th St and 5th Ave in New York City on the site of a former cemetery, St. Patrick's Cathedral replaced a building of the same name in Lower Manhattan as the cathedral church of the Archdiocese of New York. The inspiration for the new cathedral came from Archbishop John J. Hughes, who laid the cornerstone on 15 Aug 1858. The architect was James Renwick Jr. Following construction, costing between $1.9 and $2.5 million, the building was dedicated by John Cardinal McCloskey on 25 May 1879. The spires were added between 1885 and 1888 and the Lady Chapel between 1901 and 1906, by which time the cost exceeded $4 million. The new main altar was installed in 1942. In the late 1940s the exterior was restored, a new rose window was added, and new bronze doors were installed. The Gothic-style building measures 400 ft x 174 ft (122 m x 53 m) and seats about 2,400. It was visited by Pope Paul VI in 1965 and by Pope John Paul II in 1979 and 1995. Buried in the crypt under the main altar are the eight deceased archbishops of New York, several church dignitaries, including Archbishop Fulton J. Sheen, and Pierre Toussaint, a former slave whose cause for canonization has been introduced in Rome.

Carthy, Margaret. *A Cathedral of Suitable Magnificence: St. Patrick's Cathedral, New York* (Wilmington, Del: Michael Glazier, 1984)
Cohalan, Florence D. *A Popular History of the Archdiocese of New York* (Yonkers: US Catholic Historical Society, 1983)

Thomas J. Shelley

Stratford. Town (pop 640) in NW Fulton Co. Settled ?1799 by New Englanders, the town was formed in 1805 from Palatine. A sawmill (1806) and tannery (1812) became its principal industries, and by 1870 there were 5 tanneries and 16 sawmills. Other products included cheese, butter tubs, and clothespins. The town lies entirely within Adirondack Park. Lumbering and second homes were central to the economy in the early 21st century.

James Crawford

Straton, John Roach (*b* Evansville, Ind, 6 Apr 1875; *d* Clifton Springs, Ontario Co, 29 Oct 1929). Fundamentalist Baptist pastor. Son of a Baptist minister, Straton grew up in Alabama and Georgia, attending but never graduating from Mercer College and Southern Baptist Theological Seminary. Ordained in 1900, he married Georgia Hillyer in 1903 and taught oratory at Baylor College in Waco, Tex (1903–5). After pastorates in Chicago, Baltimore, and Norfolk, Va, he became pastor of Manhattan's Calvary Baptist Church in 1918. His dramatic southern oratory drew large crowds, and his sermons often appeared in New York City newspapers. He preached against the city's vices, including prostitution, political corruption, violations of Prohibition, dance halls, the theater, prizefighting, and women's fashions. He also criticized unfair working conditions, the exploitation of children, women, and minorities, and the Ku Klux Klan. He had regular pulpit exchanges with black Baptist clergy from Harlem, including Adam Clayton Powell Sr, and often preached in public places from a specially built automobile. Beginning in 1923 he broadcast Sunday services from his church's tiny 100 W radio station.

In the early 1920s he led an unsuccessful campaign to eliminate theological liberalism from the Northern Baptist Convention, which he left in 1926. In 1922 he founded the Fundamentalist League of Greater New York and Vicinity for Ministers and Laymen. He debated theological liberals, including a series of debates on the Bible, evolution, and the deity of Christ with Unitarian minister Charles Francis Potter at Carnegie Hall in Manhattan in 1923–24. A nationally recognized fundamentalist leader, Straton campaigned strenuously in the South against Democratic presidential candidate Alfred E. Smith in 1928, objecting not only to Smith's Catholicism but to his alleged political corruption. In 1924 Straton proposed a multistory church/hotel complex at the church's 57th St site. He later proposed the development of a summer conference center at Greenwood Lake (Orange Co), where a suspicious fire in 1928 burned the hotel he bought. Straton died after suffering a stroke the day the stock market crashed.

Carpenter, Joel A., ed. *Fundamentalist versus Modernist: The Debates between John Roach Straton and Charles Francis Potter* (New York: Garland Publishing, 1988)
Russell, C. Allyn. *Voices of American Fundamentalism: Seven Biographical Studies* (Philadelphia: Westminster Press, 1976)

Timothy P. Weber

Stratton, Samuel S(tuddiford) (*b* Yonkers, 27 Sept 1916; *d* Rockville, Md, 13 Sept 1990). Mayor and US congressman. Moving to Schenectady as an infant with his parents, Stratton graduated from the University of Rochester in 1937 and continued with graduate studies at Haverford (1938) and Harvard (1940). During World War II he served in the Pacific theater of operations as a US naval intelligence officer and afterward with the Far Eastern Commission from 1946 to 1948 in Washington, DC. He then returned to Schenectady, finding work as a college instructor and television newsman and serving on the Schenectady City Council (1949–56). He was elected mayor in 1956, held that office for three years, then was elected to the US Congress from Schenectady in 1959. He served for 14 consecutive terms, retiring in 1989, and was best known for supporting national defense programs. Stratton is buried at Arlington National Cemetery. In 2003 his son Brian Stratton was elected mayor of Schenectady.

Cross, Wilbur. *Samuel S. Stratton: A Story of Political Gumption* (New York: J. H. Heineman, 1964)

Wesley G. Balla

strawberries. A plant in the rose family that produces sweet, red, seed-covered fruit. Wild strawberries were found in North America when Europeans arrived; they were crossbred with varieties from Chile to create the precursors of modern strawberries. The first strawberry hybrid in the United States, the Hudson, was developed in Virginia in 1780 and was easily distinguished from Hautboys, the European varieties. Commercial production of strawberries in North America flourished with the introduction of Wilson's Albany in 1854, and between 1860 and 1885, it was the most popular variety grown in the United States. Other varieties developed in New York State in the late 19th and early 20th centuries from the Pan American in Delevan (Cattaraugus Co) to the Diadem and Emily in Flushing (Queens Co). Other significant strawberry varieties created in the state include the New York, the Austin or Shaker, the Col Ellsworth, the Golden Queen, the Hooker, and Russell's Prolific.

Strawberry fields are planted on flat, rich, well-drained fields between mid-April and mid-May, with the first harvest in late June to early July. Straw is applied to fields in early winter to protect the shallow-rooted plants from ice heaving, to retard the growth of weeds, and to protect the berries from mud. Since the late 1800s researchers at the Geneva Experiment Station (Ontario Co) have studied varieties to optimize size, taste, duration of season, tolerance against disease and poor growing conditions, and shelf life. In 1999 New York State ranked seventh nationally in strawberry production, with $8.27 million in revenues from self-pick and consumer market sales. Most (95%) strawberries grown are used as fresh fruit. In the late 1990s Erie, Onondaga, and Suffolk Cos had the largest concentrations of commercial strawberry farms. Self-pick farms are popular, though consumer market sales have increased as a percentage of the total. In 2001 recommended cultivars for New York State growers are Earliglow, Northeaster, Honeoye, Jewel, and Allstar.

Wilhelm, Stephen, and James E. Sagen. *History of the Strawberry, from Ancient Gardens to Modern Markets* (Berkeley: Univ of California, Division of Agricultural Sciences, 1974)

Marla A. Bennett

street railways. From the 1850s through the 1920s, systems of street railways emerged in cities and towns throughout New York State, strongly influencing the growth and development of these communities. Railcars hauled by horses or mules were the first true form of urban mass transportation. Beginning in the 1880s companies replaced animal-powered streetcars with larger, faster, more dependable vehicles propelled by electricity, and the street railway industry experienced extraordinary growth.

Early Years

The first horse-drawn street railway in New York State—also the first in the nation and world—inaugurated service along Manhattan's Bowery in 1832. Called the New York and Harlem Railroad, it was a specialized element within the larger, steam-powered intercity railroad that linked New York City with communities in Westchester Co and as far north as Chatham (Columbia Co). Since New York and Harlem Railroad steam locomotives were prohibited from venturing south of 42d St, the horsecar line served as a kind of shuttle carrying railroad passengers into downtown sections of the city. This street railway portion of the New York and Harlem grew to 7.5 miles (12.1 km) in length, using 162 cars and 1,159 horses. By 1890 it carried 16.6 million passengers annually, and a trip from City Hall in Lower Manhattan to Mott Haven in what is now the Bronx took a scheduled 1 h 32 min.

The nation's second street railway opened in New Orleans in 1835, but Brooklyn inaugurated the third. Brooklyn City Railroad began service in 1854 on four lines that radiated from the Union Ferry's Brooklyn terminal into Bay Ridge, Clinton Hill, Greenpoint, and other neighborhoods. By 1883 the state's street railway industry had matured to the point of generating a trade group, the Street-Railway Association of the State of New York, with 20 charter members. Ten of these member companies were from New York City, five were from Brooklyn, and the others operated in Albany, Buffalo, Rochester, and Troy (Rensselaer Co).

From the outset, the operators of New York State street railways sought a replacement for animal power. Experiments were conducted with railcars powered by small engines of steam or even of compressed air. Electricity eventually replaced draft animals, but cable power became the first alternative technology to achieve a measure of success. The state's first cable street railway opened 31 Aug 1885 when Third Avenue Railroad launched a route on Manhattan's Amsterdam Ave between 125th and 187th Sts. New York City eventually boasted two cable-car companies, Third Avenue Railroad and Metropolitan Street Railway, that laid lines principally along Broadway, Lexington, 3d, and Columbus Aves. New York City and Brooklyn were the only cities in the state to deploy cable-powered street railways.

In 1889, at the end of the era of horse-drawn streetcars, 11 of the state's 12 largest street railways were in New York City or Brooklyn. Of these the largest was Brooklyn City Railroad with annual operating expenses of over $2 million, 56 miles (90 km) of track, 1,333 cars (of which 575 were open cars for summer use only), 4,793 draft animals, and an annual patronage of 56 million. The three largest in Manhattan were, in order of size, Third Avenue Railroad, with 28 miles (45 km) of track and 31 million riders; Broadway and Seventh Avenue Railroad, with 23 miles (37 km) of track and 30 million riders; and Second Avenue Railroad, with 28 miles (45 km) of track and 17 million riders. The largest state railway outside of New York City and Brooklyn was Rochester City and Brighton Railroad, which possessed 45 miles (72 km) of track and annual patronage of 9 million. By 1889 there were 105 street railways in New York State, with 41 operating in New York City. By 1900 most street railway operations had been converted to electric traction.

The Electric Era

In 1886 the first electric street railway in New York State, and one of the first in the nation, was installed in Binghamton; it was not a success. But over the winter of 1887–88, an improved system was developed in Richmond, Va, spurring conversion to electric cars throughout New York State and elsewhere. An era of tremendous growth followed; annual patronage of US street railways increased more than 200% from 1890 to 1902, from 1.8 billion to 5.5 billion. During these years, Buffalo East Side Street Railway Co, City Railroad of Poughkeepsie, Elmira and Horseheads Railway Co, and Fulton and Oswego Falls Street Railway Co began replacing animal power with electric power.

In the early years of the 20th century New York State streetcar companies branched into complementary commercial activities. With their generating equipment, street railways in many instances provided electric power to residential and commercial customers. It was also a common practice for street railways to build and operate amusement parks, profit-making facilities that also promoted streetcar travel, at the ends of their lines. Schenectady Railway Co owned Brandywine Park, a picnic area available to social clubs for a fee; Jamestown Street Railway promoted its Celeron Park on the shores of Chautauqua Lake; and some of the companies that operated streetcars in Brooklyn owned attractions on Coney Island.

Decline

The golden age of New York State's electric-powered streetcars was brief. Mass transportation, as a whole, declined in the mid-1920s as automobiles became popular, and by the mid-1930s the motor bus functioned as a practical, less-expensive alternative to the electric streetcar; buses allowed transit companies to avoid the costs of generating plants and of track and trolley wire maintenance. Public transportation and streetcars performed well during the gasoline- and tire-rationing days of World War II, but after September 1945 the downward trend resumed. Those New York State street railways still in operation converted to motor bus operation as soon as new diesel-powered transit buses could be delivered. The last true streetcar system of the era, a small network in Brooklyn operated by the New York City Transit Authority, was motorized in 1956.

In 1985 a new light rail transit system inaugurated service in Buffalo along a single route extending 6.4 miles (10.3 km) along Main St, from the city center to the Lake Erie shore, with 5.2 miles (8.4 km) running underground. Its 27 cars carry more than 7 million passengers a year. At the beginning of the 21st century, it is New York State's only street railway.

Cudahy, Brian J. *Cash, Tokens, and Transfers: A History of Urban Mass Transit in North America* (New York: Fordham Univ Press, 1990)
Hilton, George W. *The Cable Car in America* (Stanford, Calif: Stanford Univ Press, 1997)
Middleton, William D. *The Time of the Trolley* (San Marino, Calif: Golden West Books, 1987)

Brian J. Cudahy

St. Regis Indian Reservation. See Akwesasne (St. Regis Indian Reservation).

strikes. See Labor; see also individual strikes and unions.

Strong, Augustus H(opkins) (*b* Rochester, 3 Aug 1836; *d* Rochester, 29 Nov 1921). Baptist clergyman and educator. Son of a newspaper publisher, Strong graduated from Yale College in 1857 and Rochester Theological Seminary in 1859. Ordained to the Baptist ministry at Haverhill, Mass, in 1860, he served as pastor at First Baptist in Haverhill (1860–65) and First Baptist,

Cleveland (1865–72). He returned to Rochester Seminary in 1872 to assume the position in theology vacated by Ezekiel G. Robinson, later succeeding Robinson as president of the seminary. He served as Davies Professor in Biblical Theology until his retirement in 1912, attracting a distinguished faculty and the financial resources to build an imposing campus and library. John D. Rockefeller Sr, a close friend from the Cleveland pastoral ministry, was a generous supporter.

Strong was widely published, beginning with his *Systematic Theology* (1886, rev 1908), which remains a leading resource among Baptist theologians, and later with essays such as *Christ in Creation and Ethical Monism* (1899). He attempted to bridge contemporary European thinking with his own Baptist piety. In Rochester he was a member of an intellectual circle, called the Pundits, that developed a progressive reputation. In the 1880s, for instance, with the assistance of his brother Henry, a founder of Eastman Kodak, Strong led in the adoption of individual communion cups to avoid spreading disease. As president of the American Baptist Foreign Mission Society (1892–95), he toured the mission fields of his denomination and ushered in a new era of overseas work. In a 1918 book, *A Tour of the Missions,* written after his second overseas tour in 1916, he asserted that the New Theology was undermining the missionary imperative by deemphasizing the authority of the Bible and evangelism.

Autobiography of Augustus Hopkins Strong. Ed. Crerar Douglas (Valley Forge, Pa: Judson Press, 1981)

Wacker, Grant. *Augustus Hopkins Strong and the Dilemma of Historical Consciousness* (Macon, Ga: Mercer Univ Press, 1985)

William H. Brackney

Strong, Josiah (*b* Napierville [now Naperville, Ill], 18 Jan 1847; *d* New York City, 28 Apr 1916). Author, social reformer, and theologian. In 1852 Strong's family moved to Hudson, Ohio. He attended Western Reserve College in Hudson (now Case Western Reserve University in Cleveland), then Lane Seminary in Cincinnati until 1871. After missionary service in Wyoming (1871–73), Strong held a series of posts in Ohio that included secretary of the Ohio Home Missionary Society (1881–84) and pastor of the Central Congregational Church in Cincinnati (1884–86). His best-selling book *Our Country* (1885) reconciled Protestant hopes for Christianizing the United States with Social Darwinism, envisioning a globally dominant Christian nation that would evangelize the world. Its success earned Strong a position as general secretary for the Evangelical Alliance for the United States (1886–98). Based in New York City, the alliance sought to advance religious liberty and Protestant unity, and to address social problems. Strong organized national conferences in 1887, 1889, and 1893, which developed and disseminated Social Gospel aims and methods and inaugurated his career as a leader in the movement. He resigned in 1898 to found and become president of the League for Social Service (renamed American Institute of Social Service in 1902), also in New York City, which offered lecture services and publications including two periodicals and three volumes of an encyclopedia of social progress, all edited by Strong, and also maintained a museum of safety devices. Strong published 10 more books, including *The New Era* (1893), *Expansion under the New World-Conditions* (1900), *The Challenge of the City* (1907), and *Our World: The New World-Religion* (1915).

Deichmann, Wendy Jane. "Josiah Strong: Practical Theologian and Social Crusader for a Global Kingdom" (PhD diss, Drew Univ, 1991)

Deichmann Edwards, Wendy J. "Manifest Destiny, the Social Gospel and the Coming Kingdom: Josiah Strong's Program of Global Reform, 1885–1916." In *Perspectives on the Social Gospel* (Lewiston, NY: Edwin Mellen Press, 1999)

Strong, Josiah. Papers. Burke Library, Union Theological Seminary, New York City

Wendy J. Deichmann Edwards

Strong Memorial Hospital. Part of the University of Rochester Medical Center, and adjacent to the university's campus, this 800-bed general hospital is part of the Strong Health network, which includes Highland Hospital, Golisano Children's Hospital, and four nursing homes in the Rochester area. Construction of the hospital was funded in part by sizable donations from the Strong family and George Eastman. Officially opened 4 Jan 1926, Strong Memorial is the largest hospital in the Rochester area and the leading supplier of emergency medical care on the city's south side, with about 85,000 patients having received emergency care during the 2001–2 fiscal year. With over 1,500 physicians with attending privileges and 2,000 nurses, the hospital service area encompasses a radius of 150 miles (240 km) and about 1.3 million people. Golisano Children's Hospital admits about 4,500 patients annually, and its staff delivers about 2,700 babies each year. In addition an estimated 35,000 patients annually visit the ambulatory center at the children's hospital.

To Each His Farthest Star: University of Rochester Medical Center, 1925–1975 (Rochester: Univ of Rochester Medical Center, 1975)

Martin Naparsteck

Strong Museum. Museum of American history. Established by wealthy collector Margaret Woodbury Strong in 1968 and located at 1 Manhattan Square in Rochester, it opened to the public in 1982. The more than 500,000 items in its collections are largely mass-produced consumer goods manufactured after 1820. These include the nation's most comprehensive collections of toys, dolls, home crafts, and memorabilia, as well as nationally significant holdings in home furnishings and advertising and marketing materials. The museum's mission is to explore and illustrate how these everyday objects illuminate issues of class, progress, and identity in American culture. Since the mid-1990s the museum has focused primarily on an audience of families and children, featuring hands-on exhibitions, school lessons held at the museum, and community outreach programs. In 1997 the museum added a 12,000 ft^2 (1,115 m^2) atrium entrance to its existing 156,000 ft^2 (14,493 m^2) facility. At the same time it installed an operating historical carousel, an operating diner, and a long-term exhibit based on the public television program *Sesame Street.* In 2002 attendance was nearly 400,000.

G. Rollie Adams

St. Thomas Aquinas College. Private liberal arts college. Located in Sparkill (Rockland Co), it was founded in 1952 by the Catholic Dominican Sisters of Sparkill as a three-year training institution for elementary school teachers. Permanent changes made in the school's charter in 1960 allowed it to grant BA and BS degrees. In 1962 the college accepted its first 12 laywomen, and in 1967 it became an independent, coeducational, four-year private college. The school sits on a 47-acre (19 ha) suburban campus that is 16 miles (26 km) north of New York City. In 2003 the school offered bachelor's degrees in 31 majors, two associate degrees, and three master's degrees in education and business administration. Dual-degree programs were available in conjunction with several other schools, including a part-time undergraduate extension program at the US Military Academy at West Point (Orange Co). In 2003 St. Thomas Aquinas had 2,200 full- and part-time students enrolled.

Dolan, Regina Rosaire, OP. "The First 40 Years: The History of St. Thomas Aquinas College: 1952–1992." St. Thomas Aquinas College, Sparkill, NY 1992

Marianne Rahn-Erickson

Stuyvesant. Town (pop 2,188) in NW Columbia Co. Settled *ca* 1650 by Dutch and Swedes, the town was formed from Kinderhook in 1823. Industrial development centered at Stuyvesant Falls on Kinderhook Creek, where the water dropped 45 and 26 feet (13.7 and 7.9 m) in two falls. The first paper mill in Columbia Co opened there in 1801, followed by a woolen mill (1810–75), several large cotton mills in 1827–30, and a foundry producing stoves (1855–80). Stuyvesant Falls was a busy port in the era of steamboats and canals and was served by the Hudson River Railroad (1851). A group of Volga Germans from Russia came *ca* 1900. A brickyard (1870–?1930s), three icehouses (1880), and dairy farming provided work into the 20th century. In the 1970s the population grew 33% as the town became home to Albany office workers. Stuyvesant Falls is a historic district, and the town is the site of Newton Hook National Estuarine Research Reserve.

Stuyvesant, Petrus (*b* Peperga, the Netherlands, 1612; *d* New York City, February 1672). Director General of New Netherland. He was born into an orthodox Calvinist family. In 1630 he was enrolled as a student in literature and philosophy at the University of Franeker, which he left to join the Dutch West India Co (WIC). He first served the company in a minor function around 1635 on the Brazilian island Fernando de Noronha. After returning to the Netherlands, possibly to deal with the inheritance of his father, he went in 1639 to Curaçao, where he was in charge of the stores. After the death of Jan Claeszoon van Campen in early 1642, Stuyvesant became director of the island. He lost his right leg in 1644 during an attack on St. Martin Island and returned to the Netherlands to recover.

The WIC appointed him director general of New Netherland in 1646. Whereas his predecessors were either designated commander or director, Stuyvesant had the higher rank of director general by virtue of the inclusion of Curaçao and other islands in the area under the command. When he arrived in New Amsterdam in May 1647, he found New Netherland in deplorable condition. Director Willem Kieft's ill-advised war with the Indians around New

Director General Petrus Stuyvesant; painting attributed to Hendrick Couturier, *ca* 1660.

Amsterdam had had a devastating effect on the colony's agricultural and economic progress. As a result, some colonists had left, while many of those who had stayed were opposed to the company's control. The English were encroaching on all sides, the Swedes had gained a foothold on the Delaware, and immigration had come to a standstill. Stuyvesant believed New Netherland needed strong guidance in order to develop. During the first six years of his governance, there was considerable opposition to the authoritarian way in which exercised his powers. The initial problems took time to solve, but under his able leadership, measures such as granting city rights to New Amsterdam in 1653 and the Hartford Treaty in 1650 with the English colonies ensured New Netherland would continue to develop along Dutch lines. By the mid-1650s, immigration had increased, the economy had improved, and Swedish control of the Delaware had ended.

Several problems remained, however. Stuyvesant, a devout and orthodox Calvinist, feared the religious unity of the colony was threatened by Lutheran attempts to call a minister and by the arrival of Jews and Quakers. In dealing with these problems, Stuyvesant's actions were blocked by his superiors in Amsterdam, who were more tolerant on the issue of religious diversity. In the troubles with the Indians in the Peach (1655) and Esopus Wars (1660, 1663), however, he showed both determination and flexibility, mixed with an astute judgment of the balance of power between the parties involved. The most serious threat to New Netherland remained the encroachments of the English. The inability of the WIC to supply Stuyvesant with sufficient soldiers and money seriously hampered the defense of the colony. When an English flotilla arrived in September 1664, Stuyvesant found himself under pressure from the leading burghers and reluctantly surrendered New Amsterdam. He returned to the Netherlands in 1665, where he successfully defended his conduct. Returning to New York Colony in 1668, he spent his last years on his farm (the *bouwerij*, or Bowery) in Lower Manhattan.

Under Stuyvesant the colony overcame the damage caused by Kieft's War, the economic situation improved, immigration was encouraged, and by 1664 New Netherland was the largest overseas colony of the Netherlands at that time. His inability, through no fault of his own, to prevent the English takeover gave his life a tragic twist.

Gehring, Charles. T. "Petrus Stuyvesant, directeur-generaal van Nieuw-Nederland," *Jaarboek Centraal Bureau voor Genealogie* 50 (1996): 69–87

Jensma, Goffe. "Over de jeugd van Pieter Stuyvesant," *De Vrije Fries, jaarboek uitgegeven door het Fries genootschap van Geschied-, Oudheid- en Taalkunde en de Fryske Akademy* 74 (1994): 21–41

Kessler, Henry H., and Eugene Rachlis. *Peter Stuyvesant and His New York* (New York: Random House, 1959)

Jaap Jacobs

suburbanization. Suburbs are as old as cities themselves and can be traced back at least to ancient Mesopotamia 4,000 years ago. Suburbanization as a process, however, involving the systematic growth of fringe areas at a pace more rapid than that of core cities, and as a lifestyle involving a daily commute to jobs at the center, occurred first in the United States in the early 19th century. Bucolic Brooklyn Heights began in the 1820s to attract thousands of middle-class commuters across the East River because of new steam ferry access to Lower Manhattan.

New York City Suburbanization

Suburbanization accelerated in the 1830s, when omnibuses along Broadway and other main avenues offered frequent service, low fares, and established routes to businessmen moving their families northward on Manhattan Island. The process gained strength again in the 1850s, when horsecars on steel tracks made the riding experience more pleasant and more efficient. Steam railroads brought an enormous region into commuting range. In New York City, commuter travel by steam railroad began in 1832, and by 1837 the New York and Harlem Railroad offered regular service to 125th St. The line was extended to central Westchester Co by 1844 and led to a *New York Tribune* prediction that "the line of this road will be nearly one continuous village as far as White Plains by 1860." Meanwhile, the New York and New Haven Railroad reached Port Chester (Westchester Co) in 1848, and the Hudson River line toward Albany reached Peekskill (Westchester Co) in 1849. Along these tracks population grew by more than 50% in the first decade after construction, as real estate developments sprang up in Westchester Co locations including Rye, Tarrytown, New Rochelle, and Mount Vernon. As early as 1855, English observer W. E. Baxter noted that suburban villas were "springing up like mushrooms on spots which five years ago were part of the dense and tangled forest; and the value of property everywhere, but especially along the various lines of railroad, has increased in a ratio almost incredible. Small fortunes have been made by owners of real estate at Yonkers and other places on the Hudson River."

Because annual commuting costs ($45 to lower Westchester Co in 1853) were too high for most wage earners, the railroads helped to foster the image of Westchester Co as a leafy enclave for the well-to-do. But even before the Civil War, the southernmost stations at Fordham, Morrisania, Tremont [all now in Bronx Co], and Mount Vernon were becoming centers of middle-class residence. Morrisania in particular was completely transformed between 1850 and 1865. A small village on the Boston Post Rd, Morrisania was the scene of large-scale building activity after a railroad station opened there in the mid-1840s. A particularly important 400-acre (160 ha) subdivision in the 1860s called Old Morrisania lay near the Gouverneur Morris mansion.

Westchester Co would remain the nation's most famous large suburban area until well into the 20th century. It had been a summer and weekend retreat for decades before the Civil War. Lyndhurst, the most notable of baronial houses, was built in 1838 for the merchant prince William Paulding on the banks of the Hudson River, about 25 miles (40 km) north of the city. A quarter of a century later financier Jay Gould bought the property and made it as elaborate as a castle. When Gould chose to spend the night there rather than at his Manhattan home, he either commuted down the Hudson River aboard his yacht or flagged down the New York Central, which would make a special stop. The opposite side of Westchester Co was also prime country house territory for 19th-century millionaires, especially after the New Haven Railroad pushed through the region at midcentury. In 1848 hotelier Simeon Leland built a castellated, turreted, and gabled castle of 60 rooms in New Rochelle; in 1852 another ultra-Gothic castle was built for millionaire William P. Chapman. These Westchester castles were ultimately overshadowed by the elaborate 4,500-acre (1,600 ha) estate of John D. Rockefeller Sr and his children at Pocantico Hills just northeast of Tarrytown.

Westchester's importance in the history of New York State and American suburbanization, however, derives from the upper-middle-class development of Scarsdale, Bronxville, New Rochelle, and a dozen other villages scattered among its several hundred square miles of hills and lakes. Their well-kept lawns and opulent overall ambience attracted tens of thousands of executives and businessmen from Manhattan. By 1898 the three major passenger railroad lines running along the Hudson River, the Harlem Valley, and Long Island Sound, as well as several less-important routes, were daily disgorging 118,000 commuters into Grand Central Terminal. The county's population more than doubled between 1850 and 1870, doubled again between 1870 and 1890, and yet again between 1890 and 1910, when it had 283,000 residents. Most of the development was actively encouraged by the railroads, which developed communities, advertised suburban advantages, and offered frequent and reliable service. There was in fact more and better commuter service from many of the city's northern suburbs in 1880 than in 1980.

Just as the northbound railroads opened up Westchester Co (including what would later become the Bronx), largely replacing the steamboats that had run to Yonkers and Peekskill, so too the Long Island Rail Road (LIRR) and the New York and Flushing Railroad enabled commuters to reach Manhattan from the east. The LIRR in particular was unabashedly the instrument of real estate speculators. By bringing villages in what is now the Borough of Queens within one hour of Manhattan in the late 1850s, the railroad led to an influx into Newtown, Maspeth, and Flushing.

The LIRR was a spur to the transformation of the North Shore between Great Neck [now in Nassau Co] and Huntington (Suffolk Co) after the Civil War into an area of mansions known as the Gold Coast. Nearly 1,000 were built between 1860 and 1940. Middle-class suburbanization began in the middle of the island when in 1869 A. T. Stewart began development of a model village, Garden City [now in Nassau Co]; Stewart's company built model houses, provided services, and set the rules, creating a genteel, upper-middle-class environment. However, there would be few imitators for the remainder of the century. Between 1900 and 1911 the LIRR was electrified, and it opened a tunnel to Penn Station, facilitating the suburbanization of Long Island.

The world's first thoroughfare restricted solely to the automobile and especially designed for its needs was William K. Vanderbilt's Long Island Motor Parkway (1906–11). Made of innovative concrete, it featured open speeds, bridges and tunnels to separate it from local cross traffic, and limited access through its own tollgates. Even more significant was Westchester Co's meandering Bronx River Parkway, built between 1906 and 1925. There the separation of cross-traffic from the parkway was accomplished cheaply. Because the park roadway ran through a valley, it could be bridged by crossroads without massive earthwork. The result was an enormous aesthetic success. Running 16 miles (26 km) along the New York Central tracks from Bruckner Blvd in the Bronx to White Plains, the beautifully landscaped road stimulated automobile commuting from Mount Vernon, Bronxville, Scarsdale, Hartsdale, and White Plains, the county seat. Within the next 10 years, Westchester also saw the construction of the Hutchinson River Parkway (1928), the Saw Mill River Parkway (1929), and the Cross County Parkway (1931), while on Long Island, the Southern State Parkway, begun in 1925, opened up the South Shore to auto commuting, as the South Side Rail Road (1867) had opened it by rail two generations earlier.

The suburbanization of Long Island exploded in the decades after World War II, best symbolized by the development of Levittown from 1947 to 1951. Using assembly-line techniques adapted to housebuilding, the Levitt brothers built 17,500 homes and sold them primarily to returned World War II veterans. New roads were built, such as the Long Island Expressway (1955–72). Farmlands and estates were subdivided for middle-class housing. Between 1930 and 1950 the population of Nassau Co more than doubled, then doubled again between 1950 and 1960.

The suburbanization and exurbanization of New York City is a continuing process. The growth of the inner suburbs of Westchester and Nassau Cos peaked in the 1970s, but outlying areas have continued to grow. Since 1980 Suffolk Co has overtaken Nassau Co in population and has become the fourth most populated county in the state (after Kings, Queens, and New York Cos). Rockland Co underwent great suburban growth after the opening of the Tappan Zee Bridge in 1955. The boundaries of suburbanization continue to expand, to Putnam, lower Dutchess, and Orange Cos. In 2000 the four suburban counties of Nassau, Rockland, Suffolk, and Westchester had a combined population of 3,964,125, accounting for 36% of the state's population outside New York City.

Upstate Suburbs

Suburbanization in New York State was not simply a phenomenon of the areas nearer New York City. Elite residential areas were growing on the outer edges of Buffalo by the 1860s. In the following decade similar developments occurred outside Rochester, Syracuse, and Albany. Many of these suburbs gloried in their separation from the central cities.

Albany began suburbanizing in the mid–19th century when estates were created in Menands and Loudonville. The Albany and Susquehanna Railroad opened to Altamont in 1863; it became a resort, then gradually a commuter suburb. Streetcar service in the 1890s opened up Albany Co's suburbs on the city's edge. Delmar, accessible by railroad from the late 19th century, became a fine suburb in the 1910s with subdivisions linked to Albany primarily by Delaware Ave automobile traffic. Menands Heights became the first garden apartment complex outside the New York City metropolitan area when it opened in 1940. Suburban development resumed after World War II to house veterans, chiefly in Colonie and Guilderland. The Northway (I-87) reached Latham in 1959 and Clifton Park (Saratoga Co) in 1960. Development in Clifton Park, which had begun in 1956, immediately exploded, making it the preeminent outer suburb of Albany. Suburban shopping began with Latham Circle Mall (1956) and Stuyvesant Plaza (1964). The presence of state government prevented Albany's downtown area from disappearing completely during this period. I-90 (1976) drew suburban development eastward into Rensselaer Co. In 2004 the strongest pull remained northward along I-87, with a mature suburban core in the Colonie and Guilderland (Albany Co) areas and a secondary draw along I-90. Although many workers commute on the Thruway from the south, the effect of its being a toll road has been to limit suburban development in that direction. Schenectady and Troy (Rensselaer Co) have smaller suburbanized perimeters than Albany, but those cities and their residential perimeters actually absorb some of Albany's strong suburban pressures. In 2000 Albany's population was 32% of the county's, but its suburbs were largely in Rensselaer and Saratoga Cos, and much of Albany Co, especially south of the Helderberg Escarpment, is at best exurban to the city.

Before World War II satellite villages and cities in Utica were in some respects suburbs, but they were all industrial hubs in their own right. Whitestown and New Hartford (Oneida Co) developed after World War II as the city's preeminent suburbs; Whitestown built the first shopping center (1952). Again, the Thruway had little effect because of its tolls and exit distances. Some suburban draw has taken place along arterials that run through the city, notably Rte 8, but Utica's suburbs are adjacent to the city limits and tied to it by streets and roads rather than superhighways. In 2000 only 26% of Oneida Co's population lived in Utica, but much of the county is far beyond the city's influence.

In Syracuse satellite villages predated suburban forces, notably East Syracuse, where a railroad yard and shop were the genesis of the community. The city annexed villages and unincorporated areas in the late 19th and early 20th centuries, and they became "suburban." Its modern suburbs date from the development of DeWitt and Fayetteville (Onondaga Co) about 1920. The first shopping center was Westvale Plaza (1948), built as western suburbs began to expand. The biggest force in Syracuse was the crossroads pattern of the two major highways—the Thruway (1954) and I-81 (1955–66)—which meet just north of city and extend in cardinal directions. Syracuse is the only New York State city with this pattern. It has therefore expanded in every direction except to the south, where the Onondaga Indian Reservation and topography intervene. I-690 provides an additional east-west link just north of downtown, and I-481 (1986) created a partial ring road. I-481 has helped push suburban development northward and northeastward. In 2000 Syracuse's population was 32% of Onondaga Co's. All of its suburbs are in the county.

Rochester had electric streetcars by 1890, linking the city to the port and resort community of Charlotte, which it annexed that year. Kodak Park opened in Greece in 1890, and Rochester annexed it in 1914. The planned workers' community of East Rochester opened in 1896. Highway improvements gave rise to great growth of other inner-ring suburbs in Monroe Co, such as Brighton and Irondequoit, in the interwar years. Rochester's last annexation came in 1918. Postwar growth and development of the Thruway, I-390 (1963–81), and I-490 (1963–74) caused expansion in well-to-do suburbs such as Penfield, Perinton, Victor (Ontario Co), and Pittsford to the east, and more middle-class suburbs such as Greece, Gates, and Chili to the west. In 1940, 74% of the Monroe Co's population lived within city limits, but only 30% lived there in 2000.

As with Utica, Buffalo was closely surrounded by a number of industrial villages or cities. Many had been created in the steam era rather than in the waterpower era and provided factory sites and workers' homes. But there was increased interconnection between city and outliers in Erie Co, especially after electric railroads began running. Williamsville, an old waterpower community, became suburban when trolleys were put in service in 1893 and had housing developments by 1910. Kenmore was platted as a middle-class suburb in 1889, acquired streetcars by 1893, and boomed in the 1920s, its population growing fivefold. Amherst began to suburbanize between the wars, with its University Plaza becoming the first shopping center in Western New York when it opened in 1941. The first important arterial, the Niagara Section of the Thruway (1951), was followed by the main route of the Thruway (1954), an inner- and outer-ring system, and arterials to the south and southeast, Rte 400 (1966–68) and US 219 (1968–79). In the 1950s Amherst boomed, especially after SUNY Buffalo headquartered there. Clarence, the Town of Tonawanda, and Elma were transformed from rural towns to suburbs in the 1950s. At the end of the century, Wheatfield (Niagara Co) was the booming suburb for both Buffalo and Niagara Falls. In 2000, 31% of Erie Co's population lived within Buffalo city limits, but a good many of Buffalo's suburbanites lived in Niagara Co, and many residents outside Buffalo lived in smaller cities such as Lackawanna.

Suburbanization has had, if anything, a more

pronounced effect farther away rather than closer to the New York City region. New York City remains the demographic, economic, political, and cultural core of the metropolitan region. This is not the case for other New York State cities, whose metropolitan regions are home to generally only one-quarter to one-third of the population, and much economic and political power lies in adjacent suburbs. The populations of these metropolitan areas have remained relatively stagnant in recent decades. In addition, movement from the inner suburbs to areas farther from the urban core—a phenomenon generally known as sprawl—has continued.

The suburban regions have become far more racially diverse in recent decades, though this trend is most pronounced in the New York City metropolitan area. In the 2000 census three counties had substantial minority populations: Nassau Co (20% African American; 10% Latino), Suffolk Co (15% African American, 11% Latino), and Westchester Co (27% African American, 16% Latino). This increase has challenged many facile assumptions about the inherent differences between urban and suburban populations and social problems.

See also DEPARTMENT STORES; INTERSTATE HIGHWAYS; SHOPPING CENTERS AND MALLS; URBAN PARKS; YONKERS.

Baxandall, Rosalyn F., and Elizabeth Ewen. *Picture Windows: How the Suburbs Happened* (New York: Basic Books, 2000)

Jackson, Kenneth T. *Crabgrass Frontier: The Suburbanization of the United States* (New York: Oxford Univ Press, 1985)

Kenneth T. Jackson

subways. See BUFFALO SUBWAY AND LIGHT RAIL LINE; NEW YORK CITY SUBWAY; ROCHESTER SUBWAY.

Suffern. Village (pop 11,006) in Ramapo (Rockland Co). It was known as New Antrim until 1841, when the Erie Railroad opened through the locality; the Paterson and Hudson River Railroad came through in 1848. The Suffern post office opened in 1850. By the mid-1870s Suffern attracted summer boarders. The village incorporated in 1896. California Perfume Co was formed in 1897. Renamed Avon Products in 1939, it remained an important employer in 2003. Illustrator Daniel Carter Beard (1850–1941), cofounder of the Boy Scouts of America, was a resident. The New York State Thruway opened in 1955, improving accessibility. Many Suffern residents commute to New York City using NJ Rte 17, the Thruway, or rail service.

Gardner Watts

Suffolk County (912 mi²/2,362 km²; pop 1,419,369). Created in 1683 as one of the colony's original counties and named for King Charles II, who was also Duke of Suffolk. It is subdivided into 10 towns containing 30 incorporated villages, and the Poospatuck and Shinnecock Indian Reservations. The unincorporated locality of Riverhead serves as county seat. The county extends 86 miles (138 km) from east to west, occupying roughly the eastern two-thirds of Long Island. Elevations range from sea level to the 402 ft (123 m) Jayne's Hill in the far west. Suffolk Co lies entirely within the Atlantic Coastal Lowland physiographic province. Bedrock lies between 400 and 2,200 feet (120–670 m) below sea level and is covered by a correspondingly deep mantle of unconsolidated glacial deposits. Most of the county's present landform features were created during the most recent (Wisconsinan) ice age. The most prominent topographic features are two terminal moraines that extend the length of the county. The Ronkonkoma Moraine marks the farthest southward advance of the Wisconsinan glacier and runs from the central part of the county in the west to Montauk Point in the east. The Harbor Hill Moraine extends from the north-central part of the county in the west to Orient Point and Plum and Fishers Islands in the northeast. It delineates the southern margin of the ice after it retreated, then readvanced. Huge volumes of sand- and gravel-laden meltwater from the ice fronts created outwash plains south of the moraines.

Much of the county's south coast is protected by a series of barrier islands. Over half of Fire Island is designated a national seashore. Suffolk Co contains few perennial streams. The largest is the Peconic River, which flows east into Flanders Bay. Others in order of size include the Carmans, Carlls, Nissequogue, and Connetquot Rivers. In areas that lack a surface-drainage outlet, runoff flows into shallow, closed depressions where it evaporates or percolates into the groundwater system. The largest are the Selden basin near Coram and the Lake Ronkonkoma basin, site of the island's largest kettle pond. Runoff from most housing developments and highways is collected in artificial basins (sumps) where it too percolates into the groundwater. Almost all the freshwater in Suffolk Co is supplied by three primary aquifers: the Upper Pleistocene, the Magothy, and the Lloyd Sand. Excessive pumping of groundwater is a constant concern since it can lead to saltwater contamination of the county's freshwater supply. The county's soils are, with very limited exception, well drained. Although each year fewer acres are annually devoted to crops, the outwash plain soils are especially well suited for modern commercial agriculture.

Suffolk Co's climate is humid-continental and modified by the Atlantic Ocean. The maritime influence diminishes noticeably with elevation and distance from the South Shore. Summer afternoon breezes off the ocean, for instance, reach 5–8 miles (8–13 km) inland, thereby producing cooler temperatures in the coastal areas. Mean July temperatures range from 72°F (22°C) in East Hampton to 75°F (24°C) on the North

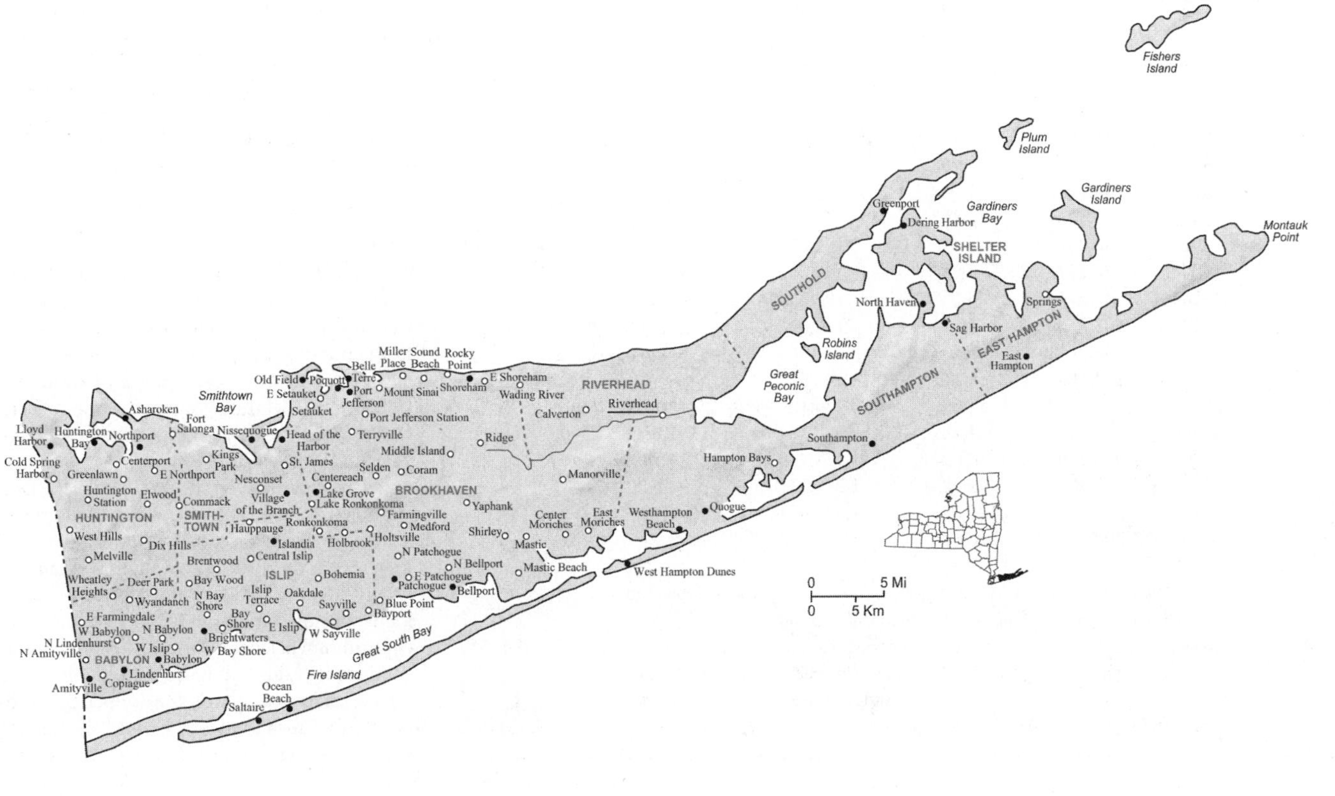

Shore and in the west. Temperatures of 90°F (32°C) or above occur every summer but most frequently in the western interior. Mean January temperatures hover at or just below freezing. The North Shore community of Setauket is the warmest winter-reporting station in the state, marginally above 32°F (0°C). In general temperatures of 0°F (-18°C) or colder occur one winter in four, except near the south-central coast where they occur twice as often. Seasonal snowfall varies significantly from a low of 13 inches (33 cm) around Setauket to 31 inches (79 cm) at Patchogue. Annual precipitation is heaviest in the west and ranges from 46 to 50 inches (117–127 cm). The sun shines more than 50% of the possible time in winter and over 60% between May and October, making this one of the sunniest parts of the state.

Primeval forest cover consisted of a central hardwood community dominated by beech, sugar maple, basswood, oak, and chestnut in the coastal zone. Sometimes referred to as the Pine Barrens, the county's interior was covered by pitch pine, dwarf post oak and scarlet oak, big tooth aspen, and huckleberry. Approximately 30% of Suffolk Co is presently forested.

Native Inhabitants

Based on the discovery of fluted projectile points in mammoth bones, it is believed that native peoples lived here for more than 12,000 years before the arrival of Europeans. The Algonquian-speaking original residents consisted of many scattered kinship groups, rather than organized into 13 tribes divided into distinct territories and governed by English standards, a persistent myth. The Indians built sturdy wigwams, lived well on fish and game, raised corn and potatoes, and gathered whales washed up on the beach or stranded offshore. The surrounding waters abounded in clams and other shellfish. Some of these shells, in particular the northern quahog, periwinkle, and knobbed whelk, became the source of currency known as wampum. The defeat of the Pequot Indians in Connecticut by the English in 1637 was soon followed by English settlement in eastern Suffolk Co. They encountered numerous bands, of which the best known were the Matinecock, Setauket, Nissequogue, and Corchaug on the North Shore and Fork; the Manhansett on Shelter Island; and the Secatogue, Unquachog (Unkechaug), Shinnecock, and Montaukett on the South Shore and Fork. After 1650 more hierarchical tribal systems emerged among the Montaukett, the Shinnecock, and possibly the Matinecock, imposed by Europeans who wanted there to be one chief empowered to sell land.

Once exposed to germs of smallpox, tuberculosis, and other diseases carried inadvertently by colonists, the indigenous population suffered almost total annihilation. An alliance between Lion Gardiner, the first English settler, and the Montaukett sachem Wyandanch spared Suffolk from much of the bloodshed that afflicted Connecticut and Massachusetts. However, Gardiner and his associates amassed fortunes by buying up land from the American Indians, whose numbers were reduced from an estimated 6,000 in 1640 to several hundred by 1700. Their only remaining lands early in the 21st century are the Shinnecock Reservation in Southampton and the Poospatuck Reservation in Mastic, but descendants of these groups as well as landless Montauketts, Matinecocks, and others determinedly survive.

Settlement

The first Europeans to settle, English soldier Lion Gardiner and his Dutch wife, Mary, acquired Gardiners Island from its Montaukett owners in 1639. The first towns, founded by small groups of English Puritans, were Southold and Southampton (no one knows which came first) in 1640, East Hampton in 1648, Shelter Island in 1652, Huntington in 1653, Brookhaven in 1655, and Smithtown in 1666. The outward feudal form of manors like Gardiners Island and St. George Manor [now in Mastic Beach] was deceiving. They lacked true feudal authority, and most land was owned in fee simple by farmers who would have been tenants in England. Though restricting first-class citizenship to Puritan coreligionists, Suffolk's self-governing Bible commonwealths endowed future generations with two building blocks of liberty: the town meeting and the independent church (owned and managed by its congregation). Later towns included Islip (1710); Riverhead (1792), split from Southold; and Babylon (1872), previously a part of Huntington. Irish, German, and Dutch immigrants augmented the population, as did later arrivals of Italian, Polish, Greek, and other immigrants, but for 250 years it remained a mixture of people of primarily English ancestry, mingled with African Americans and a dwindling number of American Indians.

African Settlement

African Americans were present from early colonial times: Nathaniel Sylvester brought slaves to Shelter Island in 1654. Some one-sixth of Suffolk's families owned slaves, ranging between 1 and 14 in a household at the time of the first federal census in 1790, which counted 2,224 black residents (13.5% of the population). Slightly more than 50% of them were free, compared to about 25% in Queens Co (which included present-day Nassau Co) and only 3% in Kings Co. After 1827, the effective date of the state's emancipation law, most freed people had to work as laborers or servants for former masters because of the lack of their own resources. Culloden Point was the landing site in 1839 of the *Amistad*, the slave ship taken over by the captives. The percentage of African Americans declined as the white population grew through immigration.

Revolutionary and Early National Period

After six generations, descendants of Puritan pioneers considered themselves American and were ready for independence. As resistance rose from protest to separation, Suffolk rallied to the patriot cause. With few loyalists or tories, the county overwhelmingly supported the Association, an agreement to boycott trade with England in 1774. William Floyd from Mastic served in the Continental Congress and signed the Declaration of Independence. After a disastrous American loss at the Battle of Long Island (27 Aug 1776), the British and their Hessian and loyalist allies occupied Suffolk for seven years. Many patriots fled to the mainland, and some engaged in whaleboat warfare, the cross-Sound commando raids on British installations. An early intelligence agency, the Culper Spy Ring in Setauket, furnished Gen George Washington with knowledge of British troop movements.

SUFFOLK CO POPULATION CENSUS FIGURES

	White	Nonwhite	Total Population	Foreign-Born
1790	14,216	2,224	16,440	—
1800	17,562	1,902	19,464	—
1810	19,327	1,786	21,113	—
1820	22,441	1,831	24,272	12
1830	24,767	2,013	26,780	83
1840	30,292	2,177	32,469	—
1850	34,805	2,117	36,922	2,095
1860	41,477	1,798	43,275	4,001
1870	44,956	1,968	46,924	4,877
1880	51,426	2,462	53,888	5,601
1890	60,061	2,430	62,491	9,990
1900	74,298	3,284	77,582	14,757
1910	93,073	3,065	96,138	22,289
1920	107,232	3,014	110,246	24,088
1930	155,217	5,838	161,055	34,634
1940	188,186	9,169	197,355	38,931
1950	262,537	13,592	276,129	44,272
1960	631,997	34,787	666,784	61,056
1970	1,066,429	58,521	1,124,950	74,790
1980	1,185,109	99,122	1,284,231	94,647
1990	1,192,236	129,628	1,321,864	104,211
2000	1,200,755	218,614	1,419,369	158,525

Notes: "Nonwhite" includes African Americans, Asians, American Indians, and Pacific Islanders and, for 2000, also the mixed race and other race categories. Through the 1960 census these figures primarily reflect the African American population. Foreign-born figures for 1820 and 1830 include only those not naturalized, and for 1930 and 1950, the foreign-born totals include Whites only. Other years include all foreign-born in the population.

POPULATIONS OF TOWNS, SUFFOLK CO

Town, Year Founded	1800	1840	1880	1920	1960	2000
Babylon, 1872	—	—	4,739	11,315	142,309	211,792
Brookhaven, 1659[a]	4,022	7,050	11,544	21,847	109,900	448,248
East Hampton, 1650[a]	1,549	2,076	2,515	4,852	8,827	19,719
Huntington, 1658[a]	3,894	6,562	8,098	13,893	126,221	195,289
Islip, 1720[b]	958	1,909	6,453	20,709	172,959	322,612
Riverhead, 1792	1,498	2,449	3,939	5,753	14,519	27,680
Shelter Island, 1730[b]	260	379	732	890	1,312	2,228
Smithtown, 1715[a]	1,413	1,932	2,249	9,114	50,347	115,715
Southampton, 1641[a]	3,670	6,205	6,352	11,614	26,861	54,712
Southold, 1654[a]	2,200	3,907	7,267	10,147	13,295	20,599

[a]Date of earliest town minutes.

[b]Formed as precinct; date of earliest precinct minutes.

After the patriots resumed control, they punished loyalists by measures as severe as banishment or confiscation, but reconciliation prevailed in the early years of the new republic. Although elected as Antifederalists to the 1788 state convention, Suffolk's delegates voted to ratify the constitution "in full confidence" that a bill of rights would be added.

Although there was strong support for the Democratic Party through the 1850s, the formation of the Republican Party in 1854–55 met with rising enthusiasm. Although Abraham Lincoln lost Kings and Queens Cos, he narrowly carried Suffolk both times he ran for president. Regardless of politics, Suffolk's sons served in the Union army and navy, and every town voted large sums to pay for enlistments and aid to soldiers' and sailors' families. Greenport editor Henry Reeves, however, was a Copperhead, favoring slavery and the South's position, and was jailed for treason during the war.

Transportation

Until roads were paved, the standard mode of transport was by water, with excellent harbors encouraging shipping by sailboat. The first land route was authorized by the colonial legislature in 1704 to run from Brooklyn to East Hampton through the center of the island; later routes paralleled it along the North and South Shores. The first post route (1764) made a full circuit in two weeks along the shores, and scheduled stagecoaches carried passengers. After 1830 steamboat service facilitated travel to and from New York City and New England. The Long Island Rail Road (LIRR) was completed from Brooklyn to Greenport in 1844, not to serve the island but rather to link New York City and Boston with a ferry across Long Island Sound. It ran inland instead of along the North and South Shores, where most people lived. Branchlines were built, and the system was completed to Montauk in 1895. In 1910, 10 years after the Pennsylvania Railroad took over the LIRR, a tunnel beneath the East River let passengers commute between Long Island and Manhattan without the inconvenience of taking a ferry. The 1920s were the start of the suburban era for Suffolk's western towns. Coinciding with the enormous increased use of automobiles, the network of parkways and expressways built by Robert Moses connected Suffolk with New York City. In the early 21st century, the L. I. MacArthur Airport at Ronkonkoma provides air transportation to all points, and the nearby LIRR station offers rapid transit to New York City.

Economic Development

Resourceful settlers, endowed with 987 miles (1,588 km) of shoreline lined with harbors and lighthouses, were as much at home on water as they were on land. They took to finfishing, shellfishing, and long-range and coastal shipping. In the first half of the 19th century, whaling and shipbuilding emerged as the rural county's only important industries. Sag Harbor was outranked in whaling only by New Bedford, Nantucket, and New London in New England. Other whaling centers were Greenport, Cold Spring Harbor, Jamesport, and New Suffolk. Related enterprises of shipbuilding, sail making, and provision of marine supplies benefited Port Jefferson, Northport, Setauket, Smithtown, and other coastal villages. Owners and captains claimed the lion's share of profits, but whaling provided a living for large numbers of seamen, including Native Americans and African Americans for whom it was a rare equal opportunity employer. Whaling ended after the discovery of petroleum in 1859, the Civil War, the overkill of whales, and the soaring cost of three-year voyages in pursuit of the ocean behemoths. There were many shipwrecks off both shores, and lighthouses and lifesaving stations became necessary features of the landscape.

Farmers learned from the American Indians that the odoriferous bony fish known as menhaden were valuable as fertilizer and for oil in the manufacture of paint, rope, and other products. Starting in the 1870s, Dutch immigrants flocked to West Sayville to engage in the oyster trade they had learned in Holland. Clams, scallops, crabs, eels, and lobsters were staples of the baymen of the Great South Bay and the East End, many of whom were equally adept at deep-sea fishing. In recent years pollution, changes in the salinity of the waters and increasing competition from sports fishers for dwindling stocks has almost shut down the shellfish industry and its hardy band of professionals. The lobster die-off in Long Island Sound has been one of the latest problems.

Ferries have long offered transportation to and from Connecticut, Fire Island, and Shelter Island. Boating remains a leading hobby and business, with every harbor providing marinas and repair services, well-patronized by amateur as well as professional skippers.

Agriculture has remained important to the county's economy throughout its history. Cordwood was one of two major cash crops before anthracite coal replaced it by the 1840s for heating homes in the city; the other was hay, the "gasoline" of horse-drawn transport. From the days of the early settlers, the county attracted farmers who raised cattle, horses, swine, and sheep; the grazing downs of Montauk were one of America's first prairies. Suffolk also led the state in the production of poultry, butter, eggs, and, once introduced in the late 19th century, Pekin ducks, a specialty that declined in the late 20th century because of pollution. In the early 21st century, Suffolk's agriculture remains economically important, based on the high wholesale value of its crops. The county has excelled in the cultivation of potatoes, strawberries, cauliflower, cucumbers, turnips, oats, and other crops. It has also been known for its orchards, nurseries, sod farms, greenhouses, and, more recently, wine grapes and wine making.

Until World War II other industry, aside from whaling and shipbuilding, was limited to a number of small cotton and woolen mills, a lace mill in Patchogue, a rubber factory in Setauket, a watch factory in Sag Harbor, and local distilleries, gristmills, sawmills, and saddle and carriage shops. Shipbuilding declined with the demise of the wooden vessel but experienced a revival in World War I and after in New Suffolk, where submarines were tested. There is still extensive small-boat building along the South Shore. The rival creators of wireless communication, Nikola Tesla and Guglielmo Marconi, both worked in Suffolk Co, competing to develop the radio during the first decades of the 20th century.

In the mid–20th century, two large government installations opened and provided thousands of jobs. At Upton, the former Camp Yaphank became Brookhaven National Laboratory in 1947. The US Navy purchased thousands of acres at Calverton in 1949 for the Calverton Naval Weapons Industrial Reserve Plant. Grumman began constructing the facility in 1952, and at its peak the facility employed 3,000 people. The plant closed, and in 1998 the land was sold to the Town of Riverhead for an industrial park.

While its economy is mainly service based, the county in the early 21st century contains such corporations as Computer Associates International, a major software producer, and Symbol Technologies, originator of the retail bar code and a manufacturer of scanning devices. Entenmann's bakery at Bay Shore and Grucci Fireworks at Bellport are distinctive Suffolk Co industries. SUNY Stony Brook's High Technology Incubator provides a startup location for new scientific companies. The county abounds in office complexes, industrial parks, hospitals, medical centers, and retail, discount, and outlet stores. Major banks include Fleet Bank and North Fork Bank. Since the early 1990s and the end of the Cold War, defense-related work largely dissipated.

Religion, Education, and Culture

Clinton Academy in East Hampton opened in 1785 and became one of the first chartered academies in the state in 1787. Other academies in Huntington (1793), Southampton (1831), Miller Place (1834), Riverhead (1835), Southold

(1837), and Sag Harbor (1848) also provided secondary education before public high schools were established later in the century. In 2003, 71 school districts served a quarter-million pupils. Fifteen institutions of higher learning included SUNY Stony Brook and three campuses of Suffolk County Community College. Cold Spring Harbor Laboratory is a world center for biological research, as Brookhaven National Laboratory, on the site of the former army induction center Camp Upton, is for the peaceful use of nuclear energy.

The first library, in East Hampton, was founded in 1753; in the early 21st century most communities have one; they are served by the Suffolk Cooperative Library System (1962). Newspapers flourished, from David Frothingham's *Long-Island Herald* in Sag Harbor in 1791, to the *Long Islander* of Huntington, founded in 1838 by Walt Whitman, to *Newsday,* Long Island's daily paper, published in Melville. William Sidney Mount (1807–68), the first artist to depict Blacks on an equal footing with Whites, is one of America's foremost genre artists; the main collection of his works is on view at the Long Island Museum at Stony Brook. Walt Whitman (1819–92), whose West Hills birthplace is a museum and cultural center, defined American democracy in his oceanic, free-verse masterpiece *Leaves of Grass* (1855). Long Island's East End was first popularized as an artistic retreat in the 1870s by the Tile Club, an association of city artists and writers. Over the next century, the East End blossomed as a haven for artists and authors, including Thomas Moran and Mary Nimmo Moran, William Merritt Chase, Jackson Pollock and Lee Krasner, Willem de Kooning, John Steinbeck, Joseph Heller, and Peter Matthiessen.

The independent congregations became Presbyterian or Congregational and remained dominant for the first 150 years, after which the Methodist Church dominated. Baptist, Lutheran, and others took root, together with African Methodist Episcopal (AME) and AME Zion congregations, and, more recently, Mormon, Unitarian Universalist, Christian Science, and Greek Orthodox. Caroline Church of Setauket, built in 1729, was the earliest of the few Anglican churches in the county. Irish immigration during the 1840s spurred rapid growth of the Catholic Church, now Suffolk's largest religious group. Jews, now well-represented, were present early on, but no synagogues were created until the late 1890s by groups of immigrants in Setauket and Sag Harbor.

Suffolk's 987 miles of coastline, deep harbors, clean sandy beaches, temperate climate, and high rate of sunshine have always appealed to devotees of bathing, sailboating, yachting, fishing, and water sports. From the mid–19th century on, vacationers and weekenders have enjoyed its hotels, boardinghouses, restaurants, camping sites, hiking trails, and abundance of parks, marinas, golf courses, tennis courts, riding stables, bowling alleys, skating rinks, and bicycle paths. Tourism now is a billion-dollar industry, and the Hamptons are among the most famed resorts in the United States. Only five counties in the nation exceed Suffolk's more than 36,000 seasonal homes.

Politics

In the 20th century, the electorate overwhelmingly supported Republicans for president; the only exceptions were Woodrow Wilson in 1912, Lyndon Johnson in 1964, and Bill Clinton in 1996. Voters sometimes chose Democrats for Congress and state and local offices, and when the county executive system started in 1959, they elected a Democrat, H. Lee Dennison, for three successive terms. W. Kingsland Macy served as Suffolk Co Republican chairman from 1926 to 1948 and remains the county's most famous political figure. In 1970 the county complied with the one person–one vote Supreme Court decision by electing a 19-district county legislature, a body that tends to maintain a Republican majority. In 1996, 7 of every 10 voters of the five eastern towns supported a nonbinding referendum to form Peconic County.

Recent History

Available land and the GI Bill attracted droves of veterans and their growing families, principally to the five western towns, where more than 80% of the people then and now reside. Between 1950 and 1960, the county's population exploded from 276,129 to 666,784, and to 1,127,030 in 1970. The five eastern towns expanded, too, from nearly 46,000 in 1950 to 125,000 in 2000. There has been an influx of second-home owners, some of whom are from the worlds of big business and big entertainment, and retirement homes and communities.

Suffolk Co pioneered in environmental concerns. In the late 1960s it became the first county to ban DDT, and it later banned detergents for 10 years until they became biodegradable. The Environmental Defense Fund was organized in 1967 in Suffolk Co. The Purchase of Development Rights strategy for farmland preservation was pioneered in the county, which passed a bond act for that purpose in 1976; it preserved nearly 8,000 acres (3,240 ha) by the early 21st century. The Islip garbage barge of 1987 dramatized some of Suffolk's environmental problems. The Long Island Pine Barrens Preservation Act was adopted by the state legislature in 1993, following lawsuits.

In the 1990 census, Suffolk's population exceeded Nassau's for the first time since 1920; this situation will endure since Nassau is at saturation while Suffolk still has land available for development. Suffolk Co is the fourth most populous county in the state. Nevertheless, the need to conserve the environment and to protect underground aquifers led Southampton, East Hampton, and other towns to invoke periodic moratoriums on residential construction. In 1997 a small tritium (radioactive hydrogen) leakage induced the Department of Energy to terminate its contract with Associated Universities, the consortium that had operated Brookhaven National Laboratory since its inception. In 1998, after the Long Island Lighting Co's (LILCO's) Shoreham Nuclear Power Plant was decommissioned for lack of confidence in the company's technical competence and the impossibility of an escape route in case of emergency, the state-created Long Island Power Authority (LIPA) took over LILCO's electric transmission and distribution system. However, despite reductions, electricity rates are still high compared with those in other parts of the country.

The county's religious and ethnic mix has shifted dramatically. After centuries of an English Protestant majority, people of Italian descent are now in the majority, followed by those of Irish and German descent. The number of Latinos is growing, and in 2000 they were 10.5% of the population; they have suffered incidents of harassment, such as the brutal 2000 beating of two laborers in Farmingville. Blacks were 6.9%, Asians, 2.5%, and Native Americans, 0.2% (excluding residents of reservations). In 1996 Suffolk Co ranked 16th in the nation in the number of business establishments, including 13 employment centers, each providing more than 10,000 jobs. At the turn of the 21st century, the expanding population exceeded 1,420,000. Of a 728,100-strong civilian labor force, 552,035 worked in Suffolk, with a 3.2% rate of unemployment. Suffolk entered the new millennium buoyed by a vibrant economy but beset by the high cost of housing, energy, and sales and property taxes.

The earliest histories of Suffolk Co covered all of geographic Long Island: Silas Wood, *A Sketch of the First Settlement of the Several Towns of Long Island, with Their Political Condition, to the End of the American Revolution* (1824); Nathaniel S. Prime, *A History of Long Island from Its First Settlement by Europeans to the Year 1845* (1845); Richard M. Bayles, *History and Descriptive Sketches of Suffolk County* (1874); and Benjamin F. Thompson, *History of Long Island from Its Discovery and Settlement to the Present Time,* 3d ed, 3 vols (1918, repr 1962). A more focused work was W. W. Munsell and Co, *History of Suffolk County* (1882, repr 1983). A mid–20th century update was provided by Paul Bailey, ed., *Long Island: A History of the Great Counties, Nassau and Suffolk,* 3 vols (1949). *Newsday,* the island's daily newspaper, published two books based on extensive research: *Long Island, Our Story* (1998), and *Home Town Long Island* (1999).

Among the scholarly works that illuminate aspects of Suffolk Co history are Lawrence J. Taylor, *Dutchmen on the Bay: The Ethnohistory of a Contractual Community* (1983); Peter Matthiessen, *Men's Lives: The Surfmen and Baymen of the South Fork* (1986); Roger Wunderlich, *Low Living and High Thinking at Modern Times, NY* (1992); and Steve Wick, *Heaven and Earth: The Last Farmers of the North Fork* (1996). Nonacademic but useful are two books on the island's famous resort: Steven Gaines, *Philistines at the Hedgerow: Passion and Property in the Hamptons* (1998), and Helen A. Harrison and Constance Ayers Denne, *Hamptons Bohemia* (2002). Articles on Suffolk Co history have been published in *Long Island Forum* (1938–), *Suffolk County Historical Society Register* (1975–), and *Long Island Historical Journal* (1988–).

Local history has been published extensively; most are adequately researched and presented. Town histories include David A. Overton, *A Brief History of Brookhaven Town* (1983); Averill D. Geus, *From Sea to Sea: 350 Years of East Hampton History* (1999); Silas Wood, *A Sketch of the Geography of the Town of Huntington* (1824); *Huntington-Babylon Town History* (1937); Patrick J. Curran, *A Brief History of the Town of Islip* (1983); Barbara Austen, *Journey through Time: The Riverhead Bicentennial* (1992); Ralph G. Duvall, *History of Shelter Island* (1932); Noel J. Gish, *Smithtown, NY, 1620–1929: Looking Back through the Lens* (1996); George R. Howell, *The Early History of Southampton, LI* (1887); James T. Adams, *History of the Town of Southampton* (1918); and James T. Adams, *History of the Town of Southampton East of Canoe Place* (1962).

Perhaps because of the size of Suffolk Co's towns, most local histories are about villages and localities. Among the best community histories are Charles E. Craven, *History of Mattituck* (1906); Henry L. Ferguson, *Fishers Island, NY, 1614–1925* (1925); *Cold Spring Harbor Soundings* (1953); Robert Payne, *The Island* (1958), about Gardiners Island; Barbara Ferris Van Liew, *50 Years, Head of the Harbor* (1978); Edward A. T. Carr, *Faded Laurels: The History of Eaton's Neck and Asharoken* (1994); Kathryn M. Pallister, *A History of the Incorporated Village of Shoreham* (1995); Harry W.

Havemeyer, *Along the Great South Bay: From Oakdale to Babylon* (1996); and Thomas Monsell and Antonia Booth, *Greenport in the Camera's Eye* (2001). A close examination of the historiography of one town is provided by the groundbreaking book by T. H. Breen, *Imagining the Past: East Hampton Histories* (1989).

Roger Wunderlich

suffrage. Now called voting rights, the word suffrage, dating from the Middle Ages, originally meant a prayer for help from the powerful. In colonial times the implied plea was for permission to choose representatives. Later suffrage was understood as a fundamental right to participate in elections.

In the Colonial Period

Both the Dutch and the English had traditions of representative government, participation being based upon demonstrating a stake in the community, normally established through property ownership. The question whether such voting was a natural right or a gift from the sovereign provoked spirited debate. Pragmatically authorities anticipated less resistance to taxes and demands for soldiers if those most affected participated in decisions. Not until 1683, under the English, were freeholders (landowners) directed to establish a general assembly in New York Colony. This body passed a Charter of Liberties and Privileges, which affirmed the right of freeholders to vote as under the laws of England, where freeholds entitling one to vote had to be worth 40s (40 shillings). Freemen of corporations (cities) could also vote under their corporate charters as granted by the king. Local authorities designated freemen, usually after payment of a small fee. King James II had approved the assembly as a proprietor but disallowed it as king. The 1688 Glorious Revolution in England, which deposed the king, opened the way for permanent representation by an assembly in 1691.

Voting requirements soon demonstrated who authorities believed could be trusted with power. In 1699 the 40s freehold requirement to vote, easy to meet in the land-rich province, increased to £40 to reduce those eligible. Catholics, viewed as placing their church above country, could vote only if they took the Test (loyalty) Oath. A 1701 law, however, permitted persons living on the great manors with estate freeholds for life to vote. Voters had to be 21 or over and male, though the sex requirement was assumed and not legislated during the colonial period. Slaves could not vote, but the small number of free African Americans who met other qualifications could. In 1737 the assembly excluded Jews from voting, a policy that continued for a decade. Quakers, suspect because of their pacifism and general antiauthoritarianism, also faced challenges when attempting to vote. Historians estimate that roughly half of adult males qualified to vote during the colonial period and that about half of these chose to participate.

Property Qualifications Challenged

In 1776 the Declaration of Independence affirmed the natural right to self-government. Facing the problem of who precisely should govern, New York State's first constitution (1777) lowered the property qualification to vote for the assembly to £20 (above debts) or a 40s renthold for six-month residents of a county. Those who had previously qualified as freemen of Albany or New York City continued to vote. A minority at the convention, however, favored a lower, taxpaying requirement, arguing that taxation without representation was unjust. This claim suggested not only that other people besides property holders contributed to the community but also that people must vote as individuals, not just as community members, and approve policies that affected their individual interests. The majority countered that only property ownership ensured independent decision making by making it difficult for the rich to buy votes or threaten voters with loss of livelihood.

To vote for governor or state senator under the 1777 Constitution required a much larger £100 freehold. Historians estimate about 60% of adult males qualified to vote for assembly and roughly 30% for senators and governor under the document, although they also suspect, because of surprisingly high vote totals in gubernatorial races, that many communities over time became careless about enforcement. The combination of democratic initiatives within a largely conservative constitutional framework suggests to some scholars that the delegates in 1777 recognized how divided the population was and attempted to offer something to everyone to maintain unity during the Revolution. As families left the land in search of new opportunities in towns or on newer lands to the west, the idea that debt-free property holders should alone participate in elections seemed increasingly unjust. Individuals pursuing their economic self-interests expected to pursue their political self-interests as well, and that meant voting. Lacking a means to amend the 1777 Constitution, a new convention, intended to make only specific alterations, assembled in 1801. Free white male citizens 21 and over chose the delegates. The law, which applied only to this convention, dropped property as a qualifier but added race and citizenship, a sign of things to come.

A new convention replaced the 1777 Constitution in 1821. An epic debate on the merits of property qualifications occurred. Facing demands for votes from the state's growing cities and indebted western farmers, delegates extended suffrage to white, taxpaying male citizens, one-year residents who were militia or firemen, and three-year residents who worked on highways. The requirements reflected service to the community, but the taxpaying provision recognized the right of individuals to protect their property from excessive levies. About 90% of adult white males now qualified to vote. The complicated record keeping required to exclude only a few Whites led to the adoption of universal white "manhood suffrage" by amendment in 1826.

African Americans and the Foreign-Born

Those who debated suffrage in 1821 did not term it a natural right. So doing would have left no leeway for excluding groups, such as Blacks and ethnic minorities, from voting in one of the most diverse states in the Union. Because many Whites viewed Blacks as permanent social outcasts who could never be accepted as fellow citizens, the struggle for the voting rights of African Americans in New York State proved more difficult than that of European immigrants. Indeed, one proposed gradual emancipation statute promised permanent disfranchisement to assure Whites that emancipation would be safe. Although slavery in New York State was in the process of gradual extermination in 1821, this did not guarantee rights for Blacks at the constitutional convention.

An attempt to restrict suffrage to white men encountered objections only from conservative Federalist and Clintonian delegates who preferred property qualifications for everyone. They accused their opponents of hypocrisy in demanding a democratic suffrage for poor white men but denying the same to black men. Attempting a compromise, the majority imposed a $250 property qualification above all debts (equivalent to the previous qualification for voting for governor) on black males, while excluding the remaining Blacks from taxation. Blacks also had to be state residents for three years to vote, a stipulation not required of Whites. Under these provisions only 5% of black men could qualify to vote. While the door was not shut entirely and over time inflating property values would increase the number of those eligible, delegates were clearly treating the African American population differently.

Immigrants were also suspect in the eyes of some delegates, who believed they were likely to succumb to bribery because of their poverty. Most immigrants, however, unlike African Americans, were supporters of the Bucktail Republicans, the majority faction at the 1821 convention, which addressed immigration by requiring voters to be citizens. While naturalization came under the jurisdiction of the US Congress, the state could increase the waiting period for voting after naturalization. Aiming to eliminate mass naturalizations on election eve, the 1846 convention required a 10-day wait, which was increased to 30 days by an 1874 amendment and to 90 days in the 1894 Constitution. The 1821 Constitution was also the first to consider disfranchisement for crime. While the constitution simply permitted the legislature to pass such laws, in 1894 the constitution required such laws. Concerns with bribery or betting on elections were specifically mentioned in 1846 and after, requiring passage of state laws calling for disfranchisement of violators; constitutional provisions that shaped the modern law date to 1874. The 1894 Constitution required personal registration for voters in cities over 5,000. This too was aimed at immigrants, who lived disproportionately in cities. While distrust of the foreign-born existed, constitutional provisions addressed specific concerns (eg, their loyalty or bribability). In a competitive, politicized, diverse state, partisan considerations shaped suffrage requirements.

The property qualification for Blacks continued. By 1846, when a new constitutional convention was held, the antiquated requirement remained because most Democrats favored a Whites-only electorate while most Whigs opposed racial discrimination in suffrage. A small but active antislavery movement drawing upon Blacks and Whites pressed determinedly for change, alarming the southern wings of both the Whigs and the Democrats nationally. In the end the politicians kept the property qualification for Blacks but submitted it for separate voter approval or rejection. It was retained by a large margin. When the Republican Party, which was purely northern, replaced the Whigs in the 1850s, its legislators pushed again for removal of the property qualification by amendment. In

1860, in the same election that Republican Abraham Lincoln sought the presidency, it was submitted for approval. It failed, although by a smaller margin. In 1867 and 1868 Republicans again backed equal suffrage for Blacks and Whites at a constitutional convention. In 1869, even though Blacks were then voting in the South, New Yorkers voted to retain the property qualification. Not until the ratification of the 15th Amendment to the US Constitution in 1870 did black men have the same voting rights as white men in New York State. A pro forma amendment to the state constitution acknowledged the change in 1874.

Woman Suffrage

New York State's 1846 Constitutional Convention was the first to receive a petition for woman suffrage, two years before the Women's Rights Convention at Seneca Falls (Seneca Co) made the same demand. Women's participation in antislavery issues taught them to analyze structures supporting discrimination, making some aware of their own peculiar status and eager to claim rights, as men did, as individuals. Their opponents drew on images of women as naturally dependent and concerned only with family matters to ridicule such claims. After the Civil War black and woman suffrage advocates united in pleas for "universal" suffrage. Pragmatic Republican politicians, however, viewed yoking black male suffrage, necessary in their eyes to govern the South, with female suffrage likely to weaken the former. Despite a majority report at the Constitutional Convention of 1867 and 1868 admitting the logic of woman suffrage, it was not recommended to the delegates, who gave it a maximum of 24 votes on the floor. This disappointment helped break the partisan bonds of some woman suffragists. Over the ensuing decades the movement would search for appropriate strategies to enlarge support for their cause. Rejected again by delegates at the 1894 convention, woman suffrage eventually was submitted for voter approval as an amendment in 1915. Defeated then 732,770 to 544,457 (1.3 to 1), it was finally approved two years later in a second referendum 703,129 to 600,776 (1.2 to 1), thus beating by two years the national adoption of the 19th Amendment.

Other Obstacles

Women were the last major addition to the electorate. Many obstacles still loomed over broad participation, however. Reflecting fears of foreigners and radicals, the legislature enacted an English literacy test in 1921, requiring future voters to be able to read and write English. Such a demand had first appeared in the 1846 convention. One 1960 estimate suggested that it kept about 100,000 from voting each year. The federal Voting Rights Act of 1965 suspended all literacy tests, and the provision became inoperative and was officially removed in 1995 by amendment. Felons have been prohibited from voting since 1821. Their voting rights can be regained via a gubernatorial or presidential pardon when they are discharged from parole or after the expiration of their maximum prison sentence.

The 1967 Constitutional Convention proposed lowering the voting age from the colonial-era requirement of 21 to 18, but the constitution itself was rejected, delaying the enfranchisement of this group until the national passage of the 26th Amendment in 1971. The wording of the New York State Constitution was not changed until 1995. The mobility of the state's diverse population also disfranchised potential voters. Beginning in 1846 a residency requirement of a year in the state, 4 months in the county, and 30 days in the electoral district was put into effect. This reflected a concern, present since colonial times, about "rootless" voters. By the 20th century such provisions increasingly affected the middle class as well as the poor. Since 1874 the state had clarified that certain groups, such as soldiers and ministers on circuits, should not be deemed to have lost residence for voting. In 1970 a national law prohibited more than a 30-day residency for presidential elections. In 1995 an amendment reduced New York State's requirement to 30 days as well. While few adults now cannot vote, political expression through voting seems less valued than ever before.

Chute, Marchette Gaylord. *First Liberty: A History of the Right to Vote in America, 1619–1850* (New York: Dutton, 1969)

Field, Phyllis F. *The Politics of Race in New York: The Struggle for Black Suffrage in the Civil War Era* (Ithaca: Cornell Univ Press, 1982)

Galie, Peter J. *Ordered Liberty: A Constitutional History of New York* (New York: Fordham Univ Press, 1996)

Keyssar, Alexander. *The Right to Vote: The Contested History of Democracy in the United States* (New York: Basic Books, 2000)

Lincoln, Charles Z. *The Constitutional History of New York from the Beginning of the Colonial Period to the Year 1905,* 5 vols (Rochester: Lawyers Cooperative Publishing, 1906)

Phyllis F. Field

sugar-refining industry. New York's extensive trade with the sugar islands of the Caribbean made it an early center of sugar refining. Nicholas Bayard opened one of the earliest sugar refineries in New York City in 1730. By 1760 there were several refineries, owned by some of the city's leading families, including the Bayards, Van Cortlandts, Cuylers, and Roosevelts. The increased production in New York and other colonies, however, prompted the British Parliament to pass the Sugar Act in 1764 to collect duties on all raw sugar coming to the colonies. The New York sugar industry survived the Sugar Act and the Revolutionary War, and in the following decades the state continued its preeminent status as a major producer of sugar in the country. The abundance of fresh water, vital to sugar refining, and proximity to busy seaports needed for the constant supply of raw sugar, kept New York City the center of the industry. Newer technologies were gradually introduced to the business through European newcomers such as William and Frederick Havemeyer, who emigrated from England in 1799 and shortly afterward opened a refinery on Vandam St in Manhattan, and domestic entrepreneurs, such as Robert and Alexander Stuart, who in 1834 patented their revolutionary system of steam refining.

During the first half of the 19th century, many manufacturers were attracted to the sugar business, and by 1868 there were 30 companies in operation producing about half of the country's sugar. Many of the largest refiners built factories in Greenpoint and other Brooklyn neighborhoods along the East River waterfront. During the second part of the century, there was a consolidation among refiners, which reached its high mark in 1887 with the creation of the Sugar Refineries Co, popularly known as the Sugar Trust, created by Henry O. Havemeyer. After being forced by New York State courts, it reorganized in 1891 as the American Sugar Refining Co (later American Sugar Co). By 1907 this enterprise had 25 refineries and was meeting 98% of the country's total sugar consumption. From this point on, although the headquarters remained in New York City, the company's operations became increasingly national, and even

Worker making cube sugar at Federal Sugar Refinery, Yonkers, *ca* 1920.

international. Despite expansion, the company's market share gradually declined throughout the 20th century as new producers emerged in the southern and western United States and overseas. Other sources of sugar emerged, and the first and only beet-sugar refinery in New York State was erected in Lyons (Wayne Co) in 1906 with limited production. In 1970, as it was diversifying into nonsugar enterprises, the American Sugar Co took the name of Amstar Corp, and in 1984, when an investment group made the company private, it was called Amstar Holdings. Four years later, the firm sold its sugar business (Amstar Sugar) to the international sugar giant based in England, Tate and Lyle PLC, for $305 million. In 1991, using one of its sugar trademarks, Amstar Sugar was renamed Domino Sugar Corp. In 2001 Tate and Lyle was acquired by an investment group headed by Alfonso and J. Pepe Fanjul of Florida, and Domino was combined with Refined Sugars, also owned by the Fanjuls, to become Domino Sugar. Domino has a refinery in Brooklyn, and Refined Sugar maintains a refinery in Yonkers.

Catlin, Daniel. *Good Work Well Done: The Sugar Business Career of Horace Havemeyer, 1903–1956* (New York: D. Catlin, 1988)

Eichner, Alfred S. *The Emergence of Oligopoly: Sugar Refining as a Case Study* (Baltimore: Johns Hopkins Press, 1969)

Mojtaba Seyedian

Sullivan. Town (pop 14,991) in NW Madison Co. Once part of the Oneida Reservation, it was settled in 1790 by squatters on reservation land. The town was organized from Cazenovia in 1803 and was crossed by the Erie Canal (1819) and the Syracuse and Utica Railroad (1839, later New York Central). Plaster, gypsum, and water lime were all quarried in town beginning about 1810. Chittenango White Sulphur Springs was a health resort (1825–late 1890s). A large cider and vinegar factory (1857) employed 40 in 1880. The Vlaie, a vast, swampy, unproductive area of muck underlain by marl, was drained by ditching (1840s, completed 1887–1900). In the 20th century the land was acquired by Italian American vegetable growers. Sullivan's Oneida Lake shore provides access for pleasure boating, fishing, and other recreational activities. Residents enjoy country living with access to Greater Syracuse for work, entertainment, shopping, and healthcare. With suburbanization, Sullivan's 1950 population of 4,905 nearly doubled to 9,369 by 1960, and its population increased an additional 40% in the remaining decades of the 20th century.

William F. Helmer

Sullivan Act. Named for its author, Timothy D. "Big Tim" Sullivan, a leading Tammany politician in Lower Manhattan and state senator, the 1911 act amended existing laws to regulate the ownership and carrying of handguns by aliens and minors. A permit was required for anyone to buy a handgun or carry a concealed weapon. Sellers were required to keep records of firearms transactions. Goaded by public outcry over rising homicide rates and the 1910 assassination attempt against Mayor William J. Gaynor, both political parties endorsed the Sullivan Act, which won passage with large majorities. The New York City police were its greatest supporters, arguing that easily concealed pistols seriously compromised the safety of law enforcement officers. There is strong evidence that it was selectively enforced against immigrants and ethnic minorities in its first years. New York State still requires a permit for the purchase of a handgun.

See also GUN CONTROL.

New York State. *Laws of the State of New York Passed at the 134th Session of the Legislature,* vol 1, chap 195 (Albany: J. B. Lyon, 1911)

Michael A. Bellesiles

Sullivan-Clinton campaign. American military engagement against the Iroquois. In 1779 Gen George Washington dispatched Maj Gen John Sullivan and an army of about 6,000 troops into New York with the tasks of punishing the Iroquois Confederacy, the Seneca Nation in particular, and of breaking their alliance with Great Britain. After the devastating raid by Britain's Indian and loyalist allies on Pennsylvania's Wyoming Valley settlements on 3 July 1778, Washington was under tremendous pressure to do something about the threat to the frontier settlements. Sullivan's immediate aim was to wage a scorched-earth campaign against the Iroquois settlements in the Finger Lakes region. Washington also specified British-held Fort Niagara [now in Porter, Niagara Co] as a target of opportunity should its possession become possible at little cost in men or time. Logistical constraints eventually rendered it impossible for Sullivan to lay siege to the fort. As part of the campaign, Washington ordered approximately 600 Continental army soldiers from Fort Pitt [now Pittsburgh] under Col Daniel Brodhead to make a diversionary attack into Seneca settlements along the Allegheny River.

Sullivan gathered most of his army at Easton, Pa, in May 1779 and began the process of cutting a road through the Pocono Mountains to the Wyoming Valley on the Susquehanna River. One brigade under Gen James Clinton assembled at Otsego Lake at the river's headwaters in what is now Otsego Co. Sullivan moved the main force of his army up the Susquehanna River to Tioga Point [now Athens, Pa] in August 1779 and he established Fort Sullivan just below the New York border. There he met up with Clinton's brigade moving down the Susquehanna. Clinton traveled with a significant supply train from New York State that Sullivan eventually found critical to operations. With approximately 4,000 of his troops and using the Chemung River as a general guide, Sullivan moved westward and northward into the Indian settlements along the Finger Lakes in late August.

Sullivan never enjoyed the benefit of secrecy. His army found itself stalked by Indian and loyalist patrols even before it departed the Wyoming Valley in July. Indian attempts to stop the campaign were brushed aside. The most noteworthy of these efforts occurred at Newtown [now Elmira] on 29 Aug 1779. Sullivan's men discovered an ambush attempt by Indians and loyalists and scattered their foes after a brief battle. Throughout the campaign his men found empty villages, most inhabitants having fled to safer parts of Iroquoia, and an abundance of food that was used to supplement their already short rations. All that was not used was burned or destroyed. The expedition moved to the north end of Seneca Lake, turning west at Kanadesaga [now Geneva, Ontario Co], and continued through the Seneca towns at Canandaigua and Honeoye [now in Ontario Co], where a small post was established before moving into the Genesee Valley. Sullivan suffered his greatest losses when Lt Thomas Boyd and 13 members of his reconnaissance patrol were killed near the present town of Geneseo (Livingston Co). The expedition then retraced its route along the north end of the Finger Lakes to the head of Cayuga Lake, where they turned south and arrived back at Fort Sullivan by the end of September 1779.

Sullivan's army burned 40 villages and destroyed at least 160,000 bushels of corn and countless quantities of other crops. The western Iroquois had been turned out of their homes, and many would spend the winter of 1779–80 huddled outside Fort Niagara, dependent on their British allies for food. Unbroken by Sullivan's army, the campaign failed to drive the Iroquois out of the war. The following year loyalists and their Iroquois allies participated in more than 50 war parties sent out from Fort Niagara.

Fischer, Joseph R. *A Well-Executed Failure: The Sullivan Campaign against the Iroquois, July–September 1779* (Columbia: Univ of South Carolina Press, 1997)

Joseph R. Fischer

Sullivan County (986 mi²/2,554 km²; pop 73,966). Formed from Ulster Co on 27 Mar 1809, the county was named in honor of Maj Gen John Sullivan, a leader in the Revolutionary War. Sullivan Co is divided into 15 towns that contain 6 incorporated villages; the county seat is Monticello. The surface of the county is mostly hilly, with some mountainous ridges, notably the Shawangunk Mountains, which run along the southeast border. Elevation ranges from a low of under 400 feet (122 m) in the Shawangunk Kill valley along the eastern edge of the county to a high of 3,053 feet (931 m) on Denman Mountain in Neversink. Most of Sullivan Co lies within the Delaware Hills subsection of the Appalachian Upland province. This deeply dissected plateau slopes gently to the southwest and is bounded to the southeast by a fairly steep, prominent escarpment. In the western part of this section, relief is generally steeper, with less relief in the southern and central areas except for the valley walls of the Delaware and lower Neversink Rivers. Two small noncontiguous areas in northern Sullivan Co lie in the Catskill Mountains subsection of the Appalachian Upland province. This area has the highest elevations, and relief is quite steep in places. The Shawangunk Mountains subsection of the Hudson-Mohawk Lowland province occupies a small area in the southeastern part of the county. Elevations of the Shawangunk Mountains range from 1,780 feet (543 m) to about 1,200 feet (366 m), and relief is very steep throughout.

Sullivan Co is underlain with bedrock of sedimentary origin. Bedrock becomes progressively younger moving in a northwesterly direction. Ordovician dark shale bedrock underlies the southeast edge of the county. Devonian shale and limestone are west of this, and rocks that are mainly red and grayish brown sandstone of the middle and upper Devonian age are farther west and continue across the rest of the county. Sullivan Co was completely glaciated, and most of the area is covered by glacial till and outwash. Many small glacial lakes formed, seen today as small deposits of peat or muck.

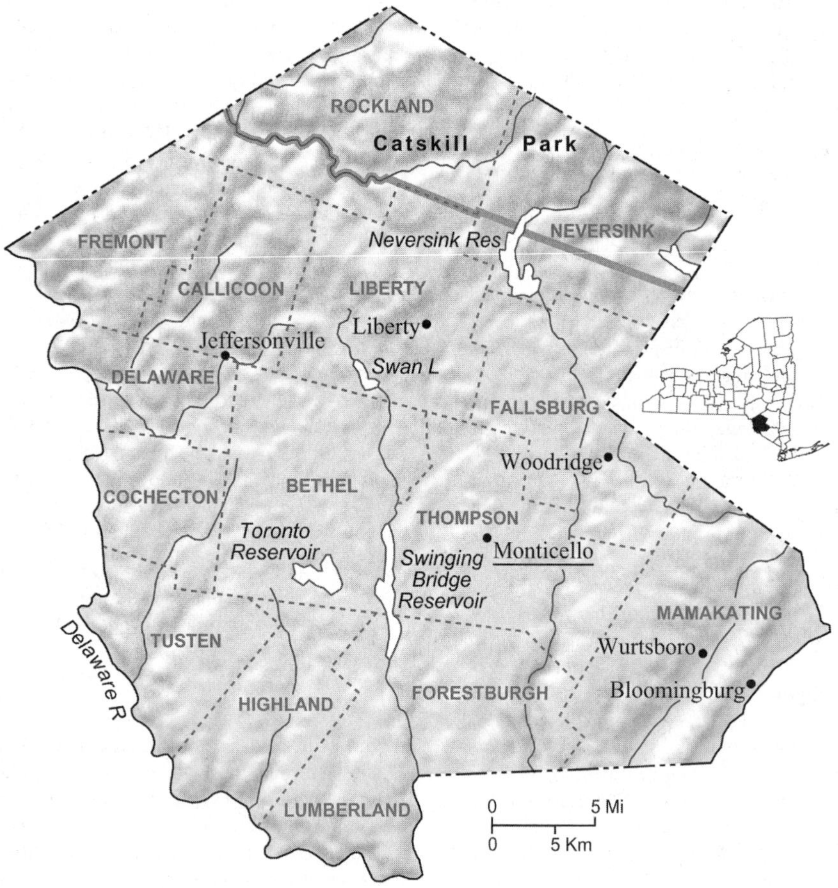

Most of the county is drained by the Delaware River and its tributaries. A small area in the east drains to the Hudson River. The Delaware River runs approximately 50 miles (80 km) along the county's western and southern edges, and its flow is now controlled by a system of dams and reservoirs in the north. The Neversink River flows nearly across the county, emptying into the Delaware in Orange Co. It has also been dammed, and two New York City water supply reservoirs lie fully or partly within the county. The Mongaup has three branches, each of which rises in the northeast part of the county; they flow southerly, emptying into the Delaware just above the county's boundary with Orange. The Swinging Bridge, Rio, and Mongaup Falls Reservoirs have been built along the Mongaup by Orange and Rockland Utilities. There are many lakes in the county, some of which were built or enlarged to serve as feeders for the Delaware and Hudson Canal (1828–98).

The climate of Sullivan County is humid-continental. Precipitation is evenly distributed throughout the year, averaging 50 inches (127 cm) annually. The average seasonal snowfall is 64 inches (163 cm) with more in the north and less in the south. The average temperature in January is 21°F (-6°C) and in July is 67°F (19°C). The primeval forest cover was primarily spruce and fir in the northern section. The Alleghenian hardwood community in the central section was made up of beech, sugar maple, hemlock, white pine, and basswood with the frequent occurrence of northern oaks, black cherry, black birch, white ash, hickories and tulip poplars. The central hardwoods of oak and chestnut dominated to the south. Farming is largely not viable in Sullivan Co except in the north and northwest.

American Indians and Early Settlement

Algonquian-speaking Indians were the first known inhabitants: the ancestors of the Munsee are believed to have been present 1,000 years ago. They lived in the area mainly in the warm-weather months, when they could hunt, fish, and farm. With the arrival of the first Europeans and the encroachment of the tribes of the Iroquois League from the north, the Munsee began to move westward to the Ohio Valley. By 1730 the Munsees' exposure to these other cultures, subsequent outbreaks of previously unknown diseases, and several wars fought with the Iroquois, left the area vacant.

The southern quarter of the county was in the Minisink Patent (1704); the remainder was in the Hardenbergh Patent (1707). Settlement by Europeans began slowly and, at first, was south of the Shawangunks and along the Delaware River. Mamakating was first settled after 1728, Neversink about 1743, and Cochecton and Tusten about 1757. The other towns were settled before the Revolution, with the exceptions of Highland, Rockland, Liberty, and Bethel, which were settled between 1789 and 1798, and Callicoon, which was not settled until 1814.

The first settlers were mostly Dutch and German. One of the first settlers of Mamakating, Manuel Gonsalus, present by 1750, was of Spanish paternity although he was culturally Dutch and his family had lived in Ulster Co since at least 1709. Enslaved Africans were present in small numbers; in 1790 Mamakating, which covered all of the present Sullivan Co, had 51 enslaved and 5 free black residents. There were 94 Blacks in Sullivan Co in 1855, over half of them in what is now the Town of Mamakating.

Sullivan Co was sparsely inhabited at the time of the Revolution. In a 1778 engagement in Neversink called the Battle of the Chestnut Woods, 18 militiamen were annihilated by a force of loyalists and their Indian allies. In 1779 about 120 patriots led by Col John Hathorn pursued the Mohawk leader Joseph Brant and a smaller group of Indians and loyalists to near the present-day Barryville, where they fought the Battle of Minisink. The patriots suffered a devastating defeat. Soon afterward, John Sullivan led his expedition against the Six Nations across Mamakating en route west.

According to a 1782 census, the population of the town or precinct of Mamakating, which encompassed what is now Sullivan Co and small parts of Delaware and Orange Cos, was 319 plus 168 refugees who came from elsewhere during the war. Immigration blossomed after the construction of the Newburgh and Cochecton Turnpike (1801–8), and the population nearly doubling from 3,222 in 1800 to 6,108 in 1810; many came from Connecticut. Irish laborers added diversity to the population and were nearly 9% of the population in 1855. By that time, Germans and Swiss were also nearly 9%, concentrated in Cochecton, Callicoon, and Fremont, having been attracted by circulars distributed beginning *ca* 1840.

Transportation

The construction of the Newburgh and Cochecton Turnpike, which connected the Hudson and Delaware Rivers, spurred the settlement of the interior. The Delaware and Hudson Canal, which traversed Highland, Lumberland, and, after passing through Orange Co, Mamakating, brought economic prosperity and led to substantial population growth. It opened in 1828, and in its first 20 years of operation, the county's population more than doubled, passing 25,000 before the 1850 census. The New York and Erie Railroad along the Delaware River was completed through the county in 1849, and the Port Jervis and Monticello and the New York and Oswego Midland Railroads (later Ontario and Western Railroad) completed the county's limited network of railroads in 1872.

Economic Development

The abundance of timber provided the earliest industry. Daniel Skinner rafted the first timber from Callicoon to Philadelphia in 1764, and others soon followed suit, providing softwoods for the shipbuilding industry. For the next 80 years, timber was Sullivan Co's primary export. Bluestone was quarried and, at first, rafted to market. Attempts were made to mine copper, lead, silver, and gold from the Shawangunk Mountains, but were all commercial failures. The Newburgh and Cochecton Turnpike carried grain, pork, butter firkins, wooden scoops and shovels, and barrel staves and hoops out of the county and brought sugar, spices, coffee, household goods, and farm tools into it. The turnpike crossed the Delaware and Hudson Canal at what was later known as Wurtsboro, providing transportation that allowed for the expansion of the tanning industry. Hides were brought in on the canal and tanned at dozens of large operations, many employing hundreds of people, and the finished product was shipped out on the canal. The tanning in-

SULLIVAN CO POPULATION CENSUS FIGURES

	White	Nonwhite	Total Population	Foreign-Born
1810	6,054	54	6,108	—
1820	8,798	102	8,900	239
1830	12,245	119	12,364	131
1840	15,549	80	15,629	—
1850	24,988	100	25,088	4,263
1860	32,291	94	32,385	5,990
1870	34,451	99	34,550	5,822
1880	32,407	84	32,491	4,262
1890	30,963	68	31,031	3,326
1900	32,219	87	32,306	3,041
1910	33,742	66	33,808	4,488
1920	33,100	63	33,163	5,498
1930	35,175	97	35,272	6,194
1940	37,520	381	37,901	6,052
1950	39,986	745	40,731	5,896
1960	43,258	2,014	45,272	4,734
1970	48,719	3,861	52,580	4,465
1980	59,071	6,084	65,155	5,392
1990	61,373	7,904	69,277	5,043
2000	63,103	10,863	73,966	5,875

Notes: "Nonwhite" includes African Americans, Asians, American Indians, and Pacific Islanders and, for 2000, also the mixed race and other race categories. Through the 1960 census these figures primarily reflect the African American population. Foreign-born figures for 1820 and 1830 include only those not naturalized, and for 1930 and 1950, the foreign-born totals include Whites only. Other years include all foreign-born in the population.

dustry peaked during the Civil War, when the demand for leather boots, belts, bridles, holsters, and saddles was at its highest. The hemlock tree, whose bark was needed for the tanning agent, was soon after depleted from the county's forests. By 1880 tanning had all but vanished from Sullivan Co.

Another industry dependent on the forests was the production of wood chemicals. "Acid factories" began with the one at Acidalia in 1878 and spread along the Willowemoc Creek in Fremont and Rockland, producing chemicals from hardwood distillates for wool cloth processing. The development of synthetics in the mid-1920s ended the industry. Agriculture, which peaked in the late 1800s, consisted mainly of dairy and poultry farming, and hay and grain crops to support the farming. In 1900 about 75% of the land was farmland.

Sullivan Co's industrial production was relatively limited. There was an early paper mill at Fallsburg, and the Long Eddy Hydraulic and Manufacturing Co (1867) attempted to dam the Delaware River for power and created the now extinct village of Douglas (1867–73). At Livingston Manor, Spalding baseball bats were made (1877–1900) and, later, bowling pins. In Tusten blasting powder (*ca* 1870–88) and excelsior (*ca* 1870–1930s) were produced. In the 19th century ironwork and cigars were made in Monticello, where, in the 20th century, workers produced gloves, Christmas tree lights, toy trucks, and flavorings.

Religion, Education, and Culture

Among the first churches were the New Vernon Baptist Church (?1785) and the Reformed Church of Mamakating (1793). In 1855 Sullivan Co had only 46 churches; like most of New York State, Methodist congregations were in the majority, with 21, but the county's mixed Yankee and Dutch population was responsible for 8 Presbyterian and 6 Reformed churches, and there was a Quaker meeting at Grahamsville. Early Irish and German immigrants had established the county's first Roman Catholic churches in Fremont and Mamakating and an Evangelical Lutheran church in Callicoon dated from 1842. The Jewish influx had just begun when the first synagogue was established in Woodridge in 1903, shortly after the beginnings of the Jewish resort business.

A school, perhaps the first in the present county, opened in Bloomingburg in 1784. The common school system developed in response to state legislation of 1812. Sullivan Co was one of the first in the state to have a teachers college, Liberty Normal Institute (1847–85). Centralization of schools began in 1915 when five common schools around Youngsville consolidated. The process was completed in 1957, at which time there were 11 districts with a handful of unattached common schools scheduled for inclusion in the Middletown Enlarged City School District. Three districts consolidated in 2000 to form Sullivan West Central School, leaving eight school districts in the county. Private elementary schools include a regional Catholic school at Liberty and a Hebrew day school at Kiamesha Lake; there is a yeshiva at Fallsburg. The only institution of higher education is Sullivan County Community College (1963) at Loch Sheldrake.

The first newspaper, the *Sullivan Whig,* was published at Bloomingburg in 1820. The weeklies *Sullivan County Democrat* (1891) at Callicoon, the *River Reporter* (1975) at Narrowsburg, and *Towne Crier* (1990) at Livingston Manor were published in 2003. Radio is broadcast from Jeffersonville, Liberty, and Monticello.

Tourism

Vacationers had discovered Sullivan Co by the mid-19th century. Its first hotel may have been the one built by J. B. Findlay at White Lake in 1846; two years later the Mansion House, the oldest hotel still standing, opened its doors. The railroads provided new access to the natural beauty of the area, which they promoted aggressively, leading to an unprecedented growth in tourism. The construction of dozens of small hotels and boardinghouses followed, catering first to sports enthusiasts and then to general summer tourists. A period of great prosperity in the area, 1890–1915, is known as the Silver Age and was typified by hotels such as the Wawonda and the Swannanoa in Liberty, the White Sulphur Springs House, the Ferndale Villa, and the Frank Leslie in Monticello. These hotels were largely wood-frame buildings of Victorian architecture and were all gentile owned. While at first they offered their guests the simple amenities of fresh air, clean water, farm fresh vegetables and milk, and plenty of shade, by 1895 lawn tennis had become an attraction. Golf also became popular, and the county's first golf course was opened in 1897 at the Trout Valley Farm on the Beaver Kill, and several more, including three official nine-hole courses, were opened by 1901.

Around the turn of the century, the fresh mountain air of Sullivan Co was promoted as a cure for people suffering from consumption; Loomis Sanitorium (1896–1938) at Liberty was a well-known establishment. Hotel owners blamed the county's budding reputation as a haven for those afflicted with tuberculosis for destroying their business, and by 1915 many of the once magnificent hotels had closed. A number burned to the ground. The county had already begun a radical change. A seasonal influx of New York City–based Jewish immigrants began in Fallsburg in 1899. Some purchased struggling hotels. Still others came to farm but soon found that they could make more by entertaining friends or relatives in the spare rooms than by working the soil. This provided Jewish vacationers, unwelcome in most other resorts, a place to spend their free time in the company of other Jews. Most notable among these early Jewish hoteliers were Selig and Malke Grossinger in Liberty, the Kutsher family near Monticello, and Fleischer and Morganstern, who purchased the Flagler House in Fallsburg. During this transition, it was not unusual to see the remaining gentile establishments identify themselves with blatant advertising copy such as "No Hebrews or Consumptives Accommodated" or the subtler, but no less discriminatory, "Conveniently Located near Catholic and Protestant Churches." Similarly, Jewish resorts identified themselves by advertising "Dietary Laws Observed." The two groups did not mix. Another type of resort was created by wealthy urban sportsmen, who developed Hartwood (1870s) and Mamakating (1893) Parks, and by artists, who established Merriewold Park (1889). Meanwhile, the Willowemoc and Beaver Kill remained major fly-fishing destinations.

By about 1935–40, the transition was complete. The county was mostly a Jewish resort area, and the resorts no longer depended on the railroads to bring in guests. The newfound freedom that the automobile provided brought about changes in both the resorts and their patrons. Now

POPULATIONS OF TOWNS, SULLIVAN CO

Town, Year Founded	1800	1840	1880	1920	1960	2000
Bethel, 1809	—	1,483	2,562	1,849	2,366	4,362
Callicoon, 1842	—	—	2,180	1,739	2,176	3,052
Cochecton, 1828	—	622	1,328	1,112	1,070	1,328
Delaware, 1868	—	—	1,830	1,740	2,141	2,719
Fallsburg, 1826	—	1,782	2,945	4,769	6,748	12,234
Forestburgh, 1837	—	433	1,058	405	356	833
Fremont, 1851	—	—	2,025	1,435	1,047	1,391
Highland, 1853	—	—	1,013	875	1,138	2,404
Liberty, 1807	—	1,569	3,209	6,030	8,676	9,632
Lumberland, 1798	733	1,205	1,050	480	538	1,939
Mamakating, 1788	1,631	3,418	3,845	2,395	3,356	11,002
Neversink, 1798	858	1,681	2,152	1,609	1,565	3,553
Rockland, 1809	—	826	2,481	3,247	4,216	3,913
Thompson, 1803	—	2,610	3,763	4,597	8,792	14,189
Tusten, 1853	—	—	1,050	881	1,087	1,415

Note: In 1800 the Towns of Lumberland, Mamakating, and Neversink were in Ulster Co.

the hotels comprised multiple buildings, mostly stucco or other masonry, in a new, distinctive architecture called Catskill Mission. Many became year-round establishments, and glitz and glamour were the goal. The hotels of this Golden Age varied greatly in size and in degree of luxury, and were as much different from each other as they were from their predecessors of the Silver Age.

Recent History

With the resort industry in full swing and with only one main highway leading from New York City to the county's vacation spots, traffic became a serious problem. Bypasses at Liberty and Bloomingburg opened in 1958; Rte 17 (I-86) as a whole was upgraded to four lanes with limited access in 1959–60 and was initially known as the Quickway. Population grew during the succeeding 40 years, chiefly in Thompson and Fallsburg, where minorities who came for hotel work settled, and in Mamakating, which received overflow from adjacent Orange Co.

This era of prosperity lasted until about 1965. Many factors played a role in the decline of the Catskill resorts. The growth of suburbia and the proliferation of air-conditioning made summers in the city more bearable. Inexpensive air travel opened up new horizons to middle- and working-class vacationers, and Jewish families became assimilated and no longer chose to vacation around other Jews to feel comfortable. Sullivan Co resorts, which had survived for decades by constantly evolving—adding tennis, golf, swimming pools, indoor swimming pools, nightclubs, harness racing—suddenly failed to adjust. Sullivan Co had fallen on hard economic times by the 1970s, and no simple solution was at hand.

In August 1969 approximately 500,000 people from all over the country converged on a field in Bethel for a three-day event that was planned for a fraction of that number. Heavy rains and inadequate facilities did little to dampen the enthusiasm of the crowd, which enjoyed "three days of peace and music." This event, the Woodstock Art and Music Festival, helped define a generation, but despite a number of halfhearted attempts, Sullivan was never able to capitalize commercially on this claim to fame. In fact, for many years after the festival, it seemed as if county officials and many residents would have preferred that the concert had never taken place. The traffic jams that paralyzed the region, the destruction of private property, and the garbage left in the festival's aftermath left a negative image in the minds of many residents. The county's Board of Supervisors enacted a strict mass gathering law to prevent a recurrence.

Despite the decline of the resorts, tourism remains the most important industry in the county, based largely on natural attractions and the recreational opportunities they afford. Hunting, fishing, eagle watching, water sports, and golf are the primary draws. Agriculture ranks second; but with only 9.4% of the county in farms, it has the smallest percentage of agricultural land upstate outside of three Adirondack counties. Poultry is the leading sector in terms of revenue, and two large operations make Sullivan Co the largest foie gras producer in the United States. The dairy industry ranks second in the county based on revenue. The number of farms increased 4% between 1992 and 1997 because of increased numbers of livestock and vegetable operations. Agriculture is concentrated in the western towns of Delaware, Bethel, and Cochecton.

As Sullivan Co enters the 21st century, a state-of-the-art performing arts center is under development at the site of the Woodstock Festival in Bethel, and gaming casinos operated under the auspices of Native American tribes have been proposed for several locations. In 2000 the highest share of jobs (37%) was in the service industry, 25% was in government, and 20% was in wholesale/retail. There was no significant manufacturing. The Center for Discovery, a residential program for children and adults with special needs, and the Catskill Regional Medical Center, both in Harris, were the county's two largest employers. Many residents worked in the nearby prisons.

The standard history is James E. Quinlan, *History of Sullivan County* (1873); a "revised edition" (a dramatic abridgement) is David M. Gold, *History of Sullivan County* (1993). The best coverage of the county's history is contained in Alf Evers, *The Catskills: From Wilderness to Woodstock* (1972). Recent works include David M. Gold, *The River and the Mountains: Readings in Sullivan County History* (1994), and John Conway, *Retrospect: An Anecdotal History of Sullivan County* (1996). The history of the county after the publication of Quinlan's 1873 work is so closely tied to the railroad that two books on that subject are central: William F. Helmer, *O and W: The Long Life and Slow Death of the New York, Ontario and Western Railway* (1959), and Manville B. Wakefield, *To the Mountains by Rail* (1970). Local histories of good quality include Andrew Neiderman, *The Sesquicentennial History of Fallsburg Township* (1976), and Erna W. Elliott, *Centreville to Woodridge: The Story of a Small Community* (1976). The literature on the area's Jewish resorts and the borscht belt is voluminous. An excellent starting place is Phil Brown, ed., *In the Catskills: A Century of the Jewish Experience in "The Mountains"* (2002).

John Conway

Sulzer, William (*b* Elizabeth, NJ, 18 Mar 1863; *d* Manhattan, 6 Nov 1941). Governor. Born of German and Scotch-Irish parents, Sulzer studied law at Columbia and passed the bar exam in 1884. After joining Tammany Hall, he represented an East Side district in Manhattan in the New York State Assembly from 1890 to 1894 and was Speaker in 1893. In November 1894 he was elected to the US Congress and served until 1912. He supported progressive labor legislation, opposed (as chairman of the House Committee on Foreign Affairs from 1910 to 1912) intervention in the Mexican Revolution, and supported efforts to force the Russian government to honor American passports issued to Jews. Elected governor of New York State in November 1912 with Tammany support, he then broke with Tammany, had several Tammany politicians investigated for graft, and pushed for an open primary law. On 13 Aug 1913 Tammany boss Charles F. Murphy had the assembly impeach Sulzer, notably for filing false campaign contribution records. Indeed, Sulzer had not reported about $60,000 in contributions and had used $40,000 of that money to play the stock market. He was found guilty on 17 October and removed from office. Anti-Tammany outrage was strong, and the following November Sulzer was elected assemblyman for the Progressive Party. Failing to gain that party's nomination for governor in 1914, he was nominated by the American Party, a short-lived party founded in 1914 by independent Democrats in New York State, and endorsed by the Prohibition Party. Receiving only 126,270 votes out of 1.49 million cast, he withdrew from active politics, declining the American Party's nomination for president in 1916. He lived in Greenwich Village in Manhattan and practiced law.

Biographical Directory of the US Congress, http://bioguide.congress.gov/scripts/biodisplay.pl?index=S001065

Dunne, John R., and Michael A. L. Balboni, "New York's Impeachment Law and the Trial of Governor William Sulzer: A Case for Reform," *Fordham Urban Law Journal* 15 (1986–87): 567–93

Wesser, Robert F. "Impeachment of a Governor: William Sulzer and the Politics of Excess," *New York History* 60 (Oct 1979): 407–38

Thomas Reimer

summer camps. New York State has been in the forefront of the children's summer camp movement since its beginnings in the late 19th century. Summer camp is defined as a residential educational program for children, and traditionally camps have been located in rural areas, primarily the Adirondacks and Catskills. Camp Dudley, considered the oldest boys' camp still operating in the nation, was founded in 1885 and moved to its location on Lake Champlain in 1892. Nearly 300 camps have existed in the Adirondacks alone. In the early 21st century that region boasts nearly 70, with more than 700 overnight camps statewide. Over the years the number of children attending has varied in line with general prosperity and changes in educational theory. Camps differ in size, accommodating anywhere from 40 to 400 children. The Canadian naturalist and illustrator Ernest Thompson Seton's interpretation of American Indian life in his Woodcraft Indian movement was particularly influential as a model for camp lifestyles. The council fires, totem poles, and Indian names of many camps are Seton's lasting mark. The early camps strongly emphasized woodcraft and outdoor exercise, but team sports, crafts, drama, and music soon became integral parts of most camp programs.

The idea of isolating a group of children in a community close to nature was originally conceived as a way of invigorating American boys so that as adults they could continue to run the country in the face of increasing "unproductive" leisure time and competition from immigrants. The movement was also fueled by America's faith in scientific parenting and education. The most rigorous period for founding camps was from about 1910 to 1930, a period of prosperity and great enthusiasm for the principles of the progressive educational movement. Urban philanthropic groups established camps for their city's underprivileged children, and the Fresh Air Fund, founded in 1877, became the most well known provider of charity camping. Jewish educators were particularly energetic in establishing their own camps, as Jewish children were not welcome in most camps until well into the 20th century. In the Adirondacks Jewish camps were generally secular, while closer to New York City many of them camps consciously worked at creating a strong Jewish community and teaching religious values and doctrine.

Children's camps in New York State fall into two major categories: private for-profit ventures and camps run by nonprofit groups. The former tend to provide summer-long (or, since the mid–20th century, month-long) sessions and emphasize interpersonal skills as much as woodcraft or sports. Camps affiliated with an organization are less expensive, have shorter sessions, and typically focus more on the instruction of skills or promotion of the organization's goals. The Boy Scouts of America and the Campfire Girls, both founded in 1910, and the YMCA, which began taking boys camping as early as the 1860s, embraced camping because it was well suited to their aims. In the mid- and late 20th century, evangelical Christian groups, educators working with children with special needs, physical education instructors, music educators, and the Department of Environmental Conservation adopted the camp model to isolate children for intensive learning experiences. Summer camps are regulated by New York State and must comply with state health codes.

Cohen, Daniel. "Outdoor Sojourn: A Brief History of the Summer Camp in the United States." In *A Worthy Use of Summer: Jewish Summer Camping in America*, ed. Jenna Weissman Joselit and Karen S. Mittelman (Philadelphia: National Museum of American Jewish History, 1993)
Eleanor Eells' History of Organized Camping: The First 100 Years (Martinsville, Ind: American Camping Association, 1986)

Hallie E. Bond

Summer Hill. Town (pop 1,098) in SE Cayuga Co. Settled in 1797, the town was formed from Locke as Plato in 1831; the name was changed to Summer Hill in 1832. In the 19th century it was a dairying and maple sugaring area. About one-sixth of the town became public forestland after the New York State Hewitt Reforestation Act in 1929. Summer Hill was the birthplace of Pres Millard Fillmore (1800–1874) and of Elbridge Gerry Spaulding (1809–97), mayor of Buffalo and later congressman from New York State. In 2003 most residents work in Cortland, Ithaca, Auburn, or Syracuse.

Gregory Reed

Summit. Town (pop 1,123) in SW Schoharie Co. Settled after the Revolution by New Englanders and Dutch migrants from the Hudson Valley, the town was formed from Jefferson and Cobleskill in 1819. A hilly upland, its central ridge is the divide between the Mohawk and Susquehanna Rivers, with beautiful vistas overlooking Summit Lake and the Charlotte River valley. Charlotteville Seminary (1850–75), also known as People's College, was a Methodist boarding school with a peak enrollment of 1,253 students in 1854. Once dominated by dairy farming and quarrying, Summit is known in the early 21st century for excellent hunting, fishing, and winter sports.

Peter Johnson and Dawn Johnson

Sun. Daily newspaper launched 3 Sept 1833 by job printer Benjamin Day "to lay before the public, at a price within the means of everyone *All the News of the Day.*" It was New York City's first penny paper when others were 6¢ and the first to be hawked by newsboys on the street. Immediately successful, it emphasized human-interest stories and achieved some notoriety for the "Moon hoax" in August 1835, when it published a series of articles purporting to relate details of lunar flora and fauna as seen through a giant telescope. Day sold it in 1838 to Moses Beach. Beach's heirs in turn sold it to Charles A. Dana and several associates in 1868. Aggressive and politically independent, Dana instituted stylish writing and instructed his staff to "stir up the animals." The *Sun* swung back and forth between attacking and backing William M. "Boss" Tweed. In 1872 the *Sun* exposed the politically scandalous Crédit Mobilier contracts with the Union Pacific Railroad Co and in 1888 published Jacob Riis's photos of life in city slums. When Rutherford B. Hayes defeated Samuel J. Tilden for president in 1876, despite getting fewer popular votes, the paper called him the "Fraudulent President" and lost circulation.

By 1883 it grew again into the largest newspaper in America, regularly exceeding 150,000 and occasionally more than 200,000. Dana dominated the city's newspapers for a time but was eventually overwhelmed in competition with Joseph Pulitzer's *World.* In 1887 Dana launched the *Evening Sun,* another penny-paper success. One of the nation's best remembered editorials appeared in 1897 when Frank P. Church responded to an 8-year-old girl's letter with a column that began, "Yes, Virginia, there is a Santa Claus." William C. Reick purchased the *Sun* papers in 1911 and sold them in 1916 to grocery tycoon Frank A. Munsey, who discontinued the morning paper. Scripps-Howard bought the *Sun* in 1950 and merged it with the *World-Telegram.* On 16 Apr 2002 a group of 15 investors launched a new paper, the *New York Sun,* editorially conservative with emphasis on New York City. Published Monday through Friday, it added "New York" to the old name and copied the old flag at the top of the front page.

O'Brien, Frank Michael. *The Story of "The Sun," New York: 1833–1928* (New York: D. Appleton, 1928)
Turner, Hy B. *When Giants Ruled: The Story of Park Row* (New York: Fordham Univ Press, 1999)

Richard E. Mooney

Sunday schools. Sunday schools in New York State started in the late 18th century as literacy training sessions by Protestants for impoverished children and adults. By 1830, however, Sunday school instruction emphasized religious training over reading and writing, volunteer teachers had replaced paid teachers, and the schools enrolled mostly children, including the offspring of middle-class church members. Remnants of the earlier prototype continued for decades in "mission" Sunday schools located in impoverished urban neighborhoods and in rural areas lacking permanent churches or schools. But in the 1830s with the emergence of common schools, the Protestant church school—attached to a congregation or parish, staffed by volunteer teachers (most of them women), providing denominational religious instruction to the members' children, and enjoying the pastor's approving gaze—became the normative version of the Sunday school.

Evangelical Protestants in New York City were among the earliest and most successful Sunday school founders. The city's Roman Catholic and Jewish congregations established equivalents of Sunday schools but never assigned them the same central role in religious education as did Protestant groups. Evangelicals linked the creation of an educated populace to the spread of evangelical religion and made Sunday schools central to the process. Early individual endeavors soon became a trend, such as the Sunday instruction that former slave Catherine (Katy) Ferguson offered to poor neighbors and almshouse residents in the 1790s, or the 1803 school in which Isabella Marshall Graham taught religion alongside her daughter Joanna Graham Bethune. The growth of the Methodist denomination spurred interest in Sunday schools, as devotees employed the institution both to instruct their own children and to evangelize non-Methodists. By 1815 Sunday schools had begun to spread to towns and villages across the state. Using religious texts to teach literacy on the Lord's day, these endeavors combined religion and reading (and occasionally writing) instruction in ways that especially met the needs of African American New Yorkers.

Sunday schools proliferated with the formation of evangelical Sunday school associations, societies, and unions. Groups such as the Female Union Society for the Promotion of Sabbath Schools (1816), the New-York Sunday-School

Union Society (1816), and the Utica-based Western Sunday School Union (1825) worked with evangelical denominations to encourage the schools' growth, held teachers meetings, distributed books and teaching materials, collected statistics, and sponsored missionaries. Once the Philadelphia-based American Sunday School Union emerged in 1824, evangelical Sunday school workers had a clearinghouse for information and a source of books, periodicals, curricular materials, and missionaries. By 1826 Sunday school unions in 17 New York counties, including some 360 schools, were affiliated with the American Sunday School Union; by 1832, the Philadelphia group claimed about 2,700 New York State Sunday schools as affiliates. In the era before the Civil War, the New York City and Western New York unions were by far the largest and most active in the state. The Western New-York Sunday School Union's book depository was a crucial supply point for library and curricular materials going to upstate schools as well as to those in Ohio and points west. Men stationed as missionaries in cities and towns such as Canandaigua (Ontario Co), Utica, and Ithaca circulated throughout their regions founding Sunday schools and supplying the American Sunday School Union with information, book orders, and publishable anecdotes.

During the mid–19th century, as denominational interests increasingly seemed to conflict with the American Sunday School Union's interests, Protestant denominational organizations and teachers conventions assumed greater prominence and leadership among Sunday school workers in the state. As early as 1816 the Methodists had formed their own "branch" of the New-York Sunday School Union; in 1827 they split off completely, forming the Methodist Episcopal Sunday School Union. The Protestant Episcopal Sunday School Union, also based in New York City, emerged in 1827. The growing importance of Sunday schools in recruiting new church members, combined with denominational and sectional tensions in the antebellum years, subtly shifted the balance of leadership between cross-denominational and denominational associations. In 1835 sectarian infighting destroyed the Western Sunday School Union; in 1842 the American Sunday School Union closed its depository in Utica, though it continued to send missionaries to the more remote parts of the state, such as the Adirondacks and the North Country. In New York City the New-York Sunday School Union increasingly focused its labors on mission schools, leaving church Sunday schools to the care of the denominations; in 1868 the members changed its name to the New York Sunday School Missionary Association. After the Civil War, when newly popular teachers conventions replaced cross-denominational organizations as the forum of choice for sharing teaching methods, the New York State Sunday School Teachers' Association, founded in 1855, became the state's leading Sunday school organization. National Sunday school teachers institutes, the first of which met in 1873 at Chautauqua Lake, inspired the formation of both the Chautauqua Institution and the National Woman's Christian Temperance Union. The increasing 20th-century emphasis on the professionalization of Sunday School instruction could be found in the Religious Education Association (1903) and the International Council of Religious Education (1950). At the turn of the 21st century, although Sunday school attendance has declined overall, most Protestant congregations in New York State still consider Sunday schools key elements in their collective mission.

Boylan, Anne M. *Sunday School: The Formation of an American Institution, 1790–1880* (New Haven: Yale Univ Press, 1988)

Lynn, Robert W., and Wright, Elliott. *The Big Little School: Sunday Child of American Protestantism* (New York: Harper & Row, 1971)

Rice, Edwin W. *The Sunday-School Movement, 1780–1917, and the American Sunday-School Union, 1817–1917* (Philadelphia: American Sunday School Union, 1917)

Wellman, Judith. "The Burned-Over District Revisited: Benevolent Reform and Abolition in Mexico, Paris, and Ithaca, New York, 1825–1842" (PhD diss, Univ of Virginia, 1974)

Anne M. Boylan

sunksquaws [Sunk Squaws]. The term comes from the Algonquian word *sauncksquuaog*, which Roger Williams translated to mean queen or female ruler. Some were the wives or widows of sachems, but others held power through the force of their personalities. Contrary to many interpretations of women's roles in Indian society, some held positions of prestige and authority. The best known on Long Island was Quashawam, the daughter of Wyandanch, a Montaukett sachem. She governed the Montaukett from 1664 until her death a few years later, negotiating a treaty in 1665 with Richard Nicolls, the English governor of the newly established Colony of New York. Nicolls affirmed Quashawam's title to the Montaukett lands lying east of East Hampton (Suffolk Co), ending, for a time, a long-standing controversy between the Montauketts and the East Hampton officials. After her death another sunksquaw, Askickotantup, assumed a similar position of authority over the tribe.

Strong, Lara, M., and Selcuk Karabag, "Quashawam: Sunksquaw of the Montauk," *Long Island Historical Journal* 3 (Spring 1991): 189–204

John A. Strong

SUNY Albany. The oldest state-chartered public institution of higher learning in New York, the institution was founded on 7 May 1844 as the New York State Normal School to train teachers for the common (free public) schools and to award diplomas for successfully completing two years of study. The school's first principal, David Perkins Page (1844–48), established a curriculum of subject instruction and pedagogy, which survived largely until 1890. Responding to the need for teachers in the expanding secondary schools, in 1890 the Board of Regents gave the school a new mission, training secondary school teachers, and a new name, the New York State Normal College. Pres William J. Milne (1889–1914) limited instruction to pedagogy in the belief that liberal arts college graduates would enroll to learn the science of teaching. The experiment failed, and to fill classes the Normal College trained both elementary and secondary school teachers.

In December 1905 Commissioner of Education Andrew S. Draper convinced the Regents to reorganize the school into a four-year liberal arts college. Dedicated exclusively to training secondary school teachers and administrators, the Normal College awarded undergraduate arts, sciences, and pedagogy degrees, adding its first master's program in 1913. A year later the school was renamed the New York State College for Teachers. Under Presidents Abram R. Brubacher (1915–39) and Evan R. Collins (1949–69), the school expanded its faculty and raised student requirements, becoming one of the foremost teacher training colleges in the state. Absorbed into SUNY in 1949, the school was renamed the State University College of Education at Albany (1959), the State University College at Albany (1961), and the State University of New York at Albany (SUNYA) (1962); it was designated by SUNY as a University Center in 1962.

The school grew rapidly during the 1960s and moved most programs to a large, new Edward Durell Stone–designed campus between Western and Washington Aves; some programs remain based at the original downtown campus. The student population increased from 2,248 in 1960 to 8,982 in 1970. A college of arts and sciences and professional schools of education, business, criminal justice, library (subsequently information) science, nursing, public affairs and policy, and social welfare were created and/or merged with SUNYA, most offering graduate programs. But contraction during the 1970s caused the loss of several academic programs, including the School of Nursing.

The university, known since the mid-1980s as the University of Albany, SUNY, began expanding again under Presidents Vincent O'Leary (1977–90), H. Patrick Swygert (1990–95), and Karen R. Hitchcock (1995–2004). It created the School of Public Health in 1985, restored lost doctoral programs, acquired a third campus in East Greenbush (Rensselaer Co) in 1996, developed sites for incubator industries in biotechnology and thin film technology, and is conducting a major building campaign. Cooperation agreements in the early 21st century with companies like International Sematech reflect the school's continuing expansion into the realm of technology research and development. In 2003 the University Center enrolled 17,426 students—11,953 undergraduates and 5,473 graduates—and offered 64 undergraduate, 84 master's, and 39 doctoral degree programs.

Birr, Kendall A. *A Tradition of Excellence: The Sesquicentennial History of the University at Albany, State University of New York, 1844–1994* (Virginia Beach, Va: Donning, 1994)

French, William Marshall, and Florence Smith French. *College of the Empire State: A Centennial History of the New York State College for Teachers at Albany* [?Albany: 1944]

Geoffrey P. Williams

SUNY Alfred. In 1908 the state legislature established the New York State School of Agriculture to serve the needs of the agriculture industry in Western New York and the Southern Tier. Originally a part of Alfred University, the school became the New York State Agricultural and Technical College at Alfred in 1941 and seven years later moved to its own nearby campus as a junior college in the newly formed SUNY system. Two long-serving presidents were instrumental in the growth of SUNY Alfred. Paul Orvis (1936–60), a leader of technical education in the state, increased enrollment, broadened program offerings, and integrated the college into the SUNY system. David Huntington (1964–86) presided over the construction of many campus buildings and expanded the vocational studies program. During the administration of William Rezak (1993–2003), the college strengthened its educational emphasis in technology, began to grant four-year baccalaureate degrees, and was renamed Alfred State College. In the early 21st century the school offers 12 baccalaureate degrees in engineering, information, and construction technologies; about 3,400 students are enrolled in agriculture, allied health, business, engineering, liberal arts and sciences, and vocational technology programs.

Hritz, Elaine B. *The First 60 Years: A History of the State University Agricultural and Technical College at Alfred* (Alfred, NY: The College, 1971)

Thomas H. Rasmussen

SUNY Binghamton. Triple Cities College in Endicott (Broome Co), the predecessor to Binghamton University, opened in 1946 as a branch of Syracuse University to educate returning veterans. Its president, Glenn G. Bartle, soon realized that Syracuse would not be able to support the college indefinitely. After two years of lobbying by local leaders, the college was accepted into the SUNY system in 1950, and the name was changed to Harpur College in honor of Robert R. Harpur, settler of Harpursville (Broome Co). Harpur College's distinction as one of only two liberal arts colleges in the SUNY system (the other, Champlain College in Plattsburgh, closed in 1953) affected its early growth. Bartle dreamed of creating a "public Swarthmore" and put in place a rigorous general education curriculum, hired top-quality faculty, and raised the standards of the school throughout the 1950s. In 1961 the campus moved to Vestal (Broome Co). By 1965, the year it became a university center, Bartle's small, undergraduate, liberal arts college was lost as the school added a graduate program, enrolled thousands of additional students, and changed its name to SUNY Binghamton. Soon after, four professional schools were added to expand the school's mission. The Decker School of Nursing was established in 1968; the School of Education and Human Development started as two separate programs in 1967 and was renamed in 1987; the School of Advanced Technology was begun in 1967 and was renamed the Thomas J. Watson School of Engineering and Applied Science in 1983; the School of Business was begun in 1970 and was renamed the School of Management in 1971. Since the late 1960s, 19 specialized research centers have been established. In 1985 the Anderson Center for the Arts was completed. Binghamton became increasingly more selective in admissions, earning a reputation as a public alternative to the Ivy League. In 1993 the school's name was changed to Binghamton University. In 2002 just under 13,000 students attended, 9,800 of them undergraduates. A significant part of the student body is from New York City and Long Island, and an increasing number are international students.

McFee, Michele. *The Cornerstone: A History of Harpur College* (Binghamton: Harpur College of Arts and Sciences, 2000)

Michele A. McFee

SUNY Brockport. Founded in 1841 as the nonsectarian Brockport Collegiate Institute in Brockport (Monroe Co), an Erie Canal boomtown 18 miles (29 km) west of Rochester. Struggling financially in its first two decades, the school was rescued by New York State, which converted it into one of the state's first normal schools, Brockport State Normal School, in 1866. Along with the other normal schools, it was granted collegiate status in 1942 by the Board of Regents and became Brockport State Teachers College. In 1948 it joined the fledgling SUNY system. A liberal arts curriculum was offered to transfer students first in 1963, then to freshmen in 1965. Also in 1965 the new president, Dr. Albert W. Brown, revised the existing plans for modest growth using large numbers of transfer students and then increased numbers of freshmen to double the projected enrollment in 1970. By the early 1970s SUNY Brockport was taking more transfers than any other school in the SUNY system. Enrollment grew from 3,353 students in 1965 to 11,696 in 1975 but declined in the late 1970s as the number of high school graduates in New York State, especially in Western New York, decreased and as other colleges and universities began to court transfer students aggressively. In 2002 enrollment was 5,797 full-time and 2,707 part-time students, mostly from the greater Rochester region, and was approximately 56% female.

Dedman, W. Wayne. *Cherishing This Heritage: The Centennial History of the State University College at Brockport, New York* (New York: Appleton-Century-Crofts, 1969)

W. Bruce Leslie and Kenneth P. O'Brien

SUNY Buffalo. Public university. The University of Buffalo (UB) was founded in 1846 as a private, nonsectarian university under a charter from New York State. Millard Fillmore, one of the founders of the university, served as chancellor from 1846 until his death in 1874. Though intended by its founders to be a comprehensive university, the Medical Department (now the School of Medicine and Biomedical Sciences) was the only functioning part of the university until it was joined by the School of Pharmacy in 1886. The university graduated its first woman physician in 1876 and the first African American in 1880. The School of Law, founded as part of Niagara University in 1887, became part of UB in 1891. The Medical Department of Niagara University, chartered in 1883, merged with UB in 1898. The School of Dentistry (now the School of Dental Medicine) was added in 1892. The School of Pedagogy existed from 1895 to 1898. In 1898 Roswell Park was largely responsible for establishing a cancer research laboratory in the medical school, which is now the Roswell Park Cancer Institute. In part to support the preprofessional education of students in medicine, courses in arts and sciences were added in 1913, forming the basis of the undergraduate College of Arts and Sciences.

In 1920 local citizens raised a $5 million endowment for the university, facilitating the move of most of the schools from several locations in downtown Buffalo to a new campus, formerly occupied by the Erie County Hospital, on the eastern boundary of Buffalo. In 1922 noted educator Samuel P. Capen became the first full-time chancellor of the university. During Capen's administration (1922–50), several new schools were added: the Evening Session, later renamed Millard Fillmore College (1922), the Schools of Management (1927), Education (1931), Social Work (1935), Nursing (1940), and Engineering (1946), and the Graduate School (1939). In the 1950s under the leadership of Chancellor Clifford C. Furnas, UB became increasingly committed to medical and scientific research. In 1962, partially because of the difficulty in raising money to support the university's programs, UB became part of the SUNY system to become one of the four SUNY University Centers. The merger brought a rapid expansion of students and faculty, from 14,360 full-time and part-time students in 1961–62 to 21,588 in spring 1970. Between 1966 and 1970 there were numerous campus protests over the war in Vietnam, culminating in spring 1970 with police on campus, the arrest of 45 members of the faculty, and the early closing of the school in May. Schools added after the SUNY merger included the School of Health Related Professions (1965), Library and Information Sciences (1966), and Architecture (1968). Ground was broken for a new campus in Amherst (Erie Co) in 1968, and the first buildings on the new North Campus opened in 1973. The older South Campus (Main St) is used primarily for the schools in the health sciences. In 2000 SUNY Buffalo had 24,830 students.

Anderson, G. Lester. "The Story of an Educational Merger: The State University of New York and the University of Buffalo," *Niagara Frontier* 18 (Winter 1971): 72–84

Park, Julian. "A History of the University of Buffalo," *Publications of the Buffalo Historical Society* 22 (1917): 1–87

Siggelkow, Richard A. *Dissent and Disruption: A University under Siege* (Buffalo: Prometheus Books, 1991)

Christopher Densmore

SUNY Buffalo School of Medicine and Biomedical Sciences. The Medical Department of the University of Buffalo was founded in 1846 as the first component of the University of Buffalo. Its creators were James Platt White, Austin Flint, Frank Hastings Hamilton, and Millard Fillmore, the school's first chancellor. Physiology, pathology, anatomy, obstetrics-gynecology, surgery, medicine, and pharmacology were the seven original chairs. Competition from Niagara University Medical School stimulated major growth and development between 1883 and 1898, when the two medical schools merged. Also in 1898 the New York State Pathological Laboratory (now Roswell Park Cancer Institute) was founded at the university. Five of the school's medical professors, led by Matthew D. Mann, operated on Pres William McKinley after he was mortally wounded at the Pan-American Exposition in 1901. The university first offered liberal arts courses in 1913 to meet the premedical education requirements of the American Medical Association, and these courses became the foundation for the College of Arts of Sciences. In 1962 the University of Buffalo and the School of Medicine joined the SUNY system. There were 574 medical students enrolled in 2001–2, and the medical school was affiliated with nearly a dozen hospitals.

Batt, Ronald E., et al. *Another Era: A Pictorial History of the School of Medicine and Biomedical Sciences, State University of New York at Buffalo, 1846–1996* (Virginia Beach, Va: Donning, 1996)

Ronald E. Batt

SUNY Buffalo State. Opened in 1871 as Buffalo Normal School, it was a training ground for public school teachers. It became a degree-granting institution in 1925 and changed its name to State College for Teachers at Buffalo in 1928. In 1931 the college moved to its current site, a 115-acre (46.5 ha) urban campus near Delaware Park and what is now Albright-Knox Art Gallery. The institution joined the newly formed SUNY system in 1948, retaining its character as a teachers college. It was reorganized as a liberal arts college in 1962, taking the name State University College at Buffalo. The college is home to the Burchfield-Penney Art Center, boasts a noted program in art conservation, and maintains the Great Lakes Center for Environmental Research and Education. Known since 1998 as Buffalo State, SUNY, it enrolled 9,500 undergraduates (1,500 part-time) and over 2,000 graduate students (1,200 part-time) in 2001.

Aiken, John R. *A History of Community: State University College at Buffalo, 1871–1996* (Buffalo: Buffalo State College Foundation, 1996)

John Aiken

SUNY Canton. Technology college. The school traces its roots to the State School of Agriculture at St. Lawrence University (1906), the first state-sponsored, two-year, postsecondary college in the state. In 1937 it broadened its offerings by introducing technical and industrial courses and in 1941 adopted the name New York State Agricultural and Technical Institute to reflect this. Joining the SUNY system in 1948, it expanded its mission further in 1997 when it began offering baccalaureate degrees in addition to associate degrees and one-year certificates. SUNY Canton has grown to an enrollment of approximately 2,300 students in more than 40 major programs of study. Among its most prominent majors are criminal investigation, engineering technology, veterinary science, technology, business, mortuary science, and nursing.

Howland, C. *Seventy Years of Change: A History of the State University of New York Agricultural and Technical College at Canton* (Ogdensburg, NY: Ryan Press, 1976)

Carl A. Westerdahl and Susan S. Clarke

SUNY Cobleskill. Technology college. The school started as the Schoharie State School of Agriculture in 1916. Programs in home economics, food service, hospitality administration, and early childhood education were added later. From 1920 to 1931 the college also offered a rural teacher training program. In 1948 it became part of SUNY and as such was renamed SUNY Agricultural and Technical College at Cobleskill. In the early 1950s its agriculture division evolved into the business division. In 1987 the school was renamed SUNY College of Agriculture and Technology at Cobleskill and since 1988 has awarded bachelor's degrees. In 1996 SUNY founded the University Colleges of Technology (UCT) sector, which links SUNY Cobleskill with the system's other colleges of agriculture and technology and other special technology colleges. In 2000 the college enrolled 2,173 full-time and 154 part-time students.

SUNY Cobleskill, http://www.cobleskill.edu

Carl A. Westerdahl and Susan S. Clarke

SUNY College of Ceramics at Alfred University. Founded in 1900 as the New York State School of Clayworking and Ceramics, it is the first institution of higher learning to combine the study of ceramic art and science. Alfred University in Allegany Co was chosen to host the college because the local area had quality clay deposits and a factory that produced ceramic roofing tiles. Renowned ceramist and ceramics scholar Charles Fergus Binns was director of the institution for its first 31 years. In 1932 the school's name was changed to New York State College of Ceramics at Alfred University, and in 1948 it became an original component of the SUNY system. The college comprises the School of Art and Design, whose plastic and visual arts curriculum includes a highly respected ceramic art program. It also includes the School of Ceramic Engineering and Materials Science, which boasts the nation's largest programs in ceramic and glass engineering. The International Museum of Ceramic Art was established on the Alfred campus in 1991. In the early 21st century the college serves a national and international body of approximately 700 undergraduate and 80 graduate students.

Bernstein, Melvin H. *Art and Design at Alfred: A Chronicle of a Ceramics College* (Philadelphia: Art Alliance Press, 1986)
McHale, Anna E. *Fusion: A Centennial History of the New York State College of Ceramics, 1900–2000* (Marceline, Mo: Walsworth Publishing, 2003)

Thomas H. Rasmussen

SUNY College of Environmental Science and Forestry. The college was founded by act of legislation in 1911 as the New York State College of Forestry at Syracuse University. Although chartered to investigate issues related to forestry, programs expanded to include environmental science, design, engineering, life sciences, and resource management. With the formation of the State University of New York (SUNY) in 1948, the college became a specialized college of the state's system. In 1972 it was rechartered as the State University of New York College of Environmental Science and Forestry (SUNY ESF). Facilities include more than 25,000 acres (10,100 ha) in six locations. The Syracuse campus on University Hill, comprising five academic buildings and the Moon Library, houses the instructional programs for the BS, MS, MPS, MF, and PhD degrees. The Tully campus (Onondaga Co) includes the Heiberg Memorial Forest, used as a teaching laboratory as well as for research. The Wanakena campus (St. Lawrence Co) is the site of the Ranger School and grants the AAS degree for forest technicians. The Warrensburg (Warren Co), Cranberry Lake (St. Lawrence Co), and Newcomb (Essex Co) campuses, and the field stations in Syracuse and Tully continue the SUNY ESF commitment to research, academic programs, and demonstration activities. SUNY ESF maintains strong ties to Syracuse University for collaboration in instruction, use of facilities, and student support services. In 2002 SUNY ESF enrolled 1,100 undergraduates and 600 graduate students.

Armstrong, George R., ed. *Essays on the Growth and Development of New York State's College of Forestry, 1911–1961* (Buffalo: Alumni Association, 1961)

Marla A. Bennett

SUNY College of Optometry. A professional school founded in Manhattan in 1971 by an act of the New York State legislature and the only institution of its type in the state. In 1975 State University of New York College of Optometry (SUNYCO) acquired the Optometric Center of New York, first chartered by the New York State Board of Regents in 1956 to maintain the clinical activity, research, and library of a defunct Columbia University optometry program. SUNYCO renamed the center, located at 100 East 24th St, to University Optometric, using it as a clinic and as part of the college's teaching program. In 1999 SUNYCO relocated its main facility from 100 East 24th St to the Aeolian Hall building, built in 1919 and twice renovated since then, at 33 West 42d St. SUNYCO offers MS and PhD degrees in vision science and the Doctor of Optometry (OD) professional degree. It also offers a residency program in optometry and a continuing professional education program. College components include the Schnurmacher Institute for Vision Research and the Center for Vision Care Policy. In 2002 the college enrolled 269 students.

Jeffrey Kraus

SUNY College of Technology at Farmingdale. Founded in 1912 as the New York State School of Agriculture and located on the Nassau Co and Suffolk Co border, it is the oldest public college on suburban Long Island. Its curriculum has mirrored the region's change from rural/agrarian to suburban/postindustrial. Director Halsey B. Knapp (1923–56) guided the institution to prominence in agricultural and technical education. It became part of the SUNY system in 1948 as SUNY Agricultural and Technical Institute. The agricultural curriculum ended in 1987, and the school became a four-year college in 1993. By the beginning of the 21st century, the college offered over 40 programs in liberal arts, science, engineering, biotechnology, health sciences, human services, and business. The school's Broad Hollow Bioscience Park, located at its main entrance, opened in 2000 in partnership with Cold Spring Harbor Laboratory to construct incubators in biotechnology, software, and other technologies. The college, commonly known as SUNY Farmingdale, enrolled 5,492 students in 2001–2.

Cavaioli, Frank J. *State University of New York at Farmingdale* (Charleston, SC: Arcadia Publishing, 1999)

Frank J. Cavaioli

SUNY Cortland. State university college. In 1866 when Cortland pledged land and nearly $100,000 to induce the state to establish a normal school, the property of Cortlandville Academy (1828) was turned over to the New York State Normal and Training School at Cortland, which opened in 1869. It drew its student body predominantly from Central New York. A 1919 fire resulted in the rebuilding of the school at its present location four years later. The school's emphasis on physical education was a result of a 1916 state law mandating exercise by schoolchildren over 8 years old. Since competent teachers were needed, Cortland initiated a pioneer program in 1922. In 1942 the school became a college offering bachelor degrees as the New York State Teachers College at Cortland. With enrollment passing 1,000 for the first time, it was incorporated into the new SUNY system in 1948. It assumed its present name in 1960. The campus elementary school closed in 1982 after 113 years. In the early 21st century, the college offered degrees in 46 majors, including elementary, secondary, and physical education, and had an enrollment of approximately 5,000 undergraduates and 1,200 graduate students.

Ralston, Leonard F. *Cortland College: An Illustrated History* (Cortland: Alumni Association of Cortland College, 1991)

Cathy A. Barber

SUNY Delhi. Technology college. The school began in 1913 as the State School for Agriculture and Domestic Science with an initial mission of providing trained farmworkers, carpenters, and builders to address regional labor force shortages. By 1941 a more diversified curriculum resulted in its renaming as the New York State Agricultural and Technical Institute at Delhi. In 1948 the college joined SUNY and in 1964 adopted its current name. New programs were introduced in practical nursing (1943), hotel technology (1957), business technology (1958), veterinary science (1961), liberal arts (1970), golf course operation (1992), and culinary arts (2001). In 2002 more than 2,000 students were enrolled in over 40 academic programs.

SUNY Delhi, http://www.delhi.edu

Carl A. Westerdahl and Susan S. Clarke

SUNY Downstate Medical Center. Located in Brooklyn, this institution dates from 1856 when two German physicians established the Brooklyn German General Dispensary in Brooklyn Heights. It soon expanded to become St. John's Hospital to reflect the changing immigrant population of the day. Other prominent Brooklyn physicians joined St. John's Hospital, which was rechartered in 1858 as the Long Island College Hospital, where medical teaching was brought to the hospital bedside. This method of teaching was practiced in Europe at the time, but the Long Island College Hospital became the first teaching hospital in the country. On 29 Mar 1860 the faculty, who had been chosen from a national search, offered the first course of study. In 1931 the school was rechartered as Long Island College of Medicine, the hospital remained Long Island College Hospital, and both began operating under separate administrative bodies. On 5 Apr 1950 the school became a unit in the recently formed SUNY system, and a new campus was opened on a site adjacent to Kings County Hospital in 1956. The Long Island College Hospital continued to operate as a voluntary facility in Brooklyn Heights. In 1966 the School of Graduate Studies, the College of Health Related Professions, the College of Nursing, and the 375-bed University Hospital were opened. In 1992 Downstate Medical Center opened the Arthur Ashe Institute for Urban Health, which focuses on urban healthcare issues by studying Brooklyn's diverse ethnic population. Downstate Medical Center is the focal point of a health education network that encompasses 26 hospitals, a 13-acre (5.3 ha) campus, a student body of 1,500, a faculty of 3,500 (including full-time, part-time, and volunteer staff), and support staff of 3,000. In 1998 one of its researchers, Dr Robert F. Furchgott, received the Nobel Prize in medicine.

Downstate Medical Center. *Medical Education in Brooklyn: The First 100 Years, 1860–1960* (Brooklyn: 1960)
Termine, Jack E. *SUNY Downstate Medical Center* (Dover, NH: Arcadia Publishing, 2000)

Jack E. Termine

SUNY Empire State College. Founded in 1971 with the help of grants from the Carnegie Corp and the Ford Foundation, and headquartered in Saratoga Springs, the college provides alternatives to undergraduate classroom-based education. It offers a liberal arts curriculum, including degree programs in business and community and human services. Distinct features are individualized degree programs, learning contracts, and assessments of college-level experiential learning for credit. In Saratoga Springs in 1979 the Center for Distance Learning opened, facilitating students' distance work with faculty and tutors using print-based materials, the telephone, the Internet, and on-line courses. The college also has degree-granting programs in Cyprus, Lebanon, Greece, and the Czech Republic for foreign and US students, and since 1983 has offered master's programs. Empire State College has over 40 locations across the state; the typical student is between 25 and 60 years old. By 2001 the college had 2,313 full-time and 6,082 part-time students.

Bonnabeau, Richard F. *The Promise Continues: Empire State College—The First 25 Years* (Virginia Beach, Va: Donning, 1996)

Richard F. Bonnabeau

SUNY Fredonia. In 1866 the state legislature authorized four normal schools for teacher training, and Fredonia (Chautauqua Co) citizens raised funds to bid successfully for one of them. The cornerstone for Fredonia Normal School was laid on 8 Aug 1867 on the campus of the former Fredonia Academy, and classes began four months later. Students had their tuition, books, and travel expenses paid. In 1900 fire destroyed most of the school's building, which was replaced (1901–3). The school began a new campus in 1939, renamed Fredonia State Teachers College in 1942, and acquired student housing in 1946. Fredonia joined the SUNY system in 1948, adopted a liberal arts curriculum in 1951, and was accredited in 1952. Dr Oscar E. Lanford became president in 1961; under his leadership Fredonia entered an aggressive building phase, expanded the curriculum, and increased enrollment. In 2000 SUNY Fredonia had over 205 full-time faculty, 90% holding doctorates. Over 5,000 students studied in more than 50 undergraduate and graduate programs. The school is particularly well known for its music, theater, and education programs.

Chazanof, William. "From Academy to State University: Fredonia's Story" [?1968]. Reed Library, SUNY Fredonia

Pam Kirst

SUNY Geneseo. Public liberal arts college. The school traces its origins to 1867, when the New York State legislature passed an act authorizing the opening of a teacher training school in the Village of Geneseo (Livingston Co), and the Wadsworth Normal and Training School opened in 1871. In 1942 it became the State Teachers College at Geneseo, in 1948 became an original campus in the SUNY system, and in 1962 changed its name to SUNY College at Geneseo. The school lies on 220 acres (89 ha) with 39 buildings and 15 residence halls and a campus sloping downhill toward the Genesee River. In addition to its long-standing mission of educating primary, secondary, and special education teachers, Geneseo has strong majors in the humanities, sciences, fine arts, and social sciences as well as professional programs in business and communicative disorders and sciences. In 2003 it offered 48 undergraduate and 6 graduate programs catering to 4,950 full-time undergraduate and some 50 graduate students.

Cook, William. *Celebrating Our Past: Livingston County in the 20th Century* (Geneseo, NY: Livingston County Board of Supervisors, 2000)

William R. Cook

SUNY Health Science Center at Brooklyn School of Medicine. See SUNY DOWNSTATE MEDICAL CENTER.

SUNY Health Science Center at Syracuse. See SUNY UPSTATE MEDICAL UNIVERSITY.

SUNY Institute of Technology. Founded in 1966 to meet the needs of area students from two-year institutions to complete bachelor's degrees in professional and technical disciplines, the institute first offered classes in Utica, Rome (Oneida Co), and Herkimer. In the 1980s it expanded its academic programs and moved to a new campus on North Horatio St in Marcy (Oneida Co), north of Utica. It offers 20 undergraduate and 11 graduate degree programs, with many courses and some degree programs offered on-line. About 2,600 students were enrolled in 2000.

SUNY Institute of Technology, http://www.sunyit.edu

Carl A. Westerdahl and Susan S. Clarke

SUNY Maritime College. Specialized college. The New York Nautical School opened in 1874 with classes on the East River aboard the sloop USS *St. Mary* as the first public institution for training merchant marine officers in the United States. It was supervised and funded by the New York City Board of Education but staffed by US Navy officers. The ship was used for an annual cruise from May to October and moored the rest of the year at the 23d St wharf on the East River. In summer 1934 the school was assigned a permanent campus at Fort Schuyler (Bronx Co) on the Throgs Neck peninsula; the campus was dedicated in 1938. In 1948 the college joined the SUNY system and in 1972 became coeducational. The *Empire State VI,* the current training ship, teaches students about operating a ship and about the maritime industry, visiting several foreign ports each summer. Courses include engineering, naval architecture, marine transportation and business administration, marine environmental sciences, and humanities. In 2000 the college enrolled 549 men and 116 women. In 2002 the New York State legislature for the first time appropriated funds to pay the tuition of 284 students to be sponsored by the governor and members of the legislature.

Brouwer, Norman G. "History of SUNY Maritime College, 1874–1974" (MA Thesis, SUNY Oneonta, 1977)
SUNY Maritime College, http://www.sunymaritime.edu

Carl A. Westerdahl and Susan S. Clarke

SUNY Morrisville. It was founded in 1908 as Morrisville Agricultural School, one of six state schools of agriculture, and classes began in 1910 in recently vacated county buildings and on adjacent farmland. Under the jurisdiction of the state commissioner of agriculture, it initially offered practical instruction in animal husbandry, crop production, blacksmithing, and related subjects, along with domestic science courses for women and, for a short period, teacher training classes. In 1917 the Agricultural Education Division of the State Education Department assumed control. With the addition of automobile mechanics in 1933, the offerings were broadened to include industrial education. After incorporation in the SUNY system as an institute of agriculture and technology in 1948, Morrisville began granting two-year associate degrees (1951) and in the late 20th century offered bachelor of technology degrees in several disciplines, including equine studies and automotive technology. The college is highly computer oriented: students in a majority of its programs are provided with laptops and classrooms are equipped with the latest in electronic learning systems. Approximately 3,000 students were enrolled in 2003.

Houghton, William. *State University of New York Agricultural and Technical College Morrisville, New York: History and Development, 1908–1968*

William F. Helmer

SUNY New Paltz. Public liberal arts college. Founded in 1828 as the New Paltz Classic Academy (Ulster Co), the school was reorganized as the New Paltz Academy in 1833. In 1885 it became a state normal school and opened the following year. In 1942 the school was granted the authority to award bachelor's degrees and was renamed and reorganized as the New Paltz State Teacher's College. In 1948 it joined the SUNY system. The name changed two more times between 1948 and 1994, when it became the State University of New York at New Paltz. The school is situated on a 216-acre (87 ha) campus, and the vast majority of students are New York State residents. In 2001 it offered 100 undergraduate and 50 graduate programs to 7,838 undergraduate and 6,053 graduate students.

Sarah E. DeSanctis

SUNY Old Westbury. Public college. Founded in 1965, the school acquired the former F. Ambrose Clark estate in Old Westbury, 604 acres (244 ha) of wooded and open land, and began campus development. Classes began in 1968 at the Planting Fields, the former William R. Coe estate, in Oyster Bay (Nassau Co). The college closed in 1970, reorganized, and reopened in 1971 at its present location. Part of the school's mission is to serve a diverse and underserved population, including adult and minority students, many of whom commute from New York City. The student body is roughly 57% female and 66% minorities. In the 1990s the college came under scrutiny for its low graduation rates and the deterioration of the physical plant. Dr Calvin Butts III, president since 1998, began a campaign to rebuild and reinvigorate the school. Enrollment in 2001 was approximately 2,995, with 72% attending full-time and 21% living on campus.

"Road Map for SUNY–Old Westbury: New President Outlines Plans Today," *Newsday*, 4 Sept 1998
State University of New York. *Sixty-Four Campuses: The State University of New York to 1985* (Albany: Author, 1985)
SUNY Old Westbury, http://www.oldwestbury.edu

Laura E. Mann

SUNY Oneonta. Public, coeducational liberal arts college. Opened as a state normal school in 1889, the school changed its name to Oneonta State Teachers College (Otsego Co) in 1942. It became part of the SUNY system in 1948 and changed its name to the State University of New York College at Oneonta in 1962. The college operates a Cooperstown Graduate Program in Museum Studies (Otsego Co) with the New York State Historical Association. In 2002 Oneonta offered 68 undergraduate majors to 5,447 undergraduates and 9 graduate programs to 251 graduate students. The main campus covers 250 acres (101 ha).

Brush, Carey Wentworth. *In Honor and Good Faith: A History of the State University College at Oneonta, New York* (Oneonta, NY: 1965)
———. *In Honor and Good Faith: Completing the First Century, 1965–1990* (Oneonta, NY: 1997)

Sarah E. DeSanctis

SUNY Oswego. Edward Austin Sheldon, superintendent of Oswego public schools, founded Oswego Primary Teachers Training School with city funds in 1861. The school received state funding beginning in 1863, and by March 1867 ownership of the Oswego State Normal and Training School's building and grounds transferred to New York State. Sheldon remained principal until his death in 1897. During his tenure Oswego became known for using object teaching methods, adapted from Swiss educator Johann Pestalozzi, whereby children learn through firsthand knowledge of objects rather than solely through textbooks. The 19th-century student was typically female, and programs usually lasted two years. Oswego competed with high schools for students. In 1913 the school moved to its current campus by Lake Ontario but by then had lost its preeminence in teacher education to university-based departments and schools of education in larger cities. Nevertheless the transformation from normal school to university had begun: it required high school diplomas for admission (1905), moved to three-year courses of study (1929), and separated liberal arts classes from instructional methods classes (1934). By 1939 the legislature permitted Oswego to issue four-year degrees, and in 1942 it became Oswego State Teachers College. Part of the SUNY system since 1948, it widened degree offerings beyond teacher education in 1962 as a college of arts and sciences. As of 1999 enrollment was 6,435 full-time and 1,365 part-time students in a variety of programs at the bachelor's and master's levels.

Rogers, Dorothy. *Oswego: Fountainhead of Teacher Education; A Century in the Sheldon Tradition* (New York: Appleton-Century-Crofts, 1961)

Jim Carl

SUNY Plattsburgh. The New York State Normal and Training School at Plattsburgh, also known as Plattsburgh Normal School (PNS), opened in 1890 and provided professionally skilled teachers for area schools. Among the original 12 faculty members were George Hawkins (principal, 1898–1933) and George Hudson, a distinguished science educator. Hawkins expanded the curriculum into pedagogy on business subjects and teacher training summer institutes. Principal Charles Ward (1933–52) developed a home economics education program in 1937 and officer training courses and a new nursing program during World War II. In 1942 PNS became Plattsburgh State Teacher's College with a four-year curriculum. Graduate studies in education and home economics were available by 1947. It became an original unit of SUNY in 1948. As SUNY College of Arts and Sciences at Plattsburgh (1962), it offered a full range of liberal arts degrees. Pres George Angell (1954–74) led the school through an era of growth. Graduate programs in liberal arts subjects started in 1966. Enrollment topped 6,700 in 1975. SUNY Plattsburgh boasts many distinctive programs, including an Adirondack Experience program that takes advantage of the school's location and complements its Canadian Studies department. In 2001 the college, commonly known as Plattsburgh State, had over 700 faculty and support staff, 5,000 full-time undergraduate students, and 290 full-time graduate students.

Cooper, Frank A. *The Plattsburgh Idea in Education, 1889–1964* (Plattsburgh: Plattsburgh College Benevolent and Educational Association, 1964)
Skopp, Douglas R. *Bright with Promise: From the Normal and Training School to SUNY Plattsburgh, 1889–1989: A Pictorial History* (Norfolk, Va: Donning, 1989)

Douglas R. Skopp

SUNY Potsdam. University college. The school traces its origins to the St. Lawrence Academy (1816) in Potsdam, which became the Potsdam Normal School in 1869. Renamed Potsdam State Teachers College in 1942, it became part of SUNY in 1948. In 1947 the college was authorized to grant master's degrees and in 1962 became a liberal arts college. Its Crane School of Music, founded in 1886 as the Crane Institute of Music, was the first such school in the country to prepare music educators for teaching in the public schools. In 2002 the college enrolled about 4,000 students.

Lahey, W. Charles. *The Potsdam Tradition: A History and a Challenge* (New York: Appleton-Century-Crofts, 1966)

Carl A. Westerdahl and Susan S. Clarke

SUNY Purchase. Opening in 1971 as a four-year liberal arts institution and now part of the SUNY system, the school sits on 500 acres (202 ha) in Harrison (Westchester Co), land once the home of the American Revolutionary war hero Thomas Thomas. Following New York State's acquisition of the property in 1966, Gov Nelson A. Rockefeller directed a group of prominent architects headed by Edward Larrabee Barnes to plan the campus. Rockefeller's vision of the college was an institution of higher learning that would promote the arts as the central part of its curriculum. The campus includes the Neuberger Museum of Art (1974) and the Performing Arts Center (1978). The museum, designed by Philip Johnson, focuses on modern art and houses at the start of the 21st century over 6,000 pieces, including Jackson Pollock's *Number 8, 1949* and Willem de Kooning's *Marilyn Monroe,* as well as the work of Milton Avery, Edward Hopper, and Jacob Lawrence. In the mid-1990s SUNY Purchase changed its name to Purchase College. In 2003 the student body numbered approximately 4,000, about 55% women and 45% men. Two-thirds were enrolled in liberal arts and one-third in arts programs, which include the School of Art + Design and Conservatories of Theater Arts and Film, Music, and Dance. Famous alumni include actors Edie Falco, Parker Posey, Wesley Snipes, and Stanley Tucci, and Pulitzer Prize–winning playwright Donald Margulies.

SUNY Purchase, http://www.purchase.edu

Lisa Keller

SUNY Stony Brook. The State University College on Long Island was founded in 1957 to address the perception that the educational needs of the growing postwar population of Long Island were not being adequately met. Temporarily housed in 9 buildings on 480 acres (194 ha) of the former Gold Coast estate of William Robertson Coe in Oyster Bay (Nassau Co), its goal was to educate secondary school teachers of science and mathematics. By 1962 the mission of this school and that of SUNY itself expanded in response to a national mandate for more training in the sciences and engineering. The school's name was changed to State University of New York Long Island Center, and it began moving to Stony Brook (Suffolk Co) on land donated by philanthropist Ward Melville. At that site, the SUNY Stony Brook campus has grown to include 123 buildings on nearly 1,200 acres (490 ha). It is a major research institute in the SUNY system and co-manages the federal Brookhaven National Laboratory. The university has an engineering school, a marine sciences research center, and a health science center with its own teaching institution, University Hospital. In 2003 SUNY Stony Brook enrolled a total of 22,355 students and with over 13,500 people on its payroll was the largest single-site employer on Long Island.

Gelber, Sidney. *Politics and Public Higher Education in New York State: Stony Brook—A Case History* (New York: Peter Lang Publishing, 2001)

Marianne Rahn-Erickson

SUNY Upstate Medical University. Professor of chemistry Edward Cutbush founded the Medical Institution of Geneva College (later Hobart College) in Geneva (Ontario Co) on 15 Sep 1834, and it opened for classes in February 1835. It graduated Elizabeth Blackwell, the first woman physician, in 1849. Through the 1850s and 1860s the school, known as Geneva Medical College from 1851 to 1871, became increasingly unable to compete with urban medical schools because it lacked nearby clinical facilities. Hobart College dissolved its medical college in 1871 and sold its library and anatomical museum to Dean John Towler. Towler and professor of surgery Frederick Hyde offered to donate these assets to the one-year-old Syracuse University on condition that its trustees immediately establish a regular medical school consistent with American Medical Association standards. The offer was accepted on 4 Dec 1871. Hyde became dean and Towler professor of chemistry. The first classes of the Syracuse University College of Medicine were held in 1872 in temporary quarters at Clinton Block, next to the Erie Canal, in Syracuse. In 1875 it occupied a remodeled carriage factory on McBride St, moving in 1896 into a new building and in 1937 to another building, subsequently named after Herman Gates Weiskotten, dean from 1922 to 1951. Syracuse University sold the College of Medicine to SUNY in 1950. Known until 1953 as the SUNY College of Medicine at Syracuse, it changed its name to the SUNY Upstate Medical Center in accord with its plans to broaden degree offerings. In 1986, after adding the College of Graduate Studies (1954), the College of Nursing (1959), and the School of Allied Health Professions (now College of Health Professions, 1965), it became the SUNY Health Science Center at Syracuse to reflect more accurately the diversity of its services. In 1999 it changed to SUNY Upstate Medical University. It is the second oldest medical school operating in New York State. In 2001–2 approximately 1,100 students were enrolled.

Luft, Eric v. d. "HSC through the Years: A Pictorial Timeline," *Alumni Journal* (Syracuse Medical Alumni Association) (Winter 1998): 13–18

Eric v. d. Luft

supermarkets. Before the advent of supermarkets, New Yorkers bought their food from thousands of small, independent, "mom and pop" neighborhood grocery stores or from the uniform outlets of large retail food chains such the national leader, the Great Atlantic and Pacific Tea Co (A&P) of New York City founded in 1869. The rapid spread of supermarkets throughout the state and nation transformed food retailing in the United States by dramatically lowering prices and broadening the selection of groceries. In creating this institution, supermarket pioneers responded to the economic constraints of the Great Depression and to shifting demographic patterns brought about by the growth of suburbs and the increased use of automobiles.

Early History

It is generally acknowledged that the American supermarket was born in Jamaica (Queens Co) in August 1930 when Michael J. Cullen opened his first King Kullen Grocery Co at 171st St and Jamaica Ave. The store's policies set the pattern for many subsequent enterprises. It was a very large-scale store that advertised national brands rather than more expensive private ones; emphasized bargain prices (the store's motto was The World's Greatest Price Wrecker); relied almost exclusively on self-service, which lowered labor costs; advertised heavily in local newspapers; piled up goods in large displays; paid lower real estate costs than urban competitors; and offered plenty of free parking. The store's mass retailing strategy of profit through low markup and high volume was reinforced by its self-service format, which encouraged impulse buying, and by its orientation to car-driving shoppers, who filled their trunks with groceries, boosting sales per customer. The first King Kullen was in an abandoned garage. Many of the early supermarkets were installed in former warehouses or automobile dealerships in less-than-prime real estate districts. They attracted hordes of customers not only with prices that appealed to depression-weary customers but also with splashy advertisements and colorful promotions, such as circus animals and kiddie carnivals. Cullen opened 15 stores in the next five years and was preparing to go national when he died in 1936. His idea caught on quickly, and by 1936 there were roughly 1,200 supermarkets in the United States, many of them in New York State.

After the effects of the Great Depression lifted, supermarkets shed their rustic appearances as their owners and designers replaced wooden cartons and sawdust floors with sleek Art Deco designs, gleaming refrigerator cases, and sparkling white tiles. Although the basic supermarket formula—low markups, self-service, national brands, and an orientation toward shoppers with cars—persisted after World War II, several new trends also took hold. Most new stores were built from the ground up rather than installed in older buildings, and many were built in suburban shopping centers. In addition, store layout and product shelf positioning became much more sophisticated, a domain of a new kind of merchandising expert, and cosmetics, pharmaceuticals, housewares, toys, and other nonfood departments became commonplace in postwar supermarkets. Moreover, a growing number of supermarket corporations were publicly traded. The average size of supermarkets continued to grow rapidly, as did their parking lots.

New York City Metropolitan Area

King Kullen soon had a number of regional rivals. After several years of hesitation, A&P committed to remaking their grocery stores as supermarkets by 1937. The same year Key Food Stores Cooperative, a group of independent grocers in Brooklyn, opened its first store. The co-op helps approximately 115 (in 2002) independently owned food stores compete with larger supermarkets by pooling their resources. Most are in Brooklyn and Queens, but there are also branches in the Bronx, Staten Island, Manhattan, and Suffolk and Nassau Cos. Members include Dan's Supreme Supermarkets, Pick Quick Foods, and Man-dell Food Stores. ShopRite (1946) is another co-op. In 2003 it was the largest in the United States, with 43 stores operating under the ShopRite banner and more than 50,000 employees. It operated 34 stores in the New York City metropolitan area and was managed by the Wakefern Food Corp out of Elizabeth, NJ. D'Agostino opened its first supermarket in Manhattan at Lexington and 83d St in 1932. In 2002 it operated 20 stores in New York City and 3 in Westchester Co, with headquarters in Larchmont (Westchester Co). Daitch-Shopwell was founded in 1955 by a merger of Daitch Crystal Dairies and Shopwell Foods. By the early 1960s it had more than 100 stores in the New York City but subsequently declined and was acquired by A&P in 1986. Some of the stores now operate under the name Food Emporium. Pathmark had 55 stores in the New York City area, and Waldbaum's, one of the many chains owned by A&P, operated 77 in the state in 2003, primarily in Nassau, Suffolk, and Richmond Cos. The original supermarket chain, King Kullen, headquartered in Bethpage (Nassau Co) still thrived, with 50 stores in Nassau, Suffolk, and Richmond Cos, 4,800 employees, and $790 million in annual sales in 2002, and was still privately owned by the Cullen family.

Elsewhere in the State

In June 1933 Henry Schaffer (president of Schaffer Stores Co) opened his first Empire Market in

Schenectady, which featured the industry's first partially self-service meat and produce departments. That same year Ben and Bill Golub (family owners of Price Chopper and its chain stores) opened their Central Market one-stop-shopping store one block from Schenectady's Central Park, followed by the opening of other stores in Watervliet (Albany Co), Glens Falls (Warren Co), and North Troy (Rensselaer Co). In 2003 Price Chopper operated a total of 68 stores in New York State. In Rochester in 1917 John and Walter Wegman opened their first grocery store, the Rochester Fruit and Vegetable Co on Clinton Ave, and in 1930 their first supermarket. By 1949 Wegmans had frozen foods and vaporized water sprays to keep foods fresh. In 1968 they expanded to Syracuse and in 1977 opened their first Buffalo store. Wegmans was one of the first stores to adopt bar-code scanning (1974) and is still privately owned by the Wegman family. In 2003 it employed 32,000 people in 66 stores (51 in New York State) and had annual sales of $3.3 billion. Wegmans has stores throughout Central and Western New York, as well as the Southern Tier.

Tops Friendly Markets, with 159 stores scattered throughout Western New York, Pennsylvania, and Ohio, originated in 1921 in Niagara Falls as a small grocery store owned by Ferrante Castellani. In 1960 Tops opened its first supermarket, a 25,000 ft^2 (2,320 m^2) store on Portage Rd in Niagara Falls and by 1984 had expanded throughout Western New York and the Rochester area. In 1991 Royal Ahold, a Netherlands corporation, acquired Tops. George W. Loft (former president of Loft Candy Stores) launched a chain of supermarkets in Mount Vernon (Erie Co) around 1934. In 1941 the Grange League Federation, a purchasing and marketing cooperative for farmers, founded the Board of Directors of Cooperative P&C (producers and consumers) Markets, and in Batavia (Genesee Co) in 1942 the first P&C Foods store opened. By the late 1940s another 20 stores had been added including stores in Auburn (Cayuga Co) and Syracuse. In 1970 P&C was bought by Pneumo Dynamics Co and acquired 18 Safeway stores in upstate New York. In 1986 P&C became a public company and in 1988 was bought by the Penn Traffic Co of Johnstown, Pa, which in 1979 also bought the Jamestown-based (Chautauqua Co) Quality markets, founded in 1913. In 2003 there were 70 P&C supermarkets, most in the Syracuse metropolitan region.

Recent Decades

There has been considerable consolidation in the supermarket business in the state and elsewhere, yet there has been very little penetration of the nation's biggest chains (Kroger's, Albertsons, and Safeway) in New York. The New York City market remains dominated by local chains, which, constrained by high real estate prices, small lots, and low levels of automobile use, are small by national standards. Outside the city, superstores increasingly dominate the supermarket landscape. The first Wegmans superstore opened in 1982, and many of its stores are larger than 100,000 ft^2 (9,300 m^2). Tops and Price Chopper also have superstores that feature dining and take-out food facilities, extensive prepared food sections, and housewares. Supermarkets have not eliminated New York State's independent corner grocery stores, still a fixture of urban neighborhoods throughout the state. But with supermarkets' wide selections and profit margins as narrow as 1%, they have been the dominant food-retailing institutions in New York State and throughout the nation for decades.

Adelman, Morris A. *A&P: A Study in Price-Cost Behavior and Public Policy* (Cambridge, Mass: Harvard Univ Press, 1959)

Seth, Andrew, and Geoffrey Randall. *The Grocers: The Rise and Rise of the Supermarket Chains* (Dover, NH: Kogan Page, 1999)

Sicilia, David B. "Supermarket Sweep," *Audacity: The Magazine of Business History* 5 (Spring 1997): 11–19

Zimmerman, M. M. *The Super Market: A Revolution in Distribution* (New York: McGraw-Hill, 1955)

Amybeth Gregory

Surveyor-General, Office of. New York State agency responsible for surveying and mapping. The Office of Surveyor-General can be traced to the Dutch position of surveyor-general *(landtmeeter)*, established in 1642. It was continued under the English, then British, government, with Cadwallader Colden serving from 1720 to 1776. In 1777 the New York State legislature authorized the Council of Appointment to name a surveyor-general to supervise the location of bounty lands promised to Revolutionary War veterans for military service. The primary duties, similar to those of the colonial office, were to preserve records of land grant maps and surveys. The position was not filled until 1782, when Gen Philip Schuyler was appointed. He was surveyor-general until his resignation in 1784. He was succeeded by Simeon DeWitt who, despite turbulent political times, continued until his death in 1834. The Surveyor-General's Office was established by law in Albany.

Although initially the surveyor-general was authorized by the commissioners of the Land Office to survey, map, and submit land claims to be certified by the secretary of state, by 1786 the designated duties were to survey and map the tracts New York State acquired, including those from seizures of forfeited estates (1788) and Indian land purchases (1789), and administer their sale. The surveyor-general was also responsible for appraising land, fixing boundaries, and appointing deputy surveyors to make surveys, maps, and appraisals. During DeWitt's tenure duties were expanded to include supervising the development of roads and canals, and the surveyor-general was appointed a commissioner of the Land Office (1803), a state canvasser (1821), and a member of the state's Canal Board (1827). DeWitt was followed in office by William Campbell (1835–38), Orville Luther Holley (1838–42), Nathaniel Jones (1842–45), and Hugh Halsey (1845–47). The 1846 New York State Constitution replaced the Surveyor-General's Office with the Office of State Engineer and Surveyor, an elected position with a two-year term, in January 1848. The commissioner of general services, acting through the Office of General Services, inherited the responsibility of mapping and selling unappropriated state lands.

Jo Margaret Mano

Susquehanna River (450 mi/724 km). Rising at the foot of Otsego Lake in Cooperstown (Otsego Co), the Susquehanna takes a meandering route through Chenango, Broome, and Tioga Cos and Pennsylvania before draining into Maryland's Chesapeake Bay at Havre de Grace. Although it rises only 14 miles (23 km) south of the Mohawk River, it has historically been a distinct river system. Hardly more than a stream at its origin, the Susquehanna is a mile wide by the time it reaches south central Pennsylvania. Over the course of its long history, shifts in topography have allowed the Susquehanna to capture other rivers, such as the Tioughnioga, Unadilla, and Chemung to the west, transforming them into tributaries. As a result, it drains approximately 27,500 mi^2 (71,220 km^2) of territory and deposits more water into the Atlantic than any other river east of the Mississippi—25 billion gallons (94.6 billion l) per day, according to one estimate. In places such as the "Grand Canyon of Pennsylvania" along the West Branch, the force of the Susquehanna has carved monumental chasms into the earth. The origin of the river's name remains uncertain, though the suffix *hanna* is an Algonquian word meaning stream or river, and the indigenous peoples of the region named places for local environmental features. To the Delaware the branch of the river flowing south from Otsego Lake was the M'chewamisipu or Mchwewarmink, "the river with extensive clear flats." Despite the river's volume of water, its frequent twists, turns, and variations in depth have made it difficult to navigate. In modern times various efforts have been made to control flooding along its banks, but like other great rivers, it has defied human attempts to confine its movements.

Early Valley Economies

The Susquehannocks, the indigenous group that controlled much of the Susquehanna Valley before European colonists arrived, had dwindled in numbers by the end of the 17th century, mostly owing to the spread of Old World epidemic diseases. The Iroquois then became dominant in the region. Without enough of their own to people the area, they encouraged other displaced Indians, such as groups of Delawares and Shawnees, to take up residence along the Susquehanna Valley. They cleared parts of the forest for fields of corn, beans, and legumes, which thrived in lowlands periodically covered by the river's floods. During the winter months, when communities tended to separate into family units, the Susquehanna Valley was conducive to fur trading, as its dense forests supported large game populations, and a series of streams and small rivers allowed access to the Susquehanna itself.

In the early 18th century European colonists began to consider the Susquehanna Valley as a place to establish new settlements. William Penn had hoped to place his colony's second city along the Susquehanna's banks, and agents for Pennsylvania and New York vied to gain control over as much of the region as possible. When colonists moved into the valley, they often clamored for lands near the Susquehanna or one of its tributaries, recognizing both the fertility of low-lying soil and the importance of the water routes that would enable them to haul their agricultural goods to distant markets. Settlers discovered that parts of the river froze from December to April, followed by spring melting that could swell the river to flood levels, threatening improvements built too close to the river's banks. Conversely, summer evaporation could reduce water volume to the point that people could walk across in places. Before canals and railroads, access to the river itself was arguably the key to economic success. Those in control of the region's economy secured their own access to the river or its tributaries and then did all they could to attract colonists to their properties. Indians were largely forced out of the valley after the Revolutionary War.

THE INDUSTRIAL ERA

The geological action that gave the river its convoluted form also created other notable features of the region: hills and valleys covered with dense forests and mountains containing anthracite (hard) or bituminous (soft) coal. During the 19th century these features made the valley a magnet for economic development. By the early 19th century coal and lumber, along with whiskey and various agricultural products, were being shipped down the river. In 1826, according to one contemporary estimate, the value of such goods descending the Susquehanna was $5 million. Lumbering became an enormous business in New York State by 1850. The state's loggers, some of whom used the north branch of the Susquehanna to send felled trees to markets, earned $13 million in profits that year, far more than their counterparts in any other state. By midcentury lumber companies developed booms—floating dams on the river itself—that could be used to store trees cut in the valley and then dragged to the water. In the early 1880s one boom held almost 1.9 million logs.

The ecological consequences of logging activity were horrendous: the water became polluted, fish could not travel upstream to spawn, and the landscape suffered from the erosion typical of overforested regions. The industry was also difficult to sustain. New York loggers produced 20% of the nation's total in 1850 but only 1% by 1920. Coal mining, the other profitable industry of the 19th-century valley, also polluted the river, arguably more significantly than lumber booms. Unlike forests that stretched across the northeast, mining was a concentrated industry. From 1800 to 1950 miners had extracted hundreds of million tons of anthracite from nine counties in northeastern Pennsylvania. By contrast, coal mining never became a significant industry along the branches of the Susquehanna in New York State.

By the late 20th century, the Susquehanna basin had become home to 18 power plants. Ten were driven by fossil fuels, five harvested the power of the river to form hydroelectric energy, and three were nuclear reactors. The worst nuclear reactor accident in the United States occurred when one of the reactors at Three Mile Island near Harrisburg, Pa, malfunctioned on 28 Mar 1979. Development of the region in the 19th and 20th centuries increased the risk of flooding, and while the US Army Corps of Engineers worked to prevent serious floods, the threat could not be eradicated. In June 1972 Tropical Storm Agnes hit the region with a fury, causing widespread destruction.

THE VALLEY OF OPPORTUNITY

Despite the problems caused by lumber and coal and the ubiquitous threat of flooding, the Susquehanna has always retained its elemental appeal. The river and its valley have attracted the attention of countless observers, including George Washington, Thomas Jefferson, and the noted French essayist Hector St. John de Crèvecoeur. James Fenimore Cooper celebrated Otsego Lake and Cooperstown, founded by his father William Cooper, in *The Pioneers* (1823), and others, like 19th-century Owego (Tioga Co) resident Nathaniel P. Willis, have written lovingly about the region. The name Susquehanna alone could inspire rapture. The English poet Samuel Taylor Coleridge wanted to establish a utopian community along the river in large part because he liked the sound of its name. By the late 20th century the Susquehanna had become, as *National Geographic* put it, "America's small-town river." Since the forests have recovered from logging boom and the river no longer contains effluvia from mining operations, the area once again provides enormous aesthetic pleasure.

Billinger, Robert D. *Pennsylvania's Coal Industry* (Gettysburg: Pennsylvania Historical Association, 1954)
Cox, Thomas R., et al. *This Well-Wooded Land: Americans and Their Forests from Colonial Times to the Present* (Lincoln: Univ of Nebraska Press, 1985)
Mancall, Peter C. *Valley of Opportunity: Economic Culture along the Upper Susquehanna, 1700–1800* (Ithaca: Cornell Univ Press, 1991)
Miller, Peter. "Susquehanna: America's Small-Town River," *National Geographic,* Mar 1985
Nash, Gary. "The Quest for the Susquehanna Valley: New York, Pennsylvania, and the 17th-Century Fur Trade," *New York History* 48 (1967): 3–27
Stranahan, Susan Q. *Susquehanna: River of Dreams* (Baltimore: Johns Hopkins Univ Press, 1993)
Taylor, Alan. *William Cooper's Town: Power and Persuasion on the Frontier of the Early American Republic* (New York: Knopf, 1995)
Willis, N. Parker. *Rural Letters and Other Records of Thought at Leisure* (New York: Baker & Scribner, 1849)

Peter C. Mancall

Susquehanna Turnpike. Officially named the Susquehanna Turnpike but commonly known as the Catskill Turnpike, it was a toll road built by the Susquehanna Turnpike Co. Beginning in 1802 it provided an improved route from Catskill (Greene Co) on the Hudson River to Wattles Ferry [now Unadilla, Otsego Co] on the Susquehanna River, passing through Greene (via Leeds and Durham), Schoharie, and Delaware Cos. The development of the Catskills and their foothills progressed rapidly as traffic along the road increased. The turnpike served the new settlements as a way to market their products and to obtain merchandise from New York City and other eastern markets. The Susquehanna Turnpike reached its peak in the 1820s and then declined, supplanted by the Erie Canal and railroads. Beginning with the abandonment in 1842 of the western section from Harpersfield (Delaware Co) to Wattles Ferry, the Susquehanna Turnpike Co gradually surrendered portions of the road. In 1901 Greene Co purchased the remaining section, and the company was dissolved. Though sections have been lost, much of the original turnpike route can be traveled today. Some of the stone walls, rows of maples that once lined the route, and a few mile markers still survive. The Susquehanna Turnpike is not to be confused with the nearby Susquehanna and Bath Turnpike, chartered in 1804, which ran from Jericho [now Bainbridge, Chenango Co] to Ithaca.

Erdmann, David George. "The Susquehanna Turnpike in Greene County, New York," *The Catskills* (Winter 1972–73)
Kubik, Dorothy. "Touring the Past: The Susquehanna Turnpike," *Kaatskill Life* (Summer 1987)
———. *West through the Catskills: The Story of the Susquehanna Turnpike* (Fleischmanns, NY: Purple Mountain Press, 2001)

Dorothy Kubik

Swallowtails Loose affiliation of wealthy men who influenced New York City politics during the 1870s and 1880s. The Swallowtails drew their name from an expensive coat worn to fancy dinners by members of the upper class. Many business and professional leaders complained that the lower classes were controlling urban government, and the Swallowtails worked to preserve the political power of the economic elite. After the fall of William M. "Boss" Tweed's administration in 1872, merchants, bankers, and lawyers controlled much of New York City's municipal government until the late 1880s. Mainly of Protestant British ancestry and high social standing, they were frightened by the rise of the working class and specifically by the eight-hour strikes of 1872. Swallowtails Samuel J. Tilden, August Belmont, and William C. Whitney each had strong connections with the national Democratic Party, but Republicans such as David Dudley Field, Sidney Howard Gay, and Robert Minturn also occasionally joined them, as well as some Mugwumps.

Swallowtail mayors—every New York City mayor during the era was linked with the group—wrenched municipal power away from neighborhood aldermen and used it to lower taxes, reduce city spending on infrastructure development and public works, and keep municipal employment to a minimum. During the 1870s and 1880s Tammany Hall often fought the Swallowtails for control of the New York City Democratic Party, but the two groups also worked together occasionally, most notably under William R. Grace (1881–82, 1885–86), New York City's first Irish Catholic mayor. In the election of 1886 Swallowtail Abram Hewitt, with the support of Tammany Hall, defeated Henry George and Theodore Roosevelt in the mayoral election. However, Hewitt's uncompromising administration (he vetoed 285 of the 920 resolutions passed by the Board of Aldermen in 1887) stamped the Swallowtails as nativist, anti-labor, and anti-immigrant. By 1896 many of the Democratic Swallowtails were so frightened by the panic of 1893 that they turned their support to Republican William McKinley. Individually, wealthy elites continued to play an important role in both major parties, but the concept of the Swallowtails as a political entity gradually disappeared.

Hammack, David. *Power and Society: Greater New York at the Turn of the Century* (New York: Columbia Univ Press, 1987)
Teaford, Jon. *The Unheralded Triumph: City Government in America, 1870–1900* (Baltimore: Johns Hopkins Univ Press, 1984)

Jon Sterngass

swamps. See WETLANDS.

Sweden. Town (pop 13,716) in W Monroe Co. Settled around 1804, the town was formed from Murray [now in Orleans Co] in 1814. Sweden is crossed by numerous streams that flow in every direction from its center. Brockport, a canal port (1823) on the town's north border, acquired rail service in 1852 from the Niagara Falls Branch of the New York Central Railroad. In the late 20th century its farms produced apples, cherries, corn, onions, and cabbages. Ledgedale Airport, a reliever airport for private flights, was modernized in 1989. An outer suburb of Rochester, its population more than doubled between 1960 and 2000.

Carolyn Vacca

Swedes. New York Colony's first Swedes arrived at New Amsterdam on Dutch ships during the mid-1600s. Jonas Bronck was the first-known person of Swedish origin to live in the area, soon removing to adjacent land in what would become the Bronx (1639). Some Swedish settlers also moved north from New Sweden, founded on the Delaware River in 1638. Prior to 1681 Mons Pieterson participated in surveying Harlem on land cleared by Swedes. Migration quickened in the 1700s and 1800s, and social and cultural organizations soon developed. The Swedish Society was established in New York City in 1836 to offer support and guidance to newcomers. In 1845 Olof G. Hedstrom formed a Scandinavian Methodist mission on the ship *Bethel* docked at New York City's Pier 11. In 1847 this mission gave birth to the Brooklyn congregation that would found Immanuel Swedish Methodist Episcopal Church in 1872. Swedes were drawn to seaport and industrial cities, especially New York City, but also to rural settings like the Adirondacks and Champlain Valley, with sizable populations emerging in Jamestown (Chautauqua Co), where the first Swedes settled in 1849, and Rochester, Buffalo, and Albany.

New York City became a key center of Swedish cultural life. Napoleon Berger published *Skandinaven,* America's first Swedish language newspaper, from 1851 to 1853. Other publications included the weekly *Nordstjernan* (The North Star) (1872–), the weekly *Arbetaren* (The Worker) (1896–1928), and the monthly magazine *Valkyrian* (1897–1909). Gustavus Adolphus at 155 East 22d St was the first Swedish Lutheran congregation organized in the city in 1865, with Baptists, Congregationalists, and other religious groups soon organizing as well. The New York City community founded Brooklyn's Swedish Hospital (1906), the Swedish Chamber of Commerce (1907), Augustana Home for the Aged (1908), and the American Scandinavian Foundation (1911). Upsala University began in a classroom in Brooklyn's Bethlehem Church in 1900, and Swedes also established theater and singing groups, such as the Lyran Singing Society of Brooklyn, during this era. Many Swedes worked in the building trades and as longshoremen. Swedish-born and Swedish-descended New Yorkers in science and engineering include John Ericsson, designer of the 1862 warship *Monitor,* Emil Swensson, who developed the frame of the city's first steel skyscraper in the 1880s, and Chester F. Carlson, who developed the xerographic copying process.

The largest Swedish community outside of New York City was in Chautauqua Co, centered in Jamestown. Many community members worked in wood and metals industries. Charles P. Dahlstorm, creator of the first fireproof door, founded a metals factory in Jamestown in 1904. In the early 20th century, local institutions there included Swedish restaurants, a weekly Swedish language newspaper, and municipally owned public utilities, reflecting Swedish ideals of cooperation. By 1930 nearly 8,000 Swedish-born persons lived in Jamestown, with many residing on Swedish Hill, and in 1940, 60% of the residents claimed some Swedish ancestry. In 1976 Sweden's King Carl XVI Gustaf visited the city. At the beginning of the 21st century, Swedes form Chautauqua Co's largest ethnic group, and traditional Swedish festivals (Midsummer and St. Lucia's Day) as well as Scandinavia Day are major events at the county's noted Chautauqua Institution.

In 1900 more than 90% of foreign-born Swedes in the state lived in Brooklyn and Manhattan. Improvement in the Swedish economy caused emigration to slow after the 1920s, and New York City Swedes increasingly moved to suburbs to the west. In 1930 Swedes constituted 1.9% of the state's population and lived in every county, with greatest numbers in Kings, New York, Chautauqua, and Westchester Cos, in this order. By the mid–20th century new immigrants were mostly professionals, heavily concentrated in New York City, which functioned both as a gateway to America and as a focus of Swedish American life. The 2000 census showed 77,045 Swedish-born persons and 133,788 persons of Swedish ancestry living in New York State.

Kastrup, Allan. *The Swedish Heritage in America* (St. Paul, Minn: North Central Publishing, 1975)

Nelson, Helge. *The Swedes and Swedish Settlements in North America,* 2 vols (New York: Bonnier, 1943)

Ann M. Legreid

Swiss. Switzerland is inhabited by four distinct ethnic groups, Germans, French, Italians, and a small Romansh group. Among the 18th-century Palatine German immigrants were German Swiss, who settled in the area of Albany and along the Mohawk River. In the 1840s Swiss dairy farmers began to move to Central New York, settling in places such as Ava (Oneida Co). Swiss also built and managed cheese factories across Central New York, such as Nickolaus Gerber, who pioneered the mass production of Limburger cheese. There were almost 8,000 Swiss in the state in 1870 and 13,678 in 1900. Most were German Swiss, divided between Catholics and Protestants, who lived primarily in urban areas, especially New York City.

German Swiss readily joined German American associations, especially before World War I, but also created local associations devoted to mutual support, benevolence, and sociability in the form of singing, gymnastics, and rifle clubs. These include the still existing Swiss Benevolent Society of New York, founded in 1846, the Swiss Society of New York, founded as Swiss Club in 1882, and the New York Schweizer Turnverein (now Swiss Gymnastic Society of New York). The nationwide Swiss association Grütli-Bund had branches in New York City, Rochester, Buffalo, Troy, and Albany in 1920. In 2000 about 23,000 Swiss-born live in New York State but many only temporarily while working for a Swiss business or organization. Many local Swiss societies have dissolved or merged into regional associations, such as the Hudson-Mohawk Swiss Society and the Swiss Club of Buffalo and Western New York. Prominent New Yorkers of Swiss birth or parentage include Henry Wisner, signer of the Declaration of Independence; Albert Gallatin, Geneva-born US secretary of the treasury (1801–13); the Italian Swiss Delmonico family, pioneering 19th-century restaurateurs; Oscar Tschirky, "Oscar of the Waldorf"; and Othmar H. Ammann, the engineer of several major New York City spans, including the George Washington and the Verrazano-Narrows Bridges.

Grüningen, John Paul von, ed. *The Swiss in the United States* (Madison, Wisc: Swiss-American Historical Society, 1940)

Schelbert, Leo. "Swiss." In *Gale Encyclopedia of Multicultural America,* vol 2, ed. Judy Galens, et al (New York: Gale Research, 1995)

Swope, Gerard (*b* St. Louis, 1 Dec 1872; *d* New York City, 20 Nov 1957). Businessman. The child of Jewish parents, Swope displayed technical aptitude from an early age. He attended the Massachusetts Institute of Technology, graduating in 1895 with a BS in electrical engineering. Swope joined Western Electric Co in Chicago in 1895, and he was named general sales manager in 1908. He moved to General Electric Co (GE) in 1919 when he was named president of its new subsidiary, International GE. In 1922 he became president of GE, with an office at 120 Broadway in New York City, and focused on making the electrical giant a highly efficient and stable producer. Swope, who managed the internal affairs of the company, while Owen D. Young, GE's board chairman, represented the company publicly, was successful in preventing labor strikes at GE by winning over the loyalty of the company's employees. To do this Swope introduced worker benefit programs, including stock ownership and annual profit-sharing bonuses, and created a company union. Pres Franklin D. Roosevelt in 1933 appointed Swope to the federal National Labor Relations Board and to the Business Advisory and Planning Council of the US Department of Commerce. In 1939 Swope retired from GE. The following year New York City mayor Fiorello La Guardia choose Swope to head the city's Housing Authority after a political scuffle emerged between city and federal officials. Swope, who had impeccable credentials in Washington, DC, ably headed the authority until 1942, when he briefly returned as GE's president (1942–44). In the decade before his death he served as board chairman for the private cooperative housing projects of Queensview, which built housing in Long Island City in Queens, and Kingsview, which constructed homes in Fort Greene in Brooklyn.

Loth, David. *Swope of GE* (New York: Simon & Schuster, 1958)

Darwin Stapleton

Sylvan Beach. Village (pop 1,071) in Vienna (Oneida Co). Although located where Wood Creek flows into Oneida Lake, on the traditional water route to the west, Sylvan Beach did not become a popular resort until the opening of Forest Home, a hotel, in 1879. The first rail line to serve Sylvan Beach, the Ontario and Western, came through in 1869. The settlement took on the character of a working- and middle-class resort for residents of Utica, Rome, Syracuse, and the surrounding farm country. Annual hop growers' picnics attracted up to 40,000. Once automobiles became common, Sylvan Beach vacations declined, though big bands at Russell's Danceland attracted crowds in the 1930s and 1940s. In 1971 Sylvan Beach incorporated (it had previously existed as a village from 1896 to

1911), and residents succeeded in reversing its deterioration. Many scenes in *The Sterile Cuckoo* (1968), starring Liza Minnelli, were filmed in Sylvan Beach. In 2003 a landmark business is the family-run Eddie's Restaurant.

Syosset. Locality (pop 18,544) in Oyster Bay (Nassau Co). Originally settled by Dutch farmers, the area took the name Syosset after the bayfront hamlet of Oyster Bay used the name from 1846 to 1848. With the arrival of the Long Island Rail Road in 1854, Syosset became a bustling hamlet. Much of the local produce, including what was processed at the local pickle works, was shipped to New York City. The population was 1,133 in 1950 but grew with extensive suburban development, particularly in the 1950s and the 1980s. Today Syosset is mainly residential, with some commercial and industrial properties.

Tom Kuehhas

Syracuse. City (pop 147,306) in central Onondaga Co. Syracuse lies in a valley formed during the last glacial retreat, about 10,000 BP, and on the hills surrounding it. Onondaga Creek flows north along the valley floor into Onondaga Lake. The city's position relative to Lake Ontario contributes to its distinction as the snowiest US city of more than 100,000 people. Syracuse occupies traditional territory of the Onondaga Nation. During the 17th-century Contact period, Onondaga villages were generally located on hills 10–12 miles (16–19 km) southeast, but in the 18th century they were concentrated in the Onondaga Creek valley immediately south of the present city. Onondaga Lake's productive fishing, however, drew natives to seasonal shoreline camps.

Colonial French and British interests were active in the area because the Onondaga were a major force in Iroquois-European relations. Evidence suggests that Samuel de Champlain's 1615 attack on the Iroquois took place on the south shore of Onondaga Lake. From 1656 to 1658 the French maintained a lakeshore mission about 1 mile (1.6 km) north of present-day Syracuse. In 1696 New France invaded with a large army under Comte de Frontenac. Within today's city limits, soldiers erected a lakeside log fort to protect their boats and marched south to attack the Onondaga. Increasingly the Onondaga fell under British influence, especially through the efforts of Sir William Johnson, who in 1751 assumed ownership of land surrounding the lake. American troops attacked and burned Onondaga settlements near the present city's southern boundary in April 1779, and several Onondaga were killed during a brief skirmish within the city.

Settlement

When the New Military Tract opened much of Central New York to non-native settlement in 1791, all of what now comprises Syracuse was reserved for the Onondaga. A 1795 treaty greatly reduced their lands, opening the site for development. Natural brine springs on Onondaga Lake's swampy south shore lured entrepreneurs intent on salt production. Some of the first settlers were squatters who boiled brine at Salt Point. The New Military Tract survey established the Onondaga Salt Springs Reservation, a public reservation of 1 mile, around Onondaga Lake to ensure state control and revenue from salt making. Parcels were leased to private parties beginning in 1797, but production was regulated by the state through an appointed salt superintendent.

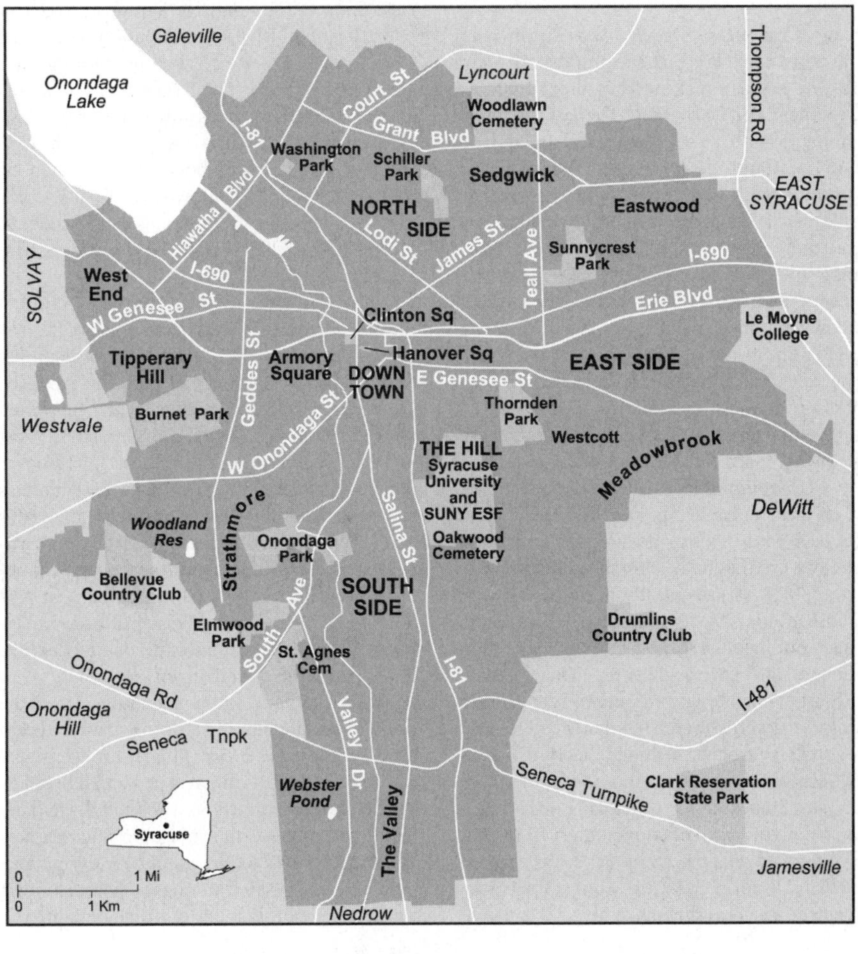

In 1798 the state authorized the platting of Salina, now Syracuse's far north side, at Salt Point. Some settlers were attracted to fertile valley soils along Onondaga Creek at Onondaga Hollow, now the most southern part of the city. Syracuse's pioneers were from eastern New York State and New England, and of Dutch, English, German, or Irish ethnicity; they were accompanied by a few dozen free and enslaved African Americans. The earliest religious organization was the First Presbyterian Church of Onondaga Hollow and Salina (1810). Over the next 20 years Baptist, Methodist, Roman Catholic, and Episcopal congregations formed.

Syracuse proper originated midway between Salina and Onondaga Hollow, near today's Clinton Square. This marshy land had been avoided by the first white settlers, but in 1804 the state legislature authorized the sale of 250 acres (101 ha) of the salt reservation for revenue needed to extend a road closer to the saltworks. The acreage included a stretch of Onondaga Creek with waterpower potential. Utica speculator Abraham Walton purchased it and erected a mill where the road, now Genesee St, crossed the creek. Another road to Salina crossed nearby. Henry Bogardus opened a tavern in 1806, and the intersection became Bogardus Corners.

A local visionary named Joshua Forman understood the potential of building a canal across the state. He bought Walton's remaining interest in 1814 and worked tirelessly to promote the young swamp-side settlement he called Corinth. Erie Canal construction, which began in 1817, was complete from Utica through Corinth and westward in 1819. A post office designation was needed in 1820, but the name Corinth had just been claimed by another town. Syracuse, the name of an ancient city in Sicily near saltworks, was substituted.

The outlet of Onondaga Lake was dredged in 1822, lowering lake levels and draining much of the surrounding wetlands, thus removing a major hindrance to the settlement's expansion. Three years later, with direct Erie Canal access, additional mills along Onondaga Creek, and a concentration of commercial activity, the settlement of 1,000 incorporated as the Village of Syracuse. Salina had incorporated as a village in 1824.

With completion of the Oswego Canal in 1828, the Erie was linked at Syracuse to Lake Ontario. Canal transportation ignited an explosion in local salt production as the bulky cargo moved to market at less expense. In 1848 Syracuse and Salina merged under a city charter, which provided greater representation in the county's legislative body and better taxing mechanisms. Leaders also hoped the new city would gain statewide recognition and increase its chances to become a new, centrally located state capital. In 1887 Syracuse annexed the adjacent industrial village of Geddes, which became Syracuse's far west side, and the suburban village of Danforth to the south. Annexation of other territory continued as the city's professional fire and police departments, expansive school services, and modern utilities beckoned: Elmwood in 1899, Eastwood in 1926, and the old Hollow, or the

Valley, in 1927. These additions boosted the city's population, which jumped to 209,326 by 1930.

Economic Development

Stimulated by canal access, the salt industry flourished from the 1820s to the 1860s. Dozens of salt-boiling structures (known as salt blocks, from the rectangular stonework that housed the brine kettles) lined the banks of both Oswego and Erie Canals. Thousands of wooden vats for solar evaporation of brine occupied hundreds of acres around Onondaga Lake's southern end. Salt brought wealth to Syracuse, capitalizing banks that financed other commercial interests; Onondaga County Bank (1830) was the first.

An east-west railroad arrived in 1839, eventually becoming part of the New York Central Railroad. Connections north and south were in place by 1854, evolving into elements of the Delaware, Lackawanna and Western system. New factories located near their tracks, especially on the city's west side, which was served by both lines.

Over time, the industrial zone expanded to produce a staggering variety of goods. During the 1850s and 1860s, Syracuse had more than 20 manufacturers of melodeons, pianofortes, and parlor, church, and pipe organs. By 1890 Marsellus Casket had a large west-side factory. R. E. Dietz shipped kerosene lanterns worldwide. Onondaga Pottery (1871, now Syracuse China) produced some of America's superior china. Syracuse Chilled Plow operated a sprawling complex, turning out agricultural machinery. Specialty steel giant Crucible has its roots there. Local inventor John Wilkinson's air-cooled engine concept matured into the Franklin automobile. At its west-side plant, H. H. Franklin Manufacturing Co (1902–34) was the city's largest employer in the early 1920s. New Process Gear (1888) and Brown-Lipe Gear evolved into major auto parts producers; by 1915 New Process moved to a second manufacturing district that was developing on abandoned salt lands north of downtown. The Syracuse Washing Machine Corp followed in 1920.

By 1900 the manufacture of typewriters had inherited the place of the waning salt industry as Syracuse's signature industry. Lyman C. Smith organized the Smith Premier Typewriter Co in 1890, later purchased by Remington. Smith and his three brothers went on in 1903 to start L. C. Smith and Bros Typewriter. By 1907 Syracuse led the nation in typewriter production. In a 1914 manufacturing census, typewriters were the city's most valuable product, followed by brewed liquors and malts, machine-shop products, autos and auto parts, and candles. In 1923 nearly 150,000 typewriters were made in Syracuse, supplying a global market.

The depression hit Syracuse hard. Between 1929 and 1933 it lost nearly half of its industrial jobs, affecting 13,000 workers and their families. Franklin Manufacturing declared bankruptcy in 1934. Some new work opportunities arose with a massive railroad track relocation project. This $23.5 million public-private effort to elevate dozens of dangerous grade crossings employed almost 1,900 men for four years. The city foreclosed on the sprawling, empty Franklin factory and used it as an incentive to lure a promising manufacturer from New Jersey. The 1937 arrival of Carrier Corp brought 1,000 jobs in the new air-conditioning field. The start of World War II ultimately revitalized local industry as many firms retooled to produce an array of armaments.

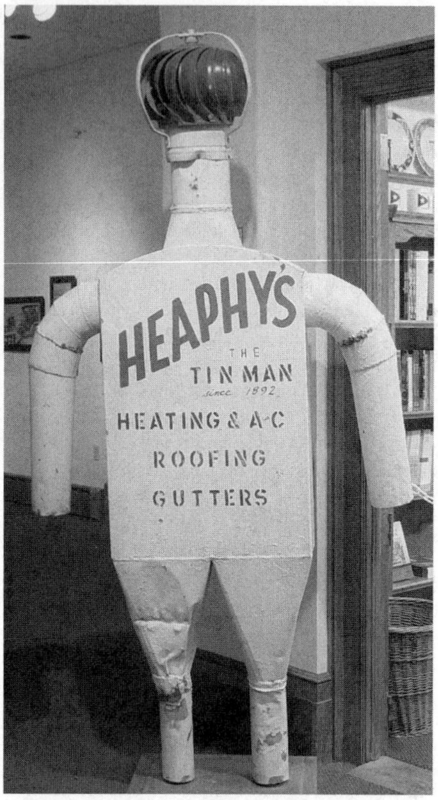

Heaphy's tin man, built in the 1920s, was a familiar site on North Geddes St in Syracuse. Since 1998 he has been on display at the Onondaga Historical Association.

Ethnicity and Immigration

Syracuse's pioneer settlers were primarily Protestants from New England and eastern New York. The population grew from about 1,000 in 1825 to nearly 6,500 by 1840. There was a flood of immigrants from Germany and Ireland in the 1840s. About the time the city charter was adopted in January 1848, the population was reported to be 13,741. It reached 25,226 by 1855, an increase of 83% in just seven years. By 1865, Germans and Irish far exceeded other foreign-born residents. If one includes their children, their combined numbers made up about a third of the city's 31,784 citizens at the end of the Civil War.

The Irish gravitated to work in salt-boiling blocks and the solar evaporation yards, congregating on Syracuse's far north end and west sides. Most Germans settled north of downtown. Their community established candle making, cigar manufacturing, and the brewing of lager beer as distinctive north-side industries. The city's first Lutheran church was organized there in 1838. Nearby, Assumption parish was established in 1843 to serve German Catholics. Smaller numbers were Jewish, primarily from Germany and central Europe. They settled southeast of downtown and worked primarily as peddlers, dry goods merchants, and grocers. The city's first synagogue, Temple Society of Concord, organized in 1841. Almost forgotten in 2003 are Francophone Canadians who emigrated south in search of employment. In 1897 it was estimated that as many as 2,500 former Canadians lived in Syracuse. Some worked as carpenters, others as shoemakers.

From 1880 to 1920 new immigrants from Italy, Poland, Russia, and Ukraine arrived, including new Jewish arrivals from eastern Europe who moved into the old Jewish district. Italians were first attracted by railroad work in the early 1880s. In 1899 an estimated 5,000 Italian-born resided in Syracuse, primarily on the near north side. Many worked in construction. Eastern European immigration was dominated by Poles, an estimated 1,500 by 1897 and 10,000 by 1924. These new arrivals were drawn to the west side, where factories and railroad yards offered employment. There were also distinct Slovak, Ukrainian, and Russian Orthodox enclaves on the far west side by 1910, and a small Greek presence. Syracuse's population jumped from 28,119 in 1860 to 137,249 by 1910, propelled by immigration and annexation. African American percentages through the late 19th and early 20th centuries remained generally under 1%. By 1920 the blocks just east of downtown housed most of the city's 1,260 Blacks, kept there by widespread discrimination in housing.

Cityscape

The city seal, in use for over 150 years, features a train, canalboat, salt blocks, and evaporation sheds: defining landmarks of 19th-century Syracuse. The Erie Canal's packet landing stood adjacent to the Genesee Turnpike; soon named Clinton Square, the landing became a public and market space. Canals also dictated locations for commercial activity, especially salt-boiling factories. The land stretching south toward downtown from Onondaga Lake filled with thousands of solar salt evaporation vats, blocking the city from its lakefront. Following the salt industry's demise in the 1920s, this area was filled by dozens of oil storage tanks. They were removed in a massive waterfront recovery effort, begun in 1990 and still underway in 2003.

Washington St served as the route for the New York Central tracks. The Delaware, Lackawanna and Western skirted downtown's west side. Until elevated, trains at street level congested the central city. The railroads built passenger stations in the 1870s on downtown's west side, stimulating development of hotels and wholesale businesses in what is now the Armory Square Historic District.

Hanover Square, just south of the junction of the Erie and Oswego Canals and north of the first railroad depot (1839), became a shopping district that spread south along Salina St. From the 1860s to 1890s, grand bank structures sprouted around Hanover and Clinton Squares, most of which survive. Blocks southeast of Hanover Square became residential. Fayette Park was ringed with several mansions during the 1840s and 1850s. As more bridges across the canals improved access toward the northeast, James St became the elite residential thoroughfare, in part because its elevated topography afforded magnificent views. More modest residential districts developed south of downtown.

Salina St remains the north-south axis of the city. The portion linking downtown with the old north side features many 19th-century commercial structures. It terminates in a small business district dating from the old Salina village days. South and east was the village's residential area where salt manufacturers and brewery owners built homes. Scattered among them were modest workers' residences, many of which remain.

Hills frame the southern half of Syracuse. Oakwood Cemetery, a rural cemetery masterpiece, was dedicated in 1859 on the rise to the southeast. Syracuse University, built north of the cemetery, created University Hill. Its robust skyline now rivals downtown's vista and features landmarks as diverse as the Victorian sandstone turrets of Crouse College (1889) and the inflated roof of the Carrier Dome (1980). Woodland Reservoir and its brick standpipe dominate the southwest. They identify the historic heart of Syracuse's present water system, a major municipal achievement first opened in 1894. Gravity draws the water from Skaneateles Lake.

The city had few parks in its early days. Modest Fayette Park was one, made over into a densely ornamental retreat in the 1870s. A true parks system began in 1886 when John B. Burnet donated sprawling west-side acreage that now bears his name. Further growth occurred with the early 20th-century development of Thornden and Onondaga Parks. In 1910 the massive Civil War Soldiers' and Sailors' Monument formalized Clinton Square's role as the city's primary civic space.

By the early 1900s electric streetcar lines and automobiles fostered new residential districts farther from downtown. Sedgwick Farms opened in 1908, followed by Berkeley Park in 1911, Scotholm in 1914, and Strathmore-by-the-Park in 1919. The 1950s and 1960s were an era of massive change to the urban landscape. Private development transformed much of James St from distinctive mansions to sober, suburban-style office buildings. The old Jewish quarter, southeast of downtown and predominantly African American by 1960, was leveled by urban renewal for a grand vision of a governmental and cultural center that was only partially fulfilled. Between 1962 and 1967, I-81 was built at the eastern edge of downtown, severing it from the growing University Hill district. Some new landmarks, such as the twin 20-story towers of the Mutual of New York complex, joined the downtown skyline.

In the 1970s historic preservation began making advances. A historic preservation ordinance passed in 1975. Hanover Square became the city's first National Register Historic District in 1976. The city's last grand movie palace, Loew's State (1928), was saved from demolition in 1978 and is now Landmark Theatre. During the 1980s visionary capitalists saw potential in the 19th-century warehouses and old railroad hotels of downtown's west side. The 1992 conversion of the neighborhood's National Guard Armory into a science museum was a further catalyst. This revitalized Armory Square Historic District has become a bright spot for downtown retail, dining, and housing. Early 20th-century brick factories of the industrial precinct along Onondaga Creek, north of downtown, are also being transformed into a mixed-use sector known as Franklin Square.

Manually operated traffic light on James and State Sts in downtown Syracuse, 1924.

Culture

By the 1850s Syracuse was hosting traveling Shakespearean dramas and light-hearted operettas. The famous "Swedish Nightingale," Jenny Lind, performed in 1851 at the National Theater, a crude affair converted from a Baptist church. Two more formal theaters opened in 1870: the Grand Opera House and its rival, the Wieting, which were joined by the Bastable Theater (1893). Each played a formative role in launching the theatrical management dynasty of Sam, Lee, and Jacob (J. J.) Shubert, who all began their careers in Syracuse. By 1900 Syracusans were enjoying a wide variety of theater and musical offerings, as it was a major stop on national performance circuits.

Intellectual and cultural organizations flowered in the late 19th and early 20th centuries. Civic Morning Musicals was started in 1890 by a group of visionary women to increase the community's access to quality performances by classical musicians. In 1903 the scientific and engineering leaders from local industries organized the Technology Club. And in 1906 the Onondaga Historical Association (1862) opened its first museum building. All three remained vital in 2003. George Fisk Comfort, former dean of Syracuse University's College of Fine Arts, steered the Syracuse Museum of Fine Arts to incorporation in 1896; following reorganization in 1959 as the Everson Museum, it moved into a world-class I. M. Pei–designed building in 1968. The Everson is noted for its collection of American art and ceramics. Syracuse enjoyed a particularly creative period in the early 20th century when several national figures in America's arts and crafts movement practiced there, including furniture maker Gustav Stickley, art historian Irene Sargent, ceramist Adelaide Alsop Robineau, and architect Harvey Ellis. Stickley's *Craftsman* magazine exerted a profound influence in promoting the movement's ideals. The Gustave Stickley Co's factory (1898) in nearby Eastwood and that of his brothers, L. and J. G. Stickley (1902) in suburban Fayetteville, shaped the Syracuse region's reputation for distinctly crafted furniture. A succession of orchestras in the first half of the 20th century struggled financially; in 1961 the modern Syracuse Symphony was born, and in 1976 it moved into the new Crouse-Hinds Concert Theater. The first radio broadcast was by station WMAC (now WSYR) in 1922. The first TV station was WHEN (1948), joined two years later by WSYR.

A variety of baseball teams from 1877 to 1927 played under the name Syracuse Stars. Baseball returned to Syracuse with the Syracuse Chiefs in 1934, along with the new Municipal Stadium, renamed after Gen Douglas MacArthur during World War II. "Big Mac" housed the franchise (1934–55, 1961–present) until P&C Stadium replaced it in 1997, when the team was renamed the SkyChiefs. The National Basketball Association's Syracuse Nationals (1946–63) inspired fierce local pride, especially in 1955 when it won the championship. Hockey teams representing the city have included the Syracuse Blazers (1967–76) and, since 1994, the American Hockey League's Syracuse Crunch. Syracuse University's teams have captured national championships in football, basketball (in 2003), and lacrosse (ninth national title in 2004).

Syracuse Music Scene. At the crossroads of I-81 and I-90, the Syracuse area has been a musical crossroads for a wide range of styles and artists, locally and nationally known. The first nationally prominent Central New York jazz figure was trombonist Spiegle Willcox from Sherburne (Chenango Co). Willcox played on several of legendary jazz cornetist Bix Beiderbecke's recordings in the 1920s. Syracuse-born clarinetist Michael "Peanuts" Hucko performed and recorded with Glenn Miller, Louis Armstrong, and Django Reinhardt. Another Syracusan, tenor saxophonist Sal Nistico, made an explosive impact on the jazz world as a featured player with Woody Herman in the 1960s.

Songwriter Jimmy Van Heusen was born and raised in Syracuse. Notable songs, including "Swinging on a Star," "Love and Marriage," and "Come Fly with Me," were recorded by Bing Crosby, Frank Sinatra, and other stars of the 1940s and 1950s. Van Heusen was inducted into the Songwriters Hall of Fame in 1971. Also local, Bob Halligan Jr had major success in the 1980s and 1990s writing songs for Judas Priest, Cher, Blue Oyster Cult, and others before forming the Celtic rock group Ceili Rain. Vocalist Mark Murphy from Fulton (Oswego Co) made three successful pop recordings for Capitol Records in the 1950s before switching to jazz in the early 1960s. He went on to release over two dozen recordings in the period 1970–2000, working with many top names in jazz. Bassist Scott LaFaro from Newark (Wayne Co) performed and recorded with Bill Evans, Ornette Coleman, and Chet Baker before dying in a 1961 automobile accident at age 25.

Syracuse rock and roll began with Jimmy Cavallo. Born in 1928, he became the first white rock and roll act to play Harlem's famed Apollo Theater in December 1956, the same year he appeared in the Alan Freed movie *Rock, Rock, Rock!* Ronnie James Dio of Cortland began recording in 1958, signed with Epic Records in 1970 with the band Elf, and went on to international fame as a heavy metal singer, first in Rainbow and Black Sabbath and later in his own band, Dio. Numerous bands from Syracuse have achieved national recognition through major label distribution. Jam Factory released *Sittin' in the Trap* in 1969 on Epic Records. Jukin' Bone, featuring singer Joe Whiting and guitarist Mark Doyle, released two albums on RCA Records: *Whiskey Woman* (1971) and *Way Down East* (1972). Progressive rockers 805 also signed with RCA Records and released the album *Stand in Line* (1982). In 1988 the Masters of Reality, with singer Chris Goss and guitarist Tim Harrington, received national attention with their self-titled album on Delicious Vinyl. The band followed with several other releases on various labels. Songwriter Ed Hamell, who fronted the band The Works in the 1980s, signed with Mercury Records in 1996 and went on to release a number of albums under the name Hamell on Trial. From the late 1970s Syracuse nurtured a vibrant alternative scene that produced the Flashcubes, Wallmen, Dracula Jones, and, most notably, Earth Crisis, which toured internationally and released seven albums between 1995 and 2001.

Cleveland-born singer-songwriter Benny Mardones became a sensation in Central New York in the 1980s when his single "Into the Night" was a top-10 hit. Even after moving to California, Mardones sold out several shows a year in New York State, where he enjoyed his greatest success. Other singer-songwriters of note include Grammy-nominated Native American artist Joanne Shenandoah of the Oneida Nation; Syracuse native Martin Sexton, who released CDs on Atlantic Records in 1998 and 2000; and Karen Savoca of Munnsville (Madison Co), who appeared on Garrison Keillor's National Public Radio (NPR) show *A Prairie Home Companion.* Syracuse-based label Blue Wave Records, founded in 1985 by Greg Spencer and still operating in 2003, nurtured a very successful regional blues scene with releases by the Kingsnakes, Kim Simmonds, and Kim Lembo. Prominent blues vocalist Roosevelt Dean, a Syracuse resident for four decades, became known as the "Voice of Syracuse."

Summer music festivals have been abundant in the area. The Syracuse M & T Jazz Fest at Onondaga Community College, founded in 1982 and produced annually by native Syracusan Frank Malfitano, features internationally known jazz artists. The Central New York Jazz Orchestra, founded in 1996, performs with national acts in a subscription-series season and hosts jazz clinics for scholastic musicians. Other music festivals include the New York State Rhythm and Blues Festival, WBBS-FM radio's B104.7 BJam country music show at the New York State Fairgrounds, Jazz in the Square, and Bill Knowlton's Bluegrass Ramble Picnic. Knowlton, host of a long-running bluegrass show on WCNY-FM, began producing the Ramble in 1973. It features bluegrass and old-time acts from across the state, including Syracuse's Tony Trischka and John Rossbach and the Cortland-based Delaney Brothers. Ithaca's Finger Lakes GrassRoots Festival, founded in 1990, features a wildly eclectic mix of folk, rock, blues, cajun, zydeco, and other ethnic styles. Area music venues include the 50,000-seat Carrier Dome and Onondaga County War Memorial in Syracuse, and the 800-seat Showroom at the Turning Stone Casino in Verona (Oneida Co). The Grandstand at the New York State Fairgrounds hosts national rock and country acts during the fair each August. The biannual SAMMY (Syracuse Area Music) Awards, beginning in 1993 and honoring Central New York musicians in all fields, is a Grammy-style event at the Landmark Theatre, Syracuse's oldest (1928) and grandest entertainment venue.

The club scene in Central New York played a major part in nurturing local talent and presenting less well-known national touring acts. Notable small venues included Styleen's Rhythm Palace, the Lost Horizon, Firebarn Tavern, and legendary Syracuse University club Jabberwocky. While these no longer operate, others remained active in 2003. Syracuse's Dinosaur Bar-B-Que, the site of live recordings by Roosevelt Dean and by well-known local rhythm and blues band Dave Hanlon's Cookbook, presents live music seven nights a week, and the Bridge Street Music Hall hosts regional and touring rock acts in a large-stage setting.

All Music Guide, http://www.allmusic.com
Syracuse Area Music Awards, http://www.syracuseareamusic.com

Gary Frenay

Politics

Syracuse reflected the mid-19th-century reform movements that surged through Central and Western New York. Syracuse's antislavery forces were led by Samuel J. May (1797–1871), a Unitarian minister who also supported women's causes, and Rev Jermain W. Loguen (?1813–1872), himself an escaped Tennessee slave. May, Loguen, and others made Syracuse an Underground Railroad stop. Local abolitionists' boldest moment came on 1 Oct 1851 when an organized citizens' assault rescued William Henry, known as Jerry, a former slave seized by federal authorities under provisions of the Fugitive Slave Law, an event known as the Jerry Rescue.

Not all Syracusans were abolitionists, and the community was often fiercely divided over the issue. During the 1850s Republicans, such as Congressman Charles B. Sedgwick, became a force because of the city's strong antislavery leadership. Democrats maintained some influence, especially among the Irish. Syracuse's first German-born mayor, Republican cigar manufacturer George Hier, took office in 1875. The Republican Party, courting new immigrants like Italians, came to dominate by the 1890s, especially under Francis Hendricks (1834–1920). Hendricks, who had previously served as mayor (1880–82), state assemblyman (1884–85), and state senator (1886–91), captured control of Onondaga Co Republicans in 1890. His influence expanded to state and national politics. In 1912 he helped broker William H. Taft's renomination for the presidency.

Democrats successfully challenged on occasion. In 1895, first-generation Irish American James Kennedy McGuire, age 27, captured the Democratic nod for mayor when a local feud resulted in two Republicans candidates, and won handily. A populist known as the "Boy Mayor," he was twice reelected. Republicans, however, reasserted control and occupied the mayor's office for all but eight years between 1902 and 1970. John Walrath in the 1920s and Thomas Corcoran in the 1950s were the Democratic exceptions and popular personalities when there was weariness with the status quo. The most successful Republican was five-term mayor Roland B. Marvin (1930–41). Marvin steered the city through the difficult depression years, in part by shepherding the massive railroad track elevation and other projects.

Democratic enrollment rose in the city during the 1960s as poor and minority voters claimed the party as their own. The 1969 mayoral election of Greek American Lee Alexander, a Democrat, marked a modern shift in urban politics. A charismatic politician, Alexander commanded city affairs for four terms (1970–85) but ended his political career in disgrace, pleading guilty to extortion in 1988. From 1970 on, Democrats have generally held city hall. The exception was the 1993–2001 term of Republican Roy Bernardi, who first gained the mayoralty after a rancorous Democratic primary.

Town and Gown

Higher education has become a factor of increasing importance to the city's economy and identity since World War II. Syracuse University (1870) expanded tremendously with the GI Bill. Renewed interest was expressed in the adjacent SUNY College of Environmental Science and Forestry (1911) with the environmental movement of the 1960s; it has expanded into a national center for the study of environmental resource management, wood products engineering, and forest biology. The Jesuits opened Le Moyne College in 1946. Financial challenges led Syracuse University to transfer its Medical College to the SUNY system in 1950; its existence had fostered a concentration of hospitals near the campus. Eventually, in 1964, the state erected its own University Hospital. Syracuse University and the SUNY Upstate Medical University were the city's top two employers in 2003, with a combined total of nearly 11,000 workers.

Despite the presence of thousands of college students within its borders, Syracuse is not generally considered a college town. However, Syracuse University provides many cultural resources for the community. Its Drama Department helps sustain the city's professional theater, Syracuse Stage. The university's School of Architecture and SUNY's School of Landscape Architecture conduct design studies for city needs. The university's Department of Public Administration at the Maxwell School and other departments offer ready access to leading professionals. At the same time, Syracuse University's physical expansion has consumed many residential blocks, converting them to tax-exempt status and creating additional pressure on the city for services. Neighborhoods bordering the university have a high concentration of both students and faculty. Although conversion of large homes into student apartments with associated lifestyles has eroded the area's once dominant single-family, middle-class nature, some faculty, choosing to live near campus, have invested in nearby houses. University-associated residents have slanted east-side politics toward a liberal perspective. The city and university negotiated an arrangement in 1990 in which, in exchange for transforming some nearby streets into limited-access campus roads, the university provides at least $250,000 annually to the city to strengthen surrounding neighborhoods. With the 1980 opening of the Carrier Dome as SU's premier athletic facility, the city's skyline gained its most recognized feature.

Recent History

In the decades since World War II, Syracuse's strong manufacturing sector has declined. Many industries like Carrier and New Process Gear abandoned their 19th-century factories in the city for more efficient, one-story plants in the suburbs. Business ownership, including that of most major banks, shifted to out-of-town conglomerates. Production lines and whole companies, including many that were started in Syracuse, were transferred to the sunbelt and foreign sites. These trends have produced an ongoing, significant loss of manufacturing jobs, increasing the proportion of employment based in services and higher education and creating a diverse economy.

In recent decades there have been sharp increases in the minority population. Following World War II, there was a great northern migration of Blacks from the South who were seeking economic opportunity. By 1960 African Americans numbered 11,210, about 5% of Syracuse's population. The 15th Ward, immediately south and east of downtown, was almost the only neighborhood open to African Americans. It was poor but vibrant and close-knit, with many businesses catering to its residents. It was eradicated by 1960s urban renewal projects. Increasing civil protest by Blacks and their supporters for improved housing and job opportunities occurred in the 1960s, but Syracuse was spared the violence that sometimes marked this era in other New York State cities. The black population expanded from 23,597 in 1970 to 33,170 by 1990. Blacks represented about 25% of Syracuse's residents in 2000.

A growing urban Native American population, mostly Mohawk, concentrated on the west side and formed about 1% of Syracuse's residents in 2000. The Asian population rose by nearly 40% during the 1990s and accounted for about 3% of city residents in 2000. Numbers are led by those of Vietnamese ancestry, followed in order by Chinese, Indian, Korean, and a small but distinct Hmong community. Most Southeast Asians are concentrated on the city's north side. Latino numbers increased too, up nearly two-thirds since 1990. Syracuse had 7,768 residents of Latino background in 2000, mostly of Puerto Rican ancestry and concentrated on the near west side.

Many residents have moved to surrounding towns with a corresponding transfer of municipal financial strength from city to county. Syracuse's population peaked in 1950 at 220,583, with the rest of the county at just 121,136. The 2000 census showed Syracuse had 147,306 residents, while the rest of the county housed over 311,000 inhabitants. The resulting growth of suburban plazas and malls drained downtown of much retail vitality. The city in the early 21st century is overloaded with abandoned houses and struggles with a declining tax base. That has reduced resources for schools, which, in turn, becomes a major factor in residential choices. Although white flight to the suburbs created neighborhoods with disproportionate concentrations of minorities, a growing number of streets sustain a more integrated mix than 40 years ago, and many neighborhoods attract residents with their architecturally diverse housing.

Onondaga Co reorganized under a new charter in 1962. Although not a metropolitan government, it has assumed many former city responsibilities. During the 1970s this included integrating Syracuse's baseball stadium, zoo, and libraries into countywide systems. Yet Syracuse remains the hub, cultural center, and source of community identity for Central New York. The locally based Pyramid Companies' 1990 transformation of a lakeside industrial brownfield into the retail giant Carousel Center mall stimulated a complete reevaluation of the city's Onondaga Lake waterfront. A massive effort to improve the lake's water quality, following decades of industrial and municipal pollution, is well underway. The former State Barge Canal terminal has been transformed into the nucleus for an attractive harbor. Work is progressing to link this area to downtown along a 1 mi (1.6 km) Onondaga Creekwalk. Other recent lakefront improvements include the 1998 opening of the William F. Walsh Regional Transportation Center, which serves as the intercity bus depot and Amtrak station. Carousel Center is linked to downtown and the University Hill district via self-propelled passenger railcars operated by the OnTrack subsidiary of the New York, Susquehanna and Western Railroad. In the early 21st century, plans are underway to extend the distinctive OnTrack system to the Regional Transportation Center.

In 2003 Pyramid was planning a massive expansion of its Carousel Center mall into a national entertainment, recreation, and retail magnet for tourism. The proposal includes an aquarium, 4,000-room hotel complex, 65-acre (26.3 ha) domed green space, stylized Erie Canal re-creation, major New York State tourism center, and 15,000-seat amphitheater. It is a controversial concept that seeks local and state tax incentives in exchange for the promise of a huge economic boost for Central New York. It has also generated debate over its potential physical impact, both positive and negative, on surrounding neighborhoods, including the city's historic north side.

Downtown, which lost the last of its major retail stores in 1992, continues to seek a new formula for vitality. One critical component is the Oncenter convention complex that opened the same year. Revitalization in Armory, Franklin, and Hanover Squares has proven the appeal of mixed-use historic structures, including a growing market for downtown area housing. Cultural activity has also grown in recent years, with an opera company, puppet museum, and numerous theater groups. The 2001 renovation of Clinton Square expanded its use for musical and ethnic festivals. A promising new element is the 2003 creation of a special municipally designed cultural district, linking museums, performing arts venues, private galleries, restaurants, and artist studios especially along Montgomery St.

See also James family; Suburbanization;

WATER SUPPLY AND USE (NON–NEW YORK CITY WATERSHED).

Beauchamp, William M. *Past and Present of Syracuse and Onondaga County* (New York: S. J. Clarke Publishing, 1908)

Bruce, Dwight H. *Memorial History of Syracuse* (Syracuse: H. P. Smith, 1891)

Chase, Franklin H. *Syracuse and Its Environs* (Chicago: Lewis Historical Publishing, 1924)

Connors, Dennis J. *Syracuse* (Dover, NH: Arcadia Publishing, 1997)

Connors, Dennis J., and John Reap. *A Guide to Sites and Related History: Society for Industrial Archeology, Fall Tour 2001* (Syracuse: Onondaga Historical Association, 2001)

Geddes, George. "Survey of Onondaga," *Transactions of the New York State Agricultural Society* 19 (1859): 219–352

Hardin, Evamaria. *Syracuse Landmarks* (Syracuse: Onondaga Historical Association and Syracuse Univ Press, 1993)

Roseboom, William F., and Henry W. Schramm. *Syracuse: From Salt to Satellite* (Woodland Hills, Calif: Windsor Publications, 1979)

Schramm, Henry W. *Central New York: A Pictorial History* (Norfolk, Va: Donning, 1987)

Strong, Gurney S. *Early Landmarks of Syracuse* (Syracuse: Times Publishing Co, 1894)

Dennis J. Connors

Syracuse China Company. Ceramics manufacturer tracing its origins to an 1841 pottery established in Geddes (Onondaga Co) by Vermont-born potter William H. Farrar. In 1857 Farrar moved his pottery, which produced stoneware and Rockingham ware, to a site on the Erie Canal. A year later he sold the business to a group that reorganized it as Empire Crockery Mfg Co, hiring skilled English potter Lyman Clark as manager. In 1871, 16 area businessmen founded Onondaga Pottery Co (OPCo) on Fayette St in Geddes; the enterprise consolidated Empire Crockery and other Syracuse area potteries into the firm that would take the name Syracuse China Co in 1966.

OPCo first produced white earthen table- and toiletware, with the pottery's raw materials, clay and coal, arriving by canal and railroad. In 1875 Richard Pass, a potter from Staffordshire, England, became manager. On his death, his son James took over as company president from 1884 to 1913 and made the firm a national leader. From 1884 Pass employed the Boston China Decorating Works, also located on Fayette St, to decorate some product and in 1886 absorbed that company. Two years later Pass developed a vitreous clay body, similar to porcelain but tougher and differing in makeup and firing requirements, which he ultimately named Syracuse China. His Imperial Geddo ware, fashioned from the new clay mix, won a medal for "translucent china" at Chicago's 1893 World Columbian Exposition. Pass oversaw further developments in technology, in 1896 installing the industry's first in-house lithographic shop for printing decals to decorate the china pieces. This same year, OPCo introduced the first American vitreous china made exclusively for restaurant use and ceased production of earthenware.

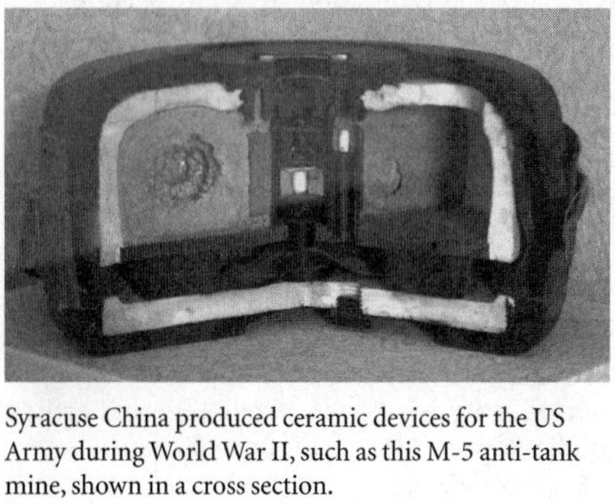

Syracuse China produced ceramic devices for the US Army during World War II, such as this M-5 anti-tank mine, shown in a cross section.

With the introduction of the chip-resistant Round-Edge shape in 1897, OPCo led the fast-growing hotelware market. In 1908 the company perfected underglaze decals that would not wear off, and OPCo designers created hundreds of stock patterns and thousands of custom designs for hotels, restaurants, hospitals, schools, fraternal orders, and transportation lines. OPCo's fine china for home use was of the same highly durable body as hotelware but of thinner dimensions, rendering it translucent. Advertising campaigns promoted this fine ware in national magazines. In 1921 the company's new factory on Court St in Syracuse became the first linear, one-floor plant in the US industry, streamlining movement of product in a single direction from clay shop mixing room to shipping department. The plant had about 1,000 employees at this time.

In 1933 the Econo-Rim shape revolutionized hotelware; its narrow rims suited the limited table space of railroad dining cars, and the firm soon supplied most of the nation's railroad china. The Pass dynasty continued under James Pass's son Richard, who headed the company from 1941 to 1958. During World War II, women, who had always worked as OPCo decorators, joined the workforce throughout the Syracuse plant, which produced ceramic shell casings in 1942–45 and again during the Korean War.

A century of private ownership ended in 1971 when Ryacuss Inc bought the company and formed Syracuse China Corp; workers unionized for the first time the same year. In 1978 Canadian Pacific Investments Ltd bought Syracuse China and then acquired two Pennsylvania potteries, Mayer China (1984) and Shenango Pottery (1988). Susquehanna-Pfaltzgraff Co of York, Pa, purchased Canadian Pacific's pottery holdings in 1989, closing Pennsylvania plants and concentrating operations in Syracuse. In 1995 Libbey Inc of Toledo, Ohio, bought Syracuse China, renaming all product lines Libbey–Syracuse China. In 2002 the Syracuse facility employed about 400 people.

Reed, Cleota, and Stanley Skoczen. *Syracuse China* (Syracuse: Syracuse Univ Press, 1998)

Cleota Reed

Syracuse Nationals. Professional basketball team. In 1946 Danny Biasone, owner of a bowling alley and liquor store in Syracuse, purchased a franchise in the National Basketball League (NBL) for $5,000. The Syracuse Nationals, or Nats, played downtown in the Jefferson Street Armory until 1949. That year the NBL merged with the Basketball Association of America to form the National Basketball Association (NBA). The team drew large audiences but had losing seasons in its early years. Player-coach Al Cervi, a Buffalo native, forward Dolph Schayes, who played college basketball at New York University, and guard Paul Seymour soon led the Nats to became one of the powers of the NBA. The Nats lost the league finals in 1950 and 1954, and won the championship in 1955 by defeating the Fort Wayne Pistons. The deciding seventh game of the series was played on Easter Sunday 1955 at the Onondaga War Memorial in downtown Syracuse. The Nats fell behind by 17 points, but a rally led by guard Billy Kenville gave Syracuse a 1-point lead in the final seconds. Guard George King clinched the victory and the title when he stole the ball from Fort Wayne's Andy Phillip. The Nats nearly returned to the championship series in 1959 when they led the Boston Celtics by 16 points in the seventh game of the Eastern Division finals, but Boston rallied to win. At the birth of the NBA, Syracuse was one of many small-city franchises along with Anderson, Ind; Waterloo, Iowa; and Sheboygan, Wisc. By 1963 those cities had lost their teams, and Syracuse was competing against markets like Los Angeles, Chicago, and New York City. After losing $39,000 in the 1962–63 season because of low attendance, Biasone sold the franchise for $500,000 to new owners in Philadelphia, who moved the team and renamed it the 76ers. The Nats had an NBA record of 576-437, and Biasone, Cervi, Schayes, guard Hal Greer, and Coach Alex Hannum were all voted into the Basketball Hall of Fame.

Ramsey, David. *The Nats: A Team, a City, an Era* (Utica: North Country Books, 1995)

David Luke Ramsey

Syracuse Post-Standard. Daily newspaper published by Advance Publications. The newspaper traces its history to the *Onondaga Standard,* which first appeared in 1829. Named the *Daily Standard* in 1850, the paper was edited by abolitionist Moses Summers and gave readers firsthand accounts of Civil War battles. The newspaper continued with minor variations in name until 1899, when it merged with the *Syracuse Post* (1894–98) to become the *Post-Standard.* Mabel G. Parker, a graduate of Syracuse University's first journalism class, became the first professionally trained staff member for a Syracuse newspaper when she was named society editor of the *Post-Standard* in 1924.

Early competition had come from the weekly *Western State Journal,* begun in 1839, which evolved into the *Syracuse Daily Journal* in 1844 and became the *Syracuse Journal* in 1899. Newspaper tycoon William Randolph Hearst bought the *Syracuse Journal* in 1925 and merged it with the *Evening Telegram* to become the city's late-afternoon paper. In 1939 S. I. Newhouse bought the *Syracuse Herald,* which dated to the 1870s, and within a few months also acquired the *Journal* and the *Sunday American* when Hearst's media empire ran into financial trouble. The *Journal* was closed and the *Herald-Journal* emerged in July. In 1942 Newhouse bought the *Post-Standard,* which moved into the same building with the *Herald-Journal* in 1965. The papers maintained a separate news staff and printing schedule but were joined under the corporate name of Syracuse Newspapers.

The staffs of these various papers merged in 1996, continuing to produce the morning *Post-Standard,* the afternoon *Herald-Journal,* and the Sunday *Herald American.* The Syracuse Newspapers building on Clinton Square was dedicated in 1971. A $30 million expansion in 2000 made room for a new press. Publication of the *Herald-Journal* and the *Herald American* ceased in 2001, dropping Syracuse off the list of 33 US cities to have both morning and afternoon newspapers. The *Post-Standard*'s electronic library, started in 1987, contains more than 1 million staff-written articles. The paper continues publication under Newhouse ownership, with daily circulation of nearly 124,000 and Sunday edition circulation of 178,000 as of 2002.

Lodder, Grace B. *Newspapers Published in Onondaga County to 1900* (Syracuse: Syracuse Public Library, 1932)

Meeker, Richard M. *S. I. Newhouse and the Business of News* (New York: Ticknor & Fields, 1983)

Matt Leingang

Syracuse SkyChiefs. Baseball team. The Syracuse Base Ball Club, formed in 1858, was the city's first organized baseball team. John Dunn formed the Syracuse Stars team eight years later, and the club's first games were played at Rose Hill Park. The Stars entered the professional ranks in 1876, and they played in the National League in 1879 until money woes forced them to disband just before the season ended. Another Stars club played in the major league American Association in 1890. Syracuse continued to host Stars teams in several leagues until 1929. Development of the modern minor league farm system began with Syracuse in 1921 when Branch Rickey, the general manager of the St. Louis Cardinals, acquired a half-interest in the Stars. Notable Stars players included Henry McCormick (a native Syracusan), Grover Cleveland Alexander, Mike Dorgan, Chick Hafey, Jim Bottomley, and Pepper Martin.

Pro baseball returned to the city in 1934 when Jack Corbett relocated his International League (IL) Jersey City franchise. Municipal Stadium at LeMoyne Park was built quickly for the 18 April opener of the new Syracuse Chiefs. A year later the Chiefs won their first IL Governors' Cup Championship as affiliates of the Boston Red Sox. The Chiefs became a farm team of the Cincinnati Reds in 1941, and the relationship lasted through the end of the decade. In June 1942 Municipal Stadium was renamed MacArthur Stadium in honor of the American general. The Chiefs won the Governors' Cup that year and the next. They reclaimed the championship in 1947 with a team led by IL Most Valuable Player Hank Sauer, who hit 50 home runs that season. In 1951 Vic Power and Nino Escalera became the team's first black players, and Manager Skeeter Newsome guided the Chiefs to another Governors' Cup in 1954. The Chiefs were sold to Miami businessmen on 5 Jan 1956. A month later the Detroit Tigers' Eastern League affiliate from Elmira (Chemung Co) moved to Syracuse and played as the Chiefs for a season and a half before the team was moved to Allentown, Pa.

In February 1961 the newly formed Community Baseball Club of Central New York purchased the IL Montreal Royals franchise from the Los Angeles Dodgers. They moved the team to Syracuse and named it the Chiefs. The new club has been affiliated with the Mets, Senators, Tigers, Yankees, and Blue Jays, and 1960s standouts included Mack Jones, Willie Horton, and Jim Northrup. On 14 May 1969 fire destroyed the center section of MacArthur Stadium, though most scheduled games were still played there. The team remained undaunted, winning three Governors' Cup titles over the next decade (1969–70, 1976) and reaching the championship round another three times (1974–75, 1979). The 1970 team, led by general manager Tex Simone and field manager Frank Verdi, also won a Little World Series title. Ron Guidry and Thurman Munson were among the renowned players of the time. Tony Fernandez, Carlos Delgado, and Shawn Green played for Syracuse in the following decades, and in 1995 construction began on a new stadium in the MacArthur Stadium parking lot. Funding came from the Toronto Blue Jays ($1 million), the SkyChiefs ($6 million), Onondaga Co ($3 million), and New York State ($16 million). In April 1997 the new P&C Stadium opened, MacArthur Stadium was demolished, and the team was renamed SkyChiefs.

Blahnik, Judith, and Phillip Stephen Schulz. *Mud Hens and Mavericks: The New Illustrated Travel Guide to Minor League Baseball* (New York: Viking Studio Books, 1995)

Syracuse SkyChiefs AAA Baseball, http://SkyChiefs.com

Ronald Gersbacher

Syracuse University. Private university. Chartered as a coeducational institution by the Methodist Episcopal Church in 1870, Syracuse University (SU) offered its first classes to 41 students in a rented building in downtown Syracuse on 4 Sept 1871. At that time the first building was begun on 50 acres (20 ha) of land donated by George F. Comstock. The Geneva Medical College was moved to SU and opened as the College of Physicians and Surgeons on 3 Oct 1872. SU dedicated its first building, the Hall of Languages, in 1873. The Holden Observatory was constructed in 1887, the College of Law opened in 1895, and the Carnegie Library, established by a $150,000 donation from Andrew Carnegie, was begun in 1905. By 1910 the university plant comprised 17 buildings on 100 acres (40 ha). In 1920 the charter was modified to define the university as nonsectarian. Syracuse University further expanded under the guidance of Chancellor James Roscoe Day, who enlisted the financial support of John D. Archbold, president of Standard Oil Co of New Jersey. Between 1894 and 1922, enrollment grew from 666 to 4,800, with commensurate growth in endowment support, the number of colleges and academic programs, and faculty. The university experienced periods of financial distress after World War I. At the height of the depression in 1933, faculty agreed to a 10% salary cut and the Joseph Slocum College of Agriculture was closed. The School of Public Communications was founded in 1934.

Under Chancellor William P. Tolley (1942–69), SU underwent major expansion. Starting in March 1943 it accepted 2,100 US Army Air Force cadets for a program combining military training with academics and bought about 50 houses and apartment buildings to accommodate them. More housing facilities were added as the university received soldiers from other branches of the armed forces, including the Women's Army Corps. At the suggestion of the Society of Friends (Quakers), SU offered 65 tuition-free scholarships to American-born Japanese (Nisei), freeing them from internment camps. Syracuse University Press began in 1943 with the publication of two technical books written by IBM personnel. The Servicemen's Readjustment Act of 1944 (GI Bill of Rights) brought 9,664 returning World War II veterans to SU in 1946. The university turned two extension centers into colleges, establishing Triple Cities College in Endicott (Broome Co) and Utica College in 1946. The university radio station, WAER-FM, began operation in 1947 and provided training for a range of broadcast journalists from Dick Clark to Ted

Hall of Languages at Syracuse University, designed by Horatio Nelson White, dedicated 8 May 1873.

Koppel. Spurred by financial considerations and the creation of the State University of New York (SUNY), the Forestry College became a specialized college of the state's system (now SUNY College of Environmental Science and Forestry) in 1948. SU sold its College of Medicine (now SUNY Upstate Medical University) and Triple Cities College (now Binghamton University) in 1950.

Social and political issues shaped Syracuse University in the postwar years. Tolley promoted racial integration and eliminated quotas for Jewish students in the professional schools. The men's student government elected its first African American president in 1958. The School of Public Communications received a donation of $15 million from publisher S. I. Newhouse in 1962. At the 1964 dedication of the S. I. Newhouse School of Public Communications, Pres Lyndon Johnson gave a speech warning of the communist threat to Southeast Asia. Protests by black students in 1969 initiated programs focused around African American academic needs.

During the 20-year tenure of Chancellor Melvin A. Eggers, the university's athletic prominence was highlighted in 1980 with the completion of the Carrier Dome, which serves NCAA Division I teams in men's basketball, football, and lacrosse. Syracuse suffered its greatest tragedy when 35 students returning home from a semester in London were killed in the 21 Dec 1988 terrorist destruction of Pan Am Flight 103 over Lockerbie, Scotland. To honor the memory of the victims, SU established the Lockerbie Scholars and Remembrance Scholars programs, as well as a stone semicircle memorial, the Place of Remembrance. The Special Collections Research Center of Syracuse University Library includes the private collection of Leopold von Ranke (1795–1886), regarded as the founder of the modern historical research, and the Rare Book and Manuscript Collections. Chancellor Kenneth A. Shaw (1991–2004) focused efforts on developing a "student-centered research university." Nancy Cantor was inaugurated as the 11th chancellor in November 2004, becoming the first woman to hold that post at SU.

Enrollment peaked in the late 1980s with 22,196 students in the university's 13 schools and colleges. Enrollment in fall 2003 comprised 11,455 full-time and 992 part-time undergraduates, and 4,096 full-time and 2,096 part-time graduate and law students. Just over 40% of its full-time undergraduates were New York State residents.

See also SYRACUSE.

Galpin, W. Freeman. *Syracuse University: The Pioneer Days* (Syracuse: Syracuse Univ Press, 1952)

———. *Syracuse University: The Growing Years* (Syracuse: Syracuse Univ Press, 1960)

Greene, John R. *Syracuse University: The Tolley Years* (Syracuse: Syracuse Univ Press, 1996)

———. *Syracuse University: The Eggers Years* (Syracuse: Syracuse Univ Press, 1998)

Tolley, William Pearson. *At the Fountain of Youth: Memories of a College President* (New York: Syracuse Univ, 1989)

Wilson, Richard, ed. *Syracuse University: The Critical Years* (Syracuse: Syracuse Univ Press, 1984)

Marla A. Bennett

Syracuse University football. The program began in 1889 with players clad in pink and blue. Orange became the official school color a year later. In 1907 the team moved into the new Archbold Stadium. Coach Frank "Buck" O'Neill's 1915 team (9-1-2) won a Rose Bowl invitation that it was unable to accept because of insufficient funds. Center and guard Joe Alexander became Syracuse's first three-time All-American (1918–20). End Vic Hanson was Syracuse's best player during the 1920s and won All-American honors in 1926. Teams of the 1930s included Olympic sprinter Marty Glickman. Syracuse University suspended sports competition during World War II, and the team had five losing seasons when play resumed. Improvement came after the arrival of Coach Floyd "Ben" Schwartzwalder (1949–73). In 1953 the Orangemen played in their first bowl game, losing the Orange Bowl to Alabama. Strong play continued with back Jim Brown, a 1956 All-American who led Syracuse to the 1957 Cotton Bowl. Brown was the first in a line of great running backs wearing number 44, and the tradition endures. He was followed by Ernie Davis, the first African American to win the Heisman Trophy (1961), and Floyd Little, a 1964–66 All-American. The hallmark season in Syracuse University football history remains 1959, when Davis ran behind a great offensive line nicknamed the Sizable Seven. Syracuse went 11-0, beating Texas in the Cotton Bowl (23-14) on 1 Jan 1960 to win the national championship. Fullback Larry Csonka starred for Syracuse during the late 1960s. Schwartzwalder retired in 1973 with a career record of 153-91-3 and was replaced by Frank Maloney (1974–80). The 1979 team won the Independence Bowl. That squad played home games at various sites while Archbold Stadium was torn down. In 1980 Syracuse University football moved into the Carrier Dome. Dick MacPherson (1981–90) coached the 1987 team to an 11-0-1 record and a tie with Auburn in the Sugar Bowl. Syracuse has fielded several outstanding quarterbacks since the mid-1980s, including Don McPherson, Marvin Graves, and Donovan McNabb. Paul Pasqualoni became head coach in 1991, and in 2001 he led the team to a victory over Kansas State in the Insight.com Bowl.

Early 20th-century Syracuse University football players.

Mullins, Michael A. *Syracuse University Football: A Centennial Celebration* (Norfolk, Va: Donning, 1989)

Snyder, Bob. *Orange Handbook: Stories, Stats, and Stuff about Syracuse Sports* (Wichita, Kans: Wichita Eagle and Beacon Publishing, 1996)

Bob Snyder

Syracuse University men's basketball. The program began in 1900 with little fanfare and no coach until the fourth season. Interest grew when the team, coached by Ed Dollard (1911–24), went undefeated in 1913–14. The Helms Foundation named the Syracuse team college basketball's national champion for 1917–18 and again under Coach Lew Andreas (1924–50) in 1925–26. Forward Vic Hanson (1925–27), enshrined in the Basketball and College Football Halls of Fame, was the 1927 college basketball Player of the Year and Syracuse's best player in its first half century. During that time the Syracuse Orangemen played home games in Archbold Gym, Jefferson Street Armory, Fairgrounds Coliseum, and the War Memorial. Syracuse played in its first NCAA tournament in 1957, but the program subsequently endured a 27-game losing streak, including the first 22 games in 1961–62. Play improved with the arrival of Dave Bing (1964–66) after the team had moved to Manley Field House in 1962. Syracuse's greatest player, Bing averaged 24.8 points per game in his career. He led Syracuse to the NCAA regional final in 1966. The program's last losing season of the century was 1968–69. Just a few years later, in 1975, Syracuse made its first NCAA Final Four appearance, under coach Roy Danforth (1969–76). Syracuse University was a charter member of the Big East Conference in 1979, and the team moved to the Carrier Dome in 1980. Fans there saw the play of Dwayne "Pearl" Washington, as well as of Rony Seikaly, Sherman Douglas, and Derrick Coleman, who led Syracuse to the 1987 NCAA finals, where they lost by one point to Indiana. In November

Reggie Powell driving to the basket, 1976.

1992 the NCAA placed the basketball program on a two-year probation for violation of recruitment rules, but the team returned to the NCAA tournament in 1994 after a one-year ban on postseason play. Billy Owens, John Wallace (leader of the 1996 NCAA runner-up team), and Etan Thomas have entertained huge crowds. In 2003 Jim Boeheim, Bing's teammate and Syracuse coach since 1976, coached the team to its first NCAA Championship and his 653d career win. Though unranked during the preseason, the team, led by freshman sensation Carmelo Anthony, defeated Kansas 81-78 in the title game. The program has over 1,500 victories.

Snyder, Bob. *Syracuse Basketball: A Century of Memories* (Champaign, Ill: Sports Publishing, 1999)

Bob Snyder

Syro-Lebanese. The first wave of immigrants from Arabic-speaking countries to New York State arrived from the late 1870s until 1924 and intermittently thereafter until 1965. These people were largely Maronite, Melkite, or Orthodox Christians from present-day Lebanon and Syria; all were called Syrian, according to the usage of both the Ottoman Empire and the government of the French Mandate (1920–43). For the most part, these immigrants came to better themselves economically, settling in New York City in various occupations, with a significant number in peddling and small business trades, including dealing in dry goods, laces, kimonos, needlework, and embroideries. The 1909 *Syrian Business Directory* shows 357 businesses in New York City, many in the Washington St area of Lower Manhattan and then later in the 1930s along Atlantic Ave in downtown Brooklyn. From these locations, the new immigrants, many of whom were coreligionists from the same villages in Lebanon and Syria, spread out through New York State, setting up networks of dry goods stores and peddling routes.

A sizable community developed in Utica, where by 1900 there were two dry goods stores on Bleecker St that each functioned as centers for villagers from two different Lebanon towns. Each store provided upstairs dormitories for more than 20 men, all listed on the 1900 census as peddlers. The era of dry goods peddling waned in the 1920s as many Syro-Lebanese outside New York City established corner grocery stores; Utica had 3 Syro-Lebanese groceries in 1910 and 66 in 1940. The New York City—based Mokarzel brothers launched the newspaper *Al-Hoda* (1898–1992), which served Arabic-speaking communities both within and outside the state. These communities also provided an audience for Syro-Lebanese intellectuals writing in English, including Kahlil Gibran, author of *The Prophet* (1923), and other New York City writers of the late 1910s and 1920 in the "Pen-Bond" club. Other writers published in the *Syrian World* (1926–32), edited by Salloum Mokarzel. By the 1920s children of immigrants began to attain higher education.

The state's Syro-Lebanese communities grew across the 20th century. The Utica area, which had counted 2,500 individuals of Syro-Lebanese origin in 1920, contained perhaps 5,000—including the grandchildren of immigrants—by 2000. Brooklyn remained the home of many descendants of the first wave of Arab immigrants from Lebanon and Syria. The Maronite Catholic parish of Our Lady of Lebanon in Brooklyn was founded in 1903 in Brooklyn Heights. Since 1977 it has been the see of the Eparchy of St. Maron of Brooklyn. The Church of the Virgin Mary is a Melkite Byzantine Catholic congregation in Park Slope in Brooklyn. Brooklyn also has two Syrian or Antiochian Orthodox parishes, St. Nicholas Antiochan Orthodox Cathedral and St. Mary's Orthodox Church.

After 1965 many Syro-Lebanese students and professionals left their homeland for the United States due to political, economic, and social unrest. Although many were Christian, several were Muslim. A number of Islamic mosques have opened, serving growing numbers of Muslims from Lebanon, Egypt, Palestine, and other Arab nations. There is also a substantial Jordanian Christian community in Yonkers, making up the majority of the approximately 10,000 Arabs who live in the city. The Melkite Christ the Savior Church in Yonkers is attended by many of these Jordanian Christians. Since the 1960s there has been a substantial immigration of Syrian Jews to New York City, with many living in Brooklyn, where there are at least 17 synagogues, with the population concentrated in the Flatbush and Gravesend neighborhoods. Among prominent Syro-Lebanese in New York City are the actor F. Murray Abraham, the former president of Hunter College Donna Shalala, and in Utica, James Zogby, director of the Arab American Institute, and his brother, John Zogby, president of Zogby International, a polling firm.

Benson, Kathleen, and Philip M. Kayal, eds. *A Community of Many Worlds: Arab Americans in New York City* (Syracuse: Syracuse Univ Press, 2002)
Kayal, Philip M., and Joseph M. Kayal. *The Syrian-Lebanese in America: A Study in Religion and Assimilation* (Boston: Twayne Publishers, 1975)
Moses, John G. *From Mount Lebanon to the Mohawk Valley: The Story of Syro-Lebanese Americans of the Utica Area* (Utica: Author, 1981)
Nassar, Eugene P. *Wind of the Land: Two Prose Poems* (Detroit: Association of Arab-American University Graduates, 1979)
Younis, Adele L. *The Coming of the Arabic-Speaking Peoples to the United States* (Staten Island: Center for Migration Studies, 1995)
Zogby, John. *Arab America Today* (Washington, DC: Arab American Institute, 1990)

Eugene Paul Nassar and John Zogby

Szasz, Thomas (Stephen) (*b* Budapest, Hungary, 15 Apr 1920). Psychiatrist and philosopher of medicine. He immigrated to the United States in 1938 and attended the University of Cincinnati, where he received an MD (1944), and subsequently trained in psychiatry and was on staff at the Chicago Institute for Psychoanalysis. He served from 1954 to 1956 in the Medical Corps of the US Naval Reserve. Szasz became a psychiatry professor at Upstate Medical Center (now SUNY Upstate Medical University) in Syracuse (1956–90). In 1961 he received international fame with his revolutionary work *The Myth of Mental Illness,* in which he argues that "mental illness" does not exist and that psychiatric practice, which deals with unacceptable behavior rather than "disease," is not medical treatment—it is a personal service if voluntary and a method of social control if not. Szasz's libertarian views include abolishing the insanity defense, prohibiting involuntary mental hospitalization, and decriminalizing drugs and suicide. Among his numerous books are *The Manufacture of Madness* (1970) and *Pharmacracy: Medicine and Politics in America* (2001).

Vatz, Richard E., and Lee S. Weinberg, eds. *Thomas Szasz: Primary Values and Major Contentions* (Buffalo: Prometheus Books, 1983)

Eric v. d. Luft

T

Taconic Range. A mountain range of about 140 miles (225 km) running north-south along New York State's eastern border. It is part of the Appalachian Mountains and runs from Dutchess Co northward to southwest of Brandon, Vt, forming New York's border with Massachusetts and with parts of Connecticut and Vermont. The range's name is derived from the Mohican word *taghkanick,* generally believed to mean wooded mountains. In 1839 State Geologist Ebenezer Emmons proposed his Taconic theory, according to which the range broke loose from the Berkshire Hills and Green Mountains some 445 million years ago in a geological event known as a klippe and drifted westward. The theory sparked long-standing debate among Emmons's colleagues, who had previously regarded the range as much younger. In general the Taconic Range is heavily wooded, steep, and narrow. It is broken by a few significant valleys, where the Hoosic River, Batten Kill, Kinderhook Creek, and smaller streams have cut broad channels. I-90 follows one of these valleys. The highest point along the range in New York State is Berlin Mountain (Rensselaer Co) with an elevation of 2,798 feet (852.8 m). Some of the most spectacular views are seen along the Taconic Trail (Rte 2), which was opened in 1920 over Petersburgh Pass, between Petersburgh (Rensselaer Co) and Williamstown, Mass. Considerable acreage along the Taconic Range has been preserved in all four states as part of public park and forest and private conservation lands, thus protecting the range's highly scenic character. Since the late 1980s, land preservation activity in New York and Massachusetts has protected much of the land along a ridge-top corridor, where the Taconic Crest Trail runs north for 30 miles (48 km) from US 20 to Rte 346. Another significant area has been preserved at Bashbish Falls, near the intersection of the New York, Massachusetts, and Connecticut state lines.

Roseberry, C. R. *From Niagara to Montauk: The Scenic Pleasures of New York State* (Albany: SUNY Press, 1982)

Warren F. Broderick

Taconic State Parkway. A 105 mi (169 km) scenic highway that begins at Kensico Dam in Valhalla (Westchester Co), extends north through the centers of Putnam, Dutchess, and Columbia Cos, and ends at the Berkshire Spur of the New York State Thruway near Chatham (Columbia Co). An important component of the New York State park system, the Taconic State Parkway (TSP) began as two separate projects. The southern section, the Bronx Parkway Extension (BPE), was proposed in the 1922 state park plan. This 30 mi (48 km) road extended the new Bronx River Parkway from Valhalla to Peekskill (Westchester Co), where drivers could cross the Bear Mountain Bridge (1924) into Bear Mountain and Harriman State Parks before heading south on the west side of the river. Funded by the state, the BPE was designed and built between 1923 and 1932 by the Westchester County Park Commission. A 4 mi (6 km) spur north connected the BPE to the Eastern State Parkway (ESP).

The northern component, the ESP, was planned, designed, and built between 1926 and 1963 by the Taconic State Park Commission (TSPC) and the New York State Department of Public Works. The TSPC had been created in 1925 to develop the state's recreational program in Putnam, Dutchess, Columbia, and Rensselaer Cos. Led by Franklin D. Roosevelt from 1925 to 1928, the commission embraced construction of a parkway as its primary recreational initiative in the region. Although it never reached Rensselaer Co, the 70 mi (113 km) drive linked four state parks, scenic overlooks, and recreational facilities throughout the eastern Hudson Valley. In 1941 the BPE and the ESP were combined as the Taconic State Parkway.

Following the model established by the Bronx River Parkway, the TSP was designed as a limited-access pleasure drive through a landscaped corridor. Like its predecessor, the southern Taconic was small in scale, following a narrow right-of-way landscaped to obscure dense outside development. The northern Taconic, built over three decades beginning in 1931, also followed this model but used improved road-building technology to create broader banked curves, wide rights-of-way and medians, and independent drives at different elevations. Its landscape design, however, was strikingly different. Leaving Westchester, the parkway traversed the steep Hudson Highlands and the open agricultural landscape of the eastern Hudson Valley. In the 21st century the parkway is a busy commuter highway. To improve safety the State Department of Transportation began closing numerous grade crossings in 2001. The parkway carries approximately 65,000 vehicles per day through Westchester Co, 25,000 through Putnam and southern Dutchess Cos, and 10,000 north of I-84.

Historic American Engineering Record. National Park Service, US Department of the Interior. "Taconic State Parkway. HAER No. NY-316." Prints and Photographs Division, Library of Congress, 1999

Kathleen LaFrank

Taghkanic [TOK-KON-IK]. Town (pop 1,118) in S central Columbia Co. Settled by Dutch and Germans probably by 1714, the town was formed from Livingston in 1803 as Granger and renamed in 1814. It was the site of two Marysburgh forges established by the Livingstons in 1760 and *ca* 1772, and of a plow foundry from *ca* 1820. While not prosperous farming country, it produced rye and lesser amounts of oats and corn; its residents were active in the antirent movement in 1844. A group of interrelated families in the hills near West Taghkanic have long been renowned for distinctive basketry. The Taconic State Parkway was built across Taghkanic in 1954. The town is the site of part of Lake Taghkanic State Park, New Forge State Forest, and Churchtown Reservoir (1905, Hudson water supply). The West Taghkanic Diner (1953) is a vintage eatery and landmark.

Tajiks. See CENTRAL ASIANS.

Talbert, Mary Burnett (*b* Oberlin, Ohio, 17 Sept 1866; *d* Buffalo, 15 Oct 1923). Civil and women's rights advocate and educator. Daughter of free-born Blacks from North Carolina, she graduated from Oberlin College in 1886. Family tradition holds she was a descendant of Richard Nicolls, the first English governor of New York Colony. She taught school in Little Rock, Ark, until 1891 when she married William H. Talbert, an accountant and prominent realtor. They moved to Buffalo, where they were active members of the Michigan Street Baptist Church and leaders of Buffalo's African American community. She was a cofounder of the Phyllis Wheatley Club in 1899, Buffalo's affiliate of the National Association of Colored Women's Clubs (NACW). W. E .B. DuBois, John Hope, and William Monroe Trotter met at her house in 1905 to organize the Niagara Movement, a civil rights organization and precursor to the NAACP. Talbert was elected president of the Empire Federation of Colored Women's Clubs in 1911 and of the NACW in 1916, serving until 1920. During her administration the NACW purchased and restored Cedar Hill, the Anacostia, Washington, DC, home of Frederick Douglass, as a historical site. During World War I Talbert served as a Red Cross nurse in France. In 1920 she was elected NACW delegate to the International Council of Women's conference in Christiana, Norway, and was appointed to the League of Nations Women's Committee on International Relations. As NAACP vice president Talbert chaired its antilynching campaign in 1921. Women's clubs, hospitals, and a University at Buffalo building have been named in her honor.

Talbert, Mary B. "Did the Negro Make in the 19th Century Achievements along the Lines of Wealth, Morality, Education, etc., Commensurate with His Opportunities? If So, What Achievements Did He Make?" In *20th-Century Negro Literature,* ed. Daniel Wallace Culp (New York: Arno Press, 1969)
Williams, Lillian S. "Talbert, Mary Morris Burnett." In *Black Women in America: An Historical Encyclopedia,* ed. Darlene Clark Hine (Brooklyn: Carlson Publishing, 1993)

Lillian S. Williams

Tallmadge, Nathaniel P(arker) (*b* Chatham, Columbia Co, 8 Feb 1795; *d* Battle Creek, Mich, 2 Nov 1864). US senator. An 1815 graduate of Union College, he studied law in Poughkeepsie, where he was admitted to the bar 1818. Tallmadge was elected to the state assembly in 1827. He served as Poughkeepsie's postmaster in 1830 and in the state senate from 1830 to 1833. He served two terms in the US Senate, 1833–44. Initially an enthusiastic supporter of Martin Van Buren for governor and then for president, he became an outspoken critic of Van Buren's fiscal policies. He joined the Whig Party in 1837. Accepting a presidential appointment as governor of Wisconsin Terr, he resigned from the Senate. Removed from the governorship the following year by Pres James K. Polk, he never held political office again. He spent his last years studying and writing tracts on spiritualism.

William P. McDermott

Tammany Hall. Democratic Party organization in New York Co that dominated New York City politics from the 1850s through the 1930s. The Tammany Society was founded on 12 May 1789 as a nonpolitical patriotic and fraternal organization. It was named after a 17th-century Delaware Indian and used pseudo-Indian ritual at meetings at its headquarters in Lower Manhattan for its "braves" and "sachems." It entered politics in support of Aaron Burr in 1800 and would support a number of Democratic-Republican and Democratic politicians, among them Martin Van Buren. Its support of Democratic Party issues, such as opposition to nativism and anti-Catholicism, forged an enduring link with the immigrant Irish.

Tammany Hall emerged as a major force in New York City politics with the election of Fernando Wood as mayor in 1854. William M. "Boss" Tweed became its leader in 1863, dominating the city's politics for the remainder of the decade. He embarked on an ambitious rebuilding plan for New York City, which badly needed new infrastructure, but the bribery and kickbacks that accompanied the new construction would forever associate Tammany Hall with the heights of municipal corruption. The downfall of the Tweed Ring came in 1871 through an alliance between anti-Tammany Democrats and Republicans.

Tammany Hall rebounded quickly from the debacle. Tweed's replacement, "Honest John" Kelly, the first of 10 consecutive Irish American leaders, built the machine, modeling it on the Catholic archdiocese and dividing Manhattan into districts of some thousand or so voters, roughly the size of a parish. Supervising the districts were captains, who functioned like auxiliary bishops, and over them was the party chair, equivalent to the archbishop. Kelly's successor, Richard Croker, developed the principle of trading favors for votes. Whenever Tammany did a favor for a business, it exacted one in return, often in the form of cash but also in jobs. The district leaders distributed these jobs to party faithful. If a loyal voter had a problem, he took it to the leader. If his son got into minor trouble with the law, the leader would have a word with the judge, often also a member of Tammany. If he fell behind in the rent, the leader would have a word with the landlord. If someone died, the leader went to the wake and the funeral, sent the biggest bouquet, and, if needed, supplied money to meet expenses. At the same time, those in the city's flourishing commercialized vice industries, especially gambling and prostitution, often sought and found Tammany's protection, and organized crime developed an enduring relationship with Tammany Hall. All of these services, legal and illegal, were subordinate to the dispensing of patronage, which was Tammany's raison d'être. By the turn of the 20th century, by one estimate, Tammany controlled 60,000 government jobs, with salaries totaling $90 million a year.

The Lexow Committee's 1894 investigation of municipal corruption contributed to Tammany's defeat in the New York City mayoral races in 1894 and 1901. Charles F. Murphy, Croker's successor, headed Tammany from 1902 until his death in 1924. While Murphy remained committed to Tammany's usual patronage prerogatives, he tried to broaden the appeal of Tammany to good government supporters and non-Irish voters with a newfound commitment to Progressive era reform. In doing so he advanced the careers of Tammany politicians like Robert F. Wagner Sr and Alfred E. Smith, both of whom developed national reputations as progressives. Tammany's political power remained formidable, not just in New York City, but in the state as a whole, where all Democrats had to define their relation to Tammany, which had immense power in the legislature. Tammany's leverage was perhaps most clearly demonstrated in 1913 when Democratic governor William Sulzer, elected the previous year with Tammany support, broke with Tammany and was promptly impeached and removed from office.

The Seabury Committee's investigations, which uncovered a skein of municipal corruption and in 1932 forced Tammany stalwart and New York City mayor Jimmy Walker from office, marked the end of the heyday of Tammany Hall. The end came in part because the Seabury Investigations engendered much bad blood between Tammany and Gov Franklin D. Roosevelt. The former's mistrust continued under Roosevelt's presidency, when he funneled city patronage to Mayor Fiorello La Guardia (1933–45), a resolute opponent of Tammany Hall. Tammany Hall never regained its former power but still played a major role in mayoral and state politics. Carmine DeSapio emerged as Tammany Hall's leader in the 1950s, though his repudiation by Mayor Robert F. Wagner Jr in 1961 and defeats in a comeback by young Reform Democrat Ed Koch ended his political career. DeSapio's successor, J. Raymond Jones, was the first African American head of Tammany Hall and its last significant leader before changes in the city's politics reduced its position to one of relatively minor importance. Among Jones's protégés was David Dinkins, New York City's first black mayor (1990–93) and one of the many mayors to emerge from the regular Democratic organization of New York Co.

See also CARTOGRAPHY AND MAPPING; PROSTITUTION; SEABURY INVESTIGATIONS; TWEED RING.

McClymer, John F. "Of 'Mornin' Glories' and 'Fine Old Oaks': John Purroy Mitchel, Al Smith, and Reform as an Expression of Irish-American Aspiration." In *The New York Irish*, ed. Ronald H. Bayor and Timothy J. Meagher (Baltimore: Johns Hopkins Univ Press, 1996)

Mushkat, Jerome. *Tammany: The Evolution of a Political Machine, 1789–1865* (Syracuse: Syracuse Univ Press, 1971)

Weiss, Nancy Joan. *Charles Francis Murphy, 1858–1924: Respectability and Responsibility in Tammany Politics* (Northampton, Mass: Smith College Press, 1968)

John McClymer

Tannersville. Village (pop 448) in Hunter (Greene Co). Named for the men of the tanneries that dominated the area in the early 19th century, by midcentury the boardinghouse resort business had grown. From 1887 through 1889 three large cottage parks—residential developments of summer homes—were constructed nearby, providing extensive employment. Jewish vacationers started arriving around 1893 and were soon dominant in the village, which was incorporated in 1895. Synagogues were organized in 1899 and 1911. Beginning in the 1920s Armenians, Greeks, Syrians, and Italians began patronizing specific resorts. Much of its resort trade depends on nearby Hunter Mountain.

Field Horne

tanning industry. Leather tanning once was a ubiquitous component of American manufacturing. Shoes, clothing, saddles, and industrial machinery all derived some of their raw materials from tanned leather. Prior to 1800 most leather was tanned in cottage industry tanneries on family farms or in small town tanneries. Dutch settlers established New York's first tanneries in the 17th century to make leather from deer- and calfskins. The earliest tanneries were little more than a few pits in which tanners, many of whom also made shoes, immersed locally slaughtered animal hides and skins to produce leather for household and community use. As New York State's population increased during the 18th century, the demand for leather, especially shoe leather, also increased. By the first decade of the 19th century, there were 867 tanneries in the state. Higher demand, increased supplies of domestic and foreign hides and skins, improved technology, and innovative integration strategies contributed toward making New York State the cradle of the American tanning industry.

From Farm to Factory

Before the War of 1812, most tanneries were small workshops where tanners, some of whom were also farmers and cordwainers, transformed perishable hides into durable leather. Using tannin-rich bark from oaks and hemlocks for tanning liquors and animal hides, tanners relied on two commodity flows for raw materials: forest products (bark) and the by-products of meat-animal slaughter (hides). Tanners generally purchased ground bark from a bark miller and used hides from family-owned livestock, or they engaged in community exchange systems in which hides and skins belong to neighbors were tanned in return for other agricultural commodities or labor. By 1820 many tanneries had integrated bark mills into their facilities, reducing the need to rely on third-party millers for the great quantities of tanbark necessary to make leather.

New York State's tanning industry followed an uneven trajectory from farm to factory. During the 17th and 18th centuries, small tanneries were distributed throughout the state. By the turn of the 19th century, tannery concentrations began to appear in New York City and regionally. Driven by access to raw materials, mainly tanbark, and increased demand, tanners took up the trade full-time and spread across New York State's landscape and its borders, building tanneries and towns. Five tanning regions developed as a result of this expansion: the Hudson River, Catskill Mountain, Southern Tier, Mohawk River valley, and Adirondack Mountain regions. New York City also had its own tannery district (and later leather industry financial center) called the Swamp. Although all five regions played an important role in making New York State the leading producer of tanned leather in the United States by the Civil War, the Swamp and the Catskill Mountains were the cultural hearths from which most technological innovations and business practices flowed.

New York City

During the colonial period, tanners plied their trade along Ferry, Frankfort, Gold, Jacob, and Spruce Sts in Manhattan's Swamp. They also made leather along the margins of Collect Pond. As nuisance trades such as tanning were regulated further away from urban cores, the Swamp's tanners became hide and leather merchants, and this group included some of New

York City's earliest power brokers. Jacob Lorillard entered the leather trade in 1800, and future New York City mayor Gideon Lee began brokering leather in New York City in 1807 and pioneered leather trade mercantilism; these two men were among the Swamp's earliest and most widely known tanners and leather merchants. Many of the entrepreneurs who set up shop in the Swamp had begun tanning on family farms. Cousins George and William Palen, Swamp mainstays throughout much of the 19th century, were third-generation tanners whose grandfather, Ezekiel Palen, was a Dutchess Co farmer, cordwainer, and tanner. Their fathers learned to tan on Ezekiel's farm and in 1802 opened their own independent tannery in Ulster Co. Greene Co tanner Zadock Pratt, whose son George went to work in the Swamp, tanned leather alongside his father and brothers on a Rensselaer Co farm. Cottage industry tanneries were fertile training fields for second-generation industrial tanners.

Manhattan's Swamp became the financial hub of the American leather industry. Tanners-turned-merchants contracted with tanners throughout New York State, Pennsylvania, and beyond to tan hides the merchants owned and to return the leather to New York City for sale. Prior to 1800 most of New York State's leather was light upper leather, but many tanners produced both light and heavy leather; after the turn of the 19th century, specialization in heavy sole leather characterized the industry.

Catskills

With their hemlock-covered mountainsides and clear streams, the five-county Catskills region (Delaware, Greene, Schoharie, Sullivan, and Ulster Cos) attracted former cottage industry tanners, such as the Palens, who founded Palenville (Greene Co), and the Pratts, who founded Prattsville (Greene Co), as well as master tanners from other regions. Massachusetts tanner William Edwards moved to Greene Co in 1816 and founded a tannery where he developed innovative tanning methods, such as heaters for tanning liquors and conveyance systems for filling and draining tanning vats, that decreased the time required for tanning and facilitated economies of scale in the industrialization of tanning. Edwards's methods were rapidly adopted by tanners statewide.

Catskill Mountain tanners specialized in heavy sole leather, produced from Swamp merchants' hides, which was shipped back to New York City for sale. The height of Catskills tanning lasted approximately from 1815 to 1850. Between 1835 and 1860, more than 40% of the leather produced in New York State was tanned in the Catskills. Success in the area was limited by a finite supply of hemlock trees. By 1850 intensive tanning had deforested much of the five-county region, and tanners sought new locations in environmentally similar regions. They set their sights on the Adirondack Mountains or the Southern Tier, and many either left New York altogether for Pennsylvania or opened satellite tanneries in the Pocono and Allegheny Mountains.

The migration northward from the Catskills to the Adirondacks began in the 1840s as Catskills tanners discovered rapid deforestation, the downside of the economies of scale they enjoyed. By 1850 large Catskills-like tanneries were operating in the same pattern crystallized in the southern counties. Hides were shipped from New York City and were tanned on contract in the Adirondacks; Swamp merchants then sold the finished leather. Benjamin Burhans, who in 1836 bought a large tannery in Warrensburg (Warren Co), began his tanning career as a partner of Jonathan Palen in an Ulster Co tannery near the Greene Co line. Burhans sold his interest in the Plattekill tannery in 1836 and moved north to Warren Co. Tanning for Swamp merchants throughout its ownership by the Burhans family, the tannery at Warrensburg produced sole leather until it closed in 1885.

Large Catskills tanning families bought and built tanneries in the hemlock-rich Alleghenies and neighboring mountain groups. Catskills tanners, starting in the late 1830s, began buying and building tanneries from Broome to Cattaraugus Cos. Lewis Northrup started his career working alongside Peter Palen in one of Palen's Greene Co tanneries. In 1828, after becoming his partner, Northrup married Palen's daughter. Within a decade Northrup had moved to Broome Co, where he built the first of three tanneries that produced sole leather until the 1880s.

In Cattaraugus Co brothers Gilbert W., Arthur, and Edward Palen in 1867 bought and enlarged a decade-old tannery in Limestone. Located in the heart of hemlock country, the Limestone Tannery produced sole leather until it was sold by the Union Leather Co, the operating company of United States Leather Co, in 1917. As New York State's hemlock trees disappeared, so too did the state's tanneries. The tanbark along the Southern Tier and in Central New York began to disappear around the turn of the 20th century, as did the bark in the Adirondacks. In 1893, when many of New York State's tanning families merged their plants into the United States Leather (along with their holdings in Pennsylvania and other states), the state's leadership role in the American leather industry was on the wane. Raw material costs and increasing concerns over stream pollution pushed tanners farther west to Wisconsin and ultimately the Pacific Northwest. By the middle of the 20th century, there were few tanneries left in New York State. Small concentrations of specialized tanners, such as those at Gloversville (Fulton Co), remained active, and the tanneries associated with the sprawling Endicott Johnson shoe operation in Broome Co continued to produce leather.

Ellsworth, Lucius. *Craft to National Industry in the 19th Century: A Case Study of the Transformation of the New York State Tanning Industry* (New York: Arno Press, 1975)

McMartin, Barbara. *Hides, Hemlock, and Adirondack History* (Utica: North Country Books, 1992)

Rotenstein, David S. "Tanbark Tycoons: Palen Family Sullivan County Tanneries, 1832–1871," *Hudson Valley Regional Review* 15 (Sept 1998): 1–42

David S. Rotenstein

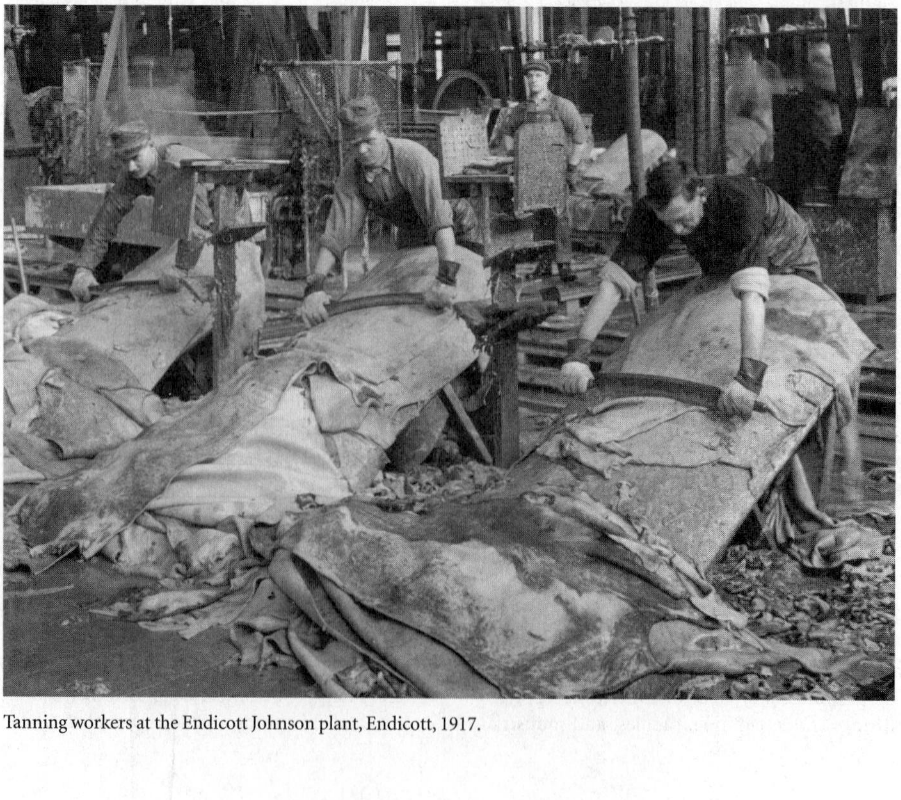

Tanning workers at the Endicott Johnson plant, Endicott, 1917.

tap dance. American dance characterized by rhythmic and often improvisational footwork. The form originated in West African rhythms and dances brought by slaves and was combined with the European-rooted folk dances of white southern plantation owners, specifically the Lancaster clog from England and the Irish jig. The body, through stamping, clapping, and thigh whacking, was made a rhythmic instrument.

In the early 1800s, minstrel shows featured predominantly Irish and English immigrants in blackface makeup impersonating African American song and dance. Minstrelsy's heyday was from the 1840s to the late 19th century but began roughly in 1828 when Thomas Dartmouth "Daddy" Rice impersonated a singing and dancing black slave called "Jim Crow." Jigs and clog dances were peppered with imitations of shuffling steps done by slaves, resulting in a form known as the soft shoe. A master of this style was George W. Primrose, a white performer from Mount Vernon (Westchester Co). Black dancer Master Juba (William Henry Lane) learned to incorporate intricate Irish footwork while dancing in street corner dance "challenges" in the Irish Paradise Square neighborhood of the Five

Points section of Lower Manhattan. Living very near Irish immigrants, Juba learned and adapted the Irish jig to his own style of dance, and by 1845 he was the first black dancer to receive top billing over white minstrel performers. As minstrelsy began to wane, many tap performers went on to make careers in vaudeville, which would remain popular until around 1920.

In Manhattan *Darktown Follies* (1913) featured the tapping of black dancers Toots Davis and Eddie Rector, while Eubie Blake and Noble Sissle's *Shuffle Along* (1921) featured an all-black cast including Josephine Baker. Both productions helped catapult the popularity of tap and other black dance and musical theater, sparking a marked increase of dancing in musical comedies. Touring in New York State by vaudeville and dance revues included performances at the Town Casino and Shea's Theater in Buffalo. Other venues for tap were found in Harlem, such as the Hoofer's Club (1920–mid-1940s), Connie's Inn (1929–32), and the Cotton Club (1923–39). The Cotton Club featured the Nicholas Brothers (Harold and Fayard), who were regulars at the club from 1932 until it closed in 1939.

In the early 1900s "King" Rastus Brown pioneered the "buck" dance style, with flat-footed shuffling and rhythmic steps and a low stance. His rival, Bill "Bojangles" Robinson, developed a lighter, more vertical style dance on the toes, becoming famous for a stair dance in Broadway's *Blackbirds of 1928*. After his death in 1949 a group of veteran tappers formed the Copasetics to preserve Robinson's steps. John "Bubber" Sublett founded rhythm tap, using the toe and the heel separately to make complex rhythms. Clayton "Peg Leg" Bates developed a unique style that merged soft shoe and rhythm tap with unique techniques and sounds made possible by his wooden leg. In the 1950s he established the Peg Leg Country Club in Kerhonkson (Ulster Co), the largest black-owned and -operated resort in the country, featuring numerous jazz musicians and tap dancers. Laurence Donald Jackson, known as Baby Laurence, used rhythm tap techniques to emulate the improvisations of jazz musicians in the 1940s. The Hoofer's Club in Harlem served as both an informal school and a proving ground for aspiring tap dancers. Dancers such as Charles "Honi" Coles and Charles "Cholly" Atkins taught at Coles's school in Manhattan in the 1950s.

In the 1960s the popularity of tap waned, although it revived with Broadway productions such as *The Wiz* (1975), *Sugar Babies* (1979), *The Tap Dance Kid* (1983), and *Jelly's Last Jam* (1992), featuring Savion Glover and his mentor, Gregory Hines. In 1996 Glover incorporated hip-hop and funk rhythms into tap in *Bring in Da Noise, Bring in Da Funk*. Brenda Bufalino founded the Dancing Theater in 1975, a tap school, in New Paltz (Ulster Co), and Manhattan's American Tap Orchestra (1986). In 1986 Heather Cornwell founded Manhattan Tap in New York City.

Haskins, Jim, and N. R. Mitgang. *Mr. Bojangles: The Biography of Bill Robinson* (New York: William Morrow, 1988)

Stearns, Marshal, and Jean Stearns. *Jazz Dance* (New York: DaCapo Press, 1968)

Patricia Beaman

Tappan. Locality (pop 6,757) in Orangetown (Rockland Co). Settled *ca* 1680, Tappan was patented in 1687 to 16 purchasers, most of whom were Dutch, but three were of African origin. Tappantown, as it was called, was the Orange Co seat until 1773. Its oldest house, the DeClark-DeWint House (1700), is operated as the George Washington Masonic Historic Site in recognition of Washington having stayed there on four occasions. Maj John André was imprisoned in the Mabie House (often called the Old '76 House) before his execution on Andre Hill nearby on 2 Oct 1780. Tappan acquired stations on the Erie (1841) and West Shore (1883) Railroads, and development accelerated after World War II. The Palisades Interstate Parkway (1958) improved communter's travels. The hamlet contains a National Historic District (1990).

Mary R. Cardenas

Tappan Indians. A Munsee-speaking community centered around the wide cove bordered by the upper reaches of the Palisades Escarpment on the west shore of the Hudson River around what is now the Village of Nyack (Rockland Co) and adjacent regions of New Jersey. Of uncertain linguistic derivation, the name Tappan first appeared on Dutch maps in 1616. Sparkill Creek, flowing into the Hudson River at the Village of Piermont (Rockland Co), was originally known as Tappan Creek. Surviving documents indicate that the people of Tappan were closely connected with their Hackensack and Haverstraw neighbors. Several Tappans were among those killed or taken captive by a large Mohican (Mahican) war party that swept through lower Hudson Valley Indian towns in the winter of 1642–43 during Kieft's War. Still others died in the fighting that followed before peace was restored on 30 Aug 1645. Maintaining close connections with their Indian neighbors, Tappan people surviving the war and the many epidemic outbreaks that devastated Indian communities throughout the region finally sold their lands to English colonists in a series of deeds beginning in 1671. Led by Mindawassa, their war captain, and Memshe, a Minisink man also identified as a Tappan sachem, most Tappans moved to Minisink after selling the last of their lands in 1681. Shortly thereafter, colonists stopped using the name to identify Indians living at Tappan.

Esposito, Frank J. "Indian-White Relations in New Jersey" (PhD diss, Rutgers Univ, 1976)

Grumet, Robert S. " 'We Are Not So Great Fools': Changes in Upper Delawaran Socio-Political Life, 1630–1758" (PhD diss, Rutgers Univ, 1979)

Robert S. Grumet

Tappan Zee Bridge. One of the nation's longest bridges, this 3.03 mi (4.88 km) cantilever truss span is the centerpiece of the New York State Thruway, carrying the roadway across the Hudson River from South Nyack (Rockland Co) to Tarrytown (Westchester Co). Construction began in March 1952 and cost $80.8 million. Gov W. Averell Harriman officially opened the bridge on 15 Dec 1955. The span is revolutionary in design: because the underlying bedrock is too far beneath the river bottom to make economically feasible a traditional design, in which supports are fixed directly to the bedrock, the Tappan Zee floats upon buoyant air-filled caissons buried in the river's silt. The siting of the bridge was highly controversial. The Tappan Zee was placed at one of the widest points of the river because the Port Authority of New York and New Jersey, since its inception in 1921, holds monopoly rights to Hudson River crossings from the Statue of Liberty north 25 miles (40 km). Seeking to operate its own bridge independently, the New York State Thruway Authority situated it outside of the Port Authority's zone of control. The crossing could have been placed much further upriver; however, this would have required the Thruway to traverse the entire length of the New York City suburb of Westchester Co, making it prohibitively expensive to condemn the necessary lands. Therefore the Thruway was carried down through the farming region of Rockland Co on the river's opposite side. Once opened the bridge had an extraordinary impact on Rockland, rapidly transforming its communities into suburbs, with the county's population increasing from 89,276 in 1950 to 229,903 in 1970. In 1994 the span was renamed the Governor Malcolm Wilson Tappan Zee Bridge in honor of the former governor. The success of the Tappan Zee has sown the seeds of its own possible demise. With Rockland now a densely populated suburb, traffic over the span has greatly increased, and by 2001 traffic loads exceeded by 30% the bridge's original design specifications for a maximum capacity of 100,000 vehicles per day. The heavy usage has led to the rapid physical deterioration of the crossing. Since 1997 Thruway engineers have called to replace the current span with a much larger structure.

New York State Thruway Authority. "The Governor Malcolm Wilson Tappan Zee Bridge," http://www.thruway.state.ny.us/factbook/tz/index.html

Tod M. Ottman

Tarrytown. Village (pop. 11,090) in Greenburgh (Westchester Co). The site of Maj John André's capture in 1780, Tarrytown originated in the 18th century as a landing and trading center and became increasingly busy in the 19th century. The Hudson River Railroad came through in 1849. The village incorporated in 1870. Among Tarrytown's industrial products between the Civil War and World War I were shoes, hats, silk, wallpaper, and eggbeaters. Until it closed in 1997, the General Motors plant in Sleepy Hollow was the largest employer of Tarrytown residents. In 2003 largely a suburban commuter village, its largest employers were Hitachi America (electronics marketing), Kraft Foods, and Hilton Inn. Landmarks include the Gothic Revival estate Lyndhurst (1838–65), Washington Irving's home Sunnyside (1835), and the Tarrytown Music Hall (1885), Westchester Co's oldest operating theater. The Hackley School (1899) and Marymount College (1907) are in Tarrytown.

J. Brooks Flippen

Taughannock Falls. Waterfall and popular natural attraction in the Taughannock State Park near Ulysses (Tompkins Co). The falls plunge through a scenic, mist-shrouded glen with walls nearly 400 ft high (122 m). The gorge into which the water flows was formed by a combination of erosion caused by Taughannock Creek and glacial activity carving away shale. The cataract has a drop of 215 feet (65.5 m), 33 feet (10.1 m) more than Niagara Falls, making it the highest free-falling waterfall in the United States east of the Rocky Mountains. The name originates from the Delaware word *taghkanic,* meaning great waterfall in the forest. It is easily accessible and offers nearby trails, campsites, cabins, and recreational facilities. The Taughannock Falls State Park was created in 1925.

Halsey, Lewis. *The Falls of Taughannock* (New York: J. A. Gray and Green, 1866)
Taughannock Falls, http://www.taughannock.com

Barry Mowell

taxation. New York State has the powers of a sovereign entity to levy and collect taxes. Within the American system of dual sovereignty, however, a state's exercise of this power is limited by certain provisions of the US Constitution, including the commerce clause and due process clause. In addition, New York State has adopted provisions in its own constitution that guide and constrain the exercise of its inherent powers of taxation. New York State not only establishes and administers its own taxes, but also determines the taxes that its local governments may levy. The state has delegated great responsibility to its local governments for both the delivery of services and the raising of revenues to pay for those services. In 2000 New York was the only state in which local governments raised more tax revenues than the state government. Local governments raised 52% of all state-local tax revenue; for the other 49 states collectively, this figure was 36.3%. Half of all local tax revenues were raised by New York City, even though it has only 42% of the state's population. New York City, with its huge daily influx of commuters, its many business and leisure visitors from throughout the world, and its unusual mix of wealth and poverty, has service responsibilities that are disproportionate to its residential population. The state has authorized New York City to levy a far broader range of taxes than other local governments. As a consequence, New York City's tax system is more akin to a state tax system than to those of other localities within New York or elsewhere in the country.

The US Constitution does not contain any explicit limitations on the states' power to tax, but a number of its provisions have been interpreted to limit the states' use of the taxing power. For example, a state cannot levy a tax that discriminates against interstate commerce in favor of local business interests or that treats residents of other states more harshly than its own residents. New York State has been the subject of a number of landmark court decisions in this regard, including *Boston Stock Exchange et al v State Tax Commission et al* (1977) and *Westinghouse Electric Corporation v Tully* (1984), in which the US Supreme Court struck down New York State tax laws on these grounds. The power to tax rests inherently with the state legislature as part of its lawmaking power. As with other laws, the legislature can enact laws imposing taxes by a simple majority with the concurrence of the governor or by a two-thirds majority over the governor's veto. The state constitution does provide, however, that neither the senate nor the assembly may give final passage to tax legislation unless at least three-fifths of the members of that house are present. In addition to this extra "quorum" requirement, tax bills, like other bills, require the affirmative vote of a majority of all elected members, not just a majority of those present and voting, to become a law.

Unlike the US Constitution, which requires that revenue bills originate in the House of Representatives, the state constitution provides that tax bills may originate in either house of the legislature. The state constitution prohibits the imposition of a property tax on intangible personal property and legislation granting exemptions from real property tax to specific individuals or businesses. It also prohibits tax legislation drafted to incorporate other legislation by reference. In 1959 the voters of the state approved an amendment to this constitutional provision allowing the legislature to incorporate provisions of federal income tax laws by reference.

Historical Perspective

Until the 1840s, New York State was able to operate with little or no direct taxation. Instead, the state financed its expenditures through lotteries, the sale of state lands, canal tolls, auction fees, taxes on saltworks, and investment of state funds. The state resorted to general property taxation only twice in this period, from 1799 to 1802 and again from 1815 to 1826. In both instances, the imposition of a general property tax was motivated by the need for increased military spending in light of hostile relations between the United States and foreign nations. Like that of most states, the state's property tax was originally imposed on all property, both real and personal. Collecting revenues was largely the responsibility of the comptroller. A state property tax was reinstated in 1842, at the rate of 1 mill (one-tenth of 1¢) per dollar of assessed value. This rate ranged between 1/4 mill and 1 mill per dollar for the next 12 years. Today, real property tax rates in New York are expressed relative to each $1,000 of assessed value; 1 mill per dollar of assessed value is the same as $1 per $1,000 of assessed value. Constitutional amendments adopted on the recommendation of the 1846 Constitutional Convention to improve state financial practices also increased the need for taxation, as did the American Civil War. As a result, the property tax rate was increased in 1855 to 1.25 mills per dollar, and by 1862 it had grown to 4.75 mills per dollar, with 2 mills of that rate raising funds for the national treasury. The property tax continued to serve as the primary source of both state and local revenue until the beginning of the 20th century.

During the late 1800s and the early 1900s the activities of state and local governments grew in response to the challenges of urbanization and industrialization. So too did the recognition that the increased tax burden should not be borne entirely by property taxes, which measured only one kind of wealth. In response, the state began to diversify its tax system. During the 1880s it established a corporate franchise tax (1880) and a tax on the organization of corporations (1886), and began to tax inheritances (1885). A stock transfer tax was added in 1905 and a mortgage recording tax in 1906. The State Tax Department, headed by a three-member State Tax Commission, was created in 1915. A net income–based corporate franchise tax was imposed beginning in 1917 and a personal income tax in 1919. By 1921 the Tax Department had assumed most of the state's tax collection responsibilities. In 1927 the Tax Department was renamed the Department of Taxation and Finance (DTF) and assigned the duties of the state treasurer. Meanwhile, real property taxes continued to decline as a source of revenue for the state government and were abandoned entirely for this purpose by 1929. The modern tax system and its administration had begun to take shape. Over the next three decades, the state added taxes on motor fuel (1929), alcoholic beverages (1933), the income of unincorporated businesses (1935), cigarette sales (1939), a pari-mutuel tax on horse-race wagering (1940), a bank tax (1940), and a truck mileage tax (1952). Over the same period the taxation of personal property was abolished by statute (1934), and the taxation of intangible personal property was prohibited by constitutional amendment (1938). The personal income tax emerged as the single largest source of state revenues over this period.

In 1960 the state enacted its current personal income tax. In 1965 it adopted a statewide sales and use tax of 2%, which immediately became the second leading source of state revenue. New York's top personal income tax rate reached its peak in 1972 under Gov Nelson A. Rockefeller: 15% on taxable income over $25,000, plus a 2 1/2% surcharge, making the top effective marginal rate 15.375%. Corporate franchise tax rates peaked in 1976 at 10%, with a 20% surcharge, for an effective rate of 12%. In the second half of the 1970s, following a New York City fiscal crisis, the state's tax policy increasingly focused on its competitive position vis-à-vis other states. The fact that New York State's combined state and local tax collections at this time, on both a per capita basis and relative to personal income, were among the highest of the 50 states was seen as a negative factor in attracting and retaining business. The result was a turning point in the state's tax policy, with economic development becoming a primary concern.

In the late 1970s the state began a series of substantial reductions in its top personal income tax rates and by 1982 had eliminated its stock transfer and unincorporated business taxes. In addition, the state accelerated the use of targeted tax incentives to encourage business activity within its borders. While controversial, this use of the tax system has proliferated through the end of the 20th century and into the current one.

In 1983 facing a revenue shortfall as a result of the national recession and the personal income tax cuts of the previous several years, the state cut spending and increased taxes. Among the tax increases was the imposition, on a statewide basis, of a 10% tax on gains realized on sales of real property in which the consideration exceeded $1 million. This tax generated substantial revenue through the boom years of the late 1980s but far less in the early 1990s during a deep downturn in the real estate market. It was repealed in 1996 under Gov Mario M. Cuomo's successor, George E. Pataki. Significant structural changes in New York State's personal and corporate income taxes were enacted in 1987 in the wake of major reforms in these taxes at the federal level. In addition to reducing the top personal income tax rates substantially, the 1987 changes to the personal income tax also eliminated the distinction between earned and unearned income that had been introduced a decade earlier, made joint returns standard for federal joint filers, altered the delivery of low-income relief, and revamped the taxation of nonresidents.

DURATION OF MAJOR NEW YORK STATE REVENUE SOURCES

Tax	Commenced	Terminated
Personal Income Tax	1919	—
Corporation Organization Tax	1886	—
Corporation Franchise Tax	1880	—
Income Basis	1917	—
Bank Tax[a]	1940	—
Insurance Tax[b]	1974	—
Direct Writings Tax	1990	—
Unincorporated Business Tax	1935	1980[c]
Sales Tax	1965	—
Motor Fuel Tax	1929	—
Highway Use Tax		
Truck Mileage Tax	1952	—
Fuel Use	1968	—
Cigarette Tax	1939	—
Other Tobacco Products	1989	—
Alcoholic Beverage Tax	1886, 1933	1919
Estate Tax[d]	1885	—
Gift Tax[e]	1972	2000
Stock Transfer Tax[f]	1905	—
Real Estate Transfer Tax	1968	—
Mortgage Recording Tax	1906	—
Pari-Mutuel Tax	1940	—
OTB	1978	—
Lottery	1967	—
Petroleum Business Tax	1983	—
Real Property Gains Tax[g]	1983	1996
Container Tax[h]	1990	1998
Hotel Occupancy Tax	1990	1994
Auto Rental Tax	1990	—
Lubricating Oils Tax	1990	1994
Hudson River Valley Greenway Fee	1992	1994
Paging Device Fee[i]	1992	1993

Source: NYS Department of Taxation and Finance, Office of Tax Policy Analysis, *New York State Tax Sourcebook* (2003), App B.

[a]Banks were subject to tax before 1940, but all revenue went to local governments.

[b]Until 1974 insurance companies were taxed under Article 9.

[c]UBT was imposed in 1981 but at 0%.

[d]Before 1930 the estate tax was preceded by an inheritance tax. Effective for decedents dying on or after 1 Feb 2000, New York imposes a "pickup tax" equal to the maximum federal credit for a state death tax.

[e]Repealed effective 1 Jan 2000.

[f]Since 1977 nonresident taxpayers were eligible for 100% rebate. Resident taxpayers became eligible for rebates in 1979 with a 100% rebate in 1981.

[g]Applies to transfers occurring before 15 June 1996.

[h]Repealed effective 1 Oct 1998.

[i]Declared unconstitutional by state supreme court in June 1993.

New York's version of an enterprise zones program, originally called Economic Development Zones, was established in 1986. Renamed Empire Zones in 2000 and restructured to provide more lucrative tax benefits, this program has become an increasingly important but controversial economic development tool. The program was originally designed to attract business activities to economically disadvantaged areas within the state. Over the years, the restrictions that limited the geographic scope of the program were eased even as benefits were enhanced, with the result that lucrative tax benefits were available not only to businesses undertaking new activities in disadvantaged neighborhoods but also to those engaging in ongoing business activities in locations that were not economically disadvantaged. By 2003 the program was receiving increased media scrutiny in light of perceived abuses in its operations. The 1987 income tax rate reductions, which were scheduled to be phased in over a four-year period, were designed to return to New York State taxpayers the "windfall" that the state government would otherwise receive from the broadening of the tax base resulting from federal tax reform and to reduce state taxes in light of the strong economic growth that the state was then experiencing. The state was hit particularly hard by the recession that began in 1989, however, and over the next several years delayed the implementation of the remaining steps of the 1987 tax cuts while balancing its budgets in large part through cuts in local aid programs such as revenue sharing. This placed substantial pressure on the local sales and real property tax bases. Local real property tax levies went up at an average annual rate of almost 8% per year between 1987 and 1993, sales tax rates were increased by all of the state's large counties and many of the smaller ones, and New York City increased its local personal income tax rates.

The Current Tax System

In the second half of the 1990s and into 2000, a vibrant national economy and a stock market surge produced revenues in quantities that allowed for both increased spending and significant tax cuts, including further reductions in personal and corporate income tax rates, the elimination of a number of minor taxes, the exemption of items of clothing and footwear costing less than $110 from the state sales tax, and a variety of new business tax incentives. The personal income tax continued to play a dominant role, accounting for more than $20 billion by fiscal year 1999 and approximately 60% of all state tax revenue during the first several years of the new century. In contrast, the share of revenue from business taxes shrank as New York State and its sister states responded to competitive concerns by reducing taxes on business. In the 1999–2000 fiscal year, New York State raised approximately $41.7 billion in tax revenues. This figure included motor vehicle registration fees but excluded most other user fees imposed by the state, including SUNY and CUNY tuition. Local governments, including school districts, raised more than $45 billion in taxes, the vast majority from real property and local sales taxes. In 2001, with the national economy in recession and the stock market "bubble" burst, the state's revenue picture, along with those of most other states, began to darken. Revenues continued to deteriorate in 2002 and 2003, and for the 2003–4 fiscal year the state faced a revenue shortfall of record proportions. In response, the legislature enacted a host of new revenue measures, including temporary increases in the rates of both the personal income tax and the sales tax, and the temporary suspension of the clothing exemption.

Tax Administration and Adjudication

The DTF, led by the commissioner of taxation and finance, administers all state taxes with the exception of the alcoholic beverage tax, which is under the jurisdiction of the State Liquor Authority. It maintains an expansive tax collection infrastructure, disseminating tax forms, promoting voluntary compliance, undertaking audits, and enforcing tax assessments. In 1986 the three-member State Tax Commission was abolished and an independent three-member Tax Appeals Tribunal was created. The president of the tribunal also serves as the chief executive of the Division of Tax Appeals, an independent division within the DTF responsible for the adjudication of tax disputes. The Division of Tax Appeals provides taxpayers an opportunity to contest actions of the DTF through quasi-formal hearings conducted by administrative law judges. The Tax Appeals Tribunal sits in review of these administrative law judges' determinations. Taxpayers may appeal an adverse ruling by the tribunal to the Appellate Division of State Supreme Court in Albany. The DTF does not have a similar right to appeal decisions of the tribunal.

Personal Income Tax

New York State imposes a personal income tax on the income from all sources of resident individuals, estates, and trusts. Nonresident individuals, estates, and trusts are subject to tax on income derived from or connected with New York State sources. The state's personal income tax incorporates many of the features of the federal income tax. Federal adjusted gross income is the starting point for the calculation of the tax, which is then subject to modifications that may increase or decrease the amount of income subject to tax. A taxpayer's federal filing status generally dictates state filing status. The state does not allow a personal exemption but does grant an exemption for dependents and either a standard or itemized deduction. The tax offers a variety of credits, including an earned income credit tied to the federal earned income credit. The highest rate in the permanent rate structure is 6.85%, imposed on the taxable income of single individuals in excess of $20,000 and on the amount in excess of $40,000 for married joint filers. High-income taxpayers also face the recapture of the benefits of the lower brackets and a reduction in the value of their itemized deductions. In 2003, two temporary tax rates, the higher of which was 7.7% on taxable income in excess of $500,000, were imposed for a three-year period. New York City imposes a personal income tax on residents that piggybacks on the state tax. The highest rate, calculated to include a 14% surcharge, is 3.648%. In 2003 temporary increases in the New York City income tax were also put into place for a three-year period. The City of Yonkers imposes both a personal income tax on its residents and an earnings tax on nonresidents. A tax imposed by New York City on the earnings of nonresidents, often referred to as the "commuter tax," was eliminated in 1999.

Sales and Use Tax

The state sales tax is imposed at the rate of 4% on retail sales of tangible personal property and statutorily enumerated services. Exemptions from the tax are provided for most food items and for articles of clothing up to $110. In 2003 legislation was enacted increasing the state rate to 4.25% from 1 June 2003 through 31 May 2005 and suspending the exemption for articles of clothing under $110 from 1 June 2003 through 31 May 2004. Counties and cities may piggyback their own sales taxes on the state tax, all of which are administered by the state. Local rates run as high as 4.25%. Sales in New York City and the surrounding counties served by the Metropolitan Transportation Authority (MTA) are subject to an additional 0.25% tax. A use tax is imposed to complement the sales tax, theoretically ensuring that taxpayers cannot avoid sales tax by purchasing goods out-of-state for use in the state. As part of its 2003 revenue-raising package, the legislature enacted measures to improve enforcement of the use tax. The legal imposition of the sales tax is on the purchaser, but vendors are obligated to assist in the collection of the tax, and both parties face liability if the proper tax is not collected and remitted. New York City imposes its local sales and use tax on a slightly broader range of services than the state, including such personal services as beauty and hair care. The New York City rate, set at 4%, was temporarily increased to 4.125% for the period 1 June 2003 through 31 May 2005.

Business Taxes

New York State imposes an annual franchise tax on domestic and foreign corporations for the privilege of exercising their corporate franchise, doing business, employing capital, owning or leasing property, or maintaining an office in the state. The determination of the tax requires the computation of tax under four alternative bases, including 7.5% of the portion of a corporation's entire net income allocated to New York on the basis of a formula that takes into consideration the location of a firm's property, payroll, and sales. In an effort to help small businesses, corporations with less than $200,000 of entire net income pay at a reduced rate of 6.85%. Corporations pay the highest tax calculated under the four bases, plus a tax on subsidiary capital of 0.9 mill on each dollar of allocated subsidiary capital. Under each of the four bases other than the state's "fixed dollar minimum tax" (which varies from $100 to $1500 depending on gross payroll, with an $800 minimum tax imposed on inactive "shell" corporations), corporations must allocate their income or capital within and without New York. The entire net income base is closely related to the federal income tax base, which serves as the starting point in the calculation of entire net income. The tax offers a variety of incentives to encourage business activity in the state, including an investment tax credit available to manufacturers and segments of the financial services sector. Corporations doing business within the Metropolitan Commuter Transportation District (MCTD), the region served by the MTA, also pay a surcharge on the portion of their tax liability that is allocated to that region on the basis of the location of their property, payroll, and sales. New York City imposes an 8.85% general corporation tax on the portion of a corporation's net income allocated to the city. This tax is modeled on but is not identical to the state's corporate income tax. Significant differences exist, for example, with respect to the provisions of credits rewarding investment and other activities. In addition, New York City imposes an unincorporated business tax at the rate of 4%.

The state imposes a franchise tax on every banking corporation doing banking business or exercising its corporate franchise in New York. A banking corporation's tax liability is the highest tax calculated under four different computations, including a tax on allocated entire net income imposed at a rate of 7.5% and a fixed dollar minimum tax of $250. Banks doing business within the MCTD are subject to a surcharge on their state tax liability allocable to activity within that region. New York City imposes a bank tax at the rate of 9% that closely tracks the state's tax. All domestic, foreign, and alien insurance companies that do business in the state are taxed at a rate of 1.75% of receipts from accident and health insurance premiums and 2.0% on all other nonlife premiums. Life insurers pay the greater of a 1.5% tax on premiums or the amount due under a tax modeled closely on the general corporate franchise tax. Taxpayers doing insurance business in the MCTD are subject to an MCTD surcharge. Insurance companies doing business in New York are also subject to premium taxes and retaliatory taxes.

New York State imposes a variety of taxes measured by gross receipts on businesses in specific industries, including energy and telecommunications. These taxes include a franchise tax on the capital stock of corporations principally engaged in a transportation or transmission business (not including the transmission of gas, electricity, or steam); a franchise tax on the gross receipts of corporations principally engaged in a transportation or transmission activity (except for long-distance telephone carriers); a tax on gross income or gross operating income for entities furnishing water, gas, electricity, or steam, whether or not it is their principal business, and

NEW YORK STATE AND LOCAL SALES AND USE TAX RATES, 1933–2002

Year	State Rate (%)	Additional MCTD Tax[a] (%)	Top Local Rate (%)	Maximum State and Local Rate (%)
1933	1.00	—	—	1.00
1934–40	—	—	2.00	2.00
1941–44	—	—	1.00	1.00
1945–50	—	—	2.00	2.00
1951–64	—	—	3.00	3.00
1965–68	2.00	—	3.00	5.00
1969–70	3.00	—	3.00	6.00
1971–73	4.00	—	3.00	7.00
1974–80	4.00	—	4.00	8.00
1981–90	4.00	0.25	4.00	8.25
1991–2002	4.00	0.25	4.25	8.50

Source: NYS Department of Taxation and Finance, Office of Tax Policy Analysis, *New York State Tax Sourcebook* (2003), Table 52.

[a]The Metropolitan Commuter Transportation District (MCTD) includes 12 counties: New York, Bronx, Kings, Queens, Richmond, Dutchess, Nassau, Orange, Putnam, Rockland, Suffolk, and Westchester.

for local telephone companies subject to the supervision of the Public Service Commission; an excise tax on telecommunications services for all companies engaged in the furnishing of telecommunication services; a franchise tax on the capital stock of farmers' or other agricultural cooperatives; and a privilege tax on the importation of natural gas for consumption for all companies importing natural gas for self-use in the state. Certain local governments, including New York City, impose gross receipts taxes on utilities authorized by the state. New York City's tax on utilities is at the rate of 2.35%. The state imposes a set of related taxes, known collectively as the Petroleum Business Tax, on a variety of petroleum products and aviation fuel imported into or produced in New York State. Though formally structured as a tax on the privilege of doing business in the state, the tax is imposed on a cents-per-gallon basis, with different rates, indexed annually, applying to different products such as motor fuel, diesel motor fuel, nonautomotive diesel fuel, and residual petroleum products.

Property Transfer Taxes

As of 1 Feb 2001 New York's estate tax was designed to impose a tax equal to the maximum credit allowed against the federal estate tax for state death taxes paid. Under this form of state estate tax, the tax imposed never exceeds the credit allowed against the federal tax. However, as a result of subsequent federal estate tax changes, New York State's estate tax no longer operates in this fashion. Instead, for deaths in 2002 and thereafter the estate tax is based on the maximum federal credit for state death taxes as it existed in 2001, while the actual federal state death tax credit available has diminished since 2001 and will be eliminated in 2005. The threshold for liability for New York State estate tax is $1 million.

New York State imposes a real estate transfer tax on every conveyance of real property in the state where the consideration exceeds $500. A conveyance includes any method of transfer of any interest in real property, including the acquisition of a controlling interest in an entity with an interest in real property located in the state. The tax specifically applies to the conveyance of shares in a cooperative housing corporation. An interest in real property includes titles in fee, certain leasehold interests, beneficial interests, encumbrances, development rights, air space and air rights, and any other interest with the right to use or occupy real property or the right to receive rents, profits, or other income derived from real property. It also includes an option or contract to purchase real property but not a right of first refusal to purchase property. The basic rate is $2 for every $500 of consideration or fractional part thereof. The tax is imposed on the grantor, but in the event the grantor fails to pay in a timely fashion, grantor and grantee become jointly and severally liable for the tax. New York City, Erie and Broome Cos, and the cities of Yonkers and Mount Vernon (Westchester Co) all impose additional transfer taxes that apply to real property located in their respective jurisdictions.

The state imposes a tax on recording mortgages on real property located in the state, generally at the rate of $1 per $100 of principal debt secured. The tax is actually three separate taxes: a basic tax, an "additional" tax, and a "special additional" tax. Instruments subject to the tax include almost every type of mortgage and all deeds of trust that impose a lien on or affect the title to real property, as well as executory contracts for the sale of real property under which the purchaser has or is entitled to possession of the property. A contract or agreement by which the debt secured by a mortgage is increased is also deemed a taxable mortgage. New York City, the City of Yonkers and selected counties impose local mortgage recording taxes.

Excise and User Taxes

The state imposes a cigarette excise tax through the sale of tax stamps to licensed agents. Agents must affix the tax stamps to each package of cigarettes before sale can occur in New York State. The tax rate is $1.50 per pack of 20 cigarettes. In addition, a prepaid sales tax is paid by the agent at the time the cigarette tax stamp is purchased. Distributors of other tobacco products such as cigars, snuff, chewing tobacco, pipe, and loose tobacco pay a 37% excise tax on the wholesale price. New York City imposes a separate excise tax of $1.50 per pack, which brings the combined per pack tax in New York City to $3. The alcoholic beverage tax imposes liquor, beer, and wine taxes at various rates, ranging from 11¢ per gallon for beer to $6.43 per gallon for liquors with alcohol contents of over 24%. New York City imposes taxes of 12¢ per gallon on beer and 26.4¢ per liter on liquor, but no tax on wine. New York State also imposes a motor fuel tax, highway use taxes on truck travel, a wireless communication service surcharge, boxing and wrestling exhibition taxes, and pari-mutuel taxes on horse racetracks and off-track betting operators. New York City also imposes a taxicab license transfer tax, a commercial rent tax in Manhattan south of 96th St, a hotel room occupancy tax, a horse race admission tax, and a tax on foreign and alien insurers.

Real Property Taxes

The real property tax is by far the leading source of local tax revenue in New York State and competes with the personal income tax as the largest source of tax revenue overall. In 1999–2000, the property tax accounted for $25.2 billion of the $45.1 billion in tax revenue raised by local governments in the state. The real property tax system has been shaped over many decades by the state and by hundreds of local taxing jurisdictions with varying approaches to property taxation that operate within the broad framework of state law. In 1958 the state enacted the Real Property Tax Law (RPTL), which consolidated all the laws relating to the assessment and taxation of real property. The RPTL establishes basic standards of taxation, collection, and administration throughout the state. Real property taxation remains largely a function of local governments, with the state role limited to that of broad oversight. The Office of Real Property Services is the state agency assigned to assist localities in the taxation of real property. It has general supervision of the assessment process throughout the state, assesses special franchises, sets equalization rates for localities, and approves assessments of state lands. Overlapping units of government may impose tax on the same piece of real property, referred to as a parcel. Except in New York City, every parcel of property in the state is subject to taxation by at least two units of government (a county and a city) and by many more, such as county, town, school district, fire district, and sometimes library and other special districts, in most of the state. Outside of the state's largest cities, school districts are by far the largest users of the property tax.

Until 1981 state law required all properties to be assessed at their true market value. At that time, in response to the 1975 State Court of Appeals decision in *Hellerstein v Assessor, Town of Islip* requiring conformance with this longstanding requirement, the legislature amended the law to authorize so-called fractional assessment. Under this law, properties must be assessed at a uniform percentage of full value. The 1981 law also authorized special assessment procedures for New York City and Nassau Co, allowing them to assess each of four different classes of property differently. Other localities must assess all property at the same percentage of full value but are allowed to establish different rates for homestead and nonhomestead properties. All real property is subject to tax unless specifically exempt. Separate taxes are established in the RPTL for special franchises, forestlands, and shellfish grounds. Classes of exempt or potentially exempt property may be authorized in the first instance only by the state, and exemptions may be created only by general laws. The authorization to grant exempt status, however, is in many instances placed in the hands of the localities by state enabling laws. Mandatory exemptions are accorded to property owned by certain nonprofit corporations, including religious and educational institutions, while permissive exemptions may be provided to certain other nonprofit corporations. Unlike other taxes, property tax rates are not written into law. Instead, local governments, as part of their budget processes, annually determine the total amount of money (called the tax levy) to be raised from property taxes by estimating the revenue available from all other sources and then subtracting that estimate from the total amount of expenditures being authorized for the coming year. The property tax rate for the coming year is then determined by dividing the total levy by the taxable value of the properties within the locality's jurisdiction.

Looking Forward

Since the late 1800s New York State's tax system has gone from one that was based almost entirely on the taxation of one form of wealth (real and personal property) to a more diverse mix of taxes on various measures of income, consumption, and wealth. By the late 1990s the personal income tax had surpassed the property tax as the single largest source of state and local tax revenue. With the bursting of the Wall Street and "dot com" bubbles in the year 2000 and the subsequent precipitous decline in personal income tax revenues, the property tax may well regain its place as the state's primary tax source. However, current debates over the funding of education and Medicaid could lead the state to take responsibility for funding a larger portion of these services. This in turn could lead to an attempt to reform the corporate income tax system or to restore some of the personal income tax brackets that were eliminated during the 1977–97 period. Such policy changes could also alter the distributional impact of New York's state-local tax system. Because of the state's high degree of reliance on property and sales taxes, its tax system, like that of most other states, is relatively regressive,

NEW YORK STATE TAX COLLECTIONS, FISCAL YEARS 1988–2002

Fiscal Year	Total State Collections	Personal Income	Corporation and Business	Sales, Excise, and User	Property Transfers
2002	$43,370,339,957	$27,413,649,936	$4,656,708,249	$10,118,248,304	$1,143,026,295
2001	43,664,205,694	26,892,084,122	5,243,970,082	10,320,567,873	1,169,451,636
2000	38,306,238,399	21,533,217,882	5,544,609,092	9,772,951,716	1,409,723,589
1999	37,165,396,956	20,662,375,214	5,820,785,763	9,224,443,948	1,412,773,448
1998	33,927,730,471	17,758,697,181	5,957,475,493	8,879,450,323	1,284,470,485
1997	32,076,909,740	16,370,887,332	5,920,605,026	8,609,791,751	1,126,165,580
1996	32,178,839,324	16,998,212,766	5,709,784,799	8,330,926,856	1,086,847,097
1995	32,704,550,205	17,589,489,166	5,689,177,572	8,310,519,743	1,050,356,853
1994	31,254,356,521	16,033,524,352	6,229,073,291	7,862,010,220	1,054,582,023
1993	29,826,321,068	15,318,849,593	5,707,269,896	7,653,003,325	1,019,403,278
1992	28,594,999,541	14,913,380,341	5,190,949,381	7,374,501,861	1,030,726,198
1991	26,887,360,839	14,527,036,203	4,075,702,297	7,076,991,545	1,119,385,965
1990	26,930,157,402	15,240,467,249	3,378,609,123	7,125,785,027	1,097,369,979
1989	25,213,562,059	13,844,385,434	3,416,726,760	6,617,919,692	1,240,460,359
1988	25,182,394,770	13,920,987,777	3,537,482,785	6,422,049,268	1,195,450,080

Source: NYS Department of Taxation and Finance, Office of Tax Policy Analysis, *2001–2002 New York State Tax Collections: Statistical Summaries and Historical Tables* (2003), Table 1.

Note: The fiscal year runs 1 April through 31 March.

taking a larger percentage of the income of low-income families than of upper-income families. The most recent comprehensive study of this issue found that New York's state-local tax system, as of 2002, accounted for 12.7% of the family income of the lowest quintile of nonelderly taxpayers, 11.9% of the income of the middle quintile, and 9.1% of the income of the top 1%. After taking the federal deductibility of state and local income and property taxes into consideration, these differences were even greater: 12.6% for the lowest quintile, 11.6% for the middle quintile, and 6.5% for the top 1%.

See also AMERICAN INDIANS: POLICIES SINCE 1776.

Nelson A. Rockefeller Institute of Government. *2002 New York State Statistical Yearbook* (Albany: SUNY, 2002)

New York City Department of Finance. *The NYC Tax Guide* (New York: Author, 1998)

New York State Archives. "New York State Department of Taxation and Finance" (agency history)

New York State Commission for the Revision of the Tax Laws. *Preliminary Report* (Albany: J. B. Lyon, 1931)

New York State Division of the Budget. *New York State Statistical Yearbook* (Albany, 1979–1980)

———. *2003–2004 New York State Executive Budget, Appendix II* (Albany, Jan 2003)

New York State Department of Taxation and Finance. *Handbook of New York State and Local Taxes* (Albany: Author, 2002)

Plattner, Robert D. *The New York State Tax Handbook* (Rochester: Winterman Ink Publishing, 2003)

Robert D. Plattner and Frank J. Mauro

Taxation and Finance, Department of. New York State agency established on 1 Jan 1927 that administers the state's tax laws, revenue collections, treasury, and lottery. After the Revolutionary War the state legislature elected a treasurer annually, and from 1846, biannually. Most state revenue came from land sales, canal tolls, lotteries, taxes on saltworks, and investments, with the treasurer holding and disbursing funds and a comptroller collecting the taxes. By 1845 the state instituted widespread property taxation, and town and county officers assessed and collected these monies, which accounted for 98% of state revenues by 1879. In 1859 the legislature created the Board of Equalization of Assessments to devise a standard assessment formula. Commissioners of the Land Office (appointed by the governor with the consent of the state senate) and three state assessors (also appointed by the governor) served on this board. In 1896 the Board of Tax Commissioners (three gubernatorial appointees) replaced the assessors and also heard and decided appeals by local tax districts protesting county assessment decisions. State government dependence on property tax decreased after 1880 and would end completely in 1930 as other revenue programs were introduced, such as taxes on alcohol and racing tickets, corporation franchise taxes, estate taxes, motor vehicle registrations, and, from 1919, personal income tax.

In 1915 a newly formed State Tax Department assumed the duties of the now defunct Board of Tax Commissioners and the state comptroller regarding corporate taxes, except their collection. In 1921 it took over most of that as well, including inheritance, personal income, stock transfer, and corporate franchise taxes. In 1927 it became the Department of Taxation and Finance (DTF), headed by a governor-appointed commissioner; it acquired all remaining collection duties of the state's treasurer and comptroller. The commissioner, along with two other gubernatorial appointees, formed the State Tax Commission. This constituted the Board of Equalization until 1949, when the board became the autonomous State Board of Equalization and Assessment.

In 1960 taxation lost its Bureau of Motor Vehicles, which became independent, and in 1965 oversaw implementation of a sales tax that by the 1980s would become the state's second largest source of income after personal income tax. In 1967 DTF gained authority over the state's new lottery but would lose control from 1973 to 1976 and then regain a semiautonomous Division of the Lottery. In 1986 the state legislature replaced the State Tax Commission with a Tax Appeals Tribunal consisting of three gubernatorial appointees, with the tribunal president also serving as head of the newly created Division of Tax Appeals. This division, though located within DTF, operates independently to resolve disputes between taxpayers and DTF. In 1994 DTF privatized the processing of personal income tax returns due the state with Fleet Services Corp, a subsidiary of Fleet Bank and Bank of America, which was given a 10-year contract. In 1997 DTF began getting overdue child-support payments by tax warrants and levies on the assets of delinquent parents, and collected $238 million from March 1997 to May 2003.

In 2001 DTF collected $43.6 billion, about 94% of the state's general fund revenue exclusive of federal assistance. DTF also collects income taxes for New York City and Yonkers. Its treasury division receives and disburses state funds, issues unemployment insurance, workers' compensation, and tax refund checks, and acts as a joint custodian with the comptroller of state securities. Other major DTF components include the Office of Tax Operations, which enforces the state's tax laws; the Office of Tax Policy Analysis, which develops and evaluates tax policy; and the Office of Tax Enforcement, which investigates and prosecutes tax fraud cases. The DTF is headquartered at W. Averell Harriman State Office Campus in Albany, and its treasury division is located in the Alfred E. Smith Building. DTF also maintains 13 district offices dealing primarily with audit and tax compliance. The terrorist attack of 11 Sept 2001 destroyed the Manhattan office at World Trade Center 2 and killed 40 agency employees.

New York State. Assembly. *Tax Processing Banking Arrangements* (Albany: Legislative Commission on Expenditure Review, 1990)

State of New York Management Resources Project. *Governing the Empire State: An Insider's Guide* (Albany: Author, 1988)

Jeffrey Kraus

taxi and car services. Private businesses offering motor vehicle transport to individuals or small groups, usually on a one-time basis. They operate most prominently in New York State's major cities. In 2002 New York City boasted 12,187 taxis to Buffalo's 350 and Rochester's 260. Taxis are the sole vehicles legally entitled to cruise for fares. Livery services run sedans that serve a similar function, but drivers respond only to radio dispatch calls and are barred by law from picking up fares on the street. Neighborhood-based liveries serve a range of clients on a cash basis; luxury or "black car" liveries primarily serve corporate accounts, charging zone-based fares payable by voucher. Another category of car service, jitneys, use vans or sedans to pick up multiple passengers along fixed or semifixed routes. Liveries and jitneys are an almost exclusively New York City phenomenon.

New York City Taxis

A young entrepreneur, Harry Allen, originated the city's taxicab industry in 1907 with a fleet of 65 French-made automobiles. His new motorized taxicabs quickly replaced horse-drawn hansom cabs with their faster service and more accurate fares (computed by mechanical meter). By 1923 the industry had grown to 15,000 vehicles and was dominated by several large fleets: Checker Co with 3,750 taxis, Yellow Cab Co with 3,000, and National Transportation Co with 1,500. During the 1920s and 1930s, easy entry into this all-cash business led to an oversupply of taxis, resulting in traffic congestion, fare-cutting wars, low driver wages, inadequately insured vehicles, and other unsafe and sometimes illegal activities. The Great Depression created an influx of unemployed workers, making these problems more acute, and the number of cabs spiraled to 21,000 in 1931. A 1937 city ordinance sponsored by Alderman Lew Haas froze the number of taxi licenses at 13,595, the number then outstanding. As taxi companies continued to cut fares to attract riders, some vehicle permits lapsed. By the late 1940s, there were only 11,787 licenses, 6,818 for fleet-operated taxis and 4,969 for owner-driven ones.

Demand for taxis soared after World War II, but under pressure from taxi owners, the city issued no new licenses. The existing transferable licenses or medallions rose in value from $2,500 in 1947 to over $25,000 in 1963. In the 1950s and 1960s taxi drivers increasingly serviced Manhattan's growing demand, with trips originating in Manhattan accounting for 78% of the total in 1963. Drivers sought to benefit from the industry's rising profitability and were aided by the city council, which tied each fare increase of the 1950s and 1960s to increases in driver commissions. With Mayor Robert F. Wagner Jr's support, Electrical Workers Union and Central Labor Council head Harry Van Arsdale led a unionization drive, and in 1965 won the right to organize 82 fleet garages.

Challenge of the Liveries and Jitneys

During the 1950s and early 1960s, as medallioned taxis concentrated on servicing downtown and central Manhattan, nonmedallioned car services sprang up in poor and minority areas in upper Manhattan and the city's other boroughs. These included liveries—both "gypsy" cabs that illegally cruised for fares and cars that responded to telephone calls for service through radio dispatch bases—and jitneys, also illegal at this period, that serviced major avenues feeding subway stations.

Liveries and jitneys were a source of contention from their beginning. While many elected officials defended them as community businesses providing needed transportation, the taxi industry attacked them as unregulated, unsafe, and encroaching on taxi owners' rights. In 1968 the New York City Council mandated that all medallioned cabs be painted yellow to distinguish them from the gypsies. The nonmedallioned car services continued to grow rapidly, from an estimated 2,000 to 3,000 vehicles in 1964. They operated 14,000 vehicles by 1971, the founding year of the city's comprehensive regulatory authority for taxis and all car services, the Taxi and Limousine Commission (TLC). Although many of the nonmedallioned vehicles were properly insured and operated legally by radio dispatch, approximately 40% were true gypsies cruising for street hails and lacking proper insurance.

Late 20th to 21st Century

Economic recession in the 1970s led to sharp declines in demand for taxis. About 75% of the taxi fleets, which together owned 58% of the city's taxis, sold their medallions to individual nonunion drivers, dramatically weakening the union. Drivers' positions were further weakened in 1979 when the TLC permitted taxi owners to lease cabs to drivers for flat per-shift fees. At the same time that liveries and jitneys were increasing their numbers (to 35,000 vehicles in 1983), taxi fleets dropped employee benefits, and taxi driving became a transient job, filled by a changing mix of immigrants from over 80 countries.

In the early 1980s the TLC ordered the 3,200 medallioned taxis using radio-dispatch technology to remove their radios and respond to street hails only. Owner-drivers of these taxis then switched their radio operations to luxury cars, creating the class of vehicles called black cars; these owners generally leased their medallioned cabs to other operators. Rapidly growing business demand and fear of crime in the subways raised the number of black cars to 8,000 by the mid-1980s. The city's economic growth in the 1980s and 1990s buoyed all parts of the industry. The value of a medallion reached $100,000 in 1986. A year later, a new TLC-administered ordinance resulted in the licensing of a large proportion of livery owners, drivers, and bases. Full compliance, implemented through vigorous enforcement that included seizing unlicensed vehicles and padlocking unlicensed bases, required base dispatch, insurance, and driver background checks. Taxi activity further concentrated in Manhattan; in 1988 over 94% of all taxi rides originated there. In 1991, 10% of new drivers were native-born and 41% were from South Asia. In 1992 the TLC licensed 29,400 livery vehicles and in 1994 gained authority to license the jitneys or "commuter vans." In 1996–97 the city auctioned 400 new medallions, resisting a larger number because of environmental concern over emissions. The final collapse of union activity in the fleet garages came in 1997. Demand for the medallions quickly outpaced the added supply; a single medallion sold for $250,000 in 1998. In 1999 taxi ridership rose to 660,000 on an average weekday, generating a total of $1.4 billion in fares.

During the 1990s the TLC mandated driver training, newer vehicles, and other reforms, including installation of partitions, trouble lights (flashers usually located near the rear license plate and easily activated from the driver's seat), and cameras to protect drivers from crime. Drivers' reluctance to go outside Manhattan for safety and economic reasons also made service refusals to black and Hispanic riders a persistent issue, only partly alleviated by enforcement crackdowns. In 2000 New York City's 12,187 taxis served about 240 million passengers, its 11,000 black cars served 30–40 million, and its 30,000 other liveries 140–160 million. In addition, 400 licensed jitneys or commuter vans, plus some illegally operating jitneys, together served a substantial but unknown number of people.

In 1999–2001 taxi owners and drivers contested efforts to tighten standards and increase the number of taxis in Albany and to adopt a regional fare structure. For the most part, however, taxis in Albany, Buffalo, Rochester, Syracuse, and other cities in Northern, Central, and Western New York generate little controversy. They provide service primarily to lower-income individuals without private cars and to visitors, especially business travelers, using the local airports.

Gilbert, Gorman. *The Taxicab: An Urban Transportation Survivor* (Chapel Hill: Univ of North Carolina Press, 1982)

Schaller, Bruce. *New York City For-Hire Vehicle Fact Book* (New York: New York City Taxi and Limousine Commission, 1993)

Schaller Consulting. "Taxi Regulation and Policy," http://www.schallerconsult.com/taxi

Bruce Schaller

Tayler, John (*b* New York City, ?28 July 1742; *d* Albany, 19 Mar 1829). Merchant and lieutenant and acting governor. He moved to Albany in 1759, followed the army as a trader during the French and Indian War, farmed at Stillwater [now in Saratoga Co] from 1771 to 1773, and thereafter advanced as a politically astute and ingratiating trader, Albany merchant, land investor, and banker. Tayler married Margarita van Valkenburgh in 1764. During the Revolution he represented Albany Co in the Third and Fourth Provincial Congresses and sat in five sessions of the New York State Assembly, including its first meeting in 1777. Acting often as an agent for the commissioners of Indian Affairs, Tayler contributed to the state's acquisition of Native American land in Central and Western New York and procured substantial real estate. He then served as an original director of the Western Inland Lock Navigation Co (1792) and as Albany Co judge (1797). A political adherent of George Clinton, reputedly his distant relative, Tayler was elected to 11 sessions of the state senate (1802, 1804–13) and became president of the senate in 1811. His service on the Board of Regents began in 1802 and continued until his death. When serving in the 1805 senate, he sought to block the creation of the anti-Clintonian Merchants' Bank of New York City, an institution that would compete with the New-York State Bank of Albany, which he helped to create and over which he presided. In 1812 Tayler opposed the creation of the Federalist-backed Bank of America and supported Gov Daniel D. Tompkins's decision to prorogue the legislature. Adept at legislative management, he contributed to a wide range of laws, including the statutes that fostered New York State's turnpikes and shaped its local government, including that of New York City. He served as lieutenant governor under both Tompkins (1813–17) and De Witt Clinton (1817–22), and he briefly acted as governor in 1817 when Tompkins became US vice president. As an ex-officio member of the Council of Revision,

Tayler voted against the Erie Canal bill. He presided over the 1824 People's Party convention, a body in which upstate business banking interests had strong representation. In 1824 he substituted for an absent John Quincy Adams elector and in 1828 voted for Andrew Jackson as an elector-at-large.

Hammond, Jabez D. *The History of Political Parties in the State of New-York from the Ratification of the Federal Constitution to December, 1840,* 2 vols (Albany: Van Benthuysen, 1842)

Tayler, John. Papers. New York State Archives, Albany

Craig and Mary L. Hanyan

Taylor. Town (pop 500) in E Cortland Co. Settled in 1793, the town formed from Solon in 1849. Its land is hilly and broken. Butter and cheese were its staple agricultural products, and its first cheese factory was built in 1866. Dairy farming continued in the early 21st century, while other residents commuted to Cortland, Syracuse, or Binghamton. A nuclear waste dump targeted for Taylor was prevented by a 1992 decision of the US Supreme Court that declared the siting process unconstitutional.

Cathy A. Barber

Taylor, Anna Edson (*b* Auburn, Cayuga Co, ?1838; *d* Lockport, Niagara Co, 30 Apr 1921). Daredevil. Born to Lucretia Waring and Merick Edson, Taylor grew up in Auburn where her father operated a mill. Her early life remains a mystery. She claimed to have married at 18 and been widowed by 20. On 24 Oct 1901 Taylor ventured over Niagara Falls in a barrel, the first person to do so and survive. Onlookers labeled the schoolteacher a publicity seeker but were amazed when she climbed into the oak barrel she designed, plummeted over the falls, and emerged with only minor cuts. Her daring feat arose from her desire for financial security, but the self-proclaimed Queen of the Mist never attracted the attention she sought and died a pauper.

Parish, Charles Carlin. *Queen of the Mist* (Interlaken, NY: Empire State Books, 1987)

Nancy E. Frazier

Taylor Law. New York State legislation of 1967, also known as the Public Employees' Fair Employment Act (Civil Service Law §§ 200–214), guaranteeing public employees the right to join unions and bargain collectively. In 1947 the state legislature passed the Condon-Wadlin Act, which continued a common-law prohibition of strikes by public employees. Under this act violators could be terminated and, if reinstated, suffer a three-year ban on pay increases. The penalties were rarely enforced. Through 1964 Condon-Wadlin was invoked seven times in the course of 21 strikes with only 18 employees statewide terminated. In 1963 the legislature amended the law to impose fines of two days' pay for each day a public employee was on strike, but this provision lapsed in 1965. After the legislature granted amnesty to striking transit workers who had shut down New York City subways and buses for 12 days in January 1966, Gov Nelson A. Rockefeller formed the Committee on Public Employee Relations with University of Pennsylvania professor George W. Taylor as chair. This was to ensure operation of vital public services while providing for labor-management negotiations.

Anna Edson Taylor with barrel she rode over Horseshoe Falls in 1901.

Repeal of Condon-Wadlin led to the Taylor Law, which became effective 1 Sept 1967 and was one of the first US statutes to establish a comprehensive framework for labor relations in the public sector. It requires that the state and all its political subdivisions negotiate with unions on terms and conditions of employment, and sets procedures for the resolution of collective bargaining disputes; it also established a state agency called the Public Employment Relations Board (PERB) to administer the law. The Taylor Law prohibits strikes by public employees and prescribes sanctions for violators that include loss of two days' pay for every day on strike, loss of "dues check-off" (direct remittance of union dues from employee paychecks to the union), and forfeit of contract coverage for workers and unions. It specifies no penalties for employers. Two notable amendments followed within a decade: negotiation over retirement benefits was prohibited from 1973, and binding arbitration in police and firefighter impasses was required from 1974.

Passage of the law decreased, but did not eliminate, public employee strikes. In 1979, 6,400 corrections officers went on strike for 15 days, forcing Gov Hugh Carey to use the National Guard in the state's prisons. Their union, the District Council 182 of the American Federation of State, County, and Municipal Employees (AFSCME), lost their dues check-off for 18 months, and their original fine of $4 million was eventually reduced to $150,000. A year later, the Transport Workers Union Local 100 struck against the Metropolitan Transportation Authority (MTA) and as a result was fined $1 million and lost dues check-off for 18 months, with its 33,000 members individually fined. Further amendments to the law stipulated that employers adhere to an expired contract with any nonstriking union until negotiation of a new agreement (1982) and prohibited use of state funds to discourage union organization (1998). In 2000 some 4,000 Buffalo teachers each lost four days' pay for a two-day strike, and their union president spent 15 days in jail for defying a court injunction.

Donovan, Ronald. *Administering the Taylor Law: Public Employee Relations in New York* (Ithaca: Cornell Univ Press, 1990)

Jeffrey Kraus

teachers' associations and unions. Teachers in New York State rely on unions, which began as teachers' associations, to represent them in contract negotiations and other work-related matters. The first association in the state, the Society of Associated Teachers, was formed in New York City in 1794, and the New York State Teachers' Association (NYSTA) was created in 1845. Large cities and regions each had affiliated local associations, which offered educational seminars and support for teachers, but they had no influence over contracts or working conditions as teachers were hired annually. The NYSTA was involved in the creation of the National Teachers' Association in 1857, along with teachers' associations from nine other states, all of which became state affiliates. The organization changed its name to the National Education Association (NEA) in 1870. From its beginning, male school administrators and normal school professors dominated the National Teachers' Association, with little power given to the female grammar school teachers.

In 1916 teachers in several large cities, including New York, Chicago, Washington, DC, and Gary, Ind, organized the American Federation of Teachers (AFT) and joined the American Federation of Labor. *American Teacher,* published by the New York City high school teachers' organization, became the national journal for the new union. The AFT attempted to gain greater rights for teachers but had limited impact until the 1960s. The NEA, controlled by school administrators, successfully portrayed union activity as unprofessional, and the fledgling AFT had its own organizational problems.

The role of teachers' unions expanded in the 1960s and 1970s as teachers used their combined power to press for collective bargaining, improved working conditions, and a larger role in educational decisions. In 1960 the United Federation of Teachers (UFT) was created, joining together 106 diverse organizations that represented teachers in New York City. New York State public employees, including teachers, won collective bargaining rights in 1967 with passage of the Taylor Law, although the law prohibited strikes.

During the same time period, efforts were made to create a separate statewide teachers' union that would better represent teachers' interests because NYSTA continued to be controlled by school administrators. What would become the United Teachers of New York underwent several name changes, and in 1971 Albert Shanker, the UFT president, became its first president. Initially, the NYSTA and United Teachers of New York were rivals, but they merged in 1972 to become the New York Congress of Teachers, renamed New York State United Teachers (NYSUT) in 1973. NYSUT has affiliations with both the AFT and the NEA. Shanker and Thomas Y. Hobart Jr were the first co-presidents, and Hobart continues to serve as NYSUT's president into the early 21st century.

Despite the antistrike legislation, teachers' unions called for strikes throughout the state during the 1960s, 1970s, and 1980s, with salaries and class sizes as key issues. Striking teachers were heavily penalized, losing two days of pay for every day on strike, and in some cases union leaders were jailed. The strikes, plus lobbying by NYSUT, led to passage of the Triborough Amendment to the Taylor Law in 1982, which maintains the provisions of an expired contract until a new contract has been approved. With teachers assured that their old contract would be in effect during negotiations, the number of strikes decreased dramatically.

In the early 21st century NYSUT has more than 400,000 members, with local affiliates in every school district across the state and a number of healthcare organizations. NYSUT is a powerful voice for teachers on legislative issues and endorses candidates for public office at all levels. The union provides a wide range of professional and educational services for its members and is active in addressing concerns such as school safety and higher standards. Local associations, such as the Rochester Teachers' Association (RTA), have been active in promoting agendas that support teacher professionalization. Since the mid-1980s, the RTA has been successful in raising teachers' salaries, implementing a mentoring program for new teachers, and addressing poor teaching through a peer intervention program.

The first labor organization for college professors, the United Federation of College Teachers (now United College Employees of the Fashion Institute of Technology) was founded in 1967. That year, the union negotiated the first public higher education collective bargaining agreement in the United States. In 1972 City University of New York employees formed the Professional Staff Congress to represent them. United University Professions, representing faculty and staff at SUNY campuses, was created in 1973. These groups are affiliated with NYSUT. The most recent unionization efforts have been among university graduate assistants. New York University was the first private university to negotiate an agreement with newly organized graduate assistants in 2002. Graduate assistants at the City University of New York and the SUNY are also unionized.

Murphy, Marjorie. *Blackboard Unions: The AFT and the NEA 1900–1980* (Ithaca: Cornell Univ Press, 1990)

New York State United Teachers, http://www.nysut.org

New York State United Teachers 25th Anniversary, 1973–1998 (Albany: NYS United Teachers, 1998)

Christine E. Murray

teacher training and certification. Before the advent of formal teacher-education programs, many teachers were young men who taught temporarily while preparing for other occupations. The New York State Board of Regents began holding teacher-training classes in private high schools and academies by 1820, and the state legislature provided a small amount of funding for this effort in 1827 and 1834. In 1832 the University of the City of New York (now New York University) added a teacher-training course, and in 1844 the state designated funds for a normal school in Albany. Private colleges such as Elmira College in Elmira and Vassar College in Poughkeepsie began to provide postsecondary teacher training in the 1850s and 1860s.

Emma Willard, founder of the Troy Seminary for Women (now Emma Willard School), promoted one-day teachers' institutes that combined academic subjects with motivational lectures on teaching and the shaping children's characters. The first "pedagogical convention" for teachers was held in Ithaca in 1843. Within two years, 39 counties were holding similar institutes, which were offered until 1912.

During the 1860s the state established and funded several normal schools to educate teachers, and cities began to establish their own teacher-training schools. The Female Normal and High School (now Hunter College) for women was founded in 1869 in New York City. Private universities also added programs. In Ithaca, Cornell University founded its Department of Pedagogy in 1886, and a year later the New York College for the Training of Teachers (now Teachers College at Columbia University) was established in New York City. In 1889 the state funded tuition-free, one-year courses for rural teachers at selected high schools.

Prior to 1864, teacher certification was the responsibility of each school district. No formal tests were required, and local school commissioners evaluated applicants' character and abilities. In 1843 the state superintendent for education was authorized to give life certificates to teachers recommended by local school officials. The 1864 School Law required that local commissioners give formal examinations. As public education centralized, the state began to license teachers in 1888. At that time 50% of teachers had locally issued certificates, 25% had high school training certificates, and 25% were normal school graduates. By the 1890s New York State had assumed responsibility for certification and encouraged formal teacher education. The Education Law of 1895 established minimum requirements for entry into teaching based on experience and standardized examinations.

Between 1895 and 1915, the number of high schools in the state increased from 373 to 740. The growing demand for teachers could not be fully met by private institutions, and there was a push to extend and standardize training requirements. In 1926 teachers were granted certification after completion of a state-approved program of study—a system that has continued to exist for initial certification—and a four-year degree became mandatory in 1936. By 1943 a fifth year of study was required for high school teachers, and in 1966 this requirement was extended to include elementary teachers. State normal schools became four-year teachers colleges in 1942 and were incorporated into the newly created SUNY system in 1948.

New York State has 96 institutions with teacher-education programs. Regulations adopted by the Board of Regents in 1999 require that all programs provide an academic concentration in a relevant subject area, 100 hours of field experience, and student teaching at two grade levels. Programs must be accredited by an external agency, such as the National Council for the Accreditation of Teacher Education, the Teacher Education Accreditation Council, or the Regents' Accreditation Organization. These provisions reflect an ongoing increase in the requirements for certification. Since 1978 New York State teachers have been required to complete a master's degree within five years for permanent certification, but after 2004 the time limit may be shorter. Beginning in 1984, teachers were required to pass the National Teachers Exam, which was subsequently replaced by several New York State teachers' examinations, including a general knowledge test, written and performance tests of teaching skills, and content-specific tests.

In 1998 the Professional Standards and Practices Board, made up of public school teachers, higher education faculty, and the public, was created to advise the Board of Regents on teacher-education and certification policies. As of 2004, teachers were no longer granted permanent certification but would receive a renewable five-year professional certificate after completion of the master's degree. Teachers with the new professional certificate are required to complete 175 hours of professional development every five years to maintain certification.

New certification areas include early childhood (birth–grade 2), childhood (grades 1–6), and adolescence (grades 7–12) for specific subject areas. There are also special certifications for bilingual education, special education, reading, technology, art, dance, home economics, health, music, physical education, recreation, speech, and vocational subjects.

See also HIGHER EDUCATION.

Folts, James D. *History of the University of the State of New York and the State Education Department, 1784–1996* (Albany: NYS Education Department, 1996)

Horner, Harlan Hoyt, ed. *Education in New York State, 1784–1954* (Albany: Univ of the State of New York, State Education Department, 1954)

New York State Education Department, Office of Teaching Initiatives, http://www.highered.nysed.gov/tcert

Christine E. Murray

teasels *[Dipsacus fullonum].* A burrlike plant used in the woolen industry. The plant heads contain very strong bracts, curved downward, that "tease" the wool fibers of woven cloth up, raising the nap. Dr John Snook of Skaneateles (Onondaga Co) is credited with first planting English teasel seeds there in 1833 and harvesting them in 1835. The soil and weather of Skaneateles and Marcellus (Onondaga Co) were conducive to teasel culture, and in 1899 the district supplied all the teasels used in the US market except for a small quantity produced in Oregon.

The crop became the greatest asset of Skaneateles area farmers. The teasel is a biennial plant with the burrs growing on 6 ft (1.8 m) stalks in the second year. The main stalk produces the largest and strongest teasel, called the king; smaller ones on the bush are the queens and buttons. The crop was harvested in August and dried in barns with doors that could be opened for air circulation or closed against dampness. In the winter the burrs were trimmed and sized, then delivered to Skaneateles teasel merchants for storage and marketing.

In woolen mills, teasels were mounted on a rotating cylindrical drum called a gig; the dampened woven wool cloth was drawn over the drum in the opposite direction, the teasel penetrating and raising the fibers of the cloth to produce a fine finish with a minimum of injury. Teasels were replaced on the cylinder every three to five days. The Skaneateles Teasel Growers Cooperative Association (1927) contracted to sell its production to a New Jersey teasel merchant. When local merchants offered a higher price, the co-op demanded that price from the New Jersey merchant and lost the contract. The development of mechanical nappers and of synthetic fibers, a New Deal policy of duty-free wool combined with cheap labor in English mills, and the reduction in demand for fine grades of wool cloth all contributed to the ultimate loss of the teasel industry. The last crop was planted in 1956; F. and J. McLaughlin, the last merchant, closed in 1960.

Leslie, Edmund N. *Skaneateles: History of Its Earliest Settlements and Reminiscences of Later Times* (New York: Andrew H. Kellogg, 1902)

Spain, Barbara B., and Karen R. Anklin. *Skaneateles:*

Glimpses of the Past (Moravia, NY: Village Printer, 1987)

Patricia Blackler

technology. Technology is the application of scientific knowledge for practical purposes, and its importance to New York State dates at least to the middle of the 18th century. Technology can manifest itself in many ways and at different levels but has been most conspicuous as industrial production. One of the earliest examples is iron manufacturing, and the state's natural resources of large reserves of iron ore, dense forests that could be turned into fuel, and an abundant supply of water that could be harnessed for power made iron smelting possible. By the mid–18th century there were at least three iron furnaces in operation in the colony, including the Ringwood Ironworks (1741) [now in Rockland Co], a furnace at the Philip Livingston estate (1750) [now in Columbia Co], and the Forest of Dean furnace on Popolopen Creek (1756) (Orange Co). The laws governing iron manufacture were such that New York State producers could make some castings, but the bulk of the pig iron coming from the furnaces was sent to British factories. The list of legal domestically made goods included pots and pans, firebacks, grates, horseshoes, nails, wheel rims, and cannons.

The power to operate equipment essential to the process of iron making came from the streams and rivers that were plentiful in the state. Starting in the 1830s the Mohawk River proved especially important in this early stage of industrial development. The energy needs of most industries far exceeded that which could be produced by human beings or animals. For areas without the benefit of waterpower, there was, eventually, the steam engine. Introduced to North America in 1755, these engines were used initially for pumping water. It was not until 20 years later that the first such engine, designed to power the municipal waterworks, was produced in New York City by Irish-born Christopher Colles. Not long after 1800 there were several engine builders at work in the city, including the Allaire Ironworks (*ca* 1815) on Cherry St in Manhattan. The manufacture of steam engines was New York State's first heavy industry.

The region at the confluence of the Mohawk and Hudson Rivers, now in modern-day Albany and Saratoga Cos, became a center of industrial development at the beginning of the 19th century and has been referred to as the birthplace of the industrial revolution in America. Although some of the early efforts, such as the Cohoes Manufacturing Co, a waterpowered factory built in 1811 to produce wood screws, and several cotton mills erected during the 1820s, were short-lived, manufacturing began in earnest in the region in the early 1830s. Experienced textile workers from New England settled, and the textile mills of Harmony Manufacturing Co in Cohoes (Albany Co) began operation in 1838.

The 19th Century to World War II

For New York State, the 19th century was a period of remarkable advances in technology. Institutions of higher learning, especially those devoted to teaching science and technology, enhanced the industrial growth taking place. The state leaders' attitude toward internal developments—particularly in the construction of canals—contributed to the growth of industry by providing the means for moving both raw materials and finished goods. Municipal improvements were encouraged as well. Gas lighting was introduced to New York City in 1823. In Fredonia (Chautauqua Co) the means for capturing and using natural gas were just being devised, although the experiments had little immediate impact. The opening of what became Rensselaer Polytechnic Institute in 1825 in Troy (Rensselaer Co) was the first of several civilian institutions of higher learning in New York State devoted to instruction and research in science and engineering. In 1829 a similar institution, the forerunner of the Rochester Institute of Technology, was organized; a third school, Cooper Union for the Advancement of Science and Art, was founded by industrialist Peter Cooper at Astor Place in Manhattan in 1859.

At midcentury technology was taking many new forms and exerting a great influence on everyday life. The event that may have had the most impact for introducing the public to all manner of consumer goods and industrial technology was the Crystal Palace exhibition held in New York City in 1853. Although it was an international event, a great many of the products and participants were from New York State. An exhibitor to make a lasting impression was Elisha Graves Otis of Yonkers. He provided fairgoers with dramatic demonstrations of his soon-to-be-patented safety elevator. Opening a factory in Yonkers to manufacture his new invention in 1853, Otis's elevator would be an essential element of the tall buildings that would eventually define New York City.

During this period, the New York State led the country in heavy industry, both in extent and in the technical skill of its workers. Heading a list of four or five large-scale producers (each employing several hundred people) and manufacturing a wide range of heavy industrial machinery was the Novelty Iron Works of New York City. The variety of goods manufactured in the state included steam engines, machine tools, carriages, wagons, bicycles, and mechanical instruments, among other things. Some companies came to be known for their broad range of products. None was more varied than E. Remington and Sons of Ilion (Herkimer Co), established *ca* 1815 and later known as Remington Arms. This firm, aside from making firearms, produced mowing machines, cultivators, bridge spans, sewing machines, and typewriters.

New York State was the site of a number of important technological developments during the 19th century. Typical of the diversity of these inventions were the locks of inventor Linus Yale Jr of Salisbury (Herkimer Co) and the steam-heating system of Birdsill Holly. Holly developed a commercial hydraulic power company, Holly Manufacturing and in 1877 introduced district steam heating, consisting of a boiler that forced steam through a network of underground pipes, to his hometown of Lockport (Niagara Co). The town was the first place in the world to have such a system, which became particularly important in the development of large cities and the standard method of heating extensive areas of commercial structures.

Until the 1870s water and steam were the primary sources of power. In 1879 the first waterpowered Edison electric generator was installed in a piano factory in Dolgeville (Herkimer Co). But New York State's premier electrical event took place when an Edison generating station began operating on Pearl St in Lower Manhattan in 1882. This installation, though at first supplying only 85 customers, ushered in a new age in power distribution and lighting. To supply the materials needed by the new electrical industry, Thomas Edison bought several existing buildings in Schenectady and established his factory, the Edison Machine Works, in 1886; it became part of the General Electric Co six years later.

The state's association with hydraulic power continued in the late 19th century. In 1885 Thomas Evershed, an engineer for the New York State canal system, was asked to devise a plan for the further development of waterpower at Niagara Falls. Water from the Niagara River was already being diverted to power several factories. The plan suggested that all future development be toward producing electricity rather than apply waterpower directly to run machinery. With the opening of the Adams generating station in 1897, located in Niagara Falls and operated by the Niagara Falls Power Co, the power of the Niagara River was turned into electricity that could be distributed to customers far from the source.

Developments in transportation technology were not neglected in New York State. Railroads that crisscrossed the state brought in materials for industry and enabled New York–made products to reach distant markets. New York City's first experimental subway line was built under Broadway in the 1870s by Alfred Ely Beach. His greatest contribution, however, was to the advancement of technology during the middle and late 19th century through his editorship of *Scientific American* magazine. The popular weekly journal, which was based in New York City, was written for the layperson and did much to promote public acceptance and understanding of the latest inventions and developments in science and technology.

New York State's relationship with the new fields of automotive transportation and flight began early in the 20th century. Although the state was home to a number of automobile builders, perhaps the best remembered vehicle was that manufactured by Herbert H. Franklin of Syracuse. Franklin's firm, H. H. Franklin Manufacturing (known as Franklin Automobile Co after 1917), was the first US company to mass-produce passenger cars powered by air-cooled engines; production began in 1902 and continued until 1934. Hammondsport (Steuben Co) was the home of air pioneer Glenn H. Curtiss, an early rival of the Wright brothers. In the 1910s Curtiss developed and produced some of the first successful flying boats in Hammondsport and Buffalo.

After World War II

New forms of technology flowed from advances made during World War II, and none had a greater impact than atomic energy. One immediate result was the creation of the Knolls Atomic Power Laboratory at Niskayuna (Schenectady Co) in 1946. Initially the facility conducted research toward the development of a nuclear plant to generate electricity for civilian purposes. In 1950, however, the laboratory's efforts were redirected toward designing nuclear propulsion systems for the US Navy, and this work continues in the 21st century. In 2003 Knolls was operated by the Lockheed-Martin

Corp and employed 2,600. Atomic energy–related activities were also the impetus for the creation of the Brookhaven National Laboratory when it was organized on a former US Army base at Upton (Suffolk Co) in 1947. Begun as a regional laboratory by an educational consortium under contract to the US Atomic Energy Commission, it provided facilities that were too costly for its individual members. Research at Brookhaven continues in the early 21st century; topics have varied over the years but include physics, medicine, and the environment.

Where heavy industry and manufacturing were the hallmarks of the state's 19th- and early 20th-century technology, what has followed is a focus on electronics. By the mid-1980s New York State had as many as 1,400 private and commercial research testing laboratories employing thousands. Typical of the growth of postwar electronics-based industries was the Haloid Co of Rochester. Work by Chester F. Carlson in the late 1930s came to fruition when Haloid put the first photocopying machines he devised on the market in late 1948. The invention transformed Haloid into a major corporation, and in 1962 it became Xerox Corp. International Business Machines Corp (IBM) was created in 1924 in New York City when three moderate-sized companies specializing in tabulating and time-keeping machines joined forces. Like most industries, the company converted to military production during World War II, but following the war it resumed its research activities. These yielded the first large-scale digital calculating machine in the late 1940s, a progression of computing machines in the 1950s, and full-time computer production in the 1960s. In 1961 New York State became the home of IBM's industrial research laboratory, the Thomas J. Watson Research Center in Yorktown Heights (Westchester Co), one of the largest labs of its type in the world. In 1981 the company introduced the IBM personal computer, which set the industry standard.

The state's history of fostering technical education continued in 1965 with the creation of the National Technical Institute for the Deaf at the Rochester Institute of Technology. The institute, with approximately 1,100 deaf or hard-of-hearing students enrolled in 2002, was the world's largest technological college for the deaf and prepared its students with state-of-the-art technical and professional education programs.

Industries in New York State have embraced the latest advances in technology and in some cases have become major contributors. Glass producer Corning Inc (Steuben Co), founded in 1851, is one such company. Over the decades its products have ranged from glassware to lightbulbs and television picture tubes. In 2003 the company was a major producer of telecommunications materials—including optical fibers, cables, and related components—and liquid crystal displays for computer screens. Among the company's other products are pollution-control devices, lighting, and materials relating to the manufacture of semiconductors. Early in 2001 Corning entered a new area of medical research when it began manufacture of glass slides imprinted with genetic material.

See also SCIENTIFIC CULTURE (17TH–18TH CENTURIES).

Crease, Robert P. *Making Physics: A Biography of Brookhaven National Laboratory, 1946–1972* (Chicago: Univ of Chicago Press, 1999)

Giedion, Siegfried. *Mechanization Takes Command* (New York: Norton, 1975)

Kelly, Virginia B., et al. *Wood and Stone: Landmarks of the Upper Mohawk Valley Region* (Utica: Central New York Community Arts Council, 1974)

Pursell, Carroll W., Jr. *Early Stationary Steam Engines in America* (Washington, DC: Smithsonian Institution Press, 1969)

Vogel, Robert M. ed. *A Report of the Mohawk-Hudson Area Survey* (Washington, DC: Smithsonian Institution Press, 1973)

White, Norval. *New York: A Physical History* (New York: Atheneum, 1987)

William E. Worthington Jr

Teed, Cyrus Reed (*b* Trout Creek, Delaware Co, ?Oct 1839; *d* Estero, Fla, 22 Dec 1908). Utopian religious leader. Teed grew up in Utica and left school at age 11 to work on the Erie Canal. In 1859 he began studying medicine with his uncle, Samuel Teed, in Utica, graduating from the Eclectic Medical College of the City of New York in 1868 and returning to Utica to establish a practice. In the years that followed he claimed to have discovered cellular cosmogony, a term used to describe his theory of a concave earth. Moving to Moravia (Cayuga Co) in 1880, he assumed the name Koresh and established his first commune, which later moved to Chicago, where it prospered and established a newspaper and publishing house. In 1893 Teed moved to Estero, Fla, where he built another commune and conducted experiments to prove his theory that the earth is hollow and that we are living on the inside, publishing *The Cellular Cosmogony* in 1899. Although some people still followed Teed's teachings after his death, the commune dwindled in size and the last Koreshan died in 1982.

Landing, James E. "Cyrus Reed Teed and the Koreshan Unity." In *America's Communal Utopias,* ed. Donald E. Pitzer (Chapel Hill: Univ of North Carolina, 1997)

David B. Malone

Tekakwitha, Kateri (*b* Ossernenon [now Auriesville, Montgomery Co], 1656; *d* LaPrairie de la Madelaine, Canada, 17 Apr 1680). Mohawk religious figure. Child of a marriage between a Mohawk father and Algonquin mother, she was left deeply scarred by smallpox at the age of 4 in an outbreak that killed her parents. She was thereafter raised by her uncle at a village called Ganadawage, near what is now known as Fonda (Montgomery Co). Various translations of her name include "Who Walks Groping for Her Way," which may allude to the fact that disease had left her partially physically disabled and nearly blind. She became acquainted with Christianity in 1675 through the efforts of the Jesuit Jacques de Lamberville and was baptized on Easter Day the following year. Her christening name was Kateri, for Catherine. Likely long-standing hostility from her village and foster family, exacerbated by her conversion, persuaded her by 1677 to seek refuge among other native converts who lived under Jesuit influence at Kahnawake, Canada. During the remaining three years of her life there, Tekakwitha became renowned for piety, self-sacrifice, and intense devotionalism. Following a model set by nuns in Montreal and Quebec, she led a small group of Iroquoian women in severe penitential and ascetic practices. Her emulation of French monastic virtue simultaneously worked to preserve pre-contact ideals regarding the power of virginity among Native Americans. But physical austerities such as scourging, walking barefoot in winter, and frequent fasting weakened her already frail health. Having received last rights during Holy Week of 1680, she died at the age of 24. Since then her memory has edified Jesuit communities and generations of Indians who visit her shrine, now located at Fonda. In 1932 she was formally nominated for sainthood; Pope Pius XII declared her venerable in 1943; and the penultimate step was taken on 22 June 1980 when she became the first North American Indian beatified by the Roman Catholic Church.

Kateri Tekakwitha, painted after her death by Fr Chauchetière in the 1680s.

Bechard, Henri. *Kaia'tanoiron Kateri Tekakwitha.* Trans Antoinette Kinlough (Quebec: Kateri Center, 1976)

Shoemaker, Nancy. *Kateri Tekakwitha: Mohawk Maid* (San Francisco: Ignatius Press, 1991)

Weiser, Francis X. *Kateri Tekakwitha* (Quebec: Kateri Center, 1972)

Henry Warner Bowden

telegraph industry. The first patent for the electromagnetic telegraph was granted to Samuel F. B. Morse, a professor of art at the University of the City of New York (now New York University), in 1838. After receiving a government subsidy Morse completed an experimental line between Baltimore and Washington, DC, in 1844. In 1846 the telegraph linked New York City with Washington, Boston, and Buffalo. Scottish scientist Alexander Bain and Royal E. House of Vermont introduced new telegraph patents in the late 1840s, providing competition for the original Morse lines. By 1850, 10 main lines ran from New York City: 4 to Buffalo, 3 to Philadelphia, and 3 to Boston. The telegraph network was filled in with feeder companies, such as the Ithaca and Binghamton Telegraph Co and the Syracuse and Oswego Telegraph Co. Buffalo connected with cities in the Midwest.

In April 1851 the New York and Mississippi Valley Printing Telegraph Co, controlled by a group of investors from Rochester, was incorporated in New York State. The company, led by Hiram Sibley, was to connect Buffalo with St. Louis by either building new or buying existing lines. Because they had control of the House patent for the entire region, the investors thought that they could compete effectively with the multitude of shorter Morse lines. Through a series of aggressive tactics, Sibley purchased many bankrupt lines and "divided and conquered" the remaining important ones. One conquest was of a network of companies controlled by Ezra Cornell and his associates. Cornell had been involved with the telegraph since 1844 when he worked on Morse's experimental line. Starting in 1853, he attempted to create a network of companies under one management that connected Buffalo, Pittsburgh, Chicago, and St. Louis. Sibley was able to split Cornell's partnership and buy his interests in the telegraph. Cornell later used his telegraph fortune to found Cornell University (1865). During this merger with Cornell, and to reflect the integration of the western lines, the company changed its name to Western Union Telegraph Co in April of 1856.

Other companies also created regional monopolies, changing the industry's structure dramatically by the late 1850s. Of the six major telegraph companies in the eastern half of the nation, three operated in New York State. Western Union controlled much of the Midwest with lines extending west from Buffalo; the American Telegraph Co connected New York City to Maine and New Orleans; and the New York, Albany and Buffalo Telegraph Co controlled the remainder of New York State. In 1861 the first transcontinental line was completed, and in 1866 the first permanent transatlantic telegraph was laid. Ultimately strategic considerations and the impact of the Civil War led to further consolidation until Western Union had a national monopoly and moved its headquarters from Rochester to New York City in 1866.

The telegraph revolutionized several industries that required coordination across long distances and contributed to the general acceleration of daily life in the United States. In 1849 the Associated Press opened its first foreign bureau in Halifax, Nova Scotia, to relay news to New York City from steamers arriving from Europe. Newspapers around the country received news from the Associated Press, and by the 1870s it generated over 10% of Western Union revenues. In 1851 Charles Minot, the superintendent of the New York and Erie Railroad, was the first railroad manager in the United States to use the telegraph. The telegraph was used to coordinate the scheduling and loading of trains. A subsidiary technology, the stock ticker, was first installed in 1868 by Gold and Stock Reporting Telegraph Co of New York City, allowing for the widespread dispersion of information from the New York Stock Exchange.

Although one can point to the patenting of the telephone in 1876 as the beginning of the end of the industry, the telegraph remained common through the 1970s. But from its peak of over 236 million domestic messages in 1945, traffic declined to 69 million by 1970. In 1960 a three-minute station-to-station daytime telephone call between New York City and Chicago cost $1.45, as much as a 15-word telegraph message. In 2004 Western Union was a subsidiary of First Data Corp and generated the majority of its revenues through money transfers.

Blondheim, Menahem. *News over the Wires: The Telegraph and the Flow of Public Information in America, 1844–1897* (Cambridge, Mass: Harvard Univ Press, 1994)

Thompson, Robert L. *Wiring a Continent: The History of the Telegraph Industry in the United States, 1832–1866* (Princeton, NJ: Princeton Univ Press, 1947)

Tomas Nonnenmacher

telephone industry. Alexander Graham Bell conducted his research in Boston and, after securing the first of two key patents for the telephone in 1876, chartered the original Bell Telephone Co in Massachusetts (1877). But the telephone industry in the United States, dominated by the Bell monopoly until its breakup in 1984, came of age in the friendlier business climate of New York State. American Telephone and Telegraph Co (AT&T), initially a Bell subsidiary providing long-distance telephone service, was chartered in New York State in 1885. On 31 Dec 1899 the Bell Co was reorganized so that AT&T became the parent. New York City became the financial center of the telephone industry in 1907, when J. P. Morgan and several other New York bankers wrested control of the company from Boston-based financiers and moved corporate headquarters. Several critical early innovations in the industry were associated with New York City, from the first major long-distance line, which linked New York City and Boston in 1884, to the first school to train the "telephone girls" working switchboards (1902), to the invention by a Columbia professor of the loading coil, which greatly enhanced long-distance transmission, to the first transcontinental line (linking New York and San Francisco in 1915).

The First Bell Monopoly

The Bell Telephone Co of New York was formed in 1878 and bought out Western Union's telephone business in 1879, enjoying a patent-based monopoly over telephone service in the United States until 1894, leasing equipment and the right to use its network to a host of local companies in which it also held equity. New York State was served by an assortment of Bell licensees, including the Metropolitan Telephone and Telegraph Co in the New York City area, the Central New York Telephone and Telegraph Co (1882), and the New York and Pennsylvania Telephone Co (1882).

With antimonopolism percolating throughout 1880s America, New York State became a center of telephone industry patent wars. Several concerns launched patent suits against Bell, and the *New York Times* editorial board engaged in an ongoing campaign against Bell and its patents. Relations with customers also soured as a result of the initial high cost of telephone service and the ugly and dangerous mazes of telephone wires that blanketed city streets. In November 1886 all telephone users in Rochester canceled service after the Bell Telephone Co of Buffalo (1879), which served Rochester, switched to measured service (as opposed to flat-rate service, an innovation successfully launched in Buffalo). The boycott held until Bell capitulated on the rate structure 18 months later. In 1888 the New York State legislature conducted an investigation of the Bell system. The committee report criticized Bell's monopolistic practices and proposed regulating telephone rates directly. However, it also concluded that only the federal government could effectively regulate the telephone industry and even hinted at the possibility of nationalizing the industry. The US Supreme Court affirmed the Bell patents in the same year and proposed rate legislation disappeared quietly.

Competition and the Second Bell Monopoly

In 1894 the second of Alexander Graham Bell's original patents expired, and thousands of independent telephone companies emerged in the United States, offering primarily local service. Bell tried to crush the independents by refusing most interconnection to its network, buying or suing some, engaging in price wars, and above all, further consolidating its own system. Nevertheless, some independents thrived, particularly in Western New York, led by the Rochester Telephone Co (1899) and Frontier (1901) in Buffalo. In New York City, however, the independents were thwarted by local regulators, the Merchants' Association of New York and New York Telephone, the new name for the Metropolitan Co, after 1896.

By 1907 independent phone companies accounted for half the telephones in the United States. Bell then seized on a brilliant strategy to regain its monopoly position. It embarked on a buyout spree of independents with which its local companies directly competed. It absorbed many more noncompeting independents into the Bell system, thereby allowing their survival but ensuring its dominant position. Arguing that the telephone industry was a natural monopoly, one in which a single provider is most efficient, and promising to work toward "universal service," it embraced government regulation in exchange for monopoly protection. Ever since, historians and economists have vigorously debated the merits of Bell's natural monopoly argument, but regardless, the new policies worked. In 1913 Bell did agree to stop acquiring competing independents to stave off a federal antitrust lawsuit hastened by the independent Home Tele-

Telephone pole workers in Syracuse, 1911.

phone Co (1901) in Jamestown (Chautauqua Co). But this was only a brief pause on the way to regulated monopoly. The desire of many consumers for unified service, consolidation induced by World War I, and finally a federal law in 1921 permitting Bell to buy its direct competitors all aided Bell's return to dominance by the 1920s.

Consolidation accelerated within New York State as well. Between 1906 and 1909 the various Bell companies merged into a new statewide New York Telephone Co. In 1909 and 1910 the New York State legislature again investigated and chided the Bell monopoly, yet its report also suggested that the largest consortium of independents in the state, organized as the Federal Telephone Co, was trying to replace one monopoly with another. By the time of the next investigation, in 1914, the New York Telephone Co controlled 90% of the state market. Shortly thereafter Bell did surrender the Rochester market to the independents, leading to a newly reorganized Rochester Telephone Corp (1921), but as part of the same agreement gained control over Buffalo. New York State's Public Service Commission, created in 1907, had jurisdiction over the telephone industry but preferred a single provider to competition and in regulating rates actually helped consolidate Bell's dominant position.

From the 1920s through the 1960s, "Ma Bell" dominated local service and enjoyed an airtight monopoly over long-distance service. From its creation in 1934 the Federal Communications Commission (FCC) embraced the view that a regulated monopoly telephone provider would best serve the public. In 1949 the Justice Department initiated antitrust proceedings against AT&T, but a lukewarm Eisenhower administration dropped the case in 1956. New York State's Public Service Commission continued to play a role in regulating phone rates and promoting access to telephone service in the underdeveloped rural areas.

The Bell Breakup and the Current Industry

In the late 1950s and 1960s, new technologies and firms, especially Microwave Communications Inc (MCI), which tried to establish a competing long-distance network, renewed suspicion of big business, and economists' rejection of regulation and natural monopoly theory all challenged the Bell monopoly. The FCC and the courts gradually shifted from pro-monopoly to pro-competition. In 1974 the federal government sued AT&T for antitrust violations. After a protracted legal battle, the company agreed to merge its local-service providers into seven regional holding companies or "Baby Bells," effective 1 Jan 1984; AT&T remained the long-distance company. New York Telephone merged with New England Telephone to form NYNEX, though the two kept their old names for another decade. Almost immediately after the Bell breakup a competitor, Teleport Communications, an initiative of the Port Authority of New York and New Jersey, began offering local service in New York City, primarily to businesses. In 1989 the Public Service Commission demanded that New York Telephone provide interconnection with Teleport and other firms.

Telephone operators at dial assistance switchboard, New York City, mid–20th century.

The 1996 Federal Telecommunications Act encouraged local and long-distance providers to enter each other's markets and, along with the late 1990s stock market bubble and rapid advances in technology, led to a frantic wave of mergers and acquisitions. In 1997 NYNEX merged with Bell Atlantic, another Baby Bell, to form Bell Atlantic. AT&T entered the local-service market the following year by buying Teleport. In 2000 Bell Atlantic merged with GTE, founded in 1959 from a merger of previously existing companies and the largest independent in New York State and the nation for most of the 20th century, to form Verizon, which as of 2004 dominated New York State's local-service market. However, competition in the long-distance and cellular markets was wide open. Rochester's Frontier Corp, the descendant of the old Rochester Telephone Co, is owned by Citizens Communications. Several local independents survive: Chautauqua and Erie Telephone Corp of Westfield (Chautauqua Co); Warwick Valley Telephone Co in Warwick (Orange Co); Middleburgh Telephone Co (Schoharie Co); and Nicholville Telephone Co (St. Lawrence Co).

Cohen, Jeffrey E. *The Politics of Telecommunications Regulation: The States and the Divestiture of AT&T* (Armonk, NY: M. E. Sharpe, 1992)

Garnet, Robert W. *The Telephone Enterprise: The Evolution of the Bell System's Horizontal Structure, 1876–1909* (Baltimore: Johns Hopkins Univ Press, 1985)

Mosher, William E. "Public Utilities and Their Early Regulation." In *Wealth and Commonwealth*, vol 8 of *History of the State of New York,* 10 vols, ed. Alexander C. Flick (1933; repr Port Washington, NY: I. J. Friedman, 1962)

Derek Hoff

television, cable. By the end of the 20th century, this billion-dollar national communications industry, which makes use of satellite communications technology to offer subscribers hundreds of channels of video and data services, was available in almost every community in New York State.

Early Years

Before 1953 the Federal Communications Commission had issued only 108 television station licenses, pending agreement on certain technical standards. Most of these were in the nation's larger cities, including New York City, Rochester, and Buffalo in New York State. Outside of these areas, it was nearly impossible to receive any television with a standard roof-top or set-top antenna. Community antenna television (CATV), a technology implemented in 1950 by Lansford, Pa, appliance dealer Frank Tarlton, was first developed to reach potential viewers in the more remote areas of the country. Hoping to initiate sales of television sets, Tarlton built a large outdoor master antenna capable of picking up Philadelphia stations some 70 miles (113 km) away. In return for a one-time installation fee and a monthly service charge, he ran 75-ohm coaxial cable from his antenna to his customers' homes, bringing television to an area otherwise beyond its reach.

Hornell TV Service (Steuben Co) built New York State's first cable system in 1951. Other franchises in Chemung and Steuben Co were granted in Elmira (1954) and Corning (1955). Ideally situated less than 100 miles (161 km) from New York City atop the high ground overlooking southern New York State's coastal plain, the mid-Hudson region became home to a cluster of pioneering systems, including the Ellenville CATV Association (1952) in Ulster Co; Margaretville Tel-Viz (1953) in Delaware Co; and the Roundtop TV Club of Livingston Manor (1954) in Sullivan Co. In the geographically isolated Finger Lakes region, systems were built in Ithaca and Moravia (Cayuga Co) in 1952. The City of Oneonta (Otsego Co) initiated a system in 1954.

During the mid-1950s new television broadcasting stations took to the air across the state in Albany, Binghamton, Buffalo, Elmira, Rochester, Syracuse, Utica, and Watertown. Even though most New Yorkers could now receive television with conventional home antennas, CATV continued to thrive as a source of programming diversity. Nearly all of the new channels were affiliates of the three major networks, CBS, NBC, and ABC. Cable systems, however, offered "independent" channels from New York City that aired classic feature films, reruns of off-network series, and live coverage of New York City's major league baseball, basketball, and hockey teams. They also offered public television stations, which were uncommon in the state before the 1970s. These offered viewers the noncommercial programs of National Educational Television, the forerunner of PBS.

While CATV became commonplace elsewhere in the state, little interest developed in New York City. All existing viewing options (network, independent, and noncommercial) were available free of charge from New York City's eight over-the-air broadcast stations. Demand grew, however, among residents of Manhattan, where skyscrapers interfered with reception. In 1965 New York City designated its first cable districts, dividing Manhattan into two zones, north and south of 96th St, and awarded franchises for the difficult task of wiring the island. By the end of the 1960s growth in the state's cable television industry leveled. Most viewers wanting it lived upstate and had service readily available, while little potential for expansion was seen in New York City. The cable operators lacked new options to stimulate demand. It was not until the 1970s that interest in cable began to accelerate rapidly as evolving technologies, especially satellite transmission to cable ground stations, revolutionized the industry.

GROWTH WITH PREMIUM SERVICES

In 1972 Time Inc (now Time Warner) initiated the first pay-cable service, Home Box Office (HBO). Cable subscribers were given the opportunity of paying an additional monthly fee over their basic subscription rate for a channel offering recent feature films, live sports events, and original programming, all without commercial interruption. Known as a "tiered" cable service, this kind of multiple pricing structure eventually became standard in the industry. In 1975 Time began transmitting HBO to cable operators by satellite. Large dish antennas sprang up in the parking lots of local cable companies as they transformed themselves into satellite ground stations. In the years that followed, scores of satellite-delivered television channels, which viewers could only get through cable subscription, were developed. Unlike HBO most of the new cable channels were advertiser-supported services directed at specific niche audiences: CNN (news), ESPN (sports), BET (African American programming), and New York City–based MTV (music and youth culture). Although most of the satellite services sought national or even international audiences, several regional New York State news channels, including Long Island 12 and NY1, and sports channels, such as MSG and Fox Sports–Western NY (now Empire Sports Network), also came into being.

With so much additional programming available, demand for cable service increased steadily during the 1980s and 1990s. New subscribers signed on in areas that already had cable, and for the first time there was a general clamor for service in areas of New York City that had never been wired. Although it took years of political wrangling, cable franchises were awarded and systems built during the 1980s and 1990s covering all of New York City's boroughs, leaving only the state's remotest areas of the Adirondacks without service.

INDUSTRY REGULATION

Treated much like a public utility, cable television in New York State began in 1972 as a heavily regulated industry overseen by the New York State Commission on Cable Television. In 1996 regulatory authority shifted to the New York State Public Service Commission. In the early 1990s, however, as part of a general trend in American telecommunications, cable television was increasingly viewed as an internally competitive industry and as a technology that was itself vulnerable to external competition. At the start of the 21st century increasing numbers of New Yorkers could choose from among several cable operators in their franchise districts. Those wishing to circumvent cable systems completely have direct broadcast satellite (DBS) receiving dishes installed on their property. In remote areas of New York State and elsewhere, DBS became the standard technology, with backyard and rooftop satellite dishes as common as the roof antennas of the 1950s.

Franchises to operate cable television systems in New York State are awarded at the municipal and town levels, but the federal government wields most of the regulatory power affecting rates and technical standards. The state government can assert authority in the areas of taxation and civil law. New York is one of only two states in which it is illegal for a landlord to deny a tenant access to cable service. New York State government has actively supported local cable access channels, which carry government proceedings and other forms of locally produced programming that would not otherwise be broadcast. Cable franchise operators, represented by the Cable Television and Telecommunications Association of New York (CTTANY), have provided several free educational services to local communities, including the Cable in the Classroom channel for schools and various distant learning projects. CTTANY, founded in 1956, sponsors statewide talk and call-up shows with the governor and other leading state officials and commits its members to carry special events, such as the governor's annual State of the State address.

In 2002 there were 213 systems serving approximately 4.7 million subscribing households in 1,783 New York State communities. Franchise operators pay close to $100 million to local governments in franchise fees and employ upward of 10,000 workers across the state. Competition has led to more innovation and diversification in the industry, such as the offering of cable-linked home security systems and cable-delivered Internet data services.

Baldwin, Thomas F., and D. Stevens McVoy. *Cable Communication* (Englewood Cliffs, NJ: Prentice-Hall, 1983)

New York State. Assembly. Committee on Oversight, Analysis and Investigation. *Cable Picture: Staff Report Examining the Industry and Regulators,* by Anthony J. Genovesi (1994)

New York State. Public Service Commission. *Regulation of Cable Television by the State of New York: Report to the Commission,* by William K. Jones (1970)

Phillips, Mary Alice Mayer. *CATV: A History of Community Antenna Television* (Evanston, Ill: Northwestern Univ Press, 1972)

David Marc

television broadcasting. See BROADCASTING (RADIO AND TELEVISION); PUBLIC BROADCASTING (RADIO AND TELEVISION).

temperance movement. One of the major reform movements of the 19th and early 20th centuries, temperance found both strong support and strong opposition in New York State. Many New Yorkers viewed alcohol as the road to ruin and a national menace, and these residents remained at the heart of the temperance movement as organizers and theorists throughout the 100-year battle against strong drink. But for many other New Yorkers, the consumption of alcohol was an integral part of their cultural and religious heritage.

ORIGINS

The consumption of large amounts of alcohol was commonplace and acceptable in colonial America, but attitudes toward drink began to change with the opening of the 19th century. As the nation began to industrialize, the new economy required disciplined, sober workers, and in 1808 the history of the temperance movement began in New York State with the founding of Saratoga Co's Moreau and Northumberland Temperance Society by physician Dr Billy J. Clark and congregational minister Rev Lebbeus Armstrong. Within a short span of time, other temperance groups sprang up, including the short-lived Canal Temperance Society (1829–?1834), which aimed to serve men employed in barge crews and as tow drivers on the Erie Canal. In February 1826 the American Temperance Society (ATS), a Massachusetts group, opened its first New York chapter under the guidance of Rev Gardiner Spring of New York City. The ATS would mount the first sustained effort to organize temperance societies throughout the nation.

During the 1820s and 1830s few temperance organizations gained wide attention or support. Often these societies aimed at the suppression of vice and focused on temperance as a means to promote morality. Temperance preachers, who frequently employed the techniques of religious revivals, singled out drunkenness as the most devastating sin of the day. But temperance also linked church or moral concerns with a new, science-inspired desire to improve people. By eliminating intemperance, reformers believed they would also reduce insanity, economic decay, poverty, and the risk of social upheavals. The economic advantages of abstinence helped the societies gain recruits. Much of the success of the temperance movement in New York State came through the work of the American Tract Society, an interdenominational—though exclusively Protestant—reform organization that published uplifting pamphlets. The advent of the steam printing press and the expansion of roads, canals, and rails made such literature both inexpensive to produce and easy to distribute. Much of the output of the tract society centered on temperance, and such tales as *The Well-Conducted Farm* (*ca* 1825) by Justin Edwards, describing the prosperity of a "dry" homestead, enjoyed a circulation of almost 1,500,000.

Temperance initially referred to the philosophy of moral suasion, not to prohibition. Temperance advocates sought to persuade heavy drinkers of the error of their ways rather than to end all consumption of alcoholic beverages. This moderate approach helped the movement in New York City, where several local societies combined to form the New York City Temperance Society in 1827. With a high population of immigrants who regularly consumed the alcoholic drinks native to and approved by their cultures, New York City had long been considered the greatest site of intemperance in the state as well as a bastion of the liquor interests. In 1829 temperance received a further boost with the formation in Albany of the New York State Temperance Society (NYSTS), a federation of ATS groups. Founded by a wealthy retired merchant, Edward C. Delavan, who had been converted by a temperance pamphlet placed under his plate at an Albany restaurant, the NYSTS urged moderate drinking and remained the most important temperance society in New York State until Delavan's death in 1871. In addition to amalgamating existing temperance groups, the NYSTS organized new local groups and persuaded employers to stop supplying distilled liquors to workers and merchants to stop selling them. The NYSTS, typical of most early temperance societies, did not condemn the use of beer or wine. As some temperance reformers began to categorize all intoxicating beverages as dangerous, the movement suffered a serious breach.

Beginning in the early 1830s, local societies started adopting an abstinence pledge that proscribed the use of wine, hard cider, and beer as well as distilled spirits. The pledge became known as the "teetotal" pledge, presumably in reference to *Ts* placed by a Hector [now in Schuyler Co] temperance secretary next to the names of members who took the pledge. A national convention of ATS, parent organization of the NYSTS, met at Saratoga Springs in 1836 and formally recommended teetotalism, at the same time changing the name of the group to American Temperance Union. When radicals sought to ban churches from employing fermented wines at communion services, over 2,000 New York State chapters disbanded. While the NYSTS attracted wealthier members, the Baltimore-based Washington Temperance Benevolent Society appealed to blue-collar workers. The Washingtonians, who established their first New York State chapter in New York City in 1841, used personal testimonies in recruiting, and the group soon gained a reputation for vulgarity. By requiring members to pledge total abstinence from alcohol and by excluding religious observances from meetings, the Washingtonians found it difficult to sustain the initial burst of interest that had swelled their membership rosters. In addition, many did not want to join the group for fear that membership would serve as an admission that they had been closet drinkers. Washingtonian acceptance of anyone who signed the abstinence pledge, regardless of moral conduct, also hindered recruitment, and the group's temperance efforts gradually stilled until legislation in Maine revitalized the movement.

Prohibition

By the 1850s prohibition had gained so many supporters that a ban on alcohol became the clear goal of the movement. To achieve prohibition, the state's reformers tried a number of strategies—without significant success. Inspired by an 1846 Maine law banning all liquor sales except those approved by local governments and, later, by a more stringent 1851 Maine law also banning liquor manufacture, they hurried to push a similar law through the New York State legislature. The NYSTS organized a statewide alliance of all prohibitionists to lobby for the legislation, and "Maine Law" associations sprang up throughout the state. In 1855 a law equivalent to Maine's substantial ban on the sale of alcohol took effect in New York State. It dictated that intoxicating liquors could not be kept for sale except for chemical, medical, or sacramental purposes, and, if transactions occurred, they had to be carried out through the offices of a liquor agent and with the approval of local authorities and the courts. Violations of the new law were punishable by fines and imprisonment, but lawbreakers did not always receive equal treatment. In New York City, as well as in a number of other localities, the law was met with open defiance. Weakened by legal challenges, the prohibition received a fatal blow in March 1856 when the Court of Appeals ruled the legislation unconstitutional since it did not clearly distinguish between property or alcohol held before it took effect and such property acquired after its passage. The Maine Law marked the high point of the antebellum temperance movement. With the battle over slavery pushing the country into war, abolition overwhelmed all other reform subjects for some years. But when the guns fell silent, temperance once again seized center stage.

Women

Most temperance societies directed their attentions to stamping out intemperance among men. Women received little attention, as drinkers or as activists. Martha Washington societies, adjuncts of the Washingtonians, provided clothing to families of drunkards and tried to influence female drinkers but did not succeed in establishing an important or influential network. The Woman's New York State Temperance Society did not fare much better. After the Civil War women flooded the temperance movement, seeking to protect home and family. Sparked by the speeches of male physician Dio Lewis, the women of Fredonia (Chautauqua Co) organized bands and visited saloons to pray with patrons. Their Women's Crusade soon turned into the nucleus of the Woman's Christian Temperance Union (WCTU) with Fredonia forming the first chapter in 1874. By the end of that year, the WCTU had spread throughout the state.

Victory

The WCTU worked closely with the male-dominated Prohibition Party, formed in Oswego in 1869, which sought to place the question of prohibition in the political arena by running its own third party male candidates for public office. The Prohibition Party never enjoyed much success and soon found itself surpassed by the Anti-Saloon League (ASL), founded in Oberlin, Ohio, in 1893. The ASL quickly established chapters throughout New York State, and in 1899 members began ringing doorbells and lobbying legislators on a nonpartisan basis on behalf of Prohibition. These tactics slowly began to bear fruit. In 1896 the state legislature passed the Raines Law, which allowed localities to limit the sale of alcohol entirely or partially, according to majority vote. A year later, although some towns had voted to forbid alcohol sales, it was apparent that Raines would not stop the liquor trade. In 1914 a number of New York State temperance groups launched a drive for statewide Prohibition, while ALS continued to push for the local option. The temperance movement received an enormous boost when World War I heightened both patriotism and ethnic tensions. All things German, including breweries and beer, became suspect, while supporters of Prohibition maintained that the use of alcohol weakened the war effort by producing drunken workers and soldiers. To protect the country from foreign menaces, New York State passed statewide Prohibition in December 1917 and supported efforts for a national prohibition law. With the adoption of the 18th Amendment in 1919, New Yorkers could boast of having played a significant role in temperance reform.

Gusfield, Joseph R. *Symbolic Crusade: Status Politics and the American Temperance Movement* (Urbana: Univ of Illinois Press, 1966)

Murdock, Catherine Gilbert. *Domesticating Drink: Women, Men, and Alcohol in America, 1870–1940* (Baltimore: Johns Hopkins Univ Press, 1998)

Tyrrell, Ian R. *Sobering Up: From Temperance to Prohibition in Antebellum America, 1800–1860* (Westport, Conn: Greenwood, 1979)

Caryn E. Neumann

Temporary Emergency Relief Administration (TERA). New York State's unemployment relief program was an effort to deal with the crisis of the depression, during which the number of unemployed New Yorkers in nonagricultural jobs rose from 656,000 in 1929 to 2.06 million in 1933. Facing dire numbers and increasingly urgent requests for state action, Gov Franklin D. Roosevelt called the legislature into special session on 28 Aug 1931. On its final day, 20 September, the legislature unanimously approved the bill establishing TERA, making New York the first state to create a comprehensive, multimillion dollar program of unemployment relief. The legislature appropriated $20 million—to be raised by a one-year, 50% increase in the state income tax—for TERA to spend between 1 Nov 1931 and 1 June 1932. TERA worked with local officials in the more than 100 welfare districts by reimbursing 40% of the districts' home relief expenditures and discretionary amounts for work relief, thereby preserving considerable local autonomy. TERA also provided to local governments free milk and lunches for schools, supplied equipment for subsistence gardens, sponsored budgeting and parenting classes, and contributed to Camp TERA at Lake Tiorati in Orange Co, a rest camp for impoverished single women who also received some job training.

Although TERA originally was meant to be temporary, the initial $20 million evaporated in five months, and the agency existed for nearly six years, until 30 June 1937. It provided public assistance to an estimated 5 million people, about 40% of the state's population, and spent $1.16 billion in local, state, and federal funds. TERA also became the prototype for agencies associated with the federal New Deal, such as the Works Progress Administration and the Federal Emergency Relief Administration, whose chief administrator, Harry Hopkins, was TERA's first director.

TERA was a major component of New York State's "Little New Deal," a contemporary period term referring to a series of relief and reform programs implemented during the Great Depression. After 1933 about 80% of the funds spent by TERA came from federal funds for emergency relief and projects. Yet the leadership of Gov Herbert H. Lehman as well as the state's reform history, urbanization, and wealth allowed New York to develop a comprehensive welfare state that was in many respects independent of the federal government. In the 1930s the state adopted unemployment relief and work assistance, granted public aid to the elderly and to people with disabilities, established a minimum wage system, provided for some collective bargaining, created public housing, and initiated farm price supports. Both TERA and the Little New Deal contributed significantly to New York becoming the first state, in 1938, to provide a constitutional guarantee of public relief and care.

Bremer, William. *Depression Winters: New York Social Workers and the New Deal* (Philadelphia: Temple Univ Press, 1984)

Ingalls, Robert P. *Herbert H. Lehman and New York's Little New Deal* (New York: New York Univ Press, 1975)

New York State. Temporary Emergency Relief Administration. *Five Million People, One Billion Dollars: Final Report of the Temporary Emergency Relief Administration, 1 Nov 1931–30 June 1937* (Albany: J. B. Lyon, 1937)

William Rainbolt

tenant farming and sharecroppers. Farming by nonlandowners who pay for the use of the land with cash or a portion of their agricultural output. New York Colony had a long history of tenant farming concentrated primarily in the large manors along the Hudson River that were reminiscent of quasi-feudal estates. The endemic tensions between landlord and tenant on the manors periodically erupted before the Revolutionary War, in 1751–57, in 1766, and then finally and decisively in the 1840s when the antirent movement forced the issue and resulted in the breakup of the leasehold system on the former manorial estates.

Hundreds of thousands, perhaps millions, of other New York State farmers worked outside the manor system in the 19th and 20th centuries. In the early 1800s most were sharecroppers who allocated part of their harvest to the landlord. Typically the landowner furnished the seed, basic tools, and stock, for which the cropper would give back two-thirds of the total output. If the tenant owned tools and animals, as much as one-half of what was produced may be kept. Some tenants working the land for wealthier farmers were allowed to farm a small lot for their own consumption and trade. Later, as the market economy gained ground, these rental payments were sometimes made in cash. By the early 20th century about 45% of all New York State farm tenants settled their accounts that way.

In addition to sharecroppers and cash tenants were three groups of "farmers without farms," agricultural laborers who neither owned nor rented land as tenants. The first included young sons and relatives of farm owners who received room and board for their labor and perhaps the promise of a share of an inheritance. The second consisted of farmworkers who were paid a modest wage. This group grew steadily in the 19th and 20th centuries, until it represented about 35% of all farmers in the state at beginning of the 21st century. The third were the increasing number of 20th-century migrant farmworkers who provided seasonal labor for the state's growing agricultural industries.

See also MANOR SYSTEM.

Hedrick, U. P. *A History of Agriculture in the State of New York* (New York: Hill & Wang, 1966)
Parkerson, Donald H. *The Agricultural Transition in New York State: Markets and Migration in Mid-19th-Century America* (Ames: Iowa State Univ Press, 1995)

Donald H. Parkerson

tenement reform. New York was the first state in the nation to undertake serious reform aimed at improving living conditions in multifamily homes of the working class. In the 1840s middle-class New Yorkers recognized the problems of overcrowding and poor sanitation in the dwellings known as tenements. At this time, tenements were mainly older, single-family homes divided to accommodate six or more "tenants." Newer buildings, designed for multiple tenancy, were on the increase; these typically featured five floors, each divided into four small apartments—sometimes housing a dozen persons each—with the single water source for the building next to the cellar privy. Groups such as the Association for Improving the Condition of the Poor sought legal regulation of existing tenements as well as construction of healthier buildings.

While minor pieces of legislation affecting housing were passed in the 1850s, New York State did not enact a comprehensive housing law until 1867; this measure legally defined a tenement for the first time and also required one fire ladder and one toilet per 20 tenants. During the 1870s reformers' attention shifted from legislation to construction of philanthropy-funded "model tenements." In 1878 the *Sanitary Engineer* sponsored a design competition for the best tenement plan for a standard New York City lot of 25 x 100 feet (8 x 30 m). The winning entry, James A. Ware's dumbbell plan (so named because interior air shafts made the building's footprint look like a dumbbell), became the state's legally authorized style of tenement the next year.

Increased immigration and the extension of transportation networks in the 1880s multiplied the number of tenement districts in New York City and State. No longer solely interested in regulating how tenements were built, reformers—through private groups such as New York City's Tenement House Committee—sought to control activities within them, attempting to ban garment production and at-home childbirths, in particular. New York State enacted housing legislation throughout the late 19th century, but with almost no enforcement provisions, the laws had little effect on housing conditions. This changed with the state's Tenement House Act of 1901, judged one of the most significant regulatory acts in US history. As the first retroactive housing reform, the "New Law" of 1901 required indoor plumbing and lighting; it also established tenement house departments, city agencies responsible for enforcing the law's provisions. The depression essentially ended the era of tenement reform in New York State. Starting in the 1930s, the state government, with federal aid, assumed more direct responsibility for housing working-class New York State residents through construction of public housing projects.

See also ARCHITECTS AND ARCHITECTURE, NEW YORK CITY; *LOCHNER V NEW YORK*.

Day, Jared N. *Urban Castles: Tenement Housing and Landlord Activism in New York City, 1890–1943* (New York: Columbia Univ Press, 1999)
Plunz, Richard. *A History of Housing in New York City: Dwelling Type and Social Change in the American Metropolis* (New York: Columbia Univ Press, 1990)

Stephen Long

Room in a tenement flat, New York City. Photograph by Jessie Tarbox Beals, 1910.

tennis. Lawn tennis was introduced to New York State (and the United States) by Mary Ewing Outerbridge, who brought the game from Bermuda and arranged the construction of the first courts on a corner of the Staten Island Cricket and Baseball Club grounds in 1874. Although limited mostly to the wealthy, the game caught on quickly, and the first "Championship of America" was held on the Staten Island courts in 1880.

THE AMATEUR ERA

The US National Lawn Tennis Association or USNLTA (US Lawn Tennis Association, 1920–75; US Tennis Association, 1975–), formed in New York City in 1881 and established the specifications and rules for amateur tennis. New Yorker Julian Myrick, one of the most influential organizers of amateur tennis and a president of the USLTA (1920–22), is remembered for his aggressive advocacy of junior tennis and of opening the sport to all classes. Other notable administrators were Larry Baker, founder and president (1948–50) of the National Tennis Foundation, and Bob Kelleher, progressive USTA president who brought the United States into the open era in 1968. The West Side Tennis Club (1892), which began as a men's club and continues to limit female membership, rented courts at various Manhattan locations until 1913, when it acquired property at Forest Hills in Queens. The club hosted tournaments—including, from 1915, the US National Championships—and in 1923 built the only tennis stadium in the country, which opened with the first Wightman Cup, a women's competition between teams from the United States and Great Britain. The club also hosted the finals of the international Davis Cup for men 11 times from 1902 to 1959.

African Americans were excluded from the tennis circuit. In 1916 the oldest African American sports organization in the United States, the American Tennis Association, was formed. It held matches at the Cosmopolitan Tennis Club on West 138th St in Harlem, where interracial matches between top players first took place in 1940. In 1948 Dr Reginald Weir became the first black man to play in a USLTA tournament, the National Indoor Championship at the Seventh Regiment Armory in Manhattan. Weir won the event in 1956, 1957, and 1959. Althea Gibson, raised in Harlem, made history in 1950 as the first African American admitted to a US National Championship, going on to win singles titles at Forest Hills in 1957 and 1958.

PROFESSIONAL TENNIS

As long as amateur tennis was the most prestigious tennis venue, there was a concerted effort to keep the best players there and under control. As early as the 1920s tennis officials connived at "shamateurism": amateur players were given secret payments to cover their expenses to play in tournaments. Despite this effort, players did turn professional, and the men's segment of the first tour began at Madison Square Garden on 9 Oct 1926, culminating with the US Pro Championship held at the Notlek Tennis Club in Manhattan (1927). In succeeding decades, many of the best tennis players, such as Bill Tilden and Ellsworth Vines, turned professional after successful amateur careers and played memorable matches at Madison Square Garden and other venues. These one-night tours and small purses kept spectator interest low until the 1950s, when Jack Kramer's tours gained recognition. Excessive shamateur payments to compete with the pros fostered discontent among the players and helped set the stage for the open era.

In 1968 the open era began in the United States when the first US Open was hosted at Forest Hills. The event drew a mix of amateur and professional players, with Arthur Ashe becoming the first African American and only amateur to win a major title. In 1975 Forest Hills added night play and introduced the 12-point tie-breaker; during that year Martina Navratilova announced her defection from Czechoslovakia at the Open. Dr Renee Richards' yearlong battle for acceptance of the transgendered in women's tournaments ended with a 1976 New York State Supreme Court ruling that she could not be barred from the US Open for failing a chromosome test. In 1978 the National Tennis Center opened at Flushing Meadows in Queens, and the US Open has been played there since. Jimmy Connors and Pete Sampras have won the most men's singles championships during the open era with five; Chris Evert has won the most women's titles with six.

World Team Tennis, launched in 1974, renewed professional tennis with city team franchises and a new format. The New York franchise won championships in 1976 and 1977. The league folded after five years but reappeared in 1981. In 2004 there were two New York teams, based in Schenectady and Mamaroneck (Westchester Co).

Some of the professional game's most accomplished contributors have New York State connections. Since 1955, 18 of the 186 inductees to the International Tennis Hall of Fame have been native New Yorkers, including Gladys Heldman, founder of *World Tennis* magazine (1953) and organizer of the Virginia Slims women's tournaments (1970). Additional members with strong ties to the state include Althea Gibson, winner of 11 Grand Slam events; John McEnroe, raised in Queens and the winner of four singles titles at the US Open between 1979 and 1984; Arthur Ashe, a native of Richmond, Va, who was instrumental in forming the Association of Tennis Professionals (ATP) and after whom the US Open stadium is named; Allison Danzig, who covered the sport for the *New York Times* and the *Brooklyn Daily Eagle* from 1922 to 1967; and Al Laney, journalist and author of *Covering the Court* (1968). Other New York State notables are player and broadcaster Mary Carillo of Queens; Brooklyn-born Australian Open champion (1977) Vitas Gerulaitis; and Theodore Roosevelt, an avid recreational player who incorporated the younger members of his administration into a "tennis cabinet."

In 2003 in New York State there were 1,790,000 players, of whom 1,190 were ranked, playing on 6,875 public courts or in the 319 clubs with 2,470 private courts and competing in 469 annual tournaments. Today the USTA depends on the US Open to support its amateur development programs and tournament sponsorship nationwide. In 2003 there were 937 varsity high school tennis teams, with more than 20,400 students participating in tennis programs (junior varsity, varsity, and modified).

PLATFORM TENNIS

In 1928 Fessenden Blanchard and James Cogswell of Scarsdale (Westchester) built a platform to provide opportunities for winter outdoor play. Modifications were made to playing surface, equipment, and rules, the main difference being the ability to play the ball off the court's wire enclosure. The first club court was built and the first official tournament held at Fox Meadow in Scarsdale in 1931. The American Paddle Tennis Association (now American Platform Tennis Association) was founded in 1934 with Blanchard as president. National championships were first held at Fox Meadow in 1935 and continued to be played there until 1973. The finals of the Tribuno World Championship, the first professional tour (1975–80), were held on temporary courts installed at Forest Hills. The Apple Platform Tennis Club opened in 1977 atop an apartment building on East 24th St in New York City. In 2004 there were approximately 500 platform tennis courts and 60 clubs in New York State, along with 20 tournaments and 5 junior tournaments.

PADDLE TENNIS

Frank P. Beal created paddle tennis as a children's game in 1898 and in 1921 brought it to New York City, where its small courts were conducive to the limited spaces of the urban environment. Althea Gibson began her tennis career playing the game on West 143d St in Harlem before becoming a lawn tennis champion. The first citywide tournament was held in 1922, and a year later the American Paddle Tennis Association (later US Paddle Tennis Association) was established. Interest in the sport peaked in the late 1980s.

Collins, Bud, and Zander Hollander. *Modern Encyclopedia of Tennis* (Detroit: Gale Research, 1994)
Danzig, Allison, and Peter Schwed, comps. *The Fireside Book of Tennis* (New York: Simon & Schuster, 1972)
Talbert, William F. *Tennis Observed: The USLTA Men's Singles Champions, 1881–1966* (Barre, Mass: Barre Publishers, 1967)

Cynthia B. Childs

10,000 Maniacs. Singer Natalie Merchant, keyboardist Dennis Drew, and bassist Steven Gustafson met in 1980–81 at the community college radio station WJWK in Jamestown (Chautauqua Co) and frequented nearby Broadhead Mills, a former warehouse that housed painting studios and held art exhibitions, film screenings, and live music. There they joined with guitarist John Lombardo, and with the names Still Life and then Burn Victims they performed punk and new wave cover songs, before adopting, in 1981, the name 10,000 Maniacs, derived from the horror film *2000 Maniacs*. Their eclectic mix of folk, rock, world music, and socially topical lyrics was captured on their first album, *Human Conflict Number Five* (1982), recorded at nearby SUNY Fredonia. Drummer Jerry Augustyniak joined the group in 1983, and in 1985 they were signed to a major label, Elektra Records, where they enjoyed considerable success. Merchant left the group in 1993 to pursue a solo career, though 10,000 Maniacs, with singer Mary Ramsey, continued to perform and record through 1999.

10,000 Maniacs, http://www.maniacs.com

Hugh W. Foley Jr

terrorism. Though acts of politically motivated violence have a long history in New York State, the term terrorism came into common usage in the early 20th century in connection with the violent acts of anarchists and military saboteurs. The explosion of a munitions plant on Black Tom Island in New York Harbor along the Jersey City, NJ, waterfront on 30 July 1916 was blamed on German saboteurs and helped speed the entry of the United States into World War I. On the morning of 16 Sept 1920, a bomb in a horse-drawn cart exploded in front of the offices of J. P. Morgan and Co at the corner of Wall and Broad Sts in the heart of Manhattan's financial district; 30 people were killed and over 300 injured. No one took credit for the explosion, though it was widely believed to be the work of anarchists. Despite a substantial federal investigation, no arrest was ever made in the case. The ensuing decades were relatively free of political terrorism. The best-known case during this period was that of George Metesky, who became known in the press as the Mad Bomber. He terrorized New York City with over 30 bombings in the 1950s before his capture in 1957. His original motivation was losing a disability claim against Consolidated Edison.

The domestic unrest of the 1960s and 1970s brought a new level of political violence to New York City. The Weather Underground, a radical offshoot of Students for a Democratic Society, claimed responsibility for approximately a dozen small bombings in the city, most notably that of the New York City Police Department's headquarters. The unintended explosion in 1970 of the Weathermen's bomb-making workshop in the basement of a Greenwich Village townhouse killed three members of the group and sent the rest underground. The Puerto Rican terrorist group Fuerzas Armadas de Liberación Nacional (FALN) carried out a campaign of almost 50 bombings around New York City in the mid-1970s, including the 1975 bombing of historic Fraunces Tavern in Lower Manhattan, which killed four. Also in 1975 a bomb in La Guardia Airport killed 11; the attack remains unsolved. The following year Croatian ultranationalists hijacked a plane en route from New York City to Paris and left a bomb in a locker in Grand Central Terminal that killed a police officer. Puerto Rican nationalists planted a bomb in a men's washroom in Kennedy Airport in 1981, killing one person. New Yorkers have also been touched by terrorist acts occurring far outside the state's borders. Pan Am Flight 103 exploded over Lockerbie, Scotland, on 21 Dec 1988, killing 35 Syracuse University students. Timothy McVeigh, a native of Pendleton (Niagara Co), was responsible for the bombing of an Oklahoma City federal building in 1995 that resulted in 168 deaths.

Terrorists operating at the behest of Sheik Omar Abdel-Rahman, an Egyptian Muslim cleric living in New Jersey, set off a powerful car bomb in a garage under the World Trade Center on 26 Feb 1993, intending to topple the structures. Though the towers held, six people were killed and dozens injured while escaping. This prefigured the worst act of terrorism in the nation's history, the destruction of the World Trade Center on 11 Sept 2001 by two hijacked airliners. The attack brought down the two towers in less than two hours, with an estimated death toll of 2,819.

See also CARTOGRAPHY AND MAPPING; SEPTEMBER 11TH, 2001; WORLD TRADE CENTER: THE 1993 WORLD TRADE CENTER BOMBING.

Jacobs, Ron. *The Way the Wind Blew: A History of the Weather Underground* (New York: Verso, 1997)

Laquer, Walter, and Yonah Alexander, eds. *The Terrorism Reader: A Historical Anthology,* rev ed. (New York: NAL Penguin, 1987)

Matthew Taylor Raffety

Terryville. Locality (pop 10,589) in Brookhaven (Suffolk Co). Terryville had its own post office from 1888 to 1918 and from 1924 to 1958, but has otherwise been served by the one at Port Jefferson Station. Long an agricultural district, its farms were first developed for suburbs extensively in 1959.

Tesla, Nikola (*b* Smiljan [now in Croatia], 9 July 1856; *d* New York City, 7 Jan 1943). Electrical engineer and inventor. Tesla studied at the polytechnic school in Graz, Austria, and the University of Prague before joining the Continental Edison Co in Paris in 1882. Already well along with his work on alternating current technology, Tesla emigrated to New York City in 1884 and briefly worked for Thomas Edison. Tesla did pioneering research into the nature of electricity, magnets, and the transmission of electrical power for practical applications. In 1888 he sold his work on alternating-current dynamos, transformers, and motors to the Westinghouse Electric Co. Tesla did experiments on electromagnetic radiation, various wireless lighting systems, and other subjects in the laboratory he opened in Greenwich Village in Manhattan. The Tesla coil, a transformer he invented in 1891, is common in radio and television transmission equipment. A generating station using Tesla's patents was built in 1895 at Niagara Falls and carried power to Buffalo by 1896. He also worked on radio-controlled model airplanes and boats, giving public demonstrations, one at Madison Square Garden in 1897, to prove his theories. In the late 1890s Tesla discovered that the earth itself was a conductor of electricity. He began work in 1900 on a wireless broadcasting system near Shoreham (Suffolk Co) that could transmit signals anywhere in the world. A tower was built, but the project was never completed because of insufficient funds. Tesla had few close friends. Though some of Tesla's ideas were considered eccentric and were ridiculed by other scientists, his writings are still consulted.

Cheney, Margaret. *Tesla: Man Out of Time* (New York: Dell Publishing, 1981)

Childress, D. H. *The Fantastic Inventions of Nikola Tesla* (Stelle, Ill: Adventures Unlimited Press, 1993)

Brian Regal

textile industry. Textile manufacturing in New York State has been concentrated primarily in an east-west corridor between Albany and Buffalo, with the majority of activity between Albany and Syracuse.

Domestic Production

In the colonial period textile production was a vertical, domestic enterprise, that is, the entire process was performed within the household. First, fibers had to be cleaned and prepared for yarn spinning. Natural fibers occur in nonlinear, amorphous masses. Yarn, however, requires a parallel, uniform arrangement, which was achieved by carding, a highly labor-intensive process. Carding mills performed some of this work for client families from about 1775. After carding, the fiber was spun into yarn. Woven fabric, the bulk of domestically produced cloth, required arranging individual strands of yarn into a warp, a long parallel formation set up onto a loom for weaving. A class of itinerant weavers who would weave family-spun yarn for various forms of payment, including room and board, eventually arose. Because New York State was climatically ill suited to growing cotton, late 18th- and early 19th-century farm families converted wool and flax into clothing and home goods, generally for personal use rather than for sale or trade. Before the mechanical gin was invented in 1793, cotton was a luxury fabric.

Transition to Industry

The transition from domestic production to industrial manufacture of textile goods was protracted and not technologically smooth. By the end of the 18th century there was yet little industrialization of textile production, though hand-ginned cotton, shipped to New York State from southern states and the Caribbean, was being processed into cloth by a number of early mills. Mechanized equipment like the spinning jenny and weaving machines were invented in England in the late 18th century and were in limited use in New England from approximately 1814. However, widespread industrial application of these advances had to await refinements in fiber preparation technology. Samuel Slater came to Rhode Island around 1789 having memorized plans for carding machinery already in use in England. Slater's innovations were responsible for an upsurge in the number of carding mills catering to domestic spinners and allowed for dramatic increases in productivity. Whereas in a completely manual process, 5 to 8 carders were needed to prepare fiber for each handspinner, a single early carding machine could outpace 12 to 15 spinners.

Industrial Production

Between 1823 and 1830, Slater made considerable progress in establishing fully mechanized textile mills in New York State and contributed significantly to the increasingly specialized personnel makeup of the early factory system; tasks

New York City Textile Marketing. The historical vitality of the textile industry of New York State owes much to the textile selling and marketing agents who were congregated from about 1850 in a very small area around Worth St in Lower Manhattan. Rail transportation, which had expanded dramatically in the second quarter of the 19th century, and relatively easy road access to docks along both the Hudson and East Rivers opened the Worth St market to the entire textile-producing and -consuming world. Among the significant early occupants of the Worth St textile market were Bates Fabrics, Chicopee Mills, Pacific Mills, Pepperell Manufacturing Co, J. P. Stevens and Co, Wellington Sears Co, Cannon Mills, Fieldcrest Mills, and Dan River Mills. A. D. Juilliard and Co, founded in 1874, began as a selling agent for New York Mills in Oneida Co and owned and operated the mills from around 1906 to 1953. Some of the Worth St merchants were, like Juilliard, exclusive selling agents for one particular company, while others were independent commission agents representing noncompeting lines from several companies. Worth St began to decline after 1925, as mills turned increasingly to in-house sales forces and as the apparel and fashion industry, the largest consumer of textile mill output, concentrated in the Midtown area. By the late 1940s the center of textile marketing had shifted northward, to 7th Ave and cross streets from 30th to 40th.

Walton, Frank L. *Tomahawks to Textiles: The Fabulous Story of Worth Street* (New York: Appleton-Century-Crofts, 1953)

Allen Fannin

Harmony Mills in Cohoes; detail from panoramic map, 1879.

like warping, formerly the weavers' responsibility, were transferred to workers who did little or nothing else. By 1845, 325 woolen mills were operating in the state, and within a few years all operations in cloth production, from initial preparation of fiber through dyeing and finishing, could be performed in a factory setting using powered equipment. The 1855 census revealed 114 "carding and cloth dressing establishments" widely dispersed throughout the state. They were most numerous in Chenango Co (9), Jefferson Co (7), and St. Lawrence and Schoharie Cos (5 each). The same census listed 184 "woolen cloth and yarn factories," with 13 in Oneida Co, 9 in Erie Co, and 8 in both Orange and Washington Cos. By 1868, 476 carding, weaving, knitting, dyeing, and finishing mills across the state produced cotton, woolen, silk, and linen goods.

The topography of New York State has had a significant effect on the location of milling operations. While New England provided considerable waterpower for its mills, New York mills relied primarily on steam boilers to run their equipment. The Erie Canal and the railroads that eventually replaced it were oriented east-west, leading to a concentration of textile mills in the Mohawk Valley, the Capital District, and New York City and the Hudson Valley.

Regional Textile Production

Textile production in Western and Central New York tended to favor woolen mills, which were smaller on average than cotton operations. In 1860 Auburn (Cayuga Co) and Oswego each had five shops producing woolen goods. In the first half of the 20th century the industry declined statewide as the development of electric power allowed manufacturers to take advantage of lower labor costs in southern states. Despite this downturn, in 1958 there were wool weaving, finishing, and spinning mills with over 100 employees in Niagara, Chautauqua, Cattaraugus, Seneca, and Onondaga Cos.

Textile operations significant in size and importance evolved around Utica in Oneida, Madison, and Herkimer Cos. By 1845, 21 woolen mills running a total of 41 carding machines operated in this three-county area. The Wool-Growers Manufacturing Co of Little Falls (Herkimer Co) ran three cards, and Frederick Hollister of New Hartford (Oneida Co) eight. Cotton, silk, and linen mills added their yardage to the primary industry in woolen cloth. During the 1920s some of Utica's textile manufacturers joined the southern migration of the industry. Postwar decline led to 10 plant closures between 1952 and 1959, with local textile employment dropping from 9,700 jobs in 1947 to 1,700 in 1957. In 2004 only three plants still operated in the Utica area. The oldest, Waterbury Felt in Oriskany (Oneida Co), has operated continuously since 1869.

At the confluence of the Hudson River and the Erie Canal and close to New England, the Capital District once boasted New York State's largest textile enterprise, Harmony Mills. Established in Cohoes (Albany Co) in 1836–37, Harmony Mills reached a spindle capacity of 285,000 by the early 20th century. There were 46 smaller woolen mills producing wovens, knits, and hosiery in 1845, and by 1888 there were 80. Because of the waterpower available from area waterways, many of the Capital District's textile mills were equipped with both steam boilers and waterwheels or turbines. Harmony Mills operated until it was liquidated between 1932 and 1937. In the early 21st century the Capital District textile industry consists of a producer of industrial fabrics and two small fiber processors.

Although New York City has been the center of textile marketing and selling in the state and at times the world, the high cost of space in the city has generally discouraged textile manufacturing. Nevertheless, by the late 19th century there were around 100 mills within what are now the five boroughs of New York City, many of them involved in supporting industries such as dyeing, knitting, and printing. In 2004 the Scalamandré silk company, a manufacturer of high-end interior fabrics that operated the only remaining textile mill in New York City, moved its manufacturing facility to North Carolina, leaving just its design studios in place. In addition there were a number of small knitting mills, many with no more than 40 employees. As of 2004 most of Brooklyn's textile operations consisted of small knitting mills employing fewer than 100 workers. In 1997 the value of textiles produced in New York State mills was nearly $3 billion.

See also Carpet industry; Utica.

Davison's Textile Blue Book (1966)

The Dry Goods Trade, and Cotton, Woolen, Silk, and Linen Manufacture of the United States (Boston: C. A. Dockham, 1868)

Kane, Nancy F. *Textiles in Transition: Technology, Wages, and Industry Relocation in the US Textile Industry, 1880–1930* (New York: Greenwood Press, 1988)

Thomas, Alexander R. *In Gotham's Shadow: Globalization and Community Change in Central New York* (Albany: SUNY Press, 2003)

Walkowitz, Daniel J. *Worker City, Company Town: Iron and Cotton Worker Protest in Troy and Cohoes, New York, 1855–84* (Urbana: Univ of Illinois Press, 1978)

Allen Fannin

theater, Albany and the Capital District. The first known play performed in Albany was by British soldiers in 1760 at the military hospital. A professional company visited Albany and performed Thomas Otway's *Venice Preserved* at the Masonic Lodge in 1769. The first organized theater was the Green Street Theater, which opened in 1813 and closed in 1818. The South Pearl Street Theater opened in 1825, and the nearby Albany Museum held theatrical performances that included freak shows. In the 1870s Albany's Leland Opera House was the largest theater and hosted major professional companies. The most celebrated theater in Albany was Harmanus Bleecker Hall, on Pearl St, which opened in 1889. By the 1890s many theaters opened on or near North and South Pearl Sts, and as the area became a theater district it featured plays, burlesque, and vaudeville houses. By the early 1900s theaters were being converted into movie houses, but vaudeville and burlesque still survived.

Amateur theater troupes in the Capital District include the Bellevue Young People's Chorus (1926; now the Schenectady Light Opera Company), the Schenectady Civic Players (1928), and the Albany Civic Theater, formed by the merger of the Ilium Players of Troy and the Albany Dramatic Group. The Albany Civic Theater staged its first show, Noël Coward's *Blithe Spirit,* in 1955. Albany's Palace Theatre (1931), formerly a movie house, presents concerts, dance programs, and occasional theater pieces by local and national groups. The Empire State Center for the Performing Arts, called the Egg because of its architectural design, opened in 1978 and houses two theaters in the Empire State Plaza. It presents notable touring theater productions and a youth theater. Albany's Capital Repertory The-

Tweddle Hall, Albany.

atre (1980) has a year-long season, a summer drama program for young people, and play-reading events for the community. In 2003 popular theater in Albany included the outdoor Park Playhouse, where a troupe performs Broadway musicals during the summer in Washington Park.

Outside Albany, the Troy Savings Bank Music Hall (Rensselaer Co) opened in 1870 above bank offices. In Cohoes (Albany Co) entrepreneurs established a Cohoes Music Hall (1874), a theater/music hall above stores and a post office. The hall provided an early stage for vaudevillian Eva Tanguay, raised in Cohoes, who achieved fame as the "I Don't Care Girl." A bank bought the building in 1905, but the city acquired the Music Hall and reopened it in 1974. Frederick Francis Proctor created Schenectady's first theater in 1912 close to the Erie Canal but later built Proctor's Theatre in 1926, which was a larger facility and featured Broadway productions, musical groups, and dance programs. Amateur and professional theaters in the region include Curtain Call, opened in 2000 in Latham (Albany Co); Spa Little Theater, founded in 1985 in Saratoga Spa State Park (Saratoga Co); and the New York State Theatre Institute (1974), a troupe whose offerings are pitched mainly at adolescents who attend with their school groups.

Howell, George, and Jonathan Tenney. *History of the County of Albany from 1609 to 1886* (New York: W. W. Munsell, 1886)

Kennedy, William. *O Albany! Improbable City of Political Wizards, Fearless Ethnics, Spectacular Aristocrats, Splendid Nobodies, and Underrated Scoundrels* (New York: Viking, 1983)

Paul Lamar

theater, Buffalo. As the terminus of the Erie Canal, Buffalo connected the Northeast to the Midwest and was therefore a strategically important stop on every theatrical tour during the years of the canal's operation and a giant of the vaudeville era. In the early 1840s, at a theater on the Buffalo waterfront, Edwin P. Christy developed the prototypical minstrel show featuring "Mr. Interlocutor," a master-of-ceremonies character who would lead a line of performers arranged in a semicircle. Christy's minstrel show, featuring a three-part parade-olio-musicale format, would become the model for all subsequent minstrel shows in America. In 1889 William Gillette staged the world premiere of his signature role in *Sherlock Holmes* in Buffalo, and major 19th-century stars from Lola Montez to Jenny Lind to Edwin Booth to Sarah Bernhardt performed there.

By 1900 Buffalo was the eighth largest city in the United States and during the vaudeville era represented such a lucrative market that Buffalo presenter Michael Shea, who also ran theaters in nearby Toronto, was able to operate with relative independence from the powerful Keith/Albee vaudeville circuit in New York City. Although the population and importance of Buffalo declined after World War II, the local taste for live entertainment endured. The Erlanger Theater, built in 1927 by Ellsworth M. Statler of hotel fame, continued to book tours featuring major stars through the 1950s. Today Shea's Performing Arts Center, a former movie palace built in 1926 as Shea's Buffalo and the last of Michael Shea's many theaters to survive, serves as a venue for touring productions of Broadway shows. Buffalo is also home to Studio Theatre School (1927), renamed Studio Arena Theatre in 1965, when it became a professional Actors' Equity theater. Studio Arena is the oldest such institution in the country associated with a resident Equity theater. The richness of today's Buffalo theater scene, however, derives from its numerous small independent non-Equity theaters. Among the most established are the Alleyway Theatre, Buffalo Ensemble Theatre, Buffalo United Artists, Irish Classical Theatre Co, Kavinoky Theatre, MusicalFare Theatre, Paul Robeson Theatre, Shakespeare in Delaware Park, Theatre of Youth, and Ujima Theatre Co.

Smith, Ardis, and Kathryn Smith. "Theater in Early Buffalo." In *Adventures in Western New York History*, vol 23 (Buffalo: Buffalo & Erie County Historical Society, 1975)

Stein, Charles W. *American Vaudeville as Seen by Its Contemporaries* (New York: Da Capo Press, 1984)

Anthony Chase

theater, musical. See MUSICAL THEATER.

theater, New York City. New York City is widely considered to be the theater capital of the United States, a distinction it has held since the early 19th century, when theatergoing became a major tourist activity. Today more than 1 million visitors from across the world flock each year to the Broadway theater district in and around Times Square and to the many important producing theaters in other areas of Manhattan, as well as in the other boroughs, especially Brooklyn. There is also a large theatrical support industry clustered in and around New York City, including builders and suppliers of scenery, costumes, makeup, and lighting and sound equipment; agents and managers; labor unions; photographers; publishers; and acting schools.

GEOGRAPHY

Theater in New York City developed in tandem with the geographic development of Manhattan Island, roughly following Broadway, the borough's principal thoroughfare, from the southerly tip northward to its present locus at Times Square. Although the earliest theaters arose in the 1730s, the first important playhouse, the John Street Theatre, opened in 1767 and served as the city's principal theater for the next 30 years. It was replaced in 1798 by the more fashionably appointed Park Theatre at 21–25 Park Row. Between 1810 and 1840, more than 25 theaters were built from Park Row northward to Astor Place to house both legitimate theatricals and burgeoning popular entertainments such as minstrelsy and vaudeville.

The first bona fide theater district developed in Union Square at the confluence of Broadway, 4th Ave, and 14th St in the 1870s and 1880s. It boasted major performing venues such as the Academy of Music, the home of grand opera; the Union Square Theatre, the most prestigious theater in the area; and Tony Pastor's New 14th Street Theatre, widely considered the birthplace of vaudeville; as well as many theatrical support

Broadway Theatre, 1859, by Samuel Hollyer, early 20th century.

businesses. There also were hotels, restaurants, and boardinghouses established to accommodate swelling numbers of stage personnel and audiences.

The current Broadway theater district at Times Square began when two impresarios, Charles Frohman and Oscar Hammerstein I, built theaters on Broadway surrounding what was then known as Long Acre Square. Frohman's Empire Theatre at 40th St (1893) and Hammerstein's Olympia at 44th (1895) initiated a surge of theater construction between 39th and 52d Sts that generated nearly 80 theaters by 1928, the peak of Broadway's heyday. The number has declined so that now there are fewer than 40 legitimate theaters in the Times Square district. There are, however, many off- and off-off-Broadway theaters thriving elsewhere in Manhattan. Of the other boroughs, only Brooklyn actively developed a professional theater. The first Brooklyn Academy of Music (BAM) was built in 1861, with several others, including the renowned Park Theatre (1863–98), following within the next several decades. The original BAM burned in 1903 but was replaced in 1908 by the present building at 30 Lafayette St, which, with four auditoriums, was the first multiple-theater facility in the United States.

The Colonial Era through 1850

Theater was introduced via traveling troupes of British players, led most notably by Lewis and William Hallam and later by David Douglas in the 18th century. During the Revolutionary War all professional theater ceased, but Douglas's American Co returned in 1785 to instigate a great period of theater expansion. William Dunlap managed the city's leading theater, the Park, in the early 19th century, featuring distinguished British actors and encouraging native American talent. Consequently, the "star system" quickly developed as popular British and English-speaking European actors and an increasing number of Americans, notably Edwin Forrest, Charlotte Cushman, and Edwin Booth, drew eager audiences.

"Yankee" plays were also developed in the early 19th century, extolling the virtues of the fledgling nation, as well as formulaic melodramas designed for working-class audiences. By the 1840s popular entertainment forms, especially minstrelsy and vaudeville, soon to be followed by English-style burlesques, early musical comedies and spectacles, comic opera, and other variety shows, rivaled the legitimate stage for audiences.

Development of the Theater Industry, 1850–2002

A theater industry developed in response to the changing modes of production in the latter half of the 19th century. Traditional stock companies, which had been the staple of the legitimate theater, were disbanding in favor of combination companies. These developed in the wake of the phenomenal success of a stage production of *Uncle Tom's Cabin,* which ran for more than 300 performances in 1853–54 at the National Theatre in Washington, DC. Unlike stock companies, which featured a resident company of actors who owned their own scenery and costumes and produced multiple plays each season, combination companies were created to produce a single production that, it was hoped, would enjoy a long run in New York City and then tour to other cities, touted as being "direct from New York." Since these companies always were created from scratch, everything, from actors through scene paint, needed to be procured afresh. Hence specialty businesses designed to meet every production need abounded. This mode of production, as well as the desire for long-running hit shows, continues to be the standard for commercial theater to this day.

By the end of the 19th century, savvy entrepreneurs realized the economic advantages of consolidating combination companies under large producing organizations. In 1896 producer Charles Frohman, booking agents Marc Klaw and A. L. Erlanger, and Alfred Hayman, Frederick G. Nixon, and Fred Zimmerman, all of whom owned or leased a large number of theaters nationwide, created the Theatrical Syndicate, which controlled first-class production throughout the country for the next 15 years. This was the first of several New York City–based monopolies that developed in the early 20th century to manage and control live entertainment. The power of the syndicate was finally broken by the Shubert brothers, who created an even more powerful monopoly that controlled theater nationwide until 1930 and Broadway until 1950. In 2002 the Shubert Organization owned 16 of the major Broadway producing houses outright and half of the Music Box, co-owned by the estate of Irving Berlin; 9 are controlled by the Nederlander Organization, 5 by the Jujamcyn Co, and at least 7 others, such as the refurbished Selwyn (built in 1918 and renovated in 2000 as the Roundabout Theatre Co's American Airlines Theatre), are independently owned and operated.

The power of the syndicate and other monopolistic producing collectives gave rise to theatrical labor unions in the early 20th century. Actors, stagehands, designers, publicists, and other theatrical workers who felt oppressed by employment constraints, poor working conditions, and unfair labor practices founded individual craft unions, which eventually became affiliated with the AFL-CIO. These include the International Alliance of Theatrical Stage Employees (1893), Actors' Equity Association (1913), United Scenic Artists (1918), and the Association of Theatrical Press Agents and Managers (1928). Dramatic writers formed a professional collective in 1920, the Dramatists Guild, to maintain artistic control of their work and to regularize royalty payments from producers.

Musical Theater

New York City theater is most readily associated with the big splashy Broadway musical, which had its genesis with *The Black Crook,* a four-act extravaganza that opened at Niblo's Garden Theatre in September 1866 and ran for 474 performances. Thereafter, musical shows of many types, including comic opera, operetta, musical comedy, and revue, became the dominant forms of entertainment. The most famous productions of the era included Florenz Ziegfeld's series of *Follies* beginning in 1907, which inspired many imitators, and comic operettas like *Babes in Toyland* (1903) by Victor Herbert. Notable developments in musical theater began in the 1910s with a series of intimate musicals cowritten by Jerome Kern, Guy Bolton, and P. G. Wodehouse for the Princess Theatre on West 39th St, while the 1920s heralded the successful collaborations of George and Ira Gershwin in such shows as *Lady, Be Good!* (1924) and *Funny Face* (1927). Kern's landmark 1927 musical *Showboat,* with lyrics by Oscar Hammerstein II, inspired the more serious musical plays of the 1940s and 1950s, many of which were collaborations between Hammerstein and composer Richard Rodgers. Their first effort, *Oklahoma!* (1943), with its deft integration of plot, music, and dance, is widely considered to be the prototype for the modern American musical. Successful imitators, many of whom focused on New York City themes and characters, included Frank Loesser *(Guys and Dolls,* 1950) and Leonard Bernstein, the composer of *On the Town* (1944), *Wonderful Town* (1953), and *West Side Story* (1957).

Since the mid–20th century Broadway producers have focused on developing new musicals that offer innovative twists on the traditional successful formulas. Although there have been many expensive failures, there also have been monumental triumphs that established the musical as America's unique contribution to world theater. These include Jerry Bock and Sheldon Harnick's *Fiddler on the Roof* (1964); *Hello, Dolly!* (1964), by Jerry Herman; the 1968 rock musical *Hair,* which introduced nudity to the Broadway stage; and Michael Bennett's paean to the Broadway gypsy dancer, *A Chorus Line* (1975). Since the 1960s Stephen Sondheim has reinvented the Broadway musical as a complex dramatic genre via his brilliant yet often controversial music and lyrics in such shows as *Company* (1970), *A Little Night Music* (1973), and *Sunday in the Park with George* (1984).

A dearth of new American musicals in the 1980s and 1990s was filled by blockbuster musical hits imported from London. Andrew Lloyd Webber's *Cats* (1982) was the most successful, although several others, including *Les Misérables* (1987) and *Phantom of the Opera* (1988) continue to attract large audiences into the 21st century. The American musical is still alive and well, demonstrated by several recent hits produced by Disney, such as *The Lion King* (1998) and *Beauty and the Beast* (1999); Mel Brooks's smash 2001 hit musicalization of his 1968 film, *The Producers;* and a series of successful revivals, including *Chicago* (1996), *Cabaret* (1998), *42nd Street* (2001), and *Oklahoma!* (2002).

Major Playwrights

Although the musical has garnered much of the popular press, New York City has also hosted premieres of straight plays and comedies by America's most important playwrights. The art or little theater movement of the 1910s, which was heavily influenced by European modernist playwriting, spurred the founding of important Greenwich Village and other downtown theaters, such as the Washington Square Players (1914), Neighborhood Playhouse at the Henry Street Settlement (1915), and the Provincetown Players (1915). These theaters specialized in experimental and serious dramas by major European and up-and-coming American playwrights like Eugene O'Neill, Elmer Rice, and Maxwell Anderson. By the 1920s these playwrights had found a home on Broadway, largely because of the efforts of Lawrence Langner and the Theatre Guild that evolved out of the Washington Square Players. The Great Depression furthered the cause of serious American playwriting through the work of ideological theater collectives promulgating political agendas. The most famous of these, the Group Theatre, introduced the plays of Clifford Odets and the talents of many actors, directors, and producers, including Stella Adler, Harold Clurman, Elia Kazan, and Lee Strasberg. New York City also was the biggest production center and eastern regional headquarters for the Works Progress Administration's Federal Theatre Project, established by an act of Congress in 1935 to provide meaningful employment to thousands of out-of-work theater professionals across the country during the depression. It is estimated that more than 12 million people attended performances in New York City alone between 1935 and 1939, the four years of the project's duration, including the premiere of the "living newspaper" *One Third of a Nation* (1938) and the innovative productions of the Negro Theater Unit, notably the "voodoo" *Macbeth* (1936), *Haiti* (1938), and *The Swing Mikado* (1939).

While musicals were being touted as the great new American art form during the 1940s and 1950s, there was equally important development in straight playwriting, which varied from escapist froth, such as Joseph Kesselring's *Arsenic and Old Lace* (1941) and Mary Chase's *Harvey* (1944), to the serious dramas of Arthur Miller (*Death of a Salesman,* 1949), Tennessee Williams (*A Streetcar Named Desire,* 1947), William Inge (*Picnic,* 1953), and the later work of Eugene O'Neill (*Long Day's Journey into Night,* 1956). In the 1960s Neil Simon (*The Odd Couple,* 1965) and Edward Albee (*Who's Afraid of Virginia Woolf?,* 1962) had major Broadway premieres. From the 1970s onward, however, many important playwrights like Christopher Durang, David Mamet, and Sam Shepard had most of their work produced off Broadway and off-off Broadway, where production costs were lower and producers were more willing to take a chance on experimental, nontraditional work.

Alternative Theater

Alternative theaters grew out of a widespread dissatisfaction with the artistic offerings, business practices, and exorbitant prices common to commercial theater. The earliest of these were art or little theaters of the 1910s, soon to be followed by the political theaters spawned by the depression. The major plays and theater artists produced by these theaters tended eventually to end up on Broadway. This was not so often the case, however, from the 1950s onward with the development of noncommercial producing organizations such as Circle in the Square, credited with beginning the off-Broadway movement with its 1952 production of Tennessee Williams's *Summer and Smoke.* Soon thereafter, many other like-minded producers and theaters emerged, most notably Joseph Papp, whose free summer Shakespeare in New York City parks, which began in 1954, evolved into the New York Shakespeare Festival at the Public Theatre (1967) in Manhattan East Village.

The term off-off Broadway evolved in the early 1960s to describe the plethora of noncommercial performances presented in alternative spaces, such as churches, lofts, and art galleries in Greenwich Village and on the Lower East Side. These theaters developed in reaction to escalating production costs off Broadway and a desire for freer experimentation in production types and styles. Joe Cino, who presented plays by then unknown writers John Guare, Marie Irene Fornes, and Lanford Wilson in his small coffeehouse, Caffe Cino, in 1958, is widely regarded as the movement's first impresario. Other producers quickly followed, including Al Carmines, the assistant minister at the Judson Memorial Church in the heart of Greenwich Village who began the Judson Poets' Theatre in 1961, and Ellen Stewart, founder in 1962 of La MaMa Experimental Theatre Club on East 4th St, which is still a leading venue of provocative new work. Producing theater companies also evolved, most notably Julian Beck and Judith Malina's Living Theatre, founded in 1948, 10 years before the opening of Caffe Cino; the Open Theatre (1963) featuring the work of Joseph Chaikin; Richard Schechner's Performance Group (1967), which evolved into the Wooster Group (1975); Ridiculous Theatrical Co, founded in 1967 by Charles Ludlam; Richard Foreman's Ontological-Hysteric Theatre (1968); and Mabou Mines (1970), a theatre collective founded by JoAnne Akalaitis, Lee Breuer, Philip Glass, Ruth Maleczech, and David Warrilow.

Ethnic Theater

Ethnic theaters, created by and for the many immigrant groups moving to the city during the 19th and 20th centuries, have been an important component of the city's cultural milieu. Germans founded the Stadt Co in 1854 at the Amphitheater while Irish newcomers flocked to the Bowery and National Theaters. The Bowery would later host Italian vaudeville in the 1910s and Chinese dramas in the 1920s as local immigrant populations began to shift around the city. The Irving Place and French theaters offered a variety of foreign-language dramas, while Yiddish theater, transplanted to New York City by Russian and Polish Jewish refugees in the late 19th century, enjoyed its own theater district along 2d Ave on the Lower East Side and flourished through the mid–20th century. Two companies offering Spanish-language theater, INTAR Hispanic American Arts Center and the Puerto Rican Traveling Theatre, were founded in 1966, while several Asian American theaters, including the Pan Asian Repertory Theatre, were established in the 1970s. The first African American theater company of record, William Henry Brown's African Theatre, established in 1821 on lower Broadway, produced internationally acclaimed actor Ira Aldridge. Later companies included the Lafayette Players (1915) and the Negro Ensemble Co, founded by Douglas Turner Ward in 1967.

Brown, Thomas A. *A History of the New York Stage* (New York: Dodd, Mead, 1903)
Frick, John W., and Martha S. LoMonaco. "Theater." In *The Encyclopedia of New York City,* ed. Kenneth T. Jackson (New Haven, Conn: Yale Univ Press, 1995)
Henderson, Mary C. *The City and the Theatre: New York Playhouses from Bowling Green to Times Square* (Clifton, NJ: James T. White, 1973)
———. *Theater in America* (New York: Harry N. Abrams, 1986)
Langley, Stephen. *Theatre Management and Production in America: Commercial, Stock, Resident, College, Community, and Presenting Organizations* (New York: Drama Book Publishers, 1990)
Wilmeth, Don B., and Christopher Bigsby, eds. *The Cambridge History of American Theatre,* 3 vols (Cambridge: Cambridge Univ Press, 1998–2000)
Wilmeth, Don B., and Tice L. Miller, eds. *Cambridge Guide to American Theatre* (Cambridge: Cambridge Univ Press, 1993)

Martha S. LoMonaco

theater, Rochester. Theater was not popular in Rochester, aside from traveling shows, until Edwin Dean opened a theater in Concert Hall on Exchange St in 1840. Dean's company included his daughter, Julia, who would later become a nationally acknowledged actress. Religious revivals in the area in the 1840s made theater unpopular, and theaters struggled to survive, many only lasting one season, many sharing actors and managers with companies in Buffalo. In the 1870s theaters suffered from the depression, relying on traveling shows rather than on resident companies. In 1887 Hiram Sibley, H. H. Warner, and W. H. Kimball backed the Lyceum Theater, built on South Clinton St just off Main St, which attracted national stars and prospered until the depression of the 1890s. At the turn of the 20th century Rochester theaters became good places to try out a new play. The Lyceum hosted the American premier of Henrik Ibsen's *When We Dead Awake* in 1905.

By the beginning of the 21st century four commercial companies were thriving. In 1950 the Catholic Theatre of Rochester was established, changing its name in 1962 to the Blackfriars. Geva Theatre Center, established in 1972 by William and Cynthia Mason Selden, is now housed in a 500-seat theater in the renovated Naval Armory Building in downtown Rochester. The Downstairs Cabaret, which offered its first play in 1983, specializes in comedy and musicals and in 2002 announced plans to add two stages in the downtown east-side area, bringing its total downtown stages to four. Shipping Dock Theatre also has a downtown location. The Rochester Theatre League brings in out-of-town plays, and local colleges also regularly offer dramas, comedies, and musicals.

McKelvey, Blake. "The Theater in Rochester during Its First Nine Decades," *Rochester History,* July 1954

Martin Naparsteck

theological education. Before the 19th century, there were no separate institutions for training ministers; they had to study in Europe or in colleges such as King's College (now Columbia University) in Manhattan or Union College in Schenectady (1795). After the Revolutionary War settlers, many of them Presbyterians and Congregationalists from New England, streamed into the northern and western parts of the state. Under the 1801 Plan of Union these denominations agreed to cooperate, sharing pastors to further expansion. Plan of Union ministers established Auburn Seminary (Cayuga Co) in 1818, to maintain (and tame) the burgeoning revival spirit in central and western New York State. Although founded by Presbyterians, the school's charter provided that Christians of all denominations be admitted. In 1939 it moved to New York City and became affiliated with Union Theological Seminary. In 1819 Baptists, also beneficiaries of the revival, established the Hamilton Literary and Theological Institution (Madison Co). The school admitted its first nonministerial students in 1839 and changed its name first to Madison University and again in 1890 to Colgate University. As American education became more differentiated, the school separated its liberal arts and professional studies. By 1928 the seminary detached from the university and merged with the Rochester Theological Seminary to become the Colgate Rochester Divinity School.

In 1817 the General Convention of the Episcopal Church voted to establish a theological seminary in New York City, partially because of the wealth of Trinity Church. The Chelsea campus of General Theological Seminary was built in 1827, and it became the American center of the Anglo-Catholicism favored by the English John Henry Newman. Presbyterians established Union Theological Seminary in 1836, using New York City's missions and churches as part of ministerial preparation. Union quickly became a primary American interpreter of European Protestant theology.

Catholic history in the state was shaped by successive waves of immigration, initially Irish and German in the 19th century, followed by eastern Europeans and Hispanics in the 20th. Ethnic immigrants preferred priests who spoke their language, and many priests were immigrants who had received their training abroad. After 1810 the Irish arrived in New York City in great numbers. As young Irish Americans entered the priesthood, the diocese experimented with a location for its major seminary, St. Joseph's. The school was at Nyack (Rockland Co) from 1833 to 1834, La fargeville (Jefferson Co) from 1838 to 1840, Fordham [now in Bronx Co] from 1840 to 1861, and Troy (Rensselaer Co) from 1864 to 1896 before moving to its present location in the Dunwoodie section of Yonkers. Fordham University still has undergraduate programs in religious studies and theology, and maintains a graduate school of religion and religious studies. In 1893 Bernard J. McQuaid of Rochester established St. Bernard's Seminary, which became St. Bernard's Institute in 1981. Christ the King, the diocesan seminary of Buffalo, was founded in 1857.

Although Jewish immigrants entered New York in the colonial period, they founded their first theological schools in the 19th century. In New York City the Orthodox established Rabbi Isaac Elchanan Theological Seminary (RIETS) in 1897. Now affiliated with Yeshiva University (incorporated 1946), RIETS is the largest center for higher education in the Orthodox Jewish tradition in the Western Hemisphere. Yeshiva also maintains undergraduate and graduate schools of Jewish studies. The Conservatives founded the Jewish Theological Seminary of America (JTS) in 1886. Both RIETS and JTS stressed knowledge of the Hebrew language, and JTS became a center for training Hebrew teachers. JTS's first president, Solomon Schechter, was an important figure in the development of the American rabbinate. The Jewish Institute of Religion (JIR) opened in Manhattan in 1922. Despite initial ideological differences, the JIR merged with Hebrew Union College of Cincinnati in 1950 to form the Hebrew Union College–Jewish Institute of Religion. Today the school is a center for the study of Reform Judaism and has campuses in Manhattan, Cincinnati, Los Angeles, and Jerusalem.

Theological modernism challenged Protestant seminaries in the late 19th and early 20th centuries in different ways. A controversy over the historical criticism of the Bible in 1893 led to Union Theological Seminary severing its ties with the Presbyterian Church and becoming interdenominational. Although both Colgate and Rochester adopted similar modernist theological innovations with less controversy, both seminaries also made moves toward an interdenominational faculty. At the same time more conservative Protestants established their own seminaries. Dr A. B. Simpson, an energetic New York City pastor, established a training school in Manhattan in 1882, the Missionary Training Institute, to meet the needs of urban church workers. He moved his school to Nyack in 1897. Like many training schools, it developed into an accredited college, Nyack College, and a closely related theological school, Alliance Theological Seminary. In 1900 Dr Wilbert White founded the Biblical Teachers' College in Montclair, NJ, to teach "inductive Bible study," which interpreted scriptural text by internal criteria. The school moved to New York City in 1902, and by the 1920s it had become a more standard theological school. In the 1970s it discontinued its traditional program to concentrate on theological education for minorities.

Theological education in New York became even more diverse as the 20th century progressed. St. Vladimir's Orthodox Theological Seminary opened in the parish house of Christ Our Savior Church in Brooklyn in 1938 and in 1939 moved to the campus of General Theological Seminary. Post–World War II immigration from eastern Europe created a distinguished faculty, and in 1961 the school moved to Crestwood (Westchester Co). St. Nersess Armenian Seminary, which moved to New York from Evanston, Ill, in 1967 affiliated with St. Vladimir's.

Although each of the state's theological programs is distinctive, since the mid–20th century their curricula have become more standardized with accreditation by the New York State Board of Regents and with the national standards set by the Association of Theological Schools.

Handy, Robert T. *A History of Union Theological Seminary in New York* (New York: Columbia Univ Press, 1987)

Miller, Glenn T. *Piety and Intellect: The Aims and Purposes of Antebellum Theological Education* (Atlanta: Scholars Press, 1990)

Shelley, Thomas J. *Dunwoodie: The History of St. Joseph's Seminary* (Westminster, Md: Christian Classics, 1993)

Wertheimer, Jack, ed. *Tradition Renewed: A History of the Jewish Theological Seminary* (New York: Jewish Theological Seminary of America, 1997)

Glenn T. Miller

theosophical societies. Founded in New York City on 17 Nov 1875 by Helena Petrovna Blavatsky (1831–91), Henry Steel Olcott (1832–1907), and others, the Theosophical Society has since early in its history had three central aims: to create a universal brotherhood based on the equality of humanity; to promote the comparative study of religion, philosophy, and science; and to promote individuals' investigation of their own latent potential. The society's leading theorist was Madame Blavatsky, a charismatic, Russian-born aristocrat who claimed to have received her philosophy from holy men (mahatmas) she had met in India. Her first book, *Isis Unveiled,* was published in New York City in 1877, followed a decade later by the 1888 publication of her major work, *The Secret Doctrine,* which tried to recover some of the tenets of ancient wisdom and knowledge. Olcott, a New York lawyer, became the society's president, a position he held until his death in 1907. In 1878 he and Mme Blavatsky left for India, where they established the society's headquarters in Madras. In their absence, Gen Abner Doubleday, a distinguished Civil War veteran and the alleged inventor of baseball, served as president from 1879 to 1882.

The Madras community remained the organization's center of activity for many years, but by 1886 there were enough branches throughout the United States to start the American Section of the Theosophical Society. William Q. Judge (1851–96), a young Irish immigrant who had been present at the society's founding, was elected general secretary of the American Section. Under his leadership, the movement flourished in the United States, although a controversy over Judge's honesty led to a split with the European and Indian branches of the movement. In April 1895 the American Section declared its autonomous status, changing its name to the Theosophical Society in America. After Judge's death in 1896, Katherine Tingley (1847–1929) rose to a position of prominence in the society. In 1898 she started the Universal Brotherhood, a fraternal organization that merged with the Theosophical Society in America and moved its headquarters to Point Loma, Calif, where it flourished well into the 1930s.

The New York City members who remained loyal to Olcott's society were chartered as the New York Theosophical Society on 4 Apr 1897, and the American Section was re-formed under General Secretary Alexander Fullerton, a former Episcopalian minister. Prominent New York members of this group included Claude Bragdon, a noted architect, Fritz Kunz, the editor of *Main Currents in Modern Thought,* and Dora Kunz, Fritz's wife, who helped establish the healing therapy Therapeutic Touch. Branches of the Theosophical Society exist today in Buffalo and New York City. Although relatively small, the movement has done much to popularize ideas from Asia such as karma and reincarnation.

Gomes, Michael. *The Dawning of the Theosophical Movement* (Wheaton, Ill: Quest Books, 1987)

———. *Theosophy in the 19th Century: An Annotated Bibliography* (New York: Garland Publishing, 1994)

Michael Gomes

Theresa [THREE-SAH]. Town (pop 2,414) and village (pop 912) in N Jefferson Co. James Le Ray de Chaumont, the proprietor, began improvements to the land in 1810–11, but permanent settlement began in 1817. The town was formed from Alexandria in 1841. The Indian River provided good waterpower for the manufacture of chairs, cheeseboxes, stoves, farm tools, and textiles. The village was incorporated in 1871. The Clayton and Theresa Railroad began service in 1873. The town was chiefly agricultural until the mid–20th century, when tourism evolved as the primary industry. With 12 lakes, Theresa has abundant cottage sites and excellent hunting, fishing, boating, and water sports. Theresa is the birthplace of Gov Roswell P. Flower (1835–99).

Laura Lynne Scharer

Thiells. Locality (pop 4,758) in Haverstraw (Rockland Co). Jacob Thiell, a Dane, bought 3,000 acres (1,210 ha) along the Minisceongo Creek before the Revolution, establishing a farm and a forge. A needle factory (1850–80), a tannery, and a candle factory (1862–66) provided employment. The New Jersey and New York Railroad came through in 1874, and a post office opened in 1879. Letchworth Village, a state residential facility for people with developmental disabilities, operated near Thiells from 1907 to

THIRD PARTIES IN NEW YORK STATE, 1900–2002

Party	Election Years on the Ballot
American	1914–16
American Labor	1936–54
Citizens	1980
Civil Service Independents	1970
Communist	1930–36; 1942; 1970–80; 1984
Constitution	2000–2002
Constitutional	1934
Conservative	1962–[a]
Courage	1968, 1974
Farmer Labor	1920–22
Free Libertarian	1974–84
Freedom[b]	1996
Freedom and Peace	1968
Greater NY Democrat	1902
Green	1996–2002
Independence[c]	1996–[a]
Independence Alliance	1970
Independence Fusion[c]	1994
Independence League	1906–16
Independent Progressive	1938; 1988
Independent Republican	1926
Independent Socialist	1958
Industrial Government	1938; 1942–44; 1948–54
Labor	1974–78
Law Preservation	1930–34
Liberal	1944–2002
Liberal Democrat	1902
Libertarian	1988–2002
Marijuana Reform	1998
National Progressive (Bull Moose)[d]	1912; 1916
Natural Law	1992–96
New Alliance	1982–92
People's	1904
Progressive (Bull Moose)[d]	1914
Progressive (La Follette)	1924
Prohibition	1900–1922; 1926; 1940
Reform	2000
Right to Life	1978–82; 1986–2002
Social Democratic[e]	1900–1904
Socialist[e]	1906–44; 1948; 1952
Socialist Labor	1900–34; 1962–74
Socialist Workers	1948–54; 1960–2000
Statewide Independent	1982
Tax Cut Now[b]	1994
Unity	1982; 1998
Workers	1924–28
Working Families	1998–[a]
Workers World	1980; 1984; 1988; 1996

Sources: NYS Board of Elections; *Manual for the Use of the Legislature of the State of New York.*

Notes: Table includes parties with candidates on the ballot for governor, president, or US senator. Inclusive date span indicates that the party had a candidate on the ballot for all even-numbered years within that span.

[a] Party held an automatic ballot line after the 2002 gubernatorial election.

[b] The Tax Cut Now Party was renamed the Freedom Party after the 1994 gubernatorial election.

[c] The Independence Fusion Party was renamed the Independence Party after the 1994 gubernatorial election.

[d] Candidates for the Progressive (or Bull Moose) Party were listed on the ballot in New York State on a National Progressive line in 1912 and 1916 and on a Progressive line in 1914.

[e] The Socialist Party of America was organized in 1901, but ballots in New York State through 1904 listed the party's candidates on a line for the Social Democratic Party. From 1906 ballots listed these candidates on a line for the Socialist Party.

1996. North Rockland High School, which serves the Towns of Haverstraw and Stony Point, is located in Thiells.

third parties. Minor or third parties have played an important role in New York State politics since the end of the 19th century, being surprisingly persistent and influential without successfully placing candidates in office because of the state's political culture and vagaries of state law. The Antimasonic Party, which started in New York State in the late 1820s and is generally recognized as the first national third party, had considerable success for several years before it largely became absorbed by the new Whig Party. The most successful of the abolitionist political parties was the New York State–based Liberty Party, which in 1840 and 1844 ran James G. Birney, a Kentucky native living in New York City, for president. In 1844 the Liberty Party in New York State was likely the first American third party to play the role of spoiler, its 15,812 votes for Birney perhaps responsible for James K. Polk defeating Henry Clay in the state by some 5,000 votes, thereby swinging the election to Polk. Peter Cooper of New York City was the Greenback Party candidate for president in 1876, and the party had some success in attracting local voters. The Populist Party of the 1880s and 1890s had less success in the state.

After the Civil War, opponents of New York City's Tammany Hall political machine joined together in short-lived "fusion" movements that incorporated multiple party endorsements. Such actions were common nationally in the 19th century but declined in the 1890s when most states banned multiple endorsements. Fusion politics continued in New York State, however, and were codified into state law under a cross-endorsement rule that allows parties to endorse candidates already nominated by other parties. A candidate can get on a state ballot with 20,000 supporting signatures in petition prior to a current election, but a party can get an automatic ballot line for the next four years if it endorses an existing candidate for governor who receives 50,000 votes or more. Votes for a candidate on all lines are added together to determine the winner, so mixed endorsements don't harm a contender although they can harm a major party. These critical features of the law allow minor parties to attract voters and to bargain with major parties by offering their endorsement in exchange for ideological concessions or patronage. Sixteen minor parties have won automatic ballot recognition: Prohibition (1892–1922), Socialist Labor (1896–1904), Socialist (1900–1938), Independence League (1906–16), Progressive (1912–16), American (1914–16), Farmer Labor (1920–22), Law Preservation (1930–34), American Labor (1936–54), Liberal (1944–2002), Conservative (1962–), Right to Life (1978–2002), Independence (1994–), Freedom (1994–98), Green (1996–2002), and Working Families (1998–).

The American Labor Party was founded in 1936 by supporters of Pres Franklin D. Roosevelt who wanted to avoid supporting the Tammany-dominated regular Democratic line. It had considerable influence for several years, but increasing dominance by communist members led to the founding of the Liberal Party in 1944, a party with significant force in state politics for many decades. Its greatest electoral success was likely the victory of Mayor John Lindsay in 1969 against Democratic and Republican candidates. It declined rapidly in the 1980s and 1990s and lost its slot on the ballot when its candidate for governor, Andrew Cuomo, pulled out of the 2002 election.

The mirror of the Liberal Party was the Conservative Party, founded in 1962 as a result of dissatisfaction with liberal Republicanism, embodied by Gov Nelson A. Rockefeller. Conservative Party members hoped to pressure Republicans to move to the right and generally sided with conservative Republicans, especially after Rockefeller's departure, with occasional support from conservative Democrats. In some areas of the state the Conservative endorsement is pursued equally by both Democrats and Republicans. The Right to Life Party (RTLP) began among a group opposed to state and national liberalized abortion practices, but its single-issue stand resulted in few links with other parties and candidates. The party's endorsement was the only one routinely avoided by candidates in a state where support for abortion rights is high. The RTLP lost its ballot line in 2002 when gubernatorial candidate Gerard Cronin received 43,000 votes. The Freedom Party, initially called the Tax Cut Now Party, was a short-lived party created in 1994 by state Republican Party leaders to boost the run of gubernatorial candidate George E. Pataki. He received 54,000 votes on this line, qualifying it as an established party for four more years. The Freedom Party was directed by party leaders in Albany and was available only to Republican candidates. It disappeared in 1998 because it fielded no candidate for governor.

In 1994 millionaire businessman B. Thomas Golisano from Victor (Ontario Co), in suburban Rochester, ran for governor on the Independence Fusion Party ticket. Emulating the 1992 independent presidential campaign of businessman Ross Perot, Golisano spent his own money on an extensive advertising campaign and gained over 217,000 votes, enough for his party (renamed the Independence Party after the election) to win the fourth spot on New York State ballots below Democrats, Republicans, and Conservatives. In 1998 Golisano again ran for governor, garnering 364,000 votes and winning third-line position for the party on the next ballot. His 633,000 votes in 2002 reinforced the party's standing.

Two left-wing third parties emerged in the 1990s, in part filling the vacuum created by the demise of the Liberal Party. The New York State Green Party was formed in 1996. Named and known for support of environmental issues, Greens espoused other liberal causes including consumer protection, universal healthcare, opposition to the death penalty, increase in the minimum wage, and repeal of the state's tough Rockefeller Drug Laws. In 1998 its ploy of naming actor Al Lewis, best known as Grandpa Munster from the 1960s *Munsters* television show, as its gubernatorial candidate helped the party gain the 50,000 votes it needed for automatic ballot status. The party's 2002 candidate, Stanley Aronowitz, failed to garner enough votes to keep the Green's ballot line.

The Working Families Party also emerged in 1998. The product of union activism among communications workers, auto workers, teamsters, and teachers, its leaders felt that neither Democrats nor Liberals were adequately responsive to progressive concerns. State party formation paralleled a similar national effort to form a labor party. The party endorsed Democratic gubernatorial nominee Peter Vallone, who received 51,325 votes. The party retained its line in 2002 by endorsing Democratic gubernatorial nominee H. Carl McCall. Despite the disappearance of three formerly recognized third parties after the 2002 elections, New York State minor parties such as the Marijuana Reform and Libertarian Parties continue to vie aggressively for official recognition, and candidates for office at all levels continue to welcome endorsements from third parties.

Scarrow, Howard A. *Parties, Elections, and Representation in the State of New York* (New York: New York Univ Press, 1983)

Schneier, Edward, and John Brian Murtaugh. *New York Politics: A Tale of Two States* (Armonk, NY: M. E. Sharpe, 2001)

Spitzer, Robert J. "Third Parties in New York." In *Governing New York State*, ed. Jeffrey M. Stonecash (Albany: SUNY Press, 2001)

Robert J. Spitzer

Thomas, Norman (Mattoon) (*b* Marion, Ohio, 20 Nov 1884; *d* Huntington, Suffolk Co, 19 Dec 1968). Socialist. Raised from a long line of Presbyterian ministers, Thomas attended Princeton University, graduating in 1905. He moved to New York City that same year and enrolled in the Union Theological Seminary, becoming interested in social work. A pacifist, after America's entry into World War I he became a defender of conscientious objectors, cofounding in 1917 the National Civil Liberties Bureau, the forerunner of the American Civil Liberties Union (ACLU). His opposition to the war led to his forced resignation from his ministerial post at the East Harlem Presbyterian Church in 1918. That same year Thomas joined the New York City–based Socialist Party, and he quickly became an influential member as both a critic of capitalism, which he saw as un-Christian, and communism, which he viewed as totalitarian. Thomas ran for a series of local and state offices on the Socialist ticket, including governor of New York State in 1924, mayor of New York City in 1925, state senator from Manhattan in 1926, and Manhattan borough president in 1931. After becoming the party head in 1926, Thomas ran for the US presidency as the Socialist Party nominee in every election from 1928 to 1948. As an anticommunist, however, Thomas opposed the Progressive Party, a left-wing third party that threw its support behind Henry A. Wallace's 1948 bid for the presidency. Aghast at the US atomic bombings of Japan, Thomas became a critical spokesman for the postwar antinuclear movement. In 1957 he and others formed the Committee for a Sane Nuclear Policy (SANE) in New York City, an organization dedicated to raising public consciousness about the growing nuclear arms race. True to his pacifist convictions, Thomas later opposed America's military involvement in Indochina. A prolific author and a highly influential Socialist and peace activist, Thomas lived his final years in Cold Spring Harbor (Suffolk Co).

Duram, James C. *Norman Thomas* (New York: Twayne Publishers, 1974)

Stephen Burwood

Thomas Indian School. Founded in 1855 by Philip Thomas and Asher and Laura Wright as the Thomas Asylum for Orphan and Destitute Indian Children, the school opened in 1856 on the Seneca Nation of Indians' Cattaraugus Reservation [loc in Cattaraugus, Chautauqua, and Erie Cos]. The tribal council gave 15 acres (6 ha) of its land to the school, whose expanded grounds eventually included 9 main buildings in Georgian Revival (including a decorative administration center featuring Indian motifs and themes) and 25 lesser constructions. Various philanthropic organizations, as well as New York State and the federal Bureau of Indian Affairs, provided funding. It was renamed the Thomas Indian School in 1905. Many of the early orphans' parents died fighting in the Civil War.

In 1862 an Indian Board of Managers was established to oversee the institute. The original focus was to promote self-sufficiency. Girls were taught home economics and boys agricultural skills. At the age of 16, the children began working for local non-Indian families. The school was run in military fashion and reflected the assimilation policy of the 19th-century United States. It imposed Christianity and forbade the speaking of the children's native Indian tongue. In 1875 New York State became the owner of the school, which was placed under the jurisdiction of the State Board of Charities. The school held eight grades by 1905, and the Regents exams were given there for the first time in 1908. By 1919 it had 200 students, and there continued to be a waiting list for admission. In 1927 supervision of the institute was transferred to the Department of Charities (later Department of Social Welfare). One more grade was added in 1930, making it a junior high school.

Many of the graduates became significant leaders in their communities. The school housed children from all six Iroquois nations and Algonquian-speaking children from Long Island, but most were from the Cattaraugus Reservation. At the request of Indian families, in 1954 the school became part of the Gowanda public school system. The Thomas Indian School was closed in 1957.

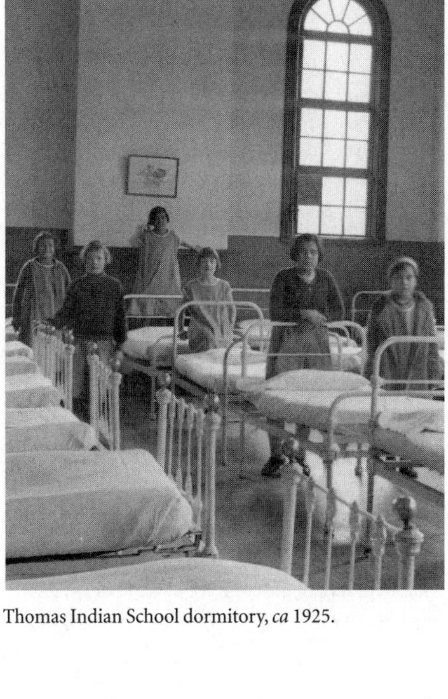

Thomas Indian School dormitory, *ca* 1925.

Hauptman, Laurence M. *The Iroquois and the New Deal* (Syracuse: Syracuse Univ Press, 1981)
Upton, Helen M. *The Everett Report in Historical Perspective: The Indians of New York* (Albany: NYS American Revolution Bicentennial Commission, 1980)

Randy A. John

Thomas-Morse Aircraft Corporation. Early aircraft manufacturer. The company originated when William T. Thomas, an engineer for Glenn Curtiss, built his own airplane in Hammondsport (Steuben Co) in 1909. The following year Thomas moved operations to Hornell (Steuben Co), also recruiting Curtiss employee Walter E. Johnson, who, after teaching himself to fly, became an expert pilot and exhibitor of planes. In 1911 the company relocated to Bath (Steuben Co), where William's brother Oliver W. Thomas, a former engineer at Schenectady's General Electric, joined the firm. The young company opened a cut-rate flying school, and their machines repeatedly set endurance and altitude records. The Thomas brothers, along with Johnson and Cummings M. Cox incorporated the business in 1912 as Thomas Bros Aeroplane Co. Throughout this period their aircraft, including water fliers, were of the general Curtiss type and usually powered by Kirkham engines made in Bath. With the outbreak of World War I, the firm moved to Ithaca, where more factory space was available. The arrival of former Curtiss and Sopwith engineer B. Douglas Thomas (no relation to the Thomas brothers) led to creation of the Model T2 biplane and a British order for 24 units. In 1917 a merger with Morse Chain Co formed Thomas-Morse Aircraft Corp, which soon employed 1,200 people and ranked as the nation's fourth most productive aircraft maker. Thomas-Morse's S-4 Scout or "Tommy" was its most successful aircraft, and the flying school trained scores of US and Canadian pilots. Business shrank after the war, and both brothers left the firm by 1922. Consolidated Aircraft Corp of Buffalo bought the company in 1929.

Dunn, Lindsley. "The Thomas Brothers." In *The Heritage of Bath, NY, 1793–1993: Discovering the Facts, Families, and Folklore,* ed. Thomas E. Stackpole (Bath: Historical Foundation of Bath, NY, 1998)

Kirk W. House

Thomaston. Village (pop 2,607) in North Hempstead (Nassau Co). Businessman and future mayor of New York City William R. Grace acquired land on the Great Neck peninsula in the 1870s, part of which he subdivided to create Thomaston, naming it after his wife's home in Maine. The village incorporated in 1931. Its population grew gradually, but there has been little new housing built in the village since 1960. In the early 21st century it is upper middle class and predominantly a residential community.

Richard A. Winsche

Thompson. Town (pop 14,189) in central Sullivan Co. First settled before the Revolutionary War, the town's permanent settlement dates from 1795 and the arrival of Judge William Thompson. The town was formed from Mamakating in 1803. Its economy was based on lumbering, tanning (beginning 1831), and stock raising, and centered on Monticello, the county seat, with its rail link to Port Jervis (1871–1953). That service and the Ontario and Western Railroad nearby (1871–1953) created the town's resort industry; it was the site of two of the largest and best-known Jewish resort hotels, the Concord (1935–99) and Kutsher's Country Club (1907). Automobile traffic on Rte 17 (I-86) grew in the 1920s, and the road became a limited-access highway, completed between 1956 and 1958. Thompson is the site of the county's two largest private employers: the Center for Discovery, for people with developmental disabilities, and Catskill Regional Medical Center, both in Harris and each employing about 900 in 2003.

John Conway

Thompson, Harold W(illiam) (*b* Buffalo, 5 June 1891; *d* Cortland, 21 Feb 1964). Folklorist and educator. Reared in Westfield (Chautauqua Co), Thompson graduated from Hamilton College in Clinton (Oneida Co) in 1912 and earned a PhD from Harvard University in 1915. While on the faculty of the New York State College for Teachers at Albany (1915–40), he pioneered the teaching of American folk culture. Thompson's landmark work, *Body, Boots, and Britches* (1939), made a vast reservoir of New York State folklore available to the reading public for the first time. He was president of the American Folklore Society in 1942 and two years later founded the New York Folklore Society with Louis C. Jones. Thompson served as the society's first president (1945–49) and helped launch its journal, *New York Folklore Quarterly.* He concluded his teaching career at Cornell University (1940–59). With the help of his students he amassed an extensive folklore archive, now housed at the library of the New York State Historical Association in Cooperstown (Otsego Co).

Walker, Warren S., ed. *Whatever Makes Papa Laugh: A Folklore Sheaf Honoring Harold W. Thompson* (Cooperstown, NY: New York Folklore Society, 1958)

Frank K. Lorenz

Thompson, Smith (*b* Amenia, Dutchess Co, 17 Jan 1768; *d* Poughkeepsie, 18 Dec 1843). US Supreme Court justice. A 1788 graduate of the College of New Jersey (now Princeton University), Thompson prepared for the bar with James Kent in Poughkeepsie and was admitted to practice in 1793. That year he replaced Kent as Gilbert Livingston's partner and in 1794 married Livingston's daughter Sarah. Thompson served in the assembly (1800–1801) and was a member of the 1801 Constitutional Convention. He rejected appointment as a district attorney before accepting a seat in 1802 on the state supreme court, where his work was marked by judicial restraint and fairly close adherence to precedent. He became chief justice in 1814. Though committed to the state's Jeffersonian Republican Party, Thompson was partly responsible for that party's 1804–5 split between Lewisites and Clintonians, and he became allied with Martin Van Buren's Bucktail faction. Bucktail support led to his 1818 appointment as Pres James Monroe's secretary of the navy, and he was Monroe's only candidate when the "New York seat" on the US Supreme Court became vacant in 1823. During 20 years on the Court, Thompson was responsible for shifting interpretation of the commerce clause toward a concurrent approach, allowing states to regulate commerce in the absence of a specific federal law. Thompson's dissent in *Cherokee Nation v Georgia* (1831), arguing that Indian tribes remained sovereign nations, became the accepted rule the following year and is perhaps his most important opinion. He married Eliza Livingston in 1837, three years after his first wife's death.

Roper, Donald M. *Mr. Justice Thompson and the Constitution* (New York: Garland Publishing, 1987)

Donald M. Roper

Thomson, Virgil (Garnett) (*b* Kansas City, Mo, 25 Nov 1896; *d* New York City, 30 Sept 1989). Composer and music critic. Thomson was active as a church organist in Kansas City; he studied music at Harvard from 1919 to 1925, with two years' study in Paris during that time. Thomson returned to Paris in 1925, living there until 1940. He belonged to the city's large circle of expatriate American artists, including the writer Gertrude Stein, with whom he collaborated on two operas: *Four Saints in Three Acts* (1927–28) and *The Mother of Us All* (1946). The former was produced on Broadway in 1934 with an all-black cast and striking sets and costumes designed by New York City artist Florine Stettheimer. Returning to the United States in 1940, he lived much of the rest of his life in the Chelsea Hotel on 23d St in Manhattan. From 1940 to 1954 Thomson was the music critic for the *New York Herald-Tribune.* His reviews challenged the complacency of local music institutions, notably the New York Philharmonic. Arguably the most brilliant American music critic of the 20th century, his collected reviews are still enjoyable and worth reading. As a composer Thomson was strongly influenced by the simplicity of the French composer Erik Satie and by the direct expression of American hymns, jazz, and other vernacular music. He was especially adept at setting English verse of all kinds to music and at writing brief musical "portraits" of friends while they sat for him. Thomson's other important works include the film scores *The Plow That Broke the Plains* (1936), *The River* (1937), and *Louisiana Story* (1948), the latter being the first film score to win a Pulitzer Prize. He also wrote another opera, *Lord Byron,* which premiered at the Juilliard School in 1972, and three symphonies.

Thomson, Virgil. *Virgil Thomson* (New York: Knopf, 1966)
Thomson, Virgil, and John Rockwell. *A Virgil Thomson Reader* (New York: Dutton, 1984)
Tommasini, Anthony. *Virgil Thomson: A Composer on the Aisle* (New York: Norton, 1997)

David Raymond

Thomsonism. See Alternative medicine.

Thornwood. Locality (pop 5,980) in Mount Pleasant (Westchester Co). Nanegeekin, an outpost of Philipsburgh Manor, was first settled around 1695 by the Huguenot See family. Snowflake Lime Works and the adjacent marble quarry started providing employment about 1865. From 1891 to 1894 Lewis Smadbeck platted Sherman Park, marketing it to German Americans in New York City, some of whom became commuters. From 1906 to 1914 it was an incorporated village, Hillside, which was dissolved; the post office and train station names became Thornwood. Extensive suburban development followed World War II.

Field Horne

thoroughbred racing. Horse racing was an established English pastime when the first colonial racetrack opened on Long Island in 1665, a year after the Dutch surrendered New Amsterdam. Gov Richard Nicolls ordered a 2 mi (3.2 km) oval laid out on Salisbury Plain (later Hempstead Plain). He named it Newmarket, after the English racing center, and offered a silver cup to be run for each spring and fall. At least three other tracks were built in the next century in Manhattan. Among the leaders of the New York City turf were the landed aristocrat Lewis Morris (1726–98), a signer of the Declaration of Independence, and James DeLancey, a tory who operated a prominent racing stable.

Increased selectivity by colonial breeders began in 1730 when Bulle Rock, the first English "blood" or "bred" horse, arrived in Virginia. But after the Revolution the sport faded in the northern states, where religious opponents deemed it too sinful. The heaviest blow in New York State came in 1802 when the legislature banned horse racing as a form of gambling. Still, northern racing had its significant antebellum moments, especially after 1821, when the state ban was lifted for Queens Co. That allowed construction of the famous Union Course west of Jamaica (Queens Co), which hosted the "race of the century" on 27 May 1823. The New York–bred American Eclipse defeated Virginia's Henry before at least 25,000 fans in the first of many North versus South races over the next two decades.

GROWTH AND DECLINE

As the Civil War destroyed racing in the South, it rose again in the North. With the fighting at a safe distance, several northern racing meetings opened in 1863, the most important at Saratoga Springs. A loophole in the state law had allowed racing to resume as a method for "improvement of the breed." The first Saratoga meeting was so successful that its backers, Cornelius Vanderbilt and friends, built a new track in 1864. Today it is America's oldest major professional sporting venue, and its inaugural race, the Travers Stakes, the oldest major event in American spectator sports. Jerome Park near Fordham [now in Bronx Co] opened in 1866. Kings Co had thoroughbred tracks at Brighton Beach (1879), Sheepshead Bay (1880), and Gravesend (1886). Major New York racetracks opening in and around Queens included Aqueduct (1894), Jamaica (1903), and Belmont Park (1905). In 1895 the legislature formed a racing commission to monitor horse racing in the state and the revenues it generated. A year earlier several prominent New Yorkers had formed the Jockey Club in Manhattan to organize the sport. Club members set racing dates, established rules, and licensed jockeys; they retained licensing powers in New York State until 1951.

It was open to question whether the sport would last. Early in the 20th century antigambling forces again crippled the sport, as states moved to wipe out betting operations. The number of tracks nationwide fell from 314 to just 25 by 1908. That year the New York State legislature made it illegal to solicit or record bets in a fixed place. New York City tracks struggled for three years and closed in 1911 along with Saratoga. They reopened two years later, circumventing the law with a system of "oral betting." A "bookie," or bookmaker, still not allowed to solicit bets, could quote odds to anybody who inquired orally, and the inquirer could then write the bets on a slip of paper, hand it over to the bookie, and pay up or collect winnings the next day. The most celebrated horse of the oral days was Man o' War, who won 20 of 21 races, 18 of which were run in New York State. The antibetting law was repealed in 1934, and the bookies returned in force but not for long.

THE PARIMUTUEL ERA

In 1939 New York voters approved a constitutional amendment permitting parimutuel betting, to be taxed at 10%, with the revenue split between the tracks and the state. The implementing legislation outlawed bookmaking. The colorful bookies with their booths and little boards advertising their odds were replaced by an impersonal system of adding machines and ticket windows. Fans lined up to bet a horse to win, place (finish second), or show (third). A large tote board in a track's infield revealed the totals wagered on each horse and its odds. The total that was bet to win, or "win pool," was divided among the bettors who had the winner; the place and show pools were similarly split. It was a huge success. New York's first parimutuel season, 1940, boosted attendance by about 30%.

World War II did not shut down racing until late 1944, when the Office of War Mobilization asked the racetracks to suspend operations. But the next summer they reopened to record crowds. The star of the period was Citation, winner of the 1948 Triple Crown and 32 out of 45 races. In 1955 the nonprofit New York Racing Association (NYRA) was formed and bought out the state's main tracks from private shareholders: Saratoga, Aqueduct, Jamaica, and Belmont Park. NYRA built a new Aqueduct on the original site for $33 million. It opened in 1959 with accommodations for 80,000, and the Jamaica track was shut down. A new Belmont Park costing $31 million opened in 1968. However, the NYRA did not quite have a monopoly. The first modern thoroughbred track in western New York State, independent Finger Lakes, opened in 1962 at Farmington (Ontario Co) and staged racing from April to December.

A major challenge to the NYRA appeared in 1971 when OTB, a public benefit corporation, began operating off-track betting parlors. It expanded from 5 parlors in New York City during its first year to 113 statewide two years later and threatened to wipe out track attendance and handles. Officials countered in 1973 by creating the State Racing and Wagering Board to supervise the tracks and OTB, extending the racing season to 12 months and introducing Sunday racing.

The New York City–area tracks could still lure crowds for big events, such as the 69,138 who attended the 1973 Belmont Stakes, won by Secretariat, and the 85,818 who saw Lemon Drop Kid win the Belmont in 1999. But on some days only a few thousand hardened bettors congregated in the vast emptiness of Belmont and Aqueduct. The exception was Saratoga, once in danger of being shut down as a needless detour for New York City's bettors, but now offering $1 million purses and luring daily crowds reaching 50,000, with most people out to savor the place's rare country charm and antique traditions. Saratoga Springs is the site of the National Museum of Racing and Hall of Fame, founded in 1950.

Hervey, John. *Racing in America, 1665–1865* (New York: Scribner's, 1944)

Hotaling, Edward. *They're Off! Horse Racing at Saratoga* (Syracuse: Syracuse Univ Press, 1995)

Manning, Landon. *The Noble Animals; A Look into the Past of Events of the Turf at Saratoga, New York* (Saratoga Springs: Author, 1973)

Robertson, William H. P. *The History of Thoroughbred Racing in America* (New York: Bonanza Books, 1964)

Edward Hotaling

Thousand Island dressing. Salad dressing made with mayonnaise, chili sauce, chives, green pepper, and chopped hard-boiled eggs. Though its history is debated, in all versions of its story George Boldt, manager of the Waldorf-Astoria Hotel in New York City, is credited with popularizing it nationally by serving it in his hotel around the turn of the 20th century. Boldt was a regular summer visitor to the Thousand Islands, and for years local guides have said that the recipe was invented there by Oscar Tschirky, maître d' of the Waldorf, when he ran out of his usual dressing ingredients while he and Boldt were cruising on Boldt's yacht. Boldt liked the mixture so much, the story goes, that he insisted Tschirky add it to the menu at the hotel. The owners of the Thousand Islands Inn in Clayton (Jefferson Co) claim instead that the recipe was created in the early 1900s by Sophia LaLonde, wife of a fishing guide who served it to customers at his shore dinners. In this version May Irwin, a renowned actress of the time, tasted the dressing on one of George LaLonde's expeditions, then took the recipe home to New York City and introduced it to George Boldt.

Lynn Ekfelt

Grandstand at Belmont Park during the Belmont Stakes, 1965.

Thousand Island shore dinner. This picnic has been a traditional part of a guided fishing trip in the Thousand Islands since the early 1900s. Initially guides put their groups ashore at random sites and began to cook. More recently several of the area's fishing guides associations have set up permanent locations with picnic tables and fireplaces for members to use. Early meals could take several hours. Since modern anglers are less willing to give up fishing time for eating, the dinner has been shortened, but the menu has not varied. The main course consists of the fish caught by those in the guide's boat. The guide begins by rendering fatback in a large pot over a wood fire. While that is cooking down, potatoes and corn are boiled in separate pots. The first course includes sandwiches of tomatoes and the cracklings left from the fatback. Breaded fish fillets, deep-fried in the fatback oil, are cooked to be ready at the same time as the corn and potatoes, and salad topped with Thousand Island dressing is also served. Dessert is french toast: thick slices of Italian bread dipped in eggs and cream, deep-fried in the same oil as the fish, and served drizzled with local maple syrup, brandy, or Grand Marnier, and a bit more cream.

Ekfelt, Lynn. "Shore Dinner." In *Good Food, Served Right: Traditional Recipes and Food Customs from New York's North Country* (Canton, NY: Traditional Arts in Upstate New York, 2000)

Lynn Ekfelt

Thousand Islands resorts. Recreational development began in the 1850s on the islands in the St. Lawrence River on the northern border of New York State. At the mid–19th century, a few of the larger islands supported farms, but because of rocky terrain and thin soil most were useful only to supply wood sold as fuel for passing steamboats. Once cleared of timber, most islands had little marketability. Because early sportsmen came without families, few erected cottages. Through the mid–19th century water transport provided the main access to the region. Prominent visitors of the 1840s included Pres Martin Van Buren and Albany and Washington legislators who came to fish during their recess, accompanied by clergy on leave during the summer months.

With arrival in 1852 of the Watertown and Rome Railroad at Cape Vincent (Jefferson Co) more business owners and their families began to visit, especially after the American Civil War. Azariah Walton, an Alexandria Bay (Jefferson Co) merchant, owned many of the islands, which his younger partner, Andrew Cornwall, subsequently acquired. Cornwall had vision and initiative to lead development of the resort, and he sold islands to summer visitors at reasonable prices. George M. Pullman was the most prominent industrialist to become a summer resident, acquiring an island near Alexandria Bay in 1864. The Chicago manufacturer of railroad cars was a native of Albion (Orleans Co), and his son attended nearby St. Lawrence University. Pullman's mother became particularly attached to her summer home, a place of reunion for her family. At a modest frame cottage in August 1872 Pullman entertained Pres Ulysses S. Grant and other Civil War heroes. Their visit coincided with an excursion of national journalists to the resort. Perhaps no mere coincidence, the conjunction of events proved to be a public relations triumph. Pullman's gala reception for the president and his party at his island was reported in many national newspapers. The exposure triggered the "Rush of '72," when Alexandria Bay was overwhelmed with new visitors. Grand hotels suddenly appeared. Cornwall donated prime waterfront property at Alexandria Bay for construction of the Thousand Island House (1872–73). Charles Crossmon simultaneously expanded his old inn nearby into an elegant modern hotel, Crossmon House. Other new hostelries and many whole cottage communities like Thousand Island Park (1875), a Methodist camp meeting facility, soon appeared.

Clayton (Jefferson Co) was less exclusively a seasonal resort community than Alexandria Bay was. With year-round commercial activities, Clayton has always been the larger village. Its inns served early fishermen as well as other transients. Establishment in 1873 of a railroad terminus at Clayton also gave that community more prominence. Clayton increasingly vied with Alexandria Bay as the dominant resort community. Eventually the largest of the region's grand hotels, the Frontenac, opened in 1899 near Clayton rather than Alexandria Bay.

Cape Vincent, a village near the confluence of lake and river, had a railroad terminus earlier, but because the community was less central to the Thousand Islands, it did not develop so extensively as a resort. Hotels likewise served summer visitors, some of whom regarded the nearby waters as superior for bass fishing. For a few years Ithaca native William Wyckoff's summer home, Carleton Villa (1893) on Carleton Island, near Cape Vincent, was regarded as the region's most ambitious residence, surpassing even Pullman's second summer home near Alexandria Bay, Castle Rest, the first of the Thousand Islands castles built in 1888. Soon vying with both was Charles Emery's Calumet Island, with its sandstone castle across from Clayton, built in 1893. That property in turn was surpassed in 1900 by Boldt Castle built on Heart Island. The last of the Thousand Islands castles was Frederick Bourne's granite summer home on Dark Island, near Chippewa Bay, built in 1903 shortly before the incomplete Boldt Castle was abandoned in January 1904.

Many other splendid villas were built at the Thousand Islands, largely by New York City residents. The US islands developed more rapidly than the Canadian, in part because a question of American Indian title to the Canadian islands had not been clearly resolved. The Canadian government eventually auctioned off groups of islands periodically, allowing them to be acquired by private owners, but in the main they did not experience the same rapid development at the end of the 19th century through the early 20th century that the US islands did. Tourism in the latter fluctuated with the economy. The high point came over the turn of the 20th century, subsiding with a cooling of the economy in the first decade and declining abruptly after disastrous fires in 1911 and 1912. Also, the failure to develop good highway access to the Thousand Islands area after the decline of railroad service made the resorts more inaccessible.

Prior to automobiles early in the 20th century, steamboats provided regular communication and transportation between river ports. Many lines served various island cottage colonies, some with resort hotels. Large steamboats picked up excursion parties at railroad depots and

Boldt Castle, Alexandria Bay.

provided cruises of the islands. Smaller tour boats competed with the steamboats, advertising themselves as being better able to pass through narrow and shallow passages. The St. Lawrence skiff, which evolved during the 19th century, has become recognized as a classic type of rowboat, used by fishing guides and produced locally. Regional shipyards and boat works have built various sorts of craft, from huge schooners of the early 19th century to canoes and competition race boats. From 1904 through 1913 the international races of the American Power Boat Association were held in the Thousand Islands area for several consecutive seasons after the Gold Cup was won by local yacht clubs that sponsored the entries.

Many yacht clubs flourished in the region during the early 20th century. The three major organizations were the Thousand Islands Yacht Club at Alexandria Bay, the Chippewa Bay Yacht Club, and the Frontenac Yacht Club near Clayton. Prior to World War I a feature of the region was its astonishing fleet of magnificent steam yachts, many more than 100 feet (30 m) in length, carrying tall masts and rigging. Huge yacht houses, built to shelter long, masted boats, became distinctive landmarks of the Thousand Islands. Island residents were served by an array of boats, providing utilitarian service as well as sport and entertainment. Commercial boat tours have been a major business for well over a century and in 2002 remained the mainstay of tourism, which in recent years has increased markedly. Boldt Castle attracts more than 200,000 visitors each summer, and luxury hotels operate year around.

Haddock, John A. *A Souvenir: The Thousand Islands of the St. Lawrence River* (Albany: Weed-Parsons Printing, 1895)

Hough, Franklin Benjamin, ed. *The Thousand Islands of the River St. Lawrence* (Syracuse: Davis & Bardeen, 1880)

Malo, Paul. *Fools' Paradise: Remembering the Thousand Islands* (Fulton, NY: Laurentian Press, 2003)

Paul Malo

Three Village. Area in Brookhaven and Smithtown (Suffolk Co). The designation was coined in 1929 and originally included the Village of Old Field and the localities of Setauket and Stony Brook. The Three Village Central School District (1966) expanded its boundaries by including East Setauket, the Village of Poquott, parts of the Villages of Head of the Harbor and Port Jefferson, and the campus of SUNY Stony Brook.

Beverly C. Tyler

Throop. Town (pop 1,824) in central Cayuga Co. Settled in 1790, the town was formed from Aurelius, Mentz, and Sennett in 1859 and was named after Gov Enos T. Throop (1784–1874), a prominent county resident. Along its eastern border, Throop was served by the Southern Central Railroad (1869). Nineteenth-century manufacturing included forks, wool cloth, and springs; gravel for roads has been mined through the years.

Laurel Auchampaugh

Throop, Enos T(hompson) (*b* Johnstown [now in Fulton Co], 21 Aug 1784; *d* Owasco, Cayuga Co, 1 Nov 1874). Governor. While reading law in Albany from 1798 to 1801, he became friends with future governor and president Martin Van Buren. Throop passed the bar in 1806 and began practicing law in Auburn (Cayuga Co). In 1811 he became county clerk. The following year he purchased and operated mill property along the Owasco Lake Outlet near Auburn with his sister's husband, establishing the community of Throopsville (Cayuga Co). He was elected to Congress from New York's 20th district in 1814 as a Republican. In 1816 Throop returned to Auburn to farm and to practice law. He served as a state circuit court judge from 1823 to 1827. With Van Buren's support Throop was elected lieutenant governor in 1828 as a Democrat and became acting governor in March 1829, when Gov Van Buren resigned to become Pres Andrew Jackson's secretary of state. Throop was elected governor in his own right in 1830. In that position he initiated legislation providing asylum for the insane poor, ended imprisonment for debt, and led the state's response to an outbreak of cholera. He did not run for reelection in 1832. Jackson appointed Throop naval officer of the Port of New York in 1833, and from 1838 to 1842 he was chargé d'affaires to the Kingdom of the Two Sicilies [now in Italy]. Throop served in this capacity until 1842 then returned to his farm, Willowbrook, on the northeast shore of Owasco Lake. In 1847 he moved to Kalamazoo, Mich, where he speculated in real estate before retiring to Willowbrook once again in 1857.

Hammond, Jabez D. *The History of Political Parties in the State of New-York from the Ratification of the Federal Constitution to December, 1840*, 2 vols (Albany: C. Van Benthuysen, 1842)

Scott W. Anderson

Thurman. Town (pop 1,199) in W Warren Co. Settled *ca* 1783, the town was formed from the extinct town of Athol in 1852. Settlers came from New England, Dutchess Co, and Blair Atholl in Scotland. Lumbering began *ca* 1820, and timber was floated down the Hudson to Jessup's Landing and Glens Falls. Hemlock bark was harvested for tanneries. In 1869 the Adirondack Railroad (later Delaware and Hudson) reached Thurman. In the 20th century, marginal farmlands were reforested for timber and Christmas trees, and resorts and dude ranches were developed. The Fiddler's Jamboree is held annually in Thurman.

Marilyn J. Van Dyke

Thurston. Town (pop 1,309) in central Steuben Co. Settled in 1813, the town was formed from Cameron in 1844. A huge sawmill, built in 1852, at Risingville harvested 2,000 acres (809 ha) of heavy pineland and employed 30. Dairy farming supported several small cheese factories. Goodhue Lake became a resort in the 1920s. Tanglewood Lake, with 60 lots, was developed in the 1980s. The annual Thomas Homestead Folk Festival drew thousands in the 1980s.

Virginia L. Wright and Jerry Wright

Ticonderoga. Town (pop 5,167) in SE Essex Co. The French, who built Fort Carillon in 1755, settled around it, and then destroyed it as they withdrew. It was rebuilt by the British (1758–60) as Fort Ticonderoga. British grantees followed from about 1764 to 1767. After the Revolution the community was resettled by New Englanders. The town was formed from Crown Point in 1804. Lumbering, tanning, boatbuilding, and iron- and clothmaking were early industries. Graphite was mined as early as 1818; the Ticonderoga Graphite Co incorporated in 1863 and merged with Joseph Dixon Co in 1873, refining graphite for "lead" pencils until 1921. Pulp papermaking started in 1877, and International Paper Co remains a major employer. Since 1908 the restoration of Fort Ticonderoga by the Pell family has provided employment and stimulated tourism.

Thomas A. Rumney

Ticonderoga, Battle of (1758). The most important French victory of the French and Indian War. In an attempt to drive the French out of the Champlain Valley in 1758, British major general James Abercromby assembled a force of 16,000 troops at the southern end of Lake George, the largest army assembled in North America at that time. To the north a force of 3,400 men under the command of the Marquis de Montcalm occupied Fort Carillon at Ticonderoga [now in Essex Co]. In 48 hours the French fortified the heights of Carillon near the fort with earthworks and abatis, a tangle of sharpened tree limbs. After the death of British field commander Lord George Augustus Howe in a skirmish on 6 July, the British regrouped and struck the French lines on 8 July, attacking relentlessly for six hours but without success. Even though outnumbered almost five to one, the French prevailed. With approximately 3,000 combined French and British casualties, this was the bloodiest battle in North America until the Civil War.

Hamilton, Edward P. *Fort Ticonderoga: Key to a Continent* (1964; repr Ticonderoga, NY: Fort Ticonderoga Association, 1995)

Nicholas Westbrook

Tiffany, Louis C(omfort) (*b* New York City, 18 Feb 1848; *d* New York City, 17 Jan 1933). Artist and businessman. Son of Harriet Olivia Young and Charles Lewis Tiffany, owner of the silver and jewelry store Tiffany and Co, he attended Flushing Academy in Queens and Eagleswood Military Academy in Perth Amboy, NJ, before enrolling in New York City's National Academy of Design in 1866. He frequented the studio of painter Charles Inness while a student and traveled abroad in the late 1860s and 1870s. He painted genre scenes based on his travels as well as local landscapes, such as the realistic *Duane Street, New York* (1878). In 1879 he helped found Louis C. Tiffany and Associated Artists, a New York City interior decorating business. Prestigious commissions included the home of New Yorker Cornelius Vanderbilt II (1881–82) and Pres Chester A. Arthur's White House (1882–83). Interested in glass production since 1873, he founded the Tiffany Glass Co, which produced stained-glass windows for homes and churches in 1885. By 1892 Tiffany changed his firm's name to the Tiffany Glass and Decorating Co and established a glass factory at Corona in Queens. Tiffany hired Arthur Nash, an English glassmaker, to run the glasshouse and to experiment with vessel glass production. The vessel glass, which Tiffany called Favrile, became popular with collectors and museum curators. Tiffany presented a group of glassware to the Smithsonian Institution. The Metropolitan Museum of Art, among others, acquired Tiffany pieces in the

Photograph of Ticonderoga, by Seneca Ray Stoddard, late 19th century.

1890s. In 1893 the Tiffany firm drew critical acclaim after showing stained-glass windows and a chapel at the World's Columbian Exposition in Chicago. Henceforth, Tiffany's company, which became Tiffany Studios in 1902, was the most prestigious producer of stained-glass windows in the United States and eventually garnered considerable appeal abroad. The firm decorated numerous churches in New York City and throughout the state, including the Willard Chapel in Auburn (Cayuga Co) and the First Presbyterian Church in Bath (Steuben Co). The leaded floral shades he created for electric lamps also became popular among Americans and Europeans, who were accustomed to the dimmer light generated by kerosene and gas lamps. The lamps, with shade designs featuring flowers, birds, and insects, diffused the light as well as provided it. Tiffany became design director of Tiffany and Co after his father's death in 1902, enabling him to move into jewelry design after already expanding his company's production to include glass mosaics (1878), metalwork (1893), enamels (1898), ceramics (1900), and woodwork (1905). Although the Corona glass factory, renamed Tiffany Furnaces around 1902, remained open until 1924 and Tiffany Studios operated until 1932, Tiffany retired in 1919. He established the Tiffany Foundation shortly before his retirement and set up his Cold Spring Harbor (Suffolk Co) home, Laurelton Hall, as a retreat for young artists. He lived there until his death. Curators and collectors have come to recognize Tiffany as the foremost American designer in the international Art Nouveau style.

Duncan, Alastair, Martin Eidelberg, and Neil Harris. *Masterworks of Louis Comfort Tiffany* (New York: Abrams, 1989)

Koch, Robert. *Louis C. Tiffany: Rebel in Glass*, 3d ed. (New York: Crown Publishers, 1982)

Jane Shadel Spillman

Tilden, Samuel J(ones) (*b* New Lebanon, Columbia Co, 9 Feb 1814; *d* Yonkers, 4 Aug 1886). Governor and presidential candidate. Tilden graduated from the law school of the University of the City of New York (now New York University) in 1841, became a successful corporate lawyer specializing in railroad finance, and acquired a considerable fortune. He served a term in the state assembly in 1846 and was the same year a delegate to the state constitutional convention. A Free Soil Democrat in the late 1840s, Tilden returned to the Democratic Party in the 1850s. He gave lukewarm support to the Civil War and spoke against perceived Republican abuses of power. As New York State Democratic chairman from 1866 to 1874, Tilden managed Horatio Seymour's unsuccessful 1868 run for the presidency. He then moved into the spotlight when he belatedly joined the forces battling the Tweed Ring, becoming a member of the Committee of Seventy in 1871, a group that helped gather and publicize the evidence that brought down William M. "Boss" Tweed. In 1874 Tilden rode a wave of positive publicity to the governor's mansion, where he further enhanced his reputation by successfully attacking New York State's corrupt Canal Ring, a bipartisan group of politicians who profited from the repair of the state canal system.

Tilden's attacks on corruption earned him a national reputation and made him the logical

Samuel J. Tilden.

choice to oppose a Republican Party tainted by the two scandal-ridden terms of Ulysses S. Grant. He campaigned on the platform of "Tilden and Reform," advocating limited government, states' rights, and an end to Republican Reconstruction. In the general election, Tilden received a majority of the popular vote (4.2 million, 51%), but there were conflicting returns on electoral votes from Florida, Louisiana, and South Carolina, where white terror had prevented African Americans from voting, and there was a contest over one Oregon elector. Congress created a 15-person electoral commission to resolve these issues. After several months of turmoil the commission on 2 Mar 1877, by a party-line vote, awarded Tilden's Republican opponent Rutherford B. Hayes all the disputed electoral votes, giving Hayes the presidency by one electoral vote, 185 to 184.

Tilden remained the logical Democratic candidate for the presidency in 1880 but declined to run, in part because of ill health. He moved from his long-time residence in Gramercy Park in New York City and retired to a new estate in Yonkers. At his death, more than half of his $5 million estate helped establish a free public library in New York City. In 1895 this trust was joined with the Astor and Lenox Libraries to form the New York Public Library.

Flick, Alexander. *Samuel Jones Tilden: A Study in Political Sagacity* (New York: Dodd, Mead, 1939)

Mushkat, Jerome. *The Reconstruction of the New York Democracy, 1861–1874* (Rutherford, NJ: Fairleigh Dickinson Univ Press, 1981)

Polakoff, Keith. *The Politics of Inertia: The Election of 1876 and the End of Reconstruction* (Baton Rouge: Louisiana State Univ Press, 1973)

Jon Sterngass

timber. See LUMBER AND TIMBER PRODUCTS.

Timbucto. A settlement of African American homesteaders established in 1846 by Peterboro (Madison Co) reformer and philanthropist Gerrit Smith in the Adirondacks. With enclaves of settlers in Essex and Franklin Cos, Timbucto was situated in and around the Town of North Elba (Essex Co), although its exact location remains unknown. Partly in response to New York State voters' overwhelming rejection of an equal suffrage referendum and the continuation of a $250 property requirement for African American voters in 1846, Smith devised a plan to give away 120,000 acres (48,560 ha) to 3,000 black New Yorkers. Smith's vision of a colony of self-sufficient black farmers expressed his deep-felt agrarianism and his expectation that the improved value of the land grants would help gain the deed holders access to the ballot. To identify 3,000 eligible (free, African American, non-drinking, able-bodied, and male) grantees, Smith appealed to black allies long engaged in political affairs: urban powerbrokers like Theodore S. Wright, Henry H. Garnet, James McCune Smith, and Charles Bennett Ray. From 1846 to 1853 these New York State activists promoted the land grants at pulpits, meetings, and conventions. The grantees, disturbed by rumors of the poor quality of the land, hobbled by their poverty and their lack of farming expertise, and discouraged by reports of tricks being played on black deed holders by unscrupulous white guides, failed to respond to Gerrit Smith's offer. Still, some small, short-lived enclaves formed; Smith's largesse may have drawn some 100 Blacks to the Adirondack region. The settlement, which was informally called Timbucto (or Timbuctoo) after the West African city, attracted abolitionist John Brown and his family to North Elba in 1849 and references to Timbucto figure in Brown's and others' correspondence. The guide and farmer Lyman Epps, best known of the Timbucto black settlers, helped found the local library and Baptist church; his son, Lyman Jr, last known descendant of a "Gerrit Smith grantee," died in North Elba in 1942.

Smith, Gerrit. Papers. Bird Library, Syracuse Univ, Syracuse

Stauffer, John. *Black Hearts of Men: Radical Abolitionists and the Transformation of Race* (Cambridge, Mass: Harvard Univ Press, 2002)

Amy Godine

Times Square. Formally the Midtown Manhattan intersection of 7th Ave and 42d St, the square is more generally considered bounded by 42d and 47th Sts and Broadway and 8th Ave. Called Longacre Square in the 19th century, the area was dominated by carriages, stables, and blacksmiths. The majority of the west part of the district was owned by the Astor family, the parcel having been purchased by John Jacob Astor in the early 19th century. From 1878 to 1910 it was the site of William H. Vanderbilt's American Horse Exchange, where urban dwellers came to purchase horses, buggies, and fresh milk. The area was renamed Times Square when the *New York Times* relocated its offices to the Times Tower at 43d St and 7th Ave on 31 Dec 1904. Helping to spur the area's growth, the same year the city completed the first segment of the Interborough Rapid Transit Co subway line, running from City Hall to 42d St then west to Times Square and north on Broadway to 145th St. In 1907 the New Year's tradition of lowering a brightly lit ball at midnight in Times Square began.

The theater district, then centered on 14th St, gradually moved to the Times Square area beginning at the turn of the 20th century. Charles Frohman's Empire Theatre (1893), at 1430 Broadway and West 40th St, and Oscar Hammerstein I's Republic Theater, at 207 West 42d St, were instrumental in the northward shift. The Times Square theater district has long maintained the heaviest concentration of live theater in the United States. In 2003 there were approximately 40 theaters in the Broadway theater district, which is bordered by 41st and 53 Sts and 6th and 9th Aves.

O. J. Gude, a designer of advertising displays, is said to have dubbed the area in 1901 the Great White Way to describe the glow of white lights along Broadway (and later the neon and electric advertising and oversized billboards that illuminate the thoroughfare). Strauss Signs, established in 1897 and since 1931 Artkraft Strauss, has been responsible for much of the spectacular Times Square billboard and electronic scenery over the past century. In 1917 the first large electric display billboard was installed, advertising Wrigley's P. K. chewing sweet, and in 1928 the first moving electric sign wrapped around the Times Tower broadcasting Herbert Hoover's victory in the presidential elections. Many notable advertising events followed, including the Camel sign with its smoking rings (1941), the Bond clothing sign with nearly 2 miles (3 km) of neon (1948), and more recently the world's largest Coca-Cola bottle at 42 feet (12 m) tall (1991). Times Square's illuminated billboards have achieved such prominence that a 1987 zoning ordinance requires new buildings in the area to be covered with them.

In the 1930s the depression led to a sharp decline in theater attendance, and many businesses in the area were replaced by burlesque and peep shows. After World War II the neighborhood declined in its overall prosperity because it no longer could sustain itself as purely an entertainment district. In 1969, in an effort to create incentives to restore the decaying theaters and to encourage residential housing, the Times Square Special Theater District Zoning was created. Despite these efforts, by the mid-1970s many tourists avoided Times Square, which had become a seedy, crime-ridden, and drug-infested place. The Broadway shows went on, but Times Square was no longer a popular destination for recreation and commercial exchange. The 1969 film *Midnight Cowboy,* much of it shot in Times Square, is a graphic illustration of the neighborhood's deterioration.

The first abortive attempt at revitalization, the 42d Street Redevelopment Plan, came in the early 1980s with the never realized plans for four buildings, designed by Philip Johnson and John Burgee, with 4.1 million ft² (381,000 m²) of office space. In the 1990s the revival developed in earnest, with the erection of the Reuters, Conde Nast, and Bertelsmann AG buildings, and the Walt Disney Co reopening the New Amsterdam Theatre in 1997. At the same time most of the X-rated cinemas and peep shows were forced to close. Although some critics feel that the new Times Square has exchanged some of its former gritty vitality for a new faceless corporate facade, there can be no doubt that by most measures the renewal has been a great success, with millions of out-of-towners again flocking there annually.

Delany, Samuel. *Times Square Red, Times Square Blue* (New York: New York Univ Press, 2001)

Reichl, J. Alexander. *Reconstructing Times Square: Politics and Culture in Urban Development* (Lawrence: Univ Press of Kansas, 2000)

Sagalyn, B. Lynne. *Times Square Roulette: Remaking the City Icon* (Cambridge, Mass: MIT Press, 2001)

Taylor, William R. *Inventing Times Square: Commerce and Culture at the Crossroads of the World* (Baltimore: Johns Hopkins Univ Press, 1996)

Leonard Benardo

Timon, John (*b* Conewago, Pa, 12 Feb 1797; *d* Buffalo, 16 Apr 1867). Roman Catholic bishop. Timon and his family moved frequently during his childhood, from Baltimore to Louisville, Ky, to St. Louis. After he was ordained in 1826, Timon was a missionary in Missouri and parts of the Southwest, and in 1835 he became the national superior of the Vincentian religious order in the United States. In 1847 Timon was named the first bishop of Buffalo. A brash, dogmatic administrator, Timon clashed with both the German Catholic community and the Protestants in Buffalo. He was devoted to children and to the poor and established three orphanages, a hospital, two colleges, and a number of parish schools. These institutions survive in the work of the Sisters of Charity, Sisters of Mercy, and other religious orders. During the Civil War Timon was an ardent Unionist and helped to stifle draft riots in his diocese. He died from an illness contracted while visiting the hospital he had established.

Deuther, Charles G. *The Life and Times of the Rt. Rev. John Timon, D.D., First Roman Catholic Bishop of the Diocese of Buffalo* (Buffalo: Author, 1870)

Timothy Walch

Tin Pan Alley. Manhattan district where the music publishing industry was concentrated, originally (*ca* 1895–1910) West 28th St between 6th Ave and Broadway. The term also refers to the industry itself and the types of light entertainment music it produced, especially from 1890 to 1940. Supposedly coined by songwriter and journalist Monroe Rosenfeld, the name was inspired by the sound of many tinny pianos being played simultaneously by "song pluggers" (demonstrators) in the offices lining the street. Tin Pan Alley represented a great intensification of the post–Civil War era music industry. Its first golden age was from about 1892 through the 1920s, and the major publishers included M. Witmark and Sons; Leo Feist, Inc; Shapiro, Bernstein and Co; and Jerome Remick and Co. The music industry gradually followed the theaters uptown, relocating to the Times Square area around 1910. Songwriters penning major hits included brothers Harry ("Wait Till the Sun Shines Nellie," 1905) and Al ("Take Me Out to the Ballgame," 1908) Von Tilzer, George M. Cohan ("Give My Regards to Broadway," 1904), Paul Dresser ("My Gal Sal," 1905), Jack Norworth ("Shine on Harvest Moon," 1908), Jerome Kern, and Irving Berlin. Great African American songwriters of the period included Bob Cole and the brothers James Weldon and J. Rosamond Johnson ("Under the Bamboo Tree," 1902), and Shelton Brooks ("Some of These Days," 1910).

By the mid-1930s, as most of the major firms sold out, Tin Pan Alley began to disperse and, with the rise of rock and roll in the 1950s, began to fade into insignificance. A final group of important Tin Pan Alley songwriters produced hits for singing groups such as the Coasters and the Drifters *ca* 1955–60. At that time the stretch of Broadway from 49th to 53d St, including the famous Brill Building at 1619 Broadway, headquartered songwriters including the teams of Gerry Goffin and Carole King, Barry Mann and Cynthia Weil, and Jerry Leiber and Mike Stoller.

Goldberg, Isaac. *Tin Pan Alley* (New York: John Day, 1930)

Jasen, David A. *Tin Pan Alley* (New York: Donald Fine, 1988)

Witmark, Isidore. *From Ragtime to Swingtime* (New York: Leo Furman, 1939)

Elliott S. Hurwitt

Tioga. Town (pop 4,840) in S central Tioga Co. Settled *ca* 1785, the town was formed in 1791 as Owego; the name was changed to Tioga in 1813. Lumbering and tanneries were early industries, but both had largely ended by the late 19th century. The Erie Railroad came through in 1849 and the Southern Central Railroad in 1872. Pruning shears were a Tioga product, manufactured by Tiffany Pruner (1891–1947) and Coleman Pruning Shears (1947–90). Landmarks have included the Glenmary Sanitarium (1889–1941), the Shangri-La Motor Speedway (1946–; now Tioga Speedway), and the Skyline Amusement Park (1962–84). While land use for farms continues, most residents commute to Elmira and the area of the Triple Cities (Binghamton, Endicott, and Johnson City in Broome Co).

Joann Lindstrom

Tioga County (519 mi²/1,344 km²; pop 51,784). Created in 1791, Tioga Co originally included all of Broome and Chemung and parts of Chenango and Tompkins Cos. The most recent boundary change occurred in 1836. The county is divided into nine towns containing six incorporated villages. The Village of Owego serves as county seat. The county lies entirely within the Susquehanna Hills subregion of the extensive Appalachian Upland physiographic region. Elevations range from 750 feet (229 m) east of Waverly, where the Susquehanna River exits the county, to more than 1,995 feet (608 m) in the Town of Richford. Bedrock consists of Devonian shale and sandstone. The county was glaciated in its entirety, as evidenced by several substantial valleys that run north-south and join the more imposing, glacially modified Susquehanna Valley cutting east-west across the region. These same valleys contain areas of rich alluvial soils that are the most arable in the county. In contrast, the thin upland soils derived from glacial till are of limited agricultural value. Located within the Susquehanna watershed, surface waters flow south via Catatonk, Cayuta, and Owego Creeks and numerous lesser streams to the southwesterly flowing Susquehanna River.

The county's climate is humid-continental. The southwest corner near Waverly tends to have the warmest temperatures: the mean January temperature is 23°F (-5°C), but nighttime lows will on occasion drop below 0°F (-18°C); the mean July temperature is 70°F (21°C), but a few afternoon highs above 90°F (32°C) can be expected every summer. Elsewhere averages are typically a few degrees cooler, depending largely upon elevation. Average seasonal snowfall

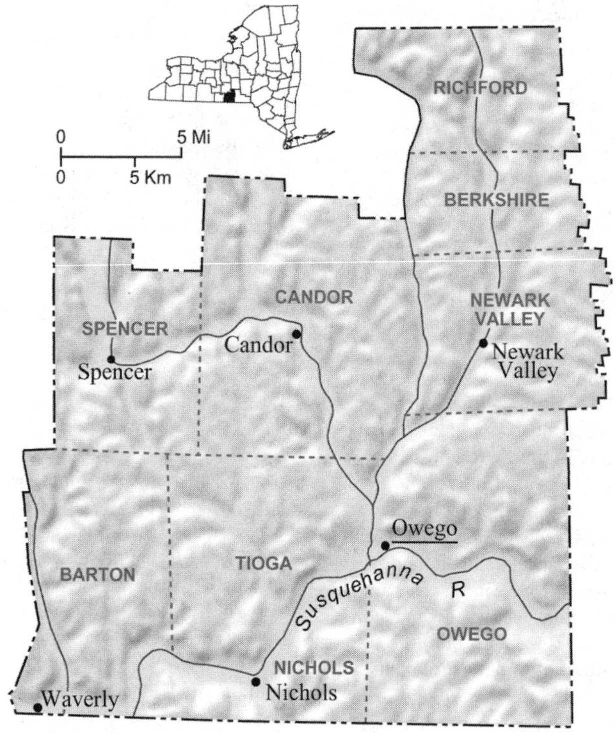

ranges from 39 inches (99 cm) in the southwest to 74 inches (188 cm) in the higher elevations of the northeast. Primeval forest cover varied with elevation and soils. An Alleghenian hardwood community dominated by beech, sugar maple, hemlock, white pine, and basswood blanketed all of the uplands and the smaller valleys, while a deciduous oak-chestnut forest with red maple and tulip poplar covered the Susquehanna and Cayuta Valleys. In the early 21st century nearly 60% of Tioga Co is covered by hardwood forest, parts of which are being selectively harvested.

American Indians and Early Settlement

Archaeological evidence discovered in Nichols indicates the earliest human activity in Tioga Co took place 11,000–12,000 BP. Owasco culture flourished in the area from AD 1100 to 1350, when it was supplanted by the forerunners of the modern Iroquois. By the early 18th century there was an Onondaga village at Ahwaga [now in Owego], while smaller Cayuga settlements were noted nearby during the Sullivan-Clinton campaign. In August 1779 Gen James Clinton's troops burned Ahwaga and destroyed its apple orchards and standing crops, some of which were destined to feed British troops. Lt Erkuries Beatty and other diarists among the troops noted the Fitzgerald farm on the south side of the Susquehanna in the present-day Town of Nichols, though no house remained there at the time they passed through. Forced to flee the region, the native inhabitants made a strong effort to return at war's end, but few remained after 1800. The Onondaga and Cayuga ceded their lands in what is now Tioga Co to the State of New York in 1788 and 1789, respectively.

In 1786 the dispute between New York and Massachusetts concerning ownership of lands west of the Proclamation Line of 1763 was resolved, and Massachusetts acquired a large tract of land that became known as the Boston Purchase or Boston Ten Towns. Roughly half of the 230,400-acre (93,240 ha) Ten Towns tract lies within northeastern Tioga Co. Massachusetts quickly sold the entire tract to a 60-member company led by Samuel Brown. The northwestern part of the county was within the Watkins and Flint Purchase (1794), the southwest part was in the township of Chemung, and the southeast part was encompassed by four small grants, one of which, Coxe's Manor (1775), had been given to the Coxe family before the Revolution in exchange for their rights to lands in Georgia and the Carolinas.

The first permanent white settlers preceded most of the land grants. A vanguard of Connecticut Yankees migrated north from Pennsylvania's Wyoming Valley in 1785 and settled along Pipe Creek in the Town of Tioga. Other settlers soon followed, taking up land by 1794 in each of the county's towns except Richford, which was unoccupied until some time before 1808. Settlers from Connecticut, western Massachusetts, Pennsylvania, New Jersey, and New York's Hudson Valley were substantial in the early wave of immigration. Nearly all were drawn to the quality alluvial soils of the larger valley bottoms, especially the Susquehanna's. Clusters of settlement were soon evident at Owego and at sites of other future villages in the region. By 1800 the county's population was nearly 7,000. As the central places grew, some, like Richford, Berkshire, and Newark Valley, with their central green spaces, took on characteristics reminiscent of many settlers' home region of New England. Population growth continued, most dramatically during the 1810s and 1820s. Irish and German ethnic communities took root during the 1840s: the Irish in thriving villages like Owego and Waverly, the Germans, from the French-governed provinces of Alsace and Lorraine, on farms near Tioga Center. By the mid–19th century the population of the county approached 25,000.

Economic Development

Agriculture and forest exploitation were the basis of the economy during the first half of the 19th century. Settlers focused on growing wheat and feed crops and raising livestock. Timber, plaster, and some surplus crops were shipped

TIOGA CO POPULATION CENSUS FIGURES

	White	Nonwhite	Total Population	Foreign-Born
1800	6,829	50	6,879	—
1810	7,799	100	7,899	—
1820	16,835	136	16,971	59
1830	27,527	163	27,690	66
1840	20,365	162	20,527	—
1850	24,683	197	24,880	973
1860	28,500	248	28,748	1,697
1870	30,206	366	30,572	1,902
1880	32,228	445	32,673	1,637
1890	29,572	363	29,935	1,434
1900	27,641	310	27,951	1,049
1910	25,379	245	25,624	925
1920	24,051	161	24,212	1,212
1930	25,329	151	25,480	1,329
1940	26,907	165	27,072	1,199
1950	29,984	182	30,166	1,233
1960	37,588	214	37,802	964
1970	46,076	437	46,513	894
1980	49,192	620	49,812	1,043
1990	51,646	691	52,337	990
2000	50,501	1,283	51,784	872

Notes: "Nonwhite" includes African Americans, Asians, American Indians, and Pacific Islanders and, for 2000, also the mixed race and other race categories. Through the 1960 census these figures primarily reflect the African American population. Foreign-born figures for 1820 and 1830 include only those not naturalized, and for 1930 and 1950, the foreign-born totals include Whites only. Other years include all foreign-born in the population.

POPULATIONS OF TOWNS, TIOGA CO

Town, Year Founded	1800	1840	1880	1920	1960	2000
Barton, 1824	—	2,324	5,825	6,746	8,365	9,066
Berkshire, 1808	—	956	1,304	805	953	1,366
Candor, 1811	—	3,370	4,323	2,639	3,488	5,317
Newark Valley, 1823[a]	—	1,616	2,577	1,889	2,880	4,097
Nichols, 1824	—	1,986	1,709	1,392	1,998	2,584
Owego, 1791	1,284	5,340	9,884	6,707	14,710	20,365
Richford, 1831[b]	—	939	1,477	831	804	1,170
Spencer, 1806	—	1,532	2,382	1,526	1,790	2,979
Tioga, 1800	751	2,464	3,192	1,677	2,814	4,840

Note: In 1800 Tioga Co included the Towns of Chenango, Lisle, and Union [now in Broome Co]; the Towns of Chemung and Elmira [then Newtown; now in Chemung Co]; and the Town of Catharine [now in Schuyler Co].

[a]Westville until 1824.

[b]Arlington until 1832.

down the Susquehanna to Pennsylvania and Chesapeake markets. Some livestock followed the same route, while some was driven east over turnpikes and other roads to Hudson Valley markets. Timber was harvested and shipped as rafts down the Susquehanna both "in the round" and as sawn lumber and shingles; stands of hemlock were felled and stripped of their bark for use in tanneries. As late as 1840 Tioga Co ranked among the state's top three counties in the value of furs harvested. Ginseng was also gathered and sold. The Susquehanna River was a primary southward transportation artery for bulk goods from the time of initial settlement until after the mid–19th century. Besides the Susquehanna and Bath Turnpike, locally known as the Catskill Turnpike, early roads included the Ithaca and Owego Turnpike, which opened in 1808 and was reported to have carried upward of 500 wagon loads a day of lumber, gypsum, salt, and farm products destined for points south on the Susquehanna. Although not a turnpike, the River Rd followed the Susquehanna. In 1834 the Ithaca and Owego Railroad, the second railroad chartered in the state, began operating using horses for motive power. The main line of the New York and Erie Railroad was built across the county in 1849, providing a connection to New York City. In 1850 there were 2,026 farms operating in Tioga Co. The Bank of Tioga, the first in the county, opened in Owego in 1856.

The economy expanded and diversified after midcentury. Additional rail lines were built during the 1870s: Waverly to Ithaca (1870), Waverly to Owego and northward (1871–72), a line from Elmira to Ithaca crossing the county's northern towns (1874), and the Delaware, Lackawanna and Western (1882), running parallel to the Erie. Most of the lines were eventually sold to the Lackawanna or the Lehigh Valley Railroads. Expanded rail service prompted increasing numbers of farmers to turn to fluid-milk production, and creameries were built along the rail network beginning in the 1870s. One of the largest was the Borden Co (1906–51, then Crowley until 1971) in Nichols; at its height it received as much as 2 million pounds (900,000 kg) of milk monthly. The Standard Butter Co (1888–1921) in Owego produced as much as 3 million pounds (1.4 million kg) annually, using milk supplied in part by 20 company-owned creameries. Some farmers in the Owego area began cultivating tobacco for local cigar production. The tanning industry declined after 1850, but a variety of manufacturing firms began about the same time. Late 19th-century products included wooden goods such as rakes, butter tubs, and chairs. Iron bridges, pianos, and wagons were made in Owego. The county's population fluctuated between 25,000 and 33,000 during the period.

Religion, Education, and Culture

Congregations organized in several of the county's present-day towns in 1796. In 1855 there were 18 Methodist, 11 Baptist, 5 Congregational, and 3 Presbyterian churches. The first Roman Catholic church, St. Patrick's, was organized by 1844 by Irish immigrants. While there is no synagogue in the county, there have long been Jewish residents; in 1941 Congregation Beth Israel served Jews living in four communities on both sides of the state line near Waverly. School centralization began in 1930 with the Newark Valley Central School District. Five other central districts followed, the last being Waverly in 1957. The county has no colleges within its borders.

The first newspaper was the *American Farmer,* published at Owego in 1810. In the early 21st century local news is provided by the *Tioga County Courier,* published at Owego, the *Candor Chronicle,* and the *Random Harvest Weekly,* which covers the northern towns. WEBO-AM (1957) in Owego is the only radio station. The Tioga County Historical Society operates a museum in Owego, and the Newark Valley Historical Society's maintains the Bement-Billings Farmstead living history museum in Newark Valley, along with a historic railroad depot, a stop on the Tioga Scenic Railroad excursions. The Tioga County Council on the Arts, based in Owego, presents cultural programs.

Politics

Tioga Co has a longstanding record of voting Republican. In 1972 the Board of Supervisors, an original feature of the county government, was replaced by a nine-member legislature elected from seven districts. Daily operations are overseen by a manager appointed by the county legislature. Two Tioga Co natives rose to national political influence during the second half of the 19th century. Thomas C. Platt (1833–1910) was a two-term state congressman (1873–77), chairman of the Republican state convention (1877), and US senator (1881, 1897–1909). Known as the "Easy Boss" of the state's Republican Party, he became one of the most influential figures in Republican national politics. Benjamin Franklin Tracy (1830–1915), Platt's lifelong friend, was a Tioga Co district attorney (1853–59) and state assemblyman (1862) before joining the 109th New York Volunteers; he later served as commandant of the Elmira Prison Camp and was named secretary of the navy in Benjamin Harrison's administration (1889–93). Other prominent natives and residents have included Woodbridge Ferris (1853–1928), governor of Michigan (1913–16) and US senator (1923–28), born in Spencer; industrialist John D. Rockefeller Sr (1839–1937), born in Richford; and Henry M. Robert (1837–1923), author of *Robert's Rules of Order,* who resided in Owego from the 1890s until his death.

The 20th Century

In 1900 Tioga Co had over 3,000 farms. Most were dairy operations producing fluid milk, which was shipped to creameries for processing into butter and cheese. Potatoes, buckwheat, and honey were other important cash crops. But there were some major changes in the agricultural sector in the 20th century. Total farm acreage dropped by two-thirds, but the number of active farm operations declined far more precipitously, to 497 in 1997. This meant that the average farm doubled in size at the same time that extensive areas of the countryside reverted to second-growth forest. Farm sales early in the century resulted in the establishment of rural ethnic enclaves. Finntown in Spencer began when Finns were actively recruited to settle starting in 1910. The Finnish presence remains evident in the saunas many built on their farmsteads. During the same period Poles settled on farms in the northeastern part of the county. In 1919 there were 186 Polish and Ukrainian families there, and an Owego agent was advertising for more.

Factories producing consumer goods were scattered across the county in the early 20th century. In Newark Valley, J. S. Kemp (later International Harvester Co) made manure spreaders (1901–12) and Chesebro Whitman Co made ladders (1922–93). Nichols Knitting Mills (*ca* 1900–1920) and Johnson and Son Furniture Co (1908–48) provided employment in Nichols. Candor boasted the Wands Glove Co (1895–1958) and the Ironclad blanket factory, which closed *ca* 1920 after a long history. Tiffany Pruner (1891–1947) and Coleman Pruning Shears (1947–90) were located in Tioga. In 1925 Endicott Johnson (shoes and leather) opened a factory in Owego, and Stakmore Chair Co began operations there the following year.

Clark Seed Farms of Richford was established in 1941 and ultimately grew 100,000 bushels (3,525,000 l) of seed potatoes on 400 acres (160 ha) of hilltop land. Operations ceased around 1972. Despite the general contraction of farming in this agriculturally oriented county, the population nearly doubled during the 20th century, to more than 50,000 residents. The most dramatic increases occurred during the 1950s and 1960s, when small factories like Wands Glove Co and Borden's milk plant in Newark Valley were closing. The population increase was partly because of the opening of a large IBM military products facility at Owego in 1958 that grew to employ 5,000 people and contributed to the electronics and computer guidance systems used in the Gemini, Saturn I, and Apollo space programs. Ingersoll-Rand (tools) opened a plant at Waverly in 1974 but closed it 10 years later.

Other county residents commuted to jobs in Broome Co, Ithaca, Elmira, Cortland, or Sayre, Pa, a travel pattern reinforced by the opening of the Southern Tier Expressway (Rte 17/I-86) from Binghamton as far as Nichols in 1969, and on to Waverly in 1973. In more recent years rail lines have been abandoned and service curtailed; in 2003 Norfolk Southern Railway and a short line, the Owego and Harford, remained in operation. Closure of the Endicott Johnson factory at Owego in 1986 was counterbalanced in part by IBM subcontractors such as Hadco and Sanmina-SCI Corp (printed circuit boards), which established production facilities in the area. The IBM plant changed hands twice in the 1990s, becoming the Lockheed Martin Systems Integration Facility in 1996. Tioga Co experienced a decline in population—the first since World War I—of just over 1% in the 1990s.

The standard source is [Henry B. Peirce and D. Hamilton Hurd], *History of Tioga, Chemung, Tompkins and Schuyler Counties* (1879), the so-called Four County History. Additional material is found in W. B. Gay, *Historical Gazetteer of Tioga County* (1888) and Leroy W. Kingman, ed., *Our County and Its People* (1897). Tioga is one of the few counties with a modern and comprehensive history: Thomas C. McEnteer, ed., *Seasons of Change: An Updated History of Tioga County* (1990). Old but useful town histories include LeRoy W. Kingman, *Owego* (1907) and Charles L. Albertson, *History of Waverly, NY and Vicinity* (1943). Hilda R. Watrous, *Owego Reflections 1887–1987* (1994) adopts the device of surveying the community's history at 10-year intervals. The region's early development is placed in a broader context by Peter Mancall, *Valley of Opportunity: Economic Culture along the Upper Susquehanna, 1700–1800* (1991). Somewhat dated but still a very useful and comprehensive description of the county's physical environment is Clarence Lounsbury, et al, *Soil Survey of Tioga County, New York* (1953).

Richard E. Quest and Heidi Canavan

Tivoli. Village (pop 1,163) in Red Hook (Dutchess Co). Settled *ca* 1715, it became an important landing for a ferry that operated until 1938 and a site for brick making, small textile mills, and a modest freighting business. A French immigrant, Peter de Labigarre, planned a 60-acre (24.3 ha) plat in the 1790s. While never fully developed, it became home to commercial fishers and, after the Hudson River Railroad came through in 1851, to railroad workers. Later it had box, barrel, and hat factories. The village incorporated in 1872, joining the old hamlets of Tivoli and Madalin (formerly Myersville). In decline since the late 19th century, its recent rejuvenation has attracted new residents and tourist-related businesses.

William P. McDermott

tobacco industry and smoking. Tobacco is a crop that grows natively in New York State. Iroquois ceremonials often include the use of special locally grown tobacco. The Dutch West India Co used the abundance of tobacco to encourage migration to New Amsterdam. In what is now Brooklyn the first recorded property sale was for a Gowanus tobacco plantation (1639), a Dutch governor resided on a Canarsie tobacco farm, and tobacco trading flourished in Greenpoint and Gravesend. New York soils did not produce sweet tobacco, but the strong, glossy, and smooth leaf of the Connecticut Broadleaf, Duck Island, and Spanish Seed varieties were ideal for wrapping cigars.

SNUFF, CHEW, AND CIGARS

Colonial era farmers were unable to alter geography to make tobacco growing as profitable in New York as in the Chesapeake region; instead, attention turned to creating tobacco products for mass consumption using leaf grown elsewhere. Manhattan boasted several tobacconists during the 18th century, and in 1760 Pierre Lorillard opened a snuff manufactory near present-day Park Row in Lower Manhattan. Lorillard was the first to use tanned animal bladder to ensure snuff's freshness, and he launched the nation's first tobacco advertising campaign during the late 1780s. A later Lorillard snuff mill in what is now the New York Botanical Gardens in the Bronx is a city landmark. By the 1830s snuff use began to wane, and the company pioneered direct-mail selling of plug tobacco; its "eating" chews included the famed Sailors Delight. Lorillard sold 10% of all American plug tobacco by the 1870s, and the state ranked second only to Virginia in plug production until 1900. As with the cotton trade, New York City's money, skilled labor, and sales ability facilitated its control of tobacco distribution in America before 1860. Metropolitan tobacco factors provided finished products to wholesalers throughout the nation. Their defaults during the Panic of 1857 caused production shutdowns in Virginia and fostered anti-Yankee outrage. During the Civil War border states redirected their tobacco crops to Manhattan cigar makers, and after 1865 New York agents continued to purchase prime leaf at Danville, Lynchburg, and Richmond, Va.

Gradually the cigar became New York City's major tobacco product. Using a workforce composed largely of European immigrants (first German, then Russian and Bohemian), Manhattan replaced Philadelphia as the prime cigar manufacturing site by 1865 and dominated America's trade for 50 years. Cigar making was decentralized work, literally thousands of small firms participated, employing molders in both overcrowded workshops and tenement apartments. Appalling working conditions fostered labor organization, and the Cigar Makers International Union led strike actions in 1869, 1873, and 1877. In 1886 Samuel Gompers, head of Local #144 of the cigar makers in New York City, became the first president of the American Federation of Labor (AFL); a third of the AFL's original members were cigar makers. Jacob Riis's *How the Other Half Lives* (1890) documented, with regard to cigar making, "slavery as real as any that ever disgraced the South."

The industry thrived, though, and New Yorkers created machinery that quickened the cigar-making process, including the mold, the bunch maker, and the suction table. Inventions patented by Oscar Hammerstein I financed his theatrical endeavors, and the sale proceeds from the *United States Tobacco Journal* (now *US Distribution Journal*), which he founded and edited from 1874 to 1888, financed a Manhattan opera house. Beyond New York City, cigar manufacturing reinvigorated the cultivation of tobacco, and the Chemung Valley, Onondaga Co, and Binghamton areas provided substantial quantities of hard-to-grow wrapping leaf. In 1880 New York State workers rolled one-third of all American cigars, and as late as 1900 Binghamton factories employed 5,000 cigar makers. New York in 1900 manufactured 20% of all tobacco products sold in the nation.

THE CIGARETTE INDUSTRY

Perhaps New York State's most dramatic role in the history of smoking was its decisive part in creating the cigarette industry. The first American cigarettes, hand rolled in Manhattan after 1860 by immigrant laborers using Turkish leaf, soon became popular enough to be taxed by the government (1864). In 1868 the Bedrossian Brothers blended American-grown Bright tobacco with Turkish, creating a cigarette favored by Manhattan's carriage trade. Elite city residents preferred aromatic Turkish blends for another 50 years, but most smokers selected cigarettes with mostly domestic tobacco. William Kimball's Peerless Tobacco Works in Rochester soon dominated that market, and his

Workers in tobacco field near Fitch's Bridge in Chemung Valley, *ca* 1890.

several brands accounted for one-sixth of all cigarette sales by 1880. America's single largest brand was Frank Kinney's Sweet Caporals, offering a hint of Turkish leaf amid domestic Bright. Kinney created Sweet Caps in Manhattan, but by 1880 he and Lewis Ginter, another New York cigarette entrepreneur, relocated closer to supplies in Richmond. Nevertheless, New York dominated the cigarette portion of tobacco usage, in 1880 producing 385 million of the 500 million smoked by Americans.

Like cigars, cigarettes were largely a hand-rolled product until the 1880s. Mechanizing the industry was the accomplishment of James Buchanan Duke, owner-manager of a prosperous North Carolina company who moved to Manhattan in 1884. Duke himself smoked only cigars and considered cigarettes a fad, but his products included Duke of Durham cigarettes hand rolled by Jewish workers he had recruited in New York City. Duke first experimented with machine production in Durham, and in April 1885 he installed Bonsack cigarette machines at his Rivington St factory on the Lower East Side. Although cigarettes constituted only 1% of national tobacco use, Duke believed they were particularly suited to the rapid pace of metropolitan living. He offered a variety of brands—Cameo, Cyclone, Cross-Cut, and Duke of Durham—and spent $800,000 in 1889 alone to advertise them. He also placed free "Sporting Girls" trading cards in cigarette packages. Mechanization and advertising made Duke America's largest manufacturer of cigarettes, and in 1890 he forced four major rivals (Kinney, Kimball, Ginter, and Goodwin and Co) to unite. Duke's American Tobacco Co then waged plug and snuff wars to obtain control of the rest of the industry. Only cigar making, insulated by brand loyalty and decentralized hand processing, resisted Duke's cartelization. By 1904 the "tobacco trust" manufactured 88% of US cigarettes, 90% of snuff, 80% of chew, and 75% of pipe tobacco. In 1911 the federal government ordered the corporation dissolved and appointed Duke to restructure it into 16 "competing" firms. Manhattan remained the corporate headquarters for industry giants like American Tobacco and Lorillard, but manufacturing facilities gradually shifted southward.

From 1910 to 1920 cigarette production increased sevenfold. Taking advantage of mechanization, wartime, and changing social customs, the "fag" became practically universal and the preferred mode of tobacco use. In the mature industry of the 1920s no single company dominated sales, but all manufacturers used Madison Ave advertising techniques to compete for an ever increasing market. Advertising genius George Washington Hill promoted American Tobacco's Lucky Strikes against R. J. Reynolds's Camels and Liggett and Myers's Chesterfields. In an era of national brands, the Big Three often sold 90% of all cigarettes virtually without price competition. Hill, who proudly grew tobacco at his Irvington (Westchester Co) mansion, was also responsible for introducing Pall Mall, the first king-size cigarette (1939). A latecomer to the competition was the Philip Morris Co and, in a unique advertising campaign beginning in 1933, page boy Johnny Roventini of the New Yorker hotel became a living trademark for its name brand. By 1950 advertising made Philip Morris so successful that it held 11% of the national market. Although the Supreme Court in *American Tobacco Co v United States* (1946) upheld fines against an industry that operated in price lockstep, it did not order corporate breakups. Cigarette manufacturing operated and prospered essentially without price competition.

Health Concerns

From colonial times some New Yorkers opposed the use of tobacco for both moral and health reasons. Dutch director Willem Kieft issued a no-smoking edict in 1639, but over the next two centuries tobacco use became ingrained in American culture. During the 19th century temperance advocates always condemned tobacco use. The Woman's Christian Temperance Union called for the prohibition of cigarettes as early as 1887, and in 1892 the *New York Times* reported that the state senate was deluged with "petitions against cigarettes." Although the Anti-Cigarette League was founded in Manhattan in 1894, New York State never joined 13 other states in a total ban on cigarette sales. However, in 1898 the New York City Board of Aldermen did ban the sale of cigarettes to minors under 18. Agitation continued until an attempt to extend the prohibition to women failed because of a mayoral veto in 1908. The work of Charles Pease and his Non-Smoker Protective League in the early 20th century led to smoking bans on public transportation, but further limitations failed as Americans smoked their way through two world wars.

Not until the 1950s was tobacco effectively linked to deteriorating health. Cigarette advertising often emphasized health advantages from smoking, but accumulating medical studies and constant articles in the New York–based *Reader's Digest* raised troubling questions. Filtered Marlboros, introduced by New York–based Philip Morris in 1955, became the nation's favorite smoke by 1975 and the world's best-selling consumer product by the 1990s. After 1964 a succession of surgeon general reports documented the relationship between smoking and various diseases, and the *New York Times* led a campaign to place health warnings on cigarette packages. The beleaguered industry voluntarily ended radio and television advertising on 1 Jan 1971. After 1970 "Big Tobacco" companies evolved into multiproduct conglomerates and sought respectability through sponsorship of cultural and sporting events. The word tobacco was excised from corporate names, and public concern led to the elimination of advertisements directed at teenagers. From the 1980s New York State led efforts to regulate tobacco sales and use, and legislated the nation's highest cigarette tax ($1.50 per pack in 2002). The state participated when the industry settled healthcare claims in 1998 and will receive $25 billion over 20 years, with 26.7% of the money going to New York City.

See also Binghamton.

Downey, Fairfax Davis. *Lorillard and Tobacco* ([New York]: P. Lorillard, 1951)

Kluger, Richard. *Ashes to Ashes: America's 100-Year Cigarette War, the Public Health, and the Unabashed Triumph of Philip Morris* (New York: Vintage Books, 1997)

Robert, Joseph C. *The Story of Tobacco in America* (Chapel Hill: Univ of North Carolina Press, 1967)

Tate, Cassandra. *Cigarette Wars: The Triumph of "The Little White Slaver"* (New York: Oxford Univ Press, 1999)

George J. Lankevich

NEW YORK STATE CIGARETTE TAX RATES

Effective Dates	Cents per Pack[a]
1939–31 Mar 1959	2
1 Apr 1959–31 Mar 1965	5
1 Apr 1965–31 May 1968	10
1 Jun 1968–31 Jan 1972	12
1 Feb 1972–31 Mar 1983	15
1 Apr 1983–30 Apr 1989	21
1 May 1989–31 May 1990	33
1 Jun 1990–31 May 1993	39
1 Jun 1993–29 Feb 2000	56
1 Mar 2000–2 Apr 2002	111
3 Apr 2002–31 Dec 2002	150

Source: NYS Department of Taxation and Finance, Office of Tax Policy Analysis, *New York State Tax Sourcebook* (2003), Table 60.

[a]For a pack of 20 cigarettes.

Tompkins. Town (pop 1,105) in W Delaware Co. Settled *ca* 1785, the town was formed from Walton in 1806 as Pinefield and renamed Tompkins in 1808. Settlers were occupied with lumbering and rafting and later with dairy farming, quarrying, and wood acid factories. In 1875 Tompkins led the county in population, with 4,138 inhabitants, but the population began to decline in 1880 when the Town of Deposit was formed. The acid factories failed early in the 20th century. Cannonsville Reservoir (1966) inundated several communities and the most fertile and level land, but a few farms have survived. Most residents travel to work in neighboring areas.

Dorothy Kubik

Tompkins, Daniel D. (*b* Fox Meadow [now Scarsdale, Westchester Co], 21 June 1774; *d* Tompkinsville, Richmond Co, 11 June 1825). Governor and US vice president. Later known as the "farmer's boy," he was the son of Sarah Ann Hyatt and Jonathan Griffin Tompkins, a landowning Westchester Co farmer and patriot leader. After attending the Academy of North Salem, Tompkins was admitted to Columbia College as a sophomore and graduated as valedictorian in 1795. Two years later he was admitted to the bar and in 1798 married Hannah Minthorne, daughter of Mangle Minthorne, a wealthy Republican merchant and Tammany leader, whose influence contributed to Tompkins's early political success.

Tompkins subsequently filled positions of increasing responsibility, including federal commissioner of bankruptcy (1800), member of the Constitutional Convention of 1801, assemblyman (1803), and member of the New York State Supreme Court (1804–7). Tompkins was elected governor in 1807, when he ran for the Clintonian sector of the Republican Party and defeated the incumbent Morgan Lewis. Tompkins, an ingratiating man who paid little heed to social distinctions, proved an ideal and enduring candidate. Subsequently he overcame three Federalist contenders: Jonas Platt (1810), Stephen Van Rensselaer (1813), and Rufus King (1816). Though the Jeffersonian-backed Embargo of 1807 proved unpopular in New York State, Tompkins supported the Virginian-dominated national party leadership while pushing for statewide reforms that attested a benevolent concern for poorer New Yorkers. He opposed the death penalty and condemned whipping as a punishment for petit larceny, a penalty that was dropped when the state's laws were revised in 1813. The report of a commission that he appointed in 1811 led to the passage of laws that laid the foundations for a statewide education system reaching down to the town and school district level. Pointing out the cost and inadequacy of care for the mentally ill in rural areas, Tompkins also won legislation that enabled town officers to send individuals to New York Hospital in New York City. In 1817, at his request, the legislature rounded out New York State's gradual emancipation statutes by providing that all slaves born before 4 July 1799 be freed by 4 July 1827. Mindful of the need for American Indian support in the event of hostilities with Great Britain, Tompkins tried, with little lasting success, to protect Iroquois property and land in New York State. In 1812, charging that lobbyists corrupted state legislators to vote for incorporating the Bank of America, he prorogued the state legislature for 55 days. Though the delay did not prevent the eventual chartering of the Bank of America, it did frustrate De Witt Clinton's supporters in the legislature, who could not nominate him for president in a legislative caucus before Congress renominated James Madison, whom Tompkins supported. The breach between Tompkins and Clinton, long chafing under the governor's popularity and deference to the Virginia leadership, had become complete.

Tompkins also proved a dedicated war governor, who sought to strengthen both the fortifications protecting New York City and the militia defending the state's northern and western borders. After the burning of Washington, DC, in 1814, a prowar legislature gave Tompkins the measures for which he called, including the order to raise 12,000 militia. Placed in command of the federal military district encompassing New York City, Tompkins took charge of its defenses and personally guaranteed defense loans. His gubernatorial war efforts prompted Madison to offer Tompkins the post of secretary of state in September 1814, a position he declined. Later that year Tompkins was thrown from his horse while inspecting a Brooklyn Heights fort. He sustained injuries that likely impaired his health and judgment and perhaps contributed to his subsequent drinking problem.

After his 1816 electoral victory, Tompkins sought national prominence. Though New York State's choice in the 1816 presidential contest, he wound up James Monroe's vice president and surrendered the governorship, now easily taken by his rival Clinton. Tompkins, careless about money and now heavily in debt because of his investments in Staten Island real estate and transportation projects, eagerly sought recompense for his wartime financial services to New York State, which included personally backing loans, raising money, and handling government securities. Clintonians, under attack by their Bucktail foes and given scant patronage by the Monroe administration, in 1819 launched a pamphlet assault led by State Comptroller Archibald McIntyre, who denied the integrity of Tompkins's financial accounts and sought to refute the vice president's claim that the state owed him about $130,000. In spite of Martin Van Buren's efforts to dissuade him, Tompkins accepted the Bucktail Republican nomination for governor in 1820. Narrowly defeated by Clinton but reelected vice president, Tompkins presided over the Bucktail-ordained Constitutional Convention of 1821. There he left a somewhat tangled record of support for modest changes, including the broadening of franchise for white males, the vesting of executive veto power in a vaguely defined council, and the retention of existing legislation to free slaves. Because of financial problems and frail health, Tompkins presided over the US Senate only for brief periods during 1819, 1822 and 1823, and 1824. Meanwhile he struggled to hold on to his Staten Island home and farm. Some of the financial relief he continued to seek came from New York State legislation in 1821 and from federal legislation in 1824, two years after a federal court endorsed his claims against the United States. Out of office and drinking ever more heavily, he soon died at his Staten Island home.

See also WAR OF 1812.

Hammond, Jabez D. *The History of Political Parties in the State of New-York from the Ratification of the Federal Constitution to December, 1840*, 2 vols (Albany: Van Benthuysen, 1842)

Irwin, Ray W. *Daniel D. Tompkins: Governor of New York and Vice President of the United States* (New York: New-York Historical Society, 1968)

Craig and Mary L. Hanyan

Tompkins County (476 mi^2/1,233 km^2; pop 96,501). Created in 1817 from Cayuga and Seneca Cos, it is named for Daniel D. Tompkins, governor of New York (1807–17) and US vice president (1817–25). The county's boundaries were adjusted in 1819, 1823, and 1854. Tompkins Co is divided into one city (Ithaca, the county seat) and nine towns containing six incorporated villages. It lies entirely within the Appalachian Upland; the northern half is within the Finger Lakes Hills subregion, the southern half within the Susquehanna Hills subregion. Elevations range from the summit of Connecticut Hill at 2,099 feet (640 m) to the mean water level of Cayuga Lake at 381 feet (116 m). The latter extends diagonally almost halfway across the county. Bedrock consists of southward-dipping Devonian shales and sandstones. The topography in the southern half is generally higher and decidedly more rugged, with steep-sided hills and narrow intervening valleys, while the northern half is characterized by rolling hills whose bases lie 500 or more feet (150 m) above Cayuga Lake. The lake sits in a large, deep, glacially scoured, U-shaped valley that extends well south of the present water body.

The combination of easily eroded bedrock and numerous hanging valley tributaries along the sides of the primary valley near Ithaca has resulted in an exceptional collection of deep, rock-walled, picturesque gorges and a host of impressive waterfalls, including 215 ft (66 m) high Taughannock Falls, the highest in the state. Three of these dramatic valleys are preserved as state parks, namely, Buttermilk Falls, Taughannock Falls, and Robert H. Treman State Parks. At the head of the lake the City of Ithaca lies on the composite delta of four streams: Cascadilla, Fall, and Sixmile Creeks, and Cayuga Inlet. Further south the Valley Heads moraine runs east-west across the breadth of the county, forming a high and wide natural dam across the area's deep valleys and creating a striking, hummocky topography. Surface water flows into Cayuga Lake, except for the headwaters of Owasco Inlet in Groton and portions of the southern margins of the county that lie within the Susquehanna watershed. Soils vary from highly arable limy tills to nonarable gravels. The most highly productive soils are concentrated in the northwest quarter. With few local exceptions the soils in the southern half of the county cannot support viable modern agriculture.

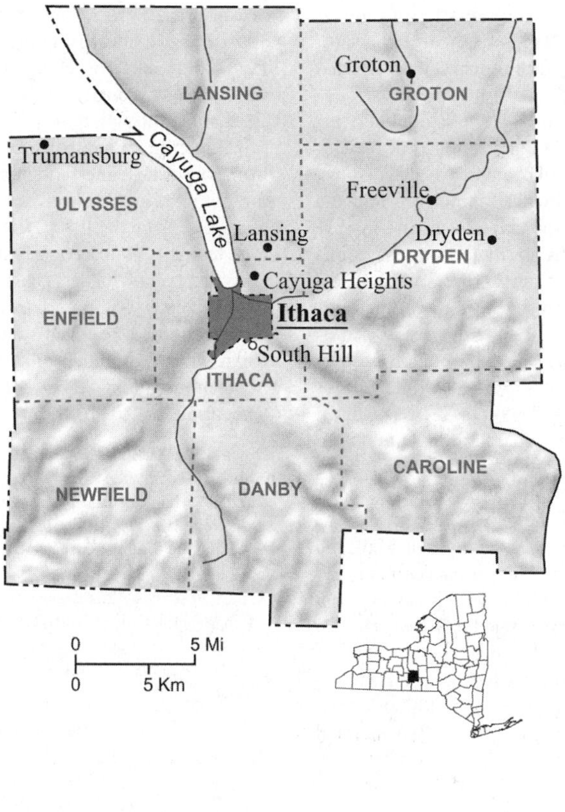

The climate is humid-continental. Mean January temperatures are in the low 20s°F (-7 to -4°C), although nighttime temperatures sometimes approach or fall below 0°F (-18°C). Average July temperatures are in the mid- to upper 60s°F (19 to 21°C), with daytime highs frequently exceeding 80°F (27°C) and sometimes 90°F (32°C). At least 50 inches (127 cm) of snow can be expected annually, more in the higher elevations. Original forest cover consisted of hardwood communities dominated by beech, sugar maple, and to a lesser extent basswood, interspersed with oak, hickory, hemlock, or white pine depending upon soil and moisture conditions.

Settlement

Archaeological evidence indicates that present-day Tompkins Co was occupied 10,000–8,000 BC. Known settlement sites are few and confined to locations near the head of Cayuga Lake and on the uplands to the west. By the early 1600s the area had become Cayuga territory, used primarily for hunting and fishing, although there were two village sites as well. In 1779 their territory was invaded and settlements destroyed by regiments led by Henry Dearborn and William Butler, who, respectively, marched down the west and east sides of Cayuga Lake as part of Maj Gen John Sullivan's campaign against the Iroquois. Few Cayuga returned afterward, and in 1789, by a treaty signed at Albany, they surrendered their Tompkins Co lands to New York State. Within a year the lands were made part of two major tracts: the New Military Tract, which encompassed the county's northern half, and the Watkins and Flint Purchase, which contained the rest. Surveying efforts started in 1790. White settlers began arriving in 1792 to stay, making their way into the area over Indian trails or rough roads ordered by the state. Cut between 1791 and 1793, the roads linked the present location of Ithaca with Owego (Tioga Co) to the south, the site of the Watkins and Flint land office, and Oxford (Chenango Co) to the east. Indian old fields (open land cultivated by the native inhabitants) near the head of Cayuga Lake attracted the first settlers. Other early arrivals were drawn to quality land in the Towns of Dryden, Lansing, and Ulysses. The rugged, less-promising portions of the Watkins and Flint tract further south were occupied last.

The early settlers were predominantly native-born white Americans from New England, New Jersey, Pennsylvania, and the Hudson Valley. The Town of Caroline, for instance, was initially called Dutch Settlement because many residents were Dutch-speaking migrants from Ulster Co. Some came with slaves. Beginning in 1803 several families from Maryland and Virginia also settled in Caroline and Danby, and they too brought slaves. Slavery existed in Tompkins Co until its abolition in New York State in 1827. In the years following, the influx of settlers continued but at a slower pace than was simultaneously occurring in the more famous and accessible Genesee Country. The most rapid growth took place in the 1820s, and by 1840 most towns had reached their highest population levels prior to 1940. There was a significant Irish migration in the 1840s. By 1855 there were 1,177 Irish and 249 Blacks living in the county. Half of each group resided in Ithaca, where they worked primarily as laborers.

Economic Development

Tompkins Co's early economy was based largely on agriculture, and, like settlement, it was slow to develop. Still by 1800 there were sawmills at Ithaca and on Taughannock Creek and gristmills on Taughannock Creek near Trumansburg and on Salmon Creek near Ludlowville. Relative isolation combined with the Embargo Act of 1807 helped prompt further road-building efforts. By 1810 new roads linked Ithaca with Bath (Steuben Co) to the southwest and Geneva (Ontario Co) and the Seneca River to the north. In 1810 the state chartered the Ithaca and Owego Turnpike. Lake traffic increased, and Ithaca became a transshipment point for goods such as salt from Salina (Onondaga Co) moving south. Traffic was substantial. To regulate the teamsters, who sometimes numbered as many as 400 at one time, residents formed the Ithaca Moral Society (?1812–23), which acted as a vigilante committee. The improved road infrastructure helped spawn the growth of central places such as Dryden, Ludlowville, and Trumansburg. By 1820 the portion of the county formerly part of the military tract contained 32 gristmills, 70 sawmills, 34 carding mills, 19 fulling mills, 3 oil mills, 1 paper mill, 1 ironworks, and 3 trip-hammer operations. In 1821 the steamboat *Enterprise* was launched at Ithaca. It made once-a-day round-trip runs the length of the lake and, after 1825, exchanged passengers and cargo bound for the Erie Canal and later the New York Central Railroad at the north end. In 1834 the Ithaca and Owego (later Delaware, Lackawanna and Western), a horse-drawn railway and the second rail line chartered in the state, connected the namesake communities. Later this line was used to haul anthracite to the lakehead, where it was transshipped to barges for distribution north and west. The county's first bank, a branch of the Bank of Newburg, opened prior to 1820. The Bank of Ithaca, the first locally organized bank, opened in 1830. Other businesses included a coverlet factory at Ithaca, which was also an early printing center. The panic of 1837 dashed dreams of a more diversified economy. To stimulate a recovery, in 1840 a group of concerned citizens sent young Ezra Cornell to scout out factories that might relocate in Ithaca, but the effort was unsuccessful. By 1850 there were more than 3,000 farms operating in the county.

The second half of the 19th and the early 20th centuries brought improved transportation, new industrialization, and a major population adjustment. During the 1870s new rail lines, most centering on Ithaca and all ultimately becoming part of the Lehigh Valley Railroad, expanded rail service southward and established three links to the north and one to the east. The rail transportation enhanced access to Cornell University, a significant economic force in the area since its opening in 1868. Ithaca's industrial base diversified in the latter 1800s with glass, paper, and other manufactories. Some succumbed to later consolidation by larger companies. One that did not was Ithaca Gun Co, which was founded in 1883 and remained in Ithaca until it moved to nearby Cayuga Co in 1989. Another well-known Tompkins Co company, Morse Chain, began as Morse Spring Co in Trumansburg in the early 1890s, manufacturing bicycle chains before moving to Ithaca in 1905. It was acquired by Borg-Warner in 1928 and continues to operate as part of the Emerson Power Transmission Corp. By the turn of the 20th century, Groton was home to several typewriter companies, which evolved into Smith Corona, and the Groton Iron Bridge Co. In 1885, while

TOMPKINS CO POPULATION CENSUS FIGURES

	White	Nonwhite	Total Population	Foreign-Born
1820	20,609	72	20,681	20
1830	36,311	234	36,545	166
1840	37,695	253	37,948	—
1850	38,421	325	38,746	1,427
1860	31,112	297	31,409	1,503
1870	32,777	401	33,178	2,127
1880	33,980	465	34,445	2,173
1890	32,520	403	32,923	2,137
1900	33,366	464	33,830	2,076
1910	33,114	533	33,647	2,487
1920	34,787	498	35,285	2,661
1930	40,723	767	41,490	3,263
1940	41,550	790	42,340	2,987
1950	57,958	1,164	59,122	3,386
1960	64,491	1,673	66,164	3,940
1970	73,834	3,045	76,879	4,209
1980	81,455	5,630	87,085	6,124
1990	85,085	9,012	94,097	8,000
2000	82,507	13,994	96,501	10,166

Notes: "Nonwhite" includes African Americans, Asians, American Indians, and Pacific Islanders and, for 2000, also the mixed race and other race categories. Through the 1960 census these figures primarily reflect the African American population. Foreign-born figures for 1820 and 1830 include only those not naturalized, and for 1930 and 1950, the foreign-born totals include Whites only. Other years include all foreign-born in the population.

POPULATIONS OF TOWNS AND CITIES, TOMPKINS CO

Town or City, Year Founded	1800	1840	1880	1920	1960	2000
Caroline, 1811	—	2,457	2,171	1,542	2,118	2,910
Danby, 1811	—	2,570	2,065	1,143	2,059	3,007
Dryden, 1803	—	5,446	4,805	3,186	7,353	13,532
Enfield, 1821	—	2,340	1,690	867	1,573	3,369
Groton, 1817[a]	—	3,618	3,450	4,122	4,469	5,794
Ithaca, 1821	—	5,650	11,198	1,480	9,072	18,198
Ithaca (city), 1888	—	—	—	17,004	28,799	29,287
Lansing, 1817	—	3,672	3,000	2,380	4,221	10,521
Newfield, 1811[b]	—	3,567	2,608	1,456	2,193	5,108
Ulysses, 1794	927	2,976	3,458	2,105	4,307	4,775

Notes: In 1800 the Town of Ulysses was part of Cayuga Co. In 1840 Tompkins Co included the Town of Hector [now in Schuyler Co].

[a]Division until 1818.

[b]Cayuta until 1822.

natural gas deposits were being explored, a large salt deposit was discovered beneath Ithaca and the surrounding area. In 1921 Cayuga Rock Salt Co began mining operations in Lansing. Cargill Corp purchased the operation in 1970, and it is presently the deepest salt mine in the country at 2,400 feet (732 m) below Cayuga Lake. In 1900 Tompkins Co contained 3,270 farms that averaged 87 acres (35 ha).

Rev John Perkins's comment of 1827 that Ithaca "is the most fluctuating place I was ever in. So much coming and going" could be said for much of the 19th and 20th centuries. Between 1850 and 1940 Tompkin Co's population fluctuated between 31,000 and 42,000 residents. Only the Village of Ithaca (a city after 1888) experienced a steady population increase over the period. Most of the towns reached their pre-1940 peak population between 1830 and 1860. The declines were often dramatic. The Town of Newfield, for example, with its marginal soil and excessive slopes, lost more than half its population between 1850 and 1930, declining from 3,816 residents to 1,451. Even towns with better land experienced a drop. Lansing had over 4,000 residents in 1830 but just 2,721 in 1930; Dryden had a peak population of 5,446 in 1840 and slipped to 3,532 by 1930.

Religion, Education, and Culture

Methodist circuit riders began to service what became Tompkins Co in 1794. Presbyterian congregations formed in Ulysses, Ithaca, and Trumansburg in 1803, 1804, and 1805 respectively. Baptists began organizing during that same period in Lansing, Dryden, and Groton. African Americans formed an African Methodist Episcopal Zion church in 1833, about the same time Irish immigrants began moving into the area, becoming its first Catholics. The first Catholic church was built in Ithaca in 1836, followed by others in McLean (1851), Trumansburg (1856), and Groton (1870). The first Jewish temple was erected in 1929 in Ithaca. In 2003 there were at least 83 functioning churches in Tompkins Co, plus various religious services at Cornell University and Ithaca College.

Tompkins Co's current public school districts evolved out of the early common school system that began in 1797. Several private academies, including Ithaca Academy (1823), Groton Academy (1837), and Trumansburgh Academy (1854), concurrently provided secondary education. School centralization efforts began in 1925 with the Trumansburg Central School District. The most recent consolidation effort involved Dryden Central in 1951. In 2003 there were five centralized school districts, Ithaca city district, and George Junior Republic. There were also a number of private and parochial schools. Two mid-19th-century events that altered the course of the educational landscape were Ezra Cornell's 1865 gift of a free public library open to all county residents and the selection of Ithaca's East Hill as the site of Cornell University. The university helped stabilize the economy by providing steady employment for local residents and by fostering commercial development; it continues to do both in the early 21st century. Ithaca College began in 1892 as the Ithaca Conservatory of Music. A third local postsecondary educational institution, Tompkins-Cortland Community College, or TC3, opened at Groton in 1968.

Numerous philanthropic efforts have also helped improve life in the county. Several were initiated during the last third of the 19th century. The Ladies' Union Benevolent Society, founded in 1869, established facilities for elderly women and orphans; the local chapter of the Woman's Christian Temperance Union (WCTU) organized the Associated Charities, predecessor of the United Way, in 1891. A YMCA opened in Ithaca in 1886 and the Salvation Army in 1892. The Ithaca City Hospital was founded in 1891.

The county's first newspaper, the *Seneca Republican* (later *Ithaca Journal*), was founded in 1814. Initially an organ of the Democratic Party, it switched political allegiance to the newly formed Republican Party in 1856. Another, the *Ithaca Democrat,* began in 1884 and lasted until 1912, leaving the *Ithaca Journal* and the *Cornell Sun* (1880) as the only daily papers in Tompkins Co. Beginning in the 1960s there has been at least one and often two alternative papers, such as the *Ithaca Times* (1977). The monthly *Bookpress* (1990) is a well-regarded literary newspaper.

Politics

In 1970 Tompkins Co government changed from a board of supervisors with a representative from each town and the City of Ithaca to the population-based Board of Representatives with 15 members, including 5 from the City of Ithaca. The name was changed to the Tompkins County Legislature in 2003. Services and facilities are overseen by a county administrator hired by the legislature. Outside the City of Ithaca, the county has traditionally voted Republican, but population growth following World War II led to the gradual expansion in the Democratic Party, and in 1993 the county board had a Democratic majority for the first time. Nationally known abortion rights advocate Constance E. Cook represented the region in the state assembly (1963–74).

Haystack in Tompkins Co, 1923.

RECENT HISTORY

World War II and the GI Bill had a tremendous impact upon Tompkins Co, largely through the expansion of Cornell. Between 1940 and 1950 the county had a 28% increase in population, with the largest gain in Ithaca. Tompkins had greater than 10% growth during each succeeding decade through 1990. Exceptionally high geographic mobility was another demographic characteristic as it consistently leads the state in population turnover, due largely to Cornell's large student enrollment. During the 1960s an additional jump in population was reflected in a shift toward more rural living, as the northeast corner of the Town of Ithaca and areas close to Cornell became heavily settled by faculty and students. Population growth also led to the creation of the Village of Lansing in 1974. As a result local governments expanded services and took a proactive role in shaping subsequent development. The face of the county's population has also changed. During the 20th century, the ethnic composition shifted. Italians, Greeks, and Hungarians appeared in the 1890s and Finns after 1910. In 1900 there were two Chinese listed in the census; in 1990 a diversified Asian community numbered over 5,000. At approximately 6% of the overall population, the African American segment has remained fairly constant for most of the century.

As a new century begins Tompkins Co's economy continues to exhibit one of the lowest unemployment rates in the state, primarily because of the nature of the employment base. Cornell University is by far the largest employer, with over 9,500 full-time personnel. As one of nation's premier educational institutions, its influence will no doubt continue to shape much of the local culture and economy. Among other roles, the university has served as incubator for a variety of successful local start-up firms in recent decades, especially technology companies, and that trend is apt to continue. Other major employers include Borg-Warner and Ithaca College. In contrast, most of the more marginal farmland has been abandoned, with large acreages in the Towns of Caroline, Danby, Dryden, and Newfield now owned by the state. In 1997 there were 447 farms, averaging 213 acres (86 ha), operating in the county; the vast majority were dairy farms. The local economy's retail base continues to display steady growth, with more of the same anticipated in the years to come.

The standard 19th-century history is [Henry B. Peirce and D. Hamilton Hurd], *History of Tioga, Chemung, Tompkins, and Schuyler Counties* (1879). Very useful is W. Glenn Norris's *The Origin of Place Names in Tompkins County* (1951). See also Carol Kammen's *The Peopling of Tompkins County: A Social History* (1985) and Jane M. Dieckmann's *A Short History of Tompkins County* (1986). Of the histories of the nine towns and the City of Ithaca, Henry Abt's *Ithaca* (1926) and George Goodrich's *The Centennial History of the Town of Dryden, 1797–1897* (1898) stand out. The most recent work on the county's history is *The Towns of Tompkins County: From Podunk to the Magnetic Springs*, edited by Jane M. Dieckmann (1998). Important repositories of county history include the DeWitt Historical Society, Cornell University, and Tompkins County Archives.

Carol Kammen

Tonawanda. Town (pop 78,155) and city (pop 16,136) in NW Erie Co. Sold by the Holland Land Co in 1797, the area was settled in 1805. Major growth began with the platting of the village (1824) in anticipation of the opening of the Erie Canal (1825). The town was formed from Buffalo in 1836, and the Buffalo and Niagara Falls Railroad began service the same year. The village was incorporated in 1853. In the mid–19th century Tonawanda became the site of huge grain elevators and the manufacture and transshipment of lumber originating in Michigan, Wisconsin, Minnesota, and Canada. Industrialization in and around the village continued throughout the 19th century. Boatbuilding was common, and water pipes (1857), bricks (1870), and boilers (1898) were among Tonawanda's products. It acquired a brewery in 1867. Much of the later growth was made possible by the expansion of the Erie Canal, the New York Central Railroad (1871), and, ultimately, the New York State Barge Canal (1918), which continued navigation on Tonawanda Creek. The Village of Kenmore in the south, on the Niagara River, incorporated in 1899. By 1903 the Village of Tonawanda became a city that attracted, among others, Polish, German, Lebanese, and Italian immigrants. In the early 20th century, many industries located in Tonawanda, including Wickwire-Spencer Steel Co (1908–64), a power plant (1916), DuPont (1920; rayon), Chevrolet (1938; engines), Frontier Oil Refinery (1952), and Dunlop Tire and Rubber Co (1923), along with producers of chemicals and telephone equipment. Western New York's first commercial airport, the Curtiss Aerodome, operated until 1926, and the Curtiss firm manufactured airplanes in the 1940s. The town's population exploded from 55,270 to 105,032 in the 1950s. Landmarks include the Evangelical and Reformed Church (1849) in the town and the Voisinet House (1828) and the New York Central Railroad Depot (1870) in the city. Tonawanda was home of Leslie L. Irvin (?1895–1966), inventor of the modern parachute harness.

Nancy B. Mingus

Tonawanda Indian Reservation. Seneca reservation in Genesee and Niagara Cos comprising some 7,549 acres (3,055 ha). Originally retained as Seneca land at the Treaty of Big Tree in 1797, it was sold after the fraudulent Treaty of Buffalo Creek in 1838. Although the Allegany and Cattaraugus Reservations were returned to the Seneca by the Compromise Treaty of 1842, the Tonawanda and Buffalo Creek Reservations were not. The Tonawanda chiefs had signed neither the 1838 nor the 1842 document, refusing to recognize the negotiations and to vacate their reservation. Not until 1856 was a reduced portion of the former Tonawanda Reservation bought back and then at a greatly inflated price. Ely S. Parker, a Seneca who was born on this reservation and who later became a Union general in the Civil War, was instrumental in the Tonawanda Senecas regaining their lands.

The Tonawanda attended the Cattaraugus convention in 1848 that created the Seneca Nation of Indians but chose not to abolish their chief system. Although sympathetic to the political revolution at the other Seneca reservations, the Tonawanda Senecas were attempting to regain their reservation and feared that a change in their government at that time might jeopardize those efforts. They are therefore still governed by a council of 16 chiefs and other office holders.

The Tonawanda Reservation is where Handsome Lake settled after leaving the Allegany Reservation and where the "preachers" of the Code of Handsome Lake are officially recognized. It is generally accepted as the major center of the Longhouse religion.

Abler, Thomas S., and Elisabeth Tooker. "Seneca." In *Northeast*, ed. Bruce G. Trigger, vol 15 of *Handbook of North American Indians*, ed. William C. Sturtevant (Washington, DC: Smithsonian Institution, 1978)
Abrams, George H. J. *The Seneca People* (Phoenix: Indian Tribal Series, 1976)

George H. J. Abrams

Tooker, William W(allace) (*b* Sag Harbor, Suffolk Co, 14 Jan 1848; *d* Sag Harbor, 2 Aug 1917). Indian linguist. A self-described pioneer "Algonkinist," he was drawn to Indian studies by the artifacts he discovered near his home. Forced to abandon his plans to enter Yale College after he completed Sag Harbor Academy, he apprenticed to a pharmacist in his hometown in 1866. Consulting colonial documents, maps, and surviving vocabulary lists, Tooker pursued the study of the extinct languages of eastern Long Island Indians. Between 1887 and 1911 he published 12 books, 50 pamphlets, and over 100 articles. He retired financially troubled in 1897 and sold his collection of artifacts to the Brooklyn Museum to raise cash. A trust fund provided around 1906–7 by Margaret Olivia Slocum Sage allowed Tooker, physically disabled and with limited means, to complete his major work, *The Indian Place Names on Long Island* (1911). Modern scholars believe that many of Tooker's translations were educated guesses and that some are completely unreliable. Nevertheless, Tooker remains respected as a trailblazer in the field of Algonquian studies.

Huden, John C. "William Wallace Tooker, Algonkinist," *Long Island Forum* 18 (1955): 143 ff

Richard F. Welch

tories. See LOYALISTS AND LOYALISM.

tornadoes. Violently rotating columns of air, dust, and debris, sometimes with a roughly funnel-shaped cloud, with wind speeds from 40 to over 300 mph (64–483 kph), often formed on the right rear flank of severe thunderstorms. Most last just a few minutes and travel under 5 miles (8 km), sometimes causing enormous damage from flying debris such as glass, broken lumber, and whole sections of buildings, and they are sometimes deadly. There have been 254 confirmed tornadoes in New York State between 1953 and 1995, about 6 per year, ranking the state 30th for frequency. They have resulted in 21 fatalities, storm damage of about $4 million a year, placing the New York at 26th among the states. Between 1989 and 1994 the frequency increased to about 17 per year. In 1989 there were 15, causing 11 deaths, 49 injuries, and property damage amounting to over $51 million. Tornadoes can occur in every area of the state but are most common in the far west, with Chautauqua (22), Erie (15), and Cattaraugus (13) Cos reporting the most between 1950 and 1995. The area with the fewest tornadoes is New York City, with only two known occurrences, one on Staten Island and one in Queens. In contrast Nassau Co (5) and Suffolk Co (10) in central and eastern Long Island have had more activity. The difference is at least in part because of these counties' greater size.

New York Disaster Center. "New York Tornadoes," http://www.disastercenter.com/newyork/tornado.html
Tornado Project Online. "All US Tornadoes," http://www.tornadoproject.com/alltorns/ustorns.htm

C. G. Rose

Torr, Helen (*b* Roxborough, Pa, 22 Nov 1886; *d* West Islip, Suffolk Co, 8 Sept 1967). Artist. Born in a Philadelphia suburb, Torr studied art at the Drexel Institute and the Pennsylvania Academy of the Fine Arts from 1903 to 1906. While living in Coleytown, Conn, with her political cartoonist husband, Clive Weed, in 1919 she met the painter Arthur Dove. Unhappy with their marriages, she and Dove left their spouses around 1920, eventually marrying in April 1932. From 1924 to 1933 they lived aboard a sailboat near Halesite (Suffolk Co) on Long Island Sound, moving to Geneva (Ontario Co) in July 1933 to settle Dove's family estate and returning to Long Island in April 1938, where they bought a one-room waterfront cottage in Centerport (Suffolk Co). Soon after moving, Dove contracted pneumonia and suffered a heart attack. He remained an invalid until his death in 1946. Torr stopped painting to care for Dove, which in turn enabled him to paint.

Torr worked both in oil and charcoal, and though she did not date her paintings, documentary evidence suggests that the majority of her extant work was executed between 1924 and 1938. None of her early work survives. Torr found inspiration in the landscape and buildings that surrounded her and in the natural and human-constructed objects she would bring home for her still lifes. Among her most notable works are *White Cloud (Light House)* a compelling view of the Lloyd Harbor Lighthouse in Huntington Harbor (Suffolk Co), painted in 1932, and *January,* a Geneva subject that effectively conveys the raw chill of winter in upstate New York, done in 1935. Both works display the rhythmic sense of design and a subtle palette that distinguish her work, which was exhibited publicly only twice during her lifetime, once with Dove's at Alfred Stieglitz's New York City gallery, An American Place, in 1933. Torr's work, reevaluated since her death, represented a distinctive voice within the modernist movement. The Heckscher Museum of Art in Huntington (Suffolk Co) owns the largest public collection and the Dove/Torr cottage, which is on the National Register of Historic Places.

DePietro, Anne Cohen. *Arthur Dove and Helen Torr: The Huntington Years.* Catalog of Exhibition at the Heckscher Museum of Art (Huntington, NY: Heckscher Museum of Art, 1989)
DePietro, Anne Cohen, et al. *Out of the Shadows: Helen Torr, a Retrospective* (Huntington, NY: Heckscher Museum of Art, 2003)

Anne Cohen DePietro

Torrey. Town (pop 1,307) in NE Yates Co. Settled in 1788 by followers of Jemima Wilkinson (1752–1819) at City Hill, the town was formed from Benton and Milo in 1851, in part to enhance Dresden's importance as a village. Mills were developed along the Crooked Lake Canal (1833–77). Torrey was served by the Northern Central Railroad (1851), the Fall Brook (1877), and its Penn Yan and Dresden Branch (1884). Danish farmers settled in the town in the 1890s. Heavy industry in the vicinity of Dresden included DuPont, which manufactured hydrogen peroxide from the World War II years through 1959; Mercury Aircraft, which closed its plant in the early 1990s; and a carbon disulfate plant near Cascade Mills, which operated from 1901 to 1967. Ferro (1978; powders for lens grinding) remained in operation in 2003. The town is otherwise primarily a farming community with two wineries.

Gwen Chamberlain

Torrey, John (*b* New York City, 15 Aug 1796; *d* New York City, 10 Mar 1873). Botanist, chemist, and physician. Torrey graduated from the College of Physicians and Surgeons in New York City in 1818. He was elected president of the Lyceum of Natural History of New York (later the New York Academy of Sciences) in 1824, the same year he became professor of chemistry and mineralogy at West Point. By 1826 Torrey's work engaged the "natural system" of classifying plants according to their features and morphology. He returned to New York City in 1827 as professor of chemistry at the College of Physicians and Surgeons, a position he held until 1853, and also served as professor of chemistry and botany at New York University beginning in 1832. Torrey was a botanist for the Natural History Survey of New York State, conducted from 1836 to 1843, and assisted Joseph Henry in creating a herbarium at the Smithsonian Institution. The Torrey Botanical Club, which John Torrey started around 1865, initiated actions that resulted in the creation of the New York Botanical Garden in 1891.

Rodgers, Andrew Denny, III. *John Torrey: A Story of North American Botany* (New York: Hafner, 1942)

Pamela Cooper

Toscanini, Arturo (*b* Parma, Italy, 25 Mar 1867; *d* New York City, 16 Jan 1957). Conductor. Trained as a cellist, he led Milan's La Scala Opera from 1898 to 1908. As principal conductor of the Metropolitan Opera (1908–15), he achieved a degree of artistic control and distinction not subsequently matched. He returned to La Scala (1914–29) but eventually made New York City his artistic home. Toscanini's peak influence and celebrity coincided with his tenure as principal conductor of the New York Philharmonic (1926–36) and of the NBC Symphony (1937–54). As the undisputed symbol of classical music for a generation of Americans, he was, according to *Time* magazine, as well known as Joe DiMaggio. Such was the Philharmonic's dependency on Toscanini for its excellence, prestige, and revenues that, when he departed, it was proposed by some that the orchestra be disbanded. NBC's David Sarnoff created the NBC Symphony expressly for Toscanini. Toscanini therefore stayed in New York City, where the orchestra performed for an invited audience at Radio City Music Hall's Studio 8H. Toscanini was an early and courageous opponent of Benito Mussolini and Adolf Hitler. During World War II he stirred patriotic fervor, leading the NBC Symphony and New York Philharmonic in such works as Beethoven's Third and Fifth Symphonies, performed as "Victory" symphonies. His antifascist crusade also included a sold-out Red Cross benefit concert at Madison Square Garden, on 25 Mar 1944, with both orchestras and the All-City High School Chorus. The net proceeds, including $11,000 for a Toscanini baton auctioned by Mayor Fiorello La Guardia, totaled over $120,000. Another wartime Toscanini specialty was "The Star-Spangled Banner," which he would conduct facing the audience, eyes blazing, singing along in his hoarse baritone. In 1950, at the age of 83, he undertook his first transcontinental US tour, with the NBC Symphony. Although this was hailed by NBC publicists as "a great and lasting monument to American culture," Toscanini's tour repertoire included no American music.

In the New York City press, Toscanini was anointed a deity. Olin Downes wrote in the *New York Times:* "If ever there was a man who justified the theory of aristocracy built upon the fundamental conception that men are not born free and equal, that some are immeasurably superior to others, and that their superiority is justification for their control of others' acts and destinies, that man is Arturo Toscanini." In certain respects Toscanini became an adoptive American. His enthusiasms for boxing and Disney cartoons were hailed in newspapers and magazines. He was observed to be self-made in the American mold. His vaunted objectivity, emphasizing the printed score over received notions of interpretive "tradition," implied that Italians and Americans could perform Beethoven as authentically as Germans could. But he never took American citizenship and was buried in the family tomb in Milan.

Horowitz, Joseph. *Understanding Toscanini: How He Became an American Culture-God and Helped Create a New Audience for Old Music* (New York: Knopf, 1987)
Sachs, Harvey. *Toscanini* (New York: J. B. Lippincott, 1978)

Joseph Horowitz

Totten and Crossfield Purchase. Land tract. Brothers Edward and Ebenezer Jessup, land speculators and lumbermen from what is now Lake Luzerne (Warren Co), bought some 1,150,000 acres (465,000 ha) encompassing most of Hamilton Co and parts of Essex, Warren, and Herkimer Cos from the Mohawk Indians in 1771. Because purchases from the Indians required royal approval and because the Jessups had an approval request pending on another large purchase, they arranged to have Manhattan shipwrights Joseph Totten and Stephen Crossfield place their names on the deal in exchange for one of the 50 townships to be created. By 1773, 24 had been surveyed and allotted to investors, but the Revolutionary War intervened before the deal could be confirmed, and the lands reverted to the possession of New York State. Crossfield petitioned the new government in 1785 for redress, and most of the townships were distributed to the original investors in 1786–87.

Donaldson, Alfred L. *A History of the Adirondacks* (1921; repr Fleischmanns, NY: Purple Mountain Press, 1992)

Francis P. Boscoe

tourism. The first major tourist area in the United States was New York State's Hudson River valley. Robert Fulton provided reliable river transportation beginning in 1807 with his *North River Steamboat.* His line fed tourists to fashionable destinations, in particular the springs at Ballston Spa (Saratoga Co) and Saratoga Springs. By 1812 the springs had the largest collection of hotels outside the major cities. Tourism began to make a cultural impact by 1820, when Washington Irving published his first book of stories, *The Sketch-Book,* some of them set in the Hudson Valley. The region spawned the first US tourist guidebook, when, in 1821, Saratoga's Gideon Minor Davison published *The Fashionable Tour,* describing the existing Grand Tour through New York and into Canada. And in 1825 on Thomas Cole's first visit to the valley, he sketched the dramatic Kaaterskill Falls just west of the Hudson River. His paintings of the falls and the Catskill region were the basis of the Hudson River school of landscape painting.

From the Hudson Valley, tourism spread westward via the Erie Canal. As early as 1819, even before the canal was completed, tourists were riding on elaborately decorated canalboats created for their travel. Through the canal (completed in 1825), thousands more people could visit what would become the state's premier tourist destination: Niagara Falls. In 1822 William Forsyth built a large tourist hotel, the Pavilion (also known as Forsyth's), on the Canadian side, and similar hotels soon sprang up on the New York State side. It was in this early era, beginning in the 1830s, that Niagara's reputation as a honeymoon spot developed.

Saratoga Springs remained quite successful in the 1830s, but Ballston Spa suffered a series of problems when its springs began flowing irregularly. Tourism spread north from Saratoga to picturesque locations like Lake George (Warren Co), where the Lake House was completed in 1828. Its spread west from the Hudson included the Catskill Mountains. The first of the Catskill hotels, the Catskill Mountain House, was completed in 1824 on the escarpment overlooking the Hudson in the Village of Catskill (Greene Co). By the 1830s competition by these new resorts required some older resorts to change. Saratoga Springs, for example, experimented with gambling in the 1830s before instituting it permanently in the 1840s. In 1847 the Saratoga Trotting Course opened; the present track for thoroughbreds opened in 1864 on Union Ave. The first railroad in the tourist region was opened in 1832 and completed in 1833. It linked Saratoga to Schenectady, where New York's first railroad, the Mohawk and Hudson, ran on to Albany. Until the 1850s, however, steamboats, stage lines, and canals would remain central to tourist travel in New York State.

Meanwhile, New York City had itself been creating a tourist world. The site of some of the nation's first hotels, it had long had accommodations for tourists. Some of the nation's first city guides for visitors had been published about the city, including Samuel Latham Mitchill's *Picture of New York* (1807). New York City's status as the nation's leading mercantile location led many travelers to there to shop, mostly in the stores of lower (now West) Broadway. Visitors saw the theater and music and the spectacles of the American Museum or P. T. Barnum's museum (1841) on lower Broadway. A few came to experience the debauchery of Five Points and the seamier side of the city. By 1850 these lures had become notorious enough that a guidebook by George G. Foster, *New York by Gas-Light,* was published. Much of what was tourist oriented in New York City, though, was obscured by the many commercial visitors to the city and by the increasing demand for recreation created by its rapid expansion. Tourist sites near New York City included Rockaway Beach (Queens Co) and, by the 1850s, Fire Island (Suffolk Co).

From 1865 to 1910

In the years after the Civil War the railroad defined tourism: it became a key factor in whether and how long people were tourists and where they went. More important, its cost allowed many in the growing middle classes to travel, and a number of resorts consequently grew. Railroads began offering lower-cost packages or scenic tours of regions, imitating earlier efforts by steamboat companies; the New York Central Railroad, for example, offered tours of the Hudson and Mohawk Valleys. Many from the earlier generation of tourists deplored the flood of this new generation and the creation of places they could afford. Some resorts, such as Saratoga Springs, sought to exclude them by becoming more expensive. Others, like Niagara Falls, created entire districts with lower-cost entertainment to serve them, as did some of the early Catskill resorts, such as the Mohonk Mountain House in New Paltz (Ulster Co), built in 1869.

One major region of New York State that opened to tourism in this era was the Adirondacks. A number of romantic writings from the 1840s and 1850s had depicted it as an unspoiled wilderness. Thousands of visitors started arriving in the 1860s, many spurred by William H. H. Murray's 1869 book, *Adventures in the Wilderness.* A railroad connected Saratoga to North Creek (Warren Co) in 1871, carrying tourists who then traveled to places like Raquette Lake (Hamilton Co) or Lake Placid (Essex Co). There they rented rooms from country homes or inns. A number of hotels were constructed, including Paul Smith's, first built on Lower St. Regis Lake (Franklin Co) in 1861, and the Prospect House on Blue Mountain Lake (Hamilton Co) opened in 1882, the first hotel to have electric lights in every room. By 1876 there was a direct rail link between Albany and Montreal. The presence of tourists was balanced by the pressures on the land, including logging. In some ways the state's creation of parts of the Adirondacks as a forest preserve in 1885 and the founding of a more formal Adirondack Park in 1892 can be seen as the triumph of the former. Another uniquely 19th-century aspect of tourism was the rise of lecture sessions at Chautauqua Lake, first held in 1874. By the mid-1880s, 60,000 to 100,000 people attended annually. The Chautauqua idea spread not only throughout the state to places like Lake George but also across the country. This combination of vacation and education appealed to those less comfortable with the idea of extended leisure. Railroads also allowed thousands to come to New York City. The expectations of the wealthy visitors in this period can be gauged by the opulence of the city's highest-priced hotels, especially the 1,000-room Waldorf-Astoria, begun in 1892.

From 1910 to World War II

The widespread availability of automobiles in the years after 1910 transformed tourism and its destinations. What was distant became accessible. The successes of the labor movement gave the working class more vacation time, and they became the newest generation of tourists. The spread of the tourist idea led to the growth of a number of local resorts. One of them, at Sag Harbor (Suffolk Co), was created to serve Blacks, who had been actively discriminated against at other resorts. Jews, too, found themselves excluded. Prior to the 1880s, the relatively small number of Jews who were from western Europe had generally been accepted at upstate resorts. But as the number of eastern European Jews grew in the late 1800s, both groups were increasingly discriminated against. Although many hotels decided to open their doors to all, some, such as the Catskill Mountain House, barred Jews for some time. Nevertheless, Jews built their own resorts in the lower regions of the Catskills, primarily in Sullivan and Ulster Cos, the foundation of the borscht belt. Outside the Catskills, however, hotels and resorts remained openly anti-Semitic until, in some cases, the early 1960s.

Post–World War II

The nation's return to prosperity in the postwar period led to an explosion of tourism. Long-established tourist sites such as Lake George moved to cater to the new tourist masses, and hundreds of thousands of hotel and motel rooms were built to accommodate them. The much wider popularity of sports such as skiing led to year-round tourism in some places, particularly in the Catskills and the Adirondacks. Belleayre Mountain State Ski Center in Highmount (Ulster Co), opened in 1950 in the Catskill Forest Preserve and was operated by the State Conservation Department [now Department of Environmental Conservation]. Following the 1980 Winter Olympic Games in Lake Placid, the state established the Olympic Regional Development Authority to manage several facilities including Whiteface Mountain State Ski Area in Wilmington (Essex Co) and, since 1984, Gore Mountain Ski Center in North Creek. The construction of the expressway system and the New York State Thruway meant that millions of tourists could visit New York State. However, some sites never recovered from the decline of the war years. The Catskill Mountain House, for example, was abandoned in 1942. Some resorts also suffered as tourists became more sophisticated in their tastes and more able to drive wherever they chose. The borscht belt area of the Catskills enjoyed a postwar bloom. An estimated 1 million visitors spent their summer vacation in the Catskills annually in the 1950s and 1960s. By the late 1960s, however, it had become unfashionable, its accommodations increasingly shabby and outdated, and the region went into perceptible decline. By the late 1980s few of its grand resorts survived. Other groups developed distinctive recreation areas. Many Irish Americans vacationed in the northern Catskills, including Catskill, East Durham, and Cairo (Greene Co), an area often called the Irish Alps. Gays and lesbians developed their own resorts as well, notably on Fire Island.

Efforts in the late 1990s to revitalize Catskills tourism most often focused on bringing legalized gambling to the region. Although casinos were rejected by residents in a 1997 vote, they have remained on the state legislature's agenda, and in 2001 Gov George E. Pataki signed legislation authorizing three Native American–run casinos in Sullivan and Ulster Cos. A smaller effort to create other attractions has been somewhat successful, including an arts center, Catskill Corners, built in Mount Tremper (Ulster Co) in 1998.

The state has also promoted tourism through various programs highlighting historic and scenic highways. Beginning in 1992 the Scenic Byways Program recognized highways notable for scenic, historic, natural, and archaeological qualities. In 2003 there were 79 designated state scenic byways, including one national scenic byway, the Seaway Trail, and one All-American Road, the Lakes to Locks Passage. The Heritage Trails Program, begun in 2001, includes the Revolutionary War Trail, the Underground Railroad Trail, Women's Heritage Trail, and Theodore Roosevelt Heritage Trail.

In the years after World War II, New York City began to cater more explicitly to tourists, who provided an important segment of the city's audiences for cultural and theater events. However, the social unrest of the late 1960s and the severe economic downturn of the early 1970s led to a steep decline in visitors. In the mid-1970s, William Doyle, senior deputy commissioner of New York, and John Dyson, New York State commissioner of commerce, proposed an advertising campaign to reinvigorate tourism in the city and the state. The legislature, under Gov Hugh Carey, allocated $4 million for the promotion, and in May 1977 the I♥NY campaign initially aired on television. The steady improvement of the quality of life in New York City through the 1980s and 1990s led to an explosion of tourists by 1999. The city's image steadily improved, helped by massive restoration of the most visited sites such as Grand Central Terminal and Times Square. Employment in the leisure and hospitality industry rose from an average of 218,000 in 1990 to more than 260,000 in 2001. That year, more than 20 million tourists spent at least one night in the city, and tourists were vital to the health of the theater industry. The tragedy of the terrorist attack on the World Trade Center on 11 Sept 2001 hit the city hard, but the basic infrastructure remained. In 2002 international and domestic visitors to the city spent more than $14 billion.

See also ADIRONDACKS; AUTOMOBILE LANDSCAPES; BORSCHT BELT; CATSKILLS; ENVIRONMENTALISM; PORT OF BUFFALO; SARATOGA SPRINGS; STEAMBOATS; THOUSAND ISLANDS RESORTS.

Aron, Cindy. *Working at Play: A History of Vacations in the United States* (New York: Oxford Univ Press, 1999)

Cocks, Catherine. *Doing the Town: The Rise of Urban Tourism in the United States, 1850–1915* (Berkeley: Univ of California Press, 2001)

Evers, Alf. *The Catskills: From Wilderness to Woodstock* (Garden City, NY: Doubleday, 1972)

Gassan, Richard. "The Birth of American Tourism: New York, the Hudson Valley, and American Culture, 1790–1835" (PhD diss, Univ of Massachusetts, 2002)

Irwin, William. *The New Niagara: Tourism, Technology, and the Landscape of Niagara Falls, 1776–1917* (University Park: Pennsylvania State Univ Press, 1996)

Kanfer, Stefan. *A Summer World: The Attempt to Build a Jewish Eden in the Catskills from the Days of the Ghetto to the Rise and Decline of the Borscht Belt* (New York: Farrar, Straus & Giroux, 1989)

Sears, John. *Sacred Places: American Tourist Attractions in the 19th Century* (New York: Oxford Univ Press, 1989)

Richard H. Gassan

tourist railroads. New York State railroads serving tourists usually run from Memorial Day through the fall foliage season. In the 1890s three inclined railways hauled tourists to mountaintops for panoramic views: Otis Elevating, Mount Beacon, and Prospect Mountain. Other non-inclined tourist lines were Catskill and Tannersville, and Saratoga and Mount MacGregor. Some year-round freight and passenger railroads ran summer tourist trains to beaches and amusement parks, such as Fonda, Johnstown, and Gloversville's seasonal one to Sacandaga Park (1898–1930). The Marion River Carry (1900–1929) and the second Fulton Chain Railroad, renamed Old Forge Branch (1896–1932), ran exclusively in the summer for Adirondack hotel guests and camp owners. In 2001, 11 tourist railroads operated in the state, carrying passengers for recreational, historic, and educational purposes: Delaware and Ulster in Arkville; Catskill Mountain in Mount Pleasant; Cooperstown and Charlotte Valley; Trolley Museum of New York in Kingston; Adirondack Scenic in Thendara and Lake Placid; Upper Hudson River in North Creek; Arcade and Attica; New York City Transit Museum; Tioga Scenic Railroad in Owego; New York Museum of Transportation in Rochester; and Northeastern New York Railroad Preservation Group in Greenwich.

Empire State Railway Museum. *36th Annual Guide to Tourist Railroads and Museums* (Waukesha, Wisc: Kalmbach Books, 2001)

Michael Kudish

Touro College. Private college. Headquartered in Manhattan and opened in 1971 by Dr. Bernard Lander, the school is named after Judah and Isaac Touro, prominent 18th-century Jewish philanthropists. Its mission is to preserve and perpetuate Jewish traditions while promoting social justice and community service. Originally a men's school, Touro College became coeducational in the mid-1970s. With its main campus on West 23d St in Manhattan, the school offers its courses in many locations around the New York City metropolitan area, including 4 in Manhattan, 12 in Brooklyn, 4 in Queens, and 2 in Suffolk Co. There are also two campuses in California as well two programs in Israel, one in Moscow, and one in Berlin. Associate, bachelor's, and master's degrees are offered with majors in the liberal arts and sciences, business, and healthcare. Touro also offers doctorate degrees in law at its Jacob D. Fuchsberg Law Center. Undergraduate enrollment in 2003 stood at 7,393.

Marianne Rahn-Erickson

Toussaint College. Proposed black college. In October 1870 a group of African Americans of fairly humble backgrounds from Dutchess, Orange, Columbia, Ulster, and Greene Cos met at Poughkeepsie to create a local college for African Americans in that city. Isaac Deyo, a local black leader, laborer, and cartman, spearheaded the group. They intended to name the college after Toussaint L'Ouverture, the leader of the Haitian Revolution. The state senate approved $500,000 in funding in 1871, and a prestigious board of black trustees was named. However, many black leaders had second thoughts and wondered whether an all-black college would institutionalize segregation, despite the reality that Blacks had limited access to higher education in the Northeast. As black and white support for the idea waned, the Toussaint College movement died.

Mabee, Carleton. "Toussaint College: A Proposed Black College for New York in the 1870s," *Afro-Americans in New York Life and History* 1 (Jan 1977): 25–36

———. *Black Education in New York State: From Colonial to Modern Times* (Syracuse: Syracuse Univ Press, 1979)

Tricia Barbagallo

town government. Towns are general-purpose municipal governments with constitutional home-rule powers serving suburban and rural New York State. Their territory encompasses the entire state except the land within cities or Indian reservations, and each town is entirely within a single county. There are no towns within the five counties of New York City; 18 towns formerly in its territory were eliminated in its consolidation in 1898. Outside of New York City, Nassau Co had the fewest towns at the turn of the 21st century, with three. At the other extreme were Cattaraugus, St. Lawrence, and Steuben Cos, each with 32.

By 1788 the state already had 119 towns. Counties were given the power to create towns and change their boundaries in 1830; this power was removed in 1950. Totaling 932 in 2003, the number of towns in New York State had changed little over the course of the 20th century. Three towns were dissolved: Wilmurt (1918, Herkimer Co), Elko (1965, Cattaraugus Co), and High Market (1973, Lewis Co). Six were created: Piercefield (1900, St. Lawrence Co); Inlet (1901, Hamilton Co); Minetto (1915, Oswego Co); North Harmony (1919, Chautauqua Co); and two with coterminous boundaries with existing villages, Mount Kisco (1978, Westchester Co) and East Rochester (1981, Monroe Co). In 2000, 8,692,132 people lived in towns, 1,871,947 of these within and 6,820,185 outside village boundaries. The 2000 federal census showed that more than five-sixths of New York State towns had populations below 10,000, with 25 below 500. Ten, with eight on Long Island, had more than 100,000 people each. The most populated was Hempstead (Nassau Co), with 755,924 residents, and the least, with 38 people, was Red House (Cattaraugus Co). If Hempstead were a city it would have been the 2d largest in the state and 14th in population nationally in 2000, between San Francisco (776,733) and Jacksonville, Fla (735,618). The largest town in land area, Webb (Herkimer Co), with 451.2 mi² (1,168.6 km²), was bigger than 11 New York counties. Green Island (Albany Co), encompassing only 0.7 mi² (18.13 km²), was the smallest.

Towns in New York State are governed by boards elected for two- or four-year terms and are composed of council members and a supervisor who presides and exercises limited executive authority. Council members number from two to six, depending on the classification of the town—as first class, second class, or suburban—in state law and/or on local choice. Other elected town officials include a highway superintendent, two justices of the peace, and a town clerk. There is also a receiver of taxes and assessments, often simultaneously the town clerk, or in some jurisdictions a board of three elected assessors and a tax collector, often the clerk. The evolution to this representative structure and partial separation of powers occurred in the late 19th and early

20th centuries. Prior to this, New York State towns were governed, like those in New England, through annual town meetings of freeholders and others qualified to vote. Even as late as 1890, except in the largest counties, it was at these town meetings that key decisions were made and local officials elected to implement them. The supervisor also represented the town on the county board of supervisors. Gradually meetings became biannual, as did the terms of officials elected at them, and were held not in the winter or early spring but simultaneous with other elections. Reformers shaped in Progressive era thinking about government restructuring in the 1920s sought to establish separation of powers in towns and to have key administrative officials appointed rather than elected. A major change in town law, advanced as a recodification in 1932, shifted power from the town meeting to the town board. According to this law, towns were placed in two classes, based largely on size. The distinct job of councilman, or legislative representative, was established, and justices of the peace were reduced from four to two and removed from town boards in larger towns. Justices' service on boards in smaller towns was barred by state law in 1976.

Over time a number of elected town offices performing administrative functions were abolished, such as commissioners of excise and overseers of the poor, with duties shifted to county government or other town elected officials or appointees. Some budgetary and management authority was given to the supervisor. State policy encouraged the replacement of elected boards of assessors with professionally trained appointed assessors. Towns were authorized to appoint professional managers. The continued choice by election, and not on the basis of training and experience, of such key administrators as the clerk and highway superintendent remain an occasional matter of controversy at the beginning of the 21st century, as does the practice of electing justices of the peace not required to have training in the law.

Towns were created by the state with limited powers to ensure the delivery of local services required in rural areas: highways, criminal justice, fence maintenance, and animal regulation. Gov David B. Hill (1885–91) regularly vetoed legislation extending the powers of some growing town governments because he believed that "towns are not safe or proper repositories for the exercise of municipal powers. When towns become so populous that they have outgrown the simple form of town government applicable to all towns, then they should be incorporated as villages." Even as Hill wrote, however, his view was giving way to the inexorable pressures arising from rapid suburbanization, as former city residents demanded the diversity of local services to which they had become accustomed. Laws passed in the 1890s extended powers to some towns to license public entertainments, establish lighting districts, dispose of garbage, build waterworks, and create sewer districts. Powers given to the Erie Co towns of Tonawanda and Amherst in 1895 were fully comparable to those given villages. In connection with the 1932 recodification, the powers generally available to first-class towns became equal to those of villages. After 1962, with further suburban growth and concomitant demands for more extensive services, towns with larger populations and those close to major cities could opt for designation as "suburban towns" and gain an even greater range of governmental power. After passage of the Home Rule Amendment to the state constitution in 1964, all towns obtained the local law powers just given to suburban towns. By 2000 distinctions in classification made little difference in the powers of town governments in New York State.

In 2000 New York State towns had in aggregate revenues of $4.348 billion and expenses of $4.643 billion. They relied on the real property tax for more than half (52%) of their income. Residents of villages (who receive services from them) pay at different rates than those who live outside villages. Extensive use of special districts, for example, for water and sewer, often links levies directly to services provided. State aid was 8% of aggregated income, and federal aid 3%. Just over 75% of town spending went directly to provide local services, with the rest for capital outlay (14%) and debt service (10%). Over a third (35.5%) of town spending was by the 10 largest towns. Hempstead alone spent $364.7 million.

See also Home rule; Village government.

New York State. Office of the Comptroller. *Special Report on Municipal Affairs, 2001,* 94th ed (Albany, 2002)

New York State. Secretary of State. Division of Local Government Services. *Local Government Handbook* (Albany, 2001)

Gerald Benjamin

town-villages and village-towns. Coterminous towns and villages sharing boundaries and government. Of the state's 554 villages, 5 fall within this category: East Rochester (Monroe Co), Green Island (Albany Co) and Harrison and Mount Kisco (Westchester Co) are town-villages; and Scarsdale (Westchester Co) is a village-town. There were a variety of motivations for becoming coterminous. Scarsdale, which was a town before its 1915 incorporation as a village, changed in part because of a threat that the neighboring city of White Plains (Westchester Co) might annex portions of it. Separate town and village governments merged in 1930, resulting in a unique structure in which the government of Scarsdale convenes as either the town or as the village, depending on its needs. The state's Village Law, Article 17, establishes provisions for structuring these governments, requiring that a referendum be held after establishment of coterminous status to determine whether the government will operate "principally as a Village or principally as a Town." If the boundaries of either government change, the boundaries of the other government must also change to agree. There are special laws for Mount Kisco, an exception to the rule of there being a single assessment roll for both the town and the village. Along with a section relating to a special tax authority, Article 17 allowed Scarsdale to abolish its town supervisor position when Westchester Co abolished its Board of Supervisors.

See also Town government.

New York State. Secretary of State. Division of Local Government Services. *Local Government Handbook* (Albany: Office of the Secretary of State, 2001)

Eric L. Kline

track and field. Running, jumping, and throwing competitions became common in New York State in the 19th century. The Great Footrace of 1835 took place on the Union Race Course west of Jamaica (Queens Co). Henry Stannard won $1,300 for running 10 miles in 59 min 48 s, possibly the first American track record. Pedestrianism, participation in running and walking races that continued for days or even weeks, was popular among 19th-century working-class men and women who competed for cash. A distance running tradition had developed among the Iroquois Confederacy; Louis Bennett, a Seneca Indian living on the Cattaraugus Reservation [loc in Cattaraugus, Chautauqua, and Erie Cos], achieved international fame under the name Deerfoot in the early 1860s. Scottish immigrants included field events such as hammer throwing, shot putting, pole vaulting, high and low jumping, and short-distance running in their Caledonian Games, which offered prize money. In 1867 the national Caledonian Clubs of the United States and Canada met at Jones's Wood in Manhattan for the International Games.

The New York Athletic Club (NYAC) was organized as a sport club for amateurs, men of middle-class or higher status who did not compete for money. On 11 Nov 1868 the NYAC held the first amateur US track and field meet in Manhattan. In addition to maintaining amateurism as a class distinction, the NYAC used stopwatches and calibrated courses to rationalize track and field meets. College runners had previously accepted money prizes, but when the first intercollegiate track and field championships were held at Saratoga Springs in 1876 under the auspices of the Intercollegiate Association of Amateur Athletes of America (IC4A), the winners received trophies. At their 1878 Thanksgiving Day meet the Westchester Hare and Hounds Club introduced Columbia College students to paper chasing, or hare-and-hounds racing, which evolved into cross-country. Pedestrians who adhered to the rules of "fair heel and toe" developed the amateur sport of racewalking. Competing as an amateur for the Manhattan Athletic Club, runner Laurence Myers set records in the sprints and middle distances from 1879 to 1885.

On 21 Jan 1888 the NYAC led the organization of clubs into the Amateur Athletic Union (AAU), which would govern US track and field from New York City for over 80 years. The first AAU indoor meet was held on 21 Nov 1888 at the 26th St Madison Square Garden. For the first international amateur track and field meet, held on 21 Sept 1895 at Manhattan Field, the NYAC recruited the best American athletes to compete against the London Athletic Club; the NYAC won all 11 events. The track events included distances up to 5 miles (8 km) and hurdles races. The field events, from the Caledonian tradition, did not include the javelin or discus throws; later the Olympic Games would popularize these events. On 9 Nov 1895 the Vassar College Athletic Association in Poughkeepsie staged the first US track meet for women. In another notable development Syracuse University's Myer Prinstein won gold in the triple jump and silver in the long jump at the 1900 Olympic Games; he won gold in both events at the 1904 Olympics. NYAC member John J. Flanagan, a New York City policeman, took Olympic gold for the hammer throw in 1900, 1904, and 1908.

Settlement houses and the Public Schools Athletic League (PSAL), established in New York

City in 1903, brought boys and girls into the sport. Talented Italian and Jewish men were accepted into the Irish-American Athletic Club (IAAC), funded by Tammany politicians who courted the immigrant vote. Abel Kiviat from Staten Island set PSAL records before joining the IAAC; he was world record holder in the 1,500 meters when he won the silver medal in that event at the 1912 Stockholm Olympics. Madison Square Garden, venue for the first AAU national indoor track and field championships on 9–10 Nov 1906, became the center of US indoor track and field. The Millrose Athletic Association, organized in 1908 by employees of Wanamaker's Department Store, initiated the Millrose Games. Held in Madison Square Garden since 1914, these games would become the most important indoor track meet in the United States. The largest number of American women ever gathered for track and field competition met at Oaksmere School in Mamaroneck (Westchester Co) on 13 May 1922 to select the US national team to compete at the International Women's Games in Paris that August. Buffalo's 174th Regiment Armory provided the venue for the 1922 and 1923 AAU national indoor championships. New York City's indoor scholastic track and field meets were held at the 102d Engineer's Armory, outdoor track was held in the Randall's Island stadium, and cross-country venues were established at Van Cortlandt Park.

The New York Pioneer Club (1936) met at the 369th Regiment Armory in Harlem (New York Co). Originally an African American club, the Pioneers were integrated by 1942 and first won the AAU national indoor championship in 1951. Pioneer member Louis Woodard Jones, born in New Rochelle (Westchester Co), graduated Manhattan College before winning gold on the 4 x 400 m relay team at the 1956 Olympics. NYAC member Al Oerter, born in Astoria (Queens Co), won the discus throw in four consecutive Olympic Games: 1956, 1960, 1964, and 1968. John Wesley Carlos, born in Harlem, was recognized for his running ability while a student at Machine Trade and Metal High School. On the victory stand after taking bronze in the 200 meters at the 1968 Olympics, Carlos raised a black-gloved fist to protest oppression. Robert Beamon, who set a national high school record for the triple jump while a student in Jamaica (Queens Co), won the 1968 Olympic long jump and set a world record that would stand for 23 years.

In 1973 the Colgate Women's Games began in New York City under the direction of Fred Thompson, founder of the Atoms Track Club in Brooklyn. Brooklyn-born Diane Dixon joined the Atoms and began competing in the Colgate Women's Games in 1977; she won silver on the 4 x 400 m relay team at the 1988 Olympic Games. The 2002 USA Track and Field Indoor National Championships were held at the newly refurbished Armory Track and Field Center in New York City. The National Track and Field Hall of Fame was relocated from Indiana to New York City and opened at the Armory in 2004.

Cumming, John. *Runners and Walkers: A 19th Century Sports Chronicle* (Chicago: Regnery Gateway, 1981)
Donovan, Wally. *A History of Indoor Track and Field* (El Cajon, Calif: Edward Jules, 1976)
Nelson, Cordner. *Track and Field: The Great Ones* (Los Altos, Calif: Tafnews Press, 1970)
Tricard, Louise Mead. *American Women's Track and Field: A History, 1895 through 1980* (Jefferson, NC: McFarland, 1996)

Pamela Cooper

Tracy, Benjamin Franklin (*b* Owego, Tioga Co, 26 Apr 1830; *d* New York City, 6 Aug 1915). Secretary of the navy, soldier, and lawyer. Passing the state bar exam in 1851, Tracy quickly became a key figure in the regional politics of the fledgling Republican Party, serving two three-year terms as district attorney for Tioga Co (1853, 1856) and winning election to the New York State Assembly in 1862 on the Unionist ticket. Tracy traveled from Albany to Owego in response to Pres Abraham Lincoln's call for 300,000 more troops to defend the Union, successfully raising the 109th and 137th New York State Volunteer Regiments in 1862, and was commissioned a colonel of the 109th. His bravery at the Battle of the Wilderness in Virginia in 1864 subsequently earned him the Medal of Honor. After recuperating from illness, he commanded the Elmira prisoner of war camp and rendezvous point. At war's end he was brevetted a brigadier general, and he moved to New York City and restarted his political career. Tracy served as US district attorney for the Eastern District of New York, appointed 1 Oct 1866 and reappointed 23 Jan 1871. From 1889 to 1893, as secretary of the US Navy, he promoted its expansion, emphasized the need for professionalism among officers and sailors, encouraged offensive strategies in tactics, and commissioned several steel-hulled ships used during the Spanish-American War in 1898. Tracy is often considered the father of the modern navy. Following his retirement, he played a key role in the framing of the Greater New York Charter in 1896, an act that consolidated the boroughs into the modern New York City.

Cooling, Benjamin F. *Benjamin Franklin Tracy: Father of the Modern American Fighting Navy* (Hamden, Conn: Archon Books, 1973)

Richard E. Quest

traffic management. The control of traffic to maximize the efficient and safe use of streets and highways, thereby ensuring a mobile populace and the transport of freight. Classic traffic engineering solutions, widely used in New York State from the 1930s through the 1970s, included adding or widening lanes or roadways, introducing turning lanes by widening intersections, and installing traffic signals, stop signs, and other traffic control devices. Parking was banned at curbs to convert parking lanes into traffic lanes. Traffic police were assigned to control busy intersections and ticket and tow illegally parked cars. In cities and towns, many streets were made one-way to increase capacity and to simplify coordination of traffic signals whereby vehicles, traveling at the speed limit, would not have to stop. By 1966, nearly every major avenue in Manhattan was made one-way. Despite these attempts, congestion returned as traffic volume increased. New York State motor vehicle registration soared from 2,454,000 in 1945 to 7,250,000 in 1970. Reliance on the automobile became even more pronounced with the mass migration from the cities to the suburbs.

In the late 1960s through the 1980s traffic authorities sought ways to entice car drivers toward public transportation or car pools, thus reducing the number of cars on the road. Exclusive bus lanes were introduced adjacent to the crowded expressways in the hopes of luring suburban drivers. In 1970, a contra-flow bus lane (a lane taken from the opposing direction) was opened at the Lincoln Tunnel entering Manhattan. The New York City Department of Traffic established a contra-flow lane on the Long Island Expressway in 1971. In 2002 bus lanes are commonplace throughout the state. Another popular strategy of the time was the introduction of park-and-ride sites at commuter rail stations and bus stops. Parking lots and garages were added, making it easier for drivers to shift modes. Some lots were built as car pool staging areas. To further encourage car pooling, lanes on highways were dedicated for cars with passengers during peak hours. In New York City the first dedicated car pool lane was on the Queensboro Bridge in 1994. Nevertheless, traffic congestion continued to worsen as car ownership increased and suburban migration continued, albeit at a slower pace.

In the 1990s and into the 21st century, traffic engineers have turned to a mixture of high-tech and historic traffic control techniques. Nearly every major city in New York State has interconnected traffic signals on major arteries linked to computers that can "sense" traffic conditions and adjust signals as needed. New York City was the first to computerize traffic signals, beginning with Northern Blvd in 1968. Other recent innovations include in-vehicle transponders, intelligent transportation systems (ITS), traffic calming, traffic demand management, and congestion or value pricing.

In 1993 E-Z Pass was established on the New York State Thruway, and as of 2002, 4.8 million tags were in use for which users had accounts with either MTA Bridges and Tunnels, the New York State Thruway Authority, or the Port Authority of New York and New Jersey. The tags allow transportation authorities to deduct tolls without having to stop vehicles. The intent of ITS is to detect traffic disruptions and to resolve congestion problems. Detector technologies include radar, magnetic induction loops, cameras, and E-Z Pass. Drivers can be reached by commercial and highway advisory radio channels. Many cars automatically alert motorists to traffic delays through in-vehicle navigation devices. Web sites allow drivers to examine traffic conditions be-

Detail from an International Railroad Co advertisement targeting Erie Co commuters in the 1950s.

fore they get into their cars, and cell phones and pagers provide drivers with traffic information.

Traffic calming techniques to slow traffic in residential areas or school zones include complex one-way patterns, speed bumps, narrowing the roadways at intersections (thereby shortening the crossing distance, also called neckdowns), lower speed limits, and roundabouts. Traffic demand management identifies congested corridors and tries to reduce the volume of traffic. Methods include car pool and bus lanes and other transit improvements to encourage drivers to switch to transit. Other techniques, often combined with ITS technologies, divert drivers around a congested corridor to alternate, less-congested routes. One of the most controversial strategies is congestion or value pricing. The concept, proposed in 1954 by the late Nobel Laureate for economics, Columbia Univ professor William Vickrey, manages demand for roadway space by setting prices for the use of congested thoroughfares during peak hours. In March 2001 the Port Authority of New York and New Jersey set higher prices for cars entering Manhattan between 6 and 10 AM and 4 and 7 PM. Traffic management took a new turn after 11 Sept 2001. Not only must traffic systems be efficient, but they need to be made secure from possible terrorist activities. Bridges and tunnels throughout New York State include regular or random security checks of trucks and other vehicles.

See also NEW YORK CITY REGIONAL TRANSPORTATION.

Carter, Everett C., and Stein Lundebye, eds. *The Traffic Safety Toolbox: A Primer on Traffic Safety* (Washington, DC: Institute of Traffic Engineers, 1993)

Dunphy, Robert T., and Ben C. Lin. *Transportation Management through Partnerships* (Washington, DC: Urban Land Institute, 1990)

Edwards, John D., ed. *Transportation Planning Handbook* (Washington, DC: Institute of Traffic Engineers, 1999)

Samuel I. Schwartz

transgendered people. See LESBIANS, GAYS, BISEXUALS, AND TRANSGENDERED PEOPLE.

Transportation, Department of. State agency responsible for developing and maintaining the state's entire transportation network, principally highways and bridges. The department, which was established in 1967, dates back to the surveyor general's office of the Dutch colonial period, whose primary function was the surveying of public lands. From 1777 to 1821 this official was selected by the Council of Appointment and after that was elected by the state legislature. In 1816 the legislature appointed five commissioners to oversee construction of the Erie Canal. The surveyor general soon took a formal role in canal affairs by serving as one of the commissioners of the Canal Fund (1817), which was a pool of toll revenues, land donations, and other state monies dedicated to canal projects. In 1846 a new state constitution replaced the surveyor general with the state engineer and surveyor, whose office was responsible for both canal engineering work and surveying and who directed the Canal Board (1825). Through 1926 the office was popularly elected. In 1876 a constitutional amendment created the post of superintendent of public works, who was chosen by the governor and served on the Canal Board in place of the previous canal commissioners. This superintendent took charge of maintenance and navigation on state-built canals—including the Champlain, Black River, Cayuga and Seneca, Chemung, Chenango, Genesee Valley, and Oswego, as well as the Erie—leaving the state engineer and surveyor in charge of maps, plans, and estimates for new construction. These two officials, together with the commissioners of the Canal Fund, formed the Canal Board, which from 1903 to 1911 oversaw improvements to the Erie, Champlain, and Oswego Canals that resulted in the new Barge Canal.

In 1907 the state legislature granted the Public Service Commission authority over economic and safety regulation of privately operated railroads and buses and a year later formed the Department of Highways to supervise state-financed bridges and highways. From 1911 to 1913 the superintendent of highways, state engineer and surveyor, and superintendent of public works all served as highway commissioners, with a single commissioner replacing them in 1913. A 1923 law consolidated a number of offices into the Department of Public Works, which had five divisions: canals and waterways, highways, public building, engineering, and architecture. In 1943 these were reorganized into three divisions: administration, construction, and operation and maintenance. In 1955 the department gained an architecture division and in 1964 a finance and planning division.

In 1967 the Department of Transportation (DOT) was created by the legislature to coordinate all development within the state, incorporating the now defunct Department of Public Works duties of transportation planning, construction, and operation, which included maintenance of the state's Barge Canal System. DOT also absorbed the State Traffic Commission (1936), responsible for traffic lights, signs, speeds, and safety programs; the Office of Transportation (1959), a gubernatorial advisory group; and the aviation functions of the Commerce Department. In 1992 the legislature transferred control of the canals to the New York State Thruway Authority, whose subsidiary, the New York State Canal Corp, operates the system. DOT coordinates annually a network of transportation that includes 110,000 highway miles (177,000 km), 17,000 bridges, 456 public and private aviation facilities, and a 5,000 mi (8,050) rail network. A gubernatorially appointed commissioner directs the department, which is headquartered at the W. Averell Harriman State Office Campus in Albany and in 2002 had 11 regional offices, 68 county offices, and 12,000 employees.

See also CARTOGRAPHY AND MAPPING; ROADS; SNOW REMOVAL.

New York State. Assembly. "Legislative Commission on Expenditure Review." In *State Highway Pavement Management* (Albany: Legislative Commission on Expenditure Review, 1992)

New York State. Public Transportation Safety Board. *Annual Report* (Albany: Department of Transportation, 1984)

Jeffrey Kraus

transportation authorities. Public benefit corporations chartered by the New York State legislature to provide transportation services on a regional basis throughout the state. Like other public benefit corporations, transportation authorities have their own autonomous governing boards. They finance themselves through fares, tolls, and revenue bonds and are tax exempt and exempt from civil service rules. In 1968 the Metropolitan Transportation Authority (MTA) was established by the state legislature, absorbing a number of existing entities, among them the New York City Transit Authority, which operated the New York City subway system; Staten Island Rapid Transit Operating Authority; Metropolitan Suburban Bus Authority; Long Island Rail Road; and Triborough Bridge and Tunnel Authority. In 1969 state legislation created four regional transportation authorities: Capital District Transportation Authority, serving the greater Albany area; Central New York Regional Transportation Authority (CENTRO), serving Onondaga, Cayuga, and Oswego Cos; Niagara Frontier Transportation Authority (NFTA), serving Erie and Niagara Cos; and Rochester-Genesee Regional Transportation Authority (RGRTA), serving Monroe, Genesee, Livingston, Wayne, and Wyoming Cos. All the regional authorities offer bus service on a local and regional basis. CENTRO manages parking facilities and Syracuse's William F. Walsh Regional Transportation Center, providing residents of Central New York with connections to intercity bus and rail transportation. NFTA operates Buffalo, Niagara, and Niagara Falls Airports, Buffalo's Metro rail system, the Port of Buffalo, the NFTA boat harbor, and transportation centers in downtown Niagara Falls and Buffalo.

Walsh, Annmarie H. *The Public's Business: The Politics and Practices of Government Corporations* (Cambridge, Mass: MIT Press, 1978)

Jeffrey Kraus

Transport Workers Union of America (TWU). In 1934 in New York City a core of Irish Americans and left-wing organizers founded the TWU as an industrial union. In January 1937 the TWU organized a sit-down strike in the Kent Ave subway powerhouse in Brooklyn, spurring a successful organizing drive among workers in two of the three subway lines and most bus lines in New York City's transit system, quickly adding over 30,000 members. After receiving a national charter from the Committee for Industrial Organization (CIO) in 1937, the TWU expanded nationally, organizing public and private transit, university, and utility workers. It established an airline division in 1942 and won national agreements on American Airlines and Pan American World Airways. The United Railroad Workers Organizing Committee affiliated in 1954, adding railroad workers from the Pennsylvania and New York Central Railroads. Locals were established throughout New York State. Despite its national presence, the TWU is perceived as a New York City–based union because of the prominence of Local 100, its largest affiliate. The local enforced its contracts for many years through economic power, strike threats, and political activity in City Hall and Albany, an unusual feat for a union with public sector members. Even after a 12-day strike in 1966 that paralyzed New York City, the union won substantial gains and convinced the state legislature to waive the heavy penalties of the Condon-Wadlin Act, which required the firing of striking public sector workers and the postponement of wage increases. The strike moved Gov Nelson A. Rockefeller to appoint a committee that recommended a new public employment statute

TRANSPORTATION AUTHORITIES (2000)

Name	Service Area	Transportation Services	Passenger Miles	Total Operating Expenses
Metropolitan Transportation Authority (MTA)	New York City, Nassau, Suffolk, Westchester, Rockland, Dutchess, Putnam, Orange in New York State; New Haven and Fairfield in Connecticut	bus, rail, subway, bridges, tunnels	14,839,000,000	$6,250,000,000
Niagara Frontier Transportation Authority (NFTA)	Erie, Niagara	bus, rail, airports, Port of Buffalo, boat harbor	85,145,079	$71,001,900
Capital District Transportation Authority (CDTA)	Albany, Rensselaer, Saratoga, Schenectady	bus, rail station	40,853,252	$35,572,600
Rochester-Genesee Regional Transportation Authority (RGRTA)	Monroe, Genesee, Livingston, Wayne, Wyoming	bus	40,815,155	$36,639,600
Central New York Regional Transportation Authority (CENTRO)	Onondaga, Cayuga, Oswego	bus, rail station, parking facilities	27,620,637	$20,781,300

Sources: National Transit Database (2000); Metropolitan Transportation Authority, *Annual Report* (2000).

known as the Taylor Law. After an 11-day transit strike in 1980, penalties invoked under the Taylor Law fined individual members and crippled the local financially. Since 1970 the TWU has expanded its organizing activities to municipal workers, school support staff, toll collectors, and airline crafts such as flight dispatchers and pilot instructors. In that same time period, the largely white male urban transit locals have been transformed in composition to locals often dominated by minorities and women. At the turn of the 21st century, the TWU represented over 110,000 members nationally in all aspects of transportation-related work.

Freeman, Joshua. *In Transit: The Transport Workers Union in New York City, 1933–1966* (New York: Oxford Univ Press, 1989)

Marmo, Michael. *More Profile Than Courage: The New York City Transit Strike of 1966* (Albany: SUNY Press, 1990)

Robert Wechsler

Trans World Airlines (TWA). International airline that dates to 1925 with the founding of Western Air Express, one of its ancestors. In 1928 Transcontinental Air Transport was launched, backed mainly by the Pennsylvania Railroad. Coast-to-coast service began on 7 July 1929, and at first, passengers took a train from Pennsylvania Station in New York City to Columbus, Ohio, where they transferred to the Ford Tri-Motor airplanes. Another rail journey was necessary from Waynoka, Okla, to Clovis, N Mex. A merger took place on 1 Oct 1930 to form Transcontinental and Western Air (TWA), and it became known as the Lindbergh Line after its technical director, Charles Lindbergh, mapped the route in detail. Full air service from Newark, NJ, to Los Angeles began on 25 Oct 1930. Though advertised as a Los Angeles–New York City air service, the eastern terminus was Newark until January 1940, when it began using North Beach Airport (now La Guardia Airport) in Queens. On 8 July 1940 TWA introduced the Boeing 307 Stratoliner, the first airliner to be pressurized and thus able to fly above the turbulence at an altitude of 20,000 feet (6,096 m). The airline flew many missions during World War II out of La Guardia Airport, across the North and South Atlantic, through its specially created Intercontinental Division. On 1 May 1945 TWA began a route from Pittsburgh to Boston, with stops at Williamsport, Pa, Binghamton, and Albany. This route was maintained until April 1964, when it was transferred to Mohawk Airlines, but a more direct Pittsburgh-Albany-Boston route was retained. The Albany stop was discontinued within two years.

After Idlewild International Airport (now John F. Kennedy International Airport) opened in Queens on 1 July 1948, TWA was one of its biggest users for many years. The company advertised itself as the Trans World Airline beginning 5 Feb 1946, when it inaugurated service to Paris from La Guardia Airport, and on 17 May 1950 this became the official name. At its zenith during the latter 1960s, TWA was the leading airline on the North Atlantic route. It overtook the hitherto dominant Pan American World Airways in June 1969, carrying 131,000 passengers against Pan Am's 128,000. The airline had thrived under the sometimes erratic but effective leadership of Howard Hughes. He had purchased 25% of the TWA stock in April 1939 and increased his share to 78% by 1940 but relinquished his interest completely on 3 May 1966. The airline's fortunes declined beginning in the 1970s. After three battles with the bankruptcy courts, TWA was sold to American Airlines on 12 Mar 2001. TWA's terminal, commissioned to Eero Saarinen in 1956 and opened in 1962, graced JFK as an architectural gem.

Davies, R. E. G. *TWA—An Airline and Its Aircraft* (McLean, Va: Paladwr Press, 2000)

Serling, Robert J. *Howard Hughes' Airline* (New York: St. Martin's/Marek, 1983)

R. E. G. Davies

Travers Stakes. A race for 3-year-olds at the Saratoga Race Course in Saratoga Springs, it is among the most prestigious events on the thoroughbred racing circuit. Sometimes called the Mid-Summer Derby, the Travers is one of the oldest stakes races in North America. It was first run on 2 Aug 1864 during the inaugural season of the present track. The stakes race is named after William R. Travers, a New York City stockbroker and first president of the Saratoga Association, the controlling body of the track. Travers's horse, Kentucky, won the initial race, held at the distance of a mile and three-quarters, in the time of 3 min 18.75 s. The Travers Stakes has been held annually except for 1896, 1898–1900, and 1911–12. From 1943–45 it was held at the Belmont Park Racetrack in Elmont (Nassau Co). Since 1904 it has been run at a mile and a quarter. Through 1975 the Travers was an allowance stakes, with the weights carried by each horse determined by its previous perfor-mance; since then it has been run with a scale weight of 126 lb (57.2 kg) for colts and 121 lb (54.9 kg) for fillies. In 2002 the purse was $1,000,000. Each victorious owner receives a small replica of the Man o' War Cup, a permanent gold trophy. Since 1961 a canoe floating in the track's infield lake is immediately painted in the colors of the Travers champion.

The list of Travers winners includes many of America's greatest racehorses, including Man o' War (1920), Whirlaway (1941)—the only Triple Crown champion to win the Travers—Native Dancer (1953), and Alydar (1978). Among the more memorable races were in 1930, when Jim Dandy came from behind to best Triple Crown winner Gallant Fox at odds of 100 to 1, and in 1962, when Jaipur and Ridan rode neck and neck the entire distance before Jaipur won by a nose. The fastest Travers champion was General Assembly (1979) in 2 min 0 s.

Hotaling, Edward. *They're off: Horse Racing at Saratoga* (Syracuse: Syracuse Univ Press, 1995)

Field Horne

Treaty of Big Tree. Negotiated in 1797, the Treaty of Big Tree [north of present-day Cuylerville, Livingston Co] marks the beginning of the reservation period for the Seneca. It established four major Seneca reservations in western New York State: the Allegany [loc in Cattaraugus Co], the Cattaraugus [loc in Erie, Chautauqua, and Cattaraugus Cos], the Buffalo Creek [now in Erie Co], and the Tonawanda [loc in Erie, Genesee, and Niagara Cos]. In addition, there was also the Canadaway Reservation [now in Cattaraugus and Chautauqua Cos] on Lake Erie. The Oil Spring Reservation [loc in Cattaraugus and Allegany], mistakenly omitted from the Treaty of Big Tree, was added to Seneca landholdings in 1801 at the request of Handsome Lake. Six smaller reservations encompassed old village sites in the Seneca homelands along the Genesee River and ranged in size from 16 mi^2 (41 km^2) at the southernmost Caneadea to 2 mi^2 (5 km^2) each for Squakie Hill, Little Beard's Town, Big Tree, Canawaugus, and Gardeau.

By this treaty the Seneca sold all of their other lands in western New York State for $100,000. This money was to be invested at 6% and an annuity was to be paid from the interest to each Seneca. In 1791 Robert Morris of Philadelphia, a major financier of the Revolutionary War, had acquired the preemption right to purchase the lands remaining to the Seneca, if they chose to sell them. Morris sold the majority of his right during 1792 and 1793 to a representative of the Dutch banking houses that would become, in 1796, the Holland Land Co. As the sale depended on extinguishing Seneca claims to the land, Morris, represented by his son, purchased the 3.3 million acres (1.3 million ha) from the Seneca at the Treaty of Big Tree. The land was then transferred to the Holland Land Co.

The ongoing loss of Seneca lands through treaties negotiated between the Treaty of Fort Stanwix in 1784 and the Treaty of Big Tree established the foundation for future political unrest among the Seneca. Major segments of the loyalist Iroquois, including some Senecas, had removed with Joseph Brant to Canada, effectively dividing the political unity of the confederacy. The treaty process, through the bribery of political leaders by gifts of land and money, created jealousy and resentment among the common people. By creating economic inequality, old rivalries reemerged and factionalism was exacerbated.

Abler, Thomas S., and Elisabeth Tooker. "Seneca." In *Northeast,* ed. Bruce G. Trigger, vol 15 of *Handbook of North American Indians,* ed. William C. Sturtevant (Washington, DC: Smithsonian Institution, 1978)

Hauptman, Laurence M. *Conspiracy of Interests* (Syracuse: Syracuse Univ Press, 1999)

Wallace, Anthony F. C. *The Death and Rebirth of the Seneca* (New York: Knopf, 1970)

George H. J. Abrams

Treaty of Buffalo Creek (1826). On 31 Aug 1826, under a treaty authorized by the United States at Buffalo Creek, some Seneca chiefs and warriors came to agreement with Ogden Land Co agents that the Seneca cede the last of their Genesee Valley lands: Big Tree, Canawaugus, and Squakie Hill Reservations [now in Livingston Co]; the remaining 2 mi^2 (5.2 km^2) at the Gardeau Reservation [now in Wyoming Co]; and the 16 mi^2 (41.4 km^2) Caneadea Reservation [now in Allegany Co]. The areas of the Buffalo Creek [now in Erie Co], Tonawanda [loc in Erie, Genesee, and Niagara Cos], and Cattaraugus Indian Reservations [loc in Cattaraugus, Chautauqua, and Erie Cos] were also reduced: Buffalo Creek by 36,638 acres (14,827 ha), Tonawanda by 33,409 acres (13,520 ha), and Cattaraugus by 5,120 acres (2,072 ha), decreasing the Seneca land base by 86,887 acres (35,162 ha). Among the Seneca signing the treaty were Big Kettle, Gov Blacksnake, Henry Two Guns, Little Billy, Pollard, Red Jacket, Seneca White, Capt Shongo, Capt Strong, White Seneca, and Young King. Some of them had narrowly defined concerns, specifically, to protect their individual reservations and immediate interests rather than to fight for all of the Seneca lands. Some of the federal officials and Seneca negotiating the treaty were bribed by the Ogden Land Co. The treaty was of doubtful legal standing also because it had never been ratified by the US Senate, but its provisions were never reversed. Red Jacket never truly supported the treaty (though he signed it), and he led the opposition to it up until his death in 1830. Opposition continued, and the Indian Claims Commission in the late 1960s and early 1970s awarded the Seneca monetary compensation for the land illegally taken under the treaty.

Densmore, Christopher. *Red Jacket: Iroquois Diplomat and Orator* (Syracuse: Syracuse Univ Press, 1999)

Hauptman, Laurence M. *Conspiracy of Interests: Iroquois Dispossession and the Rise of New York State* (Syracuse: Syracuse Univ Press, 1999)

Manley, Henry S. "Red Jacket's Last Campaign," *New York History* 31 (Apr 1950): 149–68

Laurence M. Hauptman

Treaty of Buffalo Creek (1838). With the election of Andrew Jackson to the presidency and New Yorker Martin Van Buren to the vice presidency in 1828, Washington policy makers began to consider the removal of all the Iroquois nations to lands west of the Mississippi River. This policy was promoted by land speculators, such as officials of the Ogden Land Co, and by certain Albany politicians promoting the state's economic growth. Jackson appointed first John Freeman Schermerhorn and later Ransom Gillet to help James Stryker, the federal Indian agent, negotiate the treaty. Under its terms, the Seneca would cede to the Ogden Land Co all their remaining New York State lands, with the exception of the 1 mi^2 (2.6 km^2) Oil Spring Reservation [loc in Allegany and Cattaraugus Cos]. The cession amounted to 102,069 acres (41,306 ha), comprising the Allegany [loc in Cattaraugus Co], Cattaraugus [loc in Cattaraugus, Chautauqua, and Erie Cos], Tonawanda [loc in Erie, Genesee, and Niagara Cos], and Buffalo Creek [now in Erie Co] Reservations. The Indians also relinquished their rights to Menominee lands in Wisconsin that had been purchased for them by the United States. They accepted in return from the federal government a 1,824,000-acre (738,150 ha) Kansas reservation for all six Iroquois nations and the Stockbridge-Munsee, with an obligation to occupy these eastern Kansas lands within five years or forfeit them. They also were to receive $202,000; $100,000 of this amount was to be invested in safe securities by the president of the United States with the interest earned to be returned to the Indians, plus a modest amount for help with the relocation, the establishment of schools, and agricultural purposes. One month later some of the Oneida, already in Wisconsin, signed an appendage to this treaty in Washington, DC, whereby they secured a 65,400-acre (26,466 ha) reservation. The Buffalo Creek Treaty of 1838 never received the approval of two-thirds of the US Senate, even though it was promulgated by Pres Van Buren in 1840.

The Treaty of Buffalo Creek of 1838 shaped the destinies of the New York State Iroquois for much of the 19th century. As a result of the treaty, there was a removal of many Indians from the state. A small number of the Iroquois who left for Indian Territory, primarily Cayuga who had occupied Seneca lands and a few Tuscarora, died en route or upon arrival from the consequences of governmental neglect. Anger at the chiefs who had signed the treaty and the subsequent bitter infighting led to the creation in 1848 of the Seneca Nation of Indians, a new political entity. Partly because of the blatant frauds committed in getting Indian approval of the treaty, many congressmen and missionaries questioned its binding force. A campaign led by Quakers to restore the Indian lands in New York State resulted in the US Senate's ratification of the Supplemental Treaty of 1842, also known as the Compromise Treaty of 1842. Under this treaty the Seneca regained the Allegany and Cattaraugus but not the Buffalo Creek and Tonawanda Reservations. Only in 1856 was the Tonawanda Band of Senecas finally permitted to buy back a small part of its reservation from the Ogden Land Co. A treaty the following year between the United States and the Tonawanda Band of Senecas acknowledged this purchase and the land's federal reservation status. Claims under the treaty of 1838 were not settled until a series of decisions made in the US Court of Claims from 1895 to 1906. The 1838 treaty remains one of the major frauds in American Indian history. While some of its provisions were subsequently litigated or overturned, there was no reversing the loss of the Buffalo Creek Reservation, on which more than 100,000 non-Indians settled over the next 30 years.

Hauptman, Laurence M. "Four Eastern New Yorkers and Seneca Lands: A Study in Treaty-Making," *Hudson Valley Regional Review* 13 (Mar 1996): 1–19

———. *Conspiracy of Interests: Iroquois Dispossession and the Rise of New York State* (Syracuse: Syracuse Univ Press, 1999)

Manley, Henry S. "Buying Buffalo from the Indians," *New York History* 28 (July 1947): 313–29

Laurence M. Hauptman

Treaty of Canandaigua. Also known as the Pickering Treaty, it affirmed a lasting peace and friendship between the Six Nations, or Iroquois Confederacy, and the United States. It was signed on 11 Nov 1794 in Canandaigua (Ontario Co) and negotiated by Timothy Pickering, the official representative appointed by Pres George Washington. Approximately 1,600 Iroquois delegates attended the negotiations, of which almost 800 were Seneca; the other half represented the Cayuga, Onondaga, Oneida, and Tuscarora Nations. The pro-British Mohawk sent only one representative from Canada. The treaty recognized the land reserved to the Oneida, Onondaga, and Cayuga Nations in prior treaties and detailed the boundaries of the Seneca Nation in Western New York. It did not mention the Mohawk or Tuscarora lands. One stipulation provided that the United States could build a wagon road for free passage between Lake Ontario and Lake Erie. The treaty states that the Six Nations will make no claim on lands within the boundaries of the United States. A one-time payment by the United States of goods valued at $10,000 was stated, and an annual expenditure of $4,500 for the purchase of additional goods was to be paid to the Iroquois in perpetuity. Today this takes the form of treaty cloth, an inexpensive material distributed annually to each of the Six Nations on a per capita basis. Pres Washington added his signature to the treaty on 21 Jan 1795, but the treaty was never officially ratified by the US Senate. Contemporary Iroquois hold the Treaty of Canandaigua to be the basis of their continuing sovereign status. Every year a commemoration of the treaty is held in Canandaigua on 11 November.

Jemison, G. Peter, and Anna M. Schein, eds. *Treaty of Canandaigua: 200 Years of Treaty Relations between the Iroquois Confederacy and the United States* (Santa Fe, N Mex: Clear Light Publishers, 2000)

G. Peter Jemison

Treaty of Fort Schuyler (Oneida). Agreement signed on 22 Sept 1788 at Fort Schuyler [now Rome, Oneida Co], between Oneida Nation representatives and New York State. One of a series of land treaties, its provisions included more than 5 million acres (2.02 million ha) of Oneida tribal land ceded to New York State. In return for territory from Lake Ontario to the Pennsylvania border, the state granted the Oneida a reservation of approximately 300,000 acres (121,000 ha) in what is now Madison and Oneida Cos, as well as $2,000 in cash, $2,000 in clothing and other goods, $1,000 in provisions, $500 to build grist- and sawmills, and an annuity of $600. The treaty also provided smaller tracts for the Stockbridge and Brotherton Indians. In 1978 the Oneida Nation challenged the legality of the treaty, which was made without the presence of a federal official, but the US District Court for the Northern District of New York dismissed the claim in *Oneida Indian Nation v State of New York* (1986) after finding that the land acquisitions were valid under the Articles of Confederation. The decision was upheld by the US Second Circuit Court of Appeals in 1988, and the following year the US Supreme Court denied a petition to hear the case.

"State Treaty with the Oneida Indians, 1788," 22 Sept 1788, http://www.madisoncounty.org/motf/T1788.html

Suzan D. Friedlander

Treaty of Fort Stanwix (1768). In 1768 the British government authorized Sir William Johnson, superintendent of Indian affairs and a prominent Mohawk Valley resident, to negotiate a permanent boundary line for the northern colonies to replace the temporary Proclamation Line of 1763. After the French and Indian War (1754–63), Indian nations favored a boundary line to protect their lands from colonial encroachment. Iroquois, Delaware, Shawnee, and other Indians met colonial officials from New York, New Jersey, Pennsylvania, and Virginia at Fort Stanwix [now Rome, Oneida Co] from 24 Oct to 5 Nov 1768. With more than 3,000 attending, the conference was one of the largest Indian councils held in North America. Despite Ohio Indians' objections, but with Johnson's support, the Iroquois Confederacy relinquished Indian claims to most of the Ohio River valley in an attempt to deflect colonial expansion away from Iroquoia. Johnson collaborated with land speculators, proprietors, and impoverished Indian traders to secure large tracts of Indian lands for himself. He disobeyed the British Board of Trade's instructions to end the line at the Great Kanawha River [now Kanawha River in W Va], where a similar boundary line for the southern colonies terminated. The final treaty line ran southward from New York Colony to the Delaware River, westward along the Susquehanna and Allegheny Rivers, and down the Ohio River to the mouth of the Tennessee River, near what is now Paducah, Ky. The treaty failed to resolve relations between Whites and Indians permanently, stimulated colonial settlement, and precipitated conflict with Indian nations in the Ohio Valley. By the early 1770s, the Iroquois complained that New York colonists had transgressed the treaty line. Many Indian nations continued to define their borders based on the 1768 treaty line until after the Revolutionary War.

Jones, Dorothy V. *License for Empire: Colonialism by Treaty in Early America* (Chicago: Univ of Chicago Press, 1982)

David L. Preston

Treaty of Fort Stanwix (1784). Delegates of the Iroquois Confederacy met with commissioners of the United States at Fort Stanwix [now Rome, Oneida Co] in October 1784 to settle disputes following the American Revolution. Despite some sharp divisions during the war, the majority of the Iroquois supported the British in the hope that it offered the best defense against encroaching American colonists. The American victory marked a decided defeat for the Iroquois, especially when the 1783 Treaty of Paris failed to include provisions for protecting Indian lands east of the Mississippi River and south of the Great Lakes. Rather than employ military force to facilitate white settlement on Indian land in the Ohio Valley region, American officials opted for diplomacy as a less expensive and less contentious strategy. The US commissioners at Fort Stanwix were Arthur Lee of Virginia, Gen Richard Butler of Pennsylvania, and Oliver Wolcott of Connecticut. Iroquois delegates included Seneca chief Cornplanter, Oneida chief Good Peter, and Mohawk chief Aaron Hill, who was later held hostage by the Americans pending the return of captives held by the Iroquois. The Seneca, Cayuga, Onondaga, and Mohawk were treated as defeated nations, but the Oneida and Tuscarora were confirmed as allies for their support during the war. Indian nations residing in the disputed territory had almost no voice in treaty negotiations. Despite their resolve not to part with any more land, the Iroquois delegates were powerless to fend off the commissioners' demands and agreed to cede all claims to land west of New York State and Pennsylvania to the United States. Although the treaty did not seek to limit land held by the Iroquois in New York or Pennsylvania, except to guarantee American access to Oswego, all six nations would lose substantial territory in the decades that followed. Many Iroquois refused to acknowledge the treaty's legitimacy on the grounds that their delegates were not empowered to make land cessions and that they had done so only through coercion. American attempts to settle the western lands claimed by the Iroquois led to a series of wars with western Indian nations in the late 1780s and 1790s.

Calloway, Colin G. *Crown and Calumet: British-Indian Relations, 1783–1815* (Norman: Univ of Oklahoma Press, 1987)
Graymont, Barbara. *The Iroquois in the American Revolution* (Syracuse: Syracuse Univ Press, 1972)

Gail D. MacLeitch

Treaty of 1701. Also known as the Peace of 1701, the event was marked by the conclusion of separate negotiations between the Iroquois and the French in Montreal and the Iroquois and the English in Albany. Before the French and English concluded the Treaty of Ryswick in 1697, ending their limited war in North America, the French had been pressuring the Iroquois to stop warring against them. The Iroquois had been asking for English support to fight against the French to protect against further French encroachments onto Iroquois land. When the English came to terms with the French, the Iroquois gave in to French requests for peace, recognizing their inability to pursue war unaided. To try to protect their land, the Iroquois gave to the English a vast tract in what is now southwestern Ontario and southern Michigan. The peace bought the Iroquois time to try to resolve how to deal with French encroachments onto their land.

Brandão, J. A., and William A. Starna. "The Treaties of 1701: A Triumph of Iroquois Diplomacy," *Ethnohistory* 43 (Spring 1996): 209–44
Haan, Richard. "The Problem of Iroquois Neutrality: Suggestions for Revision," *Ethnohistory* 27 (Fall 1980): 317–30
Havard, Gilles. *The Great Peace of Montreal of 1701.* Trans Phyllis Aronoff and Howard Scott (Montreal and Kingston: McGill-Queen's Univ Press, 2001)

José António Brandão

tree diseases and pests. New York State has the dubious distinction of being North America's chief port of entry for invasive tree diseases and insect pests, with the first recorded invaders of this type arriving in the 1800s. The advent of the fungus-caused chestnut blight is perhaps the most tragic example of the state's role as initial host area. The pathogen *Cryphonectria parasitica* was inadvertently introduced in 1904 when Japanese chestnuts with inconspicuous disease symptoms were transplanted to New York Zoological Park in the Bronx. Within 40 years, the disease had spread to American chestnuts throughout their natural range, and a once dominant forest tree was reduced to little more than an occasional shrub. Other tree diseases that have entered the United States through the Port of New York and had a major impact on the composition of the nation's forests and on urban landscapes include white pine blister rust *(Cronartium ribicola)* (1906), Dutch elm disease *(Ophiostoma ulmi)* (around 1932), and anthracnose *(Discula destructiva)* of flowering dogwood (1982). While native elms approach extinction, largely because an efficient insect vector, the barkbeetle *(Scolytus multistriatus),* arrived almost simultaneously with the Dutch elm pathogen, the picture is brighter for flowering dogwood because some trees seem to be anthracnose-resistant.

The state's tree population has also suffered from foreign diseases introduced elsewhere but established in New York State. For instance, beech bark disease, first found in eastern Canada in the 1930s and caused by the combined effects of an introduced insect *(Cryptococcus fagisuga)* and an introduced fungus *(Nectria coccinea* var *faginata),* has killed hundreds of thousands of American beech throughout the state. At the beginning of the 21st century, with no effective control measures available, the disease continues unabated.

Serious insect pests that have entered North America through New York State ports include elongate hemlock scale *(Fiorina externa)* (1908), European pine shoot moth *(Ryacionia buoliana)* (1914), imported willow leaf beetle *(Plagiodera versicolora)* (1915), and common pine shoot beetle *(Tomicus piniperda)* (1992). In 1996 a wood-boring beetle, the Asian longhorn *(Anoplophora glabripennis),* was found in and around New York City. These beetles make large channels as they feed in the wood of deciduous trees, weakening branches and trunks until they break. Aggressive efforts by state and federal inspectors to destroy infested trees before the beetles reproduce are slowing, but not stopping, the spread of the invaders.

Other foreign insect pests have migrated into New York's forests from nearby states. In 1870, for instance, Eastern European gypsy moths *(Lymantria dispar)* being tested for cold-climate silk production in a Massachusetts laboratory escaped and spread to New York. Their leaf consumption has killed hundreds of thousands of valuable trees, oaks in particular. Fortunately two diseases, one caused by a virus and the other by a fungus, reduced gypsy moth populations to tolerable levels by the last years of the 20th century. Hemlock wooly adelgids *(Adelges tsugae),* first found in the United States in 1927 in Connecticut, have killed thousands of eastern hemlocks in the lower Hudson Valley and on Long Island. Timely applications of pesticides prevent these insects from damaging individual landscape trees. Unfortunately they remain unchecked in forests and continue to spread north and east from that point of introduction.

Increasing international trade and travel through New York and other East Coast ports heighten the chances of more foreign pests being introduced. Careful inspection of imported products and responsible behavior by travelers are the best hopes for minimizing future threats.

Johnson, W. T., and H. H. Lyon. *Insects That Feed on Trees and Shrubs,* 2d ed. (Ithaca: Comstock Publishing, 1988)

Sinclair, W. A., H. H. Lyon, and W. T. Johnson. *Diseases of Trees and Shrubs* (Ithaca: Comstock Publishing, 1987)

Tainter, F. H., and F. A. Baker. *Principles of Forest Pathology* (New York: John Wiley & Sons, 1996)

George W. Hudler

Trenton. Town (pop 4,670) in NE Oneida Co. The town was formed from Schuyler (Herkimer Co) in 1797. Trenton's main attraction is Trenton Falls, and to serve meals to its visitors, the Rural Resort opened in 1823. Michael Moore took it over in 1831, expanding it and devoting his life to popularizing the falls; he built a larger hotel in 1851. Tourism peaked during the 1850s and 1860s with rail service provided by the Black River and Utica Railroad (1855). In 1849 a large gang sawmill was built at Hinckley and operated until the 1920s. The Hinckley Reservoir, supporting the Barge Canal, was constructed from 1911 to 1915. At South Trenton peppermint and witch hazel distilleries were in production in the 19th century. The Moore family sold its water rights to Utica Electric Light and Power Co, which began operating a hydroelectric plant in 1901, although it was the Mohawk and Malone Railroad (1892) that doomed the falls as a tourist attraction by carrying nature seekers farther north. While the falls remain intact, no public access exists at the turn of the 21st century. In 2003 Jet Sew (industrial sewing machines) employs residents; others commute to Utica and Rome.

Trenton Falls. Name given to the hamlet and to a series of three waterfalls in Oneida Co on West Canada Creek. Geologically the creek cuts through fossil-laden black limestone, from which 6 in (15 cm) trilobites have been extracted. The Trenton epoch of the Ordovician period is named for the location where these unique fossils were found. Trenton Falls was one of the earliest tourist spots in America. John Sherman, who had purchased the falls and surrounding land from the Holland Land Co, built the first hotel here in 1822. The opening of the Erie Canal in 1825 and of subsequent railway lines simplified access to Trenton Falls. Tourism peaked at roughly 7,500 visitors a year between 1850 and 1870. On 18 Aug 1863 Secretary of State William H. Seward met with diplomats from around the world at Trenton Falls as part of a successful effort to prevent their countries from recognizing the Confederacy as an independent nation.

As trains were able to carry passengers deeper into the Adirondacks, tourism decreased, and in 1888 the falls were sold to the Utica Gas and Light Co. In 1914 the top of the High Falls was dammed, a 7 ft (2.1 m) diameter pipe was installed to carry the water to four turbines for a hydroelectric plant, and public access was banned. In 1996 the falls owners, Niagara Mohawk, and the Town of Trenton discussed a land transfer that would include access to scenic overlooks of the falls, but in 1999 Niagara Mohawk sold its hydroelectric plants to Orion Power Holdings of Baltimore, and the subject was dropped. In December 2001 Orion merged with Houston-based Reliant Resources.

Schwabach, Deborah. "From Sublime to Industrious," *Adirondack Life* 27 (Dec 1996): 18–24

Thomas, Howard. *Trenton Falls Yesterday and Today* (Prospect, NY: Prospect Books, 1951)

Deborah Schwabach

Trenton Falls; detail from stereoscopic card.

Triangle. Town (pop 3,032) in N Broome Co. Settled by 1791, the town was formed from Lisle in 1831 and named for the Chenango Triangle, the land grant of which it was part. Abolitionist Gerrit Smith helped settle a few African American families in the 1840s. Pres Franklin D. Roosevelt was instrumental in building the US Army Corps of Engineers' Whitney Point Dam and Reservoir (1938–1942) following serious floods on the Otselic and Tioughnioga in 1935 and 1936; the reservoir has three county parks on its shores. Dairy farming has declined in importance. Schaeffer's Gardens (1976), wholesale growers, and the construction firm of W. and D. Smith and Sons (1973) are major employers in 2003.

Charles J. Browne

Triangle Shirtwaist Factory fire. The Triangle Shirtwaist Co, which produced formfitting women's blouses, was owned by Max Blanck and Isaac Harris. It employed 650 workers and was housed in the Asch Building (1901) on the corner of Greene and Washington Sts in Greenwich Village in New York City. At approximately 4:40 PM, just 5 minutes before quitting time, on 25 Mar 1911, a small fire started on the 8th floor. The exact cause is unknown, but the fire spread rapidly, fed by several tons of flammable fabric. Managers and owners on the 10th floor were notified and escaped across the roof, aided by students at the neighboring New York University Law School; most workers on the 8th floor rushed through the exits. Dozens of workers died on the 9th floor, where the exits were chain locked, a common practice to keep out union organizers. The fire escape collapsed, elevators seared with the heat, and piles of bodies blocked the only exit. With nowhere else to go, many workers jumped out the 9th-floor windows. A total of 146 women died, mostly young immigrant Jews and Italians. The sight of the helpless victims shocked the nation. The fire caused a commotion as workers from the Lower East Side and residents of the factory's middle-class neighborhood watched in horror. After the largest public funeral in New York City history, the public pressured the state government to act. In 1911 the legislature created the Factory Investigating Commission, and by 1915 New York State had the most advanced labor and industrial legislation in the country. The building that housed the Triangle Shirtwaist Co is now a National Historic Site occupied by New York University.

Stein, Leon. *The Triangle Fire* (Philadelphia: J. B. Lippincott, 1962)

Richard A. Greenwald

Triborough Bridge and Tunnel Authority (TBTA). The New York State legislature in 1933 established the Triborough Bridge Authority (TBA) to build the Triborough Bridge complex, joining Queens with Manhattan and Bronx Co. Construction of the bridge had been halted in 1929 with the onset of the Great Depression. The new agency, a state public authority, had the power to issue its own bonds with state backing. Robert Moses was appointed to head the TBA. Following the authority's creation, the Triborough Bridge was completed in 1936. Moses was able to exploit successfully ambiguities in the TBA's original enabling legislation and its toll revenue and bonding power to build or acquire infrastructure projects that extended far beyond the original mission of the authority. In 1939 Moses constructed the Bronx-Whitestone and the Cross Bay Bridges (later renamed Cross Bay Veterans Memorial Bridge). In 1940 the TBA absorbed the Marine Parkway Authority, builder of the Marine Parkway Bridge (later renamed Marine Parkway Gil Hodges Memorial Bridge), and the next year the Henry Hudson Parkway Authority, but ultimately retained only the Henry Hudson Bridge. Moses also incorporated the New York City Tunnel Authority into the TBA in 1946, which consisted of the Queens-Midtown Tunnel (1940) and the Brooklyn-Battery Tunnel project (completed in 1950), and renamed the authority the TBTA. Additional authority projects included the construction of the now-demolished New York Coliseum (1956) on Columbus Circle in Manhattan and the Throgs Neck (1961) and Verrazano-Narrows (1964) Bridges. In time, the power of the TBTA and Moses and the apparent lack of public oversight of their activities made the authority extremely controversial. In 1968 Gov Nelson A. Rockefeller removed Moses as TBTA chairman and incorporated the TBTA into the region's subway, rail, and bus agencies, creating the Metropolitan Transportation Authority (MTA).

Caro, Robert A. *The Power Broker: Robert Moses and the Fall of New York* (New York: Vintage Books, 1974)

Thomas A. Birkland

Trico. Automotive parts manufacturer. With auto windshield wipers yet to be invented, John R. Oishei drove his car in a Buffalo rainstorm in 1916 and knocked down and slightly injured a bicyclist. The next year he and several inventors and financial backers founded the windshield wiper company later known as Trico, or Tri-Continental Corp. The firm became dominant in its field through its patents and product innovation and through the purchase of competitors' patents in the 1920s and 1930s. At its peak in the early 1950s, the company employed up to 4,700 workers in its three Buffalo plants, controlled two-thirds of the new domestic auto wiper blade market, and branched out into other automotive accessories such as power windows.

Trico's sales doubled between 1968 and the early 1980s to $100 million, but the company's position weakened in the 1970s and 1980s due to the increasing instability of the domestic auto industry and the piecemeal sale of its owners' holdings. In 1986 Trico faced demands for a 30% cut in its wiper costs, and management shifted most of its Buffalo production to the Mexican-Texas border, decreasing the Buffalo workforce from 2,700 to 900. In 1999 the headquarters moved to Michigan. In December 2002 the Buffalo workforce was 212.

Santella, Jim. "Richard L. Wolf," *Western New York*, March 1991

Kenneth S. Mernitz

Trinidadians. Small groups of immigrants from Trinidad and Tobago came to New York City starting around 1900. By 1950 several thousand lived mainly in Harlem in Manhattan and Bedford-Stuyvesant in Brooklyn. Most had African ancestry, and many were sojourners who intended to return home with savings. They founded several organizations, such as the Trinidad Benevolent Association, the Tobago Benevolent Society, and the United Mutual Life Insurance Co. Immigration grew after 1965, with increasing numbers of Trinidadians of East Indian ancestry. In 2000 the US census tallied 98,473 people in New York State born in Trinidad; including children born in the United States and undocumented immigrants, their number is estimated at 200,000. Almost all Trinidadians live in the New York City area, those of African descent especially in the Flatbush section of Brooklyn, where they have a community center, and those of Indian ancestry in Richmond Hill in Queens. There are few specifically Trinidadian churches, mosques, or Hindu temples. Trinidadians read the weekly *Carib News.* The Trinidad and Tobago Women's Association networks professional women and supports Trinidadian young women in college. The main social event in the community is the West Indian American Day Carnival Parade, celebrated since 1967 on Labor Day in Brooklyn. Trinidadians were the main founders of the parade. Trinidadian music styles, soca and calypso, have influenced the New York City music scene since the 1930s. Black power advocate Stokely Carmichael was born in Trinidad in 1941 and grew up in the Bronx. Basketball great Kareem Abdul-Jabbar was born in New York City of Trinidadian parents.

Kasinitz, Philip. *Caribbean New York* (New York: Cornell Univ Press, 1992)

Thomas Reimer

Trinity Church. Oldest Episcopal parish church in New York City. Chartered by the royal governor on 6 May 1697, its first building was constructed in 1698 on the corner of Broadway and Wall St. In 1705 England's Queen Anne granted the parish ownership of Queen's Farm, a tract of land stretching from Fulton to Christopher Sts, which would become a source of great wealth. Trinity School was founded in 1709. In 1754 the parish gave the land on which King's College (now Columbia University) was built. Trinity expanded its mission as the city grew. Beginning in the 1760s it began to establish chapels, including St. Paul's (1766), the oldest church building in Manhattan. Trinity Church burned in 1776, and a second church was consecrated in 1790. This building was torn down in 1840–41 and replaced in 1846 with a large Gothic structure designed by Richard Upjohn. At its height Trinity managed eight chapels, but changing population currents during the 20th century led to the closing of many of these, while in 1976, St. Luke's (1820), St. Augustine's (1869), and Intercession (1908) were made independent. Trinity has been known as "the mother of churches." Owning over 6 million feet^2 (560,000 m^2) of prime commercial real estate, it uses its wealth for social causes and to assist Episcopal churches in New York and surrounding states. It has also given substantial assistance to Washington College (now Trinity College) in Hartford, Conn, and the General Theological Seminary in New York City. The terror attacks of 11 Sept 2001 forced the closing of Trinity Church for almost two months. Though the sanctuary and the churchyard were covered with debris, there was little lasting structural damage.

Meriam, Dena. *Trinity: A Church, a Parish, a People* (New York: Cross River Press, 1996)

Robert Bruce Mullin

triracial groups. A little-explored aspect of New York State's complex racial history are small communities of people with combined African, American Indian, and European ancestry. In many areas free persons of color retreated from white society and its racial laws, moved to the frontier, and resettled in frontier areas. They were often among the earliest settlers in an area and usually enjoyed a higher status in the 17th and 18th centuries than they did after that. They frequently intermarried with local Indians. Research on these groups is difficult and often controversial. Members often deny black or Indian ancestry.

There is a significant African American ancestry among the populations of the four surviving Algonquian Indian groups on Long Island: the Shinnecock, the Montaukett, the Poospatuck (Unkechaug), and the Matinecock. As Lynda Day has written, family histories of African Americans on Long Island dating back to the 19th century often show an Indian parent or grandparent. The Bonackers, a group of East Hampton (Suffolk Co) fishing families that trace their heritage back to 17th-century British immigrants, possibly have Indian, and therefore mixed, ancestry. Some of their common surnames can be found among the Shinnecock and Montaukett.

Elsewhere in the state the best-known triracial group is the Ramapo Mountain People or the Ramapo Mountain Indians in Rockland Co and in adjacent areas of New Jersey. Like many such groups their history is murky and controversial. They have been trying (as of 2003, unsuccessfully) to achieve federal recognition as an Indian tribe on the basis of intermarriage with local Munsee Indians. There are two groups named Bushwhackers in New York State. One can be found in Rockland and Orange Cos and is of partly African ancestry. The other is in Columbia Co and is also known as Pondshiners, according to some accounts of Mohican (Mahican) ancestry.

The area of Schoharie Co had an Indian and free black population in the 18th century and is home to several groups of families that may be triracial. The Clappers (the name possibly derived from German or Dutch families), the Honies, and the Arabs have all been identified as having Indian ancestry, as has the best known of the county's mixed-race groups, the Sloughters (Slaughters). There are two possibly mixed-race groups in Rensselaer Co, the Van Guilders and another group of Bonackers, both with possible Mohican ancestry.

In many areas these groups were often relegated to the most menial and difficult labors, were on the fringes of polite society, were often seen as having serious deficiencies in their personal character, and became a byword for rural poverty and improvidence. There is some evidence that the pseudonymous "Jukes" from Richard Dugdale's notorious 1877 study of an Ulster Co family were of Indian descent. Dugdale's conclusion that tendencies to social failings were inheritable provided much of the basis for the nascent eugenics movement. The term *sloughter* was defined in an 1882 history of Schoharie Co as one "whose morality was lost long ago." On the other hand, in recent decades the names of two of these groups, the Sloughters and Bonackers, have lost their connection to a specific racial ancestry and their negative connotations. Many long-term multigenerational families from Schoharie Co and East Hampton, regardless of their racial backgrounds, now consider themselves to be real or honorary Sloughters and Bonackers.

Berry, Brewton. *Almost White* (New York: Macmillan, 1963)

Brasser, T. J. "Mahican." In *Northeast,* ed. Bruce G. Trigger, vol 15 of *Handbook of North American Indians,* ed. William C. Sturtevant (Washington, DC: Smithsonian Institution, 1978)

Day, Lynda R. *Making a Way to Freedom: A History of African Americans on Long Island* (Interlaken, NY: Empire State Books, 1997)

Gilbert, William Harlen, Jr. "Surviving Indian Groups of the Eastern United States." In *Annual Report of the Board of Regents of the Smithsonian Institution for 1948* (Washington, DC: Smithsonian Institution Press, 1948)

Renate Bartl

tri-state area. Territory including 31 counties—5 in New York City; 9 elsewhere in New York State (2 on Long Island and 7 extending up the Hudson); 14 in New Jersey; and 3 in Connecticut—as defined by the Regional Plan Association (RPA). The region comprises 12,688 mi^2 (32,862 km^2) with a 2000 population of 21,491,898 tied together by an extensive system of public and highway transport. Although a single market with New York City at its core and united by regional media, sports team loyalties, and an underlying popular regional identity, the tri-state region is served and divided by a complex web of 2,179 local governments, including more than two-thirds of all the localities in New Jersey, almost half of Connecticut's, and more than a quarter of New York State's.

In the early 17th century, the Dutch governed the economically unified area at the mouth of the Hudson River as a single political unit. Several centuries later, advocates for the consolidation of greater New York City out of New York Co (Manhattan), Kings Co (Brooklyn), Richmond Co (Staten Island), and parts of Queens and Westchester Cos viewed the region as an economically integrated whole. More than a decade before the city's consolidation in 1898, the US Census Bureau remarked in 1886 that "the vast population occupying the cities of New York, Brooklyn, Jersey City, Newark and Hoboken . . . [constitute] one great metropolitan community."

The region defined by interstate compact in 1921, when the Port of New York Authority (now Port Authority of New York and New Jersey) was created, included all or parts of 17 New York and New Jersey counties within a 25 mi (40 km) radius of the Statue of Liberty in New York Harbor but no territory in Connecticut. The first regional plan, issued in 1929 by RPA's predecessor, the Committee on a Regional Plan of New York and Its Environs, defined the region as containing New York City and 16 surrounding counties—1 in Connecticut, 6 in New York, and 9 in New Jersey.

The Arbitron and Nielson Cos' designated market area for television in the tri-state region in 1997 conformed almost exactly to the RPA's definition. However, it differed somewhat from the US Census Bureau's, which has evolved over time and is very important for the administration of intergovernmental policy. In 2002 the New York Consolidated Statistical Metropolitan Area (CSMA) as defined by the national government was made up of 15 primary metropolitan statistical areas. These in aggregate exclude Ulster and Sullivan Cos in New York but include Pike Co in Pennsylvania and part of Middlesex Co in Connecticut.

Benjamin, Gerald, and Richard Nathan. *Regionalism and Realism: A Study of Governments in the New York Metropolitan Area* (Washington, DC: Brookings Institution Press, 2001)

Yaro, Robert D., and Tony Hiss. *A Region at Risk: The Third Regional Plan* (New York: The Regional Plan Association, 1996)

Gerald Benjamin

Trotskyists. Starting in 1928 followers of dissident Communist Leon Trotsky played a disproportionate role in shaping left-wing politics and intellectual life in New York City, which was the home city of the American Trotskyist movement and its principal leaders, James P. Cannon and Max Shachtman. Committed at both to revolutionary socialism and to opposition of Joseph Stalin's dictatorship in the Soviet Union, the Trotskyists often found themselves execrated by Communists and anti-Communists alike. The precarious ideological balancing that was at the heart of Trotskyism manifested itself in an array of short-lived and often tiny parties and factions; the longest-lived of these, the Socialist Workers Party (SWP), was founded in 1938. During World War II the SWP was critical of what it perceived as America's imperialist war aims and the opposition of the Communist Party—after 21 June 1941, when Nazi Germany invaded the Soviet Union—to labor strikes that might derail the war effort. By the war's end the SWP had approximately 1,500 members, and in 1946 the party participated in the many industrial strikes that swept the country. After a fallow period SWP gained new strength in the 1960s, supporting Malcolm X after his break with the Nation of Islam and protesting the US involvement in the Vietnam War. With the ebbing of revolutionary enthusiasm in the late 20th century, though, both the SWP ranks and its connection to Trotskyism have been greatly diminished.

During its heyday in the 1930s and 1940s, the broader fringe of Trotskyism touched many of the leading figures in New York City's intellectual life. The *Partisan Review,* after 1937 the central journal of the anti-Stalinist left, was imbued with Trotskyism, as were many of its leading writers and editors, such as Philip Rahv, Mary McCarthy, Dwight MacDonald, and Clement Greenberg. Others in the Trotskyist orbit at the time included Columbia University art historian Meyer Schapiro and Trinidad-born historian C. L. R. James, who was deported from the United States in 1953 during the height of the Cold War. The cafeteria in City College of New York in Upper Manhattan was a known incubator of Trotyskists; the critic Irving Howe, the founding editor of *Dissent,* and Irving Kristol are perhaps its most famous graduates. Kristol, a noted editor and political commentator, and Gertrude Himmelfarb, his wife and later librarian of Congress, are former Trotskyists who became influential anticommunists and conservatives. James Burnham, a founder of the SWP, became in 1955 a founding editor of the conservative *National Review,* as did Max Eastman, another prominent Marxist editor and former Trotskyist.

Trotskyist leader Max Shachtman's abhorrence of the Soviet Union would bring him by the 1950s close to anti-Communists in the labor movement, where his protégés included Al Shanker, later founder of New York City's powerful United Federation of Teachers. Though Shachtman remained an avowed socialist, his rightward trajectory led him to support the Vietnam War, and many onetime Shactmanites would enjoy prominent positions in Pres Ronald Reagan's administration. The broader legacy of Trotskyism, a combination of a commitment to social justice with a rejection of authoritarianism, proved a lasting and powerful inspiration to the anti-Stalinist left and, in an altered form, to the neoconservative right.

Wald, Alan. *The New York Intellectuals: The Rise and Decline of the Anti-Stalinist Left, from the 1930s to the 1980s* (Chapel Hill: Univ of North Carolina Press, 1987)

Peter Eisenstadt

Troupsburg. Town (pop 1,126) in SW Steuben Co. Settled in 1805, the town was formed from Middletown [now Addison] and Canisteo in 1808. When the timber on the hills was depleted, the town became a farming community. An annual agricultural fair was held from 1880 to 1924. In 2003 dairying and related businesses remained important, and a recently settled Amish community produced rustic furniture, quilts, and maple syrup.

Virginia L. Wright and Jerry Wright

Troy. City (pop 49,170) in NW Rensselaer Co. The county seat of Rensselaer Co is located on the east bank of the Hudson River at the head of tidal navigation. The city stretches for 7 miles (11.3 km) along the alluvial floodplain of the Hudson and the Mohawk Rivers. As the city grew, it expanded over the bluffs that line the upper valley and now extends 2.5 miles (4.0 km) east of the river at its widest point.

Settlement

The present city of Troy was the product of two separate land purchases. Abraham J. Lansing, an Albany merchant, acquired the Stone Arabia Patent and platted Lansingburgh in 1771. By the end of the Revolution, an influx of New Englanders had turned Lansingburgh into a thriving trading and manufacturing center. Its businesses included shipbuilding; milling; the shipping of livestock, produce, and potash; and, later, the manufacture of brushes and oilcloth. The first bridge spanning the Hudson River linked Lansingburgh and Waterford (Saratoga Co) in 1804. Lansingburgh incorporated as a village in 1790 and formed as a town from Troy and Petersburgh in 1807.

South of Lansingburgh, Dirck van der Heyden acquired the site of downtown Troy in 1707 on a lease that gave him the right to sell or bequeath the land, requiring only an annual ground rent payment to the Van Rensselaers. In 1731 this farmland was divided among his three heirs; the central part, along with its deeded privilege of operating a ferry across the Hudson, later descended to his grandson Jacob Vanderheyden. This Dutch family, suspicious of English influences, long held out against commercial development.

In 1787, under increasing pressure from newly arrived Yankee merchants who saw the commercial utility of the better banks and deeper river channel along the Vanderheyden land, Jacob finally had his farmland platted into city lots. Naming the site Vanderheyden (more commonly called Ashley's Ferry), Jacob watched the locality grow rapidly. However, to his intense displeasure, at a public meeting on 5 Jan 1789 residents voted to adopt the name of Troy. It incorporated as a village in 1798, and in 1800 the village population was reckoned at 1,802. In 1816, with over 4,300 residents, it was incorporated as a city. Its growth was rapid. By 1840, with 19,334 residents, it was the 21st largest city in the United States and the 5th largest city in the state.

Troy's burgeoning population included a large number of immigrants. The Irish started coming in the 1820s and in great numbers during the 1840s and 1850s. Those born in Ireland made up 21% of the total population as late as 1875. Other immigrant groups in Troy in large numbers were Francophone Canadians, Germans, and British (especially Scots), with the foreign-born of each of these groups accounting for between 3% and 4% in 1875. After 1880 Troy's population was further augmented by more Francophone Canadians coming to work in the knitting industry, along with Poles, Ukrainians, Danes, and Italians. Troy's peak population was reached in 1910 at 76,813. The 1871 election of its first Irish mayor began a period of Irish political dominance.

Economic Development

Much commercial growth occurred in the first half of the 19th century. Situated at the head of navigation on the Hudson, Troy was ideally located to ship the farm produce of northern New York, western Vermont, and Massachusetts. Its business owners helped finance several turnpikes, including the Northern Turnpike, which tapped Washington Co and Vermont farmers. The development of banks advanced capital. In 1801 the Farmers' Bank opened midway between Troy and Lansingburgh, and by the century's end 17 more followed. The waterpower of numerous streams descending over Troy's bluffs led to industry, and numerous mills, ironworks, and textile factories took advantage of this resource until it was supplanted by steam power. The river and canals and, later, railroads made possible the cheap transportation of iron ore from the Adirondacks and Pennsylvania to Troy, where the charcoal, limestone, and molding sand necessary for iron production were already available.

Beginning in 1824 Henry Burden built the Troy Nail Factory into national prominence with his invention of machines to make cut nails, hook-headed rail spikes, and horseshoes, eventually providing the vast majority of those used by Union forces in the Civil War. Congressman John A. Griswold and John F. Winslow, Troy iron makers, were instrumental in persuading the US government to build the USS *Monitor,* and acted both as financial sureties and as manufacturers of the deck plates, bars, and rivets for the ship. These same two men, in conjunction with Alexander Holley, initiated in Troy in 1865 the first US production of steel using the Bessemer process. Twenty-three iron foundries operating in 1875 employed 2,000 workers to produce tens of thousands of cast-iron stoves based on the model of Troy's Philo P. Stewart, but the stove business declined in the 1880s. Troy was the site of three bell foundries that produced almost 100,000 bells between 1808 and 1953. One of those foundries also made surveying instruments and grew into the W. and L. E. Gurley Co. Another prominent industry was the production of valves for fire hydrants and water systems; it continues in the early 21st century at the Ross Valve Manufacturing Co.

Not all of Troy's economic development was in heavy industry. Around 1827 a Troy housewife, Hannah Lord Montague, tired of having to launder her husband's shirt daily, cut off the collar and cuffs so that they could be washed separately. Her timesaving invention of detachable collars led to the birth of an industry, which earned for Troy its abiding nickname "The Collar City." The vast majority of that industry's 15,000 workers were female. Factories sprang up, and by the peak years at the turn of the 20th century, 25 Troy firms were manufacturing a total of 8 million dozen collars and cuffs a year, over 90% of the United States production. One of the industry's great inventions was Sanford Cluett's "sanforization" process (1929) for preshrinking cotton cloth. This advance, together with dynamic advertising, led to the Cluett Peabody and Co's Arrow Shirt becoming a leading international brand by 1940. Relative latecomers to Troy's industrial sector were knitting mills; between 1881 and 1884, three were built, one each in Troy, Lansingburgh, and Albia. Lansingburgh, a town of 7,774 in 1880, was in constant economic competition with Troy until it was forcibly annexed by Troy on 1 Jan 1901 with the stipulation that their school systems would remain separate.

The commercial laundries that were created in the wake of the collar industry led to the birth of the first female union in the country. Kate Mullaney (1845–1906), a teenage Irish laundress, began working in one of the shirt laundries in the 1860s. Wanting safer working conditions, she organized 200 fellow employees into the Collar Laundry Union. Following a successful strike in 1864, she became the first woman appointed national secretary of a labor union. The women were not alone in forming unions to fight for higher wages, safer and cleaner working conditions, shorter workdays, and limits on child labor. The iron industry organized early on, and Iron Molders' International Union No. 2 of Troy, formed in 1858, was said to be the largest local in the country through the early 1870s. Repeated and violent labor strife through the 1870s and 1880s radicalized the movement and led to the establishment of trade associations by owners. These eventually took most of the heavy industry to new locations in the Midwest in response to Troy's aging plants and higher wages along with the lure of cheaper ore from Minnesota.

The Civil War Era

Troy was a hotbed of antislavery and Underground Railroad activity. Rev Henry Highland Garnet, pastor from 1840 to 1848 of the Liberty Street Presbyterian Church, turned the "moral suasion" faction of the abolition movement on its ear with his call for armed slave rebellion in 1843. Troy was home to a stable African American community, numbering 894 in 1855. A Troy theater owner plagiarized and produced the first-ever stage production of Harriet Beecher Stowe's *Uncle Tom's Cabin* (1852). John Brown's widow, Mary Brown, bearing his body back from Virginia for burial, made her only overnight stay in Troy as she felt safe there. In April 1860 an escaped slave named Charles Nalle was rescued from the police by a crowd led by Harriet Tub-

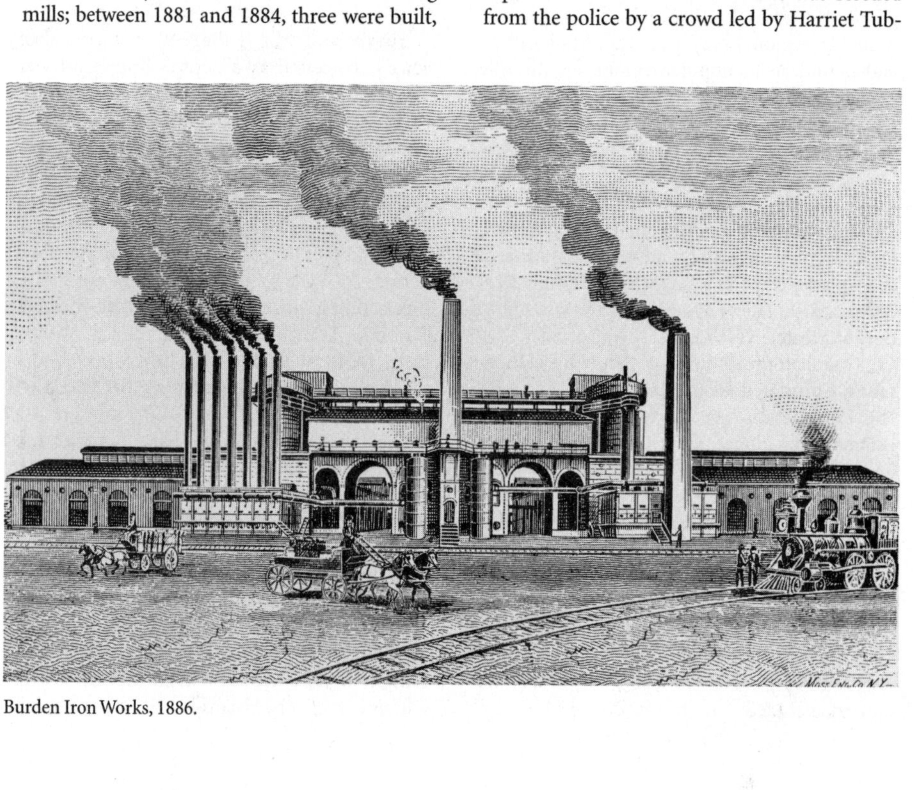

Burden Iron Works, 1886.

Collar workers in dampening room, Troy.

man. Yet on 15 July 1863, economic resentment among the working class erupted into what has been called the second most destructive draft riot in the nation, eclipsed only by New York City's riot that had begun one day earlier. Troy's Blacks fled the city, rioters attempted to destroy the Liberty Street Presbyterian Church, and the latter succeeded in destroying the property of one of the newspaper offices.

Religion, Education, and Culture

Lansingburgh's first church, Dutch Reformed, opened in 1788, and Troy's first church, Presbyterian, opened in 1791. Episcopalian churches were also founded in Lansingburgh and Troy, in 1804. The Irish, following canal construction, formed St. Peter's Church in Troy in 1824.

The Lansingburgh Academy began operating in 1791 and was chartered in 1796. The city's earliest public school dated from 1796. The Troy Academy (1816) used the Lancasterian system, in which the eldest students helped teach the youngest. By 1820 a separate school had been established exclusively for "persons of African descent" and operated for several decades. In 1849 the city charter was amended to establish 12 free public schools, one for each ward. A public high school was added in 1854.

Troy is home to three colleges, as well as the Emma Willard School, America's oldest girls boarding school. Rensselaer Polytechnic Institute (1824) is the oldest degree-granting engineering institution in the nation. Russell Sage College (1916) is located in the heart of downtown. It was founded by Margaret Olivia Slocum Sage, widow of a one-time Troy alderman who became a successful financier. Hudson Valley Community College originated as the Troy Technical Institute in 1953. Important cultural institutions include the Troy Music Hall, Arts Center of the Capital Region, Rensselaer County Historical Society, and Rensselaer County Junior Museum.

Recent History

In the World War II era Troy was an industrial powerhouse but had lost its dominant position in steel, wrought iron, and cast iron. The Burden Iron Co had closed in 1938; in 1940 Republic Steel acquired the plant and operated until 1972. Troy continued to produce valves, fire hydrants, engineering and surveying instruments, shirts and collars, and women's wear. Cluett Peabody employed 3,700 in 1940, most of them women. A new city product was the rototiller (1937). The company was purchased in 1962 by Garden Way, which consolidated its operation in 1982, making the most of its Troy Bilt trademark until sagging sales resulted in its closure in 2001. By that time almost all of Troy's historic manufacturing was gone.

Other changes affected the city during the postwar period. In 1958 rail passenger service ended, and Troy's massive Union Station was subsequently demolished. The 1963 opening of Colonie Center began the decline of Troy's grand shopping district, and in 1966 urban renewal was launched, one of its results being the unsuccessful Uncle Sam Atrium (1978). Troy's position as a sister city to Albany was enhanced by the construction of I-787 and the Collar City Bridge (1980). At the same time, its historic buildings, most of which survived the urban renewal onslaught, became its greatest asset. A historic preservation movement developed, and Hollywood moviemakers sought out the city for scenes in such films as *Ironweed* (1987) and *The Age of Innocence* (1993).

Troy has never been dominated for a long period by either major party, but its workforce, at times, has voted Democratic. As Troy's economy began to stagnate in the 1950s, some proposed an end to the strong-mayor system, which actually reflected the strength of the county headquarters of the mayor's party. A new city charter in 1964 created a city manager, but the position's effectiveness was hindered by political interference; the system was scrapped in 1995 with a return to the strong-mayor form of government. At that time the city's finances were in dire condition, requiring a 21% tax increase, and the state stepped in with a Municipal Assistance Corp (MAC) to oversee its affairs. Despite a more stable financial situation, the erosion of the tax base still presents major problems, and the voters have responded once again with a bellwether shift in political control.

Although its population dropped 9% in the 1990s, Troy has become a bedroom community in the Capital District, and historical tourism draws people to the city. The arts, antiques, and boutique businesses are a new downtown presence. Waterfront public spaces have been redeveloped to reorient Troy to the Hudson. The entrepreneurial spirit still exists in a number of high-tech companies, many of which are offshoots from research done at the local universities. The best example is MapInfo, which originated in Troy; it is now headquartered in North Greenbush. Troy is perhaps most famous as the creator of Uncle Sam. During the War of 1812, Samuel Wilson (1766–1854) was dubbed with that name as a result of marking ration barrels with "US." Troy is also the birthplace of actress Maureen Stapleton (1925–).

See also Architects and architecture, Albany and capital district; Garment industry; Iron and steel industry; Melville, Herman.

Parker, Joseph A. *Looking Back: A History of Troy and Rensselaer County, 1925–1980* (Troy, NY: Author, 1982)

Rittner, Don. *Troy: A Collar City History* (Charleston, SC: Arcadia, 2003)

Sylvester, Nathaniel B. *History of Rensselaer County* (Philadelphia: Everts & Peck, 1880)

Turbin, Carole. *Working Women of Collar City: Gender, Class and Community in Troy, New York, 1864–1886* (Urbana: Univ of Illinois Press, 1992)

Walkowitz, Daniel J. *Worker City, Company Town: Iron- and Cotton-Worker Protest in Troy and Cohoes, New York, 1855–1884* (Urbana: Univ of Illinois Press, 1978)

Wiese, Arthur J. *Troy's 100 Years* (Troy, NY: W. H. Young, 1891)

Michael P. Barrett

Troy Haymakers. A charter member in 1871 of the National Association of Professional Base Ball Players, the first professional baseball league. The Troy (Rensselaer Co) club was backed by John Morrissey, a congressman, gambling proprietor, and former prizefighter. Sometimes called the Unions, after the Unions of Lansingburgh (Rensselaer Co) of the late 1860s, the team played at the Haymakers' Grounds on Center Island and finished its first season in sixth place with a 13-15 record. Team members included third baseman Esteban "Steve" Bellan of Havana, Cuba, professional baseball's first Latino player. Outfielder Lipman Pike, a New York City native and the professional game's first Jewish player, tied for the league lead in home runs with four. Highlights that season included playing in the first professional baseball game in Boston, beat-

Unions baseball club, Lansingburgh, *ca* 1866–71.

ing the Red Stockings 29-14, and defeating the favored New York Mutuals 25-10. The Haymakers played to a 15-10 record until financial problems caused the team to fold on 23 July 1872.

Ryczek, William J. *Blackguards and Red Stockings: A History of Baseball's National Association, 1871–1875* (Jefferson, NC: McFarland, 1992)

Richard A. Puff

Troy Music Hall. Concert hall in Troy. Located in the upper floors of the Troy Savings Bank building (1875), designed by architect George B. Post, the 69 x 106 ft (21.0 x 32.3 m) auditorium has 60 ft (18.3 m) ceilings. The orchestra, dress circle, and gallery, with 16 boxes, provide seating for 1,253. Iron staircases forged by the Architectural Iron Works Co of New York City run along both sides of the auditorium and to the upper and lower boxes, balcony, and gallery seating areas. The Beaux Arts exterior is decorated with iron balustrades and a frieze under the cornice that bears the names of great composers and authors. An impressive array of musicians from Lillian Nordica to Yo-Yo Ma have performed at the hall. The Troy Chromatics subscription series, established 1894, has presented such world-renowned orchestras as the New York Philharmonic and the Cleveland Orchestra, and most performances of the Albany Symphony Orchestra take place in the hall. In 1979 the Troy Savings Bank Music Hall Revitalization Committee was organized to raise funds for its restoration and to increase public awareness and use of the hall. It was named a National Historic Landmark in 1989. The acoustics of the hall are widely held to be among the best in the world.

Troy Savings Bank Music Hall, http://www.troymusichall.org

Kathryn T. Sheehan

Troy Trojans. The team played in baseball's National League from 1879 through 1882. Also known as the Troy Citys and occasionally the Haymakers, the club featured five future Hall of Famers in 1880: Roger Connor, Buck Ewing, Mickey Welch, Tim Keefe, and Dan Brouthers. Despite great players, the team never had a winning season, compiling records of 19-56 in 1879 (finishing in last place in the eight-team league), 41-42 in 1880 (fourth place), 39-45 in 1881 (fifth place), and 35-48 in 1882 (seventh place). Financially the club was doing even worse. Poor attendance kept income low, and at one point in 1881 the team talked of transferring to Pittsburgh. The last game of the 1881 season was played before an audience of just 12 fans, and the team resigned from the league after the 1882 season. The following year many of the Trojan players formed the nucleus of the New York Gothams, which became known as the New York Giants in 1885.

Puff, Richard A. "Haymakers and Daisycutters: Troy and the National Pastime." In *Troy's Baseball Heritage*, ed. Richard A. Puff (Troy, NY: Committee to Preserve Troy's Baseball Heritage, 1992)

Richard A. Puff

trucking industry. By 1900 trucks were being integrated into New York State's economy. In 1907 the George N. Pierce Manufacturing Co of Buffalo began producing tank trucks to transport oil products, and the renamed Pierce-Arrow Motor Car Co continued to manufacture tank cars until 1935. It took some time for trucking to muster competition for rail as a viable long-distance alternative, however. In 1916 a transcontinental road journey between New York City and Seattle took 31 days. The development of pneumatic tires, new design improvements, and the beginnings of a federal highway system around the time of World War I doubled the speed at which trucks could travel. The need to move military supplies quickly to ports for shipment overseas during the war sustained demand for truck transportation, and the Pierce-Arrow Co alone manufactured hundreds of trucks for use in England and France. When the Erie Railroad in 1921 began using trucks rather than water transportation as feeders, and other railroads followed suit, it was clear that the new industry had become vital to the state's economy and infrastructure.

By the 1930s trucking was providing increasing competition to rail freight. Despite the economic downturn of the Great Depression, semitrailer use from 1929 to 1936 increased 500% nationwide. The Port of New York Authority (now Port Authority of New York and New Jersey) had been created in 1921 to increase freight-handling capacity, and it opened the first rail and truck terminal in 1931, the Union Inland Freight Station in Manhattan. With the opening of the George Washington Bridge the same year, the Port Authority provided the first vehicular crossing of the Hudson River suitable for trucks. Trucking came in time to replace the huge lighterage traffic that ferried freight across the Hudson to Manhattan, and after World War II eventually displaced much of the rail-based freight service. In 1932, as evidence of the growing power of the industry, the New York State Motor Truck Association was formed.

Development of the Interstate Highway System after World War II further helped the industry, and changes since the mid-1970s have allowed more companies to use independent, for-hire trucking companies rather than fleets. Additionally, the 1980 federal Motor Carrier Act eliminated many significant restrictions on the trucking business, allowing existing companies to expand rapidly and new companies to flood the market. The number of companies nationwide peaked in 1986, but thereafter mergers, consolidations, and failures caused the figures to drop. Many of the new firms were undercapitalized or not flexible enough to adapt to the newly competitive marketplace. High state taxes on the industry contributed to driving some established companies out of business, like Boss-Linco of Buffalo, or to move out of state, like Red Star Express Lines of Auburn (Cayuga Co) and United Parcel Service. The number of registered New York State truck tractors dropped 43% from 1985 through 1995.

In 1998 New York State accounted for 7.5% of the value of US annual truck freight; in 2000 it ranked third in truck exports to Canada, moving $10 billion in freight. Nonmetallic minerals and petroleum or coal products are the top commodities by weight shipped to, from, and within the state. The top commodities by value are transportation equipment and instruments and photographic or optical equipment. Trucks transport over 80%, an estimated 267 million tons (242 MT), of New York State freight, though railroads continue to play an active, if diminished, role. The New York State Department of Transportation retains responsibility for the licensing, safety, and insurance of carriers operating solely within the state. Since 1996 the US Department of Transportation has regulated interstate trucking. In 2001 New York State had 4,235 trucking companies, over 50% of them employing one to four individuals.

New York State Department of Transportation, http://www.dot.state.ny.us/ts/license.html
US Department of Transportation, Federal Highway Administration, Office of Freight Management and Operations, http://www.ops.fhwa.dot.gov/freight

Janet Kaye

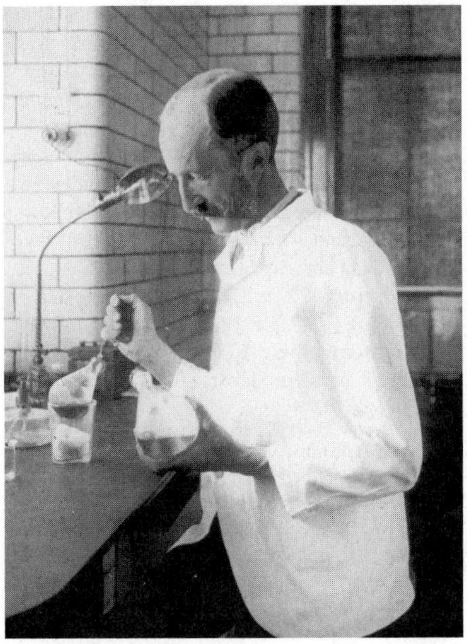

Trudeau in his laboratory, 1894.

Trudeau, Edward Livingston (*b* New York City, 5 Oct 1848; *d* Saranac Lake, Franklin and Essex Cos, 15 Nov 1915). Physician. Raised mostly in Paris, he returned to New York City in 1865. After earning his MD from the College of Physicians and Surgeons at Columbia College in 1871, he practiced medicine on Long Island and in Manhattan. When he caught tuberculosis in 1873, he went to Paul Smith's Hotel in Saranac Lake in the Adirondacks to recover and soon discovered the practical benefits of rest, clean air, wholesome food, and moderate exercise. Convinced of the merits of environment, in 1880 he resumed practicing medicine, this time in Saranac Lake, where he specialized in tuberculosis. There he founded the Adirondack Cottage Sanitarium (1884; renamed the Trudeau Sanatorium in 1917) for patient care and the Saranac Laboratory for the Study of Tuberculosis (1894) for research, the first American institutions of their kind. In 1904 he was the cofounder and first president of the National Association for the Study and Prevention of Tuberculosis (now the American Lung Association). In 1954 the Trudeau Sanatorium closed. The Trudeau Institute, a research center for immunology and infectious diseases, opened at Saranac Lake in 1964.

Trudeau, Edward Livingston. *An Autobiography* (Garden City, NY: Doubleday, Page, 1916)

Eric v. d. Luft

Trumansburg. Village (pop 1,581) in Ulysses (Tompkins Co). It was founded in 1793 by Abner Treman, who received the area of the present village for his Revolutionary War service and who built a gristmill and sold lots. Treman's Village was renamed Trumansburg when a post office was established in 1811. Incorporated in 1872, the village was home to Gregg Iron Works (1866; later Morse Chain), which employed 100 men in 1880. In the 20th century, Hartley Bros (1907–31; silk) and Cooper Bros (1946–64; fine leather) provided employment, and the 1941 opening of the Seneca Army Depot at Sampson (Seneca Co) created a huge demand for workers. Robert A. Moog began manufacture of his electric synthesizers in Trumansburg in 1964. Among village institutions are the Trumansburg Fair, an annual summer event for 150 years; the Finger Lakes Grassroots Festival, which began in 1990, of world and roots music; and the Conservatory of Fine Arts, housed in a renovated 1851 church building.

Jane Dieckmann

Truth, Sojourner [Van Wagenen, Isabella] (*b* Hurley, Ulster Co, ?1797; *d* Battle Creek, Mich, 26 Nov 1883). Preacher, abolitionist, and women's rights activist.

New York State Years

Sojourner Truth was one of 13 children of Elizabeth (or Mau-mau Bett) and James Bomefree, who were slaves of Johannis Hardenbergh, a Dutch landowner. Named Isabella (sometimes called Bell), she spoke only Dutch in her early years and received early religious training from Mau-mau Bett, who believed in direct communication with God. Johannis son Charles inherited the family but died in 1808. The aged James and Elizabeth were freed, but Isabella and her brother Peter were sold at auction. Isabella was bought by John Nealy, who refused to provide shoes during the bitter Hudson Valley winter and beat her for not understanding English. Isabella prayed for a better master, and through her father's influence was soon bought by Martins Schryver, a Dutch tavern keeper.

In 1810 she was sold to Johannes I. Dumont, a New Paltz Huguenot farmer, with whom she remained enslaved another 16 years. Indoors she nursed and cared for the Dumont's nine children, cooked, cleaned, washed, and spun. She also milked, gardened, planted, cultivated, plowed, reaped, and harvested. Dumont's wife, Elizabeth, hated Isabella and tormented her throughout those years, perhaps because Dumont had fathered Diana, Isabella's oldest child.

Isabella grew into a tall, slim, handsome woman. She had five children, four of whom reached adulthood. Her first known conjugal relationship was with Robert, owned by Charles Catton Sr. Catton and his son disapproved of Isabella and on discovering Robert at the Dumont's, beat him unmercifully with "the heavy ends of their canes," causing brain damage and eventually death. She later married Thomas, one of Dumont's slaves, and remained with him until she sought freedom.

Isabella would have been emancipated in 1827 by the gradual abolition law of 1817 but took her freedom a year early because Dumont reneged on his promise of early liberation for faithful service. Guided by the promptings of the voice of God, she fled with her infant child, seeking refuge in her old Hardenbergh neighborhood with Isaac Van Wagenen, whose name she took. Van Wagenen bought Bell's remaining time for $20 and gave Dumont $5 for the baby's freedom.

About to attend the Pinkster festival in 1827, Isabella underwent a profound religious conversion, proclaiming a spiritual rebirth, personal sanctification, and a special calling as God's messenger. The first of many tests of faith occurred when her only son, 5-year-old Peter, was sold illegally to people in the South by Dumont's brother-in-law. Isabella rallied antislavery Quakers for financial support and appealed to the

Sojourner Truth, *ca* 1870.

court through a Dutch descendant of the Hardenberghs. Peter was brought back to Ulster Co and given his freedom.

Isabella had become a member of the Kingston (Ulster Co) Methodist Church while waiting for her son's return. The Methodists recognized her remarkable speaking gifts and a Miss Gear took her to New York City about 1828. There Isabella joined the African Zion Church and was reunited with two sisters and a brother. Her English improved, and she soon became a popular revival preacher. Adopting Perfectionist beliefs, she worked among the poor and kept house for a Perfectionist merchant named Elijah Pierson. In 1832 a religious zealot calling himself Matthias appeared at Pierson's home. Both Pierson and Isabella became members of his commune until it collapsed in 1835 amid rumors of the murder of Elijah Pierson and sexual misconduct. Isabella was accused of poisoning Pierson, but she successfully won a slander suit against her accusers. The Perfectionists' emphasis on challenging oppression by setting up a Kingdom of God on earth influenced Isabella's commitment to social reform.

Called by the Spirit

On 1 June she left the city, taking the name Sojourner Truth, a woman called by the Spirit to travel the land and speak God's truth. Throughout Long Island, Connecticut, and western Massachusetts, she spoke on temperance, abolition, and the power of God and debated with followers of William Miller, who proclaimed that the end of the world was at hand. In February 1844 abolitionists in Springfield, Mass, sent her to the Northampton Association in Massachusetts. Founded in 1842 by radical abolitionists such as George W. Benson, brother-in-law of William Lloyd Garrison, it was the headquarters of Connecticut River Valley reform. Sojourner Truth was exposed there to abolitionist speakers such as Frederick Douglass, Garrison, and Abby Kelley and issues such as women's rights, the underground railroad, activism, and spiritualism. Truth became an abolitionist speaker soon after her arrival. When the community dissolved in 1846, she remained. The association became her springboard for many other reform activities, including women's rights.

In 1849 Truth dictated her life's story to abolitionist Olive Gilbert. *The Narrative of Sojourner Truth* (1850) became a classic antislavery account. In 1850 Truth bought her own Northampton home with proceeds from sales of the *Narrative,* continuing her antislavery work, traveling throughout the Northeast and Midwest along with Abby Kelley Foster, Lucy Coleman, Laura Haviland, Parker Pillsbury, Garrison, Douglass, and British abolitionist George Thompson. Unable to read or write, Truth analyzed political and social issues through the Bible and parables from everyday life. "I cannot read a book," Sojourner insisted, "but I can read the people." Always a Garrisonian abolitionist, Truth admonished her friend Douglass in 1851, when he became frustrated with pacifism and advocated violence. "Is God gone?" she asked. Truth embraced spiritualism and was a medium and trance speaker at meetings and séances conducted in New York City and in Rochester with abolitionists Amy and Isaac Post, leading spiritualist Cora Daniels, and three famous Fox sisters. Truth made a moving speech in 1851 at a women's rights convention in Akron, Ohio, which has come down to posterity as "Ar'n't I a Woman?" In 1858 a group of Indiana proslavery Democrats questioned her gender. Truth boldly exposed her bosom, insisting it was not her shame but theirs because black breasts had suckled many a white babe. In 1856 she relocated to Michigan, continuing her abolitionist activities throughout the west. By then Sojourner was a come-outer, one who dismissed traditional religion because of its ties to slavery. She retained her Perfectionist views but did not join a church.

During the Civil War, Truth spoke to black troops, had an audience with Abraham Lincoln, worked among the freed people in Arlington Heights, Va, nursed soldiers in Washington hospitals, and brought suit against a streetcar company, thereby desegregating public transportation. Although Truth initially joined Susan B. Anthony and Elizabeth Cady Stanton on universal suffrage, in 1869 she broke with them over black male suffrage. After passage of the 15th Amendment, Sojourner again supported woman suffrage. Her main crusade, however, was attempting to secure land in the west for Blacks suffering in the Washington, DC, slums and elsewhere. In 1874 her Quaker friend Frances Titus compiled a book, *Narrative of Sojourner Truth; With a History of Her Labors and Correspondence Drawn from Her "Book of Life,"* to raise money for Truth. It contained her slave narrative, autographs from prominent Americans including presidents, abolitionist remembrances, and newspaper clippings. Advocating all manner of reform, social justice, and spirituality, this towering figure of humble birth and no schooling possessed a simple eloquence, gifted wit, and common sense practicality that appealed to all people.

Mabee, Carleton, with Susan Mabee Newhouse. *Sojourner Truth: Slave, Prophet, Legend* (New York: New York Univ Press, 1993)
Painter, Nell I. *Sojourner Truth: A Life, a Symbol* (New York: Norton, 1997)
Stetson, Erlene, and Linda David. *Glorying in Tribulation: The Lifework of Sojourner Truth* (East Lansing: Michigan State Univ Press, 1994)
Titus, Frances W. *Narrative of Sojourner Truth; With a History of Her Labors and Correspondence Drawn from Her "Book of Life"* (Battle Creek, Mich, 1874)
Washington, Margaret, ed. *Narrative of Sojourner Truth* (New York: Vintage Books, 1993)

Margaret Washington

Truxton. Town (pop 1,225) in NE Cortland Co. Settled in 1793 the town was formed from Fabius (Onondaga Co) in 1808. Truxton saw an influx of Irish farmers by 1854 when St. Patrick's Church (closed 1919) was built. The town's most famous native is John McGraw (1873–1934), manager of the New York Giants baseball team (1902–32). Truxton hamlet, in the Tioughnioga Valley, was the center of a dairy region by 1860 and acquired a cheese factory (1876) and a butter tub factory. The Utica, Ithaca and Elmira Railroad came through in 1872. Labrador Mountain Ski Area is in town, as is the Labrador Hollow State Unique Area, a protected wetland featuring a quaking bog.

Cathy A. Barber

Tryon, William (*b* Norbury Park, England, 8 June 1729; *d* London, 27 Jan 1788). Royal governor and lieutenant general. The son of Charles and Lady Mary Shirley, he lived a privileged childhood and had a distinguished military career. Tryon was appointed lieutenant governor of North Carolina in 1764 and governor in 1765. He was appointed governor of New York in July 1771; Tryon Co was named for him the following year. As royal governor Tryon solidified loyalist support in the years before the Revolution by rewarding "friends of the government" with large land grants in Tryon Co and in what is now Vermont. In the turmoil leading up to the Revolution, he urged the British government to abandon efforts to tax the colonies and attempted to maintain loyal civil government. He called for an assembly election in early 1776, believing that a loyalist majority would result, but only four loyalist candidates were elected; this assembly never met. After fleeing to a Royal Navy ship in New York Harbor, Tryon continued his political duties, rallied loyalists, and established a military headquarters. He was involved in the failed plot to kidnap George Washington and his officers in 1776. In 1780 he returned to England. Tryon Co was renamed Montgomery Co in 1784, though Fort Tryon Park in Upper Manhattan, the site of a former military post, still bears his name.

See also COLONIAL NEW YORK.

Nelson, Paul David. *William Tryon and the Course of Empire: A Life in British Imperial Service* (Chapel Hill: Univ of North Carolina Press, 1990)

Edward H. Knoblauch

Tryon County. Created from Albany Co 12 Mar 1772, named after Gov William Tryon. The county encompassed all New York land west of Albany Co and the contemporaneously created Charlotte Co, and had no specific western boundary. Originally settled in the 1720s by German Palatine refugees, it was later augmented by Scots and others who were tenants and military associates of Sir William Johnson. An act of the legislature of 22 Mar 1772 divided Tryon Co into five districts: Mohawk, Stone Arabia, Canajoharie, German Flatts, and Kingsland. An Old England district was added in 1775. The county was created in response to a petition from Johnson, who built a jail and a courthouse in Johnstown [now in Fulton Co] next to his baronial hall. The courthouse is the oldest still in use in New York State. In 1775–76 the loyalists under Sir William's heir Sir John Johnson and their Mohawk Indian allies were arrested, expelled, or fled to Canada. They returned in a series of battles and raids from 1777 to 1781, including the Battle of Oriskany (1777). In 1784 the county was renamed Montgomery Co, dropping the royal governor's name in favor of a revolutionary hero.

Campbell, William W. *Annals of Tryon County: Or, the Border Warfare of New York, during the Revolution* (New York: J. & J. Harper, 1831)

Edward H. Knoblauch

tuberculosis. A contagious pulmonary disease, most often spread through airborne particles but also transmittable by touching the clothes or other personal items of infected persons. Tuberculosis, which was commonly called "consumption," became especially prevalent during the 19th century, accounting for approximately 20% of all deaths in Western Europe and the United States. Physicians prescribed a number of treatments such as complete rest or travel to more healthful climates, which was the course of action taken by New York City physician Edward Livingston Trudeau after being diagnosed with the disease in 1873. During a trip to the Adirondacks his symptoms went into remission, encouraging him to open the first sanatorium at Saranac Lake (Franklin and Essex Cos) in 1884. Two years earlier German bacteriologist Robert Koch had isolated the tubercle bacillus, which revealed the disease's communicable nature and the potential health threat posed by those infected. Overall the number of tuberculosis cases had declined among the general population but continued to flourish within certain urban neighborhoods. In 1890 only 49 per 100,000 deaths occurred from tuberculosis in Manhattan's affluent Upper West Side, compared with 776 per 100,000 in Lower Manhattan's tenement neighborhoods. One response to the prevalence of tuberculosis, often carrying with it the presumption that the ill were incapable of caring for themselves and thus prone to spread the bacteria, was mandatory reporting of those infected and institutionalization of individuals against their will if they did not cooperate. Starting in New York City in 1894, under the leadership of Hermann M. Biggs of the New York City Health Department, the policy was soon adopted elsewhere in the state; Rochester (1900), Buffalo (1902), Albany (1907), and Syracuse (1908).

Though mandatory registration was widely resented, it was likely one of the causes of a dramatic drop in tuberculosis cases in the first decades of the 20th century, along with the opening of more sanatoriums and the improvement of conditions in tenements—better ventilation and light, the installation of toilets and running water—following the Tenement House Law of 1901. The control of spitting and the proper disposal of sputum was another major health concern, resulting in New York State's anti-spitting legislation of 1908. But the real turning point in the decline of tuberculosis was the introduction of antibiotics and other therapeutics, starting with streptomycin in 1944, followed by para-aminosalicylic acid, isoniazid, and rifampin. Though the demise of the disease seemed at hand, tuberculosis never fully disappeared. By the late 1980s a new virulent form of multidrug-resistant tuberculosis (MDRTB) appeared in New York City, particularly among those infected with human immunodeficiency virus (HIV) but also among other segments of the population, such as the poor and homeless. From 1985 to 1990 the number of cases in New York City increased by 89%. Since MDRTB resulted from individuals not completing full treatment, therefore allowing the bacteria to build immunities to less toxic drugs, New York City officials implemented directly observed therapy (DOT), similar to that initiated by Biggs a century earlier. In 2000 New York State reported 1,744 per 100,000 cases of tuberculosis. By the early 21st century, the disease once again subsided within the United States, but among populations in Africa and Asia it remained a significant health threat.

Feldberg, Georgina D. *Disease and Class: Tuberculosis and the Shaping of Modern North American Society* (New Brunswick, NJ: Rutgers Univ Press, 1995)
Ott, Katherine. *Fevered Lives: Tuberculosis in American Culture since 1870* (Cambridge, Mass: Harvard Univ Press, 1996)
Rothman, Sheila M. *Living in the Shadow of Death: Tuberculosis and the Social Experience of Illness in American History* (New York: Basic Books, 1994)

Douglas McCombs

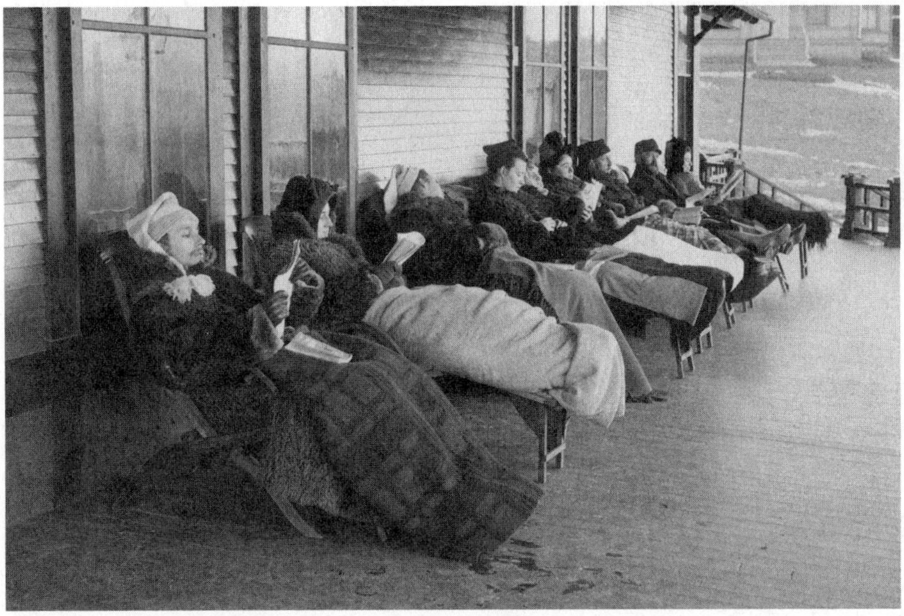

Taking the outdoors cure on steamer chairs at the Trudeau Sanatorium, Saranac Lake.

tuberculosis sanatoriums. In the 19th century physicians treating tuberculosis often advocated travel to invigorating climates, abundant nutritious food, rest, and exposure to the open air. New York City physician Edward Livingston Trudeau (1848–1915) built resistance to the disease by following this regimen in the Adirondacks. In 1884, eager to investigate the effects of this regimen and to help others, Trudeau opened in Saranac Lake (Franklin and Essex Cos) the Adirondack Cottage Sanitarium (renamed the Trudeau Sanatorium in 1917). The first facility in the country designed specifically to treat tuberculosis patients, it began with a one-room cottage named "Little Red," which featured a covered porch where its first two patients were encouraged to sit most of the day. Other cottages were built, and by 1900 the Adirondack Cottage Sanitarium consisted of 22 buildings. In a 1906 survey about one-third of 1,066 former patients reported that they were "well." Even though these results were not overly encouraging, the reputation of the climate and regimen established by Trudeau attracted increasing numbers of patients by the early 1900s. Treating the tubercular became the main industry of Saranac Lake. Local farmers increased vegetable plots and livestock; homeowners opened rooms to tuberculous boarders. In addition, commercial private sanatoriums, or "cure cottages," opened throughout the town. Some were simple rooming houses that furnished few basic services, but others provided elaborate accommodations, meals, and nurses. These private sanatoriums commonly catered to specific ethnic or occupational groups, or to particular social classes. Cure cottages often revealed their function through architectural features and design. Since exposure to the open air was essential for curing, cure cottages featured several porches and verandas, some enclosed with glass. Patients could be seen lying on these porches even during the harsh Adirondack winters. The need to rest in the open air also led to the creation of the "cure chair"; a cushioned recliner with an adjustable back, it featured a slight arch in the seat to force its occupant into the "Fowler position" to facilitate breathing. Its popularity supported five manufacturers within Saranac Lake and led to the popular name "Adirondack recliner."

Not all sanatoriums consisted of pleasant-looking cottages and not all followed the same regimen as Trudeau's. In 1906 Hermann M. Biggs, a public health officer in New York City, opened a sanatorium in Otisville (Orange Co). This sanatorium in the Catskills housed the poorest tuberculosis patients and implemented a "work cure" that emphasized manual labor. The New York State Sanatorium at Ray Brook (Essex Co) began in 1900 as a tent city, housing those too poor or too sick to find accommodations in nearby Saranac Lake. It eventually developed into a complex of several drab brick buildings. Life inside a sanatorium offered the only hope of cure for the majority of those with tuberculosis, but it also meant a sacrifice of personal freedom. Patients at most sanatoriums spent their time resting. Reading and conversing were discouraged except for very limited periods. The monotony of this existence led patients to hope for a speedy release. Even for those who did find a cure, months and sometimes years passed inside the sanatorium. The widespread use of antibiotics by the 1950s eventually eliminated the need for these institutions. The last patient at the Trudeau Sanatorium left in 1954.

Gallos, Philip L. *Cure Cottages of Saranac Lake: Architecture and History of a Pioneer Health Resort* (Saranac Lake, NY: Historic Saranac Lake, 1985)

Douglas McCombs

Tubman [née Ross], **Harriet** [Araminta] (*b* Dorchester Co, Md, ?1820; *d* Auburn, Cayuga Co, 10 Mar 1913). Abolitionist. Born a slave on Maryland's Eastern Shore, Araminta, or "Minty," Ross was one of nine children born to Benjamin and Harriet Green Ross. At age 5 she was rented out to a neighboring family as a domestic servant and later was hired out as a field hand. "I grew up like a neglected weed," she once said. At about age 13 she was struck on the head by a 2 lb (.9 kg) weight, thrown when she interposed herself between an overseer and an escaping slave. She suffered from narcolepsy or sudden blackouts for the remainder of her life. In 1844 she married John Tubman, a local free Black. They had no children. When Tubman's master, Edward Brodess, died in 1849, it raised fears that she would be sold. "Every time I saw a white man," she told an interviewer, "I was afraid of being carried away."

Underground Railroad

That same year, 1849, she escaped slavery, took the name Harriet, and made her way to Philadelphia, where she was aided by local abolitionists and the many free Blacks living there. She eventually settled in St. Catharines [now in Ont] not far from the New York State border, where there was a large African American community outside of the reach of the federal Fugitive Slave Act. This would serve as the primary residence for many of the freedom seekers she brought north; she also maintained a residence in Philadelphia in the 1850s. She soon returned to the South through her activities on the Underground Railroad. Personally fearless, she took approximately 9–11 trips south, most to the familiar Eastern Shore of Maryland, freeing 80–100 slaves. She first helped bring away her niece Kessiah and her two children in 1850 and the next year tried to persuade her husband to go north, though he had remarried and did not want to leave. Tubman brought away her aged parents in 1857, when they fell under suspicion for aiding freedom seekers. As she made her way south, news of her presence would circulate through the slave grapevine, and she would assemble slaves for the dangerous journey north. Traveling by night, hiding by day, she always carried a gun, both for defense against slave patrols and to stiffen the resolve of any wavering fugitives.

Harriet Tubman at home, Auburn, 1911.

Her early route first took her through Baltimore; later her destination was often Wilmington, Del, and then the Quaker settlements of southeastern Pennsylvania. She brought her "passengers" to New York State, sometimes to Gerrit Smith's mansion in Peterboro (Madison Co), Jermain Loguen's house in Syracuse, or destinations in Rochester, and from there on to St. Catharines and other points in Canada. Tubman made her last trip south in December 1860, just months before the outbreak of the American Civil War. Though shrouded in secrecy, Tubman's work on the Underground Railroad soon became legendary. She was lionized by abolitionists and reviled by slave owners, the latter offering a large reward for her capture. In 1858 she met in Canada with the militant abolitionist John Brown, who wanted Tubman to help him recruit former slaves to aid in his plan for a massive slave insurrection. By some accounts only Tubman's illness prevented her from joining John Brown's doomed 1859 raid on the US military arsenal at Harpers Ferry [now in W Va]. Tubman saw the Civil War as a continuation of the struggle to destroy slavery. From 1862 to 1865 she served in the Union army as a volunteer nurse in camp hospitals and as a scout in the coastal regions of South Carolina, Georgia, and Florida gathering information behind Confederate lines while enlisting slaves in the Union cause. Under the command of Col James Montgomery, Tubman conducted a secret raid up the Combahee River in South Carolina in 1863, which purportedly was the first armed expedition led by a woman in American history.

AUBURN

In 1859 Harriet Tubman's parents moved to Auburn, where the US senator and former New York State governor William H. Seward offered Tubman a plot of land on easy terms in the nearby Town of Fleming (Cayuga Co). She found herself spending increasing amounts of time in New York State, as in April 1860, when she participated in the rescue of fugitive slave Charles Nalle in Troy (Rensselaer Co). Tubman helped rescue him from the office of the US commissioner and spirited him to Niskayuna (Schenectady Co), where he remained in hiding for a month until citizens of Troy purchased his freedom for $650. After the war Tubman returned to Auburn to care for her elderly parents, and in 1869, two years after her husband John Tubman died, she married Nelson Davis, a Union army veteran and an elder in the local Parker St African Methodist Episcopal Zion (AMEZ) Church (now the Harriet Tubman Thompson Memorial AMEZ Church).

Though Tubman's financial situation was often precarious, she brought in some income from farming and support from white benefactors and local family and friends. Tubman fought for a pension for her Civil War activities but was consistently turned down because of her lack of official status with the US Army. Finally in 1890 she was awarded a partial pension of $20 per month as the widow of Davis, who had died in 1888. In 1869 Tubman cooperated with Sarah Bradford, a resident of Geneva (Ontario Co), in a biography of her life called *Scenes in the Life of Harriet Tubman,* followed by a second, expanded version, *Harriet Tubman: The Moses of Her People* (1886). In 1896 she purchased a parcel of 25 acres (10 ha) adjoining her residence straddling the Fleming-Auburn line. She converted two structures, a brick structure that she called John Brown Hall and a wooden structure into homes for aged and infirm Blacks in the Auburn area. This property, donated to the Thompson Memorial AMEZ Church in 1903, formally opened in 1908 as the Harriet Tubman Home. The wooden-frame structure is still standing and in 1974 was declared a National Historic Landmark by the US government. Tubman remained a legendary figure in her later years, attending many suffrage meetings, including the founding meeting of the National Association of Colored Women in 1896, and she was a friend and supporter of suffragist leader Susan B. Anthony. Tubman received assistance from both the AMEZ Church and the Empire State Federation of Women's Clubs until her death from pneumonia. Local Civil War veterans marched in her funeral procession, and she was buried with military honors. In 2002 New York State declared 10 March as Harriet Tubman Day for the role she played in the state and the nation. In 2003 Congress appropriated $11,750 for the Harriet Tubman Home as compensation for the widow's pension Tubman only partially received until 1913.

Bradford, Sarah. *Harriet Tubman: The Moses of Her People* (New York: Corinth Books, 1886)

Larson, Kate Clifford. *Bound for the Promised Land: Harriet Tubman, Portrait of an American Heroine* (Forthcoming)

Quarles, Benjamin. "Harriet Tubman's Unlikely Leadership." In *Black Leaders in the Nineteenth Century,* ed. Leon Litwack and August Meier (Urbana: Univ of Illinois Press, 1988)

Sernett, Milton. *North Star Country: Upstate New York and the Crusade for African American Freedom* (Syracuse: Syracuse Univ Press, 2002)

Floris Barnett Cash

Tuckahoe. Village (pop 6,211) in Eastchester (Westchester Co). Manufacturing began at Tuckahoe with the Old Stone Mill on the Yonkers side of the Bronx River, where the Eastchester Manufacturing Co began making cotton cloth *ca* 1800–1810. Rich marble deposits were discovered nearby in 1822 just as Greek Revival architecture was coming into fashion, and Tuckahoe marble found a market for many important buildings. The Harlem Railroad served the community beginning in 1844. Irish and later Italian quarrymen and their families settled in the village. In 1855 two quarries employed 750 workers, the second-largest number of stoneworkers in the state outside of New York City; quarrying ended in 1930. The Old Stone Mill became the factory of Hodgman Rubber Co (1852–1925), makers of a rubberized raincoat, and then of Burroughs Wellcome (1925–70), a pharmaceutical manufacturer. The village incorporated in 1902. In the early 21st century the village was a residential community with many commuters.

Ernest Zocchi and Jeff Zuckerman

Tucker, Luther (*b* Brandon, Vt, 7 May 1802; *d* Albany, 26 Jan 1873). Publisher and agricultural advocate. Tucker was the youngest of six children; his mother died shortly after his birth, and his father left him in the care of a neighbor when he moved west with the older siblings. Tucker had little formal schooling and apprenticed with a printer in Middlebury, Vt, at age 14. He worked in New York City, Philadelphia, Baltimore, and Washington, DC, as a journeyman-printer before establishing the *Rochester Daily Advertiser,* one of the first daily papers west of Albany, in 1826. Tucker's second newspaper, the *Genesee Farmer* (1831, Rochester), became a leading agricultural periodical containing original articles written by expert agriculturists and advocating scientific farming methods. Tucker published the *Genesee Farmer* until 1839, when he purchased the *Cultivator* (1834, Albany) and combined the publications under the latter's name. He moved to Albany the following year. In 1841 the New York State Agricultural Society adopted a constitution drafted by Tucker that provided for the holding of state fairs. Tucker established the *Horticulturist,* whose first editor was landscape gardener and architect Andrew Jackson Downing, in 1846. He sold the publication in 1852 and founded the *Country Gentleman,* which contained general and agricultural news, in 1853. In 1866 the *Cultivator* was absorbed by the *Country Gentleman.* Tucker was a model and leader in the field of agricultural journalism, an important influence on agricultural matters, and a significant promoter of agricultural literature. At his death he was succeeded in business by his sons, who both served as editors of the *Country Gentleman.*

Demaree, Albert Lowther. *The American Agricultural Press, 1819–1860* (New York: Columbia Univ Press, 1941)

Suzan D. Friedlander

tugboat companies. The Port of New York was one of the world's first to introduce steam-powered towing vessels. As early as 1818 the *Nautilus,* used as a Staten Island ferry, began diverting from its route to tow becalmed sailing ships through the Narrows. It was quickly apparent that steamers designed purely for towing were needed. The first was the *Rufus King,* which entered service in the harbor in 1825. Early tugboats were side-wheel steamers, best suited for towing ships or barges astern. The advent of the propeller led in the 1850s to the development of tugboats far more suitable for working around piers and wharves, berthing and unberthing ships, and maneuvering barges of all shapes and sizes. By the Civil War the familiar steam tugboat profile—tall stack and pilothouse forward on the upper deck—had become standard, though some side-wheel towboats were still used into the first years of the 20th century. The side-wheelers drew giant rafts of canalboats and barges between the port and the Erie Canal and other points along the Hudson River. Irish American families operated many of the private companies, creating what was popularly known as New York Harbor's Irish Navy. Two of the oldest Irish firms, Moran and McAllister, in operation since the 1860s, remain active in the Port of New York and in other East Coast ports into the 21st century.

All the major railroads serving the Port of New York also developed tugboat fleets, which moved lighterage barges and car floats back and forth across the harbor. The railroads used distinct types of tugs for specific purposes. Those for car floats had extra-high wheelhouses to allow operators to see over the freight cars on the floats; the Pennsylvania Railroad built double-ended "drill tugs" to work in close quarters, shifting barges within terminals. Diesel propulsion began to replace steam around 1930, but the characteristic tug profile remained largely unchanged. The number of tugs in the port dropped sharply after the 1950s with the decline of the railroads and lighterage following construction of the Interstate Highway System and the rise of the trucking industry. At the beginning of the 21st century, a "tractor tug," already popular in Europe, is being introduced; it uses a propulsion system allowing movement in any direction and has a wheelhouse designed for 360 degrees of visibility.

Writers' Program of the Works Progress Administration of the City of New York. *A Maritime History of New York* (Garden City, NY: Doubleday, Doran, 1941)

Norman Brouwer

Tug Hill (region). An area that spans over 2,100 mi² (5,439 km²) between the Adirondack Mountains and Lake Ontario in portions of Jefferson, Lewis, Oneida, and Oswego Cos. The region's southern boundary runs from Oneida Lake, about 10 miles (16 km) north of Syracuse, to just north of Utica. The Black River bounds the area to the east and north. Some believe that the name Tug Hill is a generic name applied to many areas settled by Europeans prior to the American Revolution. Many of these areas lost the name as they later developed, but New York State's Tug Hill may have kept it because of the relative lack of development. The "tug" probably refers to the hard work of horse or oxen making their way up steep slopes.

The Tug Hill landform, a plateau, tips up to the east. The west side at Lake Ontario has an elevation of approximately 250 feet (76 m). A gradual rise to the east culminates in a sharp escarpment of almost 2,100 feet (640 m) in elevation, dropping precipitously to the Black River. One of the most rural parts of New York State, as defined by the Tug Hill Commission, the region consists of 41 towns, containing 21 villages, with a population in 2000 of 105,028. Lake Ontario, prevailing westerly winds, and the eastward rise of Tug Hill spawn the heaviest snowfalls in the eastern United States. The average snowfall in the center of the region is 20 feet (6.1 m) a season. The record snowfall, of 1976–77, was just short of 40 feet (12.2 m). It is not uncommon for the spring snowpack to exceed 3 feet (.9 m). Tug Hill snows and summer rains make it one of the wettest parts of the state, giving birth to the Salmon River, Fish Creek, and major portions of the Black and Mohawk Rivers. Fish Creek provides the water supply for the Cities of Rome and Oneida.

Tug Hill snows have always kept its population sparse. Making a living from its forests has been the rule, and most of Tug Hill's development was probably late in the 19th century, when sawmills were the focal point of many small communities. Logging remains central to the region's economy, although now there are fewer paper mills and more furniture-manufacturing companies. In 2003 the forests contributed $80 million to the area's economy, with approximately 20 sawmills and more than 50 furniture, paper, and other secondary wood-using industries in the region. Forests and rivers have made hunting and fishing an important part of life on Tug Hill. Recreational pursuits such as skiing and snowmobiling are growing in importance. These traditions, combined with the wealth of the region's forests and rivers, make Tug Hill prominent in the state's planning for open space protection. In 1972 the state legislature designated the Tug Hill region and created the Tug Hill Commission to assist towns, villages, and community organizations in protecting the area's natural resources and strengthening its economy. Commission headquarters are in Watertown.

McNamara, Robert, ed. *Tug Hill: A Four Season Guide to the Natural Side* (Utica: North Country Books/Tug Hill Tomorrow Land Trust, 1999)

Robert R. Quinn

Tug Hill Plateau. Upland area extending from Watertown to Rome (Oneida Co). An outlier of the Appalachian Upland, the plateau is separated from the Adirondack Highlands by the Black River Valley. The land slopes gradually upward from east of Lake Ontario to a maximum elevation of almost 2,100 feet (640 m), forming a tilted mesa capped by resistant Ordovician Oswego sandstone. The steep scarp slope on the east has been dissected by retreating ice, forming several steep waterfalls and canyons, including a 3 mi (4.8 km) long gorge at Whetstone Gulf State Park, near Lowville (Lewis Co). The plateau is most famous for its winter snowfall records. Towns such as Montague (Lewis Co) and Boonville (Oneida Co) frequently record the highest seasonal snowfall tallies east of the Rocky Mountains, receiving in excess of 200 inches (500 cm). Lake effect snow occurs when cold, dry air masses from Canada warm during their passage across the lake surface and absorb moisture. When the air moves over the colder land surface on the downwind side of the lake and rises up the Tug Hill dip slope, it rapidly cools, forcing moisture to condense and fall as snow.

See also GEOLOGY AND PLATE TECTONICS.

Cadwell, D. H., and D. L. Pair. *Surficial Geologic Map of New York, Adirondack Sheet* (Albany: NYS Museum/Geological Survey, 1986)

Susan Millar

Tully. Town (pop 2,709) and village (pop 924) in S Onondaga Co. Settled in 1795, the town was formed in 1803 from Fabius. Nineteenth-century products included wool cloth (1830s–1840s), horse rakes (1870s), and novelties (1890s). It was served by the Syracuse, Binghamton and New York Railroad (1854). The village incorporated in 1875. After the Civil War, Tully became a summer resort because of a chain of lakes and glacial potholes. The Tully Lake Park Association (1888) platted lots, walks, and drives and built a hotel (1889), and Assembly Park (1892) was located on Tully Lake's west side. In the early and mid-20th century, Tully's farms shipped cabbages and seed potatoes, and ice was cut extensively until the development of refrigeration. With the completion of I-81 (1957 north, 1966 south), commuting to both Syracuse and Cortland increased, and the area around the lakes was developed for housing.

Eleanor Preston

tunnels. See BRIDGES AND TUNNELS; HOLLAND TUNNEL; LINCOLN TUNNEL.

Tupper Lake. Village (pop 3,935) in Altamont (Franklin Co). Tupper Lake was developed quickly as a sawmilling community at the junction of the New York and Ottawa Railroad (1890) and the Mohawk and Malone Railroad (1892). The "Big Mill" (1890) produced 300,000 board feet daily. Two "rossing" (de-barking) mills for pulpwood (1898–99) and the Brooklyn Cooperage (1900) stave mill added jobs. The Oval Wood Dish factory (1918–69) and the Sunmount VA Hospital (1924–65) were long the largest employers. Tupper Lake workers were drawn heavily from Quebec, and in 1955 its population was 84% Roman Catholic. The VA Hospital became Sunmount Developmental Center (1965). Tourism and resort services remain important. In 2003 the Natural History Museum of the Adirondacks was under development.

Thomas W. Perrin

Turin. Town (pop 793) and village (pop 263) in central Lewis Co. Settled in 1798, the town was formed from Mexico (Oswego Co) in 1800. Located in the eastern Tug Hill Plateau region, snowfall exceeds 200 inches (500 cm) annually. Snow Ridge Ski Area (1945), with the heaviest snowfall of any East Coast ski area, transformed Turin into a resort town with lodging, restaurants, and vacation homes. The Swiss Ski School under Rudi Kuersteiner and Otto Frei trained racers chosen for the US Olympic Alpine Teams of 1960 and 1968. The Hall Ski Lift Co (1949) produced machinery for ski areas, moving to Watertown in 1962. Turin has also become a popular destination for snowmobilers.

Emily Williams

Turkmens. See CENTRAL ASIANS.

Turks. Turkish-speaking immigrants came to New York City in small numbers in the 19th and early 20th centuries. Several thousand Turks lived in New York State in 1940, mainly in New

York City. Those who stayed in New York City tended to settle in boardinghouses around Rivington and Forsythe Sts in Lower Manhattan and in Brooklyn adjacent to neighborhoods occupied by other immigrants from the Ottoman Empire, such as along Atlantic Ave. A second wave of Turkish immigrants arrived in the United States following World War II. They tended to have more education than those in the first wave and included many students. Most settled in New York City, but there were settlements elsewhere as well. In the 1960s Bond Stores hired 200 Turkish tailors for its Rochester plant. By 1967 over 600 Turks lived in Rochester. Another group settled in Syracuse.

Turkish immigration to the United States was limited until 1965 by the quota system and by Turkish laws restricting emigration without official permission. After these laws were rescinded in the 1960s, economic hardship and political instability in the 1960s and 1970s, followed by a military coup in 1980, led to increased emigration to the United States, peaking at more than 2,000 annually in the early 1980s. This group of immigrants included a high proportion of professionals as well as students who remained in the United States following their studies. In New York City the immigrants concentrated in Brighton Beach in Brooklyn and in Sunnyside and Richmond Hills in Queens. In 2000, 23,674 people living in New York State reported Turkish ancestry. Turkish American societies, mainly in the New York City area, include branches of the Turkish Women's League of America and the Young Turks of America, and professional associations such as the Turkish-American Physicians Association. There are social and fraternal groups, such as the Club Anadolu in East Patchogue (Suffolk Co), and organizations for ethnic Turks from areas outside of Turkey proper, such as the Turkish-Cypriot Aid Society in the Bronx, the Association of Crimean Turks in Brooklyn, and the Association of Balkan Turks in Manhattan. A focus of religious and cultural activities is the American Turkish Islamic Cultural Center in Forest Hills (Queens Co), though many Turks are secular in outlook. A large number of Turkish societies in New York State have joined the Federation of Turkish-American Societies, founded in 1956, or the Association of Turkish American Associations. Since 24 Apr 1984 there has been an annual parade on 5th Ave in Manhattan on Turkish-American Day. The Turkish Society of Rochester was founded in 1969, with the annual Turkish Festival since 1987. Turkish Americans from New York State include the brothers Ahmet and Nesuhi Ertegun, cofounders of Atlantic Records.

Ahmed, Frank. *Turks in America: The Ottoman Turk's Immigrant Experience* (Washington, DC: Library of Congress, 1986)

John VanderLippe

turnpikes. Roads financed by tolls levied on users, named from the bar or "pike" used as a tollgate. Americans adopted the toll road principle in the early 1800s, and turnpikes provided the best means of overland transportation until the growth of the railroad network some 50 years later.

Turnpikes usually followed more direct, less undulating routes than common roads and were typically ditched and drained. The best featured roadbeds made of compacted broken stone, called metal, as advocated by British engineer John McAdam. Most New York State turnpikes were more cheaply made than true macadam roads. Unlike states farther south and west, New York's turnpikes were built entirely by private corporations without state aid. Local landowners purchased shares with an eye to secondary benefits, such as better access to markets and improved land values. Turnpikes made for poor direct investments, since they rarely returned more than 2% of capital investment annually over the long term. Despite some opposition to giving private companies control over public highways, turnpikes were popular and accounted for about one-third of all business charters granted by New York State between 1791 and 1830. Tolls averaged 1.2¢ per mile, with gradations based on vehicle size and number of draft animals. Tollgates were located every 10 mi (16.1 km) or sometimes every 5 mi (8.1 km). Turnpike companies granted broad concessions to local residents, who paid no tolls while attending to religious or civic duties. Turnpikes served farmers hauling their own produce, professional teamsters moving long-distance freight, drovers herding livestock to urban markets, and emigrants on treks to new homes in the West. Stagecoaches carrying passengers and mail used the turnpikes for speed. Turnpike travel nurtured its own service economy, and taverns usually lined the roads at 1 mi (1.6 km) intervals.

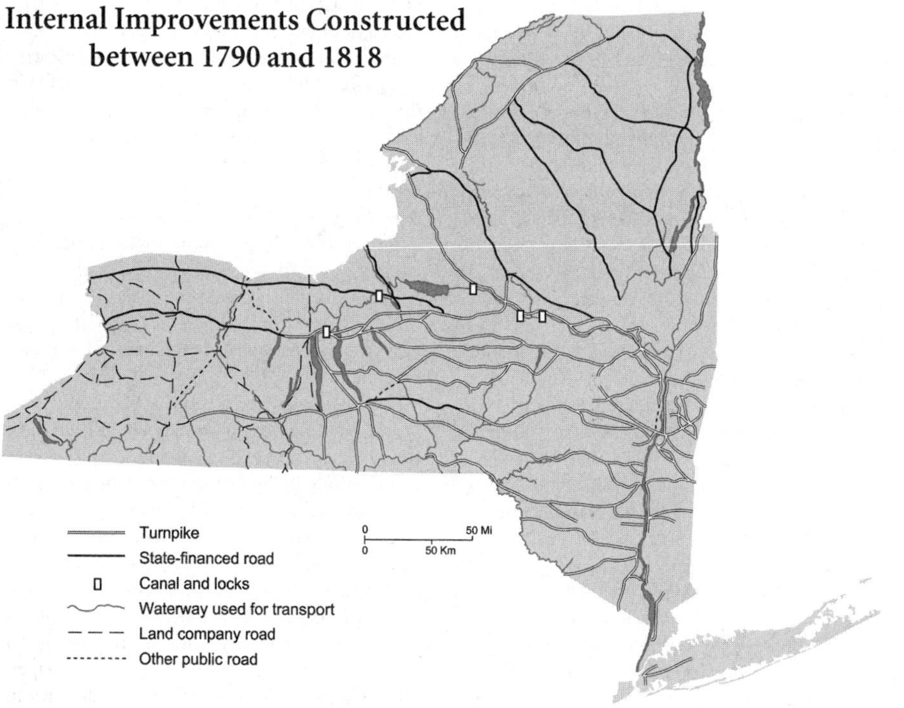

The Turnpike Network

The last of the major northeastern states to adopt the turnpike system, New York quickly gained first place in miles constructed. The state chartered its first turnpike in 1797 and by 1821 had 3,000–4,000 miles (4,800–6,400 km) of toll roads. Its turnpikes formed part of a larger network linking New England, northern New Jersey, and northeastern Pennsylvania. On a map, they are revealed as an artifact of the Yankee diaspora, linking the New England heartland with areas of Yankee settlement. In this network, turnpikes were built quickly and cheaply but had shorter life spans than those built farther south and west.

New York State turnpikes were concentrated between the Hudson and Genesee Rivers. Portions of the New York–Albany Post Road were turnpiked, and toll roads ran from all of the major towns on the east bank of the Hudson into the New England states. On the west shore of the Hudson, turnpikes led from even minor landings back toward the mountains. The Newburgh and Cochecton ran straight from Newburgh (Orange Co) to the Delaware River, where it connected with a chain of turnpikes running across the northeast corner of Pennsylvania to Bath (Steuben Co). While both of the two turnpikes running west from Kingston (Ulster Co) failed to complete their roads across the Catskill, Ramapo, and Shawangunk Mountains, Susquehanna Turnpike extended from Catskill (Greene Co) to Wattles Ferry [now Unadilla, Otsego Co], joining Susquehanna and Bath Turnpike, which then continued through Ithaca to Steuben Co. From Bath, Lake Erie Turnpike reached only as far as Angelica (Allegany Co).

Albany boasted three main routes to the west. Albany and Schenectady Turnpike and Mohawk Turnpike formed a continuous route to Utica. Seneca Road, the longest turnpike in the state at 157 miles (252.7 km), then ran from Utica to Canandaigua (Ontario Co). Genesee and Ontario failed to extend the line from Canandaigua to Black Rock (Erie Co) because the Holland Land Co lacked cash to support the project. The second route from Albany was formed by five Great Western Turnpike companies. First Great Western ran to Cherry Valley (Otsego Co). From this point Third Great Western continued to the Seneca Road at Manlius (Onondaga Co), while Second Great Western branched south from Cherry Valley to Sherburne (Chenango Co), there connecting with Fourth Great Western to

Homer (Cortland Co) and Fifth Great Western to the east shore of Cayuga Lake. The third route was formed by Albany and Delaware Turnpike and Rensselaerville and Durham Turnpike, linking Albany with Susquehanna Turnpike.

Maturity and Decline

The first wave of turnpike construction ended by 1825, with half the mileage abandoned over the next decade. Overbuilding, cheap construction, and inflated traffic estimates explained much of the decline. But it was also easy to open free roads, called shunpikes, that bypassed tollgates. Despite fines and lawsuits, shunpiking was difficult to suppress and it cut into turnpike revenue. Only a few turnpikes failed because of canal competition. Many areas remained remote from canals, and mails moved faster by road. Some long-distance turnpikes, such as the Great Westerns and the Seneca Road, continued in use, and additional short turnpikes were built in the 1830s and 1840s as feeders for canals, railroads, and market towns. Toll roads revived briefly during the plank road craze of 1846–54. Some turnpikes were converted to plank roads, and much new mileage was added. The wooden roads, however, were soon abandoned or reverted to conventional turnpikes as the wood rotted. Completion of trunk-line railroads during the 1850s doomed the last long-distance turnpikes, as passengers, mail, and even livestock began to move by rail. Parts of the Newburgh and Cochecton survived into the 1870s. A few short turnpikes, including portions of First Great Western and Delaware Turnpikes near Albany, remained economically viable, and some new turnpikes were chartered as late as 1888. A few survived into the first decades of the 20th century, when government-funded paved highways, financed by taxes rather than tolls, finally replaced them. State and US numbered highways occupy the beds of many old turnpikes.

See also AUTOMOBILE LANDSCAPES.

Durrenberger, Joseph Austin. *Turnpikes: A Study of the Toll Road Movement in the Middle Atlantic States and Maryland* (Valdosta, Ga: Southern Stationery & Printing, 1931)

Holmes, Oliver W. "The Turnpike Era." In *Conquering the Wilderness*, vol 5 of *History of the State of New York*, 10 vols, ed. Alexander C. Flick (New York: Columbia Univ Press, 1934)

Klein, Daniel B., and John Majewski. "Economy, Community, and Law: The Turnpike Movement in New York, 1797–1845," *Law and Society Review* 26 (1992): 469–512

Taylor, George Rogers. *The Transportation Revolution, 1815–1860* (New York: Holt, Rinehart & Winston, 1951)

Christopher T. Baer

turnverein. Association-based gymnastics that originated in central Europe during the Napoleonic Wars. The turnverein movement was nurtured by a Prussian-born patriot named Friedrich Ludwig Jahn, whose systematic approach to gymnastics was meant to prepare Germans physically and mentally to combat the conquering French. Jahn's *Turnplatz* (gymnastic field) included places for long- and high-jumping and for the pole vault as well as gymnastics equipment such as the balance beam, horse, and ladders. Jahn and his assistants created the parallel bars for club exercises.

Prussian political refugees brought the turnverein movement to the United States during the 1820s. Following the failed revolutions of 1848–49, many Germans immigrated to the United States, and some formed gymnastic associations. In 1848 the New York Turngemeinde initiated club gymnastics in New York City. It was followed by the New York Turnverein (1850), the Socialist Turnverein of Brooklyn (1850), the New York Social Turnverein (1851), the Albany Social Turnverein (1851), the Rochester Social Turnverein (1852), the Buffalo Turnverein (1853), the Utica Turnverein (1854), and the Poughkeepsie Social Turnverein (1854). Associations operated out of saloons and summer gardens until they could afford to buy property to build their own *Turnhallen.* At the 1855 national convention in Buffalo, northern turners voiced opposition to slavery, Sabbatarianism, and nativism. New York City hosted the gymnastics meet of the national organization in 1857. During the Civil War German gymnasts formed the 20th New York Infantry, United Turner Regiment, made of companies from New York City, Rochester, Syracuse, Brooklyn, Albany, Poughkeepsie, Morrisania, Williamsburg, College Point, and Bloomingdale. Buffalo turners joined either the 21st, 49th, or 116th New York Infantries and saw considerable action in secessionist Virginia.

Turner societies in New York State formed the Amerikanischer Turnerbund, or American Gymnastics Union. To join the federation societies organized themselves into *Bezirke,* or districts, based on geographic region; for example, the Western New York Gymnastics District was created from societies in Buffalo, Rochester, Syracuse, and Dunkirk. Created in 1891, the First Circle, or Atlantic Circle, comprised the districts of New York City, Long Island, Western New York, and Central New York. These districts held annual gymnastics festivals as well as quarterly or semiannual training days for the finest athletes in the district to learn or perfect apparatus and free exercise routines.

New York State turners were proponents for German language instruction and physical education in public school curricula. Gymnastics displays, such as the one held at Buffalo's Star Theatre in 1891, demonstrated the benefits of exercise. As a result, physical education won public funding in New York City, Brooklyn, Utica, Syracuse, Rochester, and Buffalo within the next two decades. Physical education instructors hired by the Buffalo school board in 1910 operated out of school basements until a gymnasium was built. After World War I the numbers of New York State turners dwindled; however, Buffalo hosted the gymnastics meet of the national organization in 1930 and again in 1953. These gymnastics organizations, including one on Tonawanda Ave in Kenmore (Erie Co), continue but no longer serve as German American social clubs.

Metzner, Henry. *History of the American Turners,* 3d ed. (Rochester: National Council of the American Turners, 1974)

Pumroy, Eric L., and Katja Rampelmann, comps. *Research Guide to the Turner Movement in the United States* (Westport, Conn: Greenwood, 2000)

Kevin J. Grzymala

Tuscarora. Town (pop 1,400) in SE Steuben Co. Its name is from the Tuscarora Indians who moved into the area during and after the Revolutionary War. European settlers arrived in 1804, and the town was formed from Addison in 1859. A large woolen mill with 250 spindles operated from 1844 until late in the 19th century. From 1851 to 1858 Tuscarora was the site of a tollhouse on a plank road from Addison to Elkland, Pa. A series of railroads—including the Addison and Northern Pennsylvania, the Baltimore and Susquehanna, and the Wellsville, Addison, and Galeton—served the town from 1882 to 1960. After the forests were depleted and the timber industry faltered, dairy farming became more important. Tobacco was a major crop from the mid–19th century until World War II.

Virginia L. Wright and Jerry Wright

Tuscarora Nation. The homeland of these Iroquois Indians is the Tuscarora Reservation located in Niagara Co near Lewiston, Pekin, and Sanborn. Although there are Tuscaroras living and working elsewhere in New York State and in other states, the greatest concentration remains on their reservation. According to the US Census Bureau, in 2000 the total population of the reservation was 1,338. The Tuscarora are predominantly Christian, though a number of members of the nation adhere to the Iroquois Longhouse religion. In addition to the Tuscarora community in New York State, there is one on the Six Nations Reserve in Ontario, where a number of pro-British Tuscaroras moved after the American Revolution. There has been ongoing contact between residents of the two communities over the years.

Settlement

The Tuscarora were originally a northern Iroquoian group that had migrated southward in ancient times but had maintained friendly relations with the groups in the north. They first entered New York as a result of their wars in 1711–13 with the North Carolina colonists who were severely encroaching on their territory and kidnapping Indians for sale into slavery. Badly defeated, the hostile Tuscarora fled and appealed to the Five Nations Iroquois for a place of refuge. They were accepted and sponsored for adoption by the Oneida, who welcomed them into Oneida territory. The refugees traveled by foot, horse, and canoe through Virginia, Maryland, and Pennsylvania, settling mainly south of Oneida Lake, along the east branch of the Susquehanna River on both sides of the New York–Pennsylvania border, and between the Unadilla and Chenango Rivers. By 1722 or 1723 they had been incorporated into the Iroquois Confederacy as the sixth nation. Thereafter the Tuscarora participated fully in Iroquois military and political affairs, including treaty making, but undoubtedly because their ancestors had not participated in the original formation of the confederacy, the names of their hereditary chiefs were not added to the ceremonial roll call of the founders. Tuscarora chiefs are raised to office by condolence ritual, similar to the league chiefs. The coming of the American Revolution divided the Tuscarora; those closest to the Oneida and most under the influence of missionary Samuel Kirkland favored the American cause, and those living in villages farther removed favored the British. During the war the latter moved west of the Genesee River and settled in Seneca country. Because of the sale of most of Oneida land to New York State in 1785, 1788, and 1798, the Tuscarora remaining in Oneida country were left nearly homeless and began looking westward toward the Niagara Frontier, where most of their kin were living. At the same time, the migration of Tuscaroras from North Carolina occurred at intervals over a period of 90 years and ended in 1803 when the last North Carolina immigrants arrived at the Tuscarora Reservation.

Reservation

The original Indian village was established by Tuscaroras who had fled Oneida territory and settled in Seneca territory during the American Revolution. A number of these refugees moved to Johnson's Landing [now in Porter, Niagara Co] about 4 mi (6 km) east of the Niagara River, explored the area to the south, and established a settlement in a most favorable spot along the escarpment just east of what is now Lewiston. They were gradually joined by other Tuscaroras living in villages along the west bank of the Genesee River and later by pro-American Tuscaroras from Oneida territory south of Oneida Lake. The Seneca had granted the Tuscarora a 1 mi^2 (3 km^2) area encompassing their village on the escarpment. At the Treaty of Big Tree (1797), the Seneca sold a huge amount of their country to Robert Morris, who then sold it to the Holland Land Co. Inadvertently the Seneca had not officially preserved the Tuscarora grant in the treaty. Upon complaint from the Tuscarora, Thomas Morris, on behalf of his father Robert, granted the Tuscaroras a square mile, which the company confirmed. In 1798 the Holland Land Co granted the Tuscarora another square mile east of their holdings. The Seneca later officially confirmed their original (pre-1797) square-mile grant by a deed in 1808, in total 3 mi^2 (8 km^2), or 1,920 acres (777 ha). In 1801–2 Tuscarora chiefs traveled to North Carolina to obtain payment for their original lands. The North Carolina legislature had permitted lease of these lands, for which the Tuscaroras received $13,722. Secretary of War Henry Dearborn, acting on their behalf, then purchased from the Holland Land Co an additional 4,329 acres (1,752 ha) south and east of the original 3 mi^2 reservation, bringing the total Tuscarora homeland in Niagara Co to 6,249 acres (2,529 ha).

Cultural Life

Farming and hunting were the foundations of the Tuscarora economy in their Niagara Frontier location. Visitors often noted their neat farms and extensive orchards. An interest in art, Indian history, and folklore was evident among the Tuscarora even early in the 19th century. Dennis and David Cusick, sons of Revolutionary War veteran Nicholas Cusick, were both gifted artists; David was also the first Tuscarora author, producing two editions of *David Cusick's Sketches of Ancient History of the Six Nations* in 1827 and 1828. In 1881 Elias Johnson published *Legends, Traditions, and Laws of the Iroquois,* which contains particularly valuable chapters on Tuscarora life and history. Native Tuscarora J. N. B. Hewitt was a major Iroquois linguist and ethnologist during his long tenure at the Smithsonian Institution.

As a result of the depression of the 1930s, farming as a major occupation declined but did not disappear as more and more Tuscaroras began commuting to off-reservation employment. In the early 21st century, many make their living in construction, skilled trades, office work, factory work, computer technology, nursing, and teaching. Beadwork, art, lacrosse stick manufacture, and crafts are still important reservation occupations.

The Tuscarora had received their first introduction to Christianity in their Oneida homeland through association with Oneida and Mohawk Christians and from a succession of missionaries. In 1800 the New York Missionary Society sent missionary Elkanah Holmes to the Tuscarora living in Niagara Co. A school was established, and in July 1806 a Congregational church was formally organized on the reservation. In 1861 the church became Presbyterian, later was nondenominational, and is currently known as the Mission. A Baptist church was organized in 1836 but became defunct in 1846 when most of its members migrated to Kansas Territory. It was revived in 1860 and remains vigorous. In the mid–20th century, a Roman Catholic chapel was established on the reservation. The churches have been important cultural institutions for two centuries. Over the years both Protestant churches have produced native pastors and evangelists. The Tuscarora Temperance Society, founded 19 Feb 1830 with Nicholas Cusick as its first president, has continued to be an organization of major importance, promoting its aims of temperance, industry, education, and moral reform. The unique Tuscarora New Year Day's celebration reinforces traditional kinship relations and culminates in a feast sponsored by the Tuscarora Temperance Society. The National Picnic is held on the second Friday and Saturday in July, featuring food, craft tables, and a platform for talks by Indian leaders and other dignitaries.

Preserving Land and Culture

Since their relocation to Niagara Co, the Tuscaroras have faced three crises that have involved their land and threatened their way of life. In December 1813, with the British-Indian invasion of the Niagara Frontier, Tuscarora warriors came to the aid of inhabitants of nearby Lewiston. In retaliation the British Indian allies burned the Tuscarora village, leaving its occupants homeless. The Tuscarora continued to serve faithfully with American troops during the remainder of the war. In 1838 the Treaty of Buffalo Creek would have deprived Tuscaroras of 1,920 acres (777 ha) of their reservation and forced them to migrate westward, but the Tuscarora people dissented. A lawsuit decided by the state supreme court in 1850 canceled the 1838 Tuscarora deed to the Ogden Land Co for the 1,920 acres. In 1957 the New York Power Authority sought to condemn 1,383 acres (560 ha) of the reservation for a reservoir. The Tuscarora formed an ongoing mass protest and, through their governing chiefs' council, carried the case through the courts, but by a 6-3 vote, the US Supreme Court in 1960 in *Federal Power Commission v Tuscarora Indian Nation* rejected the Indian nation's claims. The delay forced the Power Authority to redesign the reservoir and to take instead 550 acres (223 ha) of the reservation. The vigorous and widely publicized Tuscarora resistance to the State Power Authority's land seizure inspired other Indians throughout the country with a new sense of militancy and determination to preserve their land base. Also, the historic legal matters raised by attorneys in the Tuscarora case revealed the questionable and often illegal methods used by New York State in the early years of the Republic to obtain Indian lands. This knowledge helped provide a foundation for future Indian land claim cases in New York State. Despite a long history of threats against both their land and their self-determination, the Tuscarora have been resilient, maintaining their sovereignty as a nation by adopting from the general culture what is necessary for their progress while pre-

Tuscarora land dispute, 1958.

serving what is distinctive and vital in their own culture.

See also AMERICAN INDIANS IN LITERATURE: INDIGENOUS AUTHORS.

Chazanof, William. *Joseph Ellicott and the Holland Land Company: The Opening of Western New York* (Syracuse: Syracuse Univ Press, 1970)
Graymont, Barbara. "The Tuscarora New Year Festival," *New York History* 50 (Apr 1969): 143–63
Hauptman, Laurence M. *The Iroquois Struggle for Survival: World War II to Red Power* (Syracuse: Syracuse Univ Press, 1986)
Hewitt, J. N. B. "Tuscarora." In *Handbook of American Indians North of Mexico.* Bureau of American Ethnology, Bulletin 30, vol 2, ed. Frederick Webb Hodge (Washington, DC: Smithsonian Institution, 1910)
Landy, David. "Tuscarora among the Iroquois." In *Northeast,* ed. Bruce G. Trigger, vol 15 of *Handbook of North American Indians* (Washington, DC: Smithsonian Institution, 1978)

Barbara Graymont

Tusten. Town (pop 1,415) in SW Sullivan Co. Settlement began ?1757 by the Delaware Co under a Connecticut claim at the mouth of the Tenmile River but wiped out by the Lenape Indians in 1763. The town formed from Lumberland in 1853, and its residents worked at farming or lumbering. The Erie Railroad (1847) crossed the Delaware in the present Tusten, creating the hamlet of Narrowsburg; the tracks are still used by CSX. A blasting-powder factory operated from *ca* 1870 to 1888 and an excelsior mill from *ca* 1870 to the 1930s. The deepest point of the Delaware River, a hole some 113 feet (34 m) deep, is located just south of the bridge to Pennsylvania.

John Conway

Tutelo Nation. Tutelo, Totero, Todirich-roone, and several other variations were the generic Iroquoian references to all Siouan peoples, including the Catawbas, from the Virginia-Carolinas Piedmont. The precise meaning of Tutelo is uncertain, although it is generally believed that the Iroquois borrowed the name from the southern Indians. In the piedmont they were better known by their own ethnic names, such as Saponi, Tutelo, Occaneechi, and several others. During the 17th and early 18th centuries, the Siouan peoples crisscrossed the piedmont in search of safety from the Iroquoian raids from New York State. By the 1740s, increasingly besieged by the surrounding English settlements, some of the Saponi, Tutelo, and Occaneechi decided to follow the Tuscarora example and seek the protection of the Iroquois in New York. They initially settled at Shamokin [now Sunbury, Pa] on the Susquehanna River. Gradually they moved upriver to the villages of Skogari and Tioga, in Pennsylvania, and from there into New York State on the Chemung River and at Coreorgonel [now Ithaca] by 1753. That year, the Cayuga adopted the Tutelo. The Clinton-Sullivan campaign of 1779 destroyed their villages along with those of the Iroquois. The refugees streamed west toward Fort Niagara and settled at Buffalo Creek. In 1780 the Cayuga war chief Fish Carrier led a mixed band of Cayuga-Tutelo warriors on the British side during the American Revolution. The Tutelo joined the loyalist Iroquois and eventually settled at Six Nations in Ontario, although some descendants are still found in Western New York, principally among the Seneca at the Cattaraugus Indian Reservation. Tutelo songs and ceremonies have enriched Iroquoian culture. In 1999 the Town of Ithaca dedicated a park site near the remains of the main Tutelo village to commemorate the importance of the Tutelo Nation to New York State. Tutelo Park promises to rekindle a cultural revival among the many Tutelo descendants in New York State and elsewhere.

Hale, Horatio. *The Tutelo Tribe and Language* (Philadelphia: American Philosophical Society, 1883)
Speck, Frank G. *The Tutelo Spirit Adoption Ceremony: Reclothing the Living in the Name of the Dead* (Harrisburg: Pennsylvania Historical Commission, 1942)

Heriberto Dixon

Tuxedo. Town (pop 3,334) in S Orange Co. Settled in the 18th century, the town was formed in 1889 from Monroe. Its first and main industry was iron mining, which began in the 1750s with Sterling Ironworks, which had forges and furnaces in what is now Warwick. Iron-producing centers in town included the Augusta Works (1783–1813) on the Ramapo River, which produced bar iron and anchors; Southfield Ironworks (1804–87), which produced blister steel and cannons for the US government; Monroe Ironworks (1809–83) at Southfield; and the Greenwood Furnaces (1811–85) at Arden. The Erie Railroad came through in 1841. Later iron production included the Hall Bedstead Manufacturing Co in the first half of the 20th century. Much of Tuxedo's territory was incorporated into the 20,000-acre (8,000 ha) estate of E. H. Harriman (1848–1909), some of which became Harriman State Park in 1910; 43.6% of the town's land area is now in the much-enlarged park, and an additional 26.1% is in Sterling Forest State Park (1998). International Paper operates a coated-products pilot plant in Tuxedo. Clove Furnace Historic Site at Arden interprets the history of iron production.

Tuxedo Park. Village (pop 748) in Tuxedo (Orange Co). In the mid–19th century, the Erie Railroad used the region as a timber lot. The Lorillard family, tobacco manufacturers and merchants, acquired 600,000 acres (240,000 ha), and Pierre Lorillard IV began work on the community in 1885, with Bruce Price as architect and Ernest Bowditch as engineer. Lorillard imported 1,800 Italian and Slovakian workers to transform the tract into a superb private park, with 30 miles (48 km) of graded roads and 22 English cottages for employees, as well as stores, stables, lawn tennis courts, a bowling alley, a swimming tank, a boathouse, an icehouse, a dam, a trout pond and hatchery, a complete sewage and water system, and a park gatehouse. The clubhouse featured a circular ballroom 80 feet (24 m) in diameter. At the first Autumn Ball (1886) young Griswold Lorillard wore the tailless dress coat to which the resort gave its name. Over the first 30 years, more than 250 houses and stables, as well as stores, service establishments, churches, a railroad station, a library, a post office, and one of the nation's first golf courses (1889) were built in an eclectic range of styles. Emily Post, perhaps Tuxedo Park's most famous resident, wrote her treatise on etiquette there in 1925. After the depression, many of the homes were abandoned or torn down. In 1952, however, Tuxedo Park became an incorporated village, which gave tax advantages that helped restore its appeal. In the early 21st century it is an attractive residential community; the village is listed on the National Register, and the Tuxedo Club remains a prestigious country club.

Jon Sterngass

Twain, Mark [Clemens, Samuel L(anghorne)] (*b* Florida, Mo, 30 Nov 1835; *d* Redding, Conn, 21 Apr 1910). Writer. Samuel Clemens first visited New York State in 1853 as a 17-year-old itinerant typesetter-printer, passing through Buffalo, Syracuse, and Albany before arriving in New York City, where he spent several months at various printing houses. Between 1854 and 1862 Clemens adopted and set aside a series of professions, working as a typesetter-printer in Missouri and Iowa, a steamboat pilot on the Mississippi River, and a silver prospector in the Nevada and California Terrs. From 1862 to 1867 he achieved some success in the West as a reporter, writer, and lecturer under the name Mark Twain. He returned east in 1867, hoping to parlay his reputation as correspondent and humorist into a successful literary career. That year he made his first appearance in the East as a lecturer at Mercantile Hall in New York City. Clemens published his first major book, *The Innocents Abroad,* in 1869 while courting his future wife, Olivia Louise "Livy" Langdon of Elmira, and negotiating a partnership in the *Buffalo Express* newspaper. Late in 1869, with the help of his future father-in-law, Jervis Langdon, Clemens purchased a one-third interest in the *Buffalo Express* and became a contributing editor. He and Livy married on 2 Feb 1870. They lived in Buffalo for 18 months and their son Langdon, who lived just under two years, was born there. Clemens's time in Buffalo was pivotal: he used his newspaper column to experiment with a variety of approaches to contemporary political and social issues and storytelling styles.

After signing a contract for his second book, *Roughing It* (1872), Clemens left the *Express* and

Mark Twain.

became a full-time writer of travel books and novels, moving to Hartford, Conn, in 1872. From 1870 to 1890, the Clemenses spent summers in Elmira at the Langdon family's farm, where Clemens's sister-in-law had a customized, octagonal study built overlooking the Chemung River so that he could work undisturbed. These years, enriched by summers in Elmira, are considered the most productive of Clemens's literary career. He worked tirelessly to sharpen his skills as a writer and to shape his most celebrated novels: *The Adventures of Tom Sawyer* (1876), *The Prince and the Pauper* (1883), *Adventures of Huckleberry Finn* (1885), and *A Connecticut Yankee in King Arthur's Court* (1889). In 1890 Clemens moved his family to Europe to trim living expenses, a move made necessary by a series of failed investments, most notably a ruinous attempt to develop an automated typesetting machine, and poor decisions related to Clemens's publishing company, Charles L. Webster Co, founded in New York City in 1884. The family returned to New York State in 1900 after a triumphant world speaking tour of 1895–96 that saved Clemens financially but was marred by the death of his oldest daughter Susy. Clemens lived in New York City and Riverdale-on-the-Hudson [now Riverdale, Bronx Co] until shortly before his death, surviving both his wife, who died in 1904, and his youngest daughter, Jean, who died in 1909. At his death, his body lay in state in New York City's Brick Presbyterian Church before burial in Elmira's Woodlawn Cemetery. There, the family plot features a 12 ft (3.7 m) obelisk created to signify his pen name, Mark Twain, the Mississippi riverboat call indicating a depth of two fathoms. In 1952 Clemens's octagonal study was moved from the original Chemung River site to the campus of Elmira College.

Kaplan, Justin. *Mr. Clemens and Mark Twain: A Biography* (New York: Simon & Schuster, 1966)

Twain, Mark. *Mark Twain's Own Autobiography: The Chapters from the North American Review.* Ed. Michael J. Kiskis (Madison: Univ of Wisconsin Press, 1990)

Michael J. Kiskis

Tweed Ring. Loosely organized political group known for corruption. William M. "Boss" Tweed (1823–78), a native of Manhattan, entered politics as the foreman of a fire company in the 1840s and served a term in Congress (1853–55) while rising through the ranks of the Democratic Party in New York City during the 1850s and early 1860s. In 1863 he became head of the Tammany Society, and he dominated the city's politics for the remainder of the decade. Tweed's only political positions during his heyday were deputy street commissioner for New York City (1863–70) and state senator (1867–73). Other influential people associated with the ring included John T. Hoffman, mayor of New York City (1866–68) and governor of New York State (1869–73); the genteel mayor of New York City A. Oakey Hall (1868–72), a former lawyer, journalist, and pragmatic district attorney; the shrewd Irish-born comptroller Richard Connolly; and the city chamberlain (treasurer) Peter Sweeny, one of Tweed's closest advisors.

Under Tweed's direction, the city dramatically enlarged the workforce to accommodate party stalwarts. In Albany, Tweed's legislative supporters passed a series of controversial laws that included a reformed New York City charter (1870)

William M. "Boss" Tweed. Photograph by Napoleon Sarony, *ca* 1870.

to strengthen home rule and municipal government by abolishing the state commissions that had supervised city affairs and transferring their functions to departments headed by mayoral appointees. Tammany launched a grandiose and generally beneficial public works program, providing jobs for its supporters and money for politicians. Estimates of the degree of theft accomplished by the Tweed Ring vary widely and are disputed. Many were certainly guilty of padded expenses, fictitious charges, outright embezzlement and bribery, bogus contracts, vote buying, and money made through foreknowledge of the city's plans. Tweed, though, continued to receive safe majorities in New York City because Tammany provided the most effective welfare system for poor residents, many of them immigrants, when no other safety net existed. Prominent and "upright" merchants and manufacturers readily cooperated with the Tweed Ring because it cut through red tape or secured them valuable franchises or contracts.

The Republican *New York Times* carried on a protracted campaign against Tweed, and political cartoonist Thomas Nast turned the Tweed Ring into a national issue in *Harper's Weekly.* Nast vividly portrayed a corpulent "Boss" Tweed and a sinister "Mayor Haul," often appealing to anti-Catholic and nativist prejudice. In response, Hall established a committee of six businessmen with unimpeachable reputations and gave them access to municipal accounts. On the eve of the 1870 election they avowed the books had been "faithfully kept" and debt levels were manageable. Yet within a year, the Tweed Ring had been destroyed. A religious riot at the Boyne Day Parade in July 1871 killed 60 civilians and convinced many Protestant Democrats that Tweed could no longer provide political stability. Rumors that the city might not be able to meet its debt payments because of chronic mismanagement or overexpansion alienated the financial and mercantile communities. From disgruntled insiders, the *New York Times* acquired hard evidence of corruption and began publishing it in July 1871. In October the state filed a civil suit against Tweed and various contractors to recover more than $6 million in overcharges. A conservative Committee of Seventy, organized to fight Tammany Hall, elected most of its candidates in 1871, although Tweed retained his senate seat. Largely through the efforts of Samuel J. Tilden, who had previously worked agreeably with Tweed, a grand jury now indicted him; Sweeny and Connolly quickly fled the country. Tammany purged its general committee, dismissed Tweed, and appointed prominent businessman Augustus Schell as grand sachem. The new mayor of New York City, wealthy sugar merchant William F. Havemeyer, imposed a vigorous retrenchment policy on the city, laying off workers and discontinuing projects.

Tweed's first trial ended without a conviction, but in a second trial he was convicted on 204 of 220 misdemeanor counts of failing to audit claims against the city and sentenced to 13 years in prison. An appeals court ruled unanimously in 1875 that the sentence was excessive. Immediately charged with a civil suit, he was unable to come up with bail and was jailed again the day after his release. He escaped and fled to Cuba and then to Spain, was extradited to New York City in November 1876, and died in prison two years later. Hall was tried three times (1871–73) on charges that he approved fraudulent overpayments as mayor; the trials resulted in a mistrial, a hung jury, and an acquittal. Although Hall vehemently defended himself to the end of his life, his reputation and social position were destroyed. Tweed left a modest estate, and almost no one in the Tweed Ring seems to have become particularly wealthy. The story of the Tweed Ring has become the personification of Gilded Age corruption.

Callow, Alexander. *The Tweed Ring* (London: Oxford Univ Press, 1966)

Hershkowitz, Leo. *Tweed's New York: Another Look* (Garden City, NY: Doubleday, 1977)

Homberger, Eric. *Scenes from the Life of a City: Corruption and Conscience in Old New York* (New Haven, Conn: Yale Univ Press, 1994)

Mandelbaum, Seymour. *Boss Tweed's New York* (New York: John Wiley, 1965)

Mushkat, Jerome. *The Reconstruction of the New York Democracy, 1861–1874* (Rutherford, NJ: Fairleigh Dickinson Univ Press, 1981)

Pratt, John. "Boss Tweed's Public Welfare Program," *New-York Historical Society Quarterly* 45 (1961): 396–411

Jon Sterngass

Twentieth Century Limited. Deluxe passenger train of the New York Central Railroad. The Twentieth Century Limited traveled the "Water Level Route" between New York City and Chicago, crossing the state from Albany to Buffalo, from 15 June 1902 until 2 Dec 1967. The train first drew wooden cars but switched over to heavyweight, riveted-steel cars eight years later. Passenger bookings soared in the 1910s and 1920s, with the train routinely running multiple sections of cars. In 1928 the train pulled an average of three sections, each the length of an average train, per run. The Twentieth Century Limited entered the streamline era of sleek, steel-shrouded locomotives and cars in 1938. Henry Dreyfuss designed an all-private-room train featuring Art Deco interiors in blue, gray, and silver. The new model cut the timing of the New York–Chicago run to 16 hours. Pennsylvania Railroad's competing streamliner Broadway Limited sometimes raced the Twentieth Century Limited on parallel tracks for the last miles into Chicago. But the Pennsylvania train never achieved the same cachet or ridership. The Twentieth Century Limited symbolized speed and style. Its inspired name, coined by passenger agent George H. Daniels, and the red carpet rolled out for departures from New York City's Grand Central Terminal enhanced the image. The train was celebrated in a 1932 Broadway play, *Twentieth Century,* in a 1934 film of the same name starring John Barrymore and Carole Lombard, and in a successful 1978 musical adaptation, *On the Twentieth Century;* it also provided a memorable setting for Cary Grant and Eva-Marie Saint in Alfred Hitchcock's film *North by Northwest* (1959). At the beginning of the 21st century, Amtrak's Lake Shore Limited provided service on the Twentieth Century Limited's route between Chicago and New York City.

Beebe, Lucius M. *20th Century, the Greatest Train in the World* (Berkeley, Calif: Howell-North Books, 1962)

Zimmerman, Karl. *20th Century Limited* (Osceola, Wisc: Motorbooks, 2003)

Karl Zimmermann

Tyler, Julia Gardiner (*b* Gardiners Island, Suffolk Co, 4 May 1820; *d* Richmond, Va, 10 July 1889). First lady. Descended from old and wealthy New York families, Julia Gardiner grew up in East Hampton, trained from earliest childhood for a life in society. In 1839 the high-spirited Julia appeared as the "Rose of Long Island" in one of the first endorsed advertisements to appear in New York City. The Gardiners went to Washington, DC, in 1842, and Julia attracted the attention of Pres John Tyler after his wife died that September. The following year Julia and her father joined a presidential excursion on the new steam frigate *Princeton,* during which David Gardiner died when a naval gun exploded. Tyler comforted Julia and two months later won her consent to a secret engagement. They were married on 26 June 1844, making Tyler the first president to marry in office.

Julia was first lady for only eight months, but she enjoyed the position immensely and presided over official functions with vivacity. She is said to have initiated the custom of having musicians play "Hail to the Chief" when the president appears at events. On Tyler's retirement, the couple moved to Virginia, where Julia was mistress of their plantation until the Civil War intervened. She and Tyler had seven children together, the last when he was 70. Despite her New York upbringing, she enthusiastically embraced the southern position on states' rights and in 1853 published a defense of slavery. Hard times ensued—John Tyler died in 1862, and their plantation was pillaged by Union troops. She moved back to her mother's New York home in 1863, but politics divided the household, and her financial situation suffered from a protracted court battle over the Gardiner estate. In 1880 Congress voted her a pension of $1,200 a year and, after Pres James A. Garfield's assassination in 1881, passed bills to grant uniform amounts of $5,000 annually to presidents' widows. Julia Tyler converted to Catholicism in 1872 and lived out her last years comfortably in Richmond, Va.

Delaney, Theodore. "Julia Gardiner Tyler: A 19th-Century Southern Woman" (PhD diss, College of William and Mary, 1995)

Seager, Robert, II. *And Tyler Too: A Biography of John and Julia Gardiner Tyler* (New York: McGraw-Hill, 1962)

Jon Sterngass

typewriter industry. New York State's role in typewriter history began in 1852 when John M. Jones of Clyde (Wayne Co) invented a good, but slow, machine. In 1868, the year that Christopher L. Scholes of Milwaukee, Wisc, invented what would become the first mass-produced typewriter, at least three New Yorkers patented others: F. A. de May (New York City), George House (Buffalo), and Thomas Hall (Brooklyn). In 1873 the owners of most of Scholes's rights, Yates Co native and inventor George W. N. Yost and associate James Densmore, offered an improved version to Philo Remington of E. Remington and Sons of Ilion (Herkimer Co). The company had been known as a gun, sewing machine, and farm machinery maker but sold its first "Scholes and Glidden Type Writer" in 1874. This machine used only capital letters and its stand and foot pedal for carriage return resembled those of a sewing machine, but it featured the modern "qwerty" keyboard layout. In 1878 Remington introduced a new model with both capital and small letters.

In 1882 three of the company's employees—William Wyckoff, C. W. Seamans, and Henry Benedict—acquired the sales rights to Remington's typewriter, and four years later bought the whole of the business, moving it to New York City. In 1888 the company continued to operate under the Remington name at 327 Broadway in Manhattan, and in 1905 the name was changed to the Remington Typewriter Co. In 1908 Remington introduced a new hangar bar, allowing users to see what they were typing. By 1912 the company had expanded to occupy 19 floors at 325–31 Broadway, and in 1914 it offered the noiseless Model 1. In 1927 Remington merged with the Rand Kardex Co to form Remington Rand. The company survived World War II by making other products, including Browning automatic rifles and naval and aircraft fire control instruments.

Other typewriter companies were formed around the state. In 1906 New York City machinists Edward B. Hess and Lewis C. Meyers launched Royal Typewriter Co on Liberty St in Brooklyn, producing machines that allowed print visibility and featured swift, "frictionless" carriages. Royal moved to Hartford, Conn, in 1908. A substantial firm was created in 1876 by inventor Alexander Brown and Syracuse gun makers L. C. Smith and Bros Co. From a large factory in Syracuse they pressed ahead with development of "front-strike" machines, allowing the typist an immediate view of the printed letters. In 1926 Smith merged with Corona Typewriter Co, successor to Standard Typewriter Co, though the resulting company in Groton (Tompkins Co) did not officially become Smith Corona until 1946. In 1951 Smith Corona had a number of factories in the region, including Syracuse, Groton, Cortland, and Geneva, and employed 5,000.

International Business Machines (IBM), based out of Endicott (Broome Co), acquired the Electromagnetic Typewriters of Rochester in 1933, which was made the basis of Endicott's Electric Writing Machine Division. Two years later IBM introduced the first commercially successful electric typewriter and in 1944 introduced the first proportional spacing. Throughout the 1950s, IBM regularly made minor improvements in typewriter technology, and in 1961 its Selectric revolutionized the industry with a single-element mechanism, a metal typeball that held all letters and characters. Throughout the 1960s IBM developed the term word processing and offered numerous improvements to the typewriter, such as editing and pasting.

In 1958 Smith Corona acquired Marchant Calculators, and Kleinschmidt owned the combined company by the early 1970s. At that time it no longer made manual models, instead making portables in England. The company declared bankruptcy in 1995. By the early 1970s Remington, since 1955 a division of Sperry Rand Corp, was a giant manufacturer of typewriters, calculators, adding machines, and other business equipment, though it made its standard typewriters in Europe and contracted production of compact electric and portable models in Japan. Throughout the 1980s and 1990s word processors gradually became more commonly used than typewriters.

See also SYRACUSE.

Beeching, Wilfred A. *Century of the Typewriter* (New York: St. Martin's Press, 1974)

Dane S. Claussen

Smith and Corona typewriter.

Tyre. Town (pop 899) in NE Seneca Co. Settled in 1794, the town was formed from Junius in 1829. Part of the town was included in the Cayuga Reservation that was ceded by the Cayuga between 1789 and 1807. The Erie Canal (1822) crosses the town's northeastern corner. One-third of Tyre's area is composed of the Montezuma National Wildlife Refuge (1938), a major migratory stop on the Atlantic coastal flyway. The nesting bald eagles are a popular draw for bird-watchers. The New York State Thruway (1954) crosses Tyre. The vast Montezuma Swamp provided muckland for farming in the 19th century, and agriculture remains the primary occupation; corn and soybeans were the principal crops in 2003, with some orchards and dairy farms.

Lisa Compton

Tyrone. Town (pop 1,714) in NW Schuyler Co. Between Waneta and Lamoka Lakes is a prehistoric archaeological site, Lamoka Lake (*ca* 3433–2419 BC), which is listed on the National Register. Settled between 1798 and 1800, the town was formed from Wayne (Steuben Co) in 1822. An Irish colony at Wayne hamlet (1804) was dispersed in the 1810s, but its families were ultimately responsible for St. Mary's of the Lake Roman Catholic Church (1846) at Watkins Glen. In 1879 the town had a box factory, a tannery, two shingle mills, a foundry, and a machine shop. In 2003 Tyrone had a few dairy farms, and other residents commute.

Glenda Gephart

U

Ukrainians. Ukrainians began arriving in significant numbers during the last quarter of the 19th century. This first wave lasted until World War I, and a great many of the immigrants were not ethnic Ukrainian but Polish or Jewish. Most emigrated from eastern Galicia in the former Austro-Hungarian empire, now part of western Ukraine and southeastern Poland. Overpopulation, economic conditions, and the absence of an industrial base encouraged agrarian Ukrainians to emigrate temporarily, but most who left never returned. They also relocated in the state from the anthracite coal region of northeastern Pennsylvania, the first Ukrainian settlement in the United States. In New York State, they settled mainly in the most industrialized areas, finding work in heavy industries. Some became farmers. Large numbers went to Rochester, Manhattan's Lower East Side, Buffalo, and Syracuse; others settled in Auburn (Cayuga Co) and Elmira. Communities were organized around the parish church and civic or cultural organizations. Neighborhood life in New York City became more community oriented after St. George's Ukrainian Catholic Church was established in 1905.

US immigration restrictions lowered the number of arrivals during a second wave of migration from 1920 to 1939. The interwar period brought stabilization and growth to Ukrainian communities. Ukrainian Greek Catholic or Orthodox parishes, along with national homes or civic centers, were the focus of cultural, social, and political activities. Influenced by Ukraine's brief period of independence in 1918–20, these communities took a greater interest in political events in their homeland; they also became more active in the US political system. Most were still engaged in industrial labor, but increasing numbers began to operate small businesses within their ethnic enclaves. Despite limited social mobility for working-class eastern Europeans, they slowly entered middle-class professions.

A third wave arrived after World War II. Many were better educated, including a significant number of professionals. They considered themselves political rather than economic émigrés, having fled the communist takeover of their homeland. Meanwhile, the established communities had reached a balanced ethnic identity as assimilated Americans maintaining a strong attachment to their ancestral heritage. The terms "old" and "new" immigrants defined these two types of Ukrainian Americans. The third wave settled mainly in the largest urban centers of the state, setting up organizations oriented toward the liberation of Ukraine and the preservation of Ukrainian culture in America as a bulwark against Sovietization and Russification. Christian evangelicals fleeing religious persecution arrived during the 1980s.

Since the Soviet Union was dissolved in 1991, a large fourth wave of highly educated immigrants has come seeking economic opportunities. Ukrainian Americans in New York State now work in a broad spectrum of occupations, especially engineering and healthcare. Business associations are thriving, and a healthy network of credit unions is evidence of financial stability. Self Reliance New York (1951) is the world's oldest and largest Ukrainian credit union; by 2003 it had over 13,900 members and assets exceeding $465 million. The Ukrainian Federal Credit Union, headquartered in Rochester, had over 8,200 members nationwide and assets exceeding $83 million in 2003. There are about 100 Ukrainian American organizations in the state, including businesses, churches, veterans' groups, and student associations.

Manhattan's Ukrainian community, dominated by Ukrainian language speakers, is home to major cultural and political institutions including the Ukrainian Museum (1976), which has begun a large new building on East 6th St; the Ukrainian Institute of America (1948) at 5th Ave and 79th St; the Ukrainian Academy of Arts and Sciences in the United States on West 100th St; and the Shevchenko Scientific Society on 4th Ave. Periodicals include *Brama, Bandura,* and the weekly *National Tribune.* The effort to preserve Taras Shevchenko Place, off Cooper Square and East 7th St, is the focus of a major community drive. Auburn maintains a parish elementary school, and Johnson City (Broome Co) holds impressive Ukrainian festivals. Many individuals do not belong to formal organizations but attend festivals, family celebrations, or other events. Most Ukrainian New Yorkers speak English at home, but new immigrants and educational programs are reintroducing the Ukrainian language. Recently, migration from New York State to other parts of the United States has declined. The 2000 US census counted 82,238 Ukrainian-born people in the state, of whom 69,727 lived in New York City, and 148,700 of Ukrainian ancestry. New York City has one of the largest ethnic populations outside of Ukraine, and in 2000 most (55,573) of its Ukrainian-born population lived in Brooklyn.

Halich, Wasyl. *Ukrainians in the United States* (1937; repr New York: Arno Press, 1970)

Kuropas, Myron B. *The Ukrainian Americans: Roots and Aspirations, 1884–1954* (Toronto: Univ of Toronto Press, 1991)

Subtelny, Orest. *Ukrainians in North America: An Illustrated History* (Toronto: Univ of Toronto Press, 1991)

Zenon V. Wasyliw

Ulster. Town (pop 12,544) in NE Ulster Co. Settled by the Dutch in the 17th century, it was crossed by the Delaware and Hudson Canal (1828) and was known for bluestone and cement quarrying. The town was formed in 1879 from Kingston because of some residents' perceptions of government corruption in Kingston. The population was as low as 2,622 in 1920 but numbered 4,411 by 1950 and continued to climb. In 1954 the New York State Thruway was completed, and in 1955 an IBM plant opened. By 1960 the population was 8,448. The Kingston-Rhinecliff Bridge (1957) and the suburban shopping district along Albany Avenue Extension facilitated growth to the northeast part of town. The IBM facility closed in 1994. Some agriculture continues along Esopus Creek.

Ruth Piwonka

Ulster and Delaware Railroad. The line originated as New York, Kingston and Syracuse, chartered in 1868, with track built from Rondout to Phoenicia (Ulster Co) in 1870 and to Stamford (Delaware Co) in 1872. A second reincorporation in 1875 created Ulster and Delaware (U&D), which extended service in Delaware Co to Hobart (1884) and Bloomville (1889) and in Otsego Co to Oneonta (1900). The U&D carried summer tourists to Catskill hotels as well as freight carloads of coal, feed, and grain to the mountain region. The railroad also transported Delaware Co dairy products and Ulster Co bluestone, used in building construction and for sidewalks and curbstones, to New York City. Forest products shipped out of the Catskills included logs, lumber, Christmas trees, excelsior and other wood by-products, furniture, and spring water. In 1932 bankrupt U&D became New York Central Catskill Mountain Branch, which suspended passenger service in 1954. While the Oneonta-to-Bloomville track was abandoned in 1965, some freight service continued through 1976 under Penn Central and then Conrail. In 1983 two segments of line were revived as tourist lines: Catskill Mountain Railroad and Delaware and Ulster Rail Ride.

Best, Gerald M. *The Ulster and Delaware: Railroad through the Catskills* (San Marino, Calif: Golden West Books, 1972)

Michael Kudish

Ulster County (1,126 mi²/2,916 km²; pop 177,749). Created in 1683 as one of the original 12 counties in the colony and named after the Duke of York's earldom in Ireland. Five boundary changes occurred during the colonial period. Portions of Ulster Co were annexed to help form Delaware and Greene Cos in 1797 and 1800, respectively, and Sullivan Co in 1809. Lesser adjustments were made with Albany and Orange Cos (1798), Delaware Co (1801, 1812), and Greene Co (1801, 1812, 1814, 1822). Ulster Co is subdivided into 1 city, Kingston, the county seat, and 20 towns that contain 5 incorporated villages. Elevations range from sea level along the Hudson River to over 4,190 feet (1,277 m) at the summit of Slide Mountain. The county lies within two major landform provinces, the Appalachian Upland and the Hudson-Mohawk Lowland. Most of the county's northwestern half is part of the Catskill Mountains. Smaller portions in the south are part of the noticeably lower Delaware Hills. The coarsely dissected Catskills consist of extensive, uninterrupted masses separated by steep-walled, 1,000–1,500 ft (300–450 m) deep valleys. In contrast the Delaware Hills are divided by wider, shallower, more gently sloped valleys. The county's southeastern half comprises the folded and faulted lowlands, containing the Hudson and Wallkill Valleys, and the structurally related Shawangunk Mountains, which approach 2,300 feet (700 m) at Sam's Point.

Ulster Co's bedrock is principally Devonian, Ordovician, and Silurian sandstone, found sequentially from northwest to southeast. There are also significant areas of shale in the northwest and southeast, and a band of Devonian limestone and dolostone runs diagonally from the Sullivan Co border immediately west of the Shawangunks to the Greene Co border north of Kingston. Ulster Co was ice covered during the

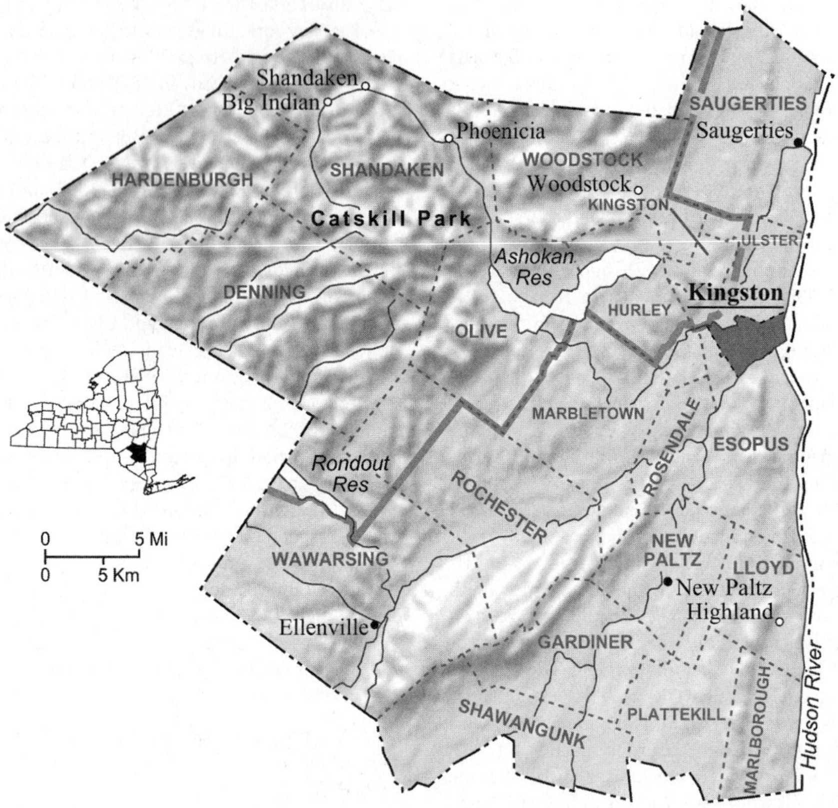

most recent continental glaciation, as attested by the rounded hilltops and a combination of widespread ground moraine and lacustrine deposits. Subsequently, mountain glaciers formed cirques, or amphitheater-like depressions, on the sides of some of the Catskill peaks. Most of Ulster Co lies within the Hudson River watershed and is drained primarily by Esopus and Rondout Creeks and the Wallkill River. Esopus Creek is dammed near Olivebridge, creating Ashokan Reservoir, the largest reservoir in New York City's water supply system. Waters in the northwest drain into the Delaware River. Agriculturally productive soils are primarily found in the valleys of Rondout Creek, Wallkill River, and Shawangunk Kill, along with scattered areas along the Hudson River.

Ulster Co's climate is humid-continental. Mean January temperatures range from 18°F (-8°C) on the slopes of Slide Mountain to 25°F (-4°C) in the southeast near the Hudson River. Temperatures in the higher elevations drop below 0°F (-18°C) on occasion every winter, less frequently in the lowlands. Mean July temperatures range from 63°F (17°C) on Slide Mountain to 73°F (23°C) in the southeast near the Hudson River. The lower elevations have temperatures of 90°F (32°C) or above most summers, but such readings are unusual in the higher Catskills. Annual average precipitation ranges from 44 inches (112 cm) at the Delaware Co border to almost 64 inches (163 cm) on Slide Mountain, the highest amount recorded anywhere in the state. Normal seasonal snowfall amounts range from 40 inches (100 cm) in the southeast near the Hudson River to over 100 inches (250 cm) in the higher Catskill elevations. Primeval forest cover consisted of four communities. The lowlands were covered by central hardwoods dominated by beech, sugar maple, basswood, oak, and chestnut. An oak-pine community grew along the Shawangunk ridge tops. Most of the Appalachian Upland supported a northern hardwood forest of beech, sugar maple, hemlock, and white pine, mixed with basswood at the lower elevations and with yellow birch at intermediate heights. A spruce-fir forest of red spruce, balsam fir, and paper birch grew in the highest areas. In the early 21st century over 80% of the county is forested. Approximately 45% of the county lies within the Catskill Park.

American Indians and Early Settlement

At the time of European settlement, present-day Ulster Co was inhabited by the Esopus Indians, Munsee speakers who grew corn and hunted and fished throughout the Hudson River tributary system. Their chief villages were located on the flats of the lower Esopus and Rondout Valleys in and around what is now Kingston; others were in Kingston's hinterland and around the present town of Wawarsing. The Esopus Wars, conflicts with the settlers who began occupying the site of Kingston in 1652, resulted in the Indians signing a treaty in 1664 in which they relinquished their most productive lands, and the new English administration negotiated a treaty of friendship the following year. By 1746 the Esopus had sold most of their traditional homeland, but a few remained in the region and sided with the British during the Revolution, after which they removed to Ontario and to several midwestern states.

Thomas Chambers (*d* 1694), an English carpenter, is thought to have been the first white settler. On 5 June 1652 he purchased land at the present site of Kingston from several Esopus Indians. Other settlers followed within a year. On 16 May 1661 the grain-producing settlement, which had been under the jurisdiction of Fort Orange [now Albany], was chartered and received its own court of justice; it was named Wiltwijck. Most early European settlers were culturally if not always ethnically Dutch, but they were joined by some British after 1664. Farms spread out slowly from Kingston: to present-day Hurley in 1662, to Marbletown in 1669, and to Rochester and Rosendale *ca* 1680. Huguenots from France settled in what is now Hurley by 1663 and founded New Paltz in 1677. Palatine Germans settled in the Town of Saugerties after 1710.

In 1683 Ulster Co's territory comprised the towns of Kingston, Hurley, Marbletown, Foxhall, and New Paltz and all non-Indian settlements on the west side of the Hudson that fell between Murderer Creek [now Moodna Creek] and Sawyer Kill. For over a century the borders fluctuated, as, for example, when large patents such as the Hardenbergh and Hurley Patents of 1708 extended them west and north. By 1723 there were 2,923 residents in the county; of these, 2,357 were white. The remainder were slaves, a population that was to remain substantial throughout the colonial period. In the late 18th century the county's population surged as New Englanders flowed in and as urban New Yorkers arrived to escape Revolutionary conflict; these movements helped settle the mountain towns of Shandaken (1770s) and Hardenburgh (1790s), but the present-day Denning remained wilderness until 1837.

In 1790 there were 16,297 residents in the towns that make up the present county. By that year the number of slaves had declined to 10% of the population. Among the 2,257 slaves recorded in the 1800 census was Isabella Van Wagenen (?1797–1883), born and raised in Hurley, who later achieved fame as the abolitionist Sojourner Truth.

Revolutionary Period

A majority of residents supported the Revolution, and farmers supplied George Washington's army with wheat and other provisions. The county remained isolated from agitation preceding the war but furnished three regiments in response to news of the Battle of Lexington in 1775. Opposition surfaced when, after the battle, the "Freemen, Freeholders and Inhabitants of New York" sent the Articles of Association to Ulster Co for signatures. Some residents declared the document treasonous, but a majority finally supported it. After the signing of the Declaration of Independence, a convention was held in Kingston to ratify the state constitution; it passed with one dissenting vote on 22 Apr 1777. In June George Clinton was elected the state's first governor. On 15 October of that year about 30 British ships under the command of Gen John Vaughan sailed up the Hudson River to Esopus; the following day they sacked and burned Kingston, partly in consequence of the town's provisioning of the American army. The state government thereafter met in Marbletown (through 18 November) and Hurley (through 17 December). In May 1779 the government ordered Fort Shandaken built on the county's northwest settlement frontier in response to threats of attack by Indians and tories.

Economic Development

Colonial settlements were agriculturally based and concentrated along the Hudson River and in the Rondout, Esopus, and Wallkill Valleys, growing wheat for export to New York City. Even in

ULSTER CO POPULATION CENSUS FIGURES

	White	Nonwhite	Total Population	Foreign-Born
1790	26,334	3,063	29,397	—
1800	22,262	2,593	24,855	—
1810	24,073	2,503	26,576	—
1820	28,814	2,120	30,934	105
1830	34,655	1,770	36,550[a]	339
1840	44,018	1,804	45,822	—
1850	57,799	1,585	59,384	8,431
1860	74,772	1,609	76,381	12,746
1870	82,638	1,437	84,075	12,740
1880	84,465	1,373	85,838	10,319
1890	85,813	1,249	87,062	10,385
1900	87,057	1,365	88,422	9,276
1910	89,737	2,032	91,769	14,233
1920	73,989	990	74,979	8,048
1930	78,793	1,362	80,155	8,819
1940	84,763	2,254	87,017	8,658
1950	90,202	2,419	92,621	9,090
1960	114,622	4,182	118,804	9,443
1970	135,351	5,890	141,241	8,611
1980	148,634	9,524	158,158	10,739
1990	153,673	11,631	165,304	9,573
2000	158,042	19,707	177,749	10,468

Notes: "Nonwhite" includes African Americans, Asians, American Indians, and Pacific Islanders and, for 2000, also the mixed race and other race categories. Through the 1960 census these figures primarily reflect the African American population. Foreign-born figures for 1820 and 1830 include only those not naturalized, and for 1930 and 1950, the foreign-born totals include Whites only. Other years include all foreign-born in the population.

[a]Total includes 125 people living in a poorhouse at New Paltz. Their races were not taken.

Kingston, where there was a concentration of artisans and shopkeepers, farming was the chief occupation of most families at the time of the Revolution. By 1830 Genesee Valley grain, brought east on the Erie Canal, undercut Ulster Co's crop. Settlers diversified with dairy farming. Butter, cheese, calves, poultry, and flaxseed were taken to Rondout for sloop transport to Manhattan. Farmers experimented with apple, peach, and pear orchards and, after 1850, with the first vineyards. Some operated distilleries.

Those not engaged in agriculture were mainly involved in the wood-products industries in the highlands or the cement and bluestone industries in Rosendale, Esopus, Ulster, Marbletown, Hurley, and Kingston. Until the depletion of hemlock in the 1850s, tanneries in northwestern towns relied on tannin produced by its bark. Sawmills and paper mills were more successful in the long term. Paper mills operated on Esopus Creek in Saugerties from 1827 to 1977. Sawmills supported barrel, tool, and furniture making throughout the 19th century. Waste wood for fuel was a byproduct.

The completion in 1828 of the Delaware and Hudson Canal, intended for the shipment of Pennsylvania coal to the Hudson watershed, strengthened the economy by stimulating the Rosendale cement industry and, from 1851 to 1865, supporting a busy coal trade at Port Ewen. The high quality of Rosendale cement created international demand, which peaked in 1895 but was soon undercut by the introduction of synthetic Portland cement. From the early 1830s the area also produced bluestone, a fine-grained sandstone that yielded cut stone suitable for urban building needs; the industry declined after 1905, again because of competition from Portland cement. Hudson River ice cutting, centered in Highland, was similarly rendered obsolete by the innovation of artificial refrigeration.

The activities of industries, boatyards, and ports that developed along the Delaware and Hudson Canal cushioned the decline of the extraction-based industries. Canal work brought new immigrant groups; in 1855, 12% of county residents were Irish and 5% were Germans. The canal transformed remote localities such as Eddyville and Ellenville into industrial centers that produced boats, iron goods, glass, and cutlery. The canal, along with spillover from the Green Co Catskills tourism boom, gave an impetus to the boardinghouse industry.

Transportation and Tourism

Ulster Co continued to utilize its river and canal for shipping and travel much later than most parts of New York State. The first railroad, the Wallkill Valley, was completed from the south to Kingston in 1869; the Ulster and Delaware ran from Rondout northwesterly into the Catskills beginning in 1870; and the Ontario and Western reached Ellenville from the south in 1871. These lines, while important for the shipment of farm produce, essentially created the county's boardinghouse industry. In addition, the Stony Clove Railroad (1881) ran from Phoenicia to important Greene Co resorts, funneling traffic through Kingston. In 1883 the West Shore Railroad was completed along the Hudson River; the Poughkeepsie Railroad Bridge (1888) made possible the east-west link of the Central New England Railroad (1889–1983), which passed through the county's southeast. The Ontario and Western completed the county's rail network when it extended northeast from Ellenville to Kingston in 1902.

The resort business began in the mid-19th century; the Mountain Inn (1848–1903) at Pine Hill was one of the earliest hotels. The business was anchored by the Mohonk Mountain House (1869) near New Paltz and the Cliff House (1879) and Wildmere House (1887) at Lake Minnewaska, developed by Quaker brothers Alfred and Albert Smiley. In the county's northwest, the Grand Hotel (1881–1960s) at Highmount depended upon the Ulster and Delaware. Jewish boardinghouses (and, later, vast resort hotels) clustered in Ellenville after 1902. In the 20th century several small villages in the county developed distinctive resort industries: Plattekill was at one time the largest Spanish resort in the eastern United States; Rifton reinvented itself as a resort in the 1920s after its mills declined; Ukrainians discovered Kerhonkson and Spring Glen; and in the early 21st century Germans continue to vacation at Oliverea. Other specialized markets developed, such as those for private cottages (Big Indian Mountain Club, Shandaken) and for celebrity vacations (Yama Farms Inn, Napanoch). In 1935 business operators began promoting winter sports with skiing in Shandaken. Belleayre Mountain State Ski Center remained in operation in 2003, though Shandaken is better known for summer "tubing" on the Esopus.

Religion, Education, and Culture

Prior to the Revolution most community institutions were local and religious. In 1659, when Esopus residents petitioned church leaders in Amsterdam in the Netherlands for permission to form a Dutch Reformed congregation. The French Huguenot settlers of New Paltz were known for their religious devotion and for their unique form of civil governance, the Council of the Twelve Men, later referred to in local histories as the Duzine.

In 1855 the Dutch Reformed Church was still the largest single denomination, with 30 congregations, but there were also 27 Methodist Episcopal congregations. Other Protestant denominations included the Baptists (8 congregations), Presbyterians (7), and Episcopalians (6). Quakers organized seven meetings (congregations), and Irish and German immigrants established seven Roman Catholic churches. Evangelical Lutheran churches, the legacy of Palatine Germans, were concentrated in Saugerties, Woodstock, and Kingston. Wawarsing had briefly been the site of America's first Jewish agricultural experiment, Sholem (1837–42). Synagogues were established at Kingston (1853), Rondout (1854), and, beginning in 1909, Ellenville and its vicinity. In 1954 the Hutterian Society of Brothers (Bruderhof), an Anabaptist communitarian sect, acquired land in Rifton and relocated there from Paraguay. In 1985 they established a second community at Ulster Park. Other religiously based societies to take hold in the 19th century included the Ulster County Bible Society, Ulster County Agricultural Society, and Ulster County Temperance Society, Ulster County Sunday School Association, Ulster County Historical Society, and the Ulster County Homeopathic Medical Society.

POPULATIONS OF TOWNS AND CITIES, ULSTER CO

Town or City, Year Founded	1800	1840	1880	1920	1960	2000
Denning, 1849	—	—	1,036	419	215	516
Esopus, 1811	—	1,939	4,736	3,913	6,597	9,331
Gardiner, 1853	—	—	1,794	1,088	1,660	5,238
Hardenburgh, 1859	—	—	801	420	252	208
Hurley, 1708	1,159	2,201	2,521	846	4,526	6,564
Kingston, 1661[a]	4,615	5,824	1,093	166	490	908
Kingston (city), 1872	—	—	18,344	26,688	29,260	23,456
Lloyd, 1845	—	—	2,713	3,079	5,842	9,941
Marbletown, 1703[b]	2,847	3,813	3,970	2,017	3,191	5,854
Marlborough, 1772[c]	1,656	2,523	3,472	3,274	4,863	8,263
New Paltz, 1738[d]	3,255	5,408	1,958	2,163	5,841	12,830
Olive, 1823	—	2,023	2,927	1,237	1,999	4,579
Plattekill, 1800	1,625	2,125	2,205	1,798	3,009	9,892
Rochester, 1703[e]	2,423	2,674	4,109	2,188	3,012	7,018
Rosendale, 1844	—	—	4,724	1,959	4,228	6,352
Saugerties, 1811	—	6,216	10,375	8,245	13,608	19,868
Shandaken, 1804	—	1,455	2,829	2,372	2,078	3,235
Shawangunk, 1703[f]	2,809	3,886	2,910	2,087	4,604	12,022
Ulster, 1879	—	—	2,806	2,622	8,448	12,544
Wawarsing, 1806	—	4,044	8,547	6,910	11,245	12,889
Woodstock, 1787	1,244	1,691	1,968	1,488	3,836	6,241

Note: In 1800 Ulster Co included the Towns of Lumberland, Mamakating, and Neversink [now in Sullivan Co].

[a]Formed under Dutch as Wiltwyck; patented as corporation 1667; recognized as town 1788.

[b]Patent date.

[c]Formed as New Marlborough Precinct; recognized as Town of Marlborough 1788.

[d]Governed by trustees until 1785.

[e]Patent date; residents chose officers by 1709.

[f]Patent date; residents chose officers by 1711; became precinct 1743; recognized as town 1788.

The first teacher, Andries van der Sluys, served Wiltwijck briefly around 1668 in the office of *voorlezer* (lay catechist for the Reformed Church). New Paltz and West Camp also put a high priority on education and employed schoolmasters in the first years of settlement. Kingston Academy (1774; incorporated 1795) was the first secondary school. The common school system was established by law in 1812. Further legislation in 1853 enabled larger communities to support high schools. Kingston incorporated its school district in 1863, and Ellenville organized a Union Free School district in 1866, but New Paltz relied on its academy (1832) for many years after the Civil War. The first consolidated districts were Highland Central, converted from a single Union Free School district in 1926, and New Paltz Central, which consolidated from 12 common schools in 1929. Kingston's enlarged city school district was not completed until after 1958. In the early 21st century, there are eight central districts in the county, along with the Kingston city district and the West Park Union Free School District, which provides special education. A state normal school was founded at New Paltz in 1886 and evolved into SUNY New Paltz; the county's other college is Ulster County Community College (1962) in Marbletown.

John Holt was forced to move his *New-York Journal; or General Advertiser* out of New York City by the British occupation. From July to October 1777 it was published at Kingston, thereby becoming Ulster Co's first newspaper. The *Farmer's Register* followed in 1792. By 1880 there were 12 newspapers in the county. In the early 21st century the *Daily Freeman* (1871), published at Kingston, is supplemented by weeklies at Ellenville, Saugerties, and Woodstock. Ulster Co has one television station, at Kingston, and more than a dozen radio stations in various localities.

Many figures of the Hudson River school painted in Ulster Co, but its most famous native artist may be the Paris-trained John Vanderlyn (1755–1852). Artists' colonies emerged at Cragsmoor (around 1882) and at Woodstock, where Englishman Ralph Whitehead founded the Byrdcliffe Arts Colony (1903). The Towns of Woodstock and New Paltz continue a tradition of artistic activity in the 21st century. The county has many historical museums. Among art attractions, Opus 40, a vast outdoor environmental sculpture in Saugerties, stands out.

Politics

Ulster Co was long governed by its Board of Supervisors, with a representative from each town and one from each ward of the City of Kingston. In 1966, following the US Supreme Court's one person–one vote decision, the board adopted a plan for reapportionment in which town supervisors would be eligible for election as county legislators but would not automatically serve as such. It went into effect on 1 Jan 1968, with 33 legislators representing 12 districts. Members elect one of their number to a one-year salaried term as chair.

The 20th Century

The transforming event for the Towns of Olive and Hurley was the construction of the Ashokan Reservoir from 1907 to 1917. That project and the Catskill Aqueduct, which ran from the Ashokan Dam to the county's southern boundary, drew thousands of laborers, about half of them Italian immigrants. It inundated much of the good valley farmland in Olive and Hurley and required the relocation of a number of hamlets and 504 homes. Infrastructure development continued to stimulate the economy in the early 20th century. What is now US 9W was gradually converted into a state highway starting in 1907. US 209, the so-called Old Mine Rd along which settlement spread from Kingston to Marbletown in the mid–17th century, was also improved, as was the Minnewaska Trail (Rte 55). The Mid-Hudson Bridge (1930) and the Kingston-Rhinecliff Bridge (1957) permitted cross-river traffic for the first time. The New York State Thruway, completed in 1954, has three exits in the county. Prisons became an economic engine in the 20th century. Napanoch's Eastern Correctional Facility (1900), the wall-less Wallkill Correctional Facility (1932), and the maximum security Shawangunk Correctional Facility (1985) have provided jobs for many residents affected by industrial decline.

In 1940 Ulster remained one of the richest agricultural counties in the state, with 3,286 farms and 280,000 acres (113,000 ha) of agricultural land valued at an average of $119 per acre, compared with the state average of $55. Fruit and vegetable production accounted for 31% of cropland, with the southern towns leading the way in apple, grape, and berry production. Italian immigrants moving south from industrial work in the county's north helped build the orchard and vineyard economy in Marlborough, Lloyd, Esopus, Gardiner, and Plattekill.

More good valley land, this time in Wawarsing, was inundated by the completion of the Rondout Reservoir in 1951. The most important economic news of the postwar period, however, was the 1955 opening of the IBM plant in the Town of Ulster. It brought in hundreds of employees and triggered moderate suburbanization of the Kingston vicinity. The county urbanized rapidly over the next 50 years. As the New York City population spread north to the mid–Hudson Valley, taking advantage of commuter corridors such as I-87, the number of residents doubled. Population density increased from 124 persons per square mile in 1970 to 141 persons per square mile in 1990. The IBM plant closed in 1994, accounting for most of the City of Kingston's 20% decline in population between its 1960 peak and 2000. Agriculture remained important, however; in 1997 there were 409 farms on 69,000 acres (27,900 ha), including 10 wineries scattered throughout the county's southeastern towns. By 2000 development pressure prompted state-level farmland protection assistance. At the same time county economic planners continued to encourage a seasonal influx of people by promoting tourist attractions such as the more than 12,000-acre (4,900 ha) Lake Minnewaska State Park Preserve (1987) and the wineries.

In 2003 the county's largest employers were the county government, the Kingston School District, and SUNY New Paltz. Uniprise (insurance services) employed 965 in Kingston. Significant manufacturers were Imperial Schrade (knives) and Hydro Aluminum North America in Ellenville; Vertis, a commercial printer in Saugerties; and Ametek Rotron, a manufacturer of military blowers and fans in Woodstock.

See also ARTS AND CRAFTS MOVEMENT.

The standard county histories are Nathaniel B. Sylvester, *History of Ulster County* (1880); Alphonso T. Clearwater, *History of Ulster County* (1907); Louise Hasbrouck Zimm, "Ulster County," in *Southeastern New York,* 3 vols (1946); and the substantial town-by-town *History of Ulster County, with Emphasis upon the Last 100 Years, 1883–1983* (1984). There are many town histories; early examples include Charles H. Cochrane, *History of the Town of Marlborough* (1887), Marius Schoonmaker, *History of Kingston* (1888), Benjamin M. Brink, *The Early History of Saugerties, 1660–1825* (1902), C. M. Woolsey, *History of the Town of Marlborough* (1908), and Ralph LeFever, *History of New Paltz,* 2d ed. (1909). One of the best New York State town histories ever published is Alf Evers, *Woodstock: The History of an American Town* (1987). Other local histories from the 20th century include Reginald Bennett, *The Mountains Look Down: A History of Chichester, a Company Town in the Catskills* (1999); *Town of Esopus Story* (1979); William C. DeWitt, *People's History of Kingston, Rondout, and Vicinity, 1820–1943* (1943); Katharine T. Terwilliger, *Napanoch: Land Overflowed by Water* (1982); Vera V. S. Sickler, *The Town of Olive through the Years* (1976); Ann Gilchrist, *Footsteps across Cement: A History of the Township of Rosendale* (1976); Lonnie and Ruth Gale, *Shandaken, New York: A Pictorial History* (1999); and Katharine T. Terwilliger, *Wawarsing: Where the Streams Wind* (1977). *Maple Lanes: The History of Woodcrest and the Rifton Valley* (1989) is an award-winning community history by elementary school students. Judith C. Renker, *Growing Up in Tillson, New York, 1900–1955* (1991), is an exemplary oral history.

Topical and academic works of note include Bob Steuding, *The Last of the Handmade Dams: The Story of the Ashokan Reservoir* (1985) and *Rondout: A Hudson River Port* (1995); Thomas S. Wermuth, *Rip Van Winkle's Neighbors: The Transformation of Rural Society in the Hudson River Valley, 1720–1850* (2001); and Marc Fried, *The Early History of Kingston and Ulster County* (1975). *Early Architecture in Ulster County* (1974) surveys important buildings; William B. Rhoads, *Kingston, New York: The Architectural Guide* (2002) covers the city in depth.

Karen Nichols

Ulysses. Town (pop 4,775) in NW Tompkins Co. Settled in 1790, the town was formed in 1794. A lead pipe factory operated in the 1830s and a nursery at Jacksonville from 1845 to 1871. The county home for people in need on Perry City Rd was open between 1827 and 1987. The town is bounded on the east by Cayuga Lake, and in its northeast corner is the 738-acre (299 ha) Taughannock Falls State Park, with a 215 ft (66 m) waterfall, unique geological formations, and extensive lakefront; it draws about a half million visitors annually. The town was site of Babcock Industries (1935), a poultry-breeding company now in France as ISA-Babcock, and of the Halsey Seed Farms (1936), which produced hybrid seed corn. The Ulysses Philomathic Library (1811) in Trumansburg moved into a new building in 2001. Many Ulysses residents in 2003 worked in nearby Ithaca.

Jane Dieckmann

Unadilla [YOU-NA-DILL-AH]. Town (pop 4,548) and village (pop 1,127) in SW Otsego Co. After several attempts, the town was settled in 1784 and formed from Otsego in 1792. Located on the Susquehanna Turnpike (1802), a main route for pioneers going westward, the village incorporated in 1827. The Albany and Susquehanna Railroad (1866; later Delaware and Hudson) fostered small manufacturing, including wagons, sash and blinds, ironwork, condensed milk, cigars, and paper. Boy Scouts of America Troop 1, one of the nation's earliest, claims an unbroken registration since its 1910 charter. In the 1960s Unadilla became a bedroom community for factories and retail enterprises in nearby Oneonta and Sidney (Delaware Co), a trend encouraged by the opening of I-88 (1976–77). In the early 21st century it is the home of several small manufacturers, including Tieco-Unadilla Corp (1892; industrial ties), Unadilla Silo (1906), and York Modern Corp (1922; rakes). St. Matthew's Episcopal Church (1845–46) is a landmark.

Hugh C. MacDougall

Uncle Sam. The most widely accepted version of the origin of Uncle Sam as a symbol of the United States attributes it to Samuel Wilson (1766–1854) of Troy (Rensselaer Co). Born in Massachusetts in 1766, Wilson fought in the American Revolution. In 1789 he moved with his brother Ebenezer to Troy, where the two established the meatpacking firm of E. and S. Wilson. When war broke out in 1812, the Wilson brothers contracted to provide provisions to US Army troops based near Troy. The barrels of rations intended for the army were labeled "U.S.," an abbreviation not yet in common use. When visiting federal inspectors asked a worker what the "U.S." stood for, the man guessed that it referred to his employer, "Uncle Sam" Wilson, beginning the legend.

Cartoonists started drawing Uncle Sam in the 1830s and early images varied: short and fat, clean shaven or bearded, tall and lanky. As the Civil War began, however, political cartoonist Thomas Nast drew Uncle Sam to resemble Abraham Lincoln, and the character eventually acquired his canonical white hair and star-spangled top hat. In 1961 the US Congress passed a resolution recognizing Samuel Wilson as the inspiration for Uncle Sam. Troy's role in inspiring the Uncle Sam legend is remembered in the names of local bowling alleys and restaurants, in delis offering Uncle Samwiches, bars that have Uncle Sam amber on tap, and an annual Uncle Sam parade in June near Flag Day, crowning a Miss Uncle Sam.

Jones, Taffy. *Who Is Uncle Sam?* (Lanham, Md: Maryland Historical Press, 1991)

J. Justin Gustainis

Underground Railroad. Routes and methods used by African Americans held in slavery to escape to freedom. The Underground Railroad, sometimes called the Freedom Trail, was a complex movement that often involved helpers who were motivated by political and religious ideals of equality. At times the Underground Railroad was a well-organized operation; at others it was haphazard; it was sometimes secret, sometimes very open. Only rarely was it associated with actual tunnels. Between 1830 and 1860 as many as 1,500 people traveled north each year. Many of them passed through New York State, headed for Canada, but many settled within the state.

FREEDOM SEEKERS AND THE ORIGIN OF THE UNDERGROUND RAILROAD

Slavery existed in New York for more than 200 years, from its establishment by the Dutch in the 1620s until its abolition by state law in 1827. Throughout that time African Americans resisted their enslavement in various ways, including running away. Many people went to nearby Native American lands. On Long Island both the Shinnecock and Poospatuck people sheltered African Americans. Iroquois homelands offered similar refuges in central and western New York State. When the US Army attacked these areas in 1779, they found one African American living among the Iroquois at Newtown [now Elmira] and one working as a doctor among the Onondaga. Chaotic conditions during the American Revolution, combined with a British offer to free enslaved people who fought against the Americans, led many freed Blacks to migrate to Nova Scotia and New Brunswick. Others settled as farmers, millers, barbers, or homemakers on former Iroquois lands. An African American who escaped enslavement was the first non-Iroquois settler in Paris [now in Oneida Co]; he settled in Paris before the first white families moved to the settlement in the 1780s. After the American Revolution, African Americans continued to seek freedom in New York, although it remained a slave state. Austin Steward, born enslaved in Virginia in the 1790s, came as a young man to Bath (Steuben Co) with his master. He escaped to Rochester and became a leader of its African American community in the 1820s. From 1831 to 1836 he and his family were pioneers in the Wilberforce colony, a black settlement in Upper Canada [now Ontario]. Thomas James, enslaved in Canajoharie (Montgomery Co), fled to Canada in 1821, stayed three months, and returned to New York State to serve as an African Methodist Episcopal Zion (AMEZ) minister in Rochester, Syracuse, and Ithaca. In *The Fugitive Blacksmith* (1849), James W. C. Pennington, a Presbyterian minister in New York City, described his 1827 exodus from slavery in Maryland.

Between 1830 and 1860, freedom seekers began to leave slavery in larger numbers, inspired by the abolition of slavery in northern states and Canada, the development of abolitionism as a major political force, and the emerging transportation networks. While the origin of the term remains obscure, "Underground Railroad" seems to have been widely used by the early 1840s. Eber Pettit, who published stories of the Underground Railroad in 1879, reported that the term, which reflected the perceived se-

Image found in the basement of Wesleyan Methodist Church (an abolitionist church in Syracuse) possibly carved by African Americans on the Underground Railroad.

crecy and speed of this movement, was first used in Washington, DC, in 1839. A Chicago abolitionist newspaper noted one instance of a freedom seeker in 1842 who was returned to slavery from Oswego and who reported that "the abolitionists had a railroad under ground." In some places and times, this "railroad" became relatively systematized. A coordinated network of sympathizers offered freedom seekers safety and shelter as they traveled to their respective destinations. In other places it was relatively haphazard, and individuals had to find their way virtually alone. An enslaved African American named Moses, for example, fled Georgia and followed the North Star all the way to New Haven (Oswego Co) before receiving any help.

GEOGRAPHY AND ROUTES

New York State became an important link in the Underground Railroad for three reasons. First, the state had a lengthy border with Canada along Lake Erie, the Niagara River, Lake Ontario, and the St. Lawrence River. Because of the state's well-developed system of rivers, roads, canals, and railroads, and its active urban centers of shipping and trade, travel across this border became physically possible. Second, the existence of African American communities in both urban and rural areas offered pockets of resistance to slavery and obvious havens for freedom seekers. Many African Americans living in New York State actively opposed slavery and worked to improve the lives of both enslaved and free Blacks. From 1830 to 1835 and again in the 1840s, for example, many African American New Yorkers participated in the national black convention movement, which provided a forum for Blacks working to end slavery and racism. Third, organized abolitionists in the state created a powerful political network that sustained community support for Underground Railroad activists in many areas.

After 1830 some freedom seekers who came to New York State went on to Canada or remained in New York State. Those traveling to Canada left through ports such as Buffalo, Rochester, Oswego, and Cape Vincent (Jefferson Co). Some people migrated to Canadian communities settled almost entirely by people of African descent. The Dawn Valcour community, organized in 1841 by white abolitionist Hiram Wilson and freedom seeker Josiah Henson, who claimed to be the model for Uncle Tom in *Uncle Tom's Cabin,* was one such community. Abolitionists from across the state sent money and supplies to its residents. Most freedom seekers who reached Canada, however, made new lives for themselves in major cities such as Toronto, Hamilton [now in Ont], and Kingston [now in Ont]. Many of Harriet Tubman's journeys from the South ended in St. Catharines [now in Ont], across the border from Buffalo, where there was a large fugitive community. By the 1850s about 20,000 people of African descent lived in Canada West [now Ontario]. On the US side of the border, Albany, Rome, Utica, Syracuse, Oswego, Auburn, Binghamton, Elmira, Bath, Geneva, Canandaigua, Rochester, Buffalo, and New York City all had sizable African American populations. According to the 1855 state census, for example, 12,000 African Americans lived in New York City, 611 in Albany, 252 in Syracuse, 140 in Oswego, 183 in Auburn, 371 in Rochester, and 784 in Buffalo. The African American population in all of these communities ranged between 1 and 2% of the total population, though many urban African Americans lived in black neighborhoods, such as Weeksville [now in Brooklyn]. It is estimated that one-third of these residents had been born in southern states and escaped slavery. It is difficult to establish how many freedom seekers came through New York State, but Amy Post, white abolitionist of Rochester, estimated that as many as 150 came through her house annually. Jermain Loguen, an AMEZ minister who escaped slavery in Tennessee, and his wife Caroline, originally from Busti (Chautauqua Co), believed that they had assisted about 1,500 people over a period of several years in Syracuse.

Freedom seekers followed several different routes into and out of New York State. From New York City many moved east to Long Island and across Long Island Sound into Connecticut. Others traveled north along the Hudson River to Albany. From Albany people followed the Erie Canal west before going to Canada through Oswego, Rochester, Buffalo, or Lewiston (Niagara Co). Others traveled north from Maryland and Virginia through Pennsylvania, following the Susquehanna River valley before entering Binghamton, Elmira, or smaller communities, then moving north along the Finger Lakes. In Western New York another stream of freedom seekers traveled from Cleveland and Fredonia (Chautauqua Co) into Buffalo. These routes converged at key nodes.

Beginning in the mid-1830s, citizens in many areas formed vigilance committees to collect food and clothing and to arrange shelter, transportation, and jobs for freedom seekers. In New York City, for example, they often found help from David Ruggles or Theodore S. Wright. In Queens and on Long Island, Quakers such as Samuel Parsons, Isaac A. Hopper, and members of the Willet, Mott, and Hicks families offered havens. Those who came through Elmira would be directed to the home of John W. Jones, formerly enslaved in Virginia. In Albany freedom seekers often found support from white abolitionists, including Abigail and Lydia Mott, Rev Abel Brown, and Charles Torrey and William Chaplin, the editors of the *Albany Patriot,* and black abolitionists, such as Stephen Myers. Gerrit and Ann Smith's home in Peterboro (Madison Co) became a way station as early as 1838. By the mid-1850s Jermain and Caroline Loguen operated a very visible way station in Syracuse, supported by people such as Samuel J. May, minister of Syracuse's Unitarian Church. By the late 1850s Harriet Tubman's home in Auburn became a focal point for her activities. William Henry and Frances Seward's home also served as an Underground Railroad stop in Auburn. In Rochester Frederick Douglass, himself a freedom seeker from Maryland, and Amy Post operated the city's most active stations. In Buffalo William Wells Brown, born into slavery in Kentucky, was well known. Eber Pettit operated a major station in Versailles (Cattaraugus Co). Such major figures were part of a network that involved hundreds and perhaps thousands of lesser-known supporters. In Jamestown (Chautauqua Co), for example, Catherine Harris, a free African American from Pennsylvania, fed and housed many freedom seekers, while George Bragdon funneled people north to Cape Vincent.

Certainly, much Underground Railroad work remained secret, as danger to freedom seekers was very real. Those who claimed ownership of them were anxious to reclaim their "property" because a worker who escaped meant considerable financial loss. Some slave catchers found a lucrative business in kidnapping African Americans, whether free or enslaved, and selling them. In 1835 African Americans in Buffalo rescued one family that had been captured in St. Catharines. Although Underground Railroad activists were generally discreet, information about the movement was widely available from freedom seekers and abolitionists, who sought converts to their cause, and from newspaper editors who promoted sensational stories about escapes and rescues. Jermain Loguen, Samuel Ringgold Ward, Frederick Douglass, William Wells Brown, Harriet Ann Jacobs, Harriet's brother, John Jacobs, and others who had es-

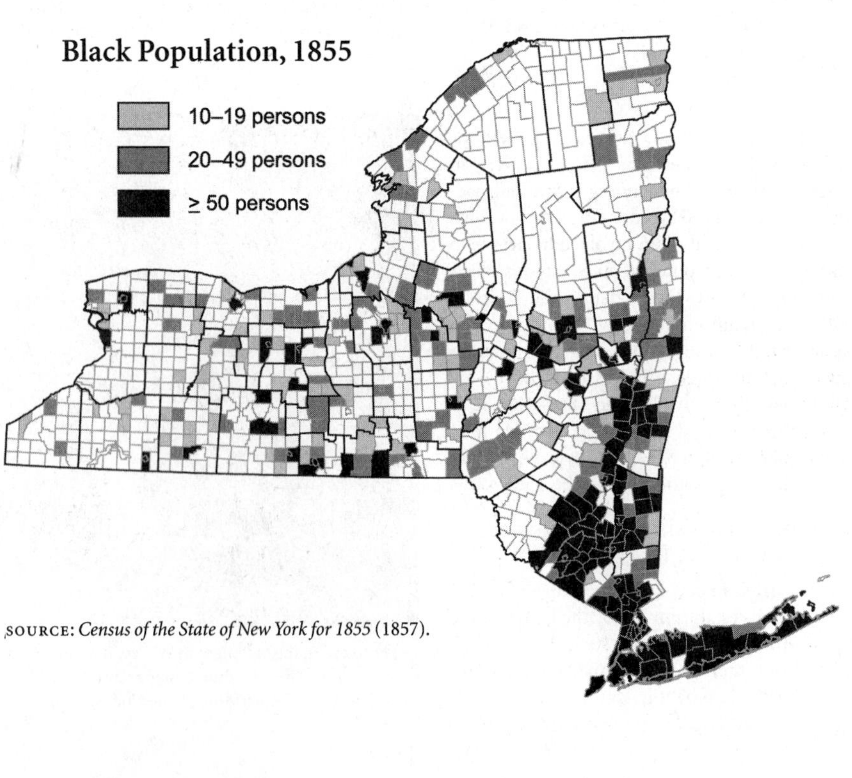

SOURCE: *Census of the State of New York for 1855* (1857).

caped slavery often lectured and wrote about their experiences. Abolitionists also publicized freedom seekers' stories as a powerful force for expanding antislavery sentiment in the North. Sometimes large groups of people, usually led by African Americans, forcibly rescued freedom seekers in dramatic street actions, as in the cases of Christopher Webb in Buffalo in 1847 and Charles Nalle in Troy (Rensselaer Co) in 1860. Newspaper editors reported these stories widely.

Demographics

Freedom seekers traveled to New York State both as single men and women, and as families with children. Amy Post in Rochester welcomed one group of 15 people, all related to the oldest woman. On Christmas Eve in 1850, Asa and Caroline Wing in Mexico (Oswego Co) sheltered the Thompson family—husband, wife, and five little girls. Asa Wing noted in his diary that the Thompsons were traveling to Canada "to save their children from the kidnappers." Census data confirm the impression that freedom seekers included women and children as well as men. In Oswego, women constituted 43% of possible freedom seekers identified in censuses from 1850 to 1865. Those who came through New York State originated primarily in the upper South. A large proportion, particularly those who traveled through eastern and central New York State, came from Maryland and Virginia. In these areas, worn out tobacco lands eroded the economic viability of slavery. As a result enslaved people faced a strong possibility that they would be sold in the New Orleans slave market. Potential sale of oneself or one's family was a powerful motive for flight. Another stream of freedom seekers, more common in Western New York, came through Ohio from Kentucky, Tennessee, and Missouri.

Underground Railroad networks were found in both rural and urban areas, and its participants included Blacks and Whites of different ages, sexes, occupations, and wealth. Men were often active in transporting individuals and identifying and arranging stops, while women frequently raised money, collected supplies, and sewed clothing, often in organized groups, such as the Rochester Ladies' Anti-Slavery Society. They also fed and housed freedom seekers who came through their homes. Both men and women came from a variety of economic circumstances. Gerrit and Ann Smith in Peterboro and James Canning Fuller, a British Quaker in Skaneateles (Onondaga Co), represented the few wealthy supporters, but most keepers of way stations had relatively modest resources and small homes. Urban sympathizers coordinated movements and provided temporary housing, but rural way stations offered a safer refuge for those requiring longer stays. Presumably slave catchers had fewer places to hide near small communities and farms, and federal marshals resisted venturing far into the countryside. Slocum Howland in Sherwood (Cayuga Co) sent freedom seekers to William Duvall in Port Byron (Cayuga Co), for example. The small size of Warsaw (Wyoming Co) and Mexico belied their importance as major Underground Railroad nodes.

Within African American communities barbers, hotel workers, and people associated with transportation appear to have been especially effective agents. As public places barbershops were useful communication centers. Similarly hotel workers had contact with a variety of people and often assisted in escapes. Tom Leonard, a black waiter in the Hotel Syracuse, helped Harriet Powell escape in 1839. Black waiters at the Cataract House in Niagara Falls were less successful in their attempt to rescue another enslaved woman in 1847. In Oswego John McKenzie promoted the Underground Railroad through his work as a carter, while William Wells Brown aided freedom seekers through his work on ships in Buffalo.

In spite of their differences, Underground Railroad supporters were united in their opposition to slavery, which was most often based on moral and religious grounds. Some religious groups—African Methodist Episcopal (AME) and AMEZ churches, Quakers, as well as some Congregationalists, Presbyterians, Methodists, and Baptists—opposed slavery, but radical abolitionism split many mainstream white churches in the late 1830s and early 1840s. Underground Railroad supporters often joined the antislavery Wesleyan Methodists, Christian Union churches, or Congregational Friends. Some of these, such as the Bristol Hill Congregational Church in Volney (Oswego Co), had a biracial membership. Many of them, including the Michigan Street Baptist Church in Buffalo, the AMEZ Church in Ithaca, and St. David's AMEZ Church in Sag Harbor (Suffolk Co), retain strong oral traditions of Underground Railroad activism. The basement of Syracuse's Wesleyan Methodist Church contained a set of sculpted faces, perhaps reflecting the use of this church as a stop on the Freedom Trail.

Liberty Party activism also correlated well with Underground Railroad activity. First organized in 1840 the Liberty Party drew so many votes from New York State in 1844 that it inadvertently threw the presidential election from Henry Clay, a moderate Whig, to James K. Polk, a proslavery Democrat. Towns such as Cazenovia (Madison Co) gave strong support to both the Liberty Party and the Underground Railroad. For the 1852 election the radical wing of the Liberty Party gathered at an Oswego convention and nominated Gerrit Smith for president and Samuel Ringgold Ward, a Congregational minister from Cortland who escaped slavery in 1820, for vice president.

Although people often associated the Underground Railroad with tunnels, no underground spaces built especially for the network have so far been documented. A few way stations contain unusual features, such as hidden rooms or scooped out areas under floors, that suggest their possible use as hiding places. Such evidence is problematic, though, without more specific proof. They may have been built as cisterns, root cellars, closets, or storage areas that were then used, or not used, as hiding places. Most freedom seekers likely stayed in barns or in the attics, bedrooms, kitchens, cellars, or parlors of homes. Martha Coffin Wright wrote in 1843 that one individual stayed overnight in the kitchen of her Auburn home. Elizabeth Cady Stanton recalled in her autobiography that those passing through Gerrit and Ann Smith's Peterboro home often stayed in their kitchen or barn. In cases of extreme danger, freedom seekers or their helpers used woods or fields as hiding places. Nine who traveled through Fulton (Oswego Co) in 1845 hid in the woods for three days.

After the Fugitive Slave Act

Passage of the federal Fugitive Slave Act in 1850 changed the nature of the Underground Railroad. The law, which mandated the recapture and return of escaped slaves and punished those who assisted freedom seekers, prompted protests in communities across the state. Often organized by African Americans, the protests publicized the danger of federal intervention. The response of African Americans in Buffalo was typical. We prefer "to die in resisting the execution of so monstrous a law," they affirmed, "rather than submit to its infamous requirements." Seizure of African Americans in New York State, including James Hamlet, who was returned to slavery in Baltimore after seizure in New York City in September 1850, made real the worst fears of

Local Antislavery Societies Established by 1840

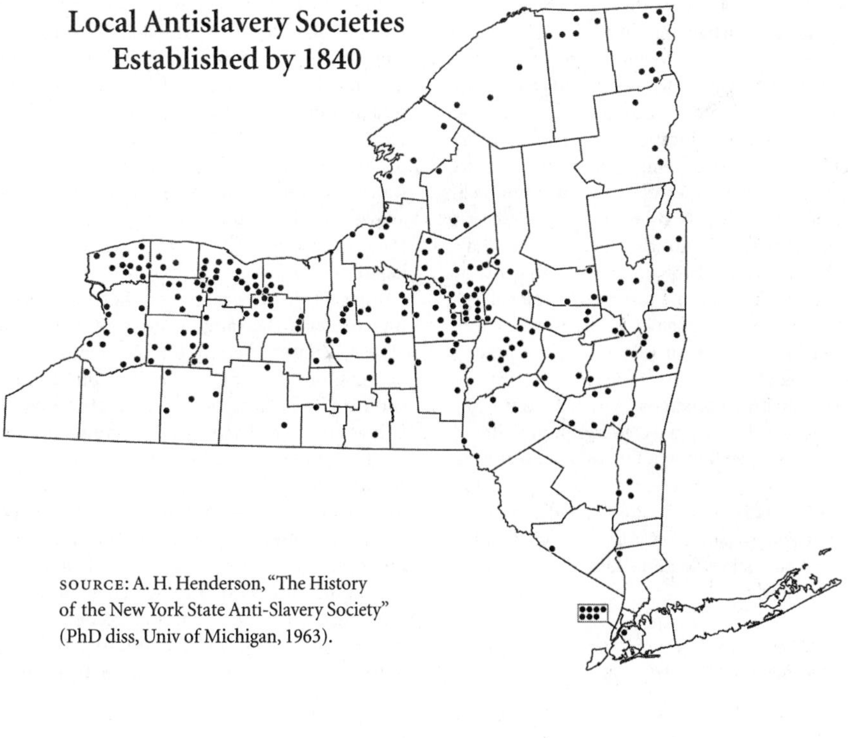

SOURCE: A. H. Henderson, "The History of the New York State Anti-Slavery Society" (PhD diss, Univ of Michigan, 1963).

African Americans. Many longtime New York State residents, including Jermain Loguen and Samuel Ringgold Ward, went to Canada. Some communities successfully challenged the federal government's ability to enforce the Fugitive Slave Law. While the case of Shadrach Minkins in Boston is perhaps the most famous, New York State's abolitionists were also vigilant. In October 1851 they coordinated the rescue of William "Jerry" Henry in Syracuse; in 1859 others rescued Charles Nalle in Troy. By the mid-1850s many freedom seekers had returned from Canada, and some Underground Railroad activists became more public about their work. In Syracuse Loguen advertised openly that freedom seekers were welcome at his home.

Perhaps the most dramatic single incident associated with the Underground Railroad was John Brown's raid on the US arsenal at Harpers Ferry [now in W Va] in 1859. With a small band of Whites and Blacks, John Brown, a white abolitionist, hoped to set up a "subterranean passageway" to bring people from slavery into freedom. This was not a new idea; Charles Torrey and William Chaplin had planned similar schemes in the 1840s. Torrey died in a Maryland prison. Chaplin escaped a similar fate only because abolitionists in New York State raised and then forfeited his $10,000 bail. Brown was no more successful. He was captured and hanged. His widow buried his body near their home in North Elba (Essex Co) in the Adirondacks. Brown's death symbolized a country increasingly divided over slavery. Abolitionists compared John Brown to Jesus Christ, while proslavery advocates viewed him as the devil. In either case he represented the perceived ability of Underground Railroad activists to undermine American slavery and ultimately to bring the country to civil war. Citizens of New York State, both black and white, had contributed powerfully to that result.

The abolition of slavery in 1865 encouraged more openness on the part of Underground Railroad participants about their activities. This is reflected in accounts of freedom seekers and their helpers, such as Pettit's *Sketches in the History of the Underground Railroad* (1879), William H. Siebert's *The Underground Railway from Slavery to Freedom* (1898), and biographies of significant participants, like Harriet Tubman. With the passing of the generation active in the antislavery struggle, interest generally waned. In some New York State communities during the 1930s, the State Education Department commemorated places of refuge with historic markers. While many other places went unmarked, community residents continued to pass down stories about a building's Underground Railroad connections throughout the 20th century, though getting accurate history about local legends was often a challenge. In the 1990s a more formal interest in documenting and interpreting the people and places associated with the Underground Railroad emerged. A year before Congress passed the National Underground Railroad Network to Freedom Act, Onondaga Co created the first countywide Freedom Trail Commission in 1997 to assist with identifying and commemorating sites locally. New York State created the nation's first statewide Freedom Trail Commission in 1999.

Driscoll, James, et al. *Angels of Deliverance: The Underground Railroad in Queens, Long Island, and Beyond.* Ed. Wini Warren (Flushing, NY: Queens Historical Society, 1999)

Gara, Larry. *The Liberty Line: The Legend of the Underground Railroad,* 2d ed. (Lexington: Univ of Kentucky Press, 1996)

National Park Service. *Underground Railroad* (Washington, DC: US Department of the Interior, 1998)

Pettit, Eber M. *Sketches in the History of the Underground Railroad* (1879; repr Westfield, NY: Chautauqua Region Press, 1999)

Sernett, Milton C. "On Freedom's Trail: Researching the Underground Railroad in New York State," *Afro-Americans in New York Life and History* 25 (Jan 2001): 7–32

———. *North Star Country: Upstate New York and the Crusade for African American Freedom* (Syracuse: Syracuse Univ Press, 2002)

Sernett, Milton C., and Judith Wellman. "Historic Resources Related to the Freedom Trail, Abolitionism, and African American Life in Central New York, 1820–1870," http://www.oswego.edu/Acad_Dept/a_and_s/history/ugrr/mpndraft.html

Siebert, Wilbur. *The Underground Railroad from Slavery to Freedom* (1898, repr New York: Arno Press, 1968)

Wellman, Judith. "This Side of the Border: Fugitives from Slavery in Three Central New York Communities," *New York History* 79 (Oct 1998): 359–92

———. "Larry Gara's *Liberty Line* in Oswego County, New York, 1838–1854: A New Look at the Legend," *Afro-Americans in New York Life and History* 25 (Jan 2001): 33–55

Judith Wellman

underwater archaeology. New York State's submerged archaeological resources constitute an incredible variety of material, reflecting many aspects of society and technology. These include artifacts, shipwrecks, docks, breakwaters, bridge remains, and battlefields. On land, New York State archaeology has yielded extraordinary information about American Indians, Dutch, French, British, and American inhabitants. In recent years a parallel collection of underwater sites has revealed additional information.

As early as the mid–19th century, people fascinated with naval history were locating shipwrecks in shallow water. Efforts to remove them often led to their destruction. The 1776 gunboat *Philadelphia,* raised in Valcour Bay (Clinton Co) in 1935, is a rare survivor of this early approach. It is now on permanent exhibit at the Smithsonian Institution in Washington, DC. In an effort to improve the management of underwater cultural resources, Congress passed the Abandoned Shipwreck Act in 1987. This act transfers much of the management role to the states in whose waters the sites are located. In New York this has allowed for the creation of Underwater Historic Preserves in Lake Champlain, Lake George, and Lake Ontario.

In recent decades there have been numerous underwater archaeology projects in New York State. During excavations for a Manhattan office building on Water St in 1982, the builders encountered what has been dubbed the Ronson Shipwreck, an early 18th-century vessel eventually filled in to create more land on the east side of Manhattan. The practice of creating new land by filling up discarded vessels and marine structures was common. The Ronson shipwreck, however, was a rare archaeological discovery. Additional surveys of submerged vessels have been made in Sackets Harbor (Jefferson Co) from 1985 to 1987 on the War of 1812 brig *Jefferson* and in Lake Ontario near the location of Fort Niagara [now in Porter, Niagara Co] in 1988.

In Lake George, Bateau Below, Inc has located and documented the *Land Tortoise,* a British-built *radeau* from 1758, as well as dozens of bateaux from this same period. In Lake Champlain, archaeologists from the Lake Champlain Maritime Museum (Vergennes, Vt) have used a sonar survey to locate almost 300 shipwrecks. This collection includes military vessels from the French and Indian War, the Revolutionary War, and the War of 1812, as well as commercial schooners, steamboats, and a rare horse-powered ferry.

Bellico, Russell P. *Sails and Steam in the Mountains: A Maritime and Military History of Lake George and Lake Champlain,* 2d ed. (Fleischmanns, NY: Purple Mountain Press, 2001)

Cohn, Arthur B. *Lake Champlain's Sailing Canal Boats: An Illustrated Journey from Burlington Bay to the Hudson River* (Vergennes, Vt: Lake Champlain Maritime Museum, 2003)

Lundeberg, Philip K. *The Gunboat "Philadelphia" and the Defense of Lake Champlain in 1776* (Vergennes, Vt: Lake Champlain Maritime Museum, 1995)

Arthur B. Cohn

undocumented immigration. The problem of aliens entering the United States without official authorization first arose when Washington lawmakers moved away from an open-door immigration policy by barring the entry of prostitutes and criminals in 1875 and of Asian groups in 1882. The Buffalo–Niagara Falls region became an area of considerable illegal Chinese immigration from Canada in the following decades. In the 1920s immigration quotas were set to curtail the flow of Europeans, especially from southern and eastern Europe. Many entered New York State as stowaways. Some were brought in on the ships of rum smugglers and others through the connivance of corrupt steamship employees and inspectors on Ellis Island. The nationalities of unauthorized immigrants have changed but little else has. One of the best known stories is that of the *Golden Venture,* a ship with a cargo of nearly 300 undocumented Chinese that ran aground in June 1993 off New York City's Rockaway Peninsula.

In recent decades undocumented immigrants have for the most part entered the country illegally from Mexico. Undocumented immigrants to New York State, however, usually entered legally, with a visitor, student, or other temporary visa but stayed beyond the required departure date. While some of them did not have the family ties, job skills, or refugee status entitling them to an immigrant visa, others were eligible, but getting such visas often entailed a wait of more than a decade in their home countries. They thus chose to enter legally with temporary visas and overstay their authorization. In the 1990s alone, as the number of these temporary entrants to New York State burgeoned from 2.5 million in 1992 to 4.3 million in 2000, so has the undocumented population.

One of the first attempts to estimate the number of undocumented immigrants focused on comparing records from the now defunct national alien registration system with data on the foreign-born from the 1980 census. This method yielded 2.1 million undocumented immigrants counted in the 1980 census, of whom 234,000 (11%) lived in New York State. Congress sought to address concerns over the large number of undocumented immigrants by cutting off the employment opportunities encouraging this situation. In 1986 it passed the Immigration Reform and Control Act (IRCA), which for the first time imposed civil and criminal penalties on employers who knowingly hired undocumented immigrants. The law also granted legal status to approximately 2.7 million undocumented immigrants already living in the United States. There were 171,000 applicants for legalization from New York State, nearly 90% of whom lived in New York City. The largest sources of legal immigrants to New York State in the previous decade (1977–86)—the Dominican Republic, Jamaica, China, Guyana, and Haiti—were among the major sources of legalized immigrants. But the list of legalized immigrants also included people from Mexico, Pakistan, Bangladesh, Peru, Ghana, Nigeria, and Honduras.

Despite the amnesty and employer sanctions, the undocumented population in New York State increased. Estimates for 2000 climbed to an estimated 489,000, which amounts to roughly 2.6% of New York State's total population and 7% of the approximately 7 million undocumented immigrants in the United States. While undocumented immigrants often operate on the margins of society, they are bound by a web of economic and social ties to other Americans. They are employed across the occupational spectrum but particularly in service occupations that are frequently part of the underground economy. Many live in households where other family members are documented. Indeed, when an undocumented woman gives birth in the United States, the child is an American citizen. Through these ties many undocumented immigrants eventually become legal residents. However, the 1996 Illegal Immigration Reform and Immigrant Responsibility Act makes this transition to legal status much more difficult. Moreover, the environment since 11 Sept 2001 has been very harsh on undocumented immigrants, with many of those from Arab and Muslim countries facing deportation. A consequence of these measures may be a further marginalization of the undocumented population.

Bean, Frank, Barry Edmonston, and Jeffrey S. Passel, eds. *Undocumented Migration to the United States: IRCA and the Experience of the 1980s* (Washington, DC: Urban Institute Press, 1990)

Estimates of the Unauthorized Immigrant Population Residing in the United States: 1990 to 2000 (Washington, DC: Office of Policy and Planning, US Immigration and Naturalization Service, 2003)

Lobo, Arun Peter, Joseph J. Salvo, and Vicky Virgin. *The Newest New Yorkers: 1990–1994* (New York: Department of City Planning, New York City, 1996)

Passel, Jeffery S., and Karen A. Woodrow. "Geographic Distribution of Undocumented Immigrants: Estimates of Undocumented Aliens Counted in the 1980 Census by State," *International Migration Review* 18 (1984): 642–71

Salvo, Joseph J., and Arun Peter Lobo. "Immigration and the Changing Demographic Profile of New York." In *The City and the World: New York's Global Future,* ed. Margaret Crahan and Alberto Vourvoulias-Bush (New York: Council on Foreign Relations Press, 1997)

Warren, Robert. *Estimates of the Undocumented Immigrant Population Residing in the United States: October 1996* (Washington, DC: US Immigration and Naturalization Service, 1997)

Joseph J. Salvo and Arun Peter Lobo

Unification Church. Religious denomination. Founded in 1954 by Sun Myung Moon (*b* 1920) in Seoul, South Korea, the Holy Spirit Association for the Unification of World Christianity had a handful of followers in the West by 1973, when Moon set up his home and a training center in Tarrytown (Westchester Co). According to Moon's *Divine Principle,* Unification's core theological text, the biblical Fall is a consequence of a sexual relationship between Eve and Lucifer, then between Adam and Eve, resulting in humanity's Satan-centered, rather than God-centered, lineage. Jesus was meant to marry and reestablish God's ideal family but was prematurely murdered. At Jesus' request, however, Moon and his wife, the "True Parents," are completing Jesus' mission and establishing God's Kingdom of Heaven on Earth.

From 1972 Moonies, as followers came to be known, were a familiar sight in New York City and elsewhere as they witnessed and raised funds by selling literature, candles, candy, roses, and other high-profit wares. Moon became a public figure, preaching at rallies nationwide, two of the largest being in Madison Square Garden (1974) and Yankee Stadium (1976). During the 1970s the movement acquired property of considerable value in the state, including Manhattan's New Yorker hotel, the former Columbia Club, and the Tiffany Building (which was later resold). The Unification Theological Seminary was established in Barrytown (Dutchess Co). In 1975 there was a mushrooming of projects under numerous names, including conferences, and from 1977 to 1991 the church owned the daily newspaper *News World* (later *New York City Tribune*). This activity gave Unificationists a high profile, but due largely to a high turnover of converts leaving (voluntarily) after a few months, there have rarely been more than 2,000 core-member Americans at one time, although these have frequently been supplemented by Japanese and Korean members.

From the mid-1970s distrust and antagonism was being directed toward the movement. How, it was asked, could young, middle-class Americans give up everything to work for a Korean "Messiah" who chose their partner for a mass wedding? At Madison Square Garden in 1982 Moon married 2,075 couples from more than 70 countries. A popular explanation was that the movement used brainwashing or mind-control techniques. Some parents thought this justified forcible "deprogramming." In 1980 the state legislature ratified the Lasher Amendment, a bill allowing the state to appoint conservators for the victims of such groups, but this was vetoed by Gov Hugh Carey. Anti-Unification sentiment peaked around 1983, when Moon was convicted of tax fraud and sentenced to 18 months imprisonment. By the 1990s the Unification Church in the United States was attracting less negative publicity and had come to resemble a more conventional religion, with most members living with their families and working outside the movement. Activity increasingly focused on promoting family values, and the movement's name was changed to the Family Federation for World Peace and Unification in 1996. A mass blessing in 1998 at Madison Square Garden included nonmembers and enjoyed the support of influential black leaders such as Al Sharpton and Louis Farrakhan.

Barker, E. *The Making of a Moonie: Brainwashing or Choice?* (1984; repr Aldershot, England: Gregg Revivals, 1993)

Eileen Barker

Union. Town (pop 56,298) in SW Broome Co. Settled in 1785, the town was formed in 1791. A hamlet had developed by 1810, when a Union post office opened; streets for a larger community were laid out in 1846. The Erie Railroad came through in 1849. The village incorporated in 1871 but merged with Endicott in 1921. In town, the Villages of Endicott and Johnson City were dominated by the Endicott Johnson Co, whose corporate actions formed Union's landscape, including four carousels. In the early 21st century, Glendale Technology Park and Airport Road Industrial Park house a variety of industrial plants, and the Tri-Cities Airport (1936) services the area.

Charles J. Browne

Union Carbide Corporation. Chemical company. The Union Carbide Co was founded in 1898 to produce calcium carbide, by smelting lime and coke. The action of water on calcium carbide produces acetylene, a combustible gas suitable for illumination. By 1900 the company, then headquartered in Chicago, was capitalized at $6 million. The first of Union Carbide's New York State plants was a carbide facility in Niagara Falls, originally operated by Acetylene Light and Power Co and acquired by Union Carbide in 1905. The Niagara plant took advantage of the falls' low-cost electric power, soon producing 20 tons (18 MT) of carbide per day. In 1917 Union Carbide merged with several other chemical manufactures to become Union Carbide and Carbon Corp and began supplying the US military with helium, activated carbon, and other chemical products. Union Carbide would later open a plant in Tonawanda (Erie Co), and there were other facilities in Arcade (Wyoming Co), Warwick (Orange Co), and Tarrytown (Westchester Co). By the 1930s the company was producing petrochemical products. The New York State plants, which had turned largely to the production of consumer items such as antifreeze and batteries after World War I, returned to the production of defense materials during World War II. In 1957 the company became Union Carbide Corp (UCC). During the latter half of the 20th century, it grew into a $9 billion corporation producing a wide range of chemicals and polymers, both for the US military and for the civilian market. Consumer goods included plastic wrap and floor waxes. Divestment followed in the mid-1980s; the two UCC plants at Niagara Falls became part of Praxair, producer of liquid hydrogen for the aerospace industry. In 2001 Dow Chemical Co, a Michigan-based corporation, acquired UCC along with its remaining New York State properties but had no production facilities in the state.

Jack Westbrook

Union College. Private liberal arts college. Rev Dirck Romeyn, pastor of the Schenectady Dutch Reformed Church, began the school as Schenectady Academy in 1785. With the support of Gen Philip Schuyler and Gov George Clinton, Rev Romeyn and others convinced the Regents of the State of New York to convert the academy to a college in 1795. The original charter provided that a majority of trustees could not be from the same denomination and the president could not simultaneously hold a pastorate. The name, Union, symbolized the school's pan-Protestant support and national aspirations. The first president, John Blair Smith (1795–99), added French to the curriculum and purchased library books more heavily weighted to sciences than had been customary. Pres Jonathan Edwards Jr (1799–1801) devised the 1801 Plan of Union between Congregationalists and Presbyterians for the development of frontier churches.

Union's innovative tenor was broadened by Eliphalet Nott, president from 1804 to his death in 1866. From the 1820s through the 1850s, Union rivaled Yale and Harvard in enrollment and influence. Nott moved the college to the grounds on Nistiquona Hill in 1814, in buildings designed the previous year by Joseph Jacques Ramée. Nott pushed Union's curriculum in scientific and secular directions, hiring the first chemistry professor (1809), moving to an elective system and adding a parallel scientific course (1827–28), and establishing a civil engineering department (1845). He also adopted less punitive forms of student discipline, established New York State's first chapter of Phi Beta Kappa (1817), and tolerated students' secret societies and fraternities, six of which began at Union from 1825 to 1847. From Nott's long tenure, 86 former students became college presidents. Nott funded Union's growth primarily through a series of state lotteries that he eventually directed. His reliance on lotteries and, after their 1833 abolition, other risky ventures ultimately tipped the college into decline. Nott and the Board of Trustees had settled out of court in a dispute with the lottery partners in 1837, but in the early 1850s Nott again stood accused of misappropriating funds. To distance himself from such charges, in 1854 he made a donation to the college that proved of dubious value because its largest holding was Manhattan real estate under disputed ownership. Union emerged from the Civil War with little endowment and a diminished enrollment that reversed the college's nationwide reach.

Intercollegiate athletics began with rowing in the 1870s, then football in 1886. Pres Eliphalet Nott Potter (1871–83) established Union University in 1873, a loose federation with Albany Law School, Albany Medical College, Dudley Observatory, and in 1881 Albany College of Pharmacy, with the president of Union College serving as chancellor. Potter also completed the construction of the 16-sided Nott Memorial in 1875; its foundation had been laid in 1858. The college's resurgence began in the 1890s, paralleling the economic growth of Schenectady. Pres Andrew Van Vrankon Raymond (1894–1907) established a pioneering department of electrical engineering and applied physics in 1895, which was headed from 1901 to 1913 by Charles P. Steinmetz of the General Electric Co. Through the sale of Nott's remaining Brooklyn real estate and the campus's undeveloped eastern end, Union began to emerge from its fiscal problems. Alumnus Frank Bailey, treasurer from 1901 to 1953, put the college on stable financial footing, and by the interwar period it enrolled approximately 800 men. Enrollment doubled by 1969, when the trustees decided to admit women, and coeducation helped stabilize it at 2,000 students. Aggressive building programs in the post–World War II era extended the campus far beyond the original Ramée design. In 2000 Union's 174 faculty members offered courses in 20 academic departments with interdisciplinary options, including joint programs in law, medicine, and pharmacy. Under Pres Roger Hull (1990–) the college phased out the Civil Engineering Department in 2001 to devote more resources to emerging engineering technologies and created a house system, to begin in 2004, to diversify residential options beyond the social fraternities and sororities. Enrollment in 2000 was 2,439, 52% men and 48% women.

Fortenbaugh, Samuel B., Jr. *In Order to Form a More Perfect Union* (Schenectady: Union College Press, 1978)

Fox, Dixon Ryan. *Union College: An Unfinished History* (Schenectady: Graduate Council, Union College, 1945)

Somers, Wayne, comp and ed. *Encyclopedia of Union College History* (Schenectady, NY: Union College Press, 2003)

Jim Carl

Uniondale. Locality (pop 23,011) in Hempstead (Nassau Co). Variously known as East Meadow, Turtle Hook, and East Hempstead, the school district adopted the name Uniondale in 1853. A farming community, the population was only 1,100 in 1940. After rapid postwar growth, the total has been relatively stable since 1960, though diversity has increased. In 2000 African Americans were 45% of the population and persons of Latino ethnicity 23%. A residential community, Uniondale has retail stores, the county's A. Holly Patterson Geriatric Center, and portions of the Hofstra University campus, as well as the Nassau Coliseum (home of the New York Islanders), a few large multistory office buildings, and a hotel on Mitchel Field.

Natalie A. Naylor

unions. See CONDON-WADLIN ACT; LABOR; POLICE UNIONS; PUBLIC EMPLOYEES UNIONS; TAYLOR LAW; TEACHERS' ASSOCIATIONS AND UNIONS; see also individual unions.

Union Springs. Village (pop 1,074) in Springport (Cayuga Co). Settled in 1790 on the Cayuga Lake shore, Union Springs acquired a post office in 1810 and was incorporated as a village in 1848. Quakers established Friends Academy, later Oakwood Seminary (1858–1920). Howland College (1863–78) for women was also in the village. When Oakwood moved to Poughkeepsie, Seventh-Day Adventists founded the Union Springs Academy (1921), which remained in operation in 2003. The sulfur and salt springs for which Union Springs was named supported a sanatorium and hotel in the 19th century. Agricultural equipment (starting 1830), wheel hubs and milling hardware (starting 1875), and brick and tile were manufactured. From 1874 to 1916 the Cayuga Plaster Co processed gypsum. Steamboats served the village, as did the Cayuga Lake Railroad (1873–1974). In 2002 a landmark is the Stone Mill (1836), now the site of Finger Lakes Extrusion Corp, a plastics manufacturer. The village's main business in 2002 was tourism; it has four marinas on Cayuga Lake.

Laurel Auchampaugh

Union Station (Albany). Opened 17 Dec 1900, the terminal served many railroads, including the New York Central, Albany and Boston, and Delaware and Hudson. Designed by the Boston firm Shepley, Rutan and Coolidge, the station was typical of the period's grand Beaux Arts classicism. Constructed of pink Milford granite, a modern material at the time, it had an elaborate interior, including a lobby with mosaic floors, 110 ft (33.5 m) ceilings, chandeliers, and a cocktail lounge. By the 1910s Union Station was a regional crux of transportation. In 1966 the state bought the structure and spent $1 million on renovations, but in December 1968 the station closed. Although it was listed on the National Register of Historic Places in 1971, it was left to decay until 1984, when Norstar Bancorp's Peter Kiernan restored it as Norstar headquarters and it was renamed Peter D. Kiernan Plaza. In 2003 the structure, located on Broadway, was headquarters to Fleet Bank, which acquired Norstar in 1988.

Finnegan, Thomas. *Saving Union Station: An Inside Look at Historic Preservation* (Albany: Washington Park Press, 1988)

Waite, Diana S., ed., *Albany Architecture* (Albany: Mount Ida Press, 1993)

William Brandow

Union Station (Utica). The railroad passenger station in Utica opened on 14 May 1914; it replaced a station built in 1869 and became the third permanent station on the site. Fellheimer and Long, Allen H. Stem, Associated Architects designed the station in a Beaux Arts style, the exterior modeled after an Italian palace and the interior after Roman baths. Construction costs totaled $1 million, double the initial estimate. It became a union station in 1915 when the Delaware, Lackawanna and Western, and the New York, Ontario, and Western Railroads closed their respective stations and relocated with the New York Central. Though it was nearly demolished in the 1970s, it is now owned by Oneida Co and has been incrementally rehabilitated. It has been a continuously operating train station since it opened, serving Amtrak, intercity buses, and the Adirondack Scenic Railroad.

Oneida Co. Department of Planning. *Union Station, Utica, New York,* Historic Structure Report (Utica, 1978)

Michael J. Bosak

Union Theological Seminary. Founded in 1836 by a group of "new school" Presbyterian laity and clergy at 9 University Place in New York City as the New York Theological Seminary. In 1839 it adopted its current name. In 1884 Union moved to more spacious accommodations at 700 Park Ave between 16th and 17th Sts, close to the campus of Columbia College. At that time the two institutions entered into an agreement that permitted the seminary students to take courses at Columbia, an affiliation that continues today. When Columbia University moved to Morningside Heights in Upper Manhattan in 1897, Union soon followed. In the fall of 1910 its new home opened at 120th to 122d Sts between Broadway and Claremont Ave.

By this time Union was a nondenominational graduate school of Christian theology. After a controversial lecture by Union professor Charles Briggs in 1891, an adherent of the historically based Higher Criticism, the General Assembly of the US Presbyterian Church attempted to veto his appointment as professor. The controversy led Union's board to rescind its 1870 agreement of union with the Presbytery of New York, and after similar charges involving other members of the faculty, Union chose once again to become an independent theological institution.

At Morningside Heights, Union added both to its curricular offerings and its distinguished list of faculty. In 1909 the seminary created the Department of Religious Education and Psychology with George A. Coe as its senior scholar in the field. Harry F. Ward joined the seminary in 1918 to teach Christian ethics. Ward, an advocate of the social gospel, was noted as the main author of the Federal Council of Churches' Social Creed of the Churches (1908). The establishment of the School of Sacred Music in 1928 made Union the premier training ground in the United States for professional church musicians and significantly increased the seminary's female enrollment. Henry Sloane Coffin, who became president of the faculty in 1926, strengthened Union's practical theology program during his nearly two decades as president. The 1928 hiring of Reinhold Niebuhr as an ethics professor made Union a center of neo-orthodox theology in America. In addition to Niebuhr, other Union faculty members are seen as leaders in US theology. Paul Tillich arrived at Union from Germany in 1933, and his writings on theology and culture quickly made him a household name among US Christians. James Cone, the key voice in the establishment of black theology as a field, joined Union in 1969, the same year his book *Black Theology and Black Power* revolutionized US religious thought.

Handy, Robert T. *A History of Union Theological Seminary in New York* (New York: Columbia Univ Press, 1987)

Quinton H. Dixie

Union Vale. Town (pop 4,546) in S central Dutchess Co. Part of the Beekman Patent (1697), it was settled by Palatine Germans in 1727. It was formed from Beekman and Freedom [now La Grange] in 1827. In the 19th century two iron mines, a charcoal industry, and a woolen mill operated. The Dutchess and Columbia Railroad passed through town (1869). In recent years it has attracted commuters relocating from Westchester Co; they commute to that county and to New York City.

William P. McDermott

Unionville. Village (pop 536) in Minisink (Orange Co). Unionville grew up around a station on the Middletown, Unionville and Water Gap Railroad (1868) and incorporated as a village in 1871. A silk mill (1894) triggered real growth; it became the American Silk Label Co, a ribbon factory. Standard Oil Co operated a pumping station from 1906 to 1928. In the early 21st century Carnegie Industries produced fabric coatings. The Appalachian Trail passes along the village streets.

Unitarian Universalists. The 1961 merger of the Universalist Church of America (1793) and the American Unitarian Association (1825) produced this liberal religious movement that has roots in the radical wing of the Protestant Reformation. Unitarianism derives from a challenge to the doctrines of the Trinity and of human depravity, and Universalism from an assertion that eternal punishment is inconsistent with a God whose basic nature is love. Noncreedal and governed by congregational polity that rests authority in the hands of local congregations, Unitarian Universalism embraces diverse theological and social views.

Unitarianism and Universalism in North America emerged in New England but appeared soon after in New York State. John Murray, a founder of American Universalism, preached occasionally in New York City between 1770 and 1796. In 1793 the *Free Universal Magazine* was published in the city, and three years later the first Universalist congregation in New York State was established as the Society of United Christian Friends. Other congregations developed in Otsego and Oneida Cos during the first decade of the 19th century, and a congregation formed in Southold (Suffolk Co) in 1836. The New York State Convention of Universalists was organized in 1825. With annual meetings at various locations statewide, the convention supported Universalist interests and expansion, including credentialing ministers and providing financial aid for institutions.

By 1870 there were more Universalists in New York than in any other state. Throughout the 19th century, Universalism flourished in small towns, semirural locales, and such urban areas as Utica, Syracuse, Rochester, Binghamton, Cortland, Watertown, and Buffalo. In 1831, to provide nonsectarian education for women and men on equal terms, Universalists established the Clinton Liberal Institute (Oneida Co), which merged in 1900 with St. Lawrence University, a coeducational institution founded by the Universalists in 1859, in Canton. Socially and theologically liberal, Universalists actively supported the temperance movement, campaigned for women's rights, advocated prison reform, and opposed the death penalty. The first women to be ordained as ministers with full denominational approval were New York State Universalists: Lydia Jenkins in 1860 at Geneva (Ontario Co) and Olympia Brown in 1863 at Malone (Franklin Co). Horace Greeley and P. T. Barnum were among the state's other influential Universalists.

Unitarianism entered New York State almost as early as Universalism. In 1794 an English Unitarian, John Butler, lectured in New York City on the unity of God. The subsequently formed church was greeted with hostility and lasted only a few months. When Joseph Priestley, the English Unitarian preacher and scientist, visited the city the same year, he was welcomed as a scientist, but no pulpits were open to him. In 1803 under the influence of Rev Francis Adrian Van der Kemp a congregation was organized at Oldenbarneveld [now Barneveld, Oneida Co] that called John Sherman, a Unitarian from Connecticut, its minister; the congregation remains Unitarian Universalist. In 1818–19 Henry Ware Jr and William Ellery Channing, visiting New York City from Boston, preached to small gatherings. In 1819 a church was organized and in 1821 a building constructed; the congregation continues as the Unitarian Church of All Souls. The Church of the Messiah (now Community Church of New York City) was organized in 1825, followed by one in Brooklyn in 1833 and Staten Island in 1852. In the 19th century Unitarian congregations emerged in urban centers across the state, including Albany, Syracuse, Rochester, Buffalo, and Ithaca.

Unitarians in New York State, such as Susan B. Anthony, Antoinette Brown Blackwell, and William Henry Channing, were committed to crusades for temperance, women's rights, alleviation of poverty, and an end to slavery. Samuel J. May, Unitarian minister in Syracuse, led opposition to enforcing the Fugitive Slave Act in the state and supported the radical abolitionists. During the Civil War Henry Whitney Bellows, Unitarian minister from New York City, led the US Sanitary Commission, a precursor of the American Red Cross. In the 20th century, both Unitarians and Universalists focused on a social gospel ministry that, inspired by John Haynes Holmes (Unitarian) and Clarence R. Skinner (Universalist), sought to address issues of war, poverty, disease, education, and racism.

The merger of Unitarians and Universalists had been discussed as early as 1865 but did not occur for nearly a century until the creation of the Unitarian Universalist Association. Since the merger Unitarian Universalists, acting on shared religious principles including faith in the worth and dignity of every person and a concern for the interdependent web of existence, have provided leadership in movements for civil rights, gay and lesbian rights, abortion rights, economic and racial justice, and global environmental issues. In the 20th century Unitarian Universalists continued to influence the development of New York State: Holmes led Unitarians in a reform movement for honest government in New York City; Pete Seeger led a campaign to clean up the Hudson River; and Forrester Church, minister of All Souls Unitarian Church in New York City, became a national spokesman for liberal causes. Unitarian Universalist congregations are largely urban and suburban, middle class, and European American, though recent efforts have been made to welcome African American and Latino populations. As of 1999 there were 14,086 Unitarian Universalists affiliated with 62 congregations in New York State.

Bumbaugh, David E. *Unitarian Universalism: A Narrative History* (Chicago: Meadville/Lombard Press, 2001)
Kring, Walter Donald. *Liberals among the Orthodox: Unitarian Beginnings in New York City* (Boston: Beacon Press, 1974)
Robinson, David. *The Unitarians and the Universalists* (Westport, Conn: Greenwood Press, 1985)
Williams, George H. *American Universalism* (Boston: Universalist Historical Society, 1971)

David E. Bumbaugh

UNITE. See Amalgamated Clothing Workers of America; International Ladies' Garment Workers' Union (ILGWU).

United Airlines. National Air Transport organized in 1925 and started mail and express (parcel) service with open-cockpit biplanes on the New York City–Chicago route on 1 Sept 1927. At first the mail service for New York City was via Hadley Field near New Brunswick, NJ, but when passenger service began in 1930, National moved to Newark, NJ. Passengers were carried only if there was room for them to sit on the mail sacks. United Aircraft and Transport Corp (UATC) bought National on 7 May 1930, operating it as one of its four divisions until United Air

Lines was organized to combine them on 1 July 1931. During the 1930s United became one of the nation's leading airlines, and by its integration of the former companies, including Boeing Air Transport, was operating a coast-to-coast trunk line with its New York City–Chicago service generating most of the traffic. By September 1933 it was offering three daily round-trip flights from Newark Airport to Chicago.

The airline division broke clear of the Boeing-controlled UATC and became fully independent on 1 May 1934. United's new-type aircraft inaugurals were invariably made from New York City to Chicago, where it faced the stiffest competition, but with the DC-7 (1 June 1954) and the DC-8 jets (18 Sept 1959), the inaugurals from New York City were nonstop services to San Francisco. United acquired Capital Airlines on 1 June 1961. At the time, Capital was the fifth largest airline in the world, measured in passenger boardings, and United was second; the acquisition made United the largest airline in the world outside of the USSR. In 1961 United carried 7,357,000 passengers, overtaking American Airlines by more than 1 million. Through Capital, United added New York State airports to its network: Rochester and Buffalo were served from Washington, DC, and were later connected to Chicago, Pittsburgh, and all three of New York City's airports. The airline started service from New York City's John F. Kennedy International Airport with its first wide-body Boeing 747 in 1970. It bought Pan American World Airways's Pacific network in October 1985 and that airline's London routes, starting transatlantic service to the British capital on 3 Apr 1991. United Airlines (renamed 1974) headquarters are in Chicago with New York City its major hub for all main-line, long-distance routes.

Davies, R. E. G. *Airlines of the United States since 1914* (1972; repr McLean, Va: Paladwr Press, 1998)

R. E. G. Davies

United Electrical, Radio, and Machine Workers (UE). Labor union. The United Electrical and Radio Workers was founded in Buffalo on 21 Mar 1936 from a coalition of 17 local unions in the electrical industry, representing approximately 16,000 of the industry's 350,000 workers. The first national officers were James B. Carey of Philadelphia, president, and Julius Emspak of Schenectady, secretary-treasurer; they worked out of UE's first national headquarters at 1133 Broadway in New York City. UE was one of many unions in New York State that were built in the 1930s with active communist involvement. In 1937 James J. Matles merged his New York City–based Metal Workers Industrial Union into UE, renamed United Electrical, Radio, and Machine Workers of America; Matles became director of organization and the third national officer. In 1938 UE became a charter member of the Congress of Industrial Organizations (CIO) and was the CIO's third-largest union by 1943, with 600,000 members. A World War II influx of women workers generated path-breaking efforts to address employment discrimination issues, particularly wage inequities. Local 301 at General Electric's (GE's) Schenectady plant, the largest shop in the industry, pioneered with a successful grievance lodged with the federal National War Labor Board in 1945, charging discrimination against women.

With the onset of the Cold War, federal intelligence agencies and US congressional committees investigated UE, seeking to uncover connections to the Communist Party. The UE leadership was specifically targeted, including Matles and Emspak, both of whom were accused of being Communist Party members, a charge both denied. The effort set the stage for conflict within the union that ultimately decimated UE. In 1949 the CIO expelled UE and replaced it with a new anticommunist union, the International Union of Electrical Workers (IUE). UE maintained its viability until 1954, when members of the Schenectady GE local voted to transfer its affiliation to IUE by a vote of 9,005 to 5,179. By 1956 UE had few remaining members in New York State, but headquarters remained in New York City until 1987, when they were moved to Pittsburgh.

Filippelli, Ronald L., and Mark D. McColloch. *Cold War in the Working Class: The Rise and Decline of the United Electrical Workers* (Albany: SUNY Press, 1995)

Lisa Kannenberg

United Garment Workers. First national clothing workers union to represent the diverse labor force in the men's ready-made clothing industry. Chartered by the American Federation of Labor (AFL), the United Garment Workers (UGW) was formed in New York City in 1891, joining the more skilled, largely native-born Journeyman Tailors' Union of America and the less skilled, largely foreign-born Tailors' National Progressive Union. Though dominated by the skilled cutters, the union maintained a tenuous peace amidst employer attacks. The UGW successfully led an 1893 strike of 16,000 garment workers in New York City, but a number of reversals in 1896 led to a more conservative strategy of accommodation. This shift alienated more radical, primarily Jewish workers. Between 1907 and 1912, a series of strikes heightened internal divisions. Union leaders halted strikes, against the wishes of many of the rank and file, and members were disillusioned by the union's growing nativist and craft-bound parochialism following the general strike of clothing workers in New York City in 1913. Dissatisfied workers bolted the UGW convention in 1914 to establish the Amalgamated Clothing Workers of America (ACW). Despite court challenges by the AFL, the ACW quickly became the dominant national labor organization in the men's clothing industry.

Carpenter, Jesse Thomas. *Competition and Collective Bargaining in the Needle Trades, 1910–1967* (Ithaca: Cornell Univ Press, 1972)
Fraser, Steven. *Labor Will Rule: Sidney Hillman and the Rise of American Labor* (New York: Free Press, 1991)

Christopher Martin

United Jewish Appeal (UJA)–Federation of New York. In 1917 a group led by New York City banker Felix M. Warburg established the Federation for the Support of Jewish Philanthropic Societies, soon renamed the Federation of Jewish Philanthropies, to support efforts for Jewish charities in New York City. In 1934 the federation brought about the merger of six vocational assistance groups to form FEGS (Federation Employment and Guidance Services), which assisted in job training and placement and which was in 2002 the largest private nonprofit organization of its kind in the United States. In 1943 the federation expanded to the city's suburbs, establishing Jewish Community Services of Long Island and Westchester Jewish Community Services. In 1978 the Jewish Board of Guardians and Jewish Family Services, both federation agencies, merged to form the Jewish Board of Family and Children's Services, which was one of the nation's largest private mental health and social service agencies by 2002. After 1974 the federation joined with United Jewish Appeal (UJA), a Zionist philanthropy, in fund-raising efforts, known as the Joint Campaign, and in 1986 merged into the UJA, forming the UJA–Federation of New York. The UJA–Federation, consisting of over 100 local, national, and international agencies, is affiliated with United Jewish Communities, which coordinates over 150 federations in the United States. In recent decades the group has continued to support Jewish communities and resettlement efforts worldwide and provides services to 185,000 Jewish New Yorkers living near the poverty line, with many member agencies offering social services to needy clients regardless of ethnicity or religion. There are Jewish philanthropic federations in Buffalo, Poughkeepsie, Latham, Newburgh, Rochester, Syracuse, and Utica.

Goldin, Milton. *Why They Give: American Jews and Their Philanthropies* (New York: Macmillan, 1976)

Milton Goldin

United Nations (UN). An organization comprising most of the independent countries of the world, devoted to strengthening peace and international cooperation. It was founded by the Allied powers in San Francisco in 1945. In February 1946 the General Assembly, in London for its first meeting, voted to place its headquarters in the area of Westchester Co or in Fairfield Co, Conn. New York City mayor William O'Dwyer appointed a committee, chaired by city parks commissioner Robert Moses, to convince the UN to locate its headquarters in the city. The committee proposed Flushing Meadow as a permanent home, but this was rejected. Finally, in December 1946, in the days before the UN's decision was due, a deal was struck to acquire a 17-acre (6.9 ha) parcel of land in Manhattan's Turtle Bay district bounded by East 42d St, East 48th St, 1st Ave, and the East River. The city provided some adjacent properties, surrendered waterfront rights, and agreed to improve the neighborhood, including the construction of a tunnel for First Ave so that UN Plaza could be built over it. The UN headquarters, built between 1949 and 1952, was designed by a sometimes fractious international team of architects, including Wallace K. Harrison (United States), Le Corbusier (France), and Oscar Niemeyer (Brazil). The Secretariat building was the first of the glass-curtain-wall structures that would mark New York City architecture for decades to come.

As one of the 20 largest employers in the city and as a major tourist attraction drawing nearly 9 million visitors a year, the UN has contributed both materially and culturally to the city and state. The presence of the UN headquarters and

Aerial view of UN headquarters, 1951.

its 191 diplomatic missions has also complicated life for the city. The police must provide security, which is especially difficult during the opening session each autumn, when many heads of state and government attend and protesters often congregate in the Dag Hammarskjold Plaza. The US mission and the city's Division of Diplomatic and Consular Affairs must also contend with complaints of inadequate parking, attempt to enforce parking and traffic regulations among people with diplomatic immunity, and deal with failures to fulfill contractual obligations by missions of countries undergoing political and financial crises. The state legislature established the not-for-profit United Nations Development Corporation (UNDC) in 1968 to provide office space and other facilities for the UN. In the mid-1990s Gov George E. Pataki and New York City mayor Rudolph Giuliani hoped to sell off many UNDC properties and did dispose of a hotel, but UNDC continued to operate buildings at One, Two, and Three UN Plaza. In 2002 UN secretary general Kofi Annan proposed that UNDC build the UN an additional 35-story headquarters building in part of Robert Moses Park. Under his plan, the UN would compensate the city for the park space by contributing to a waterfront esplanade. The new building, designed by Fumihiko Maki in the International Style, is to be completed by 2008.

See also ROOSEVELT, (ANNA) ELEANOR.

Basic Facts about the United Nations (New York: United Nations, 2000)

Meisler, Stanley. *United Nations: The First 50 Years* (New York: Atlantic Monthly Press, 1995)

Scott C. Monje

United States Air Force. See entries for individual wars.

United States Army. See entries for individual wars.

United States Coast Guard. This service dates from 1790, when the US Congress authorized 10 armed cutters for coastal patrols to collect tariffs and prevent smuggling. It was known first as the Revenue Marine and by 1863 as the Revenue Cutter Service. Duties expanded to include search and rescue, enforcing the laws against slave-carrying vessels and pirates, and serving under the US Navy in wartime. The US Life-Saving Service got its start in 1848 with the passage of the Newell Act, allotting federal funds to establish eight volunteer rescue stations along the New Jersey coast. The next year Congress allotted $20,000 more, which led to eight boathouses on Long Island and six more on the New Jersey coasts, equipped with surfboats, rockets, and cannonades, which projected a light line to a ship in distress. One of the first Life-Saving stations in New York was built on Fire Island in 1848; many more were built along the seacoast and on islands along the shore, all operated by volunteers called "surfmen." The volunteer keeper patrolled the shore, and if a shipwreck or vessel in distress were spotted, he had to assemble a rescue crew. By 1853 keepers in the houses began receiving pay, and by 1871 all crews were also paid. In 1878 the service was established as a separate agency; on 20 Jan 1915 Pres Woodrow Wilson signed legislation merging the Revenue Cutter and Life-Saving Services to form the US Coast Guard. The Lighthouse Service and Steamboat Inspection Service were merged with the Coast Guard in 1939, all under the Department of the Treasury.

The Port of New York and the state's inland waters have always had many Coast Guard facilities, especially in wartime: 30 between 1849 and 1875, 36 in 1917, down to 19 after 1950. During World War I, convoy escort cutters were based in Staten Island, horse patrols covered the beaches of Long Island against saboteurs, and port security was provided for munitions, troop, and cargo shipments. During World War II the Coast Guard operated a large training station at Manhattan Beach in Brooklyn, where more than 43,000 recruits were trained; 38,000 were apprentice seamen. The Manhattan Beach facility had the first significant number of blacks in training for the Coast Guard, more than 300 by late summer 1942. The military began training on helicopters for the first time in 1938 at the Coast Guard's Brooklyn Air Station with 21 of the Sikorsky HNS-1 and HOS-1 helicopters based at Floyd Bennett Field in Brooklyn. During World War II, the Women's Reserve of the Coast Guard, the SPARS (from an acronym created from the Coast Guard slogan, Semper Paratus, Always Ready) trained at a center at Hunter College in Manhattan.

Budget cuts and downsizing in the 1990s reduced the service's presence in New York State. The Brooklyn Air Station was deactivated in 1998 and the Coast Guard Support Center on Governors Island, which had taken over the facilities from the US Army in 1966, ceased operations there in 1997. The Marine Safety Office (MSO) Buffalo is the largest in the Ninth Coast Guard District, which encompasses the Great Lakes basin. Activities New York (ANY), in the First Coast Guard District, is the largest operational field command in the Coast Guard and is responsible for the Port of New York and the Hudson River–Champlain corridor. Station New York, located at Rosebank on Staten Island, and Station Rockaway in Queens Co are two Coast Guard stations actively engaged in search-and-rescue missions and are part of ANY. The service came under the newly formed federal Department of Transportation in 1967, and in March 2003 the Coast Guard became part of the Department of Homeland Security. The Coast Guard's duties included marine environmental protection, enforcement of laws and treaties, vessel inspections, drug and alien migrant interdiction, and search and rescue. Since 11 Sept 2001, Coast Guard units have also been charged with controlling the movement and anchorage of vessels in the country's navigable waters and up to 3 nautical miles (5.6 km) from the coast.

Johnson, Robert Erwin. *Guardian of the Sea: History of the United States Coast Guard, 1915 to the Present* (Annapolis, Md: Naval Institute Press, 1987)

Francis J. Duffy

United States Colored Troops. Men of African descent served with regular New York regiments since the early days of the Civil War. Pvt Reuben Dyer of Delhi (Delaware Co) served with the 89th New York Volunteers as early as September 1861; Pvt Bruce Anderson of Amsterdam (Montgomery Co) served with the 142d New York Volunteers and became a Medal of Honor recipient. New York State is credited with 4,125 of the black soldiers who served in the United States Colored Troops (USCT), established by the War Department on 22 May 1863.

On 3 Dec 1863 Secretary of War Edwin M. Stanton granted permission to the Union League Club of New York City to organize the 20th USCT, comprised primarily of New York residents. Seven hundred recruits trained at Rikers Island in New York City, the remaining 300 men necessary to complete the regiment at Elmira. Rev Henry Highland Garnet of the Shiloh Presbyterian Church acted as the men's temporary chaplain, while his wife, Julia Williams Garnet, supervised the Ladies Committee for the Aid of Sick Soldiers, a group of black women who provided medical care and meals to the soldiers. On 5 Mar 1864 the soldiers from Elmira joined the Rikers Island group to form the first black regiment sent to war from New York. Both *Harper's New Monthly Magazine* and *Frank Leslie's Illustrated Newspaper* recorded their departure. The men served under Col Nelson Bartram and Lt Col Andrew E. Mather. They received spiritual guidance from the black chaplain George W. LeVere. The regiment served in the Department of the East and in the Department of the Gulf's District of New Orleans and the southern Division of Louisiana.

Permission was granted by the War Department on 4 Jan 1864 for the Union League to organize its second regiment, the 26th Regiment USCT. The men of the 26th Regiment arrived at Rikers Island from multiple states, Canada, and Caribbean territories such as the Bahamas, Barbados, Haiti, Jamaica, and the Virgin Islands. Also among the rank and file were American Indians from Long Island and the New England states, and a small number of men of Asian descent. The regiment was under the command of Col William Silliman and Lt Col George B. Guernsey. The black chaplain, Benjamin F. Randolph, provided the men with spiritual guidance. On 27 Mar 1864 the men departed aboard the steamer *Warrior.* The regiment served, participating in major engagements, primarily near Beaufort, SC. The 26th Regiment lost 21 enlisted men and 5 officers killed in action, and 119 were wounded, captured, missing, or disabled. Among those killed in action were Col Silliman and Chaplain Randolph. Guernsey was promoted to colonel on 18 June 1865, approximately two months before the 26th was honorably discharged from service. The 20th USCT lost 2 officers and 283 enlisted men before mustering out in October 1865. USCT units were assigned to the unhealthiest posts and were inevitably given inferior medical care. The majority of the deaths occurred from sickness rather than from battle, with more than 106 of the 20th USCT soldiers buried in New Orleans.

About 2,000 black men from New York State enlisted in state regiments organized in Massachusetts, Connecticut, and Rhode Island, as well as with the Third USCT of Pennsylvania. Approximately 300 New York recruits were joined by three companies of the 30th Connecticut to form the 31st USCT, authorized in February 1864 and consolidated in June 1864. The 31st USCT was assigned to the 3d Brigade, 4th Division, 9th Army Corps. The regiment lost 136 officers and men on 30 July 1864 in the Battle of the Crater during the Siege of Petersburg in Virginia. The remaining soldiers were among the forces present at Gen Robert E. Lee's surrender at Appomattox. The regiment lost a total of 181 officers and men before its honorable discharge and mustering out in November 1865.

A proclamation honoring the memory of the US Colored Troops from New York was prepared by Gov George A. Pataki and presented by New York State senator James L. Seward to Harry Bradshaw Matthews in January 1998 at the USCT Memorial Symposium of Delaware and Otsego Cos. The USCT Institute for Local History and Family Research at Hartwick College in Oneonta (Otsego Co) continues the work of honoring the memory of the soldiers.

Enrollment Cards of the 26th United States Colored Troops Infantry Regiment. B0807. NYS Archives, Albany

Matthews, Harry Bradshaw. *Voices from the Front Line: New York's African American Statesmen of the Underground Railroad Freedom Trail and the United States Colored Troops Organized in the Empire State, 1863–1865, Roll Call: Men of the 20th USCT and 26th USCT* (Oneonta, NY: USCT Institute, Hartwick College, 2000)

Union League Club. *Report of the Committee on Volunteering* (New York: Author, 1864)

Harry Bradshaw Matthews

United States Constitution ratification. New York State was the 11th and final state to ratify the federal Constitution before it took effect. The remaining 2 states of the original 13, Rhode Island and North Carolina, delayed acceptance until after the new government took office. Aside from those two, New York State was the most strongly antifederal of all the states, and during the early months of 1788 it possibly was in a position to block the Constitution altogether. When it finally did ratify, the instrument declared the state's "full confidence" that amendments would follow swiftly.

Federalists, the group that favored the Constitution, were a distinct minority in New York State. When the ratifying convention gathered at Poughkeepsie in June 1788, they had only 19 delegates to the Antifederalists' 46. In an election with all free adult males eligible to vote, Federalists won only four counties: New York, Richmond, Kings, and Westchester. Arrayed against them was a coherent, well-organized group that centered on Gov George Clinton, who was serving his fourth consecutive three-year term and who once had been elected without opposition. Clinton was a delegate from his native Ulster Co, and he presided in Poughkeepsie. The forces tilting against each other in New York State had also done so in almost all the others. Federalism was the brainchild of the national elite that had emerged during the Revolution from mere provincial prominence. Its leaders had been wartime members of Congress, field-grade officers, and supply officers in the Continental army, functionaries in the wartime continental bureaucracy, and diplomats. Strangers for the most part when the Revolution unfolded, they made common cause and experienced the Revolution from the perspective of the center. Socioeconomically the leaders were men of capital, whether that took the form of urban money from law practices and businesses or rural money represented by great tenanted estates and speculative ventures. They were at home in the large world of major affairs. In New York their ranks included John Jay, Philip Schuyler, Robert R. Livingston, James Duane, Isaac Roosevelt, Lewis Morris, and Nicholas Low, whose family names were a virtual roll call of the patriot wing of the old New York elite. But they also were open to talent, as their reception of Alexander Hamilton, despite his totally obscure background, showed.

The Federalists did enjoy popular support, particularly in New York City. The city's artisans, seafarers, dockworkers, and small traders supported the Federalists because they understood that their future lay in being connected to the outside world, with the protection and stability that a strong government could provide. But they were not humble followers. They had learned during the Revolution to think for themselves and to calculate their own interests. They had clashed in the past with the Federalist leadership group and would do so again. But they understood that they were enmeshed in an ocean-spanning world, reaching to Europe, the rest of the Americas, and even as far as China. Their coalition with the Federalist leaders was precisely the configuration that held in Boston, Philadelphia, Baltimore, and Charleston. In fact every American city except Albany supported the Constitution.

Timing was a major aspect of ratification in all the states. Seeking momentum, Federalist leaders looked for the states where ratification would prove easiest, including New Jersey and Connecticut. Each resented New York State's taxing of their own trade for its sole benefit. Antifederalists sought delay, which is why New York State's convention did not convene until almost a year after the federal convention adjourned. When the Poughkeepsie meeting convened, eight states had already ratified the Constitution. Only one was therefore needed for it to take effect. But Rhode Island and North Carolina had refused to ratify it. Conventions also were sitting in Virginia and New Hampshire. A rejection by either, or by New York, might have provided enough momentum for Antifederalist triumphs in the other two, and the Constitution would have failed.

One of the great results of the ratification campaign in New York was the 85 *Federalist* essays, coauthored by Alexander Hamilton, John Jay, and Virginia's James Madison under the pseudonym Publius. Addressed to the "Considerate Citizens of the State of New York" and written to tight deadlines, *The Federalist* explored the social and political consequences of adopting the Constitution. The essays were not wholly original, but they do represent one of the triumphant moments in American political thinking and continue to be cited when courts expound the Constitution. Jay wrote only five of the essays; of the rest, Madison's contributions were focused primarily on political theory and Hamilton's on American potential for commercial development and military glory.

Despite the lopsided Antifederal majority, the convention did agree to a Federalist motion that it consider the Constitution clause by clause. The effect was a pause until either New Hampshire or Virginia acted. Copies of *The Federalist* and of Antifederal essays did circulate on the floor, but the major shift came when, against all expectations, New Hampshire ratified. That changed the problem to whether New York would participate in the new federal union. Talk circulated that if it

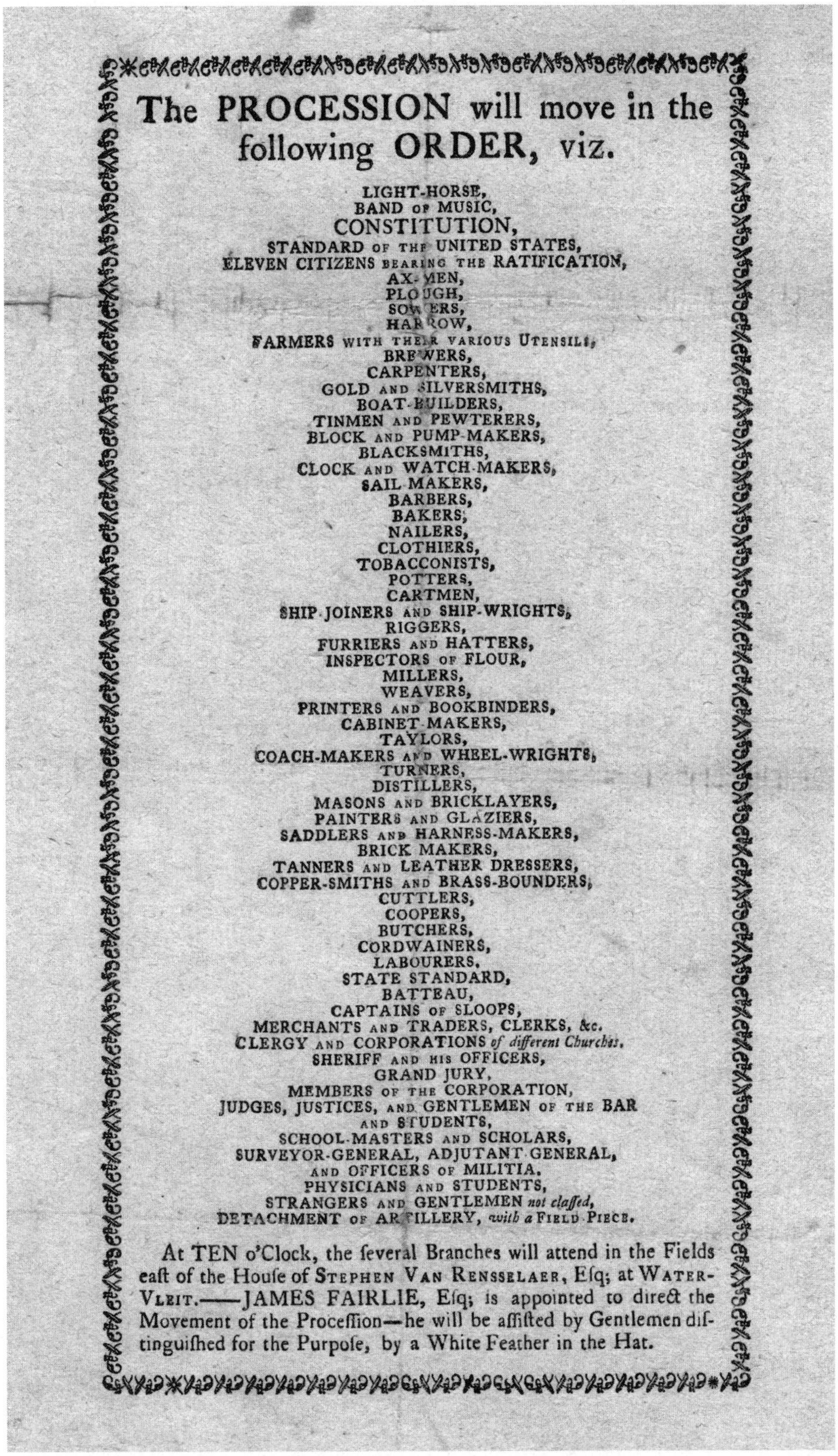

The PROCESSION will move in the following ORDER, viz.

LIGHT-HORSE,
BAND OF MUSIC,
CONSTITUTION,
STANDARD OF THE UNITED STATES,
ELEVEN CITIZENS BEARING THE RATIFICATION,
AX-MEN,
PLOUGH,
SOWERS,
HARROW,
FARMERS WITH THEIR VARIOUS UTENSILS,
BREWERS,
CARPENTERS,
GOLD AND SILVERSMITHS,
BOAT-BUILDERS,
TINMEN AND PEWTERERS,
BLOCK AND PUMP-MAKERS,
BLACKSMITHS,
CLOCK AND WATCH-MAKERS,
SAIL-MAKERS,
BARBERS,
BAKERS,
NAILERS,
CLOTHIERS,
TOBACCONISTS,
POTTERS,
CARTMEN,
SHIP-JOINERS AND SHIP-WRIGHTS,
RIGGERS,
FURRIERS AND HATTERS,
INSPECTORS OF FLOUR,
MILLERS,
WEAVERS,
PRINTERS AND BOOKBINDERS,
CABINET-MAKERS,
TAYLORS,
COACH-MAKERS AND WHEEL-WRIGHTS,
TURNERS,
DISTILLERS,
MASONS AND BRICKLAYERS,
PAINTERS AND GLAZIERS,
SADDLERS AND HARNESS-MAKERS,
BRICK MAKERS,
TANNERS AND LEATHER DRESSERS,
COPPER-SMITHS AND BRASS-BOUNDERS,
CUTTLERS,
COOPERS,
BUTCHERS,
CORDWAINERS,
LABOURERS,
STATE STANDARD,
BATTEAU,
CAPTAINS OF SLOOPS,
MERCHANTS AND TRADERS, CLERKS, &c.
CLERGY AND CORPORATIONS *of different Churches*,
SHERIFF AND HIS OFFICERS,
GRAND JURY,
MEMBERS OF THE CORPORATION,
JUDGES, JUSTICES, AND GENTLEMEN OF THE BAR
AND STUDENTS,
SCHOOL-MASTERS AND SCHOLARS,
SURVEYOR-GENERAL, ADJUTANT-GENERAL,
AND OFFICERS OF MILITIA,
PHYSICIANS AND STUDENTS,
STRANGERS AND GENTLEMEN *not claffed*,
DETACHMENT OF ARTILLERY, *with a* FIELD PIECE.

At TEN o'Clock, the feveral Branches will attend in the Fields eaft of the Houfe of STEPHEN VAN RENSSELAER, Efq; at WATER-VLEIT.——JAMES FAIRLIE, Efq; is appointed to direct the Movement of the Proceffion—he will be affifted by Gentlemen diftinguifhed for the Purpofe, by a White Feather in the Hat.

Broadside announcing parade in Albany to celebrate New York State's ratification of the federal constitution, 1788.

rejected the Constitution, the Southern District of Long Island, Manhattan, Staten Island, and Westchester would secede and ratify on its own. That may have had some effect, but amendments were the real problem.

The great Federalist fear was a conditional ratification, which raised the specter of reconvening the constitutional convention. Many possible amendments had been bruited in the press and raised in one state convention or another. The theme repeated most often was the need for a bill of rights. But the other states that accepted the Constitution did so unconditionally. New York's Federalist leaders proposed a formula of ratifying the Constitution "in full confidence" that amendments would be made later. A split developed within the Antifederalist majority. Some, including all the delegates from Albany, Columbia, and Ulster Cos, were absolutists. But another group was willing to accept the compromise. The final vote, on July 26, was 30 for ratification and 27 against.

Countryman, Edward. *A People in Revolution: The American Revolution and Political Society in New York, 1760–1790* (Baltimore: Johns Hopkins Univ Press, 1981)

De Pauw, Linda Grant. *The 11th Pillar: New York State and the Federal Constitution* (Ithaca: Cornell Univ Press, 1966)

Lynd, Staughton. *Anti-Federalism in Dutchess County, New York: A Study of Democracy and Class Conflict in the Revolutionary Era* (Chicago: Loyola Univ Press, 1962)

Young, Alfred F. *The Democratic Republicans of New York: The Origins, 1763–1797* (Chapel Hill: Univ of North Carolina Press, 1967)

Edward Countryman

United States House of Representatives.

From 1810 to 1970, New York State's delegation to the House of Representatives was the largest in that body. In the early 21st century it is still near the top in number of delegates.

Antebellum Representatives

During the first half of the 19th century representatives from New York State led the antislavery faction in the debate over the continuation and expansion of slavery in the United States. James Tallmadge Jr (1817–19), a Clintonian Republican, offered important antislavery amendments to the bill for Missouri statehood, prohibiting any more slaves brought into the territory. Fellow Clintonian John W. Taylor (1813–33) tried to extend Tallmadge's antislavery efforts and served as Speaker of the House in 1819 and 1825. Taylor is the only New Yorker to hold that position for more than one day. Whig representative Seth Gates (1839–43) opposed the "gag rule" that prevented antislavery petitions from being read on the floor of Congress. In 1846 Democrat Preston King (1843–47, 1849–53) helped draft and introduce the Wilmot Proviso, which attempted to outlaw slavery in territory gained during the Mexican-American War, along with Martin Grover (1845–47) and Timothy Jenkins (1845–49, 1851–53). King changed party allegiance and was elected as a Republican to the Senate in 1856. Whig Daniel Gott (1847–51) sought to eliminate the slave trade in Washington, DC, while Free Soil Party representative Gerrit Smith (1853–54) was perhaps the most radical New York State opponent of slavery in Congress.

Notable Republican Representatives

Conservative New Yorkers and Republican Party leaders in the House of Representatives include Sereno E. Payne (1883–87, 1889–1914), Bertrand Snell (1915–39), John Taber (1923–63), Daniel A. Reed (1919–59), Gerald Solomon (1979–99), and Jack Kemp (1971–89). Each of these men used their positions to urge less government action, less spending, and lower taxes. Hamilton Fish (1920–45) and James W. Wadsworth Jr (1933–51), as well as Reed, Snell, and Taber, vociferously opposed New Deal programs. Taber, as chair of the Appropriations Committee, deployed the largest staff the committee had to that date to search for spending cuts, and Kemp pursued a bill lowering tax rates titled the Kemp-Roth Bill in 1978.

Notable Democratic Representatives

New Yorkers have elected many influential liberals to the House of Representatives. During the 1930s Joseph Gavagan (1929–43) led the defense

SIZE AND RANK OF NEW YORK DELEGATION IN US HOUSE OF REPRESENTATIVES, 1788–2000

Census Year	NY Members	House Membership	% of Total	Rank
1788[a]	6	65	9.2	4[b]
1790	10	105	9.5	4[b]
1800	17	141	12.0	3
1810	27	181	14.9	1
1820	34	213	16.0	1
1830	40	240	16.7	1
1840	34	223	15.0	1
1850	33	234	14.1	1
1860	31	241	12.9	1
1870	33	292	11.3	1
1880	34	325	10.5	1
1890	34	356	9.6	1
1900	37	386	9.6	1
1910	43	435	9.9	1
1930[c]	45	435	10.3	1
1940	45	435	10.3	1
1950	43	435	9.9	1
1960	41	435	9.4	1
1970	39	435	9.0	2
1980	34	435	7.8	2
1990	31	435	7.1	2
2000	29	435	6.7	3

Source: K. Martis and G. Elmes, *The Historical Atlas of State Power in Congress, 1790–1990* (1993).

[a]1788 figures indicate apportionment prescribed by 1787 federal constitutional convention.

[b]Tie.

[c]There was no reapportionment after 1920 census.

Compiled by David I. Wells

of civil rights and proposed antilynching legislation. Adam Clayton Powell Jr (1945–67, 1969–71), the state's first African American member of Congress, worked to prevent the allocation of federal funds to those who discriminate. Shirley Chisholm (1969–83), the first African American woman to seek a major party presidential nomination, was also the first African American woman elected to Congress. A former daycare director, Chisholm, with Bella Abzug (1971–77), introduced legislation to provide extensive federal support for childcare. Abzug drew attention to a wide range of liberal causes, including civil rights, gay rights, decriminalization of marijuana, and opposition to the Vietnam War. Other opponents of the war included William Fitts Ryan (1961–72), Elizabeth Holtzman (1973–81), Allard Lowenstein (1969–71), and John Dow (1965–69, 1971–73), founder of Americans against Nuclear War.

Other Notables

At times, New York politicians blurred party lines. Not all Republican representatives, for example, were conservatives. Some supported organized labor. Republican Robert Bacon (1923–38) cosponsored the Davis-Bacon Act, which required payment of prevailing wages on government construction projects; Fiorello La Guardia (1917–33) cosponsored legislation restricting antiunion tactics. First elected as Republicans, La Guardia and his protégé Vito Marcantonio (1935–37, 1939–51) were closer politically to Socialist Meyer London (1915–19, 1921–23), advocating government action on behalf of the less fortunate, civil liberties, and civil rights. Marcantonio won reelection only after he left the Republican Party and accepted the American Labor Party (ALP) candidacy. Diligent constituent service ensured his repeated reelection as the ALP candidate through the 1940s.

Other party shifts involved John Lindsay (1959–65), Ogden Reid (1963–75), Peter Peyser (1971–77, 1979–83), and Michael Forbes (1995–2001); they had been elected originally as Republicans but later switched to the Democratic Party. Sherwood Boehlert (1983–) remains a Republican, while challenging his party's positions, particularly on environmental issues. Some Democrats have opposed their party, notably John J. O'Connor (1923–39), who obstructed New Deal proposals as Rules Committee Chair, leading to Franklin Roosevelt's successful campaign for O'Connor's defeat in the 1938 Democratic primary.

Four generations of the Hamilton Fish family served in the House of Representatives. Whig Hamilton Fish (1843–45) went on to become governor of New York State; his son Hamilton Fish culminated a distinguished political career with a House term (1909–11); and his grandson Hamilton Fish (1920–45) and great-grandson Hamilton Fish Jr (1969–95) each played important leadership roles in Congress during the 20th century.

Significant Events

Representatives from New York State played key roles in some of the House's most memorable proceedings. In the only presidential election decided in the House of Representatives, Stephen Van Rensselaer (1822–29) cast the decisive vote for John Quincy Adams on 9 Feb 1825. John Churchill (1867–71) cast the decisive vote in the Judiciary Committee to impeach Andrew Johnson in February 1868, and a century later Republican Hamilton Fish Jr voted in the Judiciary Committee to impeach Richard M. Nixon, as did Democrat Elizabeth Holtzman. Additionally, she urged the addition of impeachment charges related to the bombing of Cambodia and went to court seeking limitation of the president's war powers. Chairing a House Select Committee on Intelligence, Democrat Otis Pike (1961–79) led a controversial investigation into misdeeds of the Central Intelligence Agency, and Democrat Jerrold Nadler (1992–) prominently defended Bill Clinton on the Judiciary Committee during consideration of impeachment proceedings in 1998.

Not all New Yorkers have gained distinction in the House. During the 1850s William Gilbert (1855–57), Francis Edwards (1855–57), and Orsamus Matteson (1849–51, 1853–59) resigned after being implicated in bribery schemes. The House censured James Brooks (1849–53, 1863–66, 1867–73) after the Crédit Mobilier scandal in 1873. John Murphy (1963–81) was caught in the FBI's Abscam sting, and Mario Biaggi (1969–88) resigned because of a bribery case. Adam Clayton Powell Jr, Martin McKneally (1969–71), and Frederick Richmond (1975–82) were each charged with income tax evasion. Powell was cited for contempt of court in 1966 after refusing to pay damages from a previous lawsuit, and in 1967 the House voted to remove him from his seat.

Stepping Stone to Higher Office

Many New York State representatives went on to higher political office. Fernando Wood (1841–43, 1863–65, 1867–81), Abram Hewitt (1875–79, 1881–86), La Guardia, Lindsay, and Ed Koch (1969–77) won elections as mayors of New York City. William A. Wheeler (1861–63, 1869–77), Levi P. Morton (1879–81), and James S. Sherman (1887–91, 1893–1909) became vice presidents, and Millard Fillmore (1833–35, 1837–43), after being elected vice president, became president in 1850 to complete Zachary Taylor's term.

The last three New Yorkers to serve on a national ticket, all as vice presidential candidates in losing causes, were members (or former members) of the House of Representatives: William E. Miller (1951–65), the Republican candidate in 1964; Geraldine A. Ferraro (1979–85), the Democratic candidate in 1984; and Jack Kemp, the Republican candidate in 1996. Ferraro was the first woman, and through the 2004 election the only woman, nominated for a national office by a major political party.

MacNeil, Neil. *Forge of Democracy: The House of Representatives* (New York: D. McKay, 1963)

Ragsdale, Bruce A., ed. *Origins of the House of Representatives: A Documentary Record* (Washington, DC: Government Printing Office, 1990)

Joel Lefkowitz

United States Marines. See entries for individual wars.

United States Merchant Marine Academy (USMMA). Federal service academy in Kings Point (Nassau Co). Dedicated in 1943 by Pres Franklin D. Roosevelt on 82 acres (33 ha) of the former Walter P. Chrysler estate, it is operated by the US Department of Transportation's Maritime Administration. Fronting Little Neck Bay the campus includes 28 buildings, more than 120 vessels and small craft, and the US Merchant Marine Museum. The USMMA offers a four-year military and college curriculum, with BS degrees, merchant marine licenses, and Naval Reserve commissions awarded upon graduation. In 1974 the USMMA became the first federal service academy to enroll women. The student body numbered approximately 950 men and women in 2001.

"U.S. Merchant Marine Academy: A Half Century of Service," *Journal of Commerce* (Special Supplement), 30 Sept 1993

Joan Gay Kent

United States Military Academy (West Point).

Beginnings

In the years after the Revolutionary War, George Washington, Alexander Hamilton, Henry Knox, Baron Friedrich von Steuben, and others argued for the creation of a military academy to ensure that Americans acquired the technical skills of artillery and engineering. In 1802 Pres Thomas Jefferson signed legislation establishing a military academy at the site of the military post and Revolutionary War fortress at West Point (Orange Co), a site designed by French and Polish engineers and considered the key to the strategic Hudson River valley during the Revolution. The

View of the Hudson River from Battle Monument at Trophy Point at West Point.

US Military Academy, often known simply as West Point, became the nation's first service academy and engineering school. In its first decade, however, inadequate funding limited development. Sylvanus Thayer, who served as the commanding officer, or superintendent (1817–33), gathered a faculty who achieved national renown in the fields of mathematics, science, and engineering. He also established a four-year prescribed courses of study taught in small classes with daily recitations, academic practices that would persist at the academy well into the 20th century. Not only did cadets at West Point receive a technical education, but graduates wrote widely used texts and helped develop the nation's initial railroad lines, harbors, canals, roads, and bridges. Beginning in 1843 Congress required the academy to maintain a geographically representative student body, or Corps of Cadets.

The 19th Century

The military skills of graduates were demonstrated first in the War of 1812, the Seminole Indian Wars, and, particularly, the Mexican War. Many graduates, serving as junior officers in the Mexican War, won accolades for their skill and service to the nation. Hundreds of academy graduates served as general officers for both the Union and Confederacy during the Civil War. Gens Ulysses S. Grant, William Sherman, and Philip Sheridan were leaders of the Union forces, while Gens Robert E. Lee and Thomas "Stonewall" Jackson were leaders of the Confederate armies. Jefferson Davis, class of 1828, became president of the Confederacy.

In the decades after the Civil War, the academy, once at the forefront of American institutions, began to fall behind because it relied on established practices and did not keep up with advances in science and technology. At the same time the quality and variety of military instruction offered was inhibited by the inadequacy of land to conduct training.

The first African Americans attended West Point after the Civil War but faced hostility and ostracism from their fellow cadets. In 1877 Henry Ossian Flipper became the first black graduate. Charles Young, who in 1889 became the third black graduate, was subsequently the highest-ranking African American officer in the army until World War I. He was the last African American West Point graduate until Benjamin O. Davis Jr, class of 1936, who later would become the first Black to reach the rank of lieutenant general.

From 1900 to the 1930s

By the turn of the century, although academic and military practices became bound to tradition, the academy expanded in the area of physical fitness. Spurred by Pres Theodore Roosevelt's advocacy of the vigorous life, physical development was required of cadets throughout their cadetship. The superintendency of Douglas MacArthur (1919–22) further enhanced the recognition of the importance of physical proficiency just after World War I. He advocated the concept of "every cadet an athlete" and sought to expand on previous efforts to broaden the curriculum beyond math, science, and engineering. He also formalized the cadet honor system, further enhancing a vital component of military professionalism that had been promoted from the earliest days of the institution. During the 1930s limitations posed by the physically constricted environment were overcome when the federal government acquired thousands of undeveloped acres to the south in the neighboring Town of Highlands (Orange Co). The additional land enabled the academy to expand greatly on-site military training opportunities. At the same time, much of the territory was kept in a relatively natural state, and it provided for a generally undeveloped buffer with other park areas in the Hudson Highlands. Annual federal impact aid compensated for the loss of tax base, and the academy made its facilities available to the surrounding communities for activities such as regional tournaments for local athletic teams and blood drives.

Since the 1940s

By World War II contributions of the graduates of the Reserve Officer's Training Corps provided thousands of officers. Yet, once again, academy graduates like MacArthur, Dwight D. Eisenhower, Omar N. Bradley, and George Patton were the most powerful generals. After the war, during the superintendency of Maxwell Taylor (1945–49), the curriculum was expanded, enhancing leadership training and providing instruction, for the first time, in the psychology of the American soldier. In the last decades of the 20th century, the curriculum was further broadened to provide a balance between traditional mathematics, science, and engineering courses and humanities and public affairs courses. The first female cadets entered the academy in 1976. During the 1980s cadets, who are prepared to become second lieutenants in the US Army, gained the opportunity to select academic majors. The Military Academy's Corps of Cadets began with 10 cadets in 1802 and grew to 250 by 1812 and to 500 by 1900. Enrollment reached a high of 4,400 in the 1960s and since the 1990s has been about 4,000.

The academy has become a major tourist destination in the mid–Hudson Valley, receiving over 2.5 million visitors annually. Notable structures on the campus include the superintendent's residence, known as Quarters 100 (1820), the Greek- and Roman-styled Old Cadet Chapel (1836); the Gothic-styled New Cadet Chapel (1910), which houses the world's largest church organ; the Headquarters building (1909); and Michie Stadium (1924), the site of Army football games, which seats 40,000 people. Statuary on the Parade Ground includes monuments honoring Sylvanus Thayer (1883), George Washington (1916), and Dwight D. Eisenhower (1983). A monument honoring Thaddeus Kosciuszko (1828, 1913) overlooks the Hudson River at the site of the Revolutionary Era Fort Clinton that he helped construct (1778–80). The West Point Museum, housed on academy grounds and first opened to the public in 1854, holds over 45,000 artifacts related to the nation's military history.

See also Army football.

Ambrose, Stephen. *Duty, Honor, Country* (1966; repr Baltimore: Johns Hopkins Univ Press, 1999)
Crackel, Theodore J. *West Point: A Bicentennial History* (Lawrence: Univ Press of Kansas, 2002)

Stephen B. Grove

United States Navy. See entries for individual wars.

United States Sanitary Commission. Civilian medical relief organization during the Civil War. At a time when more soldiers died from disease than from enemy weapons, disease prevention was the self-appointed task of the United States Sanitary Commission (USSC). In April 1861 Dr Elizabeth Blackwell, with the support of Unitarian minister Henry Whitney Bellows, founded the New York City–based Women's Central Association of Relief (WCAR). Bellows traveled to Washington, DC, in May to seek government recognition for the WCAR and to establish a link between the organization and the army. While there, his plans for the aid organization evolved to include a sanitary commission, inspired by the British commission that had reduced British army mortality and morbidity during the Crimean War. On 9 June 1861 Secretary of War Simon Cameron approved the USSC. Bellows served as president.

The standard of medical care within the army was low. Army hospitals were overcrowded, undersupplied, and generally inadequate. The soldiers' diet was poor, infectious disease epidemics were common, and little attention was given to sanitary arrangements within the camps. The USSC targeted each of these deficiencies and lobbied successfully for improvements within the Army Medical Bureau, including the appointment of its preferred candidate as surgeon general. The organization also distributed relief supplies, trained nurses, transported wounded soldiers, produced medical monographs, constructed and administered hospitals and soldiers' homes, and kept a directory of wounded soldiers.

The USSC board, whose members included lawyer George Templeton Strong and municipal public health leader Dr Elisha Harris, held weekly meetings in Manhattan. Louisa Schuyler chaired the WCAR, which centralized the collection of relief supplies and money for distribution by the USSC. During the later war years, women organized sanitary fairs locally to raise money for the USSC. Fairs in Rochester, Brooklyn, Albany, and Poughkeepsie in 1863–64 raised hundreds of thousands of dollars. The largest New York fair, the April 1864 Metropolitan Fair in Manhattan, raised over $1 million. A USSC representative attended the Geneva convention of 1864 that resulted in the founding of the International Red Cross and shared information about the activities and organization of the USSC. After the war USSC branches closed, and unused supplies were distributed to the poor in New York State and the southern states. The USSC itself was formally dissolved on 8 May 1878.

Maxwell, William Q. *Lincoln's Fifth Wheel: The Political History of the United States Sanitary Commission* (New York: Longmans, Green, 1956)

The Sanitary Commission of the United States Army: A Succinct Narrative of Its Works and Purposes (1864; repr New York: Arno Press and New York Times, 1972)

Ellen Sexton

United States Senate. The US Constitution initially provided for the election of two senators by the legislature from each state. Since passage of a 1913 constitutional amendment, senators have been directly elected by the people of their state.

Early Senators and Scandals

Rufus King (1789–96, 1813–25) and Philip Schuyler (1789–91, 1797–98), the first two senators from New York State, were prominent in early national politics and supported the Federalist policies of Alexander Hamilton. In his second stint as a senator, King was a forceful supporter of the antislavery movement and in 1820 led opposition to the Missouri Compromise. Other senators from New York State were also involved in debates over slavery. Although better remembered as US secretary of state, William H. Seward (1849–61) led opposition to the Compromise of 1850.

New York senators have often been concerned with patronage appointments, as exemplified by William Marcy and his famous declaration: "nothing wrong with the rule that to the victor belongs the spoils." In 1881 Sens Roscoe Conkling (1867–81) and Thomas C. Platt (1881,

US SENATORS FROM NEW YORK

Name	Dates of Service	Residence
Philip Schuyler (F)	1789–91; 1797–98	Albany
Rufus King (F)	1789–96; 1813–25	New York City
Aaron Burr (DR)	1791–97	New York City
John Laurance (F)	1796–1800	Queens
John Sloss Hobart (F)	1798	Huntington (Suffolk Co)
William North (F)	1798	Duanesburg (Schenectady Co)
James Watson (F)	1798–1800	New York City
Gouverneur Morris (F)	1800–1803	Morrisania (Westchester Co)
John Armstrong Jr (JR)	1800–1804	Rhinebeck (Dutchess Co)
De Witt Clinton (JR)	1802–3	Newtown (Queens Co)
Theodorus Bailey (JR)	1803–4	Poughkeepsie
John Smith (JR)	1804–13	Brookhaven (Suffolk Co)
Samuel Latham Mitchill (JR)	1804–9	New York City
Obadiah German (JR)	1809–15	Norwich (Chenango Co)
Rufus King (F)	1813–20	Jamaica (Queens Co)
Nathan Sanford (CR, A, AJ)	1815–21; 1826–31	New York City
Martin Van Buren (VBR, JD)	1821–28	Kinderhook (Columbia Co)
Charles Dudley (JD)	1829–33	Albany
William L. Marcy (JD)	1831–33	Albany
Silas Wright (JD, D)	1833–44	Canton (St. Lawrence Co)
Nathaniel P. Tallmadge (JD, W)	1833–44	Poughkeepsie
Henry A. Foster (D)	1844–45	Rome (Oneida Co)
Daniel S. Dickinson (D)	1844–51	Binghamton
John Adams Dix (D)	1845–49	Albany
William H. Seward (W, O, R)	1849–61	Auburn (Cayuga Co)
Hamilton Fish (W, O)	1851–57	New York City
Preston King (R)	1857–63	Ogdensburg (St. Lawrence Co)
Ira Harris (R)	1861–67	Albany
Edwin D. Morgan (R)	1863–69	New York City
Roscoe Conkling (R)	1867–81	Utica
Reuben E. Fenton (R, LR)	1869–75	Jamestown (Chautauqua Co)
Francis Kernan (D)	1875–81	Utica
Thomas C. Platt (R)	1881; 1897–1909	Owego (Tioga Co)
Warner Miller (R)	1881–87	Herkimer
Elbridge G. Lapham (R)	1881–85	Canandaigua (Ontario Co)
William M. Evarts (R)	1885–91	New York City
Frank Hiscock (R)	1887–93	Syracuse
David B. Hill (D)	1892–97	Elmira
Edward Murphy Jr (D)	1893–99	Troy (Rensselaer Co)
Chauncey M. Depew (R)	1899–1911	New York City
Elihu Root (R)	1909–15	New York City
James A. O'Gorman (D)	1911–17	New York City
James W. Wadsworth Jr (R)	1915–27	Geneseo (Livingston Co)
William M. Calder (R)	1917–23	Brooklyn
Royal S. Copeland (D)	1923–38	New York City
Robert F. Wagner Sr (D)	1927–49	New York City
James M. Mead (D)	1938–47	Buffalo
Irving M. Ives (R)	1947–59	Norwich (Chenango Co)
John Foster Dulles (R)	1949	New York City
Herbert H. Lehman (D)	1949–57	New York City
Jacob K. Javits (R)	1957–81	New York City
Kenneth B. Keating (R)	1959–65	Rochester
Robert F. Kennedy (D)	1965–68	New York City
Charles E. Goodell (R)	1968–71	Jamestown
James L. Buckley (C)	1971–77	New York City
Daniel Patrick Moynihan (D)	1977–2001	West Davenport (Delaware Co)
Alfonse M. D'Amato (R)	1981–99	Island Park (Nassau Co)
Charles Schumer (D)	1999–	Brooklyn
Hillary Rodham Clinton (D)	2001–	Chappaqua (Westchester Co)

Abbreviations: A: Adams; AJ: Anti-Jacksonian; C: Conservative; D: Democrat; DR: Democratic-Republican; F: Federalist; J: Jacksonian; JD: Jacksonian Democrat; JR: Jeffersonian Republican; LR: Liberal Republican; O: Opposition; R: Republican; W: Whig.

SENATORIAL ELECTIONS

1914	James W. Gerard (Dem/Ind League)	**James W. Wadsworth Jr** (Rep)	Bainbridge Colby (Prog)	Charles Edward Russell (Soc)	Other	Total
NYC	311,576	191,241	22,506	35,647	56,818	617,788
Downstate Suburban	35,957	43,688	4,832	1,382	5,963	91,822
Upstate Urban	69,061	128,407	9,953	5,897	22,619	235,937
Upstate Nonurban	154,825	275,776	24,686	12,340	48,808	516,435
Total State	571,419	639,112	61,977	55,266	134,208	1,461,982

1916	William F. McCombs (Dem/Amer)	**William M. Calder** (Rep)	Joseph D. Cannon (Soc)	Other	Total
NYC	281,698	309,058	44,927	76,803	712,486
Downstate Suburban	36,353	62,394	1,547	9,197	109,491
Upstate Urban	90,047	143,807	5,804	30,110	269,768
Upstate Nonurban	197,835	324,055	8,889	81,513	612,292
Total State	605,933	839,314	61,167	197,623	1,704,037

1920	Harry C. Walker (Dem)	**James W. Wadsworth Jr** (Rep)	Jacob Panken (Soc)	Ella Boole (Proh)	Other	Total
NYC	452,085	562,361	145,498	18,625	93,391	1,271,960
Downstate Suburban	55,780	122,616	7,417	8,310	18,482	212,605
Upstate Urban	130,184	237,996	28,124	25,763	33,980	456,047
Upstate Nonurban	263,261	511,420	27,116	106,925	73,473	982,195
Total State	901,310	1,434,393	208,155	159,623	219,326	2,922,807

1922	**Royal S. Copeland** (Dem)	William M. Calder (Rep)	Algernon Lee (Soc/Farmer Labor)	Other	Total
NYC	697,728	290,328	75,422	58,056	1,121,534
Downstate Suburban	80,907	87,731	5,927	13,366	187,931
Upstate Urban	179,744	180,976	19,202	35,892	415,814
Upstate Nonurban	318,288	436,386	17,377	80,094	852,145
Total State	1,276,667	995,421	117,928	187,408	2,577,424

1926	**Robert F. Wagner Sr** (Dem)	James W. Wadsworth Jr (Rep)	F. W. Cristman (Ind Rep)	Other	Total
NYC	769,998	392,244	19,456	95,218	1,276,916
Downstate Suburban	86,380	129,331	13,397	14,988	244,096
Upstate Urban	181,063	238,594	38,586	43,554	501,797
Upstate Nonurban	284,022	445,077	160,467	61,885	951,451
Total State	1,321,463	1,205,246	231,906	215,645	2,974,260

1928	**Royal S. Copeland** (Dem)	Alanson B. Houghton (Rep)	Other	Total
NYC	1,178,649	631,248	165,158	1,975,055
Downstate Suburban	148,503	230,194	25,155	403,852
Upstate Urban	301,860	363,365	56,125	721,350
Upstate Nonurban	455,261	809,207	100,637	1,365,105
Total State	2,084,273	2,034,014	347,075	4,465,362

1932	**Robert F. Wagner Sr** (Dem)	George Z. Medalie (Rep)	Other	Total
NYC	1,440,544	517,991	296,734	2,255,269
Downstate Suburban	214,206	229,708	32,012	475,926
Upstate Urban	361,401	317,653	67,207	746,261
Upstate Nonurban	516,754	685,834	128,693	1,331,281
Total State	2,532,905	1,751,186	524,646	4,808,737

1934	**Royal S. Copeland** (Dem)	E. Harold Cluett (Rep)	Norman Thomas (Soc)	Other	Total
NYC	1,124,219	383,206	128,824	69,901	1,706,150
Downstate Suburban	159,709	185,139	14,105	5,929	364,882
Upstate Urban	342,707	248,171	20,546	7,108	618,532
Upstate Nonurban	419,742	546,924	31,477	10,090	1,008,233
Total State[a]	2,046,377	1,363,440	194,952	93,028	3,932,601

continued on page 1614

SENATORIAL ELECTIONS (continued)

1938[b]	**James M. Mead** (Dem/Amer Labor)	Edward F. Corsi (Rep/Ind Prog)	Harry W. Laidler (Soc)	Total
NYC	1,487,423	673,744	19,475	2,180,642
Downstate Suburban	164,702	303,381	1,608	469,691
Upstate Urban	359,978	362,346	2,675	724,999
Upstate Nonurban	426,801	744,195	3,403	1,174,399
Total State[a]	2,438,904	2,083,666	27,161	4,813,039

1938[c]	**Robert F. Wagner Sr** (Dem/Amer Labor)	John Lord O'Brien (Rep/Ind Prog)	Other	Total
NYC	1,551,993	625,015	18,778	2,195,786
Downstate Suburban	173,232	298,925	1,519	473,676
Upstate Urban	337,157	385,240	2,850	725,247
Upstate Nonurban	434,647	749,435	4,257	1,188,339
Total State[a]	2,497,029	2,058,615	27,404	4,815,533

1940	**James M. Mead** (Dem/Amer Labor)	Bruce Barton (Rep)	Other	Total
NYC	1,997,698	1,152,189	162,528	3,312,415
Downstate Suburban	229,146	401,801	10,381	641,328
Upstate Urban	466,874	423,253	26,620	916,747
Upstate Nonurban	581,048	891,609	64,842	1,537,499
Total State	3,274,766	2,868,852	264,371	6,407,989

1944	**Robert F. Wagner Sr** (Dem/Lib/Amer Labor)	Thomas J. Curran (Rep)	Other	Total
NYC	2,050,818	1,226,116	11,046	3,287,980
Downstate Suburban	231,120	412,030	632	643,782
Upstate Urban	451,663	432,024	1,417	885,104
Upstate Nonurban	560,975	829,327	2,149	1,392,451
Total State[a]	3,294,576	2,899,497	15,244	6,415,918

1946	Herbert H. Lehman (Dem/Lib/Amer Labor)	**Irving M. Ives** (Rep)	Other	Total
NYC	1,493,553	1,008,269	96,808	2,598,630
Downstate Suburban	148,196	379,876	14,353	542,425
Upstate Urban	303,463	425,882	25,723	755,068
Upstate Nonurban	362,900	745,338	41,810	1,150,048
Total State	2,308,112	2,559,365	178,694	5,046,171

1949	**Herbert H. Lehman** (Dem/Lib)	John Foster Dulles (Rep)	Other	Total
NYC	1,586,316	797,857	272,151	2,656,324
Downstate Suburban	190,972	372,852	18,188	582,012
Upstate Urban	375,258	422,350	35,469	833,077
Upstate Nonurban	429,892	791,322	68,466	1,289,680
Total State	2,582,438	2,384,381	394,274	5,361,093

1950	**Herbert H. Lehman** (Dem/Lib)	Joe R. Hanley (Rep)	W. E. B. DuBois (Amer Labor)	Other	Total
NYC	1,534,917	821,572	165,599	183,148	2,705,236
Downstate Suburban	242,834	382,994	10,484	17,505	653,817
Upstate Urban	392,752	392,437	11,986	25,371	822,546
Upstate Nonurban	461,810	770,350	17,660	41,629	1,291,449
Total State	2,632,313	2,367,353	205,729	267,653	5,473,048

1952	John Cashmore (Dem)	**Irving M. Ives** (Rep)	George S. Counts (Lib)	Other	Total
NYC	1,418,601	1,421,074	404,769	99,103	3,343,547
Downstate Suburban	246,931	679,204	37,779	7,413	971,327
Upstate Urban	402,109	609,065	16,981	3,346	1,031,501
Upstate Nonurban	454,095	1,144,591	30,246	4,936	1,633,868
Total State[a]	2,521,736	3,853,934	489,775	114,798	7,216,054

SENATORIAL ELECTIONS (continued)

1956	Robert F. Wagner Jr (Dem/Lib)	**Jacob K. Javits** (Rep)	Other	Total
NYC	1,783,008	1,340,730	97,440	3,221,178
Downstate Suburban	425,390	741,176	23,867	1,190,433
Upstate Urban	485,674	571,463	28,803	1,085,940
Upstate Nonurban	571,087	1,070,564	48,206	1,689,857
Total State	3,265,159	3,723,933	198,316	7,187,408

1958	Frank S. Hogan (Dem/Lib)	**Kenneth B. Keating** (Rep)	Other	Total
NYC	1,423,608	849,600	119,959	2,393,167
Downstate Suburban	389,239	640,871	33,578	1,063,688
Upstate Urban	402,318	498,598	35,624	936,540
Upstate Nonurban	494,785	853,873	53,576	1,402,234
Total State	2,709,950	2,842,942	242,737	5,795,629

1962	James B. Donovan (Dem)	**Jacob K. Javits** (Rep)	Other	Total
NYC	977,539	1,228,142	276,168	2,481,849
Downstate Suburban	312,907	730,162	85,491	1,128,560
Upstate Urban	394,035	470,397	71,122	935,554
Upstate Nonurban	429,291	843,716	102,533	1,375,540
Total State	2,113,772	3,272,417	535,314	5,921,503

1964	**Robert F. Kennedy** (Dem/Lib)	Kenneth B. Keating (Rep)	Other	Total
NYC	1,779,992	1,068,943	225,263	3,074,198
Downstate Suburban	647,703	709,193	83,422	1,440,318
Upstate Urban	593,344	492,339	23,599	1,109,282
Upstate Nonurban	802,710	833,581	44,401	1,680,692
Total State	3,823,749	3,104,056	376,685	7,304,490

1968	Paul O'Dwyer (Dem)	**Jacob K. Javits** (Rep/Lib)	James L. Buckley (Cons)	Other	Total
NYC	906,663	1,112,353	475,665	225,096	2,719,777
Downstate Suburban	356,585	764,354	352,223	51,013	1,524,175
Upstate Urban	404,715	520,276	122,021	47,983	1,094,995
Upstate Nonurban	482,732	872,789	189,493	75,649	1,620,663
Total State	2,150,695	3,269,772	1,139,402	399,741	6,959,610

1970	Richard L. Ottinger (Dem)	Charles E. Goodell (Rep/Lib)	**James L. Buckley** (Cons)	Other	Total
NYC	979,328	439,452	731,023	209,425	2,359,228
Downstate Suburban	430,942	269,372	609,812	48,787	1,358,913
Upstate Urban	342,996	279,124	322,037	37,258	981,415
Upstate Nonurban	417,966	446,524	516,768	69,663	1,450,921
Total State	2,171,232	1,434,472	2,179,640	365,133	6,150,477

1974	Ramsey Clark (Dem)	**Jacob K. Javits** (Rep/Lib)	Barbara A. Keating (Cons)	Other	Total
NYC	718,295	683,360	241,808	202,842	1,846,305
Downstate Suburban	397,175	590,447	258,327	61,994	1,307,943
Upstate Urban	366,059	384,864	121,269	55,839	928,031
Upstate Nonurban	492,252	681,517	201,180	86,426	1,461,375
Total State	1,973,781	2,340,188	822,584	407,101	5,543,654

1976	**Daniel P. Moynihan** (Dem/Lib)	James L. Buckley (Rep/Cons)	Other	Total
NYC	1,427,434	598,410	204,483	2,230,327
Downstate Suburban	776,334	761,960	58,582	1,596,876
Upstate Urban	530,737	515,583	58,745	1,105,065
Upstate Nonurban	688,089	960,680	85,838	1,734,607
Total State	3,422,594	2,836,633	407,648	6,666,875

continued on page 1616

SENATORIAL ELECTIONS (continued)

1980	Elizabeth Holtzman (Dem)	**Alfonse M. D'Amato** (Rep/Cons/RTL)	Jacob K. Javits (Lib)	Other	Total
NYC	1,065,788	568,958	208,731	169,597	2,013,074
Downstate Suburban	601,200	744,752	145,162	46,188	1,537,302
Upstate Urban	393,498	500,029	128,903	56,357	1,078,787
Upstate Nonurban	558,175	885,913	181,748	103,273	1,729,109
Total State	2,618,661	2,699,652	664,544	375,415	6,358,272

1982	**Daniel P. Moynihan** (Dem/Lib)	Florence Sullivan (Rep/Cons/RTL)	Other	Total
NYC	1,146,137	296,958	243,559	1,686,654
Downstate Suburban	719,197	500,559	79,660	1,299,416
Upstate Urban	578,311	288,281	69,834	936,426
Upstate Nonurban	788,501	610,963	117,007	1,516,471
Total State	3,232,146	1,696,761	510,060	5,438,967

1986	Mark Green (Dem)	**Alfonse M. D'Amato** (Rep/Cons/RTL)	Other	Total
NYC	649,071	464,618	176,928	1,290,617
Downstate Suburban	379,249	639,345	52,934	1,071,528
Upstate Urban	299,864	460,950	60,874	821,688
Upstate Nonurban	395,032	813,284	92,710	1,301,026
Total State	1,723,216	2,378,197	383,446	4,484,859

1988	**Daniel P. Moynihan** (Dem/Lib)	Robert R. McMillan (Rep/Cons)	Other	Total
NYC	1,485,651	348,071	292,546	2,126,268
Downstate Suburban	879,954	606,467	123,262	1,609,683
Upstate Urban	720,595	271,766	108,597	1,100,958
Upstate Nonurban	962,449	649,480	186,615	1,798,544
Total State	4,048,649	1,875,784	711,020	6,635,453

1992	Robert Abrams (Dem/Lib)	**Alfonse M. D'Amato** (Rep/Cons/RTL)	Other	Total
NYC	1,202,725	741,113	267,635	2,211,473
Downstate Suburban	664,364	905,734	134,700	1,704,798
Upstate Urban	497,676	515,423	161,111	1,174,210
Upstate Nonurban	721,435	1,004,724	262,165	1,988,324
Total State	3,086,200	3,166,994	825,611	7,078,805

1897–1909) resigned their seats in a prolonged losing battle with Pres James A. Garfield over appointment, particularly the nominee for the position of collector of the Port of New York. The 1906 *Cosmopolitan* magazine exposé "Treason of the Senate" began by attacking New York senator Chauncey Depew (1899–1911) for his corporate connections and his role in insurance scandals. Although Theodore Roosevelt derided this journalistic effort in coining the term "muckraker," the series was well received in the era of Progressive reform. The articles espoused the benefits of direct election of senators by the general population, which would make them accountable to their constituents and prevent corruption. Despite much popular support for changing the mode of selection, Depew pursued legislative tactics that delayed the 17th Amendment, which was ultimately adopted in 1913.

Modern Liberalism

Some of the most influential liberal senators of the 20th century have hailed from New York State. Among them Robert F. Wagner Sr (1927–49) is the only New Yorker among the Famous Seven senators whose importance has been acknowledged with official portraits in the Senate Reception Room. Wagner won his first term by defeating conservative Republican James W. Wadsworth Jr (1915–27) in a three-way race in 1926. Wagner authored many New Deal legislative initiatives and is best known for the 1935 National Labor Relations Act (Wagner Act), which committed the federal government to protecting the right of workers to form unions and to opposing unfair employer practices. Wagner also sponsored major legislation to assist retirees, the unemployed, and veterans, and to fund public housing. Democrat Herbert H. Lehman (1949–57), elected to fill the seat vacated by Wagner in 1949, maintained a liberal stance, criticizing McCarthyism during his tenure.

During the 1960s liberal senators from New York State maintained influence. Robert F. Kennedy (1965–68) sought to advance the federal commitment to supporting the poor. Kennedy held Senate subcommittee hearings in Mississippi documenting poverty and hunger there. He also drew attention to the plight of Native Americans and the cause of striking farmworkers in California. After Kennedy's assassination, his successor, Charles E. Goodell (1968–70), became a leading Republican critic of the Vietnam War. In response to the conduct of the war, liberal Republican Jacob Javits (1957–81) promoted passage of the War Powers Act, intended to reassert congressional authority over war making, and also advanced federal support for the arts. In the last two decades of the 20th century, Daniel P. Moynihan (1977–2001) drew attention to the extent to which New York State residents' federal tax contributions outweighed the state's share of national spending. Best known as a critic of welfare policy, Moynihan also criticized welfare changes adopted in 1996 for abandoning federal commitments to the poor.

Modern Conservatism

Republican conservative Elihu Root became a senator (1909–15) after having already served as US secretary of war and of state. During his term in the Senate, Root took an active role in settling

SENATORIAL ELECTIONS (continued)

1994	**Daniel P. Moynihan** (Dem/Lib)	Bernadette Castro (Rep/Tax Cut Now/Cons)	Other	Total
NYC	957,178	322,735	297,975	1,577,888
Downstate Suburban	586,270	564,641	110,767	1,261,678
Upstate Urban	462,759	345,684	97,807	906,250
Upstate Nonurban	640,334	755,248	187,088	1,582,670
Total State	2,646,541	1,988,308	693,637	5,328,486

1998	**Charles Schumer** (Dem/Lib/Ind)	Alfonse M. D'Amato (Rep/Cons/RTL)	Other	Total
NYC	1,045,175	354,529	137,306	1,537,010
Downstate Suburban	551,815	576,785	47,626	1,176,226
Upstate Urban	411,515	352,716	73,387	837,618
Upstate Nonurban	542,560	774,958	121,505	1,439,023
Total State	2,551,065	2,058,988	379,824	4,989,877

2000	**Hillary Rodham Clinton** (Dem/Lib/Wrkg Fam)	Rick Lazio (Rep/Cons)	Other	Total
NYC	1,604,949	548,460	114,863	2,268,272
Downstate Suburban	742,758	876,998	58,022	1,677,778
Upstate Urban	579,036	483,605	40,752	1,103,393
Upstate Nonurban	820,567	1,006,667	82,985	1,910,219
Total State	3,747,310	2,915,730	296,622	6,959,662

Sources: ICPSR Election Returns for New York; *Manual for the Use of the Legislature of the State of New York;* New York State Board of Elections; *New York Red Book.*

Notes: Winners' names appear in bold. Regional designations are as follows: NYC: Bronx , Kings (Brooklyn), New York (Manhattan), Richmond (Staten Island), Queens Cos; Downstate Suburban: Nassau, Rockland, Suffolk, Westchester Cos; Upstate Urban: Albany, Erie, Monroe, Onondaga Cos; Upstate Nonurban: remainder of counties.

[a]Sources did not print the breakdown of the blank, void, and scattered vote by county for this election. As a result, these votes are not included in the "other" column or the regional total columns, but are counted in the total state vote tally.

[b]Unexpired term ending 1940.

[c]Full term.

North Atlantic fishery disputes and pressed for international arbitration; in 1912 he won the Nobel Peace Prize for his efforts at international understanding. James W. Wadsworth Jr represented New York State conservatives in the Senate during World War I and the 1920s. Wadsworth, a strong proponent of limiting federal powers, did not think it was within the national government's purview to ban lynching, child labor, or alcohol. He lost his seat when a Prohibition candidate drew more than the difference in votes between him and liberal Democrat Robert F. Wagner Sr in traditionally Republican areas of New York State. However, three-way races led to victory for Conservative James L. Buckley (1971–77) in 1970 and for Republican Alphonse D'Amato (1981–99) in 1980. Buckley successfully opposed campaign finance legislation in court. D'Amato was criticized by the Senate Ethics Committee and the press for ethical lapses, and his efforts at bringing benefits to New York State led to the nickname Senator Pothole.

New York State Notables

Four senators—King, Wagner, Javits, and Moynihan—share the record for New Yorkers of serving four terms in the US Senate. King and Gouverneur Morris (1800–1803) represented other states at the constitutional convention, and then—as Buckley, Kennedy, and Hillary Rodham Clinton (2001–) did some 200 years later—moved to New York State before being elected to the US Senate. Among those senators better known for other activities are Gov De Witt Clinton (1802–3), Pres Martin Van Buren (1821–28), Vice Pres Aaron Burr (1791–97), First Lady Hillary Clinton, and US Secretaries of State John Foster Dulles (1949) and Elihu Root. Three US senators—William L. Marcy (1831–33), Hamilton Fish (1851–57), and Seward—also served as both New York State governor and US secretary of state.

Huthmacher, J. Joseph. *Senator Robert F. Wagner and the Rise of Urban Liberalism* (New York: Atheneum, 1968)

Mayhew, David R. *America's Congress: Actions in the Public Sphere, James Madison through Newt Gingrich* (New Haven, Conn: Yale Univ Press, 2000)

Joel Lefkowitz

United States Supreme Court. The nation's highest court held its first term in New York City in 1790, and for more than two centuries the Court has been closely tied to New York State's legal and political culture. Reflecting the state's heavy and complex legal business, as well as its one-time Electoral College predominance, 14 New Yorkers have sat on the Court, more than from any other state, beginning with the first chief justice, John Jay, who was appointed for his statesmanship rather than his brief tenure as chief justice of the state supreme court. A lack of cases and the difficulties in beginning a new institution prevented Jay from realizing his vision of the Court becoming an instrument for maintaining a national moral order, and he resigned in 1795 to become governor of New York State. The 11 years following his resignation mark the longest absence of a New Yorker from the Court.

The 1802 Federal Judiciary Act assigned justices to specific circuits, and New York State's inclusion with Vermont and Connecticut in the Second Circuit meant that a New Yorker would be designated to the Court. The six justices who occupied the "New York seat" almost consecutively from 1807 to 1909 were career judges who were acceptable to the political powers in both Albany and Washington, DC. Only Samuel Blatchford was not a state judge, though he had served as a federal judge in New York State for 15 years. The only gaps in the 102-year skein occurred when Pres John Tyler in the 1840s and Pres Grover Cleveland in the 1890s each failed to get a New Yorker immediately confirmed to the vacant New York seat. Roscoe Conkling was considered for the Court but refused a nomination for the chief justiceship in 1873 and declined a confirmed appointment in 1882. However, his position as a US senator and head of the New York State Republican Party gave him considerable control over appointments to the New York seat.

While the elimination of circuit duties in the 1890s removed the reason for the New York seat, as late as the 1950s the Eisenhower administration felt the need to appoint a New Yorker, John Marshall Harlan II. With seats no longer as-

US SUPREME COURT JUSTICES FROM NEW YORK STATE

Justice	Tenure[a]
John Jay	1789–95[b]
Brockholst Livingston	1807–23
Smith Thompson	1823–43
Samuel Nelson	1845–72
Ward Hunt	1873–82
Samuel Blatchford	1882–93
Rufus W. Peckham	1896–1909
Charles Evans Hughes	1910–16; 1930–41[c]
Harlan Fiske Stone	1925–46[d]
Benjamin N. Cardozo	1932–38
Robert H. Jackson	1941–54
John Marshall Harlan II	1955–71
Thurgood Marshall	1967–91
Ruth Bader Ginsburg	1993–

[a]Unless otherwise indicated, tenure refers to service as an associate justice.

[b]Jay served his whole tenure as chief justice.

[c]Hughes served as associate justice 1910–16 and as chief justice 1930–41.

[d]Stone served as associate justice 1925–41 and as chief justice 1941–46.

signed by circuit, more than one New Yorker could serve simultaneously—in the 1930s they made up one-third of the Court: Chief Justice Charles Evans Hughes and associate justices Benjamin Cardozo and Harlan Fiske Stone. The 20th-century justices also had more varied professional lives than their 19th-century predecessors and included a two-term governor, a former dean of Columbia Law School, two US attorneys general, and two US solicitors general. Of the New Yorkers who served on the Court in the 20th century, only Cardozo was involved in New York State jurisprudence, serving as chief judge of the Court of Appeals. Distinguished 20th-century jurist Learned Hand is the most notable among the many other New Yorkers considered for, but never appointed to, the Court.

With their near continuous presence on the Court, New Yorkers have contributed much to its jurisprudence. In general the contributions of the 20th-century justices overshadow those of their predecessors. A memorable contribution by a 19th-century appointee was Rufus W. Peckham's opinion in *Lochner v New York* (1905), which elevated liberty of contract to a constitutional right. In the 20th century Harlan Fiske Stone was a voice for judicial restraint and preferred rights and perhaps the most influential New Yorker to serve on the Court.

See also APPORTIONMENT AND DISTRICTING.

Friedman, Leon, and Fred L. Israel, eds. *The Justices of the United States Supreme Court, 1789–1969: Their Lives and Major Opinions,* 5 vols (New York: Chelsea House, in association with Bowker, 1969–78)

Hall, Kermit L., ed. *The Oxford Companion to the Supreme Court of the United States* (New York: Oxford Univ Press, 1992)

The Oliver Wendell Holmes Devise. *History of the Supreme Court of the United States,* 9 vols (New York: Macmillan, 1971)

Donald M. Roper

Universalists. See UNITARIAN UNIVERSALISTS.

Universal Negro Improvement Association. See BLACK NATIONALISM; GARVEY, MARCUS.

University at Albany. See SUNY ALBANY.

University at Buffalo. See SUNY BUFFALO.

University of Rochester. Private university. In 1850 a rift within Madison University (now Colgate University) at Hamilton (Madison Co) prompted a nucleus of faculty and students to move to what they believed was a more propitious location in Rochester, founding their own university under Baptist auspices. Its first home was the former United States Hotel. The university's first president (1853–88), Martin B. Anderson, oversaw its move to the Prince St campus in 1861. For its first 50 years the university remained small and male, with the exception of one female student in 1893–95. In 1900 women students were first admitted, due in large part to the efforts of Susan B. Anthony. In the same year Rush Rhees was inaugurated as its third president. During his 35-year administration the school evolved into a true university, partly because of his friendship with George Eastman of Eastman Kodak, whose gifts to the university ultimately exceeded $51 million.

The first school added to the university was the Eastman School of Music (ESM) in 1921. As a result of Eastman's personal interest in music, he endowed the school and built the Eastman Theatre, designed by McKim, Mead and White. Howard Hanson was appointed director in 1924 and, over the next 40 years, developed the ESM into one of the major music schools in the country. The ESM has maintained a distinct identity on a downtown campus. The School of Medicine and Dentistry and the Strong Memorial Hospital opened in 1925, funded by gifts from Eastman and from John D. Rockefeller Sr's General Education Board. Founding dean Dr George Hoyt Whipple served until 1953. At the start of the 21st century, the Arthur Kornberg Medical Research Building and the Aab Institute of Biomedical Sciences are the latest additions to the school's facilities, supporting increased research.

An unprecedented fund-raising campaign was undertaken in 1924, supported by Eastman, the General Education Board, former students and friends, to buy and construct the River Campus, the university's present location on a bend in the Genesee River just south of downtown. Eastman Quadrangle, with the Rush Rhees Library at its head and four imposing academic halls on two sides, forms the heart of this campus. The men's college moved from Prince St in 1930, leaving the women's college at the former site. This period of "coordinate" education continued for 25 years, during which some students attended classes on both campuses. In 1955 the women moved to the River Campus, and most of the Prince St buildings were sold, a notable exception being the Memorial Art Gallery (1913), a part of the university since its inception.

The university is known for its strengths in the sciences. Henry Augustus Ward, explorer and naturalist, sold his 40,000-specimen collection to the university in 1862. The Institute of Optics (1929) has been preeminent in optics research, which is also carried out in the Laboratory for Laser Energetics. The university was the home of several early cyclotrons that advanced research in particle physics. Prof Robert Marshak developed the Physics Department into a leading research center of high-energy physics and founded the series of Rochester Conferences that attracted researchers from all over the world. Significant achievements in the humanities were made at the university during the second half of the 20th century. Eugene Genovese, Stanley Engerman, and Herbert Gutman produced groundbreaking work on the institution of American slavery. Historian Christopher Lasch's *Culture of Narcissism* (1978) established him as a leading social critic of American life in the age of consumer culture. As a relatively small research university, Rochester has a very large endowment, surpassing the $1 billion mark at the end of the 20th century. At one time the university's endowment was the fourth largest in the country, but during the 1990s the university suffered a financial shortfall, and the management of the endowment was criticized. In 2002 the university is the second largest employer in the Rochester area. In addition to the schools previously mentioned, it includes the School of Nursing, the William E. Simon Graduate School of Business Administration, and the Margaret Warner Graduate School of Education and Human Development. In 2001 there were 4,435 full-time undergraduates, 2,560 full-time graduate students, and 1,345 part-time students.

May, Arthur J. *A History of the University of Rochester, 1850–1962* (Rochester: Univ of Rochester, 1977)

Waxman, Jan L. *Beside the Genesee: A Pictorial History of the University of Rochester* (Rochester: Univ of Rochester, 2000)

Nancy Martin

University of the State of New York. See EDUCATION DEPARTMENT AND UNIVERSITY OF THE STATE OF NEW YORK.

Upland County. See EXTINCT COUNTIES.

Upper Brookville. See BROOKVILLE.

Upper Nyack. Village (pop 1,863) in Clarkstown (Rockland Co). Settled in the 1680s, the village was initially supported by farming. Boatbuilding and quarrying got underway by the end of the 18th century. In the 19th century boatyards operated at Van Houten's Landing, which was served by a marine railway. Farms along Broadway were divided for estates, and the village incorporated in 1872 to circumvent the Village of Nyack's plans to encompass it. During World Wars I and II Petersen's Boatyard employed hundreds. Since 1957 Upper Nyack has been the national headquarters of the interreligious pacifist organization the Fellowship of Reconciliation. Upper Nyack's nickname, Goosetown, and motto, Goosetown Against the World, survive in local usage. It is the site of Nyack Beach and Hook Mountain State Parks.

Winston C. Perry Jr

upright and wing house. Modest dwelling type of two gable-roof pavilions abutting perpendicularly to form a T- or L-shaped plan. The "upright" presents its gable end to the street and is usually one and one-half stories high. The "wing" is typically lower, but in late examples both pavilions may be two stories tall. The form developed in the upper Hudson Valley. Small, one-and-one-half story, gable-end houses built during the former Dutch colony were altered, beginning in the mid–18th century, by the addition of kitchen wings placed at right angles to the original houses. Examples include the Winne-Creble House in Bethlehem (Albany Co), the Jacob G. Lansing House formerly in Albany, and the Abraham Yates House in Schenectady's Stockade District. From the 1820s builders created all-new upright and wing houses, with the style reaching its peak popularity during the mid–19th century. Many examples can be found along the major transportation corridors of that era, now Rte 5 and US 20. The house form was carried westward by migrating Yorkers and Yankees and through pattern books; it continued to be built until the beginning of the 20th century.

Mattson, Richard Leonard. "The Gable Front and Upright-and-Wing: An Historical Geography of Two Common American House Types" (PhD diss, Univ of Illinois at Urbana-Champaign, 1988)

Upton, Dell. "Pattern Books and Professionalism: Aspects of the Transformation of Domestic Architecture in America, 1800–1860," *Winterthur Portfolio* 19 (Summer/Autumn 1984): 107–50

Walter Richard Wheeler

upstate and downstate. The terms upstate and downstate refer to the two main regions of New York State. Downstate is New York City and often is extended to include the greater metropolitan area. Upstate is the rest of the state, although the border between the two regions is a matter of great contention. But while they are rather vague as geographic terms, they do serve to reflect diversity in what embodies the "New York State of mind" by distinguishing the urban culture and diversity of New York City from the more traditional norms and values of upstate communities. Like all generalizations, the terms upstate and downstate both illumine and obscure aspects of the reality they are trying to describe.

Definitions

Regional relationships in New York State have been defined historically by the singular nature of New York City and the distinctive cultures of the rest of the state. From its earliest days as a trading post founded by a quasi-public corporation through its later decades as a manufacturing base to its most recent incarnation as a world financial center, New York City has always been primarily a center of commerce. The economic development built on the city's commercial base generated immense personal fortunes and financed the development of a large public sector. But the extraordinary nature and unparalleled extent of New York City's development exacerbated traditional urban-rural tensions that have long served to separate cities from the hinterlands. For much of New York State's history, the term downstate emphasized big-city cultural values and referred to New York City and the City of Brooklyn. The geographic area encompassed by the term downstate evolved as New York City expanded, first northward to include all of Manhattan Island and the Bronx, and after the 1898 consolidation, to encompass all five boroughs of Greater New York. Eastern Long Island has never been considered part of downstate, though because of its geography, neither has it been considered part of upstate.

Conversely the traditional economy in upstate New York was based largely on agriculture and small business. And broadly speaking upstate was more Protestant, more northern European, and generally whiter than its neighbor to the south. In the 19th century New York City was shaped by the waves of European immigration to the United States, while the defining moment for upstate was the Yankee migration of 1800–1830 and the westward movement of Protestant New Englanders. Upstate New York is not monolithic, and especially along the Erie Canal corridor, in Rochester, Buffalo, Utica, and other cities, there was much heavy industry and considerable Irish and German immigration. Nevertheless, when viewed as a whole and, particularly, when compared to New York City, the more rural and Protestant character of upstate becomes clear.

As a consequence of these overall social and cultural differences, upstate-downstate relationships in New York State have often reflected regional stereotypes. To many in upstate communities, downstaters were either too focused on the economic bottom line or overly fond of social programs. To many in New York City, people upstate maintained attachments to pre-modern values that made them economically and socially backward. Their dramatic cultural and socioeconomic differences notwithstanding, the two regions have been forced to interact within a web of political relationships. Because politics concerns choices about "the authoritative allocation of values" (resources) and one group's share is often perceived as another's loss, political relationships inevitably involve conflict. When political relationships reflect spatial settlement patterns, as they most certainly do in New York State, political conflicts assume regional bases.

Roots of the Dichotomy

Historically the Hudson River has served to connect and define upstate and downstate New York. Most of the North American colonies slowly expanded from coastal settlements inland. But because of the navigability of the river far inland, from the time of the earliest settlement under the Dutch there was a downstate center in New Amsterdam [now New York City], and an upstate center 150 miles (240 km) away in Beverwijck [now Albany]. The Dutch influence on Albany continued for years after the beginning of English rule in 1664, and New York City slowly acquired a more cosmopolitan and English character. Albany and New York City had a tense but generally peaceful relationship during the colonial period.

Although the history of New York State is replete with examples of conflict between upstate and downstate interests, three are of particular note because they occurred during critical junctures in the nation's history: the American Revolution, the Civil War, and the industrial revolution. In the decade prior to the American Revolution, downstate merchants, with profitable financial arrangements with England, sought to moderate the opposition to the Crown emerging from tenant farmers upstate and city radicals like the Sons of Liberty. During the war itself upstate New York saw numerous critical battles for control of the Hudson River; the city, having been abandoned by George Washington's army early in the conflict, served as a safe haven for tories.

After the Revolution, the commercially friendly, centralizing impulses of the Constitution written in Philadelphia in 1787 found much greater support among downstate business interests, particularly creditors, than among the farmers and artisans of upstate New York. In the election to select delegates to the state's ratification convention, candidates supporting the new Constitution received large majorities of the downstate vote. So intense was the regional conflict on ratification, however, that the Federalist landslide downstate was more than countered by an Antifederalist tide upstate, and the Constitution's opponents wound up with a majority of convention seats. The convention's upstate majority eventually agreed to ratification but only after securing the promise of a Bill of Rights attachment to the Constitution and under the threat of downstate secession. New York State's birth in an upstate-downstate compromise extended to the site of the state capital. It did not return to its colonial location in New York City; in part because of fear of domination by downstate interests, it was permanently located in Albany.

In the middle of the 19th century, the national debate over slavery divided the regions in New York State. There was a long history of upstate support, nurtured by the Protestant clergy, for an abolitionist or a Free Soil position on slavery. When the Whig Party was finally marginalized by passage of the Kansas-Nebraska Act in 1854 and the country's second major party system unraveled, upstate was dominated by the new Republican Party. In the 1856 elections, with overwhelming upstate support, the new Republican Party not only carried New York State for its presidential candidate, John C. Frémont, but it also succeeded in electing its first governor, John A. King.

In New York City, however, the issues of the day were less clearly defined. The city's economic role as one axis in the cotton triangle that united the American South with Europe—a role serving the economic interests of the city's ship owners, bankers, as well as the immigrant working classes who depended on them—confused the local political situation. Despite the best efforts of anti-slavery advocates and other proponents of the union position within the Democratic Party in the antebellum years, the city's commercial ties to the southern economy and therefore unavoidably to slavery kept New York as that "most southern of northern cities." In the 1860 election only another overwhelming Republican vote upstate allowed Abraham Lincoln, who lost the New York City vote to Stephen Douglas, to carry the state's electors. Fernando Wood, mayor of New York City in 1861, floated an abortive idea of downstate as a neutral free port. Downstate divisions over the emancipation issue during the war years culminated in the violence of the draft riots of 1863, which was largely directed at the city's black population and its Republican commercial and civic elite. In 1864 Lincoln lost the downstate vote to Democrat George B. McClellan but carried the state's electors once again based on a decisive Republican majority upstate.

The cultural, economic, and political divisions in New York State evident during the nation's founding and the Civil War solidified in the late 19th century as industrialization downstate acted to enhance regional stereotypes and institutionalize regional conflicts. To many upstate, as well as to "old wealth" in the city, the new class of industrial entrepreneurs represented the worst of the downstate business stereotype: the crude robber baron type who was given to conspicuous consumption and concerned only with profits. Moreover, the flood tide of immigrants, increasingly from southern and eastern Europe to fill the unprecedented demands for unskilled labor occasioned by industrialization, reaffirmed existing negative stereotypes about the foreign-born. It was the downstate response to coping with these developments through the urban political machine, however, that institutionalized regional divisions in the modern party system.

American cities undergoing industrial transformations had government structures designed to deal with the commercial economies of earlier periods. Indeed, through control of city charters and the use of state commissions to administer local services, upstate interests in the legislature had limited New York City's governance capacity for decades. Many upstate-downstate political battles in New York State would also reflect tensions between New York City Democrats and their outnumbered but elite Republican opponents who often called on upstate Republican allies for support. An example of this was in 1857 when upstate interference came to a head as the city-controlled Municipal Police force engaged in pitched battles in City Hall Park with the state-appointed Metropolitan Police, and federal troops were necessary to restore order. State controls encouraged efforts to secure increased home rule (ie, greater local autonomy over local affairs), which helped to further empower Democrats in the city at a point when the nativist Whigs were already in political retreat and Republicans were in ascendance upstate.

By default then, as much as by design, the political machine emerged as the extragovernmental mechanism for coordinating industrial urbanization. As the industrial era began, however, New York City's political machine, Tammany Hall, was more a fragmented collection of competing, often violently hostile, factions than a structured political operation. In the late 1860s William M. Tweed, leader of one of the political factions within Tammany, managed to seize control of the machine, the city government, and eventually the state legislature; he exercised virtually unchecked power in the first two venues and substantial influence in Albany. Following the Tweed Ring's downfall in 1873 in the wake of investigations of massive corruption, new Tammany bosses fashioned a more structured machine. The era of institutional machine politics, initiated by "Honest John" Kelly and continued by Richard Croker and Charles F. Murphy, was characterized by a process where politicians secured control over divisible material resources for the price of party loyalty; industrialists secured favorable treatment for the price of contributions to machine coffers; and immigrants obtained the services of a primitive and informal welfare state for the price of a vote.

During the late 19th century upstate Republicans regularly sought to neutralize Tammany's power and downstate's influence. The 1894 state constitution, for example, included reapportionment provisions limiting the number of downstate districts and therefore downstate representation in the state legislature. The negative political impact of these provisions on downstate interests continued until the 1960s when the US Supreme Court mandated legislative representation based on districts with equal population. During the 1890s upstate Republicans also organized a series of three legislative investigations that uncovered evidence of widespread corruption downstate. In an example of the regional politics around such investigations, the Chamber of Commerce of the State of New York provided money for the Lexow Committee investigation after the legislative allocation of funds for the committee had been vetoed by Democratic Gov Roswell P. Flower. Even an issue as fundamental as the consolidation of Greater New York in 1898 was supported by upstate Republican boss Thomas C. Platt, who saw it as an opportunity to dilute the Manhattan machine's power while capturing downstate patronage opportunities for his own organization.

The restructured Tammany machine, however, was resilient in the face of upstate assaults. It maintained its power into the 1930s by integrating new interests without upsetting the balance in the political game it had established. Even as atypical Tammany politicians like Gov Alfred E. Smith and Robert F. Wagner Sr, for example, fought for and eventually won the kind of social reforms in Albany that politically co-opted progressive forces downstate, the machine maintained its mutually profitable interactions with the business community. During this extended period regional conflicts over home rule, prohibition, aid to parochial schools, and legislative malapportionment served to widen and deepen the upstate-downstate dichotomy as the political leadership in each section used such controversies to rally their respective bases.

Tammany's hold on power was perennially challenged downstate by a reform coalition comprising an eclectic blend of religious reformers, political progressives, Protestant "nativists," and Republican politicians. Although reformers had periodic electoral successes during these five decades of Tammany rule, their challenge took on particular salience as a consequence of two events in the early 20th century. The depression crippled Tammany's ability to maintain its various quid pro quo operations around the city. And in 1931 yet another investigation of downstate politics, this time into the magistrate courts, evolved into a broader examination of corruption in city government. Led by Judge Samuel Seabury, the expanded investigation uncovered evidence of substantial wrongdoing. As a result, in 1932 New York City Mayor Jimmy Walker was pressured by Democratic presidential candidate and governor Franklin D. Roosevelt to resign. In the wake of the depression and the Seabury investigations, the 1933 election of reform candidate Fiorello La Guardia as mayor signaled the end of Tammany's downstate dominance.

Although La Guardia was nominally a Republican, the progressive direction of his fusion administration, coupled with its close ties to New Deal Democrats in Washington, served to marginalize Tammany. In the years following World War II, downstate Democratic politicians, even many of those associated with what was still referred to as Tammany Hall, embraced the social programs of the welfare state. Downstate voters too continued to send large majorities of Democrats, usually elected by large majorities of votes, to represent them in the state legislature and Congress. The trend has lasted into the early 21st century, as no Republican gubernatorial candidate has carried New York City since consolidation, and no presidential candidate has carried New York City since Calvin Coolidge in 1924.

During this postwar period, upstate politicians and voters remained firmly committed to the Republican Party, representing one faction in the party's internal conflicts between its largely upstate "Main Street" and its more corporate and socially progressive "Wall Street" faction downstate. For a time some prominent New York State Republicans of the day, notably Gov Nelson A. Rockefeller, established national reputations as leaders of the liberal wing of the party. However, the founding of the Conservative Party in 1962 and Rockefeller's declining support among Republicans upstate began to push the governor and the party in a more conservative direction. By the early 1970s Tammany was gone, but New York City was as Democratic as ever. Republican leaders, under pressure from the party faithful, were backing away from their accommodations with a welfare-state worldview; and upstate-downstate divisions, evident since the nation's founding and politically institutionalized in the years after the Civil War, were as rock solid as ever.

Changing Demographics and Regionalism

Two developments in the second half of the 20th century muddied the analytical waters around the notion of the upstate-downstate dichotomy: the suburbanization of city populations around the state and the spread of what were thought of as only downstate urban problems to cities upstate. In the 1950s, as part of a larger national movement encouraged by federal housing, tax, and transportation policies, an eastern and, to a lesser extent, northern exodus from New York City began to accelerate. Spreading initially into Nassau and Westchester Cos, the migration eventually expanded into Suffolk Co to the east and into outlying counties north and west of the city. Suburbanization had dramatic economic and political impacts. The rapid development of large residential tracts required substantial investment in the public infrastructure necessary to support suburban lifestyles. When the Supreme Court issued its reapportionment decisions in the middle 1960s, the suburbs emerged as a third force in New York State politics, a force that was neither downstate Democrat nor upstate Republican.

While white families were heading to the suburbs, the mechanization of agricultural and the brutality of racism in southern states resulted in an African American migration to northern cities. As this dual migration proceeded, manufacturing jobs, historically the base for upward mobility among incoming groups to New York City, were being moved from cities to outlying areas. The out-migration of the tax base coupled with the in-migration of a population facing fewer available jobs put substantial pressure on city resources. The pattern was not just a downstate phenomenon, as upstate cities increasingly became troubled fiscally as their surrounding metropolitan areas grew.

As in the past, the modern-day political relationships between and among regions in New York State are constrained by their socioeconomic and cultural characteristics. The emergence of the suburban counties around New York City and the evolution of urban and metropolitan areas upstate have resulted in increasingly complex regional patterns. At the dawn of the 21st century, New York City remains more demographically diverse than the rest of the state. With nonwhites making up more than 55% of the city's population, however, the ethnic and religious differences of previous years have been superseded by racial distinctions between an increasingly African American, Latino, and Asian New York City and the largely European American rural areas and suburbs. To be sure, racial diversity has also been increasing in other areas of the state. In 2000 nonwhites accounted for over 25% of the total downstate suburban population and nearly 45% of the population in upstate cities.

New York City's experience with foreign-born residents remains sui generis in the state and the nation. For nearly four centuries, the city has been the port of entry for immigration around the globe. At the turn of the 20th century, more than 35% of the city's population was foreign-born. Indeed the post-1965 immigration has been far more concentrated in New York City than the great waves of 19th- and early 20th-century immigration. In 1920, 25% of the state's foreign-born population lived outside of New York City. In 2000 only 14% of the foreign-born lived outside of New York City, and much of that 14% was in the downstate suburbs. In 1920 there were many upstate counties with substantial foreign-born populations. In both Erie and Monroe Cos, for example, the foreign-born made up about 23% of the total county population; the figures for 2000 were about 5% and 7% respectively. This unbalanced representation of the foreign-born might well serve to keep the upstate-downstate relationship current in the 21st century.

Historically New York City has served a bifurcated economic role, acting as a regional center of both wealth creation and seemingly intransigent social problems. While the city's capabilities of generating wealth provide state governments with large amounts of revenues, its social problems demand large amounts of state expenditures. As a result, the city's relationship with the rest of the state has ebbed and flowed depending on economic circumstances. In the period after the 1975 New York City fiscal crisis, there was resentment expressed by many in the rest of the state about the fiscal burdens imposed on state taxpayers because of the city's financial mess. During the 1990s the resentments were returned as the city's economy flourished while upstate New York continued to close factories and lose jobs. Such geopolitical divides often provide intense political conflicts among the groups involved and the public officials representing them.

Governance and Modern Regionalism

Modern regional politics in New York State is constrained by a system of constitutional and statutory limits on local autonomy that defines the basic rules of the state governance process. A 1923 amendment to the state constitution and the 1924 City Home Rule Law codified home rule in New York State by establishing local authority over local "property, affairs and government." However, if principles of state preeminence and home rule conflict, state courts have consistently ruled that a "state concern" doctrine preempts home rule. As a result, modern regional politics in New York State still occurs within a context where state government limits local governments' revenue authority, mandates local expenditures on state programs, and maintains administrative supervision of local agencies.

Given the centrality of governance in New York State, the political conflicts occasioned by modern regional differences play out in the state legislature and in elections for statewide office. In these twin venues, an urban agenda, once defined narrowly in downstate terms but increasingly inclusive of upstate cities, competes with the political demands of the suburbs and upstate rural areas. Since 1974 control of the state legislature has been divided between the Democrats who run the assembly and the Republicans who hold a majority in the senate. Under a highly partisan, strong-leadership system, majority party conferences develop policy positions and charge their leaders with representing them in negotiations with the other house and the governor. In general, the makeup of the majority conferences clearly reflects regional politics in the state. The Republican senate majority includes mostly suburban and rural members, while there is a decided downstate and urban cast to the Democratic conference in the state assembly.

Since the Democrats gained control of the assembly, 60% of their majority conference and all five of the speakers elected by the conference have come from New York City. It is not surprising that, during the last quarter of the 20th century and beginning of the 21st century, assembly policy proposals have tended to emphasize a socially activist approach to governance that is often associated with New York City politics. Party conferences, however, are neither ideologically nor regionally monolithic; they reflect the diversity of interests in the electorate. As a result, conference positions are usually the result of accommodations among factions representing diverse regional interests, including upstate-downstate divisions. Democrats from upstate cities and their surrounding suburbs are generally, though not universally, more conservative than their downstate colleagues. Indeed, during reelection campaigns, upstate Democrats often need to counter their opponents' attempts to connect them with the downstate party leadership. The New York City delegation itself includes a number of moderates from outer borough districts who, reflecting their constituencies, emphasize a less socially activist agenda. In conference the leadership cannot ignore the interests of its more conservative members, particularly those from upstate, if the party is to maintain its majority in the assembly.

The Republican senate conference, comprising mostly upstate rural conservatives and suburban moderates, also has internal regional tensions. Despite the party's philosophical and rhetorical association with smaller state government, tax cuts, and local government autonomy, for example, suburban Republicans demand substantial state spending on education and transportation to help hold down the already high property tax burdens on their constituents in Nassau and Suffolk Cos. Moreover, the Republican leadership is aware that the party's small legislative majority is, in part, based on the presence of several Republican senators from New York City and that maintaining its majority requires addressing at least some of their downstate constituents' demands. In extraordinary cases, this small city delegation can gain political leverage by threatening to act as a swing vote by joining their votes with those of the minority party and creating a new majority on the floor.

The unwritten rule for winning statewide elections in New York requires that Republicans maximize their winning margins upstate, secure the suburban vote, and hold down their losing margins in New York City; Democratic candidates, on the other hand, need to carry the city by a wide margin, run close in the suburbs, and hold down their losing margins upstate. Since the end of World War II, most successful gubernatorial candidates have heeded this rule, although suburbanization and the proportionately smaller turnout of the city's low-income voters have decreased the political impact of New York City over the years. In 1950 city voters accounted for nearly 50% of the votes cast in statewide elections; in the 1990s that total dropped to barely 30%, while the suburban vote has risen from 12% to nearly 25% of the total.

In an era when the New York City generated nearly 50% of the statewide vote, Republican governors Thomas E. Dewey and Nelson A. Rockefeller attended to downstate interests and received sufficient support, often 40% and more, from city voters to win seven elections between them. Rockefeller, in particular, developed working relationships with union leaders and prominent Democrats in the city, which served him well in his four gubernatorial campaigns. However, until the 2002 election, when George E. Pataki courted the city vote as a strategy to counter problems upstate, he had adapted to the diminishing import of the city's electoral base and won his previous two elections with a smaller percentage of the city vote than any other governor in modern history. Conversely, and not surprisingly, Democrats W. Averell Harriman, Hugh Carey, and Mario M. Cuomo based their six gubernatorial victories in part on the overwhelming support of New York City voters.

Conclusions

At the beginning of the 21st century, the upstate-downstate division in New York State has been complicated by suburban growth downstate and the appearance of kindred economic and social problems in New York City and upstate cities. Nevertheless, there are constancies. New York City is still the most heterogeneous area in the state although the nature of the heterogeneity has changed; the city continues to generate wealth for the state although it makes expensive demands on state social service resources; and it continues to be a center of the state's Democratic Party. Rural areas of the state are still racially and to a great extent ethnically homogeneous and remain a center for the Republican Party in the state. There has also been change. The city retains an important though no longer dominant role in state politics as the rise of the suburban voter has shifted the political balance in the state. Upstate New York as a whole has become more diverse as the rural population has shrunk to less than 10% of the state total and the metropolitan areas around upstate cities continue to grow and differentiate themselves from their urban cores.

In state government, representatives of these diverse regional forces contest for their constituents' share of resources. Politics in Albany continues to manifest a strong, at times seemingly unbridgeable, upstate-downstate cultural divide. There are reasons to wonder, however, whether at some point socioeconomic commonalities among people from around the state will supersede long-standing regional divisions and thereby redefine overall state culture and politics. Such a scenario, however, consigning the notion of an upstate-downstate dichotomy to the annals of New York State history, does not seem likely anytime soon.

See also APPORTIONMENT AND DISTRICTING.

Burrows, Edwin G., and Mike Wallace. *Gotham: A History of New York City to 1898* (New York: Oxford Univ Press, 1999)

Connable, Alfred and Edward Silberfarb. *Tigers of Tammany: Nine Men Who Ran New York* (New York: Holt, Rinehart & Winston, 1967)

Ellis, David M. *New York: State and City* (Ithaca: Cornell Univ Press, 1979)

Liebschutz, Sarah F. *New York Politics and Government: Competition and Compassion* (Lincoln: Univ of Nebraska Press, 1998)

Sayre, Wallace, and Herbert Kaufman, *Governing New York City: Politics in the Metropolis* (New York: Russell Sage Foundation, 1960)

Schneier, Edward, and John Brian Murtaugh. *New York Politics: A Tale of Two States* (Armonk, NY: M. E. Sharpe, 2001)

Stonecash, Jeffrey, ed. *Governing New York State*, 4th ed. (Albany: SUNY Press, 2001)

Straetz, Ralph, and Frank Munger. *New York Politics* (New York: New York Univ Press, 1960)

Zimmerman, Joseph F. *The Government and Politics of New York State* (New York: New York Univ Press, 1981)

Robert F. Pecorella

Urbana. Town (pop 2,546) in NE Steuben Co. Settled in 1793, the town was formed from Bath in 1822. It is divided, northeast to southwest, by Keuka Lake and Pleasant Valley. Hills bordering the lake are largely devoted to grape culture, begun in 1829. By the close of the 19th century local viniculture had expanded to include Pleasant Valley Wine Co (1860; America's first bonded winery), Urbana Wine Co (1865), and Taylor Wine Co (1880). Urbana was the site of early flight tests, including the first preannounced flight of over .62 mile (1 km) on 4 July 1908, by which Glenn H. Curtiss became a competitor of the Wright brothers. Many large commercial wine producers had closed by the 1990s, but by 2002 several small estate wineries, including Dr. Frank's Vinifera Wine Cellars, had become well established. A New York State fish hatchery is located at Cold Springs.

Virginia L. Wright and Jerry Wright

urban gangs. In the early 19th century, groups of young men allied through a common trade roamed the streets of New York City. These bands of butcher's boys, bookbinders, printers, and watermen fought each other in the streets after working hours. As immigrants poured into the city, fighting between ethnic gangs mirrored the political contests between immigrants and the native-born population. One battle between the nativist American Guards and Irish immigrants in 1835 was so fierce that intervention by 200 policemen was ordered. Five Points was especially rife with gang activity. That notorious neighborhood was near what was originally the intersection of Orange, Anthony, and Cross Sts, just north of City Hall and below Canal St. One of the first organized Irish gangs, called the Forty Thieves, was founded in 1826 by Edward Coleman.

Although this subject has often been viewed by the somewhat romanticized and unreliable vision of Herbert Asbury's 1927 classic, *The Gangs of New York*, the source of Martin Scorcese's 2002 film, there indeed was much Irish-inspired gang activity in the Five Points. The best-known names are the Dead Rabbits, Shirt Tails, and the Plug Uglies. Faction fighting was imported by Irish immigrants. Gangs were territorial, with border transgressions by rivals initiating brawls. Volunteer firefighting companies also provided a focus for the formation of fighting gangs. By the mid–19th century the Bowery had become the hub of a youthful counterculture; young men dressed in extravagant costumes and proclaimed their separateness from both bourgeois New York City society and their immigrant parents. These Bowery "b'hoys" were primarily native-born and full of patriotic fervor, and not all of them were involved in gang activity. Some of it was merely a social and stylistic convention, proclaiming their working-class status by wearing their hair in long "soap tails" and speaking in their own youth lingo. Some of their invented slang ("crusher" for policeman, "roughs" for someone always ready to fight, and "star-gazer" for prostitute) later came into use in mainstream America. Gang activity in Five Points essentially became a proxy war for various American political factions. Young men of the Bowery who did become involved in gangs (Bowery Boys and American Guards) were nativists who sided with the Whigs or Know-Nothing Party, whereas Irish gangs ultimately aligned themselves with Tammany Hall.

Professional thieves formed criminal gangs to ensure their livelihoods. New York City's police chief claimed in 1850 that there were more than 50 gangs of river pirates operating around the wharves. In the decade before the Civil War, the line between criminal and political activity, protection and patronage, began to blur. After the war, gangs of thieves specialized in targeting banks and cash transporters, while juvenile gangs in the slums engaged in petty crime and violence. The Whyos became infamous for providing assault and murder for pay services. Politicians used gangs for their own advancement, most notably the Democrats of Tammany Hall, some of whom started out in public life as gang members.

In the early 20th century there were gangs among many immigrant communities, among them Jewish and Italian immigrants on the Lower East Side and Little Italy; Chinatown, in the same area, hosted a number of tongs—sophisticated, hierarchical organizations with business networks crossing the country and extending to China.

After World War II the youth gang phenomenon attracted the attention of city authorities and the media. New York City was losing blue-collar jobs and attracting Puerto Rican immigrants and African American migrants from the South. Urban renewal efforts destroyed old neighborhoods, massive segregated housing projects appeared, and middle-class Whites left for the suburbs. Fighting between ethnic gangs became common in demographically changing neighborhoods. Fights among schoolboys were sensationalized in the media as full-scale riots, but actual gangs were indeed becoming more violent and better armed. The New York City Youth Board (1947) and the Council of Social and Athletic Clubs (1950) were established in attempts to control gang activities. A new practice, employing "detached workers," became popular. It involved trying to move gang activity from perceived antisocial to more acceptable activities; workers advocated for gang members in securing healthcare, recreation, and employment, and acted as liaisons with the legal system.

In 1957 seven members of a gang called the Egyptian Kings attacked and killed a 15-year-old polio victim named Michael Farmer. The trial of his assailants was a sensational trial that attracted much media attention, including a one-hour radio documentary subsequently produced and narrated by journalist Edward R. Murrow, entitled "Who Killed Michael Farmer?" Also in 1957 the musical *West Side Story*, with music by Leonard Bernstein and lyrics by Stephen Sondheim, opened on Broadway. Loosely based on Shakespeare's *Romeo and Juliet*, it involved members of rival gangs, one white and one Puerto Rican, in the area of what is now Lincoln Center.

There was also gang activity elsewhere in the state, such as the *Canadiana* incident, which took place near Buffalo on Memorial Day in 1956. Early in the day violence between youths, both black and white, began at Crystal Beach, an amusement park on the Canadian side of the border. Knives and other weapons were used, and four people were hospitalized; nine people, all from Buffalo, were arrested. Later in the day more than 1,000 mostly young people boarded the passenger ferry *Canadiana*. Violence erupted that was to some degree interracial harassment between youths wearing jackets identifying them as members of various gangs. Three people were arrested, and the incident was later considered a portent of escalating racial tensions and violence in the years that followed.

During the 1960s and early 1970s gang activity became intertwined with the political and social turmoil of the period. Organizations such as the Black Panthers and Young Lords emerged with agendas of racial and ethnic advancement. In Chinatown gang violence erupted again during the seventies. In 1985 the Chinese Ghost Shadows became the first gang to be convicted under the federal Racketeer Influenced and Corrupt Organizations Act (RICO) of 1970. In the 1980s there was a marked change in street gang activities, as drugs, particularly crack cocaine, infested the cities. Street crews of young men formed to sell drugs, acting as intermediaries between the wholesale drug suppliers and consumers. Battles for territory, and thus customers, were lethal, with prison, drug addiction, and murder common fates for crew members.

During the 1990s the extent of networks linking gangs across the country became apparent. The Latin Kings, originally a Chicago gang, had members in New York State and held national meetings. The jails on Rikers Island were short-term homes for members of over 40 different gangs, including the Crips, Bloods, Netas, Five Percenters, and Trinitarians. The Netas started out as a self-help organization for Puerto Rican prisoners during the 1980s, though New York State members were subsequently convicted of murder, drugs, and arms dealing. A 1990 report by the New York State Task Force on Juvenile Gangs identified 37 active street gangs in New York City, with another 51 "under investigation." Rochester, Syracuse, Albany, Mount Vernon, and Buffalo were also identified as having gangs. The

1998 National Youth Gang survey reported that law enforcement agencies in 16 New York cities with populations of over 25,000 admitted to having problems with gangs. In 2004 urban gangs continued to relocate to smaller jurisdictions.

Jamaican and Dominican gangs existed in most urban areas in the state, although there was also a significant influx of Mexicans. Originating in El Salvador, the Mara Salvatrucha grew to include other *sureños* (southerners), including Ecuadorean, Guatemalan, Honduran, and Mexican factions. Mara Salvatrucha made significant inroads on other gangs in Suffolk and Nassau Cos in an attempt to control the drug trade there. Upstate, local drug dealers allied more closely with Jamaican and Dominican gangs, with the Jamaicans dominating marijuana sales. Other gangs branched into more sophisticated money-raising schemes; the Netas in Albany, for example, were active in cellular phone fraud.

Asbury, Herbert. *The Gangs of New York: An Informal History of the Underworld* (1927; repr, frwd Jorge Luis Borges, New York: Thunder's Mouth Press, 2001)

Brotherton, David C. "The Evolution of New York City's Street Gangs." In *Crime and Justice in New York City: An Area Handbook,* 2001–2 ed., vol 1, ed. Andrew Karmen (Cincinnati: Wadsworth/Thomson Learning, 2001)

National Youth Gang Center. *1998 National Youth Gang Survey* (Washington, DC: US Department of Justice, Office of Justice Programs, Office of Juvenile Justice and Delinquency Prevention, 2000)

New York State. Task Force on Juvenile Gangs. *Reaffirming Prevention: Report of the Task Force on Juvenile Gangs* (Albany: NYS Division for Youth, 1990)

Schneider, Eric C. *Vampires, Dragons, and Egyptian Kings: Youth Gangs in Postwar New York* (Princeton, NJ: Princeton Univ Press, 1999)

Ellen Sexton

urban hotels. During the 19th century urban hotels evolved from inns and boardinghouses. Hotel owners created top-of-the-line and multiservice facilities with advertised prices and rules. Their amenities came to include public rooms, restaurants, entertainment, cleaning services, the latest lighting and plumbing, and eventually elevators and private bathrooms. While their facades and public rooms were elegant, their sleeping arrangements left much to be desired. In the first decades sleeping chambers were spare and small because crowding as many rooms into a structure as possible was standard practice. Only at the end of the century did the chamber become as luxurious as the rest of the hotel as visitors sought privacy and rest rather than the social display of the public rooms. Restaurants were not common until the 1890s, and even the most expensive hotels featured a table d'hôte, a single multicourse menu served at a specified hour to guests seated at long communal tables. The only other sitting was for servants. Hotels were most prolific in New York City, but on a smaller scale Albany and then Buffalo, Rochester, and Syracuse came to have hotels that served as civic social centers as much as travelers' accommodations.

New York City's earliest hotel, the 73-room City Hotel, opened in 1794 on Broadway north of Trinity Church. It offered either the American plan, room and meals for one price, or the European plan, room without meals. The City Hotel eventually had a bar, cloakroom, three gentlemen's parlors, two ladies' parlors, and offices. By 1818 New York City had eight hotels. In 1836 the six-story Park Hotel, with an astounding 300 rooms, was built. It was renamed Astor House for its proprietor, John Jacob Astor. He insisted that ladies who stayed there have a gentleman escort. This was to avoid the possibilities of liaisons with the accomplished prostitutes who inhabited the parlor houses that mushroomed around hotels. Astor House was one of the first to offer the latest refinement, a restaurant where individuals could have their own small tables and choose from a list of dishes on a menu. It also had an art gallery that included Adolphe William Bouguereau's scandalous *Nymphs and Satyr* (1873). By midcentury a definite tourist trade had appeared in New York City, and the St. Nicholas Hotel (1853) was the latest deluxe establishment, with a marble facade, gas lighting, elegant chandeliers and ceiling frescoes, walnut wainscoting, hot running water, central heat, and a telegraph in the lobby.

Post–Civil War and Early 20th-Century Expansion

After the Civil War hotels expanded their services. The Hoffman House in New York City (1870) contained the headquarters of the famous brokerage firm run by two emancipated women, Victoria Woodhull and her sister, Tennessee Claflin. The Grand Union Hotel, erected in 1871 in New York City, took advantage of its location in the heart of the city opposite the Grand Central Depot, providing free baggage service to and from the hotel. In 1893 the Waldorf Hotel in New York City was built, and four years later the Astoria rose next to it. They merged into the Waldorf-Astoria, the largest hotel in the world, with 1,000 rooms, 750 with private baths. It was torn down in 1930 to make way for the Empire State Building. In 1931 the firm of Schultze and Weaver designed the second Waldorf-Astoria on Park Ave at 49th and 50th Sts, continuing the tradition of comfort set by its predecessor. The Plaza Hotel was twice built on the same plot at 5th Ave and 59th St, first in 1890 and again in 1907; architect Henry J. Hardenbergh's 800-room masterpiece is the best surviving example of the turn-of-the-century grand hotel in New York City. Other prominent hotels built at the time, catering to the Midtown Manhattan business traveler, included the Hotel McAlpin (1912), the Biltmore Hotel (1914), the Commodore (1919), and the Pennsylvania (1919).

Urban hotels in the state outside of New York City in the late 19th century rarely had more than five or six stories. Notable in Syracuse was the Yates Hotel, completed in 1892, which had its own electric light plant and an ice machine. Although completed in 1878, Albany's Kenmore Hotel on North Pearl St peaked in popularity after an addition was built in the 1890s. Adam Blake Jr, a wealthy African American, initially operated it. Typical guests were politicians and businessmen. It had more than 600 rooms, the first floor had retail stores, and the roof had tennis, squash, and handball courts. In the 1940s guests and residents were entertained by big bands at the Kenmore's famous nightclub, the Rain-Bo Room. After being abandoned for years it was converted into offices in the early 1980s. Early 20th-century hotels upstate were taller than their predecessors. The Buffalo Touraine was completed in 1901 for the Pan-American Exposition. It had 250 rooms and 100 private bathrooms with tiled walls and showers. The 14-story Hotel Utica was built in 1912. Albany's De Witt Clinton, a block-long structure with 11 floors, was completed in 1927. George B. Post's three-tower Hotel Syracuse (1924) was both a high-rise and a hotel complex. He completed another version of the structure in Buffalo and called it the Statler Towers (1927). In Rochester the Hotel Rochester (1908) and the Hotel Seneca (1926) were the most famous high-rises and also were in the center of downtown areas to serve business clientele.

After World War II

By the 1950s many of the old-line urban hotels went into a decline. The rise of motels, changes in travel patterns, and the growth of suburbs all contributed. Only those hotels with the greatest resources survived because of the new mixture of downtown activities such as conventions, business meetings, and sports events. Many hotels were converted to office space, or they were

Hotel Utica reception lobby, Utica, early 20th century.

abandoned. By the early 21st century few of the older large urban hotels remain in upstate cities, largely replaced with more generic chains such as Sheraton or Hilton Hotels. Many of the older hotels closed in New York City as well, but they were replaced by a new generation of opulent hotels, many of architectural distinction. The New York Hilton (1963) was built in the International Style. The Helmsley Palace (1981; now New York Palace) followed a popular trend of using historical structures for hotels. In this case a private mansion, the Villard House, was integrated into the base of the hotel, preserving the old-world flavor of the Italian palazzo.

After the early 1960s hotel towers were built in every major city in the state and were part of national hotel chains such as Omni, Marriott, and Sheraton. They were hotels and conference centers, and had restaurants and bars, business conference rooms, and ballrooms for wedding receptions. The Midtown Tower in Rochester (1962, additions 1980) was constructed as an independent hotel in the center of the city's crowded business area and is a notable round and green-glass structure similar to the University Tower Hotel (1969; now the Marx Hotel and Conference Center) in Syracuse. An alternative to chain hotels in New York City in the 1980s and 1990s were boutique hotels: small, architecturally distinguished, and catering to an elite clientele, such as Morgans (1984) and Mercer (1998) in SoHo.

Burrows, Edwin G., and Mike Wallace. *Gotham: A History of New York to 1898* (New York: Oxford Univ Press, 1999)

Dorsey, Leslie, and Janice Devine. *Fare Thee Well: A Backward Look at Two Centuries of Historic American Hostelries, Fashionable Spas, and Seaside Resorts* (New York: Crown Publishers, 1964)

Hardin, Evamaria. *Syracuse Landmarks: An AIA Guide to Downtown and Historic Neighborhoods* (Syracuse: Syracuse Univ Press, 1993)

Stern, Robert A. M., Gregory Gilmartin, and John Montague. *New York 1900: Metropolitan Architecture and Urbanism, 1890–1911* (New York: Rizzoli, 1983)

Theodore Corbett

urban parks. Before the mid–19th century New Yorkers devoted little time to creating elaborate public landscapes. By the mid-1800s, however, rapid growth from an increase in immigration and advances in industrialization, combined with a growing interest in leisure activities, had New York State residents looking to public lands as places to escape from the emerging ills of the urban centers. These cultural changes began a movement that would transform the state's urban landscapes.

The Romantic Influence

The influence of 19th-century Romantic ideology, in which the untamed wilderness became a foil to the increasing density, filth, and crime characterizing cities, first influenced public burial grounds. As these facilities were often in the city proper, their worsening condition because of overuse and mismanagement became a cause for alarm. In response, citizen and political leaders advocated for the purchase of large tracts for new burial sites at or just beyond city boundaries. By the 1850s many cities in the state had developed new rural cemeteries that contained curvilinear road and path systems, profuse use of both native and exotic plantings, and elaborate displays of funerary art. It was the popular appeal of these cemeteries that inspired Romantic reformers, most notably Andrew Jackson Downing and William Cullen Bryant, who led the charge to establish public parks. The City of New York in 1857 announced a design competition for the proposed Central Park. The winning Greensward plan by Frederick Law Olmsted and Calvert Vaux followed the Romantic style exhibited in the cemeteries. Its popularity proved that public parks not only offered citizens a place for recreation but also spurred the physical expansion, economic growth, and social progress of a city.

Following New York City's lead, several other cities in the state planned parks during the latter half of the 19th century. Olmsted and Vaux were among the most prolific designers. They collaborated on many commissions, including the 526-acre (213 ha) Prospect Park in Brooklyn (deemed their masterpiece by the pair themselves); the 35-acre (14 ha) Downing Park in Newburgh (Orange Co), designed and created in honor of Downing in 1870; and the elaborate park and parkway system of Buffalo, begun in 1868, the first such in the country. Other design professionals created parks along similar lines, including John Bogart and John Yapp Cuyler's 1870 Washington Park in Albany, with 90 acres (36 ha) and 5 miles (8 km) of tree-lined driveways, and Downing Vaux's College Hill Park in Poughkeepsie, with its sweeping greensward. In some communities park superintendents were appointed, and these individuals—many trained as horticulturists or gardeners—also laid out municipal parks in the pleasure ground tradition. Eldridge Park in Elmira and Lakeside Park in Auburn (Cayuga Co) were developed privately but became quasi-public parks laid out on the same principles. The 300 acres (121 ha) that constitute Eldridge Park (1876) include a series of artificial ponds and lakes, and the 1893 Lakeside Park offered visitors meandering walks along the shores of Owasco Lake. Gernet Baltimore's 1903 Prospect Park in Troy (Rensselaer Co), with its extensive pedestrian path system and contrived views and vistas, was a late example of Romantic public landscapes.

Pleasure grounds were often developed on newly acquired land of little commercial value and often at the city boundary. In some cases, however, new parks were former residential estates or agricultural properties. Land speculators and real estate developers capitalized on the leisure and public health benefits attributed to these pleasure grounds as they promoted new residential areas along park borders, ultimately contributing to the physical expansion of cities. These early, often outlying parks shared many features, such as dramatic topography (natural or otherwise), abundant indigenous and introduced vegetation, buildings and structures integrated into the landscape, controlled vistas and views, and sequential spatial order.

Municipal Parks and Progressive Reform

The social thinking of the Progressive era played a role in the evolution of municipal parks. In principle these public spaces had to not only provide for leisure activities but also offer structured programs, staff, and facilities for organized play encompassing a wide range of civic, social, and athletic opportunities. Activities for mothers and young children were thus offered throughout the day, late afternoon events were scheduled for school-age children, and evening and weekend offerings catered to working men and women.

Landscape architects and other park builders responded to these well-ordered functions by creating reform parks that, unlike their pleasure ground predecessors, were laid out formally and symmetrically. The need to accommodate organized field games, many of which supported routine competitions and tournaments, required flat or nearly flat topography. Vegetation was used sparingly, rolling open greenswards giving way to level lawns and gravel-paved areas. Complex mass plant groupings were replaced by perimeter vegetation, specialty gardens, and decorative flower plantings. Park roads, now economic in alignment and length, were no longer integrated into the landscape and emphasized the axial arrangement of field, playgrounds, and recreational buildings. Of these buildings, one was often centrally located, large and classically decorated, and housed administrative services as well as recreational programming.

Some Romantic era pleasure grounds were modified to accommodate regimented programs and related buildings. By the 1920s, however, proponents of public parks advocated development of separate new reform parks for daily use, while retaining the older pleasure grounds in their unaltered form for special outings. Olmsted's successor firms, overseen by Frederick Law Olmsted Jr and John C. Olmsted, led the way in this new wave of park building. Thousands of acres in the state were made into reform parks, such as Thornden Park in Syracuse (1921), with its amphitheater and specialty gardens; F. T. Proctor Park in Utica (1923), offering 50 acres (20 ha) with playing fields and courts; and Johnson Park (*ca* 1925) in Binghamton, which contained a carousel, bandstand, and bathhouse.

With citizens' increased time and energy devoted to play, park administrators were forced to respond to popular demands rather than to develop and administer structured programs based on overarching social reform principles. Gradually municipal leaders and park advocates began speaking of "recreation" instead of "play," and "facilities" instead of "parks" because both terms better reflected the growing diversity of park activities and the broadening constituency. Furthermore, establishing parks such as Thornden Park in Syracuse offered jobs for the growing number of unemployed amidst the depression. It was only after World War II, however, that development of these new recreation facilities began in earnest.

The Growth of Suburbs and the Changed Cityscape

Mid-20th-century recreational facilities were typically small, generally 10 acres (4 ha) or less, and served their immediate contiguous neighborhoods. Many were affiliated with the vast number of housing developments and schools that appeared during the postwar years of urban renewal and suburban expansion. Notably absent was the spatial order of previous park designs, as large informal spaces and multiuse buildings and structures offered unrestricted and unprogrammed recreational activities. Vegetation was used sparingly, primarily in perim-

Maypole dance at Seneca Park in Rochester, early 20th century.

eter hedgerows emphasizing boundaries rather than adding to scenic value, and roads were limited for direct access and ample room for parking, with no thought toward experience of place. Materials and features were simplified and standardized, resulting in a uniformity that contrasted with the more finely detailed pleasure grounds and reform parks. The greatest variety often came from the new features, which included lively signs and rambling play equipment, that together supported a vast array of traditional recreation activities.

By the mid-1960s municipal parks fell victim to the mass exodus of the urban middle class to the suburbs. For many of those who remained, there were more reasons not to frequent municipal parks than to use them. Parks lost the vibrancy attendant with human interaction and soon were perceived as unsightly, unsafe places best avoided. Yet this was also an age rife with social, cultural, and environmental awareness demanding venues for celebrations, protests, and other public gatherings. These events focused attention on many older parks and awakened citizen interest in retaining and protecting them. Beginning with Central Park and Prospect Park, supporters called for official recognition of the historical significance of municipal parks. They also encouraged increased input in developing park policy as well as more creativity and flexibility in programming, giving rise to the term "open space," signifying the infinite number of ways parks could and should be used. Definitions of what constituted a new open space park were equally original, as this period led to the development of vest-pocket parks, pedestrian malls, raised and sunken public plazas, and cultural and heritage trails.

Although these new park types were not necessarily similar in size or scale, they were designed with some common characteristics. Most were in city centers and attracted users because of their convenient locations and the opportunity for both solitude and social gathering. Surrounding buildings were integral to defining park boundaries and sense of place. Vegetation was limited and used for both visual relief from the immediate structural context and physical relief from sun and wind. Materials were tough and durable but used creatively. Water features, whether still or moving, served as focal points. Adventure playgrounds perpetuated the importance of addressing play in municipal parks; and public art, though not often appreciated as such, was used literally and figuratively as place markers. Paley Park in Manhattan, Manhattan Square Park in Rochester, and the Commons in Ithaca were three early examples incorporating these characteristics. The 4,000 ft^2 (371 m^2) Paley Park at 53d St between 5th Ave and Madison Ave was designed by Zion and Breen in 1965 and used a wall of cascading water and the dappled shade of honey locust to provide a soothing and comfortable open space. Noted landscape artist Lawrence Halprin's 5-acre (2 ha) Manhattan Square Park integrated play and water in an elaborate fountain and stage (1975). The design for the Commons in 1976, by Anton Egner Associates with landscape architect Marvin Adelman, adapted several blocks of a major downtown Ithaca street into a pedestrian mall that included public art and seating enclaves accented by vegetation.

See also ARCHITECTS AND ARCHITECTURE, SARATOGA COUNTY; SCULPTURE, PUBLIC; WORLD'S FAIRS; ZOOS.

Capella Peters, Christine, and George W. Curry. "A Framework for the 21st Century: Frederick Law Olmsted Jr's 1908 Report for Utica, NY." In *Book of Texts for the International Symposium for the Conservation of Urban Squares and Parks* (Montreal, 1992)

Cranz, Galen. *The Politics of Park Design: A History of Urban Parks in America* (Cambridge, Mass: MIT Press, 1982)

Pregill, Philip, and Nancy Volkman. *Landscapes in History: Design and Planning in the Western Tradition* (New York: Van Nostrand Reinhold, 1993)

Schuyler, David. *The New Urban Landscape: The Redefinition of City Form in 19th-Century America* (Baltimore: Johns Hopkins Univ Press, 1986)

Christine Capella Peters

Uruguayans. The number of Uruguayans immigrating to the United States has remained moderately stable throughout the 1990s, and most are professionals. They do not represent a sizable population when compared to other groups with South American origins, but many factors point toward a growing Uruguayan presence in the United States. Uruguayans have developed some transnational projects in New York State, such as Reaching U, whose objective is to improve the quality of life of marginalized communities in Uruguay. In addition, a statue of the Uruguayan national hero, General José Gervasio Artigas, was unveiled in SoHo on 6th Ave and Broome St in the late 1990s. Uruguayans in New York State celebrate their Independence Day on 25 August with social gatherings. The 2000 census indicates that there were approximately 18,804 Uruguayans living in the United States. An independent report favors a higher estimate of 30,010. In New York State there are approximately 3,366 Uruguayans, with the majority of them residing in Queens Co (1,255), primarily in the Jackson Heights area, as well as in Westchester Co (690).

International Organization for Migration. *World Migration Report: 2000* (Geneva, Switzerland: UN Publications, 2000)

Ana Margarita Cervantes-Rodríguez and Michael C. English

USAir. See ALLEGHENY AIRLINES.

US 9. As trading posts became settlements in the dense forests along the Hudson River, the Kings' Highway, now US 9 (commonly known as Rte 9), was created by law on 19 June 1703. Early settlements served as campsites for Gen George Washington's troops during the Revolutionary War. In addition, numerous battles along US 9 occurred during the French and Indian War, Revolutionary War, and War of 1812. A national highway, it begins as US 9 near Laurel, Del, entering New York State at the New York–New Jersey state line at the George Washington Bridge, and extends 325 miles (523 km) to the Canadian border, exiting the state at the Northway (I-87) in Champlain (Clinton Co). The major retail corridor for hundreds of communities, US 9 served as the primary south-north corridor for automobiles and trucks until the New York State Thruway and Northway were built in the late 1950s and early 1960s. Afterward many downtown business districts and roadside businesses suffered a severe decline of patronage as more people opted for the freeways over the scenic byways and two-lane roads going directly through towns and cities.

Matthew J. Lindstrom

US Open. A tennis tournament held in New York City since 1924, when it was known as the US National Singles Championship. The men's competition originated in 1881 at Newport, RI, and the women's in 1887 at Philadelphia. In 1915 the US National Lawn Tennis Association, now the United States Tennis Association (USTA), moved the men's singles tournament to the West Side Tennis Club in Forest Hills in Queens, where it remained except for three years from 1921 through 1923. The women's event came to Forest Hills as a separate tournament in 1921. The name of the tournament changed to US Open in 1968, with competition open to both professionals and amateurs. Arthur Ashe, the first African American man to become amateur champion, won the 1968 men's singles tournament. The US Open consolidated five major competitions—men's and women's singles, men's and women's doubles, and mixed doubles—offering a total of $100,000 to the winners. The tournament was held on grass courts until the Forest Hills venue was changed to clay in 1975. In 1978 the US Open moved to Flushing Meadows–Corona Park and the asphalt composition hard courts at the USTA National Tennis Center, making the tournament the only Grand Slam event that has been played on three types of court surfaces. The proximity of the stadium to La Guardia Airport as well as the need for additional seating and other renovations threatened the tournament's continued existence in the city. In 1993 New York City mayor and tennis enthusiast David Dinkins signed legislation for the construction of a 23,000-seat stadium as part of a $254 million transformation financed by USTA-guaranteed bonds. The Arthur Ashe Tennis Stadium was dedicated in 1997, and additional renovations of the USTA complex increased the number of courts to 47, open to the public 300 days each year. The US Open receives television and press coverage in more than 160 countries. The 2002 match offered more than $16.2 million in prize money.

Collins, Bud, and Zander Hollander. *Bud Collins' Modern Encyclopedia of Tennis* (Washington, DC: Gale Research, 1994)

Williams, Roger M. *The US Open: Game, Set, Unmatched* (New York: Time-Life Books, 1997)

Kristen L. Allen-Hanks

USS *San Diego*. On 19 July 1918 the largest warship lost by the US Navy during World War I sank about 11 miles (18 km) southeast of Fire Island Inlet. The *San Diego*, a 14,000-ton (12,700 MT) armored cruiser traveling from Portsmouth, NH, to Staten Island, was ripped by an explosion on its port side. It sank in about 20 minutes, but only 6 of 1,183 men and officers were lost. The vessel's commander, Capt Harley H. Christy, believed that a German U-boat had torpedoed his ship. Possibly to calm public fears, the Naval Court of Inquiry declared that a mine had sunk the *San Diego*. However, acting on declassified British intercepts of German naval communications, the US Navy reversed the determination in 1959 and attributed the loss to a torpedo fired by a German U-156, thus confirming Christy's conviction. The *San Diego* lies inverted in the sand 115 feet (35 m) below the surface. Six divers have died investigating the wreck.

Gentile, Gary. *The U.S.S.* San Diego*: The Last Armored Cruiser* (Gary Gentile Productions, 1989)

Hausrath, Ralph. "The Sinking of the USS *San Diego*," *Long Island Forum* 53 (Spring 1990): 52–58

USS San Diego, http://www.geocities.com/Yosemite/5609/sandiego.html

Richard F. Welch

US 20. An east-west highway from Boston to Newport, Ore, more than 3,200 mi (5,150 km) long, which enters New York State at New Lebanon (Columbia Co) on the Massachusetts border and exits at State Line (Chatauqua Co) into Pennsylvania, a distance of 400 mi (644 km). Formed from Native American trails and earlier turnpikes, US 20 marked the route of migration that fueled the western expansion of the United States through New York State and was instrumental in the state's economic growth. At the beginning of the 19th century, commerce developed rapidly in interior New York, aided by migrants from New England. The initial developed portion of the route, known as the First Great Western Turnpike, was chartered by the New York State legislature on 10 Apr 1792 to run from Albany to Cherry Valley (Otsego Co). However, a wagon road was not completed until 1806, allowing commerce and people to move easily on its path from Albany to Cazenovia (Madison Co). The first tollgate stood west of Manning Blvd in Albany. The road continued to play an important role in the economic life of the state throughout the 1800s and into the 1900s. West of Cazenovia to LaFayette (Onondaga Co), the highway reflects its 1934 alignment. With the rise in automobile travel, auto camps, tourist attractions, and small restaurants proliferated on US 20. The Tepee, a souvenir shop near Cherry Valley, is known for its distinctive architecture.

The completion of the New York State Thruway in 1956 had a negative impact on US 20 as travelers chose the faster toll road. In the first year of the Thruway's opening, revenues for US 20's roadside businesses dropped 30%. In 1999, recognizing US 20's importance to New York State commerce and the unique architecture found along the route, the Preservation League of New York State named the roadway as one of its Seven to Save.

Lape, Fred. *A Farm and Village Boyhood* (Syracuse: Syracuse Univ Press, 1980)

US Route 20, http://www.usroute20.com/

Ellen McHale

Utica. City (pop 60,651) in E Oneida Co. Located at a ford on the Mohawk River, the locality was a natural place for fortification and settlement. In 1758 Fort Schuyler (later Old Fort Schuyler) was constructed as a protective outpost, but it was never garrisoned. In 1772 four prominent New Yorkers, including Gen Philip Schuyler, purchased the lapsed 1734 grant of Gov William Cosby, but it was not until after the end of the Revolutionary War that the tract was surveyed into lots (1786) and settlement commenced (1788) by a mixture of westward-moving Yankees, Dutch, Germans, and in the late 1790s Welsh. Its location in the gap and at a ford was a strong asset to traders. It quickly became a market town, and in 1797 Bryan Johnson began purchasing produce for cash, a business previously monopolized by Kane and Van Rensselaer of Canajoharie (Montgomery Co). When the latter partnership moved to Utica, a vital competition was set in motion, and Utica became a center of trade. Having acquired a post office in 1795 under the name Old Fort Schuyler, it incorporated as Utica in 1798 after its name was chosen at random from a hat, and the post office followed suit. A town surrounding the village was later formed, in 1817, from Whitestown.

Capital from trade accumulated and the Bank of Utica was chartered in 1812. Utica merchants invested in mills in nearby towns on the Oriskany and Sauquoit Creeks. Along with trade and industries not requiring waterpower, such as glass (1809–36) and stoneware (1825–1910), Utica businesses quickly specialized in transportation and accommodation. The Erie Canal opened westward in 1819 and eastward in 1821, and created a demand for overnight lodging, meals, and provisions. Business increased when the canal became a through route in 1825; in the succeeding 10 years population almost doubled to 10,183. Utica incorporated as a city in 1832.

Continuing transportation improvements ultimately impacted Utica's business community. The Utica and Schenectady Railroad (1836) and the Syracuse and Utica (1839)—merged in 1853 as the New York Central—carried travelers past Utica without stopping and forced Utica's capitalists to look closely at New England cities for a replacement for lost business. Utica had no waterpower, but with coal cheap because of the Chenango Canal (1837), there was great potential in textile mills. In 1847 the Utica Steam Cotton-Mill Co and Globe Woolen Co began operation, followed by other textile mills and factories producing ironwork, screws, millstones, shoes and shoe lasts, clothing, and cigars.

Utica was chosen as the site of the New York State Lunatic Asylum (1843; now Mohawk Valley Psychiatric Center) and became the site of the first commercial telegraph company in the United States (1845). It acquired rail links north and south: the Black River and Utica Railroad (1855) and the Utica, Clinton and Binghamton Railroad (1870, later Ontario and Western Railroad). In 1863 it became the fifth US city with a horse-drawn trolley system.

The factories drew immigrant workers in large numbers. Despite its early influx of Yankee and New World "Dutch," Utica soon became a markedly ethnic city. It and its environs were the home of one of the largest concentrations of Welsh in North America. The national Welsh newspaper, *Y Drych*, was published weekly from 1860 to 1940 and continued as a monthly until 1960. The first Irish came with canal construction and built St John's Church as early as 1819; more came during the famine, and they numbered 15% of the city's population in 1855. German speakers from Germany, Austria, Alsace, and Switzerland followed in the 1830s, numbering 11% in 1855, and they too published a Utica newspaper (1853–1934). Jews, especially from Poland, arrived as peddlers, established Beth Israel Synagogue (1848), and grew in numbers in the 1870s. Italians, including a community of Italian Baptists, arrived starting in the 1870s. Later groups included Poles, western Ukrainians, and Syrian Lebanese, their immigration taking place generally from the 1890s to the early 1920s.

Although makers of heaters (International Heater, 1889) and guns (Savage Arms, 1900) also became large employers, textiles came to represent industrial Utica, especially knit goods beginning in the late 1850s. Utica's 19 knitting mills in 1902 employed 20,000 workers and earned it recognition as the Knit Goods Capital of the World. World War I brought flush times, as Utica supplied knit underwear and machine guns for the war effort, but labor unrest soon followed. A 1919 strike by Polish and Italian operatives at the Oneita Knitting Co lasted five months and was the cause of an incident during which police fired 250 rounds at peaceful protesters outside City Hall.

The city, located on a plain south of the Mohawk River and the Erie Canal, pushed outward, annexing territory on 16 occasions, beginning with a tract taken from New Hartford in 1862. In 1891 and 1916 territory was taken north of the

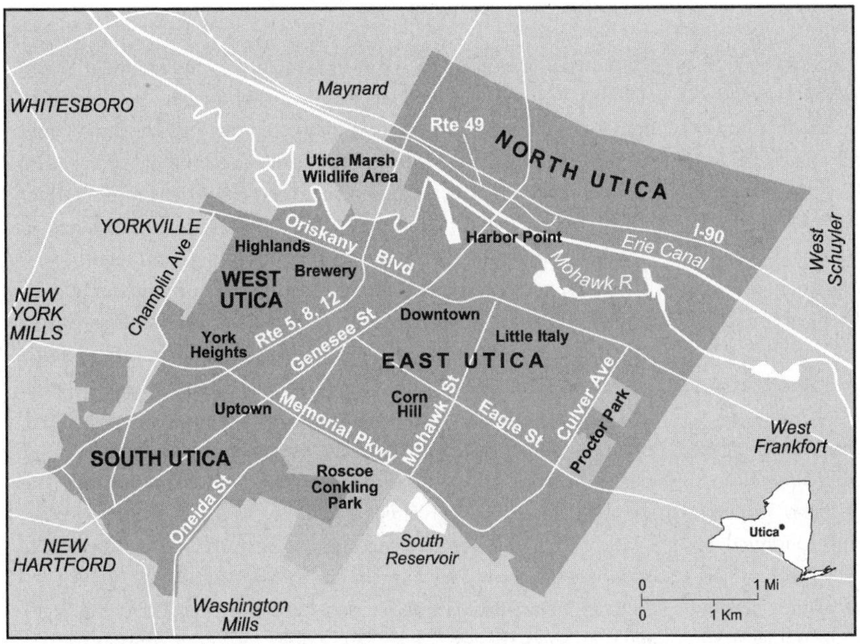

Mohawk from Deerfield; in 1911 the canal was moved northward and rebuilt as the New York State Barge Canal. The last annexation took place in 1967.

Culture

A common school was in operation by 1797. As befitting a rising mercantile class, the Utica Academy (1814) and Utica Female Seminary (1837) provided secondary education; the former joined the public system as its high school in 1853. Charles Grandison Finney held his first successful urban revival in Utica over the winter of 1825–26 and helped make the city a center of evangelical Protestantism in the decades before the Civil War. Utica was a pioneer in the pictorial press: in 1881, the *Saturday Globe* was the first illustrated newspaper in the United States. Successor to many earlier papers, the modern *Observer-Dispatch* was formed by Frank E. Gannett in 1922, the same year that the first radio station, WIBX, went on the air.

For a city its size, Utica has a distinguished literary history. Alexander Bryan Johnson (1786–1867), a banker, published a series of pathbreaking works on philosophy, linguistics, and semiotics that have only recently been rediscovered. Harold Frederic (1856–98), editor of the *Utica Daily Observer* from 1880 to 1882, set many of his works in and around a lightly disguised Utica, including his best-known novel, *The Damnation of Theron Ware* (1896). Late 20th century works include several novels set among Utica Italians in the 1950s by the well-known literary critic Frank Lentricchia and memoirs of the Arab community by Eugene Nassar. The city's distinguished art museum, the Munson-Williams-Proctor Arts Institute (1919), its historic house museum, Fountain Elms, the Oneida County Historical Society (1876), the Children's Museum at Utica (1963), Central New York Arts Council, the restored Stanley Theater (1928), its resident Utica Symphony Orchestra, and the Mohawk Valley Ballet make up an unusual concentration of fine arts in a small city. Utica is also the home of the National Distance Running Hall of Fame and the annual Good Old Summertime Festival. The Utica Boilermaker, a 15 km race started in 1976, is the largest race of its distance in the United States. Utica is a center of the sport of curling, although the main curling facility moved to a suburban location in 1997.

Higher education in Utica and vicinity has been largely a postwar development. Utica College (originally Utica College of Syracuse University) and Mohawk Valley Community College (originally the New York State Institute of Applied Arts and Sciences at Utica) both opened in 1946. The Utica School of Commerce (1896), the St. Elizabeth College of Nursing (1904), and the Munson-Williams-Proctor School of Art (1941; affiliated with Pratt Institute) are smaller but significant.

Politics

In 1835 a Utica lawyer, Alvan Stewart, was instrumental in calling for a meeting of some 600 abolitionists who formed what would become the New York State Anti-Slavery Society. On 21 October a crowd of some 300 antiabolitionists, mostly day laborers but backed by many of the leading citizens of Utica, broke into the meeting, and a bloody riot ensued. The riot is an example of how divided the city was on the political questions of the day. The city was represented by nationally influential figures on both sides of the political spectrum. Democrat Horatio Seymour (1810–86), mayor in 1843, was governor 1853–55 and 1863–65, and the unsuccessful 1868 Democratic candidate for president. His brother-in-law, Roscoe Conkling (1829–88) was mayor in 1858 and a powerful US senator. Republican James S. Sherman (1855–1912) of Utica was elected US vice president in 1908.

Ethnic politics created two strong political machines during the 19th and 20th centuries. In the 1870s a political machine came to control both local parties. By the 1880s insurgent Irish and members of other immigrant groups wrested control of the Democratic Party, leaving the machine to run the Republican Party. During the presidential campaign of Alfred E. Smith in 1928, when Republicans capitalized on anti-Catholic feeling to defeat the Catholic Smith, the Republican machine lost its dominance in Utica politics. This paved the way for the rise of the Democratic machine that had strong connections with both federal and state legislators. As a result, Utica benefited from considerable patronage in the 1930s and 1940s. The machine's leader, Democrat Rufus Elefante (1903–94), worked city politics to the benefit of his constituents. But after a 1959 state investigation into crime and vice embarrassed Uticans, they ousted old guard Democrats and elected Republican Frank M. Dulan to the mayoralty. The first Italian-American mayor, Dominick Assaro, assumed office in 1967. Controversial international businessman Edward Hanna was elected on the Democratic ticket in 1973, but, when his party refused to renominate him two years later, he formed an independent Rainbow Party and won; he was again elected in 1995 and 1999. At the turn of the 21st century, Hanna, in his fourth term, cooperated with Rome's city government and with the Oneida county executive to attract new business.

Detail from a panoramic map of Utica, *ca* 1850.

Bosnians in Utica. New York State has long been a haven for refugees from war. More than 100,000 refugees from the horror that descended on the former Republic of Yugoslavia in the 1990s found sanctuary in the United States. Of the approximately 12,000 Bosnian refugees in New York State, about one-third have been resettled in Utica by the federal Office of Refugee Resettlement in the US Department of Health and Human Services. Approximately three-quarters of the state's Bosnian refugees are Muslim (targeted in the war for ethnic cleansing), almost one-quarter are Serbs, and a small number are Croats or of mixed or other ancestries.

By the end of August 2001, approximately 4,200 Bosnian refugees had officially resettled in Utica. While some have since left the area, Utica has attracted Bosnians moving from other parts of the United States, drawn to reunification with families and friends, inexpensive housing, and a strong center for refugee services, the Mohawk Valley Resource Center for Refugees. Significant numbers of Bosnians continued to arrive under the Family Reunification Act—15,777 in 2001 with projections for 6,000 more in 2002 and 2,500 more in 2003, as immigration rules become increasingly restrictive. Immigrating Bosnian refugees are much younger on average than the resident population of the city as a whole. Bosnian families are repopulating the city and its schools, with 1,068 (approximately one-quarter of all Utica's Bosnian refugees) of public school age (5–17 years old) when they immigrated, and another 450 under 5 years old. More than one-third of the Bosnians were under age 18 on arrival, compared with less than one-quarter of all residents citywide in 2000.

Bosnian refugees arrived in the United States after an interim period in Croatian refugee camps or in countries of first asylum such as Germany, Austria, Sweden, or Pakistan. Most came with few belongings and no means of support, although some had been able to work in countries of first asylum and accumulate modest savings. Most Bosnian refugees found employment within three or four months of arriving in Utica. Entry-level jobs for refugees with beginning English offer low pay and demand low skills, even though the refugees may have held managerial or professional positions in Bosnia. In a sample of 100 Bosnian families interviewed in 1999, 60% of women and 68% of men were working as machine operators, fabricators, or laborers. Many are frustrated by the loss of professional and economic status, but as their English language skills improve, they are moving into better positions as teachers, city planners, insurance sellers, financial planners, laboratory technicians, and supervisors. There are also 15–20 Bosnian entrepreneurs running construction, restaurant, discotheque, barber shop, and beauty salon businesses in Utica. The Bosnian community has a privately published newspaper, Cross Atlantic, a radio broadcast in their native Bosnian language on a rural network station on Sunday mornings, and a private karate school for its youth. Several Bosnian soccer teams have helped raise the level of play in the regional men's league.

Many refugees purchased homes just two or three years after arriving in Utica. According to recent estimates, nearly 400 Bosnian families in Utica own homes, most clustered in East Utica, in and around the Corn Hill area. Bosnians have helped rebuild neighborhoods by purchasing homes and improving them, and they often buy two- or three-family homes to provide housing for relatives or as an additional source of income. Following Bosnian tradition, they try to avoid debt, often working more than one job to save money. Families tend to pool their incomes, rapidly accumulating savings for housing, furnishings, and cars.

Bosnian family relationships remain strong in both nuclear and extended kin groups. Respect for elders and social traditions of hospitality are carried over in home life. About 80% of the Bosnian refugees in Utica are Muslims. The other 20% may be partners in mixed marriages of Catholic, Orthodox, or Muslim religions, or children of parents of different religions. Although most Bosnian Muslims consider themselves secular, there is regular participation in a mosque in Utica, with two imams serving the diverse local Islamic community.

There are significant differences among Bosnians in Utica, depending on where and how they lived in the former Yugoslavia. About two-thirds of Utica's Bosnian population came from small towns, villages, and rural areas; the rest lived in larger cities, including Sarajevo, Mostar, and Zenica. Refugees from major cities had good jobs and enjoyed travel and middle-class amenities before the war, a lifestyle that was abruptly cut off. Many of those from small towns and rural villages were subsistence farmers, and men in rural households typically sought wage employment to supplement household income. Social, political, and economic differences were embedded in the Muslim, Catholic, and Orthodox cultural traditions, creating an extremely diverse society. Some of these differences undoubtedly survived the move to America, but the disruptions of war and adjustment to a new society may have lessened the social cleavages of the past.

The refugees face the challenges of adjustment and starting over after the losses of war and in a new environment; the situation is particularly difficult for the elderly. Most families lost close relatives and friends during the war; family separations continue to be a hardship for many as immigration rules have become more restrictive. Frustration and anxiety are compounded by the economic and political plight of relatives and friends in Bosnia. While acknowledging that conditions are not excellent, many of Utica's Bosnians describe Utica and the United States as places offering support and opportunity. In planning for the future they emphasize their children's education and investment in economic stability for their families. Most anticipate applying for US citizenship.

Coughlan, Reed, and Judith Owens-Manley. "Adaptation of Refugees during Cross-cultural Transitions: Bosnian Refugees in Upstate New York." In *Crossing Borders, Changing Minds*, ed. Jorunn Fure and Line Alice Ytrehus (Bergen, Norway: Kulturstudier, the Norwegian Research Council, 2002)

——. "The New Face of Immigration: Bosnian Refugees in Transition." In *Ethnic Utica*, ed. J. Pula (Utica: Oneida County Historical Society, 2002)

——. *New Communities, New Cultures* (New York: Kluwer Academic/Plenum Publishers, forthcoming)

Reed Coughlan and Judith Owens-Manley

Recent History

Utica's population passed 100,000 in 1930 and held steady through 1960 before a precipitous decline set in, caused by industrial transformation. The city's textile works again supplied the armed forces during World War II, as did Utica Cutlery (bayonets), Brunner Manufacturing (pumps, freezer units), Divine Bros (fuses), and Bossert Co (cartridge cases). As late as 1950 soft goods employed 9,500 workers, but seven years later so many firms had moved south that only 1,100 people still had jobs in the sector. Nearby Griffiss Air Force Base (1948) compensated in part for the lost jobs, but it was recognized from the beginning as an impermanent source.

City leaders began actively soliciting new manufacturers soon after World War II, drawing Chicago Pneumatic Tool Co (1948), Bendix (1951), General Electric (GE; 1953), Sperry-Rand Univac (1957), and Kelsey-Hayes Co, among others. GE, with its 6,500 workers in 1965, was the leader, but each firm employed 1,000 or more. Utica also benefited from easy Thruway access (1954) and a continuing influx of eager workers, including African Americans from the South and more Poles and Ukrainians.

With the end of the textile industry, Utica's tired infrastructure encouraged a flight to the suburbs. Shopping centers opened in Whitestown and North Utica; in the late 1970s the city's flagship department store, the Boston Store, closed. During the late 1950s, a 12-block site on the western edge of downtown became an urban renewal pilot project. Several subsequent urban renewal projects leveled deteriorated blocks, but in many cases nothing rose in their place. In the last quarter of the century, Utica lost most of the hard-goods plants that had replaced textiles between 1948 and 1957. As had happened so many times before, new groups of people seeking a better life moved into the space left by those who had succeeded and moved on to follow the jobs. In the 1970s refugees from Vietnam, Cambodia, and Laos, and beginning in 1993 refuges from Bosnia and immigrants from Russia brought their aspirations to Utica. Nevertheless, the city's population fell to around 60,000 and that of the metropolitan area fell from its 1970 peak of 340,000 to 300,000 in 2000.

At the very end of the 20th century, new life was coming to the center city. A post–urban renewal era City Hall and county and state office buildings still anchored the downtown cityscape, but newer positive signs were seen in the conversion of the old Bankers Trust Building in 1998 for corporate offices and, especially, in the $13 million restoration of the Hotel Utica. Zogby International (1984), an important public opinion firm founded by a Utica native, was based in the city and growing in size and importance. Other attractions include the Saranac Brewery and the historic Amtrak station, which serves as the southern terminus of the Adirondack Scenic Railroad. Utica today has more acres of parkland per capita than any other city in the United States.

See also ARCHITECTS AND ARCHITECTURE, SYRACUSE AND CENTRAL NEW YORK; GUNS AND ORDNANCE INDUSTRY; SUBURBANIZATION; TEXTILE INDUSTRY.

Bagg, M. M. *Memorial History of Utica, N.Y.* (Syracuse: D. Mason, 1892)

Bean, Philip A. "The Irish, the Italians, and Machine Politics," *Journal of Urban History* 20 (1994): 205–39

"History of the Village and City of Utica." In *History of Oneida County* (Philadelphia: Everts and Fariss, 1878)

Thomas, Alexander R. *In Gotham's Shadow: Globalization and Community Change in Central New York* (Albany: SUNY Press, 2003)

Tomaino, Frank. "Utica." In *Exploring 200 Years of Oneida County History,* ed. Donald F. White (Utica: Oneida County Historical Society, 1998)

Field Horne and Alex Thomas

Utica College. Private liberal arts college. Originally Utica College of Syracuse University, it opened as a two-year college at Oneida Square in downtown Utica in September 1946 and became a four-year school in 1949. The campus relocated to Burrstone Rd in 1961, and ground was broken for the first dormitory in 1963. In 1995 Utica College's charter was revised, granting it independent status from Syracuse University; the two institutions, however, maintain their academic relationship and students still receive a Syracuse University diploma. Along with its 27 undergraduate programs, Utica College offers 4 master's degree programs. In 2003 Utica College enrolled 2,175 undergraduate and 215 graduate students.

Behrens, John C., and Michael K. Simpson. *Pioneering Generations: The Utica College Story, 1946–1996* (Utica: Utica College Press, 1997)

Sarah E. DeSanctis

Utica Observer-Dispatch. Eliasaph Dorchester founded the weekly *Oneida Observer,* which was sometimes published under the title *Utica Observer,* in 1817. When Dorchester became Oneida Co clerk, printer Augustus Dauby took over and in 1826 became partners with Eli Maynard. The name formally changed to *Utica Observer* in 1831. In 1834 the *Observer* began a daily edition, and the paper acquired the *Utica Democrat* in 1852. The weekly edition continued through 1916 under a series of different names. Rochester-based newspaper publisher Frank E. Gannett purchased the daily paper in 1922, the same year he purchased the *Herald-Dispatch,* which he combined into the *Utica Observer-Dispatch.* Unlike the Democratic-leaning *Observer* and the Republican-oriented *Herald-Dispatch,* the combined newspaper was nonpartisan. In 1935 Gannett purchased another competing daily, the *Utica Daily Press.* The *Observer-Dispatch* and *Daily Press* jointly received a Pulitzer Prize in 1959 for meritorious service for their investigation of official corruption in Utica, which sparked reforms of city government. The two papers combined operations in 1987, publishing since as the *Observer-Dispatch.* At the beginning of the 21st century it had a Monday-to-Saturday circulation averaging 49,000 and a Sunday circulation of 60,000. It publishes regional editions for the Utica, Rome (Oneida Co), and Herkimer Co markets.

Williamson, Samuel T. *Imprint of a Publisher: The Story of Frank Gannett and His Independent Newspapers* (New York: Robert M. McBride, 1948)

Martin Naparsteck

utopian and intentional communities. The formation of experimental communities to exemplify specific social goals and ideals has found fertile ground in New York State since the early 19th century. Although there are exceptions to every generalization about utopian and other intentional communities, common characteristics include collective decision making, some form of communal ownership of property, and the belief that the forms of social interaction practiced were a model for others and perhaps in time would be adopted more generally.

RELIGIOUS COMMUNITIES: 19TH CENTURY

The most common impulse for the formation of utopian communities has been religious or spiritual. During the 19th century the combination of available land, thriving commerce, the general toleration of heterodox spirituality, and the proximity to large urban centers made New York State one of the centers of American communalism. The state's earliest utopian community was the first Shaker settlement at Mount Lebanon (Columbia Co) in 1787, which operated until 1947, the longest lasting of all intentional communities in the state. The Shakers also established three other sites in New York State: Watervliet (Albany Co), Groveland (Livingston Co), and Sodus Bay (Wayne Co). Jemima Wilkinson, a charismatic preacher who styled herself the "Publick Universal Friend," founded Jerusalem [now in Yates Co], which existed from 1788 to 1820. The Ebenezer Society, or the Community of True Inspiration, was a German immigrant religious community near Buffalo from 1843 to 1855. Crowded by the growth of Buffalo, they moved to Amana, Iowa, in 1855.

Probably the best-known utopian community in 19th-century New York State was the Oneida Community (1848–81) in Madison Co, led by religious Perfectionist John Humphrey Noyes (1811–86) and organized around his unique brand of Bible communism. He argued for the possibility of sinless perfection in this life and, notoriously, for a rejection of monogamous marriage in favor of regulated couplings between consenting adults. This evolved in 1869 into an experiment in selective breeding. The community lasted until 1881, when internal tensions over sexual practices and external hostility led to its breakup. There were short-lived branches in Manlius (Onondaga Co) and Brooklyn from 1851 to 1855. With 300 members at its height, it was one of the few financially successful utopian experiments. It left behind a silverware manufactory that became the well-known concern Oneida Ltd. The community's Mansion House is a National Historic Landmark.

Modern spiritualism had its origins in New York State in the 1840s, and the state was home to a number of spiritualist communities. The members of Harmonia (1853–63) at Kiantone (Chautauqua Co), led by former Unitarian minister John Murray Spear (1804–87), hoped to create a city of universal harmony. Thomas Lake Harris (1823–1906), born in England, raised in Utica, and minister of a spiritualist church in New York City in the 1840s, was the founder of three spiritualist communities in the state. Known as the Brotherhood of the Good Life, they were in Amenia (Dutchess Co) from 1861 to 1863, Wassaic (Dutchess Co) from 1863 to 1867, and Brocton (Chautauqua Co) from 1867 to 1875, when Harris and his closest followers moved to California. The Brotherhood's members, which included both men and women, were largely celibate and practiced various breathing techniques to achieve higher states of consciousness. Because of contributions from wealthy members, they were able to start a successful vineyard at Brocton. Of the approximately 60 members at Brocton, there were about 20 Japanese Christians, who had come to America to study with Harris. The short-lived Dawn Valcour community (1874–75) was on Valcour Island in Clinton Co and in western Vermont. It combined elements of spiritualism with Fourierist socialism.

SOCIALIST AND SECULAR COMMUNITIES: 19TH CENTURY

Perhaps the nation's first nonreligious utopian community was the Union in Clark's Crossing [now Potsdam, St. Lawrence Co], extant from 1804 to 1810. About 12 families under the leadership of William Bullard held property in common. The Union was a forerunner of the Owenite and Fourierist utopian socialist communities that would flourish from the 1820s to the 1840s. Scottish industrialist and reformer Robert Owen, who established a model community at New Harmony, Ind, in 1825, had followers in New York City who established the New York Society for Promoting Communities. They created two Owenite communities in 1826: the Franklin Community at Haverstraw (Rockland Co), which lasted about five months, and the Forestville Community at Coxsackie (Greene Co), which survived only slightly longer. Disputes between radical freethinkers influenced by the sermons of the radical preacher Abner Kneeland and those of more conventional religious views hastened the demise of the Owenite experiments. In 1827 about half the membership of the Forestville Community moved farther west to Ohio to join another colony.

During the late 1830s and early 1840s, the writings of the eccentric French philosopher Charles Fourier began to attract an audience among New York State intellectuals, especially through the efforts of Albert Brisbane, a native of Batavia (Genesee Co). Starting in 1841 a series of Fourierist communities were established across the country, with several organized in New York City. Six phalanxes, or industrial associations, were created in the mid-1840s at Sodus Bay, North Bloomfield, Clarkson [now Hamlin], Bates Mills [now Littleville], Mixville [now Wiscoy], and Cold Creek, the first four in what is now considered the greater Rochester metropolitan area. Fourier's phalanxes emphasized joint-stock holding of property, the achievement of individual needs and desires within the context of a community, and the throwing off of restraints of civilized life and labor (as epitomized by the factory system) in favor of "passional attraction." None lasted more than two years. A related venture was the Skaneateles Community (Onondaga Co), the product of several reform meetings held in Syracuse in 1843 and of the work of an antislavery agent and agitator named John Collins. Collins issued a statement in 1843 stressing anarchist principles and Fourierist practices that emphasized common ownership of land and a prohibition on alcohol and meat eating, and that hinted at a free-love philosophy. Disputes between Collins and a Syracuse lawyer, Quincy Johnson, led to the breakup of the community in 1846. An anarchist or libertarian philosophy animated Modern Times [now Brentwood, Suffolk Co], which was founded in 1851 and lasted until 1864. It developed out of the social and economic theories of Josiah Warren and Stephen Pearl Andrews, both advocates of liberal divorce and equitable labor. Reports of the practice of "free love" dogged its existence.

Communities in the 20th-Century

In the late 19th and early 20th centuries utopian and intentional communities continued to be founded, though they tended to be smaller, lacking in charismatic figures, looser in organizational form, and more diverse in type than their predecessors. One of the new forms in the early decades of the 20th century were artists' colonies. The best known in the state was Roycroft in East Aurora (Erie Co), founded by Elbert Hubbard, who from around 1895 to 1915 produced fine furniture and other handcraft. Roycroft combined aspects of a cooperative association of craftsworkers and a commercial enterprise operated by Hubbard. Two artists' communities in Woodstock (Ulster Co)—Byrdcliffe, opened in 1903, and the Maverick, opened in 1908—drew numerous artists and gave Woodstock a continuing legacy as a center for artists.

Many intentional communities founded in New York State in the 20th century had a religious orientation. The Catholic Worker movement, founded by Dorothy Day in New York City in 1933, operated both urban communal houses and rural farms in Newburgh (Orange Co) from 1947 to 1955, in Pleasant Plains (Richmond Co) from 1950 to 1964, and in Tivoli (Dutchess Co) from 1964 to 1979. The Anabaptist-inspired Bruderhof movement, founded by anti-Nazi German refugees, established its first American community at Rifton (Ulster Co) in 1953; they later formed four others in the state that continue into the early 21st century.

In the mid–20th century there was a revival of traditional monasticism in the state. In 1951 two traditional Roman Catholic monasteries were founded: the Trappist Abbey of the Genesee at Piffard (Livingston Co) and the Benedictine Mount Saviour Monastery in Pine City (Chemung Co). The monasteries of New Skete (1966) in Cambridge (Washington Co), associated with the Orthodox Church of America, has separate monasteries for men, women, and married couples. It is best known for its best-selling text on dog training. Non-Western religious communities have also flourished. Some of the more enduring are the Hindu Ananda Ashram (1964) in Monroe (Orange Co), the Zen Center of Rochester (1966), and the Tibetan Buddhist Namgyal Monastery (1992) in Ithaca. A Sufi community, the Abode of the Message, opened in 1975 on hallowed communal grounds in Mount Lebanon, on the site of the old Shaker settlement.

The state's most significant political communitarian movement in the middle decades of the 20th century was inspired by Ralph Borsodi (1888–1977), a New York City writer who advocated small-scale subsistence farming and homesteading. He founded several communal homesteads in Rockland Co, including the Dogwoods Homestead (?1923–?45), Bayard Lane Homestead Association (?1936–?45), and School of Living (1934–45) at Suffern, and the Van Houten Fields Community (1939–?1945) at West Nyack.

Communes in the 1960s

Far more intentional communities were formed between 1960 and 1975 than in any other period in US history. Historian Timothy Miller in *The 60s Communes* documented 126 New York State communes formed during these 15 years. One of the earliest and most influential of all was Millbrook (Dutchess Co), which from 1963 to 1966 was a collective experiment in psychedelic drug use and general abandon, and its excesses helped make its leader, Timothy Leary, one of the decade's icons. Although many of the 1960s communes were influenced by the counterculture and a desire to return to nature and simplicity and to throw off what were perceived as the shackles of societal restriction, these communes varied widely. By no means were all founded by those who might be described as hippies. There were urban and rural communes, communes inspired by Eastern and Western religions, and secular communes. Some were committed to radical political action; many more sought only a simpler lifestyle. Most proved ephemeral, though their influence on trends in politics, ecology, interpersonal relationships, diet, and spiritual expression belied their relatively short duration. Some formed during this period were extant in 1999, including two established by followers of anthroposophist Rudolf Steiner: the Fellowship Community, founded in 1967 in Spring Valley (Rockland Co), and Triform, founded in 1977 in Hudson (Columbia Co). Others to survive to the end of the 20th century included the Rochester Folk Art Guild, begun in 1967; the Farm, opened in Canaan (Columbia Co) in 1971; and Birdsfoot Farm, opened in 1972 in Canton (St. Lawrence Co).

Bestor, Arthur, Jr. *Backwoods Utopia*, 2d ed. (Philadelphia: Univ of Pennsylvania Press, 1970)

Fogarty, Robert S. *Dictionary of American Communal and Utopian History* (Westport, Conn: Greenwood Press, 1980)

———. *All Things New: American Communes and Utopian Movements, 1860–1914* (Chicago: Univ of Chicago Press, 1990)

Guarneri, Carl. *The Utopian Alternative: Fourierism in 19th-Century America* (Ithaca: Cornell Univ Press, 1991)

Miller, Timothy. *The Quest for Utopia in 20th-Century America: 1900–1960* (Syracuse: Syracuse Univ Press, 1998)

———. *The 60s Communes: Hippies and Beyond* (Syracuse Univ Press, 1999)

Robert Fogarty

Uzbeks. See Central Asians.

V

Valatie [VA-LAY-SHA]. Village (pop 1,712) in Kinderhook (Columbia Co). A sawmill and gristmill were operating by 1763, but Valatie's industrial development began *ca* 1820 with Kinderhook Manufacturing Co (cotton goods). Within a decade there were three cotton factories and two iron foundries. Later products included weaving machinery, cotton wadding, knit goods, and wrapping paper. The village was incorporated in 1856. Valatie was served by the Kinderhook and Hudson Railroad (1890). In the 20th century Rielly Mills (1917) produced underwear and outerwear. In the early 21st century Valatie is residential. The High Victorian Gothic and Stick-style First Presbyterian Church (1878) is listed on the National Register, as is the Wild's Mill Complex (1846). Valatie resident Rensselaer Reynolds (1807–72) invented a practical machine gun in 1837, and Martin H. Glynn (1871–1924) became the state's first Roman Catholic governor (1913–15) when William Sulzer was removed by impeachment.

Valcour Island, Battle of. American naval defeat in Revolutionary War. In June 1776, following the failed American invasion of Canada the previous winter, the Americans began building boats at Skenesborough [now Whitehall, Washington Co] for the defense of Lake Champlain and an expected British invasion led by Gen Guy Carleton. By late September, Brig Gen Benedict Arnold moored his 15-boat fleet on the west side of Valcour Island, now part of Clinton Co. The British fleet moving south from St. Jean, Que, consisted of 25 or more small ships and gunboats commanded by Capt Thomas Pringle. It carried nearly twice the weight in cannons as the American fleet and was manned by more experienced sailors.

When the British squadron was sighted on the morning of 11 October, Arnold formed his fleet into a line across Valcour Bay and sent several vessels forward to entice the enemy into the bay. The battle began midmorning, and for the next several hours the British and American crews engaged in a duel as cannons fired solid shot, barshot, and grapeshot. Shortly after the start of the battle, the American ship *Royal Savage* ran aground on the southwestern corner of Valcour Island. Hampered by adverse winds, the larger British vessels were unable to engage the American fleet effectively. By midafternoon the British schooner *Carleton* managed to sail into Valcour Bay but was disabled by American fire. By the end of the day the American fleet had been badly damaged and the gunboat *Philadelphia* sunk. The British fleet formed a blockade just south of Valcour Island to prevent the American fleet from escaping, but in the darkness and a dense fog, the crippled American vessels moved south along the western shore and passed by the British fleet, scuttling two of the gunboats, the *New Jersey* and the *Spitfire*. The *New Jersey*, however, did not sink and was later recovered by the British. Arnold took his fleet to Schuyler Island [now in Essex Co], 7.5 miles (12.1 km) south of Valcour Island, and remained long enough to stop leaks and mend sails. The American cutter *Lee* crossed the lake to what is now Vermont and was abandoned by her crew in the Winooski River.

On 13 October, with Arnold's fleet making slow progress toward the American forts to the south, the British caught up with the galley *Washington* and forced its surrender. On the deck of the galley *Congress*, Arnold directed a return fire on the British vessels. With no hope of escape on the lake, Arnold ran the *Congress* and four gunboats into a shallow bay that is now Arnold's Bay in Panton, Vt, and set them on fire. Four other vessels made it safely to the American-held fort at Ticonderoga [now in Essex Co]. Because of the approaching winter and a large number of American troops at Ticonderoga and Mount Independence [now in Vt], Carleton ordered his men into winter quarters in Canada by early November. Although the American fleet was defeated at Valcour Island, the mere existence of the flotilla delayed the British invasion of the United States until the following year when Lt Gen John Burgoyne led the expedition that resulted in his surrender at Saratoga.

In 1935 the *Philadelphia* was recovered from Valcour Bay. It was acquired by the Smithsonian Institution in 1961 and is on display in the National Museum of American History. The *Spitfire* was discovered intact and upright at the bottom of the lake in 1997 by the Lake Champlain Maritime Museum.

Bellico, Russell P. *Sails and Steam in the Mountains: A Maritime and Military History of Lake George and Lake Champlain,* 2d ed. (Fleischmanns, NY: Purple Mountain Press, 2001)

Lundeberg, Philip K. *The Gunboat Philadelphia and the Defense of Lake Champlain in 1776* (Basin Harbor, Vt: Lake Champlain Maritime Museum, 1995)

Russell P. Bellico

Benedict Arnold's gondola, *Philadelphia*, sunk during the Battle of Valcour Island.

Valhalla. Locality (pop 5,379) in Mount Pleasant (Westchester Co). As a station stop for nearby Kensico, it was originally called Kensico Station. The present name was chosen when the post office was established in 1861. The Bronx Reservoir (1871) and its enlargement, Valhalla Lake (1885), were between Valhalla and Kensico. When 1905 plans for the Kensico Reservoir were implemented between 1913 and 1917, Kensico Dam flooded the old Kensico, resulting in housing growth at Valhalla. Kensico Cemetery (1889) and other large cemeteries stretch north and west from the hamlet.

Field Horne

Valley Cottage. Locality (pop 9,269) in Clarkstown (Rockland Co). Valley Cottage developed as a suburban commuter hamlet on the West Shore Railroad (1883). Countess Alexandra Tolstoy (1884–1979), daughter of Leo Tolstoy, moved to a 72-acre (29 ha) farm in 1941; her Tolstoy Foundation (1939), which serves international refugees, remains headquartered there. St. Sergius of Radonezh Church (1957) is built in the old Russian style.

Valley Falls. Village (pop 491) in Pittstown and Schaghticoke (Rensselaer Co). By the early 1800s a number of saw, cotton, woolen, and flax mills were in operation. The successes of these industries stimulated development, as did the construction of two rail lines in 1853, both of which were later operated by the Boston and Maine. Thomas Lape purchased several farms in 1863 and platted the Valley Falls Extension, later called Promised Land. The village incorporated in 1904. Many residents worked at the Schaghticoke Powder Mills, located just outside village limits, from 1849 to 1928, or at a paper mill within the limits. In the early 21st century Valley Falls is a quiet residential village.

Kathryn T. Sheehan

Valley Stream {North Valley Stream, locality (pop 15,789) in Hempstead, Nassau Co; South Valley Stream, locality (pop 5,638) in Hempstead; Valley Stream, village (pop 36,368) in Hempstead}. The Rockaway Indians used this fertile area with its many ponds and streams for hunting and fishing. In the 1670s European settlers established farms. In 1868 Electus B. Litchfield of Babylon purchased land for development, creating a wholly new community. A railroad station was established in 1869, followed by the first post office, called Valley Stream, a year later. In 1922 another developer, Charles Gibson from Queens, built hundreds of homes in the southern part of Valley Stream to serve commuters; the village incorporated in 1925 and a Gibson railroad station was built in 1929. From 1929 to 1933 Curtiss Aircraft operated Curtiss Field, the largest commercial airport on Long Island. In 1936 a New York City developer, William Chanin, created the Green Acres community of 1,800 homes, giving shape to the present South Valley Stream. Green Acres Shopping Center, one of the first on Long Island, was built in 1956. Valley Stream grew rapidly in the 1930s through the 1950s and peaked in 1970. South Valley Stream is racially diverse, with 8% of the population black and 14% Asian in 2000. North Valley Stream was, in part, opened up for residential purposes by the Southern State Parkway (1927), which runs through it; in 2000 its racial composition was 37% black and 9% Asian. An additional 10.8% were of Latino ethnicity. The Valley Streams are bedroom communities and the site of Valley Stream State Park. Snapple Beverages and actor/filmmakers Ed Burns and Steve Buscemi got their starts in Valley Stream.

Georgina Martorella

Van Buren. Town (pop 12,667) in NW Onondaga Co. Jacks Reef on the Seneca River was a landmark and a fishing spot when explorers arrived. The first settlers arrived in 1789, occupying land along the river; the town was formed in 1829 from Camillus. Bounded on three sides by the river and the Erie (1819) and later Barge (1918) Canals, Van Buren was physically isolated until the late 20th century. The New York State Thruway opened across town in 1954, and its population increased nearly 60% during the 1950s. I-690 provides easy access to this residential suburb of Syracuse, as well as to regional distribution warehouses and related businesses such as Sysco (1984; food products distribution) concentrated near the Thruway.

Barbara S. Rivette

Van Buren, John (*b* Hudson, Columbia Co, 10 Feb 1810; *d* at sea, Atlantic Ocean, 13 Oct 1866). Democratic factional leader. The son of Pres Martin Van Buren and Hannah Hoes Van Buren, he graduated from Yale College (1828), was admitted to the bar (1831), and opened a law practice in Albany. During his father's vice presidency and presidency (1833–41), "Prince John" emerged as a powerful Democratic Party leader representing his father's political interests in New York State. When the depression of 1837 threatened the latter's presidency, Van Buren helped form the Barnburner faction, which favored drastic spending reductions and curbs on banks. The factionalism nearly cost him appointment by the state legislature as state attorney general (1845). Upset when James K. Polk won the presidential nomination from his father in 1844, Van Buren hoped the Wilmot Proviso, banning slavery from territory acquired in Polk's war with Mexico, would restore his faction to power. Instead it led to a factional exodus to the Free-Soil Party in 1848, with Martin Van Buren its reluctant presidential nominee and John Van Buren its most inspired political speaker. John's return to the Democrats by 1850, placing loyalty to their program of states' rights and limited government above antislavery, left him trusted fully by no group. He declined in political significance until his death aboard the *Scotia* while returning from Europe. He never held elective office.

Donovan, Herbert D. A. *The Barnburners* (1925; repr Philadelphia: Porcupine Press, 1974)

Phyllis F. Field

Van Buren, Martin (*b* Kinderhook, Columbia Co, 5 Dec 1782; *d* Kinderhook, 24 July 1862). Lawyer, governor, US president.

EARLY LIFE

Nicknamed the Little Magician or the Red Fox of Kinderhook for his political dexterity, he was the first son and third of six children born to Abraham Van Buren, a farmer and tavern keeper, and Maria Hoes Van Buren, a widow with three children. Reared in a large Dutch American family, Van Buren was educated in local schools and never attended college. In 1796 he began studying law with Francis Silvester, a Kinderhook Federalist, and completed his training in New York City with William Van Ness, Aaron Burr's close ally. Admitted to the bar in 1803, Van Buren opened a successful practice in Kinderhook with James Van Alen; it dissolved with Van Alen's 1808 election to Congress. Having moved to Hudson (Columbia Co) in 1808 and then to Albany in 1816, Van Buren associated with other partners and achieved broader statewide success and a greater reputation. He established key legal precedents, grounded on republican principles, in a series of mainly appellate cases, which confirmed his reputation as an elite attorney. Van Buren reached the peak of his profession by serving as state attorney general (1815–18). Van Buren, a slim redhead standing 5 feet 6 inches (168 cm) tall and having a flair for fashionable clothing, became a wealthy man by practicing law. On 21 Feb 1807 he married distant cousin Hannah Hoes. The couple had four sons before she died in 1819. Van Buren did not remarry.

Silhouette of Martin Van Buren, by Augustin Edouart, 1841.

POLITICAL CAREER IN NEW YORK STATE

Attracted by the principles of Jeffersonianism, he joined the Republican Party and used his intelligence and skills in public affairs and party organization to gain eminence without having the benefits of great wealth or family connections usually needed for political advancement in early 19th-century New York State. After breaking with Burr (1804), Van Buren aligned with New York City mayor and future governor De Witt Clinton and gained appointments as Columbia Co's fence viewer (1806) and surrogate (1808–13). In 1812 voters of the senate's Middle District elected him to the first of three terms as state senator. Although Van Buren backed Clinton's 1812 presidential bid, they split over political and wartime issues. Believing in the importance of party regularity and political organization, he opposed Clinton's personal and dictatorial style of politics. Van Buren also backed the War of 1812, while Clinton questioned its necessity. Van Buren allied with Gov Daniel D. Tompkins and formed the Bucktails, an anti-Clinton faction. A state senator with growing political stature, Van Buren lobbied for a prowar classification bill (1814) that set guidelines for a prototype military draft, and, though his supporters opposed it, he endorsed a bill (1817) authorizing construction of Clinton's Erie Canal. From 1817 on Van Buren was leader and chief organizer of the Albany Regency, which regularized the chaotic nature of party politics. A model for future political machines, it included many of the state's most talented politicians, such as Silas Wright and William L. Marcy, and reflected Van Buren's belief that politics was a career, not a part-time job. Under his leadership the Regency used patronage, ideology, campaign acumen, and tight organization to control the legislature and pass laws reflecting Van Buren's commitments to limited federal government, New York State–sponsored economic development, and enlightened public service.

A moderate delegate at the 1821 Constitutional Convention, he helped modernize state government by backing changes allowing the governor to veto legislation subject to a two-thirds override and by sponsoring efforts to abolish the councils of appointment and revision. He backed efforts to revamp senatorial districts to reflect the state's population growth and to expand the number of districts to ensure the Regency's control of the legislature. Acknowledging his achievements the legislature named him to the state's Board of Regents (1816–29), a position that gave him great personal satisfaction given his lack of formal education. In 1821 the Bucktail-controlled legislature also elected him to the US Senate, where he supported issues he thought critical to New York State: limited federal government, states' rights, low tariffs, and no federal aid for internal improvements. After John Quincy Adams became president in 1825, Van Buren assembled a diverse coalition around Andrew Jackson, including John C. Calhoun,

OK. This phrase originated in the late 1830s as part of a vogue among some writers for unusual misspellings of common terms. "O.K." likely first appeared in print in the *Boston Morning Post* on 23 Mar 1839 as an abbreviation for "oll korrect," or "all correct." The term soon made its way to New York City, where a Democratic O.K. Club was organized by March 1840. Democrats that year sought the reelection of Pres Martin Van Buren, whose nickname, Old Kinderhook, derived from his hometown of Kinderhook (Columbia Co). As a result, the cheer "OK!" took on added resonance to his supporters. Van Buren lost, but his campaign helped propel the new catchphrase to widespread acceptance. It is arguably the most popular and ubiquitous American contribution to the English language.

Flexner, Stuart Berg. *I Hear America Talking: An Illustrated History of American Words and Phrases* (New York: Simon & Schuster, 1979)

Peter Eisenstadt

William H. Crawford, and followers of Clinton; this group became the Democratic Party. Van Buren resigned from the Senate in 1828 and won election as New York State's governor. Although serving barely 12 weeks before becoming Jackson's secretary of state, Van Buren helped stabilize state banking through the Safety Fund Law, which created a regulatory commission to monitor banks' activities. In 1831 Van Buren resigned his cabinet post, served briefly as minister to Great Britain, became Jackson's vice president in 1833, and solidified his position as Jackson's political heir. In 1836 Van Buren won the presidency, the first New Yorker to do so, defeating four Whig opponents—William Henry Harrison, Hugh White, Daniel Webster, and Willie Mangum—in the electoral college, 170 to 124. In the popular election Van Buren received 764,176 votes, while Harrison, the leading Whig candidate, garnered 550,816.

PRESIDENT VAN BUREN

Inaugurated just before the Panic of 1837, Van Buren failed to understand its multiple causes. He ignored calls for federal stimulation of the economy, retarded recovery through his Independent Treasury Bill, and increased unemployment by cutting spending for internal improvements. In foreign policy he preserved peace with Great Britain during the Canadian Rebellion of 1837 and when disputes arose over the area along the Maine–New Brunswick border in 1839. On the western border Van Buren continued Pres Jackson's harsh policy of pushing native people west of the Mississippi. Though he couched his American Indian removal program in humanitarian terms, the army rounded up unprepared Cherokees, thousands of whom died on the trek west along the Trail of Tears in 1838. A consistent nationalist Van Buren sought to avoid sectional fractures over slavery. He opposed both slavery's abolition in the District of Columbia without the concurrence of slave states and interference with slavery where it existed. He also refused to back freedom for Africans in the *Amistad* case (1839). Even so he alienated proslavery interests by refusing to support the annexation of Texas, which would have resulted in the spread of slavery. This refusal, coupled with the futile Second Seminole War and the continued downward economic spiral, eroded his popularity and led to his defeat to William Henry Harrison, 234 to 60, in the bitter "Log Cabin Campaign"; Harrison received 1,275,390 popular votes to Van Buren's 1,128,854. Before leaving office Van Buren issued an executive order limiting labor on federal projects to a 10-hour day.

AFTER THE PRESIDENCY

Believing that Whigs had distorted his record and maligned his character, Van Buren sought vindication, but he forfeited the 1844 presidential nomination when he refused to endorse annexation of Texas without Mexico's approval. Although he retired to Lindenwald, the Kinderhook estate he acquired in 1839, Van Buren remained active in New York State politics. After first siding with tenants in their disputes with landlords in Columbia and Rensselaer Cos in 1811, Van Buren opposed tenants who used violence against landholders attempting to collect unpaid rents and supported state efforts to subdue antirent rioting in the early 1840s. When conflict developed among Democratic factions, he supported the Barnburners over the Hunkers. In 1848 he accepted the Free-Soil Party's nomination for president on a platform opposed to slavery's expansion. Though his strong second-place finish in New York State caused Democrat Lewis Cass to lose the state, Van Buren failed to carry any state and finished an embarrassing third nationally. He then retired from active politics, spent time at Lindenwald, and traveled overseas. During this period Van Buren wrote a historically valuable but incomplete autobiography and an analytic political history of political parties in the United States. In the Civil War's early days, he supported Pres Abraham Lincoln, but chronic heart problems left him weak; he died in 1862. His Kinderhook estate became the Martin Van Buren National Historic Site maintained by the National Park Service.

See also LIBERALISM.

Cole, Donald B. *Martin Van Buren and the American Political System* (Princeton, NJ: Princeton Univ Press, 1984)

Mushkat, Jerome, and Joseph G. Rayback. *Martin Van Buren: Law, Politics, and the Shaping of Republican Ideology* (DeKalb: Northern Illinois Univ Press, 1997)

Niven, John. *Martin Van Buren: The Romantic Age of American Politics* (New York: Oxford Univ Press, 1983)

Remini, Robert Vincent. *Martin Van Buren and the Making of the Democratic Party* (New York: Columbia Univ Press, 1959)

Jerome Mushkat

Van Buren Republicans. See BUCKTAILS; DEMOCRATIC PARTY.

Van Cortlandt, Pierre (*b* New York City, 21 Jan 1721; *d* Croton [now Croton-on-Hudson, Westchester Co], 1 May 1814). Politician and landholder. He was the son of Philip van Cortlandt and Catherine De Peyster van Cortlandt, and his family was politically influential. At 27 he married Joanna Livingston, a second cousin, with whom he had eight children. Upon his father's death in 1748 he inherited manor lands in Westchester Co. He moved there in 1749–50 and developed the land for commerce, agriculture, and milling. His political career began in 1768 when he won an assembly seat as the representative of Cortlandt Manor. During the Revolutionary War he helped organize and preside over several provincial congresses and committees of safety. In 1777 he was appointed state senator from the Southern District and served as lieutenant governor (1777–95). Van Cortlandt handled administrative duties while Gov George Clinton pursued military activities. After retiring in 1795 he settled in Peekskill (Westchester Co) and in 1803 moved to the Van Cortlandt manor house.

Judd, Jacob. "Biographical Sketch of Pierre Van Cortlandt, 1721–1814." In *Correspondence of the Van Cortlandt Family of Cortlandt Manor, 1748–1800*, ed. Jacob Judd (Tarrytown, NY: Sleepy Hollow Restorations, 1977)

Jacob Judd

Van Cortlandt Manor. See CORTLANDT MANOR.

Van Cortlandt Manor House. Mansion homestead of the Van Cortlandt family located at the confluence of the Croton and Hudson Rivers in Croton-on-Hudson (Westchester Co). A small structure existed on the property in the early 18th century. Pierre van Cortlandt (1721–1814) and his family moved into the one-story structure *ca* 1749–50. He remodeled the building and added a second floor made of brick and a veranda that wrapped around the house on three sides. The house then had two entrances, one on the ground level and the other from the veranda. When the Revolutionary War commenced, the family abandoned the estate and fled to safety in Peekskill (Westchester Co), but they reclaimed their property in 1783 and later added two wings. Descendants lived there until 1945. The mansion was slated to be demolished, but preservationist John D. Rockefeller, Jr acquired the house and 184 acres (74 ha) in 1953. He retained staff from Colonial Williamsburg in Virginia to restore the house and grounds to their 18th-century appearance. During restoration two wings were removed from the mansion, and the house was furnished with original family fixtures. In 1959 Rockefeller transferred ownership

Van Cortlandt Manor House, Croton-on-Hudson.

of the manor house to Sleepy Hollow Restorations (now Historic Hudson Valley). In 2003 the house, grounds, and a reconstructed ferry house served as a living museum under the auspices of Historic Hudson Valley.

Brown, Charles H. *Van Cortlandt Manor* (Tarrytown, NY: Sleepy Hollow Restorations, 1965)

Butler, Joseph T. *The Family Collections at Van Cortlandt Manor* (Tarrytown, NY: Sleepy Hollow Restorations, 1967)

Jacob Judd

Van Cott [née Newton], **Maggie** [Margaret Ann] (*b* New York City, 25 Mar 1830; *d* Catskill, Greene Co, 29 Aug 1914). Evangelist and preacher. She was born an Episcopalian and lived in a religious household in New York City until the age of 12. She officially became a Methodist in 1866 after several years of affiliation with the religion. Married to merchant Peter Van Cott in 1847 and widowed in 1866, she first achieved fame as a home missionary in the notorious Five Points district in Manhattan. In 1868 clergy friends persuaded Van Cott to take up full-time evangelistic work. The following year she became the first woman in the Methodist Episcopal Church licensed to preach. Though she was not allowed to administer the sacraments, a right reserved for the ordained, she carried on an extensive and successful evangelistic ministry across the nation until her retirement in 1902.

Foster, John O. *Life and Labors of Mrs. Maggie Newton Van Cott* (Cincinnati: Hitchcock & Walden, 1872)

Charles Yrigoyen Jr

Van Curler, Arent (*b* Nijkerck, the Netherlands, 1620; *d* Lake Champlain, July 1667). Colonial official and intercultural negotiator. In December 1637, Van Curler was sent to New Netherland as a minor official in his great-uncle Kiliaen van Rensselaer's colony of Rensselaerswijck [now in Albany, Columbia, and Rensselaer Cos]. In May 1639 he was appointed bookkeeper and secretary of the colony and held the office of *commies* (chief mercantile agent) from 1642 to 1644. Van Curler left for Holland in October 1644 and returned to Rensselaerswijck in late 1647. During the early 1640s he had established important trade and diplomatic relations with the Mohawk, which continued on his return to the colony. In 1661 Van Curler and several other Dutch colonists obtained a tract of Indian land west of Fort Orange [now Albany] and founded what is now the City of Schenectady. From 1666 to 1667 Van Curler maintained relations with Richard Nicolls, governor of New York; Alexander Prouville, Seigneur de Tracy, viceroy of New France; and the Mohawk. He drowned during a storm in Lake Champlain on the way to Canada in the summer of 1667. The term "Corlaer," another spelling of his last name, was later used by the Iroquois as a symbolic name for the colonial governors of New York.

Burke, Thomas E., Jr. *Mohawk Frontier: The Dutch Community of Schenectady, New York, 1661–1710* (Ithaca: Cornell Univ Press, 1991)

Mark Meuwese

Vandalia. The first propeller-driven steamship on the Great Lakes, built in 1841 at Oswego by Sylvester Doolittle for himself and several partners. The 138-ton (125 MT), single-decked, sloop-rigged vessel had one mast and twin propellers and measured 91 feet (27.7 m) long, with a 20 ft 2 in (6.15 m) beam, and an 8 ft 3 in (2.51 m) depth. It had an Ericsson patent steam engine of 25 horsepower built by C. C. Dennis at Auburn (Cayuga Co). The ship could make 9 mph (14 kph). It proved faster and more reliable than contemporary sailing craft and revolutionized the transport of commodities on the Great Lakes. The ship was operated in the New York, Oswego and Chicago Line. "Propellers" superseded side-wheel steamers by 1855, by which time there were more than 200 of the former in service. *Vandalia* was enlarged in 1846 and renamed *Milwaukee.* She was lost in a collision, without fatalities, with the schooner *Fashion* on Lake Erie 27 Oct 1851.

Palmer, Richard F., and Anthony Slosek. "The *Vandalia*—First Screw Propeller on the Lakes," *Inland Seas* 44 (Winter 1988): 236–52

C. Patrick Labadie

Van Dam, Rip (*b* Beverwijck [now Albany], *ca* 1660; *d* New York City, 10 June 1749). Politician. Van Dam moved to New York City by 1680 and became a merchant. He served as an alderman from 1693 to 1696 and was part of the anti-Leisler faction. In 1702 Gov Edward Hyde, Viscount Cornbury, appointed him to the governor's council. He was a senior councilor under Gov John Montgomerie, and when Montgomerie died in 1731, Van Dam became interim governor and served for 11 months. When William Cosby arrived in the colony to take his post as governor, he demanded that Van Dam turn over one-half of his salary. Van Dam refused, and Cosby pursued the issue in court in 1733. Because Lewis Morris (1671–1746), one of the chief justices who heard the case, supported Van Dam, Cosby fired him. During the trial, Van Dam and Morris supporters politically attacked Cosby by publishing virulent commentaries in John Peter Zenger's *New-York Weekly Journal.* Cosby tried to expel Van Dam from the council and brought a libel suit against Zenger. On his deathbed in 1736, Cosby named George Clarke acting governor. The move hindered Van Dam from serving as governor, a position he was entitled to as senior councilor. Van Dam assumed the position of governor in March 1736, but was ousted that October when England officially recognized George Clarke as governor. Van Dam was removed from the council, and he permanently retired from politics.

Bonomi, Patricia U. *A Factious People: Politics and Society in Colonial New York* (New York: Columbia Univ Press, 1971)

Goodfriend, Joyce D. *Before the Melting Pot: Society and Culture in Colonial New York City, 1664–1730* (Princeton, NJ: Princeton Univ Press, 1992)

Jennifer Steenshorne

Van den Bogaert, Harmen Meyndertsz (*b* The Netherlands, ?1612; *d* Hudson River, winter 1647–48). Dutch West India Company (WIC) official. Van den Bogaert arrived in New Netherland as a barber-surgeon in May 1630. Best known as leader of a WIC trade mission to several Mohawk and Oneida communities in the winter of 1634–35, his journal of this expedition is an important source for Dutch-Iroquois relations as well as one of the earliest ethnographic documents about the Iroquois peoples. Van den Bogaert was appointed as *commies* (chief mercantile agent) for the WIC at Fort Orange [now Albany] in 1645. In the fall of 1647, however, he was accused of committing sodomy with a young black slave. To escape prosecution, Van den Bogaert fled to Mohawk country. He was eventually apprehended by a Rensselaerswijck employee and returned to Fort Orange. Van den Bogaert escaped from the fort and subsequently drowned when falling through the ice on the Hudson River.

Gehring, Charles T., and William A. Starna, eds. *A Journey into Mohawk and Oneida Country, 1634–1635: The Journal of Harmen Meyndertsz van den Bogaert* (Syracuse: Syracuse Univ Press, 1988)

Mark Meuwese

Vanderbilt, Cornelius (*b* Port Richmond, Richmond Co, 27 May 1794; *d* New York City, 4 Jan 1877). The son of poor farmers, Vanderbilt purchased a $100 sailboat at age 16, using it to operate a ferry and freight business between Staten Island and Manhattan. During and after the War of 1812, he expanded his business, running both coastal and Hudson River schooners. In 1813 he married his cousin Sophia Johnson; the couple would have 13 children. By 1818 the superiority of steam power led him to sell his sailing vessels and to take a job as a steamboat captain on Thomas Gibbons's New York City–New Brunswick, NJ, line. A tough and resourceful captain, he also built several boats for Gibbons, leaving the company in 1829 with personal capital of $30,000. In 1830 he established his own Hudson River steamboat line and engaged Daniel Drew's rival service in a price war. Paid off by Drew to leave the Hudson, he established a new New York City–Providence, RI, line on Long Island Sound, eventually extending this to Boston and to Portland, Maine. By 1838 he had established another line in the nation's southeast, returned his boats to the Hudson, acquired large tracts of land on Staten and Coney Islands, and gained the unofficial title Commodore Vanderbilt.

After gold was discovered in California, he built seagoing steamers in East River shipyards to operate to Nicaragua, providing an alternative to the long sailing ship voyage around Cape Horn. In 1853, a year after he began construction of his mansion at Manhattan's 10 Washington Place, Vanderbilt outfitted the steamship *North Star* as a private yacht and cruised to Europe. Two years later he used this ship to enter the transatlantic trade, providing service between New York City and Le Havre, France. Crossings were also made to Bremen, Germany, but in 1860 Vanderbilt withdrew from the North Atlantic route. He would continue service to Central America until 1865.

In the later 1850s he began to buy railroad stock, by 1857 holding a majority interest in the New York and Harlem Railroad, which followed Manhattan's 4th Ave north from 23d St. He next acquired control of the Hudson River Railroad, which carried passengers between a Manhattan depot at 30th St and 11th Ave and East Greenbush (Rensselaer Co), just across the Hudson from Albany. He enhanced this line by double-tracking it and building an East Greenbush–Albany bridge. In 1867–68 he tried to establish a New York State railroad monopoly by acquiring the Erie Railroad running through the Southern Tier but was thwarted by rivals Jim Fisk and

Daniel Drew in the "Great Erie Railroad War," a duel of court injunctions and phony stock issues. But Vanderbilt achieved some of his goals by merging the Hudson River Railroad and the New York Central Railroad, under Vanderbilt control from 1867, to form the New York Central and Hudson River Railroad (NYC&HRRR). In 1871 he completed construction of the $3 million Grand Central Depot, precursor of Grand Central Terminal, in Manhattan and two years later acquired Lake Shore and Michigan Southern Railroad, which allowed NYC&HRRR to offer New York City–Chicago service.

In the mid-1870s, his second wife, a woman named Frank Crawford whom he had married after Sophia's death in 1868, inspired him to give $1 million to found Vanderbilt University in Nashville, Tenn. His son William inherited his leadership of the NYC&HRRR and most of his $100 million estate.

Lane, Wheaton J. *Commodore Vanderbilt: An Epic of the Steam Age* (New York: Knopf, 1942)

Patterson, Jerry E. *The Vanderbilts* (New York: Harry N. Abrams, 1989)

Norman Brouwer

Vanderbilt Cup race. Automobile race founded by William K. Vanderbilt II, great-grandson of Cornelius Vanderbilt, that sought to capture the spirit of the popular European road races. Nearly 50,000 spectators watched the inaugural race on 6 Oct 1904, with 17 cars competing on a 28.4 mi (45.71 km) road course in Nassau Co. Beginning in Westbury, drivers raced 10 laps on a triangular course over portions of the Jericho Turnpike, Massapequa Rd (now Rte 106), and Hempstead Turnpike. The race was sponsored by the new American Automobile Association. In 1905 several accomplished European drivers competed, and by 1906 a quarter of a million spectators attended. Crowd-control problems forced the race's cancellation in 1907, but it was revived in 1908 on a course that included a 9 mi (14.5 km) section of the new Long Island Motor Parkway. In 1909 and 1910 the race attracted far fewer spectators and the Vanderbilt Cup moved out of New York State. In 1936 the race was revived with the 300 mi (482.8 km) George Vanderbilt Cup, held on a twisting course at the new Roosevelt Raceway near Westbury. Tazio Nuvolari won the race, averaging by modern standards a modest 64 mph (103 kph). The final Vanderbilt Cup race was held the following year with a redesigned course, enabling winner Bernd Rosemeyer of Germany a top speed of 159 mph (256 kph).

Long Island Motor Parkway, http://www.fortunecity.com/silverstone/wiper/388/

Phil McCray

Van der Donck, Adriaen (*b* Breda, Netherlands, 1618; *d* New Netherland, 1655). Lawyer and author. Adriaen van der Donck enrolled as a student of law at Leiden University on 24 Sept 1638. He was recruited in 1641 by Kiliaen van Rensselaer to serve as *schout* (sheriff) for the Rensselaerswijck patroonship. He left this position in 1645 to settle in New Amsterdam, where he married Mary Doughty. He became a spokesman for the commonalty of New Amsterdam [now New York City] in its conflict with the West India Co and returned to the Netherlands in 1649 to argue their case before the States General. In that capacity he published *The Remonstrance of New Netherland (Vertoog van Nieu Nederlandt)* in 1650. While in the Netherlands he also obtained his doctorate in both civil and canon law (Juris Utriusque Doctor) from Leiden University in 1653 and published his *Description of the New Netherlands (Beschryvinge van Nieuw-Nederlandt)* in 1655, which was reprinted in 1656, one of the earliest accounts of the colony, and his best-known work. Van der Donck returned to New Netherland in 1653 and settled on his patroonship, Colendonck [now at Yonkers]. The city took its name from Van der Donck's honorific, *Jonkheer* (squire) Van der Donck.

Van der Donck, Adriaen. *A Description of the New Netherlands.* Trans Jeremiah Johnson (1841; repr, ed. Thomas F. O'Donnell, Syracuse: Syracuse Univ Press, 1968)

———. "Remonstrance of New Netherland." In vol 1 of *Documents Relative to the Colonial History of the State of New York,* 15 vols, trans and ed. E. B. O'Callaghan and B. Fernow (Albany: Weed, Parsons, 1856)

Van Gastel, Ada. "Adriaen van der Donck, New Netherland, and America" (PhD diss, Pennsylvania State Univ, 1985)

———. "Adriaen van der Donck in Rensselaerswijck: 1641–1643," *de Halve Maen* 60 (1987): 14–19.

Jaap Jacobs

Vanderlyn, John (*b* Kingston, Ulster Co, 15 Oct 1775; *d* Kingston, 23 Sept 1852). Painter. Son of Nicholas and Sarah Tappen, and grandson of artist Pieter Vanderlyn, he made toys in his youth and attended the Kingston Academy in 1791. At 17 he moved to New York City and worked for an engraver. He studied at the Columbian Academy of Painting and with Gilbert Stuart by duplicating Stuart portraits for clients. Aaron Burr recognized Vanderlyn's talent and financed his education. In 1796 he traveled to Paris to study with neoclassical artist François-André Vincent. Vanderlyn returned to New York City in 1801. His association with Burr afforded him opportunities as a portraitist for notable politicians. He returned to Paris and painted his first historical work, *The Death of Jane McCrea* (1804), illustrating Native Americans killing a British officer's fiancée during the Revolutionary War near Fort Edward (Washington Co). In 1809 he started his famous nude *Ariadne Asleep on the Island of Naxos* and began panoramas. He returned to New York City in 1815 to show his work. His *Palace and Gardens of Versailles,* two paintings 165 feet (50 m) long, are in the collection of the Metropolitan Museum of Art. His exhibition hall in New York City, Rotunda, failed, which led him to tour his art in Saratoga Springs and elsewhere. His last commission, *The Landing of Columbus,* was placed in the US Capitol rotunda (1847). His agent defrauded his finances, and after 1846 he encountered financial problems but sustained himself by doing portraits of James Monroe, New York City mayor Philip Horne, and Gov Joseph C. Yates. He retired to Kingston, continued as a copyist and portraitist, and advocated unsuccessfully for a national gallery.

Lindsay, Kenneth C. *The Works of John Vanderlyn: From Tammany to the Capitol* (Binghamton: Univ at Binghamton Art Gallery; distributed by Worldwide Books, 1970)

Nancy Knechtel

Van Etten. Town (pop 1,518) and village (pop 581) in NE Chemung Co. Settled in 1795, the town was formed in 1854 from Cayuta [now in Tompkins Co] and Erin. Lumber was the town's first industry but was later supplanted by dairy farming. It was served by three railroads completed between 1871 and 1891. The village was incorporated in 1876 and was known in the late 19th century for its small industries, including textiles, firearms, and swords. After World War I, Finnish immigrants developed poultry farms and built feed mills. In August 1930 a Communist-run youth camp in town was the site of conflict between Communists and patriotic and civic organizations. During the 1930s Van Etten had a reforestation project at a Civilian Conservation Corps camp, which housed German prisoners of war in 1944–45. Anti-Nazi prisoners and American specialists published a German language newspaper in Van Etten entitled *Der Ruf* (The Call), aimed to foster democratic ideals in the returning prisoners. The town remains predominantly agricultural.

Heather A. Wade

Van Olinda [née van Slyck], **Hilletie** (*b* ?Canajoharie [now in Montgomery Co], ?1645; *d* ?Schenectady, 1707). Interpreter. Her father was Cornelis Antoniseen van Slyck, a Dutch fur trader, and her mother Otstock was a Mohawk. Hilletie van Slyck grew up among the Mohawk but in her teens went to live with a woman trader in Schenectady and Albany, where she learned Dutch and was baptized in the Dutch Reformed Church. Around 1665 she married Peter Danielse van Olinda. Beginning in the 1680s she interpreted for the minister Godfridius Dellius and worked with him to translate Dutch religious texts into Mohawk. She rose in prominence when appointed official interpreter for the provincial government in 1690. Her career was nearly ended by 1699 when she was made a scapegoat for unwittingly helping Dellius negotiate a fraudulent land deal with eight Mohawk men. She returned to her post in 1700, sharing official interpreting duties with Lawrence Claes and Jan Baptist van Eps, but never regained prominence.

Hagedorn, Nancy L. "Brokers of Understanding: Interpreters as Agents of Cultural Exchange in Colonial New York," *New York History* 76 (Winter 1995): 379–408

Sivertsen, Barbara J. *Turtles, Wolves, and Bears: A Mohawk Family History* (Bowie, Md: Heritage Books, 1996)

Alison Duncan Hirsch

Van Rensselaer, Kiliaen (*b* Hasselt, the Netherlands, *ca* 1585; *bur* Amsterdam, 7 Oct 1643). Patroon. Orphaned in his teens, Van Rensselaer was apprenticed to Wolfert van Bijler, a relative in Amsterdam who ran a jewelry business. By 1614 he was in a position to merge the business with the firm of Johan van Wely, after whose death he formed his own company in 1616. When the newly chartered Dutch West India Co (WIC) sought operating funds in 1621, Van Rensselaer was financially able to subscribe 6,000 guilders as a chief participant. At some point he developed an interest in agriculture and pursued his avocation with the purchase and cultivation of a country estate in Het Gooi called Crailo.

As a director of the WIC, Van Rensselaer wanted to see New Netherland develop into a self-sustaining province, and this made him a leader of a faction within the company that promoted colonization and the formation of agricultural settlements rather than the mere exploitation of natural resources. These efforts led to the Charter of Freedoms and Exemptions, which established patroonships in the New World. Van Rensselaer was one of the first directors to apply. Through knowledgeable contacts in New Netherland he was able to acquire the rights to land from Indian owners on both sides of the Hudson River, approximately the present-day north and south boundaries of Albany and Rensselaer Cos. Not only was it excellent agricultural land, but it also had the WIC trading post of Fort Orange nearly in its geographical center.

Van Rensselaer's experience in land reclamation and management of agricultural production procedures in Het Gooi served him well in his new venture. Although he never visited his patroonship he paid close attention to its growth and development. In detailed letters to his managers he expressed concern for every phase of agricultural development and production. As a testament to his ability, Rensselaerswijck was the only patroonship to survive. Although its success stemmed partly from its superior location, most of the credit must go to the energy and patience of its major investor.

De Vries, W. "De Van Rensselaer's in Nederland," *De Nederlanddsche Leeuw* 66 (1949): 150–72, 194–211

De Roever, N. "Kiliaen van Rensselaer en zijne kolonie Rensselaerswijck," *Ous-Holland* 8 (1890): 29–74, 241–96

Van Laer, A. J. F., trans and ed. *Van Rensselaer Bowier Manuscripts, Being the Letter of Kiliaen van Rensselaer, 1630–1643, and Other Documents Relating to the Colony of Rensselaerswijck* (Albany: SUNY, 1908)

Charles T. Gehring

Van Rensselaer, Martha (*b* Randolph, Cattaraugus Co, 21 June 1864; *d* New York City, 26 May 1932). Educator. After graduating from the Chamberlain Institute in Randolph in 1884, Van Rensselaer taught in local schools and also at the Chautauqua Summer School from 1894 through 1903. In 1893 and 1896 she was elected school commissioner of Cattaraugus Co. In this capacity, she noted the need for practical information for farmers' wives, and after her second term ended in 1899 she began making connections at Cornell University to provide such materials. She helped establish the Department of Home Economics in Cornell's College of Agriculture in 1907, serving as the department's co-chair. The department, by 1917, included a four-year degree, extensions courses, and 200 study clubs. In 1919 it became a school in 1919 and the New York College of Home Economics in 1925 with Van Rensselaer as co-director. Head of the American Home Economics Association from 1914 to 1916 and director of the Home Conservation Division of the US Food Administration during World War I, Van Rensselaer also served on the American Relief Commission to Belgium in 1923 and was honored with Belgium's Order of the Crown for her work. New York State allocated $1 million in 1929–30 for construction of the Martha Van Rensselaer Hall at Cornell to honor the founder of modern home economics education in the state.

Percival, Caroline M. *Martha Van Rensselaer* (Ithaca: Alumnae Association of the NYS College of Home Economics at Cornell Univ, 1957)

Joseph N. Prenoveau

Van Rensselaer, Stephen, III (*b* New York City, 1 Nov 1764; *d* Albany, 26 Jan 1839). Politician and philanthropist. The son of Stephen Van Rensselaer II and Catherine Livingston, he became heir to a fortune at age 4. He was known by his family's Dutch title, Patroon of the Manor of Rensselaerswijck. Considered one of the largest landholders in the state, he owned 700,000 acres (280,000 ha) in Rensselaer, Albany, and Columbia Cos. After graduating from Harvard in 1782, he settled at the family homestead, Van Rensselaer Manor in Albany Co. He fathered 3 children with his first wife, Margarita Schuyler, and 10 children with his second wife, Cornelia Patterson, and began a career in politics and the military. Van Rensselaer was a major in the state militia (1786) and was promoted to colonel (1788) and major general (1801). A Federalist, he served in the state assembly (1789, 1807–10, and 1817) and state senate (1791–96). Van Rensselaer was lieutenant governor from 1795 to 1801. As a Federalist he ran unsuccessfully for governor in 1801 and 1813. During the War of 1812 he served as major general of volunteers. Inexperienced in command and leading unmotivated and underequipped troops, he led an attack at Queenston Heights [now Queenston, Ont] in October 1812 that ended in defeat and embarrassment.

Van Rensselaer returned to politics, supported the Erie Canal, and was a Canal Commission member (1816–39), serving as president for 14 years. He backed state improvements, including the Great Western Turnpike and the state's first railroad, the Mohawk and Hudson (1831). President of the state's first Board of Agriculture (1820), he financed the periodicals *Plough Boy* and *Cultivator.* He was a delegate to the state's 1821 Constitutional Convention before winning a seat in Congress (1822–29), where he chaired the Committee on Agriculture and cast the deciding vote that elected John Quincy Adams president in 1825.

Van Rensselaer served on the State Board of Regents for 26 years, becoming chancellor in 1835. He established, with Amos Eaton, the Rensselaer School (now Rensselaer Polytechnic Institute) in 1824, demonstrating his interest in applying science to advance agriculture and commerce. He was a founder of the Albany Academy, a trustee of Union College, and a benefactor for Hamilton College. He cofounded the Society for the Promotion of Useful Arts (1804) and Albany Lyceum of Natural History (1823). Both merged in 1824 under his leadership, forming the Albany Institute of History and Art. The mineral Rensselaerite, a talc, was named for him after it was discovered in St. Lawrence Co in 1837. He influenced the founding of the American Bible Society (1816), the American Tract Society (1825), and the American Home Missionary Society (1826). He also was a leader in the Masonic Order and invested in banking, industry, and insurance. As patroon of his family estate, Van Rensselaer managed perpetual leases for over 3,000 tenant farms but rarely requested rent. His sons attempted to collect past due payments after his death, which sparked protests and led to the antirent wars and the breakup of the family's holdings.

Stephen Van Rensselaer III, by Gilbert Stuart, 1795.

See also SCIENTIFIC CULTURE (19TH–21ST CENTURIES); WAR OF 1812.

Fink, William B. "Stephen Van Rensselaer: The Last Patroon" (PhD diss, Columbia Univ, 1950)

Westerdahl, Carl A. "Stephen Van Rensselaer: Catalyst for Progress," *Rensselaer Alumni Magazine* (Sept 1998)

Carl A. Westerdahl

Van Rensselaer Manor House. Patroon Jeremias van Rensselaer built a two-story manor house in 1668 on the northern outskirts of Albany. In 1765 Stephen van Rensselaer II constructed a brick Georgian mansion near the site. It was considered one of the largest in America and boasted an enormous 47 ft (14 m) long hall. Stephen III employed Philip Hooker in 1819 to design a piazza and east and west wings, and in 1843 architect Richard Upjohn completed brownstone trims and modified the wings for Stephen IV. Industrialization of the area and the death of Stephen IV in 1868 prompted descendants to abandon the house by 1875. The structure was demolished in 1893, but interior elements were salvaged and the furnishings dispersed. The famed hallway was reconstructed and is exhibited in the Metropolitan Museum of Art. Marcus T. Reynolds incorporated wooden and stonework elements from the manor house into the Sigma Phi Fraternity House at Williams College in Williamstown, Mass, in 1893. When the fraternity house was demolished in 1973, Dr D. Joseph Demis of Albany salvaged stone and woodwork. He donated remains to Rensselaer Polytechnic Institute and the Historic Albany Foundation in 1995–96.

Bucher, Douglas G., and W. Richard Wheeler. *A Neat Plain Modern Stile: Philip Hooker and His Contemporaries, 1796–1836* (Clinton, NY: Hamilton College, 1992; distributed by Univ of Massachusetts Press)

Carl A. Westerdahl

Van Schaick, Goose (*b* Albany, 5 Sept 1736; *d* Albany, 4 July 1789). Military officer. Born into a privileged family, Van Schaick was lieutenant of the New York Provincial Regiment during the French and Indian War. In a 1758 campaign at Fort Ticonderoga [now in Essex Co], he was permanently disfigured after a French soldier struck him in the face with the butt of a musket. In the 1759 siege on Fort Niagara [now in Porter, Nia-

Van Rensselaer Manor House, *ca* 1843.

gara Co], he served as field officer. Returning to Albany in 1770 he married Mary ten Broeck, with whom he had seven children. In the early 1770s Van Schaick joined the Albany Sons of Liberty and in 1776 accepted command of the First New York Regiment as colonel. He led a campaign in 1779 against the Onondagas southwest of present-day Syracuse and destroyed their villages despite protests by his Oneida allies. His superiors praised his actions, which they considered more effective than the Sullivan-Clinton campaign in taking prisoners. Although a respected officer, Van Schaick never received the promotion to brigadier general he desired. In 1783 he retired to manage his family's extensive landholdings. He died from his old face injury, which had turned cancerous. His unusual first name was a variation of the Netherlands name Gosa or Gozen, but had been Anglicized in the colonies.

Egly, T. W., Jr. *Goose Van Schaick of Albany (1736–1789): The Continental Army's Senior Colonel* (1992)

Kathryn Clippinger Kosto

Van Twiller, Wouter (*bap* Nijkerk, Netherlands, 22 May 1606; *bur* Amsterdam, 29 Aug 1654). Director of New Netherland. Formerly a clerk of the Dutch West India Co, he arrived in New Netherland in 1633 as the new director, replacing Bastiaen Jansz Krol. Van Twiller quickly got into conflict with the minister Everardus Bogardus and the fiscal Lubbert van Dincklagen over the way the colony should be governed. He also had run-ins with David Pietersz de Vries, who considered him too inexperienced and too weak in leadership. De Vries's opinion resulted in a rather unfavorable report in his book, *Short Historical and Journal-Notes of Various Voyages Performed in the Four Quarters of the Globe,* published in 1655, which, perhaps unfairly, adversely affected Van Twiller's reputation. Van Twiller's resistance to the English intrusions on the Connecticut and Delaware Rivers, for instance, was as strong as New Netherland's military force permitted. Recalled in 1637 Van Twiller returned to the Netherlands after July 1638 and lived mainly in Amsterdam. His involvement in New Netherland continued both through his own trade and as trustee of the inheritance of his uncle, Kiliaen Van Rensselaer.

Hoffman, William J. "An Armory of American Families of Dutch Descent: Van Rensselaer–Van Twiller–Van Doorn–Van Curler–Van Vlierden–De Sille," *New York Genealogical and Biographical Record* 64 (1933), 3–15

Van Laer, Arnold J. F., trans and ed. "Letters of Wouter van Twiller and the Director General and Council of New Netherland to the Amsterdam Chamber of the Dutch West India Company, August 14, 1636," *New York History* (1969), 44–50 (supplement)

Jaap Jacobs

Van Vechten, Abraham (*b* Catskill [now in Greene Co], 5 Dec 1762; *d* Albany, 6 Jan 1837). Lawyer and politician. After attending King's College (now Columbia University), Van Vechten received legal training in John Lansing Jr's Albany office. Admitted to the bar in 1785 he practiced for a short time in Johnstown [now in Fulton Co] before moving to Albany, where he enjoyed exceptional success as an appellate lawyer. He was opposed to change, and his conservatism was an apt fit for the Federalist Party. Because Albany Co remained a Federalist stronghold, it guaranteed him a political base. Appointed as a district attorney in 1796, a position he shortly resigned, Van Vechten rejected appointment to the state supreme court in 1798 but served in the state senate (1798–1805, 1816–19), in the assembly (1806, 1808–13), as state attorney general (1810–11, 1813–15), and as a delegate to the Constitutional Convention of 1821, where he was a determined opponent of universal white male suffrage. Van Vechten's reputation among judges was one of no-nonsense thoroughness. In one of his most notable arguments, *Goodell v Jackson* (1823), he successfully contended for American Indian sovereignty. He was married to Catharine Schuyler, and they had 15 children.

Hammond, Jabez D. *The History of Political Parties in the State of New-York from the Ratification of the Federal Constitution to December, 1840,* 2 vols (Albany: C. Van Benthuysen, 1842)

Roper, Donald M. "The Elite of the New York Bar as Seen from the Bench: James Kent's Necrologies," *New-York Historical Society Quarterly* 56 (July 1972): 199–237

Donald M. Roper

Varèse, Edgard [Edgar Victor Achille Charles] (*b* Paris, 22 Dec 1883; *d* New York City, 6 Nov 1965). Composer. Born in Paris and educated there and in Berlin, Varèse moved to New York City in 1915. In 1917 he conducted a landmark performance of the Berlioz *Requiem* in honor of the fallen soldiers of World War I. In 1921 he cofounded the International Composers Guild, which promoted new music, including his own. He became an American citizen on 9 June 1927. In 1928, with composer Henry Cowell, Varèse founded the Pan-American Association of Composers, whereupon he returned to Paris for five years. *Ionisation* (1931), written in Paris, was one of the first works for percussion ensemble, and his use of a siren foreshadowed his later electronic compositions. *Ecuatorial* (1934) was written for an ensemble that included two electronic cellos made to his specifications by Russian inventor Leon Theremin. From 1936 to 1940 Varèse lived in Santa Fe, N Mex, and in San Francisco and Los Angeles. Back in New York in 1942, he founded the Greater New York Chorus, an amateur choral group based in Lower Manhattan's Greenwich House Music School. After 1948 the importance of Varèse's work was increasingly recognized, championed by influential *New York Herald Tribune* critic Virgil Thomson. *Déserts* (1954) was the first work to combine a live orchestra with recorded sounds. *Poème électronique,* composed for the Philips Pavilion at the 1958 Brussels World's Fair, incorporated nine recorded tracks with visual projections, activating more than 400 speakers in patterns and enabling Varèse to realize his concept of moving sound masses. This work brought Varèse wide acclaim in the last years of his life.

Mattis, Olivia. "The Physical and the Abstract: Varèse and the New York School." In *The New York Schools of Music and Visual Arts,* ed. Steven Johnson (New York: Garland Publishing, 2002)

Ouellette, Fernand. *Edgard Varèse.* Trans Derek Coltman (1968; repr New York: Da Capo Press, 1981)

Olivia Mattis

Varick. Town (pop 1,729) in central Seneca Co. Settled *ca* 1790, the town was formed from Junius in 1830. Part of the town was included in the Cayuga Reservation ceded by the Cayuga between 1789 and 1807. An 800-acre (324 ha) cranberry swamp in the center of town was harvested in the 19th century. The Burroughs Hotel at East Varick (early 1860s–1909) was one of the earliest resorts; others followed, along with many private summer cottages. The town was served by the Geneva and Ithaca Railroad, later the Lehigh Valley (1873–1960s), and by its Seneca Lake Line (1892). Part of Seneca Army Depot (1941–2000) was in Varick. Amish farmers from Pennsylvania began buying farms in the 1990s. In 2003 grain corn was the principal crop, with some poultry and dairy.

Lisa Compton

Varick, James (*b* Newburgh, Orange Co, ?1750; *d* New York City, 22 July 1827). Religious leader, educator, and abolitionist. Likely freeborn to a slave mother and a free father, Varick moved to New York City early in his childhood. He joined the predominantly white congregation of John Street Methodist Episcopal Church in New York City around age 16, supporting himself as a shoemaker. In 1796 he and 30 of his fellow black members from John St left the church because of racial tensions. This group built African Methodist Episcopal Church, or Zion Church, officially known as African Methodist Episcopal Zion (AMEZ) after 1848, a black church with an independent charter as part of the Methodist Episcopal denomination in 1801. Yet most of the preachers who served the church were white, causing members to pressure the church hierarchy to allow Varick and two of his colleagues to become the first black deacons ordained in New York State in 1806. On 21 July 1820 the AMEZ Church officially separated from the Methodist Episcopal Church, and Varick became the first superintendent consecrated by the new denomination on 30 July 1822, serving until his death. Varick spoke out politically for black suffrage in New York State and in 1827 helped form *Freedom's Journal,* the first black newspaper in the United States.

American National Biography, vol 22, sv "James Varick"

Jason E. Bernth

Vassar College. Private college. Located in Poughkeepsie, it was chartered as Vassar Female College on 18 Jan 1861 and opened in the fall of 1865 with 353 students. Founded and endowed by Matthew Vassar, a Poughkeepsie businessman, "to create a monument to benefit mankind," the school modified its name to Vassar College in 1867 after complaints about the vulgarity of the word female. Challenged to offer the same educational advantages to women as those already offered to men at Yale or Harvard, the original nine professors quickly discovered that only one-third of the entering students were adequately prepared for college-level study. This deficiency was immediately accommodated by adding preparatory classes. From the beginning the college was housed in a large building designed by James Renwick Jr and modeled after the Tuileries in Paris. The multifunctional building provided an environment in which the students were protected by the adult presence, as if in a large family. Between 1865 and 1890, during the presidencies of Rev John Raymond (1864–78) and Rev Samuel Caldwell (1878–85), the college offered both certificates and bachelor's degrees in music and art. In the early 1880s the alumnae encouraged the trustees to cease offering preparatory work because secondary education had become mandatory and earlier student deficiencies largely eradicated. When Rev James Monroe Taylor was president (1886–1914), the college expanded its offerings, enlarged physical resources, and strengthened teaching. By 1914 enrollment was near 1,000 students.

With Henry Noble MacCracken's presidency (1915–46), America's adoption of woman suffrage, and entry into World War I, the mission of the college changed. Believing that traditional liberal arts education must be broadened to meet the needs of students, MacCracken encouraged students to become members of the larger local, national, and international communities. He introduced new majors, including a renowned drama department, began admitting foreign students, and included émigré scholars on the faculty. A model college constitution of 1922 democratized college governance. During World War II the college responded to wartime exigencies by introducing a temporary accelerated degree program and in 1946, for about five years, admitted male veterans. Under Sarah Gibson Blanding (1946–64), the college established programs such as a Vassar-Wellesley summer internship in Washington, DC. A grant from Paul Mellon promoted a residential system of house fellows, which articulated and enlarged relationships between students and faculty. In the late 1960s under Pres Alan Simpson (1964–77), the college turned down an offer from Yale University for a coeducational merger in New Haven. At that time, however, Vassar's trustees decided to educate men as well as women, and the school's charter was so amended in 1968. The first class to admit men as freshmen graduated in 1974, and during the next administration, under Pres Virginia Smith (1977–86), coeducation was solidified. Vassar College entered the 21st century under Pres Frances Fergusson (1986–), fully coeducational with a student body of approximately 2,270. Its traditional emphases on individual growth in a demanding educational environment have persisted.

Daniels, Elizabeth A. "History of Vassar College, http://faculty.vassar.edu/daniels

Daniels, Elizabeth A., and Clyde Griffin. *Full Steam Ahead in Poughkeepsie: The Story of Coeducation at Vassar, 1966–1974* (Poughkeepsie: Vassar College, 2000)

Linner, Edward R. *Vassar: The Remarkable Growth of a Man and His College, 1855–1865.* Ed. Elizabeth A. Daniels (Poughkeepsie: Vassar College, 1984)

Elizabeth A. Daniels

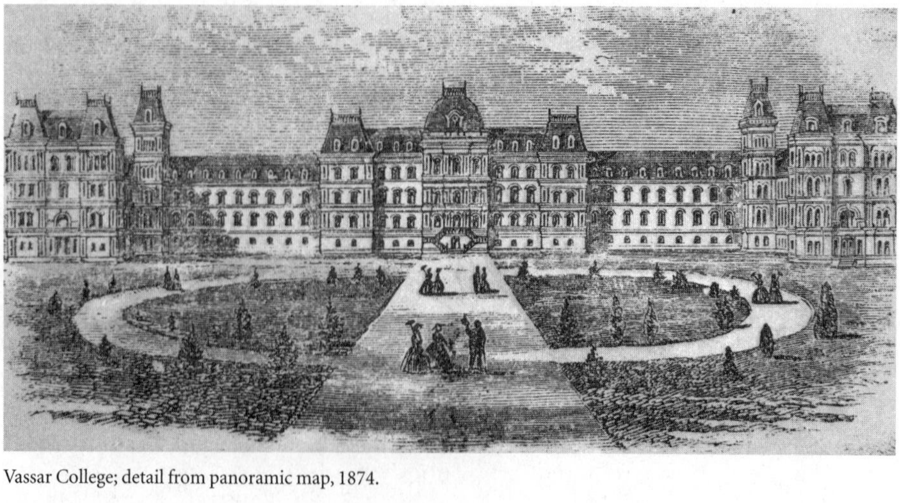

Vassar College; detail from panoramic map, 1874.

vaudeville. A series of acts by different performers strung together to form a complete bill of entertainment, emerging in New York State during the 1880s. From the Palace Theatre in Manhattan to Michael Shea's theaters in Buffalo, vaudeville had a broad audience and was a vital element in both local culture and the rise of national entertainment industries. It was variety theater, a staple of the 19th-century stage. Vaudeville was grounded in the search for a wide and lucrative audience, which pushed showmen to accommodate a variety of tastes in one theater: men and women, the rough and the refined, native-born and immigrant, middle class and working class.

The founders of New York State vaudeville emerged from the world of popular theater. Shea was born in Canada West [now Ontario, Wayne Co] and first worked as a sailor, stevedore, and ironworker before breaking into American theater in 1882 and directing the opening of Shea's Music Hall in Buffalo. Frederick Francis Proctor, acrobat and gymnast, ran theaters in Albany and Rochester in the early 1880s before moving to Brooklyn and Manhattan in the latter part of the decade. Tony Pastor appeared at dime museums and sang in Bowery concert saloons before presenting vaudeville shows at a theater near Union Square in New York City in 1881.

New York State vaudeville was distinguished by the relationship between New York City and the rest of the state. Early vaudevillians exploited the city's prominence as a center for theater, theatrical bookings, song publishing, commerce, and transportation to make it the capital of the vaudeville industry. New York City became a magnet for performers and showmen with aspirations, such as Proctor from the Albany region and B. F. Keith and E. F. Albee, circus managers from New England. Keith and Albee opened a theater on Union Square in 1893 and organized a national vaudeville booking system in 1900.

The Keith and Albee system grew powerful, but it was not the only face of vaudeville. In 1911 Marcus Loew began to open less expensive, less prestigious "small-time" theaters that offered vaudeville and film combinations in the neighborhoods around New York City. The Shubert Organization, founded in Syracuse in the late 19th century, twice challenged Keith and Albee's dominance. In Buffalo the Shea theaters had a distinct regional identity. In small towns and cities around the state, modest theatrical halls like the Earlville Opera House (Madison Co) and the Palace Theater of Lockport (Niagara Co) made businesses for themselves by presenting vaudeville shows as one element in an eclectic range of offerings that covered everything from movies to local pageants to high school graduations. Showmen also staged vaudeville shows at amusement parks, from Sacandaga Park (Fulton Co) in the Adirondacks to South Beach in Staten Island. However, through their control of bookings and aggressive dealings with rivals, Keith and Albee established circuits of theaters across the state that presented their acts. In the 1920s the Keith circuit controlled some 20 theaters in New York City and 18 more around the state, including Proctor's in Albany, the Temple in Rochester, and the Crescent in Syracuse.

Touring performers typically spent one week

at a theater before moving on to the next. Vaudevillians, especially performers that came from working-class and ethnic backgrounds, such as Eddie Cantor and Belle Baker, learned to adapt their routines to local preferences and customs. At the same time, audiences in far corners of the New York State were introduced to big-city style and humor. Out of this interaction emerged a statewide audience that would later be exploited by film, radio, and television. The summit of every vaudevillian's ambitions was the Palace Theatre in Manhattan's Times Square district. The theater, built by impresario Martin Beck, opened in 1913. After some sharp maneuvers by Albee, it came under the control of the Keith circuit. Soon it was the most prestigious vaudeville house in the United States and a testament to New York City's stature as the capital of vaudeville. Once there, performers used the cachet of having played the Palace to gain bookings at other theaters and to increase their wages.

The glory days of the Palace cast a glow over the declining years of vaudeville. By the 1920s movies and radio were both winning the loyalty of former vaudeville fans. Many theaters hung on by presenting combination bills of film and vaudeville, but by late in the decade vaudeville was fading. Its symbolic death came in 1932, when the Palace became a motion picture theater. Other vaudeville houses followed suit. Many former vaudevillians who had graced New York State theaters made a similar transition to film, radio, and television, among them Fred Allen, Milton Berle, and George Burns and Gracie Allen.

In recent years "new vaudeville"—a hybrid performance that can combine comedy, music, acrobatics, juggling, magic, and more—has attracted audiences. Although they are 21st-century performers who do not necessarily re-create the earlier generations of vaudevillians, they do perpetuate the eclectic, improvisatory style of the earlier era. More tangible connections can be formed by visiting old vaudeville theaters now enjoying second lives as showcases for legitimate theater and as performing arts centers. Among these are the Palace in New York City, the Bardavon 1869 Opera House in Poughkeepsie, the Tarrytown Music Hall (Westchester Co), and Proctor's Theatre in Schenectady.

See also BURLESQUE; FILM, SILENT.

Slide, Anthony. *The Encyclopedia of Vaudeville* (Westport, Conn: Greenwood, 1994)
Snyder, Robert W. *The Voice of the City: Vaudeville and Popular Culture in New York* (1989; repr Chicago: Ivan R. Dee, 2000)

Robert W. Snyder

vegetable farming. More than 20 types of crops are cultivated throughout the state, and dozens more are grown on small acreage. Until after the Revolutionary War, growers concentrated on field and forage crops, and vegetables were relegated to small garden-like plots. The most common vegetables included cabbage, turnips, cucumbers, beans, peas, pumpkins, and squash.

Commercial vegetable farming appeared by the mid–19th century and was a prosperous venture for many reasons: soils were ideal, especially in the Genesee River valley, and were deep loams that were uniform and rich; the climate was moderate, affected by the Great Lakes, and produced a relatively long frost-free season; and rainfall was usually consistent throughout the growing season. Farming also became more successful as cultivation tools were developed, as canals and railroads appeared, and as greenhouses and cold frames made early cultivation of seedlings possible.

In the latter half of the 19th century, there were two types of vegetable operations, market gardens and truck farms. Market gardens were located on the fringes of major cities and raised high-value, perishable crops on 5–10 acres (2–4 ha) of very expensive land. Typical crops on these labor-intensive farms included asparagus, celery, lettuce, spinach, and out-of-season crops grown in heated greenhouses. Many of these operations were on Long Island and provided vegetables for the burgeoning population of New York City. In the late 19th century, Kings Co was, for the brief time before urbanization eroded the county's agricultural base, the nation's leading county for vegetable production.

Truck farmers grew less perishable crops on less valuable land far from markets. These operations were usually larger than those near cities and often grew only two or three commodities, including root crops such as onions, beets, and carrots as well as cabbage, potatoes, snap beans, sweet corn, and peas. Cold winters allowed farmers to store cabbage, onions, potatoes, and carrots and to sell commodities off-season, a practice still common today. Truck farms were generally in the central Genesee River valley and the northern Finger Lakes region. As the ability to process vegetables cheaply and efficiently was realized in the late 19th century, the vegetable-processing industry expanded.

The largest vegetable farms today are primarily in Western New York and continue to produce low-value crops such as processing vegetables and wholesale commodities. Smaller farms with a diversity of vegetables are no longer limited by proximity to cities and thus scattered statewide. Acreage for all other vegetables has increased by about 30,000 acres (12,000 ha) since 1900, with the 2001 statewide total at about 160,000 acres (64,700 ha), sixth nationwide in vegetable acreage.

Becker, Robert F. "Vegetable Gardening in the United States, 1565–1900," *HortScience* 19 (Oct 1984): 624–29
Burritt, Maurice C. "An Account of the History and Development of Agriculture in Western New York" (MS thesis, Cornell Univ, 1910)
Hedrick, U. P. *A History of Agriculture in the State of New York* (New York: Hill & Wang, 1933)
Linder, Marc, and Lawrence S. Zacharias. *Of Cabbages and Kings County: Agriculture and the Formation of Modern Brooklyn* (Iowa City: Univ of Iowa Press, 1999)

Stephen Reiners

vegetation. See FLORA AND VEGETATION.

Velveeta. A process cheese developed around 1920 by innovative cheese maker Emil Frey of the Monroe Cheese Co (Orange Co). When the company's large cheese wheels became misshapen or broken, they could not be sold to the public. For years Frey experimented in his home kitchen, steaming and adding other ingredients to unsalable Swiss cheese, to develop a process cheese. The product that resulted was given the brand name Velveeta and registered with the US Patent and Trademark Office in 1923. A new business, the Velveeta Cheese Co, was created and incorporated 23 Feb 1923, with Frey as one of the company directors. When Monroe Cheese Co—along with Frey, who retained his position there—moved to Van Wert, Ohio, in 1926, Velveeta Cheese purchased the Monroe plant and operated until 1927, when the business was sold to Kraft Cheese Co. The success of Velveeta encouraged development of similar cheese foods, but at the beginning of the 21st century Velveeta was the single most popular brand of process cheese, controlling 20% of the $300 billion US process cheese market. Kraft Foods is headquartered in Northfield, Ill.

James Nelson

Velvet Underground. Avant-garde rock group. John Cale, Sterling Morrison, Maureen Tucker, and Brooklyn-born Syracuse University graduate Lou Reed (Louis Firbank) formed the Velvet Underground in New York City in 1965. Their association with artist Andy Warhol helped them become a fixture in the city's downtown art scene, and they appeared in Warhol's multimedia Exploding Plastic Inevitable events. Warhol provided a cover image of a banana for their first album, *The Velvet Underground and Nico* (1967), in which they were joined by the German singer Nico. *Loaded* (1970) produced several of the group's best-known songs, including "Sweet Jane." The group disbanded shortly after its release, reuniting briefly in 1993. Noted for Reed's incisive, sometimes harsh urban lyrics in such songs as "Heroin" (1967) and their use of noise and distortion, the influence of the Velvet Underground on successive generations of experimental rockers has been greater than their commercial success. Lou Reed's successful solo career included the song "Walk on the Wild Side" from *Transformer* (1972) and the album *New York* (1989). The group was inducted into the Rock and Roll Hall of Fame in 1996.

Bockris, Victor, and Gerard Melanga. *Uptight: The Velvet Underground Story* (New York: Quill, 1983)

Hugh W. Foley Jr

venereal disease. See SEXUALLY TRANSMITTED DISEASE (STD).

Venezuelans. Venezuelans started arriving in the United States in significant numbers in the 1970s, with those in New York State for the most part professionals and entrepreneurs. Not until the 1990s, however, did their presence in New York State become particularly visible. Of the four populations originating in the Andean region, Venezuelans number after Peruvians, Ecuadoreans, and Colombians. According to the 2000 census the foreign-born Venezuelan population in New York was 10,645, second to Florida's 47,351. Venezuelans in New York State settle primarily in Jackson Heights, an area of Queens rich in populations from South America, with smaller numbers also in the Morningside Heights area of Manhattan. Many Venezuelans celebrate their homeland country's Independence Day of 5 July.

International Organization for Migration. *World Migration Report: 2000* (Geneva, Switzerland: UN Publications, 2000)

Ana Margarita Cervantes-Rodríguez and Michael C. English

Venice. Town (pop 1,286) in SE Cayuga Co. Settled in 1800, the town was formed from Scipio in 1823. Slate was quarried *ca* 1830, and at Poplar

Ridge there was a sawmill. Where Venice touches Owasco Lake, the Cascade Hotel (1872) attracted vacationers. It was served by the Southern Central Railroad (1872) and by short lines running from Scipio to Ithaca. Mastodon bones were unearthed in town in 1957. Residents were alarmed by the "Venice Booms" (1966–68), loud noises that were never explained, and by the craters apparently resulting from them, but no meteorite activity was discovered. Poplar Ridge is the site of the Southern Cayuga Atmospherium-Planetarium (1968), which is owned by Southern Cayuga Central School District.

Laurel Auchampaugh

Vermont Sufferers Tract. Approximately 41,000 acres (16,600 ha) in what are now Bainbridge and Afton (Chenango Co), the tract was granted individually to 135 men in 1786 as compensation for being expelled from what was then Cumberland Co [now in Vermont] for serving in a New York State militia regiment during the Revolution. During the last years of the war, before New York State acknowledged Vermont's independence, Vermont attempted to remain neutral, and an active militia under New York State command in Vermont was a threat to both Vermont's neutrality and its claim to New York lands. The Vermonters attacked the militiamen, killed one, wounded some, imprisoned others, drove the rest from their homes, confiscated their land, and sold their personal property. Several sufferers, including the son of the New York State Militia colonel, are counted as early settlers of the tract, but most sold their land without occupying it.

Benton, R. C. *The Vermont Settlers and the New York Land Speculators* (Minneapolis: Housekeeper Press, 1894)

Michele A. McFee

Vernon. Town (pop 5,335) and village (pop 1,155) in SW Oneida Co. Settled in 1794, the town was formed from Augusta, Westmoreland, and Oneida Indian Reservation land in 1802. The town was on Seneca Turnpike (incorporated 1800; now Rte 5). Three glass factories began operating in 1809–10. The last one, Mount Vernon Glass Co, closed in 1845 and moved to Saratoga. The village incorporated in 1827. The industries of the Oneida Community and its successors were economically important to the town from 1864 until Sherrill incorporated as a city in 1916. Vernon Downs racetrack opened in 1952. Employers in 2003 include HP Hood (milk processors), Oneida Containers, and Kuhn Farm Machinery. Dairy farming continues in the southern and northern parts of Vernon.

Vernon, Lillian [Menasche, Lilly] (*b* Leipzig, Germany, 18 Mar 1927). Entrepreneur. After flight from Nazi-menaced Europe, her Jewish family settled in New York City in 1937. There teenaged Lillian worked as a theater usher and in a candy store before enrolling in New York University in 1947. After marriage to Samuel Hochberg in 1950, she left college and moved to Mount Vernon (Westchester Co). While awaiting the birth of her first child in 1951, she launched her direct-mail retailing career by advertising a monogrammed belt and bag in a popular teenage magazine. In 1954 she converted a Mount Vernon storefront into a warehouse and two years later mailed more than 100,000 copies of the first Lillian Vernon catalog. In 1965 she established Lillian Vernon Corp and in 1970 married Lucite manufacturer Robert Katz. In 1990, following divorce from Katz, the founder of Lillian Vernon Corp legally changed her name to Lillian Vernon. In 1993 corporate headquarters moved to New Rochelle (Westchester Co) and five years later to Rye (Westchester Co). In 1998 Vernon married Paolo Martino, a hairdresser, and in 1999, New York University's Lillian Vernon Foundation established an endowed chair for entrepreneurship. Following diminished catalog sales, Vernon agreed to sell the business to entrepreneur Strauss Zelnick in April 2003. She has served on the boards of cultural institutions, including that of Lincoln Center.

Vernon, Lillian. *An Eye for Winners* (New York: Harper Business, 1997)

Marilyn E. Weigold

Verona. Town (pop 6,425) in W Oneida Co. Settled by Europeans in 1791, it was mostly within the original Oneida Indian Nation Reservation. The town was formed from the reservation and Westmoreland in 1802. A part of the Erie Canal opened through town in 1819; later two Oneida Lake canals (1835–63, 1877–78) and the Barge Canal (1918) also passed through Verona. Nineteenth-century industries included extensive boatbuilding along the Erie Canal, especially at New London, and glassmaking at Dunbarton (*ca* 1825–95) and Durhamville (1845), which was also home to a clay pipe factory. A hotel was built *ca* 1830 at Verona Springs. The canning of local produce by Oneida Canning (?1892–1958) and three other shorter-lived plants provided an important source of employment. Verona Beach State Park (1947), Verona Military Reservation (SONAR installation, 1951), and the Thruway (1954) opened in town, bringing changes that proved minor compared with those caused by Turning Stone Casino and Resort (1993). The profits from this Oneida Indian Nation enterprise allowed the tribe to purchase nearly 40% of the town's land by 2002. Many residents of Verona commute to Syracuse, Utica, Rome, and Oneida (Madison Co).

Verrazano-Narrows Bridge. A two-level, 12-lane suspension bridge spanning the Narrows, the entrance to New York Harbor, between Staten Island and Brooklyn. Named for Giovanni da Verrazano, thought to be the first European to pass through this gateway, the structure provided the first vehicular crossing between Staten Island and the other New York City boroughs. Built by the Triborough Bridge and Tunnel Authority (TBTA), it opened in 1964 as part of I-278 and together with its approaches created a southern bypass around Manhattan that led to more rapid residential and commercial development of Staten Island. Its 4,260 ft (1,298.5 m) main span was the longest suspension bridge in the world until 1981. The Brooklyn-Queens Expressway and Belt Parkway serve as the main Brooklyn approaches, with the Staten Island Expressway connecting at the other end of the bridge. The Metropolitan Transportation Authority's (MTA) Bridges and Tunnels agency, the successor agency of the TBTA, operates Verrazano-Narrows. Since 1986 tolls have been collected from westbound traffic only, with MTA introducing an electronic (E-Z Pass) toll system in the 1990s. The annual New York City Marathon begins from the Staten Island toll plaza. In 1999 about 68 million vehicles crossed the structure. The bridge is also a primary public transit link used by express buses between Staten Island and Manhattan.

Leon Goodman

Vestal. Town (pop 26,535) in SW Broome Co. Cultivated fields and the Tuscarora settlement of Chugnutt were destroyed in 1779 during the Sullivan-Clinton campaign. Amos Draper established a trading post in 1782, and settlement followed in 1785. The town was formed from Union in 1823 and is bordered on the north by the Susquehanna River. Lumbering and agriculture were important early industries, and much of the town remains rural, although suburbanization from the Triple Cities metropolitan area (Binghamton, Endicott, and Johnson City) began in the north part of town in the 1920s. The suburban development is considerable, and a number of shopping malls line Vestal Parkway (1951). SUNY Binghamton (1946), whose campus was built starting in 1955, and Kopernik Observatory are located in town. Vestal was the birthplace of David R. Locke (1833–88), who, under the pen name Petroleum Vesuvius Nasby, wrote influential Northern propaganda during the Civil War.

Charles J. Browne

Veteran. Town (pop 3,271) in N Chemung Co. Settled in 1798, the town was formed from Catharine [now in Schuyler Co] in 1823. Lumbering was its first important industry. The Chemung Canal (1833–78) passed through town, with locks at Pine Valley and Millport, as did the Northern Central Railroad (1849; later Pennsylvania Railroad). Farming overtook the lumber industry after the canal closed. In the 1920s a group of Czech immigrants purchased farms in the eastern part of Veteran. When farming declined, the town became increasingly residential, and Fran Court (1961) was the first housing development. Veteran is the site of the golden domes of Elmira College's J. Ralph Murray Athletic Education Center (1973) and Mark Twain State Park.

Heather A. Wade

Veterans' Affairs, Division of. Executive branch agency created in 1945 to aid veterans, members of the military, their families, dependents, and survivors in securing entitlement benefits. Established by Gov Thomas E. Dewey in response to the large number of returning World War II veterans, the agency works as an advocate and service provider to those deemed eligible through military service. In the years after the war the agency assisted New York State veterans in applying for various programs under the GI Bill of Rights. The agency offers three core programs as well as other general services. Its Counseling and Claims Service assists veterans in filing the necessary applications to receive benefits from the US Department of Veterans' Affairs (VA). The Blind Annuity Program provides an annual $1,000 benefit to blind veterans and spouses, offering support to roughly 3,800 recipients in 2002. Its Veterans' Education Program approves and certifies higher education, job training, and apprenticeship programs to those eligible for educational benefits. The agency is headed by a director who is appointed by the governor and must be a veteran. The Veterans' Affairs Commission, made up of 13 members who are appointed by the governor and legislature to three-year terms and the state's adjutant general, who is an ex-officio member, assists the director in policy planning. In 2003 the agency operated in 70 locations, including 12 VA hospitals throughout the state. With an appropriated budget of close to $11 million, its staff of roughly 110 employees was responsible for serving the more than 1.2 million veterans in New York State. In 2003 nearly 125,000 veterans (as well as dependents and survivors) received over $1.1 billion in benefits through the agency's efforts.

New York State. Division of Veterans' Affairs. *2002 Annual Report* (Albany, 2003)

Jeffrey Kraus

veterans' healthcare and hospitals. The oldest veterans' hospital in New York State is the Bath VA Medical Center in Bath (Steuben Co). Sponsored by the Grand Army of the Republic, it opened in 1878. Known initially as the New York State Soldiers' and Sailors' Home, the center reached its peak resident population of 2,143 by 1907. In 1929 the hospital was turned over to the federal government and in 1930 became part of the Veterans' Administration (VA), which in 1989 became the Department of Veterans Affairs. It is adjacent to the Bath National Cemetery.

Two major networks served New York State veterans in 2003: Veterans Integrated Service Network 2 (VISN2) for upstate New York and VISN3 for downstate New York and New Jersey. VISN2 served 47 counties in New York and 2 in Pennsylvania and had 5 major medical centers providing outpatient care to surrounding towns and villages, for a total of 28 clinic sites around the state. Besides Bath, the most important medical centers in VISN2 included Syracuse, primarily a full-service inpatient hospital. Affiliated with SUNY Upstate Medical University and Syracuse University, it had a 50-bed short-term transitional care nursing home unit. The VA Western NY Health Care System included medical centers in Batavia (Genesee Co) and in Buffalo. The Batavia campus was built in 1933. In 1995 the New York State Veterans Home moved to the campus to house long-term care patients. The Batavia facility provided geriatric care, rehabilitation, and outpatient service and housed a post-traumatic stress care unit. The Buffalo VA opened in 1950 and provided multiple medical services, including a cardiac center. Both Batavia and Buffalo were affiliated with SUNY Buffalo's School of Medicine and Biomedical Sciences. A VA hospital opened in Albany in 1951 and became known as the Stratton VA Medical Center in 1990, serving 22 counties in upstate New York, western Massachusetts, and Vermont. Designated a Comprehensive Cancer Center by the American College of Surgeons, the facility had fully integrated residency programs with its affiliate, the Albany Medical College. The Canandaigua VA Medical Center (Ontario Co) opened in the 1940s, and in 2003 its campus included 14 buildings on 150 acres (61 ha). It provided primary and outpatient care, and acute and long-term psychiatric treatment. Its academic affiliates included the University of Rochester, three SUNY campuses, and six private colleges. At the end of 2003 strenuous local political opposition led the Department of Veterans Affairs to reverse their decision to close the Canandaigua facility.

VISN3 included six major medical centers in Brooklyn, the Bronx, Castle Point (Dutchess Co), Montrose (Westchester Co), Manhattan, and Northport (Suffolk Co). There were also facilities in East Orange and Lyons, NJ. The Bronx VA Medical Center is the oldest VA hospital in New York City. Occupying a site used as an orphanage in the late 19th century, the VA began operating the Bronx hospital in 1922, moving it to its current location on Kingsbridge Rd in 1981. With 1,663 beds, it was the second largest VA facility in the country. The Brooklyn VA Medical Center in Bay Ridge was originally called the Manhattan Beach VA Hospital and was developed on the site of Fort Hamilton in 1950. By 2003 it was affiliated with SUNY Downstate and provided full-service care, including surgical, psychiatric, and residential substance-abuse care. It is maintained by the VA New York Harbor Healthcare System, along with facilities on Manhattan's East Side and in St. Albans (Queens Co). The Northport VA Medical Center was affiliated with the SUNY Stony Brook Medical School and specialized in general medicine and surgery, as well as serving as a point of reentry for recent combat veterans. Founded in 1924, the Castle Point Campus of the VA Hudson Valley Health Care System was a primary and secondary care facility by 2003. The Montrose Campus was originally known as the Franklin D. Roosevelt VA Hospital when it opened in 1950. It subsequently provided full-service care for acute and chronic psychiatric patients, with special programs for Agent Orange and Persian Gulf issues. It maintained one of most extensive community home-care programs for veterans in the country.

Although veterans hospitals provide a vast array of services including cutting-edge cardiac surgery and research, as well as psychiatric, medical, and primary care, there has been a shift in recent years to an emphasis on outpatient care. Many of the VA hospitals, however, still have domiciliaries and provide nursing home care for elderly veterans. In 2000 New York State was home to 1,361,164 civilian veterans or 10% of the total civilian population of the state.

See also CEMETERIES.

VA Healthcare Network Upstate New York, http://www1.va.gov/visns/visn02/facilities.html
VA NY/NJ Veterans Healthcare Network, http://www.appc1.va.gov/visns/visn03/visn3fac.asp

Jane M. DeLuca

veto power. The word *veto* is Latin and means "I forbid." It is used in a governmental context to refer to the power of the executive to prevent a bill passed by a legislature from becoming law. Its origin in US history dates from the power exercised by the royal governors to invalidate laws passed by the colonial legislatures. Because of this, the framers of postcolonial state constitutions avoided giving veto power to their chief executives. The 1777 New York State Constitution did not give the governor veto power but instead vested the power in a body called the Council of Revision. Comprising the governor and the state's principal judges, the council was given the power to veto bills "inconsistent with the spirit of the constitution or with the public good." The council was abolished by the Constitutional Convention of 1821, which adopted provisions giving the governor veto power and the legislature the power to override the veto by a two-thirds vote of the members present.

The issue of the veto power remained central in constitutional reform. From 1847 it became the practice of New York governors to sign bills after the legislature had adjourned. The Constitutional Convention of 1867 favored a provision that limited the time the governor had to sign bills to 10 days and required a two-thirds vote of elected legislative members to override the veto; these provisions were adopted by amendment in 1874. In addition, the convention rejected the idea of giving the governor the power to veto only specific portions of bills, known as the line-item veto. The 1872 Constitutional Commission revived that issue and proposed that the governor be allowed to use an item veto on appropriation bills, a measure voters approved in 1874.

The frequency of the use of the veto power changes from governor to governor. Grover Cleveland (1883–85) and Theodore Roosevelt (1899–1901) used the power fairly heavily in their relatively short terms, with 288 and 287 vetoes respectively. Charles Evans Hughes (1907–10) recorded 919, Mario M. Cuomo (1982–94) 969, and Hugh Carey (1974–82) 1,209. Impeached governor William Sulzer (1913) recorded 384 in his one year.

Although the legislature retains the power of override, successful use of that power has been infrequent. Between 1823 and 1975, for example, only 16 gubernatorial vetoes were overridden. However, in May 2003 Gov George E. Pataki vetoed $3.2 billion in tax increases and spending additions the legislature added to the 2003–4 budget, which using his line-item power amounted to 119 separate vetos. That same month a unanimous state senate and 104 of 150 members of the assembly voted to override all of the governor's vetoes. The line-item veto was further considered in the case of *Silver v Pataki*, brought by Sheldon Silver, the speaker of the assembly, against Gov Pataki, which challenged both the long-standing tradition of separation of powers between state government branches and the veto powers specific to the governor. The suit alleged that Pataki used the line-item veto unconstitutionally 55 times on nonappropriation bills the legislature proposed. The December 2003 ruling by the Appellate Division of the New York Supreme Court favored the governor, based on the 1927 constitutional amendment that transferred budget responsibilities from the legislature to the executive.

Prescott, Frank W., and Joseph F. Zimmerman. *The Politics of the Veto of Legislation in New York State* (Washington, DC: Univ Press of America, 1980)

Philip Lance

Vick, James (*b* Chichester, England, 23 Nov 1818; *d* Rochester, 16 May 1882). Horticulturist and seedsman. Vick immigrated to New York City with his family in 1833, moving in 1837 to Rochester and finding work as a printer in various newspaper offices. By the late 1840s he had become interested in floriculture and contributed articles to the *Genesee Farmer*, becoming an editor in 1850. In 1853 Vick bought the *Horticulturist* and published it in Rochester.

During the late 1850s he propagated flowers from seed in a small garden on Union St in Rochester. By 1860 he had founded a seed business and introduced the practice of receiving orders and sending packets by mail instead of through vendors. In 1866 he established an extensive nursery along East Ave and later transferred seed production to a large expanse of land near Lake Ontario. His name became well known in American homes through *Vick's Illustrated Catalogue and Floral Guide* and chromolithographic prints of floral displays introduced in 1870. Vick is credited with developing new flower varieties, among them white double phlox and the fringed petunia.

McKelvey, Blake. "The Flower City: Center of Nurseries and Fruit Orchards," *Rochester Historical Society Publications* 18 (1940): 121–69

Paul Grebinger

Victor. Town (pop 9,977) and village (pop 2,433) in NW Ontario Co. Ganondagan State Historic Site (1987) is on the site of Ganondagan, a Seneca village burned by the Marquis de Denonville in July 1687. Victor was settled in 1789, and the town was formed from Bloomfield in 1812. The first railroad, the Auburn and Rochester, came through in 1840. Gypsum mining was important from the 1830s to 1940, and crops included grain, apples, and seed potatoes. The Irish established a Catholic church in 1850; German and Italian immigrants arrived later in the century. The village was incorporated in 1879. Victor Insulator Co (1893; now Victor Insulators) manufactures glass insulators. A 4 mi (6 km) section of the Thruway built between 1946 and 1948 was the first stretch opened for public use. Notable landmarks are Ganondagan, the Valentown Museum (built 1879–81), and Eastview Mall (1970). The population of this popular suburb of Rochester increased 38% from 1990 to 2000.

Marla A. Bennett

Victory. Town (pop 1,838) in N Cayuga Co. Settled in 1800, the town was formed from Cato in 1821. Blue limestone deposits were quarried for building material, and there was a tannery at Westbury in the late 19th century, but the town did not thrive as a mill town because the Red and Little Sodus Creeks furnished only meager waterpower. In the early 21st century its agricultural crops are corn, soybeans, and hay; many residents commute to Oswego, Auburn, Syracuse, and Rochester.

Laurel Auchampaugh

Victory. Village (pop 544) in E Saratoga Co. In 1846 the Saratoga Victory Manufacturing Co, named in allusion to the Battle of Saratoga and owned by three Bostonians, built a cloth mill on Fish Creek that produced cotton cloth for retail. It included dyeing and finishing works and employed up to 700 hands, many of them living in company housing. The village was incorporated in 1849. By 1860 a quarter of its 637 residents were Irish-born; later they were joined by a significant French Canadian population. The manufacturing company moved out of state in 1928. From 1937 to 1972 United Board and Carton used the facility. Although some small companies have moved into the old mill buildings, most residents find work elsewhere. Victory is the site of the Saratoga Battle Monument.

Field Horne

Videofreex. One of the first collectives of artists, activists, and aspiring producers that created the video movement in the early 1970s. Videofreex formed when Parry Teasdale and David Cort met while videotaping the August 1969 Woodstock Art and Music Fair in Bethel (Sullivan Co). Joined by Mary Curtis Ratcliff, the group worked together in Lower Manhattan from 1969 to 1971. Two other New York City groups, People's Video Theater and Raindance Corp, also explored various forms of expression made possible by the first relatively inexpensive, portable videotape recorders. In 1971 the New York State Council on the Arts (NYSCA) granted approximately $40,000 through the Rochester Museum and Science Center to Videofreex to fund its work in video and film. After Videofreex created a nonprofit corporation called Media Bus, the group moved to the hamlet of Lanesville (Greene Co) to satisfy NYSCA's wishes that its funds help stimulate the group's work beyond New York City. The nine members of Freex traveled to Syracuse, Rochester, Binghamton, Cooperstown (Otsego Co), and other cities and rural communities around the state, introducing new video technology and teaching people how to use it. In 1973 the group published *Spaghetti City Video Manual: A Guide to Use, Repair and Maintenance.* Neither cable television nor broadcast stations reached Lanesville in the heart of the Catskills, so Videofreex built and operated its own unlicensed television transmitter. Lanesville TV, Channel 3, broadcast weekly to the few hundred homes in the vicinity from 1972 to 1977. It was the nation's first pirate television station. The station aired local events and programs that would showcase the work of the artists who visited Maple Tree Farm, the Videofreex house in Lanesville. Local residents participated in the programs and often joined in video improvisations. The Lanesville facility closed in 1978, although a few members of the group continued to operate as Media Bus. In 2001 the bulk of the original Videofreex videotapes were taken to Chicago, where attempts are being made to preserve them. Videofreex stretched the boundaries of handheld productions, inserting the camera as active participant rather than as passive observer. The group also showed that television could function collectively and within a community without relying on the corporate model.

Teasdale, Parry D. *Videofreex: America's First Pirate TV Station and the Catskills Collective that Turned It On* (Hensonville, NY: Black Dome Press, 1999)

Parry D. Teasdale

Vienna [VY-AN-NA]. Town (pop 5,819) in W Oneida Co. The area was settled around 1797, and the town was formed from Camden in 1807 as Orange; it changed to Bengal in 1808 and to Vienna in 1816. Natural resources included lumber, fuller's earth, and wintergreen oil. With the Ontario and Western Railroad (1869), greater accessibility created North Bay and Sylvan Beach summer resorts. The former is no longer a resort, although Sylvan Beach continues to draw vacationers. Several canning factories operated from *ca* 1880. A landmark is the Stone Barn, constructed from 1899 to 1906 for the dairy farm of Charles W. Knight of Rome and measuring 120 feet (36.6 m) by 42 feet (12.8 m). In 2003 many residents worked in McConnellsville, Camden, Rome, and Syracuse.

Vietnamese. A few Vietnamese students lived in New York City before 1975, but the vast majority of Vietnamese in New York State came after 1975 as refugees. The first wave included military and government officials who had worked with the United States during the Vietnam War. The second wave began in the late 1970s and continued into the early 1980s as hundreds of thousands of ethnic Chinese, farmers, fisher families, and relatives of those who had left earlier fled Vietnam. Because many, but not all, left Vietnam by sea, they were sometimes called "boat people." Starting in the mid-1980s, many who came to the United States were former political prisoners or children of Vietnamese mothers and US servicemen. A modest migration continues into the 21st century, usually through family reunification. The federal government and nonprofit agencies resettled the early refugees, many of whom came with nothing. World Relief and Catholic Charities settled Vietnamese refugees in Broome Co, while the Mohawk Valley Resource Center for Refugees brought Vietnamese to Oneida Co.

In 2000, 23,818 people of Vietnamese birth or parentage lived in New York State, an increase of almost 50% since 1990. About 13,500 live in the New York City area; 3,000 in the Rochester area, and 2,000 in the Syracuse vicinity. Smaller numbers live near Buffalo and Albany. Perhaps three-quarters of the Vietnamese in the state are Buddhists, and one-fifth are Catholic. Regardless of religion many Vietnamese practice some form of ancestor worship in which they honor parents, grandparents, and deceased family members, and many celebrate Tet (Lunar New Year). The Vietnamese American Cultural Organization at 113 Baxter St in Manhattan and the Greater New York Vietnamese-American Community Association on Ocean Parkway in Brooklyn provide cultural activities and social services. In Rochester Vietnamese Catholics worship at St. Anthony of Padua.

Haines, D., ed. *Refugees in America in the 1990s: A Reference Handbook* (Westport, Conn: Greenwood, 1996)

Irene Bloemraad

Vietnam War. Although the period of conflict is usually given as 1960 to 1975, US military presence in Vietnam began during World War II. Lt Col A. Peter Dewey, nephew of New York State Gov Thomas E. Dewey, went to Vietnam in August 1945 as head of an Office of Strategic Services (OSS) team sent to rescue American prisoners of war held by the Japanese near Saigon. On 26 Sept 1945 Dewey was on his way to the Tan Son Nhut Airport, northeast of Saigon, when he was caught in an ambush in the hostilities between the French and the Vietnamese and became the first American serviceman killed in Vietnam. By 1964 the US military presence in Vietnam had grown to more than 15,000. On 6 July 1964 Capt Roger Hugh C. Donlon, US Army Special Forces, was serving as commanding officer at Camp Nam Dong near the 17th parallel when the North Vietnamese launched an attack. Donlon, born in Saugerties

(Ulster Co), distinguished himself in the five hours of battle that followed and received the first congressional Medal of Honor of the Vietnam War.

Antiwar Protest

New York City became a major venue for protests against the intervention in Vietnam. At a 2 May 1964 march to the UN Plaza, hundreds of students demonstrated their objection to the American presence in Vietnam. Antiwar activity increased after Pres Lyndon Johnson asked that monthly draft calls be increased in July 1965. At a 15 Oct 1965 pacifist rally outside the Whitehall Examining and Entrance Station in Lower Manhattan, David J. Miller was among the first objectors to burn his draft card and later served two years in prison for doing so. A protest at Manhattan College in Riverdale (Bronx Co) ended in a violent confrontation between students for and against the war. The Fifth Avenue Peace Parade Committee in New York City drew a diverse crowd to march behind the slogan Stop the War in Vietnam Now on 16 Oct 1965 and went on to organize semiannual protests until 1973.

About 50,000 people marched in antiwar protests on 5th Ave in March 1966, and Gov Nelson A. Rockefeller, Sen Jacob K. Javits, and New York City mayor John Lindsay openly expressed their objections to the Vietnam War. Fifty-two were arrested at a 15 Dec 1966 blockade of 39 Whitehall St in Manhattan, probably the busiest induction center on the East Coast. Folksinger Arlo Guthrie recounted his own experience at Whitehall in the satirical talking-blues composition "Alice's Restaurant." At the Village Gate in New York City's Greenwich Village, Barbara Garson's play "MacBird!" satirized Lyndon Johnson as a MacBeth-like assassin of the ideals of the Kennedy era.

At the Spring Mobilization on 15 Apr 1967 more than 130,000 participants gathered in Central Park to witness over 100 men burn their draft cards. They then followed Rev Martin Luther King Jr and Dr Benjamin Spock to demonstrate before the United Nations. Speaking at Riverside Church a few days beforehand, King had joined the peace movement to the civil rights movement when he noted that working-class men and black men were markedly overrepresented among those sent to fight in Vietnam. The December 1967 Stop the Draft Week resulted in hundreds of arrests around the Whitehall induction center, which was by then processing about 250 men each day.

Service in the Armed Forces

Potential soldiers continued to be processed at Whitehall throughout the protest. "If I have to go to Vietnam, I'll go," 19-year-old Pedro Anton Baez told the *New York Times* on 6 Dec 1967. In *Working-Class War* Christian Appy noted that about 80% of draftees came from working-class or poor families. Ron Kovic of Massapequa (Nassau Co), son of working-class parents, joined the Marine Corps after high school and served two tours in Vietnam. In 1968 he, by then a sergeant, was paralyzed from the neck down in combat. He came home to an indifferent and occasionally hostile public and to substandard conditions in Veterans' Administration (VA) hospitals in New York City. Kovic's memoir, *Born on the Fourth of July,* was published in 1976 and made into a film in 1989. African Americans made up about one-ninth of US troops in Vietnam and about one-fifth of combat troops. The usual avenues of avoiding the draft, such as college deferments, were often not available to them.

The Marine Corps' Fr Vincent R. Capodanno became famous in 1966 as the "Chaplain on a Hill" who went into the field on patrol. Capodanno, born the son of Italian immigrants on Staten Island, volunteered for the Navy Chaplain Corps in 1965 and was sent to Vietnam. On 4 Sept 1967 he was with a routine search-and-destroy mission about 50 miles (80 km) south of Danang when the company was hit by North Vietnamese fire. Although a mortar round blew off part of his leg, Fr Capodanno continued to give last rites and pray with the wounded until he died. He was posthumously awarded the congressional Medal of Honor. Jan Barry, born in Ithaca, had served in Vietnam in 1962 and 1963, then became a cadet at the United States Military Academy at West Point (Orange Co) in 1964, but he dropped out in 1965, critical of US intervention in Vietnam. He was working as a journalist in New York City when he and five other Vietnam veterans established the Vietnam Veterans against the War (VVAW) on 1 June 1967. The VVAW condemned US actions but supported the men fighting there: its goal was to bring them home alive. The presence of VVAW marchers lent new gravity and validity to peace events.

The Tet Offensive

Many Americans turned against the war after the 30 Jan 1968 Tet Offensive. The offensive galvanized opposition to Pres Johnson among the Democrats, leading Sen Robert F. Kennedy to announce his candidacy for president on 16 Mar 1968. This led to widespread protests. On April 23, under the aegis of Columbia University's Students' Afro-American Society (SAS) and the Students for a Democratic Society (SDS), students occupied five buildings, including the university's administrative headquarters. The takeover ended on 30 April, when more than 1,000 police drove the students out in a violent confrontation that led to further national and international student protests. In late 1968 students at Cornell University used physical force to express their objections to corporate recruiters and the policies of the president of Cornell. The Woodstock Festival of 15–17 Aug 1969 in Ulster Co was in part an antiwar gathering, heralding the apogee of the protest movement in 1969–1970. On Vietnam Moratorium Day, 15 Oct 1969, when thousands across the nation took the day off from work or classes to protest the war, Mayor Lindsay ordered flags flown at half-staff in New York City.

On 30 Apr 1970 Pres Richard M. Nixon announced that US troops were going into Cambodia, and protest tore across the nation. New York University students occupied school buildings from 4 to 22 May 1970. On 8 May they joined with students from Hunter College and other local colleges and high schools to demonstrate near Wall St, where they were chased and beaten by construction workers. Peter J. Brennan, president of New York Building and Construction Trades Council, a leader of the "hardhats" who supported the war, later served as Pres Nixon's secretary of labor.

On 13 June 1971 the *New York Times* began publishing excerpts from the Pentagon Papers, a secret archive of government documents pertaining to the Vietnam War. When the government tried to stop it, the Supreme Court ruled in favor of the *Times.* The United States resumed bombing of North Vietnam in April 1972, and the most intense bombing of the war occurred 18–29 Dec 1972. On 23 Jan 1973 US and North Vietnamese representatives reached a peace agreement. Judge Orin Judd, Federal District Court of New York, tried to stop the bombing of Cambodia by issuing an injunction on 15 July 1973. The injunction was suspended, and the bombing of Cambodia continued through 14 Aug 1973. On 30 Apr 1975, Saigon, the capital of South Vietnam, fell to the communists.

Vietnam Veterans

In 1970 New York physician Robert Jay Lifton MD started therapy groups among the VVAW in New York. Lifton's work created the Veterans Centers within the VA system. He published *Home from the War,* a major study on post-traumatic stress disorder (PTSD), in 1973. In addition to PTSD and medical problems from combat injuries and other sources, such as exposure to the herbicide Agent Orange, returning Vietnam veterans often lacked marketable skills and education as well as social support. In 1994 there were an estimated 9,000 homeless veterans of the Vietnam War in New York State.

The New York State Vietnam Memorial in Albany was dedicated in 1984, the Vietnam Veterans Memorial of Greater Rochester opened in 1996, and the New York State Women Veterans Memorial, also in Albany, was dedicated in 1998. Of the 4,033 lost from New York State in the Vietnam War, the 1,741 who entered the service in New York City are honored at the Vietnam Veterans Plaza, which opened in 1985 at 55 Water St in Lower Manhattan.

Appy, Christian. *Working-Class War: American Combat Soldiers and Vietnam* (Chapel Hill: Univ of North Carolina Press, 1993)

Steinman, Ron. *Women in Vietnam* (New York: TV Books, 2000)

Wells, Tom. *The War Within: America's Battle over Vietnam* (Berkeley: Univ of California Press, 1994)

Pamela Cooper

War protester in Syracuse, 1972.

village government. Villages are incorporated general-purpose local governments. For much of New York State history they were established in response to local need for an enhanced level of public services in more densely settled places. Villages were initially created by special acts of the legislature. Lansingburgh, incorporated in 1790, is generally recognized as the state's first village. (It is now a neighborhood in Troy, Rensselaer Co.) Seven trustees were named "to enable them to regulate their internal police, and to secure the benefits of certain commonable lands." The first use of the term "village" in state law came with the incorporation of Waterford (Saratoga Co) and Troy (Rensselaer Co) in 1794. The first general village law was passed in 1847 after a call for it by the 1846 Constitutional Convention. Reacting to the frequent hamstringing of the legislative process by the volume of special legislation to adopt and amend village charters, governors in the mid–19th century called regularly for reform, which led to an 1874 constitutional amendment barring villages from incorporating by special legislative act. Changes in the Village Law in 1897 subjected already incorporated villages to it when not inconsistent with their charters and allowed them to reincorporate under general law. All but 12 have done so. Those still operating under special act charters are: Alexander (Genesee Co), Carthage (Jefferson Co), Catskill (Greene Co), Cooperstown (Otsego Co), Deposit (Delaware and Broome Cos), Fredonia (Chautauqua Co), Ilion (Herkimer Co), Mohawk (Herkimer Co), Ossining (Westchester Co), Owego (Tioga Co), Port Chester (Westchester Co), and Waterford.

There were 554 villages in New York State in 2000, most chartered between the Civil War and World War I. Village creation waned with the extension of the powers of town government in the 1930s. By the end of the 20th century the few villages being established involved attempts to benefit by shifting the locus of land-use decision making or by reducing property taxes. Occasionally, unique local purposes were involved, such as the Village of Kiryas Joel (Orange Co), chartered in 1977, an Orthodox Jewish religious community. In 2000, 1,834,159 New Yorkers lived in villages that ranged widely in size, more than three-fifths with fewer than 2,500 people. The state's largest and smallest villages in 2000 were both on Long Island: 11 people lived in West Hampton Dunes (Suffolk Co) and 56,554 in Hempstead (Nassau Co). A quarter of New York State's villages were in the four suburban counties closest to New York City: Nassau had 64, Suffolk 31, Westchester 23, and Rockland 19. In contrast, Hamilton and Warren Cos in the Adirondack Forest Preserve had only one each. Cities do not contain villages, and thus the five counties of New York City are without villages; 10 were dissolved in Queens and 5 in Staten Island in 1898 in the consolidation of the greater city.

Villages may have boundaries that overlap or align with those of other general-purpose governments: 70 villages are in two or more towns and 7 are in two counties. The Village of Saranac Lake is in three towns and two counties (Essex and Franklin). Five villages are coterminous with towns: Green Island (Albany Co), East Rochester (Monroe Co), and Scarsdale, Harrison, and Mount Kisco (Westchester Co). Village officers in East Rochester, Scarsdale, and Mount Kisco also serve as town officers and must approve the town budget. The town and village governments in Green Island and Harrison deliver distinct services and function independently.

Villages are governed by an elected board of trustees, most commonly five members, one of whom is a mayor. Elections, usually held in early spring, are commonly without major party involvement and are rarely competitive. The village mayor exercises limited executive authority and, with board approval, appoints the village clerk and treasurer; duties of these positions are sometimes held and discharged by a single person. A village justice may also be appointed. In 1999, reflecting a national trend toward professional management in local government, 65 villages had appointed administrators. Collectively, state villages raised $1.67 billion in revenues in 2000, about half from local taxes, predominantly the real property tax. State aid accounted for 6% of total village revenues; federal aid provided 5%. The same year villages spent $1.78 billion with 74% allocated for such local services as police and fire protection, street and highway lighting and maintenance, parks, water and sewer systems, code enforcement, and community planning. The balance was spent for capital purposes (18%) and to service debt (8%).

Villages are the only general-purpose local governments in New York State that may be created and dissolved entirely by local action. A village may be created based on a petition to a town or towns by 20% of the qualified voters or by owners of half the assessed value of property in an area of less than 5 mi^2 (13 km^2) with at least 500 inhabitants, though the territorial limit may be larger if coterminous with an existing town, school district, or fire district. (After the 2000 federal census there were 73 villages in New York State that did not meet the minimum population requirement for new villages.) If the petition is found sufficient as prescribed by state law, a referendum is held. A village is created if supported by an affirmative majority voting in the area to be within the village or, if more than one town is affected, distinct majorities from the part of each town to be within the village. In the last half of the 20th century villages were most likely to be created in suburban areas, with Kaser and Airmont (Rockland Co), East Nassau (Rensselaer Co) and West Hampton Dunes created in the 1990s. Villages may be dissolved on the initiative of the village board of trustees or as a result of a citizen petition. Although those living in adjacent areas are also affected, only qualified village residents may participate in a referendum on dissolution. Dissolution proposals, often advanced by those who seek less local government jurisdictional overlapping and greater efficiency, are frequently controversial; they challenge fundamental local loyalties and may threaten the jobs and status of community leaders and employees. During the 1990s dissolution efforts were most likely to succeed in rural areas: the Villages of Fillmore (Allegany Co), Henderson (Jefferson Co), Mooers (Clinton Co), Pine Valley (Chemung Co), Schenevus (Otsego Co), Ticonderoga (Essex Co), and Westport (Essex Co) were dissolved during this decade.

New York State. Office of the Comptroller. *Special Report on Municipal Affairs, 2001,* 94th ed. (Albany, 2002)

New York State. Secretary of State. Division of Local Government Services. *Local Government Handbook* (Albany, 2001)

Gerald Benjamin

Village of the Branch. Village (pop 1,895) in Smithtown (Suffolk Co). Named for the northeast branch of the Nissequogue River, the area was settled in 1690. The Long Island Rail Road came through in 1872. Debate over the need for a public water system resulted in incorporation of the village in 1927. In 2003 it encompassed both residential and business development and was the site of a number of historic structures along Middle Country Rd: the Epenetus Smith Tavern, the Caleb Smith House, the Judge J. Lawrence Smith Homestead, the Rockwell Cottage, and the Franklin A. Arthur Farm. All were operated by the Smithtown Historical Society and the First Presbyterian Church.

Noel J. Gish

Villenova. Town (pop 1,121) in NW Chautauqua Co. Settled in 1810 the town was formed in 1823 from Hanover. It has been a farming community throughout its history, and the rugged hills and broad valleys shelter small family farms into the early 21st century. In town the headwaters of the Conewango Creek flow from the outlets of East and West Mud Lakes. Most residents commute to surrounding areas to work.

Michelle Henry

viniculture. See WINE INDUSTRY AND VITICULTURE.

Viola. Locality (pop 5,931) in Ramapo (Rockland Co). The locality was originally named Mechanicsville due to its many small workshops, including a tannery, a wheelwright shop, and a silver-plating operation. The name was changed to Viola when a post office (1882–1905) was established. The County Almshouse opened in 1883; in 1959 it became the administration building of Rockland Community College. Aside from the 8,000-student college, Viola is residential.

Virgil. Town (pop 2,287) in SW Cortland Co. It was settled in 1792 by Joseph Chaplin, who surveyed the state road through Virgil, running from Oxford (Chenango Co) to Ludlowville (Tompkins Co). The town was formed from Homer in 1804. It is located on the divide between Seneca Lake and the Susquehanna River and contains the county's highest elevation, Virgil Mountain, at 2,132 feet (649.8 m). As early as 1828 a resident developed a plan for a railroad through the town; the Syracuse, Binghamton and New York Railroad was completed in 1854. In the 1860s a 500 lb (227 kg) cheese was made in town to promote its agricultural fair. Greek Peak (1958) is a ski area on Virgil Mountain.

Cathy A. Barber

visiting nurse associations. Established statewide, visiting nurse associations (VNAs) provide care in the home and attend to community healthcare needs. During the later 19th century, women's religious groups began organizing the care of people with sickness or disability, and philanthropic individuals provided funds. New York City's Bellevue Hospital, responding to the need for trained nurses, began the country's first formal nursing program in 1873. Bellevue's inaugural class included Francis Root, hired by the New York City Mission in 1877 as a salaried missionary nurse to provide nursing care and religious instruction. As scientific principles blended with humanitarian efforts, most agencies assigned an experienced nurse to direct the activities of nurse subordinates. Nurses in Buffalo began providing care without religious affiliation in 1885, thus initiating the visiting nurse movement. In 1888 Red Cross Society nurses began visits in Brooklyn, leading to the incorporation of the Brooklyn VNA in 1919. In 1893 the staff of three Brooklyn nurses each week earned $11.55 and made 15 home visits. That same year Lillian D. Wald and Mary Brewster began visiting on New York City's Lower East Side and expanded the concept of visiting to involve the community in disease prevention. The Henry Street Settlement was established in 1893 as a settlement solely maintained by visiting nurses. The Visiting Nurse Service of New York grew out of the Henry Street Settlement in 1946 and has continued this public health tradition.

Other nurse services developed around the state. The Visiting Nurses Association of Central New York, serving the Syracuse area, dates to 1890. Responding to high infant mortality in 1915, the Baby Welfare Committee of Utica (now Utica VNA) set up milk stations, and nurses taught mothers how to store fresh milk safely. Rochester established its Visiting Nurse Service in response to the 1918 influenza epidemic. In 1919 its 13 nurses made home visits and educated families for 70¢ a visit. This agency was among the first to provide Meals on Wheels to elderly homebound, and 2,000 volunteers continue providing that service. The number of VNAs declined during the depression, then increased sharply after 1965, when expansion of the Social Security Act provided home visits to qualified persons over age 65. Many VNAs educate nurses by providing clinical experience to students.

Executive officers of agencies in the 21st century administrate large businesses. The crucial addition of strong business principles has allowed VNAs to provide humanitarian service to the community and receive reimbursement for service from a variety of funders. Home care remains their basic service, and they also conduct public clinics, staff dispensaries, and present community education. Some schools and employment sites contract VNAs to provide nursing services. In 2003 New York State had nearly 30 visiting nurse associations, located in such communities as Albany, Elmira, Rochester, Johnstown, Poughkeepsie, Utica, Syracuse, New Rochelle, and Yonkers; the New York City–area Visiting Nurse Service of New York is the largest home care association in the world.

Buhler-Wilkerson, Karen. *No Place Like Home: A History of Nursing and Home Care in the United States* (Baltimore: Johns Hopkins Univ Press, 2001)

Lundy, Karen Saucier, and Sharyn Janes. *Community Health Nursing: Caring for the Public's Health* (Sudbury, Mass: Jones & Bartlett Publishers, 2001)

Anne Slyer Oboyski

Vocational and Educational Services for Individuals with Disabilities (VESID). Office within the New York State Education Department that coordinates policy and services for those with disabilities, including coordination of services for infants and toddlers, special education for school-age children, vocational rehabilitation for teens age 16 and older, and independent living services for adults. In 1921 New York State opened a Bureau of Rehabilitation in the Education Department, using funds from the 1920 federal Smith Fess Act, which provided reimbursement for 50% of vocational rehabilitation services. The bureau's functions were expanded in 1943 to include services to emotionally and mentally handicapped persons. The program continued to grow, with more than 20,000 cases in the 1950s and more than 100,000 clients in the mid-1970s. Oversight and complaints led to the creation of VESID in 1989.

VESID provides direct services to individuals with disabilities age 16 and older through administration of the Vocational Rehabilitation (VR) program in its local district offices. Services provided through VESID include vocational assessment, vocational counseling, assistance with transition from school to work, job training and placement, follow-up, driver evaluation and training, and adaptive devices needed for rehabilitation. VESID also works with the business community, vocational rehabilitation service agencies, other state agencies, labor organizations, and schools to help individuals with disabilities live independent, self-determined lives in their chosen communities. VESID places more than 15,000 people with disabilities in employment each year. The deputy commissioner, who heads the office, is appointed by the Board of Regents. In 2003 VESID had 15 district offices throughout the state with 1,000 employees, 105,000 clients, and an annual budget of $130 million.

Sarah E. DeSanctis

vocational services. See VOCATIONAL AND EDUCATIONAL SERVICES FOR INDIVIDUALS WITH DISABILITIES (VESID).

Volney. Town (pop 6,094) in W central Oswego Co. Settled in 1795 the town was formed as Fredericksburgh in 1806 from Mexico; the name was changed to Volney in 1811. Residents from 1812 until about 1825 furnished spars and masts for oceangoing ships. After the Oswego Canal opened (1828) the town was home to canal workers in the summer who lumbered in the winter. Extensive dairying began during the Civil War with the construction of butter and cheese factories. In the last quarter of the 19th century Volney was a flour-milling center. In the late 20th century it was the site of a Miller brewery (1974–94) and an Owens-Illinois glass factory (1975–2001). A truck body fabricator (Crysteel) and a business park moved onto the brewery site. Interface Solutions manufactures felt products.

Barbara J. Dix

Vonnegut, Kurt (*b* Indianapolis, 11 Nov 1922). Author. Vonnegut attended local schools in Indianapolis and in 1941 enrolled at Cornell University as a biochemistry major. He enlisted in the US Army in 1943 and the following year was captured during the Battle of the Bulge. In 1947 he moved to Schenectady, where he worked in public relations for the General Electric (GE) Research Laboratory until 1951, when he moved to Massachusetts and began to write full time. His first novel, *Player Piano* (1952), the first of several set in a fictionalized Schenectady he called Ilium, was a satire on modern automation and corporate control based on his experience at GE. Ilium was also a setting in *Cat's Cradle* (1963) and *Hocus Pocus* (1990). Vonnegut's fictional character, Kilgore Trout, who appears in several novels, lives in Cohoes (Albany Co). *Slaughterhouse-Five* (1969), his most acclaimed novel, drew on his wartime experience and his presence in Dresden, Germany, in early 1945 at the time of the devastating Allied firebombing of that city.

In 1971 Vonnegut moved to New York City, which remains his home. Later novels include *Galapagos* (1985) and *Timequake* (1997); all of his 14 novels are still in print, and many have been best-sellers. The New York State Writers Institute named him New York State Author, a post he held from 2001 to 2003. The central motif of Vonnegut's writing has been the importance of human compassion and kindness, even in a chaotic and painful world.

Marvin, Thomas F. *Kurt Vonnegut: A Critical Companion* (Westport, Conn: Greenwood Press, 2002)

John R. Deitrick

Voorheesville. Village (pop 2,705) in New Scotland (Albany Co). First known as New Scotland Station on the Albany and Susquehanna Railroad (1863, later Delaware and Hudson), the village arose at a junction with the Saratoga and Hudson River Railroad (1865, later West Shore). The Voorheesville post office opened in 1868. It was a shipping point for hay and straw and a summer resort with three hotels, many boardinghouses, and attractions including the Helderberg Caves and LaGrange Falls. In the 1890s the community began industrializing, producing cider (Empire Cider and Vinegar Co, 1891–1956, Duffy-Mott after 1917; Voorheesville Canning and Preserving Co, 1899), shirts (1896–1902), and iron (Phoenix Foundry, 1895–1916; Albany Malleable Iron, 1908–68). The village was incorporated in 1899. In the early 21st century Voorheesville is primarily a Capital District residential suburb with some industry, including Atlas Copco Compressors (1980).

Cynthia B. Childs

voter turnout. Participation in elections is conventionally calculated as the percentage of registrants who vote. Registration as a requirement for voting was first enacted in a short-lived law of 1840. Registration laws from the late 1850s were a response to charges of voter fraud in urban

Youthful voter at the polls in Syracuse in 1971, the year the 26th Amendment to the US Constitution granted the vote to 18-year-olds.

VOTER TURNOUT IN US PRESIDENTIAL AND GUBERNATORIAL ELECTIONS IN NEW YORK STATE

Year	Registered to Vote	Voted	Turnout (%)
1960	7,881,203	7,290,823	92.5
1962	7,032,478	5,921,503	84.2
1964	7,781,760	7,166,015	92.1
1966	7,170,001	6,159,578	85.9
1968	7,647,766	6,790,066	88.8
1970	7,354,240	6,150,477	83.6
1972	8,687,414	7,161,830	82.4
1974	7,356,385	5,543,654	75.4
1976	7,672,584	6,525,225	85.0
1978	6,856,204	4,929,426	71.9
1980	7,870,000	6,176,293	78.5
1982	7,460,696	5,437,367	72.9
1984	9,044,208	6,805,973	75.3
1986	8,078,779	4,481,719	55.5
1988	8,581,276	6,485,683	75.6
1990	8,201,532	4,290,261	52.3
1992	9,193,391	6,926,481	75.3
1994	8,818,691	5,325,323	60.4
1996	10,162,156	6,439,129	63.4
1998	10,740,788	4,985,932	46.4
2000	11,262,816	6,960,215	61.8
2002	11,246,362	4,579,078	40.7

Sources: Manual for the Use of the Legislature of the State of New York; New York Red Book.

Note: Presidential elections were held in 1960 and every four years subsequently; gubernatorial elections were held in 1962 and every four years subsequently.

Compiled by Jeffrey M. Stonecash

areas such as New York City. These laws, to verify that those voting were members of the community, were opposed by urban politicians, repealed, and then reenacted several times through the end of the century. The issue generally was whether laws should apply just to urban areas or to all areas of the state. The 1894 state constitution required personal registration in cities with populations over 5,000; elsewhere local officials compiled poll-based registry lists; personal registration was eventually extended throughout the state. In 1967 permanent registration was required statewide, allowing people to remain registered unless they did not vote regularly. The 1993 federal Motor Voter legislation, which took effect in 1995, made it easier for people to register, allowing anyone who visited various government offices to fill out and submit a registration form. It also made it more difficult to remove nonvoters, leading to a significant increase in the number of registrants in the last decade or so.

These changes make it difficult to compare turnout rates over time. Although historians sometimes speak of very high turnouts in 19th-century elections, hard statistics are difficult to come by. The evidence on the last several decades suggests that turnout has declined since the 1960s. Much of the apparent decline is because over the years the laws regulating registration encourage more people to be registered by making it easier to register and more difficult for local boards of elections to eliminate people from the rolls for infrequent voting. These changes have increased the pool of eligible voters, meaning a lower percentage of those on the rolls who actually vote. While it does appear that voting is declining, it is not entirely clear how much is because of registration and how much is because of more general causes.

Turnout varies significantly by election type in New York State. It is highest in US presidential elections and is lower for "off" years, in elections for members of the US Congress and the statewide officials of governor, comptroller, and attorney general. Turnout is even lower for "off-off" years, in local elections for county executives, district attorneys, mayors, and local legislators. The lowest turnout occurs in village and school budget elections, often held in the spring.

Perhaps most important for representation in the state's political process is who votes. Groups that consistently vote gain the most attention from politicians. In general, voting is greater among those who are older, have more education, have lived in a community longer, and are white. These individual differences create regional variations. New York City, with a more mobile and less affluent population, had a turnout rate of 33.3% in 2002, while areas in the rest of the state had a turnout rate of 46.7%. These variations have less impact in US presidential elections because turnout rates across groups are more similar. In contrast, in local elections, where overall turnout is much lower, those who are older with longer residency dominate.

Beginning in the 1980s county boards of election gradually took advantage of new technologies and began to store voter registration files in computer formats. Currently, all counties retain their records of such files. These voter registration files, which record voting frequency, are available to politicians and pollsters in electronic format and therefore make it possible for those seeking office to determine who votes regularly and then target them. Political polls tend to be conducted among those who vote regularly, and campaign efforts such as direct mail, door-to-door visits, and telephone calls are directed to them.

Conway, M. Margaret. *Political Participation in the United States,* 3d ed. (Washington, DC: Congressional Quarterly Press, 2000)

Jeffrey M. Stonecash

voting. See SUFFRAGE.

Voudon. See SANTERIA AND VOUDON.

Vreeland, Ellwyne Mae (*b* Stockbridge, Mass, 28 Nov 1909; *d* Riviera Beach, Fla, 12 May 1971). Nurse administrator. From 1934 to 1942 she served in a variety of nursing positions at hospitals in Saranac (Clinton Co), Lake Kushaqua (Franklin Co), Rochester, and Schenectady. After receiving an MA in 1949 from Columbia University's Teachers College, she served as assistant director of nursing and nurse education at Russell Sage College in Troy (Rensselaer Co) and at Albany Hospital. During the next 23 years she served as an officer of the US Public Health Service, where she was a strong voice for nursing in the federal government and laid the foundation for federal support for postgraduate education and nursing research. She developed and administered the first extramural federal research program for nursing. She retired from the Public Health Service in 1968.

Julie M. Pavri

W

Wachtler, Sol(omon) (*b* Brooklyn, 29 Apr 1930). Chief judge of the New York State Court of Appeals. Raised in Brooklyn and in several southern states, Wachtler attended a boarding school in Milford, Conn, and earned his law degree from Washington and Lee University in 1952. After serving in the US Army, Wachtler practiced law in Queens, and in 1963 he entered politics when he was elected to the town council of North Hempstead (Nassau Co). He became town supervisor in 1965 and gained the attention of the Nassau Co Republican Party. Three years later Wachtler was appointed to the state supreme court in Nassau Co. By the late 1960s he considered running for governor, in 1972 was elected to the state Court of Appeals, and 13 years later was appointed chief judge of that body by Democratic Gov Mario M. Cuomo. An expert in court administration, Wachtler's legal decisions were highly influential, including his strong support for free speech and civil rights for women and people with disabilities. Wachtler entertained political ambitions until 1983, when he chose not to seek the Republican nomination for governor. His career ended in disgrace in 1993 when he was convicted and imprisoned on federal charges stemming from his harassment of Joy Silverman, a former lover. After his release Wachtler became a strong advocate for the rights of prisoners and published a book in which he attributed his behavior to mental illness.

Caher, John M. *King of the Mountain: The Rise, Fall, and Redemption of Chief Judge Sol Wachtler* (New York: Prometheus Books, 1998)

Thomas A. Birkland

Waddington. Town (pop 2,212) and village (pop 923) in NW St. Lawrence Co. Settled before 1797 by Vermonters and Scots, the town was formed in 1859 from Madrid. Nineteenth-century products included paper, iron, leather, and woolens; the Thayer, Whitcomb and Wales paper mill (1826–46) was the county's first. The village was incorporated in 1839. Rail service was provided by the Norwood and St. Lawrence (1909). In the early 20th century, Runkles Bros manufactured cocoa and chocolate. The town's landscape, flat to rolling with numerous wetlands, is largely agricultural. The village lost a number of businesses and small industries when the riverfront was inundated in 1959 by the St. Lawrence Seaway project, and some farms were acquired and flooded. With the exception of Coles Creek State Park and some land leased to farmers, New York Power Authority lands remain mostly idle, including Ogden Island, across from the village. The Italianate Chase Mills Inn (*ca* 1865) is listed on the National Register. St. Paul's Episcopal Church (1818) is the oldest church building in the county.

Richard E. Mooers

Wading River. Locality (pop 6,668) in Riverhead and Brookhaven (Suffolk Co). Settlers from Brookhaven arrived in 1671. The river, in which Indians fished for clams, supported boatyards and mills. Eastern European immigrants from countries such as Poland and Lithuania were drawn to the area at the end of the 19th century to farm. The Long Island Rail Road, which served the community from 1895 to 1935, operated an experimental farm (1905–14) in Wading River. The area's rural character, along with available land, drew renewed development in the late 20th century. It is the site of Wildwood State Park.

Chris Kretz

Wadsworth, James (*b* Durham, Conn, 20 Apr 1768; *d* Geneseo, Livingston Co, 7 June 1844), and **Wadsworth, William** (*b* Durham, 1761; *d* Geneseo, 6 Mar 1833). Land proprietors. The Wadsworth brothers came to Big Tree, north of present-day Cuylerville (Livingston Co), in 1790 to serve as agents for their cousin, Jeremiah Wadsworth of Hartford, Conn, managing his land on the east bank of the Genesee River; the land was part of the Phelps and Gorham Purchase. In 1801 they acquired his holdings to create one of the largest landholdings in western New York State, some 20,000 acres (8,100 ha). The Wadsworth Homestead in Geneseo was a showcase for the brothers' scientific farming experiments. They grew corn, wheat, hemp, tobacco, and fruit, and operated a dairy. Their herds of livestock were improved by crossbreeding with imported European breeds, such as the merino sheep. They worked to improve American agriculture through their model farm, state fairs, and the New York State Agricultural Society. James was also an educational reformer and, through his position on the state Board of Regents, actively supported the development of district schools, normal schools, libraries, and the dissemination of textbooks throughout the state. William was unmarried and left no heirs, but James's descendants continued to own and manage in 2002 a large tract of farmland in the Genesee Valley.

McNall, Neil. *An Agricultural History of the Genesee Valley* (Philadelphia: Univ of Pennsylvania Press, 1952)
Newman, James J. "To Plow the Same Five Times: Estate Management and Agricultural Change in the Genesee Valley of New York State, 1816–1865" (PhD diss, Univ of Rochester, 1988)
Turner, Orsamus. *History of the Pioneer Settlement of Phelps and Gorham's Purchase and Morris' Reserve* (1851)

William H. Siles

Wadsworth, James S. (*b* Geneseo, Livingston Co, 30 Oct 1807; *d* Chancellorsville, Va, 8 May 1864). General and politician. Born to one of the wealthiest families in New York State, he attended Harvard and studied law. At the onset of the Civil War he volunteered to serve in the Union army. After a brief apprenticeship in the army's command staff, in August 1861 he was commissioned a brigadier general and seven months later was placed in command of the defense of Washington, DC. While in the field with his troops, he ran unsuccessfully for governor of New York in 1862 as the Union Party candidate, the label used by the state's Republican Party during the Civil War. He participated in the campaigns at Chancellorsville and Gettysburg, and after a brief leave of absence from the army, he returned to active duty in March 1864 as the commander of the Fourth Division of the Army of the Potomac. On May 6 during the Battle of the Wilderness while rallying his troops, he received a gunshot wound to the head and died two days later in a Confederate field hospital.

Mahood, Wayne. *General Wadsworth: The Life and Times of Brevet Major General James S. Wadsworth* (New York: Da Capo Press, 2003)
Rhea, Gordon. *The Battle of the Wilderness, May 5–6, 1864* (Baton Rouge: Louisiana State Univ Press, 1994)

Barry Mowell

Wadsworth, James W(olcott), Jr (*b* Geneseo, Livingston Co, 12 Aug 1877; *d* Washington, DC, 21 June 1952). Politician. Born to a family with vast farm holdings in the Genesee Valley and a history of public service, Wadsworth was raised with an understanding and appreciation of agriculture and hard work. He graduated from Yale University in 1898. A Republican, he began his political career in the state assembly in January 1905 and was elected its Speaker in 1906. Under Wadsworth's leadership the assembly was reorganized to diminish the power exercised by political machines and bosses. His influence contributed to the success of bills such as that which created the New York State Public Service Commission (1907) and stalled the direct primary initiative (1910). Wadsworth did not seek state reelection in 1910 but won a New York State seat in the US Senate in 1914, where he was a dominant figure in shaping national military policy. He was a vocal opponent of woman suffrage and national Prohibition, his criticism of which contributed to his failure to win reelection in 1926. Wadsworth was elected to the US House of Representatives for the 39th Congressional District (West Rochester and the Genesee Valley) in 1932 and served until his retirement in 1950, acquiring a reputation for conservative economic views.

Fausold, Martin L. *James W. Wadsworth, Jr.: The Gentleman from New York* (Syracuse: Syracuse Univ Press, 1978)

Lenora M. Henson

Wagner, Robert F(erdinand), Jr (*b* New York City, 20 Apr 1919; *d* New York City, 12 Feb 1991). Mayor of New York City. Son of a longtime US senator from New York State, Wagner graduated from Yale Univiversity in 1933 and Yale Law School four years later. He began his political career in the state assembly (1938–41) but left Albany after the attack on Pearl Harbor to enlist in the US Army Air Corps. After World War II Wagner returned to New York City, serving in the administration of Mayor William O'Dwyer in a series of posts, including chair of the City Planning Commission. Wagner served as Manhattan borough president from 1950 to 1953 and in 1953 won election as mayor of New York City. In his three terms of office (1954–65) Wagner expanded social services, reformed the civil service, and initiated an expansive program of housing for the middle class. He instituted collective bargaining and pattern contracts for most of the city's municipal unions. In his successful 1961 reelection campaign, Wagner broke with the leadership of Tammany Hall and its leader Carmine DeSapio. With the support of such prominent state Democrats as former Gov Herbert H. Lehman, Wagner defeated Tammany's candidate Arthur Levitt in the Democratic primary that year. As mayor, Wagner was criticized by some for an overly cautious political style; however, he had the lasting impact of strengthening the administrative powers of the office of mayor. After 1965 Wagner remained active, serving as an advisor to Gov Hugh L. Carey and the New York City mayors Abe Beame and Ed Koch.

McNickle Chris. *To Be Mayor of New York* (New York: Columbia Univ Press, 1993)

Richard M. Flanagan

Wagner, Robert F(erdinand), Sr (*b* Nastätten, Germany, 8 June 1877; *d* New York City, 5 May 1953). US senator. The youngest of nine children, he immigrated with his family to New York City in 1886 and graduated from City College in 1898 and New York Law School in 1900. In Yorkville, on Manhattan's Upper East Side, he became involved, through a friend, in several local campaigns of Tammany Hall, New York Co's Democratic machine. In 1904 he won election to the state assembly and was reelected in 1906. A protégé of Tammany boss Charles F. Murphy, Wagner was a leader of a wing of the machine that embraced progressive reform. He served in the state senate from 1909 to 1918, the last eight years as Democratic floor leader. Following the Triangle Shirtwaist Factory fire in 1911, Wagner, as chair of the Factory Investigating Commission (1911–15) and with vice chair and fellow Democrat Alfred E. Smith, pushed through a series of much needed reforms. In a period of three years they passed 56 new laws to protect the rights of working-class New Yorkers. This legislation—on child labor, safety standards, sanitary regulations, and protection of workers' rights—made him immensely popular in the state and helped make New York one of the most progressive states in the nation in labor reform. He was a justice on the New York Supreme Court (1919–26) and in 1926 was elected to the US Senate. One of a handful of reformers in Washington, DC, at the time, Wagner became one of the most important legislators in Congress after the election of Franklin D. Roosevelt in 1932. Roosevelt referred to Wagner as "the copilot of the New Deal" because he was active in drafting and sponsoring much of the significant legislation of the era: National Industrial Recovery Act (1933), National Labor Relations Act (the Wagner Act) (1935), and Social Security Act (1935). He served in the senate until 1949. His son, Robert F. Wagner Jr, was mayor of New York City from 1954 to 1965.

Huthmacher, J. Joseph. *Senator Robert F. Wagner and the Rise of Urban Liberalism* (New York: Atheneum, 1968)

Richard A. Greenwald

Wagner College. Liberal arts college. Founded as the Lutheran Proseminary in Rochester in 1883, it had six students enrolled under director Rev Alexander Richter. Three years later the school was renamed Wagner Memorial Lutheran College in memory of ministerial student George Wagner, whose parents gave a gift of $12,000 on his death. In 1918 Wagner moved to its present location in Grymes Hill (Richmond Co) at the urging of alumnus Rev Frederic Sutter. The 105-acre (42 ha) site includes portions of the 19th-century estates of Cornelius Vanderbilt and Edward Cunard of the shipping line. The school has been coeducational since 1933, and the current name was adopted in 1959. Curriculum changes during the 1990s emphasized experiential and interdisciplinary learning with a focus on internship experiences. In 2003 Wagner offered more than 30 academic programs to approximately 1,750 undergraduate students, and graduate programs including business, education, microbiology, and nursing enrolled 350 students.

Rowen, William Albert. "The Emerging Identity of Wagner College" (EdD diss, Indiana Univ, 1972)
Wagner College, http://wagner.edu/prosstud/location/

John Ross

Wagner Palace Car Company. Manufacturer of railway sleeping cars and parlor cars, headquartered in New York City with production facilities in Buffalo. The company grew from the initiative of Webster Wagner, who was born in Palatine Bridge (Montgomery Co) 2 Oct 1817 and worked as station agent at the Utica and Schenectady Railroad depot there during the 1840s. Wagner recognized a need for improved sleeping cars. In 1858, with the assistance of several wealthy backers, Wagner built four sleeping cars under a licensing agreement with Theodore Tuttle Woodruff and contracted with New York Central Railroad to operate his cars between Albany and Buffalo. In 1859 he improved the Woodruff-designed cars by raising and ventilating the roofs. Ten cars were in operation by 1860, and the business grew rapidly. In 1866 Wagner and several partners established New York Central Sleeping Car Co, with Wagner taking over the whole business after a few years. The company's capitalization reached $600,000 in 1870. Cornelius Vanderbilt, who controlled New York Central Railroad and other railroads at this time, demanded and received majority shares in Wagner's company. In 1875 the firm was reorganized as a joint-stock company that operated nearly 200 cars. These included both sleeping cars and the luxury day suites called parlor cars that Wagner had introduced in 1867. As Vanderbilt acquired lines in the Midwest and New England, he banished the sleeping cars of rival companies, mostly those of George M. Pullman. The rivalry with Pullman heated up in 1875 when Vanderbilt interests gained control of Michigan Central Railroad and ousted Pullman's service. Pullman retaliated with a series of lawsuits charging patent infringement, but New York Central Sleeping Car Co continued to thrive. Webster Wagner died in a train collision at Spuyten Duyvil [now in Bronx Co] 13 Jan 1882. Vanderbilt's son-in-law, William Seward Webb, succeeded Wagner as company president and in the mid-1880s reorganized the business as Wagner Palace Car Co. He also enlarged the workshops at Buffalo and built new rolling stock. In the early 1890s the firm had 3,000 workers and 600 cars running on 20,000 miles of railroad. Pullman remained a powerful competitor though. He bought Wagner Palace Car Co for $36 million, effective 1 Jan 1900.

White, John H. *The American Railroad Passenger Car* (Baltimore, Md: Johns Hopkins Univ Press, 1978)

Albert S. Eggerton Jr

Wald, Lillian D. (*b* Cincinnati, 10 Mar 1867; *d* Westport, Conn, 1 Sept 1940). Nurse, settlement house founder, Progressive reformer. Wald moved to Rochester at age 11 and always considered it her hometown. Her family, German and Polish Jewish professionals, had arrived in the United States in 1848 and prospered in Rochester's garment and optical goods industries. The Walds belonged to Temple B'rith Kodesh, a center of Reform Judaism, and Lillian attended private schools. Wald's vision of mutuality, where "no one class of people lives independent of another," as she wrote in the *Cleveland Women's Journal* 4 May 1918, derived from her family's successful assimilation and inspired her commitment to social reform. Refused entry into Vassar College at age 16 because of her youth, she moved to Manhattan in 1889 and graduated from the New York Hospital School of Nursing in 1891. After a year at the New York Juvenile Asylum, she enrolled at the Woman's Medical College of the New York Infirmary.

While teaching home nursing classes to immigrants on the Lower East Side, Wald witnessed industrial poverty for the first time. She moved there, founding the Nurses' Settlement in 1893. Relying on her nursing connections for professional support, Wald enlisted the funding of financier and philanthropist Jacob Schiff, who introduced her to the city's elite networks. Wald's institution grew into the Henry Street Settlement, offering home nursing, citizenship classes, club work, and theater. She fought for child labor laws, protective legislation for working women, and woman suffrage. In 1909 Wald served on the New York State Immigration Commission, inspecting labor camps along the Erie and Barge Canals. In response to the commission's report, the state established a Bureau of Industries and Immigration. In 1910 both sides of the massive garment workers' strike elected Wald to be a public representative on the Joint Board of Sanitary Control. The board monitored working conditions and was one of the first industry-wide collective bargaining agreements in US history. Wald helped establish the Department of Nursing and Health at Columbia University's Teachers College in 1910. In 1912 she was elected first president of the National Organization for Public Health Nursing.

Alongside other antimilitarist Progressives, Wald protested American involvement in World War I. She nonetheless trained nurses for the war effort and chaired the New York City Nurses' Emergency Council during the 1918 influenza epidemic. She never married but formed close friendships that continued to sustain her after her retirement in 1933. Wald was one of the first Jewish Americans chosen for the New York University Hall of Fame for Great Americans. The Henry Street Settlement and the Visiting Nurse Service of New York continue to serve the needs of New Yorkers.

Daniels, Doris G. *Always a Sister: The Feminism of Lillian D. Wald* (1989; repr New York: Feminist Press at the City Univ of New York, 1995)
Wald, Lillian D. *The House on Henry Street* (New York: Henry Holt, 1915)

Marjorie N. Feld

Walden. Village (pop 6,164) in Montgomery (Orange Co). Located at the High Falls on the Wallkill River, it is named for Jacob T. Walden who, with others, planned in 1813 an industrial textile complex using the falls for power. Important woolen mills included the Franklin Co (1823) and the Orange Co (1827). The village incorporated in 1855, and it was served by the Wallkill Valley Railroad (1872). Walden's distinctive industry, the manufacture of knives, began with the New York Knife Co (1856) and included Walden Knife Co (1870) and Schrade Cutlery Co (1904–57). Other 19th-century products were condensed milk (1864), hot-air pumping engines (1870), bricks, soap, files, cigars, and overalls. In the 20th century knives remained paramount, but new products included hatters' fur, silk, undergarments, dresses, pocketbooks, paper shopping bags, lighting fixtures, toys, metal goods, ball bearings, and slicing machines. Among manufacturers in 2003 were Spence Engineering (steam-regulating valves), Ampac Paper (paper bags), and Amthor Welding (truck bodies).

Marcus H. Millspaugh

Wales. Town (pop 2,960) in E Erie Co. Settled in 1806 by Ethan and William Allen, grandsons of the Revolutionary War hero, the town was formed in 1818 from Willink [now Aurora] and acquired a post office in 1821. Its railroad station was South Wales, served by the Buffalo, New York and Philadelphia (1872; later Pennsylvania Railroad). Buffalo's WGR-TV built a transmission tower in 1968. In the early 21st century, dairy and maple sugar are its main agricultural products.

Andrew C. Maines

Walker [née Breedlove], **Madam C(harles) J(oseph)** [Sarah] (*b* Delta, La, 23 Dec 1867; *d* Irvington, Westchester Co, 25 May 1919). Businesswoman and philanthropist. Born Sarah Breedlove to plantation laborers, she lived an impoverished childhood and married as a teenager; she was widowed at age 20. While she was working as a washerwoman in St. Louis, she began to lose her hair. Using a formula that came to her in a dream, she developed a hair treatment product that inspired a thriving cosmetic enterprise, the Madam C. J. Walker Manufacturing Co, which she established in Denver in 1905. Charles J. Walker, whom she married that year, assisted in marketing her products. Despite her lack of formal education, Walker ran the business, which employed thousands of women who sold her products as agent-operators. Her company's success spurred her to expand, including to New York City in 1913, a year after she divorced her husband. In Harlem she purchased a town house in which she opened a Walker Salon and a branch of Lelia College, a training center founded for her beauticians. One of the nation's richest self-made businesswomen, her company grossed over $1 million in 1914. She moved to a lavish estate, Villa Lewaro, in Irvington in 1916. Walker, who participated in campaigns against lynching and Jim Crow laws, enjoyed a prominent presence in Harlem's progressive social and political life. She sought numerous opportunities to help her race and community, including support of the NAACP and the National Association of Colored Women. She died of kidney disease in 1919. Her daughter A'Lelia Walker succeeded her mother as president of the cosmetics company and became a leading figure in the Harlem Renaissance. Villa Lewaro was named a National Historic Landmark in 1976.

Bundles, A'Lelia Perry. *On Her Own Ground: The Life and Times of Madam C. J. Walker* (New York: Scribner's, 2001)

Audrey M. Wilson

Walker, Mary Edwards (*b* Oswego, 26 Nov 1832; *d* Oswego, 21 Feb 1919). Physician and social reformer. After schooling at home and Falley Seminary in Fulton (Oswego Co), she enrolled in Syracuse Medical College, Stephen Hollister Potter's proprietary eclectic medical school, where she received her MD in 1855. She practiced medicine in Columbus, Ohio, and in Rome (Oneida Co) with her husband Albert Miller until 1859, when the couple separated. During the Civil War she served as a Union army nurse and volunteer surgeon at First Bull Run, Chickamauga, Atlanta, and Washington, DC's Patent Office Hospital, and was a prisoner of war in Richmond, Va, from 10 Apr to 12 Aug 1864; she was commissioned as acting assistant surgeon in October 1864. Pres Andrew Johnson awarded her the congressional Medal of Honor in 1865, but the Department of War rescinded it in 1917 because of her civilian status. She refused to return it and continued to wear it throughout her lifetime. After the Civil War Walker primarily concentrated on dress reform—in 1866 she was arrested in New York City for disturbing the peace by wearing bloomers—and other women's rights issues. She authored the autobiographical *Hit* (1871) and the treatise *Unmasked, or The Science of Immorality* (1878). Arguing that the Constitution already granted women voting rights, she broke with activists seeking a constitutional amendment. In 1890 she returned to her family's Oswego farm, where she lived until her death. After a lobbying campaign initiated by her great grandniece Ann Walker, Pres Jimmy Carter restored the congressional Medal of Honor to Walker in 1977; in 2002 she remained its only female recipient.

Hall, Marjory. *Quite Contrary: Dr. Mary Edwards Walker* (New York: Funk & Wagnalls, 1970)

Eric v. d. Luft

Walk-in-the-Water. The first steamship to operate on the upper Great Lakes (above Niagara Falls). The vessel was built in 1818 at Black Rock [now in Erie Co] by Noah Brown for a group of "subscribers," or partners, from Albany and New York City, operating as the Lake Erie Steamboat Co. The ship was a side-wheeler measuring 135 feet (41.2 m) in length, 32 feet (9.8 m) beam (width), and 8 feet 6 inches (2.6 m) depth. Built for passengers and freight, it measured 338 tons (306.6 MT) and carried two masts with sails and a crosshead steam engine with a 40 in (101.6 cm) cylinder and 15 ft (4.6 m) paddle wheels. Robert McQueen built the machinery in New York City. The craft made its maiden voyage from Buffalo to Detroit in September 1818, averaging 7.5 mph (12 kph). *Walk-in-the-Water* was wrecked a few miles west of Buffalo on the Lake Erie shore on 1 Nov 1821; all people aboard made it safely ashore. The machinery was salvaged and installed in the new steamer *Superior* the following year.

Rennie, Joe. "The Walk-in-the-Water, First Steamship on Lake Erie," *Lower Lakes Marine Historical Society Newsletter* 14, no. 1 (Jan–Feb 2001): 4–7; no. 2 (Mar–Apr 2001): 3–7

C. Patrick Labadie

Wallkill. Town (pop 24,659) in Orange Co. The territory was bought from local Indians between 1703 and 1761 and created as a precinct in 1743. It was formed as a town in 1788 as part of Ulster Co and annexed to Orange Co in 1798. Industry was centered in Mechanicstown, where there was a trip-hammer and forge, a woolen factory, and a glove factory. The dog power, a treadmill by which a dog could power a churn or other small machine, is believed to have been invented in Wallkill by George F. Reeve in the early 1820s. Farmers were served by the Erie (1843), Crawford (1871), and Ontario and Western (1873) Railroads, which also shipped milk to city markets; the town led the county in milk production in 1874. Suburbanization dates to 1950 when Edmund S. Lloyd opened a grocery store on Rte 211 that grew into a supercenter, a prototype for the "big box" retailer. More critically, the limited-access Rte 17 (I-86), built in 1951 and 1958, and I-84, built in 1969, intersect in Wallkill, making it a transportation hub and encouraging both retail business and industry. In the early 21st century its residents commute to the greater New York City/New Jersey metropolitan area. The Mechanicstown Elementary School contains within it the innovative Micro-Society Magnet School, in which students run more than 20 businesses and services, helping them bridge the worlds of school and work. Wallkill is the site of the Orange County Fair (1841) and Highland Lakes State Park. In 2000, 9% of the population of Wallkill was black, and people of Latino ethnicity made up 13% of the total.

Dorothy Hunt-Ingrassia

Walloons. See ALBANY; NEW NETHERLAND.

Wall Street Journal. In 1885 Wall St financial journalists Charles Dow and Edward Jones began publishing the *Customers' Afternoon News Letter,* the forerunner of the *Wall Street Journal,* which first appeared on 8 July 1889. The *Journal* featured an index of the closing prices of leading securities, which after several transformations became the Dow Jones Industrial Transportation and Utilities Average. Published Monday through Friday, the paper was in danger of folding during the depression because of declines in advertising and subscriptions, but it survived through the perseverance of Jane Bancroft, former publisher Clarence Barron's daughter. After World War II the *Wall Street Journal* came under the leadership of Bernard "Barney" Kilgore, who had previously worked as the paper's managing editor. The *Journal* is widely considered the authoritative business newspaper in the nation, and it is often a leader in national policy debates. The paper began publishing editions in Asia in 1976 and in Europe in 1983. An Internet edition appeared in 1996 and a print Sunday supplement debuted in 1998. In 2002 the paper was headquartered at 200 Liberty St, with major operations in New Jersey, and had an average daily edition circulation of 1.8 million.

Scharff, Edward E. *Worldly Power: The Making of the Wall Street Journal* (New York: Beaufort Books, 1986)
Wendt, Lloyd. *The Wall Street Journal: The Story of Dow Jones and the Nation's Business Newspaper* (Chicago: Rand McNally, 1982)

Lloyd Chiasson Jr

Walton. Town (pop 5,607) and village (pop 3,070) in W Delaware Co. Settled in 1785, the town was formed from Franklin in 1797. Settlers rafted lumber on the Delaware for the Philadelphia market; later tanning, quarrying, and dairy farming became common occupations. The village was incorporated in 1851 and was served by the Ontario and Western Railroad (1872–1957), which provided access to markets for farmers and manufacturers, including Walton Novelty Works (1876–1930s; wooden toys) and Munn Piano Factory (1901). A community of Italians, the first of whom arrived as a railroad worker in 1882, grew by immigration of friends and relatives from Chiaramonte, Italy. Twentieth-century industries included S. J. Bailey and Sons (1939; pine and oak furniture) and Del-Met Corp (1946; automobile accessories). The loss of these industries late in the 20th century forced many residents to seek work in surrounding areas. Breakstone made soft cheeses in Walton by 1912; in 2003 two dairy processing plants, one a Breakstone facility, operated as part of Kraft Foods. Gardiner Place in the village is a National Historic District. Walton has been the site of the annual Delaware County Fair since 1925.

Dorothy Kubik

Walworth. Town (pop 8,402) in W Wayne Co. Settled in 1799, the town was formed from the Town of Ontario in 1829. A prominent citizen was Theron G. Yeomans (1815–1901), an agricultural innovator who received an award for his experiments in tile drainage, introduced dwarf pear trees and Holstein-Friesian cattle to the area, and was the first president of the Holstein-Friesian Association of America. Since the 1950s, owing to its proximity to Rochester, Walworth has experienced significant suburban development, including the building of Gananda, an early 1970s residential community with its own central school district, which opened in 1974. Between 1950 and 2000, Walworth's population increased by 260%.

Scott C. Monje

Walworth, Reuben Hyde (*b* Bozrah, Conn, 26 Oct 1788; *d* Saratoga Springs, 28 Nov 1867). Jurist. Raised on a family farm near Hoosick (Rensselaer Co) with little formal education, Walworth was admitted to the bar in 1809, having prepared at John Russell's Troy (Rensselaer Co) office, and began practice in Plattsburgh in 1810. As an adjutant general in the state militia he was involved in the Lake Champlain battles of the War of 1812. Walworth served one term in the House of Representatives (1821–23), when as a loyal supporter of Martin Van Buren he was appointed to a newly created state district judgeship and moved to Saratoga Springs to be closer to his work. Five years later former congressional colleague and then governor Nathaniel Pitcher appointed Walworth the state's chancellor—he would be the last one as the position was abolished in 1846. In his 20 years as chancellor, New York State's legal business dramatically increased in volume and complexity, and Walworth's reputation was mixed. A mistaken notion that he opposed slavery led to his failure to be confirmed to the US Supreme Court in 1844, and Walworth unsuccessfully ran for governor in 1848 as a regular Democrat to thwart the radical Barnburner candidate. In retirement Walworth worked as an arbitrator on federal and state court cases and as an inspector general for the War Department. His wife, Maria Ketchum Averrill, with whom he had five surviving children (most notably Clarence and Mansfield), died in 1847, and in 1851 he married Sarah Ellen Hardin. In July 1873, nearly six years after Walworth's death, his grandson shot Mansfield in a notorious patricide case, for which Walworth was held indirectly responsible: his will had only continued the misunderstandings between him and Mansfield and further fueled Mansfield's stormy marital relationship, which prompted the murder.

Dougal, Mary E. "An American Victorian Family: The Walworths of Saratoga" (Master's thesis, SUNY Oneonta, 1979)

Donald M. Roper

Wampsville. Village (pop 561) in Lenox (Madison Co). The post office, established in 1825, was named after tavern keeper Myndert Wemple. The county seat moved from Morrisville to Wampsville in 1910 in recognition of the greater population in the northern section of the county. Both Oneida and Canastota had contended for the honor, so Wampsville, a compromise location midway between the two, was chosen. The village is the site of a Hot Air Balloon and Tractor Festival in June.

William F. Helmer

wampum. Tubular shell beads used in ornament, ritual, and exchange. Although shell ornaments were made in what is now New York State from at least the Late Archaic period, approximately 3,000–5,000 years ago, American Indians needed the iron drills and awls European traders offered to make wampum. Wampum are small cylindrical beads about .25–.40 inches (.64–1.02 cm) long, with average diameters of .10 inches (.25 cm) and bores of less than .05 inches (.13 cm). White beads were made from clam *(Mercenaria mercenaria)* and whelk *(Busycon carica, B canaliculatum);* purple beads came from the hard mantle of the clam. These shells were plentiful in Long Island Sound, and wampum was manufactured regularly in this area by Algonquian-speaking groups, including the Shinnecock, Corchaug, and Montaukett. The term "wampum" is derived from the Algonquian word *wampumpeak,* which means "string of white (shell) beads." In the 17th century, wampum was referred to as *sewan* or *sewant,* from an Algonquian term for scattered or loose beads.

To make the beads, sections of shell were broken off in roughly square shapes, then knapped into strips. These strips were ground smooth into beadlike cylinders and then bored, using small iron drills. Some were drilled all the way through from one side, others from both sides. The pierced beads were threaded on string or wire to be held to a grindstone for a final smoothing and finishing. Both Indians and Europeans used this process.

In the 17th century, wampum produced by Algonquians in the Long Island area was traded to the English for manufactured goods. With Algonquian men spending more time making wampum than following their customary hunting rounds, Algonquian communities became more sedentary. More permanent settlements and reduced hunting may have influenced the rise of agriculture, with corn becoming an important nutritional source. Increased reliance on agriculture may have made women's roles more significant, as agriculture was part of Algonquian women's work and hunting was the men's.

The Mohawk were the first nation of the Iroquois Confederacy to become involved in wampum exchange because of their proximity to the Dutch outposts at Fort Nassau (1614–18) [now Gloucester City, NJ] and Fort Orange (1624–64) in the vicinity of what is now Albany. Wampum became a powerful medium of communication and ceremonial exchange for the Iroquois, as shell beads fit into existing Iroquois belief systems. Shell was considered a gift from the spirit world, imbued with *orenda* (supernatural power). White shell represented light and life, and dark shell the opposite. Wampum exchange was tied to life-cycle events and marked activities of the Iroquois Council. Wampum belts are the best-known uses of wampum. These were woven, with white and purple beads creating particular patterns, for a variety of reasons: to record agreements, to ratify treaties, to establish alliances, or to commemorate events. Some belts were kept as records; others were disassembled and altered. The belts served as mnemonic devices, and their patterns carried specific messages.

Despite the common misconception that wampum was used by the Indians as money, Europeans actually used it as such. Within the Dutch colonial community in New Netherland, it took the place of hard currency to alleviate a severe shortage in coin. The Dutch also used it in their lucrative fur trade with the Iroquois. Wampum was linked to Dutch currency rates, with the purple beads worth twice as much as

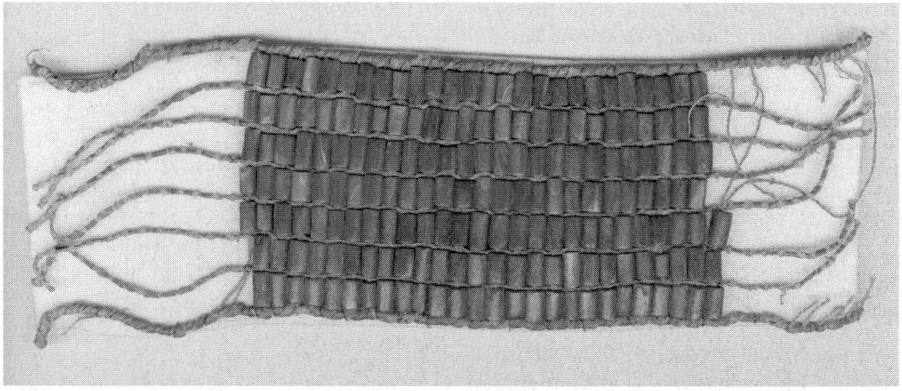

Fragment of wampum belt owned by Joseph Brant, from the collection of Lewis Henry Morgan at the Rochester Museum and Science Center.

the white. New Netherlanders exchanged wampum loose, in strings, or by the standard measure of a fathom, which measured approximately 6 feet (1.8 m) in length and contained some 360 beads.

By the mid–18th century, wampum manufacture at coastal Algonquian mints had given way to a different mode of production and distribution. The center of manufacture shifted from Long Island to Albany as colonial traders oversaw production. Archaeological evidence from 18th-century Albany in the form of shell debris, unfinished wampum beads, and tools has demonstrated that soldiers on guard duty, as well as poor people in the almshouse, made wampum. By this time, the need for wampum in both the fur trade and diplomacy had moved far from Albany. The Albany wampum probably was purchased by local businessmen who sold it to northern traders by way of the Hudson-Champlain corridor, as well as to western markets via the Mohawk Valley and the Niagara Frontier.

Wampum production continued in the 19th century as a more commercial operation, undertaken by New Jersey entrepreneurs who supplied beads to explorers and settlers of western North America. Although this manufacturing created specialized products, wampum did not carry symbolic significance in the Midwest and the West, and wampum use gradually subsided. Today wampum remains an important element of Iroquois culture. Many belts that had been owned by museums in New York, Canada, and elsewhere have been returned to the Iroquois, as they preserve their cultural patrimony for the future.

Ceci, Lynn. "Tracing Wampum's Origins: Shell Bead Evidence from Archaeological Sites in Western and Coastal New York." In *Proceedings of the 1986 Shell Bead Conference,* ed. Charles F. Hayes III (Rochester: Rochester Museum and Science Center, 1989)

Peña, Elizabeth S. "Wampum Production at the Albany Almshouse," *International Journal of Historical Archaeology* 5 (2001): 155–74

Snyder, Gary S. "Wampum: A Material Symbol of Cultural Value to the Iroquois Peoples of Northeastern North America." In *Material Symbols: Culture and Economy in Prehistory,* ed. John E. Robb (Carbondale: Southern Illinois Univ Center for Archaeological Investigations, 1999)

Elizabeth S. Peña

Wantagh {North Wantagh, locality (pop 12,156) in Hempstead, Nassau Co; Wantagh, locality (pop 18,971) in Hempstead}. Wantagh, which is bounded on the south by East Bay, a part of Great South Bay, was settled in 1644. North Wantagh was settled in 1666 and called Jerusalem; it later had a substantial Quaker community. As Ridgewood, Wantagh became a stop on the South Side Rail Road (now Long Island Rail Road) in 1867 and acquired a post office in 1868; both were changed to Wantagh in 1891. "The Poinsettia King," August Dauerheim, built hothouses that supported a cut-flower industry from *ca* 1850 to 1960; the site is now the Willow Wood housing and shopping complex. Grain, vegetables, and dairy products were cultivated *ca* 1875 to 1905. The first portion of the Wantagh State Parkway opened in 1929 and reached Jones Beach State Park. Wantagh, which had a 1940 population of 2,780, experienced rapid suburban growth in the two decades after World War II, with some homes built by William J. Levitt. The Wantagh High School was built in 1952; North Wantagh students attend Levittown and North Bellmore schools. Landmarks include Jackson House (?1644), Birdsall Miller's house and sluiceway (?1794), Friends Meeting House (1827), Seaman-Venier House (?1871), and Wantagh Railroad Complex (1885, 1912).

Kenneth M. Foreman

Wappinger. Town (pop 26,274) in SW Dutchess Co. The Wappinger Indians established seasonal hunting and fishing camps along Wappinger Creek, especially at its mouth. Part of the Rombout Patent (1685), the area was settled in the 1730s by freeholders from elsewhere in the county. The town was formed from Fishkill in 1875. Except for Wappingers Falls, a manufacturing village, it remained agricultural until suburbanization in the 20th century. Two IBM plants in nearby towns, established in 1948 and 1963, fueled a 433% population increase (1950–70). It is the site of the Dutchess County Airport and Castle Point VA Hospital.

William P. McDermott

Wappinger Indians. An eastern Algonquian-speaking people whose homeland extended from the east bank of the Hudson River in present-day Putnam and Dutchess Cos. Compelled to give up much of their best land by the 1680s, most Wappingers took up a wandering life along a line of less-habitable rocky upland valleys stretching from western New England to more remote parts of the lower Hudson Valley, northern New Jersey, and northwestern Pennsylvania. Their presence in so many places led local historian Edward Ruttenber to suggest, erroneously, that a Wappinger Confederacy extended throughout the lower Hudson Valley. Although many dispossessed Munsee and Mohican (Mahican) people joined the Wappinger at upland locales, they never formed a single political group. The mobile and polyglot nature of Wappinger communities continues to perplex modern investigators, who are unsure whether they spoke Munsee or Mohican, or if their name meant easterner or opossum. Wappinger people played significant roles in early Hudson Valley history, fighting against the Dutch during Kieft's War and covertly maintaining close ties in Canada while openly supporting the British in their wars with France between 1689 and 1762. During more peaceful times Wappinger men traveled far into Canada and the midwestern interior, bartering European goods for furs wanted by New York and New England merchants. In company with elders, the young, and visiting spouses, Wappinger women maintained households at Stockbridge, Mass, and Schaghticoke, Conn, at Fishkill (Dutchess Co) and Wikapy [now Putnam Valley, Putnam Co] within their traditional homeland, at Pompton along the upper Passaic Valley in northern New Jersey, along the upper Delaware River around Cochecton (Sullivan Co), and at Chenango and Oquaga (Broome Co) along the upper Susquehanna River in Pennsylvania.

Some Wappingers also joined Christian mission communities established in or near many of these places between the 1730s and 1760s. The Wappinger, led by their leader Nimham, conveyed their last rights to lands in New Jersey in 1758. His son, Daniel Nimham (*fl* 1725–78), tried to regain Wappinger holdings in Dutchess Co in the mid-1760s, claiming the deed of 1703 was invalid, and went to London to press his claims, which came to nothing. Daniel's son, Abraham Nimham, commanded a company of Stockbridge Indian riflemen during the Revolutionary War. Both Abraham and Daniel Nimham were killed by British troops at the battle of Cortlandt's Ridge on 31 Aug 1778. Despite their support of the American cause, most Wappingers joined other Munsee and Mohican expatriates into exile in the years after the war. Some went north to Canada. Others moved farther west into a wandering exile that finally ended in Wisconsin, Kansas, and Oklahoma, where most descendants of Wappingers live today. Still others clung to homes in and around the Hudson Highlands.

Brasser, Ted J. C. "Mahican." In *Northeast,* ed. Bruce G. Trigger, vol 15 of *Handbook of North American Indians,* ed. William C. Sturtevant (Washington, DC: Smithsonian Institution, 1978)

Grumet, Robert S. "The Nimhams of the Colonial Hudson Valley, 1667–1783," *Hudson Valley Regional Review* 9 (Sept 1992): 80–99

Ruttenber, Edward Manning. *History of the Indian Tribes of Hudson's River* (Albany: J. Munsell, 1872)

Smith, J. Michael. "The Highland King Nimhammaw and the Native Proprietors of Land in Dutchess County, NY: 1712–1765," *Hudson Valley Regional Review* 17 (Sept 2000): 69–108

Robert S. Grumet

Wappingers Falls. Village (pop 4,929) in Wappinger and Poughkeepsie (Dutchess Co). With power from the steady flow of Wappinger Creek (75 ft/23 m fall), it became a center for production, printing, and textile dyeing beginning in 1827. The mills and the nearby railroad drew Irish Catholics in midcentury. Combs, mahogany veneer, and metal products were also made, and from 1871 to 1958 the nationally known Sweet-Orr Co manufactured work clothing. The village incorporated in 1871. During the second half of the 20th century large manufacturing declined and was replaced by small manufacturing, trade, and housing for IBM employees.

William P. McDermott

War Council. A temporary state agency that coordinated activities for the defense effort in New York State during World War II. The organization grew out of the State Council of Defense, created on 1 Aug 1940 by Gov Herbert H. Lehman. With the passage of the New York State War Emergency Act in April 1942, the New York State War Council replaced the Council of Defense. The governor, legislative leaders, and 10 gubernatorial appointees made up the leadership of the council. The War Council offered civil defense training, oversaw federal and state rationing and price control programs, recruited labor for war production industries, and studied defense issues, especially those relating to supplying matériel for the war. New York State's counties and cities formed 107 local war councils, which coordinated with and were responsible to the state council in Albany. The War Council developed over 30 agencies and programs during its life span. Air-raid defense, metal and paper salvage, childcare programs (allowing mothers to work in defense factories), and physical fitness campaigns all fell under the council's auspices. More than 150,000 New Yorkers participated in council activities during the agency's six-year life. The council's greatest legacy may have been the State Commission against Discrimination, established on 12 Mar 1945, which sprang from its Committee on Discrimination in Employment, formed on 29 Mar 1941. The council was not without its critics. Some state politicians, including Assemblyman and War Council member Abbot Low Moffat (R-Manhattan), initially criticized many of the agency's programs as overzealous. The council was officially terminated on 1 Apr 1946, although the agency's childcare program continued for another year under the aegis of the State Youth Commission.

Hartzell, Karl Drew. *The Empire State at War* (Albany: State of New York, 1949)

New York State War Council. Papers. New York State Archives, Albany

Tod M. Ottman

Ward. Town (pop 390) in E central Allegany Co. Settled in 1817, the town was formed in 1856 from Alfred and Amity. Ward became a dairying town after its first cheese factory was built in 1865 and was a Populist enclave in the 1890s, with a county supervisor from that party. It is the site of the Phillips Creek (2,709 acres/1,096 ha) and Vandermark (2,384 acres/965 ha) State Forests. In 2003 all of the roads in town were gravel except one county road and one state highway. Dairy cows and cattle are no longer raised. Residents are either retirees or work in Alfred or Wellsville. Ward also has many seasonal hunting camps.

Ward, John Quincy Adams (*b* Urbana, Ohio, 29 June 1830; *d* New York City, 1 May 1910). Sculptor. Unlike most aspiring sculptors of the period, who pursued classical training abroad, Ward studied in Brooklyn, where he began a seven-year apprenticeship under Henry Kirke Brown in 1849. Ward developed a distinctly American sculptural style that explored American subjects with unprecedented naturalism. His first sculpture, *The Indian Hunter* (1866), was the first by an American placed in Central Park, while later casts survive in Cooperstown (Otsego Co) (1898) and Buffalo (1926). His *Henry Ward Beecher* (1891, Cadman Plaza in Brooklyn) and *George Washington* (1883, Federal Hall in Manhattan) are hallmarks of the American Renaissance. A founder and trustee of the Metropolitan Museum of Art, Ward also served as the first president of the National Sculpture Society. His equestrian monument of *General Philip Henry Sheridan* (1906–10) at the New York State Capitol was cast and dedicated posthumously in 1916.

Sharp, Lewis I. *John Quincy Adams Ward: Dean of American Sculpture* (Newark: Univ of Delaware Press, 1985)

Brian Edward Hack

Ward, Samuel Ringgold (*b* Maryland's Eastern Shore, 17 Oct 1817; *d* St. George Parish, Jamaica, ?1866). Minister and abolitionist. In 1820 Ward's family escaped slavery and eventually settled in New York City. Ward was educated at an African American grammar school before attending the multiracial Oneida Institute in Whitesboro (Oneida Co). A gifted orator and rhetorician often compared to Daniel Webster, he became a well-known antebellum spokesperson for African American rights. He was an American Anti-Slavery Society traveling agent (1839–41), a vice president of the American Missionary Association (1846), and the pastor of two all-white Congregational churches in South Butler (Wayne Co) (1841–43) and Cortland (1846–51). Ward edited two antislavery newspapers, the *True American* (1847–48) in Cortland and the *Impartial Citizen* (1849–51) in Syracuse. A supporter of the Liberty Party, he served as its nominee for state assemblyman and vice president during the 1850s. After assisting in the Jerry Rescue in Syracuse in 1851, Ward feared his own arrest. He fled to Canada and, in 1855, to Jamaica, where he was a pastor and farmer.

Burke, Ronald K. *Samuel Ringgold Ward: Christian Abolitionist* (New York: Garland Publishing, 1995)

Ward, Samuel Ringgold. *Autobiography of a Fugitive Negro* (1855; repr New York: Arno Press, 1968)

Douglas M. Strong

Warfield, William [Caesar] (*b* West Helena, Ark, 22 Jan 1920; *d* Chicago, 25 Aug 2002). Singer. Warfield was raised in Rochester, where he earned his bachelor's degree from the Eastman School of Music in 1942. After serving in the army and pursuing further studies at Eastman, he made his New York City recital debut at Town Hall in 1950, after which his deep baritone voice received national attention. A distinguished recitalist in the works of Aaron Copland and others, he is best known for his performances in George Gershwin's opera *Porgy and Bess,* and the role of Joe in Jerome Kern's *Show Boat.* At the behest of the US State Department he toured Africa and the Middle East in 1956, Europe with the Philadelphia Orchestra in 1956, and Asia in 1958, often with his wife at the time, soprano Leontyne Price. In a nonsinging role Warfield played De Lawd in the 1957 Hallmark Hall of Fame production of Marc Connelley's *Green Pastures.* In 1974 he was appointed to the faculty at the University of Illinois at Champaign-Urbana and in 1994 to Northwestern University in Evanston, Ill.

Warfield, William, and Alton Miller. *William Warfield: My Music and My Life* (Champaign, Ill: Sagamore Press, 1991)

Vincent Lenti

war memorials. Erecting memorials to those who have died in war is not a new custom, but it has gained in importance in recent decades. Before the Civil War only sporadic attempts were made to provide physical commemorations for the war dead. Few memorials were erected by the contemporaries of those in New York's numerous colonial wars. Revolutionary War engagements were sometimes commemorated, but the relatively few markers often deteriorated. Painted pine boards at Sackets Harbor (Jefferson Co) during the War of 1812 indicated a mass grave for several officers. This marker, however, quickly rotted, and its exact location is hardly remembered. In 1777 Congress authorized the construction of a monument to Brig Gen Nicholas Herkimer at the cost of $500. It was not until 1883 that the 122 ft (37.2 m) high granite shaft was erected near his home, 3 miles (4.8 km) below Little Falls (Herkimer Co), largely at the sponsorship of the Oneida Historical Society. The soldiers who defended Fort Plain [now in Montgomery Co] in the 1770s were not commemorated until 1907, when Daughters of the American Revolution placed an inscribed boulder near the site of the conflict.

Civil War Memorials

The Civil War renewed interest in war commemoration. New York was the first state in the country officially to recognize Memorial Day, with the Village of Waterloo (Seneca Co) claiming to be the holiday's birthplace. In 1866 a local apothecary, Henry C. Welles, convinced Seneca Co clerk Gen John B. Murray to create an organizing committee to decorate the graves of the Civil War dead. In May 1866 a parade featuring flags and mourning streamers terminated at the three existing cemeteries. The celebration quickly became popular, and in 1868 the Grand Army of the Republic called for an annual "Decoration Day" to be held on 30 May. In 1873 New York was the first state to proclaim Memorial Day a legal holiday. Numerous towns and villages around the state erected monuments to the Union dead. Most were of little lasting artistic significance, though there were noteworthy exceptions. One of the earliest monuments developed from an 1869 proposal by sculptor John Quincy Adams Ward for the Seventh Regiment National Guard Monument and features a base by architect Richard Morris Hunt. The statue of Adm David G. Farragu in Madison Square in Manhattan, unveiled on Memorial Day 1881, has an exedra base by architect Stanford White and figure sculpted by Augustus Saint-Gaudens. An equestrian statue of Gen Philip Sheridan (1916) by Ward and Daniel Chester French dominates the eastern approach to the State Capitol Building in Albany. New York City has two prominent Grand Army Plazas. One, near Prospect Park in Brooklyn, is dominated by a triumphal arch (1892) by John H. Duncan in the spirit of Paris's Etoile. The other, near the southeast corner of Central Park in Manhattan, features an equestrian statue of Gen William T. Sherman by Saint-Gaudens (1907).

Memorials of the 20th Century

The brevity of the Spanish-American War seems to have worked against a widespread spirit of commemoration. More often, as in Binghamton, that memorial is absorbed in a larger scheme. There "The Skirmisher," a lone rifleman by sculptor Robert Aitken, is mounted in a circular plaza at the eastern approach to the Memorial Bridge to Soldiers and Sailors of World War I. That war, with its enormous impact on civilian life, inspired in its wake a renewed focus upon memorials of all kinds, with a strong emphasis on the common social bond of people and the passage of time. This imperative for commemorative monuments demanded increased production and standardization, much to the dismay of the artistic community. Throughout the state a plethora of statues, tablets, gateways, flagstaffs, clocks, bridges, memorial greens, and highways were constructed to honor the war's veterans. The Memorial Clock Tower on Pier A, Battery Park Place SW, at the corner of West St in Manhattan, installed in 1919, is believed to be the nation's first World War I memorial. Other monuments include Philip Martiny's Abingdon Square Doughboy (1921) in Manhattan and Karl Illava's 107th Infantry Memorial (1927), standing at 5th Ave at East 67th, representing the Seventh Street Regiment National Guard.

Though war monument building continued, World War II engendered a more marked shift away from the purely aesthetic war memorial in favor of the more functional "living memorial." The rejection of sentimentality, class differences, and ornamental work, complete with a desire to renew and rehabilitate society with lasting structures dedicated to community building, were all part of this shift. To this end, gymnasiums, swimming pools, playgrounds, auditoriums, and even museums became war memorials. The trend began before World War II. An early example is a Gothic complex of twin residential towers, the Army Tower and the Navy Tower, at Cornell University, a practical acknowledgment of the 237 Cornell alumni slain in World War I, designed by architects Day and Klauder of Philadelphia and dedicated in 1926. The Onondaga County War Memorial (1949), a thin-shell concrete roof sheltering entertainment events of every description, containing a hall with an honor roll of war losses in its interior and major battles depicted in bas-relief on its exterior, is a much celebrated example of New York State's multifunctional designs. Buffalo's Roesch Memorial Stadium (1937), almost immediately renamed the Civic Stadium, was rededicated the War Memorial Stadium in 1959 and demolished in 1988. Rochester's Community War Memorial, built in 1955 with a hall of honor and rebuilt in 1998, also hosted sports and entertainment events. A more traditional monument is the East Coast Memorial (1963) to the 4,596 military personnel who died in the Atlantic during World War II; in Manhattan's Battery Park, the memorial by Gehron and Seltzer contains 4 pairs of granite monoliths centered on a 13 ft (3.4 m) bronze eagle.

The World War II honor roll memorials that blossomed during the late 1940s and 1950s, with, at a minimum, lists of individual's names mounted on signboards at the entrance to a community, seem to have provided the hallowed ground to be rededicated to other wars, for lists of Korean and Vietnam war dead have been added to the same location. The painful legacy of the Vietnam War inspired a vogue for separate memorials. At the Empire State Plaza, the New York State Vietnam Memorial (1984) was the first state memorial to the war in the nation. This was followed by New York State Korean War Veterans Memorial (1990), and New York State Women Veterans Memorial (1998). Finally, in Albany, an impressive 2002 World War II Veterans Memorial opened, containing some of the same elements of the new monument under construction on the Mall in Washington, DC. The scheme centers on an eagle, surrounded by a large round pool of water divided into segments, symbolizing how World War II divided the world.

Borg, Alan. *War Memorials: From Antiquity to the Present* (London: Leo Cooper, 1991)
Dahir, James, comp. *Community Centers as Living War Memorials* (New York: Russell Sage Foundation, 1946)
Mayo, James. *War Memorials as Political Landscape* (New York: Praeger, 1988)
Waterloo Memorial Day Centennial Committee. *The History and Origin of Memorial Day in Waterloo, New York* (Waterloo, 1966)

Michael A. Tomlan

New York State World War II Veterans Memorial, Albany, opened in 2002.

Warner, Anna Bartlett (*b* New York City, 11 Aug 1824; *d* Highland Falls, Orange Co, 22 Jan 1915), and **Warner, Susan Bogert** (*b* New York City, 11 July 1819; *d* Highland Falls, 17 Mar 1885). The sisters enjoyed luxurious childhoods in New York City, but the family suffered in the panic of 1837 and relocated in 1838 to Constitution Island in the Hudson River near Cold Spring (Putnam Co), where they lived in increasing isolation and poverty. With the encouragement of her aunt, Frances Warner, Susan turned to fiction writing, and her first novel *The Wide, Wide World* (1850), which dramatized the spiritual and temporal trials of a young girl in rural Columbia Co, became an immediate bestseller. Susan followed with another best-seller, *Queechy* (1852), a masterpiece of early realism, and Anna published her first novel, *Dollars and Cents* (1852), which dramatized episodes from the family's fall from wealth. Their first joint production, *Say and Seal* (1860), included their popular children's hymn "Jesus Loves Me." Devout evangelical Christians, the Warners combined vivid local color with sophisticated theological argument in the many novels that followed. Susan and Anna continued to write in collaboration and separately; Susan wrote 29 novels and an anthology of biblical texts. Anna wrote 41 books, including novels, children's stories, devotional manuals, and two charming gardening manuals. The sisters co-authored 14 additional novels and children's books.

Following their father Henry's death in 1875, Susan and Anna, with their aunt Frances, took up annual winter residence in Highland Falls, forging closer ties with the nearby US Military Academy at West Point. Susan began popular Bible study sessions for cadets, which Anna continued after Susan's death. She cultivated such warm friendships with cadets that she won the nickname "the Mother of the Academy."

Foster, Edward Halsey. *Susan and Anna Warner* (Boston: Twayne Publishers, 1978)

Jane Weiss

Warner, H(ulbert) H(arrington) (*b* Van Buren, Onondaga Co, 18 Jan 1842; *d* Minneapolis, 27 Jan 1923). Patent medicine entrepreneur. Warner attended Dr. Wright's Academy in Elbridge (Onondaga Co) and was apprenticed to a tinsmith at 15. He later moved to Michigan, where he sold hardware and stoves. He arrived in Rochester in 1870 as a salesman of safes, and within a short time he opened his own office safe factory. In 1877 he sampled a patent medicine invented by a local doctor, Charles Craig, and manufactured by a group of New York City speculators. He found it so beneficial he bought the patent and brought the business to Rochester, where he renamed the product Warner's Safe Kidney and Liver Cure. Although Warner offered various formulas for different afflictions, the Safe Kidney and Liver Cure sold best. It contained 14% alcohol, 8% glycerin, saltpeter, water, plus the herbs Virginia bugleweed *(Lycopus virginiana),* hepatica, and oil of wintergreen. He proceeded to make a fortune, largely due to marketing savvy. He used a picture of an iron safe on his medicine bottle to inspire consumer confidence, and he sponsored a puzzle contest (perhaps the first widely circulated one of its kind) to promote his product. Because of the huge volume of Warner mail, the Rochester post office acquired its first automatic canceling machine.

Warner's most important contribution to Rochester—and biggest promotional move—was the Warner Observatory, opened in 1883 to house the telescope of Lewis Swift, a prominent amateur astronomer who discovered several comets in the 1870s and 1880s. Unlike most observatories of its time, Warner's was open to the public; the price of admission was 25¢ or the label of a Warner's product. Always restless, Warner expanded his medicine business overseas and became involved in politics, mining, and stock promotion. He spent increasing amounts of time outside Rochester. In 1893 a severe recession, coupled with Warner's own financial missteps, resulted in the loss of his medicine business. In 1894 Swift took the telescope and relocated to California. Warner left Rochester permanently and spent the next 30 years trying to match his earlier successes with a series of advertising and patent medicine businesses in New York, Philadelphia, and Minneapolis.

Atwater, Edward C. "Hulbert Harrington Warner and the Perfect Pitch: Sold Hope; Made Millions," *New York History* 56 (Apr 1975): 154–90

Joann Minor

Warner, Pop [Glenn Scobey] (*b* Springville, Erie Co, 5 Apr 1871; *d* Palo Alto, Calif, 7 Sept 1954). Football coach. Raised in Springville, Warner attended the local Griffith Institute and Cornell University Law School, from which he graduated in 1894. He participated in football, baseball, track, and boxing at Cornell, where his football teammates named him Pop because he was an older student. Warner's legal career began in Buffalo in 1895, when he also started coaching football at both Iowa State University and University of Georgia (1895–96), performing preseason work and then leaving his assistants in charge. His major coaching stints include those at Cornell (1897–98, 1904–6); Carlisle Indian School (1899–1903, 1907–14), where he coached Jim Thorpe; University of Pittsburgh (1915–23); Stanford University (1924–32); and Temple University (1933–38). Warner's teams were national champions in 1915, 1916, 1918, and 1926, and played three times in the Rose Bowl and once in the Sugar Bowl. His football innovations include the single wing, the screen pass, the rolling block, shoulder and thigh pads, the three-point stance, and uniform numbers. The Pop Warner League (now the Pop Warner Little Scholars), founded in 1929, combines athletic competition with academic performance. New York State has teams anchored in more than 75 localities. The US Postal Service issued a stamp honoring Warner in 1997. The Pop Warner Museum is in Springville.

Bynum, Mike, ed. *Pop Warner, Football's Greatest Teacher: The Epic Autobiography of Major College Football's Winningest Coach, Glenn S. (Pop) Warner* (Birmingham, Ala: Gridiron Football Properties, 1993)

Dave Wohlhueter

War of 1812. In the years leading up to America's second war with Great Britain, the United States had attempted to remain neutral in the conflicts that embroiled Europe. Both Great Britain and France limited trade with the United States, and US ships were harassed and seized. Because they refused to recognize any claims of neutrality, and because American sailors continued to be impressed into service on British ships, the British were seen as a greater threat to America. Diplomatic efforts and a trade embargo were unsuccessful in avoiding conflict, and war was declared with Great Britain on 18 June 1812. New York State residents were bitterly divided over the war from its start.

Political Response

During the April 1812 election campaign for the state legislature, Federalists championed peace, neutrality, and free trade. Republican supporters of Pres James Madison's reelection endorsed the embargo and war. Those supporting De Witt Clinton's presidential bid criticized the timing of the 90-day embargo before the outbreak of war and blamed Madison for the state of Anglo-American relations. Republicans received a shock when they lost 19 seats in the state assembly and the Federalists won an 8-seat majority. When Congress voted on the declaration of war in June 1812 only three Republican New York State congressmen and Republican senator John Smith voted for war. Seven Republicans and four Federalists in the US House of Representatives voted against war. With the exception of Samuel Latham Mitchill of New York City, the antiwar Republicans were followers of Clinton, who feared that war would solidify the Federalist victory in the April election and would keep them out of power as long as the war lasted.

When the state legislature met in 1813, a confrontation developed between Republicans and Federalists. The Federalist-controlled assembly killed a proposal from New York governor Daniel D. Tompkins to loan the federal government $500,000 to prosecute the war. Pro-war resolutions passed by the Republican-controlled senate contrasted with antiwar resolutions approved by the Federalist assembly. The war remained the major issue in the 1813 legislative and gubernatorial elections. Republicans renominated Gov Tompkins for a third term but dropped Clinton as lieutenant governor. Federalists allowed Clinton to remain mayor of New York City, but Clintonian Republican attacks on Tompkins and his alliance with the Federalists undermined Clinton's political base within the Republican Party for the duration of the war. The Federalists nominated Stephen Van Rensselaer for governor and campaigned against the war and the governor's callout of the militia.

Tompkins won reelection, but his majority dropped by half from 1810—hardly a ringing endorsement of the war, especially given that the Federalists won another majority in the assembly and captured 17 of the 27 seats in the congressional delegation. The deadlock in the legislature continued through 1813. During the 1814 spring campaign for Congress and the state legislature, the Federalists railed against the war and taxes. Republicans carried 21 of 27 congressional seats, however, and picked up two-thirds of the assembly seats. This change appeared to be an endorsement of the war and a repudiation of Federalism. In the spring 1815 elections, after the war ended, Federalists emphasized opposition to conscription and higher taxes, and the futility of the war. Republicans argued that the war proved a republican government could wage war. This time the Federalists gained 22 seats in the assembly for a tie. Republicans disqualified one Federalist to give them a 64–62 majority. No other state entered or left the war as politically divided over the War of 1812 as New York did.

Military Events

Shortly after war was declared, Gov Tompkins appointed Stephen Van Rensselaer commander of the state's militia. New York had an army of 95,000 militiamen, but most lacked adequate training and equipment, and a majority of the officers lacked military experience. By 1813 many militiamen proved reluctant to show up and were often unwilling to participate in military service. The shortage of food, winter clothing, and shelter led to mutinies and mass desertions during the winter of 1812–13. Widespread evasion of the militia draft in 1812 led Tompkins to favor special courts to try militia delinquents, but New York State residents continued to resist the call-up of the militia in 1813.

On 13 Oct 1812 Gen Van Rensselaer ordered the attack on Queenston Heights [now Queenston, Ont] on the Canadian side of the Niagara River. He quarreled with Brig Gen Alexander Smyth, commander of the regular army troops at Fort Niagara [now in Porter, Niagara Co], who refused to launch a simultaneous attack on Fort George [now in Niagara-on-the-Lake, Ont]. The initial attack on Queenston Heights by both militia and regular army troops was unsupported by reinforcements. When ordered to cross the river from New York State and to support the attack, the remaining militiamen refused. This forced Lt Col Winfield Scott to surrender to the British with a loss of almost 1,000 captured, killed, and wounded. Van Rensselaer resigned his command soon after the battle. Smyth took command of the forces in the Niagara region and led two aborted assaults on Fort Erie [now in Ont] in late November and early December.

Known for his successful raids across the northern New York–Canadian border, Maj Benjamin Forsyth attacked Elizabethtown [now Brockville, Ont] on 6 Feb 1813 to release 52 American prisoners and British deserters. British lieutenant colonel George Macdonnell, commander at Prescott [now in Ont], raided Oswegatchie [now Ogdensburg, St. Lawrence Co] on 22 February to end Forsyth's raids on British supply lines and to retaliate for his assault on Elizabethtown. With a force of Canadian militia and Indian allies, Macdonnell surprised Forsyth, capturing Oswegatchie and forcing Forsyth to withdraw. After looting the town and seizing equipment and stores, the British withdrew. The Americans did not reestablish a military presence there for the remainder of the war, and the citizens of Oswegatchie traded actively with the British over the border.

In April–May 1813 Commander Isaac Chauncey, American naval commander on Lakes Ontario and Erie, used his fleet out of Sackets Harbor (Jefferson Co) to support Maj Gen Henry Dearborn's attacks and subsequent victories at York [now Toronto] and Fort George. While Chauncey's fleet was away, Sir George Prevost ordered an attack on Sackets Harbor from Kingston [now in Ont]. His attack on 28–29 May 1813 was met by Gen Jacob Brown in command of approximately 800 militiamen and regulars who defended Sackets Harbor. Although many of the militia fled, Brown's forces repulsed the British, who returned to Kingston after destroying naval supplies reserved for Chauncey's fleet.

On 11 July 1813 British lieutenant colonel Cecil Bisshopp and 250 regulars and militia crossed into the United States from Canada and raided Black Rock [now in Erie Co]. Bisshopp's forces burned a schooner, barracks, and blockhouse, and captured supplies. With a force of regulars, militia, and Seneca Indians, Brig Gen Peter B. Porter repulsed the attack in which Bisshopp was mortally wounded. On 31 July, a British force sailed into American waters on Lake Champlain and reached and briefly occupied Plattsburgh; there they destroyed the arsenal, blockhouse, and several storehouses and looted private homes before withdrawing. Lt Col John Murray commanded the British forces. A second part of the raiding force attacked Swanton, Vt, briefly dueled with American naval forces off Burlington, Vt, and captured eight vessels on Lake Champlain. En route back to

Gen. Peter B. Porter, by Lars Sellstedt, 1873.

Canada they destroyed two blockhouses, the barracks, and a warehouse at Champlain (Clinton Co), and captured a company of Clinton Co Militia on 3 Aug 1813.

Dearborn's failures following the capture of York and Fort George led to his replacement as commanding general by Maj Gen James Wilkinson. On 17 Oct 1813 Wilkinson left Sackets Harbor with a force of about 8,000 men to travel down the St. Lawrence River and seize Montreal as part of a two-pronged attack. After his forces were repulsed at the Battle of Chrysler's Farm [now in South Dundas Township, Ont] on 11 November he abandoned the invasion and returned for winter quarters at French Mills [now Fort Covington, Franklin Co]. Simultaneously Maj Gen Wade Hampton, who had assumed command of forces near Plattsburgh in July 1813, was to attack Montreal from the south. His invasion force was 4,000 inexperienced troops; almost all of the 1,400 New York militiamen refused to cross the border. After a skirmish with British and Canadian forces along the Chateauguay River near what is now Howick, Que, on 25–26 October, Hampton abandoned the invasion and withdrew to Plattsburgh.

The failed campaigns along the northern border of New York shifted most regulars away from the Niagara Frontier. When British troops threatened to retake Fort George on the Canadian side of the Niagara River in December 1813, American militia commander brigadier general George McClure withdrew, burning Newark [now Niagara-on-the-Lake] and part of Queenston Heights. In retaliation the British, under Maj Gen Sir Gordon Drummond, captured Fort Niagara on 19 December. Sixty-five Americans out of the 400-man garrison were killed; the British retained control of Fort Niagara until the end of the war. Simultaneously a British force under Brig Gen Phineas Riall reached Lewiston (Niagara Co) on 18 December and destroyed all buildings, and Canadian Indians serving with Riall killed 10 civilians. The militia fled, and Riall's forces burned Lewiston and settlements south to Tonawanda Creek. Riall followed up with another assault on Black Rock and Buffalo on 29–30 Dec 1813, and once again the militia did little to defend the settlements. News of the British raids led thousands of civilians to flee eastward to Batavia (Genesee Co) and Canandaigua (Ontario Co), where they depended on public and private contributions during the winter of 1813–14.

In the spring of 1814, Sir James L. Yeo, commander of British naval forces on the Great Lakes, attacked Oswego to capture supplies intended for Sackets Harbor. Yeo's squadron arrived off Oswego on 5 May 1814. British troops (800 men) landed and forced the 400 American defenders of Fort Ontario (Oswego Co) under Lt Col George Mitchell to withdraw 8 miles (13 km) upriver, where additional supplies and cannon were secured. After seizing over 2,000 barrels of food and salt at Oswego, the British withdrew. The raid slowed the shipbuilding at Sackets Harbor for several weeks.

Along the Niagara Frontier in July 1814, Jacob Brown successfully led almost 5,000 troops to capture Fort Erie, the British post at the mouth of the Niagara River. Riall defeated Brig Porter's brigade near the Chippewa River on 5 July, but that day Scott's brigade defeated Riall's troops at the Battle of the Chippewa. Three weeks later, on 25 July, Brown and Riall fought an indecisive battle at Lundy's Lane [now in Niagara Falls, Ont]. Brown fell back to Fort Erie with his troops. British forces under Drummond followed and laid siege to the fort. Hoping to draw out the Americans, he sent Lt Col John Tucker to attack Black Rock on 2 August, but American forces blocked the raid. On 15 Sept 1814, in a sortie against British artillery positions ordered by Brown, New York militia played a major role in breaking Drummond's siege, effectively ending military action on the Niagara Frontier.

In the summer of 1814, Prevost decided to invade northern New York in what would be one of the last military engagements of the war in New York State. On 3 September he led 10,300 troops across the border in two wings and quickly occupied Plattsburgh north of the Saranac River. Regular US Army troops and militia destroyed two bridges and occupied defensive positions south of the river. Prevost delayed the attack to wait for the arrival of a fleet of 4 warships and 12 gunboats on Lake Champlain under Capt George Downie. An American fleet of 4 warships and 10 gunboats under Capt Thomas Macdonough made a stand in Plattsburgh Bay on 11 September. Downie attacked, allowing Macdonough to rake the British fleet, especially the British flagship *Confiance.* The British surrendered after less than two hours; Downie was killed early in the battle. British soldiers in Plattsburgh advanced south across the Saranac River. Prevost halted the attack, however, when he learned of his fleet's surrender and ordered the troops to return to Canada. The treaty ending the war was signed three months later.

Broadside condemning British encouragement of scalping during War of 1812.

The Iroquois and the War

Early in the war, Iroquois leaders did not want to participate or take sides in the conflict; Seneca prophet Handsome Lake was among them. Initially American officials encouraged Iroquois neutrality, and New York Iroquois encouraged their brethren in Upper Canada [now Ontario] to remain at peace. The Canadian Iroquois, however, supported the British, and by the end of 1812, the Americans had recruited support from the New York State Iroquois. By coming to the aid of Black Rock in July 1813, the Senecas effectively ended the neutrality of the Iroquois. From this point New York Iroquois actively joined the war effort, and a civil war developed as Iroquois from Canada fought against those from New York in several engagements. By December 1813 British raids on the Niagara Frontier led to the burning of homes on the Tuscarora Indian Reservation [loc in Niagara Co]. For the most part, the Americans failed to make the most of the military ability of the Iroquois. Despite the importance of the Iroquois in the Battle of the Chippewa in 1814, American military leaders gave little credit to their Iroquois allies. Iroquois contributions to the American war effort did not prevent the continued loss of their lands once the war ended.

Impact of the War on New York City

New York City emerged as a privateering base for 102 vessels. Within three months of the declaration of war, the city sent out 26 privateers. During the war, New York City privateers captured 275 prizes. On 9 Sept 1814 the brig *General Armstrong,* commanded by Samuel Chester Reid, left New York City at night to avoid detection by a British blockading squadron. In the Azores Islands, the brig battled with a British squadron, which delayed reinforcements for the British attack on New Orleans. Upon Reid's return to New York, the state legislature and New York City merchants honored him. Reid served as a harbormaster after the war.

In May 1813 the British blockaded the Port of New York, harassed ships passing through Long Island Sound, and seized vessels sailing from Sag Harbor and eastern Suffolk Co for cattle. The problems at Sag Harbor proved a boon to the whaling industry in Hudson River communities such as Newburgh (Orange Co) and Poughkeepsie. Congressman Ebenezer Sage informed Secretary of War John Armstrong Jr of Suffolk Co residents' anxiety about British plundering and about a possible assault by the British on Sag Harbor.

Although some New York City merchants prospered from the city's role as a major military supply base, the war created widespread poverty for others. Trade restrictions and the British blockade increased unemployment and led to a sharp rise in the prices of flour, sugar, coffee, tea, firewood, and coal, placing them beyond the means of many residents. During the last year of the war, the city provided cash, food, and firewood to 19,000 people, one-fifth of its population. Of those receiving assistance, more than 16,400 were living independently and not in the city almshouse. During the war relief for the poor became the largest item in the municipal budget.

State residents also contributed in early 1814 to the victims of the British attacks in the Niagara region. The New York State legislature contributed $50,000 to help the refugees who fled the Niagara Frontier for the comparative safety of Batavia and Canandaigua. The attacks on the frontier raised the concern that New York City might become a victim as well. New York State depended on fortifications on Staten Island, Governors Island, and Lower Manhattan. In spring 1814 Gov Tompkins, Mayor Clinton, and chief of engineers, Col Joseph G. Swift, inspected the northern approaches to the city and recommended additional fortifications.

Concern for the city's safety increased in 1814. The British raided Riverhead (Suffolk Co), but Long Islanders repulsed the attack; they were, however, unable to stop a raid on Gardiners Island (Suffolk Co). News of a British fleet off Sandy Hook, NJ, on 6 July 1814 spurred New York City residents to action. The Common Council appealed to Gov Tompkins and Pres Madison for funds to complete the new fortifications around New York City at Harlem Heights, Hell Gate, and Brooklyn Heights. The council appealed to the public to volunteer their labor. The Tammany Society held public meetings to encourage volunteers, and in August 1814 citizens established a Committee of Defense to supervise them. Thousands of militiamen from as far as Saratoga Co were at the fortifications. As fall turned to winter, some people sent their families out of the city, but the British did not attack.

On 11 Feb 1815 word arrived in New York City of the Treaty of Ghent. Thousands of people carrying candles gathered in a spontaneous parade down Broadway to celebrate the war's end. A few nights later, despite a foot of snow on the ground, many crowded the streets for an official celebration but even that was marred by a dispute between Federalists and Republicans over whether the war achieved anything.

See also ERIE CANAL.

Barbuto, Richard. *Niagara 1814: America Invades Canada* (Lawrence: Univ Press of Kansas, 2000)

Benn, Carl. *The Iroquois in the War of 1812* (Toronto: Univ of Toronto Press, 1998)

Benn, Carl, and R. Arthur Bowler, eds. *War along the Niagara Frontier: Essays on the War of 1812 and Its Legacy* (Youngstown, NY: Old Fort Niagara Association, 1991)

Burdick, Virginia. *Captain Thomas McDonough: Delaware-Born Hero of the Battle of Lake Champlain* (Wilmington: Delaware Heritage Press, 1991)

Everest, Allan. *The War of 1812 in the Champlain Valley* (Syracuse: Syracuse Univ Press, 1981)

Morris, John D. *Sword of the Border: Major General Jacob Jennings Brown, 1775–1828* (Kent, Ohio: Kent State Univ Press, 2000)

Wilder, Patrick. *The Battle of Sackett's Harbour: 1813* (Baltimore: Nautical and Aviation Publishing, 1994)

Harvey Strum

Warren. Town (pop 1,136) in S Herkimer Co. Settled prior to 1758, it was the site of an Indian raid led by Joseph Brant on the Andrustown settlement on 18 July 1778. The town was formed from German Flatts in 1796. In 1834–36 town native Harriet Douglas Cruger (1790–1872) of New York City built Gelston Castle on her 1,500-acre (607 ha) estate northwest of Jordanville; the castle is now a ruin, but her more modest Henderson Home is owned by cellist and conductor Mstislav Rostropovich, who has built a contemporary house nearby. Jordanville is the site of the Holy Trinity Russian Orthodox Monastery (1928) and its 1950 cathedral, and is the center of a rural Russian community. In the early 21st century, dairy farming continues to predominate.

Susan R. Perkins

Warren, Sir Peter (*b* Warrenstown, Ireland, 10 Mar 1703; *d* Dublin, Ireland, 29 July 1752). British naval officer. Warren entered the navy in 1716 and advanced quickly due to the patronage of his uncle, Lord Matthew Aylmer, Admiral of the Fleet. By 1730 he was stationed in New York City. A year later he married Susannah DeLancey, sister of James DeLancey, and received large land tracts with her dowry. These included his estate, Warren Farm on Manhattan, near the present location of Greenwich Village, and a 14,000-acre (5,670 ha) Mohawk Valley tract. He entrusted these to his nephew William Johnson, who became an influential Mohawk Valley landowner. Warren's substantial personal wealth derived from prizes taken in military victories, land speculation, and money lending. He was an important source of patronage and support for the DeLancey family. During King George's War, his defeat of the French at Louisbourg on Cape Breton Island [now in Nova Scotia] in 1745 and at Cape Finisterre, Spain, in 1747 made him a celebrity in England and earned him a knighthood and promotion to rear admiral of the blue. Returning to England in 1747, he served in the British House of Commons until his death.

Gwyn, Julian. *The Enterprising Admiral: The Personal Fortune of Admiral Sir Peter Warren* (Montreal: McGill-Queen's Univ Press, 1974)

Jennifer Steenshorne

Warren County (869 mi²/2,251 km²; pop 63,303). Created in 1813 from Washington Co and named for Revolutionary War general Joseph Warren. The county is divided into 1 city, Glens Falls, and 11 towns, which contain one incorporated village, Lake George. The Town of Queensbury has served as county seat since 1963. Elevations range from less than 220 feet (67 m) where the Hudson River leaves the county to 3,583 feet (1,092 m) at the summit of Gore Mountain. Warren Co lies within two major physiographic provinces. Queensbury and adjacent Glens Falls are situated in the Hudson Valley subregion of the Hudson-Mohawk Lowland. Here relief is generally less than 100 feet (30 m). The rest of the county falls within the Adirondack Low Mountains subregion of the Adirondack Upland, except for the northwest quadrant, which enters into the Adirondack Mountain Peaks subregion. Upland relief ranges from 1,200 to 2,500 feet (370–760 m) and is partly the result of substantial geologic faulting, deepened in places by streams. Lowland bedrock is composed of Ordovician limestone and dolo-

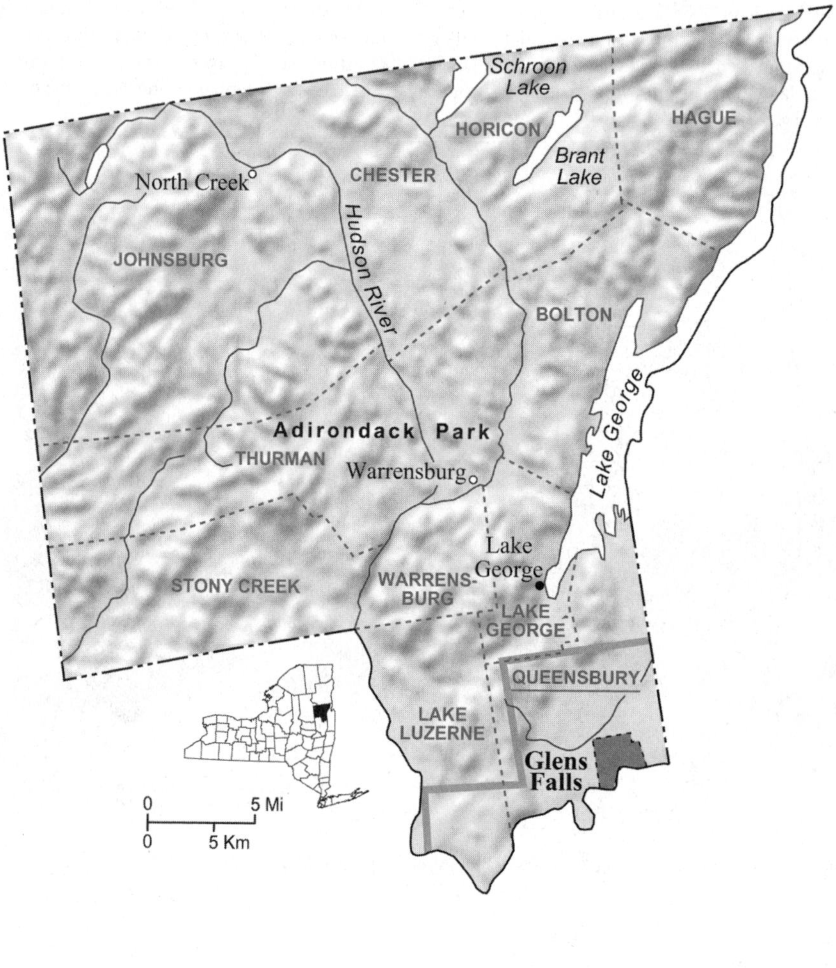

WARREN CO POPULATION CENSUS FIGURES

	White	Nonwhite	Total Population	Foreign-Born
1820	9,436	17	9,453	19
1830	11,774	22	11,796	97
1840	13,390	32	13,422	—
1850	17,153	46	17,199	1,356
1860	21,376	58	21,434	2,648
1870	22,528	64	22,592	2,578
1880	25,115	64	25,179	2,497
1890	27,765	101	27,866	2,592
1900	29,849	94	29,943	2,628
1910	32,179	44	32,223	2,978
1920	31,644	29	31,673	2,443
1930	34,085	89	34,174	2,318
1940	35,918	117	36,035	2,071
1950	39,060	145	39,205	1,984
1960	43,802	200	44,002	1,741
1970	49,075	327	49,402	1,491
1980	54,343	511	54,854	1,933
1990	58,328	881	59,209	1,646
2000	61,705	1,598	63,303	1,541

Notes: "Nonwhite" includes African Americans, Asians, American Indians, and Pacific Islanders and, for 2000, also the mixed race and other race categories. Through the 1960 census these figures primarily reflect the African American population. Foreign-born figures for 1820 and 1830 include only those not naturalized, and for 1930 and 1950, the foreign-born totals include Whites only. Other years include all foreign-born in the population.

stone. The highly complex Precambrian rocks of the Adirondacks consist primarily of crystalline silicates, including gneiss, schist, anorthosite, and granite, occasionally interrupted by narrow bands of marble.

Continental glaciation covered all and sculpted much of Warren Co's landscape. Mile-high ice caused the supporting bedrock to deform, creating a northward tilt as the ice retreated. This facilitated the creation of multiple lakes and the establishment of postglacial drainage patterns. Various unconsolidated deposits were left behind, including an end moraine and a thin ground moraine cover in the higher areas. A large complex of kame terraces exist between Glens Falls and Lake George. About 80% of the county is contained within the Hudson River watershed, where waters flow generally south. The remainder, including Lake George (the eastern boundary for much of the county), Glen Lake, and Halfway Brook, with its many tributaries, drain the county's eastern margins north into Lake Champlain. Very little of the county's soil is considered arable by modern agricultural standards.

Warren Co's climate is humid-continental. Mean January temperatures range from 14°F (-10°C) or below in the mountainous northwest to 20°F (-7°C) near Glens Falls. Comparable mean July temperatures are 64°F (18°C) or lower and 71°F (22°C). Temperatures below 0°F (-18°C) are expected every winter, while daytime summer temperatures reach 90°F (32°C) or above at Glens Falls once every two years on average; similar temperatures are less frequent in the Adirondack Upland. Average annual precipitation varies from 39 inches (99 cm) at Glens Falls Airport to around 45 inches (115 cm) in some of the higher elevations. Seasonal snowfall varies from 66 inches (168 cm) near Glens Falls to over 100 inches (254 cm) in the higher mountains.

Fully 90% of the county's primeval forest cover consisted of a northern hardwood community dominated by beech, sugar maple, hemlock, and white pine. The exceptions were a small area in the far northwest made up of red spruce, balsam fir, paper birch, and hardwoods, and a band of central hardwoods, composed largely of beech, sugar maple, and basswood, located south of Lake George. In the early 21st century over 95% of the county is forested, with 93% lying inside the Adirondack Park Blue Line.

Precolonial, Colonial, and Revolutionary Periods

Native Americans made no permanent settlements but hunted and fished seasonally. Archaeological finds, such as stone implements, potsherds, pipes, arrowheads, and spearheads, show evidence of aboriginal encampments dating back to the early Archaic period (7000–6000 BC). In 1642–43 Fr Isaac Jogues (1607–46) became the first recorded European to see Lake George. He came to the region to gain converts among the Mohawk and in 1646 bestowed the name Lac du Saint Sacrement on the lake. During the French and Indian War, the American Revolution, and the War of 1812, military expeditions passed along the Lake Champlain corridor from Albany to Montreal. Wars in Europe played out on the frontier, with the Algonquin aligning with the French and the British frequently recruiting the Iroquois—particularly the Mohawk, who formed an allegiance with Sir William Johnson. Forts William Henry, Gage, George, William, and Amherst were built in present-day Warren Co. The stage was set for some of the bloodiest battles of the French and Indian War (1754–63). Mohawk leader King Hendrick and Col Ephraim Williams were killed just south of Bloody Pond in the southeast corner of the present Town of Lake George during the Battle of Lake George. After the 1757 fall of Fort William Henry and the surrender of its garrison, the defeated were guaranteed passage to Fort Edward (Washington Co) only to be massacred by native tribes that Marquis de Montcalm could not control. Armies under Gen James Abercromby and later Gen Jeffery Amherst were mounted and sent down Lake George to take Fort Carillon [now Fort Ticonderoga, Essex Co]. The defeat of the French opened the land for permanent settlement, and speculators sought land grants from the province. In 1763 Abraham Wing, a Dutchess Co Quaker, brought a band of settlers to Queensbury, and Edward and Ebenezer Jessup acquired lands in Luzerne in 1768.

The present Warren Co was a lightly settled frontier during the Revolutionary War. Queensbury residents fled to Dutchess Co with the onslaught of Gen John Burgoyne's campaign. Fort George and the site at Fort William Henry served as places for the Hessian general Friedrich von Riedesel to gather artillery for Burgoyne to be moved over the Old Military Rd to Fort Edward. In 1780 Carleton's Raiders sacked and burned Queensbury. Citizens requisitioned the state for the loss of their property and goods.

Transportation

Many town and county roads followed the routes of Native American trails and of military roads. The first steamboat on Lake George, the *James Caldwell,* served from 1816 to 1820; such boats carried passengers and goods the length of the lake until the Champlain (1823) and Feeder (1832) Canals gradually shifted commerce to Glens Falls. In 1848 a plank road was built from Glens Falls to Caldwell [now Lake George], Warrensburg, and Chestertown, facilitating stagecoach service between those towns; other stages met the train at Fort Edward beginning in the same year. As late as 1880, 85 canalboats plied the Feeder Canal with 120–150 tons (110–135 MT) of merchandise per load.

The Adirondack Railroad reached Thurman in 1869 and North Creek in 1871. The Delaware and Hudson Railroad connected Glens Falls to Fort Edward in 1869 with 11 passenger cars that made 11 round trips daily. In 1882 the Delaware and Hudson Railroad was completed to Lake George and remained in operation until 1957. Horse-drawn (1885) and electric (1892) trolleys transported tourists and local residents. The automobile came into use at the turn of the 20th century and became widely available, especially after World War I. Public bus transportation replaced the trolleys in 1928 around Glens Falls, connecting the city to Queensbury, Hudson Falls (Washington Co), and Fort Edward throughout World War II.

Aviation in Warren Co began with the 1919 landing of a barnstormer on a field at Miller Hill in Glens Falls. By 1928 the Glens Falls Chamber of Commerce spearheaded construction of the Floyd Bennett Field, later deeded to Glens Falls. In 1938 the first air mail left the field for Albany. In 1941 commercial service to New York City was initiated by Colonial Airways. The field was abandoned in 1946 when the Warren County Airport (now Floyd Bennett Memorial Airport) was built off County Line Rd in Queensbury.

Economic Development

At the end of the Revolution present-day Warren Co was opened for permanent settlement, chiefly from New England. John Thurman, like other speculators, arrived to develop his patent

POPULATIONS OF TOWNS AND CITIES, WARREN CO

Town or City, Year Founded	1800	1840	1880	1920	1960	2000
Bolton, 1799	959	937	1,132	1,184	1,417	2,117
Chester, 1799	508	1,633	2,247	1,572	1,974	3,614
Glens Falls (city), 1908	—	—	—	16,638	18,580	14,354
Hague, 1807[a]	—	610	807	1,028	771	854
Horicon, 1838	—	659	1,633	754	833	1,479
Johnsburg, 1805	—	1,139	2,742	2,242	2,250	2,450
Lake George, 1810[b]	—	693	1,223	1,297	2,429	3,578
Lake Luzerne, 1792[c]	591	1,284	1,438	1,018	1,830	3,219
Queensbury, 1762[d]	1,435	3,789	9,805	2,584	10,004	25,441
Stony Creek, 1852	—	—	1,253	651	459	743
Thurman, 1792[e]	1,332	1,210	1,174	680	548	1,199
Warrensburg, 1813	—	1,468	1,725	2,025	2,907	4,255

Note: In 1800 the Towns of Bolton, Chester, Lake Luzerne, Queensbury, and Thurman were in Washington Co.

[a]Rochester until 1808.

[b]Caldwell until 1962.

[c]Fairfield until 1808; Luzerne until 1963.

[d]Patent date; recognized as town 1788.

[e]Thurman dissolved by dividing into Warrensburg and Athol 1813; Athol dissolved by dividing into Stony Creek and new Town of Thurman 1852.

in a town that took his name, and James Caldwell began promoting development of Lake George. As land became available, settlers arrived to farm or to cut lumber. By 1800 the population of the county had reached 4,317, and it nearly tripled in 30 years to 12,212. In 1820, 2,360 out of a total of 9,453 residents were engaged in farming.

African American slaves were not brought to the county in any significant numbers. Independent farmers on small tracts had little money or need for slave labor. John Thurman had one slave in 1790; there were two slaves in Warren Co in 1800 and a peak of seven in 1820. The number of free African Americans grew from 10 in 1820 to 58 in 1860. In the antebellum period, the Liberty Party and the Wesleyan Methodist Church became active in the abolition movement. The Joseph Leggett House in Chestertown was a site of Underground Railroad activity, and numerous other houses were safe havens.

Land improved for agriculture increased gradually, from 71,410 acres (28,899 ha) in 1835 to 136,981 acres (56,648 ha) in 1875, much of it in Queensbury and Johnsburg. Grazing increased in importance during the century; pasture and meadow were always dominant over plowed land and accounted for 75% of improved acreage in 1875. In the last quarter of the 19th century, agriculture in the southern part of the county, where it had been most viable, began to decline. There were 2,121 farms in 1900 but 547 in 1950. By 2000 there were only 58 farms occupying 1.7% of the county's land, the lowest figure of any county outside the New York City area except for Hamilton.

Soon after 1763 Abraham Wing constructed a sawmill on the Hudson River to process logs floated downstream. The logging industry became dominant, with 94 sawmills producing 123,246 board feet of lumber by 1835. Other early woods industries included potash production and tanning. By contrast there were only 17 gristmills in Warren Co in 1835, and a single ironworks located in Athol. Black marble, lime and cement, and feldspar were quarried; garnet and graphite were mined. During the late 19th century and into the 20th, wood products, textiles, woolens, shirts, dresses, gloves, wallpaper, pigments, chemicals, catheters, and papermaking machinery were manufactured in the county.

Banking and insurance grew in response to these industries. The Glens Falls Bank (now Glens Falls National Bank) opened in 1851. By the end of the century Glens Falls had four banks. In 1849 Russell M. Little organized the Glens Falls Dividend Mutual Insurance Co (later Glens Falls Insurance Co), whose business would expand far beyond the local market. In 1883 A. C. and L. W. Emerson organized the Emerson and Co bank in Warrensburg.

Zenas Van Dusen generated the first electricity for Glens Falls around 1880 near Feeder Dam. In 1897 a generator in John G. Smith's sawmill on the Schroon River furnished electricity for Warrensburg homes. In 1900 the Hudson River Power Co organized to "tap the unused power of the Hudson where it plunges" and constructed Spier Falls Dam, completed in 1903; this marked the beginning of large-scale electrical generation in eastern New York.

At Warren Co's formation Lake George was widely known for its natural beauty, and those who could afford to travel for pleasure began coming to enjoy the scenery and to fish. Some travelers used Lake George en route to Lake Champlain and Canada. The first inn at the present Village of Lake George catered to such travelers, but the Trout Pavilion in Queensbury was built for sports enthusiasts in 1810. The smaller Lake Luzerne was attracting visitors by 1832, when the Rockwell House was built. Stagecoach service for the Canada-bound traveler was established from Saratoga to Whitehall (Washington Co) and Caldwell, the latter popular with the first generation of landscape painters. With the 1849 construction of railroad lines north from Saratoga Springs, the journeys became more practicable.

A growing leisure class with fortunes made in the Civil War sought out Warren Co. Large "cottages" were built along Lake George's southern reaches, while big wooden hotels catered to less-affluent vacationers; the best known were the United States Hotel (*ca* 1850), the Fort William Henry Hotel (1855), and the Sagamore Hotel (1883). The books of William H. H. "Adirondack" Murray helped focus interest on Warren Co's mountains, lakes, and wilderness areas. The county became part of the Adirondack Forest Preserve in 1885, and when the Adirondack Park was established in 1892 most of the county fell within its Blue Line. A railway to the summit of Prospect Mountain (1890–1903) was another attraction for tourists.

With the increased availability of automobiles, a new form of vacationing developed around dude ranches, which were concentrated in Luzerne and a few other places. Following the 1932 Winter Olympics at Lake Placid (Essex Co), the first commercial ski area in the eastern United States opened in North Creek in 1933, and the state developed the Gore Mountain ski area in 1964. With the pent-up demand of the World War II era, Warren Co tourism expanded greatly beginning in 1946, almost entirely because of the automobile. Motels began replacing the interwar tourist cabins. Hotels, except for the Sagamore on Lake George, faded, and highway-based amusement parks such as Storytown USA in Queensbury (1954) were constructed.

Religion, Education, and Culture

Protestant Christianity was dominant among the settlers. Quakers came to Queensbury in 1762. Baptist and Methodist churches were established after the American Revolution. Irish and French Canadian immigrant families brought their Catholic faith, founding churches in Glens Falls in 1848 and 1853, respectively. By 1855 Warren Co had 12 Methodist, 7 Baptist, and 6 Presbyterian congregations; no other denomination had more than 2. Jewish families settled in the Glens Falls area in the late 19th century, organizing the first synagogues in 1925 and 1926.

The first newspaper, the *Warren Republican,* appeared in 1813 and the first daily, the *Glens Falls Times,* in 1879. In the early 21st century the daily paper is the *Glens Falls Post-Star* (1909), and weeklies are the *Chronicle* (1980) of Glens Falls, the *Lake George Mirror* (1890), the *Adirondack Journal* (1987) of Warrensburg, and the *North Creek News-Enterprise* (1924). The county has a number of small community libraries such as the Mountainside Library in Queensbury, built with money from the Carnegie family. The large Crandall Public Library (1892) in Glens Falls is a regionally significant institution.

Common schools developed following 1812 legislation. In 1844–45 Lemon Thompson, the county superintendent of schools, reported 112 school districts in the county. Private schools were established in Caldwell, Chester, Johnsburg, Warrensburg, and Glens Falls. Beginning in 1853 common schools were combined into Union Free School districts for the support of high schools. The first in the county was at Glens Falls in 1881, but its first high school class did not graduate until 1891. Glens Falls also supported St. Mary's (1883) and St. Alphonsus (1893) parochial schools. School systems were centralized throughout the county beginning in 1926 at Hague, a district later annexed by Ticonderoga (Essex Co). Central school districts include Glens Falls, Bolton (1927), Hadley-Luzerne (1937), Warrensburg (1938), Johnsburg (1946), Queensbury (1948), Lake George (1950), and North Warren (after 1958). A single common school, the Abraham Wing School (1842), continues independent of the surrounding Glens Falls district in a 1937 building. A BOCES program began in the late 1960s. From 1946 to 1952, Skidmore College operated its Glens Falls Division for returning veterans. In 1961 Adirondack Community College, serving Warren and Washington Cos, was established; it opened its Queensbury campus in 1963.

The county is home to 18 historical and art museums, notably the Hyde Collection Art Museum with its small but world-class collection of European masters. The Lake George Arts Project promotes the work of contemporary artists. Many artists have painted the county's scenery, thereby helping to lure tourists to the area. In the late 1910s and early 1920s, Georgia O'Keeffe (1887–1986) summered and painted in Lake George. The Bolton Landing home of opera star Marcella Sembrich has been a museum since 1937. The county has created or supported the Lake George Opera Festival, Glens Falls Symphony, Glens Falls Community Theater (formerly Glens Falls Operetta Club), and Lake Luzerne Music Festival. The Lower Adirondack Regional Arts Council supports many cultural efforts.

Politics

The county court and jail were located at Caldwell, the first county seat, but by 1928 the facilities were overcrowded and rented space became necessary. The modern Warren County Municipal Center in Queensbury opened in 1963. A 20-member Board of Supervisors governs the county with one representative for each of 10 towns, five from the City of Glens Falls and five from Queensbury. Weighted voting was instituted in 1966. Elected mayors administer the City of Glens Falls and the Village of Lake George. Elected supervisors and town boards administer each town.

Since the middle of the 19th century the county has had a consistent ratio of two Republicans for each Democratic voter. The only time in the 20th century that the county voted for a Democratic presidential candidate was in 1964, when it supported Lyndon Johnson. Significant political figures from Warren Co include Gov John Alden Dix (1860–1928); Charles Evans Hughes (1862–1948), governor of New York State and chief justice of the US Supreme Court; and Robert P. Patterson (1891–1952), secretary of war under Pres Harry S. Truman. Another native, Charles Reed Bishop (1822–1915) was a banker and cabinet minister in Hawaii before it was annexed by the United States. Gerald Solomon (1930–2001), a US congressman, was the county's best-known politician in the late 20th century, rising to chairman of the House Ways and Means Committee.

Recent History

The change from an agrarian society to a modern suburban way of life was led by Queensbury, which experienced great changes following World War II and again with the completion of the southern part of the Northway (I-87) in 1963. A host of shopping malls along US 9 were developed. Other towns in the county have been stable in population, while receiving benefits from summer tourism. Warren Co has 160 lakes and vast stretches of river for fishing and boating. There is downhill skiing at Gore and West Mountains. Approximately 100 miles (160 km) of cross-country ski trails are groomed, while the International Trail is located in Crandall Park in Glens Falls. The Glens Falls Civic Center (1978) hosts sporting events. The Americade Motorcycle Rally in Lake George, the Adirondack Hot Air Balloon Festival, and the Adirondack Regional Chambers of Commerce Quality of Life Expo are held annually. As changes bring retirees and others seeking seasonal homes and recreation, planning and zoning have been enacted by most communities to protect growth and open spaces.

See also Logging and lumbering; Welsh.

The standard 19th-century county history is H. P. Smith, *History of Warren County* (1885). An update by William H. Brown, ed., *History of Warren County* (1963), is good though unannotated. Warren Co is unusual in having been the subject of a Work Projects Administration guidebook, *Warren County: A History and Guide* (1942). There are two histories of Glens Falls: Louis F. Hyde, *History of Glens Falls, New York and Its Settlement* (1936), and *Bridging the Years: Glens Falls, New York, 1763–1978* (1978). Other town histories include A. W. Holden's pioneering *History of the Town of Queensbury* (1874); Lester S. Thomas, *Timber, Tanneries, and Tourists* (1979), on Lake Luzerne; *Rivers, Roads, and Ski Trails: The History of the Town of Johnsburg* (1994); Janice M. Whipple, *Stony Creek: Then and Now* (1980); David C. Haskell and Edythe L. Haskell, *A History of Stony Creek, New York,* 2 vols (1991–96); and Bea Greenwood, comp, *Reflections and Recollections of the Town with a Past: Warrensburg* (2002). Also of interest is Ann Breen Metcalfe, *The Schroon River: A History of an Adirondack Valley and Its People* (2000).

Marilyn J. Van Dyke

Warrensburg. Town (pop 4,255) in central Warren Co. Settled in 1786, the town was formed from the extinct town of Thurman in 1813. Warrensburg developed as an industrial center for northern Warren Co. Waterpower, hemlock bark, and the Adirondack Railroad (1905, later Delaware and Hudson) enabled the A. C. Emerson sawmill and B. P. Burhans and Co tannery to become big producers of lumber and leather. Other factories produced shirts, ladies' shirtwaists, pants, paper, and wooden pegs. Whitby, Emerson, and Eldridge made the well-known Warrensburg Woolens (1899). Aviator Floyd Bennett (1899–1928), who flew over the North Pole in 1926, spent his youth in Warrensburg. Tourism gradually replaced manufacturing in the 20th century. The "World's Largest Garage Sale" (1979) is held every fall.

Marilyn J. Van Dyke

Warsaw. Town (pop 5,423) and village (pop 3,814) in central Wyoming Co. Settled in 1803, the town was formed from Batavia (Genesee Co) in 1808. The village, surveyed in 1816 and 1836, became the county seat in 1841 and was incorporated in 1843. Nineteenth-century industrial products included wool cloth, stoves, and carpets; Martin and Co manufactured map rollers beginning in 1853. Rail service was provided by the Erie Railroad (1852) and the Rochester and State Line Railroad (1877). The Warsaw Salt Co (1882) drilled 22 wells in three years, and later the Warsaw Salt Sanitarium (1891–97) claimed to be the first in the United States to offer salt baths. Warsaw Elevator Co, later part of Otis Elevator (1892–1966), was an important employer in the 20th century. Marr and Colton Co made pipe organs from 1915 to 1932. The largest employer in the early 21st century is the regional Wyoming County Community Hospital, and dairy farming continues. A well-documented Underground Railroad rescue ended in Warsaw in 1851, when Mrs Jones and her child were literally crated in the District of Columbia and driven in a leisurely and open way as far as Warsaw. Trinity Church (1853), a frame Gothic Revival building, and the cobblestone Greek Revival–style Warsaw Academy are on the National Register of Historic Places. Barber B. Conable Jr (1922–2003), president of the World Bank, is a Warsaw native.

Warwick. Town (pop 30,764) and village (pop 6,412) in S central Orange Co. Settled permanently in 1712, the town was formed in 1788. Sterling Furnace (1751) was a main industry for many years; a forge began operating in 1752. The town was famed for its butter in the first quarter of the 19th century. The village was incorporated in 1867, and industrial products included knives and fire hoses. Bypassed by the Erie Railroad, it later acquired service from the Warwick Valley Railroad (1862), the Pine Island Branch of the Erie (1869), and the Lehigh and Hudson River Railroad (1881), allowing farmers to ship produce and fluid milk to city markets and encouraging the construction of summer homes for the wealthy beginning in the 1880s. In the same decade the Drowned Lands along the Wallkill were drained, creating the Black Dirt region, which was farmed by Polish and German Russian farmers. Its onion and other muckland crops remain important, tended in the early 21st century by Mexican migrants.

In the late 1950s Sterling Forest Corp acquired title to 20,000 acres (8,100 ha), half of it in Warwick. Sterling Forest State Park (1998) obtained much of this land and protects 15,000 acres (6,070 ha) of the tract. In the early 21st century Warwick continues to support farms, apple orchards, and wineries, while many residents commute to New York City. The Warwick Village Historic District, the Gen John Hathorn House, and the Boulders at Greenwood Lake are on the National Register of Historic Places. Famous residents include painter Jasper Francis Cropsey (1823–1900). Statesman William H. Seward (1801–72) was a native. Part of the Wallkill River National Wildlife Refuge is in town. Residents of Pine Island hamlet, the heart of the Black Dirt region, and other Black Dirt farmers organize Onion Harvest Festivals every few years in August.

Sue Gardner

Washington. Town (pop 4,742) in central Dutchess Co. Part of the Great Nine Partners Patent (1697), it was settled in the late 1730s by freeholders, some of them New England Quakers. It was formed as a town in 1788. In early years farmers raised grain and then stock before finally turning to dairying. It was the site of the Quaker-operated Nine Partners Boarding School (1796–1864) and the Dutchess County Fair. Millbrook, its commercial center, developed when the Dutchess and Columbia Railroad (1869) headquartered there. In the late 19th century it attracted wealthy summer residents and by the 21st century became a weekend-home community. It was the home of Hamilton Fish Jr (1926–96), member of the US House of Representatives (1969–95).

William P. McDermott

Washington, George (*b* Bridges Creek, near Fredericksburg, Va, 22 Feb 1732; *d* Mount Vernon, Va, 14 Dec 1799). Revolutionary War general and first US president. Son of a wealthy Virginia plantation family, Washington was commissioned as a lieutenant colonel in 1754 in the Virginia Regiment and served in the French and Indian War before resigning his commission in 1758. He was elected commander in chief of the Continental army in May 1775. New York Colony was the site of both the darkest and the brightest moments of Washington's life. Washington arrived in New York City early in the Revolutionary War on 13 Apr 1776, but his underequipped and poorly disposed force was routed by the British army in the Battle of Long Island on 27 August and at Kip's Bay in Manhattan on 15 September. The skirmish at Harlem Heights (18 October) in Upper Manhattan was near the location where the George Washington Bridge (1931) would be built across the Hudson River. Washington's retreat was marked by another battle defeat at White Plains (Westchester Co) on 28 October.

Washington appreciated the strategic importance of New York State in the war, particularly the Hudson River and Highlands. As the Continental army's commander, he spent much of the latter half of the war with his troops in the colony: from July to December 1778 in the area of White Plains, Fredericksburg [now Patterson, Putnam Co], and Fishkill (Dutchess Co); from June to November 1779 at New Windsor and West Point (Orange Co); from November 1780 through June 1781, with some interruptions, in New Windsor; and from March 1782 until August 1783 in the Hasbrouck House at Newburgh (Orange Co). He made numerous visits to other parts of the state as well and maintained a constant correspondence throughout the war with his friend and supporter Gov George Clinton. After the British evacuation of New York City on 25 Nov 1783, Gov Clinton accompanied Washington on his victorious return to the city, and on 4 December Washington said farewell to his officers at Fraunces Tavern on Queen St (now Pearl St). In November 1784 Gov Clinton, on behalf of himself and Washington, bought a parcel of 6,071 acres (2,457 ha) on the Mohawk River in Montgomery Co for £1,062 5s. Washington was unable to pay for his half of this speculative purchase until 1787, but by 1793 Clinton had succeeded in selling about 4,000 acres (1,600 ha) of the tract for £3,400 3s New York currency; the rest remained unsold at Washington's death.

After being chosen as the nation's first president, Washington left his home at Mount Vernon on 16 Apr 1789, beginning his inaugural journey to New York City, the nation's first capital. On 23 April he boarded a barge at Elizabeth Town Point, NJ, prepared in his honor by 46 wealthy citizens of New York City. His craft entered New York Harbor escorted by dozens of smaller vessels, landing early in the afternoon among large crowds at Murray's Wharf at the end of Wall St. Washington, accompanied by Gov Clinton and other officials, made slow progress through the adoring crowds along Queen St to his presidential mansion at Frank-

Peace medal given to Red Jacket by Pres George Washington in 1792 at a meeting with Seneca leaders in Philadelphia.

lin House, 3 Cherry St, previously used by the president of the congress. On inauguration day, 30 April, Washington's carriage moved slowly through the crowds down Cherry St to Queen, Great Dock, and Broad Sts, where it halted, allowing the new president to walk the remaining 600 feet (183 m) to Wall St and Federal Hall. Here he took the oath of office and delivered his inaugural address. Washington would leave the city for Mount Vernon and ultimately Philadelphia for the last time on 30 Aug 1790.

Freeman, Douglas Southall. *George Washington: A Biography,* 6 vols (New York: Charles Scribner's Sons, 1948–1954)

Edward G. Lengel

Washington Benevolent Society. Isaac Sebring, a prosperous merchant living in New York City, hatched a plan in 1808 to unite the Federalist Party in opposition to Pres Thomas Jefferson's foreign policy. Jefferson had implemented an embargo on trade with Great Britain and France in an effort to curb their hostility to American commerce and shipping. Jefferson's successor, James Madison, pursued the policy further, seriously damaging the American economy. The policy had little effect on Britain and France but encouraged revitalized Federalist opposition to the administration. In 1808 Sebring, aided by Gulian Crommelin Verplanck and Richard Varick, organized the Washington Benevolent Society, which was nominally founded to promote fellowship and patriotism, and to relieve distress, especially of old Revolutionary War soldiers. The society held its meetings secretly but celebrated Washington's birthday and the Fourth of July publicly, the first public celebration occurring 22 Feb 1809. Federalists around the state formed chapters soon after, sometimes serving a town, sometimes a county, and occasionally both.

The society's political nature was obvious because its members regularly criticized the administration's policies and supported Federalist candidates for local and national positions. With no Federalist leader able to rival Jefferson in popularity, the society benefited from its attachment to the growing reputation of the recently deceased first president. Between 1808 and 1820 hundreds of locally run and funded clubs were established in New York State, Pennsylvania, New Jersey, and New England. Members usually paid a $1 initiation fee and 50¢ in annual dues. Membership was open to men except atheists, deists, drunkards, and those who used profane language or refused to keep the Sabbath. There was a separate club for African Americans. Members received a ribbon affixed with George Washington's picture and a book containing his portrait and the text of his 1796 farewell address, the Declaration of Independence, the US Constitution, and the constitution of their local chapter. The local chapters often held patriotic parades with Federalist oratory on Washington's birthday and on the Fourth of July.

Clubs provided philanthropic services, but the political agenda was always paramount. The New York City chapter raised money for the construction of a great political hall named for Washington. Soon other local chapters, including those of Albany and Troy (Rensselaer Co), built similar, though less elaborate, buildings. Before the conclusion of the War of 1812, the chapters experienced some political successes. In New York City, Federalists regained control of the Common Council that they had lost in 1804. With the end of the war and the nationalistic fervor that followed, opposition politics declined and the "era of good feelings" emerged. By 1820 most of the clubs had dissolved.

Fox, Dixon Ryan. *The Decline of Aristocracy in the Politics of New York, 1801–1840* (1919; repr New York: Harper Torchbooks, 1965)

John P. Kaminski

Washington County (837 mi²/2,168 km²; pop 61,042). Created as Charlotte Co in 1772 and named for Princess Charlotte, consort of George III. It was renamed in honor of George Washington in 1784. Subsequently territory was surrendered to create Clinton Co in 1788; other parts were ceded to Vermont in 1790; area was annexed to Albany Co in 1791; and Warren Co was split off in 1813. Washington Co is subdivided into 17 towns that contain 9 incorporated villages. Hudson Falls serves as the county seat. The highest elevation is the 2,646 ft (807 m) summit of Black Mountain, overlooking Lake George in the Town of Dresden; the lowest is approximately 85 feet (26 m) on the banks of the Hudson in the south. The mountainous northwest, the highest and most rugged section of the county, is part of the Adirondack Low Mountains subregion of the Adirondack Upland, where bedrock consists of Precambrian gneisses, schists, and granites. In the east the more gentle, folded Taconic Mountains, a subregion of the New England Upland, extend the full length of the county and are composed of Cambrian and Ordovician slate, phyllite, quartzite, and graywacke. In between lies the clearly defined Hudson Valley subregion of the Hudson-Mohawk Lowland. It also runs the county's full length, in the south as a narrow plain along the Hudson River, then broadening out and ending at Lake Champlain in the north. It is underlain by nearly level strata of Ordovician and Devonian shale, sandstone, and limestone.

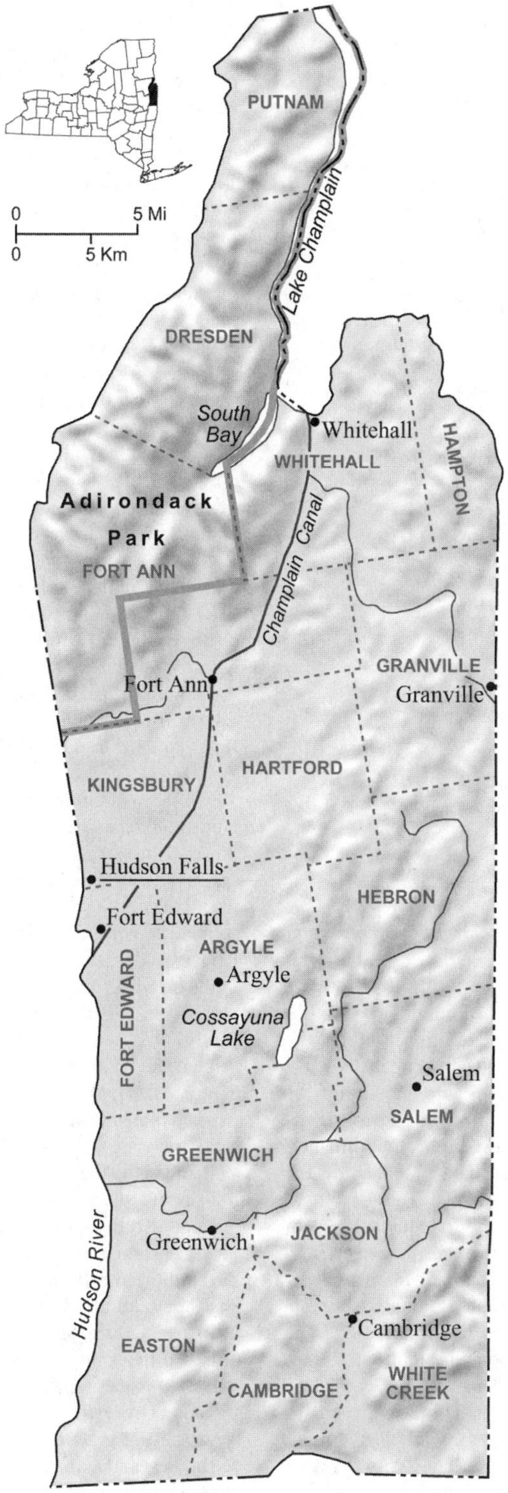

Surface waters in the northern half drain into Lakes George and Champlain and ultimately the St. Lawrence River. The southern half drains to the Hudson River by way of Batten Kill or tributaries of the Hoosic River. During the most recent continental glaciation, bedrock was eroded and smoothed, and a layer of unconsolidated drift of varying thickness was laid down across the entire county. Most of the Hudson Lowland was later occupied by glacial Lakes Albany and Vermont and covered with a layer of lacustrine material as a result. With the exception of the unproductive lands of the Adirondack region, most Washington Co soils can support modern agricultural activity.

Washington Co's climate is humid-continental. The average normal temperature in January hovers around 20°F (-7°C). Nevertheless, readings below 0°F (-18°C) are a significant part of every winter, especially in the north and higher elevations. July temperatures range from less than 70°F (21°C) in some of the higher country to 73°(23°C) at Whitehall. Daytime highs of 90°F (32°C) or above are likely to occur once or twice every summer in the lower elevations. Mean annual precipitation ranges from less than 35 inches (89 cm) along the Vermont line to over 41 inches (104 cm) in the south central part of the county, while mean seasonal snowfall varies from less than 55 inches (140 cm) in the lower parts of the south to around 70 inches (178 cm) in the high country east of Lake George. Primeval forest cover consisted predominantly of varieties of northern hardwoods. An Alleghenian hardwood community dominated by beech, sugar maple, hemlock, white pine, and basswood blanketed the Taconic Mountains and the lower elevations between Lake Champlain and Fort Edward, while an Adirondack hardwood community dominated by beech, sugar maple, yellow birch, hemlock, white pine, red spruce, and balsam fir cloaked the high country east of Lake George. The Hudson Lowland south of Fort Edward supported a central hardwood forest of beech, sugar maple, basswood, oak, and chestnut, except for a narrow band of oak-pine forest along the Hudson. Presently, over 55% of Washington Co is forested. The mountainous region east of Lake George lies within the Adirondack Park.

American Indians and Early Settlement

Archaeologists have dated the Little Wood Creek site along the Hudson River at Fort Edward to *ca* 6000 BC. Over 2,000 years of habitation ended around 3100 BC because of incessant flooding but resumed around AD 1000. In the Contact period, the present Washington Co was used for hunting by the Mohawks from the west and perhaps the Mohicans (Mahicans) from the south, but is thought to have been largely uninhabited. By the Revolution most native people were gone; the few who remained were intermarried with non-natives.

In 1709 during Queen Anne's War the British built three fortifications in the area: Fort Saraghtoga at Easton, Fort Nicholson, and Fort Anne [now Fort Ann]. The first European settler was Col John Henry Lydius, who built a house and a fur-trading post (*ca* 1730) near the ruins of Fort Nicholson to support his land claim. His settlement was attacked and burned by the French in 1745. The French and Indian War was the defining event of the colonial period. In 1755 the British rebuilt Fort Anne and Fort Nicholson. The latter, renamed Fort Edward, was the most important of that war's fortifications in the present county. Some veterans of the war received land as bounties and, with the end of hostilities in 1760, became permanent settlers. The first important settlement was Skenesborough [now Whitehall], founded by Maj Philip Skene in 1759. Scots and Scots-Irish settled Argyle and New Perth [now Salem]; German Moravians settled the Camden Valley; and those of Dutch descent settled in Easton. English immigrants and New England migrants settled throughout the county. By 1770 initial settlement had been made except in the northwestern towns of Dresden and Putnam and the interior town of Hartford, all of which were occupied immediately after the Revolution. The 1790 census recorded 46 slaves and 3 free Blacks in the county. The latter number increased to 119 in 1800, by which time Slyboro, a substantial free black community, had formed in Granville.

The Revolution severely divided the county's residents. A large number were loyalists, especially in Whitehall, Kingsbury, and Fort Edward. Gen John Burgoyne's 1777 campaign was waged throughout the county, with major battles at Skenesborough (the campaign's only naval battle), Fort Ann, and Fort Edward. The last was

WASHINGTON CO POPULATION CENSUS FIGURES

	White	Nonwhite	Total Population	Foreign-Born
1790	13,992	50	14,042	—
1800	35,375	199	35,574	—
1810	41,159	3,130[a]	44,289	—
1820	38,427	404	38,831	233
1830	42,242	393	42,635	749
1840	40,808	272	41,080	—
1850	44,400	350	44,750	6,004
1860	45,645	259	45,904	6,656
1870	49,186	382	49,568	8,294
1880	47,523	348	47,871	6,354
1890	45,438	252	45,690	5,864
1900	45,379	245	45,624	5,220
1910	47,576	202	47,778	6,106
1920	44,646	242	44,888	4,217
1930	46,087	395	46,482	3,803
1940	46,189	537	46,726	2,963
1950	46,640	504	47,144	2,264
1960	47,916	560	48,476	1,739
1970	51,906	819	52,725	1,197
1980	53,429	1,366	54,795	1,215
1990	56,665	2,665	59,330	1,284
2000	57,973	3,069	61,042	1,153

Notes: "Nonwhite" includes African Americans, Asians, American Indians, and Pacific Islanders and, for 2000, also the mixed race and other race categories. Through the 1960 census these figures primarily reflect the African American population. Foreign-born figures for 1820 and 1830 include only those not naturalized, and for 1930 and 1950, the foreign-born totals include Whites only. Other years include all foreign-born in the population.

[a]This anomalous figure appeared as such in the original census data.

the site of the murder of Jane McCrea in 1777, presumably at the hands of Indians allied to the British. This became a patriot cause célèbre. In raids of 1780 Maj Guy Carleton seized Fort Ann and set properties afire belonging to patriot, loyalist, and neutral residents alike. Much of Charlotte Co's territory was lost to Vermont independence on 15 Jan 1777. Cambridge, Easton, Salem, Hebron, Granville, Skenesborough, Fort Edward, and Kingsbury voted to unite with Vermont in May 1781, but with New York State's arrest of several leaders and threat of war with Vermont, the towns reversed their vote.

Transportation

The earliest transportation routes in Washington Co were the Hudson River and the Lake George–Lake Champlain corridor. Fort Edward, long referred to as the Great Carrying Place, was the critical link between the Mohawk and Hudson Rivers and Lakes George and Champlain. Native Americans and Europeans alike carried canoes around the falls at Fort Edward, Hudson Falls, and Glens Falls as they made their way along the Hudson into the deep Adirondacks or to Lake George, or north from Fort Edward along Little Wood and Wood Creeks to Lake Champlain. Routes that existed in colonial times as trade routes became toll roads in the early 19th century. The Post Rd [now Rte 40] went from Lansingburgh (Rensselaer Co) to Whitehall; the Great Northern Turnpike [now Rte 22] connected Cambridge, Salem, and Granville; and the road from Schuylerville (Saratoga Co) to Sandy Hill [now Hudson Falls] is now Rte 4. A steamboat connected Whitehall with the north end of Lake Champlain beginning in ?1809. The natural water routes were improved by the Champlain Canal (1823) from Whitehall to Waterford (Saratoga Co). This gradually shifted the economic and political power to canal towns, especially Fort Edward, Kingsbury, and Whitehall.

From 1848 to 1875 railroads spread across the county. The Saratoga and Washington Railroad (1848) linked Fort Edward to Whitehall. Salem developed as the county's eastern rail center beginning with the establishment of the Albany Northern Railroad (1853). Both lines became part of the Delaware and Hudson in 1871. The Greenwich and Johnsonville Railroad began service in the southern part of the county in 1870. Finally, Whitehall was linked by rail in 1875 to Ticonderoga (Essex Co), Plattsburgh, and beyond. Interurban lines and trolleys were acquired by the Delaware and Hudson Railroad in 1906 and forged into a system called the Hudson Valley Railway, which operated until 1928. Rail, both as a means of transportation and as a source of employment, remained important through the 1920s but declined drastically after 1945. In the early 21st century Amtrak provides passenger service to Fort Edward and Whitehall on tracks of the Canadian Pacific Railroad. The Batten Kill Railroad freight and excursion short line began operations in the southern towns in 1994.

Economic Development

Agricultural, mineral, and timber-related industries have consistently made up the largest sectors of the economy. Industry was shaped by available resources and abundant waterpower for sawmills and gristmills. Clearing the forests in the late 18th and the 19th centuries created a thriving lumber industry, especially in the areas near the Hudson River and Lake Champlain, where logs could be rafted to market. Early industry included iron ore mining and smelting in Fort Ann, and quarrying, lime production, and brickmaking elsewhere. The construction of toll roads and bridges between 1800 and 1820 opened the interior of the county to development and to increased communication among market towns and with the blossoming shipping trade in Lansingburgh. Although flax, grain, cheese, wool, and lumber were at first produced for local consumption, they soon went south to Lansingburgh and north to Whitehall for shipment. Wool from Cambridge, Salem, and Granville was the county's chief export until the 1840s. There were sawmills and cabinet shops in many towns. In Granville, Hampton, Hebron, Kingsbury, Salem, and Whitehall, slate and other stone quarries emerged. Granville's slate industry began about 1853 and continues to flourish in the early 21st century. Graphite, iron, and flint were mined in Dresden in the 19th century, while stoneware was an important 19th-century industry in Fort Edward, Greenwich, and Kingsbury. Hilfinger Bros Pottery in Fort Edward survived until 1942.

By 1785 wing dams were constructed on the Hudson River at Sandy Hill and Fort Edward for power. Later dams diverted water to the canal system and attracted paper mills, foundries, and machine shops. From the 1870s on, wood pulp supplanted cotton rags for papermaking. George Underwood's paper mill at Fort Edward was one of the original consortium of 19 that formed International Paper Co. Between 1875 and 1910, Sandy Hill became the county's largest industrial center. The Sandy Hill Iron and Brass Co (later Sandy Hill Corp) became a national producer of papermaking machinery.

Merino sheep, introduced around 1810, were well suited to the county's rugged, thin-soiled hill pastures. Granville, Hartford, Salem, Greenwich, and other towns had woolen mills, employing women and children as carders. Wool, flax, imported cotton, and, later, silk became the basis for a countywide textile industry that was at its peak from 1850 to 1930. The Manhattan Shirt Co had mills in Salem and Fort Edward, while Dunbarton Flax Mill manufactured linen thread in Greenwich from 1880 to 1952.

Agriculture grew rapidly from 1840 to 1900. Turnpikes and canals facilitated shipment of cheese, butter, apples, and wool. By 1870 beef and dairy cattle had replaced sheep as the most numerous farm animal. In 1875 there were 346,518 acres (140,231 ha) of farmland producing grains, apples, maple sugar, pork, beef, dairy products, poultry, and eggs. Cheese manufacturing proliferated after the Civil War, with 11 factories producing 749,876 pounds (340,138 kg) of cheese in 1874. Fluid-milk production rose as a result of faster rail transportation and pasteurization. The county was also a center of potato cultivation. Agriculture-related businesses included Greenwich's W. Eddy Plow Co (1835–1956), a major producer of farm machinery in the state, and Cambridge's Rice Seed Co (1832), which closed in 1976.

A limited resort business developed in the late 19th century on the eastern shore of Lake

POPULATIONS OF TOWNS, WASHINGTON CO

Town, Year Founded	1800	1840	1880	1920	1960	2000
Argyle, 1771[a]	4,597	3,111	2,775	1,535	1,898	3,688
Cambridge, 1772[b]	6,187	2,005	2,324	1,620	1,610	2,152
Dresden, 1822[c]	—	679	730	495	426	677
Easton, 1789	3,069	2,988	2,740	1,851	1,681	2,259
Fort Ann, 1786[d]	2,502	3,559	3,263	2,357	3,124	6,417
Fort Edward, 1818	—	1,726	4,680	5,845	6,523	5,892
Granville, 1786	3,175	3,846	4,149	4,966	5,015	6,456
Greenwich, 1803	—	3,382	3,860	4,268	3,969	4,896
Hampton, 1786	700	972	833	552	469	871
Hartford, 1793	2,108	2,164	1,760	1,102	1,058	2,279
Hebron, 1786	2,528	2,498	2,383	1,184	1,026	1,773
Jackson, 1815	—	1,730	1,562	836	795	1,718
Kingsbury, 1762[a]	1,651	2,773	4,614	7,336	11,012	11,171
Putnam, 1806	—	784	611	528	490	645
Salem, 1764[a]	2,861	2,855	3,498	2,235	2,258	2,702
White Creek, 1815	—	2,195	2,742	2,170	2,365	3,411
Whitehall, 1763[a]	1,604	3,813	5,347	6,008	4,757	4,035

Note: In 1800 Washington Co included the Towns of Bolton, Chester, Lake Luzerne [then Fairfield], Queensbury, and Thurman [now in Warren Co].

[a]Date of first town meeting.

[b]Formed as district; recognized as town 1788.

[c]South Bay when formed; renamed same year.

[d]Westfield until 1808.

George. Later, cottages were built around Summit Lake, Cossayuna Lake, Hedges Lake, and Lake Lauderdale. The sole survivor among the era's grand hotels is the recently renovated Cambridge Hotel (1884), which claims to be the place of origin of pie à la mode.

Immigration and Ethnicity

Washington Co's population increased steadily in the first half of the 19th century, peaking in 1870 at 49,568. Thereafter, through 1960, the population stayed between 44,000 and 49,000. Immigrant populations concentrated in the villages that were rail centers. There were substantial influxes of Francophone Canadians (1820s–1850s) and Irish (1840s–1880s). In 1875 the county was 3% Canadian-born and 9.5% Irish-born. Welsh settled in Granville in the 1850s to work the slate quarries and amounted to 7% of the town's population in 1865; they were joined later by Ruthenians. From 1890 to 1930 Poles, Czechs, Hungarians, Greeks, Scots, Italians, and Lithuanians predominated on immigrant rolls. Italians, settling most heavily in the corridor along the Champlain Canal, made up 10–20% of the Villages of Fort Edward, Hudson Falls, and Whitehall. A small Finnish community formed in Shushan in the early 20th century, and the saunas they built are still in evidence a century later.

Religion, Education, and Culture

In the colonial and federal periods religious communities abounded, including a Scots-Irish Presbyterian community that settled in Salem in 1764. Presbyterians from Scotland settled the Argyle Patent the same year. Moravians settled in the Camden Valley [now in Salem] about 1770 and maintained a congregation with a settled pastor until 1869. Quakers from Rhode Island settled in the Towns of Easton and White Creek. Philip Embury and Barbara Heck, founders of Methodism in North America, settled Ash Grove [now in White Creek]. The county's first Roman Catholic congregation was established by Quebecois immigrants to Whitehall in the late 1830s; a church was built in 1841. Rev William Miller started the Millerite movement, the forerunner of Seventh-day Adventism, in Low Hampton in 1843. His chapel and home are maintained as a museum. In 1855 the county had 28 Methodist, 22 Presbyterian, and 19 Baptist churches. Episcopal and Quaker congregations, at five each, were next. New Skete (1967) in White Creek is a community affiliated with the Orthodox Church in America.

The *Northern Centinel* (1798) was the county's first newspaper, published at Salem; it became the *Washington County Post* in 1814 and continued until 1988. In the early 21st century there are four weeklies: the *Eagle* in Cambridge, the *Whitehall Times,* the *Granville Sentinel,* and the *Greenwich/Salem Journal Press.* One of the earliest formally incorporated libraries was the Argyle Library (1805). Hubbard Hall (1878) in Cambridge has been restored and is an active performing arts and community center. Other cultural institutions include the Fort Salem Theater (1971) and the Mettawee Valley Theater Co (1975). Museums include the Pember Museum (natural history) and the Slate Valley Museum, both in Granville; the Georgi Museum in Shushan; the Skenesborough Museum in Whitehall; and the Old Fort House in Fort Edward.

The first private school was Salem Academy (1791). The largest was the Fort Edward Institute (1854–1910), which had over 500 students at the time of its destruction by fire in 1910. The earliest Union Free School was in Sandy Hill in 1867. By 1910 most villages had formed Union Free Schools, resulting in the loss of private schools. Centralization began in Putnam in 1928; Whitehall was the last central district created, shortly after 1958. In 2003 there were 10 central districts in the county, along with Fort Edward Union Free School district.

Politics

Masonic lodges influenced town government and the formation of political organizations. Fort Edward's Washington Lodge was the first of 17 founded between 1785 and 1813. Abolitionism was a political force in Greenwich and Easton, and the woman suffrage movement had strongholds in Fort Edward, Easton, and Kingsbury. Significant labor unions included, by 1900, the Bricklayers International Union and the International Brotherhood of Pulp, Sulfite, and Paper Mill Workers.

Fort Edward was the original county seat, but courts were established at Salem in 1787. Fort Edward lost its designation to Sandy Hill in 1797. The half-shire system continued until 1991 when all courts were again held in Fort Edward. A board composed of the 17 town supervisors governs the county, with voting weighted according to population. The board employs a professional county manager for day-to-day operations.

Recent History

County government emerged as a political and economic force after World War I, with establishment of county health and veterans' programs, the building of county highways, and rural electrification. County government expanded further under New Deal programs. The paper industry expanded during World War II and the postwar years, notably with Decora (1945–2002) in Fort Edward; the catheter industry emerged in 1955; and General Electric plants were established in Hudson Falls and Fort Edward. Sandy Hill Corp (1857–1990) continued a substantial business in Hudson Falls. This renewed industry was relatively short-lived, and by the 1970s the county's manufacturing base was in decline. In 2000 the county had half the manufacturing jobs of 50 years earlier. By 1975 most independent dairies and cheese plants had closed. The county's last private bus line closed in 1964, and its last movie theater, the Strand in Hudson Falls, closed in the 1970s. Many churches, granges, and other social organizations countywide were discontinued.

Although the county remains primarily agricultural, farms are fewer and larger because of consolidation. Between 1950 and 1997 the number of farms dropped from 2,349 to 738, and the agricultural acreage from 384,889 (155,759 ha) to 194,962 (78,898 ha). Nevertheless, the county still ranks 12th in the state in agricultural production. Dairy accounts for 75% of agricultural sales. Bentley Seeds and Rice Seed Co continue packing seeds in Cambridge in the early 21st century. Specialty farmers serving the Saratoga Springs market have been increasingly successful; there were more than 20 such operations in 2003. Manufacturing is less concentrated and mostly smaller in scale, but it still provides many jobs. General Electric and Irving Tissue Co remain industrial employers in Fort Edward. Hollingsworth and Vose Co (paper) has locations at Clark Mills and Center Falls. The Toy Works at Middle Falls, Phantom Laboratories (prosthetic devices) in the Town of Greenwich, and Telescope Folding Furniture Co in Granville employ a significant number of county residents, as do two prisons at Comstock. The Willard Mountain ski area (1957) operates in Easton.

Suburbanization, first in the areas nearest Glens Falls (Warren Co) and then more generally throughout Washington Co, led to a 20% increase in population between 1960 and 2000, and many areas became bedroom communities for the Capital District. Abandoned farmland, coupled with minimal or no zoning, has fueled unplanned growth. This growth and the decay or loss of several county landmarks have spurred grassroots preservation efforts, which are buttressed by the increasing conversion of older homes to seasonal residences by weekenders from the Capital District and the New York City area. Sharp philosophical divisions are emerging over the issues of planning and zoning.

Prominent persons raised in the county include Pres Chester A. Arthur (1829–86) from Greenwich; suffragist Susan B. Anthony (1820–1906) from Battenville; Solomon Northup (1808–60), author of a well-known slave captivity narrative and resident of Granville, Kingsbury, and Fort Edward at various times; engineer George Henry Corliss (1817–88) from Easton; pioneer American diplomat to Japan Townsend Harris (1804–78) from Hudson Falls; and artist Grandma Moses (1860–1961) from Greenwich.

The standard reference is Crisfield Johnson, *History of Washington County* (1878). Other sources include *History and Biography of Washington County* (1894) and William L. Stone, *Washington County, New York: Its History to the Close of the 19th Century* (1901). Early community histories include Elisha P. Thurston, *History of the Town of Greenwich* (1876); Robert O. Bascom, *The Fort Edward Book* (1903); and William Henry Hill, *Old Fort Edward before 1800* (1929), with addenda (1957). Isabella Brayton with John B. Norton, *The Story of Hartford* (1929) is quite comprehensive. Valuable local histories from the late 20th century include Hebron Preservation Society, *Hebron: A Century in Review* (1987); *Old Cambridge* (1988); Katharine Tomasi, *The Village of Salem, 1761–1994* (1995); James MacNaughton Jr, *The Argyle Patent and Its Early Settlers* (1999); and two collections of personal reminiscences by the Argyle History Group, *I Remember Argyle* (1996) and *Argyle, My Argyle* (1998).

Among notable topical works is William H. Hill, *History of Washington County, NY: The Gibson Papers; The History of Washington Academy; The Bench and Bar of Washington County for a Century* (1932). Alice R. Loughlin, *Sto Lat: 100 Years on River Street* (1996) is the history of a Lithuanian colony in Hudson Falls. William A. Cormier, *Next Year in Salem: A Chronicle of the Home Front During World War II* (1996) is among the best of its kind, and William T. Ruddock, *Linen Threads and Broom Twines*, 2 vols (1997) is an extraordinary study that reconstructs the labor force of the Dunbarton Mill at Greenwich. Additionally, see Joseph A. Cutshall-King and the Italian Heritage Committee, *Con Amore: The Italian History of Fort Edward, NY* (2001). The county's architectural heritage is documented in Washington County Planning Department, *An Introduction to Historic Resources in Washington County*, 2d ed (1984), which updates the century-old county histories. Also useful is Kenneth A. Parry, comp, *The Fitch Gazetteer: An Annotated Index to the Manuscript History of Washington County, New York*, 4 vols (1999).

Joseph A. Cutshall-King

Washington's Headquarters State Historic Site. Located in Newburgh (Orange Co) and known as the Hasbrouck House, it served as George Washington's residence from April 1782 to August 1783, longer than any of his other Revolutionary War headquarters. The 8.5-acre (3.4 ha) property features a colonial stone house built possibly as early as 1718 and added to in stages by merchant and mill owner Jonathan Hasbrouck between 1750 and 1770. Washington's notable accomplishments while in residence at Newburgh included his rejection of the suggestion that the new nation become a monarchy with him as its head and his brilliant suppression of the upheaval provoked by the Newburgh Addresses. Beginning in the 1830s national attention focused on preserving the old house. In 1849 the state loan commissioners acquired the property, which in 1850 became the nation's first publicly owned historic site. In 1886–87 the Tower of Victory was erected to commemorate the Revolutionary War events of 1783, and in 1910 a brick museum building was added to the property. Today the site is maintained and operated by the Palisades Interstate Park Commission and the State Office of Parks, Recreation, and Historic Preservation.

Anthony, Walter C. *Washington's Headquarters, Newburgh, New York* (Newburgh, NY: Historical Society of Newburgh Bay and the Highlands, 1928)

Paul R. Huey

Washingtonville. Village (pop 5,851) in Blooming Grove (Orange Co). Settled in 1731 and called Little York in its early days, it acquired a post office in 1813 named Blooming Grove. Although the community was renamed Washingtonville in 1818, the post office was not until 1875. The Brotherhood Winery (1839) is the oldest in the United States in continuous operation and produced communion wines during Prohibition. The Newburgh Branch of the Erie Railroad provided service beginning in 1850. A creamery and a wood-products factory were in operation in the 1880s. The village incorporated in 1895. The Moffat Library (1887), with its Tiffany windows, is listed on the National Register. The Grape Harvest Festival has been an annual October event since 1997.

Anthony Knipp

water and hydrology. New York State is a well-watered land with a rich and varied array of water resources. Partially bounded by Lake Champlain, Great Lakes Erie and Ontario, and the Atlantic Ocean, the state contains thousands of waterbodies that range from farm dugout ponds to the many Adirondack lakes and the renowned Finger Lakes. Similarly the state is drained by some of the largest or otherwise most important rivers in the eastern United States like the Allegheny, Niagara, Susquehanna, St. Lawrence, Delaware, Mohawk, and Hudson, along with a dense web of lesser rivers and tributaries. In addition the state is underlain by numerous groundwater aquifers. Sustained by precipitation amounts that average nearly 100 billion gallons (378.5 billion l) a day, these fresh and saline waters flow in prodigious quantities, contribute to a myriad of uses, and are increasingly well managed for a sustainable future.

HYDROGRAPHY AND FORMATION

New York State contains all or part of 17 major watersheds, geographical surface areas that drain to a stream, river, wetland, lake, and coastal water. These 17 watersheds are part of 3 of the 18 first-order watersheds delineated in the conterminous United States by the US Geological Survey, known by Hydrologic Unit Codes (HUCs) 02, 04, and 05, or Mid-Atlantic, Great Lakes, and Ohio. Seventeen watershed regions were established by the New York State Department of Environmental Conservation (DEC) as an aid in conserving and developing the state's water. The watersheds typically extend into two or more of New York's nine primary physiographic provinces whose distinct geology strongly influences their form and character.

Below the earth's surface, subsurface or groundwater reserves are also affected by physiographic structure. Reserves capable of supplying wells with substantial amounts of water are called aquifers. The principal aquifers are found in three types of environment: unconsolidated glacial deposits, unconsolidated coastal plain sediments, and consolidated bedrock. The un-

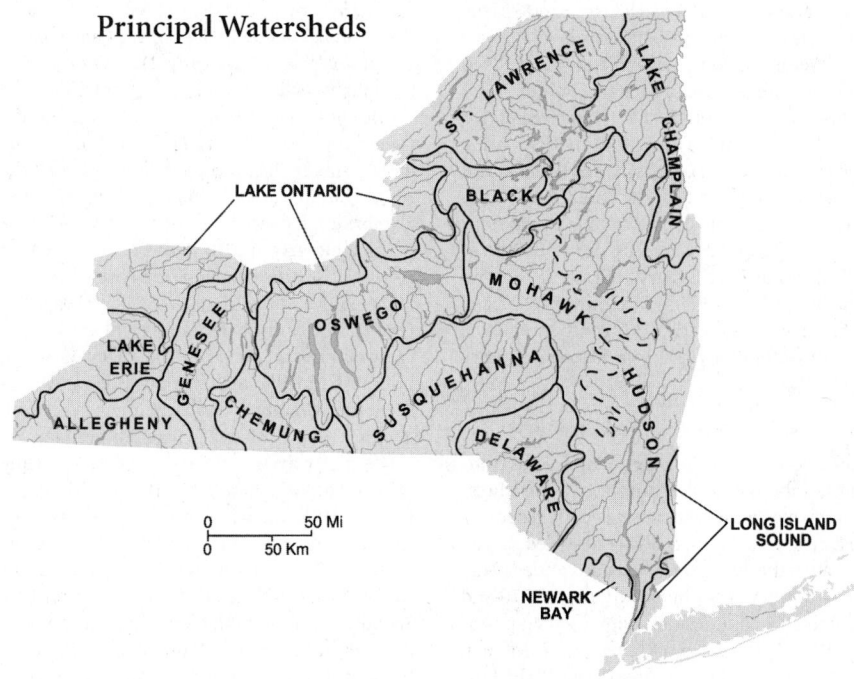

Principal Watersheds

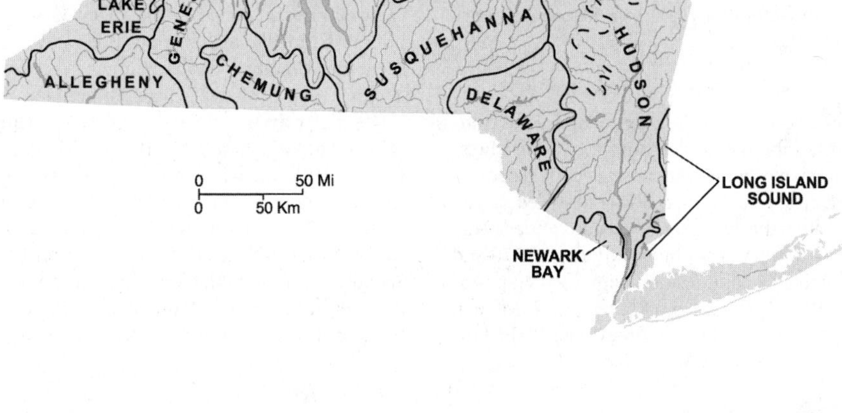

GEOGRAPHICAL EXTENT OF WATER RESOURCES

Surface Water Resources	
Perennial rivers/streams	46,266 mi (74,458 km)
Intermittent rivers/streams	5,075 mi (8,167 km)
Canals/ditches	547 mi (880 km)
Rivers bordering Pa, Vt, NJ, and Canada	448 mi (721 km)
Lakes/reservoirs/ponds (7,849)	790,782 acres (320,018 ha)
Bays/estuaries/harbors	979,200 acres (396,268 ha)
Wetland Resources	
Freshwater wetlands	2,400,000 acres (971,246 ha)
Tidal wetlands	25,000 acres (10,117 ha)
Groundwater Resources	
Primary Long Island aquifers (2)	951,859 acres (385,204 ha)
Primary upstate aquifers (18)	1,269,146 acres (513,605 ha)
Principal aquifers[a]	3,553,608 acres (1,438,094 ha)
Shoreline and Coastline Resources	
Great Lakes shoreline	577 mi (929 km)
Ocean coastline	120 mi (193 km)

Source: NYS Department of Environmental Conservation, Division of Water, *New York State Water Quality 2000* (2000).

Note: New York State has a surface area of 49,576 mi^2 (128,401 km^2), or 31,728,640 acres (12,840,125 ha).

[a]Highly productive aquifers not presently intensively used.

Compiled by Theodore A. Endreny

consolidated glacial deposits were formed in four general classes: ice-deposited unsorted and unstratified till ranging from clay to boulders; meltwater-deposited outwash materials of stratified sand and gravel; ice-contact deposits of poorly stratified sand and gravel; and glacial lake deposits consisting of clay, silt, and fine clay. The coastal plain aquifer is principally fine to medium sand with some clay and coarse sand and gravel. Consolidated bedrock aquifers are formed in limestone, dolomite, and marble carbonate rocks; in sandstone, conglomerate, siltstone, and shale; in pegmatite, granite, granodiorite, diorite, and gabbro igneous rocks; and in argillite, slate, quartzite, schist, and gneiss metamorphic rocks.

Study of a New York State topographical map illustrates the basic fluvial networks, where most of the Appalachian Plateau and much of the Adirondacks drain southward, and the interior lowlands and western and northern Adirondacks drain north; in-between lies the east-west-oriented Erie Canal. Nearly all of the state's natural waterbodies were influenced by the erosional and depositional actions of continental glaciation. Glacial debris and meltwater formed Long Island, while advancing ice and huge quantities of meltwater helped create the 11 Finger Lakes and alter the forms of Lake Erie, Lake Ontario, Lake Champlain, and St. Lawrence River drainage patterns. In New York's mountainous areas, glacial scouring and meltwater forces accentuated the already present steep river drainage systems, while melting of remnant ice blocks helped form numerous Adirondack lakes and ponds.

Human intervention has also affected the extent of New York's surface water–resource features by creating an extensive canal system, draining and filling thousands of acres of wetland, damming dozens of large rivers for drinking water, hydropower, and flood control, altering the course of thousands of smaller streams, and constructing thousands of farm and recreational ponds. Natural forces of erosion and beaver activity continue to alter the surface hydrography. Well drilling and the pumping of freshwater groundwater reserves have created linkages between distinct aquifers, sometimes mixing saline and fresh water.

Bisecting and connecting each watershed are complex fluvial and lacustrine networks, many with well-known names such as Niagara, St. Lawrence, Delaware, Hudson, Mohawk, and Susquehanna. New York State streams often take the generic name of Brook, Creek, or Kill, a pattern that suggests the varied cultural backgrounds of explorers and early settlers. Larger streams and lakes often function as political boundaries. Conversely watersheds do not normally conform to political boundaries, and only a portion of the state's 17 watersheds lie entirely within the state. The arrangement and ratio of land area to waterbody area in each watershed affects the magnitude and rate of water-level response to rainfall-runoff events. Differences vary tremendously across the state and sometimes within a single watershed, a circumstance that compounds water-management concerns.

SUPPLIES

New York State receives on average 40 inches (102 cm) of liquid-equivalent precipitation each year, which amounts to a supply of 98.4 billion gallons (372.4 billion l) daily from rain and snow. The average flow into Lake Ontario from the upper four Great Lakes brings an additional 1.4 trillion gallons (5.3 trillion l) daily. These precipitation inputs are measured by using a network of roughly 200 gaging stations and a handful of overlapping radar sites. Historic weather records of more than 105 years of state precipitation and snow events, referred to as climate data, are available through the Northeast Regional Climate Center at Cornell University. The range of precipitation values across New York is wide because of significant differences in topography, which encourage, trigger, or block storms, from sea-level beaches to windward and leeward sides of high mountains. Annual precipitation amounts, both rain and liquid equivalent snow (about 10% of snow depth), range from 30 to 66 inches (76–168 cm). Peak values reflect orographic processes within the Catskill and Adirondack Mountains; overall, frontal and convectional precipitation processes cause rain amounts to increase from the north to the south. Snow constitutes between 6 and 30% of these totals. Annual nonliquid snow depths range on average from less than 30 inches (76 cm) along the Atlantic coast of Long Island to nearly 300 inches (762 cm) of lake effect snows atop the Tug Hill Plateau, a range that makes statewide averages of limited value.

The temporal distribution of these events is familiar to most state residents, with summer convective showers, autumnal frontal storms, winter lake effect and midlatitude cyclone snows, and spring frontal storms. The distribution of liquid-equivalent monthly precipitation is nearly constant at 3.3 inches (8.4 cm) throughout the year. El Niño Southern Oscillation events that disrupt distant Pacific Ocean temperatures and pressures through teleconnections impact New York weather, generally causing a 5–15% decrease in precipitation and an increase of a few degrees in winter temperatures. The colder La Niña events cause increases in winter precipitation.

Precipitated water may be temporarily stored or detained at the ground surface but is ultimately divided between storm runoff, evaporation, and infiltration processes into surface water, atmospheric water, and groundwater storage. Evaporation amounts range across the state between 16 and 24 inches (41–61 cm) annually, with an average of 20 inches (51 cm), or 50% of average precipitation. The remaining water, both surface and subsurface storage, is considered runoff and varies from 10 to 40 inches (25–102 cm) across the state. An average of 49.2 billion gallons (186.2 billion l) go into recharging New York's surface- and subsurface-water supplies each day; an equivalent amount is returned to the atmosphere. The temporal distribution of runoff and evaporation is not as even as precipitation, with low evaporation in the winter allowing for large spring and early summer snowmelts causing the greatest flows, and high evaporation throughout the spring and summer causing the lowest flows at the end of summer.

The geographical extent of New York State's surface-water and groundwater resources is impressive, with nearly 8,000 lakes, reservoirs, and ponds covering 2.5% of the state, and a far greater number of inland wetlands covering 7.6%. The distribution of surficial sand and gravel aquifers trends closely with major rivers and valleys. The Magothy and Lloyd aquifers underlie the coastal plain of Long Island; carbonate rock aquifers outline the Appalachian Plateau, Adirondack, and Hudson Valley physiographic provinces; and sandstone aquifers are principally located in the Great Lakes Lowland and St. Lawrence Valley regions.

DEMANDS

New York State's public policy is to conserve and develop state waters for all beneficial uses. An enormous average volume of 16.8 billion gallons (63.6 billion l) of water is withdrawn each day from state water resources. Of this 54% is from surface-freshwater sources and 6% from groundwater. The remaining 40% is saline water and is used principally for thermoelectric power generation. Conversely average daily recharge is 49.2 billion gallons (186.2 billion l) with excess draining to the Atlantic Ocean.

While nonconsumptive withdrawals return 10.1 billion gallons (38.2 billion l) of freshwater to the natural system, they may adversely affect water functions (eg, fish migration) and quality (eg, discharge of wastewater). Water is central to the state's power generation, operated in part by the New York State Power Authority and private firms. Major hydropower facilities are the St. Lawrence–Franklin D. Roosevelt Power Project (800,000 kW), the Niagara Power Project (2.4 million kW), and the Blenheim-Gilboa Pumped Storage Power Project (1.04 million kW). The Indian Point, James A. FitzPatrick, and Nine Mile Point Nuclear Power Plants use significant amounts of water for cooling purposes.

Recreation, ecological, and wildlife uses of the state's waters are mostly unmetered, but occur regularly in more than hundreds of state and county parks, wetlands, lakes, and rivers. Management of aquatic ecological resources is supervised by the DEC's Division of Fish, Wildlife, and Marine Resources, which oversees programs ranging from fishing and boating to protecting endangered species and restoration programs. Beginning in the 1950s state government has codified the management of water resources by balancing competing needs, such as flood protection and irrigation, commercial and recreational fishing, and navigation. Newer initiatives are expanding management to include ecological users, such as wetland communities.

Nearly 90% of New York's 18.2 million residents are served by roughly 3,200 public water supply (PWS) systems, and 73% of these supplies use surface-water sources. Nearly 67% of state households are supplied from surface waters, the remaining 33% by groundwater. The PWS is supplied by more than 5,200 wells, many grouped in productive well fields. More rural populations, including schools, cottages, and farms, are self-supplied or served by private water-supply systems, including over 13,000 groundwater wells. Water yield from groundwater wells is affected by numerous geophysical factors but generally range from 10 to 1,000 gallons (38–3,800 l) per minute in surficial aquifers, 50 to 1,200 gallons (190–4,540 l) per minute in Coastal Plain aquifers, and 10 to 100 gallons (38–380 l) per minute in carbonate aquifers.

US Environmental Protection Agency Safe Drinking Water Act requires most PWS systems to filter, flocculate, settle, and chlorinate the water prior to its distribution. The New York City and the City of Syracuse surface-fed PWS systems are among a half-dozen in the nation permitted to use unfiltered water. Nearly 90% of New York City's pristine drinking waters are collected in large reservoirs located in the Catskills and the Delaware Hills; Skaneateles Lake supplies most of Syracuse.

PRINCIPAL RIVERS OF NEW YORK STATE

	Length of Main Stream		Drainage Area	
Name	mi	km	mi^2	km^2
Great Lakes–St. Lawrence System	—	—	22,000	57,000.0[a]
Cattaraugus Creek	64	103.0	560	1,450.4
Buffalo River	8	12.9	420	1,087.8
Cazenovia Creek	37	59.6	141	365.2
Buffalo Creek	40	64.4	145	375.6
Cayuga Creek	34	54.7	127	328.9
Tonawanda-Ellicott Creeks	84	135.2	610	1,579.9
Genesee River	144	231.8	2,446	6,335.1
Black Creek	46	74.0	212	549.1
Oatka Creek	51	82.1	208	538.7
Caneadea Creek	14	22.5	63	163.2
Canaseraga Creek	36	57.9	341	883.2
Honeoye Creek	36	57.9	263	681.2
Oswego River	24	38.6[b]	5,002	12,955.1
Seneca River	60	96.6	3,433	8,891.4
Oneida River	18	29.0	1,404	3,636.3
Salmon River	44	70.8	285	738.1
Black River	112	180.3	1,930	4,998.7
Deer River	26	41.8	102	264.2
Moose River	53	85.3	416	1,077.4
Independence River	31	50.0	99	256.4
Beaver River	59	94.9	338	875.4
Oswegatchie River	133	214.0	1,609	4,167.3
Indian River	97	156.1	544	1,409.0
West Branch Oswegatchie River	35	56.3	272	704.5
Grass River	112	180.3	637	1,649.8
Raquette River	163	262.3	1,240	3,211.6
St. Regis River	77	123.9[c]	910	2,356.9
Deer River	46	74.0	212	549.1
West Branch St. Regis River	59	94.9	280	725.2
East Branch St. Regis River	32	51.5	347	898.7
Salmon River	46	74.0[c]	452	1,170.7[c]
Chateaugay River	30	48.3[c]	199	515.4[c]
Lake Champlain Drainage	—	—	2,950	7,640.5[c]
Great Chazy River	48	77.3	300	777.0
Saranac River	86	138.4	628	1,626.5
Ausable River	57	91.7	519	1,344.2
Boquet River	43	69.2	—	—
Lake George Outlet	2	3.2	229	593.1
Hudson River System	306	492.5	12,200	31,597.9[c]
Croton River	57	91.7	378	979.0
Fishkill Creek	32	51.5	204	528.4
Wappinger Creek	37	59.6	182	471.4
Rondout Creek	50	80.5	1,148	2,973.3
Wallkill River	53	85.3	567	1,468.5[c]
Esopus Creek	48	77.3	417	1,080.0
Catskill Creek	37	59.6	394	1,020.5
Kinderhook Creek	42	67.6	305	790.0[c]
Normans Kill	30	48.3	168	435.1
Poesten Kill	21	33.8	89	230.5
Mohawk River	148	238.2	3,400	8,806.0
Schoharie Creek	83	133.6	947	2,452.7
Otsquago Creek	15	24.1	60	155.4
East Canada Creek	34	54.7	286	740.7
West Canada Creek	75	120.7	569	1,473.7
Oriskany Creek	27	43.5	146	378.1
Hoosic River	57	91.7	730	1,890.7[d]
Batten Kill	53	85.3	460	1,191.4[d]
Fish Creek (to Saratoga Lake)	8	12.9	253	655.3
Kayaderosseras Creek	32	51.5	—	—
Sacandaga River	84	135.2	1,055	2,732.4
East Stony Creek	23	37.0	212	549.1
East Branch Sacandaga River	31	49.9	124	321.2
West Branch Sacandaga River	29	46.7	240	621.6
Middle Branch Sacandaga River	23	37.0	115	297.9
Schroon River	45	72.4	550	1,424.5
Indian River	35	56.3	160+	414.4+
Cedar River	35	56.3	—	—

PRINCIPAL RIVERS OF NEW YORK STATE *(continued)*

	Length of Main Stream		Drainage Area	
Name	mi	km	mi^2	km^2
Allegheny River System	325	523.0	2,100	5,439.0[b]
Allegheny River	47	75.6[a]	1,330	3,444.7[b]
Great Valley Creek	23	37.0	145	375.6
Conewango Creek	36	57.9[a]	770	1,994.3[e]
Chadakoin River	6	9.7[b]	343	888.4
Susquehanna River System	444[a]	714.6	6,267	16,231.5[b]
Chemung River	41	66.0[f]	2,518	6,521.6
Cohocton River	50	80.5	472	1,222.5
Tioga River	12	19.3	1,370	3,548.3[e]
Newtown Creek	16	25.8	—	—
Susquehanna River	158	254.3[b]	3,749	9,709.9[b]
Cayuta Creek	33	53.1	148	383.3
Owego Creek	30	48.3	391	1,012.7
Chenango River	85	136.8	1,582	4,097.4
Unadilla River	55	88.5	561	1,453.0
Otego Creek	26	41.8	110	284.9
Oaks Creek	24	38.6	103	266.8
Schenevus Creek	26	41.8	127	328.9
Charlotte Creek	31	49.9	178	461.0
Ouleout Creek	26	41.8	115	297.9
Delaware River System	140	225.3[b]	2,580	6,682.2
Neversink River	61	98.2	346	896.1
Mongaup River	30	48.3	204	528.4
Tenmile River	10	16.1	46	119.1
Callicoon Creek	19	30.6	112	290.1
West Branch Delaware River	73	117.5	685	1,774.1
Oquaga Creek	12	19.3	66	170.9
Trout Creek	14	22.5	50	129.5
Little Delaware River	15	24.1	53	137.3
East Branch Delaware River	62	99.8	919	2,380.2
Beaver Kill	37	59.6	322	834.0
Tremper Kill	11	17.7	35	90.6
Platte Kill	11	17.7	35	90.7
Long Island Streams	—	—	—	—
Connetquot Brook	9	14.5	24	62.2
Peconic River	18	29.0	75	194.3
Nissequogue River	10	16.1	30	77.7
Carmans River	11	17.7	71	183.9
Swan River	4	6.4	10	25.9
Patchogue River	4	6.4	15	38.9
Sampawams Creek	4	6.4	24	62.2
Carlls River	7	11.3	35	90.6
Massapequa Creek	6	9.7	38	98.4
East Meadow Brook	8	12.9	31	80.3
Long Island Sound–East River Drainage	—	—	—	—
Mamaroneck River	10	16.1	24	62.2
Tenmile River	24	38.6	204	528.4
Blind Brook	9	14.5	10	25.9
New York City Area (tidal estuaries)	—	—	—	—
East River	16	25.8	—	—
Harlem River	8	12.9	—	—
Arthur Kill	12	19.3	—	—

Source: J. H. Thompson, *Geography of New York State* (1977).

[a]Approximate.

[b]To junction of Oneida and Seneca Rivers.

[c]In New York State.

[d]Partly in Vermont.

[e]Partly in Pennsylvania.

[f]Between mouth and Painted Post.

Once used, drinking water is often treated, discharged, and reused by another community downstream. In 1999 there were 605 wastewater treatment plants (WTPs) in New York State regulated by the DEC with a daily total design flow of 3.7 billion gallons (14.0 billion l) of wastewater, or nearly 34% of the state's total daily freshwater demands. Secondary treatment of wastewater is achieved by 68% of the WTP facilities, which process 84% of the total design flow, and 28% of the WTPs provide tertiary treatment, processing only 7% of the total design flow. Residents without access to WTPs use on-site wastewater treatment, such as small septic systems or large galley systems, regulated by the DEC but inspected by county health offices.

Issues of Quantity

Persistent weather patterns can create a few sequential years that are wetter or drier than normal, but for the most part regular precipitation, runoff, and evaporation keep the hydrologic cycle churning, with little noted loss to water quantity. An exception to this is the loss of the state's wetland areas (including the burying of many urban streams), which are critical for flood- and storm-water control, erosion and sediment control, pollution treatment, groundwater replenishment, fish and wildlife habitat maintenance, and nutrient cycling. Since colonization, New York has seen nearly 50%, or 2.5 million acres (1.0 million ha) of wetlands drained or filled primarily for agriculture and development. More recently programs have been established to re-create wetlands. Between 1985 and 1995 the state constructed 37,000 acres (15,000 ha) while losing 22,000 acres (8,900 ha) of wetland.

Floods and droughts have affected human activities since initial occupance, and the science of managing for both remains inexact. The National Flood Insurance Program has required that any post-1979 construction be designed to avoid at least the 100-year floodwater level; most coastal communities and interstate highways are designed for 500-year maximum flood events. Many older homes and businesses, along with lesser roads, are not adequately protected from floodwaters. DEC's Bureau of Flood Protection works with the State Emergency Management Office to administer community outreach, flood mitigation, flood mapping, flood modeling, and flood insurance programs, plus rehabilitation, flood-control structure inspection, channel clearing, ice-jam response, coastal shore protection, coastal beach renewal, and emergency preparedness. The monitoring of stream discharge, actual and predicted precipitation, and flood watch and warning forecasting are done through the collaborative efforts of the US Geological Survey and the National Weather Service (NWS).

Droughts do not carry the alarm or sudden urgency of floods, but the gradual decline in water availability typically affects a much larger region. New York State's Drought Management Task Force (DMT) compares current stream flows, precipitation amounts, lake and reservoir storage levels, and groundwater levels with historic levels to anticipate the impact on drinking water supply. The agency uses the NWS Palmer Drought Severity Index to measure the impact that water shortages are having on agriculture. The four stages of drought include "watch" (to begin voluntary water conservation), "warning" (to intensify voluntary conservation and to develop local contingency plans), "emergency" (to impose mandatory conservation measures and to tap alternative supplies), and "disaster" (to try to obtain federal assistance). NYS Environmental Conservation Law requires use of water-saving plumbing fixtures to reduce water losses, and the DMT suggests numerous other indoor and outdoor conservation measures, such as filling the washer before running to maximize efficiency and watering gardens in the early morning to minimize evaporation losses.

Issues of Quality

Deterioration of water quality may result from altering the physical, chemical, or biological aquatic systems of a stream or watershed. New York State agencies regularly monitor water quality, and report their findings to the EPA and the STORET database. Surface fresh and saline waters and groundwaters are classified based on best use, such as drinking, bathing, fish propagation, fish survival, and recreation. Waters not meeting their classified best use because of physical, biological, or chemical pollutants are considered impaired. Water quality is monitored and assessed in using a rotating intensive basin study (RIBS) approach. This system coordinates the efforts of multiple agencies to sample a broad set of indicators in all of New York State's 17 watersheds within a five-year period. Some random "probabilistic" sampling is also done to reduce the bias of monitoring known polluters. RIBS also supports volunteer monitoring networks, such as the Hudson River Basin Watch.

Water-quality data are analyzed to determine and document the severity of water-use impairments in categories of aquatic life, water supply, fish consumption, shellfishing, public bathing, recreation, and aesthetics. When water uses that are precluded, impaired, stressed, or threatened, the waterbody is added to the Waterbody Inventory/Priority Waterbodies List, a program designed to track progress toward solutions. Drinking waters receive additional monitoring to ensure that maximum contaminant levels, set nationally under the Safe Drinking Water Act, are not exceeded. In 2002 it was determined that 312 of New York State wells, delivering 417 million gallons (1.58 billion l) per day and serving 93 PWS, were contaminated by organic pollutants.

Monitoring programs identify both sources and causes for surface and groundwater waterbody impairment. Categories for groundwater sources include material stockpiles, storage tanks, waste tailings, septic systems, landfills, hazardous waste spills, and saltwater intrusion. Groundwater contaminants are principally microbial, organic chemicals, nitrate, pesticides, petroleum products, and radon. Categories for surface-water sources include industrial point sources like industry, municipal wastewater plants, concentrated animal-feeding operations, combined sewer overflows, and urban stormwater runoff, while nonpoint sources (NPS) include agriculture, silviculture, construction, landfills, septic systems, habitat modification, atmospheric deposition, highway salt runoff, and erosion. Causes of water impairment include unknown toxics, pesticides, priority organics (polychlorinated biphenyls), metals, ammonia, chlorine, other inorganics, nutrients, pH, siltation, organic enrichment (low dissolved oxygen),

MAJOR LAKES AND RESERVOIRS OF NEW YORK STATE

Name	County	Area in mi^2 (km^2)	Maximum Depth in ft (m)
Lake Ontario[a]	—	3,446.0 (8,925.10)	802 (244.5)
Lake Erie[a]	Chautauqua, Erie	553.1 (1,432.52)	210 (64.0)
Lake Champlain[b]	Essex, Clinton	439.0 (1,137.00)	399 (121.6)
Oneida Lake	Oneida, Oswego	79.9 (206.94)	55 (16.8)
Seneca Lake	Seneca, Schuyler, Ontario, Yates	66.7 (172.75)	618 (188.4)
Cayuga Lake	Cayuga, Seneca, Tompkins	66.4 (171.98)	435 (132.6)
Lake George	Essex , Warren, Washington	44.4 (115.00)	187 (57.0)
Sacandaga Reservoir	Fulton, Saratoga	41.7 (108.00)	70 (21.3)
Chautauqua Lake	Chautauqua	20.9 (54.13)	77 (23.5)
Keuka Lake	Steuben, Yates	17.4 (45.07)	186 (56.7)
Black Lake	St. Lawrence	17.2 (44.55)	30 (9.1)
Canandaigua Lake	Ontario, Yates	16.6 (42.99)	274 (83.5)
Skaneateles Lake	Cortland, Cayuga, Onondaga	13.8 (35.74)	300 (91.4)
Ashokan Reservoir	Ulster	12.8 (33.15)	98 (29.9)
Cranberry Lake	St. Lawrence	10.7 (27.71)	38 (11.6)
Owasco Lake	Cayuga	10.3 (26.68)	177 (54.0)
Carry Falls Reservoir	St. Lawrence	10.1 (26.16)	50 (15.2)
Pepacton Reservoir	Delaware	8.9 (23.05)	180 (54.9)
Raquette Lake	Hamilton	8.5 (22.01)	96 (29.3)
Upper Saranac Lake	Franklin	8.2 (21.24)	100 (30.5)
Indian Lake	Hamilton	6.9 (17.87)	80 (24.4)
Saratoga Lake	Saratoga	6.8 (17.61)	96 (29.3)
Schroon Lake	Essex, Warren	6.6 (17.09)	121 (36.9)
Otsego Lake	Otsego	6.2 (16.06)	168 (51.2)
Big Tupper Lake	St. Lawrence, Franklin	6.1 (15.80)	90 (27.4)
Long Lake	Hamilton	6.0 (15.50)	45 (13.7)
Conesus Lake	Livingston	5.1 (13.21)	66 (20.1)
Hinckley Reservoir	Herkimer, Oneida	5.1 (13.21)	75 (22.9)
Redfield Reservoir (Salmon River Reservoir)	Oswego	5.0 (12.95)	50 (15.2)
Onondaga Lake	Onondaga	4.8 (12.43)	73 (22.3)
Lake Placid	Essex	4.4 (11.40)	150 (45.7)
Beaver River Flow (Stillwater Reservoir)	Herkimer	4.2 (10.88)	60 (18.3)
Delta Reservoir	Oneida	4.0 (10.36)	60 (18.3)
Piseco Lake	Hamilton	4.0 (10.36)	129 (39.3)
Little Tupper Lake	Hamilton	3.8 (9.84)	42 (12.8)
Upper Chateaugay Lake	Clinton	3.8 (9.84)	78 (23.8)
Kensico Reservoir	Westchester	3.5 (9.06)	155 (47.2)
Lower Saranac Lake	Franklin	3.5 (9.06)	65 (19.8)
Otisco Lake	Onondaga	3.5 (9.06)	66 (20.1)
Fourth Lake	Herkimer, Hamilton	3.3 (8.55)	85 (25.9)
Rondout Reservoir	Ulster, Sullivan	3.3 (8.55)	175 (53.3)
Canadarago Lake	Otsego	3.1 (8.03)	42 (12.8)
Cross Lake	Onondaga, Cayuga	3.0 (7.77)	65 (19.8)
Greenwood Lake	Orange	3.0 (7.77)	57 (17.4)
Hemlock Lake	Livingston	2.9 (7.51)	90 (27.4)
Tomhannock Reservoir	Rensselaer	2.7 (6.99)	—
Honeoye Lake	Livingston, Ontario	2.6 (6.73)	30 (9.1)
Sacandaga Lake	Hamilton	2.5 (6.47)	60 (18.3)
Lake Pleasant	Hamilton	2.4 (6.22)	65 (19.8)
Chazy Lake	Clinton	2.3 (5.96)	70 (21.3)
Lake Lila	Hamilton	2.3 (5.96)	—
Neversink Reservoir	Sullivan	2.3 (5.96)	175 (53.3)
Blue Mountain Lake	Hamilton	2.1 (5.44)	102 (31.1)
Brant Lake	Warren	2.1 (5.44)	60 (18.3)
Middle Saranac Lake	Franklin	2.1 (5.44)	17 (5.2)
Big Moose Lake	Hamilton, Herkimer	2.0 (5.18)	70 (21.3)
Lake Bonaparte	Lewis	2.0 (5.18)	69 (21.0)
Forked Lake	Hamilton	1.9 (4.92)	74 (22.6)
Meacham Lake	Franklin	1.9 (4.92)	62 (18.9)
Alcove Reservoir	Albany	1.8 (4.66)	—
Schoharie Reservoir	Delaware, Schoharie	1.8 (4.66)	150 (45.7)
Cazenovia Lake	Madison	1.7 (4.40)	48 (14.6)
Raquette Pond	Franklin	1.7 (4.40)	12 (3.7)
Woodhull Lake	Herkimer	1.7 (4.40)	197 (60.1)
Lake Clear	Franklin	1.6 (4.14)	45 (13.7)

MAJOR LAKES AND RESERVOIRS OF NEW YORK STATE (continued)

Name	County	Area in mi² (km²)	Maximum Depth in ft (m)
Follensby Pond	Franklin	1.4 (3.63)	100 (30.5)
Honnedaga Lake	Herkimer	1.4 (3.63)	—
Paradox Lake	Essex	1.4 (3.63)	52 (15.9)
Brandreth Lake	Hamilton	1.3 (3.37)	—
Silver Lake	Clinton	1.3 (3.37)	50 (15.2)
Waneta Lake	Schuyler	1.3 (3.37)	29 (8.8)
Wolf Pond	Franklin	1.3 (3.37)	76 (23.2)
Cossayuna Lake	Washington	1.2 (3.11)	25 (7.6)
Round Lake	Hamilton	1.2 (3.11)	—
Silver Lake	Wyoming	1.2 (3.11)	37 (11.3)
Peck Lake	Fulton	1.1 (2.85)	60 (18.3)
Rainbow Falls Reservoir	St. Lawrence	1.1 (2.85)	55+ (16.8+)
Upper St. Regis Lake	Franklin	1.1 (2.85)	90 (27.4)
Blake Falls Reservoir	St. Lawrence	1.0 (2.59)	49+ (14.9+)
Canadice Lake	Ontario	1.0 (2.59)	84 (25.6)
Little Moose Lake	Herkimer	1.0 (2.59)	129 (39.3)
Nehasane Lake	Hamilton	1.0 (2.59)	—

Source: J. M. Swart and J. A. Bloomfield, *Characteristics of New York State Lakes: Gazetteer of Lakes, Ponds, and Reservoirs* (1987)

[a]The figures provided are for the New York State portion of the lakes. The total sizes of Lake Erie and Lake Ontario are 9,940 mi² (25,744.9 km²) and 7,500 mi² (19,424.9 km²), respectively.

[b]The figures provided for Lake Champlain correspond to the total area and depth of the lake, not the New York State portion.

salinity, thermal modification, flow alterations, pathogens, oil and grease, and aesthetics.

Point sources of pollutants that come through a pipe must be limited by best conventional, available, or economical control technologies, and may undergo toxicity testing on organisms. NPS and storm-water runoff are the primary sources of pollution for 90% of the state's impaired waters. Once pollutants enter a waterbody, they may become incorporated, accumulated, and magnified along the food chain; settle into bottom sediments, for example, the PCBs at the bottom of the Hudson River; or enter groundwater reserves. Point and NPS pollutants have closed nearly 16% of New York State's 1.2 million acres (486,000 ha) of marine shellfishing beds, many of which were highly productive and near shore.

Almost 50% of New York fish kills between 1984 and 1998 were traced to industrial and municipal discharges; another 24% were attributed to agricultural or road runoff. Most New York fish consumption advisories are linked to contamination by mercury, PCBs, cadmium, or chlordane. Restoration of impaired waters depends on compliance, enforcement, and, for NPS controls, integrated watershed approaches involving all landowners. The DEC has adopted distinct watershed restoration approaches in the Great Lakes, the New York–New Jersey Harbor, Long Island Sound, the Peconic Estuary, the Lake Champlain Basin, Onondaga Lake, and the New York City drinking supply area. The state recognizes the value of all water resources, and uses the Wild, Scenic and Recreational Rivers Act to protect special waters. As of 2000 there were12 segments of Wild River (comprising 142 mi/229 km), 49 segments of Scenic River (551 mi/887 km), and 42 segments of Recreational River (604 mi/972 km) in New York State.

Acidification of New York lakes poses a major threat to water quality and has been recorded for 1,850 lakes and ponds, covering 503,400 acres (203,720 ha), primarily in the Adirondacks, and representing nearly 50% of that region's waterbodies. Less than 2% of the area sampled, represented by 365 lakes and ponds, had acidities below 5.0 and were considered impaired, while less than 4% of the studied area (289 waterbodies), was between a pH of 5 and 6 and considered threatened. Deterioration is caused by wet and dry deposition of sulfate and, to a lesser extent, nitric acids. Sulfur dioxide is estimated to come primarily from Ohio, Pennsylvania, and West Virginia, and constitutes 23% of the Adirondack and 36% of the Catskill acid-producing contaminants. New York State is estimated to contribute 14% and 31% respectively. Vehicular traffic in the state contributes upward of 32% of the nitrogen-related oxides; Canadian cities like Toronto and Montreal, and urban centers in western Pennsylvania and eastern Ohio also contribute significant portions.

Invasive species present a relatively new form of pollution to New York State's surface waters. Thick zebra mussel colonies have choked closed water-delivery intakes and outlets, spiny water fleas are creating an unwanted stiffening of recreational and commercial fishing lines and nets, and dense stands of purple loosestrife have blocked access to ground-nesting birds. Eurasian water milfoil has clogged numerous ponds and lakes, but innovative biological controls such as sterile hybrid grass carp and several grazing insects have shown promise as controls.

Allan, J. D. *Stream Ecology: Structure and Function of Running Waters* (Boston: Kluwer Academic Publishers, 1995)

Dingman, L. *Physical Hydrology* (Upper Saddle River, NJ: Prentice-Hall, 1994)

Division of Water, New York State Department of Environmental Conservation, "Descriptive Data of Municipal Wastewater Treatment Plants in New York State" (1999), http://www.dec.state.ny.us/website/dow/descdata.pdf

———. "New York State Water Quality 2000," http://www.dec.state.ny.us/website/dow/305b98.pdf

Eschner, Arthur R. "Water." In *Geography of New York State,* ed. John H. Thompson (Syracuse: Syracuse Univ Press, 1966)

Great Lakes Regional Assessment Group. *Preparing for*

TOTAL DAILY WATER WITHDRAWALS AND CONSUMPTION

Water Use Category	Total Withdrawal %	Total Withdrawal million gal (l)	Consumptive Use[a] million gal (l)
Public and Private Supply			
Domestic	11.8	1,954 (7,396)	107 (405)
Commercial	3.6	609 (2,305)	61 (231)
Industrial	3.7	615 (2,328)	62 (235)
Public Use	2.5	424 (1,605)	—
Agricultural and Mining			
Irrigation	0.2	30 (114)	26 (98)
Livestock	0.2	34 (129)	30 (114)
Mining	0.4	62 (235)	17 (64)
Thermoelectric Power			
Fossil Fuel	63.1	10,600 (40,121)	212 (802)
Nuclear	14.5	2,440 (9,235)	88 (333)
Total		16,800 (63,588)	603 (2,282)

Source: NYS Department of Environmental Conservation, Division of Water, *New York State Water Quality 2000.*

[a]Water not returned to water supply because of evapotranspiration, incorporation in products, or other processes.

Compiled by Theodore A. Endreny

AVERAGE MONTHLY RIVER FLOWS, THROUGH 2000

River, Location of Measurement	1st Year Measured	Measurement in ft^3 per sec (m^3 per sec)			
		Jan	Apr	Aug	Nov
Allegheny, Salamanca	1903	3,336 (94.5)	5,834 (165.2)	715 (20.2)	2,522 (71.4)
Ausable, Sable Forks	1910	457 (12.9)	1,892 (53.6)	287 (8.1)	611 (17.3)
Black, Watertown	1920	4,123 (116.7)	10,000 (283.1)	1,773 (50.2)	4,343 (123.0)
Chemung, Chemung	1903	2,392 (67.7)	6,206 (175.7)	715 (20.2)	1,913 (54.2)
Chenango, Chenango Forks	1912	2,636 (74.6)	5,760 (163.1)	634 (18.0)	2,235 (63.3)
Delaware, Callicoon	1975	2,480 (70.2)	5,776 (163.6)	1,288 (36.5)	2,577 (73.0)
Genesee, Mount Morris	1903	1,838 (52.0)	3,905 (110.6)	429 (12.1)	1,324 (37.5)
Hudson, Green Island	1946	13,480 (381.7)	31,140 (881.8)	5,783 (163.8)	13,089 (370.6)
Mohawk, Cohoes	1917	5,571 (157.8)	14,000 (396.4)	1,748 (49.5)	5,446 (154.2)
Oneida, Euclid	1996	3,786 (107.2)	4,912 (139.1)	641 (18.2)	2,158 (61.1)
Oswego, Oswego	1900	7,917 (224.2)	13,220 (374.3)	2,595 (73.5)	6,066 (171.8)
Raquette, Piercefield	1908	1,113 (31.6)	3,151 (89.2)	591 (16.7)	1,172 (33.2)
Saranac, Plattsburgh	1903	699 (19.8)	2,005 (56.8)	474 (13.4)	736 (20.8)
Seneca, Baldwinsville	1950	3,917 (110.9)	6,006 (170.1)	1,522 (43.1)	3,347 (94.8)
Susquehanna, Conklin	1913	3,933 (111.4)	8,476 (240.0)	978 (27.7)	3,341 (94.6)

Source: US Geological Survey, "Surface Water Statistics," http://nwis.waterdata.usgs.gov/ny/nwis/annual.

Note: Data are given for select rivers and for select months based on high and low flows. Averages are based on annual measurements beginning with the first year of measurement.

Compiled by Theodore A. Endreny

a Changing Climate: The Potential Consequences of Climate Variability and Change: Great Lakes Overview (Ann Arbor: Univ of Michigan, 2000)

Maidment, D. *Handbook of Hydrology* (New York: McGraw-Hill, 1992)

Randall, A. D. *Mean Annual Runoff, Precipitation, and Evapotranspiration in the Glaciated Northeastern United States, 1951–1980,* map (Troy, NY: US Geological Survey, 1996)

Sawyer, C., P. McCarty, and G. Parkin. *Chemistry of Environmental Engineering* (New York: McGraw-Hill, 1994)

Theodore A. Endreny

water cure. See ALTERNATIVE MEDICINE; SPAS.

Waterford. Town (pop 8,515) and village (pop 2,204) in SE Saratoga Co. Dutch traders settled in the area in the mid–17th century. It was formed from Halfmoon in 1816. Surveyed in 1784 the village was incorporated in 1794. Located at the confluence of the Hudson and Mohawks Rivers, its destiny was determined by them and the Champlain and Erie Canals; it remains the eastern entrance of the Barge Canal. The Mohawk was bridged in 1795 and the Hudson in 1804. Trade and manufacturing were well established when a hydraulic canal was built from 1828 to 1829 to provide waterpower. Enterprises included foundries; cooperages; tool and die factories; knitting mills; paper mills; ink, soap, and candle manufactories; and especially the Button Fire Engine Works (1834) and Eddy Valve Co (1847). Peebles Island, a state park since 1973, was the site of the Cluett Peabody Bleachery (1910). Grand Union's warehouse (?1947) and the General Electric Specialty Materials Silicones plant (1947) provided a strong industrial base for accelerating suburbanization.

Field Horne

Waterford bridge. Designed and built by Theodore Burr in 1804, this four-span, arch-truss wooden bridge, called the Union Bridge at Waterford, was the first to cross the Hudson River. The Union toll bridge connected Waterford (Saratoga Co) and Lansingburgh (Rensselaer Co). Built from hand-hewn pine, the 800 ft (243.8 m) bridge had pine plank siding and its four spans measured 154 feet (46.9 m), 161 feet (49.1 m), 176 feet (53.6 m), and 180 feet (54.9 m). Originally uncovered but given a shingled roof in 1814, the bridge carried pedestrian and carriage traffic and later trolley lines connecting the same communities. In 1909 it was destroyed by fire, having served for more than 105 years. The toll bridge company immediately replaced it with a steel bridge built on the same piers by Boller and Hodge Engineers and fabricated by the Phoenix Bridge Co. This bridge, with little change, continues to serve pedestrian and automobile traffic across the river.

Frank E. Griggs Jr

waterfronts. Europeans settled New York State largely along navigable waterways. Dutch and British colonizing began during periods of mercantile long-distance trade, which made strategic port locations important geographic factors in eras of slow overland transportation. New York Harbor's incomparable series of sheltered bays, river outlets, straits, and sounds afforded deepwater anchorage for oceangoing vessels, while the Hudson and Mohawk Rivers provided continental access. From their bustling waterfronts, seaports and inland river ports gave rise to the commercial, industrial, and financial prowess of the Empire State.

URBAN SETTLEMENT AND WATERFRONT DEVELOPMENT

Nowhere has the urban landscape experienced more constant and dramatic alteration than the water's edge. For reasons ranging from convenient dumping ground to technological innovation, waterways have been deepened, widened, and sometimes created from scratch. The emergence of shipping and other maritime functions prompted the construction of permanent piers and ferry slips; early public structures included municipal docks, public markets, and customhouses. Many nearby businesses provisioned the ships and provided lodging, food, drink, and recreation in "sailor's town." On the waterfront diverse social worlds overlapped in the service of shipping and commerce: laborers unloaded merchandise, often repackaging it for further transport or processing it further in local mills; financial transactions involved factors, brokers, and insurance companies; urban trades provided the wide variety of tasks necessary in such a cosmopolitan milieu. With the proliferation of taverns and other institutions catering to footloose migrant populations, reformers identified waterfronts as places of questionable morals and established Protestant missions. Given the waterfront's common association with unsavory sailors, dockworkers, and vice districts, the middle and upper classes sought to avoid the industrial waterfront.

By the mid–19th century, as vessels evolved from sailing ships to steamships, the major ports began to develop separate docking, warehouse, industrial, financial, commercial, housing, and entertainment districts. New Amsterdam [now New York City] grew as a mercantile town at one of the world's greatest natural deepwater ports. After the English assumed control in 1664, the city remained thoroughly commercial, dominated by its bustling East River port on lower Manhattan Island. The piers, warehouses, countinghouses, insurance offices, stores, and other commercial venues were concentrated along South St and constituted the heart of the New York waterfront until the late 19th century. By 1812 a roughly 2 mi (3 km) stretch known as the Street of Ships, along the East River of Lower Manhattan, encompassed more than 50 numbered piers and was filled with docked ships from distant locations. Taverns sprang up there to serve all sectors of society, and coffeehouses often served as mercantile meeting places. The Tontine Coffee House, at Wall and Water Sts, became the epicenter of the city's financial activity when a group of brokers, traders, underwriters, and other commercial interests began trading upstairs in 1796; this group evolved into the New York Stock Exchange, founded in 1817.

By 1900 the focus of New York City's shipping had relocated from Manhattan's Lower East Side to the Hudson River and Brooklyn waterfronts, where modernized shipping facilities, deepwater anchorages, and connecting railways permitted larger steamships. For example, the Chelsea Piers included nine large docks between 12th and 22d Sts. The Transatlantic Steamship Terminal (Piers 88, 90, 92), which opened between 48th and 52d Sts in 1936, received such ocean liners as the *Normandie* and the *Queen Mary.* South St remained a center for sailing vessels through the 19th century but subsequently sank into decay, although some waterfront activities, like the Fulton Fish Market, remained on the East Side.

The development of Brooklyn's waterfront made it New York City's most populated borough. The success of the Atlantic Docks, built in the 1850s for transshipment of cargo from the Erie Canal and the Atlantic trade, preceded development of the Erie Basin complex in Red Hook. By the late 19th century Brooklyn's wharves and piers carried considerably more cargo than Manhattan's. In addition, the New York Naval Ship Yard (1800) popularly known as the Brooklyn Navy Yard, manufactured many of the country's most famous warships. Activity at the Brooklyn Navy Yard peaked in 1944, when more than 70,000 employees built much of the US wartime fleet. After World War II shipbuilding gradually declined until the yard finally closed in 1966. New York City bought 265 acres (107 ha) of it as an industrial park. Waterfront areas of Williamsburg, Red Hook, and the Gowanus Canal also grew up as manufacturing and warehouse areas, only to face postwar industrial decline and closing.

Other cities in New York State also underwent rapid growth in the 19th century. Such Hudson Valley cities as Poughkeepsie, Kingston, Hudson, Newburgh, and Troy grew from river ports with inland seaport functions, stimulated by the growth of steamboat traffic. Albany benefited from its strategic location at a convenient portage on the west side of the Hudson River, which facilitated land communication with the interior. The Erie Canal encouraged the growth of trade, industry, and population throughout the region—most notably in important cities such as Schenectady, Utica, Rome, Syracuse, and Rochester. With the arrival of railroads after 1850, however, these inland waterfronts often declined as active shipping centers and evolved primarily into industrial and commercial centers.

Major ports of call developed on the state's portions of the Great Lakes, initially stimulated by important transportation and commercial linkages with the Erie Canal. Buffalo, located on the eastern end of Lake Erie at a natural east-west transportation juncture, emerged on the Niagara Frontier in the early 1800s. Subsequent development of railroads and industries in the late 19th century made Buffalo a major metropolis and the leading grain-handling port of the United States. Buffalo's waterfront became a vibrant zone of docks, grain elevators, factories, and transportation facilities. On Lake Ontario, the Port of Oswego grew with the completion of the Oswego Canal in 1828. Ogdensburg (St. Lawrence Co) on the St. Lawrence River became an important port of entry for the Great Lakes.

Industrial and Postindustrial Adaptations

As railroads developed and increasingly absorbed the shipment of passengers and freight, waterfront sites often became less significant than locations along railroad lines; small Hudson Valley cities, for example, generally suffered a decline in their status as river ports. In contrast, as the shipping of bulk freight and passengers continued to grow in major ports such as New York City and Buffalo, major urban waterfronts became more functionally specialized in adjacent areas dedicated to cargo, warehouses, industry, transportation, commerce, and worker housing. The laying of railroad tracks behind the piers during the late 19th century and the construction of elevated roadways after World War II, however, often impeded access to the water's edge and further isolated the waterfront. Transportation congestion and outmoded docks also remained major problems. The Port Authority of New York (now Port Authority of New York and New Jersey), a two-state agency formed in 1921, subsequently dedicated itself largely to improving metropolitan transportation links and modernizing shipping facilities. The 1954 film *On the Waterfront,* directed by Elia Kazan and featuring actor Marlon Brando, depicted the New York–New Jersey urban waterfront as it began a postwar decline, beset by labor conflicts, organized crime, corruption, and human pathos. The rise of the automobile and trucking further altered waterfronts as many industries moved away from urban locations to take advantage of cheaper suburban land. Technological changes in shipping also changed the waterfront. Starting in the 1960s, the advent of container shipping required larger loading areas, modernized facilities, and improved transportation access. Shipping abandoned many central areas, leaving behind waterfront districts of rotting piers, empty warehouses, and largely vacant factories. Container shipping in New York City is now restricted to facilities at the Brooklyn–Port Authority Marine Terminal and at Howland Hook in Staten Island; port functions have moved largely to state-of-the-art container facilities in outlying Jersey City, Port Newark, and Elizabeth, NJ.

As once vibrant port districts in central areas fell into disuse during the late 20th century, New York State's major cities lost factory jobs and blue-collar positions in trucking, warehousing, wholesale, and shipping. While port and industrial functions decentralized, cities attempted to attract leading service-sector and financial operations to sustain their economies. As part of this economic restructuring, urban renewal projects tried to convert waterfront districts to highways, housing, and recreational and commercial activities. In recent years the once gritty urban waterfronts, previously among the least salubrious areas in town, have been gentrified by affluent residents and fashionable businesses.

Emergence of the postindustrial waterfront is nowhere more evident than in New York City, where large-scale redevelopment along 770 linear miles (1,239 km) of waterfront has become the subject of public controversy. Contemporary renovation of the deteriorated Manhattan waterfront began in the late 1960s. Against a backdrop of widespread urban renewal in massive modernist office and apartment complexes, the incorporation of the South Street Seaport Museum in 1967 signaled an alternative approach with an emphasis on historical preservation, rehabilitated tall ships, and commercial ventures in restored buildings along the East River. On the other hand, the Port Authority of New York and New Jersey completed the twin 110-story World Trade Center towers and an adjacent plaza by the mid-1970s. In the 1980s Battery Park City added a complex of high-rise office buildings and mid-rise residential blocks for affluent residents on the Hudson River adjacent to the financial district, along with boat marinas and public parks on a riverfront esplanade. Plans to redevelop more of the Hudson River waterfront in large-scale residential and commercial projects were derailed in 1982 and 1985, when environmental lawsuits filed by local activists blocked the federal government's proposed Westway, an ambitious 4.2 mi (6.8 km) six-lane roadway on about 180 acres (73 ha) of landfill along the Hudson River.

Defeat of the Westway project opened the way for renovation of the existing piers, starting with the completion of the Chelsea Piers complex in 1995. Where ocean liners used to dock, the Chelsea Piers created a vast athletic center with a golf range, a sports fitness center, Olympic-size pools and skating rinks, and restaurants. In 1998 state legislation mandated a 550-acre (223 ha) Hudson River Park along a 5 mi (8 km) stretch of Lower Manhattan, scheduled for completion in approximately 2005, featuring a redesigned roadway, areas of recreational space, and more than a dozen renovated piers for public use. The first of the Hudson River Park's planned six segments opened in 2003 along the Greenwich Village waterfront; work is underway on other segments of the $400 million project. On the East River, Stuyvesant Cove Park—a narrow, 2-acre (.8 ha) swath of land between 23d and 18th Sts—opened in 2002.

Similar plans for park, commercial, and residential development are afoot as other boroughs of New York City also rediscover the allure of the water's edge. In Brooklyn waterfront projects include the redevelopment of 1.3 miles (2.1 km) around the Manhattan and Brooklyn bridges, revitalization of the 1.6 mi (2.6 km) industrial waterfront of Williamsburg, and creation of a Brooklyn Waterfront Greenway between Red Hook and Brooklyn Bridge Park. A remarkable cleanup of the Gowanus Canal in South Brooklyn followed the reactivation of the Gowanus Canal Flushing Tunnel in 1999. Other projects comprise renovation of the waterfront near Yankee Stadium in the Bronx, and the Bronx River, adaptive reuse of the former Homeport Navy site in Staten Island, and several projects in Queens, including the Queens West residential towers and proposals to improve public access to the waterfronts in Jamaica Bay and the Flushing River. Formation of the Metropolitan Waterfront Alliance in 1999, a network of concerned governmental, civic, educational, business, environmental, labor, and media groups in the Greater New York City region, signaled new and widespread interest in waterfront issues. This active nongovernmental organization focused on creating public access to the water's edge, reconnecting waterfront communities with waterborne transportation, cleaning up polluted areas, and revitalizing waterfront communities.

Although on a scale smaller than New York City, similar waterfront redevelopment projects have been planned across New York State, generally with an emphasis on historical preservation, recreational facilities, boating marinas, housing, and retail-restaurant development. Buffalo's decline in importance as a rail and canal link to the Great Lakes after the St. Lawrence Seaway was completed in 1959 prompted large-scale waterfront redevelopment. By the mid-1990s this multiphase project had yielded the Marine Midland Center (now HSBC Center), several large office buildings, a 500-room hotel, and Waterfront Village with marinas, restaurants, and townhouses. Buffalo's waterfront also boasts a small flotilla of retired warships: a cruiser, a destroyer, and a submarine. In the early 21st century the Buffalo Waterfront Corridor Initiative focuses on economic redevelopment, neighborhood revitalization, improvement of direct access from Riverside to South Buffalo, and the creation of an International Gateway at and around the Buffalo Peace Bridge. In Rochester it is hoped the opening of the fast ferry to Toronto in 2004 will revitalize the waterfront area of Charlotte.

Contemporary waterfront redevelopment along the Erie Canal has emphasized pleasure boating, fishing, and cycling on the former towpaths where mules once trudged. For example, North Tonawanda (Niagara Co) became a popular recreational area with boathouses and pleasure craft after World War II; contemporary development plans call for museums, retail outlets, restaurants, new docks, and historical ships. Similar development of the canal front in Pittsford and Fairport (Monroe Co) was also undertaken.

The Hudson River Valley Greenway Act of 1991 created a framework for voluntary regional cooperation among communities to promote the creation of riverside parks and the Greenway Trail System with links to local natural and cultural resources. For example, Poughkeepsie is typical of the 191 Greenway communities in 13 counties in the Hudson River valley in 2003. Poughkeepsie's Waterfront Advisory Committee encouraged the redevelopment of a public promenade along the city's 2.5 mi (4.0 km) waterfront with enhanced amenities at Waryas Park, riverfront restaurants, parking and boating facilities, and permanent open space for Kaal Rock.

The significance of these efforts to integrate the waterfront in contemporary redevelopment projects became tragically clear with the destruction of the World Trade Center on 11 Sept 2001, which prompted the evacuation of nearly 500,000 people from Lower Manhattan by a flotilla of more than 100 boats, many of them crewed by volunteers. This dramatic episode, reminiscent of the impromptu evacuation of some 300,000 Allied troops from Dunkirk in 1940, heightened awareness of the importance of ensuring waterfront access and regular waterborne transportation service.

See also HUDSON RIVER FERRIES.

Bone, Kevin, Mary Beth Betts, and Stanley Greenberg, eds. *The New York Waterfront: Evolution and Building Culture of the Port and Harbor* (New York: Monacelli Press, 1997)

Buttenwieser, Ann L. *Manhattan Water-Bound: Planning and Developing Manhattan's Waterfront from the 17th Century to the Present* (New York: New York Univ Press, 1987)

Gastil, Raymond W. *Beyond the Edge: New York's New Waterfront* (New York: Princeton Architectural Press, 2002)

Hudson River Park Conservancy. *Hudson River Park: Concept and Financial Plan* (New York: author, 1995)

Brian J. Godfrey

Waterloo. Town (pop 7,866) and village (pop 5,111) in N central Seneca Co. Settled ?1789 as New Hudson, its name was changed in 1816, and it became the location of one of the county's two courthouses in 1818. The village incorporated in 1824, and the town was formed from Junius in 1829. The Seneca Lock Navigation Co (1813) opened canal transport through Waterloo in 1816, which was improved by the state as the Cayuga and Seneca Canal (1828) but was soon challenged by the Auburn and Rochester Railroad (1841). Waterloo Manufacturing Co (woolen cloth), Waterloo Wagon Co, and Waterloo Organ Co were important 19th-century industries; in 1895 they employed 657 workers. A member of the family that owned Coe-Genung Funeral Home (1852) developed a modern embalming method in the 1890s that is still in use. The first Memorial Day was observed in Waterloo on 5 May 1866, an event recognized by presidential proclamation in 1966. Alone among Seneca Co towns, Waterloo's population nearly doubled between 1920 and 2000. The Seneca County Fair takes place in Waterloo each July. Women's Rights National Historical Park owns the homes of Jane Hunt and Mary Ann McClintock, who were among the organizers of the first women's rights convention. The Scythe Tree, a large poplar along Rte 5/US 20, has embedded in it the scythe that young farmer James W. Johnson hung there in 1861 when he joined the Union army in the Civil War; he died of wounds in 1864.

Lisa Compton

water supply and use (New York City watershed). New York City obtains water from three watersheds covering almost 2,000 mi^2 (5,200 km^2) in Schoharie, Delaware, Sullivan, Greene, Ulster, Dutchess, Putnam, and Westchester Cos. Water is collected in 19 reservoirs and 3 controlled lakes and delivered by 3 gravity-fed aqueducts to storage reservoirs in Westchester and Bronx Cos for distribution by city tunnels. The system, begun in 1837, has a storage capacity of 600 billion gallons (2.27 trillion l), with an average daily consumption in the city of 1.2 billion gallons (4.54 billion l); another 120 million gallons (454 million l) a day are supplied outside the city to Westchester, Putnam, Orange, and Ulster Cos.

ORIGINAL SUPPLIES

For two centuries New York City's public water supply came from street wells; after the first public well was dug in 1666, hundreds of pump-equipped wells were eventually sunk. Geological conditions beneath the community, founded at the low-lying southern tip of salt-ringed Manhattan, caused well water to be, initially, merely distasteful. As the population spread north up the island, the wells became increasingly polluted by protoindustrial, animal, and human wastes. Christopher Colles's 1774 plan for a public water supply piped from a deep, high-ground well beyond the city's settled area was abandoned during the Revolution. Aaron Burr's Manhattan Co, chartered as a water business by the legislature in 1799, quickly evolved into a monopoly that thrived as a bank, eventually becoming Chase Manhattan (now Chase Bank) but provided little water and frustrated other private and public efforts aimed at the water problem. A palatable but limited and expensive supply was available from carted spring and private pump water. After an 1832 cholera epidemic killed over 3,500 residents (1 in 60) of the notoriously filthy and ill-watered city, alderman and state senator Myndert Van Schaick led an effort to tap the pure waters of the Croton River in then remote northern Westchester Co. State-appointed commissioners oversaw the planning and construction of Croton Aqueduct, opened in 1842 and quickly ending the city's reputation for poor water. Delivering 90 million gallons (341 million l) a day, the aqueduct became the model for urban American water supplies, and Croton became a byword for excellent water. As larger systems became operational in the 20th century, the aqueduct was gradually cut back and then closed in 1955.

THE MODERN SYSTEM

As New York City's population surged past 1.5 million in the early 1890s, the city completed New Croton Aqueduct, which quadrupled the daily supply from the Croton watershed. This Croton system—still in use at the beginning of the 21st century—involved the construction of a landmark dam on lower Croton River, opened in 1905, to operate in conjunction with 11 other reservoirs on dammed upper branches and tributaries, opened from 1866 to 1911.

The creation of Greater New York in 1898, which expanded the city to its current five boroughs and nearly doubled its population, prompted the building of an aqueduct from the Catskill Mountains west of the Hudson River and 100 miles (161 km) northwest of the city. Begun in 1907, opened in 1917, and completed in 1927, the Catskill system features two reservoirs—123 billion gal (465.6 billion l) Ashokan in Ulster Co and 18 billion gal (68.1 billion l) Schoharie at the intersection of Schoharie, Delaware, and Greene Cos—as well as the 92 mi (148 km) aqueduct. This aqueduct passes through a tunnel running between Storm King and Breakneck Mountains, 1,100 feet (335 m) below the Hudson River, and transmits up to 800 million gallons (3 billion l) a day. As the city's population grew to near 8 million, planning began for an aqueduct from the Delaware River's source waters in Delaware Co. A US Supreme Court decision (*New Jersey v New York,* 283 US 336) settled water rights litigation with down-river states in 1931, but the depression delayed the start of construction until 1937. Completed in 1965 the Delaware system features two reservoirs in Delaware Co: 96 billion gal (363.4 billion l) Cannonsville, 120 miles (193 km) from the city; and 140 billion gal (529.900 billion l) Pepacton, the largest of the city's reservoirs. It

Spillway, New Croton Dam, Croton-on-Hudson, early 20th century.

also claims 35 billion gal (132.5 billion l) Neversink Reservoir in Sullivan Co, 50 billion gal (189.3 billion l) Rondout Reservoir on the border of Sullivan and Ulster Cos, and 84 mi (135 km) Delaware Aqueduct, the world's longest continuous tunnel. At the beginning of the 21st century, Delaware Aqueduct supplied 50%, Catskill Aqueduct 40%, and New Croton Aqueduct 10% of New York City's water. The major ongoing work of this era was a massive new tunnel for distribution of existing supplies within the city, City Water Tunnel No. 3. At a projected cost of $6 billion, it was the largest capital construction project in the city's history.

New York City and Its Watershed Region

Since 1837, when landowners unsuccessfully petitioned the legislature to halt the "invasion" of Westchester Co by Croton Aqueduct, the relationship between New York City and the populations of its watershed has been uneasy. Construction of the Croton, Catskill, and Delaware systems between the mid–19th and mid–20th centuries flooded at least 40 communities, displaced over 10,000 residents, and required the reinterment of nearly 12,000 graves from over 80 cemeteries. Since the city stopped building new supply facilities in the 1960s, it has sought to preserve supply quality with watershed land purchases and environmental regulation, engendering new resentment. Increasing commercial and residential development in the watershed counties, in part the result of city water projects in the latter, has compounded the threat to water purity, especially in the suburbanized Croton watershed counties of Westchester and Putnam.

Conservation measures since the late 1980s within the city—introduction of water meters in place of flat-rate charges based on street frontage and replacement of old toilets with low-flow models—reduced per capita daily water consumption from over 200 gallons (757 l) in the early 1990s to 155 gallons (587 l) in 2001. Despite lower demand, tensions over New York City's vast extraterritorial water supply will likely continue.

See also Catskills.

Galusha, Diane. *Liquid Assets: A History of New York City's Water System* (Fleischmanns, NY: Purple Mountain Press, 1999)
Koeppel, Gerard T. *Water for Gotham: A History* (Princeton, NJ: Princeton Univ Press, 2000)
Marx, Robin, and Eric A. Goldstein. *A Guide to New York City's Reservoirs and Their Watersheds* (New York: Natural Resources Defense Council, 1993)

Gerard T. Koeppel

water supply and use (non–New York City watershed). Geology and climate have provided New York State with an ample water supply, but scientific ignorance, politics, and economic considerations have conspired to make potable water a relatively recent phenomenon in urban areas. During settlement years backyard wells, public cisterns and pumps, and nearby surface water served as the first water supplies. Because sewers did not exist, groundwater and surface water were inevitably contaminated and outbreaks of waterborne illnesses such as cholera, yellow fever, typhoid fever, and dysentery recurred. By the early- to mid–19th century citizens turned to private water companies to satisfy demand, but these firms were undercapitalized and unable to meet the demands of rapidly growing populations. By the Civil War, municipalities had started assuming control of waterworks, usually resulting in improved supply as projects were undertaken to pump nearby river water, draw water from area lakes, or dam mountain streams to create upland reservoirs. Improvement in water quality depended on how removed the sources were from human settlement.

Water-treatment techniques first appeared in 1872 when the first filtration plant in the United States was built in Poughkeepsie. Water was percolated through a bed of sand primarily to improve its clarity, taste, and smell, but health improvements were readily noted as well. Between 1900 and 1910 the filtration process was mechanized and other innovations were introduced, including construction of sedimentation basins to remove solids before filtration, use of chemical additives to promote further removal of solids, and addition of chlorine to kill waterborne pathogens. This last technique, adopted by most cities during the 1910s, all but eliminated the risk of waterborne infectious disease. Further technological enhancements, expansion of existing facilities, and tapping of underground aquifers and new surface sources were explored in the 20th century. Many public water systems began adding fluoride to their supplies in the 1950s and 1960s to protect against tooth decay. The requirement of lower levels of chlorination by-products beginning in the 1990s resulted in public water systems reducing the amount of chlorine used or changing the entry point of chlorine into the treatment process. Chlorination by-products, the most abundant class of which are trihalomethanes, form when chlorine reacts with naturally occurring organic matter and are suspected of contributing to cancer and birth defects.

Countywide water authorities created in the second half of the 20th century, different from municipal or private water systems, helped provide economies of scale that allowed low-density suburban towns to obtain or improve the public water supply. For administrative and maintenance purposes, some towns and counties created water districts, a term describing water-supply service areas. In 2002 there were over 10,000 public water systems in the state outside the New York City area that served a large majority of the population; private wells in rural areas made up the balance. Most of these public water systems were very small, and 176 systems served about 70% of public water-supply customers. Of these large systems, 101 used surface-water sources and 75 used groundwater sources. Approximately 150 used chlorination.

Albany

Archaeological evidence hints at the existence of waterworks during Dutch colonial rule, but in 1748 Albany citizens were drinking from private wells and nearby surface-water sources, described by one visitor as "generally quite muddy." In 1802 the Albany Water-Works Co was chartered and developed a water-supply system drawing from nearby streams. As the city grew rapidly during the first half of the 19th century, the system proved inadequate, and improvements and upkeep were neglected. In 1850 Albany took over the system and expanded it, drawing water from streams west of the city. By the 1870s this system was also inadequate, and attention turned to the Hudson River. A pumping station was built to deliver river water to a reservoir at a high point in the city. As Albany residents began consuming the sewage discharge of Troy (Rensselaer Co) and other upstream locales, the typhoid mortality rate surged. When a filtration system was established in 1898, the typhoid rate dropped significantly but water quality remained poor. In 1926 a new source was chosen in the Helderberg Mountains in southern Albany Co. Hannacrois Creek was impounded to form the Alcove Reservoir in Coeymans (Albany Co) in 1929, submerging 2,000 acres (810 ha) including the hamlet of Indian Fields. This reservoir continues to supply the vast majority of Albany's water needs in the 21st century.

Syracuse

An 1829 act of the New York State legislature gave Capt Oliver Teall the exclusive rights to supply water to the nascent village of Syracuse.

These lapsed but were renewed in 1834 after the state increased the rates he was permitted to charge. Teall founded the Syracuse City Waterworks Co, whose original patchwork system drawing from nearby springs and streams was inadequate by the Civil War. In 1871 the company impounded Onondaga Creek, but this water was poor because of nearby tanneries and other industries. The city attempted to establish a public waterworks in 1885, but a court upheld the private monopoly. Four years later, waterworks were established by the City of Syracuse by nearly unanimous referendum, and Skaneateles Lake, 20 miles (32 km) southwest of the city, was tapped as the new supply. The system went into service in 1894, giving Syracuse one of the purest water supplies in the nation. Skaneateles Lake water, which remains the principal source for Syracuse, is so clean that it is one of the few large-system surface-water supplies not requiring filtration. In the 1970s a connection was made to Lake Ontario to supply water during drought conditions. Otisco Lake is the largest single source of water for the Onondaga County Water Authority, which serves suburban towns such as Camillus.

Rochester

Rochester citizens relied on wells and nearby springs for their water supply for much of the 19th century. The private Rochester Water Co was founded in 1852 in the wake of a cholera epidemic but made little progress before going bankrupt in the 1860s. In the early 1870s the city decided to build two separate, municipally owned water supplies, one for firefighting and one for general use. The high-pressure firefighting system used water from the Genesee River and made use of pumps, hydrants, and other technological innovations of the Holly Manufacturing Co in Lockport (Niagara Co). For the domestic supply, Hemlock Lake, 28 miles (45 km) south of the city, was chosen and later augmented by a link to nearby Canadice Lake. In 1940 the two systems were accidentally cross-contaminated, triggering an outbreak of over 34,000 cases of dysentery and diarrhea, and prompting the firefighting system to switch to treated Lake Ontario water. In 1955 the city began increasing its domestic supply with Lake Ontario water following the defeat of a plan to impound the entire Honeoye Creek watershed, which would have inundated Honeoye (Ontario Co).

Buffalo

The first water system in Buffalo was provided by the Jubilee Water Works Co, organized in 1826 and using the water of Jubilee Springs in what is now Buffalo's Forest Lawn Cemetery. In 1849 the Buffalo City Water Works Co was established and began construction of a system to draw water from the Niagara River to a hilltop reservoir. Beset by financial difficulties, the company was taken over by the city after the Civil War. In about 1910 a circular water-intake crib was installed in Lake Erie near the mouth of the Niagara River in a swift-flowing area known as the Emerald Channel. This source, combined with water-treatment technologies then emerging, gave Buffalo a safe and inexhaustible supply. In 1997, in response to fiscal difficulties, the city entered a five-year contract, subsequently renewed, with a private firm to manage its waterworks and provide other services. The Emerald Channel intake structure is still in use, restored to its original appearance in 2002. With its red conical roof and navigation light, it is a distinctive Buffalo landmark.

Long Island

Most of Long Island consists of glacial deposits of sand and gravel up to 2,000 feet (610 m) thick. Rainwater percolates through this soil and forms subsurface aquifers that are the primary water source for Nassau and Suffolk Cos. The island has a very limited amount of surface water. The vast underground supply means these counties are not vulnerable to drought, but the aquifers are vulnerable to pollution and urban development. The Upper Glacial aquifer near the surface has been substantially degraded by agricultural and industrial runoff. Most of the current supply comes from the larger and deeper Magothy aquifer. Population growth on Long Island has reduced the ability of aquifers to recharge, as rainwater falling on paved or roofed areas is often routed into sewer systems rather than allowed to find its way back into the ground.

In 2003 Suffolk and Nassau Cos were served by some 500 public water systems. Among the larger systems was the Suffolk County Water Authority (SCWA), the first public benefit corporation for water service, chartered by New York State in 1951. Run like a private enterprise but with profits accruing to the state treasury, SCWA served as a model followed by numerous other counties, including Onondaga, Monroe, Erie, Saratoga, and Orange.

Fluoridation

In the 1930s animal studies and chemical analyses showed that fluoride protected against tooth decay (though sometimes producing mottling of the teeth), leading dentists and public health officials to advocate fluoridating the water supply. In 1945 Newburgh (Orange Co) was selected by the US Public Health Service (USPHS) for experimental fluoridation, with Kingston (Ulster Co) providing a nonfluoridated control population. Early results were striking, and by 1950 the USPHS, American Dental Association, and American Medical Association all endorsed fluoridation. In most communities the issue was contentious, and in some it remains so, with opposition centered on the propriety of "compulsory mass medication" and concern over possible health risks such as osteoporosis. Rochester (1952) and Buffalo (1955) were early adopters; Syracuse, Binghamton, and Utica began fluoridation in the mid-1960s. Albany, where a referendum on the issue was defeated in 1994, is the state's largest city never to have fluoridated its water. A similar referendum in Ithaca was defeated in 2000.

Barnes, Joseph W. "Water Works History: A Comparison of Albany, Utica, Syracuse, and Rochester," *Rochester History* 39 (July 1977): 1–23

Blake, Nelson M. *Water for the Cities: A History of the Urban Water Supply Problem in the United States* (Syracuse: Syracuse Univ Press, 1956)

Fagin, Dan. "Ancient, Clean, Controversial: Preserving Deep Reserves of Water Is LI's Chief Environmental Issue," http://www.newsday.com/community/guide/lihistory/ny-history-hs103a,0,5257146.story

Galishoff, Stuart. "Triumph and Failure: The American Response to the Urban Water Supply Problem, 1860–1923." In *Pollution and Reform in American Cities, 1870–1930,* ed. Martin V. Melosi (Austin: Univ of Texas Press, 1980)

Martin, Brian. *Scientific Knowledge in Controversy: The Social Dynamics of the Fluoridation Debate* (Albany: SUNY Press, 1991)

McKelvey, Blake. "Water for Rochester," *Rochester History* 34 (July 1972): 1–23

United States. *Fluoridation Census* (1963–)

Francis P. Boscoe

Watertown. Town (pop 4,482) and city (pop 26,705) in central Jefferson Co. Settled in 1800, the town was formed that year from Mexico [now in Oswego Co] and in 1805 became the county seat. It was incorporated as a village in 1816. The site, on the south bank of the Black River, was chosen for its waterpower potential; dams were built in 1803, 1805, 1814, and 1835. A paper mill began operations in 1808, and the Black River Cotton and Woolen Manufacturing Co opened in 1814. Textiles were the most important early industry. Early settlers, mostly New Englanders and first-generation New Yorkers, were joined by Irish, Germans, French, and Quebecois; the population reached 5,207 by 1840. The Rome, Watertown and Ogdensburg Railroad (1851 south, 1857 north) provided transportation for heavy industry, and a rail link to Cape Vincent was completed in 1852. The Carthage, Watertown and Sackets Harbor Railroad (1870 east, 1874 west) completed Watertown's position as a regional transportation hub. With the railroad, papermaking became the village's most important industry. Remington Paper (1854) and Taggart Bros (1865–1949) were the largest mills. By 1860 Watertown was heavily industrial, producing cotton and woolen goods, leather, flour, paper, iron castings, machinery, agricultural implements, lead pipe, sash and blind, and furniture.

In 1869 Watertown incorporated as a city, and by 1920 the population had grown from 10,697 to 31,285. New residents included English and French Canadians, Italians, Greeks, eastern European Jews, and a number of African Americans from rural Jefferson Co. All were attracted by flourishing industries. The most important of these during this period were the paper mills, steam engine companies, carriage and wagon manufactories like H. H. Babcock and Sons (1879–1921), New York Air Brake (1890), and Bagley and Sewall Co (1882–1999), paper-machine makers.

The industrial boom made the city very wealthy, which is evident in streets lined with elegant mansions, the white marble Flower Memorial Library (1902), the Augustus Saint-Gaudens statue of Gov Roswell P. Flower (1903), the Olmsted Bros–designed Thompson Park (1904), the beautiful Brookside Cemetery (1854), and impressive churches like Trinity Episcopal (1890). One of the oldest landmarks is the Paddock Arcade (1850), believed to be America's oldest enclosed shopping mall. It was in Watertown that Frank W. Woolworth (1852–1919) introduced the 5¢ counter while he was employed as a sales clerk (1878).

After 1920 Watertown industries began to decline. Depleted resources, rising transportation costs, and decreased demand for some products were all contributing factors. World War II brought a temporary boost, both from war manufacturing and from the presence of several thousand soldiers at nearby Pine Camp (now Fort Drum), but it did not last. I-81 provided a

Public Square in Watertown, early 20th century.

limited-access highway link to Syracuse in 1959, but the impact was not extensive. In the 1960s and 1970s the local economy was sluggish, and urban renewal left downtown devastated. Unemployment rates were some of the highest in the state. A former air base (1951–79) was made into Watertown Correctional Facility (1982), boosting local employment. The 10th Mountain Division, with its thousands of soldiers, was stationed at Fort Drum in the 1980s, and the economy bounced back with new construction, businesses, and jobs. Many people moved into the city. For the first time there were significant numbers of Blacks and Latinos; enough Koreans settled to support two churches. The boost from Fort Drum ebbed after 1989, and many urban problems persist into the 21st century.

Watertown adopted the city manager form of government in 1920. It has an elected mayor and four council members. Though staunchly Republican since the Civil War, the city's new mix of residents helped to elect a Democratic assemblyman and sheriff in 2001. Watertown's religious congregations reflect the area's ethnic diversity, with a range of Protestant churches, including Korean Presbyterian and Episcopalian congregations, Irish (1856), French (1857), and Italian Roman Catholic churches, Greek Orthodox (*ca* 1920), AME Zion (1878), and a synagogue (1903). There are six church-related day schools in Watertown; only one of them is non-Catholic.

The *American Eagle* (1809–12), Watertown's first newspaper, was founded by Henry Coffeen, one of the community's founders. In 2003 the *Watertown Daily Times* (1970) had a circulation of 32,662, and the city's first radio station, WANT (1941), remained in operation. WCNY television began in 1954, and in 2003 there were five stations. Watertown is home to the semi-pro Red and Black football club (1896). In 2000 the racial composition of the city was 89% white, 5% black; 4% of the population was of Latino ethnicity. The town was 83% white and 11% black; 7% was of Latino ethnicity.

See also CANADIANS, ANGLOPHONE.

Laura Lynne Scharer

Waterville. Village (pop 1,721) in Sangerfield and Marshall (Oneida Co). Settled in 1789, the locality supported many shops, including a distillery (1802, later a brewery), cotton and woolen mills, foundry, paint factory, potato starch factory, and boot and shoe factory. At the center of a huge trade in hops during the late 19th century, when that crop was grown extensively, Waterville was called the "hops capital" because prices were set there. The Utica, Chenango and Susquehanna Valley Railroad came through in 1869. Passenger service ended in 1951, but freight service continues in the 21st century. The village incorporated in 1870. The Waterville Knitting Mills (1922–71) became Barclay Sportswear, and in 1995 the building was taken over by C and H Plastics. Waterville was the birthplace of George Eastman (1854–1932), founder of Eastman Kodak.

Watervliet [WAT-ER-VLEET]. City (pop 10,207) in NE Albany Co. Located on the Hudson River at the junction of the Erie and Champlain Canals (1823), the three distinct village plats of Gibbonsville (1804), West Troy (1823), and Port Schuyler (1827) merged into the village of West Troy in 1836. Hanks (1808) was the first bell foundry in the United States, and Meneely bell foundry (1826–1950) was also important. The lumber trade was significant from 1830 to 1845, but the village turned to manufacturing, producing woolen goods, hinges, castings, carriages, and malt. It drew Francophone Canadian workers and, by the 1870s, Ukrainians. In 1896 it incorporated as the City of Watervliet. Throughout most of the 20th century its factories produced metal goods. In the 1970s, I-787 cut the city off from the Hudson River. The main industry remains the historic Watervliet Arsenal (1813), America's oldest continuous armament manufacturer. Its 91 buildings are listed on the National Register, and it operates the Museum of the Big Guns (1975).

See also ERIE CANAL IN FOLKLORE AND THE ARTS; SHAKERS.

Watervliet Arsenal. US government armament manufacturer founded in Watervliet (Albany Co) in 1813. Owned and operated by the US Army, the arsenal is the oldest continuously active armament manufacturer in the United States. Established to support the War of 1812, the arsenal has produced matériel for the US military and its allies through all subsequent conflicts. Conveniently located on the Hudson River and near the confluence of the Hudson and Mohawk Rivers, it produced cannonballs, gunshot, leather goods, wooden carriages, and limbers during the 19th century. Ebbs and flows of employment and production followed times of peace and war. During the Civil War the workforce rose to more than 2,000 to manufacture weapons for the Union army. After World War I nearly two-thirds of the workers were let go. With the onset of World War II, the facility produced the famous 16-inch guns for the US Navy's North Carolina, South Dakota, and Iowa class battleships, and employment spiraled to nearly 10,000. In more recent decades, Watervliet has produced a variety of howitzers, mortars, and tank guns for the US Army and Marine Corps. In the 1950s research and development of new artillery systems was added to the arsenal's mission. In the early 1960s Building 40 was dedicated as the Benet Research and Engineering Laboratories, and by 1980 the Benet labs had become part of a consolidated army research and development command. During the mid-1980s spike in defense spending, nearly 3,000 were employed at the arsenal. A series of layoffs following the end of the Cold War in 1991 left employment at less than 800, including tenant activities, in 2002. The 120 mm cannon for the M1A2 Abrams, the army's current main battle tank, was the principal item manufactured in 2002. The arsenal site encompasses 142 acres (57 ha). A museum located on-site is open to the public year-round and contains exhibits on arsenal history and the evolution of cannon design.

For illustration see CAST-IRON ARCHITECTURE.

Swantek, John, ed. *The Watervliet Arsenal: A Chronology of the Nation's Oldest Arsenal, 1813–2002* (Watervliet, NY: Watervliet Arsenal Public Affairs Office, 2002)

John Swantek

Watkins and Flint Purchase. In 1791 New York City investors John W. Watkins, Royal W. Flint, and associates approached the commissioners of the State Land Office about buying a tract bounded by the New Military Tract, the Town of Chemung (Chemung Co), the New Preemption Line and the Boston Ten Townships. For a mere 3s 4d per acre, the speculators purchased 336,380 acres (136,128 ha) in the present Towns of Spencer and Candor (Tioga Co); Veteran and Catlin, and parts of Horseheads, Erin, Van Etten, and Big Flats (Chemung Co); Dix, Montour, Catharine, and Cayuta, and part of Orange (Schuyler Co); and Newfield, Danby, and Caroline (Tompkins Co). The 1794 patent specified that all gold and silver mines belonged to the state, 5 acres of every 100 (2 ha of every 40) were set aside for highways, and settlers were to occupy "certain areas" within seven years. A year later one man, Robert C. Johnson, had purchased more than one-third of the land.

Hurd, Henry B. *History of Tioga, Chemung, Tompkins, and Schuyler Counties* (Philadelphia: Everts and Ensign, 1879)

Margaret D. Costello

Watkins Glen. Village (pop 2,149) in Dix and Reading (Schuyler Co). John W. Watkins and several partners purchased 350,000 acres (141,640 ha) of state land in 1794 and began development of the village around the outlet of Seneca Lake. Its post office, founded 1823, was known as Catlin and then Salubria; the village was incorporated in 1842 as Jefferson. In 1852 the names of the post office and village were changed to Watkins and in 1926 to Watkins Glen. The village was served by the Chemung Canal (1833), by lake steamers, and by the Northern Central Railroad (1849, later Pennsylvania Railroad). The Glen Springs Sanitarium and hotel operated from 1890 to 1942. Basket-making machinery was manufactured in the village in the 1890s. Located just outside village limits, the Watkins Salt Co, owned by US Salt Corp, employed 110 people in 2003. Tourism is important to Watkins Glen, given its easy access to Seneca Lake, the Watkins Glen State Park, and Watkins Glen International raceway. An Italian festival is held in August.

Elizabeth Barnaskey

Watkins Glen International. American automobile road racing was reborn after World War II in Watkins Glen (Schuyler Co). Cameron Argetsinger of Ohio, who summered in Burdett (Schuyler Co), and village civic leaders founded the Grand Prix of Watkins Glen chiefly as a way to prolong the tourist season. Sanctioned by the Village of Watkins Glen and the Sports Car Club of America (SCCA), racing took place on a 6.6 mi (10.62 km) course along the village streets and on outlying roads around the glen. The inaugural race was 2 Oct 1948. Following the death of a spectator in 1952, the races moved out of the village the next year to a temporary 4.6 mi (7.4 km) course on county roads in the Town of Dix (Schuyler Co). Also in 1953 the Watkins Glen Grand Prix Corp was formed to own and manage the race. In 1956 racing took place on a 2.3 mi (3.7 km) permanent road course designed in part by Cornell University engineers. From 1958 to 1960 Formula Libre races were held on the course each year.

From 1961 to 1980 the course hosted the US Grand Prix, attracting Formula 1 drivers from around the world. On 28 July 1973 the track was the site of one of the largest rock concerts in history, Summer Jam featuring the Grateful Dead, the Allman Brothers, and the Band. An estimated 650,000 music fans occupied the track and effectively closed down traffic in Schuyler Co. After 1980 the track was used only for amateur and professional sports car, stock car, and, rarely, motorcycle racing. By 1982 the track entered receivership, and no professional races were held. The following year it was purchased by Corning Enterprises and reopened in 1984. Since 1986 the National Association for Stock Car Auto Racing's (NASCAR's) Winston Cup (now Nextel Cup) series has staged an annual August event at Watkins Glen, attended by as many as 180,000 fans. SCCA events, vintage racing, and professional sports car racing also take place each year. International Speedway Corp (ISC) of Daytona Beach, Fla, parent company of NASCAR, acquired a half-interest in the track from Corning and in 1997 purchased the remaining half.

O'Malley, J. J., and Bill Green. *Watkins Glen from Griswold to Gordon: 50 Years of Competition at the Home of American Road Racing* (Watkins Glen, NY: Watkins Glen International Speedway, 1998)

Phil McCray

Detail of Cavern Cascade and Long Stairs at Watkins Glen State Park.

Watkins Glen State Park. Located in Dix (Schuyler Co), the park is centered on a 2 mi (3 km) gorge created by glacial advance and retreat, with 19 waterfalls as well as cascades and rock chutes. The walls of the gorge rise upward of 200 feet (61 m). The 832 steps of the gorge trail and its bridges are all made of native stone. Originally called Freer's Glen, the park opened to the public on 4 July 1863 under private ownership with newspaper editor Morvalden Ells as manager; it was sold to the state in 1906. The park encompasses approximately 1,000 acres (405 ha) with a swimming pool, campsites, picnic areas, and hiking trails, including a section of the Finger Lakes Trail. Average annual attendance in 2003 was approximately 1 million.

New York State Parks, Recreation, and Historic Preservation, http://nysparks.state.ny.us

Glenda Gephart

Watson. Town (pop 1,987) in E Lewis Co. First settled in 1799, it was not permanently settled until 1811. The town was formed from Leyden in 1821. Potatoes were a successful crop during the heyday of the Black River Canal (1851–1924), when low freight costs made marketing profitable. Bog iron was mined for the furnace at Carthage (Jefferson Co), and hemlock extract for tanning was produced from ?1871 to 1898. Dairy farms once supplied cheese factories, but most of the town has been reforested and lies within the Adirondack Park. It supports lumbering, summer resorts, and children's camps; an influx of new permanent and summer residents around Beaver, Francis, Crystal, and Chase Lakes increased the population by 339% between 1950 and 2000.

Arthur Einhorn

Watson, Elkanah (*b* Plymouth, Mass, 22 Jan 1758; *d* Port Kent, Essex Co, 5 Dec 1842). Entrepreneur and agricultural reformer. Watson attended common school in Plymouth, Mass, until 1773, when he entered an apprenticeship with a Providence, RI, merchant. After his apprenticeship, from 1779 to 1784 he traveled first to Nantes, France, forming a brief business there, but also lived in England and North Carolina. In 1789 he moved to Albany, where he helped found that city's first two banks, and successfully advocated for the 1792 incorporation of the Western Inland Lock Navigation Co and the Northern Inland Lock Navigation Co (both firms sought to build a canal system). With his banking connections he speculated heavily in lands throughout the state, particularly townsites. In 1807 he moved to Pittsfield, Mass, where he raised merino sheep and helped launch the Berkshire Agricultural Society and its fair in 1811. Watson returned to Albany six years later, promoted the idea of agricultural fairs throughout New York State, and successfully lobbied the state legislature to create the Board of Agriculture (1819). Over the period 1825–28 period he moved, in a gradual process while his house was being built, to Port Kent. Watson made and lost several fortunes during his lifetime, always managing to combine self-interest with a vision of the greater good.

Flick, Hugh Meredith. "Elkanah Watson: Gentleman-Promoter, 1758–1842" (PhD diss, Columbia Univ, 1947)

Richard Schein

Watson, James D(ewey) (*b* Chicago, 6 Apr 1928). Scientist. An enthusiastic bird-watcher as a child, Watson entered the University of Chicago at age 15. After receiving his BS in 1947, he enrolled in graduate school at Indiana University where he studied under microbiologist Salvatore Luria. Watson spent summers researching at Cold Spring Harbor Laboratory (Suffolk Co), and in 1950 he received his PhD from Indiana. From 1951 to 1953 Watson worked in the Cavendish Laboratory at the University of Cambridge in England, where he collaborated with Francis Crick. In 1953 their research developed the double helix model for the structure of deoxyribonucleic acid (DNA), which has proved to be one of the key events in modern biology. This accomplishment earned Watson the shared Nobel Prize in physiology or medicine in 1962. As a member of Harvard University's faculty from 1956 to 1976, Watson continued to make contributions to molecular biology and became publicly known for publishing *The Double Helix* (1968), an inside view of the highly competitive world of science. In 1968 Watson became director of the Cold Spring Harbor Laboratory; he modernized and expanded the institution, secured funding, and directed the laboratory into tumor virology research. From 1989 to 1992 Watson also headed the National Center for Human Genome Research at the National Institutes of Health in Bethesda, Md. Since 1994 Watson has served as Cold Spring Harbor Laboratory's president.

Watson, James D. *A Passion for DNA* (Cold Spring Harbor, NY: Cold Spring Harbor Laboratory Press, 2000)
———. *Genes, Girls, and Gamow: After the Double Helix* (New York: Knopf, 2002)

Darwin Stapleton

Watson, Thomas J(ohn), Sr (*b* Campbell, Steuben Co, 17 Feb 1874; *d* New York City, 19 June 1956). Business executive. Son of a lumber dealer, Watson grew up in Elmira, attending the Miller School of Commerce. At age 18 he began in business as a bookkeeper and traveling salesman; in 1895 he joined National Cash Register Co (NCR) as a salesman in Buffalo. He moved to company headquarters in Ohio in 1903 and rose to general sales manager in 1913, the year he was indicted and convicted, with others, of illegal sales practices. Watson appealed the outcome, which was overturned on technical grounds in 1915, and left NCR in 1914 for the Computing-Tabulating-Recording Co (C-T-R) of Endicott (Broome Co), a recently formed company with 1,300 employees. Hired as general manager, he became president in 1915.

In 1917 Watson consolidated activities of C-T-R in Canada, then expanded business to four other continents by 1923. When the name International Business Machines was adopted in 1924, new manufacturing sites in France and Germany were supplementing production at the original plants in Endicott, Washington, DC, and Dayton, Ohio. Under Watson's energetic and demanding leadership, the company doubled in size—in number of employees, manufacturing capacity, sales offices, and territorial scope—about every five or six years from 1914 to the mid-1930s, when employees numbered about 10,000. Watson and IBM maintained controversial relationships with Nazi Germany until the eve of America's entrance into World War II. Later, when IBM began producing wartime matériel, Watson declared the company would take only a 1% profit on those products. He offered the company's services in 1950 for Korean War assistance as well.

Growth of IBM in any decade could be linked to Watson's efforts to build an informed, motivated, and loyal sales force driven by a variety of morale-boosting rewards. This continued as product focus changed in the 1950s from card-based calculating machines to fully electronic devices with memory storage and as government work changed from conventional to cold-war interests in air defense, missile tracking, and space flight. With the help of federal contracts, IBM more than tripled in size between 1946 and 1956, from 22,500 employees to more than 72,500. Watson passed the presidency to his son Tom Jr in 1952, then full control in 1956, the year he died.

Maney, Kevin. *The Maverick and His Machine: Thomas Watson, Sr and the Making of IBM* (New York: John Wiley, 2003)

John Tepper Marlin

Waverly. Town (pop 1,118) in W Franklin Co. Settled *ca* 1858–59 at St. Regis Falls, the town was formed in 1880 from Dickinson, and Altamont was taken off in 1890. The first mills were built to market the local hardwoods; there was also a tannery (1865–1901) and a paper company. In 1883 the Northern Adirondack Railroad provided greater access to the timber. During the town's zenith in the 1890s, woodenware factories produced boxes, chairs, clapboard, lath, barrel staves, and broomsticks, but with the reduction of the hardwood supply, the mills closed. A mica factory operated for a time after 1911. Rail service ended in the mid-1930s, and the town went into a decline. The southern third of town is a part of the William Rockefeller private park.

Thomas W. Perrin

Waverly. Village (pop 4,607) in Barton (Tioga Co). Growth followed the completion of the Erie Railroad in 1849, and a post office opened the same year. The village was incorporated in 1853. The Elmira, Cortland and Northern Railroad (1869) and Southern Central Railroad (1872) helped foster industries, including furniture, butter pails, and toys, but many employers were outside the village limits, such as Waverly Paper Mills in East Waverly and Cayuta Car-Wheel Works across the Pennsylvania border in Sayre. From 1940 to 1955 the Manoil Toy Co's headquarters were in the village. Ingersoll-Rand operated a plant from 1974 to 1983; employees bought it and renamed it Twin Tier Casting (1985–88). Iroquois Tool Systems bought the plant in 1989. LePrino Cheese Factory opened in 1979. In 1973, Rte 17 (I-86) detoured heavy traffic out of the village center. Many residents work in the village, but others commute to Elmira, Sayre, or Athens, Pa.

Joann Lindstrom

Wawarsing [WA-WARS-ING]. Town (pop 12,889) in SW Ulster Co. Settled in 1708 by the Dutch, the town was formed from Rochester in 1806. The Delaware and Hudson Canal (1828–98) facilitated the growth of industries, the largest of which were Ellenville Glass Co (1836) and Ulster Knife Co (1871), along with a furnace and forge, paper mill, and axe factory at Napanoch. Sholem (1837–42) was North America's first Jewish agricultural colony. The Ontario and Western Railway came as far north as Ellenville in 1871 and stimulated the development of resorts in the succeeding decade and of Jewish resorts beginning just after 1900, especially in the western part of town. An Ellenville synagogue opened in 1909, and six rural synagogues followed in the 1920s. Cragsmoor was an artists' colony begun by painter E. L. Henry about 1882. The Japanese-theme Yama Farms Inn (1913–44) at Napanoch attracted celebrities. With industrial decline, the Eastern New York Correctional Facility (1900) at Napanoch became an increasingly important employer. The Merriman Dam (1951) impounded the Rondout Reservoir in western Wawarsing. In addition to surviving Jewish resorts such as the huge Nevele Hotel, there are Ukrainian summer colonies at Kerhonkson and Spring Glen. Wawarsing is the site of Sam's Point Dwarf Pine Ridge Preserve and Ice Caves Mountain. In 2000 the population was 12% black; 18% of the total population was of Latino ethnicity.

Ruth Piwonka

Wawayanda. Town (pop 6,723) in central Orange Co. Fort Gardner at Gardnerville sat on the disputed New Jersey claim line during the French and Indian War. The town was formed in 1849 from Minisink. Railroad service was provided by both the Erie (1843) and the New Jersey Midland (1868) Railroads. Hats were manufactured at Slate Hill until an 1876 fire destroyed the factory, and in the 1900s Crescent Manufacturing Co produced printers' type. I-84 opened across the town in 1970. In 2003 the Slate Hill plant of Balchem (1967) provided microencapsulation for the food and dairy industries, and Pillar manufactured interruptible power supplies for computers. Crop farming continued on the muck soils in the town's southeast corner, along with several dairy farms and orchards. Wawayanda is the site of the Mid-Hudson Forensic Psychiatric Center, a facility for the criminally insane. The Primitive Baptist Church of Brookfield (1792) is listed on the National Register.

Wawayanda Patent. In 1703, 12 New York Co residents fronted by Dr John Bridges bought land in Orange Co from 12 Munsee Indians. Supposedly 60,000 acres (24,000 ha), it was patented to them later that year by Gov Edward Hyde. Bounded on the southwest by New Jersey, the tract was actually more than 150,000 acres (61,000 ha) and included the present town of Warwick and parts of Chester, Goshen, Minisink, and Tuxedo. It was divided among the grantees in 1706, and lot sales followed. Dr James Staats had been promised land in the area and had built a house in what is now Warwick in 1700; left out of the patent, he litigated and was awarded a 13th share in 1713.

Ruth Piwonka

Wayland. Town (pop 4,314) and village (pop 1,893) in NW Steuben Co. Settled in 1806, the town was formed from Cohocton and Dansville in 1848. Beginning in the 1830s Wayland attracted many German immigrants, and by 1855 approximately two-thirds of the residents were German by birth or parentage. Rail service first came to Wayland through the Rochester Division of the Erie Railroad (1852) and later by the Delaware, Lackawanna and Western (1882). Lumbering was succeeded by dairying after the 1850s. Loon Lake was developed as a resort, and a hotel was built in 1870. The village was incorporated in 1877. From 1892 to 1912 local deposits of marl were used to make Portland cement. From 1907 to 1946 a silk mill manufactured various specialty fabrics. In the early 21st century the Gunlocke Chair Co (1902) continues to manufacture office furniture. Agriculture remains important, with potatoes and milk the principal products.

Virginia L. Wright and Jerry Wright

Wayne. Town (pop 1,165) in NE Steuben Co. Settled in 1791 and formed as Fredrickstown in 1796, Wayne adopted its current name in 1808. Francis M. McDowell (1831–94), one of the founders of the National Grange of the Patrons of Husbandry (1868), was a native. Keuka Lake was the site of the Grove Springs Hotel (1867–1915) and of the Keuka Hotel (1894–1974). Summer cottages have lined the shore since the 1920s. The lake provides a climate suitable for grape culture, and by 2002 a number of small estate wineries were flourishing in Wayne.

Virginia L. Wright and Jerry Wright

Wayne County (604 mi²/1,564 km²; pop 93,765). Created on 11 Apr 1823 from Ontario and Seneca Cos, it was named after Gen "Mad" Anthony Wayne. Lake Ontario bounds Wayne Co on the north. Sodus Bay and Port Bay, both

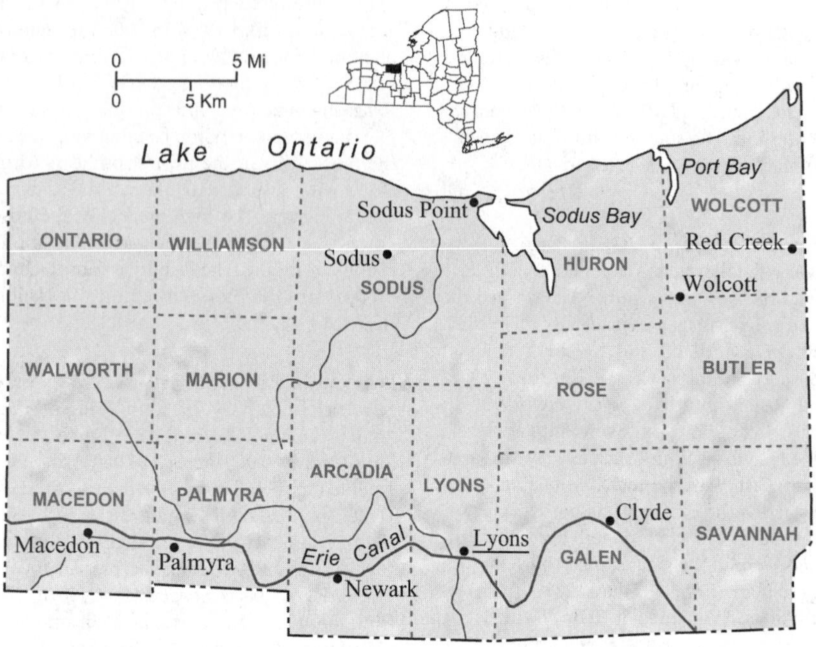

submerged estuaries, interrupt an otherwise unindented shoreline. The most recent glaciation was the primary force shaping the county's geography. Aside from a few small areas of exposed bedrock, a thick mantle of loose glacial material covers the area. The most prominent topographic features include hundreds of drumlins scattered throughout the county. Marshes in the southeastern quarter include parts of the Montezuma National Wildlife Refuge and two state wildlife management areas, all remnants of the once more extensive Cayuga Marshes. Another wildlife management area dots the northeastern shore. There are other poorly drained areas, including Zurich Bog, a habitat unchanged since the Ice Age and designated a National Natural Landmark. The county's highest point, Brantling Hill, rises 681 feet (207.6 m) above sea level. A partially eroded drumlin is the primary feature at Chimney Bluffs State Park. A subtler topographic feature is the beach ridge of glacial era Lake Iroquois running parallel to Lake Ontario's shoreline, about 5 miles (8 km) to the south; it served as a natural highway, especially from Sodus Bay west. Stones from the lakeshore supplied much of the material for Wayne Co's cobblestone buildings, the largest concentration of such buildings in the nation.

Annual precipitation approximates 36 inches (91 cm). Waters south of a second, midcounty ridge drain south and then east via Ganargua Creek and Clyde River, emptying into the Seneca River. Water north of the ridge flows directly into Lake Ontario. Aside from the marshes, the vegetation at the time of settlement consisted of maple, beech, and birch forests, or elm, ash, and cottonwood forests, depending on soils and drainage. Mastodon remains have been unearthed at several locations in the county, most recently in 1973.

American Indians, Settlement, and Ethnicity

There is archaeological evidence of human habitation, particularly near the Clyde River, dating back at least 5,000–6,000 years. The Seneca and the Cayuga, who lived to the south, included the area within their hunting and fishing ranges. French traders began visiting the lakeshore from at least the late 1600s, and about 1722 they built a blockhouse inland near Clyde; otherwise, white settlement did not begin until 1789, near Palmyra and Lyons. The Preemption Line extends south from Sodus Bay, splitting the county's lands into two major parcels. The eastern third was surveyed as part of the New Military Tract, and the rest was part of the Phelps and Gorham Purchase (later Pulteney Purchase).

Charles Williamson, Pulteney land agent, anticipating major trade routes to run north and south between Lake Ontario and the Susquehanna River, projected an important commercial role for Sodus Bay. In 1794 he planned a city and ordered roads cut from the bay to Palmyra and Lyons, but the east-west routes that developed favored other localities. Williamson hoped to attract "substantial farmers," but most initial settlers were small farmers from the Hudson Valley, Long Island, New England, and New Jersey who paid by installment for small tracts. Williamson attracted a few substantial buyers between 1795 and 1810, mostly from Maryland, who brought enslaved African Americans with them. Slavery did not take hold, however, and those brought in were soon manumitted. By 1799 there was a community of freemen near Palmyra. The 1820 census records no slaves, but there were 142 "free persons of color." That population grew slowly, reaching a peak of 379 in 1880, when it was concentrated in Sodus and Lyons, then declining to 89 in 1925.

Settlement was gradual because of disease, relative isolation, and drier and flatter lands to the south and west. During the War of 1812, the British destroyed Sodus Point (1813) and Pultneyville (1814) and seized the military supplies, but both were rebuilt; settlement was arrested by the war and to an extent reversed. Irish immigrants began arriving in the 1820s and then came in larger numbers, along with German and Dutch settlers, from the 1840s to the early 20th century. The Irish and the Germans settled mainly in canal villages. In 1850 nearly 10% of Lyons' population was German-born. The Dutch immigrants tended to farm, initially in Williamson, Sodus, and Marion; they appear as the largest foreign-born population in the county in the 1910 census.

Italians began settling in the canal towns after 1880, especially in Clyde. Starting in the 1930s, but especially after 1945, African Americans came as migrant farmworkers. Some stayed,

WAYNE CO POPULATION CENSUS FIGURES

	White	Nonwhite	Total Population	Foreign-Born
1830	33,455	188	33,643	410
1840	41,835	222	42,057	—
1850	44,685	268	44,953	4,063
1860	47,492	270	47,762	7,304
1870	47,355	355	47,710	7,411
1880	51,300	400	51,700	7,891
1890	49,429	300	49,729	7,654
1900	48,401	259	48,660	6,899
1910	49,980	199	50,179	7,425
1920	48,687	140	48,827	6,639
1930	49,860	135	49,995	6,167
1940	52,613	134	52,747	4,902
1950	56,859	464	57,323	4,096
1960	66,440	1,549	67,989	3,528
1970	76,671	2,733	79,404	2,654
1980	81,035	3,546	84,581	2,443
1990	85,234	3,889	89,123	1,815
2000	87,954	5,811	93,765	2,157

Notes: "Nonwhite" includes African Americans, Asians, American Indians, and Pacific Islanders and, for 2000, also the mixed race and other race categories. Through the 1960 census these figures primarily reflect the African American population. Foreign-born figures for 1830 include only those not naturalized, and for 1930 and 1950, the foreign-born totals include Whites only. Other years include all foreign-born in the population.

POPULATIONS OF TOWNS, WAYNE CO

Town, Year Founded	1800	1840	1880	1920	1960	2000
Arcadia, 1825	—	4,980	5,702	9,266	15,836	14,889
Butler, 1826	—	2,271	2,161	1,452	1,441	2,277
Galen, 1812	—	4,234	5,461	4,172	4,419	4,439
Huron, 1826[a]	—	1,943	2,036	1,416	1,356	2,117
Lyons, 1811	—	4,302	5,762	5,559	6,147	5,831
Macedon, 1823	—	2,396	2,871	2,202	3,617	8,688
Marion, 1825[b]	—	1,903	2,100	2,158	2,785	4,974
Ontario, 1807[c]	—	1,889	2,962	2,620	4,259	9,778
Palmyra, 1796	994	3,549	4,435	4,040	6,179	7,672
Rose, 1826	—	2,038	2,244	1,928	2,122	2,442
Savannah, 1824	—	1,718	1,867	1,524	1,667	1,838
Sodus, 1796	416	4,472	5,285	4,408	6,587	8,949
Walworth, 1829	—	1,734	2,338	1,997	2,782	8,402
Williamson, 1802	—	2,147	2,745	3,293	5,294	6,777
Wolcott, 1807	—	2,481	3,731	2,792	3,498	4,692

Note: In 1800 the Towns of Palmyra and Sodus were in Ontario Co.

[a]Port Bay until 1834.

[b]Winchester until 1826.

[c]Freetown until 1808.

concentrating initially in Sodus and Williamson and later in Lyons. More recently Puerto Ricans and, in the 1990s, Mexicans arrived as seasonal labor in canneries, horticultural enterprises, and orchards. Some settled, especially in Newark. On the whole, however, the county's population remains non-Latino white at 92.5% of the 2000 population, with African Americans at 3.4%. Those of Latino ethnicity make up 2.4%.

Transportation

Despite Williamson's plans, most traffic moved east and west. The first turnpikes bypassed Wayne Co to the south. The available routes within the county were the Clyde River–Ganargua Creek waterway (roughly the route of the Erie Canal) and the Ridge Road. Some produce was shipped by way of Lake Ontario, and for this purpose a Canadian firm established a purchasing office at Sodus Bay about 1806. The Ridge Road was extended eastward after 1817, regular coach service was soon in place, and other roads were built, but all of this development was overshadowed by the Erie Canal, completed in Wayne Co in 1822. The canal spurred settlement, commercial agriculture, and industry, and stimulated growth in existing settlements (Clyde, Lyons, and Palmyra) and the creation of Newark. As a result, the county population grew 65% between 1820 and 1830 and 25% between 1830 and 1840.

Rail service began in 1853 with the New York Central Railroad, parallel to the Erie Canal. During the 1870s two additional lines were built: the Lake Ontario Shore Railroad linked the county's northern reaches with Oswego and Lewiston (Niagara Co), and a north-south route connected Sodus Bay and Newark to the Pennsylvania coalfields (1872). Other lines came later, along with two electric interurban lines by 1906. Due in part to its canal and rail connections, Newark became the county's largest village by 1900. Wayne Co is still served by the Ontario Midland Railroad and by CSX Transportation. Rail passenger service ended in 1967.

Economic Development

Agriculture, agriculture-related industries, and small- and medium-scale manufacturing are the core of Wayne Co's economy. Initially, products included potash, grain, flour, and whiskey. The drop in shipping costs because of the Erie Canal transformed the county's relationship to markets. Wheat became the principal cash crop. As the Midwest came to dominate the wheat market, Wayne Co farmers placed greater emphasis on fruit, ideally suited to its soil and lake-moderated climate. Other 19th-century crops were tobacco and peppermint. In the mid-1800s Wayne Co produced approximately 50% of the nation's peppermint oil.

Early industry tended to be ancillary to agriculture, beginning with asheries, gristmills, and distilleries. Canneries, which began in Newark in 1863, and evaporators proliferated by the early 20th century. According to the *Cyclopedia of American Agriculture* (1907), Wayne Co "undoubtedly produce[d] more evaporated apples than any state outside of New York, except perhaps California" early in the 20th century. Many of these dried apples were exported. Other 19th-century industries included iron mining and founding, coverlet weaving, pottery and glass manufacture, and cigar making. The county's first newspaper was the *Palmyra Register* (1817), and its first bank was the Wayne County Bank of Palmyra (1829).

In the 20th century, fruit grew in economic importance while its region shifted northward, closer to the lake. (In 1997 Wayne Co ranked first in the state and fifth nationwide in apple production.) Dairying, vegetable farming, and horticulture thrived in the south. Mucklands in central and southeastern Wayne Co produce potatoes and onions. Farms became larger, less numerous, and more specialized. Wegman's Egg Farm in Wolcott produces 550,000 eggs a day, making it the largest in the state. Marshall Farms, in Huron, is the nation's largest supplier of pet ferrets. Mott's apple-processing plant in Williamson is one of the largest in the United States. Wayne Co ranks fifth in the state in overall agricultural production.

Industry consolidated and expanded, eventually far outstripping agriculture in sales. In addition to food processing, products came to include wood and paper goods, plastics, machinery, and electronics. Recent additions include custom-designed batteries for industrial and military use, porous ceramics for filtration systems, and shipboard navigation systems. From 1990 to 1999, 736 patents were issued to Wayne Co companies.

Labor

The most persistent issue regarding labor in Wayne Co has been about the seasonal needs of the fruit harvest. In the 19th century, help was found locally, if only by closing school for two weeks in autumn to allow students and teachers to participate. In the 20th century, the need for outside labor grew with the expansion of the fruit industry and with laws limiting women's and children's hours. During World War I, men and boys were recruited from nearby cities. In the 1920s and 1930s there was increased seasonal use of "hoboes," "drifters," and Indians from Onondaga Reservation. During severe World War II labor shortages, farmers and manufacturers used German prisoners of war. In the decades after 1945, African American migrant workers, primarily from Florida, became important to the fruit industry. In the 1990s those migrants were being displaced by workers from Mexico.

Manufacturing is Wayne Co's largest source of employment, but 46% of its workforce commutes to jobs outside the county. The median household income approximately matches the statewide average, although per capita income is lower. The county's poverty rate, at 8.6%, was half the state average in 1999. Union activity has never been strong. Railroad workers were organized but not as a result of local efforts. The first local industry to be unionized was Bloomer Bros, a Newark manufacturer of cardboard boxes in the 1930s. Unions with offices in Wayne Co represent letter carriers, rural letter carriers, papermakers, railroad signalers, cannery workers, and security guards. In 2002 union leaders in Wayne, Ontario, Seneca, and Yates Cos formed the Finger Lakes Labor Council for the area's estimated 19,000 union members.

Religion and Social Movements

Churches were organized in Palmyra and Lyons in the 1790s and throughout the county in the first decades of the 19th century. Methodist, Baptist, and Presbyterian congregations predominated, and there were smaller numbers of Episcopalians and Quakers. Toward midcentury, with the arrival of European immigrants came Lutheran and Dutch Reformed Churches; the first Catholic Church was in Palmyra in 1849.

As part of the Burned-over District, Wayne Co experienced many of the new religions, religious revivals, and social reform movements of the Second Great Awakening in the early 1800s. The most famous of the religious events in the area relates to the establishment of the Church of Latter-Day Saints (Mormons). In 1830 Joseph Smith Jr published the first edition of the Book of Mormon in Palmyra. In 1826 the Shakers founded a community on the south shore of Sodus Bay, but it relocated to Livingston Co in

1838. The site was soon used by a Fourierist utopian community, the Sodus Bay Phalanx (1844–46). Modern Spiritualism had its roots in the hamlet of Hydesville, where in 1848 the Fox sisters reported hearing "rappings."

Other social movements included the Antimasonic movement of the 1820s and 1830s and abolitionism. Rallies were held to denounce Freemasonry, and Masonic lodges were forced to close, including those in Clyde, Lyons, Newark, Palmyra, and Pultneyville. Myron Holley, editor of the *Lyons Countryman,* was a leader of the Antimasonic Party and delivered the main address at its Philadelphia convention in 1830. The Palmyra Anti-Slavery Society (1834) was one of the earliest of such organizations in the state. Samuel C. Cuyler operated an Underground Railroad station in Pultneyville, and Pliny Sexton, a Quaker, did so in Palmyra. H. N. Throop and other lake captains ferried escaped slaves to Canada. Samuel Ringgold Ward, who had escaped slavery in Maryland as a child, pastored an all-white Congregational church in South Butler in 1841–43 and became a well-known lecturer and the author of *Autobiography of a Fugitive Negro* (1855). The Liberty League, the uncompromising faction of the abolitionist Liberty Party, selected Gerrit Smith as its presidential candidate at its 1847 convention in Macedon. In 1853 at the South Butler church Antoinette Brown (later Blackwell) became the first ordained woman minister in the nation.

Education and Social Welfare

The first schools in what became Wayne Co were log structures built in Palmyra in 1793 and in Macedon soon afterward. Early secondary schools included the Clyde High School (1834), one of the state's earliest union schools, and Lyons Academy (1837–43), which merged into the public system as a union school. Specialized and advanced institutions included the Lyons Musical Academy (1853-late 1880s) and the Marion Collegiate Institute (1855–1904). In the 20th century rural and village districts consolidated. The first central school district was formed in Rose (1926); consolidation was completed in 1969, but the Gananda district was a new formation in 1974. The county had two church-affiliated schools in 2003: St. Michael's School in Newark (Roman Catholic, K–8) and East Palmyra Bible School (K–8). The Newark Developmental Center (1878–1991), under various names, was the home of the state's second-oldest institution for people with developmental disabilities. The site now houses the Finger Lakes Developmental Disabilities Services branch office, local BOCES headquarters, and a Finger Lakes Community College branch. There is a 280-bed hospital in Newark that has a branch in Sodus.

Politics

Rivalry between Canandaigua and Rochester influenced the creation of Wayne Co. For five years from 1816 Canandaigua's representatives stalled the formation of Monroe Co, and when the division of Ontario Co could no longer be delayed, they sought to hem in Rochester by supporting Palmyra's aspirations to form a county extending from Sodus to Irondequoit Bays. Nathaniel Rochester then supported Lyons as the seat of an alternative county farther east. When Wayne Co was formed in 1823, with Lyons as county seat, it extended neither so far west as Canandaigua wanted nor so far east as Rochester proposed. In 1854 construction of the present county courthouse was completed. It was substantially renovated in 1898.

As a noncharter county under the state's County Law, Wayne has no elected executive. The Board of Supervisors elected by the county's 15 towns governs. In the 1960s the courts determined that the arrangement of each supervisor having one vote violated the US Constitution, so Wayne Co adopted a weighted voting system, in proportion to the population of the supervisor's town, ranging (in 2002) from 86 for Savannah to 630 for Arcadia. An appointed county administrator oversees day-to-day operations.

Recent History

Population growth has been persistent. Wayne Co as a whole has not experienced a decline since 1920. After World War II the pace of growth quickened, growing 63.6% from 1950 to 2000, with the fastest rate between 1950 and 1970. Looking more closely, the picture is mixed. Several eastern and central towns and villages have suffered significant declines in population. The most striking growth has occurred in the west, in the three towns nearest Rochester and bordering Monroe Co, where suburbanization since the 1950s has been marked. As a result, the western towns are younger and more affluent than those of the east.

A high dependence on manufacturing (26.4% of the workforce in 2000) has left the county exposed to fluctuations in the business cycle. As a consequence, employment levels can be unsteady. To bolster economic activity, the Wayne Economic Development Corp promotes the county's 10 industrial parks. In October 2002 the state established the Wayne County Empire Zone, concentrated in Newark, to provide tax incentives to investors, and active exploration for natural gas is under way in the eastern portion of the county. Tourism, including heritage and agricultural tourism, is also being encouraged, especially along the lakeshore and the Erie Canal corridor. In addition, Wayne Co has played an active role in the development of "Smart Growth" policies, including those intended to reconcile suburbanization and agriculture.

The standard histories are W. H. McIntosh, *History of Wayne County* (1877), and George W. Cowles, *Landmarks of Wayne County* (1895). Stephen W. Jacobs, *Wayne County: The Aesthetic Heritage of a Rural Area* (1979) is without peer as a study of the landscape and built environment. The county's most distinctive form of agriculture is discussed in James Kerr, *The Fruit Industry in Wayne County, 1823–1984* (1985). There are many community histories of towns and villages in the county; one of the oldest, by Alfred S. Roe, *Rose Neighborhood Sketches* (1893), is unusually detailed. On archaeology, see Harold Secor, *Prehistory of the Savannah NY Area, 9000 BC to 1700 AD* (1987). Wayne Co figures prominently in Olaf William Shelgren, et al, *Cobblestone Landmarks of New York State* (1978).

Scott C. Monje

weather. See Climate and weather.

Weavers. Pioneering folk music group. New York City–born Pete Seeger (*b* 1919), Arkansas-born Lee Hays (1913–81), and Ronnie Gilbert (*b* 1926) and Fred Hellerman (*b* 1927), both born in Brooklyn, first began performing for People's Songs concerts in New York City in late 1948. With Seeger playing banjo and guitar, Hellerman on guitar, and vocals by Gilbert and Hays, they recorded briefly for Charter and Hootenanny Records in 1949. An engagement at the Village Vanguard in Greenwich Village in late 1949 soon led to numerous popular recordings for Decca Records (1950–53), particularly the Hebrew song "Tzena, Tzena, Tzena," Lead Belly's "Goodnight Irene," the traditional "On Top of Old Smoky," and Woody Guthrie's "So Long (It's Been Good to Know Yuh)." Increasing political attacks because of band members' involvement in left-wing politics caused them to stop playing together in 1952, but a 1955 Christmas Eve concert at Manhattan's Carnegie Hall led to a renewed concert career and recordings for Vanguard Records. Beginning in 1958 Seeger was replaced by Erik Darling, Frank Hamilton, and finally Bernie Krause before the group disbanded in 1964. The original members reunited in 1980 for a final concert at Carnegie Hall, documented by an album and a film, both entitled *Weavers: Wasn't That a Time!*

Cohen, Ronald D. *Rainbow Quest: The Folk Music Revival and American Society, 1940–1970* (Amherst: Univ of Massachusetts Press, 2002)

Ronald D. Cohen

Webb. Town (pop 1,912) in N Herkimer Co. Settlement was attempted in 1790 by Arthur Noble, a Scot, on the Nobleborough tract, and by John Brown of Rhode Island, who tried to open an iron mine near Thendara on 210,000 acres (85,000 ha) he acquired in 1798. Permanent settlement followed in 1837, and lumbering became the chief industry. The Mohawk and Malone Railroad (1892) opened up the town for tourist facilities, such as the Eagle Bay Hotel (1896–1945), and private camps. The town was formed from Wilmurt in 1896; Wilmurt dissolved in 1918 and was divided between Webb and Ohio. Moss Lake was the site of the Ganienkeh Mohawk occupation of state land from 1974 to 1978. In the early 21st century Webb is a major summer and winter destination for hikers, campers, sports enthusiasts, and snowmobilers; skiing is offered at McCauley Mountain. Created by the lumbering industry, Stillwater Reservoir (1876) had been enlarged three times by 1924; since 1922 it has been managed by the Hudson–Black River Regulating District. Webb, at 466 mi^2 (1,207 km^2), has the largest area of any town in the state.

Susan R. Perkins

Webb, James Watson (*b* Claverack, Columbia Co, 2 Feb 1802; *d* New York City, 7 June 1884). Newspaper editor. Orphaned at 5, Webb lived with and was educated by relatives in Cooperstown (Otsego Co). In 1819 Webb was granted a commission as a second lieutenant in the US Army. He married Helen Lispenard Stewart, the daughter of New York City merchant Alexander L. Stewart, in 1823. Webb resigned his commission in 1827 and moved to New York City, where Stewart hired him as editor of the *New York Morning Courier* newspaper. In 1829 Webb merged the *Courier* and *New York Enquirer* into the *Morning Courier and New-York Enquirer,* which by 1832 became New York City's largest daily newspaper. Initially Webb made the paper an organ of the emerging Democratic Party, but in 1832 he broke with the Democrats, and in the 1834 campaign he aligned with the Whig Party. Later a Republican, he was a strong supporter of

Abraham Lincoln in 1860. Pres Lincoln appointed Webb minister to Brazil in 1861. Webb sold the newspaper in 1861 and remained in diplomatic service until 1869. He purchased a home in New York City in 1874 and often spent summers in Bay Shore (Suffolk Co).

Crouthamel, James L. *James Watson Webb: A Biography* (Middletown, Conn: Wesleyan Univ Press, 1969)

Thomas D. Beal

Webb, William Seward (*b* New York City, 31 Jan 1851; *d* Shelburne, Vt, 29 Oct 1926). Railroad builder. From a wealthy family, Webb studied medicine at the College of Physicians and Surgeons of Columbia College in New York City and graduated in 1875. After several years of private medical practice, he entered the world of finance as a stockbroker with the Wall St firm Worden and Co, which became the W. S. Webb Co in 1888. After his 1881 marriage to Eliza "Lila" Vanderbilt, daughter of railroad entrepreneur William H. Vanderbilt, Webb joined the family railcar-building business in 1885 and the following year became president of the newly reorganized Wagner Palace Car Co, with headquarters in New York City and a factory in Buffalo. To open and access land that he had bought in the Adirondacks, Webb built a railroad from Herkimer in the Mohawk Valley to Montreal, completed in just 18 months and opened in October 1892. Called the Adirondack and St. Lawrence Railroad and later the Mohawk and Malone Railroad, it was leased by the New York Central and Hudson River Railroad in 1893. Webb purchased 250,000 acres (101,000 ha) in the central Adirondacks in 1891 in what is now the Town of Webb (Herkimer Co). There he built a luxurious summer estate on an 8,000-acre (3,200 ha) parcel at Lake Lila, named after his wife, and called it Nehasane, a Native American term meaning "Beaver Crossing River on Log." This area is now part of the Adirondack Park.

Foreman, John, and Robbe Pierce Stimson. *The Vanderbilts and the Gilded Age* (New York: St. Martin's Press, 1991)

Harter, Henry. *Fairy Tale Railroad: The Mohawk and Malone; from the Mohawk, through the Adirondacks to the St. Lawrence* (Sylvan Beach, NY: North Country Books, 1979)

Jim Shaughnessy

Webb Institute. Private college in Glen Cove (Nassau Co). A unique institution devoted solely to teaching naval architecture and marine engineering, it was founded in 1894 by William H. Webb, New York City's preeminent shipbuilder of the mid–19th century. Believing that technological changes necessitated a more formal and sophisticated shipbuilding education than had previously existed, Webb opened it as the Webb Academy and Home for Shipbuilders in Fordham [now in Bronx Co] with an initial enrollment of eight. All students received full-tuition scholarships, a practice that continues into the 21st century. Renamed Webb Institute, it moved in 1947 to a 26-acre (11 ha) estate on Long Island Sound. At the start of the 21st century, it had 11 full-time faculty and an enrollment of 70–100 students.

Webb Institute, http://www.webb-institute.edu

Richard F. Welch

Webster. Town (pop 37,926) and village (pop 5,216) in NE Monroe Co. Permanently settled in 1805, the town was formed from Penfield in 1840. German farmers arrived before the Civil War, and berries were a major crop. As a result, Webster had large basket factories from 1875 to 1964. By the end of the 19th century there was a substantial trade in dried apples. Other products included sashes, doors, moldings, and caskets. The village incorporated in 1905. In the 1950s it annexed 182 acres (73.7 ha), which became the main Xerox complex beginning in 1956. This spurred rapid suburbanization; Webster increased in population from 7,174 in 1950 to 16,434 a decade later. Other large employers are Lawyers Cooperative Publishing Co (1971), the Paychex data center, and Trident Precision Manufacturing. The town's population increased 17% from 1990 to 2000 because of high-tech industries, a strong school system, and developable farmland. Growth has been supported by the expansion of parks, public services, and new facilities like the Webster Aquatic Center. The cobblestone Webster Baptist Church (1855) is a landmark.

Carolyn Vacca

Webster, (Alice) Jean (Chandler) (*b* Fredonia, Chautauqua Co, 24 July 1876; *d* New York City, 11 June 1916). Author. Jean Webster was the great niece of Mark Twain and the daughter of Charles Webster, with whom Twain quarreled bitterly over business concerns. She graduated from the Lady Jane Grey School in Binghamton in 1896, attended the college division of Fredonia Normal School, and graduated from Vassar College in 1901. Webster's first book, *When Patty Went to College* (1903), was well received, and Webster went on to write several more books and plays. She is best remembered for *Daddy Long-Legs* (1912), the story of an orphaned girl sent to college by an unknown benefactor. Webster rewrote it as a play script and toured with the company producing it in 1914, the same year its sequel, *Dear Enemy*, was published. *Daddy Long-Legs* was made into several movies (the 1955 version starred Fred Astaire) and a British musical comedy, *Love from Judy*. After marrying her longtime love, Webster died tragically in childbirth.

Simpson, Alan, and Mary Simpson. *Jean Webster, Storyteller* (LaGrangeville, NY: Tymor Associates, 1984)

Pam Kirst

Weed, (Edward) Thurlow (*b* Cairo [now in Greene Co], 15 Nov 1797; *d* New York City, 22 Nov 1882). Politician and newspaper publisher. The son of unsuccessful farmers, he left school at age 8 to help support his family and developed an interest in politics while working in Albany and New York City (1815–17). He became a foreman at the *Albany Register* in 1817 and wrote his first editorials; he then launched two unsuccessful papers of his own. Moving to Rochester as assistant editor of the *Telegraph* in 1822, he became part owner by 1825. He went to Albany to lobby for a bank charter in 1824 and was elected later that year to the assembly as a Clintonian Republican. Weed eventually gravitated to the Antimasonic Party, which was emerging in western New York State, and in 1828 launched the *Anti-Masonic Enquirer* in Rochester. Arguing that the party was not yet ready to act on its own, he pragmatically favored supporting the National Republican candidate for governor in 1828. When the Antimasons rejected his advice, ran their own candidate, and failed, Weed's position in the party was strengthened. Elected to the assembly in 1829, he founded the *Albany Evening Journal* in 1830 and made the newspaper his power base for the next 30 years.

In 1834, as Antimasonic excitement waned, Weed helped form the New York State branch of the Whig Party. Benefiting from the panic of 1837, Weed successfully promoted William H. Seward for the governorship in 1838 and led the move to replace Henry Clay with William Henry Harrison as the Whig candidate for the presidential election of 1840. Weed's use of political influence for personal gain, his openness to Catholics, and his refusal to support the outright abolition of slavery alienated various factions and set him back within the party. Following Clay's loss in the 1844 presidential election, in 1848 Weed successfully promoted Zachary Taylor for president, New Yorker Millard Fillmore for vice president, and Seward for senator. After Taylor's death, however, the Compromise of 1850 divided Fillmore, Seward, and the party as a whole.

The transition from Whig to Republican was delayed in New York State because Weed believed Seward's chances for reelection in 1854 were better as a Whig. Once Seward was elected, Weed helped form New York State's Republican Party in 1855. Believing the time not right, he held Seward back from the presidential nomination of 1856. Weed then promoted him unsuccessfully in 1860, when Seward's position was harmed in part by his long association with Weed. Still, Pres Abraham Lincoln sought Weed's advice on patronage issues and in 1861 included him in an informal diplomatic mission to curb support for the Confederacy in Britain and France. Increasingly at odds with the Radical Republicans, Weed left the *Evening Journal* in 1863 to engage in lucrative war-related business deals in New York City. He backed the Union (Republican) ticket in 1864 in the state and after the war supported Pres Andrew Johnson. He was the publisher of the *New York Commercial Advertiser* from 1867 to 1869. He toyed with the idea of starting a new party but gradually faded from active political life.

Weed, a controversial figure admired for his political skills, came to be known to both friend and foe as "the Dictator." Although he never held office apart from two brief terms in the assembly, he was the behind-the-scenes leader of three successive parties in New York State. Charming and persuasive, he was also secretive by nature and rarely spoke above a whisper. He was adept at identifying and supporting popular issues but on the whole was less interested in issues than in the mechanics of party organization, candidate selection, and patronage.

See also ANTIMASONRY.

Van Deusen, Glyndon G. *Thurlow Weed: Wizard of the Lobby* (Boston: Little, Brown, 1947)

Scott C. Monje

Weedsport. Village (pop 2,017) in Brutus (Cayuga Co). Settled in 1802 and named for the Weed family, Weedsport developed rapidly after the Erie Canal came through in 1819; from that year until 1838, it served as Auburn's canal port. The village was incorporated in 1831. In the 19th century Weedsport's factories included a foundry, bending works, brewery, and distillery;

shops produced pumps, hoopskirts, cigars, and patent medicines. The New York Central Railroad (1853) and the Southern Central Railroad (1869–1957; after 1888, Lehigh Valley Railroad) ran through the village and were later joined by the West Shore Railroad (1883). Starting in 1865 Weedsport had a famed baseball team, the Watsons. Harry "Zip" Northup (1882–1944), grandson of Solomon Northup (the famed free man tricked into slavery), pitched for the Watsons and went on to play three years for the Cuban Giants. A Thruway exit just north of the village (1954) gave it excellent highway access. In 2002 Weedsport is the site of the Cayuga County Fairgrounds, the DIRT Motorsport Hall of Fame and Classic Car Museum, and the Weedsport Speedway.

Jeanne L. Baker

Wegmans Food Markets. In 1916 John Wegman opened the Rochester Fruit and Vegetable Co after having worked for his parents' grocery. In 1921 he and his brother Walter E. Wegman purchased the Seel Grocery Co and in 1930 opened their first supermarket, a 20,000 ft^2 (1,860 m^2) store with a cafeteria for 300 diners, in Rochester. It was incorporated in 1931, and in 1949 Robert Wegman started to convert his grocery stores into self-service supermarkets and over the course of the 1950s and 1960s expanded throughout Rochester and nearby suburbs. In 1968 Wegmans opened its first store in Syracuse, and since then throughout Western and Central New York, entering the Buffalo market in 1977 and Corning (Steuben Co) in the Southern Tier in 1992. In 1974 Wegmans purchased a Rochester-based chain of home and garden stores, Bilt-Rite Chase-Pitkin. Renamed Chase-Pitkin, these stores are usually located adjacent to Wegmans Food Markets. Also in 1974 Wegmans became one of the first supermarkets in the country to scan products through the use of universal product codes (UPCs). Wegmans Food Markets opened their first 100,000 ft^2 (9,300 m^2) store in 1982 and have opened similar "superstores" in a number of locations, including the 130,000 ft^2 (12,100 m^2) flagship store in Pittsford (Monroe Co). The superstores often feature dining facilities, which serve as convenient meeting places. Still privately owned, Wegmans had more than 60 supermarkets with annual revenues of $2.9 billion, and about 29,000 employees in 2001. Of those, approximately 20 were in the Rochester region, 12 in metropolitan Buffalo, 9 in the Syracuse area, and 10 in the Finger Lakes and Southern Tier. The Chase-Pitkin chain had 15 stores, with more than 2,000 employees. Wegmans Food Market opened its first store outside of New York State in 1993 in Erie, Pa, and its first store in New Jersey in 1999.

Wegmans, http://www.wegmans.com

Martin Naparsteck

Weight Watchers International. Weight loss company with headquarters in Woodbury (Nassau Co), founded in New York City by Jean Nidetch and Albert Lippert in 1963. After obtaining Dr Norman Jolliffe's dietary plan from the New York City Department of Health Obesity Clinic, Nidetch began a support group for overweight friends in her Queens apartment in 1962. After the support group spread throughout the New York City area, Lippert, an executive in the garment business, suggested in April 1963 that Nidetch organize a weight loss business, and the following month the company, Weight Watchers, began. The first franchise opened in Providence, RI, in 1964 and within a decade franchises were operating throughout the United States and Europe with well over half a million members attending the weekly meetings. By 1978, when Nidetch sold Weight Watchers to H. J. Heinz Co for $71.2 million, the company had begun selling its own brand of food scales, created *Weight Watchers* magazine, a cookbook series, and a prepared foods line. By the end of the 1980s Weight Watchers prepared foods were the second largest selling brand item at Heinz. Nidetch, who served as president until 1973, stepped down to become consultant to the business until 1998. Lippert, who was chairman of the board of Weight Watchers from its inception, served as president after Nidetch retired and remained chairman of the board after the company was sold to Heinz. In 1999 Heinz sold Weight Watchers diet centers, with sales of $400 million, to the European investment firm Artal Luxembourg for $735 million while retaining the prepared foods line. Weight Watchers went public 15 Nov 2001.

Nidetch, Jean, and Joan Rattner Heilman. *The Story of Weight Watchers* (New York: New American Library, 1979)
Weight Watchers International, http://www.weightwatchers.com

Timothy W. Kneeland

Weill, Kurt (Julian) (*b* Dessau, Germany, 2 Mar 1900; *d* New York City, 3 Apr 1950). Composer. Weill's father, a Jewish cantor, taught him piano, and by his teens he was working as accompanist and musical coach at a nearby theater. He studied with Ferruccio Busoni in Berlin and soon emerged as the most innovative German composer of theater music and opera during the Weimar period. He collaborated with dramatist Bertolt Brecht on his two most famous German works, the operas *Dreigroschenoper* (Threepenny Opera, 1928) and *Aufstieg und Fall der Stadt Mahagonny* (Rise and Fall of the City of Mahagonny, 1930). In 1926 he married actress and singer Lotte Lenya [Karoline Blamauer] (1898–1981), who became the most renowned interpreter of his music. Weill left Germany in 1933 for Paris, then London. He moved to the United States in 1935, began composing for Broadway, and became a citizen in 1945. Weill and Lenya moved in 1941 to Nyack (Rockland Co), which would remain their home for much of their lives.

Though his American musical style was somewhat less harmonically audacious than the style of his German works, his musicals were still adventurous musically and dramatically. *Johnny Johnson* (1937), his first Broadway musical, produced by the Group Theater, had an antiwar theme. A vast pageant of Jewish history, *The Eternal Road* (1937) with a libretto by Franz Werfel and staged by Max Reinhardt, appeared at the Manhattan Opera House. In *Knickerbocker Holiday* (1938), loosely based on Washington Irving's *Knickerbocker History of New York,* Petrus Stuyvesant's character sings what is perhaps Weill's best-known American show tune, "September Song." *Lady in the Dark* (1941) explored psychoanalysis, *Love Life* (1948) was a satirical look at American marriage, and *Lost in the Stars* (1949) was a powerful indictment of apartheid. Weill's crowning Broadway achievement was his American opera *Street Scene* (1947) with a libretto by Langston Hughes. Weill's European works were almost unknown in this country at the time of his death, and few took his Broadway shows seriously. A revival of *Three-Penny Opera* (1954–59) and Lenya's tireless advocacy helped raise awareness of Weill's music.

Taylor, Ronald. *Kurt Weill: Composer in a Divided World* (New York: Simon & Schuster, 1991)

David Raymond

Welch Allyn. Medical equipment manufacturer. Dr. Francis A. Welch and William N. Allyn developed the first handheld, direct-illuminating ophthalmoscope, which is used by doctors to examine the eye, and a process for manufacturing it. In 1915 they formed Welch Allyn in Auburn (Cayuga Co) to produce and distribute the instrument. Other medical equipment followed. In 1924 Welch Allyn invented a locking mechanism with interchangeable tool heads, allowing multiple tools and accessories to be attached to the same handle; the device would become standard in the industry. Welch Allyn was the first company to manufacture disposable tips for diagnostic in-struments, helping to prevent cross-contam-ination and infection (1956). It developed the disposable sigmoidoscope, a hollow tubular device used to inspect the rectum (1969), and invented a color-imaging technique for video endoscopy, giving physicians a more accurate picture of the body's hollow organs (1977).

The company relocated to nearby Skaneateles Falls (Onondaga Co) in 1953. It has diversified with an electronic bar code reading company, Hand Held Products (1972), and now has divisions that work exclusively in vital signs monitoring and high-quality lighting systems. In the early 21st century, Welch Allyn has a global workforce of over 2,300, including about 1,000 people in Central New York. It continues to rely heavily on local providers from around the state for many of its materials.

Welch Foods. Producer of juices and other products from Concord grapes. Thomas Branwell Welch, a Vineland, NJ, dentist, wanted an unfermented grape "wine" for use at his church's communion services in 1869. With his wife, Lucy, and his son, Charles, he harvested several baskets of Concord grapes, cooked them briefly, strained them through cheesecloth, and poured the juice into 12 glass bottles, applying pasteurization techniques to the juice. When the bottled juice had not fermented after several weeks, Welch began marketing the product to churches in southern New Jersey. In 1873 Charles E. Welch purchased his father's interest in the enterprise; growth was very slow. In 1890 Welch changed the name of the business from Dr. Welch's Unfermented Wine to Dr. Welch's Grape Juice. The first major breakthrough came at the 1893 Chicago World's Fair. Thousands of visitors sampled and enjoyed the product. Charles gave up dentistry and devoted himself solely to the juice business. In 1896 Thomas Welch reinvested in the business. Since a better source of grapes was needed, the father-son team moved operations to Watkins Glen (Schuyler Co) and began their first vigorous advertising campaign. They outgrew the site almost immediately and moved the following year to Westfield (Chautauqua Co), in the largest Concord grape–producing belt in the country, organizing the Welch Grape Juice Co.

Welch's got a tremendous national boost when Secretary of State William Jennings Bryan served the juice instead of wine at a state dinner. The national press lampooned the gesture, making the juice a household name. Welch's added jam to its product list after it produced Grapelade for the US Army; soldiers demanded it when they returned home, and it was manufactured for retail sale. Charles Welch died in 1927 and his son Edgar assumed the presidency, selling the company the following year to a Nashville, Tenn, syndicate, which did not expand the business. Depression years brought a decline in demand for Welch's products. The trend continued into the 1940s. Jacob "Jack" Kaplan bought the company in 1945 and began the process of selling it to the National Grape Co-operative Association, completing the transaction in 1956. Welch's sales have increased every year since its purchase by the association, and its product line has diversified. Welch's changed its name to Welch Foods in 1969 to represent its varied product line. The company operates plants in Westfield; North East, Pa; Lawton, Mich; and Kennewick and Grandview, Wash. In 1983 headquarters moved from Westfield to the grape's birthplace in Concord, Mass. Welch's employed 1,300 people in the United States and had sales of $553.5 million in 2002.

Chazanof, William. *Welch's Grape Juice: From Corporation to Co-operative* (Syracuse: Syracuse Univ Press, 1977)

Pam Kirst

Wells. Town (pop 737) in SE Hamilton Co. Settled before 1792 by Joshua and Mary Wells from Long Island, the town was formed from Northampton and Mayfield [now in Fulton Co] in 1805. Although well within the Adirondacks, Wells is flat and low and, with the Military Rd built through the valley in 1812, attractive to farmers. Tanning began in 1820, and the town's two large tanneries at Griffin and at Wells did not close until 1896 and 1898. Lumbering peaked in the 1880s; other industries included a hemlock-extract mill (1872) at Griffin, a hardwood veneer mill (1899–1917), and the sewing of gloves at home (46 women in 1925). Serfis Glove Corp (1941–65) operated a factory in Wells. A public campsite on the Sacandaga River opened in 1920, and Rte 30 was improved in 1925. After Lake Algonquin was created in 1925, summer residences proliferated. Old Home Days is an annual event in August. Wells is the birthplace of Vic Kibler (1918–), the last of the great Adirondack fiddlers who learned traditionally before the advent of radio.

Wells, Henry (*b* Thetford, Vt, 12 Dec 1805; *d* Glasgow, Scotland, 10 Dec 1878). Express company entrepreneur and philanthropist. Raised in a Presbyterian family, his father a minister, Wells moved to Central New York with them in 1814. He attended school in Fayette (Seneca Co) and apprenticed in tanning and shoemaking in Palmyra (Wayne Co). After undergoing therapy for a speech defect in the early 1820s, he opened schools for treatment of such disorders in Rochester, Buffalo, New York City, Pittsburgh, Cincinnati, and Cleveland. During the 1840s Wells was instrumental in forming several express companies to service Buffalo, New York City, Cincinnati, St. Louis, and Chicago. His New York City–based firm of Wells and Co united with two competing firms, owned by John Butterfield and William G. Fargo, to create the American Express Co in 1850; Wells became its first president and served until 1868. The company was founded in Buffalo, but later in the 1850s its headquarters were moved to New York City. Taking advantage of the California gold rush, in 1852 he organized Wells, Fargo and Co, initially based in New York City, to fulfill his longtime dream of an express service to the West Coast. He moved from New York City to Aurora (Cayuga Co) in 1850 and founded the Wells Seminary for the Higher Education of Young Women, which opened in 1868 and became Wells College in 1870. Wells died en route to Sicily and is buried in Aurora.

Grossman, Peter Z. *American Express: The Unofficial History of the People Who Built the Great Financial Empire* (New York: Crown Publishers, 1987)

Sharon Ann Murphy

Wellsburg. Village (pop 631) in Ashland (Chemung Co). Settled in 1787–88, the village was laid out in 1848 and, beginning in 1849, served by the Erie Railroad. A tannery (1859) and creamery (1879) provided employment. The village incorporated in 1872. The business district was ravaged by Hurricane Agnes flooding in 1972 and was rebuilt throughout the 1970s. In the early 21st century, Wellsburg industry includes contract grinding and the manufacture of precision-turned parts.

Heather A. Wade

Wells College. American Express and Wells Fargo Cos entrepreneur Henry Wells established in 1866 the Wells Seminary for the Higher Education of Young Women in Aurora (Cayuga Co). The school was incorporated in 1868 and in 1870 became a four-year chartered college for women, renamed Wells College, and is the oldest women's college in the state. Influenced by Wells's dream to create a distinct institution that would meaningfully educate women, the college has provided career-oriented training. Five graduates obtained their doctorates before 1900. In 1976 Frances T. "Sissy" Farenthold became the school's first female president, improved the school's finances, and erected an athletic building. In 1995 Lisa Marsh Ryerson became the first alumna president; her initiatives included a 30% reduction of tuition fees as of 1999, resulting in a 51% increase in the size of the entering class. Prominent graduates include Dr Ruth Barnhart (1923), first woman physician in the city of Roanoke, Va; Margie Filter Hostetter (1962), vice president of Xerox Corp; *American Girl* entrepreneur Pleasant Thiele Rowland (1962); Margaret Pericak-Vance (1973), director of the Duke Center for Human Genetics; and Emily Hsu Landau Quach (1983), engineer on the Brooklyn Bridge reconstruction. As of 2001, 468 students were enrolled.

Dieckmann, Jane Marsh. *Wells College: A History* (Aurora, NY: Wells College Press, 1995)

Jane R. Plitt

Wellsville. Town (pop 7,678) and village (pop 5,171) in SE Allegany Co. Settled in 1795, the town was formed in 1855 from Scio, Andover, and Willing. The village, where commercial activity began in 1832, was incorporated in 1857 and changed its name to Genesee from 1871 to 1873. It acquired rail service westward with the Erie (1851) and southward to Pennsylvania with the Wellsville, Coudersport and Pine Creek Railroad (1882). Developing into a manufacturing village, with 20 factories in 1896, Wellsville produced plows, horse powers (treadmills on which a horse powers machinery), iron-building fronts, boilers, engines, mill machinery, leather, wood novelties, and cigars. In the early 1880s it began to benefit from the oil boom set off by the Triangle No. 1 well in nearby Scio (1879) and became the wealthy village it is in the early 21st century. In the 20th century its industry was anchored by Wellsville Refining Co (1902–58; later Sinclair Refining Co) and the Air Preheater Co (1925, now Alstom Power Air Preheater Corp). In 2003 Dresser Rand's steam turbine/motor division employed 800 workers; other manufacturers were Alstom (620 employees), Current Controls (electronics; 120 employees), LC Whitford Co (construction; 400 employees), and Northern Lights Candles (250 employees). Wellsville's Allegany County Nitros play baseball in the New York Collegiate League. Wellsville was the birthplace of Charles M. Sheldon (1857–1946), author of the best-selling inspirational novel *In His Steps* (1896), which was the origin of the expression "What would Jesus do?" It is also the birthplace of actor George "Gabby" Hayes (1885–1969). Wellsville has a branch campus of the SUNY College of Technology at Alfred.

Welsh. Culturally distinct from other British immigrants, the Welsh hailed from the principality of Wales, spoke a Celtic language, and practiced indigenous forms of nonconformist Protestantism. Although the Welsh were among the early colonial population, there were no population concentrations.

SETTLEMENT

In the late 18th century, poor harvests in Wales and a desire for landownership led many Welsh farmers to move to Oneida Co, which had become the cultural center of Welsh American life by 1830. First arriving in 1795 the Welsh established a strong presence in Steuben, Utica, Remsen, and other towns. Adapting their traditional agricultural methods, they became the first to introduce dairying into the region, and Welsh butter became a valued commodity on the New York City market. In 1900 the US Census recorded 6,676 Welsh immigrants and their American-born children in Oneida Co, though the total figure for persons of Welsh ancestry, including those of second and third generations, was no doubt considerably higher.

There was also a midcentury migration to the slate mines in Washington Co along the Vermont border, centering on Granville and neighboring Vermont villages. Slate miners from North Wales were heavily recruited, and they dominated the mining and finishing industries in the slate valley. By the late 19th century, the Welsh dominated the more privileged positions in the industry, with bands of eastern European and Italian workers carrying out the unskilled labor of the quarries. Fluctuations in levels of Welsh immigration to the area tended to follow the relative fortune of the slate industries in Wales and America; labor troubles in Wales tended to increase the flow to Washington Co.

New York City also had a substantial Welsh population in the middle of the 19th century, and in 1835 the local community established the St. David's Society of the State of New York, which still exists in the early 21st century. Smaller Welsh communities developed in Cattaraugus, Chemung, Herkimer, Lewis, Madison, Otsego, and St. Lawrence Cos.

CULTURE

Welsh culture in New York State was rooted in its linguistic and religious distinctiveness. The Welsh population in Oneida Co supported a Welsh American publishing industry, including 19 publishers that produced 240 Welsh language imprints, 4 denominational periodicals, and the influential newspaper *Y Drych.* The nonconformist "chapel" was integral to Welsh American culture. Religious worship was conducted in the Welsh language, and the chapel provided guidance on almost every aspect of immigrants' lives. The three leading denominations—Calvinistic Methodists (a distinctly Welsh sect), Baptists, and Congregationalists—established a firm presence within the Welsh American communities of New York. Although congregations tended to remain small, chapel construction flourished. There were 5 chapels in New York City, 13 in the New York–Vermont slate valley, and 43 in Oneida Co. Central to worship was the tradition of four-part congregational singing of Welsh hymns. Highlights of the year in any Welsh American community included all-day events such as the *gymanfa ganu* (hymn-singing festival) and *gymanfa pregethu* (preaching festivals). These cultural institutions were rivaled only by the *eisteddfod,* a musical and literary competition devoted to poetry and choral singing, usually in the Welsh language. In addition to the several *eisteddfodau* organized locally, Utica was the site of a grand *eisteddfod* that began in 1854 and continued for over a century. As in New York City, local St. David's Societies were established in most areas of Welsh settlement. The societies stressed charitable, social, and cultural activities, most notably the annual St. David's Day (1 March) banquet. In New York City it was an elegant affair, featuring the presence of local dignitaries, elaborate toasts, performance of Welsh poetry and song, and reception of delegates from the societies of other ethnic groups.

With the decline of immigration in the early 20th century, the Welsh in New York State—highly literate, economically successful, and familiar with English—slowly lost their cultural uniqueness. From the mid–19th century, many Welsh farmers in central New York State migrated to cities or to farms farther west. A similar process occurred in the slate valley of Washington Co when the slate industry declined after World War I and collapsed during the depression of the 1930s. Welsh immigration slowed to a trickle after the First World War, and in 1919 the decline of Welsh speakers in Welsh American communities prompted the majority of Calvinistic Methodist Churches in the United States to join with the Presbyterian Church. Nevertheless, a strong sense of Welsh American identity remains in areas of the state with large communities of Welsh ancestry (85,356 New Yorkers identified themselves in the 2000 census as being of Welsh heritage). These communities are marked by the continuing traditions of *gymanfa ganu,* concerts by visiting Welsh choirs, and St. David's Day banquets. Prominent Welsh Americans from New York State include Revolutionary War era patriots Morgan Lewis and Francis Lewis; US Supreme Court Chief Justice Charles Evans Hughes; Samuel Ellis, the last private owner of Ellis Island; abolitionist Robert Everett, editor of *Y Cenhadwr,* an antislavery journal in Utica; Welsh language publisher Thomas J. Griffiths; and the distinguished historian of New York State, David Maldwyn Ellis.

Ellis, David Maldwyn. "The Assimilation of the Welsh in Central New York," *New York History* 53 (1972): 299–333

Hartmann, Edward George. *Americans from Wales* (New York: Octagon Books, 1983)

Roberts, Gwilym R. *New Lives in the Valley: Slate Quarries and Quarry Villages in North Wales, New York and Vermont, 1850–1920* (Somersworth: New Hampshire Printers, 1998)

Robert Huw Griffiths and John S. Ellis

Wende, Ernest (*b* Mill Grove, Erie Co, 23 July 1853; *d* Buffalo, 11 Feb 1910). Public health reformer. Wende obtained his first medical degree at the University of Buffalo (1878), took additional courses at Columbia College (1881–82), and obtained his second MD (1884) and BS (1885) degree from the University of Pennsylvania. Wende studied in Berlin with Robert Koch, the discoverer of the causes of cholera and tuberculosis. In 1891 Buffalo mayor Charles Bishop appointed Wende to be the first commissioner of the city's Health Department. He served from 1892 to 1902 and 1907 to 1910, applying his training in microbiology and germ theory to public health issues. Wende established public health rules, sanitary inspections, enforcement routines, and laboratory research programs. He led efforts to eliminate sewage practices that spread typhoid, and he successfully campaigned to end the use of unsanitary baby bottles and to regulate milk sold in urban markets. Wende's contemporaries credited him with halving Buffalo's mortality rate during an era of rapid population growth. He died of cancer.

Moot, Adelbert. "Ernest Wende: A Memoir." In *Buffalo Historical Society Publications,* vol 22 (Buffalo: Buffalo Historical Society, 1918)

Pendleton, M. Stephen. "Pestilence and Public Policy: The Rise of Public Health Regulation and the Growth of Public Authority in Buffalo, NY, 1832–1910." Paper presented at the annual meeting of the American Political Science Association, Washington, DC, Aug 1997)

M. Stephen Pendleton

Wendt, Margaret L(ouise) (*b* Buffalo, 1 Sept 1885; *d* Buffalo, 9 Jun 1972). Philanthropist. Wendt grew up in Buffalo and attended local schools, graduating from Buffalo Seminary in 1903. Her father, William F. Wendt, was cofounder of the Buffalo Forge Co. She was involved in many Buffalo organizations, including the Graduates Association of the Buffalo Seminary, the Twentieth Century Club, the Bristol Home, the Niagara Lutheran Home, and Holy Trinity Lutheran Church. When her father died in 1923, his estate, valued at $500,000–$1,500,000, was left to his wife and daughter. Margaret Wendt lived in Buffalo and managed the family cattle and horse farm in Lockport (Niagara Co). She contributed to local organizations and was a benefactor of the Buffalo Philharmonic Orchestra. In 1956 she established the Margaret L. Wendt Foundation. After her death, the majority of her $14.5 million estate went to that foundation, which has supported Buffalo and Western New York social service, cultural, religious, and educational organizations, including the Buffalo and Erie County Historical Society, Buffalo Seminary, and the Frank Lloyd Wright Graycliff estate.

Vogel, Mike. "The Continuing Legacy of Margaret L. Wendt," *Western New York Heritage Magazine* 5 (Spring 2002): 9–13

Varney Spaulding Greene

Wenro Indians. Iroquoian speakers, similar in language and culture to the tribes of the Five Nations to their east, and associated at one point with the Neutral Nation, the Wenros lived close to the shore of Lake Ontario, between the Genesee and Niagara Rivers, in what is now Niagara and Orleans Cos. Little is known about the Wenros. They are not represented on any surviving map. The scant evidence gleaned by the Jesuit fathers secondhand from the Neutrals and the Five Nations suggests that the Wenros received protection from the Neutrals that allowed them to stave off aggression from the Senecas. In 1638, apparently after some planning (including the dispatch of ambassadors), they left their homeland, marched through the Neutrals' territory, and relocated among the Huron confederacy in what is now Ontario. According to the Jesuits, the Wenros became "a prey to their enemies," pummeled by epidemic disease and plundered by the Senecas. It has been suggested that the abundance of beavers in the Wenro homeland led to the Senecas' expanding their fur-gathering territory, to the Wenros' loss. After the conquest of the Hurons by the Five Nations in 1649, the Wenros are not heard from or of, though individual members of the tribe almost certainly lived scattered among the neighboring Iroquois communities.

Engelbrecht, William. *Iroquoia: The Development of a Native World* (Syracuse: Syracuse Univ Press, 2003)

White, Marian. "Neutral and Wenro." In *Northeast,* ed. Bruce G. Trigger, vol 15 of *Handbook of North American Indians,* ed. William C. Sturtevant (Washington, DC: Smithsonian Institution, 1978)

Michael Leroy Oberg

Wesley Hills. Village (pop 4,848) in Ramapo (Rockland Co). In the 19th century the locality was known as Furmanville, Sherwoodville, and Wesley Chapel, after a Methodist chapel (1829) there. Cigars were made by the Forshay family in the late 19th and early 20th centuries. It was an area of summer homes until development accelerated in the 1960s. The village incorporated in 1982 to control zoning and development. The name Wesley Hills was selected as a nod to the historic Wesley Chapel.

West Almond [AL-MOND]. Town (pop 353) in central Allegany Co. Settled in 1816, it was formed in 1833 from Alfred, Almond, and Angelica. Located on the Lake Erie Turnpike from Bath to Olean, the town in its early years experienced heavy westward migration. Later it was served by the Pittsburgh, Shawmut and Northern Railroad (1903–46). In 1974 it acquired an expressway exit when Rte 17 (I-86) was completed. About half the town's land area is contained in the 3,645-acre (1,475 ha) Palmer's Pond State Forest. Aside from three commercial dairy farms (one with 600 head), employment is found outside of town.

West Babylon. See BABYLON.

West Bay Shore. See BAY SHORE.

West Bloomfield. Town (pop 2,549) in NW Ontario Co. Settled in 1789, the town was formed from East Bloomfield in 1833. The state road from Utica to Avon (authorized 1794) passed through the region. In 1865 a vein of natural gas was discovered, and in 1872 a 25 mi (40 km) wood pipeline was built to Rochester but was unsuccessful. West Bloomfield remains a farming community and has large dairy farms, vegetable stands, fruit tree nurseries, and an American Beefalo ranch.

Marla A. Bennett

Westbury. Village (pop 14,263) in North Hempstead (Nassau Co). Quakers established a meeting here in 1671. The first Catholic mass in the present Nassau Co was held in 1851 at what became Westbury's St. Brigid's Church. Westbury remained agricultural until the 1880s when estates were created in neighboring Old Westbury, giving rise to service businesses and workers' housing in Westbury. Breezy Hills (1914) was a subdivision for Italian estate gardeners. The village incorporated in 1932. Westbury is a racially diverse bedroom community, nearly 25% African American and 19% Latino in 2000. Hicks Nursery, in business in 2003, has been operated by successive generations of the Hicks family since 1853.

Georgina Martorella

West Carthage. Village (pop 2,102) in Champion (Jefferson Co). Settled in 1798, the village was platted in 1833. It briefly had a blast furnace (1834–36). West Carthage grew in the 1840s because of good waterpower and proximity to Carthage across the river. Products included pails and tubs, map rollers, sash and blinds, pumps, and leather. The village was incorporated in 1889. Beginning *ca* 1900 pulp and paper mills began to dominate the economy; these included West End Paper (1901–28), St. Regis (1925–63), and Carthage Paper (1932; in 2003 part of Climax Manufacturing). Many residents commute to Fort Drum and Watertown.

Laura Lynne Scharer

Westchester County (450 mi^2/1,165 km^2; pop 923,459). Created in 1683 as one of the colony's original 12 counties. The county annexed several islands in Long Island Sound in 1768. Parts of Westchester Co were annexed by New York Co in 1874 and 1895 and by Bronx Co in 1917. The county is presently divided into 6 cities and 19 towns that contain 23 incorporated villages. White Plains serves as county seat. Elevation ranges from sea level on the Hudson River and Long Island Sound to 982 feet (299 m) at the summit of Mt Bailey in the Town of North Salem. Westchester Co extends across two subregions of the New England Upland physiographic province: the Hudson Hills in the northern quarter and the Manhattan Hills elsewhere.

The topography is broken throughout and is greatly influenced by the character of the underlying bedrock, which is composed of a complex mix of middle Proterozoic, Cambrian, and Ordovician gneiss and schist formations. Local relief typically varies between 200 and 300 feet (60–90 m). Continental glaciers scoured and eroded the bedrock, leaving behind a significant mantle of till and water-laid deposits. Over 500 feet (150 m) thick in places, these deposits include moraines, terraces, and outwash plains that create a number of marshes and small lakes. Surface drainage is largely determined by the location of softer, more easily eroded bedrock in conjunction with rock fractures and faults. The northern section of the county is drained by the Saw Mill and Croton Rivers and their tributaries, which empty into the Hudson River. Extensive portions of the Croton watershed are impounded in a series of large reservoirs that serve New York City. The east and central parts of the county drain into Long Island Sound via small streams that flow east into Connecticut. The southern portion is also drained by small streams that flow into either the Sound or the Hudson River. Soils vary considerably in character; present agricultural use is confined to some horse pasturage and high-value, specialty farming.

The climate of Westchester County is humid-continental, although winter temperatures are moderated by nearby Long Island Sound and the Atlantic Ocean. Winters tend to be short and sunny compared to areas to the north and west. Mean January temperatures range from 26°F (-3°C) at Yorktown Heights to 31°F (-1°C) at Dobbs Ferry. A typical winter brings lows of 0°F (-18°C) or below 5–10 times in the northern interior, much less often near the Sound. Mean July temperatures range from 72°F (22°C) at Yorktown Heights to 76°F (24°C) at Dobbs Ferry. Daytime highs usually reach or exceed 90°F (32°C) 20–25 days a year, sometimes more often. Average annual precipitation varies from 46 inches (117 cm) at Scarsdale to more than 52 inches (132 cm) in the northeast. Seasonal snowfall amounts range from 29 inches (74 cm) at Westchester County Airport near White Plains to 35 inches (89 cm) in the north. Primeval forest cover consisted primarily of a central hardwood community dominated by beech, sugar maple, basswood, plane, oak, and chestnut.

American Indians and Early Settlement

Communities of Munsee speakers (Wiechquaeskecks in Greenburgh, Rechgawawanks in Yonkers, Sinsinks around Ossining, and Kicktawanks in the northern parts of the county) inhabited the area at the time of European contact.

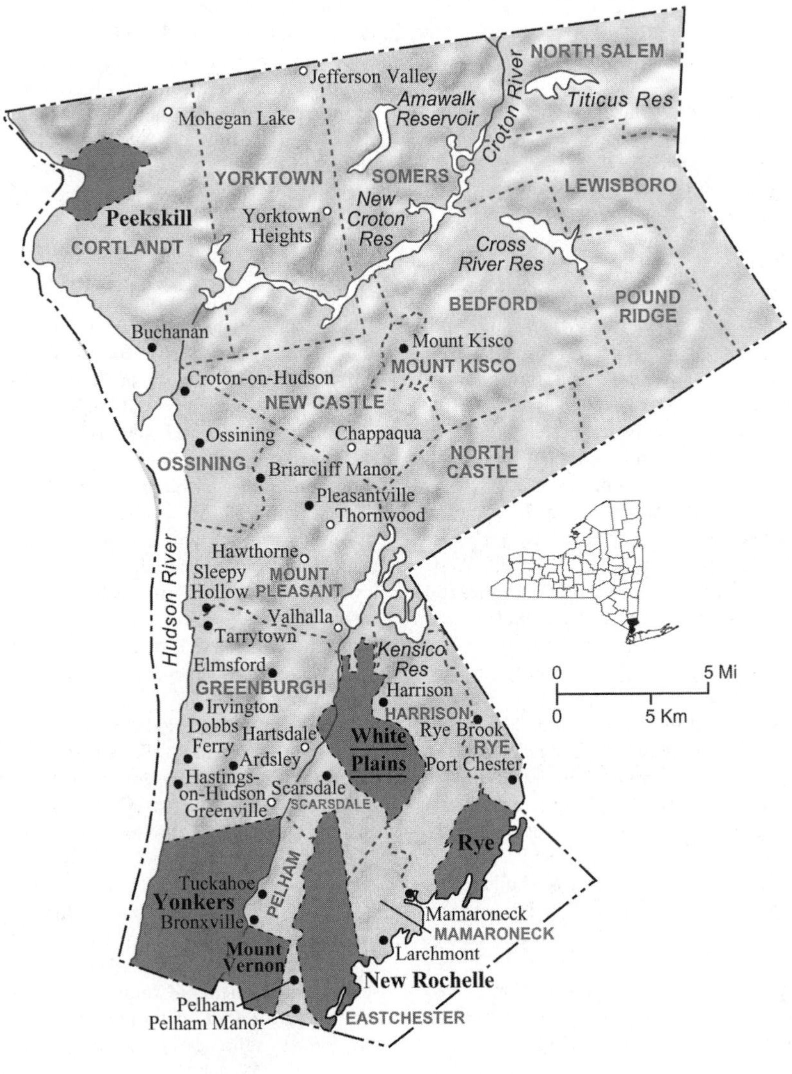

WESTCHESTER CO POPULATION CENSUS FIGURES

	White	Nonwhite	Total Population	Foreign-Born
1790	22,227	1,776	24,003	—
1800	25,687	1,741	27,428	—
1810	28,342	1,930	30,272	—
1820	30,795	1,843	32,638	270
1830	34,341	2,115	36,456	885
1840	46,386	2,300	48,686	—
1850	56,188	2,075	58,263	11,225
1860	97,227	2,270	99,497	27,823
1870	128,830	2,518	131,348	37,344
1880	106,364	2,624	108,988	23,710
1890	143,272	3,500	146,772	38,392
1900	178,742	5,515	184,257	46,682
1910	273,827	9,228	283,055	81,285
1920	333,110	11,326	344,436	80,265
1930	497,247	23,700	520,947	120,712
1940	541,680	31,878	573,558	105,682
1950	587,100	38,716	625,816	96,069
1960	746,406	62,485	808,891	103,981
1970	802,722	91,382	894,104	106,629
1980	729,831	136,768	866,599	126,866
1990	695,738	179,128	874,866	158,597
2000	658,858	264,601	923,459	205,429

Notes: "Nonwhite" includes African Americans, Asians, American Indians, and Pacific Islanders and, for 2000, also the mixed race and other race categories. Through the 1960 census these figures primarily reflect the African American population. Foreign-born figures for 1820 and 1830 include only those not naturalized, and for 1930 and 1950, the foreign-born totals include Whites only. Other years include all foreign-born in the population.

Archaeological remains demonstrate that fishing and farming played a key role in their economy. Early resistance to white settlement subsided by the mid–17th century as natives were driven out. Kieft's War (1640–45), during which an estimated 1,000 Indians were killed, ended with a peace agreement between the Indians and the Dutch. By the late 17th century, the Indian proprietors had traded most of their lands to white settlers and moved on. A small remaining group joined the patriots in 1778 in a battle at Tibbet's Brook, where more than 40 were killed. The Ward Pound Ridge Reservation, a county-owned nature preserve at Cross River, contains a significant collection of Indian artifacts.

Beginning in 1639 both Dutch and English settlers occupied Westchester Co territory to take advantage of farming opportunities. After capturing the colony in 1664, the English awarded patents to political favorites, while settlers bought up the lands that had not already been occupied. Westchester's settlers included large landowners, small freeholders, tenant farmers, and slaves. In the mid–18th century about half the county consisted of six manors: Cortlandt, Philipsburg, Scarsdale, Pelham, Fordham, and Morrisania. The Philipse and Van Cortlandt manor lords dominated until the American Revolution. The eastern part of the county consisted of freeholds. Rich soil and many watercourses made farming attractive and facilitated transport both locally and to the important New York City markets. The county was also a haven for religious dissenters in the late 17th century: Huguenots planted a substantial community in New Rochelle, while Quakers settled in Harrison, Scarsdale, Chappaqua, and elsewhere. The first documented Jewish residents lived in Rye in 1716. Early records show a significant number of women landowners.

Revolutionary War

On 9 July 1776 participants of the Fourth Provincial Congress met in White Plains and, declaring themselves representatives of New York State, endorsed the Declaration of Independence, which was publicly read on the county courthouse steps on 11 July 1776. But county residents were split in their loyalties, and 21,000 of them became embroiled in the Revolutionary War in several ways. Formally a neutral ground between the British in New York City and the Americans north of Peekskill, Westchester was the scene of constant skirmishes and two major battles, the Battle of White Plains and the Battle of Pell's Point, both in October 1776. The 1780 capture of Benedict Arnold's co-conspirator Maj John André at Tarrytown was one of the war's most dramatic events. Westchester Co also served as the military's breadbasket and supply center, though raiders on both sides circumvented the formal supply systems by looting, pillaging, and burning. Destruction by the "Cowboys" (loyalists) and "Skinners" (patriots) was so intense that it took years to rebuild towns and to restore farms. Until 1787 the county was divided into two shires, with courthouses in White Plains and Bedford, both of which had been burned during the Revolution. Confiscated loyalist lands, including the extensive Philipse Manor, were redistributed after 1783.

African Americans

In the mid–18th century African Americans accounted for about 13% of the population, most of them slaves brought in to work on the manors. In the same period some Westchester Co schools were among the first in New York State to educate African Americans. On the eve of the American Revolution they accounted for about 15% of the population, and African American troops participated in various aspects of the war. By 1779 Westchester Co Quakers manumitted their slaves and were responsible for the establishment of the county's first significant free black community, Stoney Hill in Harrison. All that physically remains from this community, which survived until the 1930s, is a 6-acre (2.4 ha) cemetery, the site of the original Mount Hope African Methodist Episcopal Zion Church. Another free black community was established in Bedford. In the 19th century African Americans also established neighborhoods in New Rochelle, Ossining, Rye, and Yonkers and played a key role in the county's active Underground Railroad.

Transportation and Infrastructure

Facilitating the county's expansion was the creation of a significant transportation and infrastructure system between 1850 and 1950. Before the early 19th century the county was serviced by the Boston, Albany, and Danbury post roads. Since the beginning of the century, the Westchester Turnpike from Somers to Sing Sing [now Ossining] and a number of active ports on both the Hudson and the Sound served the area. Transportation was revolutionized by midcentury when three major railroads connected the county to New York City and the rest of the state: the Harlem line to White Plains in 1844, the New Haven line in 1848, and the Hudson line to Peekskill in 1849. Two other lines operated for shorter periods. The New York and Putnam (1881), renamed the Putnam Division (1893–1958) after acquisition by the New York Central, carried commuters and milk from the Saw Mill River valley in the eastern part of the county to 155th St in the Bronx. (Westchester had previously been linked to Putnam Co through the 7 mi (11 km) New York and Mahopac line in 1871.) The heavily used New York, Westchester and Boston short line (1911–38) connected the south central area to the Bronx but fell victim to the automobile. Street railways and trolleys were common in most towns; the one in Pelham became the inspiration for the "Toonerville Trolley" cartoon strip in the early 20th century. Interurban lines, such as those connecting New York City with New Rochelle, Mount Vernon, White Plains, Tarrytown, and Connecticut, also proliferated.

During the same period New York City's demand for water reshaped Westchester. The Croton Dam, the first large masonry dam in the United States, was constructed between 1837 and 1842, creating Croton Lake and requiring a 33 mile (53 km) aqueduct. Bronx Reservoir (1871) was enlarged to become Kensico Reservoir (1915). Enlargements of the Croton system produced Titicus (1893), Amawalk (1897), and Cross River (1908) Reservoirs, as well as a substantial enlargement of Croton Lake (1905). The construction displaced thousands of residents and forced the relocation of villages and con-

POPULATIONS OF TOWNS AND CITIES, WESTCHESTER CO

Town or City, Year Founded	1800	1840	1880	1920	1960	2000
Bedford, 1682[a]	2,404	2,822	3,731	5,905	14,656	18,133
Cortlandt, 1737[b]	2,752	5,592	12,664	21,023	26,336	38,467
Eastchester, 1665[c]	738	1,502	8,737	9,372	33,613	31,318
Greenburgh, 1788	1,581	3,361	8,934	23,881	76,213	86,764
Harrison, 1774	855	1,139	1,494	5,006	19,201	24,154
Lewisboro, 1747[d]	1,696	1,619	1,612	1,069	4,165	12,324
Mamaroneck, 1697[e]	503	1,416	1,863	7,801	29,107	28,967
Mount Kisco, 1978	—	—	—	—	—	9,983
Mount Pleasant, 1742[a]	2,744	7,307	5,450	14,004	34,955	43,221
Mount Vernon (city), 1892	—	—	—	42,726	76,010	68,381
New Castle, 1791	1,468	1,529	2,297	3,639	14,388	17,491
New Rochelle, 1699[a]–1899	692[f]	1,816	5,276	—	—	—
New Rochelle (city), 1899	—	—	—	36,213	76,812	72,182
North Castle, 1721[g]	1,168	2,058	1,818	1,705	6,797	10,849
North Salem, 1784	1,150	1,161	1,693	934	2,345	5,173
Ossining, 1845	—	—	8,769	12,358	26,199	36,534
Peekskill (city), 1940	—	—	—	—	18,737	22,441
Pelham, 1666[h]	234	789	2,540	5,195	13,404	11,866
Pound Ridge, *ca* 1750[i]	1,266	1,407	1,034	515	2,573	4,726
Rye, 1665[j]	1,074	1,803	6,576	25,819	38,147	43,880
Rye (city), 1942	—	—	—	—	14,225	14,955
Scarsdale, 1783	258	255	614	3,506	17,968	17,823
Somers, 1788[k]	1,578	2,082	1,630	1,117	5,468	18,346
White Plains, 1727[a]–1916	571	1,087	4,094	—	—	—
White Plains (city), 1916	—	—	—	21,031	50,485	53,077
Yonkers, 1756–1872	1,176	2,968	—	—	—	—
Yonkers (city), 1872	—	—	18,892	100,176	190,634	196,086
Yorktown, 1788	1,806	2,819	2,481	1,441	16,453	36,318

Note: The Westchester Co Towns of West Farms (1846), Morrisania (1855), and Kingsbridge (1873) were dissolved by annexation to New York Co in 1874; the Town of Westchester (1655) was dissolved by annexation to New York Co in 1895. All are now in the Bronx.

[a]Date of first meeting minutes.

[b]As Cortlandt Manor, elected town officers and functioned as a town.

[c]Date of Articles of Agreement; surviving minutes begin 1671.

[d]Date of first minute book; named Salem until 1806–8, then South Salem until 1840.

[e]Date first town officers elected.

[f]1790 population; 1800 population not available.

[g]Earliest reference to Town of North Castle in provincial records.

[h]Date created a manor; reorganized as a town in 1788.

[i]Date uncertain; officers were appointed by North Castle through 1746.

[j]Date settlements were merged under Connecticut authority; minutes began by 1672.

[k]Stephentown until 1808.

Detail of Croton Aqueduct.

struction of 32 miles (52 km) of new roads and 19 bridges. Much of the county's best farmland in the north was submerged, accelerating the decline of agriculture.

The last element of infrastructure came after World War I with the development of the county's extensive road system, one of the oldest in the nation. The Bronx River Parkway was dedicated in 1925, its construction accompanied by a restoration of the river. This was followed by the Saw Mill River (first section, 1926), Hutchinson River (1928), Taconic (1931–32), and Cross County (1932) Parkways. Road construction in the 1950s made Westchester one of the most transportation-friendly counties in the nation: the New York State Thruway opened in 1955; the New England Thruway in 1958; the county's first major east-west artery, the Cross-Westchester Expressway, in 1960; and I-684 in 1967. Two bridges connect Westchester to the west side of the Hudson: the Bear Mountain Bridge (1924), the first vehicular bridge south of Albany, and the Tappan Zee Bridge (1955), which provided the first Westchester-Rockland link and completed the Thruway from New York City to Albany. Westchester's only airport, in Rye, was originally a World War II test ground that was converted into a commercial strip in 1944.

Economics and Suburbanization

Westchester experienced two great booms in the 19th century: farming in the first half and industry in the second. They were accompanied by population surges, increased ethnic diversity, urbanization, and massive infrastructure development. Wheat, rye, oats, corn, potatoes, hay, buckwheat, wool, potatoes, and dairy products were produced extensively; orchards proliferated; sawmills, gristmills, and cider mills thrived. Other industries also flourished: iron foundries in Port Chester, Peekskill, and Morrisania; brickyards in Croton-on-Hudson; marble quarries in Tuckahoe, Hastings-on-Hudson, Thornwood, and Sing Sing, the latter offering the materials for construction of one of New York State's oldest prisons, now called Sing Sing Correctional Facility (1828). New transportation modes made Westchester a major supplier of food and building materials to New York City. In the second half of the century, agricultural production declined significantly and was replaced by an extensive manufacturing sector. At the same time the growth and incorporation of villages and cities, accessible transportation, plentiful housing, and a surging population made Westchester an attractive commercial center. The 1880 census recorded 500 manufacturing establishments, many of which employed large numbers of women.

Westchester doubled in population between 1800 and 1850 and more than tripled between 1850 and 1900 (despite losing its southern portion to New York City), reaching 184,257, which made it the fifth most populated county in New York State. Population growth reflected suburban migration and the influx of immigrant labor. Railroad suburbs exploded in Westchester after 1865, long before suburban development had taken place elsewhere in the nation, and historians credit Westchester as the first suburbanized county in America. While the new suburbs, such as Irvington, Hastings-on-Hudson, Ardsley, and Larchmont, catered to upper-middle-class residents, the rest of the county became a magnet for working-class job seekers in such communities as Yonkers, New Rochelle, Port Chester, Dobbs Ferry, and Peekskill. The growing manufacturing and construction sectors drew huge numbers of immigrants, and by 1870 more than a quarter of the county's residents (37,344) were foreign-born, a level sustained through the early 20th century. Irish immigrants in the 1830s and 1840s worked on railroad construction, and in the second half of the century Italian stonemasons were among the skilled and unskilled attracted to the many construction and manufacturing jobs. Jews established a sizable presence in both retailing and manufacturing. By the end of the century, the county's growing network of benevolent and fraternal organizations reflected its ethnic, religious, and racial diversity: Little Russians Citizens Social Club of Yonkers, Roccaseccani Benevolent Association of Mount Vernon, Hebrew Free Burial Society of

Yonkers, St. Joseph's Lithuanian Society of Port Chester, Hastings First Hungarian Society, West New Rochelle Freundschafts Bund, Dorcas Society of Peekskill, Yonkers Free Circulating Library for Self-Supporting Women, New Rochelle United Colored Democracy, Colored Chauffeurs Association of New Rochelle, and Young Men's Colored Social Club of Mount Vernon.

Westchester's geopolitical boundaries were finalized when New York City annexed by popular referendum the lower portions of the county in two stages: Morrisania, West Farms, and Kingsbridge in 1874, and the Town of Westchester and parts of Eastchester and Pelham in 1895. The population dropped 17% after the first change but increased by 25% after the second, an indication of the county's increasing popularity as a work and residential center.

Just as the county shifted from agriculture to manufacturing in the 19th century, it shifted from manufacturing to residential housing and white-collar business in the 20th century. In 1900 Westchester was a major manufacturing county, producing everything from pianos to minerals, hats to bottle caps, wicker to chemicals, buttons to heavy machinery. An extensive retail and wholesale sector also thrived. Tarrytown was a center of automobile manufacturing for most of the 20th century, starting with the Fleming Motor Vehicle Co (1901) and the Maxwell Briscoe Co (1904). Dozens of other auto-manufacturing and automotive-related businesses were created. Yonkers reigned in carpet and elevator manufacturing from mid–19th to mid–20th century; Irvington was known for greenhouses; Hastings-on-Hudson for conduits; Port Chester and Peekskill for foundries; Ossining for medicines and metal files. Demand for property from the last quarter of the 19th century to the first quarter of the 20th led to the creation of almost 1,000 real estate–related businesses, accompanied by hundreds of associated ones: utility companies, banks, debt collection agencies, bond trading, credit reporting, title guaranty companies, and construction companies.

The depression helped accelerate the decline in manufacturing and heavy industry. By the mid–20th century, they were replaced by real estate as the county's most important commodity. The housing subdivision explosion, which started in the southern part of Westchester, extended into the central and northern sectors as farms were sold. Manufacturers, beset by increasing operating costs, moved out, and land values soared. Known for its outstanding school systems, the county became a premier commuting destination for New York City workers looking for a more pastoral setting. The population nearly doubled between 1920 and 1950, and reached 800,000 in 1960, the baby boom peak. In the 1950s General Foods and Nestlé, and in the 1960s IBM, paved the way for corporate relocation into the county; the "Platinum Mile," a strip of corporate headquarters in White Plains and Harrison, also contributed. By mid–20th century every major New York City department store had opened a branch in Westchester, and one of the nation's first suburban shopping malls, the Cross County Shopping Center, opened in 1954.

Culture and Recreation

The legend of the Headless Horseman, perhaps known to many children from the Disney cartoon, was a reworking of a European folktale penned by the county's most famous 19th-century personality, Washington Irving. At Sunnyside, his home on the Hudson, Irving attracted a constant stream of visitors. An adoring public worshiped Irving's "Legend of Sleepy Hollow" and *Knickerbocker History of New York* well after his death in 1859, transforming his home into a major US historic site. Also famous was *New York Tribune* editor and Chappaqua resident Horace Greeley, who won the presidential vote in the county in 1872 but lost the election and died a few weeks later.

By the second half of the 19th century, Westchester's proximity to New York City, its waterways, and its idyllic landscape helped make it a popular recreation destination. Day-trippers came by water to resorts and beaches on the Long Island Sound. New Rochelle's islands, such as Starin's Glen Island, were among the most popular destinations. Ice skating, bicycling, baseball, and stock-car racing were featured recreational activities, and the nation's first golf course, St. Andrews, opened in 1888. Clubs abounded, including social clubs, country clubs, and boating, golf, tennis, and gun clubs. Westchester Co has the only publicly owned amusement park in the nation, Playland Amusement Park (1928). For a century after the Civil War, opera houses and theaters were common; some remain today but few serve their original purposes. The Westchester County Center, still in operation, opened in 1930 for all-purpose recreation. In the early 20th century more than a dozen filmmaking companies were established in the Sound area, including All Star Studios, Thanhauser Films, and Sphinx Films. A particularly flourishing studio was D. W. Griffith's in Mamaroneck, where the Gish sisters often filmed. The nation's first pet burial ground, Hartsdale Pet Cemetery, opened in 1896.

While the county has always contained a sizable working-class population, by the second half of the 19th century it had become a popular address for the wealthy and the artistic. Artists' colonies in Bronxville and Croton-on-Hudson thrived. Hudson River school artist Jasper Francis Cropsey lived in Hastings-on-Hudson from 1885 until his death in 1900. Many 20th-century residents were artists and writers; Gordon Parks (1912–), America's most prominent African American photographer, stands out.

Department store magnate A. T. Stewart's land in Purchase was not far from Ophir Hall, home to the *New York Herald Tribune*'s Reid family. Madame C. J. Walker, who became American's first black female millionaire by selling hair-care products, built a mansion in Irvington. Woman suffrage leader Carrie Chapman Catt continued her battles from her New Rochelle home. Amelia Earhart practiced flying over her home in Harrison, while multimillionaire John D. Rockefeller's hilltop home, Kykuit, dominated the Pocantico Hills vista. Middle-class subdivisions, accelerating in the post–World War II era, took over much abandoned farmland and some estates, but it did not eradicate the large estates and wealthy enclaves that remain in the 21st century. In 1999 First Lady Hillary Rodham Clinton, along with Pres Bill Clinton, bought a house in Chappa-qua, and in 2000 home-decorating guru Martha Stewart moved to Katonah.

The county's rich historical legacy survives in two dozen sites open to the public, including the Rockefeller reconstruction of 17th-century Philipsburg Manor in Sleepy Hollow, St. Paul's National Historic Site in Mount Vernon, and the Thomas Paine Cottage and Museum in New Rochelle. Westchester's three dozen major cultural facilities include the Hudson River Museum in Yonkers, the Performing Arts Center at SUNY Purchase, the Katonah Museum, and Caramoor. The county contains nine four-year accredited colleges and universities, including Sarah Lawrence, Pace, Iona, Manhattanville, and Mercy Colleges and SUNY Purchase, as well as the county-operated Westchester Community College and numerous other specialized and technical colleges.

Politics

Westchester established its own governance under the independent state and nation by 1788, when supervisors were elected by its then 21 towns and began meeting as a Board of Supervisors to oversee county business. Until 1868 it operated on a half-shire system, with courts held at both White Plains and Bedford. A county executive position was created in 1939; the Board of Supervisors was replaced by a reapportioned 17-member Board of Legislators in 1970. A Democratic stronghold in the 19th century, the county switched to Republican control by 1896, the year its present geographical borders were established. As the head of the Westchester County Republican Committee for 37 years, William "Boss" Ward (1856–1933) cemented the party's dominance in county politics, broken only twice in the 20th century by Democratic county executives Alfred Delbello and Andrew Spano. The state's last three Republican governors (Rockefeller, Wilson, and Pataki) were from Westchester Co.

The politics of dissent also emerged in Westchester in the 20th century. Violence erupted during a 1900 strike by Croton Dam workers and the National Guard was sent. A training facility for labor leaders, Brookwood Labor College, operated in Katonah for nearly two decades in the 1920s and 1930s, and at the same time in northern Westchester a number of summer colonies catered to New York City leftists. The 1949 Peekskill Riots, an attempted repression of a Paul Robeson concert attended by 15,000 people, resulted in a riot in which 100 people were hospitalized after 1,000 police and state troopers did little to prevent violence. From 1949 to 1954 Scarsdale residents led an unusual resistance to an attempted purge of district teachers accused by a local "Committee of Ten" of assigning communist reading material.

In the first half of the 20th century, Westchester ranked third in New York State in the number of African American residents. While the county's overall African American presence ranged from 2% to 7% between 1790 and 1960, it was unevenly distributed, with some central Westchester communities as high as 15%. In the early 1960s New Rochelle became the "Little Rock of the North" when the city integrated its school system and bused black students to the predominantly white schools. In the mid-1980s the Yonkers desegregation case set a national precedent when a federal court ruled that the county's largest city had purposefully segregated its black population and forced the city to take corrective measures. In 2000 the African American population, at 14%, once again neared its pre–Revolutionary War proportion.

Political controversy in the early 21st century erupted over Indian Point in Buchanan, a nuclear energy facility built in 1962. Opponents to the power plant maintained it was not safe and should be decommissioned. As a result of a report finding major problems with the plant's safety systems, County Executive Andrew Spano announced in late 2002 that the county would begin steps to take over nuclear plants and replace them with an alternative energy source. Since 1998 the county has actively pursued "green" policies, allocating $10 million annually for protecting open space and increasing the amount of land so designated. In 2003 one-fifth of its land area was preserved in parks, nature preserves, private recreation facilities and watershed.

RECENT HISTORY

Westchester's population reached its peak in 2000, at 923,459, up 5.6% from a decade earlier. The demographic trend in the last three decades of the 20th century illustrated significant and unprecedented shifts in the county's constituency. Its elderly and white populations declined, and its Asian, African American, and Latino populations grew. In 2000 Blacks were 14.2% of the population, and Asians were 4.5%. The growth of the Latino community was most striking, from a little over 2% in 1970 to more than 15% in 2000. These changes occurred despite soaring real estate prices and a critical lack of affordable housing. In a county where more than 40% of residents live in low-density housing (fewer than six persons per acre), there has been slow progress toward meeting affordable housing targets. Only 45% of a projected 5,000 units were built between 1990 and 2000. In the same decade the number of families living under the poverty line reached 6%. Westchester Co ranked third nationally in per capita income in 2000.

By the start of the 21st century, Westchester had succeeded in recovering its white-collar business sector from the slump of the late 20th century. Approximately 64% of its working population was employed within the county. White-collar work had shifted from the 1960s megacorporations to smaller companies occupying subdivided office parks; 90% of businesses had fewer than 20 employees. The county's 19 hospitals were among the largest employers, and two-thirds of all business enterprises were in the service and retail/wholesale sectors. Part of the county's effort to attract big business was evidenced after the 11 Sept 2001 tragedy; Westchester enticed a number of New York businesses to relocate, most significantly Morgan Stanley, which moved 2,500 employees to Harrison in 2004. Major corporations in the county include IBM, Kraft Foods, Reader's Digest, ATT Corp, MasterCard, and PepsiCo.

See also COOPER, JAMES FENIMORE; SUBURBANIZATION; WATER SUPPLY AND USE (NEW YORK CITY WATERSHED).

The standard histories are Robert Bolton, *History of the County of Westchester,* 2d ed. (1881); J. Thomas Scharf, *History of Westchester County* (1886); Frederic Shonnard and W. W. Spooner, *History of Westchester County* (1900); Alvah P. French, *History of Westchester County* (1925–27); and Ernest F. Griffin, *History of Westchester County* (1946). Visual works include Susan Cochran Swanson and Elizabeth Fuller, *Westchester County: A Pictorial History,* rev ed. (1998), and Renoda Hoffman, *It Happened in Old White Plains* (1989).

There have been scores of town and village histories, including Charles W. Baird, *Chronicles of a Border Town: History of Rye* (1871), which also covers Harrison and White Plains through 1788; C. E. Allison, *History of Yonkers* (1896); Frances R. Duncombe, *Katonah: The History of a New York Village and Its People* (1961); Carol O'Connor, *A Sort of Utopia: Scarsdale, 1891–1981* (1983); and Bruce D. Haynes, *Red Lines, Black Spaces: The Politics of Race and Space in a Black Middle-Class Suburb* (2001). Old but still indispensable is Otto Hufeland, *A Check List of Books, Maps, Pictures and Other Printed Matter Relating to the Counties of Westchester and Bronx* (1929). Topical works include Otto Hufeland, *Westchester County during the American Revolution* (1926); William S. Hadaway, ed., *The McDonald Papers,* 2 vols (1926–27); Roger Arcara, *Westchester's Forgotten Railway, 1912–1917* (1962); and Frank Sanchis, *American Architecture: Westchester County* (1977). *The Westchester Historian* has been published quarterly under various titles since 1925.

Lisa Keller

Westchester County Park System. The Westchester County Park Commission (WCPC) was established in 1922 to extend the recreational, planning, and economic benefits of the Bronx River Parkway (BRP), which terminated in Valhalla (Westchester Co), to the entire county. The role of parkways in local planning became an important consideration in the mid-1920s with the explosion of unplanned suburban growth. Led by Jay Downer, BRP chief engineer, the WCPC developed a countywide system of recreational facilities connected by boulevards or parkways. The extensive network was laid out to preserve open land and dedicate recreational facilities in rapidly developing areas. The system is noteworthy for its variety of recreational features: scenic roads, parks, picnic areas, trails, beaches, bridal paths, and an amusement park (Rye Playland, 1928). In 1924 the county plan was expanded, and the commission was incorporated into the New York State Park System. With state funding, the WCPC from 1923 to 1932 extended the Bronx River Parkway 30 miles (48 km) north to Peekskill (Westchester Co), connecting with the new Bear Mountain Bridge (1924) and the proposed Eastern State Parkway. The Bronx Parkway Extension and the Eastern State were combined in 1941 as the Taconic State Parkway. By 1934 the WCPC had developed more than 17,000 acres (6,900 ha) of parkland. In 2003 there were 51 county parks including 15,900 acres (6,430 ha). Principal parks included the Ward Pound Ridge Reservation (1925), 4,700 acres (1,900 ha) in Cross River, and Tibbetts Brook Park (1923), 161 acres (65 ha) in Yonkers. The parks and the Bronx River Parkway are county owned; all the other parkways are state owned.

Weigold, Marilyn E. "Pioneering in Parks and Parkways: Westchester County, New York, 1895–1945." In *Essays in Public Works History* (Chicago: Public Works Historical Society, 1980)

Kathleen LaFrank

Westcott, Edward Noyes (*b* Syracuse, 27 Sept 1846; *d* Syracuse, 31 Mar 1898). Banker and author. Westcott, educated in Syracuse schools, at age 16 began a 30-year career in business at Mechanics Bank in Syracuse. His career encompassed work in insurance, finance, and government. He served as secretary of the Syracuse Water Commission until he was diagnosed with tuberculosis in 1895. While at Lake Meacham in the Adirondacks, Westcott wrote his first and only fiction, inspired by the colorful David Hannum of Homer, a friend of Westcott's father. (In 1869 Hannum and Westcott's father held an interest in the infamous Cardiff Giant, vying with P. T. Barnum for ownership.) An ailing Westcott rewrote much of the copy while in Naples, Italy. Six publishers rejected the work before it was accepted by D. Appleton and Co late in 1897. Westcott died six months before publication. An instant best-seller, *David Harum: A Story of American Life* sold over 400,000 copies within two years. Hannum's witty phrases were incorporated into the work and earned it instant popularity with the public. The innovative style of the book set a standard for professional acceptance of regional literature. In 1934 Will Rogers portrayed the title role in the film version.

"Edward Noyes Westcott's David Harum: A Forgotten Cultural Artifact," *Syracuse University Library Associates Courier* 32 (1996)

Vance, Arthur T. *The Real David Harum* (New York: Baker & Taylor, 1900)

Cathy A. Barber

West Elmira. Locality (pop 5,136) in Elmira (Chemung Co). Covered mostly by land cultivated by tobacco and ginseng farmers in the late 19th century, the area began suburban residential growth in the 1920s and 1930s. Beginning in the 1950s it has developed independent water, sewage, and fire protection systems. Agriculture declined throughout the 20th century. In the early 21st century West Elmira is a suburb.

Heather A. Wade

Westerlo. Town (pop 3,466) in S Albany Co. Settled before the Revolutionary War, the town was formed in 1815 from Coeymans and Rensselaerville. A woolen factory at South Westerlo (1830) operated to the end of the century. Westerlo was otherwise a farming town, especially fruit, which was dried in evaporators. In 1933 a resident invented a practical hose reel; his company, Clifford B. Hannay and Son, employed 145 workers in 2003. Westerlo is the site of the Basic Creek Reservoir (1932), supplying Albany city water, and of the Big Bear and Little Bear Swamps, owned by the Nature Conservancy.

Western. Town (pop 2,029) in N Oneida Co. Settled in 1789 the town formed from Steuben in 1797. The town was served by the Black River Canal (1849–1924). Many cheese factories produced cheddar and Limburger cheeses; the last closed in the 1950s. Canneries at Delta and Westernville packed local produce. In 1912 the Mohawk River was dammed to provide a water source for the Barge Canal, and the hamlet of Delta was abandoned and submerged. George J. Olney Machine Shop employed 30 workers in 1978 to manufacture food-processing machines. Many residents in 2003 worked in Utica and Rome. Western is the site of Delta Lake State Park (1968) and Woods Valley Ski Resort (1964). The home (1803) of Gen William Floyd (1734–1821) is a landmark.

Western Inland Lock Navigation Company. This private corporation was organized in May 1792 and given the mission by the state legislature to improve a network of waterways that comprised the approximately 200 mi (320 km) long inland navigation route connecting the Hudson River at Albany with Lake Ontario at Oswego. As a way to the interior of North America, this was a transport route of international significance, and its improvement was critical for development of the nation after the American Revolution. Between 1792 and 1820 the company cleared debris from natural channels, deepened rapids with stone dams, cut channels across necks of land in meandering streams, and completed the first canals in New York State. These were short bypass canals around falls and the headwaters of the Mohawk River at Little Falls (Herkimer Co), German Flatts (Herkimer Co), and Rome (Oneida Co). Passage normally obstructed by rapids and interrupted by portages was converted into a continuous deep-water channel capable of carrying boats several times the capacity of those used previously. Debris was also removed from Wood Creek [now in Oneida Co], and its course was straightened by more than 7 miles (11 km). The company's work, however, never progressed west beyond Oneida Lake. After April 1808, the company ceded its rights to all lands west of that lake. All of the company's lands and works were purchased by New York State in 1820 to make way for the Erie Canal.

Gen Philip Schuyler of Albany presided over this company from its inception until his death in 1804. He also oversaw the Northern Inland Lock Navigation Co, a sister company focused on the route from the Hudson River to Lake Champlain. Under his direct guidance, experiments in American canal engineering were applied along the corridor, often in wilderness conditions, including stone and wood canal locks of innovative design. The company became one of the first in the nation to sell stock as a means to raise funds for construction. Although the company was not profitable and never fully established a cleared route to Lake Ontario, it reduced the time and cost of transport across New York State.

Lord, Philip L., Jr. *The Navigators: A Journal of Passage on the Inland Waterways of New York, 1793* (Albany: NYS Museum, 2003)

Whitford, Noble E. *History of the Canal System of the State of New York,* vol 1 (Albany: Brandow Printing, 1906)

Philip L. Lord Jr

Westfield. Town (pop 5,232) and village (pop 3,481) in NW Chautauqua Co. Settled in 1802 the town was formed in 1829 from Portland and Ripley; the village was incorporated in 1833. Barcelona became a port of entry in 1826 and surveyed in streets in 1831; once a flourishing commercial fishing port, the hamlet is the site of the Barcelona Lighthouse, first in the United States to use natural gas for illumination (1830). In 1860, 12-year-old Grace Bedell wrote Abraham Lincoln suggesting he grow a beard, and on his inaugural tour, he stopped at Westfield station and asked to meet her. Located in the heart of the Concord grape belt, the first plant in the area to produce grape juice was built in Westfield in 1897, and it was the headquarters of Welch's Grape Juice Co until 1983; a Welch's plant remains in town. The Thruway was built through town in 1957.

See also ARCHITECTS AND ARCHITECTURE, SOUTHERN TIER (WESTERN).

Sharon Gollnitz

Westford. Town (pop 784) in E central Otsego Co. Settled in 1786 by Robert Roseboom from New Jersey, who was followed by other settlers from Vermont, the town was formed from Worcester in 1808. The population peaked at 1,645 in 1830, and the town was the site of Westford Literary Institute from 1830 to 1880). In 2003 agriculture was still the predominant land use. Griggs Store (*ca* 1830) has an intact Greek Revival interior. Westford was the birthplace of Andrew S. Draper (1848–1913), the influential first head of the State Commission of Education (1904).

Hugh C. MacDougall

Westhampton Beach. Village (pop 1,902) in Southampton (Suffolk Co). Settled by 1727 and known as Catchaponack, its residents farmed, fished, or went on whaling voyages. P. T. Barnum financed the first resort hotel, the Howell House (1868). The Long Island Rail Road arrived in 1879, and Seafield, the summer home of Gov John Adams Dix, became Westhampton Beach's first summer cottage in the same year. The future village became famous for Hampton ware, a class of art pottery invented by T. A. Brouwer in 1888. Polish immigrants arrived at the end of the 19th century. The village was incorporated in 1928. Chronically troubled by beach erosion, it was ravaged by the 1938 hurricane, which left 28 residents dead. After World War II the Westhampton Beach became an attractive resort town with a strong economic base; it was also home to C and R Duck Farm, the world's largest duck egg hatchery, and a US air force base (1940s–1969). Westhampton Beach is the site of the Long Island Aeronautical Museum.

Bronwyn Hannon

West Hampton Dunes. Village (pop 11) in Southampton (Suffolk Co). Located on a barrier island, the area became separated from land to the east when a 1993 storm created an inlet. The village was incorporated in 1994 to protect the property interests of landholders on the threatened sandbar. It is the site of the 296-acre (120 ha) Cupsogue Beach County Park (1915).

West Haverstraw. Village (pop 10,295) in Haverstraw (Rockland Co). Garnerville, a hamlet in the village, was settled around millsites on the Minisceongo Creek. During the Revolutionary War Benedict Arnold handed over plans to West Point to the British spy Maj John André at the so-called Treason House. Demolished in the 1930s, its site is on the grounds of Helen Hayes Hospital (founded in 1900 as the State Rehabilitation Hospital, renamed in 1974). At various times in the 19th century, mills produced rolled iron, printed cloth, needles, locks, percussion caps, carpets, and chemicals. The village was incorporated in 1883. Garnerville Holding Co (1934) manages the old mill buildings, leasing space to more than 25 manufacturers. Approximately 30% of the village's population was of Latino ethnicity in 2000.

West Hempstead. Locality (pop 18,713) in Hempstead (Nassau Co). The first settlers moved west in the Town of Hempstead in the mid–17th century. The Long Island Rail Road established a West Hempstead station on a branchline in 1893. The school district was established in 1912. The 1940 population of 3,384 had increased sixfold by 1960, and the total has since remained relatively stable. Primarily a residential community, West Hempstead includes the county's Halls Pond Park and the northern part of Hempstead Lake State Park.

Natalie A. Naylor

West Hills. Locality (pop 5,607) in Huntington (Suffolk Co). Taking its name from the rolling hills of the Harbor Hill moraine, West Hills was one of Huntington's earliest settlements. It is the site of Walt Whitman's birthplace, now a state historic site. Pioneer Long Island historian Silas Wood (1769–1847) was also born in West Hills, and Secretary of State and War Henry L. Stimson was a resident. Much of its area, including Jayne's Hill, the highest elevation on Long Island at 400 feet (122 m), is contained in West Hills County Park. The residential areas are zoned for low-density houses, which have attracted professionals.

Richard F. Welch

Westinghouse, George (*b* Central Bridge, Schoharie Co, 6 Oct 1846; *d* New York City, 12 Mar 1914). Inventor and manufacturer. As a boy in Schenectady, George Westinghouse spent hours in the family's machine shop. By age 15 he had invented and built a rotary engine. Westinghouse served in the Union army and navy during the Civil War. In 1865 he entered Union College in Schenectady, where he perfected two inventions: a rerailing device for railroad cars and an improved rail crossover mechanism. Westinghouse left Union after a year and a half to work on his inventions. After unsuccessful business ventures in Schenectady, Westinghouse in 1868 moved to Pittsburgh and arranged for a steel firm there to manufacture the railroad devices. His further work on rail safety led to the founding of Westinghouse Air Brake Co in 1869 and Union Switch and Signal Co in 1881. After purchasing and improving Nikola Tesla's inventions of alternating current (AC) electric motors, Westinghouse established Westinghouse Electric Co in 1886. Thomas Edison, who developed direct current (DC) electric power, tried to brand Westinghouse's new alternating current technology as too dangerous for everyday use. In 1889, to make this point, Edison arranged for the world's first electric chairs located at New York State's Sing Sing, Dannemora, and Auburn prisons to receive Westinghouse AC generators despite Westinghouse's objection. The tactic failed to discredit AC power, though. In 1891 Westinghouse Electric Co was reorganized as Westinghouse Electric and Manufacturing Co and by 1895 was generating and transmitting power from a facility at Niagara Falls. Westinghouse became one of the world's largest employers, held 361 US patents, and received many honors from scientific societies.

Levine, Israel E. *Inventive Wizard: George Westinghouse* (New York: Messner, 1962)

Prout, Henry G. *A Life of George Westinghouse* (New York: Scribner, 1922)

Albert S. Eggerton Jr

West Islip. Locality (pop 28,907) in Islip (Suffolk Co). Most of West Islip was patented to brothers Thomas and Richard Willetts in 1695. A Presbyterian church (*ca* 1730) was destroyed by British soldiers in 1788, but a mill on Sumpawams Creek (1750) survived until the early 20th century. The LaGrange Inn was an important stagecoach stop on the Montauk Highway for a century beginning in the 1780s. Many Ukrainian immigrants arrived in the early 20th century. Facilities built to serve the post–World War II population boom include the Robert Moses Causeway (1953–64), the high school (1957), the newly designated post office (1958), and Good Samaritan Hospital (1959).

Daria E. Merwin

Westmere. Locality (pop 7,188) in Guilderland (Albany Co). The locality's main artery is US 20, which began as the First Great Western Turnpike in 1799. After World War I, suburban bungalows were built along the route, but real growth followed World War II, when housing for returning servicemen was built. Crossgates Mall, the region's largest indoor shopping facility, opened on what had been vacant land in 1984. Westmere residents work in Albany or adjacent suburban towns.

West Monroe. Town (pop 4,428) in central Oswego Co. Settled in 1806 the town was formed in 1839 from Constantia. Much of the town is marshy and unfit for cultivation; the largest wetland in the county is located at Three Mile Bay. A colony of Cape Cod fishers came for lake salmon in 1810, and some stayed to farm. Lumbering, succeeded by dairying, and cranberry culture were 19th century industries, aided by the Ontario and Western Railroad (1869). The town is the site of Big Bay Wildlife Management Area. Most residents commute to work, especially greater Syracuse.

Barbara J. Dix

Westmoreland [WEST-MIR-LAND]. Town (pop 6,207) in central Oneida Co. Settled in 1786, the town was formed from Whitestown in 1792. The first industry was Westmoreland Furnace at Hecla, which began processing iron in 1800. The Westmoreland Malleable Iron Co Ltd (1850) closed after 1976. Several mineral springs in town attracted health seekers beginning in the 1830s. After the Civil War the southern part of Westmoreland was devoted to hop growing, while the north was a dairy region. The first cheese factory opened in 1861. Rail service was provided by the Rome and Clinton Railroad (1871) and the West Shore Railroad (1883). A Borden condensery opened in 1907. In 1954 Gov Thomas E. Dewey opened 115 miles (185 km) of the Thruway at a ceremony in town. In the late 20th century the town's dairy farms tended toward consolidation, and Westmoreland residents commuted as far as Syracuse and Albany. ABC-MCI Steel (sheet steel), Norbco (farm gates and stalls), and Harding Manufacturing (molded plastics) were employers in 2003.

West Point. Locality (pop 7,138) in Highlands (Orange Co). Part of a 1723 land grant of 1,463 acres (592 ha) to Charles Congreve, the granite bluff high above the Hudson River was fortified in 1778 under the direction of Thaddeus Kosciuszko, a Polish military engineer serving in the American army. The fortress was never captured despite Gen Benedict Arnold's plan to surrender West Point to the British in 1780. In 1790 the US government purchased it, and in 1802 the US Military Academy was established. The entire site, including Constitution Island (part of Philipstown, Putnam Co), is a military reservation. Of West Point's 2000 population, some 4,000 were cadets at the academy, which occupies approximately 16,080 acres (6,510 ha). A landmark is the Hotel Thayer (1926), designed to resemble a Gothic fortress.

See also HUDSON HIGHLANDS FORTIFICATIONS.

Barbara J. Dunlap

Westport. Town (pop 1,362) in E Essex Co. Settled in 1770 by tenants of William Gilliland, who had received a vast grant from the British government, it was first called Bessboro. The settlers left during the Revolution, and it was resettled after 1783. Westport developed its lumber and iron resources and was a lake port during the 19th century. In the 20th century the economy was shaped by summer tourism and outdoor recreation, boosted by the Northway (1967) passing through the northwest corner of town.

Thomas A. Rumney

West Sayville. See SAYVILLE.

West Seneca. Town (pop 45,920) in central Erie Co. A part of the Buffalo Creek Reservation, its first white settlers arrived in 1826. The German immigrant Community of True Inspiration, after settling in 1843, took the name Ebenezer, the name given to the town when it was formed from Hamburg and East Hamburg [now Orchard Park] in 1851. It was renamed West Seneca a year later. Rich soil and proximity to Buffalo made for good farming in the early years. Heavy industry came in the 20th century and included manufacturers of wire, pipe, and industrial equipment. An industrial park was created in the 1960s to diversify the economy. Schwabl's Restaurant is one of the traditional birthplaces of the regional specialty beef on weck. Residents have included artist Charles Burchfield (1893–1967) and Wilson Greatbatch (1919–), inventor of the implantable pacemaker. The town is the site of the West Seneca Developmental Center (1962).

Andrew C. Maines

West Shore Railroad. The New York, West Shore, and Buffalo Railroad (NYWS&B) was built between 1881 and 1883 to connect the Port of New York with Buffalo, duplicating the route of New York Central Railroad on the opposite shore of the Hudson River. The eastern terminus of the line was at Weehawken, NJ, across the river from Manhattan. From here the line went north, partly inland and partly along the west shore of the Hudson, to the Albany region and then west to Buffalo, still paralleling New York Central track but on the opposite or south side of the Mohawk River and Erie Canal waterway. George M. Pullman and the Jay Gould interests promoted this expensive and unnecessary railroad, possibly in an attempt to force New York Central to buy the line at an exorbitant price. Instead, a ruinous competition began, and NYWS&B went bankrupt in June 1884. Even then it represented a danger to New York Central, as arch-competitor Pennsylvania Railroad threatened to acquire complete control of the line. In retaliation New York Central invested in a competing line in Pennsylvania. J. P. Morgan halted the war by inviting the rival magnates aboard his yacht *Corsair* in July 1885; he sailed it up and down the Hudson River until the heads of both railroads agreed to stop supporting their respective "blackmail" lines. New York Central acquired NYWS&B's bonds and took a 450-year lease on the line, changing its name to West Shore Railroad and, at first, keeping the "unwanted stepchild" in operation primarily for local traffic. Around 1900, to handle great increases in traffic, New York Central began to use the portion south of Albany to deliver much of its eastbound freight traffic. All passenger service ended by 1959. After Conrail absorbed the eastern trunk lines in 1976, the line (now River Division) became the chief north-south freight route in the region.

Crawford, Thomas M., and Frederick A. Kramer. *Rails along the Hudson* (New York: Quadrant Press, 1979)

Thomas R. Flagg

West Sparta. Town (pop 1,244) in S central Livingston Co. Settled in 1792, the town was formed from Sparta in 1846. Millard Fillmore worked at a wool-carding mill in West Sparta as a young man in 1814–15. The Erie and Genesee Valley Railroad came through in 1872. I-390 was completed through town in 1979. A variety of nondairy farms exist in the early 21st century, and many residents work in neighboring towns. The Canaseraga Swamp lies in the northeast part of town.

Mary Jo Marks

West Turin. Town (pop 1,674) in S Lewis Co. Settled in 1796, the town was formed from Turin in 1830. West Turin lies on the east base of the Tug Hill Plateau. The two main activities are dairy farming and maple sugaring. The Village of Constableville, named for proprietor William Constable, is the site of his Georgian mansion (1810–19), which is now a museum. A Welsh colony established a church at Collinsville in 1846; Polish and Hungarian farmers arrived after World War I. In 1973 the adjacent Town of Highmarket (1852) was dissolved and its territory added to West Turin.

Arthur Einhorn

West Union. Town (pop 399) in SW Steuben Co. Settled in 1821, the town was formed from Greenwood in 1845. Catholics from the Ulster region of Ireland settled in the town beginning about 1830. After the forests were cleared, dairy farming became important. Cheese making for market began in 1842, and cheese factories were built in West Union in the 1870s. A commercial maple sugar works produced approximately 500 gallons (1,890 l) of syrup annually until the mid-1960s. The New York and Pennsylvania Railroad (1876) served the town. West Union lies on the edge of the Pennsylvania oil pool. In the early 21st century numerous active wells pump modest amounts of marketable crude oil in the Fulton Valley.

Virginia L. Wright and Jerry Wright

Westvale. Locality (pop 5,166) in Geddes (Onondaga Co). Residential subdivisions began in the 1930s and expanded rapidly after World War II. Westvale is the site of Onondaga Co's first suburban shopping center, Westvale Plaza (1948), which remained in operation in 2003 with two original tenants, P&C Foods and Geddes Federal Savings and Loan.

Barbara S. Rivette

Westville. Town (pop 1,823) in N Franklin Co. Settled *ca* 1800, chiefly by Vermonters, the town was formed in 1829 from Constable. A forge for the manufacture of bar iron from local bog ore was in operation from *ca* 1810 until midcentury. Other products included lime, potato starch (*ca* 1850–*ca* 1900), and cheese. In the southern part of town, market gardening for nearby Malone was popular. The town's population grew 12% between 1990 and 2000.

Thomas W. Perrin

West Winfield. Village (pop 862) in Winfield (Herkimer Co). The community developed as a commercial center on the Third Great Western Turnpike (1803) and the Richfield Springs Branch of the Utica, Chenango and Susquehanna Valley Railroad (1870–1987). A tannery (*ca* 1820–1968, with gaps) was the principal village employer; in recent years its site has been identified as the locus of hazardous wastes. The village incorporated in 1898. In the early 21st century West Winfield's businesses serve local residents and farmers.

James Crawford

Wethersfield. Town (pop 891) in central Wyoming Co. The area was settled in 1809, and the town was formed in 1823 from Orangeville. Grain culture gave way to dairying, especially after the development of cheese factories in the Civil War era. At the turn of the 21st century, a 6.6 MW wind farm was a new addition to the town's landscape, with its 213 ft (64.9 m) towers.

wetlands. According to the US Environmental Protection Agency (EPA), wetlands are areas saturated by surface or groundwater at a frequency and duration sufficient to support vegetation typically adapted for life in saturated soil conditions. Wetlands are ephemeral, with their creation and disappearance based on a number of factors that vary with time.

Although wetlands are now recognized as important, they were not so recognized historically. From colonial times many thought them undesirable: unhealthy breeding grounds for insects that carried diseases and otherwise just "unproductive" waste areas. Because of these attitudes, wetlands were drained to convert land for other, usually agricultural, uses. Before Europeans arrived in what is now the New York City metropolitan area, there were vast reaches of wetlands. Most by far were gradually drained and filled. One surviving remnant is the Jamaica Bay Wildlife Refuge, part of the Gateway National Recreation Area, in Brooklyn and Queens. Beginning in the 1820s in Madison, Orange, and Oswego Cos, wetlands were turned into highly productive mucklands used to cultivate lettuce and onions. Overall, about 40% of coastal wetland habitat was lost from 1780 to 1980 in the Northeast, with New York State losing closer to 60%, according to T. E. Dahl in *Wetland Losses in the United States, 1780s to 1980s*. New York State's losses were from agricultural and other developments promoted further by a public health fear of diseases exacerbated by areas of standing water. Beginning in the 1970s major federal and state laws on wetland preservation came into force. The federal Clean Water Act (1972) regulates discharge of dredged and fill material into US waters, including wetlands; the EPA has ultimate enforcement authority although the permitting authority is under the US Army Corps of Engineers. The state legislature enacted the Tidal Wetlands Act (1973) to regulate activities such as construction and dredging in wetland areas and the Freshwater Wetlands Act (1975) to protect wetlands of 12.4 acres (5.02 ha) or larger. The Adirondack Park Agency oversees and enforces the latter act within the park.

There are generally four types of wetlands in New York State: marshes (tidal and nontidal), swamps (forested and shrub), bogs, and fens, each with its own unique characteristics. Tidal marshes can be freshwater, brackish, or saline, and provide a vital habitat for clams, crabs, small fish, plant life, and migratory waterfowl. Tidal wetlands can be found in the 9,155 acre (3,705 ha) Jamaica Bay Wildlife Refuge. Great South Bay (Suffolk Co), with nearly 70,000 acres (28,000 ha) and extensive tidal salt marshes, is the largest shallow estuarine bay in the state. Other tidal wetlands are the salt marshes in the Hudson River north to near the Tappan Zee Bridge at Tarrytown (Westchester Co). Nontidal marshes are primarily freshwater, but some are brackish or alkaline, and these are the most prevalent, usually found along streams, lakes, rivers, and ponds. They have highly organic, mineral-rich soils and provide an excellent habitat for waterfowl, mammals, and plant life. Two are in the eastern Lake Ontario region: Thousand Acre Swamp (Monroe Co) and the 36,000-acre (14,600 ha) Montezuma Wetlands Complex (Cayuga, Seneca, and Wayne Cos). These are the most spectacular remaining wetlands from a vast system that arose during the draining of glacial Lake Iroquois and the forming of the much smaller Lake Ontario.

Swamps are dominated by woody plants and support many species. Forested swamps are inundated with floodwater from rivers and streams. Shrub swamps are similar to forested swamps, but shrubby vegetation is predominant in the former. Forested and shrub swamps are often found adjacent to one another, along slow-moving streams or floodplains. A good example is the area along Sterling Creek (Cayuga Co) where there is both an open area of shrubby wetlands and an extensive red maple wooded wetland. The Great Swamp of the Croton River (Dutchess and Putnam Cos) is another example of the co-occurrence of these types of wetlands.

Bogs are characterized by spongy peat deposits, acidic waters, and a floor covered by a thick carpet of sphagnum moss. Almost all of the water in a bog comes from precipitation. Bogs prevent downstream flooding by absorbing precipitation, support various species of plant life, and provide a habitat for animals. Because carbon is stored in the peat deposits, they also play a role in regulating the global climate. Notable bogs in New York include the calcareous meadows around Quaker Pond in Mendon Park Ponds (Monroe Co) and Zurich Bog (Wayne Co), a National Natural Landmark.

Fens are peat-forming wetlands that receive nutrients from sources other than precipitation. With lower acidity and higher nutrient levels and therefore different from bogs, fens can support a more diverse plant and animal community. The eastern Lake Ontario region has many acres of fens. Other fen habitats include parts of the Amagansett National Wildlife Refuge (Suffolk Co) and along the Taconic Ridge borderlands of New York, Massachusetts, and Connecticut.

The New York State Department of Environmental Conservation estimates there are approximately 2.4 million acres (970,000 ha) of freshwater wetlands in the state, with the Adirondack and Lake Plains regions in Western New York encompassing 74% of the total. From the mid-1980s until the mid-1990s, there was a net gain of 15,500 acres (6,270 ha) of freshwater wetlands, mostly because agriculture use of those acres was abandoned. Many of New York's endangered or threatened species require or prefer wetlands for at least part of their life cycle, including the bog turtle, Northern harrier, Hooker's orchid, and the crested fringed orchid. The state of wetlands is improving as society begins to recognize the important functions of their natural systems. Federal and state permitting processes require "mitigation" for any wetland due to construction activities. These mitigation projects often result in the creation of new wetlands. One example is the wetland built to mitigate the loss of wetland with the construction of Rte 17 (I-86) in the western Southern Tier. Other efforts create wetlands for treating wastes, such as the planned demonstration project for treating combined sewer discharges into Harbor Brook in the City of Syracuse.

Chabreck, Robert A. *Coastal Marshes: Ecology and Wildlife Management* (Minneapolis: Univ of Minnesota Press, 1988)

Dahl, T. E. *Wetland Losses in the United States, 1780s to 1980s* (Washington, DC: US Department of Interior, Fish and Wildlife Service, 1990)

Keddy, Paul A. *Wetland Ecology: Principles and Conservation* (Cambridge, UK: Cambridge Univ Press, 2000)

Samuel H. Sage

whaling. For nearly three centuries whaling was a significant facet of the New York State fishing industry.

Colonial Shore Whaling, 1644–1800

New York's whaling industry likely began on the eastern shores of Long Island, in what is now Suffolk Co. As early as 1644 English and Dutch settlers combed beaches and maintained watchtower-type platforms to spot stranded whales. The whales were dissected for their layers of insulating fatty tissue, called blubber. Colonials boiled the fat into a smooth oil useful for tanning leather, lubricating machinery and making soap and lamp oil. Whales were also hunted for baleen, a substance sometimes referred to as whalebone, a dense yet flexible material made of keratin that hangs from the upper jaw of non-toothed species of whales. Baleen was the raw material of choice in Europe for riding whips, carriage springs, umbrella spokes, corsets, and hoopskirt frames. As early as 1650, residents of Southampton [now in Suffolk Co] were enlisting for their whaling companies the skills and labor of the local Montaukett and Shinnecock peoples. These early shore whale hunters skillfully pursued their prey (predominantly North Atlantic right whales, *Eubalaena glacialis*) using dugout canoes, stone-tipped arrows, and hemp towing lines. Following a kill, crews would tow the whale to whaling stations on shore where its baleen was dried and blubber boiled in enormous iron kettles to render what was called trayn oil, which was packed in barrels and shipped to larger markets in Boston and New Amsterdam [now New York City] for sale and export.

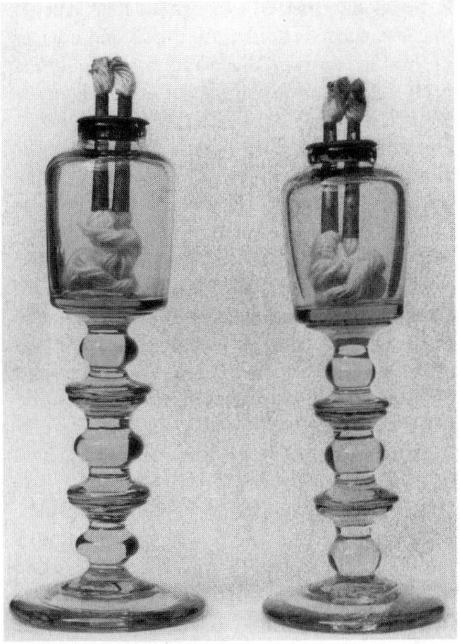

Whale oil lamps, *ca* 1815–30.

Most shore whaling occurred along the southeastern shorelines of Suffolk Co between December and April, consistent with the North Atlantic right whale's migratory patterns. Active whaling stations continued to operate until the late 19th century in Amagansett, Southampton, Bridgehampton, East Hampton, Wainscott, Fire Island, and as far west as Jamaica in Queens Co. At the height of the industry, between 1620 and 1725, whaleboat crews were typically a combination of farmers looking to supplement their winter incomes and Indians trading their labor for food and supplies. Shore whaling was second only to agriculture on Long Island as a source of income and employment.

New Techniques for Deep-Sea Whaling

In 1712 a new species known as the sperm whale *(Physeter macrocephalus)* was first hunted far off the coast of Massachusetts. Whalers discovered that its blubber created a fine-grade, low-sediment oil considered superior to right whale oil. By the mid–18th century overhunting of the North Atlantic right whale had thinned its herds and forced shore whale hunters to undertake more distant expeditions, causing many whaling companies to modify their operations and labor force to accommodate the new sperm whale fishery. In 1784 the first Long Island whale ship, the *Hope,* was sent to sea prepared to hunt for sperm whales. The sperm whale industry required long journeys to new hunting grounds because sperm whales are deep-sea feeders. Whale ship crews were therefore expected to make whaling their primary business, as it required extended leaves from home for three to four years at a time.

Larger, specially equipped ships were needed to haul tons of whale products, crew members, provisions, and specialized equipment necessary for the kill and onboard processing. Hunting for sperm whales made 400-ton (363 MT) ships a whaler's base of operations. Novice whalers, known as greenhands, spied for whales from lookout hoops fastened to the highest points on the masts. When a whale was sighted, one or more of the ship's four whaleboats pursued it, each with a crew of five oarsmen, one officer, and a boatsteerer/harpooner. Using harpoons, crews struck and tethered their boats to the injured whale until the animal exhausted itself and the final, deadly lance could be applied. The crew then towed the whale back to the main ship, where it was butchered and its blubber boiled in a brick furnace on deck known as a try works.

Whale ships required deep harbors to dock, shifting Long Island's whaling industry from the sandy beaches of its south shores to the deep-water harbors on the north shore along Long Island Sound. Whaling ports developed in Cold Spring Harbor, Greenport, New Suffolk, Amagansett, East Hampton, and South Hampton. The whaling industry in Sag Harbor (Suffolk Co) was particularly successful, ranking it sixth in the nation for vessels registered and voyages, according to statistics gathered for the period from the 1780s to the 1870s. New York City also profited significantly from whaling. During the same period, it ranked 13th in the nation for vessels registered and was a major supplier of whale ships, forged whaling equipment, labor, and investors for whaling companies along the Atlantic coast, as well as a marketplace for oil and bone when ships returned. Whaling was so profitable a business venture that even small ports like Staten Island with access to the Atlantic's feeding grounds sought to enter the industry.

Hudson Valley Whaling

The first Hudson River–based whaling company was established in Claverack Landing [now Hudson, Columbia Co] in 1783 by a community of Nantucket Quaker families that had fled harassment from American and British raiders. The transplanted community built a whaling center that launched 24 voyages from 18 vessels between 1786 and 1841. The success of the Hudson Whaling Co inspired further upriver community investment in whaling ventures. The Poughkeepsie Whaling Co and Dutchess Whaling Co were incorporated in Poughkeepsie in 1832 and 1833, respectively, and by 1833 Newburgh (Orange Co) hosted the Newburgh Whaling Co and the North River Whaling Co. The difficulty of navigating ships up the ice-clogged Hudson River, combined with disappointing profits, the financial depression of 1837, and a series of bizarre and unfortunate disasters, ultimately led to the demise of Hudson River whaling. By 1844 the last of the Hudson River whaling voyages had left and its spermaceti candle factories had burned to the ground.

Effects and Accomplishments

The whale fishery stimulated the growth of cities, towns, and communities in the Hudson Valley and Long Island with the creation of settlements of shipbuilders, craftsmen, and sailors who supported the industry. Shipbuilding villages like Port Jefferson, Setauket, and Northport (Suffolk Co) grew around whaling centers and thrived from their business. During the boom years of the whaling industry, fortunes were made in New York State by whaling company stockholders, whaling captains, and industry agents. Sailors from the state also earned fame for their voyages. Capt Mercator Cooper of the Sag Harbor whaleship *Manhattan* earned the double distinction of being the first whaler to explore and work the Okhotsk Sea and the first American to be received by the Japanese empire in 1845. Thomas Welcome Roys, also a Sag Harbor captain, commanded the first whaler, the *Superior,* to cross the Bering Strait in mid-July 1848, where he discovered the Arctic bowhead whale *(Balaena mysticetus).*

Young whalemen who signed to extended cruises discovered that their new careers guaranteed little more than poor food, dangerous and exhausting labor, and disappointing pay. During inactive portions of the voyage, whalemen honed their energies into scrimshaw, a form of folk art created by etching designs and drawings onto whales' teeth, baleen, wood, and jawbone or carving these materials into functional or decorative items like canes, umbrellas, keepsake boxes, and knitting tools. Whalemen also composed sea chanteys, or work tunes, to entertain them through their difficult, unpleasant labor. Desertions and death were common, and captains often filled empty slots with willing natives from foreign shores, giving New York's whaling ports a reputation as melting pots for international languages and customs from whalemen of many nationalities who routinely disembarked when their voyages had ended.

Whaling became one of the 19th century's few careers where men of different races and ethnicities mixed in common living and working quarters. A whaler's promotion and pay depended largely on skill and experience, making whaling an appealing career for many African Americans who took this opportunity to earn a modest living and be rewarded with some measure of respect and responsibility. Yet relatively few nonwhite sailors ever rose to officer status, and the industry is marred by the participation of several of its ships in illegal slave trade operations between the African and Brazilian coasts between 1845 and 1862.

Decline of the Industry

New York City and Long Island's deep-sea whale fishery reached its peak during the late 1840s and the early 1850s and declined steadily after that. Several factors contributed to the extinction of New York State's commercial whale fishery. First, cheaper synthetic substitutes, such as petroleum and spring steel, nearly eliminated the demand for whale products. Second, significant overhunting depleted whale populations, making voyages even longer. As whalers ventured into harsh climates such as the Arctic Ocean, whaling cruises came to be viewed as prohibitively risky, less profitable, and achingly long to wait for returns. Third, whaling companies lost many of their reliable investors, sources of labor, and ships to moneymaking ventures like the California gold rush of 1847. Finally, the collateral destruction that accompanied the American Civil War increased the whaling industry's troubles as potential greenhands were drafted into service in the Union army and many whale ships were either scuttled by Confederate raiders or commandeered by the Union navy.

Cold Spring Harbor and Greenport saw their last whaling voyages depart in 1857. Sag Harbor dispatched its last whale ship, the *Myra,* in 1871. Although New York City continued its business relationships with ports that whaled, its last registered whale ship was dispatched in 1874. Shore whaling continued on Long Island in varying degrees until 1924. Though commercial whaling has long disappeared from the state, visitors may learn about the now defunct industry in whaling museums in Cold Spring Harbor and Sag Harbor.

See also MELVILLE, HERMAN.

Bolster, W. Jeffrey. *Black Jacks: African American Seamen in the Age of Sail* (Cambridge, Mass: Harvard Univ Press, 1997)

Creighton, Margaret S. *Rites and Passages: The Experience of American Whaling, 1830–1870* (New York: Cambridge Univ Press, 1995)

Ellis, Richard. *Men and Whales* (New York: Lyons Press, 1999)

Lund, Judith Navas. *Whaling Masters and Whaling Voyages Sailing from American Ports* (New Bedford, Mass: New Bedford Whaling Museum and Ten Pound Book, 2001)

Jill Wright

Wharton, Clifton R., Jr (*b* Boston, 14 Sept 1926). Economist and educator. He is the son of diplomat Clifton Wharton, the first black US ambassador to a European country (Norway), and graduated from Harvard at 16 with a degree in history. In 1958 he received a PhD in economics from the University of Chicago. He became president of Michigan State University in 1970, making him the first African American in the 20th century to serve as president of a predominately white university. He was appointed chancellor of the State University of New York System in 1978 and served until 1987, overseeing 64 campuses and 380,000 students. Wharton became the first African American to head a Fortune 500 company when he became chairman and chief executive officer of Teachers Insurance and Annuity Association–College Retirement Equities Fund (TIAA-CREF) from 1987 through 1993. He retired in 1987 and moved to Cooperstown (Ostego Co) but continues to serve on numerous institutional boards. He was appointed deputy secretary of state (1993) under Pres Bill Clinton.

Blinken, Donald B. Papers. Univ at Albany Archives, Albany, New York

Tricia A. Barbagallo

Wharton [née Jones], **Edith (Newbold)** (*b* New York City, 24 Jan 1862; *d* St.-Brice-sous-forêt, France, 11 Aug 1937). Writer. The daughter of a wealthy and socially prominent New York City family, Edith Jones was bookish and shy, and, like many young women of her class, schooled at home. She spent her childhood at the family home on 14 West 23d St and traveled to residences in Newport, RI, and Paris. She began writing at an early age. In 1885 she married Edward "Teddy" Robbins Wharton, a banker from Boston 12 years her senior. The couple had a home in Newport and, until 1889, at 28 West 25th St. In 1891 Wharton bought a home at 884 Park Ave. Her first book, *The Decoration of Houses* (1897), coauthored with architect Ogden Codman, presented her views on design and was an immediate success. Thereafter, she was committed to a writing career. Her early efforts were short stories, the first collection of which, *The Greater Inclination,* was published in 1899. Her first novel, *Valley of Decision* (1902), set in the 18th century, sold very well and also brought Wharton to the attention of Henry James, who became her friend and mentor.

Wharton's privileged upbringing gave her insights into the social elite, and she created multifaceted characters, vividly drawn, with irony and wit. *The House of Mirth* (1905) was a popular and critical success. Set in New York City, Lily Bart, the heroine, is prevented by social constrictions from finding true love and eventually commits suicide. The strictures of social class would be a major theme throughout Wharton's writing. Much of her work would also be critical of American culture, which she saw as provincial and lacking appreciation for art in any form. In 1909 she took up residence in France, where she would ultimately make her home. In 1911 Wharton published the highly popular novel *Ethan Frome,* a tragic tale of love gone wrong set in rural New England. She divorced Teddy in 1913 and never remarried.

Wharton was a prolific writer, averaging nearly a book a year for most of her career. She was awarded the Pulitzer Prize for her historical novel *The Age of Innocence* (1920), which explored the social conventions of New York City's elite in the 1870s. New York City was also the setting for *The Custom of the Country* (1913), *Hudson River Bracketed* (1929), *The Gods Arrive* (1932), and *Old New York* (1924), and for much of her autobiography, *A Backward Glance* (1933).

Lewis, R. W. B. *Edith Wharton: A Biography* (New York: Harper & Row, 1975)

Wolff, Cynthia Griffin. *A Feast of Words: The Triumph of Edith Wharton* (New York: Addison-Wesley, 1995)

J. Justin Gustainis

wheat. This old world grain came to New York Colony with the earliest European settlers. The English, in particular, preferred wheat over rye or corn for bread. From the settlement period, both winter and spring wheat, named for their planting times, were grown, but the former predominated. Winter wheat was planted in the late autumn and left to germinate under the snow. It sprouted early in spring and was harvested between the first and second cuttings of hay, usually in mid-July. Spring wheat was planted as soon as the ground could be worked and was harvested later in the year. Winter wheat fit into the evolving agricultural calendar, slipping between June and August hayings. Also, if an autumn-sown crop failed in a harsh winter, the field could be replanted with buckwheat, turnips, or spring wheat, crops that would mature before frost. Because wheat played a large role in the diet, a surplus could always be sold, and from the mid–17th century, wheat was planted both as a domestic staple and as a cash crop in colonial New York. Historically, red and white, bearded and unbearded, varieties were grown. Wheat is a demanding crop, preferring the mellow ground of oft-tilled soil, but it frequently failed in old, nutrient-impoverished fields until farmers began manuring in the 1800s.

Within a generation of its earliest planting in America, disease and pests plagued wheat crops. Fungal disease, variously known as blast, rust, or smut, blackened stems and hollowed out grains, making the wheat useless as a crop. In a pattern established by the mid-1700s, the predictable appearance of fungal disease in old fields helped drive the opening of new lands. Wheat usually followed potatoes in the crop rotation on new land; in older fields, wheat was often the first crop in a field left fallow for several seasons. As new lands opened, landlords in the pre-Revolutionary period encouraged their tenants to grow wheat. Indeed, until the second quarter of the 18th century, the colony levied quitrents from landholders in bushels of wheat. The valleys of the Schoharie Creek, the Hudson River, and the Mohawk River became breadbasket regions by the mid-1700s. The Schoharie Valley was plundered by British troops during the Revolution because it was among the most important suppliers of wheat flour to the Continental army. In the Hudson Valley, wheat was grown on a large scale to meet the demands of large landholders who collected rents from tenants in wheat. By the late 1700s the Hessian fly, named for the German mercenaries used by the British during the Revolutionary War, infested and blighted crops on Long Island and in the Hudson River valley, spreading northward.

Early barns in both the English and Dutch building traditions were designed for grain threshing and storage, with large central areas with double-laid threshing floors. English barns, common until the mid-1800s in Central New York, were three-bay, gable-roofed, frame structures with doors in the long walls, which were opened for cross ventilation when winnowing (separating the grain from the chaff). Dutch barns with steeply pitched roofs and doors in the gable walls were characteristic of Dutch- and German-settled areas in the Hudson and Mohawk Valleys.

After the Revolution, land speculators encouraged newly settled farmers to grow wheat to pay their mortgages or rents. As land in Central New York opened for settlement, farmers grew wheat for their own use and for a salable surplus. Thus, wheat growing continued west. Wheat's importance made it one of the earliest crops to receive serious attention from agricultural inventors. By 1810 hand-cranked fanning mills were already replacing the older winnowing baskets, known as corn fans, in Central New York. In addition to problems with the Hessian fly and fungal diseases, midges damaged the wheat crop in the 1820s and 1830s. While writers of the early 1800s did not understand the mechanism of fungal contagion, they advocated moving fields often and discouraged the use of cradle scythes as ways to diminish disease. It was difficult to discourage the use of the efficient cradle scythes, however, which cut three times as quickly as a sickle; farm labor beyond the family workforce was scarce through the Civil War period, and a skillful cradler also laid out the stalks in neat piles for bundling and drying before storage. Mechanical reapers, first patented in the 1840s, did not gain immediate acceptance, and while draught animals drew plows and harrows for field preparation, broadcast sowing and harvesting with scythes continued into the 1850s and 1860s.

By the second quarter of the 19th century, the rich lands of the Genesee Valley became the nation's most important wheat-growing section. Rochester, at the mouth of the valley, achieved a quarter century of prominence as the nation's largest milling center after the opening of the Erie Canal (1825) and improvement of the city's access to Lake Ontario via canal in the early 1830s. Known as the Flour City, Rochester ground 500,000 barrels in 1840, processing both Genesee and Canadian wheat. The city's 1855 flour output certainly surpassed this amount, because the same year Monroe Co grew 810,000 bushels (28.5 million l) and neighboring Livingston Co more than 1 million (35.2 million l). The Genesee Valley wheat economy declined during the third quarter of the 19th century, with the decrease beginning in the 1850s as large-scale wheat growing moved to the upper Midwest.

For a brief period in the mid–19th century, horse-drawn mechanical reapers upset the balance in production because they could cut more grain than could be sown by hand. But the patenting of economical seed drills in the 1850s and their increasing use in the post–Civil War era allowed farmers to plant and harvest roughly equal acreages. Also in the 1850s, entomologist Dr Asa Fitch of Salem (Washington Co) helped solve the problem of Hessian fly blight through his identification of a common weed that harbored the fly during a portion of its life cycle. Binders, developed in the 1870s, decreased labor needs still further. Combines, common by 1920, could reap and thresh grain in one pass over the field. All these horse-drawn machines operated best on relatively flat land, and each innovation hastened the decline of upland-area arable farms, encouraging the movement of grain growing to the Midwest's Great Plains. But as late as the 1870s, the number of winter wheat bushels harvested in the state greatly exceeded the number of spring wheat bushels. In 1875 Genesee Co produced 618,157 bushels (21,783,240 l); Cayuga Co, 709,442 bushels (25,000,030 l); Niagara Co, 653,524 bushels (23,029,530 l); Seneca Co, 507,405 bushels (17,880,450 l); Erie Co, 340,540 bushels (12,000,290 l); and Livingston Co, 633,148 bushels (22,311,510 l). Overall New York State wheat production peaked in 1878 with a harvest of 15.2 million bushels (535.6 million l). Wheat growing continued in New York State through the succeeding century, with western counties being the largest producers, but on a declining scale. In 2000 New York State harvested 7,420,000 bushels (261.47 million l) of wheat from 140,000 acres (56,700 ha).

Hurt, R. Douglas. *American Farm Tools from Hand-Power to Steam-Power* (Manhattan, Kans: Sunflower Univ Press, 1982)

Quick, Graeme, and Wesley Buchele. *The Grain Harvesters* (St. Joseph, Mich: American Society of Agricultural Engineers, 1978)

Schlebecker, John T. *Whereby We Thrive: A History of American Farming, 1607–1972* (Ames: Iowa State Univ Press, 1975)

Jessie Ravage

Wheatfield. Town (pop 14,086) in SW Niagara Co. Settled in 1824, the town was formed in 1836 from Niagara. Originally it was a wheat-growing town, but by 1900 potatoes and berries, with garden vegetables in the south, were its chief products. German Lutherans arrived in 1843, forming the communities of Bergholz, Martinsville, St. Johnsburg, and New Walmore. Parts of Niagara Falls International Airport (1929) and Niagara Falls Air Force Base are located in town. During World War II and after, Bell Aircraft manufactured fighter planes at its plant adjacent to the airport. Wheatfield is the fastest-growing town in the county, up 26.6% between 1990 and 2000 because of suburban development. Much of the town remains agricultural, especially in garden produce. The German Heritage Museum preserves Das Haus (1843), a log house from the beginning of German settlement.

Nancy B. Mingus

Wheatland. Town (pop 5,149) in SW Monroe Co. Settled in 1786, the town was formed from Caledonia (Livingston Co) in 1821 as Inverness and was renamed Wheatland immediately afterward. The first important industry was distilling, to convert grain into a more shippable product. The Remington and Allen woolen mill at Mumford operated from 1829 to 1902. Gypsum mining and milling began in the mid-1830s. Scottsville citizens initiated both canal and railroad construction in 1837, connecting to the Genesee Valley Canal (1840–78). Wheat declined after five bad harvests (1855–59), and general farming succeeded it. After the Civil War a number of free African Americans came to Wheatland to work, forming Belcoda Baptist Church (1891; now Second Baptist Church, Mumford). Mumford Mills (1905–39) produced toilet tissue. By the 1920s some residents commuted to Rochester, but Wheatland remains essentially rural. It is the site of the Genesee Country Village and Museum and of the Cedar Springs State Fish Hatchery.

Carolyn Vacca

Wheatley Heights. Locality (pop 5,013) in Babylon (Suffolk Co). Built on pine barrens, its name comes from a 1913 residential development but was not official until 1976 when the area was given its own postal designation as a substation of Wyandanch. A predominantly white community until the 1960s, it is a racially mixed community of ranch homes; its population in 2000 was more than 48% African American and 11.7% were of Latino ethnicity. In 2003 it retained a rural character with two campgrounds and a working farm.

Laura E. Mann

Wheeler. Town (pop 1,263) in N central Steuben Co. Settled in 1799, the town formed from Bath and Prattsburgh in 1820. After the forests were cleared from its high rolling hills, farming predominated. From the mid-1800s to World War II tobacco was an important crop. The Kanona and Prattsburgh Railroad served the town from 1882 to 1961. Amish farmers established a community in the 1980s. Mucklands drained in the 1930s continue to support truck farming in the early 21st century.

Virginia L. Wright and Jerry Wright

Wheeler [née Thurber], Candace (*b* Delhi, Delaware Co, 24 Mar 1827; *d* New York City, 5 Aug 1923). Designer. Thurber was educated in Delhi, where she was home schooled by her father and studied at the Delaware Academy. On 28 June 1844 she married Thomas M. Wheeler, and the couple moved to Brooklyn. With a lifelong interest in painting and decorative arts, Candace began studying textiles and was committed to creating American designs in domestic arts. In 1877 she organized the Society of Decorative Art. Wheeler joined Louis C. Tiffany's design firm, Associated Artists, in 1879, serving as head of the textile department. In 1883 she began her own firm, retaining the name Associated Artists, and focused on textiles made by women. During this time Wheeler became the director of the Bureau of Applied Arts for New York State, a lecturer of the New York Institute for Artist-Artisans, and a consultant to the Woman's Art School of Cooper Union. By 1900, having relinquished control of her design firm to her son, Wheeler was writing articles and books on American decorative arts, including *Principles of Home Decoration* (1903). Wheeler spent her summers in Onteora Park (Greene Co), in the Catskill Mountains, where she began designing cottages, which she regarded as aesthetically pleasing residences for persons of modest income. Although by the end of her life textile designs were machine made and the demand for handmade fabrics significantly diminished, Wheeler's work opened new doors for women in interior design and decorative arts.

Peck, Amelia, and Carol Irish Peck. *Candace Wheeler: The Art and Enterprise of American Design, 1875–1900* (New Haven, Conn: Yale Univ Press, 2001)

Kerry Delaney

Wheeler, William A(lmon) (*b* Malone, Franklin Co, 30 June 1819; *d* Malone, 4 June 1887). US vice president. Wheeler lived and taught in Franklin Co schools before being admitted to the bar in 1845. After four years as Franklin Co district attorney (1846–50), he served as a Whig in the state assembly (1850–51) and thereafter as counsel for St. Lawrence Valley banking and railroad corporations; he became president of the New York Northern Railroad. He joined the new Republican Party in 1855, was elected to the state senate in 1858, and served a term in the House of Representatives (1861–63), where he was an advocate for emancipation. In 1867 he presided over the New York State Constitutional Convention, where he opposed an amendment to guarantee racially equal suffrage. Reelected to Congress (1869–77), he chaired key committees on southern affairs and appropriations and in 1874–75 organized the "Wheeler Compromise" among different factions in Louisiana politics following widespread white intimidation of Republican voters; his report criticized the implementation of black suffrage without black education. Wheeler's reputation for honesty and his increasingly conciliatory attitudes to Whites in the South made him an ideal running mate for Rutherford B. Hayes in 1876. His term as vice president passed quietly, and in 1879 he temporarily healed the rift between the Stalwart and Half-breed factions of New York State's Republican Party. When Hayes's administration ended, however, Wheeler declined a run for the US Senate and retired to Malone, where he resided until his death.

Howells, William Dean. *Sketch of the Life and Character of Rutherford B. Hayes: Also a Biographical Sketch of William A. Wheeler* (1876; repr Norwood, Pa: Norwood Editions, 1978)

Williams, T. Harry, ed. *Hayes: The Diary of a President, 1875–1881* (New York: David McKay, 1964)

Jon Sterngass

Whig Party. A major party that opposed Democrats in New York State from 1834 to 1855. While less often in power than the Democrats, the Whigs helped shape state policies regarding banks, canals, and reform, and attracted many politicians, such as William H. Seward and Millard Fillmore, who would serve the nation.

Origins

Party organizers of the congressional opponents of Pres Andrew Jackson chose the name Whig to highlight Jackson's alleged similarity to King

George III, whom the English Whigs had opposed. In New York State the National Republicans and the Antimasons, who opposed the successful Democratic effort to get Jackson elected in 1828, were the logical recruits for a Whig Party. From the Antimasons came the Whigs' critique of the Democrats as hypocrites who appealed to the common man while conspiratorially advancing the interests of their elite members instead of pursuing equality of opportunity. From the National Republicans came a belief that government should advance the growth, prosperity, and well-being of society by promoting transportation, banks, tariffs, public schools, and moral reform generally. Attracted to this agenda tended to be those of New England ancestry, business people, evangelical Protestants whether native-born or immigrant, African Americans, and a disproportionate number of the middle class, although there were numerous exceptions in all of these categories. The strongest Whig support came from Western New York, where newspapers such as the *Rochester Telegraph* developed party ideology.

New Yorkers Thurlow Weed, Horace Greeley, and Seward were the party's early national and state leaders. Editor of the *Albany Evening Journal,* Weed established communications among Whigs throughout the state and through his knowledge of local conditions advised Whig officeholders on patronage and on policy matters for a generation. Greeley, editor of the *New York Tribune,* portrayed Whig policies in a favorable light to national and state audiences. Seward served as the state's first Whig governor (1839–42) and as senator (1849–61). Other party notables included Hamilton Fish, Millard Fillmore, Francis Granger, and John Young.

Policy Challenges

The Whigs and the Democrats were of comparable strength in this era, leaving neither with a popular mandate and both subject to defeat due to factional dissatisfaction. The Whigs, who first gained power at the state level in the election of 1838, initially criticized the Democrats' handling of the aftermath of Jackson's Bank War and joined with conservative Democrats to prevent a "no banks" position, which favored removing public funds from banks, from prevailing at the state level. During his tenure Seward attempted to continue canal and railroad construction in New York State despite an ongoing depression, because he believed that the economic stimulus would bring in revenues to offset the costs. Having frightened the state's investors, who bought state bonds only when they were deeply discounted, the Democrats regained the governorship in 1842 and enacted the Stop and Tax Law to defer spending until revenues were available; most Whigs opposed this measure. Young played on the Democrats' factional differences, however, to revive canal spending as governor. Whig Washington Hunt, governor from 1851 through 1853, also oversaw enlarging the canal system only to have his efforts ruled unconstitutional. In pursuit of expanded public education, Seward proposed giving state money to parochial schools. This shocked Protestants and prevented enactment. Fish, governor from 1849 through 1850, was more successful in reforming public education by proposing a bureaucracy independent of partisan politics to expend increased state aid. Fish was also successful in reforming the tax and criminal codes during his administration.

The Whigs' promise to use government to improve society made them a target for more controversial reform groups, including advocates of antislavery, temperance, and antirentism. Seeking to turn "feudal" leaseholds along the Hudson River into freeholds, antirenters challenged both Whigs and Democrats, who largely agreed with the outcome but struggled over how to realize it without disrespecting existing property rights. Neither party was able to solve the dilemma, but both tried to appear helpful. Democrats crafted an 1846 law somewhat limiting landlords' prerogatives. Under Young, governor from 1847 through 1848, the attorney general investigated claims that the original titles of New York State's landlords were faulty, and Young also pardoned some antirenters convicted of crimes. The leases remained, however. Temperance reform, whose advocates associated crime, poverty, and violence directly with alcohol and wished to end its use, appealed to evangelical Protestants but was anathema to many immigrants. Whigs like Seward were reluctant to alienate the growing immigrant bloc and to threaten the property rights of distillers and others. The issue grew in importance with the upsurge of immigration after 1846. In 1853 Whig state senator Myron H. Clark masterminded passage of a law forbidding the manufacture and sale of alcoholic beverages, which was vetoed by Horatio Seymour, the Democratic governor. Clark used the issue to become governor but was unable to achieve legislation that the courts would accept.

Counterpoising property rights to human rights, slavery also proved a major problem for Whigs and Democrats, who faced an antislavery third party alternative, first the Liberty Party and then the Free Soil Party, beginning in 1840. The state's close division between the major parties heightened the importance of the antislavery issue. Even symbolic acts of support of antislavery, such as Gov Seward's denunciation of Virginia's slave laws in 1839, could be troublesome. Southern states retaliated against New York City merchants, heightening their awareness of antislavery as a threat to the Union and to their trade. In 1850 a major factional split between the Silver Grays and the Wooly Heads occurred within the Whig Party over the passage of the Compromise of 1850. Seward, of the Wooly Heads, opposed the Fugitive Slave Act and any expansion of slavery, while Millard Fillmore as a Silver Gray and who became president in 1850 upon the death of Pres Zachary Taylor, favored it. Controlling federal patronage, Fillmore rewarded Silver Grays who refused to support anticompromise platforms and candidates of the numerically stronger Seward faction.

Party Decline

Any flirting with antislavery alarmed Whigs from the southern states, lessening Whig chances to win national office. Disagreements over how to handle other controversial issues, such as temperance and immigration, exacerbated matters. Willingness to compromise de-

Center painting of a Whig political banner, by Terence J. Kennedy, *ca* 1839, capturing the spirit of home industry as protected by Whig tariff policy.

clined. In 1854 Clark's gubernatorial victory was by 300 votes in a four-candidate race. Many Whigs joined former Democrats in a new Republican Party. In 1855 Whigs and Republicans symbolically united by choosing the same candidates and platform and by Whig delegates taking seats at the Republican state convention. Not all Whigs followed this path; some moved to the American (Know-Nothing) Party and others to the Democrats.

See also ANTIRENT MOVEMENT.

Barkan, Elliott R. "The Emergence of a Whig Persuasion: Conservatism, Democratism, and the New York State Whigs," *New York History* 52 (1971): 367–95

Benson, Lee. *The Concept of Jacksonian Democracy: New York as a Test Case* (Princeton, NJ: Princeton Univ Press, 1961)

Holt, Michael F. *The Rise and Fall of the American Whig Party: Jacksonian Politics and the Onset of the Civil War* (New York: Oxford Univ Press, 1999)

Van Deusen, Glyndon G. *William Henry Seward* (New York: Oxford Univ Press, 1967)

Phyllis F. Field

Whipple, George Hoyt (*b* Ashland, NH, 28 Aug 1878; *d* Rochester, 1 Feb 1976). Pathologist and medical school dean. The son and grandson of physicians, Whipple graduated from Phillips Academy in Andover, Mass, and received his AB degree (1900) from Yale University and his MD degree (1905) from Johns Hopkins Medical School. Continuing at Johns Hopkins as a researcher and educator, he identified in 1907 what became known as Whipple's disease, a rare disorder involving the inability to metabolize fat. In 1914 he became professor of research medicine and director of the Hooper Foundation for Medical Research at the University of California Medical School, serving as dean of the medical school from 1920 to 1921. In 1921 University of Rochester president Rush Rhees approached Whipple to help him start a new medical school. Initially, Whipple resisted, but Rhees traveled to San Francisco to promise him full support for his research efforts. In 1921 Whipple became professor of pathology and dean of the School of Medicine and Dentistry at the University of Rochester. In 1934 Whipple shared the Nobel Prize in physiology or medicine for his work on the treatment of pernicious anemia, a disease that until then was fatal. Esteemed as one of New York State's great medical educators, Whipple was appointed in 1946 by Gov Thomas E. Dewey to serve on the Temporary Commission on the Need for a State University; the commission explored policy solutions to help alleviate overcrowding in the state's private colleges and in 1948 recommended the creation of a public community college system. Whipple retired as dean of the medical school in 1953, but he continued as professor of pathology. After retiring from the pathology chair two years later, he conducted a weekly lecture with students until 1960.

Corner, George W. *George Hoyt Whipple and His Friends: The Life Story of a Nobel Prize Pathologist* (Philadelphia: J. B. Lippincott, 1963)

Joann Minor

Whipple, Squire (*b* Hardwick, Mass, 16 Sept 1804; *d* Albany, 15 Mar 1888). Engineer, mathematical instrument maker, and author. Whipple was exposed to construction at an early age because his father had built and run and cotton-spinning mill in Massachusetts. In 1817 the family moved to New York State and settled just north of Cooperstown (Otsego Co). Whipple graduated from Union College in Schenectady in 1830, served an apprenticeship on the Baltimore and Ohio Railroad, and then worked for Holmes Hutchinson on the expansion of the Erie Canal. In 1841 he designed and built the first successful iron bridge over the Erie Canal in Newville, near Rome (Oneida Co). Whipple relied on scientific formulation to determine the specific stresses on the trusses used in construction, determining loads so he could size its members using the best materials, cast and wrought iron.

His scientific approach to bridge building was unique in the 1840s, and in 1841 he patented the truss design. In 1847 he published *A Work on Bridge Building*, the first book describing the mathematical methods used in designing truss bridges and offering original plans and details for iron and wooden bridges. Whipple's patented truss became the foundation of later designs, including the Bowstring Truss Bridge (1851). The New York State Canal Commissioners adopted it as the standard canal bridge in 1855. In 1873 he published an enlarged version of his earlier work, *An Elementary and Practical Treatise on Bridge Building*, and it was one of the standard manuals for railroad bridge construction for decades. In 1874 he designed, patented, and built the first iron lift bridge in the United States; it was over the Erie Canal at Utica. One of his extant bridges, a bowstring overhead truss design at Union College in Schenectady, is a National Historic Civil Engineering Landmark.

Griggs, Francis E. "Squire Whipple: Father of Iron Bridges," *Journal of Bridge Engineering (ASCE)* 7 (May–June 2002): 146–55

Frank E. Griggs Jr

Whitcher [née Berry], Frances Miriam (*b* Whitesboro, Oneida Co, ?1811; *d* Whitesboro, 4 Jan 1852). Writer. She was the child of a New Jersey man who settled among the mostly New England–born inhabitants of Whitesboro, where he kept a hotel on the village green across from the county courthouse. Her two older brothers graduated from Hamilton College, and Frances grew up in a cultured home with tutors in literature and art. She developed an early talent for satiric drawings and verbal sketches, and her comic pieces on "The Widow Spriggens," written in the upstate Yankee dialect, were soon serialized in local newspapers. By 1846 she won national fame with additional satiric, vernacular pieces on the irascible "Widow Bedott" and her more benign sister, "Aunt Maguire," which appeared in *Neal's Saturday Gazette* and *Godey's Lady's Book*, among the most popular magazines of the period. She married Episcopal minister B. W. Whitcher in 1847, moving to a parish in Elmira. There, her writing aroused disapproval, with one local man threatening Rev Whitcher with a lawsuit over the Aunt Maguire stories; the angry man believed Frances Miriam Whitcher had portrayed his wife as "Mrs Samson Savage." Whitcher died of consumption in 1852. The *Gazette* and *Godey* sketches were published in 1855 as *The Widow Bedott Papers*, with their editor Alice Neal acclaiming them "the most popular of any humorous articles written by an American author." The Widow Spriggens sketches and others were collected in 1867.

Morris, Linda. *Women's Humor in the Age of Gentility: The Life and Works of Frances Miriam Whitcher* (Syracuse: Syracuse Univ Press, 1992)

Eugene Paul Nassar

White, Andrew Dickson (*b* Homer, Cortland Co, 7 Nov 1832; *d* Ithaca, 4 Nov 1918). College president, diplomat, and historian. Educated in schools in Syracuse before graduating from Yale in 1853, White served in St. Petersburg as an attaché to the American legation (1854–55), studied history at the University of Berlin for a year, then returned to Yale to complete an MA in 1857. From 1857 to 1863 he taught European history at the University of Michigan, marrying Mary Outwater in 1859. An ardent abolitionist, he wrote several antislavery articles for *Atlantic Monthly* in 1862. White relocated to Syracuse and won election to the New York State Senate as a Republican, serving from 1864 to 1867. White supported equal political and civil rights for African Americans and fought unsuccessfully for integration of New York State's public schools in 1864.

Along with his fellow state senator Ezra Cornell of Tompkins Co, he advocated using New York State's share of money available under the Morrill Land Grant Act of 1862 to establish one state college, which became Cornell University. While in the senate White developed the educational principles for the new institution: nondenominationalism, coeducation, a cooperative relationship between students and faculty, and academic freedom. The university emerged as a model for combining agricultural education, industrial skills, and liberal arts disciplines on an equal footing. When Cornell opened in 1868, White became president and served until 1885. His ideas made him one of the leading higher education reformers of the time. As president he kept Cornell afloat during financial difficulties in the 1870s. Despite his avowed vision of the university as a nonsectarian institution, White in 1877 gave in to a demand by the Board of Trustees to terminate Felix Adler, of Jewish background, who founded the Society for Ethical Culture and taught comparative religion at Cornell. White further compromised in 1881 by terminating an iconoclastic scholar of history, William Channing Russel, for teaching that churches were social institutions. Nevertheless, under White's leadership Cornell developed a uniquely flexible curriculum, introducing programs in architecture and electrical engineering and endorsing the use of free electives rather than required courses. Many of White's innovations were widely adopted in higher education.

Leaves of absence from Cornell allowed White to remain active in local, national, and international politics. He served in 1871 on a presidential commission to investigate the possibility of annexing Santo Domingo and was minister to Germany in 1879–81. In 1884 White became the first president of the American Historical Association, and he was a delegate to several Republican National Conventions between 1864 and 1912. Following the death of his wife in 1887, he met Helen Magill, the first woman to earn a PhD in the United States; they married in 1890.

White's diplomatic and academic connections to Germany made him popular with German Americans in Onondaga Co, who endorsed him for governor in 1891; however, internal party politics derailed the campaign at the state convention and White's name was withdrawn. He served as minister to Russia from 1892 to 1894, then as a member of the Venezuela Boundary Commission, formed to arbitrate a territorial dispute between Venezuela and Great Britain in 1896. While ambassador to Germany (1897–1902) he headed the American delegation to the First International Peace Conference at the Hague, Netherlands, in 1899. His publications include *Paper-Money Inflation in France* (1876), *A History of the Warfare of Science with Theology in Christendom* (1896), an autobiography (1905), and *Seven Great Statesmen in the Warfare of Humanity with Unreason* (1910). He was an advocate of civil service reform in the 1870s and 1880s, international arbitration in the 1890s, and neutrality and arbitration during World War I.

Altschuler, Glenn. *Andrew D. White: Educator, Historian, Diplomat* (Ithaca: Cornell Univ Press, 1979)

Harvey Strum

White, Canvass (*b* Whitestown [now Whitesboro, Oneida Co], 8 Sept 1790; *d* St. Augustine, Fla, 18 Dec 1834). Civil engineer. Raised in Whitestown he studied at Fairfield Academy (Herkimer Co) and served in the War of 1812. White joined the Erie Canal engineer corps in 1816 and a year later traveled to Great Britain to study engineering works. In 1819 he discovered that crushed Madison Co limestone and similar argillaceous limestones could be made into a waterproof cement that was essential for canal construction. His family manufactured this cement at Chittenango (Madison Co), and in 1820 he obtained a patent for it. In 1822 White designed the Glens Falls (Warren Co) feeder and a lock and dam between Troy (Rensselaer Co) and Waterford (Saratoga Co). White also worked on harnessing the waterpower at Cohoes (Albany Co) for manufacturing purposes and conducted an early survey for Croton Aqueduct, which would carry Croton-on-Hudson (Westchester Co) water to New York City. White's later career was spent outside of New York State where he spread knowledge gained on the state canals and trained a new generation of civil engineers. He was chief engineer of the Union (1825–26) and Lehigh (1827–29) Canals in Pennsylvania and the Delaware and Raritan Canal in New Jersey (1830–34), the last two being models of their kind, before ill health caused him to move south.

Stuart, Charles B. *Lives and Works of Civil and Military Engineers of America* (New York: D. Van Nostrand, 1871)

Christopher T. Baer

White, Horace (*b* Buffalo, 7 Oct 1865; *d* New York City, 26 Nov 1943). Lawyer, businessman, and governor. Horace White was a nephew of Andrew Dickson White, first president of Cornell University. He moved with his family to Syracuse, where he attended public schools and later practiced law. He entered politics with a successful run for a state senate seat in 1896. White remained in the senate until 1908, when he was nominated to run for lieutenant governor on the Republican ticket. He was elected and became governor for 86 days in 1910–11 when Charles Evans Hughes resigned to join the US Supreme Court. However, White was not picked to run again because of his involvement in a scandal over the illegal sale of a Syracuse insurance company. When his term expired he returned to Syracuse to practice law. He was named president of the Syracuse Post-Standard Co in January 1942.

Branche, Lewis. *Governors of New York* (Watertown: Watertown Daily Times, 1958)

Dick Case

White Creek. Town (pop 3,411) in SE Washington Co. Settled 1761–65, the town was formed from Cambridge in 1815. Merino sheep were introduced to the community in 1809, and sheep raising peaked in the mid–19th century, giving way to dairy, potatoes, and flax. During the 19th century White Creek had many small shops producing chairs, hats, mittens, farm tools, handles, and leather. In 1852 the town was crossed by a railroad that later became the Delaware and Hudson Railroad. New Skete (1967) is a community affiliated with the Orthodox Church of America. The town's most famous resident was artist Anna Mary Robertson (Grandma Moses) (1860–1961). White Creek hamlet is a National Register historic district.

R. Paul McCarty

Whitehall. Town (pop 4,035) and village (pop 2,667) in NE Washington Co. It was settled in 1759 by about 30 families under the direction of Maj Philip Skene, who patented it in 1765 as Skenesborough. The first known town meeting was held in 1778. Whitehall is often called the birthplace of the US Navy on the basis of Skene's trading schooner being captured by American forces in 1775 and renamed *Liberty.* Shipbuilding later became an industry. In 1786 Skenesborough was recognized as a town and renamed Whitehall. The steamboat *Vermont* provided service to St. John [now in Que], beginning around 1809. The Champlain Canal (1819) and a railroad (from the south, 1848; to Vermont, 1850; to Canada, 1875) also served the town. The village incorporated in 1820. By 1841, when its Catholic Church organized, Whitehall drew Francophone Canadians to work in its lumber mills and tanneries. Italians arrived later and in 1940 constituted one-third of the population. Late 19th- and early 20th-century employers included the Delaware and Hudson Railroad, a silk mill, and a clothing factory. Slate was quarried in the southeast; the lands in other areas of town were better suited for livestock grazing. In 2003 the village was a tourist destination with the Skenesborough Museum (1959) and an urban cultural park, and the town's land was mainly agricultural.

R. Paul McCarty

White Plains. City (pop 53,077) in central Westchester Co. In 1683, 18 Indians sold 4,435 acres (1,795 ha) to New Englanders who had settled nearby in Rye. The land was known to the Indians as Quaroppas (white marshes or plains) because of heavy fogs in the area. White Plains was patented in 1721 and became the county seat in 1759. On 9 July 1776 the New York Provincial Congress, meeting there, adopted a resolution approving the Declaration of Independence and referring for the first time to the "State of New York." On 28 Oct 1776 Gen George Washington and his troops met British and Hessian troops in the Battle of White Plains; confronted by a much superior army, the Americans were forced to retreat, but this pivotal battle blocked the British campaign into Westchester Co.

In 1790 White Plains had 505 inhabitants, including 49 enslaved Africans. With the Harlem Railroad (1844) a period of growth began, and by 1870 the population exceeded 2,500. White Plains incorporated as a village in 1866 and became a city in 1916. As the county seat it became an important legal and banking center by the early 20th century. Urban renewal changed the face of the downtown area between 1966 and 1980; a substantial portion (130 acres/53 ha) was redeveloped to facilitate growth of a modern central business district. In 2000, 16% of the population was black, and 4.5% were Asian. In addition, 23.5% were of Latino ethnicity. In 2003 White Plains was undergoing a construction boom, with $650 million in new development underway. In the early 21st century, tens of thousands of workers come daily to work in corporate headquarters, offices, stores, and federal, state, and county courts. The city is a center for shopping and home to the Westchester County Center, several major medical centers, and the Jacob Purdy House (1720).

Elaine Massena

White Plains, Battle of. American defeat during Revolutionary War. On 12 Oct 1776 forces of British general William Howe landed at Throgs Neck [now in Bronx Co] in an attempt to cut Gen George Washington's line of communications to Connecticut. In response, Washington began withdrawing his troops from Harlem Heights on Manhattan on 16 October, with the majority of the army departing for White Plains (Westchester Co) two days later. After receiving Hessian reinforcements on 18 October at Pell's Point [now Rodman's Neck in Bronx Co], Howe's army made a slow march toward White Plains. On the morning of 28 October, Washington's army of 14,500 soldiers faced Howe's of more than 13,000 to the north, west, and east of White Plains. After crossing the Bronx River, 4,000 Hessians and British attacked Washington's undermanned right flank at Chatterton Hill, where they met resistance from about 1,600 men commanded by Brig Gen Alexander McDougall. The massed fire of 12 British cannons and attack by the British and Hessian troops forced the American regiments off the hill. Howe inexplicably failed to execute a simultaneous attack against Washington's main position during the assault on Chatterton Hill. He planned such an attack for 31 October, but it was rained out, giving Washington the chance to withdraw his forces to the heights at North Castle [now North White Plains, Westchester Co].

American casualties were about 150 men killed and wounded. The British and their Hessian allies claimed the field of battle but may have had as many as 313 men killed and wounded. When Howe turned from Dobbs Ferry (Westchester Co) back toward New York City on 12 November to attack Fort Washington on the north end of Manhattan, he abandoned an aggressive strategy that might have destroyed Washington's army. Although the battle was technically a defeat for Washington, he checked Howe's advance and saved his army, which crossed the Delaware River two months later to take Trenton, NJ, on 25 December.

Hoffman, Renoda. *The Battle of White Plains* (White Plains, NY: White Plains Historical Society, 1999)

James M. Johnson

Whitesboro. Village (pop 3,943) in Whitestown (Oneida Co). An important Mohawk River landing became the site of the 1798 Whitestown post office at the present Whitesboro. From 1802 to 1850 it was the half-shire of Oneida Co, with some courts. Manufacturing was launched by cotton and woolen factories (1811, 1813). The village attempted incorporation as early as 1813 and has been incorporated since 1829. First called the Oneida Academy (1827–29), the Oneida Institute (1829–44), an integrated school with an abolitionist agenda, became the Whitestown Seminary (1844–84). From 1819 to 1918 the Erie Canal passed through Whitesboro, which was also served by the Syracuse and Utica Railroad (1839, later New York Central). Later in the 19th century Whitesboro produced iron, canned goods, furniture, felt, and weavers' reeds. Two knitting mills, Anchor (*ca* 1890) and Alliance (1898), produced underwear through the 1930s; Alliance employed 350 workers. The last factory, Utica Drop Forge, left the village in the 1970s. In the early 21st century Whitesboro was a suburb of Utica, with some commuting to Syracuse and elsewhere.

Whitestown. Town (pop 18,635) in E Oneida Co. Whitestown was the site of the Battle of Oriskany (1777), one of the bloodiest confrontations of the Revolutionary War. Settled in 1785 by its proprietor, Judge Hugh White, the town was formed in 1788. The Erie Canal opened through the town in 1819, and the Syracuse and Utica Railroad in 1839. Industries, aside from the many Whitesboro mills, included the manufacturing of woolens by Dexter Manufacturing Co (1832) at Pleasant Valley and cotton and paper by mills at Walesville. The Oneida County Airport opened in 1951, the region's first shopping center in 1952, and the Thruway in 1954. Whitestown's population increased by 33% during the 1950s. Much of the town remains rural, but the four villages and the southeastern area are all Utica suburbs. The Utica Corp, an aerospace firm, is a large employer. Whitestown is the site of the Oriskany Flats State Wildlife Management Area and, since 1997, of the rink of the Utica Curling Club.

Whitman, Charles S(eymour) (*b* Hanover, Conn, 28 Aug 1868; *d* New York City, 29 Mar 1947). Governor. Graduating from Amherst College in 1890 and New York University Law School in 1894, Whitman opened a legal practice in New York City and participated in local Republican politics. As district attorney of New York Co, his 1912 campaign against police corruption won him statewide prominence and catapulted him into the state governorship in 1914 with a victory over Democrat Martin H. Glynn. Whitman served two terms in Albany, winning reelection in 1916 against Democrat Samuel Seabury. Whitman's gubernatorial administrations were marked by a concern for fiscal and bureaucratic efficiency and the implementation of modest reforms. He also oversaw the state's 1915 Constitutional Convention and the adoption of prohibition and woman suffrage (both of which he supported) and guided the state through the tumultuous years of World War I. Defeated for reelection in 1918 by Democrat Alfred E. Smith, Whitman returned to private legal practice in New York City and remained influential in Republican and Fusion politics.

See also WORLD WAR I.

Public Papers of Charles Seymour Whitman, Governor, 4 vols (Albany: J. B. Lyon, 1916–19)

Christopher Capozzola

Whitman, Walt(er) (*b* West Hills, Suffolk Co, 31 May 1819; *d* Camden, NJ, 26 Mar 1892). Poet. Born in a simple farmhouse to a Dutch mother and English father, Whitman moved with his family to Brooklyn at the age of 4. At 12 he left school to become a printer's apprentice in New York City. He maintained contact with friends and relatives on Long Island through visits and correspondence, and Long Island figures prominently in his poems where it is given an Algonquian name, Paumanok. Whitman was, by turn, a printer, schoolteacher in Suffolk Co and what is now Nassau Co, owner of the *Long Islander* newspaper in Huntington (Suffolk Co), house builder, author of short fiction and the temperance novel *Franklin Evans* (1842), and journalist and editor of the *New York Aurora* and *Brooklyn Daily Eagle* before publishing the breakthrough first edition of *Leaves of Grass* (1855). It contained 12 untitled poems, the longest (later titled "Song of Myself") an autobiographical account of a representative American living and working in New York City. Whitman's aims were to describe and extol life in a democratic society, to raise the working class to the level of poetic subjectivity, and to break with existing concepts of poetic form and content. To bring attention to his work Whitman wrote his own reviews, oversaw the sale of the book, and solicited a response from one of the nation's leading intellectuals, Ralph Waldo Emerson. With a letter of praise from Emerson affixed to the 1856 second edition, Whitman was on his way to a long and stormy career that would see a total of six editions of *Leaves of Grass* (1860, 1867, 1871, 1881) as well as prose writings.

During the Civil War Whitman served as a hospital visitor to the sick and wounded in Washington, DC, army hospitals. Writing as a war correspondent, he dispatched articles to New York City and Brooklyn newspapers with news of their regiments. "Drum-Taps," a section of *Leaves of Grass,* contains poems that reflect these years, as does the major portion of his autobiographical prose work, *Specimen Days*

Walt Whitman; detail from print by Samuel Hollyer, *ca* 1855.

(1882). At this time Whitman worked as a clerk in the army paymaster's office and later in the Department of the Interior. In 1865 he was fired from the latter position, allegedly because some, including Secretary of the Interior James Harlan, found *Leaves of Grass* obscene in its frankness on human sexuality. Almost immediately Whitman was granted a post in the attorney general's office. A strong admiration for Pres Abraham Lincoln led to the composition of two poems marking Lincoln's assassination, "O Captain! My Captain!" and "When Lilacs Last in the Dooryard Bloom'd." Known as the "poet of democracy," in his final years he published many poems in New York City newspapers, thus returning to the scene of his initial inspiration. One of his poems, "Crossing Brooklyn Ferry," recounts his musings on a daily commute between Brooklyn and New York City in the years he lived and worked in both places. "Mannahatta" employs for its title the name by which he consistently denoted New York City in his poems. "Song of Myself" contains numerous descriptions of New York City workers of all kinds, with considerable attention paid to the city's firefighters. Notable places of interest, such as the burial place of the Wallabout martyrs (Continental soldiers who died on British prison ships docked in Wallabout Bay in Brooklyn during the Revolution), and significant events in New York's history are commemorated in Whitman's poems. Whitman's health was affected by his hospital service, and in 1873 he suffered a severe stroke that partially paralyzed him and forced him to live with his brother and sister-in-law in Camden, NJ. In 1884 Whitman purchased a house in Camden and resided there until his death. Whitman has been commemorated in differing ways; the Walt Whitman Mall lies across the street from his birthplace, a New York State Historic Site.

Allen, Gay Wilson, and Sculley Bradley, eds. *The Collected Writings of Walt Whitman* (New York: New York Univ Press, 1963–75)

Krieg, Joann P. *A Whitman Chronology* (Iowa City: Univ of Iowa Press, 1998)

LeMaster, J. R., and Donald D. Kummings, eds. *Walt Whitman: An Encyclopedia* (New York: Garland, 1998)

Joann P. Krieg

Whitney Museum of American Art. Gertrude Vanderbilt Whitney founded the Whitney Museum in 1930 to display the work and launch the careers of American artists. Whitney had sponsored experimental studios and galleries since 1914, but these were disbanded to make way for the permanent museum, which opened in 1931 on West 8th St. Whitney and director Juliana Reiser Force established a collection that included works by John Sloan, George Luks, Everett Shinn, and Maurice Prendergast of the Ashcan school (artists who painted realistic city scenes), as well as American Scene painters such as Thomas Hart Benton. The Whitney has traditionally bought works from its Biennial Exhibition and by this route has acquired works by Stuart Davis, Reginald Marsh, and Jasper Johns. The Whitney boasts the largest collection of Alexander Calder's works in any museum, as well as one of the most extensive collections of post–World War II American sculpture. The Whitney also holds the largest collection of Edward Hopper's art, a full range of John Marin's paintings, and significant examples of Georgia O'Keeffe's work. In 1966 the Whitney moved to a

My city's fit and noble name resumed,
Choice aboriginal name, with marvelous beauty, meaning,
A rocky founded island shores where ever gayly dash the coming, going, hurrying sea waves.
—*from* "Mannahatta"

Sea-beauty! strech'd and basking!
One side thy inland ocean laving, broad, with copious commerce, steamers, sails,
And one the Atlantic's wind caressing, fierce or gentle—mighty hulls dark-gliding in the distance.
Isle of sweet brooks of drinking-water—healthy air and soil!
Isle of the salty shore and breeze and brine!
—*from* "Paumanok"

The Complete Writings of Walt Whitman, vol 2
(New York: G. P. Putnam's Sons, 1902)

granite building designed by Bauhaus architect Marcel Breuer on Madison Ave and 75th St. At the beginning of the 21st century the Whitney has an endowment of $43.5 million and receives about 608,000 visitors annually.

Berman, Avis. *Rebels on Eighth Street: Juliana Force and the Whitney Museum of American Art* (New York: Atheneum, 1990)
McCarthy, Kathleen D. *Women's Culture: American Philanthropy and Art, 1830–1930* (Chicago: Univ of Chicago Press, 1991)
Whitney Museum of American Art, http://www.whitney.org

Dorothy M. Browne

Whitney Point. Village (pop 965) in Triangle (Broome Co). The site of the village was settled in 1791. The Catskill Turnpike came through in ?1806. Early products included artificial teeth (1865), sleighs (1876), and carriages (1883). The village was incorporated in 1871, the same year it became the home of the Broome County Fair. Floods on the Otselic River devastated the village until the Whitney Point Dam was completed in 1942. I-81 (1968) provided easy access for commuting to the Triple Cities (Binghamton, Endicott, Johnson City) and to Cortland. Whitney Point is the commercial hub of northern Broome Co, and the school district is the largest employer.

Charles J. Browne

Wickersham, George W(oodward) (*b* Pittsburgh, 19 Sept 1858; *d* New York City, 25 Jan 1936). US attorney general. Wickersham studied civil engineering at Lehigh University (1873–75) in Bethlehem, Pa, and graduated from the University of Pennsylvania Law School in Philadelphia in 1880. He moved to New York City, joining the law firm of Strong and Cadwalader in 1883 and becoming a partner in 1887. In 1909 Pres William H. Taft appointed Wickersham US attorney general. He initiated antitrust actions against Standard Oil Co, US Steel, International Harvester Co, and many other corporations. He served as attorney general until 1913, when he returned to his law firm (Cadwalader, Wickersham, and Taft since 1914), remaining a partner until his death. He was a member of the 1915 New York State Constitutional Convention, chair of the Judiciary Committee, and a member of the Committee for the Reorganization of New York State Government in 1925. In 1929 he was appointed chairman of the National Commission on Law Observance and Enforcement, commonly known as the Wickersham Commission, established to study federal law enforcement, especially the policing of Prohibition. Its final report of 7 Jan 1931 stated that while Prohibition could not be enforced, it should nonetheless be preserved as national law.

Link, Arthur S. *Woodrow Wilson and the Progressive Era, 1910–1917* (New York: Harper & Row, 1963)

James R. Belpedio

Wiechquaeskeck Indians. Wiechquaeskeck was originally the Indian name of the Dobbs Ferry locale, where it is preserved as the name of a local stream in its anglicized form as Wickers Creek. Thought to derive from a Munsee expression for marshy or boggy uplands, Wiechquaeskeck became a general term identifying all Indians living in Westchester Co and adjacent parts of Connecticut. They numbered between 1,000 and 2,000 when Europeans first encountered them. Colonial chroniclers recorded names of a number of local communities in Wiechquaeskeck territory, including Alipkonck [now Tarrytown], Singsing [now Ossining], Poningo [now Rye], and the Sachus, Shippan, and Toquams locales around Greenwich and Stamford in Fairfield Co, Conn. Writers in the 19th century divided this territory into three parts: Wiechquaeskeck in the northeast, Rechgawawanck in the southeast, and Siwanoy in the east. Although still widely accepted, reexamination of written records documenting this tripartite division indicates that Rechgawawanck was another term for Haverstraw. Siwanoy, evidently from the Algonquian word for southerner, is only mentioned three times: at Rhode Island on a 1614 map; as the name for Indians living along Long Island Sound 8 leagues (24 mi) east of Hell Gate in a 1625 account; and as one of two Long Island Indian tribes, the other being Sinnecox (Shinnecocks), in 1628.

Whatever they called themselves, Indians living between the east bank of the Hudson River and Long Island Sound were gradually squeezed between Dutch settlers moving north from Manhattan and English colonists pressing west from Connecticut. Worsening relations led to open violence when Wiechquaeskeck warriors, avenging the murder of friends and relations by the Dutch on the night of 25 Feb 1643, destroyed all settlements within their territories. They captured many settlers and killed 18, including the exiled New England dissenter Anne Hutchinson and most of her family. A mixed Dutch-English force led by John Underhill, one of the officers responsible for the Pequot massacre at the Mystic Fort in Connecticut six years earlier, killed all but a few of a reported 600 Wiechquaeskeck and other Indians gathered for a festival near Bedford (Westchester Co) during the first days of 1644. Devastated by these losses but unwilling to capitulate openly, Wiechquaeskecks refusing to attend the 30 Aug 1645 meeting ending the war allowed Mohican (Mahican) sachem Aepjen to sign the treaty on their behalf.

Many Wiechquaeskecks subsequently moved farther north away from settlers to Kichtawank communities along the Croton River valley. Others left Westchester entirely, moving among relatives to Raritan country [now central New Jersey] and returning home only after signing a separate peace costing them the western half of their territories in 1649. On their remaining lands, they were joined by expatriates from other Indian communities who moved to the area after conveying their last lands to colonists. One of these, a former Canarsee sachem named Sauwenaro (*fl* 1636–66), became a key intermediary with colonial authorities, representing Wiechquaeskecks at treaties and putting his mark on 10 deeds to lands in east Westchester Co at Rye, Mamaroneck, and Harrison, and in West Farms [now in Bronx Co] between 1650 and 1666. A prominent Ramapo sachem from the Pequannock Valley in nearby Connecticut named Katonah (*fl* 1680–1708) presided over 18 sales conveying the last tracts of Wiechquaeskeck land in northern Westchester to English buyers. A village in Westchester Co bears his name. Most Wiechquaeskeck ultimately moved farther north to Indian towns in remote Berkshire Mountain valleys along contested borderlands between New York and New England. Some settled in Dutchess Co among Wappinger people. Others joined Christian mission communities at Shekomeko (Dutchess Co), Kaunaumeek [now Nassau, Rensselaer Co], Schaghticoke [now Schaghticoke Reservation loc in Kent, Conn), and Stockbridge, Mass, established during the 1730s and 1740s. Although most of these people supported their American neighbors during the Revolutionary War, nearly all were finally compelled to leave the region by 1800. Today, many of their descendants live on Ontario Indian reserves at Moraviantown and Munceytown and on the Stockbridge-Munsee Reservation in Bowler, Wisc.

Brawer, Catherine, ed. *Many Trails: Indians of the Lower Hudson Valley* (Katonah, NY: Katonah Gallery, 1983)
Ruttenber, Edward Manning. *History of the Indian Tribes of Hudson's River* (Albany: J. Munsell, 1872)
Trelease, Allen W. *Indian Affairs in Colonial New York: The 17th Century* (Ithaca: Cornell Univ Press, 1960)

Robert S. Grumet

Wilder, Alec [Alexander Lafayette Chew] (*b* 16 Feb 1907, Rochester; *d* 24 Dec 1980, Gainesville, Fla). Composer and author. Though mostly self-trained, Wilder did study intermittently at the

Eastman School of Music in Rochester between 1926 and 1933. Wilder moved to New York City in 1934, contributing songs to Broadway revues and working as an arranger for many radio shows, starting with the *Ford Hour* in 1936. He attracted notice in the late 1930s and early 1940s with a series of octets, short pieces with whimsical titles like "Sea Fugue Mama" and "The Neurotic Goldfish," scored for an idiosyncratic ensemble of wind instruments and harpsichord. Several of Wilder's songs, including "While We're Young" (1943), "It's So Peaceful in the Country" (1941), and "I'll Be Around" (1942), have become standards. Wilder's chamber music, which falls between popular and classical styles, includes ensembles and sonatas for brass instruments, several operas and ballets, *Carl Sandburg Suite* for orchestra (1960), and the choral *Children's Plea for Peace* (1969). Wilder was lyricist for many of his songs and the author of the influential *American Popular Song: The Great Innovators, 1900–1950* (1972) and *Letters I Never Mailed* (1975). Wilder lived a nomadic life, often staying with friends, but his home base in New York City was the Algonquin Hotel. An annual Wilder birthday concert at the Eastman School of Music celebrates his diverse musical legacy.

Stone, Desmond. *Alec Wilder in Spite of Himself* (New York: Oxford Univ Press, 1996)

David Raymond

wildflowers. New York State ranks second after Texas among the contiguous 48 states in the diversity of its trees and wildflowers. The systematic compilation of the state's flora was largely the work of four botanists: Amos Eaton (1776–1842); John Torrey (1796–1873) Asa Gray (1810–88), one of the most famous botanists of the 19th century; and Arthur Cronquist (1919–92), a senior curator at the New York Botanical Garden in the Bronx. This institution's vast herbarium remains the cornerstone of botanical inventory in the state, though the New York State Herbarium in Albany and the collections of several state colleges and universities provide additional information.

New York State's 3,022 recorded species reflect the complex interactions of climate and soil in the state, resulting in seven distinct zones, each with unique flora: the St. Lawrence lowlands; the northern boreal and alpine areas of the Adirondacks; the valley and ridge terrain of the Capital District and Mid-Hudson and Mohawk Valleys; the "New England" and maritime areas of the lower Hudson and New York City; the piedmont plateau reaching into New York City and Long Island's coastal plain; the Appalachian plateau of Central New York and the Southern Tier; and the central lowlands including Western New York's lake plains.

Many of the state's wild flowering plants bear inconspicuous, often overlooked blossoms, including most grasses (Gramineae or Poaceae), sedges (Cyperaceae), and rushes (Juncaceae), as well as many tree species. Other wild plants present showy blossoms, such as early spring's trillium *(Trillium grandiflorum)*, late spring's lady's slipper *(Cypripedium acaule)*, early summer's rhodora *(Rhododendron canadense)*, midsummer's cardinal flower *(Lobelia cardinalis)*, late summer's bonesets *(Eupatorium maculatum* and *E perfoliatum)* and ironweed *(Vernonia noveboracensis)*, fall's New England aster *(Aster novae-angliae)*, and the singular, fall-flowering shrub witch hazel *(Hamamelis virginiana)*.

New York State's wildflowers were important to Native Americans for food, flavorings, medicinals, and dyes long before the influx of Europeans, with early colonists adopting many for similar or novel functions. Those flora that developed valuable fruits that were consumed fresh or dried for later use included cranberry *(Vaccinium macrocarpon* and *V oxycoccus)*, blackberry, raspberry or bramble *(Rubus* spp), elderberry *(Sambucus canadensis)*, and blueberry *(Vaccinium* spp). Others gave rise to easily collected and stored edible nuts, such as black walnut *(Juglans nigra)*, butternut *(Juglans cinera)*, pignut hickory *(Carya* spp), and acorns produced by oaks, notably the white oak *(Quercus alba)*, which served as either human or animal food. Both Indian cucumber *(Medeola virginiana)* and American cattail *(Typha americana)* boasted edible rhizomes. Numerous herbaceous species such as fireweed *(Epilobium angustifolium)* supplied edible leaves and shoots, with medicinals derived from the roots of ginseng *(Panax quinquefolium)*, Kentucky coffee tree *(Gymnocladus dioica)*, sassafras *(Sassafras albidum)*, sarsaparilla *(Aralia nudicaulis)*, wild geranium *(Geranium maculatum)*, and sweet flag *(Acorus calamus)*. Indian ginger *(Asarum canadense)* was another valued flavoring, and Indian hemp *(Apocynum cannabinum)* provided strong vegetable fibers for cordage.

Approximately 36% of New York State's flora is nonindigenous, the highest level of such imports of any state in the continental United States. Some species—especially ornamentals, medicinals, food and flavoring plants, and those useful for cordage—were deliberately introduced. Most arrived in the ballast of ships that made the passage from Europe to New York City, and most have added diversity to the native flora without negative impact. Among these are the great hairy willowherb *(Epilobium hirsutum)* and the only introduced orchid, helleborine *(Epipactus helleborine)*. Others have become familiar lawn and garden weeds: dandelion *(Taraxacum officinale)*, garlic mustard *(Alliaria officinalis)*, sow thistle *(Sonchus arvensis)*, and chicory *(Cichorium intybus)*. Additional species have functioned as noxious, invasive weeds, eliminating native flora and providing little wildlife value: ornamental bittersweet *(Celastrus orbiculatus)* and purple loosestrife *(Lythrum salicaria)* introduced in the late 1800s, multiflora rose *(Rosa multiflora)* introduced in the early 1900s, and Eurasian water milfoil *(Myriophyllum spicatum)* introduced in the 1940s. Water chestnut *(Trapa natans)* has recently invaded the Hudson River's backwaters, portions of the Mohawk River, and sites across Central New York to Oneida Lake. The plant shades out everything in the water below, and its multispined fruit can easily pierce skin, including the feet of wildlife.

The aggressive nature of some introduced species, coupled with loss of habitat through agriculture and urban sprawl, has meant the decline and disappearance of native species. In 2002 New York State's Natural Heritage Program listed 68 plant species as extinct in the state, with 610 on its New York Rare Plants Status List, of which 77 are indicated as endangered. In addition to these pressures, many of New York State's rare wildflowers grow in limited habitats. Low nut rush *(Scleria verticillata)* is restricted to fen habitats; alpine woodsia *(Woodsia alpina)* and Lapland rosebay *(Rhododendron lapponicum)* to the high peaks of the Adirondacks; hart's tongue fern *(Phylitis scolopendrium)* to a few limestone sites in Onondaga and Madison Cos; and twinleaf *(Jeffersonia diphylla)* to sites in Western New York.

Gardening with wildflowers, an activity that has recently become popular, benefits native species. Wildflower gardens are an important component of the major botanical gardens as well as of many private and public gardens and arboretums in New York State.

Barkley, Theodore, Luc Brouillet, and Richard Spellenberg, eds. *Introduction*, vol 1 of *Flora of North America: North of Mexico* (New York: Oxford Univ Press, 1993)

McGrath, Anne, and Joanne Treffs. *Wildflowers of the Adirondacks* (Sylvan Beach, NY: North Country Books, 1981)

Marinelli, Janet, ed. *Native Perennials* (Brooklyn: Brooklyn Botanic Garden, 1989)

David Moore

Wildlife Conservation Society. See Zoos.

Wilkeson, Samuel (*b* Carlisle, Pa, 1 June 1781; *d* Kingston, Tenn, 7 July 1848). Businessman and mayor of Buffalo. Wilkeson was the son of Scots-Irish immigrant parents, and as a youth he worked on the family farm near Pittsburgh, receiving little formal education. After 1802 he moved to Pittsburgh. Between 1807 and 1810 in Portland (Chautauqua Co) he engaged in shipbuilding and the salt trade. During the War of 1812 he served as a volunteer militiaman along the Niagara Frontier. In 1814 Wilkeson settled in Buffalo, becoming freight forwarder, vessel owner, and merchant. Through his efforts Buffalo became the Erie Canal's western terminus, defeating rival Black Rock (Erie Co). To secure this, without engineering training, he organized efforts in 1820 to create Buffalo's harbor, improvising the necessary tools and working alongside the laborers. Wilkeson served as judge of Erie Co Court of Common Pleas (1821–24), was elected to the state assembly in 1822, and served in the state senate (1825–28) and as mayor of Buffalo (1836–37). As mayor he sought to build up the police force and enforce the law. He is remembered for his work in developing Buffalo as a transshipment center. In the late 1830s Wilkeson opened a small cotton textile mill and erected Buffalo's first iron foundry, establishing the manufacture of steam engines and stoves in the city. Around 1838 he relocated to Washington, DC, to become the general agent of the American Colonization Society.

Gerber, David. *The Making of an American Pluralism, Buffalo, New York, 1825–1860* (Urbana: Univ of Illinois Press, 1989

Jean Richardson

Wilkinson, Jemima (*b* Cumberland, RI, 29 Nov 1752; *d* Jerusalem [now in Yates Co], 1 July 1819). Religious leader. She was raised as a Quaker but joined the New Light Baptists in 1776. In October of that year she became seriously ill and claimed that the old Jemima Wilkinson had died and that a reborn spirit of the "Publick Universal Friend" occupied her body. "The Friend," as her followers now called her, began preaching in 1776, gaining converts in Rhode Island, Connecticut, and Pennsylvania. In addition to preaching repentance and avoidance of evil, she interpreted dreams, opposed war and slavery, and advocated celibacy but did not require it of her followers. By 1784 Wilkinson's followers were making plans to establish a separate community, and after a few years of exploring sites in Western New York, in 1788 they established the Friends Settlement on the west side of Seneca Lake, southwest of Dresden [now in Yates Co]. She joined the community in 1790 but four years later moved with some of her followers several miles west to Jerusalem. Though not communal the Friends Society did provide for the poorer members of the community. Wilkinson was controversial during and after her lifetime, both for her religious claims of individual, divinely sanctioned authority, claims made on her behalf that she was the female Christ, and for her alleged demands on the property of her followers. Wilkinson was the subject of two hostile and inaccurate biographies by David Hudson, published in 1821 and 1844. Wilkinson died, or "left time" in 1819, and the Friends Society dwindled away with the passing of the generation that had personally known Jemima Wilkinson. Her career prefigures the religious enthusiasm and perfectionist tendencies of what came to be characterized as the Burned-over District of New York State.

Wisbey, Herbert A., Jr. *Pioneer Prophetess: Jemima Wilkinson, the Publick Universal Friend* (Ithaca: Cornell Univ Press, 1964)

Christopher Densmore

Willard [née Hart], Emma (*b* Berlin, Conn, 23 Feb 1787; *d* Troy, Rensselaer Co, 15 Apr 1870). Educator. She became the proprietor of a Middlebury, Vt, girls academy in 1807 and married John Willard in 1809. Convinced that girls needed both academic study and training in deportment and the domestic arts, in 1814 she opened the Middlebury Female Seminary, the nation's first intellectually rigorous girls school. In 1818 she petitioned Gov De Witt Clinton and the New York State legislature to fund a girls seminary. Her petition was published as *Plan for Improving Female Education* in 1819, and that same year she moved the school to Waterford (Saratoga Co) in hopes of securing state funding. The legislature refused her request, but a $4,000 allocation from the Troy Common Council enabled her to move the school to Troy in 1821. Willard, whose husband died in 1825, remained headmistress of the Troy Female Seminary (now Emma Willard School) until 1838, when she remarried and moved to Boston. The marriage failed, and she returned to Troy in 1844. She spent the remainder of her life campaigning for better schooling for both girls and boys. One of the first American women to publish studies of human physiology and a lifelong champion of women's education, Willard was in other respects socially conservative: she opposed abolitionism and until the 1860s was ambivalent about woman suffrage.

Lutz, Alma. *Emma Willard: Pioneer Educator of American Women* (Boston: Beacon Press, 1964)

Bonita L. Weddle

Willard, Sylvester (*b* Saybrook [now Old Saybrook, Conn], 24 Dec 1798; *d* Auburn, Cayuga Co, 12 Mar 1886). Physician and industrialist. Born to a prominent Connecticut family, Willard studied medicine at the College of Physicians and Surgeons (now part of Columbia University) in New York City before establishing a practice in Sennett (Cayuga Co), near Auburn, around 1823. Willard married Jane Frances Case and joined her father, clock manufacturer and entrepreneur Erastus Case, in a number of business enterprises in Connecticut and Chicago. The Case and Willard families settled permanently in Auburn in 1843, purchasing the residence that came to house the Cayuga County Museum. In 1848 Willard, Case, and others established the Oswego Starch Co under the management of Thomas Kingsford, inventor of a cornstarch extraction process. With Willard as president for the next 25 years, Oswego Starch produced over 10,500 tons (9,530 MT) of cornstarch annually, or about one-third of the world total. Willard was also a founder (1847) and president of Auburn Savings Institution. In 1894 Willard's daughters Georgiana and Carolina donated the Willard Memorial Chapel, with interior decoration by Louis C. Tiffany, to Auburn Theological Seminary.

See also MENTAL HEALTH CARE.

Biographical Review: The Leading Citizens of Cayuga County, New York (Boston: Biographical Review Publishing, 1894)

Scott W. Anderson

Willard Psychiatric Center. New York State's second psychiatric facility. In 1865 the state legislature passed the Willard Law, named for psychiatrist Sylvester D. Willard, providing a mental health facility for the care of the "chronic pauper insane." When it opened on 13 Oct 1869 on the grounds of the former State Agricultural College in Seneca Co, Willard Asylum for the Insane was the first US institution for chronically ill patients and reflected sophisticated diagnosis and treatment methods. By the late 19th century the Willard Asylum had grown to become the largest institution of its kind in the United States, encompassing more than 1,100 acres (445 ha) and over 100 buildings. After the State Care Act of 1890, it was renamed Willard State Hospital. It reached a peak census of more than 3,000 by the mid–20th century, with more than 1,000 employees and its own nursing school, farm, and fire department. Despite declining in-patient numbers by 1974, the hospital was renamed the Willard Psychiatric Center. Its closure in 1995, because of budget cuts and declining numbers, ended 125 years of care for the mentally disabled. The New York State Department of Corrections subsequently began using the buildings and grounds for a drug rehabilitation facility. In 2004 the New York State Museum created a major exhibit using hundreds of old patient suitcases found in the attic when the center closed. The project pieces together the life stories of those admitted to the center between 1898 and 1952.

Grob, Gerald N. *Mental Illness and American Society, 1875–1940* (Princeton, NJ: Princeton Univ Press, 1983)

New York State Department of Mental Hygiene. *History of the Department of Mental Hygiene* (Albany, 1955)

Willet. Town (pop 1,011) in SE Cortland Co. Settled in 1797 the town was formed from Cincinnatus in 1818. The land is composed of high ridges and the valley of the Otselic River. As late as 1860, one-third of its area was unsettled. It remains agricultural in the early 21st century. The Otselic River runs through the center of town and is protected as a wetland area.

Cathy A. Barber

Willett, Marinus (*b* Jamaica, Queens Co, 31 July 1740; *d* New York City, 22 Aug 1830). Military officer. Willett's family moved to New York City in 1749, and he grew up in Manhattan. Willett was a junior officer in a New York regiment commanded by Oliver DeLancey during the French and Indian War. Although his father remained a confirmed loyalist, Willett was active in the Sons of Liberty in New York City from the outset, beginning with the Stamp Act crisis of 1764–65. When fighting broke out against England, Willett accepted a commission as captain and served in the 1775 invasion of Canada. As lieutenant colonel of the Third New York Regiment in 1777, Willett won fame during the siege of Fort Stanwix [now Rome, Oneida Co] by defying British demands to surrender, leading a successful raid on the British camp, and venturing on a hazardous mission to bring relief. Willett's most valuable service came in 1781–82, when he commanded militia and levies in the Mohawk Valley. His leadership inspired the devastated region to resist tory and Indian raids. After the war he was active in New York politics as a fervent Antifederalist and also led a peace mission to the Creek Indians. Under the patronage of Gov George Clinton he served two terms as sheriff of New York City from 1784 to 1788 and 1791 to 1795 and was later mayor (1807–8). Willett became quite prosperous because of income from his position as sheriff, extensive land speculation, and development. He was overwhelmingly defeated as a candidate for lieutenant governor in 1811, after which he largely retired from public life. He made a notable speech in New York City on 10 Aug 1814 to rally support for the War of 1812.

Lowenthal, Larry. *Marinus Willett: Defender of the Northern Frontier* (Fleischmanns, NY: Purple Mountain Press, 2000)

Willett, William M. *Narrative of the Military Actions of Colonel Marinus Willett, Taken Chiefly from His Own Manuscript* (1831; repr New York: New York Times, 1969)

Larry Lowenthal

William Freeman case. Murder trial. The case originated in the fatal stabbing of four members of the Van Nest family by Freeman, a man of mixed African and Native American descent, in Fleming (Cayuga Co) on 12 Mar 1846. The victims were a respected town supervisor, his pregnant wife, two-year-old son, and elderly mother-in-law. The community was so outraged that Freeman, an Auburn (Cayuga Co) resident in his early 20s, was nearly lynched by an angry mob as he was escorted to jail. The press throughout New York State reported the crime, and a heated debate ensued. Numerous commentators admonished the movement to abolish capital punishment for meddling in recent murder trials and thereby inspiring Freeman to commit murder without fear of punishment. Other reports deemed Freeman's violent behavior consistent with the natural tendencies of the races from which he descended, while a small group of antigallows reformers held American society in some measure responsible given the long-standing mistreatment of people not of European descent.

Freeman's trial hinged upon the jury's interpretation of the legal definition of insanity. A matter of common rather than statutory law, insanity was defined in the majority of antebellum American courts in accordance with the McNaughtan Rules, which emphasized defendants' ability to understand that their actions were wrong. William H. Seward, former governor and Freeman's defense attorney, argued that Freeman lacked the moral and emotional capacity to control behavior that he understood to be wrong. State Atty Gen John Van Buren, prosecuted the case. Freeman was convicted on 23 July 1846, but the New York State Supreme Court reversed that judgment and ordered a new trial. In the process, however, the higher court upheld the McNaughtan Rules as the proper means of defining insanity in criminal cases. Suffering from tuberculosis, Freeman died on 21 Aug 1847 without receiving a new trial.

Arpey, Andrew W. "The Van Nest Killings and the Trial of William Freeman: Insanity, Politics, and Race in Antebellum New York" (PhD diss, SUNY Albany, 2000)

Dimon, David. *The Freeman Trial: Presenting the Testimony Given in This Remarkable Case, with Comments* (Auburn, NY: Dennis Bros & Thorne, 1871)

"The Trial of William Freeman for the Murder of John G. Van Nest, Auburn, New York, 1846." In *American State Trials,* vol 16, ed. John D. Lawson (St. Louis: Thomas Law Book, 1928)

Andrew W. Arpey

Williams, Frank M(artin) (*b* Durhamville, Oneida Co, 11 Apr 1873; *d* Albany, 20 Feb 1930). State engineer and surveyor. After earning a law degree from Syracuse University in 1897, he entered the Office of State Engineer and Surveyor (now Department of Transportation) as a rodman, helping with the failed "Nine Million Dollar" canal improvement project and Edward A. Bond's 1901 study that became the blueprint for the Barge Canal. In 1908 he became state engineer and surveyor for the first of five two-year terms. He made decisions on important canal issues, such as the Terminal Act, which directed construction of freight houses, grain elevators, and harbors; adding the Cayuga and Seneca Canal to the Barge system; establishing the "blue line" surveys that defined state canal lands; and experimenting with concrete for canal structures. He also lobbied the federal government to return the canal to New York State control after World War I, an important step in the Barge Canal's early growth. After leaving the Office of the State Engineer and Surveyor in 1922, he worked on the Holland and Lincoln Tunnels in New York City.

McFee, Michele A. *A Long Haul: The Story of the New York State Barge Canal* (Fleischmanns, NY: Purple Mountain Press, 1998)

Orzell, Bill. "Frank M. Williams, State Engineer and Surveyor," *Bottoming Out* 33 (1996)

Michele A. McFee

Williams, John A(lfred) (*b* Jackson, Miss, 5 Dec 1925). Writer. Williams spent most of his childhood in Syracuse, served in the US Navy during World War II, earned a BA in journalism from Syracuse University (1950), and worked in the insurance industry and as a publicist and journalist before publishing his first novel, *The Angry Ones* (1960). Here and in his next two novels, *Night Song* (1961) and *Sissie* (1963), he created characters whose struggles resulted from their being compartmentalized by society because of their race. Williams won his first mass acclaim with *The Man Who Cried I Am* (1967), which centers on a scheme involving Western countries to thwart the unification of Blacks in Africa. *Sons of Darkness, Sons of Light* (1969) charts the events that spiral from the murder of a young, unarmed black man by a white police officer, to the contracting by a civil rights leader of a hit man to kill the policeman. Williams's nonfiction includes *Africa: Her History, Lands, and People* (1962), *This Is My Country Too* (1965), *Minorities in the City* (1975), and studies of Richard Wright, Martin Luther King Jr, and Richard Pryor.

Williams taught at several New York schools, including the City University of New York and Sarah Lawrence College, and was Paul Robeson Professor of English at Rutgers University (1990). A novelist, essayist, editor, and biographer, Williams is one of the most gifted African American writers of his generation. His fictional characters are African Americans who, despite their aptitudes and aspirations, fail to live satisfying lives because of racism. His most recent novel, *Clifford's Blues* (1999), tells of a black jazz musician in the Dachau concentration camp. Williams retired from Rutgers University in 1994 and lives in Teaneck, NJ.

Muller, Gilbert H. *John A. Williams* (Boston: Twayne Publishers, 1984)

William Smith College. See HOBART AND WILLIAM SMITH COLLEGES.

Williamson. Town (pop 6,777) in NW Wayne Co. Bounded on the north by Lake Ontario, Williamson was formed from Sodus in 1802; the first settlement within its present boundaries began around 1805. Pultneyville, a 19th-century lake port and port of entry, was raided by a British squadron in 1814. East Williamson was founded by Dutch immigrants; its Reformed Church was organized in 1854. The Rome, Watertown and Ogdensburg Railroad opened through town in 1873. In the early 21st century, apples and other fruits were grown. Mott's (now part of Cadbury-Schweppes) operates one of the nation's largest apple-processing plants in Williamson, and an apple blossom festival is held each May.

Scott C. Monje

Williamson, Charles (*b* Balgray, Scotland, 12 July 1757; *d* at sea, 8 Sept 1808). Military officer and land developer. Captured on the high seas in 1781 as he was on his way to join British forces in Virginia, Williamson returned to Scotland in 1782 after a brief imprisonment in Boston. Nine years later he was chosen as the general agent of the former, unsold lands of the Phelps and Gorham Co, property then owned by a London investment group later known as Pulteney Associates. The bulk of the lands he was to manage lay in the present-day counties of Steuben, Allegany, Livingston, Yates, Monroe, Schuyler, and Wayne. Because foreigners could not, by state law, own land in New York State, Williamson became a US citizen in January 1792, enabling him to hold his employers' properties in trust. Moving to New York State shortly afterward to undertake his duties, Williamson also exerted leadership in local politics. He was appointed a judge for Ontario Co in 1793 and 1795 and was elected to the state assembly from Steuben Co in 1796, holding that office until 1800. Replaced as the Pulteney Associates' land agent in 1801, Williamson returned to England two years later. He visited Cuba some time after that and died of yellow fever en route back to England.

Cowan, Helen I. *Charles Williamson, Genesee Promoter* (1941; repr Clifton, NJ: A. M. Kelley, 1973)

William H. Siles

Williamson Tract. See PULTENEY PURCHASE.

Williamstown. Town (pop 1,350) in E Oswego Co. Settled in 1801 the town was formed in 1804 from Mexico. The Rome-Oswego Plank Road (1847) and the Rome, Watertown and Ogdensburg Railroad (1851) opened the town for lumbering and tanning. Between 1860 and 1876 a contract for firewood for the New York Central Railroad was filled in town, requiring the construction of a short-line railroad north from the hamlet of Williamstown. Forest industries were succeeded by dairying. The Case Wall, a 6 ft wide, 12 ft high, and 2 mi long mortarless wall, was built from 1854 to 1890 by Jonathan Case to "keep the boys and animals out of his orchard." In 2002 Omega Wire employed almost 400 people. Residents also commute to Rome (Oneida Co), Utica, Oswego, and Syracuse.

Barbara J. Dix

Williamsville. Village (pop 5,573) in Amherst (Erie Co). Settled in 1800, Williamsville developed around sawmills and gristmills on Ellicott Creek and tributaries. The village was incorporated in 1850. Products included brooms, chairs, leather, and iron; limestone was quarried and burned for hydraulic cement use. The Chalmers Gelatin Co (1872–1974) was a village industry. Williamsville acquired an electric railroad in 1893, encouraging Buffalo residents to move to the village; the Lehigh Valley Railroad followed in 1896. Landmarks include the Church of Christ, Disciples (1871), known as the Williamsville Meeting House, and the Williamsville Water Mill complex (1811), listed on the National Register.

Nancy B. Mingus

Willing. Town (pop 1,371) in SE Allegany Co. The present hamlet of Shongo was home of a Seneca chief of the same name. Settled in 1819, the town was formed in 1851 from Independence and Scio. West of the Genesee River, it supported lumbering until late in the 19th century, at the end of which its farm economy was equally based on dairy products and potatoes. David Beecher Marks (Dr Job Quincy Smythe) (1819–81) invented an improved articulated artificial leg (patent 1854) and operated the Botanic Distillery in the 1860s and 1870s. Willing was served by the Wellsville, Coudersport and Pine Creek Railroad (1882). A cyclone in 1884 killed 3 residents and injured 22, destroying the hamlet of Willing. In 2003 residents work in Wellsville, Rochester, or Coudersport, Pa; a few families run dairy farms, and maple syrup is produced.

Williston Park. Village (pop 7,261) in North Hempstead (Nassau Co). In 1926 the area known as East Williston was divided and two villages were incorporated, the second being Williston Park. In that year William Chatlos bought 195 acres (79 ha) and built 1,000 homes; by 1930 its initial population of 495 had grown to about 4,500. Its population peaked in 1970 at 9,154. In the early 21st century, Williston Park is a suburban, residential community.

Richard A. Winsche

Willsboro. Town (pop 1,903) in E Essex Co. It was settled in 1765 under the direction of William Gilliland, who received a large land grant. The settlement was abandoned during the Revolution, but Gilliland returned in 1784 with new settlers. Iron and lumber businesses prospered during the 19th century and were strengthened by freight transport on the Delaware and Hudson Railroad (1875) but declined after 1900. In the 19th century blue limestone was quarried in town; a pulp paper mill was built in 1884, operating until the 1970s. The NYCO Minerals wollastonite mine (1953) was the first such operation worldwide. In the early 21st century, the mine, farming, lumbering, and tourism were the mainstays of its economy. The living history Homestead Farm Museum is open seasonally.

Thomas A. Rumney

Wilmington. Town (pop 1,131) in N Essex Co. Settled in the 1790s the town was formed as Dansville in 1821 from Jay; its name was changed to Wilmington in 1822. Rye for local distilleries was grown during the War of 1812, and there was an iron forge *ca* 1815–20. Otherwise, residents were lumbermen and farmers until the town began to draw tourists in the 1880s. Today it is widely known for the trout fishing on the Ausable River and is the site of Whiteface Mountain State Ski Center, Whiteface Mountain Memorial Highway, and Wilmington Notch State Campground. Santa's Workshop (1949), a Christmas-themed amusement park in the hamlet of North Pole, sends out letters to children from "North Pole, New York."

Thomas A. Rumney

Wilna. Town (pop 6,235) in E Jefferson Co. Settled in 1794 under the Castorland Co, the town was formed from Le Ray and Leyden (Lewis Co) in 1813 and named for a battle that took place in Russia. Settlers were a mix of French and New Englanders, but by 1855 nearly 9% of its residents were Irish-born. A steamboat provided service on the Black River beginning in 1832. The town was agricultural aside from the manufacturing at Carthage and the paper mills at Deferiet and Herrings. In 1941 the federal government annexed nearly 58% of the town for the Pine Camp military reservation (now Fort Drum). In 2003 residents work at Watertown or Fort Drum or in Wilna's schools and medical facilities. The hamlet of Natural Bridge, platted in 1818, is an artists' colony; its caverns were formerly a tourist attraction. In the 1830s Natural Bridge was the summer home of Joseph Bonaparte, the former king of Spain.

Laura Lynne Scharer

Wilson. Town (pop 5,840) and village (pop 1,213) in N central Niagara Co. Settled in 1808, the town was formed from Porter in 1818. Laid out in 1842 and designated a port of entry in 1846, the village was incorporated in 1858. Beginning 1876, the Rome, Watertown and Ogdensburg Railroad provided ready access from Rochester and Buffalo, and lake resorts were created, including Lake Island Park (?1887) and Sunset Beach (*ca* 1890). Steamboat excursions brought Torontonians on holiday across the lake. The harbor was also used to ship apples and receive Canadian lumber. Just after 1900, automobiles were briefly made in town, and the Fredonia Preserving Co operated an evaporator, cabbage storage, pickle company, and fruit storage facilities in the village. Agriculture, especially fruit growing, remains important in the early 21st century. The 395-acre (160 ha) Wilson-Tuscarora State Park is in Wilson, and the Wilson Historical Society has gathered a number of endangered structures, including a schoolhouse (1861) and a caboose (1903), and exhibits a classic car collection.

Nancy B. Mingus

Wilson, (Charles) Malcolm (*b* New York City, 24 Feb 1914; *d* New Rochelle, Westchester Co, 13 Mar 2000). Governor and lieutenant governor. The son of Charles H. Wilson, a patent lawyer, and Agnes Wilson, both active in the Republican Party, Wilson was raised in Yonkers, to which his family had moved in 1920. Graduating from Fordham Preparatory School in 1929, he received an AB degree from Fordham College in 1933 and an LLB from Fordham Law School in 1936. In 1933 he joined the White Plains (Westchester Co) law firm that would become Kent, Hazzard, Jaeger, Greer, Wilson, and Faye as a clerk, becoming a partner in 1946.

Wilson, a Republican, began 36 consecutive years of service in state elected office in 1938, when he won a race for a state assembly seat from Yonkers by 238 votes. Under a little-known state constitutional provision, he continued in elective office (and was reelected in absentia) while serving as a naval ensign in the European theater of operations during World War II (1943–45). Wilson later often joked that his victory margins grew in reverse relationship to his proximity to his district. This self-deprecating humor was typical. Colleagues of all political persuasions admired Wilson for his understated wit, great intelligence, political acumen, command of the details of state government, and extraordinary personal probity. Wilson described himself as "an economic conservative and a human rights liberal." He was a party organization and legislative man, at his best in smaller groups of peers but less effective with large audiences on the campaign trail, where his occasional ventures into Latin, a legacy of his Fordham education and a sign of his scholarly temperament, did not serve him well. He served much of his tenure in the assembly (1939–58) as chair of the Codes Committee, where he developed a reputation as a legislative craftsman and gained credit for the passage of 432 laws.

Frustrated by his failure to rise to leadership in the assembly or to gain his party's nomination for attorney general, and interested in the governorship, Wilson gave way to Westchester Co's favorite son, Nelson A. Rockefeller, for the nomination in 1958. Wilson then drove the candidate across the state in his Buick, introducing Rockefeller to his vast array of contacts among Republican leaders and activists to secure their support for his nomination. In gratitude, Rockefeller invited Wilson to accept the Republican nomination for lieutenant governor, and their partnership was sealed. He served as Rockefeller's lieutenant governor from 1959 to 1973 and was involved in virtually every major political and governmental decision, playing an especially important role in the administration's relationship with the legislature. Loyal to a fault, he rarely publicly differed from the governor. An exception was his opposition to legalizing abortion, a matter of conscience for this devout Roman Catholic.

Wilson became the 50th governor of New York on 18 Dec 1973 when Rockefeller resigned. Defeated by Democratic representative Hugh Carey the following year in his attempt to win the governorship in his own right, Wilson returned to his law firm in White Plains. Between 1977 and 1988 he was chairman and chief executive officer of the Manhattan Savings Bank. He later served New York on the Commission on Judicial Nominations in 1991, where he assisted in vetting nominees for the New York State Court of Appeals and the Constitution Revision Commission (1993–95). In 1994 the Tappan Zee Bridge was renamed the Gov Malcolm Wilson Tappan Zee Bridge in his honor.

Wilson, Malcolm. "The Man and Public Servant." In *Rockefeller in Retrospect: The Governor's New York Legacy,* eds. Gerald Benjamin and T. Norman Hurd (Albany: Nelson A. Rockefeller Institute, 1984)

Gerald Benjamin

Wilson, Edmund (*b* Red Bank, NJ, 8 May 1895; *d* Talcottville, Lewis Co, 12 June 1972). Writer, editor, and literary critic. Wilson was educated at the Hill School in Pottstown, Pa, graduated from Princeton in 1916, and began writing as a reporter. After serving with the US Army in France during World War I from 1917 to 1919, he resumed his journalism career as an editor, reviewer, and writer for such publications as *Vanity Fair, New Republic,* and *New Yorker.* Living in Manhattan, he immersed himself in Greenwich Village's Bohemian world, becoming a friend of F. Scott Fitzgerald, among other literary figures, and having an affair with Edna St. Vincent Millay.

An eclectic thinker and writer, he had interests straddling many subjects and languages, including the origins of modern literature (*Axel's Castle,* 1931) and of communism (*To The Finland Station,* 1940). New York State was a continuing theme in his work. His collection of reportage of the 1920s and 1930s, *The American Earthquake* (1957), includes vignettes of radicals in New York City and milk strikers in Herkimer Co. His controversial and sexually frank novel, *Memoirs of Hecate County* (1946), was set in a fictionalized New York suburb. By the 1950s he was making extended stays at his family's summer house in Talcottville, which influenced two books. *Apologies to the Iroquois* (1960) is an account of the Seneca, Tuscarora, and other Iroquois nations in the early days of the Indian civil rights movement. His last work, *Upstate: Records and Recollections of Northern New York* (1971), was a diary and history of his time in Talcottville and of his friends and travels in the region, particularly in Lewis and Oneida Cos.

Groth, Janet. *Edmund Wilson: A Critic for Our Time* (Athens: Ohio Univ Press, 1989)
Meyers, Jeffrey. *Edmund Wilson: A Biography* (Boston: Houghton Mifflin, 1995)

Arthur Einhorn

Wilton. Town (pop 12,511) in central Saratoga Co. Its western border is along the Palmertown range and much of the town is a sandy plain. It was settled in 1764 and taken from Northumberland in 1818. Developments on Mt McGregor have been chief points of interest since the first hotel was built in 1872, although the summit itself is divided among the Towns of Wilton, Corinth, and Moreau. A narrow-gauge railroad from Saratoga Springs served the Hotel Balmoral (1884–96); Pres Ulysses S. Grant died at a cottage on its grounds in 1885. The site became the Metropolitan Life Insurance Co Sanitorium for tuberculosis patients (1913–45), later the Wilton Developmental Center, and then the Mount McGregor Correctional Facility (1976). Land surrounding McGregor Links golf course (1921) was developed for suburban housing starting in 1970; in 1974 Pyramid Mall opened in the southern part of town, the first of extensive automobile-dependent retail development. The town is the chief bedroom suburb of Saratoga Springs, and its population increased more than sixfold from 1960 to 2000.

Field Horne

Windham. Town (pop 1,660) in NW Greene Co. The first settlement was in the Batavia Kill valley in 1785. The town was formed from Woodstock (Ulster Co) in 1798. Much of the town is on high, steep hills. In the mid–19th century, woodenware shops, which made shaving boxes, combs, and broom handles, supplemented the farming economy. Early in the 20th century, dairy, poultry, and potatoes were the chief products. Summer boarders became important by the Civil War era, and tourism remains significant. Many vacation houses and condominiums have been built since the 1980s. Ski Windham (1963) became a private club in 1967, attracting wealthy New York City residents.

Field Horne

windmills. Wind-powered mills for grinding grain were built from the earliest years of settlement of New Amsterdam and Long Island. Those from the 1600s into the late 1700s were of a type called post mills, and in them millstones and wooden gearing were contained in a small house that sat on top of a massive post. The house itself was turned on top of this post by a large lever, called a tailpole, so that the sails could be kept faced into the wind. No early American post mills survive. Only on eastern Long Island, where there were few streams or suitable tidal inlets for water mills, did the windmill continue as the predominant type of gristmill.

A new type of windmill, the smock mill, appeared on Long Island in the late 18th century. This type has a stationary octagonal, timber-framed tower housing the millstones, surmounted by a cap, which can be revolved, on which the sails are built. The earliest smock mill surviving on Long Island was built on Gardiners Island in the Town of East Hampton (Suffolk Co) in 1795. The Hook Windmill, built in East Hampton in 1806 by Nathaniel Dominy, displays sophisticated wooden gearing that drives two pairs of millstones and revolves the cap as well. The Beebe Windmill (1820) in Bridgehampton (Suffolk Co) introduced cast-iron gearing made possible by the production of accurate iron castings. Wind-powered gristmills began to be replaced by steam-powered mills in the middle of the 19th century and were finally replaced on eastern Long Island by the railroad in 1895, which brought processed flour from New York City.

Windmill in East Hampton. Photograph by Robert L. Harrison.

Windmills of different types and for different uses were built sporadically in other parts of New York State during the 19th century. The McConnell's Windmill (*ca* 1825) in Morristown (St. Lawrence Co) is a masonry tower gristmill. Eleven smock mills built between 1795 and 1820 survive in the Towns of East Hampton, Southampton, and Shelter Island (all in Suffolk Co). In East Hampton the Gardiner, Hook, and Pantigo Windmills are open to the public. In recent decades windmills have found new uses as ecologically friendly generators of electricity. In 2000 the first commercial wind farm (11.55 MW) opened in New York State near the Town of Hamilton (Madison Co). By 2003 wind turbine projects were also located in Wethersfield (Wyoming Co), Fenner (Madison Co), Calverton (Suffolk Co), and Ontario (Wayne Co).

Hefner, Robert J. *Windmills of Long Island* (Setauket, NY: Society for the Preservation of Long Island Antiquities and Norton, 1983)

Robert J. Hefner

Windsor. Town (pop 6,451) and village (pop 901) in SE Broome Co. By 1712 the intra-Indian settlement of Oquaga (Onaquaga), populated by, among others, Tuscarora, Oneida, Nanticoke, and Delaware Indians, stood on the Susquehanna about a mile north of the present village, and a Christian mission operated from 1748 to 1777. Sir William Johnson traded in furs and ordered a fort built in 1756. The fort was destroyed by American troops in 1778. White settlement began in 1788, and the town was formed from Chenango in 1807. Lumbering was important in early years. After 1830 population and industry concentrated at Windsor hamlet, the Erie Railroad came through in 1849, and the village incorporated in 1897. From 1854 on, buggy whip manufacture was the leading industry, with one firm making them as a novelty until 1950. In 2003 farming continues in the valleys, and bluestone quarrying has increased. Residents commute to Kirkwood, Conklin, and the Triple Cities (Binghamton, Endicott, Johnson City).

Charles J. Browne

wine industry and viticulture. New York State has 33,500 acres (13,550 ha) in grape cultivation in four regions: the Lake Erie area in the west, the Finger Lakes in Central New York State, the Hudson River valley in the east, and an area on Long Island Sound in the southeast. In 2002 about 60% of the production was grape juice and 40% was wine. New York State's terrain was sculpted during the last Ice Age, which created large, deep bodies of water and steep slopes, conditions necessary for quality viticultural, combined with good drainage of water and cold air. The state is the third-largest total grape and wine producer in the United States, and the second-largest wine producer.

The Pioneer Period

Though grapes were native to the region, New Netherland director general Petrus Stuyvesant tried to introduce European grapevines into New Amsterdam [now New York City], as did the English on Long Island, and French Huguenots in New Paltz (Ulster Co) by the 1670s. The Huguenots' attempts failed because of New York Colony's harsh climate and a small but devastating grape louse, *Phylloxera vastatrix*, which attacked the roots of the European varieties. In response, the Huguenots began cultivating a cold-hardy and insect-resistant indigenous species, *Vitis labrusca*, but were not pleased with its strong "foxy" flavor. Eventually growers located, named, and planted other grape varieties throughout New York State, such as the red Catawba (1801) and the Isabella (1816). Many of these were second-generation native varieties, random hybrids with other native varieties, which became the *Vitis labruscanas* commonly planted since the 19th century. Niagara (1872) is the most important white-wine grape in this species.

New York State's diverse array of *V labruscana*, French American hybrids, New York hybrids, and European *Vitis vinifera* are the foundation of its viticultural and vinicultural history. The ubiquitous Concord grape, which had its beginning in the native blue-black variety that grew wild in New England, is a *V labruscana*. Introduced first in 1853 by Ephraim Bull in Concord, Mass, to fill the need for a grape that would be as successful for juice and jellies as for wine, Concord grapes grew well in New York. The French American hybrids were created in France beginning in the 1880s to protect French vineyards after the *Phylloxera* grape louse had been inadvertently exported to France 20 years earlier. French hybridizers crossed hardy native American varieties, carefully selected for their resistance to cold and insects, but without strong foxy flavors, with the more familiar tender European varieties, to salvage their own vineyards. These hybrids were later used in the northeast United States, particularly in the Finger Lakes. By the end of the 19th century, New York State had a number of active wineries. Brotherhood Winery of Washingtonville (Orange Co) in the Hudson Valley, established in 1837, is America's oldest continuously operated winery.

Federal Prohibition (1920–33) significantly retarded the development of the wine industry. Many of the state's wineries closed, but others sold grape juice to stay in business. Because home wine makers were allowed to make 200 gallons (757 l) per year, some of the state's wineries made wine concentrates for that market. Others were able to stay in business by making wine for religious services, still permitted by federal law.

The Rise of Premium Wines

Following the repeal of Prohibition, the wine industry in New York was permanently altered by the introduction of European hybrid varieties. Many tender European varieties were made resistant to insects and severe cold by grafting them onto resistant native rootstocks. When carefully selected and matched, the rootstocks did not contribute any native flavors to the European scions. Among the most famous of the scientists in France developing hybrids that became important to the vintners of New York State were Albert Seibel, who created the Chancellor and the red Chelois; J. F. Ravat, best known for the white Vignoles; and Joannes Seyve, who created the red Chambourcin. Charles Fournier, a French Champagne maker, immigrated to the United States in 1934 to become a wine maker at Urbana Wine Co (now Gold Seal Vineyards) in Hammondsport (Steuben Co). He introduced some French American hybrid varieties to the state from his native France to make sparkling wines.

In 1953 Fournier met Ukrainian plant scientist Dr Konstantin Frank, also a recent immigrant to the United States, and hired him to work at Gold Seal Vineyards, lending his expertise in grafting European *V vinifera* scions to cold-hardy rootstocks. Frank is credited with bringing the first experimental *V vinifera* plantings to the Finger Lakes. Riesling, chardonnay, sauvignon blanc, and gewurztraminer were successful whites, and red cabernet sauvignon, cabernet franc, pinot noir, and merlot survived as well. The first commercial *V vinifera* wines were produced in 1961 at Gold Seal Vineyards and have continued to flourish with improved techniques for winter survival. Frank left Gold Seal in 1962 to establish his own company, Dr. Frank's Vinifera Wine Cellars, and in the 1980s he started a second winery, Chateau Frank, to produce sparkling wines, both on Keuka Lake. The New York State Agricultural Experiment Station at Geneva (Ontario Co) created hybrids, such as Cayuga white (1972), melody (1986), and, in 1990, chardonel, a hybrid of *V vinifera* chardonnay and the French American hybrid seyval blanc. The hybrids brought from Europe and developed in New York State changed the focus of the wine industry that had previously been dominated by wine companies such as Taylor Wines, which relied on native grape varieties to produce inexpensive table wines, often called jug wines. As wine drinkers' tastes moved to more expensive varietals, the demand for cheaper table wines declined.

Aside from success in producing European grape varieties, probably the biggest boon to the New York State wine industry in the postwar period was an act by the state government. Promoted by Commissioner of Agriculture John Dyson, the Farm Winery Act was an effort by the state to allow small farm wineries (provided that they produced at least 51% of their wine on their own or on leased land) to sell their wines directly to the public, have tasting rooms, and pay reduced state taxes and licensing fees. Gov Hugh Carey signed the act into law in 1976. Benmarl Winery of Marlboro (Ulster Co) in the Hudson Valley was the state's first winery to take advantage of this act. Between 1976 and 2000 the number of wineries in New York State climbed from 20 to 153. This growth was concentrated in the small premium winery sector. Commercial wineries, those that produce more than 150,000 gallons (567,750 l) annually, do not fall under the purview of the act. One result is that smaller wine companies merged and were purchased by other wineries, such as Canandaigua Wine Co, which began as a family business in 1945 in Canandaigua (Ontario Co) in the Finger Lakes region and is now a division of Constellation Brands, the world's largest wine company.

New York State has made its mark on table wines, sparkling wines, dessert wines such as sherries, wine coolers, and kosher wines (which must be made under rabbinical supervision). With wineries in 32 of New York State's 62 counties, the average annual production is 30 million gallons (114 million l), yielding more than $300 million in gross sales. About 18,000 people work directly with the grape and wine industry, making vineyards and wineries significant factors in the state's rural economy. The New York Wine and Grape Foundation, created in 1985 by the state legislature, finances promotion and research to support the state's grape industry (which includes all grape products). The emphasis is on quality, social responsibility, forging links to business-related industries and research institutions, wine exports, and an increase in tourism, which by 2000 was up to 900,000 tourists a year.

Viticultural Areas

New York State's four main viticultural areas were officially designated American Viticultural Areas (AVAs) after proponents described and demonstrated those regions' unique qualities. Subappellations have been added within them. The value of large bodies of water can be seen by understanding the lake effect, specifically important to the Finger Lakes and Lake Erie, which provides for less severe extremes of temperature in winter and summer. The lakes retain their summer warmth in winter, warding off early frosts, and warm any cold air descending from the slopes. That air then rises, permitting more cold air down the hillside in turn to be warmed. In spring the lakes are cold, and the cold air given off by them cools the climate against early warm spells and retards bud-break until the danger of frost is past. The "ocean effect," important to Long Island, works in the same way—ocean breezes moderate both the heat in summer and the cold in winter.

The Lake Erie District is the largest geographic grape-growing region in New York State, with viticulture situated on the southern shore of the lake in Erie and Chautauqua Cos. Early settler and farmer Elijah Fay planted the first vineyard in this region in Chautauqua Co in 1818. The Lake Erie AVA was established in 1983 and includes 20,000 acres (8,100 ha) in New York State and smaller portions in Ohio and Pennsylvania. This area of the Great Lakes provides the most protection against extremes of weather, being downwind from Arctic air masses over Lakes Superior and Huron. Because Chautauqua Co was also a center of temperance activity during the 19th and early 20th centuries, public pressure encouraged growers in this area to cultivate table and juice grapes, rather than wine grapes. The most notable growers were Thomas Welch and his son Charles, who sold grapes, juices (pasteurized), jams, and jellies as the Welch Grape Juice Co. The company was a phenomenal financial success, and in 1928 the Welches sold their firm. In 1933 the National Grape Co-operative was begun, which comprised many Chautauqua Co growers, including Welch's; the co-op produced bottled and frozen juices, mostly the popular purple Concord and white Niagara grape juices, and "nonfermented wine" for church services. The Concord grape accounts for 90% of all grapes planted here, and Lake Erie is the largest grape juice–producing area in the state. Despite this region's emphasis on grapes grown for juice, it boasted 10 wineries by 2000.

The Finger Lakes AVA, established in 1982, has been the center of the state's wine industry since the Civil War. It is the second-largest grape-growing area in the state and, with 14,000 acres (5,700 ha) planted and 61 bonded wineries, is America's largest wine region outside California. About 90% of Finger Lakes grape production is devoted to wine. The lakes important to viticulture are Canandaigua, Keuka, Seneca, and Cayuga, whose significant depth moderates the climate and permits a 190- to 200-day growing season. The Village of Hammondsport, at the southern end of Cayuga Lake, was the center of the earliest wine-making activities in this region, with William Taylor's winery on Bully Hill in 1878, and is still significant. Many of the farm wineries in this region began as grape growers, selling much of their harvest to the nearby Taylor Wine Co in the first half of the 20th century. Changing tastes and the shifting fortunes of Taylor Wine, however, led to a loss of that market. Many growers set up their own wineries and vinified their grapes themselves. All types of still, sparkling, and fortified dessert wines are produced from native, hybrid, and *V vinifera* grapes in the Finger Lakes. Some of the state's largest

At Bully Hill Vineyards, Hammondsport.

wineries are here, notably the Widmer Wine complex on Lake Keuka, which includes Taylor Wine Co, Pleasant Valley Wine Co, and Gold Seal. Now a division of Constellation Brands, the Canandaigua Wine Co also has interests in California, Europe, and the Southern Hemisphere. In 1986 Canandaigua purchased the Manischewitz brand of kosher wines, of which the Concord wine is the most famous. Because of increased demand, however, this wine is no longer made only from New York State grapes. Seneca Lake is the largest and deepest of the Finger Lakes and has smaller wineries on its eastern and western sides. Founded in 1977, Glenora Wine Cellars was the first winery on Seneca Lake and produces sparkling wines from *V vinifera* grapes. Hermann J. Wiemer, a wine maker and vineyardist, used his grafting skills to create a *V vinifera* nursery in 1973. His grapevines provide the fruit for vineyards in every major winery on America's East Coast. By 2000, 79 wineries were operating in the Finger Lakes.

The Hudson Valley AVA begins about 40 miles (64 km) north of New York City. The steep Hudson River valley draws warm maritime air from the Atlantic Ocean, giving a growing season of 180 to 196 days. It is the oldest wine region in New York State, with plantings originally concentrated around the Town of New Paltz; it became an AVA in 1982. Brotherhood America's Oldest Winery still makes many styles of wine and has the largest underground cellars in the state. The Royal Kedem Wine Co, founded on Manhattan's Lower East Side but now with wineries in Milton (Ulster Co) and Marlboro, produces kosher wines from *V vinifera* and native varieties, and kosher grape juice from native varieties. The Schapiro Wine Co, another producer of kosher wines, dates from the late 19th century and operated in New York City through the 20th century. Its wines are now made in Monticello (Sullivan Co), and the company maintains a retail shop on the Lower East Side. There were 27 bonded wineries in the region as of 2000, growing mostly hybrids and *V vinifera* varieties. Besides wines from grapes, some wineries in this area, such as the Regent Champagne Cellars in Highland (Ulster Co) and Warwick Valley Winery (Orange Co), also produce wines from other fruits.

Established in 2001, the Long Island AVA, concentrated in an area of Suffolk Co 90 miles (145 km) east of New York City, encompasses North Fork of Long Island and the Hamptons. New York State's newest and fastest-growing wine region is flanked by the Long Island Sound to the north, Peconic Bay to the east, and the Atlantic Ocean to the south. It enjoys the longest growing season in the state, from 215 to 230 days, which enables the *V vinifera* varietals to ripen; hybrids are also grown here. Alex and Louisa Hargrave established the first commercial *V Vinifera* vineyard and winery in 1973, the Hargrave Vineyards (now Long Island Vineyard) in Cutchogue, replanting potato fields with grapes. Long Island wines must use a minimum of 85% Long Island grapes. For farm wineries, the balance of wine may come from other officially designated regions of New York State. Commercial wineries may use wine from New York or other states; demand is exceeding production and making this practice necessary. By 2000 Long Island had 28 bonded wineries.

Many of New York State's wineries can be visited for both tours and complimentary tastings. In the Finger Lakes the Pleasant Valley Wine Co contains a collection of antique wine-making equipment, while Bully Hill Vineyards also contains a museum; both wineries are in Hammondsport. In the Hudson Valley, Brotherhood America's Oldest Winery Wine Museum in Washingtonville and Mark Miller's Museum for Preservation of Illustrative Art at Benmarl Winery in Marlboro are open to the public. New York Wine Trail signs are posted in the state's major wine regions to help guide visitors.

See also FRUIT FARMING.

Adams, Leon D. *The Wines of America* (New York: McGraw-Hill, 1978)
Dial, Tom. *The Wines of New York State* (Utica: North Country Books, 1986)
Gianotti, Peter M. *Guide to the Wines of Long Island* (Melville, NY: Newsday, 1998)
Klees, Emerson. *Wineries of the Finger Lakes Region* (Rochester: Friends of the Finger Lakes, 2000)
Morton, Lucy. *Winegrowing in Eastern America* (Ithaca: Cornell Univ Press, 1985)
Robinson, Jancis. *Vines, Grapes, and Wines* (New York: Knopf, 1986)

Harriet Lembeck

Winfield. Town (pop 2,202) in SW Herkimer Co. The Unadilla River traverses the town. Settled *ca* 1790, the town was formed in 1816 from Litchfield, Richfield (Otsego Co), and Plainfield (Otsego Co), and named for Gen Winfield Scott, a hero of the War of 1812. The town benefited from its location on the Third Great Western Turnpike (1803). Sheep raising for wool production dominated *ca* 1820–50. In the late 19th century Winfield became a dairy town, with 11 cheese factories in 1878. In the early 21st century, Winfield remains a farming town.

James Crawford

Winged [WING-ED] **Foot Golf Club.** The group of New York Athletic Club members who formed Winged Foot in 1920 hired A. W. Tillinghast to design two 18-hole layouts in Mamaroneck (Westchester Co), the East Course (1921) and the West Course (1923). The West Course, with its long and narrow tree-lined fairways and steep bunkers, is routinely ranked among the nation's best. The course has hosted the 1940 US Amateur competition, four men's US Opens (1929, 1959, 1974, 1984), and the 1997 PGA Championship. The East Course has hosted two women's US Opens (1957, 1972). Winged Foot was again the site of the US Amateur tournament in 2004. Members also claim to have originated one of golf's most enduring terms: when club member David B. Mulligan in 1937 insisted on rehitting poor shots, he gave his name to the "do over" shot, or the "Mulligan."

McCarthy, John Francis. *The Beauty of Golf in New York State* (Auburn, NY: Summerfield House, 1989)

Sal Maiorana

wire manufacture industry. Though the Troy Iron and Nail Factory, established in 1813, manufactured wire for nail making, significant production of wire in New York State—and in the United States—did not occur until the 1830s. During the antebellum period, wire was used primarily to make pins, hoops for petticoats, and telegraph line. Following the American Civil War, its applications expanded, including fencing, mattress springs, nails, suspension bridge cable, and reinforcements for plaster walls, among other uses. In 1868 the largest New York State ferrous wire manufacturer was Eagleton Manufacturing Co of New York City and Brooklyn. The Wests, Bradley and Carys Hoop Skirt Works, located in New York City, employed up to 2,000 persons in the 1860s. In 1909 General Electric Co (GE) in Schenectady developed the method of making tungsten wire for lamp filaments, a process still in use at the beginning of the 21st century. In the 1960s and 1970s GE and a spin-off company, Intermagnetics General of Schenectady, developed new processes for producing superconducting wire. At the beginning of the 21st century, the state is no longer a significant site of ferrous wire drawing. The largest remaining companies—those with more than 100 employees—are AL Tech Specialty Steel in Dunkirk (Chautauqua Co), which manufactures fencing and reinforcements for concrete, and Strandflex, a division of Maryland Specialty Wire, in Oriskany (Oneida Co). In contrast, the making of nonferrous wire of copper, aluminum, and other metals is an important New York State industry. It generated $172 million of the $933 million value of total US production in 1997 and employs thousands in the state. Superior-Essex, the largest producer of wire and cable in the United States, operates 1 of its more than 100 plants in Hudson (Columbia Co). Rome Cable Co (Oneida Co) produces a range of nonferrous wire and cable; Endicott Machine (Broome Co) manufactures wire forms or springs. Camden Wire Co (Oneida Co), Omega Wire in Williamstown (Oswego Co), and Owl Wire and Cable Co in Canastota (Madison Co) specialize in copper goods. Alcoa Wire Rod in Massena (St. Lawrence Co) produces aluminum rod and wire; Chester Alcatel (Orange Co) makes electronic and specialty wire; and Oswego Wire Co in Fulton (Oswego Co) manufactures telecommunication and electronic conductors.

Jack Westbrook

Wirt. Town (pop 1,215) in SW Allegany Co. Settled in 1812, the town was formed in 1838 from Bolivar and Friendship. Located on the divide between the Allegheny and Genesee watersheds, it was a farming town until oil was drilled in 1881; in the mid–20th century the oil was extracted by the flooding method. The town was served by the Pittsburgh, Shawmut and Northern Railroad (1903–46). Between 1912 and 1926 three firms in Wirt manufactured gasoline. In 2003 the town has one large dairy farm, and most residents work in Olean or Wellsville.

Wise [Weiz], **Isaac Mayer** (*b* Steingrub [now Lomnice in Czech Republic], 29 Mar 1819; *d* Cincinnati, 26 Mar 1900). Reform rabbi. Educated in yeshivas and the Universities of Prague and Vienna and influenced by European reform movements, Wise moved to New York City in 1846. Shortly after his arrival Wise became rabbi at Congregation Beth El in Albany, where his controversial reforms included choral singing, the introduction of confirmation, and the unprecedented experiment of mixed seating of men and women for services. These radical innovations did not find favor with the more traditionally minded members of the congregation, who dismissed Wise. Wise and his supporters did not accept his firing, and on Rosh Hashanah in 1850, when Wise tried to speak from the pulpit, a riot ensued between pro- and anti-Wise factions. The pro-Wise faction thereafter formed a new congregation, Anshe Emeth. In 1854 Wise took a pulpit in Cincinnati, where he would remain for the rest of his career. The leader of the Reform movement, in 1875 he became the first president of Hebrew Union College, the nation's first Jewish seminary.

Temkin, Sefton D. *Isaac Mayer Wise: Shaping American Judaism* (New York: Oxford Univ Press, 1992)

Susan Roth Breitzer

Wise, Stephen S(amuel) (*b* Eger [Erlau], Hungary, 17 Mar 1874; *d* New York City, 19 Apr 1949). Religious leader. Wise moved to the United States in 1875 when his father became rabbi of Congregation Beth Elohim in Brooklyn. He studied at the College of the City of New York, the Jewish Theological Seminary, and Columbia University, and he was ordained in 1893. Wise became assistant rabbi to Henry F. Jacobs at Congregation B'nai Jeshurun in New York City, and in 1905 he was a candidate to become the senior rabbi at Congregation Emanu-El, a prestigious New York City Reform congregation. When the board offered him the position but made it clear that they would need to approve his sermons in advance, Wise declined the position and affirmed his commitment to freedom of the pulpit. In 1907 he founded the Free Synagogue, whose services were held in the Hudson Theatre and later in Carnegie Hall, with a branch on the Lower East Side at Clinton Hall. The tragic fire at the Triangle Shirtwaist Factory in 1911 compelled him to increase his efforts on behalf of exploited immigrants. He worked closely with Louis Brandeis in establishing the Provisional Executive Committee for General Zionist Affairs in 1914. In 1918 Wise was elected president of the Zionist Organization of America, an organization he had helped found in 1898. In 1921 he established the Jewish Institute of Religion, a multidenominational rabbinic school in New York City. Wise was politically active in city and state politics, challenging corruption under Mayor Jimmy Walker and canvassing for prominent politicians like Alfred E. Smith, Fiorello La Guardia, and Franklin D. Roosevelt. A leader of the American Jewish opposition to Adolf Hitler, he has nonetheless been criticized for not pushing Roosevelt harder to save European Jewry at the earlier stages of Nazi persecution. A brilliant speaker and passionate advocate for social justice, Wise was one of the most important American Jewish leaders of the 20th century.

Urofsky, Melvin I. *A Voice That Spoke for Justice: The Life and Times of Stephen S. Wise* (Albany: SUNY Press, 1981)

Dana Evan Kaplan

Wisner, Henry (*b* near Florida, Orange Co, *ca* 1720; *d* Goshen, Orange Co, 4 Mar 1790). Politician and businessman. Raised on his parents' farm near Goshen, Wisner acquired land and a gristmill in the Goshen area, in 1739 marrying Sarah Norton. By the 1760s Wisner served as justice of the peace, sat in the New York Colonial Assembly, and was assistant justice of the Court of Common Pleas of Orange Co. After Sarah's death he married Sarah Cornell Waters in 1769. Wisner was elected to the First Continental Congress in 1774 and signed the nonimportation agreement. A delegate to the Second Continental Congress in 1775, he planned secret actions to obtain saltpeter to make gunpowder. On 2 July 1776 he voted for the Declaration of Independence but, as an active member of New York State's provincial congress, was absent when it was signed on 2 Aug 1776. He built gunpowder mills, one in Ulster Co and two in Orange Co, and supplied critically needed powder for Washington's army during the Revolution. Called a "tyrant" and "malefactor" by the English press for preventing suppression of the rebellion, Wisner formed part of the state's Commission for Detecting and Defeating Conspiracies and secured the arrest of hundreds of loyalists in Orange, Dutchess, and Ulster Cos. He participated in framing the first constitution of New York State (1777) and in fortifying the Hudson River (1777–78). His efforts led to the building of Fort Arnold and Fort Putnam in West Point (Orange Co). Wisner was a member of the state senate (1777–82) and of the first Board of Regents of the University of the State of New York (1784–87). A delegate to the 1788 New York State Constitutional Convention, Wisner voted against ratification, fearing that too strong a federal government would overpower state and individual rights.

Burdge, Franklin. "A Memorial of Henry Wisner." In *The Wisners in America and Their Kindred: A Genealogical and Biographical History,* ed. George Franklin Wisner (Baltimore, Md, 1918)

Frank Price

Wolcott. Town (pop 4,692) and village (pop 1,712) in NE Wayne Co. Bounded on the north by Lake Ontario, the town was formed from Junius (Seneca Co) in 1807. The village, part of which lies in the Town of Butler, was incorporated in 1852. Settlement within the present town and village began in 1806 with the arrival of Jonathan Melvin Sr, who built the first mills on Wolcott Creek. Iron deposits attracted another early industry; a blast furnace was built around 1825 and a foundry in 1845. Roads extending east, west, and south and, after 1873, the Rome, Watertown and Ogdensburg Railroad made the Village of Wolcott a transportation and trading hub. In the early 21st century, apples and other fruits were grown and processed. Wegmans Egg Farm, producing 550,000 eggs a day, is the largest egg farm in the state. Electromark is a national manufacturer of safety-warning signage. Part of the Lake Shore Marshes State Wildlife Management Area lies in the town. A cast-iron fountain, *Venus Rising from the Sea* (1913), is a landmark in the village, which is the trading center for a sizable farming district.

Scott C. Monje

Woman's Christian Temperance Union (WCTU). First national women's organization in the United States, established in 1874. The WCTU developed from the involvement of antebellum women in the temperance movement, evangelical revivalism, and local charitable works. The organization emerged out of a series of spontaneous prayer meetings and demonstrations against public drinking that occurred in the United States during the winter of 1873–74. Women in Fredonia (Chautauqua Co) held their first public prayer meeting on 15 Dec 1873 and established a formal organization of 208 members on 22 December, adopting the name Woman's Christian Temperance Union. Fredonia's meeting was among the earliest in the United States, if not the first, of these women's crusades against the saloon. In October 1874, 90 delegates representing 25 counties attended the first New York State WCTU convention in Syracuse. In November of that year the national organizing convention for the WCTU was held in Cleveland.

The WCTU is credited with pioneering modern lobbying techniques, particularly the use of the petition drive. The national WCTU focused on legislation and education, and the first generation of leadership moved rapidly beyond a temperance agenda to support a broad reform program. National president Frances Willard (1879–98), born in Churchville (Monroe Co), set the broad goal of "Home Protection" and endorsed a "Do Everything" policy that allowed unions to set local priorities. New York State women participated actively in prison reform, social purity, temperance education, and suffrage campaigns, and published their own state journal, *Woman's Temperance Work.* Members also campaigned for separate prison facilities for women and for the appointment of women prison guards, resulting in the 1888 Prison Matron Law. New York State WCTU women secured social purity legislation in 1877 and legislation to raise the age of consent from 10 to 18 in 1895. Following the national union's endorsement of woman suffrage in 1881, the state WCTU established its own Franchise Department in 1886. By 1900 national membership was more than 200,000, and the state organization had more than 22,000 members registered in 793 local unions. An estimated 1,500 people attended an assembly week at the WCTU temperance camp in Cuba (Allegany Co) that year. In 1917, with state membership exceeding 45,000, members actively participated in that year's successful state campaign for woman suffrage.

The active WCTU membership provided crucial support for the organization's final legislative campaign for national prohibition through ratification of the 18th Amendment in 1919. Ella Boole of Brooklyn, then president of the New York State WCTU, led the allied forces of state prohibition groups and testified before Congress and the state legislature in support of the amendment for prohibition. Boole served as New York State's first president of the national WCTU (1925–33). During Prohibition the entire WCTU campaigned for stringent law enforcement but increasingly lost influence as public support for Prohibition eroded and popular culture moved away from the organization's religious and family-centered conservatism. After Prohibition repeal in 1933, the WCTU shifted more toward international temperance work through its missionary programs. New York continued to have the largest single state enrollment into the 1940s and generated another national president, Mamie White Colvin (1944–53) of New York City. In 2003 the WCTU was a much smaller federation of unions committed to total personal abstinence from all addictive substances. National membership was approximately 5,000, and New York State had 150 members with 11 local unions.

Bordin, Ruth. *Women and Temperance: The Quest for Power and Liberty, 1873–1900* (Philadelphia: Temple Univ Press, 1981)

Graham, Frances. *Sixty Years of Action, 1874–1934: A History of Sixty Years' Work of the Woman's Christian Temperance Union of the State of New York* (Lockport, NY, 1935)

Laurie Kozakiewicz

Woman's New York State Temperance Society (WNYSTS). Antebellum organization that sought to end alcohol consumption and promote women's rights. Inspired by an 1851 Maine law that made it illegal to manufacture or sell liquor, temperance supporters in New York State mobilized for a similar law. During this period men dominated most temperance societies. Although women were generally welcome at these gatherings, they could not speak or take an active role. In response, women inclined to the temperance cause gathered in Rochester on 20–21 Apr 1852. Organized by Elizabeth Cady Stanton of Seneca Falls (Seneca Co), this gathering, attended by 500 women, created WNYSTS and elected Stanton as its president. Stanton rejected the then current notion that men and women inhabited separate spheres and that only men should play public roles. She asked women to withdraw from all temperance societies that did not allow them a voice, also proposing that drunkenness become legal grounds for divorce and that wives refuse conjugal rights to drunken husbands. Many officers of the new society came from the Rochester area and included Susan B. Anthony and Mary H. Post Hallowell of Rochester, Amelia Bloomer of Seneca Falls, and Antoinette Brown Blackwell of Henrietta and Hannah S. Shute of Fairport (Monroe Co). The society sent lecturers, particularly Anthony and Emily Clark, to Albany and throughout the state to urge women to work for the "Maine law"; it also purchased and distributed temperance literature at public meetings. WNYSTS's efforts did not win any new antiliquor legislation in the state, and internal disagreements over women's rights resulted in Stanton's ouster from the presidency in 1853. The society faded away within the next few years, probably dissolving when Bloomer's temperance newspaper, the *Lily*, ceased publication in 1856. After WNYSTS's demise politically radical women and conservative, "dry" women never joined together again.

Gordon, Ann D., ed. *The Selected Papers of Elizabeth Cady Stanton and Susan B. Anthony: In the School of Anti-Slavery, 1840–1866*, vol 1 (New Brunswick, NJ: Rutgers Univ Press, 1997)

Caryn E. Neumann

Woman Suffrage Party (WSP). Suffrage organization. Carrie Chapman Catt, leader of the National American Woman Suffrage Association (NAWSA), launched the WSP on 29 Oct 1909. The WSP drew a diverse array of suffrage groups into a compact, active organization. Catt believed that woman suffrage on the federal level could be achieved only by winning suffrage first in New York State and that New York City as a large media center held the key to winning the state. One thrust of WSP was educational, appealing to voters' sense of justice to gain their support for a woman's right to the ballot, thereby creating a grassroots demand for policy change. Politically savvy, WSP remained—like its parent NAWSA—strictly nonpartisan in order to appeal to all political stripes. Although the party billed itself as a state organization and created 12 campaign districts in the state, all of its officers hailed from New York City and its efforts were almost exclusively focused on that area. Prominent WSP members included historian Mary Ritter Beard and longtime NAWSA leader Mary Garrett Hay, who served as WSP president. Beard was vice chair of the Manhattan branch before becoming editor of the *Woman Voter* (1910–17), the WSP's official organ. After strong WSP pressure the state legislature authorized a voter referendum on woman suffrage for November 1915. New York City's 20 WSP chapters, claiming over 100,000 members, campaigned hard, orchestrating thousands of rallies, bonfires, and torchlight parades in the city, but the 1915 referendum lost by a 26% margin. Undeterred, WSP immediately pressured the legislature to establish a new state referendum, which passed by a 15% margin on 6 Nov 1917. In the city the initiative was carried by a 29% margin whereas the referendum lost by 1% elsewhere in the state. The referendum's success can be credited to both the WSP's efforts in New York City and the endorsement of the metropolis's Tammany Hall, which backed the initiative under WSP pressure just a few days prior to the vote. With New York State won, the WSP continued to work for national woman suffrage, disbanding after this was achieved in 1920.

Peck, Mary Gray. *Carrie Chapman Catt: A Biography* (New York: H. W. Wilson, 1944)

Caryn E. Neumann

Women, Division for. In 1967 Gov Nelson A. Rockefeller, acting on recommendations from the 1966 Governor's Conference on Women, established the Women's Unit—an information clearinghouse for state agencies dealing with issues of interest to women—within the Office of the Secretary to the Governor. In 1975, through Executive Order 8, Gov Hugh Carey established the Division for Women in the Executive Department, with a charge to advocate for women's issues within state government. The division reviews and monitors proposed legislation and state policies for their impact on women. It also sponsors programs and conferences designed to increase women's participation in New York State's government and economy and publishes newsletters: *Women New York* (1975–85; 1985–95, *New York Women*); *Women and AIDS Project* (1987–91), issued with the New York State Division of Alcoholism and Alcohol Abuse; *Women in Focus* (1997–2000); and *Focus* (2000–). A director heads the division, aided by 12 regional advisory councils. In November 1996 the councils met for the first time in conference, and since that date they have met jointly once a year. Since 1996 the Division for Women has presented Women of Excellence Awards and High School Achievement Awards, and it sponsors a Women's History Month reception. In 1997 Gov George E. Pataki established the Commission Honoring the Achievements of Women, charged with commemorating the 150th anniversary of the first women's rights convention in Seneca Falls. This Division for Women–staffed commission funded Ken Burns's film *Not for Ourselves Alone: The Story of Elizabeth Cady Stanton and Susan B. Anthony* (1998) and a July 1998 sesquicentennial celebration at the Women's Rights National Historical Park in Seneca Falls. In 2003 the division's offices were at 633 3rd Ave in Manhattan.

Dangler, Jamie. *Hidden in the Home: The Role of Waged Homework in the Modern-World Economy* (Albany: SUNY Press, 1994)

Jeffrey Kraus

women-owned businesses. The number and growth of women-owned businesses in New York State historically reflect women's changing civil rights, skills and training, and opportunities to pursue entrepreneurial ambitions. In the colonial era, women faced common-law obstacles that assumed they were economically dependent on their husbands or fathers for support, though women often had to care for themselves and their dependents. The early household economy found women farming and managing home production, as well as manufacturing household products such as candles, cloth, and soap. Some women pursued midwifery, writing, or the arts, and others ran boardinghouses, dry goods or other retail establishments, and even print shops. Historians have estimated that 10% to 25% of American women were engaged in some entrepreneurial activity before industrialization and that in urban centers half of all retailers were women.

During the 19th century, industrialization and women's rights opened more business opportunities for women. From 1848 to 1862, a series of married women's property acts, including New York State's 1860 Earnings Act, provided legislative impetus for economic advancement and an increased ability of women, particularly married women, to retain their earnings and to make contracts in their own names. Hundreds of women ran small manufacturing operations, as well as bookstores, groceries, dry goods shops, and hair businesses. Other women generated needed money through boardinghouses and saloons. The death of a male relative made it more permissible for women to assume leadership over nontraditional businesses such as manufacturing and construction-related enterprises. Rose Knox took over control of the Knox Gelatine Co in 1890 in Johnstown (Fulton Co) upon the death of her husband, and by 1936 it was the country's largest producer of unflavored gelatin. Amanda Lougees became head of a rubber "gossamer" factory with the death of her brother, employing 275 people with offices in New York City, Chicago, and Boston. Following her husband's death, Nellie Rusell Kimball ran a coal and wood yard near Dunkirk (Chautauqua Co). Women, however, often succeeded in business on their own. Women found independent business opportunity as milliners and dressmakers. The Curtis sisters, Ellen and Katherine, operated a millinery shop in Troy (Rensselaer Co), and later in New York City in 1850, where they designed innovative crinolines and corsets. With Ellen's marriage to William Demorest, she took a less public role but continued to innovate by creating paper patterns, an idea she copied from her black servant. At the peak of their business, during the 1870s, the Demorests sold 3 million paper patterns through distribution agencies in the United States and Europe.

Hair and beauty care was another untapped market that women seized. In 1891 Martha Matilda Harper of Rochester initiated modern retail franchising of healthy hair and skin care salons, creatively financing her business expansion and providing working-class women the opportunity to own a franchise. Helena Rubinstein, Florence Graham, whose firm went under the name of Elizabeth Arden, and the African American Madam C. J. Walker led some of the more famous beauty operations in New York State. Capital has been an obstacle for women entrepreneurs. Milliners and dressmakers, for example, had small operations because of their inability to obtain credit. As men increasingly recognized the market potential of the clothing industry with prefabrication and wholesaling, they took over the industry. Similarly, in the 1920s, as men saw the market potential of the beauty industry, they bought out many female-run businesses. Women seeking venture capital continue to struggle, and the federal government has set up a small loan program to help women through the US Small Business Administration. Women in the 21st century represent the fastest growing segment of entrepreneurs. According to the *1999 Facts on Women-Owned Businesses,* in New York State women owned 600,000 businesses, or 37% of all businesses. They employed nearly 1.9 million people and generated over $304 billion in sales. Estimates indicate that from 1992 to 1999 employment among these businesses increased 88% and sales rose by 107%. As of 1999 New York City led the nation as the top metropolitan area when measuring women-owned firms. These firms employed more than 1 million people and generated approximately $194 billion in sales. Most New York women-owned firms are in the service (54%) and retail trade (15%) sectors. However, from 1992 to 1999, there were sizable increases in nontraditional sectors: the number of women business owners included increases of 69% in construction, 61% in transportation/communications businesses, and 61% in agriculture/mining businesses.

Kwolek-Folland, Angel. *Incorporating Women: A History of Women and Business in the United States* (New York: Twayne Publishers, 1998)

1999 Facts on Women-Owned Businesses: Trends in the United States and the Fifty States (Silver Springs, Md: National Foundation for Women Business Owners, 1999)

Plitt, Jane R. *Martha Matilda Harper and the American Dream: How One Woman Changed the Face of Modern Business* (Syracuse: Syracuse Univ Press, 2000)

Jane R. Plitt

women's clubs. Benevolent societies, usually supporting missionaries and orphans, were the most common form of women's organizations following the American Revolution. New York City's Orphan Asylum Society, formed in 1806, provided moral and religious training, as well as housing to the city's youth. During the antebellum period reform societies organized, such as New York City's Female Moral Reform Society, founded in 1834 to try to rescue women from prostitution, and the New York Asylum for Lying-In Women, formed in 1823 to provide poor women with medical care during pregnancy. In Rochester the Female Charitable Society was established in 1822, while in Utica the local Female Charitable Society formed in 1806 and the Female Moral Reform Society in 1837. Some reform-minded women transferred their activity to political issues, such as antislavery before the Civil War and women's suffrage and temperance after the war. Self-improvement, literary, and culture clubs existed in New York State prior to the Civil War but proliferated in its aftermath. They drew to their ranks mostly white, married, middle-class women with grown children and fewer domestic responsibilities. Members also gained valuable experiences in organization, serving as club leaders and on committees.

The Sorosis club was organized in 1868 in New York City by Jane Cunningham Croly, a journalist. When Croly and other women journalists were refused entrance to a dinner in honor of Charles Dickens by the New York Press Club, they banded together to organize a club. Sorosis members came mainly from the city's female professional ranks, including physicians, editors, lawyers, and ministers. In 1890 Sorosis helped form the General Federation of Women's Clubs. In 1894 clubs in the state formed the New York State Federation of Women's Clubs; there were 99 clubs in the federation on its first anniversary. Community participation and civic reform became an increasingly important focus. Women's clubs established public libraries in many towns, including those in Corning (Steuben Co), where the Clionian Circle reopened the library in 1897; New Paltz (Ulster Co) in 1907; Boonville (Oneida Co) in 1911; and Delmar (Albany Co) in 1912, courtesy of the Delmar Progress Club. Women's clubs also investigated school conditions and started reading and public health programs, and college scholarships for women. An attempt to establish a state industrial school for girls in Amsterdam (Montgomery Co) in 1903 proved abortive.

Suffrage was not a main focus of club activities, though the clubs were concerned with abolishing child labor, implementing pure food and drug laws, and conserving the environment. Through their size and national scope, they became effective lobbyists. At their peak, around 1920, membership in New York State Federation of Women's Clubs reached over 250,000. Ethnic and racial minorities formed parallel organizations. African American women formed the Empire State Federation of Women's Clubs in 1908, which concentrated on providing scholarship funds for African American girls. If the women's club movement waned in the decades after World War II, many of the traditional women's clubs remain active, including Sorosis, Brooklyn Women's Club, Corning Area Women's Club, Syracuse Federation of Women's Clubs, Ithaca Women's Clubs, Travel Club of Elmira, Study Club of New Paltz, and Century Club of Amsterdam, and continue to exert influence in their communities. New York State Federation of Women's Clubs' membership in 2002 numbered 2,376 women in 63 clubs.

Blair, Karen J. *The Clubwoman as Feminist: True Womanhood Redefined, 1868–1914* (New York: Holmes & Meier Publishers, 1980)

Lisa C. Mangiafico

women's education. In the early years of colonial settlement, most children were educated primarily within the family. Parents taught their children to read and write, and mothers taught their daughters "housewifery." Some women provided rudimentary education for young children in their homes in what were called dame schools. When towns hired schoolmasters, they offered an elementary education for girls and boys. Beginning in the second half of the 18th century, entrepreneurial teachers operated private venture schools, mainly in the cities. Those catering to young women usually advertised the availability of instruction in dancing, painting, and ornamental needlework as well as in academic subjects. Literacy rates were higher for males, although by the late 1700s the gender gap had considerably narrowed. The greatest disparity in educational opportunity was in advanced education. Female students were not admitted to the colonial Latin grammar schools or to colleges until the mid–19th century. They were excluded because some thought a woman's intellect was inferior. Advanced education was not thought necessary or proper for women, and they were not allowed in the learned professions, particularly the ministry, which required college. The arguments for women's education that began to be advanced in the late 18th century were based on what historians have called "Republican motherhood": mothers needed to instruct their sons to be good citizens.

Beginning in 1787, New York State incorporated quasi-public academies under boards of trustees; most accepted boarding students. Academies were the dominant institution of higher schooling for nearly a century, and the majority of their students were female. Ninety percent of the academies were coeducational (some with "female departments"), and many provided elementary as well as higher schooling. Emma Willard was the pioneer women's educator, and her *Plan for Improving Female Education* (1819) is the seminal statement. Her Troy Female Seminary (1821; now Emma Willard School) in Rensselaer Co was the preeminent women's educational institution in the nation for decades. Willard educated hundreds of teachers who spread her influence throughout the country.

When New York State established its system of public education in 1812, common schools offered elementary education to both girls and boys. Some had separate entrances, designated rows, or even different classrooms for girls and boys, but most had mixed classes. After state legislation in 1853 and 1867 encouraged districts to establish high schools or academic departments, academies (including the female seminaries) began to decline. Some became public high schools, but many closed. By the late 1870s, the number of students in public high schools surpassed those in academies and seminaries. Most high schools were coeducational, although New York City established some girls high schools, and Catholic religious orders continued to organize single-sex schools. Almost all the surviving private secondary schools for girls in New York State in 2002 were in cities, and the majority were under Roman Catholic auspices. The Emma Willard School (renamed in 1895) was the only remaining girls boarding school in 2002. The Albany Academy for Girls (1814), the Buffalo Seminary (1851), and Brearley (1884) and Spence Schools (1892), both in Manhattan, are the oldest independent day schools. The oldest Catholic schools in the state are the Academy of Mount St. Ursula (1855) in the Bronx, Buffalo Academy of the Sacred Heart (1877), and Convent of the Sacred Heart (1881) in Manhattan.

The first state normal school was established in Albany in 1844 to train teachers. Existing academies became state normal schools: Brockport (1867), Fredonia (1868), Cortland (1869), and Potsdam (1871). As public institutions, normal schools offered inexpensive advanced education, and women students predominated (two-thirds of the state's teachers were women by 1860). New York City established a normal school in 1869 (now Hunter College), which enrolled only women until 1964. The state normal schools evolved into teachers colleges by 1942 and became the foundation for the 1948 establishment of the State University of New York. The first women's colleges whose curriculum and admission standards were comparable to the men's colleges of the day were in New York State. Elmira Female College, which conferred its first degrees in 1859, originated in 1852 as Auburn Female University. Ingham Collegiate Institute at Le Roy (Genesee Co) became Ingham University in 1857. Vassar College opened in 1865, and Wells in Aurora (Cayuga Co) received its college charter in 1870. Elmira, Vassar, and Wells benefited from large endowments from their founders. Of these pioneering institutions, Ingham closed in 1892, Elmira and Vassar became coeducational in 1969, and Wells continues as a women's college. The earliest coeducational colleges in New York State were Genesee (1850; the antecedent of Syracuse University), St. Lawrence (1856), and Alfred (1857). Early Catholic women's colleges included the College of New Rochelle (1904) and D'Youville in Buffalo (1908). Elizabeth Blackwell graduated from Geneva Medical College (Ontario Co) in 1849, the first American woman to receive a medical degree. Opportunities opened for other women when Blackwell established the Woman's Medical College of the New York Infirmary in New York City in 1868. Bellevue Hospital in New York City opened a nurses' training school in 1873. Beginning in the late 19th century, vocational education became available in the commercial courses in high schools and private business and secretarial schools.

Title IX of the federal Education Amendments of 1972, which prohibits discrimination on the basis of sex in educational programs or activities receiving federal aid, has had an important impact on women's education. It ended single-sex public schools and sex-segregated home economics, shop, and gym classes, and it led to greater opportunities in athletics and sports in high schools and colleges. The women's movement in the 1960s and 1970s led to women's studies courses and programs in colleges and also women's centers beginning in the late 1960s. Reentry programs for older women were established at some colleges beginning in the 1960s. The federal Women's Educational Equity Act (1974) has promoted gender equity in curricula, particularly in math and science. In the 1990s it also addressed sexual harassment issues. Women are the majority of students, at 58%, in colleges and universities in New York State in 2001. Women's colleges in 2003 include Barnard College (1889; coordinate college with Columbia), Russell Sage College (1916), and the College of New Rochelle (1904).

See also ACADEMIES; HIGHER EDUCATION; HOME ECONOMICS; JEWISH EDUCATION; MEDICAL EDUCATION.

Solomon, Barbara Miller. *In the Company of Educated Women: A History of Women and Higher Education in America* (New Haven, Conn: Yale Univ Press, 1985)

"Symposium: Reappraisals of the Academy Movement," *History of Education Quarterly* 41 (Summer 2001): 216–70

Woody, Thomas. *A History of Women's Education in the United States* (1929; repr New York: Octagon Books, 1974)

Natalie A. Naylor

"New York City—Medical College for Women, East Twelfth Street and Second Avenue—The Anatomical Lecture-Room," from *Frank Leslie's Illustrated Newspaper,* 16 Apr 1870.

Women's Joint Legislative Conference. Formed in September 1918 the Women's Joint Legislative Conference (WJLC) attempted to continue the progressive reforms initiated by the Factory Investigating Commission. At its peak in the early 1920s, the WJLC had 16 member organizations, including working-class women's groups such as the New York Women's Trade Union League, the Women's City Club of New York (a major organization of middle- and upper-class professionals), the Consumers' League of New York, and the state branch of the Woman's Christian Temperance Union. Because of strong conservative feelings in New York State's rural areas the WJLC never extended its organizational membership beyond the New York City region, although it did garner support from working women's groups in Buffalo and Syracuse. In the 1919 New York State legislative session the WJLC propounded a six-part agenda that included a minimum wage measure for working women and a health insurance bill for all private employers. But opposition from a network of women's antilabor legislation groups, Republican state legislators, and business people largely frustrated the WJLC's agenda in the 1920s. Successful WJLC lobbying for a 48-hour bill in 1927 and a minimum wage measure in 1933 came through new alliances with working-class women and with the New York State Democratic Party. The WJLC effectively ceased to exist in April 1933 when leaders such as Molly Dewson, Frances Perkins, and Rose Schneiderman left the state to work in the administration of Pres Franklin D. Roosevelt.

McGuire, John Thomas. "A Catalyst for Reform: The Women's Joint Legislative Conference (WJLC) and Its Fight for Labor Legislation in New York State, 1918–1933" (PhD diss, SUNY Binghamton, 2001)

John Thomas McGuire

women's rights and feminism

COLONIAL NEW YORK, 1621–1776

Native American women in New York State have always held a high position. Clan mothers in Iroquois society are powerful economically, politically (with the responsibility to appoint chiefs), and socially. Mohawk clan mother Molly Brant became famous for encouraging the Iroquois Confederacy to remain allied with the British.

Women in the Dutch colony of New Netherland benefited from the legal system based on Roman-Dutch law, which was the jurisprudence for both Holland and the New World colony. Spinsters and widows held the same legal rights as men, and while in some marriages a woman put herself and her property under her husband's control, in other cases antenuptial contracts allowed women to retain full rights and privileges. These included the ability to appear unaided in court, own and run businesses, and buy and sell property. Adult women, regardless of marital status, could make their own wills and inherit real property. If either a husband or wife died intestate, the survivor inherited half the estate, with the other half divided equally among children, regardless of sex. Their inheritance practices were guaranteed to the Dutch when the English took over the colony in 1664, and both Dutch and English women continued to participate actively in almost all aspects of social and economic life in the early 18th century. These included appearing in court, engaging in business, inheriting real property, and making wills. By the mid–18th century women's legal status declined as English practices began to hamper the rights married women had come to enjoy in the colonies.

The Early Republic, 1776–1828

Following the Revolution, New York State based much of its legal system on William Blackstone's 1765 *Commentaries on the Laws of England*, which declared that the "very being or legal existence" of a married woman was "consolidated into that of her husband, under whose wing, protection, and cover, she performs everything." Legally, married women could not own property, sue or be sued, or testify in court. Families of property could often bypass these provisions by establishing trusts, administered through equity courts, which allowed women to control property independently from their husbands. Under the 1828 Revised Statutes, however, New York State abolished these equity courts and prevented parents from making special property provisions for their married daughters.

Voting rights were denied to women under the 1777 New York State Constitution. Black or white males, however, could vote at 21 years of age if they owned at least $250 worth of property. According to republican theory, voting rights belonged to those who gave up part of their own resources to benefit the larger whole. Because married women did not serve in the military, could not own property, and did not pay taxes, it was deemed that they were not entitled to vote or hold office. Single women who owned property remained an anomaly, paying taxes without political or legal recognition. When New York State adopted a new constitution in 1821, delegates removed nearly all property requirements for white men, retained property requirements for black men, and shut the door to suffrage for women or Native Americans.

Even as legal and political discrimination solidified, women's roles were changing. Beginning in 1821, Emma Willard offered a program at Troy Female Seminary (Rensselaer Co) similar to those available at men's colleges. Women found work outside the home as teachers and at textile factories.

Beginnings of the Women's Rights Movement, 1828–60

The political and legal limitations that women faced began to gain some public attention. In the late 1820s Frances Wright, an English radical associated with the Workingmen's Party in New York City, spoke out for the abolition of slavery and the rights of women. During the 1830s Thomas Herttell represented the views of this group in the New York State legislature, introducing a bill for married women's property rights in 1836. Five women, led by Paulina Wright Davis of Utica and Ernestine Rose of New York City, supported his efforts with a petition. The issue was widely discussed for the next several years. Some people realized that granting married women the right to own property could open the door to political rights, yet discussion at the 1846 New York State Constitutional Convention brought no immediate results. In February 1848, 44 "married ladies" from Darien (Genesee Co) and Covington (Wyoming Co) sent state legislators a petition arguing that women had no more legal rights than "infants, idiots, and lunatics." The legislature finally passed a Married Women's Property Act in April 1848.

Abolitionist activity also nurtured women's rights. In the mid-1830s, under the direction of the New York City–based American Anti-Slavery Society, women and men throughout New York State and the North organized societies, petitioned Congress, lectured, and printed pamphlets and newspapers. Opposition to women in public roles, combined with divisions over political abolitionism, forced a split in the abolitionist movement in 1840. Some opposed women's activism, while others, including Quakers and those affiliated with William Lloyd Garrison in Boston, asserted the right of women to speak in public. In New York State many abolitionists, including those associated with Gerrit Smith of Peterboro (Madison Co), chose to create a third party, known as the Liberty Party, which endorsed both women's rights and political abolitionism.

It was in this context in 1840 that Elizabeth Cady Stanton spent her honeymoon with Henry Brewster Stanton, a major political abolitionist, at the World Anti-Slavery Convention in London and met Lucretia Mott, Quaker minister and abolitionist from Philadelphia. In 1848, when the Stantons lived in Seneca Falls (Seneca Co), Mott was visiting Quakers in nearby Waterloo (Seneca Co) and once reunited, Stanton and Mott decided to hold a convention, which met on 19–20 July 1848, to highlight the oppression of women. Their Declaration of Sentiments, modeled after the Declaration of Independence, asserted that "all men and women are created equal." At the convention Stanton argued for the right of women to vote and hold office. With the support of Frederick Douglass, an advocate of women's rights throughout his life, this resolution passed.

The Seneca Falls Declaration of Sentiments acted as a catalyst for emerging state and national debates about women's rights. In 1850 the first national women's rights convention was held in Worcester, Mass. From 1850 to 1860 women held national as well as statewide conventions every year except one. Susan B. Anthony, from Rochester, organized a number of conventions, many being held in New York State, including several in the Albany area and one national convention in 1852 in Syracuse, where Matilda Joslyn Gage gave her first speech. The conventions addressed a wide range of issues, including education, jobs, the double standard of morality, unequal marriage laws, divorce, political rights, domestic violence, and a woman's right to her own body. Dress reform attracted many women, who donned a short dress with pants, called the Bloomer costume once Amelia Bloomer publicized it in the pages of her Seneca Falls temperance newspaper, the *Lily*. In 1854 Anthony traversed New York State lobbying for women's right to control their own earnings, keep custody of their children in the case of divorce, and to vote. New York State expanded its Married Women's Property Act in 1860 to include women's right to keep their wages as well as to own real property, although the legislature rescinded this act in 1862.

Maturing of the Women's Rights Movement, 1860–96

During the Civil War women supported military efforts by nursing, providing supplies through the US Sanitary Commission, and operating farms and factories at home. Stanton and Anthony organized the National Woman's Loyal League, headquartered in New York City, to generate support for the abolition of slavery. Harriet Tubman, a major conductor on the Underground Railroad and, beginning in the late 1850s, a resident of Auburn (Cayuga Co), worked as a nurse, scout, and spy with Union troops. Dr Mary Edwards Walker, from Oswego, worked as a military surgeon and became the first woman to win the Congressional Medal of Honor. Sojourner Truth, born enslaved in Dutchess Co, became a lecturer for both abolitionism and women's rights.

At the end of the war, women made progress in many areas. Some women from New York State, both black and white, including Edmonia Highgate, Emily Howland, and Myrtilla Miner, worked as teachers with the Freedman's Bureau in the South. More women entered the workforce in such occupations as printers, post office workers, and teachers. Both before and after the war, new opportunities opened for women in higher education, especially in coeducational colleges such as Alfred University and St. Lawrence University, and in single-sex colleges such as Vassar. Women's clubs often appealed to middle-class women and included Sorosis in New York City, American Association of University Women, Woman's Loyal League, the National Association of Colored Women, YWCA, National Council of Jewish Women, and women's literary clubs. Some working-class women became union leaders, including Kate Mullaney of the Collar Laundry Union in Troy. The Woman's Christian Temperance Union was founded in Fredonia (Chautauqua Co) in 1874 and became one of the largest women's organizations in the country.

Political rights for women, however, proved elusive. During the late 1860s debates over the 14th and 15th Amendments split the women's movement. The 14th Amendment introduced the word "male" into the Constitution for the first time, and the 15th Amendment granted male citizens, "without regard to race, color, or previous condition of servitude," the right to vote. Some women's rights advocates, including Stanton and Anthony, refused to support any suffrage amendment that did not include women. Others, such as Frederick Douglass and Lucy Stone, believed that supporting the right of African American males to vote was crucial and could be a steppingstone toward woman suffrage.

In 1869 the New York–based group, led by Stanton and Anthony, organized the National Woman Suffrage Association, while the New England–based group, led by Lucy Stone and others, organized the American Woman Suffrage Association. In 1872 Victoria Woodhull, editor of *Woodhull and Claflin's Weekly* in New York City, became the first woman to run for president, and in that same year a number of women, including Anthony and 12 others in Rochester, cast ballots in the presidential election. Anthony was arrested three weeks later on a voting fraud charge. At her trial in early 1873 the judge directed the jury to find Anthony guilty. She was ordered to pay a $100 fine, which she refused to do. *Minor v Happersett*, an 1874 Supreme Court case originating in Missouri, indicated that suffrage was not an inherent right of citizenship. Proponents lobbied unsuccessfully to include woman suffrage in the New York State constitutional revisions in both 1867 and 1894.

In spite of these problems, there were encouraging advances in women's position. In 1870, prodded by Esther Morris from Owego (Tioga Co), Wyoming became the first US territory to incorporate woman suffrage, and in 1879 Belva Ann Lockwood, a native of Royalton (Niagara Co), became the first woman to practice law before the US Supreme Court. The two national suffrage organizations joined into the National American Woman Suffrage Association (NAWSA) in 1890, the same decade that four states came into the union allowing woman suffrage: Wyoming (1890), Colorado (1893), Utah (1896), and Idaho (1896).

Progressive Reform and Suffrage, 1896–1920

By the early 20th century, the death of the first generation of women's rights leaders and changing national priorities brought the organized suffrage movement close to a standstill. Additionally, Americans who were concerned with problems relating to urban growth, industrialism, and immigration turned to other kinds of reform. Many women in urban areas became social workers, nurses, or advocates for working women. They worked in settlement houses, such as Henry Street Settlement in New York City, and with organizations such as the Consumers' League of the City of New York, the Urban League, the National Women's Trade Union League, and labor unions. In 1885 Elizabeth Marshall of Buffalo hired a nurse to distribute care to the city's poor, and thus the first visiting nurses' association in the country was founded.

Working outside the formal political system, these women found allies among male politicians, creating the foundation of the Progressive reform movement. Progressive reformers in New York State influenced national policy, especially after Theodore Roosevelt became president in 1901. Social workers such as Lillian D. Wald and Frances Perkins became politically influential. Crystal Eastman was at the center of a group of socialists and intellectuals in New York City who fought for women's rights, socialism, and peace. Emma Goldman, who had emigrated from Russia first to Rochester and then to New York City, became a leading anarchist and reform advocate. Mary Burnett Talbert, from Buffalo, was one of the founders of the NAACP. Verina Harris Morton-Jones was president of the Brooklyn Equal Suffrage League and a member of both the Brooklyn chapter of the NAACP and the National Urban League. Margaret Sanger and her sister Virginia Byrne, born in Corning (Steuben Co), made sensational headlines with their public advocacy of birth control and later with the organization of the American Birth Control League in 1921 (now Planned Parenthood).

In the context of Progressive reform, advocates of woman suffrage formed new cross-class coalitions. In 1907 Harriet Stanton Blatch formed the Equality League of Self-Supporting Women (later Women's Political Union), designed to appeal to all working women. Suffrage parades attracted wealthy women, such as Alvah Vanderbilt Belmont, and middle-class and working women. By 1916, energized by younger leaders and the approval of suffrage in several western states, NAWSA took on new life. Carrie Chapman Catt, based in New York City, made New York State a key component of her "winning plan."

In 1915, despite an extremely well organized campaign, voters defeated proposed amendments for woman suffrage in New Jersey, Massachusetts, Pennsylvania, and New York. Opponents included liquor interests, who feared that women would vote against the sale of alcohol, and conservatives in general, who feared drastic changes in women's roles. New Yorkers finally approved woman suffrage in 1917. Working-class immigrants in New York City voted heavily for suffrage, while upstate areas were generally opposed it. On 16 Aug 1920, the 19th Amendment to the US Constitution was ratified, giving suffrage to women across the country.

Suffragists in dominoes and masks parade through Rochester, carrying placards of states that had already given women the right to vote. Photograph by Albert R. Stone, 15 Aug 1914.

Practicing Women's Rights, 1920–60

Although women did not vote as a bloc in the 1920s, they did take an active part in politics. Women's organizations were centers of political power. Eleanor Roosevelt acted as a liaison among the League of Women Voters, the Women's Trade Union League, the Women's Division of the New York State Democratic Committee (headed by Harriet May Mills of Syracuse), and the Women's City Club of New York. Between 1912 and 1926, Maria C. Lawton of Brooklyn helped expand the Empire State Federation of Women's Clubs, originally only including a small number of African American women's clubs in New York City and Buffalo, to include 103 black women's clubs across the state. Women campaigned for improvements in communities, schools, and conditions for workers, as well as for political rights, such as the right of women to serve on juries. Several women also ran for statewide office. In 1919 Marion Dickerman from Fulton (Oswego Co) unsuccessfully challenged Speaker Thaddeus Sweet in the assembly. Through these activities, Roosevelt and others learned how to create a politically powerful movement and enlisted the help of male politicians such as Gov Alfred E. Smith. In 1923 Alice Paul, founder of the National Woman's Party, traveled to Seneca Falls to announce a campaign for an Equal Rights Amendment. When Franklin D. Roosevelt became president in 1932, the Woman's Committee of the Democratic Party, strongly influenced by New York State women, successfully lobbied for a cabinet post for Frances Perkins. She was the first female cabinet member in US history, serving as secretary of labor from 1933 to 1945.

During World War II women enlisted in the armed forces and worked on the home front in defense-related industries. At the Grumman aircraft plants in Nassau Co, for example, women made up 30% of the workforce. Postwar government aid, like Federal Housing Administration loans, spurred many families to move to expanding suburbs, such as Levittown (Nassau Co).

Feminism, 1960–Present

Women involved in the Civil Rights Movement began the second wave of the women's movement in the 1960s. In 1961 Pres John F. Kennedy appointed Eleanor Roosevelt as chair of the Commission on the Status of Women. In 1963 Betty Friedan, a journalist and housewife from Sneden's Landing (Rockland Co), published *The Feminine Mystique,* identifying the "problem that had no name" and arguing that middle-class women lived under a patriarchal system that prevented them from becoming fully themselves. In 1966 she cofounded the National Organization for Women (NOW), and organizations formed all across the state, with Karen DeCrow, from Syracuse, serving as the fourth national president. In 1971 Gloria Steinem, Letty Cottin Pogrebin (a native of Queens), and others founded *Ms.* magazine, which became a major voice for the new feminist movement. Political women in 1971 formed the National Women's Political Caucus. The caucus included Shirley Chisholm of Brooklyn, who became the first African American woman elected to Congress (1968) and a presidential candidate (1972),

VOTE ON WOMAN SUFFRAGE IN NEW YORK STATE, BY COUNTY, 1915 AND 1917

	1915			1917		
	Yes	No	% in Favor	Yes	No	% in Favor
Albany	12,263	23,604	34.2	15,026	21,375	41.3
Allegany	3,851	4,372	46.8	4,172	3,248	56.2
Bronx	34,307	40,991	45.6	52,660	36,346	59.2
Broome	8,022	7,607	51.3	9,449	6,861	57.9
Cattaraugus	5,319	6,338	45.6	6,744	4,943	57.7
Cayuga	4,467	5,870	43.2	5,587	5,160	52.0
Chautauqua	9,887	7,086	58.3	9,448	5,784	62.0
Chemung	6,371	5,910	51.9	5,684	6,517	46.6
Chenango	3,358	3,802	46.9	3,473	2,682	56.4
Clinton	2,657	4,126	39.2	2,985	3,657	44.9
Columbia	2,030	5,610	26.6	3,099	4,658	40.0
Cortland	2,822	2,848	49.8	3,644	2,564	58.7
Delaware	4,242	5,701	42.7	5,224	4,492	53.8
Dutchess	6,839	10,220	40.1	6,207	6,817	47.7
Erie	25,669	36,491	41.3	31,952	27,617	53.6
Essex	2,853	3,433	45.4	2,891	2,869	50.2
Franklin	2,113	3,136	40.3	2,125	2,265	48.4
Fulton	3,145	3,561	46.9	3,785	3,654	50.9
Genesee	3,027	3,453	46.7	3,076	3,065	50.1
Greene	2,264	3,999	36.2	2,834	3,305	46.2
Hamilton	464	663	41.2	453	541	45.6
Herkimer	3,819	5,182	42.4	4,835	5,348	47.5
Jefferson	5,648	9,476	37.3	6,442	8,822	42.2
Kings	87,402	121,679	41.8	129,601	92,315	58.4
Lewis	1,604	3,768	29.9	2,120	3,235	39.6
Livingston	2,320	3,934	37.1	1,655	2,967	35.8
Madison	3,776	5,188	42.1	4,171	3,988	51.1
Monroe	18,297	24,843	42.4	18,362	22,428	45.0
Montgomery	3,661	4,642	44.1	4,208	4,520	48.2
Nassau	7,097	8,295	46.1	8,008	5,848	57.8
New York	88,886	117,610	43.0	129,412	89,124	59.2
Niagara	6,832	9,214	42.6	7,460	7,699	49.2
Oneida	8,891	15,562	36.4	9,487	12,279	43.6
Onondaga	19,190	21,901	46.7	17,877	16,276	52.3
Ontario	4,032	6,603	37.9	4,118	5,731	41.8
Orange	9,433	11,838	44.4	9,064	8,536	51.5
Orleans	2,301	3,201	41.8	2,295	2,804	45.0
Oswego	5,915	6,358	48.2	6,497	5,189	55.6
Otsego	4,205	5,925	41.5	5,268	5,243	50.1
Putnam	1,062	1,441	42.4	1,373	1,119	55.1
Queens	21,395	33,104	39.3	34,125	26,794	56.0
Rensselaer	6,875	11,630	37.2	7,156	9,406	43.2
Richmond	6,108	7,469	45.0	7,868	5,224	60.1
Rockland	3,810	4,559	45.5	4,238	3,735	53.2
St. Lawrence	5,599	7,300	43.4	6,395	8,142	44.0
Saratoga	5,020	7,349	40.6	6,855	5,862	53.9
Schenectady	7,351	6,006	55.0	6,955	5,628	55.3
Schoharie	2,061	3,540	36.8	2,501	3,067	44.9
Schuyler	1,413	1,918	42.4	1,576	1,725	47.7
Seneca	2,139	3,346	39.0	2,376	3,016	44.1
Steuben	7,226	9,740	42.6	6,760	6,866	49.6
Suffolk	7,219	8,962	44.6	7,188	5,746	55.6
Sullivan	2,415	4,992	32.6	3,351	3,775	47.0
Tioga	1,945	2,573	43.1	1,909	1,795	51.5
Tompkins	3,266	3,157	50.9	3,739	2,410	60.8
Ulster	5,035	10,099	33.3	5,769	9,447	37.9
Warren	2,297	4,369	34.5	3,147	3,156	49.9
Washington	4,138	5,456	43.1	4,821	4,573	51.3
Wayne	3,508	6,700	34.4	4,086	5,827	41.2
Westchester	20,165	23,930	45.7	25,340	17,284	59.5
Wyoming	2,622	3,981	39.7	2,759	3,160	46.6
Yates	1,410	2,671	34.6	1,444	2,247	39.1
Total	553,358[a]	748,332	42.5	703,129	600,776	53.9

Sources: Manual for the Use of the Legislature of the State of New York (1916); *New York Red Book* (1918).

[a]Total given in sources is 553,348.

and Bella Abzug, an outspoken activist for social justice who served three terms in the House of Representatives (1970–76). In 1974 Betty Bone Schiess of Syracuse was one of the first women ordained as an Episcopal priest, and Mary Anne Krupsak was New York State's first female lieutenant governor (1975–78).

During the 1970s feminism became increasingly diverse, with the formation of such groups as Coalition of Labor Union Women (CLUW) and the National Black Feminist Caucus. Lesbians became vocal, as did women with disabilities and survivors of rape, incest, and domestic violence. All of these groups found a voice in 1976 in Houston, Tex, where a conference ended the International Year of Women with runners carrying a torch from Seneca Falls, symbolizing how modern feminism traced its roots back to 19th-century New York State. In 1982 the Women's Rights National Historical Park opened in Seneca Falls.

In the last part of the 20th century, feminist issues such as equal pay, access to education and jobs, domestic partnerships and same-sex marriages, contraception and abortion, domestic violence, child daycare, and parental leave became part of mainstream political debates. New state laws strengthened penalties for sexual assault, assisted women and minority business owners, improved childcare, created programs relating to breast cancer and family healthcare, and helped save abandoned babies by giving amnesty to mothers who left them at the appropriate institutions. NOW-NYS, the largest women's political action organization in the state, had 24 chapters representing over 14,000 members.

In 2000, New Yorkers elected former first lady Hillary Rodham Clinton as the state's first female US senator, but overall the state ranked only 38 in the nation for women elected to public office. Nevertheless, politically active women were well organized, and a Legislative Women's Caucus consisted of all the female members of the New York State legislature, while the New York State Women's Advisory Council operated from the governor's office. Think tanks such as the Center for Women and Government, the Civil Society at SUNY Albany, and the Institute for Women and Work at Cornell University focused on women's issues.

See also DIVORCE; SUFFRAGE; WORLD WAR II.

Biemer, Linda. *Women and Property in Colonial New York: The Transition from Dutch to English Law, 1643–1727* (Ann Arbor, Mich: UMI Research Press, 1983)

Cott, Nancy, ed. *No Small Courage: A History of Women in the United States* (New York: Oxford Univ Press, 2000)

Flexner, Eleanor. *Century of Struggle*, 2d ed. (New York: Atheneum, 1968)

Narrett, David E. *Inheritance and Family Life in Colonial New York City* (Ithaca: Cornell Univ Press, 1992)

Rosen, Ruth. *The World Split Open: How the Modern Women's Movement Changed America* (New York: Viking, 2000)

Wellman, Judith. *The Road to Seneca Falls: Elizabeth Cady Stanton and the First Woman's Rights Convention* (Urbana: Univ of Illinois Press, 2004)

Judith Wellman

Wood, Fernando (*b* Philadelphia, 14 June 1812; *d* Hot Springs, Ark, 14 Feb 1881). Mayor and congressman. Wood was the son of a merchant, and his family moved to New York City in 1821.

At 13 he left school and began a business career. He aligned with the Democratic Party and became a member of Tammany Hall in 1836. In 1840 he was elected to the House of Representatives and served one term. From 1842 to 1847, he was dispatch agent for the Port of New York. Wood returned to politics and was elected mayor of New York City in 1854 and reelected in 1856. His measures to improve public services made him popular with the working class, but his reforms of the Police Department angered Tammany Hall and the Republican-controlled state legislature. In 1857 the legislature revised the municipal charter to limit his power, and Tammany Hall abandoned him. Wood lost the mayoral election that year, but he formed a rival Democratic Party organization, Mozart Hall, in 1858. With the help of Mozart Hall and support from Irish and German immigrant communities, he was elected mayor in 1859. Wood openly defended slavery, and in early 1861 his pro-southern leanings led him to urge the Common Council to declare New York City a "free city" and to secede from the state so that merchants could continue their profitable trade with southern states. He was defeated in his mayoral bid in 1861. Throughout the Civil War, he remained a Peace Democrat. He returned to the House of Representatives (1863–65, 1867–81).

Mushkat, Jerome. *Fernando Wood: A Political Biography* (Kent, Ohio: Kent State Univ Press, 1990)

Pleasants, Samuel Augustus. *Fernando Wood of New York* (New York: Columbia Univ Press, 1948)

Thomas D. Beal

Wood, Jethro (*b* ?Dartmouth, Mass, 16 Mar 1774; *d* Ledyard, Cayuga Co, 18 Sept 1834). Inventor. Possibly born in White Creek (Washington Co) where his Quaker family moved prior to 1783, he established a successful farm near Scipio (Cayuga Co) in 1800. Wood, who tinkered with plows from early childhood, received his first plow patent in 1814. On 1 Sept 1819 he was granted a patent for a cast-iron plow featuring curved moldboard and interchangeable parts, with advantages of balance, strength, durability, light weight, and low cost over existing iron plows. Wood began manufacture this same year in Moravia (Cayuga Co), but competing firms took advantage of weak national patent laws to avoid royalty payments. As a result litigation during the 14 years of the original patent and one 14-year extension impoverished Wood and his eldest son, who won a favorable decision in federal circuit court in Albany in 1845 but died soon thereafter. Wood's daughters failed in several efforts to gain renewed rights or substantial relief from Congress. The inventor was hailed by Wood family counsel William H. Seward and others as the country's greatest unrewarded benefactor; his invention was among the most significant agricultural innovations of the 19th century.

Gilbert, Frank. *Jethro Wood, Inventor of the Modern Plow* (Chicago: Rhodes & McClure, 1882)

Gerard T. Koeppel

Woodbury. Locality (pop 9,010) in Oyster Bay (Nassau Co). A post office opened in 1836 but moved to West Hills (Suffolk Co) four years later; the present post office opened in 1858. Walt Whitman taught in the local school in 1837–38. Turn-of-the-century estate builders included Andrew Mellon, whose property is now a town golf course. After World War II farms and estates were subdivided for housing. Population has continued to grow; in the 1980s and 1990s the increase was about 1,000 per decade. In the early 21st century there is considerable commercial development, but some farms remain.

Richard A. Winsche

Woodbury. Town (pop 9,460) in SE Orange Co. The town was formed in 1889 from Monroe. The Erie Railroad (1866) ran through Woodbury. Tomás Estrada Palma (1832–1908), first president of Cuba, operated a boarding school for Cuban boys at Central Valley from 1890 to 1902. Arden House (1905), the home of railroad magnate E. H. Harriman (1848–1909), overlooks the Ramapo Valley. Hall fishing line (1850–1940s) and the Leonard fly fishing rod (1880s–1960s) were manufactured in town. Woodbury's greatest change occurred when the New York State Thruway (1954) was built through town, making it readily accessible to the metropolitan area by automobile. The Thruway also attracted Woodbury Common Premium Outlets (1985) at Central Valley, which draws 11 million visitors annually.

Alan Hunter

wood chemical industry. During the 19th century the wood chemical industry in New York State produced wood chemicals including potassium carbonate (potash) and charcoal, the principal fuel in metal smelting. Wood was piled and burned and the ashes passed through water to recover the potash, a key ingredient in soap. To make charcoal, wood was covered with soil, restricting air intake during burning; after extinguishing the fire charcoal remained. Other useful wood acids were discovered in the gases discharged during a wood fire. A flourishing industry developed in the Catskill Mountains, where useful hardwoods including maple, ash, and beech were readily available. Trees were cut to 4 ft (1.2 m) lengths and hauled to an acid wood factory, where the wood was then "cooked" in large retorts. Gases and accompanying water vapor from the cooking wood were captured, distilled, and refined to create wood alcohol, acetic acid, and other chemicals. At the industry's height during the late 19th century, an estimated 190,000 cords of wood were consumed each year and 3,000 men employed in over 100 plants in Delaware and Sullivan Cos. The acid wood industry declined after the 1930s because of the development of synthetic chemicals as substitutes for chemicals produced from wood as a raw material. Forests for acid wood were cut over often every 20 years, but following the decline of the industry the multiple clear-cuts ceased. Today the forests of the Catskills have regrown many fine stands of maple, birch, cherry, oak, and other species.

Myers, F. D. *The Wood Chemical Industry in the Delaware Valley* (Middletown, NY: Prior King Press, 1986)

Panshin, A. J., E. S. Harrar, W. J. Baker, and P. B. Proctor. *Forest Products: Their Sources, Production, and Utilization* (New York: McGraw-Hill, 1950)

Hugh O. Canham

Wood Creek (22.4 mi/36.1 km). Flowing west from what is now Rome (Oneida Co) into Oneida Lake, Wood Creek represented an important link in the chain of inland waterways connecting the Hudson River and the Great Lakes. In spite of its narrow, twisting channel and generally low water level, its clay-lined bed was free of large rocks and supported boat navigation during the 18th and early 19th centuries. Without Wood Creek, travelers heading west on the Mohawk River would have faced 30 miles (48 km) of difficult, overland portage to reach Oneida Lake and the network of rivers entering Lake Ontario at Oswego. The Western Inland Lock Navigation Co improved passage in 1793 by removing fallen trees and making cuts across 13 of the many sharp meanders, shortening its length by more than 7 miles (11 km). Improvements were made again in 1802–3 with the construction of four mini-canals in the upper shallows of the creek. The changes made the creek navigable for the large capacity Durham boats and preserved the viability of navigation between Albany and the Great Lakes in the era before the Erie Canal. In a 1794 treaty of questionable legality, the Oneida Indians ceded much of the Wood Creek area to New York State.

Schuyler, Philip, and William Weston. "Report of the Directors of the Western and Northern Inland Lock Navigation Companies" (1796). In *Publications of the Buffalo Historical Society*, vol 2 (Buffalo: Bigelow Brothers, 1880)

Philip L. Lord Jr

Woodhull. Town (pop 1,524) in S central Steuben Co. Settled in 1804, the town was formed from Troupsburg and Addison in 1828. Lumbering was succeeded by farming and ultimately by dairying, with some emphasis on tobacco and hops. The town's first cheese factory was built in 1874. Golden Age Cheese Co, begun in 1895, was by 2002 the state's largest independently owned cheese factory. The Village of Woodhull was incorporated in 1899 but dissolved in 1987. Natural gas was discovered in the town in 1938, and the Municipal Gas Co formed in 1949. In 2002 Woodhull was the site of both stock-car racing at Woodhull Raceway (1999) and the Kwan-Yin Zen Buddhist Temple. As of 2003 Dominion Transmission, formerly Municipal Gas, operated a large natural gas storage field and a compressor station in the town.

Virginia L. Wright and Jerry Wright

Woodhull, Nathaniel (*b* Mastic, Suffolk Co, 30 Dec 1722; *d* New Utrecht, Kings Co, 20 Sept 1776). Revolutionary War officer. After service in the French and Indian War, Woodhull entered politics, representing Suffolk Co in the assembly (1769–75). He opposed British economic and political policy, and became a member of the local Committee of Correspondence in 1774. Woodhull represented Suffolk at New York's provincial congress in May 1775 and served as its president from August 1775 to July 1776. In the face of imminent British invasion, Woodhull, a brigadier general and commander of the Suffolk and Queens Co militias, was given the assignment of driving livestock and carting provisions from the western parts of the island. On 27 August he was captured by a unit of Light Dragoons near Jamaica (Queens Co). The wounds he suffered at his capture became gangrenous and he died in a hospital set up in New Utrecht. He became the subject of myth making; it was alleged that the fatal wound was deliberately inflicted after his capture.

Cartelli, A. "The Murder of Nathaniel Woodhull," *Long Island Forum* 70 (Spring 1997): 25–33

Richard F. Welch

Woodmere. Locality (pop 16,447) in Hempstead (Nassau Co). When the Rockaway Branch Railroad came through in 1869, Samuel Wood purchased farms on Brower's Point, surveyed streets, and built the Woodsburgh Pavilion, a hotel. The railroad station and post office (1873) were named Woodsburgh, but the post office was changed to Hewlett's in 1888. When a new post office was created near Woodsburgh station in 1897 both were designated Woodmere. In 1901 New York City investor Robert Burton demolished the hotel and subdivided 300 acres (121 ha) into smaller building lots. Although Woodmere has never incorporated, it grew after World War II to be the most populous locality of the Five Towns. Film producer David Brown and designer Donna Karan grew up in Woodmere.

John A. Hewlett

Woodridge. Village (pop 902) in Fallsburg (Sullivan Co). The Ontario and Western Railway came through in 1871, and a post office named Centreville was established in the same year. Its resort industry grew with railroad access, becoming predominantly Jewish around 1900. The first synagogue was founded in 1903. Many of the year-round residents were also Jewish and were employed in support services for the local resorts, such as laundry, meat cutting, dairy, and insurance. The village was incorporated in 1911 and began to decline when the railroad ceased operation in 1953. Today it consists of just a handful of businesses. It has a large year-round Orthodox Jewish population that swells considerably in the summer and through growth has displaced older African American and Latino populations.

John Conway

Woodsburgh. Village (pop 831) in Hempstead (Nassau Co). One of the wholly residential villages in the Five Towns, Woodsburgh was originally called Brower's Point. It incorporated in 1912, and by 1940 it reached a population of 702. Movie mogul William Fox lived in Woodsburgh from 1917 until his death in 1952. His estate, Fox Hall, complete with movie theatre and lakeside guest cottages, faced the Woodmere Golf Club, which occupies the southern third of the village. A local landmark is the monument Abraham Hewlett erected in 1888 to Culluloo Telewana (*d* 1818), whom Hewlett believed to be the last of the Rockaway Indians.

John A. Hewlett

Woodstock. Town (pop 6,241) in N Ulster Co. Settled in 1762 by Palatine German tenants of Robert Livingston, the town was formed from Hurley in 1787; the Zena district, settled by Kingston Dutch *ca* 1720, was annexed in 1879. Located in the eastern Catskill Mountains, Woodstock benefited in the 18th and 19th centuries from the extraction of natural resources such as fur and timber. Local industries included glassmaking (1809–54) and tanning. Irish immigrants quarried bluestone from the 1840s until about 1900. By the late 19th century, when the mountains around Woodstock had been logged off and the land was found to be good only for grazing, the region had already developed a tourist industry.

Initially, Woodstock owed its popularity among tourists to nearby Overlook Mountain, which offers stunning views of the Catskills and Hudson River valley. Thomas Cole, who climbed Overlook Mountain in 1846, helped create interest in the region just as railroads and steamboats made the Catskills more accessible to tourists. The Ulster and Delaware Railroad reached nearby West Hurley in 1870, and a hotel, the Overlook Mountain House, opened atop the mountain in 1871, operating until 1929. In the first decade of the 20th century Woodstock began to attract artist colonies. In 1903 the Byrdcliffe Arts Colony opened, first as a summer painting school and later offering year-round instruction in decorative design, furniture making, metalworking, weaving, and pottery. With the success of the Byrdcliffe school, the Art Students League of New York in 1906 opened a summer landscape painting school in the center of the hamlet. Its students linked Woodstock to the New York City art world, but the use of nude models by the Art Students League caused a stir in Woodstock and beyond. Rifts developed over theories of social reform and matters of control, and artists left the original two schools to form new art schools and colonies. One such colony, the Maverick, developed in the next decade into another important center of the arts in Woodstock, becoming famous for its lively and bohemian summer festivals (1915–31) and outdoor concerts. By the 1920s the performing arts began attracting tourists to Woodstock, and the Woodstock Playhouse opened in 1929. Art galleries, restaurants, hotels, and other businesses followed.

The art colony experienced new life in the mid-1940s. The town also began to be a summer residence for city dwellers. In the 1960s Woodstock's reputation for summer revelry attracted folk and rock musicians. In 1966 Bob Dylan moved to Woodstock after a motorcycle accident. Dylan's *Basement Tapes* were recorded in Woodstock, as was the Band's 1968 album, *Music from Big Pink,* which paid tribute to their Woodstock residence in its title. Dylan's manager, Albert Grossman, moved to Woodstock and in 1969 opened Bearsville Studios at Bearsville. Paul Butterfield, Tim Hardin, and Jimi Hendrix also moved there, and Woodstock became a popular gathering place for musicians. If the 1969 Woodstock Art and Music Fair brought the town international recognition, it is also something of a misnomer. Organized by Woodstock Ventures, a group of young men with ties to the local music community, the concert was actually held in Bethel (Sullivan Co), some 45 miles (72 km) away, because no site in Woodstock could accommodate the crowds. Woodstock remains an active arts community and is a popular tourist destination known for live music and theater, art galleries, restaurants, summer festivals, and boutiques. It has also become a significant weekend and summer retreat for New York City residents. The Byrdcliffe Theatre offers summer performances, as does the Maverick Concert Hall and the newly rebuilt Woodstock Playhouse. The Bearsville Theater provides year-round concerts and performances.

Evers, Alf. *Woodstock: History of an American Town* (Woodstock, NY: Overlook Press, 1987)

Randal Angiel

Woodstock Festival. The Woodstock Music and Arts Fair held 15–18 Aug 1969, did not take place in Woodstock (Ulster Co) and was not a music and arts fair. It was instead an unprecedented phenomenon that has become an icon for the 1960s. Four New Yorkers in their 20s—an unlikely coalition of two wealthy young investors, John Roberts and Joel Rosenman, and two representatives of a new generation of equally young rock entrepreneurs, Arthur Kornfeld and Michael Lang—formed Woodstock Ventures to sponsor a huge weekend rock and roll festival near the Town of Woodstock, home to the already legendary Bob Dylan. The intended Woodstock site and a substitute in nearby Wallkill (Orange Co) were not possible once local people learned what was planned. At the last moment, dairy farmer Max Yasgur, offered a 600-acre (240 ha) site on his farm in Bethel (Sullivan Co).

A team of professionals in their mid- to late 20s, all solidly grounded in the rock festival business, worked feverishly to prepare, merging communal hippie kitchens in the woods and logistics drawn from US Army field manuals. Security was directed by a retired California policeman and provided largely by the Hog Farm, a commune from New Mexico. The flood of converging young people, however, swelled so far beyond expectations that all preparations were overwhelmed. Rte 17B leading to Bethel quickly became a 13 mi (21 km) parking lot. "The situation is hopeless," one state trooper reported, "and getting worse." Nearly 500,000 people arrived, making for, at that point, the largest mass entertainment event in history. All attempts to collect tickets and charge the audience soon ceased, although the promoters more than made back their initial investments through subsequent repackagings of the Woodstock experience.

Drawn by a constellation of more than 30 top musicians and bands—ranging from Joan Baez, Arlo Guthrie, and Ravi Shankar to Jefferson Airplane, the Who, Sly and the Family Stone, Richie Havens, Janis Joplin, Jimi Hendrix, and Santana—attendees also sought something more. After a decade of conflict with parents, teachers, and neighbors about hair, drugs, sex, race relations, urban crisis, and the war in Vietnam, young people were drawn by advertisements promising a pastoral retreat for youth: "Three Days of Peace and Music." What they found was more urban than pastoral, an intragenerational stream of diversity, from hippies to teenyboppers to clean-cut suburban collegians to bikers and rockers and Hell's Angels. The environment rapidly presented a free-form museum of urban problems: litter and garbage, disintegrating communications, water and food shortages, and inadequate sewage and healthcare facilities. Looming in the shadows was the specter of violence, all too familiar after the "long hot summers" of the 1960s. But instead, a remarkable ethic of mutuality took hold. Voices from the state urged calm and tolerance. Exhilarated by the sight of 500,000 filling the natural hillside amphitheater, the young people rose to the challenge, sharing scarce food with strangers, shepherding those freaking out on bad drug trips, gathering in the rising tide of garbage, and linking themselves into chains of volunteer workers.

As the festival closed, with an enigmatic solo version of the "Star-Spangled Banner" by Jimi Hendrix, the image of Woodstock was already contested. For local residents, it had been a great nuisance and confirmed the less than flattering views that many had of the new youth culture. For many outsiders, the initial reaction was often somewhat hysterical. The *New York Times,* in an editorial 18 Aug 1969, observed that the "dreams of marijuana and rock music" that drew concert-goers to Woodstock "had little more sanity than the impulses that drive the lemmings to march to their deaths in the sea." But different images soon prevailed. As the world came to appreciate the triumph over chaos, Woodstock's diverse cultural mix and complexity of interdependence came quickly to be celebrated as what the *Times* editorial on 19 Aug 1969 then called "essentially a phenomenon of innocence." More broadly, Woodstock soon came to represent the cultural and political potential for an energized and connected youth culture, a Woodstock Nation, as proclaimed in the title of a popular book by Abbie Hoffman, released several months after the festival. And when a youth was murdered by Hell's Angels motorcycle gang members entrusted with security at another outdoor event only months later (the Rolling Stones concert in Altamont, Calif) Woodstock became remembered as a temporary Garden of Eden inhabited by a dreamy flower-child youth culture soon to face reality. In the song "Woodstock," which became a Woodstock Nation anthem, Joni Mitchell sang, "We've got to get ourselves back to the Garden." An Academy Award–winning documentary, *Woodstock* (1970), helped solidify and perpetuate the notions of the festival as a peak moment of the decade's wistful effort to achieve "peace, love, and understanding."

But Joni Mitchell had not been there, and for most of those who had been present, the real experience of Woodstock was not one of innocence or naïveté, but rather one of struggle, process, and challenge. The threat of chaos and the music-mediated response of strangers linked by self-discipline and collective self-help served to create a political, cultural, and musical generational community where none had quite existed. As process, Woodstock helped to crystallize and fuse the values of culture, politics, and community at the core of generational change in the 1960s. The festival also revealed how dependent this vision was on extraordinary circumstances: how hard it was for the same unity, struggle, and spirit to survive without confrontation, whether that confrontation involved the emergency of food and healthcare at Woodstock or the government's policy on the war in Vietnam.

The generational innocence story seemed confirmed by anniversary festivals organized by promoters of the original Woodstock Festival and held in Saugerties (Ulster Co) in 1994, and at the former Griffiss Air Force Base in Rome (Oneida Co) in 1999. The events presented some similar challenges: overwhelmed facilities, sewage and filth, and uncontrollable crowds. But at Woodstock '99 violence erupted as marauding youths set fires and vandalized and looted the premises. The disaster provided instant confirmation-by-contrast for those still focused on either celebrating or condemning the generation of the 1960s. Almost lost in such debate was the real lesson of the original Woodstock—a lesson not about facile generational images, but about how imposed emergencies can bring the best out of people, creating community and potentially profound social, cultural, and political change in the process.

Frisch, Michael. "Woodstock and Altamont." In *True Stories from the American Past,* ed. William Graebner (New York: McGraw-Hill, 1993)
Makower, Joel. *Woodstock: The Oral History* (New York: Doubleday, 1989)
Pilpel, Robert, Joel Rosenman, and John Roberts. *Young Men with Unlimited Capital* (1974; repr New York: Bantam Books, 1989)
Samuels, David. "Rock Is Dead (Woodstock 1999)," *Harper's Magazine,* Nov 1999

Michael Frisch

Woolworth, Frank W(infield) (*b* Rodman, Jefferson Co, 13 Apr 1852; *d* Glen Cove, Nassau Co, 8 Apr 1919). Businessman. Woolworth attended business classes in Watertown and was clerking at a small grocery when he introduced a profitable counter selling 5-cent goods. On 22 Feb 1879 he opened a 5-cent store in Utica. This store failed, but four months later, on 21 June 1879, he introduced a five-and-ten-cent store to Lancaster, Pa. The success of this venture led Woolworth and his partners to open a chain of similar stores in Pennsylvania and New York. On 16 Oct 1886 he opened a store in Elmira in partnership with Earl Northrup. In 1886 Woolworth transferred his executive office to Manhattan, where F. W. Woolworth and Co was incorporated on 15 Dec 1911. In 1913 headquarters moved to the new Gothic-style Woolworth Building at 233 Broadway. At Woolworth's death in 1919, there were 1,057 Woolworth stores in North America and 175 in Great Britain. The Woolworth Building, at 792 feet (241.4 m) the tallest building in the world until 1930, is a historic landmark. The Woolworth stores closed in 1997, and the company, renamed Foot Locker in 2001, operates a chain of athletic specialty stores.

Brough, James. *The Woolworths* (New York: McGraw-Hill, 1982)
Nichols, John P. *Skyline Queen and the Merchant Prince: The Woolworth Story* (New York: Trident Press, 1973)

R. Jake Sudderth

Worcester. Town (pop 2,207) in SE Otsego Co. Settled ?1787–88, the town was formed from Cherry Valley in 1797. After the Albany and Susquehanna Railroad (1865; later Delaware and Hudson Railroad) opened the town to markets, the town grew rapidly, its population peaking at 2,741 in 1890. Worcester's small factories produced paper, chairs, and shirts. Hops were produced in quantity until the 1910s and were succeeded by potatoes and finally by dairying. Slovenians came to town before World War I. By the early 1950s workers commuted to Cobleskill (Schoharie Co) or Schenectady; out-of-town work was encouraged by the 1979–80 completion of I-88 through the town. The Worcester Creameries Co (1970) tests and ships milk from area dairy farms. The hamlet of Worcester is a National Register historic district and includes the Smith and Swarthout Building (1884) and Wieting Opera House (1909).

Hugh C. MacDougall

workers' compensation. In 1910 New York State passed the nation's first law guaranteeing partial wages and money for medical expenses to workers injured on the job in a range of occupations. The measure mandated payment of half wages to such workers whether they had been negligent, their employers had been negligent, or any person could be directly blamed for an accident. Before 1910 injured workers had only limited rights when they sued for damages caused by employer negligence. From the 1840s New York State courts had allowed employers many common-law defenses against liability for worker injuries; the smallest amount of negligence by a worker involved in an accident invalidated a worker's claim for compensation, even in the face of overwhelming employer negligence. Courts hearing negligence suits also gave rights to owners of business property but denied them to injured workers. In cases of coach or ship collisions, the state's courts awarded damages to the vehicle or vessel owners in proportion to the negligence of each driver or captain; the courts also awarded damages to railroad passengers hurt in train wrecks caused by the negligence of a railroad employee but denied damages to other employees injured by the same negligent act.

By the early 20th century these double standards had convinced many workers as well as business owners, academics, and politicians that the laws were unjust. Reformers concluded that business enterprises could afford to treat injured workers more fairly. Some also believed that workers' compensation programs would prevent blue-collar workers from listening to socialist politicians who proclaimed capitalism incapable of treating workers fairly. In 1909 Gov Charles Evans Hughes appointed a special commission that investigated industrial accidents in the state and drafted the 1910 law. Chaired by Jonathan M. Wainwright, a Republican state senator from Westchester Co, the committee drew on the talents of its secretary, Crystal Eastman, a democratic socialist lawyer, and Columbia University economist Henry R. Seager to draft the legislation. Seager and Eastman spoke at New York City labor union meetings to explain the advantages of workers' compensation to workers suspicious of reform proposals supported by business owners, and by June 1910 most labor groups in the state, including the state chapter of the American Federation of Labor (AFL), backed the measure.

In 1911 the New York State Court of Appeals declared the compensation law in violation of the due process clauses of the New York and US Constitutions and therefore unconstitutional. Within another two years, however, the state legislature passed and voters ratified a constitutional amendment making workers' compensation legal. In 1914 the legislature passed a law giving injured workers more generous benefits—the basic compensation scale at the time was 66% of lost wages—and created a state insurance fund to offer employers low-cost insurance for their workers' compensation liabilities. This fund competed with private insurance companies for the business of employers. The 1914 law also created the Industrial Commission (from 1971, the Workers' Compensation Board), which held hearings to determine the amount of compensation due injured workers and achieved nationwide fame for administrative excellence. The state's pioneering workers' compensation laws enacted between 1911 and 1917 cost the typical employer three times as much as it had formerly paid for casualty insurance or in direct payments to injured workers.

During the 1920s the Industrial Commission, under the leadership of Frances Perkins, led the nation in developing vocational rehabilitation programs for injured industrial workers. In 1922 the legislature authorized compensation payments to workers who contracted some occupational diseases, including anthrax and poisoning by metal, acid, alcohol, and formaldehyde. Willful self-injuries or those resulting from intoxication were specifically exempted from coverage.

Full-time, though not part-time, domestic workers won coverage in 1962. At the beginning of the 21st century, agricultural workers also enjoy coverage, and the compensation law addresses a much wider range of occupational diseases. These include silicosis, suffered by quarry workers who inhale silica dust, and byssinosis, or brown lung disease, affecting textile workers who inhale hemp, flax, or cotton fibers. Injured workers receive all their medical expenses and, while disabled, 66% of their wages, up to $400 a week or $20,000 a year. An official hears complaints by injured workers who disagree with rulings of the Workers' Compensation Board.

Page, Joseph A., and Mary-Win O'Brien. *Bitter Wages: Ralph Nader's Study Group Report on Disease and Injury on the Job* (New York: Grossman Publishers, 1973)

Yellowitz, Irwin. *Labor and the Progressive Movement in New York State, 1897–1916* (Ithaca: Cornell Univ Press, 1965)

Robert Asher

workers' education. In the early 1920s, trade unionists and pro-labor intellectuals launched "labor colleges" across the United States, aiming to strengthen the labor movement by training working men and women to think, speak, and write confidently about problems they faced as individuals and union members. The movement was particularly strong in New York State. Brookwood Labor College was organized in 1921 on a 53-acre (21 ha) site near Katonah (Westchester Co) and offered a two-year residential program along with shorter summer institutes and conferences. Rochester Labor College, also founded in 1921, with the endorsement of 15 unions and the city's AFL Central Labor Council, offered classes, lectures, and choral and dramatic clubs to the city's workers. Unions and the Industrial YWCA, a division serving industrial workers, also offered workers' education classes during the 1920s in Syracuse, Poughkeepsie, Mount Vernon (Erie Co), Yonkers, and Buffalo. New York City was the headquarters of the Workers' Education Bureau, an umbrella organization of labor colleges around the country and programs organized by the International Ladies' Garment Workers' Union (ILGWU), the Presbyterian Labor Temple, and the New York branch of the Women's Trade Union League, an organization of working women and their pro-union women allies.

Over its 16-year history, Brookwood, which called itself "labor's own school," offered college-level courses in history, economics, sociology (or "social problems"), English and journalism, union organization, and dramatics to about 450 students, about one-quarter of whom were from New York State. Particularly in the early years, most of the miners, machinists, clothing workers, textile workers, railroaders, and others who attended had left regular school in the early grades to work full time as industrial workers. Although Brookwood offered no credits or degrees, its program was highly praised by academics, writers, and other intellectuals, many of whom visited the school and gave lectures. In his book *The Goose-Step: A Study of American Education* (1923), Upton Sinclair described Brookwood as "a place where the true spirit of comradeship prevails, where men and women, middle-aged and young, consecrate themselves with fervor, and also with fun, to the service of freedom and social justice." Sinclair Lewis stayed at the school for several weeks in 1929 as part of his research on a planned (but never completed) novel about labor. Brookwood's one- to three-week summer institutes, begun in 1924, centered on problems facing workers in specific industries, such as railroads or textiles. The school also held pathbreaking conferences in 1927 and 1930 on black workers in industry, the labor movement, and workers' education. Brookwood graduates included many who became well known in the labor movement, among them Rose Pesotta, a vice president of the ILGWU and an organizer of the Congress of Industrial Organizations (CIO), Roy Reuther, one of the three Reuther brothers who helped found the United Automobile Workers and served in its leadership for a generation, and Len DeCaux, the editor of *CIO News* from 1935 to 1947.

Rochester's workers' education activities were spearheaded by the Amalgamated Clothing Workers of America (ACW), which had some 13,000 members in 9 locals in the city in 1920. Paul Blanshard, a former minister and union organizer, was ACW education director in Rochester during the 1920s and organized a course in Principles of Unionism for every new union member. The union also held Friday night forums attended by an average audience of 1,000–1,500 weekly, in part by providing child-care for up to 150 children. Rochester Labor College brought the ACW together with other unions to offer a program of classes in labor unionism, public speaking, English, and social problems, taught by local college professors and public school teachers.

Residential summer schools for women workers were another important component of the workers' education movement. Hilda Worthington Smith, a native of West Park (Ulster Co), directed the first of these programs, Bryn Mawr Summer School for Women Workers in Industry (established 1921) at Bryn Mawr College in Pennsylvania. In 1929 Smith launched a winter residential program, Vineyard Shore School for Women Workers, on the grounds of her family home. This small program (14–15 students per year) ran for four years until depression conditions forced it to close. Smith was a neighbor and friend of Franklin and Eleanor Roosevelt, and from 1933 to 1942, she headed workers' education programs under the Federal Emergency Relief Administration and Works Progress Administration.

Workers' education programs suffered severe financial problems and declined in New York and elsewhere during the mid- to late 1930s. However, in 1945 New York became the first of 46 states to establish a state-sponsored labor education program, the New York State School of Industrial and Labor Relations at Cornell University (NYSSILR). Recognizing the arrival into full legitimacy of the labor movement, the ILR School, as it was known, offered training programs for unionists in collective bargaining, labor law, labor history, and other subjects. In addition, SUNY Empire State College established an accredited Labor Studies Center in 1971, renamed the Harry Van Arsdale Jr Center for Labor Studies in 1986 and popularly known as the Labor College, offering associate, bachelor's, and master's degrees. These institutions, along with educational programs offered by New York's unions and independent allied organizations, continue the spirit of the 1920s workers' education pioneers.

Bloom, Jon. *189 at 75: The Voice of Labor Educators* (Katonah, NY: Brookwood Labor College, 1997)

Rohfeld, Rae Wahl. *Breaking New Ground: The Development of Adult and Workers' Education in North America* (Syracuse: Syracuse Univ Kellogg Project, 1990)

Jon Bloom

Working Families Party. Political party formed in June 1998 by union members (especially those representing the Communications Workers of America, the United Automobile Workers, the Teamsters, various teacher and transportation unions, and the Association of Community Organizations for Reform Now [ACORN]) and activists seeking to advance a liberal pro-union political agenda. The party gained official party status after statewide elections of 1998 in which it cross-endorsed the Democratic candidate for governor. The party backs candidates who support economic issues favorable to workers, such as increasing the minimum wage and indexing it to inflation, and promotes issues such as universal healthcare, job growth, creation of a living wage, additional funding for childcare and housing, and investment in public schools. It frequently cross-endorses candidates from both the Democratic and Republican Parties based on the candidate's support for the Working Families platform. In 2000 the party cross-endorsed Al Gore, the Democratic candidate for president. With the demise of the Liberal Party, the Working Families Party has become the most influential left of center political party in the state. Letitia James of Brooklyn, who won a seat on the New York City Council in 2003, is the first person elected to public office solely on the Working Families Party line. The party had a statewide enrollment in 2003 of 19,214, of whom 7,029 were New York City residents.

Sifry, Micah L. *Spoiling for a Fight: Third-Party Politics in America* (New York: Routledge, 2002)

Working Families Party, http://www.workingfamiliesparty.org

John Evers

Workingmen's Assembly of New York State. First state federation of workers in the nation, established in February 1865 at a statewide convention of trade union leaders in Albany. The Trades Assembly of New York State was organized labor's response to the state legislature's proposed 1864 Folger Anti-Strike Bill, which provided for fining and/or imprisoning strikers. In spring 1864 labor unions in major cities across the state held rallies, including 15,000 people at Tompkins Square in New York City, as union delegates in Albany lobbied against the bill. The measure eventually died in the Senate Judiciary Committee, and the victory signaled to state trade union leaders the need for lobbying.

At the first convention in 1865, delegates elected Henry Rockefeller of the Troy Typographical Union as president. In September 1865 the Trades Assembly changed its name to the Workingmen's Assembly of New York State and elected as president John Jacobs of the New York Ship Builders Union; he served until 1867. At the 1869 convention representatives of the New York City Women's Typographical Union No. 1 and Troy's Collar Laundry Union successfully lobbied for an amendment to the assembly's constitution that would allow for women delegates. Throughout the 1870s and 1880s the assembly's president and delegates lobbied the state legislature regarding laws that affected organized labor and the working classes. In 1870 under Pres William J. Jessup of the New York City Ship Builders Union, the assembly secured a bill establishing an eight-hour day for state and county employees. Under George Blair, president from 1874 to 1883, the assembly lobbied for passage of legislation aimed at improving the working conditions for women.

Until 1882 lobbying delegates were those who lived in the Capital District; thereafter, the assembly established a statewide committee for lobbying. State conventions were held in Albany until 1890, when they took place in different parts of the state. The assembly remained committed to labor issues throughout the state, which is reflected in the rotation of the leadership, including Samuel Gompers as president (1886–87), representing many trades. Gompers was able to lobby for enactment of a proposal calling for the inspection of working and health conditions in factories. In 1888 the New York State branch of the American Federation of Labor (AFL) was created, and in 1898 the assembly and the New York AFL merged to create the Workingmen's Federation of the State of New York.

Hurwitz, Howard L. *Theodore Roosevelt and Labor in New York State, 1880–1900* (New York: Columbia Univ Press, 1943)

New York State AFL-CIO. *A Tradition of Leadership: A History of the New York State AFL-CIO* (New York: Author, 1990)

Brian Keough

Working Men's Party. Political party. With universal suffrage for adult white men established in New York State by the late 1820s, both national and local politicians, from Andrew Jackson to those involved with Tammany Hall, began to court the common man. However, some radical factions within the working class believed their concerns were not being addressed directly. In New York City in 1829, a radical journeyman's protest erupted in response to low wages and unemployment. Rumors of a unified effort by large employers to extend the workday to 11 hours circulated throughout the city, and a general strike was anticipated. One of the leaders of this movement was Thomas Skidmore, a machinist, who was profoundly influenced by Thomas Paine and who offered a radical critique of the existing social system and private property in *The Rights of Man to Property!* (1829). At a meeting on 23 Apr 1829, Skidmore urged his fellow mechanics to organize politically for a 10-hour workday and decent wages and working conditions, and also called for the redistribution of property. On 28 Apr 1829 the Committee of Fifty was formed to help strikers and to develop a unified political strategy. By the summer of 1829, it was decided that they would run their own candidates in local elections. A platform was developed that opposed the credit and banking system; sought to abolish licensed auctioneers and imprisonment for debt; and favored taxation for clerics and churches, reform of electoral procedures, and the 10-hour workday. As nonlabor elements joined the movement, some of the more radical ideas about property reform were modified. Symbolic of this change was the involvement of Noah Cooke, a commission merchant.

These activities attracted the attention of other reformers. In 1828 Frances Wright, a writer and lecturer on social issues, and Robert Dale Owen, the son of industrialist and reformer Robert Owen, opened their Hall of Science as a lecture hall and educational facility in a converted church near the Bowery in Manhattan. They began publication of the *Free Enquirer* to disseminate their ideas, chief among them being the power of education to uplift the working class. They were attracted to the budding Working Men's Party but rejected radical property reform. Owen in particular sought to influence the new party. Their associate, George Henry Evans, founded the *Workingman's Advocate* in 1829 as a mouthpiece for the Owen-Wright faction. In October 1829 a compromise between the moderates and radical followers resulted in a ticket of 11 candidates running for seats in the state assembly. In the November election, this new Working Men's Party successfully elected Ebenezer Ford, a carpenter, to the assembly. The moderate Owen-Evans-Cooke faction took over the party shortly thereafter, and Skidmore's ideas were marginalized. He died in the cholera epidemic of 1832. During the 1830s, the Jacksonians and Tammany Hall adopted some of the party's most popular ideas. The Working Men's Party ceased to exist after the early 1830s, but its experiences influenced future labor movements.

Wilentz, Sean. *Chants Democratic: New York City and the Rise of the American Working Class, 1788–1850* (New York: Oxford Univ Press, 1984)

Jennifer Steenshorne

Works Progress Administration (WPA). Federal relief agency created 6 May 1935 to employ people able to work but unable to find jobs. Replacing earlier 1930s employment programs that had focused almost exclusively on the construction industry, the Works Progress Administration (after 1939 the Work Projects Administration) continued to build and improve public facilities and to employ construction workers, while also providing jobs for professional and white-collar workers. In New York State the WPA was administered by two agencies, one covering New York City, the other the rest of the state.

Construction Activities

New York State, with about 10% of the US population and an estimated 37% of its nonfarm workers unemployed in 1932–33, was a major beneficiary of the WPA's construction activities. Of the approximately $1.4 billion the WPA spent in the state, about $1.2 billion was for construction. In Albany the WPA built the Loudonville Reservoir, doubling the city's water supply, and converted an obsolete reservoir to the 20,000-seat Bleecker Stadium. In Buffalo the WPA constructed the Clearwater Reservoir, converted a reservoir to Roesch Memorial Stadium, and modernized the Zoological Gardens. Other New York State projects included the development of Bear Mountain State Park along the Hudson River and Jones Beach and Sunken Meadow State Park on Long Island, and the construction of a bathing beach in Plattsburgh. In New York City the WPA erected or renovated 391 buildings for public use, including fire and police stations, libraries, and hospitals; completed 17 municipal swimming pools; and expanded and renovated beaches and other parks, including Orchard Beach in the Bronx and Jacob Riis Park in Queens. The WPA also assisted with the construction of 13 municipal airports and the improvement of 26 others in the state, including

WPA workers tearing up streetcar tracks on St. Paul St, Rochester.

those in Jamestown, Buffalo, Wainscott, Glens Falls, Syracuse, and a tri-city airport serving Binghamton, Endicott, and Johnson City, and under the New York City WPA, North Beach Airport (now La Guardia Airport). Total WPA expenditures in the state on airports were $68.2 billion. WPA construction projects in New York State and New York City also included water main and sewage facility installations and road construction, including a section of Manhattan's FDR Drive.

Social Programs

The WPA also supplied diverse social services including school lunches, nursery schools, and adult education. A Syracuse program employed 300 teachers offering evening instruction to 15,000 adults, while in Buffalo 300 courses were provided to more than 30,000 students. The New York State WPA also employed 537 nurses, working in 53 cities and 50 rural districts, and supported the Housekeepers' Aides Project to provide emergency assistance to families in need. In New York City WPA social services included preventative medical programs, such as chest X rays and diphtheria immunizations, recreational therapy in hospitals, housekeeping services to the sick and indigent, teaching and library staff for prisons, and free in-school lunches for the poor. The WPA sponsored the building of the Tonawanda Indian Community House, and a special program based in Rochester helped revive interest in Seneca arts and crafts on the Tonawanda and Cattaraugus Reservations, and produced about 5,000 baskets, masks, jewelry, and other crafts, and more than 3,000 watercolor and oil paintings.

Arts Projects

Among the most novel WPA programs were those employing artists: the Federal Art Project (FAP), Federal Music Project (FMP), Federal Theatre Project (FTP), and Federal Writers' Project (FWP). While the artists' programs received only a small percentage of the funds expended by the WPA and employed relatively few people, they were among the most prominent of the WPA programs. The approximately 250 artists employed in the New York State FAP were scattered throughout the state, with groups in Buffalo, Rochester, Syracuse, Dutchess Co, Westchester Co, Long Island, and the largest number in Woodstock (Ulster Co), the well-known artists' colony. They produced easel paintings, murals, photographs, and prints, typically exhibited in public spaces such as schools, hospitals, and museums. The New York City FAP, which accounted for just under half of FAP expenditures nationwide and received approximately $16.2 billion (compared to the $600,000 expended by the FAP elsewhere in New York State), employed over 2,000 artists. In addition to producing thousands of paintings, prints, and sculptures, the New York City FAP held hundreds of art classes throughout the city, attended by more than 2 million students.

The FMP developed musical groups, especially symphony orchestras, to perform for public audiences. By 1938, 34 FMP-organized or -assisted symphony orchestras, including one each in Buffalo and Syracuse, and two in New York City, employed over 2,500 musicians nationwide. The Buffalo Philharmonic Orchestra was one of the few WPA-assisted orchestras to become a successful, privately supported institution after termination of the WPA. Among New York State FTP projects, the Buffalo Historical Marionettes offered programs for both children and adults, Syracuse had both a popular vaudeville unit and an ambitious legitimate theater company, and there were smaller FTP units in Westchester Co and Long Island, including a critically acclaimed repertory group at the Theatre of the Four Seasons in Roslyn (Nassau Co). Nationwide the FTP employed an average of 10,000 people annually in 33 states. In May 1936 more than 5,300 individuals were employed in the New York City FTP compared to just over 450 elsewhere in the state. The concentration of FTP employment in New York City, Chicago, and Los Angeles, as well as congressional concern over the political leanings of many of its productions and performers, led to termination of the FTP in June 1939. During their existence, the FTP projects in New York City and New York State entertained more than 14 million people.

The major task of FWP employees was the preparation of visitor guidebooks for each state. New York State writers compiled *New York: A Guide to the Empire State* (1940), a reference tool still in use, as is *The New York City Guide* (1939), produced by the New York City FWP. The state program also compiled city and county guides for Dutchess Co, Rochester and Monroe Co, and Warren Co, among others. The Historical Records Survey (HRS) was created as a part of the FWP before becoming an independent project in October 1936. The HRS inventoried, transcribed, and preserved county and town records, and published guides and inventories to such things as county archives, church archives, maps, and vital statistics records across the state and within New York City.

Legacy

WPA employment peaked in 1939. Congressional opposition to its supposed left-wing bias and the shift to preparedness spending after 1939 limited WPA appropriations. The WPA's emphasis shifted to defense projects, and as the economy strengthened, a government employment program was no longer necessary. The WPA was liquidated, ceasing to exist on 30 June 1943. In New York City alone, more than 700,000 had been employed by the WPA. In its eight years of existence, it provided work for about 8.5 billion people nationwide, at a cost of nearly $1.1 billion.

Herzog, Lester W. *WPA in the Empire State* ([Albany?]: WPA, [1938?])

Millett, John D. *The Works Progress Administration in New York City* (Chicago: Public Administration Service, 1938)

United States. Federal Works Agency. *Final Report on the WPA Program, 1935–1943* (Washington, DC: Government Printing Office, 1947)

Reba White Williams

world music. A commercial designation created in the 1980s to encompass the vast diversity of international musical traditions and styles that fall outside conventional Western music categories such as classical and rock. At the start of the 21st century, the world music rubric covered roughly three major areas: commercial recordings, performance series and artists, and music created and maintained within ethnic communities.

Recordings

New York City–based record companies recorded and marketed world music from the early 20th century under such headings as race (blues and other African American genres) and ethnic (eg, Jewish/Yiddish, Irish, Caribbean, Spanish, Greek, and Middle Eastern). These records sold mainly to immigrants who saw the music as an opportunity to bring the best artists from their homelands into their living rooms. The production of these recordings diminished significantly by the 1930s. In 1945 record producer Moses "Moe" Asch and ethnomusicologist Harold Courlander published five albums of Caribbean, American Southern, and Central Asian field recordings as part of a new ethnic series on Asch's Disc label. Three years later Asch brought these recordings into the catalog of his new company, Folkways Records. Along with other small New York City–based labels such as Stinson Records, Monitor, and Vanguard Records, Folkways promoted music of the world's cultures as an expression of the common people. Although international artists such as Bob Marley gained fame by the 1960s, it was only in the 1980s that globalized trade routes and a trend toward multiculturalism helped foster a world music market. Labels begun in New York State such as Shanachie Entertainment Corp, Lyrichord Discs, Putumayo World Music, and Ellipsis Arts gained great success marketing compact discs to the general public, and larger conglomerates such as Sony began to purchase smaller world music companies and promote world music artists. At the end of the 20th century, world music had its own market niche and an international audience; meanwhile mainstream pop, rap, and club artists incorporated samples of world music to create new sounds and genres of music.

Performance Series and Artists

A number of nonprofit organizations have arisen that actively support and promote world music performances throughout New York State. The World Music Institute, founded in 1985, grew out of a series of world music programs held at the New York Alternative Museum. The Manhattan-based organization has brought commercial and nonprofit musical acts from more than 70 countries, including Turkey, Puerto Rico, Bulgaria, Brazil, India, Pakistan, Ireland, and Korea, to perform in front of paying audiences. The Center for Traditional Music and Dance, founded in 1968, sponsors traditional performing artists in the New York City area. Summer concert series such as Central Park's Summerstage and Prospect Park's Celebrate Brooklyn often feature local world music performers, including New York City's Chinese Music Ensemble and Los Pleneros de 21.

Music within Ethnic Communities

While communities frequently perform and negotiate their musical traditions privately at religious and life-cycle occasions or at local gathering places, several communities throughout New York State put their cultures on display to show national and religious pride. Native American nations hold annual public powwows and festivals featuring dance, drum, and song in Barryville (Sullivan Co), Binghamton, Syracuse, at the Shinnecock Reservation [loc in Suffolk Co], and at the Seneca Nation's Allegany Reservation [loc in Cattaraugus Co]. The Greek American community in Buffalo celebrates its cultural heritage with traditional music and dance each May. Polish communities in Buffalo and Riverhead (Suffolk Co) celebrate with polka music and dance. Bagpipe band performances and competitions take prominent roles at the Scottish Games held in Albany each September. In June Altamont (Albany Co) holds its Old Songs Festival of Traditional Music and Dance, focusing on northeastern American folk arts and music. New York City, a center for numerous ethnic communities, hosts annual festivals celebrating countries including Greece, India, Ukraine, Israel, Puerto Rico, Brazil, Ecuador, Ireland, Africa, Norway, Czechoslovakia, the West Indies, and Korea.

Goldsmith, Peter D. *Making People's Music: Moe Asch and Folkways Records* (Washington, DC: Smithsonian Institution Press, 1998)
Levin, Theodore. *The Hundred Thousand Fools of God: Musical Travels in Central Asia (and Queens, New York)* (Bloomington: Indiana Univ Press, 1996)
New York City: Global Beat of the Boroughs (Smithsonian Folkways Recordings 40493)

Judah Cohen

world's fairs. New York City has hosted three world's fairs, most notably those in 1939–40 and 1964–65. The tradition of bringing together exhibitors and visitors from the United States and around the globe started with the 1853 New York World's Fair at the Crystal Palace in Midtown Manhattan, a site now occupied by Bryant Park. Critics were quick to derogate this exhibition, the first in the United States, as a rather overt emulation of the 1851 London World's Fair.

In sharp contrast, the 1939 fair in New York City was welcomed as the embodiment of a technologically refined future. The 150th anniversary of Pres George Washington's inauguration served well as an official stimulus. Selecting the site proved to be a more delicate task since Manhattan would not be able to offer adequate open space. A former refuse dump in Queens was earmarked instead. The fairgrounds later became the site of Flushing Meadow Park, covering an area of 1,255 acres (507.9 ha). A nonprofit organization, the World's Fair of 1939 Corp, headed by former New York City police commissioner Grover A. Whalen, issued bonds backed by revenues from rents, permits, and admissions. Success in recruiting international exhibitors, however, was severely limited as the world found itself on the verge of a new war; only 36 nations participated in the fair. Political turmoil also forced a change in the fair's theme, from the original Building the World of Tomorrow to For Peace and Freedom. With its stylized symbols—the Trylon, a pinnacle measuring about 700 feet (210 m), and the Perisphere, a polished globe 200 feet (61 m) in diameter—the fair introduced a series of innovative products ranging from color film (by Eastman Kodak) to the dishwasher (by Westinghouse). Other items still unfamiliar at the time but to come out of the fair included nylon stockings, air-conditioning, cloverleaf highways, and television. Pres Franklin D. Roosevelt's opening address was one of the first events aired live on television. The credo of the constant progress of technology constituted one of the fair's hallmarks and was expressed in the general layout and in the many futuristic attractions. The widely patronized Futurama by General Motors, depicting the world in 1960 as dependent on the automobile, later proved to have been very prescient. The fair opened on 30 Apr 1939, and 44,931,681 visitors—a number far below the projected 100 million—had passed the turnstiles before the gates were closed on 26 Oct 1940. For some visitors the fair's endeavors in the fine arts may have generated a shock of modernity, as exemplified by Finland's pavilion designed by architect Alvar Aalto or the Dream of Venus Surrealist pavilion by Salvador Dalí. For others these visualizations demonstrated a decent attempt to integrate art with the everyday hodgepodge at the fairgrounds. More than 100 painters and sculptors were on hand, presenting some 158 murals and 173 sculptures. Beyond this point, the fair worked as a catalyst for the future in many other ways, the most important of which was imagining a positive outlook after a decade of economic depression.

Trylon and Perisphere under construction for the World's Fair, New York City, 1939.

The critical success of the 1939 fair could not be reiterated in 1964. More conservative in its conception, the 1964 fair predominantly developed around the ideas of Triborough Bridge and Tunnel Authority Chairman Robert Moses, who headed the World's Fair Corp. The fair, running 22 Apr–18 Oct 1964 and 21 Apr–17 Oct 1965, registered attendance at 51 million. The Bureau of International Expositions did not sanction the 1964 fair, as it had the 1939 fair. By reusing the 1939 site, Moses hoped to save money for the construction of public facilities that would outlive the fair's pavilions and furnish the later Flushing Meadow Park with architectural remnants of the fair. Features retained from the first fair included the New York City Building (later Queens Museum), a lake, a boathouse, and paths. Pres Lyndon Johnson attended the fair's opening, as did New York State governor Nelson A. Rockefeller and former president Harry S. Truman. The Unisphere, a giant steel globe 140 feet (42.7 m) high, was a central symbol and stood for one of the many themes with which the fair was marketed: Peace through Understanding. Eighty nations participated in the fair. General Motors presented Futurama II, portraying the world of 2064 dominated by pure technology conquering the ultimate niches of nature—on the moon, in Antarctica, on the seafloor, in the desert, and in the concrete city of the future. The US Atomic Energy Commission rejected a request by fair organizers to erect a mobile nuclear fission plant on the fairgrounds and instead exhibited a simulated reactor. Some of the innovations introduced were a rudimentary computer, the Information Machine, at the IBM Pavilion and the Picturephone at the AT&T Pavilion. Even though Pop Art, by Roy Lichtenstein, Robert Rauschenberg, Andy Warhol, and others, obtained a highly visible stage, the iconic impact generated by the 1939 fair was never felt in 1964. Remnants of the 1964 fair include the Unisphere, Space Park (later New York Hall of Science), and the Winston Churchill Pavilion (later aviary of Queens Zoo).

See also BROADCASTING (RADIO AND TELEVISION).

Bletter, Rosemarie Haag. *Remembering the Future: The New York World's Fair from 1939–1964* (New York: Rizzoli, 1989)

Gelernter, David Hillel. *1939, The Lost World of the Fair* (New York: Free Press, 1995)

Zim, Larry, Mel Lerner, and Herbert Rolfes. *The World of Tomorrow: The 1939 New York World's Fair* (New York: Harper & Row, 1988)

Werner Gamerith

World Trade Center (WTC). The World Trade Center has become a symbol of national tragedy. Its Twin Towers are best known now for the terrifying spectacle of their destruction, the target of international terrorism. Yet the WTC, as originally conceived and built, was intended as a magnet for international commerce and reflected the flush of post–World War II prosperity. Walter Gropius, one of the first architects asked to offer a conception for the complex, cited philosopher John Stuart Mill's belief that if people were to trade, they would end wars. "By its very nature," wrote Gropius, "trade is cosmopolitan and liberating to society." Perhaps those very qualities made the WTC a logical target for the fundamentalist ideologues who destroyed it.

As built, the Trade Center reflected major trends in cities across the country: superblocks, giant plazas, and the steel and glass towers of major corporate headquarters. The Twin Towers joined that small but illustrious group of New York City skyscrapers claiming the title of world's tallest building. Yet unlike the rest of the Wall Street District and its skyscrapers, the Trade Center was built not by private developers but by an arm of government, and the primary impetus behind its construction was the fear that downtown itself might become economically irrelevant.

With commercial development rebounding in New York City during the years following the two-decade hiatus of the Great Depression and World War II, the Wall Street District experienced a crisis in confidence, as development of a new business district in Midtown picked up speed. Chase Manhattan Bank took the lead in recommitting to Lower Manhattan by building Chase Manhattan Plaza, which opened in 1960. Chase Manhattan's vice chairman David Rockefeller went further, organizing a group of business interests in 1958 as the Downtown–Lower Manhattan Association (DLMA) to pursue strategies for reversing the Wall Street District's decline.

The DLMA retained the architectural firm of Skidmore, Owings and Merrill (SOM) to study the district. SOM's vision was shaped by International-Style thinking and the values of urban renewal current in the 1950s and 1960s: massive clearance of older buildings and the construction of superblocks with modern towers. Accordingly, SOM recommended leveling and rebuilding almost all of the Wall Street District. The report's suggestions for new construction included a World Trade Center complex.

The Port of New York Authority (now Port Authority of New York and New Jersey), a bistate, public authority jointly controlled by the states of New York and New Jersey, took over responsibility for the project, with the goal of bringing under one roof all the region's international trade–related businesses and government agencies. The Port Authority initially selected a site on the East Side, a stretch along the East River just south of the Brooklyn Bridge, today occupied largely by the South Street Seaport. To design the proposed project—the country's biggest skyscraper complex since Rockefeller Center—the Port Authority initially turned to a team of three of New York City's most prominent architects: Gordon Bunshaft of SOM, the designer of Chase Manhattan Plaza; Wallace K. Harrison of Harrison and Abramovitz, who had worked on Rockefeller Center; and Edward Durell Stone, architect of the Rockefeller-backed Museum of Modern Art. The team in 1960 and 1961 proposed a collection of glass towers in a plaza that, had it been built, might well have become the ultimate International-Style complex in America.

New Jersey, however, did not see how it would gain from the Port Authority building a Manhattan office tower, and the project stalled until the suggestion was made in 1962 to move the project to a site bounded by Vesey, Church, Liberty, and West Sts on the West Side, and for the Port Authority to take over the financially ailing Hudson and Manhattan Railroad that operated between New Jersey and Manhattan (now the PATH [Port Authority Trans-Hudson] system). A PATH station would become a part of the WTC complex. Bunshaft, Harrison, and Stone unexpectedly fell out of the running to be the project architects. The Port Authority then conducted an in-house survey of a dozen potential replacements. To the surprise of many, the commission in August 1962 went to Michigan-based Minoru Yamasaki (1912–86). Yamasaki was an unusual choice. Not only did he have little skyscraper experience, he had earned a reputation as a rebel against International-Style orthodoxy, becoming known for a delicate ornamental style not generally associated with the Modern movement. Because Yamasaki maintained too small an office to handle such a huge project, the Port Authority brought in the highly experienced firm of Emery Roth and Sons as associate architects to prepare the hundreds of thousands of working drawings the project would require.

Even before Yamasaki's selection, the Port Authority's studies had identified the project's general parameters: 10 million ft² (930,000 m²) of

Twilight, view toward the East River from the 104th floor of the north tower of the World Trade Center, by Marcia Clark, 1984.

The verticality of the towers could be overwhelming. In the foreground is St. Nicholas Greek Orthodox Church, also destroyed on September 11th.

office space, a number of skyscrapers, an underground shopping concourse, a hotel, and a large open plaza. The WTC complex as finally designed represented a compromise between the Port Authority's desire for 10 million ft^2 of space and Yamasaki's fascination with ornament and plazas. Yamasaki originally envisioned his plaza ringed by reflecting pools and surrounded by interconnecting buildings, high and low, with an overlay of pointed arches so reminiscent of Venetian Gothic that several critics likened it to a new "St. Mark's on the Hudson." In this scheme, the towers perched uneasily on the plaza's edge, almost as an afterthought. Then Yamasaki turned to the towers' design. He experimented with large-scale models to find the right combination: three, four, five towers, even a wall of towers, finally settling on twin towers set at an angle to, rather than parallel with, each other. In the final design, the plaza became subordinated to the towers, losing much of its original detail. Inevitably, the Twin Towers replaced the plaza as the Trade Center's focus.

Though Yamasaki's towers were extremely tall, the idea of making them the world's tallest came from the Port Authority. Port Authority officials wanted the Trade Center to become a major monument, not just for New York City but for the world, and pushing the height of the towers to 1,350 feet (411.5 m), just 100 feet (30.5 m) higher than the Empire State Building, was part of that effort. The Twin Towers held the title of world's tallest only briefly, however, losing it to the Sears Tower in Chicago.

There were many who tried to stop the building of the Trade Center. Commercial developers, such as the owners of the Empire State Building, brought suit to halt the construction, disliking the idea of government-sponsored rivals. Most immediately threatened were the owners of small businesses on the site, especially the biggest cluster, "Radio Row" on Cortlandt St, New York City's discount electronics center since the 1920s. All efforts to block the project were ultimately unsuccessful.

Unlike most post–World War II International-Style skyscrapers that approach the appearance of glass boxes, Yamasaki's towers seemed to be boxes made of metal: solid, like the models from which they were designed. He created this effect by using narrow windows and deep aluminum facing. That all-metal appearance reflected the towers' novel structure. The sheer cliffs of aluminum did not look like the kind of insubstantial, non-weight-bearing, glass-curtain walls hung on the outside of a steel cage that Harrison or Bunshaft might have designed, because they were not curtain walls at all but rather load-bearing walls, a remarkable innovation devised by the center's engineers, John Skilling and Leslie Robertson of the firm Worthington, Skilling, Helle and Jackson. Together with the elevator core at the center of each building, the walls helped support the towers' enormous weight. The surrounding plaza, defined by the towers and three low buildings, had its main entrance via a flight of steps from Church St. Said to be the size of five football fields, the plaza was a classic 1960s-style attempt to open up urban centers to light and air. In the end, the plaza served more as a stage for the Twin Towers. On the plaza, visitors could walk right up to either one and look up 110 stories of aluminum and glass.

Building the world's tallest buildings involved extraordinary feats of engineering beyond the load-bearing walls. The flow of materials to the site was so huge that no roadway could handle it; materials were floated in via the Hudson River. Site excavation posed an enormous hurdle. Bedrock lay 70 feet (21 m) below landfill, making excavation nearly impossible. The WTC's engineers imported a slurry trench technology from Italy that enabled them to sink a reinforced concrete perimeter wall six stories down to bedrock and then excavate a 500,000 ft^2 (46,500 m^2) concrete-lined hole dubbed the bathtub. The 1.2 million yd^3 (918,000 m^3) of excavated rubble were dumped into the Hudson River to create the landfill now underlying Battery Park City.

Although conceived in the booming economy of the 1960s, by the time the WTC opened its doors to the still unfinished complex in 1970, the recession of the early 1970s was well underway, leaving it unclear who would rent all that space. In a deal with New York State, roughly half the complex was leased to state agencies. The WTC soon was functioning as a city within a city, with an estimated working population of 50,000 people joined by some 80,000 daily visitors. Eventually, almost all of the state offices moved out, though the Port Authority retained offices in the complex.

The Trade Center quickly became a major tourist destination. The rooftop observatory hosted as many as 10,000 visitors in a single day coming to marvel at the extraordinary views of New York City and surroundings. Windows on the World, the 107th floor restaurant, became a major attraction in its own right. Aerialist Philippe Petit made headlines on 7 Aug 1974 by walking on a tightrope between the two towers. Three years later, on 26 May 1977, George Willig, a mountain climber, scaled the exterior wall of one of the towers. Neither would have attracted such attention attempting to conquer less famous structures. Two buildings joined the center in the 1980s: the Vista Hotel (1981), on the plaza, and World Trade Center 7 (1987), a distinct office building separated from the complex by Vesey St but officially part of it. Following the recession of the early 1990s the WTC joined the general downtown boom, filling up with financial services firms. In April 2001 the Port Authority leased the complex to real estate developer Larry Silverstein.

In the years after its construction, architecture critics, and New York City residents generally, had little good to say about the WTC. Visitors, on

1993 World Trade Center Bombing. On Friday, 26 Feb 1993, at 12:18 PM, a bomb weighing between 1,200 and 1,500 pounds (550–680 km) exploded in a van parked in the World Trade Center (WTC) underground parking garage in Lower Manhattan. The explosion, which many said felt like an earthquake, knocked out power and created a crater 150 feet (46 m) across and five floors deep, killing six persons in the immediate vicinity. Evacuation of the WTC, in dark, smoke-filled stairways, took more than six hours. More than 1,000 persons were treated for smoke inhalation, and estimated damage was more than $500 million. In the wake of the 1993 bombing, the Port Authority of New York and New Jersey, owners of the WTC, undertook a multimillion dollar upgrading of the security of the WTC, including battery-operated light fixtures in the stairwells and installation of a public address system. Visitors entering the trade complex were checked far more carefully, and fire drills were taken more seriously by the tenants and workers. A new evacuation plan was devised, which, when used in 2001, was credited with saving thousands of lives.

A few days after the 1993 bombing, the rented van in which the homemade fertilizer bomb had been placed was traced to Jersey City, NJ. Four persons with ties to radical Islamic fundamentalist groups were convicted in 1994 and each sentenced to 240 years in prison. In 1996 a Muslim cleric from Jersey City, Sheik Omar Abdel-Rahman, one of the planners of the bombing, received the same sentence. Another leader of the plot, Ramzi Ahmed Yousef, was arrested in Pakistan in 1995. He had become an explosives expert at a terrorist training camp in Afghanistan. At his 1998 trial in New York City he was also sentenced to 240 years in prison. Most experts concluded that the goal of the perpetrators was to weaken the structural integrity of the 110-story twin towers and adjacent buildings in the complex and cause their collapse, with maximum loss of life.

the other hand, adopted it as *the* symbol of New York City. Today, given the circumstances of its destruction, it is probably impossible to form a fair judgment of its architectural value. But millions of people—remembering how, especially when lit at night, the towers appeared as gleaming, evanescent, abstract sculptures floating in the skyline—miss the Twin Towers' presence.

See also ART, NEW YORK CITY AREA; SEPTEMBER 11TH, 2001.

Gillespie, Angus Kress. *Twin Towers: The Life of New York City's World Trade Center* (1999; rev ed, Brunswick, NJ: Rutgers Univ Press, 2001)

Glanz, James, and Eric Lipton. *City in the Sky: The Rise and Fall of the World Trade Center* (New York: Times Books/Henry Holt, 2003)

Robins, Anthony. *Classics of American Architecture: The World Trade Center* (Englewood, Fla: Pineapple Press, 1987)

Stein, Abraham. "The Port Authority of New York and New Jersey and the 1962 PATH–World Trade Center Project" (PhD diss, New York Univ, 1980)

Anthony Robins

World War I

The Coming Storm

After the outbreak of war in Europe in August 1914, New York State officials shared Pres Woodrow Wilson's official position of neutrality. Responses to the war in local communities, however, varied from indifference to strident nationalism, particularly among recent immigrants from the warring European countries. In Utica, city residents of English ancestry enlisted in the British and Canadian armed forces, while German immigrants raised funds for their homeland. The state's economy shifted toward war production after 1914 even though the United States was not a combatant. Factories produced military equipment and munitions, many of them shipped through the Port of New York. Initially, the outbreak of war shocked the New York City financial markets; the New York Stock Exchange was closed for the second half of 1914 in response to the unsettled European situation. Eventually these markets emerged from the war far stronger than before. Financial institutions, particularly the J. P. Morgan Bank in New York City under the direction of the vigorously pro-British J. P. Morgan Jr, funded the Allied war effort.

The outbreak of the war led to a division among Progressive reformers as peace organizations expanded into a full-fledged movement to stop the war. Most prominent were two New York City–based organizations, the American Union Against Militarism (AUAM) and the Woman's Peace Party (WPP), both founded in 1915. At the same time, other New York State residents pressed the government to strengthen its military power and to enter the war on the side of the Allies. Prominent among the interventionists were former president Theodore Roosevelt and Walter Hines Page, president of Doubleday, Page publishers in Garden City (Nassau Co), who served as US ambassador to Great Britain from 1913 to 1918. Advocates of military preparedness set up an officer training camp at the Plattsburgh Barracks in the summer of 1915 for college students and businessmen and gathered some 1,300 recruits from the country's elite in its first session; by the next summer, 16,000 men attended similar camps nationwide. The program became known as the Plattsburgh Idea and laid the groundwork for the US Army's ROTC program.

Naval warfare severely curtailed international travel by civilians and brought an end to the steady stream of immigrants who had shaped New York State life for decades. Attacks on American ships and travelers also eroded support for neutrality; the sinking of the *Lusitania* on 7 May 1915, during a run from New York City to Liverpool, England, killed nearly 1,200 people. A massive explosion on 30 July 1916 at the munitions factories on Black Tom Island in New York Harbor fostered fears of German sabotage, although the true cause of the explosion remains unknown. Tensions over the war also surfaced in the state during the hotly contested presidential election of 1916; Wilson defeated US Supreme Court justice and former New York State governor Charles Evans Hughes, but Hughes won New York State by more than 100,000 votes. Although Wilson was reelected on the slogan He Kept Us Out of War, world events soon pressed the country into an official declaration of war on 6 Apr 1917.

Mobilization

Within days, New York State began to mobilize troops. State residents reported to cantonments across the country: more than 25,000 went to Camp Wadsworth in South Carolina, while a handful traveled as far as Camp Lewis in Washington State. More than 73,000 New Yorkers, mostly inductees from New York City and Long Island, trained as part of the US Army 77th Division at Camp Upton, near Yaphank (Suffolk Co). Among them was songwriter Irving Berlin, who commemorated the experience in the wartime musical *Yip! Yip! Yaphank* (1918). By war's end, 367,864 New Yorkers had served in the armed forces. Among the state's military regiments was the 369th US Infantry, also known as the Harlem Hellfighters. During the war African American men mobilized in segregated units under the command of white officers. The 369th gathered black soldiers from across New York State. Cpl Henry Johnson of Albany earned America's first Croix de Guerre for service in combat in France. The regiment's band, under director James Reese Europe, was the first to play live jazz in Europe. At home, the migration of African Americans to northern urban areas brought increasing numbers to New York State cities. More moved to Harlem than anywhere else, and by the end of the war Harlem had emerged as the unofficial capital of black America.

With the United States officially in the war, the state's industries turned dramatically toward a war footing. In the Mohawk Valley, Remington Arms in Ilion (Herkimer Co) produced rifles while Utica's Savage Arms factory provided the US military with machine guns. The huge plant of the Lackawanna Iron and Steel Co (Erie Co) produced steel for the war effort, while in nearby Buffalo, National Aniline manufactured explosives, and the Curtiss Aeroplane Co produced thousands of military aircraft. In 1916 a subsidiary, the Curtiss Engineering Corp, opened a factory in Garden City, marking the beginning of Long Island's aviation industry. In Rochester Bausch and Lomb produced range finders, gun sights, trench periscopes, and other optical equipment with military uses. During the spring and summer of 1918, the Boys' Working Reserve excused thousands of state schoolchildren (both boys and girls) from classes to fill shortages of agricultural labor. Finance continued from New York City banks, now supplemented with federal funds. Reformers in the American Committee on War Finance, founded in March 1917 by Amos Pinchot, pressed for progressive taxation and against war profiteering.

A Divided Home Front

Mobilizing New York State's home front required intellectual support as well as industrial and agricultural production. Gov Charles S. Whitman established home defense committees at the county level across the state. Hundreds of thousands volunteered with local chapters of the American Red Cross. Food conservation drew the New York State Federation of Women's Clubs. Volunteer public speakers known as "Four Minute Men" roused audiences in rallies and at movie theaters; film stars Douglas Fairbanks, Charlie Chaplin, and Mary Pickford participated in bond drives. Motivational speakers in Albany included the Hip Hip Hooray Girls, a burlesque troupe from the city's Empire Theatre. Whitman appointed James Montgomery Flagg the state's official military artist; he would later go on to fame with his US Army recruiting poster of Uncle Sam featuring the words "I Want You." In Rochester, George Eastman took charge of the Patriotic and Community Fund Drive in May 1918.

Not all efforts on the home front were so upbeat. Immigrants came under special scrutiny. Citizens of Germany, Austria-Hungary, and the Ottoman Empire were required to register as enemy aliens and forbidden to enter areas of military importance. German Americans in particular were targets of repression. Buffalo's German-American Bank renamed itself Liberty Bank; in 1918 in New York City the Germania Life Insurance Co became the Guardian Life Insurance Co of America. Italian and French composers replaced Germans in the lineup of the Metropolitan Opera in New York City. More serious episodes occurred as well. The state's vibrant German language press all but disappeared under wartime strictures that required submitting English translations to postal inspectors before publication; German newspapers in Utica, Buffalo, Albany, and Troy (Rensselaer Co) either ceased or significantly reduced publication. Schools across the state eliminated German from the curriculum; the school board in Mount Vernon (Westchester Co) even voted to destroy the German language textbooks that had been used in the school before the war. A German immigrant in Utica who refused to purchase war bonds was arrested on charges of sedition. Germans were not the only subjects of surveillance. Irish Americans with ties to the rebellious home country were also suspect; the *Irish World and American Industrial Liberator*, published in New York City, was censored. On the other hand, for immigrants who found their national aspirations in tune with American policy, the war was a welcome chance to express their views. Most Jews, of whatever political ideology, were reluctant to align themselves with the notoriously anti-Semitic regime in Russia. By the time America declared war, the overthrow of the czar and Wilson's promises of a new order in eastern Europe made the war effort more popular. After Italy joined the Allies in 1915, most Italian immigrants supported the war effort.

Banner displayed on a streetcar in Albany during World War I.

During the war political radicals and pacifists found themselves the subject of investigation and numerous schoolteachers were relieved of their positions, including Mary McDowell, a Quaker teacher in Brooklyn charged with "conduct unbecoming a teacher." Columbia University professor James McKeen Cattell was dismissed in October 1917 for opposing the war; the furor among academics over his dismissal led to other resignations, including Charles A. Beard, who left to help found the New School for Social Research in New York City. Police in Buffalo visited 55,000 homes to gather "voluntary" purchases of war bonds. Conscientious objectors faced ridicule and harassment, and all the state's draft-age men were subject to "slacker raids" conducted by the American Protective League. This volunteer draft-enforcement organization detained over 50,000 men (only 8 of whom turned out to be draft dodgers) during the nation's largest raid in New York City in early September 1918.

Despite formal and informal repression, antiwar activism continued throughout the war. The New York City branch of the WPP was among the nation's most active women's peace organizations; after the war, it would merge into the Women's International League for Peace and Freedom. The AUAM unraveled, but many of its leading figures turned their attention to protecting the rights of draftees, immigrants, and radicals as the union's Bureau of Conscientious Objectors. This group became the National Civil Liberties Bureau in 1917 and merged with several other organizations to form the American Civil Liberties Union in 1920. Several key free-speech cases were heard in federal courts in New York City, among them the trial of Jacob Abrams and four others charged for distributing seditious materials. Although the Abrams convictions were upheld by the US Supreme Court in *Abrams v United States* (1919), dissents in that case by Justices Oliver Wendell Holmes and Louis D. Brandeis laid the groundwork for modern understandings of free speech.

Political radicalism continued as well, despite significant repression. On 28 July 1917, a parade of 8,000 African Americans marched down New York City's 5th Ave in silent protest of a recent race riot in East St. Louis, Ill. The Socialist Party (the only national political party to take an official stand against the war) reaped marked gains across the state in the 1917 elections, sending 10 candidates to the state assembly. Mayoral elections in New York City voted in Tammany functionary John F. Hylan and pushed out John Purroy Mitchel, whose strident pro-war stance had alienated ethnic German American and Irish American voters. The unpopular Mitchel finished just ahead of Morris Hillquit, who ran on the Socialist Party ticket.

Faced with wartime inflation (prices rose 79% over the course of the war), housing shortages, and increased working hours, workers pushed for bargaining rights, higher wages, and better working conditions. The National War Labor Board, a federal agency, urged companies with war contracts to bargain with organized labor and to meet minimal workplace requirements; in return, many major labor unions pledged not to strike for the duration of the war. Moderate labor leader Samuel Gompers of the American Federation of Labor succeeded in his quest to bring Pres Wilson before the union's convention in Buffalo in November 1917. Labor protest did not disappear, though. The more radical Amalgamated Clothing Workers, under the leadership of Sidney Hillman, achieved a significant wartime victory in Rochester.

Supporters of woman suffrage pressed their case throughout the war. New York State women, under the leadership of Carrie Chapman Catt, won the right to vote in a state referendum in November 1917. On 4 June 1919, New York State's congressional delegation voted overwhelmingly to submit the 19th Amendment to the states, although Sen James W. Wadsworth Jr of Geneseo (Livingston Co) continued his lifelong opposition. The state legislature adopted the amendment on 16 June 1920 in a unanimous vote. The movement for Prohibition also gained momentum during the war; residents who sought to conserve foodstuffs urged restrictions on whiskey (produced from valuable corn); others supported the legislation in response to wartime propaganda that demonized the political power of the German-dominated brewing industry. Temporary wartime measures set the stage for the adoption on 29 Jan 1919 of the 18th Amendment, which passed with strong support from Protestant communities outside of the New York City area.

Victory and Postwar Adjustment

Meanwhile, New York State troops in France contributed to the Armistice, achieved on 11 Nov 1918. That day, the streets of Albany filled with at least 50,000 people. Victory celebrations, however, were mostly postponed by the global epidemic of Spanish influenza. The disease first appeared in New York City in September 1918 and spread rapidly throughout the state. Perhaps as many as 500,000 took ill and more than 60,000 died. Elections that fall were also disrupted by the epidemic; those who made it to the polls joined a nationwide reaction against the wartime leadership of the Democratic Party, although Democrat Alfred E. Smith won the governor's race. Wartime victory celebrations would wait until the fall of 1919, after troops returned from Europe. New York City's Victory Parade that September, led by Gen John Pershing and Pres Wilson, drew massive crowds. Wilson marched in the Victory Parade as part of his effort to win support for the Treaty of Versailles and American participation in the League of Nations. The proposed treaty was voted down on 19 Nov 1919.

Wartime anti-Germanism subsided almost as quickly as it had risen (though German American culture never returned to its prewar vibrancy), but it was soon replaced by concerns over labor unrest. Postwar economic dislocation, which hit war-industry workers particularly hard, spurred a wave of strikes in the fall of 1918, beginning on the docks of New York City in November and among trolleymen in Buffalo in December. The nationwide steel strike of 1919 crippled plants in Erie Co and elsewhere. When New Yorkers heard news of the Bolshevik Revolution in Russia in November 1917 and learned its leader Vladimir Lenin had been supported by the imperial German government (which was true, but not the sole reason for his success), fears of conspiracy in the United States exploded into the nation's first Red Scare. Socialist radicals, beleaguered by wartime repression and fragmented by internal ideological divisions over developments in Russia, faced formidable enemies in New York State.

New York City mayor Hylan refused to allow the display of the red flag, a banner of socialism, on city streets; other cities followed. The Lusk Committee, chaired by Sen Clayton Lusk of Cortland, investigated "seditious activities" of hundreds of state organizations. US Att Gen A. Mitchell Palmer launched his crusade against un-American radicals with raids in New York City in November 1919; further raids took place in Buffalo, Rochester, and Utica in December. Many foreign-born radicals were deported, among them anarchists Emma Goldman and Mollie Steimer, the latter one of the *Abrams* case defendants. In January 1920 the state assembly refused to seat five legitimately elected assemblymen who were members of the Socialist Party. A September 1920 bomb in the Wall St area of New York City, which killed 35 people and injured 130 others, further fanned the flames, although the responsible party was never found.

Monuments to approximately 14,000 New Yorkers killed in the war were soon constructed across the state to honor their service. In later years, accounts of the state's experience during World War I highlighted unity and patriotic togetherness and erased many memories of genuine discord and tumult. The war marked an important turning point in the state's history, putting an end to mass immigration and political progressivism, and ushering in a new era of prohibition and antiradicalism along with postwar economic growth.

See also ESPIONAGE; FREE SPEECH; ITALIANS; SCULPTURE, PUBLIC; SOCIALIST EXPULSION; WAR MEMORIALS.

Bean, Philip A. "The Great War and Ethnic Nationalism in Utica, New York, 1914–1920," *New York History* 74 (Oct 1993): 383–413

Bristow, Nancy K. *Making Men Moral: Social Engineering during the Great War* (New York: New York Univ Press, 1996)

Clifford, J. Garry. *The Citizen Soldiers: The Plattsburgh Training Camp Movement, 1913–1920* (Lexington: Univ Press of Kentucky, 1972)

Early, Frances H. *A World without War: How US Feminists and Pacifists Resisted World War I* (Syracuse: Syracuse Univ Press, 1997)

Harris, Bill. *The Hellfighters of Harlem: African-American Soldiers Who Fought for the Right to Fight for Their Country* (New York: Carroll & Graf Publishers, 2002)

Jaffe, Julian F. *Crusade against Radicalism: New York during the Red Scare, 1914–1924* (Port Washington, NY: Kennikat, 1972)

Kennedy, David M. *Over Here: The First World War and American Society* (New York: Oxford Univ Press, 1980)

Polenberg, Richard. *Fighting Faiths: The Abrams Case, the Supreme Court, and Free Speech* (New York: Viking Press, 1987)

Summerscales, William. *Affirmation and Dissent: Columbia's Response to the Crisis of World War I* (New York: Teachers College Press, 1970)

Witcover, Jules. *Sabotage at Black Tom: Imperial Germany's Secret War in America, 1914–1917* (Chapel Hill, NC: Algonquin Books of Chapel Hill, 1989)

Christopher Capozzola

World War II. New York State had a significant role in the country's war effort; by September 1945 it led all states both in the production of war material and in the number of men and women enlisted in the US armed forces.

Military Preparedness

Eighteen months prior to the Japanese attack on Pearl Harbor, New York State's government, under Gov Herbert H. Lehman, was gearing up for war. Following the German army's sweeping attack on Western Europe in the spring of 1940, Pres Franklin D. Roosevelt on 16 May called for the annual production of 50,000 planes and for movement of the United States to a war footing. Responding to Roosevelt's call, Lehman created the New York State Defense Council through an executive order on 1 Aug 1940. Dedicated to preparing the state for war, the council was a temporary state agency administered by commissioners from a series of state governmental departments. Lt Gov Charles Poletti served as its chair. Some branches of the Defense Council focused on civil defense, some focused on assisting state industry in war production, and some maintained services to a war-stressed civilian population. Following America's entry into the war in December 1941, the New York State Defense Council was renamed the New York State War Council. This agency functioned through 1945, and with an annual budget of $2 million it aided New Yorkers in almost every aspect of the war effort.

War Industry Production

One of the most significant contributions of New York State to the national war effort was in defense production. With a highly industrialized economy, New York State played a pivotal role in federal rearmament. Between June and November 1940 alone, New York State manufacturers received $1 billion in federal war contracts, and by war's end New York led the nation in the total amount of contracts awarded per state, with $21.5 billion.

The most critical war industry in the state was aviation. Together the Long Island and Buffalo/Niagara regions had served as the center of the US aeronautical industry since the 1910s. Following Pres Roosevelt's May 1940 order to rearm, federal aircraft contracts poured into these areas. The four largest aviation firms in the state were Grumman Aircraft of Bethpage (Nassau Co), Republic Aviation of East Farmingdale (Suffolk Co), Bell Aircraft, and the Curtiss-Wright Corp, the latter two of Buffalo. Grumman employed 22,000 workers during the war, while the massive Curtiss-Wright Corp was New York State's most prolific aircraft producer. Curtiss-Wright's production facility at the Buffalo Municipal Airport was the largest combat plane plant in the nation. Combined with its other Erie Co plants, Curtiss-Wright had a staggering 85,000 employees by the summer of 1945. By V-J Day more than 15,000 P-40 fighters had rolled off the Curtiss assembly lines.

Other important New York State war industries included General Electric (GE) of Schenectady. With its 40,000 employees GE had a monopoly on the production of radio equipment, radar systems, and steam turbines for ships. Nearly 20% of all war contracts for New York State firms were awarded to GE. Eastman Kodak Co of Rochester was another crucial state defense firm, producing photographic apparatuses as well as optical equipment. The Brooklyn Navy Yard also contributed significantly to the war effort. A massive ship repair and construction facility, the yard employed 75,000 workers and was most noted for construction of the US Navy's battleship USS *Missouri,* launched 29 Jan 1944. Yet aviation remained as New York's most significant defense industry: from 1940 through June 1945, New York State ranked second nationally, after California, in the number of federal aviation contracts received. These contracts totaled $7.5 billion, or 35% of all federal contracts awarded to New York State firms during the war.

Mobilization

Similar to its efforts as America's leader in war production, New York State was again the leader in providing personnel for the US armed forces. On 16 Sept 1940 Pres Roosevelt signed the Burke-Wadsworth bill into law, creating the selective service. Under this law each state was required to create local draft, advisory, and appeal boards, as well as to provide examining physicians to evaluate draftees. In addition to the selective service's establishment, Roosevelt, by presidential proclamation, on 16 Oct 1940 called for all males 35 years and younger to register for the draft. According to the 1940 federal census, 10.2% of the total US population lived in New York State, and of the nation's total male population, 6,690,326, or 10%, were New York State residents. Accordingly the state provided more personnel for military service than any other state in the union. By 1 Sept 1945, 14,673,089 males either enlisted or were drafted into the US armed forces. Of this total, 1,553,094, or 10.5%, were from New York State. New York City provided 885,928 men, or 57%, of New York State's total contribution. By 1 Sept 1945 New York City, when compared with US states, ranked

Scrap drive in Syracuse, 1942.

This "canning caravan" trailer traveled throughout Broome Co to educate homemakers on canning the products of their World War II victory gardens.

fourth in the total number of men contributed to the war effort. By war's end the conflict had claimed the lives of 27,659 New Yorkers, both women and men, who had served in the US armed forces.

Home Front Life

For those New York State residents who did not serve in the armed forces, life on the home front was characterized by scrap drives, rationing programs, and in the agricultural regions the ominous presence of large numbers of Italian and German prisoners of war. Beginning in the summer of 1941, various salvage drives were undertaken in the state to prepare for war. With the boom in defense production, raw material shortages began to appear. Thus the State Advisory Committee on Conservation of Waste Materials, a Defense Council bureau, responded with scrap collections on the town level. These proceeded at a constant pace through the spring of 1945. More than 300,000 people participated, mostly New York State schoolchildren, in collecting used rags, rubber, and wastepaper for the war effort.

In summer 1941 the state government also began a voluntary gasoline conservation program, which became compulsory in 1942. These rationing programs were administered by the Bureau of Rationing, a Defense Council agency. By the time the US government took over rationing in May 1942, New York State had rationing programs for gas, rubber, automobiles, and sugar. In 1940 New York was the seventh largest food-producing state in the United States, and people in rural agricultural regions felt the impact of the war most severely. In June 1940 Gov Lehman created the Agricultural Defense Committee to coordinate state agricultural efforts with defense needs. With the committee's aid, for the 1941 and 1942 harvests, the state experienced tremendous production totals. Following 1942, however, as most farmworkers were drafted into the military, a state agricultural crisis loomed. To solve this harvest labor crisis for 1943, the federal War Food Administration brought 3,000 Jamaican laborers to the regions of Buffalo/Niagara and Western New York. The workers were housed in more than a dozen old federal Civilian Conservation Corps camps. After large numbers of Axis soldiers were captured following the Allied landings in North Africa, 800 Italian prisoners of war were also added in 1943, provided by the federal War Department. The Italian prisoners were housed at separate camps in these same regions. In 1944, however, the Jamaican labor program was abolished, and the Italians were relocated to similar agricultural labor camps in Staten Island and Suffolk Co. In their place the War Department provided more than 4,500 German prisoners to the labor-starved areas of Buffalo/Niagara and Western New York. These German workers remained through the end of 1946, providing vitally needed field labor as well as labor in food processing centers, including the H. J. Heinz Co in Medina (Orleans Co).

Shifts in Public Policy

Most aspects of life in the state were only temporarily affected by the war, but for state government the conflict brought significant and lasting change, notably in its policies on labor and higher education. Reflecting national trends it had long been accepted practice in industrial firms to discriminate against ethnic Whites, African Americans, and Asian Americans. Efforts by state and local governments and private organizations to rectify these practices prior to the war continually failed. Yet as war contracts poured into plants in 1940, labor shortages, exacerbated by discriminatory practices, quickly emerged. In March 1941 Gov Lehman was forced to create the Committee on Discrimination in Employment, a temporary Defense Council agency dedicated to eradicating employment discrimination. On 12 Mar 1945 Gov Thomas E. Dewey signed the Ives-Quinn bill into law, banning employment discrimination.

New York State's higher education policy had long consisted of generous public subsidies to private colleges because the state lacked a public university. By the Great Depression this system failed to address higher educational needs. World War II ushered in permanent changes. In 1944 Pres Roosevelt signed into law the Servicemen's Readjustment Act (commonly known as the GI Bill), enabling state veterans to attend college in numbers far exceeding the capacity of the state's private colleges. The war also brought about cultural changes that rendered current college admission practices unacceptable. Before the war the private colleges used a quota system to accept limited numbers of ethnic Whites and Blacks. Starting in 1945 critics compared these practices to the policies of Nazi Germany, and public outrage over the quotas led Gov Dewey to appoint a commission in July 1946 to explore new policy options. On 4 Apr 1948 Dewey signed legislation both creating the State University of New York (SUNY), a system dedicated to nondiscriminatory admissions practices, and banning discrimination in private college admissions.

Women and Ethnic and Racial Minorities

World War II significantly altered the lives of women and ethnic minorities in New York State. For both groups the war provided new opportunities, though the changes for ethnic minorities proved to have much greater resilience than did those for women. The war brought about profound new employment opportunities for women in the state. Starting in 1943 New York's defense industries turned to women, traditionally shut out of industrial jobs in large numbers, as more men were drafted. By August 1945, 100,000, or 40%, of the employees in New York State's aeronautical industries were women. The introduction of large numbers of women into the workplace was aided by state government. Beginning in September 1941 the State Education Department administered a large statewide program for the Committee on Child Care, which provided childcare services for all mothers employed in defense industries. The program was tremendously successful, and by June 1945 over 251 centers in 42 communities were taking care of more than 7,000 children daily. Yet these changes for women lasted only for the war's duration. In the fall of 1945 almost all state industrial plants shut down for reconversion. When the plants reopened, through seniority rules, returning male veterans received preference over women for rehiring. As a result, demand for the state's childcare program plummeted, leading to its termination on 1 Oct 1947.

If attitudinal changes toward female industrial employment lasted only to 1945, war-driven changes toward ethnic Whites and African Americans were more permanent. For ethnic Whites, particularly Italian and Jewish Americans, war-induced labor shortages and new state antidiscrimination policies led to the near elimination of workplace bias by 1943, and workplace barriers to Blacks lessened somewhat. Racial tensions between Blacks and Whites, however, remained strained throughout the war. On the night of 1 Aug 1943 the shooting of an African American soldier by a white New York City police officer in Harlem sparked two days of violence in that neighborhood. The rioting left 5 dead, 400 injured, and 180 arrested, and led to the looting of many of Harlem's white-owned stores. Nevertheless World War II did result in far-reaching policy changes in state government that aided black advancement in the postwar period.

EMIGRES AND REFUGEES

Even before the outbreak of World War II, New York State served as a haven for a significant number of German academics. In September 1933 Director Alvin S. Johnson organized the University in Exile at the New School for Social Research in Manhattan. The new program offered teaching positions to German academics who had been fired by their own universities for their opposition to the Nazi regime. The German émigrés who came to the New School included economists Karl Brandt and Emil Ledrer, sociologist Hans Speier, and Gestalt psychologist Max Wertheimer. By summer 1941, 170 scholars, refugees from European fascism, had taken up residence at the New School; 50 of the program's émigrés became permanent faculty there after the University in Exile was closed in 1945. Additionally, the Institute of Social Research relocated to Columbia University, and a number of leading European art historians joined New York University's Institute of Fine Arts.

In 1944 New York State became home to America's only refugee camp during the war. Established at Fort Ontario in Oswego, the Fort Ontario Emergency Refugee Shelter housed 982 European refugees, of whom 874 were Jews. Pres Roosevelt had long resisted efforts to establish facilities in the United States for war refugees, but following the British and US invasion of Italy, when large numbers of displaced persons fell into Allied hands and pressure by international aid agencies increased, the president relented. A US Army base, Fort Ontario began receiving war refugees in August 1944. The shelter remained open until February 1946, when the federal government granted 853 of the refugees permanent visas to stay.

DEMOBILIZATION AND LASTING CHANGE

The conclusion of World War II on 2 Sept 1945 was quickly felt in New York State, particularly in defense industries. Even by the fall of 1944 the US military slowed the pace of its purchase orders, leading to slowdowns and layoffs at some state war plants. With V-J Day hundreds of thousands of New York State defense workers were laid off. Layoffs affected women the most because there was little likelihood that they were going to be rehired. Gains made by women during the war in industrial employment were driven only by wartime necessity. In New York State women made up 35% of the workforce in the summer of 1945; they would not reach that percentage again until the early 1970s. Defense spending helped catalyze the last great industrial age for New York State and in places like Westchester, Nassau, and Suffolk Cos paved the way for rapid postwar suburbanization. World War II did bring a number of other significant and lasting changes, however, particularly in the areas of ethnicity and race by reversing some of the prewar discrimination in employment and education. Advocates who broke down these barriers used the rhetoric of the war and of the struggle between American democracy and Nazi racism to bring lasting change. On 4 Nov 1947, as a token of gratitude to the sacrifices made by veterans, the electorate approved a state constitutional amendment authorizing the state government to issue a $400 million bond to pay a $250 "veteran bonus" to each New Yorker who had been a member of the US armed forces during World War II. In 2002 a memorial to honor the war's New York State veterans opened beside the Empire State Plaza in Albany.

See also AVIATION; ELMIRA; ESPIONAGE; ITALIANS; JAPANESE; LABOR; WAR MEMORIALS.

Capeci, Dominic J., Jr. "Wartime Fair Employment Practices Committees: The Governor's Committee and the First FEPC in New York City, 1941–1943," *Afro-Americans in New York Life and History* 9 (1985): 45–63

Dewey, Thomas E. Papers. Univ of Rochester Library

Hartzell, Karl Drew. *The Empire State at War* (Albany: State of New York, 1949)

Kessner, Thomas. *Fiorello H. La Guardia and the Making of Modern New York* (New York: McGraw-Hill, 1989)

Knapp, Gretchen Elizabeth. "Home Front Maneuvers: Civilian Mobilization and Social Problem-Solving in Western New York during World War II" (PhD diss, SUNY Buffalo, 1995)

Mazuzan, George T., and Nancy Walker. "Restricted Areas: Prisoner-of-War Camps in Western New York, 1944–1946," *New York History* 59 (Jan 1978): 55–72

Nevins, Allan. *Herbert H. Lehman and His Era* (New York: Scribners, 1963)

New York State War Council. Papers. NYS Archives, Albany

Smith, Richard Norton. *Thomas E. Dewey and His Times* (New York: Simon & Schuster, 1982)

Ottman, Tod M. " 'Government That Has Both a Heart and a Head': The Growth of New York State Government during the World War II Era, 1930–1950" (PhD diss, SUNY Albany, 2001)

Tod M. Ottman

Worth. Town (pop 234) in SE Jefferson Co. Settled in 1802 by an association from Litchfield (Herkimer Co), it was abandoned in 1816–17 but resettled several years later. The town was formed in 1848 from Lorraine. Uncertainty over land titles retarded development, a situation from which the town never recovered. Agriculture and lumbering were its principal industries. At 1,200–1,600 feet (365–490 m) above sea level, Worth is the most elevated town in Jefferson Co, cut by wide gorges and subject to early frosts and deep snows. In the early 21st century the town is known for hunting camps, snowmobiling, and four-wheeling trails.

Laura Lynne Scharer

WPA. See FEDERAL ART PROJECT; FEDERAL DANCE PROJECT; FEDERAL THEATRE PROJECT; FEDERAL WRITERS' PROJECT; WORKS PROGRESS ADMINISTRATION.

Wright. Town (pop 1,547) in NE Schoharie Co. Palatines settled the lower Fox Creek area *ca* 1735, and New Englanders filled in the eastern area before the Revolution. The town was formed from Schoharie in 1846. A hilly upland with good soils, most of the town's land is used for agriculture, especially dairying. The hamlet of Gallupville includes a number of fine Greek Revival houses.

Peter Johnson and Dawn Johnson

Wright, Archie (*b* Westville, Franklin Co, 25 July 1891; *d* Ogdensburg, St. Lawrence Co, 24 Dec 1967). Farmer and labor activist. After graduating from the Ogdensburg Free Academy in 1911, Wright, a socialist, refused to register for the draft during World War I (1917). He served one day in jail and was compelled to register, although he was never drafted. After the war Wright traveled the world with the Merchant Marine. From 1921 to 1926 he was a member of the Industrial Workers of the World (IWW). In 1928 he returned to his father's small dairy farm (of 39 cows) near Ogdensburg, just as milk prices collapsed with the onset of the Great Depression. In the 1930s Wright gained prominence in state and national politics. Drawing upon his experience as an IWW organizer, in 1936 he founded the Dairy Farmers Union (DFU), the only farmers' organization in US history explicitly in the model of a trade union. Under Wright's leadership as president, the DFU led two major milk strikes in New York State: in 1937 it organized a boycott of milk deliveries to Sheffield Farms, a major New York City dealer; in 1939 the 25,000 members of the DFU shut down the New York City milk market for nine days. In a settlement negotiated with help from Mayor Fiorello La Guardia, DFU farmers received a 45% increase in wholesale prices. The DFU's successful strikes, however, led its opponents to mount a well-financed red-baiting campaign, which specifically targeted Wright's draft resistance and leftist politics. At their urging the FBI began an investigation of Wright. After a congressional investigation and many critical news stories, the DFU was torn apart by conflict in 1941. Many of Wright's supporters joined him in a new organization, the Farmers Union of the New York Milkshed (FUNY). He continued as head of the FUNY until 1958, although it was never as politically effective as the DFU.

Dyson, Lowell K. *Red Harvest* (Lincoln: Univ of Nebraska Press, 1982)

Kriger, Thomas J. "Syndicalism and Spilled Milk: The Origins of Dairy Farmer Activism in New York State, 1936–1941," *Labor History* 38 (Spring–Summer 1997): 266–86

———. "A Very Unusual Partnership: The Consumer-Farmer Milk Cooperative in New York City, 1938–1971," *New York History* 80 (July 1999) 305–32

Thomas J. Kriger

Wright, Asher (*b* Hanover, NH, 1803; *d* Cattaraugus Indian Reservation [loc in Cattaraugus, Chautauqua, and Erie Cos], 13 Apr 1875). Missionary to the Seneca Indians. Attending first Dartmouth College and then Andover Theological Seminary, Wright graduated in 1831 and was ordained the same year. He began his missionary work for the American Board of Commissioners for Foreign Missions and moved to the Buffalo Creek Reservation [now in Erie Co], where he translated biblical texts and hymns into Seneca. In 1833 he married Laura Sheldon, who joined him at the mission. The Wrights produced language-teaching materials, including the *Spelling Book in the Seneca Language with English Definitions* (1842), and later translated the Gospels into Seneca. Wright opposed the Treaty of Buffalo Creek of 1838 in which the Seneca lost all of their major New York State reservations. Together with the Society of Friends he helped secure the Compromise Treaty of 1842. Under this treaty the Seneca retained ownership of the Allegany and Cattaraugus Reservations but were displaced from the Buffalo Creek and Tonawanda reservations. In 1845 the Wrights relocated to the Cattaraugus Reservation and in 1855 established the Thomas Indian School.

Fenton, William N. "Toward the Gradual Civilization of the Indian Natives: The Missionary and Linguistic Work of Asher Wright (1803–1875) among the

Senecas of Western New York," *American Philosophical Society Proceedings* 100 (1956): 567–81

Ute Ferrier

Wright, Benjamin (*b* Wethersfield, Conn, 10 Oct 1770; *d* New York City, 24 Aug 1842). Surveyor and civil engineer. As a teenager Wright learned law and surveying from his uncle, Maj Joseph Wright, and by 1790 followed his parents to Fort Stanwix [now at Rome, Oneida Co]. Between 1791 and 1812 Wright surveyed land in central and northern New York State for speculators, including George Scriba, Baron Frederick Von Steuben, William Constable, and the French-owned Castorland Co. Wright subdivided more than 2 million acres (800,000 ha) in Oswego, Oneida, Lewis, Jefferson, and St. Lawrence Cos. On 27 Sept 1798 Wright married Philomela Waterman, and between 1800 and 1810 he built locks and other canal structures west of Rome for Western Inland Lock Navigation Co. He also represented Oneida Co in the state legislature in 1808–9 as a Federalist, becoming a county judge in 1813. From 1817 to 1825 Wright served as chief engineer of the Erie Canal where he supervised construction and trained engineers as well as conferred with the state's canal commissioners. Expanding his projects Wright conducted the initial survey for Connecticut's Farmington Canal (1822) and became chief engineer both of the Chesapeake and Delaware Canal (1824) and of the Delaware and Hudson Canal (1825). From the mid-1820s he consulted on various Virginia transportation projects and on New England's Blackstone Canal, and served as chief engineer of the Chesapeake and Ohio Canal (1828–31). Wright then became the streets commissioner of New York City (1831–34), planning Manhattan's northward expansion and proposing Croton Aqueduct, later built by Wright trainee John B. Jervis. While Streets Commissioner Wright worked in Canada as chief engineer of the St. Lawrence Ship Canal and as consultant on the Welland Canal between Lakes Ontario and Erie. In 1834 Wright resigned the New York City job to plan a route for the New York and Erie Railroad and a year later became chief engineer of the James River and Kanawha Canal in Virginia, aided by his student Charles Ellet Jr. Wright collaborated with his son Benjamin H. Wright on Cuba's first railroad for one of his final projects. In 1968 the American Society of Civil Engineers hailed Wright as the "Father of American Civil Engineering."

Larkin, F. Daniel. *John B. Jervis: An American Engineering Pioneer* (Ames: Iowa State Univ Press, 1990)

F. Daniel Larkin

Wright, Frank Lloyd (*b* Richmond Center, Wisc, 8 June 1867; *d* Phoenix, 9 Apr 1959). Architect. Wright established himself as a leading architect in Chicago after working as a draftsman and designer for Louis Sullivan from 1888 to 1893. Wright's style in his first decades of prominence is characterized by strong horizontal lines and interpenetrating spaces, and his Prairie-style houses were innovative integrations of architecture with interior design. Some of Wright's most important early commissions were in Buffalo, including the Barton House (1904), the Darwin D. Martin House (1904), the Larkin Administration Building (1906; razed 1950), the Heath House (1906), and, in Rochester, the E. E. Boynton House (1908). The Francis Little House living room, originally built to overlook Lake Minnetonka in Minnesota (1913) was re-created and permanently installed at the Metropolitan Museum of Art in New York City in the early 1980s. In the 1930s he developed a low-cost style called Usonian, examples of which include the Sol Friedman House (1948), the Edward Serlin House (1949), and the Roland Reisley House (1951), all in Pleasantville (Westchester Co). Late works include the interior remodeling of the Hoffman Auto Showroom (1954), the home of Mercedes Benz Manhattan since 1957, and the city's Solomon R. Guggenheim Museum (1959), in what Wright termed a "ziggurat" design, a spiraling organic shape devoid of all surface embellishment.

Twombly, Robert C. *Frank Lloyd Wright: His Life and His Architecture* (New York: John Wiley & Sons, 1979)

Nancy E. Green

Wright, Silas (Jr) (*b* Amherst, Mass, 24 May 1795; *d* Canton, St. Lawrence Co, 27 Aug 1847). Governor and US senator. Born into a New England farm family, he attended Middlebury College in Vermont, studied law, and opened a practice in Canton. Active in local politics Wright was elected to the New York State Senate in 1823 and worked closely with Martin Van Buren as the Albany Regency's second in command. Wright served one term in the US House of Representatives (1827–29) and was reelected but opted against serving when he was appointed state comptroller (1829–33). He was elected to the US Senate (1832–44) and married Clarissa Moody in 1833. He backed Pres Andrew Jackson's war against the Second Bank of the United States and led the Democrats in support of Pres Van Buren's program, including the Independent Treasury plan, which would remove government funds from commercial banks to a federal institution, during the depression of 1837. When the Democrats denied Van Buren, who had lost his 1840 reelection bid, the renomination in 1844, winning candidate James K. Polk offered Wright the vice presidential spot. Because of the convention's abandonment of his close friend and leader, Wright refused, but he agreed to run for governor to bolster Polk's chances in New York State. Both were successful. As governor Wright was hurt by Democratic Party infighting, caused initially by differences over banking and state funding for canal construction, by Pres Polk's mistreatment of Van Buren's faction, and by Polk's commitment to expand slavery. The Van Burenites, now called Barnburners, supported Wright's reelection in 1846, but he lost, his friends believed, because of opposition by his Democratic foes; his harsh stance against the violent antirent agitation in the Hudson Valley also cost him many votes there. Wright retired to his Canton farm in 1847 and was a possible Democratic presidential nominee for the 1848 election, when he suffered a sudden, fatal stroke. Wright's home in Canton is now a museum and library.

Garraty, John Arthur. *Silas Wright* (New York: Columbia Univ Press, 1949)

Joel H. Silbey

Wurtsboro. Village (pop 1,234) in Mamakating (Sullivan Co). Under the name Rome, it became a prosperous company town when the Delaware and Hudson Canal (1828–98) was built and was renamed after the company president, Maurice Wurts, when it acquired a post office in 1830. Washington Irving wrote of Wurtsboro's quaint beauty after an 1834 visit with Vice Pres Martin Van Buren. Wurtsboro incorporated in 1866 and, beginning in the 1870s, was a trading village for resorts on the surrounding Shawangunk Mountains. When the automobile became the preferred means of transportation to Sullivan Co resorts in the 1920s, the road through the village was designated a main highway, adding to its growth, but Wurtsboro was bypassed by the rebuilt Rte 17 between 1956 and 1958. It is home to the oldest soar-plane (glider) airport in the United States (1927).

John Conway

Wyandanch (*b* Montauk [now in Suffolk Co], *ca* 1600; *d* ?Montauk, 1659). Sachem of the Montaukett. The Montaukett homelands were located on the far eastern end of Long Island, only a short canoe trip from southern Connecticut. In 1637, shortly after the Pequot massacre in Connecticut, Wyandanch approached Lion Gardiner, the commander of Fort Saybrook [now Old Saybrook, Conn], at the mouth of the Connecticut River and accepted English jurisdiction over his people in exchange for military protection. The two men established a bond of friendship that served as an important diplomatic bridge between the two cultures. In 1642 Wyandanch rejected an appeal from Miantonomo, the Narragansett sachem, to break his ties with the English and join him in an alliance. Wyandanch was convinced that Montaukett interests would be better served by maintaining friendly relations with the English, who could provide military protection and access to such highly valued trade goods as guns, metal tools, and blankets. Two years later Wyandanch signed a formal alliance with the English colonial authorities. In 1648 he invited settlers from Massachusetts to establish the town of East Hampton [now in Suffolk Co] near his villages. Wyandanch's growing ties with the English increased his status among the sachems on eastern Long Island. The English valued his friendship because he successfully negotiated many disputes between them and the Long Island Indian communities. He was also called upon to endorse land sales by other sachems. In the summer of 1657 Wyandanch was in Setauket [now in Suffolk Co] to endorse the sale of two necks of land by Wenecoheage, the local sachem. The sachem acknowledged Wyandanch's authority and gave him a share of the settlement. As Wyandanch's influence grew, proprietors from all over Long Island sought him out to endorse their purchases from local Indians. After Wyandanch's death, Gardiner suggested in his journal that the sachem may have been poisoned, but this is not corroborated in the colonial records. It is possible that Wyandanch died in the plague that took the lives of an estimated two-thirds of the Algonquian people on Long Island between 1659 and 1664.

Strong, John A. "Wyandanch, Sachem of the Montauks." In *Northeastern Indian Lives,* ed. Robert Grumet (Amherst: Univ of Massachusetts Press, 1996)

John A. Strong

Wyandanch. Locality (pop 10,546) in Babylon (Suffolk Co). West Deer Park post office, which opened in 1875, was renamed Wyandanch in 1888, and the Long Island Rail Road established a station in 1903. An early industry was Wyandance Brick and Terra Cotta Co, which burned in 1894. The area was served by the Long Island Motor Parkway (1908–38) and, since 1941, the Southern State Parkway. Lots were platted in 1926, many sold originally to working-class Irish Americans and soon after to African Americans as well. After World War II the black population increased significantly. A former industry was Fairchild Engine and Airplane Corp (1952; guided missiles). The racial composition in 2000 was 78% African American, and 16% of the population was of Latino ethnicity.

Wyoming. Village (pop 513) in Middlebury (Wyoming Co). Settled in 1809, the village was incorporated in 1916. A furnace, a woolen factory, and a tannery all started about 1816. Middlebury Academy was founded in 1817; its building is the town museum. The Wyoming Water Cure (1851) was short-lived, though its 55 ft (16.8 m) polygonal gymnasium is still standing. After World War II the Barlow-Welker Knitting Mill was an employer. In the early 21st century, Wyoming was known as Gaslight Village because its streets were still lit by the original gaslight. The center of the village, including 70 buildings, is on the National Register of Historic Places, and tourism is a growing industry. The AppleUmpkin Festival (1986) in September celebrates the harvest.

Wyoming County (601 mi²/1,557 km²; pop 44,189). Created from Genesee Co in 1841 with Warsaw as its county seat, its name means broad, open, flat lands. Eagle, Pike, and part of Portage (Livingston Co) were annexed from Allegany Co in 1846. It is divided into 16 towns and has 9 incorporated villages. The county is located entirely within the Appalachian Upland, more specifically, within the subregion sometimes referred to as the Cattaraugus Hills. Relief is more pronounced in the north, where valleys are more clearly defined and 300–600 feet (91–183 m) below the surrounding highlands. Although higher, the land farther south is more gently rolling, and the valleys are not as sharply outlined. An exception is along the county's southeast border, where the Genesee River has carved a postglacial canyon whose floor lies as much as 800 feet (244 m) below the adjacent upland. The lowest elevation can be found here at approximately 615 feet (187 m); the highest elevation is slightly above 2,100 feet (640 m) near the southern boundary. Bedrock consists of Devonian shales, sandstones, and siltstones. Sizable pockets of natural gas are scattered under the western third and northeast quarter, and salt deposits underlie all but the extreme northwest corner. The entire county was glaciated and is covered with a mantle of glacial till of variable quality and thickness. Consequently the soils vary substantially in character, although those that support viable agriculture far exceed those that do not.

Wyoming Co's climate is humid-continental. Normal July temperature at Warsaw is 67°F (19°C), and normal January temperature is 20°F (-7°C). The summer daytime maximum fails to reach 90°F (32°C) in about half the summers, while the coldest winter temperature usually ranges between -10°F (-23°C) and -20°F (-29°C). Annual precipitation normals are near 43 inches (109 cm), with about 19 inches (48 cm) falling during the growing season. Figures are slightly higher for the western portions because of Lake Erie. Seasonal snowfall normals lie generally in the 110–120-inch (279–305 cm) range, with highest amounts in the northwest quarter. Surface drainage flows outward from the center of the county with the largest streams being Oatka, Tonawanda, Cayuga, Buffalo, and Wiscoy Creeks. The region's primeval forest consisted of Alleghenian hardwoods, a community made up principally of beech, sugar maple, hemlock, white pine, and basswood. Letchworth State Park occupies the land bordering the Genesee River north of Portageville.

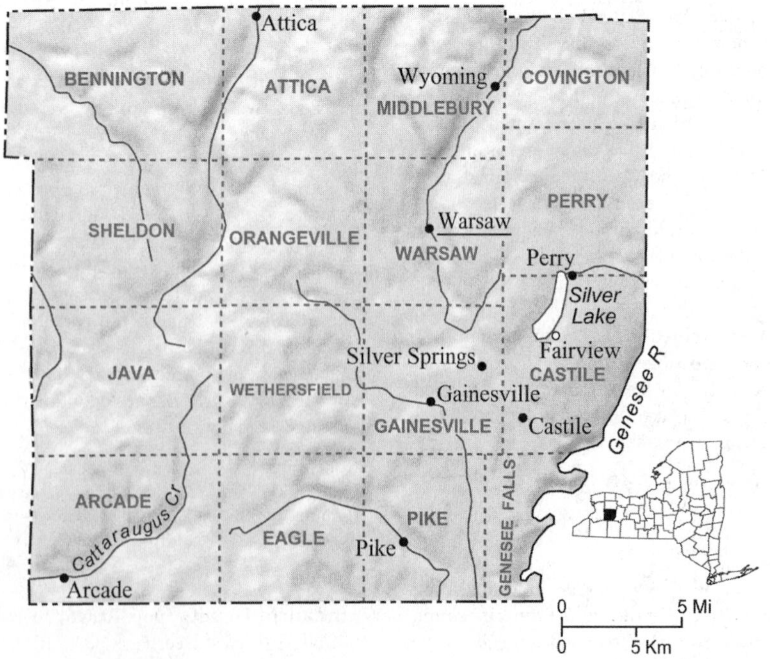

Settlement

In June 2001 the discovery of the remains of an Ice Age mastodon was a reminder of the climate at the time of first settlement by native peoples. In the Contact period the area was used by the Seneca Nation as a hunting and fishing ground. The Seneca remained in possession of the land until 1797, when, at the Treaty of Big Tree, they relinquished claim to all but a few parcels of their once extensive tribal lands. Among these parcels was the Gardeau Reservation, a modest tract (17,927 acres/7,255 ha) partly in Castile and straddling the Genesee River granted to Mary Jemison, who sold it in 1822–23 and 1831.

Robert Morris had purchased the right to negotiate with the Iroquois for ownership of essentially all of the land west of the Genesee River. After acquiring title, Morris in turn sold the western part of the present county to a consortium of Dutch investors, the Holland Land Co, reserving to himself the four eastern towns. Once the Holland Land Co holdings were surveyed, permanent settlement began in 1802 in the Towns of Attica, Middlebury, and Sheldon. By 1810 the territory of all of Wyoming Co's future towns was inhabited, and the population had grown to 2,724 persons, mostly from New England, particularly Massachusetts and Vermont; others came from eastern New York State. By 1850 after Irish and German immigrants had been added to the mix, the population had increased to 31,981.

Economic Development

One of the first roads built by the Holland Land Co linked Batavia (Genesee Co) with Attica in 1802; it was soon joined by another from Batavia to Middlebury. By 1811 these roads extended north-south the full length of Wyoming Co, while the Old Buffalo Rd (now US 20A from Varysburg west) traversed east-west its full breadth. The railroad first arrived when Attica became the southern terminus of a line from Rochester in 1842. The first modern transportation artery, the Attica-Hornellsville Railroad (later Erie Railroad), began operations in 1852. The Genesee Valley Canal (1856) linked eastern towns to the Erie Canal at Rochester. Other railroads followed: the Rochester and State Line (1878; later Buffalo, Rochester and Pittsburgh) and the Attica and Arcade (1881) following north-south routes like the first line, while the Buffalo, New York and Pennsylvania (1871) did the same but crossed only the county's southwest corner.

The first roads were far more efficient at allowing settlers access to the land than they were at providing farmers access to markets. Indeed, limited markets combined with primitive transportation enforced a subsistence agriculture on the first generation of farmers, for whom potash was the most reliable cash generator. Saw- and gristmills began to dot the landscape shortly after initial settlement, sometimes with the financial assistance of the land proprietors. In 1855 there were 30 gristmills, 77 sawmills, and 16 tanneries. A few woolen mills using locally grown wool, a few furnaces and foundries catering mostly to the need for agricultural implements and machinery, and a paper mill were the exceptions to the farm-centered economy during the first three-quarters of the 19th century.

WYOMING CO POPULATION CENSUS FIGURES

	White	Nonwhite	Total Population	Foreign-Born
1850	31,917	64	31,981	3,822
1860	31,916	52	31,968	4,929
1870	29,082	82	29,164	4,051
1880	30,809	98	30,907	3,946
1890	31,132	61	31,193	3,912
1900	30,366	47	30,413	3,287
1910	31,790	90	31,880	3,397
1920	30,220	94	30,314	2,669
1930	28,683	81	28,764	2,220
1940	31,059	335	31,394	2,034
1950	32,194	628	32,822	1,657
1960	33,962	831	34,793	1,118
1970	36,434	1,254	37,688	762
1980	38,499	1,396	39,895	868
1990	39,622	2,885	42,507	928
2000	39,880	3,544	43,424	982

Notes: "Nonwhite" includes African Americans, Asians, American Indians, and Pacific Islanders and, for 2000, also the mixed race and other race categories. Through the 1960 census these figures primarily reflect the African American population. For 1930 and 1950, the foreign-born totals include Whites only. Other years include all foreign-born in the population.

Agriculture dominated, with an emphasis on grains, sheep, and cattle. As late as 1855 there were more sheep than cows. As farmers turned to dairying due to competition from western grain and dips in the price of wool, a milk surplus resulted in the creation of cheese and butter factories. These flourished well into the early 20th century. The nonindustrial economy was slow to demand banking facilities. The Wyoming County Bank (1851) has been owned and operated by Warsaw's Humphrey family for generations, while the Bank of Castile (1869) was owned by the VanArsdale family for over a century. Both remained independent community banks in 2003.

The county's first large industry focused on salt, beginning in the 1870s. The Warsaw Salt Co (1882), Worcester Salt Co (1883) in Silver Springs, Pearl Salt Co (1886–99) in Covington, and Perry Salt Co (1886–1909) were all relatively large producers. When the salt industry declined, textile manufacturing expanded in Arcade, Perry, Warsaw, and Wyoming. Italian immigrants gravitated toward the salt and cut-stone industries and railroad jobs, while Polish immigrant concentrated in the textile industry. The Attica State Prison (1929) was an entirely new employment sector and grew to be a significant employer, especially in the county's northwest. In 1971 a riot in the prison became international news, but the state opened a second prison, Wyoming Correctional Facility, in 1985, and the two facilities employed 1,460 in 2003. The need for all-weather, hard-surface roads came with the automobile. About 1905 the highway system and its maintenance became based on taxes rather than on local labor; tax revenues were used to purchase equipment and to maintain roads. After 1910 construction of brick, macadam and concrete highways began. Road improvements created jobs and helped the local economy, directly influencing the growth of the dairy industry.

Religion, Education, and Culture

One-room log schoolhouses began to appear in Wyoming Co soon after the settlers arrived. These simple structures were later replaced by frame buildings. After 1814 a permanent system of common school districts was established in each town. Private academies and seminaries followed; the first, Middlebury Academy in the Village of Wyoming, was incorporated in 1819. The transition from private academies to public high schools began in the 1850s. Following the Civil War, social and economic conditions, coupled with a growing middle-class population, supported expansion of the tax-based school system. Wyoming Central (1936) and Arcade Central (1938) became the first central districts, and the movement proceeded rapidly after World War II. In the early 21st century, there are six central school districts. Student population decreased in the late 20th century, but the services offered became more diverse.

The First Baptist Church of Attica (1806) was the first church organized in Wyoming Co. Eventually a variety of religious congregations took root. Nearly all of the earliest settlers were Protestants, many of them Baptists. A small Quaker settlement was formed in Orangeville in the 1820s. In Sheldon, where German immigrants first settled in 1823, a Catholic church was organized in 1840. Religion and reform were closely aligned. Antislavery societies were established, and temperance reformers linked social ills, such as crime, disease, and poverty, with the consumption of alcohol. In the 1840s an innovative approach to physical and mental well-being was advocated by water-cure enthusiasts; Castile's Dr Jabez Greene operated a sanatorium (1849) that was continued to be run by two generations of female Dr Greenes until World War II. The Warsaw Salt Sanitarium (1891–97) is believed to have been the first salt bath establishment in North America. Wyoming Co's first newspaper was Warsaw's *Genesee Register* (1828); papers were also published at various times at Arcade, Attica, Perry, and, briefly, Pike. In 2003 three weeklies were published: *Country Courier* (Warsaw), *Arcade Herald*, and *Perry Herald.*

Politics

In 1839 Myron Holley of Perry was a lead organizer of the first convention of the Liberty Party, held in Warsaw. Although that party soon disappeared, the Free Soil and later the Republican Parties had strong support. Republicans have tended to dominate local elections for the past century and a half. Since its 1841 formation,

POPULATIONS OF TOWNS, WYOMING CO

Town, Year Founded	1840	1880	1920	1960	2000
Arcade, 1818[a]	—	2,000	2,412	2,861	4,184
Attica, 1811	2,710	3,099	2,743	5,781	6,028
Bennington, 1818	2,368	2,365	1,557	1,983	3,349
Castile, 1821	2,833	2,315	2,290	2,609	2,873
Covington, 1817	2,438	1,176	788	827	1,357
Eagle, 1823	1,187	1,203	1,059	896	1,194
Gainesville, 1814[b]	2,367	1,787	2,276	2,032	2,333
Genesee Falls, 1846	—	860	542	397	460
Java, 1832	2,331	1,953	1,469	1,757	2,222
Middlebury, 1812	2,445	1,822	1,204	1,416	1,508
Orangeville, 1816	1,949	1,164	838	633	1,301
Perry, 1814	3,082	2,571	5,400	5,372	6,654
Pike, 1818	2,176	1,797	1,003	878	1,086
Sheldon, 1808	2,353	2,257	1,593	1,898	2,561
Warsaw, 1808	2,841	3,227	4,396	4,803	5,423
Wethersfield, 1823	1,728	1,311	744	650	891

Notes: In 1840 the Towns of Pike and Eagle were in Allegany Co. The Towns of Arcade, Attica, Bennington, Castile, Covington, Gainesville, Java, Middlebury, Orangeville, Perry, Sheldon, Warsaw, and Wethersfield were in Genesee Co.

[a]China until 1866.

[b]Hebe until 1816.

Wyoming Co has been governed by a board of supervisors elected directly from the towns by county residents. Voting power is determined by population. A chairperson, elected by the Board of Supervisors, is the chief executive, and the full board meets monthly. The position of county administrator oversaw county business from 1994 until it was eliminated in 2002.

Recent History

The depression's impact on Wyoming Co was considerable. The Civilian Conservation Corps (CCC) put people to work improving roads and parks; there was a camp off Rte 98 between Varysburg and Attica. Public utilities expanded in the 1930s, and electricity became available to more rural residents. World War II strengthened local manufacturing. Textile mills produced uniforms, and factories made elevator hoists and ramps for US Navy LSTs (tank landing ships), as well as tools and hydraulic presses. In 1954 the New York State Thruway opened through Genesee Co, a few miles north of the Wyoming Co border. At the same time, rail service was being cut back. By the end of the decade, the loss of large manufacturing firms had begun. In Perry, Borden's closed in 1959, Perry Knitting Co in 1969, and Robeson Cutlery Co in 1974; Champion and Kaustine survived until the 1990s. Warsaw lost Otis Elevator in 1966, Attica lost Westinghouse Castings in 1986, and Arcade lost Motorola about 1990. Other closures included Lucas Rule Co in Silver Springs and Barlow-Welker Knitting in the Village of Wyoming.

Nevertheless, Wyoming Co has retained a significant manufacturing sector, which employed 13.5% of its workers in 2000, ranking 21 of 62 counties in the state. However, in that same year the county ranked last in the state in service sector jobs. Major industrial employers in 2003 were Prestolite Electric (600 workers) and American Precision Industries (255), both in Arcade; Archway Bakery (165) in Perry; and Morton Salt (175) in Silver Springs. At the turn of the century, the county's fastest growing business was Pioneer Credit Recovery (550), with facilities in Perry and Arcade. The county-owned Wyoming County Community Hospital (1931) employed 560 workers.

Wyoming Co remains an important agricultural region, although the number of farms has dropped considerably in recent decades. From 3,519 farms in 1900 to 2,217 farms in 1950, there were 702 farms in 1997, with the acreage declining from 325,661 (131,790 ha) to 194,902 (78,874 ha). Many of the farms that remain are large-scale factory farms. The county is third in the state for percentage of the workforce in agriculture (9.4%). It produced 935 million pounds (424,108,500 kg) of milk, placing 1st in the state and 20th in the nation. Other important farm products include potatoes (2,300 acres/931 ha planted), wheat, corn, peas, beans, apples, berries, and hay. Christmas trees are growing in importance, and maple sugar remains a side product of many farms.

Tourism is growing, with established destinations like Letchworth State Park (1907), its William Pryor Letchworth Museum (1913), and the gaslight village of Wyoming, where street lights are powered by natural gas. In the late 20th century the Arcade and Attica Railroad began operating excursion trains, and the Arts Council for Wyoming County developed ambitious arts offerings, including a leading folk arts program. A newly built YMCA opened in Warsaw in 2002.

William Wyckoff, *The Developer's Frontier* (1988), provides fairly extensive discussion of the early and subsequent cultural landscape in Wyoming Co. The standard history of the county is *History of Wyoming County, NY* (1880). See also the fine chapters on Wyoming Co in John T. Horton, Edward T. Williams, and Harry S. Douglass, *History of Northwestern New York,* 3 vols (1947). Andrew W. Young, *History of the Town of Warsaw* (1869) is outdated but useful, as is Frank D. Roberts, *History of the Town of Perry* (1915). More recent are [Harry Douglass], *Progress with a Past: Arcade NY 1807–1957* (1957) and *Perry, NY, As It Was and Is* (1976). Two excellent architectural studies are available: James R. Yarrington, *Wyoming County, NY: An Architectural Tour* ([1985]) and Jeffrey C. Mason, *Around Arcade: An Architectural Study of the Town of Arcade* (1985). Mark D. Herman, *Images of the Past: A Pictorial History of Wyoming County* (1991), updates the county history through illustrations with intelligent captioning. *Historical Wyoming* is published quarterly.

X

Xerox Corporation. Manufacturer of document technology products. The Haloid Co incorporated on 18 Apr 1906 with 12 employees and manufactured a proprietary brand of photographic paper invented by founder Joseph C. Wilson. In 1912 Rochester financier Gilbert E. Mosher purchased a controlling share of the company. Joseph R. Wilson, son of the founder, opened sales offices in New York City, Boston, and Chicago. The first Haloid plant was built in Rochester on what would become known as Haloid St. A third-generation Wilson family member, another Joseph C. Wilson, joined the company in 1935. That year Haloid made its first public stock offering in order to finance the purchase of the Rectigraph Co, another Rochester firm. In 1937 Haloid workers organized, joining the Amalgamated Clothing Workers of America, which had a strong local presence. Now known as the Union of Needletrades, Industrial and Textile Employees, the union continues to represent the company's Monroe Co workforce.

The second Joseph C. Wilson was named president of the company in 1945 and led a concerted effort to develop and market new products in the photoreproduction field. In April 1945 John Dessauer, a research engineer at Haloid, found an abstract of an article describing Chester F. Carlson's experiments in electrophotography. Dessauer and Wilson traveled to the Battelle Memorial Institute in Columbus, Ohio, which had a licensing arrangement with Carlson and was supporting further research. Haloid purchased the rights to develop an electrophotographic machine from Battelle. A research grant from the Army Signal Corps enabled the small company to devote a large part of its resources toward development. The name xerography (from the Greek for "dry writing") was coined to describe the photoduplication process.

Thus the Xerox Model A (the second *x* added in imitation of rival photographic manufacturer Kodak) debuted in October 1948. As Haloid had only 889 employees, the first machines were manufactured by the Todd Equipment Co in Rochester. Haloid devised a novel marketing method, retaining ownership of the machines and licensing them to users on a per-use fee schedule. The Model A required 13 separate hand processes to make a single copy and was rejected by the office market; but a secondary use was found for it in the offset reproduction industry, where its paper copies were used to replace the more expensive metal plates that had been standard until then. This market provided income for further research. In 1950 Haloid revisited its original agreement with Battelle and purchased an exclusive license to make and sell all equipment and supplies. In 1955 a new machine, the Copyflo, was unveiled. It used a rotating drum that became standard on all future Xerox copiers. The first commercially successful office copy machine, the Xerox 914, was introduced in 1959. The company became Haloid Xerox in 1958 and simply Xerox in 1962.

Xerox became a major presence within the Greater Rochester area. Construction started in 1955 for a 105-acre (42 ha) industrial park in Webster (Monroe Co) that would eventually grow to include two sites of over 400 acres (162 ha) each, 40 factory buildings, and a 29-story skyscraper in downtown Rochester. The company reached 55,000 employees worldwide in 1969, while the Town of Webster grew from a population of just over 7,000 in 1950 to nearly 25,000 in 1970. The Wilson family became major philanthropists in the Rochester area; their benefactions include the Wilson Health Center (1973) and the Wilson Commons at the University of Rochester (1974).

Corporate headquarters were transferred to Stamford, Conn, in 1970. Manufacturing and sales remained in the Rochester area, however, and only about 150 employees were transferred. Xerox expanded into computer and publishing technology markets, but most of the ventures were failures. The most celebrated was the Palo Alto Research Center (PARC) in California, which in the 1970s developed the first practical personal computers with graphical user interfaces, but Xerox never benefited commercially from these innovations. At the same time the company faced expensive legal challenges to its market position. In 1972 the Federal Trade Commission (FTC) charged Xerox with restraint of trade related to its vigorous protection of patent rights. A wave of antitrust suits from rivals followed. Xerox's settlement with the FTC in 1975 and the expiration of some of its patents allowed competitors to introduce their own office copiers. Xerox's share of the market dropped from 80% in 1976 to 13% in 1982. The company was in danger of going out of business.

Xerox responded in the early 1980s by eliminating 12,000 jobs and diversifying its business with the acquisition of financial services companies. Nevertheless, the corporation's return to health over the course of the 1980s was mainly based on successful competition in its core business of photoreproduction technologies, and most of the financial services holdings were eventually divested. Xerox's legal and financial difficulties resumed in the 1990s, and a series of layoffs beginning in 1993 reduced its workforce by over 30,000. In 2000 the federal Securities and Exchange Commission opened an investigation of Xerox, resulting in allegations of accounting fraud and numerous shareholder lawsuits. This and heavy corporate losses caused the company's stock price to drop from a high of $64 per share in May 1999 to around $5 per share late in 2000. Following the investigation the company announced it would restate its earnings for 1997–2001, lowering its reported pretax income by $1.4 billion. At the end of 2001, the company employed 78,900 people worldwide, including 46,600 in the United States. Of these, 13,350 worked in the Rochester area. The company's financial situation had improved somewhat by 2003.

Dessauer, John H. *My Years with Xerox: The Billions Nobody Wanted* (Garden City, NY: Doubleday, 1971)
Dunn, Esther A. *Webster . . . Through the Years* (Webster, NY: Webster Town Board, 1971)
Hiltzik, Michael. *Dealers of Lightning: Xerox PARC and the Dawn of the Computer Age* (New York: Harper Collins, 1999)

Laura Zelasnic

Y

yachting and yacht clubs. Yacht is a general term for any watercraft used for pleasure. When American yachting developed during the 19th century, most racing was limited to the waters around New York City and Boston, where there was sufficient wealth and leisure to support the sport. Early yacht design followed existing plans for commercial vessels such as keel pilot boat schooners and fishing sloops. In 1839 Robert L. Stevens of Hoboken, NJ, designed the centerboard schooner *Onkahye* specifically as a sailing yacht; as the anchorages and racing courses of early New York yachters were in shoal water, the favored vessel was a shallow centerboard yacht. The following year Stevens and his brothers John C. and Edwin A. engaged George Steers to design a smaller racing schooner, *Gimcrack,* which Steers built in Brooklyn. John C. Stevens and eight other men founded the New York Yacht Club (NYYC) aboard the *Gimcrack* on 30 July 1844. Steers's most famous ship was the 1851 schooner-yacht *America,* commissioned by the Stevens brothers and built at the William H. Brown shipyard in Manhattan. On 22 Aug 1851 the *America* entered a race around the Isle of Wight, United Kingdom, winning the Royal Yacht Squadron trophy cup against more than a dozen British cutters and schooners. The 101 ft (31 m) long yacht's speed was largely due to its fine hull lines. Innovative sails designed by R. H. Wilson of Port Jefferson (Suffolk Co) also contributed to *America*'s victory. On 8 July 1857 the winner's trophy was renamed the America's Cup and given to the NYYC, along with a set of rules to govern the contest in the future. Yachts flying the NYYC pennant successfully defended the America's Cup in 23 races beginning in 1870 until losing to Australia in 1983.

In the early 20th century yacht clubs flourished throughout the state. The NYYC moved to a landmark Beaux Arts–style building at 37 West 44th St in Manhattan in 1901. Other important clubs founded in this period and remaining active include the Buffalo Yacht Club (1860), Seawanhaka Corinthian Yacht Club (1871) in Oyster Bay, Rochester Yacht Club (1877), Larchmont Yacht Club (1880) in Westchester Co, Lake George Yacht Club (1888), Sodus Bay Yacht Club (1893), and Ithaca Yacht Club (1907). As early as the 1840s various handicapping systems attempted to level the playing field for variously sized yachts. Builders responded with new hull forms designed to skirt handicapping rules. In 1896 small boat builder Nathaniel Herreshoff suggested racing duplicate yachts. Herreshoff designed the locally successful New York Yacht Club 35 ft (11 m) class in 1905. The first nationally successful boat-racing class, the Star Class, debuted in 1911 at the Seawanhaka Corinthian Yacht Club.

Long Island Sound became a focal point of yachting after World War II, when commercial traffic and polluted waters drove recreational sailors from New York Harbor. In 1987 a consortium brought yachting back to New York Harbor by organizing the new Manhattan Yacht Club around a fleet of 12 J/24 sailboats docked at facilities rented from the South Street Seaport Museum. Larchmont Yacht Club's annual Race Week, instituted in 1898, continues to be a premier yachting event in Long Island Sound. The NYYC holds an annual cruise and has sponsored several transatlantic races since 1866, including the Atlantic Challenge Cup race from New York Harbor to England in 1997.

See also THOUSAND ISLANDS RESORTS.

Chapelle, Howard I. *The History of American Sailing Ships* (New York: Norton, 1935)
Johnson, Peter. *The Encyclopedia of Yachting* (Auckland, New Zealand: Angus & Robertson, 1989)

Daria E. Merwin

Yaddo. An estate retreat for creative artists in Saratoga Springs. In 1893 Spencer Trask, a New York City investment banker, and his wife, poet Katrina Trask, built a mansion on their 400-acre (162 ha) estate. After the early deaths of their children in 1900, the Trasks decided to incorporate Yaddo as a retreat for artists. Artists were chosen to live there on the basis of work completed, work in progress, or the promise of notable work. In 1909 Spencer Trask died in a train crash. Katrina Trask died in 1922. In 1926 their friend George Foster Peabody supervised the establishment of Yaddo; Elizabeth Ames was its executive director from its opening until 1969. Since 1926 over 5,000 writers, composers, visual artists, performance artists, and choreographers have lived and worked there for stays ranging from a few weeks to a few months. Studios and meals were provided and a period of quiet was in effect every day. Langston Hughes, Leonard Bernstein, Sylvia Plath, Katherine Anne Porter, and Clyfford Still are among famous artists who have done important work at Yaddo. In the early 21st century Yaddo is funded by private contributions, including donations from artists who lived at the mansion. Yaddo visual artists have their work on permanent exhibit in public spaces in New York City, Albany, Cleveland, and San Pedro, Calif. In 2000 Yaddo celebrated its centennial with arts festivals in New York City and Saratoga Springs, where they raised $8.5 million. There are 10 acres (4 ha) of public gardens, maintained by volunteers of the Yaddo Garden Association, formed in 1991. The Trask Society was founded in 1999 to manage estate donations.

Yaddo, http://www.yaddo.org

Paul Lamar

Yankee migration. During its peak years from 1783 to 1820, the exodus of New Englanders into New York State was one of the earliest and most significant internal migrations in the nation's history. The shift was dramatic; New York State's population grew fourfold from 1790 to 1820, largely fueled by New Englanders and their children. Census figures indicate that over 15% (more than 206,000) of New York's population was Yankee by birth in 1850 and far more were descended from New Englanders. In 1855 there were almost 64,000 Connecticut natives in New York State, 57,000 from Massachusetts, and 54,000 from Vermont (at a time when Vermont had about 315,000 residents). There were smaller numbers from New Hampshire, Rhode Island, and Maine. New Englanders did not always remain on the land they first purchased, and within a few years many families continued moving farther west until they were satisfied with their surroundings or something prevented them from traveling farther. Spreading across New York State and then into the Midwest, New Englanders' politics, agricultural practices, sense of community, and manners became the cultural norm for life in the North during the 19th century.

Migration and Settlement

Boundary issues and different concepts of property ownership created a tense relationship between New York and New England during the colonial era. New Englanders moved into the Hudson Valley, some to Livingston Manor, where they clashed with existing landlords and tenets over settling on unimproved lands. Under Massachusetts law, squatters could claim title to land. Yankee settlers therefore petitioned Massachusetts for rights to these borderlands, prompting Robert Livingston to evict them in 1751–53 with support from New York Colony's government. By 1755 matters had escalated: settlers rioted and burned crops, resulting in the imprisonment of dozens of men by Livingston. Yankee-landlord tensions were not resolved, and similar uprisings occurred in 1766 and in the 1770s, when settlers in the Green Mountains revolted against land titles issued by New York. These Green Mountain Boys seceded from New York, forming the independent republic of Vermont in 1777, and entered the union as the 14th state in 1791.

For years New Englanders had been eyeing lands even farther west, especially those lands adjacent to the Genesee River. During the Revolutionary War, many New England soldiers on the 1779 Sullivan-Clinton campaign wrote letters home praising the fertile soils of the Finger Lakes country, and their envy was increased by the abundant Iroquois farms. Colonial charters also whetted interest in the region as Connecticut and Massachusetts each claimed vast tracts of what is now Central and Western New York via colonial charters that granted them land from "sea to sea," bounded only by latitudinal boundaries.

Massachusetts renounced its claim of sovereignty to lands in Central and Western New York at the Hartford Convention of 1786 but retained preemption rights west of a north-south line running from Sodus Bay on Lake Ontario to the Pennsylvania border. New York State law was to prevail in all of the ceded territories, but Massachusetts reserved the right to sell the land and retain the proceeds.

When treaties with the Iroquois opened millions of acres in Central and Western New York for settlement in the 1790s, it devalued the older Hudson Valley tracts, and Yankees flooded New York State, buying land at bargain prices. New Englanders settled first in the Hudson Valley, then in the Mohawk, and then spread to Central and Western New York. Moving in small nuclear family units or in groups of relatives, up to 20 boats of settlers navigated up the Mohawk River daily in 1796 and then crossed the Oneida Carrying Place into the Oswego River watershed for westward destinations. Most traveled overland, often in winter, trudging along the well-traveled Genesee Road or newly opened turnpikes. Between 1800 and 1820, several thousand New England families settled in the northern New

York counties of Essex, Clinton, Franklin, St. Lawrence, and Jefferson.

Yankees migrated into New York State for many reasons, including proximity to New England, rich soils, and modest land prices. Glowing reports from kin and neighbors of their burgeoning farms enticed many to follow in the footsteps of the initial migrants, a process known as chain migration. Portions of New England towns gradually transplanted to New York as extended families and previous neighbors settled in the same community to provide mutual support. When Vermonters began migrating in the 1790s, much of the prime land in Central New York was claimed, so they sought land in the North Country at first, with the region around Lake Champlain eventually being referred to as "New Vermont." Later Vermonters settled in the region centering around Cattaraugus Creek in Erie and Cattaraugus Cos and in the Holland Land Co territory.

Most New England migrants did not cast a fond glance backward. In New England, firewood was scarce, soils depleted, and crop pests proliferated. Because of inheritance customs, the average southern New England farm had but 50 acres (20 ha) by 1775, barely enough to support a family averaging six to seven children. At the same time, the agricultural market economy was expanding. Europe needed wheat in the late 1780s and 1790s because of a spate of bad harvests, economic depression, and war, and the increased prices made even distant farms cost effective. By 1800 New York State farmers could turn a profit living 143 miles (230 km) from a market center, over twice the range of the early 1770s. Albany was a hub for this wheat boom as sleighs and wagons brought loads for shipment down the Hudson River while manufactured goods and textiles made the return trip.

Land companies also fanned Yankees' desire, as agents distributed handbills in New England villages, offering splendid new lands on long credit at low prices. Land speculators, such as Jeremiah James and William Wadsworth, traveled through the New England countryside, with maps and ready-to-sign deed forms. William Cooper sold eager migrants plots on the Otsego Patent five times the size of the average New England farm for pennies an acre. Both the Pulteney group and the Holland Land Co encouraged New Englanders to settle in planned towns by building roads, taverns, stores, and mills. Though land companies often preferred wealthier settlers from Pennsylvania, Yankees were willing to settle where Yorkers and Pennsylvanians would not. Hilly, forested terrain, often shunned by Dutch and German settlers for valley plots, posed less concern to New Englanders. Confronted with thick woods, they tapped maple sugar trees or cleared fields by burning, turning the ashes into a cash crop of potash. In turn, Yankees often found the Mohawk and Hudson bottomlands crowded and too expensive, though they settled in the Genesee Valley lands when available. Cultural and agricultural differences could lead to mutual animosity. Yankees sometimes labeled the Dutch lazy dullards and the Dutch thought the migrant hilltop farmers greedy busybodies trying to draw blood from a stone.

Cultural Imprint

Although most New Englanders sought farms, Yankees also changed New York State's cities. By 1803 Yankees outnumbered the original inhabitants of Albany and dominated its business life. New England investors founded Troy (Rensselaer Co) as a model city in 1787, and inhabitants often contrasted themselves to tradition-bound Albany with pride. Yankees often sided with the Federalist Party, supporting John Jay rather than Gov George Clinton. With the notable exception of Martin Van Buren, by the 1830s almost all of New York State's major political leaders came from New England stock. Ideas of reform were often tied to the political culture of upstate New York, reflecting New England's commonwealth ideology. New York City drew the younger sons of New England mercantile families, such as A. A. Low of Salem, Mass; Preserved Fish and Joseph Grinnell of New Bedford, Mass; and J. P. Morgan of Hartford, Conn. The nature and nativity of the city's elite changed with their influx.

New Englanders also left a strong imprint on the land. They laid out villages in a "town green" pattern, bordering a shared meadow with churches and home sites; this can be seen in many New York towns especially in the Chenango Twenty Townships tract (Chenango, Madison, and Oneida Cos). New Englanders brought their own ways of building houses, preferring wood-framed, central hall houses of a full two stories for their residences rather than the one-and-a-half-story stone and wood houses more common among Dutch and German settlers. New place-names reflected New England roots, including Berkshire (Tioga Co), North Boston (Erie Co), and Bennington (Wyoming Co). New Englanders tended to identify towns using north, south, east, and west, drawing on their English heritage in designating places. Many of upstate New York's dialect features, such as using pail instead of bucket, reflect New Englander's linguistic patterns.

In contrast with New Yorkers' diverse roots, Yankees were ethnically homogenous. Those with Dutch, German, or French ancestry made up scarcely 2% of New England's population in 1790, compared to almost 30% of New York State's. The majority of Yankees descended from New England Puritans, though some families had Scots-Irish, Welsh, or Indian heritage. Although few skilled craftsmen migrated, most Yankees were middling to poor and sought independent means as freehold farmers, artisans, and peddlers. Few owned slaves, unlike wealthier Dutch families. They were known for their delight in success and eagerness to achieve it. With Calvinist roots, they interpreted good fortune as God's blessing. Yorkers might deride them as hypocritical, callous, or needlessly competitive, but Yankees had important community-based traditions. More than any other 18th-century group, they supported tax-funded public education and communal charitable groups.

From the nation's most literate region, scores of Yankee schoolmasters and schoolmarms taught New Yorkers. Gideon Hawley, a New England native, directed the first successful program of state-aided neighborhood schools in New York, and the majority of antebellum college presidents and faculty were alumni of New England colleges, following New England curricula. Singing societies, small-town newspapers, county fairs, and agricultural societies were also Yankee imports. Yankee migration also inspired a cultural efflorescence among older New York City families. Elite members of Dutch descent organized the St. Nicholas and Knickerbocker Societies as centers of "authentic" culture to counter the New England Society established by newly settled Yankees in 1805.

New York's literature reflected this tension: Washington Irving's Yankee schoolmaster Ichabod Crane is constantly at odds with Dutch burghers but bewitched by their fetching daughters. James Fenimore Cooper's novels distilled the Yankee essence in characters like Hiram Doolittle in *The Pioneers* (1823), though his later works took a harsher view, portraying transplanted New Englanders as covetous and scheming. In turn, New Englanders derided New Yorkers, such as Yale president Timothy Dwight, who when traveling through the region in 1820 found Yankee settlements such as New Hartford (Oneida Co) pristine havens of educated, hardworking farmers, in contrast to the untidy villages of churlish and slothful Yorkers.

Boundaries began to dissolve with time as intermarriage and the increased political activity of the 1840s and 1850s revealed avenues of commonality. The arrivals of new immigrant groups made more established groups coalesce, united by prejudice and class consciousness. Irish immigration shifted many New Yorkers' perception of difference and when contrasted to the swell of poor, Catholic immigrants, many Yorkers and Yankees found they had more in common than initially supposed. Political causes created new alliances: Yankees often supported abolition, forging bonds with African American leaders.

Religious traditions changed as well. Although most New England migrants were Congregationalists, after the 1802 Plan of Union between the Presbyterian and Congregational Associations, new settlements united into a single congregation to select a minister. Others joined interdenominational groups such as the American Bible Society, finding common ground in faith. The outpouring of religious expression in Central and Western New York in the antebellum period, when the area was often known as the Burned-over District, was fostered by migrating New Englanders looking for new religious directions. Among the era's most significant religious figures of New England birth who came of age in New York State were the revivalist Charles Grandison Finney (born in Warren, Conn), the minister Henry Ward Beecher (born in Litchfield, Conn), and Mormon leaders Joseph Smith Jr (born in Sharon, Vt) and Brigham Young (born in Whittingham, Vt).

Indeed, the very meaning of Yankee reveals how New York State defined New England. The term probably arose in the 17th century from the Dutch *janke,* a diminutive of the common first name, Jan (John) to designate a shrewd trader. During the 18th and 19th centuries, Yankee came to be applied to New Englanders. By the time of the Civil War the term was used for all Northerners, and Europeans used the term for Americans as a whole. Yorkers' and Yankees' initial assessment of irreconcilable difference softened with time, and the two melded to become what many deemed the quintessential upstate New Yorker.

Darlington, James W. "Peopling the Post-Revolutionary New York Frontier," *New York History* 74: 340–81

Ellis, David Maldwin. "The Yankee Invasion of New York, 1783–1850," *New York History* 32 (1951): 3–17

Fink, Daniel. *Barns of Genesee Country, 1790–1915,*

Including an Account of Settlement and Changes in Agricultural Practices (Geneseo, NY: James Brunner, 1987)
Fox, Dixon Ryan. *Yankees and Yorkers* (New York: New York Univ Press, 1940)
Higgins, Ruth L. *Expansion in New York: With Especial Reference to the 18th Century* (Columbus: Ohio State Univ, 1931)
Holbrook, Stewart H. *The Yankee Exodus: An Account of Migration from New England* (New York: Macmillan, 1950)
Taylor, Alan. *William Cooper's Town: Power and Persuasion on the Frontier of the Early American Republic* (New York: Vintage Books, 1995)
Wyckoff, William. *The Developer's Frontier: The Making of the Western New York Landscape* (New Haven, Conn: Yale Univ Press, 1988)

Kathryn Clippinger Kosto

Yaphank. Locality (pop 5,025) in Brookhaven (Suffolk Co). Originally called Millville, it acquired a station on the new Long Island Rail Road in 1844, and the Yaphank post office opened in the following year. During World War I, it was the site of the 19,990-acre (8,090 ha) Camp Upton, a military training facility, that was immortalized in Irving Berlin's 1917 all-soldier revue *Yip! Yip! Yaphank.* In 1937–38, a Nazi-sympathizing German American Bund camped at Upper Lake. Camp Upton became Brookhaven National Laboratory in 1947. Landmarks include Yaphank Presbyterian (1851) and St. Andrew's Episcopal (1853) Churches, and is the site of the Suffolk County Farm and Education Center.

Suzanne Johnson

Yates. Town (pop 2,510) in NW Orleans Co. Settled in 1809, the town was formed in 1822 as Northton but changed its name the following year. In 1836 the first beans grown as a New York State field crop were harvested in town. A harbor at Shadigee was improved with a 275 ft (84 m) pier built by a stock company *ca* 1850; it became less important after 1876 when the Rome, Watertown and Ogdensburg Railroad (called Ho-Jack) began service to the town. Farmers grew hay, wheat, fruits, and vegetables, and chief industries were canning, drying, vinegar making, and cold storage. In the early 21st century the town remains agricultural, growing grain and apples; Dobbins Cold Storage and Oakes Apple Depots store the orchard harvests.

Virginia W. Cooper

Yates, Abraham, Jr (*b* Albany, 23 Aug ?1724; *d* 30 June 1796). Politician. Son of blacksmith Christoffel Yates and Catalina Winne, he apprenticed as a shoemaker before reading law as a clerk for attorney Peter Silvester. About 1747 he married Anna De Ridder of Schaghticoke [now in Rensselaer Co]. His legal practice embraced less advantaged clients and paralleled his public ascendancy to the Albany Common Council (1753–73), as Albany Co sheriff (1754–59), and as a local leader of the Revolutionary movement. Elected to the First Provincial Congress in 1775, Yates served as president (1776) and as chairman of the committee that wrote the first New York State Constitution (1777). He was state senator and member of the Council of Appointment (1777–90), Albany city recorder (1778–79), state loan officer (1779–83), and a delegate to the Continental Congress (1787–88). From 1783 to 1792 Yates articulated his Antifederalist views and opposition to the new federal constitution in a series of essays, gaining renown under the pseudonyms of Cato and A Rough Hewer. He was appointed mayor of Albany in 1790.

Bielinski, Stefan. *Abraham Yates, Jr. and the New Political Order in Revolutionary New York* (Albany: NYS American Revolution Bicentennial Commission, 1975)

Stefan Bielinski

Yates, Joseph C(hristopher) (*b* Schenectady, 9 Nov 1768; *d* Schenectady, 19 Mar 1837). Governor. Son of patriot merchant and surveyor Christopher Yates and Jane Bradt, he studied with tutors and at local schools before clerking with Albany attorney Peter W. Yates. In 1791 he began a Schenectady law practice. Yates helped found Union College and served as mayor of Schenectady (1798–1808) and New York State senator (1805–7) before becoming a New York State Supreme Court justice in 1808. A presidential elector for De Witt Clinton in 1812, Yates refused to run for governor against Clinton in 1817. Shifting toward Clinton's Bucktail Republican opposition in 1821, Yates supported revision of the 1777 Constitution; he appeared comfortable with the constitutional convention's elimination of the Council of Appointment and Council of Revision. Nominated for governor by an 1822 Bucktail caucus, he won easily. Yates subsequently incurred opposition by failing initially to endorse the popular election of presidential electors under a state law, by recommending two anti-Bucktails to the supreme court, and because he was obliged to settle disputed nominations of justices of the peace. When the Bucktails rejected him as their gubernatorial candidate in 1824, Yates called a special session to pass an electoral law, but it failed. The People's Party successfully backed De Witt Clinton, and Yates retired to Schenectady. He served as a presidential elector for Andrew Jackson in 1828 and presided over a meeting called in 1832 to protest the rejection of Martin Van Buren's nomination as minister to Great Britain. Yates's last years were spent in retirement, disturbed, according to James Kent, by a ward's charges that he had behaved fraudulently as a guardian.

Hanyan, Craig, with Mary Hanyan. *De Witt Clinton and the Rise of the People's Men* (Montreal: McGill-Queen's Univ Press, 1996)

Craig and Mary L. Hanyan

Yates, Robert (*b* Schenectady, 27 Mar 1738; *d* Albany, 8 Sept 1801). Politician and jurist. Son of merchant Joseph Yates and Maria Dunbar, he was a law clerk for William Livingston in New York City and was admitted to the bar in 1760. Yates prospered in Albany as an attorney and surveyor. He produced the first civilian map of Albany in 1770, was elected city alderman (1771–75), and compiled and published *Laws and Ordinances of the City of Albany* (1773). From 1775 to 1778 he served on the Albany Committee of Correspondence and was secretary to the Board of Indian Commissioners. Representing Albany in all four provincial congresses, he served on the committee that drafted the state constitution (1776–77) and was appointed to the state supreme court in October 1777. Although primarily a sitting judge, he accepted surveying commissions and continued a modest legal practice. Yates, with John Lansing Jr and Alexander Hamilton, represented New York State at the Philadelphia constitutional convention in 1787. He and Lansing left Philadelphia 5 July when the convention moved to create a centralized government, which they felt was dangerous. Yates's notes from the meeting were published in 1821. It is believed he authored a series of essays, called the Brutus Letters, in the *New York Journal,* which opposed the Constitution. In 1788 he was elected an Antifederalist delegate to the state ratifying convention. When the Constitution was ratified, he supported it but only out of patriotic obligation.

He was the Federalist candidate for governor in 1789 but was defeated by Gov George Clinton. In September 1790 he was chosen chief justice of the state supreme court. Federalists asked him to be their candidate in the 1792 governor's race, but he declined, saying that the financial strains were too taxing. He ran for governor against John Jay in 1795 and was narrowly defeated. In 1798 he retired from the bench and returned to his modest Albany home.

Bielinski, Stefan. "Robert Yates," http://www.nysm.nysed.gov/albany/bios/y/ryates.html
Young, Alfred F. *Democratic Republicans of New York: The Origins, 1763–1797* (Chapel Hill: Univ of North Carolina, 1967)

Stefan Bielinski

Yates County (338 mi²/875 km²; pop 24,621). Created in 1823 from Ontario Co and named for Joseph Yates, the New York State governor who signed the act establishing the county. A portion of Steuben Co was annexed in 1826, but sections were lost to Seneca and Tompkins Cos in 1828. Parts of Seneca Lake were gained from Schuyler and Seneca Cos in 1946. Yates Co is divided into nine towns containing four incorporated villages. Penn Yan serves as county seat.

Elevation ranges from 445 feet (136 m) at the Seneca Lake shoreline to over 2,140 feet (652 m) in the Town of Italy. Yates Co lies completely within the Finger Lakes Hills subregion of the Appalachian Upland physiographic province. Relief and average elevation increase from north to south and east to west. The southern part of the county consists of a rolling upland broken by a series of deep, U-shaped, north-south trending valleys whose sides rise 800 feet (245 m) or more in places. Four valleys contain large lakes. Seneca and Canandaigua Lakes form all or part of the county's east and west boundaries. The northern forks of Keuka Lake occupy two more of the valleys. Three others are, from east to west, Crystal, Italy, and West River valleys. Bedrock consists of slightly southward dipping strata of Devonian-age sandstone and shale.

All of Yates Co was glaciated, as evidenced by an extensive till plain in the north and deeply scoured valleys and ice rounded hills in the upland. Some of the valleys are filled with deep till deposits. Aside from a few square miles in the Towns of Italy and Jerusalem contained within the greater Susquehanna watershed, surface drainage flows into one or another lake (Canandaigua, Keuka, or Seneca) or into the Canandaigua Lake Outlet and ultimately into Lake Ontario via the Oswego River. The most significant stream is the short but rapid Keuka Lake Outlet, historically the site of much early industry. Soils throughout the northern half and most of the eastern half of Yates Co are of superior agricultural quality. Most of the land

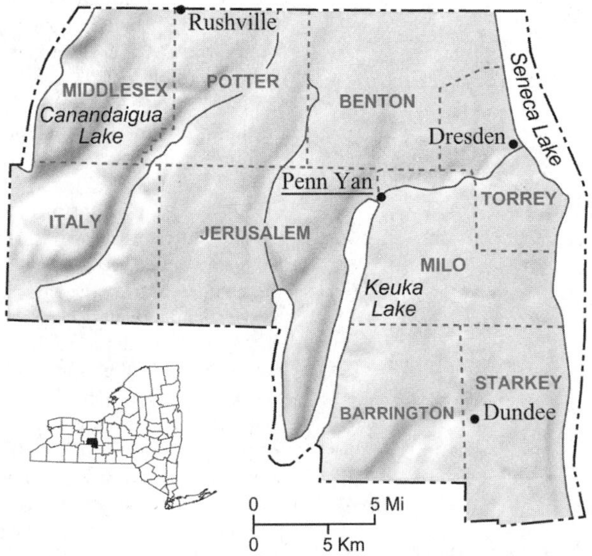

in the southwest is not suited for commercial farming.

Yates Co's climate is humid-continental. Mean January temperatures are fairly uniform, ranging from 23°F (-5° C) at Penn Yan to 24°F (-4°C) in the northwest. Temperatures fall below 0°F (-18°C) a few times nearly every winter. Mean July temperatures in the county are almost uniform as well, ranging from about 70°F (21°C) in the southeast to 71°F (22°C) in the northwest. Daytime highs reach 90°F (32°C) or above for a few days every summer. The lakes and their surrounding steep-walled valleys combine to generate local microclimates advantageous to grape growing. Average annual precipitation ranges from 32 inches (81 cm) at Penn Yan to several inches more in the higher southwest corner. Seasonal snowfall varies from about 50 inches (127 cm) at Penn Yan to over 80 inches (203 cm) in the highest parts of the southwest. The primeval forest cover varied in composition. A central hardwood community dominated by beech, sugar maple, and basswood occupied most of the county, but an oak-hickory forest grew along the shores of Keuka Lake and its outlet to Seneca Lake. An Alleghenian hardwood community of beech, sugar maple, hemlock, white pine, and basswood grew along the upper portions of Flint Creek, while a wetland forest of elm, black ash, and hemlock bordered its lower reaches.

American Indians and Early Settlement

Before the first European settlers arrived, the Seneca occupied what is now Yates Co. Their creation myth says the nation "broke forth from the earth" at Bare Hill in Middlesex, but ruins and artifacts found in other areas point to earlier inhabitants, dating back to nomadic hunters who passed through the region after the Ice Age. The last Seneca community left the area in 1815; one family remained in Jerusalem until 1838.

Many Seneca villages, including one near Kashong in Benton, were destroyed by Gen John Sullivan's troops in 1779 in retaliation for their support of the British during the Revolutionary War. New York's Genesee Co took a long lease of land from the Seneca in 1787–88 but it was quickly disallowed by the state which, instead, confirmed the Phelps and Gorham Purchase. It covered all of the present Yates Co except a narrow strip near Seneca Lake south of Dresden, which fell east of the final Preemption Line and was surveyed in 1788–89. The land east of the line was granted by the state in relatively small parcels after the line was resurveyed in 1792.

The first known white inhabitants were two French Canadian traders who settled near Kashong and a hunter/fisherman who lived farther south on Seneca Lake's shore, both around 1787. A number of families, including many women who left families in Rhode Island and Pennsylvania, came to what is now Yates Co in August 1788 with Jemima Wilkinson (1752–1819), who called herself the Public Universal Friend. Wilkinson's followers created "New Jerusalem," near the Keuka Lake Outlet in Torrey. In 1792 the Torrey tax roll lists 30 heads of households who were members of the community. It relocated in 1794 to an even more remote area, called Friend, in the present Jerusalem. Other settlers followed, many of them former soldiers under Gen Sullivan, and took deeds from Phelps and Gorham or later proprietors.

In 1820 the population of the five towns that later became Yates Co stood at 11,000; the number doubled by 1850. Settlers came from Pennsylvania, New Jersey, and other New England states. Alsatians settled in Potter between about 1815 and 1860. Danes began arriving about 1872, ultimately farming much of Benton, Milo, and Torrey. The 1892 census counted 76 Danes, and the county's population was 15% foreign-born.

The African American population of Yates Co has always been fairly small and did not exceed 200 until 1970. Before the Civil War, most Yates Co Blacks were former slaves from the South. John Nichols of Hopeton freed a slave couple named Mingo and Mariah in 1808; they settled nearby and became the nucleus of a small settlement of free Blacks.

Transportation

In the early 19th century, stage lines ran through Yates Co between Geneva (Ontario and Seneca Cos) and Bath (Steuben Co) or Elmira, but most long-distance travel was by water. The completion of the Erie Canal (1825) and of the Crooked Lake Canal (1833–77) between Keuka and Seneca Lakes linked the area to other regions via Seneca Lake. Beginning in 1851 rail service connected Penn Yan to Canandaigua (Ontario Co) and Elmira. Later lines were the Fall Brook Railroad (1877, later New York Central) and the Middlesex Valley Railroad (1892, later Lehigh Valley), while a short line, the Penn Yan and Dresden Branch of the Fall Brook, connected those villages in 1884. An electric line, the Penn Yan, Keuka Park and Branchport Railroad, operated from 1897 to 1927. Although state highways pass through Yates Co, there are no expressways

YATES CO POPULATION CENSUS FIGURES

	White	Nonwhite	Total Population	Foreign-Born
1830	18,903	106	19,009	125
1840	20,310	134	20,444	—
1850	20,425	165	20,590	831
1860	20,133	157	20,290	1,512
1870	19,429	166	19,595	1,755
1880	20,941	146	21,087	1,799
1890	20,858	143	21,001	1,878
1900	20,185	133	20,318	1,630
1910	18,507	135	18,642	1,411
1920	16,520	121	16,641	1,150
1930	16,741	107	16,848	1,051
1940	16,242	139	16,381	814
1950	17,505	110	17,615	639
1960	18,480	134	18,614	611
1970	19,606	225	19,831	441
1980	21,228	231	21,459	406
1990	22,514	296	22,810	305
2000	24,103	518	24,621	565

Notes: "Nonwhite" includes African Americans, Asians, American Indians, and Pacific Islanders and, for 2000, also the mixed race and other race categories. Through the 1960 census these figures primarily reflect the African American population. Foreign-born figures for 1830 include only those not naturalized, and for 1930 and 1950, the foreign-born totals include Whites only. Other years include all foreign-born in the population.

POPULATIONS OF TOWNS, YATES CO

Town, Year Founded	1800	1840	1880	1920	1960	2000
Barrington, 1822	—	1,868	1,478	822	754	1,396
Benton, 1803[a]	—	3,911	2,413	1,797	2,093	2,640
Italy, 1815	—	1,634	1,444	731	428	1,087
Jerusalem, 1790	1,219	2,935	2,626	2,025	2,847	4,525
Middlesex, 1796[b]	483	1,439	1,457	951	817	1,345
Milo, 1818	—	3,986	5,755	5,817	6,965	7,026
Potter, 1832	—	2,245	1,940	1,200	1,106	1,830
Starkey, 1824	—	2,426	2,729	2,382	2,597	3,465
Torrey, 1851	—	—	1,245	916	1,007	1,307

Note: In 1800 the Towns of Jerusalem and Middlesex were in Ontario Co.

[a] Vernon until 1808, then Snell until 1810.

[b] Augusta until 1808.

or interstate highways; the county airport near Penn Yan offers chartered flight service.

Economic Development

Yates County's industries have always been tied to agriculture, such as the Seneca Foods plant (1940–2002) at Dundee. The pattern that began with the first settlers seeking good land continued with new generations of family farmers. Through the World War I era, farming was the dominant activity: Yates Co's lakeside slopes were ideal for grape growing (first planted 1855), and fertile muckland that emerged from centuries-old swamps was productive for vegetables. Yates Co's flat, fertile plains were ideal for cash crops and grains. The first cash exports were potash and whiskey, followed by wheat, rye, and corn. The terrain contributed to industrial and business development. One of the first mills in western New York State was built on the Keuka Outlet in 1790, and other waterpowered mills were scattered along the major tributaries of Keuka and Seneca Lakes. As many as 30 manufacturers of grain, timber, oil, potash, plaster, tools, wheel spokes, wooden hoops, handles, and shingles were strung along the 8 mi (13 km) Keuka Lake Outlet in the mid–19th century. After rail service replaced canal transport, paper mills pumped out 60 tons (54 MT) of paper daily. Birkett Mills in Penn Yan was established in 1801 and was in 2003 the world's largest producer of buckwheat products, using some of the mill's original equipment. Other products were straw paper, fruit baskets, agricultural machinery, malt, and flour from Penn Yan; woolen cloth from Dresden; plows from Dundee; iron, shoes, steel springs, spokes, and fruit baskets from Branchport; and woolen cloth and agricultural machinery from Starkey.

In the 20th century, Penn Yan's busy manufacturing sector produced wooden store fixtures, clothing, shoes, brass door hardware, boats, electrical conduit, wine, vinegar, carriages, and bus bodies. Boats, canned goods, and fruit juice were produced in Dundee. A chemical plant near Cascade Mills in Torrey manufactured carbon disulfate from 1900 to 1966; also in Torrey, DuPont made hydrogen peroxide from World War II until 1959. The hamlet of Himrod experienced a brief economic boom when Morton Salt opened a modern rock-salt mining facility in 1970, but environmental concerns forced it to close nine years later, leaving abandoned structures and vast, deep mines.

Agriculture remained the backbone of Yates Co's economy, with dairy, livestock, and field crop farms working nearly 115,000 acres (46,500 ha) of the nearly 216,000 acres (87,400 ha) of the county and generating over $40 million annually in 1998. Responding to changes in wine production laws and declining prices for the native grapes used for jams, jellies, juices, and sweet wines in the mid-1970s, many grape growers began planting vinifera and opening wineries. More than 5,500 acres (2,230 ha) of vineyard in Yates Co produce more wine grapes than any other county in the eastern United States. As the number of wineries in the county grows, tourism and related employment are also on the rise. In the late 1990s tourism-related payroll increased by nearly 14%.

Adjacent to these modern wineries, one finds agricultural growth of a different sort. In 1940, 1,548 farms operated on 177,516 acres (71,838 ha) of farmland. After World War II the number of farms declined to 1,183 in 1950 and to 741 in 1969. But when the Groffdale Conference Mennonite farmers in Pennsylvania saw land prices in their region rising, they came to Yates Co seeking land suitable for agriculture and for community growth. The first Mennonite farm in the county was established in Milo in 1974. Since then, many more families have come to the area, and their communities have grown, establishing additional farms, dotting the countryside with churches and one-room schoolhouses, particularly in Barrington, Jerusalem, Milo, Potter, and Starkey. The Mennonite population increased 89% between 1990 and 2000, and there were roughly 345 Mennonite families in Yates in 2003. Dairy farming continues to be the primary industry in terms of both land use and economic impact. In 1980 there were only 100 dairy farms operating in Yates Co; this number increased by 58% between 1990 and 2000, at which time Mennonites owned over 90% of the 224 dairy farms.

Religion, Education, and Culture

Religion has been important to life in Yates Co since Jemima Wilkinson and her followers arrived. Marcus Whitman (1802–47), a Rushville native, went to the Pacific Northwest with his wife Narcissa in 1835 as Presbyterian missionaries to the Cayuse Indians. An exponent of unconventional religious ideas was the famous agnostic and orator Robert Green Ingersoll (1833–99), a Dresden native, who influenced thousands with his speeches in the 19th century. The 1855 census counted 17 Methodist, 14 Baptist, and 8 Presbyterian churches in Yates Co, along with 7 other Protestant bodies and 2 Roman Catholic parishes. In 1998 there were 52 churches in Yates Co, most of them Protestant (including Mennonite) and Roman Catholic.

Three central school districts—Penn Yan (1952), Dundee (1937), and Marcus Whitman (1938)—educate Yates Co children early in the 21st century. A private residential school for troubled youths, Freedom Village, is located in the Dundee district; the campus was originally Starkey Seminary and later Lakemont Academy. St. Michael's Catholic School and Emmanuel Baptist Academy are located in Penn Yan. More than 30 one-room schools are operated by the Mennonite community. Keuka College (1888), a private coeducational college at Keuka Park, serves just over 1,000 students and offers bachelor's and master's programs. The first newspaper published in the county was the *Penn Yan Herald* (1818). In 2003 there were two weekly newspapers: the *Penn Yan Chronicle-Express* and the *Dundee Observer.*

Politics

In the county's first election in 1823, the full Republican (forerunner of the Democratic Party) ticket was elected to office. Since the Civil War, Yates Co politics have been strongly Republican, The Republic Party continues to have a robust political voice in the early 21st century (more than 54% of registered voters, compared with 24% Democrat and 15% Independent). A board of supervisors administered county government until 1973, when it was reorganized as a board of 14 legislators elected from four districts. Supervisors, council members, clerks, and highway superintendents are elected in each of the nine towns. Mayors and trustees are elected in the four incorporated villages.

Recent History

Changes in Yates Co's agricultural and recreational land use have affected much of its recent history and have influenced the local economy and political environment. While the numbers of full-time farmers and total farm acreage increased modestly through the 1990s, the average acreage of a farm shrank slightly, reflecting the small family farms of the Mennonites. In 1997, 657 farms occupied 48.4% of its land area, ranking eighth in the state.

Summer cottages were built on Keuka Lake as early as 1878 and later along the Seneca Lake shoreline. In the second half of the 20th century the county's economy became increasingly based on tourism, recreation, and agriculture because of the loss during that period of much of its manufacturing. As suburban sprawl pushes more Rochester-area workers southward, some have chosen Yates Co for their homes, and retirees have moved to lakeside dwellings, converted from simple cottages to larger year-round homes. This has resulted in land-use concerns around the lakes.

County and town lawmakers work to balance the needs of farmers and their nonfarming neighbors. Concerns about the environmental impact of concentrated animal feeding operations (CAFOs) pushed the Towns of Milo and Barrington to pursue government controls on the size and operations of such businesses. In 2003 the manufacturing sector consisted of Coach and Equipment Co (buses), Silgan Plastics, and Iron Age Shoes, all in Penn Yan; Ferro

Inc (powders for lens grinding) in Torrey; and the Greenidge Plant, a large coal-fired electrical plant at Dresden.

The earliest historical account is Orsamus Turner, *History of the Pioneer Settlement of Phelps and Gorham's Purchase, and Morris' Reserve* (1851). It was followed by two county histories: Stafford C. Cleveland, *History and Directory of Yates County,* 2 vols (1873) and Lewis Cass Aldrich, *History of Yates County* (1892). Miles Davis, *History of Jerusalem* (1912) covers part of the county in greater depth. Frances Dumas, *A Good Country, A Pleasant Habitation* (1990) explores the physical environment and the economy at regular intervals, beginning 1892, closely analyzing maps and other primary sources. The county's most significant ethnic minority was studied in Varick Chittenden, *The Danes of Yates County* (1985).

Gwen Chamberlain

Y Drych [The Mirror]. Welsh American newspaper. This weekly paper was established in New York City to provide information to monoglot Welsh speakers on particular aspects of cultural, political, religious, and social life. The first issue was published on 2 Jan 1851; it contained eight pages and cost subscribers $1 a year. In 1861 the paper was transferred to Utica. Its circulation was estimated at 5,000 in the late 1860s and may have been 10,000 by the end of the century. A major factor in its success was its policy of buying up rival publications around the United States, including *Y Gwyliedydd* (1855), *Baner America* (1877), *Y Wasg* (1890), and *Y Columbia* (1894). In 1941 it became a monthly publication, and during the 1940s the language of the publication gradually changed from Welsh to English. In 1962 the publication offices of *Y Drych* were transferred to Milwaukee; in the early 21st century it was published in St. Paul. It is one of the oldest continuously published ethnic newspapers in the United States.

Hopkin, Deian. "Welsh Immigrants to the United States and their Press." In *The Press of Labour Migrants in Europe and North America 1880's to 1930's* (Bremen, Germany: Univ of Bremen, 1985)

Jones, Aled, and Bill Jones. *Welsh Reflections: "Y Drych" and America, 1851–2001* (Llandysul, Wales: Gomer Press, 2001)

Robert Huw Griffiths and John S. Ellis

Yeshiva University. Private university. The oldest and largest Jewish school in the United States, Yeshiva University traces its origins to 1886, when Yeshiva Etz Chaim was founded to teach Talmud, Bible, and secular studies according to the "strict Orthodox and Talmudical law" to boys ages 9 to 15 on the Lower East Side of Manhattan. In 1897 the Rabbi Isaac Elchanan Theological Seminary (RIETS) was founded to teach the Talmud to more advanced students. In 1915 Etz Chaim and RIETS merged to create the Rabbinical College of America. In 1928 Yeshiva College was established, providing students with a full undergraduate program, and in 1937 a graduate school was created. Yeshiva University was incorporated in 1946. The university's main campus on 185th St in Washington Heights in Manhattan houses the men's undergraduate program and the rabbinical school. Yeshiva also includes the Stern College for women and coeducational graduate and professional programs: Albert Einstein College of Medicine, Benjamin N. Cardozo School of Law, Sy Syms School of Business, Wurzweiler School of Social Work, Ferkauf Graduate School of Psychology, Bernard Revel Graduate School, and Azrieli Graduate School of Education and Administration. The university provides an educational focus for much of the Orthodox Jewish community of the United States while offering several programs in secular studies to a pluralistic student body. Total campus enrollment in 2002 was approximately 6,350, including about 2,000 undergraduates, 1,700 professional students (including law and medicine), and 300 rabbinical students.

Gurock, Jeffrey S. *The Men and Women of Yeshiva: Higher Education, Orthodoxy, and American Judaism* (New York: Columbia Univ Press, 1988)

Dana Evan Kaplan

YIVO Institute for Jewish Research. Research institute, library, and archives in New York City. The only pre-Holocaust scholarly institution to transfer its mission from Europe to the United States, YIVO is devoted to the study of the history and culture of East European Jewry. YIVO is the acronym for Yidisher visnshaftlekher institut, or Yiddish Scientific Institute, the name under which the organization was founded in 1925 in Wilno [now Vilnius, Lithuania]. In 1940, with World War II raging and Wilno under Soviet occupation, YIVO's directors relocated the organization's headquarters to New York City, where an affiliate of YIVO had already existed. After Wilno fell to German forces in 1941, the Nazis began the systematic looting of Jewish institutions in the area. Thousands of YIVO books and documents were confiscated and sent to Frankfurt am Main to the anti-Semitic Institute for the Study of the Jewish Question. In 1947, with the help of the US Army, YIVO managed to recover some of the looted items. In 1989 other materials, long thought lost or destroyed, were discovered in the Lithuanian National Book Chamber, where they had been hidden for safekeeping by Lithuanian librarians. Soon after, the Lithuanian government granted YIVO permission to move these archives to New York City for microfilming. In 1995 YIVO cofounded the Center for Jewish History, a partnership of five Jewish cultural organizations and in 1999 became the first of the partners to move into the center's newly renovated complex on 16th St. The institute's library holds one of the world's most extensive collections of Yiddish books and periodicals, and its archives contain over 12 million documents and other artifacts related to Jewish history. YIVO offers instruction in Yiddish as well as graduate-level Jewish studies courses, publishes scholarly journals and books, and sponsors public programs and conferences.

Dawidowicz, Lucy. *From That Place and Time: A Memoir, 1938–1947* (New York: Norton, 1989)

Mohrer, Fruma, and Marek Web, eds. *Guide to the YIVO Archives* (New York: YIVO Institute for Jewish Research, 1998)

Roberta Newman

YMCA. In 1844 London dry goods clerk George Williams formed the first Young Men's Christian Association (YMCA) as a prayer and self-improvement society for other young, single clerks. By 1851 Great Britain claimed 24 YMCAs serving 2,700 members. In May 1852, shortly after the Montreal and Boston associations were established, New York City merchant George Petrie founded the New York City YMCA (from the 1950s, YMCA of Greater New York) at 659 Broadway in Manhattan. Petrie was concerned with the moral welfare of new arrivals in the city, both native rural migrants and European immigrants, and with their adaptation to metropolitan life. In its first years the Manhattan YMCA focused on evangelism, Bible studies, and charity work, and also supplied some short-term boarding facilities. The Brooklyn YMCA was created in 1854 (from 1920, Brooklyn and Queens YMCA.) It is said to have admitted the first female member in the late 1850s, perhaps in 1858, the founding year of the Manhattan-located Ladies' Christian Association, precursor of the Young Women's Christian Association (YWCA).

By 1857 both the Manhattan and Brooklyn YMCAs offered classes in foreign languages, music, and gymnastics. During the Civil War, the Manhattan association's Army Committee published and distributed the pocket-sized *Soldier's Hymn Book* (1861) to military posts and naval stations, pioneered armed services canteens, and recruited a regiment of African American troops. The all-white organization encouraged that separate YMCAs be formed for Blacks, with one of the first opening in the city in 1866. The Broadway association constructed a new building in 1869 on 23d St, featuring a star-shaped ground plan with central reception area leading to seven departments: classrooms, library, gymnasium, bowling alley, dormitory, reading rooms, and recreation rooms. This design would be repeated in YMCA buildings into the mid–20th century.

By the post–Civil War decades, the state's YMCAs offered day and night classes, some affiliated with institutions of higher learning such as Columbia University, in liberal arts subjects as well as instruction in work skills; the associations also provided short- and long-term lodging and a structured environment for working youth. By 1874 the movement had inspired formation of a Young Men's Hebrew Association (YMHA), located at 1395 Lexington Ave (the "92d Street Y") in Manhattan and from 1902 associated with a Young Women's Hebrew Association (YWHA) on the same premises, with the two organizations merging in 1945.

During the 1880s associations across the nation focused on programs for underprivileged boys, with Buffalo's 1852-founded YMCA the first to employ a full-time, salaried executive to oversee boys' activities. In 1885 Brooklyn's YMCA pioneered an aquatics program, opening the nation's first swimming hall at its Fulton St branch, as YMCA volunteer Sumner F. Dudley pioneered the boys camp movement at Newburgh (Orange Co). Creation of Camp Dudley, the nation's oldest supervised boys camp, at Champlain (Clinton Co) soon followed. In 1887 Luther Gulick, a physical examiner at Manhattan's 23d St branch, created the symbol for the national organization, a red triangle signifying the three dimensions—body, mind, and spirit—of the complete man. By the close of the 19th century, the YMCA had adopted its mission of "the improvement of the spiritual, mental, social, and physical condition of young men" and completed the transformation from religious shelter to semipublic, civic institution.

In the early 1900s many towns in Northern, Central, and Western New York acquired YMCAs, and additional boys camps were established: Putnam Co's Camp Osawana (1903) and the Harlem branch's camp at Westchester Co's Lake Waccabuc (1904). In 1919 the Commission on Interracial Co-operation of the YMCA called for desegregation of all facilities. Staten Island obtained its first YMCA in 1946. In 1979 the organization received a fond tribute in the international hit *YMCA* by New York City disco group Village People. In 2001 New York City's YMCA of Greater New York, with branches in all five boroughs, served 419,000. New York State claims 48 corporate-member YMCAs and about 68 other YMCA branches—camps and program centers—all of which accept members regardless of race, age, gender, or religious affiliation. In 2001 New York State's YMCAs served 989,840 people. A recent initiative is the Virtual Y, which provides after-school learning enhancement at 105 public elementary schools in the New York City area.

See also BIRTH CONTROL.

Donoghue, Terry. *An Event On Mercer Street: A Brief History of the YMCA of the City of New York* (New York, 1952)

Hopkins, Charles Howard. *History of the YMCA in North America* (New York: Association Press, 1951)

Maria Kiriakova

Yonkers. City (pop 196,086) in SW Westchester Co. The Rechgawawank Indians, who inhabited the area when Adriaen van der Donck purchased the present Yonkers in 1646, made ample use of the Hudson River for fishing and transportation. Originally called Nepperhaem (rapid water settlement), the place became known as Yonkers, a derivation of the Dutch *jonkheer,* meaning young gentleman or squire (a reference to Van der Donck). After serving as *schout* (chief law enforcement officer) of the patroonship of Rensselaerswijck [now in Albany, Columbia, and Rensselaer Cos] and assisting with a treaty between the Mohawk Indians and the Dutch, in 1646 Van der Donck received permission to buy a large tract in the present Yonkers and Bronx Co. The tract was made a patroonship called Colendonck. He soon erected a sawmill, and several dozen settlers took up residence. On his death in 1655 the property went to his widow and, following her remarriage, was subdivided and sold over several decades.

Much of Yonkers was purchased by Frederick Philipse I in 1672 and became part of Philipsburg Manor. Following his death in 1702, his grandson, Frederick II, presided over the manor and enlarged the Philipse Manor Hall, an imposing residence built by Frederick I in the 1680s on the Nepperhan or Saw Mill River near its confluence with the Hudson. The Philipse gristmill nearby processed tenants' grain, which was then shipped on board sloops.

Revolution and Early National Period

The economy of Yonkers and the rest of Westchester Co was devastated by the Revolutionary War. Much of the county constituted the Neutral Ground lying between patriot-controlled territory north of the Croton River and British-dominated Manhattan. The area was overrun by both sides. For a brief time in 1776 George Washington had a headquarters in Yonkers. In 1778 an American force of about 100 men, half of them Indians, was defeated by enemy troops who had previously been forced to retreat when confronted by the Indians. Father and son chiefs named Ninham were slain, along with several dozen others at Kingsbridge [now in Bronx Co], then part of Yonkers. A British camp located at Mile Square in southeast Yonkers served as a base of operations for a 1779 raid on northern Westchester.

With the cessation of hostilities came dramatic changes for Yonkers. The seizure of loyalist Frederick Philipse III's manor and subsequent sale of the property resulted in the rise of a class of small freeholders. The areas surrounding Philipse Manor Hall, Mile Square, and Tuckahoe [now Crestwood and vicinity] emerged as distinct communities with churches, taverns, and mills. Yonkers was recognized as a town in 1788. Its 1790 population was 1,125, including 170 slaves, most of whom worked on farms. New York City continued to be a major market for the bounty of local farms, which was transported by sloops and, beginning in the early 1830s, by steamboats. Two decades later, in 1852, flames engulfed the *Henry Clay* as it steamed downriver past Yonkers, following a race with the *Armenia.* St. John's Episcopal Church in Yonkers is the final resting place of some of the 60 victims of that disaster. Perceived by the public as a safe alternative to steamboats, railroads, such as the Harlem (1844) running from Manhattan through central Westchester Co, including the eastern part of Yonkers, and the Hudson River Railroad, completed along the river shore in 1849, positioned Yonkers for an economic transformation.

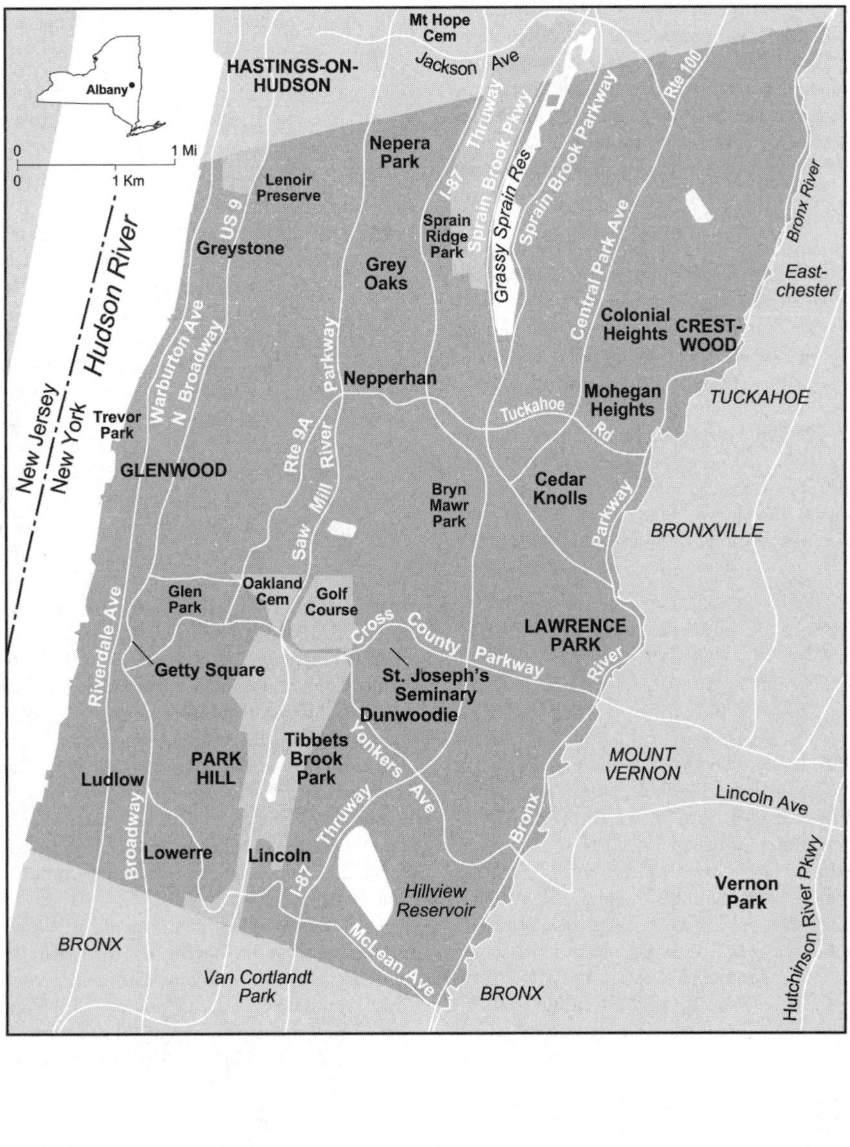

Economic Development

Although large-scale industrialization did not take hold until the second half of the 19th century, Yonkers had one of the earliest cotton mills in the United States. Located on the eastern edge of town in a sturdy, three-story building erected between 1800 and 1810 for the Eastchester Manufacturing Co, the business survived until 1821 when legal difficulties forced the sale of the mill. Textile manufacturing continued under new ownership, but the building was vacant at the time of its 1852 sale to the Hodgman Rubber Co, manufacturers of products ranging from life preservers to rubber knapsacks for miners and raincoats for American troops during World War I.

When Hodgman relocated to Yonkers from New York City it joined a small number of industries, including hat, veneer, and carpet companies that were beginning to transform the local economy. It was not until 1864, however, that the Alexander Smith and Sons Carpet Co relocated to Yonkers after two disastrous fires at its West Farms [now in Bronx Co] plant. By this time Alexander Smith and Halcyon Skinner had patented a new type of power loom that transformed the industry. Their companies' rapid expansion necessitated a larger workforce, mainly composed of immigrants from Ireland and southern and eastern Europe. John Masefield, who later became England's poet laureate, wrote *In the Mill* (1941) about his experiences as a worker in the Alexander Smith mills in the 1890s. The influx of immigrants helped swell the population, and Yonkers became the county's largest municipality in 1860, with 11,484 residents. In 1872 the downtown area, which had incorporated as the Village of Yonkers in 1855, joined the rest of the town to form Westchester Co's first city. The area known as South Yonkers, or Kingsbridge, became a town under the latter name and soon afterward was annexed by New York City. By the time the City of Yonkers was incorporated, elevator manufacturing, begun in Yonkers in 1852 by Elisha Graves Otis, was rivaling carpet production as an economic force. Like the carpets woven at Alexander Smith and Sons, including the custom rugs for the Winter Palace in St. Petersburg, Otis elevators became world famous. Less celebrated but nonetheless important were such firms as Waring, Belknap and Co, which was turning out 800 hats a day in 1877, Skinner and Co, manufacturer of sewing silk and embroideries, W. H. Copcutt Manufacturing Co, producers of ribbons and spool silk, Osterheld and Eckemeyer Machine Co, American Gear Co, Hepworth and Co, manufacturers of machinery for sugar refineries, and Underhill's Brewery.

Despite economic panics in 1857, 1873, and 1893 and the shutdown of Alexander Smith and Sons by an 1885 strike organized by the Knights of Labor, the city's industrial base continued its expansion. Aiding this growth were such financial institutions as the Yonkers Savings Bank, Citizens National Bank, and People's Savings Bank. Nonfinancial institutions also played important roles in the life of the community. This was especially true of the city's churches. St. John's Episcopal Church had been welcoming worshipers since 1752. By the mid–19th century there were other Episcopal churches in various parts of town, as well as Methodist, Presbyterian, and Roman Catholic churches, including the Church of the Immaculate Conception (1848, popularly known as St. Mary's). Jewish services were held beginning in 1870; Teutonia Hall became a synagogue 20 years later. By the late 1800s Catholicism and Judaism were well established because of the new influx of European immigrants. In 1890, when the population reached 32,033, 34% of the city's residents were foreign-born. By the turn of the 20th century, neighborhoods and churches reflected the ethnicity of their immediate area to the extent that Yonkers appeared to be not one city but many, especially in the industrialized area near the Hudson River, where workers lived close to their places of employment. Irish and Jews settled in the Flats, Slovaks in the Hollow, and Italians southeast of Getty Square. This situation persisted into the 20th century with additional ethnic enclaves created by Poles and a small African American community that made up 3.2% of the population in 1950.

Cityscape

In contrast with the densely populated area near the Hudson, the eastern part of the city was suburban. Although such neighborhoods as Park Hill in the western part of Yonkers constituted pockets of suburbia and afforded residents who worked in New York City an easy commute by rail, suburbanization was most pronounced in the Bronx River corridor after the Bronx River Parkway was completed in 1925. Land values soared on both sides of the roadway, and attractive homes were built in Crestwood, Colonial Heights, and other neighborhoods. The completion of the Yonkers section of the Saw Mill River Parkway in 1929 and the Cross County Parkway in 1932 spurred further development, as did the new county-owned Tibbets Brook Park and Dunwoodie Golf Course. Golf had been played in Yonkers since 1888, when the St. Andrew's Golf Club was organized. One of the earliest courses in the country, it hosted the first US Open in 1894 but abandoned Yonkers for Hastings-on-Hudson. Yonkers Raceway, however, known originally as the Empire City Trotting Club when it opened in 1899, remained a premier Yonkers sporting venue. Recreational amenities and improved transportation were instrumental in spurring suburbanization; so, too, were developers. The Lawrence family, who had transformed the nearby Village of Bronxville into a haven for artists and commuters, developed the Lawrence Park West residential enclave in Yonkers and established Sarah Lawrence College (1926). Other institutions of higher education in the city are St. Joseph's Seminary, established in 1896 to educate future Roman Catholic priests, St. Vladimir's Orthodox Theological Seminary, which opened in Crestwood in 1962, and Mercy College of Dobbs Ferry, which established its first satellite campus in Yonkers in 1977. Newspapers included the *Statesman* (1863–1932) and the *Herald Statesman* (1932–1998); in 2003 the *Yonkers Home News and Times* fills the need for city reportage.

Boys ready for work, each with a hoe or a rake, at the Fairview Garden School, Yonkers, 1904.

Recent History

Although Yonkers factories made valuable contributions to the military effort, including the submarine pipeline that delivered gasoline for the D-Day invasion during World War II and the coaxial cable for the distant early warning system used in the Cold War, the city declined as a manufacturing center in the second half of the 20th century. The Alexander Smith and Sons moved away in 1955 and Otis Elevator, which had benefited from incentives granted in conjunction with the city's urban renewal effort, announced its withdrawal in 1983. The Boyce Thompson Institute for Plant Research (1924) became part of Cornell University and moved to Ithaca in the 1970s. Although Yonkers had fallen on hard times, the area bordered by Broadway and the Saw Mill River Parkway benefited from the building of the South Westchester Executive Park in the 1970s. A few miles away the Hudson River Museum was flourishing. South of the museum, however, Getty Square, once the retail hub of the city, was affected by competition from the Cross County Shopping Center (1955), a mall adjacent to the Thruway (1955) and the Cross County Parkway. Strip shopping centers on Central Ave and big box stores, erected in the 1990s along the Thruway and accessible from the Sprain Brook Parkway (1963), accelerated the shift of retailing away from downtown.

Adding to the challenge of revitalizing the old industrial heart of the city was the concentration of public housing near this area, which became increasingly occupied by minority populations in the last half of the 20th century. Arguing that school segregation was the result of the city's practice of siting public housing in western Yonkers, the NAACP and the US Justice Department sued the city in 1980. Five years later Yonkers was ordered to integrate its schools and erect affordable housing in white neighborhoods on the east side of the city. Appeals and additional suits followed, and the school component was settled only in 2002. From 1980 to 2000 the African American population increased from 10.5% to 16.6%, and people of Latino ethnicity from 8.7% to 25.9%.

In the early 21st century, although the affordable housing initiative was behind schedule, the western part of the city was being transformed. The Hudson River waterfront, inaccessible for so long because of the industry along the shoreline, was being reclaimed. The ferry from Yonkers to Alpine, NJ, an important transportation link from 1893 until 1956, was gone, but there was a new sense of vitality along the Yonkers waterfront. Near a power plant that was converted to condominiums in 1988, a market-rate apartment complex was under construction. Other integral components of the area's revitalization are a parking garage for 600 vehicles, a refurbished railroad station, a 1.5 mi (2.4 km) long public park along the river, and the Larkin

Center, housing the Yonkers Public Library and Board of Education in a restored and expanded building once part of Otis Elevator. The Hudson Valley National Bank, a commercial bank established in 1972, continues to operate.

Notable residents have included Edwin Armstrong, who invented FM radio in 1912 while living in Yonkers, and Lee H. Baekeland, who invented Velox paper and Bakelite, a synthetic plastic, in 1906. At various times Yonkers was home to prominent political figures, including Gov Malcolm Wilson, Lt Gov (and Westchester Co Executive) Alfred B. DelBello, and Gov Samuel J. Tilden, 1876 Democratic presidential candidate. The city acquired Tilden's estate in 1946 and converted it to a park overlooking the Hudson.

See also CARPET INDUSTRY.

Allison, Charles E. *The History of Yonkers* (New York: Wilbur B. Ketchum, 1896)
Bolton, Robert. *The History of the Several Towns, Manors, and Patents of the County of Westchester,* 2d ed. (New York: Charles F. Roper, 1881)
Rebic, Michael P. *Landmarks Lost and Found: An Introduction to the Architecture and History of Yonkers* (Yonkers: Yonkers Planning Bureau, 1986)

Marilyn E. Weigold

York. Town (pop 3,219) in NW Livingston Co. The town was formed from Caledonia and Leicester in 1819. At Fowlerville, the Livingston Agricultural Works made implements from *ca* 1835 to 1881; its plant was later a bolt factory. The Genesee Valley Canal operated 1840–78, and two railroads served the town beginning in the 1870s and 1880s. A salt spring was discovered in 1835. In 1884 the Retsof Mining Co—named for the company president, Foster, spelled backward—began mining salt in the first deep (1,170 ft/356.6 m) salt mine in the United States. Italians came for employment, especially in the 1890s. In 2003 salt mined in Groveland was being trucked to Retsof for packaging. Atofina Inc manufactures chemicals at Piffard. Agriculture is the predominant land use. A stay at Abbey of the Genesee (1951) in Piffard inspired Henri Nouwen's spiritual classic, *The Genesee Diary: Report from a Trappist Monastery* (1976). Monk's Bread, produced by the abbey's bakery, is sold widely in the region.

Joyce Rapp

York College. Public college, part of the City University of New York (CUNY). The school was created in 1966 to accommodate increasing numbers of students seeking admission to CUNY institutions. York became the fifth senior college in the CUNY system in 1967, when just over 370 students began attending classes in temporary quarters in Bayside (Queens Co). Led by Milton G. Bassin, who would serve as college president for 20 years, York moved to temporary quarters in Jamaica (Queens Co) in 1971. Permanent facilities opened in 1986 on the 50-acre (20 ha) Jamaica campus at 94–20 Guy R. Brewer Blvd, where the academic core building houses lecture halls, laboratories, classrooms, and studios. This liberal arts college offers a wide choice of baccalaureate programs, emphasizing accounting, education, and nursing. Designated a center for cooperative education in health and business professions, York is the only CUNY institution where undergraduates can major in occupational therapy, gerontology, or biotechnology. York offers a major in information systems management and a physician assistant program. In fall 2002 enrollment was 3,180 full-time and 2,534 part-time students.

Roff, Sandra Shoiock, Anthony M. Cucchiara, and Barbara J. Dunlap. *From the Free Academy to CUNY: Illustrating Public Higher Education in New York City, 1847–1997* (New York: Fordham Univ Press, 2000)

Pamela Cooper

Yorkers. The colloquial term for individuals claiming New York State as their home. Although settlement, with its accompanying cultural-geographic similarities, did occur between New England and New York State, the western border of Vermont, Massachusetts, and Connecticut demarcates an area that is distinctively unlike New England. Within New York Colony the cultural influences of German, Dutch, and English settlement gave rise to distinctive speech and settlement patterns. "Yorkers" has come to denote residents of the State of New York, recognizing these unique cultural expressions. One example of the various uses of the term include the naming of a Canadian regiment of loyalists raised by Sir John Johnson in June 1776, the King's Royal Yorkers, most of whom were from the Mohawk and Schoharie Valleys of New York State. The increasing presence of New Englanders in New York State after 1770 provided a neat dichotomy between Yankees and Yorkers, and the term "Yorkers" remained popular in the mid–19th century. Writers such as Washington Irving referred to New York as the York State and its residents as York Staters. The term Yorker retains some currency, though residents of New York City almost never use it, and it can have a subtle anti–New York City bias. The New York State Historical Association founded a Yorker program in 1942 to promote the interest in New York State history within school settings.

Fox, Dixon Ryan. *Yankees and Yorkers* (New York: New York Univ Press, 1940)
Zelinsky, Wilbur. *The Cultural Geography of the United States* (Englewood Cliffs, NJ: Prentice-Hall, 1973)

Ellen McHale

Yorkshire. Town (pop 4,210) in NE Cattaraugus Co. Settled in 1810, the town was formed from the old town of Ischua [now Franklinville] in 1820. Industries in the 19th century included a foundry, plow factory, and cheese box and shingle mill. The Buffalo, New York and Philadelphia Railroad (1872; later Pennsylvania Railroad) crossed the town. The Rock Environmental Center (230 acres/93 ha) supports research of pond and forest ecosystems and encourages its visitors to understand and appreciate their relationship with the environment. The town's population doubled between 1960 and 2000.

Bruce D. Fredrickson and Madelynn P. Fredrickson

Yorkshire County. See EXTINCT COUNTIES.

Yorktown. Town (pop 36,318) in N Westchester Co. Settled *ca* 1728 and known as Hanover, the town was formed from Cortlandt Manor under its present name in 1788. Most settlers, who rented or purchased land from the Van Cortlandt family, were from New England, White Plains, or Rye; a Quaker meeting formed in 1774. There was considerable action in Yorktown during the Revolutionary War. Earthworks on Crow Hill were dug in 1779 to strengthen the defense of Pines Bridge from possible British advances. In 1781 and 1782 six French regiments under the command of Comte de Rochambeau camped in the town. On 14 May 1781 as many as 20 black and Indian soldiers of the First Rhode Island Regiment and 2 white officers, encamped at the Davenport House in Croton Heights, were killed by Col James DeLancey's Refugees; the officers are buried in the Yorktown Presbyterian Churchyard.

Yorktown, although home to Bailey's Wire Mill (?1831–69), was primarily agricultural. Croton Lake, created by the Croton Dam in 1842, inundated farmland and physically divided the town; it was enlarged by the New Croton Dam in 1904. With the advent of the railroad in 1881, the Yorktown's business center shifted to the railroad station in what is now Yorktown Heights. Hotels at Mohegan Lake, Croton Heights, and Yorktown Station accommodated summer vacationers. The Mohegan Quarry, active during the first half of the 20th century, provided granite for the Cathedral of St. John the Divine; the quarry is now the site of Sylvan Glen Park. Construction of the Taconic Parkway (1932) allowed easy access to hotels and made commuting convenient. The town began to grow rapidly in the 1950s, when large tracts of farmland were subdivided and the Thomas J. Watson Research Center of IBM was constructed (1959). The 2000 population was almost 10 times that of 1940.

Monica Doherty

Yorktown Heights. Locality (pop 7,972) in Yorktown (Westchester Co). The hamlet developed after the construction of the New York City and Northern Railroad (1881); a post office named Underhill opened in 1881 and was renamed Yorktown Heights in 1889. The Taconic Parkway (1932) provided a limited-access highway connection. Housing subdivisions followed World War II, and the hamlet gradually became the business center of the town, with a population of 2,478 in 1960. Its commercial position was solidified in 1965 by the Triangle Shopping Center.

Amy Surak

Yorkville. Village (pop 2,675) in Whitestown (Oneida Co). Yorkville grew to house the workers in the woolen and cotton mills of adjacent New York Mills. After the Civil War it had a pork-packing plant. The Yorkville post office opened in 1889, and the village incorporated in 1902. In the early 21st century it is a Utica suburb, and the Media Corp manufactured Tiffany-style stained-glass lamps.

Young, John (*b* Chelsea, Vt, 12 June 1802; *d* New York City, 23 Apr 1852). Governor. Young's family moved to Conesus [now in Livingston Co] when he was 4. He was admitted to the bar in 1827. Young shifted from the Jacksonians to the Antimasons, under whose banner he was elected to the state assembly in 1832, to the Whigs, with whom he was elected to Congress in 1836 and 1840. After Pres William Henry Harrison's death, Young led the Whig opposition to John Tyler in Congress and returned in 1844–45 to the state assembly, where he competed with William H. Seward for party leadership. In 1846 Young defeated Silas Wright for governor in a close election, winning by 5,000 votes. He horrified many conservatives by pardoning antirent rioters on the grounds that their crimes had been political. As governor, Young, like many Whigs, hedged on issues such as the Mexican War and the Wilmot Proviso. By supporting Zachary Taylor for president in 1848 and later the Compromise of 1850, he received the lucrative patronage appointment as assistant US treasurer in New York City. Young continued to lead conservative New York State Whigs who disliked Seward but died of tuberculosis before the collapse of the Whig Party.

Holt, Michael. *The Rise and Fall of the American Whig Party: Jacksonian Politics and the Onset of the Civil War* (New York: Oxford Univ Press, 1999)

Hutson, Reeve. *Land and Freedom: Rural Society, Popular Protest, and Party Politics in Antebellum New York* (New York: Oxford Univ Press, 2000)

Jon Sterngass

Young, Owen D. (*b* Van Hornesville, Herkimer Co, 27 Oct 1874; *d* St. Augustine, Fla, 11 July 1962). Business executive. Young graduated as valedictorian from the Academy of East Springfield (near Van Hornesville) at 14. In 1890 he entered St. Lawrence University in Canton (St. Lawrence Co), and in 1894 he enrolled at Boston University Law School, graduating two years later. Young joined the Boston law firm of Charles H. Tyler, and by 1913 he had become one of the country's most knowledgeable advisers on electric utilities. That year he joined the General Electric Co (GE) in Schenectady as general counsel and vice president. His first major accomplishment was the establishment, at government request, of Radio Corporation of America (RCA) in 1919. Young became increasingly involved in work for the government. In 1921 he served on a presidential Unemployment Conference and in 1924 was chairman of the American delegation to the International Chamber of Commerce's International Court of Arbitration. In 1922 Young became chairman of the board of GE. In 1923 he was appointed to the Committee of Representatives of World War I powers that designed plans for German reparation payments, and he helped devise the Dawes Plan (1924) to rescue Germany from financial ruin. In 1930 a modified reparation scheme, known as the Young Plan, was introduced. He was a director of the Federal Reserve Bank of New York (1923–40) and a trustee of St. Lawrence University (1912–34). Young retired from GE in 1939 and went into public service, chairing numerous committees. He served on the New York Regional Committee of the War Manpower Commission (1942–45) and in 1946 chaired the New York Temporary Commission on the Need for a State University, which led to the creation of the state's university system. In later years he divided his time between tending his orange groves in Florida and supervising the family dairy business in Van Hornesville.

See also COMMUNITY COLLEGES.

Case, Josephine Young, and Everett Case. *Owen D. Young and American Enterprise: A Biography* (Boston: David R. Godine, 1986)

Mojtaba Seyedian

Youngstown. Village (pop 1,957) in Porter (Niagara Co). Named in 1808 for John Young, it became a customs port in 1811 but was destroyed by the British and the Indians in 1813. In early years, lumber was shipped from Youngstown to Montreal. The village incorporated in 1854. Orchard produce and commercial fishing became important, and in the late 19th century, the Eldorado Hotel offered resort accommodations. The electric Lewiston and Youngstown Frontier Railway (1896) made the village more accessible. Landmarks include the Ontario House (1842), still an operating hotel; the Fort Niagara Light (1871–72); and the Carpenter Gothic St. John's Episcopal Church (1878). Old Fort Niagara State Park, just outside village limits, creates tourist traffic for Youngstown.

Nancy B. Mingus

Youth, Division for. See CHILDREN AND FAMILY SERVICES, OFFICE OF.

YWCA of the USA. Its origins date to 1858 in New York City, where 35 women formed a prayer union circle that became the first Ladies Christian Association in the United States. Responding to the needs of young women working in manufacturing industries, the Ladies Christian Association of New York City opened its first boardinghouse for young women in 1860. Soon services expanded to include an employment bureau and classes in cooking, calisthenics, and typing. Associations were organized in Buffalo and Utica during the 1870s, and in Poughkeepsie, Rochester, Albany, Jamestown, Schenectady, Brooklyn, and Newburgh during the 1880s. The Syracuse association began working with younger girls in 1889, the Brooklyn association opened the first school in the state to train women for practical nursing in 1893, and the Rochester association reported a strong focus on Traveler's Aid Work, a program intended to meet the needs of transient women in large cities. In 1905 African American women formed a branch in New York City to benefit black women, many of whom migrated north seeking better opportunity.

In December 1906 the various associations and student groups united to form a national organization called the YWCA (Young Women's Christian Association) of the USA, making its headquarters in New York City. From 1906 to 1914 Grace H. Dodge of Manhattan served as president of the newly created National Board, which was incorporated in New York State in 1907. Although black branches were still segregated, in 1907 Addie Hunton, an African American, joined the staff of the National Board and reorganized the administrative structure of New York City's black branch. The industrial department was formed in 1910 to improve recreational opportunities for young women working in manufacturing industries. Camp Altamont (Albany Co) was the site of one of the YWCA's first national industrial conferences. In spring 1917, with the formation of the National Board's War Work Council, the federal government designated the YWCA as one of seven official war service organizations. That summer the first of what would be 140 hostess houses, which provided recreational and social programs for soldiers, was established near the army camp at Plattsburgh. The first of 16 hostess houses for segregated black troops was at Camp Upton in Yaphank (Suffolk Co). Among the YWCA workers assisting women in foreign countries during World War I were women of Polish American descent, many from Erie Co, who became known as the Polish Grey Samaritans. The YWCA resumed war work in World War II as part of the United Service Organizations (USO). In 1946 the YWCA adopted the Interracial Charter, which called for the integration of all YWCA associations. By 1960 the previously white association of Buffalo employed as executive director Mary E. Wood, the first African American to head a metropolitan YWCA. The organization in 1970 adopted the One Imperative, which aimed at eliminating racism wherever it existed. In 2002, the year the new National Coordinating Board was established, there were 23 local YWCA associations in New York State offering programs for the physical and social betterment of women and children.

Sims, Mary S. *The YWCA: An Unfolding Purpose* (New York: Woman's Press, 1950)

Weisenfeld, Judith. *African American Women and Christian Activism: New York's Black YWCA, 1905–1945* (Cambridge, Mass: Harvard Univ Press, 1997)

Ilene Magaras

Z

zebra mussels. Freshwater bivalve species in the genus *Dreissena.* East European in origin, they are named for the often striking stripes on their shells. In the 1980s two species, *D. polymorpha* and *D. bugensis*—also known as the quagga mussel—crossed the Atlantic, probably in ballast water, to have significant adverse economic and ecological impacts within New York State and elsewhere in North America. Zebra mussels are thought to have arrived in New York State from Lake Erie and the Erie Canal in early 1989. They quickly colonize hard substrates after introduction into a water body and can develop extremely high population densities because of their fecundity, high growth rate, and tolerance of a range of environmental conditions. Although small in size—adults are typically less than .8 inch (2 cm) long—they have caused damage and increased operating expenses by hundreds of millions of dollars in North America. It is usually the dead organisms, dislodged from walls or rocks, that foul or clog the screens of raw-water conduits within municipal and industrial facilities. Their ecological impacts include decreasing phytoplankton productivity, increasing water clarity and creating other water quality changes, increasing native bivalve mortality, and restructuring bottom-dwelling communities. At the beginning of the 21st century, they are present in the Hudson and Mohawk Rivers, in the Finger Lakes, Lake Champlain, and Oneida Lake, among other New York State water bodies. In August 2003 a state task force was created to combat the problems caused by invasive species, including zebra mussels.

D'Itri, Frank M., ed. *Zebra Mussels and Aquatic Nuisance Species* (Chelsea, Mich: Ann Arbor Press, 1997)

Clifford A. Siegfried and Daniel P. Molloy

Zebra mussels will attach to any hard surface underwater. Photograph by Shannon P. Quinn.

Zenger trial. John Peter Zenger (1697–1746), printer and editor of the opposition newspaper *New York Weekly Journal,* attacked the administration of Gov William Cosby. Indicted on the charge of seditious libel, Zenger went to trial on 4 Aug 1735 at City Hall in New York City. He was primarily represented by Andrew Hamilton, a prominent Philadelphia lawyer. Hamilton's defense focused on the status of the common law of seditious libel in the colonies. That law limited the jury's role to the factual question of whether the defendant had printed the suspect material and whether the material was directed at his majesty or his principal ministers. The judge decided whether the words were libelous; the truth of the words in question was not a legal defense. Admitting that his client did indeed publish the articles, Hamilton attempted to discredit the law itself. His argument rested on four propositions: the material was true and accurate; true statements could not be libelous; the jury should determine both law and facts; and, as American politics and society differed so greatly from those in England, the law must likewise be different. The jury deliberated only a few minutes to reach a verdict of not guilty. An act of jury nullification, the decision had no legal standing (because juries only decided innocence or guilt, and in that capacity set no legal precedent) and did not alter the law of libel in England or the colonies. Nevertheless it provoked a significant debate, and *A Brief Narrative of the Case and Trial of John Peter Zenger* (1736), initially published by Zenger and later reprinted in Boston, became the most popular publication issued in America before the Revolution. The law did not change, but the practice did. Colonial publishers in the 18th century acted as if seditious libel did not exist, and there were few prosecutions for it. The Zenger trial provides a dramatic snapshot of the movement toward a theory of free speech that would eventually lead to the elimination of seditious libel from American law.

Katz, Stanley Nider, ed. *A Brief Narrative of the Case and Trial of John Peter Zenger, Printer of the New York Weekly Journal,* by James Alexander, 2d ed. (Cambridge, Mass: Belknap Press of Harvard Univ Press, 1972)

Levy, Leonard W. *Emergence of a Free Press* (New York: Oxford Univ Press, 1985)

Smith, William J., Jr. *The History of the Province of New York.* Ed. Michael Kammen, 2 vols (Cambridge, Mass: Belknap Press of Harvard Univ Press, 1972)

Peter J. Galie

Zippy Chippy. Racehorse foaled in New York State on 20 Apr 1991. He started his racing career in 1994, never placing better than third in 11 starts. Fearing the horse would end up at the meat market, trainer Felix Monserrate traded an old horse van for the winless gelding in 1995. Zippy Chippy continued to lose, and in 1998, after he refused to leave the starting gate for the third time, officials at Finger Lakes Racetrack in Farmington (Ontario Co), his home base, banned him from racing there. Racing at tracks outside of New York State proved no easier; at a Northampton, Mass, track on 6 Sept 1999, he lost his 86th consecutive race, setting the record for lost races among thoroughbreds. His record won him throngs of fans and a spot in *People* magazine's list of the 50 most fascinating personalities in 2000. Despite his losses, he had accumulated $29,167 in winnings by placing second in 7 races and third in 12 races through 2001. Although winless against horses, Zippy Chippy won his first race in August 2001, when he narrowly defeated a Rochester Red Wings baseball player in a 120 ft (37 m) race. In December 2004 Monserrate announced that he was retiring the horse from racing. Zippy Chippy, who finished with 100 losses, was to become an outrider pony at the Finger Lakes Racetrack in 2005.

Kane, Mike. "He Just Can't Win," *The Blood-Horse,* 10 Oct 1998, 5582

Elizabeth Redkey

zoning. Local regulation of land use. Before fire building codes it was not uncommon for entire blocks of wood-frame buildings in urban areas to be destroyed by fire. Beginning in 1835, after a disastrous fire in New York City, local ordinances to promote fire-safe construction of new buildings were enacted, initially in that city and shortly thereafter in numerous others throughout New York State. In 1909 the state legislature authorized villages to establish and regulate construction in fire zones or districts. In further response to the dangers of fire, as well as to combat unhealthy sanitary conditions, to systematize future construction to general standards, and to promote increased property values, a 1914 act by the state legislature empowered New York City's Board of Estimate and Apportionment to draw up a comprehensive array of zoning regulations for the city. Completed and implemented two years later, New York City's zoning regulations controlled the height and bulk of buildings, mandated setbacks for taller buildings, required minimum amounts of light and ventilation for buildings, and regulated the use of open spaces. They allowed for the division of the city into districts, with regulations for permissible types of business differing between them. New York City was the first city in the United States to have a comprehensive set of zoning regulations. Consequently these ordinances became the model for other cities and permitted the creation and enforcement of much sharper differentiations between commercial and residential neighborhoods.

In 1917 the state legislature, through an amendment to General City Law, empowered all other cities in New York State, except Rochester, to have zoning regulations similar to those of New York City. Rochester was given the power to zone through an amendment made to its charter by the state legislature in 1919. To further strengthen zoning in cities in 1920, the legislature, in another amendment to the General City Law, provided for the formulation of a board of appeals, giving those who disagreed with a zoning decision of a city an appropriate venue to apply for relief. Five years later the legislature, again in an amendment to the General City Law, acted to allow all cities in the state the power to regulate population densities.

Other local governments in New York State soon were authorized to establish zoning regulations similar to those of cities. This was partly due to the explosion of motor vehicle traffic throughout the state during and after World War I, leading to billboard advertising along roadsides and to community debates on issues of taste. Traffic spurred the move of gas stations and other types of retail and manufacturing establishments to residential areas outside the confines of the traditional downtown, developments many saw as endangering the health and safety of their communities. In 1921 the state legislature empowered villages with the right to zone, and in 1923 an amendment to this law made a village's zoning power comparable to that of cities. Towns gained the right in 1922 and had powers similar to those of villages by 1926. Since the 1930s the legislature has enabled cities, towns, and villages throughout the state with similar zoning powers and rights.

Even though all local governments in New York State had the ability by 1926 to impose a comprehensive set of zoning regulations within their jurisdictions, many failed to enact such laws. By 1939 only 44 of the 60 cities and 160 of the 555 villages within New York State had zoning regulations; even more striking, only 50 of the 932 towns were zoned. One of the prime reasons for the absence of zoning in so many areas was a deep-seated belief in private property.

In 2003 zoning existed in the more populated areas of New York State. Many rural areas remained unzoned, even though various branches of state government have called for zoning regulations there since the 1930s. Rural landowners frequently believe zoning prohibits them from full control over the use of their lands, although well-written regulations can protect land from despoliation by neighboring property owners without limiting activity, unless it is harmful to others.

See also PLANNING AND REGIONAL PLANNING ASSOCIATIONS.

New York State. Secretary of State. *A Guide to the Planning and Zoning Laws of New York State* (Albany: Office of the Secretary of State, 1996)

Eric L. Kline

ZOOS. The nation's first zoological gardens, permanent exhibitions of captive animals designed for public education and enjoyment, opened during the mid–19th century. Most European zoos were founded by private zoological societies, but American zoos tended to develop as adjuncts of municipal parks departments. The first such "public menagerie" was established in New York City's Central Park in the early 1860s. As a city-run facility competing with other civic responsibilities, the Central Park Menagerie never matched the size or sophistication of its European counterparts, but it did not charge admission, and a pleasant Sunday would often attract tens of thousands of visitors.

Although more formal, privately run zoological gardens opened in Philadelphia and Cincinnati during the 1870s, the municipal model remained dominant well into the 20th century, and parks in New York State generally followed this trend. Animal collections established at Ross Park in Binghamton (1875), Delaware Park in Buffalo (1875), Prospect Park in Brooklyn (1893), Seneca Park in Rochester (1894), and Burnet Park in Syracuse (1914) were all part of their cities' existing parks departments. They were relatively modest affairs, averaging less than 20 acres (8 ha). Although they depended on the often fickle support of local officials, they were enthusiastically supported by the public. Only the New York Zoological Park, opened in 1899 and popularly known as the Bronx Zoo, diverged from the prevailing model. With substantial private and public funding, a spacious wooded site, and a staff of experts, the Bronx Zoo had the resources to compete with New York City's other major cultural attractions.

During the first half of the 20th century, the state's zoos enjoyed a remarkable boom. In 1920 new municipal facilities opened in Utica and what is now the New York State Living Museum opened in Watertown, as advocates convinced city officials of the civic benefits of a local zoo. Other unusual animal parks that began operations during this time include the Bear Mountain Trailside Museum and Zoo (1927) in Rockland Co, a project of the Palisades Interstate Park Commission; the Catskill Game Farm (1933) in Greene Co, a family-run breeding facility and tourist attraction; and Trevor Zoo (1936), an addition to the private Millbrook School in Dutchess Co. Further stimulus came with the Great Depression, because the state's zoos benefited from New Deal relief programs, especially the Works Progress Administration. Federal dollars supported the expansion of zoos in Buffalo and Rochester, the reconstruction of New York City's dilapidated menageries in Central and Prospect Parks, and the creation of a new "educational zoo" under the auspices of the Staten Island Zoological Society (1936). Such government largesse reinforced the image of zoos as a civic necessity, a vital element of urban culture.

In the decades after World War II, however, New York State's zoological parks endured difficult times. Although the postwar era brought some important new construction—notably the city-owned Flushing Meadows Zoo in Queens (1968; now Queens Wildlife Center)—there was an overall reduction of municipal support, as city governments, facing shrinking tax bases, sharply curtailed funding for zoos and other recreational facilities. At many parks, financial neglect led to physical decay, which in turn discouraged attendance and precipitated a further decline in income. Moreover, underfunded zoos could endanger the resident animals, sparking criticism from the increasingly vocal animal welfare movement. Patrons of several zoos organized private zoological societies to provide fund-raising and public relations assistance for their struggling municipal facilities. During the 1960s and 1970s overburdened city authorities took themselves out of the zoo business; the management of several municipal zoos was transferred to private societies, as in Utica, Buffalo, and Binghamton, or to more financially secure county governments, as in Rochester and Syracuse.

By the late 20th century, though, many New York State zoos had begun to reinvent themselves, physically, politically, and philosophically. In the early 1980s, for instance, the New York Zoological Society (renamed Wildlife Conservation Society in 1993) negotiated a partnership with the New York City Department of Parks and Recreation, whereby the society agreed to renovate and operate the municipal zoos in Central Park, Prospect Park, and Flushing Meadows. After extensive remodeling, these parks reopened in the late 1980s and early 1990s as "wildlife centers," a title that reflected American zoos' emerging interest in environmental education, naturalistic design, and species conservation. Individual exhibits at other zoos likewise demonstrated a growing ecological awareness, as designers sought to immerse both animals and visitors in realistic replicas of the creatures' native habitats.

Building and maintaining such exhibits proved extremely expensive, though, and while municipal governments still provided some subsidies, most late 20th-century zoos perpetuated the postwar trend toward privatization. Even the Wildlife Conservation Society saw its government support decline; by the 1990s just one-quarter of its operating funds came from New York City, down from 71% in 1951. In fact, in 2003 Mayor Michael Bloomberg tried unsuccessfully to withdraw all city subsidies from the Queens and Prospect Park zoos. Several zoological parks in the state undertook major capital campaigns during the 1990s, urging private citizens, foundations, and corporations to underwrite the costs of expansions and improvements in return for such perks as naming privileges; the Syracuse zoo, for instance, was renamed the Rosamond Gifford Zoo at Burnet Park in 1999. In addition, rising costs meant the end of free admission at several parks, including the Central Park Zoo (successor to the Central Park Menagerie), which began charging visitors in 1988.

The state also has two aquariums. The New York Aquarium, now managed by the Wildlife Conservation Society, opened at Castle Garden

Elephants at Burnet Park Zoo in Syracuse, 1990.

in Lower Manhattan's Battery Park in 1896. It remained there until 1941, then was housed temporarily in the Bronx Zoo before moving to its permanent home in Brooklyn's Coney Island in 1957. The Aquarium of Niagara in Niagara Falls, a pioneer in the use of synthetic seawater, opened in 1965. New York State zoos remain powerful attractions, receiving more than 5 million visitors annually in the early 21st century.

Croke, Vicki. *The Modern Ark: The Story of Zoos, Past, Present, and Future* (New York: Scribner's, 1997)

Kisling, Vernon N., Jr, ed. *Zoo and Aquarium History: Ancient Animal Collections to Zoological Gardens* (Boca Raton, Fla: CRC Press, 2001)

Mullan, Bob, and Garry Marvin. *Zoo Culture,* 2d ed. (Urbana: Univ of Illinois Press, 1999)

Jeffrey Hyson

Zoroastrians (Parsis). Religious group that adheres to the monotheistic ethical and religious teachings of the Iranian prophet Zarathustra (*ca* 1400–1250 BC). After the Muslim conquests, Zoroastrians were largely displaced from Persia [now Iran] to neighboring countries, especially India, where they were known as Parsis. Zoroastrians worship in what is called a fire-temple, using a fire-urn as an altar. According to Zarathustra, the Divinity, Ahura-Mazda, had a vision of the universe evolving toward an ideal of perfection, or Asha. It is humanity's function to assist in this enterprise. Zoroastrians hold that, upon death, the soul is separated from the body for its moral character to be judged; the corpse is a piece of matter subject to corruption and must be disposed of without polluting the elements. Because the religion imposes no social or dietary requirements, members of the Zoroastrian community have been able to assimilate easily into Western society. Some Zoroastrians immigrated to New York State in the 1920s, most notably the Soroushian family, which established major business concerns in the state. In 2002 about 2,000 Zoroastrians lived in New York State, of about 6,000 in the United States and about 140,000 worldwide. Most Zoroastrians in New York State are professionals and business people. Their families arrived around the middle of the 20th century, approximately one-third from Iran and two-thirds from India. The Zoroastrian Association of Greater New York was founded in 1973. In 1977 it opened a fire-temple, Darbe Meher, in New Rochelle (Westchester Co), which moved for space reasons to Suffern (Rockland Co). Their festivals are essentially seasonal, the Zoroastrian New Year being 21 March, the spring equinox.

Boyce, Mary. *Zoroastrians: Their Religious Beliefs and Practices* (New York: Routledge, 2001)

Hinnels, John R. "The Zoroastrian Diaspora." In *The South Asian Religious Diaspora in Britain, Canada, and the United States,* ed. Harold G. Coward, John R. Hinnels, and Raymond Brady Williams (Albany: SUNY Press, 2000)

Kaikhosrov D. Irani

Contributors

A

Kenneth Aaron is a reporter with the *Albany Times-Union* who has covered energy and utilities. He is also a journalism instructor at the College of St. Rose.

George H. J. Abrams is an enrolled full-blood member of the Seneca Nation of Indians. An anthropologist by training, he is former director of the Yager Museum, Hartwick College. He has been a college professor, founding director of the Seneca-Iroquois National Museum, and special assistant to the director at the National Museum of the American Indian, Smithsonian Institution.

Rudy Abramson is coeditor of the *Encyclopedia of Appalachia* and author of *Spanning the Century: The Life of W. Averell Harriman, 1891–1986.* He is former Washington correspondent for the *Los Angeles Times.*

Edna Acosta-Belén (PhD) is Distinguished Service Professor of Latin American and Caribbean Studies, SUNY Albany. She is director of the Center for Latino, Latin American, and Caribbean Studies and author of *The Puerto Rican Woman: Perspectives in Culture, History, and Society* and coauthor of *"Adiós, Borinquen querida": The Puerto Rican Diaspora, Its History, and Contributions.*

Arthur G. Adams is a transportation and planning consultant and regional historian. He is founding president of the Hudson River Maritime Museum, Kingston, and fellow at Carmer Center for Catskill and Hudson River Studies, SUNY New Paltz.

G. Rollie Adams (PhD Univ of Arizona) has been president and CEO of Strong Museum since 1987. Previously he served in various capacities at the American Association for State and Local History and as director of the Buffalo and Erie County Historical Society and the Louisiana State Museum. He is author of *General William S. Harney: Prince of Dragoons* (2001).

Ralph M. Aderman is professor emeritus of English at the Univ of Wisconsin, Milwaukee. He edited *The Letters of James Kirke Paulding* (1962) and was senior editor of *The Letters of Washington Irving* (1978–82).

Rohit T. Aggarwala (PhD Columbia Univ) is a consultant with McKinsey and Co in Florham Park, NJ.

John Aiken is professor emeritus at SUNY Buffalo and author of *A History of Community: SUNY College at Buffalo, 1871–1996* (1996).

James R. Albanese (PhD) is associate professor of earth sciences at SUNY Oneonta. He is coauthor of "Aggregate and Heavy-Mineral Resources of the Continental Shelf in the Eastern New York Bight" (1993) and "Bluestone: Geology and Resource Identification in the Southwestern Catskill Delta of New York State" (1995) in *Geological Society of America.*

Reynaldo Gamboa Alejandro is research librarian at the New York Public Library. He was the choreographer/artistic director of the Philippine Dance Company of New York and the Reynaldo Alejandro Dance Theater. He has written more than 20 books on cuisine, dance, design, and history and is president of the Filipino American National Historical Society, Metropolitan New York Chapter.

David Yehling Allen (PhD Columbia Univ) was geosciences and map librarian at SUNY Stony Brook. His publications include *Long Island Maps and Their Makers: Five Centuries of Cartographic History* (1997).

Elizabeth K. Allen is a writer and editor of works on history and art. She is coauthor of *A Tradition of Change: Albany Law School, 1851–2001* (2001).

Maury Allen is a prizewinning sportswriter and author of more than 30 books on baseball. He is a contributor to television documentaries on baseball and is a member of several sports halls of fame.

Richard Sanders Allen is a historian and compiler. He was director of the NYS American Revolution Bicentennial Commission.

Kristen L. Allen-Hanks is a graduate student of European and modern American history at the Univ of Cincinnati, and has interests in the Plattsburgh officers' training camp (WWI) and the film collection of Theodore Roosevelt.

Elena Ames is Village of Lyndonville historian.

Tyler Anbinder is associate professor of history at George Washington Univ. He has published books on the Know-Nothing Party and the Five Points slum in 19th-century New York City.

Jonathan G. Andelson (PhD Univ of Michigan) is professor of anthropology at Grinnell College. His teaching and research specialties are intentional communities, religion, and ecology. His dissertation was on the Amana colonies.

Donna K. Anderson was professor of music and chair of the Department of Performing Arts at SUNY Cortland until her retirement in 1997. She has written on the life and career of Charles Tomlinson Griffes and performs his music.

Scott W. Anderson teaches courses on historical geography, the state, and the American landscape at SUNY Cortland. He writes about the early economic development of postrevolutionary New York State.

Anthony D. Andreassi (MDiv St. Joseph's Seminary, Yonkers; MA Georgetown Univ) is a native of White Plains and lives in Washington, DC. He teaches history at Gonzaga College High School.

Richard Andress (MLS Univ of Maryland) is senior archivist at the NYS Archives. He specializes in reference, photographs, and correctional services records.

Dorothy Angell (PhD American Univ) has lived in Bangladesh and conducted ethnographic research there and in several US-Bangladeshi communities. She coauthored *Bangladeshis in the United States: Community Dynamics and Cultural Continuity.*

Randal Angiel is working on a PhD in history at SUNY Albany. His family settled in Woodstock in 1815, where he remains today, pursuing his interest in regional history.

Christopher Angus is a newspaper columnist and commentator. He is book review editor of *Adirondac* magazine and author of *Reflections from Canoe Country: Paddling the Waters of the Adirondacks and Canada* (1997) and *The Extraordinary Adirondack Journey of Clarence Petty: Wilderness Guide, Pilot, and Conservationist* (2002).

Maboud Ansari (PhD Graduate Faculty, New School for Social Research) is professor of sociology at William Paterson Univ, NJ. He has written on Iranian and Muslim communities in the US, including *The Making of the Iranian Community in America,* and coauthored *Sociological Theory* (in Farsi, 1979).

Terry Ariano is curator of the Somers Historical Society. She was assistant curator of prints and photographs at the Museum of the City of New York.

Christopher R. Armstrong (MA Gordon-Conwell Theological Seminary) is a PhD candidate at Duke Univ. His dissertation explores the emotional culture of the postbellum camp meeting Holiness movement.

Andrew W. Arpey (PhD SUNY Albany) is historian and archivist for the NYS Archives. He is author of *The William Freeman Murder Case* (2003).

Robert Asher is professor of history at the Univ of Connecticut. He is editor of *Connecticut History* and is finishing a book on the history of workers' compensation in the US, 1840–1980.

Victoria R. Aspinwall is a freelance copy editor and proofreader. She is also office manager at the Long Island Studies Institute of Hofstra Univ, where she edits institute publications.

Laurel Auchampaugh is Town of Owasco historian.

Richard E. Austic is professor of nutrition in the Department of Animal Science at Cornell Univ and author of *Poultry Production* (1991).

Barbara B. Avery was born in the Town of Columbus and is its historian.

B

David Babson is a historical archaeologist and a PhD candidate in the Department of Anthropology at Syracuse Univ. In addition to studies of plantation, farmstead, and industrial archaeological sites, he has pursued his interest in the history, development, and operations of railroads, especially those of the northeastern US.

Christopher T. Baer is assistant curator of manuscripts and archives at the Hagley Museum and Library. He has supervised the Pennsylvania Railroad Archive since 1984 and is author of *Canals and Railroads of the Mid-Atlantic States, 1800–1860* (1981) and *The Trail of the Blue Comet* (1994).

Rita Bahren is a member of the Chester Historical Society and is Village of Chester historian. She was president of the American Legion Ladies Auxiliary, the St. Columba's Ladies Auxiliary, and the St. Columba Mother's Club.

Eli Bail is author of *From Railway to Freeway* (1984) and contributor to *A Historical Survey of Transit Buses in the United States* (1990). His subjects have included both transit and over-the-road operations. He also writes articles for magazines.

Sallie Naatz Bailey is an artist and freelance writer working from her home studio in Syracuse.

Stella Bailey is president of the Town of Highlands Historical Society. She is also secretary and charter board member of the Fort Montgomery Revolutionary Battle Site Association and trustee of the Constitution Island Association.

Jeanne L. Baker is Town of Brutus historian.

Wesley G. Balla is curator of history at the Albany Institute of History and Art. He is the author of essays and museum exhibitions about the social history and material culture of Albany and the upper Hudson River valley region.

Martin Bannan is a military journalist for the New York Air National Guard and volunteer for the NYS Military Heritage Institute. He is former researcher for the Colonial Albany Social History Project.

Stuart A. Banner is professor of law at Washington Univ. He is author of *Dangling between Heaven and Earth: A History of Capital Punishment in the United States* (2002) and *Anglo-American Securities Regulation: Cultural and Political Roots, 1690–1860* (1998).

Tricia A. Barbagallo (PhD candidate SUNY Albany) is historian, fellow, and research associate at the Colonial Albany Social History Project at the NYS Museum. She published a short history of Albany and an article on James Caldwell, and her dissertation analyzes poverty through the lives of paupers in postrevolutionary Albany. She is assistant editor of *The Encyclopedia of New York State.*

Cathy A. Barber is Cortland County historian.

David Barclay is assistant professor of geology at SUNY Cortland. His research over the past decade has focused on glacial geology, geomorphology, and climate change in Alaska, Antarctica, and New York State.

Eileen Barker (OBE, FBA) is professor of sociology with special reference to the study of religion at the London School of Economics. In 1988 she founded INFORM and she is author of 170 publications, including *New Religious Movements: A Practical Introduction.*

Elizabeth Barnaskey is from Syracuse and a graduate of Cazenovia College.

Jeffrey K. Barnes (PhD Cornell Univ) was curator and research entomologist at the NYS Museum for 20 years and is a research entomologist with the Univ of Arkansas Arthropod Museum. He is writing a guide to the Albany Pine Bush.

Georgia B. Barnhill is the Andrew W. Mellon Curator of Graphic Arts at the American Antiquarian Society, Worcester, Mass. She is author of *Wild Impressions: The Adirondacks on Paper* (1995).

Michael P. Barrett is a graduate of Russell Sage College and Western New England School of Law. He is a fan of Troy history and lectures on it. He also leads historical tours for various organizations.

Stephanie Barrett has worked in a variety of units at the NYS Library since 1988. She majored in archaeology at SUNY Albany, with minors in English and history.

Paul J. Bartczak is a bank examiner employed by the Federal

Deposit Insurance Corp. He is an amateur historian with a special interest in transportation and industrial topics, particularly for New York State.

Renate Bartl (MA Ludwig-Maximilians-Univ of Munich, Germany) focuses her research on the triracial groups in the eastern US.

Lynn A. Bassanese is director of public programs at the Franklin D. Roosevelt Presidential Library.

Ronald E. Batt is professor of clinical gynecology at the SUNY School of Medicine and Biomedical Sciences, Buffalo. He is author of *Another Era: A Pictorial History of the School of Medicine and Biomedical Sciences, State Univ of New York at Buffalo, 1846–1996* (1996).

Henry H. Baxter (PE) is a planner and designer of grain mills and schoolhouses.

Patricia Bayer, a writer and editor specializing in architecture, design, and decorative arts of the 19th and 20th centuries, is author of *Art Deco Interiors* (1990) and *Art Deco Architecture* (1992). Since 1993 she has been the arts editor of *Encyclopedia Americana.*

Ronald Bayer (PhD) is professor of public health at the Joseph L. Mailman School of Public Health at Columbia Univ. He is also co-director of the program in the history of medicine and public health. He is coauthor of *AIDS Doctors: Voices from the Epidemic.*

Nancy Beadie is a historian of education and associate professor of educational leadership and policy studies in the College of Education at the Univ of Washington, Seattle. Her areas of expertise include history of school funding in the US, women's education, community–school relations, and 19th-century academies.

Thomas D. Beal is assistant professor of American history and urban studies at SUNY Oneonta.

David Beale has a PhD from Bob Jones Seminary, where he teaches. His dissertation is titled "Ante-Nicene Eschatology: An Historical and Theological Analysis." He is author of *In Pursuit of Purity: American Fundamentalism since 1850* (1986) and *The Mayflower Pilgrims: Roots of Puritan, Presbyterian, Congregationalist, and Baptist Heritage* (2000).

Patricia Beaman teaches dance history at New York Univ's Tisch School of the Arts and is on the dance faculty at Wesleyan Univ, Conn.

Philip A. Bean earned degrees from Union College, Oxford Univ, and the Univ of Rochester. He has published articles on state immigration history in the *Journal of Ethnic Studies, Journal of Urban History,* and *New York History.* He is associate dean and director of academic resources at Haverford College, Pa.

G. William Beardslee (JD Univ of Denver) received his master's in history after practicing law for several years. He is author of "The Otsego Frontier Experience" (*New York State Historical Society Journal,* 1998) and writes a weekly local history column for *New Berlin Gazette.* He is associate professor in the College of Health and Human Services at the Univ of Northern Colorado.

Michael L. Beardsley, a graduate of SUNY Oswego, was director of marketing for the Marsellus Casket Co, Syracuse. He is a writer for *Antique Week* magazine and has been a featured lecturer for the National Funeral Directors Association, National Foundation of Funeral Service, mortuary science colleges, and State Funeral Director Associations.

Mildred L. Becker is Village of Forestville historian.

Jean Bedient is Town of Gerry historian.

David W. Beebe (DDS Univ of Pennsylvania) is director of the Erie Canal Park, Camillus, and the Camillus Canal Society. He is a member of the board of directors for the Canal Society of New York State.

Raymond Beecher (MCS Boston Univ) is Greene Co historian and president and chair of the Greene County Historical Society. He is a local history author and librarian of the Vedder Research Library, and is involved in saving Thomas Cole's Cedar Grove Estate (Catskill).

Michael A. Bellesiles is author of *Revolutionary Outlaws: Ethan Allen and the Struggle for Independence on the Early American Frontier* (1993) and *Arming America: The Origins of a National Gun Culture* (2000). He won the Organization of American Historians' Louis Pelzer Award (1986) and Binkley-Stephenson Award (1996). He is founding director of Emory's Violence Studies Program.

Russell P. Bellico is professor of economic history at Westfield State College. He is author of *Chronicles of Lake George* (1995) and *Chronicles of Lake Champlain* (1999).

Lynne Belluscio has been the director of the Le Roy Historical Society since 1988 and served as the chair of the Western New York Association of Historical Agencies. She is a graduate of SUNY Oswego and was lead interpreter and coordinator of special events for the Genesee Country Museum. An authority on open-hearth cooking and brick breadovens, she is author of articles on western state history.

James R. Belpedio (DA Univ of North Dakota) is professor of history, government, and humanities at Becker College, Mass.

Leonard Benardo is a devotee of state architecture and history and is author of two chapters in *Big Onion Guide to New York City: Ten Historic Tours* (2002).

Daniel E. Bender (PhD New York Univ) is visiting assistant professor at Michigan State Univ. His dissertation is entitled "From Sweatshop to Model Shop: Anti-Sweatshop Campaigns and Languages of Labor and Organizing, 1880–1934."

Gerald Benjamin (PhD) is Distinguished Teaching Professor and dean of the College of Arts and Sciences at SUNY New Paltz. He is coauthor of *Regionalism and Realism: A Study of Governments in the New York Metropolitan Area* (2001) and *Decision 1997: Constitutional Change in New York* (1997). He is consultant to the Governor's Office of Employee Relations.

Marla A. Bennett (PhD Syracuse Univ) is a senior staff assistant at SUNY-ESF, Syracuse. Her dissertation was on black students at Syracuse Univ, 1942–69, and her postdoctoral research and teaching are on race and gender issues in higher education. She is coordinator of the ESF Honors Program and adjunct instructor.

Thomas E. Bergler (PhD Univ of Notre Dame) is assistant professor of educational ministries and associate director at Link Institute for Faithful and Effective Youth Ministry, Huntington College, Ind.

Jerry Bergman (PhD Wayne State Univ) has taught behavioral sciences for over 20 years. His master's thesis was on community and the Jehovah's Witnesses, and he has published several books and over 100 articles on the Witness movement in popular and scholarly journals.

Frank Bergmann (PhD) is associate dean for arts and sciences at Utica College. He is author of *Upstate Literature: Essays in Memory of Thomas F. O'Donnell* (1985) and *Robert Grant* (1982). At the Regional Conference of Historical Agencies he received the John Ben Snow manuscript prize (1985).

S. (Sam) Berliner III writes technical manuals on filtration and consults on the application of ultrasonics to filtration. He is a graduate of Adelphi Univ trained in mechanical engineering. He lectures on the history of technology as it applies to ultrasonics and transportation and is the convener of the Motor Parkway Panel.

Jason E. Bernth (BA Webster Univ) is a graduate student in the Department of Religious Studies at Indiana Univ. He has contributed original research to the Warner Sallman Archives, Anderson, Ind.

Al Berr joined the NYS Council on the Arts in 1975 and became director of the Performing Arts Fiscal Department in 1976. He has been deputy director since 1980 and was acting executive director for most of 1995–96.

Jake Besterman is a PhD student in the Department of Geography and Anthropology at Louisiana State Univ.

Charles E. Beveridge is research professor and series editor of the Frederick Law Olmsted Papers in the Department of History at American Univ. He is author of *Frederick Law Olmsted: Designing the American Landscape.*

Robert Beyfuss (MA Cornell Univ) is agriculture and natural resources program lead for Cornell Cooperative Extension of Greene County and the state specialist on American ginseng for the Department of Natural Resources at Cornell Univ. He is author of *American Ginseng Production in NY State* and *The Practical Guide to Growing Ginseng,* among other fact sheets.

Bharat L. Bhatt (PhD Syracuse Univ) is an independent scholar of Indian culture and literature. He taught at the Univ of Texas, Austin, and held a Fulbright faculty fellowship in India. He has been associated with ethnic media and was consultant for a documentary on Asian Indians in Texas.

Stefan Bielinski is founder and director of the Colonial Albany Social History Project, a model community history program at the NYS Museum. For more than 30 years he has been a teacher, author, student, and advocate of the "history of the people, by the people, and for the people" approach of the community historian.

Joy A. Bilharz is associate professor of sociology and anthropology at SUNY Fredonia. She is author of *The Allegany Senecas and Kinzua Dam: Forced Relocation through Two Generations* (1998) and is project director of the Mohawk Valley Battlefield Ethnography Project for the National Park Service.

Daniel Bille is City of North Tonawanda historian. He is a retired technical writer and is researching Niagara frontier history.

Frederick M. Binder is professor emeritus of history at the College of Staten Island CUNY and coauthor of *All the Nations under Heaven: An Ethnic and Racial History of New York City* (1995).

Thomas A. Birkland (PhD Univ of Washington) is associate professor of public administration and policy and political science, and director of the Graduate School of Public Affairs at the Nelson A. Rockefeller College of Public Affairs and Policy of SUNY Albany. He is author of *An Introduction to the Policy Process: Theories, Concepts, and Models of Public Policy Making* (2001).

Don Bissell has published historical narratives, computer product reviews, book reviews, and company profiles, and has provided computer show reportage as a freelance journalist. He was contributing technical editor for *Design Technologies* and *Design Management* magazines, and his work has appeared in regional and national magazines, including *BYTE.*

Patricia Blackler is historian of the Village of Skaneateles. She is a graduate of the Univ of New Hampshire and was employed by Eastman Kodak Co.

Barbara J. Bloemink (PhD) is an independent curator and art historian. She was director and chief curator for the Kemper Museum of Contemporary Art, the Contemporary Art Center of Virginia, and the Hudson River Museum. She co-curated the Florine Stettheimer exhibition at the Whitney Museum. She has authored five books and organized over 70 museum exhibitions.

Irene Bloemraad (PhD candidate Harvard Univ) is author of "The North American Naturalization Gap" (*International Migration Review,* 2002) and "Citizenship and Immigration: A Current Review" (*Journal of International Migration and Integration,* 2000). Her dissertation compares the political incorporation of immigrants and refugees in the US and Canada.

Amanda Blohm (BA Western Kentucky Univ) is a graduate student and associate instructor in religious studies at Indiana Univ. Her interests include 19th-century American religious history and Buddhism in America.

Jon Bloom (PhD New York Univ) has taught labor history and labor studies at Rutgers Univ, SUNY Old Westbury, and CUNY Center for Worker Education. He is executive director of the Workers Defense League, an educational and advocacy organization based in New York City.

Kenneth J. Blume (PhD SUNY Binghamton) is associate professor of history at Albany College of Pharmacy. His biography of Rear Adm Richard W. Meade is forthcoming, and he is writing a book about the naval efficiency boards of 1855–57.

Edith L. Blumhofer (PhD Harvard Univ) is professor of history and director of the Institute for the Study of American Evangelicals at Wheaton College, Ill.

Kathryn A. Boardman is a trainer, consultant, and music performer for historical societies, outdoor museums, and schools. She was founder of the Cherry Valley Group and First Frost Traditions and has been associate curator and associate director of interpretation for the Farmers' Museum, Cooperstown. She was adjunct professor of history museum studies for the Cooperstown Graduate Program.

Sarah E. Boehme is John S. Bugas Curator of the Whitney Gallery of Western Art at the Buffalo Bill Historical Center, Cody, Wyo. She is coauthor of *John James Audubon in the West: The Last Expedition: Mammals of North America* (2000) and *Powerful Images: Portrayals of Native America* (1998).

Erin Bohen graduated from South Colonie Central High School and is a student of mass communications at Drake Univ, Iowa.

Hallie E. Bond (MA, Hagley Fellow, Univ of Delaware) is curator of boats at the Adirondack Museum, Blue Mountain Lake. She is author of *Boats and Boating in the Adirondacks* (1995) and other works on recreational history and material culture.

Richard F. Bonnabeau joined Empire State College in November 1974. He is associate director for international programs and is the college historian and archivist.

Patricia U. Bonomi is professor emerita of history at New York Univ. She is author of *The Lord Cornbury Scandal: The Politics of Reputation in British America* (1998).

Antonia Booth is Town of Southold historian. She is a professionally trained historian and social scientist. A former news editor, she has published essays on local history.

Joe Bopp is a state native who has been interested in mammals since childhood, which led him to study wildlife biology at SUNY-ESF. He is collections manager for birds and mammals at the NYS Museum.

Michael J. Bosak is a NYS-registered architect. He is a railroad and railroad-station historian and photographer.

Francis P. Boscoe (PhD Pennsylvania State Univ) is a research scientist with the NYS Department of Health, Albany.

Adam Bostanci (MPhil Univ of Cambridge) is a science writer interested in the sociology of science and technology.

Henry Warner Bowden is professor of religion at Rutgers Univ, NJ. A graduate of Baylor and Princeton Univs, he is author of several books on historiography, biography, and Indian missions. He is also executive secretary of the American Society of Church History.

Brian Boyd is professor of English literature at the Univ of Auckland, New Zealand. He has edited much of Nabokov's work and is author of *Vladimir Nabokov: The Russian Years* (1990) and *Vladimir Nabokov: The American Years* (1991).

Anne M. Boylan is associate professor of history and women's studies at the Univ of Delaware and author of *Sunday School: The Formation of an American Institution, 1790–1880* (1988). She is working on a comparative study of women's organizations in New York City and Boston, 1797–1840.

William H. Brackney is professor of the history of Christianity, director of the program in Baptist studies, and chair of the Department of Religion at Baylor Univ, Tex.

James C. Bradford (PhD Univ of Virginia) taught at the US Naval Academy, Annapolis, before going to Texas A&M Univ, where he teaches courses in naval and US history. He is author or editor of eight books including *The Papers of John Paul Jones, Command under Sail: Makers of the American Naval Tradition, 1775–1850* and *Quarterdeck and Bridge.*

Michael T. Bradley Jr is an adjunct instructor in the Department of Religion at Emory Univ.

Amy Braig-Lindstrom attended Loras College, Clark College, the College of St. Benedict, and Northern Arizona Univ for education and pottery training. She operates Every-Ware Populist Pottery.

José António Brandão is assistant professor of history at Western Michigan Univ. He teaches the history of northeastern North Americans with a focus on the history and culture of native people.

William Brandow is project architect at John G. Waite Associates, an Albany architectural firm specializing in historic preservation.

Elizabeth Brayer writes about Rochester area history. Her works include *George Eastman: A Biography* (1996; nominated for a Pulitzer Prize) and *MAGnum Opus: The Story of the Memorial Art Gallery* (1988).

Alvin R. Breisch is amphibian and reptile specialist in the endangered species unit of the NYS Department of Environmental Conservation, Division of Fish, Wildlife, and Marine Resources.

Helen Moore Breitbeck (PhD Syracuse Univ) is former research associate for the Heritage Foundation of Oswego. She is a freelance writer specializing in historic preservation and local history.

Susan Roth Breitzer is a PhD candidate at the Univ of Iowa. Her dissertation is entitled "Class, Ethnicity, and Community: The Jewish Working Class of Chicago, 1886–1928."

Virginia Lieson Brereton teaches at Tufts Univ and is author of *Training God's Army: The American Bible School, 1880–1940* and *From Sin to Salvation: Stories of Women's Conversions, 1800 to the Present.*

Jennifer R. Breslin (MA Univ of Virginia) is an associate with John G. Waite Associates, Architects, PLLC, in charge of marketing and business development.

Jerry R. N. Brisco (PhD candidate Arizona State Univ) is a retired retail executive. His specialties are business and economic history and his master's thesis was on early department stores in Phoenix.

Warren F. Broderick is senior archives and records management specialist at the NYS Archives. He has published on local history and folklore, American literature, and American ceramics.

Ray Bromley (PhD Cambridge Univ) taught international development studies at the Univ of Wales, Swansea, and worked for USAID in a regional development program in Peru. He is professor of planning, geography, and Latin American studies at SUNY Albany and member of the American Institute of Certified Planners specializing in urban studies, community development, and planning history.

Simon J. Bronner is Distinguished Professor of Folklore and American Studies at Pennsylvania State Univ, Harrisburg. He is author of over a dozen books, including *Old-Time Music Makers of New York State* (1987) and *Following Tradition: Folklore in the Discourse of American Culture* (1998).

Charles E. Brooks is associate professor of history at Texas A&M Univ. He is author of *Frontier Settlement and Market Revolution: The Holland Land Purchase* (1996).

Chris Brooks is a postgraduate researcher at the Univ of Edinburgh.

Norman Brouwer is marine historian and acting librarian of the Melville Library and South Street Seaport Museum. He is a member of the board of advisors of the North River Historic Ship Society and coauthor of *A Mariner's Fancy: The Whaleman's Art of Scrimshaw* (1992).

Pamela A. Brown is Village of Panama historian.

Phil Brown is professor of sociology at Brown Univ. He is author of *Catskill Culture: A Mountain Rat's Memories of the Great Jewish Resort Area* and cofounder and president of the Catskills Institute, an organization that documents and preserves the Jewish experience in the Catskills.

Charles J. Browne is deputy historian of Broome Co, officer of the Broome County Historical Society, and collections specialist at the Roberson Museum and Science Center. He has served as curator for three exhibits at the Binghamton Visitors Center, Roberson.

Dorothy M. Browne (PhD candidate Graduate School and Univ Center CUNY) works at the Center for the Study of Philanthropy on its curriculum guides. Her dissertation examines the history of New York museums.

Joseph W. Brownell (PhD) attended schools throughout the state during the Great Depression, then served in noncombat roles in the US Navy during World War II and Korea. After graduating from Syracuse Univ he spent 45 years at SUNY Cortland, retiring in 2001.

Joan Jacobs Brumberg is the Stephen H. Weiss Presidential Fellow and professor at Cornell Univ, where she teaches history in the NYS College of Human Ecology.

Stephan F. Brumberg is professor of education at Brooklyn College and the Graduate Center CUNY. He is author of *Going to America, Going to School: The Jewish Immigrant Public School Encounter in Turn-of-the-Century New York City* (1986), among other works.

Charles Brumley was an Adirondack guide for 10 years. He has taught Adirondack history at North Country Community College and has written a book of Adirondack short stories and one on Adirondack guides.

Jack A. Bucco (PhD Bowling Green State Univ) is professor at Austin Community College. He is a former professional hockey player with the Troy Slapshots.

Gary Bugh (PhD SUNY Albany) teaches courses in American politics and political theory and served as consultant for the 2000 NYS Electoral College.

David E. Bumbaugh holds degrees from Wilmington College, Ohio, and Meadville/Lombard Theological School, Chicago, where he is associate professor of ministry and director of field education. He served Unitarian Universalist churches in numerous states and was named minister emeritus of the Unitarian Church in Summit, NJ.

Ronald J. Burch is curator of art and architecture at the NYS Museum, Albany.

Wanda Burch (MA SUNY Oneonta) has worked in museums since 1974 and is site manager of Johnson Hall State Historic Site, Johnstown. She has published articles in history journals and wrote the historic district nomination for the hamlet of Glen.

Edwin G. Burrows is Distinguished Professor of History at Brooklyn College and coauthor of *Gotham: A History of New York City to 1898,* winner of the Pulitzer Prize in history.

Linnea Goodwin Burwood is assistant professor of history at SUNY Delhi. Her doctoral dissertation is on Alexander Berkman, a Russian American anarchist from Binghamton Univ.

Stephen Burwood is director of study abroad and associate dean at SUNY Geneseo. He is author of *American Labor, France, and the Politics of Intervention, 1945–1952* (1999).

Ann L. Buttenwieser is author of *Manhattan Water-Bound* (1999) and the introduction to *The Lower Manhattan Plan* (2002). She is a waterfront planning consultant and adjunct professor at Columbia Univ. She worked in the NYC Departments of City Planning and Parks and Recreation and the city's Economic Development Corp.

Richard Byron (BS Rensselaer Polytechnical Institute) was metallurgical engineer for Republic Steel Corp and owner/president of CH Byron Co, Inc Industrial Contractors. He is executive director of the Niagara Aerospace Museum, Niagara Falls.

C

Joel S. Cadbury is a graduate student at Cornell Univ.

Timothy Calabrese is research associate in the Population Division of the NYC Department of City Planning, where he does historical census work. He is a GIS specialist and is completing his master's degree in geography at CUNY's Hunter College.

Alexander V. Campbell completed his PhD dissertation, " 'Still in Service': The 60th (Royal American) Regiment of Foot, 1755–1772" at the Univ of Western Ontario.

Nancy D. Campbell, assistant professor in the Department of Science and Technology Studies at Rensselaer Polytechnic Institute, Troy, is author of *Using Women: Gender, Drug Policy, and Social Justice* (2000).

Heidi Canavan is a high school history teacher at Candor Central School.

Hugh O. Canham (PhD) has taught forest and resource economics and conducted research at SUNY-ESF, Syracuse, on forest ownership, land taxation, the impact of forestry activities, and issues facing the forest products industry. He served as consultant to the NYS Governor's Task Force on Forest Industry, the NYS Department of Environmental Conservation, and the US Forest Service.

Charles H. Canon III (MLS SUNY Geneseo) has been associated with Roberts Wesleyan College since the fall of 1966, when he arrived on campus as a freshman and a cross-country runner. He has been the archivist since 1982.

Christine Capella Peters (MLA SUNY-ESF) is a member of the technical staff for the NYS Historic Preservation Office responsible for reviewing physical undertakings affecting historic and cultural resources. She is coeditor of *The Secretary of the Interior's Standards for the Treatment of Historic Properties and the Guidelines for the Treatment of Cultural Landscapes* (1996).

Christopher Capozzola (PhD Columbia Univ) is assistant professor of history at the Massachusetts Institute of Technology. He is completing a book on the American home front during WWI.

Malio J. Cardarelli, after his retirement as chief of labor and employee relations in the Civilian Personnel Division of Griffiss AFB, began preserving on paper the people and events that exemplify some of Utica's past. He is author of *The Historic WPA Murals of Egbert Norman Clark at Utica's Thomas R. Proctor High School* (1997) and *Utica's Mother Lavender; I'll See You in Heaven* (1999).

Maren Lockwood Carden (PhD Harvard Univ) is professor of sociology at Long Island Univ, Brooklyn. She is author of *Oneida: Utopian Community to Modern Corporation* (1998) and *The New Feminist Movement* (1974). She is working on an institutional history of Long Island Univ.

Mary R. Cardenas became Orangetown historian in 1993. She is museum director of the Orangetown Historical Museum and Archives. She was president of the Tappantown Historical Society, 1987–91.

Jim Carl is assistant professor of curriculum and foundations at Cleveland State Univ.

Gerald L. Carr (PhD Univ of Michigan) is an art and architectural historian, photographer, and instructor. He was visiting art historian at Olana State Historic Site and is author of *In Search of the Promised Land: Paintings by Frederic Edwin Church* (2000) and *Frederic Edwin Church: Catalogue Raisonné of Works of Art at Olana State Historic Site* (1994).

Elisa Carrillo is professor emerita of history at Marymount College. She is author of *Alcide De Gasperi: The Long Apprenticeship* (1965).

Cynthia Carrington Carter (MA) was born on a dairy farm in northeastern Pennsylvania.

Bret E. Carroll (PhD Cornell Univ) is assistant professor of history at California State Univ, Stanislaus. He is author of *Spiritualism in Antebellum America* (1997) and *The Routledge Historical Atlas of Religion in America* (2000).

Kerry Dean Carso (PhD Boston Univ) is assistant professor of art history at James Madison Univ.

Robert Allan Carter is senior librarian at the NYS Library. He is author of *The New York State Constitution: Sources of Legislative Intent*, 2d ed. (2001).

Dick Case is a columnist for the *Syracuse Post-Standard* and author of *Good Guys, Bad Guys, Big Guys, Little Guys: Upstate New York Stories from the "Syracuse Herald Journal/Herald American"* (1994). He is also a trustee of the Rosamond Gifford Charitable Corp and Syracuse University Library Associates.

Marion R. Casey is assistant professor of history and Faculty Fellow in Irish American Studies at New York Univ.

Thomas W. Casey was professor of philosophy and regional history at Marist College. He was former chair of the Department of Philosophy and Religious Studies, director of American studies, and chair of the faculty.

William Casey works as an organic dairy farmer and agricultural historian from his home in Apulia Station. He has a web site.

Floris Barnett Cash is associate professor of Africana studies and history at SUNY Stony Brook. She is author of *African American Women and Social Action: The Clubwomen and Volunteerism from Jim Crow to the New Deal, 1896–1936* (2001) and "Gender and Race Consciousness: Verina Morton Jones Inspires a Settlement House in Suburbia" (*Long Island Women Activists and Innovators,* 1998).

John Cashman is a Teaching Fellow at Boston College, Mass. His research and published work focus on Baltimore's maritime workers.

Jay Cassel (PhD Univ of Toronto) has taught at Canadian universities and worked on historical documentaries for television with the Canadian Broadcasting Corp and National Geographic.

Stephanie Cassidy (PhD candidate Univ of California, San Diego) is archivist at the Art Students League of New York.

Frank J. Cavaioli is professor emeritus at SUNY College of Technology, Farmingdale, and consultant in ethnic and Italian American studies. He is editor of *The Italian American Experience: An Encyclopedia* (2000) and contributor to *Long Island Historical Journal.*

Ana Margarita Cervantes-Rodríguez (PhD) is professor of international migration, transnationalism, and Latinos in the US at SUNY Albany and research associate at the Center for Social and Demographic Analysis. She is author of *From Bozales to Balseros: International Migration in Cuba* (forthcoming).

Gwen Chamberlain, a lifelong resident of Yates Co, is a freelance writer and owner of Write Now Promotions, Dundee. She is former editor of the *Chronicle-Express,* Penn Yan.

Thomas A. Chambers is assistant professor of history at Niagara Univ. He is author of *Drinking the Waters: Creating an American Leisure Class at 19th-Century Mineral Springs.*

Carolle Charles (PhD Univ of Binghamton) is associate professor of sociology at Baruch College. Her research and work concentrate on processes and agencies in Haitian society and in the Haitian immigrant communities of North America.

Anthony Chase (MA SUNY Buffalo) is theater editor for *Artvoice* in Buffalo, assistant to the president of Buffalo State College, and member of its theater faculty. He is author of articles on American theater.

Joyce Chase is Town of Cherry Creek historian.

David Chenkin (MA Yale Univ) is academic services coordinator for the continuing and professional studies program at Baruch College.

Lloyd Chiasson Jr (PhD Southern Illinois) is journalism professor at Nicholls State Univ, La. He has published articles and book chapters and is coauthor of *Reporter's Notebook,* an interactive computer simulation for reporting courses. He is coauthor and editor of *Crime, Justice, and the Media: Press Coverage of Socially Significant American Trials* (2001).

Cynthia B. Childs (BS Rider Univ) is a research assistant of *The Encyclopedia of New York State.*

John J. Chiment (PhD) is professor of paleontology and geology in the Department of Earth and Atmospheric Sciences at Cornell Univ. He excavated two mammoths in the state and performs chemical analysis on wood and fossils from archaeological, historic, and artistic sites, and collects fossils worldwide. He is editor of *PaleoBios* and *Cornell Plantations Quarterly.*

Victoria J. Chiment resides in Schuyler Co with her husband, John.

Florence A. Christoph is a certified genealogist and historical editor. She is author of *The Van Voorhees Family in America* (2000).

Peter R. Christoph is director and senior editor of the New York Historical Manuscripts publication project and serves as archivist for the Upstate New York Synod of the Evangelical Lutheran Church in America. He was curator of manuscripts at the NYS Library, 1968–88, and director of the New Netherland Project, 1974–84.

Yayin Chu-Reimer graduated from Hubei Univ in Wuhan, China, and studied urban planning at SUNY Albany. She works for the NYS Education Department.

Nicholas P. Ciotola is curator at the Historical Society of Western Pennsylvania's Senator John Heinz Pittsburgh Regional History Center and teaches at the Univ of Pittsburgh.

Mary Ann Clark is an independent scholar working in the field of Afro-Caribbean religious beliefs and practice. Her book on the material culture of Santería focuses on religious displays as theological statements.

Susan S. Clarke (MBA Boston Univ) is principal in Unconventional Wisdom, a consulting firm for creative approaches and institutional histories. She is administrative coordinator for the National Consortium for Continuous Improvement in Higher Education. She helped edit *Rensselaer: Where Imagination Achieves the Impossible* and *The Albany Academy: Its History, Its Words and Faces.*

Dane S. Claussen (PhD) is associate professor and director of the graduate program in the Department of Journalism and Mass Communication at Point Park Univ, Pa. He edited *The Promise Keepers* (2000) and *Sex/Religion/Media* (2001). He is writing a history of the US newspaper industry's marketing practices from 1920 to 1970 and a media management textbook.

Beth Cleary is associate professor of dramatic arts at Macalester College, Minn, and author of articles and reviews on puppetry, women's performance, and performing race.

Kathryn Clippinger Kosto is a graduate student in early American history at Cornell Univ.

Stacey Coburn is a graduate of Scotia-Glenville High School and resides in Scotia. She is attending Ithaca College as a Park Scholar and is studying journalism.

Carolyn E. Cocca is assistant professor of politics at SUNY Old Westbury. She is writing a book about statutory rape laws across the US.

Craig Richard Coenen is adjunct assistant professor of history at Rider and Lehigh Univs. He has authored articles on urban and sports history.

Sean Coffey was an on-line and contributing editor before serving as staff writer for *Bicycling* magazine and is a lifelong cyclist.

David Steven Cohen (PhD Univ of Pennsylvania) taught history and American studies at Rutgers Univ, NJ, before serving as senior research associate and director of the Ethnic History Program at New Jersey Historical Commission. He is author of *Folk Legacies Revisited* (1995) and *The Dutch-American Farm* (1992).

Jocelyn Cohen (PhD Univ of Minnesota) is coeditor and translator on the American Immigrant Autobiographies Project at the YIVO Institute for Jewish Research, New York City.

Judah Cohen (PhD candidate Harvard Univ) is studying musical practice in American Reform Judaism.

Ronald D. Cohen is professor of history at Indiana Univ Northwest Gary. He is author of *Rainbow Quest: The Folk Music Revival and American Society, 1940–1970* (2002) and *Golden Threads: An Illustrated History of Folk Music in the United States, 1900–1970* (2001).

Arthur B. Cohn is cofounder and executive director of the Lake Champlain Maritime Museum, Ferrisburgh, Vt. He has been involved in nautical archaeological studies on Lake Champlain and other state waters for more than two decades and advises local, state, and national officials on underwater resource management issues.

Kathleen Collins (MA New York Univ Journalism School) was research coordinator at the Freedom Forum Media Studies Center. She wrote about Irish Americans in television for the *American Irish Desk Reference* and about radio critics for the *Encyclopedia of Radio* (2001).

Gould Colman (PhD) was Cornell Univ archivist for 23 years. His thesis, *Education and Agriculture: A History of the New York State College of Agriculture at Cornell University,* was published in 1963.

Lisa Compton has served as curator and executive director of historical museums and national landmarks in Massachusetts, Oregon, and New York, and is executive director of the Seneca Falls Historical Society. She has published articles on local history, historic preservation, museum practice, and early American music and dance.

Susan L. Conklin (BA SUNY Geneseo) has served as Genesee Co historian since 1980 and as records management officer since 1989. She works with the Genesee County Historians Association to write, edit, and publish books including *Bridges: A Collection of Senior Reminisces,* and *Batavia Walking Tour.*

John H. Conlin (MA SUNY Buffalo) is editor in chief of *Western New York Heritage* magazine. He is an architectural historian and historic preservationist, author of *Buffalo City Hall: Americanesque Masterpiece* (1993), and recipient of the Buffalo Historical Society's Owen Augspurger Award for local history.

Dennis J. Connors is curator of history at the Onondaga Historical Association. He is author of *Images of America: Syracuse* (1997) and *Echoes of Our Past: The Historic Landscapes of Syracuse's Cemeteries* (1994). He is former chair of the Syracuse Landmark Preservation Board and lectures on Syracuse's history.

John Conway has been the Sullivan Co historian since 1993. He is adjunct professor of history at SUNY Sullivan and has written four books. He is quoted on Catskills and resort history and on gambling, and won a NYS Broadcasters Association award for *A Look Back,* a series of historical vignettes on WVOS Radio.

William R. Cook (PhD Cornell Univ) is Distinguished Teaching Professor of History at SUNY Geneseo. He is author of *Celebrating Our Past: Livingston County in the 20th Century* (2000).

Brad Coon is reference librarian with Montana State Univ. His research interests include environmentalism and Native American linguistics.

Pamela Cooper (PhD) specializes in 20th-century American history and is author of *The American Marathon* (1998). She is assistant editor of *The Encyclopedia of New York State.*

Virginia W. Cooper is Town of Yates historian.

John J. Coppola (MA) is executive director of the New York Association of Alcoholism and Substance Abuse Providers, Inc. He served on the executive committee of the NYS Association of Substance Abuse Programs, chair of the NYS Catholic Conference Alcoholism and Substance Abuse Committee, and as advisor with the Office of National Drug Control Policy.

Theodore Corbett is director of the Better Bennington Corp and is former director of the Saratoga Springs Preservation Foundation. He has published books and articles on resort history.

Alison M. Cornish is an architectural historian. She is curator of *Castles in the Sand: The Design of Long Island's State Parks* (Society for the Preservation of Long Island Antiquities) and co-curator of *Robert Moses's New York and Long Island* (Museums of Stony Brook).

Margaret D. Costello is a writer and editor in the Syracuse Univ Publications office. A former daily newspaper reporter, she received several awards from Gannett Corp and the Associated Press, and has contributed to *The Insider's Guide to the Colleges* (1995–96).

Reed Coughlan is professor of sociology at Empire State College, SUNY. He has published work on ethnicity and the state, theories of ethnic identity, and conflict, and coedited

The Economic Dimensions of Ethnic Conflict. He is working on a study of the breakup of Yugoslavia and a project on the Bosnian refugee communities in upstate New York.

Edward Countryman (PhD) is director of graduate studies in history at Southern Methodist Univ. He is author of *Americans: A Collision of Histories* (1996) and *The American Revolution* (1985). He was recipient of the Royal Historical Society Fellowship (1987–91) and the Bancroft Prize (1982).

Walter C. Cowles (BS Univ of Michigan) was employed by the American Ship Building Co, Cleveland, as draftsman, chief hull draftsman, and naval architect. He is a member of maritime history organizations and life member of the Society of Naval Architects and US Naval Institute. He is author of several maritime history articles.

Thomas H. Cox is a PhD candidate in history at the SUNY Buffalo. His dissertation is entitled "Courting Commerce: *Gibbons v Ogden* and the Legal Transformation of Interstate Trade in the Early Republic."

James Crawford has been curator of Canajoharie Library and Art Gallery since 1994. He holds graduate degrees from East Stroudsburg and New York Univs.

Robert P. Crease is professor of philosophy at SUNY Stony Brook and historian of Brookhaven National Laboratory. His books include *Making Physics: A Biography of Brookhaven National Laboratory, 1946–1972* (1999).

Brian J. Cudahy (PhD St. Bonaventure Univ) has written about transportation subjects from subway trains to cruise ships.

John J. Curran has been Peekskill City historian since 1994. He is author of articles, books, and publications, including *Attack at Peekskill by the British in 1777* (1998) and has scripted and directed three local historic videotape productions.

Beatrice Houck Curtin is Town of Arkwright historian.

Joseph A. Cutshall-King is a published writer and historian. He was museum director for 15 years and Washington Co historian for 5 years. He is coordinator of grants at Orange Community College, Middletown, and writes a weekly column on local history for the *Post-Star.*

D

Janet Daley (MA Univ of North Dakota) is a freelance editor and was editor at the State Historical Society of North Dakota, 1992–2002. She is assistant editor of *The Encyclopedia of New York State.*

Elizabeth A. Daniels has been Vassar College historian since 1985, when she retired from the Helen D. Lockwood Chair of English there after 37 years of teaching and administration. She is coauthor of *Full Steam Ahead in Poughkeepsie: The Story of Coeducation at Vassar, 1966–1974* (2000).

Robert A. Daniels is curator of ichthyology at the NYS Museum. His research focuses on ecology and zoogeography of freshwater fish. He has conducted research programs in the Northeast, Pacific Slope, Antarctica, and India.

James W. Darlington is geography and map editor for *The Encyclopedia of New York State.*

Thomas E. Darlington is a student in the Westhill School District and enjoys playing soccer, piano, and trumpet.

William J. Darlington is a student at Onondaga Hill Middle School. He is an architecture and soccer enthusiast.

R. E. G. Davies, FRAeS, FRGS, FRSA, was economist at the British Ministry of Civil Aviation, and British European Airways, and at Bristol, de Havilland, and Hawker Siddeley aircraft companies. He was Lindbergh Chair of Aerospace History at the National Air and Space Museum, Smithsonian Institution, where he is curator of air transport. He has written 20 books on airlines and air transport history.

Chad P. Dawson is professor in forest and natural resources management at SUNY-ESF, Syracuse.

Lynda R. Day (PhD Univ of Wisconsin, Madison) is associate professor of Africana studies at Brooklyn College, CUNY. She is author of *Making a Way to Freedom: A History of African Americans on Long Island,* which received a certificate of commendation from the Association of State and Local History (1998).

Marsha DeFilipps is Village of Holley and Town of Murray historian.

Gregory Dehler received his PhD from Lehigh Univ.

Wendy J. Deichmann Edwards (PhD Drew Univ) teaches theology and church history at United Theological Seminary, Buffalo. She has published several articles about the history of Christian missions and the Social Gospel movement and is writing a biography of Social Gospel leader Josiah Strong.

John R. Deitrick is professor of English at Becker College, Mass, and senior lecturer in English at Northeastern Univ College.

Ellen M. deLalla is local historian of the Saratoga Room, the local history collection of the Saratoga Springs Public Library. She is a freelance photographer.

Kerry Delaney (BA SUNY Albany) is executive director of the Albany County Historical Association. Her interests include women's history, legal history, and 19th-century decorative arts.

Jane M. DeLuca (RN, doctoral candidate) is coordinator of the inborn errors of metabolism clinic at Golisano Children's Hospital/Strong Memorial Hospital.

Janet Dempsey is Town of Cornwall historian and author of *Images from the Past* (1989) and *Cornwall Revisited* (1994).

Jim Denn (MA Nelson A. Rockefeller College of Public Affairs and Policy, SUNY Albany) is NYSTAR's director of public information specializing in analyzing and writing about business and high technology–related issues in the state.

Christopher Densmore (MA Univ of Wisconsin) is curator at the Friends Historical Library at Swarthmore College. He is author of *Red Jacket: Iroquois Orator and Diplomat* (1999) and articles on Quakers, Iroquois, and archival management in *Quaker History, Canadian Quaker History Journal,* and *New York History.*

Anne Cohen DePietro is chief curator of the Heckscher Museum of Art. She also directs the Newsday Center for Dove/Torr Studies, which will be housed in the cottage once owned by Arthur Dove and Helen Torr.

Amy DeRogatis is assistant professor of American religion and culture in the Religious Studies Department at Michigan State Univ.

Anne M. Derousie (PhD candidate SUNY Binghamton) is park historian at the Women's Rights National Historical Park in Seneca Falls.

Sarah E. DeSanctis (MA Univ of Rochester) is manuscripts assistant in the Department of Rare Books, Special Collections, and Preservation at the Univ of Rochester. Her publications include "Victory Girls, Cuddle Bunnies, and Patriotutes: World War II and the Crisis of White Female Sexuality" (2003). She is assistant editor of *The Encyclopedia of New York State.*

Jane Dieckmann is an indexer, editor, and writer living in Ithaca. She is author of *A Short History of Tompkins County* (1986) and *Wells College: A History* (1995)

J. Herbie DiFonzo (JD, PhD Univ of Virginia) is professor of law at Hofstra Univ School of Law. Born in Buenos Aires and raised in New York City, he is a legal historian who has written on issues involving family history and criminal law.

Thomas Dimitroff taught history and English in Corning public schools for 35 years. He is a Fellow at the Corning Museum of Glass and honorary curator of Carder glass at the Rockwell Museum of Western Art. He is author of *Frederick Carder and Steuben Glass: American Classics* and coauthor of *History of the Corning–Painted Post Area: 200 Years in Painted Post Country.*

Hasia R. Diner is Paul S. and Sylvia Steinberg Professor of American Jewish History at New York Univ. She is author of *Lower East Side Memories: The Jewish Place in America* (2000).

Victor DiSanto (PhD) is historic preservation program analyst for the NYS Office of Parks, Recreation, and Historic Preservation.

Barbara J. Dix is Oswego Co historian and records manager.

Quinton H. Dixie (PhD Union Theological Seminary) is assistant professor of religious studies at Indiana Univ, Bloomington.

Heriberto Dixon (PhD) is an enrolled tribal member of the Saponi Nation of Ohio. He is researching the migration history and development of the eastern Siouan peoples. He is senior lecturer in strategic management at SUNY New Paltz and former associate professor of human resources management at the Milano Graduate School of Management and Urban Policy of the New School Univ.

Joseph Doherty (MA SUNY Albany) is a licensed professional engineer in Colorado and New York State. He has been with the NYS Department of Transportation since 1984 and program manager for snow and ice removal since 1994.

Monica Doherty is Yorktown Historical Society Board trustee and former president of Yorktown Historical Society. She is a historical research enthusiast and field-trained archaeologist and lecturer.

The Doing History class at SUNY Fredonia (Spring 2001) included Jay Bachmann, Zachary Ballard, Adam Connelly, Cory Eno, Nicholas Fattey, Joelle Grimm, Brian Isaac, Matthew Perry, Jesse Pletts, Kathryn Reagan, Joseph Scalzo, Wesley Smith, and Patrick Yandow.

Wayne D. Drummond is president of the New Haven Railroad Historical and Technical Association. He is an author and historian and is retired from the New York Police Department.

David A. Dudley is Town of Cato historian.

Francis J. Duffy is a state-based writer and aerial photographer. He is vice president and one of the founders of the Maritime Industry Museum on the campus of SUNY Maritime College, Fort Schuyler. He covers the maritime scene in the US for the UK publications *Fairplay, Ships Monthly,* and *Marine News.*

Ruth DuMont (BA Gordon College) is library assistant in the Basil G. Bibby Library, Univ of Rochester Eastman Dental Center. She has been organizing the Eastman Dental Center Archives and participated in an arrangement and description grant by the NYS Archives and Records Administration Documentary Heritage Program with the Rochester Health Care Archives Network (1997–98).

Janice K. Dunham is social science librarian and associate chief librarian of John Jay College Library, CUNY. She has contributed articles to the *Encyclopedia of Crime and Punishment* and reviews for *Library Journal.*

Anthony L. Dunlap is a graduate of Washington Univ, St. Louis, and works in publishing in New York City.

Barbara J. Dunlap (MS Columbia Univ) is professor emerita at City College, CUNY, where she was chief of the Division of Archives and Special Collections. She is coauthor of *From the Free Academy to CUNY: Illustrating Public Higher Education in New York City* (2000) and has published articles such as "Reading Charlotte M. Yonge into the Novels of Barbara Pym" (*All This Reading,* 2003).

Edward T. Dunn (PhD Univ of Rochester) is professor of history at Canisius College. He is author of *Railroads of Western New York* (1996) and *Buffalo's Delaware Avenue: Mansions and Families* (2003).

Shirley W. Dunn (MA) has studied Hudson Valley Native Americans and is a historic preservation consultant and interpreter/assistant manager in a historic house museum. She teaches a course on Native American research at Columbia-Greene Community College. She is author of *The Mohicans and Their Land, 1609–1730* (1994) and *The Mohican World, 1680–1750* (2000).

Brian Leigh Dunnigan is curator of maps at William L. Clements Library, Univ of Michigan. He was executive director (1979–96) of the Old Fort Niagara Association and wrote monographs about it.

E

Charlotte B. Eaton is a retired elementary school art teacher. She created exhibits and was curator of the Foundry School Museum and Putnam County Historical Society where she volunteers.

Helen Ebersole is Village of Lakewood historian.

Brad Edmondson is a graduate of Cornell Univ and member of the Finger Lakes Land Trust. He is author of *Environmental Affairs in New York State: A Historical Overview,* a project of the NYS Archives Environmental Affairs Documentation Project.

Sheila Edmunds is Village of Aurora historian.

R. A. R. Edwards is assistant professor of history at Rochester Institute of Technology.

Eileen Effrat is a librarian.

Michael Egan is a PhD student in environmental history at Washington State Univ.

Albert S. Eggerton Jr, former manager of corporate communications at Norfolk Southern Corp, is volunteer researcher at the Smithsonian Museum of American History.

Ronald Ehmke, a Buffalo-based writer and performer, edited *Consider the Alternatives: 20 Years of Contemporary Art at Hallwalls* (1996). He is minister of communications for Righteous Babe Records.

Arthur Einhorn (American Anthropological Association

Fellow) was associate professor of anthropology at Jefferson Community College and chair of the Social Science Department at Lowville Academy. He was also associate director of Indian Education Institutes at St. Lawrence Univ and adjunct professor of anthropology. He served as Lewis Co historian and director of the Historical Society Museum.

Peter Eisenstadt is editor in chief of *The Encyclopedia of New York State.*

Lynn Ekfelt retired after 28 years as librarian and archivist at St. Lawrence Univ. She is a professional folklorist. Her book *Good Food, Served Right: Traditional Recipes and Food Customs from New York's North Country* (2000) was the national winner in the 2000 Tabasco competition.

Eric A. Eliason (PhD Univ of Texas, Austin) is assistant professor of English at Brigham Young Univ, where he teaches folklore and Mormon literature. He has written on pioneers in Mormon popular historical expression, Western American folk heroes, conversion narratives, the civil rights of Mormons, and the economics of women's handicrafts on the Dutch Caribbean island of Saba.

Evelyn Ellis is Village of Lindenhurst historian. In the 1880s her maternal grandparents settled in Breslau [now Lindenhurst], where she was born in 1920. In 1942 she was appointed deputy village clerk, and she also served as treasurer and village clerk.

John S. Ellis (PhD) is assistant professor at the Univ of Michigan–Flint. He has published articles in *Welsh History Review, Journal of British Studies,* and *Albion and Eire.* He is member of the Welsh American community of the New York–Vermont State Valley.

Louis R. Eltscher is professor emeritus of history and politics at the Rochester Institute of Technology. He is coauthor of *Curtiss-Wright: Greatness and Decline.*

Theodore A. Endreny (PhD), PH, PE, is assistant professor at SUNY-ESF in the Department of Environmental Resources and Forest Engineering and in the Department of Forest and Natural Resources Management.

William Engelbrecht is professor of anthropology at Buffalo State. He is author of *Iroquoia: The Development of a Native World* (2003).

Steven Engelhart (MA Univ of Vermont) is executive director of Adirondack Architectural Heritage (AARCH). He is author of *Crossing the River: Historic Bridges of the AuSable River* and lectures on Adirondack architecture and historic preservation throughout the region.

Robert Englert received his bachelor's degree in geography and urban studies and studied city planning, with an emphasis on historic preservation, at Cornell Univ. He is the national register and survey representative for the Historic Preservation Field Services Bureau/SHPO, covering the five counties around Rochester.

Michael C. English (MA SUNY Albany) has done research on 16th- and 18th-century French literature in Strasbourg, France, and is a freelance writer.

Jonathan Entin, professor of law and political science at Case Western Reserve Univ, is working on a book on the law of equal protection. He has written on constitutional law and history, the regulatory process, civil rights and civil liberties, and legal aspects of the census.

Philip B. Eppard is professor at the School of Information Science and Policy at SUNY Albany. He teaches and does research in the areas of archives, preservation, and the history of the book.

Harry Eskew (PhD Tulane Univ) is professor emeritus of New Orleans Baptist Theological Seminary, where he served for 36 years as professor of music history and hymnology and as music librarian. He is coauthor of *Singing Baptists: Studies in Baptist Hymnody in America.*

Suzanne Etherington holds a doctorate in history from Syracuse Univ. She teaches a graduate course in NYS history at SUNY Cortland. She has been the NYS Archives government records regional advisory officer for the 10-county Region 6 since 1996.

Christopher H. Evans is associate professor of church history at Colgate Rochester/Crozer Divinity School. He is author of publications including *Social Gospel Liberalism and the Ministry of Ernest Fremont Tittle* (1996). He is editor of *Perspectives on the Social Gospel* (1999) and *The Social Gospel Today* (2001).

John Evers (MA SUNY Albany), legislative analyst for the Business Council of New York State, Inc, is former historian of the NYS Assembly.

F

Firth Haring Fabend is an independent historian. She is author of *A Dutch Family in the Middle Colonies, 1660–1800* (1991) and *Zion on the Hudson: Dutch New York and New Jersey in the Age of Revivals* (2000).

Mike Fabricant (PhD Brandeis Univ) is professor in the Hunter College School of Social Work. He is author of *Besieged Social Services: Settlements at the Close of the 20th Century* (forthcoming).

Duncan Faherty is a PhD candidate in English at the Graduate Center CUNY.

Robert H. Fakundiny (PhD Univ of Texas, Austin) is state geologist and chief scientist of geology for the NYS Geological Survey at the NYS Museum. He has written for *Northeastern Geology, State Geologists Journal* and *Geological Society of America.*

Allen Fannin was owner/manager of a commission weaving mill, 1965–95. He is author of technical works and adjunct professor of textile design technology at Syracuse Univ.

Kelly A. Yacobucci Farquhar is Montgomery Co historian and records management officer. She is also head of the county's Department of History and Archives, a genealogical and historical research library in Fonda.

Grant Farr is professor and chair of the Department of Sociology at Portland State Univ. He is author of a number of books including *Global Societies* (2000) and *Modern Iran* (1999).

David H. Fasser (RLA) is director of landscape architecture for the NYS Department of Transportation, responsible for planning, design, development, and management of the Scenic Byways Program. He is an American Society of Landscape Architecture Fellow.

H. William Feder (PhD SUNY Buffalo) is former Niagara Co historian. He is author of *The Evolution of an Ethnic Neighborhood That Became United in Diversity: The East Side, Niagara Falls, NY 1880–1930* and contributing author of *Welcome to the Niagara Historic Trail.* He was a county legislator representing the area around Niagara Falls.

Loren Butler Feffer (PhD Univ of Chicago) was an independent scholar and taught at the Univ of Chicago, Rutgers Univ, and the Univ of Pennsylvania. She authored articles on the history of physics/mathematics in *Isis, Historia Mathematica* and *Historical Studies in the Physical Sciences.*

Michael R. Fein (PhD candidate Brandeis Univ) is research associate at Harvard Business School. His dissertation is on the politics of state highway construction.

Marjorie N. Feld (PhD student Brandeis Univ) is instructor in the American Studies Department at Univ of Massachusetts, Boston, and serves as manuscript editor for *Radical Teacher.*

Larry Felser, sports editor of the *Buffalo News,* has been a journalist for nearly half a century, covering the World Series, the first 34 Super Bowls, and the Olympic Games, including the 1980 Winter Games in Lake Placid.

Susan E. Ferrara (PhD Univ of Maryland, College Park) is author of *The Family of the Wizard: The Baums of Syracuse* (2000). She lives in Princeton, NJ.

Ute Ferrier (PhD candidate SUNY Binghamton) has taught college-level history courses and published articles.

Phyllis F. Field is associate professor of history at Ohio Univ. She is author of *The Politics of Race in New York* (1982).

Erwin Fineout is Village of Fair Haven historian.

Paul Finkelman (PhD Univ of Chicago) is a Fellow in law and humanities at Harvard Law School and Chapman Distinguished Professor of Law at the Univ of Tulsa College of Law. He is author of *Slavery and the Founders: Race and Liberty in the Age of Jefferson* (2002) and editor of *The Library of Congress Civil War Desk Reference* (1996).

Joseph R. Fischer (PhD Pennsylvania State Univ) authored *A Well-Executed Failure: The Sullivan Campaign against the Iroquois* as well as articles on the American Revolution. He has taught at the US Military Academy, Pennsylvania State Univ, Bloomsburg Univ, and Fayetteville State Univ. He teaches advanced placement American history at Shikellamy Senior High School, Sunbury, Pa.

Donald M. Fisher is associate professor of history at Niagara County Community College. He is author of *Lacrosse: A History of the Game* (2002).

John K. Fitzer (PhD SUNY Buffalo) is program director for English as a Second Language programs at SUNY Buffalo.

Tracy Schpero Fitzpatrick (PhD candidate Rutgers Univ) is former assistant curator at the National Museum of Women in the Arts, Washington, DC. Her dissertation is entitled "Tunnel Vision: Images of the New York City Subway, 1904–1941."

Thomas R. Flagg (MPhil Columbia Univ) is an industrial archaeologist in New York City. He is author of *New York Harbor Railroads in Color* (2000).

Kathleen Flanagan (PhD Union Theological Seminary) is professor of religious studies at the College of Saint Elizabeth, NJ, and member of the Sisters of Charity of St. Elizabeth. Her dissertation was entitled "The Influence of John Henry Hobart on the Life of Elizabeth Bayley Seton."

Richard M. Flanagan (PhD Rutgers Univ) teaches American politics in the political science program at the College of Staten Island CUNY.

Richard F. Fleck is dean of language, arts, and behavioral sciences at Community College of Denver. In addition to editing *Deep Woods* (1998), he is author of *Clearing of the Mist* (2001).

Thomas Fletcher (PhD McGill Univ) is assistant professor of environmental studies and geography at Bishop's Univ, Quebec. His research on the politics of hazardous waste has been supported by the NYS Archives Partnership Trust and the Canada-US Fulbright Foundation. He is executive board member of the Sierra Club of Canada, Quebec Group.

J. Brooks Flippen (PhD Univ of Maryland) is associate professor of history at Southeastern Oklahoma State Univ, where he has taught since 1995. He is author of *Nixon and the Environment* (2000) and articles on modern American political history.

Maribeth Flynn is an art historian and educator. She directs the docent program at the Brooklyn Museum of Art.

Gerald P. Fogarty SJ (PhD Yale Univ) is William R. Kenan Jr Professor of Religious Studies and History at the Univ of Virginia. He specializes in American Catholic history. Among his published works are *The Vatican and the American Hierarchy from 1870 to 1965* (1982) and *Commonwealth Catholicism: A History of the Catholic Church in Virginia* (2001).

Robert Fogarty is professor of history at Antioch College, editor of *Antioch Review,* and author of *Special Love/ Special Sex* (1994) and *Desire and Duty at Oneida* (2000). He has been Visting Fellow at All Souls College, Oxford, and several other institutions.

Eva C. Fognell is assistant curator at the NYS Historical Association, Cooperstown, and is writing her master's thesis on the material culture at the Auriesville Shrine.

Denis Foley (PhD) is research professor of cultural anthropology at Union College. His specialties are Iroquois, Mohican, and northwest Native Americans. He is author of "The Iroquios Condolence Business" (*Man in the Northeast,* 1973) and *Lemuel Smith and the Compulsion to Kill: The Forensic Story of a Multiple Personality Serial Killer* (2003).

Hugh W. Foley Jr is assistant professor of communications and fine arts at Rogers State Univ, Okla.

Jeff Foley is a freelance writer and participatory journalist who played for the Arena Football League's Albany Firebirds in 1999 and 2000. He is author of *War on the Floor: An Average Guy Plays in the Arena Football League and Lives to Write about It.*

James D. Folts (PhD) is archivist III and head of researcher services at the NYS Archives. He is author of *History of the University of the State of New York and the State Education Department, 1784–1996* (1996) and *Bicentennial History of Cohocton, New York, 1794–1994* (1994).

Paul E. Fontenoy is curator of maritime research at the North Carolina Maritime Museum. He is author of *The Sloops of the Hudson River* and journal articles on naval and maritime history and nautical archaeology.

Kenneth M. Foreman is a retired aerospace research engineer and curator of the Historical Society of the Bellmores. He has authored over 130 technical papers and articles and holds five US patents. He is contributor to the *Long Island Forum* and *Bellmore Life.*

Richard Forliano is Town of Eastchester historian and public school social studies teacher. He has written a booklet on the town's role in the freedoms in the Bill of Rights and is working on a book on its role in the Civil War.

Brett Forman (BA Columbia Univ) is the founder of a music and humor web site and the copy chief of *Waters.* He is also a writer, editor, and musician living in New York City.

Sherrill Foster is a graduate of Brown Univ, Villa Schifanoia, and SUNY Binghamton. She has done history exhibits for Guild Hall Museum, East Hampton, and architectural inventory work in Connecticut. She writes a history column for the *East Hampton Independent.*

Cynthia A. Fox (PhD Indiana Univ), a Buffalo native, is associate professor of French studies at SUNY Albany.

Gino Francesconi was an usher with Carnegie Hall in 1974 while in college. He worked in the house manager's office, box office, and administration office, and became the artist assistant backstage for more than 3,000 performances. In 1984 he established Carnegie Hall's first archives, locating enough material to curate nine exhibitions during the 100th anniversary season (1990–91).

Timothy Frazer is professor emeritus of English at Western Illinois Univ. He was a fieldworker for the *Dictionary of American Regional English* and has published *"Heartland" English.*

Nancy E. Frazier is reference librarian at E. H. Butler Library, SUNY Buffalo State.

Bruce D. Fredrickson is a retired elementary school teacher and City of Lockport historian.

Madelynn P. Fredrickson is a foreign language teacher. She is City of Lockport deputy historian and author of *The Life and Times of Birdsill Holly.*

Laura E. Free (PhD candidate Cornell Univ) is completing her dissertation, "Gendering the Constitution: Masculinity, Woman Suffrage, and the Politics of Citizenship, 1865–1869."

Robert J. Freeman is executive director of the Committee on Open Government and has discussed open government throughout the state, the US, Canada, Japan, and Hong Kong. In 1999 he was selected by *Empire State Report* as one of the 25 individuals who in the past quarter century contributed most to the operation of state government.

Gary Frenay has been a professional musician in Syracuse for over 25 years. He was honored with two SAMMY (Syracuse Area Music) Awards for best songwriter, has toured internationally, and has appeared on over 50 releases.

Suzan D. Friedlander is an independent historian and museum consultant, specializing in 19th-century New York State. Her exhibitions include *Upon Good Lands: A Look at New York State Agriculture from the Colonial Period to the Present* (Syracuse) and *It Must Begin as Fantasy: The Genesis and Growth of Glimmerglass Opera, 1975–2000* (Cooperstown).

Tami J. Friedman (PhD Columbia Univ) is senior associate for communications at the Center of Wisconsin Strategy. Her dissertation examines the causes and consequences of capital flight in the post–World War II US carpet industry.

Michael Frisch teaches history and American studies at SUNY Buffalo. He is author or editor of four books, including *A Shared Authority: Essays on the Craft and Meaning of Oral and Public History* (1990) and *Portraits in Steel* (1993), winner of the Oral History Association Book Prize for 1993–95.

Andrea E. Frohne (PhD candidate SUNY Binghamton) focuses on the African Burial Ground in New York City.

Lou Fuller is Town of Shelby historian.

Elisabeth Paling Funk (PhD Fordham Univ) taught college-level English literature and composition. Born in the Netherlands, her articles on early American and Dutch American literature have been published in the US and the Netherlands.

James Futrell is historian for the National Amusement Park Historical Association. He is author of *Amusement Parks of Pennsylvania* (2002) and amusement industry–related articles.

G

John Allen Gable (PhD Brown Univ) has been executive director of the Theodore Roosevelt Association, Oyster Bay, since 1974. He is adjunct professor at Hofstra Univ.

Loretta J. Gabriel is an elementary school teacher and librarian from Pennsylvania.

Mary E. Gabriel is a preschool teacher who enjoys learning about people and events of the US.

Michael P. Gabriel (PhD Pennsylvania State Univ) is assistant professor of history at Kutztown Univ of Pennsylvania. The author of *Major General Richard Montgomery* (2002), he has contributed articles to reference works and has reviewed books for journals and web sites such as *New York History, The Historian,* and H-SHEAR.

Peter J. Galie is professor of political science and director of the Raichle Pre-Law Center at Canisius College. He is author of *The New York State Constitution: A Reference Guide* (1991) and *Ordered Liberty: A Constitutional History of New York* (1996).

Mary A. Y. Gallagher is adjunct professor at Queens College, CUNY. She is author of *The American Revolution: A Short History* (2001) and coeditor of *The Papers of Robert Morris.*

Bill Gallo is associate sports editor for the *New York Daily News.* He was named to Yonkers and Westchester Halls of Fame and received a New York Press Association Award and National Cartoonists Society's Lifetime Achievement Award. He is author of *Drawing a Crowd: Bill Gallo's Greatest Sports Moments.*

Werner Gamerith is assistant professor of geography at the Univ of Heidelberg, Germany. His research focuses on urban social geography. He is the author of articles on the social geography of New York City published in German geography journals.

Eric Gansworth (Onondaga) is associate professor of English at Canisius College. His work is anthologized, and his books include *Smoke Dancing* (2004) and a collection of poems and paintings, *Nickel Eclipse: Iroquois Moon* (2000).

Randy Garbin published and edited *Roadside Magazine,* a publication covering the back roads and Main Streets of America 1990–2001, for which he traveled a quarter million miles and dined in almost 400 diners. He is publisher of a similar magazine, *By the Way Magazine* and its companion web site.

Alejandro Garcia (PhD) is professor in the School of Social Work at Syracuse Univ.

Deborah S. Gardner is a former commissioner of the NYC Landmarks Preservation Commission. She is author of *Privilege and Responsibility: A Life of I. N. Phelps Stokes, Architect, Philanthropist, and Civic Leader* (forthcoming) and *A Family Foundation: Looking to the Future, Honoring the Past* (1997).

Sue Gardner (MS Columbia Univ) is local history librarian at Albert Wisner Public Library and archivist for the Historical Society of the Town of Warwick. She is author of the web site Warwick Valley History.

Jonathan Garlock (PhD) is professor emeritus, Monroe Community College, and is a labor historian and coordinates unions in schools programs. He is a member of NYS United Teachers and officer of the Rochester Labor Council.

George W. Garner is director and curator of the National Speedskating Museum and Hall of Fame in Saratoga Springs.

Stanton Garner (PhD) is a retired professor of English in the Univ of Texas system. He is secretary of the Melville Society, author of *The Civil War World of Herman Melville* (1993), and editor of *The Captain's Best Mate: The Journal of Mary Chipman Lawrence on the Whaler "Addison," 1856–1860.*

Dee Garrison is historian of modern America at Rutgers Univ.

Richard H. Gassan is a historian, writer, and researcher living in Amherst, Mass. His main field of research is early 19th-century tourism with an emphasis on the state.

William Preston Gates is a retired teacher and Lake George steamboat captain aboard the M/V *Mohican.* He is author and publisher of books relating to the history of the Lake George region, including *History of the Sagamore Hotel* and *Lake George Boats and Steamboats.*

Carol Gayle is associate professor of history at Lake Forest College. She is coauthor of *Cast-Iron Architecture in America: The Significance of James Bogardus* (1998) among other publications.

Margot Gayle, whose career is historic preservation, founded the Friends of Cast-Iron Architecture in 1970 during the fight to save SoHo in New York City. She is coauthor of *Cast-Iron Architecture in America: The Significance of James Bogardus* (1998).

Charles T. Gehring (PhD Indiana Univ) is director of the New Netherland Project and a fellow of the Holland Society of New York. His dissertation was a linguistic investigation of Dutch language survival in colonial New York. In 1994 Her Majesty Queen Beatrix of the Netherlands conferred on him the distinction of Officer in the Order of Orange-Nassau.

Noah L. Gelfand is a PhD candidate at New York Univ. His dissertation is on religious toleration in 17th-century Dutch Atlantic colonization.

Glenda Gephart of Reading Center in Schuyler Co, is a newspaper journalist with experience in reporting and editing.

Don R. Gerlach is professor emeritus of history at the Univ of Akron, Ohio. A graduate of the Univ of Nebraska and 1956–57 Fulbright Scholar, he is a Fellow of the Royal Historical Society and historiographer of the Anglican Catholic Church.

Ronald Gersbacher has written articles about baseball history in central New York State for the past 20 years. He is historian for the Syracuse SkyChiefs Baseball Club, Greater Syracuse Sports Hall of Fame, and Syracuse Area Music Awards. He is also chair of the Syracuse Baseball Wall of Fame.

Gary Gershman (PhD Duke Univ) is professor of history and legal studies at Nova Southeastern Univ, Fla. The title of his dissertation is "Hamilton Ideals and the Bill of Rights: American Rejection and Canadian Compromise."

Kristina Gibson is a graduate student in the Department of Geography at Pennsylvania State Univ. She is conducting research on the evolution of public space in New York City.

Chris Gilbert is a PhD candidate at Virginia Commonwealth Univ. His art criticism has been published in *New Art Examiner, Sculpture,* and *64.*

Paul A. Gilje (PhD Brown Univ) is professor in the History Department at Univ of Oklahoma. He is author of *The Road to Mobocracy: Popular Disorder in New York City 1763–1834* (1987) and *Rioting in America* (1996).

Jonathan Gill teaches American literature and culture at Columbia Univ and the Manhattan School of Music.

Angus Gillespie has covered hockey from junior, intercollegiate, and Olympic programs to the NHL's Buffalo Sabres and Toronto Maple Leafs for print and broadcast. A publisher and editor, he writes for *Hockey Magazine* and was contributing editor of *Kings of the Ice* and *Canadian Gold 2002.*

Michael Patrick Gillespie is Louise Edna Goeden Professor of English at Marquette Univ. He has written books on the works of James Joyce, Oscar Wilde, and William Kennedy.

Noel J. Gish is teacher of American history and Long Island studies at Hauppauge High School. He is author of *Smithtown, 1660–1929: Looking Back through the Lens* (1996).

Brian J. Godfrey is professor of geography at Vassar College. He is author of *Neighborhoods in Transition: The Making of San Francisco's Ethnic and Nonconformist Communities* (1988) and coauthor of *Rainforest Cities: Urbanization, Development, and Globalization of Brazilian Amazonia* (1997).

Amy Godine is a writer and social historian who has published on Adirondack social and ethnic history in regional magazines and journals. Curator of the traveling exhibition, *Dreaming of Timbuctoo,* her book on Timbuctoo is forthcoming.

Kenneth M. Gold (PhD Univ of Michigan, Ann Arbor) is assistant professor at the College of Staten Island, CUNY. He is author of *School's In: The History of Summer Education in American Public Schools* (2002).

Liliana R. Goldín is associate professor of anthropology at SUNY Albany and author of publications on the social and economic life of rural populations of Guatemala.

Milton Goldin (MA New York Univ) was president of the Milton Goldin Co, a member of the National Coalition of Independent Scholars' fund-raising counsel, and a writer. In addition to articles, he was author of *The Music Merchants* and *Why They Give: American Jews and Their Philanthropies.*

Kathy Goldman is Village of Sloatsburg historian and member of Sloatsburg Historical Society.

Sharon Gollnitz is Town of Westfield historian.

Joseph Golombek Jr is a member of the Buffalo Common Council. He teaches at SUNY Buffalo and is editing a biography of Dr Francis E. Fronczak.

Michael Gomes, a Canadian writer, is author of *The Dawning of the Theosophical Movement* and *Theosophy in the 19th Century* (1994). He is a member of the American Academy of Religion.

Susan Goodier (PhD candidate SUNY Albany) focuses on 19th- and early 20th-century women's political movements in the US.

Leon Goodman (PE) is principal transportation engineer with Parsons Transportation Group. He was manager of transportation planning for the Port Authority of New York and New Jersey, served as international president of the Institute of Transportation Engineers, and taught transportation engineering and planning courses at colleges in the New York–New Jersey area.

Monette Goodridge is owner/operator of Meadowview Nursery and Meadowview LLC. In conjunction with Soil and Water Conservation and Natural Resource Conservation district programs, the nursery provides over 1 million trees for planting in the state annually.

Timothy P. Gordinier (PhD SUNY Albany) teaches at area colleges including Union, Siena, and SUNY New Paltz and specializes in constitutional law and American political theory. He is public policy director of the Institute for Humanist Studies, a think tank that promotes the rights and interests of the nonreligious.

David R. Gould (PhD SUNY Albany) was a high school history and social studies teacher and had a part-time railroad career until 1970, when he joined the NYS Museum planning staff and was responsible for researching and writing exhibit plans. He continues as a consultant to museums and historic preservation organizations while working as assistant conductor for Amtrak Empire Service.

William Graebner is professor of history at SUNY Fredonia. He is author of *Coming of Age in Buffalo: Youth and Authority in the Postwar Era* (1990).

H. Roger Grant is professor of history at Clemson Univ. He is author of more than a dozen books on railroads and transportation history, including *Ohio on the Move: Transportation in the Buckeye State* (2000).

Thomas X. Grasso is a retired professor of geology at Monroe Community College. He has been president of the Canal Society of New York State since 1978 and president of Inland Waterways International, based in the UK, since 2002.

Steve Graves teaches geography at California State Univ, Northridge. His research interests are popular culture and social justice issues.

Barbara Graymont (PhD Columbia Univ) is professor emerita of History at Nyack College. She is author of books and articles on the Iroquois, including four volumes in the series *Early American Indian Documents: Treaties and Laws.* Her book *The Iroquois in the American Revolution* was cited in the 1985 US Supreme Court decision upholding the Oneida Indian Nation land claim.

Paul Grebinger is professor of anthropology in the College of Liberal Arts at Rochester Institute of Technology. He is coauthor of *To Dress and Keep the Earth: The Nurseries and Nurserymen of Geneva, New York* (1993).

Nancy E. Green is chief curator at Herbert F. Johnson Museum of Art, Cornell Univ. She is author of *Arthur Wesley Dow and American Arts and Crafts* (1999) and *A Handbook of the Collection: Herbert F. Johnson Museum of Art* (1998).

Brian Greenberg (PhD Princeton Univ) is Jules Plangere Chair in American Social History at Monmouth Univ. He is author of *Worker and Community: Response to Industrialization in a 19th-Century American City, Albany, New York, 1850–1884* and coauthor of *Upheaval in the Quiet Zone: A History of Hospital Workers' Union, Local 1999.*

John Robert Greene is Paul J. Schupf Professor of History and Humanities at Cazenovia College. He is author of 15 books, including *The Presidency of George Bush* (2000).

Varney Spaulding Greene is reference librarian in the Special Collections Department of the Buffalo and Erie County Library.

Richard A. Greenwald is assistant professor of history at the US Merchant Marine Academy, Kings Point.

Amybeth Gregory is completing her master's degree in American history with a minor in public history at SUNY Brockport. She is assistant editor for *The Encyclopedia of New York State.*

James Clifford Greller is a transportation executive for the New Jersey Department of Transportation and NJ TRANSIT. He is cofounder and managing editor of *Electriclines* magazine and author of works on electric rail service in the NYC region, including *New York City Subway Cars* (1997).

Robert Huw Griffiths (PhD student Univ of Wales, Cardiff) is researcher and historical consultant to independent television producers. He has taught at schools and universities in South Wales.

Frank E. Griggs Jr is professor emeritus of civil engineering at Merrimack College, Mass. He is member of the American Society of Civil Engineers' Committee of History and Heritage of American Civil Engineering and edited *A Biographical Dictionary of Civil Engineers* (1991).

Nancy Groce (PhD Univ of Michigan) is folklorist and ethnomusicologist. She works as a folklorist/curator at the Smithsonian Center for Folklife and Cultural Heritage, Washington, DC. She is author of *New York: Songs of the City* (1999) and is writing *Heart of Gotham* on the occupational folklife of contemporary New York.

Tammis Groft is chief curator at the Albany Institute of History and Art.

Paul Grondahl is feature writer for the *Albany Times-Union,* where he has worked since 1984. He is author of *That Place Called Home* (2000) and *I Rose Like a Rocket: The Political Education of Theodore Roosevelt* (2004).

Sara Stidstone Gronim teaches history at C. W. Post Campus, Long Island Univ. Her research is in the knowledge of the natural world in colonial New York State.

Stephen B. Grove (PhD Univ of Pennsylvania) is US Military Academy at West Point historian.

Robert S. Grumet (PhD) is author of *Historic Contact* (1995) and *Journey on the Forbidden Path* (1999).

Kevin J. Grzymala teaches, writes, and lives in northern California. A graduate of SUNY Buffalo, he is completing a book on the relationship between sports and ethnicity in 19th-century Buffalo and a children's picture book on the meanings of friendship.

J. Justin Gustainis is professor of communication at SUNY Plattsburgh. He is author of *American Rhetoric and the Vietnam War* (1993) and several shorter works of scholarship and fiction.

K. R. Constantine Gutzman (PhD Univ of Virginia) has published articles in *Journal of Southern History, Journal of the Early Republic,* and other journals. He has contributed articles to historical encyclopedias and popular publications and scholarly reviews to academic and popular journals. He is assistant professor of history at Western Connecticut State Univ.

H

Brian Edward Hack (PhD candidate CUNY Graduate School and Univ Center) is adjunct lecturer at Kingsborough Community College and afflliated instructor with Hofstra Univ. He specializes in 19th- and early 20th-century American painting and sculpture and in the visual and philosophical impact of Darwinism, monism, and eugenics on the art and architecture of this period.

Evan Haefeli (PhD Princeton Univ) studies New Netherland and early colonial New York.

John Haines is associate scientist in mycology at the NYS Museum, Albany.

Thomas C. Haley (PhD) is nuclear engineering and applied mathematics consultant and adjunct professor at Rensselaer Polytechnic Institute, Troy. His expertise is in Monte Carlo methods, criticality safety, and statistical analysis.

Frederick J. Halik (DDS), FICD, FACD, is associate professor of clinical dentistry at the Univ of Rochester School of Medicine and Dentistry. He is president of the Pierre Fauchard Academy and former president of the NYS Dental Association and member of the American Academy of the History of Dentistry.

Donna L. Halper (MA Northeastern Univ) hopes to complete a PhD in American Studies. She runs a radio programming and management consulting firm and is author of *Invisible Stars: A Social History of Women in American Broadcasting* (2001) and two textbooks on broadcasting.

Eugene Halton lives in South Bend, Ind, where he teaches sociology and humanities at the Univ of Notre Dame. He is author of *Bereft of Reason* and *Meaning and Modernity,* and is preparing a collection of essays on American culture.

Charles E. Hambrick-Stowe (PhD Boston Univ) is pastor of the Church of the Apostles, United Church of Christ, Lancaster, Pa, and adjunct professor of church history at Lancaster Theological Seminary. He is author of books and articles on New England Puritanism and the history of Congregationalism and of *Charles G. Finney and the Spirit of American Evangelicalism* (1996).

Marsha Hamilton is assistant professor in the Department of History at the Univ of South Alabama. She has researched the barrier beaches for the exhibit *Shifting Sands: Long Island's Ocean Beaches* (2003).

Thomas D. Hamm is archivist and professor of history at Earlham College, Ind. He is author of three books and articles on Quaker and American religious history and contributed a chapter to *Quaker Crosscurrents: A History of Friends in the New York Yearly Meetings* (1995).

David C. Hammack is Haydn Professor of History at Case Western Reserve Univ. He is author of *Making the Nonprofit Sector in the United States: A Reader* (1998) and *Power and Society: Greater New York at the Turn of the Century* (1982; nominated for a Pulitzer Prize). He is president-elect of the Association for Research on Nonprofit Organizations and Voluntary Action.

Bronwyn Hannon is associate curator of rare books and Long Island studies at Hofstra Univ. She is on the board of the Empire Performing Arts Center at the Egg, Albany, and is a member of the NYS Commission on the Restoration of the State Capitol.

Mary Anne Hansen (MLS Univ of Arizona) has been reference librarian at Montana State Univ since 1996. Her work includes three entries for the *Encyclopedia of Marches and Demonstrations* (forthcoming) and "The Academic Reference Librarian at the Land Grant University: Requisite Characteristics" (*Librarianship in the 21st Century: What Do We Want?,* forthcoming).

R. Scott Hanson (PhD Univ of Chicago) did fieldwork in New York City for the Pluralism Project at Harvard Univ. His dissertation, "City of Gods: Religious Freedom, Immigration, and Pluralism in Flushing, Queens–New York City, 1945–2000," is under review at Oxford Univ Press. He is visiting assistant professor of history at Philadelphia Univ.

Craig Hanyan is professor emeritus in the History Department of Brock Univ, Ont.

Mary L. Hanyan is an independent researcher living in St. Catharines, Ont.

Keith J. Hardman (PhD) is professor of philosophy and religion at Ursinus College, Pa. He is author of *Charles Grandison Finney, 1792–1875: Revivalist and Reformer* (1987).

Sidney L. Harring (PhD Univ of Wisconsin) teaches undergraduate sociology and law and researches and writes on juries, police, American Indians, and the social history of American law. He is author of *Crow Dog's Case* (1994) and *White Man's Law: Native People in 19th-Century Canadian Jurisprudence* (1998).

April Harris (PhD candidate Syracuse Univ) is interested in the history of African American schooling in colonial America.

Helen A. Harrison is director of the Pollock-Krasner House and Study Center, East Hampton, and columnist for the *New York Times,* Long Island section. She is author of *Such Desperate Joy: Imagining Jackson Pollock* (2000).

D. G. Hart is academic dean and professor of church history at Westminster Theological Seminary, Escondido, Calif. He is author of *The University Gets Religion: Religious Studies and American Higher Education* (1999) and coeditor of *The Dictionary of the Presbyterian and Reformed Tradition in America* (1999).

Nasim Hassan writes for Pakistani newspapers on issues relevant to Pakistani living in the US. He served as president of the Pakistani American Society of Delaware Valley, 1997–98. He is a chemical engineer specializing in technology transfer as it relates to chemical industries.

Laurence M. Hauptman (PhD) is professor of history at SUNY New Paltz. He is author of *Conspiracy of Interests: Iroquois Dispossession and the Rise of New York State* (1998), *Between Two Fires: American Indians in the Civil War* (1995), and several other titles on American Indians. He received the NYS Board of Regents Award for Excellence in Archival Research in 1992.

William Hausman (PhD Univ of Illinois) teaches at the College of William and Mary and is Chancellor Professor of Economics. He is editor of *Enterprise and Society* and coauthor of articles including "The Market for Capital and the Origins of State Regulation of Electric Utilities in the United States" (2002).

William M. Healy is an antiquarian bookseller, writer, photographer, and musician from Schenectady. He is author of *The Adirondacks: A Special World* (1986) and *The High Peaks of Essex: The Adirondack Mountains of Orson Schofield Phelps* (1993).

Leslie Heaphy (PhD Univ of Toledo, Ohio) is assistant professor at Kent State Univ, Stark. She is author of "Sports, Women In" (*Ready Reference: Women's Issues,* 1997) and "Althea Gibson" (*Encyclopedia of Sports in American Culture,* 2001).

Robert J. Hefner is a historic preservation consultant in East Hampton.

Bernadette Zbicki Heiney (MA Pennsylvania State Univ) is information services technician at the George B. Stevenson Library, Lock Haven Univ of Pennsylvania.

M. J. Heisey is assistant professor of American, labor, and women's history at SUNY Potsdam. Her research includes Anabaptist and peace history.

William F. Helmer retired as professor of English at SUNY Morrisville, where he headed the Liberal Arts Division. He is village historian and author of *O&W: The Long and Slow Death of the New York, Ontario and Western Railway* (1959, 2000) and *Rip Van Winkle Railroads* (1970, 1999).

William S. Helmer is an attorney concentrating in environmental and energy law, and his works dealing with law, politics, and history have appeared in various publications of the NYS Bar Association. From 1995 to 1999 he was chief of the Environmental Protection Bureau in the State Attorney General's office and continues to lecture on environmental subjects.

Penny Helzer is Village of Port Byron historian.

Keith Henderson (PhD) is professor of political science at SUNY Buffalo. He previously taught overseas and at the Robert Wagner Graduate School of Public Service at New York Univ. He has published in the field of public administration.

Brian M. Henehan is senior extension associate in the Department of Applied Economics and Management in the College of Agriculture and Life Sciences at Cornell Univ. He is also secretary of the Northeast Cooperative Council.

Thomas C. Hennessy SJ is professor emeritus of education, as well as counselor and educator in the School of Education at Fordham Univ. He was dean of the School of Education at Marquette Univ.

James A. Henretta is Priscilla Alden Burke Professor of History at the Univ of Maryland and author of a forthcoming study, *The Liberal State in America: New York, 1820–1970.*

Michelle Henry (MA Arizona State Univ) is Chautauqua Co historian and former director of the Chautauqua County Historical Society. She also implemented the county's records management program.

Lenora M. Henson (MA) worked with the Livingston County Historian's Office, Strawbery Banke Museum, Society for the Preservation of New England Antiquities, and the Wright Museum. She is curator at the Theodore Roosevelt Inaugural National Historic Site, Buffalo.

Rita G. Herrington (PhD Indiana State Univ) is assistant professor of education at the Univ of Evansville, Ind.

Robert H. Herzog is sportswriter for *Newsday.* His primary beats are college basketball and major league baseball.

John A. Hewlett taught and wrote about Long Island history for 40 years, an interest he gained from his father, who was Town of Hempstead historian.

R. Ashley Hibbard has been librarian for the NYS Department of Labor since 1974, first in New York City and since 1994 in Albany. She is producing web pages for a virtual resource room to enable job seekers to find print and electronic material on choosing and finding the right job.

Alan Hicks is mammal specialist with the endangered species unit of the NYS Department of Environmental Conservation.

George W. Hilton is professor emeritus of economics at the Univ of California, Los Angeles. He is coauthor of *The Electric Interurban Railways in America* and author of *The Cable Car in America.*

H. F. Hintz is professor of animal science at the College of Agriculture and Life Sciences at Cornell Univ. He has conducted equine research and taught equine courses since 1967.

Alison Duncan Hirsch (PhD) is author of "The Celebrated Madame Montour: 'Interpretress' across Early American Frontiers" (*Explorations in Early American Culture,* 2000).

Bernard Hirschhorn (PhD) is a historian and author of *Democracy Reformed: Richard Spencer Childs and His Fight for Better Government.* He is adjunct assistant professor of history at Bernard Baruch College, CUNY.

Richard Hite is head of processing in the state archives of the Ohio Historical Society. He is coauthor of three articles on the archival profession and author of two genealogy books.

Graham Russell Hodges is professor of history at Colgate Univ. He is author of *Root and Branch: African Americans in New York and East Jersey, 1613–1863* (1999) and *Slavery and Freedom in the Rural North: African Americans in Monmouth County, New Jersey, 1665–1870* (1997).

Derek Hoff (PhD candidate Univ of Virginia) is completing his dissertation on the political economy of population in 20th-century America.

Lysbeth Hoffman is Town of Carlton historian.

A. William Hoglund is retired professor of history at the Univ of Connecticut. His bibliographical publications include a union list of Finnish American newspapers. He is compiling a union list of all Finnish American books and pamphlets.

Eric Homberger (PhD) is head of American studies and reader in American literature at the Univ of East Anglia, UK. He is author of *Mrs. Astor's New York: Money and Social Power in a Gilded Age* (2000).

Clifton Hood (PhD) is associate professor of history at Hobart and William Smith Colleges. He is author of *Capitalist City: The Political Economy of New York City, 1664–1987* (forthcoming) and *722 Miles: The Building of the Subways and How They Transformed New York* (1993) for which he received the Manuscript Award from the NYS Historical Association.

Field Horne, a 12th-generation New Yorker, is a graduate of Williams College. A writer and historian, he is best known for *The Greene County Catskills: A History* (1994). He is assistant editor of the locality entries of *The Encyclopedia of New York State.*

Joseph Horowitz is author of five books about the history of classical music in the US. He is artistic advisor to American orchestras on both coasts and director of historical projects for the American Symphony Orchestra League. He teaches at the Eastman School of Music.

Gerald Horton is a retired business manager pursuing his avocation as an independent historian.

Edward Hotaling is author of *They're Off! Horse Racing at Saratoga* and *The Great Black Jockeys* and has written on the history of thoroughbred racing in the US for the *New York Times* and other publications.

Kirk W. House, a former educator, is director/curator of the Glenn Curtiss Museum in Hammondsport. He holds degrees from Rhode Island College and Lehigh Univ.

Edward T. Howe is professor of economics at Siena College. He is author of several articles on state and local taxation.

George W. Hudler is professor of plant pathology at Cornell Univ. His research focuses on improving methods for detecting and managing tree diseases. He is author of *Magical Mushroom, Mischievous Molds* (1998).

Paul R. Huey (PhD Univ of Pennsylvania) is a graduate of Hartwick College. From 1969 to 1995 he developed and directed the historical archaeology program of the Bureau of Historic Sites in the NYS Office of Parks, Recreation, and Historic Preservation.

Robert C. Hughes (law degree, Fordham Univ) was appointed Huntington Town historian in 2002. He volunteered for, served six years on the board of trustees of, and was executive director and president of the Huntington Historical Society. After three years as an attorney in New York City, he retired from law practice to raise his daughters.

Michael W. Hughey (PhD) is professor of sociology at Minnesota State Univ, Moorhead. He is editor of *The Resurgence of Race and Ethnicity* (1998).

Alan Hunter lives in Harriman, where he was a postmaster for 18 years. For the last 15 years he has been a dealer in old and rare books.

Christopher Hunter (MA SUNY Albany) is archivist at the Schenectady Museum.

Thomas A. Hunter has been the senior curator of collections at Onondaga Historical Association since 1989, managing local history collections, including sculpture. He is author of articles on artists and artwork of Onondaga Co.

Dorothy Hunt-Ingrassia retired from the NYS court system as personal secretary to a Supreme Court justice in Goshen. She has been historian for the Town of Wallkill since 1987.

Elliott S. Hurwitt (PhD) is author of "William Christopher Handy" (*International Dictionary of Black Composers,* 1999) and articles in *Fanfare.*

Reeve Huston is associate professor of history at the Univ of Arizona. He is author of *Land and Freedom: Rural Society, Popular Protest, and Party Politics in Antebellum New York* (2000).

Jeffrey Hyson is assistant professor of history at Saint Joseph's Univ in Philadelphia. He is completing a social and cultural history of American zoos.

I

Kaikhosrov D. Irani is professor emeritus and former chair of the Department of Philosophy at City College, CUNY and was president of the Zoroastrian Association of Greater New York.

Adrienne M. Israel (PhD Johns Hopkins Univ) is professor of history at Guilford College, NC, and author of a historical biography of Amanda Berry Smith.

Maurice Isserman (PhD) teaches history at Hamilton College. He is author of *The Other American: The Life of Michael Harrington* (2000) and other books.

Paul E. Ivey is professor of art history at the Univ of Arizona. His research interests include religious architecture in the American built environment.

J

Kenneth T. Jackson is chair of the History Department at Columbia Univ. He is editor of *The Encyclopedia of New York City* (1995) and author of *Crabgrass Frontier: The Suburbanization of the United States* (1985). He was president of the Organization of American Historians in 1999–2000.

Harold Jacobs is professor of sociology at SUNY New Paltz. He is editor of *Weatherman* (1971) and numerous articles on the New Left.

Jaap Jacobs (PhD Leiden Univ) is affiliated with the Gemeentearchief Amsterdam. He has published articles on New Netherland in Dutch and American journals and the book *Een zegenrijk gewest: Nieuw-Nederland in de zeventiende eeuw* (1999 Hendricks Manuscript Award). A translation is in progress.

Michael L. James, a teacher of history and government in East Aurora, writes and lectures on arts and crafts in western New York State. He is author of *Drama in Design: The Life and Craft of Charles Rohlfs* (1994).

Frank S. Jazzo (PE) graduated from Clarkson College in 1958 and was civil engineer for the Westchester Co for 37 years. He is Town of Greenburgh historian and vice president of the Ardsley Historical Society.

G. Peter Jemison, a member of the Heron Clan of the Seneca Nation of Indians, is the historic site manager for Ganondagan State Historic Site, a 17th-century Seneca town located in Victor. He is an artist, a curator of Native American art, and a coeditor of *Treaty of Canandaigua 1794: 200 Years of Treaty Relations between the Iroquois Confederacy and the United States.*

George M. Jenks is a retired Bucknell Univ librarian. He was advisory editor for *Railroad History* and book reviewer of *Library Journal.*

Randy A. John (PhD Syracuse Univ) is associate professor in St. Bonaventure Univ's Department of Sociology and Social Science. He is author of *Social Integration of an Elderly Native American Population* (1995) and is completing a second book on the Salamanca leases of the Allegany Indian Reservation of the Seneca Nation of Indians.

Dawn Johnson, resident of Schoharie, is a retired NYC history teacher.

James M. Johnson (PhD) was head of the military history program at the US Military Academy. He is military historian of the Hudson River Valley National Heritage Area and visiting professor of history at Marist College. He is author of *Militiamen, Rangers, and Redcoats: The Military in Georgia, 1754–1776.*

Jamie W. Johnson (PhD candidate, Graduate Center, CUNY) is completing her dissertation, "The Viewer Viewed: Representations of the Art Public in the Victorian Era."

Marie Johnson (PhD geology, Brown Univ) attended Harvard College and majored in geology. She is associate professor at the US Military Academy, where she volunteers as head coach of the Army women's lacrosse team.

Paul E. Johnson (PhD Univ of California, Los Angeles) is professor in the Department of History at the Univ of South Carolina. He is author of *Sam Patch, the Famous Jumper* (2003) and coauthor of *The Kingdom of Matthias: A Story of Sex and Salvation in 19th-Century America* (1994).

Peter Johnson is a historian who works for the Rockefeller family. He lives in Schoharie.

Suzanne Johnson is assistant director of the Longwood Public Library in Middle Island. She is author of *Longwood Long Ago* (1991).

William J. Johnston is a retired educator. He has held leadership roles in Nassau-Suffolk historical organizations since the 1970s and has been historian of the Village of Farmingdale since 1990.

Jacob Judd is professor emeritus at Herbert H. Lehman College and the Graduate School and Univ Center, CUNY. He is editor of the four-volume *Van Cortlandt Family Papers (1976–1981)* and *Colonial America: A Basic History* (1998).

Benjamin Justice is a graduate student in the history of education at Stanford Univ and a Charlotte W. Newcombe Fellow. His dissertation examines the history of religion in state public schools.

K

Karl S. Kabelac is a retired special collections librarian from the Univ of Rochester.

John P. Kaminski directs the Center for the Study of the American Constitution in the History Department at the Univ of Wisconsin, Madison. He is director and coeditor of the multivolume *Documentary History of the Ratification of the Constitution.*

Carol Kammen is a local historian and senior lecturer in history at Cornell Univ. She is author of *The Peopling of Tompkins County: A Social History* (1985) and editor of *The Encyclopedia of Local History* (2000).

Lisa Kannenberg (PhD Rutgers Univ) is assistant professor of history at the College of Saint Rose.

Dana Evan Kaplan is Oppenstein Brothers Assistant Professor of Judaic and Religious Studies in the Department of History at the Univ of Missouri, Kansas City, and Research Fellow at the Miller Center for Contemporary Judaic Studies at the Univ of Miami. His works include *Contemporary American Reform Judaism* (2003) and *Cambridge Companion to American Judaism* (2004).

Andrew Karmen (PhD Columbia Univ) has been a member of the Sociology Department at John Jay College of Criminal Justice since 1978. He is author of *New York Murder Mystery: The True Story behind the Crime Crash of the 1990s* (2000), and his textbook *Crime Victims: An Introduction to Victimology* (2004) is in its fifth edition.

Christine Karpiak is senior archivist at the NYS Archives.

Esther Katz is adjunct associate professor of history at New York Univ. She is director of the Margaret Sanger Papers Project and editor of *The Margaret Sanger Microfilm Edition* (1995–96) and *The Selected Papers of Margaret Sanger* (4 vols, 2002–).

Janet Kaye is assistant professor of communication at SUNY Buffalo. She is a former journalist and federal government attorney.

Roland W. Kays (PhD) is curator of mammals at the NYS Museum.

Lisa Keller is associate professor of history at SUNY Purchase. The recipient of an NEH grant for local history, she is writing a monograph on comparative urban history.

Barbara M. Kelly is associate professor in the School of Communications and former director of the Long Island Studies Institute at Hofstra Univ. She writes on the history of suburbanization and its expression on Long Island.

Mary C. Kelly teaches modern US and Irish history at Franklin Pierce College, NH. Her research interests include the New York Irish and Irish American famine memory.

William M. Kelly (PhD) has studied the mines and mineral resources of the state for 20 years as a member of the NYS Geological Survey. He is also curator of geology for the NYS Museum.

Samuel V. Kennedy III is a retired associate professor at Syracuse Univ and former editor of the *Auburn Citizen-Advertiser.* He is author of *Samuel Hopkins Adams and the Business of Writing.*

Paul Kens is professor of political science and history at Southwest Texas State Univ. He is author of *"Lochner v New York": Economic Regulation on Trial* (1998) and *Justice Stephen Field: Shaping Liberty from the Gold Rush to the Gilded Age* (1997).

Joan Gay Kent is historian for the Town of North Hempstead, vice chairman of its Historic Landmarks Preservation Commission, president of the Cow Neck Peninsula Historical Society, and author of *Discovering Sands Point: Its History, Its People, Its Places* (2000).

Ronni Kent (MA SUNY Albany) is instructor for New Visions: Public Communications, a program at the *Albany Times-Union.*

Brian Keough is curator of manuscript collections at the M. E. Grenander Department of Special Collections and Archives at SUNY Albany.

Robert P. Kerker (MA Columbia Univ) served with the NYS Division of the Budget as management analyst in research, 1955–92. He is editor and principal author of *The Executive Budget in New York State: A Half-Century Perspective* (1981) and of articles on budgeting, budget history, and public management.

William C. Ketchum (JD Columbia Univ) is author of 40 books on American art and antiques, including *Potters and Potteries of New York State, 1650–1900* (1987). He is on the faculty of New York Univ and the Folk Art Institute of the Museum of Folk Art.

James K. Kettlewell is professor emeritus of history of art at Skidmore College and author of *Saratoga Springs: An Architectural History* (1991).

Cynthia A. Kierner is professor of history at the Univ of North Carolina Charlotte. She is author of *Traders and Gentlefolk: The Livingstons of New York, 1675–1790* (1992).

Katherine B. Killoran is reference librarian and assistant professor at John Jay College of Criminal Justice.

Vitaut Kipel is author of *Belarusians in the United States* (1999).

Maria Kiriakova (MLS Queens College, CUNY) is reference librarian and assistant professor at John Jay College of Criminal Justice. She has written for *Encyclopedia of Crime and Punishment* and *International Journal of Legal Information.*

George B. Kirsch is professor of history and chair of the History Department at Manhattan College. He specializes in 19th-century American baseball and cricket and has written and edited books on US sport history. He is coeditor of the *Encyclopedia of Ethnicity and Sports in the United States* (2000).

Matt Kirsch is a graduate student at Temple Univ.

Anne Taylor Kirschmann (PhD Univ of Rochester) studies and writes on history of medicine, including homeopathy and women in the health professions.

Pam Kirst is a member of the professional staff and English faculty at SUNY Fredonia. She was reviewer of local interest books for the *Chautauqua Mirror.*

Michael J. Kiskis is associate professor at Elmira College, where he teaches courses in American literature, primarily of the 19th century. He is editor of *Mark Twain's Own Autobiography: The Chapters from the "North American Review"* (1990).

Nadieszda Kizenko is associate professor of history at SUNY Albany. She is author of *A Prodigal Saint: Father John of Kronstadt and the Russian People* (2000).

Chuck Klaus has been involved in arts broadcasting for over a quarter century. He reviews classical music concerts for the *Syracuse Post-Standard.*

Milton M. Klein was Alumni Distinguished Service Professor of History Emeritus at the Univ of Tennessee, Knoxville. He was former president of the American Society for Legal History and editor of *The Empire State: History of New York* (2001).

Christine Kleinegger is senior historian at the NYS Museum. She is author of "The Janes Who Made the Planes" (*Long Island Historical Journal,* 1999.) She is researching the social history of sleep, for which she received a Winterthur Research Fellowship.

Christopher Klemek is a PhD candidate in history at the Univ of Pennsylvania. His dissertation is entitled "Great American Cities: Jane Jacobs, Modernist Planning, and the Crisis of Urban Liberalism, 1945–1975."

Eric L. Kline is regional service and marketing coordi-nator for Business Management Systems, Inc, and has worked with local governments since 1982. He is author of articles on local legislation and information management.

Robert A. Klump, an attorney in Buffalo, is associate director of the Raichle Pre-Law Center at Canisius College, where he also teaches constitutional law.

Joette Knapp is Town of Kendall historian.

Nancy Knechtel is professor of art history at Niagara County Community College and adjunct professor at Niagara Univ.

Timothy W. Kneeland (PhD Univ of Oklahoma) teaches history and political science at Nazareth College. He is author of *Pushbutton Psychiatry: A History of Electroshock in America* (2002).

Anthony Knipp was Village of Washingtonville historian.

Edward H. Knoblauch is former managing editor of *The Encyclopedia of New York State.*

Heidi Knoblauch is research assistant for *The Encyclopedia of New York State.*

Gerard T. Koeppel is a writer and editor. He is author of *Water for Gotham: A History* (2000) and a book on the building of the Erie Canal (forthcoming).

Lee Kogan is director of the Folk Art Institute and curator of special projects for the Contemporary Center of the American Museum of Folk Art. She is adjunct professor of art and art education at New York Univ.

Mark Kohan of Hamburgh, is editor in chief of the *Polish American Journal.* He has written articles and essays on the history of the polka and its components. He has served as a consultant to and performed on numerous Polish American cultural projects for the NYS Council on the Arts, the National Endowment for the Arts, and public and private regional cultural organizations.

Virginia L. Koon is Town of Scipio historian.

Giacinta Bradley Koontz is director of the Harriet Quimby Research Conference and founder and director of the Portal of the Folded Wings Shrine to Aviation and Museum in California. She edits the annual *Harriet Quimby Research Conference Journals* and is author of *The Harriet Quimby Scrapbook: The Life of America's First Birdwoman, 1875–1912* (2004).

Connie Kopelov (Fulbright Scholar, London) has served as instructor of trade women's studies at Cornell Univ and is an executive board member of the New York Labor History Association. She helped found the national Coalition of Labor Union Women and served as vice president of its NYC chapter.

Laurie Kozakiewicz (PhD student SUNY Albany) specializes in public policy history in 19th- and 20th-century America and the intersection of gender and American state development. She has presented papers at various women's studies, political science, and history conferences and is co-founder and co-organizer of the Researching New York conference.

Herbert C. Kraft (PhD) was professor emeritus of anthropology and director of the Seton Hall Univ Museum, NJ. He was recognized worldwide as a Lenape–Delaware Indian scholar. A Fellow of the NYS Archaeological Association and of the Holland Society, he authored 13 books and over 200 professional articles.

John P. Kraljic (JD Georgetown Univ) is an attorney practicing in New York and is completing an MA in history with a thesis on South Slavic–American Spanish Civil War volunteers. He is author of works on Croatian history and Croatian American history.

Daniel C. Kramer is professor emeritus of political science at the College of Staten Island, CUNY. He has written five books, including *The Days of Wine and Roses Are Over: Governor Hugh Carey and New York State* (1997) and *Workplace Sabbaticals: Bonus or Entitlement?* (2001).

Jeffrey Kraus is professor of political science at Wagner College. He has served twice as president of the NYS Political Science Association.

Chris Kretz is faculty librarian at Dowling College.

Joann P. Krieg is professor of English at Hofstra Univ. She is author of *A Whitman Chronology* (1999) and *Whitman and the Irish.*

Thomas J. Kriger (PhD CUNY) has taught American politics at St. Lawrence Univ, Providence College, and the Univ of Northern Colorado. He has written and lectured on dairy politics in New York State. He is associate director of research and legislation at United University Professions.

Jeffrey A. Kroessler is author of *New York, Year by Year: A Chronology of the Great Metropolis* (2002) and *Lighting the Way: A Centennial History of the Queensborough Public Library* (1996). He is historian with Archives and Special Collections at the College of Staten Island.

Claus-Dieter Krohn is professor of modern history at the Univ of Lüneburg and editor of the yearbook *Exilforschung.* He is author of *Intellectuals in Exile: Refugee*

Scholars and the New School for Social Research (1993) and coeditor of the *Handbuch der deutschsprachigen Emigration, 1933–1945* (1998).

Hadley Kruczek-Aaron (PhD candidate Syracuse Univ) is assistant managing editor of *The Encyclopedia of New York State.* She is also a historical archaeologist specializing in 19th-century New York State.

Margaret Kruesi received her PhD in folklore from the Univ of Pennsylvania, where she works in the Annenberg Rare Book and Manuscript Library.

Dorothy Kubik is a freelance writer living in Hamden. She is author of *West through the Catskills: The Story of the Susquehanna Turnpike* (2001) and *A Free Soil—A Free People: The Anti-Rent War in Delaware County, New York* (1997).

Michael Kudish (PhD) is professor in the Division of Forestry at Paul Smith's College. He is author of *Railroads of the Adirondacks: A History* (1996) and *The Catskill Forest: A History* (2000).

Tom Kuehhas (MA St. John's Univ) has served as director of the Oyster Bay Historical Society since 1992 and editor of its quarterly history magazine, the *Freeholder.* Active in the Long Island historical community, he serves on the boards of several historical and community organizations.

Jonathan Kuhn (MA Columbia Univ) was appointed New York City's park historian in 1987. He is director of art and antiquities for the City of New York Parks and Recreation and author of *Historic Houses in New York City Parks* (1989–92) and *Queens' Parks* (2002).

Richard S. Kujawa is a broadly trained geographer with research and teaching interests related to Lake Champlain and the Champlain Valley. In addition to teaching geography and planning at Saint Michael's College, Vt, he is cocoordinator of the Vermont Geographic Alliance.

Amy Kurlander (PhD Harvard Univ) specializes in the history of photography. She is curator at the New York Transit Museum, Brooklyn.

Kathleen Smith Kutolowski is professor of history at SUNY Brockport. She is author of "Freemasonry Revisited: Another Look at the Grass-Roots Bases of Antimasonic Anxieties" (*Freemasonry on Both Sides of the Atlantic,* 2002).

L

C. Patrick Labadie is retired director of the Lake Superior Maritime Museum, Duluth, Minn, and author of articles on the archaeology of Great Lakes watercraft.

Kathleen LaFrank (MA Parsons School of Design) is historian with the NYS Historic Preservation Office with expertise in rural cultural landscapes, state parks, and parkways, on which she writes and lectures.

Robin Lakes is professor in the Department of Dance and Theater Arts at the Univ of North Texas. Her research encompasses dance history and dance pedagogy and has appeared in *Medical Problems of Performing Artists* and *Dancer.*

Paul Lamar (MAT Harvard) is adjunct instructor at the College of St. Rose, theater critic for the *Daily Gazette,* and GED teacher in an Albany recovery program. He was a resident at Yaddo in 1974–75.

Evan Lampe is a graduate student at SUNY Albany. He presented his research on the 1930 anti–venereal disease campaign at the 2001 Researching New York conference.

Philip Lance (JD Albany Law School) is a family court hearing examiner for the NYS Office of Court Administration. He has taught at Hudson Valley Community College and Russell Sage College.

Ed Landing (PhD) is NYS paleontologist and author of more than 100 articles and editor of 11 books on early life and earth history.

Doris Lange is a broom maker at Farmers' Museum in Cooperstown. She is a former teacher, Peace Corps volunteer, and farmer.

Randy Lange has covered the Giants, Jets, and pro football for the *Record* since 1990 and for newspapers in the metropolitan area since 1979. He is a contributor to *Sports Illustrated, USA Today,* and WFAN-AM radio.

William R. D. Lange (BS East Stroudsburg Univ) is park ranger for the National Park Service of the US Department of Interior at Fort Stanwix National Monument, Rome. Since 1988 he has worked in Pennsylvania, California, and New York City.

George J. Lankevich is professor emeritus of history at Bronx Community College, CUNY. He is author or editor of more than 20 volumes of history including *American Metropolis: A History of New York City* (1998).

F. Daniel Larkin (PhD) is SUNY Distinguished Service Professor and interim provost and vice president for academic affairs at SUNY Oneonta. He is author of *Pioneer American Railroads: The Mohawk and Hudson and the Saratoga and Schenectady* (1995) and *New York State Canals: A Short History* (1998).

Mitch Lawrence (graduate, Temple Univ) is *New York Daily News* NBA columnist. He has been covering the NBA since 1987. He also worked for the *Syracuse Post-Standard* and *Rochester Democrat and Chronicle.*

William M. Leary is E. Merton Coulter Professor of History at the Univ of Georgia. He has written histories of the China National Aviation Corp, Civil Air Transport, and the US Air Mail Service, 1918–27. In 1996–97 he was Charles A. Lindbergh Professor of Aerospace History at the National Air and Space Museum.

Susan A. Lee (PhD) is director of the Department of Theatre's Dance Program at Northwestern Univ. She is author of articles on the life course development of women artists and dance in education.

Joel Lefkowitz teaches political science at SUNY New Paltz.

Ann M. Legreid is professor of geography at Central Missouri State Univ.

Teresa K. Lehr teaches advanced composition at SUNY Brockport. She is author of *Let the Art of Medicine Flourish: The Centennial History of the Rochester Academy of Medicine* (2000) and *Lighting the Way: A History of the First 100 Years of St. John's Home, Rochester, New York* (2002).

Matt Leingang (BA Kent State Univ) is a reporter for the *Rochester Democrat and Chronicle.*

Harriet Lembeck is wine director for the New School Univ and director of the Wine and Spirits Program, both in New York City.

Edward G. Lengel (PhD Univ of Virginia) is assistant editor at *Papers of George Washington,* Charlottesville, Va.

Arthur Lennig is a former professor of film at SUNY Albany and author of *The Count* (1973) and *Stroheim* (2000).

Vincent Lenti is a member of the piano faculty at the Eastman School of Music of the Univ of Rochester. He is a writer and commentator on the history of Rochester.

W. Bruce Leslie is professor of history at SUNY Brockport. He has published more than 15 articles on the history of higher education, as well as *Gentlemen and Scholars: College and Community in the "Age of the University"* (1993). He is coauthoring a book on the last 50 years of SUNY Brockport's history.

Michelle Leung-Elder (PhD candidate Univ of Toronto) is author of "Baroness Friederike von Riedesel: 'Mrs. General' " (*The Human Tradition in the American Revolution,* 2000).

Jeff Levine, a former award-winning journalist in the Hudson Valley, is media relations coordinator at the Culinary Institute of America.

Herbert S. Levinson is a transportation planning and engineering consultant in the New York metropolitan area. He is a member of the National Academy of Engineering, a University Transportation Research Center mentor at CUNY, and a published author.

James G. Lewis (PhD) is an independent scholar and visiting scholar at the Forest History Society in Durham, NC. He has published articles on the history of forestry education.

Susan Ingalls Lewis (PhD SUNY Binghamton) is assistant professor of history at SUNY New Paltz, where she teaches state history. Her dissertation focused on businesswomen in mid-19th-century Albany.

Tom Lewis is professor of English and Quadracci Professor of Social Responsibility at Skidmore College. His books include *Empire of the Air: The Men Who Made Radio* (1991) and *Divided Highways: The Interstate Highway System and the Transformation of American Life* (1997) He has researched, written, and produced documentary films for Hott Productions and Florentine Films.

W. David Lewis is Distinguished University Professor of History at Auburn Univ, Ala. He is coauthor of *Delta: The History of an Airline* (1979) and *The Airway to Everywhere: A History of All American Aviation* (1988), and is writing a biography of Edward V. Rickenbacker.

Laurence Libin is research curator of musical instruments at the Metropolitan Museum of Art. He is author of *American Musical Instruments in the Metropolitan Museum of Art* (1985).

Don Liddick (PhD Pennsylvania State Univ) is associate professor of criminal justice and criminology at the Univ of Pittsburgh, Greensburg. He has written articles and three books on organized crime and governmental misconduct.

Sarah F. Liebschutz is Distinguished Service Professor Emeritus at SUNY Brockport and adjunct professor of political science at the Univ of Rochester. She is author of four books, including *New York: Politics and Government* (1998) and *Managing Welfare Reform in Five States: The Challenge of Devolution* (2000).

Joni Lincoln is Town of Conquest historian.

Charles Lindner is a professor at John Jay College of Criminal Justice and teaches in the Department of Law, Police Science, and Criminal Justice Administration. He served as executive assistant to the commissioner of the NYC Department of Probation. He has written articles for criminal justice journals.

Joann Lindstrom (BA SUNY New Paltz) is a native of New York's Southern Tier and collections consultant for history museums throughout the state.

Matthew J. Lindstrom (PhD Northern Arizona Univ) teaches political science at Siena College and is director of the Program for Sustainable Land Use and Just Communities. He is coauthor of *The National Environmental Policy Act: Judicial Misconstruction, Legislative Indifference, and Executive Neglect* (2001) and coeditor of *Suburban Sprawl: Culture, Theory, and Politics* (2003).

Jon Lines (PhD candidate SUNY Buffalo) is lecturer in the Department of Political Science at SUNY Buffalo State. He specializes in and teaches urban government, ethnic and racial politics, and civil rights law.

Daniel J. Linke is archivist at Princeton Univ's Seeley G. Mudd Manuscript Library and former senior archivist at the NYS Archives.

Steve Litwin is editor of the Polka Magazine section of the *Polish American Journal.* A columnist for over 30 years, he has written for *Polka World, Polka News,* and other publications.

Greg Livadas started ballooning as a teenager in 1978 and operates High Hopes Balloon Co around Rochester and the Finger Lakes. He flies in numerous states but believes New York State has some of the most beautiful scenery.

Karen E. Livsey is Town of Ellicott historian.

Cindy R. Lobel is a PhD candidate in US history at the Graduate Center, CUNY. Her dissertation focuses on the cultural impact of changing food habits in 19th-century New York City.

Arun Peter Lobo is deputy director of the Population Division at the NYC Department of City Planning. He is lead author of *The Newest New Yorkers* (1996) and author of articles on the occupational background and residential patterns of immigrants.

Martha S. LoMonaco (PhD) is chair of the Department of Visual and Performing Arts and associate professor of theater at Fairfield Univ, Conn. She is author of *Every Week, A Broadway Revue: The Tamiment Playhouse, 1921–1960* (1992). She premieres new work in New York City, New England, the Edinburgh Festival Fringe, Scotland, and Fairfield Univ, where she is resident director.

Kathryn T. Long (PhD Duke Univ) is associate professor of history at Wheaton College, Ill. She is author of *The Revival of 1857–58: Interpreting an American Religious Awakening* (1998) and writes articles on the history of revivals, Methodist Holiness teacher Phoebe Palmer, and evangelical missionary martyrs.

Stephen Long is curator of the Lower East Side Tenement Museum managing collections and research activities, after serving as program coordinator. He attended graduate school in the History Department at New York Univ.

Richard Longstreth is professor of American civilization at George Washington Univ. He is author of *The Drive-In, the Supermarket, and Transformation of Commercial Space in Los Angeles, 1914–1941* (1999) and is completing *The Department Store Transformed, 1920–1960.*

Cheryl Longyear is Town of Montezuma historian.

Philip L. Lord Jr (MA SUNY Albany) is former director of the Division of Museum Services, NYS Museum. His research projects have focused on waterways-linked systems of transportation and technology, 1790–1830, and inland waterway improvements known as the Durham Project.

He is manager for the state historic marker program and the state lands research permit program.

Frank K. Lorenz (MLS SUNY Albany) is curator of special collections and publications and editor emeritus of Hamilton College. He is former president of the Clinton Historical Society. He is also author of articles on the history and alumni of Hamilton College, where he is editor emeritus.

Howard Lowe is former assistant general manager of WLIW-TV, Plainview, and president and CEO of Mountain Lake Public Television, Plattsburgh. He produces programs distributed by PBS and for public radio nationally. He is author of *History of Public Broadcasting in New York State.*

Larry Lowenthal is a retired National Park Service historian and author.

Eric v. d. Luft (PhD Bryn Mawr College) is curator of historical collections in the Health Sciences Library of SUNY Upstate Medical Univ. He taught philosophy at Villanova Univ and was historical collections assistant at the College of Physicians of Philadelphia.

David E. Lunde is professor of English and director of creative writing at SUNY Fredonia. He is a member of Science Fiction and Fantasy Writers of America and the Science Fiction Poetry Association. He is author of *Blues for Port City* and *Nightfishing in Great Sky River.*

Marian Lupulescu (PhD) is acting curator of mineralogy at the NYS Museum. He is former associate professor of geology and chair of the Mineralogy Department at Bucharest Univ, Romania. He was a Senior Fulbright Scholar at California Institute of Technology.

Mary Lou Lustig (PhD Syracuse Univ) is associate professor at West Virginia Univ. She is author of *Privilege and Prerogative: New York's Provincial Elite, 1710–1776* (1995), and *The Imperial Executive in America: Sir Edmund Andros, 1637–1714* (2002).

John F. Lyons (PhD Univ of Illinois, Chicago) is assistant professor in history at Joliet Junior College and is writing a book on the history of labor activism among Chicago public schoolteachers.

M

James Maas is personnel program manager for New York State. He is author of works on the Brewster Aeronautical Corp and its products. He completed a history of state aviation under a grant from the NYS Department of Parks, Recreation, and Historic Preservation.

Carleton Mabee is professor emeritus of history at SUNY New Paltz. He won a Pulitzer Prize for his biography of Samuel F. B. Morse.

Hugh C. MacDougall is a retired diplomat living in Cooperstown. He is founder and secretary/treasurer of the James Fenimore Cooper Society. He is author of *Cooper's Otsego County* (1989), writes a local history column for *Cooperstown Crier,* and lectures on Otsego Co local history.

Nannette V. Maciejunes is director of exhibitions and collections and senior curator at the Columbus Museum of Art. She is author of *The Early Works of Charles E. Burchfield, 1915–1921* (1987) and co-curator of *The Paintings of Charles Burchfield: North by Midwest* (1997). She received a grant from the Charles E. Burchfield Foundation to write his biography.

Mary Alice Mackay is research curator at the Albany Institute of History and Art. She is coeditor and contributing author of *Albany Institute of History and Art: 200 Years of Collecting.*

Robert B. MacKay (PhD) is director of the Society for the Preservation of Long Island Antiquities and chair of the NYS Board for Historic Preservation.

Jane Mackintosh is assistant editor of *The Encyclopedia of New York State.*

Gail D. MacLeitch is assistant professor in American studies at King's College, London. She is completing a study on the cultural history of the Iroquois in the late 18th century.

Ilene Magaras is a librarian/archivist residing in Brooklyn. She was librarian/archivist for the National Board and project archivist for the YWCA Digital Archive.

Paul Robert Magocsi is professor of history and political science at the Univ of Toronto. He is author of *A History of Ukraine* (1996) and editor in chief of *An Encyclopedia of Canada's Peoples* (1999).

Sarah J. Mahler received her graduate degrees from Columbia Univ and is associate professor of anthropology at Florida International Univ. She is author of *American Dreaming: Immigrant Life on the Margins* (1995) and "Engendering Transnational Migration: A Case Study of Salvadorans" (*American Behavioral Scientist,* 1999).

Dennis J. Maika (PhD New York Univ) writes articles and papers on colonial state history. He is coordinator of the Social Studies/Business Department at Fox Lane High School, Bedford.

Andrew C. Maines is librarian at Buffalo and Erie County Public Library.

Sal Maiorana is sports writer for the *Rochester Democrat and Chronicle,* covering the Buffalo Bills and local sports. He is author of books on the Buffalo Bills and one on the Buffalo Sabres. He is a freelance contributing writer for *Sporting News* and CBS Sportsline.

Jon C. Malinowski is associate professor of geography at the US Military Academy at West Point. He is coauthor of *The Spirit of West Point: Celebrating 200 Years* (2001) and *The Summer Camp Handbook* (2000).

Bill Mallon (MD) is president of the International Society of Olympic Historians. He has written 23 books on the Olympics Games.

Paul Malo is professor emeritus of architecture at Syracuse Univ. He has written books and articles about historic places and buildings of the state, including *Boldt Castle: In Search of the Lost Story* (2001).

David B. Malone (PhD student Northern Illinois Univ, DeKalb) is head of special collections at Wheaton College and college archivist at Buswell Memorial Library. He is coordinator of the Association of Christian Librarians' liberal arts section committee. His articles have been published in *The Encyclopedia of Fundamentalism* (2001) and *The Historical Encyclopedia of World Slavery.*

John B. Manbeck (professor emeritus) has served as Brooklyn Borough historian since 1993. He taught English and journalism for 32 years at Kingsborough Community College CUNY and served two years as Fulbright lector at Helsinki Univ, Finland. He is author of *Coney Island Kaleidoscope* and consulting editor of *The Neighborhoods of Brooklyn* (rev ed. 2004).

Peter C. Mancall is professor of history at the Univ of Southern California. He is author of *Valley of Opportunity: Economic Culture along the Upper Susquehanna, 1700–1800* (1991) and *Deadly Medicine: Indians and Alcohol in Early America* (1995).

Lisa C. Mangiafico is archivist for Soroptimist International of the Americas. She worked in the archives of the General Federation of Women's Clubs and has written historical publications for both organizations.

Laura E. Mann is librarian at *Newsday* in Melville on Long Island.

Susan Manning is Grierson Professor of English Literature at the Univ of Edinburgh. She is author of *Fragments of Union* (2002) and editor of J. Hector St. John de Crèvecoeur's *Letters from an American Farmer.* She is a board member and past president of the 18th-Century Scottish Studies Society.

Jo Margaret Mano is associate professor of geography at SUNY New Paltz. Her research investigates the historical cartography of New York State.

Vincenza Rose Marash (PhD) is continuing graduate studies in the School of Social Work at Syracuse Univ.

David Marc is a freelance writer. He is author of articles and four books concerning radio, television, film, and net surfing, including *Bonfire of the Humanities: Essays on Television, Subliteracy and Long-Term Memory Loss* (1995).

Maxine L. Margolis is professor of anthropology at the Univ of Florida, Gainesville. She is author or editor of seven books including *An Invisible Minority: Brazilians in New York City* (1998) and *True to Her Nature: Changing Advice to American Women* (2000).

John Marino (MA Fordham Univ) is a historian working for HarpWeek. He specializes in city and state government and politics during the Gilded Age. He teaches college-level history.

Mary Jo Marks (BS SUNY Geneseo) is board member and archivist/historian for the American Red Cross and Town of Sparta historian. She is a member of the historical societies of Dansville and Livingston Co, the Livingston County Federation of Historical Societies, and the Dansville Association for Historic Preservation.

John Tepper Marlin (PhD George Washington Univ) is chief economist at the NYC Office of the Comptroller and adjunct professor at Stern School of Business, New York Univ, and Lubin School of Business, Pace Univ. He is author of 15 books including *The Livable Cities Almanac* and *Building a Peace Economy.*

John D. Marsellus is former president of the Marsellus Casket Co.

Glenn T. Marshall (MPA John Jay School of Criminal Justice) has been government historian for the Town of New Windsor since 1996.

Christopher Martin (PhD Univ of Rochester) has taught at the Univ of Rochester and Rochester Institute of Technology. His dissertation title is "New Unionism at the Grassroots: The Amalgamated Clothing Workers of America in Rochester, New York, 1914–1929."

David F. Martin is an independent arts researcher specializing in women and minority artists active in western New York State and the Pacific Northwest during 1890–1950. He is co-owner of Martin-Zambito Fine Art.

Nancy Martin is manuscripts librarian and archivist in the Department of Rare Books, Special Collections, and Preservation in Rush Rhees Library at the Univ of Rochester.

Timothy Martinson has been regional grape specialist with the Finger Lakes Grape Program of Cornell Cooperative Extension, Penn Yan, since 1997.

Vincent Martonis is Town of Hanover historian.

Georgina Martorella is assistant professor and librarian at Hofstra Univ. She is former research librarian at *Newsday* and chief researcher for *Long Island: Our Story.*

Benedict R. Maryniak has been a social worker for 33 years. President of the Buffalo Civil War Roundtable since 1985, his research on Civil War army chaplains is part of *Faith in the Fight* (2003). In 1991 he led a Canada-US committee that orchestrated a 125th anniversary celebration of the Irish nationalist Fenian Brotherhood's 1866 raid that culminated in the Battle of Ridgeway, Ont.

Mark S. Massa SJ (ThD Harvard Univ) is director of the American Studies program and associate professor of theology at Fordham Univ, Bronx. He is author of *Charles Briggs and the Crisis of Historical Criticism* and *Catholics and American Culture: Fulton Sheen, Dorothy Day, and the Notre Dame Football Team.* He is working on a history of anti-Catholicism in the US in the 20th century.

Elaine Massena is principal archivist at the Westchester County Archives, Elmsford, and serves as archivist for the City of White Plains.

Helen Mathes is Town of Barre historian.

Cathy Matson is professor of history at the Univ of Delaware and director of the program in early American economy and society at the Library Company of Philadelphia. She is author of articles on NYC commercial life and political economy within the wider region in the 18th century. She is writing on the comparative economic cultures of the Hudson River and Delaware River valleys.

Bob Matthews (graduate, Gettysburg College) is sports columnist with the *Rochester Times-Union* and *Rochester Democrat and Chronicle.* He is a sports talk-show host at WHAM.

Harry Bradshaw Matthews (MA Northern Michigan Univ) teaches history and is associate dean of the Center for Interdependence at Hartwick College. He is also president and senior fellow of the US Colored Troops Institute for Local History and Family Research.

Jeffrey J. Matthews (PhD) teaches business, leadership, and history at the Univ of Puget Sound. He is author of articles in *Presidential Studies, Business and Economic History,* and *Mid-America: An Historical Review.*

Olivia Mattis (PhD Stanford Univ) is a musicologist specializing in 20th-century music. She has served on the faculties of the Eastman School of Music and the Univ of New Hampshire. She is author of articles in the *Musical Quarterly, The New Grove Dictionary of Music,* and *Keyboard Magazine.*

Kevin Mattson (PhD Univ of Rochester) is associate professor of American history at Ohio Univ, Athens. He is author of *Intellectuals in Action: The Origins of the New Left and Radical Liberalism, 1945–1970* (2002).

Thomas J. Mauhs-Pugh is associate professor of education and chair of the Education Department at Green Mountain College, Vt. He is author of *Rural School Consolidation in New York State, 1795–1993* (1994).

Frank J. Mauro (MPA Syracuse Univ) is director of the Fiscal Policy Institute. He holds the honorary rank of Public Service Professor at SUNY Albany's Nelson A. Rockefeller

College of Public Affairs and Policy, where he teaches state government and politics.

Thomas C. McCarthy is director of historical services for the City Correction Department and general secretary/webmaster of the New York Correction History Society, which he helped found. He is a former newspaper reporter, columnist, and editor, and had a long career in government public information service.

R. Paul McCarty is instructor and department head for technology education at the Saratoga Springs City School District. He was appointed town and village historian of Fort Edward in 1975 and is executive director of the Fort Edward Historical Association, which operates the Old Fort House Museum.

Laura J. McClusky is assistant professor of sociology and anthropology at Wells College. She is author of *"Here, Our Culture Is Hard": Stories of Domestic Violence from a Mayan Community in Belize* (2001).

John McClymer is professor of history at Assumption College, Mass, and co-director of the American History and Culture on the Web Project. He is author of *The Triangle Strike and Fire* (1998) and *"This High and Holy Moment": The First National Woman's Rights Convention, Worcester, 1850* (1999).

Douglas McCombs (PhD candidate Kent State Univ) is assistant curator at the Historical Society of Western Pennsylvania. His dissertation is on the therapeutic aspects of wilderness vacationing for the late 19th- and early 20th-century urban middle class. He is author of "Therapeutic Rusticity: Antimodernism, Health, and the Wilderness Vacation" (*New York History,* 1995).

Kimberly McCray (BA Saint Michael's College) is public programs coordinator at the Smithsonian Institution's National Postal Museum.

Phil McCray is archival consultant and founder of Upstate Archival Consultants of Ithaca and Rome. He is former director and curator of the International Motor Racing Research Center, Watkins Glen, and associate archivist at Cornell Univ's Division of Rare and Manuscript Collections.

Marie McCutcheon is Town of Ripley historian.

William P. McDermott is Town of Clinton historian. He has published articles on Dutchess Co history and is editor of *18th-Century Documents of the Nine Partners Patent* (1979) and *Clinton, Dutchess County, NY: A History of a Town* (1987).

Douglas B. McDonald is director of economic development for the City of Ithaca. He is former director of planning and development for the City of Ogdensburg. He taught geography at St. Lawrence Univ.

Michele A. McFee is a freelance writer. She is author of *A Long Haul: The Story of the New York State Barge Canal* (1998) and *Cornerstone: Harpur College of Binghamton Univ* (2000).

Larry McGill is a baseball researcher and resides in New Jersey.

Patrick McGreevy is professor of geography and chair of the Department of Anthropology, Geography, and Earth Science at Clarion Univ, Pa. He is author of *Imagining Niagara: The Meaning and the Making of Niagara Falls* (1994).

John Thomas McGuire is adjunct professor of American history at SUNY Oneonta. He completed his doctoral dissertation, "A Catalyst for Reform: The Women's Joint Legislative Conference (WJLC) and Its Fight for Labor Legislation in New York State, 1918–1933," at SUNY Binghamton.

Ellen McHale (PhD Univ of Pennsylvania) is executive director of the New York Folklore Society. She served as Fulbright Scholar to the Institutet for Folklivsforskning at the Univ of Stockholm, Sweden.

Catherine A. McKeen (PhD SUNY Stony Brook) is an independent historian. She teaches American history at Suffolk County Community College and Long Island history at SUNY Stony Brook.

Scott A. McLaughlin is an archaeologist working in the Champlain Valley and coauthor of archaeological studies on the region's canalboats.

Thelma C. McLester (MA Univ of Wisconsin, Madison) is an Oneida tribal member of the Oneida Tribe of Indians of Wisconsin and is area manager of education and training. She is author of articles in the *Encyclopedia of North American Indians* (1996) and *Oneida Indian Experience* (1988). She is regent board member of Haskell Nations Univ, Kans, and director of Brown County Historical Society.

Barbara McMartin (PhD) has written 23 books on the Adirondacks, starting with guides to the region. In recent years she has focused on historical topics such as forests, hemlock-bark tanning, early vacationers, local history, and the political scene.

Jan R. McTavish (PhD York Univ, Toronto) is assistant professor of history at Alcorn State Univ and has publications including "What Did Bayer Do before Aspirin? Early Pharmaceutical Marketing Practices in America" (*Pharmacy in History,* 1999).

Joseph F. Meany Jr (PhD) is former senior historian at the NYS Museum and former acting state historian. He is author of "Port in a Storm: The Port of New York in World War II" (*To Die Gallantly: The Battle of the Atlantic,* 1994).

Tracy N. Meehan is collection manager at the Adirondack Museum, Blue Mountain Lake. She has studied basketry for more than 20 years and in 1994 won a NYSCA grant to apprentice in pack-basket making.

Thomas Mellins is an architectural historian and coauthor of three award-winning books on the architecture and urbanism of New York City. He has written for the *New York Times, Architectural Record,* and other publications. He has served as a guest curator at the National Building Museum, Washington, DC.

Lloyd J. Mercer is professor of economics at the Univ of California, Santa Barbara. He is author of *E. H. Harriman: Master Railroader* (1985).

Kenneth S. Mernitz is associate professor of history at SUNY Buffalo and author of professional articles and presentations on the history of US business and technology.

Thomas E. Mertes is administrator of the Center for Social Theory and Comparative History and teaches at the Univ of California, Los Angeles Extension.

Daria E. Merwin (PhD candidate SUNY Stony Brook) is project director at the Institute of Long Island Archaeology.

Arpena S. Mesrobian (MSSc Syracuse Univ) is director emerita of Syracuse Univ Press. Her book *"Like One Family": The Armenians of Syracuse* is the first comprehensive historical study of a specific Armenian community in America.

Penny Messinger (PhD Ohio State Univ) works for the Higher Education Opportunity Program at St. Bonaventure Univ. Her dissertation was on gender and reform in the Appalachian South.

Mark Meuwese (PhD candidate Univ of Notre Dame) is writing his dissertation on negotiators between the Dutch and native peoples in New Netherland and Dutch Brazil.

Nathan R. Meyer teaches history and is a graduate student at George Mason Univ. He has been a research assistant on two encyclopedias and has written for five reference books.

Dennis J. Michalski has been assistant director for community affairs for the NYS Emergency Management Office since 1996. He was a reporter and editor at upstate daily newspapers, most recently at the *Albany Times-Union* and *Knickerbocker News.*

Peter Mickulas (PhD candidate Rutgers Univ) is a freelance writer.

Susan Millar is associate professor of geography at Syracuse Univ. She has conducted research in Quaternary geomorphology in New York State and Alaska.

Benjamin Miller, former director of policy planning for the NYC Department of Sanitation, is an environmental policy consultant. He is author of *Fat of the Land: Garbage in New York, the Last 200 Years* (2000).

Glenn T. Miller (ThD Union Theological Seminary) is Waldo Professor of Ecclesiastical History and dean at Bangor Theological Seminary. He is author of *Piety and Learning: A History of Ante-Bellum Theological Education in America* (1990) and *The Modern Church* (1997).

Norton G. Miller is principal botany scientist at the NYS Museum and adjunct professor of biological sciences at SUNY Albany. He has published in taxonomic and floristic botany and on the Quaternary paleobotanical and paleoecological history of eastern North America.

Thomas Ross Miller (PhD Columbia Univ) is assistant editor of *The Encyclopedia of New York State* and contributing author to *Life on Earth: An Encyclopedia of Biodiversity, Ecology, and Evolution* (2002) and *The Rolling Stone Jazz and Blues Album Guide* (1999).

Brett Michael Mills is history instructor at San Jacinto College and director of the Spring History Educator's Institute.

Quincy T. Mills is a PhD candidate at the Univ of Chicago. His dissertation examines the social and political history of black barbershops from slavery to the Civil Rights Movement.

Marcus H. Millspaugh Jr is a lifelong resident of Walden.

Pyong Gap Min is professor of sociology at Queens College and the Graduate Center, CUNY. He is author of three books, including *Caught in the Middle: Korean Communities in New York and Los Angeles* (1996), winner of two national book awards, and editor or coeditor of three books.

Gwendolyn L. Miner is supervisor of domestic arts at the Farmers' Museum, Cooperstown.

Nancy B. Mingus is president of Mingus Associates, Inc, a writing, training, and consulting company specializing in historic preservation and project management. She is author of *Teach Yourself Project Management in 24 Hours* (2001).

David Minor (MA New School for Social Research) is a freelance writer, researcher, and broadcaster. Much of his work, including an extensive timeline of New York City and State, can be found at his web page.

Joann Minor is a writer of advertising, promotional, technical, business, and instructional materials. She is an alumna of Nazareth College and Rochester Institute of Technology and former employee of Doubleday, Harcourt Brace Jovanovich, and General Electric. She operates her own consulting business.

Nancy Raquel Mirabal is assistant professor of Raza Studies at San Francisco State Univ. She is on a Chancellor's Post-doctoral Fellowship at the Univ of California, Berkeley, where she is completing a manuscript on the early history of Afro-Cuban migrants in the US. She has published articles on Cubans, including a community oral history project on the San Francisco Latino community.

Edwin A. Mirand (PhD) is an internationally known oncologist. He has been associated with Roswell Park Cancer Institute for more than 54 years as scientist and administrator. He is senior advisor to the president and CEO at the institute. He was vice president and dean of the Roswell Park Graduate Division of SUNY Buffalo for more than 30 years.

Paul C. Mishler is historian and labor educator. He is author of *Raising Reds: Young Pioneers, Radical Summer Camps, and Communist Political Culture* (1999). He has taught at Vassar College, Empire State College, and Univ of Massachusetts, Amherst, and is assistant professor of labor studies at Indiana Univ, South Bend.

Richard S. Mitchell (PhD Univ of California) is state botanist at the NYS Museum. His books include two checklists of state plants and monographs of state plant families. He is founder of the New York Flora Association and is finishing a botanical exploration of the Hudson Highlands and compendium of wild-growing state plants, their habitats, distributions, and medical and economic uses.

Daniel P. Molloy is aquatic biologist with the NYS Museum. His research focuses on diseases of invertebrates, particularly pest species such as zebra mussels and black flies. He studies the taxonomy and biology of disease-causing agents and evaluates their potential use as environmentally safe biological control agents.

Scott C. Monje (PhD Columbia Univ) is senior editor for area studies at the *Encyclopedia Americana* and historical interpreter at Philipsburg Manor, Sleepy Hollow. He has taught political science at Rutgers and New York Univs.

Thomas Monsell is cohistorian of the Village of Greenport. He is a retired high school English teacher and drama coach and is author of *Shakespeare in Performance: Hamlet and Nixon on Stage and Screen.*

Richard E. Mooers (AM Syracuse Univ) was a local government planner for 24 years, retiring in 2001 as director of planning for St. Lawrence Co. He is a former naval officer and teacher and is chair of the board for SOAR at SUNY Potsdam. He has climbed and hiked in the Northeast and elsewhere.

Richard E. Mooney is retired from the *New York Times,* where he was member of the editorial board. He was executive editor of the *Hartford Courant,* 1976–81.

David Moore (PhD) is coordinator and professor of biology at Utica College. His research in aquatic vascular plants focuses on the floristics of the wetlands associated with Lake Erie and is detailed in *Great Lakes Research Review* (2000).

Rue Moore has been associate professor of the history of medicine at Albany Medical College since 1965. He is Albany Medical Center archivist.

Sean T. Moore (PhD student Univ of Connecticut) is author of "National Prohibition in Northern New York" (*New York History,* 1996).

Paul Moreno is assistant professor of history at Hillsdale College.

John Moriello covered a variety of sports topics for the *Rochester Democrat and Chronicle,* 1982–95, and works in the company's on-line publishing department. He was vice president of the NYS Sports Writers Association for several years and has been its president since 1999.

Joan Morris has recorded 22 albums of American popular songs, from Civil War era to cabaret songs. With Bolcom and Morris she concertized throughout the US and Europe, performing for the US Supreme Court in 2000. She is working on a book on singing popular songs.

Christopher Morton is assistant curator for collections management at the NYS Military Museum and Veterans Research Center. He is a graduate of the public history master's degree program at SUNY Albany.

Daniel N. Moses has taught at Nazareth College and the Univ of Rochester. He is completing his dissertation, entitled "Tom Sawyer Nation: Lewis Henry Morgan and the Discourse of Savagery."

Laura-Eve Moss (PhD Univ of Connecticut) is managing editor of *The Encyclopedia of New York State.* She specializes in NYS constitutional and political history.

Barry Mowell is associate professor of geography and history in the Department of Social Sciences at Broward Community College, Fla.

Nan Mullenneaux (PhD student SUNY Albany) is a research fellow at the Colonial Albany Social History Project.

Robert E. Mulligan Jr (MA SUNY Albany) volunteers for the Irish American Heritage Museum of East Durham. He is former curator of Fort Ticonderoga. He is involved with the NYS Military Heritage Museum and Veterans Resource Center.

Robert Bruce Mullin (PhD Yale Univ) is Society for the Promotion of Religion and Learning Professor of History at the General Theological Seminary of the Episcopal Church. He is author or editor of five books, including *The Puritan as Yankee: A Life of Horace Bushnell* (2002) and *Miracles and the Modern Religious Imagination* (1996).

Arlene Murphy is Town and Village of Moravia historian.

Sharon Ann Murphy is completing her PhD at the Corcoran Department of History at the Univ of Virginia. Her dissertation analyzes the cultural, financial intermediary, and regulatory impact of the rise of the life insurance industry in the US, 1830s–1930s.

Christine E. Murray is associate dean for the School of Professions and associate professor in the Department of Education and Human Development at SUNY Brockport. She is coauthor of *Teaching in America: The Slow Revolution* (1999).

Jerome Mushkat is professor emeritus of history at the Univ of Akron. His books include *The Reconstruction of the New York Democracy, 1861–1874* (1981) and *Martin Van Buren: Law Politics and the Shaping of Republican Ideology* (1997).

N

Stan Nadel (PhD Columbia Univ) is a social historian who has taught history at more than a dozen US colleges and universities. He has published a book and numerous articles in the areas of immigration, labor, and urban history, many of them focused on New York City.

Martin Naparsteck is author of the novels *War Song* and *A Hero's Welcome.*

David Nasaw is professor of history at the Graduate Center, CUNY and author of books on the social and cultural history of the US.

Eugene Paul Nassar (PhD Cornell Univ) is professor and director of the Ethnic Heritage Studies Center at Syracuse Univ. He is author of *Wind of the Land: Two Prose Poems* (1979) and other books and articles.

Natalie A. Naylor is professor emerita of Hofstra Univ, where she taught US and Long Island history and was director of the Long Island Studies Institute (1985–2000). She has published articles and edited books and conference volumes. Since 1996 she has been editor of the *Nassau County Historical Journal.*

James Nelson has been historian of the Town of Monroe since 1981, vice president of the Orange County Historical Society, and charter member of the Monroe Historical Society. He contributed articles to the Orange County Historical annual journal, newspapers, and the Village of Monroe centennial book. He is working on the publication of the Town of Monroe Bicentennial book.

Caryn E. Neumann is a PhD candidate in women's history at Ohio State Univ.

Richard Newman teaches history at the Rochester Institute of Technology. He is coeditor of *Pamphlets of Protest: An Anthology of African American Protest Literature, 1790–1860* and author of *The Transformation of American Abolition, 1780–1840.*

Roberta Newman is a media producer and writer specializing in Jewish culture and history. In 2000 she became the director of new media at the YIVO Institute for Jewish Research. She is assistant editor of *The Encyclopedia of New York State.*

Eric Newton was founding managing editor of the Newseum in Arlington, Va. He is editor of *Crusaders, Scoundrels, Journalists* (1999) and coeditor of *Capture the Moment: The Pulitzer Prize Photographs* (2003) and is director of journalism initiatives at the John S. and James L. Knight Foundation in Miami.

Mitchell C. Newton-Matza (PhD Catholic Univ of America) specializes in the history of law and labor and teaches at the Univ of St. Francis and Roosevelt Univ, both in Illinois.

Karen Nichols is assistant professor of geography at SUNY Geneseo.

Michael I. Niman (PhD) is assistant professor of journalism and media studies at SUNY Buffalo State, syndicated freelance journalist, and editorial columnist. He is also an ethnographer and author of *People of the Rainbow: A Nomadic Utopia.*

Tomas Nonnenmacher is assistant professor of economics at Allegheny College. He is author of "State Promotion and Regulation of the Telegraph Industry, 1845–1860" *(Journal of Economic History).*

Mark Noon is English instructor at the Univ of Pennsylvania, Bloomsburg. His dissertation, " 'Nothing to Arbitrate': The Strike in the American Novel, 1888–1915" (1998) has chapters on two radical novels set in New York City: Theresa Serber Malkiel's *The Diary of a Shirtwaist Striker* (1910) and Ernest Poole's *The Harbor* (1915).

David J. Nordloh is professor of English at Indiana Univ and coeditor of *American Literary Scholarship: An Annual.*

Hans Norman earned his PhD from the Univ of Uppsala, where he is associate professor of history. He is author of "Swedes in North America" (*From Sweden to America: A History of the Migration,* 1976) and coauthor of *The Rise and Fall of New Sweden: Governor Johan Risingh's Journal, 1654–1655, in Its Historical Context* (1988).

Linda Norris is managing partner of Riverhill, a museum consulting firm. She served as director of the Delaware County Historical Association from 1982 to 1994.

Elizabeth M. Nuxoll (PhD Graduate Center, CUNY) was project director and coeditor of *The Papers of Robert Morris, 1781–1784.* She is associate editor of the *Papers of Clarence Mitchell, Jr.*

O

Brian Obach is professor of sociology at SUNY New Paltz.

Michael Leroy Oberg is associate professor of history at SUNY Geneseo. He is author of *Uncas: First of the Mohegans* (2003) and *Dominion and Civility: English Imperialism and Native America, 1585–1685* (1999).

Elizabeth A. Obomsawin (PhD candidate Syracuse Univ) is a Wolf Clan member of the Oneida Indian Nation. She has written articles, been involved in the production of documentaries, and lectured on Iroquois history and culture.

Anne Slyer Oboyski (PhD SUNY Albany) is associate professor in the School of Nursing at SUNY Institute of Technology at Utica/Rome. She researches nursing history with an emphasis on public policy and professionalism and as Larry J. Hackman Research Resident continues her research at the NYS Archives.

Kenneth P. O'Brien is associate professor of history at SUNY Brockport. He is coeditor of *The Home-Front War: American Society and World War II* (1995) and author of several articles on modern film. He is completing a book on the last 50 years of SUNY Brockport's history.

E. Dale Odom is a retired professor of history at the Univ of North Texas. He is author of scholarly articles on railroads and the dairy industry.

Carl Oechsner is a graduate of Ithaca College and Columbia Univ. He is author of three books and president of the Croton-on-Hudson Historical Society.

Christine A. Ohl is a PhD student in the Higher Education Program at Syracuse Univ.

Thomas H. Olbricht (PhD Univ of Iowa; STB Harvard Divinity School) has taught at several universities, including Pepperdine Univ, where he is Distinguished Professor of Religion, Emeritus. He has published 10 books, essays in 50 others, and journal articles in church history and biblical studies.

Andrea Olmstead is chair of the Department of Music History at the Boston Conservatory. She is author of three books on Roger Sessions (1985, 1987, 1992) and of *Julliard: A History* (1999).

Robert A. Olmsted (PE) holds civil engineering degrees from Cornell Univ and the Polytechnic Institute of Brooklyn. He has over 50 years of experience in transportation engineering and history.

Sean M. O'Mara (MA SUNY Albany) is a teacher of American history in Keene, NH, a former intern with the Colonial Albany Social History Project, and two-time presenter at the Conference on New York State History.

David H. Onkst (PhD candidate American Univ) is writing a book about the Grumman engineers and production workers who designed and built the Apollo lunar modules. He has been a Smithsonian Institution Fellow at the National Air and Space Museum, the American Historical Association's Aerospace History Fellow in residency at NASA, and a National Science Foundation Fellow.

Sandra Opdycke is associate director of the Fordham Institute for Innovation in Social Policy, Tarrytown. She is author of *No One Was Turned Away: The Role of Public Hospitals in New York City since 1900* (1999).

Kimberly A. Orcutt is a PhD student in American art at the Graduate Center, CUNY.

Cheryl Orlick has been public information officer at the Albright-Knox Art Gallery since 1988.

Bill Orzell is editor of *Bottoming Out,* the journal of the Canal Society of New York State. He is an avid boater on the canals and waterways of the Empire State.

Peter Osborne is executive director of the Minisink Valley Historical Society and City of Port Jervis historian.

Tod M. Ottman (PhD SUNY Albany) is founder of the annual conference Researching New York: Perspectives on Empire State History. He is assistant managing editor of *The Encyclopedia of New York State.*

Paul Otto is associate professor of history at Dordt College. His research focuses on Dutch–Native American interaction in New Netherland.

Susan M. Ouellette (PhD) is assistant professor in the Department of History and American Studies at Saint Michael's College. She is author of *Conflict and Accommodation in the North Country, 1850–1930* (forthcoming) and *All Hands Are Enjoined to Spin: A Social History of Textile Production in New England, 1630–1730* (forthcoming).

Judith Owens-Manley (PhD SUNY Albany) is associate director for community research at the Arthur Levitt Center for Public Affairs at Hamilton College. She has published journal articles on community human service issues such as welfare and domestic violence and is working on a book about refugees in New York State.

P

Dominique Padurano (PhD candidate Rutgers Univ) graduated magna cum laude from Harvard College. She has published in the *Dictionary of American History, Latin American Art* magazine, and newspapers in the NYC area.

Jean M. Pardo has been an Orangetown resident since 1957 and Village of Nyack historian since 1996. In 2000 she directed publication of *Nyack in the 20th Century.*

Donald H. Parkerson is Distinguished Professor of Teaching and Professor of History at East Carolina Univ. He is author of three books including *The Agricultural Transition in New York State* (1995).

Jon Parmenter is assistant professor of history at Cornell

Univ. His research deals with the history of eastern Native Americans, especially the Iroquois Confederacy.

Rebecca Partise is a graduate of Hartwick College. She is former education coordinator for the Le Roy Historical Society and is working on a book about the 1971 Attica prison rebellion.

Christine Sternberg Patrick (PhD) is assistant editor for *The Papers of George Washington.*

Julie M. Pavri is former associate director of the library of the NYS Nurses Association and former archivist for the Foundation of the NYS Nurses Association's Center for History. She has written articles on nursing history and the management of historical nursing materials and is author of a forthcoming history of the NYS Nurses Association.

James Paxton is a PhD candidate at Queen's Univ, Kingston.

Phillip G. Payne is assistant professor of history at St. Bonaventure Univ, where he teaches American and public history.

Chad Pearson (PhD student SUNY Albany) is interested in the history of employer organizations and in the ways they fought unions and unionization campaigns in the early 20th century. He is union organizer for the Communications Workers of America (CWA) and business agent for CWA Local 1104.

Robert F. Pecorella (PhD) is associate professor with the Department of Government and Politics at St. John's Univ and is professor in residence with the NYS Assembly Intern Programs. He is author of *Community Power in the Post-reform City: Politics in New York City* and coauthor of *Politics and Structure.*

Robert Pedersen is an independent scholar in Washington, DC, specializing in education policy and history. He maintains the web site junior-college-history.org.

Elizabeth S. Peña (PhD) is anthropologist and curator of anthropological collections at the Buffalo Museum of Science. She conducts archaeological research at Old Fort Niagara, Youngstown.

M. Stephen Pendleton is associate professor of economics at SUNY Buffalo State. He is author of "Pipe Dream Come True: Buffalo's Decision to Supply Water through the Public Sector" *(The Middle State Geographer).*

Susan R. Perkins (AS Cazenovia College) is administrative director of the Herkimer County Historical Society.

Thomas W. Perrin is a native of northern New York State and author of *I Am an Adult Who Grew Up in an Alcoholic Family* (1992).

Elisabeth Israels Perry is John Francis Bannon Professor of History at St. Louis Univ.

Winston C. Perry Jr is Village of Upper Nyack historian.

Susan Persia is Town of Clarendon historian.

F. Charles Petrillo is a graduate of Wilkes College, Pa, and the Dickinson School of Law, Pa. He is a writer and lecturer on the canal and steamboat history of the North Branch of the Susquehanna River.

Todd Pfannestiel is instructor of history at Clarion Univ of Pennsylvania.

Daniel A. Piazza is a PhD student in early American history at Syracuse Univ.

Dana Pilson (PhD student Graduate Center, CUNY) is research assistant in the American Paintings and Sculpture Department at the Metropolitan Museum of Art.

Darrell Pinckney is archaeologist and field conservationist with Hartgen Archeological Associates, Rensselaer. He is former president of the Massachusetts Archaeological Society.

Douglas J. Pippin (PhD candidate Syracuse Univ) is assistant editor for *The Encyclopedia of New York State* and instructor in the Department of Anthropology at SUNY Oswego.

John C. Pitarresi has been a sportswriter at the *Utica Observer-Dispatch* since 1973 and outdoor columnist since 1980. He is a graduate of Hamilton College.

John Pitcher is classical music critic for the *Rochester Democrat and Chronicle.* He has been a cultural commentator on National Public Radio, and his views and reviews have appeared in the *Washington Post* and the *Newark Star-Ledger,* among other publications.

Scott Pitoniak is sports columnist for the *Rochester Democrat and Chronicle.* He is author of *Playing Write Field: Selected Works by Scott Pitoniak* (1997) and *Silver Seasons: The Story of the Rochester Red Wings* (1996).

Donald E. Pitzer (PhD Ohio State Univ) is professor of history and director of the Center for Communal Studies at Univ of Southern Indiana. He is editor of *America's Communal Utopias.*

Ruth Piwonka is Town of Kinderhook historian and member of the Village of Kinderhook Board of Trustees. She is author of *A Portrait of Livingston Manor, 1686–1850* and coauthor of *A Visible Heritage, Columbia County, New York: A History in Art and Architecture.*

Robert D. Plattner (JD Stanford Law School) is Of Counsel to the Albany law firm McNamee, Lochner, Titus and Williams, PC, where he concentrates in state and local taxation. He is adjunct professor at Albany Law School, author of the annual *New York State Tax Handbook,* and principal state correspondent for *State Tax Notes.*

Jane R. Plitt is visiting scholar at the Univ of Rochester. She is author of *Martha Matilda Harper and the American Dream: How One Woman Changed the Face of Modern Business.*

Jerald E. Podair (PhD Princeton Univ) is assistant professor of history at Lawrence Univ, Wisc. He is author of *Like Strangers: Blacks, Whites, and New York City's Ocean Hill–Brownsville Crisis* (2002).

Andrew Podnieks is author of books on hockey, including *A Day in the Life of the Maple Leafs* and *Players: The Complete Hockey Biographies.*

Julie Polhemus is a master's student in environmental studies at the Univ of Oregon. Her thesis is a collection of writing and photography about her childhood home in New York State.

Tammy Popejoy (BA Bethany College) is library supervisor at the American Institute of Baking, Manhattan, Kans. She is a student in the Library Services Certificate program at Emporia State Univ, Kans.

Ned Pratt, a preservation consultant in Troy, is former adjunct professor of the history of architecture and furniture, and of interior design, at the Sage Colleges. He is president of the Turpin Bannister Chapter, Society of Architectural Historians, and of the Dutch Barn Preservation Society.

Joseph N. Prenoveau is professor of education at the Sage Colleges. He served as assistant superintendent of schools in the South Colonie Central School District for 23 years.

David L. Preston is a PhD candidate at the College of William and Mary. His dissertation is entitled "The Texture of Contact: Indians and European Settlers on the New York and Pennsylvania Frontiers, 1720–1780."

Eleanor Preston is a graduate of the Central City Business Institute. She volunteers for the Tully Area Historical Society as president and administrator of its headquarters and museum. She is former Village of Tully historian.

William S. Pretzer is curator at the Henry Ford Museum and Greenfield Village, Dearborn, Mich. He is author of articles on the history of printing labor and technology.

Frank Price is a motion picture producer and writer and former president of Columbia Pictures and Universal Pictures. He is best known for *Out of Africa, Tootsie,* and *Ghandi,* and his production of *The Tuskegee Airmen* received the George Foster Peabody Award.

Marvin Pritts (PhD) is professor and chair of the Department of Horticulture at Cornell Univ. His specialty is berry crop production and management.

Ellen Prokop is a graduate student at New York Univ.

Stephanie Przybylek (MA Univ of Delaware) is director of collections at the Schenectady Museum.

Richard A. Puff was a member of the board of directors of the Society for American Baseball Research. His articles have been included in *National Pastime, Baseball Weekly,* and *Giants Magazine.* He is assistant director of public relations for Albany Medical Center.

James S. Pula (PhD Purdue Univ) is dean of graduate and continuing education at Utica College. The author of several books on Polish Americans, he has twice been awarded the Oskar Halecki Prize for outstanding books on Polonia, as well as being honored with the Mieczyslaw Haiman Award for scholarly contributions in Polish studies.

Q

Richard E. Quest was Tioga Co historian, 1994–2001. A former history teacher at Candor Central School, he is a high school principal. The Daughters of the American Revolution named him NYS History Teacher of the Year in 2000.

D. Michael Quinn (PhD) was Beinecke Senior Fellow and postdoctoral associate in the History Department at Yale Univ. He is author of *The Mormon Hierarchy: Origins of Power* (1994) and *Early Mormonism and the Magic World View* (1998), and he received a best book award from the American Historical Association in 1997.

Robert R. Quinn (MS SUNY-ESF) is executive director and former natural resource coordinator of the NYS Tug Hill Commission. He was assistant director of the NYS Senate Research Service, executive director of the Adirondack Mountain Club, and National Park Ranger at Denali National Park, Alaska.

William Quirin (PhD) is author of *Golf Clubs of the MGA* (1997) and *America's Linksland* (2002).

R

Gregory P. Rabb (JD SUNY Buffalo) is associate professor of political science and director of international studies at Jamestown Community College.

Peter Rachleff is professor of history at Macalester College. He is author of *Black Labor in Richmond, Virginia, 1865–1890* (1989) and essays and articles on race, class, and ethnicity.

Matthew Taylor Raffety (PhD Columbia Univ) is author of articles in *Encyclopedia of American History* and *Violence in America: An Encyclopedia.*

Ethan S. Rafuse (PhD) is associate professor of military history at the US Army Command and General Staff College, Fort Leavenworth, Kans. He is author of *A Single Grand Victory: The First Battle and Campaign of Manassas* (2002) and of essays, articles, and reviews in scholarly and popular history journals.

Enayetur Rahim (PhD Georgetown Univ) taught South Asia history. He was a native of Bangladesh who settled in the US and wrote books and articles on the history of South Asia and the Middle East.

Marianne Rahn-Erickson (MS Rensselaer Polytechnic Institute) is an independent writer and audio documentary producer raising sheep, boys, and taxes in Washington Co. She is also assistant editor for *The Encyclopedia of New York State.*

William Rainbolt teaches at SUNY Albany and is working on a book about the NYS Temporary Emergency Relief Administration.

Karl Raitz (PhD Univ of Minnesota) is professor and chair of geography at the Univ of Kentucky. He is editor of *National Road* and *A Guide to the National Road.*

David Luke Ramsey is a graduate of Abilene Christian Univ, Tex, and author of *The Nats: A Team, A City, An Era.*

Gary Allen Randall (BA) taught cabinetmaking, carpentry, and architecture for 26 years. He is Village of Florida historian, president of the Florida Historical Society, and vice president of the Town of Warwick Historical Society. He is coauthor of *Florida, New York, Orange County: An Early Look at Its Faces, Places, and Winding Staircases.*

Richard Ranieri is an earth science teacher at Unatego High School in Otego. He is a volunteer consultant at the NYS Civilian Conservation Corps Museum at Gilbert Lake State Park, Laurens.

Joyce Rapp is Town and Village of Lima historian. She graduated from Univ of Rochester in 1983, when she was elected to Phi Beta Kappa.

Joseph Raskin (MA Queens College, CUNY) lives in Brooklyn with his wife, Karli Kelber, and their children, Nicholas and Natalie.

Thomas H. Rasmussen is professor of political science at Alfred Univ. Among his research interests are early settlement patterns in western New York State and the social history of American architecture.

John David Rausch Jr is assistant professor of political science at West Texas A&M Univ. He has published articles and book chapters on legislative studies issues.

Jessie Ravage is a historical research consultant in Cooperstown, specializing in the agricultural and architectural history of central New York State and the Southern Tier.

Kathy Ray is a physician assistant.

David Raymond is a graduate of SUNY Binghamton and the Eastman School of Music. He is on staff of the Rochester alternative weekly *City* and is a freelance writer.

John Recchiuti (PhD Columbia Univ) is associate professor of history and political science at Mount Union College. He writes on intellectuals and reform politics in New York State, 1900–1917.

Elizabeth Redkey (PhD student SUNY Albany) is studying

American cultural history. She is also a lifelong horsewoman.

Cleota Reed is ceramic historian and Scholar Affiliate of the Department of Fine Arts at Syracuse Univ. She is coauthor of *Syracuse China* (1998).

Gregory Reed is Town of Summer Hill historian.

Brian Regal studied intellectual history at Drew Univ and is historian with the Mary Baker Eddy Library, Boston. He is author of *Henry Fairfield Osborn: Race and the Search for the Origins of Man* (2002).

Daniel D. Reiff is professor of art history at SUNY Fredonia. During the 1970s he headed six architectural surveys of Chautauqua Co for a local arts council. Two of his five published books deal in whole or in part with architecture in that county.

Philip R. Reilly (MD JD) is executive director of the Shriver Center for Mental Retardation, assistant professor of pediatrics at Tufts Univ School of Medicine, and president of the American Society of Law, Medicine, and Ethics. He is a board-certified clinical geneticist and attorney who consults with biotech companies, the pharmaceutical industry, universities, and nonprofit organizations.

Thomas Reimer (PhD Syracuse Univ) is assistant editor of *The Encyclopedia of New York State* and instructor at Empire State College–CDL.

Stephen Reiners is associate professor of horticultural sciences at Cornell Univ's NYS Agricultural Experiment Station.

Barbara Reinfeld (PhD Columbia Univ) is professor of history and chair of social sciences at the New York Institute of Technology, Westbury. She was president of the Czechoslovak History Conference in 1990–92. Her dissertation was published as *Karel Havlicek (1821–1856): A National Liberation Leader of the Czech Renascence* (1982).

Glenn Reynolds is working on a PhD dissertation at SUNY Stony Brook entitled "Picture Power: Film for Education and Uplift in Sub-Saharan Africa, 1920–40."

William T. Reynolds is director of the New Netherland Museum and captain of the *Half Moon,* the fully operational replica of the Dutch East India Co ship.

Suzanne Rhebergen is Town of Clymer historian.

Sarah K. Rich (PhD Yale Univ) is assistant professor of art history at Pennsylvania State Univ. She has published reviews in *Art Bulletin* and *Afterimage.* She is completing a book on Barnett Newman in the sixties.

Frederick S. Richards is chief of the Fire and Life Safety Education Bureau at the NYS Department of State, Office of Fire Prevention and Control, and serves on training manual committees for the International Fire Service Training Association and a technical committee for the National Fire Protection Association. His graduate work is in public administration.

Jean Richardson is assistant professor of history at SUNY Buffalo State and has written "A Tale of Two 19th-Century Hospitals: Buffalo Hospital of the Sisters of Charity and Buffalo General Hospital" (*Medical History in Buffalo, 1846–1996,* 1996) and "Sisterhood Is Powerful: Sister Nurses Confront the Modernization of Nursing" (*Florence Nightingale and Her Era,* 1990).

Daniel K. Richter is professor of history at the Univ of Pennsylvania. He is author of *The Ordeal of the Longhouse: The Peoples of the Iroquois League in the Era of European Colonization* (1992) and coeditor of *Beyond the Covenant Chain: The Iroquois and Their Neighbors in Indian North America, 1600–1800* (1987).

Whitman H. Ridgway is associate professor of history at the Univ of Maryland, College Park. He is writing a book on the Alien and Sedition Act crisis in the 1790s.

Andrew C. Rieser (PhD Univ of Wisconsin, Madison) is assistant professor of history at St. Cloud State Univ. He is author of a forthcoming book and of articles on Chautauqua, including "Secularization Reconsidered: Chautauqua and the De-Christianization of Middle-Class Authority, 1880–1920" (*Middling Sorts: Essays in the History of the American Middle Class,* 2001).

Christina Rieth is archaeologist with the cultural resource survey program at the NYS Museum. She is coeditor of *Early Late Prehistoric Settlement and Subsistence Diversity in the Northeast,* AD *700–1300.*

James A. Riley is president of the Society for American Baseball Research and director of research for the Negro Leagues Baseball Museum, Kansas City, Mo. He is author of six books on baseball, including *The Biographical Encyclopedia of the Negro Baseball Leagues,* and contributor to baseball books and sports publications.

Kathleen L. Riley (PhD Univ of Notre Dame) is assistant professor of history at Ohio Dominican College and adjunct assistant professor of history at Canisius College. Her dissertation is "Bishop Fulton J. Sheen: An American Catholic Response to the 20th Century," and she is working on a manuscript entitled "The American Catholic Odyssey of Bishop Fulton Sheen."

Michael Riley is Town of Mentz historian. He is former director of the Canal Society of New York State.

Barbara S. Rivette is Town of Manlius and Village of Fayetteville historian. She spent 50 years as a newspaper reporter, photographer, and editor. She is a historical researcher and author specializing in women's rights, roads and settlement patterns prior to 1830, and legal procedures and documents before 1840.

Warren Roberts is Distinguished Teaching Professor in the Department of History at SUNY Albany.

Anthony Robins is an architectural historian and author of *Classics of American Architecture: The World Trade Center.* He is former deputy director of research and director of survey at the NYC Landmarks Preservation Commission.

Greg Robinson (PhD) is a professor at the Univ of Montreal and is author of *By Order of the President: FDR and the Internment of Japanese Americans* (2001) and of articles and book chapters. He is associate editor of the *Encyclopedia of African American Culture and History.*

Scott Rochette (PhD) is assistant professor of meteorology in the Department of the Earth Sciences and Weather Center director at SUNY Brockport. He is technical editor of *National Weather Digest.*

E. Burke Rochford Jr is professor of sociology and religion at Middlebury College, Vt. He has studied the Hare Krishna movement for over 25 years and published articles on the movement's North American development. He is now focusing on women, children, and family life.

Kathleen Roe (MLS Wayne State Univ) is chief of archival services at the NYS Archives. She manages the operation of the facility as well as statewide programs to provide training and advisory services to local government archives and historical records programs.

Rachel Rojanski (PhD) is lecturer at the Department of Jewish History, Univ of Haifa. She is author of *Conflicting Identities: Poalei-Zion in North America, 1905–1931* (2003) and of articles on the politics and culture of East European Jewish immigrants in America.

Lomarsh Roopnarine (PhD candidate SUNY Albany) is researching Indo-Caribbean indenture, resistance, and accommodation on the sugar plantations in the 19th century. He is author of "Politics, Economics, and Environmental Policy in Guyana" (*Journal of Caribbean History,* 2000) and "Environmental Policy Challenges and Development in Guyana" (*Issues in Sovereignty and Government,* forthcoming).

Donald M. Roper is a retired associate professor of history at SUNY New Paltz. He is preparing a study of the New York Supreme Court, 1798–1823.

C. G. Rose teaches at Bishop's Univ of Environmental Studies and Geography. He coauthor of "Nitrogen Loading to Green Pond, Falmouth, MA: Sources and Evaluation of Management Options" (*Environment Cape Cod,* 1999).

Ruth Rosenberg-Naparsteck is City of Rochester historian. She is author of *Runnin' Crazy: A Portrait of the Genesee River* (1996) and *Rochester: A Pictorial History* (1989; rev ed. 1994).

Reuben Skye Rose-Redwood is a graduate student in the Department of Geography at Pennsylvania State Univ. He is a US Environmental Protection Agency Fellow and is conducting research on the environmental history of New York City.

John Ross is director of alumni relations at Wagner College.

Mary Ellen Ross (MLS Case Western Reserve Univ) was City of Fulton historian, 1989–2002.

Brian W. Rossmann is government information specialist librarian at Montana State Univ. He is on the editorial boards of the *Journal of Government Information* and *Documents to the People.*

David S. Rotenstein (PhD Univ of Pennsylvania) is a historic preservation consultant in Bethesda, Md. His dissertation was on New York and Pennsylvania leather tanners, and he has written articles on history of American livestock and the leather industry.

Mark Rothenberg (MS C. W. Post) works for the Suffolk Cooperative Library System as reference librarian in the local history room at the Patchogue-Medford Library. He is researching the Town of Brookhaven's history for its upcoming 350th anniversary.

Peggy Rotton is a member of the Utica and Albany Curling Clubs, director of the US Curling Association, and Grand National Curling Clubs' women's event chair. She is past president of the US Women's Curling Association.

David L. Rowe (PhD Univ of Virginia) is author of *Thunder and Trumpets: Millerites and Dissenting Religion in Upstate New York, 1800–1850* and of articles in *Church History* and other publications.

John Rowen is a writer and broadcaster. He has won awards for his essays and broadcasts, and in 2001 he completed his 500th book and author interview.

Paul Roxin became a licensed pilot in 1936. From 1938 to 1955 he was Civil Aeronautics Administration airway traffic controller and aircraft communicator. He is owner of Roxin Radio Systems and cofounder of Geriatric Pilots Association.

Anya Peterson Royce is professor of anthropology at Indiana Univ, Bloomington, and author of *The Anthropology of Dance* (1977) and *Movement and Meaning: Creativity and Interpretation in Ballet and Mime* (1984). She danced professionally in ballet companies before becoming an anthropologist.

Rachel Rubin compiled many of the tables that appear in *The Encyclopedia of New York State.* She has an undergraduate degree in urban studies and planning from SUNY Albany and is studying law at Brooklyn Law School.

Joshua Ruff is history curator of the Long Island Museum of American Art, History, and Carriages, Stony Brook. He is adjunct professor of American history at St. Joseph's College.

Thomas A. Rumney (PhD Univ of Maryland) is professor of geography at SUNY Plattsburgh. He is author of 110 publications and coauthor of *A Scholar's Guide to Geographical Writing on the American and Canadian Past* (1993).

Phillip M. Runkel is Catholic Worker archivist in the Department of University Archives and Special Collections at Marquette Univ Libraries, Wisc.

Thaddeus Russell (PhD Columbia Univ) is visiting assistant professor of history at Barnard College and author of *Out of the Jungle: Jimmy Hoffa and the Remaking of the American Working Class.*

Joan Ryan CSJ is assistant professor and reference librarian at St. Joseph's College.

Lynne Ryan is executive director of the Bedford Historical Society.

S

Deborah Woeckner Saavedra is a PhD candidate in US Latino cultural studies at SUNY Albany, where she has worked as research assistant. Her dissertation explores the educational challenges faced by urban youth with focus on ethnicity, identity, and immigration.

Samuel H. Sage is president and senior scientist for Atlantic States Legal Foundation, Syracuse, and adjunct professor at SUNY-ESF, where he teaches urban environmental policy and works with students on urban projects in the Onondaga Lake basin. He is a physical inorganic chemist with degrees from Cornell Univ and the Univ of Minnesota.

Gaspare J. Saladino (PhD) is coeditor of *The Documentary History of the Ratification of the Constitution* (16 vols to date) at the Univ of Wisconsin, Madison. He has published articles on the ratification of the Constitution in New York State and Delaware and on the Bill of Rights.

Matt T. Salo is former research anthropologist at the US Bureau of the Census. He has done ethnographic and historical research on several gypsy and traveler populations in North America.

Sheila Salo is an independent researcher and former editor of the *Journal of the Gypsy Lore Society.* She has written ethnographical and historical studies of gypsy groups in North America.

Joseph J. Salvo is director of the Population Division at the NYC Department of City Planning. He is author and editor for the *Encyclopedia of the US Census* (2000) and has published on the demography of immigrants in New York State.

Robert D. Sampson (PhD Univ of Illinois, Urbana-Champaign) is a former newspaper reporter and congressional aide. He is author of *John L. O'Sullivan and His Times* (2003) and of journal articles on 19th-century US history.

Shirley S. Samuels has taught writing and American literature since 1959 at Herkimer County Community College and Utica College.

David W. Sawicki is reference librarian at E. H. Butler Library, SUNY Buffalo State.

Daniel A. Scalberg (PhD Univ of Oregon) is professor of history and chair of the Department of Historical Studies at Multnomah Bible College, Oreg. He is author of *The Kregel Pictorial Guide to Christian Heritage in England* (2002).

Bruce Schaller is principal of Schaller Consulting and author of papers and reports on the taxi and livery industries.

Laura Lynne Scharer was Jefferson County historian and author of *An Old-Fashioned Christmas.*

Alexandra Schein (PhD candidate Graduate Center, CUNY) is teaching introductory art history classes as adjunct lecturer.

Richard Schein is geographer at the Univ of Kentucky. His doctoral dissertation explored the colonization of the New Military Tract after the American Revolution. He is interrogating the American cultural landscape as "discourse materialized."

John L. Scherer (MA Cooperstown Graduate Program) is curator of decorative arts at the NYS Museum. He lectures on antiques, teaches a graduate course on material culture at SUNY Albany, and has published museum catalogs, brochures, and articles in *Connoisseur, Antiques the Magazine, Art and Antiques Magazine,* and other publications.

William Scheuerman (PhD) is president of the United University Professions. He is author of *The Steel Crisis* and coauthor of *Private Interests, Public Spending.* He has written in scholarly journals and popular periodicals, including the *Nation.*

Joseph G. Schmidt has been public relations manager at Munson-Williams-Proctor Arts Institute since 1990. He is a graduate of Utica College, and his works have appeared in national and regional publications.

Robert F. Scholz (PhD Univ of Minnesota) is pastor of Holy Trinity Lutheran Church, New York City, and historian of the Metropolitan New York Synod, Evangelical Lutheran Church in America. He was a member of the history faculties of the Univ of Washington and Wagner College, and has also taught at other universities.

Jeff Schramm is a PhD candidate at Lehigh Univ. His dissertation is on the dieselization of North American railroads.

Dorothy Moses Schulz is associate professor of law, police science, and criminal justice administration at John Jay College of Criminal Justice. She writes on a number of police topics and is the author of *From Social Worker to Crimefighter: Women in United States Municipal Policing* (1995).

Deborah Schwabach teaches writing at SUNY Oneonta.

Joel Schwartz teaches history at Montclair State Univ. He is author of *The New York Approach: Robert Moses, Urban Liberals, and Redevelopment of the Inner City* (1993) and of chapters in *The Empire State: History of New York* (2001).

Samuel I. Schwartz was New York City's traffic commissioner, 1982–86. He is CEO of Sam Schwartz LLC, a traffic engineering firm, and adjunct professor at Cooper Union. He is author of a traffic column for the *New York Daily News* (under his nom de plume, Gridlock Sam) and *New York Shortcuts and Traffic Tips* (1994).

Paul A. Schweizer is a graduate aeronautical engineer who founded Schweizer Aircraft Corp with his brothers. He is retired, has written several books on soaring, and is writing his memoirs.

Chris Matthew Sciabarra is visiting scholar in the Department of Politics at New York Univ. He is author of *Ayn Rand: The Russian Radical* (1995).

Alice Scourby (PhD) is professor of sociology at Long Island Univ, Brookville. She is author of *The Greek Americans,* coeditor of *The Greek Community in Transition,* and author of articles including "The Greeks of New England" (*Encyclopedia of New England Culture,* 2001).

Richard Hughes Seager (PhD Harvard Univ) is author of *The World's Parliament of Religions: The East/West Encounter, Chicago 1893* and *Buddhism in America.* He is associate professor at Hamilton College, Clinton.

Milton C. Sernett is professor of African American studies and history and adjunct professor of religion at Syracuse Univ. He is author of *Abolition's Axe: Beriah Green, Oneida Institute, and the Black Freedom Struggle* (1986), and *North Star Country: Upstate New York and the Crusade for African American Freedom* (2000).

Vincent Serravallo (PhD Graduate Center, CUNY) teaches in the Department of Sociology and Anthropology at Rochester Institute of Technology. He is author of "Class and Gender in Recreational Marathon Running" (*Race Gender and Class,* 2000) and "Brick Foundations: Continuity and Change in an Italian Working-Class Rural Community" (*Differentia,* 1994).

David P. Setran (PhD Indiana Univ) is assistant professor of educational ministries at Wheaton College, Ill. His areas of interest are the history of Christianity in the US, history of religious education, and history of moral education.

Ellen Sexton (MS Hunter College) is reference and reserve librarian at John Jay College of Criminal Justice. She is author of "Stachybotrys: Media Hype or True Hazard?" (*Library and Archival Security,* 2001) and articles for the *Encyclopedia of Crime and Justice* (2001).

Mojtaba Seyedian is professor of finance at SUNY Fredonia. He has published biographies on prominent figures in business and economics.

Vincent F. Seyfried (MA Fordham Univ) is author of 7 histories of street railways, a 7-volume history of the Long Island Rail Road, 5 volumes of community histories, 3 pictorial histories of Queens, and 15 newspaper indexes. He is a historian of Garden City.

Ruth Shackelford is professor of history at Long Island Univ, Brooklyn. She is author of "Poor Relief in Nassau County, 1899–1999" (*Nassau County: From Rural Hinterland to Suburban Metropolis,* 2000).

Timothy J. Shannon is associate professor of history at Gettysburg College. He is author of *Indians and Colonists at the Crossroads of Empire: The Albany Congress of 1754* (2000).

Martha Dickinson Shattuck (PhD Boston Univ) is assistant editor to the New Netherland Project and is New Netherland and colonial editor of *The Encyclopedia of New York State.* She is author of *A Civil Society: Court and Community in Beverwijck, New Netherland* (forthcoming).

Jim Shaughnessy (PE) is a civil engineer alumni of Rensselaer Polytechnic Institute. He is a writer, historian, photographer, and author of *Delaware and Hudson* (1967) and *The Rutland Road* (1964).

Barbara Shay (PhD Hofstra Univ) is an educator and freelance educational consultant. She has 30 years experience in education and worked as a bureau chief in the NYS Education Department for 18 years, supervising and administering state and federal programs.

Kathryn T. Sheehan began working as an intern at the Rensselaer County Historical Society in 1987 while a history student at SUNY Albany. As registrar, volunteer coordinator, and local historian, she has provided information on Rensselaer County history and has presented her research on local television and on the History Channel, C-Span, and the Russian Network.

Martin Shefter is professor in the Government Department of Cornell Univ. Among his books are *Political Crisis/Fiscal Crisis: The Collapse and Revival of New York City* and *Capital of the American Century: The National and International Influence of New York City.*

Thomas J. Shelley (PhD Catholic Univ of America) is a priest of the Archdiocese of New York and associate professor of theology at Fordham Univ. His publications include *Dunwoodie: The History of St. Joseph's Seminary* (1993) and *The History of the Archdiocese of New York* (1999).

Doug Sherman is sports editor for the *Niagara Gazette.*

Sylvia Berry Shoebridge (MA Syracuse Univ) is Town of Pompey historian. She has done research in provincial museums in France and was a garment designer in New York City and London. She taught dress design and tailoring.

George H. Shriver (PhD Duke Univ) is professor emeritus of history at Georgia Southern Univ. His specialty is Western religious history with an emphasis on dissent and heresy. He is author of 10 books, chapters in books, and articles.

Stephanie Shultes (MA SUNY Albany) has been curator at the Iroquois Indian Museum, Howes Cave, since 1992.

John Shy (PhD Princeton Univ) is professor emeritus of history at the Univ of Michigan. He is a graduate of the US Military Academy and is author of *A People Numerous and Armed* (1990).

David B. Sicilia is associate professor of history at Univ of Maryland, College Park. He is coauthor and coeditor of six books on business and economic history including *Constructing Corporate America: History, Politics, Culture* (2003).

Clifford A. Siegfried (PhD Univ of California, Davis) was appointed assistant commissioner for museums and director of the NYS Museum in 1999. He has published his scientific research results in more than 100 articles, books, and reports and is a reviewer for the American Association of Museums, the National Science Foundation, and scholarly journals.

William H. Siener is a historian and museum curator. He is executive director of the Buffalo and Erie County Historical Society and Erie County historian.

Igor I. Sikorsky Jr (LLB Yale Univ) is founder and first chairman of the board of directors of the New England Air Museum and has written and lectured on aviation history. He has expertise in WWI aviation history, the amphibian era, and the pioneering of the helicopter as related to the career of Igor Sikorsky Sr.

Joel H. Silbey is President White Professor of History at Cornell Univ. He has written about 19th-century party politics, including *The American Political Nation, 1839–1893* (1991).

William H. Siles is associate professor in history at the Univ of Illinois at Springfield. He is author of *A Vision of Wealth: Speculators and Settlers in the Genesee Country* and other works on state frontier.

Deborah Anders Silverman (PhD) is a folklorist and author of *Polish-American Folklore* (2000). She serves as executive assistant to the provost at SUNY Buffalo.

Erin Melissa Silverman is an alumna of the Emma Willard School and undergraduate student at the Johns Hopkins Univ, Md.

Ron Simon has been curator of television at the Museum of Television and Radio since the early 1980s. Among the exhibitions he has curated are *Witness to History* and *Worlds without End: The Art and History of the Soap Opera.* Simon is associate professor at Columbia Univ and Hunter College, where he teaches courses in the history of the media.

William M. Simons is chair and professor of history at SUNY Oneonta. He edited *The Cooperstown Symposium on Baseball and American Culture* (2000, 2001). His work has been published in *Baseball History from Outside the Lines* (2001) and *Encyclopedia of Ethnic Sports in the United States* (2000).

Roberta L. Singer (PhD Indiana Univ) is director of music programs at City Lore: The New York Center for Urban Folk Culture in New York City. Her dissertation was on Latin popular music and identity in the city. She produced a documentary video about the Afro-Puerto Rican bomba and is coproducing a documentary on mambo to hip hop in the south Bronx.

Patricia Siska (PhD student Graduate Center, CUNY) is associate cataloger at the Frick Art Reference Library of the Frick Collection.

Douglas R. Skopp is SUNY Distinguished Teaching Professor of History, specializing in the history of Europe and of education. He is author of a pictorial history of SUNY Plattsburgh commemorating the college's first century.

Wanda Slawinska is editor of a biography of Dr. Francis E. Fronczak. She is also librarian and curator of the Fronczak Room of the E. H. Butler Library at SUNY Buffalo.

Robert A. Slayton is associate professor at Chapman Univ and author of *Back of the Yards* and *Empire Statesman.*

Myrna Sloam is archivist of the Bryant Library, Roslyn. She is editor of the second edition of *Roslyn Then and Now* and author of feature articles on the history of Roslyn for the *Bryant Library Newsletter.*

David C. Sloane is associate professor in the School of Policy, Planning, and Development at the Univ of Southern California. He is author of *The Last Great Necessity: Cemeteries in American History* (1991) and coauthor of *Medicine Moves to the Mall* (2002).

Peter Slocum is a writer and former journalist who served as senior staff adviser in the executive and legislative branches of state government and as a public policy advocate. He is coauthor of *From Rocky to Pataki: Character and Caricatures in New York Politics* (1998).

Charles R. Smith (PhD Cornell Univ) is a naturalist, educator, and conservationist employed by Cornell Univ as senior research associate for the Department of Natural Resources. He has more than 40 years of experience in teaching, research, and science-based conservation related to plants and terrestrial vertebrates of eastern North America.

Eve P. Smith is a social worker and social welfare historian. She is retired from the School of Social Work, Univ of Windsor, Ont. She edited *A History of Child Welfare* (1996) and is author of six articles on the history of child welfare in New York State.

Gerald R. Smith is Broome Co historian and oversees the Local History and Genealogy Center in the Broome County Public Library. He is author of over 200 articles and *The Valley of Opportunity: A Pictorial History of the Greater Binghamton Area.*

John Howard Smith (PhD candidate SUNY Albany) has presented conference papers that focus on the relationship between religion, loyalism, and neutrality during the American Revolution. He is author of " 'Sober Dissent' and 'Spirited Conduct': The Sandemanians and the American Revolution, 1765–1783" (*Historical Journal of Massachusetts,* 2000).

Robert C. Smith is assistant professor of sociology at Barnard College and associate editor of *Global Networks: A Journal of Transnational Affairs.* He is finishing a book manuscript, "Migration, Settlement, and Transnational Life," and has received grants from the National Science Foundation, the Spencer Foundation/National Academy of Education, and other organizations.

Edward J. Smits is historian of Nassau Co and leading Long Island preservationist. He was director of the Nassau Co Division of Museum Services and is planner of the Museums at Mitchel.

Kevin Smyth took a lifelong love of film and turned it into 20 years of experience behind the camera as a rigging technician on movies such as *Leaving Las Vegas* and *Kama Sutra.* He has worked on commercials, videos, and feature films in the US and Asia.

Stuart Smyth (PhD SUNY Albany) is professor at Mount Saint Mary College. He is author of *Definitions* and articles in the *Asia Journal of Theology: Syncretism and Rejection* and *Muscular Christianity.*

Dean R. Snow is an archaeologist who taught for 26 years at SUNY Albany, during which time he directed the multiyear Mohawk Valley Project. He is professor and head of the Department of Anthropology at Pennsylvania State Univ.

Bob Snyder has been a sports writer/columnist for Syracuse newspapers since 1965. A native of Albany and graduate of Syracuse Univ, he was the university's basketball beat writer from the mid-1960s to the 1980s. He covers the national and Big East basketball and football scene, and for 14 years he has cohosted *SU Overtime,* a basketball postgame TV show.

Robert W. Snyder is a historian interested in New York City. He is director of the journalism and media studies program at Rutgers Univ, Newark. He is also author of *The Voice of the City: Vaudeville and Popular Culture in New York* and *Transit Talk: New York's Bus and Subway Workers Tell Their Stories.*

Jonathan Soffer is assistant professor of history at Polytechnic Univ. He is author of *General Matthew B. Ridgway: From Progressivism to Reaganism, 1895–1993* (1998) and is working on a biography of Mayor Ed Koch.

Miriam Steinhardt Soffer is managing editor of the *New York State Library News.* She is a writer and was manag-ing editor of magazines and other publications for the NYS Health Department, Governor's Office, and NYS Museum.

Winton U. Solberg (PhD Harvard Univ) is professor emeritus of history at the Univ of Illinois. He has published in American intellectual and cultural history and is author of *Redeem the Time: The Puritan Sabbath in Early America.*

Geri Solomon (MA New York Univ) has been university archivist/conservator at Hofstra Univ since 1988 and is interim director of the Long Island Studies Institute. She is former president of the Long Island Archives Conference (1990–95) and chair of the Conservation/Preservation Committee of the Long Island Libraries Resource Council.

Elisabeth Sommer (PhD Univ of Virginia) is author of *Serving Two Masters: Moravian Brethren in Germany and North Carolina, 1727–1801* (2000). She is working on her certification in museum studies/public history at the Univ of North Carolina, Greensboro.

Dorothy Southard is Town of Ira historian.

Daniel Soyer teaches history at Fordham Univ. He is a collector of political buttons.

Mark G. Spencer is a PhD candidate in the Department of History at the Univ of Western Ontario.

Jane Shadel Spillman is deputy director for collections of the Corning Museum of Glass and in her 35-year career has published and lectured on the history of American glass. She is author of *The American Cut Glass Industry: T. G. Hawkes and His Competitors* (1996).

Robert J. Spitzer is Distinguished Service Professor of Political Science at SUNY Cortland and is author or editor of 10 books, including *President and Congress* (1993) and *The Politics of Gun Control* (1998).

Hannah M. Springer (AAS Fashion Institute of Technology) is administrative assistant at *The Encyclopedia of New York State* and is pursuing her bachelor's degree in social work at SUNY Albany. She also custom-designs wedding gowns.

Martin Stack (PhD Univ of Notre Dame) is author of "Local and Regional Breweries in America's Brewing Industry, 1865 to 1920" (*Business History Review,* 2000). He is writing an article on pre-Prohibition beer quality and an essay on the introduction and spread of pasteurization in the US. He is assistant professor of economics at Saint Mary College, Kans.

Martin Stahl (MA Columbia Univ) has been lecturer/tutor/mentor in the Business, Management, and Economics Group at Empire State College since 1995. He has written entries for the *Scribner Encyclopedia of American Lives.*

Mary Jane Stahley is Village of Bemus Point historian.

Cheryl Staines is Town of Albion historian.

Howard R. Stanger is associate professor in the Department of Management and Marketing at Canisius College. He has published articles on the Larkin Co and newspaper industry labor relations.

Darwin Stapleton is director of the Rockefeller Archive Center, Sleepy Hollow. His is author or editor of 7 books and 40 articles on the history of technology and science.

Myra Starr (MS Hunter College, CUNY) is South Nyack historian and member of the administrative staff of Nyack Library. She is on the board of trustees of the Historical Society of the Nyack's Edward Hopper House Art Center, Friends of the Library, and she volunteers in the library's local history room.

Ryan Staude (PhD student SUNY Albany) studies colonial and early American history.

John G. Staudt is instructor of American history at Hofstra Univ. He is author of several reviews and articles on Long Island and early American history.

Edith J. Steblecki is curator at the Paul Revere Memorial Association, Boston. She is author of *Paul Revere and Freemasonry* (1985).

David Warren Steel is associate professor of music and southern studies at the Univ of Mississippi. He has published works on early American music, including editions of the music of Stephen Jenks and Daniel Belknap.

Ian K. Steele, whose books include *Betrayals* (1990) and *Warpaths* (1994), is professor of history at the Univ of Western Ontario.

Ivan D. Steen is associate professor of history at SUNY Albany, where he directs the oral history program. He has interviewed individuals who were important in Albany politics from the 1930s to the 1980s. He has written and lectured about Erastus Corning 2d.

Jennifer Steenshorne (PhD candidate Univ of California Irvine) specializes in state cultural and political history. She works at La Guardia College Archives.

Francis B. Stein is Village of Buchanan historian. She served as elementary school president of the Hendrick Hudson School District for 24 years.

Geoffrey N. Stein has been history curator at the NYS Museum since 1967. He is curator of *The Great New York Motorcycle Show,* a loan exhibit of 47 New York–built motorcycles, and author of *The Motorcycle Industry in New York State: A Concise Encyclopedia of Inventors, Builders, and Manufacturers* (2001).

Stephen J. Stein is Chancellor's Professor of Religious Studies and adjunct professor of history at Indiana Univ. His research is on 18th-century America and alternative religious communities. He is author of *The Shaker Experience in America: A History of the United Society of Believers* (1992) and editor of volumes in *The Works of Jonathan Edwards.*

Henry Steiner is Village of Sleepy Hollow historian. He is author of *The Place Names of Historic Sleepy Hollow and Tarrytown* (1998).

Michael J. Stenzel (MPA SUNY Brockport) is federal technician with the Division of Military and Naval Affairs and deputy chief of staff for the New York Guard. He spent 24 years with the NYS Office of General Services Design and Construction Group and 31 years in NYARNG. He has developed and maintains web pages on state forts for the DMNA web site and a USS *Slater* web site.

William M. Sternberg (BS Syracuse Univ) writes and consults on television as a mass medium in the 500 Channel Universe. He formerly worked at American Home Products, Ogilvy and Mather, and ABC.

Jon Sterngass is visiting assistant professor at Union College and author of *First Resorts: Pursuing Pleasure at Saratoga Springs, Newport, and Coney Island* (2001).

Robert H. Stockman (ThD Harvard Univ) is author of *The Bahá'í Faith in America* (1985, 1995) and *Thornton Chase: A Biography of the First American Bahá'í* (2000), as well as articles. He is director of the Institute for Bahá'í Studies, Wilmette, Ill, and instructor in religious studies at DePaul Univ.

Gaynell Stone (PhD SUNY Stony Brook) is museum director of the Suffolk County Archaeological Association. She has published articles about American Indians on Long Island in *Material Culture* (1991) and *Between Ocean and Empire: An Illustrated History of Long Island* (1985, 2000).

Jeffrey M. Stonecash is professor of political science at the Maxwell School, Syracuse Univ. He is author of *Class and Party in American Politics* (2000) and *Diverging Parties* (2002) and is editor of *Governing New York State,* 4th ed. (2001).

Mark Storey teaches philosophy at Bellevue Community College, Wash. He is editor at large for *Nude and Natural* magazine and is on the boards of Naturist Action Committee and Naturist Education Foundation.

Dale C. Storms is Chenango Co historian.

Sue Stoyell is Town of Niles historian.

Jean Strawser is Town of Sheridan historian.

Dan Streever is deputy managing editor of *The Encyclopedia of New York State.*

Douglas M. Strong is professor of the history of Christianity at Wesley Theological Seminary, Washington, DC. He is author of *Perfectionist Politics: Abolitionism and the Religious Tensions of American Democracy* (1999).

John A. Strong is professor emeritus at the Southampton College of Long Island Univ. He is author of *The Algonquian Peoples of Long Island from Earliest Times to 1700* (1997) and *"We Are Still Here!" The Algonquian Peoples of Long Island Today* (1998).

Harvey Strum is professor of history and political science at Sage Colleges.

Roger W. Stump is professor of geography and religious studies at SUNY Albany. He is the author of *Boundaries of Faith: Geographical Perspectives on Religious Fundamentalism* (2000).

R. Jake Sudderth (MA Univ of Idaho) has published articles addressing American business and urban history. He is a graduate student at Columbia Univ and coauthor of *The St. Ann's Kid: A Seattle Memoir* (2001).

Larry E. Sullivan (PhD Johns Hopkins Univ) is chief librarian of the John Jay College of Criminal Justice and professor of Criminal Justice in the Graduate School and Univ Center, CUNY. He is author or editor of books and articles, including *Bandits and Bibles: Convict Literature in 19th-Century America* (2003) and *The Prison Reform Movement: Forlorn Hope* (1990, 2002).

Timothy Sullivan is a PhD student in American history at the Univ of Maryland, College Park. His dissertation is entitled "Crashing the Party: The New York State Conservative and Republican Parties, 1962–1980."

Amy Surak is archivist for Manhattan College and De La Salle Christian Brothers of the New York and Long Island–New England Districts. She worked at the New York Public Library and New York Univ.

John Swantek (MA Norwich Univ) is public affairs officer of Watervliet Arsenal. He also serves as director/curator of the Museum of the Big Guns. He is former reporter and editor with the *Troy Record.*

Hallie A. Sweeting is Town of Sterling historian.

Margaret Sweetman is Village of Cato historian.

Robert F. Swift (PhD Eastman School of Music) is professor of music and chair of the Music, Theatre, and Dance Department at Plymouth State College of the Univ System of New Hampshire. He is a composer, clinician, adjudicator, and choral conductor whose choirs have toured several countries.

Richard Sylla is professor of economic and financial history at the Stern School of Business, New York Univ. He is coauthor of *A History of Interest Rates* (3d ed. rev, 1996).

Martha Symes is an archaeologist and senior grants officer at Hartwick College. She has taught at Western Washington Univ and Jamestown Community College and is former administrative director of the Seneca-Iroquois National Museum and director of the Salamanca Rail Museum.

Sallie S. Sypher (PhD Cornell Univ) is a graduate of Mount Holyoke College. She has been a college teacher, town supervisor, and Putnam Co historian.

T

Harold Takooshian (PhD CUNY) has been on the faculty of Fordham Univ, where he is director of the Fordham Institute. His writings on the Armenian community include the chapter on Armenian Americans for the *Gale Encyclopedia of Multicultural America* (1995).

David Tatham is professor of fine arts at Syracuse Univ and author of six books and articles concerning 19th- and 20th-century American art.

Devon Taylor is Village of Mayville historian.

Parry D. Teasdale is editor of the *Independent,* a twice-weekly newspaper serving Columbia and Rensselaer Cos. He is also author of two books on the video movement and former consultant to the Federal Communications Commission.

Harvey M. Teres is associate professor of English at Syracuse Univ. He is author of *Renewing the Left: Politics, Imagination, and the New York Intellectuals* (1996) and *American Beauty: Aesthetics and Ordinary Life* (forthcoming). He has written articles on 20th-century American literature and culture.

Jack E. Termine is archivist at SUNY Downstate Medical Center and head of the Special Collections and Archives Department of the Medical Research Library of Brooklyn. He is author of *SUNY Downstate Medical Center,* a photographic history in Arcadia's College History series.

Philip G. Terrie is professor of American culture studies at Bowling Green State Univ. A former assistant curator at the Adirondack Museum, he is author of books and articles on Adirondack history, including *Contested Terrain: A New History of Nature and People in the Adirondacks* (1997).

Alex Thomas is coordinator of the Center for Social Science Research and chair of the Department of Sociology at SUNY Oneonta. He is author of articles and *In Gotham's Shadow: Globalization and Community Change in Central New York* (2003), a study of economic and social change in the Utica and Cooperstown areas.

Laura Dickstein Thompson (EdD) is director of education and public programs at the Schenectady Museum. Her dissertation was on museum mission statements and their impact on interpretive practices and includes a chapter on the history and role of museums in New York City.

Esther Thornton is Town of Locke historian.

Timothy N. Thurber is professor of history at SUNY Oswego and author of *The Politics of Equality: Hubert Humphrey and the African American Freedom Struggle* (1998).

Joseph S. Tiedemann is professor of history at Loyola Marymount Univ, Los Angeles, and author of *Reluctant Revolutionaries: New York City and the Road to Independence* (1997).

Karim M. Tiro is assistant professor of history at Xavier Univ. His essays on native peoples of the Northeast have appeared in *American Quarterly, New York History,* and *Explorations in Early American Culture.*

Amy Ruth Tobol (Esq) is assistant professor at SUNY Empire State College. She teaches legal studies, sociology, and criminal justice.

Andrew D. Todd is a graduate student of history at West Virginia Univ. He has degrees in engineering and anthropology and specializes in the history of computers. He has also done research in artificial intelligence and in the anthropology of war.

Kathryn Tomasek teaches at Wheaton College, Mass. She has published articles on women and utopia in 19th-century America, and she is at work on a study of women, Fourierism, and the public sphere.

Michael A. Tomlan is associate professor and director of the graduate program in historic preservation planning in the College of Architecture, Art, and Planning at Cornell Univ. He is author of two books and editor of five others, and has contributed to the *Association for Preservation Technology Bulletin* and other journals.

Silvio Torres-Saillant (PhD New York Univ) is associate professor of English and director of the Latino–Latin American Studies Program at Syracuse Univ. He is coauthor of *The Dominican-American* (1998).

Veronica F. Towers is humanities editor for *The Encyclopedia Americana.*

Georgianna Tracy is Town of Sempronius historian.

Hans L. Trefousse is Distinguished Professor of History at Brooklyn College and the Graduate Center, CUNY. He is author of biographies of radical Republicans and Andrew Johnson and works on Abraham Lincoln and Reconstruction.

Paul Trela (DH student SUNY Albany) is student adviser and instructor at the Center for Distance Learning at Empire State College.

James W. Trent Jr is professor and director of the Master of Social Work Program at Southern Illinois Univ, Edwardsville. He is author of *Inventing the Feeble Mind: A History of Mental Retardation in the United States* (1994).

Wendell Tripp was editor of *New York History* and director of publications at the NYS Historical Association from 1964 to 2000. He was also mayor of Cooperstown from 1996 to 2002.

Frances Trix (PhD) is a linguistic anthropologist specializing in discourse analysis of interactions in Albanian, Turkish, Arabic, and English. She is author of *Spiritual Discourse: Learning with an Islamic Master* (1993), which is based on 20 years of study with an Albanian Bektashi Baba. She is associate professor of anthropology at Wayne State Univ.

Sheila Tucker is Town of Fleming historian.

Beverly C. Tyler is education chair of the Three Village Historical Society. He is author of *Discover Setauket: Brookhaven's Original Settlement* (2000) and *Village Green Program: A Teacher's Guide* (2002).

U

Lloyd Ultan is professor of history at Fairleigh Dickinson Univ and has been Bronx Borough historian since 1996. He has written or coauthored eight books, including *Bronx Accent: A Literary and Pictorial History of the Borough* (2000) and *The Birth of the Bronx, 1609–1900* (2000).

Brad L. Utter (MA SUNY Albany) is director of the Waterford Historical Museum and Cultural Center.

V

Carolyn Vacca is Monroe Co historian and a published author. She is visiting assistant professor at St. John Fisher College and has taught at SUNY Brockport.

Nicholas J. Vagianelis (MPA Rockefeller College of Public Affairs) is responsible for the administration of the Statewide Classification and Compensation Program.

Erik van den Berg teaches American history and American studies in the Department of History at Utrecht Univ, Netherlands. He is completing his PhD dissertation on the political career of Franklin D. Roosevelt Jr.

Jos van der Linde (PhD candidate Univ of Leiden, Netherlands) is administrative director at the New England Conservatory of Music, Boston.

John VanderLippe is associate professor of history at SUNY New Paltz. He is author of works on modern Turkish history and Turkish-American relations.

Marilyn J. Van Dyke (PhD) is an educator, author, and historical and genealogical researcher. She is Town of Queensbury historian and executive director of the Warren County Historical Society.

Cynthia Van Ness is a writer, librarian, and web master in Buffalo. She is author of *Victorian Buffalo: Images from the Buffalo and Erie County Public Library* (1999).

Mark C. Van Sluyters has been a teacher and Yorker adviser for 30 years at Hoosic Valley Central School, Schaghticoke. He is author and editor of *Present Meets Past* (1988) and education consultant to the NYS Education Department, museums, and school districts.

Abigail A. Van Slyck is Dayton Associate Professor of Architectural History at Connecticut College. She is author of *Free to All: Carnegie Libraries and American Culture, 1890–1920* (1995).

William E. Van Vugt is professor of history at Calvin College, Mich. His publications include *Britain to America: The Mid-19th-Century Immigrants to the United States* (1999) and *Race and Reconciliation in South Africa: A Multicultural Dialogue in Comparative Perspective* (2000).

Steven Béla Várdy (PhD) is McAnulty Distinguished Professor of European History at Duquesne Univ. He is author or coauthor of 17 books and nearly 500 articles, essays, and reviews. His works include *Historical Dictionary of Hungary* (1997) and *Hungarian-Language Hungarians in the New World* (2000; English, 2003).

Victor A. Varis, a Lithuanian American, is an international AIDS/HIV education consultant and freelance writer. He has traveled extensively in eastern Europe.

Ren Vasiliev (PhD) is chair of the Geography Department at SUNY Geneseo. She is author of *From Abbotts to Zurich: New York State Placenames* (2004).

Jeanne Versweyveld is a lifelong resident of Orange Co. She is Town of Blooming Grove historian.

Heidi Solberg Viar (MS Univ of Wisconsin, River Falls) is a PhD candidate in history at Western Michigan Univ. Her research interests include sport in culture, cross-cultural political relations in Canada, and linguistic and cultural preservation.

Milton Vickerman is associate professor of sociology at the Univ of Virginia. He researches immigration and issues pertaining to race. He has conducted fieldwork among West Indian immigrants in New York City and among Blacks in Prince William Co, Va. He has written *Crosscurrents: West Indian Immigrants and Race* (1999) and chapters and articles on West Indian immigrants in the US.

Jeffrey S. Victor (PhD SUNY Buffalo) is professor of sociology at Jamestown Community College. He received the H. L. Mencken Award from the Free Press Association for the best book of 1994.

Jacqueline Villarrubia-Mendoza (PhD student SUNY Albany) is researching the role of race and class in the residential segregation of neighborhoods in Puerto Rico. She is assistant editor of *The Encyclopedia of New York State.*

Laura Viscome is a retired reporter/photographer. She writes a weekly column and freelance articles. She served as board member and editor of the US Bobsled and Skeleton Federation for four years.

Dan Vogel (BA California State Univ, Long Beach) is an independent researcher whose first volume of *Early Mormon Documents* (1996) received the Mormon History Association's Steven F. Christensen Award for Best Documentary. He is working on a biography of Joseph Smith's early life and teachings.

David William Voorhees is director of the Papers of Jacob Leisler Project at New York Univ and editor of *de Halve Maen,* the journal of the Holland Society of New York. He is translator of the Flatbush Church Records (1999).

George Vrtis is a PhD candidate and lecturer in the Department of History at Georgetown Univ.

W

Heather A. Wade (MA George Mason Univ) is an archivist.

Diana S. Waite is president and founder of Mount Ida Press, Albany, which conducts historical research, writing, editing, and publication projects. She served as executive director of the Preservation League of New York State for 10 years and since 1991 has been editor of the *APT Bulletin: The Journal of Preservation Technology.*

John G. Waite, FAIA, is senior principal of John G. Waite Associates, Architects, PLLC of Albany and New York City, a nationally recognized practice that has been responsible for the restoration of many significant buildings in the US. He has written over 50 books and articles, including *Metals in America's Historic Buildings: Uses and Preservation Treatments.*

Timothy Walch is director of the Herbert Hoover Presidential Library. He is associate editor of the *US Catholic Historian* and author of *Parish School: American Catholic*

Parochial Education from Colonial Times to the Present (1996).

John Waldman is senior scientist with the Hudson River Foundation for Science and Environmental Research, New York City. He is author of *The Dance of the Flying Gurnards: America's Coastal Curiosities and Beachside Wonders* (2002).

Daniel J. Walkowitz is professor of history at New York Univ, where he directs the Metropolitan Studies Program. He is author of *Working with Class: Social Workers and the Politics of Middle-Class Identity* (1999).

Richard C. Wandel (MA New York Univ) is founding archivist/historian of the Lesbian, Gay, Bisexual and Transgender Community Center National History Archive in New York City.

Xinyang Wang (PhD Yale Univ) is assistant professor in the Division of Humanities at the Hong Kong Univ of Science and Technology. He is author of *Surviving the City: The Chinese Immigrant Experience in New York, 1890–1970* (2001) and articles in *New York History, Labor History* and other publications.

Robert B. Ward is director of research for the Public Policy Institute and author of *New York State Government: What It Does, How It Works* (2002).

Eric K. Washington is a tour guide in New York City. He is author of *Manhattanville: Old Heart of West Harlem* (2002).

Margaret Washington is professor of history at Cornell Univ. She has published and edited an annotated version of the *Narrative of Sojourner Truth* and is writing a biography entitled *Sojourner Truth: Her Life and Times* (forthcoming).

Zenon V. Wasyliw (PhD SUNY Binghamton) has been associate professor of history at Ithaca College since 1989.

Bryan Waterman (PhD Boston Univ) is working on a book about the Friendly Club and New York City in the 1790s.

Deborah Dependahl Waters is curator of decorative arts and manuscripts, and acting deputy director and chief curator, Division of Collections and Exhibitions at the Museum of the City of New York. She is editor of *Elegant Plate: Three Centuries of Precious Metals in New York City* (2000) and contributor of entries to *Albany Institute of History and Art: 200 Years of Collecting* (1998).

Gardner Watts is Village of Suffern historian.

Timothy P. Weber (PhD Univ of Chicago) is president of the Memphis Theological Seminary. He also taught the history of Christianity at Denver Seminary and Southern Baptist Theological Seminary and was dean at Northern Baptist Theological Seminary, Ill.

Harold S. Wechsler (PhD Columbia Univ) is professor at the Margaret S. Warner Graduate School of Education and Human Development, Univ of Rochester. He is author of *The Qualified Student: A History of Selective College Admission in America, 1870–1970* (1977) and coauthor of *Jewish Learning in American Universities: The First Century* (1994).

Robert Wechsler (PhD Columbia Univ) is director of education for the Transport Workers Union of America, AFL-CIO. He is past president of the New York Labor History Association and serves on the boards of Robert F. Wagner Labor Archives and the NYC Transit Museum.

Bonita L. Weddle (MA Kent State Univ) is archives and records management specialist I at the NYS Archives. She is assistant editor for *The Encyclopedia of New York State.*

Nancy Weekly is head of collections and the Charles Cary Rumsey Curator of the Burchfield-Penney Art Center, Buffalo State College. Previously she directed the art gallery at Fredonia State College, designed exhibits for SUNY Buffalo's Poetry/Rare Books Collection, and was an adjunct lecturer at SUNY Buffalo State and SUNY Buffalo.

Veronica A. Weigand holds degrees in fisheries and wildlife technology and environmental studies. She is employed with Community Planning and Environmental Associates and teaches at SUNY Cobleskill. Publications include an article in *Sialia* and poetry writings in the literary magazine *Many Waters.*

Marilyn E. Weigold is professor of history at Pace Univ. She is author of *Silent Builder: Emily Warren Roebling and the Brooklyn Bridge* (1984) and *Opportunitas* (1991).

Paul O. Weinbaum is the National Park Service's program lead for history in its Northeast Region. He is author of *Statue of Liberty: Heritage of America* (1979).

Jane Weiss (PhD CUNY) is assistant professor at SUNY Old Westbury. She is editing Susan Warner's journals for publication and writing her biography.

Luise Weiss is coordinator of adult reference at the Middle Country Public Library, Centereach, and adjunct professor at the Palmer School of Library and Information Science. She is author of *Reflections on 1788: Long Island and the Constitution* and *The Hamlet of Selden.* She has graduate degrees from SUNY Stony Brook and Long Island Univ/C. W. Post.

Vicki Weiss is senior librarian at the NYS Library and a weekend/lunchtime historian. She serves as president of the Friends of the NYS Newspaper Project.

Patrick Weissend (BA SUNY Brockport) started at the Holland Land Office Museum in 1998 and became director in 2001.

Richard F. Welch (PhD SUNY Stony Brook) is author of *Memento Mori: The Gravestones of Early Long Island* (1983) and *An Island's Trade: 19th-Century Shipbuilding of Long Island* (1993). He has been editor of *Long Island Forum* since 1991.

Judith Wellman is professor emerita from SUNY Oswego and author of books and articles relating to 19th-century New York State, women's rights, and abolitionism.

David I. Wells retired in 1995 as associate director of the Political Department of the International Ladies' Garment Workers' Union. He has written and lectured on apportionment and districting and was successful plaintiff in *Wells v Rockefeller.* He was consultant in *WMCA v Lomenzo* and served as member of the 1991 NYC Districting Commission.

Caroline M. Welsh is chief curator, curator of art, and director of operations at the Adirondack Museum, Blue Mountain Lake. She lectures, publishes, and exhibits on Adirondack art and history. She is coauthor of *The View from Asgaard: Rockwell Kent's Adirondack Legacy* (2000) and *In Search of a National Landscape: William Trost Richards in the Adirondacks* (2002).

Simon R. E. Werrett is postdoctoral research fellow at the Max Planck Institute for the History of Science, Berlin, and the Getty Center, Los Angeles. He is writing a book on the history of pyrotechnics and the sciences since the Renaissance.

Jack Westbrook (PhD) is principal consultant with Brookline Technologies of Ballston Spa. He is a metallurgist with interests in the history of science and technology. He has published more than 15 papers in addition to a bibliography in materials research and information technology.

Nicholas Westbrook has been director of Fort Ticonderoga since 1989.

Carl A. Westerdahl is principal of Unconventional Wisdom. He is coauthor of histories of Rensselaer Polytechnic Institute and the Albany Academy and has researched the lives of over 100 accomplished graduates. He is especially interested in the life and times of Stephen Van Rensselaer III.

Chad Wheaton is a PhD candidate in history at Syracuse Univ.

Barbara G. Wheeler is president of Auburn Theological Seminary and director of the Auburn Center for the Study of Theological Education.

Walter Richard Wheeler is a practicing architect and architectural historian. He has coauthored *In a Neat, Plain, Modern Stile: The Architecture of Philip Hooker and His Contemporaries, 1796–1836* (1993) and *The Marble House in Second Street* (2000).

W. Richard Whitaker (PhD) is professor of journalism and broadcasting at SUNY Buffalo State.

Gordon S. White Jr is former sports reporter for the *New York Times.* He was elected to the Basketball Writers Association Hall of Fame in 1992. He is author of *Tom Cahill: A Man for the Corps.*

John White is a retired librarian who worked for the NYS Library and was library director at Hudson Valley Community College.

Carol Whittaker is an employee of the NYS Health Department and faculty member of the Graduate School of Public Health, SUNY Albany.

Randy William Widdis (PhD Queen's Univ) is full professor at the Univ of Regina. He is author of over 40 publications, including *With Scarcely a Ripple: Anglo-Canadian Migration into the United States and Western Canada, 1880–1920* (1998).

William M. Wiecek is Congdon Professor of Law and professor of history at Syracuse Univ. He is editor of *Oxford Companion to the Supreme Court of the United States.*

Tim Wiles is director of research at the National Baseball Hall of Fame Library. He is coeditor of *Line Drives: 100 Contemporary Baseball Poems* (2002) and articles.

Mark N. Wilhelm is associate director of the Auburn Center for the Study of Theological Education at Auburn Theological Seminary.

Debra A. Willett is associate director of the Long Island Studies Institute at Hofstra Univ.

Emily Williams is coauthor of *Stagecoach Country, Cherry Valley Country,* and *Canal Country,* as well as magazine articles.

Geoffrey P. Williams (MLS Univ of Illinois, Urbana-Champaign) is university archivist at SUNY Albany and chair of the NYS Historical Records Advisory Board.

Lillian S. Williams (PhD) is Chair of the African American Studies Department at SUNY Buffalo. She is author of *Strangers in the Land of Paradise: The Creation of an African American Urban Community, Buffalo, New York, 1900–1940* (1999) and *A Bridge to the Future: The History of Diversity in Girl Scouting* (1996).

Reba White Williams (PhD) writes about early 20th-century New York State.

Robert Williams is Town of Montgomery historian.

Alan Scot Willis (PhD Syracuse Univ) is assistant professor of history at Northern Michigan Univ. He has published articles on racism and religion in the *Georgia Historical Quarterly* and *Proteus.* His forthcoming publications include essays on Malcolm X for *The Encyclopedia of Malcolm X.*

Annys Wilson graduated from Bard College in 1948. She served as director of publications and public relations, 1967–75, and as registrar, 1975–93. She was a college archivist and historian.

Audrey M. Wilson (PhD) is assistant professor of public relations and marketing communications at Indiana Univ School of Journalism.

William Wilson taught in the Division of Languages and Literatures of Bard College and was editor of the *Hudson Valley Regional Review.*

Richard L. Wing (PhD SUNY Buffalo) is professor emeritus at Houghton College, where he spent 20 years as an administrator and teacher of writing. He is a 21-year US Air Force veteran and has visited over 40 countries and logged over 6,500 flying hours.

Richard A. Winsche is retired historian for the Nassau County Museum System. He is author of the *History of Nassau County Community Place-Names* (1999).

Diane Winston is program officer at Pew Charitable Trusts. She is author of *Red-Hot and Righteous: The Urban Religion of the Salvation Army.*

Peter A. Wisbey is executive director of the Seward House in Auburn.

George Wise (PhD Boston Univ) is administrator of the Dudley Observatory. He served as communications specialist for the GE Research and Development Center, Schenectady, where he published *Willis Whitney, General Electric, and the Origins of US Industrial Research* (1985) and articles on the history of science and technology.

Laura Wittern-Keller (MA Pennsylvania State Univ) is a PhD candidate in American history at SUNY Albany.

Dave Wohlhueter, a graduate of Ithaca College, worked as sports information director at Bucknell Univ and Cornell Univ for 33 years before going into semiretirement in 1998. He is treasurer and member of the College Sports Information Directors of America, as well as Ithaca College and Cornell Halls of Fame.

Richard Wojtowicz (MS Univ of Illinois, Urbana-Champaign) is reference librarian at Montana State Univ Library.

Eric Wolf (PhD Harvard Univ) has worked as an architectural historian, archivist, and librarian.

William E. Worthington Jr specializes in the history of mechanical and civil engineering at the National Museum of American History, Smithsonian Institution. He is author of articles on the history of technology.

Peter J. Wosh (PhD) is director of the archives program in the History Department at New York Univ. He is author of *Protestants at Play: Religion, Recreation, and Resorts in Modern America* (forthcoming) and *Spreading the Word: The Bible Business in 19th-Century America* (1994).

Glenn Wright (PhD Univ of Michigan) is assistant editor

with *The Encyclopedia of New York State.* He has taught at the Univ of Michigan and the Univ at Albany and has published articles in *Modern Philology, English Studies,* and *Genre.*

Jerry Wright is retired from Corning, Inc, where he was a consumer-product designer. He is co-chair of Steuben Co's US Bicentennial Project.

Jill Wright (MA, SUNY Oneonta) is curator of the Whaling Museum at Cold Spring Harbor.

Virginia L. Wright, a reference librarian, is retired from the Rakow Library of the Corning Museum of Glass.

Roy A. Wright-Tekastiaks (PhD candidate) has taught linguistics, anthropology, and Native American Indian studies at McGill, Trent, and Cornell Univs, and is semiretired from Marlboro College. He was etymologist for the *American Heritage Dictionary* (1969) and author of articles and contributions in linguistics and ethnohistory and a monograph on the Erie Indians (1974).

Roger Wunderlich was research associate professor of history at SUNY Stony Brook, where he taught Long Island history. He was founder and editor of the *Long Island Historical Journal* and author of *Low Living and High Thinking at Modern Times, New York* (1992).

Y

Edward Yadzinski (Master of Music Eastman School of Music) was clarinetist in the Buffalo Philharmonic Orchestra, 1963–90, and is its program annotator and historian. Since 1964 he has served on the performance faculty at SUNY Buffalo. He is a composer and arranger whose music is published by Alphonse Leduc, Paris.

Richard Yakman was appointed town historian of North Salem in 1994.

Rebecca Yamin (PhD New York Univ) is principal archaeologist/project manager with John Milner Associates, Philadelphia. She was principal investigator for the analysis of material from the Five Points site in Lower Manhattan. She is coeditor of *Landscape Archaeology: Reading and Interpreting the American Historical Landscape* and author of technical papers.

Allan E. Young is professor of finance and chair of the Department of Finance in the School of Management at Syracuse Univ and senior researcher in the Michael J. Falcone Center for Entrepreneurship. He is author or coauthor of 7 books and 80 articles and chapters in academic and professional publications.

Andrew P. Yox is professor of history at Northeast Texas Community College. He has published articles on Buffalo, German Americans, and art in the US.

Charles Yrigoyen Jr is general secretary of the General Commission on Archives and History of the United Methodist Church and editor of *Methodist History.* He is affiliate professor of church history at Drew Univ and adjunct professor at Moravian Theological Seminary, Philadelphia Lutheran Theological Seminary, and Union Theological Seminary.

Z

Gerald Zahavi (PhD) is associate professor of history at SUNY Albany. He is author of *Embers on the Land: Studies in the Local and Regional History of Labor and US Communism, 1918–1955* (forthcoming) and *Workers, Managers, and Welfare Capitalism: The Shoemakers and Tanners of Endicott Johnson, 1890–1950* (1988).

Joseph W. Zarzynski is underwater archaeologist with Bateaux Below, Inc. He is author of *Monster Wrecks of Loch Ness and Lake Champlain* (1986) and coauthor of *The Radeau Land Tortoise: North America's Oldest Intact Warship* (1993).

Laura Zelasnic is project cataloger with the NYS Newspaper Project.

Martin Fedor Ziac is a social studies teacher at Scotia-Glenville High School.

Patrick Ziegler (PhD student SUNY Albany) specializes in US foreign policy.

Joseph F. Zimmerman is professor of political science at SUNY Albany. He is author of more than 20 books including *The Government and Politics of New York State* (1981).

Karl Zimmermann is author of books and articles about railroads.

Ernest Zocchi owned and operated two businesses in Tuckahoe until his retirement in 2000. He is an unofficial village historian who has pictorially documented the past 50 years.

John Zogby is president of Zogby International and author of *Arab America Today* (1990).

Zion Zohar is professor at the Religious Studies Department of Florida International Univ. He is associate director of Institute for Judaic and Near Eastern Studies, Sephardic/Oriental Studies Program. He is author of *Song of My People* (1994).

Jeff Zuckerman serves on the Tuckahoe Village Planning Board. He teaches high school in a neighboring village.

Illustration Credits

A

Abbott, Berenice: Museum of the City of New York. abolitionism: Madison County Historical Society. Adirondack guideboat: New York State Library, Maitland DeSormo and North Country Books. Adirondack guides: Sterling and Francine Clark Art Institute. Adirondack lean-to: New York State Library, Maitland DeSormo and North Country Books. Adirondacks: New York State Archives; New York State Library, Maitland DeSormo and North Country Books; New York State Library. African Americans: New-York Historical Society; New York State Historical Association; New-York Historical Society; New York State Historical Association. agriculture: The Post-Standard and the Onondaga Historical Association; New York State Historical Association. airports: The Post-Standard and the Onondaga Historical Association. Albany: Albany Institute of History and Art. Albany County: New York State Archives. Albany Medical Center: New York State Archives. Allen, Ethan: New York State Library. American Revolution: Military History: Library of Congress; Library of Congress. Ames, Ezra: Albany Institute of History and Art. Amsterdam: New York State Archives. ancient life: New York State Museum. Anthony, Susan B.: New York State Library. antirent movement: Albany Institute of History and Art. Ararat: Buffalo and Erie County Historical Society. architects and architecture, Adirondacks and North Country: New York State Library, Maitland DeSormo and North Country Books. architects and architecture, Albany and Capital District: Albany Institute of History and Art. architects and architecture, Long Island: photograph by Robert L. Harrison, Hofstra University Archives. architects and architecture, Mid-Hudson: Metropolitan Museum of Art. architects and architecture, Mohawk Valley: New York State Historical Association. architects and architecture, Saratoga County: New York State Library. architects and architecture, Syracuse and Central New York: Onondaga Historical Association. art, Albany and the Capital District: Albany Institute of History and Art. art, Buffalo and the Niagara Frontier: New York State Library. art, New York City area: New York State Department of Economic Development. art, Syracuse, Ithaca, Utica, and Central New York: Onondaga Historical Association. art museums, collecting, and patronage: New York State Historical Association. Athens: New York State Historical Association. Auburn: New York State Department of Economic Development. automobile racing: New York State Department of Economic Development. aviation: Buffalo and Erie County Historical Society.

B

baking industry: The Post-Standard and the Onondaga Historical Association. Ball, Lucille: The Post-Journal of Jamestown. baseball: National Baseball Hall of Fame and Museum; Vassar College Archives. Bausch and Lomb: Rochester City Hall Photo Lab and Rochester Online. bear, black: New York State Museum. beaver: New York State Museum. beer and brewing: Albany Institute of History and Art. Binghamton: Broome County Historical Society. bird decoy art: New York State Historical Association. birds: New York State Archives. birth control: Library of Congress. blackouts: Reuters NewMedia, Inc./Corbis. blizzard of 1888: Albany Institute of History and Art. botanical gardens: New York State Department of Economic Development. Brant, Joseph: New York State Historical Association. brasher doubloon: Smithsonian Institution, NNC, Douglas Mudd. brick industry: Manuscripts and Special Collections of the New York State Library. bridges and tunnels: Museum of the City of New York. Bronx: New York State Library. Bronx Zoo: New York State Department of Economic Development. Brooklyn: New-York Historical Society; Museum of the City of New York. Broome County: Broome County Historical Society. Brown, Jim: Syracuse University Archives. Buffalo: Buffalo and Erie County Historical Society; Buffalo and Erie County Historical Society. Burned-over District: New York State Library.

C

Canada: New York State Library. Canal Board: Canal Society of New York State and New York State Library. canals: New York State Museum. capital punishment: New York State Archives. Cardiff Giant: New York State Historical Association. carnivores: WCS/NYSM Adirondack Carnivore Project. carousels: Museum of the City of New York. Carrier Dome: SUA. cartography and mapping: Library of Congress; Library of Congress; New York State Library; New York State Library; New York State Museum. cast-iron architecture: Library of Congress. Catholic education: The Post-Standard and the Onondaga Historical Association. Catholics: The Post-Standard and the Onondaga Historical Association. Catskill Mountain House: Albany Institute of History and Art. Central Park: New York State Library. ceramics and pottery: New York State Archives. Champlain: New York State Library. Chautauqua County: New York State Department of Economic Development. Chautauqua Institution: New York State Department of Economic Development. Chemung County: Chemung County Historical Society, Elmira. Chenango Canal: Canal Society of New York State. Chinese: St. Lawrence County Historical Association. citizenship education: Onondaga Historical Association. civil service: New York State Department of Civil Service. Civil War: New York State Library; Onondaga Historical Association. *Clermont:* New York State Library. Clinton, De Witt: New York State Historical Association. Cohoes: New York State Library. Cold War and McCarthyism: The Post-Standard and the Onondaga Historical Association. colonial New York: New York State Historical Association; Historic Hudson Valley Library. communists: Museum of the City of New York. Coney Island: Museum of the City of New York. Cooper, James Fenimore: New York State Library. Cornell University: New York State Archives. Corning, Erastus: New York State Archives. Cortland County: Cortland County Historical Society. courts, federal: Library of Congress. covered bridges: New York State Department of Economic Development. Crane, Stephen: Syracuse University Special Collections Research Center. crime: New-York Historical Society. Croton Reservoir and Aqueduct: New York State Library. Cuomo, Mario M.: The Post-Standard and the Onondaga Historical Association.

D

dairy industry: New York State Historical Association; New-York Historical Society. Davis, Ernie: Syracuse University Archives. Day, Dorothy: National Portrait Gallery, Smithsonian Institution/Art Resource, NY. deer, white-tailed: New York State Archives. Delaware and Hudson Railroad: New York State Archives. Democratic Party: Office of the Honorable Hillary Rodham Clinton. dentistry: St. Lawrence County Historical Association. department stores: The Post-Standard and the Onondaga Historical Association. Dewey, Thomas E.: New York State Archives. DeWitt Clinton: Albany Institute of History and Art. Douglass, Frederick: Onondaga Historical Association. draft riots: New-York Historical Society. Durand, Asher B.: Metropolitan Museum of Art. Dutch: Elizabeth Sullivan; Albany Institute of History and Art; New York State Museum. Dutch barn: New World Dutch Barn Survey 2000 and Gigi Miner. Dyngus Day: Buffalo and Erie County Historical Society and Malczewski Poultry Co.

E

Education Department and University of the State of New York: New York State Archives. Ellis Island: Museum of the City of New York. Elmira: New York State Department of Economic Development. Empire State Building: New York State Archives. Empire State Express: New York State Library. Empire State Plaza, Governor Nelson A. Rockefeller: The Post-Standard, Onondaga Historical Association, and Bergan & Klineberg, Inc. English: Albany Institute of History and Art. environmentalism: New York State Archives. Episcopalians: Museum of the City of New York. Erie Canal: New York State Museum; New York State Library; New York State Library; Albany Institute of History and Art; New-York Historical Society; New York State Museum. Erie Canal in folklore and the arts: New York State Library; Onondaga Historical Association, gift of Rev. Dr. Herbert G. Coddington. Erie County: Buffalo and Erie County Historical Society. Evans, Walker: Metropolitan Museum of Art. exploration: New York State Library.

F

Factory Investigating Commission: New York State Archives. Fairchild Aviation Corporation: New York State Archives. Farmers' Museum: New York State Historical Association. farmsteads: Buffalo and Erie County Historical Society; Buffalo and Erie County Historical Society. film, silent: Fort Ticonderoga Museum. firefighting: Chemung County Historical Society, Elmira; New York State Museum. fish: New York State Museum; New York State Museum. fishing, commercial: Long Island Studies Institute. fishing, recreational (freshwater): New York State Library, Maitland DeSormo and North Country Books. fishing, recreational (saltwater): Lionel Green and Long Island Studies Institute. folk art: New York State Historical Association. forest fires: New York State Archives. Fort Drum: The Post-Standard and the Onondaga Historical Association. Fort Niagara: Buffalo and Erie County Historical Society. Fort Orange: L. F. Tantillo. Fort Ticonderoga: Fort Ticonderoga Museum. Four Indian Kings: Albany Institute of History and Art. Fox sisters: Wayne County Historical Society. French and Indian War: Fort Ticonderoga Museum. furniture making: New York State Museum.

G

garment industry: Rochester Museum and Science Center. Gehrig, Lou: National Baseball Hall of Fame and Museum. *General Slocum:* New York State Library. Genesee River: New York State Library. Geneva: New York State Library. Germans: Buffalo and Erie County Historical Society. Gilboa: New York State Museum. Glens Falls: New York State Library. Gold Coast: Museum of the City of New York. Goldman, Emma: Library of Congress. goldsmithing and silversmithing: Albany Institute of History and Art. golf: New York State Library. governor: New York State Library. grain elevators: Buffalo and Erie County Historical Society. Grand Army of the Republic: New York State Library. Grand Central Terminal: Metropolitan Museum of Art. Great Lakes shipping lines and watercraft: Buffalo and Erie County Historical Society. Greene County: New York State Library. gun control: Museum of the City of New York.

H

Hamilton, Alexander: National Portrait Gallery, Smithsonian Institution/Art Resource, NY. Harlem: Museum of the City of New York. Harlem Renaissance: Metropolitan Museum of Art. healthcare and hospitals: The Post-Standard and the Onondaga Historical Association. Henry, Joseph: National Portrait Gallery, Smithsonian Institution/Art Resource, NY. Herkimer, Nicholas: New York State Department of Economic Development. Herkimer County: New York State Department of Economic Development. higher education: Library of Congress. Hill, David B.: Duke University Rare Book, Manuscript, and Special Collections Library. historical preservation and restoration: Fort Ticonderoga Museum. Holland Land Company: Buffalo and Erie County Historical Society. homelessness: New-York Historical Society. hops: New York State Historical Association. Howe Caverns: Howe Caverns. Hudson: New York State Library. Hudson-Fulton Celebration of 1909: New York State Library. Hudson Highlands fortifications: New York State Archives. Hudson River: Library of Congress; New York State Museum; New York State Library. Hudson River school: The Warner Collection of Gulf States Paper Corporation, Tuscaloosa, Ala. hunting: New York State Historical Association.

I

ice boating: New York State Library. ice hockey: The Post-Standard and the Onondaga Historical Association. ice industry: New York State Archives. I♥NY: New York State Department of Economic Development. immigration: Museum of the City of New York. Influenza Pandemic, 1918–19: Buffalo and Erie County Historical Society. Irish: New-York Historical Society. Iroquois art: Historic Hudson Valley Library; New York State Museum; New York State Museum. Iroquois Confederacy: Rochester Museum and Science Center. Iroquois government and religion: Rochester Museum and Science Center; New York State Museum. Iroquois wars: New York State Museum. Italians: New-York Historical Society. Ithaca: New York State Library.

J

Japanese: Bancroft Library, University of California, Berkeley. Jell-O: Le Roy Historical Society. Jerry Rescue: Onondaga Historical Association. Jews and Judaism: The Post-Standard and the Onondaga Historical Association; New-York Historical Society. Johnson, Sir William: National Archives of Canada. Johnson Hall: New York State Library. Jones Beach State Park: Long Island State Park Commission and Long Island Studies Institute.

K

Kingston: Library of Congress. Koch, Ed: The Post-Standard and the Onondaga Historical Association.

L

labor: The Post-Standard and the Onondaga Historical Association. lacrosse: New York State Museum. Lake Erie: New York State Library. Lake George: Metropolitan Museum of Art. Lake Placid Winter Olympics 1980: New York State Department of Economic Development; New York State Department of Economic Development. land companies and patents: New York State Library. landforms: New York State Archives. lawyers and law firms: New York State Archives. legislature: National Portrait Gallery, Smithsonian Institution/Art Resource, NY. Le Roy: New York State Library. Levittown: New York State Archives. libraries: New York State Archives. lighthouses: New York State Department of Economic Development. limners: Albany Institute of History and Art. literacy: New York State Archives. literature, beyond New York City: Historic Hudson Valley Library. Little Falls: Herkimer County Historical Society. Livingston, Robert R., Jr: National Portrait Gallery, Smithsonian Institution/Art Resource, NY. Livingston Manor: New York State Library. Lockport: New York State Museum. logging and lumbering: The Streever family; New York State Archives. Long Island: Metropolitan Museum of Art. Long Island Rail Road: Hofstra University Archives. Long Island Sound: Robert L. Harrison, Hofstra University Archives. lumber and timber products: The Streever family. Lutherans: The Post-Standard and the Onondaga Historical Association. lynching: New-York Historical Society. Lyons: Canal Society of New York State.

M

Madison County: Fryer Memorial Museum. mammals: New York State Museum. Manhattan: Library of Congress; New York State Library. maple syrup: DeWitt Historical Society of Tompkins County. Marcy, William L.: National Portrait Gallery, Smithsonian Institution/Art Resource, NY. McCrea, Jane: Fordham University Archives. meatpacking industry: New York State Archives. Mechanicville: New York State Library. medical education: University at Buffalo. Melville, Herman: Berkshire Athenaeum, Pittsfield, Mass. mental retardation and developmental disabilities: New York State Archives. migrant farmworkers: BOCES Geneseo Migrant Center. mining and mineral industry: New York State Museum. modern dance: National Portrait Gallery, Smithsonian Institution/Art Resource, NY. Mohonk Mountain House: New York State Library. Montgomery County: Montgomery County Archives. Mormons: New York State Archives. motorcycling: Buffalo and Erie County Historical Society. motor vehicle industry: Onondaga Historical Association. Mount, William Sydney: Metropolitan Museum of Art. Mount Vernon: New York State Library.

N

Nabokov, Vladimir: New York State Museum. Negro Leagues: National Baseball Hall of Fame and Museum. New France: New York State Library. New Netherland: New York State Library; Mashantucket Pequot Museum and Research Center, Archives & Special Collections; Albany Institute of History and Art. newspapers: New York State Library; Metropolitan Museum of Art. New York Central Railroad: New York State Library. New York City: New York State Library; Metropolitan Museum of Art; New York State Archives; New York State Library; New York State Archives; Museum of the City of New York. New York City subway: Museum of the City of New York. New York State Museum: New York State Archives. New York State Thruway: New York State Department of Economic Development. New York Stock Exchange: New-York Historical Society. New York Yankees: New York State Department of Economic Development. Niagara Falls: Library of Congress; New York State Library. Niagara Falls (city): New York State Library. Niagara Mohawk: The Post-Standard and the Onondaga Historical Association. Niagara River: Library of Congress. North Country: New York State Library. North Elba: New York State Library, Maitland DeSormo and North Country Books. nurses: The Post-Standard and the Onondaga Historical Association.

O

oats: New York State Archives. Olean: New York State Library. Oneida Community: New York State Historical Association. Onondaga County: Onondaga Historical Association. Onondaga Nation: New York State Archives. Otsego Lake: New York State Historical Association.

P

Pan-American Exposition: New York State Library. parkways: New York State Archives. Pataki, George E.: Office of the Governor. Patch, Sam: Rochester Historical Society and Rochester Public Library. patroonships: New York State Library. philanthropy: New York State Library. Philipsburg Manor: Metropolitan Museum of Art. physicians: Onondaga Historical Association. Pierce-Arrow Motor Car Company: Buffalo and Erie County Historical Society. Poles: Buffalo and Erie County Historical Society. policing: Carrie Diesend; Rochester Museum and Science Center. pollution: The Post-Standard and the Onondaga Historical Association. Port of Buffalo: Buffalo and Erie County Historical Society. Port of New York: New York State Library. Poughkeepsie Railroad Bridge: New York State Library. poverty: Metropolitan Museum of Art. power and lighting: The Post-Standard and the Onondaga Historical Association. prehistoric archaeology: New York State Museum. prisoner of war facilities: Rochester Democrat and Chronicle and Rochester Public Library. prison industry and labor: New York State Archives. Prohibition: Rochester Museum and Science Center. public education: New York State Library. public employees union: The Post-Standard and the Onondaga Historical Association.

Q

quilting: American Folk Art Museum, gift of the J. M. Kaplan Fund 1991.3.1.

R

railroads: Onondaga Historical Association. Red Cross: New York State Archives. Red Jacket: New York State Library. Reformed Churches: Albany Institute of History and Art. religion: New-York Historical Society. Remington, Frederic: New York State Department of Economic Development. Rensselaer County: Staats family. Rensselaerswijck: Albany Institute of History and Art and New York State Museum. Republican Party: Buffalo and Erie County Historical Society; The Post-Standard and the Onondaga Historical Association. riots and civil disturbances: New-York Historical Society. Rip Van Winkle: Albany Institute of History and Art. roads: Albany Institute of History and Art. Rochester: New York State Library; Rochester City Hall Photo Lab and Rochester Online; New York State Archives. Rockefeller, Nelson A.: New York State Archives. Rogers' Rangers: Fort Ticonderoga Museum. Rome: New York State Library. Roosevelt, Eleanor: Franklin D. Roosevelt Presidential Library and Museum. Roosevelt, Franklin D.: Franklin D. Roosevelt Presidential Library and Museum. Roosevelt, Theodore: New York State Library, Maitland DeSormo and North Country Books. Rossie: St. Lawrence County Historical Association. Roycroft: New York State Museum. Rushton, J. Henry: St. Lawrence County Historical Association. Rye: New York State Library.

S

salt industry: New York State Library. Sand Lake: Rensselaer County Historical Society. sanitation and sewage: Buffalo and Erie County Historical Society. Saranac Lake: Trudeau Institute Archives. Saratoga Race Course: New York State Department of Economic Development. savings banks: Albany Institute of History and Art. Schenectady: New York State Department of Economic Development. Schenectady County: New York State Library. Schoharie County: Beverly T. Lavick. Schuyler, Philip: Albany Institute of History and Art. Seneca County: Seneca Falls Historical Society. Seneca Nation: New York State Historical Association. September 11th, 2001: Woody Woodworth/New Netherland Museum. Serling, Rod: Broome County Historical Society. Setauket: New York State Historical Association. Seton, Elizabeth Ann: National Portrait Gallery, Smithsonian Institution/Art Resource, NY. Seward, William H.: National Portrait Gallery, Smithsonian Institution/Art Resource, NY. Shakers: Library of Congress. shopping centers and malls: Hofstra University Archives. Sing Sing Correctional Facility: New York State Archives. skiing: Library of Congress. slavery: Albany Institute of History and Art. snow removal: Onondaga Historical Association. Sodus Bay: New York State Department of Economic Development. spas: New York State Library. stagecoach lines: Albany Institute of History and Art. state government and services: New York State Archives. Staten Island: New York State Department of Economic Development. state parks: New York State Department of Economic Development. State Police, Division of: The Post-Standard and the Onondaga Historical Association. state seal and state flag: Albany Institute of History and Art. Statue of Liberty: New York State Library. Steuben Glass: Metropolitan Museum of Art. St. Lawrence River: New York State Department of Economic Development. St. Nicholas: Ohio State University Cartoon Research Library. Stuyvesant, Petrus: New-York Historical Society. sugar-refining industry: New York State Archives. Syracuse: Onondaga Historical Association; Onondaga Historical Association. Syracuse China Company: Courtesy of the Pass family and the Onondaga Historical Association. Syracuse University: Syracuse University Archives. Syracuse University football: Syracuse University Archives. Syracuse University men's basketball: Syracuse University Archives.

T

tanning industry: New York State Archives. Taylor, Anna Edson: Niagara Falls Public Library. Tekakwitha, Kateri: St. Francis Xavier Church and Mission. telephone industry: Onondaga Historical Association; Museum of the City of New York. tenement reform: Museum of the City of New York. textile industry: New York State Library. theater, Albany and the Capital District: Albany Institute of History and Art. theater, New York City: New York State Library. Thomas Indian School: New York State Archives. thoroughbred racing: New York Racing Association and Long Island Studies Institute. Thousand Islands resorts: New York State Department of Economic Development. Ticonderoga: New York State Library, Maitland DeSormo and North Country Books. Tilden, Samuel J.: New York State Library. tobacco industry and smoking: Chemung County History Museum, Elmira. Tompkins County: DeWitt Historical Society of Tompkins County. traffic management: Buffalo and Erie County Historical Society. Trenton Falls: New York State Library. Troy: Library of Congress; Rensselaer County Historical Society. Troy Haymakers: National Baseball Hall of Fame and Museum. Trudeau, Edward Livingston: Trudeau Institute Archives. Truth, Sojourner: National Portrait Gallery, Smithsonian Institution/Art Resource, NY. tuberculosis sanatoriums: Trudeau Institute Archives. Tubman, Harriet: Library of Congress. Tuscarora Nation: Buffalo and Erie County Historical Society. Twain, Mark: Buffalo and Erie County Historical Society. Tweed Ring: National Portrait Gallery, Smithsonian Institution/Art Resource, NY. typewriter industry: Onondaga Historical Association.

U

Underground Railroad: Syracuse University Archives. United Nations: New York State Archives. United States Constitution ratification: Albany Institute of History and Art. United States Military Academy: New York State Archives. urban hotels: New York State Library. urban parks: New York State Library. Utica: New York State Library.

V

Valcour Island, Battle of: Vermont Historical Society. Van Buren, Martin: National Portrait Gallery, Smithsonian Institution/Art Resource, NY. Van Cortlandt Manor House: Historic Hudson Valley Library. Van Rensselaer, Stephen, III: Albany Institute of History and Art. Van Rensselaer Manor House: Albany Institute of History and Art. Vassar College: New York State Library. Vietnam War: The Post-Standard and the Onondaga Historical Association. voter turnout: The Post-Standard and the Onondaga Historical Association.

W

wampum: Rochester Museum and Science Center. war memorials: New York State Office of General Services. War of 1812: Buffalo and Erie County Historical Society; New York State Library. Washington, George: Buffalo and Erie County Historical Society. water supply and use (New York City watershed): New York State Library. Watertown: New York State Archives. Watkins Glen State Park: New York State Library. Westchester County: New York State Library. whaling: Metropolitan Museum of Art. Whig Party: New York State Historical Society. Whitman, Walt: New York State Library. windmills: Robert L. Harrison, Hofstra University Archives. wine industry and viticulture: New York State Department of Economic Development. women's education: New-York Historical Society. women's rights and feminism: Rochester Museum and Science Center. Works Progress Administration: Rochester Public Library. world's fairs: Museum of the City of New York. World Trade Center: Albany Institute of History and Art; New York State Department of Economic Development. World War I: New York State Library. World War II: The Post-Standard and the Onondaga Historical Association; New York State Archives.

Y

Yonkers: New York State Archives.

Z

zebra mussels: New York State Museum. zoos: The Post-Standard and the Onondaga Historical Association.

Index

Page numbers in bold indicate encyclopedia main entries; page numbers in italic indicate illustrations or tables.

C

D

H

J